HANDWÖRTERBUCH DEUTSCH-ENGLISCH ENGLISCH-DEUTSCH GERMAN-ENGLISH ENGLISH-GERMAN DICTIONARY

KLETT HANDWÖRTERBUCH DEUTSCH-ENGLISCH ENGLISCH-DEUTSCH

Collins
London • Glasgow • Toronto

Klett
Stuttgart

Check out the first two titles featuring Laurie Holbrook!

Miss Match

ISBN-13: 978-1-60006-095-3
ISBN-10: 1-60006-095-1

Lauren Holbrook has found her life's calling: matchmaking for the romantically challenged. When her foolproof plans begin to unravel, she learns that a simple introduction between friends can bring about complicated results. And as Lauren reconsiders her new role as Cupid (as well as her vow to stay single forever), will she finally decide that God's plan is always good enough?

Rematch

ISBN-13: 978-1-60006-096-0
ISBN-10: 1-60006-096-X

With two successful matches under her belt, Lauren's thrown for a loop when her dad announces that he's heading out of town for a singles' retreat. And in the midst of panicking about her dad and potential future stepmom, there's the matter of Ryan: Love interest or friend? Only time, vats of coffee, and pounds of chocolate will tell!

To order copies, visit your local Christian bookstore, call NavPress at 1-800-366-7788, or log on to www.navpress.com.
To locate a Christian bookstore near you, call 1-800-991-7747.

About the Author

ERYNN MANGUM plans her life around caffeine, but when she's not tipping the coffee mug, she's spending time with her husband, Jon, who she met and married since writing *Miss Match* and *ReMatch*. She also works as an intern at her church and loves hanging out with her family and friends. She's twenty-three years old and a graduate of both Christian Writers Guild courses. Learn more at: www.erynnmangum.com.

WEBSTER'S NEW WORLD®

GERMAN DICTIONARY

CONCISE EDITION

GERMAN-ENGLISH
ENGLISH-GERMAN

HOUGHTON MIFFLIN HARCOURT
BOSTON NEW YORK

EDITORS/REDAKTEURE
Peter Terrell & Horst Kopleck

ASSISTANT EDITORS/MITARBEITER
Jimmy Burnett
Andrea Ender
Philip Ladd
Reinhold Trou

COPY EDITOR/REDAKTIONSASSISTENTIN
Daphne Trotter

Words are included in this dictionary on the basis of their usage. Words that are known to have current trademark registrations are shown with an initial capital and are also identified as trademarks. No investigation has been made of common-law trademark rights in any word, because such investigation is impracticable. The inclusion of any word in this dictionary is not, however, an expression of the publisher's opinion as to whether or not it is subject to proprietary rights. Indeed, no definition in this dictionary is to be regarded as affecting the validity of any trademark.

Trademarks: Webster's New World, the Webster's New World logo, We Define Your World, and related trade dress are trademarks or registered trademarks of Houghton Mifflin Harcourt.

ISBN 978-0-544-94482-4

Visit our website: hmhco.com

Manufactured in the United States of America

17 18 19 20 21 22 - DOC - 22 21 20 19 18 17

4500648880

INTRODUCTION

This dictionary provides the user wishing to learn, read and understand German with a detailed and clearly structured analysis of the German and English languages and of the correspondence between them. Emphasis is placed on current usage–from the colloquial to the more formal–and there is extensive treatment of all areas relevant to the modern world.

To facilitate communication and self-expression in the foreign language, the basic, most frequently used words in the language are treated in depth, so that the user may express himself correctly and idiomatically–both orally and in writing. A unique guiding system of indicating words helps the user to pinpoint meaning and identify the correct translation from among all the possible translations given.

Compiled by a team of experienced German and English linguists and lexicographers, this reference book combines comprehensive coverage with outstanding clarity, simplicity and economy, making it an efficient and ideal working tool for school, self-study and professional life.

EINLEITUNG

Dieses Wörterbuch bietet dem Benutzer für das Lernen, Lesen und Verstehen des Englischen eine detaillierte und klar strukturierte Analyse der englischen und der deutschen Sprache und der Wechselbeziehungen zwischen beiden. Das Hauptgewicht liegt auf dem modernen Sprachgebrauch–von der Umgangssprache bis zur förmlicheren Ausdrucksweise–und alle für die heutige Zeit relevanten Bereiche werden eingehend behandelt.

Um die Verständigung und Ausdrucksfähigkeit in der Fremdsprache zu erleichtern, werden die grundlegenden und am häufigsten gebrauchten Wörter ausführlich behandelt, so daß dem Benutzer eine mündlich wie schriftlich korrekte und idiomatisch richtige Verwendung der Sprache ermöglicht wird. Ein einzigartiges Kennzeichnungssystem hilft dem Benutzer, Bedeutungsunterschiede zu erkennen und die jeweils richtige Übersetzung unter allen angegebenen Übersetzungsmöglichkeiten herauszufinden.

Dieses Nachschlagewerk wurde von einem Team erfahrener englischer und deutscher Linguisten und Lexikographen zusammengestellt und verbindet Ausführlichkeit mit außerordentlicher Klarheit, Einfachheit und Prägnanz. Hierdurch wird es zu einem leistungsstarken und vorzüglichen Arbeitsmittel für die Schule, zum Selbststudium und im Beruf.

CONTENTS

INHALT

How to use the dictionary

Layout and order

1.1 Alphabetical order is followed throughout. Where a letter occurs in brackets in a headword, this letter is counted for the alphabetical order, eg **Beamte(r)** will be found in the place of **Beamter, vierte(r, s)** in the place of **vierter**.

1.2 Abbreviations, acronyms and proper nouns will be found in their alphabetical place in the word list.

1.3 Superior numbers are used to differentiate between words of like spelling.

rowing[1], **rowing**[2]; **durchsetzen**[1], **durchsetzen**[2].

1.4 Compounds will be found in their alphabetical place in the word list. The term "compound" is taken to cover not only solid and hyphenated compounds (eg **Bettwäsche, large-scale**) but also attributive uses of English nouns (eg **defence mechanism**) and other set collocations (eg **long jump**). Where the alphabetical order permits, compounds are run on in blocks with the first element printed in boldface type at the beginning of each block. Where possible a general translation has been given for the compound element.

Silber- *in cpds* silver.

From this the user can derive the translation for compounds not given in the word list.

1.5 Phrasal verbs (marked ♦) will be found immediately after the main headword entry.

1.6 Idioms and set phrases will normally be found under the first meaningful element or the first word in the phrase which remains constant despite minor variations in the phrase itself. Thus 'to throw out the baby with the bathwater' is included under '**baby**' whereas 'to lend sb a hand' is treated under '**hand**' because it is equally possible to say 'to give sb a hand'.
Certain very common verbs such as be, get, have, make, put, bringen, haben, geben, machen, tun, which form the basis of a great many phrases, eg to make sense, to make a mistake, etw in Ordnung bringen, etw in Gang bringen, have been considered as having a diminished meaning and in such cases the set phrase will be found under the most significant element in the phrase.

Benutzungshinweise

Aufbau und Anordnung der Einträge

1.1 Die alphabetische Anordnung der Einträge ist durchweg gewahrt. In Klammern stehende Buchstaben in einem Stichwort unterliegen ebenfalls der Alphabetisierung, so findet man z.B. **Beamte(r)** an der Stelle von **Beamter, vierte(r, s)** unter **vierter**.

1.2 Abkürzungen, Akronyme und Eigennamen sind in alphabetischer Ordnung im Wörterverzeichnis zu finden.

1.3 Hochgestellte Ziffern werden verwendet, um zwischen Wörtern gleicher Schreibung zu unterscheiden.

1.4 Zusammengesetzte Wörter stehen an ihrer Stelle im Alphabet. Der Begriff „zusammengesetzte Wörter" bezeichnet nicht nur zusammengeschriebene oder durch Bindestrich verbundene Komposita (z.B. **Bettwäsche, large-scale**) sondern auch die attributive Verwendung englischer Substantive (z.B. **defence mechanism**) und andere feste Verbindungen (z.B. **long jump**). Wo die alphabetische Ordnung es gestattet, werden die Zusammensetzungen in Blöcken angeordnet, wobei der erste Bestandteil am Kopf jedes Blocks in Fettdruck erscheint. Wo immer möglich, ist für das erste Element eine allgemeine Übersetzung angegeben.

Daraus kann der Benutzer die Übersetzung hier nicht angegebener Zusammensetzungen erschließen.

1.5 *Phrasal verbs* (durch ♦ gekennzeichnet) folgen unmittelbar auf das Hauptstichwort.

1.6 Redensarten und feste Wendungen sind im allgemeinen unter dem ersten bedeutungstragenden Element oder dem ersten Wort der Wendung, das trotz leichter Abwandlungen in der Wendung selbst unverändert bleibt, zu finden. So ist 'to throw out the baby with the bathwater' unter '**baby**' aufgenommen, 'to lend sb a hand' dagegen wird under '**hand**' abgehandelt, weil es ebenfalls möglich ist, 'to give sb a hand' zu sagen.
Bei als Funktionsverben gebrauchten Verben wie be, get, have, make, put, bringen, haben, geben, machen und tun, werden die meisten festen Wendungen, wie z.B. to make sense, to make a mistake, etw in Ordnung bringen, etw in Gang bringen, unter dem bedeutungstragenden Bestandteil der Wendung behandelt.

Indicating material

General indicating material in the dictionary is printed in italics and takes the following forms:

2.1 Indicators in parentheses:

2.1.1 synonyms and partial definitions

gefühlvoll *adj (empfindsam)* sensitive; *(ausdrucksvoll)* expressive; *(liebevoll)* loving.

2.1.2 within verb entries, typical subjects of the headword

peel 3 *vi (wallpaper)* sich lösen; *(paint)* abblättern; *(skin, person)* sich schälen *or* pellen *(col)*.

2.1.3 within noun entries, typical noun complements of the headword

Schar *f* **-en** crowd, throng *(liter)*; *(von Vögeln)* flock; *(von Insekten etc)* swarm.

2.2 Collocators, not in parentheses:

2.2.1 within transitive verb entries, typical objects of the headword

dent 2 *vt car* eindellen, verbeulen; *(col) pride* anknacksen *(col)*.

2.2.2 within adjective entries, typical nouns modified by the headword

neu *adj* new; *Kräfte, Hoffnung auch* fresh; *Wäsche* clean; *Wein* young.

2.2.3 within adverb entries, typical verbs or adjectives modified by the headword

vaguely *adv* vage; *remember also* dunkel; *speak also* unbestimmt; *understand* ungefähr, in etwa.

2.3 Field labels are used:

2.3.1 to differentiate various meanings of the headword

Jungfrau *f* virgin; *(Astrol)* Virgo.

2.3.2 when the meaning in the source language is clear but may be ambiguous in the target language.

Virgo *n (Astrol)* Jungfrau *f*.

A full list of labels is given on pages xviii–xix.

2.4 Style labels are used to mark all words and phrases which are not neutral in style level or which are no longer current in the language. This labelling is given for both source and target languages and serves primarily as an aid to the non-native speaker.
When a style label is given at the beginning of an entry or category it covers all meanings and phrases in that entry or category.

(col) denotes colloquial language typically used in an informal conversational context or a chatty letter, but which would be inappropriate in more formal speech or writing.

(col!) denotes words which are potentially offensive.

(col!!) denotes words which are highly offensive.

(sl) combined with a field label eg *(Mil sl)*, *(Sch sl)* it denotes that the expression belongs to the jargon of that group.

Erklärende Zusätze

Allgemeine erklärende Zusätze im Wörterbuch sind kursiv gedruckt und erscheinen in folgender Form:

2.1 Indikatoren, in Klammern stehend:

2.1.1 Synonyme und Teildefinitionen

2.1.2 typische Substantiv-Ergänzungen in Verb-Einträgen

2.1.3 typische Substantiv-Ergänzungen des Stichworts in Substantiv-Einträgen

2.2 Kollokatoren, ohne Klammern stehend:

2.2.1 typische Objekte des Stichworts bei transitiven Verb-Einträgen

2.2.2 typische, durch das Stichwort näher bestimmte Substantive in Adjektiv-Einträgen

2.2.3 typische, durch das Stichwort näher bestimmte Verben oder Adjektive bei Adverb-Einträgen

2.3 Sachbereichsangaben werden verwendet:

2.3.1 um die verschiedenen Bedeutungen des Stichworts zu unterscheiden

2.3.2 wenn die Bedeutung in der Ausgangssprache klar ist, jedoch in der Zielsprache mehrdeutig sein könnte.

Eine vollständige Liste dieser Sachbereichsangaben befindet sich auf den Seiten xviii und xix.

2.4 Stilangaben werden verwendet zur Kennzeichnung aller Wörter und Wendungen, die keiner neutralen Stilebene oder nicht mehr dem modernen Sprachgebrauch angehören. Die Angaben erfolgen sowohl in der Ausgangs- als auch in der Zielsprache und sollen in erster Linie dem Nicht-Muttersprachler helfen.
Stilangaben zu Beginn eines Eintrages oder einer Kategorie beziehen sich auf alle Bedeutungen und Wendungen innerhalb dieses Eintrages oder dieser Kategorie.

(col) bezeichnet umgangssprachlichen Gebrauch, wie er für eine formlose Unterhaltung oder einen zwanglosen Brief typisch ist, in förmlicherer Rede oder förmlicherem Schriftverkehr jedoch unangebracht wäre.

(col!) bezeichnet Wörter, an denen unter Umständen Anstoß genommen wird.

(col!!) bezeichnet Wörter, die allgemein als anstößig gelten.

(sl) weist in Verbindung mit einer Sachbereichsangabe, z.B. *(Mil sl)*, *(Sch sl)*, auf die Zugehörigkeit des Ausdrucks zum Jargon dieser Gruppe hin.

(geh)	denotes elevated style of spoken or written German such as might be used by an educated speaker choosing his words with care.	*(geh)*	bezeichnet einen gehobenen Stil sowohl im gesprochenen wie geschriebenen Deutsch, wie er von gebildeten, sich gewählt ausdrückenden Sprechern verwendet werden kann.
(form)	denotes formal language such as that used on official forms, for official communications and in formal speeches.	*(form)*	bezeichnet förmlichen Sprachgebrauch, wie er uns auf Formularen, im amtlichen Schriftverkehr oder in förmlichen Ansprachen begegnet.
(spec)	indicates that the expression is a technical term restricted to the vocabulary of specialists.	*(spec)*	gibt an, daß es sich um einen Fachausdruck handelt, der dem Wortschatz von Fachleuten angehört.
(dated)	indicates that the word or phrase, while still occasionally being used especially by older speakers, now sounds somewhat old-fashioned.	*(dated)*	weist darauf hin, daß solche Wörter bzw. Wendungen heute recht altmodisch klingen, obwohl sie besonders von älteren Sprechern noch gelegentlich benutzt werden.
(old)	denotes language no longer in current use but which the user will find in reading.	*(old)*	bezeichnet nicht mehr geläufiges Wortgut, das dem Benutzer jedoch noch beim Lesen begegnet.
(obs)	denotes obsolete words which the user will normally only find in classical literature.	*(obs)*	bezeichnet veraltete Wörter, die der Benutzer im allgemeinen nur in der klassischen Literatur antreffen wird.
(liter)	denotes language of a literary style level. It should not be confused with the field label *(Liter)* which indicates that the expression belongs to the field of literary studies, or with the abbreviation *(lit)* which indicates the literal as opposed to the figurative meaning of a word.	*(liter)*	bezeichnet literarischen Sprachgebrauch. Es sollte nicht mit der Sachbereichsangabe *(Liter)* verwechselt werden, die angibt, daß der betreffende Ausdruck dem Gebiet der Literaturwissenschaft angehört, und ebensowenig mit der Abkürzung *(lit)*, die die wörtliche im Gegensatz zur übertragenen Bedeutung eines Wortes bezeichnet.

Grammatical Information

Gender

3.1 All German nouns are marked for gender in both sections of the dictionary.

3.2 Where more than one German noun of the same gender are given consecutively as interchangeable translations, the gender is given only after the last translation.

Grammatische Angaben

Geschlecht

3.1 Alle deutschen Substantive sind in beiden Teilen des Wörterbuches mit der Geschlechtsangabe versehen.

3.2 Wo mehrere deutsche Substantive gleichen Geschlechts als austauschbare Übersetzungen hintereinander stehen, wird das Geschlecht nur nach der letzten Übersetzung angegeben.

computer *n* Computer, Rechner *m*.

3.3 Where a German translation consists of an adjective plus a noun, the adjective is given in the indefinite form which shows gender and therefore no gender is given for the noun.

3.3 Wenn eine deutsche Übersetzung aus einem Adjektiv und einem Substantiv besteht, wird das Adjektiv in der unbestimmten Form angegeben, die das Geschlecht erkennen läßt. Für das Substantiv erfolgt daher keine Geschlechtsangabe.

große Pause; zweites Frühstück.

3.4 Nouns of the form **Reisende(r)** *mf decl as adj* can be either masculine or feminine and take the same declensional ending as adjectives.

3.4 Substantive nach dem Muster **Reisende(r)** *mf decl as adj* können sowohl männlich wie weiblich sein und haben die gleichen Deklinationsendungen wie Adjektive.

m **der Reisende, ein Reisender, die Reisenden** *pl*
f **die Reisende, eine Reisende, die Reisenden** *pl*

3.5 Nouns of the form **Beamte(r)** *m decl as adj* take the same declensional endings as adjectives.

3.5 Substantive nach dem Muster **Beamte(r)** *m decl as adj* haben die gleichen Deklinationsendungen wie Adjektive.

der Beamte, ein Beamter, die Beamten *pl*

3.6 Adjectives of the form **letzte(r, s)** do not exist in an undeclined form and are only used attributively.

3.6 Adjektive nach dem Muster **letzte(r, s)** haben keine unflektierte Form und werden nur attributiv verwendet.

der letzte Mann, ein letzter Mann
die letzte Frau, eine letzte Frau
das letzte Kind, ein letztes Kind

3.7 Nouns of the form **Schüler(in** *f***)** *m* are only used in the bracketed form in the feminine.

3.7 Substantive nach dem Muster **Schüler(in** *f***)** *m* werden nur im Femininum in der eingeklammerten Form benutzt.

der/ein Schüler
die/eine Schülerin

3.8 The feminine forms are shown, where relevant, for all German noun headwords; unless otherwise indicated, the English translation will be the same as for the masculine form.
Where there is no distinction between the translations given for the masculine and feminine forms and yet the context calls for a distinction, the user should prefix the translation with 'male/female *or* woman *or* lady ...'

3.8 Für alle deutschen Substantive, die ein natürliches Geschlecht haben, wird die weibliche neben der männlichen Form angegeben. Wenn nicht anders angegeben, lautet die englische Form für beide gleich.
Wo die für die männliche und die für die weibliche Form angegebene Übersetzung dieselbe ist, im entsprechenden Zusammenhang aber betont werden soll, daß es sich um einen Mann bzw. eine Frau handelt, sollte der Benutzer der Übersetzung 'male/female *or* woman *or* lady' voranstellen.

male teacher, female *or* **woman** *or* **lady teacher**

Nouns

4.1 Nouns marked *no pl* are not normally used in the plural or with an indefinite article or with numerals.

4.2 Nouns marked *no art* are not normally used with either a definite or an indefinite article except when followed by a relative clause.

4.3 The plural endings are given for all German noun headwords except for certain regular noun endings. A complete list of these is given on page xvi.
The plural endings of German compound nouns are only given where the final element does not exist as a headword in its own right.

4.4 Irregular plural forms of English nouns are given on the English-German side.

4.4.1 Most English nouns take *-s* in the plural.

Substantive

4.1 Substantive mit der Angabe *no pl* werden im allgemeinen nicht im Plural, mit dem unbestimmten Artikel oder mit Zahlwörtern verwendet.

4.2 Mit *no art* bezeichnete Substantive stehen im allgemeinen weder mit dem unbestimmten noch mit dem bestimmten Artikel, außer wenn ein Relativsatz von ihnen abhängig ist.

4.3 Bei allen deutschen Substantiv-Stichwörtern ist der Plural angegeben, mit Ausnahme bestimmter regelmäßiger Endungen. Diese sind in einer vollständigen Liste auf Seite xvi erfaßt.
Der Plural ist bei zusammengesetzten Substantiven nur dann angegeben, wenn das letzte Element der Zusammensetzung nicht als Einzelwort vorkommt.

4.4 Unregelmäßige Pluralformen englischer Substantive sind im englisch-deutschen Teil angegeben.

4.4.1 Die meisten englischen Substantive bilden den Plural durch Anhängen von *-s*.

bed -s, site -s, key -s, roof -s

4.4.2 Nouns ending in *-s, -z, -x, -sh, -ch* take *-es*.

4.4.2 Substantive, die auf *-s, -z, -x, -sh, -ch* enden, erhalten die Endung *-es*.

gas -es, box -es, patch -es

4.4.3 Nouns ending in *-y* preceded by a consonant change the *-y* to *ie* and add *-s* in the plural, except in the case of proper nouns.

4.4.3 Substantive, die auf Konsonant + *-y* enden, verwandeln im Plural das auslautende *-y* in *-ie*, auf das die Pluralendung *-s* folgt. Ausnahmen bilden Eigennamen.

lady – ladies, berry – berries
Germany – the two Germanys

Adjectives and adverbs

Adjektive und Adverbien

5.1 As a general rule, adjective translations consisting of more than one word should be used after not before the noun.

5.1 Grundsätzlich sollten Übersetzungen von Adjektiven, die aus mehreren Wörtern bestehen, nur nachgestellt oder adverbial gebraucht und nicht dem Substantiv vorangestellt werden.

ordnungsgemäß *adj* in accordance with the rules

5.2 On the German-English side of the dictionary adverbs have only been treated as separate grammatical entries distinct from adjective entries:

(a) when their use is purely adverbial

5.2 Im deutsch-englischen Teil des Wörterbuches sind Adverbien als selbständige grammatische Einträge von Adjektiven nur dann unterschieden worden,

(a) wenn es sich um echte Adverbien handelt

höchst, wohl, sehr

(b) when the adverbial use is as common as the adjective use

(b) wenn der adverbiale Gebrauch genauso häufig ist wie der adjektivische

schön

(c) when the English translation of the adverbial use cannot be derived from the adjectival translations by the rules of adverb formation.

(c) wenn die englische Übersetzung eines adverbial verwendeten Adjektivs nicht mit Hilfe der Regeln erschlossen werden kann, nach denen im Englischen Adverbien aus Adjektiven gebildet werden.

gut

Where no separate entry is given for the adverbial use of a German adjective, the user should form the English adverb from the translations given according to the rules given on page xv.

Wo für den adverbialen Gebrauch eines deutschen Adjektivs kein gesonderter Eintrag vorliegt, ist es dem Benutzer selbst überlassen, aus den angegebenen Übersetzungen die englischen Adverbien nach den auf Seite xv angeführten Regeln zu bilden.

5.3 On the English-German side of the dictionary adverbs have only been entered when separate translations are necessary, which differ from those of the related adjective. Normally the German translation of an English adverb takes the same form as the translation of the related adjective. For example:

5.3 Im englisch-deutschen Teil des Wörterbuchs sind Adverbien nur dann als gesonderte Einträge aufgenommen worden, wenn eine eigenständige Übersetzung erforderlich ist. Normalerweise ist die deutsche Übersetzung eines englischen Adverbs gleichlautend mit der des entsprechenden Adjektivs. Zum Beispiel:

he is astute er ist scharfsinnig
..., he remarked astutely ..., bemerkte er scharfsinnig

Verbs

Verben

6.1 All German verbs which form the past participle without *ge-* are marked with an asterisk in the text.

6.1 Alle Verben im Deutschen, die das 2. Partizip ohne *ge-* bilden, sind im Text durch Sternchen gekennzeichnet.

umarmen* *vt insep ptp* **umarmt**
manövrieren* *vti ptp* **manövriert**

6.2 All German verbs beginning with a prefix which can allow separability are marked *sep* or *insep* as appropriate.

6.2 Alle deutschen Verben, die mit einer oft trennbaren Vorsilbe beginnen, werden durch *sep* oder *insep* (= trennbar/untrennbar) bezeichnet.

unterliegen *vi insep* es unterliegt keinem Zweifel, daß ...
umschalten *vti sep* wir schalten jetzt um nach Hamburg

Verbs beginning with the prefixes *be-, er-, ver-, zer-* are always inseparable.

Verben mit den Vorsilben *be-, er-, ver-, zer-* sind immer untrennbar.

6.3 All German verbs which take 'sein' as the auxiliary are marked *aux sein.*

6.3 Alle deutschen Verben, die die zusammengesetzten Zeiten mit „sein" bilden, sind durch *aux sein* gekennzeichnet.

gehen *pret* **ging,** *ptp* **gegangen** *aux sein*

Where the auxiliary is not stated, 'haben' is used.

Erfolgt keine Angabe, ist „haben" zu verwenden.

6.4 German irregular verbs composed of prefix and verb are marked *irreg*, and the forms can be found under the simple verb. For example, the irregular forms of 'eingehen' will be found under 'gehen'.

6.4 Zusammengesetzte unregelmäßige Verben im Deutschen sind durch *irreg* bezeichnet, ihre Stammformen sind beim Simplex angegeben. So sind beispielsweise die Stammformen von „eingehen" unter „gehen" zu finden.

6.5 If the present or past participle of a verb has adjectival value it is treated as a separate headword in its alphabetical place.

6.5 Wenn 1. oder 2. Partizip eines Verbs den Status eines Adjektivs haben, werden sie als eigenständige Stichwörter in alphabetischer Reihenfolge aufgeführt.

gereift *adj (fig)* mature.
growing *adj (lit, fig)* wachsend; *child* heranwachsend.

Phrasal verbs

7.1 Phrasal verbs are covered in separate entries marked ♦ following the main headword.

7.2 Phrasal verbs are treated in four grammatical categories:

7.2.1 *vi*

Phrasal verbs

7.1 *Phrasal verbs* sind in eigenen Einträgen abgehandelt. Sie sind durch ♦ gekennzeichnet und folgen dem Stichworteintrag für das Simplex.

7.2 *Phrasal verbs* werden unter vier grammatischen Kategorien abgehandelt:

7.2.1 *vi*

♦ **grow apart** *vi (fig)* sich auseinanderentwickeln.

7.2.2 *vi +prep obj*
This indicates that the verbal element is intransitive but that the particle requires an object.

7.2.2 *vi + prep obj*
Hiermit soll gezeigt werden, daß das Verbelement intransitiv ist, daß aber die Partikel ein Objekt erfordert.

♦ **hold with** *vi + prep obj (col)* **I don't ~ ~ that** ich bin gegen so was *(col).*

7.2.3 *vt*
This indicates that the verbal element is transitive. In most cases the object can be placed either before or after the particle; these cases are marked *sep.*

7.2.3 *vt*
Dies gibt an, daß das Verbelement transitiv ist. In den meisten Fällen kann das Objekt vor oder hinter der Partikel stehen; diese Fälle sind mit *sep* bezeichnet.

♦ **hand in** *vt sep* abgeben; *forms, resignation* einreichen.

In some cases the object must precede the particle; these cases are marked *always separate.*

In einigen Fällen muß das Objekt der Partikel vorangehen; solche Fälle sind durch *always separate* bezeichnet.

♦ **get over with** *vt always separate* hinter sich *(acc)* bringen.
let's ~ it ~ (~) bringen wir's hinter uns.

Occasionally the object must come after the particle; these cases are marked *insep.*

Gelegentlich muß das Objekt der Partikel nachgestellt werden; solche Fälle sind durch *insep* bezeichnet.

♦ **strike up** *vt insep* **(a)** *(band) tune* anstimmen.
(b) *friendship* schließen; *conversation* anfangen.

7.2.4 *vt + prep obj*
This indicates that both the verbal element and the particle require an object.

7.2.4 *vt +prep obj*
Hiermit wird gezeigt, daß sowohl das Verbelement wie die Partikel ein Objekt verlangen.

♦ **take upon** *vt +prep obj* **he has taken it ~ himself to ...**
er hat die Verantwortung auf sich genommen, zu ...

In cases where a prepositional object is optional its translation is covered under *vi* or *vt*.

In Fällen, wo ein Präpositionalobjekt möglich, aber nicht nötig ist, findet man die entsprechende Übersetzung unter *vi* oder *vt*.

♦ **get off** *vi (from bus, train etc)* aussteigen *(prep obj* aus*)*; *(from bicycle, horse)* absteigen *(prep obj* von*)*.
♦ **go down** *vi* hinuntergehen *(prep obj acc)*.

For example:

Zum Beispiel:

he got off er stieg aus/ab
he got off the bus er stieg aus dem Bus aus
he got off his bicycle er stieg von seinem Fahrrad ab
she went down sie ging hinunter
she went down the street sie ging die Straße hinunter

8.1 Punctuation and Symbols

, between translations indicates that the translations are interchangeable; between source language phrases indicates that the phrases have the same meaning.

; between translations indicates a difference in meaning which is clarified by indicating material unless:
(**a**) the distinction has already been made within the same entry;
(**b**) the distinction is self-evident.

: between a headword and a phrase indicates that the headword is normally only used in that phrase.

~ is used within an entry to represent the headword whenever it occurs in an unchanged form.
In German headwords of the form **Reisende(r)** *mf decl as adj*, and **höchste(r, s)** *adj* it only replaces the element outside the bracket.
In German compound blocks it represents the compound element exactly as given at the beginning of the block. If it is given with a capital, any occurrence in a compound or phrase where it requires a small letter is clearly shown eg **Wochen-**: ...; **w~lang** *adj, adv* ...

— separates two speakers.

≃ indicates that the translation is the cultural equivalent of the term and may not be exactly the same in every detail.

* after a German verb indicates that the past participle is formed without *ge-*.

also, auch used after indicating material denotes that the translation(s) following it can be used in addition to the first translation given in the respective entry, category or phrase.

8.1 Satzzeichen und Symbole

, zwischen Übersetzungen zeigt an, daß die Übersetzungen gleichwertig sind;
zwischen Wendungen in der Ausgangssprache zeigt an, daß die Wendungen die gleiche Bedeutung haben.

; zwischen Übersetzungen zeigt einen Bedeutungsunterschied an, der durch erklärende Zusätze erläutert ist, außer:
(**a**) wenn die Unterscheidung innerhalb desselben Eintrags schon gemacht worden ist;
(**b**) wenn die Unterscheidung offensichtlich ist.

: zwischen Stichwort und Wendung gibt an, daß das Stichwort im allgemeinen nur in der aufgeführten Wendung vorkommt.

~ wird innerhalb von Einträgen verwendet, um das unveränderte Stichwort zu ersetzen.
Bei deutschen Stichwörtern des Typs **Reisende(r)** *mf decl as adj* und **höchste(r, s)** *adj* ersetzt der Strich den außerhalb der Klammer stehenden Teil des Wortes.
In deutschen Komposita-Blöcken ersetzt der Strich den Bestandteil der Zusammensetzung genau, wie er am Kopf des Blocks erscheint. Soll von Großschreibung auf Kleinschreibung übergegangen werden, ist dies angegeben, z.B. **Wochen-**: ...; **w~lang** *adj, adv* ...

— unterscheidet zwischen zwei Sprechern.

≃ weist darauf hin, daß die Übersetzung eine Entsprechung ist, die auf Grund kultureller Unterschiede nicht in allen Aspekten deckungsgleich ist.

* nach einem deutschen Verb gibt an, daß das 2. Partizip ohne *ge-* gebildet wird.

also, auch nach erklärenden Zusätzen gibt an, daß die folgende(n) Übersetzung(en) zusätzlich zu der ersten Übersetzung, die in dem Eintrag oder der Kategorie angegeben ist, benutzt werden kann/können.

Phonetic Symbols Zeichen der Lautschrift

Vowels/Vokale

matt	[a]	
Fahne	[aː]	
Vater	[ɐ]	
	[ɑː]	calm, part
	[æ]	sat
	[ɒ]	cot
Chanson	[ã]	
Chance	[ãː]	
	[ɑ̃ː]	double entendre
Etage	[e]	egg
Seele,Mehl	[eː]	
Wäsche, Bett	[ɛ]	
zählen	[ɛː]	
Teint	[ɛ̃ː]	
mache	[ə]	above
	[ɜː]	burn, earn
Kiste	[ɪ]	pit, awfully
Vitamin	[i]	
Ziel	[iː]	peat
Oase	[o]	
oben	[oː]	
Fondue	[õ]	
Chanson	[õː]	
Most	[ɔ]	
	[ɔː]	born
ökonomisch	[ø]	
blöd	[øː]	
Götter	[œ]	
Parfum	[œ̃ː]	
zuletzt	[u]	
Mut	[uː]	pool
Mutter	[ʊ]	put
Typ	[y]	
Kübel	[yː]	
Sünde	[ʏ]	

Diphthongs/Diphthonge

weit	[ai]	
	[aɪ]	buy, die, my
Haus	[au]	
	[aʊ]	house, now
	[eɪ]	pay, mate
	[ɛə]	pair, mare
	[əʊ]	no, boat
	[ɪə]	mere, shear
Heu, Häuser	[ɔy]	
	[ɔɪ]	boy, coin
	[ʊə]	tour, poor

Consonants/Konsonanten

Ball	[b]	ball
mich	[ç]	
denn	[d]	den
fern	[f]	field
gern	[g]	good
Hand	[h]	hand
ja, Million	[j]	yet, million
Kind	[k]	kind
links, Pult	[l]	left, little
matt	[m]	mat
Nest	[n]	nest
lang	[ŋ]	long
Paar	[p]	put
rennen	[r]	run
fassen	[s]	sit
Stein, Schlag	[ʃ]	shall
Tafel	[t]	tab
	[θ]	thing
	[ð]	this
wer	[v]	very
	[w]	wet
Loch	[x]	loch
singen	[z]	pods, zip
genieren	[ʒ]	measure

Other signs/Andere Zeichen

|	glottal stop/Knacklaut
[ʳ]	[r] pronounced before a vowel/vor Vokal ausgesprochenes [r]
[ˈ]	main stress/Hauptton
[ˌ]	secondary stress/Nebenton

The Pronunciation of German

German pronunciation is largely regular, and a knowledge of the basic patterns is assumed.
A list of the symbols used is given on page xiii.

Stress

1. The stress and the length of the stressed vowel are shown for every German headword.
2. The stressed vowel is usually marked in the headword, either with a dot if it is a short vowel
 eg **sofọrt, Mạtte**
or a dash if it is a long vowel or diphthong
 eg **họchmütig, kaufen**

Glottal Stop

1. A glottal stop (*Knacklaut*) occurs at the beginning of any word starting with a vowel.
2. A glottal stop always occurs in compounds between the first and second elements when the second element begins with a vowel.
3. When a glottal stop occurs elsewhere it is marked by a hairline before the vowel
 eg **Be|ạmte(r)**

Vowel length

1. When phonetics are given for the headword a long vowel is indicated in the transcription by the length mark after it
 eg **Chemie** [çe'miː]
2. Where no phonetics are given a short stressed vowel is marked with a dot in the headword
 eg **Mụtter**
and a long stressed vowel is marked with a dash
 eg **Vạter**
3. Unstressed vowels are usually short; if not, phonetics are given for that vowel
 eg **Ạlmosen** [-oː-]

Diphthongs and double vowels

1. Where phonetics are not given, vowel combinations which represent a stressed diphthong or a stressed long vowel are marked with an unbroken dash in the headword
 eg **beiderlei, Haar, sieben**
2. *ie*
Stressed *ie* pronounced [iː] is marked by an unbroken line
 eg **sieben**
When the plural ending *-n* is added, the pronunciation changes to [-iːən]
 eg **Allegorie**, *pl* **Allegorien** [-iːən]
When *ie* occurs in an unstressed syllable the pronunciation of that syllable is given
 eg **Hortensie** [-iə]
3. *ee* is pronounced [eː]
When the plural ending *-n* is added, the change in pronunciation is shown
 eg **Allee** *f* **-n** [-eːən]

Consonants

Where a consonant is capable of more than one pronunciation the following rules have been assumed:

1. *v*
 (i) *v* is generally pronounced [f]
 eg **Vater** ['faːtɐ]
 Where this is not the case phonetics are given
 eg **Sklave** [sklaːvə]
 (ii) Words ending in *-iv* are pronounced [iːf] when undeclined, but when an ending is added the pronunciation changes to [iːv]
 eg **aktiv** [ak'tiːf]
 aktive (as in '**der aktive Sportler**') [ak'tiːvə]
2. *ng*
 (i) *ng* is generally pronounced [ŋ]
 eg **Finger** ['fɪŋɐ]
 Where this is not the case phonetics are given
 eg **Angora** [aŋ'goːra]
 (ii) In compound words where the first element ends in *-n* and the second element begins with *g-* the two sounds are pronounced individually
 eg **Eingang** ['aingaŋ]
 ungeheuer ['ʊngəhɔyɐ]
3. *tion* is always pronounced [-tsioːn] at the end of a word and [-tsion-] in the middle of a word
 eg **Nation** [na'tsioːn]
 national [natsio'naːl]
4. *st, sp*
 (i) Where *st* or *sp* occurs in the middle or at the end of a word the pronunciation is [st], [sp]
 eg **Fest** [fɛst], **Wespe** ['vɛspə]
 (ii) At the beginning of a word or at the beginning of the second element of a compound word the standard pronunciation is [ʃt] [ʃp].
 eg **Stand** [ʃtant], **sperren** ['ʃpɛrən]
 Abstand ['ap-ʃtant], **absperren** ['ap-ʃpɛrən]
5. *ch*
 (i) *ch* is pronounced [ç] after *ä-, e-, i-, ö-, ü-, y-, ai-, ei-, äu, eu-* and after consonants
 eg **ich** [ɪç], **Milch** [mɪlç]
 (ii) *ch* is pronounced [x] after *a-, o-, u-, au-*
 eg **doch** [dɔx], **Bauch** [baux]
 Phonetics are given for all words beginning with *ch.*
6. *ig* is pronounced [ɪç] at the end of a word.
 eg **König** ['køːnɪç]
When an ending beginning with a vowel is added, it is pronounced [ɪg]
 eg **Könige** ['køːnɪgə]
7. *h* is pronounced [h]
 (i) at the beginning of a word
 (ii) between vowels in interjections
 eg **oho** [o'hoː]
 (iii) in words such as **Ahorn** ['aːhɔrn] and **Uhu** ['uːhu].
It is mute in the middle and at the end of non-foreign words
 eg **leihen** ['laiən], **weh** [veː]
Where *h* is pronounced in words of foreign origin, this is shown in the text.
8. *th* is pronounced [t].
9. *qu* is pronounced [kv].
10. *z* is pronounced [ts].

Phonetics are given where these rules do not apply and for foreign words which do not follow the German pronunciation patterns.

Adjectives and Adverbs

Declension of German adjectives
Adjectives ending in *-abel, -ibel, -el* drop the *-e-* when declined.

miserabel **ein miserabler Stil**
eine miserable Handschrift
ein miserables Leben
heikel **ein heikler Fall**
eine heikle Frage
ein heikles Problem

Adjectives ending in *-er, -en* usually keep the *-e-* when declined, except:
(*a*) in language of an elevated style level
finster **seine finstren Züge**
(*b*) in adjectives of foreign origin
makaber **eine makabre Geschichte**
integer **ein integrer Beamter**

Adjectives ending in *-auer, -euer* usually drop the *-e-* when declined.
teuer **ein teures Geschenk**
sauer **saure Gurken**

Comparison of German adjectives and adverbs
Irregular comparative and superlative forms are given in the text, including those of adjectives and adverbs with the vowels *-a-, -o-, -u-* which take an umlaut.
hoch *adj comp* **höher**, *superl* **höchste(r, s)** *or (adv)* **am höchsten**

Where no forms are given in the text, the comparative and superlative are formed according to the following rules:
(*a*) Both adjectives and adverbs add *-er* for the comparative before the declensional endings.
schön – schöner
eine schöne Frau – eine schönere Frau
(*b*) Most adjectives add *-ste(r, s)* for the superlative.
schön – schönste(r, s)
ein schöner Tag – der schönste Tag
(*c*) Most adverbs form the superlative according to the following pattern.
schön – am schönsten
schnell – am schnellsten
(*d*) Adjectives and adverbs of one syllable or with the stress on the final syllable add *-e* before the superlative ending:
(i) always if they end in *-s, -ß, -st, -tz, -x, -z*
(ii) usually if they end in *-d, -t, -sch*
spitz *adj* **spitzeste(r, s)**
adv **am spitzesten**
gerecht *adj* **gerechteste(r, s)**
adv **am gerechtesten**
The same applies if they are used with a prefix or in compounds, regardless of where the stress falls.
unsanft *adj* **unsanfteste(r, s)**
adv **am unsanftesten**

Adjektive und Adverbien

Adverbialbildung im Englischen
(*a*) Die meisten Adjektive bilden das Adverb durch Anhängen von *-ly*:
strange -ly, odd -ly, beautiful -ly
(*b*) Adjektive, die auf Konsonant +*y* enden, wandeln das auslautende *-y* in *-i* um und erhalten dann die Endung *-ly*:
happy – happily
merry – merrily
(*c*) Adjektive, die auf *-ic* enden, bilden normalerweise das Adverb durch Anhängen von *-ally*:
scenic -ally
linguistic -ally

Steigerung der englischen Adjektive und Adverbien
Adjektive und Adverbien, deren Komparativ und Superlativ im allgemeinen durch Flexionsendungen gebildet werden, sind im Text durch *(+er)* bezeichnet, z.B.
young *adj (+er)*

Komparativ und Superlativ aller nicht durch *(+er)* bezeichneten Adjektive und Adverbien sind mit *more* und *most* zu bilden. Das gilt auch für alle auf *-ly* endenden Adverbien, z.B.
grateful more grateful most grateful
fully more fully most fully

Unregelmäßige Formen des Komparativs und Superlativs sind im Text angegeben, z.B.
bad *adj comp* **worse**, *superl* **worst**
well *adv comp* **better**, *superl* **best**

Die flektierten Formen des Komparativs und Superlativs werden nach folgenden Regeln gebildet:
(*a*) Die meisten Adjektive und Adverbien fügen *-er* zur Bildung des Komparativs und *-est* zur Bildung des Superlativs an:
small smaller smallest
(*b*) Bei auf Konsonant +*y* endenden Adjektiven und Adverbien wird das auslautende *-y* in *-i* umgewandelt, bevor die Endung *-er* bzw. *-est* angefügt wird:
happy happier happiest
(*c*) Mehrsilbige Adjektive auf *-ey* wandeln diese Endsilbe in *-ier, -iest* um:
homey homier homiest
(*d*) Bei Adjektiven und Adverbien, die auf stummes *-e* enden, entfällt dieser Auslaut:
brave braver bravest
(*e*) Bei Adjektiven und Adverbien, die auf *-ee* enden, entfällt das zweite *-e*:
free freer freest
(*f*) Adjektive und Adverbien, die auf einen Konsonanten nach einfachem betontem Vokal enden, verdoppeln den Konsonanten im Auslaut:
sad sadder saddest
Nach Doppelvokal wird der auslautende Konsonant nicht verdoppelt:
loud louder loudest

Regular German Noun Endings

The genitive and plural of a large number of German nouns is formed according to regular patterns. These patterns are:

nom		*gen*	*pl*
-ade	*f*	-ade	-aden
-ant	*m (wk)*	-anten	-anten
-anz	*f*	-anz	-anzen
-ar	*m*	-ars	-are
-är	*m*	-ärs	-äre
-at	*nt*	-at(e)s	-ate
-atte	*f*	-atte	-atten
-chen	*nt*	-chens	-chen
-ei	*f*	-ei	-eien
-elle	*f*	-elle	-ellen
-ent	*m (wk)*	-enten	-enten
-enz	*f*	-enz	-enzen
-esse	*f*	-esse	-essen
-ette	*f*	-ette	-etten
-eur	*m*	-eurs	-eure
-eurin	*f*	-eurin	-eurinnen
-euse	*f*	-euse	-eusen
-graph	*m (wk)*	-graphen	-graphen
-heit	*f*	-heit	-heiten
-ie	*f*	-ie	-ien
-ik	*f*	-ik	-iken
-in	*f*	-in	-innen
-ine	*f*	-ine	-inen
-ion	*f*	-ion	-ionen
-ist	*m (wk)*	-isten	-isten
-ium	*nt*	-iums	-ien
-ius	*m*	-ius	-iusse
-ive	*f*	-ive	-iven
-ivum	*nt*	-ivums	-iva
-keit	*f*	-keit	-keiten
-lein	*nt*	-leins	-lein
-ling	*m*	-lings	-linge
-ment	*nt*	-ments	-mente
-mus	*m*	-mus	-men
-nis	*f*	-nis	-nisse
-nis	*nt*	-nisses	-nisse
-nom	*m (wk)*	-nomen	-nomen
-oge	*m (wk)*	-ogen	-ogen
-or	*m*	-ors	-oren
-rich	*m*	-richs	-riche
-schaft	*f*	-schaft	-schaften
-sel	*nt*	-sels	-sel
-tät	*f*	-tät	-täten
-tiv	*nt, m*	-tivs	-tive
-tum	*nt*	-tums	-tümer
-ung	*f*	-ung	-ungen
-ur	*f*	-ur	-uren

On the German-English side of the dictionary we have not shown plural endings where these regular patterns apply. All other plural endings are shown in the entry

Fang *m* **¨e**
Norm *f* **-en**

Genitive endings are formed

for masculine and neuter nouns by adding *-s* or *-es*

der Mann: *(gen)* **des Mann(e)s**
das Rad: *(gen)* **des Rad(e)s**

for feminine nouns: no change

die Frau: *(gen)* **der Frau**

Masculine or neuter nouns ending in *-s*, *-ß*, *-x* and *-z* always take the full form of *-es* for the genitive

das Glas: *(gen)* **des Glases**
das Maß: *(gen)* **des Maßes**
der Komplex: *(gen)* **des Komplexes**
der Geiz: *(gen)* **des Geizes**

Masculine or neuter nouns ending in *-sch* or *-st* normally take the full form of *-es*, as do those ending in a double consonant

der Wunsch: *(gen)* **des Wunsches**
der Gast: *(gen)* **des Gastes**
das Feld: *(gen)* **des Feldes**
der Kampf: *(gen)* **des Kampfes**

Masculine or neuter nouns ending in *-en*, *-em*, *-el*, *-er* and *-ling* always take the short form of *-s*

der Regen: *(gen)* **des Regens**
der Atem: *(gen)* **des Atems**
der Mantel: *(gen)* **des Mantels**
der Sänger: *(gen)* **des Sängers**
der Flüchtling: *(gen)* **des Flüchtlings**

Masculine or neuter nouns ending in *-ß* preceded by a short vowel will change the *ß* to *ss*

der Fluß: *(gen)* **des Flusses**

If the genitive is not formed according to these patterns it will be shown in the entry after the gender and before the plural ending

Herz *nt* **-ens, en**
Klerus *m* **-,** *no pl*

If only one ending is given this will be the plural, unless otherwise indicated.

Weak nouns

Weak nouns (marked as *wk*) have the same *-en* ending in the accusative, genitive and dative cases in both singular and plural forms

der Mensch: *(acc)* **den Menschen**
(gen) **des Menschen**
(dat) **dem Menschen**

Abbreviations Abkürzungen

Abkürzung	*abbr*	abbreviation
Akkusativ	*acc*	accusative
Adjektiv	*adj*	adjective
Verwaltung	*Admin*	administration
Adverb	*adv*	adverb
Landwirtschaft	*Agr*	agriculture
Anatomie	*Anat*	anatomy
Archäologie	*Archeol*	arch(a)eology
Architektur	*Archit*	architecture
Artikel	*art*	article
Kunst	*Art*	art
Astrologie	*Astrol*	astrology
Astronomie	*Astron*	astronomy
attributiv	*attr*	attributive
österreichisch	*Aus*	Austrian
australisch	*Austral*	Australian
Kraftfahrzeugwesen	*Aut*	automobiles
Hilfsverb	*aux*	auxiliary
Luftfahrt	*Aviat*	aviation
Kindersprache	*baby-talk*	
biblisch	*Bibl*	biblical
Biologie	*Biol*	biology
Botanik	*Bot*	botany
Bundesrepublik Deutschland	*BRD*	Federal Republic of Germany
britisch	*Brit*	British
Hoch- und Tiefbau	*Build*	building
Kartenspiel	*Cards*	
Chemie	*Chem*	chemistry
Schach	*Chess*	
umgangssprachlich	*col*	colloquial
derb	*col!*	potentially offensive
anstößig	*col!!*	highly offensive
Handel	*Comm*	commerce
Komparativ	*comp*	comparative
Computer	*Comp*	computers
Konjunktion	*conj*	conjunction
Zusammenziehung	*contr*	contraction
Kochen	*Cook*	cooking
Kompositum	*cpd*	compound
Dativ	*dat*	dative
altmodisch	*dated*	
Deutsche Demokratische Republik	*DDR*	German Democratic Republic
dekliniert	*decl*	declined
bestimmt	*def*	definite
demonstrativ	*dem*	demonstrative
Dialekt	*dial*	dialect
Verkleinerung	*dim*	diminutive
Akkusativobjekt	*dir obj*	direct object
kirchlich	*Eccl*	ecclesiastical
Volkswirtschaft	*Econ*	economics
Elektrizität	*Elec*	electricity
betont	*emph*	emphatic
besonders	*esp*	especially

etwas	*etw*	something
Euphemismus	*euph*	euphemism
Femininum	*f*	feminine
Mode	*Fashion*	
übertragen	*fig*	figurative
Finanzen	*Fin*	finance
Fischerei	*Fishing*	
Forstwesen	*Forest*	forestry
förmlich	*form*	formal
Fußball	*Ftbl*	football
gehoben	*geh*	elevated
Genitiv	*gen*	genitive
Geographie	*Geog*	geography
Geologie	*Geol*	geology
Grammatik	*Gram*	grammar
Heraldik	*Her*	heraldry
Geschichte	*Hist*	history
Gartenbau	*Hort*	horticulture
scherzhaft	*hum*	humorous
Jagd	*Hunt*	hunting
Imperativ	*imper*	imperative
unpersönlich	*impers*	impersonal
Industrie	*Ind*	industry
unbestimmt	*indef*	indefinite
Dativobjekt	*indir obj*	indirect object
Infinitiv	*infin*	infinitive
untrennbar	*insep*	inseparable
Versicherungswesen	*Insur*	insurance
Interjektion	*interj*	interjection
interrogativ	*interrog*	interrogative
unveränderlich	*inv*	invariable
irisch	*Ir*	Irish
ironisch	*iro*	ironical
unregelmäßig	*irreg*	irregular
jemand, jemandes, jemandem, jemanden	*jd, jds jdm, jdn*	somebody, somebody's
Rechtswesen	*Jur*	law
Sprachwissenschaft	*Ling*	linguistics
wörtlich	*lit*	literal
literarisch	*liter*	literary
Literatur	*Liter*	literature
Maskulinum	*m*	masculine
Mathematik	*Math*	mathematics
Maß	*Measure*	
Mechanik	*Mech*	mechanics
Medizin	*Med*	medicine
Meteorologie	*Met*	meteorology
Metallurgie	*Metal*	metallurgy
militärisch	*Mil*	military
Bergbau	*Min*	mining
Mineralogie	*Miner*	mineralogy
Straßenverkehr	*Mot*	motoring and transport
Musik	*Mus*	music
Mythologie	*Myth*	mythology
Substantiv	*n*	noun
nautisch	*Naut*	nautical
verneint	*neg*	negative
nordenglisch	*N Engl*	Northern English

norddeutsch	*N Ger*	North German
Nationalsozialismus	*NS*	Nazism
Neutrum	*nt*	neuter
Zahlwort	*num*	numeral
Objekt	*obj*	object
obsolet	*obs*	obsolete
veraltet	*old*	
Optik	*Opt*	optics
Vogelkunde	*Orn*	ornithology
Parlament	*Parl*	parliament
Passiv	*pass*	passive
pejorativ	*pej*	pejorative
persönlich/Person	*pers*	personal/person
Pharmazie	*Pharm*	pharmacy
Philosophie	*Philos*	philosophy
Phonetik	*Phon*	phonetics
Fotografie	*Phot*	photography
Physik	*Phys*	physics
Physiologie	*Physiol*	physiology
Plural	*pl*	plural
poetisch	*poet*	poetic
Dichtung	*Poet*	poetry
Politik	*Pol*	politics
Possessiv-	*poss*	possessive
prädikativ	*pred*	predicative
Vorsilbe	*pref*	prefix
Präposition	*prep*	preposition
Präsens	*pres*	present
Presse	*Press*	
Präteritum, Imperfekt	*pret*	preterite, imperfect
Pronomen	*pron*	pronoun
sprichwörtlich	*prov*	proverbial
Sprichwort	*Prov*	proverb
Partizip Präsens	*prp*	present participle
Psychologie	*Psych*	psychology
Partizip Perfekt	*ptp*	past participle
Warenzeichen	®	trademark
Rundfunk	*Rad*	radio
Eisenbahn	*Rail*	railways
selten	*rare*	
regelmäßig	*reg*	regular
Relativ-	*rel*	relative
Religion	*Rel*	religion
jemand(em, -en)	*sb*	somebody
Schulwesen	*Sch*	school
Naturwissenschaften	*Sci*	science
schottisch	*Scot*	Scottish
Bildhauerei	*Sculpt*	sculpture
trennbar, veränderbare Folge	*sep*	separable
Handarbeiten	*Sew*	sewing
süddeutsch	*S Ger*	South German
Singular	*sing*	singular
Skisport	*Ski*	skiing
Slang, Jargon	*sl*	slang
Sozialwissenschaften	*Sociol*	social sciences
Raumfahrt	*Space*	space flight
Fachausdruck	*spec*	specialist term
Börse	*St Ex*	Stock Exchange
etwas	*sth*	something
Konjunktiv	*subjunc*	subjunctive
Nachsilbe	*suf*	suffix
Superlativ	*superl*	superlative
Landvermessung	*Surv*	surveying
schweizerisch	*Sw*	Swiss
Technik	*Tech*	technology
Nachrichtentechnik	*Telec*	telecommunications
Textilien	*Tex*	textiles
Theater	*Theat*	theatre, theater
Fernsehen	*TV*	television
Typographie, Buchdruck	*Typ*	typography and printing
Hochschule	*Univ*	university
(nord)amerikanisch	*US*	(North) American
gewöhnlich	*usu*	usually
Verb	*vb*	verb
Tiermedizin	*Vet*	veterinary medicine
intransitives Verb	*vi*	intransitive verb
reflexives Verb	*vr*	reflexive verb
transitives Verb	*vt*	transitive verb
schwache Deklination	*wk*	weak declension
Zoologie	*Zool*	zoology
ptp ohne ge-	*	ptp without ge-

Trademarks

Words which we have reason to believe constitute registered trademarks are designated as such. However, neither the presence nor the absence of such designation should be regarded as affecting the legal status of any trademark.

Warenzeichen

Wörter, die unseres Wissens eingetragene Warenzeichen darstellen, sind als solche gekennzeichnet. Es ist jedoch zu beachten, daß weder das Vorhandensein noch das Fehlen derartiger Kennzeichnungen die Rechtslage hinsichtlich eingetragener Warenzeichen berührt.

A

A, a [aː] *nt* **-, -** A, a. **das A und O** the be-all and end-all; *(eines Wissensgebietes)* the basics *pl*; **von A bis Z** *(fig col)* from beginning to end; **wer A sagt, muß auch B sagen** *(prov)* in for a penny, in for a pound *(prov)*.

à [a] *prep (esp Comm)* at.

Aal *m* **-e** eel. **sich winden wie ein ~** to wriggle like an eel.

aalen *vr (col)* to stretch out. **sich in der Sonne ~** to bask in the sun.

aalglatt *adj (pej)* slippery (as an eel), slick.

Aas *nt* **-e (a)** *(Tierleiche)* carrion, rotting carcass. **(b)** *pl* **Äser** *(col: Luder)* bugger *(col!)*. **kein ~** not a single bloody person *(col)*.

aasen *vi (col)* to be wasteful. **mit etw ~** to waste sth.

Aasgeier *m (lit, fig)* vulture.

ab [ap] **1** *prep +dat (räumlich)* from; *(zeitlich auch)* as of. **Kinder ~ 14 Jahren** children from (the age of) 14; **Soldaten ~ Gefreitem** soldiers from private up; **~ Werk** *(Comm)* ex works; **~ sofort** as of now/then. **2** *adv* off. **die nächste Straße rechts ~** the next street off to the right; **München ~ 12^{20} Uhr** *(Rail)* leaving Munich 12.20; **~ wann?** from when?, as of when?; **~ nach Hause** off you go home; **~ ins Bett mit euch!** off to bed with you; **Tell ~** *(Theat)* exit Tell; **N und M ~** *(Theat)* exeunt N and M; **~ durch die Mitte!** *(col)* beat it! *(col)*, hop it! *(col)*; **~ und zu** from time to time, now and then.

ab|ändern *vt sep* to alter *(in +acc* to*)*; *Gesetzentwurf* to amend *(in+acc* to*)*; *Strafe, Urteil* to revise *(in+acc* to*)*.

Ab|änderung *f siehe vt* alteration *(gen* to*)*; *(Parl, Jur)* amendment; revision.

Ab|änderungsantrag *m (Parl)* proposed amendment. **einen ~ einbringen** to submit an amendment.

ab|arbeiten *sep* **1** *vt Schuld* to work off. **2** *vr* to slave (away).

Ab|art *f* variety *(auch Biol)*; *(Variation)* variation *(gen* on*)*.

ab|artig *adj* abnormal, deviant.

Abbau *m no pl* **(a)** *(von Personal, Produktion etc)* reduction *(gen* in, of*)*, cutback *(gen* in*)*. **(b)** *(von Kohlen etc)* mining. **(c)** *(Chem)* decomposition. **(d)** *(lit, fig: Demontage)* dismantling.

abbauen *sep* **1** *vt* **(a)** *(demontieren) Gerüst, System* to dismantle; *Gerüst auch, Zelt* to take down; *Lager* to break, to strike. **(b)** *(verringern) Produktion, Personal, Bürokratie* to cut back, to reduce. **Arbeitsplätze ~** to make job cuts. **(c)** *Kohle etc* to mine. **(d)** *(Chem)* to break down, to decompose. **2** *vi (col: erlahmen)* to flag, to wilt.

abbeißen *sep irreg* **1** *vt* to bite off. **2** *vi* to take a bite.

abbekommen* *vt sep irreg* to get. **etwas ~** to get some (of it); *(beschädigt werden)* to get damaged; *(verletzt werden)* to get hurt; **das Auto/er hat dabei ganz schön was ~** *(col)* the car/he really copped it *(col)*; **nichts ~** not to get any (of it); *(nicht beschädigt werden)* not to get damaged; *(nicht verletzt werden)* to come off unscathed; **sein(en) Teil ~** *(lit, fig)* to get one's fair share.

abberufen* *vt sep irreg Diplomaten etc* to recall.

Abberufung *f* recall.

abbestellen* *vt sep* to cancel; *jdn* to put off.

Abbestellung *f* cancellation.

abbezahlen* *vt sep Raten, Auto etc* to pay off.

abbiegen *sep irreg* **1** *vt* **(a)** to bend; *(abbrechen)* to bend off. **(b)** *(col: verhindern) Frage, Thema* to head off, to avoid. **das Gespräch ~** to change the subject; **zum Glück konnte ich das ~** luckily I managed to stop that. **2** *vi aux sein* to turn off *(in +acc* into*)*; *(Straße)* to bend. **nach rechts ~** to turn (off to the) right.

Abbild *nt (Kopie)* copy, reproduction; *(Spiegelbild)* reflection; *(Wiedergabe)* picture, portrayal. **er ist das genaue ~ seines Vaters** he's the spitting image of his father.

abbilden *vt sep (lit, fig)* to depict, to portray; *(wiedergeben)* to reproduce.

Abbildung *f* **(a)** *(Illustration)* illustration; *(Schaubild)* diagram. **(b)** *(Wiedergabe)* reproduction.

abbinden *vt sep irreg* **(a)** *(losbinden)* to undo, to untie. **(b)** *(Med) Arm, Bein etc* to ligature.

Abbitte *f* apology. **(bei jdm wegen etw) ~ tun** to make *or* offer one's apologies (to sb for sth).

abblasen *vt sep irreg* **(a) eine Hauswand mit Sandstrahl ~** to sandblast a house wall. **(b)** *(col) Veranstaltung, Feier, Streik* to call off.

abblättern *vi sep aux sein (Putz, Farbe)* to flake (off).

abblenden *vt sep Lampe* to shade, to screen; *Scheinwerfer* to dip *(Brit)*, to dim *(US)*.

Abblendlicht *nt (Aut)* dipped *(Brit) or* dimmed *(US)* headlights *pl*.

abblitzen *vi sep aux sein (col)* to be sent packing *(bei* by*) (col)*. **jdn ~ lassen** to send sb packing.

abblocken *vt sep (Sport, fig)* to block.

abbrausen *vt sep* to give a shower. **sich ~** to have *or* take a shower.

abbrechen *sep irreg* **1** *vt* **(a)** to break off. **etw von etw ~** to break sth off sth; **sich** *(dat)* **einen ~** *(col) (Umstände machen)* to make heavy weather of it *(col)*; *(sich sehr anstrengen)* to bust a gut *(col)*. **(b)** *Zelt* to take down; *Lager* to strike; *(niederreißen)* to demolish, to pull down. **(c)** *(beenden)* to break off; *Streik* to call off. **2** *vi* **(a)** *aux sein* to break off; *(Bleistift, Fingernagel)* to break. **(b)** *(aufhören)* to break off, to stop.

abbremsen *vt sep Motor* to brake; *(fig)* to curb.

abbrennen *sep irreg* **1** *vt Gehöft, Dorf* to burn down; *Feuerwerk, Rakete* to let off; *Kerze etc* to burn. **ein Feuerwerk ~** to have a fireworks display. **2** *vi aux sein* to burn down.

abbringen *vt sep irreg* **jdn davon ~, etw zu tun** to stop sb doing sth; *(abraten auch)* to persuade sb not to do sth; **jdn von etw ~** to make sb change his/her mind about sth; **jdn vom Rauchen ~** to get sb to stop smoking.

abbröckeln *vi sep aux sein* to crumble away; *(fig)* to fall off. **der Ruf der Firma ist am A~** the firm's reputation is gradually declining.

Abbruch *m no pl* **(a)** *(das Niederreißen)* demolition. **(b)** *(Beendigung)* breaking off; *(von Veranstaltung etc)* stopping. **es kam zum ~ des Kampfes** the fight had to be stopped. **(c)** *(Schaden)* harm, damage. **einer Sache** *(dat)* **~ tun** to do (some) harm *or* damage to sth.

Abbruch-: ~arbeiten *pl* demolition work; **a~reif** *adj* only fit for demolition; **~unternehmer** *m*

demolition contractor.
abbrühen *vt sep* to scald; *siehe* **abgebrüht.**
abbuchen *vt sep (im Einzelfall)* to debit *(von* to, against*)*; *(durch Dauerauftrag)* to pay by standing order *(von* from*)*.
Abbuchung *f siehe vt* debit; (payment by) standing order.
abbürsten *vt sep Staub* to brush off *(von etw* sth*)*; *Schuhe* to brush.
abbüßen *vt sep Strafe* to serve.
Abc [aːbeːˈtseː] *nt* **-, -** *(lit, fig)* ABC. **Namen nach dem ~ ordnen** to put names in alphabetical order.
abchecken [ˈaptʃɛkn] *vt sep* to check.
Abc-Schütze *m (hum)* school-beginner.
ABC-Waffen *pl* atomic, biological and chemical weapons.
Abdampf *m* exhaust steam.
abdampfen *vi sep aux sein (fig col: losgehen, -fahren)* to hit the road *(col)*.
abdanken *vi sep* to resign; *(König etc)* to abdicate.
Abdankung *f (Thronverzicht)* abdication; *(Rücktritt)* resignation.
abdecken *vt sep* **(a)** *(freilegen) Tisch* to clear; *Bett* to turn down; *Haus* to tear the roof off. **(b)** *(zudecken) Grab, Loch* to cover (over). **(c)** *(ausgleichen, einschließen)* to cover.
Abdeckung *f* cover.
abdichten *vt sep (isolieren)* to insulate; *Loch, Leck, Rohr* to seal (up); *Ritzen* to stop up. **gegen Luft/Wasser ~** to make airtight/watertight.
Abdichtung *f (Isolierung)* insulation; *(Verschluß, Dichtung)* seal.
abdienen *vt sep (Mil: ableisten)* to serve.
abdrängen *vt sep* to push away *(von* from*)*. **einen Spieler vom Ball ~** to push a player off the ball.
abdrehen *sep* **1** *vt* **(a)** *Gas, Wasser, Hahn* to turn off; *Licht, Radio auch* to switch off. **(b)** *Film* to shoot, to film. **(c)** *Hals* to wring. **jdm den Hals ~** to wring sb's neck *(col)*; *(col: ruinieren)* to bankrupt sb. **2** *vi aux sein or haben (Richtung ändern)* to change course. **nach Osten ~** to turn east.
abdriften *vi sep aux sein* to drift (away).
abdrosseln *vt sep Motor* to throttle down; *(fig) Produktion* to cut down (on).
Abdruck[1] *m, pl* **Abdrücke** imprint, impression; *(Stempel~)* stamp; *(Finger~, Fuß~)* print. **einen ~ machen** to take *or* make an impression.
Abdruck[2] *m* **-e** *(Kopie)* copy; *(Nachdruck)* reprint.
abdrucken *vt sep* to print. **wieder ~** to reprint.
abdrücken *sep* **1** *vt* **(a)** *Gewehr* to fire. **(b)** *Vene* to constrict. **jdm die Luft ~** *(col) (lit)* to squeeze all the breath out of sb; *(fig)* to force sb into bankruptcy, to squeeze the lifeblood out of sb. **2** *vi* to pull *or* squeeze the trigger.
abdunkeln *vt sep Lampe* to dim; *Zimmer auch* to darken.
abduschen *vt sep siehe* **abbrausen.**
ab|ebben *vi sep aux sein* to die *or* fade away.
Abend *m* **-e** evening. **am ~** in the evening; *(jeden ~)* in the evening(s); **am ~ des 4. April** on the evening *or* night of April 4th; **gegen ~** towards (the) evening; **~ für ~** every evening *or* night, night after night; **eines ~s** one evening; **den ganzen ~ (über)** the whole evening; **guten ~** good evening; **letzten ~** yesterday evening, last night; **zu ~ essen** *(geh)* to have supper *or* dinner, to dine *(form)*; **je später der ~, desto schöner** *or* **netter die Gäste** *(prov)* the best guests always come late; **man soll den Tag nicht vor dem ~ loben** *(Prov)* don't count your chickens before they're hatched *(Prov)*.
abend *adv* **gestern/morgen/Mittwoch ~** yesterday/tomorrow/Wednesday evening, last/tomorrow/Wednesday night.
Abend- **~andacht** *f* evening service; **~anzug** *m* dinner jacket, DJ *(col)*, tuxedo *(US)*; **~brot** *nt* supper; **~brot essen** to have (one's) supper; **~dämmerung** *f* dusk, twilight; **~essen** *nt* supper, evening meal, dinner; **mit dem ~essen auf jdn warten** to wait supper *or* dinner for sb; **a~füllend** *adj* taking up the whole evening; *Film, Stück* full-length; **~gymnasium** *nt* night school; **~kasse** *f (Theat)* box office; **~kleid** *nt* evening dress *or* gown; **~kleidung** *f* evening dress *no pl*; **~kurs(us)** *m* evening classes *pl (für* in*)*; **~land** *nt no pl (geh)* West, western world; **a~ländisch** *(geh) adj* western, occidental *(liter)*.
abendlich *adj no pred* evening *attr*. **die ~e Stille** the quiet of the evening; **es war schon um drei Uhr ~ kühl** at three it was already as cool as in the evening.
Abend-: **~mahl** *nt (Eccl)* (Holy) Communion; **~mahlzeit** *f* evening meal; **~programm** *nt (Rad, TV)* evening('s) programmes *(Brit) or* programs *(US) pl*; **~rot** *nt* sunset.
abends *adv* in the evening; *(jeden Abend)* in the evening(s). **spät ~** late in the evening; **~ um neun** at nine in the evening.
Abend-: **~schule** *f* night school; **~schüler** *m* night-school student; **~stern** *m* evening star; **~stunde** *f* evening (hour); **sich bis in die ~stunden hinziehen** to go on (late) into the evening; **~vorstellung** *f* evening performance; **~zeitung** *f* evening paper.
Abenteuer *nt* **-** adventure; *(Liebes~ auch)* affair. **ein militärisches ~** a military venture; **auf ~ aussein** to be looking for adventure.
abenteuerlich *adj* **(a)** adventurous; *(erlebnishungrig auch)* adventuresome. **(b)** *(phantastisch)* bizarre; *Erzählung auch* fantastic.
Abenteuer-: **~lust** *f* thirst for adventure; **~roman** *m* adventure story; **~spielplatz** *m* adventure playground.
Abenteurer *m* **-** adventurer *(auch pej)*.
Abenteu(r)erin *f* adventuress.
aber **1** *conj* **(a)** but. **~ dennoch** *or* **trotzdem** but still; **schönes Wetter heute, was? — ja, ~ etwas kalt** nice weather, eh? — yes, a bit cold though; **da er ~ nicht wußte ...** however, since he didn't know ...; **oder ~** or else. **(b)** *(zur Verstärkung)* **~ ja!** oh, yes!; *(sicher)* but of course; **~ selbstverständlich!** but of course; **~ nein!** oh, no!; *(selbstverständlich nicht)* of course not!; **~ Renate!** but Renate!; **~, ~!** tut, tut!; **das ist ~ schrecklich!** but that's awful!; **das mach' ich ~ nicht!** I will *not* do that!; **das ist ~ heiß/schön!** that's really hot/nice; **du hast ~ einen schönen Ball** you've got a nice ball, haven't you?; **bist du ~ braun!** aren't you brown!; **das geht ~ zu weit!** that's really going too far!
2 *adv (liter)* **tausend und ~ tausend** thousands upon thousands.
Aber *nt* **-** *or (col)* **-s** but. **kein ~!** no buts (about it); **die Sache hat ein ~** there's just one snag.
Aberglaube(n) *m* superstition; *(fig auch)* myth.
abergläubisch *adj* superstitious.
Aberhunderte *pl* hundreds upon hundreds *pl*.
ab|erkennen* *vt sep or (rare) insep irreg* **jdm etw ~** to strip sb of sth.
Ab|erkennung *f* deprivation, stripping.
aber-: **~malig** *adj attr* repeated; **~mals** *adv* once more.
ab|ernten *vti sep* to harvest.
Abertausende *pl* thousands upon thousands *pl*.
aberwitzig *adj (liter) siehe* **wahnwitzig.**
abfackeln *vt Erdgas* to burn off.
abfahrbereit *adj* ready to leave.
abfahren *sep irreg aux sein* **1** *vi* **(a)** to leave, to depart *(form)*; *(Schiff auch)* to sail. **der Zug fährt um 8^{00} von Bremen ab** the train leaves Bremen at 8 o'clock; **der Zug ist abgefahren** *(lit)* the train has left; *(fig)* we've/you've *etc* missed the boat. **(b)** *(col: abgewiesen werden)* **jdn ~ lassen** to tell sb to get lost *(col)*.
2 *vt* **(a)** *Stück von Mauer etc* to knock off. **der**

Trecker hat ihm ein Bein abgefahren the tractor severed his leg. **(b)** *aux sein or haben Strecke (bereisen)* to cover; *(Polizei etc)* to patrol. **wir mußten die ganze Strecke noch einmal ~, um ... zu suchen** we had to go over the whole stretch again to look for ... **(c)** *(abnutzen)* to wear out; *Reifen auch* to wear down; *(benutzen) Fahrkarte* to use. **abgefahrene Reifen/Schienen** worn tyres/ rails. **(d)** *(Film, TV) Kamera* to roll; *Film* to start. **bitte ~!** roll 'em!

3 *vr (Reifen etc)* to wear down.

Ạbfahrt *f* **(a)** *(von Zug, Bus etc)* departure. **bis zur ~ sind es noch fünf Minuten** there's still five minutes before the train/bus goes; **Vorsicht bei der ~ des Zuges!** stand clear, the train is about to leave! **(b)** *(Ski) (Talfahrt)* descent; *(~sstrecke)* (ski-)run. **(c)** *(Autobahn~)* exit. **die ~ Gießen** the exit for Gießen.

Ạbfahrts-: **~lauf** *m (Ski)* downhill; **~zeit** *f* departure time.

Ạbfall *m, pl* **Abfälle (a)** waste; *(Haus~)* rubbish, garbage *(esp US)*; *(Straßen~)* litter *(Brit)*, trash *(US)*. **(b)** *no pl (Lossagung)* break *(von* with*)*. **(c)** *no pl (Rückgang)* drop *(gen* in*)*, fall *(gen in)*; *(Verschlechterung auch)* deterioration.

Ạbfall-: **~beseitigung** *f* refuse *or* garbage *(US)* disposal; **~eimer** *m* rubbish bin, trashcan *(US)*.

ạbfallen *vi sep irreg aux sein* **(a)** *(herunterfallen)* to fall *or* drop off; *(Blätter, Blüten etc)* to fall. **(b)** *(col: herausspringen)* **wieviel fällt bei dem Geschäft für mich ab?** how much do I get out of the deal? **(c)** *(fig: übrigbleiben)* to be left (over). **(d)** *(schlechter werden)* to go downhill; *(Sport: zurückbleiben)* to drop back. **(e) alle Unsicherheit/ Furcht fiel von ihm ab** all his uncertainty/fear left him. **(f)** *(Fraktion: von Partei etc)* to break away *(von* from*)*. **vom Glauben ~** to leave the faith. **(g)** *(sich senken: Gelände)* to fall away; *(sich vermindern: Druck, Temperatur)* to fall.

ạbfällig *adj Bemerkung, Kritik* disparaging; *Lächeln* derisive; *Urteil* adverse. **über jdn ~ reden/ sprechen** to be disparaging about sb.

Ạbfall-: **~produkt** *nt (lit, fig)* waste-product; **~verwertung** *f* waste utilization.

ạbfälschen *vti sep (Sport)* to deflect.

ạbfangen *vt sep irreg* **(a)** *Flugzeug, Funkspruch, Brief, Ball* to intercept; *Menschen auch* to catch *(col)*; *Schlag* to block; *(col: anlocken) Kunden* to lure away. **(b)** *(bremsen) Fahrzeug* to bring under control; *Flugzeug auch* to pull out; *Aufprall* to absorb; *Trend* to check.

Ạbfangjäger *m (Mil)* interceptor.

ạbfärben *vi sep* **(a)** *(Wäsche)* to run. **paß auf, die Wand färbt ab!** be careful, the paint comes off the wall. **(b)** *(fig)* **auf jdn ~** to rub off on sb.

ạbfassen *vt sep (verfassen)* to write; *Entwurf* to draft.

ạbfaulen *vi sep aux sein* to rot away *or* off.

ạbfeiern *vt sep (col)* **Überstunden ~** to take time off in lieu of overtime pay.

ạbfertigen *sep* **1** *vt* **(a)** *(versandfertig machen) Pakete, Waren* to prepare for dispatch, to process; *Gepäck* to check (in); *(be- und entladen) Flugzeug* to make ready for take-off. **(b)** *(bedienen) Kunden etc* to attend to; *(col: Sport) Gegner* to deal with. **jdn kurz ~** *(col)* to snub sb. **2** *vti (kontrollieren) Waren, Reisende* to clear.

Ạbfertigung *f* **(a)** *siehe vt (a)* making ready for dispatch, processing *(form)*; checking; making ready for take-off. **(b)** *(~sstelle)* dispatch office. **(c)** *(Bedienung) (von Kunden)* service; *(von Antragstellern)* dealing with. **(d)** *(von Waren, Reisenden)* clearance. **die ~ an der Grenze** customs clearance.

ạbfeuern *vt sep* to fire.

ạbfinden *sep irreg* **1** *vt* to pay off; *Gläubiger auch* to settle with; *(entschädigen)* to compensate. **er wurde von der Versicherung mit 20.000 DM abgefunden** he was paid DM 20,000 (in) compensation by the insurance company; **jdn mit leeren Versprechungen ~** to fob sb off with empty promises. **2** *vr* **sich mit jdm/etw ~** to come to terms with sb/sth; **er konnte sich nie damit ~, daß ...** he could never accept the fact that ...

Ạbfindung *f (von Gläubigern)* paying off; *(Entschädigung)* compensation.

ạbflachen *sep* **1** *vt* to level (off), to flatten (out). **2** *vr (Land)* to flatten out. **3** *vi (fig: sinken)* to decline.

ạbflauen *vi sep aux sein* **(a)** *(Wind)* to die down. **nach (dem) A~ des Windes** when the wind had died down. **(b)** *(fig) (Erregung)* to die away; *(Interesse auch)* to wane; *(Börsenkurse)* to drop; *(Geschäfte, Konjunktur)* to fall off.

ạbfliegen *sep irreg* **1** *vi aux sein (Aviat)* to take off *(nach* for*)*; *(Zugvögel)* to migrate. **sie sind gestern nach München abgeflogen** they flew to Munich yesterday. **2** *vt Gelände* to fly over.

ạbfließen *vi sep irreg aux sein (wegfließen)* to drain *or* flow away; *(durch ein Leck)* to leak away. **ins Ausland ~** *(Geld)* to flow out of the country.

Ạbflug *m* take-off; *(von Zugvögeln)* migration.

ạbflugbereit *adj* ready for take-off.

Ạbfluß *m* **(a)** *(Abfließen)* draining away; *(durch ein Leck)* leakage. **dem ~ von Kapital ins Ausland Schranken setzen** to impose limits on the (out)flow of capital out of the country. **(b)** *(~stelle)* drain; *(von Teich etc)* outlet; *(~rohr)* drainpipe; *(von sanitären Anlagen)* wastepipe.

Ạbfluß-: **~rinne** *f* gutter; **~rohr** *nt* outlet; *(im Gebäude)* wastepipe; *(außen am Gebäude)* drainpipe; *(unterirdisch)* drain.

Ạbfolge *f (geh)* sequence, succession.

ạbfordern *vt sep* **jdm etw ~** to demand sth from sb.

ạbfragen *vt sep* **(a)** *(esp Sch)* **jdn etw ~** to question sb on sth; *(Lehrer)* to test sb orally on sth. **(b)** *(Comp)* to call up; *Datei* to interrogate.

ạbfrieren *sep irreg* **1** *vi aux sein* **ihm sind die Füße abgefroren** his feet got frostbite; **abgefroren sein** *(Körperteil)* to be frostbitten. **2** *vt* **sich** *(dat)* **einen ~** *(col)* to freeze to death *(col)*.

Ạbfuhr *f* **-en (a)** *no pl (Abtransport)* removal. **(b)** *(col: Zurückweisung)* snub, rebuff. **jdm eine ~ erteilen** to snub *or* rebuff sb; *(Sport)* to thrash sb *(col)*; **sich** *(dat)* **eine ~ holen** to meet with a snub.

ạbführen *sep* **1** *vt* **(a)** *(wegführen)* to lead away; *(ableiten) Gase etc* to draw off. **~!** away with him/her *etc*! **(b)** *(abgeben) Betrag* to pay *(an+acc* to*)*. **2** *vi* **(a)** *(wegführen)* **der Weg führt hier (von der Straße) ab** the path leaves the road here; **das würde vom Thema ~** that would take us off the subject. **(b)** *(den Darm anregen)* to have a laxative effect.

ạbführend *adj* laxative *no adv*. **~ wirken** to have a laxative effect.

Ạbführmittel *nt* laxative.

Ạbfüll-: **~anlage** *f* bottling plant; **~betrieb** *m* bottling factory.

ạbfüllen *vt sep* **(a)** *(in Flaschen)* to bottle; *Flasche* to fill. **Wein in Flaschen ~** to bottle wine. **(b) jdn ~** *(col)* to get sb pickled *(col) or* sloshed *(col)*.

Ạbgabe *f* **(a)** *no pl (Abliefern)* handing in; *(von Gepäck auch)* depositing; *(Übergabe: von Brief etc)* delivery. **zur ~ von etw aufgefordert werden** to be told to hand sth in. **(b)** *no pl (Verkauf)* sale. **(c)** *no pl (von Wärme etc)* giving off; *(von Schuß, Salve)* firing; *(von Erklärung etc)* giving; *(von Stimme)* casting. **(d)** *(Sport: Abspiel)* pass. **(e)** *(Steuer)* tax; *(auf Tabak etc auch)* duty; *(soziale ~)* contribution.

Ạbgabetermin *m* closing date; *(für Dissertation etc)* submission date.

Ạbgang *m no pl* **(a)** *(Absendung)* dispatch. **vor ~ der Post** before the post goes. **(b)** *(Abfahrt)* departure. **(c)** *(aus einem Amt)* departure; *(Schul~)* leaving. **seit seinem ~ vom Gymna-**

sium since he left the grammar school. **(d)** *(Theat, fig)* exit.

Abgangszeugnis *nt* leaving certificate.

Abgas *nt* exhaust *no pl*, exhaust fumes, waste gas *(esp Tech)*.

Abgas-: a~frei *adj Motor, Fahrzeug* exhaust-free; **a~frei verbrennen** to burn without producing exhaust; **~wolke** *f* cloud of exhaust.

abge|arbeitet *adj (verbraucht)* workworn; *(erschöpft)* exhausted.

abgeben *sep irreg* **1** *vt* **(a)** *(abliefern)* to hand in; *Gepäck* to deposit; *(übergeben)* to deliver; *(weggeben)* to give away; *(gegen Gebühr)* to sell; *(an einen anderen Inhaber)* to hand over; *(überlassen) Auftrag* to pass on *(an+acc* to*)*; *(abtreten) Posten* to hand over *(an+acc* to*)*. **Kinderwagen abzugeben** pram for sale; **jdm etw von seinem Kuchen ~** to give sb some of one's cake. **(b)** *(Sport) Punkte, Rang* to concede; *(abspielen)* to pass. **(c)** *Schuß, Salve* to fire; *Erklärung* to give; *Stimmen* to cast. **(d)** *Rahmen, Hintergrund, Stoff, Material etc* to provide; *(verkörpern)* to make. **den Vermittler ~** *(col)* to act as mediator. **2** *vr* **sich mit jdm/etw ~** *(sich beschäftigen)* to bother oneself with sb/sth; *(sich einlassen)* to associate with sb/sth. **3** *vi (Sport)* to pass.

abgebrannt *adj pred (col)* broke *(col)*.

abgebrochen *adj (nicht beendet) Studium* uncompleted. **er ist ~er Mediziner** *(col)* he broke off his medical studies.

abgebrüht *adj (col: skrupellos)* hard-boiled *(col)*, hardened.

abgedroschen *adj (col)* hackneyed, well-worn; *Witz auch* corny *(col)*. **eine ~e Phrase** a cliché.

abgefeimt *adj* cunning, wily.

abgegriffen *adj Buch* (well-)worn; *(fig) Phrasen etc* hackneyed.

abgehackt *adj* clipped. **~ sprechen** to clip one's words.

abgehangen *adj* **(gut) ~** well-hung.

abgehärtet *adj* tough, hardy; *(fig)* hardened. **gegen Erkältungen ~ sein** to be immune to colds.

abgehen *sep irreg aux sein* **1** *vi* **(a)** *(abfahren)* to leave, to depart *(form) (nach* for*)*. **(b)** *(Theat: abtreten)* to exit. **(c)** *(ausscheiden)* to leave. **von der Schule ~** to leave school. **(d)** *(sich lösen: Knopf etc)* to come off; *(herausgehen: Farbe etc auch)* to come out. **(e)** *(abgesandt werden)* to be sent *or* dispatched; *(Funkspruch)* to be sent. **etw ~ lassen** to dispatch sth. **(f)** *(col: fehlen)* **jdm geht Verständnis/Taktgefühl ab** sb lacks understanding/tact. **(g)** *(abgezogen werden)* **(von etw) ~** *(von Preis* to be taken off (sth); *(von Verdienst auch)* to be deducted (from sth); **davon gehen 5% ab** 5% is taken off that. **(h)** *(abzweigen)* to branch off; *(bei Gabelung auch)* to fork off. **(i)** *(abweichen)* **von einem Plan/einer Forderung ~** to give up a plan/demand; **von seiner Meinung ~** to change one's opinion. **(j)** *(verlaufen)* to go. **es ging nicht ohne Streit ab** there was an argument.

2 *vt (entlanggehen)* to walk along; *(Mil) Gelände* to patrol.

abgehetzt *adj* out of breath.

abgekämpft *adj* exhausted.

abgeklärt *adj* serene, tranquil.

abgelagert *adj Wein* mature; *Holz, Tabak* seasoned.

abgelegen *adj (entfernt) Dorf, Land* remote; *(einsam)* isolated.

abgeleiert *adj (pej)* banal, trite.

abgelten *vt sep irreg Ansprüche* to satisfy.

abgemacht 1 *interj* OK, that's settled; *(bei Kauf)* it's a deal. **2** *adj* **eine ~e Sache** a fix *(col)*.

abgemagert *adj (sehr dünn)* thin; *(ausgemergelt)* emaciated.

abgemergelt *adj* emaciated.

abgemessen *adj Schritt, Worte* measured, deliberate.

abgeneigt *adj* adverse *pred (dat* to*)*. **ich wäre gar nicht ~** *(col)* actually I wouldn't mind.

abgenutzt *adj* worn, shabby; *Besen* worn-out; *Reifen* worn-down; *(fig) Klischees* well-worn.

Abge|ordnete(r) *mf decl as adj* (elected) representative; *(von Parliament)* member of parliament.

abgeraten *vi sep irreg aux sein (geh)* **vom Weg ~** to lose one's way.

abgerissen *adj Kleidung* tattered; *Worte, Gedanken* disjointed.

Abgesandte(r) *mf decl as adj* envoy.

abgeschieden *adj (geh: einsam)* secluded. **~ leben/wohnen** to live in seclusion.

Abgeschiedenheit *f* seclusion.

abgeschlagen *adj* **(a)** *(besiegt)* defeated. **er landete ~ auf dem 8. Platz** he finished up way down in 8th place. **(b)** *(erschöpft)* shattered *(col)*.

abgeschlossen *adj (einsam)* isolated; *(attr: geschlossen) Wohnung* self-contained.

Abgeschlossenheit *f* isolation.

abgeschmackt *adj* fatuous; *Witz auch* corny; *Preise* outrageous.

abgesehen 1 *ptp of* **absehen. es auf jdn ~ haben** to have it in for sb *(col)*; *(interessiert sein)* to have one's eye on sb; **du hast es nur darauf ~, mich zu ärgern** you're only trying to annoy me. **2** *adv:* **~ von jdm/etw** apart from sb/sth; **~ davon, daß ...** apart from the fact that ...

abgespannt *adj* weary, tired.

abgespielt *adj Schallplatte* worn.

abgestanden *adj Luft, Wasser* stale; *Bier, Limonade etc* flat.

abgestorben *adj Glieder* numb; *Pflanze, Ast, Gewebe* dead.

abgestumpft *adj (gefühllos) Person* insensitive; *Gefühle, Gewissen* dulled.

abgetakelt *adj (pej col)* worn out, shagged out *(col!)*.

abgetan *adj pred* finished with. **damit ist die Sache ~** that settles the matter.

abgetragen *adj* worn. **~e Kleider** old clothes.

abgewinnen *vt sep irreg* **(a)** *(lit)* **jdm etw ~** to win sth from sb. **(b)** *(fig)* **jdm ein Lächeln ~** to persuade sb to smile; **dem Meer Land ~** to reclaim land from the sea; **einer Sache keinen Reiz ~ können** to be unable to see anything attractive in sth.

abgewogen *adj Urteil, Worte* balanced.

abgewöhnen *vt sep* **jdm etw ~** to cure sb of sth; *das Rauchen, Trinken* to get sb to give up sth; **sich** *(dat)* **das Trinken ~** to give up drinking; **noch einen zum A~** *(hum)* one last one; *(von Alkohol auch)* one for the road; **das/die ist ja zum A~** *(col)* that/she is enough to put anyone off.

abgewrackt *adj (abgetakelt) Mensch* worn-out.

abgezehrt *adj* emaciated.

abgießen *vt sep irreg* **(a)** *Flüssigkeit* to pour off; *Kartoffeln* to strain. **(b)** *(Art, Metal)* to cast.

Abglanz *m* reflection *(auch fig)*. **nur ein schwacher** *or* **matter ~** *(fig)* a pale reflection.

abgleiten *vi sep irreg aux sein (geh: abrutschen)* to slip; *(Gedanken)* to wander; *(Fin: Kurs)* to drop, to fall. **von etw ~** to slip off sth.

Abgott *m*, **Abgöttin** *f* idol. **jdn zum ~ machen** to idolize sb.

abgöttisch *adj* idolatrous. **jdn ~ lieben** to idolize sb; **jdm ~ lauschen** to listen adoringly to sb.

abgrasen *vt sep Feld* to graze; *(fig col) Geschäfte* to scour, to comb; *Thema* to do to death *(col)*.

abgrenzen *sep* **1** *vt Gelände* to fence off; *(fig) Rechte, Befugnisse, Begriff* to delimit *(gegen, von* from*)*. **etw durch einen Zaun/eine Mauer/Hecke ~** to fence/wall/hedge sth off. **2** *vr* to dis(as)sociate oneself *(gegen* from*)*.

Abgrenzung *f* **(a)** *no pl siehe vt* fencing/walling/hedging off; *(fig)* delimitation. **(b)** *siehe vr* dis-

(as)sociation *(gegen* from*)*. **(c)** *(Zaun)* fencing *no pl.*

Abgrund *m* precipice; *(Schlucht, fig)* abyss, chasm. **sich am Rande eines ~es befinden** *(lit, fig)* to be on the edge of a precipice; **in einen ~ von Verrat blicken** *(fig)* to stare into a bottomless pit of treason.

abgründig *adj Humor, Ironie* cryptic.

abgrundtief *adj Haß, Verachtung* profound.

abgucken *vti sep* to copy. **jdm etw ~** to copy sth from sb; **bei jdm (etw) ~** *(Sch)* to copy (sth) from *or* off *(col)* sb.

Abguß *m* **(a)** *(Art, Metal) (Vorgang)* casting; *(Form)* cast. **(b)** *(dial: Ausguß)* sink.

abhaben *vt sep irreg (col)* **(a)** *Brille, Hut* to have off; *(abgemacht haben)* to have got off. **(b)** *(abbekommen)* to have. **willst du ein Stück ~?** do you want a bit?

abhacken *vt sep* to chop off, to hack off; *siehe* **abgehackt.**

abhaken *vt sep (markieren)* to tick *or (esp US)* check off; *(fig)* to cross off.

abhalten *vt sep irreg* **(a)** *Kälte, Hitze, Fliegen* to keep off. **(b)** *(hindern)* to stop, to prevent. **jdn von etw/von der Arbeit ~** to keep sb from sth/from working; **jdn davon ~, etw zu tun** to prevent sb from doing sth; **laß dich nicht ~!** don't let me/us *etc* stop you. **(c)** *(veranstalten)* to hold.

Abhaltung *f no pl (Durchführung)* holding.

abhandeln *vt sep* **(a)** *Thema* to treat, to deal with. **(b)** *(abkaufen)* **jdm etw ~** to do a deal with sb for sth. **(c) jdm 8 Mark ~** to beat sb down 8 marks.

abhanden *adv:* **~ kommen** to get lost; **jdm ist etw ~ gekommen** sb has lost sth.

Abhang *m* slope, incline.

abhängen *sep* **1** *vt* **(a)** *Bild* to take down; *(Rail) Wagen* to uncouple; *Anhänger* to unhitch. **(b)** *(col: hinter sich lassen) jdn* to shake off *(col)*. **2** *vi* **(a)** *irreg (Fleisch etc)* to hang; *siehe* **abgehangen. (b)** *irreg* **von etw ~** to depend on sth, to be dependent on sth; **das hängt ganz davon ab** it all depends. **(c)** *(Telec col)* **er hat abgehängt** he hung up (on me *etc*).

abhängig *adj* dependent *(auch euph: süchtig)*; *Satz auch* subordinate; *Rede* indirect. **von etw ~ sein** to be dependent on sth; *(Gram)* to be governed by sth; **voneinander ~ sein** to be dependent on each other.

Abhängigkeit *f* **(a)** *no pl (Bedingtheit)* dependency *no pl (von* on*)*; *(Gram: von Sätzen)* subordination *(von* to*)*. **(b)** *(Angewiesensein, euph: Sucht)* dependence *(von* on*)*. **gegenseitige ~** interdependence.

abhärten *sep* **1** *vt* to toughen up. **2** *vi* **das härtet ab** that toughens you up. **3** *vr* to toughen oneself up. **sich gegen etw ~** to toughen oneself against sth; *(fig)* to harden oneself to sth; *siehe* **abgehärtet.**

Abhärtung *f siehe vb* toughening up; hardening.

abhauen *sep irreg* **1** *vi aux sein (col)* to clear out; *(verschwinden auch)* to push off. **hau ab!** beat it *(col)*. **2** *vt Kopf* to chop off; *Baum* to chop down; *Verputz, Schicht* to knock off.

abheben *sep irreg* **1** *vti* **(a)** *(anheben)* to lift (up), to raise; *(abnehmen)* to take off; *Telefonhörer* to pick up, to lift; *Telefon* to answer; *(Sew) Masche* to slip. **(b)** *Geld* to withdraw. **wenn Sie ~ wollen** if you wish to make a withdrawal. **2** *vi* **(a)** *(Flugzeug)* to take off; *(Rakete)* to lift off. **(b)** *(Cards: vor Spielbeginn etc)* to cut. **3** *vr* **sich von jdm/etw** *or* **gegen jdn/etw ~** to stand out from/against sb/sth; **sich wohltuend gegen etw ~** to contrast pleasantly with sth.

abheften *vt sep* **(a)** *Rechnungen etc* to file away. **(b)** *(Sew)* to tack, to baste.

abhelfen *vi sep irreg +dat* to remedy; *einem Fehler auch* to rectify.

abhetzen *sep* **1** *vt Tiere* to exhaust, to tire out. **hetz' mich nicht so ab!** *(col)* stop hustling me like that! *(col)*. **2** *vt* to wear *or* tire oneself out; *siehe* **abgehetzt.**

abheuern *sep (Naut)* **1** *vi* to be paid off. **2** *vt* to pay off.

Abhilfe *f no pl* remedy, cure. **~ schaffen** to take remedial action.

abholen *vt sep* to collect *(bei* from*)*; *Bestelltes auch* to call for *(bei* at*)*; *Fundsache* to claim *(bei* from*)*; *jdn* to call for; *(mit dem Wagen auch)* to pick up. **jdn am Bahnhof/Flughafen ~** to meet sb at the station/airport; *(mit dem Wagen auch)* to pick sb up from the station/airport; **etw ~ lassen** to have sth collected; **„Geldbörse gefunden, abzuholen bei ...“** “purse found, claim from ...”.

Abholung *f* collection.

abholzen *vt sep Wald* to clear, to deforest.

Abhör|anlage *f* bugging system.

abhorchen *vt sep* to sound, to listen to. **einen Patienten ~** to listen to a patient's chest.

abhören *vt sep* **(a)** *(auch vi: überwachen) Gespräch* to bug; *(mithören)* to listen in on; *Telefon* to tap. **abgehört werden** *(col)* to be bugged. **(b)** *(zuhören) Schallplatte etc* to listen to. **(c)** *(Med)* to sound, to listen to. **einen Patienten ~** to listen to a patient's chest. **(d)** *(Sch: abfragen)* **einem Schüler etw ~** to test a pupil orally on sth.

Abhörgerät *nt* bugging device.

abhungern *vr sep* **er mußte sich** *(dat)* **sein Studium ~** he had to starve his way through college *etc*; **sich** *(dat)* **10 Kilo ~** to lose 10 kilos by going on a starvation diet.

Abi *nt* **-s** *(Sch col)* = **Abitur.**

ab|irren *vi sep aux sein (geh)* to lose one's way; *(fig: Gedanken)* to wander. **vom Weg(e) ~** to wander off the path. **vom Thema ~** to digress.

Abitur *nt* **-e** *school-leaving exam and university entrance qualification,* ≈ A-levels *pl (Brit)*. **(das) ~ machen** to take (one's) school-leaving exam *or* A-levels *(Brit)*.

Abiturient(in *f*) *m person who is doing/has done the Abitur.*

Abiturzeugnis *nt certificate of having passed the Abitur,* ≈ A-level certificate *(Brit)*.

abjagen *vt sep* **jdm etw ~** to get sth off sb.

abkämmen *vt sep (fig)* to comb, to scour.

abkämpfen *vr sep* to fight hard; *siehe* **abgekämpft.**

abkanzeln *vt sep (col)* **jdn ~** to give sb a dressing-down.

abkapseln *vr sep (fig)* to cut oneself off.

abkarten *vt sep* to rig *(col)*, to fix. **die Sache war von vornherein abgekartet** the whole thing was a put-up job *(col)*.

abkassieren* *vti sep (col)* to cash up *(col)*. **bei jdm ~** to get sb to pay; **darf ich (bei Ihnen) ~?** could I ask you to pay now?

abkauen *vt sep Fingernägel* to bite; *Bleistift* to chew.

abkaufen *vt sep* **jdm etw ~** to buy sth from sb; *(col: glauben)* to buy sth *(col)*.

Abkehr *f no pl* turning away *(von* from*)*; *(von Glauben etc)* renunciation *(von* of*)*.

abkehren *sep* **1** *vt (geh) Blick, Gesicht* to avert, to turn away. **2** *vr (fig)* to turn away *(von* from*)*.

abklappern *vt sep (col) Läden, Straße* to scour, to comb *(nach* for*)*; *Kunden* to call on.

abklären *sep* **1** *vt (klarstellen)* to clear up, to clarify. **2** *vr* **(a)** *(sich setzen)* to clarify. **(b)** *(sich beruhigen)* to calm down; *siehe* **abgeklärt.**

Abklatsch *m* **-e** *(Art)* cast, casting; *(fig pej)* poor imitation *or* copy.

abklemmen *vt sep Nabelschnur, Leitung* to clamp.

abklingen *vi sep irreg aux sein* **(a)** *(leiser werden)* to die *or* fade away. **(b)** *(nachlassen)* to wear off, to abate; *(Erregung, Fieber auch)* to subside.

abklopfen *vt sep* **(a)** *Staub etc* to brush off; *Teppich, Polstermöbel* to beat. **(b)** *(beklopfen)* to tap; *(Med)* to sound, to percuss *(form)*.

abknabbern *vt sep (col)* to nibble off; *Knochen* to gnaw at.

abknallen *vt sep (col)* to shoot down *(col)*.

abknappen, abknapsen *vt sep (col)* **sich** *(dat)* **jeden Pfennig ~ müssen** to have to scrimp and save; **er hat mir 20 Mark abgeknapst** he got 20 marks off me.

abknicken *sep* **1** *vt (abbrechen)* to break *or* snap off; *(einknicken)* to break. **2** *vi aux sein (abzweigen)* to fork *or* branch off.

abknöpfen *vt sep* **(a)** *(lit)* to unbutton. **(b)** *(col: ablisten)* **jdm etw ~** to get sth off sb.

abkochen *vt sep (keimfrei machen)* to sterilize (by boiling).

abkommandieren* *vt sep (Mil) (zu Einheit)* to post; *(zu bestimmtem Dienst)* to detail *(zu* for*)*.

abkommen *vi sep irreg aux sein* **(a) von etw ~** *(abirren)* to wander off sth; **vom Kurs ~** to deviate from one's course; **(vom Thema) ~** to get off the subject, to digress. **(b)** *(aufgeben)* **von etw ~** to drop sth; *(von Angewohnheit)* to give sth up; *(von Idee, Plan)* to abandon sth; **von einer Meinung ~** to revise one's opinion.

Abkommen *nt* - agreement *(auch Pol)*.

abkömmlich *adj* available. **nicht ~ sein** to be unavailable.

Abkömmling *m (Nachkomme)* descendant; *(fig)* adherent.

abkönnen *vt sep irreg (col)* **(a)** *(trinken)* **er kann nicht viel ab** he can't take much (drink). **(b)** *(mögen)* **das kann ich nicht ab** I can't stand it.

abkoppeln *vt sep (Rail)* to uncouple; *Anhänger* to unhitch; *(Space)* to separate; *Pferd* to untie.

abkratzen *sep* **1** *vt Schmutz etc* to scratch off; *(mit einem Werkzeug)* to scrape off. **2** *vi aux sein (col: sterben)* to kick the bucket *(col)*.

abkriegen *vt sep (col) siehe* **abbekommen.**

abkühlen *sep* **1** *vt* to cool; *Speise auch* to cool down. **2** *vi aux sein* to cool down. **3** *vr* to cool down; *(Beziehungen)* to become cool(er).

Abkühlung *f* cooling.

Abkunft *f no pl (liter)* descent, origin; *(Nationalität auch)* extraction.

abkürzen *sep* **1** *vt* **(a)** *(abschneiden)* **den Weg ~** to take a short cut. **(b)** *(verkürzen)* to cut short; *Verfahren* to shorten; *Aufenthalt, Urlaub auch* to curtail. **(c)** *Namen* to abbreviate. **2** *vi (verkürzt schreiben)* to use abbreviations.

Abkürzung *f* **(a)** *(Weg)* short cut. **(b)** *(von Wort)* abbreviation.

abladen *vti sep irreg Last, Wagen* to unload; *Schutt* to dump; *(esp Comm) Passagiere, Ware* to offload; *(fig col) Ärger auch* to vent *(bei jdm* on sb*)*.

Ablage *f* **-n** place to keep/put sth. **wir brauchen eine ~ für die Akten** we need somewhere for our files; **etw als ~ benutzen** *(für Akten, Bücher etc)* to use sth for storage.

ablagern *sep* **1** *vt (deponieren)* to leave, to store. **2** *vi aux sein or haben (ausreifen)* to mature; *(Holz auch)* to season. **~ lassen** to allow to mature; *Holz auch* to (allow to) season. **3** *vr* to be deposited.

Ablagerung *f (abgelagerter Stoff)* deposit.

ablassen *sep irreg* **1** *vt* **(a)** *(herauslaufen lassen) Wasser, Luft* to let out; *Motoröl auch* to drain off; *Dampf* to let off. **(b)** *(ermäßigen)* to knock off *(col)*. **er hat mir 20 Mark abgelassen** he knocked 20 marks off for me *(col)*. **2** *vi (liter)* **(a)** *(mit etw aufhören)* to desist. **von einem Vorhaben** *etc* **~** to abandon a plan *etc*. **(b)** *(jdn in Ruhe lassen)* **von jdm ~** to leave sb alone.

Ablauf *m* **(a)** *(Abfluß)* drain; *(Rinne)* drainage channel. **(b)** *(Verlauf)* course; *(von Verbrechen)* sequence of events *(gen* in*)*; *(von Handlung in Buch etc)* development. **der ~ der Ereignisse** the course of events; **es gab keinerlei Störungen im ~ des Programms** the programme went off without any disturbances. **(c)** *(von Zeitraum, Frist etc)* expiry. **nach ~ von 4 Stunden** after 4 hours (have/had passed *or* gone by*)*; **nach ~ des Jahres/dieser Zeit** at the end of the year/this time.

ablaufen *sep irreg* **1** *vt* **(a)** *(abnutzen) Schuhsohlen, Schuhe* to wear out; *Absätze* to wear down. **sich** *(dat)* **die Beine** *or* **Hacken nach etw ~** *(col)* to walk one's legs off looking for sth. **(b)** *aux sein or haben (entlanglaufen) Strecke* to go *or* walk over; *Stadt, Straßen, Geschäfte* to comb, to scour. **2** *vi aux sein* **(a)** *(abfließen: Flüssigkeit)* to drain *or* run away *or* off; *(trocken werden: Geschirr)* to dry off. **(b)** *(vonstatten gehen)* to go off. **(c) ~ lassen** *(abspulen, abspielen) Platte, Tonband* to play; *Film* to run. **(d)** *(ungültig werden: Paß etc)* to expire, to run out; *(enden: Frist, Vertrag etc auch)* to run out, to be up. **(e)** *(Zeitraum)* to pass, to go by.

Ableben *nt no pl (form)* demise *(form)*.

ablecken *vt sep* to lick; *Teller* to lick (clean).

ablegen *sep* **1** *vt* **(a)** *(niederlegen)* to put down; *Last, Waffen auch* to lay down; *(Zool) Eier* to lay. **(b)** *Schriftwechsel* to file (away). **(c)** *(ausziehen) Kleider* to take off, to remove. **(d)** *(nicht mehr tragen) Anzug, Kleid* to discard, to cast off. **abgelegte Kleider** cast-off clothes. **(e)** *(aufgeben) Mißtrauen, Scheu, Stolz* to lose, to shed; *Namen* to give up. **(f)** *Schwur, Eid* to swear; *Gelübde auch* to make; *Zeugnis* to give; *Bekenntnis, Beichte* to make; *Prüfung* to take, to sit; *(erfolgreich)* to pass. **2** *vi* **(a)** *(Schiff)* to cast off; *(Space auch)* to separate. **(b)** *(Garderobe ~)* to take one's things off.

Ableger *m* - *(Bot)* layer; *(fig: Zweigunternehmen)* branch, subsidiary.

ablehnen *vt sep* **(a)** *auch vi (zurückweisen, nein sagen)* to decline; *Antrag, Vorschlag, Bewerber* to reject; *(Parl) Gesetzentwurf* to throw out. **eine ~de Antwort** a negative answer; **ein ~der Bescheid** a rejection; **dankend ~** to decline with thanks. **(b)** *(mißbilligen)* to disapprove of.

Ablehnung *f* **(a)** *(Zurückweisung)* refusal; *(von Antrag etc)* rejection. **(b)** *(Mißbilligung)* disapproval. **auf ~ stoßen** to meet with disapproval.

ableiern *vt sep (col) Gedicht etc* to reel off.

ableisten *vt sep (form) Zeit* to serve; *Wehrdienst* to do.

ableiten *sep vt* **(a)** *(herleiten)* to derive; *(logisch folgern auch)* to deduce *(aus* from*)*. **(b)** *(umleiten) Fluß* to divert; *(herausleiten) Rauch, Flüssigkeit* to draw off *or* out; *(ablenken) Blitz* to conduct.

Ableitung *f* **(a)** *siehe vt* derivation; deduction; diversion; drawing off *or* out; conduction. **(b)** *(Wort, Math)* derivative.

ablenken *sep* **1** *vt* **(a)** *(ab-, wegleiten)* to deflect *(auch Phys)*, to turn aside. **(b) er ließ sich durch nichts ~** he wouldn't let anything distract him; **das lenkt mich ab** *(zerstreut mich)* it takes my mind off things; **jdn von seinem Schmerz/seinen Sorgen ~** to take sb's mind off his pain/worries. **(c)** *(abbringen)* to divert; *Verdacht* to avert. **2** *vi* **(a) (vom Thema) ~** to change the subject. **(b) das lenkt ab** *(zerstreut)* it takes your mind off things; *(stört)* it's distracting. **3** *vr* to take one's mind off things.

Ablenkung *f* **(a)** *(Ab-, Wegleitung)* deflection *(auch Phys)*. **(b)** *(Zerstreuung)* diversion, distraction. **~ brauchen** to need something to take one's mind off things.

Ablenkungsmanöver *nt* diversionary tactic; *(um von Thema abzulenken auch)* red herring.

ablesen *vt sep irreg* **(a)** *(auch vi: vom Blatt)* to read. **er muß (alles/seine Rede) ~** he has to read everything/his speech (from notes *etc*); **(jdm) etw von den Lippen ~** to lip-read sth (that sb says). **(b)** *(auch vi: registrieren) Meßgeräte, Barometer, Strom* to read. **nächste Woche wird abgelesen** the meter(s) will be read next week. **(c)** *(herausfinden, erkennen, folgern)* to see. **jdm etw vom Gesicht ~** to read sth in sb's face; **das**

konnte man ihr vom Gesicht ~ it was written all over her face; **jdm jeden Wunsch von den Augen** ~ to anticipate sb's every wish.
ableugnen *vt sep Schuld, Tat* to deny.
Ableugnung *f* denial.
ablichten *vt sep (form)* to photocopy; *(fotografieren)* to photograph.
Ablichtung *f (form) siehe vt* photocopy; photograph.
abliefern *vt sep* to hand in *(bei* to*)*; *(liefern)* to deliver *(bei* to*)*; *(col) Kinder* to deposit *(col) (bei* with*)*.
Ablieferung *f (von Waren)* delivery.
abliegen *vi sep irreg (entfernt sein)* **das Haus liegt weit ab** the house is quite a distance away; *siehe* **abgelegen.**
ablisten *vt sep* **jdm etw** ~ to trick sb out of sth.
ablocken *vt sep* **jdm etw** ~ to get sth out of sb.
ablöschen *vt sep* **(a)** *(mit dem Löschblatt)* to blot. **(b)** *(Cook)* to add water to.
ablösen *sep* **1** *vt* **(a)** *(abmachen)* to take off, to remove; *Etikett etc auch* to detach. **(b)** *(Fin) Schuld, Hypothek* to pay off, to redeem. **(c)** *(ersetzen) Wache* to relieve; *Amtsinhaber* to replace. **(d)** *(fig: an Stelle treten von)* to take the place of; *(Methode, System)* to supersede. **2** *vr* **(a)** *(abgehen)* to come off; *(Lack etc auch)* to peel off. **(b)** *(auch* **einander** ~*)* to take turns; *(Fahrer, Kollegen auch, Wachen)* to relieve each other.
Ablösesumme *f (Sport)* transfer fee.
Ablösung *f* **(a)** *(von Hypothek, Schuld)* paying off, redemption. **(b)** *(Wache)* relief; *(Entlassung)* replacement. **bei dieser Arbeit braucht man alle zwei Stunden eine** ~ you need relieving every two hours in this work.
abluchsen *vt sep (col)* **jdm etw** ~ to get *or* wangle *(col)* sth out of sb.
Abluft *f no pl (Tech)* used air.
ablutschen *vt sep* to lick.
abmachen *vt sep (col)* **(a)** *(entfernen)* to take off. **(b)** *(vereinbaren) Termin etc* to agree (on). **(c)** *(besprechen)* to settle. **etw mit sich allein** ~ to sort sth out for oneself.
Abmachung *f* agreement.
abmagern *vi sep aux sein* to get thinner, to lose weight.
Abmagerung *f no pl* emaciation.
Abmagerungskur *f* diet. **eine** ~ **machen** to be on a diet, to be dieting; *(anfangen)* to go on a diet.
abmalen *vt sep (abzeichnen)* to paint.
Abmarsch *m* departure; *(von Soldaten auch)* march-off. **beim** ~ when marching off; **zum** ~ **antreten** *(Mil)* to fall in for the march-off.
abmarschbereit *adj* ready to move off.
abmarschieren* *vi sep aux sein* to move off.
abmelden *sep* **1** *vt* **(a)** *Telefon* to have disconnected; *(bei Verein) jdn* to cancel the membership of. **sein Auto** ~ to take one's car off the road; **ein Kind von einer Schule** ~ to take a child away from a school. **(b)** *(col)* **er/sie ist bei mir abgemeldet** I don't want anything to do with him/her. **2** *vr* to ask for permission to be absent; *(im Hotel)* to check out. **sich bei jdm** ~ to tell sb that one is leaving; **sich polizeilich** ~ to notify the police that one is moving away.
Abmeldung *f (von Telefon)* disconnection; *(bei der Polizei)* cancellation of one's registration. **seit der** ~ **meines Autos** since I took my car off the road.
abmergeln *vr sep* to slave away.
abmessen *vt sep irreg* **(a)** to measure; *(fig) Worte* to weigh. **(b)** *(abteilen)* to measure off.
Abmessung *f usu pl* measurement; *(Ausmaß)* dimension.
abmildern *vt sep Geschmack, Worte* to tone down; *Aufprall* to cushion, to soften; *Schock* to lessen.
abmontieren* *vt sep Räder, Teile* to remove *(von etw* from sth*)*; *Maschine* to dismantle.
abmühen *vr sep* to struggle (away).
abmustern *sep (Naut)* **1** *vt Besatzung* to pay off. **2** *vi* to sign off, to leave the ship.
abnagen *vt sep* to gnaw off; *Knochen* to gnaw.
Abnahme *f* **-n** **(a)** *(Wegnahme)* removal; *(Amputation)* amputation. **(b)** *(Verringerung)* decrease *(gen* in*)*; *(bei Anzahl, Menge auch)* drop *(gen* in*)*; *(von Kräften, Energie, Interesse, Nachfrage)* decline *(gen* in*)*. **(c)** *(von Prüfung)* holding; *(von Neubau, Fahrzeug etc)* inspection. **(d)** *(Comm)* purchase. **bei** ~ **von 50 Exemplaren** if you/we *etc* purchase *or* take 50 copies; **keine/gute** ~ **finden** not to sell/to sell well.
abnehmbar *adj* removable, detachable.
abnehmen *sep irreg* **1** *vt* **(a)** *(herunternehmen)* to take off, to remove; *Hörer* to lift, to pick up; *Obst* to pick; *(lüften) Hut* to raise; *Vorhang, Bild, Wäsche* to take down; *Maschen* to decrease; *(amputieren)* to amputate.
(b) *(an sich nehmen)* **jdm etw** ~ to take sth from sb; *(fig) Arbeit, Sorgen* to relieve sb of sth; **darf ich Ihnen den Mantel** ~? can I take your coat?; **kann ich dir etwas** ~? *(tragen)* can I take something for you?; *(helfen)* can I do anything for you?; **jdm die Beichte** ~ to hear confession from sb; **jdm ein Versprechen** ~ to make sb promise sth.
(c) *(wegnehmen)* to take away *(jdm* from sb*)*; *(rauben, abgewinnen)* to take *(jdm* off sb*)*.
(d) *(begutachten) Gebäude, Auto* to inspect; *(abhalten) Prüfung* to hold.
(e) *(abkaufen)* to take *(dat* off*)*, to buy *(dat* from, off*)*.
(f) *(fig col: glauben)* to buy *(col)*. **dieses Märchen nimmt dir keiner ab!** nobody'll buy that!
(g) *Fingerabdrücke* to take.
2 *vi* **(a)** *(sich verringern)* to decrease; *(Niveau, Kräfte)* to decline; *(Fieber)* to go down; *(Mond)* to wane; *(beim Stricken)* to decrease. **(an Gewicht)** ~ to lose weight. **(b)** *(Telec)* to answer.
Abnehmer *m* **-** *(Comm)* buyer, customer. **viele/wenige** ~ **finden** to sell well/badly.
Abneigung *f* dislike *(gegen* of*)*; *(Widerstreben)* aversion *(gegen* to*)*.
abnorm, abnormal *adj* abnormal.
Abnormität *f* abnormality.
abnötigen *vt sep (geh)* **jdm etw** ~ to force sth from sb; **jdm Respekt** ~ to gain sb's respect.
abnutzen *vtr sep* to wear out.
Abnutzung *f* wear (and tear).
Abonnement [abɔnə'mã:] *nt* **-s** *or* **-e** **(a)** *(Zeitungs~)* subscription. **eine Zeitung im** ~ **beziehen** to subscribe to a newspaper. **(b)** *(Theater~)* season ticket.
Abonnent(in *f***)** *m (Zeitungs~)* subscriber; *(Theater~)* season-ticket holder.
abonnieren* *vt Zeitung* to subscribe to; *Konzertreihe etc* to have a season ticket to.
ab|ordnen *vt sep* to delegate.
Ab|ordnung *f* delegation.
Abort[1] *m* **-e** *(dated)* lavatory, toilet.
Abort[2] *m* **-e** *(Fehlgeburt)* miscarriage; *(Abtreibung)* abortion.
abpacken *vt sep* to pack. **ein abgepacktes Brot** a wrapped loaf.
abpassen *vt sep* **(a)** *(abwarten) Gelegenheit* to wait for. **den richtigen Zeitpunkt** ~ to wait for the right time; **etw gut** ~ to time sth well. **(b)** *(auf jdn warten)* to catch; *(jdm auflauern)* to waylay.
abpausen *vt sep* to make a tracing of.
abpfeifen *sep irreg (Sport)* **1** *vi (Schiedsrichter)* to blow one's whistle. **2** *vt* **das Spiel/die erste Halbzeit** ~ to blow the whistle for the end of the game/for half-time.
Abpfiff *m (Sport)* final whistle.
abpflücken *vt sep* to pick.

abplagen *vr sep* to struggle (away).
abprallen *vi sep aux sein* **von** *or* **an etw** *(dat)* ~ *(Ball)* to bounce *or (Kugel)* to ricochet off sth; **an jdm** ~ *(fig)* to make no impression on sb.
Abpraller *m* - *(Sport)* rebound.
abputzen *sep vt* to clean; *Schmutz* to clean off. **sich** *(dat)* **die Nase/den Hintern** ~ to wipe one's nose/bottom; **putz dir die Schuhe ab!** wipe your feet!
abquälen *sep* **1** *vr* to struggle (away). **2** *vt* **sich** *(dat)* **ein Lächeln** ~ to force a smile.
abqualifizieren* *vt sep* to dismiss, to write off.
abquetschen *vt sep* to crush. **sich** *(dat)* **den Arm** ~ to get one's arm crushed.
abrackern *vr sep (col)* to slave away. **sich mit etw** ~ to struggle with sth.
abrasieren* *vt sep* to shave off; *(col) Gebäude* to flatten.
abraten *vti sep irreg* **jdm (von) etw** ~ to advise sb against sth.
abräumen *vti sep* to clear up *or* away. **den Tisch** ~ to clear the table.
abreagieren* *sep* **1** *vt Spannung, Wut* to work off, to get rid of. **seinen Ärger an anderen** ~ to take it out on others. **2** *vr* to work it off. **er war ganz wütend, aber jetzt hat er sich abreagiert** he was furious, but he's simmered down now.
abrechnen *sep* **1** *vi* **(a)** *(Kasse machen)* to cash up. **darf ich** ~? would you like your bill *(Brit) or* check *(US)* now? **(b) mit jdm** ~ to settle up with sb; *(fig)* to get even with sb. **2** *vt (abziehen)* to deduct.
Abrechnung *f* **(a)** *(Aufstellung)* statement *(über +acc* for*)*; *(Rechnung)* bill, invoice; *(Bilanz)* balancing; *(fig: Rache)* revenge. **der Tag der** ~ *(fig)* the day of reckoning. **(b)** *(Abzug)* deduction. **nach** ~ **von** after (the deduction of); **in** ~ **stellen** *(form)* to deduct.
Abrede *f* **etw in** ~ **stellen** to deny *or* dispute sth.
abregen *vr sep (col)* to calm *or* cool down. **reg dich ab!** relax!, cool it! *(col)*.
abreiben *vt sep irreg Schmutz, Rost* to clean *or* rub off; *(trocknen)* to rub down.
Abreibung *f (col: Prügel)* hiding, thrashing.
Abreise *f* departure *(nach* for*)*. **bei meiner** ~ on my departure.
abreisen *vi sep aux sein* to leave *(nach* for*)*.
abreißen *sep irreg* **1** *vt* **(a)** *(abtrennen)* to tear off; *Tapete, Blätter auch* to strip (off). **er hat sich** *(dat)* **den Knopf abgerissen** he's torn his button off; **er wird dir nicht (gleich) den Kopf** ~ *(col)* he won't bite your head off *(col)*. **(b)** *(niederreißen) Gebäude* to pull down. **2** *vi aux sein (sich lösen)* to come off; *(fig: unterbrochen werden)* to break off. **das reißt nicht ab** *(fig)* there is no end to it; **den Kontakt** *etc* **nicht** ~ **lassen** to stay in touch.
Abreißkalender *m* tear-off calendar.
abrichten *vt sep* to train. **der Hund ist auf Einbrecher abgerichtet** the dog is trained to go for burglars.
Abrichtung *f* training.
abriegeln *vt sep (verschließen) Tür* to bolt; *(absperren) Straßen, Gebiet* to cordon off.
abringen *vt sep irreg* **jdm etw** ~ to wring *or* force sth out of sb; **sich** *(dat)* **ein Lächeln** ~ to force a smile; **dem Meer Land** ~ *(liter)* to wrest land away from the sea *(liter)*.
Abriß *m* **(a)** *(Abbruch)* demolition. **(b)** *(Übersicht)* outline, summary. **(c)** *(von Eintrittskarte etc)* tear-off part.
abrollen *sep* **1** *vt (abwickeln)* to unwind; *Stoff* to unroll. **2** *vi aux sein* **(a)** *(abfahren: Züge, Waggons)* to roll off *or* away. **(b)** *(col: vonstatten gehen) (Programm)* to run; *(Veranstaltung)* to go off; *(Ereignisse)* to unfold. **mein ganzes Leben rollte noch einmal vor meinen Augen ab** my whole life passed before me again.
abrücken *sep* **1** *vt (wegschieben)* to move away. **2** *vi aux sein* **(a)** *(fig: sich distanzieren)* to dissociate oneself *(von* from*)*. **(b)** *(Mil etc)* to move out.
Abruf *m* **(a) sich auf** ~ **bereit halten** to be ready to be called (for); **auf** ~ **zur Verfügung stehen** to be available on call. **(b)** *(Comm)* **etw auf** ~ **bestellen/kaufen** to order/buy sth (to be delivered) on call. **(c)** *(Comp)* retrieval.
abruf-: ~**bar** *adj Daten* retrievable; ~**bereit** *adj* **(a)** *Arzt etc* on call; *(abholbereit)* ready to be called for; **(b)** *(Comm, Fin)* ready on call.
abrufen *vt sep irreg* **(a)** *(wegrufen)* to call away. **(b)** *(Comm)* to request delivery of; *(Fin: abheben)* to withdraw. **(c)** *Daten* to retrieve.
abrunden *vt sep (lit, fig)* to round off. **eine Zahl nach oben/unten** ~ to round a number up/down.
Abrundung *f (lit, fig)* rounding off. **zur** ~ **von etw** to round sth off.
abrupt *adj* abrupt.
abrüsten *sep vi (Mil, Pol)* to disarm.
Abrüstung *f no pl (Mil, Pol)* disarmament.
abrutschen *vi sep aux sein (abgleiten)* to slip; *(fig) (Leistungen)* to go downhill; *(moralisch)* to let oneself go.
absäbeln *vt sep (col)* to hack *or* chop off.
absacken *vi sep aux sein (sinken)* to sink; *(Boden, Gebäude auch)* to subside; *(fig col: nachlassen)* to fall off; *(verkommen)* to go to pot *(col)*.
Absage *f* **-n** refusal; *(auf Einladung auch)* negative reply. **das ist eine** ~ **an die Demokratie** that's a denial of democracy; **jdm/einer Sache eine** ~ **erteilen** to reject sb/sth.
absagen *sep* **1** *vt (rückgängig machen) Veranstaltung, Besuch* to cancel, to call off; *(ablehnen) Einladung* to decline. **2** *vi* to decline. **jdm** ~ to tell sb that one can't come; **in letzter Minute** ~ to cry off at the last minute.
absägen *vt sep* **(a)** *(abtrennen)* to saw off. **(b)** *(fig col)* to chuck *or* sling out *(col)*.
absahnen *sep (fig col)* **1** *vt Geld* to rake in; *(sich verschaffen)* to cream off. **2** *vi* to make a killing *(col)*.
absatteln *vti sep* to unsaddle.
Absatz *m, pl* **Absätze (a)** *(Abschnitt)* paragraph; *(Jur)* section. **einen** ~ **machen** to start a new paragraph. **(b)** *(Treppen~)* half-landing. **(c)** *(Schuh~)* heel. **spitze Absätze** stiletto heels; **auf dem** ~ **kehrtmachen** to turn on one's heel. **(d)** *(Verkauf)* sales *pl*. **guten** ~ **finden** to sell well.
Absatz-: **a**~**fähig** *adj* marketable, saleable; ~**gebiet** *nt* sales area; ~**schwierigkeiten** *pl* sales problems *pl*; ~**steigerung** *f* increase in sales.
absaufen *vi sep irreg aux sein (col) (ertrinken)* to drown; *(Motor)* to flood; *(Schiff etc)* to go down.
absaugen *vt sep Flüssigkeit* to suck out *or* off; *Teppich, Sofa* to hoover ®, to vacuum.
abschaben *vt sep* to scrape off.
abschaffen *sep vt* **(a)** to abolish, to do away with. **(b)** *(nicht länger halten)* to get rid of.
Abschaffung *f* abolition.
abschälen *vtr sep* to peel off.
abschalten **1** *vti sep (lit, fig col)* to switch off. **2** *vr* to switch itself off.
abschätzen *vt sep* to estimate; *Menschen, Fähigkeiten* to assess. **seine Lage** ~ to take stock of one's position; **ein** ~**der Blick** an appraising look.
abschätzig *adj* disparaging. **sich** ~ **über jdn äußern** to make disparaging remarks about sb.
Abschätzung *f siehe* **Schätzung.**
Abschaum *m no pl* scum. **der** ~ **der Menschheit** the scum of the earth.
abscheiden *vt sep irreg (ausscheiden)* to give off, to produce; *(Biol auch)* to secrete.
Abscheu *m or f no pl* repulsion, abhorrence *(vor +dat* at*)*. **vor jdm/etw** ~ **haben** *or* **empfinden** to loathe sb/sth; **jdm** ~ **einflößen** to fill sb with loathing.
abscheuern *vt sep* **(a)** *Schmutz* to scrub off. **(b)**

(abschürfen) Haut to rub *or* scrape off. **(c)** *Kleidung* to wear thin.

abscheulich *adj* abominable, loathsome; *Verbrechen auch* heinous; *Anblick auch* repulsive. **wie ~!** how awful!; **~ kalt** hideously cold.

Abscheulichkeit *f (Untat)* atrocity, abomination; *(no pl: Widerwärtigkeit)* loathsomeness; *(von Verbrechen auch)* heinousness; *(von Geschmack, Anblick)* repulsiveness.

abschicken *vt sep* to send; *Paket, Brief* to send off, to dispatch.

abschieben *sep irreg* **1** *vt* **(a)** *(wegschieben)* to push away *(von* from*)*; *(fig) Verantwortung, Schuld* to shift *(auf+acc* onto*)*. **(b)** *(ausweisen) Ausländer* to deport. **(c)** *(col: loswerden)* to get rid of. **jdn in eine andere Abteilung ~** to shunt sb off to another department *(col)*. **2** *vi aux sein (col)* to clear off *(col)*.

Abschiebung *f (Ausweisung)* deportation.

Abschied *m* **-e (a)** *(Trennung)* farewell, parting. **von jdm/etw ~ nehmen** to say goodbye to sb/sth, to take one's leave of sb/sth; **ein ... zum ~** a farewell ...; **es war ein ~ für immer** it was goodbye for ever; **beim ~ meinte er, ...** as he was leaving he said ...; **ihr ~ von der Bühne/vom Film** her farewell from the stage/from film; *(letzte Vorstellung)* her farewell performance; **der ~ von der Vergangenheit** the break with the past. **(b)** *(von Beamten)* resignation; *(von Offizieren)* discharge. **seinen ~ nehmen** to hand in one's resignation/to apply for a discharge.

Abschieds-: ~besuch *m* farewell visit; **~brief** *m* farewell letter; **~feier** *f* farewell party; **~schmerz** *m* pain of parting; **~stunde** *f* hour of parting; **~szene** *f* farewell scene.

abschießen *vt sep irreg (auf+acc* at*)* **(a)** *Geschoß, Gewehr* to fire; *Pfeil* to shoot; *Rakete* to launch; *(auf ein Ziel)* to fire. **(b)** *(außer Gefecht setzen) Flugzeug* to shoot down. **(c)** *(totschießen) Wild* to shoot. **(d)** *(fig col: abschieben)* to get rid of.

abschirmen *sep* **1** *vt* to shield; *(schützen auch)* to protect; *(vor Licht auch)* to screen. **2** *vr* to shield oneself *(gegen* from*)*; *(sich schützen)* to protect oneself *(gegen* from *or* against*)*; *(sich isolieren)* to cut oneself off *(gegen* from*)*.

Abschirmung *f no pl* **(a)** *(Schutz)* protection. **(b)** *(fig: Isolierung)* isolation.

abschlachten *vt sep* to slaughter.

Abschlachtung *f* slaughter.

abschlaffen *vi sep aux sein (col)* to flag.

Abschlag *m* **(a)** *(Preisnachlaß)* reduction. **(b)** *(Zahlung)* part payment *(auf+acc* of*)*.

abschlagen *vt sep irreg* **(a)** *(mit Hammer etc)* to knock off; *(mit Beil etc)* to chop off; *Baum* to chop down; *(herunterschlagen)* to knock down. **etw vom Preis ~** to knock sth off the price. **(b)** *(ablehnen)* to refuse; *Einladung, Bitte auch, Antrag* to turn down. **jdm etw ~** to refuse sb sth. **(c)** *(zurückschlagen) Angriff, Feind* to drive off. **(d)** *siehe* **abgeschlagen.**

abschlägig *adj* negative. **jdn/etw ~ bescheiden** *(form)* to turn sb/sth down.

Abschlag(s)zahlung *f* part payment.

abschleifen *sep irreg* **1** *vt Unebenheiten* to grind down; *Holzboden* to sand (down). **2** *vr (fig) (Angewohnheit etc)* to wear off; *(Mensch)* to have the rough edges taken off. **das schleift sich (noch) ab** *(fig)* that'll wear off.

Abschleppdienst *m* breakdown service *(Brit)*, (vehicle) recovery service.

abschleppen *sep* **1** *vt* **(a)** *Fahrzeug, Schiff* to tow, to take in tow; *(bei widerrechtlichem Parken)* to tow away. **(b)** *(col) Menschen* to drag along; *(aufgabeln)* to pick up *(col)*. **2** *vr* **sich mit etw ~** *(col)* to struggle with sth.

Abschlepp-: ~fahrzeug *nt* breakdown *(Brit) or* recovery vehicle, wrecker *(US)*; **~seil** *nt* towrope.

abschließbar *adj* lockable.

abschließen *sep irreg* **1** *vt* **(a)** *(zuschließen)* to lock. **(b)** *(beenden) Sitzung, Vortrag etc* to conclude, to bring to a close. **sein Studium ~** to graduate; **mit abgeschlossenem Studium** with a degree. **(c)** *(vereinbaren) Geschäft* to transact; *Versicherung* to take out; *Wette* to place. **einen Vertrag ~** *(Pol)* to conclude a treaty; *(Jur, Comm)* to conclude a contract. **2** *vr (sich isolieren)* to cut oneself off. **sich von der Außenwelt ~** to shut oneself off from the outside world; *siehe* **abgeschlossen. 3** *vi* **(a)** *(zuschließen)* to lock up. **sieh mal nach, ob auch abgeschlossen ist** will you see if everything's locked? **(b)** *(enden)* to come to a close. **(c)** *(Comm: Vertrag schließen)* to conclude the deal. **(d)** *(Schluß machen)* to finish, to end. **mit der Vergangenheit ~** to break with the past.

abschließend 1 *adj* concluding. **2** *adv* in conclusion, finally.

Abschluß *m* **(a)** *(Beendigung)* end; *(col: ~prüfung)* final examination; *(Univ)* degree. **zum ~ möchte ich ...** finally *or* to conclude I would like ...; **zum ~ kommen** to come to an end; **etw zum ~ bringen** to finish sth. **(b)** *no pl (Vereinbarung)* conclusion. **bei ~ des Vertrages** on completion of the contract. **(c)** *(Rand etc)* border.

Abschluß-: ~feier *f (Sch)* speech *or* prizegiving day; **~prüfung** *f (Sch)* final examination; *(Univ auch)* finals *pl*; **~zeugnis** *nt (Sch)* leaving certificate, diploma *(US)*.

abschmecken *vt sep (kosten)* to taste; *(würzen)* to season.

abschmettern *vt sep (col) (Sport)* to smash; *(fig: zurückweisen)* to throw out.

abschmieren *vt sep (Tech) Auto* to grease.

abschminken *vt sep* **(a)** *Gesicht, Haut* to remove the make-up from. **sich ~** to remove one's make-up. **(b)** *(col: aufgeben)* **sich** *(dat)* **etw ~** to get sth out of one's head.

abschmirgeln *vt sep* to sand down.

abschnallen *sep* **1** *vt* to unfasten, to undo. **2** *vr* to unfasten one's seat belt. **3** *vi (col)* **(a)** *(nicht mehr folgen können)* to give up. **(b)** *(fassungslos sein)* to be staggered *(col)*.

abschneiden *sep irreg* **1** *vt (lit, fig)* to cut off; *Blumen, Fingernägel, Haar* to cut. **jdm das Wort ~** to cut sb short. **2** *vi* **bei etw gut/schlecht ~** *(col)* to come off well/badly in sth.

Abschnitt *m* **(a)** section; *(Math)* segment; *(Mil)* sector, zone; *(Geschichts~, Zeit~)* period. **(b)** *(Kontroll~) (von Scheck etc)* counterfoil; *(von Karte)* section; *(von Papier)* slip.

abschnitt(s)weise *adv* in sections.

abschnüren *vt sep* to cut off *(von* from*)*. **jdm das Blut ~** to cut off sb's circulation; **jdm die Luft ~** *(lit)* to stop sb breathing; *(fig)* to ruin sb.

abschöpfen *vt sep Fett* to skim off; *(fig)* Ruhm to reap. **den Gewinn ~** to siphon off the profits.

abschotten *vt sep* **sich gegen etw ~** *(fig)* to cut oneself off from sth.

abschrägen *vt sep* to slope; *Holz, Brett* to bevel. **ein abgeschrägtes Dach** a sloping roof.

abschrauben *vt sep* to unscrew.

abschrecken *sep* **1** *vt* **(a)** *(fernhalten)* to deter, to put off; *(verjagen: Hund, Vogelscheuche)* to scare off. **ich lasse mich dadurch nicht ~** I won't be deterred by that. **(b)** *(abkühlen) Stahl* to quench; *(Cook)* to rinse with cold water. **2** *vi (Strafe)* to act as a deterrent.

abschreckend *adj (warnend)* deterrent. **ein ~es Beispiel** a warning; **eine ~e Wirkung haben, ~ wirken** to act as a deterrent.

Abschreckung *f* deterrent.

Abschreckungs-: ~mittel *nt* deterrent; **~waffe** *f* deterrent (weapon).

abschreiben *sep irreg* **1** *vt* **(a)** to copy *(bei, von* from; *(kopieren)* to copy out. **(b)** *(Comm: absetzen, abziehen)* to deduct. **(c)** *(verlorengeben)* to write off. **er ist bei mir abgeschrieben** I'm finished with him. **2** *vi* **(a)** *(Sch)* to copy, to crib *(col)*. **(b) jdm ~** to write to sb to tell him/her that one cannot come *etc*.

Abschreibung *f (Comm)* deduction.

abschreiten *vt sep irreg (entlanggehen) Gelände* to patrol; *(inspizieren) Front* to inspect.

Abschrift *f* copy.

abschrubben *vt sep (col) Schmutz* to scrub off; *Rücken, Fußboden* to scrub (down).

abschuften *vr sep (col)* to slog one's guts out *(col)*.

abschürfen *vt sep* to graze.

Abschürfung *f (Wunde)* graze.

Abschuß *m* **(a)** *(das Abfeuern)* firing, shooting; *(von Rakete)* launch(ing). **(b)** *(das Außer-Gefecht-Setzen)* shooting down; *(von Panzer)* knocking out. **die Luftwaffe erzielte zwölf Abschüsse** the air force shot down twelve planes. **(c)** *(von Wild)* shooting. **Fasanen sind jetzt zum ~ freigegeben** pheasant-shooting is now permitted; **zum ~ freigegeben sein** *(fig)* to be fair game.

abschüssig *adj* sloping. **eine sehr ~e Straße** a steep road.

Abschuß-: ~liste *f* **er steht auf der ~liste** *(col)* his days are numbered; **~rampe** *f* launch(ing) pad.

abschütteln *vt sep (lit, fig)* to shake off.

abschütten *vt sep Flüssigkeit etc* to pour off; *(Cook)* to drain off; *Kartoffeln etc* to drain.

abschwächen *sep* **1** *vt* to weaken; *Formulierung* to tone down. **2** *vr* to fall off, to diminish; *(Lärm)* to decrease; *(Preisauftrieb, Andrang)* to ease off.

Abschwächung *f siehe vb* weakening; toning down; decrease; easing off.

abschweifen *vi sep aux sein (lit, fig) (von* from*)* to stray, to wander (off); *(Redner auch)* to digress.

Abschweifung *f* digression.

abschwellen *vi sep irreg aux sein (Entzündung, Fluß)* to go down; *(Lärm)* to die away.

abschwenken *sep* **1** *vi aux sein* to turn away; *(Kamera)* to pan. **er ist nach links abgeschwenkt** *(lit)* he turned off to the left; *(fig)* he swung (over) to the left; **(nach rechts) ~** *(Mil)* to wheel (right). **2** *vt* **(a)** *(abschütteln) Tropfen* to shake off. **(b)** *(Cook)* to drain (off).

abschwindeln *vt sep* **jdm etw ~** to swindle sb out of sth.

abschwirren *vi sep aux sein* to whirr off; *(fig col: weggehen)* to buzz off *(col)*.

abschwören *vi sep irreg (old, liter)* to renounce *(dat* sth*)*. **dem Glauben/Teufel ~** to renounce one's faith/the devil; **dem Alkohol ~** *(col)* to give up drinking.

Abschwung *m (Sport)* dismount; *(Econ)* downward trend, recession.

absegnen *vt sep (col)* to give one's blessing to.

absehbar *adj* forseeable. **in ~er/auf ~e Zeit** in/for the forseeable future; **die Folgen sind noch gar nicht ~** there's no telling what the consequences will be.

absehen *sep irreg* **1** *vt* **(a)** *(abgucken)* **(bei) jdm etw ~** to pick sth up from sb. **(b)** *(voraussehen)* to foresee. **es ist ganz klar abzusehen, daß ...** it's easy to see that ...; **das Ende läßt sich noch nicht ~** the end is not yet in sight; *siehe* **abgesehen 1.**
2 *vi* **von etw ~** *(verzichten)* to refrain from sth; *(nicht berücksichtigen)* to disregard sth; **davon ~, etw zu tun** to dispense with doing sth; *siehe* **abgesehen 2.**

abseifen *vt sep* to soap down.

abseilen *sep* **1** *vt* to lower down on a rope. **2** *vr* *(Bergsteiger)* to abseil (down).

absein *vi sep irreg aux sein (col)* **(a)** *(weg sein)* to be off. **die Farbe/der Knopf ist ab** the paint/button has come off. **(b)** *(abgelegen sein)* to be far away.

abseitig *adj* **(a)** *(ausgefallen)* esoteric. **(b)** *(pervers)* perverse.

abseits *adv (abgelegen)* out of the way, remote; *(Sport)* offside. **~ vom Wege** off the beaten track; **~ stehen** *(fig)* to be on the outside; *(Sport)* to be offside; **~ bleiben, sich ~ halten** *(fig)* to keep to oneself.

Abseits *nt* **-** *(Sport)* offside. **im ~ stehen** to be offside; **im ~ leben** *(fig)* to live in the shadows.

Abseits-: ~position, ~stellung *f* offside position; **~tor** *nt* offside goal.

absenden *vt sep* to send; *(mit der Post auch)* to post *(Brit)*, to mail *(esp US)*.

Absender(in *f***)** *m* **-** sender; *(Adresse)* (sender's) address.

abservieren* *sep* **1** *vi* to clear the table. **2** *vt* **(a)** *Geschirr, Tisch* to clear. **(b)** *(col: entlassen, kaltstellen)* **jdn ~** to push sb out, to get rid of sb. **(c)** *(col: umbringen)* to do in *(col)*. **(d)** *(Sport col: besiegen)* to thrash *(col)*.

absetzbar *adj Ware* saleable; *Betrag* deductible.

absetzen *sep* **1** *vt* **(a)** *(abnehmen) Hut, Brille* to take off; *(hinstellen) Gepäck, Glas* to set *or* put down. **(b)** *(aussteigen lassen) Fahrgast* to drop. **(c)** *Theaterstück* to take off; *Fußballspiel, Versammlung, Termin* to cancel; *Punkt von der Tagesordnung* to delete. **(d)** *(entlassen)* to dismiss; *König* to depose. **(e)** *(Med) Medikament* to stop taking; *Behandlung* to discontinue. **(f)** *(Comm) Waren* to sell. **sich gut ~ lassen** to sell well. **(g)** *(abziehen) Betrag* to deduct. **das kann man ~** that is tax-deductible.
2 *vr* **(a)** *(Chem, Geol)* to be deposited; *(Feuchtigkeit, Staub etc)* to collect. **(b)** *(col: weggehen)* to get *or* clear out *(aus* of*)* *(col)*; *(Sport: Abstand vergrößern)* to pull ahead. **sich nach Brasilien ~** to clear off to Brazil.
3 *vi* **er trank das Glas aus, ohne abzusetzen** he emptied his glass in one.
4 *vt impers* **es setzt etwas ab** *(col)* there'll be trouble.

Absetzung *f* **(a)** *(Entlassung) (von Beamten)* dismissal; *(von König)* deposing, deposition. **(b)** *(von Theaterstück etc)* withdrawal; *(von Fußballspiel, Termin etc)* cancellation; *(von Punkt auf der Tagesordnung)* deletion.

absichern *sep* **1** *vt* to safeguard; *(garantieren)* to cover; *Bauplatz, Gefahrenstelle* to make safe. **2** *vr* *(sich schützen)* to protect oneself; *(sich versichern)* to cover oneself.

Absicht *f* **-en** *(Vorsatz)* intention; *(Zweck)* purpose; *(Jur)* intent. **in der besten ~** with the best of intentions; **die ~ haben, etw zu tun** to intend to do sth; **eine ~ mit etw verfolgen** to have something in mind with sth; **ernste ~en haben** *(col)* to have serious intentions; **das war nicht meine ~!** I didn't intend that; **etw mit/ohne ~ tun** to do/not to do sth deliberately *or* on purpose.

absichtlich *adj* deliberate, intentional. **etw ~ tun** to do sth on purpose *or* deliberately.

absinken *vi sep irreg aux sein (Schiff)* to sink; *(Boden auch)* to subside; *(Interesse, Leistungen)* to fall *or* drop off; *(fig: moralisch ~)* to go downhill.

absitzen *sep irreg* **1** *vt* **(a)** *(verbringen) Zeit* to sit out; *(verbüßen) Strafe* to serve. **(b)** *(abnutzen) Hose etc* to wear thin. **2** *vi aux sein* **(vom Pferd) ~** to dismount (from a horse).

absolut *adj* absolute; *(völlig auch)* complete, total. **~ nicht/nichts** absolutely not/nothing; **das ist ~ unmöglich** that's quite *or* absolutely impossible.

Absolutheits|anspruch *m* claim to absolute right. **einen ~ vertreten** to claim absoluteness.

Absolution *f (Eccl)* absolution. **jdm die ~ erteilen** to grant *or* give sb absolution.

Absolvent(in *f***)** [apzɔl'vɛnt(ɪn)] *m (Univ)* graduate. **die ~en eines Lehrgangs** the students who have completed a course.

absolvieren* [apzɔl'viːrən] *vt insep Studium, Probezeit* to complete; *Schule* to finish, to graduate from *(US)*; *Prüfung* to pass.

absonderlich *adj* peculiar, strange.

absondern *sep* **1** *vt* **(a)** *(trennen)* to separate;

(isolieren) to isolate. **(b)** *(ausscheiden)* to secrete. **2** *vr (Mensch)* to cut oneself off. **sie sondert sich immer sehr ab** she always keeps herself very much to herself.

Absonderung *f* **(a)** *siehe vt* separation; isolation; secretion. **(b)** *(abgeschiedener Stoff)* secretion.

absorbieren* *vt insep (lit, fig)* to absorb.

Absorption *f* absorption.

abspalten *vtr sep* to split off; *(Chem)* to separate (off).

abspannen *sep* **1** *vt Pferd, Wagen* to unhitch. **2** *vi (fig: entspannen)* to relax; *siehe* **abgespannt.**

absparen *vt sep* **sich** *(dat)* **ein Auto vom Lohn ~** to save up for a car from one's wages; **sich** *(dat)* **etw vom Munde ~** to scrimp and save for sth.

abspecken *sep (col)* **1** *vt* to shed. **2** *vi* to lose weight.

abspeisen *vt sep (fig: abfertigen)* **jdn mit etw ~** to fob sb off with sth.

abspenstig *adj* **jdm jdn/etw ~ machen** to lure sb/sth away from sb; **jdm die Freundin ~ machen** to pinch sb's girlfriend *(col)*.

absperren *sep* **1** *vt* **(a)** *(versperren)* to block off. **(b)** *Strom etc* to turn *or* shut off. **(c)** *(zuschließen)* to lock. **2** *vi* to lock up.

Absperrung *f* **(a)** *(Abriegelung)* blocking *or* closing off. **(b)** *(Sperre)* barrier.

Abspiel *nt (Sport)* pass.

abspielen *sep* **1** *vt* **(a)** *Tonband etc* to play; *(vom Blatt) Musik* to sight-read; *siehe* **abgespielt. (b)** *(Sport) Ball* to pass. **2** *vr (sich ereignen)* to happen.

absplittern *vti sep (vi: aux sein)* to chip off; *Holz auch* to splinter off.

Absprache *f* arrangement. **ohne vorherige ~** without prior consultation.

absprechen *sep irreg* **1** *vt* **(a) jdm etw ~** *(verweigern) Recht* to deny sb sth; *(in Abrede stellen) Begabung* to dispute sb's sth; **er ist wirklich sehr klug, das kann man ihm nicht ~** there's no denying that he's very clever. **(b)** *(verabreden) Termin* to arrange. **2** *vr* **sich mit jdm ~** to make an arrangement with sb; **die beiden hatten sich vorher abgesprochen** they had agreed on what to do/say *etc* in advance.

abspringen *vi sep irreg aux sein* **(a)** *(herunterspringen)* to jump down *(von* from*)*; *(herausspringen)* to jump out *(von* of*)*; *(Aviat)* to jump *(von* from*)*; *(bei Gefahr)* to bale out. **(b)** *(sich lösen)* to come off; *(Farbe, Lack auch)* to flake *or* peel off. **(c)** *(fig col: sich zurückziehen)* to get out; *(von Partei, Kurs etc)* to back out.

abspritzen *vt sep* **etw/jdn ~** to spray sth/sb down; *Schmutz* to spray off *(von etw* sth*)*.

Absprung *m* jump *(auch Aviat)*, leap; *(Sport)* take-off. **den ~ schaffen** *(fig)* to make the break *(col)*; **er hat den ~ gewagt** *(fig)* he took the leap.

abspulen *vt sep Kabel, Garn* to unwind.

abspülen *sep* **1** *vt Hände, Geschirr* to rinse; *Fett etc* to rinse off. **2** *vi* to wash up.

abstammen *vi sep no ptp* to be descended *(von* from*)*.

Abstammung *f* descent; *(Abkunft auch)* origin. **ehelicher/unehelicher ~** *(Jur)* of legitimate/illegitimate birth; **französischer ~** of French extraction *or* descent.

Abstand *m* **(a)** *(Zwischenraum)* distance; *(kürzer)* gap, space; *(Zeit~)* interval; *(fig: Distanz)* distance. **mit ~** by far, far and away; **~ von etw gewinnen** *(fig)* to distance oneself from sth; **in Abständen von 10 Minuten** at 10 minute intervals; **~ halten** to keep one's distance; **mit großem ~ führen** to lead by a wide margin. **(b)** *(form: Verzicht)* **davon ~ nehmen, etw zu tun** to refrain from doing sth.

Abstandssumme *f (form)* indemnity.

abstatten *vt sep (form)* **jdm einen Besuch ~** to pay sb a visit; **jdm seinen Dank ~** to give thanks to sb.

abstauben *vti sep* **(a)** *Möbel etc* to dust. **(b)** *(col) (wegnehmen)* to nick *(col)*; *(schnorren)* to cadge *(von, bei, dat* off, from*)*.

Abstauber *m* - *(Ftbl col)* **(a)** *(auch* **~tor***)* easy goal. **(b)** *(Spieler)* goal-hanger *(col)*.

Abstecher *m* - *(Ausflug)* trip; *(Umweg)* detour, side-trip.

abstecken *vt sep* **(a)** *(lit, fig) Gelände, Verhandlungsposition* to mark out. **(b)** *Kleid, Naht* to pin.

abstehen *sep irreg* **1** *vi (entfernt stehen)* to stand away; *(nicht anliegen)* to stick out. **~de Ohren** ears that stick out; *siehe* **abgestanden. 2** *vt (col)* **sich** *(dat)* **die Beine ~** to stand for hours.

Absteige *f* **-n** cheap hotel.

absteigen *vi sep irreg aux sein* **(a)** *(heruntersteigen)* to get off *(von etw* sth*)*. **(b)** *(abwärts gehen)* to make one's way down; *(Bergsteiger auch)* to climb down. **in ~der Linie** in the line of descent; **auf dem ~den Ast sein** *(col)* to be going downhill, to be on the decline; **gesellschaftlich ~** to go down in society. **(c)** *(einkehren)* to stay; *(im Hotel auch)* to put up *(in +dat* at*)*. **(d)** *(Sport: Mannschaft)* **aus der ersten Liga ~** to be relegated from the first division.

Absteiger *m* - *(Sport)* relegated team.

abstellen *vt sep* **(a)** *(hinstellen)* to put down. **(b)** *(unterbringen)* to put; *(Aut: parken auch)* to park. **(c)** *(abrücken, entfernt stellen)* to put away from. **(d)** *(abkommandieren)* to order off, to detail; *Offizier auch* to second. **(e)** *(abdrehen)* to turn off. **(f)** *(sich abgewöhnen)* to give up, to stop. **(g)** *(unterbinden) Mangel, Unsitte etc* to bring to an end. **das läßt sich nicht/läßt sich ~** nothing/something can be done about that.

Abstell-: ~gleis *nt* siding; **jdn aufs ~gleis schieben** *(fig)* to cast sb aside; **~raum** *m* storeroom.

abstempeln *vt sep* to stamp; *Post* to postmark; *(fig)* to brand *(zu, als* as*)*.

absterben *vi sep irreg aux sein (eingehen, Med, fig)* to die; *(gefühllos werden: Glieder)* to go *or* grow numb; *siehe* **abgestorben.**

Abstieg *m* **-e** *(das Absteigen)* way down, descent; *(Niedergang)* decline; *(Sport)* relegation.

abstimmen *sep* **1** *vi* to take a vote. **über etw** *(acc)* **~** to vote on sth; **über etw** *(acc)* **~ lassen** to put sth to the vote; **geheim ~** to have a secret ballot. **2** *vt Instrumente* to tune *(auf +acc* to*)*; *Farben, Kleidung* to match *(auf+acc* with*)*; *Termine* to coordinate *(auf+acc* with*)*; *(anpassen)* to suit *(auf +acc* to*)*. **gut auf etw** *(acc)***/aufeinander abgestimmt sein** *(Instrumente)* to be in tune with sth/with each other; *(Farben, Speisen etc)* to go well with sth/to go well together; *(Termine)* to fit in well with sth/with each other; *(einander angepaßt sein)* to be well-suited to sth/(to each other); **etw miteinander ~** *(vereinbaren)* to settle sth amongst ourselves/themselves *etc.* **3** *vr* **sich ~ (mit jdm/miteinander)** to come to an agreement (with sb/amongst ourselves/themselves *etc*).

Abstimmung *f (Stimmabgabe)* vote; *(geheime ~)* ballot. **eine ~ durchführen** to take a vote.

Abstimmungs|ergebnis *nt* result of the vote.

abstinent *adj* teetotal.

Abstinenz *f no pl* teetotalism, abstinence.

Abstinenzler(in *f)* *m* - teetotaller *(Brit)*, teetotaler *(US)*.

abstoppen *vti sep (auch Sport)* to stop; *(mit Stoppuhr)* to time.

Abstoß *m (Ftbl)* goal kick; *(nach Fangen des Balls)* clearance.

abstoßen *sep irreg* **1** *vt* **(a)** *(wegstoßen) Boot* to push off *or* out; *(abschlagen) Ecken* to knock off. **(b)** *(zurückstoßen)* to repel; *(Comm) Ware, Aktien* to sell off; *(fig: anwidern)* to repel. **dieser Stoff stößt Wasser ab** this material is water-repellent; **gleiche Pole stoßen sich ab** like poles repel (each other). **(c)** *(Ftbl)* **den Ball ~** to take the goal kick; *(nach Fangen)* to clear (the ball). **2** *vr (esp Sport: Mensch)* **sich mit den Füßen vom Boden ~** to push oneself off. **3** *vi (anwidern)* to be repulsive. **sich von etw abgestoßen fühlen** to find sth repulsive.

abstoßend *adj Aussehen, Äußeres* repulsive.

Abstoßung *f (Phys)* repulsion.

abstottern *vt sep (col)* to pay off.

abstrahieren* [apstra'hi:rən] *vti insep* to abstract *(aus* from*)*.

abstrahlen *vt sep Wärme etc* to emit.

abstrakt [ap'strakt] *adj* abstract.

abstrampeln *vr sep (fig col)* to sweat (away) *(col)*.

abstreichen *vt sep irreg (wegstreichen)* to wipe off.

abstreifen *vt sep* **(a)** *(abtreten) Schuhe, Füße* to wipe. **(b)** *(abziehen) Kleidung, Schmuck* to take off, to slip off; *(entfernen) Haut* to shed; *(fig) Gewohnheit, Fehler* to get rid of.

abstreiten *vt sep irreg (leugnen)* to deny. **das kann man ihm nicht ~** you can't deny it.

Abstrich *m* **(a)** *(Kürzung)* cutback. **~e machen** to cut back *(an+dat* on*)*; *(weniger erwarten etc)* to lower one's sights. **(b)** *(Med)* swab; *(Gebärmutter~)* smear. **einen ~ machen** to take a swab/smear.

abstrus [ap'stru:s] *adj (geh)* abstruse.

abstufen *vt sep Gelände* to terrace; *Farben* to shade; *Gehälter, Steuern, Preise* to grade.

Abstufung *f (Nuance)* shade; *(Stufe)* grade.

abstumpfen *sep* **1** *vt Mensch* to dull; *siehe* **abgestumpft. 2** *vi aux sein (fig: Geschmack etc)* to become dulled. **diese Arbeit stumpft ab** this work dulls the mind.

Absturz *m siehe vi* crash; fall. **ein Flugzeug zum ~ bringen** to bring a plane down.

abstürzen *vi sep aux sein (Flugzeug)* to crash; *(Bergsteiger)* to fall.

abstützen *sep* **1** *vt* to support *(auch fig)*; *Haus, Mauer auch* to shore up. **2** *vr* to support oneself.

absuchen *vt sep* to search; *Gegend auch* to comb, to scour; *Himmel* to scan; *(Scheinwerfer)* to sweep.

absurd *adj* absurd. **~es Drama** *or* **Theater** theatre of the absurd.

Absurdität *f* absurdity *(auch Philos)*.

Abszeß *m* **-sse** abscess.

Abt *m* **¨-e** abbot.

abtakeln *vt sep Schiff* to unrig; *siehe* **abgetakelt.**

abtasten *vt sep* to feel; *(Elec)* to scan; *(bei Durchsuchung)* to frisk *(auf+acc* for*)*.

abtauen *sep* **1** *vt* to thaw out; *Kühlschrank* to defrost. **2** *vi aux sein* to thaw.

Abtei *f* abbey.

Abteil *nt* **-e** compartment.

abteilen *vt sep (abtrennen)* to divide off.

Abteilung *f (in Firma, Kaufhaus)* department; *(in Krankenhaus, Jur)* section; *(Mil)* unit, section.

Abteilungsleiter *m* head of department.

abtelefonieren* *vi sep* to telephone to say one can't make it.

abtippen *vt sep (col)* to type out.

Äbtissin *f* abbess.

abtönen *vt sep Farbe* to tone down.

Abtönung *f (Farbton)* tone, shade.

abtöten *vt sep (lit, fig)* to destroy, to kill (off); *Nerv* to deaden.

abtragen *vt sep irreg* **(a)** *(abbauen) Gebäude, Mauer* to take down; *(Fluß) Ufer* to erode. **(b)** *(abbezahlen) Schulden* to pay off. **(c)** *(abnutzen) Kleider* to wear out; *siehe* **abgetragen.**

abträglich *adj* detrimental *(dat* to, for*)*; *Kritik etc* adverse.

Abtragung *f (Geol)* erosion.

Abtransport *m* transportation; *(aus Katastrophengebiet)* evacuation. **beim ~ der Gefangenen** when the prisoners were being taken away.

abtransportieren* *vt sep* to transport; *(aus Katastrophengebiet)* to evacuate.

abtreiben *sep irreg* **1** *vt* **(a) vom Kurs ~** to carry off course. **(b)** *Kind* to abort. **sie hat das Kind abgetrieben** *or* **~ lassen** she had an abortion. **2** *vi* **(a)** *aux sein* **(vom Kurs) ~** to be carried off course. **(b)** *(Abort vornehmen)* to carry out an abortion; *(Abort vornehmen lassen)* to have an abortion.

Abtreibung *f* abortion. **eine ~ vornehmen lassen** to have an abortion.

abtrennen *vt sep* **(a)** *(lostrennen)* to detach; *Knöpfe, Besatz etc* to remove; *Bein, Finger etc (durch Unfall)* to sever, to cut off. **„hier ~"** "detach here". **(b)** *(abteilen)* to separate off; *(mit Zwischenwand etc auch)* to partition off.

abtreten *sep irreg* **1** *vt* **(a)** *Teppich* to wear (out); *Schnee, Schmutz* to stamp off. **sich** *(dat)* **die Füße ~** to wipe one's feet. **(b)** *(überlassen) (jdm or an jdn* to sb*)* to hand over; *Gebiet, Land auch* to cede; *Ansprüche* to transfer. **2** *vi aux sein (Theat)* to go off (stage); *(Mil)* to dismiss; *(col: zurücktreten) (Politiker)* to resign; *(Monarch)* to abdicate. **~!** *(Mil)* dismiss!

Abtreter *m* **-** *(Fuß~)* doormat.

Abtretung *f (an+acc* to*)* transfer; *(von Ansprüchen auch, von Gebiet)* ceding, cession.

Abtritt *m (Theat)* exit; *(Rücktritt) (von Minister)* resignation; *(von Monarch)* abdication.

abtrocknen *sep* **1** *vt* to dry. **2** *vi* to dry up, to do the drying-up.

abtropfen *vi sep aux sein* to drip; *(Geschirr)* to drain. **etw ~ lassen** to let sth drain.

abtrotzen *vt sep* **jdm etw ~** *(geh)* to wring sth out of sb.

abtrünnig *adj* renegade; *(rebellisch)* rebel. **jdm/einer Gruppe ~ werden** to desert sb/a group.

abtun *vt sep irreg (fig: beiseite schieben)* to dismiss. **etw mit einem Achselzucken/einem Lachen ~** to shrug/laugh sth off; **etw kurz ~** to brush sth aside; *siehe* **abgetan.**

abtupfen *vt sep Tränen* to dab away; *Gesicht, Wunde* to dab.

ab|urteilen *vt sep* to pass sentence *or* judgement on.

abverlangen* *vt sep siehe* **abfordern.**

abwägen *vt sep irreg* to weigh up; *Worte* to weigh. **er wog beide Möglichkeiten gegeneinander ab** he weighed up the two possibilities; *siehe* **abgewogen.**

Abwahl *f* voting out. **es kam zur ~ des gesamten Vorstands** the whole committee was voted out.

abwählen *vt sep* to vote out (of office); *(Sch) Fach* to give up.

abwälzen *vt sep Schuld, Verantwortung* to shift *(auf+acc* onto*)*; *Arbeit* to unload *(auf+acc* onto*)*; *Kosten* to pass on *(auf+acc* to*)*. **die Schuld von sich ~** to shift the blame onto somebody else.

abwandeln *vt sep Melodie* to adapt; *Thema auch* to modify.

abwandern *vi sep aux sein* to move (away) *(aus* from*)*; *(Kapital)* to be transferred *(aus* out of*)*. **viele Spieler/Abonnenten** *etc* **wandern ab** a lot of players/subscribers *etc* are transferring.

Abwandlung *f* adaptation, variation; *(von Thema etc auch)* modification.

Abwärme *f* waste heat.

abwarten *sep* **1** *vt* to wait for. **das Gewitter ~** to wait till the storm is over; **er kann es nicht mehr ~** he can't wait any longer; **das bleibt abzuwarten** that remains to be seen. **2** *vi* to wait. **warten Sie ab!** just wait a bit!; **~ und Tee trinken** *(col)* to wait and see; **eine ~de Haltung einnehmen** to play a waiting game.

abwärts *adv* down; *(nach unten auch)* downwards. **„~!"** *(im Fahrstuhl)* "going down!".

abwärtsgehen *vi impers sep aux sein (fig)* **mit ihm/dem Land geht es abwärts** he/the country is going downhill.

Abwärtstrend *m* downwards *or* downhill trend.

Abwasch *m no pl* washing-up *(Brit)*. **den ~ machen** to do the washing-up *(Brit)*, to wash the dishes; **dann kannst du das auch machen, das ist (dann) ein ~** *(col)* then you could do that as well and kill two birds with one stone *(prov)*.

abwaschbar *adj Tapete* washable.

abwaschen *sep irreg* **1** *vt Gesicht* to wash; *Geschirr* to wash; *Schmutz* to wash off; *Auto* to wash down. **den Schmutz (vom Gesicht) ~** to wash the dirt off (one's face). **2** *vi* to wash up *(Brit)*, to do the washing-up *(Brit)*, to wash the dishes.

Abwaschwasser *nt* washing-up water *(Brit)*, dishwater; *(fig col)* dishwater *(col)*.

Abwasser *nt* sewage *no pl*.

Abwasserkanal *m* sewer.

abwechseln *vir sep* to alternate. **sich** *or* **einander ~** to alternate; *(Menschen auch)* to take turns; **sich mit jdm ~** to take turns with sb.

abwechselnd *adv* alternately. **er war ~ fröhlich und traurig** he alternated between being happy and sad.

Abwechslung *f* change; *(Zerstreuung)* diversion. **eine angenehme/schöne ~** a pleasant/nice change; **zur ~** for a change; **für ~ sorgen** to provide entertainment; **hier haben wir wenig ~** there's not much variety in life here.

abwechslungs-: ~halber *adv* for a change; **~los** *adj* monotonous; **~reich** *adj* varied.

Abweg ['apve:k] *m* **jdn auf ~e führen** to lead sb astray *(auch moralisch)*; **auf ~e geraten** *or* **kommen** to go astray; *(moralisch auch)* to stray from the straight and narrow.

abwegig ['apve:gıç] *adj (geh)* erroneous; *(bizarr)* eccentric; *Verdacht* groundless.

Abwehr *f no pl* **(a)** defence *(Brit)*, defense *(US)* *(gen* against*)*; *(~truppen)* defence *(Brit) or* defense *(US)* troops; *(Spionage~)* counter-intelligence (service); *(Schutz)* protection *(gen* against*)*. **der ~ von etw dienen** to provide *or* give protection against sth. **(b)** *(Zurückweisung)* repulse; *(Abweisung)* rejection. **die ~ des Feindes** repelling the enemy; **auf ~ stoßen** to be repulsed.

abwehrbereit *adj (Mil)* ready for defence *(Brit) or* defense *(US)*.

abwehren *sep* **1** *vt* **(a)** *Gegner* to fend *or* ward off; *Ball* to clear; *Schlag* to parry, to ward off. **(b)** *(fernhalten)* to keep away; *Krankheitserreger* to protect against; *Gefahr, üble Folgen* to avert. **(c)** *(abweisen) Anschuldigung* to dismiss. **eine ~de Geste** a dismissive wave of the hand. **2** *vi (Sport)* to clear; *(Torwart auch)* to make a save. **mit dem Kopf ~** to head clear; **zur Ecke ~** to clear and concede a corner.

Abwehr-: ~kampf *m (Mil, Sport)* defence *(Brit)*, defense *(US)*; **~reaktion** *f (Psych)* defence *(Brit) or* defense *(US)* reaction; **~spieler** *m* defender.

abweichen *vi sep irreg aux sein (sich entfernen)* to deviate; *(sich unterscheiden)* to differ. **voneinander ~** *(Theorien)* to diverge, to differ; **vom Kurs ~** to deviate *or* depart from one's course; **vom Thema ~** to digress; **vom rechten Weg ~** *(fig)* to wander off the straight and narrow; **ich weiche erheblich von seiner Meinung ab** I hold quite a different view from him; **~des Verhalten** *(Psych, Sociol)* deviant behaviour.

Abweichler(in *f***)** *m* **-** *(Pol)* deviant.

abweichlerisch *adj (Pol)* deviant.

Abweichung *f siehe vi* deviation; difference; *(von Theorien)* divergence. **zulässige ~** *(Tech)* tolerance; *(zeitlich, zahlenmäßig)* allowance.

abweisen *vt sep irreg* to turn down; *(wegschicken)* to turn away; *(Jur) Klage* to dismiss. **er läßt sich nicht ~** he won't take no for an answer.

abweisend *adj Ton, Blick* cold, chilly.

abwenden *sep reg or irreg* **1** *vt* **(a)** *(zur Seite wenden)* to turn away; *Blick* to avert; *Kopf* to turn. **(b)** *(verhindern) Unheil* to avert. **2** *vr* to turn away.

abwerben *vt sep irreg* to woo away *(dat* from*)*.

abwerfen *sep irreg* **1** *vt* to throw off; *Reiter* to throw; *Bomben, Flugblätter etc* to drop; *Ballast* to jettison; *Blätter, Nadeln* to shed; *(Cards)* to discard; *(Comm) Gewinn* to yield. **2** *vti (Sport) Ball* to throw out; *Latte* to knock off *or* down.

abwerten *vt sep* **(a)** *auch vi (Fin)* to devalue. **(b)** *(fig) Ideale* to debase, to cheapen.

abwertend *adj* pejorative.

Abwertung *f (Fin)* devaluation.

abwesend *adj (form)* absent; *(iro: zerstreut auch)* far away. **die A~en** the absentees.

Abwesenheit *f* absence. **in ~** *(+gen)* in the absence of; **durch ~ glänzen** *(iro)* to be conspicuous by one's absence.

abwickeln *sep* **1** *vt* **(a)** *(abspulen)* to unwind; *Verband auch* to remove. **(b)** *(fig: erledigen)* to deal with, to handle; *(abschließen)* to conclude. **2** *vr* to unwind; *(vonstatten gehen)* to go *or* pass off.

Abwicklung *f (Erledigung)* handling; *(Abschluß)* completion, conclusion. **die Polizei sorgte für eine reibungslose ~ der Veranstaltung** the police made sure that the event went *or* passed off smoothly.

abwiegeln *sep* **1** *vt* to appease. **2** *vi* to calm things down.

abwiegen *vt sep irreg* to weigh out.

abwimmeln *vt sep (col) jdn* to get rid of; *Auftrag* to get out of. **die Sekretärin hat mich abgewimmelt** his secretary turned me away; **laß dich nicht ~** don't let them get rid of you.

abwinken *sep* **1** *vi (col) (abwehrend)* to wave it/him *etc* aside; *(fig: ablehnen)* to say no. **als er merkte, wovon ich reden wollte, winkte er gleich ab** when he realised what I wanted to talk about he immediately put me off. **2** *vti* **ein Rennen ~** to wave the chequered *(Brit) or* checkered *(US)* flag.

abwirtschaften *vi sep (col)* to go downhill. **endgültig abgewirtschaftet haben** to have eventually reached rock bottom.

abwischen *vt sep Staub, Schmutz etc* to wipe off *or* away; *Augen, Tränen* to dry.

abwracken *vt sep Schiff, Auto* to break (up); *siehe* **abgewrackt.**

Abwurf *m* throwing off; *(von Reiter)* throw; *(von Bomben etc)* dropping; *(von Ballast)* jettisoning; *(Sport: von Speer etc)* throwing. **ein ~ vom Tor** a goal-throw, a throw-out.

abwürgen *vt sep (col)* to scotch; *Motor* to stall. **etw von vornherein ~** to nip sth in the bud.

abzahlen *vt sep* to pay off.

abzählen *vt sep* to count. **das läßt sich an den (fünf) Fingern ~** *(fig)* any fool can see that *(col)*; **abgezähltes Geld** exact money; *(Fahrgeld)* exact fare.

Abzählreim *m* counting rhyme *(such as "eeny meeny miney mo", for choosing a person)*.

Abzahlung *f* **(a)** *(Rückzahlung)* repayment, paying off. **(b)** *(Ratenzahlung)* hire purchase *(Brit)*, HP *(Brit)*, installment plan *(US)*; *(Rate)* (re)payment, instalment *(Brit)*, installment *(US)*. **etw auf ~ kaufen** to buy sth on HP *(Brit) or* on hire purchase *(Brit) or* on the installment plan *(US)*.

abzapfen *vt sep* **jdm Blut ~** to take blood from sb; **jdm Geld ~** to get some money out of sb.

Abzeichen *nt* badge; *(Mil)* insignia *pl*.

abzeichnen *sep* **1** *vt* **(a)** to draw. **(b)** *(signieren)* to initial. **2** *vr* to stand out; *(fig) (deutlich werden)* to emerge, to become apparent; *(drohend bevorstehen)* to loom (on the horizon).

Abziehbild *nt* transfer, decal *(US)*.

abziehen *sep irreg* **1** *vt* **(a)** to skin; *Fell, Haut* to remove, to strip off. **(b)** *Bett* to strip. **(c)** *Ring etc* to take off. **(d)** *Schlüssel* to take out, to remove. **(e)** *(zurückziehen) Kapital* to withdraw; *Truppen auch* to pull out; *(subtrahieren) Zahlen* to take away, to subtract; *Steuern* to deduct. **DM 20 vom Preis ~** to take DM 20 off the price. **(f)** *(Typ: vervielfältigen)* to run off; *(Phot) Bilder* to make prints of. **etw zwanzigmal ~** to run off twenty copies of sth. **(g)** *(schleifen)* to sharpen; *Parkett* to sand (down). **2** *vi* **(a)** *aux sein (sich verflüchtigen: Rauch)* to escape, to go away. **(b)** *aux sein (Soldaten)* to pull out *(aus* of*)*, to withdraw *(aus* from*)*; *(col: weggehen)* to go off *or* away. **zieh ab!** *(col)* clear off! *(col)*. **(c)** *(abdrücken)* to pull the trigger, to fire.

abzielen *vi sep* **auf etw** *(acc)* **~** *(Mensch)* to aim at sth; *(in Rede)* to get at sth; *(Bemerkung, Maßnahme etc)* to be aimed *or* directed at sth.

Abzug ['aptsu:k] *m* **(a)** *no pl (von Truppen, Kapital etc)* withdrawal. **jdm freien ~ gewähren** to give *or* grant sb a safe conduct. **(b)** *(usu pl: vom Lohn etc)* deduction; *(Rabatt)* discount. **(c)** *(Typ)* copy; *(Korrekturfahne)* proof; *(Phot)* print. **(d)** *(Öffnung für Rauch, Gas)* flue. **(e)** *(am Gewehr)* trigger.

abzüglich *prep+gen (Comm)* minus, less.

Abzweig *m* junction.

abzweigen *sep* **1** *vi aux sein* to branch off. **2** *vt (col)* to set *or* put on one side.

Abzweigung *f* junction, turn-off; *(Gabelung)* fork.

abzwingen *vt sep irreg* **jdm Respekt** *etc* **~** to gain sb's respect *etc*; **er zwang sich** *(dat)* **ein Lächeln ab** he forced a smile.

ach [ax] *interj* oh. **~ nein!** oh no!; *(überrascht)* no!, really!; *(ablehnend)* no, no!; **~ so!** I see!; **~ was** *or* **wo!** of course not; **~ was** *or* **wo, das ist doch nicht so schlimm!** come on now, it's not that bad; **~ wirklich?** oh really?

Ach *nt*: **mit ~ und Krach** *(col)* by the skin of one's teeth *(col)*.

Achat *m* **-e** agate.

Achillesferse *f* Achilles heel.

Achse ['aksə] *f* **-n (a)** axis. **(b)** *(Tech)* axle. **auf ~ sein** *(col)* to be out and about.

Achsel ['aksl] *f* **-n (a)** shoulder. **die ~n** *or* **mit den ~n zucken** to shrug (one's shoulders). **(b)** *(~höhle)* armpit.

Achsel-: **~haare** *pl* underarm hair; **~höhle** *f* armpit; **~klappe** *f*, **~stück** *nt* epaulette; **~zucken** *nt* shrug; **mit einem ~zucken** with a shrug (of one's shoulders); **a~zuckend** *adj* **er stand a~zuckend da** he stood there shrugging his shoulders; **er nahm es a~zuckend zur Kenntnis** he acknowledged it with a shrug of his shoulders.

Achsen-: **~bruch** *m* broken axle; **~kreuz** *nt* coordinate system; **~mächte** *pl (Hist)* Axis powers *pl*.

Achs-: **~lager** *nt* axle bearing; **~last** *f* axle weight.

acht[1] *num* eight. **für** *or* **auf ~ Tage** for a week; **heute/morgen in ~ Tagen** a week today/tomorrow, today/tomorrow week; **heute vor ~ Tagen war ich ...** a week ago today I was ...; *siehe* **vier.**

acht[2]: **sich in ~ nehmen** to take care, to look out; **etw außer ~ lassen** to disregard sth.

Acht[1] *f* **-en** eight; *(beim Eislaufen etc)* figure (of) eight; *siehe* **Vier.**

Acht[2] *f no pl (Hist)* outlawry, proscription.

achtbar *adj (geh)* worthy.

Acht|eck *nt* octagon.

acht|eckig *adj* octagonal, eight-sided.

achtel *adj* eighth; *siehe* **viertel.**

Achtel *nt* **-** eighth.

Achtelnote *f* quaver, eighth note *(US)*.

achten 1 *vt* to respect. **2** *vi* **auf etw** *(acc)* **~** to pay attention to sth; **auf die Kinder ~** to keep an eye on the children; **darauf ~, daß ...** to see that ..., to take care that ...

ächten *vt (Hist)* to outlaw, to proscribe; *(fig)* to ostracize.

achtenswert *adj Person* worthy; *Bemühungen, Handlung auch* commendable.

achte(r, s) *adj* eighth; *siehe* **vierte(r, s).**

Achte(r) *mf decl as adj* eighth; *siehe* **Vierte(r).**

Achter *m* **-** *(Rudern)* eight.

Achter-: **~bahn** *f* big dipper *(Brit)*, roller coaster; **~deck** *nt (Naut)* afterdeck.

achtfach *adj* eightfold; *siehe* **vierfach.**

achtgeben *vi sep irreg* to take care, to be careful *(auf+acc* of*)*; *(aufmerksam sein)* to pay attention *(auf+acc* to*)*. **auf jdn/etw ~** *(beaufsichtigen)* to keep an eye on sb/sth, to look after sb/sth.

acht-: **~hundert** *num* eight hundred; **~kantig** *adj* **jdn ~kantig rausschmeißen** *(col)* to fling sb out on his/her ear *(col)*.

achtlos *adj* careless, thoughtless. **viele gehen ~ daran vorbei** many people just pass by without noticing.

Achtlosigkeit *f* carelessness, thoughtlessness.

achtmal *adv* eight times.

achtsam *adj (sorgfältig)* careful. **mit etw ~ umgehen** to be careful with sth.

Acht-: **~stundentag** *m* eight hour day; **a~tägig** *adj* lasting a week, week-long.

Achtung *f no pl* **(a) ~!** watch out!, look out!; *(Mil: Befehl)* attention!; **~, ~!** (your) attention please!; **„~ Hochspannung!"** "danger, high voltage"; **„~ Stufe!"** "mind the step"; **~, fertig, los!** ready, steady, go! **(b)** *(Wertschätzung)* respect *(vor+dat* for*)*. **die ~ vor sich selbst** one's self-respect; **bei aller ~ vor jdm/etw** with all due respect to sb/sth; **jdm ~ einflößen** to command *or* gain sb's respect; **sich** *(dat)* **~ verschaffen** to make oneself respected; **alle ~!** good for you/him *etc*!

Ächtung *f no pl (fig: gesellschaftlich)* ostracism.

Achtungserfolg *m* reasonable success.

achtzehn *num* eighteen; *siehe* **vierzehn.**

achtzig *num* eighty. **jdn auf ~ bringen** *(col)* to make sb's blood boil *(col)*; **auf ~ sein** *(col)* to be livid, to be hopping mad *(col)*; *siehe* **vierzig.**

ächzen *vi* to groan *(vor +dat* with*)*. **~ und stöhnen** to moan and groan.

Acker *m* **¨** *(Feld)* field. **den ~/die ¨~ bestellen** to till the soil/plough the fields.

Acker-: **~bau** *m* agriculture, farming; **~bau betreiben** to farm the land; **~bau und Viehzucht** farming; **~furche** *f* furrow; **~gaul** *m (pej)* farm horse, old nag *(pej)*; **~gerät** *nt* agricultural implement; **~krume** *f* topsoil; **~land** *nt* arable land.

ackern *vi (col)* to slog away *(col)*.

a conto *adv (Comm)* on account.

Action ['ækʃən] *f no pl* action.

ad absurdum *adv* **~ führen** *Argument etc* to reduce to absurdity.

ad acta *adv*: **etw ~ legen** *(fig)* to consider sth finished; *Frage, Problem* to consider sth closed.

Adam *m* **seit ~s Zeiten** *(col)* since the year dot *(col)*; **bei ~ und Eva anfangen** *(col)* to start right from scratch *(col) or* from square one *(col)*.

Adams-: **~apfel** *m (col)* Adam's apple; **~kostüm** *nt (col)* **im ~kostüm** in one's birthday suit *(col)*.

Adapter *m* **-** adapter, adaptor.

adäquat *adj (geh) Belohnung, Übersetzung* adequate; *Stellung, Verhalten* suitable; *Kritik* valid. **einer Sache** *(dat)* **~ sein** to be adequate to sth.

addieren* *vti* to add (up).

Addition *f* addition.

Adel *m no pl (Geschlecht, Stand)* nobility; *(Brit auch)* peerage; *(hoher auch)* aristocracy. **von ~ sein** to be a member of the nobility; **er stammt aus altem ~** he comes from an old aristocratic family; **~ verpflichtet** noblesse oblige.

adeln *vt (lit, fig)* to ennoble; *(den Titel „Sir" verleihen)* to knight; *(niedrigen Adel verleihen)* to give a title to.

Adels-: ~**prädikat** *nt* mark of nobility *(in a name)*; ~**stand** *m* nobility; *(Brit auch)* peerage; *(hoher auch)* aristocracy; **in den ~stand erheben** *siehe* **adeln;** ~**titel** *m* title.
Ader *f* **-n** vein; *(fig: Veranlagung)* bent. **eine ~ für etw haben** to have feeling for sth; **eine poetische/musikalische ~ haben** to have a feeling for poetry/music, to have a poetic/musical bent; **jdn zur ~ lassen** *(old, fig col)* to bleed sb.
Adhäsion *f (Phys)* adhesion.
Adhäsionsverschluß *m* adhesive seal.
ad hoc *adv (geh)* ad hoc.
Adjektiv *nt* adjective.
Adjutant *m* adjutant; *(von General)* aide(-de-camp).
Adler *m* - eagle.
Adler-: ~**auge** *nt (fig)* ~**augen haben** to have eyes like a hawk, to be eagle-eyed; ~**blick** *m (fig)* eagle eye; ~**horst** *m* eyrie.
adlig *adj (lit, fig)* noble. ~ **sein** to belong to the aristocracy.
Adlige(r) *mf decl as adj* member of the nobility, nobleman/woman; *(Brit auch)* peer/peeress; *(hoher auch)* aristocrat.
Administration *f* administration.
administrativ *adj* administrative.
Admiral *m, pl* **-e** *or* **Admiräle (a)** admiral. **(b)** *(Zool)* red admiral.
Admiralität *f* **(a)** *(die Admirale)* admirals *pl.* **(b)** *(Marineleitung)* admiralty.
adoptieren* *vt* to adopt.
Adoption *f* adoption.
Adoptiv-: ~**eltern** *pl* adoptive parents *pl*; ~**kind** *nt* adopted child.
Adrenalin *nt no pl* adrenalin.
Adreßbuch *nt* directory; *(privat)* address book.
Adresse *f* **-n** *(Anschrift, Comp)* address. **eine Warnung an jds ~** *(acc)* **richten** *(fig)* to address a warning to sb; **dieser Vorwurf geht an Ihre ~** this reproach is directed at *or* addressed to you (personally); **an der falschen ~ sein** *(col)* to have gone/come to the wrong person.
adressieren* *vt* to address *(an +acc* to*)*.
adrett *adj (dated)* neat.
Adria *f* Adriatic (Sea).
Adriatisches Meer *nt (form)* Adriatic Sea.
Advent [at'vɛnt] *m* **-e** Advent. **erster/vierter ~** first/fourth Sunday in Advent.
Advents-: ~**kalender** *m* Advent calendar; ~**kranz** *m* Advent wreath; ~**sonntag** *m* Sunday in Advent; ~**zeit** *f* Advent.
Adverb [at'vɛrp] *nt* **-(i)en** adverb.
Advokat [atvo'kaːt] *m (wk)* **-en, -en** *(old Jur, fig)* advocate.
Aerobic *nt* aerobics *sing.*
Aero-: ~**dynamik** *f* aerodynamics; **a~dynamisch** *adj* aerodynamic.
Affäre *f* **-n (a)** *(Angelegenheit)* affair, business *no pl*; *(Liebesabenteuer)* affair. **in eine ~ verwickelt sein** to be mixed up in *or* involved in an affair; **sich aus der ~ ziehen** *(col)* to get (oneself) out of it. **(b)** *(Zwischenfall)* incident, episode.
Affe *m (wk)* **-n, -n (a)** monkey; *(Menschen~)* ape. **der Mensch stammt vom ~n ab** man is descended from the apes; **klettern wie ein ~** to climb like a monkey; **einen ~n haben** *(col)* to have had one over the eight *(col)*. **(b)** *(col: Kerl)* clown *(col)*, berk *(Brit col)*.
Affekt *m* **-e** emotion, affect *(form)*. **im ~ handeln** to act in the heat of the moment.
Affekthandlung *f* act committed under emotional stress.
affektiert *adj (pej)* affected. **sich ~ benehmen** to be affected, to behave affectedly.
Affektiertheit *f* affectation, affectedness.
Affen-: **a~artig** *adj* like a monkey; *(wie ein Menschenaffe)* apelike; **mit a~artiger Geschwindigkeit** *(col)* like greased lightning *(col)*, in a flash *(col)*; ~**haus** *nt* ape house; ~**hitze** *f (col)* sweltering heat; ~**käfig** *m* monkey's/ape's cage; ~**liebe** *f* blind adoration *(zu* of*)*; ~**schande** *f (col)* crying shame *(col)*; ~**tempo** *nt (col)* **in** *or* **mit einem ~tempo** at breakneck speed *(col)*; *(laufen auch)* like the clappers *(col)*; ~**theater** *nt (col)* carry-on *(col)*, fuss; **ein ~theater aufführen** to make a fuss; ~**zahn** *m (col) siehe* ~**tempo.**
affig *adj (col) (eitel)* stuck-up *(col)*, conceited; *(geziert)* affected; *(lächerlich)* ridiculous, ludicrous.
Äffin *f* female monkey/ape.
Affront [a'frõː] *m* **-s** *(geh)* affront, insult *(gegen* to*)*.
Afghane *m (wk)* **-n, -n, Afghanin** *f* Afghan.
afghanisch *adj* Afghan.~**er Windhund** Afghan (hound).
Afghanistan *nt* Afghanistan.
Afrika *nt* Africa.
Afrikaans *nt* Afrikaans.
Afrikaner(in *f***)** *m* - African.
afrikanisch *adj* African.
Afro-: ~**-Amerikaner** *m* Afro-American; ~**-Asiat** *m* Afro-Asian; ~**-Look** *m* Afro-look.
After *m* - *(form)* anus.
AG [aː'geː] *f* **-s** = **Aktiengesellschaft** (public) limited company, plc *(Brit)*, corporation, inc. *(US)*.
Ägäis [ɛ'gɛːɪs] *f* Aegean (Sea).
ägäisch [ɛ'gɛːɪʃ] *adj* **Ä~es Meer** Aegean Sea.
Agent *m* agent.
Agenten-: ~**ring** *m* spy ring; ~**tätigkeit** *f* espionage; **ihre ~tätigkeit** her activity as an agent.
Agentur *f* agency.
Agenturbericht *m* (news) agency report.
Aggregat *nt (Geol)* aggregate; *(Tech)* unit, set of machines.
Aggregatzustand *m* state.
Aggression *f* aggression *(gegen* towards*)*. **~en gegen jdn empfinden** to feel aggressive *or* aggression towards sb.
Aggressions-: **a~geladen** *adj* charged with aggression; ~**trieb** *m (Psych)* aggressive impulse.
aggressiv *adj* aggressive.
Aggressivität *f* aggression, aggressiveness.
Aggressor *m* aggressor.
agieren* *vi* to operate, to act; *(Theat)* to act. **als jd ~** *(Theat)* to act *or* play the part of sb.
agil *adj (körperlich)* agile, nimble. **(geistig) ~** sharp, mentally agile.
Agitation *f (Pol)* agitation. **~ treiben** to agitate.
Agitator(in *f***)** [-'toːrɪn] *m (Pol)* agitator.
agitatorisch *adj (Pol) Rede* inflammatory, agitating *attr.*
agitieren* *vi* to agitate.
agnostisch *adj* agnostic.
Agonie *f (lit, fig geh)* death throes *pl.* **in (der) ~ liegen** to be in the throes of death.
Agrar-: ~**land** *nt* agrarian country; ~**politik** *f* agricultural policy.
Ägypten *nt* Egypt.
Ägypter(in *f***)** *m* - Egyptian.
ägyptisch *adj* Egyptian.
ah [aː] ah, oh.
äh [ɛː] *interj (beim Sprechen)* er, um; *(Ausdruck des Ekels)* ugh.
aha *interj* aha; *(verstehend auch)* I see.
Aha-Erlebnis *nt* sudden insight.
Ahn *m (wk)* **-en, -en** *(geh)* ancestor, for(e)father *(liter)*.
ahnden *vt (geh) Freveltat, Verbrechen* to avenge; *Übertretung, Verstoß* to punish.
Ahndung *f siehe vt* avenging; punishment.
Ahne *f* **-n** *(geh: weiblicher Vorfahr)* ancestress.
ähneln *vi+dat* to resemble. **sich** *or* **einander** *(geh)* **~** to resemble one another; **in diesem Punkt ähnelt sie sehr ihrem Vater** she's very like her

father in this respect.
ahnen *vt (voraussehen)* to foresee, to know; *Gefahr, Tod etc* to have a presentiment *or* premonition of; *(vermuten)* to suspect; *(erraten)* to guess. **das kann ich doch nicht ~!** how am I expected to know that!; **nichts Böses ~** to be unsuspecting; **nichts Böses ~d** unsuspectingly; **ohne es zu ~** without suspecting; **davon habe ich nichts geahnt** I didn't have the slightest inkling of it.
Ahnen-: ~forschung *f* genealogy; **~galerie** *f* ancestral portrait gallery; **~reihe** *f* ancestral line.
Ahn-: ~frau *f (liter)* ancestress; **~herr** *m (liter)* ancestor.
ähnlich *adj* similar *(+dat* to*)*. **ein dem Rokoko ~er Stil** a style similar to rococo, a similar style to rococo; **~ wie er/sie** like him/her; **sie sind sich ~** they are similar *or* alike; **ein ~ aussehender Gegenstand** a similar-looking object; **ich denke ~** I think likewise; **jdm ~ sehen** to be like sb, to resemble sb; **das sieht ihm (ganz) ~!** *(col)* that's just like him!, that's him all over! *(col)*; **(etwas) Ä~es** something similar, something like it/that.
Ähnlichkeit *f* similarity *(mit* to*)*. **mit jdm/etw ~ haben** to resemble sb/sth, to be like sb/sth.
Ahnung *f* **(a)** *(Vorgefühl)* hunch, presentiment; *(düster)* foreboding, premonition. **(b)** *(Vorstellung, Wissen)* idea; *(Vermutung)* suspicion. **keine ~!** *(col)* no idea! *(col)*, I haven't a clue! *(col)*; **er hat keine blasse** *or* **nicht die geringste ~** he hasn't the faintest idea *(col)*; **ich hatte keine ~, daß ...** I had no idea that ...; **hast du eine ~, wo er sein könnte?** have you any idea where he could be?; **du hast keine ~, wie schwierig das ist** you have no idea how difficult it is; **hast du eine ~!** *(iro col)* a (fat) lot you know (about it)! *(col)*.
Ahnungs-: a~los *adj (nichtsahnend)* unsuspecting; *(unwissend)* clueless *(col)*; **~losigkeit** *f (Unwissenheit)* ignorance; **a~voll** *adj (geh)* full of presentiment *or (Böses ahnend)* foreboding.
ahoi [a'hɔy] *interj (Naut)* **Schiff ~!** ship ahoy!
Ahorn *m* **-e** maple.
Ahornblatt *nt* maple leaf.
Ähre *f* **-n** ear; *(allgemeiner, Gras~)* head.
Aids [e:ts, e:dz] *nt* **-**, *no pl* AIDS.
Airbus ['ɛːɐbʊs] *m (Aviat)* airbus.
ais, Ais ['a:ɪs] *nt* **-** A sharp.
Akademie *f* academy; *(Fachschule)* college.
Akademiker(in *f***)** *m* **-** person with a university education; *(Student)* (university) student; *(Hochschulabsolvent)* (university) graduate; *(Universitätslehrkraft)* academic.
akademisch *adj (lit, fig)* academic. **das ~e Proletariat** (the) jobless graduates *pl*; **~ gebildet sein** to have (had) a university education.
Akazie [-iə] *f* acacia.
Akelei *f* columbine.
Akklamation *f (form)* **Wahl per** *or* **durch ~** election by acclamation.
akklimatisieren* *vr (lit, fig)* to become acclimatized *(in+dat* to*)*.
Akkord *m* **-e (a)** *(Mus)* chord. **(b)** *(Stücklohn)* piece rate. **im ~ arbeiten** to do piecework.
Akkord-: ~arbeit *f* piecework; **~arbeiter** *m* piece-worker.
Akkordeon [-eɔn] *nt* **-s** accordion.
Akkord-: ~lohn *m* piece wages *pl*, piece rate; **~zuschlag** *m* piece rate bonus.
akkreditieren* *vt (Pol)* to accredit *(bei* to, at*)*.
Akkreditierung *f (Pol)* accrediting, accreditation *(bei* to, at*)*.
Akku ['aku] *m* **-s** *(col)* = **Akkumulator.**
Akkumulation *f* accumulation.
Akkumulator *m* accumulator.
akkumulieren* *vtir* to accumulate.
akkurat *adj* precise; *(sorgfältig auch)* meticulous.
Akkusativ *m* accusative.
Akkusativ|objekt *nt* accusative *or* direct object.
Akne *f* **-n** acne.
Akontozahlung *f* payment on account.
Akquisition [akvizitsi'o:n] *f (old)* acquisition; *(Comm)* canvassing.
Akribie *f no pl (geh)* meticulousness.
akribisch *adj (geh)* meticulous, precise.
Akrobat(in *f***)** *m (wk)* **-en, -en** acrobat.
Akrobatik *f no pl* acrobatics *pl*.
akrobatisch *adj* acrobatic.
Akt *m* **-e (a)** *(Tat)* act; *(Zeremonie)* ceremony. **(b)** *(Theat, Zirkus~)* act. **(c)** *(Art: ~bild)* nude. **(d)** *(Geschlechts~)* sexual act, coitus *no art (form)*.
Akt|aufnahme *n* nude (photograph).
Akte *f* **-n** file, record. **die ~ Schmidt** the Schmidt file; **das kommt in die ~n** this goes on file *or* record; **etw zu den ~n legen** to put sth on file.
Akten-: ~deckel *m* folder; **~koffer** *m* attaché case; **a~kundig** *adj* on record; **~mappe** *f* **(a)** *(Umschlag)* folder, file; **(b)** *siehe* **~tasche**; **~notiz** *f* memo(randum); **~ordner** *m* file; **~schrank** *m* filing cabinet; **~tasche** *f* briefcase, portfolio; **~zeichen** *nt* reference.
Aktfoto *nt* nude (photograph).
Aktie ['aktsi] *f* share; *(~nschein)* share certificate. **~n** shares, stock *sing;* **die ~n fallen/steigen** share prices are falling/rising; **die ~n stehen gut** shares are buoyant; **wie stehen die ~n?** *(hum col)* how are things?
Aktien-: ~besitz *m* shareholdings *pl*; **~gesellschaft** *f* joint-stock company; **~kapital** *nt* share capital; **~kurs** *m* share price; **~markt** *m* stock market.
Aktion *f (Handlung)* action *(auch Mil)*; *(Kampagne)* campaign; *(geplantes Unternehmen, Einsatz)* operation *(auch Mil)*. **in ~** in action.
Aktionär(in *f***)** *m* shareholder, stockholder *(esp US)*.
Aktionärsversammlung *f* shareholders' meeting.
Aktions-: ~einheit *f (Pol)* working unity; **a~fähig** *adj* capable of action; **~radius** *m (Aviat, Naut)* range; *(fig: Wirkungsbereich)* scope.
aktiv *adj* active; *(Econ) Bilanz* positive; *(Mil) Soldat etc* on active service. **sich ~ an etw** *(dat)* **beteiligen** to take an active part in sth.
Aktiv *nt (Gram)* active.
Aktiva *pl* assets. **~ und Passiva** assets and liabilities.
Aktive(r) *mf decl as adj (Sport)* active participant.
aktivieren* [akti'vi:rən] *vt* to activate; *(fig) Arbeit, Kampagne* to step up; *Mitarbeiter* to get moving.
Aktivist(in *f***)** *m* activist.
Aktivität *f* activity.
Aktiv-: ~posten *m (lit, fig)* asset; **~seite** *f* assets side.
Aktmodell *nt* nude model.
aktualisieren* *vt* to make topical.
Aktualität *f* relevance (to the current situation), topicality. **~en** *pl (geh: neueste Ereignisse)* current events.
aktuell *adj* relevant (to the current situation); *Frage auch* topical; *Buch, Film auch* of topical interest; *Problem, Theorie* current; *(Fashion: modern) Mode* latest *attr*, current. **von ~em Interesse/~er Bedeutung** of topical interest/of relevance to the present situation; **dieses Problem ist nicht mehr ~** this is no longer a problem; **eine ~e Sendung** *(Rad, TV)* a current-affairs programme.
Aktzeichnung *f* nude (drawing).
Akupunktur *f* acupuncture.
Akustik *f no pl* acoustics *pl*.
akustisch *adj* acoustic. **ich habe dich rein ~ nicht verstanden** I simply didn't catch what you said (properly).
akut *adj (Med, fig)* acute; *Frage auch* pressing.
Akzent *m* **-e** accent; *(Betonung)* stress. **den ~ auf etw** *(acc)* **legen** *(lit)* to stress sth. **~e setzen** *(fig)* to bring out *or* emphasize the main points.

akzentfrei *adj* without an accent.
akzentuieren* *vt* to articulate, to enunciate; *(betonen)* to stress; *(fig: hervorheben)* to accentuate.
Akzentverschiebung *f (fig)* shift of emphasis.
akzeptabel *adj* acceptable.
akzeptieren* *vt* to accept.
Akzeptierung *f* acceptance.
à la [a la] *adv* à la.
Alabaster *m* - alabaster.
Alarm *m* **-e** *(Warnung)* alarm; *(Flieger~)* air-raid warning; *(Zustand)* alert. **~!** fire! *etc*; **~ schlagen** to give *or* raise the alarm.
Alarm-: ~anlage *f* alarm system; **a~bereit** *adj* on the alert; **~bereitschaft** *f* alert; **in ~bereitschaft sein** *or* **stehen** to be on the alert; **in ~bereitschaft versetzen** to put on the alert, to alert; **~glocke** *f* alarm bell.
alarmieren* *vt Polizei etc* to alert; *(fig: beunruhigen)* to alarm. **~d** *(fig)* alarming.
Alarm-: ~ruf *m* warning cry; **~signal** *nt* alarm signal; **~stufe** *f* alert stage; **~übung** *f* practice exercise *or* drill; **~zustand** *m* alert; **im ~zustand sein** to be on the alert.
Alaska *nt* Alaska.
Albaner(in *f*) *m* - Albanian.
Albanien [-iən] *nt* Albania.
albanisch *adj* Albanian.
Alben *pl of* **Album.**
albern *adj* silly. **sich ~ benehmen** to act silly; **~es Zeug** (silly) nonsense.
Albernheit *f* **(a)** *no pl* silliness, foolishness. **(b)** *(Tat)* silly prank; *(Bemerkung)* inanity.
Album *nt, pl* **Alben** album.
alert *adj (geh)* vivacious, lively.
Alge *f* **-n** alga.
Algebra *f no pl* algebra.
Algerien [-iən] *nt* Algeria.
Algerier(in *f*) [-iɐ, -iərin] *m* - Algerian.
algerisch *adj* Algerian.
alias *adv* alias, also *or* otherwise known as.
Alibi *nt* **-s** *(Jur, fig)* alibi.
Alimente *pl* maintenance *sing.*
Alkohol ['alkohoːl, alko'hoːl] *m* **-e** alcohol; *(Getränke auch)* drink. **seinen Kummer im ~ ertränken** to drown one's sorrows; **unter ~ stehen** to be under the influence (of alcohol *or* drink).
Alkohol-: a~arm *adj* low in alcohol; **~ausschank** *m* sale of alcohol; **~einfluß** *m* **unter ~einfluß** under the influence of alcohol *or* drink; **a~frei** *adj* non-alcoholic; *Getränk auch* soft; **~gehalt** *m* alcohol(ic) content; **~genuß** *m* consumption of alcohol; **a~haltig** *adj* alcoholic.
Alkoholiker(in *f*) *m* - alcoholic.
alkoholisch *adj* alcoholic.
Alkoholismus *m* alcoholism.
Alkohol-: ~konsum *m* consumption of alcohol; **~spiegel** *m* **jds ~spiegel** the level of alcohol in sb's blood; **~steuer** *f* duty *or* tax on alcohol; **~sünder** *m (col)* drunk(en) driver; **~verbot** *nt* ban on alcohol; **der Arzt hat ihm ~verbot verordnet** the doctor told him not to touch alcohol; **~vergiftung** *f* alcohol(ic) poisoning.
all *indef pron* **all mein/sein Geld** all my/his money.
All *nt no pl (Sci, Space)* space *no art*; *(außerhalb unseres Sternsystems)* outer space *no art*; *(liter, geh)* universe. **Spaziergang im ~** space walk.
alle 1 *pron siehe* **alle(r, s). 2** *adv (col)* all gone. **die Milch ist ~** the milk's all gone, there's no milk left; **etw ~ machen** to finish sth off.
alledem *pron* **bei/trotz** *etc* **~** with/in spite of *etc* all that; **von ~ stimmt kein Wort** there's not a word of truth in any of it; **zu ~** moreover.
Allee *f* **-n** [-eːən] avenue.
Allegorie *f* allegory.
allegorisch *adj* allegorical.
allein 1 *adj pred* alone; *Gegenstand, Wort auch* by itself, on its own; *(ohne Begleitung, Hilfe auch)* by oneself, on one's own; *(einsam)* lonely. **von ~** by oneself/itself; **ganz ~** *(einsam)* all alone; *(ohne Begleitung, Hilfe)* all by oneself, all on one's own. **2** *adv (nur)* alone. **das ist ~ seine Verantwortung** that is his responsibility alone; **~ schon der Gedanke** the very *or* mere thought ..., the thought alone ...; **das Porto ~ kostet ...** the postage alone costs ..., just the postage is ...
Allein-: ~erbe *m* sole *or* only heir; **~gang** *m (col) (Sport)* solo run; *(von Bergsteiger)* solo climb; *(fig: Tat)* solo effort; **etw im ~gang machen** *(fig)* to do sth on one's own; **~herrscher** *m* autocrat, absolute dictator.
alleinig *adj attr* sole, only.
Allein-: ~sein *nt* being on one's own *no def art*, solitude; *(Einsamkeit)* loneliness; **a~stehend** *adj* living alone; **~stehende(r)** *mf decl as adj* single person; **~unterhalter** *m* solo entertainer; **~vertretung** *f (Comm)* sole agency.
allemal *adv (ohne Schwierigkeit)* without any problem *or* trouble. **was er kann, kann ich noch ~** anything he can do I can do too; **ein für ~** once and for all.
allenfalls *adv (nötigenfalls)* if need be; *(höchstens)* at most; *(bestenfalls)* at best.
alle(r, s) 1 *indef pron* **(a)** *attr* all; *(bestimmte Menge, Anzahl)* all the. **~ Kinder unter 10 Jahren** all children under 10; **im Geschäft war ~s Brot ausverkauft** all the bread in the shop was sold out; **wir haben ~n Haß vergessen** we have forgotten all (our *or* the) hatred; **~ Anwesenden** all those present; **mit ~m Nachdruck** with every emphasis; **trotz ~r Mühe** in spite of every effort; **ohne ~n Grund** without any reason, with no reason at all; **mit ~r Deutlichkeit** quite distinctly; **in ~r Unschuld** in all innocence; **ohne ~n Zweifel** without any doubt.
(b) *(substantivisch)* **~s** *sing* everything; **~** *pl* all; *(alle Menschen)* all, everybody, everyone; **~s, was ...** all *or* everything that/everybody *or* everyone who ...; **das ~s** all that; **~s Schöne** everything beautiful; **~s Gute** all the best; **~s und jedes** anything and everything; **in ~m** *(in jeder Beziehung)* in everything; **~s in ~m** all in all; **trotz ~m** in spite of everything; **vor ~m** above all; **das ist ~s, das wäre ~s** that's all, that's it *(col)*; **das ist ~s andere als ...** that's anything but ...; **das geht dich doch ~s nichts an!** none of (all) that has anything to do with you!; **es hat ~s keinen Sinn mehr** nothing makes sense any more; **was habt ihr ~s gemacht?** what did you get up to?; **wer war ~s da?** who was there?; **was er (nicht) ~s weiß!** the things he knows!; **die haben mir ~ nicht gefallen** I didn't like any of them; **~ beide/drei** both of them/all three of them; **~ diejenigen, die ...** all (those) who ...; **diese ~** all (of) these; **der Kampf ~r gegen ~** the free-for-all; **~ für einen und einer für ~** all for one and one for all; **sie kamen ~** they all came, all of them came; **sie haben ~ kein Geld mehr** none of them has any money left.
(c) *(mit Zeit-, Maßangaben) usu pl* every. **~ fünf Minuten/fünf Meter** every five minutes/five metres; **~ Jahre wieder** year after year.
2 *adv siehe* **alle.**
aller-: ~beste(r, s) *adj* very best, best ... of all; **ich wünsche Dir das A~beste** (I wish you) all the best; **der/die/das A~beste** the very best/the best of all; **~dings** *adv* **(a)** *(einschränkend)* though, mind you; **das ist ~dings wahr, aber ...** that may be true, but ...; **(b)** *(bekräftigend)* certainly; **~erste(r, s)** *adj* very first; **~frühestens** *adv* at the very earliest.
Allergie *f (Med, fig)* allergy. **eine ~ gegen etw haben** to be allergic to sth *(auch fig hum)*; *(fig auch)* to have an aversion to sth.
allergisch *adj (Med, fig)* allergic *(gegen* to*)*. **auf etw** *(acc)* **~ reagieren** to be allergic to sth.
Aller-: a~hand *adj inv (substantivisch) (allerlei)* all

kinds of things; *(ziemlich viel)* rather a lot; *(attributiv)* all kinds *or* sorts of; rather a lot of; **das ist ja a~hand!** *(zustimmend)* that's quite something!, not bad at all! *(col)*; *(empört)* that's too much! **~heiligen** *nt* All Saints' Day; **a~höchste(r, s)** *adj* **von a~höchster Stelle** from the very highest authority; **es wird a~höchste Zeit, daß ...** it's really high time that ...; **a~höchstens** *adv* at the very most; **a~lei** *adj inv (substantivisch)* all sorts *or* kinds of things; *(attributiv)* all sorts *or* kinds of; **a~letzte(r, s)** *adj* very last; *(a~neueste)* very latest; *(col: unmöglich)* most awful *attr (col)*; **der/das ist das ~letzte** *(col)* he's/it's the absolute end! *(col)*; **~liebste(r, s)** *adj* **es wäre mir das a~liebste** *or* **am a~liebsten, wenn ...** I would much prefer it if ...; **a~meiste(r, s)** *adj* most ... of all; **die ~meisten** the vast majority; **a~nächste(r, s)** *adj (in Folge)* very next; *(räumlich)* nearest; *Verwandte* very closest; **in a~nächster Zeit** in the very near future; **a~neu(e)ste(r, s)** *adj* very latest; **a~seits** *adv* on all sides, on every side; **guten Abend a~seits!** good evening everybody; **a~spätestens** *adv* at the very latest.

Allerwelts- *in cpds (Durchschnitts-)* common; *(nichtssagend)* commonplace; **~kerl** *m* Jack of all trades.

Aller-: a~wenigstens *adv* at the very least; **a~wenigste(r, s)** *adj* least ... of all; *(pl)* fewest ... of all; *(äußerst wenig)* very little; *(pl)* very few; **die a~wenigsten Menschen wissen das** very few people know that; **das ist doch das ~wenigste, was man erwarten könnte** but that's the very least one could expect; **das am a~wenigsten!** least of all that!; **~werteste(r)** *m decl as adj (hum)* posterior *(hum)*.

alles *indef pron siehe* **alle(r, s).**

allesamt *adv* all (of them/us *etc*). **ihr seid ~ Betrüger!** you're all cheats!

Alles-: ~fresser *m* omnivore; **~kleber** *m* all-purpose adhesive; **~wisser** *m* - *(iro)* know-all *(col)*, know-it-all *(US col)*.

allgegenwärtig *adj* omnipresent, ubiquitous.

allgemein 1 *adj* general; *Feiertag* public; *Wahlrecht* universal; *Wehrpflicht* compulsory. **im ~en** in general, generally; **im ~en Interesse** in the common interest; **auf ~en** Wunsch by popular request; **die ~e Meinung** the general opinion; **zur ~en Überraschung** to everyone's surprise. **2** *adv* generally; *(ausnahmslos von allen)* universally; *(nicht spezifisch)* in general terms. **es ist ~ bekannt** it's common knowledge; **es ist ~ üblich** it's the general rule; **~ verbreitet** widespread; **~ zugänglich** open to all.

Allgemein-: ~bildung *f* general *or* all-round education; **a~gültig** *adj attr* general, universal; **~heit** *f (no pl: Öffentlichkeit)* general public; *(alle)* everyone, everybody; **~medizin** *f* general medicine; **Arzt für ~medizin** general practitioner, GP; **a~verständlich** *adj no pred* generally intelligible; **~wohl** *nt* public good *or* welfare.

Allheilmittel *nt* cure-all, panacea *(esp fig)*.

Allianz *f* alliance.

Alliierte(r) *mf decl as adj* ally. **die ~n** *(im 2. Weltkrieg)* the Allies.

Alliteration *f (Poet)* alliteration.

All-: a~jährlich *adj* annual, yearly; **~macht** *f (esp von Gott)* omnipotence; **a~mächtig** *adj* all-powerful, omnipotent; **~mächtige(r)** *m decl as adj (Gott)* **der ~mächtige** Almighty God, the Almighty; **~mächtiger!** good Lord!

allmählich 1 *adj attr* gradual. **2** *adv* gradually; *(col: endlich)* at last. **es wird ~ Zeit** *(col)* it's about time; **ich werde (ganz) ~ müde** *(col)* I'm beginning to get tired; **hoffentlich kommst du ~!** *(col)* are you coming at last?; **wir sollten ~ gehen** *(col)* shall we think about going?

allmonatlich *adj* monthly.

Allotria *nt no pl (col) (Unfug)* monkey business *(col) no indef art; (Lärm)* racket *(col)*, din.

Allradantrieb *m* all-wheel drive.

allseitig *adj (allgemein)* general; *(ausnahmslos)* universal; *(vielseitig)* all-round *attr*. **~ begabt sein** to be an all-rounder; **zur ~en Zufriedenheit** to the satisfaction of all *or* everyone.

allseits *adv (überall)* everywhere, on all sides; *(in jeder Beziehung)* in every respect.

Alltag *m (fig)* everyday life. **der ~ der Ehe** the mundane *or* day-to-day side of married life.

alltäglich *adj* **(a)** *(tagtäglich)* daily. **(b)** *(üblich)* everyday *attr*, ordinary; *Gesicht, Mensch* ordinary; **es ist ganz ~** it's nothing unusual.

allumfassend *adj* all-embracing, global.

Allüren *pl* odd behaviour *(Brit) or* behavior *(US)*; *(geziertes Verhalten)* affectations *pl*; *(eines Stars etc)* airs and graces *pl*.

all-: ~wissend *adj* omniscient; **A~wissenheit** *f* omniscience; **~wöchentlich** *adj* weekly; **~zeit** *adv (geh)* always.

allzu *adv* all too; *(+neg)* too. **~ viele Fehler** far too many mistakes.

allzu-: ~gern *adv mögen* only too much; *(bereitwillig)* only too willingly; **nicht ~gern** not all that much/willingly, not too much/willingly; **er ißt Muscheln nur ~gern** he's only too fond of mussels; **~sehr** *adv* too much; *mögen* all too much; *sich freuen* only too; *versuchen* too hard; *sich ärgern, enttäuscht sein* too; **nicht ~sehr mögen/enttäuscht sein** not to like too much/not to be too disappointed; **~viel** *adv* too much; **~viel ist ungesund** *(Prov)* you can have too much of a good thing *(prov)*.

Allzweck- *in cpds* all-purpose.

Alm *f* **-en** alpine pasture.

Almosen [-oː-] *nt* **-** *(geh: Spende)* alms *pl (old)*. **~** *pl (fig)* charity.

Alpdruck *m (lit, fig)* nightmare. **wie ein ~druck auf jdm lasten** to weigh sb down, to oppress sb.

Alpen *pl* **die ~** the Alps *pl*.

Alpen- ~glühen *nt* **-** alpenglow; **~paß** *m* alpine pass; **~rose** *f* Alpine rose; **~veilchen** *nt* cyclamen; **~vorland** *nt* foothills *pl* of the Alps.

Alphabet *nt* **-e** alphabet. **nach dem ~** alphabetically, in alphabetical order.

alphabetisch *adj* alphabetical. **~ geordnet** arranged in alphabetical order.

alphabetisieren* *vt* to make literate.

Alphastrahlen *pl* alpha rays *pl*.

Alphorn *nt* alp(en)horn.

alpin *adj* alpine.

Alpinist(in *f***)** *m* alpinist.

Alptraum *m (lit, fig)* nightmare.

als *conj* **(a)** *(nach comp)* than. **ich kam später ~ er** I came later than he (did) *or* him.

(b) *(bei Vergleichen)* **soviel/soweit ~ möglich** as much/far as possible; **nichts/niemand/nirgend anders ~** nothing/nobody/nowhere but; **eher** *or* **lieber ... ~** rather ... than; **anders sein ~** to be different from; **das machen wir anders ~ ihr** we do it differently from you; **alles andere ~** anything but.

(c) es sieht aus, ~ würde es bald schneien it looks as if *or* though it will snow soon; **~ ob ich das nicht wüßte!** as if I didn't know!

(d) sie ist zu alt, ~ daß sie das noch verstehen könnte she is too old to understand; **die Zeit war zu knapp, ~ daß wir ...** the time was too short for us to ...

(e) *(in Temporalsätzen)* when; *(gleichzeitig)* as. **damals, ~** (in the days) when; **gerade, ~** just as.

(f) *(in der Eigenschaft)* as. **~ Beweis** as proof; **~ Antwort/Warnung** as an answer/a warning; **sich ~ wahr/falsch erweisen** to prove to be true/false; **~ Kind/Mädchen** *etc* as a child/girl *etc*.

also 1 *conj (folglich)* so, therefore. **2** *adv* so; *(nach*

Unterbrechung anknüpfend) well; *(zusammenfassend, erklärend)* that is. ~ **doch** so ... after all; **du machst es** ~? so you'll do it then?; ~ **wie ich schon sagte** well (then), as I said before. **3** *interj* well. **na** ~! there you are!, you see?; ~ **gut** *or* **schön** well all right then; ~ **so was/so eine Frechheit!** well (I never)/what a cheek!

alt *adj, comp* ¨**er**, *superl* ¨**este(r, s)** *or (adv)* **am** ¨**esten (a)** old; *(sehr ~) Sage, Aberglaube auch, Griechen, Geschichte* ancient; *Sprachen* classical. **das ~e Rom** ancient Rome; **das A~e Testament** the Old Testament; **die A~ Welt** the Old World; ~ **und jung** (everybody) old and young; **ein drei Jahre ~es Kind** a three-year-old child; **wie ~ bist du?** how old are you?; **etw ~ kaufen** to buy sth second-hand; **ich werde heute nicht ~ (werden)** *(col)* I won't last long today/tonight *etc (col)*; **~e Liebe rostet nicht** *(Prov)* true love never dies *(prov)*. **(b)** *(dieselbe, gewohnt)* same old. **sie ist ganz die ~e (Ingrid)** she's the same old Ingrid; **er ist nicht mehr der ~e** he's not what he was *or* the man he was; **alles beim ~en lassen** to leave everything as it was.

Alt *m* **-e** *(Mus)* alto; *(von Frau auch)* contralto.

Altar *m, pl* **Altäre** altar.

Alt-: a~backen *adj (fig) Mensch, Ansichten* old-fashioned; **~bau** *m* old building; **~bauwohnung** *f* old flat; **a~bekannt** *adj* well-known; **a~bewährt** *adj Methode etc* well-tried; *Tradition etc* long-standing; **~bier** *nt top-fermented German dark beer*; **~bundeskanzler** *m* former German/Austrian Chancellor; **a~deutsch** *adj* old German; *Möbel, Stil* German Renaissance.

Alte *siehe* **Alte(r), Alte(s).**

Alt-: a~ehrwürdig *adj* venerable; *Bräuche* time-honoured *(Brit)*, time-honored *(US)*; **a~eingesessen** *adj* old-established; **~eisen** *nt* scrap metal.

Alten-: ~heim *nt* old people's home; **~pfleger** *m* old people's nurse; **~tagesstätte** *f* old people's day home; **~teil** *nt* **sich aufs ~teil setzen** *or* **zurückziehen** *(fig)* to retire from public life.

Alte(r) *mf decl as adj (alter Mann, col: Ehemann, Vater)* old man; *(alte Frau, col: Ehefrau, Mutter)* old woman; *(col: Vorgesetzter)* boss. **die ~n** *(Eltern)* the folk(s) *pl (col)*; *(Tiereltern)* the parents *pl*; *(ältere Generation)* the old people *pl or* folk *pl*.

Alter *nt* **-** age; *(letzter Lebensabschnitt)* old age. **im ~** in one's old age; **in deinem ~** at your age; **er ist in deinem ~** he's your age; **im ~ von 18 Jahren** at the age of 18; **45, das ist doch kein ~** *(col)* 45, that's no age at all.

älter *adj* **(a)** *comp of* **alt** older; *Bruder, Tochter etc auch* elder. **werden Frauen ~ als Männer?** do women live longer than men?; **Holbein der Ä~e** Holbein the Elder. **(b)** *attr (nicht ganz jung)* elderly.

altern *vi aux sein* to age; *(Mensch auch)* to get older; *(Wein)* to mature.

alternativ *adj (geh)* alternative.

Alternativ- *in cpds* alternative.

Alternative *f* alternative *(etw zu tun* of doing sth*)*.

alternierend *adj* alternate; *Strom, Verse* alternating.

alt|erprobt *adj* well-tried.

alters *adv (geh)*: **von** *or* **seit ~ (her)** from time immemorial.

Alters-: a~bedingt *adj* related to a particular age; related to *or* caused by old age; **~erscheinung** *f* sign of old age; **~forschung** *f* gerontology; **~fürsorge** *f* care of the elderly; **~genosse** *m* contemporary; **~grenze** *f* age limit; *(Rentenalter)* retirement age; **~gründe** *pl* **aus ~gründen** for reasons of age *pl*; **~gruppe** *f* age-group; **~heim** *nt* old people's home; **~klasse** *f (Sport)* age-group; **~präsident** *m* president by seniority; **~prozeß** *m* ageing process; **~rente** *f* old age pension; **~ruhegeld** *nt* retirement benefit; **a~s chwach** *adj Mensch* old and infirm; *Auto, Möbel* decrepit; **~schwäche** *f siehe adj* infirmity; decrepitude; **~sitz** *m* **sein ~sitz war München** he spent his retirement in Munich; **~stufe** *f* age group; *(Lebensabschnitt)* age; **~werk** *nt* later works *pl*.

Altertum *nt no pl* antiquity *no art*.

Altertümer *pl* antiquities *pl*.

altertümlich *adj (aus dem Altertum)* ancient; *(altehrwürdig)* old-world; *(altmodisch)* old-fashioned *no adv; (veraltet)* antiquated.

Altertums-: ~forscher *m* archeologist; **~forschung** *f* archeology; **~wert** *m*: **das hat schon ~wert** *(hum)* it has antique value *(hum)*.

Alte(s) *nt decl as adj* **das ~** *(das Gewohnte, Traditionelle)* the old; *(alte Dinge)* old things *pl*; **er hängt sehr am ~n** he clings to the past.

Älteste(r) *mf decl as adj* oldest; *(Sohn, Tochter auch)* eldest.

älteste(r, s) *adj superl of* **alt** oldest; *Bruder etc auch* eldest.

Alt-: ~griechisch(e) *nt* classical Greek; **a~hergebracht** *adj* traditional; **~herrenmannschaft** *f (Sport) team of players over thirty*; **~hochdeutsch(e)** *nt* Old High German.

Altist(in *f***)** *m (Mus)* alto.

alt-: ~jüngferlich *adj* old-maidish; **~klug** *adj* precocious; **A~klugheit** *f* precociousness.

ältlich *adj* oldish.

Alt-: ~material *nt* scrap; **~meister** *m* doyen; *(Sport)* ex-champion; **~metall** *nt* scrap metal; **a~modisch** *adj* old-fashioned; *(rückständig)* outmoded; **~papier** *nt* wastepaper; **~philologie** *f* classical philology; **a~rosa** *adj* old rose; **~schlüssel** *m (Mus)* alto clef; **~schnee** *m* old snow; **~stadt** *f* old town; **die Ulmer ~stadt** the old part of Ulm; **~steinzeit** *f* Palaeolithic Age, Old Stone Age; **~stimme** *f (Mus)* alto *(von Frau auch)* contralto; **a~testamentarisch** *adj* Old Testament *attr*; **a~väterlich** *adj Bräuche* ancestral; *(altmodisch)* old-fashioned *no adv; Erscheinung etc* patriarchal; **~waren** *pl* second-hand goods *pl*; **~warenhändler** *m* second-hand dealer.

Altweiber-: ~geschwätz *nt* old woman's talk; **~sommer** *m (Nachsommer)* Indian summer.

Alufolie *f* tin foil.

Aluminium *nt no pl* aluminium, aluminum *(US)*.

Aluminiumfolie *f* tin foil.

am *prep* = **an dem (a)** *(zur Bildung des Superlativs)* **er war ~ tapfersten** he was (the) bravest; **er hat ~ tapfersten gekämpft** he fought (the) most bravely; **sie war ~ schönsten** she was (the) most beautiful; **~ besten machen wir das morgen** it would be best to do it tomorrow; **~ seltsamsten war ...** the strangest thing was ... **(b)** *(als Zeitangabe)* on. **~ letzten Sonntag** last Sunday; **~ 8. Mai** on the eighth of May, on May *(the Brit)* eighth; *(geschrieben)* on May 8th; **~ Morgen/Abend** in the morning/evening. **(c)** *(als Ortsangabe)* on the; *(bei Gebirgen)* at the foot of the. **(d)** *(col: als Verlaufsform)* **ich war gerade ~ Schlafen** I was just sleeping.

Amateur [-'tøːɐ] *m* amateur.

amateurhaft [ama'tøːɐ-] *adj* amateurish.

Amber *m* **-(n)** ambergris.

Ambition *f (geh)* ambition. **~en auf etw** *(acc)* **haben** to have ambitions of getting sth.

ambivalent [-va'lɛnt] *adj* ambivalent.

Ambivalenz [-va'lɛnts] *f* ambivalence.

Amboß *m* **-sse** anvil.

ambulant *adj (Med) Versorgung, Behandlung* out-patient *attr*. **~e Patienten** out-patients.

Ambulanz *f (Klinikstation)* out-patient department, out-patients *sing*.

Ambulanzwagen *m* ambulance.

Ameise *f* **-n** ant.

Ameisen-: ~bär *m* anteater; **~haufen** *m* anthill; **~säure** *f* formic acid; **~staat** *m* ant colony.

amen *interj* amen.
Amen *nt* - amen. **sein ~ zu etw geben** to give one's blessing to sth; **das ist so sicher wie das ~ in der Kirche** *(col)* you can bet your bottom dollar on that *(col).*
Amerika *nt* America.
Amerikaner(in *f*) *m* - **(a)** American. **(b)** *(Gebäck) flat iced cake.*
amerikanisch *adj* American.
amerikanisieren* *vt* to Americanize.
Amerikanisierung *f* Americanization.
Amerikanistik *f* American studies *pl.*
Ami *m* **-s** *(col)* Yank *(col)*; *(Soldat)* GI *(col).*
Amme *f* **-n** *(old)* foster-mother; *(Nährmutter)* wet nurse.
Ammenmärchen *nt* fairy tale *or* story.
Ammoniak *nt no pl* ammonia.
Amnesie *f (Med)* amnesia.
Amnestie *f* amnesty.
amnestieren* *vt* to grant an amnesty to.
Amöbe *f* **-n** *(Biol)* amoeba.
Amok *m*: **~ laufen** to run amok *or* amuck.
Amok-: ~fahrer *m* mad *or* lunatic driver; **~läufer** *m* madman; **~schütze** *m* crazed gunman.
Amor *m* - Cupid.
Amortisation *f (Econ)* amortization.
amortisieren* *vr* to pay for itself.
amourös [amu'rø:s] *adj (geh)* amorous.
Ampel *f* **-n (a)** *(Verkehrs~)* (traffic) lights *pl (Brit)*, (traffic) light *(US).* **(b)** *(geh: Hängeblumentof)* hanging flowerpot.
Ampelphase *f* traffic light sequence. **die langen ~n an dieser Kreuzung** the length of time the lights take to change at this junction.
Ampere [am'pe:ɐ] *nt* - amp.
Amperemeter [am'pe:ɐ-] *nt* ammeter.
Amphibie [-iə] *f (Zool)* amphibian.
Amphibienfahrzeug *nt* amphibious vehicle.
amphibisch *adj* amphibious.
Amphitheater *nt* amphitheatre *(Brit)*, amphitheater *(US).*
Ampulle *f* **-n** *(Behälter)* ampoule.
Amputation *f* amputation.
amputieren* *vt* to amputate. **jdm den Arm ~** to amputate sb's arm.
Amsel *f* **-n** blackbird.
Amt *nt* **¨er (a)** *(Stellung)* office; *(Posten)* post. **im ~ sein** to be in office; **jdm aus einem ~ entfernen** to remove sb from office. **(b)** *(Aufgabe)* duty, task. **seines ~es walten** *(geh)* to carry out *or* discharge *(form)* one's duties. **(c)** *(Behörde) (Einwohnermelde~, Finanz~)* registration/tax office; *(Stadtverwaltung)* council offices *pl.* **zum zuständigen ~ gehen** to go to the relevant authority; **von ~s wegen** *(auf behördliche Anordnung hin)* officially. **(d)** *(Telefon~)* operator; *(Zentrale)* exchange. **geben Sie mir bitte ein ~** could you give me a line please. **(e)** *(Eccl: Messe)* High Mass.
amtieren* *vi* **(a)** *(Amt innehaben)* to be in office. **~d** incumbent; **als Außenminister ~** to hold the post of foreign minister. **(b)** *(fungieren)* **als ... ~** to act as ...
amtlich *adj* official; *(wichtig) Miene, Gebaren* officious; **~es Kennzeichen** registration (number), license number *(US).*
Amtmann *m, pl* **-männer** *or* **-leute, Amtmännin** *f (Admin)* senior civil servant.
Amts-: ~anmaßung *f* unauthorized assumption of authority; **~arzt** *m* medical officer; **a~ärztlich** *adj Zeugnis* from the medical officer; **a~ärztlich untersucht werden** to have an official medical examination; **~bereich** *m* area of competence; **~dauer** *f* term of office; **~deutsch(e)** *nt* officialese; **~eid** *m* oath of office; **den ~eid ablegen** to be sworn in, to take the oath of office; **~einsetzung** *f* inauguration; **~enthebung** *f* dismissal from office; **~geheimnis** *nt* **(a)** *(geheime Sache)* official secret; **(b)** *(Schweigepflicht)* official secrecy; **~gericht** *nt* county *(Brit) or* district *(US)* court; **~geschäfte** *pl* official duties *pl*; **~handlung** *f* official duty; **~hilfe** *f* cooperation between authorities; **~leitung** *f (Telec)* exchange line; **~mißbrauch** *m* abuse of one's position; **~periode** *f* term of office; **~richter** *m* ≃ county *(Brit) or* district *(US)* court judge; **~schimmel** *m (hum)* officialdom; **der ~schimmel wiehert** officialdom rears its ugly head; **~sprache** *f* official language; **~vorstand, ~vorsteher** *m* head *or* chief of a/the department *etc*; **~weg** *m* **auf dem ~weg** through official channels; **~zeichen** *nt (Telec)* dialling tone *(Brit)*, dial tone *(US)*; **~zeit** *f* period of office; **~zimmer** *nt* office.
Amulett *nt* **-e** amulet, charm.
amüsant *adj* amusing.
amüsieren* **1** *vt* to amuse. **amüsiert zuschauen** to look on with amusement. **2** *vr (sich vergnügen)* to have a good time, to have fun. **sich über etw** *(acc)* **~** to find sth funny; *(unfreundlich)* to make fun of sth.
Amüsierviertel *nt* nightclub district.
an 1 *prep+dat* **(a)** *(räumlich: wo?)* at; *(~ etw dran)* on. **am Haus/Bahnhof** at the house/station; **am Fenster sitzen** to sit at *or* by the window; **am Tatort** at the scene of the crime; **~ der Tür/Wand** on the door/wall; **~ der Donau/Autobahn/am Ufer** by *or (direkt ~ gelegen)* on the Danube/motorway/bank; **zu nahe ~ etw stehen** to be too near to sth; **~ der gleichen Stelle** at *or* on the same spot; **jdn ~ der Hand nehmen** to take sb by the hand; **unten am Fluß** down by the river; **sie wohnen Tür ~ Tür** they live next door to one another; **sich** *(dat)* **die Hand am Tuch abwischen** to wipe one's hand on the cloth.
(b) *(zeitlich)* on. **~ diesem Abend** (on) that evening; **~ dem Abend, als ich ...** the evening I ...; *siehe* **am.**
(c) jung ~ Jahren sein to be young in years; **fünf ~ der Zahl** five in number; **~ etw arbeiten/schreiben/kauen** to be working on/writing/chewing sth; **~ etw sterben** to die of sth; **arm ~ Fett/reich ~ Kalorien** low in fat/high in calories; **was haben Sie ~ Weinen da?** what wines do you have?; **~ der ganzen Sache ist nichts** there is nothing in it; **es ~ der Leber** *etc* **haben** *(col)* to have liver *etc* trouble; **das gefällt mir nicht ~ ihm** that's what I don't like about him; **sie hat etwas ~ sich, das ...** there is something about her that ...; **es ist ~ ihm, etwas zu tun** *(geh)* it's up to him to do something.
2 *prep+acc* **(a)** *(räumlich: wohin?)* to; *(gegen)* on, against. **etw ~ die Wand/Tafel schreiben** to write sth on the wall/blackboard; **etw ~ etw hängen** to hang sth on sth; **A~ den Vorsitzenden ...** *(bei Anschrift)* The Chairman ... **(b)** *(zeitlich: woran?)* **~ die Zukunft/Vergangenheit denken** to think of the future/past; **bis ~ mein Lebensende** to the end of my days. **(c) ~ die Arbeit gehen** to get down to work; **ich habe eine Bitte/Frage ~ Sie** I have a request to make of you/question to ask you; **ein Gruß/eine Frage ~ jdn** greetings/a question to sb; **~ (und für) sich** actually; **dagegen ist ~ (und für) sich nichts einzuwenden** there are really no objections to that.
3 *adv* **(a)** *(ungefähr)* about. **~ (die) hundert** about a hundred. **(b)** *(Ankunftszeit)* **Frankfurt ~: 18.30** *(Rail)* arriving Frankfurt 18.30. **(c) von diesem Ort ~** from here onwards; **von diesem Tag/heute ~** from this day/today on(wards). **(d)** *(col: angeschaltet, angezogen)* on. **Licht ~!** lights on!; **ohne etwas ~** with nothing on.
Anachronismus [-kr-] *m (geh)* anachronism.
anachronistisch [-kr-] *adj (geh)* anachronistic.
Anagramm *nt (Liter)* anagram.

analog *adj* **(a)** analogous *(+dat, zu* to*)*. **(b)** *(Comp)* analogue *attr.*

Analogie *f* analogy.

Analogrechner *m* analogue computer.

Analphabet(in *f)* *m (wk)* **-en, en** illiterate (person).

Analyse *f* **-n** analysis *(auch Psych).*

analysieren* *vt* to analyze.

Analytiker(in *f)* *m* **-** analyst.

analytisch *adj* analytical.

Anämie *f* anaemia *(Brit)*, anemia *(US).*

Ananas *f* **-** *or* **-se** pineapple.

Anarchie *f* anarchy.

Anarchismus *m* anarchism.

Anarchist(in *f)* *m* anarchist.

anarchistisch *adj* anarchistic.

Anästhesie *f* anaesthesia *(Brit)*, anesthesia *(US).*

Anästhesist(in *f)* *m* anaesthetist *(Brit)*, anesthesiologist *(US).*

Anatomie *f* **(a)** anatomy. **(b)** *(Institut)* anatomical institute.

anatomisch *adj* anatomical.

anbahnen *sep* **1** *vt* to initiate. **2** *vr (sich andeuten)* to be in the offing; *(Unangenehmes)* to be looming; *(Möglichkeiten, Zukunft etc)* to be opening up. **zwischen den beiden bahnt sich etwas an** *(Liebesverhältnis)* there is something going on between those two.

Anbahnung *f* initiation *(von, gen* of*)*.

Anbau[1] *m no pl (Anpflanzung)* cultivation, growing.

Anbau[2] *m* **-ten** *(Nebengebäude)* extension; *(freistehend)* annexe.

anbauen *sep* **1** *vt* **(a)** to grow. **(b)** *(Build)* to add, to build on. **etw ans Haus ~** to build sth onto the house. **2** *vi* to build an extension.

Anbau-: ~fläche *f* (area of) cultivable land; **~gebiet** *nt* **ein gutes ~gebiet für etw** a good area for growing sth; **~möbel** *pl* unit furniture.

anbehalten* *vt sep irreg* to keep on.

anbei *adv (form)* enclosed. **~ schicken wir Ihnen ...** please find enclosed ...

anbeißen *sep irreg* **1** *vi (Fisch)* to bite; *(fig auch)* to take the bait. **2** *vt Apfel etc* to bite into. **ein angebissener Apfel** a half-eaten apple; **sie sieht zum A ~ aus** *(col)* she looks nice enough to eat.

anbelangen* *vt sep* to concern. **was das/mich anbelangt ...** as far as that is/I am concerned ...

anbellen *vt sep* to bark at.

anbeten *vt sep* to worship.

Anbetracht *m:* **in ~** *(+gen)* in consideration *or* view of; **in ~ dessen, daß ...** in consideration *or* view of the fact that ...

anbetreffen* *vt sep irreg siehe* **anbelangen.**

anbetteln *vt sep* **jdn ~** to beg from sb; **jdn um etw ~** to beg sth from sb.

anbiedern *vr sep (pej)* **sich (bei jdm) ~** to get pally (with sb) *(col).*

anbieten *sep irreg* **1** *vt* to offer *(jdm etw* sb sth*)*. **2** *vr* **(a)** *(Mensch)* **sich (als etw) ~** to offer one's services (as sth); **du darfst dich den Männern nicht so ~** you shouldn't make yourself so available; **der Ort bietet sich für die Konferenz an** that is the obvious place for the conference. **(b)** *(in Betracht kommen: Gelegenheit)* to present itself. **das bietet sich als Lösung an** that would provide a solution.

Anbieter *m* **-** supplier.

anbinden *vt sep irreg (an+acc or dat* to*)* to tie (up); *Pferd auch* to tether; *siehe* **angebunden.**

Anblick *m* sight. **beim ersten ~** at first sight; **du bist ein ~ für die Götter** you really look a sight.

anblicken *vt sep* to look at. **jdn lange/feindselig ~** to gaze/glare at sb.

anblinzeln *vt sep* **(a)** *(blinzelnd ansehen)* to squint at. **(b)** *(zublinzeln)* to wink at.

anbraten *vt sep irreg* to brown.

anbrechen *sep irreg* **1** *vt Packung, Flasche etc* to open; *Vorrat, Ersparnisse, Geldsumme* to break into; *siehe* **angebrochen. 2** *vi aux sein (Epoche etc)* to dawn; *(Tag auch)* to break; *(Nacht)* to fall; *(Jahreszeit)* to begin; *(Winter)* to close in.

anbrennen *vi sep irreg aux sein* to catch fire; *(Holz, Kohle etc)* to catch light; *(Essen)* to burn; *(Stoff)* to get scorched. **mir ist das Essen angebrannt** I burnt the food; *siehe* **angebrannt.**

anbringen *vt sep irreg* **(a)** *(befestigen)* to fix, to fasten *(an+dat* (on)to*)*; *(aufstellen, aufhängen)* to put up; *Telefon, Feuermelder etc* to put in, to install. **(b)** *(äußern) Bemerkung, Beschwerde* to make *(bei* to*)*; *Kenntnisse, Wissen* to display; *Argument* to use. **er konnte seine Kritik/seinen Antrag nicht mehr ~** he couldn't get his criticism/motion in; *siehe* **angebracht. (c)** *(col: loswerden) Ware* to get rid of.

Anbruch *m no pl (geh: Anfang)* beginning; *(von Zeitalter, Epoche)* dawn(ing). **bei ~ des Tages/Morgens** at daybreak, at break of day; **bei ~ der Nacht/Dunkelheit** at nightfall.

anbrüllen *vt sep (Löwe etc)* to roar at; *(col: Mensch)* to shout *or* bellow at.

Anchovis [an'ço:vis, an'ʃo:vis] *f* **-** anchovy.

Andacht *f* **-en (a)** *no pl (das Beten)* (silent) prayer *or* worship. **(b)** *(Gottesdienst)* prayers *pl.* **(c)** *(Versenkung)* rapt interest; *(Ehrfurcht)* reverence. **in tiefe(r) ~ versunken sein** to be completely absorbed.

andächtig *adj* **(a)** *(im Gebet)* in prayer. **(b)** *(versunken)* rapt; *(ehrfürchtig)* reverent.

andauern *vi sep* to continue; *(anhalten)* to last. **das dauert noch an** that is still going on; **der Regen dauert noch an** the rain hasn't stopped.

andauernd *adj (ständig)* continuous; *(anhaltend)* continual. **wenn du mich ~ unterbrichst ...** if you keep on interrupting me ...

Anden *pl* **die ~** the Andes.

Andenken *nt no pl* **(a)** memory. **zum ~ an jdn/etw** *(an Verstorbenen etc)* in memory *or* remembrance of sb/sth; *(an Freunde/Urlaub etc)* to remind you/us *etc* of sb/sth. **(b)** *(Reise~)* souvenir *(an +acc* of*)*; *(Erinnerungsstück)* memento, keepsake *(an+acc* from*)*.

ander(e)nfalls *adv* otherwise.

andere(r, s) *indef pron* **1** *(adjektivisch)* different; *(weiterer)* other. **ein ~r Mann/ein ~s Auto/eine ~ Frau** a different man/car/woman; *(ein weiterer etc)* another man/car/woman; **jede ~ Frau hätte ...** any other woman would have ...; **das machen wir ein ~s Mal** we'll do that another time; **er ist ein ~r Mensch geworden** he is a changed man.

2 *(substantivisch)* **(a)** *(Ding)* **ein ~r** a different one; *(noch einer)* another one; **etwas ~s** something *or (in Fragen)* anything else; **alle ~n** all the others; **das ist etwas ganz ~s** that's something quite different; **hast du etwas ~s gedacht?** did you think otherwise?; **ich habe ~s zu tun** I've other things to do; **nichts ~s** nothing else; **nichts ~s als ...** nothing but ...; **es blieb mir nichts ~s übrig, als selbst hinzugehen** I had no alternative but to go myself; **alles ~ als zufrieden** anything but pleased, far from pleased; **unter ~m** among other things; **es kam eins zum ~n** one thing led to another; **sie hat sich eines ~n besonnen** she changed her mind; **von einem Tag zum ~n** overnight.

(b) *(Person)* **ein ~r/eine ~** a different person; *(noch einer)* another person; **jeder ~/kein ~r** anyone/no-one else; **niemand ~s** no-one else; **das haben mir ~ auch schon gesagt** other people *or* others have told me that too; **die ~n** the others; **alle ~n** all the others, everyone else; **jemand ~s** somebody *or (in Fragen)* anybody else; **sie hat einen ~n** she has someone else; **der eine oder der ~ von unseren Kollegen** one or other of our colleagues; **einer nach dem ~n** one after the other; **eine schöner als die ~** each one more beautiful than the next.

and(e)rerseits *adv* on the other hand.

andermal *adv:* **ein ~** some other time.

ändern 1 *vt* to change, to alter; *Kleidungsstück* to alter. **ich kann es nicht ~** I can't do anything about it; **das ändert nichts an der Tatsache, daß ...** that doesn't alter the fact that ... **2** *vr* **(a)** to change, to alter. **(b)** *(Mensch)* to change; *(sich bessern)* to change for the better. **wenn sich das nicht ändert ...** if things don't improve ...

andernfalls *adv* otherwise.

anders *adv* **(a)** *(sonst)* else. **jemand/niemand ~** somebody *or* anybody/nobody else; **wer/wo ~?** who/where else?; **irgendwo ~** somewhere else. **(b)** *(verschieden)* differently; *(andersartig) sein, aussehen, klingen, schmecken* different *(als* to*)*. **~ als jd denken/reagieren/aussehen** to think/react differently/look different from sb; **~ als jd** *(geh: im Gegensatz zu)* unlike sb; **~ ausgedrückt** to put it another way; **das machen wir so und nicht ~** we'll do it this way and no other; **wie nicht ~ zu erwarten** as was to be expected; **sie ist ~ geworden** she has changed; **wie könnte es ~ sein?** how could it be otherwise?; **es geht nicht ~** there's no other way; **ich kann nicht ~** *(kann es nicht lassen)* I can't help it; *(muß leider)* I have no choice.

Anders-: a~artig *adj no comp* different; **~denkende(r)** *mf decl as adj* dissident, dissenter; **a~farbig** *adj* of a different colour *(Brit) or* color *(US)*; **a~(he)rum** *adv* the other way around; **a~lautend** *adj attr (form)* contrary; **a~lautende Berichte** reports to the contrary; **a~wo** *adv* elsewhere; **a~woher** *adv* from elsewhere; **a~wohin** *adv* elsewhere.

anderthalb *num* one and a half. **~ Pfund Kaffee** a pound and a half of coffee.

Änderung *f* change, alteration *(an +dat, gen* in, to*)*; *(an Kleid, Gebäude)* alteration *(an+dat* to*)*.

Änderungs-: ~antrag *m (Parl)* amendment; **~schneider** *m* tailor (who does alterations); **~vorschlag** *m* suggested change *or* alteration; **einen ~vorschlag machen** to suggest a change *or* an alteration.

anderweitig 1 *adj attr (andere, weitere)* other. **2** *adv (anders)* otherwise; *(an anderer Stelle)* elsewhere. **~ vergeben/besetzt werden** to be given to/filled by someone else; **etw ~ verwenden** to use sth for a different purpose.

andeuten *sep* **1** *vt (zu verstehen geben)* to hint, to intimate *(jdm etw* sth to sb*)*; *(kurz erwähnen) Problem* to mention briefly; *(erkennen lassen)* to indicate. **2** *vr* to be indicated; *(Gewitter)* to be in the offing.

Andeutung *f (Anspielung, Anzeichen)* hint; *(flüchtiger Hinweis)* brief mention; *(Spur)* sign, trace. **eine ~ machen** to hint *(über+acc* at*)*, to drop a hint *(über+acc* about*)*.

andeutungsweise *adv (als Anspielung, Anzeichen)* by way of a hint; *(als flüchtiger Hinweis)* in passing. **jdm ~ zu verstehen geben, daß ...** to hint to sb that ....

andichten *vt sep* **jdm etw ~** *(col) Fähigkeiten* to credit sb with sth.

Andrang *m no pl (Zustrom, Gedränge)* crowd, crush.

andrehen *vt sep* **(a)** *(anstellen)* to turn on. **(b) jdm etw ~** *(col)* to palm sth off on sb.

androhen *vt sep* to threaten *(jdm etw* sb with sth*)*.

Androhung *f* threat. **unter ~ von Gewalt** with the threat of violence; **unter ~** *(Jur)* under penalty *(von, gen* of*)*.

Andruck *m (Typ)* proof.

andünsten *vti sep (Cook)* to braise lightly.

an|ecken *vi sep aux sein (col)* **(bei jdm/allen) ~** to rub sb/everyone up the wrong way.

an|eignen *vr sep* **sich** *(dat)* **etw ~** *(etw erwerben)* to acquire sth; *(etw wegnehmen)* to appropriate sth; *(sich mit etw vertraut machen)* to learn sth.

An|eignung *f siehe vr* acquisition; appropriation; learning.

an|einander *adv* **~ denken** to think of each other; **sich ~ gewöhnen** to get used to each other; **~ vorüber-/vorbeigehen** to go past each other; **~ befestigen** to stick together; **zu dicht ~** too close together.

an|einander- *in cpds* together; **~geraten*** *vi sep irreg* to come to blows *(mit* with*)*; *(streiten)* to have words *(mit* with*)*; **~grenzen** *vi sep* to border on each other; **~hängen** *vi sep irreg* **(a)** *(zusammenhängen)* to be linked (together); **(b)** *(fig: Menschen)* to be attached to each other; **~kleben** *sep* **1** *vt* to stick together; **2** *vi* to be stuck together; *(col: unzertrennlich sein)* to be glued together *(col)*; **~reihen** *vt sep* to string together.

Anekdote *f* **-n** anecdote.

an|ekeln *vt sep (anwidern)* to disgust, to nauseate.

Anemone *f* **-n** anemone.

an|erkannt *adj* recognized; *Tatsache auch* established; *Werk* standard; *Experte* acknowledged.

an|erkennen* *vt sep or insep irreg Staat, König, Rekord* to recognize; *Forderung auch* to accept; *Vaterschaft* to accept, to acknowledge; *(würdigen) Leistung, Bemühung* to appreciate. ..., **das muß man ~** *(zugeben)* ... you can't argue with that; *(würdigen)* ... one has to appreciate that; **als gleichwertiger Partner anerkannt sein** to be accepted as an equal partner.

an|erkennenswert *adj* commendable.

An|erkennung *f siehe vt* recognition; acceptance; acknowledgement; appreciation.

an|erziehen* *vt insep irreg:* **jdm etw ~** *(Kindern)* to instil sth into sb.

an|erzogen *adj* acquired. **das ist alles ~** she *etc* has just been trained to be like that.

anfahren *sep irreg* **1** *vi aux sein (losfahren)* to start (up). **angefahren kommen** *(Wagen, Fahrer)* to drive up; *(Zug)* to pull up; **beim A~** when starting (up); **das A~ am Berg üben** to practice a hill start. **2** *vt* **(a)** *(liefern) Kohlen, Kartoffeln* to deliver. **(b)** *(ansteuern) Ort* to stop *or* call at; *Hafen auch* to put in at. **(c)** *(anstoßen) Passanten, Baum etc* to run into, to hit.

Anfahrt *f (~sweg, ~szeit)* journey; *(Zufahrt)* approach.

Anfall *m* **(a)** attack; *(Wut~, epileptisch)* fit. **einen ~ haben/bekommen** *(lit)* to have an attack/fit; *(fig col)* to have *or* throw a fit *(col)*; **in einem ~ von** *(fig)* in a fit of. **(b)** *(Ertrag, Nebenprodukte)* yield *(an+dat* of*)*; *(von Zinsen auch)* accrual. **(c)** *(von Reparaturen, Kosten)* amount *(an+dat* of*)*; *(form: Anhäufung)* accumulation. **bei ~ von Reparaturen** if repairs are necessary.

anfallen *sep irreg* **1** *vt (überfallen)* to attack; *(Sittenstrolch etc)* to assault. **2** *vi aux sein (Zinsen)* to accrue; *(Nebenprodukte)* to be obtained; *(sich anhäufen)* to accumulate. **die ~den Kosten/Reparaturen** the costs/repairs incurred; **die ~de Arbeit** the work which comes up.

anfällig *adj (nicht widerstandsfähig)* delicate; *Motor, Maschine* temperamental. **für etw/eine Krankheit ~ sein** to be susceptible to sth/prone to an illness.

Anfälligkeit *f siehe adj* delicateness; temperamental nature; susceptibility; proneness.

Anfang *m, pl* **Anfänge** *(Beginn)* beginning, start; *(Ursprung)* beginnings *pl*, origin. **zu** *or* **am ~** to start with; *(anfänglich)* at first; **~ Fünfzig** in one's early fifties; **~ Juni/1978** *etc* at the beginning of June/1978 *etc;* **von ~ an** (right) from the beginning *or* start; **von ~ bis Ende** from start to finish; **den ~ machen** to start *or* begin; *(den ersten Schritt tun)* to make the first move; **einen neuen ~ machen** to make a new start; **aller ~ ist schwer** *(Prov)* the first step is always the most difficult; **das ist der ~ vom Ende** it's the beginning of the end.

anfangen *sep irreg* **1** *vt* **(a)** *(beginnen)* to start, to begin; *Streit* to start. **(b)** *(anstellen, machen)* to do. **das mußt du anders ~** you'll have to go about it differently; **nichts mit sich/jdm anzufangen wissen** not to know what to do with oneself/sb; **damit kann ich nichts ~** *(nützt mir nichts)* that's no good to me; *(verstehe ich nicht)* it doesn't mean a thing to me; **mit dir ist heute (aber) gar nichts anzufangen!** you're no fun at all today! **2** *vi* to begin, to start. **du hast angefangen!** *(bei Streit)* you started it!; **es fing zu regnen an** *or* **an zu regnen** it started raining *or* to rain; **das fängt ja schön an!** *(iro)* that's a good start!; **jetzt fängt das Leben erst an** life is only just beginning; **mit etw ~** to start sth; **bei einer Firma ~** to start working for a firm.

Anfänger(in *f***)** *m* - beginner; *(Neuling)* novice; *(Aut)* learner; *(col: Nichtskönner)* amateur *(pej)*.

Anfängerkurs(us) *m* beginners' course.

anfänglich 1 *adj attr* initial. **2** *adv* at first, initially.

anfangs 1 *adv* at first, initially. **wie ich schon ~ erwähnte** as I mentioned at the beginning. **2** *prep +gen* **~ der zwanziger Jahre/des Monats** in the early twenties/at the beginning of the month.

Anfangs-: ~buchstabe *m* first letter; **kleine/große ~buchstaben** small/capital initials; **~gehalt** *nt* starting salary; **~stadium** *nt* initial stage; **meine Versuche sind schon im ~stadium steckengeblieben** my attempts never really got off the ground.

anfassen *sep* **1** *vt* **(a)** *(berühren)* to touch. **(b)** *(bei der Hand nehmen)* **jdn ~** to take sb's hand *or* sb by the hand; **sich ~** to take each other by the hand. **(c)** *(fig: anpacken) Problem* to tackle, to go about. **2** *vi* **(a)** *(berühren)* to feel. **nicht ~!** don't touch! **(b)** *(mithelfen)* **mit ~** to give a hand.

anfauchen *vt sep (Katze)* to spit at; *(fig col)* to snap at.

anfechtbar *adj* contestable.

anfechten *vt sep irreg (nicht anerkennen)* to contest; *Aussage auch* to challenge; *Urteil* to appeal against; *Vertrag* to dispute.

Anfechtung *f* **(a)** *siehe vt (a)* contesting; challenging; appeal *(gen* against*)*; disputing. **(b)** *(Versuchung)* temptation.

anfeinden *vt sep* to treat with hostility.

Anfeindung *f* hostility. **trotz aller ~en** in spite of all the hostility.

anfertigen *vt sep* to make; *Schriftstück* to draw up; *Hausaufgaben* to do; *Protokoll* to take down. **sich** *(dat)* **einen Anzug** *etc* **~ lassen** to have a suit *etc* made.

Anfertigung *f siehe vt* making; drawing up; taking down.

anfeuchten *vt sep* to moisten.

anfeuern *vt sep (fig: ermutigen)* to spur on.

Anfeuerung *f (fig)* spurring on.

Anfeuerungsruf *m* cheer.

anflehen *vt sep* to beseech, to implore *(um* for*)*. **ich flehe dich an, tu das nicht!** I beg you, don't!

anfliegen *sep irreg* **1** *vi aux sein (auch* **angeflogen kommen***) (Flugzeug)* to come in to land; *(Vogel, Geschoß)* to come flying up. **2** *vt (Flugzeug) Flughafen, (Mil) Stellung* to approach; *(landen)* to land *(in/auf* in/on*)*. **diese Fluggesellschaft fliegt Bali an** this airline flies to Bali.

Anflug *m* **(a)** *(Flugweg)* flight; *(das Heranfliegen)* approach. **wir befinden uns im ~ auf Paris** we are now approaching Paris. **(b)** *(Spur)* trace.

anfordern *vt sep* to request; *Waren* to order.

Anforderung *f* **(a)** *no pl (das Anfordern)* request *(gen, von* for*)*. **bei der ~ von Ersatzteilen** when ordering spare parts. **(b)** *(Anspruch)* requirement; *(Belastung)* demand. **große ~en an jdn/etw stellen** to make great demands on sb/sth.

Anfrage *f* inquiry; *(Parl)* question.

anfragen *vi sep* to inquire *(bei jdm* of sb*)*, to ask *(bei jdm* sb*)*.

anfressen *vt sep irreg* **(a)** *(Maus)* to nibble at; *(Vogel)* to peck (at). **(b)** *(zersetzen)* to eat away.

anfreunden *vr sep* to make *or* become friends. **sich mit etw ~** *(fig)* to get to like sth.

anfügen *vt sep* to add.

anfühlen *sep* **1** *vt* to feel. **2** *vr* to feel. **sich glatt/weich** *etc* **~** to feel smooth/soft *etc*.

Anfuhr *f* **-en** transport(ation).

anführen *vt sep* **(a)** *(vorangehen; befehligen)* to lead. **(b)** *(zitieren)* to quote, to cite; *Tatsachen, Beispiel auch* to give; *Grund, Beweis* to give, to offer; *(benennen) jdn* to name, to cite. **(c) jdn ~** *(col)* to have sb on *(col)*, to take sb for a ride *(col)*.

Anführer *m* leader; *(pej: Anstifter)* ringleader.

Anführung *f* **(a)** leadership; *(Befehligung auch)* command. **unter ~ von ...** under the leadership of ... **(b)** *(Zitat)* quotation.

Anführungs-: ~zeichen *nt* quotation mark, inverted comma; **~zeichen unten/oben** quote/unquote.

anfüllen *vt sep* to fill (up). **mit etw angefüllt sein** to be full of sth, to be filled with sth.

Angabe ['anga:-] *f* **-n (a)** *usu pl (Aussage)* statement; *(Zahl, Detail)* detail. **~n über etw** *(acc)* **machen** to give details about sth; **laut ~n** *(+gen)* according to; **~n zur Person** *(form)* personal details *or* particulars. **(b)** *(Nennung)* giving. **wir bitten um ~ der Einzelheiten/Preise** please give *or* quote details/prices; **ohne ~ von Gründen** without giving any reasons. **(c)** *no pl (col: Prahlerei)* showing off; *(Reden auch)* boasting.

angeben ['ange:-] *sep irreg* **1** *vt* **(a)** *(nennen)* to give; *(als Zeugen)* to name, to cite; *(erklären)* to explain; *(beim Zoll)* to declare; *(anzeigen) Temperatur etc* to indicate; *(aussagen)* to state; *(behaupten)* to maintain. **(b)** *(bestimmen) Tempo, Kurs* to set; *(Mus) Tempo, Note* to give. **den Takt ~** *(klopfen)* to beat time. **2** *vi (prahlen)* to show off; *(durch Reden auch)* to boast, to brag *(mit* about*)*.

Angeber ['ange:-] *m (Prahler)* show-off, poser *(col)*.

Angeberei [ange:-] *f no pl (Prahlerei)* showing-off, posing *(col) (mit* about*)*; *(verbal auch)* boasting, bragging *(mit* about*)*.

angeberisch ['ange:-] *adj Reden* boastful; *Benehmen, Tonfall* pretentious, showy.

angeblich ['ange:-] **1** *adj attr* so-called, alleged. **2** *adv* supposedly, allegedly. **er ist ~ Musiker** he's supposed to be a musician.

angeboren ['angə-] *adj* innate, inherent; *(Med, fig col)* congenital *(bei* with*)*.

Angebot ['angə-] *nt* **(a)** offer; *(bei Auktion)* bid; *(Comm: Offerte auch)* tender *(über +acc, für* for*)*. **(b)** *no pl (Comm, Fin)* supply *(an+dat, von* of*)*; *(Auswahl)* selection *(an + dat* of*)*. **~ und Nachfrage** supply and demand; **im ~** *(col)* on special offer.

angebracht ['angə-] *adj* appropriate; *(sinnvoll)* reasonable.

angebrannt ['angə-] *adj* burnt. **es riecht hier so ~** there's a smell of burning here.

angebrochen ['angə-] *adj Packung, Flasche* open(ed). **was sollen wir mit dem ~en Abend machen?** what shall we do with the rest of the evening?; **das Parken kostet für jede ~e Stunde eine Mark** parking costs one mark for every hour or part of an hour.

angebunden ['angə-] *adj* **kurz ~ sein** *(col)* to be abrupt *or* curt.

angegossen ['angə-] *adj* **wie ~ sitzen** *or* **passen** to fit like a glove.

angegraut ['angə-] *adj* grey; *Haar auch* greying.

angegriffen ['angə-] *adj Gesundheit* weakened; *Mensch, Aussehen* frail; *(nervlich)* strained.

angehalten ['angə-] *adj* **~ sein, etw zu tun** to be required *or* obliged to do sth.

angehaucht ['angə-] *adj* **links/rechts ~ sein** to have left-/right-wing tendencies *or* leanings.
angeheiratet ['angə-] *adj* related by marriage. **ein ~er Cousin** a cousin by marriage.
angeheitert ['angə-] *adj (col)* merry *(col)*, tipsy.
angehen ['ange:-] *sep irreg* **1** *vi* **(a)** *(col: beginnen) (Feuer)* to start burning, to catch; *(Licht)* to come on, to go on. **(b)** *(entgegentreten)* **gegen jdn/etw ~** to fight sb/sth; *gegen Mißstände, Zustände* to take measures against sth. **2** *vt* **(a)** *(anpacken) Aufgabe* to tackle. **(b)** *(bitten)* to ask *(jdm um etw* sb for sth*)*. **(c)** *(betreffen)* to concern. **was mich angeht** as far as I'm concerned; **das geht ihn gar nichts an** that's none of his business. **3** *vi impers* **das geht nicht/keinesfalls an** that's quite out of the question.
angehend ['ange:-] *adj Musiker, Künstler* budding; *Lehrer, Ehemann, Vater* prospective.
angehören* ['angə-] *vi sep+dat* to belong to; *(einer Partei, einer Familie auch)* to be a member of.
Angehörige(r) ['angə-] *mf decl as adj* **(a)** *(Mitglied)* member. **(b)** *(Familien~)* relative, relation. **der nächste ~** the next of kin.
Angeklagte(r) ['angə-] *mf decl as adj* accused, defendant.
angeknackst ['angə-] *adj (col) Mensch* uptight *(col)*; *Selbstbewußtsein* weakened. **er/seine Gesundheit ist ~** he is in bad shape.
angekratzt ['angə-] *adj (col)* seedy *(col)*.
Angel *f* **-n (a)** *(Tür~, Fenster~)* hinge. **die Welt aus den ~n heben** *(fig)* to turn the world upside down. **(b)** *(Fischfanggerät)* fishing rod, fishing pole *(US)*. **die ~ auswerfen** to cast (the line).
Angelegenheit ['angə-] *f* matter; *(politisch, persönlich)* affair; *(Aufgabe)* concern. **das ist nicht meine ~** that's not my concern *or* business.
angelegt ['angə-] *adj* calculated *(auf+acc* for*)*.
angelernt ['angə-] *adj Arbeiter* semi-skilled.
Angel-: ~gerät *nt* fishing tackle *no pl*; **~haken** *m* fish-hook.
angeln 1 *vi* **(a)** to fish. **~ gehen** to go angling *or* fishing. **(b)** *(zu greifen versuchen, hervorziehen)* to fish. **nach etw ~** to fish (around) for sth. **2** *vt Fisch* to fish for; *(fangen)* to catch. **sich** *(dat)* **einen Mann ~** *(col)* to catch (oneself) a man.
Angel-: ~punkt *m* crucial *or* central point; *(Frage)* key *or* central issue; **~rute** *f* fishing rod, fishing pole *(US)*.
Angelsachse *m decl as adj* Anglo-Saxon.
angelsächsisch *adj* Anglo-Saxon.
Angel-: ~schein *m* fishing permit; **~schnur** *f* fishing line.
angemessen ['angə-] *adj (passend)* appropriate *(dat* to, for*)*; *(adäquat)* adequate *(dat* for*)*; *Preis* reasonable, fair. **eine der Leistung ~e Bezahlung** payment commensurate with input.
angenehm ['angə-] *adj* pleasant, agreeable. **das wäre mir sehr ~** I should be very grateful; **es ist mir gar nicht ~, daß er mich besuchen will** I don't like the idea of him wanting to visit me; **wenn Ihnen das ~er ist** if you prefer; **(sehr) ~!** *(form)* delighted (to meet you); **das A~e mit dem Nützlichen verbinden** to combine business with pleasure.
angenommen ['angə-] **1** *adj* assumed; *Kind* adopted. **2** *conj* assuming.
angepaßt ['angə-] *adj* conformist.
Angepaßtheit ['angə-] *f* conformism.
angeregt ['angə-] *adj* lively, animated. **~ diskutieren** to have a lively *or* an animated discussion.
angereichert ['angə-] *adj* enriched.
angeschlagen ['angə-] *adj (col) Mensch, Aussehen, Nerven* shattered *(col)*; *Gesundheit* poor.
angeschlossen ['angə-] *adj* affiliated *(dat* to *or* with*)*, associated *(dat* with*)*.
angeschmiert ['angə-] *adj pred (col)* in trouble. **der/die A~e sein** to have been had *(col)*.
angeschrieben ['angə-] *adj (col)* **bei jdm gut/schlecht ~ sein** to be in sb's good/bad books.
angesehen ['angə-] *adj* respected.
Angesicht ['angə-] *nt* **-er** *(geh)* face. **von ~ zu ~** face to face; **im ~** *+gen (fig)* in the face of.
angesichts ['angə-] *prep+gen* in the face of; *(im Hinblick auf)* in view of.
angespannt ['angə-] *adj Nerven, Lage* tense, strained; *Aufmerksamkeit* close, keen; *(Comm) Markt, Lage* tight, overstretched.
angestammt ['angə-] *adj (überkommen)* traditional; *(ererbt) Rechte* hereditary; *Besitz* inherited.
angestellt ['angə-] *adj pred* **~ sein** to be an employee *or* on the staff *(bei* of*)*; **fest ~ sein** to be a permanent employee.
Angestellte(r) ['angə-] *mf decl as adj* (salaried) employee; *(Büro~)* office-worker, white-collar worker.
Angestellten- ['angə-]: **~gewerkschaft** *f* white-collar union; **~versicherung** *f* (salaried) employee's insurance.
angestrengt ['angə-] *adj Gesicht* strained; **~ arbeiten/denken** to work/think hard; **~ diskutieren** to have an intense discussion.
angetan ['angətan] *adj pred* **(a) von jdm/etw ~ sein** to be taken with sb/sth; **das Mädchen hat es ihm ~** he has fallen for that girl. **(b) dazu ~ sein, etw zu tun** *(geh)* to be suitable for doing sth; *(Atmosphäre, Benehmen etc)* to be apt to do sth.
angetrunken ['angə-] *adj* inebriated.
angewandt ['angə-] *adj attr Wissenschaft etc* applied.
angewidert ['angə-] *adj* nauseated, disgusted. **vom Leben ~** sick of life.
angewiesen ['angə-] *adj* **auf jdn/etw ~ sein** to have to rely on sb/sth, to be dependent on sb/sth; **auf sich selbst ~ sein** to be left to one's own devices; **darauf bin ich nicht ~** I don't need it.
angewöhnen ['angə-] *vt sep* **jdm etw ~** to get sb used to sth, to accustom sb to sth; **sich** *(dat)* **etw ~/es sich** *(dat)* **~, etw zu tun** to get into the habit of sth/of doing sth.
Angewohnheit ['angə-] *f* habit.
angewurzelt *adj* **wie ~ dastehen** to be rooted to the spot.
angiften ['angı-] *vt sep (pej inf)* to snap at.
Angina [aŋ'gi:na] *f, pl* **Anginen** *(Med)* angina. **~ pectoris** angina (pectoris).
angleichen ['angl-] *sep irreg* **1** *vt* to bring into line, to align *(dat, an+acc* with*)*. **2** *vr (gegenseitig: Kulturen, Geschlechter, Methoden)* to grow closer together. **sich jdm/einer Sache ~** *(einseitig)* to become like sb/sth.
Angleichung *f* alignment *(an +acc* with*)*.
Angler(in *f*) *m* **-** angler.
angliedern ['angl-] *vt sep (dat, an+acc* to*) (Verein, Partei)* to affiliate; *Land* to annex.
Angliederung *f siehe vt* affiliation; annexation.
anglikanisch [aŋgli-] *adj* Anglican. **die A~e Kirche** the Anglican Church, the Church of England.
Anglist(in *f*) [aŋ'glı-] *m* English specialist, Anglicist; *(Student)* English student; *(Professor etc)* English lecturer/professor.
Anglistik [aŋ'glı-] *f* English (language and literature).
Angora- [aŋ'go:ra]: **~katze** *f* Angora cat; **~wolle** *f* Angora (wool).
angreifbar ['angr-] *adj* open to attack.
angreifen ['angr-] *sep irreg* **1** *vt* **(a)** to attack. **(b)** *(schwächen) Organismus, Nerven* to weaken; *Gesundheit, Pflanzen* to affect. **2** *vi* to attack.
Angreifer ['angr-] *m* **-** attacker *(auch Sport, fig)*.
angrenzen ['angr-] *vi sep* **an etw** *(acc)* **~** to border on sth, to adjoin sth.
angrenzend *adj attr* adjacent *(an +acc* to*)*, adjoining *(an etw (acc)* sth*)*.
Angriff ['angr-] *m (Mil, Sport, fig)* attack *(gegen, auf*

+*acc* on); *(Luft~)* (air) raid. ~ **ist die beste Verteidigung** *(prov)* attack is the best means of defence; **etw in ~ nehmen** to tackle sth.

Angriffs-: ~**fläche** *f* target; **jdm/einer Sache eine ~fläche bieten** *(lit, fig)* to provide sb/sth with a target; ~**krieg** *m* war of aggression; ~**lust** *f* aggressiveness, aggression; **a~lustig** *adj* aggressive; ~**spiel** *nt (Sport)* aggressive *or* attacking game; ~**spieler** *m (Ftbl)* forward.

angrinsen ['angr-] *vt sep* to grin at.

Angst *f* ¨**e** *(innere Unruhe, Psych)* anxiety *(um* about*)*; *(Sorge)* worry *(um* about*)*; *(Befürchtung)* fear *(um* for, *vor+dat* of*)*; *(Existenz~)* angst. **(vor etw** *dat***)** ~ **haben** to be afraid *or* scared (of sth); ~ **um jdn/etw haben** to be anxious *or* worried about sb/sth; ~ **bekommen** *or* **kriegen** to become afraid *or* scared; **aus ~, etw zu tun** for fear of doing sth; **keine ~!** don't worry; **jdm ~ einflößen** *or* **einjagen** to frighten sb.

angst *adj pred* **ihr wurde ~ (und bange)** she became worried *or* anxious.

Angsthase *m (col)* scaredy-cat *(col)*.

ängstigen 1 *vt* to frighten; *(unruhig machen)* to worry. **2** *vr* to be afraid; *(sich sorgen)* to worry. **sich vor etw** *(dat)* ~ to be afraid of sth; **sich wegen etw** ~ to worry about sth.

ängstlich *adj (verängstigt)* anxious, apprehensive; *(schüchtern)* timid, timorous.

Ängstlichkeit *f siehe adj* anxiety, apprehension; timidity, timorousness.

Angst-: ~**macher** *m (col)* scaremonger; ~**schrei** *m* cry of fear; ~**schweiß** *m* cold sweat; **mir brach der ~schweiß aus** I broke out in a cold sweat; **a~voll** *adj* apprehensive, fearful; ~**zustand** *m* state of panic; ~**zustände bekommen** to get into a state of panic.

angucken ['angʊ-] *vt sep* to look at.

angurten ['angʊ-] *vtr sep siehe* **anschnallen.**

anhaben *vt sep irreg* **(a)** *(angezogen haben)* to have on, to wear. **sie hatte ein schwarzes Kleid an** she was wearing a black dress, she had on a black dress. **(b)** *(zuleide tun)* to do harm. **die Kälte kann mir nichts ~** the cold doesn't worry *or* bother me. **(c)** *(am Zeuge flicken)* **Sie können/die Polizei kann mir nichts ~!** *(col)* you/the police can't touch me.

anhaften *vi sep* **(a)** *(lit)* to stick *(an+dat* to*)*. **(b)** *(fig)+dat* to stick to, to stay with.

anhalten *sep irreg* **1** *vi* **(a)** *(stehenbleiben)* to stop. **(b)** *(fortdauern)* to last. **(c)** *(werben)* **um die Hand eines Mädchens ~** to ask for a girl's hand in marriage. **2** *vt* **(a)** *(stoppen)* to stop. **(b)** *(anleiten)* to urge, to encourage; *siehe* **angehalten.**

anhaltend *adj* continuous, incessant.

Anhalter(in *f***)** *m* **-** hitch-hiker. **per ~ fahren** to hitch-hike, to hitch *(col)*.

Anhaltspunkt *m (Vermutung)* clue *(für* about*)*; *(für Verdacht)* grounds *pl.* **ich habe keinerlei ~e** I have no idea.

anhand, an Hand *prep+gen siehe* **Hand (d).**

Anhang *m, pl* **Anhänge (a)** *(Nachtrag)* appendix. **(b)** *no pl (Gefolgschaft)* following; *(Angehörige)* family.

anhängen *sep* **1** *vt* **(a)** *(an+acc* to*) (ankuppeln)* to attach; *(Rail auch)* to couple on; *Anhänger* to hitch up; *(fig: anfügen)* to add *(dat, an +acc* to*)*. **(b)** *(col)* **jdm etw ~** *(nachsagen, anlasten)* to blame sb for sth, to blame sth on sb; *schlechten Ruf, Spitznamen* to give sb sth; *Verdacht, Schuld* to pin sth on sb. **2** *vi irreg (fig)* **(a)** *(anhaften)* **jdm** ~ to stay with sb; *(schlechter Ruf, Gefängnisstrafe auch)* to stick with sb. **(b)** *(sich zugehörig fühlen)+dat* to adhere to, to subscribe to.

Anhänger(in *f***)** *m* **- (a)** supporter; *(von Sportart auch)* fan; *(von Partei auch)* follower. **(b)** *(Wagen)* trailer. **(c)** *(Schmuckstück)* pendant. **(d)** *(Koffer~ etc)* tag, label.

Anhängerschaft *f siehe* **Anhänger (a)** supporters *pl*; fans *pl*; followers *pl.*

anhänglich *adj Kind, Freundin* clinging; *Haustier* devoted.

Anhänglichkeit *f siehe adj* tendency to cling to one; devotion.

Anhängsel *nt* **(a)** *(Überflüssiges, Mensch)* appendage *(an+dat* to*)*. **(b)** *(Schildchen)* tag; *(an Kette)* pendant.

anhauchen *vt sep* to breathe on; *siehe* **angehaucht.**

anhauen *vt sep (col: ansprechen)* to accost *(um* for*)*. **jdn um etw ~** to (try to) touch sb for sth *(col)*.

anhäufen *sep* **1** *vt* to accumulate, to amass; *Vorräte, Geld* to hoard. **2** *vr* to pile up, to accumulate; *(Zinsen)* to accumulate, to accrue.

Anhäufung *f siehe vt* accumulation, amassing; hoarding.

anheben *vt sep irreg* **(a)** *(hochheben)* to lift (up); *Glas* to raise. **(b)** *(erhöhen)* to raise.

Anhebung *f* increase *(gen, von* in*)*.

anheften *vt sep* to fasten (on) *(an +acc or dat* to*)*.

anheimelnd *adj (geh)* homely; *Klänge* familiar.

anheimfallen *vi sep irreg aux sein+dat (liter)* to pass *or* fall to; *einem Betrug* to fall victim to.

anheizen *vt sep* **(a)** *Ofen* to light. **(b)** *(fig col) Wirtschaft* to stimulate; *(verschlimmern) Krise* to aggravate.

anheuern *vti sep (Naut, fig)* to sign on *or* up.

Anhieb *m*: **auf ~** *(col)* straight *or* right away, first go *(col)*; **das kann ich nicht auf ~ sagen** I can't say offhand.

anhimmeln *vt sep (col)* to idolize, to worship.

Anhöhe *f* hill.

anhören *sep* **1** *vt* **(a)** to hear; *Schallplatten, Konzert* to listen to. **(b)** *(zufällig mithören)* to overhear. **ich kann das nicht mehr mit ~** I can't listen to that any longer. **(c)** *(anmerken)* **man konnte ihr/ihrer Stimme die Verzweiflung ~** one could hear the despair in her voice. **2** *vr* **(a) sich** *(dat)* **etw ~** to listen to sth; **das höre ich mir nicht mehr länger mit an** I'm not going to listen to that any longer. **(b)** *(klingen)* to sound. **das hört sich ja gut an** *(col)* that sounds good.

Anhörung *f* hearing.

animalisch *adj* animal; *(pej auch)* bestial, brutish.

Animierdame *f* nightclub *or* bar hostess.

animieren* *vt* **(a)** *(anregen)* to encourage. **jdn zu einem Streich ~** to put sb up to a trick; **durch das schöne Wetter animiert** prompted by the good weather. **(b)** *(Film)* to animate.

Animier-: ~**lokal** *nt* hostess bar, clipjoint *(pej)*; ~**mädchen** *nt* nightclub *or* bar hostess.

Animosität *f (geh: Feindseligkeit)* animosity, hostility *(gegen* towards*)*.

Anis [a'niːs] *m* **-e** *(Gewürz)* aniseed; *(Pflanze)* anise.

Anisett *m* **-s** *m* anisette, aniseed liqueur.

ankämpfen *vi sep* **gegen etw ~** to fight (against) sth; *gegen Wind, Strömung* to battle against sth.

ankarren *vt sep (col)* to cart along.

Ankauf *m* purchase. **An- und Verkauf von ...** we buy and sell ...

ankaufen *vti sep* to purchase, to buy.

Anker *m* **-** *(Naut, Archit, fig)* anchor. **vor ~ gehen** to drop anchor; **vor ~ liegen** to lie *or* ride at anchor; **den/die ~ lichten** to weigh anchor.

ankern *vi (Anker werfen)* to anchor; *(vor Anker liegen)* to be anchored.

Anker-: ~**platz** *m* anchorage; ~**winde** *f* capstan.

anketten *vt sep* to chain up *(an +acc or dat* to*)*. **angekettet sein** *(fig)* to be tied up.

ankläffen *vt sep (pej)* to bark at; *(kleiner Hund)* to yap at.

Anklage *f* **(a)** *(Jur)* charge; *(~vertretung)* prosecution. **gegen jdn ~ erheben** to bring *or* prefer charges against sb; **(wegen etw) unter ~ stehen** to have been charged (with sth). **(b)** *(fig) (Beschuldigung)* accusation; *(Anprangerung)*

indictment *(an+acc* of*)*.
Anklagebank *f* dock. **auf der ~ (sitzen)** *(lit, fig)* (to be) in the dock.
anklagen *vt sep (Jur)* to charge, to accuse. **jdn einer Sache** *(gen) or* **wegen etw ~** to charge sb with sth, to accuse sb of sth.
anklagend *adj Ton* accusing; *Blick* reproachful.
Anklagepunkt *m* charge.
Ankläger *m* - *(Jur)* prosecutor.
Anklage-: ~schrift *f* indictment; **~vertreter** *m* (public) prosecutor, counsel for the prosecution.
anklammern *sep* **1** *vt (mit Büroklammer)* to clip *(an+acc or dat* (on)to*)*; *(mit Heftmaschine)* to staple *(an+acc or dat* on(to), to*)*. **2** *vr* **sich an jdn/etw** *(acc or dat)* **~** to cling to sb/sth.
Anklang *m* **(a)** *no pl (Beifall)* approval. **~ (bei jdm) finden** to meet with (sb's) approval; **großen/wenig/keinen ~ finden** to be very well/poorly/badly received. **(b)** *(Reminiszenz)* **Anklänge an etw** *(acc)* **enthalten** to be reminiscent of sth.
ankleben *vt sep* to stick up *(an +acc or dat* on*)*. **Plakate ~ verboten** stick no bills.
Ankleidekabine *f* changing cubicle.
ankleiden *vtr sep (geh)* to dress.
Ankleideraum *m* dressing-room; *(im Schwimmbad, Geschäft)* changing room.
anklingen *vi sep aux sein (erinnern)* to be reminiscent *(an+acc* of*)*; *(angeschnitten werden)* to be touched (up)on.
anklopfen *vi sep* to knock *(an +acc or dat* at, on*)*.
anknabbern *vt sep (col) (annagen)* to gnaw *or* nibble (at). **zum A~ (aussehen)** *(fig)* (to look) good enough to eat.
anknacksen *vt sep (col) Knochen* to crack; *Fuß, Gelenk etc* to crack a bone in.
anknipsen *vt sep* to switch on; *Schalter* to flick.
anknüpfen *sep* **1** *vt Beziehungen* to establish; *Gespräch* to start up. **2** *vi* **an etw** *(acc)* **~** to take sth up.
Anknüpfung *f (fig) siehe vt* establishing; starting up. **in ~ an etw** *(acc)* following on from sth.
Anknüpfungspunkt *m* link.
ankommen *sep irreg aux sein* **1** *vi* **(a)** to arrive. **bist du gut angekommen?** did you arrive safely *or* get there all right?; **bei etw angekommen sein** to have reached sth, to have got to sth; **das Kind soll in 6 Wochen ~** the baby is due (to arrive) in 6 weeks. **(b)** *(sich nähern)* to approach. **(c)** *(Anklang, Resonanz finden) (bei* with*)* to go down well; *(Mode, Neuerungen)* to catch on. **damit kommst du bei ihm nicht an!** you won't get anywhere with him like that; **es ist erstaunlich, wie er bei Mädchen ankommt** it's amazing what a success he is with the girls. **(d)** *(sich durchsetzen)* **gegen etw ~** *gegen Gewohnheit, Sucht etc* to be able to fight sth; **er ist zu stark, ich komme gegen ihn nicht an** he's too strong, I'm no match for him.

2 *vi impers* **(a)** *(wichtig sein)* **es kommt auf etw** *(acc)* **an** sth matters; **es kommt darauf an, daß wir ...** what matters is that we ...; **darauf soll es mir/uns** *etc* **nicht ~** that doesn't matter. **(b)** *(abhängig sein)* to depend *(auf +acc* on*)*. **es kommt darauf an** it (all) depends; **es käme auf einen Versuch an** we'd have to give it a try. **(c)** *(col)* **es darauf ~ lassen** to chance it; **laß es nicht drauf ~!** don't push your luck! *(col)*; **er ließ es auf einen Streit/einen Versuch ~** he was prepared to argue about it/to give it a try.
ankoppeln *vt sep (Rail)* to couple up *(an+acc* to*)*; *(Space)* to link up *(an +acc* with, to*)*.
ankotzen *vt sep (col: anwidern)* to make sick *(col)*.
ankratzen *vt sep (fig) jds Ruf etc* to damage; *siehe* **angekratzt.**
ankreiden *vt sep (fig)* **jdm etw (dick** *or* **übel) ~** to hold sth against sb.
ankreuzen *vt sep* to mark with a cross.
ankündigen *sep* **1** *vt* **(a)** *(ansagen, anmelden)* to announce; *(auf Plakat, in Zeitung etc)* to advertise. **(b)** *(auf etw hindeuten)* to be a sign of. **2** *vr (fig)* to be heralded *(durch* by*)*. **der Frühling kündigt sich an** spring is in the air.
Ankündigung *f* announcement; *(vorherige Benachrichtigung)* advance notice.
Ankunft *f, pl* **Ankünfte** arrival.
Ankunftszeit *f* time of arrival.
ankuppeln *vt sep siehe* **ankoppeln.**
ankurbeln *vt sep Maschine* to wind up; *(fig) Wirtschaft, Konjunktur* to boost, to reflate.
Ankurbelung *f (fig)* reflation.
anlächeln *vt sep* to smile at.
anlachen *vt sep* to smile at. **sich** *(dat)* **jdn ~** *(col)* to pick sb up *(col)*.
Anlage *f* **-n (a)** *(Fabrik~)* plant. **(b)** *(Grün~, Park~)* (public) park; *(um ein Gebäude herum)* grounds *pl.* **(c)** *(Einrichtung) (Mil, Elec)* installation(s); *(Sport~ etc)* facilities *pl.* **(d)** *(col: Stereo~)* (stereo) system *or* equipment. **(e)** *(usu pl: Veranlagung)* aptitude, gift *(zu* for*)*; *(Neigung)* predisposition, tendency *(zu* to*)*. **(f)** *(Kapital~)* investment. **(g)** *(Beilage zu einem Schreiben)* enclosure. **als ~** *or* **in der ~ erhalten Sie ...** please find enclosed ...
Anlageberater *m* investment consultant.
anlangen *sep* **1** *vi aux sein (an einem Ort)* to arrive. **am Gipfel angelangt sein** to have reached the summit. **2** *vt (betreffen)* to concern. **was mich anlangt** as far as I am concerned.
Anlaß *m, pl* **Anlässe (a)** *(Veranlassung)* (immediate) cause *(zu* for*)*. **welchen ~ hatte er, das zu tun?** what prompted him to do that?; **es besteht kein ~ ...** there is no reason ...; **etw zum ~ nehmen, zu ...** to use sth as an opportunity to ...; **beim geringsten/bei jedem ~** for the slightest reason/at every opportunity; **das gibt ~ zur Sorge** this gives cause for concern. **(b)** *(Gelegenheit)* occasion. **aus diesem ~** on this occasion.
anlassen *sep irreg* **1** *vt* **(a)** *Motor* to start (up). **(b)** *(col) Mantel* to keep on; *Wasserhahn, Motor, Licht, Radio* to leave on. **2** *vr* **sich gut/schlecht ~** to get off to a good/bad start.
Anlasser *m* - *(Aut)* starter.
anläßlich *prep +gen* on the occasion of.
anlasten *vt sep* **jdm etw ~** to blame sb for sth; **jdm etw als Schwäche ~** to regard *or* see sth as a weakness on sb's part.
Anlauf *m, pl* **Anläufe (a)** *(Sport)* run-up. **mit/ohne ~** with a run-up/from standing; **~ nehmen** to take a run-up. **(b)** *(fig: Versuch)* attempt, try. **beim ersten/zweiten ~** at the first/second attempt.
anlaufen *sep irreg* **1** *vi aux sein* **(a)** *(beginnen)* to begin, to start; *(Saison auch, Film)* to open; *(Motor)* to start. **(b) rot/blau ~** to turn *or* go red/blue. **(c)** *(Sport: Anlauf nehmen)* to take a run-up. **2** *vt (Naut) Hafen etc* to put into, to call at.
Anlaufzeit *f (fig)* time to get going *or* started.
Anlegebrücke *f* landing stage, jetty.
anlegen *sep* **1** *vt* **(a)** *Leiter* to put up *(an+acc* against*)*; *Brett, Karte* to lay (down) *(an+acc* next to, beside*)*; *Lineal* to position, to set. **das Gewehr ~** to raise the gun to one's shoulder; **strengere Maßstäbe ~** to lay down *or* to impose stricter standards *(bei* in*)*. **(b)** *Kartei, Akte* to start; *Vorräte* to lay in; *Garten etc* to lay out. **(c)** *(investieren) Geld* to invest; *(ausgeben)* to spend *(für* on*)*. **(d) es darauf ~, daß ...** to be determined that ...; *siehe* **angelegt. 2** *vi* **(a)** *(Naut)* to berth. **(b)** *(Gewehr ~)* to aim *(auf+acc* at*)*. **3** *vr* **sich mit jdm ~** to pick an argument with sb.
Anlegeplatz *m* berth.
Anleger *m* - *(Fin)* investor.
anlehnen *sep* **1** *vt* to lean *or* rest *(an+acc* against*)*. **angelehnt sein** *(Tür)* to be ajar; *(Fenster)* to be slightly open. **2** *vr (lit)* to lean *(an+acc* against*)*;

sich an etw *(acc)* ~ *(fig)* to follow sth.

Anlehnung *f* **(a)** *(Anschluß)* dependence *(an+acc* on*)*. **~ an jdn suchen** to seek sb's support. **(b)** *(Imitation)* **in ~ an jdn/etw** following sb/sth.

Anlehnungs-: ~bedürfnis *nt* need of loving care; **a~bedürftig** *adj* needing loving care.

Anleihe *f* **-n** *(Fin)* loan; *(Wertpapier)* bond. **eine ~ aufnehmen** to take out a loan; **bei jdm eine ~ machen** to borrow (money) from sb.

anleinen *vt sep (festmachen)* to tie up. **den Hund ~** to put the dog's lead on.

anleiten *vt sep* **(a)** *(unterweisen)* to teach, to instruct. **(b)** *(erziehen)* **jdn zu etw ~** to teach sb sth.

Anleitung *f (Erklärung, Hilfe)* instructions *pl.* **unter der ~ seines Vaters** under his father's guidance *or* direction.

anlernen *vt sep (ausbilden)* to train; *siehe* **angelernt.**

anlesen *vt sep irreg (aneignen)* **sich** *(dat)* **etw ~** to learn sth by reading.

anliefern *vt sep* to deliver.

Anlieferung *f* delivery.

Anliegen *nt* **-** **(a)** *(Bitte)* request. **(b)** *(wichtige Angelegenheit)* matter of concern.

anliegen *vi sep irreg* **(a)** *(anstehen, vorliegen)* to be on. **(b)** *(Kleidung)* to fit closely *or* tightly *(an etw (dat)* sth*)*; *(Haar)* to lie flat *(an+dat* against, on*)*.

anliegend *adj* **(a)** *Ohren* flat. **(eng) ~** *Kleidung* tight- *or* close-fitting. **(b)** *(in Briefen)* enclosed. **(c)** *Grundstück* adjacent.

Anlieger *m* **-** neighbour *(Brit)*, neighbor *(US)*; *(Anwohner)* (local) resident. **~ frei** no thoroughfare — residents only.

Anlieger-: ~staat *m* **die ~staaten des Schwarzen Meers** the countries bordering (on) the Black Sea; **~verkehr** *m* (local) residents' vehicles.

anlocken *vt sep* to attract; *Tiere* auch to lure.

Anlockung *f* attraction.

anlügen *vt sep irreg* to lie to, to tell lies to.

anmachen *vt sep* **(a)** *(col: befestigen)* to put up *(an +acc or dat* on*)*. **(b)** *(zubereiten)* to mix; *Salat* to dress. **(c)** *(anstellen) Radio, Licht, Heizung etc* to put *or* turn on; *Feuer* to light. **(d)** *(col: ansprechen)* **er versuchte ständig, sie anzumachen** he kept trying to chat her up *(col)*.

anmahnen *vt sep* to send a reminder about.

anmalen *sep* **1** *vt* to paint. **2** *vr (pej: schminken)* to paint one's face *or* oneself.

Anmarsch *m no pl (Mil)* advance. **im ~ sein** to be advancing *(auf+acc* on*)*; *(hum)* to be on the way.

anmarschieren* *vi sep aux sein (Mil)* to advance.

anmaßen *vr sep* **sich** *(dat)* **etw ~** *Befugnis, Recht* to claim sth (for oneself); *Titel, Macht, Autorität* to assume sth; **sich** *(dat)* **ein Urteil über etw** *(acc)* **~** to presume to pass judgement on sth.

anmaßend *adj* presumptuous.

Anmaßung *f* presumption, presumptuousness. **es ist eine ~ zu meinen, ...** it is presumptuous to maintain that ...

Anmeldeformular *nt* application form.

anmelden *sep* **1** *vt* **(a)** *(ankündigen) Besuch* to announce. **(b)** *(bei Schule, Kurs etc)* to enrol *(bei* at, *zu* for*)*. **(c)** *(eintragen lassen) Patent* to apply for; *neuen Wohnsitz, Auto* to register *(bei* at*)*; *Fernseher* to get a licence *(Brit) or* license *(US)* for. **Konkurs ~** to declare oneself bankrupt. **(d)** *(Telec)* **ein Gespräch nach Deutschland ~** to book a call to Germany. **(e)** *(geltend machen) Recht, Ansprüche, (zu Steuerzwecken)* to declare. **ich melde starke Bedenken an** I have serious doubts about that. **2** *vr* **(a)** *(ankündigen: Besucher)* to announce one's arrival. **(b)** *(an Schule, zu Kurs etc)* to enrol (oneself) *(an+dat* at, *zu* for*)*. **sich polizeilich ~** to register with the police. **(c)** *(sich einen Termin geben lassen)* to make an appointment.

Anmeldung *f (an Schule, zu Kurs etc)* enrolment *(an+dat* at, *zu* for*)*; *(bei Polizei)* registration. **nur nach vorheriger ~** by appointment only.

anmerken *vt sep (sagen)* to say; *(als Fußnote)* to note. **jdm seine Verlegenheit** *etc* **~** to notice sb's embarrassment *etc;* **sich** *(dat)* **etw ~ lassen** to let sth show.

Anmerkung *f* note.

anmieten *vt sep* to rent.

anmustern *vti (Naut)* to sign on.

Anmut *f no pl* grace; *(Grazie auch)* gracefulness; *(Schönheit)* beauty, loveliness.

anmuten *sep* **1** *vt (geh)* to appear, to seem *(jdn* to sb*)*. **2** *vi* **eine eigenartig ~de Geschichte** a story that strikes one as odd.

anmutig *adj (geh) (geschmeidig) Bewegung* graceful; *(hübsch anzusehen)* lovely, charming.

annageln *vt sep* to nail on *(an +acc* or *dat* -to*)*. **er stand wie angenagelt da** he stood there rooted to the spot.

annagen *vt sep* to gnaw (at).

annähen *vt sep* to sew on *(an +acc or dat* -to*)*; *Saum* to sew up.

annähern *sep* **1** *vt* to bring closer *(dat, an+acc* to*)*. **2** *vr* **(a)** *(lit, fig: sich nähern)* to approach *(einer Sache (dat)* sth*)*. **(b)** *(sich angleichen, näherkommen)* to come closer *(dat, an+acc* to*)*.

annähernd 1 *adj (ungefähr)* approximate, rough. **2** *adv (etwa)* roughly; *(fast)* almost. **nicht ~ soviel** not nearly as much.

Annäherung *f (lit, fig)* approach *(an+acc* towards*)*; *(von Standpunkten)* convergence *(dat, an +acc* with*)*. **die ~ zwischen Ost und West** the rapprochement of East and West.

Annäherungsversuch *m* overtures *pl.*

Annahme *f* **-n** **(a)** *(Vermutung, Voraussetzung)* assumption. **in der ~, daß ...** on the assumption that ...; **von einer ~ ausgehen** to work on an assumption. **(b)** *siehe* **annehmen (a)** acceptance; taking; approval; passing; adoption. **~ an Kindes Statt** *(child)* adoption.

Annahme-: ~frist *f* **~frist bis zum 17. Juli** closing date 17th July; **die ~frist einhalten** to meet the deadline; **~stelle** *f (für Pakete, Telegramme)* counter; *(für Lotto etc)* (national lottery *etc)* agency; *(für Reparaturen)* reception; *(für Material)* delivery point; **~verweigerung** *f* refusal.

Annalen *pl* annals *pl.* **in die ~ eingehen** *(fig)* to go down in the annals *or* in history.

annehmbar *adj* acceptable; *(nicht schlecht)* reasonable, not bad.

annehmen *sep irreg* **1** *vt* **(a)** to accept; *einen Rat* to take; *(billigen)* to approve; *Gesetz* to pass; *Resolution* to adopt. **(b)** *(vermuten, voraussetzen)* to assume. **von jdm etw ~** *(erwarten)* to expect sth of sb; *(glauben)* to believe sth of sb; **was nehmen Sie denn von mir an!** what do you take me for?; *siehe* **angenommen. (c)** *(sich aneignen)* to adopt; *Gewohnheit etc auch* to pick up; *Staatsangehörigkeit auch* to take on; *Gestalt, Namen* to assume, to take on. **jdn an Kindes Statt ~** to adopt sb. **2** *vr* **sich jds/einer Sache ~** to look after a person/a matter.

Annehmlichkeit *f (Bequemlichkeit)* convenience. **~en** *pl* comforts *pl.*

annektieren* *vt* to annex.

Annexion *f* annexation.

anno *adj* in the year. **von ~ dazumal** *(col) or* **Tobak** *(col)* from the year dot *(col)*; **ein Überbleibsel von ~ dazumal** *(col)* a hangover from the olden days.

Anno Domini *adv* in the year of Our Lord.

Annonce [a'nõːsə] *f* **-n** advertisement, advert *(Brit col)*, ad *(col)*.

annoncieren* [anõ'siːrən] *vti* to advertise.

annullieren* *vt (Jur)* to annul.

Anode *f* **-n** anode.

an|öden *vt sep (col: langweilen)* to bore stiff.

anomal *adj (regelwidrig)* unusual, abnormal; *(nicht normal)* strange, odd.
Anomalie *f* anomaly.
anonym *adj* anonymous.
Anonymität *f* anonymity.
Anorak *m* **-s** anorak *(Brit)*, parka.
an|ordnen *vt sep* **(a)** *(befehlen, festsetzen)* to order. **(b)** *(nach Plan ordnen, aufstellen)* to arrange; *(systematisch)* to order.
An|ordnung *f* **(a)** *(Befehl)* order. **laut (polizeilicher)** ~ by order (of the police); **auf ~ des Arztes** on doctor's orders; **~en treffen** to give orders. **(b)** *(Aufstellung)* arrangement; *(systematische ~)* order; *(Formation)* formation.
an|organisch *adj (Chem)* inorganic.
anormal *adj (col)* = **anomal.**
anpacken *sep (col)* **1** *vt* **(a)** *(anfassen)* to take hold of, to grab. **(b)** *(handhaben, beginnen)* to tackle, to set about. **(c)** *(umgehen mit) jdn* to treat. **2** *vi (helfen: auch* **mit** *~)* to lend a hand.
anpassen *sep* **1** *vt* **(a)** *Kleidung* to fit *(dat* on*)*. **(b)** *(abstimmen)* **etw einer Sache** *(dat)* ~ to suit sth to sth. **(c)** *(angleichen)* **etw einer Sache** *(dat)* ~ to bring sth into line with sth. **2** *vr* to adapt (oneself) *(dat* to*)*; *(einer Situation etc)* to adjust *(dat* to*)*; *(gesellschaftlich)* to conform. **wir mußten uns (ihren Wünschen)** ~ we had to fit in with their wishes *or* them; *siehe* **angepaßt.**
Anpassung *f (an+acc* to*)* adaptation; *(an Gesellschaft, Normen etc)* adjustment.
Anpassungs-: a~fähig *adj* adaptable; **~fähigkeit** *f* adaptability; **~schwierigkeiten** *pl* difficulties *pl* in adapting.
anpeilen *vt sep (mit Radar, Funk etc)* to take a bearing on. **etw** ~ *(fig inf)* to have one's sights on sth.
anpeitschen *vt sep* to force.
anpfeifen *sep irreg (Sport)* **1** *vi* to blow the whistle. **2** *vt* **das Spiel** ~ to start the game (by blowing one's whistle).
Anpfiff *m (Sport)* (starting) whistle; *(Spielbeginn)* kick-off.
anpflanzen *vt sep (bepflanzen)* to plant; *(anbauen)* to grow.
Anpflanzung *f* **(a)** *siehe vt* planting; growing. **(b)** *(Fläche)* cultivated area.
anpirschen *vr sep* to creep up *(an +acc* on*)*.
anpöbeln *vt sep (col)* to pester.
Anprall *m* impact. **beim ~ gegen** on impact with.
anprangern *vt sep* to denounce.
anpreisen *vt sep irreg* to extol *(jdm etw* sth to sb*)*. **sich (als etw)** ~ to sell oneself as sth.
Anprobe *f* fitting.
anprobieren* *vt sep* to try on.
anpumpen *vt sep (col)* to borrow from. **jdn um 50 Mark** ~ to touch sb for 50 marks *(col)*.
anquatschen *vt sep (col)* to speak to; *Mädchen* to chat up *(col)*.
Anrainer *m* **-** neighbour *(Brit)*, neighbor *(US)*. **die ~ der Nordsee** the countries bordering (on) the North Sea.
anraten *vt sep irreg* **jdm etw** ~ to recommend sth to sb; **auf A~ des Arztes** *etc* on the doctor's *etc* advice *or* recommendation.
anrechnen *vt sep* **(a)** *(in Rechnung stellen)* to charge for *(jdm* sb*)*. **(b)** *(gutschreiben)* to count, to take into account *(jdm* for sb*)*. **das alte Auto rechnen wir (Ihnen) mit DM 500 an** we'll allow (you) DM 500 for the old car. **(c)** *(bewerten)* **jdm etw hoch** ~ to think highly of sb for sth; **jdm etw als Fehler** ~ *(Lehrer)* to count sth as a mistake; *(fig)* to consider sth as a fault on sb's part; **ich rechne es ihm als Verdienst an, daß ...** I think it is greatly to his credit that ...
Anrecht *nt (Anspruch)* right, entitlement *(auf +acc* to*)*. **ein ~ auf etw** *(acc)* **haben** to be entitled to sth, to have a right to sth.
Anrede *f* form of address; *(Brief~ auch)* salutation *(form)*.
anreden *vt sep* to address. **jdn mit „du"** ~ to address sb as "du"; **jdn mit seinem Titel** ~ to address sb by his title.
anregen *vt sep* **(a)** *(ermuntern)* to prompt *(zu* to*)*. **jdn zum Denken** ~ to make sb think. **(b)** *(geh: vorschlagen) Verbesserung* to propose, to suggest. **(c)** *(beleben)* to stimulate; *Appetit auch* to whet, to sharpen. **Kaffee regt an** coffee has a stimulating effect; *siehe* **angeregt.**
anregend *adj* stimulating.
Anregung *f* **(a)** *(Antrieb, Impuls)* stimulus. **(b)** *(Vorschlag)* idea. **auf ~ von** *or +gen* at *or* on the suggestion of. **(c)** *(Belebung)* stimulation.
Anregungsmittel *nt* stimulant.
anreichen *vt sep* to pass, to hand.
anreichern *vt sep (gehaltvoller machen)* to enrich.
Anreise *f (Anfahrt)* journey there/here. **die ~ zu diesem abgelegenen Ort ist sehr mühsam** it is very difficult to get to this remote place.
anreisen *vi sep aux sein* **(a)** *(ein Ziel anfahren)* to make a/the journey *or* trip (there/here). **(b)** *(eintreffen) (auch* **angereist kommen***)* to come.
anreißen *vt sep irreg* **(a)** *(kurz zur Sprache bringen)* to touch on. **(b)** *(pej col) Kunden* to attract.
Anreiz *m* incentive. **ein ~ zum Lernen** a learning incentive.
anreizen *sep* **1** *vt (anspornen)* to encourage. **2** *vi* to act as an incentive *(zu* to*)*.
anrempeln *(anstoßen)* to bump into; *(absichtlich) Menschen* to jostle.
anrennen *vi sep irreg aux sein* **gegen etw** ~ *gegen Wind etc* to run against sth; *(Mil)* to storm sth.
Anrichte *f* **-n** *(Schrank)* dresser; *(Büfett)* sideboard.
anrichten *vt sep* **(a)** *Speisen* to prepare. **es ist angerichtet** *(form)* dinner *etc* is served *(form)*. **(b)** *(fig) Unheil etc* to cause, to bring about. **da hast du aber etwas angerichtet!** *(col) (verursacht)* you've started something there all right; *(angestellt)* you've really made a mess there.
anrosten *vi sep aux sein* to get (a bit) rusty.
anrüchig *adj (von üblem Ruf)* of ill repute; *Lokal etc* notorious.
anrücken *vi sep aux sein (Truppen)* to advance; *(Polizei etc)* to move in.
Anruf *m* call; *(Mil: eines Wachtpostens)* challenge. **etw auf ~ tun** to do sth when called.
Anrufbe|antworter *m* (telephone) answering machine, answerphone.
anrufen *sep irreg* **1** *vt* **(a)** to shout to; *(Telec)* to call, to phone, to ring *(Brit)*; *(Mil: Posten)* to challenge. **darf ich dich ~?** can I give you a ring? *(Brit)*, can I call you? **(b)** *(fig: appellieren an)* to appeal to *(um* for*)*. **2** *vi (col: telefonieren)* to phone, to make a (phone) call. **bei jdm** ~ to phone sb; **kann man Sie ~?** are you on the phone?
Anrufer *m* caller.
Anrufung *f (Gottes, der Heiligen etc)* invocation; *(Jur)* appeal *(gen* to*)*.
anrühren *vt sep* **(a)** *(berühren, sich befassen)* to touch; *(fig) Thema* to touch on. **er rührt kein Fleisch/keinen Alkohol an** he doesn't touch meat/alcohol. **(b)** *(mischen) Farben* to mix; *Sauce* to blend; *(verrühren)* to stir.
ans = **an das.**
Ansage *f* **-n** announcement; *(Cards)* bid.
ansagen *sep* **1** *vt* **(a)** to announce. **jdm den Kampf** ~ to declare war on sb. **(b)** *(Cards)* to bid; *(Skat)* to declare. **2** *vr (Besuch ankündigen)* to say that one is coming.
Ansager(in *f***)** *m* **-** *(Rad etc)* announcer.
ansammeln *sep* **1** *vt* **(a)** *(anhäufen)* to accumulate. **(b)** *(zusammenkommen lassen)* to gather together; *Truppen* to concentrate. **2** *vr* **(a)** *(sich versammeln)* to gather, to collect. **(b)** *(aufhäufen)* to accumulate; *(Staub, Wasser auch)* to collect; *(Druck, fig: Wut)* to build up; *(Zinsen)* to build up.

Ansammlung *f* **(a)** *(Anhäufung)* accumulation; *(Sammlung)* collection; *(von Druck, Wut)* build-up; *(Haufen)* pile. **(b)** *(Auflauf)* gathering, crowd; *(von Truppen)* concentration.

ansässig *adj (form)* resident. **alle in diesem Ort A~en** all local residents.

Ansatz *m* **(a)** *(von Hals, Arm, Henkel etc)* base. **(b)** *(Tech) (Zusatzstück)* attachment; *(zur Verlängerung)* extension; *(Naht)* join. **(c)** *(erstes Anzeichen, Beginn)* first sign(s *pl*), beginning(s *pl*); *(Ausgangspunkt)* starting-point.

Ansatz-: **~punkt** *m* starting-point; **~stück** *nt (Tech)* attachment; *(zur Verlängerung)* extension.

ansaugen *vt sep* to suck *or* draw in.

anschaffen *sep* **1** *vt* **(sich** *dat***) etw ~** to get oneself sth; *(kaufen)* to buy sth; **sich** *(dat)* **Kinder ~** *(col)* to have children. **2** *vi (col: durch Prostitution)* **~ gehen** to be on the game *(col)*.

Anschaffung *f* acquisition. **ich habe mich zur ~ eines Autos entschlossen** I have decided to buy a new car. **~en machen** to acquire things; *(kaufen)* to make purchases.

Anschaffungs-: **~kosten** *pl* cost *sing* of purchase; **~preis** *m* purchase price.

anschalten *vt sep* to switch on.

anschauen *vt sep* to look at; *(prüfend)* to examine. **sich** *(dat)* **etw ~** to have a look at sth.

anschaulich *adj* clear; *(lebendig, bildhaft)* vivid; *Beschreibung* graphic; *Beispiel* concrete. **etw ~ machen** to illustrate sth.

Anschauung *f (Ansicht, Auffassung)* view; *(Meinung)* opinion. **nach neuerer ~** according to the current way of thinking.

Anschauungsmaterial *nt* illustrative material, visual aids *pl*.

Anschein *m* appearance; *(Eindruck)* impression. **allem ~ nach** to all appearances, apparently; **den ~ erwecken, als ...** to give the impression that ...; **es hat den ~, als ob ...** it appears that *or* seems as if ...

anscheinend *adv* apparently.

anschicken *vr sep* **sich ~, etw zu tun** *(geh: im Begriff sein)* to be about to do sth.

anschieben *vt sep irreg Fahrzeug* to push.

anschießen *sep irreg* **1** *vt* **(a)** *(verletzen)* to shoot (and wound); *Vogel (in Flügel)* to wing; *siehe* **angeschossen. (b)** *(col: kritiseren)* to hit out at *(col)*. **2** *vi aux sein (col) (heranrasen)* to shoot up. **angeschossen kommen** to come shooting along *or (auf einen zu)* up.

anschimmeln *vi sep aux sein* to (start to) go mouldy.

Anschiß *m* **-sse** *(col)* bollocking *(col!)*.

Anschlag *m* **(a)** *(Plakat)* poster; *(Bekanntmachung)* notice. **einen ~ machen** to put up a poster/ notice. **(b)** *(Überfall)* attack *(auf+acc* on*)*; *(Attentat)* attempt on sb's life. **einem ~ zum Opfer fallen** to be assassinated. **(c)** *(von Klavier(spieler), Schreibmaschine)* touch. **200 Anschläge in der Minute** ≃ 40 words per minute. **(d)** *(bei Hebel, Knopf etc)* stop. **etw bis zum ~ durchdrücken** to push sth right down. **(e)** *(Mil)* **ein Gewehr im ~ haben** to have a rifle at the ready.

Anschlagbrett *nt* notice-board *(Brit)*, bulletin board *(US)*.

anschlagen *sep irreg* **1** *vt* **(a)** *(befestigen)* to fix on *(an+acc* -to*)*; *(mit Nägeln)* to nail on *(an+acc* -to*)*; *(aushängen) Plakat* to put up, to post *(an+acc* on*)*. **(b)** *Taste, Akkord* to strike. **eine schnellere Gangart ~** *(fig)* to speed up; **einen anderen Ton ~** *(fig)* to change one's tune. **(c)** *(beschädigen, verletzen) Geschirr* to chip. **2** *vi* **(a)** *(Welle)* to beat *(an+acc* against*)*. **(b)** *(Laut geben) (Hund)* to give a bark; *(Vogel)* to give a screech. **(c)** *(wirken: Arznei etc)* to work, to take effect.

anschleichen *sep irreg* **1** *vi aux sein* to creep along *or (auf einen zu)* up. **angeschlichen kommen** *(col)* to come creeping along/up. **2** *vr* **sich an jdn/etw ~** to creep up on sb/sth; *(sich anpirschen)* to stalk sth.

anschleppen *vt sep* **(a)** *Auto* to tow-start. **(b)** *(col: unerwünscht mitbringen)* to bring along; *(nach Hause)* to bring home; *Freund etc auch* to drag along *(col)*.

anschließen *sep irreg* **1** *vt* **(a)** *(an+acc* to*)* *(Tech, Elec, Telec etc: verbinden)* to connect; *(in Steckdose)* to plug in. **(b)** *(fig: hinzufügen)* to add; *siehe* **angeschlossen. 2** *vr* **sich jdm** *or* **an jdn ~** *(folgen)* to follow sb; *(zugesellen)* to join sb; *(beipflichten)* to side with sb; **sich einer Sache** *(dat) or* **an etw** *(acc)* **~** *(folgen)* to follow sth; *(beitreten, sich beteiligen)* to join sth; *(beipflichten)* to endorse sth; *(angrenzen)* to adjoin sth; **sich an ein Datennetz ~** to link up with a data network. **3** *vi* **an etw** *(acc)* **~** to follow sth.

anschließend **1** *adv* afterwards. **2** *adj* following. **Essen mit ~em Tanz** dinner with a dance afterwards.

Anschluß *m* **(a)** *(Verbindung)* connection; *(Beitritt)* entry *(an+acc* into*)*; *(an Klub)* joining *(an +acc* of*)*. **~ haben nach** *(Rail)* to have a connection to; **den ~ verpassen** *(Rail etc)* to miss one's connection; *(fig)* to miss the boat *(col)*. **ihm gelang der ~ an die Spitze** *(Sport)* he managed to catch up with the leaders. **(b)** *(Telec)* connection; *(weiterer Apparat)* extension. **~ bekommen** to get through; **kein ~ unter dieser Nummer** number unobtainable. **(c) im ~ an** *(+acc) (nach)* subsequent to, following. **(d)** *(fig: Kontakt)* contact *(an+acc* with*)*; **~ finden** to make friends *(an +acc* with*)*; **er sucht ~** he wants to make friends.

Anschlußzug *m (Rail)* connecting train, connection.

anschmiegen *vr sep* **sich an jdn/etw ~** *(Kind, Hund)* to snuggle *or* nestle up to *or* against sb/sth; *(Kleidung)* to cling to sb/sth.

anschmiegsam *adj Wesen* affectionate; *Material* smooth.

anschmieren *vt sep* **(a)** *(bemalen)* to smear. **(b)** *(col) (betrügen)* to con *(col)*; *(Streiche spielen)* to play tricks on; *siehe* **angeschmiert.**

anschnallen *sep* **1** *vt Rucksack* to strap on; *Skier* to clip on. **2** *vr (Aviat, Aut)* to fasten one's seat belt. **bitte ~!** fasten your seat belts, please!

Anschnallpflicht *f* **in Taxis ist jetzt ~** you now have to wear a seat belt in taxis.

anschnauzen *vt sep (col)* to yell at.

anschneiden *vt sep irreg* **(a)** *Brot etc* to (start to) cut. **(b)** *(fig) Frage, Thema* to touch on. **(c)** *(Aut) Kurve, (Sport) Ball* to cut.

Anschovis [an'ʃo:vɪs] *f* - anchovy.

anschrauben *vt sep* to screw on *(an +acc* -to*)*.

anschreiben *sep irreg* **1** *vt* **(a)** *(aufschreiben)* to write up *(an+acc* on*)*. **etw mit Kreide ~** to chalk sth up; *siehe* **angeschrieben. (b)** *(col: in Rechnung stellen)* to chalk up. **(c)** *Behörde, Versandhaus etc* to write to. **2** *vi (col)* **sie läßt immer ~** she always buys on tick *(col)*.

anschreien *vt sep irreg* to shout *or* yell at.

Anschrift *f* address.

anschuldigen *vt sep* to accuse *(gen* of*)*.

Anschuldigung *f* accusation.

anschwärzen *vt sep (fig col)* **jdn ~** to blacken sb's name *(bei* with*)*.

anschweißen *vt sep* to weld on *(an +acc* -to*)*.

anschwellen *vi sep irreg aux sein* to swell (up); *(Lärm)* to rise. **dick angeschwollen** very swollen.

anschwemmen *vt sep* to wash up *or* ashore.

anschwimmen *sep irreg* **1** *vt* to swim towards. **2** *vi aux sein* **gegen etw ~** to swim against sth.

anschwindeln *vt sep (col)* **jdn ~** to tell sb fibs *(col)*.

ansehen *vt sep irreg* **(a)** *(betrachten)* to look at. **er sah mich ganz böse an** he gave me an angry look; **hübsch** *etc* **anzusehen** pretty *etc* to look at; **das sehe sich einer an!** just look at that!

(b) *(fig)* to regard, to look upon *(als, für* as*)*. **ich sehe es als meine Pflicht an** I consider it to be my duty; *siehe* **angesehen.**

(c) (sich *dat)* **etw ~** to (have a) look at sth; *Fernsehsendung* to watch sth; *Film, Stück, Veranstaltung* to see sth; **sich** *(dat)* **jdn/etw gründlich ~** *(lit, fig)* to take a close look at sb/sth.

(d) das sieht man ihm an/nicht an he looks it/doesn't look it; **man kann ihm die Strapazen der letzten Woche ~** he's showing the strain of the past week; **man sieht ihm sein Alter nicht an** he doesn't look his age; **jdm etw an den Augen** *or* **an der Nasenspitze** *(hum)* ~ to tell *or* guess sth by looking at sb.

(e) etw (mit) ~ to watch sth, to see sth happening; **ich kann das nicht länger mit ~** I can't stand it any more.

Ansehen *nt no pl* **(a)** *(Aussehen)* appearance. **jdn vom ~ kennen** to know sb by sight. **(b)** *(guter Ruf)* good reputation, standing. **großes ~ genießen** to enjoy a good reputation; **an ~ verlieren** to lose credit *or* standing. **(c)** *(Jur)* **ohne ~ der Person** without respect of person.

ansehnlich *adj (beträchtlich)* considerable; *Leistung* impressive.

anseilen *vt sep* **jdn/sich ~** to rope sb/oneself up.

ansein *vi sep irreg aux sein (col)* to be on.

ansetzen *sep* **1** *vt* **(a)** *(in Stellung bringen)* to place in position. **das Glas ~** to raise the glass to one's lips; **an welcher Stelle muß man den Wagenheber ~?** where should the jack be put *or* placed? **(b)** *(festlegen) Kosten, Termin* to fix *(mit* at, *auf+acc* for*)*. **(c)** *(einsetzen)* **jdn auf jdn/etw ~** to put sb on(to) sb/sth. **(d)** *(entstehen lassen)* **Fett ~** to put on weight; **Rost ~** to get rusty. **(e)** *(Cook) (vorbereiten)* to prepare; *(auf den Herd setzen)* to put on. **2** *vr (Rost)* to form; *(Kalk etc)* to be deposited. **3** *vi* **(a)** *(beginnen)* to start, to begin. **zur Landung ~** *(Aviat)* to come in to land; **zum Sprung/Spurt ~** to get ready to jump/to start one's spurt. **(b)** *(Cook: sich festsetzen)* to stick.

Ansicht *f* **-en (a)** view. **~ von hinten/vorn** rear/front view; **~ von oben/unten** view from above/below, top/bottom view *(Tech)*. **(b)** *(das Betrachten, Prüfen)* inspection. **zur ~** *(Comm)* for (your/our *etc)* inspection; **jdm Waren zur ~ schicken** *(Comm)* to send sb goods on approval. **(c)** *(Meinung)* opinion, view. **nach ~** *+gen* in the opinion of; **meiner ~ nach** in my opinion *or* view; **anderer/der gleichen ~ sein** to be of a different/the same opinion, to disagree/agree; **ich bin ganz Ihrer ~** I entirely agree with you; **die ~en sind geteilt** opinions differ, opinion is divided.

Ansichts-: ~karte *f* picture postcard; **~sache** *f* **das ist ~sache** that is a matter of opinion.

ansiedeln *sep* **1** *vt* to settle; *Tierart* to introduce. **2** *vr* to settle; *(Industrie etc)* to set up.

Ansiedlung *f* settlement.

Ansinnen *nt (dated, geh: Vorschlag)* suggestion.

ansonsten *adv* otherwise.

anspannen *vt sep* **(a)** *(straffen)* to tauten, to tighten; *Muskeln* to tense. **(b)** *(anstrengen)* to strain, to tax; *Geduld, Mittel auch* to stretch. **alle seine Kräfte ~** to strain every nerve; *siehe* **angespannt. (c)** *Wagen, Pferd* to hitch up.

Anspannung *f (fig)* strain; *(körperliche Anstrengung auch)* effort.

Anspiel *nt (Sport)* start of play. **das ~ haben** to start play; *(Ftbl)* to kick off.

anspielen *sep* **1** *vt (Sport)* to play the ball *etc* to; *Spieler* to pass to. **2** *vi* **auf jdn/etw ~** to allude to sb/sth; **worauf wollen Sie ~?** what are you driving at?, what are you insinuating?

Anspielung *f* allusion *(auf +acc* to*)*; *(böse)* insinuation, innuendo *(auf+acc* regarding*)*.

anspitzen *vt sep Bleistift etc* to sharpen.

Ansporn *m no pl* incentive.

anspornen *vt sep (fig)* to spur on, to encourage *(zu* to*)*.

Ansprache *f (Rede)* address, speech. **eine ~ halten** to make a speech.

ansprechbar *adj* **(a) er ist beschäftigt/wütend und zur Zeit nicht ~** he's so busy/angry that you can't talk to him just now. **(b)** *Patient* responsive.

ansprechen *sep irreg* **1** *vt* **(a)** *(anreden)* to speak to; *(belästigend)* to accost. **jdn auf etw** *(acc)* **~** to ask *or* approach sb about sth; **damit sind Sie alle angesprochen** this is directed at all of you. **(b)** *(gefallen)* to appeal to; *(Eindruck machen auf)* to make an impression on. **2** *vi (auf +acc* to*) (reagieren) (Patient, Gaspedal etc)* to respond; *(Meßgerät auch)* to react. **diese Tabletten sprechen bei ihr nicht an** these tablets don't have any effect on her.

ansprechend *adj (reizvoll) Äußeres, Verpackung etc* attractive, appealing.

anspringen *sep irreg* **1** *vt (anfallen)* to jump; *(Raubtier)* to pounce on; *(Hund: hochspringen)* to jump up at. **2** *vi aux sein (Motor)* to start. **das Auto springt nicht an** the car won't start.

Anspruch *m, pl* **Ansprüche (a)** *(esp Jur)* claim; *(Recht)* right *(auf+acc* to*)*. **~ auf Schadenersatz erheben/haben** to make a claim for damages/to be entitled to damages. **(b)** *(Anforderung)* demand; *(Standard)* standard, requirement. **große** *or* **hohe Ansprüche stellen** to be very demanding; *(hohes Niveau verlangen)* to demand high standards; **den Ansprüchen gerecht werden** to meet the requirements. **(c)** *(Behauptung)* claim. **diese Theorie erhebt keinen ~ auf Unwiderlegbarkeit** this theory does not claim to be irrefutable. **(d) etw in ~ nehmen** *Recht* to claim sth; *jds Hilfe* to enlist sth; *Möglichkeiten, Kantine etc* to take advantage of sth; *Zeit, Kräfte* to take up sth; **darf ich Ihre Aufmerksamkeit in ~ nehmen?** may I have your attention?; **das nimmt mich sehr in ~** it keeps me very busy.

anspruchslos *adj (bescheiden)* modest, unassuming; *(wenig Pflege etc erfordernd)* undemanding; *Literatur, Musik* low-brow.

anspruchsvoll *adj (viel verlangend)* demanding; *(übertrieben ~)* hard to please, fastidious; *(hohe Ansprüche stellend) Stil, Buch* ambitious; *(kultiviert)* sophisticated.

anspucken *vt sep* to spit at *or* on.

anspülen *vt sep* to wash up *or* ashore.

anstacheln *vt sep* to spur (on); *(antreiben)* to drive *or* goad on.

Anstalt *f* **-en (a)** institution *(auch euph)*; *(Institut)* institute. **(b) ~en** *pl (Maßnahmen)* measures *pl*; *(Vorbereitungen)* preparations *pl*; **~en/keine ~en machen, etw zu tun** to make a/no move to do sth.

Anstand *m no pl (Schicklichkeit)* decency, propriety; *(Manieren)* (good) manners *pl*. **keinen ~ haben** to have no sense of decency/no manners.

anständig 1 *adj* decent; *Witz auch* clean; *(ehrbar)* respectable; *(col: beträchtlich)* sizeable, large. **das war nicht ~ von ihm** that was pretty bad of him; **eine ~e Tracht Prügel** *(col)* a good hiding. **2** *adv* decently. **sich ~ benehmen** to behave oneself; **sich ~ hinsetzen** to sit properly.

Anständigkeit *f* decency; *(Ehrbarkeit)* respectability.

Anstands-: ~formen *pl* manners *pl*; **a~halber** *adv* out of politeness; **a~los** *adv* without difficulty.

anstarren *vt sep* to stare at.

anstatt 1 *prep+gen* instead of. **2** *conj* **~ zu arbeiten** instead of working.

anstauen *vr sep* to accumulate; *(Blut in Adern etc)* to congest; *(fig auch: Gefühle)* to build up. **angestaute Wut** pent-up rage.

anstechen *vt sep irreg* to make a hole in, to pierce;

Kartoffeln, Fleisch to prick; *Reifen* to puncture; *Faß* to tap, to broach.

anstecken *sep* **1** *vt* **(a)** *(befestigen)* to pin on; *Ring* to put *or* slip on. **(b)** *(anzünden)* to light; *(in Brand stecken)* to set fire to. **(c)** *(Med, fig)* to infect. **2** *vr* **sich (mit etw)** ~ to catch sth *(bei* from*)*. **3** *vi (Med, fig)* to be infectious *or* catching; *(durch Berührung, fig)* to be contagious.

ansteckend *adj (Med, fig)* infectious, catching *pred (col)*; *(durch Berührung, fig)* contagious.

Anstecknadel *f* pin, badge.

Ansteckung *f (Med)* infection; *(durch Berührung)* contagion.

Ansteckungsgefahr *f* danger of infection.

anstehen *vi sep irreg* **(a)** *(in Schlange)* to queue (up) *(Brit)*, to stand in line *(nach* for*)*. **(b)** *(Verhandlungspunkt)* to be on the agenda. **anstehende Probleme** problems facing us/them *etc.*

ansteigen *vi sep irreg aux sein* to rise; *(Temperatur, Preis, Zahl auch)* to go up, to increase.

anstelle *prep+gen* instead of, in place of.

anstellen *sep* **1** *vt* **(a)** to place; *(anlehnen)* to lean *(an+acc* against*)*. **(b)** *(beschäftigen)* to employ, to take on; *siehe* **angestellt. (c)** *(anmachen, andrehen)* to turn on; *(in Gang setzen auch)* to start. **(d)** *Betrachtung, Vermutung etc* to make; *Vergleich auch* to draw. **(e)** *(machen, unternehmen)* to do; *(fertigbringen)* to manage. **(f)** *(col: Unfug treiben)* to get up to. **etwas** ~ to get up to mischief; **was hast du da wieder angestellt!** what have you done now?, what have you been up to now? **2** *vr* **(a)** *(Schlange stehen)* to queue (up) *(Brit)*, to stand in line. **(b)** *(col: sich verhalten)* to act, to behave. **sich dumm/ungeschickt** ~ to act stupid/clumsily, to be stupid/clumsy. **(c)** *(col: sich zieren)* to make a fuss, to act up *(col)*. **stell dich nicht so an!** don't make such a fuss!

Anstellung *f* employment.

ansteuern *vt sep* to make *or* steer *or* head *(auch hum)* for.

Anstich *m (von Faß)* tapping, broaching.

Anstieg *m* **-e (a)** *(Aufstieg)* climb, ascent; *(Weg)* ascent. **(b)** *(von Temperatur, Kosten, Preisen etc)* rise, increase *(gen* in*)*.

anstiften *vt sep (anzetteln)* to instigate; *(verursachen)* to cause. **jdn zu etw** ~ to incite sb to (do) sth, to put sb up to sth *(col)*.

Anstifter *m* instigator *(+gen, zu* of*)*.

Anstiftung *f (von Mensch)* incitement *(zu* to*)*; *(von Tat)* instigation.

anstimmen *vt sep* **(a)** *(singen)* to begin singing; *(Chorleiter) Grundton* to give; *(Kapelle)* to strike up, to start playing. **(b)** *(fig)* **ein Geschrei/Proteste** *etc* ~ to start crying/protesting *etc.*

Anstoß *m* **(a)** impetus, impulse. **den (ersten)** ~ **zu etw geben** to initiate sth, to get sth going; **den** ~ **zu etw bekommen** to be prompted *or* encouraged to do sth; **es bedurfte eines neuen** ~**es** new impetus was needed. **(b)** *(Ftbl)* kick-off. **(c)** *(Ärgernis)* annoyance *(für* to*)*. ~ **erregen** to cause offence *(bei* to*)*; **ein Stein des** ~**es** *(umstrittene Sache)* a bone of contention.

anstoßen *sep irreg* **1** *vi* **(a)** *aux sein* **(an etw** *acc***)** ~ to bump into sth. **(b) (mit den Gläsern)** ~ to clink glasses; **auf jdn/etw** ~ to drink to sb/sth. **(c)** *(Ftbl)* to kick off. **(d)** *(angrenzen)* **an etw** *(acc)* ~ to adjoin sth; *(Land auch)* to border on sth. **2** *vt jdn* to knock (into); *(mit dem Fuß)* to kick; *(in Bewegung setzen)* to give a push.

anstößig *adj* offensive; *Kleidung* indecent.

anstrahlen *vt sep* to floodlight; *(im Theater)* to spotlight; *(strahlend ansehen)* to beam at.

anstreben *vt sep* to strive for.

anstreichen *vt sep irreg* **(a)** *(mit Farbe etc)* to paint. **(b)** *(markieren)* to mark. **(jdm) etw als Fehler** ~ to mark sth wrong.

Anstreicher *m* **-** (house) painter.

anstrengen *sep* **1** *vt* **(a)** to strain; *Muskel, Geist* to exert; *(strapazieren) jdn* to tire out; *esp Patienten* to fatigue. **das viele Lesen strengt meine Augen/mich an** all this reading puts a strain on my eyes/is a strain (for me); *siehe* **angestrengt. (b)** *(Jur)* **eine Klage** ~ to initiate *or* institute proceedings *(gegen* against*)*. **2** *vr* to make an effort; *(körperlich auch)* to exert oneself. **sich mehr** ~ to make more of an effort.

anstrengend *adj (körperlich)* strenuous; *(geistig)* demanding; *(erschöpfend)* exhausting, tiring. **das ist** ~ **für die Augen** it's a strain on the eyes.

Anstrengung *f* effort; *(Strapaze)* strain. **große** ~**en machen** to make every effort.

Anstrich *m (das Anmalen, Tünchen)* painting; *(Farbüberzug)* paint; *(fig: Anflug)* touch. **ein zweiter** ~ a second coat of paint.

Ansturm *m* onslaught; *(auf Kaufhaus etc)* rush; *(auf Bank)* run; *(Menschenmenge)* crowd.

anstürmen *vi sep aux sein* **gegen etw** ~ *(Mil)* to attack *or* storm sth; *(Wellen, Wind)* to pound sth; *(fig: ankämpfen)* to attack sth.

Antagonismus *m* antagonism.

antanzen *vi sep aux sein (col)* to turn *or* show up *(col)*.

Antarktis *f no pl* Antarctic.

antarktisch *adj* antarctic.

antasten *vt sep* **(a)** *Ehre, Würde* to offend; *Rechte* to infringe. **(b)** *(berühren)* to touch.

Anteil *m* **-e (a)** share. **(b)** *(Beteiligung)* ~ **an etw** *(dat)* **haben** *(beitragen)* to contribute to sth; *(teilnehmen)* to take part in sth. **(c)** *(Teilnahme: an Leid etc)* sympathy *(an+dat* with*)*. **an etw** *(dat)* ~ **nehmen** *an Leid etc* to be deeply sympathetic over sth; *an Freude etc* to share in sth. **(d)** *(Interesse)* interest *(an+dat* in*)*, concern *(an+dat* about*)*. **regen** ~ **an etw** *(dat)* **nehmen** to take a lively interest in sth.

anteilig *adj* proportionate, proportional.

Anteilnahme *f no pl (Beileid)* sympathy *(an+dat* with*)*.

antelefonieren* *vti sep (col)* to phone. **bei jdm** ~ to phone sb up.

Antenne *f* **-n** *(Rad, TV)* aerial, antenna *(US)*; *(Zool)* feeler, antenna. **eine/keine** ~ **für etw haben** *(fig inf)* to have a/no feeling for sth.

Anthologie *f* anthology.

Anthrazit *m* **-e** anthracite.

anthrazit(farben) *adj* charcoal-grey, charcoal.

Anthropologe *m*, **Anthropologin** *f* anthropologist.

Anthropologie *f* anthropology.

anthropologisch *adj* anthropological.

Anti- *pref* anti; ~**alkoholiker** *m* teetotaller *(Brit)*, teetotaler *(US)*; **a**~**autoritär** *adj* anti-authoritarian; ~**babypille** *f (col)* (contraceptive) pill; ~**biotikum** *nt, pl* ~**biotika** antibiotic; **a**~**demokratisch** *adj* antidemocratic; ~**faschismus** *m* antifascism; ~**faschist** *m* antifascist; **a**~**faschistisch** *adj* antifascist; ~**held** *m* antihero; ~**heldin** *f* antiheroine.

antik *adj (Hist)* ancient; *(Comm, col)* antique.

Antike *f no pl* antiquity. **die Kunst der** ~ the art of the ancient world.

Anti-: ~**kommunismus** *m* anticommunism; ~**kommunist** *m* anticommunist; **a**~**kommunistisch** *adj* anticommunist; ~**körper** *m (Med)* antibody.

Antilope *f* **-n** antelope.

Anti-: ~**pathie** *f* antipathy *(gegen* to*)*; ~**pode** *m (wk)* **-n, -n** antipodean; **die Engländer sind die** ~**poden Australiens** the English live on the opposite side of the world from Australia.

antippen *vt sep* to tap; *Pedal, Bremse* to touch; *(fig) Thema* to touch on.

Antiquar(in *f***)** *m* antiquarian *or (von moderneren Büchern)* second-hand bookseller.

Antiquariat *nt* antiquarian *or (modernerer Bücher)* second-hand bookshop *(Brit) or* bookstore

(US). **modernes ~** remainder bookshop.

antiquarisch *adj* antiquarian; *(von moderneren Büchern)* second-hand. **ein Buch ~ kaufen** to buy a book second-hand.

antiquiert *adj (pej)* antiquated.

Antiquität *f usu pl* antique.

Antiquitäten-: ~geschäft *nt* antique shop *(Brit) or* store *(US)*; **~handel** *m* antique business *or* trade; **~händler** *m* antique dealer.

Anti-: ~semit *m* antisemite; **a~semitisch** *adj* antisemitic; **a~septisch** *adj* antiseptic; **a~statisch** *adj* antistatic; **~teilchen** *nt (Phys)* antiparticle; **~these** *f* antithesis.

Antlitz *nt* **-e** *(poet)* countenance *(liter)*, face.

Antrag *m, pl* **Anträge (a)** *(auf+acc* for*)* application; *(Gesuch auch)* request; *(Formular)* application form. **einen ~ auf etw** *(acc)* **stellen** to make an application for sth. **(b)** *(Jur)* petition; *(bei Gericht)* claim. **einen ~ auf etw** *(acc)* **stellen** to file a petition/claim for sth. **(c)** *(Parl)* motion.

Antragsformular *nt* application form.

Antragsteller(in *f***)** *m* **-** claimant; *(für Kredit etc)* applicant.

antreffen *vt sep irreg* to find; *Situation auch* to meet. **er ist schwer anzutreffen** it's difficult to catch him in; **ich habe ihn in guter Laune angetroffen** I found him in a good mood.

antreiben *vt* **(a)** *(vorwärtstreiben) Tiere, Gefangene* to drive; *(fig)* to urge. **jdn zur Eile/Arbeit ~** to urge sb to hurry up/to work; **ich lasse mich nicht ~** I won't be pushed. **(b)** *(bewegen) Rad etc* to drive; *(mit Motor auch)* to power.

Antreiber *m (pej)* slave-driver *(pej)*.

antreten *sep irreg* **1** *vt Reise, Strafe* to begin; *Stellung, Amt* to take up; *Erbe, Erbschaft* to come into. **den Beweis ~, daß ...** to prove that ...; **seine Lehrzeit ~** to start one's apprenticeship. **2** *vi aux sein* **(a)** *(sich aufstellen)* to line up; *(Mil)* to fall in. **(b)** *(erscheinen)* to assemble; *(bei einer Stellung)* to start; *(zum Dienst)* to report. **(c)** *(zum Wettkampf)* to compete.

Antrieb *m* **(a)** impetus *no pl*; *(innerer)* drive. **aus eigenem ~** on one's own initiative, off one's own bat *(col)*. **(b)** *(Triebkraft)* drive. **Auto mit elektrischem ~** electrically driven *or* powered car.

Antriebs-: ~kraft *f (Tech)* power; **~rad** *nt* drive wheel.

antrinken *vt sep irreg (col)* to start drinking. **sich** *(dat)* **einen (Rausch/Schwips) ~** to get (oneself) drunk/tipsy; **sich** *(dat)* **Mut ~** to give oneself Dutch courage; **eine angetrunkene Flasche** an opened bottle; *siehe* **angetrunken.**

Antritt *m no pl (Beginn)* beginning. **bei ~ der Reise** when beginning one's journey; **nach ~ der Stellung** after taking up the post.

antun *vt sep irreg* **(a)** *(erweisen)* **jdm (große) Ehre ~** to pay (great) tribute to sb. **(b)** *(zufügen)* **jdm etw ~** to do sth to sb. **sich** *(dat)* **ein Leid ~** to injure oneself; **jdm Schaden/Unrecht ~** to do sb an injury/injustice. **(c)** *(Sympathie erregen)* **es jdm ~** to appeal to sb; *siehe* **angetan.**

anturnen ['antœrnən] *sep (col)* **1** *vt (Drogen, Musik)* to turn on *(col)*. **2** *vi* to turn you on *(col)*.

Antwort *f* **-en (a)** answer, reply; *(Lösung, bei Examen)* answer. **sie gab mir keine ~ auf die Frage** she didn't reply to *or* answer my question; **in ~ auf etw** *(acc) (form)* in reply to sth; **um umgehende ~ wird gebeten** please reply by return. **(b)** *(Reaktion)* response. **als ~ auf etw** *(acc)* in response to sth.

antworten *vti* **(a)** to answer, to reply. **jdm ~** to answer sb, to reply to sb; **was soll ich ihm ~?** what should I tell him?; **mit Ja/Nein ~** to answer yes/no. **(b)** *(reagieren)* to respond *(auf+acc* to, *mit* with*)*.

anvertrauen* *sep* **1** *vt* **jdm etw ~** *(übergeben)* to entrust sth to sb *or* sb with sth; *(vertraulich erzählen)* to confide sth to sb. **2** *vr* **sich jdm ~** *(sich mitteilen)* to confide in sb.

Anverwandte(r) *mf decl as adj (geh)* relative, relation.

anvisieren* ['anvi-] *vt sep (fig)* to set one's sights on.

anwachsen *vi sep irreg aux sein* **(a)** *(festwachsen)* to grow on; *(Pflanze etc)* to take root; *siehe* **angewachsen. (b)** *(zunehmen) (auf+acc* to*)* to increase, to grow.

Anwachsen *nt* increase, growth. **im ~ sein** to be on the increase, to be growing.

Anwalt *m, pl* **Anwälte (a)** *siehe* **Rechtsanwalt. (b)** *(fig: Fürsprecher)* advocate.

Anwaltsbüro *nt* **(a)** lawyer's office. **(b)** *(Firma)* firm of lawyers *or* solicitors *(Brit)*.

Anwalts-: ~kammer *f professional association of lawyers* ≈ Law Society *(Brit)*; **~kosten** *pl* legal expenses *pl*; **~praxis** *f* legal practice; *(Räume)* lawyer's office.

Anwandlung *f (Laune)* mood; *(Drang)* impulse. **aus einer ~ heraus** on (an) impulse.

anwärmen *vt sep* to warm up.

Anwärter(in *f***)** *m (Kandidat)* candidate *(auf+acc* for*)*; *(Sport)* contender *(auf +acc* for*)*; *(Thron~)* heir *(auf+acc* to*)*.

anwehen *vt sep Sand* to blow; *Schnee* to drift.

anweisen *vt sep irreg* **(a)** *(anleiten) Schüler* to instruct; *(befehlen auch)* to order. **(b)** *(zuweisen) (jdm etw* sb sth*)* to allocate; *Zimmer auch* to give. **jdm einen Platz ~** to show sb to a seat. **(c)** *Geld* to transfer. **(d)** *siehe* **angewiesen.**

Anweisung *f* **(a)** *(Fin)* payment; *(auf Konto etc)* transfer. **(b)** *(Anordnung)* instruction, order. **(c)** *(Zuweisung)* allocation. **(d)** *(Anleitung)* instructions *pl*.

anwendbar *adj Theorie, Regel* applicable *(auf +acc* to*)*. **das ist in der Praxis nicht ~** that is not practicable.

anwenden *vt sep auch irreg* **(a)** *(gebrauchen)* to use *(auf+acc* on*)*. **(b)** *Theorie, Prinzipien* to apply *(auf+acc* to*)*; *Erfahrung, Einfluß* to use, to bring to bear *(auf+acc* on*)*. **sich auf etw** *(acc)* **~ lassen** to be applicable to sth; *siehe* **angewandt.**

Anwender *m (esp Comp)* user.

Anwendung *f siehe vt* use; application. **etw zur ~ bringen** *(form)* to use/apply sth.

anwerben *vt sep irreg* to recruit *(für* to*)*.

Anwerbung *f* recruitment.

anwerfen *vt sep irreg (Tech)* to start up.

anwesend *adj (form)* present. **ich war nicht ganz ~** *(hum col)* my thoughts were elsewhere.

Anwesende(r) *mf decl* as *adj* person present. **die ~n** those present.

Anwesenheit *f* presence. **in ~** *+gen or* **von** in the presence of.

Anwesenheitsliste *f* attendance list.

anwidern *vt sep* **jdn ~** *(Essen, Anblick)* to make sb feel sick; **es/er widert mich an** I can't stand it/him; *siehe* **angewidert.**

Anwohner *m* **-** resident. **die ~ des Rheins** the people who live along *or* on the Rhine.

Anzahl *f no pl* number. **eine ganze ~** quite a number.

anzahlen *vt sep Ware* to pay a deposit on, to make a down payment on. **100 DM ~** to pay DM 100 down *or* DM 100 as a deposit.

Anzahlung *f* deposit, down payment *(für, auf +acc* on*)*; *(erste Rate)* first instalment *(Brit) or* installment *(US)*. **eine ~ machen** *or* **leisten** *(form)* to pay a deposit.

anzapfen *vt sep Faß* to broach; *Telefon, elektrische Leitung* to tap. **jdn (um Geld) ~** *(col)* to touch sb (for money); **jdn ~** *(col: Telec)* to tap sb's phone.

Anzeichen *nt* sign; *(Med auch)* symptom. **alle ~ deuten darauf hin, daß ...** all the signs are that ...

Anzeige *f* **(a)** *(bei Behörde)* report *(wegen* of*)*; *(bei Gericht)* legal proceedings *pl*. **jdn/etw zur ~ bringen** *(form) (bei Polizei)* to report sb/sth to the police; *(bei Gericht)* to take sb/bring sth to court. **(b)** *(Bekanntgabe) (Karte, Brief)* announcement; *(in Zeitung auch)* notice; *(Inserat, Reklame)* advertisement. **(c)** *(~tafel etc)* display.

anzeigen *vt sep* **(a) jdn ~** *(bei der Polizei)* to report sb (to the police); *(bei Gericht)* to institute legal proceedings against sb. **(b)** *(bekanntgeben) Heirat etc* to announce. **(c)** *(angeben) Temperatur, Zeit, Geschwindigkeit* to show, to indicate.

Anzeigen-: ~blatt *nt* advertiser; **~teil** *m* advertisement section.

anzeigepflichtig *adj* notifiable.

Anzeiger *m (Tech)* indicator.

Anzeigetafel *f* indicator board.

anzetteln *vt sep* to instigate.

anziehen *sep irreg* **1** *vt* **(a)** *Kleidung* to put on. **sich** *(dat)* **etw ~** to put sth on. **(b)** *(straffen)* to pull (tight); *Bremse (betätigen)* to apply, to put on; *Zügel* to pull; *Schraube* to tighten. **(c)** *(Magnet, fig)* to attract; *Geruch, Feuchtigkeit* to absorb. **sich von etw angezogen fühlen** to feel attracted to sth. **2** *vi* **(a)** *(beschleunigen)* to accelerate. **(b)** *(Chess etc)* to make the first move. **(c)** *(Fin: Preise)* to rise. **3** *vr* **(a)** *(sich kleiden)* to get dressed. **(b)** *(fig: Gegensätze)* to attract each other.

anziehend *adj (ansprechend)* attractive.

Anziehung *f* attraction.

Anziehungskraft *f (Phys)* force of attraction; *(fig)* attraction, appeal. **eine große ~ auf jdn ausüben** to attract sb strongly.

Anzug *m, pl* **Anzüge (a)** *(Herren~)* suit. **(b)** *(das Heranrücken)* approach. **im ~ sein** to be coming; *(Gewitter, Gefahr)* to be in the offing; *Krankheit)* to be coming on. **(c)** *(Chess etc)* opening move. **Weiß ist als erster im ~** white has first move.

anzüglich *adj* lewd, suggestive. **~ werden** to get personal.

Anzüglichkeit *f* lewdness, suggestiveness. **~en** lewd *or* suggestive remarks.

anzünden *vt sep Feuer* to light. **das Haus ~** to set fire to the house, to set the house on fire.

Anzünder *m* lighter.

anzweifeln *vt sep* to question, to doubt.

apart *adj* distinctive, unusual; *Mensch, Aussehen, Kleidungsstück auch* striking.

Apartheid [a'pa:ɐthait] *f no pl* apartheid.

Apartment [a'partmənt] *nt* **-s** flat *(Brit)*, apartment *(esp US)*.

Apathie *f* apathy; *(von Patienten)* listlessness.

apathisch *adj* apathetic; *Patient* listless.

Aperitif *m* **-s** *or* **-e** aperitif.

Apfel *m* ⸚ apple. **in den sauren ~ beißen** *(fig col)* to swallow the bitter pill; **etw für einen ~ und ein Ei kaufen** *(col)* to buy sth dirt cheap *(col) or* for a song *(col)*; **der ~ fällt nicht weit vom Stamm** *(Prov)* it's in the blood.

Apfel-: ~baum *m* apple tree; **~blüte** *f* **(a)** apple blossom; **(b)** *(das Blühen)* blossoming of the apple trees; **~kompott** *nt* stewed apples; **~kuchen** *m* apple cake; **~mus** *nt* apple purée *or (als Beilage)* sauce; **~saft** *m* apple juice; **~schimmel** *m* dapple-grey (horse).

Apfelsine *f* orange.

Apfel-: ~strudel *m* apfelstrudel; **~tasche** *f* apple turnover; **~wein** *m* cider.

Apokalypse *f* **-n** apocalypse.

apokalyptisch *adj* apocalyptic.

apolitisch *adj* non-political, apolitical.

Apostel *m* **-** apostle.

Apostel-: ~brief *m* epistle; **~geschichte** *f* Acts of the Apostles *pl.*

Apostroph *m* **-e** apostrophe.

Apotheke *f* **-n** chemist's *(Brit)*, pharmacy *(US)*.

apothekenpflichtig *adj* available only at a chemist's *(Brit) or* pharmacy *(US)*.

Apotheker(in *f*) *m* **-** pharmacist, (dispensing) chemist *(Brit)*.

Apparat *m* **-e (a)** apparatus *no pl*, appliance; *(kleineres, technisches, mechanisches Gerät auch)* device, gadget; *(Röntgen~ etc)* machine. **(b)** *(Radio)* radio; *(Fernseher)* set. **(c)** *(Telefon)* (tele)phone; *(Anschluß)* extension. **am ~** on the phone; *(als Antwort)* speaking; **wer war am ~?** who did you speak to?; **bleiben Sie am ~!** hold the line. **(d)** *(Personen und Hilfsmittel)* set-up; *(Verwaltungs~, Partei~)* machinery, apparatus; *(technischer etc)* equipment, apparatus.

Apparatur *f* equipment *no pl*, apparatus *no pl.*

Appartement [apartə'mɑ̃:] *nt* **-s (a)** *siehe* **Apartment. (b)** *(Zimmerflucht)* suite.

Appell *m* **-e (a)** *(Aufruf)* appeal *(an+acc* to, *zu* for*)*. **einen ~ an jdn richten** to (make an) appeal to sb. **(b)** *(Mil)* roll call. **zum ~ antreten** to line up for roll call.

appellieren* *vi* to appeal *(an +acc* to*)*.

Appetit *m no pl (lit, fig)* appetite. **~ auf etw** *(acc)* **haben** to feel like sth; **guten ~!** enjoy your meal; **jdm den ~ verderben** to spoil sb's appetite.

Appetit-: a~anregend *adj Speise etc* appetizing; **a~lich** *adj (lit, fig)* appetizing; **~losigkeit** *f* lack of appetite; **~zügler** *m* **-** appetite suppressant.

applaudieren* *vti* to applaud.

Applaus *m no pl* applause.

apportieren* *vti* to retrieve, to fetch.

Appretur *f (Mittel)* finish; *(Tex)* starch; *(Wasserundurchlässigkeit)* waterproofing.

approbiert *adj Arzt* registered, certified.

Après-Ski [apre'ʃi:] *nt* **-s** après-ski.

Aprikose *f* **-n** apricot.

Aprikosenmarmelade *f* apricot jam.

April *m no pl* April. **~, ~!** April fool!; **der erste ~** April Fool's Day; **jdn in den ~ schicken** to make an April fool of sb; *siehe* **März.**

April-: ~scherz *m* April fool's trick; **das ist doch wohl ein ~scherz** *(fig)* it's got to be a joke; **~wetter** *nt* April weather.

apropos [apro'po:] *adv* by the way, that reminds me. **~ Afrika** talking about Africa.

Aqua-: ~marin *nt* **-e** aquamarine; **~planing** *nt no pl (Aut)* aquaplaning.

Aquarell *nt* **-e** watercolour *(Brit)*, watercolor *(US)*.

Aquarell-: ~farbe *f* watercolour *(Brit)*; watercolor *(US)*; **~maler** *m* watercolourist *(Brit)*, watercolorist *(US)*; **~malerei** *f* watercolour *(Brit) or* watercolor *(US)* painting.

Aquarium *nt* aquarium.

Äquator *m no pl* equator.

Aquavit [akva'vi:t] *m* **-e** aquavit.

Äquivalent [-va'lɛnt] *nt* **-e** equivalent; *(Ausgleich)* compensation.

Äquivalenz [-va'lɛnts] *f* equivalence.

Ar *nt or m* **-e** *(Measure)* are *(100 m²)*.

Ära *f* **Ären** era. **die ~ Adenauer** the Adenauer era.

Araber *m* **-** *(auch Pferd)*, **Araberin** *f* Arab.

Arabien [-iən] *nt* Arabia.

arabisch *adj* Arab; *Ziffer, Sprache etc* Arabic.

Arbeit *f* **(a)** work; *(~stelle, Aufgabe)* job; *(Pol, Econ, Lohn für ~)* labour *(Brit)*, labor *(US)*. **~ und Kapital** capital and labour; **Tag der ~** Labour Day; **die ~en an der Autobahn** the work on the motorway; **viel ~ machen** to be a lot of work *(jdm* for sb*)*; **das ist/kostet viel ~** it's a lot of work *or* a big job; **an** *or* **bei der ~ sein** to be working; **sich an die ~ machen, an die ~ gehen** to get down to work, to start working; **an die ~!** to work!; **etw ist in ~** work on sth is in progress; **erst die ~, dann das Vergnügen** *(prov)* business before pleasure *(prov)*; **ganze** *or* **gründliche ~ leisten** *(lit, fig iro)* to do a good job.

(b) *no pl (Mühe)* trouble, bother. **jdm ~ machen** to put sb to trouble; **machen Sie sich keine ~!** don't go to any trouble *or* bother; **einer (geregelten) ~ nachgehen** to have a (steady) job;

ohne ~ sein to be out of work; **zur ~ gehen/von der ~ kommen** to go to/come back from work; **seine ~ besteht darin, zu ...** his job is to ...
(c) *(Produkt)* work; *(handwerkliche)* piece of work; *(Prüfungs~)* (examination) paper; *(wissenschaftliche)* paper; *(Sch)* test. **~en korrigieren** to mark test papers; **eine ~ schreiben/schreiben lassen** to do/set a test.

arbeiten 1 *vi* to work *(an +dat* on*)*. **die Zeit arbeitet für/gegen uns** time is on our side/against us; **er arbeitet für zwei** *(col)* he does the work of two; **die Anlage arbeitet elektrisch/mit Kohle** the plant runs on electricity/coal; **bei einer Firma/Zeitung ~** to work for a firm/newspaper; **die ~de Bevölkerung** the working population. **2** *vr* **(a) sich zu Tode ~** to work oneself to death. **(b)** *(sich fortbewegen)* to work oneself *(in + acc* into, *durch* through, *zu* to*)*. **sich nach oben/an die Spitze ~** *(fig)* to work one's way up/to the top. **(c)** *impers* **es arbeitet sich gut/schlecht** you can/can't work well.

Arbeiter(in *f***)** *m* **-** worker; *(im Gegensatz zum Angestellten)* blue-collar worker; *(auf Bau, Bauernhof)* labourer *(Brit)*, laborer *(US)*; *(bei Straßenbau, im Haus)* workman. **~ und ~innen** male and female workers.

Arbeiter-: ~bewegung *f* labour *(Brit) or* labor *(US)* movement; **~familie** *f* working-class family; **~führer** *m (Pol)* leader of the working classes; **~gewerkschaft** *f* blue-collar (trade) union, labor union *(US)*; **~jugend** *f* young workers *pl*; **~kind** *nt* child from a working-class family; **~klasse** *f* working class(es *pl*); **~lied** *nt* workers' song; **~partei** *f* workers' party; **~schaft** *f* work force; **~-und-Bauern-Staat** *m (DDR)* workers' and peasants' state; **~viertel** *nt* working-class area; **~wohlfahrt** *f* workers' welfare association.

Arbeitgeber *m* employer.

Arbeitgeber-: ~anteil *m* employer's contribution; **~verband** *m* employers' federation.

Arbeitnehmer *m* employee.

Arbeitnehmer-: ~anteil *m* employee's contribution; **~schaft** *f* employees *pl*.

Arbeitsablauf *m* work routine; *(von Fabrik)* production *no art*.

arbeitsam *adj* industrious, hard-working.

Arbeitsamkeit *f* industriousness.

Arbeits-: ~amt *nt* employment exchange, job centre *(Brit)*; **~anzug** *m* working suit; **~atmosphäre** *f* work(ing) atmosphere, work climate; **~auffassung** *f* attitude to work; **~aufwand** *m* expenditure of energy; *(Ind)* use of labour *(Brit) or* labor *(US)*; **mit geringem/großem ~aufwand** with little/a lot of work; **~ausfall** *m* loss of working hours; **~bedingungen** *pl* working conditions *pl*; **~beginn** *m* start of work; **~beschaffung** *f (Arbeitsplatzbeschaffung)* job creation; **~besuch** *m* working visit; **~eifer** *m* enthusiasm for one's work; **~erlaubnis** *f* work permit; **~erleichterung** *f* **das bedeutet eine große ~erleichterung** that makes the work much easier; **~essen** *nt (esp Pol)* working lunch/dinner; **a~fähig** *adj Person* able to work; *(gesund)* fit to work; **~friede(n)** *m* peaceful labour *(Brit) or* labor *(US)* relations *pl, no art;* **~gang** *m (Abschnitt)* operation; **~gebiet** *nt* field of work; **~gemeinschaft** *f* team; *(Sch, Univ)* study-group; **~genehmigung** *f* work permit; **~gericht** *nt* industrial tribunal; **~gruppe** *f* team; **a~intensiv** *adj* labour-intensive *(Brit)*, labor-intensive *(US)*; **~kampf** *m* industrial action; **~kleidung** *f* working clothes *pl*; **~klima** *nt* work climate, work(ing) atmosphere; **~kollege** *m (bei Angestellten etc)* colleague; *(bei Arbeitern)* fellow worker, workmate; **~kosten** *pl* labor *(Brit) or* labour *(US)* costs *pl*; **~kraft** *f* **(a)** *no pl* capacity for work; **seine ~kraft verkaufen** to sell one's labour *(Brit) or* labor *(US)*; **(b)** *(Arbeiter)* worker; **~lager** labour *(Brit) or* labor *(US)* camp; **~leistung** *f (quantitativ)* output; *(qualitativ)* performance; **~lohn** *m* wages *pl*.

arbeitslos *adj* unemployed, out of work. **~ werden** to be made redundant *(Brit)*, to lose one's job.

Arbeitslosen-: ~geld *nt* unemployment benefit; **~hilfe** *f* supplementary benefit; **~unterstützung** *f* unemployment benefit, dole money *(Brit col)*; **~versicherung** *f* ≃ National Insurance *(Brit)*, social insurance *(US)*; **~zahlen** *pl*, **~ziffer** *f* unemployment figures *pl*.

Arbeitslose(r) *mf decl as adj* employed person/man/woman *etc*. **die ~n** the umemployed; **die Zahl der ~n** the number of unemployed *or* of people out of work.

Arbeits-: ~mangel *m* lack of work; **~markt** *m* labour *(Brit) or* labor *(US)* market; **~material** *nt* material for one's work; *(Sch)* teaching aids *pl*; **~methode** *f* method of working; **~minister** *m* Employment Secretary *(Brit)*, Labor Secretary *(US)*; **~mittel** *nt siehe* **~material; ~moral** *f* attitude to work; *(in Betrieb)* work climate; **~niederlegung** *f* walkout; **~papiere** , *pl* cards, employment papers *(form) pl*.

arbeitsparend *adj* labour-saving *(Brit)*, labor-saving *(US)*.

Arbeits-: ~platz *m* **(a)** *(~stätte)* place of work; *(im Großraumbüro)* work station; **am ~platz** at work; **(b)** *(Stelle)* job; **freie ~plätze** vacancies **~platzcomputer** *m* business computer; **~probe** *f* sample of one's work; **~prozeß** *m* work process; **~raum** *m* workroom; *(für geistige Arbeit)* study; **~recht** *nt* industrial law; **~rhythmus** *m* work rhythm; **a~scheu** *adj* work-shy; **~schluß** *m* end of work; **nach ~schluß** after work; **a~sparend** *adj* = **arbeitsparend; ~stätte** *f* place of work; **~stelle** *f* **(a)** place of work; **(b)** *(Stellung)* job; **~stil** *m* work-style, style of working; **~suche** *f* search for work *or* a job; **auf ~suche sein** to be looking for a job, to be job-hunting; **~tag** *m* workday; **~takt** *m (Tech)* **(a)** *(von Motor)* power stroke; **(b)** *(bei Fließbandarbeit)* time for an/the operation, phase time; **~tätigkeit** *f* work; **~technik** *f* technique of working; **~teilung** *f* division of labour *(Brit)* or labor *(US)*; **~tempo** *f* rate of work; **~tier** *nt (fig)* glutton for work; *(Geistesarbeiter auch)* workaholic *(col)*; **~tisch** *m* work-table; *(für geistige Arbeit)* desk; *(für handwerkliche Arbeit)* workbench; **~überlastung** *f (von Mensch)* overworking.

Arbeit-: ~suche *f* = **Arbeitssuche**; **~suchende(r)** *mf decl as adj* person *etc* looking for a job.

Arbeits-: a~unfähig *adj* unable to work; *(krank)* unfit for work; **~unfähigkeit** *f siehe adj* inability to work; unfitness for work; **~unfall** *m* industrial accident; **a~unwillig** *adj* reluctant *or* unwilling to work; **~verhältnis** *nt* employee-employer relationship; **ein ~verhältnis eingehen** to enter employment; **~verhältnisse** *pl* working conditions *pl*; **~vermittlung** *f (Amt)* employment exchange; *(privat)* employment agency; **~vertrag** *m* contract of employment; **~weise** *f (Praxis)* way *or* method of working; *(von Maschine)* mode of operation; **die ~weise dieser Maschine** the way this machine works; **~welt** *f* working world; **die industrielle ~welt** the world of industry; **~wut** *f* work mania; **a~wütig** *adj* **~wütig sein** to be a workaholic *(col)*; **~zeit** *f* working hours *pl*; **während der ~zeit** in *or* during working hours; **~zeitverkürzung** *f* reduction in working hours; **~zeugnis** *nt* reference from one's employer; **~zimmer** *nt* study.

archaisch *adj* archaic.

Archäologe *m*, **Archäologin** *f* archaeologist *(Brit)*, archeologist *(US)*.

Archäologie *f* archaeology *(Brit)*, archeology *(US)*.

archäologisch *adj* archaeological *(Brit)*, archeological *(US)*.
Arche *f* **-n die ~ Noah** Noah's Ark.
Archipel *m* **-e** archipelago.
Architekt(in *f*) *m (wk)* **-en, -en** *(lit, fig)* architect.
architektonisch *adj* architectural.
Architektur *f* architecture.
Archiv *nt* archives *pl*.
Archivar(in *f*) [-'vaːɐ, -'vaːrɪn] *m* archivist.
archivieren* [-'viːrən] *vt* to put into the archives.
Areal *nt* **-e** area.
Arena *f, pl* **Arenen** *(lit, fig)* arena; *(Zirkus~, Stierkampf~)* ring.
arg *comp* **¨er**, *superl* **¨ste(r, s)** *or (adv)* **am ¨sten 1** *adj (esp S Ger) (schlimm)* bad; *Wetter auch, Gestank, Katastrophe, Verlust, Blamage, Verlegenheit, Schicksal* terrible; *Enttäuschung* bitter. **sein ¨ster Feind** his worst enemy; **etw liegt im ~en** sth is at sixes and sevens. **2** *adv* **(a)** *(schlimm)* badly. **er hat sich ~ vertan** *(col)* he's made a bad mistake; **es zu ~ treiben** to go too far. **(b)** *(col: sehr)* very.
Argentinien [-iən] *nt* Argentina, the Argentine.
Argentinier(in *f*) [-iɐ, iərɪn] *m* Argentinean.
argentinisch *adj* Argentine, Argentinean.
Ärger *m no pl* **(a)** annoyance; *(stärker)* anger. **wenn ihn der ~ packt** when he gets annoyed/angry. **(b)** *(Unannehmlichkeiten)* trouble; *(Erlebnisse auch)* bother. **jdm ~ machen** *or* **bereiten** to cause sb a lot of trouble *or* bother; **~ bekommen** *or* **kriegen** *(col)* to get into trouble; **mach keinen ~!** *(col)* don't cause any trouble!; **so ein ~!** *(col)* what a nuisance!; **es gibt ~** *(col)* there'll be trouble.
ärgerlich *adj* **(a)** *(verärgert)* annoyed, cross. **~ über** *or* **auf jdn/über etw** *(acc)* **sein** to be annoyed with sb/about sth. **(b)** *(unangenehm)* annoying; *(stärker)* maddening, infuriating.
ärgern 1 *vt* to annoy, to irritate; *(stärker)* to make angry. **jdn krank/zu Tode ~** to drive sb mad. **2** *vr (ärgerlich sein/werden)* to be/get annoyed; *(stärker)* to be/get angry *(über jdn/etw* with sb/about sth*)*. **über so etwas könnte ich mich krank/zu Tode ~** that sort of thing drives me mad.
Ärgernis *nt* **(a)** *no pl (Anstoß)* offence, outrage. **wegen Erregung öffentlichen ~ses angeklagt werden** to be charged with offending public decency. **(b)** *(etwas Anstößiges)* outrage; *(etwas Ärgerliches)* terrible nuisance.
Arglist *f no pl (Hinterlist)* cunning, craftiness; *(Boshaftigkeit)* malice; *(Jur)* fraud.
arglistig *adj* cunning, crafty; *(böswillig)* malicious. **~e Täuschung** fraud.
arglos *adj* innocent.
Arglosigkeit *f* innocence.
Argument *nt* argument.
argumentieren* *vi* to argue.
Argus|auge *nt (geh)* eagle eye. **mit ~** eagle-eyed.
Argwohn *m no pl* suspicion. **jds ~ erregen** to arouse sb's suspicions; **~ gegen jdn hegen** to be suspicious of sb; **mit** *or* **voller ~** suspiciously.
argwöhnisch *adj* suspicious.
Arie [-iə] *f (Mus)* aria.
Aristokrat(in *f*) *m (wk)* **-en, -en** aristocrat.
Aristokratie *f* aristocracy.
aristokratisch *adj* aristocratic.
Arithmetik *f no pl* arithmetic.
arithmetisch *adj* arithmetic(al).
Arkade *f (Bogen)* arch(way). **~n** *pl (Bogengang)* arcade.
Arktis *f no pl* Arctic.
arktisch *adj* arctic.
arm *adj, comp* **¨er**, *superl* **¨ste(r, s)** *or (adv)* **am ¨sten** *(lit, fig)* poor. **die A~en** the poor *pl*; **du machst mich noch mal ~** *(col)* you'll be the ruin of me; **~ an etw** *(dat)* **sein** to be somewhat lacking in sth; **der Boden ist ~ an Nährstoffen** the soil is poor in nutrients; **~ an Vitaminen** low in vitamins; **um jdn/etw ¨er werden/sein** to lose/have lost sb/sth; **um 55 Mark ¨er sein** to be 55 marks worse off *or* poorer; **ach, du/Sie A~er!** *(iro)* you poor thing!; **~ dran sein** *(col)* to have a hard time of it.
Arm *m* **-e** *(Anat, Tech, fig)* arm; *(Fluß~ auch)* branch; *(Ärmel)* sleeve. **~ in ~** arm in arm; **jdn im ~** *or* **in den ~en halten** to hold sb in one's arms; **jdn in die ~e nehmen** to take sb in one's arms; **sich in den ~en liegen** to lie in each other's arms; **jdn auf den ~ nehmen** *(fig col)* to pull sb's leg *(col)*; **jdm unter die ~e greifen** *(fig)* to help sb out; **jdn mit offenen ~en empfangen** *(fig)* to welcome sb with open arms; **der ~ des Gesetzes** the long arm of the law; **einen langen/den längeren ~ haben** *(fig)* to have a lot of/more pull *(col) or* influence.
Armaturenbrett *nt* instrument panel; *(Aut)* dashboard.
Arm-: ~band *nt* bracelet; *(von Uhr)* (watch)strap; **~banduhr** *f* wristwatch; **~beuge** *f* **(a)** inside of one's elbow; **(b)** *(Sport)* arm bend; **~binde** *f* armband; *(Med)* sling; **~bruch** *m (Med)* broken arm; **~brust** *f* crossbow.
Armee *f* **-n** [-eːən] *(Mil, fig)* army; *(Gesamtheit der Streitkräfte)* (armed) forces *pl*.
Ärmel *m* **-** sleeve. **sich** *(dat)* **die ~ hochkrempeln** *(lit, fig)* to roll up one's sleeves; **etw aus dem ~ schütteln** to produce sth just like that.
Ärmelkanal *m* (English) Channel.
ärmellos *adj* sleeveless.
Armen-: ~haus *nt (old)* poorhouse; **~recht** *nt (Jur)* legal aid; **~viertel** *nt* poor district *or* quarter.
Arm-: ~gelenk *nt* elbow joint; **a~lang** *adj* arm-length; **~lehne** *f* armrest; **~leuchter** *m (pej col: Dummkopf)* twit *(Brit col)*, fool; *(euph: Arschloch)* bastard *(col!)*.
ärmlich *adj (lit, fig)* poor; *Kleidung, Wohnung* shabby; *Verhältnisse* humble. **einen ~en Eindruck machen** to look poor/shabby; **aus ~en Verhältnissen** from a poor family.
armselig *adj (dürftig)* miserable; *(mitleiderregend)* pathetic, pitiful; *Summe, Ausrede* paltry.
Armut *f no pl (lit, fig)* poverty. **~ an etw** *(dat)* lack of sth; **charakterliche ~** lack of character; **geistige ~** *(von Mensch)* lack of intellect.
Armutszeugnis *nt (fig)* **jdm/sich ein ~ ausstellen** to show sb's/one's shortcomings; **das ist ein ~ für ihn** that shows him up.
Aroma *nt, pl* **Aromen** *or* **-s (a)** *(Geruch)* aroma. **(b)** *(Geschmack)* flavour *(Brit)*, flavor *(US)*. **(c)** *no pl* flavouring *(Brit)*, flavoring *(US)*.
aromatisch *adj* aromatic; *(wohlschmeckend)* savoury *(Brit)*, savory *(US)*.
Arrangement [arãʒə'mãː] *nt* **-s** arrangement.
arrangieren* [arã'ʒiːrən] **1** *vti* to arrange *(jdm* for sb*)*. **2** *vr* **sich mit jdm ~** to come to an arrangement with sb; **sich mit etw ~** to come to terms with sth.
Arrest *m* **-s** *(Mil, Jur)* detention.
Arrestzelle *f* detention cell.
arretieren* *vt (Tech)* to lock (in place).
Arretierung *f* **(a)** locking. **(b)** *(Vorrichtung)* locking mechanism.
arriviert [-'viːɐt] *adj* successful; *(pej)* upstart.
arrogant *adj* arrogant.
Arroganz *f no pl* arrogance.
Arsch *m* **¨e** *(col!)* arse *(col!)*, ass *(US col!)*. **auf den ~ fallen** *(fig: scheitern)* to fall flat on one's face; **leck mich am ~!** *(laß mich in Ruhe)* get stuffed! *(col)*, fuck off! *(col!!)*; *(verdammt)* bugger! *(col!)*, fuck! *(col!!)*; **jdm in den ~ kriechen** to lick sb's arse *(col!)*; **am ~ der Welt** *(col)* in the back of beyond; **im** *or* **am ~ sein** to be screwed up *(col)*.
Arsch-: ~backe *f (col!)* buttock, cheek; **~kriecher** *m (col!)* arse-licker *(col!)*; **~loch** *nt (col!)*

(Mensch) bastard *(col!)*; *(Dummkopf)* stupid bastard *(col!)*.

Arsen *nt no pl* arsenic.

Arsenal *nt* **-e** *(lit, fig)* arsenal.

Art *f* **-en (a)** kind, sort, type; *(von Pflanze, Insekt etc auch)* variety; *(Biol)* species. **diese ~ Leute/Buch** that kind *or* sort of person/book; **ein Heuchler schlimmster ~** the worst type *or* kind of hypocrite; **einzig in seiner ~ sein** to be the only one of its kind, to be unique; **aus der ~ schlagen** not to take after anyone in the family; *(pej)* to be the black sheep of the family. **(b)** *(Methode)* way; *(Stil)* style. **die einfachste ~, etw zu tun** the simplest way to do sth *or* of doing sth; **auf diese ~ und Weise** in this way; **es entspricht nicht meiner ~** it's not my nature; **das ist eigentlich nicht seine ~** it's not like him; **Schnitzel nach ~ des Hauses** schnitzel à la maison. **(c)** *(Benehmen)* behaviour *(Brit)*, behavior *(US)*. **das ist doch keine ~!** that's no way to behave!

Arterie [-iə] *f* artery.

arteriell *adj* arterial.

Arteriosklerose *f* arteriosclerosis.

Art-: **~genosse** *m* animal/plant of the same species; *(Mensch)* person of the same type; **a~gleich** *adj* of the same species; *Mensch* of the same type.

Arthritis *f, pl* **Arthritiden** arthritis.

arthritisch *adj* arthritic.

artig *adj Kind, Hund etc* good, well-behaved *no adv*. **sei schön ~** be a good boy/dog *etc*!, be good!

Artikel *m* **-** *(auch Gram)* article; *(Comm auch)* item.

artikulieren* *vti* to articulate.

Artillerie *f* artillery.

Artillerist *m* artilleryman.

Artischocke *f* **-n** (globe) artichoke.

Artist(in *f***)** *m* (circus/variety) artiste *or* performer.

Artistik *f* artistry; *(Zirkus-, Varietékunst)* circus/variety performing.

artistisch *adj* **(a) sein ~es Können** his ability as a performer; **eine ~e Glanzleistung** a feat of circus *etc* artistry. **(b)** *(geschickt)* masterly *no adv*. **(c)** *(formalkünstlerisch)* artistic.

Arznei *f (lit, fig)* medicine.

Arzneimittel *nt* drug.

Arzt *m* **¨-e** doctor. **praktischer ~** general practitioner, GP *abbr*.

Ärzte-: **~kammer** ≈ General Medical Council *(Brit)*, State Medical Board of Registration *(US)*; **~schaft** *f* medical profession.

Arzthelferin *f* (doctor's) receptionist; nurse.

Ärztin *f* woman doctor; *siehe* **Arzt.**

ärztlich *adj* medical. **er ließ sich ~ behandeln** he got medical treatment.

Arzt-: **~praxis** *f* doctor's practice; **~rechnung** *f* doctor's bill.

As[1] *nt* **-se** *(lit, fig)* ace.

As[2] *nt (Mus)* A flat.

Asbest *nt no pl* asbestos.

aschblond *adj* ashblonde.

Asche *f no pl* ash(es *pl*); *(von Zigarette, Vulkan)* ash; *(sterbliche Überreste)* ashes *pl*. **zu ~ werden** to turn to dust.

Aschen-: **~bahn** *f* cinder track; **~becher** *m* ashtray; **~brödel, ~puttel** *nt* **-** *(Liter, fig)* Cinderella.

Aschermittwoch *m* Ash Wednesday.

asch-: **~fahl** *adj* ashen; **~grau** *adj* ash-grey.

äsen *(Hunt) vir* to graze, to browse.

Asiat(in *f***)** *m (wk)* **-en, -en** Asian.

asiatisch *adj* Asian, Asiatic.

Asien [-iən] *nt* Asia.

Asket *m (wk)* **-en, -en** ascetic.

asketisch *adj* ascetic.

asozial *adj* antisocial.

Asoziale(r) *mf decl as adj (pej)* antisocial man/woman *etc*. **~** *pl* antisocial elements.

Aspekt *m* **-e** aspect. **unter diesem ~ betrachtet** looking at it from this aspect; **einen neuen ~ bekommen** to take on a different complexion.

Asphalt *m* **-e** asphalt.

Asphaltdecke *f* asphalt surface.

asphaltieren* *vt* to asphalt.

asphaltiert *adj* asphalt.

Aspik *m* **-e** aspic.

Aspirant(in *f***)** *m (geh)* candidate *(auf+acc* for*)*.

aß *pret of* **essen.**

Assel *f* **-n** woodlouse.

Assessor(in *f***)** *m graduate civil servant who has completed his/her traineeship.*

Assistent(in *f***)** *m* assistant.

Assistenz *f* assistance.

Assistenz|arzt *m* houseman *(Brit)*, intern *(US)*.

assistieren* *vi* to assist *(jdm* sb*)*.

Assoziation *f* association.

assoziieren* *vt (geh)* to associate. **mit Grün assoziiere ich Ruhe** I associate green with peace.

Ast *m* **¨-e (a)** branch. **den ~ absägen, auf dem man sitzt** *(fig)* to dig one's own grave. **(b)** *(im Holz)* knot. **(c)** *(col)* **sich** *(dat)* **einen ~ lachen to double up (with laughter).**

Aster *f* **-n** aster, Michaelmas daisy.

Astgabel *f* fork (in a branch).

Ästhet(in *f***)** *m (wk)* **-en, -en** aesthete *(Brit)*, esthete *(US)*.

Ästhetik *f* aesthetics *(Brit)*, esthetics *(US) sing; (eines Bildes)* aesthetics *pl*; *(Schönheitssinn)* aesthetic sense.

ästhetisch *adj* aesthetic *(Brit)*, esthetic *(US)*.

Asthma *nt no pl* asthma.

Asthmatiker(in *f***)** *m* **-** asthmatic.

Astloch *nt* knothole.

astral *adj* astral.

astrein *adj (col)* **(a)** *(fig col: moralisch einwandfrei)* straight *(col)*, on the level *(col)*. **(b)** *(fig: echt)* genuine. **(c)** *(prima)* fantastic.

Astro-: **~loge** *m*, **~login** *f* astrologer; **~logie** *f* astrology; **a~logisch** *adj* astrological; **~naut(in** *f***)** *m (wk)* **-en, -en** astronaut; **~nom(in** *f***)** *m* astronomer; **~nomie** *f* astronomy; **a~nomisch** *adj (lit)* astronomical; *(fig auch)* astronomic; **~physik** *f* astrophysics *sing*; **~physiker(in** *f***)** *m* astrophysicist.

Asyl *nt* **-e** *(politisch)* (political) asylum *no art*; *(geh: Schutz)* sanctuary *no art*. **um ~ bitten** to ask for (political) asylum.

Asylant(in *f***)** *m* person seeking (political) asylum.

Asylrecht *nt (Pol)* right of (political) asylum.

asymmetrisch *adj* asymmetric(al).

Atelier [-'lie:] *nt* **-s** studio.

Atelierwohnung *f* studio apartment.

Atem *m no pl* **(a)** *(das Atmen)* breathing. **den ~ anhalten** *(lit, fig)* to hold one's breath; **mit angehaltenem ~** *(lit)* holding one's breath; *(fig)* with bated breath; **wieder zu ~ kommen** to get one's breath back; **den längeren ~ haben** *(fig)* to have more staying power; **jdn in ~ halten** to keep sb in suspense *or* on tenterhooks; **das verschlug mir den ~** it took my breath away. **(b)** *(lit, fig: ~luft)* breath. **~ holen** *or* **schöpfen** *(lit)* to take a breath; *(fig)* to get one's breath back.

Atem-: **a~beraubend** *adj* breathtaking; **~beschwerden** *pl* trouble in breathing; **a~los** *adj (lit, fig)* breathless; **~losigkeit** *f* breathlessness; **~not** *f* difficulty in breathing; **~pause** *f (fig)* breathing space; **eine ~pause einlegen/brauchen** to take/need a breather; **~wege** *pl (Anat)* respiratory tracts *pl*; **~zug** *m* breath; **in einem/im selben ~zug** *(fig)* in one/the same breath.

Atheismus *m* atheism.

Atheist(in *f***)** *m* atheist.

atheistisch *adj* atheist(ic).

Athen *nt* Athens.

Athener(in *f***)** *m* Athenian.

Äther *m no pl* **(a)** ether. **(b)** *(Rad)* air.

Ätherwellen *pl (Rad)* radio waves *pl.*

Äthiopien [ɛ'tio:piən] *nt* Ethiopia.

Äthiopier(in *f*) *m* [-piɐ, -iərin] - Ethiopian.

Athlet(in *f*) *m (wk)* **-en, -en** athlete.

athletisch *adj* athletic.

Atlantik *m* Atlantic.

atlantisch *adj* Atlantic. **der A~e Ozean** the Atlantic Ocean.

Atlas *m, pl* **Atlanten** *or* **-se** atlas.

atmen *vi* to breathe. **frei ~** *(fig)* to breathe freely.

Atmosphäre *f* **-n** *(Phys, fig)* atmosphere.

atmosphärisch *adj* atmospheric. **~e Störungen** atmospherics *pl.*

Atmung *f no pl* breathing; *(Med)* respiration.

Atmungs|organe *pl* respiratory organs *pl.*

Atoll *nt* **-e** atoll.

Atom *nt* **-e** atom.

Atom-: **~angriff** *m* nuclear attack; **~antrieb** *m* nuclear propulsion; **ein U-Boot mit ~antrieb** a nuclear-powered submarine.

atomar *adj* atomic, nuclear; *Struktur* atomic; *Drohung* nuclear.

Atom-: **~bombe** *f* atomic *or* atom bomb; **a~bombensicher** *adj* atomic *or* nuclear blast-proof; **~bombenversuch** *m* atomic *or* nuclear test; **~bunker** *m* atomic *or* nuclear blast-proof bunker; **~energie** *f* nuclear energy; **a~getrieben** *adj* nuclear-powered; **~kern** *m* atomic nucleus; **~kraft** *f* nuclear power; **~kraftwerk** *nt* atomic *or* nuclear power station; **~krieg** *m* atomic *or* nuclear war; **~macht** *f* nuclear power; **~meiler** *m* nuclear reactor; **~müll** *m* nuclear *or* radioactive waste; **~physik** *f* nuclear physics *sing*; **~physiker** *m* nuclear physicist; **~pilz** *m* mushroom cloud; **~rakete** *f* nuclear-powered rocket; *(Waffe)* nuclear missile; **~reaktor** *m* atomic *or* nuclear reactor; **~rüstung** *f* nuclear armament; **~spaltung** *f* nuclear fission; **die erste ~spaltung** the first splitting of the atom; **~sprengkopf** *m* atomic *or* nuclear warhead; **~strahlung** *f* nuclear radiation; **~streitmacht** *f* nuclear capability; **~strom** *m (col)* electricity generated by nuclear power; **~test** *m* nuclear test; **~waffe** *f* nuclear *or* atomic weapon; **a~waffenfrei** *adj* nuclear-free; **~waffensperrvertrag** *m* nuclear *or* atomic weapons non-proliferation treaty; **~zeitalter** *nt* atomic *or* nuclear age.

ätsch *interj (col)* ha-ha.

Attacke *f* **-n** *(Angriff)* attack. **eine ~ gegen jdn/etw reiten** *(fig)* to attack sb/sth.

attackieren* *vt (angreifen)* to attack.

Attentat [-ta:t] *nt* **-e** assassination; *(~sversuch)* assassination attempt. **ein ~ auf jdn verüben** to assassinate sb; to make an attempt on sb's life.

Attentäter(in *f*) *m* - assassin; *(bei gescheitertem Versuch)* would-be assassin.

Attest *nt* **-e** certificate.

attestieren* *vt (form)* to certify.

Attraktion *f* attraction.

attraktiv *adj* attractive.

Attraktivität *f* attractiveness.

Attrappe *f* **-n** dummy; *(fig: Schein)* sham. **bei ihr ist alles ~** everything about her is false.

Attribut *nt* **-e** *(geh, Gram)* attribute.

atypisch *adj (geh)* atypical.

ätzen *vti* **(a)** to etch. **(b)** *(Säure)* to corrode.

ätzend *adj* **(a)** *(lit) Säure* corrosive. **(b)** *Geruch* pungent; *Spott* caustic.

au, aua *interj* ow, ouch.

Aubergine [obɛr'ʒi:nə] *f* aubergine, eggplant.

auch *adv* **(a)** *(zusätzlich, gleichfalls)* also, too, as well. **~ nicht** not ... either; **das ist ~ nicht richtig** that's not right either; **er kommt — ich ~** he's coming — so am I, me too; **ich mag das nicht — ich ~ nicht** I don't like that — nor *or* neither do I; **nicht nur ..., sondern ~** not only ... but also ...; **~ das noch!** that's all I needed!

(b) *(tatsächlich)* too, as well. **du siehst müde aus — das bin ich ~** you look tired — (so) I am; **das müßt ihr aber ~ tun** but you have to do it; **so ist es ~** (so) it is.

(c) *(sogar)* even. **~ wenn du Vorfahrt hast** even if you (do) have right of way; **ohne ~ nur zu fragen** without even asking.

(d) *(emph)* **so was Ärgerliches aber ~!** it's really too annoying!; **wozu ~?** whatever for?

(e) *(~ immer)* **wie dem ~ sei** be that as it may; **was er ~ sagen mag** whatever he might say; **so schnell er ~ laufen mag** however fast he runs *or* may run, no matter how fast he runs.

Audienz *f (bei Papst, König etc)* audience.

Audimax *nt no pl (Univ col)* main lecture hall.

audiovisuell *adj* audiovisual.

Auditorium *nt* **(a)** *(Hörsaal)* lecture hall. **(b)** *(geh: Zuhörerschaft)* audience.

Auerhahn *m* capercaillie.

Auer|ochse *m* aurochs.

Auf *nt inv*: **das ~ und Ab** the up and down; *(fig)* the ups and downs.

auf 1 *prep* **(a)**+*dat* on. **~ (der Insel) Skye** on the island of Skye; **~ See** at sea; **~ meinem Zimmer** in my room; **~ der Bank/Post/Party** at the bank/post office/party; **mein Geld ist ~ der Bank** my money is in the bank; **~ der Straße** on *or* in the street; **etw ~ der Geige spielen** to play sth on the violin; **~ einem Ohr taub/einem Auge kurzsichtig sein** to be deaf in one ear/short-sighted in one eye; **was hat es damit ~ sich?** what does it mean?; **~ der Fahrt/dem Weg** *etc* on the journey/way *etc.*

(b)+*acc* on, onto. **etw ~ etw stellen** to put sth on(to) sth *or* on top of sth; **sich ~ etw setzen/legen** to sit/lie (down) on sth; **er fiel ~ den Rücken** he fell on(to) his back; **etw ~ einen Zettel schreiben** to write sth on a piece of paper; **er ist ~ die Orkney-Inseln gefahren** he has gone to the Orkney Islands; **geh mal ~ die Seite** go to the side; **~ sein Zimmer/die Post/eine Party** *etc* **gehen** to go to one's room/the post office/a party *etc*; **~s Gymnasium gehen** to go to (the) grammar school; **die Uhr ~ 10 stellen** to put the clock to 10; **die Sitzung ~ morgen verschieben** to postpone the meeting until tomorrow.

(c)+*acc* **~ 10 km/drei Tage** for 10 km/three days; **~ eine Tasse Kaffee/eine Zigarette(nlänge)** for a cup of coffee/a smoke; **ein Manuskript ~ Fehler prüfen** to check a manuscript for errors; **~ seinen Vorschlag (hin)** at his suggestion; **~ meinen Brief hin** because of *or* on account of my letter.

(d) **es geht ~ Weihnachten zu** Christmas is approaching; **er kam ~ mich zu und sagte ...** he came up to me and said ...; **die Nacht (von Montag) ~ Dienstag** Monday night; **~ einen Polizisten kommen 1.000 Bürger** there is one policeman to every 1,000 citizens; **~ den Millimeter/die Sekunde genau** to within one millimetre/second; **~ ein glückliches Gelingen** *etc*! here's to a great success *etc*!; **die Dauer ~ ein Jahr reduzieren** to reduce the duration to one year.

2 *adv* **(a)** *(offen)* open. **Mund/Fenster ~!** open your mouth/the window. **(b)** *(hinauf)* up. **~ und ab** *or* **nieder** *(geh)* up and down. **(c)** **Helm ~!** helmets on; **ich war die halbe Nacht ~** I've been up half the night; **~ nach Chicago!** let's go to Chicago; **~ geht's!** let's go!; **~ und davon** up and away, off; **~, an die Arbeit!** come on, let's get on with it; *siehe* **aufsein.**

3 *conj (old, liter)* **~ daß** that *(old, liter).*

auf|arbeiten *vt sep* **(a)** *(erneuern)* to refurbish, to do up; *Möbel etc auch* to recondition. **(b)** *(erledigen) Korrespondenz etc* to catch up with.

Auf|arbeitung *f siehe vt* refurbishing; reconditioning; catching up.

auf|atmen *vi sep (lit, fig)* to breathe *or* heave a sigh of relief. **ein A~** a sigh of relief.

aufbacken *vt sep* to warm *or* crisp up.

aufbahren *vt sep Sarg* to lay on the bier; *Leiche* to lay out. **einen Toten feierlich ~** to put a person's body to lie in state.

Aufbau *m* **(a)** *no pl (das Aufbauen)* construction, building; *(das Wiederaufbauen)* reconstruction. **der wirtschaftliche ~** the building up of the economy. **(b)** *no pl (Struktur)* structure.

aufbauen *sep* **1** *vt* **(a)** *(errichten)* to put up; *(hinstellen) Ausstellungsstücke, Brettspiel etc* to set *or* lay out. **(b)** *(fig: gestalten) Organisation, Angriff, Spannung* to build up; *Zerstörtes* to rebuild; *Theorie* to construct. **sich** *(dat)* **eine (neue) Existenz ~** to build a new life for oneself. **(c)** *(fig: fördern) Gesundheit* to build up; *Star etc auch* to promote. **(d)** *(fig: gründen)* **etw auf etw** *(dat or acc)* **~** to base sth on sth. **(e)** *(strukturieren)* to construct; *Aufsatz, Rede auch, Komposition* to structure. **2** *vi (sich gründen)* to be based *(auf +dat or acc* on*)*. **3** *vr* **(a)** *(inf: sich postieren)* to take up position. **sich vor jdm ~** to draw oneself up to one's full height in front of sb. **(b)** *(sich bilden)* to build up. **(c)** *(sich gründen)* **sich auf etw** *(dat or acc)* **~** to be based on sth.

aufbäumen *vr sep (Tier)* to rear. **sich gegen jdn/etw ~** *(fig)* to rebel *or* revolt against sb/sth.

aufbauschen *vt sep (fig)* to blow up, to exaggerate.

aufbegehren* *vi sep (geh)* to rebel *(gegen* against*)*.

aufbekommen* *vt sep irreg (col)* **(a)** *(öffnen)* to get open. **(b)** *Aufgabe* to get as homework.

aufbereiten* *vt sep* to process; *Trinkwasser auch* to purify; *Text etc* to work up.

aufbessern *vt sep* to improve; *Gehalt etc auch* to increase.

Aufbesserung *f siehe vt* improvement; increase.

aufbewahren* *vt sep* to keep; *(in Lager)* to store; *(behalten) alte Zeitungen etc auch* to save. **kann ich hier mein Gepäck ~ lassen?** can I leave my luggage here?

Aufbewahrung *f siehe vt* keeping; storage; saving. **jdm etw zur ~ anvertrauen** to entrust sth to sb's safekeeping.

aufbieten *vt sep irreg Menschen, Mittel* to muster; *Kräfte auch* to summon (up); *Polizei* to call in.

Aufbietung *f* **unter ~ aller Kräfte ...** summoning (up) all his/her *etc* strength ...

aufbinden *vt sep irreg* **(a)** *Schuh etc* to undo, to untie. **(b) laß dir doch so etwas nicht ~** *(fig)* don't fall for that.

aufblähen *sep* **1** *vt* to blow out; *(fig)* to inflate. **2** *vr* to blow out; *(Segel auch)* to billow out; *(Med)* to become swollen; *(fig pej)* to puff oneself up.

aufblasbar *adj* inflatable.

aufblasen *vt sep irreg* to blow up; *siehe* **aufgeblasen.**

aufbleiben *vi sep irreg aux sein* **(a)** to stay up. **(b)** *(geöffnet bleiben)* to stay open.

aufblenden *vi sep (Phot)* to increase the aperture; *(Aut)* to turn the headlights on full (beam).

aufblicken *vi sep* to look up. **zu jdm/etw ~** *(lit, fig)* to look up to sb/sth.

aufblitzen *vi sep (Licht)* to flash.

aufblühen *vi sep aux sein (lit, fig)* to blossom out; *(Blume auch)* to bloom; *(Kultur etc auch)* to (begin to) flourish.

aufbocken *vt sep Auto* to jack up.

aufbrauchen *vt sep* to use up.

aufbrausen *vi sep aux sein* **(a)** *(Brandung etc)* to surge; *(fig: Beifall, Jubel)* to break out. **(b)** *(fig: Mensch)* to flare up, to fly off the handle *(col)*.

aufbrausend *adj Temperament* irascible; *Mensch auch* quick-tempered, liable to flare up.

aufbrechen *sep irreg* **1** *vt* to break *or* force open; *Tresor auch, Auto* to break into; *Boden, Oberfläche* to break up. **2** *vi aux sein* **(a)** *(sich öffnen)* to open; *(Straßenbelag etc)* to break up. **(b)** *(fig: Konflikte etc)* to break out. **(c)** *(sich auf den Weg machen)* to start *or* set out *or* off.

aufbringen *vt sep irreg* **(a)** *(beschaffen)* to find; *Geld auch* to raise; *Kraft, Mut auch* to summon up. **(b)** *(erzürnen)* to make angry. **jdn gegen jdn/etw ~** to set sb against sb/sth; *siehe* **aufgebracht. (c)** *(Naut) Schiff* to seize.

Aufbruch *m no pl (Abreise, das Losgehen)* departure. **das Zeichen zum ~ geben** to give the signal to set out *or* off.

aufbrummen *vt sep (col)* **jdm die Kosten ~** to land sb with the costs *(col)*; **eine Haftstrafe aufgebrummt bekommen** to get a sentence.

aufbügeln *vt sep* **(a)** *Kleidungsstück* to iron out. **(b)** *Flicken, Bild etc* to iron on.

aufbürden *vt sep (geh)* **jdm etw ~** *(fig)* to encumber sb with sth; **jdm die Schuld für etw ~** to put the blame for sth on sb.

aufdecken *vt sep* **(a)** *jdn* to uncover; *Bett(decke)* to turn down; *Spielkarten* to show. **(b)** *(fig) Wahrheit etc* to uncover; *Verbrechen auch* to expose; *Schwäche* to lay bare; *Geheimnis* to solve.

Aufdeckung *f siehe vt (b)* uncovering; exposure; laying bare; solving.

aufdrängen *sep irreg* **1** *vt* **jdm etw ~** to impose *or* force sth on sb. **2** *vr* to impose. **sich jdm ~** *(Mensch)* to impose oneself on sb; *(fig: Erinnerung)* to come involuntarily to sb's mind; **dieser Gedanke/Verdacht drängte sich mir auf** I couldn't help thinking/suspecting that.

aufdrehen *sep* **1** *vt* **(a)** *Wasserhahn* to turn on; *Ventil* to open; *Schraubverschluß* to unscrew; *Radio etc* to turn up. **(b)** *Haar* to put in rollers. **2** *vi (col: beschleunigen)* to open up; *siehe* **aufgedreht.**

aufdringlich *adj Benehmen, Tapete* obtrusive; *Geruch, Parfüm* powerful; *Farbe auch* loud; *Mensch* insistent, pushy *(col)*.

Aufdringlichkeit *f siehe adj* obtrusiveness; powerfulness; loudness; insistence, pushiness.

Aufdruck *m (Aufgedrucktes)* imprint.

aufdrucken *vt sep* **etw auf etw** *(acc)* **~** to print sth on sth.

aufdrücken *vt sep* **(a) etw auf etw** *(acc)* **~** to press *or (mit Stempel etc)* stamp sth on sth. **(b)** *(öffnen) Tür etc* to push open.

auf|einander *adv* **(a)** on (top of) each other *or* one another. **(b) sich ~ verlassen können** to be able to rely on each other *or* one another; **~ zufahren** to drive towards each other.

auf|einander-: ~folgen *vi sep aux sein* to follow each other; **~folgend** *adj* successive; **drei schnell ~folgende Tore** three goals in quick succession; **~prallen** *vi sep aux sein (Autos etc)* to collide; *(Truppen, Meinungen)* to clash; **~stellen** *vt sep* to put on top of each other; **~stoßen** *vi sep irreg aux sein* to bump into each other, to collide; **~treffen** *vi sep irreg aux sein (Mannschaften, Gruppen etc)* to meet; *(Meinungen)* to clash; *(Kugeln, Gegenstände etc)* to hit each other.

Aufenthalt *m* **-e (a)** stay; *(das Wohnen)* residence. **(b)** *(esp Rail)* stop; *(bei Anschluß)* wait. **wie lange haben wir ~?** how long do we stop for?

Aufenthalts-: ~erlaubnis *f* residence permit; **~ort** *m* whereabouts *sing or pl*; *(Jur)* residence; **~raum** *m* day room; *(in Betrieb)* recreation room.

auf|erlegen* *vt sep or insep (geh)* to impose *(jdm etw* sth on sb*)*.

auf|erstehen* *vi sep or insep irreg aux sein* to rise from the dead. **Christus ist auferstanden** Christ is (a)risen.

Auf|erstehung *f* resurrection.

auffädeln *vt sep* to thread *or* string (together).

auffahren *sep irreg* **1** *vi aux sein* **(a)** *(aufprallen)* **auf jdn/etw ~** to run *or* drive into sb/sth; **auf eine Sandbank ~** to run aground on a sandbank. **(b)**

(näher heranfahren) to drive up. **zu dicht** ~ to drive too close behind (the car in front). **(c)** *(auf Autobahn)* to enter. **(d)** *(aufschrecken)* to start. **aus dem Schlaf** ~ to awake with a start. **(e)** *(aufbrausen)* to flare up, to fly into a rage. **2** *vt (herbeischaffen) Truppen etc* to bring up; *(col) Speisen etc* to serve up.

Auffahrt *f* approach road; *(Autobahn~ auch)* slip road; *(bei Haus etc)* drive.

Auffahr|unfall *m* collision.

auffallen *vi sep irreg aux sein* **(a)** *(sich abheben)* to stand out; *(unangenehm ~)* to attract attention; *(sich hervortun)* to be remarkable *(durch* for*)*. **er ist schon früher als Extremist aufgefallen** he has already got a reputation for being an extremist; **angenehm/unangenehm** ~ to make a good/bad impression; **nur nicht ~!** just keep a low profile. **(b)** *(bemerkt werden)* **jdm fällt etw auf** sb notices sth, sth strikes sb; **was fällt dir an dem Satz auf?** what do you notice *or* what strikes you about this sentence?; **das muß dir doch aufgefallen sein!** surely you must have noticed (it).

auffallend *adj* conspicuous, noticeable; *Schönheit, Ähnlichkeit, Farbe, Kleider* striking. **er ist ~ intelligent** he is remarkably intelligent; **stimmt ~!** *(hum)* too true!, how right you are!

auffällig *adj* conspicuous; *Farbe, Kleidung* loud.

auffangen *vt sep irreg* **(a)** *Ball, Gesprächsfetzen* to catch; *(Telec) Nachricht* to pick up. **(b)** *(abfangen) Aufprall etc* to cushion, to absorb; *Faustschlag* to block; *(fig) Preissteigerung etc* to offset. **(c)** *(sammeln) Regenwasser etc* to collect, to catch; *(fig) Flüchtlinge etc* to assemble.

auffassen *vt sep* to interpret, to understand. **etw als etw** *(acc)* ~ to take sth as sth; **etw falsch/richtig** ~ to take sth the wrong way/in the right way.

Auffassung *f* view. **nach meiner/christlicher** ~ in my view/according to Christian belief.

Auffassungs-: ~gabe *f* intelligence, grasp; **~sache** *f (col)* question of interpretation; *(Ansichtssache)* matter of opinion.

auffegen *vt sep* to sweep up.

auffindbar *adj* **es ist nicht** ~ it can't be found.

auffinden *vt sep irreg* to find, to discover.

auffischen *vt sep* to fish up; *(col) Schiffbrüchige* to fish out.

aufflammen *vi sep aux sein (lit, fig: Feuer, Unruhen etc)* to flare up.

auffliegen *vi sep irreg aux sein* **(a)** *(hochfliegen)* to fly up. **(b)** *(fig col) (Konferenz etc)* to break up; *(Rauschgiftring etc)* to be busted *(col)*. **einen Schmugglerring/eine Konferenz ~ lassen** to bust a ring of smugglers *(col)*/to break up a meeting.

auffordern *vt sep* **(a)** to ask. **wir fordern Sie auf, ...** you are required to ... **(b)** *(bitten)* to ask, to invite; *(zum Wettkampf etc)* to challenge. **(c)** *(zum Tanz bitten)* to ask to dance.

Aufforderung *f* request; *(nachdrücklicher)* demand.

aufforsten *vt sep Gebiet* to reafforest; *Wald* to restock.

Aufforstung *f siehe vt* reafforestation; restocking.

auffressen *vt sep irreg (lit, fig)* to eat up. **er wird dich deswegen nicht gleich ~** *(col)* he's not going to eat you *(col)*.

auffrischen *sep* **1** *vt* to freshen (up); *Anstrich auch* to brighten up; *(ergänzen) Vorräte* to replenish; *(fig) Erinnerungen* to refresh; *Kenntnisse* to brush up; *persönliche Beziehungen* to renew; *Impfung* to boost. **2** *vi aux sein or haben (Wind)* to freshen. **3** *vi impers aux sein* to get fresher.

Auffrischung *f siehe vt* freshening (up); brightening up; replenishment; refreshing; brushing up; renewal; boosting.

aufführen *sep* **1** *vt* **(a)** to put on; *Drama, Oper auch* to stage, to perform. **(b)** *(auflisten)* to list; *(nennen) Zeugen* to cite; *Beispiel* to give. **einzeln ~** to itemize. **2** *vr* to behave.

Aufführung *f* performance.

auffüllen *vt sep* **(a)** *(vollständig füllen)* to fill up; *(nachfüllen)* to top up. **(b)** *(ergänzen) Flüssigkeit* to dilute; *Vorräte* to replenish; *Öl* to top up.

Aufgabe *f* **(a)** *(Arbeit, Pflicht)* job, task. **es ist nicht ~ der Regierung, ...** it is not the job *or* task of the government to ...; **sich** *(dat)* **etw zur ~ machen** to make sth one's job *or* business. **(b)** *(Zweck, Funktion)* purpose, job. **(c)** *(esp Sch) (Problem)* question; *(Math auch)* problem; *(zur Übung)* exercise; *(usu pl: Haus~)* homework *no pl*. **(d)** *(von Koffer, Postsendung)* handing in. **(e)** *(Verzicht auf weiteren Kampf etc) (Sport)* retirement; *(Mil etc)* surrender. **die Polizei forderte die Geiselnehmer zur ~ auf** the police appealed to the kidnappers to give themselves up *or* to surrender. **(f)** *(von Gewohnheit, Geschäft)* giving up; *(von Plänen, Forderungen auch)* dropping; *(von Hoffnung, Studium)* abandoning.

aufgabeln *vt sep (fig col) jdn* to pick up *(col)*; *Sache* to get hold of.

Aufgabenbereich *m* area of responsibility.

Aufgang *m* **(a)** *(von Sonne, Mond)* rising; *(von Stern auch)* ascent. **(b)** *(Treppen~)* staircase.

aufgeben *sep irreg* **1** *vt* **(a)** *Hausaufgaben* to give; *Problem* to pose *(jdm* for sb*)*. **jdm viel/nichts ~** *(Sch)* to give sb a lot of/no homework. **(b)** *Koffer, Gepäck* to hand in; *Brief* to post *(esp Brit)*, to mail; *Anzeige, Bestellung* to place. **(c)** *Kampf, Hoffnung, Arbeitsstelle, Patienten etc* to give up. **gib's auf!** why don't you give up? **2** *vi (sich geschlagen geben)* to give up *or* in.

aufgeblasen *adj (fig)* puffed up, self-important.

Aufgebot *nt* **(a)** *(zur Eheschließung)* **das ~ bestellen** to give notice of one's intended marriage; *(Eccl)* to put up the banns. **(b)** *(Ansammlung) (von Menschen)* contingent; *(von Material etc)* array.

aufgebracht *adj* outraged, incensed.

aufgedonnert *adj (pej col)* tarted up *(pej col)*.

aufgedreht *adj (col)* in high spirits.

aufgedunsen *adj* swollen, bloated; *Gesicht auch* puffy.

aufgehen *vi sep irreg aux sein* **(a)** *(Sonne, Mond, Sterne)* to come up, to rise. **(b)** *(sich öffnen)* to open; *(Theat: Vorhang)* to go up; *(Knopf, Knoten etc)* to come undone. **(c)** *(aufkeimen)* to come up. **(d)** *(Cook)* to rise. **(e)** *(klarwerden)* **jdm geht etw auf** sb realizes sth, sth dawns on sb. **(f)** *(Math, fig)* to work out. **20 durch 6 geht nicht auf** 20 divided by 6 doesn't go. **(g) in etw** *(dat)* ~ *(fig)* to be wrapped up in sth, to be taken up with sth; **in Flammen** ~ to go up in flames.

aufgehoben *adj*: **(bei jdm) gut/schlecht ~ sein** to be/not to be safe (with sb).

aufgekratzt *adj (col)* in high spirits, full of beans *(col)*.

aufgelegt *adj* **gut/schlecht** ~ in a good/bad mood.

aufgelöst *adj* **(a)** *(außer sich)* beside oneself *(vor +dat* with*)*, distraught; *(bestürzt)* upset. **in Tränen** ~ in tears. **(b)** *(erschöpft)* exhausted.

aufgeräumt *adj (geh: gutgelaunt)* light-hearted.

aufgeregt *adj (erregt)* excited; *(nervös)* nervous; *(durcheinander)* flustered.

Aufgeregtheit *f no pl siehe adj* excitement; nervousness; flustered state.

aufgeschlossen *adj (nicht engstirnig)* open-minded *(für, gegenüber* about, as regards*)*; *(empfänglich)* receptive, open *(für, gegenüber* to*)*.

Aufgeschlossenheit *f no pl siehe adj* open-mindedness; receptiveness, openness.

aufgeschmissen *adj pred (col)* in a fix, stuck.

aufgeschwemmt *adj* bloated, swollen.

aufgetakelt *adj (pej)* dressed up to the nines *(col)*.

aufgeweckt *adj* bright, quick, sharp.

aufgewühlt *adj (geh)* agitated, in a turmoil *pred*;

Gefühle auch, Meer turbulent.
aufgießen *vt sep irreg* **(a) etw (auf etw** *acc*) ~ to pour sth on (sth). **(b)** *Kaffee, Tee* to make.
aufgliedern *sep* **1** *vt (in+acc* into) to split up, to (sub)divide; *(in Kategorien auch)* to break down. **2** *vr (in+acc* into) to (sub)divide, to break down.
aufgreifen *vt sep irreg* **(a)** *(festnehmen)* to pick up, to apprehend. **(b)** *Thema* to take up.
aufgrund *prep+gen*, **auf Grund** *siehe* **Grund.**
Aufguß *m* brew, infusion; *(fig pej)* rehash.
Aufgußbeutel *m* sachet (containing coffee/herbs etc) for brewing; *(Teebeutel)* tea bag.
aufhaben *sep irreg* **1** *vt* **(a)** *Hut, Brille* to have on. **(b)** *Tür, Augen* to have open. **(c)** *(Sch: als Hausaufgabe)* **ich habe heute viel auf** I've got a lot of homework today. **2** *vi (Laden etc)* to be open.
aufhalsen *vt sep (col)* **jdm/sich etw** ~ to saddle *or* land sb/oneself with sth *(col)*.
aufhalten *sep irreg* **1** *vt* **(a)** *Fahrzeug, Entwicklung* to stop, to halt; *(verlangsamen)* to hold up, to delay; *(abhalten, stören) (bei* from) to hold back, to keep back. **ich will dich nicht länger** ~ I don't want to keep *or* hold you back any longer. **(b)** *(col: offenhalten)* to keep open. **die Hand** ~ to hold one's hand out. **2** *vr* **(a)** *(an einem Ort bleiben)* to stay. **(b)** *(sich befassen)* **sich bei etw** ~ to dwell on sth.
aufhängen *sep* **1** *vt* **(a)** to hang up; *(Aut) Rad* to suspend. **(b)** *(töten)* to hang *(an+dat* from). **2** *vr (sich töten)* to hang oneself *(an +dat* from).
Aufhänger *m* tag, loop. **ein** ~ **(für etw)** *(fig col)* a peg to hang sth on.
Aufhängung *f (Tech)* suspension.
aufhäufen *vtr sep* to pile up, to accumulate.
aufheben *sep irreg* **1** *vt* **(a)** *(vom Boden)* to pick up; *größeren Gegenstand auch* to lift up. **(b)** *(nicht wegwerfen)* to keep. **jdm etw** ~ to keep sth for sb; *siehe* **aufgehoben. (c)** *(ungültig machen)* to abolish, to do away with; *Urteil* to reverse, to quash. **(d)** *(beenden) Blockade, Belagerung* to raise, to lift; *Beschränkung* to remove, to lift. **(e)** *(ausgleichen)* to offset, to make up for; *Schwerkraft* to neutralize, to cancel out. **2** *vr (sich ausgleichen)* to cancel each other out *(auch Math)*, to offset each other.
Aufheben *nt no pl* fuss. **viel ~(s) (von etw) machen** to make a lot of fuss (about *or* over sth).
Aufhebung *f* **(a)** *siehe vt (c)* abolition; reversal, quashing. **(b)** *siehe vt (d)* raising, lifting; removal, lifting.
aufheitern *sep* **1** *vt jdn* to cheer up; *Rede, Leben* to brighten up *(jdm* for sb). **2** *vr (Himmel, Wetter)* to clear up, to brighten up.
Aufheiterung *f (Met)* brighter period.
aufheizen *sep* **1** *vt* to heat (up). **die Stimmung** ~ to stir up feelings. **2** *vr* to heat up; *(fig)* to hot up *(col)*, to intensify.
aufhelfen *vi sep irreg (lit: beim Aufstehen)* to help up *(jdm* sb).
aufhellen *sep* **1** *vt* to brighten (up); *Haare* to lighten; *(fig: klären)* to throw *or* shed light upon. **2** *vr (Himmel, Wetter, fig: Miene)* to brighten (up).
aufhetzen *vt sep* to stir up, to incite. **jdn gegen jdn/etw** ~ to stir up sb *or* incite sb against sb/sth; **jdn zu etw** ~ to incite sb to (do) sth.
Aufhetzung *f* incitement, agitation.
aufheulen *vi sep* to howl *(vor* with); *(Sirene)* to (start to) wail; *(Motor)* to (give a) roar.
aufholen *sep* **1** *vt Zeit, Vorsprung* to make up; *Lernstoff* to catch up on. **2** *vi (Mannschaft, Schüler, Arbeiter)* to catch up.
aufhorchen *vi sep* to prick up one's ears, to sit up (and take notice).
aufhören *vi sep* to stop; *(bei Firma)* to finish; *(Musik, Lärm auch, Freundschaft)* to (come to an) end. **hör doch endlich auf!** (will you) stop it!; **mit etw** ~ to stop sth; **da hört sich doch alles auf!** *(col)* that's the (absolute) limit!
aufjagen *vt sep* to disturb.
aufjauchzen *vi sep* **vor Freude** ~ to give a shout of joy.
aufkaufen *vt sep* to buy up.
Aufkäufer *m* buyer.
aufkeimen *vi sep aux sein* to germinate, to sprout; *(fig) (Hoffnung, Liebe)* to burgeon *(liter)*, to form; *(Zweifel)* to (begin to) take root.
aufklappbar *adj Verdeck* fold-back.
aufklappen *vt sep* to open up; *Klappe* to let down; *Verdeck* to fold back; *Messer* to unclasp; *Fenster, Buch* to open; *(hochschlagen) Kragen* to turn up.
aufklaren *vi sep (Met)* to clear (up).
aufklären *sep* **1** *vt* **(a)** *Mißverständnis, Irrtum* to clear up; *Verbrechen* to solve; *Ereignis, Vorgang* to throw light upon. **(b)** *jdn* to enlighten. **Kinder** ~ *(sexuell)* to tell children the facts of life; *(in der Schule)* to give children sex education; **jdn über etw** *(acc)* ~ to inform sb about sth. **2** *vr (Irrtum, Geheimnis)* to be cleared up; *(Himmel)* to clear up; *(fig: Gesicht)* to brighten (up).
Aufklärung *f* **(a)** *(Philos)* **die** ~ the Enlightenment. **(b)** *siehe vt (a)* clearing up; solution; *(von Vorgang)* elucidation. **(c)** *(Information)* enlightenment. **(d) (sexuelle)** ~ *(in Schulen)* sex education. **die** ~ **von Kindern** explaining the facts of life to children. **(e)** *(Mil)* reconnaissance.
Aufklärungs-: **~arbeit** *f* educational work; **~film** *m* sex education film; **~flugzeug** *nt* reconnaissance plane; **~kampagne** *f* information campaign; **~schiff** *nt (Mil)* reconnaissance ship.
aufkleben *vt sep (auf+acc* to) to stick on; *(mit Leim, Klebstoff auch)* to glue on.
Aufkleber *m* sticker.
aufknacken *vt sep Nüsse etc, (col) Tresor* to crack; *Auto* to break into.
aufknöpfen *vt sep (öffnen)* to unbutton, to undo.
aufknoten *vt sep* to untie, to undo.
aufknüpfen *vt sep* **(a)** to hang *(an+dat* from), to string up *(col) (an+dat* on). **(b)** *(aufknoten)* to untie, to undo.
aufkochen *vt sep* to bring to the boil.
aufkommen *vi sep irreg aux sein* **(a)** *(lit, fig: entstehen)* to arise; *(Nebel)* to come down; *(Wind)* to spring *or* get up; *(auftreten: Mode etc auch)* to appear (on the scene). **etw** ~ **lassen** *(fig) Zweifel, Kritik* to give rise to sth; **endlich kam Stimmung auf** at last things livened up. **(b)** ~ **für** *(Kosten tragen)* to bear the costs of, to pay for; *(Haftung tragen)* to be liable for. **für die Kinder** ~ *(finanziell)* to pay for the children's upkeep; **für die Kosten** ~ to bear the costs; **für den Schaden** ~ to pay for the damage.
Aufkommen *nt* **(a)** *no pl (das Auftreten)* appearance; *(von Methode, Mode etc auch)* advent, emergence. **(b)** *(Fin) (Summe, Menge)* amount; *(von Steuern)* revenue *(aus* from).
aufkreischen *vi sep (Mensch)* to scream, to shriek; *(Bremsen, Maschine)* to screech.
aufkrempeln *vi sep* **(sich) die Ärmel/Hose** ~ to roll up one's sleeves/trousers.
aufkreuzen *vi sep aux sein (col: erscheinen)* to turn *or* show up.
aufkriegen *vt sep (col) siehe* **aufbekommen.**
aufkündigen *vt sep Vertrag etc* to terminate.
auflachen *vi sep* to (give a) laugh.
aufladen *sep irreg* **1** *vt* **(a) etw (auf etw** *acc*) ~ to load sth on(to) sth. **jdm/sich etw** ~ *(fig)* to saddle sb/oneself with sth. **(b)** *(elektrisch)* to charge; *(neu* ~*)* to recharge. **emotional aufgeladen** *(fig)* emotionally charged. **2** *vr (Batterie etc)* to be charged; *(neu)* to be recharged.
Auflage *f* **(a)** *(Ausgabe)* edition; *(Druck)* impression; *(~höhe)* number of copies; *(von Zeitung)* circulation. **(b)** *(Bedingung)* condition. **jdm etw zur** ~ **machen** to impose sth on sb as a condition; **jdm zur** ~ **machen, etw zu tun** to make it a

condition for sb to do sth; **die ~ haben, etw zu tun** to be obliged to do sth. **(c)** *(Überzug)* plating *no pl*, coating.

Auflage(n)-: **~höhe** *f (von Buch)* number of copies published; *(von Zeitung)* circulation; **~ziffer** *f* circulation (figures *pl*); *(von Buch)* number of copies published.

auflassen *vt sep irreg (col) (offenlassen)* to leave open; *(aufbehalten) Hut* to keep *or* leave on. **die Kinder länger ~** to let the children stay up (longer).

auflauern *vi sep+dat* to lie in wait for.

Auflauf *m* **(a)** *(Menschen~)* crowd. **(b)** *(Cook)* (baked) pudding *(sweet or savoury)*.

auflaufen *vi sep irreg aux sein* **(a)** *(auf Grund laufen: Schiff)* to run aground *(auf +acc or dat* on*)*. **(b)** *(aufprallen)* **auf jdn/etw ~** to run into sb/sth, to collide with sb/sth; **jdn ~ lassen** *(Ftbl)* to bodycheck sb.

Auflaufform *f (Cook)* ovenproof dish.

aufleben *vi sep aux sein* to revive; *(munter, lebendig werden)* to liven up, to come to life again; *(neuen Lebensmut bekommen)* to find a new lease of life. **Erinnerungen wieder ~ lassen** to revive memories.

auflecken *vt sep* to lick up.

auflegen *sep* **1** *vt* **(a)** to put on; *Gedeck* to lay; *Hörer* to put down, to replace. **(b)** *(herausgeben) Buch* to publish, to print. **ein Buch neu ~** to reprint a book; *(neu bearbeitet)* to bring out a new edition of a book. **2** *vi (Telec)* to hang up.

auflehnen *vr sep* **sich gegen jdn/etw ~** to revolt *or* rebel against sb/sth.

Auflehnung *f* revolt, rebellion.

auflesen *vt sep irreg (lit, fig col)* to pick up. **jdn/etw von der Straße ~** to pick sb/sth up off the street.

aufleuchten *vi sep aux sein or haben (lit, fig)* to light up.

auflisten *vt sep* to list.

Auflistung *f* listing; *(Liste auch)* list.

auflockern *sep* **1** *vt* **(a)** *Boden* to break up, to loosen (up). **(b)** *Unterricht, Stoff, Vortrag* to make less monotonous, to give relief to *(durch* with*)*. **(c)** *(entspannen)* to make relaxed; *Atmosphäre auch* to ease. **in aufgelockerter Stimmung** in a relaxed mood. **2** *vr* **(a)** *(Sport)* to limber *or* loosen up. **(b)** *(Bewölkung)* to break up.

Auflockerung *f* **(a)** *(von Boden)* breaking up, loosening (up). **ihm gelang die ~ einer gespannten Atmosphäre** he succeeded in easing a tense atmosphere. **(b)** *(von Bewölkung)* breaking up.

auflodern *vi sep aux sein (Flammen, fig)* to flare up; *(lodernd brennen)* to blaze.

auflösen *sep* **1** *vt* **(a)** *(in Flüssigkeit)* to dissolve; *(in Bestandteile zerlegen)* to break down *(in+acc* into*)*; *(Math) Gleichung* to (re)solve; *siehe* **aufgelöst**. **(b)** *(aufklären) Widerspruch etc* to clear up, to resolve; *Rätsel* to solve. **(c)** *(zerstreuen) Wolken, Versammlung* to disperse, to break up. **(d)** *(aufheben)* to dissolve *(auch Parl)*; *Einheit, Gruppe* to disband; *Verlobung* to break off; *Vertrag* to cancel; *Konto* to close; *Haushalt* to break up. **2** *vr* **(a)** *(in Flüssigkeit)* to dissolve; *(Zweifel, Probleme)* to disappear. **(b)** *(sich zerstreuen)* to disperse; *(Wolken auch)* to break up; *(Nebel auch)* to lift. **(c)** *(auseinandergehen) (Verband)* to disband; *(formell: esp Parl)* to dissolve.

Auflösung *f siehe vt* **(a)** dissolving; breaking down; (re)solving. **(b)** clearing up, resolving; solving; *(fertige Lösung: von Rätsel etc)* solution. **(c)** dispersal. **(d)** dissolving; disbanding; breaking off; cancellation; closing; breaking up; *(von Parlament)* dissolution. **(e)** *(von Bildschirm)* resolution.

aufmachen *sep* **1** *vt* **(a)** *(öffnen)* to open; *(lösen, aufknöpfen etc)* to undo. **(b)** *(eröffnen, gründen) Geschäft, Unternehmen* to open (up). **(c)** *(gestalten) Buch, Zeitung* to make up; *(in Presse) Ereignis, Prozeß etc* to feature. **2** *vi (Tür öffnen)* to open the door; *(Geschäft (er)öffnen)* to open (up). **3** *vr* **(a)** *(sich zurechtmachen)* to get oneself up. **(b)** *(sich anschicken)* to get ready, to make preparations; *(aufbrechen)* to set out.

Aufmacher *m (Press)* lead.

Aufmachung *f* **(a)** *(Kleidung)* turn-out. **in großer ~ erscheinen** to turn up dressed up to the nines. **(b)** *(Gestaltung)* presentation, style; *(von Buch)* presentation, make-up; *(Press etc)* layout.

aufmalen *vt sep* to paint on *(auf etw (acc)* sth*)*.

Aufmarsch *m (Mil)* marching; *(Parade)* marchpast; *(in Stellung, Kampflinie)* deployment.

aufmarschieren* *vi sep aux sein (heranmarschieren)* to march up; *(Mil: in Stellung gehen)* to deploy; *(vorbeimarschieren)* to march past.

aufmerksam *adj* **(a)** *Zuhörer, Beobachter, Schüler* attentive; *Blicke auch, Augen* keen; *(scharf beobachtend)* observant. **jdn auf etw** *(acc)* **~ machen** to draw sb's attention to sth; **auf etw** *(acc)* **~ werden** to become aware of sth. **(b)** *(zuvorkommend)* attentive. **(das ist) sehr ~ von Ihnen** (that's) most kind of you.

Aufmerksamkeit *f* **(a)** *no pl* attention, attentiveness. **das ist meiner ~ entgangen** it escaped my attention. **(b)** *no pl (Zuvorkommenheit)* attentiveness. **(c)** *(Geschenk)* token (gift).

aufmöbeln *vt sep (col) Gegenstand* to do up *(col)*; *jdn (beleben)* to buck up *(col)*, to pep up *(col)*.

aufmucken *vt sep (col)* to protest *(gegen* at, against*)*.

aufmuntern *vt sep (aufheitern)* to cheer up; *(beleben)* to liven up.

Aufmunterung *f siehe vt* cheering up; livening up.

aufmüpfig *adj (col)* rebellious.

aufnähen *vt sep* to sew on *(auf +acc* to*)*.

Aufnahme *f* **-n** **(a)** *(Empfang, fig: Reaktion)* reception. **bei jdm freundliche ~ finden** *(lit, fig)* to meet with a warm reception from sb; **die ~ in ein Krankenhaus** admission (in)to hospital; **wie war die ~ beim Publikum?** how did the audience receive it *or* react? **(b)** *(in Verein)* admission *(in +acc* to*)*. **(c)** *no pl (lit, fig: Absorption)* absorption. **(d)** *no pl (von Kapital etc)* raising. **(e)** *no pl (Beginn: von Gespräch etc)* start, commencement. **(f)** *(Foto)* photo(graph); shot *(col)*; *(Film~)* take. **(g)** *(auf Tonband etc)* recording.

Aufnahme-: **~antrag** *m* application for membership *or* admission; **a~bereit** *adj Kamera* ready to shoot; *(fig)* receptive, open *(für* to*)*; **~bereitschaft** *f (fig)* receptiveness; **a~fähig** *adj* **für etw a~fähig sein** to be able to take sth in; **~gebühr** *f* enrolment fee; *(in Verein)* admission fee; **~leiter** *m (Film)* production manager; *(Rad, TV)* producer; **~prüfung** *f* entrance examination; **~studio** *nt* (film/recording) studio.

aufnehmen *vt sep irreg* **(a)** *(vom Boden)* to pick up. **(b)** *(lit: empfangen, fig: reagieren auf)* to receive. **(c)** *(unterbringen)* to take (in); *(fassen)* to take, to hold; *Einwanderer* to absorb. **(d)** *(in Verein)* to admit *(in+acc* to*)*; *(Schule auch)* to take on. **(e)** *(absorbieren)* to absorb, to take up; *(fig: eindringen lassen) Eindrücke* to take in; *(begreifen auch)* to grasp. **(f)** *(mit einbeziehen)* to include, to incorporate; *(aufgreifen) Thema* to take up. **(g)** *(esp Ftbl) Ball* to take, to receive. **(h)** *(beginnen) Beziehung* to establish; *Tätigkeit, Studium* to begin, to take up. **den Kampf ~** to commence battle; *(fig auch)* to take up the struggle. **(i)** *Hypothek etc* to raise; *Kredit auch* to get. **(j)** *(niederschreiben) Protokoll, Diktat* to take down; *Personalien* to take (down); *Telegramm* to take. **(k)** *(fotografieren)* to take (a photograph of), to photograph; *(filmen)* to film, to shoot *(col)*. **(l)** *(auf Tonband)* to record, to tape. **(m)** *(beim Stricken) Maschen* to increase, to make. **(n) es mit jdm/etw**

~ **können** to be a match for sb/sth.
aufnötigen *vt sep* **jdm etw ~** to force sth on sb.
auf|oktroyieren* *vt sep* **jdm etw ~** *(geh)* to impose *or* force sth on sb.
auf|opfern *vr sep* to sacrifice oneself.
auf|opfernd *adj* self-sacrificing.
Auf|opferung *f* **(a)** *(Aufgabe)* sacrifice. **(b)** *(Selbst~)* self-sacrifice.
aufpassen *vi sep* **(a)** *(beaufsichtigen)* **auf jdn/etw ~** to keep an eye on sb/sth. **(b)** *(aufmerksam sein, achtgeben)* to pay attention. **paß auf!, aufgepaßt!** look, watch; *(sei aufmerksam)* pay attention; *(Vorsicht)* look out, watch out, mind (out).
Aufpasser(in *f)* *m* - *(pej: Aufseher, Spitzel)* spy *(pej)*, watchdog *(col)*; *(Beobachter)* supervisor; *(Wächter)* guard.
aufpeitschen *vt sep Meer, Wellen* to whip up; *(fig) Sinne* to inflame, to fire; *Menschen* to work up; *(stärker)* to whip up into a frenzy.
aufpflanzen *sep* **1** *vt (Mil) Bajonett* to fix. **2** *vr* **sich vor jdm ~** to plant oneself in front of sb.
aufpicken *vt sep (Vogel)* to peck up.
aufplatzen *vi sep aux sein* to burst open.
aufplustern *sep* **1** *vt Federn* to ruffle up. **2** *vr (Vogel)* to ruffle (up) its feathers; *(Mensch)* to puff oneself up.
aufpolieren* *vt sep (lit, fig)* to polish up.
aufprägen *vt sep* **jdm/einer Sache seinen Stempel ~** *(fig)* to leave one's mark on sb/sth.
Aufprall *m* **-e** impact.
aufprallen *vi sep aux sein* **auf etw** *(acc)* **~** to strike *or* hit sth; *(Fahrzeug auch)* to collide with sth.
Aufpreis *m* extra *or* additional charge. **gegen ~** for an extra *or* additional charge.
aufpumpen *vt sep* to pump up, to inflate; *Fahrrad* to pump up the tyres *(Brit) or* tires *(US)* of.
aufputschen *sep* **1** *vt* **(a)** *(aufwiegeln)* to rouse; *Gefühle, öffentliche Meinung* to stir up. **(b)** *(durch Reizmittel)* to stimulate. **~de Mittel** stimulants. **2** *vr* to pep oneself up *(col)*, to dope oneself *(Sport col)*.
Aufputschmittel *nt* stimulant.
aufquellen *vi sep irreg aux sein (anschwellen)* to swell (up). **aufgequollen** swollen; **etw ~ lassen** to soak sth (to allow it to swell up).
aufraffen *sep* **1** *vr* to force oneself to do sth. **sich zu einer Entscheidung ~** to force oneself to make a decision. **2** *vt Papiere, Eigentum* to gather up; *(schnell aufheben)* to snatch up.
aufragen *vi sep aux sein or haben (in die Höhe ~)* to rise; *(sehr hoch, groß auch)* to tower (up) *(über +dat* above, over*)*. **die hoch ~den Türme** the soaring towers.
aufrappeln *vr sep (col)* **(a)** *siehe* **aufraffen 1. (b)** *(wieder zu Kräften kommen)* to recover, to get over it.
aufrauchen *vt sep (zu Ende rauchen)* to finish (smoking).
aufrauhen *vt sep* to roughen; *(Tex) Stoff* to nap.
aufräumen *sep* **1** *vt* to tidy *or* clear up; *(wegräumen auch)* to clear *or* put away. **2** *vi* **mit etw ~** to do away with sth; *siehe* **aufgeräumt.**
Aufräumungs|arbeiten *pl* clearing-up operations *pl*.
aufrechnen *vt sep* **etw gegen etw ~** to offset sth against sth.
aufrecht *adj (lit, fig)* upright; *Körperhaltung, Gangart auch* erect.
aufrecht|erhalten* *vt sep irreg* to maintain; *Kontakt, Bräuche auch* to keep up; *Behauptung auch* to stick to; *(moralisch) jdn* to keep going.
Aufrecht|erhaltung *f siehe vt* maintenance, maintaining; keeping up; sticking *(gen* to*)*.
aufregen *sep* **1** *vt (ärgerlich machen)* to irritate, to annoy; *(nervös machen)* to make nervous; *(beunruhigen)* to agitate; *(bestürzen)* to upset; *(erregen)* to excite. **du regst mich auf!** you're getting on my nerves. **2** *vr* to get worked up *(col)* or excited *(über+acc* about*)*; *siehe* **aufgeregt.**
aufregend *adj* exciting.
Aufregung *f* excitement *no pl*; *(Beunruhigung)* agitation *no pl*. **nur keine ~!** don't get excited, don't get worked up *(col)*; **jdn in ~ versetzen** to get sb in a state *(col)*.
aufreiben *vt sep irreg* **(a)** *Haut etc* to chafe, to rub sore. **(b)** *(fig: zermürben)* to wear down. **(c)** *(Mil: völlig vernichten)* to wipe out, to annihilate.
aufreibend *adj (fig)* wearing, trying; *(stärker)* stressful.
aufreihen *sep* **1** *vt (in Linie)* to line up; *Perlen* to string. **2** *vr* to line up.
aufreißen* *sep irreg* **1** *vt* **(a)** *(aufbrechen)* to tear *or* rip open; *Straße* to tear *or* rip up. **(b)** *Tür, Fenster* to fling open; *Augen, Mund* to open wide. **(c)** *(col) Mädchen* to pick up *(col)*. **2** *vi aux sein (Naht)* to split, to burst; *(Hose)* to tear, to rip; *(Wunde)* to tear open; *(Wolkendecke)* to break up.
aufreizen *vt sep (herausfordern)* to provoke; *(aufwiegeln)* to incite.
aufreizend *adj* provocative.
aufrichten *sep* **1** *vt* **(a)** *Gegenstand* to put upright; *jdn* to help up; *Oberkörper* to straighten (up). **(b)** *(fig: moralisch)* to put new heart into. **2** *vr (gerade stehen)* to stand up (straight); *(gerade sitzen)* to sit up (straight); *(aus gebückter Haltung)* to straighten up. **sich im Bett ~** to sit up in bed.
aufrichtig *adj* sincere *(zu, gegen* towards*)*; *(ehrlich auch)* honest.
Aufrichtigkeit *f siehe adj* sincerity; honesty.
aufrollen *vt sep* **(a)** *(zusammenrollen)* to roll up; *Kabel* to coil *or* wind up. **(b)** *(entrollen)* to unroll; *Fahne* to unfurl; *Kabel* to uncoil, to unwind. **(c)** *(fig) Problem* to go into. **einen Fall/Prozeß wieder ~** to reopen a case/trial.
aufrücken *vi sep aux sein (lit, fig)* to move up. **zum Geschäftsleiter ~** to be promoted to manager.
Aufruf *m* **(a)** appeal *(an +acc* to*)*. **(b)** *(von Namen)* **nach ~** when called.
aufrufen *sep irreg* **1** *vt* **(a)** *Namen* to call. **Sie werden aufgerufen** your name *or* you will be called; **einen Schüler ~** to ask a pupil (to answer) a question. **(b) jdn zu etw ~** *(zu Mithilfe, Unterstützung etc)* to appeal to *or* call upon sb for sth. **(c)** *(Jur) Zeugen* to summon. **(d)** *(Comp)* to call up. **2** *vi* **zum Streik** *etc* **~** to call for a strike *etc*.
Aufruhr *m* **-e (a)** *(Auflehnung)* revolt, rebellion, uprising. **(b)** *(Bewegtheit, fig: Erregung)* tumult, turmoil. **in ~ sein** to be in a turmoil; **jdn in ~ versetzen** to throw sb into a turmoil.
aufrühren *vt sep (lit, fig)* to stir up.
Aufrührer(in *f)* *m* - rabble-rouser.
aufrührerisch *adj* **(a)** *Rede, Pamphlet* rabble-rousing, inflammatory. **(b)** *attr (in Aufruhr)* rebellious; *(meuternd)* mutinous.
aufrunden *vt sep Zahl* to round up *(auf +acc* to*)*.
aufrüsten *vti sep* to arm.
Aufrüstung *f* armament. **atomare ~** nuclear armament.
aufrütteln *vt sep* to rouse *(aus* from*)*. **jdn/jds Gewissen ~** to stir sb/sb's conscience.
aufs = auf das.
aufsagen *vt sep Gedicht etc* to recite, to say.
aufsammeln *vt sep (lit, fig)* to pick up.
aufsässig *adj* rebellious.
Aufsässigkeit *f* rebelliousness.
Aufsatz *m* **(a)** *(Abhandlung)* essay; *(Schul~ auch)* composition. **(b)** *(oberer Teil)* top *or* upper part.
aufsaugen *vt sep irreg Flüssigkeit* to soak up; *(fig)* to absorb. **etw mit dem Staubsauger ~** to vacuum sth up.
aufscheuchen *vt sep* to startle.
aufscheuern *vt sep* to rub sore, to chafe.
aufschichten *vt sep* to stack, to pile up; *Stapel* to build up.
aufschieben *vt sep irreg Fenster, Tür* to slide open;

Riegel to push *or* slide back; *(fig: verschieben)* to put off, to postpone. **aufgeschoben ist nicht aufgehoben** *(prov)* putting something off does not mean it's cancelled.

Aufschlag *m* **(a)** *(das Aufschlagen)* impact. **(b)** *(Tennis etc)* service, serve. **sie hat** ~ it's her service *or* serve. **(c)** *(Preis~)* surcharge, extra charge. **(d)** *(Ärmel~)* cuff; *(Hosen~)* turn-up *(Brit)*, cuff *(US)*; *(Mantel~ etc)* lapel.

aufschlagen *sep irreg* **1** *vi* **(a)** *aux sein (auftreffen)* **auf etw** *(dat)* ~ to hit sth; **mit dem Kopf** *etc* **auf etw** *(acc or dat)* ~ to hit one's head *etc* on sth. **(b)** *aux haben or sein (Waren, Preise)* to rise, to go up *(um* by*)*. **(c)** *(Tennis etc)* to serve. **2** *vt* **(a)** *(durch Schlagen öffnen)* to crack. **jdm/sich den Kopf** ~ to crack sb's/one's head open. **(b)** *(aufklappen)* to open. **schlagt Seite 111 auf** open your books at page 111. **(c)** *Augen* to open. **(d)** *(aufbauen) Bett, Liegestuhl* to put up; *Zelt auch* to pitch; *Lager* to set up, to pitch. **(e)** *(Comm) Preise* to put up.

aufschließen *sep irreg* **1** *vt (öffnen)* to unlock. **jdm die Tür** *etc* ~ to unlock the door *etc* for sb; *siehe* **aufgeschlossen. 2** *vi* **(a)** *(öffnen)* **(jdm)** ~ to unlock the door (for sb). **(b)** *(heranrücken)* to close up; *(Sport)* to catch up *(zu* with*)*.

aufschlitzen *vt sep* to rip open; *(mit Messer auch)* to slit open.

Aufschluß *m* · *(Aufklärung)* information *no pl*. **(jdm)** ~ **über etw** *(acc)* **geben** to give (sb) information about sth.

aufschlüsseln *vt sep* to break down *(nach* into*)*; *(klassifizieren)* to classify *(nach* according to*)*.

aufschlußreich *adj* informative, instructive.

aufschnappen *vt sep* to catch; *(col) Wort etc* to pick up.

aufschneiden *sep irreg* **1** *vt* **(a)** to cut open; *Braten* to carve. **(b)** *(in Scheiben schneiden)* to slice. **2** *vi (col: prahlen)* to brag, to boast.

Aufschneider *m (col)* boaster, show-off *(col)*.

Aufschnitt *m no pl* (assorted) sliced cold meats, cold cuts.

aufschnüren *vt sep (lösen)* to untie, to undo; *Schuh auch* to unlace.

aufschrauben *vt sep Schraube etc* to unscrew; *Flasche etc* to take the top off.

aufschrecken *sep* **1** *vt* to startle; *(aus Gleichgültigkeit)* to jolt *(aus* out of*)*. **2** *vi aux sein* to start (up), to be startled. **aus dem Schlaf** ~ to wake up with a start.

Aufschrei *m* yell; *(schrill)* scream, shriek. **ein** ~ **der Empörung** *(fig)* an outcry.

aufschreiben *vt sep irreg* **(a)** *(niederschreiben)* **etw** ~ to write *or* note sth down. **(b)** *(notieren)* **sich** *(dat)* **etw** ~ to make a note of sth.

aufschreien *vi sep irreg* to yell out; *(schrill)* to scream *or* shriek out.

Aufschrift *f* inscription; *(Etikett)* label.

Aufschub *m (Verzögerung)* delay; *(Vertagung)* postponement. **die Sache duldet keinen** ~ *(geh)* the matter must not be delayed; **jdm** ~ **gewähren** to grant sb an extension.

aufschürfen *vt sep* **sich** *(dat)* **die Haut/das Knie** ~ to graze *or* scrape oneself/one's knee.

aufschütteln *vt sep Kissen* to shake *or* plump up.

aufschütten *vt sep* **(a)** *Flüssigkeit* to pour on. **Kaffee** ~ to make coffee. **(b)** *Kohle* to put on (the fire). **(c)** *Damm, Deich* to throw up.

aufschwatzen *vt sep (col)* **jdm etw** ~ to talk sb into taking sth.

aufschwingen *vr sep irreg* to swing oneself up; *(Vogel)* to soar (up). **sich zu etw** ~ *(sich aufraffen)* to bring oneself to do sth.

Aufschwung *m* **(a)** *(Antrieb)* lift; *(der Wirtschaft etc)* upturn, upswing *(gen* in*)*. **durch diese Erfindung hat die Firma einen** ~ **genommen** this invention gave the firm a boost. **(b)** *(Turnen)* swing-up.

aufsehen *vi sep irreg* = **aufblicken.**

Aufsehen *nt no pl* sensation. **großes** ~ **erregen** to cause a sensation *or* stir; **ich möchte jedes** ~ **vermeiden** I want to avoid any fuss.

aufsehen|erregend *adj* sensational.

Aufseher(in *f***)** *m (allgemein)* supervisor; *(Gefängnis~)* warder *(Brit)*, guard *(US)*; *(Park~, Museums~ etc)* attendant.

aufsein *vi sep irreg aux sein* **(a)** *(aufgestanden sein)* to be up. **(b)** *(geöffnet sein)* to be open.

aufsetzen *sep* **1** *vt* **(a)** *Brille etc, Miene etc* to put on; *Fuß* to put down. **(b)** *(verfassen)* to draft. **2** *vr* to sit up. **3** *vi (Flugzeug)* to touch down, to land.

Aufsetzer *m* - *(Sport)* bouncing ball.

aufseufzen *vi sep* **(tief)** ~ to heave a (deep) sigh.

Aufsicht *f no pl (Überwachung)* supervision *(über +acc* of*)*; *(Obhut)* charge. **unter jds** ~ *(dat)* under the supervision of sb; **bei einer Prüfung** ~ **führen** to invigilate an exam; **jdn ohne** ~ **lassen** to leave sb unsupervised.

Aufsichts-: ~**beamte(r)** *m (in Museum, Zoo etc)* attendant; ~**rat** *m* board (of directors).

aufsitzen *vi sep irreg* **(a)** *(aufgerichtet sitzen)* to sit up. **(b)** *aux sein (auf Reittier)* to mount; *(auf Fahrzeug)* to get on. **(c)** *aux sein (col: hereinfallen)* **jdm/einer Sache** ~ to be taken in by sb/sth.

aufspalten *vtr sep* to split; *(fig auch)* to split up.

aufspannen *vt sep* **(a)** *Netz, Sprungtuch* to stretch *or* spread out; *Schirm* to put up, to open. **(b)** *(aufziehen) Leinwand* to stretch *(auf +acc* onto*)*; *Saite* to put on *(auf etw (acc)* sth*)*.

aufsparen *vt sep* to save (up), to keep.

aufsperren *vt sep Tür, Schnabel* to open wide. **die Ohren** ~ to prick up one's ears.

aufspielen *sep* **1** *vi (dated)* to play; *(anfangen)* to strike up. **2** *vr (col)* **(a)** *(sich wichtig tun)* to give oneself airs. **(b) sich als etw** ~ to set oneself up as sth; **sich als Boß** ~ to play the boss.

aufspießen *vt sep* to spear; *(durchbohren)* to run through; *(mit Hörnern)* to gore; *Fleisch (mit Spieß)* to skewer.

aufsplittern *vti sep (vi: aux sein) (Holz)* to splinter; *(Gruppe)* to split (up).

aufspringen *vi sep irreg aux sein* **(a)** *(hochspringen)* to jump up. **auf etw** *(acc)* ~ to jump onto sth. **(b)** *(auftreffen)* to bounce. **(c)** *(sich öffnen) (Tür)* to burst open; *(platzen)* to burst; *(Haut, Lippen etc)* to crack, to chap.

aufspüren *vt sep (lit, fig)* to track down.

aufstampfen *vi sep* to stamp. **mit dem Fuß** ~ to stamp one's foot.

Aufstand *m* rebellion, revolt.

aufständisch *adj* rebellious, insurgent.

Aufständische(r) *mf decl as adj* rebel, insurgent.

aufstauen *sep* **1** *vt Wasser* to dam. **etw in sich** *(dat)* ~ *(fig)* to bottle sth up inside (oneself). **2** *vr* to collect; *(fig: Ärger)* to be bottled up.

aufstecken *sep* **1** *vt* **(a)** *(auf etw stecken)* to put on *(auf+acc* -to*)*. **(b)** *(mit Nadeln)* to pin up; *Haar auch* to put up. **2** *vi (col: aufgeben)* to pack it in *(col)*; *(bei Rennen etc)* to drop out.

aufstehen *vi sep irreg aux sein* **(a)** *(sich erheben)* to get *or* stand up; *(morgens aus dem Bett)* to get up. ~ **dürfen** *(Kranker)* to be allowed (to get) up; **da mußt du früher** *or* **eher** ~**!** *(fig col)* you'll have to do better than that! **(b)** *(col: offen sein)* to be open. **(c)** *(sich auflehnen)* to rise (in arms).

aufsteigen *vi sep irreg aux sein* **(a)** *(auf Berg, Leiter)* to climb (up); *(Flugzeug)* to climb; *(Nebel, Gefühl)* to rise; *(Gewitter, Wolken)* to gather. **einen Ballon** ~ **lassen** to release a balloon; **an die Oberfläche** ~ to rise to the surface; **in jdm** ~ *(Haß, Verdacht, Erinnerung etc)* to well up in sb. **(b)** *(auf Fahrrad etc)* to get on *(auf etw (acc)* (-to) sth*)*. **(c)** *(fig: im Rang etc)* to rise *(zu* to*)*; *(beruflich, Sport)* to be promoted *(in +acc* to*)*.

Aufsteiger *m* **(a)** *(Sport)* promoted team. **(b)** **(sozialer)** ~social climber.

aufstellen *sep* **1** *vt* **(a)** *(aufrichten)* to put up *(auf*

+*dat* on); *Maschine* to install; *Falle* to set; *(Mil)* to deploy; *(postieren) Wachposten* to post. **(b)** *Truppe* to raise; *Spieler, Mannschaft* to select; *Kandidaten* to nominate. **(c)** *(erzielen) Rekord* to set (up). **(d)** *Forderung, Behauptung* to put forward; *System* to establish; *Programm, Rechnung, Liste* to draw up. **(e)** *Essen etc (auf Herd)* to put on. **2** *vr (sich postieren)* to stand; *(hintereinander)* to line up; *(Soldaten)* to fall into line. **sich im Karree/Kreis** *etc* ~ to form a square/circle *etc.*

Aufstellung *f siehe vt* **(a)** putting up; installation; setting; deployment; posting. **(b)** raising; selecting; nomination; *(Mannschaft)* line-up *(col)*, team. **(c)** setting. **(d)** putting forward; establishing; drawing up; *(Liste)* list; *(Tabelle)* table.

aufstemmen *vt sep* to force open.

Aufstieg *m* **-e (a)** *no pl (auf Berg)* climb, ascent; *(von Flugzeug, Rakete)* climb; *(von Ballon)* ascent. **(b)** *(fig)* rise; *(Sport, beruflich)* promotion *(in +acc* to*)*. **den ~ ins Management schaffen** to work one's way up into the management. **(c)** *(Weg)* way up *(auf etw (acc)* sth*)*, ascent *(auf+acc* of*)*.

Aufstiegs:- **~chance, ~möglichkeit** *f* prospect of promotion.

aufstöbern *vt sep Wild* to start, to flush; *(col: entdecken)* to run to earth.

aufstocken *vt sep Vorräte* to build up.

aufstöhnen *vi sep* to give a loud groan.

aufstoßen *sep irreg* **1** *vt (öffnen)* to push open; *(mit dem Fuß)* to kick open. **2** *vi aux sein* **(a) auf etw** *(acc)* ~ to hit (on *or* against) sth. **(b)** *(rülpsen)* to burp.

Aufstoßen *nt no pl* burping, flatulence.

aufstrebend *adj (fig) Land, Volk* striving for progress; *junger Mann* ambitious.

Aufstrich *m (auf Brot)* spread.

aufstützen *sep* **1** *vt Kranken etc* to prop up; *Arme* to rest *(auf +acc or dat* on*)*. **2** *vr* to support oneself; *(im Bett, beim Essen)* to prop oneself up.

aufsuchen *vt sep Bekannten* to call on; *Arzt, Ort, Toilette* to go to.

auftakeln *vt sep (Naut)* to rig up. **sich ~** *(pej col)* to tart oneself up *(col)*; *siehe* **aufgetakelt.**

Auftakt *m* **(a)** *(Beginn)* start. **den ~ zu etw bilden** to mark the beginning of sth. **(b)** *(Mus)* upbeat.

auftanken *sep* **1** *vi* to fill up; *(Aviat)* to refuel. **2** *vt 10 Liter* to put in.

auftauchen *vi sep aux sein* **(a)** *(aus dem Wasser)* to surface; *(Taucher etc auch)* to come up. **(b)** *(fig) (sichtbar werden)* to appear; *(aus Nebel etc auch)* to emerge. **(c)** *(gefunden werden, kommen)* to turn up. **(d)** *(sich ergeben)* to arise.

auftauen *sep* **1** *vi aux sein* to thaw; *(fig auch)* to unbend. **2** *vt* to thaw; *Tiefkühlkost* to thaw (out).

aufteilen *vt sep* **(a)** *(aufgliedern)* to divide *or* split up *(in+acc* into*)*. **(b)** *(verteilen)* to share out *(an +acc* between*)*.

Aufteilung *f siehe vt* division; sharing out.

auftischen *vt sep* to serve up; *(fig col)* to come up with.

Auftrag *m, pl* **Aufträge (a)** *no pl (Anweisung)* orders *pl*, instructions *pl*; *(zugeteilte Arbeit)* job, task; *(Jur)* brief. **einen ~ ausführen** to carry out an order; **ich habe den ~, Ihnen mitzuteilen** ... I have been instructed to tell you ...; **in jds ~** *(dat) (für jdn)* on sb's behalf; *(auf jds Anweisung)* on sb's instructions; **im ~** *or* **i.A.: J. Burnett** pp J. Burnett. **(b)** *(über+acc* for*) (Comm)* order; *(bei Künstlern etc)* commission. **etw in ~ geben** to order/commission sth *(bei* from*)*.

auftragen *sep irreg* **1** *vt* **(a)** *(servieren)* to serve. **(b)** *Farbe, Salbe* to apply, to put on. **etw auf etw** *(acc)* ~ to apply sth to sth. **(c) jdm etw ~** *(form)* to instruct sb to do sth. **(d)** *Kleider* to wear out. **2** *vi (übertreiben)* **dick ~** *(col)* to lay it on thick *(col)*.

Auftraggeber(in *f***)** *m* client, customer.

Auftrags-: **~bestätigung** *f* confirmation of order; **a~gemäß** *adj, adv* as instructed; *(Comm)* as per order; **~rückgang** *m* drop in orders.

auftreffen *vi sep irreg aux sein* **auf etw** *(dat or acc)* ~ to hit *or* strike sth.

auftreiben *vt sep irreg (col: ausfindig machen)* to find, to get hold of *(col)*.

auftrennen *vt sep* to undo.

auftreten *sep irreg* **1** *vi aux sein* **(a)** *(lit)* to tread. **(b)** *(erscheinen, Theat)* to appear. **als Zeuge ~** to appear as a witness; **gegen jdn/etw ~** to stand up *or* speak out against sb/sth; **geschlossen ~** to put up a united front. **(c)** *(fig: eintreten)* to occur; *(Schwierigkeiten etc)* to arise. **(d)** *(sich benehmen)* to behave. **als Vermittler** *etc* ~ to act as intermediary *etc.* **2** *vt Tür etc* to kick open.

Auftreten *nt no pl* **(a)** *(Erscheinen)* appearance. **(b)** *(Benehmen)* manner. **(c)** *(Vorkommen)* occurrence.

Auftrieb *m no pl* **(a)** *(Phys)* buoyancy; *(Aviat)* lift. **(b)** *(fig)* impetus; *(Preis~)* upward trend *(gen* in*)*; *(Ermunterung)* lift. **das wird ihm ~ geben** that will give him a lift.

Auftritt *m* entrance; *(Theat: Szene)* scene.

auftrumpfen *vi sep (seine Leistungsstärke zeigen)* to show how good one is.

auftun *sep irreg* **1** *vt (col: ausfindig machen)* to find. **2** *vr (sich öffnen)* to open (up).

auftürmen *sep* **1** *vt* to pile up. **2** *vr (Gebirge etc)* to tower up; *(Schwierigkeiten)* to pile up.

aufwachen *vi sep aux sein (lit, fig)* to wake up. **aus einer Narkose ~** to come out of an anaesthetic.

aufwachsen *vi sep irreg aux sein* to grow up.

Aufwand *m no pl* **(a)** *(von Geld)* expenditure *(an +dat* of*)*. **das erfordert einen großen ~ an Zeit/Energie/Geld** that requires a lot of time/energy/money. **(b)** *(Luxus, Prunk)* extravagance. **(großen) ~ treiben** to be (very) extravagant.

Aufwands|entschädigung *f* expense allowance.

aufwärmen *sep* **1** *vt* to heat *or* warm up; *(col: wieder erwähnen)* to bring up. **2** *vr* to warm up.

aufwarten *vi sep (zu bieten haben)* **mit etw ~** to offer sth.

aufwärts *adv* up, upward(s); *(bergauf)* uphill. **den Fluß ~** upstream.

Aufwärts-: **~entwicklung** *f* upward trend *(gen* in*)*; **a~gehen** *vi impers sep irreg aux sein* **mit dem Staat/der Firma geht es a~** things are improving for the country/firm; **~haken** *m (Boxen)* uppercut; **~trend** *m* upward trend.

aufwecken *vt sep* to wake (up); *(fig)* to rouse; *siehe* **aufgeweckt.**

aufweichen *sep* **1** *vt* to soften; *Brot* to soak. **2** *vi aux sein* to become soft.

aufweisen *vt sep irreg* to show. **das Buch weist einige Fehler auf** the book has some mistakes in it; **etw aufzuweisen haben** to have sth to show for oneself.

aufwenden *vt sep irreg* to use; *Energie* to expend; *Geld, Zeit* to spend. **viel Mühe/Zeit ~, etw zu tun** to take a lot of trouble/spend a lot of time doing sth.

aufwendig *adj* costly; *(üppig)* lavish.

Aufwendungen *pl* expenditure.

aufwerfen *vt sep irreg* **(a)** *(aufhäufen)* to pile up. **(b)** *Frage, Probleme* to raise, to bring up.

aufwerten *vt sep* **(a)** *(auch vi) Währung* to revalue. **(b)** *(fig)* to increase the value of.

Aufwertung *f (von Währung)* revaluation; *(fig)* increase in value.

aufwickeln *vt sep* **(a)** *(aufrollen)* to roll up; *(col) Haar* to put in curlers. **(b)** *(lösen)* to untie; *Windeln, Verband* to take off.

aufwiegeln *vt sep* to stir up. **jdn zum Streik/Widerstand ~** to incite sb to strike/resist.

aufwiegen *vt sep irreg (fig)* to offset. **das ist nicht mit Geld aufzuwiegen** that can't be measured in terms of money.

Aufwiegler(in *f*) *m* - agitator; *(Anstifter)* instigator.
aufwieglerisch *adj* seditious; *Rede, Artikel auch* inflammatory.
Aufwind *m (Aviat)* upcurrent. **neuen ~ bekommen** *(fig)* to get new impetus.
aufwirbeln *vti sep (vi: aux sein)* to swirl *or* whirl up. **(viel) Staub ~** *(fig)* to cause a (big) stir.
aufwischen *vti sep* to mop up.
aufwühlen *vt sep* **(a)** *(lit) Erde, Meer* to churn (up). **(b)** *(geh) Gefühle* to stir; *siehe* **aufgewühlt.**
aufzählen *vt sep* to list.
aufzeichnen *vt sep* **(a)** *Plan etc* to draw, to sketch. **(b)** *(notieren, Rad, TV)* to record.
Aufzeichnung *f* **(a)** *usu pl (Notiz)* note; *(Niederschrift auch)* record. **(b)** *(Tonband~, Film~)* recording.
aufzeigen *vt sep* to show.
aufziehen *sep irreg* **1** *vt* **(a)** *(hochziehen)* to pull *or* draw up; *Flagge, Segel* to hoist. **(b)** *(öffnen) Reißverschluß* to undo; *Schublade* to (pull) open; *Gardinen* to draw (back). **(c)** *(aufspannen) Saite, Reifen* to put on. **(d)** *(spannen) Feder, Uhr etc* to wind up. **(e)** *(großziehen)* to raise; *Kind auch* to bring up; *Tier auch* to rear. **(f)** *(col: veranstalten)* to set up; *Fest* to arrange. **(g)** *(verspotten)* **jdn ~** *(col)* to tease sb *(mit* about*)*. **2** *vi aux sein (dunkle Wolke)* to come up; *(Gewitter, Wolken auch)* to gather; *(aufmarschieren)* to march up.
Aufzucht *f no pl (das Großziehen)* rearing, raising.
Aufzug *m* **(a)** *(Fahrstuhl)* lift *(Brit)*, elevator *(US)*; *(Güter~)* hoist. **(b)** *(von Gewitter etc)* gathering. **(c)** *(Theat)* act. **(d)** *no pl (pej col: Kleidung)* get-up *(col)*.
aufzwingen *sep irreg* **1** *vt* **jdm etw/seinen Willen ~** to force sth on sb/impose one's will on sb. **2** *vr* **das zwingt sich einem doch förmlich auf** it's the only possible conclusion.
Aug|apfel *m* eyeball. **jdn/etw wie seinen ~ hüten** to cherish sb/sth like life itself.
Auge *nt* **-n** **(a)** eye. **gute/schlechte ~n haben** to have good/bad eyesight *or* eyes; **mit den ~n zwinkern/blinzeln** to wink/blink; **jdn mit** *or* **aus großen ~n ansehen** to look at sb wide-eyed; **mit bloßem** *or* **nacktem ~** with the naked eye; **mit verbundenen ~n** *(lit, fig)* blindfold; **etw im ~ haben** *(fig)* to have one's eye on sth; **ein sicheres ~ für etw haben** to have a good eye for sth; **ich kann doch meine ~n nicht überall haben** I can't see everything at once; **er machte große ~n** his eyes popped out of his head *(col)*; **ich konnte kaum aus den ~n sehen** I could hardly see straight; **geh mir aus den ~n!** get out of my sight!; **unter jds ~n** *(dat) (fig)* before sb's very eyes; **vor aller ~n** in front of everybody, for all to see; **jdn/etw mit anderen ~n (an)sehen** to see sb/sth in a different light; **seine ~n waren größer als sein Magen** *(col)* his eyes were bigger than his stomach; **aus den ~n, aus dem Sinn** *(Prov)* out of sight, out of mind *(Prov)*; **das ~ des Gesetzes** the law; **soweit das ~ reicht** as far as the eye can see; **er hatte nur ~n für sie** he only had eyes for her; **ich habe kein ~ zugetan** I didn't sleep a wink; **da blieb kein ~ trocken** *(hum)* there wasn't a dry eye in the place; **ein ~ auf jdn/etw geworfen haben** to have one's eye on sb/sth; **ein ~/beide ~n zudrücken** *(col)* to turn a blind eye; **etw im ~ behalten** to keep *or* bear sth in mind; **sie ließen ihn nicht aus den ~n** they didn't let him out of their sight; **jdn/etw aus den ~n verlieren** to lose sight of sb/sth; *(fig)* to lose touch with sb/sth; **das springt einem gleich ins ~** it hits you right in the face *(col)*; **jdm etw vor ~n führen** *(fig)* to make sb aware of sth; **etw ins ~ fassen** to contemplate sth; **etw noch genau** *or* **lebhaft vor ~n haben** to remember sth clearly *or* vividly; **jdm die ~n öffnen** *(fig)* to open sb's eyes; **ein ~ riskieren** *(hum)* to have a peep *(col)*; **das kann leicht ins ~ gehen** *(fig col)* it might easily go wrong; **in meinen ~n** in my opinion *or* view; **mit einem lachenden und einem weinenden ~** with mixed feelings; **~ in ~** face to face; **~ um ~, Zahn um Zahn** *(Bibl)* an eye for an eye and a tooth for a tooth; **dem Tod ins ~ sehen** to look death in the face.
(b) *(bei Kartoffel)* eye.
(c) *(Punkt bei Spielen)* point.
Augen-: **~arzt** *m* eye specialist, ophthalmologist; **~aufschlag** *m* look.
Augenblick *m* moment. **jeden ~** any time *or* moment; **einen ~, bitte** one moment please!; **~ mal!** *(col)* just a minute *or* second! *(col)*; **im ~** at the moment; **im ersten ~** for a moment.
augenblicklich **1** *adj (sofortig)* immediate; *(gegenwärtig)* present, current. **2** *adv (sofort)* immediately; *(zur Zeit)* at the moment.
Augen-: **~braue** *f* eyebrow; **~entzündung** *f* inflammation of the eyes; **~farbe** *f* colour *(Brit) or* color *(US)* of eyes; **ihre ~farbe** the colour of her eyes; **~höhe** *f*: **in ~höhe** at eye level; **~höhle** *f* eye socket; **~klappe** *f* **(a)** eye patch; **(b)** *(für Pferde)* blinker, blinder *(US)*; **~krankheit** *f* eye disease; **~licht** *nt no pl* (eye)sight; **~lid** *nt* eyelid; **~maß** *nt* eye; *(für Entfernungen)* eye for distance(s); *(fig)* perceptiveness; **nach ~maß** by eye; **ein gutes/schlechtes ~maß haben** to have a good eye/no eye for distance(s); **~merk** *nt no pl (Aufmerksamkeit)* attention; **jds/sein ~merk auf etw** *(acc)* **lenken** to direct sb's/one's attention to sth; **~operation** *f* eye operation; **~optiker** *m* optician; **~paar** *nt* pair of eyes; **~ränder** *pl* rims of the/one's eyes; **~schein** *m no pl* **(a)** *(Anschein)* appearance; **dem ~schein nach** by all appearances; **(b)** **jdn/etw in ~schein nehmen** to have a close look at sb/sth; **a~scheinlich** *adj* obvious, evident; **~tropfen** *pl* eyedrops *pl*; **~weide** *f* feast *or* treat for the eyes; **~wimper** *f* eyelash; **~winkel** *m* corner of the/one's eye; **~wischerei** *f (fig)* eyewash; **~zeuge** *m* eyewitness *(bei* to*)*; **~zeugenbericht** *m* eyewitness account; **~zwinkern** *nt no pl* winking; **a~zwinkernd** *adj* winking *attr; (fig)* sly.
August *m* **-e** August; *siehe* **März.**
Auktion *f* auction.
Auktionator(in *f*) [-'toːrɪn] *m* auctioneer.
Aula *f, pl* **Aulen** *(Sch, Univ)* (assembly) hall.
Au-pair- [o'pɛːɐ]: **~-Mädchen** *nt* au-pair (girl); **~-Stelle** *f* au-pair job.
aus **1** *prep+dat* **(a)** *(räumlich)* from; *(aus dem Inneren von)* out of. **~ dem Fenster/der Tür** out of the window/door; **~ unserer Mitte** from our midst.
(b) *(Herkunft, Quelle bezeichnend)* from. **~ dem Deutschen** from (the) German; **~ guter Familie** from a good family; **er ist ~ Köln** he's from Cologne; **~ der Goethezeit** from the time of Goethe.
(c) *(auf Ursache deutend)* out of. **~ Haß/Mitleid** out of hatred/sympathy; **~ Erfahrung** from experience; **~ Furcht vor/Liebe zu** for fear/love of; **~ dem Grunde, daß ...** for the reason that ...; **~ Spaß** for fun; **~ Versehen** by mistake; **~ sich heraus** of one's own accord.
(d) *(beschaffen ~)* (made out) of. **ein Herz ~ Stein** a heart of stone.
(e) **einen anständigen Menschen ~ jdm machen** to make sb into a decent person; **was ist ~ ihm/dieser Sache geworden?** what has become of him/this?; **~ ihm wird einmal ein guter Arzt** he'll make a good doctor one day.
(f) **~ dem Gleichgewicht** out of balance; **~ der Mode** out of fashion.
2 *adv siehe auch* **aussein** **(a)** *(col: vorbei, zu Ende)* over. **~ und vorbei** over and done with. **(b)** *(gelöscht)* out; *(an Geräten)* off. **Licht ~!** lights out! **(c)** *(Sport)* out, out of play. **(d)** *(in Verbin-*

dung mit von) **von München** ~ from Munich; **von sich** *(dat)* ~ of one's own accord; **von ihm** ~ as far as he's concerned; **ok, von mir** ~ OK, if you like.

Aus *nt no pl (Sport)* touch *no art.*

aus|arbeiten *vt sep* to work out; *(vorbereiten)* to prepare.

Aus|arbeitung *f siehe vt* working out; preparation.

aus|arten *vi sep aux sein (Party etc)* to get out of control. ~ **in** *(+acc) or* **zu** to degenerate into.

aus|atmen *vti sep* to breathe out, to exhale.

ausbaden *vt sep (col)* to carry the can for *(col).*

Ausbau *m* **-ten** *siehe vt* removal; extension *(zu* into*)*; conversion *(zu* (in)to*)*; building up.

ausbauen *vt sep* **(a)** *(herausmontieren)* to remove *(aus* from*)*. **(b)** *(lit, fig: erweitern)* to extend *(zu* into*)*; *(umbauen)* to convert *(zu* (in)to*)*; *Freundschaft* to build up.

ausbaufähig *adj Position* with good prospects; *Produktion, Markt* that can be extended; *Beziehungen* that can be built up.

ausbeißen *vr sep irreg* **sich** *(dat)* **an etw** *(dat)* **die Zähne** ~ *(fig)* to have a tough time of it with sth.

ausbessern *vt sep* to repair; *Wäsche etc auch* to mend.

Ausbesserung *f siehe vt* repair; mending.

Ausbesserungs-: ~**arbeiten** *pl* repair work *sing;* **a**~**bedürftig** *adj* in need of repair *etc.*

ausbeulen *vt sep Auto* to knock the dent(s) out of; *Kleidung* to make baggy; *siehe* **ausgebeult.**

Ausbeute *f (Gewinn)* profit, gain; *(Ertrag einer Grube etc)* yield *(an+dat* in*)*; *(fig)* result(s); *(Einnahmen)* proceeds *pl.*

ausbeuten *vt sep (lit, fig)* to exploit.

Ausbeuter(in *f)* *m* **-** exploiter.

Ausbeutung *f* exploitation.

ausbezahlen* *vt sep Geld* to pay out.

ausbilden *vt sep* to train; *(unterrichten auch)* to instruct; *(akademisch)* to educate; *Fähigkeiten* to develop. **sich in etw** *(dat)***/als** *or* **zu etw** ~ **lassen** *(esp Arbeiter, Lehrling)* to train in sth/as sth; **ein ausgebildeter Übersetzer** a qualified translator.

Ausbilder(in *f)* *m* **-** instructor, instructress.

Ausbildung *f siehe vt* training; instruction; education; development. **er ist noch in der** ~ he's still a trainee; he hasn't finished his education.

Ausbildungs-: ~**beihilfe,** ~**förderung** *f* grant; ~**platz** *m (Stelle)* training vacancy; ~**stand** *m* level of training; ~**zeit** *f* training period.

ausbitten *vr sep irreg* **sich** *(dat)* **(von jdm) etw** ~ *(geh)* to request sth (from sb) *(form)*; **ich bitte mir Ruhe aus!** I will have silence!

ausblasen *vt sep irreg* to blow out; *Ei* to blow.

ausbleiben *vi sep irreg aux sein (fortbleiben)* to stay out; *(nicht erscheinen: Gäste)* to fail to appear; *(nicht eintreten: Erwartung etc)* to fail to materialize; *(aufhören: Puls, Atmung etc)* to stop. **es konnte nicht** ~**, daß ...** it was inevitable that ...

ausblenden *vti sep (TV etc)* to fade out; *(plötzlich)* to cut out.

Ausblick *m* **(a)** view *(auf +acc* of*)*. **(b)** *(fig)* prospect, outlook *(auf+acc* for*)*.

ausblicken *vi sep (geh)* **nach jdm** ~ to look for sb.

ausbooten *vt sep (col) jdn* to kick *or* boot out *(col).*

ausbrechen *sep irreg* **1** *vt (herausbrechen) Steine* to break off *(aus* from*)*. **2** *vi aux sein* **(a)** *(lit, fig: sich befreien)* to break out *(aus* of*)* *(auch Mil)*, to escape *(aus* from*)*. **(b)** *(Richtung ändern: Pferd, Wagen)* to swerve. **(c)** *(Krieg, Feuer, Schweiß etc)* to break out; *(Jubel, Zorn etc)* to erupt, to explode; *(Vulkan)* to erupt. **in Gelächter/Tränen/Jubel** ~ to burst out laughing/crying/cheering.

Ausbrecher(in *f)* *m* **-** *(col: Gefangener)* escaped prisoner, escapee.

ausbreiten *sep* **1** *vt* to spread (out); *Arme* to stretch out; *(ausstellen, fig: zeigen)* to display; *Licht, Wärme* to spread. **2** *vr* **(a)** *(sich verbreiten)* to spread. **(b)** *(col: sich breitmachen)* to spread oneself out. **(c) sich über etw** *(acc)* ~ *(fig)* to dwell on sth.

Ausbreitung *f* spread, spreading.

ausbrennen *sep irreg* **1** *vi aux sein* **(a)** *(zu Ende brennen)* to burn out. **(b)** *(völlig verbrennen)* to be burnt out, to be gutted. **er ist ausgebrannt** *(fig)* he's burnt out. **2** *vt (Med)* to cauterize.

Ausbruch *m* **(a)** *(aus* from*)* *(aus Gefängnis)* breakout *(auch Mil)*, escape *(auch fig)*. **(b)** *(Beginn)* outbreak; *(von Vulkan)* eruption. **zum** ~ **kommen** to break out. **(c)** *(fig: Gefühls~)* outburst.

ausbrüten *vt sep* to hatch; *(esp in Brutkasten)* to incubate; *(fig col) Plan etc* to cook up *(col).*

Ausbuchtung *f* bulge; *(von Strand)* (small) cove.

ausbügeln *vt sep* to iron out; *(col) Fehler, Verlust* to make good.

Ausbund *m no pl:* **ein** ~ **an** *or* **von Tugend/Sparsamkeit** a paragon of virtue/a model of thrift.

ausbürgern *vt sep* **jdn** ~ to expatriate sb.

Ausbürgerung *f* expatriation.

Ausdauer *f no pl* staying power, stamina; *(Beharrlichkeit)* perseverance.

ausdauernd *adj (Mensch)* with staying power, with stamina; *(im Ertragen)* with endurance; *(beharrlich)* persevering; *Bemühungen etc* untiring.

ausdehnbar *adj* expandable; *(fig)* extendable *(auf+acc* to*)*.

ausdehnen *sep* **1** *vt* **(a)** *(vergrößern)* to expand. **(b)** *(fig)* to extend; *(zeitlich auch)* to prolong *(auf +acc* to*)*. **2** *vr* **(a)** *(größer werden)* to expand; *(sich erstrecken)* to extend, to stretch *(bis* as far as*)*. **der Krieg dehnte sich über das ganze Land aus** the war spread over the whole country. **(b)** *(fig)* to extend *(über+acc* over, *bis* as far as, to*)*; *(zeitlich)* to go on *(bis* until*)*; *siehe* **ausgedehnt.**

Ausdehnung *f* **(a)** *siehe vt* expansion; extension; prolongation. **(b)** *(Umfang)* expanse.

ausdenken *vt sep irreg* **sich** *(dat)* **etw** ~ *(erfinden)* to think sth up; *(in Einzelheiten)* to think sth out; *Wunsch* to think of sth; *Überraschung* to plan sth; *(sich vorstellen)* to imagine sth; **eine ausgedachte Geschichte** a made-up story; **das ist nicht auszudenken** *(unvorstellbar)* it's inconceivable.

ausdienen *vi sep* **ausgedient haben** *(fig col)* to have had its day.

ausdiskutieren* *vt sep Thema* to discuss fully.

ausdrehen *vt sep (ausschalten)* to turn *or* switch off; *Licht auch* to turn out.

Ausdruck[1] *m, pl* **Ausdrücke (a)** *no pl* expression. **als** ~ **meiner Dankbarkeit** as an expression of my gratitude; **mit dem** ~ **des Bedauerns** *(form)* expressing regret; **etw zum** ~ **bringen** to express sth, to give expression to sth. **(b)** *(Wort)* expression; *(Fach~ auch)* term. **sich im** ~ **vergreifen** to use the wrong word.

Ausdruck[2] *m* **-e** *(Comp)* printout.

ausdrucken *vt sep (Comp)* to print out.

ausdrücken *sep* **1** *vt* **(a)** to press out, to squeeze out; *Pickel* to squeeze; *Zigarette* to stub out. **(b)** *(zum Ausdruck bringen)* to express *(jdm* to sb*)*. **anders ausgedrückt** in other words; **einfach ausgedrückt** put simply. **2** *vr (Mensch)* to express oneself. **in ihrem Gesicht/Verhalten drückte sich Verzweiflung aus** her face/behaviour showed her despair.

ausdrücklich 1 *adj attr Wunsch* express, explicit. **2** *adv* explicitly; *(besonders)* particularly.

Ausdrucks-: **a**~**fähig** *adj* expressive; *(gewandt)* articulate; ~**fähigkeit** *f siehe adj* expressiveness; articulateness; **a**~**los** *adj* inexpressive; *Gesicht, Blick auch* expressionless; ~**losigkeit** *f siehe adj* inexpressiveness; lack of expression; ~**mittel** *nt* means of expression; **a**~**voll** *adj* expressive; ~**weise** *f* way of expressing oneself.

ausdünsten *vt sep Geruch* to give off.

Ausdünstung *f (Dampf)* vapour *(Brit)*, vapor

(*US*); (*Geruch*) smell.

aus|einander *adv* (*getrennt*) apart. **weit ~** far apart; *Meinungen* very different; **etw ~ schreiben** to write sth as two words; **die beiden sind (im Alter) ein Jahr ~** there is a year between the two of them; **~ sein** (*col: Paar*) to have split up.

aus|einander-: ~brechen *sep irreg* **1** *vt* to break in two; **2** *vi aux sein* (*lit, fig*) to break up; **~fallen** *vi sep irreg aux sein* (*zerfallen*) to fall apart; (*fig auch*) to collapse; **~ gehen** *vi sep irreg aux sein* **(a)** (*lit, fig: sich trennen*) (*Menschen*) to part, to separate; (*Menge*) to disperse; (*Versammlung, Ehe etc*) to break up; **(b)** (*sich verzweigen: Weg etc*) to divide; (*zwei Wege*) to diverge; (*fig: Ansichten etc*) to differ; **~halten** *vt sep irreg* to keep apart; (*unterscheiden*) *Begriffe* to distinguish between; *esp Zwillinge etc* to tell apart; **~klaffen** *vi sep aux sein* to gape open; (*fig: Meinungen*) to be far apart, to diverge (wildly); **~laufen** *vi sep irreg aux sein* **(a)** (*zerlaufen*) to melt; (*Farbe*) to run; **(b)** (*col: sich trennen*) to break up; (*Menge*) to disperse; **~leben** *vr sep* to drift apart; **~nehmen** *vt sep irreg* to take apart; *Maschine etc auch* to dismantle; (*kritisch*) to tear apart *or* to pieces; **~setzen** *sep* **1** *vt* (*fig*) (*jdm* to sb) to explain; (*schriftlich auch*) to set out; **2** *vr* **sich mit etw ~setzen** (*sich befassen*) to work on; **sich kritisch mit etw ~setzen** to have a critical look at sth; **sich mit jdm ~setzen** to talk *or* (*sich streiten*) to argue with sb.

Aus|einandersetzung *f* **(a)** (*Diskussion*) discussion, debate (*über+acc* about, on); (*Streit*) argument; (*feindlicher Zusammenstoß*) clash (*wegen* over). **(b)** (*das Befassen*) examination (*mit* of); (*kritisch*) analysis (*mit* of).

aus|erkoren *adj* (*liter*) chosen, selected.

aus|erlesen *adj* (*ausgesucht*) select; *Speisen, Weine auch* choice *attr*.

aus|ersehen* *vt sep irreg* (*geh*) **dazu ~ sein, etw zu tun** to be chosen to do sth.

Aus|erwählte(r) *mf decl as adj* (*geh*) chosen one.

ausfahrbar *adj* extendable; *Antenne, Fahrgestell* retractable.

ausfahren *sep irreg* **1** *vi aux sein* **(a)** (*spazierenfahren*) to go for a ride *or* (*im Auto auch*) drive. **(b)** (*abfahren*) (*Zug*) to pull out (*aus* of), to leave; **aus dem Hafen ~** (*Schiff*) to leave harbour. **2 (a)** (*ausliefern*) *Waren* to deliver. **(b) ein Auto** *etc* **(voll) ~** to drive a car *etc* flat out. **(c)** (*Tech*) to extend; *Fahrgestell etc auch* to lower.

Ausfahrt *f* **(a)** (*auch Autobahn~*) exit. **~ Gütersloh** Gütersloh exit. **(b)** *no pl* (*Abfahrt*) departure. **der Zug hat keine ~** the train has not been cleared for departure. **(c)** (*Spazierfahrt*) drive, ride.

Ausfall *m* **(a)** (*Verlust*) loss; (*das Versagen*) (*Tech, Med*) failure; (*von Motor*) breakdown; (*Produktionsstörung*) stoppage. **(b)** *no pl* (*von Sitzung, Unterricht etc*) cancellation. **(c)** *no pl* (*das Ausscheiden*) dropping out.

ausfallen *vi sep irreg aux sein* **(a)** (*herausfallen*) to fall out. **mir fallen die Haare aus** my hair is falling out. **(b)** (*nicht stattfinden*) to be cancelled. **etw ~ lassen** to cancel sth; **die Schule fällt morgen aus** there's no school tomorrow. **(c)** (*nicht funktionieren*) to fail; (*Motor*) to break down. **(d)** (*wegfallen: Verdienst*) to be lost. **(e)** (*ausscheiden*) to drop out. **(f) gut/schlecht** *etc* **~** to turn out well/badly *etc*; **die Bluse fällt zu eng aus** the blouse is too tight. **(g)** *siehe* **ausgefallen.**

ausfallend *adj* abusive.

Ausfälligkeit *f* abusiveness; (*Bemerkung*) abusive remark.

Ausfallstraße *f* arterial road.

ausfechten *vt sep irreg* (*fig*) to fight (out).

ausfegen *vt sep* *Zimmer* to sweep out.

ausfeilen *vt sep* to file (out); *siehe* **ausgefeilt.**

ausfertigen *vt sep* (*form*) *Dokument* to draw up; *Rechnung etc* to make out; *Paß* to issue.

Ausfertigung *f* (*form*) **(a)** *no pl siehe vt* drawing up; making out; issuing. **(b)** (*Abschrift*) copy. **in doppelter/dreifacher ~** in duplicate/triplicate.

ausfetten *vt sep* to grease.

ausfindig *adj*: **~ machen** to find; (*Aufenthaltsort feststellen*) to trace.

ausfliegen *sep irreg* **1** *vi aux sein* **ausgeflogen sein** (*fig col*) to have gone out; **der Vogel ist ausgeflogen** (*fig col*) the bird has flown. **2** *vt* (*Aviat*) *Verwundete etc* to fly out (*aus* from).

ausfließen *vi sep irreg aux sein* (*herausfließen*) to flow out (*aus* of); (*auslaufen: Öl etc*) to leak (*aus* out of); (*Eiter etc*) to be discharged.

ausflippen *vi sep aux sein* (*col*) to freak out (*col*); *siehe* **ausgeflippt.**

Ausflucht *f, pl* **Ausflüchte** excuse. **Ausflüchte machen** to make excuses.

Ausflug *m* trip, outing; (*esp mit Reisebüro*) excursion; (*Betriebs~, Schul~*) outing; (*Wanderung*) walk, hike. **einen ~ machen** to go on a trip *etc*.

Ausflügler(in *f*) *m* - tripper.

Ausflugs-: ~dampfer *m* pleasure steamer; **~lokal** *nt* tourist café; (*am Meer*) seaside café; **~verkehr** *m* (*an Feiertagen*) holiday traffic; (*am Wochenende*) weekend holiday traffic; **~ziel** *nt* destination (of one's outing).

Ausfluß *m* **(a)** (*das Herausfließen*) outflow. **(b)** (*~stelle*) outlet. **(c)** (*Med*) discharge.

ausforschen *vt sep* **(a)** *Sache* to find out; (*erforschen*) to investigate. **(b)** *jdn* to question.

ausfragen *vt sep* to question, to quiz (*col*) (*nach* about); (*strenger*) to interrogate.

ausfransen *vi sep aux sein* to fray.

ausfressen *vt sep irreg* (*col: anstellen*) **etwas ~** to do something wrong; **was hat er denn wieder ausgefressen?** what's he done now? (*col*).

Ausfuhr *f* **-en** *no pl* (*das Ausführen*) export; (*~handel*) exports *pl*.

Ausfuhr- *in cpds* export; *siehe auch* **Export-.**

ausführbar *adj* *Plan* feasible, practicable. **schwer ~** difficult to carry out.

ausführen *vt sep* **(a)** *jdn* to take out; *Hund auch* to take for a walk. **(b)** (*durchführen*) to carry out; *Gesetz* to implement; (*Sport*) *Freistoß* to take. **die ~de Gewalt** (*Pol*) the executive. **(c)** (*erklären*) to explain; (*darlegen*) to set out; (*argumentierend*) to argue. **(d)** (*Comm*) *Waren* to export.

Ausfuhr-: ~güter *pl* export goods *pl*, exports *pl*; **~hafen** *m* port of exportation.

ausführlich 1 *adj* detailed, full. **2** *adv* in detail, in full. **sehr ~** in great detail.

Ausführlichkeit *f* detail, fullness.

Ausführung *f* **(a)** *no pl siehe vt (b)* carrying out; implementation; taking. **zur ~ gelangen** to be carried out. **(b)** (*Erklärung*) explanation; (*von Thema etc*) exposition. **(c)** (*von Waren*) design; (*Tech: äußere ~*) finish; (*Qualität*) quality; (*Modell*) model.

Ausfuhrzoll *m* export duty.

ausfüllen *vt sep* to fill; *Platz* to take up; *Formular* to fill out. **jdn (ganz) ~** (*Zeit in Anspruch nehmen*) to take (all) sb's time; **ein ausgefülltes Leben** a full life.

Ausgabe *f* **-n (a)** *no pl* (*Austeilung*) (*von Proviant etc*) distribution, giving out; (*von Befehl, Fahrkarten etc*) issuing; (*von Essen*) serving. **(b)** (*Schalter*) counter. **(c)** (*von Buch etc*) edition; (*von Zeitschrift auch, von Aktien*) issue. **(d)** (*Ausführung*) version. **(e)** (*Geldaufwand*) expense, expenditure *no pl*. **~en** *pl* (*Geldverbrauch*) expenditure *sing* (*für* on); (*Kosten*) expenses *pl*, costs *pl*. **(f)** (*Comp*) printout.

Ausgang *m* **(a)** (*Auslaß, Weg nach draußen*) exit, way out (*gen, von* from). **(b)** (*Erlaubnis zum Ausgehen*) permission to go out; (*Mil*) pass. **~ haben** to have the day off *or* (*am Abend*) the evening off; (*Mil*) to have a pass. **(c)** *no pl* (*Ende*) end; (*von Epoche auch*) close; (*von Roman, Film auch*) ending; *(Ergebnis)* outcome, result. **ein Unfall mit tödlichem ~** a fatal accident. **(d)** *no pl (Ausgangspunkt)* starting point; *(Anfang)* beginning.

Ausgangs-: ~basis *f* basis, starting point; **~position** *f* initial *or* starting position; **~punkt** *m* starting point; **~sperre** *f* ban on going out; *(esp bei Belagerungszustand)* curfew; *(für Soldaten)* confinement to barracks; **~sperre haben** to be forbidden to go out; *(Mil)* to be confined to barracks; **~stellung** *f (Sport)* starting position; *(Mil)* initial position.

ausgeben *vt sep irreg* **(a)** *(austeilen) Proviant etc* to distribute, to give out; *(aushändigen) Dokumente, Fahrkarten, Aktien etc* to issue; *Befehl* to issue, to give; *Essen* to serve; *(Cards)* to deal; *(ausdrucken) Text* to print out. **(b)** *Geld* to spend *(für* on*)*. **eine Runde ~** to stand a round; **ich gebe heute abend einen aus** *(col)* it's my treat this evening; **darf ich dir einen Whisky ~?** would you like a whisky? **(c) jdn/etw als** *or* **für jdn/etw ~** to pass sb/sth off as sb/sth; **sich als jd/etw ~** to pose as sb/sth.

ausgebeult *adj Kleidung* baggy; *Hut* battered.

ausgebucht *adj Reise etc* booked up.

Ausgeburt *f (pej) (der Phantasie etc)* monstrous product; **eine ~ der Hölle** a fiendish monster.

ausgedehnt *adj (breit, groß, fig: weitreichend)* extensive; *(zeitlich)* lengthy; *Spaziergang* long.

ausgedörrt *adj* dried up; *Boden, Kehle* parched; *Pflanzen* shrivelled; *Land, Gebiet* arid.

ausgefallen *adj (ungewöhnlich)* unusual; *(übertrieben)* extravagant.

ausgefeilt *adj (fig)* polished.

ausgeflippt *adj (col)* freaky *(col)*, freaked-out *(col)*. **~er Typ** *(Hippie etc)* drop-out *(col)*.

ausgefuchst *adj (col)* clever; *(listig)* crafty *(col)*.

ausgeglichen *adj* balanced; *Spiel, Klima* even; *Torverhältnis* equal.

Ausgeglichenheit *f siehe adj* balance; evenness.

ausgehen *vi sep irreg aux sein* **(a)** *(weggehen)* to go out; *(spazierengehen auch)* to go (out) for a walk. **(b)** *(ausfallen: Haare, Federn, Zähne)* to fall out. **(c)** *(seinen Ausgang nehmen)* to start *(von* at*)*; *(herrühren: Idee etc)* to come *(von* from*)*. **(d)** *(abgeschickt werden: Post)* to be sent off. **die ~de Post** the outgoing mail. **(e)** *(zugrunde legen)* to start out *(von* from*)*. **gehen wir einmal davon aus, daß ...** let us assume that ... **(f) auf etw** *(acc)* **~** to be intent on sth. **(g)** *(enden)* to end. **gut/schlecht ~** to turn out well/badly; *(Film etc)* to have a happy/sad ending; *(Abend, Spiel)* to end well/badly; **leer ~** *(col)* to come away empty-handed. **(h)** *(zu Ende sein: Vorräte etc)* to run out. **ihm ist die Luft** *or* **der Atem ausgegangen** *(lit)* he ran out of breath; *(fig col)* he ran out of steam *(col)*. **(i)** *(aufhören zu brennen)* to go out.

Ausgeh|erlaubnis *f* permission to go out; *(Mil)* pass.

ausgehungert *adj* starved; *(abgezehrt) Mensch etc* emaciated.

Ausgeh-: ~uniform *f* walking-out uniform; **~verbot** *nt siehe* **Ausgangssperre.**

ausgeklügelt *adj (col)* ingenious.

ausgekocht *adj (pej col: durchtrieben)* cunning.

ausgelassen *adj (heiter)* lively; *Stimmung* happy; *(wild) Kinder, Stimmung, Party* wild.

Ausgelassenheit *f siehe adj* liveliness; happiness; wildness.

ausgelastet *adj Mensch* fully occupied; *Maschine, Anlage* working to capacity.

ausgeleiert *adj Gummiband etc* worn.

ausgemacht *adj* **(a)** *(abgemacht)* agreed. **es ist eine ~e Sache, daß ...** it is agreed that ... **(b)** *attr (col: vollkommen)* complete, utter.

ausgemergelt *adj Gesicht* emaciated, gaunt.

ausgenommen *conj* except, apart from, aside from *(esp US)*. **alle, du** *or* **dich ~** everyone except (for) *or* apart from you; **Anwesende ~** present company excepted.

ausgeprägt *adj Gesicht* distinctive; *Eigenschaft* distinct; *Interesse* marked, pronounced.

ausgerechnet *adv* **~ du/er** *etc* you/he *etc* of all people; **~ heute/gestern** today/yesterday of all days; **~ jetzt kommt er** he would have to come just now.

ausgereift *adj* mature.

ausgeruht *adj* (well) rested.

ausgeschlossen *adj pred (unmöglich)* impossible; *(nicht in Frage kommend)* out of the question. **es ist nicht ~, daß ...** it's just possible that ...; **jeder Irrtum ist ~** there is no possibility of a mistake.

ausgeschnitten *adj Bluse, Kleid* low-cut. **ein tief ~es Kleid** a dress with a plunging neckline.

ausgesorgt *adj siehe* **aussorgen.**

ausgesprochen 1 *adj Schönheit* outstanding; *Vorliebe* definite; *Begabung* particular; *Ähnlichkeit auch* marked. **~es Pech haben** to be really unlucky. **2** *adv* really.

ausgestorben *adj Tierart* extinct; *(fig)* deserted. **der Park war wie ~** the park was deserted.

Ausgestoßene(r) *mf decl as adj* outcast.

ausgesucht *(erlesen) Wein* choice, select; *Gesellschaft* select; *Worte* well-chosen.

ausgetreten *adj Schuhe, Stufe* well-worn; *Pfad auch* well-trodden.

ausgewachsen *adj* fully-grown; *(col) Skandal* full-blown.

ausgewählt *adj* select; *Satz etc* well-chosen; *Werke* selected.

ausgewogen *adj* balanced; *Maß* equal. **ein ~es Kräfteverhältnis** an equal balance of powers.

Ausgewogenheit *f* balance.

ausgezeichnet *adj* excellent. **es geht mir ~** I'm feeling marvellous.

ausgiebig 1 *adj Mahlzeit etc* substantial, large; *Mittagsschlaf* long; *Gebrauch* extensive. **2** *adv* **~ frühstücken** to have a substantial breakfast; **~ schlafen** to have a good (long) sleep; **etw ~ gebrauchen** to use sth extensively.

ausgießen *vt sep irreg (aus einem Behälter)* to pour out; *(weggießen)* to pour away; *Behälter* to empty.

Ausgleich *m* **-e (a)** *(Gleichgewicht)* balance; *(von Konto)* balancing; *(von Schulden)* settling; *(von Verlust, Fehler)* compensation; *(von Unterschieden)* balancing out; *(von Konflikten etc)* reconciliation. **zum/als ~ für etw** in order to compensate for sth; **er treibt zum ~ Sport** he does sport for exercise. **(b)** *no pl (Ballspiele)* equalizer; *(Tennis)* deuce.

ausgleichen *sep irreg* **1** *vt Unterschiede* to even out; *Unebenheit* to level out; *Konto* to balance; *Schulden* to settle; *Fehler* to make good; *Verlust, Mangel* to offset, to compensate for; *Konflikte etc* to reconcile. **~de Gerechtigkeit** poetic justice; *siehe* **ausgeglichen. 2** *vi (Sport)* to equalize. **zum 1:1 ~** to equalize to make it 1 all. **3** *vr* to balance out; *(Einnahmen und Ausgaben)* to balance.

Ausgleichs-: ~sport *m* keep-fit activity; **als ~sport** to keep fit; **~tor** *nt*, **treffer** *m* equalizer.

ausgraben *vt sep irreg (lit, fig)* to dig up; *Grube* to dig out; *Altertümer auch* to excavate; *(hervorholen)* to dig out; *alte Geschichten* to bring up.

Ausgrabung *f* excavation, dig; *(Fund)* find.

Ausguck *m* **-e** lookout.

Ausguß *m (Becken)* sink; *(Abfluß)* drain.

aushaben *sep irreg (col)* **1** *vt (fertig sein mit) Buch etc* to have finished; *(ausgezogen haben)* to have taken off. **2** *vi (Schule etc beendet haben)* to finish.

aushalten *vt sep irreg* **(a)** to bear, to stand. **es läßt sich ~** it's bearable; **das ist nicht auszuhalten** *or* **zum A~** it's unbearable; **ich halte es vor Hitze/zu Hause nicht mehr aus** I can't stand the heat/being at home any longer; **wie kann man es bei der Firma bloß ~?** how can anyone stand working for that firm?; **er hält viel/nicht viel aus** he can take a lot/can't take much. **(b)** *Ton* to hold. **(c)** *(col: unterhalten)* to keep. **sich von jdm ~**

lassen to be kept by sb.
aushandeln *vt sep* to negotiate.
aushändigen *vt sep* **jdm etw/einen Preis** ~ to hand sth over to sb/give sb a prize.
Aushändigung *f* handing over.
Aushang *m, pl* Aushänge notice, announcement; *(das Aushängen)* posting. **etw durch** ~ **bekanntgeben** to put up a notice about sth.
aushängen *sep* **1** *vt* **(a)** *(bekanntmachen) Nachricht etc* to put up. **(b)** *(herausheben) Tür* to unhinge. **2** *vi irreg* **am Schwarzen Brett** ~ to be on the noticeboard *(Brit) or* bulletin board *(US).*
ausharren *vi sep (geh)* to wait. **auf seinem Posten** ~ to stand by one's post.
ausheben *vt sep irreg* **(a)** *Tür etc* to take off its hinges. **(b)** *Erde* to dig out; *Graben* to dig. **(c)** *(fig) Diebesnest* to raid; *Bande* to make a raid on.
aushecken *vt sep (col) Plan* to cook up *(col).*
ausheilen *sep* **1** *vt Krankheit* to cure; *Organ, Wunde* to heal. **2** *vi aux sein (Krankheit)* to be cured; *(Organ, Wunde)* to heal.
aushelfen *vi sep irreg* to help out *(jdm sb).*
Aushilfe *f* **(a)** help, aid. **jdn zur** ~ **haben** to have sb to help out. **(b)** *(Mensch)* temporary worker; *(esp im Büro auch)* temp *(col).* **als** ~ **arbeiten** to help out; *(im Büro auch)* to temp *(col).*
Aushilfs-: ~**kraft** *f* temporary worker; *(esp im Büro auch)* temp *(col);* ~**lehrer** *m* supply teacher; ~**personal** *nt* temporary staff.
aushöhlen *vt sep* to hollow out; *(fig: untergraben)* to undermine.
Aushöhlung *f* **(a)** *(ausgehöhlte Stelle)* hollow. **(b)** *no pl siehe vt* hollowing out; undermining.
ausholen *vi sep (zum Schlag)* to raise one's hand/arm *etc; (zum Wurf)* to reach back. **weit** ~ *(zum Schlag, beim Tennis)* to take a big swing; *(fig: Redner)* to go far afield; **zum Gegenschlag** ~ *(lit, fig)* to prepare for a counter-attack.
aushorchen *vt sep (col) jdn* to sound out.
aushungern *vt sep* to starve out; *siehe* **ausgehungert.**
auskennen *vr sep irreg (an einem Ort)* to know one's way around; *(auf einem Gebiet)* to know a lot *(auf or in+dat* about). **man kennt sich bei ihm nie aus** you never know where you are with him.
auskippen *vt sep (col)* to empty (out).
ausklammern *vt sep Problem* to ignore.
Ausklang *m (geh)* conclusion, end.
ausklappbar *adj* folding. **dieser Tisch ist** ~ this table can be opened out.
auskleiden *vt sep (beziehen)* to line.
ausklingen *vi sep irreg aux sein (Feier etc)* to end.
ausklopfen *vt sep Teppich* to beat; *Pfeife* to knock out.
ausknobeln *vt sep (col) Plan* to figure out *(col).*
auskochen *vt sep (fig col: sich ausdenken)* to cook up *(col); siehe* **ausgekocht.**
auskommen *vi sep irreg aux sein* **(a)** *(genügend haben, zurechtkommen)* to get by *(mit* on), to manage *(mit* on, with). **ohne jdn/etw** ~ to manage *or* do without sb/sth. **(b) mit jdm (gut)** ~ to get on *or* along well with sb.
Auskommen *nt no pl (Einkommen)* livelihood. **sein** ~ **haben/finden** to get by; **mit ihr ist kein** ~ she's impossible to get on with.
auskosten *vt sep (genießen)* to make the most of; *Leben* to enjoy to the full.
auskramen *vt sep (col)* to dig out, to unearth; *(fig) alte Geschichten etc* to bring up.
auskratzen *vt sep (auch Med)* to scrape out. **jdm die Augen** ~ to scratch sb's eyes out.
auskugeln *vr sep* **sich** *(dat)* **den Arm/die Schulter** ~ to dislocate one's arm/shoulder.
auskühlen *sep* **1** *vt* to cool down. **2** *vi aux sein (abkühlen)* to cool down; *(Körper, Menschen)* to chill through. **etw** ~ **lassen** to leave sth to cool.
auskundschaften *vt sep* to find out; *Versteck* to spy out; *(esp Mil)* to reconnoitre.
Auskunft *f, pl* **Auskünfte (a)** *(Mitteilung)* information *no pl (über+acc* about). **nähere** ~ further details; **eine detaillierte** ~ a detailed piece of information; **jdm eine** ~ **erteilen** *or* **geben** to give sb some information. **(b)** *(Schalter)* information office/desk; *(am Bahnhof auch)* enquiry office/desk; *(Telec)* directory enquiries *no art (Brit),* directory assistance *no art (US).*
Auskunfts-: ~**beamte(r)** *m* information officer; *(am Bahnhof)* information clerk; ~**person** *f* informer; *(Beamter)* information clerk; ~**schalter** *m* information desk.
auskuppeln *vi sep* to disengage the clutch.
auskurieren* *vt sep (col)* to cure; *Krankheit auch* to get rid of *(col).*
auslachen *vt sep jdn* to laugh at.
ausladen *vt sep irreg* **(a)** *Ware, Ladung* to unload. **(b)** *(col)* **jdn** ~ to tell sb not to come.
ausladend *adj Gebärden, Bewegung* sweeping.
Auslage *f* **(a)** *(von Waren)* display; *(Schaufenster)* window; *(Schaukasten)* showcase. **(b)** *usu pl* expense. **seine** ~**n für Essen** his outlay for food.
Ausland *nt no pl* foreign countries *pl; (fig: die Ausländer)* foreigners *pl.* **ins/im** ~ abroad; **aus dem** *or* **vom** ~ from abroad; **wie hat das** ~ **darauf reagiert?** what was the reaction abroad?; **Handel mit dem** ~ foreign trade.
Ausländer(in *f***)** *m* - foreigner; *(Admin, Jur)* alien.
ausländerfeindlich *adj* hostile to foreigners.
Ausländerfeindlichkeit *f* hostility to foreigners, xenophobia.
ausländisch *adj attr* foreign; *Erzeugnisse, Freunde etc auch* from abroad.
Auslands-: ~**aufenthalt** *m* stay abroad; ~**deutsche(r)** *mf* expatriate German; ~**gespräch** *nt* international call; ~**investition** *f* foreign investment; ~**korrespondent** *m* foreign correspondent; ~**reise** *f* journey *or* trip abroad; ~**schutzbrief** *m* international motoring cover; ~**vertretung** *f* agency abroad; *(von Firma)* foreign branch.
auslassen *sep irreg* **1** *vt* **(a)** *(weglassen, übergehen)* to leave *or* miss out; *(versäumen) Chance* to miss. **(b)** *(abreagieren)* to vent *(an+dat* on). **seine Gefühle** ~ to let off steam *(col).* **(c)** *Butter, Fett* to melt. **(d)** *Kleider etc* to let out; *Saum* to let down. **(e)** *siehe* **ausgelassen. 2** *vr* to talk *(über+acc* about). **sich über jdn/etw** ~ *(pej)* to go on about sb/sth *(pej).*
Auslassung *f* **(a)** *(Weglassen)* omission. **(b)** ~**en** *pl (pej: Äußerungen)* remarks *pl.*
auslasten *vt sep* **(a)** *Fahrzeug* to make full use of; *Maschine auch* to use to capacity. **(b)** *jdn* to occupy fully; *siehe* **ausgelastet.**
Auslauf *m, pl* **Ausläufe (a)** *no pl (für Kinder, Tiere)* room to run about. **(b)** *no pl (das Auslaufen)* discharge; *(das Lecken)* leakage.
auslaufen *vi sep irreg aux sein* **(a)** *(Flüssigkeit)* to run out *(aus* of); *(Behälter)* to empty; *(undicht sein)* to leak. **(b)** *(Naut: Schiff)* to sail. **(c)** *(enden) (Modell, Serie)* to be discontinued; *(Vertrag etc)* to run out. **(d)** *(zum Stillstand kommen: Motor etc)* to come to a stop. **(e)** *(Farbe)* to run.
Ausläufer *m* **(a)** *(Met) (von Hoch)* ridge; *(von Tief)* trough. **(b)** *(Vorberge)* foothill *usu pl.*
auslaugen *vt sep (lit, fig)* to exhaust.
auslecken *vt sep* to lick out.
ausleeren *vt sep Gefäß* to empty.
auslegen *vt sep* **(a)** *(ausbreiten)* to lay out; *Waren etc auch* to display; *Köder* to put down. **(b)** *(bedecken)* to cover; *(auskleiden)* to line. **den Boden/das Zimmer (mit Teppichen)** ~ to carpet the floor/room. **(c)** *(deuten)* to interpret. **etw falsch** ~ to misinterpret sth. **(d)** *Geld* to lend *(jdm etw* sb sth). **sie hat die 5 Mark für mich ausgelegt** she paid the 5 marks for me.
Ausleger *m* - **(a)** *(von Kran etc)* jib, boom. **(b)** *(Deuter)* interpreter.

Auslegung *f (Deutung)* interpretation. **falsche ~** misinterpretation.
ausleiern *vti sep (col)* to wear out; *siehe* **ausgeleiert.**
Ausleihe *f (Schalter)* issue desk. **eine ~ ist nicht möglich** it is not possible to lend out anything.
ausleihen *vt sep irreg (verleihen)* to lend *(jdm, an jdn* to sb); *(von jdm leihen)* to borrow.
auslernen *vi sep (Lehrling)* to finish one's apprenticeship. **man lernt nie aus** *(prov)* you live and learn *(prov).*
Auslese *f* **-n (a)** *no pl (Auswahl)* selection. **natürliche ~** natural selection; **eine ~ treffen** *or* **vornehmen** to make a selection. **(b)** *(Wein) high-quality wine made from selected grapes.*
auslesen *vti sep irreg (col) Buch* to finish reading.
ausliefern *vt sep* **(a)** *Waren* to deliver. **(b)** *jdn* to hand over *(an+acc* to); *(an anderen Staat)* to extradite *(an+acc* to); *(fig: preisgeben)* to leave *(jdm* in the hands of). **jdm/einer Sache ausgeliefert sein** to be at sb's mercy/the mercy of sth.
Auslieferung *f siehe vt* **(a)** delivery. **(b)** handing over; extradition.
Auslieferungs|abkommen *nt* extradition treaty.
ausliegen *vi sep irreg (zur Ansicht)* to be displayed; *(Zeitschriften etc)* to be available (to the public); *(Liste)* to be up.
auslöffeln *vt sep* **~ müssen, was man sich eingebrockt hat** *(col)* to have to take the consequences.
auslöschen *vt sep* **(a)** *Feuer etc* to put out, to extinguish. **(b)** *(auswischen) Spuren, Erinnerung* to wipe out; *Schrift* to erase *(an +dat* from).
auslosen *vt sep* to draw lots for; *Preis, Gewinner* to draw.
auslösen *vt sep Mechanismus, Alarm* to trigger off; *Kameraverschluß* to release; *(fig) Wirkung* to produce; *Begeisterung etc* to arouse.
Auslöser *m* **- (a)** trigger; *(für Bombe)* release button; *(Phot)* shutter release. **(b)** *(Anlaß)* cause.
Auslosung *f* draw.
Auslösung *f siehe vt (a)* triggering off; release; producing; arousing.
ausloten *vt sep (Naut) Tiefe* to sound; *(fig geh)* to plumb.
ausmachen *vt sep* **(a)** *Feuer, Kerze, Zigarette* to put out; *elektrisches Licht auch, Radio, Gas* to turn off. **(b)** *(ermitteln, sichten)* to make out. **(c)** *(vereinbaren)* to agree. **etw mit sich selbst ~ (müssen)** to (have to) sort sth out for oneself; *siehe* **ausgemacht. (d)** *(bewirken, darstellen)* (to go) to make up. **all der Luxus, der ein angenehmes Leben ausmacht** all the luxuries which go to make up a pleasant life. **(e)** *(bedeuten)* **viel/ wenig** *or* **nicht viel ~** to make a big/not much difference; **das macht nichts aus** that doesn't matter. **(f)** *(stören)* to matter *(jdm* to). **macht es Ihnen etwas aus, wenn ...?** would you mind if ...?
ausmalen *vt sep* **sich** *(dat)* **etw ~** to imagine sth.
ausmanövrieren* *vt sep* to outmanoeuvre *(Brit),* to outmaneuver *(US).*
Ausmaß *nt (Größe: von Gegenstand, Fläche)* size; *(Umfang: von Katastrophe)* extent. **ein Verlust in diesem ~** a loss on this scale.
ausmerzen *vt sep Unkraut, Fehler* to eradicate.
ausmessen *vt sep irreg* to measure (out).
ausmisten *vt sep Stall* to muck out; *(fig col) Schrank etc* to tidy out; *Zimmer* to clean out.
ausmustern *vt sep Maschine, Fahrzeug etc* to take out of service; *(Mil: entlassen)* to invalid out.
Ausnahme *f* **-n** exception. **mit ~ von Horst** with the exception of Horst; **~n bestätigen die Regel** *(prov)* the exception proves the rule *(prov).*
Ausnahme-: ~erscheinung *f* exception; **~fall** *m* exception, exceptional case; **~zustand** *m (Pol)* state of emergency; **den ~zustand verhängen** to declare a state of emergency.
ausnahmslos 1 *adv* without exception. **2** *adj Bewilligung, Zustimmung* unanimous.
ausnahmsweise *adv* **darf ich das machen? — ~** may I do that? — just this once; **er darf heute ~ früher von der Arbeit weggehen** as an exception he may leave work earlier today.
ausnehmen *sep irreg* **1** *vt* **(a)** *Fisch, Kaninchen* to gut; *Geflügel* to draw. **(b)** *(ausschließen) jdn* to make an exception of. **(c)** *(col) jdn* to fleece; *(beim Kartenspiel)* to clean out. **2** *vr (geh: wirken)* **sich schön** *or* **gut/schlecht ~** to look good/bad.
ausnehmend *adj (geh)* exceptional. **das gefällt mir ~ gut** I like that very much indeed.
ausnüchtern *vti sep* to sober up.
Ausnüchterung *f* sobering up.
Ausnüchterungszelle *f* drying-out cell.
ausnutzen *vt sep* to make use of; *(ausbeuten)* to exploit; *Gelegenheit* to make the most of; *jds Gutmütigkeit etc* to take advantage of.
Ausnutzung *f* use; *(Ausbeutung)* exploitation.
auspacken *sep* **1** *vti Koffer* to unpack; *Geschenk* to unwrap. **2** *vi (col: alles sagen)* to talk *(col).*
auspeitschen *vt sep* to whip.
auspfeifen *vt sep irreg* to boo.
ausplaudern *vt sep* to let out.
ausposaunen* *vt sep (col)* to tell the world about *(col).*
ausprägen *vr sep (Begabung, Charaktereigenschaft etc)* to reveal *or* show itself; *siehe* **ausgeprägt.**
Ausprägung *f no pl (von Charakter)* shaping.
auspressen *vt sep Saft, Schwamm etc* to squeeze out; *Zitrone etc* to squeeze.
ausprobieren* *vt sep* to try out.
Auspuff *m* **-e** exhaust.
Auspuff-: ~gase *pl* exhaust fumes *pl*; **~rohr** *nt* exhaust; **~topf** *m* silencer *(Brit),* muffler *(US).*
auspumpen *vt sep* to pump out.
ausputzen *vi sep (Ftbl)* to clear (the ball); *(Ausputzer sein)* to play sweeper.
Ausputzer *m* **-** *(Ftbl)* sweeper.
ausquartieren* *vt sep* to move out.
ausquetschen *vt sep Zitrone etc* to squeeze; *(col: ausfragen)* to grill *(col)*; *(aus Neugier)* to pump *(col).*
ausradiern* *vt sep* to rub out, to erase; *(fig: vernichten)* to wipe out.
ausrangieren* *vt sep Kleider* to throw out; *Maschine, Auto* to scrap. **ein altes ausrangiertes Auto** an old disused car.
ausrauben *vt sep* to rob.
ausraufen *vt sep* **ich könnte mir die Haare ~** I could kick myself.
ausräumen *vt sep* to clear out; *(fig) Mißverständnisse, Konflikt* to clear up; *Vorurteile, Bedenken* to dispel; *(col: ausrauben)* to clean out *(col).*
ausrechnen *vt sep* to work out; *(ermitteln) Gewicht, Länge auch* to calculate. **sich** *(dat)* **große Chancen ~** to reckon that one has a good chance; *siehe* **ausgerechnet.**
Ausrede *f* excuse.
ausreden *sep* **1** *vi* to finish speaking. **er hat mich nicht mal ~ lassen** he didn't even let me finish (speaking). **2** *vt* **jdm etw ~** to talk sb out of sth.
ausreichen *vi sep* to be sufficient *or* enough. **die Zeit reicht nicht aus** there is not sufficient time.
ausreichend 1 *adj* adequate; *(Sch)* satisfactory. **2** *adv* adequately.
Ausreise *f* **bei der ~** on leaving the country; *(Grenzübertritt)* on crossing the border; **jdm die ~ verweigern** to prohibit sb from leaving the country.
Ausreise|erlaubnis *f* exit permit.
ausreisen *vi sep aux sein* to leave (the country).
Ausreisevisum *nt* exit visa.
ausreißen *sep irreg* **1** *vt Haare, Blatt* to tear out; *Zahn* to pull out; *Blumen* to pull up. **er hat sich** *(dat)* **kein Bein ausgerissen** *(col)* he didn't ex-

actly overstrain himself. **2** *vi aux sein (+dat* from*) (col: davonlaufen)* to run away; *(Sport)* to break away.
Ausreißer(in *f)* *m* - *(col)* runaway; *(Sport)* runner/cyclist who breaks away.
ausreiten *vi sep irreg aux sein* to go riding.
ausrenken *vt sep* to dislocate. **sich (fast) den Hals ~** *(col)* to crane one's neck.
ausrichten *vt sep* **(a)** *(aufstellen)* to line up. **jdn/etw auf etw** *(acc)* **~** *(abstellen)* to gear sb/sth to sth. **(b)** *(veranstalten)* to organize. **(c)** *(erreichen)* to achieve. **ich konnte bei ihr nichts ~** I couldn't get anywhere with her. **(d)** *(übermitteln)* to tell; *Nachricht* to pass on. **kann ich etwas ~?** can I take a message?; **bitte richten Sie ihm einen Gruß aus** please give him my regards.
Ausrichtung *f siehe vt* **(a)** lining up. **(b)** organization. **(c)** *(fig) (auf Ideologie etc)* orientation *(auf +acc* towards*)*; *(auf Bedürfnisse etc)* gearing *(auf +acc* to*)*.
Ausritt *m* ride (out).
ausrollen *vt sep Teig, Teppich* to roll out.
ausrotten *vt sep* to wipe out; *Volk auch, Ungeziefer* to exterminate; *Religion, Ideen auch* to stamp out.
Ausrottung *f siehe vt* wiping out; extermination; stamping out.
ausrücken *vi sep aux sein* **(a)** *(Mil)* to move out; *(Polizei, Feuerwehr)* to turn out. **(b)** *(col: ausreißen)* to make off; *(von zu Hause)* to run away.
Ausruf *m (Ruf)* cry, shout.
ausrufen *vt sep irreg* to exclaim; *Schlagzeilen* to shout out; *(verkünden)* to call out; *Haltestellen, Streik* to call. **jdn zum König ~** to proclaim sb king; **jdn ~ (lassen)** *(über Lautsprecher etc)* to page sb.
Ausrufezeichen *nt* exclamation mark *(Brit) or* point *(US)*.
Ausrufung *f* proclamation. **die ~ eines Streiks** a strike call.
ausruhen *vtir sep* to rest; *(Mensch auch)* to have a rest; *siehe* **ausgeruht.**
ausrüsten *vt sp (lit, fig)* to equip. **ein Fahrzeug mit etw ~** to fit a car with sth.
Ausrüstung *f (~sgegenstände)* equipment; *(esp Kleidung)* outfit.
Ausrüstungsgegenstand *m* piece of equipment.
ausrutschen *vi sep aux sein* to slip; *(Fahrzeug)* to skid. **das Messer/die Hand ist mir ausgerutscht** my knife/my hand slipped.
Ausrutscher *m - (col: lit, fig)* slip.
Aussaat *f no pl (das Säen)* sowing.
aussäen *vt sep (lit, fig)* to sow.
Aussage *f* **-n** statement; *(Behauptung)* opinion; *(Bericht)* report; *(Jur) (eines Angeklagten)* statement; *(Zeugen~)* evidence *no pl.* **eine eidliche/schriftliche ~** a sworn/written statement; **der Zeuge verweigerte die ~** the witness refused to give evidence; **eine ~ machen** to make a statement.
aussagen *sep* **1** *vt* to say *(über+acc* about*)*; *(behaupten)* to state; *(unter Eid)* to testify. **2** *vi (Jur) (Zeuge)* to give evidence; *(Angeklagter)* to make a statement; *(unter Eid auch)* to testify. **für/gegen jdn ~** to give evidence for/against sb.
Aussatz *m no pl (Med)* leprosy.
Aussätzige(r) *mf decl as adj (lit, fig)* leper.
aussaugen *vt sep Saft etc* to suck out; *Wunde* to suck the poison out of; *(fig: ausbeuten)* to drain dry. **jdn bis aufs Blut ~** to bleed sb white.
ausschachten *vt sep* to dig, to excavate.
Ausschachtung *f* excavation.
ausschalten *vt sep* **(a)** *(abstellen)* to switch *or* turn off. **(b)** *(fig)* to eliminate.
Ausschaltung *f siehe vt* switching off; elimination.
Ausschank *m, pl* **Ausschänke** bar; *(no pl: Getränkeausgabe)* sale of drinks.
Ausschank|erlaubnis *f* licence *(Brit)*, license *(US)*.
Ausschau *f no pl*: **~ halten** to look out *(nach* for*)*.
ausschauen *vi sep (geh)* to be on the look-out *(nach* for*)*.
ausscheiden *sep irreg* **1** *vt (aussondern)* to take out; *(Physiol)* to excrete. **2** *vi aux sein* **(a)** *(aus einem Amt)* to retire *(aus* from*)*; *(aus Firma)* to leave *(aus etw* sth*)*; *(Sport)* to be eliminated; *(wegen Verletzung etc)* to drop out. **(b)** *(nicht in Betracht kommen: Möglichkeit etc)* to be ruled out. **das/er scheidet aus** that/he has to be ruled out.
Ausscheidung *f* **(a)** *no pl (das Aussondern)* removal; *(Physiol)* excretion. **(b)** *(Sport)* elimination; *(Vorkampf)* qualifying contest.
Ausscheidungs-: ~kampf *m* qualifying contest; *(Leichtathletik, Schwimmen)* heat; **~spiel** *nt* qualifying match *or* game.
ausschenken *vti sep* to pour (out).
ausscheren *vi sep aux sein (Fahrzeug)* to leave the line *or* convoy; *(zum Überholen)* to pull out.
ausschicken *vt sep* to send out.
ausschiffen *vt sep* to disembark; *Ladung, Waren* to unload.
Ausschiffung *f siehe vt* disembarkation; unloading.
ausschildern *vt sep* to signpost.
ausschimpfen *vt sep* to tell off.
ausschlachten *vt sep* **(a)** to gut, to dress. **(b)** *(fig) Fahrzeuge, Maschinen etc* to cannibalize. **(c)** *(fig col: ausnutzen) Skandal, Ereignis* to exploit.
ausschlafen *sep irreg* **1** *vt Rausch etc* to sleep off. **2** *vir* to have a good sleep.
Ausschlag *m* **(a)** *(Med)* rash. **(b)** *(von Zeiger etc)* swing; *(von Kompaßnadel)* deflection. **(c)** *(fig)* **den ~ geben** *(fig)* to be the decisive factor; **die Stimme des Vorsitzenden gibt den ~** the chairman has the casting vote.
ausschlagen *sep irreg* **1** *vt* **(a)** *(herausschlagen)* to knock out. **(b)** *Feuer* to beat out. **(c)** *(auskleiden)* to line. **(d)** *(ablehnen)* to turn down. **jdm etw ~** to refuse sb sth. **2** *vi* **(a)** *aux sein or haben (Baum, Strauch)* to start to bud. **(b)** *(Pferd)* to kick. **(c)** *aux sein or haben (Zeiger etc)* to swing; *(Kompaßnadel)* to be deflected.
ausschlaggebend *adj* decisive; *Stimme auch* deciding. **das ist von ~er Bedeutung** that is of prime importance.
ausschließen *vt sep irreg* **(a)** *(aussperren)* to lock out. **(b)** *(ausnehmen)* to exclude; *(aus Gemeinschaft)* to expel; *(vorübergehend)* to suspend; *(Sport)* to disqualify; *Fehler, Möglichkeit etc* to rule out. **das eine schließt das andere nicht aus** the one does not exclude the other; **die Öffentlichkeit ~** *(Jur)* to exclude the public; *siehe* **ausgeschlossen.**
ausschließlich *adj attr* exclusive.
ausschlüpfen *vi sep aux sein* to slip out; *(aus Ei, Puppe)* to hatch out.
Ausschluß *m siehe* **ausschließen (b)** exclusion; expulsion; suspension; disqualification. **unter ~ der Öffentlichkeit stattfinden** to be closed to the public.
ausschmücken *vt sep* to decorate; *(fig) Erzählung* to embellish.
Ausschmückung *f siehe vt* decoration; embellishment.
ausschneiden *vt sep irreg (herauschneiden)* to cut out; *siehe* **ausgeschnitten.**
Ausschnitt *m* **(a)** *(Zeitungs~)* cutting, clipping. **(b)** *(Kleid~)* neck. **ein tiefer ~** a low neckline. **(c)** *(fig: Teil)* part; *(aus Film)* clip.
ausschöpfen *vt sep* **(a)** *Wasser etc* to ladle out *(aus* of*)*. **(b)** *(leeren)* to empty; *(fig)* to exhaust.
ausschreiben *vt sep irreg* **(a)** to write out; *(ungekürzt schreiben)* to write (out) in full. **(b)** *Rechnung etc* to make out. **(c)** *(bekanntmachen)* to announce; *Wahlen* to call; *Stelle* to advertise.

Ausschreibung *f (Bekanntmachung) (von Wahlen)* calling; *(von Stelle)* advertising.
Ausschreitung *f usu pl (Aufruhr)* rioting *no pl.*
Ausschuß *m* **(a)** *(Komitee)* committee. **(b)** *no pl (Comm)* rejects *pl*; *(fig col)* trash.
ausschütten *vt sep* **(a)** *(auskippen)* to tip out; *Eimer, Glas* to empty. **jdm sein Herz** ~ *(fig)* to pour out one's heart to sb. **(b)** *(Fin) Dividende etc* to distribute.
Ausschüttung *f (Fin)* distribution.
ausschwärmen *vi sep aux sein (Bienen, Menschen)* to swarm out; *(Mil)* to fan out.
ausschweifend *adj Leben* dissipated; *Phantasie* wild.
Ausschweifung *f (Maßlosigkeit)* excess; *(in Lebensweise)* dissipation.
ausschweigen *vr sep irreg* to remain silent *(über +acc, zu* about*)*.
ausschwenken *vi sep aux sein* **(a)** *(Mil)* to wheel. **(b)** *(Kran etc)* to swing out.
ausschwitzen *vt sep* to sweat out.
aussehen *vi sep irreg* to look. **gut** ~ to look good; *(hübsch)* to be good-looking; *(gesund)* to look well; **gesund/elend** ~ to look healthy/wretched; **es sieht nach Regen aus** it looks like rain; **wie jd/etw** ~ to look like sb/sth; **wie sieht's aus?** *(col: wie steht's)* how's things? *(col)*; **es soll nach etwas** ~ it's got to look good; **es sieht danach** *or* **so aus, als ob ...** it looks as if ...; **so siehst du aus!** *(col)* that's what you think!; **es sieht nicht gut mit ihm aus** things don't look good for him.
Aussehen *nt no pl* appearance. **dem** ~ **nach** by the looks of it; **etw dem** ~ **nach beurteilen** to judge sth by appearances.
aussein *sep irreg aux sein.* **1** *vi (col)* **(a)** *(zu Ende sein) (Schule)* to finish; *(Krieg, Stück)* to have ended; *(nicht ansein) (Feuer, Ofen)* to be out; *(Radio, Fernseher etc)* to be off. **die Schule ist aus** school has finished *or* is out. **(b) auf etw** *(acc)* ~ to be (only) interested in sth; **auf jdn** ~ to be after sb *(col)*. **2** *vi impers* **es ist aus (und vorbei) zwischen uns** it's (all) over between us; **es ist aus mit ihm** he is finished, he has had it *(col)*.
außen *adv* ~ **bemalt** painted on the outside; ~ **an der Windschutzscheibe** on the outside of the windscreen; **von** ~ **sieht es gut aus** on the outside it looks good; **das Fenster geht nach** ~ **auf** the window opens outwards.
Außen-: ~**antenne** *f* outdoor aerial *(Brit) or* antenna *(US)*; ~**arbeiten** *pl* work on the exterior; ~**aufnahme** *f* outdoor shot; ~**bahn** *f* outside lane; ~**bezirk** *m* outlying district; ~**bordmotor** *m* outboard motor.
aussenden *vtr sep irreg* to send out.
Außen-: ~**dienst** *m* external duty; **im** ~**dienst sein** to work outside the office; ~**handel** *m* foreign trade; ~**minister** *m* foreign minister, foreign secretary *(Brit)*, secretary of state *(US)*; ~**ministerium** *nt* foreign ministry, foreign office *(Brit)*, state department *(US)*; ~**politik** *f (Gebiet)* foreign politics *sing; (bestimmte)* foreign policy/policies; ~**politiker** *m* foreign affairs politician; **a**~**politisch** *adj* foreign policy *attr*; *Sprecher* on foreign affairs; ~**seite** *f* outside.
Außenseiter(in *f) m - (Sport, fig)* outsider.
Außenseiterrolle *f* role as an outsider. **eine** ~ **spielen** to play the role of an outsider.
Außen-: ~**spiegel** *m (Aut)* outside mirror; ~**stände** *pl (esp Comm)* outstanding debts *pl*, arrears *pl*; ~**stehende(r)** *mf decl as adj* outsider; ~**stelle** *f* branch; ~**stürmer** *m (Ftbl)* wing; ~**temperatur** *f* outside temperature; ~**wand** *f* outer wall; ~**welt** *f* outside world.
außer 1 *prep+dat or (rare) gen* **(a)** *(räumlich)* out of. ~ **Sicht** out of sight; ~ **sich** *(acc)* **geraten** to go wild; ~ **sich** *(dat)* **sein** to be beside oneself; ~ **Haus sein/essen** to be/eat out; ~ **Atem** out of breath. **(b)** *(ausgenommen)* except (for); *(abgesehen von)* apart from, aside from. **alle** ~ **mir** everyone except (for) me. **(c)** *(zusätzlich zu)* in addition to. **2** *conj* except. ~ **daß ...** except that ...; ~ **wenn ...** unless ...
außerdem *adv* besides; *(dazu)* in addition, as well; *(überdies)* anyway.
außerdienstlich *adj (nicht dienstlich) Angelegenheit* private; *(außerhalb der Arbeitszeit)* social.
außer|ehelich 1 *adj* extramarital; *Kind* illegitimate. **2** *adv* outside marriage.
äußere(r, s) *adj (außerhalb gelegen, Geog)* outer; *Verletzung* external; *Schein, Eindruck* outward.
Äußere(s) *nt decl as adj* exterior; *(fig: Aussehen auch)* outward appearance.
außer-: ~**europäisch** *adj attr* non-European; ~**gewöhnlich 1** *adj* unusual, out of the ordinary; **2** *adv (sehr)* extremely.
außerhalb 1 *prep+gen* outside. ~ **der Stadt** outside the town, out of town. **2** *adv (außen)* outside; *(~ der Stadt)* out of town. ~ **stehen** *(fig)* to be on the outside.
außer|irdisch *adj* extraterrestrial.
äußerlich *adj* **(a)** external. **(b)** *(fig) (oberflächlich)* superficial; *(scheinbar)* outward. **„nur zur ~en Anwendung!"** for external use only; **rein** ~ **betrachtet** on the face of it.
Äußerlichkeit *f (fig)* triviality; *(Oberflächlichkeit)* superficiality; *(Formalität)* formality. ~**en** (outward) appearances.
äußern 1 *vt (sagen)* to say; *Wunsch etc* to express; *Worte* to utter; *Kritik* to voice. **seine Meinung** ~ to give one's views. **2** *vr (Mensch)* to speak; *(Krankheit, Symptom)* to show itself.
außer-: ~**ordentlich 1** *adj* extraordinary; *(ungewöhnlich auch)* exceptional; *(bemerkenswert auch)* remarkable; **2** *adv (sehr)* exceptionally, extremely; ~**parlamentarisch** *adj* extraparliamentary; ~**planmäßig** *adj Besuch, Treffen* unscheduled; ~**sinnlich** *adj* ~**sinnliche Wahrnehmung** extrasensory perception.
äußerst *adv* extremely, exceedingly.
außerstande *adv (unfähig)* incapable; *(nicht in der Lage)* unable. ~ **sein, etw zu tun** to be incapable of doing sth.
äußerstenfalls *adv* at most.
äußerste(r, s) *adj (räumlich)* furthest; *Schicht* outermost; *Norden etc* extreme; *(zeitlich)* latest possible; *(fig)* utmost. **mein** ~**s Angebot** my final offer; **im** ~**n Falle** if the worst comes to the worst; **mit** ~**r Kraft** with all one's strength.
Äußerste(s) *nt decl as adj* **bis zum** ~**n gehen** to go to extremes; **er hat sein** ~**s gegeben** he gave his all.
Äußerung *f (Bemerkung)* remark, comment; *(Behauptung)* statement; *(Zeichen)* expression.
aussetzen *sep* **1** *vt* **(a)** *Kind, Haustier* to abandon; *Pflanzen* to plant out; *(Naut) Passagiere* to maroon. **(b) jdn/etw einer Sache** *(dat)* ~ to expose sb/sth to sth; **jdm/einer Sache ausgesetzt sein** *(ausgeliefert)* to be at the mercy of sb/sth. **(c)** *Belohnung, Preis* to offer. **(d)** *(unterbrechen)* to interrupt; *Debatte, Prozeß* to adjourn. **(e)** *(vertagen) Verfahren* to suspend. **(f) an jdm/etw etwas auszusetzen haben** to find fault with sb/sth; **daran ist nichts auszusetzen** there is nothing wrong with it; **was haben Sie daran auszusetzen?** what's your objection to it?

2 *vi (aufhören)* to stop; *(bei Spiel)* to sit out; *(Herz)* to stop (beating); *(Motor auch)* to fail. **mit der Pille/Behandlung** ~ to stop taking the pill/to interrupt the treatment; **ohne auszusetzen** without a break.
Aussetzung *f* **(a)** *siehe vt (a)* abandonment; planting out; marooning. **(b)** *(Jur: von Verfahren)* suspension.
Aussicht *f* **(a)** *(Blick)* view *(auf+acc* of*)*. **mit** ~ **auf den Park** overlooking the park. **(b)** *(fig)* prospect *(auf +acc* of*)*. **die** ~**, daß etw geschieht**

the chances of sth happening; **unser Plan hat große ~en auf Erfolg** our plan has every chance of succeeding; **etw in ~ haben** to have good prospects of sth; **jdm etw in ~ stellen** to promise sb sth; **das sind ja schöne ~en!** *(iro col)* what a prospect!

Aussichts-: a~los *adj* hopeless; *(zwecklos)* pointless; *(völlig hoffnungslos)* desperate; **~losigkeit** *f siehe adj* hoplessness; pointlessness; desperateness; **a~reich** *adj* promising; *Stellung* with good prospects; **~turm** *m* lookout tower.

aussiedeln *vt sep* to resettle.

Aussiedler *m (Auswanderer)* emigrant.

Aussiedlung *f* resettlement.

aussöhnen *sep* **1** *vt* **jdn mit jdm/etw ~** to reconcile sb with sb/to sth. **2** *vr* **sich mit jdm/etw ~** to become reconciled with sb/to sth; **wir haben uns wieder ausgesöhnt** we have made it up again.

Aussöhnung *f* reconciliation *(mit jdm* with sb, *mit etw* to sth*)*.

aussondern *vt sep* to select; *Schlechtes* to separate out.

aussorgen *vi sep:* **ausgesorgt haben** to have no more money worries.

aussortieren* *vt sep* to sort out.

ausspannen *sep* **1** *vt* **(a)** *Tuch, Netz* to spread out; *Schnur, Leine* to put up. **(b)** *Pferde* to unhitch; *(aus Schreibmaschine) Bogen* to take out. **(c)** *(fig col)* **jdm die Freundin** *etc* **~** to pinch sb's girlfriend *etc (col)*. **2** *vi (sich erholen)* to have a break.

aussparen *vt sep (fig)* to omit.

Aussparung *f (Lücke)* gap.

aussperren *vt sep* to lock out.

Aussperrung *f (Ind)* lockout.

ausspielen *sep* **1** *vti* **(a)** *Karte* to play. **(b)** *(fig)* **jdn/etw gegen jdn/etw ~** to play sb/sth off against sb/sth. **(c)** *Gewinne* to give as a prize/as prizes. **2** *vi (Cards)* to lead. **wer spielt aus?** whose lead is it?

Ausspielung *f (im Lotto)* draw.

ausspionieren* *vt sep Pläne etc* to spy out; *Person* to spy on.

Aussprache *f* **(a)** pronunciation; *(Akzent)* accent. **(b)** *(Meinungsaustausch)* discussion, talks *pl*.

aussprechen *sep irreg* **1** *vt Wörter, Urteil etc* to pronounce; *Scheidung* to grant; *(äußern)* to express *(jdm* to sb*)*; *Verdächtigung* to voice; *Warnung* to give. **der Regierung das Vertrauen ~** to pass a vote of confidence in the government. **2** *vr (Partner)* to talk things out; *(sein Herz ausschütten)* to say what's on one's mind. **sich für/gegen etw ~** to come out in favour of/against sth. **3** *vi (zu Ende sprechen)* to finish (speaking); *siehe* **ausgesprochen.**

Ausspruch *m* remark; *(geflügeltes Wort)* saying.

ausspucken *sep* **1** *vt* to spit out. **2** *vi* to spit.

ausspülen *vt sep* to rinse (out).

ausstaffieren* *vt sep (col)* to rig out; *(herausputzen)* to dress up.

Ausstand *m* **(a)** *(Streik)* strike. **in den ~ treten** to (go on) strike. **(b) seinen ~ geben** to hold a leaving party.

ausstatten *vt sep* to equip; *(versorgen)* to provide; *(möblieren)* to furnish. **mit Humor** *etc* **ausgestattet sein** to be endowed with a sense of humour *etc.*

Ausstattung *f* **(a)** *siehe vt* equipping; provision. **(b)** *(Ausrüstung)* equipment; *(Tech auch)* fittings *pl*; *(von Zimmer etc)* furnishings *pl*; *(Theat)* décor and costumes.

ausstechen *vt sep irreg* **(a)** *Torf, Plätzchen etc* to cut out. **(b)** *Augen* to gouge out. **(c)** *(fig) jdn (verdrängen)* to push out; *(übertreffen)* to outdo.

ausstehen *sep irreg* **1** *vt (ertragen)* to endure; *Sorge, Angst* to go through, to suffer. **ich kann ihn/so etwas nicht ~** I can't stand him/anything like that. **2** *vi* **(a)** to be due; *(Antwort)* to be still to come; *(Entscheidung)* to be still to be taken. **(b)** *(Schulden)* to be outstanding.

aussteigen *vi sep irreg* **(a)** *aux sein* to get out *(aus* of*)*; *(aus Bus, Zug etc auch)* to get off *(aus etw* sth*)*. **alles ~!** everybody out!; *(von Schaffner)* all change! **(b)** *(col) (aus Geschäft etc)* to get out *(aus* of*)*; *(aus Gesellschaft)* to drop out *(aus* of*)*.

Aussteiger(in *f***)** *m* **-** *(col)* drop-out.

ausstellen *vt sep* **(a)** *(zur Schau stellen)* to display; *(auf Messe, in Museum etc)* to exhibit. **(b)** *(ausschreiben)* to make out *(jdm* to sb*)*. **einen Scheck auf jdn ~** to make out a cheque to sb. **(c)** *(ausschalten) Gerät* to turn off.

Aussteller(in *f***)** *m* **- (a)** *(auf Messe)* exhibitor. **(b)** *(von Scheck)* drawer.

Ausstellung *f* **(a)** *(Kunst~, Messe)* exhibition. **(b)** *no pl (von Scheck etc)* making out; *(behördlich)* issuing.

Ausstellungs-: ~datum *nt* date of issue; **~gelände** *nt* exhibition site; **~stück** *nt (in Ausstellung)* exhibit; *(in Schaufenster etc)* display item.

Aussterben *nt no pl* extinction. **vom ~ bedroht sein** to be threatened by extinction.

aussterben *vi sep irreg aux sein* to die out; *(esp Spezies, Geschlecht auch)* to become extinct; *siehe* **ausgestorben.**

Aussteuer *f* **-n** dowry.

aussteuern *vt sep Verstärker* to adjust.

Ausstieg *m* **-e (a)** *(Ausgang)* exit. **(b)** *(fig)* dropping out *(aus* of*)*.

ausstopfen *vt sep Kissen etc, Tiere* to stuff.

Ausstoß *m* **(a)** *(esp Phys, Tech: das Ausstoßen)* expulsion, discharge. **(b)** *(Produktion)* output.

ausstoßen *vt sep irreg* **(a)** *(herausstoßen)* to discharge; *Atem* to expel; *(herstellen) Teile, Stückzahl* to turn out, to produce. **(b)** *(ausschließen) (aus Verein, Armee etc)* to expel *(aus from)*; *(verbannen)* to banish *(aus* from*)*. **(c)** *(äußern)* to utter; *Schrei* to give.

ausstrahlen *sep* **1** *vt* to radiate *(auch fig)*; *esp Licht, Wärme auch* to give off; *(Rad, TV)* to transmit, to broadcast. **2** *vi* to radiate; *(Schmerz)* to spread *(bis in+acc* as far as*)*.

Ausstrahlung *f* radiation; *(Rad, TV)* transmission, broadcast(ing); *(fig: von Mensch, Ort)* aura.

ausstrecken *sep* **1** *vt* to extend *(nach* towards*)*; *Fühler auch* to put out; *Hand auch, Beine etc* to stretch out. **2** *vr* to stretch (oneself) out.

ausstreuen *vt sep* to scatter; *(fig) Gerücht* to spread.

ausströmen *sep* **1** *vi aux sein* **(a)** *(herausfließen)* to stream out *(aus* of*)*; *(entweichen)* to escape *(aus* from*)*. **(b)** *(ausstrahlen)* **etw strömt von jdm/etw aus** *(fig)* sb/sth radiates sth. **2** *vt Duft, Gas* to give off; *Wärme, Ruhe etc* to radiate.

aussuchen *vt sep (auswählen)* to choose; *(esp iro)* to pick; *siehe* **ausgesucht.**

Austausch *m* exchange; *(von Gedanken etc auch)* interchange; *(Ersatz)* replacement; *(Sport)* substitution. **im ~ für** *or* **gegen** in exchange for.

austauschbar *adj* (ex)changeable; *(untereinander ~)* interchangeable; *(ersetzbar)* replaceable.

Austausch-: ~motor *m* replacement engine; **~student** *m* exchange student.

austeilen *vt sep* to distribute *(an +acc* among*)*; *(aushändigen auch)* to hand out *(an +acc* to*)*; *Spielkarten* to deal (out); *Essen* to serve; *Befehle* to give, to issue.

Austeilung *f* distribution; *(Aushändigung auch)* handing out; *(von Essen etc)* serving.

Auster *f* **-n** oyster.

austoben *vr sep (Mensch)* to let off steam; *(sich müde machen)* to tire oneself out. **ein Garten, wo sich die Kinder ~ können** a garden where the children can romp about.

austragen *sep irreg vt* **(a)** *Waren, Post etc* to deliver. **(b)** *Duell, Wettkampf etc* to hold. **einen Streit mit jdm ~** to have it out with sb. **(c) ein**

Kind ~ *(nicht abtreiben)* to have a child. **(d)** *(löschen) Zahlen, Daten* to take out. **jdn** ~ *(aus Liste)* to cancel sb's name. **2** *vr* to sign out; *(in Hotel)* to check out.

Austragung *f (Sport)* holding.

Austragungs|ort *m (Sport)* venue.

Australien [-iən] *nt* Australia.

Australier(in *f***)** [-iɐ, -iərɪn] *m* - Australian.

australisch *adj* Australian.

austräumen *vt sep* **sein Traum von Reichtümern ist ausgeträumt** his dreams of riches are over.

austreiben *sep irreg* **1** *vt (vertreiben)* to drive out; *Teufel etc auch* to exorcize, to cast out *(esp old, liter)*. **jdm etw** ~ to cure sb of sth; *(esp durch Schläge)* to knock sth out of sb. **2** *vi (sprießen)* to sprout.

austreten *sep irreg* **1** *vi aux sein* **(a)** *(herauskommen)* to come out *(aus* of*)*; *(Gas etc)* to escape *(aus* from, through*)*. **(b)** *(col: zur Toilette gehen)* to go to the loo *or* john *(US) (col)*; *(Sch auch)* to be excused *(euph)*. **(c)** *(ausscheiden)* to leave *(aus etw* sth*)*. **2** *vt Pfad, Feuer etc* to tread out; *Schuhe* to wear out; *siehe* **ausgetreten.**

austricksen *vt sep (col: Sport, fig)* to trick.

austrinken *vti sep irreg* to finish. **trink (deine Milch) aus!** drink (your milk) up.

Austritt *m* **(a)** *no pl (von Flüssigkeit)* outflow; *(das Entweichen)* escape; *(von Blut)* issue. **(b)** *(das Ausscheiden)* leaving *no art (aus etw* sth*)*.

austrocknen *sep* **1** *vi aux sein* to dry out; *(Fluß etc)* to dry up; *(Kehle)* to become parched. **2** *vt* to dry out; *(trockenlegen) Sumpf auch* to drain.

austüfteln *vt sep (col)* to work out; *(ersinnen)* to think up.

aus|üben *vt sep* **(a)** *Beruf, Kunst* to practise *(Brit)*, to practice *(US)*; *Gewerbe auch* to carry on; *Aufgabe, Funktion* to perform; *(innehaben) Amt* to hold. **(b)** *Druck, Einfluß* to exert *(auf+acc* on*)*; *Macht, Recht* to exercise; *Wirkung* to have *(auf +acc* on*)*.

Aus|übung *f siehe vt* **(a)** practice; performance. **in** ~ **seines Dienstes/seiner Pflicht** *(form)* in the execution of his duty. **(b)** exertion; exercise.

aus|ufern *vi sep aux sein (fig)* to get out of hand; *(Konflikt etc)* to escalate *(zu* into*)*.

Ausverkauf *m* (clearance) sale; *(wegen Schließung)* closing-down sale; *(fig: Verrat)* sell-out.

ausverkauft *adj* sold out. **vor ~em Haus spielen** to play to a full house.

auswachsen *sep irreg* **1** *vi aux sein* **das ist (ja) zum A** ~ *(col)* it's enough to drive you mad *(col)*; *siehe* **ausgewachsen. 2** *vr* **sich zu etw** ~ *(fig: Streit etc)* to turn into sth.

Auswahl *f no pl* selection *(an +dat* of*)*; *(Angebot auch)* range; *(Wahl)* choice; *(die Besten)* pick. **viele Sachen zur ~ haben** to have many things to choose from; **eine ~ treffen** to make a choice; *(mehrere auswählen)* to make a selection.

auswählen *vt sep* to select, to choose *(unter+dat* from among*)*; *siehe* **ausgewählt.**

Auswahl-: ~mannschaft *f* representative team; **~möglichkeit** *f* choice.

Auswanderer *m*, **Auswanderin** *f* emigrant.

auswandern *vi sep aux sein* to emigrate *(nach, in +acc* to*)*; *(Volk)* to migrate.

Auswanderung *f* emigration; *(Massen~)* migration.

auswärtig *adj attr* **(a)** *(nicht ansässig)* non-local; *Schüler, Mitglied* from out of town. **(b)** *(Pol)* foreign. **das A~e Amt** the Foreign Office *(Brit)*, the State Department *(US)*.

auswärts *adv (außerhalb der Stadt)* out of town; *(Sport)* away. ~ **essen** to eat out.

Auswärtsspiel *nt (Sport)* away (game).

auswaschen *vt sep irreg* to wash out; *(spülen)* to rinse (out).

auswechselbar *adj* (ex)changeable; *(untereinander)* interchangeable; *(ersetzbar)* replaceable.

auswechseln *vt sep* to change; *(esp gegenseitig)* to exchange; *(ersetzen)* to replace; *(Sport)* to substitute *(gegen* for*)*. **er ist wie ausgewechselt** *(fig)* he's a changed *or* different person.

Auswechselspieler(in *f***)** *m* substitute.

Ausweg *m* way out; *(fig: Lösung auch)* solution. **der letzte** ~ the last resort.

Ausweg-· a~los *adj (fig)* hopeless; **~losigkeit** *f (fig)* hopelessness.

ausweichen *vi sep irreg aux sein* to get out of the way *(+dat* of*)*; *(fig)* to evade the point/issue *etc.* **jdm/einer Begegnung** ~ to avoid sb/a meeting; **eine ~de Antwort** an evasive answer.

Ausweich-: ~manöver *nt* evasive action; **~möglichkeit** *f (lit)* possibility of getting out of the way; *(fig)* alternative.

ausweinen *vr sep* **sich bei jdm** ~ to have a cry on sb's shoulder; **sich** *(dat)* **die Augen** ~ to cry one's eyes out *(nach* over*)*.

Ausweis *m* **-e** *(Mitglieds~/Leser~/Studenten~ etc)* (membership/library/student *etc)* card; *(Personal~)* identity card; *(Berechtigungsnachweis)* pass. **~, bitte** your papers please.

ausweisen *sep irreg* **1** *vt (aus Land)* to expel, to deport. **2** *vr* to identify oneself. **können Sie sich ~?** do you have any means of identification?

Ausweis-: ~kontrolle *f* identity check; **~papiere** *pl* identity papers *pl.*

Ausweisung *f* expulsion, deportation.

ausweiten *sep* **1** *vt* to widen; *(fig)* to expand *(zu* into*)*. **2** *vr* to widen; *(esp Dehnbares)* to stretch; *(fig) (Thema, Bewegung)* to expand *(zu* into*)*; *(sich verbreiten)* to spread.

Ausweitung *f* widening; *(Ausdehnung)* stretching; *(fig)* expansion; *(Verbreitung)* spreading.

auswendig *adv* by heart, from memory. **etw ~ können/lernen** to know/learn sth (off) by heart.

auswerfen *vt sep irreg* **(a)** *Anker, Netz* to cast. **(b)** *(hinausschleudern) Lava, Asche* to throw out.

auswerten *vt sep (bewerten)* to evaluate; *(analysieren)* to analyse.

Auswertung *f siehe vt* evaluation; analysis.

auswickeln *vt sep Paket, Bonbon etc* to unwrap.

auswiegen *vt sep irreg* to weigh (out); *siehe* **ausgewogen.**

auswirken *vr sep* to have an effect *(auf+acc* on*)*. **sich negativ** ~ to have a negative effect.

Auswirkung *f (Folge)* consequence; *(Wirkung)* effect; *(Rückwirkung)* repercussion.

auswischen *vt sep* to wipe out. **jdm eins** ~ *(col)* to get one over on sb *(col)*; *(aus Rache)* to get one's own back on sb.

auswringen *vt sep irreg* to wring out.

Auswuchs *m* **(a)** (out)growth; *(Mißbildung)* deformity. **(b)** *(fig) (Erzeugnis)* product; *(Mißstand, Übersteigerung)* excess.

auswuchten *vt sep Räder* to balance.

auszahlen *sep* **1** *vt Geld etc* to pay out; *Arbeiter, Gläubiger* to pay off. **2** *vr (sich lohnen)* to pay (off).

auszählen *sep* **1** *vt Stimmen* to count (up); *(Boxen)* to count out. **2** *vi (bei Kinderspielen)* to count out.

Auszählung *f (von Stimmen etc)* counting (up), count.

auszeichnen *sep* **1** *vt* **(a)** *(mit Preisschild versehen)* to price. **(b)** *(ehren)* to honour *(Brit)*, to honor *(US)*. **jdn mit einem Orden** ~ to decorate sb (with a medal); **jdn mit einem Preis/Titel** ~ to award a prize/title to sb. **(c)** *(hervorheben)* to distinguish (from all others); *(kennzeichnen)* to be a feature of. **2** *vr* to stand out *(durch* due to*)*. **der Wagen zeichnet sich durch ... aus** one of the car's main features is ...; *siehe* **ausgezeichnet.**

Auszeichnung *f* **(a)** *no pl (das Auszeichnen) (von Waren)* pricing; *(mit Orden)* decoration. **(b)** *(Markierung: an Ware)* ticket. **(c)** *(Ehrung)* honour *(Brit)*, honor *(US)*, distinction; *(Orden)* decoration; *(Preis)* award, prize. **mit ~ bestehen** to pass with distinction.

ausziehbar *adj* extendible; *Antenne* telescopic. **ein ~er Tisch** a pull-out table.
ausziehen *sep irreg* **1** *vt* **(a)** *(herausziehen)* to pull out; *(verlängern auch)* to extend. **(b)** *Kleider* to take off; *jdn* to undress. **2** *vr (sich entkleiden)* to undress, to take off one's clothes. **3** *vi aux sein (aufbrechen, abreisen)* to set out; *(aus einer Wohnung)* to move *(aus* out of*)*.
Auszubildende(r) *mf decl as adj* trainee; *(als Handwerker auch)* apprentice.
Auszug *m* **(a)** *(das Weggehen)* departure; *(aus der Wohnung)* move. **(b)** *(Ausschnitt)* excerpt; *(aus Buch auch)* extract; *(Konto~)* statement.
autark *adj* self-sufficient *(auch fig)*, autarkical *(Econ)*.
authentisch *adj* authentic.
Auto *nt* **-s** car, automobile *(esp US, dated)*. **~ fahren** *(selbst)* to drive (a car); *(als Mitfahrer)* to go by car; **mit dem ~ fahren** to go by car.
Autobahn *f* motorway *(Brit)*, highway *(US)*.
Autobahn-: ~ausfahrt *f* motorway *(Brit) or* highway *(US)* exit; **~dreieck** *nt* motorway *(Brit) or* highway *(US)* junction; **~kreuz** *nt* motorway *(Brit) or* highway *(US)* intersection; **~raststätte** *f* motorway *(Brit) or* highway *(US)* services *pl*.
Auto-: ~batterie *f* car battery; **~biographie** *f* autobiography; **~bus** *m* bus; *(Reiseomnibus)* coach *(Brit)*, bus; **~diebstahl** *m* car theft; **~fähre** *f* car ferry; **~fahren** *nt* driving (a car); *(als Mitfahrer)* going by car; **~fahrer** *m* (car)driver; **~fahrt** *f* drive; **~friedhof** *m (col)* car dump.
autogen *adj* autogenous. **~es Training** *(Psych)* relaxation through self-hypnosis.
Autogramm *nt* **-e** autograph.
Autogramm-: ~jäger *m* autograph hunter; **~stunde** *f* autograph(ing) session.
Auto-: ~industrie *f* car *or* automobile industry; **~karte** *f* road map; **~kino** *nt* drive-in cinema; **~knacker** *m (col)* car thief; **~krat** *m (wk)* **-en, -en** autocrat; **~marke** *f* make (of car).
Automat *m (wk)* **-en, -en** *(auch fig: Mensch)* machine; *(Verkaufs~)* vending machine; *(Spiel~)* slot-machine.
Automatic, Automatik[1] *m* **-s** *(Aut)* automatic.
Automatik[2] *f* automatic mechanism *(auch fig)*; *(Gesamtanlage)* automatic system.
automatisch *adj* automatic.
Automatisierung *f* automation.
Automechaniker *m* motor mechanic.
Automobil-: ~ausstellung *f* motor *(Brit) or* auto *(US)* show; **~club** *m* automobile association.
Auto-: a~nom *adj* autonomous *(auch fig)*; **~nomie** *f* autonomy *(auch fig)*; **~nummer** *f* (car) number.
Autopsie *f (Med)* autopsy.
Autor *m* author.
Auto-: ~radio *nt* car radio; **~reifen** *m* car tyre *(Brit) or* tire *(US)*; **~reisezug** *m* ≈ motorail train; **~rennbahn** *f* motor-racing circuit; **~rennen** *nt* (motor) race.
Autorin *f* authoress.
autorisieren* *vt* to authorize.
autoritär *adj* authoritarian.
Autorität *f* authority.
Auto-: ~schlange *f* queue *(Brit) or* line of cars; **~schlosser** *m* panel beater; **~schlosserei** *f* body shop; **~stop(p)** *m (esp S Ger)* hitch-hiking; **per ~stop(p) fahren** to hitch(-hike); **~unfall** *m* car accident; **~ verkehr** *m* motor traffic; **~verleih** *m*, **~vermietung** *f* car hire *(Brit) or* rental; *(Firma)* car hire *(Brit) or* rental firm; **~werkstatt** *f* garage, car repair shop *(US)*; **~zoom** [-'zuːm] *nt (Phot)* automatic zoom (lens); **~zubehör** *nt* motor accessories *pl*.
avancieren* [avã'siːrən] *vi aux sein (dated, geh)* to advance *(zu* to*)*.
Avant- [avã]: **~garde** *f (geh) (Art)* avant-garde; *(Pol)* vanguard; **a~gardistisch** *adj* avant-garde.
Avocado, Avocato [avo'kaːdo, -to] *f* **-s** avocado.
Axiom *nt* **-e** axiom.
Axt *f* **⸚e** axe *(Brit)*, ax *(US)*. **die ~ im Haus erspart den Zimmermann** *(Prov)* self-help is the best help; **die ~ an etw/an die Wurzel einer Sache legen** *(fig)* to strike at the very roots of sth.
Azalee [-'leːə] *f* **-n** *(Bot)* azalea.
Azoren *pl (Geog)* Azores *pl*.
Azteke *m (wk)* **-n, -n, Aztekin** *f* Aztec.
Azubi *m* **-s** *(col)* = **Auszubildende(r).**
azurblau *adj* azure.

B

B, b [beː] **-, -** B, b. **B-dur/b-Moll** (the key of) B flat major/minor.
Baby ['beːbi] *nt* **-s** baby.
Baby-: b~sitten *vi insep* to babysit; **~sitter(in** *f*) *m* **-** babysitter; **~speck** *m (col)* puppy fat.
Bach *m* **-̈e** *(lit, fig)* stream.
Bachstelze *f* **-n** wagtail.
Backblech *nt* baking tray.
Backbord *nt no pl (Naut)* port (side).
backbord(s) *adv (Naut)* on the port side.
Backe *f* **-n (a)** cheek. **mit vollen ~n kauen** to eat away heartily. **(b)** *(col: Hinter~)* buttock, cheek.
backen *vt* to bake; *Brot, Kuchen auch* to make; *(braten) Fisch, Eier etc* to fry. **frisch/knusprig gebackenes Brot** fresh/crusty bread; **gebackener Fisch** fried fish; *(im Ofen)* baked fish.
Backen-: ~bart *m* sideboards *pl*, sideburns *pl*; **~knochen** *m* cheekbone; **~zahn** *m* molar.
Bäcker *m* **-** baker.
Bäckerei *f* baker's *(Brit)*, baker *(US)*; *(Backstube)* bakery.
Bäcker-: ~junge *m (Lehrling)* baker's apprentice; **~laden** *m* baker's *(Brit)*, baker *(US)*; **~meister** *m* master baker.
Back-: b~fertig *adj* oven-ready; **~fett** *nt* cooking fat; **~fisch** *m* **(a)** fried fish; **(b)** *(dated)* teenager; **~form** *f* baking tin; **~obst** *nt* dried fruit; **~ofen** *m* oven *(auch fig)*; **~pflaume** *f* prune; **~pulver** *nt* baking powder.
Backstein *m* brick.
Back-: ~stube *f* bakery; **~waren** *pl* bread, cakes and pastries *pl*.
Bad *nt* **-̈er (a)** *(Wannen~, Phot)* bath; *(das Baden)* bathing. **ein ~ nehmen** to have *or* take a bath. **(b)** *(im Meer)* bathe, swim; *(das Baden)* bathing, swimming. **(c)** *(Badezimmer)* bathroom. **Zimmer mit ~** room with (private) bath. **(d)** *(Schwimm~)* (swimming) pool *or* baths. **die städtischen ~̈er** the public baths. **(e)** *(Heil~)* spa; *(See~)* (seaside) resort.
Bade-: ~anstalt *f* (public) swimming baths *pl*; **~anzug** *m* swimming costume; **~gast** *m* **(a)** *(im Kurort)* spa visitor; **(b)** *(im Schwimmbad)* bather, swimmer; **~(hand)tuch** *nt* bath towel; **~hose** *f* swimming trunks *pl*; **~kappe** *f* swimming cap; **~mantel** *m* bathrobe, dressing gown *(Brit)*; **~matte** *f* bathmat; **~meister** *m (im Schwimmbad)* (pool) attendant; *(am Strand)* lifeguard.
baden 1 *vi* **(a)** to have a bath. **(b)** *(im Meer, Schwimmbad etc)* to swim, to bathe. **~ gehen** to go swimming. **(c)** *(col)* **~ gehen** to come a cropper *(col)*; **wenn das passiert, gehe ich ~** I'll be for it if that happens *(col)*. **2** *vt* **(a)** *Kind etc* to bath. **(b)** *Augen, Wunde etc* to bathe.
Bade-: ~sachen *pl* swimming things *pl*; **~saison** *f* swimming season; *(in Kurort)* spa season; **~salz** *nt* bath salts *pl*; **~strand** *m* (bathing) beach; **~wanne** *f* bath(tub); **~wasser** *nt* bath water; **~zimmer** *nt* bathroom.
Bagage [ba'gaːʒə] *f no pl (dated col: Gesindel)* crowd *(col)*.
Bagatelle *f* trifle, bagatelle.
Bagatellsache *f (Jur)* minor case.
Bagger *m* **-** excavator; *(für Schlamm)* dredger.
baggern *vti Graben* to excavate; *Fahrrinne* to dredge.
Baggersee *m artificial lake in gravel pit etc.*
Bahn *f* **-en (a)** *(lit, fig)* path; *(von Fluß)* course; *(Astron auch)* orbit. **jdm/einer Sache die ~ frei machen** *(fig)* to clear the way for sb/sth; **die ~ ist frei** *(fig)* the way is clear; **sich** *(dat)* **~ brechen** *(fig)* to make headway; *(Mensch)* to forge ahead; **in gewohnten ~en verlaufen** *(fig)* to continue as before; **von der rechten ~ abkommen** *(geh)* to stray from the straight and narrow; **jdn auf die rechte ~ bringen** *(fig)* to put sb on the straight and narrow; **jdn aus der ~ werfen** *(fig)* to shatter sb.
(b) *(Eisen~)* railway *(Brit)*, railroad *(US)*; *(Straßen~)* tram, streetcar *(US)*; *(Zug)* train; *(Verkehrsnetz, Verwaltung)* railway *(Brit) usu pl*, railroad *(US)*. **mit der ~** by train *or* rail/ tram; **frei ~** *(Comm)* carriage free to station of destination.
(c) *(Sport)* track; *(für Pferderennen auch)* course; *(in Schwimmbecken)* pool; *(für einzelne Teilnehmer)* lane.
(d) *(Stoff~, Tapeten~)* length, strip.
Bahn-: ~arbeiter *m* railwayman, railroader *(US)*; **~beamte(r)** *m* railway *(Brit) or* railroad *(US)* official; **b~brechend** *adj* pioneering; **~brechendes leisten** to pioneer new developments; **~bus** *m* railway *(Brit) or* railroad *(US)* bus.
Bahndamm *m* (railway *(Brit) or* railroad *US*) embankment.
bahnen *vt* **jdm/einer Sache den/einen Weg ~** *(fig)* to pave the way for sb/sth; **sich** *(dat)* **einen Weg ~** to fight one's way through.
Bahn-: ~fahrt *f* rail journey; **~fracht** *f* rail freight.
Bahnhof *m* station. **am** *or* **auf dem ~** at the station; **~ Schöneberg** Schöneberg station; **ich verstehe nur ~** *(hum col)* it's all Greek to me *(col)*; **er wurde mit großem ~ empfangen** he was given the red carpet treatment.
Bahnhofs- *in cpds* station; **~gaststätte** *f* station restaurant; **~halle** *f* (station) concourse; **~mission** *f charitable organization for helping rail travellers in difficulties.*
Bahn-: b~lagernd *adj (Comm)* to be collected from the station; **~linie** *f* railway *(Brit) or* railroad *(US)* line *or* track; **~polizei** *f* railway *(Brit) or* railroad *(US)* police; **~schranke** *f* level *(Brit) or* grade *(US)* crossing barrier; **~steig** *m* platform; **~steigkarte** *f* platform ticket; **~übergang** *m* level *(Brit) or* grade *(US)* crossing; **beschrankter/unbeschrankter ~übergang** crossing with gates/unguarded level crossing; **~wärter** *m* gatekeeper.
Bahre *f* **-n** *(Kranken~)* stretcher; *(Toten~)* bier.
Baiser [bɛ'zeː] *nt* **-s** meringue.
Baisse ['bɛːs(ə)] *f* **-n** *(St Ex)* fall; *(plötzliche)* slump.
Bajonett *nt* **-e** bayonet.
Bajuware *m (wk)* **-n, -n, Bajuwarin** *f (old, hum)* Bavarian.
Bake *f* **-n** *(Verkehrszeichen)* distance warning signal; *(an Autobahn auch)* countdown marker.
Bakterie [-riə] *f* **-n** *usu pl* germ. **~n** germs *pl*, bacteria *pl*.
bakteriell *adj* bacterial, bacteria *attr*.
Bakteriologe *m*, **Bakteriologin** *f* bacteriologist.

bakteriologisch *adj* bacteriological; *Krieg* biological.
Balance [ba'lã:s(ə)] *f* **-n** balance, equilibrium. **die ~ halten/verlieren** to keep/lose one's balance.
Balance|akt [ba'lã:s(ə)-] *m (lit, fig)* balancing act.
balancieren* [balã'si:rən] **1** *vi aux sein* to balance. **über etw** *(acc)* ~ to balance one's way across sth. **2** *vt* to balance.
bald 1 *adv, comp* **eher,** *superl* **am ehesten (a)** soon. **er kommt ~** he'll be coming soon; **~ darauf** soon afterwards; **nicht so ~** not in the near future; **bis ~!** see you soon. **(b)** *(fast)* almost, nearly. **sie platzt ~ vor Neugier** she's just about dying with curiosity. **2** *conj (geh)* **~ hier, ~ da** now here, now there; **~ so, ~ so** now this way, now that.
baldig *adj attr, no comp* quick, speedy; *Antwort, Wiedersehen* early.
baldmöglichst *adv* as soon as possible.
Baldrian *m* **-e** valerian.
Baldriantropfen *pl* valerian (drops *pl*).
Balearen *pl* **die ~** the Balearics *pl.*
Balg[1] *m* **⸗e (a)** *(Tierhaut)* pelt, skin. **(b)** *(Blase~)* bellows *pl.*
Balg[2] *m or nt* **⸗er** *(pej col: Kind)* brat *(pej col).*
balgen *vr* to scrap *(um* over*).*
Balgerei *f* scrap, tussle.
Balkan *m (~länder)* **der ~** the Balkans *pl;* **auf dem ~** in the Balkans.
Balken *m* **- (a)** *(Holz~, Schwebe~)* beam; *(Stütz~)* prop; *(Quer~)* joist, crossbeam. **lügen, daß sich die ~ biegen** *(col)* to tell a pack of lies. **(b)** *(Strich)* bar; *(Uniformstreifen)* stripe. **(c)** *(an Waage)* beam.
Balkon [bal'kɔŋ, bal'ko:n] *m* **-s** *or* **-e** balcony; *(Theat)* (dress) circle.
Balkon-: ~möbel *pl* garden furniture *sing;* **~tür** *f* French window(s).
Ball[1] *m* **⸗e** ball. **~ spielen** to play ball; **am ~ sein** *(lit)* to have the ball; **immer am~ sein** *(fig)* to be on the ball; **am ~ bleiben** *(lit)* to keep (possession of) the ball; *(fig)* to stay on the ball; **bei jdm am ~ bleiben** *(fig)* to keep in with sb; **jdm den ~ zuspielen** *(lit)* to pass (the ball) to sb; **jdm/sich gegenseitig die ⸗~e zuspielen** *(fig)* to feed sb/each other lines.
Ball[2] *m* **⸗e** *(Tanzfest)* ball. **auf dem ~** at the ball.
Ballade *f* ballad.
Ballast [*auch* -'-] *m (rare)* **-e** *(Naut, Aviat)* ballast; *(fig)* burden, encumbrance. **~ abwerfen** *(lit)* to discharge ballast; *(fig)* to get rid of a burden.
Ballaststoffe *pl (Med)* roughage *sing.*
Ballen *m* **- (a)** bale; *(Kaffee~)* sack. **in ~ verpacken** to bale. **(b)** *(Anat: an Daumen, Zehen)* ball; *(an Pfote)* pad.
ballen *vt Faust* to clench; *siehe* **geballt.**
Ballerina *f, pl* **Ballerinen** ballerina.
ballern *vi (col)* to shoot, to fire.
Ballett *nt* **-e** ballet. **beim ~ sein** *(col)* to be a ballet dancer.
Ballettänzer(in *f***)** *m* ballet dancer.
Ballführung *f (Sport)* ball control.
Ballistik *f no pl* ballistics *sing.*
ballistisch *adj* ballistic.
Ball-: ~junge *m (Tennis)* ball boy; **~kleid** *nt* ball gown.
Ballon [ba'lɔŋ, ba'lo:n] *m* **-s** *or* **-e** balloon.
Ball-: ~saal *m* ballroom; **~spiel** *nt* ball game.
Ballung *f* concentration; *(von Truppen auch)* massing.
Ballungs-: ~gebiet *nt,* **~raum** *m* conurbation; **~zentrum** *nt* centre *(Brit) or* center *(US)* (of population, industry *etc*).
Balsam *m* **-e** balsam; *(fig)* balm.
balsamieren* *vt* = **einbalsamieren.**
Balte *m (wk)* **-n, -n, Baltin** *f* **er/sie ist ~** he/she comes from the Baltic.
Baltikum *nt* **das ~** the Baltic States *pl.*
baltisch *adj* Baltic *attr.*
Balz *f* **-en (a)** *(Paarungsspiel)* courtship display. **(b)** *(Paarungszeit)* mating season.
Balz-: ~ruf *m* mating call; **~zeit** *f* mating season.
Bambus *m* **-ses** *or* **-, -se** bamboo.
Bambus-: ~rohr *nt* bamboo cane; **~sprossen** *pl* bamboo shoots *pl.*
Bammel *m no pl (col)* **(einen) ~ vor jdm/etw haben** to be scared of sb/sth.
banal *adj* banal, trite.
banalisieren* *vt* to trivialize.
Banalität *f* banality.
Banane *f* **-n** banana.
Bananen-: ~dampfer *m* banana boat; **~republik** *f (Pol pej)* banana republic; **~schale** *f* banana skin; **~stecker** *m* jack plug.
Banause *m (wk)* **-n, -n** *(pej)* peasant *(col)*; *(Kultur~ auch)* philistine.
band *pret of* **binden.**
Band[1] *nt* **⸗er (a)** *(Seiden~ etc)* ribbon; *(Isolier~, Maß~, Ziel~)* tape; *(Haar~, Hut~)* band; *(Schürzen~)* string. **(b)** *(Ton~)* tape. **etw auf ~ aufnehmen** to tape *or* record sth. **(c)** *(Fließ~)* conveyor belt; *(als Einrichtung)* production line; *(Montage~)* assembly line. **am ~ arbeiten** to work on the production line; **am laufenden ~** *(fig)* non-stop, continuously. **(d)** *(Rad)* **auf dem 44m-~** on the 44m band. **(e)** *(Anat) usu pl* ligament.
Band[2] *nt* **-e** *(liter)* **das ~ der Freundschaft/Liebe** *etc* the bonds *or* ties of friendship/love *etc.*
Band[3] *m* **⸗e** *(Buch~)* volume. **darüber könnte man ⸗~e schreiben/erzählen** you could write a book about it; **das spricht ⸗~e** that speaks volumes.
Band[4] [bɛnt] *f* **-s** *(Mus)* band.
Bandage [-'da:ʒə] *f* **-n** bandage. **mit harten ~n** *(fig col)* with no holds barred.
bandagieren* [-'ʒi:rən] *vt* to bandage (up).
Band-: ~aufnahme *f* tape-recording; **~breite** *f* *(von Meinungen etc)* range.
Bande[1] *f* **-n** gang; *(col: Gruppe)* bunch *(col).*
Bande[2] *f* **-n** *(Sport) (von Eisbahn)* barrier; *(Billiard)* cushion.
Banden-: ~chef *(col),* **~führer** *m* gang-leader; **~diebstahl** *m (Jur)* gang robbery.
Banderole *f* **-n** tax *or* revenue seal.
bändigen *vt* to control; *(zähmen)* to tame.
Bändigung *m no pl siehe vt* controlling; taming.
Bandit *m (wk)* **-en, -en** bandit; *(fig pej)* brigand.
Band-: ~maß *nt* tape measure; **~nudeln** *pl* ribbon noodles *pl;* **~scheibe** *f (Anat)* disc; **~scheibenschaden** *m* slipped disc; **~wurm** *m* tapeworm.
bang(e) *adj* **(a)** *(ängstlich)* scared, frightened. **mir ist ~e vor ihm** I'm scared or frightened of him. **(b)** *(geh: beklommen)* uneasy *(um* about*).* **es wurde ihr ~ ums Herz** her heart sank.
Bange *f no pl (esp N Ger)* **nur keine ~!** *(col)* don't worry.
bangen *vi (geh)* **um jds Leben** *etc* **~** to fear for sb's life *etc.*
Banjo ['bɛndʒo, 'bandʒo] *nt* **-s** banjo.
Bank[1] *f* **⸗e (a)** bench; *(Kirchen~)* pew; *(Anklage~)* dock. **auf** *or* **in der ersten/letzten ~** on the front/back bench *etc;* **(alle) durch die ~** *(col)* every single one; **etw auf die lange ~ schieben** *(col)* to put sth off. **(b)** *(Arbeitstisch)* (work) bench.
Bank[2] *f* **-en (a)** *(Comm)* bank. **Geld auf der ~ liegen haben** to have money in the bank; **bei der ~** at the bank. **(b)** *(bei Glücksspielen)* bank. **(die) ~ halten** *(col)* to be banker; **die ~ sprengen** to break the bank.
Bank-: ~angestellte(r) *mf* bank employee; **~anweisung** *f* banker's order; **~direktor** *m* director of a/the bank; **~einbruch** *m* bank raid.
Bänkelsänger *m* ballad-singer, minstrel.
Bankett[1] *nt* **-e** *(an Straßen)* shoulder.
Bankett[2] *nt* **-e** *(Festessen)* banquet.
Bank-: ~fach *nt* **(a)** *(Beruf)* banking **(b)** *(Schließ-*

fach) safe-deposit box; ~**geheimnis** *nt* confidentiality in banking; ~**geschäft** *nt no pl (~wesen)* banking world; ~**guthaben** *nt* bank balance; ~**halter** *m (bei Glücksspielen)* banker.
Bankier [-'kie:] *m* **-s** banker.
Bank-: ~**kaufmann** *m* (qualified) bank clerk; ~**konto** *nt* bank account; ~**leitzahl** *f* bank code number; ~**note** *f* banknote, bill *(US)*; ~**raub** *m* bank robbery; ~**räuber** *m* bank robber.
bankrott *adj (lit, fig)* bankrupt. ~ **gehen** to go bankrupt; **jdn** ~ **machen** to bankrupt sb.
Bankrott *m* **-e** *(lit, fig)* bankruptcy. ~ **machen** to go bankrupt; **den** ~ **anmelden** *or* **erklären** to declare oneself bankrupt.
Bankrott|erklärung *f* declaration of bankruptcy; *(fig)* sellout *(col)*.
Bank|überfall *m* bank raid.
Bann *m* **-e (a)** *no pl (geh)* spell. **im** ~ **eines Menschen/einer Sache stehen** *or* **sein** to be under sb's spell/the spell of sth; **sie zog** *or* **zwang ihn in ihren** ~ she cast her spell over him. **(b)** *(Hist: Kirchen~)* excommunication.
bannen *vt* **(a)** *(geh: bezaubern)* to bewitch, to entrance. **(wie) gebannt** fascinated; *(stärker)* spellbound. **(b)** *Geister* to exorcize; *Gefahr* to ward off.
Banner *nt* **-** *(geh)* banner.
Bannmeile *f* inviolable precincts *pl (of city, Parliament etc)*.
Bantamgewicht *nt* bantamweight.
Baptist(in *f***)** *m* Baptist.
bar *adj no comp* **(a)** cash. ~**es Geld** cash; **eine Summe in** ~ a sum in cash; **(in)** ~ **bezahlen** to pay (in) cash; ~ **auf die Hand** cash on the nail; **etw für** ~**e Münze nehmen** *(fig)* to take sth at face value. **(b)** *attr Unsinn* absolute. **(c)** *pred+gen (liter)* ~ **aller Hoffnung** devoid of hope, completely without hope. **(d)** *(liter: bloß)* bare. ~**en Hauptes** bareheaded.
Bar *f* **-s** bar.
Bär *m (wk)* **-en, -en** bear. **stark wie ein** ~ *(col)* (as) strong as an ox; **der Große/Kleine** ~ *(Astron)* the Great/Little Bear, Ursa Major/Minor; **jdm einen** ~**en aufbinden** *(col)* to have sb on *(col)*.
Baracke *f* **-n** hut, shack; *(pej: kleines Haus)* hovel.
Barbar(in *f***)** *m (wk)* **-en, -en** *(pej)* barbarian.
Barbarei *f (pej)* barbarity; *(no pl: Kulturlosigkeit)* barbarism.
barbarisch *adj* **(a)** *(pej)* barbaric, barbarous. **(b)** *(col: fürchterlich)* terrible.
bärbeißig *adj (col)* grouchy *(col)*, grumpy.
Bardame *f* barmaid.
Barde *m (wk)* **-n, -n** *(Liter)* bard; *(iro)* minstrel.
Bären-: ~**dienst** *m* **jdm einen** ~**dienst erweisen** to do sb a disservice; ~**hunger** *m (col)* **einen** ~**hunger haben** to be famished *(col)*; ~**jagd** *f* bear hunt/hunting; ~**kräfte** *pl* the strength of an ox; **b**~**stark** *adj* strapping, strong as an ox.
Barett *nt* **-e** *or* **-s** cap; *(für Richter etc)* biretta.
barfuß *adj pred* barefoot(ed). ~ **gehen** to go/walk barefoot(ed).
barfüßig *adj* barefooted.
barg *pret of* **bergen.**
Bar-: ~**geld** *nt* cash; **b**~**geldlos 1** *adj* cashless; **b**~**geldloser Zahlungsverkehr** non-cash *or* credit transactions *pl*; **2** *adv* without using cash; ~**hocker** *m* (bar) stool.
Bärin *f* (she-)bear.
Bariton [-tɔn] *m* **-e** [-to:nə] baritone.
Barkasse *f* **-n** launch; *(Beiboot auch)* longboat.
Barkauf *m* cash purchase.
Barke *f* **-n** *(Naut)* skiff; *(liter)* barque *(liter)*.
Barkeeper ['ba:ɐki:pɐ] *m* **-** barman, bartender.
Barkredit *m* cash loan.
barmherzig *adj (liter, Rel)* merciful; *(mitfühlend)* compassionate.
Barmherzigheit *f (liter, Rel)* mercy, mercifulness; *(Mitgefühl)* compassion.
barock *adj* baroque.
Barock *nt or m no pl* baroque.
Barock- *in cpds* baroque; ~**zeit** *f* baroque period.
Barometer *nt* **-** *(lit, fig)* barometer. **das** ~ **steht auf Sturm** *(fig)* things look stormy.
Baron(in *f***)** *m* **-e** baron/baroness.
Barren *m* **- (a)** *(Metall~)* bar; *(esp Gold~)* ingot. **(b)** *(Sport)* parallel bars *pl*.
Barriere *f* **-n** *(lit, fig)* barrier.
Barrikade *f* barricade. **auf die** ~**n gehen** *(lit, fig)* to go to the barricades.
Barsch *m* **-e** perch.
barsch *adj* brusque, curt; *Befehl auch* peremptory. **jdn** ~ **anfahren** to snap at sb.
Barschaft *f no pl* **meine ganze** ~ **bestand aus 10 Mark** all I had on me was 10 marks.
Barscheck *m* uncrossed cheque *(Brit)* or check *(US)*.
barst *pret of* **bersten.**
Bart *m* **¨-e (a)** beard; *(Schnurr~)* moustache *(Brit)*, mustache *(US)*; *(von Katze, Robbe etc)* whiskers *pl*. **(b)** *(fig col)* **(sich** *dat***) etw in den** ~ **murmeln** to mutter sth in one's beard *(col)*; **jdm um den** ~ **gehen** to butter sb up *(col)*; **der Witz hat einen** ~ that's a real oldie *(col)*. **(c)** *(Schlüssel~)* bit.
Barthaar *nt* facial hair; *(Bart auch)* beard.
bärtig *adj* bearded.
Bart-: **b**~**los** *adj* beardless; *(glattrasiert)* clean-shaven; ~**stoppeln** *pl* stubble *sing;* ~**wuchs** *m* beard; *(esp weiblicher)* facial hair *no indef art*; **er hat starken** ~**wuchs** he has a heavy growth of beard.
Bar-: ~**verkauf** *m* cash sales *pl;* ~**vermögen** *nt* liquid assets *pl;* ~**zahlung** *f* cash payment; **(Verkauf) nur gegen** ~**zahlung** cash (sales) only.
Basar *m* **-e** bazaar.
Base[1] *f* **-n** *(old, dial)* cousin.
Base[2] *f* **-n** *(Chem)* base.
Baseball ['be:sbo:l] *m no pl* baseball.
basieren* *vi* to be based *(auf +dat* on*)*.
Basilikum *nt no pl* basil.
Basis *f, pl* **Basen (a)** *(Archit, Mil, Math)* base. **(b)** *(fig)* basis. **auf breiter** ~ on a broad basis. **(c)** *(Pol, Sociol)* ~ **und Überbau** foundation and superstructure; **die** ~ *(col)* the grass roots.
Basis|arbeit *f (Pol)* groundwork.
Basisgruppe *f* action group.
Baske *m (wk)* **-n, -n, Baskin** *f* Basque.
Basken-: ~**land** *nt* Basque region; ~**mütze** *f* beret.
Basketball *m no pl* basketball.
baskisch *adj* Basque.
Baß *m* **¨-sse (a)** bass. **(b)** *(Instrument)* double bass.
Baßbariton *m* bass baritone.
Baßgeige *f (col)* (double) bass.
Bassin [ba'sɛ̃:] *nt* **-s** *(Schwimm~)* pool.
Bassist(in *f***)** *m* **(a)** *(Sänger)* bass. **(b)** *(im Orchester etc)* (double) bass player.
Baß-: ~**schlüssel** *m* bass clef; ~**stimme** *f* bass (voice); *(Partie)* bass (part).
Bast *m (rare)* **-e** *(zum Binden, Flechten)* raffia.
basta *interj* **(und damit)** ~**!** (and) that's that.
Bastard *m* **-e (a)** *(pej)* bastard. **(b)** *(Tier)* cross.
Bastelei *f (col)* handicraft; *(pej)* botched job *(col)*.
basteln 1 *vi* **(a)** *(als Hobby)* to make things with one's hands. **sie kann gut** ~ she is good with her hands. **(b) an etw** *(dat)* ~ to make sth, to work on sth; *(an etw herumbasteln)* to tinker with sth; **mit Holz** *etc* ~ to make things out of wood *etc*. **2** *vt* to make; *Geräte etc auch* to build.
Bastion *f (lit, fig)* bastion.
Bastler(in *f***)** *m* **-** *(von Modellen etc)* modeller; *(von Möbeln etc)* do-it-yourself enthusiast. **ein guter** ~ **sein** to be clever with one's hands.
bat *pret of* **bitten.**
Bataillon [batal'jo:n] *nt* **-e** *(Mil, fig)* battalion.
Batik *f or m* **-en** batik.
Batist *m* **-e** batiste, cambric.

Batterie *f (Elec, Mil)* battery; *(Reihe von Flaschen etc auch)* row.
Batteriegerät *nt* battery-powered radio *etc.*
Batzen *m* - *(col)* **ein ~ Geld** a tidy sum *(col)*.
Bau *n* **(a)** *no pl (das Bauen)* building, construction. **im ~** under construction; **der ~ des Hauses dauerte ein Jahr** it took a year to build the house. **(b)** *no pl (Auf~)* structure; *(von Satz, Apparat auch)* construction; *(Körper~)* build. **von kräftigem ~ sein** to be powerfully built. **(c)** *no pl (~stelle)* building site. **auf dem ~ arbeiten** to work on a building site. **(d)** *pl* **-ten** *(Gebäude)* building. **(e)** *pl* **-e** *(Erdhöhle)* burrow, hole; *(Biber~)* lodge; *(Fuchs~)* den; *(Dachs~)* set(t). **(f)** *no pl (Mil sl)* guardhouse. **4 Tage ~** 4 days in the guardhouse.
Bau-: **~arbeiten** *pl* building *or* construction work *sing; (Straßen~)* roadworks *pl (Brit)*, roadwork *sing (US)*; **~arbeiter** *m* building *or* construction worker.
Bauch *m, pl* **Bäuche** **(a)** *(von Mensch)* stomach, belly *(col)*; *(Anat)* abdomen; *(Fett~)* paunch. **ihm tat der ~ weh** he had stomach-ache; **sich** *(dat)* **den ~ vollschlagen** *(col)* to stuff oneself *(col)*; **sich** *(dat)* **(vor Lachen) den ~ halten** *(col)* to split one's sides (laughing); **einen ~ ansetzen** *or* **kriegen** to get a paunch; **mit etw auf den ~ fallen** *(col)* to come a cropper with sth *(col)*. **(b)** *(Hohlraum: von Schiff etc)* belly, bowels *pl.*
Bauch-: **~ansatz** *m* beginning of a paunch; **~höhle** *f* abdomen.
bauchig *adj Gefäß* bulbous.
Bauch-: **~laden** *m* tray; **~landung** *f (col) (Aviat)* belly landing; *(bei Sprung ins Wasser)* belly-flop; **~muskel** *m* stomach muscle; **~nabel** *m* navel, belly-button *(col)*; **~redner** *m* ventriloquist; **~schmerzen** *pl* stomach-ache; **~speck** *m (Cook)* belly of pork; **~speicheldrüse** *f* pancreas; **~tanz** *m* belly-dance/dancing; **~tänzerin** *f* belly-dancer; **~weh** *nt* stomach-ache.
bauen 1 *vt* **(a)** to build, to construct; *(anfertigen auch)* to make; *Höhle* to dig. **seine Hoffnung auf jdn/etw ~** to build up one's hopes on sb/sth; **die Betten ~** *(esp Mil)* to make the beds; *siehe* **gebaut. (b)** *(col: verursachen) Unfall* to cause. **da hast du Mist gebaut** *(col)* you really messed that up *(col)*. **(c)** *(col: machen, ablegen) Prüfung etc* to pass. **seinen Doktor ~** to get one's doctorate. **2** *vi* **(a)** to build. **wir haben neu gebaut** we built a new house; **hier wird viel gebaut** there is a lot of building going on around here. **(b)** *(vertrauen)* **auf jdn/etw ~** to rely *or* count on sb/sth.
Bauer *m (wk)* **-n, -n** **(a)** *(Landwirt)* farmer; *(als Vertreter einer Klasse)* peasant; *(pej)* country bumpkin, yokel. **die dümmsten ~n haben die dicksten Kartoffeln** *(prov col)* fortune favours fools *(prov)*. **(b)** *(Chess)* pawn; *(Cards)* jack.
Bäuerchen *nt (baby-talk)* burp. **(ein) ~ machen** to burp.
Bäuerin *f* farmer's wife; *(Landwirtin)* farmer; *(als Vertreterin einer Klasse)* peasant (woman).
bäuerlich *adj* rural; *(ländlich) Fest, Sitten* rustic, country *attr.*
Bauern-: **~brot** *nt* coarse rye bread; **~dorf** *nt* farming *or* country village; **~fängerei** *f (col)* con *(col)*; **~frühstück** *nt* bacon and potato omelette *(Brit) or* omelet *(US)*; **~haus** *nt* farmhouse; **~hof** *m* farm; **~kriege** *pl (Hist)* Peasant War(s); **~regel** *f* country saying; **~schläue** *f* native cunning.
Bauersfrau *f* farmer's wife.
Bau-: **b~fällig** *adj* dilapidated; *Decke, Gewölbe* unsafe; **~firma** *f* building contractor; **~genehmigung** *f* planning and building permission; **~gerüst** *nt* scaffolding; **~grube** *f* excavation; **~handwerk** *nt* building trade; **~handwerker** *m* (trained) building worker; **~herr** *m* client *(for whom sth is being built)*; **~holz** *nt* building timber; **~ingenieur** *m* civil engineer.
Bauj. = **Baujahr.**
Bau-: **~jahr** *nt* year of construction; *(von Auto)* year of manufacture; **mein Auto ist ~jahr 80** my car is a 1980 model; **~kasten** *m* construction kit; *(mit Holzklötzen)* box of bricks; **~klotz** *m*, **~klötzchen** *nt* (building) block; **~klötze(r) staunen** *(col)* to gape (in astonishment); **~kolonne** *f* gang of building workers *or (bei Straßenbau)* navvies; **~kosten** *pl* building *or* construction costs *pl;* **~land** *nt* building land; *(für Stadtplanung)* development area; **b~lich** *adj* structural; **in gutem b~lichem Zustand** structurally sound.
Baum *m, pl* **Bäume** tree. **auf dem ~** in the tree; **heute könnte ich ~e ausreißen** I feel full of energy today.
Baum-: **~grenze** *f* tree line; **~krone** *f* treetop; **b~lang** *adj* **ein b~langer Kerl** *(col)* a beanpole *(col)*; **~rinde** *f* tree bark; **~schule** *f* tree nursery; **~stamm** *m* tree-trunk; **~stumpf** *m* tree stump.
Baumwolle *f* cotton. **ein Hemd aus ~** a cotton shirt.
Bau-: **~platz** *m* site (for building); **~polizei** *f* building control department; **~ruine** *f (col)* unfinished building; **~satz** *m* construction kit.
Bausch *m, pl* **Bäusche** *or* **-e** *(Papier~, Wolle~)* ball. **in ~ und Bogen** lock, stock and barrel.
bauschen 1 *vr (Segel)* to billow (out); *(Bluse etc)* to bunch (up). **2** *vt Segel, Vorhänge* to fill.
Bausparer *m* saver with a building society *(Brit) or* savings and loan association *(US)*.
Bauspar-: **~kasse** *f* building society *(Brit)*, savings and loan association *(US)*; **~vertrag** *m* savings contract with a building society *(Brit) or* savings and loan association *(US)*.
Bau-: **~stein** *m* stone (for building); *(fig: Bestandteil)* constituent; **~stelle** *f* building *or* construction site; *(bei Straßenbau)* roadworks *pl (Brit)*, roadwork *sing (US)*; *(bei Gleisbau)* railway *(Brit) or* railroad *(US)* construction site; **~stil** *m* architectural style; **~stoff** *m* building material; **~unternehmen** *nt (Firma)* building contractor; **~unternehmer** *m* building contractor, builder; **~weise** *f* type of construction; *(Stil)* style; **~werk** *nt* construction; *(Gebäude auch)* edifice, building; **~zaun** *m* hoarding, fence; **~zeit** *f* time taken for building *or* construction; **die ~zeit betrug drei Jahre** it took three years to build.
Bayer(in *f*) ['baiɐ, -ərɪn] *m (wk)* **-n, -n** Bavarian.
bay(e)risch ['bai(ə)rɪʃ] *adj* Bavarian.
Bayern ['baiɐn] *nt* Bavaria.
Bazillus *m, pl* **Bazillen** **(a)** bacillus, microbe; *(Krankheitserreger auch)* germ. **(b)** *(fig)* cancer, growth.
Bd., Bde = **Band, Bände.**
be|absichtigen* *vti* to intend. **eine Reise ~** *(form)* to intend to go on a journey; **das hatte ich nicht beabsichtigt** I didn't intend that to happen; **wie beabsichtigt** as planned *or* intended.
be|achten* *vt* **(a)** *(befolgen)* to observe; *Gebrauchsanweisung* to follow. **(b)** *(berücksichtigen)* to take into consideration. **(c)** *(Aufmerksamkeit schenken) jdn* to notice, to pay attention to. **jdn nicht ~** to ignore sb, to take no notice of sb.
be|achtenswert *adj* noteworthy, remarkable.
be|achtlich *adj* **(a)** *(beträchtlich)* considerable; *Erfolg* notable. **(b)** *(bedeutend) Ereignis* significant; *Leistung* considerable, excellent. **er hat im Leben/Beruf B~es geleistet** he has achieved a considerable amount in life/his job.
Be|achtung *f siehe vt* **(a)** observance; following. **unter ~ der Vorschriften** in accordance with the rules. **(b)** consideration. **(c)** notice, attention *(gen to)*. **~ finden** to receive attention; **jdm keine ~ schenken** to take no notice of sb.
Be|amten-: **~apparat** *m* bureaucracy; **~laufbahn** *f* career in the civil service; **die ~laufbahn einschlagen** to enter the civil service; **~tum** *nt no pl* civil service; **~verhältnis** *nt* **im ~verhält-**

nis stehen to be a civil servant.

Be|amte(r) *m decl as adj* official; *(Staats~)* civil servant; *(Zoll~ auch, Polizei~)* officer; *(dated: Büro~, Schalter~)* clerk. **er ist ein typischer ~r** he is a typical bureaucrat.

be|amtet *adj (form)* appointed on a permanent basis *(by the state)*.

Be|amtin *f siehe* **Beamte(r).**

be|ängstigend *adj* alarming. **sein Zustand ist ~** his condition is giving cause for concern.

be|anspruchen* *vt* **(a)** *(fordern)* to claim. **etw ~ können** to be entitled to sth. **(b)** *(erfordern)* to take; *Zeit, Platz auch* to take up. **(c)** *(ausnützen)* to use; *jds Geduld* to demand; *jds Hilfe* to ask for. **(d)** *(strapazieren) Maschine etc* to use; *jdn* to keep busy. **etw stark ~** to put sth under a lot of stress.

Be|anspruchung *f* **(a)** *(Forderung)* claim *(gen* to*)*. **(b)** *(Ausnutzung: von jds Geduld etc)* demand *(gen* on*)*. **(c)** *(Belastung)* use; *(von Beruf)* demands *pl*.

be|anstanden* *vt* to object to; *Rechnung* to query; *Ware* to complain about. **er hat an allem etwas zu ~** he complains about everything.

Be|anstandung *f* complaint *(gen* about*)*.

be|antragen* *vt* to apply for *(bei* to*)*; *(Jur) Strafe* to demand, to ask for; *(vorschlagen: in Debatte etc)* to move, to propose. **er beantragte, versetzt zu werden** he applied for a transfer.

Be|antragung *f siehe vt* application *(gen* for*)*; demand *(gen* for*)*; proposal.

be|antworten* *vt* to answer; *Anfrage, Brief auch* to reply to; *Gruß, Beleidigung auch* to respond to.

Be|antwortung *f siehe vt (gen* to*)* answer; reply; response.

be|arbeiten* *vt* **(a)** *(behandeln)* to work on; *Stein, Holz* to work, to dress. **(b)** *(sich befassen mit)* to deal with; *Fall auch* to handle; *Bestellungen etc* to process. **(c)** *(redigieren)* to edit; *(neu ~)* to revise; *(umändern) Roman etc* to adapt; *Musik* to arrange. **(d)** *(col: einreden auf) jdn* to work on. **(e)** *Land* to cultivate.

Be|arbeiter(in *f***)** *m siehe vt (c)* editor; reviser; adapter; arranger.

Be|arbeitung *f siehe vt* **(a)** working (on); dressing. **(b)** dealing with; handling; processing. **die ~ meines Antrags hat lange gedauert** it took a long time to deal with my claim. **(c)** editing; revising; adapting; arranging; *(bearbeitete Ausgabe etc)* edition; revision; adaptation; arrangement. **neue ~** *(von Film etc)* new version; **die deutsche ~** the German version. **(d)** *(von Land)* cultivation.

Be|arbeitungsgebühr *f* handling fee.

be|argwöhnen* *vt* to be suspicious of.

Beat [bi:t] *m no pl* **(a)** *(Musik)* beat *or* pop music. **(b)** *(Rhythmus)* beat.

be|atmen* *vt* to give artificial respiration to. **jdn künstlich ~** to keep sb breathing artificially.

Be|atmung *f* **künstliche ~** artificial respiration.

Beatmusik ['bi:t-] *f* beat *or* pop music.

be|aufsichtigen* *vt* to supervise; *Kind* to mind; *Prüfung* to invigilate at.

Be|aufsichtigung *f siehe vt* supervision; minding; invigilation.

be|auftragen* *vt* **(a)** *(heranziehen)* **jdm mit etw ~** to give sb the job of doing sth; *(geschäftlich)* to commission sb to do sth. **(b)** *(anweisen) Untergebenen etc* to instruct.

Be|auftragte(r) *mf decl as adj* representative.

be|äugen* *vt (col)* to gaze *or* look at.

bebauen* *vt* **(a)** *Grundstück* to build on, to develop. **(b)** *(Agr)* to cultivate; *Land* to farm.

Bebauung *f no pl* **(a)** *(Vorgang)* building *(gen* on*)*; *(von Gelände)* development. **(b)** *(Agr)* cultivation; *(von Land)* farming.

beben *vi* to tremble.

Beben *nt* **-** trembling; *(Erd~)* earthquake.

bebildern* *vt Buch, Vortrag* to illustrate.

Becher *m* **-** cup; *(esp Porzellan~, Ton~ auch)* mug; *(Plastik~ auch)* beaker.

bechern *vi (hum col)* to have a few *(col)*.

Becken *nt* **- (a)** *(Wasch~, Geol)* basin; *(Abwasch~)* sink; *(Toiletten~)* bowl, pan; *(Schwimm~)* pool. **(b)** *(Anat)* pelvis. **ein breites ~** broad hips. **(c)** *(Mus)* cymbal.

Becken- *(Anat, Med)*: **~bruch** *m* fractured pelvis; **~knochen** *m* hip-bone.

bedacht *adj* **(a)** *(überlegt)* cautious. **(b) darauf ~ sein, etw zu tun** to be concerned about doing sth.

Bedacht *m no pl (geh)* **mit ~** *(vorsichtig)* prudently, carefully; *(absichtlich)* deliberately; **ohne ~** without thinking.

bedächtig *adj Schritt, Sprache* measured *no adv*, deliberate; *(besonnen)* thoughtful.

bedanken* *vr* to say thank-you. **sich bei jdm (für etw) ~** to thank sb (for sth); **ich bedanke mich herzlich** thank you very much; **dafür können Sie sich bei Herrn Weitz ~** *(iro col)* you can thank Mr Weitz for that *(iro)*; **dafür wird er sich ~** *(iro)* he'll just love that *(iro)*.

Bedarf *m no pl* **(a)** *(Bedürfnis)* need *(an+dat* for*)*; *(~smenge)* requirements *pl*. **bei ~** as required; **Dinge des täglichen ~s** basic *or* everyday necessities; **alles für den häuslichen ~** all household requirements; **seinen ~ an Wein/Lebensmitteln** *etc* **einkaufen** to buy the wine/food *etc* one needs; **an etw** *(dat)* **~ haben** to need sth, to be in need of sth. **(b)** *(Comm: Nachfrage)* demand *(an+dat* for*)*. **(je) nach ~** according to demand; **den ~ übersteigen** to exceed demand; **über ~** in excess of demand.

Bedarfs-: **~deckung** *f* satisfaction of the/sb's needs; **~fall** *m (form)* **im ~fall** if necessary; *(wenn gebraucht)* as necessary *or* required; **~haltestelle** *f* request stop *(Brit)*, flag stop *(US)*.

bedauerlich *adj* regrettable, unfortunate.

bedauerlicherweise *adv* regrettably, unfortunately.

bedauern* *vt* **(a)** *etw* to regret. **wir ~, Ihnen mitteilen zu müssen, ...** we regret to have to inform you ...; **(ich) bedau(e)re!** I'm sorry. **(b)** *(bemitleiden) jdn* to feel sorry for. **er ist zu ~** he is to be pitied.

Bedauern *nt no pl* regret. **(sehr) zu meinem ~** (much) to my regret.

bedauernswert *adj Mensch* pitiful; *Zustand* deplorable.

bedecken* **1** *vt* to cover. **2** *vr (Himmel)* to become overcast, to cloud over.

bedeckt *adj* **(a)** covered. **(b)** *(bewölkt)* overcast, cloudy. **bei ~em Himmel** when the sky is overcast *or* cloudy.

bedenken* *vt irreg* **(a)** *(überlegen)* to consider, to think about. **wenn man es recht bedenkt, ...** if you think about it properly ... **(b)** *(in Betracht ziehen) Umstand, Folgen etc* to consider. **das hättest du vorher ~ sollen** you should have thought about that before; **ich gebe zu ~, daß ...** *(geh)* I would ask you to consider that ... **(c)** *(geh: beschenken)* **jdn mit einem Geschenk ~** to give sb a present; **jdn reich ~** to be generous to sb; **mit etw bedacht werden** to receive sth.

Bedenken *nt* **- (a)** *usu pl (Zweifel, Einwand)* doubt, reservation, misgiving. **moralische ~** moral scruples; **~ haben** to have one's doubts *(bei* about*)*; **ihm kommen ~** he is having second thoughts. **(b)** *no pl (das Überlegen)* consideration *(gen* of*)*. **nach langem ~** after much thought.

bedenkenlos *adj* **(a)** *(ohne Zögern)* unhesitating. **(b)** *(skrupellos)* thoughtless.

Bedenkenlosigkeit *f no pl* **(a)** *(Bereitwilligkeit)* readiness, promptness. **(b)** *(Skrupellosigkeit)* unscrupulousness.

bedenkenswert *adj* worth considering.

bedenklich *adj* **(a)** *(zweifelhaft)* dubious, questionable. **(b)** *(besorgniserregend)* serious. **(c)** *(besorgt)* apprehensive, anxious. **jdn ~ stimmen** to

make sb apprehensive.
Bedenkzeit *f* **um ~ bitten** to ask for time to think about it.
bedeuten* *vt* **(a)** to mean. **das hat nichts zu ~** it doesn't mean anything; *(macht nichts aus)* it doesn't matter; **das bedeutet nichts Gutes** that means trouble; **Geld bedeutet mir nichts** money means nothing to me. **(b)** *(geh: einen Hinweis geben)* to indicate. **man bedeutete mir, daß ...** I was given to understand that ...
bedeutend 1 *adj* **(a)** *(wichtig) Persönlichkeit* important, eminent; *Leistung, Rolle* major. **(b)** *(groß) Summe, Erfolg* considerable. **2** *adv (beträchtlich)* considerably.
bedeutsam *adj* significant; *(vielsagend auch)* meaningful.
Bedeutsamkeit *f siehe adj* significance; meaningfulness.
Bedeutung *f* **(a)** *(Sinn, Wortsinn)* meaning. **(b)** *(Wichtigkeit)* importance, significance. **von ~ sein** to be of significance.
Bedeutungs-: ~lehre *f (Ling)* semantics *sing* **b~los** *adj* **(a)** *(unwichtig)* insignificant, unimportant; **(b)** *(nichts besagend)* meaningless; **~losigkeit** *f* insignificance, unimportance; **zur ~losigkeit verurteilt sein** to be condemned to insignificance; **b~voll** *adj* = **bedeutsam.**
bedienen* 1 *vt* **(a)** to serve; *(Kellner auch)* to wait on. **werden Sie schon bedient?** are you being served?; **hier wird man gut bedient** the service is good here; **er läßt sich gern ~** he likes to be waited on; **damit sind Sie sehr gut bedient** that should serve you very well; **ich bin bedient!** *(col)* I've had enough. **(b)** *(handhaben) Maschine etc* to operate. **(c)** *(Cards)* **eine Farbe/Karo ~** to follow suit/to follow suit in diamonds. **2** *vi* **(a)** to serve. **(b)** *(Cards)* **du mußt ~** you must follow suit; **falsch ~** to fail to follow suit. **3** *vr* **(a) bitte ~ Sie sich** please help *or* serve yourself. **(b)** *(geh: gebrauchen)* **sich jds/einer Sache ~** to use sb/sth.
Bedienstete(r) *mf decl as adj* public employee.
Bedienung *f* **(a)** *no pl (in Restaurant etc)* service; *(von Maschinen)* operation. **die ~ der Kunden** serving the customers. **(b)** *(~sgeld)* service (charge). **(c)** *(~spersonal)* staff; *(Kellner etc)* waiter/waitress.
Bedienungs-: ~anleitung *f* operating instructions *pl;* **~zuschlag** *m* service charge.
bedingen *vt* **(a)** *(bewirken)* to cause; *(notwendig machen)* to necessitate; *(bestimmen: auch Psych, Physiol)* to condition. **sich gegenseitig ~** to be mutually dependent. **(b)** *(voraussetzen, verlangen)* to call for, to demand.
bedingt *adj* **(a)** *(eingeschränkt)* limited; *Lob auch* qualified. **(nur) ~ gelten** to be (only) partially valid; **~ tauglich** *(Mil)* fit for limited duties. **(b)** *(an Bedingung geknüpft) Straferlaß* conditional.
Bedingung *f* condition; *(Erfordernis)* requirement. **mit** *or* **unter der ~, daß ...** on condition that ...; **unter keiner ~** on no condition; **es zur ~ machen, daß ...** to make it a condition that ...; **zu günstigen ~en** *(Comm)* on favourable terms.
bedingungslos *adj Kapitulation* unconditional; *Hingabe, Gehorsam* unquestioning.
bedrängen* *vt Feind* to attack; *gegnerische Mannschaft, Schuldner* to put pressure on; *(belästigen)* to plague. **sich in einer bedrängten Lage befinden** to be in dire straits.
Bedrängnis *f (geh: seelisch)* distress, torment. **in ~ geraten** to get into difficulties.
bedrohen* *vt* to threaten; *Gesundheit* to endanger. **vom Tode/von Überschwemmung bedroht** in mortal danger/in danger of being flooded.
bedrohlich *adj (gefährlich)* dangerous, alarming; *(unheilverkündend)* ominous, menacing.
Bedrohung *f* threat *(gen* to*).* **in ständiger ~ leben** to live under a constant threat.
bedrucken* *vt* to print on. **bedruckter Stoff** print, printed fabric.
bedrücken* *vt* to depress. **was bedrückt dich?** what's getting you down?
bedrückend *adj* depressing.
bedrückt *adj (niedergeschlagen)* depressed, dejected; *Schweigen* oppressive.
Beduine *m (wk)* **-n, -n, Beduinin** *f* Bedouin.
bedürfen *vi irreg+gen (geh)* to need, to require. **es bedarf einiger Mühe** it needs *or* requires some effort; **ohne daß es eines Hinweises bedurft hätte, ...** without having to be asked ...
Bedürfnis *nt* need; *(no pl: form: Anliegen)* wish. **die ~se des täglichen Lebens** everyday needs; **ich hatte das dringende ~, das zu tun** I felt an urgent need to do it; **das ~ nach Schlaf haben** to be in need of sleep.
Bedürfnis-: ~anstalt *f (dated form, hum)* public convenience *(Brit)*, comfort station *(US)*; **~befriedigung** *f* satisfaction of one's/sb's needs; **b~los** *adj Mensch etc* undemanding, modest in one's needs.
bedürftig *adj (hilfs~)* needy, in need. **die B~en** the needy *pl.*
Bedürftigkeit *f no pl* need.
Beefsteak ['bi:fste:k] *nt* steak. **deutsches ~** hamburger.
be|ehren* *vt (iro, geh)* to honour *(Brit)*, to honor *(US).*
be|eiden* *vt (beschwören) Aussage* to swear to.
be|eilen* *vr* to hurry (up), to get a move on *(col).*
Be|eilung *interj (col)* get a move on *(col).*
be|eindrucken* *vt* to impress. **davon lasse ich mich nicht ~** I won't be impressed by that.
be|eindruckend *adj* impressive.
be|einflußbar *adj* impressionable, suggestible. **er ist nur schwer ~** he is hard to influence.
be|einflussen* *vt jdn* to influence. **er ist leicht/schwer zu ~** he is easily influenced/hard to influence.
Be|einflussung *f (das Beeinflussen)* influencing; *(Einfluß)* influence *(durch* of*).*
be|einträchtigen* *vt (stören)* to spoil; *Konzentration auch* to disturb; *Rundfunkempfang* to interfere with; *(vermindern) Sehvermögen, Reaktionen, Leistung* to impair. **jdn in seiner Freiheit ~** to restrict sb's freedom.
Be|einträchtigung *f siehe vt* spoiling; disturbance; interference *(gen* with*)*; impairment.
be|enden* *vt* to end; *Arbeit, Studium etc* to finish, to complete. **etw vorzeitig ~** to cut sth short.
Be|end(ig)ung *f no pl* ending; *(Ende)* end; *(Fertigstellung)* completion; *(Schluß)* conclusion.
be|engen* *vt (fig)* to stifle, to inhibit. **~de Kleidung** restricting clothing.
be|engt *adj* cramped; *(fig)* stifled. **~ wohnen** to live in cramped conditions.
Be|engtheit *f (von Räumen)* cramped conditions *pl.*
be|erben* *vt* **jdn ~** to be sb's heir.
be|erdigen* *vt* to bury.
Be|erdigung *f* burial; *(~sfeier)* funeral. **auf der falschen ~ sein** *(hum)* to have come to the wrong place.
Be|erdigungs- *in cpds siehe auch* **Bestattungs-** funeral; **~feier** *f* funeral service.
Beere *f* **-n** berry; *(Wein~)* grape. **~n sammeln** to go berry-picking.
Beeren-: ~auslese *f wine made from specially selected grapes;* **~obst** *nt* soft fruit.
Beet *nt* **-e** *(Blumen~)* bed; *(Gemüse~)* patch.
befähigen* *vt (jdn zu etw* sb to do sth*)* to enable; *(Ausbildung)* to qualify, to equip.
befähigt *adj* **(a)** *(durch Ausbildung)* qualified. **(b) zu etw ~ sein** to be capable of doing sth.
Befähigung *f no pl* **(a) die ~ zum Richteramt** the qualifications to become a judge. **(b)** *(Können, Eignung)* capability, ability *(zu etw* to do sth*).*

befahl *pret of* **befehlen.**

befahrbar *adj Straße* passable; *Seeweg, Fluß* navigable. ~ **sein** *(Straße)* to be open to traffic; **nicht** ~ **sein** *(Straße, Weg)* to be closed (to traffic); *(wegen Schnee etc auch)* to be impassable.

befahren¹* *vt irreg* **(a)** *Straße, Weg* to use. **der Paß kann nur im Sommer** ~ **werden** the pass is only open to traffic in summer; **diese Straße wird stark/wenig** ~ this road is used a lot/isn't used much. **(b)** *(Schiff, Seemann)* to sail.

befahren² *adj* **eine viel** *or* **stark/wenig ~e Straße** a much/little used road.

Befahren *nt no pl* use *(gen* of*)*.

Befall *m no pl* attack; *(mit Schädlingen)* infestation.

befallen¹* *vt irreg* **(a)** *(geh: überkommen)* to overcome; *(Angst auch)* to grip; *(Fieber, Krankheit)* to strike. **(b)** *(angreifen, infizieren)* to affect; *(Schädlinge, Ungeziefer)* to infest.

befallen² *adj* affected *(von* by*)*; *(von Schädlingen)* infested *(von* with*)*.

befangen *adj* **(a)** *Lächeln* bashful; *Schweigen* awkward. **(b)** *Richter* prejudiced, bias(s)ed.

Befangenheit *f no pl siehe adj* **(a)** bashfulness, awkwardness. **(b)** bias, prejudice; *(Jur)* interest.

befassen* **1** *vr* **sich** ~ **mit** to deal with; *mit Forschungsbereich* to work on; **sie hat keine Zeit, sich mit ihren Kindern zu** ~ she has no time for her children. **2** *vt (form)* **mit etw befaßt sein** to be dealing with sth.

Befehl *m* **-e (a)** *(Anordnung)* order, command *(an +acc* to, *von* from*)*; *(Comp)* command. **wir hatten den ~, ...**we had orders *or* were ordered to...; **auf seinen** ~ **(hin)** on his orders; **auf** ~ **handeln** to act under orders; **auf höheren** ~ on orders from above; **zu ~, Herr Hauptmann** *(Mil)* yes, sir; ~ **ausgeführt!** mission accomplished; ~ **ist** ~ orders are orders; **dein Wunsch ist mir** ~ *(hum)* your wish is my command. **(b)** *(Befehlsgewalt)* command. **den** ~ **haben** *or* **führen** to be in command *(über+acc* of*)*.

befehlen *pret* **befahl,** *ptp* **befohlen 1** *vi* to order; *(Befehle erteilen)* to give orders; *(den Befehl haben)* to be in command *(über+acc* of*)*. **er befahl, den Mann zu erschießen** he ordered the man to be shot. **2** *vt* to order. **du hast mir gar nichts zu** ~ I won't take orders from you; **wie Sie** ~ as you wish.

befehligen* *vt (Mil)* to command.

Befehls-: **~empfänger** *m* **~empfänger sein** to follow orders *(gen* from*)*; **~form** *f (Gram)* imperative; **b~gemäß** *adj* as ordered; **~gewalt** *f (Mil)* command; **~gewalt haben** to be in command *(über+acc* over*)*; **~haber** *m* - commander; **~notstand** *m (Jur)* obligation to obey orders; **~ton** *m* peremptory tone; **~verweigerung** *f (Mil)* refusal to obey orders.

befestigen* *vt* **(a)** *(an+dat* to*)* *(anbringen)* to fasten; *Boot* to tie up. **etw durch Nähen/Kleben** *etc* ~ to sew/glue *etc* sth. **(b)** *(fest, haltbar machen) Böschung, Deich* to reinforce; *Fahrbahn, Straße* to make up. **(c)** *(Mil)* to fortify.

Befestigung *f* **(a)** *(das Befestigen)* fastening; *(das Festmachen auch)* securing; *(von Boot)* tying up. **(b)** *(das Haltbarmachen)* reinforcement. **(c)** *(Mil)* fortification.

Befestigungs|anlage *f* fortification.

befeuchten* *vt* to moisten; *Wäsche* to dampen.

befeuern* *vt* **(a)** *(beheizen)* to fuel. **(b)** *(lit, fig: mit Geschossen)* to bombard.

befinden* *irreg* **1** *vr* **(a)** *(sein)* to be; *(liegen auch)* to be situated; *(esp in Maschine, Körper etc auch)* to be located. **unter ihnen befanden sich einige, die ...** there were some amongst them who ... **(b)** *(form: sich fühlen)* to feel. **2** *vt (form: erachten)* to deem *(form)*, to find. **etw für nötig/gut** ~ to deem *or* find sth (to be) necessary/good; **jdn für schuldig** ~ to find sb guilty. **3** *vi (geh: entscheiden)* to decide *(über+acc* about*)*. **darüber hat der Arzt zu** ~ that is for the doctor to decide.

Befinden *nt no pl* **(a)** *(form: Gesundheitszustand)* (state of) health; *(eines Kranken)* condition. **(b)** *(geh: Meinung)* **nach meinem** ~ in my view.

befindlich *adj usu attr (form) Gebäude, Park* situated, located; *(in Behälter)* contained. **der an der Tür ~e Haken** the hook on the door; **das im Umbau ~e Hotel** the hotel which is being renovated.

beflaggen* *vt Häuser* to decorate with flags; *Schiff* to dress.

beflecken* *vt* **(a)** *(lit)* to stain. **er hat sich mit Blut befleckt** *(fig)* he has blood on his hands. **(b)** *(fig geh) Ruf, Ehre* to besmirch.

befleißigen* *vr (geh)* **sich einer Sache** *(gen)* ~ to cultivate sth; **sich ~, etw zu tun** to make a great effort to do sth.

beflissen *adj (geh) (bemüht)* zealous, keen; *(pej: unterwürfig)* obsequious.

Beflissenheit *f siehe adj* zeal, keenness; obsequiousness.

beflügeln* *vt (geh)* to inspire.

befohlen *ptp of* **befehlen.**

befolgen* *vt* to follow; *Vorschrift auch* to comply with.

Befolgung *f siehe vt* following *(gen* sth*)*; compliance *(gen* with*)*.

befördern* *vt* **(a)** *Waren* to transport, to carry; *Personen* to carry. **etw mit der Post/per Bahn** ~ to send sth by post/rail. **(b) er wurde zum Major befördert** he was promoted to major.

Beförderung *f siehe vt* **(a)** transportation; carriage. **die** ~ **eines Briefes dauert 3 Tage** a letter takes 3 days (to arrive). **(b)** promotion.

Beförderungs-: **~bedingungen** *pl* conditions *pl* of carriage; **~mittel** *nt* means of transport.

befrachten* *vt (lit, fig geh)* to load.

befragen* *vt* **(a)** *(über +acc, zu* about*)* to question; *Zeugen auch* to examine. **auf B**~ when questioned. **(b)** *(um Stellungnahme bitten)* to consult *(über+acc, nach* about*)*.

Befragte(r) *mf decl as adj* person asked; *(in Umfrage auch)* interviewee. **alle ~n** all those asked.

Befragung *f siehe vt* **(a)** questioning; examining. **(b)** consultation *(gen* with *or* of*)*. **(c)** *(Umfrage)* survey.

befreien* **1** *vt* **(a)** *(frei machen)* to free, to set free. **jdn aus einer schwierigen Lage** ~ to rescue sb from a tricky situation. **(b)** *(freistellen) (von* from*)* to excuse; *(von Militärdienst, Steuern)* to exempt. **(c)** *(reinigen) (von* of*)* *(von Ungeziefer etc)* to rid; *(von Schnee, Eis)* to free. **2** *vr* **(a)** *(Volk, Land)* to free oneself; *(entkommen)* to escape *(von, aus* from*)*. **(b)** *(erleichtern)* to rid oneself *(von* of*)*, to free oneself *(von* from*)*.

Befreier(in *f***)** *m* - liberator.

befreit *adj (erleichtert)* relieved.

Befreiung *f siehe vt* **(a)** freeing, setting free. **(b)** excusing; exemption. **um** ~ **von etw bitten** to ask to be excused/exempted from sth. **(c)** ridding; freeing. **(d)** *(Erleichterung)* relief.

Befreiungs-: **~bewegung** *f* liberation movement; **~front** *f* liberation front; **~kampf** *m* struggle for liberation; **~krieg** *m* war of liberation; **~versuch** *m* escape attempt.

befremden* *vt* to amaze. **es befremdete mich zu hören, ...** I was taken aback to hear ...

Befremden *nt no pl* amazement.

befremdet *adj* taken aback.

befreunden* *vr* to make *or* become friends; *(fig: mit einem Gedanken etc)* to get used to.

befreundet *adj* **wir sind schon lange (miteinander)** ~ we have been friends for a long time; **gut** *or* **eng** ~ **sein** to be good *or* close friends; **ein ~er Staat** a friendly nation.

befriedigen* **1** *vt* to satisfy; *Gelüste auch* to gratify. **2** *vi* to be satisfactory. **3** *vr* **sich (selbst)**

~ to masturbate.
befriedigend *adj* satisfactory; *Verhältnisse, Leistung, Antwort auch* adequate; *Gefühl* satisfying.
Befriedigung *f siehe vt* satisfaction; gratification. **sexuelle ~** sexual satisfaction.
befristen* *vt* to limit, to restrict *(auf +acc* to*)*.
befristet *adj Genehmigung, Visum* restricted; *Arbeitsverhältnis, Anstellung* temporary. **~ sein/auf zwei Jahre ~ sein** *(Paß etc)* to be valid for a limited period/for two years.
befruchten* *vt (lit) Eizelle* to fertilize; *Blüte* to pollinate; *(fig: geistig anregen)* to stimulate.
Befruchtung *f siehe vt* fertilization; pollination; stimulation. **künstliche ~** artificial insemination.
Befugnis *f (form)* authority. **eine ~ erhalten/erteilen** to receive/give authority.
befugt *adj (form)* **~ sein(, etw zu tun)** to have the authority (to do sth).
Befund *m* **-e** results *pl*, findings *pl*. **ohne ~** *(Med)* (results) negative.
befürchten* *vt* to fear. **es ist zu ~, daß ...** it is (to be) feared that ...; **das ist nicht zu ~** there is no fear of that.
Befürchtung *f* fear *usu pl*. **die schlimmsten ~en haben** to fear the worst.
befürworten* *vt* to approve.
Befürworter(in *f*) *m* **-** supporter; *(von Idee auch)* advocate.
Befürwortung *f* approval.
begabt *adj* talented; *(esp geistig, musisch auch)* gifted. **für etw ~ sein** to be talented at sth.
Begabung *f (Anlage)* talent; *(esp geistig, musisch auch)* gift. **er hat ~ zum Lehrer** he has a gift for teaching; **mangelnde ~** a lack of talent.
begann *pret of* **beginnen.**
begatten* *(esp Zool)* **1** *vt* to mate with. **2** *vr* to mate; *(geh, hum)* to copulate.
Begattung *f (esp Zool)* mating; *(geh, hum)* copulation.
begeben *vr irreg* **(a)** *(geh)* to go. **sich nach Hause ~** to make one's way home; **sich auf eine Reise ~** to go on a journey; **sich zu Bett/zur Ruhe ~** to retire; **sich in ärztliche Behandlung ~** to undergo medical treatment; **sich an die Arbeit ~** to commence work; **sich in Gefahr ~** to expose oneself to danger. **(b)** *(old liter: geschehen)* to come to pass *(old liter)*.
Begebenheit *f (geh)* occurrence, event.
begegnen* *vi aux sein+dat* **(a)** *(treffen)* to meet. **sich** *or* **einander** *(geh)* **~** to meet. **(b)** *(stoßen auf)* to encounter. **(c)** *(widerfahren)* **es war mir schon einmal begegnet, daß ...** it had happened to me once already that ... **(d)** *(geh: entgegentreten) einer Krankheit, der Not* to combat; *Angriff* to resist; *einer Gefahr, Schwierigkeiten* to meet, to face. **man begegnete mir nur mit Spott** I only met with derision.
Begegnung *f* encounter; *(Treffen auch)* meeting; *(Sport auch)* match.
begehen* *vt* **(a)** *(verüben) Verbrechen, Ehebruch* to commit; *Fehler* to make. **einen Mord an jdm ~** to murder sb; **eine Dummheit/Unvorsichtigkeit ~** to do something stupid/careless; **an jdm ein Unrecht ~** to wrong sb; **Verrat an jdm/etw ~** to betray sb/sth. **(b)** *(entlanggehen) Weg* to use. **(c)** *(geh: feiern)* to celebrate.
begehren* *vt (geh, old)* to desire.
Begehren *nt* **- (a)** *(geh: Verlangen)* desire *(nach* for*)*. **(b)** *(old: Wunsch, Forderung)* wish.
begehrenswert *adj* desirable.
begehrlich *adj (geh)* covetous.
begehrt *adj* much sought-after; *Partner etc auch, Ferienziel* popular; *Posten auch* desirable.
Begehung *f (form: eines Verbrechens)* committing.
begeistern* **1** *vt* to fill with enthusiasm. **er ist für nichts zu ~** he's not interested in doing *anything*. **2** *vr* to get enthusiastic *(an +dat, für* about*)*.
begeisternd *adj* inspiring; *Rede auch* stirring.
begeistert *adj* enthusiastic *(von* about*)*.
Begeisterung *f no pl* enthusiasm *(über +acc* about, *für* for*)*. **in ~ geraten** to become enthusiastic.
Begeisterungs-: b~fähig *adj Publikum etc* quick to show one's enthusiasm; **~fähigkeit** *f* capacity for enthusiasm; **~sturm** *m* storm of enthusiasm.
Begierde *f* **-n** *(geh)* desire *(nach* for*)*; *(Sehnsucht)* longing, yearning. **vor ~ brennen, etw zu tun** to be longing to do sth.
begierig *adj (voll Verlangen)* hungry, greedy; *(gespannt)* eager, keen.
begießen* *vt irreg* **(a)** *(mit Wasser)* to pour water on; *Blumen, Beet* to water; *(mit Fett) Braten etc* to baste; *siehe* **begossen. (b)** *(fig col) freudiges Ereignis etc* to celebrate. **das muß begossen werden!** that calls for a drink!
Beginn *m no pl* beginning, start. **zu ~** at the beginning.
beginnen *pret* **begann,** *ptp* **begonnen** *vti* to start, to begin. **mit der Arbeit ~** to start *or* begin work; **es beginnt zu regnen** it's starting to rain; **eine ~de Erkältung** the beginnings of a cold.
beglaubigen* *vt* **(a)** *Testament, Unterschrift* to witness; *Abschrift* to authenticate; *Echtheit, Übersetzung* to certify. **(b)** *Botschafter* to accredit *(bei* to*)*.
Beglaubigung *f siehe vt* **(a)** witnessing, authentication; certification. **(b)** accrediting.
begleichen* *vt irreg (lit, fig)* to settle. **mit Ihnen habe ich noch eine Rechnung zu ~** *(fig)* I've a score to settle with you.
Begleichung *f* settlement.
Begleitbrief *m* covering letter.
begleiten* *vt* to accompany *(auch Mus)*.
Begleiter(in *f*) *m* **- (a)** companion; *(zum Schutz)* escort. **(b)** *(Mus)* accompanist.
Begleit-: ~erscheinung *f* side-effect; **das ist eine ~erscheinung des Alters** it's a symptom of old age; **~musik** *f* accompaniment; *(in Film etc)* incidental music; **~papiere** *pl (Comm)* accompanying documents *pl*; **~schein** *m* dispatch note; **~schreiben** *nt* covering letter; *(für Waren auch)* advice note; **~umstände** *pl* attendant circumstances *pl*.
Begleitung *f* **(a)** *no pl* company. **in ~ seines Vaters** accompanied by his father; **ich bin in ~ hier** I'm with someone. **(b)** *(Begleiter)* companion; *(zum Schutz)* escort. **ohne ~** unaccompanied. **(c)** *(Mus: Begleitmusik)* accompaniment.
beglücken* *vt* **jdn ~** to make sb happy; **er hat uns gestern mit seinem Besuch beglückt** *(iro)* he honoured *(Brit)* or honored *(US)* us with a visit yesterday; **ein ~des Gefühl** a cheering feeling.
beglückwünschen* *vt* to congratulate.
begnadet *adj* gifted.
begnadigen* *vt* to pardon.
Begnadigung *f* pardon.
begnügen* *vr* **sich damit ~, etw zu tun** to be content *or* satisfied to do sth.
Begonie [-niə] *f* begonia.
begonnen *ptp of* **beginnen.**
begossen *adj* **er stand da wie ein ~er Pudel** *(col)* he looked so sheepish.
begraben* *vt irreg* **(a)** to bury. **dort möchte ich nicht ~ sein** *(col)* I wouldn't like to be stuck in that hole *(col)*; **damit kannst du dich ~ lassen** *(col)* you can stuff that *(col!)*. **(b)** *(aufgeben) Hoffnung* to abandon; *(beenden) Streit etc* to end.
Begräbnis *nt* burial; *(~feier)* funeral.
begradigen* *vt* to straighten.
Begradigung *f* straightening.
begreifbar *adj* conceivable.
begreifen* *irreg* **1** *vti* to understand. **~, daß ...** *(einsehen)* to realize that ...; **es ist kaum zu ~** it's quite incomprehensible; **schnell/langsam ~** to

be quick/slow on the uptake; *siehe* **begriffen. 2** *vr* to be understandable. **es begreift sich, daß ...** it is understood that ...

begreiflich *adj* understandable. **ich kann mich ihm nicht ~ machen** I can't make myself clear to him.

begreiflicherweise *adv* understandably.

begrenzen* *vt* **(a)** *(Grenze sein von)* to mark the boundary of; *Straße etc* to line. **(b)** *(beschränken)* to restrict, to limit *(auf+acc* to*)*.

begrenzt *adj (beschränkt)* restricted, limited.

Begrenztheit *f no pl (von Möglichkeiten, Talent)* limited nature; *(von Menschen)* limitations *pl*.

Begrenzung *f* **(a)** *(das Begrenzen) (von Gebiet, Straße etc)* demarcation; *(von Geschwindigkeit, Redezeit)* restriction. **(b)** *(Grenze)* boundary.

Begriff *m* **-e (a)** concept; *(Terminus)* term. **etw in ~e fassen** to put sth into words; **sein Name ist mir ein/kein ~** his name means something/doesn't mean anything to me. **(b)** *(Vorstellung, Eindruck)* idea. **sich** *(dat)* **einen ~ von etw machen** to imagine sth; **du machst dir keinen ~ (davon)** *(col)* you've no idea *(col)*; **für meine ~e** in my opinion. **(c) im ~ sein, etw zu tun** to be on the point of doing sth, to be about to do sth. **(d) schwer von ~ sein** *(col)* to be slow on the uptake.

begriffen *adj* **ein noch in der Entwicklung ~er Plan** a plan still in the process of being developed.

begrifflich *adj* conceptual.

Begriffs-: ~bestimmung *f* definition; **b~stutzig** *adj (col)* dense *(col)*.

begründen* *vt* **(a)** *(Gründe anführen für)* to give reasons for; *(rechtfertigend) Forderung, Ansicht* to justify; *Verhalten* to account for; *Verdacht, Behauptung* to substantiate. **etw näher ~** to give specific reasons for sth; *siehe* **begründet. (b)** *(beginnen, gründen)* to establish; *Geschäft etc auch* to found.

Begründer *m* founder.

begründet *adj* well-founded; *(berechtigt)* justified. **es besteht ~e Hoffnung, daß ...** there is reason to hope that ...; **sachlich ~** founded on fact.

Begründung *f* **(a)** grounds *pl (für, gen* for*)*. **etwas zur** *or* **als ~ sagen** to say something in explanation. **(b)** *(Gründung)* establishment; *(von Geschäft etc auch)* foundation.

begrüßen* *vt* **(a)** to greet; *(als Gastgeber auch)* to welcome. **(b)** *Kritik, Entschluß etc* to welcome.

begrüßenswert *adj* welcome.

Begrüßung *f* greeting; *(der Gäste)* welcoming; *(Zeremonie)* welcome.

Begrüßungs- *in cpds* welcoming.

begucken* *vt (col)* to (have a) look at.

begünstigen* *vt* to favour *(Brit)*, to favor *(US)*; *Wachstum, Handel* to encourage; *Pläne, Beziehungen* to further; *(Jur)* to aid and abet. **durch die Dunkelheit begünstigt** assisted by the darkness.

Begünstigung *f* **(a)** *(Jur)* aiding and abetting. **(b)** *(Bevorzugung)* preferential treatment. **(c)** *(Förderung)* favouring *(Brit)*, favoring *(US)*; *(von Wachstum, Handel)* encouragement; *(von Plänen, Beziehungen)* furthering.

begut|achten* *vt* to give expert advice about; *Kunstwerk* to examine; *Projekte, Leistung* to judge; *(col: ansehen)* to have a look at.

Begut|achtung *f* (expert) assessment.

begütert *adj (reich)* wealthy, affluent.

begütigend *adj Worte etc* soothing. **~ auf jdn einreden** to calm sb down.

behaart *adj* hairy. **dicht ~** (thickly) covered with hair.

Behaarung *f* hairs *pl (+gen, an+dat* on*)*.

behäbig *adj Mensch* portly; *(phlegmatisch, geruhsam)* stolid; *(fig) Leben* comfortable; *Sprache, Ton* complacent.

behaftet *adj:* **mit etw ~ sein** *mit Krankheit etc* to be afflicted with sth; *mit Fehlern* to be full of sth; *mit Makel* to be tainted with sth.

Behagen *nt no pl* contentment. **mit ~ essen** to eat with relish.

behagen* *vi* **etw behagt jdm** sth pleases sb.

behaglich *adj* cosy; *(bequem)* comfortable. **es sich** *(dat)* **~ machen** to make oneself comfortable.

Behaglichkeit *f no pl siehe adj* cosiness; comfortableness.

behalten *vt irreg* to keep; *(nicht vergessen)* to remember. **~ Sie (doch) Platz!** please don't get up!; **den Hut auf dem Kopf ~** to keep one's hat on; **im Gedächtnis/im Kopf ~** to remember; **ich habe seine Adresse nicht ~** I've forgotten his address; **etw für sich ~** to keep sth to oneself.

Behälter *m* - container.

behämmert *adj (col)* screwy *(col)*.

behandeln* *vt* to treat; *Thema, Frage etc* to deal with; *(umgehen mit)* to handle. **er weiß, wie man Kinder/die Maschine ~ muß** he knows how to handle children/the machine; **der ~de Arzt** the doctor in attendance.

Behandlung *f* treatment. **wir sind jetzt bei der ~ dieses Themas** we are now dealing with this theme; **die schlechte ~ seiner Frau und Kinder** the maltreatment of his wife and children; **bei wem sind Sie in ~?** who's treating you?

Behandlungs-: b~bedürftig *adj* in need of treatment; **~kosten** *pl* cost *sing* of treatment; **~methode** *f* (method of) treatment; **~raum** *m* treatment room; **~weise** *f* treatment.

Behang *m* **¨e** *(Vorhang)* curtain; *(Wand~)* hanging; *(Schmuck)* decorations *pl*.

behängen* *vt* to decorate; *Wände auch* to hang.

beharren* *vi (hartnäckig sein)* to insist *(auf+dat* on*)*; *(nicht aufgeben)* to persist *(bei, auf+dat* in*)*.

Beharren *nt no pl siehe vi* insistence *(auf* on*)*; persistence *(bei, auf* in*)*.

beharrlich *adj (hartnäckig)* insistent; *(ausdauernd)* persistent. **~ fortfahren, etw zu tun** to persist in doing sth.

Beharrlichkeit *f siehe adj* insistence; persistence.

behauen* *vt Holz* to hew; *Stein* to cut; *(mit dem Meißel)* to carve.

behaupten* **1** *vt* **(a)** to claim, to maintain. **von jdm ~, daß ...** to say (of sb) that ... **(b)** *Stellung, Recht* to maintain. **2** *vr* to assert oneself; *(bei Diskussion)* to hold one's own *(gegenüber, gegen* against*)*. **sich auf dem Markt ~** to establish itself/oneself on the market.

Behauptung *f* **(a)** claim; *(esp unerwiesene ~)* assertion. **(b)** *(Aufrechterhaltung)* assertion; *(von Stellung)* successful defence *(Brit) or* defense *(US)*.

Behausung *f (geh, hum: Wohnung)* dwelling.

beheben* *vt irreg (beseitigen)* to remove; *Mißstände* to remedy; *Schaden* to repair; *Störung* to clear.

Behebung *f no pl siehe vt* removal; remedying; repairing; clearing.

beheimatet *adj (Mensch)* resident *(in+dat* in*)*; *(Pflanzen, Tiere)* native *(in +dat* to*)*.

beheizbar *adj* heatable; *Heckscheibe* heated.

beheizen* *vt* to heat.

Behelf *m* substitute; *(Notlösung)* makeshift.

behelfen* *vr irreg* to manage.

Behelfsheim *nt* temporary home.

behelfsmäßig *adj* makeshift.

behelligen* *vt* to bother.

behend(e) *adj (geh) (flink)* swift, quick; *(gewandt)* nimble, agile.

beherbergen* *vt (lit, fig)* to house; *Gäste* to accommodate; *Flüchtlinge* to give shelter to.

beherrschen* **1** *vt* **(a)** *(herrschen über)* to rule, to govern; *(fig: dominieren)* to dominate. **(b)** *(zügeln)* to control. **(c)** *Handwerk, Tricks* to master; *Fahrzeug, Situation* to have control of. **er**

beherrscht drei Sprachen/das Klavier he has a command of three languages/he's a skilled pianist. **2** *vr* to control oneself. **ich kann mich ~!** *(iro col)* not likely! *(col)*.

beherrscht *adj (fig)* self-controlled.

Beherrschung *f no pl* control; *(Selbst~)* self-control; *(des Markts)* domination; *(eines Fachs)* mastery. **die ~ verlieren** to lose one's temper.

beherzigen* *vt* to take to heart, to heed.

beherzt *adj (geh)* courageous, brave.

Beherztheit *f no pl (geh)* courage, bravery.

behilflich *adj* helpful. **jdm (bei etw) ~ sein** to help sb (with sth).

behindern* *vt* to hinder; *Sicht* to impede; *(bei Sport, im Verkehr)* to obstruct.

Behinderte(r) *mf decl as adj* handicapped person. **die ~n** the handicapped *pl*.

Behinderung *f* hindrance; *(im Sport, Verkehr)* obstruction; *(körperlich, Nachteil)* handicap.

Behörde *f* **-n** authority *usu pl; (Amtsgebäude)* office *usu pl*.

behördlich *adj* official. **~ genehmigt** officially approved.

behüten* *vt* to look after. **jdn vor etw** *(dat)* **~** to save *or* protect sb from sth; **(Gott) behüte!** *(col)* God forbid!; **behütet** *(Jugend etc)* sheltered.

behutsam *adj* cautious, careful; *(zart auch)* gentle. **man muß es ihr ~ beibringen** it will have to be broken to her gently.

Behutsamkeit *f no pl* care(fulness), cautiousness; *(Zartheit auch)* gentleness.

bei *prep+dat* **(a)** *(in der Nähe von)* near; *(zum Aufenthalt)* at, with; *(Tätigkeitsbereich angebend, in Institutionen)* at; *(in Werken)* in; *(jdn betreffend)* with; *(Teilnahme bezeichnend)* at; *(unter, zwischen Menge)* among. **die Schlacht ~ Leipzig** the battle of Leipzig; **dicht ~ dem Ort, wo ...** very near the place where ...; **der Wert liegt ~ tausend Mark** the value is around a thousand marks; **~ seinen Eltern wohnen** to live with one's parents; **ich war ~ meiner Tante** I was at my aunt's; **~ Müller** *(auf Briefen)* c/o Müller; **sie sind ~ uns eingeladen** they're invited to our house; **er ist** *or* **arbeitet ~ der Post** he works for the post office; **~m Militär** in the army; **~m Fleischer** at the butcher's *(Brit)*, at the butcher; **~ Collins erschienen** published by Collins; **das war ~ ihm der Fall** that was the case with him; **~ einer Hochzeit sein** to be at a wedding; **ich habe kein Geld ~ mir** I have no money on me.

(b) *(Zeitspanne: während)* during; *(Zeitpunkt)* (up)on, at. **~m letzten Gewitter** during the last storm; **~ meiner Ankunft** on my arrival; **~m Erscheinen der Königin ...** when the queen appeared ...; **ich habe ihm ~ der Arbeit geholfen** I helped him with the work; **~ der Arbeit** when I'm *etc* working; **~ dem Zugunglück** in the train crash; **er verliert ~m Kartenspiel immer** he always loses at cards.

(c) *(Zustand, Umstand bezeichnend)* in. **~ Kerzenlicht** by candlelight; **etw ~ einer Flasche Wein bereden** to discuss sth over a bottle of wine; **~ guter Gesundheit sein** to be in good health; **~ zehn Grad unter Null** when it's ten degrees below zero; **~ offenem Fenster schlafen** to sleep with the window open; **~ Feuer Scheibe einschlagen** in case of fire break glass; **~ Nebel und Glatteis** when there is fog and ice; **~ solcher Hitze/solchem Wind** in such heat/such a wind; **~ seinem Talent** with his talent; **~ aller Vorsicht** in spite of all one's caution; **~ Gott** by God.

beibehalten* *vt sep irreg* to keep; *Bräuche, Regelung auch* to retain; *Leitsatz, Richtung* to keep to; *Gewohnheit* to keep up.

Beibehaltung *f no pl siehe vt* keeping; retention; keeping to; keeping up.

Beiboot *nt (Naut)* dinghy.

beibringen *vt sep irreg* **(a)** *(unterweisen in)* to teach *(jdm etw* sb sth*)*. **(b) jdm etw ~** *(mitteilen)* to break sth to sb; *(zu verstehen geben)* to get sth across to sb. **(c)** *(zufügen) Wunde, Niederlage* to inflict *(jdm etw* sth on sb*)*. **(d)** *(herbeischaffen)* to produce; *Beweis, Geld etc* to furnish, to supply.

Beichte *f* **-n** confession. **zur ~ gehen** to go to confession.

beichten *vti (lit, fig)* to confess *(jdm etw* sth to sb*)*.

Beicht-: ~geheimnis *nt* seal of the confessional; **~stuhl** *m* confessional; **~vater** *m* father confessor.

beide *pron* **(a)** *(adjektivisch) (ohne Artikel)* both; *(mit Artikel)* two. **alle ~n Teller** both plates; **seine ~n Brüder** both his brothers, his two brothers; **ihr ~(n)/euch ~** you two; **euch ~n herzlichen Dank** many thanks to both of you. **(b)** *(substantivisch) (ohne Artikel)* both (of them); *(mit Artikel)* two (of them). **alle ~** both (of them); **keiner/keines** *etc* **von ~n** neither of them; **ich habe ~ nicht gesehen** I haven't seen either of them. **(c) ~s** both; **(alles) ~s ist erlaubt** both are permitted.

beidemal *adv* both times.

beider-: ~lei *adj attr inv* both; **~lei Geschlechts** of both sexes; **~seitig** *adj (auf beiden Seiten)* on both sides; *(gegenseitig) Vertrag etc* bilateral; *Einverständnis etc* mutual; **~seits 1** *adv* on both sides; **2** *prep+gen* on both sides of.

beidhändig *adj* ambidextrous.

beidrehen *vi sep (Naut)* to heave to.

beidseitig *adj (auf beiden Seiten)* on both sides; *(gegenseitig)* mutual.

bei|einander *adv* together. **du hast sie nicht alle ~** *(col)* you can't be all there *(col)*.

bei|einander-: ~halten *vt sep irreg* to keep together; **~sein** *vi sep irreg aux sein (col) (gesundheitlich)* to be in good shape *(col)*; *(geistig)* to be all there *(col)*.

Beifahrer *m (Aut)* (front-seat) passenger; *(beim Motorrad)* pillion passenger; *(berufsmäßiger Mitfahrer, Sport)* co-driver.

Beifahrersitz *m* passenger seat; *(auf Motorrad)* pillion.

Beifall *m no pl (Zustimmung)* approval; *(Händeklatschen)* applause; *(Zuruf)* cheering, cheers *pl*. **~ finden** to meet with approval; **~ spenden/klatschen** to applaud.

beifällig *adj* approving. **~e Worte** words of approval.

Beifalls-: ~ruf *m* cheer; **~sturm** *m* storm of applause.

Beifilm *m* short.

beifügen *vt sep (mitschicken)* to enclose *(dat* with*)*.

Beigabe *f* addition. **unter ~ eines Löffels Senf** adding a spoonful of mustard.

beige [beːʃ, 'beːʒə] *adj* beige.

beigeben *sep irreg* **1** *vt (zufügen)* to add *(dat* to*)*; *(mitgeben) jdn* to assign *(jdm* to sb*)*. **2** *vi*: **klein ~** *(col)* to give in.

Beigeschmack *m* taste; *(fig: von Worten)* flavour *(Brit)*, flavor *(US)*.

Beiheft *nt* supplement.

beiheften *vt sep* to append, to attach.

Beihilfe *f* **(a)** *(finanziell)* financial assistance *no indef art; (Zuschuß)* allowance; *(Studien~)* grant; *(Subvention)* subsidy. **(b) wegen ~ zum Mord** *(Jur)* because of being an accessory to the murder.

Beiklang *m (fig)* overtone *usu pl*.

beikommen *vi sep irreg aux sein* **jdm ~** *(zu fassen bekommen)* to get hold of sb; *(fertig werden mit)* to get the better of sb; **einer Sache** *(dat)* **~** *(bewältigen)* to deal with sth.

Beil *nt* **-e** axe *(Brit)*, ax *(US)*; *(kleiner)* hatchet; *(Fleischer~)* cleaver; *(Fall~)* blade (of a/the guillotine).

Beilage *f* **-n (a)** *(Gedrucktes)* insert; *(Beiheft)* supplement. **(b)** *(das Beilegen)* enclosure; *(in Buch)* insertion. **(c)** *(Cook)* side-dish.
beiläufig *adj* casual; *Bemerkung auch* passing *attr.* **etw ~ erwähnen** to mention sth in passing.
Beiläufigkeit *f (von Bemerkung etc)* casualness; *(Nebensächlichkeit)* triviality. **~en** trivia *pl.*
beilegen *vt sep* **(a)** *(hinzulegen)* to insert *(dat* in*)*; *(einem Brief)* to enclose *(dat* with, in*)*. **(b)** *(schlichten)* to settle. **(c) = beimessen.**
Beilegung *f siehe vt* **(a)** insertion; enclosure. **(b)** settlement.
beileibe *adv*: **das darf ~ nicht passieren** that mustn't happen under any circumstances; **~ kein ...** by no means a ..., certainly no ...
Beileid *nt no pl* condolences *pl.* **jdm sein ~ aussprechen** to offer sb one's condolences.
Beileids- *in cpds* of condolence; **~karte** *f* sympathy *or* condolence card.
beiliegend *adj* enclosed. **~ senden wir Ihnen ...** please find enclosed ...
beim = bei dem.
beimessen *vt sep irreg* **jdm/einer Sache Bedeutung ~** to attach importance to sb/sth.
beimischen *vt sep* to add *(dat* to*)*.
Bein *nt* **-e** leg. **sich kaum auf den ~en halten können** to be hardly able to stay on one's feet; **er ist noch gut auf den ~en** he's still sprightly; **jdm ein ~ stellen** *(lit, fig)* to trip sb up; **jdm wieder auf die ~e helfen** *(lit, fig)* to help sb back on his feet; **auf den ~en sein** *(nicht krank)* to be on one's feet; **wir sollten uns auf die ~e machen** *(col)* we ought to be making tracks *(col)*; **jdm ~e machen** *(col) (antreiben)* to make sb get a move on *(col)*; *(wegjagen)* to make sb clear off *(col)*; **die ~e in die Hand nehmen** *(col)* to take to one's heels; **sich** *(dat)* **die ~e in den Bauch stehen** *(col)* to stand about until one is fit to drop; **mit beiden ~en auf der Erde stehen** *(fig)* to have both feet firmly on the ground; **mit einem ~ im Grab/im Gefängnis stehen** *(fig)* to have one foot in the grave/to be likely to end up in jail; **auf eigenen ~en stehen** *(fig)* to be able to stand on one's own two feet; **auf einem ~ kann man nicht stehen!** *(fig col)* you can't stop at one!; **etw auf die ~e stellen** *(fig)* to get sth off the ground.
beinah(e) *adv* almost, nearly.
Beiname *m* epithet; *(Spitzname)* nickname.
Beinbruch *m* fracture of the leg. **das ist kein ~** *(fig col)* it could be worse *(col)*.
be|inhalten *vt* to contain.
Bein-: ~kleid *nt usu pl* breeches *pl (old, hum)*; **~schiene** *f (Sport)* shin pad; *(Med)* splint.
beipflichten *vi sep* **jdm/einer Sache (in etw** *dat)* **~** to agree with sb/sth (on sth).
Beiprogramm *nt* supporting programme *(Brit) or* program *(US)*.
Beirat *m* advisory council *or* committee.
be|irren* *vt* to disconcert. **sich nicht in etw** *(dat)* **~ lassen** not to let oneself be shaken in sth; **er läßt sich nicht ~** he won't be put off.
beisammen *adv* together.
beisammen- *pref* together; **~haben** *vt sep irreg (col) Geld, Leute* to have got together; **seinen Verstand ~haben** to have all one's wits about one; **er hat (sie) nicht alle ~** he's not all there; **~sein** *vi sep irreg aux sein (fig) (körperlich)* to be in good shape; *(geistig)* to be all there; **B~sein** *nt* get-together.
Beischlaf *m (Jur)* sexual intercourse.
Beisein *nt* presence. **in/ohne jds ~** in sb's presence/without sb being present.
beiseite *adv* aside *(auch Theat)*. **Spaß ~!** joking apart!; **jdn/etw ~ schaffen** to get rid of sb/sth.
beisetzen *vt sep (beerdigen)* to bury; *Urne* to install (in its resting place).
Beisetzung *f* funeral; *(von Urne)* installing in its resting place.
Beisitzer(in *f*) *m* **-** *(Jur)* assessor; *(bei Prüfung)* observer.
Beispiel *nt* **-e** example. **zum ~** for example *or* instance; **wie zum ~** such as; **sich** *(dat)* **ein ~ an jdm/etw nehmen** to take a leaf out of sb's book/to take sth as an example; **mit gutem ~ vorangehen** to set a good example.
beispiel-: ~haft *adj* exemplary; **~los** *adj* unprecedented; *(unerhört)* outrageous.
beispielsweise *adv* for example *or* instance.
beißen *pret* **biß,** *ptp* **gebissen 1** *vti* to bite; *(brennen: Geschmack, Schmerzen)* to sting. **in den Apfel ~** to take a bite out of the apple; **der Hund hat mich ins Bein gebissen** the dog has bitten my leg *or* me in the leg; **der Rauch beißt in den Augen** the smoke makes your eyes sting; **etwas/nichts zu ~** *(col: essen)* something/nothing to eat; **an etw** *(dat)* **zu ~ haben** *(fig)* to have sth to chew over. **2** *vr (Farben)* to clash.
beißend *adj (lit, fig)* biting; *Bemerkung* cutting; *Geschmack, Geruch* pungent, sharp; *Schmerz* gnawing; *Ironie, Spott* bitter.
Beißzange *f* (pair of) pincers *or* pliers.
Beistand *m* **¨e (a)** *no pl* help, assistance; *(moralisch)* support; *(von Priester)* presence. **jdm ~ leisten** to give sb assistance/give sb one's support. **(b)** *(Jur)* legal adviser.
Beistands-: ~pakt, ~vertrag *m* mutual assistance agreement.
beistehen *vi sep irreg* **jdm ~** to stand by sb.
Beistell- *in cpds* side; **~tisch** *m* occasional table.
beisteuern *vt sep* to contribute.
beistimmen *vi sep* = **zustimmen.**
Beitrag *m* **¨e (a)** *(Anteil)* contribution; *(Aufsatz auch)* article. **einen ~ zu etw leisten** to make a contribution to sth. **(b)** *(Betrag)* contribution; *(Versicherungs~)* premium; *(Mitglieds~)* fee.
beitragen *vti sep irreg* to contribute *(zu* to*)*.
Beitrags-: b~frei *adj* non-contributory; **b~pflichtig** *adj* contributory; **b~pflichtig sein** *(Mensch)* to have to pay contributions; **~satz** *m* membership rate.
beitreten *vi sep irreg aux sein+dat* to join; *einem Pakt* to enter into; *einem Vertrag* to accede to.
Beitritt *m siehe* **beitreten** joining *(zu etw* sth*)*; entering into *(zu etw* sth*)*; accession *(zu* to*)*. **seinen ~ erklären** to become a member.
Beitritts|erklärung *f* confirmation of membership.
Beiwerk *nt* additions *pl; (modisch)* accessories *pl.*
beiwohnen *vi sep +dat (geh: dabeisein)* to be present at.
Beize *f* **-n** *(Beizmittel)* corrosive fluid; *(Metall~)* pickling solution; *(Holz~)* stain.
beizeiten *adv* in good time.
beizen *vt* to steep in corrosive fluid; *(Metal)* to pickle; *Holz* to stain.
Beizmittel *nt* = **Beize.**
bejahen* *vti* to answer in the affirmative; *(gutheißen)* to approve of.
bejahend *adj* positive; *Antwort* affirmative.
bejahrt *adj* elderly, advanced in years.
bejammern* *vt* to lament.
bejammernswert *adj* deplorable, lamentable; *Mensch, Schicksal* pitiable.
bejubeln* *vt* to cheer; *Ereignis* to rejoice at.
bekämpfen* *vt* to fight; *(fig auch)* to combat; *Ungeziefer* to control.
Bekämpfung *f* fight, battle *(von, gen* against*)*; *(von Ungeziefer)* controlling. **zur ~ der Terroristen** to fight *or* combat the terrorists.
bekannt *adj* **(a)** well-known *(wegen* for*)*; *Mensch auch* famous. **die ~eren Spieler** the better-known players; **sie ist mir ~** I know her; **es ist allgemein ~, daß ...** it is common knowledge that ... **(b)** *(nicht fremd)* familiar. **jdn mit etw ~ machen** to familiarize sb with sth; **jdn (mit jdm) ~ machen** to introduce sb (to sb); **wir sind mit-**

einander ~ we already know each other.
Bekanntenkreis *m* circle of acquaintances.
Bekannte(r) *mf decl as adj* friend; *(entfernter ~)* acquaintance.
Bekanntgabe *f* announcement.
bekanntgeben *vt sep irreg* to announce.
Bekanntheit *f* **wegen seiner ~** because of his being well-known.
Bekanntheitsgrad *m* degree of fame.
bekanntlich *adv* **~ gibt es ...** it is known that there are ...; **er hat ~ eine Schwäche für Frauen** he is known to have a weakness for women.
bekanntmachen *vt sep* to announce; *(der Allgemeinheit mitteilen)* to publicize; *siehe* **bekannt (b).**
Bekanntmachung *f* **(a)** *siehe vt* announcement; publicizing. **(b)** *(Anschlag etc)* announcement.
Bekanntschaft *f* acquaintance; *(mit Materie, Gebiet)* knowledge *(mit* of*)*. **jds ~ machen** to make sb's aquaintance; **mit etw ~ machen** to come into contact with sth; **meine ganze ~** *(col)* all my friends.
bekanntwerden *vi sep irreg aux sein* to become known; *(Geheimnis)* to leak out.
bekehren* *vt* to convert *(zu* to*)*.
Bekehrung *f* conversion.
bekennen *irreg* **1** *vt* to confess, to admit; *Sünde* to confess. **2** *vr* **sich (für) schuldig ~** to admit *or* confess one's guilt; **sich als ... ~** to declare oneself to be a ...; **sich zu einem Glauben ~** to profess a faith; **sich zu jdm/etw ~** to declare one's support for sb/sth.
Bekenntnis *nt* **(a)** confession *(zu* of*)*. **sein ~ zum Sozialismus** his declared belief in socialism; **ein ~ zur Demokratie ablegen** to declare one's belief in democracy. **(b)** *(Rel: Konfession)* denomination.
Bekenntnis-: ~freiheit *f* freedom of religious belief; **~schule** *f* denominational school.
beklagen* **1** *vt* to lament; *Tod, Verlust* to mourn. **Menschenleben sind nicht zu ~** there are no casualties. **2** *vr* to complain *(über +acc, wegen* about*)*. **sich bei jdm ~** to complain to sb; **ich kann mich nicht ~** I can't complain.
beklagenswert *adj Mensch* pitiful; *Zustand* lamentable, deplorable; *Unfall* terrible.
Beklagte(r) *mf decl as adj (Jur)* defendant.
beklatschen* *vt (applaudieren)* to clap.
bekleben* *vt* **etw mit Papier/Plakaten** *etc* **~** to stick paper/posters *etc* on sth.
bekleckern* *(col)* **1** *vt* to stain. **2** *vr* **sich mit Saft** *etc* **~** to spill juice *etc* all over oneself; **er hat sich nicht gerade mit Ruhm bekleckert** *(iro)* he didn't exactly cover himself with glory.
bekleiden* *vt (geh)* **(a)** *(anziehen)* to dress *(mit* in*)*. **(b)** *Amt etc* to occupy, to hold.
Bekleidung *f* **(a)** clothes *pl*, clothing; *(Aufmachung)* dress. **(b)** *(form: eines Amtes)* tenure.
beklemmend *adj* oppressive.
Beklemmung *f usu pl* feeling of oppressiveness; *(Gefühl der Angst)* feeling of apprehension.
beklommen *adj* apprehensive, anxious.
bekloppt *adj (col)* crazy *(col)*.
beknackt *adj (col)* lousy *(col)*.
beknien* *vt (col) jdn* to beg.
bekommen *irreg* **1** *vt* **(a)** to get; *Geschenk, Brief, Lob, Belohnung auch* to receive; *Zug, Krankheit auch* to catch; *gutes Essen, Schlaganfall, ein Kind, Besuch* to have; *Spritze, Tadel auch* to be given. **wir ~ anderes Wetter** the weather is changing; **wir ~ Regen/Schnee** we're going to have *or* get rain/snow; **einen Stein/Ball an den Kopf ~** to be hit on the head by a stone/ball; **kann ich das schriftlich ~?** can I have that in writing?; **ich bekomme bitte ein Glas Wein** I'll have a glass of wine, please; **was ~ Sie dafür/von mir?** how much is that/how much do I owe you?; **er bekam es einfach nicht über sich, ...** he just could not bring himself to ...
(b) Flecken/Risse ~ to get *or* become spotty/cracked, to develop spots/cracks; **Heimweh ~** to get *or* become homesick; **graue Haare/eine Glatze ~** to go grey/bald; **Hunger/Durst/Angst ~** to get *or* become hungry/thirsty/afraid.
(c) etw zu sehen ~ to get to see sth; **das bekommt man hier nicht zu kaufen** you can't buy that here; **es mit jdm zu tun ~** to get into trouble with sb; **wenn ich ihn zu fassen bekomme ...** if I get my hands on him ...; **etw gemacht ~** to get *or* have sth done; **seine Arbeit fertig ~** to get one's work finished.
2 *vi aux sein+dat (zuträglich sein)* **jdm (gut) ~** to do sb good; **das Essen ist mir gut ~** I enjoyed the meal; **jdm nicht** *or* **schlecht ~** not to do sb any good; *(Essen)* not to agree with sb; **wie bekommt ihm die Ehe?** how is he enjoying married life?; **wohl bekomm's!** your health!
bekömmlich *adj Mahlzeit, Speisen* (easily) digestible; *Klima* beneficial. **schwer ~ sein** to be difficult to digest.
beköstigen* *vt* to cater for.
Beköstigung *f* catering *(gen* for*)*; *(Kost)* food.
bekräftigen* *vt* to confirm; *Vorschlag* to back up. **etw nochmals ~** to reaffirm sth.
Bekräftigung *f* confirmation. **zur ~ seiner Worte** to reinforce his words.
bekreuzigen* *vr* to cross oneself.
bekritteln* *vt* to find fault with.
bekümmern* *vt* to worry.
bekümmert *adj* worried *(über +acc* about*)*.
bekunden* *vt* to show, to express. **~, daß ...** *(Jur)* to testify that ...
Bekundung *f* expression, manifestation; *(Jur)* testimony.
belächeln* *vt* to smile at.
belachen* *vt* to laugh at.
beladen* *irreg* **1** *vt* to load; *(fig: mit Sorgen etc)* to burden. **2** *vr (mit Gepäck etc)* to load oneself up. **sich mit Verantwortung ~** to take on responsibilities. **3** *adj* loaded; *(fig: Mensch)* burdened.
Belag *m* **-̈e** coating; *(Schicht)* layer; *(auf Pizza, Brot)* topping; *(auf Tortenboden, zwischen Brotscheiben)* filling; *(auf Zahn)* plaque; *(Zungen~)* fur; *(Fußboden~)* covering; *(Straßen~)* surface.
Belagerer *m* **-** besieger.
belagern* *vt (Mil, fig)* to besiege.
Belagerung *f* siege.
Belagerungszustand *m* state of siege.
Belang *m* **-e (a)** *(no pl: Wichtigkeit)* **von/ohne ~ (für jdn/etw) sein** to be of importance/of no importance (to sb/sth). **(b) ~e** *pl* interests.
belangen* *vt (Jur)* to prosecute *(wegen* for*)*; *(wegen Beleidigung, Verleumdung)* to sue.
belanglos *adj* inconsequential, trivial. **das ist für das Ergebnis ~** that is irrelevant to the result.
Belanglosigkeit *f* **(a)** *no pl* inconsequentiality, triviality. **(b)** *(Bemerkung)* triviality.
belassen* *vt irreg* to leave. **wir wollen es dabei ~** let's leave it at that.
belastbar *adj* **(a) bis zu 500 kg ~ sein** to have a maximum load of 500 kg. **(b)** *(fig) Mensch* resilient. **(c) wie hoch ist mein Konto ~?** what is the limit on my account?; **der Etat ist nicht unbegrenzt ~** the budget is not unlimited.
Belastbarkeit *f* **(a)** *(von Brücke, Aufzug)* load-bearing capacity. **(b)** *(von Menschen, Nerven)* ability to take stress. **(c)** *(von Stromnetz etc)* maximum capacity; *(von Menschen, Organ)* maximum resilience.
belasten* **1** *vt* **(a)** *(lit)* **etw mit 50 Tonnen ~** to put a 50 ton load on sth; **die Brücke/das Fahrzeug zu sehr ~** to put too great a load on the bridge/to overload the vehicle. **(b)** *(fig)* **jdn mit etw ~** *mit Arbeit* to load sb with sth; *mit Verantwortung, Sorgen* to burden sb with sth; **von Sorgen belastet** weighed down with cares. **(c)** *(beanspruchen)*

Stromnetz, Leitung to put a load on; *Atmosphäre* to pollute; *(Med) Körper, Menschen* to put a strain on, to strain. **jdn/etw zu sehr** *or* **stark** ~ to overstrain sb/sth. **(d)** *(Jur) Angeklagten* to incriminate. **(e)** *(Fin) Konto* to debit. **steuerlich belastet** taxed; **etw (mit einer Hypothek)** ~ to mortgage sth; **jdn mit den Kosten** ~ to charge the costs to sb. **2** *vr* **(a) sich mit etw** ~ to take sth on; *mit Sorgen* to burden oneself with sth. **(b)** *(Jur)* to incriminate oneself.

belästigen* *vt* to bother; *(zudringlich werden)* to pester; *(körperlich)* to molest.

Belästigung *f* annoyance; *(durch Lärm etc)* irritation; *(Zudringlichkeit auch)* pestering; *(körperlich)* molesting. **etw als eine** ~ **empfinden** to find sth annoying.

Belastung *f* **(a)** *(Last)* weight; *(von Fahrzeug etc)* load; *(fig: Bürde)* burden. **(b)** *(von Nerven, Körper)* strain *(gen* on*)*; *(von Umwelt)* pollution *(gen* of*)*; *(von Stromnetz)* load *(gen* on*)*. **(c)** *(Jur)* incrimination. **(d)** *(Fin) (von Etat, steuerlich)* burden *(gen* on*)*; *(mit Hypothek)* mortgage *(gen* on*)*.

Belastungs-: ~**material** *nt (Jur)* incriminating evidence; ~**probe** *f* endurance test; ~**zeuge** *m (Jur)* witness for the prosecution.

belaubt *adj* **dicht** ~ **sein** to have thick foliage.

belaufen* *vr irreg* **sich auf etw** *(acc)* ~ to amount to sth.

belauschen* *vt* to eavesdrop on.

beleben* **1** *vt* **(a)** *(anregen)* to liven up; *(neu ~)* to revive; *Konjunktur, jds Hoffnungen* to stimulate. **(b)** *(zum Leben erwecken)* to bring to life. **2** *vr (Konjunktur)* to be stimulated; *(Augen, Gesicht)* to light up; *(Natur, Stadt)* to come to life. **3** *vi* **das belebt** it livens you up.

belebend *adj* invigorating.

belebt *adj Straße etc* busy.

Belebung *f* revival; *(der Konjunktur)* stimulation.

Beleg *m* **-e (a)** *(Beweis)* piece of evidence; *(Quellennachweis)* reference. **(b)** *(Quittung)* receipt.

belegbar *adj* verifiable.

belegen* *vt* **(a)** *(bedecken)* to cover; *Brote, Tortenboden* to fill. **etw mit Fliesen/Teppich** ~ to tile/carpet sth; *siehe* **belegt. (b)** *(besetzen) Wohnung, Hotelbett* to occupy; *(reservieren)* to reserve; *(Univ) Fach* to take; *Vorlesung* to enrol for. **den fünften Platz** ~ to come fifth. **(c)** *(beweisen)* to verify. **mit Beispielen** ~ to illustrate.

Belegschaft *f (Beschäftigte)* staff; *(esp in Fabriken etc)* workforce.

belegt *adj Zunge* furred; *Stimme* hoarse; *Zimmer* occupied. ~**e Brote** open sandwiches.

belehren* *vt (unterweisen)* to teach, to instruct; *(aufklären)* to inform *(über +acc* of*)*. **jdn eines anderen/Besseren** ~ to teach sb otherwise; **er ist nicht zu** ~ he won't be told; **ich bin belehrt!** I've learned my lesson.

Belehrung *f* explanation, lecture *(col)*; *(Anweisung)* instruction *(über+acc* about*)*; *(von Zeugen, Angeklagten)* caution.

beleibt *adj* stout, portly.

beleidigen* *vt jdn* to insult; *(Verhalten, Anblick)* to offend; *(Jur) (mündlich)* to slander; *(schriftlich)* to libel.

beleidigt *adj* insulted; *(gekränkt)* offended. ~ **weggehen** to go off in a huff *(col)*; **die ~e Leberwurst spielen** *(col)* to be in a huff *(col)*; **bist du jetzt ~?** have I offended you?

Beleidigung *f* insult; *(Jur) (mündliche)* slander; *(schriftliche)* libel. **etw als** ~ **auffassen** to take offence at sth.

beleihen* *vt irreg (Comm)* to lend money on.

belemmert *adj (col) (betreten)* sheepish; *(niedergeschlagen)* miserable; *(scheußlich)* lousy *(col)*.

belesen *adj* well-read.

Belesenheit *f* wide reading.

beleuchten* *vt* to light up, to illuminate; *Straße, Bühne etc* to light.

Beleuchter(in *f***)** *m* - lighting technician.

Beleuchtung *f* **(a)** lighting; *(fig)* examination. **(b)** *(Licht)* light; *(Lichter)* lights *pl*.

beleumdet, beleumundet *adj* **gut/schlecht** ~ **sein** to have a good/bad reputation.

Belgien [-iən] *nt* Belgium.

Belgier(in *f***)** [-iɐ, -iərɪn] *m* - Belgian.

belgisch *adj* Belgian.

belichten* *vt (Phot)* to expose.

Belichtung *f (Phot)* exposure.

Belichtungs-: ~**messer** *m* light meter; ~**zeit** *f* exposure (time).

Belieben *nt no pl* **nach** ~ just as you/they *etc* like.

belieben* **1** *vi impers (geh)* **wie es Ihnen beliebt** as you wish. **2** *vt* **er beliebt zu scherzen** *(iro)* he must be joking.

beliebig 1 *adj* any. **eine/jede ~e Farbe** any colour at all, any colour you like; **in ~er Reihenfolge** in any order whatever; **die Auswahl ist** ~ the choice is free. **2** *adv* as you *etc* like. **Sie können** ~ **lange bleiben** you can stay as long as you like.

beliebt *adj* popular *(bei* with*)*.

Beliebtheit *f* popularity.

beliefern* *vt* to supply.

Belieferung *f* supplying.

bellen *vi* to bark.

bellend *adj Husten* hacking; *Stimme* gruff.

Belletristik *f* fiction and poetry.

belobigen* *vt (form)* to commend.

belohnen* *vt* to reward.

Belohnung *f* reward; *(das Belohnen)* rewarding. **zur** *or* **als** ~ **(für)** as a reward (for).

belüften* *vt* to ventilate.

Belüftung *f* ventilation.

belügen* *vt* to lie to. **sich selbst** ~ to deceive oneself.

belustigen* **1** *vt* to amuse. **2** *vr (geh)* **sich über jdn/etw** ~ to make fun of sb/sth.

belustigt 1 *adj* amused. **2** *adv* in amusement.

bemächtigen* *vr (geh)* **sich eines Menschen** ~ to seize hold of sb; *(Gefühl, Gedanke)* to come over sb.

bemalen* **1** *vt* to paint. **2** *vr (pej: schminken)* to put on one's war paint *(col)*.

Bemalung *f* painting.

bemängeln* *vt* to find fault with, to fault.

bemannen* *vt U-Boot, Raumschiff* to man.

Bemannung *f* manning; *(Mannschaft)* crew.

bemerkbar *adj* noticeable, perceptible. **sich** ~ **machen** *(sich zeigen)* to make itself felt, to become noticeable; *(auf sich aufmerksam machen)* to draw attention to oneself.

bemerken* *vt* **(a)** *(wahrnehmen)* to notice. **(b)** *(äußern)* to remark, to comment. **nebenbei bemerkt** by the way.

bemerkenswert *adj* remarkable.

Bemerkung *f* remark, comment.

bemessen* *irreg* **1** *vt (zuteilen)* to allocate; *(einteilen)* to calculate. **meine Zeit ist knapp** ~ my time is limited. **2** *vr (form)* to be proportionate *(nach* to*)*.

bemitleiden* *vt* to pity, to feel sorry for. **er ist zu** ~ he is to be pitied; **sich selbst** ~ to feel sorry for oneself.

bemitleidenswert *adj* pitiable, pitiful.

bemittelt *adj* well-to-do, well-off.

bemogeln* *vt (col)* to cheat.

Bemühen *nt no pl (geh)* endeavours *pl (Brit)*, endeavors *pl (US) (um* for*)*.

bemühen* **1** *vt* to trouble, to bother; *Rechtsanwalt etc* to engage. **jdn zu sich** ~ to call in sb. **2** *vr* **(a)** to try hard, to endeavour *(Brit)*, to endeavor *(US)*. **sich um eine Stelle** ~ to try to get a job; **sich um jdn** ~ to look after sb; *(um jds Gunst)* to court sb; **bitte** ~ **Sie sich nicht** please don't trouble yourself. **(b)** *(geh: gehen)* **sich zu jdm** ~ to go to sb.

bemüht *adj* **(darum)** ~ **sein, etw zu tun** to

endeavour *(Brit)* *or* endeavor *(US)* *or* be at pains to do sth.
Bemühung *f* effort.
bemüßigt *adj* **sich ~ fühlen/sehen** *(geh, usu iro)* to feel called upon.
bemuttern* *vt* to mother.
benachbart *adj* neighbouring *(Brit)*, neighboring *(US)*; *Haus, Familie auch* next door.
benachrichtigen* *vt* to inform *(von* of); *(amtlich auch)* to notify *(von* of).
Benachrichtigung *f* notification; *(Comm)* advice note.
benachteiligen* *vt* to put at a disadvantage; *(wegen Geschlecht, Rasse, Glauben etc)* to discriminate against; *(körperliches Leiden auch)* to handicap. **benachteiligt sein** to be at a disadvantage/discriminated against/handicapped.
Benachteiligung *f siehe vt (das Benachteiligen)* disadvantaging; discrimination *(gen* against); *(Zustand)* disadvantage; discrimination *no pl*.
benebeln* *vt (col)* **jds Sinne ~** to make sb's head swim; **benebelt sein** to be feeling dazed *or (von Alkohol auch)* muzzy *(col)*.
Benediktiner *m* - *(Eccl auch* **~in** *f)* Benedictine.
Benefiz-: ~konzert, ~spiel *nt* benefit.
Benehmen *nt no pl* behaviour *(Brit)*, behavior *(US)*. **kein ~ haben** not to know how to behave.
benehmen* *vr irreg* to behave. **benimm dich!** behave yourself!; **sich gut ~** to behave oneself, to behave well; **sich schlecht ~** to behave (oneself) badly, to misbehave; *siehe* **benommen.**
beneiden* *vt* to envy. **jdn um etw ~** to envy sb sth; **er ist nicht zu ~** I don't envy him.
beneidenswert *adj* enviable.
Benelux-: ~länder, ~staaten *pl* Benelux countries *pl*.
benennen* *vt irreg* to name. **jdn/etw nach jdm ~** to name sb/sth after *or* for *(US)* sb.
Benennung *f (das Benennen)* naming; *(Bezeichnung)* name, designation *(form)*.
Bengel *m* **-(s)** boy, lad; *(frecher Junge)* rascal.
Benimm *m no pl (col)* manners *pl*.
benommen *adj* dazed.
benoten* *vt* to mark.
benötigen* *vt* to need, to require. **das benötigte Geld** the necessary money, the money needed.
Benotung *f* mark; *(das Benoten)* marking.
benutzbar *adj* usable; *Weg* passable.
benutzen* *vt* to use.
Benutzer *m* - user; *(von Leihbücherei)* borrower.
benutzerfreundlich *adj* user-friendly.
Benutzung *f* use. **jdm etw zur ~ überlassen** to put sth at sb's disposal.
Benzin *nt* **-e** petrol *(Brit)*, gas(oline) *(US)*; *(Reinigungs~)* benzine; *(Feuerzeug~)* lighter fuel.
Benzin-: ~feuerzeug *nt* petrol *(Brit) or* gasoline *(US)* lighter; **~gutschein** *m* petrol *(Brit) or* gasoline coupon *(US)*; **~kanister** *m* petrol *(Brit) or* gasoline *(US)* can; **~motor** *m* petrol *(Brit) or* gasoline *(US)* engine; **~pumpe** *f* fuel pump; **~uhr** *f* fuel gauge; **~verbrauch** *m* fuel consumption.
be|obachten* *vt* to observe; *(bemerken auch)* to notice, to see; *(genau verfolgen, betrachten auch)* to watch. **etw an jdm ~** to notice sth in sb; **jdn ~ lassen** *(Polizei etc)* to put sb under surveillance.
Be|obachter(in *f)* *m* - observer.
Be|obachtung *f* observation; *(polizeilich)* surveillance. **die ~ habe ich oft gemacht** I've often noticed that.
Be|obachtungs-: ~gabe *f* **er hat eine gute ~gabe** he has a very observant eye; **~station** *f* **(a)** *(Med)* observation ward; **(b)** *(Met)* weather station.
be|ordern* *vt* to order. **jdn zu sich ~** to send for sb.
bepacken* *vt* to load (up).
bepflanzen* *vt* to plant.
Bepflanzung *f* **(a)** *(das Bepflanzen)* planting. **(b)** *(die Pflanzen)* plants *pl* *(gen* in).
bepinkeln* *(col)* **1** *vt* to pee on *(col)*. **2** *vr* to wet oneself.
bequatschen* *vt (col)* **(a)** *etw* to talk over. **(b)** *(überreden)* to persuade.
bequem *adj* comfortable; *Weg, Methode* easy; *Ausrede* convenient; *(träge) Mensch* idle. **es sich** *(dat)* **~ machen** to make oneself comfortable.
bequemen* *vr* **sich (dazu) ~, etw zu tun** to bring oneself to do sth.
Bequemlichkeit *f no pl (Behaglichkeit)* comfort; *(Trägheit)* idleness.
berappen* *vti (col)* **er mußte schwer ~** he had to fork out a lot *(col)*.
beraten* *irreg* **1** *vt* **(a) jdn ~** to advise sb; **gut/schlecht ~ sein** to be well-/ill-advised; **sich von jdm ~ lassen(, wie...)** to ask sb's advice (on how ...), to consult sb (about how...). **(b)** *(besprechen)* to discuss. **2** *vir* to discuss. **sich mit jdm ~** to consult (with) sb *(über+acc* about).
beratend *adj* advisory, consultative. **jdm ~ zur Seite stehen** to act in an advisory capacity to sb.
Berater(in *f)* *m* - adviser, consultant.
Beratervertrag *m* consultancy contract.
beratschlagen* *vti insep* to discuss.
Beratung *f* **(a)** *(das Beraten)* advice; *(geschäftlich: bei Rechtsanwalt, Arzt etc)* consultation. **(b)** *(Besprechung)* discussion.
berauben* *vt* to rob. **jdn einer Sache** *(gen)* **~** to rob sb of sth; *seines Rechtes* to deprive sb of sth.
Beraubung *f* robbery; *(fig)* deprivation.
berauschen* **1** *vt (lit, fig)* to intoxicate; *(Droge auch)* to make euphoric. **2** *vr* **sich an etw** *(dat)* **~** *(lit, fig)* to become intoxicated with sth.
berauschend *adj* intoxicating. **das war nicht sehr ~** *(iro)* that wasn't very exciting.
Berberteppich *m* Berber carpet.
berechenbar *adj Kosten* calculable; *Verhalten* predictable.
Berechenbarkeit *f siehe adj* calculability; predictability.
berechnen* *vt* **(a)** *(ausrechnen)* to calculate. **(b)** *(in Rechnung stellen)* to charge. **jdm zu viel ~** to overcharge sb. **(c)** *(vorsehen)* to intend, to mean.
berechnend *adj (pej) Mensch* calculating.
Berechnung *f siehe vt* **(a)** calculation. **meiner ~ nach, nach meiner ~** according to my calculations; **aus ~ handeln** to act in a calculating manner. **(b)** charge. **ohne ~** without any charge.
berechtigen* *vti* to entitle. **(jdn) zu etw ~** to entitle sb to sth; **das berechtigt zu der Annahme, daß ...** this justifies the assumption that ...
berechtigt *adj* justifiable; *Frage, Hoffnung, Anspruch* legitimate; *Forderung, Einwand auch* justified. **~ sein, etw zu tun** to be entitled to do sth.
berechtigterweise *adv* legitimately, justifiably.
Berechtigung *f* **(a)** *(Befugnis)* entitlement; *(Recht)* right. **die ~/keine ~ haben, etw zu tun** to be entitled/not to be entitled to do sth. **(b)** *(Rechtmäßigkeit)* legitimacy, justifiability.
bereden* *vt* **(a)** *(auch vr: besprechen)* to discuss, to talk over. **(b)** *(überreden)* **jdn zu etw ~** to talk sb into sth.
beredsam *adj (liter)* eloquent; *(iro: redefreudig)* talkative.
Beredsamkeit *f (liter)* eloquence; *(iro)* talkativeness.
beredt *adj (geh)* eloquent.
Beredtheit *f (geh)* eloquence.
Bereich *m* **-e (a)** area. **im ~ der Innenstadt** in the town centre area. **(b)** *(Einfluß~, Aufgaben~)* sphere; *(Sach~)* area, field; *(Sektor)* sector. **im ~ des Möglichen liegen** to be within the bounds of possibility.
bereichern* **1** *vt (lit, fig)* to enrich; *Sammlung etc* to enlarge. **2** *vr* to make a lot of money *(an+dat*

out of*)*. **sich auf Kosten anderer ~** to feather one's nest at the expense of other people.

Bereicherung *f* **(a)** *(das Bereichern)* enrichment; *(von Sammlung)* enlargement. **(b)** *(Gewinn)* boon. **eine wertvolle ~** a valuable addition.

bereifen* *vt (Aut)* to put tyres *(Brit) or* tires *(US)* on.

Bereifung *f (Aut)* set of tyres *(Brit) or* tires *(US)*. **die ~ bei diesem Auto** the tyres on this car.

bereinigen* *vt* to clear up.

Bereinigung *f* clearing up.

bereisen* *vt ein Land* to travel around; *(Comm) Gebiet* to travel, to cover.

bereit *adj usu pred* **(a)** *(fertig)* ready; *(vorbereitet auch)* prepared. **sich ~ machen** to get ready. **(b)** *(willens)* willing, prepared. **sich ~ erklären, etw zu tun** to agree to do sth.

bereiten *vt* **(a)** *(zu~)* to prepare *(dat* for*)*. **(b)** *(verursachen)* to cause; *Überraschung, Empfang, Freude, Kopfschmerzen* to give. **einer Sache** *(dat)* **ein Ende ~** to put an end to sth.

bereit-: ~halten *sep* **1** *vt irreg Fahrkarten etc* to have ready; *(für den Notfall)* to keep ready; *Überraschung* to have in store; **2** *vr* to stand by; **~legen** *vt sep* to lay out ready; **~liegen** *vi sep irreg* to be ready; **~machen** *vtr sep* to get ready.

bereits *adv* already. **~ vor drei Wochen** even three weeks ago; **das haben wir ~ gestern gemacht** we did that yesterday; **~ am nächsten Tage** on the very next day.

Bereitschaft *f* **(a)** *no pl* readiness; *(Bereitwilligkeit auch)* willingness. **in ~ sein, ~ haben** *(Polizei, Soldaten etc)* to be on stand-by; *(Arzt)* to be on call. **(b)** *(Mannschaft)* squad.

Bereitschafts-: ~arzt *m* doctor on call; *(im Krankenhaus)* duty doctor; **~dienst** *m* emergency service; **~dienst haben** *siehe* **Bereitschaft.**

Bereit-: b~stehen *vi sep irreg* to be ready; *(Flugzeug auch, Truppen)* to stand by; **Ihr Wagen steht b~** your car is waiting; **b~stellen** *vt sep* to provide, to supply; **~stellung** *f* provision, supply.

Bereitung *f* preparation.

Bereit-: b~willig *adj* willing; **~willigkeit** *f* willingness.

bereuen* *vt* to regret; *Schuld, Sünden* to repent of. **~, etw getan zu haben** to regret having done sth; **das wirst du noch ~!** you'll regret it!

Berg *m* **-e (a)** mountain; *(esp kleiner auch)* hill. **~e versetzen (können)** to (be able to) move mountains; **mit etw hinterm ~ halten** *(fig)* to keep quiet about sth; **in die ~e fahren** to go to the mountains; **über den ~ sein** *(col)* to be out of the woods; **über alle ~e sein** *(col)* to be miles away *(col)*; **da stehen einem ja die Haare zu ~e** it's enough to make your hair stand on end. **(b)** *(große Menge)* heap, pile; *(von Sorgen)* mass.

Berg- *in cpds* mountain; *(Bergbau-)* mining; **b~ab** *adv* downhill; **es geht mit ihm b~ab** *(fig)* he is going downhill; **~arbeiter** *m* miner; **b~auf** *adv* uphill; **es geht wieder b~auf** *(fig)* things are getting better *or* looking up; **~bau** *m* mining.

bergen *pret* **barg,** *ptp* **geborgen** *vt* **(a)** *(retten) Menschen* to save, to rescue; *Leichen* to recover; *Ladung, Fahrzeug* to salvage. **aus dem Wasser tot/lebend geborgen werden** to be brought out of the water dead/alive. **(b)** *(geh: enthalten)* to hold. **diese Möglichkeit birgt die Gefahr in sich, daß ...** this possibility involves the danger that ... **(c)** *siehe* **geborgen.**

Berg-: ~führer *m* mountain guide; **~gipfel** *m* mountain top *or* peak; **~hang** *m* mountain slope; **b~hoch** *adj Wellen* mountainous; **~hütte** *f* mountain hut.

bergig *adj* mountainous.

Berg-: ~kamm *m* mountain ridge; **~kette** *f* mountain range; **~kristall** *m* rock crystal; **~kuppe** *f* (round) mountain top; **~land** *nt* mountainous region; **das schottische ~land** the Scottish mountains *or* hills.

Bergmann *m, pl* **-leute** miner.

Berg-: ~not *f* **in ~not sein/geraten** to be in/get into difficulties while climbing; **~predigt** *f (Bibl)* Sermon on the Mount; **~rettungsdienst** *m* mountain rescue service; **~rücken** *m* mountain ridge; **~rutsch** *m* landslide *(auch fig)*, landslip; **~spitze** *f* mountain peak; **b~steigen** *vi sep irreg aux sein or haben* to go mountain climbing *or* mountaineering; **(das) ~steigen** mountaineering; **~steiger** *m* mountaineer; **~steigerei** *f (col)* mountaineering; **~-und-Tal-Bahn** *f* big dipper, roller-coaster; **~-und-Tal-Fahrt** *f* ride on the big dipper.

Bergung *f no pl siehe* **bergen (a)** saving, rescue; recovery; salvage, salvaging.

Bergungs-: ~mannschaft *f,* **~trupp** *m* rescue team.

Berg-: ~wacht *f* mountain rescue service; **~wand** *f* mountain face; **~wanderung** *f* walk *or* hike in the mountains; **~werk** *nt* mine; **im ~werk arbeiten** to work down the mines.

Bericht *m* **-e** report *(über +acc* about, on, *von* on*)*; *(Erzählung auch)* account; *(Zeitungs~ auch)* story. **jdm über etw** *(acc)* **~ erstatten** to give sb a report (on sth).

berichten* *vti* to report; *(erzählen)* to tell. **jdm über etw** *(acc)* **~** to report to sb about sth; to tell sb about sth; **mir ist (darüber) berichtet worden, daß ...** I have received reports that ...; **er berichtete von der Reise** he told us *etc* about his journey.

Bericht-: ~erstatter *m* reporter; *(Korrespondent)* correspondent; **~erstattung** *f* reporting; **die ~erstattung über diese Vorgänge in der Presse** press coverage of these events; **zur ~erstattung zurückgerufen werden** to be called back to make a report.

berichtigen* *vt* to correct; *Fehler auch, (Jur)* to rectify.

Berichtigung *f siehe vt* correction; rectification.

berieseln* *vt* **(a)** to spray with water *etc; (durch Sprinkleranlage)* to sprinkle. **(b)** *(fig col)* **von etw berieselt werden** *(fig)* to be exposed to a constant stream of sth.

Berieselung *f* watering. **die ~ mit** *or* **durch etw** *(fig)* the constant stream of sth.

Berieselungs|anlage *f* sprinkler (system).

beritten *adj* mounted, on horseback.

Berlin *nt* Berlin.

Berliner[1] *adj attr* Berlin.

Berliner[2] *m* **-** *(Cook)* jam doughnut.

Berliner(in *f***)** *m* **-** Berliner.

berlinerisch *adj (col) Dialekt* Berlin *attr.*

Bermudas *pl* **auf den ~** in Bermuda.

Bernhardiner *m* **-** Saint Bernard (dog).

Bernstein *m no pl* amber.

Berserker *m* **- wie ein ~ arbeiten/kämpfen** to work/fight like mad *or* fury.

bersten *pret* **barst,** *ptp* **geborsten** *vi aux sein (geh)* to crack; *(auf~, zerbrechen)* to break; *(zerplatzen)* to burst. **vor Neugier/Zorn** *etc* **~** to be bursting with curiosity/anger *etc.*

berüchtigt *adj* notorious, infamous.

berückend *adj* charming, enchanting.

berücksichtigen* *vt (beachten, bedenken)* to take into account *or* consideration; *(in Betracht ziehen) Antrag, Bewerber* to consider. **das ist zu ~** that must be taken into account *or* consideration.

Berücksichtigung *f* consideration. **in** *or* **unter ~ der Tatsache, daß ...** in view of the fact that ...

Beruf *m* **-e** occupation; *(akademischer auch)* profession; *(handwerklicher)* trade; *(Stellung)* job. **was sind Sie von ~?** what is your occupation *etc?*, what do you do for a living?; **von ~ Arzt/Bäcker/Hausfrau sein** to be a doctor by profession/baker by trade/housewife by occupation; **seinen ~ verfehlt haben** to have missed one's vocation; **von ~s wegen** on account of one's job.

berufen* *irreg* **1** *vt* **(a)** *(ernennen, einsetzen)* to appoint. **zum Minister/auf einen Lehrstuhl ~ werden** to be appointed minister/to a chair. **(b)** = **beschreien. 2** *vr* **sich auf jdn/etw ~** to refer to sb/sth. **3** *adj (ausersehen)* **zu etw ~ sein** to have a vocation for sth; *(esp Rel)* to be called to sth.

beruflich *adj (esp auf akademische Berufe bezüglich)* professional. **~e Aussichten** job prospects; **verschiedene ~e Tätigkeiten** different jobs; **~ ist sie sehr erfolgreich** she is very successful in her career; **er ist ~ viel unterwegs** he is away a lot on business.

Berufs-: **~aussichten** *pl* job prospects *pl;* **b~bedingt** *adj* occupational; **~berater** *m* careers adviser; **~beratung** *f* careers guidance; **~bezeichnung** *f* job title; **~boxen** *nt* professional boxing; **~erfahrung** *f* (professional) experience; **~feuerwehr** *f* fire service; **~fußball** *m* professional football; **~geheimnis** *nt* professional secret; *(Schweigepflicht)* professional secrecy, confidentiality; **~heer** *nt* professional *or* regular army; **~kleidung** *f* working clothes *pl;* **~krankheit** *f* occupational disease; **~leben** *nt* working *or* professional life; **im ~leben stehen** to be working *or* in employment; **b~mäßig** *adj* professional; **etw b~mäßig betreiben** to do sth on a professional basis; **~risiko** *nt* occupational hazard; **~schule** *f* vocational school, ≃ technical college *(Brit)*; **~schüler** *m* student at vocational school *etc*; **~sport** *m* professional sport; **~sportler** *m* professional sportsman; **b~tätig** *adj* working; **b~tätig sein** to be working, to work; **~tätige(r)** *mf decl as adj* working person; **b~unfähig** *adj* unable to work; **~unfähigkeit** *f* inability to work; **~verband** *m* professional/trade organization; **~verbot** *nt* exclusion from a profession; **jdm ~verbot erteilen** to ban sb from his/her profession; *einem Arzt, Anwalt* to strike sb off; **~verkehr** *m* rush-hour traffic; **~wahl** *f* choice of occupation; **~wechsel** *m* change of occupation.

Berufung *f* **(a)** *(Jur)* appeal. **in die ~ gehen/~ einlegen** to appeal *(bei* to*)*. **(b)** *(in ein Amt etc)* appointment *(auf or an+acc* to*)*. **(c)** *(innerer Auftrag)* vocation; *(Rel auch)* calling. **(d)** *(form)* **unter ~ auf etw** *(acc)* with reference to sth.

Berufungs-: **~frist** *f* period in which an appeal must be lodged; **~gericht** *nt* appeal court, court of appeal; **~klage** *f* appeal.

beruhen* *vi* to be based *or* founded *(auf+ dat* on*)*. **das beruht auf Gegenseitigkeit** *(col)* the feeling is mutual; **etw auf sich ~ lassen** to let sth rest.

beruhigen* **1** *vt* to calm (down); *Baby* to quieten; *(trösten)* to comfort; *(versichern)* to reassure; *Magen* to settle; *Nerven auch* to soothe; *Gewissen* to appease. **na, dann bin ich ja beruhigt** well I must say I'm quite relieved; **~d** soothing; *(tröstlich)* reassuring. **2** *vr* to calm down; *(Krise auch)* to ease off; *(Verkehr, Kämpfe)* to subside; *(Börse, Magen)* to settle down; *(Sturm)* to die down, to abate.

Beruhigung *f no pl* **(a)** *siehe vt* calming (down); quietening; comforting; reassuring; settling; soothing; appeasement. **zu Ihrer ~ kann ich sagen ...** you'll be reassured to know that ... **(b)** *siehe vr* calming down, easing off; subsiding; settling down.

Beruhigungs-: **~mittel** *nt* sedative, tranquillizer; **~spritze** *f* sedative (injection).

berühmt *adj* famous. **das war nicht ~** *(col)* it was nothing to write home about *(col)*.

berühmt-berüchtigt *adj* infamous, notorious.

Berühmtheit *f* **(a)** fame. **~ erlangen** to become famous. **(b)** *(Mensch)* celebrity.

berühren* **1** *vt* **(a)** to touch; *(erwähnen) Thema, Punkt* to touch on. **B~ verboten** do not touch. **(b)** *(seelisch bewegen)* to move; *(auf jdn wirken)* to affect; *(betreffen)* to affect, to concern. **das berührt mich gar nicht!** that's nothing to do with me; **von etw peinlich berührt sein** to be embarrassed by sth. **2** *vr* to touch.

Berührung *f* touch; *(von Drähten etc, menschlich)* contact; *(Erwähnung)* mention. **mit jdm/etw in ~ kommen** to come into contact with sb/sth.

Berührungspunkt *m* point of contact.

besagen* *vt* to say; *(bedeuten)* to mean, to imply.

besagt *adj attr (form)* said *(form)*.

besaiten* *vt* to string. **etw neu ~** to restring sth.

besamen* *vt* to fertilize; *(künstlich)* to inseminate.

Besamung *f siehe vt* fertilization; insemination.

besänftigen* *vt* to soothe; *Menge auch* to pacify.

Besänftigung *f siehe vt* soothing; pacifying.

besät *adj* covered; *(mit Blättern etc)* strewn.

Besatz *m* **¨e** edging, trimming.

Besatzer *m* - *(pej col)* occupying forces *pl*.

Besatzung *f* **(a)** *(Mannschaft)* crew; *(Verteidigungstruppe)* garrison. **(b)** *(~sarmee)* occupying forces *pl*.

Besatzungs-: **~armee** *f* army of occupation; **~macht** *f* occupying power; **~truppen** *pl* occupying forces *pl;* **~zone** *f* occupied zone.

besaufen* *vr irreg (col)* to get plastered *(col)*.

Besäufnis *nt (col)* booze-up *(col)*.

beschädigen* *vt* to damage. **beschädigt** damaged.

Beschädigung *f* damage *(von* to*)*.

beschaffen* **1** *vt* to get (hold of), to obtain *(jdm etw* sth for sb*)*. **2** *adj (form)* **so ~ sein wie ...** to be the same as ...; **das ist so ~, daß ...** that is such that ...; **sie ist nun mal so ~** that is the way she is.

Beschaffenheit *f no pl* composition; *(körperlich)* constitution; *(Art, seelisch)* nature, qualities *pl*. **je nach ~ der Lage** according to the situation.

Beschaffung *f no pl* obtaining.

beschäftigen* **1** *vr* **sich mit etw ~** to occupy oneself with sth; *(sich befassen, abhandeln)* to deal with sth; **sich mit Literatur ~** to study literature; **sich mit jdm ~** to devote one's attention to sb. **2** *vt* **(a)** *(innerlich)* **jdn ~** to be on sb's mind. **(b)** *(anstellen)* to employ. **(c)** *(eine Tätigkeit geben)* to keep occupied.

beschäftigt *adj* **(a)** busy. **mit Nähen/jdm ~ sein** to be busy sewing/with sb; **mit sich selbst ~ sein** to be preoccupied with oneself. **(b)** *(angestellt)* employed *(bei* by*)*.

Beschäftigte(r) *mf decl as adj* employee.

Beschäftigung *f* **(a)** work *no indef art*, job; *(Anstellung, Angestelltsein)* employment. **einer ~ nachgehen** *(form)* to be employed. **(b)** *(Tätigkeit)* activity, occupation. **jdm eine ~ geben** to give sb something to do. **(c)** *(geistige ~)* preoccupation; *(mit Frage)* consideration *(mit* of*)*.

Beschäftigungs-: **b~los** *adj* unoccupied; *(arbeitslos)* unemployed; **~therapie** *f* occupational therapy.

beschämen* *vt* to put to shame. **es beschämt mich, zu sagen ...** I feel ashamed to have to say ...

beschämend *adj* shaming; *(schändlich)* shameful.

beschämt *adj* ashamed.

beschatten* *vt* **(a)** *(überwachen)* to shadow, to tail. **(b)** *(Sport)* to mark closely. **(c)** *(geh: Schatten geben)* to shade.

Beschatter *m* - *(Polizist etc)* tail; *(Sport)* marker.

Beschattung *f siehe vt* **(a)** tailing. **(b)** marking.

Beschauer *m* - *(Betrachter)* spectator.

beschaulich *adj Leben, Abend* quiet, tranquil; *Charakter, Mensch* pensive, contemplative.

Beschaulichkeit *f siehe adj* quietness, tranquillity; pensiveness.

Bescheid *m* **-e (a)** *(Auskunft)* information; *(Nachricht)* notification; *(Entscheidung auf Antrag etc)* decision. **jdm (über etw** *acc or* **von etw) ~ sagen/geben** to let sb know (about sth), to tell sb (about sth); **jdm ordentlich ~ sagen** *(col)* to tell sb where to go *(col)*. **(b) (über etw** *(acc) or* **in etw** *dat*) **~ wissen** to know (about sth); **er weiß schon ~** he knows all about it.

bescheiden[1]* *irreg* **1** *vt* **(a)** *(form: entscheiden)* to decide upon. **etw abschlägig ~** to turn sth down. **(b)** *(geh)* **es war ihr nicht beschieden, ...** it was not to be her lot to ... **2** *vr (geh)* to be content.

bescheiden[2] *adj* modest. **darf ich mal ~ fragen, ob ...** may I venture to ask whether ...; **eine ~e Frage** one small question.

Bescheidenheit *f* modesty. **nur keine falsche ~** no false modesty now.

bescheinen* *vt irreg* to shine on. **vom Mond/von der Sonne beschienen** moonlit/sunlit.

bescheinigen* *vt* to certify; *Empfang* to confirm, to acknowledge; *(durch Quittung)* to give a receipt for. **hiermit wird bescheinigt, daß ...** this is to certify that ...; **jdm äußerste Kompetenz ~** to confirm sb's extreme competence.

Bescheinigung *f siehe vt (das Bescheinigen)* certification; confirmation; *(Schriftstück)* certificate; written confirmation; *(Quittung)* receipt.

bescheißen* *vt irreg (col!) jdn* to cheat *(um* out of*)*.

beschenken* *vt jdn* to give presents/a present to. **jdn mit etw ~** to give sb sth (as a present).

bescheren* *vti* **jdn ~** to give sb a Christmas present/Christmas presents; **jdm eine Überraschung ~** to give sb a nice surprise; **ihnen waren fünf Kinder beschert** they were blessed with five children.

Bescherung *f* **(a)** giving out of Christmas presents. **(b)** *(iro col)* **das ist ja eine schöne ~!** this is a nice mess; **da haben wir die ~!** what did I tell you!

bescheuert *adj (col)* stupid.

beschichten* *vt (Tech)* to coat, to cover.

beschicken* *vt* **(a) eine Ausstellung mit jdm/etw ~** to send sb/sth to an exhibition. **(b)** *Hochofen* to charge.

beschießen* *vt irreg* to shoot *or* fire at; *(mit Geschützen, Phys)* to bombard.

Beschießung *f siehe vt* shooting *(gen* at*)*, firing *(gen* on, at*)*; bombardment *(gen* of*)*.

beschildern* *vt* to put a sign/signs on; *(mit Verkehrsschildern)* to signpost.

Beschilderung *f siehe vt* putting a sign *(von* on*)*; signposting; *(Schilder)* signs *pl*; signposts *pl*.

beschimpfen *vt jdn* to swear at.

Beschimpfung *f* **(a)** swearing *(gen* at*)*. **(b)** *(Schimpfwort)* insult.

beschirmen* *vt (geh: beschützen)* to shield.

Beschiß *m no pl (col!)* swindle, rip-off *(col)*.

beschissen *adj (col!)* bloody awful *(Brit col)*, lousy *(col)*.

Beschlag *m* ⸗**e** **(a)** *(an Koffer, Truhe)* fitting; *(an Tür, Möbelstück)* mounting; *(von Pferd)* shoes *pl*. **(b)** *(auf Glas, Spiegel etc)* condensation. **(c) jdn/etw in ~ nehmen** to monopolize sb/sth; **mit ~ belegt sein** to be occupied.

beschlagen* *irreg* **1** *vt* **(a)** *Möbel, Türen* to put (metal) fittings on; *Huftiere* to shoe; *Schuhe* to put metal tips on. **(b)** *(anlaufen lassen: Dampf)* to steam up. **2** *vir (vi: aux sein) (Brille, Glas, Fenster)* to steam up, to mist up; *(Wand)* to get covered in condensation. **3** *adj (erfahren)* **in etw** *(dat)* **(gut) ~ sein** to be (well-)versed in sth.

Beschlagenheit *f no pl* sound knowledge *or* grasp *(in+dat* of*)*.

Beschlagnahme *f* **-n** confiscation, seizure.

beschlagnahmen* *vt insep* **(a)** to confiscate, to seize. **(b)** *(col: in Anspruch nehmen) (Mensch)* to monopolize, to hog *(col)*; *(Arbeit) Zeit* to take up.

beschleunigen* **1** *vtr* to accelerate, to speed up; *Tempo auch* to increase; *Verfall* to hasten, to accelerate. **2** *vi (Fahrzeug, Fahrer)* to accelerate.

Beschleunigung *f* acceleration *(auch Aut, Phys)*, speeding up; *(von Tempo auch)* increase; *(von Verfall etc)* hastening.

beschließen* *irreg* **1** *vt* **(a)** to decide on; *Gesetz* to pass. **~, etw zu tun** to decide to do sth. **(b)** *(beenden)* to end. **2** *vi* **über etw** *(acc)* **~** to decide on sth.

beschlossen *adj (entschieden)* decided, agreed. **das ist ~e Sache** that's been settled.

Beschluß *m* ⸗**sse** decision, resolution. **einen ~ fassen** to pass a resolution; **auf ~ des Gerichts** by order of the court.

Beschluß-: b~fähig *adj* **b~fähig sein** to have a quorum; **~fähigkeit** *f no pl* quorum; **~fassung** *f* (passing of a) resolution; **b~unfähig** *adj* **b~unfähig sein** not to have a quorum.

beschmeißen* *vt irreg (col: lit, fig)* to bombard.

beschmieren* **1** *vt Kleidung* to smear; *Wand* to bedaub; *Tafel* to scribble *or* scrawl all over. **2** *vr* to get (all) dirty.

beschmutzen* **1** *vt* to (make *or* get) dirty, to soil; *(fig) Ruf, Namen* to besmirch. **2** *vr* to make *or* get oneself dirty.

beschneiden* *vt irreg* **(a)** *(stutzen)* to trim; *Sträucher etc* to prune. **(b)** *(Med, Rel)* to circumcise. **(c)** *(fig: beschränken)* to cut back, to curtail.

Beschneidung *f no pl siehe vt* **(a)** trimming; pruning. **(b)** circumcision. **(c)** *(von Unterstützung etc)* cut-back; *(von Rechten)* curtailing.

beschneit *adj* snow-covered; *Berge auch* snow-capped.

beschnuppern* **1** *vt* to sniff at; *(fig col)* to sniff out; *jdn* to size up. **2** *vr (Hunde)* to sniff each other; *(fig col)* to size each other up.

beschönigen* *vt* to gloss over. **~der Ausdruck** euphemism.

beschränken* **1** *vt (auf+acc* to*)* to limit, to restrict. **2** *vr (auf+acc* to*)* to be limited *or* restricted; *(esp Jur, Rede, Aufsatz etc auch)* to confine oneself; *(sich einschränken)* to restrict oneself.

beschrankt *adj Bahnübergang* with gates.

beschränkt *adj* **(a)** *(eingeschränkt, knapp)* limited; *Gebrauch auch* restricted. **wir sind zeitlich/finanziell ~** we have only a limited amount of time/money; **Gesellschaft mit ~er Haftung** limited company *(Brit)*, corporation *(US)*. **(b)** *(pej) (geistig) Mensch* dim; *Intelligenz* limited; *(engstirnig auch)* narrow-minded.

Beschränktheit *f siehe adj* **(a)** limited nature. **(b)** limited intelligence; narrow-mindedness.

Beschränkung *f* limitation, restriction. **jdm ~en auferlegen** to impose restrictions on sb.

beschreiben* *vt irreg* **(a)** *(auch Kreis)* to describe. **sein Glück/Schmerz war nicht zu ~** his happiness/pain was indescribable. **(b)** *(vollschreiben)* to write on. **ein eng beschriebenes Blatt** a closely written sheet.

Beschreibung *f* **(a)** description. **(b)** *(Gebrauchsanweisung)* instructions *pl*.

beschreien* *vt irreg (col)* **ich will es nicht ~, aber ...** I don't want to tempt fate, but ...

beschreiten* *vt irreg (lit geh, fig)* to follow.

beschriften* *vt* to write on; *(mit Aufschrift)* to label.

Beschriftung *f* **(a)** *(das Beschriften)* labelling. **(b)** *(Aufschrift)* writing; *(Etikett)* label.

beschuldigen* *vt* to accuse; *(esp Jur auch, liter)* to charge. **jdn einer Sache** *(gen)* **~** to accuse sb of sth; to charge sb with sth.

Beschuldigte(r) *mf decl as adj* accused.

Beschuldigung *f* accusation; *(esp Jur auch, liter)* charge.

beschummeln* *vt (col)* to cheat. **jdn um etw ~** to cheat *or* diddle *(col)* sb out of sth.

Beschuß *m no pl (Mil)* fire; *(Phys)* bombarding. **jdn/etw unter ~ nehmen** *(Mil)* to (start to) bombard *or* shell sb/sth; *Stellung auch* to fire on sth; *(fig)* to attack sb/sth.

beschützen* *vt* to protect *(vor +dat* from*)*.
Beschützer(in *f*) *m* - protector/protectress.
beschwatzen* *vt (col)* **(a)** *(überreden)* to talk over. **(b)** *(bereden)* to chat about.
Beschwerde *f* **-n (a)** *(Mühe)* hardship. **(b) ~n** *pl (Leiden)* trouble; **das macht mir immer noch ~n** it's still giving me trouble. **(c)** *(Klage)* complaint; *(Jur)* appeal. **~ einlegen** *(form)* to lodge a complaint.
Beschwerde-: b~frei *adj* fit and healthy; **~frist** *f (Jur)* period of time during which an appeal may be lodged.
beschweren* **1** *vt (mit Gewicht)* to weigh(t) down; *(fig) (Kummer)* to weigh on; *(Mensch)* to burden. **2** *vr (sich beklagen)* to complain.
beschwerlich *adj* arduous.
Beschwerlichkeit *f* difficulty; *(von Reise, Aufgabe auch)* arduousness *no pl*.
beschwichtigen* *vt jdn* to appease, to pacify; *Kinder, jds Zorn, Gewissen* to soothe.
Beschwichtigung *f siehe vt* appeasement, pacification; soothing.
beschwindeln* *vt (col)* **(a)** *(belügen)* **jdn ~** to tell sb a lie *or* a fib *(col)*. **(b)** *(betrügen)* to swindle.
beschwingt *adj* lively.
Beschwingtheit *f* liveliness.
beschwipst *adj (col)* tipsy.
beschwören* *vt irreg* **(a)** *(beeiden)* to swear to; *(Jur auch)* to swear on oath. **(b)** *(anflehen)* to implore, to beseech. **(c)** *(Geister, Erinnerung)* to conjure up; *Schlangen* to charm.
Beschwörung *f* **(a)** *(das Flehen)* entreaty. **(b)** *siehe vt (c)* conjuring up; charming.
beseelen* *vt (erfüllen)* **neuer Mut beseelte ihn** he was filled with fresh courage.
besehen* *vt irreg* to (take a) look at.
beseitigen* *vt* **(a)** *(entfernen)* to remove, to get rid of; *Schwierigkeiten auch* to sort out; *Fehler auch* to eliminate; *Mißstände* to get rid of, to do away with. **(b)** *(euph: umbringen)* to get rid of.
Beseitigung *f no pl siehe vt* **(a)** removal, getting rid of; sorting out; elimination; getting rid of, doing away with. **(b)** getting rid of.
Besen *m* **- (a)** broom. **ich fresse einen ~, wenn das stimmt** *(col)* if that's right, I'll eat my hat *(col)*; **neue ~ kehren gut** *(Prov)* a new broom sweeps clean *(Prov)*. **(b)** *(pej col: Frau)* old bag *(col)*.
Besen-: ~kammer *f*, **~schrank** *m* broom cupboard; **~stiel** *m* broom-stick.
besessen *adj (von bösen Geistern)* possessed *(von* by*)*; *(von einer Idee etc)* obsessed *(von* with*)*. **wie ~** like one possessed.
Besessene(r) *mf decl as adj* one possessed *no art*. **die ~n** the possessed.
Besessenheit *f no pl siehe adj* possession; obsession.
besetzen* *vt* **(a)** *(dekorieren)* to trim; *(mit Edelsteinen)* to stud. **(b)** *(belegen)* to occupy; *(reservieren)* to reserve; *(füllen) Plätze, Stühle* to fill. **ist dieser Platz besetzt?** is this place taken?; *siehe* **besetzt. (c)** *(esp Mil)* to occupy. **(d)** *Stelle* to fill; *(Theat) Rolle* to cast. **eine Stelle neu ~** to find a new person for a job.
besetzt *adj (belegt) Leitung* engaged *(Brit)*, busy; *WC* occupied, engaged *(Brit)*; *Abteil, Tisch* full (up); *(vorgebucht)* booked; *Abteil etc* taken.
Besetztzeichen *nt (Telec)* engaged *(Brit) or* busy tone.
Besetzung *f* **(a)** *(von Stelle)* filling; *(von Rolle)* casting; *(Theat: Schauspieler)* cast; *(Sport: Mannschaft)* team. **die Nationalelf in der neuen ~** the new line-up for the international side; **zweite ~** *(Theat)* understudy. **(b)** *(esp Mil)* occupation.
besichtigen* *vt (ansehen) Stadt, Kirche* to have a look at, to visit; *Betrieb* to tour; *(zur Prüfung) Haus* to view; *Ware, Truppen* to inspect.
Besichtigung *f (von Sehenswürdigkeiten)* sightseeing tour; *(von Museum etc)* tour; *(zur Prüfung) (von Haus)* viewing; *(von Truppen)* inspection.
besiedeln* *vt (ansiedeln)* to populate, to settle *(mit* with*)*; *(kolonisieren)* to colonize. **dicht/dünn besiedelt** densely/thinly populated.
Besied(e)lung *f no pl siehe vt* settlement; colonization. **dichte/dünne ~** dense/thin population.
besiegeln* *vt* to seal.
besiegen* *vt (schlagen)* to defeat, to beat; *(überwinden)* to overcome.
besingen* *vt irreg* **(a)** *Schallplatte* to record. **(b)** *(rühmen)* **jdn/etw ~** to sing the praises of sb/sth.
besinnen* *vr irreg (überlegen)* to reflect, to think; *(erinnern)* to remember *(auf jdn/etw* sb/sth*)*; *(es sich anders überlegen)* to have second thoughts. **sich anders ~** to change one's mind; **ohne sich zu ~** without a moment's thought *or* hesitation.
besinnlich *adj* thoughtful, contemplative.
Besinnlichkeit *f no pl* thoughtfulness, contemplativeness.
Besinnung *f no pl* **(a)** consciousness. **bei/ohne ~ sein** to be conscious/unconscious; **die ~ verlieren** to lose consciousness; *(fig)* to lose one's head; **wieder zur ~ kommen** to regain consciousness; *(fig)* to come to one's senses; **jdn zur ~ bringen** *(fig)* to bring sb to his senses. **(b)** *(das Sich-Besinnen)* contemplation *(auf+acc* of*)*.
Besinnungs-: b~los *adj* unconscious; *(fig)* blind; **~losigkeit** *f no pl (lit)* unconsciousness.
Besitz *m no pl* **(a)** possession. **im ~ von etw sein** to be in possession of sth; **etw in ~ nehmen** to take possession of sth; **von etw ~ ergreifen** to seize possession of sth; **in privatem ~** in private ownership. **(b)** *(Eigentum)* property; *(Landgut)* estate.
Besitz-: ~anspruch *m* claim of ownership; *(Jur)* title; **seine ~ansprüche (auf etw** *acc***) anmelden** to lay claim to sth; **b~anzeigend** *adj (Gram)* possessive.
besitzen *vt* to possess, to own; *Narbe, grüne Augen* to have; *Fähigkeiten* to have, to possess. **die ~den Klassen** the propertied classes.
Besitzer(in *f*) *m* - owner; *(von Wertpapieren auch, von Füherschein etc)* holder; *(Laden~ etc auch)* proprietor. **den ~ wechseln** to change hands.
Besitz-: ~ergreifung *f* seizure; **b~los** *adj* having no possessions; **~nahme** *f no pl* seizure; **~tum** *nt (Eigentum)* property *no pl; (Grundbesitz)* estate(s *pl*), property.
besoffen *adj (col) (betrunken)* pissed *(Brit col)*, smashed *(col)*; *(verrückt)* crazy.
Besoffene(r) *mf decl as adj (col)* drunk.
besohlen* *vt* to sole; *(neu ~)* to resole.
besolden* *vt* to pay.
Besoldung *f* pay.
besondere(r, s) *adj* special; *(bestimmt)* particular; *(hervorragend) Qualität, Schönheit etc* exceptional. **eine ganz ~ Anstrengung** a quite exceptional effort; **unser ~s Interesse gilt ...** we are particularly *or* (e)specially interested in ...; **ohne ~ Begeisterung** without any particular enthusiasm; **im ~n** *(im einzelnen)* in particular cases; *(vor allem)* in particular.
Besonderheit *f* special feature; *(besondere Eigenschaft)* peculiarity.
besonders *adv* particularly, (e)specially. **nicht ~ viel Geld** not a particularly large amount of money; **das Essen/der Film war nicht ~** *(col)* the food/film was nothing special *or* nothing to write home about *(col)*; **wie geht's dir? — nicht ~** *(col)* how are you? — not too hot *(col)*.
besonnen *adj* considered, level-headed. **ihre ruhige, ~e Art** her calm and collected way.
Besonnenheit *f no pl* level-headedness.
besonnt *adj* sunny.
besorgen* *vt* **(a)** *(kaufen, beschaffen etc)* to get; *(euph col: stehlen)* to acquire *(euph col)*. **jdm/sich**

etw ~ to get sth for sb/oneself. **(b)** *(erledigen)* to attend *or* see to. **(c)** *(versorgen)* to take care of, to look after. **(d)** *(col)* **es jdm ~** to sort sb out *(col)*, to fix sb *(col)*. **(e)** *(col!)* **es jdm ~** *(Mann: mit jdm schlafen)* to have it off with sb *(col)*.

Besorgnis *f* anxiety, worry.

besorgnis|erregend *adj* alarming, worrying.

besorgt *adj* **(a)** *(voller Sorge)* anxious, worried *(wegen* about*)*. **(b) um jdn/etw ~ sein** to be concerned about sb/sth.

Besorgtheit *f no pl* concern.

Besorgung *f* **(a)** *(das Kaufen)* purchase. **(b) die ~ des Haushaltes** looking after the house. **(c)** *(Einkauf)* **~en machen** to do some shopping.

bespannen* *vt* **(a)** *(mit Material)* to cover; *(mit Saiten, Fäden)* to string. **(b)** *Wagen* to harness up.

Bespannung *f* **(a)** *no pl* covering; *(mit Saiten etc)* stringing; *(mit Pferden)* harnessing. **(b)** *(Material)* covering; *(Saiten, Fäden etc)* strings *pl*.

bespielbar *adj Rasen etc* playable.

bespielen* *vt* **(a)** *Tonband* to record on. **das Band ist mit klassischer Musik bespielt** the tape has a recording of classical music on it. **(b)** *(Sport)* to play on.

bespitzeln* *vt* to spy on.

Bespitz(e)lung *f* spying.

besprechen* *irreg* **1** *vt* **(a)** to discuss, to talk about. **wie besprochen** as arranged. **(b)** *(rezensieren)* to review. **(c)** *Tonband* to make a recording on. **2** *vr* **sich mit jdm ~** to confer with sb *(über +acc* about*)*.

Besprechung *f* **(a)** discussion, talk; *(Konferenz)* meeting. **er ist bei einer ~, er hat eine ~** he's in a meeting. **(b)** *(Rezension)* review, notice.

besprengen* *vt* to sprinkle.

bespringen* *vt irreg (Tier)* to mount, to cover.

bespritzen* *vt* to spray; *(beschmutzen)* to spatter.

besprühen* *vt* to spray.

bespucken* *vt* to spit at.

besser *adj, adv, comp of* **gut** better. **~e Leute** a better class of people; **er hat ~e Tage gesehen** *(iro)* he has seen better days; **du willst wohl etwas B~es sein!** *(col)* I suppose you think you're better than other people; **~ ist ~** (it is) better to be on the safe side; **um so ~!** *(col)* so much the better!; **~ (gesagt)** or rather; **sie will immer alles ~ wissen** she always thinks she knows better; **das ist auch ~ so** it's better that way; **B~es zu tun haben** to have better things to do; **das solltest du ~ nicht tun** you had better not do that; **dann geh ich ~** then I'd better go; **das Essen war nur ein ~er Imbiß** the meal was just a glorified snack.

bessergehen *vi impers sep irreg aux sein* **es geht jdm besser** sb is feeling better; **jetzt geht's der Firma wieder besser** the firm is doing better again now.

bessern 1 *vt* to improve, to make better; *Verbrecher etc* to reform. **2** *vr (moralisch, im Benehmen)* to mend one's ways.

besser-: ~stehen *vr sep irreg (col)* to be better off; **~stellen** *vt sep* **jdn ~stellen** to improve sb's financial position.

Besserung *f no pl* improvement; *(von Verbrecher etc)* reformation; *(Genesung)* recovery. **gute ~!** I hope you get better soon; **auf dem Wege der ~ sein** to be getting better, to be improving; *(Patient auch)* to be on the road to recovery.

Besser-: ~wisser *m* **-** *(col)* know-all, know-it-all *(US)*; **b~wisserisch** *adj (col)* know-all *etc attr*.

Bestand *m* **¨e** **(a)** *(Fortdauer)* continued existence, continuance. **von ~ sein/~ haben** to be permanent, to endure. **(b)** *(vorhandene Menge, Tiere)* stock *(an+dat* of*)*. **~ aufnehmen** to take stock.

bestanden *adj* **nach ~er Prüfung** after passing the/an exam; **bei nicht ~er Prüfung** if you *etc* don't pass the exam.

beständig *adj* **(a)** *no pred (dauernd)* constant, continual. **(b)** *(gleichbleibend)* constant; *Mitarbeiter* steady; *Wetter* settled. **(c)** *no adv (widerstandsfähig)* resistant *(gegen* to*)*; *(dauerhaft) Freundschaft* lasting.

Beständigkeit *f no pl siehe adj* **(a)** continual nature. **(b)** constancy; steadiness; settledness. **(c)** resistance; lastingness.

Bestands|aufnahme *f* stock-taking.

Bestandteil *m* component, part; *(fig)* integral part. **sich in seine ~e auflösen** to fall to pieces.

bestärken* *vt* to confirm. **jdn in seinem Vorsatz/Wunsch ~** to confirm sb in his intention/desire.

Bestärkung *f* confirmation.

bestätigen* 1 *vt* **(a)** to confirm; *(beurkunden auch)* to certify; *(Jur) Urteil* to uphold. **sich in etw** *(dat)* **bestätigt finden** to be confirmed in sth; **... sagte er ~d** ... he said in confirmation; **jdn (im Amt) ~** to confirm sb's appointment. **(b)** *(Comm) Empfang, Brief* to acknowledge (receipt of). **2** *vr* to be confirmed, to be proved true.

Bestätigung *f siehe vt* **(a)** confirmation; upholding. **(b)** acknowledgement (of receipt).

bestatten* *vt* to bury. **wo liegt er bestattet?** where is he buried?

Bestatter *m* **-** undertaker, mortician *(US)*.

Bestattung *f* burial; *(Feuer~)* cremation; *(Feier auch)* funeral.

Bestattungs-: ~institut, ~unternehmen *nt* undertaker's, mortician *(US)*; **~unternehmer** *m* undertaker, mortician *(US)*.

bestäuben* *vt* to dust; *(Bot)* to pollinate.

bestaunen* *vt* to marvel at, to gaze at in wonder.

beste *siehe* **beste(r, s).**

bestechen *irreg* **1** *vt* **(a)** to bribe. **ich lasse mich nicht ~** I'm not open to bribery. **(b)** *(beeindrucken)* to captivate. **2** *vi (Eindruck machen)* to be impressive *(durch* because of*)*.

bestechend *adj Schönheit, Eindruck* captivating; *Angebot* tempting.

bestechlich *adj* bribable, corruptible.

Bestechlichkeit *f no pl* corruptibility.

Bestechung *f* bribery; *(von Beamten etc auch)* corruption.

Bestechungs-: ~geld *nt usu pl*, **~summe** *f* bribe; **~versuch** *m* attempted bribery.

Besteck *nt* **-e** **(a)** *(Eß~)* knives and forks *pl*, cutlery *sing; (Set, für ein Gedeck)* set of cutlery. **(b)** *(Instrumentensatz)* set of instruments. **chirurgisches ~** (set of) surgical instruments.

Besteckkasten *m* cutlery canteen.

bestehen *irreg* **1** *vt* **(a)** *Examen, Probe* to pass; *siehe* **bestanden. (b)** *Schicksalsschläge* to withstand; *Gefahr* to overcome; *Kampf* to win.

2 *vi* **(a)** *(existieren)* to exist. **die Universität besteht seit hundert Jahren** the university has been in existence *or* has existed for a hundred years; **es besteht die Hoffnung/der Verdacht, daß ...** there is (a) hope/a suspicion that ... **(b)** *(Bestand haben)* to continue to exist; *(Zweifel, Problem etc auch)* to persist. **(c)** *(sich zusammensetzen)* to consist *(aus* of*)*. **in etw** *(dat)* **~** to consist in sth; *(Aufgabe)* to involve sth; **seine einzige Chance besteht darin, ...** his only chance is to ...; **die Schwierigkeit/das Problem besteht darin, daß ...** the difficulty/problem lies in the fact that ..., the difficulty/problem is that ... **(d)** *(standhalten, sich bewähren)* to hold one's own *(in +dat* in*)*. **vor etw** *(dat)* **~** to stand up against sth. **(e)** *(bei Prüfung etc)* to pass. **(f) auf etw** *(dat)* **~** to insist on sth.

Bestehen *nt no pl* **(a)** existence. **seit ~ der Firma** ever since the firm came into existence *or* has existed. **(b)** *(Beharren)* insistence *(auf+dat* von*)*. **(c)** *(von Prüfung etc)* passing.

bestehenbleiben *vi sep irreg aux sein* to last, to endure; *(Frage, Hoffnung)* to remain.

bestehend *adj* existing; *Gesetze auch, Preise*

present, current.

bestehlen* *vt irreg* to rob *(um etw* of sth*)*.

besteigen* *vt irreg Berg, Leiter* to climb; *Fahrrad, Pferd* to mount, to get *or* climb on(to); *Bus, Flugzeug* to get on; *Auto* to get into; *Thron* to ascend.

bestellen* **1** *vt* **(a)** *(anfordern, in Restaurant)* to order. **sich** *(dat)* **etw ~** to order sth; **das Material ist bestellt** the material has been ordered *or* is on order; **wie bestellt und nicht abgeholt** *(hum col)* like orphan Annie *(col)*. **(b)** *(reservieren)* to book, to reserve. **(c)** *(ausrichten)* **bestell ihm (von mir), daß ...** tell him (from me) that ...; **soll ich irgend etwas ~?** can I take a message?; **er hat hier nicht viel/nichts zu ~** he doesn't have much/any say here. **(d)** *(kommen lassen) jdn* to send for, to summon. **ich bin für 10 Uhr bestellt** I have an appointment for *or* at 10 o'clock. **(e)** *(einsetzen, ernennen)* to nominate, to appoint. **(f)** *(bearbeiten) Land* to till. **(g)** *(fig)* **es ist schlecht um ihn bestellt** he is in a bad way. **2** *vi (in Restaurant)* to order.

Besteller *m* - customer.

Bestell-: ~nummer *f* order number; **~schein** *m* order form.

Bestellung *f* **(a)** *(Anforderung, das Angeforderte)* order; *(das Bestellen)* ordering. **(b)** *(Reservierung)* booking, reservation. **(c)** *(Ernennung)* nomination, appointment. **(d)** *(von Land)* tilling.

besten *adv*: **am ~** *siehe* **beste(r, s) 2.**

bestenfalls *adv* at best.

bestens *adv (sehr gut)* very well.

beste(r, s) 1 *adj, superl of* **gut (a)** *attr* best. **im ~n Fall** at (the) best; **in ~n Händen** in the best of hands. **(b) das ~ wäre, wir ...** the best thing would be for us to...; **es steht nicht zum ~n** it does not look too promising *or* good; **jdn zum ~n halten** to pull sb's leg, to have sb on *(col)*; **etw zum ~n geben** *(erzählen)* to tell sth. **(c) der/die/das B~** the best; **ich will nur dein B~s** I've your best interests at heart; **sein B~s geben** to give of one's best. **2** *adv* **am ~n** best; **am ~n gehe ich jetzt** I'd *or* I had best be going now.

Beste(s) *nt siehe* **beste(r, s) 1 (c).**

besteuern* *vt* to tax.

Besteuerung *f* taxation; *(Steuersatz)* tax.

Bestform *f (esp Sport)* top *or* best form.

bestialisch *adj* bestial; *(col)* awful, beastly *(col)*.

besticken* *vt* to embroider.

Bestie [-tiə] *f* beast; *(fig)* animal.

bestimmen* **1** *vt* **(a)** to determine; *Zeitpunkt etc auch* to fix, to set; *(entscheiden auch)* to decide; *Landschaft etc* to characterize; *Pflanze, Funde* to classify. **(b)** *(vorsehen)* to intend, to mean *(für* for*)*. **er ist zu Höherem bestimmt** he is destined for higher things; **wir waren füreinander bestimmt** we were meant for each other. **2** *vi* to decide *(über+acc* on*)*. **du hast hier nicht zu ~** you don't make the decisions here; **er kann über sein Geld allein ~** it is up to him what he does with his money.

bestimmend *adj Faktor, Einfluß* determining, decisive. **für etw ~ sein** to be characteristic of sth; *(entscheidend)* to have a determining influence on sth.

bestimmt 1 *adj* **(a)** definite; *(gewiß)* certain; *(festgesetzt) Preis, Tag* set, fixed. **suchen Sie etwas B~es?** are you looking for anything in particular? **(b)** *(entschieden) Auftreten, Ton* firm, decisive. **2** *adv* **(a)** *(sicher)* definitely, certainly. **ich weiß ganz ~, daß ...** I know for sure *or* for certain that ...; **ich komme ganz ~** I'll very definitely come. **(b)** *(wahrscheinlich)* no doubt. **das hat er ~ verloren** he's bound to have lost it.

Bestimmtheit *f* **(a)** *(Sicherheit)* certainty. **ich weiß aber mit ~, daß ...** but I know for sure *or* for certain that ... **(b)** *(Entschiedenheit)* firmness. **in** *or* **mit aller ~** quite categorically.

Bestimmung *f* **(a)** *(Vorschrift)* regulation. **(b)** *no pl (Zweck)* purpose. **eine Anlage ihrer ~ übergeben** to officially open a new plant. **(c)** *(Schicksal)* destiny. **(d)** *(das Bestimmen)* determining; *(von Zeit etc)* fixing, setting; *(von Pflanze, Funden)* classification.

Bestimmungs-: b~gemäß *adj* as agreed; **~hafen** *m* (port of) destination; **~ort** *m* destination.

Best-: ~leistung *f (esp Sport)* best performance; **seine persönliche ~leistung** *f* his personal best; **b~möglich** *adj no pred* best possible.

bestrafen* *vt* to punish; *(Jur) jdn* to sentence *(mit* to*)*; *(Sport) Spieler, Foul* to penalize.

Bestrafung *f siehe vt* punishment, sentencing; penalization.

bestrahlen* *vt* to shine on; *(beleuchten) Gebäude, Bühne* to light up, to illuminate; *(Med)* to give radiotherapy to.

Bestrahlung *f* illumination; *(Med)* radiotherapy.

Bestreben *nt no pl* endeavour *(Brit)*, endeavor *(US)*.

bestrebt *adj* **~ sein, etw zu tun** to endeavour *(Brit) or* endeavor *(US)* to do sth.

bestreichen* *vt irreg* to spread; *(mit Farbe)* to paint. **etw mit Butter/Fett/Öl ~** to butter/grease/oil sth.

bestreiken* *vt* to black. **bestreikt** strikebound; **die Fabrik wird zur Zeit bestreikt** there's a strike on in the factory at the moment.

bestreiten* *vt irreg* **(a)** *(abstreiten)* to dispute, to challenge; *(leugnen)* to deny. **jdm das Recht auf ... ~** to dispute *etc* sb's right to ...; **das will ich nicht ~** I'm not disputing *or* denying it. **(b)** *(finanzieren)* to pay for, to finance; *Kosten* to carry. **(c) er hat das ganze Gespräch allein bestritten** he did all the talking; **die Mannschaft hat fünf Spiele in zwei Wochen bestritten** the team has played five games in two weeks.

bestreuen* *vt* to cover *(mit* with*)*; *(Cook)* to sprinkle.

Bestseller ['bɛst-] *m* - best-seller.

Bestseller-: ~autor *m* best-selling author; **~liste** *f* best-seller list.

bestücken* *vt* to fit, to equip; *(Mil)* to arm; *Lager* to stock.

bestürmen* *vt* to storm; *(mit Fragen, Bitten)* to bombard; *(mit Briefen, Anrufen)* to inundate.

bestürzen* *vt* to shake.

bestürzend *adj* alarming. **er sah mich bestürzt an** he looked at me in consternation.

Bestürzung *f* consternation.

Bestzeit *f (esp Sport)* best time.

Besuch *m* **-e (a)** visit *(gen* to*)*; *(von Schule, Veranstaltung)* attendance *(gen* at*)*. **bei jdm zu ~ sein** to be visiting sb; **(von jdm) ~ erhalten** to have *or* get a visit (from sb). **(b)** *(Besucher)* visitor; visitors *pl*. **er hat ~** he has visitors/a visitor.

besuchen* *vt jdn* to visit. *Vortrag, Schule, Kino etc* to go to.

Besucher(in *f*) *m* - visitor; *(pl: Publikum)* audience. **etwa 1.000 ~ waren zu der Veranstaltung gekommen** about 1,000 people went to the function.

Besuchs-: ~erlaubnis *f (für Land)* visa; **~erlaubnis haben** to be allowed to receive visitors; **~zeit** *f* visiting time.

besucht *adj* **gut/schlecht ~ sein** to be well/badly attended.

besudeln* *vt (geh) Wände* to smear; *Kleidung, Hände* to soil; *(fig) Namen, Ehre* to sully.

betagt *adj (geh)* aged, well advanced in years.

betanken* *vt Fahrzeug* to fill up; *Flugzeug* to refuel.

betasten* *vt* to feel.

Betastrahlen *pl* beta rays *pl*.

betätigen* **1** *vt* to operate; *Muskeln, Gehirn* to activate; *Bremse auch* to apply. **2** *vr* to busy oneself; *(körperlich)* to get some exercise. **sich**

politisch ~ to be active in politics; **sich literarisch/künstlerisch** ~ to do some writing/painting; **wenn er sich als Kindermädchen betätigt** when he acts as nanny.

Betätigung *f* **(a)** *(Tätigkeit)* activity. **(b)** *siehe vt (a)* operation; activation; application.

betäuben* *vt (unempfindlich machen)* to deaden; *(durch Narkose)* to anaesthetize *(Brit)*, to anesthetize *(US)*; *(fig) Kummer etc* to ease; *(fig: benommen machen)* to stun. **~der Lärm** deafening noise; **ein ~der Duft** an overpowering smell.

Betäubung *f (Narkose)* anaesthetic *(Brit)*, anesthetic *(US)*. **örtliche** ~ local anaesthetic.

Betäubungsmittel *nt* anaesthetic *(Brit)*, anesthetic *(US)*.

Bete *f* **-n** beet. **rote** ~ beetroot.

beteiligen* **1** *vt* **jdn an etw** *(dat)* ~ to involve sb in sth; *(finanziell)* to give sb a share in sth. **2** *vr* to take part, to participate *(an+dat* in); *(finanziell)* to have a share *(an+dat* in). **sich an den Unkosten** ~ to contribute to the expenses.

beteiligt *adj* **an etw** *(dat)* **~sein/werden** to be involved in sth, to have a part in sth; *(finanziell)* to have a share in sth.

Beteiligte(r) *mf decl as adj* person involved; *(an Diskussion auch)* participant; *(Teilhaber)* partner; *(Jur)* party.

Beteiligung *f no pl (Teilnahme) (an+dat* in) participation; *(finanziell)* share; *(an Unfall)* involvement.

beten 1 *vi* to pray *(um, für* for, *zu* to), to say one's prayers; *(bei Tisch)* to say grace. **2** *vt* to say.

beteuern* *vt* to declare; *Unschuld auch* to protest.

Beteuerung *f siehe vt* declaration; protestation.

betiteln* *vt* to entitle; *(anreden)* to address as.

Beton [be'tɔŋ, be'tõ:] *m* **-s** concrete.

betonen* *vt* to emphasize; *(Gewicht legen auf auch)* to stress; *siehe* **betont.**

betonieren* *vti* to concrete. **betoniert** concrete.

Beton-: **~klotz** *m* concrete block; **~mischmaschine** *f* concrete-mixer.

betont *adj Höflichkeit* emphatic, deliberate; *Kühle, Sachlichkeit* pointed. **sich ~ einfach kleiden** to dress with pronounced simplicity.

Betonung *f* **(a)** *no pl siehe vt* emphasis; stressing. **(b)** *(Akzent, fig: Gewicht)* emphasis, stress.

betören* *vt* to bewitch, to beguile.

Betr. = **Betreff** re, ref.

betr. = **betreffend** regarding

Betracht *m no pl* **etw außer ~ lassen** to leave sth out of consideration, to disregard sth; **in ~ kommen** to be considered; **nicht in ~ kommen** to be out of the question; **jdn/etw in ~ ziehen** to take sb/sth into consideration.

betrachten* *vt* **(a)** *(sehen, beurteilen)* to look at. **bei näherem B~** on closer examination. **(b) als jdn/etw** ~ to regard *or* look upon *or* consider as sb/sth.

Betrachter *m* **-** observer.

beträchtlich *adj* considerable.

Betrachtung *f* **(a)** *(das Betrachten)* contemplation. **bei näherer** ~ on closer examination. **(b)** *(Überlegung)* reflection. **über etw** *(acc)* **~en anstellen** to reflect on *or* contemplate sth.

Betrachtungsweise *f* **er hat eine andere** ~ he has a different way of looking at things.

Betrag *m* **-̈e** amount, sum.

betragen *irreg* **1** *vi* to be; *(Kosten, Rechnung auch)* to come to, to amount to. **der Unterschied beträgt 100 DM** the difference is *or* amounts to DM 100. **2** *vr* to behave.

Betragen *nt no pl* behaviour *(Brit)*, behavior *(US)*; *(esp im Zeugnis)* conduct.

betrauen* *vt* **jdn mit etw** ~ to entrust sb with sth.

betrauern* *vt* to mourn.

beträufeln* *vt* **den Fisch mit Zitrone** ~ to sprinkle lemon juice on the fish.

Betreff *m* **-e** *(form)* **~: Ihr Schreiben vom ...** re *or* reference your letter of ...

betreffen* *vt irreg (angehen)* to concern. **von dieser Regelung werde ich nicht betroffen** this rule does not concern *or* affect me; **was mich betrifft ...** as far as I'm concerned ...; **betrifft:** re; *siehe* **betroffen.**

betreffend *adj attr (erwähnt)* in question; *(zuständig, für etw relevant)* relevant. **das ~e Wort richtig einsetzen** to insert the appropriate word in the right place.

betreiben* *vt irreg* **(a)** *(vorantreiben)* to push ahead. **auf jds B~** *(acc)* **hin** at sb's instigation. **(b)** *Gewerbe, Handwerk* to carry on; *Handel auch* to do; *Politik* to pursue. **(c)** *(Tech)* to operate.

betreten[1]* *vt irreg* to enter, to go/come into; *Spielfeld, Bühne, Brücke* to step onto; *(fig) Zeitalter etc* to enter. **„B~ (des Rasens) verboten!"** "keep off (the grass)".

betreten[2] *adj* embarrassed.

Betretenheit *f* embarrassment.

betreuen* *vt* to look after.

Betreuer(in *f)* *m (Kinder~)* child-minder; *(von Alten, Kranken)* nurse. **wir suchen noch ~ für ...** we are still looking for people to look after ...

Betreuung *f* looking after; *(von Patienten, Tieren etc)* care. **er wurde mit der ~ der Gruppe beauftragt** he was put in charge of the group.

Betrieb *m* **-e** **(a)** *(Firma)* business, concern; *(Fabrik)* factory, works *sing or pl.* **(b)** *(Tätigkeit)* work; *(von Maschine, Fabrik)* working, operation. **er hält den ganzen ~ auf** he's holding everything up; **außer** ~ out of order; **die Maschinen sind in** ~ the machines are running; **eine Maschine in/außer ~ setzen** to start a machine up/to stop a machine; **eine Maschine/Fabrik in ~ nehmen** to put a machine/factory into operation. **(c)** *(Betriebsamkeit)* bustle. **in den Geschäften herrscht großer** ~ the shops are very busy.

betrieblich *adj attr* company *attr.* **eine Sache ~ regeln** to settle a matter within the company.

Betriebs- *in cpds (Fabrik-)* factory, works; *(Firmen-)* company.

betriebsam *adj* busy, bustling *no adv.*

Betriebsamkeit *f* bustle; *(von Mensch)* active nature.

Betriebs-: **~angehörige(r)** *mf* employee; **~anleitung** *f* operating instructions *pl;* **b~bereit** *adj* operational; **~blindheit** *f* organizational blindness; **b~eigen** *adj* company *attr;* **~ferien** *pl* (annual) holiday *or* vacation *(US)*; **~führung** *f* management; **~geheimnis** *nt* trade secret; **b~intern** *adj* internal company *attr;* **etw b~intern regeln** to settle sth within the company; **~klima** *nt* working atmosphere; **~kosten** *pl (von Firma etc)* overheads *pl; (von Maschine)* running costs *pl;* **~leiter** *m* (works *or* factory) manager; **~leitung** *f* management; **~prüfung** *f* (government) audit; **~rat** *m* **(a)** *(Gremium)* works committee; **(b)** *(col: Person)* works committee member; **~schluß** *m (von Firma)* end of business hours; *(von Fabrik)* end of factory hours; **nach ~schluß** after business/factory hours; **b~sicher** *adj* safe (to operate); **~störung** *f* breakdown; **~system** *nt (Comp)* operating system; **~unfall** *m* industrial accident; *(hum col)* accident; **~wirt** *m* management expert; **~wirtschaft** *f* business management.

betrinken* *vr irreg* to get drunk; *siehe* **betrunken.**

betroffen *adj* **(a)** affected *(von* by). **(b)** *(bestürzt)* taken aback; *Schweigen* awkward.

Betroffene(r) *mf decl as adj* person affected.

Betroffenheit *f* consternation.

betrüben* *vt* to sadden, to distress.

betrüblich *adj* sad, distressing; *Zustände* deplorable.

Betrug *m no pl* deceit, deception; *(Jur)* fraud. **das ist ja (alles)** ~ it's (all) a cheat *or* fraud.

betrügen *vt irreg* to deceive; *(geschäftlich auch)* to

cheat; *Freund(in), Ehepartner auch* to be unfaithful to; *(Jur)* to defraud. **jdn um etw** ~ to cheat sb out of sth; *(Jur)* to defraud sb of sth; **ich fühle mich betrogen** I feel betrayed; **sich um etw betrogen sehen** to feel deprived of sth.
Betrüger(in *f*) *m* - *(beim Spiel)* cheat; *(geschäftlich)* swindler; *(Jur)* defrauder.
Betrügerei *f* deceit; *(geschäftlich)* cheating *no pl*, swindling *no pl; (von Ehepartner)* deceiving *no pl; (Jur)* fraud.
betrügerisch *adj* deceitful; *(Jur)* fraudulent. **in ~er Absicht** with intent to defraud.
betrunken *adj* drunk *no adv*, drunken *attr*. **Fahren in ~em Zustand** drunken driving.
Betrunkene(r) *mf decl as adj* drunk.
Bett *nt* **-en** bed. **an jds ~** *(dat)* **sitzen** to sit at sb's bedside *or* by sb's bed; **im ~** in bed; **jdn ins** *or* **zu ~ bringen** to put sb to bed; **ins ~ gehen** to go to bed; **mit jdm das ~ teilen** to share sb's bed; **er hat sich ins gemachte ~ gelegt** *(fig)* he had everything handed to him on a plate.
Bett-: ~bezug *m* quilt cover; **~couch** *f* bed settee; **~decke** *f* blanket; *(gesteppt)* (continental) quilt, duvet.
Bettel-: b~arm *adj* destitute; **~brief** *m* begging letter.
Bettelei *f* begging.
Bettelmönch *m* mendicant *or* begging monk.
betteln *vi* to beg. **(bei jdm) um etw ~** to beg (sb) for sth.
Bettelstab *m*: **jdn an den ~ bringen** to reduce sb to beggary.
betten *vt (legen)* to make a bed for, to bed down; *Kopf* to lay. **wie man sich bettet, so liegt man** *(Prov)* as you make your bed so you must lie on it *(Prov)*; **er hat sich weich gebettet** *(fig)* he's done very nicely for himself.
Bett-: ~feder *f* bedspring; **~federn** *pl (Daunen)* bed feathers; **~genosse** *m (dated, iro)* bedfellow; **~gestell** *nt* bedstead; **~hupferl** *nt* - *(S Ger)* bedtime sweet; **~kante** *f* edge of the bed; **~kasten** *m* linen drawer; **b~lägerig** *adj* bedridden, confined to bed; **~laken** *nt* sheet; **~lektüre** *f* bedtime reading.
Bettler(in *f*) *m* - beggar.
Bett-: ~nässen *nt no pl* bed-wetting; **~nässer** *m* - bed-wetter; **~pfanne** *f* bedpan; **~pfosten** *m* bedpost; **~rand** *m* edge of the bed; **~ruhe** *f* bed rest; **~schwere** *f (col)* **die nötige ~schwere haben/ bekommen** to be/get tired enough to sleep.
Bettuch *nt* sheet.
Bett-: ~vorleger *m* bedside rug; **~wäsche** *f* bed linen; **~zeug** *nt* bedding.
betucht *adj (col)* well-to-do.
betulich *adj (übertrieben besorgt)* fussing *attr; Redeweise* twee.
betupfen* *vt* to dab; *(Med)* to swab.
Beuge *f* **-n** bend; *(Rumpf~)* forward bend; *(seitlich)* sideways bend; *(Knie~)* knee-bend.
Beugehaft *f (Jur)* coercive detention.
beugen 1 *vt* **(a)** to bend; *(Phys) Wellen* to diffract; *Strahlen, Licht* to deflect; *(fig) Stolz, Starrsinn* to break. **das Recht ~** to pervert the course of justice; **vom Alter gebeugt** bent *or* bowed by age; **von Kummer/Gram gebeugt** bowed down with grief/sorrow; *siehe* **gebeugt. (b)** *(Gram)* to decline; *Verb* to conjugate. **2** *vr* to bend; *(fig)* to submit, to bow *(dat* to*)*. **sich aus dem Fenster ~** to lean out of the window; **er beugte sich zu mir herüber** he leant across to me.
Beugung *f siehe vt* **(a)** bending, diffraction; deflection; breaking. **(b)** declension; conjugation.
Beule *f* **-n** *(von Stoß etc)* bump; *(Delle)* dent.
be|unruhigen* 1 *vt* to worry. **über etw** *(acc)* **beunruhigt sein** to be worried about sth. **2** *vr* to worry (oneself) *(über+acc, wegen* about*)*.
Be|unruhigung *f* concern.
be|urkunden* *vt* to certify; *Vertrag* to record; *Geschäft* to document.
Be|urkundung *f* **(a)** *siehe vt* certification; recording; documentation. **(b)** *(Dokument)* documentation.
be|urlauben* *vt* to give leave; *(von Pflichten)* to excuse *(von* from*)*. **beurlaubt sein** to be on leave; *(suspendiert sein)* to have been relieved of one's duties; **sich ~ lassen** to take leave.
Be|urlaubung *f* granting of leave *(gen* to*)*; *(Beurlaubtsein)* leave.
be|urteilen* *vt* to judge *(nach* by, from*)*; *Leistung, Wert* to assess. **etw richtig/falsch ~** to judge sth correctly/to misjudge sth.
Be|urteilung *f siehe vt* judgement; assessment.
Beute *f no pl* **(a)** *(Kriegs~, fig hum)* spoils *pl*; *(Diebes~)* haul, loot; *(von Raubtieren etc)* prey; *(Jagd~)* bag. **~ machen** *(Dieb)* to make a haul. **(b)** *(liter: Opfer)* prey. **eine ~ einer Sache** *(gen)* **sein/werden** to have fallen prey/to fall prey to sth.
Beutel *m* - **(a)** bag; *(Tabaks~, Zool)* pouch. **(b)** *(col: Geld~) (von Frau)* purse; *(von Mann)* wallet *(Brit)*, billfold *(US)*.
Beute-: ~stück *nt* booty; **~zug** *m* raid *(auch fig)*.
bevölkern* 1 *vt* **(a)** *(bewohnen)* to inhabit; *(beleben)* to crowd, to fill. **schwach/stark bevölkert** sparsely/densely populated. **(b)** *(besiedeln)* to populate. **2** *vr* to become inhabited; *(fig)* to fill up.
Bevölkerung *f (die Bewohner)* population.
Bevölkerungs-: ~dichte *f* population density; **~explosion** *f* population explosion; **~schicht** *f* social stratum; **~zahl** *f* (total) population.
bevollmächtigen* *vt* to authorize *(zu etw* to do sth*)*.
Bevollmächtigte(r) *mf decl as adj* authorized representative.
Bevollmächtigung *f* authorization *(durch* from*)*.
bevor *conj* before. **~ Sie (nicht) die Rechnung bezahlt haben** until you pay the bill.
bevormunden* *vt* to treat like a child. **jdn ~** to make sb's decisions (for him/her).
Bevormundung *f* **unsere ~ durch den Staat** the State's making up our minds for us.
bevorstehen *vi sep irreg* to be imminent; *(Winter etc)* to approach. **jdm ~** to be in store for sb; **das Schlimmste steht uns noch bevor** the worst is still to come.
bevorstehend *adj* forthcoming; *Gefahr, Krise* imminent; *Winter* approaching.
bevorzugen* *vt* to prefer; *(begünstigen)* to favour *(Brit)*, to favor *(US)*, to give preferential treatment to.
bevorzugt 1 *adj* preferred; *Behandlung* preferential; *(priviligiert)* privileged. **2** *adv* **jdn ~ bedienen** *etc* to give sb preferential treatment; **etw ~ abfertigen** *etc* to give sth priority.
Bevorzugung *f* preference *(gen* for*)*; *(vorrangige Behandlung)* preferential treatment *(bei* in*)*.
bewachen* *vt* to guard; *(Sport) Spieler* to mark.
Bewacher *m* - guard; *(Sport: von Spieler)* marker.
bewachsen *adj* overgrown *(mit* in, with*)*.
Bewachung *f* guarding; *(Wachmannschaft)* guard; *(Sport)* marking.
bewaffnen* 1 *vt* to arm. **2** *vr (lit, fig)* to arm oneself.
bewaffnet *adj* armed. **bis an die Zähne ~** armed to the teeth.
Bewaffnung *f* arming; *(Waffen)* weapons *pl*.
bewahren* *vt* **(a)** *(beschützen)* to protect *(vor +dat* from*)*. **(Gott) bewahre!** *(col)* heaven *or* God forbid! **(b)** *(beibehalten)* to keep, to retain.
bewähren* *vr* to prove oneself/itself; *(Methode, Sparsamkeit, Fleiß)* to pay off; *(Auto, Gerät etc)* to prove a good investment. **sich im Leben~** to make something of one's life; **es bewährt sich immer, das zu tun** it's always worth doing that; **ihre Freundschaft hat sich bewährt** their friend-

ship stood the test of time; *siehe* **bewährt.**

bewahrheiten* *vr* to prove (to be) well-founded; *(Prophezeiung)* to come true.

bewährt *adj* proven, tried and tested.

Bewahrung *f siehe vt* protection; retention.

Bewährung *f* **(a) bei ~ der Methode** if the method proves (to be) workable *or* valid. **(b)** *(Jur)* probation. **eine Strafe zur ~ aussetzen** to impose a suspended sentence; **ein Jahr Gefängnis mit ~** a suspended sentence of one year with probation.

Bewährungs-: ~frist *f (Jur)* probation(ary) period; **~helfer** *m* probation officer; **~probe** *f* test; **etw einer ~probe** *(dat)* **unterziehen** to put sth to the test; **~zeit** *f* time spent on probation.

bewaldet *adj* wooded.

bewältigen* *vt Schwierigkeiten* to cope with; *Arbeit, Aufgabe auch, Strecke* to manage; *Erlebnis etc* to get over; *(erledigen, beenden)* to deal with.

Bewältigung *f* **die ~ der Schwierigkeiten/der Arbeit/eines Erlebnisses** coping with the difficulties/managing the work/getting over an experience.

bewandert *adj* well-versed.

Bewandtnis *f* **damit hat es eine andere ~** there's another reason *or* explanation for that; **damit hat es folgende ~** the fact of the matter is this.

bewässern* *vt* to irrigate; *(mit Sprühanlage)* to water.

Bewässerung *f siehe vt* irrigation; watering.

Bewässerungs- *in cpds* irrigation.

bewegen[1]* **1** *vt* to move. **dieser Gedanke bewegt mich seit langem** this has been on my mind a long time; *siehe* **bewegt. 2** *vr* **(a)** to move. **(b)** *(Bewegung haben: Mensch)* to get some exercise. **(c)** *(fig: schwanken)* to vary, to range *(zwischen* between*)*. **der Preis bewegt sich um die 50 Mark** the price is about 50 marks.

bewegen[2] *pret* **bewog,** *ptp* **bewogen** *vt* **jdn zu etw ~** to induce *or* persuade sb to do sth; **sich dazu ~ lassen, etw zu tun** to let oneself be persuaded to do sth.

Beweggrund *m* motive.

beweglich *adj* **(a)** *(bewegbar)* movable; *Truppe* mobile. **(b)** *(wendig)* agile; *Fahrzeug* manoeuvrable *(Brit)*, maneuverable *(US)*. **mit einem Kleinwagen ist man in der Stadt ~er** you're more mobile in town with a small car.

Beweglichkeit *f no pl siehe adj* **(a)** movability; mobility. **(b)** agility; manoeuvrability *(Brit)*, maneuverability *(US)*.

bewegt *adj* **(a)** *Wasser, See* choppy; *Zeiten, Leben* eventful. **(b)** *Stimme, Worte* emotional.

Bewegung *f* **(a)** movement; *(Hand~ auch)* gesture; *(Sci, Tech auch)* motion. **keine ~!** don't move!; **in ~ sein** *(Fahrzeug)* to be moving, to be in motion; *(Menge)* to mill around; **sich in ~ setzen** to start moving; **etw in ~ setzen** to set sth in motion. **(b)** *(körperliche ~)* exercise. **sich** *(dat)* **~ verschaffen** to get some exercise. **(c)** *(Ergriffenheit)* emotion. **(d)** *(Pol, Art etc)* movement.

Bewegungs-: ~freiheit *f* freedom of movement; *(fig)* freedom of action; **b~los** *adj* motionless, immobile; **~losigkeit** *f* motionlessness, immobility; **b~unfähig** *adj* unable to move; *(gehunfähig)* unable to get about.

beweinen* *vt* to mourn (for), to weep for.

Beweis *m* **-e** proof *(für* of*)*; *(Zeugnis)* evidence *no pl.* **als** *or* **zum ~** as proof *or* evidence; **ein eindeutiger ~** clear evidence; **den ~ antreten** *or* **führen** to offer evidence *or* proof; **den ~ für etw erbringen** to produce evidence *or* proof of sth.

Beweis-: ~aufnahme *f (Jur)* taking *or* hearing of evidence; **b~bar** *adj* provable, demonstrable.

beweisen *vt irreg* to prove. **was zu ~ war** QED; **was noch zu ~ wäre** that remains to be seen.

Beweis-: ~führung *f (Jur)* presentation of one's case; *(Math)* proof; *(Argumentation)* argumentation, reasoning; **~grund** *m* argument; **~kraft** *f* value as evidence; **~last** *f (Jur)* onus, burden of proof; **~material** *nt* (body of) evidence; **~not** *f (Jur)* lack of evidence; **~pflicht** *f (Jur)* onus, burden of proof; **~stück** *nt* exhibit.

bewenden *vt impers:* **wir wollen es dabei ~ lassen** let's leave it at that.

bewerben* *vr irreg (um* for*)* to apply *(als* for the post/job of*)*; *(bei Wahl)* to stand; *(Comm: um Auftrag)* to quote.

Bewerber(in *f***)** *m* **-** applicant; *(Pol)* candidate; *(Sport)* contender.

Bewerbung *f* application; *(Pol)* candidacy.

Bewerbungs-: ~bogen *m* application form; **~schreiben** *nt* (letter of) application; **~unterlagen** *pl* application documents *pl.*

bewerfen* *vt irreg* **jdn/etw mit etw ~** to throw sth at sb/sth.

bewerkstelligen* *vt* to manage; *Geschäft* to bring off. **es ~, daß jd etw tut** to manage *or* contrive to get sb to do sth.

bewerten* *vt jdn* to judge; *Gegenstand* to put a value on; *Leistung auch, Schularbeit* to assess. **etw mit der Note 5 ~** to give sth a mark of 5.

Bewertung *f siehe vt* judgement; valuation; assessment.

bewilligen* *vt* to allow; *Etat etc* to approve; *Geld etc auch* to grant; *Stipendium* to award.

Bewilligung *f siehe vt* allowing; approval; granting; awarding. **die ~ für einen Kredit bekommen** to be allowed *or* granted credit.

bewirken* *vt* **(a)** *(verursachen)* to cause, to bring about. **~, daß etw passiert** to cause sth to happen. **(b)** *(erreichen)* to achieve.

bewirten* *vt* **jdn ~** to wine and dine sb; **jdn mit Kaffee und Kuchen ~** to entertain sb to coffee and cakes.

bewirtschaften* *vt Land* to farm, to cultivate.

Bewirtschaftung *f (von Land)* farming, cultivation.

Bewirtung *f (das Bewirten)* hospitality; *(im Hotel)* (food and) service. **die ~ so vieler Gäste** catering for so many guests.

bewog *pret of* **bewegen**[2].

bewogen *ptp of* **bewegen**[2].

bewohnbar *adj* habitable.

Bewohnbarkeit *f* habitability.

bewohnen* *vt* to live in; *Haus, Bau, Nest auch* to occupy; *(Volk)* to inhabit; *siehe* **bewohnt.**

Bewohner(in *f***)** *m* **-** *(von Land, Gebiet)* inhabitant; *(von Haus etc)* occupier.

bewohnt *adj* inhabited; *Haus etc auch* occupied.

bewölken* *vr (lit, fig)* to cloud over.

bewölkt *adj* cloudy.

Bewölkung *f* clouding over; *(Wolken)* cloud.

Bewölkungs-: ~auflockerung *f* break-up of the cloud; **~zunahme** *f* increase in cloud.

Bewuchs *m no pl* vegetation.

Bewund(e)rer(in *f***)** *m* **-** admirer.

bewundern* *vt* to admire *(wegen* for*)*.

bewundernswert *adj* admirable.

Bewunderung *f* admiration.

bewußt 1 *adj* **(a)** conscious. **sich** *(dat)* **einer Sache** *(gen)* **~ sein/werden** to be/become aware *or* conscious of sth, to realize sth; **es wurde ihm allmählich ~, daß ...** he gradually realized (that) ... **(b)** *(willentlich)* deliberate, intentional; *Lüge* deliberate. **(c)** *(bekannt, besagt)* **die ~e Kreuzung** the crossroads in question. **2** *adv* **(a)** consciously. **(b)** *(willentlich)* deliberately, intentionally.

Bewußt-: b~los *adj* unconscious; **b~los werden** to become unconscious; **~lose(r)** *mf decl as adj* unconscious man/woman/person *etc;* **~losigkeit** *f* unconsciousness; **bis zur ~losigkeit** *(col)* ad nauseam; **b~machen** *vt sep* **jdm etw b~machen** to make sb conscious of sth, to make sb realize sth; **sich** *(dat)* **etw b~machen** to realize sth.

Bewußtsein *nt no pl* **(a)** *(Wissen)* awareness, consciousness. **etw kommt jdm zu(m) ~** sb becomes aware *or* conscious of sth; **jdm etw zu ~ bringen/ins ~ rufen** to make sb conscious *or* aware of sth; **im ~, daß ...** in the knowledge that ...; **er tat es mit (vollem) ~** he was (fully) aware of what he was doing. **(b)** *(Philos, Psych, Med)* consciousness. **das ~ verlieren/wiedererlangen** to lose/regain consciousness; **bei ~ sein** to be conscious; **bei vollem ~** fully conscious.

Bewußtseins-: ~bildung *f (Pol)* shaping of political ideas; **b~erweiternd** *adj* **b~erweiternde Drogen** mind-expanding drugs; **~erweiterung** *f* consciousness raising; **~veränderung** *f* change in outlook.

bezahlbar *adj* affordable.

bezahlen* **1** *vt* **(a)** to pay. **(b)** *Sache, Leistung* to pay for. **etw bezahlt bekommen/für etw nichts bezahlt bekommen** to get/not to get paid for sth; **er hat seinen Fehler mit seinem Leben bezahlt** he paid for his mistake with his life. **2** *vi* to pay.

bezahlt *adj* paid. **sich ~ machen** to pay off.

Bezahlung *f* **(a)** *siehe vt* payment; paying for *(einer Sache (gen)* sth*)*. **(b)** *(Lohn, Gehalt)* pay; *(für Dienste)* payment. **ohne/gegen** *or* **für ~** without/for payment.

bezähmen* **1** *vt (fig geh) Begierden etc* to control, to curb. **2** *vr* to control *or* restrain oneself.

bezaubern* *vt (fig)* to charm, to captivate.

bezaubernd *adj* enchanting, charming.

bezeichnen* *vt* **(a)** *(kennzeichnen)* to mark; *Takt, Tonart* to indicate. **(b)** *(genau beschreiben)* to describe. **(c)** *(benennen)* to call, to describe. **ich weiß nicht, wie man das bezeichnet** I don't know what it's called. **(d)** *(bedeuten)* to mean, to denote.

bezeichnend *adj (für* of*)* characteristic, typical.

bezeichnenderweise *adv* typically (enough).

Bezeichnung *f* **(a)** *siehe vt (a, b)* marking; indication; description. **(b)** *(Ausdruck)* expression, term.

bezeugen* *vt* to attest, to testify to. **~, daß ...** to attest the fact that ..., to testify that ...

bezichtigen* *vt* to accuse *(einer Sache (gen)* of sth*)*.

beziehbar *adj* **(a)** *Wohnung etc* ready to move into. **(b)** *Waren etc* obtainable.

beziehen *irreg* **1** *vt* **(a)** *(überziehen) Polster* to cover. **die Betten frisch ~** to change the beds. **(b)** *(einziehen in) Wohnung* to move into. **(c)** *Stellung, Standpunkt* to take up. **(d)** *(erhalten)* to get. **(e)** *(in Beziehung setzen)* **etw auf jdn/etw ~** to apply sth to sb/sth; *siehe* **bezogen. 2** *vr* **(a)** *(Himmel)* to cloud over. **(b) sich auf jdn/etw ~** to refer to sb/sth.

Bezieher(in *f***)** *m* **-** *(Abonnent)* subscriber; *(von Waren)* purchaser; *(von Einkommen)* drawer.

Beziehung *f* **(a)** *(Verhältnis)* relationship. **(b)** *usu pl (Kontakt)* relations *pl*. **diplomatische ~en** diplomatic relations. **(c)** *(Zusammenhang)* connection *(zu* with*)*, relation. **etw zu etw in ~ setzen** to relate sth to sth; **etw hat keine ~ zu etw** sth has no bearing on sth *or* no relationship to sth. **(d)** *usu pl (Verbindung)* connections *pl (zu* with*)*. **seine ~en spielen lassen** to pull strings. **(e)** *(Sympathie)* feeling, affinity *(zu* for*)*. **er hat überhaupt keine ~ zu seinen Kindern** he just doesn't relate to his children. **(f) in einer/keiner ~** in one/no respect *or* way; **in jeder ~** in every respect.

beziehungslos *adj* unrelated, unconnected.

beziehungsweise *conj* **(a)** *(oder aber)* or. **(b)** *(im anderen Fall)* and ... respectively. **zwei Briefmarken, die 50 ~ 70 Pfennig kosten** two stamps costing 50 and 70 Pfennig respectively. **(c)** *(genauer gesagt)* or rather, or that is to say.

beziffern* **1** *vt (angeben)* to estimate *(auf+acc, mit* at*)*. **2** *vr* **sich ~ auf** *(+acc)* to amount to.

Bezirk *m* **-e (a)** *(Gebiet)* district. **(b)** *(Admin) (Stadt)* ≈ district; *(von Land)* ≈ region.

Bezirks-: ~klasse, ~liga *f (Sport)* regional league; **~regierung** *f* regional administration; **~stadt** *f* ≈ county town.

bezirzen* *vt (col)* to bewitch.

bezogen *adj* **auf jdn/etw ~** referring to sb/sth.

Bezogene(r) *mf decl as adj (Fin) (von Scheck)* drawee; *(von Wechsel)* acceptor.

bezug *siehe* **Bezug (g).**

Bezug *m* **¨-e (a)** *(für Kissen, Polster etc)* cover; *(für Kopfkissen)* pillow-case, pillow-slip. **(b)** *(Erwerb)* buying, purchase; *(von Zeitung)* taking. **beim regelmäßigen ~ der Zeitung ...** if you take the newspaper on a regular basis ... **(c)** *(von Einkommen, Rente etc)* drawing. **(d) ¨~e** *pl (Einkünfte)* income, earnings *pl*. **(e)** *(Zusammenhang)* = **Beziehung (c). (f)** *(form: Berufung)* reference. **~ nehmen auf** *(+acc)* to refer to; **mit** *or* **unter ~ auf** *(+acc)* with reference to. **(g) in b~ auf** *(+acc)* regarding, with regard to, concerning.

bezüglich *prep+gen (form)* regarding, with regard to, re *(Comm)*.

Bezugnahme *f* **-n** *(form)* reference. **unter ~ auf** *(+acc)* with reference to.

Bezugs-: b~bereit, b~fertig *adj Haus etc* ready to move into; **~person** *f* **die wichtigste ~person des Kleinkindes** the person to whom the child relates most closely; **~punkt** *m (lit, fig)* point of reference; **~quelle** *f* source of supply; **~schein** *m* (ration) coupon.

bezuschussen* *vt* to subsidize.

Bezuschussung *f* subsidizing; *(Betrag)* subsidy.

bezwecken* *vt* to aim at. **etw mit etw ~** *(Mensch)* to intend sth by sth.

bezweifeln* *vt* to doubt. **das ist nicht zu ~** there's no doubt about it.

bezwingen* *vt irreg* to conquer; *Feind auch* to defeat, to overcome; *(Sport)* to beat, to defeat.

Bezwinger(in *f***)** *m* **-** *(von Berg, Feind)* conqueror; *(Sport)* winner *(gen* over*)*.

BGB ['be:ge:'be:] *nt* **-**, *no pl* = **Bürgerliches Gesetzbuch.**

BH [be:'ha:] *m* **-(s)** = **Büstenhalter** bra.

bibbern *vi (col) (vor Angst)* to tremble, to shake; *(vor Kälte)* to shiver.

Bibel *f* **-n** *(lit)* Bible; *(fig)* bible.

Bibel-: b~fest *adj* well versed in the Bible; **~spruch** *m* quotation from the Bible; **~wort** *nt, pl* **~worte** biblical saying.

Biber *m* **-** beaver.

Biber-: ~bettuch *nt* flannelette; **~pelz** *m* beaver (fur).

Bibliographie *f* bibliography.

Bibliothek *f* **-en** library.

Bibliothekar(in *f***)** *m* librarian.

biblisch *adj* biblical. **ein ~es Alter** a great age, a ripe old age.

Bidet [bi'de:] *nt* **-s** bidet.

bieder *adj* **(a)** *(rechtschaffen)* honest; *Mensch, Leben auch* upright. **(b)** *(pej)* conventional.

Bieder-: ~mann *m, pl* **~männer** *(pej geh)* petty bourgeois; **b~männisch** *adj (pej geh)* petty bourgeois; *Geschmack, Gesinnung auch* philistine.

biegen *pret* **bog,** *ptp* **gebogen 1** *vt* to bend; *(fig: manipulieren)* to wangle *(col)*. **auf B~ oder Brechen** *(col)* by hook or by crook *(col)*. **2** *vi aux sein (Mensch, Wagen)* to turn; *(Weg, Straße auch)* to curve. **3** *vr* to bend; *(Holz, Plastik)* to warp; *(Metall)* to buckle. **sich vor Lachen ~** *(fig)* to double up with laughter.

biegsam *adj* flexible; *Holz auch* pliable; *Metall auch* malleable; *Glieder, Körper* supple.

Biegsamkeit *f siehe adj* flexibility; pliability; malleability; suppleness.

Biegung *f* **der Fluß/die Straße macht eine ~** the river/road curves *or* bends.

Biene *f* **-n (a)** bee. **(b)** *(dated col: Mädchen)* bird

(Brit col), chick *(esp US col)*.

Bienen-: b~fleißig *adj* industrious; **~honig** *m* real *or* natural honey; **~königin** *f* queen bee; **~korb** *m* (bee)hive; **~schwarm** *m* swarm (of bees); **~stich** *m (Cook) cake coated with sugar and almonds filled with custard or cream;* **~stock** *m* (bee)hive; **~wachs** *nt* beeswax; **~zucht** *f* bee-keeping **~züchter** *m* beekeeper.

Bier *nt* **-e** beer. **zwei ~, bitte!** two beers, please; **das ist mein ~** *(fig col)* that's my business.

Bier- *in cpds* beer; **~bauch** *m (col)* beer gut *(col)*; **~brauerei** *f* (beer-)brewing; *(Betrieb)* brewery; **~deckel** *m* beer mat; **~dose** *f* beer can; **~ernst** *m (col)* deadly seriousness; **~faß** keg; **~flasche** beer bottle; **~kasten** beer crate; **~keller** *m* beer cellar; **~krug** *m* tankard, beer mug; *(aus Steingut)* (beer) stein; **~leiche** *f (col)* drunk; **~ruhe** *f (col)* cool *(col)*; **~schinken** *m*, **~wurst** *f* ham sausage; **b~selig** *adj Mensch* boozed up *(col)*; **~zelt** *nt* beer tent.

Biest *nt* **-er** *(pej col)* **(a)** *(Tier)* creature; *(Insekt auch)* bug. **(b)** *(Mensch)* (little) wretch; *(Frau)* bitch *(col)*.

bieten *pret* **bot,** *ptp* **geboten 1** *vt* **(a)** to offer *(jdm etw* sb sth, sth to sb*)*; *(bei Auktion)* to bid *(auf+acc* for*)*; *Gelegenheit auch* to give. **jdm die Hand ~** to offer sb one's hand; **wer bietet mehr?** *(bei Auktion)* any more bids?; **diese Stadt hat nichts zu ~** this town has nothing to offer. **(b)** *(haben, aufweisen)* to have; *Problem, Schwierigkeit* to present. **das Hochhaus bietet fünfzig Familien Wohnung** the tower block provides accommodation for fifty families. **(c)** *(zeigen, darbieten) Anblick, Bild* to present; *Film* to show; *Leistung* to give. **die Mannschaft bot ein hervorragendes Spiel** the team played an excellent game. **(d)** *(zumuten)* **so etwas könnte man mir nicht ~** I wouldn't stand for that sort of thing; *siehe* **geboten. 2** *vi (Cards)* to bid. **3** *vr (Gelegenheit, Anblick etc)* to present itself *(jdm* to sb*)*.

Bieter(in *f***)** *m* **-** bidder.

Bigamie *f* bigamy.

Bigamist(in *f***)** *m* bigamist.

bigott *adj* overly pious; *(scheinheilig)* hypocritical.

Bikini *m* **-s** bikini.

Bilanz *f* **(a)** balance; *(Abrechnung)* balance sheet. **eine ~ aufstellen** to draw up a balance sheet. **(b)** *(fig: Ergebnis)* end result. **(die) ~ ziehen** to take stock *(aus* of*)*.

Bilanzprüfer *m* auditor.

bilateral *adj* bilateral.

Bild *nt* **-er (a)** *(lit, fig)* picture; *(Film)* frame. **ein ~ machen** to take a photo *or* picture; **ein ~ des Elends** a picture of misery. **(b)** *(Abbild)* image; *(Spiegel~ auch)* reflection. **sie ist ganz das ~ ihrer Mutter** she is the image of her mother. **(c)** *(Anblick, Ansicht)* sight. **das äußere ~ der Stadt** the appearance of the town. **(d)** *(Theat: Szene)* scene. **(e)** *(Metapher)* metaphor, image. **im ~ bleiben** to use the same metaphor. **(f)** *(Erscheinungs~)* character. **sie gehören zum ~ dieser Stadt** they are part of the scene in this town. **(g)** *(fig: Vorstellung)* image, picture. **im ~e sein** to be in the picture *(über+acc* about*)*; **jdn ins ~ setzen** to put sb in the picture; **sich** *(dat)* **von jdm/etw ein ~ machen** to get an idea of sb/sth; **das ~ des Deutschen** the image of the German.

Bild-: ~ausfall *m (TV)* loss of vision; **~band** *m* illustrated book; **~beschreibung** *f (Sch)* description of a picture.

bilden 1 *vt* **(a)** to form; *(fig) Charakter auch* to shape, to mould; *Vermögen* to acquire; *(ausmachen) Höhepunkt, Ausnahme, Gefahr etc* to constitute. **sich** *(dat)* **eine Meinung ~** to form an opinion. **(b)** *(erziehen)* to educate. **2** *vr* **(a)** *(entstehen)* to form, to develop. **(b)** *(lernen)* to educate oneself; *(durch Lesen etc)* to improve one's mind; *(durch Reisen etc)* to broaden one's mind. **3** *vi siehe vr (b)* to be educational; to improve the mind; to broaden the mind.

bildend *adj* **die ~e Kunst** art; **~er Künstler** artist.

Bilderbogen *m* illustrated broadsheet. **ein musikalischer ~** a musical medley.

Bilderbuch *nt* picture book.

Bilderbuch- *in cpds (fig)* perfect; **~landung** *f* **eine ~landung** a textbook landing.

Bilder-: ~geschichte *f* picture story; *(in Comic, Zeitung)* strip cartoon; **~rahmen** *m* picture-frame; **~rätsel** *nt* picture-puzzle; **b~reich** *adj Buch etc* full of pictures; *(fig) Sprache* rich in imagery.

Bild-: ~fläche *f* **(a)** *(Leinwand)* projection surface; **(b)** *(fig col)* **auf der ~fläche erscheinen** to appear on the scene; **von der ~fläche verschwinden** to disappear (from the scene); **b~haft** *adj* pictorial; *Beschreibung, Sprache* vivid; **~hauer** *m* sculptor; **~hauerei** *f* sculpture; **~hauerin** *f* sculptress; **b~hübsch** *adj Mädchen* (as) pretty as a picture; *Kleid, Garten* really lovely.

bildlich *adj* pictorial; *Ausdruck etc* figurative. **sich** *(dat)* **etw ~ vorstellen** to picture sth in one's mind's eye.

Bildnis *nt (liter)* portrait.

Bild-: ~platte *f* video disc; **~plattenspieler** *m* video disc player; **~punkt** *m (Comp)* pixel; **~qualität** *f (TV, Film)* picture quality; *(Phot)* print quality; **~reporter** *m* photojournalist; **~röhre** *f (TV)* cathode ray tube; **~schärfe** *f* definition *no indef art;* **~schirm** *m (TV, Comp)* screen; **~schirmgerät** *nt* visual display unit, VDU, monitor; **~schirmtext** *m* viewdata; **b~schön** *adj* beautiful; **~text** *m* caption.

Bildung *f* **(a)** *(Erziehung)* education; *(Kultur)* culture. **~ haben** to be cultured. **(b)** *no pl (das Formen)* formation, forming; *(fig: von Charakter etc auch)* shaping; *(von Vermögen)* acquisition. **zur ~ des Passivs** to form the passive.

Bildungs-: ~chancen *pl* educational opportunities *pl*; **~einrichtung** *f* educational institution; *(Kulturstätte)* cultural institution; **~gang** *m* school (and university/college) career; **~grad** *m* level of education; **~lücke** *f* gap in one's education; **~politik** *f* education policy; **~reise** *f* educational trip; **~roman** *m (Liter)* Bildungsroman, *novel concerned with the intellectual or spiritual development of the main character;* **~stand** *m*, **~stufe** *f* level of education; **~urlaub** *m* educational holiday; **~weg** *m* **jds ~weg** the course of sb's education; **auf dem zweiten ~weg** through night school/the Open University *etc*; **~wesen** *nt* education system.

Bild-: ~unterschrift *f* caption; **~werfer** *m* projector; **~zuschrift** *f* reply enclosing photograph.

Billard ['bıljart] *nt (Spiel)* billiards *sing.*

Billard-: ~kugel *f* billiard ball; **~stock** *m* billiard cue; **~tisch** *m* billiard table.

Billett [bıl'jɛt] *nt* **-e** *or* **-s** *(dated)* ticket.

billig *adj* **(a)** cheap. **~ abzugeben** going cheap; **~ davonkommen** to get off lightly. **(b)** *(pej: primitiv)* cheap; *Ausrede* feeble.

billigen *vt* to approve. **etw stillschweigend ~** to condone sth; **~, daß jd etw tut** to approve of sb's doing sth.

Billigpreis *m* low price.

Billigung *f* approval. **jds ~ finden** to meet with sb's approval.

Billion *f* billion *(Brit)*, trillion *(US)*.

Bimmel *f* **-n** *(col)* bell.

bimmeln *vi (col)* to ring.

Bimsstein *m* pumice stone.

bin *1. pers sing pres of* **sein.**

Binde *f* **-n (a)** *(Med)* bandage. **(b)** *(Arm~)* armband; *(Augen~)* blindfold. **(c)** *(Monats~)* (sanitary) towel *or* napkin *(US)*. **(d)** *(dated: Krawatte)* tie. **sich** *(dat)* **einen hinter die ~ gießen** *or* **kippen** *(col)* to put a few drinks away.

Binde-: **~gewebe** *nt (Anat)* connective tissue; **~glied** *nt (fig)* link; **~hautentzündung** *f* conjunctivitis; **~mittel** *nt* binder.

binden *pret* **band,** *ptp* **gebunden 1** *vt* **(a)** *(zusammen~)* to tie; *(fest~)* to bind; *(fig geh)* to bind, to unite. **(b)** *(Buch etc)* to bind; *Strauß, Kranz* to make up; *Knoten, Schal* to tie; *Krawatte* to knot. **sich** *(dat)* **die Schuhe ~** to tie (up) one's shoelaces. **(c)** *(fesseln, befestigen) (an+acc* to*)* to tie (up); *Menschen auch* to bind; *(fig) (an einen Ort)* to tie; *(Versprechen, Vertrag, Eid etc)* to bind. **jdm die Hände auf den Rücken ~** to tie sb's hands behind his back; **mir sind die Hände gebunden** *(fig)* my hands are tied; **nichts bindet mich an Glasgow** I have no special ties in Glasgow. **(d)** *(festhalten) Staub, Erdreich* to bind; *(Chem) (aufnehmen)* to absorb; *(sich vebinden mit)* to combine with; *(Cook) Soße* to bind. **2** *vr (sich verpflichten)* to commit oneself *(an+acc* to*)*.

bindend *adj* binding *(für* on*)*; *Zusage* definite.

Binder *m* **-** *(Krawatte)* tie, necktie *(US)*.

Bindestrich *m* hyphen.

Bindfaden *m* string. **es regnet ~** *(col)* it's sheeting down *(col)*.

Bindung *f* **(a)** tie *(an +acc* with*)*; *(Beziehung zu einem Partner)* relationship *(an+acc* with*)*; *(Verpflichtung: an Beruf etc, durch Vertrag)* commitment *(an+acc* to*)*. **(b)** *(Ski~)* binding.

binnen *prep+dat or (geh) gen (form)* within.

Binnen-: **~gewässer** *nt* inland water; **~hafen** *m* river port; **~handel** *m* domestic trade; **~land** *nt (Landesinneres)* interior; **b~ländisch** *adj* inland; **~markt** *m* home market; **~meer** *nt* inland sea; **~schiffahrt** *f* inland navigation; **~staat** *m* landlocked country *or* state.

Binse *f* **-n** *usu pl* rush. **in die ~n gehen** *(fig col) (mißlingen)* to be a wash-out *(col)*; *(verlorengehen)* to go west *(col)*; *(kaputtgehen)* to give out *(col)*.

Binsen-: **~wahrheit, ~weisheit** *f* truism.

Bio- *in cpds* bio-; **~chemie** *f* biochemistry; **b~dynamisch** *adj* biodynamic.

Biograph(in *f***)** *m* biographer.

Biographie *f* biography.

Bioladen *m (col)* health food shop *(Brit) or* store *(US)*.

Biologe *m*, **Biologin** *f* biologist.

Biologie *f* biology.

biologisch *adj* biological.

Biophysik *f* biophysics *sing*.

Birke *f* **-n** birch.

Birma *nt* Burma.

Birnbaum *m (Baum)* pear tree; *(Holz)* pear-wood.

Birne *f* **-n (a)** pear. **(b)** *(Glühlampe)* (light) bulb. **(c)** *(col: Kopf)* nut *(col)*.

birnenförmig *adj* pear-shaped.

bis 1 *prep+acc* **(a)** *(zeitlich)* until, till; *(bis spätestens, nicht späte als)* by. **~ Ende Mai bin ich noch in London** I'll be in London up to *or* until the end of May; **~ Ende Mai bin ich damit fertig** I'll have finished it by the end of May; **~ dahin ist er längst weg** he will have gone long before then; **~ wann gilt der Fahrplan/ist das fertig?** when is the timetable valid till/will that be finished by?; **~ wann?** till/by when?; **~ wann bleibt ihr hier?** when are you staying here till?; **~ dann!** see you then!; **von ... ~ (einschließlich) ...** from ... to *or* till *or* through *(US)* ...

(b) *(räumlich)* to; *(in Buch, Film etc auch)* up to. **ich fahre nur ~ München** I'm only going to *or* as far as Munich; **~ dorthin sind es nur 5 km** it's only 5 km there; **~ hierher und nicht weiter** *(lit, fig)* this far and no further; **~ mindestens Carlisle** at least as far as Carlisle.

(c) *(bei Zahlen)* up to; *(bis zu einer unteren Grenze von)* (down) to. **Kinder ~ sechs Jahre** children up to the age of six.

2 *adv* **(a)** *(zeitlich)* until, till; *(bis spätestens)* by. **~ zu diesem Zeitpunkt** up to this time; **das sollte ~ zum nächsten Sommer fertig sein** that should be finished by next summer; **~ auf weiteres** until further notice.

(b) *(räumlich)* to; *durch, über, unter* right. **~ an unser Grundstück** (right *or* up) to our plot; **es sind noch 10 km ~ nach Schlüchtern** it's another 10 km to Schlüchtern; **~ ins letzte/kleinste** (right) down to the last/smallest detail.

(c) *(bei Zahlen)* **~ zu** up to; *(bis zu einer unteren Grenze von)* (down) to; **Gefängnis ~ zu 8 Jahren** a maximum of 8 years' imprisonment.

(d) ~ auf *(+acc) (außer)* except (for); *(einschließlich)* (right) down to.

3 *conj* **(a)** *(beiordnend)* to. **zehn ~ zwanzig Stück** ten to twenty; **bewölkt ~ bedeckt** cloudy or overcast. **(b)** *(unterordnend: zeitlich)* until, till; *(nicht später als)* by the time. **ich warte noch, ~ es dunkel wird** I'll wait until *or* till it gets dark; **~ es dunkel wird, möchte ich zu Hause sein** I want to get home by the time it's dark.

Bisam *m* **-e** *or* **-s** *(Pelz)* musquash.

Bisamratte *f* muskrat (beaver).

Bischof *m* **⸚e** bishop.

bischöflich *adj* episcopal.

bisexuell *adj* bisexual.

bisher *adv* until *or* till now; *(und immer noch)* up to now; **~ nicht** not until *or* till now, not before; *(und immer noch nicht)* not as yet; **~ habe ich es ihm nicht gesagt** I haven't told him as yet; **ein ~ unbekannter Stern** a hitherto unknown star.

bisherig *adj attr (vorherig)* previous; *(momentan)* present, up to now. **in meiner ~en Karriere** in my career up to now.

Biskuit [bɪsˈkviːt] *nt or m* **-s** *or* **-e** sponge.

Biskuit-: **~gebäck** *nt* sponge cake/cakes; **~teig** *m* sponge mixture.

bislang *adv* = **bisher.**

Bison *m* **-s** bison.

biß *pret of* **beißen.**

Biß *m* **-sse** bite.

bißchen 1 *adj inv* **ein ~ Geld/Liebe/Wärme** a bit of *or* a little money/love/warmth; **das ~ Geld, das wir haben** what little money we have; **ich habe kein ~ Hunger** I'm not a bit hungry. **2** *adv* **ein ~** a bit, a little; **ein ~ wenig** not very much; **ein ~ mehr/viel/teuer** *etc* a bit more/much/expensive *etc;* **ein ~ zu wenig** not quite enough.

Bissen *m* **-** mouthful; *(Imbiß)* bite (to eat). **er will keinen ~ anrühren** he won't eat a thing; **sich** *(dat)* **jeden ~ vom** *or* **am Munde absparen** to watch every penny one spends.

bissig *adj* **(a)** vicious; *Bemerkung* caustic. **~ sein** to bite; **„Vorsicht, ~er Hund"** "beware of the dog". **(b)** *(übellaunig)* snappy.

Bißwunde *f* bite.

bist *2. pers sing pres of* **sein.**

Bistum [ˈbɪstuːm] *nt* diocese, bishopric.

bisweilen *adv (geh)* from time to time.

Bit *nt* **-s** *(Comp)* bit.

Bittbrief *m* petition.

Bitte *f* **-n** request; *(inständig)* plea. **ich habe eine große ~ an dich** I have a big request to make of you; **er kann ihr keine ~ abschlagen** he can't refuse her anything.

bitte *interj* **(a)** *(bittend, auffordernd)* please. **~ schön** please; **~ nicht!** no, please!, please don't; **ja ~!** yes please. **(b)** *(bei höflicher Frage etc)* **~ schön?** *(in Geschäft)* can I help you?; *(in Gaststätte)* what would you like?; **~(, Sie wünschen)?** what can I do for you?; **ja ~?** yes?; **~(, nehmen Sie doch Platz)!** *(form)* please *or* do sit down; **aber ~!** sure *(col)*; **na ~!** there you are! **(c)** *(sarkastisch: nun gut)* all right. **~, wie du willst** (all right) just as you like. **(d)** *(Dank erwidernd)* **~ (sehr** *or* **schön)** you're welcome, not at all; **aber ~!** there's no need to thank me. **(e)** *(nachfragend)*

(wie) ~? (I beg your) pardon? *(auch iro)*, pardon me *(US)*, sorry?

bitten *pret* **bat,** *ptp* **gebeten 1** *vt* **(a)** to ask; *(inständig)* to beg. **jdn um etw ~** to ask/beg sb for sth; **jdn (darum) ~, etw zu tun** to ask *etc* sb to do sth; **darf ich Sie um Ihren Namen ~?** might I ask your name?; **er läßt sich nicht (lange) ~** you don't have to ask him twice; **aber ich bitte dich!** not at all; **wenn ~ ich darf** *(form)* if you please, if you wouldn't mind; **ich bitte darum** *(form)* if you wouldn't mind; **ich muß doch (sehr) ~!** well I must say! **(b)** *(einladen)* to ask, to invite. **jdn auf ein Glas Wein ~** to invite sb to have a glass of wine. **(c)** *(bestellen)* **jdn zu sich ~** to ask sb to come and see one.

2 *vi* **(a)** to ask; *(inständig)* to plead, to beg. **um etw ~** to ask (for) *or* request sth; to plead *or* beg for sth; **bei jdm um etw ~** to ask sb for sth. **(b)** *(einladen)* **ich lasse ~** would you ask him/her to come in now?; **darf ich (um den nächsten Tanz) ~?** may I have the pleasure (of the next dance)?

bittend *adj* pleading.

bitter *adj* bitter; *Schokolade* plain; *(fig) Geschmack* nasty; *Wahrheit, Lehre, Verlust* hard, painful; *Zeit, Schicksal* hard; *Ernst* deadly; *Hohn, Spott* cruel; *Not, Notwendigkeit* dire; *Leid, Unrecht* grievous. **bis zum ~en Ende** to the bitter end; **jdn ~ machen** to embitter sb, to make sb bitter; **etw ~ nötig haben** to be in dire need of sth; **solche Fehler rächen sich ~** one pays dearly for mistakes like that.

Bitter-: b~böse *adj* furious; **b~ernst** *adj* deadly serious; **damit ist es mir b~ernst** I am deadly serious *or* in deadly earnest; **b~kalt** *adj attr* bitterly cold; **~keit** *f (lit, fig)* bitterness; **b~lich** *adv* bitterly; **b~süß** *adj (lit, fig)* bitter-sweet.

Bitt-: ~gesuch *nt*, **~schrift** *f* petition; **~steller(in** *f***)** *m* **-** petitioner.

Biwak *nt* **-s** *or* **-e** bivouac.

bizarr *adj* bizarre.

Bizeps *m* **-e** biceps.

Bj. = **Baujahr.**

Blabla *nt no pl (col)* waffle *(col)*.

Blag *nt* **-en, Blage** *f* **-n** *(pej col)* brat.

blähen 1 *vt* to swell; *Anorak, Gardine* to fill; *Nüstern* to flare. **2** *vr* to swell; *(Segel auch, Anorak, Gardine)* to billow; *(Nüstern)* to flare. **3** *vi (Speisen)* to cause flatulence *or* wind.

blähend *adj (Med)* flatulent.

Blähung *f usu pl (Med)* wind *no pl*, flatulence *no pl*.

blamabel *adj* shameful.

Blamage [bla'maːʒə] *f* **-n** disgrace.

blamieren* 1 *vt* to disgrace. **2** *vr* to make a fool of oneself.

blank *adj* **(a)** shiny, shining. **etw ~ polieren** to polish sth till it shines. **(b)** *(nackt)* bare; *Schwert* naked; *(col: ohne Geld)* broke; *(Cards: einzeln)* single. **eine Karte ~ haben** to have only one card of a suit. **(c)** *(rein)* pure, sheer; *Hohn* utter.

Blanko- *in cpds* blank; **~scheck** *m* blank cheque *(Brit) or* check *(US)*; **~vollmacht** *f* carte blanche.

Bläschen ['blɛːsçən] *nt (Med)* small blister.

Blase *f* **-n (a)** *(Seifen~, Luft~)* bubble. **(b)** *(Med)* blister. **sich** *(dat)* **~n laufen** *etc* to get blisters from walking *etc*. **(c)** *(Anat)* bladder. **(d)** *(pej col: Clique)* gang *(col)*, mob *(col)*.

Blasebalg *m (pair of)* bellows.

blasen *pret* **blies,** *ptp* **geblasen 1** *vi* to blow. **zum Rückzug ~** *(lit, fig)* to sound the retreat; **zum Aufbruch ~** *(fig)* to say it's time to go; **es bläst** *(col)* it's blowy *(col) or* windy. **2** *vt* **(a)** to blow. **(b)** *Posaune etc* to play. **(c)** *(col)* **dir/ihm werd ich was ~!** I'll give you/him a piece of my mind.

Blasen-: ~entzündung *f* cystitis; **~leiden** *nt* bladder trouble *no art*.

Bläser(in *f***)** *m* **-** *(Mus)* wind player. **die ~** the wind (section).

blasiert *adj (pej geh)* blasé.

Blasiertheit *f (pej geh)* blasé character; *(von Mensch)* blasé attitude.

Blas-: ~instrument *nt* wind instrument; **~musik** *f* brass band music.

Blasphemie *f* blasphemy.

blasphemisch *adj* blasphemous.

blaß *adj* **(a)** *Haut, Farbe, Licht* pale. **~ werden** to grow *or* go pale, to pale; *(vor Schreck auch)* to blanch; **~ vor Neid werden** to go green with envy. **(b)** *(fig) Ahnung, Vorstellung* faint, vague; *Ausdruck* weak, insipid.

blaß- *in cpds* pale.

Blässe *f* **-n** paleness, pallor.

Blatt *nt* **⸚er (a)** *(Bot)* leaf. **kein ~ vor den Mund nehmen** not to mince one's words. **(b)** *(Papier etc)* sheet. **ein ~ Papier** a sheet of paper; **(noch) ein unbeschriebenes ~ sein** *(unerfahren)* to be inexperienced; *(ohne Image)* to be an unknown quantity; **vom ~ singen/spielen** to sight-read. **(c)** *(Seite)* page. **das steht auf einem anderen ~** *(fig)* that's another story. **(d)** *(Zeitung)* paper. **(e)** *(von Säge, Ruder)* blade. **(f)** *(Cards)* hand; *(Einzelkarte)* card. **das ~ hat sich gewendet** *(fig)* the tide has turned.

blätt(e)rig *adj Teig* flaky; *Farbe etc* flaking.

blättern 1 *vi* **in einem Buch ~** to leaf through a book. **2** *vt Geldscheine, Spielkarten* to put down one by one.

Blätterteig *m* puff pastry.

Blatt-: ~feder *f (Tech)* leaf spring; **~gemüse** *nt* greens *pl*; **ein ~gemüse** a leaf vegetable; **~gold** *nt* gold leaf; **~grün** *nt* chlorophyll; **~laus** *f* greenfly, aphid; **b~los** *adj* leafless; **~schuß** *m (Hunt)* shot through the shoulder to the heart; **~silber** *nt* silver leaf; **~werk** *nt no pl* foliage.

blau *adj* **(a)** blue. **Forelle** *etc* **~** *(Cook)* trout *etc* au bleu; **ein ~es Auge** *(col)* a black eye; **mit einem ~en Auge davonkommen** *(fig)* to get off lightly; **~es Blut** blue blood; **ein ~er Brief** *(Sch) letter informing parents that their child is likely to have to repeat a year;* **ein ~er Fleck** a bruise; **er wird sein ~es Wunder erleben** *(col)* he won't know what's hit him *(col)*. **(b)** *usu pred (col: betrunken)* drunk, tight *(col)*.

Blau *nt* **-** *or (col)* **-s** blue.

Blau-: b~äugig *adj* blue-eyed; *(fig)* naïve; **~äugigkeit** *f (fig)* naïvety; **~beere** *f* = **Heidelbeere; b~blütig** *adj* blue-blooded.

Blaue *nt no pl* **(a) das ~ vom Himmel (herunter) lügen** *(col)* to tell a pack of lies; **jdm das ~ vom Himmel (herunter) versprechen** *(col)* to promise sb the moon. **(b)** *(ohne Ziel)* **ins ~ hinein** *(col)* at random; **eine Fahrt ins ~** a mystery tour.

Bläue *f no pl* blueness; *(des Himmels auch)* blue.

blau-: ~grau *adj* blue-grey; **~grün** *adj* blue-green.

bläulich *adj* bluish, bluey.

Blau-: ~licht *nt (von Polizei etc)* flashing blue light; *(Lampe)* blue light; **mit ~licht** with its blue light flashing; **b~machen** *sep (col)* **1** *vi* to skip work; **2** *vt* **den Freitag/zwei Tage b~machen** to skip work on Friday/for two days; **~mann** *m, pl* **~männer** *(col)* boilersuit; **~meise** *f* bluetit; **~pause** *f* blueprint; **~säure** *f* prussic acid; **~tanne** *f* colorado spruce; **~wal** *m* blue whale.

Blech *nt* **-e (a)** *no pl* (sheet) metal. **(b)** *(Blechstück)* metal plate. **(c)** *(Backblech)* (baking) tray. **(d)** *no pl (col: Blechinstrumente)* brass. **(e)** *no pl (col: Unsinn)* rubbish *no art (col)*.

Blech-: ~bläser the brass (section); **~blasinstrument** *nt* brass instrument; **~büchse, ~dose** *f* tin *(Brit)*, can.

blechen *vti (col)* to cough up *(col)*.

blechern *adj* **(a)** *attr* metal. **(b)** *Geräusch* tinny.

Blech-: ~instrument *nt* brass instrument; **~kanister** *m* metal can; **~kiste** *f (pej col)* (old) crate *(col)*; **~lawine** *f (pej col)* vast column of cars; **~napf** *m* metal bowl; **~schaden** *m* damage to the bodywork; ~**schere** *f* (pair of) metal shears; ~**trommel** *f* tin drum.

blecken *vt* **die Zähne** ~ to bare one's teeth.

Blei *nt* **-e (a)** *no pl (Metall)* lead. **jdm wie** ~ **in den Gliedern** *or* **Knochen liegen** *(Schreck)* to paralyze sb; *(Depression)* to weigh sb down. **(b)** *(Lot)* plumb, (plumb-)bob.

Bleibe *f* **-n** place to stay.

bleiben *pret* **blieb,** *ptp* **geblieben** *vi aux sein* **(a)** to stay, to remain. **unbeachtet** ~ to go unnoticed; **unbeantwortet** ~ to be left *or* to remain unanswered; **in Übung/Form** ~ to keep in practice/form; **wach** ~ to stay *or* keep awake; **wenn das Wetter so bleibt** if the weather stays *or* keeps like this; **sitzen/stehen** ~ to remain seated/standing; **bitte,** ~ **Sie doch sitzen** please don't get up; **von etw** ~ to stay *or* keep away from sth; **wo bleibst du so lange?** *(col)* what's keeping you?; **wo sind denn all die alten Häuser geblieben?** what happened to all the old houses?

(b) *(fig)* **bei etw** ~ to keep *or* stick *(col)* to sth; **das bleibt unter uns** that's (just) between ourselves; **wir möchten unter uns** ~ we want to keep ourselves to ourselves.

(c) *(übrigbleiben)* to be left, to remain. **es blieb keine andere Wahl** there was no other choice; **es bleibt abzuwarten** it remains to be seen; **es bleibt zu hoffen, daß ...** I/we can only hope that ...

(d) *(col: versorgt werden)* **und wo bleibe ich?** and what about me?; **sieh zu, wo du bleibst!** that's your problem!

bleibend *adj Wert, Erinnerung etc* lasting; *Schaden, Zähne* permanent.

bleibenlassen *vt sep irreg (col)* **(a)** *(unterlassen)* **etw** ~ to give sth a miss *(col)*; **das wirst du ganz schön** ~ you'll do nothing of the sort! **(b)** *(aufgeben)* to give up.

bleich *adj* pale. ~ **wie der Tod** deathly pale.

bleichen *vt* to bleach.

Bleich-: ~**gesicht** *nt* **(a)** *(col: blasser Mensch)* pasty-face *(col)*; **(b)** *(Weißer)* paleface; ~**mittel** *nt* bleach.

bleiern *adj* **(a)** *attr (aus Blei)* lead. **wie eine** ~**e Ente schwimmen** *(hum)* to swim like a brick. **(b)** *(fig)* leaden; *Verantwortung* onerous. **es lag ihr** ~ **in den Gliedern** her limbs were like lead.

Blei-: b~frei *adj* lead-free; ~**gehalt** *m* lead content; ~**gießen** *nt New Year's Eve custom of telling fortunes by the shapes made by molten lead dropped into cold water;* **b~haltig** *adj* **b~haltig sein** to contain lead; ~**kristall** *nt* lead crystal; ~**satz** *m* *(Typ)* hot-metal setting; ~**soldat** *m* ≈ tin soldier.

Bleistift *m* pencil; *(zum Malen)* crayon.

Bleistift-: ~**absatz** *m* stiletto heel; ~**spitzer** *m* pencil sharpener.

Bleivergiftung *f* lead poisoning.

Blende *f* **-n (a)** *(Lichtschutz)* shade, screen; *(an Fenster)* blind. **(b)** *(Phot) (Öffnung)* aperture; *(Einstellungsposition)* f-stop; *(Vorrichtung)* diaphragm. ~ **4 einstellen** to set the aperture to f/4. **(c)** *(Film, TV)* fade. **(d)** *(Sew)* trim.

blenden 1 *vt* **(a)** *(lit, fig: bezaubern)* to dazzle. **(b)** *(blind machen)* to blind. **2** *vi* to dazzle.

blendend *adj* splendid; *Pianist, Schüler etc* brilliant; *Stimmung* sparkling. **es geht mir** ~ I feel wonderful.

Blesse *f* **-n** *(Fleck)* blaze.

bleu [blø:] *adj inv (Fashion)* light blue.

Blick *m* **-e (a)** look; *(flüchtiger* ~*)* glance. **auf den ersten** ~ at first glance; **Liebe auf den ersten** ~ love at first sight; **auf den zweiten** ~ when one looks again; **mit einem** ~ at a glance; **jds** ~ *(dat)* **ausweichen** to avoid sb's eye; **jds** ~ **erwidern** to return sb's gaze; **jdn mit seinen** ~**en verschlingen** to devour sb with one's eyes; **sie zog alle** ~**e auf sich** everybody's eyes were drawn to her; **einen** ~ **auf etw** *(acc)* **werfen** to throw a glance at sth; **jdm keinen** ~ **schenken** not to spare sb a glance; **er hat keinen** ~ **für sie** he takes no notice of her; **wenn** ~**e töten könnten!** if looks could kill!; **mein** ~ **fiel auf sein leeres Glas** my eyes fell on his empty glass; **den** ~ **heben** to look up; **den** ~ **senken** to look down.

(b) *(Augenausdruck)* look in one's eyes. **den bösen** ~ **haben** to have the evil eye.

(c) *(Ausblick)* view. **ein Zimmer mit** ~ **auf den Park** a room overlooking the park.

(d) *(Verständnis)* **seinen** ~ **für etw schärfen** to increase one's awareness of sth; **einen (guten)** ~ **für etw haben** to have an eye for sth.

blicken *vi (auf+acc* at*)* to look; *(flüchtig* ~*)* to glance. **sich** ~ **lassen** to put in an appearance; **laß dich hier ja nicht mehr** ~! don't show your face here again!; **laß dich doch mal wieder** ~! why don't you drop in some time?; **das läßt tief** ~ that's very revealing.

Blick-: ~**fang** *m* eye-catcher; **als** ~**fang** to catch the eye; ~**feld** *nt* field of vision; **ins** ~**feld (der Öffentlichkeit) treten** to become the focus of (public) attention; ~**kontakt** *m* visual contact; ~**punkt** *m* **(a) im** ~**punkt der Öffentlichkeit stehen** to be in the public eye; **(b)** *(fig: Standpunkt)* point of view; ~**richtung** *f* line of vision; *(fig)* outlook; ~**winkel** *m (fig)* viewpoint.

blieb *pret of* **bleiben.**

blies *pret of* **blasen.**

blind *adj* **(a)** *(lit, fig)* blind *(für* to*)*; *Zufall* pure; *Alarm* false. **jdm** ~ **gehorchen** to obey sb blindly; **ein** ~**es Huhn findet auch mal ein Korn** *(Prov)* anyone can be lucky now and again; ~**er Fleck** *(Physiol)* blind spot; ~**e Gewalt** brute force; ~**er Eifer schadet nur** *(Prov)* it's not a good thing to be over-enthusiastic; **etw** ~ **herausgreifen** to pick sth at random. **(b)** *(getrübt)* dull; *Spiegel etc* clouded. **(c)** *(Archit)* false; *Fenster* blind, false. **(d) ein** ~**er Passagier** a stowaway.

Blinddarm *m (Anat)* appendix.

Blinddarm-: ~**entzündung** *f* appendicitis; ~**operation** *f* appendectomy.

Blindekuh *f no art* ~ **spielen** to play blind man's buff.

Blinden-: ~**hund** *m* guide-dog; ~**schrift** *f* braille.

Blinde(r) *mf decl as adj* blind person/man/woman *etc.* **die** ~**n** the blind; **das sieht doch ein** ~**r** *(col)* any fool can see that.

Blind-: ~**flug** *m* blind flight; ~**gänger** *m (Mil, fig)* dud; ~**heit** *f (lit, fig)* blindness; **mit** ~**heit geschlagen** *(fig)* blind; **b~lings** *adv* blindly; ~**schleiche** *f* slow-worm; **b~schreiben** *vti sep irreg* to touch-type; **b~wütig** *adj* in a blind rage.

blinken 1 *vi* **(a)** *(funkeln)* to gleam. **(b)** *(Leuchtturm)* to flash; *(Aut)* to indicate. **2** *vt Signal* to flash. **rechts/links** ~ to indicate right/left.

Blinker *m* - *(Aut)* indicator.

Blinklicht *nt* flashing light.

blinzeln *vi* to blink; *(zwinkern)* to wink; *(geblendet)* to squint.

Blitz *m* **-e (a)** *(das Blitzen)* lightning *no pl, no indef art;* *(*~*strahl)* flash of lightning; *(Lichtstrahl)* flash (of light). **vom** ~ **getroffen/erschlagen werden** to be struck by lightning; **wie vom** ~ **getroffen** *(fig)* thunderstruck; **einschlagen wie ein** ~ *(fig)* to come as a bombshell; **wie ein** ~ **aus heiterem Himmel** *(fig)* like a bolt from the blue; **wie der** ~ *(col)* like lightning. **(b)** *(Phot col)* flash; *(Blitzlichtgerät auch)* flashgun.

Blitz-: ~**ableiter** *m* lightning conductor; ~**aktion** *f* lightning operation; ~**angriff** *m (Mil)* lightning attack; **b~artig** = **b~schnell; b~(e)blank** *adj (col)* spick and span.

blitzen 1 *vi impers* **es blitzt** there's lightning; **es blitzt und donnert** there's thunder and lightning; **es fing an zu** ~ lightning began. **2** *vi* **(a)** *(strahlen)* to flash, to sparkle. **vor Sauberkeit** ~ to be sparkling clean. **(b)** *(Phot col)* to use a flash.

Blitz-: ~**gerät** *nt (Phot)* flash(gun); ~**karriere** *f* **eine ~karriere machen** to have a meteoric rise; ~**krieg** *m* blitzkrieg; ~**licht** *nt (Phot)* flash(light); **b~sauber** *adj* spick and span; ~**schlag** *m* flash of lightning; **vom ~schlag getroffen** struck by lightning; **b~schnell 1** *adj* lightning *attr;* **2** *adv* like lightning; *(plötzlich) verschwinden* in a flash; ~**strahl** *m* flash of lightning; ~**umfrage** *f* quick poll; ~**würfel** *m (Phot)* flashcube.

Block *m* ⸚**e (a)** block *(von, aus* of) **etw im ~ kaufen** to buy sth in bulk. **(b)** *pl auch* **-s** *(Häuser~)* block. **(c)** *pl* **-s** *(Rail)* block. **(d)** *(Pol) (Staaten~)* bloc; *(Fraktion)* faction.

Blockade *f (Absperrung)* blockade.

Block-: ~**bildung** *f (Pol)* formation of blocs/ factions; ~**buchstabe** *m* block letter *or* capital.

blocken *vti (Rail, Sport)* to block.

Block-: ~**flöte** *f* recorder; **b~frei** *adj* non-aligned; ~**freiheit** *f* non-alignment; ~**haus** *nt,* ~**hütte** *f* log cabin.

blockieren* **1** *vt* **(a)** to block. **(b)** *(mit Blockade)* to blockade. **2** *vi* to jam.

Blockierung *f siehe vt* blocking; blockade.

Block-: ~**politik** *f* joint policy; ~**schokolade** *f no pl* cooking chocolate; ~**schrift** *f* block capitals *pl or* letters *pl;* ~**stunde** *f (Sch)* double period.

blöd(e) *adj (col)* silly, stupid; *(ärgerlich) Sache, Situation* stupid; *Gefühl* funny.

blödeln *vi (col)* to fool around; *(Witze machen)* to make jokes.

Blödhammel *m (pej col)* idiot *(col).*

Blödheit *f* **(a)** *(Dummheit)* stupidity. **(b)** *(blödes Verhalten)* stupid thing; *(alberne Bemerkung)* silly *or* stupid remark. **(c)** *(Med)* imbecility.

Blödian *m* **-e** *(col),* **Blödmann** *m, pl* **-männer** *(col)* idiot.

Blödsinn *m no pl* nonsense. **das ist doch ~** that's nonsense; **~ machen** to fool about.

blödsinnig *adj* stupid, idiotic.

blöken *vi (Schaf)* to bleat.

blond *adj (blondhaarig)* fair(-haired); *(bei Frauen auch)* blonde; *(bei Männern auch)* blond. ~**es Gift** *(hum col)* blonde bombshell *(col).*

blond-: ~**gefärbt** *adj* dyed blonde/blond; ~**haarig** *adj* fair-haired, blonde/blond.

blondieren* *vt* to bleach.

Blondine *f* blonde.

bloß 1 *adj* **(a)** *(unbedeckt)* bare. **etw auf der ~en Haut tragen** to wear sth next to the skin; **mit ~en Füßen** barefooted, barefoot; **mit der ~en Hand** with one's bare hand; **mit ~em Auge** with the naked eye. **(b)** *attr (alleinig)* mere; *Neid, Dummheit* sheer; *Gedanke, Anblick* very. **er kam mit dem ~en Schrecken davon** he got off with no more than a fright. **2** *adv* only. **wie kann so etwas ~ geschehen?** how on earth can something like that happen?; **tu das ~ nicht wieder!** don't you dare do that again; **geh mir ~ aus dem Weg** just get out of my way.

Blöße *f* **-n** *(geh)* bareness; *(Nacktheit)* nakedness. **sich** *(dat)* **eine ~ geben** *(fig)* to reveal a weak spot.

Bloß-: **b~legen** *vt sep* to uncover; *(ausgraben auch, Med)* to expose; *(fig) Geheimnis* to reveal; *Hintergründe* to bring to light; **b~liegen** *vi sep irreg aux sein* to be uncovered; *(Ausgegrabenes auch, Med)* to be exposed; **b~stellen** *sep* **1** *vt jdn* to show up; *Lügner, Betrüger* to unmask, to expose; **2** *vr* to show oneself up; **sich als Lügner b~stellen** to show oneself to be a liar; ~**stellung** *f siehe vt* showing up; unmasking, exposing.

Blouson [blu'zõː] *m or nt* **-s** blouson, bomber jacket.

Blücher *m:* **er geht ran wie ~** *(col)* he doesn't hang about *(col).*

Bluff *m* **-s** bluff.

bluffen *vti* to bluff.

blühen *vi* **(a)** *(Blume)* to flower, to bloom; *(Bäume)* to be in blossom, to blossom. **(b)** *(col: bevorstehen)* to be in store *(jdm* for sb). **... dann blüht dir aber was** ... then you'll be in for it *(col).*

blühend *adj Baum* blossoming; *Aussehen* radiant; *Pflanze* blooming; *Garten* full of flowers; *(fig) Geschäft etc* flourishing, thriving; *Unsinn* absolute; *Phantasie* vivid, lively. **wie das ~e Leben aussehen** to look the very picture of health.

Blume *f* **-n (a)** flower; *(Topfblume)* pot plant. **jdm etw durch die ~ sagen** to say sth in a roundabout way to sb. **(b)** *(von Wein)* bouquet; *(von Bier)* head.

Blumen- *in cpds* flower; ~**bank** *f (am Fenster)* windowsill; *(~ständer)* flower stand; ~**beet** *nt* flowerbed; ~**erde** *f* potting compost; ~**geschäft** *nt* florist; ~**kasten** *m* window box; ~**kohl** *m no pl* cauliflower; ~**meer** *nt* sea of flowers; ~**muster** *nt* floral pattern; **b~reich** *adj* full of flowers; *(fig) Sprache etc* flowery; ~**strauß** *m* bouquet, bunch of flowers; ~**topf** *m* flowerpot; **damit ist kein ~topf zu gewinnen** *(col)* that's nothing to write home about *(col);* ~**zucht** *f* flower growing; ~**zwiebel** *f* bulb.

blumig *adj (lit, fig)* flowery.

Bluse *f* **-n** blouse.

Blut *nt no pl (lit, fig)* blood. **er lag in seinem ~** he lay in a pool of blood; **es ist viel ~ geflossen** there was a lot of bloodshed; **er kann kein ~ sehen** he can't stand the sight of blood; **~ geleckt haben** *(fig)* to have tasted blood; **böses ~ machen** *or* **schaffen** to cause bad blood; **jdm steigt das ~ in den Kopf** the blood rushes to sb's head; **ihnen gefror** *or* **erstarrte das ~ in den Adern** their blood froze; **heißes** *or* **feuriges ~ haben** to be hot-blooded; **kaltes ~ bewahren** to remain unmoved; **(nur) ruhig ~** keep your shirt on *(col);* **jdn/sich bis aufs ~ bekämpfen** to fight sb/fight bitterly; **frisches ~** *(fig)* new blood; **~ und Wasser schwitzen** *(col)* to sweat blood; **das liegt mir/ ihm im ~** it's in my/his blood.

Blut-: ~**ader** *f* vein; ~**alkohol(gehalt)** *m* blood alcohol level; ~**apfelsine** *f* blood orange; **b~arm** *adj (Med, fig)* anaemic *(Brit),* anemic *(US);* ~**armut** *f (Med)* anaemia *(Brit),* anemia *(US);* ~**austausch** *m (Med)* exchange transfusion; ~**bad** *nt* bloodbath; ~**bahn** *f* bloodstream; ~**bank** *f* blood bank; **b~befleckt** *adj* bloodstained; **b~beschmiert** *adj* smeared with blood; ~**bild** *nt* blood count; ~**buche** *f* copper beech; ~**druck** *m* blood pressure.

Blüte *f* **-n (a)** flower, bloom; *(von Baum)* blossom. **eine ~ seiner Phantasie** a figment of his imagination. **(b)** *(das Blühen, Blütezeit)* **in (voller) ~ stehen** to be in (full) flower/blossom; *(Kultur, Geschäft)* to be flourishing; **sich zur vollen ~ entfalten** to come into full flower; *(Mädchen, Kultur)* to blossom; **seine ~ erleben** *(Kultur etc)* to reach its peak; **in der ~ seiner Jahre** in the prime of his life. **(c)** *(col: Falschgeld)* dud *(col).*

Blut|egel *m* leech.

bluten *vi* to bleed *(an+dat, aus* from). **mir blutet das Herz** my heart bleeds.

Blüten-: ~**blatt** *nt* petal; ~**honig** *m* honey *(made from flowers);* ~**kelch** *m* calyx; ~**staub** *m* pollen.

Blut|entnahme *f* taking a blood sample.

Bluter *m* **-** *(Med)* haemophiliac *(Brit),* hemophiliac *(US).*

Blut|erguß *m* haemorrhage *(Brit),* hemorrhage *(US); (blauer Fleck)* bruise.

Bluterkrankheit *f* haemophilia *(Brit),* hemophilia *(US).*

Blütezeit *f* **(a) während der ~ der Kirschbäume** while the cherries were in blossom. **(b)** *(fig)* heyday; *(von Mensch)* prime.

Blut-: ~**farbstoff** *m* haemoglobin *(Brit),* hemoglobin *(US);* ~**fleck** *m* bloodstain; ~**gefäß** *nt* blood vessel; ~**gerinnsel** *nt* blood clot; ~**gruppe**

f blood group; ~**hund** *m (lit, fig)* bloodhound.

blutig *adj* **(a)** *(lit, fig)* bloody. **er hat ihn ~ geschlagen** he hit him and made him bleed. **(b)** *(col) Anfänger* absolute; *Ernst* deadly.

Blut-: b~jung *adj* very young; ~**konserve** *f* unit *or* pint of stored blood; ~**körperchen** *nt* blood corpuscle; ~**kreislauf** *m* blood circulation; ~**lache** *f* pool of blood; **b~leer** *adj* bloodless; ~**leere** *f no pl* lack of blood; **b~los** *adj* bloodless; *(fig)* anaemic *(Brit)*, anemic *(US)*; ~**orange** *f* blood orange; ~**probe** *f* blood test; ~**rache** *f* blood feud; ~**rausch** *m* frenzy; **b~rot** *adj (liter)* blood-red; **b~rünstig** *adj* bloodthirsty; ~**sauger** *m (lit, fig)* bloodsucker; *(Vampir)* vampire.

Blutsbruder *m* blood brother.

Blut-: ~**schande** *f* incest; ~**senkung** *f (Med)* sedimentation of the blood; **eine ~senkung machen** to test the sedimentation rate of the blood; ~**spender** *m* blood donor; ~**spur** *f* trail of blood; **b~stillend** *adj* styptic.

Blutstropfen ['blu:ts-] *m* drop of blood.

Blutsturz *m* haemorrhage *(Brit)*, hemorrhage *(US)*.

Bluts-: b~verwandt *adj* related by blood; ~**verwandtschaft** *f* blood relationship.

Blut-: ~**tat** *f* bloody deed; ~**transfusion** *f* blood transfusion; **b~überströmt** *adj* streaming with blood; ~**übertragung** *f* blood transfusion.

Blutung *f* bleeding *no pl*; *(monatliche)* period.

Blut-: b~unterlaufen *adj* suffused with blood; *Augen* bloodshot; ~**untersuchung** *f* blood test; ~**vergießen** *nt no pl* bloodshed *no indef art*; ~**vergiftung** *f* blood-poisoning *no indef art*; ~**verlust** *m* loss of blood; ~**wurst** *f* blood pudding *(US)*, black pudding *(Brit)*; ~**zuckerspiegel** *m* blood sugar level; ~**zufuhr** *f* blood supply.

Bö *f* **-en** gust (of wind); *(stärker, mit Regen)* squall.

Boa *f* **-s** *(Schlange, Schal)* boa.

Bob *m* **-s** bob(sleigh).

Bob-: ~**bahn** *f* bob(sleigh) run; ~**fahrer** *m* bobber.

Boccia ['bɔtʃa] *nt or f no pl* bowls *sing*.

Bock *m* **¨e (a)** *(Reh~, Kaninchen~)* buck; *(Schafs~)* ram; *(Ziegen~)* he-goat, billy-goat. **alter ~** *(col)* old goat *(col)*; **sturer/geiler ~** *(col)* stubborn old devil *(col)*/randy *(Brit)* or horny old goat *(col)*; **den ~ zum Gärtner machen** *(fig)* to choose the worst possible person for the job; **einen ~ schießen** *(fig col)* to boob *(Brit col)*, to goof *(US col)*. **(b)** *(Gestell)* stand; *(Stützgerät)* support; *(für Auto)* ramp; *(aus Holzbalken, mit Beinen)* trestle; *(Säge~)* sawhorse. **(c)** *(Sport)* buck. **(d)** *(col: Lust)* **¨~e** *or* **einen ~ haben, etw zu tun** to fancy doing sth.

Bockbier *nt* bock (beer) *(type of strong beer)*.

bocken *vi* **(a)** *(Zugtier etc)* to refuse to move; *(nicht springen wollen: Pferd)* to refuse. **vor einer Hürde ~** to refuse to jump. **(b)** *(col: Auto, Mensch)* to play up.

bockig *adj (col)* contrary, awkward.

Bockmist *m (col: dummes Gerede)* bullshit *(col!)*; **~ machen** to make a balls-up *(col!)*.

Bockshorn *nt*: **sich von jdm ins ~ jagen lassen** to let sb upset one.

Bock-: ~**springen** *nt* leapfrog; *(Sport)* vaulting; ~**sprung** *m* leapfrog; *(Sport)* vault; ~**wurst** *f* bockwurst *(large frankfurter)*.

Boden *m* **¨ (a)** ground; *(Erdreich auch)* soil; *(Fuß~)* floor; *(no pl: Terrain)* soil. **auf spanischem ~** on Spanish soil; **zu ~ fallen** to fall to the ground; **festen ~ unter den Füßen haben** to be on firm ground, to be on terra firma; **den ~ unter den Füßen verlieren** *(lit)* to lose one's footing; *(fig: in Diskussion)* to get out of one's depth; **ihm wurde der ~ (unter den Füßen) zu heiß** *(fig)* things were getting too hot for him; **ich hätte (vor Scham) im ~ versinken können** *(fig)* I was so ashamed that I wished the ground would swallow me up; **am ~ zerstört sein** *(col)* to be shattered *(col)*; **(an) ~ gewinnen/verlieren** *(fig)* to gain/lose ground; **~ gutmachen** *(fig)* to make up ground; **etw aus dem ~ stampfen** *(fig)* to conjure sth up out of nothing; *Häuser* to build overnight; **auf fruchtbaren ~ fallen** *(fig)* to fall on fertile ground; **jdm/einer Sache den ~ bereiten** *(fig)* to prepare the ground for sb/sth.
(b) *(unterste Fläche)* bottom; *(Torten~)* base.
(c) *(Dach~, Heu~)* loft.
(d) *(fig: Grundlage)* **auf dem ~ der Tatsachen stehen** to base oneself on fact; **auf dem ~ der Tatsachen bleiben** to stick to the facts; **sich auf unsicherem ~ bewegen** to be on shaky ground; **einer Sache** *(dat)* **den ~ entziehen** to knock the bottom out of sth.

Boden-: ~**belag** *m* floor covering; ~**ertrag** *m (Agr)* crop yield; ~**fläche** *f (Agr)* area of land; *(von Zimmer)* floor space *or* area; ~**frost** *m* ground frost; ~**haftung** *f (Aut)* road holding *no indef art*; ~**heizung** *f* underfloor heating; ~**kammer** *f* attic; ~**kontrolle** *f (Space)* ground control; **b~los** *adj* bottomless; *(col: unerhört)* indescribable, incredible; ~**personal** *nt (Aviat)* ground personnel *pl*; ~**satz** *m* sediment; *(von Kaffee auch)* grounds *pl*; ~**schätze** *pl* mineral resources *pl*; ~**schicht** *f* layer of soil; *(Geol)* stratum; ~**see** *m*: **der ~see** Lake Constance; ~**spekulation** *f* land speculation; ~**station** *f (Space)* ground station; ~**turnen** *nt* floor exercises *pl*.

bog *pret of* **biegen.**

Bogen *m* **-** *or* **¨ (a)** curve, bend; *(Math)* arc; *(Mus)* tie; *(bei verschiedenen Noten)* slur; *(Ski)* turn. **einen ~ fahren** *(Ski)* to do a turn; **den ~ heraushaben** *(col)* to have got the hang of it *(col)*; **einen ~ machen** *(Fluß etc)* to curve; **einen großen ~ um jdn/etw machen** *(meiden)* to give sb/sth a wide berth; **jdn in hohem ~ hinauswerfen** *(col)* to fling sb out. **(b)** *(Archit)* arch. **(c)** *(Waffe, Mus: Geigen~ etc)* bow. **den ~ überspannen** *(fig)* to go too far. **(d)** *(Papier~)* sheet (of paper).

Bogen-: b~förmig *adj* arched; ~**gang** *m (Archit)* arcade; ~**schießen** *nt* archery; ~**schütze** *m* archer, bowman.

Bohle *f* **-n** (thick) board.

böhmisch *adj* Bohemian. **das sind für mich ~e Dörfer** *(col)* that's all Greek to me *(col)*.

Bohne *f* **-n** bean. **dicke/grüne/weiße ~n** broad/green *or* French *or* runner/haricot beans; **blaue ~** *(col)* bullet; **nicht die ~** *(col)* not one little bit; **du hast wohl ~n in den Ohren** *(col)* are you deaf or something?

Bohnen-: ~**eintopf** *m* bean stew; ~**kaffee** *m* real coffee; **gemahlener ~kaffee** ground coffee; ~**kraut** *nt* savory; ~**stange** *f (fig col)* beanpole *(col)*; ~**stroh** *nt*: **dumm wie ~stroh** *(col)* (as) thick as two (short) planks *(col)*; ~**suppe** *f* bean soup.

bohnern *vti* to polish.

Bohnerwachs *nt* floor polish *or* wax.

bohren 1 *vt* to bore; *(mit Bohrer auch)* to drill; *(hineindrücken) Pfahl, Schwert etc* to sink *(in+acc* into*)*. **2** *vi* **(a)** to bore *(in+dat* into*)*; to drill *(nach* for*)*. **in einem Zahn ~** to drill a tooth; **in der Nase ~** to pick one's nose. **(b)** *(fig) (drängen)* to keep on; *(peinigen: Schmerz, Zweifel etc)* to gnaw. **3** *vr* **sich in/durch etw** *(acc)* **~** to bore its way into/through sth.

bohrend *adj (fig) Blick* piercing; *Schmerz, Zweifel* gnawing; *Frage* probing.

Bohrer *m* **-** *(elektrisch)* drill; *(Hand~)* gimlet.

Bohr-: ~**insel** *f* drilling rig; *(für Öl auch)* oilrig; ~**loch** *nt* borehole; *(in Holz, Metall etc)* drill-hole; ~**maschine** *f* drill; ~**turm** *m* derrick.

Bohrung *f* **(a)** *siehe vt* boring; drilling; sinking. **(b)** *(Loch)* bore(-hole); *(in Metall etc)* drill-hole.

böig *adj siehe* **Bö** gusty; squally.

Boiler ['bɔylɐ] *m* - hot-water heater.

Boje *f* **-n** buoy.

Bolivien [-iən] *nt* Bolivia.

Böller *m* - (small) cannon *(for ceremonial use).*

Bollwerk *nt (lit, fig)* bulwark.

Bolschewismus *m* Bolshevism.

Bolzen *m* **- (a)** *(Tech)* pin; *(esp mit Gewinde)* bolt. **(b)** *(Geschoß)* bolt.

bolzen *(col)* **1** *vi* to kick about. **2** *vt Ball* to slam.

Bombardement [bõbardə'mã:] *nt* **-s** bombardment; *(mit Bomben)* bombing. **ein ~ von** *(fig)* a deluge of.

bombardieren* *vt (lit)* to bomb; *(fig)* to bombard.

Bombardierung *f* bombing; *(fig)* bombardment.

bombastisch *adj* bombastic.

Bombe *f* **-n** bomb; *(Sport col: Schuß)* cracker *(col).* **wie eine ~ einschlagen** to come as a (real) bombshell; **eine ~ platzen lassen** *(fig)* to drop a bombshell.

Bomben- *in cpds (Mil)* bomb; *(col: hervorragend)* fantastic *(col)*, great *(col)*; **~angriff, ~anschlag** *m* bomb attack; **~erfolg** *m (col)* smash hit *(col)*; **b~fest** *adj (col) Klebestelle* absolutely secure; **es steht b~fest, daß ...** it's absolutely certain *or* a dead cert *(col)* that ...; **~geschäft** *nt (col)* **ein ~geschäft sein** to be a gold mine; **ein ~geschäft machen** to do a roaring trade *(col) (mit* in); **~hitze** *f (col)* sweltering heat *no indef art*; **~leger(in** *f)* *m* bomber; **~Krater** *m* bomb crater; **b~sicher** *adj* **(a)** *(Mil)* bombproof; **(b)** *(col)* dead certain *(col)*; **~splitter** *m* bomb fragment; **~teppich** *m* **einen ~teppich legen** to blanket-bomb an/the area; **~trichter** *m* bomb crater.

Bomber *m* - bomber.

Bon [bɔŋ] *m* **-s** voucher; *(Kassenzettel)* receipt.

Bonbon [bɔŋ'bɔŋ] *nt or m* **-s** sweet *(Brit)*, candy *(US).*

Bonbonniere [bɔŋbɔ'nieːrə] *f* **-n** box of chocolates.

Bongo [bɔŋgo] *nt or f* **-s** bongo (drum).

Bonus *m* **-** *or* **-se** bonus; *(Univ, Sport: Punktvorteil)* bonus points *pl.*

Bonze *m* **-n** big shot *(col).*

Boot *nt* **-e** boat. **~ fahren** to go out in a boat; **wir sitzen alle in einem ~** *(fig)* we're all in the same boat.

Boots-: ~fahrt *f* boat trip; **~haus** *nt* boathouse; **~mann** *m, pl* **~leute** *(Naut)* bo'sun, boatswain; *(Dienstgrad)* petty officer.

Bord[1] *m no pl* **an ~ (eines Schiffes)** aboard *or* on board (a ship); **alle Mann an ~!** all aboard!; **an ~ gehen** to go aboard; **Mann über ~!** man overboard!; **über ~ gehen** to go overboard; *(fig)* to go by the board; **über ~ werfen** *(lit, fig)* to throw overboard, to jettison; **von ~ gehen** to leave the ship/the plane; *(esp Passagiere am Ziel)* to disembark.

Bord[2] *nt* **-e** *(Wandbrett)* shelf.

Bord-: ~buch *nt* log(book); **~computer** *m (Space)* on-board computer.

Bordell *nt* **-e** brothel.

Bord-: ~funk *m (Naut)* (ship's) radio; *(Aviat)* (aircraft) radio equipment; **~funker** *m (Naut, Aviat)* radio operator; **~stein(kante** *f)* *m* kerb *(Brit)*, curb *(US).*

borgen *vti* **(a)** *(erhalten)* to borrow *(von* from*).* **(b)** *(geben)* to lend, to loan *(jdm etw* sb sth, sth to sb*).*

Borke *f* **-n** bark.

borniert *adj* bigoted, narrow-minded.

Börse *f* **-n (a)** *(Geld~)* purse; *(für Männer)* wallet *(Brit)*, billfold *(US).* **(b)** *(Fin)* stock market, stock exchange.

Börsen-: ~bericht *m* stock market report; **~geschäft** *nt (Wertpapierhandel)* stockbroking; *(Transaktion)* stock market transaction; **~kurs** *m* stock market price; **~makler** *m* stockbroker; **~notierung** *f* quotation (on the stock exchange); **~spekulation** *f* speculation on the stock market; **~tendenz** *f* stock market trend.

Borste *f* **-n** bristle.

Borstenvieh *nt* pigs *pl,* swine *pl.*

borstig *adj (lit, fig)* bristly.

Borte *f* **-n** braid trimming.

bös|artig *adj* malicious, nasty; *Tier* vicious; *(Med)* malignant.

Bös|artigkeit *f siehe adj* maliciousness, nastiness; viciousness; malignancy.

Böschung *f* embankment; *(von Straße auch)* bank.

böse *adj* **(a)** bad; *(stärker)* evil, wicked; *(col: unartig auch)* naughty; *Überraschung, Geschichte, Wunde* nasty. **ein ~r Geist** an evil spirit; **das war keine ~ Absicht** there was no harm intended; **das war nicht ~ gemeint** I/he *etc* didn't mean it nastily; **~ Folgen** dire consequences; **~ Zeiten** bad times; **das/es sieht ~ aus** things look/it looks bad. **(b)** *(verärgert)* angry *(+dat, auf+acc, mit* with*).* **im ~n auseinandergehen** to part on bad terms.

Böse(s) *nt decl as adj* evil; *(Schaden, Leid)* harm. **jdm ~s antun** to do sb harm; **ich will dir doch nichts ~s** I don't mean you any harm; **ich dachte an** *or* **ahnte gar nichts ~s, als ...** I was quite unsuspecting when ...

Bösewicht *m* **-e** *or* **-er** *(old, hum)* villain.

Bos-: b~haft *adj* malicious; **~haftigkeit** *f* maliciousness; **~heit** *f* malice; *(Bemerkung, Handlung)* malicious remark/thing to do.

Boß *m* **-sse** *(col)* boss *(col).*

böswillig *adj* malicious; *(Jur auch)* wilful. **in ~er Absicht** with malicious intent.

Böswilligkeit *f* malice, maliciousness.

bot *pret of* **bieten.**

Botanik *f* botany.

Botaniker(in *f)* *m* - botanist.

botanisch *adj* botanic.

Bote *m (wk)* **-n, -n (a)** messenger; *(Kurier)* courier; *(Post~)* postman *(Brit)*, mailman *(US).* **(b)** *(fig: Anzeichen)* herald.

Botengang *m* errand. **einen ~gang machen** to run an errand.

Botin *f siehe* **Bote (a)** messenger; courier; postwoman *(Brit)*, mailwoman *(US).*

Botschaft *f* **(a)** *(Mitteilung)* message; *(esp amtlich)* communication. **eine freudige ~** good news; **die Frohe ~** the Gospel. **(b)** *(Pol: Vertretung)* embassy.

Botschafter(in *f)* *m* - ambassador.

Bottich *m* **-e** tub.

Bouillon [bul'jɔn, bul'jõː] *f* **-s** stock; *(auf Speisekarte)* bouillon, consommé.

Bouillonwürfel *m* stock cube.

Boulevard- [bulə'vaːɐ-]: **~blatt** *nt (col)* tabloid; **~presse** *f (col)* popular press; **~stück** *nt* light play/comedy; **~theater** *nt* light theatre *(Brit) or* theater *(US)*; **~zeitung** *f* tabloid.

Bouquet [bu'keː] *nt* **-s = Bukett.**

Bourgeoisie [burʒoa'ziː] *f (geh)* bourgeoisie.

Boutique [bu'tiːk] **-n** boutique.

Bowle ['boːlə] *f* **-n** *(Getränk)* punch.

Bowling ['boːlɪŋ] *nt* **-s** (tenpin) bowling. **~ spielen gehen** to go bowling.

Bowlingbahn *f* bowling alley.

Box *f* **(a)** *(Behälter)* box. **(b)** *(für Pferde)* Box; *(in Großgarage)* parking place; *(für Rennwagen)* pit. **(c)** *(Lautsprecher~)* speaker.

Boxen *nt no pl (Sport)* boxing.

boxen 1 *vi* to box; *(zur Übung)* to spar; *(mit Fäusten zuschlagen)* to hit out, to punch. **gegen jdn ~** to fight sb. **2** *vt jdn* to punch, to hit. **3** *vr* **(a)** *(col: sich schlagen)* to have a punch-up *(col) or* a fight. **(b)** *(sich einen Weg bahnen)* to fight one's way.

Boxer *m* - *(Sportler, Hund)* boxer.

Boxer-: ~motor *m (Tech)* opposed cylinder engine; **~nase** *f* boxer's nose, broken nose.

Box-: ~handschuh *m* boxing glove; **~kalf** *nt no pl*

box calf; **~kampf** *m* fight, (boxing) match; **~ring** *m* boxing ring; **~sport** *m* boxing.

Boykott [bɔy'kɔt] *m* **-e** *or* **-s** boycott.

boykottieren* [bɔykɔ'ti:rən] *vt* to boycott.

brabbeln *vi (col)* to mumble, to mutter.

brach *pret of* **brechen.**

brachial *adj* **mit ~er Gewalt** with brute force.

Brach-: **~land** *nt* fallow (land); **b~liegen** *vi sep irreg (lit, fig)* to lie fallow.

brachte *pret of* **bringen.**

Branche ['brã:ʃə] *f* **-n** *(Gewerbe)* trade; *(Wirtschaftszweig)* industry. **in welcher ~ sind Sie tätig?** what line (of business) are you in?

Branchen-: **~kenntnis** *f* knowledge of the trade/industry; **b~üblich** *adj* usual in the trade/industry; **~verzeichnis** *nt* yellow pages.

Brand *m* **¨-e (a)** *(Feuer)* fire; *(lodernd auch)* blaze. **in ~ geraten** to catch fire; **in ~ stehen** to be on fire; **etw in ~ stecken** to set fire to sth. **(b)** *(von Porzellan etc)* firing. **(c)** *(fig col: großer Durst)* raging thirst. **(d)** *(Pflanzenkrankheit)* blight.

Brand-: **b~aktuell** *adj (col) Thema, Frage* red-hot *(col)*; *Buch* hot from the presses; **~bekämpfung** *f* firefighting; **~blase** *f* (burn) blister; **~bombe** *f* incendiary bomb; **b~eilig** *adj (col)* extremely urgent; **~gefahr** *f* danger of fire; **~geruch** *m* smell of burning; **~herd** *m* source of the fire; *(fig)* source; **~katastrophe** *f* fire disaster; **~mal** *nt* **-e** brand; *(fig auch)* stigma; **b~ marken** *vt insep (fig)* **jdn als etw b~marken** *(fig)* to brand sb (as) sth; **~meister** *m* fire chief; **b~neu** *adj (col)* brand-new; **~opfer** *nt* **(a)** *(Rel)* burnt offering; **(b)** *(Mensch)* fire victim; **~salbe** *f* ointment for burns; **~satz** *m* incendiary device; **~schaden** *m* fire damage; **~schutz** *m* fire protection; **~stelle** *f* fire, blaze; *(verbrannte Stelle)* burnt patch; **~stifter** *m* arsonist; **~stiftung** *f* arson.

Brandung *f* surf, breakers *pl.*

Brand-: **~ursache** *f* cause of a/the fire; **~wunde** *f* burn; **~zeichen** *nt* brand.

brannte *pret of* **brennen.**

Branntwein *m* spirits *pl.* **Whisky ist ein ~** whisky is a (type of) spirit.

Branntwein-: **~brenner** *m* distiller; **~brennerei** *f* distillery; **~steuer** *f* tax on spirits.

Brasil *f* **-(s)** Brazil cigar.

Brasilianer(in *f*) *m* **-** Brazilian.

brasilianisch *adj* Brazilian.

Brasilien [-iən] *nt* Brazil.

Brat|apfel *m* baked apple.

braten *pret* **briet,** *ptp* **gebraten 1** *vti* to roast; *(ohne Fett)* to bake; *(in der Pfanne)* to fry. **2** *vi (col: in der Sonne)* to roast.

Braten *m* **-** roast. **kalter ~** cold meat; **ein fetter ~** *(fig)* a prize catch; **den ~ riechen** *(col)* to smell a rat *(col).*

Braten-: **~fleisch** *nt* meat for roasting/frying; **~soße** *f* gravy; **~wender** *m* **-** fishslice.

Brat-: **b~fertig** *adj* oven-ready; **~fett** *nt* fat for frying/roasting; **~fisch** *m* fried fish; **~hähnchen, ~hendl -(n)** *(Aus, SGer) nt* roast chicken; **~hering** *m* fried herring; **~huhn** *nt* roast chicken; *(zum Braten)* roasting chicken; **~kartoffeln** *pl* fried potatoes; **~ofen** *m* oven; **~pfanne** *f* frying pan, skillet *(US)*; **~röhre** *f* oven; **~rost** *m* grill.

Bratsche *f* **-n** viola.

Bratwurst *f* (fried) sausage.

Brauch *m, pl* **Bräuche** custom, tradition. **das ist bei uns so ~** *(col)* that's traditional with us.

brauchbar *adj* **(a)** *(benutzbar)* useable; *Plan* workable; *(nützlich)* useful. **(b)** *(ordentlich) Mensch, Idee* reasonable.

Brauchbarkeit *f* usefulness; *(von Plan)* workability.

brauchen 1 *vt* **(a)** *(nötig haben)* to need *(für, zu* for). **es braucht alles seine Zeit** everything takes time; **wie lange braucht man, um ...?** how long does it take to ...? **(b)** *(benutzen)* to use. **wir können das/ihn nicht ~** *(col)* we've no use for that/him. **(c)** *(col: verbrauchen)* to use (up). **2** *aux* to need. **du brauchst es ihm nicht (zu) sagen** you needn't tell *or* don't need to tell him that; **du hättest das nicht (zu) tun ~** you needn't have done that, you didn't need to do that; **du brauchst nur an(zu)rufen** you only have *or* need to call; **es braucht nicht gleich zu sein** it doesn't need to be done immediately; **es hätte nicht zu sein ~** there was no need for that; *(hätte nicht geschehen müssen)* that needn't have happened.

Brauchtum *nt* customs *pl*, traditions *pl.*

Braue *f* **-n** (eye)brow.

brauen *vti Bier* to brew; *(col) Tee* to brew up; *Kaffee* to make.

Brauer *m* **-** brewer.

Brauerei *f* brewery.

braun *adj* brown; *(col: ~haarig)* brown-haired; *(pej)* Nazi. **~ werden** *(Mensch)* to get a (sun-)tan, to go *or* get brown.

Braun *nt* **-** brown.

Braun-: **b~äugig** *adj* brown-eyed; **~bär** *m* brown bear.

Bräune *f no pl* brown(ness); *(von Sonne)* (sun-)tan.

bräunen 1 *vt (Cook)* to brown; *(Sonne etc)* to tan. **2** *vi (Cook)* to go *or* turn brown; *(Mensch)* to tan, to go brown; *(Sonne)* to tan. **sich in der Sonne ~ lassen** to get a (sun-)tan.

Braun-: **b~gebrannt** *adj attr* (sun-)tanned, brown; **b~haarig** *adj* brown-haired; *Frau auch* brunette; **~kohle** *f* brown coal.

bräunlich *adj* brownish, browny.

Braunschweig *nt* Brunswick.

Bräunung *f* browning; *(von Haut)* bronzing. **eine tiefe ~ der Haut** a deep (sun-)tan.

Brause *f* **-n (a)** shower. **sich unter die ~ stellen** to have a shower. **(b)** *(~aufsatz)* shower attachment; *(an Schlauch, Gießkanne)* rose, sprinkler. **(c)** *(Getränk)* pop; *(Limonade)* (fizzy) lemonade; *(~pulver)* lemonade powder.

brausen 1 *vi* **(a)** *(tosen)* to roar; *(sprudeln: Wasser, Brandung)* to foam. **~der Beifall** thunderous applause. **(b)** *aux sein (rasen, rennen)* to race. **(c)** *auch vr (duschen)* to (have a) shower. **2** *vt Körperteil, Kinder* to put under the shower.

Brause-: **~pulver** *nt* lemonade powder; **~tablette** *f* lemonade tablet.

Braut *f, pl* **Bräute** bride; *(dated: Verlobte)* fiancée.

Brautführer *m* person who gives away the bride.

Bräutigam *m* **-e** (bride)groom; *(dated: Verlobter)* fiancé.

Braut-: **~jungfer** *f* bridesmaid; **~kleid** *nt* wedding dress; **~leute** *pl,* **~paar** *nt* bridal couple; *(dated: Verlobte)* engaged couple; **~schau** *f*: **auf ~schau sein** to be looking for a wife; **~schleier** *m* wedding *or* bridal veil.

brav *adj* **(a)** *Kind* good, well-behaved. **sei schön ~!** be a good boy/girl. **(b)** *(rechtschaffen)* worthy *(auch iro)*; *(bieder) Frisur, Kleid* plain. **~ seine Pflicht tun** to do one's duty worthily. **(c)** *(dated: tapfer)* brave.

bravo ['bra:vo] *interj* well done; *(für Künstler)* bravo.

Bravoruf *m* cheer.

Bravour [bra'vu:ɐ] *f no pl (geh)* bravura.

bravourös [bravu'rø:s] *adj (meisterhaft)* brilliant.

BRD [be:|ɛr'de:] *f* = **Bundesrepublik Deutschland** FRG.

Brech-: **b~bar** *adj* breakable; **~bohne** *f* French bean; **~eisen** *nt* crowbar; *(von Dieb)* jemmy, jimmy *(US).*

brechen *pret* **brach,** *ptp* **gebrochen 1** *vt* **(a)** to break; *(geh: pflücken) Blumen* to pluck. **sich/jdm den Arm ~** to break one's/sb's arm; **das wird ihm den Hals ~** *(fig)* that will be his downfall. **(b)** *(erbrechen)* to bring up. **2** *vi* **(a)** *aux sein* to break.

mir bricht das Herz it breaks my heart; **mit jdm/etw ~** to break with sb/sth; **~d voll sein** to be full to bursting. **(b)** *(sich erbrechen)* to be sick, to throw up. **3** *vr (Wellen)* to break; *(Lichtstrahl)* to be refracted; *(Schall)* to rebound *(an +dat* off*)*.

Brecher *m* - *(Welle)* breaker; *(Tech)* crusher.

Brech-: **~mittel** *nt* emetic; **er/das ist das reinste ~mittel** he/it makes me feel ill; **~reiz** *m* nausea; **~stange** *f* crowbar.

Brechung *f (der Wellen)* breaking; *(des Lichts)* refraction; *(des Schalls)* rebounding.

Brei *m* **-e** mush, paste; *(für Kinder, Kranke)* mash; *(Hafer~)* porridge; *(Grieß~)* semolina; *(Reis~)* rice pudding; *(Papier~)* pulp. **jdn zu ~ schlagen** *(col)* to beat sb to a pulp *(col)*; **um den heißen ~ herumreden** *(col)* to beat about the bush *(col)*.

breiig *adj* mushy.

breit 1 *adj* broad; *(esp bei Maßangabe)* wide; *Bekanntenkreis, Publikum, Interessen auch* wide; *Schrift* broadly spaced. **etw ~er machen** to broaden *or* widen sth; **die ~e Masse** the masses *pl.* **2** *adv* **~ gebaut** sturdily built; **sich ~ hinsetzen** to sit down squarely.

breitbeinig *adj* with one's legs apart.

Breite *f* **-n (a)** breadth; *(von Dialekt, Aussprache)* broadness; *(esp bei Maßangaben)* width. **der ~ nach** widthways; **etw in aller ~ erklären** to explain sth in great detail; **in die ~ gehen** *(col: dick werden)* to put it on a bit *(col)*. **(b)** *(Geog)* latitude; *(Gebiet)* part of the world. **es liegt 20° nördlicher ~** it lies 20° north.

breiten *vtr* to spread.

Breiten-: **~grad** *m* (degree of) latitude; **~kreis** *m* parallel; **~sport** *m* popular sport; **~wirkung** *f* widespread impact.

Breit-: **b~gefächert** *adj* **ein b~gefächertes Angebot** a wide range; **b~machen** *vr sep (col)* **mach dich doch nicht so b~!** don't take up so much room; **sie hat sich im Zimmer b~gemacht** she spread her things all over the room; **b~schlagen** *vt sep irreg (col)* **sich b~schlagen lassen** to let oneself be talked round; **b~schult(e)rig** *adj* broad-shouldered; **~seite** *f (Naut)* broadside; **eine ~seite abgeben** to fire a broadside; **b~treten** *vt sep irreg (col)* to go on about; *Thema, Witz* to flog to death *(col)*; **~wandfilm** *m* film for the wide screen.

Bremsbelag *m* brake lining.

Bremse[1] *f* **-n** brake. **auf die ~(n) treten/steigen** *(col)* to put on *or* apply/slam on the brake(s).

Bremse[2] *f* **-n** *(Insekt)* horsefly.

bremsen 1 *vi* to brake. **der Wind bremst** the wind slows you *etc* down; **mit etw ~** *(col)* to cut down (on) sth. **2** *vt* **(a)** *Fahrzeug* to brake. **(b)** *(fig)* to restrict, to limit; *Entwicklung* to slow down. **er ist nicht zu ~** *(col)* there's no stopping him. **3** *vr* *(col)* **ich kann mich ~** not likely!

Brems-: **~flüssigkeit** *f* brake fluid; **~klotz** *m* brake block; **~kraft** *f* braking power; **~leistung** *f* braking efficiency; **~licht** *nt* brake light; **~pedal** *nt* brake pedal; **~spur** *f* skid mark *usu pl.*

Bremsung *f* braking.

Bremsweg *m* braking distance.

brennbar *adj* combustible, inflammable. **leicht ~** highly inflammable.

brennen *pret* **brannte,** *ptp* **gebrannt 1** *vi* to burn; *(Haus, Wald auch)* to be on fire; *(Glühbirne etc)* to be on; *(Zigarette)* to be alight; *(Stich)* to sting; *(Füße)* to hurt, to be sore. **das Streichholz brennt nicht** the match won't light; **auf der Haut ~** to burn the skin; **das Licht ~ lassen** to leave the light on; **es brennt!** fire!, fire!; *(fig)* it's urgent; **wo brennt's denn?** *(col)* what's the panic?; **darauf ~, etw zu tun** to be dying to do sth. **2** *vt* to burn; *Branntwein* to distil; *Porzellan, Ziegel* to fire, to bake; *Tier* to brand; *siehe* **gebrannt.**

brennend *adj (lit, fig)* burning; *Zigarette* lighted; *Durst* raging; *Haß* consuming. **das interessiert mich ~** *(col)* I would be incredibly interested.

Brenner *m* - **(a)** *(Tech)* burner. **(b)** *(Branntwein~)* distiller.

Brennerei *f* distillery.

Brennessel *f* stinging nettle.

Brenn-: **~holz** *nt* firewood; **~ofen** *m* kiln; **~punkt** *m (Math, Opt)* focus; **im ~punkt des Interesses stehen** to be the focus of attention; **~schere** *f* curling tongs *pl;* **~spiritus** *m* methylated spirits *sing or pl;* **~stab** *m* fuel rod; **~stoff** *m* fuel.

brenzlig *adj (col) Situation etc* precarious. **die Lage wurde ihm zu ~** things got too hot for him.

Bresche *f* **-n** breach, gap. **in die ~ springen** *(fig)* to step into the breach; **für jdn/etw eine ~ schlagen** *(fig)* to stand up for sb/sth.

Bretagne [bre'tanjə] *f* **die ~** Brittany.

Brett *nt* **-er (a)** board; *(länger und dicker)* plank; *(Regal)* shelf. **hier ist die Welt mit ~ern vernagelt** this is a parochial little place; **er hat ein ~ vor dem Kopf** *(col)* he's really thick. **(b)** **~er** *pl (fig) (Bühne)* boards *pl*; *(Boden des Boxrings)* floor, canvas; *(Skier)* planks *pl (col)*; **die ~er, die die Welt bedeuten** the stage.

Bretter-: **~bude** *f* booth; *(pej)* shack; **~zaun** *m* wooden fence; *(an Baustellen auch)* hoarding.

Brettspiel *nt* board game.

Brezel *f* **-n** pretzel.

Brief *m* **-e (a)** letter; *(Bibl)* epistle. **etw als ~ schicken** to send sth (by) letter post; **jdm ~ und Siegel auf etw** *(acc)* **geben** to give sb one's word. **(b)** *(St Ex: ~kurs)* selling rate.

Brief- *in cpds* letter; **~beschwerer** *m* - paperweight; **~bombe** *f* letter bomb.

Briefchen *nt* **ein ~ Streichhölzer** a book of matches; **ein ~ Nadeln** a packet of needles/pins.

Brief-: **~drucksache** *f* circular; **~fach** *nt* pigeonhole; **~freund(in** *f)* *m* penfriend, pen-pal; **~freundschaft** *f* **eine ~freundschaft mit jdm haben** to be penfriends with sb; **~geheimnis** *nt* privacy of the post; **~ kasten** *m* letter box, mail box *(US)*; **~kopf** *m* letterhead; **~kurs** *m (St Ex)* selling rate; **~lich** *adj* by letter; **mit jdm ~lich verkehren** to correspond with sb.

Briefmarke *f* stamp.

Briefmarken- *in cpds* stamp; **~automat** *m* stamp machine; **~kunde** *f* philately; **~sammler** *m* stamp collector, philatelist; **~sammlung** *f* stamp collection.

Brief-: **~öffner** *m* letter opener, paper knife; **~papier** *nt* letter paper, notepaper; **~porto** *nt (Gebühr)* letter rate; **~sendung** *f* letter, item sent by letter post; **~tasche** *f* wallet *(Brit)*, billfold *(US)*; **~taube** *f* carrier pigeon; **~träger(in** *f)* *m* postman/-woman, mailman/-woman *(US)*; **~umschlag** *m* envelope; **~verkehr** *m* correspondence; **~wahl** *f* postal vote; **~wähler** *m* postal voter; **~wechsel** *m* correspondence.

briet *pret of* **braten.**

Brigade *f* **(a)** *(Mil)* brigade. **(b)** *(DDR)* (work) team *or* group.

Brikett *nt* **-s** briquette.

Brikettzange *f* fire tongs *pl.*

brillant [brɪl'jant] *adj* brilliant.

Brillant [brɪl'jant] *m* diamond.

Brillantschmuck *m* diamonds *pl.*

Brille *f* **-n (a)** glasses *pl*, spectacles *pl*; *(Schutz~)* goggles *pl.* **eine ~** a pair of glasses *or* spectacles; **eine ~ tragen** to wear glasses. **(b)** *(Klosett~)* (toilet) seat.

Brillen-: **~etui** *nt* glasses *or* spectacle case; **~schlange** *f (hum)* four-eyes *(hum)*, woman who wears glasses; **~träger(in** *f)* *m* **er ist ~träger** he wears glasses.

Brimborium *nt (col)* fuss.

bringen *pret* **brachte,** *ptp* **gebracht** *vt* **(a)** *(her~)* to bring; *(holen auch)* to get *(jdm* for sb*)*; *(weg~)* to take. **der Besuch hat mir Blumen**

gebracht my visitors brought me flowers; **wir haben der Gastgeberin Blumen gebracht** we took our hostess flowers; **jdn zum Bahnhof/nach Hause** ~ to take sb to the station/home; **das Essen auf den Tisch** ~ to serve the food; **er bringt es nicht übers Herz** *or* **über sich** he can't bring himself to do it; **etw an sich** *(acc)* ~ to acquire sth; **etw mit sich** ~ to involve sth; **etw hinter sich** *(acc)* ~ to get sth over and done with.

(b) *(ein~) Gewinn* to bring in; *(Boden etc)* to produce; *Ärger* to cause; *Freude, Vorteile* to give. **das bringt nichts** *(fig col)* it's pointless.

(c) *(lenken, bewirken)* to bring. **das bringt dich vors Gericht/ins Gefängnis** you'll end up in court/prison if you do that; **das Gespräch auf etw** *(acc)* ~ to bring the conversation around to sth; **jdn in Gefahr** ~ to put sb in danger; **jdn zum Lachen/Weinen** ~ to make sb laugh/cry; **jdn zur Verzweiflung** ~ to drive sb to despair; **jdn zur Vernunft** ~ to bring sb to his senses; **jdn dazu** ~, **etw zu tun** to get sb to do sth; **jdn um etw** ~ to make sb lose sth, to do sb out of sth; **jdn ums Leben** ~ to kill sb.

(d) *(leisten, erreichen)* **es auf 80 Jahre** ~ to reach the age of 80; **das Auto bringt 180 km/h** *(col)* the car can do 180 km/h; **es zu etwas/nichts** ~ to get somewhere/nowhere; **es weit** ~ to do very well, to get far; **er hat es bis zum Direktor gebracht** he made it to director.

(e) *(senden) Bericht etc* to broadcast; *(im Fernsehen auch)* to show. **was bringt das Fernsehen/Radio heute abend?** what's on television/the radio tonight?

(f) *(veröffentlichen)* to print, to publish. **alle Zeitungen brachten es auf der ersten Seite** all the papers had it on the front page.

(g) *(aufführen) Stück* to do.

(h) *(col: schaffen, können)* **das bringt er nicht** he's not up to it; **er bringt's** he's got what it takes; **das bringt's doch nicht!** that's no damn use! *(col)*.

brisant *adj (fig)* controversial.

Brisanz *f (fig)* controversial nature.

Brise *f* **-n** breeze.

Brite *m (wk)* **-n, -n, Britin** *f* Briton, Britisher *(US)*. **er ist** ~ he is British; **die ~n** the British.

britisch *adj* British. **die B~en Inseln** the British Isles.

bröckelig *adj* crumbly; *Mauer* crumbling.

bröckeln *vti* to crumble.

Brocken *m* **-** lump, chunk; *(fig: Bruchstück)* scrap; *(col: Person)* lump *(col)*. **ein paar** ~ **Spanisch** a smattering of Spanish; **ein harter** ~ a tough nut to crack.

brocken *vt Brot* to break.

brodeln *vi (Wasser, Suppe)* to bubble. **es brodelt** *(fig)* there is seething unrest.

Brokat *m* **-e** brocade.

Brokkoli *pl* broccoli *sing*.

Brom *nt no pl* bromine.

Brombeere *f* blackberry, bramble.

Bronchie [-iə] *f usu pl* bronchial tube.

Bronchitis *f, pl* **Bronchitiden** bronchitis.

Bronze ['brõ:sə] *f* **-n** bronze.

Bronzemedaille *f* bronze medal.

Brosche *f* **-n** brooch.

Broschüre *f* **-n** brochure; *(Heft)* booklet.

Brot *nt* **-e** bread; *(Laib)* loaf (of bread); *(Scheibe)* slice (of bread); *(Sandwich)* sandwich; *(fig: Unterhalt)* daily bread *(hum)*, living. **ein** ~ **mit Käse** a slice of bread and cheese; **das ist ein hartes** ~ *(fig)* that's a hard way to earn one's living.

Brot-: ~aufstrich *m* spread *(for bread)*; **~belag** *m* topping *(for bread)*.

Brötchen *nt* roll. **kleine** ~ **backen** *(col)* to set one's sights lower.

Brötchengeber *m (hum)* employer, provider *(hum)*.

Brot-: ~erwerb *m* (way of earning one's) living; **~kasten** *m* bread bin; **~korb** *m* bread basket; **jdm den ~korb höher hängen** *(fig)* to keep sb short; **~krume** *f* breadcrumb; **~kruste** *f* crust; **~rinde** *f* crust; **~schnitte** *f* sandwich; **~zeit** *f (S Ger: Pause)* tea break; **~zeit machen** to have a tea break.

Bruch *m* **⸚e (a)** *(~stelle)* break; *(in Porzellan etc auch)* crack; *(das Brechen)* breaking. **zu** ~ **gehen** to get broken; ~ **machen** *(col)* to smash *(mit etw* sth*)*. **(b)** *(fig) (mit Vergangenheit, Partei, im Stil etc)* break; *(von Gesetz)* breaking, infringement; *(von Vertrag)* breach. **in die ⸚e gehen** *(Ehe, Freundschaft)* to break up; **es kam zum** ~ **zwischen ihnen** they broke up. **(c)** *(zerbrochene Ware)* broken biscuits/chocolate *etc; (Porzellan)* breakage. **(d)** *(Knochen~)* fracture, break; *(Eingeweide~)* hernia, rupture. **sich** *(dat)* **einen** ~ **heben** to rupture oneself. **(e)** *(Math)* fraction. **(f)** *(col: Einbruch)* break-in.

Bruch-: ~band *nt* truss; **~bude** *f (pej)* hovel; **b~fest** *adj* unbreakable.

brüchig *adj* brittle, fragile; *Gestein, Ehe, Moral* crumbling; *Leder, (fig) Stimme* cracked. ~ **werden** *(Gestein, Macht etc)* to (begin to) crumble; *(Ehe, Verhältnisse auch)* to (begin to) break up; *(Leder)* to crack *or* split.

Bruch-: ~landung *f* crashlanding; **~rechnung** *f* fractions *sing or pl; (Aufgabe)* sum with fractions; **~stelle** *f* break; *(von Knochen auch)* fracture; **~strich** *m (Math)* line (of a fraction); **~stück** *nt* fragment; *(von Lied, Rede etc auch)* snatch; **b~stückhaft** *adj* fragmentary; **~teil** *m* fraction; **im ~teil einer Sekunde** in a fraction of a second; **~zahl** *f (Math)* fraction.

Brücke *f* **-n (a)** *(lit, fig, Naut, Zahn~)* bridge. **alle ~n hinter sich** *(dat)* **abbrechen** *(fig)* to burn one's bridges behind one; **jdm goldene ~n bauen** to make things easy for sb; **~n schlagen** *(fig)* to forge links. **(b)** *(Turnen)* crab; *(Teppich)* rug.

Brücken-: ~kopf *m (Mil, fig)* bridgehead; **~schlag** *m (fig)* **das war der erste ~schlag** that forged the first link.

Bruder *m* **⸚ (a)** brother. **unter ⸚n** *(col)* between friends. **(b)** *(Mönch)* friar, brother. **(c)** *(col: Mann)* guy *(col)*. **ein warmer** ~ *(dated)* a pansy *(col)*; **euch ⸚ kenn' ich** *(pej)* I know *you* lot.

Bruder-: ~krieg *m* war between brothers; **~kuß** *m (fig)* fraternal kiss.

brüderlich *adj* fraternal, brotherly *no adv.* ~ **teilen** to share and share alike.

Brüderlichkeit *f no pl* brotherliness.

Bruder-: ~mord *m* fratricide; **~mörder** *m* fratricide; **~schaft** *f (Eccl)* brotherhood; **mit jdm ~schaft trinken** to agree to use the familiar du *(over a drink)*.

Brühe *f* **-n** *(Suppe)* (clear) soup; *(als Suppengrundlage)* stock; *(pej) (schmutzige Flüssigkeit)* sludge; *(Getränk)* dishwater *(col)*, muck *(col)*.

Brüh-: b~heiß *adj* scalding (hot); **b~warm** *adj (col)* hot from the press *(col)*; **er hat das sofort b~warm weitererzählt** he promptly spread it around; **~würfel** *m* stock cube; **~wurst** *f* sausage *(to be heated in water)*.

brüllen *vti* to shout, to roar; *(pej: laut weinen)* to yell, to bawl; *(Stier)* to bellow; *(Elefant)* to trumpet. **das ist zum B~** *(col)* it's a scream *(col)*.

Brummbär *m (col)* crosspatch *(col)*.

brummen *vti* **(a)** *(Insekt)* to buzz; *(Bär)* to growl; *(Motor, singen)* to drone; *(Kreisel etc)* to hum. **mir brummt der Kopf** my head is throbbing. **(b)** *(murren)* to grumble. **(c)** *(col: in Haft sein)* to be locked up *(col)*.

Brummer *m* **-** *(col)* **(a)** fly; wasp; bee. **(b)** *(Lastwagen)* juggernaut.

brummig *adj* grumpy.

Brumm-: ~kreisel *m (col)* humming-top; **~schädel** *m (col)* thick head *(col)*.

brünett *adj* dark(-haired). **sie ist** ~ she is a

brunette.
Brünette *f* brunette.
Brunft *f* ¨-e *(Hunt)* = **Brunst.**
Brunnen *m* - **(a)** well; *(fig liter)* fountain. **(b)** *(Spring~)* fountain. **(c)** *(Heilquelle)* spring.
Brunnen-: **~kresse** *f* watercress; **~schacht** *m* well shaft; **~vergifter(in** *f)* *m* - *(fig pej)* (political) trouble-maker; **~wasser** *nt* well water.
Brunst *f* ¨-e *(von männlichen Tieren)* rut; *(von weiblichen Tieren)* heat; *(~zeit)* rutting season.
Brunst-: **~schrei** *m* mating call; **~zeit** *f* rutting season.
brüsk *adj* brusque, curt.
brüskieren* *vt* to snub.
Brüskierung *f* snub.
Brüssel *nt* Brussels.
Brust *f* ¨-e **(a)** chest; *(fig: Inneres, Cook)* breast. **einen zur ~ nehmen** *(col)* to have a quickie *(col)*; **sich in die ~ werfen** *(fig)* to puff oneself up; **mit geschwellter ~** *(fig)* as proud as a peacock; **schwach auf der ~ sein** *(col)* to have a weak chest; *(hum: an Geldmangel leiden)* to be a bit short *(col)*. **(b)** *(weibliche ~)* breast. **einem Kind die ~ geben** to breastfeed a baby. **(c)** *(~schwimmen)* breast-stroke.
Brust-: **~bein** *nt* breastbone, sternum; **~bild** *nt* half-length portrait.
brüsten *vr* to boast, to brag *(mit* about*)*.
Brust-: **~höhe** *f*: **in ~höhe** chest high; **~kasten** *(col)*, **~korb** *m* thorax; **~krebs** *m* breast cancer, cancer of the breast; **~schwimmen** *nt* breast-stroke; **b~schwimmen** *vi infin only* to swim *or* do the breast-stroke; **~stimme** *f* chest-voice; **~stück** *nt (Cook)* breast; **~tasche** *f* breast pocket; *(Innentasche)* inside (breast) pocket; **~ton** *m* **im ~ton der Überzeugung** in a tone of utter conviction; **~umfang** *m* chest measurement; *(von Frau)* bust measurement.
Brüstung *f* parapet; *(Balkon~ etc auch)* balustrade; *(Fenster~)* breast.
Brust-: **~warze** *f* nipple; **~weite** *f* = **~umfang.**
Brut *f* **-en (a)** *no pl (das Brüten)* incubating. **(b)** *(die Jungen)* brood; *(pej)* lot, mob *(col)*.
brutal *adj* brutal; *(gewalttätig auch)* violent.
Brutalität *f* **(a)** *no pl siehe adj* brutality; violence. **(b)** *(Gewalttat)* act of violence *or* brutality.
brüten 1 *vi* to incubate; *(fig)* to ponder *(über+dat* over*)*. **~de Hitze** oppressive *or* stifling heat. **2** *vt (künstlich)* to incubate; *(Tech)* to breed.
Brüter *m* - *(Tech)* breeder (reactor). **schneller ~** fast-breeder (reactor).
Brut-: **~kasten** *m (Med)* incubator; **~reaktor** *m* breeder (reactor); **~stätte** *f (lit, fig)* breeding ground *(gen* for*)*.
brutto *adv* gross.
Brutto- *in cpds* gross; **~einkommen** *nt* gross income; **~registertonne** *f* register ton; **~sozialprodukt** *nt* gross national product, GNP.
Brutzeit *f* incubation (period).
brutzeln *(col)* **1** *vi* to sizzle (away). **2** *vt* to fry (up).
Bub *m (wk)* **-en, -en** *(S Ger, Aus, Sw)* boy, lad.
Bube *m (wk)* **-n, -n** *(Cards)* jack, knave.
Bubikopf *m* bobbed hair *no pl*, bob.
Buch *nt* ¨-er **(a)** book; *(Band)* volume; *(Dreh~)* script. **er redet wie ein ~** *(col)* he never stops talking; **ein Gentleman, wie er im ~e steht** a perfect example of a gentleman; **ein Tor, wie es im ~e steht** a textbook goal; **ein ~ mit sieben Siegeln** *(fig)* a closed book. **(b)** *usu pl (Comm: Geschäfts~)* books *pl*, accounts *pl*. **über etw** *(acc)* **~ führen** to keep a record of sth. **zu ~(e) schlagen** to make a (significant) difference.
Buch-: **~binder(in** *f)* *m* bookbinder; **~druck** *m no pl* letterpress (printing); **~drucker** *m* printer; **~druckerei** *f (Betrieb)* printery.
Buche *f* **-n** beech (tree).
Buch|ecker *f* **-n** beechnut.
buchen *vt* **(a)** *(Comm)* to enter; *(Kasse, fig: registrieren)* to register. **etw als Erfolg ~** to put sth down as a success. **(b)** *(vorbestellen)* to book.
Buchen-: **~holz** *nt* beech wood; **~wald** *m* beech wood.
Bücher-: **~bord, ~brett** *nt* bookshelf.
Bücherei *f* (lending) library.
Bücher-: **~freund** *m* book-lover, **~gestell** *nt* bookcase; **~narr** *m* book-freak *(col)*; **~regal** *nt* bookshelf; **~schrank** *m* bookcase; **~verzeichnis** *nt* bibliography; **~wand** *f* wall of bookshelves; **~wurm** *m (lit, fig hum)* bookworm.
Buchfink *m* chaffinch.
Buch-: **~führung** *f* book-keeping, accounting; **~halter(in** *f)* *m* book-keeper; **~haltung** *f* **(a)** = **~führung; (b)** *(Abteilung)* accounts department; **~handel** *m* book trade; **im ~handel erhältlich** available in bookshops *(Brit) or* bookstores *(US)*; **~händler** *m* bookseller; **~handlung** *f* bookshop *(Brit)*, bookstore *(US)*; **~laden** *m* bookshop *(Brit)*, bookstore *(US)*; **~macher** *m* bookmaker, bookie *(col)*; **~prüfer** *m* auditor; **~prüfung** *f* audit; **~rücken** *m* spine.
Buchse ['buksə] *f* **-n** *(Elec)* socket; *(Tech) (von Zylinder)* liner; *(von Lager)* bush.
Büchse ['byksə] *f* **-n (a)** tin; *(Konserven~)* can, tin *(Brit)*; *(Sammel~)* collecting box. **(b)** *(Gewehr)* rifle, (shot)gun.
Büchsen-: **~fleisch** *nt* canned *or* tinned *(Brit)* meat; **~milch** *f* tinned *(Brit) or* evaporated milk; **~öffner** *m* can *or* tin *(Brit)* opener.
Buchstabe *m* **-n** letter; *(esp Druck~)* character. **kleiner ~** small letter; **großer ~** capital (letter); **dem ~n nach** *(fig)* literally; **auf den ~n genau** *(fig)* to the letter; **nach dem ~n des Gesetzes** according to the letter of the law.
buchstabieren* *vt* to spell.
buchstäblich *adv* literally.
Buchstütze *f* bookend.
Bucht *f* **-en** bay.
Buchung *f (Comm)* entry; *(Reservierung)* booking.
Buckel *m* - **(a)** hump(back), hunchback; *(col: Rücken)* back. **einen ~ machen** *(Katze)* to arch its back; **er kann mir den ~ (he)runterrutschen** *(col)* he can (go and) take a running jump *(col)*; **80 Jahre auf dem ~ haben** *(col)* to be 80 (years old). **(b)** *(col: Auswölbung)* bulge, hump.
buck(e)lig *adj* hunchbacked; *(col) Straße* bumpy.
buckeln *vi (pej)* to bow and scrape.
bücken *vr* **sich nach etw ~** to bend down *or* to stoop to pick sth up; *siehe* **gebückt.**
Bückling *m* **(a)** *(Cook)* smoked herring. **(b)** *(hum col: Verbeugung)* bow.
buddeln *vti (col)* to dig.
Buddhismus *m* Buddhism.
Buddhist(in *f)* *m* Buddhist.
buddhistisch *adj* Buddhist(ic).
Bude *f* **-n (a)** hut; *(Markt~, Verkaufs~)* stall, booth; *(Zeitungs~)* kiosk. **(b)** *(pej col: Laden, Lokal etc)* dump *(col)*. **(c)** *(col) (Zimmer)* room; *(von Untermieter auch)* digs *pl (col)*; *(Wohnung)* pad *(col)*. **Leben in die ~ bringen** to liven the place up; **jdm die ~ einrennen** to pester sb; **jdm auf die ~ rücken** to come around.
Budget [by'dʒeː] *nt* **-s** budget.
Büfett *nt* **-e** *or* **-s (a)** *(Geschirrschrank)* sideboard. **(b)** *(Schanktisch)* bar; *(Verkaufstisch)* counter. **(c) kaltes ~** cold buffet.
Büffel *m* - buffalo.
Büffelei *f (col)* swotting *(col)*, cramming *(col)*.
büffeln *(col)* **1** *vi* to swot *(col)*, to cram *(col)*. **2** *vt Lernstoff* to swot up *(col)*.
Bug *m* ¨-e *or* **-e** *(Schiffs~)* bow; *(Flugzeug~)* nose.
Bügel *m* - **(a)** *(Kleider~)* (coat-)hanger. **(b)** *(Steig~)* stirrup. **(c)** *(Brillen~)* side *or* ear-piece.
Bügel-: **~brett** *nt* ironing board; **~eisen** *nt* iron; **~falte** *f* crease in one's trousers; **b~fertig** *adj* ready for ironing; **b~frei** *adj* non-iron.
bügeln 1 *vt* to iron; *Hose* to press. **2** *vi* to iron.

bugsieren* *vt* **(a)** *(Naut)* to tow. **(b)** *(col) Möbelstück etc* to edge. **jdn aus dem Zimmer ~** to steer *or* hustle sb out of the room.

buh *interj* boo.

buhen *vi (col)* to boo.

buhlen *vi (pej: werben)* **um jds Gunst ~** to woo *or* court sb's favour.

Buhmann *m, pl* **-männer** *(col)* bogeyman *(col)*.

Bühne *f* **-n (a)** *(lit, fig)* stage; *(von Aula etc auch)* platform. **über die ~ gehen** *(col)* to go (off); **etw über die ~ bringen** *(col)* to stage sth; **hinter der ~** *(lit, fig)* behind the scenes; **von der ~ abtreten** to make one's exit. **(b)** *(Theater)* theatre *(Brit)*, theater *(US)*; *(als Beruf)* stage. **zur ~ gehen** to go on the stage.

Bühnen-: **~anweisung** *f* stage direction; **~arbeiter** *m* stagehand; **~ausstattung** *f* props *pl;* **~autor** *m* playwright, dramatist; **~bearbeitung** *f* stage adaptation; **~bild** *nt* (stage) set; **~bildner** *m* set-designer; **~erfolg** *m* success; *(Stück auch)* (stage) hit; **~personal** *nt* theatre *(Brit) or* theater *(US)* staff; **~stück** *nt* (stage) play; **~techniker** *m* stage technician.

Buhruf *m* boo, catcall.

Bukett *nt* **-s** *or* **-e** *(geh: Blumen~, von Wein)* bouquet.

Bulgare *m (wk)* **-n, -n, Bulgarin** *f* Bulgarian.

Bulgarien [-iən] *nt* Bulgaria.

bulgarisch *adj* Bulgarian.

Bull|auge *nt (Naut)* porthole.

Bulldogge *f* bulldog.

Bulldozer ['bʊldoːzɐ] *m* - bulldozer.

Bulle *m (wk)* **-n, -n (a)** bull. **(b)** *(col: starker Mann)* great ox of a man. **(c)** *(pej: Polizist)* cop *(col)*. **die ~n** the fuzz *(pej)*, the cops *(col)*.

Bullenhitze *f (col)* sweltering heat.

bullern *vi (col) (Wasser)* to bubble; *(Ofen)* to roar.

bullig *adj (col)* **(a)** brawny, beefy *(col)*. **(b)** *Hitze* sweltering, boiling *(col)*.

bum *interj* bang; *(tiefer)* boom.

Bumerang *m* **-s** *or* **-e** *(lit, fig)* boomerang.

Bummel *m* - stroll; *(Lokal ~)* pub-crawl. **einen ~ durch die Stadt machen** to go for a stroll around (the) town.

Bummelant(in *f***)** *m (wk) (col)* **(a)** *(Trödler)* slowcoach *(Brit col)*, slowpoke *(US col)*. **(b)** *(Faulenzer)* loafer *(col)*, idler.

Bummelei *f (col) (Trödelei)* dawdling; *(Faulenzerei)* loafing about *(col)*, idling.

bummeln *vi* **(a)** *aux sein (spazierengehen)* to stroll; *(ausgehen)* to go out on the town. **(b)** *(trödeln)* to dawdle. **(c)** *(faulenzen)* to laze around.

Bummel-: **~streik** *m* go-slow *(Brit)*, slowdown *(US)*; **~zug** *m (col)* slow *or* stopping train.

Bums *m* **-e** *(col: Schlag)* bang, thump.

bumsen 1 *vi impers (col: dröhnen)* **es bumste, als ...** there was a thump *or* thud when ...; **es hat gebumst** *(von Fahrzeugen)* there's been a crash. **2** *vi* **(a)** *(schlagen)* to thump. **(b)** *aux sein (prallen, stoßen)* to bump, to bang. **(c)** *(col: koitieren)* to have it off *(col)*, to have sex. **3** *vt (col)* **jdn ~** to lay sb *(col)*, to have sex with sb; **gebumst werden** to get laid *(col)*.

Bumslokal *nt (pej col)* (low) dive.

Bund[1] *m* **¨e (a)** *(Bündnis)* alliance; *(Organisation)* association. **den ~ fürs Leben schließen** to take the marriage vows. **(b)** *(Pol: Bundesstaat)* Federal Government. **(c)** *(BRD col: Bundeswehr)* **der ~** the army. **(d)** *(an Kleidern)* waist-band.

Bund[2] *nt* **-e** *(von Stroh, Reisig etc)* bundle; *(von Radieschen, Spargel etc)* bunch.

Bündel *nt* - bundle, sheaf; *(Stroh~)* sheaf; *(von Radieschen etc)* bunch; *(fig: von Problemen etc)* cluster. **sein ~ schnüren** to pack one's bags.

bündeln *vt Zeitungen* to bundle up; *Stroh* to sheave; *Karotten etc* to tie into bunches/a bunch.

bündelweise *adv* by the bundle, in bundles.

Bundes- *in cpds* federal; **~bahn** *f (BRD, Aus, Sw)* Federal Railway(s *pl*); **~bank** *f* Federal bank; **~behörde** *f* Federal authority; **~bürger** *m* West German citizen; **~deutsche(r)** *mf* West German; **~gebiet** *nt (BRD)* federal territory; **~genosse** *m* ally, confederate; **~gerichtshof** *m (BRD)* Federal Supreme Court; **~grenzschutz** *m (BRD)* Federal Border Guard; **~kabinett** *nt* Federal cabinet; **~kanzler** *m (BRD, Aus)* West German/Austrian Chancellor; **~land** *nt* state; **~liga** *f (BRD Sport)* national league; **~minister** *m (BRD, Aus)* Federal Minister; **~mittel** *pl* Federal funds *pl;* **~nachrichtendienst** *m (BRD)* Federal Intelligence Service; **~post** *f:* **die (Deutsche) ~post** the (German) Federal Post (Office); **~präsident** *m (BRD, Aus)* (Federal) President; **~rat** *m* Bundesrat *(upper house of the West German Parliament)*; **~regierung** *f (BRD, Aus)* Federal Government; **~republik** *f* Federal Republic; **~republik Deutschland** Federal Republic of Germany; **~staat** *m* federal state; **~straße** *f* trunk road *(Brit)*, main highway *(US)*.

Bundestag *m* Bundestag *(lower house of the West German Parliament)*.

Bundestags- *(BRD)*: **~abgeordnete(r)** *m* German member of Parliament, member of the *Bundestag;* **~fraktion** *f* group *or* faction in the *Bundestag;* **~präsident** *m* President of the *Bundestag or* West German Parliament; **~wahl** *f* (federal) parliamentary elections *pl*.

Bundes-: **~trainer** *m (BRD Sport)* national coach; **~verfassungsgericht** *nt (BRD)* Federal Constitutional Court; **~wehr** *f (BRD)* army, (West German) armed forces *pl;* **b~weit** *adj* nationwide.

Bundhose *f* knee breeches *pl*.

bündig *adj* **(a)** *(schlüssig)* conclusive; *(kurz, bestimmt)* concise, succinct. **(b)** *(in gleicher Ebene)* flush *pred*, level.

Bündnis *nt* alliance.

Bundweite *f* waist measurement.

Bungalow ['bʊŋgalo] *m* **-s** bungalow.

Bunker *m* - **(a)** bunker; *(Luftschutz~)* air-raid shelter. **(b)** *(Sammelbehälter)* bin; *(Kohlen~)* bunker; **(c)** *(Mil sl: Gefängnis)* guardhouse.

Bunsenbrenner *m* Bunsen burner.

bunt *adj* **(a)** *(farbig)* coloured *(Brit)*, colored *(US)*; *(mehrfarbig)* colourful *(Brit)*, colorful *(US)*; *(vielfarbig)* multi-coloured *(Brit)*, multi-colored *(US)*; *(gefleckt)* mottled, spotted. **~ gestreift** *pred* brightly striped; **~e Farben** bright colours; **~es Glas** stained glass; **etw ~ anstreichen** to paint sth colourfully *(Brit) or* colorfully *(US)*; **~ fotografieren** *(col)* to photograph in colour. **(b)** *(fig: abwechslungsreich)* varied. **eine ~e Menge** a motley crowd; **ein ~es Bild** a colourful picture. **(c) jetzt wird's mir aber zu ~!** *(col)* that's going too far!

Bunt-: **b~bemalt** *adj attr* brightly painted; **~film** *m (col)* colour *(Brit) or* color *(US)* film; **b~gemischt** *adj attr Programm* varied; **b~gestreift** *adj attr* brightly striped; **~papier** *nt* coloured *(Brit) or* colored *(US)* paper; **~specht** *m* spotted woodpecker; **~stift** *m* coloured *(Brit) or* colored *(US)* pencil; **~wäsche** *f* coloureds *pl (Brit)*, coloreds *pl (US)*.

Bürde *f* **-n** *(lit, fig)* burden.

Burg *f* **-en** castle.

Bürge *m (wk)* **-n, -n** guarantor; *(fig)* guarantee *(für* of*)*. **für jdn ~ sein** to be sb's guarantor.

bürgen *vi* **für etw ~** to guarantee sth; **für jdn ~** *(Fin)* to stand surety for sb; *(fig)* to vouch for sb.

Bürger *m* - citizen; *(Sociol, pej)* bourgeois.

Bürger-: **~initiative** *f* action group; **~krieg** *m* civil war.

bürgerlich *adj* **(a)** civil; *Pflicht* civic. **B~es Gesetzbuch** Civil Code. **(b)** *(dem Bürgerstand angehörend)* middle-class *(auch pej)*, bourgeois *(esp pej)*; *(Hist)* bourgeois. **~es Essen/Küche** good plain food/cooking; **~es Trauerspiel** *(Liter)*

domestic tragedy.
Bürgerliche(r) *mf decl as adj* commoner.
Bürger-: **~meister(in** *f*) *m* mayor; **~pflicht** *f* civic duty; **~recht** *nt usu pl* civil rights *pl;* **~rechtler** *m* - civil rights campaigner; **~rechtsbewegung** *f* civil rights movement; **~schaft** *f* citizens *pl; (Vertretung)* City Parliament; **~schreck** *m* bogey of the middle classes; **~steig** *m* pavement *(Brit),* sidewalk *(US);* **~tum** *nt no pl (Hist)* bourgeoisie *(Hist).*
Burgfriede(n) *m (fig)* truce.
Bürgin *f siehe* **Bürge.**
Bürgschaft *f (Jur) (gegenüber Gläubigern)* security, surety; *(Haftungssumme)* penalty.
Burgunder *m* - *(auch:* **~wein***)* burgundy.
Büro *nt* **-s** office.
Büro- *in cpds* office; **~angestellte(r)** *mf* office worker; **~bedarf** *m* office supplies *pl;* **~kaufmann** *m* administrative assistant; **~klammer** *f* paper clip; **~kraft** *f* (office) clerk.
Bürokrat *m (wk)* **-en, -en** bureaucrat.
Bürokratie *f* bureaucracy.
Büro-: **~schluß** *m* office closing time; **nach ~schluß** after office hours; **~stunden** *pl* office hours *pl;* **~tätigkeit** *f* office work.
Bursche *m (wk)* **-n, -n (a)** *(col: Kerl)* fellow, guy *(col).* **ein übler ~** a bad lot. **(b)** *(Lauf~)* boy.
Burschen-: **~schaft** *f* student fraternity; **~schaft(l)er** *m* - member of a student fraternity.
burschikos *adj* **(a)** *(jungenhaft)* (tom)boyish. **(b)** *(unbekümmert)* casual.
Bürste *f* **-n** brush.
bürsten *vt* to brush.
Bürsten(haar)schnitt *m* crew cut.
Bus *m* **-ses, -se** bus; *(Reise~ auch)* coach *(Brit).*
Busbahnhof *m* bus/coach *(Brit)* station.
Busch *m* **¨e** bush. **etwas ist im ~** *(col)* there's something up; **mit etw hinter dem ~ halten** *(col)* to keep sth quiet; **bei jdm auf den ~ klopfen** *(col)* to sound sb out; **sich in die ¨~e schlagen** *(col)* to slip away.
Büschel *nt* - *(von Gras, Haaren)* tuft; *(von Heu, Stroh)* bundle.
buschig *adj* bushy.
Busch-: **~messer** *nt* machete; **~werk** *nt* bushes *pl.*
Busen *m* - *(von Frau)* bust, bosom.
Busen-: **b~frei** *adj* topless; **~freund** *m (iro)* bosom friend.
Bus-: **~fahrer(in** *f*) *m* bus/coach *(Brit)* driver; **~fahrt** *f* bus/coach *(Brit)* ride; **~haltestelle** *f* bus-stop; **~linie** *f* bus route. **welche ~linie fährt zum Bahnhof?** which bus goes to the station?
Bussard *m* **-e** buzzard.
Buße *f* **-n (a)** *(Rel)* repentance, penitence; *(Auflage)* penance; *(tätige ~)* atonement. **~ tun** to do penance. **(b)** *(Jur: Geldstrafe)* fine.
büßen 1 *vt* to pay for. **das sollst du mir ~** I'll make you pay for that. **2** *vi* **für etw ~** *(auch Rel)* to atone for sth; *für Leichtsinn etc* to pay for sth.
Büßer(in *f*) *m* - penitent.
Bußgeld *nt* fine.
Bußgeldbescheid *m* notice of payment due *(for traffic offence etc).*
Buß-: **~tag, ~- und Bettag** *m* day of prayer and repentance.
Büste *f* **-n** bust; *(Schneider~)* tailor's dummy.
Büstenhalter *m* bra.
Butan *nt* **-e, Butangas** *nt* butane (gas).
Bütten(papier) *nt no pl* handmade paper *(with deckle edge).*
Büttenrede *f* carnival speech.
Butter *f no pl* butter. **alles (ist) in ~** *(col)* everything is fine *or* hunky-dory *(col);* **jdm die ~ auf dem Brot nicht gönnen** *(fig col)* to begrudge sb the very air he breathes; **wir lassen uns nicht die ~ vom Brot nehmen** *(col)* we're going to stick up for our rights.
Butter- *in cpds* butter; **~berg** *m (col)* butter mountain; **~blume** *f* buttercup; **~brot** *nt* piece of bread and butter; *(Sandwich)* sandwich; **für ein ~brot** *(col)* for next to nothing; **das mußt du mir nicht ständig aufs ~brot schmieren** there's no need to keep rubbing it in; **~brotpapier** *nt* greaseproof paper *(Brit),* oil paper *(US);* **~creme** *f* butter cream; **~cremetorte** *f* cream cake; **~dose** *f* butter dish.
Butter-: **~keks** *m* ≈ morning coffee biscuit; **~milch** *f* buttermilk.
buttern *vt* **(a)** *Brot* to butter. **(b)** *(col: investieren)* to put *(in+acc* into*).*
Butter-: **~seite** *f* **auf die ~seite fallen** *(fig col)* to fall on one's feet *(col);* **die ~seite des Lebens** the pleasant side of life; **b~weich** *adj* beautifully soft; *(Sport sl) Aufschlag* gentle.
Buxtehude *nt* **aus/nach ~** *(col)* from/to the back of beyond *(col).*
Byte [bait] *nt* **-s** *(Comp)* byte.
bzgl. = **bezüglich.**
bzw. = **beziehungsweise.**

C

(*siehe auch* **K, Z;** *für* **CH** *siehe auch* **SCH**)

C, c [tseː] *nt* **-, -** C, c. **C-Schlüssel** *m* alto *or* C clef.
C = **Celsius.**
ca. = **circa** approx.
Cabriolet [-ˈleː] *nt* **-s** *(Aut)* convertible.
Café [kaˈfeː] *nt* **-s** café.
Cafeteria *f* **-s** cafeteria.
Calais [kaˈleː] *nt* **die Straße von ~** the Straits of Dover.
Callgirl [ˈkoːlgøːɐl] *nt* **-s** callgirl.
Calvados [kalvaˈdoːs] *m* **-, -** calvados.
Calypso *m* **-s** calypso.
Camembert [ˈkaməmbeːɐ] *m* **-s** Camembert.
Camp [kɛmp] *nt* **-s** camp.
campen [ˈkɛmpn] *vi* to camp.
Camper(in *f*) [ˈkɛmpɐ, -ərɪn] *m* **-** camper.
Camping [ˈkɛmpɪŋ] *nt no pl* camping *no art.* **zum ~ fahren** to go camping.
Camping- *in cpds* camping; **~artikel** *m* piece of camping equipment; *pl* camping equipment *sing*; **~platz** *m* camping site.
Campus *m* **-,** *no pl (Univ)* campus.
Cannabis *m* **-,** *no pl* cannabis.
Cape [keːp] *nt* **-s** cape.
Caravan [ˈka(ː)ravan] *m* **-s (a)** *(Kombiwagen)* estate car *(Brit)*, station wagon. **(b)** *(Wohnwagen)* caravan *(Brit)*, trailer *(US)*.
Casanova [kazaˈnoːva] *m* **-s** *(fig)* Casanova.
Cashewnuß [ˈkɛʃu-] *f* cashew (nut).
catchen [ˈkɛtʃn] *vi* to do catch-wrestling, to do all-in wrestling.
Catcher(in *f*) [ˈkɛtʃɐ, -ərɪn] *m* **-** all-in wrestler, catch wrestler.
Cayennepfeffer [kaˈjɛn-] *m* cayenne (pepper).
CB [ˈtseːˈbeː] = **Citizen-Band** Citizen Band.
cbm = **Kubikmeter** cubic metre.
ccm = **Kubikzentimeter** cc.
CDU [ˈtseːdeːˈ|uː] *f* = **Christlich-Demokratische Union.**
Cellist(in *f*) [tʃɛˈlɪst(ɪn)] *m (wk)* cellist.
Cello [ˈtʃɛlo] *nt* **-s** *or* **Celli** cello.
Cellophan ® [tsɛloˈfaːn] *nt no pl* cellophane.
Celsius [ˈtsɛlzius] *no art, inv* Celsius.
Celsiusskala *f* Celsius scale.
Cembalo [ˈtʃɛmbalo] *nt* **-s** cembalo, harpsichord.
ces, Ces [tsɛs] *nt, gen* **-** *(Mus)* C flat.
Ceylon [ˈtsailɔn] *nt* Ceylon.
Chamäleon [kaˈmɛːleɔn] *nt* **-s** *(lit, fig)* chameleon.
Champagner [ʃamˈpanjɐ] *m* **-** champagne.
Champignon [ˈʃampɪnjɔŋ] *m* **-s** mushroom.
Chance [ˈʃãːsə] *f* **-n** chance; *(bei Wetten)* odds *pl.* **keine ~ haben** not to have *or* stand a chance; **im Beruf ~n haben** to have good career prospects.
Chancengleichheit [ˈʃãːsən-] *f* equality of opportunity.
Chanson [ʃãˈsõː] *nt* **-s** (satirical) song.
Chaos [ˈkaːɔs] *nt* **-,** *no pl* chaos.
Chaot(in *f*) [kaˈoːt(ɪn)] *m (wk)* **-en, -en (a)** *(Pol pej)* anarchist *(pej)*. **(b)** *(col)* **du bist vielleicht ein ~** you're so chaotic.
chaotisch [kaˈoːtɪʃ] *adj* chaotic. **~e Zustände** a state of (utter) chaos.
Charakter [kaˈraktɐ] *m* **-e** [-ˈteːrə] character. **ein Mann von ~** a man of character; **der vertrauliche ~ dieses Gespräches** the confidential nature of this conversation.
Charakter-: **~darsteller** *m* character actor; **~eigenschaft** *f* character trait; **c~fest** *adj* of strong character; **~festigkeit** *f* strength of character.
charakterisieren* [ka-] *vt* to characterize.
Charakterisierung *f* characterization.
Charakteristik [ka-] *f* description; *(typische Eigenschaften)* characteristics *pl.*
Charakteristikum [ka-] *nt, pl* **Charakteristika** *(geh)* characteristic.
charakteristisch [ka-] *adj* characteristic *(für* of).
Charakter-: **c~lich 1** *adj* (of) character, personal; **c~liche Stärke/Mängel** strength of character/character defects; **2** *adv* in character; **jdn c~lich stark prägen** to have a strong influence on sb's character; **c~los** *adj* **(a)** *(niederträchtig)* unprincipled; **c~los handeln** to act in an unprincipled way; **(b)** *(ohne Prägung)* characterless; *Spiel, Vortrag* insipid; **~losigkeit** *f (Niederträchtigkeit)* lack of principle; *(Handlung)* unprincipled behaviour *(Brit) or* behavior *(US) no pl*; **~merkmal** *nt* characteristic; **~rolle** *f* character part; **~schwäche** *f* weakness of character; **~stärke** *f* strength of character; **c~voll** *adj (ausgeprägt)* full of character; **~zug** *m* characteristic.
Charge [ˈʃarʒə] *f* **-n (a)** *(Mil, fig)* rank. **(b)** *(Theat)* bit part.
charmant [ʃarˈmant] *adj* charming.
Charme [ʃarm] *m no pl* charm.
Charter- [ˈtʃartɐ]: **~flug** *m* charter flight; **~(flug)gesellschaft** *f* charter(flight) company; **~maschine** *f* charter plane.
chartern [ˈtʃartɐn] *vt Schiff, Flugzeug* to charter.
Chassis [ʃaˈsiː] *nt* **-, -** [-iːs] chassis.
Chauffeur [ʃɔˈføːɐ] *m* chauffeur.
Chaussee [ʃoˈseː] *f* **-n** [-eːən] *(dated)* high road.
Chauvi [ˈʃoːvi] *m* **-s** *(col)* male chauvinist pig, MCP.
Chauvinismus [ʃovi-] *m* chauvinism.
Chauvinist(in *f*) *m* chauvinist.
chauvinistisch [ʃovi-] *adj* chauvinist(ic).
checken [ˈtʃɛkn] **1** *vt* **(a)** *(überprüfen)* to check. **(b)** *(col: verstehen)* to get *(col)*. **2** *vti (Eishockey)* to block; *(anrempeln)* to barge.
Check- [ˈtʃɛk-]: **~liste** *f* checklist; **~point** [-pɔynt] *m* **-s** checkpoint.
Chef(in *f*) [ʃɛf] *m* **-s** boss; *(von Bande, Delegation etc)* leader; *(von Organisation, col: Schuldirektor)* head; *(der Polizei)* chief; *(Mil: von Kompanie)* commander. **er ist der ~ vom ganzen** he's the boss here.
Chef-: **~arzt** *m* senior consultant; **~etage** *f* executive floor; **~koch** *m* chef, head cook; **~redakteur** *m* editor-in-chief; **~redaktion** *f* **(a)** *(Aufgabe)* (chief) editorship; **(b)** *(Büro)* main editorial office; **~sekretärin** *f* personal assistant/secretary; **~visite** *f (Med)* consultant's round.
Chemie [çeˈmiː] *f no pl (lit, fig)* chemistry; *(col: Chemikalien)* chemicals *pl.*
Chemie-: **~arbeiter** *m* chemical worker; **~faser** *f* synthetic fibre *(Brit) or* fiber *(US)*.
Chemikalie [çemiˈkaːliə] *f* **-n** *usu pl* chemical.
Chemiker(in *f*) [ˈçeː-] *m* **-** chemist.
chemisch [ˈçeː-] *adj* chemical.
Chemotechniker [çemo-] chemical engineer.
chic [ʃɪk] *adj* = **schick.**

Chicorée [ˈʃikoreː] *f or m no pl* chicory.
Chiffon [ˈʃɪfõ(ː)] *m* **-s** chiffon.
Chiffre [ˈʃifrə] *f* **-n (a)** cipher. **(b)** *(in Zeitung)* box number.
chiffrieren* [ʃif-] *vti* to encipher, to code. **chiffriert** coded.
Chile [ˈtʃiːle] *nt* Chile.
Chilene [tʃiˈleːnə] *m (wk)* **-n, -n, Chilenin** *f* Chilean.
chilenisch [tʃi-] *adj* Chilean.
Chili [ˈtʃiːli] *m no pl* chil(l)i.
China [ˈçiːna] *nt* China.
Chinakohl *m* Chinese cabbage.
Chinese [çi-] *m (wk)* **-n, -n** Chinaman; *(heutig auch)* Chinese.
Chinesin [çi-] *f* Chinese woman; *(heutig auch)* Chinese.
chinesisch [çi-] *adj* Chinese. **die C~e Mauer** the Great Wall of China.
Chinesisch(e) [çi-] *nt decl as adj* Chinese.
Chinin [çiˈniːn] *nt no pl* quinine.
Chip [tʃɪp] *m* **-s (a)** *(Spiel~, Comp)* chip. **(b)** *usu pl (Kartoffel~)* (potato) crisp *(Brit)*, potato chip *(US)*.
Chirurg(in *f***)** [çiˈrʊrg(ɪn)] *m (wk)* **-en, -en** surgeon.
Chirurgie [çirʊrˈgiː] *f* surgery.
chirurgisch [çi-] *adj* surgical. **ein ~er Eingriff** surgery *no indef art*.
Chlor [kloːɐ] *nt no pl* chlorine.
Chloro- [kloro-]: **~form** *nt no pl* chloroform; **~phyll** *nt no pl* chlorophyll.
Choke [tʃoːk] *m* **-s** choke.
Cholera [ˈkoːlera] *f no pl* cholera.
Choleriker(in *f***)** [ko-] *m* **-** hot-tempered person.
cholerisch [ko-] *adj* choleric.
Cholesterin [ko-] *nt no pl* cholesterol.
Cholesterinspiegel *m* cholesterol level.
Chor [koːɐ] *m* **¨-e (a)** choir; *(Theat)* chorus. **im ~ sprechen/rufen** to speak/shout in chorus. **(b)** *(Archit: Altarraum)* chancel, choir.
Choral [koˈraːl] *m, pl* **Choräle** *(Kirchenlied)* hymn.
Choreo- [koreo-]: **~graph(in** *f***)** *m* choreographer; **~graphie** *f* choreography.
Chor- [ˈkoːɐ]: **~gesang** *m (Lied)* choral music; *(das Singen)* choral singing; **~gestühl** *nt* choir stalls *pl*.
Chorist(in *f***)** [ko-] *m* = **Chorsänger(in).**
Chor- [ˈkoːɐ]: **~knabe** *m* choirboy; **~leiter** *m* choirmaster; **~sänger(in** *f***)** *m* member of a choir; *(im Kirchenchor)* chorister.
Chose [ˈʃoːzə] *f* **-n** *(col: Angelegenheit)* thing.
Chr. = **Christus.**
Christ [krɪst] *m (wk)* **-en, -en** Christian.
Christbaum *m* Christmas tree.
Christbaum-: ~kugel *f* Christmas tree ball; **~schmuck** *m* Christmas tree decorations *pl*.
Christ- [ˈkrɪst-]: **~demokrat** *m* Christian Democrat; **c~demokratisch** *adj* Christian Democratic.
Christen- [ˈkrɪstn-]: **~heit** *f* Christendom; **~pflicht** *f* (one's) Christian duty; **~tum** *nt no pl* Christianity.
Christi *gen of* **Christus.**
Christianisierung [krɪ-] *f* conversion to Christianity.
Christin [ˈkrɪstɪn] *f* Christian.
Christkind [ˈkrɪst-] *nt no pl* infant Jesus, Christ Child; *(das Geschenke bringt)* Father Christmas.
christlich [ˈkrɪ-] **1** *adj* Christian. **C~er Verein Junger Männer** Young Men's Christian Association. **2** *adv* as a Christian.
Christus [ˈkrɪstʊs] *m, gen* **Christi** Christ; *(~figur auch)* figure of Christ. **vor Christi Geburt, vor ~** before Christ, BC; **nach Christi Geburt, nach ~** AD, Anno Domini; **Christi Himmelfahrt** Ascension Day.
Chrom [kroːm] *nt no pl* chrome.
Chromosom [kro-] *nt* **-en** chromosome.
Chronik [ˈkroː-] *f* chronicle.
chronisch [ˈkroː-] *adj (Med, fig)* chronic.
Chronist(in *f***)** [kro-] *m* chronicler.
Chronologie [kronoloˈgiː] *f* chronology.
chronologisch [kro-] *adj* chronological.
Chrysantheme [kryzanˈteːmə] *f* **-n** chrysanthemum.
Chuzpe [ˈxʊtspə] *f no pl (col)* chutzpa(h) *(col)*.
Cineast(in *f***)** [sineˈast(ɪn)] *m (wk)* **-en, -en** cineast(e).
circa [ˈtsɪrka] *adv* = **zirka.**
Circulus vitiosus [ˈtsɪrkulʊs viˈtsioːzʊs] *m, pl* **Circuli vitiosi** *(geh: Teufelskreis)* vicious circle.
cis, Cis [tsɪs] *nt, gen* **-** *(Mus)* C sharp.
City [ˈsɪti] *f* **-s** city centre.
Clan [klaːn] *m* **-s** *(lit, fig)* clan.
clean [kliːn] *adj pred (Drogen sl)* off drugs.
Clearing [ˈkliːrɪŋ] *nt* **-s** *(Econ)* clearing.
clever [ˈklɛvɐ] *adj* clever; *(gerissen)* crafty.
Clinch [klɪntʃ] *m no pl (Boxen, fig)* clinch. **jdn in den ~ nehmen** *(lit)* to go into a clinch with sb; *(fig)* to get stuck into sb *(col)*.
Clip *m* **-s** clip; *(Ohr~)* (clip-on) earring.
Clique [ˈklɪkə] *f* **-n** group; *(pej)* clique.
Cliquen-: ~bildung *f* forming of cliques; **~wirtschaft** *f (pej inf)* cliquey set-up *(inf)*.
Clochard [klɔˈʃaːr] *m* **-s** tramp.
Clou [kluː] *m* **-s** *(von Geschichte)* (whole) point; *(von Show)* highlight, high spot. **das ist doch gerade der ~** but that's just it, but that's the whole point.
Clown [klaun] *m* **-s** *(lit, fig)* clown. **den ~ spielen** to clown around, to play the fool; **sich/jdn zum ~ machen** to make a clown of oneself/sb.
Clownerie [klaunəˈriː] *f* clowning (around) *no pl*.
Club *m* **-s** = **Klub.**
cm = **Zentimeter** cm.
Co. = **Kompanie** Co.
Coach [koːtʃ] *m* **-s** *(Sport)* coach.
Cockpit *nt* **-s** cockpit.
Cocktail [ˈkɔkteːl] *m* **-s (a)** cocktail. **(b)** *(~party)* cocktail party.
Cocktail-: ~kleid *nt* cocktail dress; **~party** *f* cocktail party.
Code [koːt] *m* **-s** = **Kode.**
Cognac ® [ˈkɔnjak] *m* **-s** cognac.
Coiffeur [koaˈføːɐ] *m*, **Coiffeuse** [koaˈføːzə] *f (geh)* hair stylist.
Cola *f* **-s** *(col)* Coke ® *(col)*.
Collage [kɔˈlaːʒə] *f* **-n** *(Art, fig)* collage.
Collie *m* **-s** collie.
Comeback [kamˈbɛk] *nt* **-(s), -s** comeback.
Compact-disc *f* compact disk.
Computer [kɔmˈpjuːtɐ] *m* **-** computer.
Computer- *in cpds* computer-; **~generation** *f* computer generation; **c~gerecht** *adj* (ready) for the computer; **c~gesteuert** *adj* computer-controlled.
computerisieren* [kɔmpjutəriˈziːrən] *vti* to computerize.
Conférencier [kõferãˈsieː] *m* **-s** compère, MC.
Container [kɔnˈteːnɐ] *m* **-** container; *(für Schutt etc)* skip.
Container- *in cpds* container; **~bahnhof** *m* container depot; **~terminal** *m or nt* container terminal; **~verkehr** *m* container traffic.
Contergankind *nt (col)* thalidomide child.
cool [ˈkuːl] *adj (col: gefaßt)* cool.
Copyright [ˈkɔpirait] *nt* **-s** copyright.
Cord *m* **-e** *or* **-s** *(Tex)* cord, corduroy.
Cord- *in cpds* cord, corduroy; **~jeans** *pl* cords *pl*.
Cordon bleu [kɔrdõˈblø] *nt* **- -, -s -s** *(Cook)* veal cordon bleu.
Cornichon [kɔrniˈʃõː] *nt* **-s** gherkin.
Corpus delicti *nt, pl* **Corpora -** corpus delicti; *(hum)* culprit *(col)*.
Couch [kautʃ] *f* **-(e)s** *or (col)* **-en** couch.
Couch-: ~garnitur *f* three-piece suite; **~tisch** *m*

coffee table.
Couleur [ku'løːɐ] *f* **-s** *(geh)* kind, sort.
Coup [kuː] *m* **-s** coup. **einen ~ (gegen jdn/etw) landen** to bring off a coup (against sb/sth).
Coupé [ku'peː] *nt* **-s** coupé.
Coupon [ku'põː] *m* **-s** coupon, voucher.
Courage [ku'raːʒə] *f no pl (geh)* courage.
couragiert [kura'ʒiːɐt] *adj (geh)* courageous.
Courtage [kʊr'taːʒə] **-n** *(Fin)* commission.
Cousin [ku'zɛ̃ː] *m* **-s, Cousine** [ku'ziːnə] *f* cousin.
Cover ['kavɐ] *nt* **-s** cover.
Cracker ['krɛkɐ] *m* **-(s) (a)** cracker. **(b)** *(Feuerwerkskörper)* banger *(Brit)*, fire-cracker *(US)*.
Creme [kreːm] *f* **-s** *(Haut~, Cook, fig)* cream. **die ~ der Gesellschaft** the cream of society.
cremefarben *adj* cream.
cremig *adj* creamy.
Crew [kruː] *f* **-s** crew.
Croupier [kru'pieː] *m* **-s** croupier.
Crux *f no pl (Schwierigkeit)* trouble, problem.
CSU [tseː|ɛs'|uː] *f* = **Christlich-Soziale Union.**
cum laude *adv (Univ)* cum laude *(form)*, with distinction.
Cup [kap] *m* **-s** *(Sport)* cup.
Curling ['køːɐlɪŋ] *nt no pl* curling.
Curriculum *nt, pl* **Curricula** *(geh)* curriculum.
Curry ['kari] *m or nt no pl* curry.
Currywurst *f* curried sausage.
Cursor [*auch:*'kœːɐsɐ] *m* **-s** *(Comp)* cursor.
Cut [kœt] *m* **-s** *(dated)* cutaway.
Cutter(in *f***)** ['katɐ, -ərin] *m* **-** *(Film, Rad, TV)* editor.
C.V.J.M. [tseːfaujɔt'|ɛm] *m* = **Christlicher Verein Junger Männer** YMCA.

D

D, d [deː] *nt* **-, -** D, d.

da 1 *adv* **(a)** *(örtlich) (dort)* there; *(hier)* here. ~ **draußen** out there; **hier und ~, ~ und dort** here and there; **he, Sie ~!** hey, you there!; ~ **bin ich/sind wir** here I am/we are; ~ **bist du ja!** there you are!; ~ **kommt er ja** here he comes; **~, wo ...** where ...; **ach, ~ war der Brief!** so that's where the letter was; ~ **hast du dein Geld!** (here you are,) there's your money; ~ **siehst du, was du angerichtet hast** now see what you've done.

(b) *(zeitlich: dann, damals)* then. **ich ging gerade aus dem Haus, ~ schlug es zwei** I was just going out of the house when the clock struck two; ~ **kommen Sie mal gleich mit** *(col)* you just come along with me.

(c) *(daraufhin) sagen* to that; *lachen* at that. **sie weinte, ~ ließ er sich erweichen** when she started to cry he softened.

(d) *(folglich)* so. **es war niemand im Zimmer, ~ habe ich ...** there was nobody in the room, so I ...

(e) *(col)* there. ~ **haben wir aber Glück gehabt!** we were lucky there!; **was gibt's denn ~ zu lachen/fragen?** what's so funny about that?/what is there to ask?; ~ **kann man nichts machen** nothing can be done about it; ~ **kann man nur lachen/sich nur wundern** you can't help laughing/being amazed.

2 *conj* **(a)** *(weil)* as, since, seeing that. **(b)** *(liter: als)* when.

dabehalten* *vt sep irreg* to keep (here/there); *Schüler* to keep behind.

dabei *adv* **(a)** *(örtlich)* with it; *(bei Gruppe von Menschen, Dingen)* there.

(b) *(zeitlich) (gleichzeitig)* at the same time; *(währenddessen, dadurch)* in the course of this. **warum arbeiten Sie im Stehen? Sie können doch auch ~ sitzen** why are you working standing up? you can sit down while you're doing it; **... orkanartige Winde; ~ kam es zu schweren Schäden** ... gale-force winds, which have resulted in serious damage.

(c) *(außerdem)* **sie ist schön und ~ auch noch klug** she's pretty, and clever as well.

(d) *(wenn, während man etw tut)* in the process; *ertappen, erwischen* at it. **hast du ~ etwas gelernt?** did you learn anything from it?; ~ **darf man nicht vergessen, daß ...** it shouldn't be forgotten that ...; **die ~ entstehenden Kosten** the expenses arising from this/that; **wir haben ihn ~ ertappt, wie er über den Zaun stieg** we caught him in the act of climbing over the fence.

(e) *(in dieser Angelegenheit)* **das Schwierigste ~** the most difficult part of it; **mir ist nicht ganz wohl ~** I don't really feel happy about it; **er hat ~ einen Fehler gemacht** he's made a mistake; **es kommt doch nichts ~ heraus** nothing will come of it.

(f) *(einräumend: obwohl)* (and) yet. **er hat mich geschlagen, ~ hatte ich gar nichts gemacht** he hit me and I hadn't even done anything.

(g) es bleibt ~, daß ihr morgen alle mitkommt we'll stick to that, you're all coming tomorrow; **ich bleibe ~** I'm not changing my mind; **lassen wir es ~** let's leave it at that!; **was ist schon ~?** so what? *(col)*, what of it? *(col)*; **was ist schon ~, wenn man das tut?** what harm is there in doing that?; **ich finde gar nichts ~** I don't see any harm in it; **was hast du dir denn ~ gedacht?** what were you thinking of?

dabeibleiben *vi sep irreg aux sein* to stay *or* stick *(col)* with it; *(bei Firma)* to stay on; *siehe* **dabei (g)**.

dabeihaben *vt sep irreg (col)* to have with one.

dabeisein *vi sep irreg aux sein* **(a)** to be there *(bei* at); *(mitmachen)* to be involved *(bei* in). **ich bin dabei!** count me in!; **er will überall ~** he wants to be in on everything. **(b)** *(im Begriff sein)* **~, etw zu tun** to be just doing sth; **ich bin (gerade) dabei** I'm just doing it.

dabeisitzen *vi sep irreg* to sit there. **bei einer Besprechung ~** to sit in on a discussion.

dabeistehen *vi sep irreg* to stand there.

dableiben *vi sep irreg aux sein* to stay (on); **(jetzt wird) dageblieben!** (you just) stay right there!

Dach *nt* **¨er (a)** roof. **mit jdm unter einem ~ wohnen** to live under the same roof as sb; **unterm ~ wohnen** *(col)* to live in an attic; *(im obersten Stock)* to live right on the top floor; **unter ~ und Fach sein** *(abgeschlossen)* to be in the bag *(col)*; *(Vertrag, Geschäft auch)* to be signed and sealed; *(in Sicherheit)* to be safe; *(Ernte)* to be safely in. **(b)** *(fig col)* **jdm eins aufs ~ geben** *(schlagen)* to smash sb on the head *(col)*; *(ausschimpfen)* to give sb a (good) talking to; **jdm aufs ~ steigen** *(col)* to get onto sb *(col)*.

Dach- *in cpds* roof; **~boden** *m* attic; **~decker** *m* **-** roofer; *(mit Ziegeln)* tiler; **~fenster** *nt* skylight; *(ausgestellt)* dormer window; **~first** *m* ridge of the roof; **~garten** *m* roof garden; **~gepäckträger** *m (Aut)* roof rack; **~geschoß** *nt* attic storey; *(oberster Stock)* top floor *or* storey; **~giebel** *m* gable; **~kammer** *f* attic room; **~luke** *f* skylight; **~organisation** *f* umbrella *or (Comm)* parent organization; **~rinne** *f* gutter.

Dachs *m* **-e (a)** badger. **(b) ein junger ~** *(col)* a young whippersnapper.

Dachsbau *m* badger's sett.

Dach-: ~schaden *m* **(a)** *(lit)* damage to the roof; **(b)** *(col)* **einen ~schaden haben** to have a screw loose *(col)*; **~stube** *f* attic (room).

dachte *pret of* **denken.**

Dach-: ~terrasse *f* roof terrace; **~verband** *m* umbrella organization; **~wohnung** *f* attic flat *(Brit) or* apartment; **~ziegel** *m* roofing tile; **~zimmer** *nt* attic (room).

Dackel *m* **-** dachshund.

dadurch *adv (emph* **dadurch***)* **(a)** *(örtlich)* through there; *(wenn Bezugsobjekt vorher erwähnt)* through it. **(b)** *(kausal)* thereby *(form)*; *(aus diesem Grund auch)* because of this/that; *(auf diese Weise)* in this/that way. **was willst du ~ gewinnen?** what do you hope to gain by that?; **meinst du, ~ wird alles wieder gut?** do you think that will make everything all right again?; **~, daß er das tat, hat er ...** by doing that he ...

dafür *adv (emph* **dafür***)* **(a)** *(für das, diese Tat etc)* for that/it. **~ war er nicht zu haben** it wasn't his scene *(col)*; *(erlaubte es nicht)* he wouldn't have it; **~ ist er immer zu haben** he never says no to that; **ich bin nicht ~ verantwortlich, was mein Bruder macht** I'm not responsible for what my brother does; ~ **bin ich ja hier** that's what I'm here for; **er ist ~ bestraft worden, daß er frech zum Lehrer war** he was punished for being cheeky to the teacher.

(b) *(Zustimmung)* for that/it, in favour (of that/it). **ich bin (ganz) ~, daß wir das machen** I'm (all) for doing that.

(c) *(als Ersatz)* instead, in its place; *(bei Tausch)* in exchange; *(als Gegenleistung)* in return.

(d) *(zum Ausgleich).* **in Mathematik ist er schlecht, ~ kann er gut Fußball spielen** he's very bad at maths but he makes up for it at football.

(e) *(im Hinblick darauf)* **~, daß er erst drei Jahre ist, ist er sehr klug** seeing *or* considering that he's only three he's very clever.

dafür-: ~halten *vi sep irreg (geh)* to be of the opinion; **nach meinem D~halten** in my opinion; **~können** *vt sep irreg* **er kann nichts ~** he can't help it; **er kann nichts ~, daß er dumm ist** he can't help being stupid.

dagegen 1 *adv (emph* **dagegen***)* **(a)** *(örtlich)* against it. **(b)** *(als Einwand, Ablehnung)* against that/it. **~ sein** to be against it; **etwas/nichts ~ haben** to object/not to object; **was hat er ~, daß wir früher anfangen?** what has he got against us starting earlier?; **haben Sie was ~, wenn ich rauche?** do you mind if I smoke?; **sollen wir ins Kino gehen?—ich hätte nichts ~ (einzuwenden)** shall we go to the cinema?— that's okay by me *(col).* **(c)** *(als Gegenmaßnahme) unternehmen* about it; *(Medikamente einnehmen etc)* for it. **~ läßt sich nichts machen** nothing can be done about it. **(d)** *(verglichen damit)* in comparison. **(e)** *(als Ersatz) eintauschen* for that/it/them. **2** *conj (im Gegensatz dazu)* on the other hand, however.

dagegen-: ~halten *vt sep irreg* **(a)** *(vergleichen)* to compare it/them with; **(b)** *(fig: einwenden)* to object; **~sprechen** *vi sep irreg* to be against it; **was spricht ~, daß wir es so machen?** what is there against us doing it that way?; **es spricht nichts ~, es so zu machen** there's no reason not to do it that way.

dagewesen *adj siehe* **dasein.**

dahaben *vt sep irreg* to have here/there; *(in Geschäft etc)* to have in stock.

daheim *adv* at home; *(nach prep)* home. **bei uns ~** back home; **~ sein** *(lit, fig)* to be at home; *(nach Reise)* to be home; **wo bist du ~?** where's your home?

Daheim *nt no pl* home.

daher 1 *adv (auch* **daher***)* **(a)** *(von dort)* from there. **(b)** *(durch diesen Umstand)* that is why. **~ weiß ich das** that's how *or* why I know that; **~ die große Eile** hence all the hurry; **~ kommt es, daß ...** that is (the reason) why ...; **das kommt ~, daß ...** that is because ... **2** *conj (deshalb)* that is why.

daher-: ~gelaufen *adj* **jeder ~gelaufene Kerl** any Tom, Dick or Harry; **~kommen** *vi sep irreg aux sein* to come along; **~reden** *sep* **1** *vi* to talk away; **red doch nicht so (dumm) ~!** don't talk such rubbish!; **2** *vt* to say without thinking; **was er alles ~redet** the things he comes out with! *(col)*; **das war nur so ~geredet** I/he *etc* just said that.

dahin 1 *adv (emph* **dahin***)* **(a)** *(räumlich)* there; *(hierhin)* here. **kommst du auch ~?** are you coming too?; **bis ~** as far as there, up to that point; **ist es noch weit bis ~?** is it far still? **(b)** *(fig: so weit)* **~ kommen** to reach such a state; **du wirst es ~ bringen, daß ...** you'll bring things to such a state that ... **(c)** *(in dem Sinne)* **er äußerte sich ~ gehend, daß ...** he said something to the effect that ...; **eine ~ gehende Aussage** a statement to that effect; **er hat den Bericht ~ (gehend) interpretiert, daß ...** he interpreted the report as saying ...; **wir haben uns ~ geeinigt, daß ...** we have agreed that ...; **seine Meinung geht ~, daß ...** he tends to the opinion that ... **2** *adj pred* **~ sein** to have gone; **das Auto ist ~** *(hum col)* the car has had it *(col).*

dahingegen *adv* on the other hand.

dahingehen *vi sep irreg aux sein (geh: Zeit etc)* to pass.

dahingehend *adv siehe* **dahin 1 (c).**

dahin-: ~gestellt *adj* **~gestellt sein lassen, ob ...** to leave it open whether ...; **es sei ~gestellt, ob ...** it is an open question whether ...; **~leben** *vi sep* to exist, to vegetate *(pej)*; **~sagen** *vt sep* to say without (really) thinking; **~schleppen** *vr sep (lit: sich fortbewegen)* to drag oneself along; *(fig: Verhandlungen, Zeit)* to drag on; **~schwinden** *vi sep irreg aux sein (geh) (Geld, Kraft)* to dwindle (away); *(vergehen: Zeit)* to go past; **~stehen** *vi sep irreg* to be debatable.

dahinten *adv (emph* **dahinten***)* over there.

dahinter *adv (emph* **dahinter***)* behind (it/that/him *etc*). **(da ist) nichts ~** *(fig)* there's nothing behind it.

dahinter-: ~klemmen, ~knien *vr sep (col)* to put one's back into it; **~kommen** *vi sep irreg aux sein (col)* to find out; **~stecken** *vi sep (col)* to be behind it/that; **~stehen** *vi sep irreg (unterstützen)* to back it/that, to be behind it/that.

Dahlie [-iə] *f* **-n** dahlia.

Dakapo *nt* **-s** encore.

da-: ~lassen *vt sep irreg* to leave (here/there); **~liegen** *vi sep irreg* to lie there.

dalli *adv (col)* **~, ~!** on the double! *(col)*; **mach ein bißchen ~!** get a move on! *(col).*

Dalmatiner *m* **-** *(Hund)* dalmatian.

damalig *adj attr* at that time; *Sitten auch* in those days. **der ~e Kanzler** the then Chancellor.

damals *adv* at that time, then. **seit ~** since then; **von ~** of that time; **~, als ...** at the time when ...

Dame *f* **-n (a)** lady. **meine ~n und Herren!** ladies and gentlemen!; **Hundert-Meter-Staffel der ~n** women's *or* ladies' hundred metre relay. **(b)** *(Spiel)* draughts *sing (Brit)*, checkers *sing (US)*; *(Doppelstein)* king; *(Cards, chess)* queen.

Damebrett *nt* draught(s)board, checkerboard *(US).*

Dämel *m* **-** *(col)* jerk *(col!).*

Damen- *in cpds* ladies'; **~bart** *m* facial hair; **~begleitung** *f*: **in ~begleitung** in the company of a lady; **~bekanntschaft** *f* female acquaintance *(col)*; **eine ~bekanntschaft machen** to make the acquaintance of a lady/young lady; **~besuch** *m* lady visitor/visitors; **~binde** *f* sanitary towel *or* napkin *(US)*; **~gesellschaft** *f* hen party *(col)*; *(gesellige Runde)* ladies' gathering; **d~haft** *adj* ladylike *no adv*; **sich d~haft benehmen** to behave in a ladylike way; **~oberbekleidung** *f* ladies' wear; **~sattel** *m* **im ~sattel reiten** to ride side-saddle; **~toilette** *f (WC)* ladies' toilet *or* restroom *(US)*; **~wahl** *f* ladies' excuse-me.

Damhirsch *m* fallow deer.

damit 1 *adv (emph auch* **damit***)* **(a)** with it/that/them. **was soll ich ~?** what am I meant to do with that?; **ist Ihre Frage ~ beantwortet?** does that answer your question?; **meint er mich ~?** does he mean me?; **was ist ~?** what about it?; **wie wäre es ~?** how about it?; **wie sieht es ~ aus?** what's happening about it?; **muß er denn immer wieder ~ ankommen?** must he keep on about it?; **~ ist nichts** *(col)* it's no go *(col)*; **hör auf ~!** *(col)* lay off! *(col)*; **~ hat es noch Zeit** there's no hurry for that; **was willst du ~ sagen?** what's that supposed to mean?; **~ will ich nicht sagen, daß ...** I don't mean to say that ...; **~ fing der Streit an** that's how the argument started; **der Streit fing ~ an, daß er behauptete ...** the argument started when he said ...

(b) *(bei Befehlen)* with it. **weg ~!** away with it;

her ~! give it here! *(col)*.

(c) *(begründend)* because of that. **~ ist es klar, daß er es war** from that it's clear that it was him.

2 *conj* so that. **~ er nicht fällt** so that he does not fall.

dämlich *adj (col)* stupid.

Dämlichkeit *f* stupidity.

Damm *m* **¨-e (a)** *(Deich)* dyke; *(Stau~)* dam; *(Hafen~)* wall; *(Ufer~, Straßen~)* embankment; *(fig)* barrier. **(b)** *(fig col)* **wieder auf dem ~ sein** to be back to normal; **nicht recht auf dem ~ sein** to be a bit under the weather *(col)*.

Dammbruch *m* breach in a/the dyke *etc*.

dämmen *vt* **(a)** *(geh) (lit)* to dam; *(fig)* to check. **(b)** *(Tech) Wärme* to keep in; *Schall* to absorb.

dämm(e)rig *adj Licht* dim, faint; *Stunden* twilight *attr*. **es wird ~** *(abends)* dusk is falling; *(morgens)* dawn is breaking.

Dämmerlicht *nt* twilight; *(abends auch)* dusk; *(Halbdunkel)* half-light.

dämmern 1 *vi* **(a)** *(Tag, Morgen)* to dawn; *(Abend)* to fall. **als der Tag** *or* **Morgen/Abend dämmerte ...** as dawn was breaking/dusk was falling; **es dämmerte ihm, daß ...** *(col)* it dawned on him that ... **(b)** *(im Halbschlaf sein)* to doze. **vor sich hin ~** *(Kranker)* to be semi-conscious. **2** *vi impers* **es dämmert** *(morgens)* dawn is breaking; *(abends)* dusk is falling; **jetzt dämmert's (bei) mir!** *(col)* now it's dawning (on me)!

Dämmer-: ~schein *m (liter)* glow; **~schoppen** *m* early evening drink; **~stunde** *f* twilight, dusk.

Dämmerung *f* twilight; *(Abend~ auch)* dusk; *(Morgen~ auch)* dawn; *(Halbdunkel)* half-light. **in der ~** at dusk/dawn.

Dämmerzustand *m (Halbschlaf)* dozy state; *(Bewußtseinstrübung)* semi-conscious state.

Dämmung *f* insulation.

Dämon *m, pl* **Dämonen** demon.

Dampf *m* **¨-e (a)** steam. **~ ablassen** *(lit, fig)* to let off steam. **(b)** *(col: Wucht, Schwung)* force. **jdm ~ machen** *(col)* to make sb get a move on *(col)*; **~ dahinter machen** to get a move on *(col)*; **mit ~** *(col)* at full tilt.

Dampf- *in cpds* steam; **~antrieb** *m* steam drive; **~bügeleisen** *nt* steam iron.

dampfen *vi* **(a)** to steam. **ein ~des Bad** a steaming hot bath. **(b)** *aux sein (Zug, Schiff)* to steam.

dämpfen *vt* **(a)** *(abschwächen)* to muffle; *Geräusch, Schall auch* to deaden; *Farbe* to mute; *Licht, Stimme* to lower; *Wut* to calm; *Freude, Stimmung* to dampen; *Aufprall* to deaden; *siehe* **gedämpft. (b)** *(Cook)* to steam.

Dampfer *m* **-** steamer, steamship. **auf dem falschen ~ sein** *(fig col)* to have got the wrong idea.

Dämpfer *m* **-** *(Mus) (bei Klavier)* damper; *(bei Geige, Trompete)* mute. **dadurch hat er einen ~ bekommen** that dampened his spirits.

Dampf-: ~kessel *m (Tech)* steam-boiler; **~kochtopf** *m* pressure cooker; **~lokomotive, ~lok** *(col) f* steam engine *or* locomotive; **~maschine** *f* steam(-driven) engine; **~schiff** *nt* steamship, steamer; **~walze** *f* steamroller.

Damwild *nt* fallow deer.

danach *adv (emph auch* **danach***)* **(a)** *(zeitlich)* after that/it; *(nachher auch)* afterwards. **zehn Minuten ~ war sie schon wieder da** ten minutes later she was back.

(b) *(in der Reihenfolge) (örtlich)* behind (that/it/him *etc*); *(zeitlich)* after that/it/him *etc*.

(c) *(dementsprechend)* accordingly; *(laut diesem)* according to that. **~ sein** *(Wetter, Stimmung etc)* to be right; **die Torte hat nur 2 Mark gekostet — ~ ist sie auch** the gateau only cost 2 marks — it tastes like it too; **sie sieht nicht ~ aus** she doesn't look (like) it; *(als ob sie so was getan hätte)* she doesn't look the type; **~ zu urteilen** judging by that; **mir war nicht ~** *(col) or* **~ zumute** I didn't feel like it.

(d) *(in bestimmte Richtung)* towards it. **er griff schnell ~** he grabbed at it.

(e) sie sehnte sich ~, ihren Sohn wiederzusehen she longed to see her son again; **~ kann man nicht gehen** you can't go by that; **wenn es ~ ginge, was mir Spaß macht, dann ...** if it were a matter of what I enjoy then ...

Dandy ['dɛndi] *m* **-s** dandy.

Däne *m (wk)* **-n, -n** Dane, Danish man/boy.

daneben *adv (emph auch* **daneben***)* **(a)** *(räumlich)* next to him/her/that/it *etc*; **links/rechts ~** to the left/right of sb/sth; **wir wohnen im Haus ~** we live in the house next door. **(b)** *(verglichen damit)* in comparison. **(c)** *(außerdem)* as well (as that); *(gleichzeitig)* at the same time.

daneben-: ~benehmen* *vr sep irreg (col)* to make an exhibition of oneself; **~gehen** *vi sep irreg aux sein* **(a)** *(verfehlen: Schuß etc)* to miss; **(b)** *(col: scheitern)* to go wrong; **~geraten*** *vi sep irreg aux sein* to go wrong; *(Übersetzung)* not to hit the mark; **~greifen** *vi sep irreg to miss; (fig col: mit Schätzung etc)* to be wide of the mark; **im Ton ~greifen** to strike the wrong note; **~hauen** *vi sep irreg* **(a)** *(beim Schlagen)* to miss; **(b)** *(col: sich irren)* to be wide of the mark; **~liegen** *vi sep irreg (col: sich irren)* to be way out *(col)*; **~raten** *vi sep irreg (col)* to guess wrong; **~sein** *vi sep irreg aux sein (col) (verwirrt sein)* to be completely confused; *(sich nicht wohl fühlen)* to be feeling out of sorts.

Dänemark *nt* Denmark.

Dänin *f* Dane, Danish woman/girl.

dänisch *adj* Danish.

Dänisch(e) *nt decl as adj* Danish.

Dank *m no pl* thanks *pl*. **herzlichen** *or* **vielen ~** many thanks, thank you very much, thanks a lot *(col)*; **vielen herzlichen/tausend ~!** many/very many thanks!, thanks a million! *(col)*; **jdm für etw ~ sagen** *(liter)* to express one's *or* give *(esp Eccl)* thanks to sb for sth; **jdm zu ~ verpflichtet sein** *(form)* to owe sb a debt of gratitude; **mit bestem ~ zurück!** many thanks for the loan; *(iro: Retourkutsche)* thank you – the same to you!; **das ist der ~ dafür** that's all the thanks you get; **zum ~ (dafür)** as a way of saying thank you.

dank *prep+gen or dat* thanks to.

dankbar *adj* **(a)** *(dankerfüllt)* grateful; *(erleichtert, froh)* thankful; *Publikum, Zuhörer* appreciative. **jdm ~ sein** to be grateful to sb *(für* for*)*; **sich ~ erweisen** to show one's gratitude *(gegenüber* to*)*. **(b)** *(lohnend) Aufgabe, Rolle* rewarding; *(haltbar)* hard-wearing.

Dankbarkeit *f* gratitude *(gegen, gegenüber* to*)*.

danke *interj* thank you, thanks *(col)*, ta *(Brit col)*; *(ablehnend)* no thank you. **~ ja, ja, ~** yes please, yes, thank you; **~ nein, nein, ~** no thank you; **~ schön** *or* **sehr** thank you *or* thanks *(col)* very much; **~ vielmals** many thanks.

danken 1 *vi* **(a)** to express one's thanks. **jdm ~** to thank sb *(für* for*)*; **danke!** yes please!; *(ablehnend)* no thank you, no thanks *(col)*; **man dankt** *(col)* thanks *(col)*, ta *(Brit col)*; **jdm ~ lassen** to send sb one's thanks; **nichts zu ~** don't mention it; **na, ich danke** *(iro)* no thank you; **~d erhalten/ablehnen** to receive/decline with thanks. **(b)** *(ablehnen)* to decline. **2** *vt* **(a)** *(geh: verdanken)* **ihm danke ich es, daß ...** I owe it to him that ... **(b) jdm etw ~** to thank sb for sth; **man hat es mir schlecht gedankt, daß ich das getan habe** I got small thanks for doing it.

dankenswert *adj Bemühung* commendable; *Hilfe* kind; *(lohnenswert) Aufgabe, Arbeit* rewarding.

Dankeschön *nt no pl* thank-you.

Dankesworte *pl* words *pl* of thanks; *(von Redner)* vote *sing* of thanks.

Dank-: ~gottesdienst *m* service of thanksgiving; **~sagung** *f (Brief)* note of thanks; **~schreiben** *nt* letter of thanks.

dann *adv* **(a)** then. ~ **und** ~ about then; ~ **und wann** now and then; **gerade** ~, **wenn ...** just when ... **(b)** *(unter diesen Umständen)* then. **wenn ...,** ~ if ..., (then); **nein, selbst** ~ **nicht** no, not even then; **selbst** ~/**selbst** ~ **nicht, wenn ...** even/not even if ...; **erst** ~, **wenn ...** only when ...; **ja,** ~! (oh) well then!; **wenn er seine Gedichte selbst nicht versteht, wer** ~? if he can't understand his own poems, who can?; ~ **eben nicht** well, in that case (there's no more to be said); ~ **erst recht nicht!** in that case no way *(col)*; ~ **will ich lieber gehen** well, I'd better be getting along (then); **also** ~ **bis morgen** see you tomorrow then. **(c)** *(außerdem)* ~ **... noch** on top of that.

dannen *adv:* **von** ~ *(liter: weg)* away.

daran *adv (auch* **daran***)* **(a)** *(räumlich) hängen* on it/that; *schieben, lehnen, stellen* against it/that; *legen* next to it/that; *kleben, machen* to it/that. **nahe** *or* **dicht** ~ right up against it; **nahe** ~ **sein, etw zu tun** to be on the point of doing sth; **zu nahe** ~ too close (to it); ~ **vorbei** past it; ~ **kommen** to touch it/that. **(b)** *(zeitlich: danach anschließend)* **im Anschluß** ~ following that/this. **(c)** *(col)* = **dran (b, c)**. **(d)** *arbeiten* on it/that; *sterben, erinnern, Bedarf, Mangel* of it/that; *sich beteiligen, arm, reich* in it/that; *sich klammern* to it/that. **wird sich etwas** ~ **ändern?** will that change at all?; **wir können nichts** ~ **machen** we can't do anything about it; ~ **sieht man, wie ...** there you (can) see how ...; **das Beste/Schönste** *etc* ~ the best/nicest *etc* thing about it; **es ist nichts** ~ *(ist nicht fundiert)* there's nothing in it; *(ist nichts Besonderes)* it's nothing special.

daran-: ~**gehen** *vi sep irreg aux sein* to set about it; ~**gehen, etw zu tun** to set about doing sth; ~**machen** *vr sep (col)* to set about it; **sich** ~**machen, etw zu tun** to set about doing sth; ~**setzen** *sep* **1** *vt* **seine ganzen Kräfte** ~**setzen, etw zu tun** to spare no effort to do sth; **2** *vr (sich ~machen)* to get down to it.

darauf *adv (emph* **darauf***)* **(a)** *(räumlich)* on it/that/them *etc*; *(in Richtung)* towards it/that/them *etc*; *schießen, zielen, losfahren* at it/that/them *etc*; *(fig) basieren, aufbauen* on it/that; *zurückführen, beziehen* to it/that. **er schlug mit dem Hammer** ~ he hit it with the hammer; **seine Behauptungen stützen sich** ~, **daß ...** his claims are based on the supposition that ...

(b) *(Reihenfolge)* after that. **die Tage, die** ~ **folgten** the days which followed; ~ **folgte ...** that was followed by ..., after that came ...

(c) *(als Reaktion) sagen, reagieren* to that. ~ **antworten** to answer that; **eine Antwort** ~ an answer to that.

(d) *bestehen, verlassen, wetten, Zeit/Mühe verschwenden, Einfluß* on that/it; *hoffen, warten, sich vorbereiten, gefaßt sein* for that/it; *trinken* to that/it; *stolz sein* of that/it. **ich bin stolz** ~, **daß sie gewonnen hat** I'm proud that she won, I'm proud of her winning; **ich bestehe** ~, **daß du kommst** I insist that you come; **wir freuen uns schon** ~, **daß du bald kommst** we're looking forward to your *or* you coming; **wir kamen auch** ~ **zu sprechen** we talked about that too; **wie kommst du** ~? what makes you think that?; ~ **willst du hinaus!** that's what you're getting at!

daraufolgend *adj attr* after him/it/that *etc*; *Tag etc* following; *Wagen etc* behind *pred*.

daraufhin *adv (emph* **daraufhin***)* *(danach)* after that, thereupon; *(aus diesem Anlaß, deshalb)* as a result (of that/this); *(im Hinblick darauf)* with regard to that/this. **wir müssen es** ~ **prüfen, ob ...** we must test it to see whether ...

daraus *adv (emph auch* **daraus***)* out of that/it/them; *(aus dieser Angelegenheit)* from that/it/them. ~ **ergibt sich, daß ...** it follows from this that ...

därben *vi (geh: hungern)* to starve.

darbieten *sep irreg (geh)* **1** *vt* **(a)** *(vorführen) Tänze etc* to perform; *(vortragen) Lehrstoff* to present. **(b)** *(anbieten)* to offer; *Speisen* to serve. **2** *vr* to present itself.

Darbietung *f* performance; *(das Dargebotene)* act.

darbringen *vt sep irreg (geh) Opfer* to offer.

darein *adv (emph auch* **darein***)* *(räumlich: hinein)* in there; *(wenn Bezugsobjekt vorher erwähnt)* in it/them.

darein- *pref siehe auch* **drein-**; ~**finden** *vr sep irreg (geh)* to come to terms with it.

darin *adv (emph auch* **darin***)* **(a)** *(räumlich)* in there; *(wenn Bezugsobjekt vorher erwähnt)* in it/them. **(b)** *(in dieser Beziehung)* in that respect. ~ **ist er ganz groß** *(col)* he's very good at that; **die beiden unterscheiden sich** ~, **daß ...** the two of them differ in that ...; **der Unterschied liegt** ~, **daß ...** the difference is that ...

darlegen *vt sep* to explain *(jdm* to sb*)*; *Theorie, Ansichten auch* to expound *(jdm* to sb*)*.

Darlegung *f* explanation.

Darleh(e)n *nt* **-** loan. **als** ~ as a loan.

Darm *m* **¨-e** intestine(s *pl*), bowel(s *pl*); *(für Wurst)* (sausage) skin; *(für Saiten, Schläger etc)* gut.

Darm- *in cpds* intestinal; ~**ausgang** *m* anus; ~**grippe** *f* gastric influenza; ~**krebs** *m* cancer of the intestine; ~**tätigkeit** *f* peristalsis *no art*; **die** ~**tätigkeit fördern** to stimulate the movement of the bowels; ~**trägheit** *f* under-activity of the intestines.

Darre *f* **-n** drying kiln *or* oven; *(Hopfen~)* oast.

darreichen *vt sep (liter: anbieten)* to offer *(jdm etw* sb sth, sth to sb*)*.

darstellbar *adj (in Literaturwerk etc)* portrayable; *(durch Diagramm etc)* representable; *(beschreibbar)* describable. **schwer/leicht** ~ hard/easy to portray/show/describe.

darstellen *sep* **1** *vt* **(a)** to show; *(ein Bild entwerfen von)* to portray, to depict; *(Theat)* to play; *(beschreiben)* to describe. **etw kurz** ~ to give a short description of sth; **er stellt nichts dar** *(fig)* he's nothing special. **(b)** *(bedeuten)* to constitute, to represent. **2** *vr (Eindruck vermitteln)* to appear *(jdm* to sb*)*; *(sich erweisen)* to show oneself.

Darsteller *m* **-** *(Theat)* actor. **der** ~ **des Hamlet** the actor playing Hamlet.

Darstellerin *f (Theat)* actress.

darstellerisch *adj* dramatic. **eine** ~**e Höchstleistung** a magnificent piece of acting.

Darstellung *f* portrayal; *(in Buch, Bild auch)* depiction; *(durch Diagramm etc)* representation; *(Beschreibung)* description; *(Bericht)* account. **eine falsche** ~ **der Fakten** a misrepresentation of the facts; **er gab eine großartige** ~ **des Hamlet** his performance as Hamlet was superb.

darüber *adv (emph* **darüber***)* **(a)** *(räumlich)* over that/it/them; *(höher als etw)* above (there/it/them); *(direkt auf etw)* on top (of it/them). **geh** ~, **nicht hierüber!** go over there, not here!; ~ **hinweg sein** *(fig)* to have got over it. **(b)** *(deswegen, in dieser Beziehung)* about that/it. **sich** ~ **beschweren/beklagen, daß ...** to complain/moan that ... **(c)** *(davon)* about that/it. **sie führt eine Liste** ~ she keeps a list of it. **(d)** *(mehr, höher)* above *or* over that. **21 Jahre und** ~ 21 years and above *or* over; ~ **hinaus** over and above that.

darüber-: ~**fahren** *vi sep irreg aux sein (fig)* to run over it; **wenn du mit der Hand** ~**fährst, ...** if you run your hand over it ...; ~**liegen** *vi sep irreg (fig)* to be higher; ~**stehen** *vi sep irreg (fig)* to be above such things.

darum *adv (emph* **darum***)* *siehe auch* **drum (a)** *(räumlich)* around that/it/him/her/them. ~ **herum** around about (it/him/her/them). **(b)** *(um diese Angelegenheit)* **es geht** ~, **daß ...** the thing is that ...; ~ **geht es mir/geht es mir nicht** that's my point/that's not the point for me; **es geht mir ~, Ihnen das klarzumachen** I'm trying to make it clear to you; **ich gäbe viel ~, die Wahrheit zu erfahren** I would give a lot to learn the truth. **(c)** *(deshalb)* that's why, because of that. **eben ~** that is exactly why; **warum willst du nicht mitkommen? — ~!** *(col)* why don't you want to come? — I just don't.

darunter *adv (emph auch* **darunter)** **(a)** *(räumlich)* under that/it/them. **~ hervorkommen** to appear from underneath. **(b)** *(weniger)* under that. **Leute im Alter von 35 Jahren und ~** people aged 35 and under; **~ macht sie's nicht** *(col)* she won't do it for less. **(c)** *(dabei)* among them. **~ waren viele Ausländer** there were a lot of foreigners among them. **(d) was verstehen Sie ~?** what do you understand by that/it?; **~ kann ich mir nichts vorstellen** that doesn't mean anything to me.

darunter-: ~fallen *vi sep irreg aux sein (fig) (dazugerechnet werden)* to be included; *(davon betroffen werden)* to come under it/them; **~mischen** *sep* **1** *vt Mehl* to mix in; **2** *vr (Mensch)* to mingle with them; **~setzen** *vt sep Unterschrift* to put to it.

das *art etc siehe* **der**[2].

Dasein *nt no pl* existence; *(Anwesendsein)* presence.

dasein *vi sep irreg aux sein* to be there. **noch ~** to be still there; *(übrig sein auch)* to be left; **wieder ~** to be back; **ich bin gleich wieder da** I'll be right back; **ist Post für mich da?** is there any mail for me?; **war der Briefträger schon da?** has the postman been yet?; **sie ist nur für ihren Mann da** she lives for her husband; **ein Arzt, der immer für seine Patienten da ist** a doctor who always has time for his patients; **voll ~** *(col)* to be all there *(col)*; **es ist alles schon mal dagewesen** it's all been done before; **ein nie dagewesener Erfolg** an unprecedented success.

Daseins-: ~berechtigung *f* right to exist; **~kampf** *m* struggle for survival.

dasitzen *vi sep irreg* to sit there. **ohne einen Pfennig ~** *(col)* to be left without a penny.

dasjenige *dem pron siehe* **derjenige.**

daß *conj* that. **ich bin überzeugt, ~ du das Richtige getan hast** I'm sure (that) you have done the right thing; **ich bin dagegen, ~ ihr alle kommt** I'm against you all coming; **das liegt daran, ~ ...** that is because ...; **~ du es mir nicht verlierst!** see that you don't lose it!

dasselbe *dem pron siehe* **derselbe.**

dastehen *vi sep irreg aux haben or sein* **(a)** to stand there. **steh nicht so dumm da!** don't just stand there looking stupid. **(b)** *(fig)* **gut/schlecht ~** to be in a good/bad position; **allein ~** to be on one's own; **einzig ~** to be unique *or* unparalleled; **jetzt stehe ich als Lügner da** now I'm left looking like a liar; **wie stehe ich jetzt da!** *(Selbstlob)* just look at me now!; *(Vorwurf)* I look a proper fool!

Datei *f* file.

Daten (a) *pl of* **Datum. (b)** *(Comp etc)* data *pl.*

Daten-: ~bank *f* database; *(größer)* data bank; **~schutz** *m* data protection *no art*; **~technik** *f* computer science; **~träger** *m* data carrier; **~typist(in** *f*) *m* terminal operator; **~übertragung** *f* data transmission; **~verarbeitung** *f* data processing; **~verarbeitungsanlage** *f* computer.

datieren* *vti* to date. **dieser Brief datiert vom 1. Januar** this letter is dated January 1st.

Dativ *m (Gram)* dative (case).

Dativ|objekt *nt (Gram)* indirect object.

dato *adv*: **bis ~** *(Comm, col)* to date.

Dattel *f* **-n** date.

Datum *nt, pl* **Daten (a)** date. **was für ein ~ haben wir heute?** what is the date today?; **das heutige ~** today's date; **ein Brief ohne ~** an undated letter; **ein Nachschlagewerk neueren ~s** a recent reference work. **(b)** *usu pl (Statistik, Comp etc)* piece of data.

Datums-: ~grenze *f (Geog)* (international) date line; **~stempel** *m* date stamp.

Dauer *f no pl (das Andauern)* duration; *(Zeitspanne)* period, term; *(Länge: einer Sendung etc)* length. **während der ~ des Vertrages/Krieges** for the duration of the contract/war; **für die ~ eines Monats** for a period of one month; **seine Begeisterung war nicht von ~** his enthusiasm was short-lived; **von langer/kurzer ~ sein** to last a long time/not to last long; **auf die ~** in the long run; **das kann auf die ~ nicht so weitergehen** it can't go on like that indefinitely; **auf ~** permanently.

Dauer- *in cpds* permanent; **~auftrag** *m (Fin)* standing order; **~belastung** *f* continual pressure *no indef art*; *(von Maschine)* constant load; **~brenner** *m* **(a)** *(Ofen)* slow burning stove; **(b)** *(col: Dauererfolg)* long runner; **~erfolg** *m* long-running success; **~gast** *m* permanent guest; *(häufiger Gast)* regular visitor, permanent fixture *(hum)*.

dauerhaft *adj Zustand, Farbe* permanent; *Frieden, Beziehung* lasting; *Stoff* durable.

Dauerhaftigkeit *f* permanence; *(von Material)* durability.

Dauer-: ~karte *f* season ticket; **~lauf** *m (Sport)* jog; *(das Laufen)* jogging; **im ~lauf** at a jog *or* trot; **einen ~lauf machen** to go jogging; **~lutscher** *m* lollipop *(Brit)*, popsicle ® *(US)*.

dauern *vi* **(a)** *(an~)* to last, to go on. **die Verhandlungen ~ schon drei Wochen** the negotiations have already been going on for three weeks. **(b)** *(Zeit benötigen)* to take a while; *(lange)* to take a long time. **das dauert noch** *(col)* it'll be some time yet; **es dauerte lange, bis er sich befreit hatte** it took him a long time to get free; **das dauert mir zu lange** it takes too long for me; **es dauert jetzt nicht mehr lange** it won't take much longer.

dauernd 1 *adj Regelung* lasting; *Wohnsitz* permanent; *(fortwährend) Unterbrechung* constant, perpetual. **2** *adv* **etw ~ tun** to keep (on) doing sth.

Dauer-: ~obst *nt* fruit suitable for storing; **~parker** *m* - long-stay parker; **~redner** *m (pej)* interminable speaker; **~regen** *m* continuous rain; **~schlaf** *m* prolonged sleep; **~stellung** *f* permanent position; **~ton** *m* continuous tone; **~welle** *f* perm, permanent wave; **~wirkung** *f* (long-)lasting effect; **~wurst** *f* salami; **~zustand** *m* permanent state of affairs.

Däumchen *nt dim of* **Daumen.**

Daumen *m* - thumb. **jdm die Daumen drücken** to keep one's fingers crossed for sb; **~ drehen** to twiddle one's thumbs; **den ~ auf etw** *(acc)* **halten** *(col)* to hold on to sth.

Daumen-: ~abdruck *m* thumbprint; **~nagel** *m* thumbnail; **~schraube** *f* **jdm die ~schrauben anlegen** *(fig, col)* to put the (thumb)screws on sb.

Daune *f* **-n** down feather. **~n** down *sing.*

Daunen-: ~bett *nt*, **~decke** *f* (down-filled) duvet; **d~weich** *adj* soft as down.

davon *adv (emph* **davon)** **(a)** *(räumlich)* from there; *(wenn Bezugsobjekt vorher erwähnt)* from it/them; *(mit Entfernungsangabe)* away (from there/it/them). **weg ~!** *(col)* get away from there/it/them.

(b) *(fig)* **ich bin weit ~ entfernt, Ihnen Vorwürfe machen zu wollen** the last thing I want to do is reproach you; **wenn wir einmal ~ absehen, daß ...** if for once we overlook the fact that ...; **und ~ kommt die rote Farbe** and that's where the red comes from; **das kommt ~!** that's what you get!; **~ hat man nur Ärger** you get nothing but trouble with it; **~ wird man müde** it makes you tired; **was habe ich ~?** what do I get out of it?

(c) *(mit Passiv)* **~ betroffen werden** to be affected by it/them.

(d) *(Anteil)* of that/it/them. **nehmen Sie doch noch etwas ~!** do have some more!; **das Doppelte ~** twice that.

(e) *(darüber) hören, wissen, sprechen* about that/it/them; *verstehen, halten* of that/it/them. **genug ~!** enough of this!

davon-: ~bleiben *vi sep irreg aux sein (col)* to keep away; *(nicht anfassen)* to keep one's hands off; **~fahren** *vi sep irreg aux sein* to drive away; *(auf Fahrrad etc)* to ride away; *(Zug)* to pull away; **~fliegen** *vi sep irreg aux sein* to fly away; **~gehen** *vi sep irreg aux sein (geh)* to walk away; **~jagen** *vt sep* to chase off *or* away; **~kommen** *vi sep irreg aux sein (entkommen)* to get away, to escape; *(nicht bestraft werden)* to get away with it; **mit dem Schrecken/dem Leben/einer Geldstrafe ~kommen** to escape with no more than a shock/ with one's life/to get off with a fine; **~lassen** *vt sep irreg* **die Finger ~lassen** *(col)* to keep one's hands *or* fingers off (it/them); **~laufen** *vi sep irreg aux sein* to run away *(jdm/vor jdm* from sb*)*; *(verlassen)* to walk out *(jdm* on sb*)*; **es ist zum D~laufen!** *(col)* it's all too much!; **die Preise sind den Löhnen ~gelaufen** prices have outstripped wages; **~machen** *vr sep* to make off; **~schleichen** *vir sep irreg (vi: aux sein)* to creep away *or* off; **~tragen** *vt sep irreg* **(a)** *(wegtragen)* to carry away; *Preis* to carry off; *Sieg, Ruhm* to win; **(b)** *Schaden, Verletzung* to suffer; **~ziehen** *vi sep irreg aux sein (liter)* to leave; *(Sport col)* to pull away *(jdm* from sb*)*.

davor *adv (emph* **davor***)* **(a)** *(räumlich)* in front (of that/it/them); *(wenn Bezugsobjekt vorher erwähnt)* in front of it/them. **(b)** *(zeitlich)* before that; *(bevor man etw tut)* beforehand. **(c)** *bewahren, schützen* from that/it; *warnen* about that/it; *Angst haben* of that/it; *sich ekeln* by that/it. **ich habe Angst ~, daß der Hund beißen könnte** I'm afraid that the dog might bite.

davor-: ~stehen *vi sep irreg aux haben or sein* to stand in front of it/them; **~stellen** *sep* **1** *vt* to put in front of it/them; **2** *vr* to stand in front of it/them.

dazu *adv (emph* **dazu***)*. **(a)** *(dabei, damit)* with it; **er ist dumm und ~ auch noch faul** he's stupid and lazy with it *or* into the bargain *(col)*; **... und ~ nicht unintelligent** ... and not unintelligent either; **noch ~** as well, too; **~ serviert man am besten Reis** it's best to serve rice with it.

(b) *(dahin)* to that/it. **das führt ~, daß weitere Forderungen gestellt werden** that will lead to further demands being made; **wie konnte es nur ~ kommen?** how could that happen?; **wie komme ich ~?** *(empört)* why on earth should I?; **... aber ich bin nicht ~ gekommen** ... but I didn't get around to it.

(c) *(dafür, zu diesem Zweck)* for that/it. **ich bin zu alt ~, noch tanzen zu gehen** I'm too old to go dancing; **ich habe ihm ~ geraten** I advised him to (do that); **~ bereit sein, etw zu tun** to be prepared to do sth; **~ ist er da** that's what he's there for; **das Recht ~** the right to do it.

(d) *(darüber, zum Thema)* about that/it. **was meinst du ~?** what do you think about that?

(e) im Gegensatz/Vergleich ~ in contrast to/comparison with that.

dazu-: ~geben *vt sep irreg* to add; **~gehören*** *vi sep* to belong (to it/us *etc*); *(als Ergänzung)* to go with it/them; *(eingeschlossen sein)* to be included (in it/them); **das gehört ~** *(versteht sich von selbst)* it's all part of it; **es gehört schon einiges ~, das zu tun** it takes a lot to do that; **~gehörig** *adj attr* which goes/go with it/them; *Schlüssel etc* belonging to it/them; *Werkzeuge, Material* necessary; **~kommen** *vi sep irreg aux sein* **(a)** *(ankommen)* to arrive (on the scene); **(b)** *(hinzugefügt werden)* to be added; **kommt noch etwas ~?** will there by anything else?; **es kommt noch ~, daß er faul ist** added to that he's lazy; **~lernen** *vt sep* **viel/nichts ~lernen** to learn a lot more/ nothing new; **schon wieder was ~gelernt!** you learn something (new) every day!

dazumal *adv (old)* in those days.

dazu-: ~rechnen *vt sep Betrag* to add on; **~schreiben** *vt sep irreg* to add; **~setzen** *vr sep* to join him/us *etc*; **~tun** *vt sep irreg (col)* to add; **er hat es ohne dein D~tun geschafft** he managed it without your doing/saying *etc* anything.

dazwischen *adv* in between; *(in der betreffenden Menge, Gruppe)* amongst them, in with them.

dazwischen-: ~fahren *vi sep irreg aux sein* **(a)** *(eingreifen)* to intervene; **(b)** *(unterbrechen)* to interrupt; **~funken** *vi sep (col: eingreifen)* to put one's oar in *(col)*; **~kommen** *vi sep irreg aux sein (störend erscheinen)* to get in the way; **... wenn nichts ~kommt!** ... if all goes well; **mir ist leider etwas ~gekommen, ich kann nicht dabeisein** something has come *or* cropped up, I'm afraid I can't be there; **~reden** *vi sep* to interrupt *(jdm* sb*)*; **~rufen** *vti sep irreg* to yell out; **~stehen** *vi sep irreg aux haben or sein* **(a)** *(lit)* to be amongst *or (zwischen zweien)* between them; **(b)** *(zwischen den Parteien)* to be neutral; **(c)** *(geh: hindernd)* to be in the way; **~treten** *vi sep irreg aux sein* to intervene; *(störend)* to come between them.

DB [deː'beː] *f* = **Deutsche Bundesbahn.**

DDR [deːdeː'|ɛr] *f* = **Deutsche Demokratische Republik** GDR, German Democratic Republic, East Germany.

DDR-Bürger *m* East German.

Dealer(in *f***)** ['diːlɐ, -ərɪn] *m* - *(col)* pusher.

Debakel *nt* - debacle. **ein ~ erleiden** *(Stück etc)* to be a debacle.

Debatte *f* **-n** debate. **etw zur ~ stellen** to put sth up for discussion *or (Parl)* debate; **das steht hier nicht zur ~** that's not the issue.

debattieren* *vti* to debate *(über etw* sth*)*.

Debet *nt* **-s** *(Fin)* debits *pl*.

Debüt [de'byː] *nt* **-s** debut. **sein ~ als etw geben** to make one's debut as sth.

Debütant(in *f***)** *m (wk)* person making his/her debut.

debütieren* *vi (Theat, fig)* to make one's debut.

Dechant *m (Eccl)* dean.

dechiffrieren* [deʃɪ'friːrən] *vt* to decode, to decipher.

Deck *nt* **-s** deck; *(in Parkhaus)* level. **an ~ gehen** to go on deck; **alle Mann an ~!** all hands on deck!

Deck-: ~adresse *f* accommodation *or* cover *(US)* address; **~anstrich** *m* top coat; **~bett** *nt* feather quilt; **~blatt** *nt (von Zigarre)* wrapper; *(Schutzblatt)* cover.

Decke *f* **-n (a)** *(lit, fig)* blanket; *(Tisch~)* cloth; *(Stepp~)* quilt. **sich nach der ~ strecken** *(fig)* to cut one's coat according to one's cloth; **mit jdm unter einer ~ stecken** *(fig)* to be hand in glove with sb. **(b)** *(Zimmer~)* ceiling; **an die ~ gehen** *(col)* to hit the roof *(col)*; **vor Freude an die ~ springen** *(col)* to jump for joy; **mir fällt die ~ auf den Kopf** *(fig col)* I feel really claustrophobic. **(c)** *(Schicht)* layer; *(Straßen~)* surface.

Deckel *m* - lid; *(von Schachtel auch, von Flasche)* top; *(Buch~)* cover. **du kriegst gleich eins auf den ~** *(col)* you're going to catch it *(col)*.

decken 1 *vt* **(a)** *(zu~, Fin, begatten)* to cover. *(Ftbl auch)* to mark; *Komplizen* to cover up for. **ein Dach mit Ziegeln ~** to roof a building with tiles; **mein Bedarf ist gedeckt** I have all I need; *(fig col)* I've had enough. **(b)** *Tisch, Tafel* to set, to lay *(Brit)*. **sich an einen gedeckten Tisch setzen** *(fig)* to be handed everything on a plate; **ein Tuch über etw** *(acc)* **~** to cover sth with a cloth. **2** *vi* to cover; *(Boxen)* to guard; *(Ftbl auch)* to mark. **3** *vr* **(a)** *(Interessen, Begriffe)* to coincide; *(Aussagen)* to correspond, to agree. **(b)** *(Boxer etc)* to cover oneself.

Deck-: ~**farbe** *f* opaque water colour; ~**hengst** *m* stud(horse), stallion; ~**mantel** *m (fig)* mask; **unter dem ~mantel von ...** under the guise of ...; ~**name** *m* assumed name; *(Mil)* code name; ~**offizier** *m (Naut)* ≈ warrant officer; ~**platte** *f (Build)* slab; ~**schicht** *f* surface layer; *(von Straße)* surface; *(Geol)* top layer.

Deckung *f* **(a)** *(Schutz)* cover; *(Ftbl, Chess)* defence; *(Boxen etc)* guard. **in ~ gehen** to take cover. **(b)** *(Verheimlichung)* **die ~ von etw** covering up for sth. **(c)** *(Comm, Fin) (von Scheck, Wechsel)* cover; *(das Decken)* covering; *(das Begleichen)* meeting. **zur ~ seiner Schulden** to meet his debts. **(d) eine ~ der Nachfrage ist unmöglich** demand cannot possibly be met. **(e)** *(Übereinstimmung)* **lassen sich diese Standpunkte zur ~ bringen?** can these points of view be reconciled?

Deckungs-: ~**fehler** *m (Ftbl)* defensive error; ~**feuer** *nt (Mil)* covering fire; **d~gleich** *adj (Math)* congruent; **d~gleich sein** *(fig)* to coincide; *(Aussagen)* to agree.

Decoder [de'ko:dɐ, dɪ'koudə] *m* - decoder.

decodieren* *vt* to decode.

Deduktion *f* deduction.

deduzieren* *vt* to deduce *(aus* from*)*.

de facto *adv* de facto.

Defätismus *m no pl* defeatism.

defätistisch *adj* defeatist *no adv*.

defekt *adj Gerät etc* faulty, defective.

Defekt *m* **-e** fault, defect; *(Med)* deficiency.

defensiv *adj* defensive.

Defensive [-'zi:və] *f no pl* defensive. **in der ~** on the defensive; **jdn in die ~ drängen** to force sb onto the defensive.

defilieren* *vi aux haben or sein (Mil)* to march past; *(fig)* to parade past.

definierbar *adj* definable.

definieren* *vt* to define.

Definition *f* definition.

definitiv *adj* definite.

Defizit *nt* **-e** deficit; *(Mangel)* deficiency *(an+dat* of*)*.

defizitär *adj* in deficit. **eine ~e Haushaltspolitik führen** to follow an economic policy which can only lead to deficit.

Deflation *f (Econ)* deflation.

deflationär *adj* deflationary *no adv*.

deflorieren* *vt* to deflower.

Deformation *f* deformation, distortion; *(Mißbildung)* deformity; *(Entstellung)* disfigurement.

deformieren* *vt (lit, fig: mißbilden)* to deform; *(entstellen)* to disfigure. **eine deformierte Nase** a misshapen nose.

Defroster *m* - *(Aut)* heated windscreen; *(Sprühmittel)* de-icer.

deftig *adj* **(a)** *Witz, Humor* ribald. **(b)** *Lüge* whopping *(col)*, huge; *Mahlzeit* solid; *Wurst etc* substantial, good solid *attr; Ohrfeige* cracking *(col)*.

Degen *m* - *(Sportfechten)* épée.

degenerieren* *vi aux sein* to degenerate *(zu* into*)*.

degeneriert *adj* degenerate.

degradieren* *vt (Mil)* to demote *(zu* to*)*; *(fig: herabwürdigen)* to degrade. **jdn/etw zu etw ~** *(fig)* to lower sb/sth to the level of sth.

Degradierung *f (Mil)* demotion *(zu* to*)*; *(fig)* degradation.

dehnbar *adj (lit, fig)* elastic.

Dehnbarkeit *f no pl* elasticity.

dehnen 1 *vt* to stretch; *(Med auch)* to dilate; *Laut, Silbe* to lengthen. **2** *vr (auch Ozean etc)* to stretch.

Dehnung *f siehe vt* stretching; dilation; lengthening.

Deich *m* **-e** dyke, dike *(esp US)*.

Deichsel [-ks-] *f* **-n** shaft; *(Doppel~)* shafts *pl*.

deichseln [-ks-] *vt (col)* to wangle *(col)*. **das werden wir schon ~** we'll wangle it somehow.

dein *poss pron (adjektivisch) (in Briefen:* **D~***)* your. **herzliche Grüße, D~e Elke** with best wishes, yours *or (herzlicher)* love Elke.

deiner *pers pron gen of* **du** *(geh)* of you.

deine(r, s) *poss pron (substantivisch)* yours. **der/die/das ~** *(geh)* yours; **die D~n** *(geh)* your family; **das D~** *(geh: Besitz)* what is yours.

deinerseits *adv (auf deiner Seite)* for your part; *(von deiner Seite)* on your part.

deinesgleichen *pron inv* people like you.

deinet-: ~**wegen** *adv (wegen dir)* because of you, on account of you; *(dir zuliebe)* for your sake; *(um dich)* about you; *(für dich)* on your behalf; ~**willen** *adv* **um ~willen** for your sake.

deins *poss pron* yours.

de jure *adv* de jure.

Dekade *f (10 Tage)* ten days; *(10 Jahre)* decade.

dekadent *adj* decadent.

Dekadenz *f no pl* decadence.

Dekan *m* **-e** *(Univ, Eccl)* dean.

Dekanat *nt (Univ)* office of dean; *(Eccl)* deanery.

Deklamation *f* declamation. ~**en** *(pej)* (empty) rhetoric *sing*.

deklamieren* *vti* to declaim.

Deklaration *f* declaration.

deklarieren* *vt* to declare.

deklassieren* *vt* **(a)** *(Sociol, herabsetzen)* to downgrade. **(b)** *(Sport: übertreffen)* to outclass.

Deklination *f (Gram)* declension.

deklinieren* *vt (Gram)* to decline.

Dekolleté [dekɔl'te:] *nt* **-s** low-cut *or* décolleté neckline.

dekolletiert [dekɔl'ti:ɐt] *adj Kleid* low-cut, décolleté.

Dekor *m or nt* **-s** *or* **-e** decoration; *(von Raum auch, Theat, Film etc)* décor.

Dekorateur(in *f***)** [dekora'tø:ɐ, -ø:rɪn] *m* interior designer; *(Schaufenster~)* window-dresser.

Dekoration *f* **(a)** *no pl (das Ausschmücken)* decorating, decoration. **(b)** *(Einrichtung)* décor *no pl; (Fenster~)* window-dressing; *(Theat: Bühnenbild)* set. **zur ~ dienen** to be decorative. **(c)** *(Ordensverleihung)* decoration.

Dekorations-: ~**maler** *m* (interior) decorator; *(Theat)* scene-painter; ~**stoff** *m (Tex)* furnishing fabric; ~**stück** *nt* piece of the décor; **das ist nur ein ~stück** that's just for decoration.

dekorativ *adj* decorative.

dekorieren* *vt* to decorate; *Schaufenster* to dress.

Dekostoff *m (Tex)* furnishing fabric.

Dekret *nt* **-e** decree.

Delegation *f* delegation.

delegieren* *vt* to delegate *(an +acc* to*)*.

Delegierte(r) *mf decl as adj* delegate.

delikat *adj* **(a)** *(wohlschmeckend)* exquisite, delicious. **(b)** *(behutsam)* delicate. **(c)** *(heikel) Problem* delicate, sensitive; *(gewagt)* risqué.

Delikateß- *in cpds* top-quality, fine.

Delikatesse *f (Leckerbissen, fig)* delicacy.

Delikatessengeschäft *nt* delicatessen.

Delikt *nt* **-e** *(Jur)* offence; *(schwerer)* crime.

Delinquent [delɪŋ'kvɛnt] *m (geh)* offender.

Delirium *nt* delirium. **im ~ sein** to be delirious; *(col: betrunken)* to be paralytic *(col)*.

Delle *f* **-n** *(col: eingedrückte Stelle)* dent.

Delphin[1] *m* **-e** *(Zool)* dolphin.

Delphin[2] *no pl*, **Delphinschwimmen** *nt* butterfly.

Delta *nt, pl* **-s** *or* **Delten** *(Geog)* delta.

dem 1 *dat of def art* **der, das (a)** to the; *(mit Präposition)* the. **(b) wenn ~ so ist** if that is the way it is; **wie ~ auch sei** be that as it may. **2** *dat of dem pron* **der, das (a)** *attr* to that; *(mit Präposition)* that. **(b)** *(substantivisch)* to that one; that one; *(Menschen)* to him; him. **3** *dat of rel pron* **der, das** to whom, that *or* who(m) ... to; *(mit Präposition)* who(m); *(von Sachen)* to which, which *or* that ... to; *(mit Präposition)* which.

Demagoge *m* demagogue.

demagogisch *adj Rede etc* demagogic.

Demarkationslinie *f (Pol, Mil)* demarcation line.

demaskieren* **1** *vt* to unmask, to expose. **2** *vr* to take off one's mask.

Dementi *nt* **-s** denial.

dementieren* **1** *vt* to deny. **2** *vi* to deny it.

dem|entsprechend **1** *adv* correspondingly; *(demnach)* accordingly. **2** *adj* appropriate.

dem-: **~gegenüber** *adv (wohingegen)* on the other hand; *(im Vergleich dazu)* in contrast; **~gemäß** *adv, adj* = **~entsprechend.**

Demission *f (Pol: Rücktritt)* resignation.

dem-: **~nach** *adv* therefore; *(~entsprechend)* accordingly; **~nächst** *adv* soon.

Demo *f* **-s** *(col)* demo *(col).*

Demographie *f* demography.

demographisch *adj* demographic.

Demokrat(in *f*) *m (wk)* **-en, -en** democrat.

Demokratie *f* democracy.

Demokratieverständnis *nt* understanding of (the meaning of) democracy.

demokratisch *adj* democratic.

demokratisieren* *vt* to democratize, to make democratic.

Demokratisierung *f* democratization.

demolieren* *vt* to wreck, to smash up; *(Rowdy auch)* to vandalize.

Demonstrant(in *f*) *m (wk)* demonstrator.

Demonstration *f* demonstration.

Demonstrations-: **~material** *nt* teaching material; **~objekt** *nt* teaching aid; **~recht** *nt* right to demonstrate; *(Gesetz)* law on demonstrations; **~zug** *m* demonstration.

demonstrativ *adj* demonstrative *(auch Gram)*; *Beifall* acclamatory; *Protest, Fehlen* pointed. **der Botschafter verließ ~ den Saal** the ambassador pointedly left the room.

demonstrieren* *vti* to demonstrate.

Demontage [-ˈtaːʒə] *f* **-n** *(lit, fig)* dismantling.

demontieren* *vt (lit, fig)* to dismantle; *Räder* to take off.

demoralisieren* *vt* to demoralize.

Demoskop(in *f*) *m (wk)* **-en -en** (opinion) pollster.

Demoskopie *f no pl* (public) opinion research.

demoskopisch *adj* **~es Institut** (public) opinion research institute; **alle ~en Voraussagen waren falsch** all the predictions in the opinion polls were wrong; **eine ~e Untersuchung** a (public) opinion poll.

demselben *dat of* **derselbe, dasselbe.**

Demut *f no pl* humility. **in ~** with humility.

demütig *adj Bitte, Blick* humble.

demütigen **1** *vt Besiegten, Volk* to humiliate; *stolzen Menschen etc* to humble. **2** *vr* to humble oneself *(vor+dat* before*).*

Demütigung *f* humiliation.

demzufolge *adv* therefore.

den **1 (a)** *acc of def art* **der** the. **(b)** *dat pl of def art* **der, die, das** the; to the. **2** *acc of dem pron* **der (a)** *attr* that. **(b)** *(substantivisch)* that one; *(Menschen)* him. **3** *acc of rel pron* **der** who(m), that; *(von Sachen)* which, that.

denen **1** *dat pl of dem pron* **der, die, das** to them; *(mit Präposition)* them. **2** *dat pl of rel pron* **der, die, das** to whom, that *or* who(m) ... to; *(mit Präposition)* whom; *(von Sachen)* to which, that *or* which ... to; which.

Denk-: **~ansatz** *m* starting point; **~anstoß** *m* **jdm ~anstöße geben** to give sb food for thought; **~art** *f* way of thinking; **d~bar 1** *adj* conceivable; **es ist durchaus d~bar, daß er kommt** it's quite likely that he'll come; **2** *adv* extremely; **der d~bar schlechteste Eindruck** the worst possible impression.

Denken *nt no pl* thinking.

denken *pret* **dachte,** *ptp* **gedacht 1** *vi (überlegen)* to think *(über+acc* about, of*).* **bei sich ~** to think to oneself; **wo ~ Sie hin!** what an idea!; **der Mensch denkt, Gott lenkt** *(Prov)* man proposes, God disposes *(Prov)*; **das gibt mir/einem zu ~** it makes you think; **wie ~ Sie darüber?** what do you think about it?; **kleinlich ~** to be petty-minded; **alle, die damals liberal gedacht haben, ...** all those who were thinking along liberal lines ...; **an jdn/etw ~** to think of sb/sth; **daran ist gar nicht zu ~** that's (quite) out of the question; **ich denke nicht daran!** no way! *(col)*, not on your life!; **ich denke nicht daran, das zu tun** there's no way I'm going to do that *(col)*; **solange ich ~ kann** (for) as long as I can remember; **denk daran!** don't forget!; **an das Geld habe ich gar nicht mehr gedacht** I had forgotten all about the money; **die viele Arbeit, ich darf gar nicht daran ~** all that work, it doesn't bear thinking about.

2 *vt* to think. **was denkst du jetzt?** what are you thinking?; **ich denke gar nichts** I'm not thinking about anything; **(nur) Schlechtes/Gutes von jdm ~** to think ill/well of sb; **wer hätte das (von ihr) gedacht!** who'd have thought it (of her)!; **was sollen bloß die Leute ~!** what will people think!; **ich denke schon** I think so; **ich denke nicht** I don't think so, I think not; **für jdn/etw gedacht sein** to be intended *or* meant for sb/sth; **so war das nicht gedacht** it wasn't meant that way.

3 *vr* **(a)** *(vorstellen)* **das kann ich mir ~** I can imagine; **ich habe mir das so gedacht: ...** this is what I had in mind: ...; **das habe ich mir gedacht** I thought so; **dachte ich mir's doch!** I knew it! **(b)** *(beabsichtigen)* sich *(dat)* **etw bei etw ~** to mean sth by sth; **ich habe mir nichts Böses dabei gedacht** I meant no harm (in it).

Denker(in *f*) *m* **-** thinker. **das Volk der Dichter und ~** the nation of poets and philosophers.

Denkerstirn *f (hum)* lofty brow.

Denk-: **d~fähig** *adj* capable of thinking; **als d~fähiger Mensch** as an intelligent person; **~fähigkeit** *f* ability to think; **d~faul** *adj* (mentally) lazy; **~faulheit** *f* (mental) laziness; **~fehler** *m* flaw in the/one's reasoning.

Denkmal [-maːl] *nt* **¨er** *or (geh)* **-e** *(lit, fig)* monument *(für* to*)*; *(Standbild)* statue. **er hat sich** *(dat)* **ein ~ gesetzt** he has earned himself a place in history.

Denkmalschutz *m* protection of historical monuments. **etw unter ~ stellen** to classify sth as a historical monument.

Denk-: **~pause** *f* **eine ~pause einlegen** to have a break to think things over; **~prozeß** *m* thought-process; **~schrift** *f* memorandum; **~sport** *m* mental exercise; **~sportaufgabe** *f* brain-teaser.

denkste *interj (col)* that's what you think.

Denk-: **~vermögen** *nt* intellectual capacity; **~weise** *f* way of thinking; **d~würdig** *adj* memorable, notable; **~würdigkeit** *f* memorability, notability; **~zettel** *m (col)* warning; **jdm einen ~zettel verpassen** to give sb a warning.

denn **1** *conj* **(a)** *(kausal)* because, for *(esp liter).* **(b)** *(geh: vergleichend)* than. **schöner ~ je** more beautiful than ever. **(c)** *(konzessiv)* **es sei ~, (daß)** unless. **2** *adv (verstärkend)* **wann/wie/wo ~?** when/how/where?; **warum ~ nicht?** why not?; **was soll das ~?** what's all this then?

dennoch *adv* nevertheless, nonetheless. **und ~, ...** and yet ...

denselben 1 *acc of* **derselbe. 2** *dat of* **dieselben.**

dental *adj (Med, Ling)* dental.

Denunziant(in *f*) *m (wk) (pej)* informer.

Denunziation *f (pej)* informing *no pl (von* on, against*)*; *(Anzeige)* denunciation *(von* of*).*

denunzieren* *vt (pej)* to inform on *or* against, to denounce *(bei* to*).*

Deodorant *nt* **-s** *or* **-e** deodorant.
Deospray *nt or m* deodorant spray.
Depesche *f* **-n** *(dated)* dispatch.
Deponie *f* dump, disposal site.
deponieren* *vt (geh)* to deposit.
deportieren* *vt* to deport.
Depot [de'po:] *nt* **-s** depot; *(Aufbewahrungsort auch)* depository; *(in Bank)* strong room.
Depp *m* **-e(n)** *(dial pej)* twit *(col)*.
Depression *f* depression. **~en haben** to suffer from depression.
depressiv *adj* depressive; *(Econ)* depressed.
deprimieren* *vt* to depress.
deprimiert *adj* depressed.
der¹ **1 (a)** *gen of def art* **die** *sing, pl* of the. **(b)** *dat of def art* **die** *sing* to the; *(mit Präposition)* the. **2** *dat of dem pron* **die** *sing* **(a)** *(adjektivisch)* to that; *(mit Präposition)* that. **(b)** *(substantivisch)* to her; her. **3** *dat of rel pron* **die** *sing* to whom, that *or* who(m) ... to; *(mit Präposition)* who(m); *(von Sachen)* to which, which ... to; which.
der², **die, das,** *pl* **die 1** *def art* the. **die Engländer** the English *pl*; **der Hans** *(col)*/**der Faust** Hans/Faust; **der Rhein** the Rhine; **der Michigansee** Lake Michigan; **die „Bismarck"** the "Bismarck"; **der Lehrer/die Frau** *(im allgemeinen)* teachers *pl*/women *pl*; **der Tod/die Liebe/das Leben** death/love/life; **das Rauchen** smoking; **das Viktorianische England** Victorian England; **in dem England, das ich kannte** in the England (that *or* which) I knew; **er hat sich den Fuß verletzt** he has hurt his foot; **10 Mark die Stunde** 10 marks an *or* per hour; **der und der Wissenschaftler** such and such a scientist.

2 *dem pron* **(a)** *(attr) (jener, dieser)* that; *pl* those. **(b)** *(substantivisch)* he/she/it; *pl* those. **der/die war es** it was him/her; **der mit der großen Nase** the one with *or* him *(col)* with the big nose; **der und schwimmen?** swimming?, (what) him?; **der und der/die und die** so-and-so; **das und das** such and such. **3** *rel pron (Mensch)* who, that; *(Gegenstand, Tier)* which, that.
der|art *adv* **(a)** *(Art und Weise)* in such a way. **sein Benehmen war ~, daß ...** his behaviour was so bad that ... **(b)** *(Ausmaß) (vor adj)* so; *(vor vb)* so much, to such an extent. **ein ~ unzuverlässiger Mensch** such an unreliable person, so unreliable a person.
der|artig 1 *adj* **bei ~en Versuchen** in such tests, in tests of that kind. **2** *adv* = **derart.**
derb *adj* **(a)** *(kräftig)* strong; *Kost* coarse. **(b)** *(grob)* coarse; *Sprache, Humor auch* earthy, crude *(pej)*.
Derbheit *f siehe adj* **(a)** strength; coarseness. **(b)** coarseness; earthiness, crudeness.
Derby ['dɛrbi] *nt* **-s** derby.
der|einst *adv (liter)* **(a)** *(in der Zukunft)* one day. **(b)** *(früher)* at one time, once.
deren 1 *gen pl of dem pron* **der, die, das** their. **2 (a)** *gen sing of rel pron* **die** whose. **(b)** *gen pl of rel pron* **der, die, das** whose, of whom; *(von Sachen)* of which.
derent-: ~wegen *adv (weswegen)* because of whom, on whose account; *(von Sachen)* because of which, on account of which; **~willen** *adv* **um ~willen** *(rel)* for whose sake; *(von Sachen)* for the sake of which.
dergestalt *adv (geh)* in such a way.
dergleichen *dem pron inv* **(a)** *(adjektivisch)* **~ Dinge** things of that kind. **(b)** *(substantivisch)* that sort of thing. **er tat nichts ~** he did nothing of the kind; **und ~ (mehr)** and suchlike.
Derivat [-'va:t] *nt (Chem, Ling)* derivative.
derjenige, diejenige, dasjenige, *pl* **diejenigen** *dem pron* **(a)** *(substantivisch)* the one; *pl* those. **du warst also derjenige, welcher!** *(col)* so you're the one! **(b)** *(adjektivisch)* the; *pl* those.
derlei *dem pron inv* = **dergleichen.**
Dermato-: ~loge *m*, **~login** *f* dermatologist; **~logie** *f* dermatology.
derselbe, dieselbe, dasselbe, *pl* **dieselben** *dem pron* the same; **es sind immer dieselben** it's always the same ones *or* the same people; **ein und derselbe Mensch** one and the same person.
derweil(en) *adv* in the meantime, meanwhile.
derzeit *adv (jetzt)* at present, at the moment.
derzeitig *adj attr (jetzig)* present, current.
des¹ *gen of def art* **der**², **das** of the.
des², **Des** *nt no pl (Mus)* D flat.
Desaster [de'zastɐ] *nt* **-** disaster.
Deserteur(in *f*) [-'tø:ɐ, -'tø:ərɪn] *m (Mil, fig)* deserter.
desertieren* *vi aux sein or haben (Mil, fig)* to desert.
Desertion *f (Mil, fig)* desertion.
desgleichen *adv (ebenso)* likewise, also.
deshalb *adv, conj* therefore; *(aus diesem Grunde)* because of that. **ich bin ~ hergekommen, weil ich dich sprechen wollte** the reason I came here was that I wanted to speak to you; **~ muß er nicht dumm sein** that does not necessarily mean he is stupid; **~ frage ich ja** that's exactly why I'm asking.
Design [di'zaɪn] *nt* **-s** design.
Designer(in *f*) [di'zaɪnɐ, -ərɪn] *m* **-** designer.
designiert [dezɪ'gni:ɐt] *adj attr* **der ~e Vorsitzende/Nachkomme** the chairman designate/prospective successor.
des|illusionieren* *vt* to disillusion.
Des|infektionsmittel *nt* disinfectant.
des|infizieren* *vt* to disinfect.
Des|infizierung *f* disinfection.
Des|interesse *nt* lack of interest *(an +dat* in*)*.
des|interessiert *adj* uninterested.
deskriptiv *adj* descriptive.
desolat *adj (geh)* desolate; *Zustand, wirtschaftliche Lage* desperate.
Des|organisation *f* disorganization; *(Auflösung auch)* disruption. **auf der Tagung herrschte eine völlige ~** there was complete chaos at the conference.
des|organisieren* *vt* to disorganize.
des|orientieren* *vt* to disorient(ate).
Despot [dɛs'po:t] *m (wk)* **-en, -en** despot.
despotisch [dɛs'po:tɪʃ] *adj* despotic.
Despotismus [dɛspo-] *m no pl* despotism.
desselben *gen of* **derselbe, dasselbe.**
dessen 1 *gen of dem pron* **der**², **das** his; *(von Sachen, Tieren)* its. **2** *gen of rel pron* **der**², **das** whose; *(von Sachen)* of which, which ... of.
dessent- = **derent-.**
dessen|unge|achtet *adv (geh)* nevertheless.
Dessert [dɛ'se:ɐ] *nt* **-s** dessert.
Dessin [dɛ'sɛ̃:] *nt* **-s** *(Tex)* pattern, design.
Destillation [dɛstɪla'tsio:n] *f* **(a)** *(Chem)* distillation. **(b)** *(Branntweinbrennerei)* distillery.
destillieren* [dɛstɪ'li:rən] *vt* to distil.
desto *conj* **~ mehr/besser** all the more/better; **~ wahrscheinlicher ist es, daß wir ...** that makes it all the more probable that we ...; *siehe* **je.**
destruktiv [dɛstrʊk'ti:f] *adj* destructive.
deswegen *adv* = **deshalb.**
Detail [de'tai] *nt* **-s** detail; *(Filmeinstellung)* big close-up. **ins ~ gehen** to go into detail(s); **im ~** in detail; **bis ins kleinste ~** (right) down to the smallest detail; **in allen ~s** in the greatest detail.
Detail-: ~frage *f* question of detail; **~kenntnis** *f usu pl* detailed knowledge *no pl*.
detailliert [deta'ji:ɐt] *adj* detailed.
Detektei *f* (private) detective agency.
Detektiv(in *f*) *m* private detective.
Detektiv-: ~büro *nt* detective agency; **~roman** *m* detective novel.
Detektor *m (Tech)* detector.
determinieren* *vt* to determine.
Detonation *f* explosion, blast. **etw** *(acc)* **zur ~**

bringen to detonate sth.
detonieren* *vi aux sein* to explode, to go off.
Deut *m* **(um) keinen ~** not one iota *or* jot; **seine Ratschläge sind keinen ~ wert** his advice is not worth tuppence; **dafür gebe ich keinen ~** I don't give a hang for it *(col)*.
deutbar *adj* interpretable. **nicht/schwer ~** impossible/difficult to interpret.
deuteln *vi (geh)* to quibble, to cavil. **daran gibt es nichts zu ~!** there are no ifs and buts about it!
deuten 1 *vt (auslegen)* to interpret; *Zukunft* to read. **etw falsch ~** to misinterpret sth. **2** *vi* **(a) (mit dem Finger) auf etw** *(acc)* **~** to point (one's finger) at sth. **(b)** *(fig: hinweisen)* to indicate. **alles deutet darauf, daß ...** all the indications are that ...
deutlich *adj* clear. **~ sichtbar** clearly visible; **ich fühle ~, daß ...** I have the distinct feeling ...; **jdm etw ~ vor Augen führen** *or* **zu verstehen geben** to make sth perfectly clear *or* plain to sb; **muß ich ~er werden?** have I not made myself clear *or* plain enough?
Deutlichkeit *f* clarity. **etw mit aller ~ sagen** to make sth perfectly clear *or* plain.
deutsch *adj* German. **~e Schrift** Gothic script; **~er Schäferhund** Alsatian *(Brit)*, German shepherd; **~e Gründlichkeit** *etc* German *or* Teutonic efficiency *etc*; **D~e Mark** deutschmark, German mark; **sich (auf) ~ unterhalten** to speak (in) German; **auf ~ heißt das ...** in German it means ...; **mit jdm ~ reden** *(fig col: deutlich)* to speak bluntly with sb; **auf gut ~ (gesagt)** *(fig col)* in plain English.
Deutsch *nt no pl* German. **gut(es) ~ sprechen** to speak good German.
Deutsch-: **~amerikaner** *m* German American; **d~-amerikanisch** *adj* German-American.
Deutsch(e) *nt* **-n,** *no pl (Sprache)* German. **aus dem ~en/ins ~e übersetzt** translated from (the)/into German.
deutsch-englisch *adj* **(a)** *(Pol)* Anglo-German. **(b)** *(Ling)* German-English.
Deutsche(r) *mf decl as adj* **er ist ~r** he is (a) German.
Deutsch-: **d~feindlich** *adj* anti-German, Germanophobic; **d~-französisch** *adj* **(a)** *(Pol)* Franco-German; **der D~-Französische Krieg** the Franco-Prussian war; **(b)** *(Ling)* German-French; **d~freundlich** *adj* pro-German, Germanophile.
Deutschland *nt* Germany.
Deutschland-: **~frage** *f (Pol)* German question; **~lied** *nt West German national anthem;* **~politik** *f* home *or* domestic policy; *(von fremdem Staat)* policy towards Germany.
Deutsch-: **~lehrer** *m* German teacher; **~schweizer** *m* German Swiss; **d~schweizerisch** *adj* German-Swiss; **d~sprachig** *adj Bevölkerung, Gebiete* German-speaking; *Zeitung, Ausgabe* German-language; *Literatur* German; **d~sprachlich** *adj* German(-language); **d~sprechend** *adj* German-speaking; **d~stämmig** *adj* of German origin; **~stunde** *f* German lesson; **~tümelei** *f (pej)* hyper-Germanness.
Deutung *f* interpretation. **eine falsche ~** a misinterpretation.
Devise [de'viːzə] *f* **-n (a)** *(Wahlspruch)* motto. **(b)** *(Fin)* **~n** *pl* foreign exchange *or* currency.
Devisen- *in cpds* foreign exchange; **~ausgleich** *m* foreign exchange offset; **~bestimmungen** *pl* foreign exchange control regulations *pl*; **~börse** *f* foreign exchange market; **~geschäft** *nt* foreign exchange dealing; **~handel** *m* foreign currency *or* exchange dealings *pl;* **~kurs** *m* exchange rate, rate of exchange.
devot [de'voːt] *adj (pej geh: unterwürfig)* obsequious.
Dezember *m* **-** December; *siehe* **März.**
dezent *adj* discreet.
dezentral *adj* decentralized.
dezentralisieren* *vt* to decentralize.
Dezernat *nt (Admin)* department.
Dezernent(in *f***)** *m (Admin)* head of department.
Dezibel ['deːtsibɛl, -'bɛl] *nt* **-** decibel.
dezidiert *adj (geh)* firm, determined.
Deziliter *m or nt* decilitre *(Brit)*, deciliter *(US)*.
dezimal *adj* decimal.
Dezimale *f* **-n** decimal.
Dezimal-: **~rechnung** *f* decimals *pl*; **~stelle** *f* **auf zwei ~stellen genau** correct to two decimal places; **~zahl** *f* decimal number.
dezimieren* *(fig)* **1** *vt* to decimate. **2** *vr* to be decimated.
Dezimierung *f (fig)* decimation.
DFB [deː|ɛf'beː] *m* = **Deutscher Fußball-Bund** German Football Association.
DGB [deːgeː'beː] *m* = **Deutscher Gewerkschaftsbund** Federation of German Trade Unions.
d.h. = **das heißt** i.e.
Dia *nt* **-s** *(Phot)* slide, transparency.
Diabetes [dia'beːtɛs] *m no pl* diabetes.
Diabetiker(in *f***)** *m* **-** diabetic.
diabetisch *adj* diabetic.
Diadem *nt* **-e** diadem.
Diadochenkämpfe *pl (fig)* power struggle.
Diagnose *f* **-n** diagnosis. **eine ~ stellen** to make a diagnosis.
diagnostizieren* *vti (Med, fig)* to diagnose.
diagonal *adj* diagonal. **ein Buch ~ lesen** *(col)* to flick through a book.
Diagonale *f* **-n** diagonal.
Diagramm *nt* **-e** diagram.
Diakon *m* **-e(n)** *(Eccl)* deacon.
Diakonie *f (Eccl)* social welfare work.
Dialekt *m* **-e** dialect.
dialektfrei *adj* without an accent.
Dialektik *f (Philos)* dialectics *sing or pl.*
dialektisch *adj (Philos)* dialectical.
Dialog *m* **-e** dialogue.
Dialogregie *f (Film)* script supervision.
Diamant *m (wk)* **-en, -en** diamond.
diamanten *adj attr* diamond.
Diamant-: **~nadel** *f* **(a)** diamond brooch; **(b)** *(an Tonarm)* diamond (stylus); **~schleifer** *m* diamond polisher; **~schmuck** *m* diamonds *pl.*
diametral *adj* **~ entgegengesetzt** *(fig)* diametrically opposed.
Diaphragma [dia'fragma] *nt, pl* **Diaphragmen** diaphragm.
Dia- *(Phot)*: **~positiv** *nt* slide, transparency; **~projektor** *m* slide projector.
diät *adv kochen, essen* according to a diet; *leben* on a special diet.
Diät *f* **-en** *(Med)* diet. **~ halten** to keep to a strict diet; **nach einer ~ leben** to be on a diet *or (wegen Krankheit)* special diet; **jdn auf ~ setzen** *(col)* to put sb on a diet.
Diäten *pl (Parl)* parliamentary allowance.
Diät-: **~kost** *f* dietary foods; **~kost bekommen** to be on a special diet; **~kur** *f* dietary *or* dietetic treatment.
dich 1 *pers pron acc of* **du** you. **2** *refl pron* yourself. **wie fühlst du ~?** how do you feel?
dicht 1 *adj* **(a)** *Gefieder, Haar, Hecke* thick; *Laub, Nebel auch, Wald, Gewühl* dense; *Verkehr auch* heavy; *Gewebe* close; *(fig: konzentriert) Programm* full. **in ~er Folge** in quick succession. **(b)** *(undurchlässig)* watertight; airtight; *Vorhänge* thick, heavy. **nicht ~ sein** to leak; **er ist nicht ganz ~** *(col)* he's crackers *(col)*. **(c)** *(col: zu)* shut, closed. **2** *adv* **(a)** *(nahe)* closely. **(~ an) ~ stehen** to stand close together; **~ gefolgt von** closely followed by. **(b)** *(sehr stark) bevölkert* densely; **~ behaart sein** to be very hairy. **(c)** *(mit Präpositionen)* **~ an/bei** close to; **~ dahinter/davor**

right behind/in front; ~ **hintereinander** right behind one another; ~ **beieinander** close together.

dicht-: ~**auf** *adv* closely; ~**auf folgen** to follow close behind; ~**behaart** *adj attr* (very) hairy; ~**bevölkert** *adj attr* densely populated.

Dichte *f* **-n (a)** *no pl siehe adj (a)* thickness; denseness; heaviness; closeness; fullness. **(b)** *(Phys)* density.

dichten[1] **1** *vt* to write. **2** *vi* to write poems.

dichten[2] *vt (undurchlässig machen)* to seal, to make watertight/airtight.

Dichter(in *f***)** *m* **-** poet; *(Schriftsteller)* writer, author.

dichterisch *adj* poetic; *(schriftstellerisch)* literary. ~**e Freiheit** poetic licence *(Brit) or* license *(US)*.

Dichter-: ~**kreis** *m* circle of poets; ~**lesung** *f* reading *(by a poet/writer from his own works)*; ~**wort** *nt* **-e** (literary) quotation.

dicht-: ~**gedrängt** *adj attr* closely packed; ~**halten** *vi sep irreg (col)* to keep one's mouth shut *(col)*.

Dichtkunst *f* art of poetry; *(Schriftstellerei)* creative writing.

dichtmachen *vti sep (col)* to shut up, to close. **(den Laden)** ~ to shut up shop.

Dichtung[1] *f* **(a)** *no pl* literature; *(in Versform)* poetry. ~ **und Wahrheit** *(fig)* fact and fantasy. **(b)** *(Dichtwerk)* poem, poetic work; literary work.

Dichtung[2] *f (Tech)* seal; *(in Wasserhahn etc)* washer; *(Mech)* gasket.

dick *adj* **(a)** thick; *Mensch, Körperteil, Buch, Brieftasche* fat; *Baum, Stamm* big, thick; *(col) Gehalt, Rechnung, Gewinn* big, fat; *(col) Tränen, Geschäft, Fehler, Auto* big; *Zigarre* big fat. **ein** ~**er Brocken** *(col)* a tough nut (to crack); ~ **machen** *(Speisen)* to be fattening; **er hat es** ~**(e)** *(col) (satt)* he's had enough of it; *(viel)* he's got enough and to spare; **das ist ein** ~**es Lob** that's high praise; **ach, du** ~**es Ei!** *(col)* bloody hell! *(Brit col!)*; **das ist ein** ~**er Hund** *(col)* that's a bit much *(col)*; **das** ~**e Ende kommt noch** *(prov)* the worst is yet to come; **eine** ~**e Suppe** *(col: Nebel)* a real peasouper *(col)*; **durch** ~ **und dünn** through thick and thin. **(b)** *(geschwollen)* swollen; *Beule* big. **(c)** *(col) Freundschaft, Freund* close. **mit jdm** ~ **befreundet sein** to be thick with sb *(col)*.

Dick-: **d**~**bauchig** *adj Vase* bulbous; **d**~**bäuchig** *adj Mensch* potbellied; ~**darm** *m (Anat)* colon.

Dicke *f* **-n (a)** thickness. **(b)** *(von Menschen, Körperteilen)* fatness.

Dicke(r) *mf decl as adj (col)* fatty *(col)*, fatso *(col)*.

dick-: ~**fellig** *adj (col)* thick-skinned; ~**flüssig** *adj* thick, viscous; ~**häutig** *adj* thick-skinned.

Dickicht *nt* **-e** thicket; *(fig)* jungle.

Dick-: ~**kopf** *m* **(a)** *(Starrsinn)* obstinacy, stubbornness; **einen** ~**kopf haben** to be obstinate *or* stubborn; **(b)** *(Mensch)* obstinate so-and-so *(col)*; **d**~**köpfig** *adj (fig)* stubborn; **d**~**leibig** *adj Buch* massive; *Mensch* corpulent; **d**~**lich** *adj* plump; ~**milch** *f (Cook)* sour milk; ~**schädel** *m (col)* = ~**kopf;** ~**wanst** *m (pej col)* fatso *(col)*.

Didaktik *f* teaching methods *pl*.

didaktisch *adj* didactic.

die *art etc siehe* **der**[2].

Dieb(in *f***)** *m* **-e** thief. **haltet den** ~! stop thief!

Diebes-: ~**bande** *f* gang of thieves; ~**gut** *nt* stolen goods *pl*; **d**~**sicher** *adj* thief-proof.

diebisch *adj* **(a)** *(lit) Gesindel etc* thieving *attr*. **(b)** *(col) Freude, Vergnügen* impish.

Diebstahl [ˈdiːp-ʃtaːl] *m* **-̈e** theft. **einfacher/schwerer** ~ petty/grand larceny; **bewaffneter** ~ armed robbery; **geistiger** ~ plagiarism.

Diebstahl-: **d**~**sicher** *adj* theft-proof; ~**versicherung** *f* insurance against theft.

diejenige *dem pron siehe* **derjenige.**

Diele *f* **-n (a)** floorboard. **(b)** *(Vorraum)* hall.

Dielenbrett *nt* floorboard.

dienen *vi* **(a)** to serve *(jdm* sb, *einer Sache (dat)* sth*)*; *dem Fortschritt, der Erforschung* to aid; *dem Verständnis* to promote; *(nützlich sein)* to be of use *or* service *(jdm* to sb*)*. **es dient einer guten Sache** it is in a good cause; **womit kann ich Ihnen** ~? what can I do for you?; *(im Geschäft auch)* can I help you?; **damit ist mir wenig gedient** that's no use *or* good to me; **als/zu etw** ~ to serve as/for sth. **(b)** *(Militärdienst leisten)* to do (one's) military service.

Diener *m* **- (a)** servant. **(b)** *(col: Verbeugung)* bow.

Dienerin *f* maid.

dienern *vi (fig pej)* to bow and scrape *(vor+dat* to*)*.

Dienerschaft *f* servants *pl*, domestic staff.

dienlich *adj* useful, helpful. **jdm/einer Sache** ~ **sein** to help sb/sth, to be of help to sb/sth.

Dienst *m* **-e (a)** service; *(Arbeitsstelle)* position. **in jds** ~**(en)** *(dat)* **stehen** to be in sb's service; **Oberst außer** ~ retired colonel; **im** ~**(e) der Menschheit** in the service of humanity; **jdm einen schlechten** ~ **erweisen** to do sb a disservice; **jdm gute** ~**e leisten** *or* **tun** to serve sb well; ~ **am Kunden** customer service; **etw in** ~ **stellen** to put sth into service; **jdm zu** ~**en stehen** to be at sb's disposal. **(b)** *(Berufsausübung, Amtspflicht)* duty; *(Arbeit, Arbeitszeit)* work. ~ **haben** *(Arzt etc)* to be on duty; *(Apotheke)* to be open; **im** ~ **sein** *(Angestellter etc)* to be working; **nach** ~ after work; ~ **tun** to serve *(bei* in, *als* as*)*.

Dienstag *m* Tuesday. ~ **abend/morgen** (on) Tuesday evening/morning; ~ **abends/vormittags** on Tuesday evenings/mornings; **am** ~ on Tuesday; **hast du** ~ **Zeit?** have you time on Tuesday?; **alle** ~**e** every Tuesday; **eines** ~**s** one Tuesday; **die Nacht von** ~ **auf Mittwoch** the night of Tuesday to Wednesday; **den (ganzen)** ~ **über** all (day) Tuesday, the whole of Tuesday; ~ **in acht Tagen** *or* **in einer Woche** a week on Tuesday, Tuesday week; ~ **vor einer Woche** *or* **acht Tagen** a week (ago) last Tuesday.

dienstags *adv* on Tuesdays, on a Tuesday. ~ **abends** on Tuesday evenings.

Dienst-: ~**alter** *nt* length of service; ~**älteste(r)** *mf* (most) senior member of staff; ~**antritt** *m* assumption of one's duties; *(jeden Tag)* commencement of work; ~**anweisung** *f* instructions *pl*, regulations *pl*; **d**~**bar** *adj* **d**~**bare Geister** willing hands; **sich** *(dat)* **etw d**~**bar machen** to utilize sth; **d**~**beflissen** *adj* zealous; **d**~**bereit** *adj* **(a)** *Apotheke* open *pred; Arzt* on duty; **(b)** *(hilfsbereit)* obliging; ~**bezüge** *pl* salary *sing*; ~**bote** *m* servant; ~**boteneingang** *m* tradesmen's *or* service entrance; ~**eid** *m* oath of service; ~**eifer** *m* zeal; **d**~**eifrig** *adj* zealous, assiduous; **d**~**frei** *adj* free; **d**~**frei haben/bekommen** to have/be given a day *etc* off; ~**gebrauch** *m (Mil, Admin)* **nur für den** ~**gebrauch** for official use only; ~**geheimnis** *nt* official secret; ~**gespräch** *nt* business call; *(von Beamten)* official call; ~**grad** *m (Mil: Rangstufe)* rank; **d**~**habend** *adj attr Arzt, Offizier* duty *attr*, on duty; ~**herr** *m* employer; ~**jahr** *nt usu pl (Mil, Admin)* year of service; ~**leistung** *f* service; ~**leistungsbetrieb** *m* service industry; **d**~**lich 1** *adj Angelegenheiten* business *attr; Schreiben, Befehl* official; **d**~**lich werden** *(col)* to become businesslike; **2** *adv* on business; **wir haben hier d**~**lich zu tun** we have business here; ~**mädchen** *nt* maid; ~**ordnung** *f (Admin)* official regulations *pl*; *(Mil)* service regulations *pl*; **d**~**pflichtig** *adj (esp Mil)* liable for compulsory service; ~**plan** *m* duty rota; ~**rang** *m* grade; *(Mil)* rank; ~**reise** *f* business trip; **auf** ~**reise** on a business trip; ~**schluß** *m* end of work; **nach** ~**schluß** *(von Arbeiter etc)* after work; ~**stelle** *f (Admin)* department; ~**stunden** *pl* working hours *pl*; **d**~**tauglich** *adj (Mil)* fit for service; **d**~**tuend** *adj Arzt* duty *attr*, on duty; **d**~**unfähig**

adj unfit for work; *(Mil)* unfit for duty; **d~untauglich** *adj (Mil)* unfit for service; **~vergehen** *nt* breach of duty; **~wagen** *m* company car; *(von Beamten)* official car; **~weg** *m* **auf dem ~weg** through official channels; **~wohnung** *f* police/army *etc* house; **~zeit** *f* **(a)** period of service; **(b)** *(Arbeitszeit)* working hours *pl*; *(Mil)* hours *pl* of duty; **~zeugnis** *nt* testimonial.
dies *dem pron inv* this; *pl* these. ~ **sind** these are; *siehe* **dieser.**
diesbezüglich *adj (form)* regarding this.
diese *dem pron siehe* **dieser.**
Diesel *m* - diesel.
dieselbe *dem pron siehe* **derselbe.**
Diesel-: **~motor** *m* diesel engine; **~öl** *nt* diesel oil.
dieser, diese, dies(es), *pl* **diese** *dem pron* this; *(~ dort, da)* that; *pl* these; *(~ dort, da)* those. **diese(r, s) hier** this (one); **diese(r, s) da** that (one); **dieser ..., jener ...** the latter ..., the former ...; **dies und das, dieses und jenes** this and that; **diese Nacht** tonight; **dies alles** all this/that.
diesig *adj Wetter, Luft* misty.
dies-: **~jährig** *adj attr* **die ~jährige Ernte** this year's harvest; **~mal** *adv* this time; **~malig** *adj attr* **der ~malige Preis** the price this time; **~seitig** *adj Ufer etc* near(side) *attr,* (on) this side; **~seits** *prep+gen* on this side of; **D~seits** *nt no pl* **das D~seits** this life.
Dietrich *m* -e skeleton key.
diffamieren* *vt* to defame.
diffamierend *adj* defamatory.
Diffamierung *f* defamation (of character); *(Bemerkung etc)* defamatory statement.
Diffamierungskampagne *f* smear campaign.
Differential [-'tsia:l] *nt* **-e** *(Aut: auch* **~getriebe** *nt)* differential (gear).
Differential- *in cpds (Tech, Math)* differential; **~rechnung** *f (Math)* differential calculus.
Differenz *f* difference; *(Abweichung)* discrepancy.
Differenzbetrag *m* difference, balance.
differenzieren* *vti* to make distinctions/a distinction *(zwischen+dat* between, *bei* in*)*; *(abändern)* to make changes/a change in, to modify; *(den Unterschied verstehen)* to differentiate *(zwischen+dat* between, *bei* in*)*. **genau ~** to make a precise distinction.
differieren* *vi* to differ.
diffus *adj Gedanken etc* confused.
digital *adj* digital.
Digital- *in cpds* digital.
Diktat *nt* **(a)** dictation. **etw nach ~ schreiben** to write sth from dictation. **(b)** *(fig: Gebot)* dictate; *(Pol auch)* diktat.
Diktator *m* dictator.
diktatorisch *adj* dictatorial.
Diktatur *f* dictatorship.
diktieren* *vt Brief, (fig) Bedingungen* to dictate.
Diktiergerät *nt* dictating machine.
Diktion *f* style.
Dilemma *nt* **-s** dilemma.
Dilettant(in *f)* *m (wk)* amateur, dilettante *(pej).*
dilettantisch *adj* amateurish.
Dill *m* **-e** *(Bot, Cook)* dill.
Dimension *f* dimension.
DIN ® [dɪn, di:n] *f no pl* = **Deutsche Industrie-Norm** German Industrial Standard. ~ **A4** A4.
Diner [di'ne:] *nt* **-s** *(form) (Mittagessen)* luncheon; *(Abendessen)* dinner.
Ding *nt* **-e** *or (col)* **-er** thing. **das ist ein ~ der Unmöglichkeit** that is totally impossible; **guter ~e sein** *(geh)* to be in good spirits; **jedes ~ hat zwei Seiten** *(Prov)* there are two sides to everything; **gut ~ will Weile haben** *(Prov)* it takes time to do a thing well; **vergangene/berufliche ~e** past events/professional matters; **so wie die ~e liegen, nach Lage der ~e** as things are; **über den ~en stehen** to be above things; **vor allen ~en** above all (things), first and foremost; **es müßte nicht mit rechten ~en zugehen, wenn ...** it would be more than a little strange if ...; **das ~(s) da** *(col)* that thing (over) there; **das ist ein ~!** now there's a thing! *(col)*; **da hast du dir aber ein ~ geleistet** that was quite something you got up to *(col)*; **was macht ihr bloß für ~er?** the things you do! *(col).*
dingfest *adj* **jdn ~ machen** to arrest sb.
Dingi ['dɪŋgi] *nt* **-s** dinghy.
dinglich *adj* material.
Dings, Dingsbums, Dingsda *nt no pl (col)* thingummyjig *(col).*
dinieren* *vi (geh)* to dine *(form).*
Dinosaurier *m* dinosaur.
Diode *f* **-n** diode.
Diözese *f* **-n** diocese.
Diphtherie [dɪfte'ri:] *f* diphtheria.
Dipl. = **Diplom.**
Dipl. Ing. = **Diplomingenieur** academically qualified engineer.
Diplom *nt* **-e** diploma. **ein ~ machen** to take *or* do one's diploma.
Diplom- *in cpds (vor Berufsbezeichnung)* qualified; **~arbeit** *f* dissertation.
Diplomat *m (wk)* **-en, -en** diplomat.
Diplomatie *f (lit, fig)* diplomacy.
diplomatisch *adj (Pol, fig)* diplomatic.
diplomiert *adj* qualified.
dir *pers pron dat of* **du** to you; *(nach Präpositionen)* you.
direkt 1 *adj* direct; *Erledigung* immediate; *(genau) Hinweis* plain; *Auskunft* clear. **eine ~e Verbindung** a through train/direct flight. **2** *adv* **(a)** *(unmittelbar)* directly; *(geradewegs auch)* straight; *übertragen* live; *telephonieren* direct. ~ **von/nach** straight *or* direct from/to; ~ **an/unter** directly *or* right by/under; **(b)** *(unverblümt)* bluntly. **jdm etw ~ ins Gesicht sagen** to tell sb sth (straight) to his face; ~ **fragen** to ask outright *or* straight out. **(c)** *(col: geradezu)* really.
Direktion *f* management; *(Direktionsbüro)* manager's office.
Direktive *f (geh)* directive.
Direktmandat *nt (Pol)* direct mandate.
Direktor *m,* **Direktorin** *f* director; *(von Gefängnis)* governor, warden *(US)*; *(von Hochschule)* principal; *(von Schule)* head (teacher), principal *(esp US).*
Direktorat *nt* **(a)** *(Amt)* directorship; *(von Schule)* headship, principalship *(esp US).* **(b)** *(Diensträume: von Schule)* head (teacher)'s *or* principal's *(esp US)* study *or* room.
Direktorium *nt* board of directors, directorate.
Direkt-: **~übertragung** *f (Rad, TV)* live transmission; **~verbindung** *f (Rail)* through train; *(Aviat)* direct flight.
Dirigent(in *f)* *m (wk) (Mus)* conductor.
dirigieren* *vt* **(a)** *(auch vi) (Mus)* to conduct; *(fig)* to lead. **(b)** *Verkehr etc* to direct.
Dirndl *nt* - *(auch* **~kleid***)* dirndl.
Dirne *f* **-n** *(Prostituierte)* prostitute.
dis, Dis *nt* **-, -** *(Mus)* D sharp.
Disco *f* **-s** disco.
Disharmonie *f (lit, fig)* discord.
disharmonisch *adj (lit, fig)* discordant.
Diskette *f* disk, diskette.
Diskettenlaufwerk *nt* disk drive.
Diskjockey ['dɪskdʒɔke] *m* **-s** disc jockey, DJ.
Diskont *m* **-e** *(Fin)* discount.
Diskontsatz *m (Fin)* discount rate.
Diskothek *f* **-en** discotheque.
diskreditieren* *vt (geh)* to discredit.
Diskrepanz *f* discrepancy.
diskret *adj* discreet; *Gespräch* confidential.
Diskretion *f* discretion; *(vertrauliche Behandlung)* confidentiality. **strengste ~ wahren** to preserve

the strictest confidence.
diskriminieren* *vt* to discriminate against.
diskriminierend *adj* discriminatory.
Diskriminierung *f* discrimination.
Diskus *m, pl* **-se** *or* **Disken** discus.
Diskussion *f* discussion. **zur ~ stehen** to be under discussion; **etw zur ~ stellen** to put sth up for discussion.
Diskussions-: ~beitrag *m* contribution to the discussion; **~teilnehmer** *m* participant (in a discussion).
Diskus-: ~werfen *nt no pl* throwing the discus; **~werfer(in** *f***)** *m* discus-thrower.
diskutabel *adj* worth discussing.
diskutieren* *vti* to discuss. **über etw** *(acc)* **~** to discuss sth; **darüber läßt sich ~** that sounds like something we could talk about.
dispensieren* [dɪspɛn'ziːrən] *vt jdn* to excuse *(von* from*)*.
disponieren* [dɪsponiːrən] *vi (geh)* **(a)** *(verfügen)* **ich kann nicht über sie ~** I can't tell her what to do; **über etw** *(acc)* **(frei) ~** to do as one wishes with sth. **(b)** *(planen)* to make arrangements.
disponiert [dɪspo'niːɐt] *adj (geh)* **gut/schlecht ~ sein** to be in good/bad form.
Disposition [dɪspozi'tsioːn] *f (geh)* **(a)** *(Verfügung)* **jdm zur** *or* **zu jds ~ stehen** to be at sb's disposal; **jdm etw zur ~ stellen** to place sth at sb's disposal. **(b)** *(Anordnung)* arrangement. **seine ~en treffen** to make (one's) arrangements.
Disput [dɪs'puːt] *m* **-e** *(geh)* dispute.
disqualifizieren* *vt* to disqualify.
Disqualifizierung *f* disqualification.
Dissertation *f (Doktorarbeit)* thesis.
Dissident(in *f***)** *m (wk)* dissident.
dissonant *adj* dissonant.
Dissonanz *f (Mus)* dissonance; *(fig)* (note of) discord.
Distanz *f* distance *(auch Sport)*; *(fig) (Abstand, Entfernung)* detachment; *(Zurückhaltung)* reserve. **~ halten** *or* **wahren** *(lit, fig)* to keep one's distance; **auf ~ gehen** *(fig)* to become distant.
distanzieren* **1** *vr* **sich von jdm/etw ~** to dissociate oneself from sb/sth. **2** *vt (Sport)* to outdistance.
distanziert *adj Verhalten* distant.
Distel *f* **-n** thistle.
Distrikt *m* **-e** district.
Disziplin *f* **-en** discipline *(auch Sport)*.
disziplinarisch *adj* disciplinary. **jdn ~ bestrafen** to take disciplinary action against sb.
Disziplinar-: ~strafe *f* punishment; **eine ~strafe bekommen** to be disciplined; **~verfahren** *nt* disciplinary proceedings *pl*.
disziplinieren* *vt* to discipline.
Disziplin-: d~los 1 *adj* undisciplined; **2** *adv* in an undisciplined manner; **~losigkeit** *f* lack *no pl* of discipline.
dito *adv (Comm, hum)* ditto.
Diva ['diːva] *f* **-s** star; *(Film)* screen goddess.
divergieren* [divɛr'giːrən] *vi* to diverge.
divers [di'vɛrs] *adj attr* various. **„D~es"** "miscellaneous".
Dividende [divi'dɛndə] *f* **-n** *(Fin)* dividend.
dividieren* [divi'diːrən] *vti* to divide *(durch* by*)*.
Division [divi'zioːn] *f (Math, Mil)* division.
Diwan *m* **-e** divan.
DKP [deːkaː'peː] *f* = **Deutsche Kommunistische Partei.**
DM ['deː'|ɛm] *no art* - = **Deutsche Mark.**
D-Mark ['deːmark] *f* - deutschmark, (West) German mark.
Dobermann *m, pl* **-männer** Doberman (pinscher).
doch 1 *conj (aber, allein)* but; *(jedoch, trotzdem)* but still, yet. **und ~ hat er es getan** but he still did it, but still he did it.
2 *adv* **(a)** *(betont: dennoch)* after all; *(trotzdem, sowieso)* anyway. **jetzt ist er ~ nicht gekommen** now he hasn't come after all; **du weißt es ja ~ besser** you know better than I do anyway; **und ~,** ... and yet ...
(b) *(betont: tatsächlich)* really. **also ~!** so it *is*/so he *did*! *etc*; **er hat es gestohlen — also ~!** he stole it — so it *was* him!; **es ist ~ so, wie ich vermutet hatte** so it (really) *is* as I thought; **das ist er ~!** (why,) that *is* him!
(c) *(als bejahende Antwort)* yes I do/it does *etc*. **hat es dir nicht gefallen? — (~,) ~!** didn't you like it? — (oh) yes I did!
(d) *(auffordernd) nicht übersetzt aber emphatisches „to do" wird oft gebraucht.* **komm ~** do come; **seid ~ endlich still!** do keep quiet!, keep quiet, can't you?; **laß ihn ~!** just leave him!; **nicht ~!** don't (do that)!
(e) sie ist ~ noch so jung but she's still so young; **das ist ~ wohl nicht wahr?** that's not true, is it?; **du hast ~ nicht etwa ...?** you haven't ..., have you?, surely you haven't ...(, have you)?; **es war ~ ganz interessant** it was really *or* actually quite interesting; **Sie wissen ~, wie das so ist** (well,) you know how it is, don't you?; **wenn ~** if only.
Docht *m* **-e** wick.
Dock *nt* **-s** dock.
docken* *vti* to dock.
Docker *m* - docker.
Dogge *f* **-n** mastiff. **deutsche ~** great Dane.
Dogma *nt, pl* **Dogmen** dogma.
dogmatisch *adj (Rel, fig)* dogmatic.
Dohle *f* **-n** *(Orn)* jackdaw.
Doktor *m (auch col: Arzt)* doctor. **den ~ machen** *(col)* to do a doctorate *or* PhD.
Doktorand(in *f***)** *m (wk)* **-en, -en** PhD student.
Doktor-: ~arbeit *f* doctoral *or* PhD thesis; **~grad** *m* doctorate, PhD; **~hut** *m (fig)* doctorate.
Doktorin *f* doctor.
Doktor-: ~prüfung *f* examination for a/one's doctorate; **~titel** *m* doctorate; **~vater** *m* supervisor; **~würde** *f* doctorate.
Doktrin *f* **-en** doctrine.
doktrinär *adj* doctrinal; *(pej: stur)* doctrinaire.
Dokument *nt* document; *(fig: Zeugnis)* record.
Dokumentar- *in cpds* documentary; **~film** *m* documentary (film).
Dokumentation *f* documentation.
dokumentieren* *vt* to document; *(fig: zu erkennen geben)* to reveal, to show.
Dolch *m* **-e** dagger; *(col: Messer)* knife.
Dolchstoß *(esp fig) m* stab *(auch fig)*. **ein ~ (von hinten)** *(fig)* a stab in the back.
Dollar *m* **-s** dollar.
dolmetschen *vti* to interpret.
Dolmetscher(in *f***)** *m* - interpreter.
Dolmetscherschule *f* school of interpreting.
Dolomiten *pl (Geog)* **die ~** the Dolomites *pl*.
Dom *m* **-e** cathedral.
Domäne *f* **-n** *(fig)* domain, province.
domestizieren* *vt* to domesticate.
dominant *adj* dominant *(auch Biol)*, dominating.
Dominante *f* **-n (a)** *(Mus)* dominant. **(b)** *(wichtigster Faktor)* dominant *or* dominating feature.
Dominanz *f (Biol, Psych)* dominance.
dominieren* **1** *vi (vorherrschen)* to predominate; *(Mensch)* to dominate. **2** *vt* to dominate.
dominierend *adj* dominating, dominant.
Domizil *nt* **-e** *(geh, hum)* domicile *(form)*.
Dompfaff *m (Orn)* bullfinch.
Dompteur [dɔmp'tøːɐ] *m,* **Dompteuse** [-'tøːzə] *f* trainer; *(von Raubtieren)* tamer.
Donau *f* **die ~** the Danube.
Donner *m (lit, fig)* thunder *no indef art, no pl*; *(~schlag)* clap of thunder. **wie vom ~ gerührt** *(fig col)* thunderstruck.
donnern 1 *vi impers* to thunder. **es donnerte in der Ferne** there was (the sound of) thunder in the

distance. **2** *vi aux haben or (bei Bewegung) sein* to thunder. **gegen etw ~** *(schlagen)* to hammer on sth; *(schimpfen)* to thunder against sth. **3** *vt (col: schleudern, schlagen)* to slam, to crash.

donnernd *adj (fig) Beifall* thunderous.

Donnerschlag *m* clap of thunder, thunderclap. **die Nachricht traf mich wie ein ~** the news left me thunderstruck.

Donnerstag *m* Thursday; *siehe* **Dienstag.**

donnerstags *adv* on Thursdays.

Donner-: ~stimme *f* thunderous voice; **~wetter** *nt (fig col: Schelte)* row; **~wetter!** *(col) (anerkennend)* my word!; *(zornig)* blast (it)! *(col).*

doof *adj (col)* stupid; *Mensch auch* thick *(col).*

dopen *(Sport)* **1** *vt* to dope. **2** *vir* to take drugs.

Doping *nt* **-s** *(Sport)* doping.

Dopingkontrolle *f (Sport)* dope check.

Doppel *nt* **- (a)** *(Duplikat)* duplicate (copy) *(gen, zu* of*).* **(b)** *(Tennis etc)* doubles *sing.*

Doppel- *in cpds* double; **~agent** *m* double agent; **~band** *m (von doppeltem Umfang)* double-sized volume; *(zwei Bände)* two volumes *pl;* **~belastung** *f* double burden *(gen* on*)*; **steuerliche ~belastung** double taxation; **~bett** *nt* double bed; *(zwei Betten)* twin beds *pl;* **d~bödig** *adj Koffer etc* double-bottomed, false-bottomed; *(d~deutig)* ambiguous; **~decker** *m* **- (a)** *(Aviat)* biplane; **(b)** *(Bus)* double-decker (bus); **d~deutig** *adj* ambiguous; **~deutigkeit** *f* ambiguity; **~fenster** *nt* double window; *(~verglasung)* double glazing; **~gänger(in** *f***)** *m* **-** double, doppelgänger *(esp Liter)*; **~haus** *nt* semi-detached house, semi *(Brit col)*, duplex (house) *(US)*; **er bewohnt eine Hälfte eines ~hauses** he lives in a semi(-detached house); **~kinn** *nt* double chin; **~korn** *m type of schnapps;* **d~läufig** *adj* double-barrelled; **~moral** *f* double standards *pl;* **~name** *m (Nachname)* double-barrelled name; **~paß** *m (Ftbl)* one-two; **~punkt** *m* colon; **d~seitig** *adj* double-sided; *Lungenentzündung* double; **d~seitige Anzeige** double page spread; **~sinn** *m* double meaning; **d~sinnig** *adj* ambiguous; **~spiel** *nt* **(a)** *(Tennis)* (game of) doubles *sing;* **(b)** *(fig)* double game; **~stecker** *m* two-way adaptor; **~stunde** *f (Sch)* double period.

doppelt 1 *adj* double; *(verstärkt) Enthusiasmus* redoubled; *(mit zwei identischen Teilen)* twin *attr;* *(zweimal soviel)* twice; *(Comm) Buchführung* double-entry; *Staatsbürgerschaft* dual. **die ~e Freude/Menge** double *or* twice the pleasure/amount; **~er Boden** false *or* double bottom; **~e Moral** double standards *pl;* **in ~er Hinsicht** in two respects; **ein ~es Spiel treiben** to play a double game. **2** *adv sehen, zählen* double; *(zweimal)* twice; *(direkt vor Adjektiv)* doubly. **~ so schön/soviel** *etc* twice as nice/much *etc;* **sie ist ~ so alt wie ich** she is twice as old as me; **die Karte habe ich ~** I have two of these cards; **~ gemoppelt** *(col)* saying the same thing twice over; **sich ~ in acht nehmen** to be doubly careful; **~ genäht hält besser** *(prov)* better safe than sorry *(prov).*

Doppelte(r) *m decl as adj (col)* double.

Doppelte(s) *nt decl as adj* double. **das ~ bezahlen** to pay twice as much; **etw um das ~ erhöhen** to double sth.

Doppel-: ~verdiener *m* **sie sind ~verdiener** they have two incomes; **~zentner** *m* 100 kilos; **~zimmer** *nt* double room; **d~züngig** *adj* two-faced; **d~züngig reden** to say one thing and mean another; **~züngigkeit** *f no pl* two-facedness.

Dorado *nt* **-s** *(fig)* eldorado.

Dorf *nt* **¨-er** village; *(fig)* backwater. **das Leben auf dem ~e** village life.

Dorf- *in cpds* village; **~bewohner** *m* villager; **~jugend** *f* young people *pl* of the village; **~krug** *m* village inn *or* pub *(Brit).*

dörflich *adj* village *attr;* *(ländlich)* rustic, rural.

Dorn *m* **-en (a)** *(Bot, fig)* thorn. **das ist mir ein ~ im Auge** *(fig)* it's a thorn in my flesh; *(Anblick)* I find it an eyesore. **(b)** *pl* **-e** *(Sporn)* spike; *(von Schnalle)* tongue; *(Tech: Werkzeug)* awl.

Dornbusch *m* briar, thornbush.

Dornen-: ~hecke *f* thorn(y) hedge; **~krone** *f (Bibl)* crown of thorns; **d~reich** *adj* thorny.

dornig *adj* thorny.

Dorn-: ~röschen *nt* Sleeping Beauty; **~röschenschlaf** *f (fig)* slumber; **aus seinem ~röschenschlaf erwachen** to awake from one's slumbers.

dörren 1 *vt* to dry. **2** *vi aux sein* to dry; *(austrocknen)* to dry up.

Dörr-: ~fleisch *nt* dried meat; **~obst** *nt* dried fruit; **~pflaume** *f* prune.

Dorsch *m* **-e** *type of cod.*

dort *adv* there; *siehe* **da 1 (a).**

dort-: ~her *adv* **von ~her** from there; **~hin** *adv* there; **bis ~hin** as far as there; **~hinauf** *adv* up there; **~hinaus** *adv* out there; **frech bis ~hinaus** *(col)* really cheeky; **das ärgert mich bis ~hinaus** *(col)* that really gets me *(col)*; **~hinein** *adv* in there; **~hinunter** *adv* down there.

dortig *adj* **die ~en Behörden** the authorities there.

Dose *f* **-n (a)** *(Blech~)* tin; *(Konserven~)* can, tin *(Brit)*; *(Bier~)* can; *(esp aus Holz)* box; *(mit Deckel)* jar; *(Pillen~, für Schmuck)* box; *(Zucker~)* bowl. **in ~n** *(Konserven)* canned, tinned *(Brit).* **(b)** *(Elec)* socket.

dösen *vi (col)* to doze.

Dosen- *in cpds* canned, tinned *(Brit)*; **~bier** *nt* canned beer; **~milch** *f* evaporated milk; **~öffner** *m* can-opener, tin-opener *(Brit).*

dosieren* *vt (lit, fig)* to measure out.

Dosierung *f (Dosis)* dosage, dose.

dösig *adj (col)* dozy *(col).*

Dosis *f, pl* **Dosen** *(lit, fig)* dose.

Dossier [dɔ'sieː] *nt* **-s** dossier.

dotieren* *vt Posten* to remunerate; *Preis* to endow.

Dotierung *f* endowment; *(von Posten)* remuneration.

Dotter *m or nt* **-** yolk.

doubeln ['duːbln] **1** *vt jdn* to stand in for; *Szene* to shoot with a stand-in. **ein Stuntman hat die Szene für ihn gedoubelt** a stuntman doubled for him in the scene. **2** *vi* to stand in; *(als Double arbeiten)* to work as a stand-in.

Double ['duːbl] *nt* **-s** *(Film etc)* stand-in.

down [daʊn] *adj pred (col)* **~ sein** to be down.

Dozent(in *f***)** *m (wk)* lecturer *(für* in*)*, (assistant) professor *(US) (für* of*).*

Dozentur *f* lectureship *(für* in*)*, (assistant) professorship *(US) (für* of*).*

dozieren* *vi (Univ)* to lecture *(über+acc* on, *an +dat* at*)*; *(pej auch)* to pontificate *(über+acc* about*).*

dpa ['deːpeː'|aː] *f* = **Deutsche Presse-Agentur.**

Dr. ['dɔktɔr] = **Doktor. Dr.rer.nat./rer.pol./phil.** PhD; **Dr. theol./jur.** DD/LLD; **Dr. med.** M.D.

Drache *m (wk)* **-n, -n** *(Myth)* dragon.

Drachen *m* **- (a)** *(Papier~)* kite; *(Sport: Fluggerät)* hang-glider. **einen ~ steigen lassen** to fly a kite. **(b)** *(pej col: zänkisches Weib)* dragon *(col).*

Drachen-: ~fliegen *nt (Sport)* hang-gliding; **~flieger** *m (Sport)* hang-glider.

Dragée [dra'ʒeː] *nt* **-s (a)** *(Bonbon)* sugar-coated chocolate sweet. **(b)** *(Pharm)* dragee, sugar-coated pill.

Draht *m* **¨-e** wire. **auf ~ sein** *(col)* to be on the ball *(col)*; **du bist wohl heute nicht ganz auf ~** *(col)* you're not quite with it today *(col).*

Draht- *in cpds* wire; **~bürste** *f* wire brush; **~esel** *m (hum)* trusty bicycle; **~gitter** *nt* wire netting; **~haardackel** *m* wire-haired dachshund; **d~haarig** *adj* wire-haired.

drahtig *adj Haar, Mensch* wiry.

Draht-: d~los *adj Telegrafie* wireless; **~schere** *f* wire cutters *pl.*

Drahtseil *nt* wire cable. **Nerven wie ~e** *(col)* nerves of steel.

Drahtseil-: ~bahn *f* cable railway; **~künstler** *m (Seiltänzer)* tightrope walker.

Draht-: ~verhau *m or nt* wire entanglement; **~zaun** *m* wire fence; **~zieher(in** *f*) *m (fig)* wire-puller.

drakonisch *adj* draconian.

drall *adj Mädchen, Arme* strapping, sturdy.

Drall *m* **-e (a)** *(von Kugel, Ball)* spin; *(Abweichung von Bahn)* swerve; *(col: von Auto)* pull. **einen ~ nach links haben** *(Auto)* to pull to the left. **(b)** *(fig: Hang)* tendency.

Drama *nt, pl* **Dramen** *(lit, fig)* drama.

Dramatik *f (lit, fig)* drama.

Dramatiker(in *f*) *m* **-** dramatist.

dramatisch *adj (lit, fig)* dramatic.

dramatisieren* *vt (lit, fig)* to dramatize.

Dramaturg(in *f*) *m (wk)* **-en, -en** artistic director; *(TV)* drama producer.

dramaturgisch *adj* dramatic; *Abteilung* drama *attr.*

dran *adv (col)* **(a)** *(an der Reihe)* **jetzt bist du ~** it's your turn now; **(wenn er erwischt wird,) dann ist er ~** (if he gets caught) he'll be for it *(col).* **(b) schlecht ~ sein** to be in a bad way; **gut ~ sein** to be well-off; **früh/spät ~ sein** to be early/late. **(c) an ihm ist nichts ~** he doesn't have much going for him; **was ist an ihm ~, daß ...?** what is there about him that ...?; **da ist alles ~!** that's got everything; **da wird schon etwas (Wahres) ~ sein** there must be something in that; **ich weiß nicht, wie ich (bei ihm) ~ bin** I don't know where I stand (with him).

dranbleiben *vi sep irreg aux sein (col)* to stay close; *(am Apparat)* to hang on. **am Gegner ~** to stick to one's opponent.

Drang *m* **¨e** *(Antrieb)* urge *(auch Physiol)*; *(Sehnsucht)* yearning *(nach* for); *(nach Wissen)* thirst *(nach* for).

drang *pret of* **dringen.**

drangehen *vi sep irreg aux sein (col)* **(a)** *(berühren etc)* to touch *(an etw (acc)* sth). **(b)** *(in Angriff nehmen)* **~, etw zu tun** to get down to doing sth.

Drängelei *f (col)* pushing, jostling.

drängeln *(col)* **1** *vi* to push, to jostle. **2** *vr* **sich nach vorne ~** to push one's way to the front.

drängen 1 *vi* **(a)** *(in Menge)* to push. **(b)** *(fordern)* to press *(auf+acc* for). **auf Antwort ~** to press for an answer; **er drängte zur Eile** he urged us/them *etc* to hurry. **(c) die Zeit drängt** time presses. **2** *vt* **(a)** *(drücken, schieben)* to push. **(b)** *(auffordern)* to press. **3** *vr (Menge)* to throng; *(fig: Termine etc)* to mount up. **sich nach vorn ~** to push *or* force one's way to the front; *siehe* **gedrängt.**

Drängen *nt no pl* urging; *(Bitten)* requests *pl*; *(Bestehen)* insistence.

drängend *adj* pressing, urgent.

drangsalieren* *vt* to pester, to plague.

dranhalten *vr sep irreg (col: sich beeilen)* to get a move on *(col).*

drankommen *vi sep irreg aux sein (col: an die Reihe kommen)* to have one's turn; *(Sch: beim Melden)* to be called; *(Frage, Aufgabe etc)* to come up. **jetzt kommst du dran** now it's your turn.

dranmachen *sep (col)* **1** *vr* = **daranmachen. 2** *vt* **etw (an etw** *acc*) **~** to put sth on (sth).

drannehmen *vt sep irreg (col) Schüler* to ask.

dransetzen *vtr sep (col)* = **daransetzen.**

drapieren* *vt* to drape.

drastisch *adj* drastic; *(deutlich)* graphic.

drauf *adv (col) siehe auch* **darauf. ~ und dran sein, etw zu tun** to be on the point of doing sth; **etw ~ haben** *(col) (können)* to be able to do sth just like that *(col)*; *Kenntnisse* to be well up on sth *(col)*; *Witze, Sprüche* to have sth off pat *(col)*; **160 Sachen ~ haben** *(col)* to be doing 160.

Drauf-: ~gänger *m* go-getter; **d~gängerisch** *adj* go-getting; *(negativ)* reckless; **d~geben** *vt irreg sep* **(a) jdm eins d~geben** *(col)* to give sb a smack; **(b)** *(dazugeben)* **noch etwas d~geben** to add some extra *(col)*; **d~gehen** *vi sep irreg aux sein (col)*; *(verbraucht werden)* to be used up; *(kaputtgehen)* to be smashed up; *(sterben)* to bite the dust *(col)*; **dabei gehen mindestens zwei Tage d~** that'll take at least two days; **d~halten** *vi sep irreg (als Ziel)* to aim for it; **d~kommen** *vi sep irreg aux sein (col) (sich erinnern)* to remember; *(begreifen)* to catch on, to get it *(col)*; **jdm d~kommen** to get on to sb *(col)*; **d~kriegen** *vt sep (col)* **etw (auf etw** *acc*) **d~kriegen** to get *or* fit sth on(to sth); **eins d~kriegen** to catch it *(col)*; **d~legen** *vti sep (col)* **20 Mark d~legen** to lay out an extra 20 marks.

drauflos *adv* **immer feste ~!** (just) keep at it!

drauflos-: ~arbeiten *vi sep (col)* to work away, to beaver away *(col)*; **~gehen** *vi sep irreg aux sein (col: auf ein Ziel)* to make straight for it.

drauf-: ~machen *vt sep (col)* **einen ~machen** to make a night of it *(col)*; **D~sicht** *f (col)* top view; **~stehen** *vi sep irreg (col)* **auf etw** *(dat)* **~stehen** to stand on sth; *(Aufschrift)* to be on sth; **~zahlen** *sep (col)* **(a)** *vti* = **~legen; (b)** *vi (fig: Einbußen erleiden)* to pay the price.

draus *adv* = **daraus.**

draußen *adv* outside; *(im Freien auch)* outdoors; *(da ~, weit weg von hier)* out there; **~ auf dem Lande/im Garten** out in the country/garden; **hier ~** out here; **nach ~** outside; **weit ~** far out.

drechseln *vt* to turn *(on a wood lathe).*

Drechsler(in *f*) *m* **-** (wood) turner.

Dreck *m no pl* **(a)** dirt; *(Schlamm)* mud; *(Kot)* muck; *(fig) (Schund)* rubbish; *(Schmutz, Obszönes)* dirt, filth. **~ machen** to make a mess; **mit ~ und Speck** *(ungewaschen)* unwashed; **im ~ sitzen** *(col)* to be in a mess *or* jam *(col)*; **aus dem gröbsten ~ heraus sein** *(col)* to be past the worst; **jdn wie den letzten ~ behandeln** *(col)* to treat sb like dirt; **der letzte ~ sein** *(pej col: Mensch)* to be the lowest of the low; **~ am Stecken haben** *(fig)* to have a skeleton in the cupboard; **etw in den ~ ziehen** *(fig)* to drag sth through the mud. **(b)** *(col) (Kram)* business, stuff *(col)*; *(Kleinigkeit)* little thing. **sich einen ~ um jdn/etw kümmern** not to give a damn about sb/sth *(col)*; **mach deinen ~ alleine!** do it yourself; **das geht ihn einen ~ an** that's none of his business.

Dreck|arbeit *f (col)* **(a)** *(lit, fig)* dirty work. **(b)** *(pej: niedere Arbeit)* donkey work.

dreckig *adj (lit, fig)* dirty; *(stärker)* filthy. **~ lachen** to give a dirty laugh; **es geht mir ~** *(col)* I'm in a bad way.

Dreck-: ~loch *nt (pej)* hole *(col)*; **~pfoten** *pl (col) (lit, fig)* dirty paws *pl*; **~sack** *m (pej col)* dirty thing *(col)*; **~sau** *f (col!)* filthy swine *(col!)*; **~schleuder** *f (pej: Mensch)* foul-mouthed person; **~schwein** *nt (col!)* dirty pig *(col!).*

Dreckskerl *m (col!)* dirty swine *(col!).*

Dreckspatz *m (col: Kind)* mucky pup *(col).*

Dreck(s)zeug *nt (col)* damn stuff *(col).* **das ist doch ein ~** damn this stuff *(col).*

Dreh *m* **-s** *or* **-e** *(List)* dodge; *(Kunstgriff)* trick. **den ~ heraushaben** to have got the hang of it.

Dreh-: ~arbeiten *pl (Film)* shooting *sing*; **~bank** *f* lathe; **d~bar** *adj* rotating, revolving *attr*; **d~bar sein** to rotate *or* revolve; **~beginn** *m (Film)* start of shooting; **~brücke** *f* swing bridge; **~buch** *nt (Film)* screenplay, (film) script; **~buchautor** *m* scriptwriter, screenplay writer; **~bühne** *f* revolving stage.

drehen 1 *vt* to turn *(auch Tech: auf Drehbank)*; *(um eine Achse auch)* to rotate, to revolve; *Kreisel* to spin; *Zigaretten* to roll; *Film* to shoot; *(fig: verdrehen)* to twist; *(col: schaffen)* to fix *(col).* **das**

Gas hoch/auf klein ~ to turn the gas up high/down low; **Fleisch durch den Wolf** ~ to put meat through the mincer; **ein Ding** ~ *(col)* to play a prank; *(Verbrecher)* to pull a job *(col)*; **wie man es auch dreht und wendet** no matter how you look at it.

2 *vi* to turn; *(Wind)* to shift, to change; *(Film)* to shoot, to film; *(Zigaretten ~)* to roll one's own. **am Radio** ~ to turn a knob on the radio.

3 *vr* **(a)** *(lit)* to turn *(um* about*)*; *(um Achse auch)* to rotate, to revolve; *(Kreisel)* to spin; *(Wind)* to shift, to change. **sich um sich (selbst)** ~ to revolve on its own axis; **mir dreht sich alles im Kopf** my head is spinning; **sich** ~ **und winden** *(fig)* to twist and turn. **(b)** *(fig)* **sich um etw** ~ *(betreffen)* to concern sth, to be about sth; *(um zentrale Frage)* to centre *(Brit) or* center *(US)* on sth; **alles dreht sich um sie** she's the focus of attention; **es dreht sich darum, daß ...** the point is that ...

Dreher(in *f*) *m* - lathe operator.

Dreh-: ~**knopf** *m* knob; ~**kran** *m* slewing *or* rotary crane; ~**kreuz** *nt* turnstile; ~**moment** *nt* torque; ~**orgel** *f* barrel-organ; ~**orgelspieler** *m* organ-grinder; ~**ort** *m (Film)* location; ~**punkt** *m* pivot; ~**scheibe** *f* **(a)** *(Rail)* turntable; **(b)** *(Töpferscheibe)* potter's wheel; ~**stuhl** *m* swivel-chair; ~**tür** *f* revolving door.

Drehung *f* turn; *(um eigene Achse auch)* rotation, revolution. **eine** ~ **um 180°** a 180° turn; **80** ~**en pro Minute** 80 revs *or* revolutions per minute.

Drehwurm *m (col)*: **einen** ~ **kriegen/haben** to get/be giddy.

Drehzahl *f* number of revolutions *or* revs.

Drehzahlmesser *m* rev counter.

drei *num* three. **aller guten Dinge sind** ~! *(prov)* all good things/all disasters come in threes!; *(nach zwei mißglückten Versuchen)* third time lucky!; **sie sieht aus, als ob sie nicht bis** ~ **zählen könnte** *(col)* she looks pretty empty-headed; *siehe* **vier.**

Drei *f* **-en** three; *siehe* **Vier.**

Drei-D- [drai'de:] *in cpds* 3-D.

dreidimensional *adj* three-dimensional.

Drei|eck *nt* **-e** triangle.

drei|eckig *adj* triangular.

Drei|ecks-: ~**tuch** *nt* triangular shawl; *(Med)* triangular bandage; ~**verhältnis** *nt* eternal triangle.

Drei|einigkeit *f* Trinity.

dreifach 1 *adj* triple. **die** ~**e Menge** three times *or* triple *or* treble the amount; **ein** ~**es Hoch!** three cheers! **2** *adv* three times. ~ **abgesichert** trebly secure; *siehe* **vierfach.**

Dreifache(s) *nt decl as adj* **das** ~ triple *or* treble the amount, three times as much; **etw um das** ~ **vermehren** to multiply sth by three.

Drei-: ~**fuß** *m* tripod; *(Schemel)* three-legged stool; ~**gangrad** *nt* three-speed bike; ~**gangschaltung** *f* three-speed gear; **d**~**hundert** *num* three hundred; ~**käsehoch** *m* **-s** *(col)* tiny tot *(col)*; ~**klang** *m* triad; ~**königstag** *m* feast of Epiphany; **d**~**mal** *adv* three times; *siehe* **viermal;** ~**meilenzone** *f* three-mile zone.

drein-: ~**blicken** *vi sep* **traurig** *etc* ~**blicken** to look sad *etc*; ~**reden** *vi sep (col) (dazwischenreden)* to interrupt; *(sich einmischen)* to interfere *(bei* in, with*)*; **ich lasse mir da von niemandem** ~**reden** I won't have anyone interfering (with this); ~**schauen** *vi sep* = ~**blicken.**

Drei-: **d**~**polig** *adj Kabel* three-core; *Steckdose, Stecker* three-pin; ~**rad** *nt* tricycle; ~**springer** *m* triple-jumper; ~**sprung** *m* triple jump, hop, step and jump.

dreißig *num* thirty; *siehe auch* **vierzig.**

dreißig- *in cpds siehe auch* **vierzig-;** ~**jährig** *adj* **der** ~ **jährige Krieg** the Thirty Years' War.

dreist *adj* bold, audacious.

Dreistigkeit *f* **(a)** *no pl* boldness, audacity. **(b)** *(Handlung)* bold *or* audacious act.

dreiteilig *adj Kostüm etc* three-piece *attr.*

dreiviertel ['drai'fɪrtl] *siehe auch* **viertel 1** *adj* threequarter. **eine** ~ **Stunde** threequarters of an hour. **2** *adv* threequarters.

Dreiviertel-: **d**~**lang** *adj* threequarter-length; ~**literflasche** *f* three-quarter litre *(Brit) or* liter *(US)* bottle; ~**mehrheit** *f* threequarters majority; ~**stunde** *f* threequarters of an hour *no indef art*; ~**takt** *m* **im** ~**takt** in three-four time.

Dreiweg- *in cpds (Elec)* three-way; ~**stecker** *m* three-way adapter.

drei-: ~**wöchentlich 1** *adj attr* three-weekly; **2** *adv* every three weeks; ~**wöchig** *adj attr* three-week; ~**zehn** *adj num* thirteen. **jetzt schlägt's aber** ~**zehn** *(col)* that's a bit much; *siehe* **vierzehn.**

Dresche *f no pl (col)* ~ **kriegen** to get a thrashing.

dreschen *pret* **drosch,** *ptp* **gedroschen 1** *vt* **(a)** *Korn* to thresh. **Skat** ~ *(col)* to play skat. **(b)** *(col: prügeln)* to thrash. **2** *vr (col: sich prügeln)* to have a fight.

Dresch-: ~**flegel** *m* flail; ~**maschine** *f* threshing machine.

Dreß *m* **-sse** *(Sport)* (sports) kit; *(für Fußball auch)* strip.

Dresseur [-'søːɐ] *m* trainer.

dressieren* *vt* **(a)** to train. **zu etw dressiert sein** to be trained *etc* to do sth. **(b)** *Geflügel* to dress.

Dressman ['drɛsmən] *m, pl* **Dressmen** male model.

Dressur *f* training; *(für* ~*reiten)* dressage.

dribbeln *vi* to dribble. **mit dem Ball** ~ to dribble the ball.

Dribbling *nt* **-s** dribbling. **ein** ~ a piece of dribbling.

Drift *f* **-en** *(Naut)* drift.

driften *vi aux sein (Naut, fig)* to drift.

Drill *m no pl (Mil, fig)* drill; *(Sch auch)* drills *pl.*

drillen *vti* to drill. **auf etw** *(acc)* **gedrillt sein** *(fig col)* to be practised at doing sth.

Drillich *m* **-e** *(Tex)* drill.

Drilling *m* **(a)** triplet. **(b)** *(Jagdgewehr)* triple-barrelled shotgun.

drin *adv (col) siehe auch* **darin, drinnen (a)** in it. **er/es ist da** ~ he/it is in there; **in der Flasche ist noch etwas** ~ there's still something in the bottle. **(b)** *(col)* **bei ihm ist alles** ~ anything's possible with him; **bis jetzt ist noch alles** ~ everything is still quite open; **das ist doch nicht** ~ *(geht nicht)* that's not on *(col)*.

dringen *pret* **drang,** *ptp* **gedrungen** *vi* **(a)** *aux sein* **(durch etw)** ~ to penetrate (sth); **an die Öffentlichkeit** ~ to leak *or* get out. **(b)** *(geh) aux sein* **in jdn** ~ to press *or* urge sb; **sich gedrungen fühlen, etw zu tun** to feel obliged to do sth. **(c)** **auf etw** *(acc)* ~ to insist on sth.

dringend *adj (eilig, wichtig)* urgent, pressing; *(nachdrücklich, zwingend)* strong; *Gründe* compelling. **ein** ~**er Fall** *(Med)* an emergency; ~ **verdächtig** strongly suspected; ~ **empfehlen** to recommend strongly.

dringlich *adj* urgent, pressing.

Dringlichkeit *f* urgency.

Dringlichkeits-: ~**antrag** *m (Parl)* emergency motion; ~**stufe** *f* priority; ~**stufe 1** top priority.

drinnen *adv* inside; *(im Haus auch)* indoors. **hier/dort** ~ in here/there; **ich gehe nach** ~ *(col)* I'm going in(side).

drinstecken *vi sep (col)* **da steckt eine Menge Geld/Arbeit** *etc* **drin** a lot of money/work *etc* has gone into it; **er steckt bis über die Ohren drin** he's up to his ears in it; **da steckt man nicht drin** you never can tell (what will happen).

dritt *adv* **wir kommen zu** ~ three of us are coming together.

dritt- *in cpds* third; ~**älteste(r, s)** *adj* third oldest.

Drittel *nt* - third; *siehe* **Viertel**[1].
drittens *adv* thirdly.
Dritte(r) *mf decl as adj* third person, third man/woman *etc*; *(Unbeteiligter)* third party. **in dieser Angelegenheit ist er der lachende ~** he comes off best from this; **im Beisein ~r** in the presence of a third party; *siehe* **Vierte(r).**
dritte(r, s) *adj* third. **von ~r Seite** from a third party; *siehe* **vierte(r, s).**
dritt-: ~größte(r, s) *adj* third-biggest; **d~klassig** *adj* third-rate *(pej)*, third-class; **d~letzte(r, s)** *adj* third from last; **d~rangig** *adj* third-rate.
DRK ['de:|ɛr'ka:] *nt* = **Deutsches Rotes Kreuz.**
droben *adv (old, dial)* up there.
Droge *f* **-n** drug.
Drogen-: d~abhängig *adj* addicted to drugs; **~abhängige(r)** *mf decl as adj* drug addict; **~abhängigkeit** *f* drug addiction *no art*; **d~süchtig** *adj* addicted to drugs; **~süchtige(r)** *mf decl as adj* drug addict; **~szene** *f* drug scene.
Drogerie *f* chemist's *(Brit)*, drugstore *(US)*.
Drogist(in *f*) *m* chemist *(Brit)*, druggist *(US)*.
Drohbrief *m* threatening letter.
drohen *vi* to threaten *(jdm* sb). **er droht mit Selbstmord** he threatens to commit suicide; **jdm droht etw** sb is being threatened by sth; **jdm droht Gefahr** sb is in danger; **es droht ein Streik** there is the threat of a strike; **das Schiff drohte zu sinken** the ship was in danger of sinking.
drohend *adj* threatening, menacing; *(bevorstehend) Gefahr, Krieg* imminent, impending.
Drohne *f* **-n** drone.
dröhnen *vi* to roar; *(Donner)* to rumble; *(Musik, Stimme)* to boom; *(Raum etc)* to resound, to echo. **mir dröhnt der Kopf** my head is ringing.
Drohung *f* threat.
drollig *adj* comical, droll; *Kätzchen etc* cute.
Dromedar [*auch:* 'dro:-] *nt* **-e** dromedary.
Drops *m or nt* - fruit drop.
drosch *pret of* **dreschen.**
Droschke *f* **-n** *(Pferde~)* (hackney) cab, hackney-carriage; *(dated: Taxi)* (taxi-)cab.
Droschkenkutscher *m* cab driver.
Drossel *f* **-n** *(Orn)* thrush.
drosseln *vt Motor etc* to throttle; *Heizung* to turn down; *Strom, Tempo, Produktion* to cut down.
Drosselung *f siehe vt* throttling, turning down; cutting down.
drüben *adv* over there; *(auf der anderen Seite, col: auf DDR/BRD bezogen)* on the other side. **hier/dort** *or* **da ~** over here/there; **nach/von ~** over/from over there.
drüber *adv (col)* = **darüber.**
Druck[1] *m* **⸚e** *(Phys, fig)* pressure. **unter ~ stehen** *(lit, fig)* to be under pressure; **jdn unter ~ setzen** *(fig)* to put pressure on sb, to pressurize sb; **durch einen ~ auf den Knopf** by pressing the button.
Druck[2] *m* **-e (a)** *(das Drucken)* printing; *(Art des Drucks, Schriftart)* print; *(Druckwerk)* copy. **das Buch ist im ~** the book is being printed; **in ~ gehen** to go to press. **(b)** *(Kunst~)* print.
Druck-: ~ausgleich *m* pressure balance; **~buchstabe** *m* printed character *or* letter; **in ~buchstaben schreiben** to print.
Drückeberger *m* - *(pej col)* shirker.
Drückebergerei *f no pl (pej col)* shirking.
druck|empfindlich *adj* sensitive (to pressure).
drucken *vti (Typ, Tex)* to print; *siehe* **gedruckt.**
drücken 1 *vt* **(a)** *Hand, Hebel* to press; *Knopf auch* to push. **jdm etw in die Hand ~** to press *or* slip sth into sb's hand; **jdn ~** to squeeze sb; *(umarmen)* to hug sb; **jdn zur Seite ~** to push sb aside. **(b)** *(Schuhe, Korsett etc)* to pinch, to nip. **mich drückt der Magen** my stomach feels heavy. **(c)** *(verringern) Leistung, Niveau* to lower. **(d)** *(Gewichtheben)* to press. **2** *vi* **(a)** to press; *(Wetter, Hitze)* to be oppressive; *(Brille, Schuhe etc)* to pinch. **auf die Stimmung ~** to dampen one's mood. **(b)** *(drängeln, stoßen)* to push. **3** *vr* **(a)** *(sich quetschen)* to squeeze. **sich aus dem Zimmer ~** to slip out of the room. **(b)** *(col) (vor etw (dat)* sth*)* to shirk; *(vor Militärdienst)* to dodge. **sich (um etw) ~** to get out of (doing) sth.
drückend *adj Last, Steuern* heavy; *Sorgen* serious; *Armut* grinding; *Wetter, Hitze* oppressive, close. **es ist ~ heiß** it's oppressively hot.
Drucker(in *f*) *m* - printer.
Drücker *m* - *(Knopf)* (push) button; *(Türklinke)* handle; *(col: von Pistole etc)* trigger. **am ~ sein** *or* **sitzen** *(fig col)* to be the key person; **auf den letzten ~** *(fig col)* at the last minute.
Druckerei *f* printing works *pl*, printery.
Drucker-: ~presse *f* printing press; **~schwärze** *f* printer's ink.
Druck-: ~fahne *f* galley(-proof), proof; **~fehler** *m* misprint; **d~fertig** *adj* ready to print; **d~fest** *adj Werkstoff* pressure-resistant; **~knopf** *m* *(Sew)* press-stud *(Brit)*, snap fastener *(US)*; *(Tech)* push-button; **~legung** *f* printing; **~luft** *f* compressed air; **~luftbremse** *f* air-brake; **~mittel** *nt (fig)* form of pressure; **~platte** *f* printing plate; **~pumpe** *f* pressure pump; **d~reif** *adj* ready for printing, passed for press; *(fig)* polished; **~sache** *f* printed matter; **~schrift** *f* **(a)** *(Schriftart)* printing; **in ~schrift schreiben** to print; **(b)** *(gedrucktes Werk)* pamphlet.
drucksen *vi (col)* to hum and haw *(col)*.
Druck-: ~stelle *f (auf Obst, Haut)* bruise; **~taste** *f* pushbutton; **~verband** *m (Med)* pressure bandage; **~welle** *f* shock wave.
drum *adv (col) siehe auch* **darum** around. **~ (he)rumreden** to beat about the bush; **da wirst du nicht ~ (he)rumkommen** there's no getting out of it; **sei's ~!** *(geh)* never mind; **das D~ und Dran** the paraphernalia; *(Begleiterscheinungen)* the fuss and bother; **mit allem D~ und Dran** with all the bits and pieces *(col)*; *(Mahlzeit)* with all the trimmings.
Drumherum *nt no pl* trappings *pl*.
drunter *adv siehe auch* **darunter** under(neath). **~ und drüber** upside down, topsyturvy.
Drüse *f* **-n** gland.
Drüsenfieber *nt* glandular fever.
Dschungel *m* - *(lit, fig)* jungle.
Dschungel-: ~fieber *nt* yellow fever; **~krieg** *m* jungle war/warfare.
Dschunke *f (Naut)* **-n** junk.
dt. = **deutsch.**
du *pers pron (familiar form of address)* you. **D~** *(in Briefen)* you; **jdn mit ~ anreden** to say "du" (to sb); **mit jdm auf ~ und ~ stehen** to be pals with sb; **mit jdm per ~ sein** to be on familiar terms with sb; **~ bist es** it's you; **~, ich muß jetzt aber gehen** listen, I have to go now; **~, ~!** *(hum: drohend)* naughty, naughty.
Du *nt* **-(s) jdm das ~ anbieten** to suggest that sb uses "du" *or* the familiar form of address.
Dualsystem *nt (Math)* binary system.
Dübel *m* - plug; *(Holz~)* dowel.
dübeln *vti* to plug.
dubios *adj (geh)* dubious.
Dublette *f* **(a)** duplicate. **(b)** *(Boxen)* one-two.
ducken 1 *vr* to duck; *(fig pej)* to cringe, to cower. **sich in eine Ecke ~** to duck *or* dodge into a corner; *siehe* **geduckt. 2** *vi (fig pej)* to cower.
Duckmäuser *m* - *(pej)* toady.
Duckmäusertum *nt (pej)* toadying.
dudeln *vti (pej col)* to tootle. **das Radio dudelt schon den ganzen Tag** the (damn) radio's been playing all day.
Dudelsack *m* bagpipes *pl*.
Dudelsack-: ~pfeifer, ~spieler *m* (bag)piper.
Duell *nt* **-e** *(lit, fig)* duel *(um* over*)*.
Duellant [duɛ'lant] *m (wk)* dueller, duellist.
duellieren* [duɛ'li:rən] *vr* to (fight a) duel.

Duett *nt* **-e (a)** *(Mus, fig)* duet. **etw im ~ singen** to sing sth as a duet. **(b)** *(fig col: Paar)* duo *(col)*.
Duft *m* **¨-e** (pleasant) smell, scent; *(von Blumen, Parfüm auch)* fragrance; *(von Essen)* smell, aroma.
dufte *adj, adv (dated col)* great *(col)*.
duften *vi* to smell *(nach* of*)*. **das duftet** that smells nice.
duftend *adj attr* nice-smelling; *Parfüm, Blumen etc* fragrant.
duftig *adj Kleid, Stoff* light, gossamery.
Duft-: **~marke** *f* scent mark; **~note** *f (von Parfüm)* scent; **~stoff** *m* scent; *(für Parfüm, Waschmittel etc)* fragrance; **~wasser** *nt, pl* **~wässer** toilet water; **~wolke** *f (iro)* cloud of perfume.
dulden *vt* **(a)** *(zulassen)* to tolerate. **etw stillschweigend ~** to connive at sth; **er ist hier nur geduldet** he's only here on sufferance. **(b)** *(geh: erdulden)* to suffer.
duldsam *adj* tolerant *(gegenüber* of, *jdm gegenüber* towards sb*)*.
Duldsamkeit *f* tolerance.
Duldung *f* toleration. **mit stillschweigender ~ der Behörden** with the (tacit) connivance of the authorities.
dumm *adj comp* **¨-er,** *superl* **¨-ste(r, s)** *or (adv)* **am ¨-sten (a)** stupid dumb *(esp US)*; *Mensch auch* thick *(col)*; *(unklug, unvernünftig auch)* silly, foolish. **der ~e August** *(col)* the clown; **~e Gans** silly goose; **~es Zeug (reden)** (to talk) nonsense *or* rubbish; **ein ~es Gesicht machen, ~ gucken** to look stupid; **jdn wie einen ~en Jungen behandeln** *(col)* to treat sb like a child; **du willst mich wohl für ~ verkaufen** you must think I'm stupid; **ich lasse mich nicht für ~ verkaufen** I'm not so stupid *(col)*; **sich ~ stellen** to act stupid; **~ fragen** to ask a silly question/silly questions; **~ dastehen** to look stupid; **der D~ sein** to be left to carry the can *(col)*; **sich ~ und dämlich reden** *(col)* to talk till one is blue in the face *(col)*; **sich ~ und dämlich verdienen** to earn the earth *(col)*; **jetzt wird's mir zu ~** I've had enough.
(b) *(ärgerlich)* annoying; *Gefühl* nasty; *Sache, Geschichte auch* silly. **es ist zu ~, daß er nicht kommen kann** it's too bad that he can't come; **so etwas D~es** how stupid; *(wie ärgerlich)* what a nuisance.
dummdreist *adj* insolent.
Dummejungenstreich *m* silly *or* childish prank.
dummerweise *adv* unfortunately.
Dummheit *f* **(a)** *no pl* stupidity; *(Unvernunft)* foolishness. **(b)** *(dumme Handlung)* stupid thing.
Dummkopf *m (col)* idiot, fool.
dümmlich *adj* silly, stupid.
dumpf *adj* **(a)** *Geräusch, Ton* muffled. **~ aufprallen** to land with a thud. **(b)** *Geruch, Geschmack etc* musty; *(fig) Atmosphäre* stifling. **(c)** *Gefühl, Ahnung* vague; *Schmerz* dull.
Dumpingpreis ['dampıŋ-] *m* give-away price.
Düne *f* **-n** (sand-)dune.
Dung *m no pl* dung, manure.
Düngemittel *nt* fertilizer.
düngen 1 *vt* to fertilize. **2** *vi* **im Garten ~** to put fertilizer on the garden.
Dünger *m* **-** fertilizer.
dunkel *adj* **(a)** dark. **im D~n** in the dark; **im Zimmer ~ machen** *(col)* to darken the room; **sich ~ kleiden** to dress in dark colours. **(b)** *(tief) Stimme, Ton* deep. **(c)** *(unbestimmt, unklar)* vague. **in dunkler Vorzeit** in the dim and distant past; **im ~n tappen** *(fig)* to be in the dark. **(d)** *(pej: zwielichtig)* shady *(col)*, dubious.
Dunkel *nt no pl (lig, fig)* darkness. **im ~ der Nacht** at dead of night.
Dünkel *m no pl (pej geh)* conceit, arrogance.
dunkel- *in cpds* dark; **~blond** *adj* light brown; **~haarig** *adj* dark-haired.
dünkelhaft *adj (pej geh)* arrogant, conceited.
Dunkel-: **d~häutig** *adj* dark-skinned; **~heit** *f (lit, fig)* darkness; **bei Einbruch der ~heit** at nightfall; **~kammer** *f (Phot)* darkroom; **~mann** *m, pl* **~männer** *(pej)* shady character.
dunkeln *vi impers* **es dunkelt** *(geh)* darkness is falling, it is growing dark.
Dunkel-: **d~rot** *adj* dark red, maroon; **~ziffer** *f estimated number of unreported/undetected cases.*
dünken *vti impers (old, geh)* **das dünkt mir gut zu sein** it seems good to me.
dünn *adj* thin; *Kaffee, Tee* watery, weak; *(fein) Schleier, Strümpfe* fine; *Besiedlung auch* sparse. **~ gesät** *(fig)* few and far between; **sich ~ machen** *(hum)* to breathe in; *siehe* **dünnmachen.**
Dünn-: **d~besiedelt** *adj attr* sparsely populated; **~darm** *m* small intestine; **d~flüssig** *adj* thin; *Teig* runny; **d~gesät** *adj attr* sparse; **d~häutig** *adj (lit, fig)* thin-skinned; **d~machen** *vr sep (col)* to make oneself scarce; **~pfiff** *(col)*, **~schiß** *(col) m* the runs *(col)*.
Dunst *m* **¨-e** mist, haze; *(Dampf)* steam; *(Smog)* smog; *(Zigaretten~)* fug; *(Geruch)* smell. **jdm blauen ~ vormachen** *(col)* to tell sb stories *(col)*.
Dunst|abzugshaube *f* extractor hood.
dünsten *vt (Cook)* to steam; *Obst* to stew.
Dunstglocke *f* haze; pall of smog.
dunstig *adj* hazy, misty; *(verräuchert)* smoky.
Dunst-: **~kreis** *m* atmosphere; *(von Mensch)* society; **~schleier** *m* veil of mist; **~wolke** *f* cloud of smog.
Dünung *f (Naut)* swell.
Duo *nt* **-s** duo.
Duplikat *nt* duplicate (copy).
Dur *nt no pl (Mus)* major. **in G-~** in G major.
durch 1 *prep+acc* **(a)** through. **~ den Fluß waten** to wade across the river; **~ die ganze Welt reisen** to travel all over the world. **(b)** *(mittels)* through, by (means of); *(in Passivkonstruktion: von)* by. **Tod ~ den Strang** death by hanging; **Tod ~ Herzschlag** death from a heart attack; **~ die Post** by post; **etw ~ die Zeitung bekanntgeben** to announce sth in the press; **er ist ~ das Fernsehen bekannt geworden** he became famous through television. **(c)** *(aufgrund, infolge von)* due to, owing to.
2 *adv* **(a)** *(hin~)* through. **die ganze Nacht ~** all through the night, throughout the night; **es ist 4 Uhr ~** it's past 4 o'clock; **~ und ~** *kennen* through and through; *verlogen, überzeugt* completely, utterly; **~ und ~ naß** wet through; **das geht mir ~ und ~** that goes right through me. **(b)** *(Cook col)* **(gut) ~** well-done. **das Fleisch ist noch nicht ~** the meat isn't done yet.
durch|ackern *sep (col) vtr* to plough through *(durch etw* sth*)*.
durch|arbeiten *sep* **1** *vti* to work through. **2** *vr* **sich durch etw ~** to work (one's way) through sth.
durch|atmen *vi sep* to breathe deeply.
durch|aus *adv (emph auch* **durch|aus***)* **(a)** *(unbedingt)* **wenn du das ~ willst** if you insist, if you absolutely must; **das ist ~ nötig** that is absolutely necessary; **er will ~ recht haben** he (absolutely) insists that he is right. **(b)** *(bekräftigend)* quite; *verständlich, richtig, möglich auch* perfectly; *gefallen* really. **das läßt sich ~ machen** that sounds feasible; **ich bin ~ Ihrer Meinung** I quite *or* absolutely agree with you; **es ist ~ anzunehmen, daß sie kommt** it's highly likely that she'll be coming. **(c)** *(in verneinten Sätzen)* **~ nicht** *(als Verstärkung)* by no means; *(als Antwort)* not at all; *(stärker)* absolutely not; **etw ~ nicht tun wollen** to refuse absolutely to do sth; **das ist ~ kein Witz** that's no joke at all; **er ist ~ kein schlechter Mensch** he is by no means a bad person.
durchbacken *vt sep Kuchen* to bake through.
durchbeißen *sep irreg* **1** *vt* to bite through. **2** *vr*

(col) to struggle through *(durch etw* sth*)*.
durchblättern *vt sep Buch* to leaf through.
Durchblick *m* vista *(auf+acc* of*)*; *(Ausblick)* view *(auf+acc* of*)*. **den ~ haben** *(fig col)* to know what's what *(col)*.
durchblicken *vi sep* **(a)** *(lit)* to look through *(durch etw* sth*)*. **(b)** *(fig)* **etw ~ lassen** to hint at sth. **(c)** *(col: verstehen)* to understand. **blickst du da durch?** do you get it? *(col)*.
Durchblutung *f* circulation (of blood) *(gen* to*)*.
durchbohren[1]* *vt insep* to drill through; *(mit Schwert)* to run through; *(Kugel)* to go through. **jdn mit Blicken ~** *(fig)* to look piercingly at sb.
durchbohren[2] *sep* **1** *vt* **etw durch etw ~** *Loch, Tunnel* to drill sth through sth. **2** *vr* to bore (one's way) through *(durch etw* sth*)*.
durchbohrend *adj* piercing.
durchboxen *vr sep (fig col)* to fight (one's way) through *(durch etw* sth*)*.
durchbraten *vti sep irreg* to cook through. **durchgebraten** well done.
durchbrechen[1] *sep irreg* **1** *vt* to break (in two). **2** *vi aux sein* **(a)** *(in zwei Teile)* to break (in two). **(b)** *(Knospen)* to appear; *(Sonne auch)* to break through *(durch etw* sth*)*.
durchbrechen[2]* *vt insep irreg* to break; *Mauer, Blockade etc* to break through.
durchbrennen *vi sep irreg aux sein (Sicherung etc)* to blow; *(col: davonlaufen)* to run away. **jdm ~** *(col)* to run away from sb.
durchbringen *vt sep irreg* **(a)** *(durch etw* sth*)* to get through; *(durch Krankheit)* to pull through; *(für Unterhalt sorgen)* to provide for. **(b)** *Geld* to get through.
Durchbruch *m* **(a)** *(Mil, fig)* breakthrough. **jdm/etw zum ~ verhelfen** to help sb/sth on the road to success. **(b)** *(von Sonne)* breaking through *(durch etw* sth*)*; *(von Charakter)* revelation. **zum ~ kommen** *(fig)* to show itself.
durchdenken* *vt irreg insep* to think out *or* through. **gut durchdacht** well thought out.
durchdrehen *sep* **1** *vt Fleisch etc* to mince. **2** *vi* **(a)** *(Aut: Räder)* to spin. **(b)** *(col)* to go mad; *(nervlich)* to crack up *(col)*. **ganz durchgedreht sein** *(col)* to be really uptight *(col) or (verwirrt)* confused.
durchdringen[1] *vi sep irreg aux sein* **(a)** to penetrate *(durch etw* sth*)*; *(Sonne)* to come through *(durch etw* sth*)*. **bis zu jdm ~** *(fig)* to get as far as sb. **(b)** *(sich verständlich machen)* **zu jdm ~** to get through to sb.
durchdringen[2]* *vt insep irreg Materie, Dunkelheit etc* to penetrate; *siehe* **durchdrungen.**
durchdringend *adj* piercing; *Kälte, Wind auch* biting; *Geruch* pungent.
durchdrücken *vt sep* **(a)** *(durch Presse)* to press through; *Creme, Teig* to pipe. **(b)** *(fig) Gesetz, Reformen etc* to push through; *seinen Willen* to get. **(c)** *Knie, Kreuz etc* to straighten.
durchdrungen *adj pred* imbued *(von* with*)*. **ganz von einer Idee ~ sein** to be taken with an idea.
durch|einander 1 *adv* muddled up, in a muddle. **alles ~ essen/trinken** to eat/drink indiscriminately. **2** *adj pred* **~ sein** *(col) (Mensch)* to be confused *or (aufgeregt)* in a state *(col)*; *(Zimmer etc)* to be in a mess *or* muddle.
Durch|einander *nt no pl (Unordnung)* mess, muddle; *(Wirrwarr)* confusion.
durch|einander-: ~bringen *vt sep irreg* to muddle *or* mix up; *(verwirren) jdn* to confuse; **~geraten*, ~kommen** *vi sep irreg aux sein* to get mixed *or* muddled up; **~reden** *vi sep* to all talk at once; **~werfen** *vt sep irreg* to muddle up.
durchfahren[1] *vi sep irreg aux sein* **(a)** to go through *(durch etw* sth*)*. **(b)** *(nicht anhalten/umsteigen)* to go straight through. **er ist bei Rot durchgefahren** he jumped the lights; **die Nacht ~** to travel through the night.
durchfahren[2]* *vt insep irreg* to travel through; *(fig: Schreck etc)* to shoot through. **ein Gedanke durchfuhr ihn blitzartig** a (sudden) thought flashed through his mind.
Durchfahrt *f* way through. **auf der ~ sein** to be passing through; **~ bitte freihalten!** please keep access free; **~verboten!** no through road.
Durchfahrts-: ~straße *f* through road; **~verbot** *nt* **seit wann besteht hier ~verbot?** since when has this been a no through road?
Durchfall *m* **(a)** *(Med)* diarrhoea *no art (Brit)*, diarrhea *no art (US)*. **(b)** *(Mißerfolg)* failure.
durchfallen *vi sep irreg aux sein* **(a)** to fall through *(durch etw* sth*)*. **(b)** *(col: nicht bestehen)* to fail; *(Theaterstück auch)* to flop; *(Wahlkandidat)* to be defeated. **jdn ~ lassen** to fail sb; **beim Publikum ~** to be a flop with the public.
durchfeiern *vi sep* to celebrate all night.
durchfinden *vir sep irreg (lit, fig)* to find one's way through *(durch etw* sth*)*. **ich finde (mich) hier nicht mehr durch** *(fig)* I am simply lost.
durchfliegen[1] *vi sep irreg aux sein* **(a)** to fly through *(durch etw* sth*)*; *(ohne Landung)* to fly non-stop *or* direct. **(b)** *(col: in Prüfung)* to fail *(durch etw, in etw (dat)* sth*)*.
durchfliegen[2]* *vt insep irreg Luft, Wolken* to fly through; *Land* to fly over; *Strecke* to cover; *(flüchtig lesen)* to skim through.
durchfließen* *vt insep irreg (lit, fig)* to flow through.
Durchflug *m* flight through. **Passagiere auf dem ~** transit passengers.
durchfluten* *vt insep (geh: Fluß)* to flow through; *(fig: Licht, Sonne)* to flood.
durchforschen* *vt insep Gegend* to search; *Land, Fachgebiet* to explore; *Akten* to search through.
durchforsten* *vt insep (fig) Akten* to go through.
durchfragen *vr sep* to ask one's way.
durchfressen *vr sep irreg (durch etw* sth*) (Säure etc, Tier)* to eat (its way) through. **sich (bei jdm) ~** *(pej col)* to live off sb.
durchfroren *adj* frozen stiff.
Durchfuhr *f* transit.
durchführbar *adj* practicable, feasible.
Durchführbarkeit *f* feasibility, practicability.
durchführen *sep* **1** *vt* **(a)** *(durchleiten) (durch etw* sth*) jdn* to take through; *Leitung* to run through. **(b)** *(verwirklichen)* to carry out; *Gesetz* to implement; *(unternehmen) Expedition* to undertake; *Messung* to take; *Kursus* to run; *Wahl, Prüfung* to hold. **2** *vi* **zwischen/unter etw** *(dat)* **~** *(Straße etc)* to go between/under sth.
Durchführung *f siehe vt* **(a)** taking through; running through. **(b)** carrying out; implementation; undertaking; taking; running; holding.
durchfüttern *vt sep (col)* to feed. **sich von jdm ~ lassen** to live off sb.
Durchgabe *f* announcement; *(telefonisch)* message (over the telephone).
Durchgang *m* **(a)** passage. **(b)** *(das Durchgehen)* **~ verboten!** no right of way; **beim ~ durch das Tal** going through the valley. **(c)** *(von Wahl, Sport)* round; *(beim Rennen)* heat.
durchgängig *adj* universal, general.
Durchgangs-: ~lager *nt* transit camp; **~stadium** *nt* transition stage; **~straße** *f* through road; **~verkehr** *m* through traffic; *(Transitverkehr)* transit traffic.
durchgeben *vt sep irreg (Rad, TV) Hinweis, Wetter* to give; *Nachricht, Lottozahlen* to announce. **jdm etw telefonisch ~** to telephone sth to sb; **es wurde im Radio durchgegeben** it was announced on the radio.
durchgefroren *adj Mensch* frozen stiff.
durchgehen *sep irreg aux sein* **1** *vi* **(a)** to go through *(durch etw* sth*)*. **(b)** *(toleriert werden)* **jdm etw ~ lassen** to let sb get away with sth; **das lasse ich nochmal ~** I'll let it pass. **(c)** *(gehalten werden für)* **für etw ~** to pass for sth, to be taken

for sth. **(d)** *(ohne Unterbrechung)* to go straight through; *(Flug, Zug)* to be direct. **(e)** *(Pferd)* to bolt. **seine Frau ist ihm durchgegangen** his wife has run off and left him; **mit etw** ~ to run *or* make off with sth. **(f)** *(außer Kontrolle geraten)* **mit jdm** ~ *(Nerven etc)* to get the better of sb. **2** *vt (durchsprechen etc)* to go *or* run through.

durchgehend 1 *adj Öffnungszeiten* round-the-clock *attr*, continuous; *Straße* straight; *Verkehrsverbindung* direct; *Zug, Fahrkarte* through *attr*. **2** *adv* throughout, right through. ~ **geöffnet** open right through; open 24 hours.

durchgeschwitzt *adj* soaked in sweat.

durchgreifen *vi sep irreg* to reach through *(durch etw* sth*)*; *(fig)* to take (strong) action.

durchgucken *vi sep (Mensch)* to look through *(durch etw* sth*)*.

durchhaben *vt sep irreg (col)* **etw** ~ to have got sth through *(durch etw* sth*)*; *(durchgelesen etc haben)* to have got through sth.

durchhalten *sep irreg* **1** *vt Zeit, Kampf etc* to survive; *Streik* to see through; *Belastung* to stand; *(Sport) Tempo* to keep up. **das Rennen** ~ to stay the course. **2** *vi* to hold out.

Durchhalte-: ~**parole** *f* rallying call; ~**vermögen** *nt* staying power.

durchhängen *vi sep irreg (lit, fig)* to sag.

durchhauen *vt sep* to chop in two; *(spalten)* to split. **jdn** ~ *(col)* to give sb a walloping *(col)*.

durchhelfen *vi sep irreg* **jdm (durch etw)** ~ to help sb through (sth).

durchhungern *vr sep* to scrape by.

durchkämmen *sep*, **durchkämmen*** *insep vt (absuchen)* to comb (through).

durchkämpfen *sep* **1** *vt* to push through. **2** *vr* to battle one's way through *(durch etw* sth*)*.

durchkauen *vt sep Essen* to chew (thoroughly); *(col: besprechen)* to go over *or* through.

durchklingen *vi sep irreg aux haben or sein (durch etw* sth*)* to sound through; *(fig)* to come through. **etw** ~ **lassen** to hint at sth.

durchkommen *vi sep irreg aux sein (durch etw* sth*)* to come through; *(durchgelangen, telefonisch, in Prüfung)* to get through; *(Patient)* to pull through; *(finanziell)* to get by; *(im Radio)* to be announced. **mit etw** ~ *(mit Forderungen)* to succeed with sth; *(mit Betrug)* to get away with sth; **er kam mit seiner Stimme nicht durch** he couldn't make his voice heard; **damit kommt er bei mir nicht durch** he won't get away with that with me.

durchkreuzen* *vt insep* **(a)** *Wüste, Ozean* to cross. **(b)** *(fig) Pläne etc* to thwart.

durchladen *vi sep irreg Gewehr* to reload.

Durchlaß *m, pl* **Durchlässe** *(Durchgang)* passage, way through; *(für Wasser)* duct.

durchlassen *vt sep irreg (durch etw* sth*)* to let through; *(eindringen lassen)* to let in.

durchlässig *adj Material* permeable; *Zelt, Schuh* leaky; *Grenze* open. **eine** ~**e Stelle** *(lit, fig)* a leak.

Durchlaucht *f* **-en (Euer)** ~ Your Highness.

Durchlauf *m* **(a)** *(das Durchlaufen)* flow. **(b)** *(Comp)* run. **(c)** *(Sport)* heat.

durchlaufen[1] *sep irreg* **1** *vt Schuhe* to go through, to wear out. **2** *vi aux sein (durch etw* sth*)* to go through; *(Flüssigkeit auch)* to run through.

durchlaufen[2]* *vt insep irreg Gebiet* to run through; *Strecke* to cover, to run; *(Astron) Bahn* to describe; *Schule, Phase* to go through.

Durchlauf-: ~**erhitzer** *m* **-** continuous-flow water heater; ~**zeit** *f (Comp)* length of a/the run.

durchleben* *vt insep* to experience; *Jugend* to have.

durchlesen *vt sep irreg* to read through. **sich** *(dat)* **etw** ~ to read sth through.

durchleuchten* *vt insep* to X-ray; *(fig) Sache* to investigate. **sich** ~ **lassen** to have an X-ray.

Durchleuchtung *f (Med)* X-ray examination; *(fig: von Angelegenheit etc)* investigation.

durchlöchern* *vt insep* to make holes in; *(fig)* to undermine completely. **(mit Schüssen)** ~ to riddle with bullets.

durchlüften *vti sep* to air thoroughly.

durchmachen *sep* **1** *vt (erdulden, durchlaufen)* to go through; *Krankheit* to have; *Lehre* to serve; *(fig) Entwicklung* to undergo. **er hat viel durchgemacht** he has been *or* gone through a lot; **eine ganze Nacht** ~ *(col: durchfeiern)* to make a night of it. **2** *vi (col) (durcharbeiten)* to work right through; *(durchfeiern)* to keep going all night/day *etc*.

Durchmarsch *m* **der** ~ **durch die Stadt** the march through the town.

durchmarschieren* *vi sep aux sein* to march through *(durch etw* sth*)*.

Durchmesser *m* **-** diameter. **120 cm im** ~ 120 cm in diameter.

durchmischen *vt sep* to mix thoroughly.

durchmüssen *vi sep irreg (col) (durch etw* sth*)* to have to get through; *(durch Unangenehmes)* to have to go through with.

durchnässen* *vt insep* to soak, to drench. **völlig durchnäßt** wet through, drenched.

durchnehmen *vt sep irreg (Sch)* to do.

durchnumerieren* *vt sep* to number consecutively.

durch|organisieren* *vt sep* to organize down to the last detail.

durchpauken *vt sep (col)* **(a)** *Lernstoff* to swot up *(col)*. **(b)** *Gesetz, Schüler* to push through.

durchpausen *vt sep* to trace.

durchpeitschen *vt sep* to flog; *(fig)* to rush through.

durchpressen *vt sep* to press through.

durchprügeln *vt sep* to thrash, to beat.

durchqueren* *vt insep* to cross.

durchrasen *vi sep aux sein*, **durchrasen*** *vt insep* to race *or* tear through.

durchrechnen *vt sep* to calculate.

durchregnen *vi sep impers* **es regnet durchs Dach durch** the rain is coming through the roof; **es hat die Nacht durchgeregnet** it rained all through the night.

Durchreiche *f* **-n** (serving) hatch *(Brit)*, pass-through *(US)*.

durchreichen *vt sep* to pass through *(durch etw* sth*)*.

Durchreise *f* journey through. **auf der** ~ **sein** to be passing through.

durchreisen *vi sep aux sein*, **durchreisen*** *vt insep* to travel through.

Durchreisende(r) *mf decl as adj* traveller (passing through), transient *(US)*.

Durchreisevisum *nt* transit visa.

durchreißen *vti sep irreg (vi: aux sein)* to tear in two.

durchringen *vr sep irreg* **sich dazu** ~, **etw zu tun** to bring *or* force oneself to do sth.

durchrosten *vi sep aux sein* to rust through.

durchrufen *vi sep irreg (col)* to ring *(bei jdm* sb*)*.

durchrutschen *vi sep aux sein (lit)* to slip through *(durch etw* sth*)*.

durchs = **durch das.**

Durchsage *f* announcement. **eine** ~ **der Polizei** a police announcement.

durchsagen *vt sep* = **durchgeben.**

durchsägen *vt sep* to saw through.

durchsausen *vi sep aux sein (col)* **(a)** to rush through. **(b)** *(col: nicht bestehen)* to fail, to flunk *(col) (durch etw, in etw (dat)* (in) sth*)*.

durchschaubar *adj (fig) Plan, Ereignisse* clear; *Lüge* transparent. **eine leicht** ~**e Lüge** a lie that is easy to see through; **schwer** ~**er Charakter** inscrutable character.

durchschauen[1]* *vt insep Absichten, Lüge, jdn* to see through; *(begreifen)* to understand. **du bist durchschaut!** you've been found out.

durchschauen[2] *vti sep* = **durchsehen.**
durchscheinen *vi sep irreg (durch etw* sth*) (lit, fig)* to shine through; *(Farbe)* to show through.
durchscheinend *adj* transparent.
durchscheuern *vt sep* to wear through. **sich** *(dat)* **die Haut** ~ to graze one's skin.
durchschieben *vt sep irreg* to push *or* shove *(col)* through *(durch etw* sth*)*.
durchschießen[1] *vi sep irreg* **durch etw** ~ to shoot through sth.
durchschießen[2]* *vt insep irreg (lit, fig)* to shoot through. **ein Gedanke durchschoß mich** a thought flashed through my mind.
durchschimmern *vi sep (durch etw* sth*)* to shimmer through; *(Farbe, fig)* to show through.
durchschlafen *vi sep irreg* to sleep through.
Durchschlag *m* **(a)** *(Kopie)* carbon (copy). **(b)** *(Küchengerät)* sieve, strainer.
durchschlagen[1] *sep irreg* **1** *vt* **etw** ~ *(entzweischlagen)* to chop through sth; *(Cook)* to sieve sth. **2** *vi* **(a)** *aux sein (durchkommen) (durch etw* sth*)* to come through; *(fig: Charakter, Eigenschaft)* to show through. **bei ihm schlägt der Vater durch** you can see his father in him. **(b)** *aux sein (Wirkung haben)* to catch on. **auf etw** *(acc)* ~ to make one's/its mark on sth; **auf jdn** ~ to rub off on sb. **(c)** *aux sein (Sicherung)* to blow, to go. **3** *vr* to fight through; *(im Leben)* to struggle through *or* along.
durchschlagen[2]* *vt insep irreg* to blast a hole in.
durchschlagend *adj Sieg* sweeping; *Erfolg* tremendous; *Beweis* decisive, conclusive. **eine ~e Wirkung haben** to be totally effective.
Durchschlagpapier *nt* flimsy; *(Kohlepapier)* carbon paper.
Durchschlagskraft *f (von Geschoß)* penetration; *(fig: von Argument)* decisiveness.
durchschlängeln *vr sep (durch etw* sth*) (Fluß)* to wind (its way) through, to meander through; *(Mensch)* to thread one's way through; *(fig)* to manoeuvre *(Brit) or* maneuver *(US)* one's way through.
durchschleusen *vt sep* **(a) ein Schiff** ~ to pass a ship through a lock. **(b)** *(fig: durch schmale Stelle)* to guide through *(durch etw* sth*)*.
durchschlüpfen *vi sep aux sein* to slip through *(durch etw* sth*)*.
durchschmecken *vt sep* to taste. **man kann den Essig** ~ the taste of vinegar comes through.
durchschneiden[1] *vt sep irreg* to cut in two.
durchschneiden[2]* *vt insep irreg* to cut through; *(Schiff) Wellen* to plough through. **jdm die Kehle** ~ to cut *or* slit sb's throat.
Durchschnitt *m* average; *(in Statistik)* mean. **der** ~ *(normale Menschen)* the average person; *(die Mehrheit)* the majority; **im** ~ on average; **im** ~ **100 km/h fahren** to average 100 kmph; **über/unter dem** ~ above/below average; **guter** ~ **sein** to be a good average.
durchschnittlich 1 *adj* average; *Wert auch* mean *attr.* **2** *adv (im Durchschnitt) verdienen, essen etc* on average. ~ **begabt/groß** of average ability/height; **die Mannschaft hat sehr** ~ **gespielt** the team played a very average game.
Durchschnitts- *in cpds* average; **~alter** *nt* average age; **~gesicht** *nt* ordinary *or* nondescript *(pej)* face; **~mensch** *m* average person; **~wert** *m* average *or* mean *(Math)* value.
durchschreiben *vt sep irreg* to make a (carbon) copy of.
durchschreiten* *vt insep irreg (geh)* to stride through.
Durchschrift *f* (carbon) copy.
Durchschuß *m (Loch)* bullet hole. **ein** ~ **durch den Darm** a gunshot wound right through the intestine.
durchschütteln *vt sep Mischung* to shake thoroughly; *(in Auto, Bus etc) jdn* to shake about.
durchschwimmen *vi sep irreg aux sein,* **durchschwimmen*** *vt insep irreg* to swim through.
durchschwitzen *vt sep* to soak with sweat.
durchsegeln[1] *vi sep aux sein* **(a)** *(Schiff)* to sail through *(durch etw* sth*)*. **(b)** *(col: nicht bestehen)* to fail, to flunk *(col) (durch etw, bei etw* sth*)*.
durchsegeln[2]* *vt insep Meer* to sail across.
durchsehen *sep irreg* **1** *vi* **(a)** *(hindurchschauen)* to look through *(durch etw* sth*)*. **ein Stoff, durch den man** ~ **kann** see-through material. **(b)** *(col: verstehen)* = **durchblicken (c). 2** *vt (überprüfen)* **etw** ~ to have a look through sth *(auf +acc* for*)*.
durchsein *vi sep irreg aux sein (col)* to be through *(durch etw* sth*)*; *(vorbeigekommen sein)* to have gone; *(Cook: Steak, Gemüse)* to be done.
durchsetzen[1] *sep* **1** *vt Maßnahmen* to put through; *Forderung* to push through; *Vorschlag, Plan* to carry through; *Ziel* to achieve. **etw bei jdm** ~ to get sb to agree to sth; **seinen Willen (bei jdm)** ~ to get one's (own) way (with sb). **2** *vr* **(a)** *(Mensch)* to assert oneself *(bei jdm* with sb*)*; *(Partei etc)* to be successful. **sich gegen etw** ~ to win through against sth; **sich mit etw** ~ to be successful with sth; **sich im Leben** ~ to make a success of one's life. **(b)** *(Idee, Neuheit)* to be accepted, to catch on.
durchsetzen[2]* *vt insep* **mit etw durchsetzt** interspersed with sth; **mit subversiven Elementen durchsetzt** infiltrated by subversive elements.
Durchsetzung *f siehe* **durchsetzen**[1] **1** putting through; pushing through; carrying through; achievement.
Durchsicht *f* examination, inspection. **jdm etw zur** ~ **geben** to give sb sth to check through; **bei** ~ **der Bücher** on checking the books.
durchsichtig *adj (lit, fig)* transparent.
Durchsichtigkeit *f no pl (lit, fig)* transparency.
durchsickern *vi sep aux sein (lit, fig)* to trickle through; *(fig: trotz Geheimhaltung)* to leak out. **Informationen** ~ **lassen** to leak information.
durchsieben[1] *vt sep* to sieve, to sift; *(fig) Bewerber etc* to sift through.
durchsieben[2]* *vt insep (col)* **von Kugeln durchsiebt** riddled with bullets.
durchsitzen *sep irreg vt Sessel etc* to wear out (the seat of).
durchspielen *vt sep* to go *or* run through.
durchsprechen *vt sep irreg Problem, Möglichkeiten* to talk over *or* through.
durchspülen *vt sep* to rinse (out) thoroughly.
durchstarten *vi sep (Aviat)* to overshoot; *(Aut)* to accelerate off again; *(beim Anfahren)* to rev up.
durchstechen[1] *sep irreg* **1** *vt Nadel, Spieß* to stick through *(durch etw* sth*)*. **2** *vi* to pierce.
durchstechen[2]* *vt insep irreg* to pierce; *(mit Degen etc)* to run through; *(mit Nadel)* to prick.
durchstecken *vt sep* to put *or* stick *(col)* through *(durch etw* sth*)*.
durchstehen *vt sep irreg Zeit, Prüfung, Situation* to get through; *Krankheit* to get over; *Tempo, Qualen* to stand; *Abenteuer* to have.
Durchstehvermögen *nt* staying power.
durchsteigen *vi sep irreg aux sein* **(a)** to climb through *(durch etw* sth*)*. **(b)** *(col: verstehen)* = **durchblicken (c).**
durchstellen *vt sep (Telec)* to put through. **ich stelle durch** I'll put you through.
durchstöbern* *insep,* **durchstöbern** *sep vt* to hunt *or* rummage through *(nach* for*)*; *(durchwühlen)* to ransack *(nach* looking for*)*.
Durchstoß *m* breakthrough.
durchstoßen[1]* *vt insep irreg* to break through.
durchstoßen[2] *vti sep irreg (vi: aux sein)* to break through *(auch Mil)*. **etw (durch etw)** ~ to push sth through (sth).
durchstreichen *vt sep irreg* to cross out.
durchstreifen* *vt insep (geh)* to roam through.
durchströmen* *vt insep (lit, fig)* to flow through.
durchsuchen* *vt insep (nach* for*)* to search

(through); *jdn* to search, to frisk.
Durchsuchung *f* search *(auf+dat* for*)*.
Durchsuchungsbefehl *m* search warrant.
durchtrainieren* *vt sep Sportler, Körper* to get fit. **(gut) durchtrainiert** in superb condition.
durchtränken* *vt insep* to soak, to saturate.
durchtrennen *sep,* **durchtrennen*** *insep vt (schneiden)* to cut (through); *Nerv, Sehne* to sever.
durchtreten *sep irreg* **1** *vt* **(a)** *Pedal* to step on; *Starter* to kick. **(b)** *(abnutzen) Schuh, Sohle* to go *or* wear through. **2** *vi aux sein (durchsickern)* to come through *(durch etw* sth*)*. **bitte weiter ~** *(form: weitergehen)* pass along please.
durchtrieben *adj* cunning, sly.
Durchtriebenheit *f no pl* cunning, slyness.
durchwachen* *vt insep* **die Nacht ~** to stay awake all through the night.
durchwachsen *adj* **(a)** *(lit) Speck* streaky; *Fleisch, Schinken* with fat running through (it). **(b)** *pred (hum col: mittelmäßig)* so-so *(col)*.
Durchwahl *f (Telec)* direct dialling; *(bei Firma)* extension.
durchwählen *vi sep (Telec)* to dial direct. **nach London ~** to dial London direct.
durchwandern* *vt insep Gegend* to walk through; *(hum) Zimmer, Straßen etc* to wander through.
durchweben* *vt insep irreg* to interweave *(mit, von* with*)*.
durchweg *adv* without exception. **~ gut** good in every way.
durchweichen *sep* **1** *vi aux sein* to get wet through; *(weich werden: Karton, Boden)* to go soggy. **2** *vt* to soak; *Boden, Karton* to make soggy.
durchwinden *vr sep irreg* = **durchschlängeln.**
durchwühlen *sep,* **durchwühlen*** *insep vt* to rummage through *(nach* for*)*; *Zimmer auch* to ransack *(nach* looking for*)*.
durchwursteln *vr sep (col)* to muddle through.
durchzählen *vt sep* to count.
durchzechen[1] *vi sep* to carry on drinking.
durchzechen[2]* *vt insep* **die Nacht ~** to spend the night drinking; **eine durchzechte Nacht** a night of drinking.
durchziehen[1] *sep irreg* **1** *vt* **(a)** to pull through *(durch etw* sth*)*. **(b)** *(col: erledigen)* **etw ~** to get sth through. **2** *vi aux sein* **(a)** *(durchkommen)* to pass through *(durch etw* sth*)*. **(b)** *(Cook)* to soak. **3** *vr* to run through *(durch etw* sth*)*.
durchziehen[2]* *vt insep irreg (durchwandern)* to pass through, to go/come through; *(Straße, Fluß, fig: Thema)* to run through; *(Geruch)* to fill, to pervade.
durchzucken* *vt insep (Blitz)* to flash across; *(fig: Gedanke)* to flash through.
Durchzug *m* **(a)** *no pl (Luftzug)* draught *(Brit)*, draft *(US)*. **(b)** *(durch ein Gebiet)* passage; *(von Truppen)* march through.
dürfen *pret* **durfte,** *ptp* **gedurft** *or (modal aux)* **dürfen** *vi* **(a)** *(Erlaubnis haben)* **etw tun ~** to be allowed to do sth, to be permitted to do sth; **darf ich? — ja, Sie ~** may I? — yes, you may; **darf ich ins Kino?** may I go to the cinema?
(b) *(verneint)* **man darf etw nicht (tun)** *(sollte, muß nicht)* one must not *or* mustn't do sth; *(hat keine Erlaubnis)* one isn't allowed to do sth, one may not do sth; **er durfte das nicht** he wasn't allowed to; **hier darf man nicht rauchen** smoking is prohibited here; **du darfst ihm das nicht übelnehmen** you must not take offence at him; **das darf doch nicht wahr sein!** that can't be true!; **da darf er sich nicht wundern** that shouldn't surprise him.
(c) *(in Höflichkeitsformeln)* **Ruhe, wenn ich bitten darf!** quiet, (if you) please!; **darf ich Sie bitten, das zu tun?** may *or* could I ask you to do that?; **was darf es sein?** can I help you?; **dürfte ich bitte Ihren Paß sehen** may *or* might I see your passport, please.
(d) *(Veranlassung haben, können)* **wir freuen uns, Ihnen mitteilen zu ~** we are pleased to be able to tell you; **man darf doch wohl fragen** one can *or* may ask, surely?
(e) das dürfte ... *(als Annahme)* that must ...; *(sollte)* that should ..., that ought to ...; *(könnte)* that could ...; **das dürfte wohl das Beste sein** that is probably the best thing.
dürftig *adj* **(a)** *(ärmlich)* wretched, miserable; *Bekleidung* poor. **(b)** *(pej: unzureichend)* miserable, pathetic *(col)*; *Kenntnisse* scanty; *Ausrede auch* feeble; *Ersatz* poor *attr*.
dürr *adj* **(a)** dry; *Boden* arid, barren; *Ast, Strauch* withered. **(b)** *(pej: mager)* scrawny, scraggy.
Dürre *f* **-n (a)** *(Zeit der ~)* drought. **(b)** *no pl (Trockensein)* dryness; *(von Boden)* aridity.
Dürre-: ~jahr *nt* year of drought; **~katastrophe** *f* drought disaster; **~periode** *f* drought.
Durst *m no pl (lit, fig)* thirst *(nach* for*)*. **~ haben** to be thirsty; **~ bekommen** to get thirsty; **den ~ löschen** to quench one's thirst; **einen über den ~ getrunken haben** *(col)* to have had one too many.
dursten *vi (geh)* to be thirsty, to thirst *(liter)*.
dürsten 1 *vt impers (liter)* **mich dürstet** I thirst *(liter)*; **es dürstet ihn nach Rache** he is thirsting for revenge. **2** *vi (fig)* to thirst *(nach* for*)*.
durstig *adj* thirsty. **diese Arbeit macht ~** this is thirsty work *(col)*, this work makes you thirsty.
Durst-: d~löschend, d~stillend *adj* thirst-quenching; **~strecke** *f* hard times *pl*.
Durtonleiter *f* major scale.
Duschbad *nt* shower(-bath).
Dusche *f* **-n** shower. **unter der ~ sein** to be in the shower; **das war eine kalte ~** *(fig)* that really brought him/her *etc* down with a bump.
duschen *vir* to have *or* take a shower, to shower. **(sich) kalt ~** to have *or* take a cold shower.
Dusch-: ~gelegenheit *f* shower facilities *pl*; **~kabine** *f* shower (cubicle); **~raum** *m* shower room, showers *pl*; **~vorhang** *m* shower curtain.
Düse *f* **-n** nozzle; *(Mech auch, von Flugzeug)* jet.
Dusel *m no pl (col)* **(a)** *(Glück)* luck. **da hat er (einen) ~ gehabt** he was lucky. **(b)** *(Trancezustand)* daze, dream; *(durch Alkohol)* fuddle.
duselig *adj (schlaftrunken)* drowsy; *(benommen)* dizzy; *(esp durch Alkohol)* befuddled.
Düsen-: ~antrieb *m* jet propulsion; **~bomber** *m* jet bomber; **~flugzeug** *nt* jet plane, jet; **d~getrieben** *adj* jet-propelled; **~jäger** *m (Mil)* jet fighter; **~triebwerk** *nt* jet power-unit.
Dussel *m* **-** *(col)* twit *(Brit col)*, twerp *(col)*.
dusselig, dußlig *adj (col)* stupid.
Dusseligkeit, Dußligkeit *f (col)* stupidity.
düster *adj* gloomy; *Bild, Gedanken* sombre *(Brit)*, somber *(US)*, dismal; *(unheimlich) Gestalten* sinister.
Düsterheit, Düsterkeit *f* gloominess; *(Dunkelheit)* gloom, dark(ness).
Dutzend *nt* **-e** dozen. **ein halbes ~** half-a-dozen, a half-dozen; **zwei/drei ~** two/three dozen; **~e** *pl (col)* dozens *pl*.
Dutzend-: d~mal *adv (col)* **(ein) d~mal** dozens of times; **~ware** *f (pej)* (cheap) mass-produced item; **d~weise** *adv* in dozens, by the dozen.
duzen *vt* **wir ~ uns** we use "du" *or* the "du"-form.
Duzfreund *m* good friend.
Dynamik *f no pl* **(a)** *(Phys)* dynamics. **(b)** *(fig)* dynamism.
dynamisch *adj (Phys, fig)* dynamic; *Renten* ≃ index-linked.
Dynamit *nt no pl (lit, fig)* dynamite.
Dynamo *m* **-s** dynamo.
Dynastie *f* dynasty.
D-Zug ['de:tsu:k] *m* fast train; *(hält nur in großen Städten)* through train. **ein alter Mann ist doch kein ~** *(col)* I am going as fast as I can.
D-Zug-Tempo *nt (col)* fantastic speed *(col)*. **im ~** like greased lightning *(col)*.

E

E, e [eː] *nt* **-, -** E, e.

Ebbe *f* **-n (a)** ebb tide; *(Niedrigwasser)* low tide. **~ und Flut** ebb and flow; **bei ~ baden** to swim when the tide is going out; *(bei Niedrigwasser)* to swim at low tide; **es ist ~** the tide is going out; *(es ist Niedrigwasser)* it's low tide, the tide is out. **(b)** *(fig)* **in meinem Geldbeutel ist ~** my finances are at a pretty low ebb at the moment.

eben 1 *adj (glatt)* smooth; *(gleichmäßig)* even; *(gleich hoch)* level; *(flach)* flat. **zu ~er Erde** at ground level. **2** *adv* **(a)** just. **mein Bleistift war doch ~ noch da** my pencil was there (just) a minute ago; **ich gehe ~ zur Bank** I'll just go to the bank; **das reicht so** *or* **nur ~ aus** it's only just enough. **(b) das ist ~ so** that's just the way it is; **dann bleibst du ~ zu Hause** then you'll just have to stay at home. **(c)** *(gerade or genau das)* exactly, precisely. **das ist es ja ~!** that's just *or* precisely it!; **nicht ~ billig** not exactly cheap.

Ebenbild *nt* image. **das genaue ~ seines Vaters** the spitting image of his father.

ebenbürtig *adj (gleichwertig)* equal; *Gegner* evenly matched. **jdm an Kraft ~ sein** to be sb's equal in strength.

eben-: ~da *adv (gerade dort)* **~da will auch ich hin** that is exactly where I am going too; **~darum** *adv* for that very reason; **~der, ~die, ~das** *pron* he; she; it; **~deshalb, ~deswegen** *adv* that is exactly why; **~diese(r, s)** *adj* this very.

Ebene *f* **-n** plain; *(Hoch~)* plateau; *(Math, Phys)* plane; *(fig)* level. **auf höchster/der gleichen ~** *(fig)* at the highest/the same level.

eben-: ~erdig *adj* at ground level; **~falls** *adv* as well, likewise; **er hat ~falls nichts davon gewußt** he knew nothing about it either.

Ebenholz *nt* ebony.

Ebenmaß *nt (von Gestalt etc)* perfect proportions *pl; (von Versen)* even flow.

ebenso *adv (genauso)* just as; *(auch, ebenfalls)* as well. **das kann doch ~ eine Frau machen** a woman can do that just as well; **er hat ein ~ großes Zimmer wie wir** he has just as big a room as we have.

ebenso-: ~gern *adv* **ich mag sie ~gern** I like her just as much; **ich komme ~gern morgen** I'd just as soon come tomorrow; **~gut** *adv* (just) as well; **~lang(e)** *adv* just as long; **~oft** *adv* just as often; **~sehr** *adv* just as much; **~viel** *adv* just as much; **~wenig** *adv* just as little.

Eber *m* **-** boar.

Eber|esche *f* rowan, mountain ash.

ebnen *vt* to level (off), to make level. **jdm den Weg ~** *(fig)* to smooth the way for sb.

Echo *nt* **-s** echo; *(fig)* response *(auf+ acc* to*)*. **ein lebhaftes ~ finden** *(fig)* to meet with a lively response *(bei* from*)*.

Echolot *nt (Naut)* echo-sounder, sonar; *(Aviat)* sonic altimeter.

Echse ['ɛksə] *f* **-n** *(Zool)* lizard.

echt 1 *adj, adv* **(a)** real, genuine; *Haar, Perlen, Gold* real; *Unterschrift, Geldschein, Gemälde* genuine. **(b)** *(typisch)* typical. **ein ~er Bayer** a real *or* typical Bavarian; **~ englisch** typically English. **2** *adv (col)* really. **ich hab' ~ keine Zeit** I really don't have any time.

Echtheit *f* genuineness; *(von Unterschrift, Dokument auch)* authenticity.

Eck- *in cpds* corner; **~ball** *m (Sport)* corner; **~bank** *f* corner seat.

Ecke *f* **-n (a)** corner *(auch Sport)*; *(Kante)* edge; *(von Kragen)* point. **Kantstraße ~ Goethestraße** at the corner of Kantstraße and Goethestraße; **gleich um die ~** just around the corner; **jdn in die ~ drängen** *(fig)* to push sb into the background; **an allen ~n und Enden sparen** to pinch and scrape *(col)*; **jdn um die ~ bringen** *(col)* to bump sb off *(col)*; **mit jdm um ein paar ~n herum verwandt sein** *(col)* to be distantly related to sb, to be sb's second cousin twice removed *(hum col)*. **(b)** *(Käse~, Kuchen~)* wedge. **(c)** *(col: Gegend)* corner, area. **aus welcher ~ kommst du?** what part of the world are you from?

Eck-: ~fahne *f (Sport)* corner flag; **~haus** *nt* corner house.

eckig *adj* angular; *Klammer* square; *(spitz)* sharp.

Eck-: ~kneipe *f (col)* pub on the corner *(Brit)*; **~pfeiler** *m (fig)* cornerstone; **~pfosten** corner post; **~schrank** *m* corner cupboard; **~stoß** *m (Ftbl)* corner kick; **~zahn** *m* canine tooth.

edel *adj* noble; *(hochwertig)* precious; *Wein, Speisen* fine.

Edel-: ~fäule *f (bei Weintrauben)* noble rot; **~frau** *f (Hist)* noblewoman; **~gas** *nt* rare gas; **~holz** *nt* precious wood; **~mann** *m, pl* **~leute** *(Hist)* noble(man); **~metall** *nt* precious metal; **~mut** *m (liter)* magnanimity; **e~mütig** *adj (liter)* magnanimous; **~pilzkäse** *m* blue (vein) cheese; **~rost** *m* patina; **~stahl** *m* high-grade steel; **~stein** *m* precious stone; *(geschliffener auch)* jewel, gem; **~tanne** *f* noble fir; **~weiß** *nt* **-e** edelweiss.

Eden *nt no pl* **der Garten ~** *(Bibl)* the Garden of Eden.

Editor(in *f*) [-'toːrɪn] *m* editor.

EDV [eːdeː'fau] *f* = **elektronische Datenverarbeitung.**

Efeu *m no pl* ivy.

Eff|eff *nt no pl (col)* **etw aus dem ~ können** to be able to do sth standing on one's head *(col)*; **etw aus dem ~ kennen** to know sth inside out.

Effekt *m* **-e** effect.

Effekten *pl (Fin)* stocks and bonds *pl.*

Effekten-: ~börse *f* stock exchange; **~handel** *m* stock dealing.

Effekthascherei *f (col)* showmanship. **das ist reine ~** it's just done for effect.

effektiv 1 *adj* **(a)** effective. **(b)** *(tatsächlich)* actual. **2** *adv* actually. **~ kein** absolutely no.

Effektivität *f* effectiveness.

Effektivlohn *m* actual wage.

effektvoll *adj* effective.

Effet [ɛ'feː] *m* **-s** spin. **den Ball mit ~ schießen** to put spin on a ball.

effizient *adj* efficient.

EG [eː'geː] *f* = **Europäische Gemeinschaft** EEC.

egal *adj, adv* **(a)** *pred* **das ist ~** that doesn't matter, that doesn't make any difference; **das ist mir ganz ~** it's all the same to me; **~ wo/wie** it doesn't matter where/how, no matter where/how. **(b)** *(col: gleichartig)* the same, identical.

egalitär *adj (geh)* egalitarian.
Egge *f* **-n** *(Agr)* harrow.
Ego *nt* **-s** *(Psych)* ego.
Egoismus *m* ego(t)ism.
Egoist(in *f***)** *m (wk)* ego(t)ist.
egoistisch *adj* ego(t)istical.
Ego-: **~zentriker(in** *f***)** *m* - egocentric; **e~zentrisch** *adj* egocentric.
eh 1 *interj* hey. **2** *adv* **(a) seit ~ und je** for ages, since the year dot *(col)*; **wie ~ und je** just as before. **(b)** *(col: sowieso)* anyway. **ich komme ~ nicht dazu** I won't get around to it anyway.
ehe *conj (bevor)* before. **~ (daß) ich mich auf andere verlasse, mache ich lieber alles selbst** rather than rely on others, I would prefer to do everything myself.
Ehe *f* **-n** marriage. **er versprach ihr die ~** he promised to marry her; **die ~ eingehen** *(form)* to enter into matrimony *(form)*; **eine unglückliche ~ führen** to have an unhappy marriage; **die ~ brechen** *(form)* to commit adultery; **sie hat drei Kinder aus erster ~** she has three children from her first marriage.
Ehe-: **e~ähnlich** *adj (form)* **in einer e~ähnlichen Gemeinschaft leben** to cohabit *(form)*; **~anbahnungsinstitut** *nt* marriage bureau; **~beratung** *f* marriage guidance; **~bett** *nt (fig)* marital bed; **~brecher** *m* - adulterer; **~brecherin** *f* adulteress; **e~brecherisch** *adj* adulterous; **~bruch** *m* adultery.
ehedem *adv (old)* formerly.
Ehe-: **~frau** *f* wife; **~gatte** *m*, **~gattin** *f (form)* spouse *(form)*; **~gemeinschaft** *f (form)* wedlock *(form)*, matrimony; **~krach** *m* marital row; **~leben** *nt* married life; **~leute** *pl (form)* married couple; *(in Briefadresse)* Mr and Mrs.
ehelich *adj* marital; *Pflichten, Rechte auch* conjugal; *Kind* legitimate.
ehelichen *vt (dated, hum)* to wed *(old)*.
ehelos *adj* unmarried, single.
Ehelosigkeit *f no pl* unmarried state; *(Rel)* celibacy.
ehemalig *adj attr* former. **~er Häftling** ex-convict; **mein E~er/meine E~e** *(hum col)* my ex *(col)*.
ehemals *adv (form)* formerly, previously.
Ehe-: **~mann** *m, pl* **~männer** married man; *(Partner)* husband; **~paar** *nt* (married) couple; **~partner(in** *f***)** *m* husband; wife; **beide ~partner** both partners (in the marriage).
eher *adv* **(a)** *(früher)* earlier, sooner. **nicht ~ als** not before. **(b)** *(lieber)* rather, sooner; *(wahrscheinlicher)* more likely; *(leichter)* more easily. **um so ~, als** the more so because; **das ist ~ möglich** that is more likely *or* probable. **(c)** *(vielmehr)* more. **er ist ~ faul als dumm** he's more lazy than stupid, he's lazy rather than stupid.
Ehe-: **~ring** *m* wedding ring; **~scheidung** *f* divorce; **~schließung** *f* marriage ceremony, wedding.
Ehestand *m no pl* matrimony, marriage. **in den ~ treten** *(form)* to enter into matrimony.
ehestens *adv* **~ morgen** tomorrow at the earliest.
eheste(r, s) 1 *adj* **bei ~r Gelegenheit** at the earliest opportunity. **2** *adv* **am ~n** *(am liebsten)* best of all; *(am wahrscheinlichsten)* most likely; *(am leichtesten)* the easiest; **am ~n würde ich mir ein Auto kaufen** what I'd like best (of all) would be to buy myself a car; **das geht wohl am ~n** that's probably the best way.
Ehe-: **~streit** *m* marital argument; **~vermittlung** *f (Büro)* marriage bureau; **~versprechen** *nt (Jur)* promise to marry.
ehrbar *adj (achtenswert)* respectable; *(ehrenhaft)* honourable *(Brit)*, honorable *(US)*; *Beruf auch* reputable.
Ehre *f* **-n** honour *(Brit)*, honor *(US)*; *(Ruhm)* glory. **etw in ~n halten** to treasure *or* cherish sth; **jdm ~/wenig ~ machen** to do sb credit/not do sb any credit; **auf ~ und Gewissen** on my/his *etc* honour; **etw um der ~ willen tun** to do sth for the honour of it; **seine Kenntnisse in allen ~n, aber ...** I don't doubt his knowledge,but ...; **sich** *(dat)* **etw zur ~ anrechnen** to count sth an honour; **das rechne ich ihm zur ~ an** I consider that a point in his honour; **mit wem habe ich die ~?** *(iro, form)* with whom do I have the honour of speaking? *(form)*; **um der Wahrheit die ~ zu geben ...** *(geh)* to be perfectly honest ...; **wir geben uns die ~, Sie zu ... einzuladen** *(form)* we request the honour of your company at ... *(form)*; **zu ~n** *(+gen)* in honour of; **~, wem ~ gebührt** *(prov)* honour where honor is due *(prov)*.
ehren *vt* to honour *(Brit)*, to honor *(US)*. **etw ehrt jdn** sth does sb credit *or* honour; **Ihr Vertrauen ehrt mich** I am honoured by your trust; **jdm ein ~des Andenken bewahren** to treasure sb's memory; *siehe* **geehrt.**
Ehren-: **~amt** *nt* honorary office *or* post; **e~amtlich 1** *adj* honorary; **2** *adv* in an honorary capacity.
Ehrenbürger *m* freeman.
Ehrenbürgerrecht *nt* **die Stadt verlieh ihr das ~** she was given the freedom of the city.
Ehren-: **~doktor** *m* honorary doctor; **~doktorwürde** *f*: **ihm wurde die ~ doktorwürde verliehen** he was made an honorary doctor *or* given an honorary doctorate; **~garde** *f* guard of honour *(Brit) or* honor *(US)*; **~gast** *m* guest of honour *(Brit) or* honor *(US)*; **~gericht** *nt* tribunal; **e~haft** *adj* honourable *(Brit)*, honorable *(US)*; **~haftigkeit** *f* honourableness *(Brit)*, honorableness *(US)*; **e~halber** *adv* **er wurde e~halber zum Vorsitzenden auf Lebenszeit ernannt** he was made honorary president for life; **~legion** *f* legion of honour *(Brit) or* honor *(US)*; **~mitglied** *nt* honorary member; **~mal** *nt* memorial; **~mann** *m, pl* **~männer** man of honour *(Brit) or* honor *(US)*; **~mitgliedschaft** *f* honorary membership; **~platz** *m (lit)* place of honour *(Brit) or* honor *(US)*; *(fig)* special place; **~rechte** *pl (Jur)* civil rights *pl;* **~rettung** *f* **zu seiner ~rettung sei gesagt, daß ...** in his favour *(Brit) or* favor *(US)* it must be said that ...; **e~rührig** *adj* defamatory; **~runde** *f (Sport)* lap of honour *(Brit) or* honor *(US)*; **~sache** *f* matter of honour *(Brit) or* honor *(US)*; **~sache!** *(col)* you can count on me; **~tag** *m (Geburtstag)* birthday; *(großer Tag)* big day; **~titel** *m* honorary title; **~tor** *nt (Sport)* consolation goal; **~tribüne** *f* VIP rostrum; **~urkunde** *f* certificate; **e~voll** *adj* honourable *(Brit)*, honorable *(US)*; **~vorsitzende(r)** *mf* honorary chairman/chairwoman; **~wache** *f* guard of honour *(Brit) or* honor *(US)*; **e~wert** *adj Mensch* honourable *(Brit)*, honorable *(US)*; **~wort** *nt* word of honour *(Brit) or* honor *(US)*; **~wort!** *(col)* cross my heart! *(col)*; **Urlaub auf ~wort** parole; **e~wörtlich** *adj Versprechen* solemn, faithful.
Ehr-: **e~erbietig** *adj* respectful, deferential; **~erbietung** *f* respect, deference.
Ehrfurcht *f no pl* deep respect *(vor +dat* for*)*; *(Scheu)* reverence *(vor +dat* for*)*.
ehrfurchtgebietend *adj Stimme* authoritative.
ehrfürchtig *adj* reverent.
Ehrgefühl *nt* sense of honour *(Brit) or* honor *(US)*.
Ehrgeiz *m no pl* ambition.
ehrgeizig *adj* ambitious.
ehrlich 1 *adj, adv* honest; *Name* good; *Wunsch* sincere. **eine ~e Haut** *(col)* an honest soul; **er hat ~e Absichten** *(col)* his intentions are honourable *(Brit) or* honorable *(US)*; **~ verdientes Geld** hard-earned money; **~ gesagt ...** quite frankly *or* honestly ...; **~ währt am längsten** *(Prov)* honesty is the best policy *(Prov)*. **2** *adv (wirklich)* honestly. **~!** honestly!, really!

Ehrlichkeit *f no pl* honesty; *(von Gefühlen etc)* sincerity.

Ehr-: e~los *adj* dishonourable *(Brit)*, dishonorable *(US)*; **~losigkeit** *f* dishonourableness *(Brit)*, dishonorableness *(US)*; *(Schlechtigkeit)* infamy.

Ehrung *f* honour *(Brit)*, honor *(US)*; *(Sieger~ etc)* honouring *(Brit)*, honoring *(US)*.

ehrwürdig *adj* venerable.

Ei *nt* **-er (a)** egg; *(Physiol auch)* ovum. **das ~ des Kolumbus finden** to come up with just the thing; **das ~ will klüger sein als die Henne** you're trying to teach your grandmother to suck eggs *(prov)*; **jdn wie ein rohes ~ behandeln** *(fig)* to handle sb with kid gloves; **wie auf ~ern gehen** *(col)* to step gingerly; **wie aus dem ~ gepellt aussehen** *(col)* to look spruce; **sie gleichen sich wie ein ~ dem anderen** they are as alike as two peas (in a pod); **das sind ungelegte ~er!** *(col)* we'll cross that bridge when we come to it. **(b) ~er** *pl (col: Geld)* marks; *(in GB)* quid *(col)*; *(in US)* bucks *(col)*. **(c) ~er** *pl (col!: Hoden)* balls *pl (col!)*.

Eibe *f* **-n** *(Bot)* yew.

Eiche *f* **-n** oak.

Eichel *f* **-n (a)** *(Bot)* acorn. **(b)** *(Anat)* glans.

Eichelhäher *m* jay.

eichen *vt* to calibrate; *(prüfen auch)* to check against official specifications. **darauf bin ich geeicht!** *(col)* that's right up my street *(col)*.

Eichenholz *nt* oak. **ein Tisch aus ~holz** an oak table.

Eichhörnchen *nt* squirrel.

Eich-: ~maß *nt* standard measure; *(Gewicht)* standard weight; **~strich** *m* line measure.

Eid *m* **-e** oath. **einen ~ leisten** *or* **schwören** to take *or* swear an oath *(auf etw (acc)* on sth*)*; **ich nehme es auf meinen ~, daß ...** I would be prepared to swear that ...; **unter ~** under oath; **eine Erklärung an ~es Statt abgeben** *(Jur)* to make a solemn declaration .

Eidechse ['aidɛksə] *f* **-n** *(Zool)* lizard.

eidesstattlich *adj* solemn. **eine ~e Erklärung abgeben** to make a solemn declaration.

Eid-: ~genosse *m*, **~genossin** *f (Schweizer)* Swiss citizen; **~genossenschaft** *f* **Schweizerische ~genossenschaft** Swiss Confederation; **e~genössisch** *adj (schweizerisch)* Swiss.

Eidotter *m or nt* egg yolk.

Eier-: ~becher *m* eggcup; **~farbe** *f paint used for colouring eggs at Easter;* **~handgranate** *f (Mil)* (pineapple) hand grenade; **~kopf** *m (col)* egghead *(col)*; **~laufen** *nt* egg and spoon race; **~likör** *m* advocaat; **~löffel** *m* eggspoon.

eiern *vi (col)* to wobble.

Eier-: ~schale *f* eggshell; **e~schalenfarben** *adj* cream, off-white; **~speise** *f* egg dish; **~stock** *m (Anat)* ovary; **~tanz** *m* **einen ~tanz aufführen** *(fig col)* to go through all kinds of contortions; **~uhr** *f* egg timer.

Eifer *m no pl (Begeisterung)* enthusiasm; *(Eifrigkeit)* eagerness, keenness. **in ~ geraten** to get agitated; **mit großem ~ bei der Sache sein** to put one's heart into it; **im ~ des Gefechts** *(fig col)* in the heat of the moment.

Eiferer *m* **-** *(liter)* fanatic; *(Rel auch)* zealot.

eifern *vi (liter)* **(a) gegen jdn/etw ~** to inveigh against sb/sth. **(b)** *(streben)* **nach etw ~** to strive for sth.

Eifersucht *f* jealousy *(auf +acc* of*)*.

eifersüchtig *adj* jealous *(auf +acc* of*)*.

Eifersuchtsszene *f* **ihr Mann hat ihr eine ~ gemacht** her husband's jealousy caused a scene.

eiförmig *adj* egg-shaped, oval.

eifrig *adj* eager; *Leser, Sammler* keen, avid; *(begeistert)* enthusiastic; *(emsig)* zealous. **sie diskutierten ~** they were involved in an animated discussion.

Eigelb *nt* egg yolk.

eigen *adj* **(a)** own; *(selbständig)* separate. **seine ~e Wohnung haben** to have a flat of one's own, to have one's own flat; **etw sein ~ nennen** *(geh)* to have sth to call one's own; **sich** *(dat)* **etw zu ~ machen** to adopt sth; **ich möchte kurz in ~er Sache sprechen** I would like to say something on my own account. **(b)** *(typisch)* typical. **das ist ihm ~** that is typical of him; **der ihm ~e Zynismus** his characteristic cynicism. **(c)** *(seltsam)* strange, peculiar. **(d)** *(ordentlich)* particular; *(übergenau)* fussy. **in Gelddingen ist er sehr ~** he is very particular about money matters.

Eigen|art *f (Besonderheit)* peculiarity; *(Eigenschaft)* characteristic; *(Eigentümlichkeit von Personen)* idiosyncrasy.

eigen|artig *adj* peculiar; *(sonderbar auch)* strange.

Eigen-: ~bau *m no pl* **er fährt ein Fahrrad Marke ~bau** *(hum col)* he rides a home-made bike; **~bedarf** *m (von Mensch)* personal use; *(von Staat)* domestic requirements *pl;* **der Hausbesitzer machte ~bedarf geltend** the landlord claimed that he needed the house/flat for himself; **~brötler(in** *f)* *m* **-** *(col)* loner, lone wolf; *(komischer Kauz)* oddball *(col)*; **e~brötlerisch** *adj (col)* solitary; *(komisch)* eccentric; **~dynamik** *f* momentum; **eine ~dynamik entwickeln** to gather momentum; **~gewicht** *nt (Comm)* net weight; *(Sci)* dead weight; **e~händig** *adj Unterschrift etc* in one's own hand, handwritten; *Übergabe* personal; **eine Arbeit e~händig machen** to do a job oneself; **~heim** *nt* one's own home; **~heit** *f* = **~art**; **~initiative** *f* initiative of one's own; **~kapital** *nt* personal captial; *(von Firma)* company capital; **~leben** *nt no pl* one's own life; *(selbständige Existenz)* independent existence; **ein ~leben entwickeln** to develop a life of its own; **~lob** *nt* self-importance; **~lob stinkt!** *(prov)* don't blow your own trumpet! *(prov)*; **e~mächtig 1** *adj (selbstherrlich)* high-handed; *(e~verantwortlich)* taken/done *etc* on one's own authority; *(unbefugt)* unauthorized; **2** *adv* high-handedly; (entirely) on one's own authority; without any authorization; **~mächtigkeit** *f (Selbstherrlichkeit)* high-handedness *no pl; (unbefugtes Handeln)* unauthorized behaviour *(Brit) or* behavior *(US) no pl;* **~name** *m* proper name; **~nutz** *m no pl* self-interest; **e~nützig** *adj* selfish.

eigens *adv* specially.

Eigenschaft *f (Attribut)* quality; *(Chem, Phys etc)* property; *(Merkmal)* characteristic, feature; *(Funktion)* capacity.

Eigenschaftswort *nt* adjective.

Eigen-: ~sinn *m no pl* stubbornness, obstinacy; **e~sinnig** *adj* stubborn, obstinate; **e~ständig** *adj* independent; **~ständigkeit** *f* independence.

eigentlich 1 *adj* real, actual. **2** *adv* actually; *(überhaupt)* anyway. **was willst du ~ hier?** what do you want here anyway?; **wissen Sie ~, wer ich bin?** do you know who I am?; **~ müßtest du das wissen** you should really know that.

Eigentor *nt (lit, fig)* own goal.

Eigentum *nt no pl* property.

Eigentümer(in *f)* *m* **-** owner.

eigentümlich *adj* **(a)** curious, odd. **(b)** *(geh: typisch)* **jdm/einer Sache ~ sein** to be characteristic of sb/sth.

eigentümlicherweise *adv* oddly enough.

Eigentümlichkeit *f* **(a)** *(Kennzeichen)* characteristic. **(b)** *(Eigenheit)* peculiarity.

Eigentums-: ~delikt *nt (Jur: Diebstahl)* theft; **~recht** *nt* right of ownership; **~wohnung** *f* owner-occupied flat *(Brit) or* apartment; **er kaufte sich** *(dat)* **eine ~wohnung** he bought a flat (of his own).

Eigen-: e~verantwortlich 1 *adj* autonomous; **2** *adv* on one's own authority; **e~willig** *adj* with a mind of one's own; *(e~sinnig)* self-willed; *(un-*

konventionell) unconventional.

eignen *vr* to be suitable *(für, zu* for, *als* as). **er eignet sich nicht zum Lehrer** he's not suited to teaching; *siehe* **geeignet.**

Eigner(in *f*) *m* - *(form)* owner.

Eignung *f* suitability; *(Befähigung)* aptitude.

Eignungs-: ~prüfung *f*, **~test** *m* aptitude test.

Eiland *nt* **-e** *(liter)* isle *(liter).*

Eil-: ~bote *m* messenger; **per** *or* **durch ~boten** express; **~brief** *m* express letter.

Eile *f no pl* hurry. **in ~ sein** to be in a hurry; **das hat keine ~** there is no hurry, it's not urgent; **in der/meiner ~** in the hurry/my haste; **nur keine ~!** don't rush!

Eileiter *m (Anat)* Fallopian tube.

eilen *vi* **(a)** *aux sein* to hurry. **er eilte dem Ertrinkenden zu Hilfe** he rushed to help the drowning man; **eile mit Weile** *(Prov)* more haste less speed *(Prov).* **(b) eilt!** *(auf Briefen etc)* urgent; **es eilt** it's urgent.

eilig *adj* **(a)** *(schnell)* quick, hurried. **es ~ haben** to be in a hurry *or* rush; **nur nicht so ~!** don't be in such a hurry *or* rush! **(b)** *(dringend)* urgent.

Eil-: ~paket *nt* express parcel; **~tempo** *nt*: **etw im ~tempo machen** to do sth in a rush; **~zug** *m* fast stopping train; **~zustellung** *f* special delivery.

Eimer *m* - bucket; *(Müll~)* (rubbish) bin. **ein ~ (voll) Wasser** a bucket(ful) of water; **es gießt wie aus ~n** *(col)* it's bucketing down *(col)*; **im ~ sein** *(col)* to be up the spout *(col) or* be ruined.

ein[1] *adv (an Geräten)* **E~/Aus** on/off; **er geht bei uns ~ und aus** he is always round at our place; **ich weiß nicht mehr ~ noch aus** I'm at my wits' end.

ein[2], **eine, ein 1** *num* one. **er ist ihr ~ und alles** he means everything to her; *siehe* **eins. 2** *indef art* a; *(vor Vokalen)* an. **~ Europäer** a European; **~ Hotel** a *or* an hotel; **der Sohn ~es Lehrers** the son of a teacher, a teacher's son; **was für ~ Wetter!** some weather.

Ein|akter *m* - *(Theat)* one-act play.

einander *pron* one another, each other.

ein|arbeiten *sep* **1** *vr* to settle in. **2** *vt jdn* to train.

Ein|arbeitungszeit *f* training period.

ein|armig *adj* one-armed.

ein|äschern *vt sep Leichnam* to cremate; *Stadt etc* to reduce to ashes.

Ein|äscherung *f (von Leichnam)* cremation.

ein|atmen *vti sep* to breathe in.

ein|äugig *adj* one-eyed.

Einbahnstraße *f* one-way street.

einbalsamieren* *vt sep* to embalm.

Einbalsamierung *f* embalming.

Einband *m* book cover.

einbändig *adj* one-volume *attr.*

Einbau *m* **-ten** installation.

einbauen *vt sep* to install, to put in.

Einbauküche *f* (fully-)fitted kitchen.

Einbaum *m* dug-out (canoe).

Einbaumöbel *pl* built-in *or* fitted furniture; *(Schränke)* fitted cupboards *pl.*

einbegriffen *adj* included.

einbehalten* *vt sep irreg* to keep back.

einbeinig *adj* one-legged.

einberechnen* *vt sep* to allow for (in one's calculations). **~, daß ...** to allow for the fact that ...

einberufen* *vt sep irreg Parlament* to summon; *Versammlung* to convene, to call; *(Mil)* to call up, to draft *(US).*

Einberufung *f* **(a)** *(einer Versammlung)* calling; *(des Parlaments)* summoning. **(b)** *(Mil)* conscription; *(~sbescheid)* call-up.

Einberufungs-: ~bescheid, ~befehl *m (Mil)* call-up *or* draft *(US)* papers *pl.*

einbetten *vt sep* to embed *(in +acc* in); *Rohr, Kabel* to lay *(in+acc* in); *siehe* **eingebettet.**

Einbettzimmer *nt* single room.

einbeziehen* *vt sep irreg* to include *(in+acc* in).

Einbeziehung *f* inclusion. **unter ~ von etw** including sth.

einbiegen *vi sep irreg aux sein* to turn (off) *(in +acc* into). **links ~** to turn (off to the) left.

einbilden *vr sep* **(a) sich** *(dat)* **etw ~** to imagine sth; **er bildet sich** *(dat)* **ein, daß ...** he's got hold of the idea that ...; **das bildest du dir nur ein** that's just your imagination; **was bildest du dir eigentlich ein?** what's got into you? **(b)** *(stolz sein)* **sich** *(dat)* **viel auf etw** *(acc)* **~** to be conceited about sth; **darauf können Sie sich etwas ~!** that's something to be proud of!; **darauf brauchst du dir nichts einzubilden** that's nothing special; *siehe* **eingebildet.**

Einbildung *f* **(a)** *(Vorstellung)* imagination; *(irrige Vorstellung)* illusion. **das sind ~en** that's pure imagination. **(b)** *(Dünkel)* conceit.

Einbildungskraft *f* (powers *pl* of) imagination.

einbinden *vt sep irreg Buch* to bind.

einblenden *sep (Film, TV, Rad)* **1** *vt* to insert, to slot in; *(nachträglich) Musik etc* to dub on. **2** *vr* **sich in etw** *(acc)* **~** to link up with sth.

einbleuen *vt sep (col)* **jdm etw ~** *(einschärfen)* to drum sth into sb.

Einblick *m (fig: Kenntnis)* insight. **~ in etw** *(acc)* **gewinnen** to gain an insight into sth; **~ in die Akten nehmen** to examine the files; **jdm ~ in etw** *(acc)* **gewähren** to allow sb to look at sth.

einbrechen *vi sep irreg aux sein* **(a)** *(einstürzen)* to fall *or* cave in. **er ist (auf dem Eis) eingebrochen** he fell through the ice. **(b)** *aux sein or haben (Einbruch verüben)* to break in. **bei mir ist eingebrochen worden** I've been burgled *or* burglarized *(US)*; **in neue Absatzmärkte** *etc* **~** to break into new markets *etc.* **(c)** *(Dämmerung etc)* to fall; *Winter* to set in. **bei ~der Nacht** at nightfall.

Einbrecher(in *f*) *m* - burglar.

einbringen *sep irreg* **1** *vt Geld, Ernte, Schiff* to bring in; *Ruhm, Nachteil* to bring; *Zinsen* to earn; *(Parl)* to introduce. **das bringt nichts ein** *(fig)* it's not worth it; **etw in die Ehe ~** to bring sth into the marriage. **2** *vr (col)* **sich (in einer Diskussion) ~** to involve oneself (in a discussion).

einbrocken *vt sep (col)* **jdm/sich etwas ~** to land sb/oneself in it *(col)*; **da hast du dir etwas Schönes eingebrockt!** you've really let yourself in for it there.

Einbruch *m* **(a)** *(~diebstahl)* burglary, break-in *(in+acc* in); *(Mil: in Front)* breakthrough *(in +acc* of). **der ~ in die Bank** the break-in at the bank. **(b)** *(von Wasser)* penetration. **(c)** *(Einsturz, Fin)* collapse. **(d)** *(des Winters)* onset. **bei/vor ~ der Nacht/Dämmerung** at/before nightfall/dusk.

Einbruch(s)-: ~diebstahl *m (Jur)* burglary, breaking and entering *(form)*; **e~sicher** *adj* burglar-proof.

Einbuchtung *f* indentation; *(Bucht)* inlet, bay.

einbürgern *sep* **1** *vt Person* to naturalize; *Fremdwort, Gewohnheit* to introduce. **2** *vr (Person)* to become *or* be naturalized; *(Brauch, Tier)* to become established; **das hat sich so eingebürgert** *(Brauch)* it's just the way we/they *etc* have come to do things.

Einbürgerung *f siehe vt* naturalization; introduction.

Einbuße *f* loss *(an +dat* in).

einbüßen *sep vt* to lose; *(durch eigene Schuld)* to forfeit.

eincremen *vt sep* to put cream on.

eindämmen *vt sep Fluß* to dam; *(fig)* to check, to contain.

Eindämmung *f* **(a)** *(Damm)* dam. **(b)** *siehe vt* damming; checking, containing.

eindecken *sep* **1** *vr* **sich (mit etw) ~** to stock up (with sth). **2** *vt (col: überhäufen)* **mit Arbeit eingedeckt sein** to be inundated with work.

eindeutig *adj* clear; *(nicht zweideutig)* unambiguous; *Witz* explicit. **jdm etw ~ sagen** to tell sb sth quite plainly.

eindeutschen *vt sep Fremdwort* to Germanize.

eindimensional *adj* one-dimensional.

eindösen *vi sep aux sein (col)* to doze off.

eindrängen *vr sep* to crowd in *(in +acc* -to*)*; *(fig)* to intrude *(in+acc* upon*)*.

eindrehen *vt sep* **(a)** to screw in *(in+acc* -to*)*. **(b)** *Haar* to put in rollers.

eindringen *vi sep irreg aux sein* **(a)** *(einbrechen)* **in etw** *(acc)* ~ to force one's way into sth; **in unsere Linien/das Land** ~ *(Mil)* to penetrate our lines/to enter the country. **(b) in etw** *(acc)* ~ *(Messer, Wasser)* to penetrate sth; *(Fremdwörter etc)* to find its way into sth. **(c)** *(bestürmen)* **auf jdn** ~ to go for sb, to attack sb *(mit* with*)*; *(mit Fragen, Bitten etc)* to besiege sb.

eindringlich *adj (nachdrücklich)* insistent; *(dringend auch)* urgent; *Schilderung* vivid. **ich habe ihn ~ gebeten ...** I urged him ...

Eindringling *m* intruder.

Eindruck *m* **-ë** impression. **den ~ erwecken, als ob** *or* **daß ...** to give the impression that ...; **großen ~ auf jdn machen** to make a big impression on sb; **er will ~ (bei ihr) machen** *or* **schinden** *(col)* he's out to impress (her).

eindrücken *vt sep* to push in; *Fenster* to break; *Tür, Mauer* to push down; *(Sturm, Explosion)* to blow in/down; *(einbeulen)* to dent; *Brustkorb* to crush; *Nase* to flatten.

eindrucksvoll *adj* impressive.

eine *siehe* **ein[2], eine(r, s).**

ein|ebnen *vt sep (lit)* to level (off); *(fig)* to level out.

Ein|ehe *f* monogamy.

ein|eiig *adj Zwillinge* identical.

ein|einhalb *num* one and a half; *siehe* **anderthalb.**

einen *vtr (geh)* to unite.

ein|engen *vt sep (lit)* to constrict; *(fig)* to restrict. **jdn in seiner Freiheit ~** to restrict sb's freedom.

Ein|engung *f (lit)* constriction; *(fig)* restriction.

eine(r, s) *indef pron adj* **(a)** one; *(jemand)* somebody, someone. **der/die/das ~** the one; **das ~ Gute war ...** the one good thing was ...; **er denkt immer nur an das ~** he only thinks of one thing; **sein ~r Sohn** *(col)* one of his sons; **die ~n sagen so, die anderen ...** some (people) say one thing and others ...; **~r für alle, alle für ~n** *(prov)* all for one and one for all *(prov)*; **du bist mir vielleicht ~(r)!** *(col)* you're a fine one *(col)*; **sieh mal ~r an!** *(iro)* well what do you know! *(col)*; **in ~m fort, in ~r Tour** *(col)* non-stop. **(b)** *(man)* one *(esp form)*, you. **wie kann ~r nur so dumm sein!** how could anybody be so stupid! **(c) ~s** *(auch* **eins***)* one thing; **~s sag' ich dir** I'll tell you one thing; **noch ~s, bevor ich's vergesse** (there's) one other thing before I forget; **es kam ~s zum anderen** it was (just) one thing after another. **(d)** *(col)* **sich** *(dat)* **~n genehmigen** to have a quick one *(col)*; **jdm ~ kleben** to thump sb one *(col)*.

Einer *m* **-** **(a)** *(Math)* unit. **(b)** *(Ruderboot)* single scull.

einerlei *adj pred inv (gleichgültig)* **das ist mir ganz ~** it's all the same to me; **~, was/wer ...** no matter what/who ...

Einerlei *nt no pl* monotony.

einerseits *adv* **~ ... andererseits ...** on the one hand ... on the other hand ...

einfach 1 *adj* **(a)** simple; *Mensch* ordinary; *Essen* plain. **(b)** *(nicht doppelt) Knoten* simple; *Fahrkarte* single *(Brit)*, one-way. **2** *adv* simply. **~ gemein** downright mean; **das ist doch ~ dumm** that's (just) plain stupid.

Einfachheit *f siehe adj* simplicity; ordinariness; plainness. **der ~ halber** for the sake of simplicity.

einfädeln *sep* **1** *vt* **(a)** *Nadel, Faden* to thread *(in +acc* through*)*. **(b)** *(col) Plan etc* to engineer. **2** *vr* **sich in eine Verkehrskolonne ~** to filter into a stream of traffic.

einfahren *sep irreg* **1** *vi aux sein (Zug, Schiff)* to come in *(in+acc* -to*)*. **2** *vt* **(a)** *(kaputtfahren) Mauer, Zaun* to knock down. **(b)** *Ernte* to bring in. **(c)** *Fahrgestell etc* to retract. **(d)** *Wagen* to run in *(Brit)*, to break in *(US)*; *siehe* **eingefahren.**

Einfahrt *f* **(a)** *no pl (das Einfahren)* entry *(in +acc* to*)*; *(Min)* descent. **Vorsicht bei (der) ~ des Zuges!** stand well back, the train is arriving. **(b)** *(Eingang)* entrance; *(von Autobahn)* sliproad.

Einfall *m* **(a)** idea; *(Grille, Laune)* notion. **es war nur so ein ~** it was just an idea; **er hat ~e wie ein altes Haus** *(hum)* he has some weird ideas. **(b)** *(Mil)* invasion *(in+acc* of*)*.

einfallen *vi sep irreg aux sein* **(a)** to collapse; *siehe* **eingefallen. (b)** *(eindringen)* **in ein Land ~** to invade a country. **(c)** *(Licht)* to fall; *(in ein Zimmer etc)* to come in *(in+acc* -to*)*. **(d)** *(mitsingen, mitreden)* to join in; *(dazwischenreden)* to break in *(in+acc* on*)*. **(e)** *(Gedanke)* **jdm ~** to occur to sb; **hast du dir etwas ~ lassen?** have you had any ideas?, have you thought of anything?; **da mußt du dir schon etwas Besseres ~ lassen!** you'll really have to think of something better; **was fällt Ihnen ein!** what are you thinking of!; **dabei fällt mir mein Onkel ein, der ...** that reminds me of my uncle, who ...; **es fällt mir jetzt nicht ein** I can't think of it *or* it won't come to me at the moment; **es wird Ihnen schon wieder ~** it will come back to you.

Einfalls-: e~los *adj* unimaginative; **e~reich** *adj* imaginative; **~reichtum** *m* imaginativeness.

Einfalt *f no pl* naivety.

einfältig *adj* naive.

Einfaltspinsel *m (col)* simpleton.

Einfamilienhaus *nt* family house.

einfangen *vt sep irreg (lit, fig)* to catch, to capture.

einfärben *vt sep Stoff, Haar* to dye.

einfarbig *adj* all one colour *(Brit) or* color *(US)*, plain; *Stoff* self-coloured *(Brit)*, self-colored *(US)*.

einfassen *vt sep Beet, Kleid* to edge; *Edelstein* to set. **ein Grundstück (mit einem Zaun) ~** to put a fence around a plot of land.

Einfassung *f (von Beet)* border; *(von Edelstein)* setting.

einfetten *vt sep* to grease; *Leder, Schuhe* to dubbin; *Haut, Gesicht* to rub cream into.

einfinden *vr sep irreg* to come; *(eintreffen)* to arrive.

einflechten *vt sep irreg* to twine; *(fig: ins Gespräch etc)* to work in *(in+acc* -to*)*.

einfliegen *vt sep irreg Proviant, Truppen* to fly in *(in+acc* -to*)*.

einfließen *vi sep irreg aux sein* to flow in. **er ließ nebenbei ~, daß ...** he let it drop that ...

einflößen *vt sep* **jdm etw ~** to pour sth down sb's throat; *Medizin auch* to give sb sth; *Ehrfurcht, Mut etc* to instil sth into sb.

Einfluß *m* **(a)** influence. **unter dem ~ von jdm/etw stehen** to be under the influence of sb/sth; **~ auf jdn haben/ausüben** to have/exert an influence on sb; **~ nehmen** to bring an influence to bear. **(b)** *(von Luft)* influx.

Einfluß-: ~bereich *m* sphere of influence; **~nahme** *f* exertion of influence *(gen* by*)*; **e~reich** *adj* influential.

einflüstern *vt sep* **jdm etw ~** to whisper sth to sb; *(fig)* to insinuate sth to sb.

einförmig *adj* uniform; *(eintönig)* monotonous.

Einförmigkeit *f siehe adj* uniformity; monotony.

einfrieren *sep irreg* **1** *vi aux sein* to freeze; *(Wasserleitung)* to freeze up. **2** *vt Nahrungsmittel, Löhne etc* to freeze; *(Pol) Beziehungen* to suspend.

einfügen *sep* **1** *vt Steine etc* to fit *(in+acc* into*)*; *(nachtragen)* to insert *(in +acc* in*)*, to add *(in +acc* to*)*. **2** *vr* to fit in *(in+acc* -to*)*; *(sich anpassen)* to adapt *(in+acc* to*)*.

Einfügung *f* insertion, addition.
einfühlen *vr sep* **sich in jdn ~** to empathize with sb; **sich in etw** *(acc)* ~ *in Situation, jds Probleme* to understand sth, to sympathize with sth; *in Gedicht, Rolle* to feel one's way into sth.
einfühlsam *adj* sensitive; *Mensch auch* understanding.
Einfühlungsvermögen *nt* empathy. **mit großem ~** with a great deal of sensitivity.
Einfuhr *f* **-en** import; *(das Einführen auch)* importing.
Einfuhr- *in cpds* import; **~artikel** *m* import.
einführen *vt sep* **(a)** to introduce *(in+acc* into*)*; *Mode, Sitte* to start; *(hineinstecken auch)* to insert. **jdn in sein Amt ~** to install sb (in office). **(b)** *(Comm) Waren* to import.
Einfuhr-: ~genehmigung *f* import permit; **~hafen** *m* port of entry; **~land** *nt* importing country; **~sperre** *f*, **~stopp** *m* ban on imports.
Einführung *f* introduction *(in +acc* to*)*; *(Amts~)* installation.
Einführungs- *in cpds* introductory.
Einfuhr-: ~verbot *nt* ban on imports; **~zoll** *m* import duty.
einfüllen *vt sep* to pour in.
Einfüllstutzen *m (Aut)* filler pipe.
Eingabe *f* **(a)** *(form: Gesuch)* petition *(an+acc* to*)*. **(b)** *(Comp)* input.
Eingang *m* **(a)** entrance *(in+acc* to*)*; *(Zutritt, Aufnahme)* entry. **„kein ~!"** "no entrance"; **in etw** *(acc)* ~ **finden** to find one's way into sth. **(b)** *(Comm: Waren~, Post~)* delivery; *(Erhalt)* receipt. **wir bestätigen den ~ Ihres Schreibens vom ...** we acknowledge receipt of your letter of the ...; **den ~** *or* **die ~e bearbeiten** to deal with the in-coming mail.
eingängig *adj Melodie, Spruch* catchy.
eingangs 1 *adv* at the beginning. **2** *prep+gen (form)* at the beginning of.
Eingangs-: ~bestätigung *f (Comm)* acknowledgement of receipt; **~datum** *nt* date of receipt; **~halle** *f* entrance hall; **~stempel** *m (Comm)* receipt stamp; **~tür** *f* entrance, door.
eingeben *vt sep irreg* **(a)** *(verabreichen)* to give. **(b)** *(einspeichern)* **dem Computer etw ~** to feed *or* input sth into the computer.
eingebettet *adj* **in** *or* **zwischen Hügeln ~** nestling among the hills.
eingebildet *adj* **(a)** *(hochmütig)* conceited. **(b)** *(imaginär)* imaginary. **ein ~er Kranker** a hypochondriac.
eingeboren *adj (einheimisch)* native; *(angeboren)* innate, inborn *(dat* in*)*.
Eingeborene(r) *mf decl as adj* native *(auch hum)*.
Eingebung *f* inspiration.
eingedenk *(old, liter) prep +gen* bearing in mind. **~ dessen, daß ...** bearing in mind that ...
eingefahren *adj Verhaltensweise* well-worn. **die Diskussion bewegte sich in ~en Gleisen** the discussion covered the same old well-worn topics.
eingefallen *adj Wangen* hollow; *Gesicht* gaunt.
eingefleischt *adj attr (überzeugt)* confirmed; *(unverbesserlich)* dyed-in-the-wool. **~er Junggeselle** *(hum)* confirmed bachelor.
eingehen *sep irreg aux sein* **1** *vi* **(a)** *(Aufnahme finden: Wort, Sitte)* to be adopted *(in +acc* in*)*. **in die Geschichte ~** to go down in history. **(b)** *(ankommen: Briefe, Waren etc)* to arrive. **eingegangene Post/Spenden** mail/donations received. **(c)** *(sterben: Tiere, Pflanze)* to die *(an+dat* of*)*; *(col: Firma etc)* to fold. **bei dieser Hitze/Kälte geht man ja ein!** *(col)* this heat/cold is just too much *(col)*. **(d)** *(behandeln)* **auf etw** *(acc)* ~ *auf Frage etc* to go into sth; **niemand ging auf meine Frage ein** nobody took any notice of my question; **auf jdn/etw ~** to give (one's) time and attention to sb/sth. **(e)** *(zustimmen)* **auf einen Vorschlag/Plan ~** to go along with a suggestion/plan. **2** *vt (abmachen, abschließen)* to enter into; *Risiko* to take; *Wette* to make.
eingehend *adj* detailed, in-depth.
eingekeilt *adj* hemmed in; *(fig)* trapped.
Eingemachte(s) *nt decl as adj* bottled fruit/vegetables; *(Marmelade)* preserves *pl*.
eingemeinden* *vt sep* to incorporate *(in+acc, nach* into*)*.
eingenommen *adj* **für jdn/etw ~ sein** to be taken with sb/sth; **gegen jdn/etw ~ sein** to be biased against sb/sth; **er ist sehr von sich** *(dat)* **selbst ~** he really fancies himself.
eingeschnappt *adj (col)* cross. **~ sein** to be in a huff.
eingeschossig ['aɪngəʃɔsɪç] *adj Haus* single-storey *(Brit)*, single-story *(US)*.
eingeschränkt *adj (eingeengt)* restricted, limited; *(sparsam)* careful.
eingeschrieben *adj Mitglied, Brief* registered.
eingeschworen *adj* confirmed; *Gemeinschaft* close. **auf etw** *(acc)* **~ sein** to swear by sth; **auf eine Politik ~ sein** to be committed to a policy.
eingesessen *adj Familie* old-established.
eingespannt *adj* busy.
eingespielt *adj Mannschaft, Team* (well-)adjusted to playing/working together. **aufeinander ~ sein** to be used to one another.
Eingeständnis *nt* admission, confession.
eingestehen* *vt sep irreg* to admit, to confess.
eingestellt *adj* **links/rechts ~ sein** to have leanings to the left/right; **wer so ~ ist wie er** anyone who thinks as he does; **gegen jdn ~ sein** to be set against sb; **ich bin im Moment nicht auf Besuch ~** I'm not prepared for visitors.
eingetragen *adj Verein, Warenzeichen* registered.
Eingeweide *nt* **-** *usu pl* entrails *pl*, innards *pl*.
Eingeweihte(r) *mf decl as adj* initiate. **ein paar ~** a chosen few.
eingewöhnen* *vr sep* to settle down *(in+dat* in*)*.
Eingewöhnung *f* settling down.
eingießen *vt sep irreg (hineinschütten)* to pour in *(in+acc* -to*)*; *(einschenken)* to pour.
eingleisig *adj* single-track. **er denkt sehr ~** *(fig)* he's completely single-minded.
eingliedern *sep* **1** *vt* to integrate *(in+acc* into*)*. **2** *vr* to integrate oneself *(in+acc* into*)*.
Eingliederung *f* integration.
eingraben *sep irreg* **1** *vt* to bury *(in+acc* in*)*; *Pflanze etc* to dig in *(in+acc* -to*)*. **2** *vr* to dig oneself in *(auch Mil)*. **dieses Erlebnis hat sich seinem Gedächtnis eingegraben** this experience has engraved itself on his memory.
eingravieren* *vt sep* to engrave *(in +acc* in*)*.
eingreifen *vi sep irreg (einschreiten, Mil)* to intervene. **in jds Rechte** *(acc)* ~ to intrude (up)on sb's rights.
Eingreifen *nt no pl* intervention.
eingrenzen *vt sep* to enclose; *(fig) Problem* to delimit.
Eingriff *m* **(a)** *(Med)* operation. **(b)** *(Übergriff)* intervention. **ein ~ in jds Rechte** an intrusion (up)on sb's rights.
einhaken *sep* **1** *vt* to hook in *(in+acc* -to*)*. **2** *vi (col: Punkt aufgreifen)* to intervene; *(in Unterhaltung auch)* to break in. **3** *vr* **sie hakte sich bei ihm ein** she put *or* slipped her arm through his.
Einhalt *m no pl* **jdm/einer Sache ~ gebieten** to stop sb/sth.
einhalten *vt sep irreg (beachten)* to keep; *Spielregeln* to follow; *Diät, Vertrag* to keep to; *Verpflichtungen* to carry out. **die Zeit ~** to keep to time *or* schedule.
Einhaltung *f siehe vt* keeping; following; keeping to; carrying out.
einhämmern *vt sep Nagel etc* to hammer in *(in +acc* -to*)*. **jdm etw ~** *(fig)* to hammer sth into sb.
einhandeln *vt sep* **(a)** *(gegen, für* for*)* to trade. **(b)**

(bekommen) **sich** *(dat)* **etw** ~ *(col)* to get sth.
einhändig *adj* one-handed.
einhängen *sep* **1** *vt Tür* to hang; *Fenster* to put in; *(Telec) Hörer* to put down. **2** *vi (Telec)* to hang up.
einheften *vt sep* **(a)** *(Sew)* to tack in. **(b)** *Akten etc* to file.
einheimisch *adj* native, indigenous; *Produkt, Mannschaft* local.
Einheimische(r) *mf decl as adj* local.
einheimsen *vt sep (col)* to collect; *Erfolg, Ruhm auch* to walk off with; *Geld auch* to rake in *(col)*.
Einheirat *f* marriage *(in +acc* into*)*.
einheiraten *vi sep* **in einen Betrieb** ~ to marry into a business.
Einheit *f* **(a)** unity; *(das Ganze)* whole. **eine geschlossene** ~ **bilden** to form an integrated whole. **(b)** *(Mil, Sci)* unit.
einheitlich *adj (gleich)* the same, uniform; *(genormt)* standard(ized); *(in sich geschlossen)* unified. **wir müssen** ~ **vorgehen** we must act in a unified fashion.
Einheitlichkeit *f siehe adj* uniformity; standardization; unity.
Einheits-: ~**front** *f (Pol)* united front; *(Volksfront)* popular front; ~**gewerkschaft** *f* unified trade *(Brit) or* labor *(US)* union; ~**kleidung** *f* uniform; ~**liste** *f (Pol)* single *or* unified list of candidates; ~**preis** *m* standard price.
einheizen *sep* **1** *vi* to put the heating on. **jdm (tüchtig)** ~ *(col) (die Meinung sagen)* to haul sb over the coals; *(zu schaffen machen)* to make things hot for sb. **2** *vt Zimmer* to heat (up).
einhellig *adj* unanimous.
einhergehen *vi sep irreg aux sein* to walk.
einholen *vt sep* **(a)** *Boot, Netz* to pull in; *Fahne, Segel* to lower. **(b)** *Rat, Erlaubnis* to get. **(c)** *(erreichen) Laufenden* to catch up; *Vorsprung, Zeit* to make up. **(d)** *auch vi* = **einkaufen.**
Einholung *f* **(a)** *(von Fahne)* lowering. **(b)** *(von Rat etc)* obtaining.
Einhorn *nt* unicorn.
einhüllen *vt sep* to wrap (up) *(in +acc* in*)*. **in Wolken eingehüllt** shrouded in clouds.
einhundert *num siehe* **hundert.**
einig *adj* **(a)** *(geeint)* united. **(b)** *(einer Meinung)* agreed, in agreement *(über+acc* on, about, *in +dat* on*)*. **sich** *(dat)* **über etw** *(acc)* ~ **werden** to agree on sth; **wir sind uns** ~**, daß ...** we are agreed that ...; **wir werden schon miteinander** ~ **werden** we will manage to come to an agreement.
einige *indef pron siehe* **einige(r, s).**
einigemal *adv* a few times.
einigen **1** *vt Volk etc* to unite; *Streitende* to reconcile. **2** *vr* to reach (an) agreement *(über+acc* about*)*. **sich auf einen Kompromiß** ~ to agree to a compromise.
einige(r, s) *indef pron* **(a)** *sing (etwas)* some; *(ziemlich viel)* (quite) some. **in** ~**r Entfernung** some distance away; **das wird** ~**s kosten** that will cost something; **dazu ist noch** ~**s zu sagen** there are still one or two things to say about that; **mit** ~**m guten Willen** *(mit Anstrengung)* with a bit of effort. **(b)** *pl* some; *(mehrere)* several; *(ein paar auch)* a few. **mit Ausnahme** ~**r weniger** with a few exceptions; ~ **hundert Menschen** a few hundred people; **in** ~**n Tagen** in a few days; **vor** ~**n Tagen** the other day, a few days ago.
einigermaßen *adv* rather, somewhat; *(vor adj)* fairly; *(ungefähr)* to some extent. ~ **Bescheid wissen** to have a fair idea; **wie geht's dir? —** ~ how are you? — all right, not too bad.
einiges *indef pron siehe* **einige(r, s).**
Einigkeit *f no pl* unity; *(Übereinstimmung)* agreement.
Einigung *f* **(a)** *(Pol)* unification. **(b)** *(Übereinstimmung)* agreement. **über etw** *(acc)* ~ **erzielen** to come to *or* reach agreement on sth.
ein|impfen *vt sep* **jdm etw** ~ to din sth into sb.
einjagen *vt sep* **jdm Furcht/einen Schrecken** ~ to give sb a fright.
einjährig *adj Kind, Tier* one-year-old; *Pflanze* annual. **nach** ~**er Pause** after a break of one year.
einkalkulieren* *vt sep* to reckon on; *Kosten* to take into account.
einkassieren* *vt sep* **(a)** *Geld, Schulden* to collect. **(b)** *(col: wegnehmen)* to take; *Dieb* to nab *(col)*.
Einkauf *m* **(a)** *(das Einkaufen)* buying, purchase. **Einkäufe machen** to go shopping; **ich muß noch ein paar Einkäufe machen** I still have a few things to buy. **(b)** *(usu pl: Gekauftes)* purchase. **(c)** *no pl (Comm: Abteilung)* purchasing (department).
einkaufen *sep* **1** *vt* to buy. **2** *vi* to shop; *(Comm)* to buy. ~ **gehen** to go shopping.
Einkäufer *m (Comm)* buyer.
Einkaufs- *in cpds* shopping; ~**bummel** *m* **einen** ~**bummel machen** to go on a shopping spree; ~**leiter** *m (Comm)* chief buyer; ~**netz** *nt* string bag; ~**preis** *m* wholesale price; ~**tasche** *f* shopping bag; ~**wagen** *m* trolley *(Brit)*, cart *(US)*; ~**zettel** *m* shopping list.
einkehren *vi sep aux sein* **(a)** *(in Gasthof)* to (make a) stop *(in+dat* at*)*. **(b)** *(geh: Ruhe, Frühling)* to come.
einkellern *vt sep* to store in a cellar.
einkerben *vt sep* to cut a notch/notches in.
einkerkern *vt sep* to incarcerate.
einkesseln *vt sep* to encircle.
einklagen *vt sep Schulden* to sue for (the recovery of).
einklammern *vt sep* to put in brackets.
Einklang *m* **(a)** *(Mus)* unison. **(b)** *(geh: Übereinstimmung)* harmony. **in** ~ **bringen** to harmonize; **im** ~ **mit etw stehen** to be in accord with sth.
einkleben *vt sep* to stick in *(in +acc* -to*)*.
einkleiden *vt sep* to fit out. **jdn/sich völlig neu** ~ to buy sb/oneself a completely new wardrobe.
einklemmen *vt sep* **(a)** *(quetschen)* to jam. **er hat sich die Hand in der Tür eingeklemmt** he caught his hand in the door. **(b)** *(festdrücken)* to clamp.
einknicken *sep* **1** *vt Papier* to crease; *Streichholz, Äste* to snap. **2** *vi aux sein (Strohhalm)* to get bent; *(Äste)* to snap; *(Knie)* to give way, to buckle.
einkochen *vt sep Gemüse* to preserve; *Obst auch, Marmelade* to bottle.
einkommen *vi sep irreg aux sein* to come in.
Einkommen *nt* - income.
Einkommens-: ~**ausfall** *m* loss of income; **e**~**schwach** *adj* low-income *attr;* **e**~**stark** *adj* high-income *attr*.
Einkommen(s)steuer *f* income tax.
Einkommen(s)steuer-: ~**erklärung** *f* income tax return; **e**~**pflichtig** *adj* liable to income tax.
Einkommensverhältnisse *pl* (level of) income.
einkreisen *vt sep Feind, Wild* to surround; *(fig) Problem* to consider from all sides.
Einkreisung *f (von Feind etc)* surrounding; *(Pol)* isolation.
einkriegen *sep (col)* **1** *vt* to catch up. **2** *vr* **sie konnte sich gar nicht mehr darüber** ~**, daß ...** she couldn't get over the fact that ...; **krieg dich mal wieder ein!** control yourself!
Einkünfte *pl* income *sing; (einer Firma auch)* receipts.
einkuppeln *vi sep (Aut)* to let the clutch in.
einladen *vt sep irreg* **(a)** to invite. **jdn zu einer Party** ~ to ask sb to a party; **jdn auf ein Bier** ~ to invite sb for a beer; **laß mal, ich lade dich ein** let me treat you; **wir sind heute abend eingeladen** we've been invited out this evening. **(b)** *Waren* to load *(in +acc* into*)*.
einladend *adj* inviting; *Speisen* appetizing.
Einladung *f* invitation.
Einlage *f* **(a)** *(in Brief etc)* enclosure. **(b)**

(Schuh~) insole; *(zum Stützen)* (arch) support. **(c)** *(Sew)* padding; *(Versteifung)* interfacing. **(d)** *(Zahn~)* temporary filling. **(e)** *(Cook) noodles, egg etc added to a clear soup.* **(f)** *(Zwischenspiel)* interlude. **(g)** *(Fin: Kapital~)* investment; *(Spar~ auch)* deposit.
einlagern *vt sep* to store.
Einlagerung *f* storage.
Einlaß *m* **(a)** *no pl (Zutritt)* admission. **jdm ~ gewähren** to admit sb. **(b)** *(Tech)* inlet.
einlassen *sep irreg* **1** *vt* to let in *(in+acc* -to); *Person auch* to admit; *Wasser* to run *(in+acc* into). **2** *vr* **(a) sich auf etw** *(acc)* ~ to get involved in sth; *(sich zu etw verpflichten)* to let oneself in for sth; **sich auf einen Kompromiß** ~ to agree to a compromise; **ich lasse mich auf keine Diskussion ein** I'm not having any discussion about it. **(b) sich mit jdm** ~ *(pej: Umgang pflegen mit)* to get mixed up *or* involved with sb; **sie läßt sich mit jedem ein** she'll go with anyone.
Einlauf *m* **(a)** *no pl (Sport) (am Ziel)* finish; *(ins Stadion etc)* entry. **beim ~ in die Zielgerade ...** coming into the final straight ... **(b)** *(Med)* enema. **jdm einen ~ machen** to give sb an enema.
einlaufen *sep irreg* **1** *vi aux sein* **(a)** to come in *(in +acc* -to); *(ankommen auch)* to arrive *(in+acc* in); *(Wasser)* to run in *(in +acc* -to). **(b)** *(eingehen: Stoff)* to shrink. **2** *vt Schuhe* to wear in. **3** *vr (Motor, Maschine)* to be run in, to be broken in *(US)*.
einläuten *vt sep neues Jahr* to ring in; *(Sport) Runde* to sound the bell for.
einleben *vr sep* to settle down *(in or an+dat* in).
einlegen *vt sep* **(a)** *(hineintun)* to insert *(in+acc* in), to put in *(in+acc* -to); *Film auch* to load *(in +acc* into); *(in Brief)* to enclose *(in+acc* in). **(b)** *Sonderschicht, Spurt* to put on; *Pause* to have; *(Aut) Gang* to engage. **(c)** *(in Holz etc)* to inlay. **(d)** *(fig) Protest* to register. **ein gutes Wort für jdn** ~ to put in a good word for sb *(bei* with); **sein Veto** ~ to use one's veto. **(e)** *(Cook) Heringe etc* to pickle. **(f)** *Haare* to set, to put in rollers.
Einlegesohle *f* insole.
einleiten *vt sep* **(a)** *(in Gang setzen)* to initiate; *Maßnahmen auch, Schritte* to introduce, to take; *neues Zeitalter* to mark the start of, to inaugurate; *(Jur) Verfahren* to institute; *(Med) Geburt* to induce. **(b)** *(beginnen)* to start; *(eröffnen)* to open. **(c)** *Abwässer etc* to discharge *(in+acc* into).
einleitend *adj* introductory. **er sagte ~, daß ...** he said by way of introduction that ...
Einleitung *f* **(a)** *siehe vt (a)* initiation; introduction; inauguration; institution; induction. **(b)** *(Vorwort)* introduction; *(Mus)* prelude. **(c)** *(von Abwässern)* discharge *(in +acc* into).
einlenken *vi sep (fig)* to yield, to give way.
einlesen *sep irreg* **1** *vr* **sich in ein Gebiet** ~ to get into a subject. **2** *vt Daten* to feed *(in+acc* into).
einleuchten *vi sep* to be clear *(jdm* to sb). **ja, das leuchtet mir ein!** yes, I see that.
einleuchtend *adj* reasonable, plausible.
einliefern *vt sep Waren* to deliver. **jdn ins Krankenhaus** ~ to admit sb to hospital; **jdn ins Gefängnis** ~ to put sb in prison.
Einlieferung *f (von Waren)* delivery; *(ins Krankenhaus)* admission *(in+acc* to); *(ins Gefängnis)* committal *(in+acc* to).
Einlieferungsschein *m* certificate of posting.
einlochen *vt sep (col: einsperren)* to lock up.
einlösen *vt sep Pfand* to redeem; *Scheck, Wechsel* to cash (in); *(fig) Wort, Versprechen* to keep.
Einlösung *f siehe vt* redemption; cashing (in); keeping.
einlullen *vt sep (fig col)* **jdn mit schönen Worten** ~ to soft-talk sb.
einmachen *vt sep* to preserve; *(in Gläser auch)* to bottle.
Einmachglas *nt* bottling jar.
einmal *adv* **(a)** *(ein einziges Mal)* once; *(erstens)* first of all, firstly. **~ sagt er dies, ~ das** sometimes he says one thing, sometimes another; **auf ~** *(plötzlich)* all at once; *(zugleich)* at once; **~ mehr** once again; **~ und nie wieder** once and never again; **noch ~** again; **wenn sie da ist, ist es noch ~ so schön** it's twice as nice when she's there; **~ ist keinmal** *(Prov)* once doesn't count. **(b)** *(früher, vorher)* once; *(später, in Zukunft)* one day. **waren Sie schon ~ in Rom?** have you ever been to Rome?; **es war ~ ...** once upon a time there was ...; **das war ~!** that was then. **(c) nicht ~** not even; **wieder ~** again; **sag ~, ist das wahr?** tell me, is it true?; **gib mir ~ das Buch** give me that book.
Einmal|eins *nt no pl* (multiplication) tables *pl; (fig)* ABC, basics *pl.* **das ~ lernen** to learn one's tables; **das kleine/große ~** (multiplication) tables up to ten/over ten.
einmalig *adj* unique; *Anschaffung, Zahlung* one-off; *(col: hervorragend)* fantastic, amazing.
Einmaligkeit *f* uniqueness.
Einmannbetrieb *m* **(a)** one-man business. **(b) etw auf ~ umstellen** to convert sth for one-man operation.
Einmarkstück *nt* one-mark piece.
Einmarsch *m* entry *(in +acc* into); *(in ein Land)* invasion *(in+acc* of).
einmarschieren* *vi sep aux sein* to march in *(in +acc* -to).
einmauern *vt sep (ummauern)* to wall in *(in+acc* in).
einmieten *vr sep* **sich bei jdm** ~ to take lodgings with sb.
einmischen *vr sep* to interfere *(in +acc* in).
Einmischung *f* interference *(in +acc* in).
einmonatig *adj attr* one-month.
einmontieren* *vt sep* to fit in *(in +acc* -to).
einmotorig *adj Flugzeug* single-engine(d).
einmotten *vt sep Kleider etc* to put in mothballs.
einmünden *vi sep aux sein* **in etw** *(acc)* ~ *(Fluß)* to flow into sth; *(Straße)* to run *or* lead into sth.
Einmündung *f (von Fluß)* confluence; *(von Straße)* junction.
einmütig *adj* unanimous.
Einmütigkeit *f* unanimity.
einnähen *vt sep* to sew in *(in +acc* -to); *(enger machen)* to take in.
Einnahme *f* **-n (a)** *(Mil)* seizure, capture. **(b) ~n** *pl* income *sing; (Geschäfts~)* takings *pl; (aus Einzelverkauf)* proceeds *pl; (eines Staates)* revenue *sing;* **~n und Ausgaben** income and expenditure.
Einnahmequelle *f* source of income; *(eines Staates)* source of revenue.
einnehmen *vt sep irreg* **(a)** to take; *(lit, fig) Platz etc* to take (up), to occupy; *Stelle (innehaben)* to have, to occupy; *Haltung, Standpunkt etc* to take up; *Steuern* to collect. **die eingenommenen Gelder** the takings. **(b) er nahm uns alle für sich ein** he won us all over; **jdn gegen sich** ~ to set sb against oneself.
einnehmend *adj* likeable, charming. **er hat ein ~es Wesen** he's a likeable character; *(hum col)* he has taking ways *(hum col)*.
einnicken *vi sep aux sein (col)* to nod off.
einnisten *vr sep (lit)* to nest; *(Parasiten, Ei)* to lodge; *(fig)* to park oneself *(bei* on).
Ein|öde *f* wilderness.
ein|ölen *sep* **1** *vt* to oil. **2** *vr* to rub oneself with oil.
ein|ordnen *sep* **1** *vt* **(a)** *Bücher etc* to (put in) order; *Akten* to file. **(b)** *(klassifizieren)* to classify. **2** *vr* **(a)** *(in Gemeinschaft etc)* to fit in *(in+acc* -to). **(b)** *(Aut)* to get in(to) lane.
einpacken *sep* **1** *vt* **(a)** *(einwickeln)* to wrap up *(in +acc* in) *(auch fig)*. **(b)** *(hineintun)* to pack *(in +acc* in). **2** *vi* to pack. **dann können wir ~** *(col)* in that case we may as well pack it all in *(col)*.
einparken *vti sep* to park. **(in eine Parklücke) ~** to get into a parking space.

Einparteien- *in cpds* one-party.

einpassen *vt sep* to fit in *(in +acc -to)*.

einpauken *vt sep (col)* **jdm etw ~** to drum sth into sb.

einpendeln *vr sep (fig)* to settle down; *(Preise etc)* to level off.

einpennen *vi sep aux sein (col)* to drop off *(col)*.

Einpfennigstück *nt* one-pfennig piece.

einpferchen *vt sep Vieh* to pen in *(in +acc -to)*; *(fig)* to coop up *(in +acc in)*.

einpflanzen *vt sep* to plant *(in +dat in)*; *(Med)* to implant *(jdm* in(to) sb*)*.

einplanen *vt sep* to plan (on), to include in one's plans; *Verzögerungen, Verluste* to allow for.

einpökeln *vt sep Fisch, Fleisch* to salt.

einprägen *sep* **1** *vt Muster, Spuren* to imprint, to impress; *Inschrift* to stamp. **sich** *(dat)* **etw ~** to remember sth; *(auswendig lernen)* to memorize sth, to commit sth to memory. **2** *vr* **sich jdm ~** to make an impression on sb.

einprägsam *adj* easily remembered; *Slogan, Melodie auch* catchy.

einprogrammieren* *vt sep Daten* to feed in.

einprügeln *sep (col)* **1** *vt* **jdm etw ~** to din sth into sb *(col)*. **2** *vi* **auf jdn ~** to lay into sb *(col)*.

einquartieren* *sep* **1** *vt* to quarter; *(Mil auch)* to billet. **Gäste bei Freunden ~** to put visitors up with friends. **2** *vr* to be quartered *(bei* with*)*; *(Mil auch)* to be billeted *(bei* on*)*; *(Gäste)* to stop *(bei* with*) (col)*.

einquetschen *vt sep* = **einklemmen (a).**

einrahmen *vt sep (lit, fig)* to frame.

einrasten *vti sep (vi: aux sein)* to engage.

einräumen *vt sep* **(a)** *Wäsche, Bücher etc* to put away; *Schrank, Regal etc* to fill. **(b)** *(zugestehen)* to concede, to admit; *Freiheiten etc* to allow; *Frist, Kredit* to grant, to allow. **die Presse räumte diesem Skandal viel Platz ein** the press devoted a lot of space to this scandal.

einrechnen *vt sep* to include. **ihn (mit) eingerechnet** including him.

einreden *sep* **1** *vt* **jdm/sich etw ~** to talk sb/oneself into believing sth, to persuade sb/oneself of sth; **das redest du dir nur ein!** you're only imagining it. **2** *vi* **auf jdn ~** to keep on and on at sb.

einreiben *vt sep irreg* **er rieb sich** *(dat)* **das Gesicht mit Creme ein** he rubbed cream into his face.

einreichen *vt sep Antrag, Unterlagen* to submit *(bei* to*)*; *(Jur) Klage* to file; *(bitten um) Versetzung, Pensionierung* to apply for, to request.

einreihen *sep* **1** *vt (einordnen, einfügen)* to put in *(in+acc -to)*; *(klassifizieren)* to classify. **2** *vr* **sich in etw** *(acc)* **~** to join sth.

Einreiher *m* - single-breasted suit/jacket/coat.

einreihig *adj Anzug etc* single-breasted.

Einreise *f* entry *(in +acc* into, to*)*. **bei der ~ in die DDR** when entering the GDR, on entry to the GDR.

Einreise|erlaubnis *f* entry permit.

einreisen *vi sep aux sein* to enter the country. **er reiste in die Schweiz ein** he entered Switzerland.

Einreise-: **~verbot** *nt* refusal of entry; **~verbot haben** to have been refused entry; **~visum** *nt* entry visa.

einreißen *sep irreg* **1** *vt* **(a)** *Papier, Nagel* to tear. **(b)** *Zaun etc* to tear *or* pull down. **2** *vi aux sein (Papier)* to tear; *(fig col: Unsitte etc)* to catch on *(col)*, to get to be a habit *(col)*.

einrenken *sep* **1** *vt Gelenk, Knie* to put back in place; *(fig col)* to sort out. **2** *vr (fig col)* to sort itself out.

einrennen *vt sep irreg (col) Tür* to break down.

einrichten *sep* **1** *vt* **(a)** *(möblieren) Wohnung* to furnish; *(ausstatten) Hobbyraum* to fit out; *Praxis, Labor* to equip, to fit out. **eine Wohnung modern ~** to furnish a flat in a modern style. **(b)** *(gründen, eröffnen)* to set up; *Konto* to open. **(c)** *(fig: arrangieren)* to arrange, to fix. **ich werde es ~, daß wir um zwei Uhr da sind** I'll arrange for us to be there at two. **2** *vr* **(a)** *(sich möblieren)* to furnish one's house *etc*. **(b)** *(sich der Lage anpassen)* to get along *or* by, to manage; *(sparsam sein)* to cut down. **(c) sich auf etw** *(acc)* **~** to prepare oneself for sth; **auf Tourismus eingerichtet sein** to be geared to tourism.

Einrichtung *f* **(a)** *(das Einrichten) (von Wohnung)* furnishing; *(von Hobbyraum)* fitting-out; *(von Labor, Praxis)* equipping. **(b)** *(Wohnungs~)* furnishings *pl; (Geschäfts~ etc)* fittings *pl; (Labor~ etc)* equipment *no pl*. **(c)** *(Gründung, Eröffnung)* setting-up; *(von Konto)* opening. **(d)** *(behördlich, wohltätig)* institution; *(öffentliche ~)* facility. **(e)** *(Gewohnheit)* **zur ständigen ~ werden** to become an institution.

Einrichtungsgegenstand *m* item of furniture.

einritzen *vt sep* to carve in *(in +acc -to)*.

einrollen *vt sep (einwickeln)* to roll up *(in+acc in)*. **sich** *(dat)* **die Haare ~** to put one's hair in rollers.

einrosten *vi sep aux sein* to rust up; *(fig: Glieder)* to stiffen up; *(Kenntnisse etc)* to get rusty.

einrücken *sep* **1** *vi aux sein (Mil: in ein Land)* to move in *(in+acc -to)*. **2** *vt Zeile* to indent; *Anzeige (in Zeitung)* to insert.

einrühren *vt sep* to stir *or* mix in *(in+acc -to)*.

eins *num* one. **es ist ~** it's one (o'clock); **~ zu ~** *(Sport)* one all; **~ mit jdm sein** *(übereinstimmen)* to be in agreement with sb; **das ist doch alles ~** *(col)* it's all one *or* all the same; **sehen und handeln waren ~** when I/he *etc* saw it I/he *etc* had to do something; **~ a** *(col)* first-rate *(col)*; *siehe* **eine(r, s) (c), vier.**

Eins *f* **-en** one; *(Sch auch)* A.

einsacken[1] *vt sep (col: erbeuten)* to grab *(col)*; *Geld, Gewinne* to rake in *(col)*.

einsacken[2] *vi sep aux sein (einsinken)* to sink; *(Boden etc auch)* to subside.

einsalzen *vt sep Fisch, Fleisch* to salt.

einsam *adj* **(a)** lonely; *(einzeln)* solitary. **~ leben** to live a lonely/solitary life. **(b)** *(abgelegen) Haus, Insel* secluded; *Dorf* isolated; *(menschenleer)* empty. **(c)** *(col)* **~e Klasse/Spitze** absolutely fantastic *(col)*.

Einsamkeit *f siehe adj* **(a)** loneliness; solitariness. **er liebt die ~** he likes solitude. **(b)** seclusion; isolation; emptiness.

einsammeln *vt sep* to collect (in).

Einsatz *m* **(a)** *(~teil)* insert; *(Schubladen~, Koffer~)* tray; *(Topf~)* compartment. **(b)** *(Spiel~)* stake; *(Kapital~)* investment. **den ~ erhöhen** to raise the stakes. **(c)** *(Mus)* entry. **der Dirigent gab den ~** the conductor raised his baton and brought in the orchestra. **(d)** *(Verwendung)* use; *(esp Mil)* deployment; *(von Arbeitskräften)* employment. **im ~** in use; **die Ersatzspieler kamen nicht zum ~** the reserves weren't used; **unter ~ aller Kräfte** by making a supreme effort. **(e)** *(Aktion) (Mil)* action; *(von Polizei)* intervention. **im ~** in action; **zum ~ kommen** to go into action; **bei seinem ersten ~** the first time he saw action; **sich zum ~ melden** to report for duty. **(f)** *(Hingabe)* commitment. **etw unter ~ seines Lebens tun** to risk one's life to do sth.

Einsatz-: **~befehl** *m* order to go into action; **e~bereit** *adj* ready for use; *(Mil)* ready for action; **e~fähig** *adj* fit for use; *(Mil)* fit for action; *Sportler* fit; **~kommando** *(Mil) nt* task force; **~leiter** *m* head of operations; **~wagen** *m (bei Straßenbahn, Bus)* extra tram/bus.

einschalten *sep* **1** *vt* **(a)** *(in Betrieb setzen)* to switch on; *Sender* to tune in to. **(b)** *(einfügen)* to interpolate. **(c) jdn ~** to bring sb in. **2** *vr* **(a)** *(Heizung etc)* to switch itself on. **(b)** *(eingreifen)* to intervene.

Einschaltquote *f (TV)* viewing figures *pl*.

einschärfen *vt sep* **jdm etw ~** to impress sth (up)on sb.
einschätzen *vt sep* to assess *(auch Fin)*, to evaluate. **falsch ~** to misjudge; **wie ich die Lage einschätze** as I see the situation; **jdn hoch/niedrig ~** to have a high/low opinion of sb; **etw zu hoch/niedrig ~** to overestimate/underestimate sth.
Einschätzung *f* assessment, evaluation. **falsche ~** misjudgement; **nach meiner ~** in my estimation.
einschenken *vt sep* to pour (out). **darf ich Ihnen noch Wein ~?** can I give you some more wine?
einscheren *vi sep aux sein* to get back (into lane).
einschicken *vt sep* to send in *(an +acc* to*)*.
einschieben *vt sep irreg* to put in *(in +acc* -to*)*. **eine Pause ~** to have a break.
einschießen *sep irreg* **1** *vt Scheibe (mit Ball etc)* to smash (in). **2** *vi* **(a)** *(Sport)* to score. **er schoß zum 1:0 ein** he scored to make it 1-0. **(b) auf jdn ~** to shoot at sb.
einschiffen *sep* **1** *vt* to ship. **2** *vr* to embark.
Einschiffung *f (von Personen)* boarding, embarkation; *(von Gütern)* loading.
einschl. = **einschließlich** incl.
einschlafen *vi sep irreg aux sein* to fall asleep, to go to sleep; *(Bein, Arm)* to go to sleep; *(fig: Freundschaft)* to peter out. **ich kann nicht ~** I can't get to sleep; **vor dem E~ zu nehmen** *(Medizin)* to be taken before retiring.
einschläfern *vt sep (schläfrig machen)* to make sleepy; *Gewissen* to soothe; *(narkotisieren)* to give a soporific; *(töten) Tier* to put to sleep.
einschläfernd *adj* soporific; *(langweilig)* monotonous.
Einschlag *m* **(a)** *(von Geschoß)* impact. **der ~ der Granate war deutlich zu sehen** the place where the grenade had landed was clearly visible. **(b)** *(Aut: des Lenkrads)* lock. **(c)** *(Zusatz, Beimischung)* element.
einschlagen *sep irreg* **1** *vt* **(a)** *Nagel* to hammer *or* knock in; *Pfahl* to drive in. **(b)** *(zertrümmern)* to smash in; *Zähne* to knock out. **(c)** *(einwickeln) Ware* to wrap up. **(d)** *(Aut) Räder* to turn. **(e)** *(wählen) Weg* to take; *Kurs* to follow; *Laufbahn etc* to enter on. **das Schiff änderte den eingeschlagenen Kurs** the ship changed from its previous course. **2** *vi* **(a) (in etw** *acc***) ~** to hit (sth); **es muß irgendwo eingeschlagen haben** something must have been struck by lightning; **gut ~** *(col)* to go down well, to be a big hit *(col)*. **(b) auf jdn/etw ~** to hit out at sb/sth. **(c)** *(zur Bekräftigung)* to shake on it.
einschlägig *adj* appropriate; *Literatur, Paragraph auch* relevant. **er ist ~ vorbestraft** *(Jur)* he has a previous conviction for a similar offence.
einschleichen *vr sep irreg (lit, fig)* to creep in *(in +acc* -to*)*. **sich in jds Vertrauen ~** *(fig)* to worm one's way into sb's confidence.
einschleppen *vt sep (fig) Krankheit etc* to bring in.
einschleusen *vt sep* to smuggle in *(in +acc* -to*)*.
einschließen *vt sep irreg* **(a)** to lock up *(in+acc* in*)*. **er schloß sich in seinem Zimmer ein** he locked himself (up) in his room. **(b)** *(umgeben)* to surround. **(c)** *(fig: beinhalten)* to include.
einschließlich **1** *prep+gen* including, inclusive of. **2** *adv* **bis S. 205 ~** up to and including p.205; **vom 1. bis ~ 31. Oktober** from 1st to 31st October inclusive.
einschlummern *vi sep aux sein (geh)* to fall asleep.
Einschluß *m* **mit** *or* **unter ~ von** *(form)* including.
einschmeicheln *vr sep* **sich bei jdm ~** to ingratiate oneself with sb; **~de Stimme** silky voice.
einschmieren *vt sep (mit Fett)* to grease; *(mit Öl)* to oil; *Gesicht (mit Creme)* to put cream on.
einschmuggeln *vt sep* to smuggle in *(in+acc* -to*)*. **er hat sich in den Saal eingeschmuggelt** he sneaked into the hall.
einschnappen *vi sep aux sein* **(a)** *(Schloß, Tür)* to click shut. **(b)** *(col: beleidigt sein)* to take offence *(Brit) or* offense *(US)*, to get into a huff *(col)*.
einschneiden *vt sep irreg* to cut. **tief eingeschnittene Felsen** steep cliffs.
einschneidend *adj (fig)* drastic, radical.
einschneien *vi sep aux sein* to get snowed in. **eingeschneit sein** to be snowed in.
Einschnitt *m* cut; *(Med)* incision; *(im Tal, Gebirge)* cleft; *(im Leben)* decisive point.
einschnüren *vt sep* **(a)** *(einengen)* to cut into. **dieser Kragen schnürt mir den Hals ein** this collar is strangling me. **(b)** *Paket* to tie up.
einschränken *sep* **1** *vt* to cut back; *Bewegungsfreiheit, Recht* to limit, to restrict; *Wünsche* to moderate; *Behauptung* to qualify. **~d möchte ich sagen, daß ...** I'd like to qualify that by saying ...; **das Rauchen ~** to cut down on smoking. **2** *vr (sparen)* to economize. **sich im Trinken ~** to cut down on one's drinking; *siehe* **eingeschränkt.**
Einschränkung *f siehe vt* cutting back; limitation, restriction; moderation; qualification; *(Vorbehalt)* reservation.
einschrauben *vt sep* to screw in *(in +acc* -to*)*.
Einschreib(e)brief *m* registered letter.
einschreiben *sep irreg* **1** *vt (eintragen)* to enter; *siehe* **eingeschrieben. 2** *vr (für Abendkurse etc)* to enrol; *(Univ)* to register.
Einschreiben *nt* registered letter/parcel. **einen Brief als ~ schicken** to send a letter by registered mail.
Einschreibung *f* enrolment; *(Univ)* registration.
einschreiten *vi sep irreg aux sein* to take action *(gegen* against*)*; *(dazwischentreten)* to intervene, to step in.
Einschreiten *nt no pl* intervention.
Einschub *m* insertion.
einschüchtern *vt sep* to intimidate.
Einschüchterung *f* intimidation.
einschulen *vti sep* to send to school. **eingeschult werden** *(Kind)* to start school.
Einschulung *f* first day at school. **die ~ findet im Alter von 6 Jahren statt** children start school at the age of 6.
Einschuß *m* **(a)** *(~stelle)* bullet hole; *(Med)* point of entry. **(b)** *(Ftbl)* (shot into) goal.
einschütten *vt sep* to tip in *(in +acc* -to*)*; *Flüssigkeiten* to pour in *(in+acc* -to*)*. **er hat sich** *(dat)* **noch etwas Kaffee eingeschüttet** he poured himself (out) some more coffee.
einschweißen *vt sep (Tech)* to weld in *(in+acc* -to*)*; *(in Plastik)* to shrink-wrap.
einschwenken *vi sep aux sein* to turn *or* swing in *(in+acc* -to*)*. **auf etw** *(acc)* **~** *(fig)* to go along with sth.
einsehen *vt sep irreg* to see; *(prüfen auch)* to inspect; *Fehler, Schuld auch* to recognize. **das sehe ich nicht ein** I don't see why.
Einsehen *nt:* **ein ~haben** to have some understanding *(mit, für* for*)*; *(Vernunft, Einsicht)* to see reason; **hab doch ein ~!** be reasonable!
einseifen *vt sep* to soap; *(col: betrügen)* to con *(col)*.
einseitig *adj* one-sided; *Ernährung* unbalanced; *(Jur, Pol) Erklärung, Kündigung* unilateral. **~e Lähmung** paralysis of one side of the body.
Einseitigkeit *f* one-sidedness; *(von Ernährung)* imbalance.
einsenden *vt sep irreg* to send in, to submit *(an +acc* to*)*.
Einsender(in *f***)** *m* sender; *(bei Preisausschreiben)* competitor.
Einsendeschluß *m* closing date (for entries).
Einsendung *f* **(a)** *(bei Wettbewerb etc)* entry. **(b)** *no pl (das Einsenden)* sending in, submission.
einsetzen *sep* **1** *vt* **(a)** *(einfügen)* to put in *(in+acc* -to*)*; *Maschinenteil auch* to insert *(in+acc* into*)*, to

fit in *(in+acc* -to); *(schreiben auch)* to enter *(in +acc* in). **jdm einen Goldzahn** ~ to give sb a gold tooth. **(b)** *(ernennen)* to appoint; *Nachfolger* to name. **jdn in ein Amt** ~ to appoint sb to an office. **(c)** *(verwenden)* to use; *Truppen, Polizei* to deploy; *Busse, Sonderzüge* to put on. **(d)** *(beim Glücksspiel)* to stake; *Leben* to risk. **2** *vi (beginnen)* to start, to begin; *(Mus)* to come in. **3** *vr* **sich (voll)** ~ to show (complete) commitment *(in+dat* to); **sich für jdn/etw** ~ to support sb/sth; **ich werde mich dafür** ~, **daß ...** I will do what I can to see that ...

Einsetzung *f* appointment *(in +acc* to).

Einsicht *f* **(a)** *(in Akten, Bücher)* inspection *(in +acc* of). ~ **in etw** *(acc)* **haben/verlangen** to look/ask to look at sth. **(b)** *(Vernunft)* sense, reason; *(Erkenntnis)* insight. **zur** ~ **kommen** to come to one's senses; **zu der** ~ **kommen, daß ...** to recognize that ...; **haben Sie doch** ~! have a heart!; *(seien Sie vernünftig)* be reasonable!

einsichtig *adj* **(a)** *(vernünftig)* reasonable; *(verständnisvoll)* understanding. **(b)** *(verständlich, begreiflich)* understandable. **jdm etw** ~ **machen** to make sb understand *or* see sth.

Einsichtnahme *f* **-n** *(form)* inspection. **er bat um** ~ **in die Akten** he asked to inspect *or* see the files; **„zur** ~**"** "for attention".

einsickern *vi sep aux sein* to seep in *(in+acc* -to); *(fig)* to filter in *(in +acc* -to).

Einsiedler(in *f***)** *m* hermit; *(fig auch)* recluse.

einsilbig *adj* monosyllabic.

einsinken *vi sep irreg aux sein (im Morast, Schnee)* to sink in *(in+acc or dat* -to); *(Boden etc)* to subside, to cave in. **eingesunkene Wangen** sunken *or* hollow cheeks.

einspannen *vt sep* **(a)** *(in Schraubstock)* to clamp in *(in+acc* -to). **(b)** *(in Schreibmaschine)* to insert *(in+acc* in, into). **(c)** *Pferde* to harness. **(d)** *(fig: arbeiten lassen)* to rope in *(für etw* to do sth). **jdn für seine Zwecke** ~ to use sb for one's own ends; *siehe* **eingespannt.**

einsparen *vt sep* to save, to economize on; *Kosten* to cut down on; *Posten* to eliminate.

Einsparung *f* **(a)** economy. **(b)** *siehe vt* saving; cutting down *(von* on); elimination.

einspeichern *vt sep Daten* to feed in *(in+acc* -to).

einsperren *vt sep* to lock up *(in +acc or dat* in).

einspielen *sep* **1** *vr (Mus, Sport)* to warm up; *(Regelung, Arbeit)* to work out. **aber das spielt sich alles noch ein** but things should sort themselves out all right; **sich aufeinander** ~ to become attuned to one another; *siehe* **eingespielt. 2** *vt (Film etc)* to bring in, to gross; *Kosten* to recover.

einsprachig *adj* monolingual.

einspringen *vi sep irreg aux sein (col: aushelfen)* to stand in; *(mit Geld etc)* to help out.

Einspritz- *(Aut)*: ~**düse** *f* injector; ~**motor** *m* injection engine; ~**pumpe** *f* injection pump.

einspritzen *vt sep (Aut, Med)* to inject. **er spritzte ihr Insulin ein** he gave her an insulin injection.

Einspruch *m* objection *(auch Jur).* ~ **einlegen** *(Admin)* to file an objection; **gegen etw** ~ **erheben** to raise an objection to sth.

Einspruchsfrist *f (Jur)* period for filing an objection.

einspurig *adj (Rail)* single-track; *(Aut)* single-lane. **die Straße ist nur** ~ **befahrbar** it's single-lane traffic only.

einst *adv (geh)* **(a)** *(früher)* once. **(b)** *(in ferner Zukunft)* one day.

einstampfen *vt sep Bücher* to pulp (down).

Einstand *m* **(a) er hat gestern seinen** ~ **gegeben** yesterday he celebrated starting his new job. **(b)** *(beim Tennis)* deuce.

einstanzen *vt sep* to stamp in *(in +acc* -to).

einstechen *vt sep irreg* to pierce; *Nadel* to put *or* stick in *(in+acc* -to); *(Cook)* to prick.

einstecken *vt sep* **(a)** *(in etw stecken)* to put *or* stick in *(in+acc* -to); *Gerät* to plug in. **(b)** *(in die Tasche etc)* **(sich** *dat***) etw** ~ to take sth; **hast du deinen Paß eingesteckt?** have you got your passport with you? **(c)** *(in den Briefkasten)* to post, to mail *(esp US).* **(d)** *(col) Kritik etc* to take; *(verdienen) Geld, Profit* to pocket *(col).* **der Boxer mußte viel** ~ the boxer had to take a lot of punishment.

einstehen *vi sep irreg aux sein* **(a)** *(sich verbürgen)* **für jdn/etw** ~ to vouch for sb/sth; **ich stehe dafür ein, daß ...** I will vouch that ... **(b)** *(Ersatz leisten)* **für etw** ~ to make good sth.

einsteigen *vi sep irreg aux sein* **(a)** *(in ein Fahrzeug etc)* to get in *(in+acc* -to); *(in Zug auch, in Bus)* to get on *(in+acc* -to). ~! *(Rail etc)* all aboard! **(b)** *(in ein Haus etc)* to climb *or* get in *(in+acc* -to). **(c)** *(col)* **in die Politik/ins Verlagsgeschäft** ~ to go into politics/publishing.

einstellbar *adj* adjustable.

einstellen *sep* **1** *vt* **(a)** *(hineinstellen)* to put in. **Bücher ins Regal** ~ to put books away on the shelves. **(b)** *(anstellen) Arbeitskräfte* to take on. **(c)** *(beenden)* to stop; *(endgültig auch)* to discontinue; *Expedition, Suche* to call off; *(Mil) Feuer* to cease. **(d)** *(regulieren)* to adjust *(auf+acc* to); *Fotoapparat (auf Entfernung)* to focus *(auf+acc* on); *Wecker* to set *(auf +acc* for); *Sender* to tune in to. **(e)** *(Sport) Rekord* to equal. **2** *vr* **(a) sich auf jdn/etw** ~ *(sich richten nach)* to adapt oneself to sb/sth; *(sich vorbereiten auf)* to prepare oneself for sb/sth; *siehe* **eingestellt. (b)** *(erscheinen)* to appear; *(Fieber, Regen)* to set in; *(Wort, Gedanke)* to come to mind; *(Jahreszeiten)* to come, to arrive.

einstellig *adj Zahl* single-digit.

Einstellplatz *m (auf Hof)* carport; *(in Großgarage)* (covered) parking space.

Einstellung *f* **(a)** *(Anstellung)* employment. **(b)** *(Beendigung) siehe vt (c)* stopping; discontinuation; calling-off; cessation. **der Sturm zwang uns zur** ~ **der Suche** the storm forced us to call off the search. **(c)** *(Film: Szene)* take. **(d)** *(Gesinnung, Haltung)* attitude; *(politisch, religiös etc)* views *pl.*

Einstellungs-: ~**gespräch** *nt* interview; ~**stopp** *m* halt in recruitment; ~**termin** *m* starting date.

Einstieg *m* **-e (a)** *no pl (das Einsteigen)* getting in; *(in Bus)* getting on; *(von Dieb: in Haus etc)* entry; *(fig: zu einem Thema etc)* lead-in *(zu* to). **kein** ~ no entrance. **(b)** *(von Bus, Bahn)* door.

einstig *adj attr* former.

einstimmen *sep* **1** *vi (in ein Lied etc)* to join in. **2** *vt (Mus) Instrument* to tune. **jdn/sich auf etw** *(acc)* ~ *(fig)* to get sb/oneself in the mood for sth.

einstimmig 1 *adv singen, rufen* in unison. **2** *adj (einmütig)* unanimous.

Einstimmigkeit *f* unanimity.

einstöckig *adj Haus* two-storey *(Brit)*, two-story *(US).*

einstöpseln *vt sep (Elec)* to plug in *(in+acc* -to).

einstreichen *vt sep irreg (col) Geld, Gewinn* to pocket *(col).*

einstreuen *vt sep* to sprinkle in *(in +acc* -to); *(fig) Bemerkung etc* to slip in *(in+acc* -to).

einströmen *vi sep aux sein* to flood in *(in+acc* -to); *(Licht, fig auch)* to stream in *(in +acc* -to). ~**de Kaltluft** a stream of cold air.

einstudieren* *vt sep Rolle* to study; *Theaterstück* to rehearse.

einstufen *vt sep* to classify. **in eine Kategorie** *etc* ~ to put into a category *etc.*

Einstufung *f* classification. **nach seiner** ~ **in eine höhere Gehaltsklasse** after he was put on a higher salary grade.

einstündig *adj attr* one-hour.

einstürmen *vi sep aux sein* **auf jdn** ~ *(Mil)* to storm sb; *(fig)* to assail sb.

Einsturz *m* collapse.

einstürzen *vi sep aux sein* to collapse. **auf jdn** ~

(fig) to overwhelm sb.
Einsturzgefahr *f* danger of collapse.
einstweilen *adv* in the meantime; *(vorläufig)* temporarily.
einstweilig *adj attr* temporary. **~e Verfügung** *(Jur)* temporary *or* interim injunction.
eintägig *adj attr* one-day.
Eintagsfliege *f (Zool)* mayfly; *(fig)* nine-day wonder.
eintauchen *sep* **1** *vt* to dip *(in+acc* in, into*)*; *(völlig)* to immerse *(in +acc* in*)*. **2** *vi aux sein (Schwimmer)* to dive in; *(U-Boot)* to dive.
Eintausch *m* exchange, swap *(col)*. **im ~ gegen** *or* **für etw** in exchange for sth.
eintauschen *vt sep* to exchange, to swap *(col) (gegen, für* for*)*; *(umtauschen) Devisen* to change.
eintausend *num siehe* **tausend.**
einteilen *vt sep* **(a)** to divide (up) *(in+acc* into*)*. **(b)** *(sinnvoll aufteilen) Zeit, Arbeit* to plan (out), to organize; *Geld* to budget. **(c)** *(dienstlich verpflichten)* to detail *(zu* for*)*. **er ist als Aufseher eingeteilt** he has been assigned the job of supervisor.
einteilig *adj Badeanzug* one-piece *attr.*
Einteilung *f siehe vt* **(a)** division. **(b)** planning, organization; budgeting. **(c)** assignment.
eintönig *adj* monotonous.
Eintönigkeit *f* monotony.
Eintopf *m* stew.
Eintracht *f no pl* harmony, concord.
einträchtig *adj* peaceable.
Eintrag *m* ⸚**e** *(schriftlich)* entry *(in+acc* in*)*.
eintragen *sep irreg* **1** *vt* **(a)** *(in Liste etc)* to enter; *(amtlich)* to register; *siehe* **eingetragen. (b) jdm Gewinn ~** to bring sb profit; **das trägt nur Schaden ein** that will only do harm. **2** *vr* to sign; *(im Hotel)* to check in. **er trug sich in die Warteliste ein** he put his name down on the waiting list.
einträglich *adj* profitable.
Eintragung *f* entry *(in +acc* in*)*.
eintreffen *vi sep irreg aux sein* **(a)** *(ankommen)* to arrive. **(b)** *(fig: wahr werden)* to come true.
eintreiben *vt sep irreg* **(a)** *Vieh* to drive in *(in+acc* -to*)*. **(b)** *Geldbeträge* to collect.
eintreten *sep irreg* **1** *vi* **(a)** *aux sein* **in etw** *(acc)* **~** to enter sth; *(in Zimmer etc auch)* to go/come into sth; *(in Verein etc)* to join sth. **(b) auf jdn ~** to kick sb. **(c)** *aux sein (sich ereignen) (Tod)* to occur; *(Zeitpunkt)* to come; *(beginnen) (Dunkelheit, Nacht)* to fall; *(Tauwetter)* to set in. **(d)** *aux sein* **für jdn/etw ~** to stand up for sb/sth. **2** *vt (zertrümmern)* to kick in.
eintrichtern *vt sep (col)* **jdm etw ~** to drum sth into sb.
Eintritt *m* **(a)** *(das Eintreten)* entry *(in+acc* (in)to*)*; *(ins Zimmer etc auch)* entrance; *(in Verein etc)* joining *(in+acc* of*)*. **beim ~ ins Zimmer** on entering the room; **der ~ ins Geschäftsleben** getting into the business world. **(b)** *(~sgeld)* admission *(in+acc* to*)*. **~ frei!** admission free; **„~ verboten"** "no admittance". **(c) bei ~ eines solchen Falles** in such an event; **der ~ des Todes** the moment when death occurs.
Eintritts-: ~geld *nt* entrance money, admission charge; **~karte** *f* (entrance) ticket; **~preis** *m* admission charge.
eintrocknen *vi sep aux sein* to dry up.
eintrudeln *vi sep aux sein (col)* to drift in *(col)*.
eintunken *vt sep Brot* to dunk *(in +acc* in*)*.
ein|üben *vt sep* to practise *(Brit)*, to practice *(US)*; *Theaterstück etc* to rehearse.
einverleiben* *vi sep and insep* **(a)** *Gebiet, Land* to annex *(dat* to*)*. **(b)** *(hum col)* **sich** *(dat)* **etw ~** *(essen, trinken)* to put sth away *(col)*.
Einvernehmen *nt no pl (Eintracht)* harmony; *(Übereinstimmung)* agreement. **in gutem ~ leben** to live in perfect harmony; **im ~ mit jdm** in agreement with sb.
einvernehmlich *adj (form) Regelung* joint.
einverstanden *adj* **~!** okay!, agreed!; **~ sein** to agree; **ich bin mit deinem Verhalten/mit dir gar nicht ~** I don't approve of your behaviour; **sich mit etw ~ erklären** to give one's agreement to sth.
Einverständnis *nt* agreement; *(Zustimmung)* consent. **wir haben uns in gegenseitigem ~ scheiden lassen** we were divorced by mutual consent; **im ~ mit jdm handeln** to act with sb's consent.
Einwaage *f no pl (Comm: Reingewicht) weight of contents of can or jar excluding juice etc.*
Einwand *m* ⸚**e** objection. **einen ~ erheben** to raise an objection.
Einwanderer *m* immigrant.
einwandern *vi sep aux sein* to immigrate *(nach, in +acc* to*)*.
Einwanderung *f* immigration *(nach, in+acc* to*)*.
Einwanderungs- *in cpds* immigration.
einwandfrei *adj* **(a)** *(ohne Fehler)* perfect; *Sprache, Arbeit auch* faultless; *Benehmen* impeccable. **er spricht ein ~es Spanisch** he speaks perfect Spanish. **(b)** *(unzweifelhaft)* indisputable; *Beweis auch* definite. **etw ~ beweisen** to prove sth beyond doubt.
einwechseln *vt sep Geld* to change *(in +acc, gegen* into*)*.
einwecken *vt sep* to preserve; *Obst auch* to bottle.
Einweckglas *nt* preserving jar.
Einweg- ['ainve:k]: **~flasche** *f* non-returnable bottle; **~verpackung** *f* disposable wrapping.
einweichen *vt sep* to soak.
einweihen *vt sep* **(a)** *(feierlich eröffnen)* to open (officially); *(fig)* to christen. **(b) jdn in etw** *(acc)* **~** to initiate sb into sth; **er ist eingeweiht** he knows all about it; *siehe* **Eingeweihte(r).**
Einweihung(sfeier) *f* (official) opening.
einweisen *vt sep irreg* **(a)** *(in Krankenhaus)* to admit *(in+acc* to*)*. **(b)** *(in Arbeit unterweisen)* **jdn ~** to introduce sb to his job *or* work. **(c)** *(Aut)* to guide in *(in+acc* -to*)*.
Einweisung *f siehe vt* **(a)** admission *(in+acc* to*)*. **(b) die ~ der neuen Mitarbeiter übernehmen** to assume responsibility for introducing new employees to their jobs *or* work. **(c)** guiding in.
einwenden *vt sep irreg* **etwas/nichts gegen etw einzuwenden haben** to have an objection/no objection to sth, to object/not to object to sth; **er hat immer etwas einzuwenden** he always has some objection to make.
Einwendung *f* objection *(auch Jur)*.
einwerfen *sep irreg* **1** *vt* **(a)** *Fensterscheibe etc* to break, to smash. **(b)** *Brief* to post, to mail *(esp US)*; *Münze* to insert. **(c)** *(fig) Bemerkung* to throw in. **2** *vi (Sport)* to throw in, to take the throw-in.
einwickeln *vt sep* **(a)** to wrap (up). **(b)** *(col: überreden)* to take in. **da hat er sich schön ~ lassen** he's really been taken for a ride *(col)*.
einwilligen *vi sep (in+acc* to*)* to consent, to agree.
Einwilligung *f (in+acc* to*)* consent, agreement.
einwinken *vt sep* to guide *or* direct in.
einwirken *vi sep* **auf jdn/etw ~** to have an effect on sb/sth; *(beeinflussen)* to influence sb/sth.
Einwirkung *f* influence; *(einer Sache auch)* effect. **unter (der) ~ von Drogen** *etc* under the influence of drugs *etc;* **unter (der) ~ eines Schocks stehen** to be suffering from shock.
einwöchig *adj* one-week *attr.*
Einwohner(in *f***)** *m* **-** inhabitant.
Einwohner-: ~meldeamt *nt residents' registration office;* **sich beim ~meldeamt (an)melden** ≈ to register with the police; **~schaft** *f no pl* population, inhabitants *pl;* **~zahl** *f* polulation.
Einwurf *m* **(a)** *(von Münze)* insertion; *(von Brief)* posting, mailing *(esp US)*. **(b)** *(Sport)* throw-in.

(c) *(Schlitz)* slot; *(von Briefkasten)* slit. **(d)** *(fig)* interjection; *(Einwand)* objection.

Einzahl *f* singular.

einzahlen *vt sep* to pay in. **Geld auf ein Konto ~** to pay money into an account.

Einzahlung *f* payment; *(auf Sparkonto auch)* deposit.

Einzahlungs- *in cpds* paying-in; **~frist** *f* payment deadline.

einzäunen *vt sep* to fence in.

Einzäunung *f* fence, fencing; *(das Umzäunen)* fencing-in.

einzeichnen *vt sep* to draw in. **ist der Ort eingezeichnet?** is the place marked?

Einzel *nt* - *(Tennis)* singles *sing*.

Einzel-: **~antrieb** *m (Tech)* independent drive; **~ausgabe** *f* separate edition; **~behandlung** *f* individual treatment; **~blattzuführung** *f* sheet-feed; **~erscheinung** *f* isolated occurrence; **~fall** *m* individual case; *(Sonderfall)* isolated *or* one-off case; **~gänger(in** *f*) *m* - loner; **~haft** *f* solitary (confinement).

Einzelhandel *m* retail trade. **im ~ erhältlich** available retail.

Einzelhandels- *in cpds* retail.

Einzel-: **~händler** *m* retailer; **~heit** *f* detail, particular; **etw in allen ~heiten schildern** to describe sth right down to the last detail; **~kind** *nt* only child.

Einzeller *m* - *(Biol)* single-celled organism.

einzeln *adj* **(a)** individual; *(getrennt)* separate; *(von Paar) Schuh etc* odd. **bitte ~ eintreten** please come in one (person) at a time; **die ~en Städte, die wir besucht haben** the individual cities which we visited; **~ aufführen** to list separately *or* individually. **(b)** *(alleinstehend) Baum, Haus* single, solitary. **(c)** *(mit pl n: einige, vereinzelte)* some. **~e Besucher kamen schon früher** one or two visitors came earlier. **(d)** *(substantivisch)* **der/die ~e** the individual; **ein ~er** an individual, a single person; *(ein einziger Mensch)* one single person; **~e** some (people), a few (people); **jeder ~e** (each and) every one of you/them *etc*; **~es** some; **~es hat mir gefallen** I liked some of it; **das ~e** the particular; **jedes ~e** each one; **etw im ~en besprechen** to discuss sth in detail.

Einzel-: **~person** *f* single person; **~radaufhängung** *f (Aut)* independent suspension; **~stück** *nt* **ein schönes ~stück** a beautiful piece; **~stücke verkaufen wir nicht** we don't sell them singly; **~teil** *nt* individual *or* separate part; *(Ersatzteil)* spare part; **etw in seine ~teile zerlegen** to take sth to pieces; **~wesen** *nt* individual; **~zelle** *f* single cell *(auch Biol)*; **~zimmer** *nt* single room.

einzementieren* *vt sep Stein* to cement.

einziehen *sep irreg* **1** *vt* **(a)** *(einfügen) Faden* to thread; *(in einen Bezug etc)* to put in; *(Build: einbauen) Wand etc* to put in. **(b)** *(zurückziehen) Krallen, Fahrgestell* to retract, to draw in; *Bauch, Netz* to pull in; *Flagge, Segel* to lower, to take down. **den Kopf ~** to duck (one's head); **der Hund zog den Schwanz ein** the dog put his tail between his legs. **(c)** *(Mil) (zu* into*) Personen* to call up, to draft *(esp US)*; *Fahrzeuge etc* to requisition. **(d)** *(einfordern) Steuern* to collect; *Banknoten* to withdraw (from circulation); *Führerschein* to take away; *Vermögen* to confiscate; *(fig) Erkundigungen* to make *(über+acc* about*)*. **2** *vi aux sein* **(a)** *(in Haus)* to move in. **(b)** *(auch Mil: einmarschieren)* to march in *(in+acc* -to*)*. **(c)** *(einkehren)* to come *(in+dat* to*)*. **wenn der Friede im Lande einzieht** when peace comes to our country. **(d)** *(eindringen)* to soak in *(in +acc* -to*)*.

Einziehung *f* **(a)** *(Mil) (von Personen)* call-up, drafting *(esp US)*; *(von Fahrzeugen)* requisitioning. **(b)** *(Einforderung) (von Vermögen)* confiscation; *(von Banknoten, Führerschein etc)* withdrawal; *(von Steuern etc)* collection.

einzig 1 *adj* **(a)** *attr* only, sole. **ich sehe nur eine ~e Möglichkeit** I can see only one (single) possibility; **kein ~es Mal** not once, not one single time. **(b)** *(emph)* absolute. **dieses Fußballspiel war eine ~e Schlammschlacht** this football match was just one big mudbath. **(c)** *pred (~artig)* unique. **(d)** *(substantivisch)* **der/die ~e** the only one; **das ~e** the only thing; **kein ~er** nobody, not a single person. **2** *adv (allein)* only, solely. **die ~ mögliche Lösung** the only possible solution; **~ und allein** solely; **das ~ Wahre** the only thing; *(das beste)* the real McCoy.

einzig|artig *adj* unique.

Einzig|artigkeit *f* uniqueness.

Einzimmer- *in cpds* one-room.

Einzug *m* **(a)** *(in Haus etc)* move *(in+acc* into*)*. **(b)** *(Einmarsch)* entry *(in +acc* into*)*. **(c)** *(fig: von Stimmung, Winter etc)* advent. **der Frühling** *etc* **hält seinen ~** spring *etc* is coming. **(d)** *(von Steuern)* collection; *(von Banknoten)* withdrawal.

Einzugs-: **~bereich** *m* catchment area; **~feier** *f* house-warming (party).

einzwängen *vt sep (lit)* to squeeze *or* jam in; *(fig) jdn* to constrict.

Eis *nt* - **(a)** *no pl* ice. **zu ~ gefrieren** to freeze, to turn to ice; **das ~ brechen** *(fig)* to break the ice; **etw auf ~ legen** *(fig col)* to put sth on ice *or* into cold storage. **(b)** *(Speise~)* ice(-cream). **~ am Stiel** ice(d)-lolly *(Brit)*, popsicle ® *(US)*.

Eis-: **~bahn** *f* ice-rink; **~bär** *m* polar bear; **~becher** *m* sundae; **e~bedeckt** *adj* ice-covered; **~bein** *nt (Cook)* knuckle of pork; **~berg** *m* iceberg; **die Spitze des ~bergs** *(fig)* the tip of the iceberg; **~beutel** *m* ice pack; **~block** *m* block of ice; **~blume** *f usu pl* frost pattern; **~brecher** *m* icebreaker.

Eischnee *m (Cook)* beaten white of egg.

Eis-: **~creme** *f* ice(-cream); **~decke** *f* sheet of ice; **~diele** *f* ice-cream parlour *(Brit) or* parlor *(US)*.

Eisen *nt* - iron. **mehrere ~ im Feuer haben** *(fig)* to have more than one iron in the fire; **zum alten ~ gehören** *(fig)* to be on the scrap heap; **man muß das ~ schmieden, solange es heiß ist** *(Prov)* strike while the iron is hot *(Prov)*.

Eisenbahn *f* railway *(Brit)*, railroad *(US)*; *(~wesen)* railways *(Brit) pl*, railroad *(US)*; *(col: Zug)* train; *(Spielzeug~)* train set. **es ist (aller) höchste ~** *(col)* it's getting late.

Eisenbahn-: **~abteil** *nt* compartment; **~brücke** *f* railway *(Brit) or* railroad *(US)* bridge.

Eisenbahner(in *f*) *m* - railwayman *(Brit)*, railway employee *(Brit)*, railroader *(US)*.

Eisenbahn-: **~fähre** *f* train ferry; **~fahrkarte** *f* rail *or* train ticket; **~fahrt** *f* train *or* rail ride; **~netz** *nt* rail network; **~schaffner** *m* (railway) guard *(Brit)*, (railroad) conductor *(US)*; **~strecke** *f* railway line *(Brit)*, railroad *(US)*; **~überführung** *f* footbridge; **~wagen** *m* railway *(Brit) or* railroad *(US)* carriage; **~waggon** *m (Güter~)* goods wagon.

Eisen-: **~erz** *nt* iron ore; **e~haltig** *adj Gestein* iron-bearing; **das Wasser ist e~haltig** the water contains iron; **~mangel** *m* iron deficiency; **~oxyd** *nt* ferric oxide; **~präparat** *nt (Med)* iron tonic/tablets *pl*; **~stange** *f* iron bar; **e~verarbeitend** *adj attr* iron processing; **~waren** *pl* ironmongery *sing (Brit)*, hardware *sing (US)*; **~warenhandlung** *f* ironmonger's *(Brit)*, hardware store *(US)*; **~zeit** *f* Iron Age.

eisern *adj* **(a)** *attr (aus Eisen)* iron. **der E~e Vorhang** the Iron Curtain; **~e Lunge** *(Med)* iron lung. **(b)** *Disziplin, Wille* iron *attr; Energie* unflagging; *Ruhe* unshakeable. **~e Gesundheit** iron constitution; **er schwieg ~** he remained resolutely silent; **er ist ~ bei seinem Entschluß geblieben** he stuck firmly to his decision; **mit ~er**

Faust with an iron hand; **in etw** *(dat)* ~ **sein** to be adamant about sth; **mit ~em Besen kehren** to make a clean sweep; ~ **sparen** to save resolutely. **(c)** *attr Reserve* emergency; *Ration auch* iron.

Eiseskälte *f* icy cold.

Eis-: **~fach** *nt* freezer compartment, ice-box; **~fläche** *f* (surface of the) ice; **e~frei** *adj* free of ice *pred;* **e~gekühlt** *adj* chilled; **~hockey** *nt* ice hockey, hockey *(US).*

eisig *adj (lit, fig)* icy.

Eis-: **~kaffee** *m* iced coffee; **e~kalt** *adj* **(a)** icy-cold; **(b)** *(fig) (abweisend)* icy, cold; *(kalt und berechnend)* cold-blooded, cold and calculating; *(dreist)* cool; **~kunstlauf** *m* figure skating; **~kunstläufer** *m* figure skater; **~lauf** *m* ice-skating; **e~laufen** *vi sep irreg aux sein* to ice-skate; **~läufer** *m* ice-skater; **~meer** *nt* polar sea; **Nördliches/Südliches ~meer** Arctic/Antarctic Ocean; **~pickel** *m* ice axe *(Brit) or* ax *(US),* ice pick.

Eisprung *m (Physiol)* ovulation *no art.*

Eis-: **~regen** *m* sleet; **~revue** *f* ice revue, ice show; **~schießen** *nt* curling; **~schmelze** *f* thaw; **~schnellauf** *m* speed skating; **~schnelläufer** *m* speed skater; **~scholle** *f* ice floe; **~schrank** *m* refrigerator; **~tanz** *m* ice-dancing; **~torte** *f* ice-cream cake; **~verkäufer** *m* ice-cream seller *or* man *(col);* **~vogel** *m (Orn)* kingfisher; **~würfel** *m* ice cube; **~zapfen** *m* icicle; **~zeit** *f* Ice Age.

eitel *adj* vain; *(eingebildet auch)* conceited.

Eitelkeit *f* vanity.

Eiter *m no pl* pus.

eit(e)rig *adj Ausfluß* purulent; *Wunde* festering.

eitern *vi* to discharge pus, to suppurate.

Eiweiß *nt* (egg-)white, white of egg; *(Chem)* protein.

Eiweiß-: **~gehalt** *m* protein content; **e~haltig** *adj* **Fleisch ist sehr e~haltig** meat is high in protein *or* contains a lot of protein; **~mangel** *m* protein deficiency; **~präparat** *nt* protein preparation.

Eizelle *f (Biol)* egg cell.

Ejakulation *f* ejaculation.

Ekel[1] *m no pl* disgust, revulsion; *(Übelkeit)* nausea. **vor jdm/etw einen ~ haben** to loathe sb/sth; **dabei empfinde ich ~** it gives me a feeling of disgust *etc;* **er hat das Essen vor ~ ausgespuckt** he spat out the food in disgust; **er konnte es vor ~ nicht tun** he was too disgusted to do it.

Ekel[2] *nt* **-** *(col)* obnoxious person, horror *(col).*

ekel|erregend *adj* nauseating, revolting.

ekelhaft, ek(e)lig *adj* disgusting, revolting; *(col) Problem, Chef* nasty *(col),* horrible.

ekeln 1 *vt* to disgust, to revolt. **2** *vt impers* **es ekelt mich vor diesem Anblick** the sight of it fills me with disgust *or* revulsion. **3** *vr* to feel disgusted. **sich vor etw** *(dat)* ~ to find sth disgusting.

EKG [eːkaːˈgeː] *nt* **-s** = **Elektrokardiogramm** ECG.

Eklat [eˈkla(ː)] *m* **-s** *(geh: Aufsehen)* sensation.

eklatant *adj Fall* sensational; *Beispiel* striking; *Verletzung* flagrant.

eklig *adj* = **ek(e)lig.**

Eklipse *f* **-n** eclipse.

Ekstase *f* **-n** ecstasy. **in ~ geraten** to go into ecstasies; **jdn in ~ versetzen** to send sb into ecstasies.

ekstatisch *adj* ecstatic.

Ekzem *nt* **-e** *(Med)* eczema.

Elan *m no pl* élan, zest.

elastisch *adj* elastic; *Gang, Metall, Holz* springy; *(fig) Muskel, Mensch* strong and supple; *(flexibel)* flexible, elastic.

Elastizität *f siehe* **elastisch** elasticity; springiness; flexibility. **die ~ seines Körpers** the supple strength of his body.

Elch *m* **-e** elk.

Elefant *m* elephant. **wie ein ~ im Porzellanladen** *(col)* like a bull in a china shop *(prov).*

elegant *adj* elegant.

Eleganz *f* elegance.

Elegie *f* elegy.

elektrifizieren* *vt* to electrify.

Elektrifizierung *f* electrification.

Elektrik *f (Anlagen)* electrical equipment.

Elektriker(in *f)* *m* **-** electrician.

elektrisch *adj* electric; *Entladung, Widerstand* electrical. **~e Geräte** electrical appliances; **~er Schlag/Strom** electric shock/current; **der ~e Stuhl** the electric chair; **wir kochen/heizen ~** we cook/heat by electricity.

Elektrische *f* **-n** *(dated)* tram, streetcar *(US).*

elektrisieren* **1** *vt (lit, fig)* to electrify. **ich habe mich elektrisiert** I got an electric shock; **wie elektrisiert** (as if) electrified. **2** *vi* to give an electric shock.

Elektrizität *f* electricity.

Elektrizitätswerk *nt* (electric) power station; *(Gesellschaft)* electric power company, Electricity (Generating) Board *(Brit).*

Elektro- [eˈlɛktro] *in cpds* electro- *(auch Sci),* electric; **~artikel** *m* electrical appliance.

Elektrode *f* **-n** electrode.

Elektro-: **~gerät** *nt* electrical appliance; **~geschäft** *nt* electrical shop *(Brit) or* store *(US);* **~herd** *m* electric cooker; **~kardiogramm** *nt (Med)* electrocardiogram; **~magnet** *m* electromagnet; **~mechaniker** *m* electrician; **e~mechanisch** *adj* electromechanical; **~motor** *m* electric motor.

Elektron *nt* **-en** [elɛkˈtroːnən] electron.

Elektronen-: **~(ge)hirn** *nt* electronic brain; **~rechner** *m* (electronic) computer.

Elektronik *f* electronics *sing; (Teile)* electronics *pl.*

elektronisch *adj* electronic.

Elektro-: **~rasierer** *m* electric shaver *or* razor; **~schock** *m (Med)* electric shock, electroshock; **~technik** *f* electrical engineering; **~techniker** *m* electrician; *(Ingenieur)* electrical engineer; **e~technisch** *adj* electrical.

Element *nt* element; *(Elec)* cell. **kriminelle ~e** *(pej)* criminal elements; **in seinem ~ sein** to be in one's element.

elementar *adj (grundlegend)* elementary; *Gewalt, Trieb* elemental.

Elementarteilchen *nt (Phys)* elementary particle.

elend *adj* **(a)** wretched, miserable; *(krank)* wretched, awful. **mir ist ganz ~** I feel really awful. **(b)** *(col: furchtbar) Hunger, Wetter* awful. **ich habe ~ gefroren** I was miserably cold.

Elend *nt no pl (Unglück, Not)* misery, distress; *(Verwahrlosung)* squalor; *(Armut)* poverty. **(wie) ein Häufchen ~** *(col)* (looking) a picture of misery; **da kann man das heulende ~ kriegen** *(col)* it's enough to make you scream *(col).*

elendig(lich) *adv (geh)* wretchedly. **~ zugrunde gehen** to come to a wretched end.

Elendsviertel *nt* slums *pl,* slum area.

elf *num* eleven; *siehe* **vier.**

Elf *f* **-en** *(Sport)* team, eleven.

Elfe *f* **-n** elf.

Elfenbein *nt* ivory.

elfenbeine(r)n *adj* ivory.

Elfenbein-: **~küste** *f* Ivory Coast; **~turm** *m (fig)* ivory tower.

elfmal *adv* eleven times; *siehe* **viermal.**

Elfmeter *m (Ftbl)* penalty (kick) *(für* to, for*).* **einen ~ schießen** to take a penalty.

Elfmeter-: **~punkt** *m (Ftbl)* penalty spot; **~schießen** *nt (Ftbl)* sudden-death play-off; **durch ~schießen entschieden** decided on penalties; **~schütze** *m (Ftbl)* penalty-taker.

Elftel *nt* **-** eleventh.

elfte(r, s) *adj* eleventh; *siehe* **vierte(r, s).**

eliminieren* *vt* to eliminate.

elitär 1 *adj* elitist. **2** *adv* in an elitist fashion.

Elite *f* **-n** elite.

Elitetruppe *f (Mil)* crack *or* elite troops *pl.*

Elixier *nt* **-e** elixir *(liter)*, tonic.

Elle *f* **-n** *(Anat)* ulna *(spec)*. **alles mit der gleichen ~ messen** *(fig)* to measure everything by the same yardstick.

Ell(en)bogen *m* **-** elbow. **die ~ gebrauchen** *(fig)* to be pushy *(col) or* ruthless.

Ell(en)bogenfreiheit *f (fig)* elbow room.

ellenlang *adj (fig col)* incredibly long *(col)*; *Kerl* incredibly tall *(col)*.

Ellipse *f* **-n** *(Math)* ellipse.

elliptisch *adj (Math)* elliptic(al).

Elsaß *nt, gen* **-** *or* **-sses das ~** Alsace.

Elsässer(in *f***)** *m* **-** Alsatian, inhabitant of Alsace.

Elsässer, elsässisch *adj* Alsatian.

Elster *f* **-n** magpie. **eine diebische ~ sein** *(fig)* to be a thief.

elterlich *adj* parental.

Eltern *pl* parents *pl.* **nicht von schlechten ~ sein** *(col)* to be quite something *(col)*.

Eltern-: ~abend *m (Sch)* parents' evening; **~haus** *nt (lit, fig)* (parental) home; **e~los** *adj* orphaned; **~sprechtag** *m* open day (for parents); **~teil** *m* parent.

Email [e'mai] *nt* **-s, Emaille** [e'maljə] *f* **-n** enamel.

emaillieren* [ema'ji:rən] *vt* to enamel.

Emanze *f* **-n** *(usu pej)* women's libber *(col)*.

Emanzipation *f* emancipation.

emanzipatorisch *adj* emancipatory.

emanzipieren* *vr* to emancipate oneself.

Embargo *nt* **-s** embargo.

Emblem *nt* **-e** emblem.

Embryo *m* **-s** *or* **-nen** [-y'o:nən] embryo.

embryonal *adj attr (Biol, fig)* embryonic.

Emigrant(in *f***)** *m* emigrant; *(politisch)* émigré.

Emigration *f* emigration. **in der ~ leben** to live in self-imposed exile.

emigrieren* *vi aux sein* to emigrate.

eminent *adj (geh) Person* eminent. **von ~er Bedeutung** of the utmost significance.

Eminenz *f (Eccl)* **(Seine) ~ (His) Eminence.**

Emirat *nt* emirate.

Emission *f* **(a)** *(Fin)* issue. **(b)** *(Phys)* emission.

Emotion *f* emotion.

emotional *adj* emotional; *Ausdrucksweise* emotive.

emotions-: ~geladen *adj* emotionally-charged; **~los** *adj* free of emotion, unemotional.

empfahl *pret of* **empfehlen.**

empfand *pret of* **empfinden.**

Empfang *m* **¨e** reception *(auch Rad, TV)*; *(von Brief, Ware etc)* receipt. **etw in ~ nehmen** to receive sth; *(Comm)* to take delivery of sth; **(zahlbar) nach/bei ~** *(+gen)* (payable) on receipt (of).

empfangen *pret* **empfing,** *ptp* **~** *vt* to receive *(auch Rad, TV)*; *(begrüßen)* to greet, to receive *(form)*; *(herzlich)* to welcome; *(abholen) Besuch* to meet.

Empfänger(in *f***)** *m* **-** recipient, receiver *(auch Rad, TV)*; *(Adressat)* addressee; *(Waren~)* consignee. **~ unbekannt** *(auf Briefen)* not known at this address.

empfänglich *adj (aufnahmebereit)* receptive *(für* to*)*; *(anfällig)* susceptible *(für* to*)*.

Empfänglichkeit *f siehe adj* receptivity; susceptibility.

Empfängnis *f* conception.

Empfängnis-: e~verhütend *adj* contraceptive; **e~verhütende Mittel** *pl* contraceptives *pl;* **~verhütung** *f* contraception.

Empfangs-: ~bereich *m (Rad, TV)* reception area; **~bestätigung** *f* (acknowledgment of) receipt; **~chef** *m (von Hotel)* head porter; **~dame** *f* receptionist; **~gerät** *nt* (radio/TV) set, receiver; **~störung** *f (Rad, TV)* interference *no pl.*

empfehlen *pret* **empfahl,** *ptp* **empfohlen 1** *vt* **(jdm) etw/jdn ~** to recommend sth/sb (to sb); **jdm ~, etw zu tun** to recommend *or* advise sb to do sth; **ich würde dir Vorsicht/Geduld ~** I would recommend caution/patience. **2** *vr* **(a)** to recommend itself/oneself. **sich als Experte** *etc* **~** to offer one's services as an expert *etc;* **es empfiehlt sich, das zu tun** it is advisable to do that. **(b)** *(dated, hum: sich verabschieden)* to take one's leave. **ich empfehle mich!** I'll take my leave.

empfehlenswert *adj* to be recommended.

Empfehlung *f* recommendation; *(Referenz)* reference; *(form: Gruß)* regards *pl.* **auf ~ von** on the recommendation of; **mit freundlichen ~en** *(am Briefende)* with best regards.

Empfehlungsschreiben *nt* letter of recommendation, testimonial.

empfinden *pret* **empfand,** *ptp* **empfunden** *vt* to feel. **etw als Beleidigung ~** to find sth insulting; **jdn als Störenfried ~** to see sb as a troublemaker.

Empfinden *nt no pl* feeling. **meinem ~ nach** to my mind.

empfindlich *adj* **(a)** sensitive *(auch Phot, Tech)*; *Gesundheit, Stoff* delicate; *(leicht reizbar)* touchy *(col)*. **~ reagieren** to be sensitive *(auf+acc* to*)*; **~e Stelle** *(lit)* sensitive spot; *(fig auch)* sore point. **(b)** *Verlust, Kälte, Strafe* severe. **deine Kritik hat ihn ~ getroffen** your criticism cut him to the quick.

Empfindlichkeit *f siehe adj (a)* sensitivity *(auch Phot, Tech)*; delicateness; touchiness *(col)*.

empfindsam *adj Mensch* sensitive.

Empfindung *f* feeling; *(Sinnes~ auch)* sensation.

empfing *pret of* **empfangen.**

empfohlen *ptp of* **empfehlen.**

empfunden *ptp of* **empfinden.**

empirisch *adj* empirical.

empor *adv (liter)* upwards, up.

empor-: ~arbeiten *vr sep (geh)* to work one's way up; **~blicken** *vi sep (liter: lit, fig)* to look up *(zu* to*)*.

Empore *f* **-n** *(Archit)* gallery.

empören* 1 *vt* to outrage; *siehe* **empört. 2** *vr* to be indignant *or* outraged *(über +acc* at*)*.

empörend *adj* outrageous.

Empor-: e~heben *vt sep irreg (geh)* to raise; **e~kommen** *vi sep irreg aux sein (geh)* to rise (up); *(fig) (aufkommen)* to come to the fore; *(vorankommen)* to go up in the world; **~kömmling** *m (pej)* upstart; **e~ragen** *vi sep aux haben or sein (geh: lit, fig)* to tower *(über+acc* above*)*; **e~steigen** *sep irreg aux sein (geh) vti* to climb (up); *(fig: Karriere machen)* to climb, to rise.

empört *adj* indignant, outraged *(über +acc* at*)*.

Empörung *f no pl (Entrüstung)* indignation *(über +acc* at*)*. **über etw in ~ geraten** to get indignant about sth.

emsig *adj* busy, industrious; *Treiben* bustling.

Emsigkeit *f siehe adj* industriousness; bustle.

Emu *m* **-s** emu.

End- *in cpds* final; **~abnehmer** *m* buyer; **~abrechnung** *f* final account; **~betrag** *m* final amount.

Ende *nt* **-n** end; *(Ergebnis)* outcome, result; *(Ausgang eines Films, Romans etc)* ending. **~ Mai/der Woche** at the end of May/the week; **er ist ~ vierzig** he is in his late forties; **er wohnt am ~ der Welt** *(col)* he lives at the back of beyond; **bis ans ~ der Welt** to the ends of the earth; **letzten ~es** in the end, at the end of the day; **einer Sache** *(dat)* **ein ~ machen** to put an end to sth; **damit muß es jetzt ein ~ haben** there has to be an end to this now, this must stop now; **ein ~ nehmen** to come to an end; **ein böses ~ nehmen** to come to a bad end; **... und kein ~ ...** with no end in sight, ... without end; **es ist noch ein gutes** *or* **ganzes ~** *(col)* there's still quite a way to go (yet); **am ~** at the end; *(schließlich)* in the end; *(col: möglicherweise)* perhaps; **am ~ sein** *(fig)* to be at the end of one's tether; **ich bin mit meiner Weisheit am ~** I'm at my wit's end; **meine Geduld ist am ~** my patience is at an end; **zu ~** finished, over; **etw zu ~ führen** to finish (off) sth; **ein Buch zu ~ lesen** to finish (reading) a book; **zu ~ gehen** to come to an end; *(Vorräte)* to run out; **~ gut, alles gut** *(Prov)* all's well that ends well *(Prov)*.

End|effekt *m*: **im ~** *(col)* in the final analysis, at the end of the day.

enden *vi* to end, to finish; *(Zug)* to terminate; *(sterben)* to meet one's end. **auf etw** *(acc)* **~** *(Wort)* to end with sth; **der Streit endete vor Gericht** the quarrel ended up in court; **wie wird das noch mit ihm ~?** what will become of him?; **das wird böse ~!** no good will come of it!

End|ergebnis *nt* final result.

endgültig *adj* final; *Antwort* definite; *Fassung* definitive.

Endivie [-viə] *f* endive.

End-: ~lagerung *f* permanent disposal; **~lauf** *m* final.

endlich 1 *adv* finally, at last; *(am Ende)* eventually, in the end. **hör ~ damit auf!** will you stop that!; **komm doch ~!** come on! **2** *adj (Math, Philos)* finite.

endlos *adj* endless. **ich mußte ~ lange warten** I had to wait for an interminably long time.

Endlosigkeit *f* endlessness.

End-: ~phase *f* final stage(s *pl*); **~produkt** *nt* end *or* final product; **~punkt** *m (lit, fig)* end.

Endrunde *f (Sport)* finals *pl; (fig)* final round.

Endrunden-: ~spiel *nt* final (match); **~teilnehmer** *m* finalist.

End-: ~spiel *nt (Sport)* final; *(Chess)* end game; **~spurt** *m (Sport, fig)* final spurt; **~station** *f (Rail etc)* terminus; *(fig)* end of the line; **~stufe** *f* final stage; **~summe** *f* (sum) total.

Endung *f (Gram)* ending.

End-: ~verbraucher *m* consumer, end-user; **~ziel** *nt* ultimate goal; **~zweck** *m* ultimate purpose.

Energie *f (Sci, fig)* energy. **mit ganzer ~** with all one's energy.

Energie-: ~bedarf *m* energy requirement; **~gewinnung** *f* generation of energy; **~krise** *f* energy crisis; **e~los** *adj* lacking in energy; **~politik** *f* energy policy/politics *sing or pl;* **~träger** *m* source of energy; **~verbrauch** *m* energy consumption; **~versorgung** *f* supply of energy; **~zufuhr** *f* energy supply.

energisch *adj (entschlossen, streng)* forceful, firm; *Protest* energetic, strong. **~ durchgreifen** to take vigorous *or* firm action; **etw ~ verteidigen** to defend sth vigorously; **etw ~ dementieren** to deny sth strenuously.

eng *adj* **(a)** *(lit, fig)* narrow; *Raum* cramped; *Kleidung* tight, close-fitting. **ein Kleid ~er machen** to take a dress in; **im ~eren Sinne** in the narrow sense; **in die ~ere Wahl kommen** to be short-listed. **(b)** *(nah, vertraut)* close. **~ nebeneinander** close together; **eine Feier im ~sten Kreise** a small party for close friends; **mit jdm ~ befreundet sein** to be a close friend of sb.

Engagement [ãgaʒə'mã:] *nt* **-s (a)** *no pl* commitment *(für* to*)*. **(b)** *(Theat)* engagement.

engagieren* [ãga'ʒi:rən] **1** *vt* to engage. **2** *vr* to be/become committed *(für* to*)*; *(in einer Bekanntschaft)* to become involved. **er hat sich sehr dafür engagiert, daß ...** he completely committed himself to ...; **ein engagierter Film** a (socially/politically) committed film.

Enge *f* **-n (a)** *no pl (lit, fig)* narrowness; *(von Wohnung)* crampedness; *(Gedrängtheit)* crush; *(von Kleid)* tightness. **(b)** *(Engpaß)* pass, defile. **jdn in die ~ treiben** *(fig)* to drive sb into a corner.

Engel *m* **-** *(lit, fig)* angel. **ein guter ~** *(fig)* a guardian angel; **wir sind alle keine ~** *(prov)* none of us is perfect.

Engelmacher(in *f***)** *m (euph col)* backstreet abortionist.

Engels-: ~geduld *f* **sie hat eine ~geduld** she has the patience of a saint; **~haar** *nt* angel's hair, *type of Christmas tree decoration;* **~zungen** *pl*: **(wie) mit ~zungen reden** to use all one's powers of persuasion.

Eng-: e~herzig *adj* petty, hidebound; **~herzigkeit** *f* pettiness.

England *nt* England.

Engländer *m* **- (a)** Englishman; English boy. **die ~** *pl* the English, the Britishers *(US)*; **er ist ~** he's English. **(b)** *(Tech)* adjustable spanner, monkey wrench.

Engländerin *f* Englishwoman; English girl.

englisch 1 *adj* English; *siehe* **deutsch. 2** *adv (Cook)* rare.

Englisch(e) *nt decl as adj* English; *siehe* **Deutsch(e).**

englisch-: ~-deutsch *etc adj* Anglo-German *etc*; *Wörterbuch* English-German *etc*; **~sprachig** *adj Gebiet* English-speaking.

Eng-: e~maschig *adj* close-meshed; **~paß** *m* (narrow) pass, defile; *(Mot, fig)* bottleneck.

en gros [ã'gro] *adv* wholesale.

engstirnig *adj* narrow-minded.

Enkel *m* **-** *(~kind)* grandchild; *(~sohn)* grandson; *(Nachfahr)* descendant.

Enkelin *f* granddaughter.

Enkel-: ~kind *nt* grandchild; **~sohn** *m* grandson; **~tochter** *f* granddaughter.

enorm *adj* enormous; *(col: herrlich, kolossal)* tremendous *(col)*. **er verdient ~ viel (Geld)** *(col)* he earns an enormous amount (of money).

en passant [ãpɑ'sã] *adv* en passant, in passing.

Ensemble [ã'sãbl] *nt* **-s** ensemble; *(Besetzung)* cast.

ent|arten* *vi aux sein* to degenerate *(zu* into*)*.

ent|artet *adj* degenerate.

Ent|artung *f* degeneration.

entbehren* *vt (vermissen)* to miss; *(auch vi: verzichten)* to do without; *(zur Verfügung stellen)* to spare. **wir können ihn heute nicht ~** we cannot spare him today.

entbehrlich *adj* dispensable.

Entbehrung *f* privation, deprivation. **~en auf sich** *(acc)* **nehmen** to make sacrifices.

entbinden* *irreg* **1** *vt* **(a)** *Frau* to deliver. **(b)** *(von Amt etc)* to release *(von* from*)*. **2** *vi (Frau)* to give birth.

Entbindung *f* delivery, birth; *(von Amt etc)* release.

Entbindungsstation *f* maternity ward.

entblößen* *vt (form)* to expose *(auch Mil)*; *Kopf* to bare; *(fig) sein Innenleben* to lay bare.

entblößt *adj* bare.

entbrennen* *vi irreg aux sein (liter) (Kampf, Streit)* to flare up; *(Liebe)* to be aroused.

entdecken* *vt* to discover; *Fehler auch* to detect; *(erspähen)* to spot.

Entdecker(in *f***)** *m* **-** discoverer.

Entdeckung *f* discovery; *(von Fehler auch)* detection.

Ente *f* **-n (a)** duck. **(b)** *(col) (Falschmeldung)* hoax, false report; *(Aut)* Citroën 2CV, deux-chevaux.

ent|ehren* *vt* to dishonour *(Brit)*, to dishonor *(US)*.

ent|eignen* *vt* to dispossess; *Besitz* to expropriate.

Ent|eignung *f siehe vt* dispossession; expropriation.

ent|eisen* *vt* to de-ice; *Kühlschrank* to defrost.

Enten-: ~braten *m* roast duck; **~ei** *nt* duck's egg.

ent|erben* *vt* to disinherit.

Enterhaken *m* grappling iron *or* hook.

Enterich *m* drake.

entern *(Naut)* *vti Schiff* to board.
entfachen* *vt (geh) Feuer* to kindle; *Krieg, Streit* to provoke.
entfahren* *vi irreg aux sein* **jdm ~** to escape sb's lips.
entfallen* *vi irreg aux sein+dat* **(a) der Name ist mir ~** the name has slipped my mind. **(b)** *(nicht in Betracht kommen)* not to apply; *(wegfallen)* to be dropped. **(c) auf jdn/etw ~** *(Geld, Kosten)* to be allotted to sb/sth; **auf jeden ~ 100 Mark** each person will receive/pay 100 marks.
entfalten* **1** *vt* **(a)** *(lit)* to unfold. **(b)** *(fig)* *(entwickeln)* to develop; *(darlegen) Plan* to unfold; *(zeigen) Pracht* to display. **2** *vr (Knospe, Blüte)* to open, to unfold; *(fig)* to develop; *(Schönheit)* to blossom (out). **hier kann ich mich nicht ~** I can't make full use of my abilities here.
Entfaltung *f* unfolding *(auch von Plan)*; *(Entwicklung)* development; *(von Schönheit)* blossoming; *(von Prunk, Tatkraft)* display. **zur ~ kommen** to develop; *(Schönheit)* to blossom.
entfärben* *vt* to take the colour *(Brit)* *or* color *(US)* out of.
entfernen* **1** *vt* to remove *(von, aus* from*)*. **das entfernt uns (weit) vom Thema** that takes us a long way from our subject. **2** *vr* **sich (von** *or* **aus etw) ~** *(weggehen)* to go away (from sth), to leave (sth); **sich unerlaubt von der Truppe ~** *(Mil)* to go absent without leave; **sich zu weit ~** to go too far away; **sich von jdm ~** *(fig)* to become estranged from sb.
entfernt **1** *adj Ort, Verwandter* distant; *Ähnlichkeit* remote. **10 km ~ von** 10 km (away) from. **2** *adv* remotely, slightly. **~ verwandt** distantly related; **das hat nur ~ mit dieser Angelegenheit zu tun** that is only vaguely related with this matter; **nicht im ~esten!** not in the slightest.
Entfernung *f* **(a)** distance. **aus kurzer/großer ~ (schießen)** (to fire) from close/long range; **aus einiger ~** from a distance; **in einiger ~** at a distance. **(b)** *(das Entfernen)* removal. **unerlaubte ~ von der Truppe** absence without leave.
Enfernungsmesser *m* - *(Phot)* rangefinder.
entfesseln* *vt (fig)* to unleash.
entfesselt *adj* unleashed; *Trieb* unbridled; *Naturgewalten* raging. **vor Begeisterung ~** wild with enthusiasm.
entfetten* *vt* to de-grease.
Entfettungskur *f* weight-reducing course.
entflammbar *adj* inflammable.
entflammen* **1** *vt (fig)* to (a)rouse. **2** *vi aux sein* to burst into flames; *(fig)* *(Streit)* to flare up; *(Leidenschaft)* to be (a)roused *or* inflamed. **in Liebe ~** to fall passionately in love.
entfliegen* *vi irreg aux sein* to fly away, to escape *(dat or aus* from*)*.
entfliehen* *vi irreg aux sein (geh)* to escape, to flee *(dat or aus* from*)*.
entfremden* **1** *vt* to alienate *(auch Sociol, Philos)*, to estrange. **jdn einer Person/Sache** *(dat)* **~** to alienate *or* estrange sb from sb/sth. **2** *vr* to become alienated *or* estranged *(dat* from*)*.
Entfremdung *f* alienation, estrangement.
entfrosten* *vt* to defrost.
Entfroster *m* - defroster.
entführen* *vt jdn* to abduct, to kidnap; *Beute etc* to carry off; *Flugzeug* to hijack; *(hum col: wegnehmen)* to make off with.
Entführer(in *f)* *m* abductor, kidnapper; *(Flugzeug~ etc)* hijacker.
Entführung *f siehe vt* abduction, kidnapping; hijack(ing).
entgegen **1** *adv (liter)* **der Sonne/der Zukunft** *etc* **~!** on towards the sun/future *etc*! **2** *prep+dat* **~ meiner Bitte** contrary to my request.
entgegenbringen *vt sep irreg* **jdm etw ~** *(fig) Achtung, Verständnis etc* to show sth for sb.
entgegengehen *vi sep irreg aux sein +dat* to go towards, to approach; *(um jdn zu treffen)* to go to meet; *(fig) einer Gefahr, dem Tode, der Zukunft* to face. **dem Ende ~** *(Leben, Krieg)* to approach its end; **Schwierigkeiten ~** to be heading for difficulties.
entgegengesetzt *adj Richtung etc* opposite. **einander ~e Interessen/Meinungen** opposing *or* conflicting interests/views; **genau ~ denken/handeln** to think/do exactly the opposite.
entgegenhalten *vt sep irreg +dat* **(a)** *(lit)* **jdm etw ~** to hold sth out towards sb. **(b)** *(fig)* **einer Sache ~, daß ...** to object to sth that ...; **dem hielt sie entgegen, daß ...** she made the objection that ...
entgegenkommen *vi sep irreg aux sein+dat* to come towards, to approach; *(fig)* to accommodate. **das kommt unseren Plänen sehr entgegen** that fits in very well with our plans.
Entgegenkommen *nt (Gefälligkeit)* obligingness; *(Zugeständnis)* concession.
entgegenkommend *adj (fig)* obliging, accommodating.
Entgegennahme *f no pl (form)* *(Empfang)* receipt; *(Annahme)* acceptance.
entgegennehmen *vt sep irreg (empfangen)* to receive; *(annehmen)* to accept.
entgegensehen *vi sep irreg (fig)* **einer Sache** *(dat)* **~** to await sth; *(freudig)* to look forward to sth; **einer Sache ~ müssen** to have to expect sth.
entgegensetzen *vt sep +dat* **etw einer Sache ~** to set sth against sth; **wir können diesen Forderungen nichts ~** we have nothing to counter these claims with; **dem habe ich entgegenzusetzen, daß ...** against that I'd like to say that ...; **jdm/einer Sache Widerstand ~** to put up resistance to sb/sth; *siehe* **entgegengesetzt.**
entgegenstehen *vi sep irreg +dat (fig)* to stand in the way of, to be an obstacle to. **dem steht nichts entgegen** there's no objection to that.
entgegenstellen *sep +dat* **1** *vt* = **entgegensetzen. 2** *vr* **sich jdm/einer Sache ~** to oppose sb/sth.
entgegentreten *vi sep irreg aux sein +dat einer Politik* to oppose; *Behauptungen* to counter; *einer Gefahr, Unsitten* to take steps against.
entgegenwirken *vi sep +dat* to counteract.
entgegnen* *vti* to reply; *(kurz, barsch)* to retort *(auf+acc* to*)*.
Entgegnung *f* reply; *(kurz, barsch)* retort.
entgehen* *vi irreg aux sein +dat* **(a)** *(entkommen)* to escape; *Verfolgern, dem Feind* to escape from. **(b)** *(fig: nicht bemerkt werden)* **dieser Fehler ist mir entgangen** I missed this mistake; **ihr entgeht nichts** she doesn't miss a thing; **sich** *(dat)* **etw ~ lassen** to miss sth.
entgeistert *adj* dumbfounded.
Entgelt *nt no pl (form)* remuneration *(form)*. **gegen ~** for a fee.
entgleisen* *vi aux sein* **(a)** *(Rail)* to be derailed. **(b)** *(fig: Mensch)* to misbehave.
Entgleisung *f* derailment; *(fig)* faux pas, clanger *(col)*.
entgräten* *vt Fisch* to fillet, to bone.
enthaaren* *vt* to remove unwanted hair from.
enthalten* *irreg* **1** *vt* to contain. **(mit) ~ sein in** *(+dat)* to be included in. **2** *vr* **(a)** *(geh)* **sich einer Sache** *(gen)* **~** to abstain from sth; **sich einer Bemerkung nicht ~ können** to be unable to refrain from making a remark. **(b) sich (der Stimme) ~** to abstain.
enthaltsam *adj* abstemious; *(geschlechtlich)* chaste.
Enthaltsamkeit *f siehe adj* abstemiousness; chastity.
Enthaltung *f* abstinence; *(Stimm~)* abstention.
enthärten* *vt Wasser* to soften; *Metall* to anneal.
enthaupten* *vt* to decapitate; *(als Hinrichtung auch)* to behead.

Enthauptung *f siehe vt* decapitation; beheading.
enthäuten* *vt* to skin.
entheben* *vt irreg* **jdn einer Sache** *(gen)* ~ to relieve sb of sth.
enthemmen* *vti* **jdn** ~ to make sb lose his inhibitions; **Alkohol wirkt ~d** alcohol has a disinhibiting effect.
enthüllen* *vt* to reveal; *Skandal, Lüge auch* to expose; *Denkmal* to unveil.
Enthüllung *f siehe vt* revealing; exposure; unveiling. **noch eine sensationelle** ~ another sensational revelation *or* disclosure.
Enthusiasmus *m* enthusiasm.
Enthusiast(in *f*) *m* enthusiast.
enthusiastisch *adj* enthusiastic.
entjungfern* *vt* to deflower.
entkalken* *vt* to decalcify.
entkernen* *vt Orangen etc* to remove the pips from; *Kernobst* to core; *Steinobst* to stone.
entkleiden* *vtr (geh)* to undress.
entkommen* *vi irreg aux sein* to escape, to get away *(+dat, aus* from*)*.
Entkommen *nt* escape.
entkorken* *vt Flasche* to uncork.
entkräften* *vt (schwächen)* to weaken; *(erschöpfen)* to exhaust; *(fig: widerlegen) Behauptung* to invalidate.
Entkräftung *f (Erschöpfung)* exhaustion; *(Widerlegung)* invalidation.
entkrampfen* *vt (fig)* to relax, to ease.
Entkrampfung *f (fig)* relaxation, easing.
entladen* *irreg* **1** *vt* to unload; *Batterie etc* to discharge. **2** *vr (Gewitter)* to break; *(elektrische Spannung, Batterie, Waffe)* to discharge; *(Sprengladung)* to explode; *(fig) (Emotion)* to vent itself; *(Spannung)* to release itself.
Entladung *f* **(a)** *(das Entladen)* unloading. **(b)** *siehe vr* breaking; discharge; explosion; venting; release.
entlang 1 *prep* along. ~ **dem Fluß, den Fluß** ~ along the river. **2** *adv* along. **hier** ~ this way.
entlang- *pref* along; **~gehen** *vti sep irreg aux sein* to walk along, to go along.
enlarven* *vt (fig)* to expose.
entlassen* *vt irreg (aus* from*) (kündigen)* to dismiss; *(nach Stellenabbau)* to make redundant; *Patienten, Soldaten* to discharge; *(aus dem Gefängnis, aus Verpflichtungen)* to release.
Entlassung *f siehe vt* dismissal; making redundant; discharge; release. **es gab 20 ~en** there were 20 redundancies.
Entlassungs-: ~gesuch *nt* (letter of) resignation; **ein ~gesuch stellen** to tender one's resignation; **~zeugnis** *nt (Sch)* school leaving certificate.
entlasten* *vt* to relieve the strain on; *(Mil, Rail)* to relieve; *Gewissen, Verkehr* to ease; *(Arbeit abnehmen)* to take some of the load off; *(Jur) Angeklagten* to exonerate; *(Comm) Vorstand* to approve the activities of; *(von Verpflichtungen) jdn* to release.
Entlastung *f* relief *(auch Mil, Rail etc)*; *(von Achse etc, Herz)* relief of the strain *(+gen* on*)*; *(Jur)* exoneration; *(Comm: des Vorstands)* approval; *(von Verpflichtungen etc)* release. **zu seiner** ~ **führte der Angeklagte an, daß ...** in his defence *(Brit) or* defense *(US)* the defendant stated that ...
Entlastungs-: ~material *nt (Jur)* evidence for the defence *(Brit) or* defense *(US)*; **~zeuge** *m (Jur)* defence *(Brit) or* defense *(US)* witness; **~zug** *m* relief *(Brit) or* extra train.
entlaufen* *vi irreg aux sein* to run away *(dat, von* from*)*. **ein ~es Kind** a runaway child; **ein ~er Sträfling** an escaped convict; **ein ~er Hund** a lost dog.
entledigen* *(form) vr* **sich einer Person/Sache** *(gen)* ~ to rid oneself of sb/sth; **sich seiner Kleidung** ~ to remove one's clothes.
entleeren* *vt* to empty; *Darm* to evacuate.
entlegen *adj* remote.
entleihen* *vt irreg* to borrow *(von, aus* from*)*.
Entleiher *m* - borrower.
Entlein *nt* duckling.
entloben* *vr* to break off one's engagement.
entlocken* *vt* **jdm/einer Sache etw** ~ to elicit sth from sb/sth.
entlohnen* *vt* to pay; *(fig)* to reward.
Entlohnung *f* pay(ment); *(fig)* reward.
entlüften* *vt* to ventilate, to air; *Bremsen* to bleed.
Entlüfter *m* - ventilator.
Entlüftung *f siehe vt* ventilation, airing; bleeding.
entmachten* *vt* to deprive of power; *(stürzen)* to topple.
entmannen* *vt* to castrate.
Entmannung *f* castration.
entmilitarisieren *vt* to demilitarize.
entmündigen* *vt (Jur)* to (legally) incapacitate, to declare incapable of managing one's own affairs; *(wegen Geisteskrankheit auch)* to certify.
Entmündigung *f siehe vt (Jur)* (legal) incapacitation; certification.
entmutigen* *vt* to discourage, to dishearten. **sich nicht ~ lassen** not to be discouraged.
Entmutigung *f* discouragement.
Entnahme *f* **-n** *(form)* removal; *(von Blut)* extraction; *(von Geld)* withdrawal.
entnehmen* *vt irreg (aus, dat)* to take (from); *(aus Kasse) Geld* to withdraw (from); *(fig: folgern)* to infer (from). **wie ich Ihren Worten entnehme, ...** I gather from what you say that ...
entnerven* *vt* to unnerve. **~d** nerve-racking.
entpuppen* *vr* **sich als Betrüger** *etc* ~ to turn out to be a cheat *etc.*
entrahmen* *vt Milch* to skim.
enträtseln* *vt* to solve; *Sinn, Schrift* to decipher.
entreißen* *vt irreg* **jdm etw** ~ *(lit, fig)* to snatch sth (away) from sb.
entrichten* *vt (form)* to pay.
Entrichtung *f (form)* payment.
entrinnen* *vi irreg aux sein (geh) +dat* to escape from; *dem Tod* to escape. **es gibt kein E~** there is no escape.
entrückt *adj (geh verzückt)* enraptured. **der Wirklichkeit ~ sein** to live in a world of one's own.
entrümpeln* *vt* to clear out.
Entrümp(e)lung *f* clear-out.
entrüsten* 1 *vt (empören)* to fill with indignation, to outrage. **2** *vr* **sich ~ über** *(+acc) (sich empören)* to be outraged at.
entrüstet *adj* indignant, outraged.
Entrüstung *f* indignation *(über +acc* at*)*.
Entsafter *m* - juice extractor.
entsagen* *vi +dat (geh)* **der Welt** ~ to renounce the world.
Entsagung *f (geh)* renunciation.
Entsatz *m no pl (Mil)* relief.
entschädigen* *vt (für* for*) (lit, fig)* to compensate, to recompense; *(Kosten erstatten)* to reimburse. **das Theaterstück entschädigte uns für das lange Warten** the play made up for the long wait.
Entschädigung *f siehe vt* compensation, recompense; reimbursement.
Entschädigungssumme *f* compensation.
entschärfen* *vt (lit, fig)* to defuse.
entscheiden* *irreg* **1** *vti* to decide. ~ **Sie, wie es gemacht werden soll!** you decide how it is to be done; **den Kampf (um etw) für sich** ~ to secure victory in the struggle (for sth); **über etw** *(acc)* ~ to decide (on) sth; **es ist noch nichts entschieden** nothing has been decided (as) yet; **darüber habe ich nicht zu** ~ that is not for me to decide. **2** *vr (Mensch)* to decide, to make up one's mind; *(Angelegenheit)* to be decided. **sich für jdn/etw** ~ to decide in favour of sb/sth.

entscheidend *adj* decisive; *Augenblick, Fehler auch* crucial. **die ~e Stimme** *(bei Wahlen etc)* the deciding *or* casting vote; **der alles ~e Augenblick** the all decisive moment; **das E~e** the decisive *or* deciding factor.

Entscheidung *f* decision. **eine ~ treffen** to make a decision; **wie ist die ~ ausgefallen?** which way did the decision go?; **es geht um die ~, ob ...** it's a question of deciding whether ...

Entscheidungs-: ~befugnis *f* decision-making powers *pl*; **~freiheit** *f* freedom of decision-making; **e~freudig** *adj* able to make decisions, decisive; **~kampf** *m* show-down *(auch fig)*; *(Sport)* decider; **~schlacht** *f* decisive battle; *(fig)* show-down *(col)*; **~spiel** *nt* decider, play-off.

entschieden *adj* **(a)** *(entschlossen)* determined, resolute; *Befürworter* staunch. **etw ~ ablehnen** to reject sth firmly. **(b)** *no pred (eindeutig)* decided, distinct. **das geht ~ zu weit** that's definitely going too far.

Entschiedenheit *f (Entschlossenheit)* determination, resolution. **etw mit aller ~ dementieren** to deny sth categorically.

entschlacken* *vt (Med) Körper* to purify.

entschlafen* *vi irreg aux sein (geh)* to fall asleep.

entschleiern* *vt (lit, fig)* to unveil.

entschließen* *vr irreg* to decide *(für, zu* on*)*. **ich entschloß mich zum Kauf dieses Hauses** I decided to buy this house; **sich zu nichts ~ können** to be unable to make up one's mind; **ich bin fest entschlossen** I am absolutely determined; **zu allem entschlossen sein** to be ready for anything; **kurz entschlossen** straight away.

Entschließung *f* resolution.

entschlossen *adj* determined, resolute. **~ handeln** to act resolutely *or* with determination.

Entschlossenheit *f* determination, resolution.

entschlüpfen* *vi aux sein (dat* from*)* to escape, to slip away; *(fig: Wort etc)* to slip out.

Entschluß *m* decision; *(Vorsatz)* resolution, resolve. **aus eigenem ~ handeln** to act on one's own initiative; **es ist mein fester ~ ...** it is my firm intention ...

entschlüsseln* *vt* to decipher; *Funkspruch auch* to decode.

Entschluß-: e~freudig *adj* decisive; **~kraft** *f* decisiveness; **e~los** *adj* indecisive.

entschuldbar *adj* excusable, pardonable.

entschuldigen* 1 *vt* to excuse. **etw mit etw ~** to excuse sth as due to sth; **das ist durch nichts zu ~!, das läßt sich nicht ~!** that is inexcusable!; **jdn bei jdm ~** to make sb's excuses *or* apologies to sb; **einen Schüler ~ (lassen)** to ask for a pupil to be excused; **ich bitte mich zu ~** I beg to be excused. **2** *vi* **~ Sie (bitte)!** excuse me; *(Verzeihung auch)* sorry; *(bei Frage etc)* sorry, pardon me *(esp US)*. **3** *vr* **sich (bei jdm) ~** to excuse oneself; *(um Verzeihung bitten)* to apologize (to sb) *(wegen etw (gen)* for sth*)*; **sich ~ lassen** to send one's apologies.

Entschuldigung *f (Grund)* excuse; *(Bitte um ~)* apology; *(Sch: Brief)* note. **~!** excuse me; *(Verzeihung auch)* sorry; **(jdn) (wegen einer Sache) um ~ bitten** to apologize (to sb) (for sth); **ich bitte vielmals um ~ (, daß ich mich verspätet habe)!** I do apologize (for being late)!

entschwefeln* *vt* to desulphurize.

Entschwef(e)lung *f* desulphurization.

entschwinden* *vi irreg aux sein (geh: lit, fig)* to vanish.

entsenden* *vt irreg or reg (geh)* to dispatch.

entsetzen* 1 *vt* **(a)** to horrify, to appal. **(b)** *(Mil)* to relieve. **2** *vr* **sich über jdn/etw ~** to be horrified *or* appalled at sb/sth; *siehe* **entsetzt**.

Entsetzen *nt no pl* horror; *(Erschrecken)* terror. **mit ~ sehen, daß ...** to be horrified/terrified to see that ...

entsetzlich *adj* dreadful, appalling.

entsetzt *adj* horrified, appalled *(über +acc* at, by*)*. **ein ~er Schrei** a cry of horror.

entsichern* *vt* to release the safety catch of.

entsinnen* *vr irreg (einer Sache (gen), an etw (acc)* sth*)* to remember, to recall. **wenn ich mich recht entsinne** if my memory serves me correctly.

entsorgen* *vt* **eine Stadt ~** to dispose of a town's refuse and sewage.

Entsorgung *f* waste management.

Entsorgungspark *m* (nuclear) waste dump.

entspannen* 1 *vt Muskeln, Nerven etc* to relax; *(fig) Lage auch* to ease. **2** *vr* to relax *(auch fig)*; *(ausruhen)* to rest; *(nach der Arbeit etc)* to unwind; *(Lage etc)* to ease.

Entspannung *f* relaxation *(auch fig)*; *(Pol)* détente, easing of tension *(+gen* in*)*.

Entspannungs-: ~politik *f* policy of détente; **~übungen** *pl (Med etc)* relaxation exercises.

entsprechen* *vi irreg +dat* to correspond to; *Vorschriften* to be in accordance with; *(genügen) Anforderungen* to meet; *Erwartungen* to come up to; *einer Beschreibung* to answer, to fit; *einer Bitte, einem Wunsch etc* to meet, to comply with. **sich ~** to correspond, to tally.

entsprechend 1 *adj* corresponding; *(zuständig)* relevant; *(angemessen)* appropriate. **2** *adv* accordingly; *(ähnlich, gleich)* correspondingly. **er wurde ~ bestraft** he was suitably *or* appropriately punished. **3** *prep+dat* in accordance with, according to; *(ähnlich, gleich)* corresponding to. **er wird seiner Leistung ~ bezahlt** he is paid according to output.

Entsprechung *f* equivalent; *(Analogie)* parallel; *(Übereinstimmung)* correspondence.

entspringen* *vi irreg aux sein* **(a)** *(Fluß)* to rise. **(b)** *(+dat: sich herleiten von)* to spring from.

entstaatlichen* *vt* to denationalize.

entstammen* *vi aux sein +dat* to stem *or* come from.

entstehen* *vi irreg aux sein (ins Dasein treten)* to come into being; *(seinen Ursprung haben)* to originate; *(sich entwickeln)* to arise *(aus, durch* from*)*; *(hervorkommen)* to emerge *(aus, durch* from*)*; *(verursacht werden)* to result *(aus, durch* from*)*; *(Kunstwerk: geschrieben/gebaut etc werden)* to be written/built *etc*. **wir wollen nicht den Eindruck ~ lassen, ...** we don't want to give rise to the impression that ...; **für ~den** *or* **entstandenen Schaden** for damages incurred.

Entstehung *f (das Werden)* genesis, coming into being; *(das Hervorkommen)* emergence; *(Ursprung)* origin; *(Bildung)* formation.

Entstehungs-: ~geschichte *f* genesis; **~ort** *m* place of origin.

entsteinen* *vt* to stone.

entstellen* *vt (lit, fig)* to distort; *(verunstalten) Gesicht* to disfigure. **etw entstellt wiedergeben** to distort *or* misrepresent sth.

Entstellung *f siehe vt* distortion; disfigurement.

entstören* *vt Radio, Telefon* to free from interference; *Staubsauger* to suppress.

enttarnen* *vt Spion* to blow the cover of *(col)*.

enttäuschen* 1 *vt* to disappoint; *Vertrauen* to betray. **enttäuscht sein über** *(+acc)***/von** to be disappointed at/by. **2** *vi* **unsere Mannschaft hat sehr enttäuscht** our team were very disappointing.

Enttäuschung *f* disappointment. **jdm eine ~ bereiten** to disappoint sb.

entthronen* *vt (lit, fig)* to dethrone.

entvölkern* *vt* to depopulate.

entwachsen* *vi irreg aux sein +dat* **(a)** to outgrow, to grow out of. **(b)** *(geh: herauswachsen aus)* to spring from.

entwaffnen* *vt (lit, fig)* to disarm.

entwaffnend *adj (fig)* disarming.

Entwaffnung *f* disarming; *(eines Landes)* disarmament.

entwarnen* *vi* to sound the all-clear.
Entwarnung *f* all-clear.
entwässern* *vt* to drain.
Entwässerung *f* drainage.
entweder [*auch:* 'ɛntweːdɐ] *conj* ~ ... **oder** ... either ... or ...; ~ **oder!** yes or no.
entweichen* *vi irreg aux sein* to escape *(+dat, aus* from*)*.
entwenden* *vt (form)* **jdm etw** ~ to steal *or* purloin *(hum, form)* sth from sb.
entwerfen* *vt irreg Zeichnung* to sketch; *Muster, Modell* to design; *Gesetz, Schreiben etc* to draft, to draw up; *Plan* to devise, to draw up; *(fig) Bild* to draw; *(in Umrissen darstellen)* to outline.
entwerten* *vt* **(a)** *(im Wert mindern)* to devalue. **(b)** *(ungültig machen)* to make invalid; *Briefmarke, Fahrschein* to cancel.
Entwerter *m* - (ticket-)cancelling machine.
Entwertung *f siehe vt* devaluation; invalidation; cancellation.
entwickeln* **1** *vt* to develop *(auch Phot)*; *Gas etc* to produce, to generate; *Mut, Energie* to show, to display. **etw zu etw** ~ to develop sth into sth. **2** *vr* to develop *(zu* into*)*; *(Gase etc)* to be produced *or* generated. **das Projekt entwickelt sich gut** the project is coming along *or* progressing nicely.
Entwicklung *f* development; *(von Gasen etc)* production, generation; *(von Mut, Energie)* show, display; *(Phot)* developing. **in der** ~ at the development stage; *(Jugendliche etc)* still developing.
Entwicklungs-: e~fähig *adj* capable of development; **diese Stelle ist e~fähig** this position has prospects; **~geschichte** *f* evolution; **~helfer** *m* VSO worker *(Brit)*, Peace Corps worker *(US)*; **~hilfe** *f* foreign aid; **~jahre** *pl* adolescent *or* formative *(auch fig)* years, adolescence; **~land** *nt* developing *or* third-world country; **~stadium** *nt*, **~stufe** *f* stage of development; **~zeit** *f* period of development; *(Phot)* developing time.
entwirren* *vt (lit, fig)* to disentangle, to unravel.
entwischen* *vi aux sein (col)* to escape, to get away *(dat, aus* from*)*.
entwöhnen* *vt* **jdn** ~ to break sb of the habit *(+dat, von* of*)*, to cure sb *(+dat, von* of*)*; *Säugling, Jungtier* to wean.
Entwöhnung *f siehe vt* cure, curing; weaning.
entwürdigen* **1** *vt* to degrade. **2** *vr* to degrade oneself.
Entwürdigung *f* degradation.
Entwurf *m* ¨**e (a)** *(Skizze, Abriß)* outline, sketch; *(Design)* design; *(Archit, fig)* blueprint. **(b)** *(Vertrags~, von Plan)* draft; *(Gesetz~)* bill.
entwurzeln* *vt (lit, fig)* to uproot.
entzerren* *vt* to correct.
entziehen* *irreg* **1** *vt (+dat* from*)* to withdraw, to take away; *Gunst etc* to withdraw; *Flüssigkeit, (Chem)* to extract. **jdm Alkohol/Nikotin** ~ to deprive sb of alcohol/nicotine; **jdm die Erlaubnis** *etc* ~ to take sb's permit *etc* away; **dem Redner das Wort** ~ to ask the speaker to stop. **2** *vr* **sich jdm/einer Sache** ~ to evade *or* elude sb/sth; **sich seiner Verantwortung** ~ to shirk one's responsibilities; **das entzieht sich meiner Kenntnis** that is beyond my knowledge; **sich jds Blicken** ~ to be hidden from sight.
Entziehung *f* withdrawal; *(Behandlung)* treatment for drug addiction/alcoholism.
Entziehungskur *f* cure for drug addiction/alcoholism.
entzifferbar *adj siehe vt* decipherable; decodable.
entziffern* *vt* to decipher; *Funkspruch auch* to decode.
entzücken* *vt* to delight. **von jdm/über etw** *(acc)* **entzückt sein** to be delighted by sb/at sth.
Entzücken *nt no pl* delight, joy. **in** ~ **geraten** to go into raptures.
entzückend *adj* delightful, charming.
Entzug *m no pl (einer Lizenz etc, Med)* withdrawal.
Entzugs|erscheinung *f* withdrawal symptom.
entzündbar *adj (lit, fig)* inflammable. **leicht** ~ highly inflammable; *(fig)* easily roused.
entzünden* **1** *vt Feuer* to light; *(fig) Streit etc* to spark off; *Haß* to inflame. **2** *vr* **(a)** to catch fire; *(fig) (Streit)* to be sparked off; *(Haß)* to be inflamed. **(b)** *(Med)* to become inflamed. **entzündet** inflamed.
entzündlich *adj Gase, Brennstoff* inflammable; *(Med)* inflammatory.
Entzündung *f* **(a)** *(Med)* inflammation. **(b)** ignition *(esp Sci, Tech)*. **Funken führten zur** ~ **des Heus** sparks led to the hay catching fire.
entzwei *adj pred* in two, in half; *(kaputt)* broken; *(zerrissen)* torn.
entzweien* *vt* to turn against each other.
entzweigehen *vi sep irreg aux sein* to break (in two *or* half).
Enzian ['ɛntsiaːn] *m* **-e** gentian; *(Branntwein) spirit distilled from the roots of gentian.*
Enzyklika *f, pl* **Enzykliken** *(Eccl)* encyclical.
Enzyklopädie *f* encyclop(a)edia.
Enzym *nt* **-e** enzyme.
Epen *pl of* **Epos.**
Epidemie *f (Med, fig)* epidemic.
epidemisch *adj (Med, fig)* epidemic.
Epik *f* epic poetry.
Epilepsie *f* epilepsy.
Epileptiker(in *f***)** *m* - epileptic.
epileptisch *adj* epileptic.
Epilog *m* **-e** epilogue.
episch *adj (lit, fig)* epic.
Episode *f* **-n** episode.
Epoche *f* **-n** epoch.
epochemachend *adj* epoch-making.
Epos *nt, pl* **Epen** epic (poem).
Equipe [e'kɪp] *f* **-n** team.
er *pers* he; *(von Dingen)* it; *(von Hund etc)* it, he. **wenn ich** ~ **wäre** if I were him *or* he *(form)*; ~ **ist es** it's him, it is he *(form)*; **sie ist größer als** ~ she is taller than he is *or* than him.
er|achten* *vt (geh)* **jdn/etw für** *or* **als etw** ~ to consider sb/sth (to be) sth.
Er|achten *nt no pl:* **meines ~s** in my opinion.
er|arbeiten* *vt* **(a)** *Vermögen etc* to work for; *Wissen etc* to acquire. **(b)** *Entwurf etc* to work out.
Erb-: ~anlage *f usu pl* hereditary factor(s *pl*); **~anspruch** *m* claim to an/the inheritance.
erbarmen* **1** *vt* **jdn** ~ to arouse sb's pity; **es kann einen** ~ it's pitiable; **er sieht zum E~ aus** he's a pitiful sight. **2** *vr (+gen)* to take pity (on) *(auch hum col)*. **Herr, erbarme dich (unser)!** Lord, have mercy (upon us)!
Erbarmen *nt no pl (Mitleid)* pity, compassion *(mit* on*)*; *(Gnade)* mercy *(mit* on*)*. **aus** ~ out of pity; **ohne** ~ pitiless(ly), merciless(ly); **er kennt kein** ~ he knows no mercy.
erbarmenswert *adj* pitiable, wretched, pitiful.
erbärmlich *adj (erbarmenswert, pej: dürftig)* pitiful, wretched; *(gemein, schlecht)* wretched, miserable.
Erbärmlichkeit *f (Elend)* wretchedness, misery; *(fig: Dürftigkeit, Gemeinheit etc)* wretchedness, miserableness.
Erbärmungs-: e~los *adj (lit, fig)* pitiless, merciless; **~losigkeit** *f (lit, fig)* pitilessness, mercilessness; **e~voll** *adj* compassionate, full of pity.
erbauen* *vt* **(a)** *(lit, fig: errichten)* to build. **(b)** *(fig: seelisch)* to edify, to uplift. **er ist von meinem Plan nicht besonders erbaut** *(col)* he isn't particularly enthusiastic about my plan.
Erbauer(in *f***)** *m* - builder; *(fig auch)* architect.
erbaulich *adj* edifying *(auch iro)*, uplifting.
Erbauung *f siehe vt* building; edification.
Erb-: e~berechtigt *adj* entitled to inherit; **e~biologisch** *adj (Jur)* **e~biologisches Gutachten**

blood test *(to establish paternity)*.

Erbe[1] *m (wk)* **-n, -n** *(lit, fig)* heir *(einer Person (gen)* of *or* to sb, *einer Sache (gen)* to sth*)*. **jdn zum** *or* **als ~n einsetzen** to make sb one's/sb's heir.

Erbe[2] *nt no pl* inheritance; *(fig)* heritage; *(esp Unerwünschtes)* legacy.

erbeben* *vi aux sein (geh)* to shudder.

erben 1 *vt (lit, fig)* to inherit *(von* from*)*; *(col: geschenkt bekommen)* to get, to be given. **bei ihm ist nichts zu ~** *(col)* you won't get anything out of him. **2** *vi* to inherit.

erbeuten* *vt (Tier) Opfer* to carry off; *(Dieb)* to get away with; *(im Krieg)* to capture.

Erb-: ~faktor *m (Biol)* hereditary factor, gene; **~feind** *m* traditional *or* arch enemy; **~folge** *f* (line of) succession.

erbieten* *vr irreg (geh)* **sich ~, etw zu tun** to offer to do sth.

Erbin *f* heiress.

erbittern* *vt* to enrage, to incense.

erbittert *adj Widerstand, Gegner etc* bitter.

Erbitterung *f* rage.

Erbkrankheit *f* hereditary disease.

erblassen* *vi aux sein* to (go) pale, to blanch. **vor Neid ~** to go green with envy.

Erblasser(in *f***)** *m* **-** *(Jur)* person who leaves an inheritance.

erblich *adj* hereditary. **er ist ~ (vor)belastet** it runs in the family.

erblicken* *vt (geh)* to see; *(erspähen)* to spot.

erblinden* *vi aux sein* to go blind.

Erblindung *f* loss of sight.

erblühen* *vi aux sein (geh)* to bloom, to blossom.

Erbmasse *f* estate; *(Biol)* genetic make-up.

erbosen* *(geh)* **1** *vt* to infuriate. **2** *vr* **sich ~ über** *(+acc)* to become infuriated at.

erbrechen* *vtir irreg* **(sich) ~** *(Med)* to vomit, to be sick *(Brit) (nicht vt)*; **etw bis zum E~ tun** *(fig)* to do sth ad nauseam.

Erbrecht *nt* law of inheritance.

erbringen* *vt irreg* to produce, to furnish.

Erbschaft *f* inheritance. **eine ~ machen** to come into an inheritance.

Erbschaftssteuer *f* estate *or* death duties *pl*.

Erbschleicher(in *f***)** *m* legacy-hunter.

Erbse *f* **-n** pea.

Erbsensuppe *f* pea soup.

Erb-: ~stück *nt* heirloom; **~sünde** *f (Rel)* original sin; **~teil** *nt (Jur: auch m)* (share of an/the) inheritance.

Erd|achse *f* earth's axis.

erdacht *adj Geschichte* made-up.

Erdball *m (liter)* globe, world.

Erdbeben *nt* earthquake.

Erdbeere *f* strawberry.

Erdboden *m* ground, earth. **etw dem ~ gleichmachen** to level sth, to raze sth to the ground; **als hätte ihn der ~ verschluckt** as if the earth had swallowed him up.

Erde *f* **-n (a)** *(Welt)* earth, world. **auf der ganzen ~** all over the world. **(b)** *(Boden)* ground. **unter der ~** underground, below ground; **du wirst mich noch unter die ~ bringen** *(col)* you'll be the death of me yet *(col)*; **über der ~** above ground. **(c)** *(Erdreich, Bodenart)* soil, earth *(auch Chem)*. **(d)** *(Elec: Erdung)* earth *(Brit)*, ground *(US)*.

erden *vt (Elec)* to earth *(Brit)*, to ground *(US)*.

erdenklich *adj attr* conceivable, imaginable. **sich** *(dat)* **alle ~e Mühe geben** to take the greatest (possible) pains; **alles E~e tun** to do everything conceivable *or* imaginable.

Erd-: ~gas *nt* natural gas; **~geschoß** *nt* ground floor, first floor *(US)*; **im ~geschoß** on the ground/first floor; **~innere(s)** *nt* interior *or* bowels *pl* of the earth; **~kruste** *f* earth's crust; **~kugel** *f* earth, globe; **~kunde** *f* geography; **~nuß** *f* peanut, groundnut; **~oberfläche** *f* earth's surface; **~öl** *nt* (mineral) oil, petroleum.

erdolchen* *vt* to stab (to death). **jdn mit Blicken ~** to look daggers at sb.

Erdreich *nt* soil, earth.

erdreisten* *vr* **sich ~, etw zu tun** to have the audacity to do sth; **wie können Sie sich ~!** how dare you!

erdrosseln* *vt* to strangle, to throttle.

erdrücken* *vt* to crush (to death); *(fig: überwältigen)* to overwhelm. **~de Übermacht/~des Beweismaterial** overwhelming superiority/evidence; **die Schuld erdrückte ihn** the sense of guilt oppressed him.

Erd-: ~rutsch *m* landslide, landslip; **~schicht** *f* layer (of the earth), stratum; **~stoß** *m* (seismic) shock; **~teil** *m* continent.

erdulden* *vt* to endure, to suffer.

Erdung *f (Elec)* earth(ing), ground(ing) *(US)*.

er|eifern* *vr* to get worked up *(über +acc* over*)*.

er|eignen* *vr* to occur, to happen.

Er|eignis *nt* event; *(Vorfall auch)* incident.

er|eignis-: ~los *adj* uneventful; **~reich** *adj* eventful.

Erektion *f (Physiol)* erection.

Eremit *m (wk)* **-en, -en** hermit.

er|erben* *vt* to inherit.

erfahren* 1 *vt irreg* **(a)** *Nachricht etc* to learn, to find out; *(hören)* to hear *(von* about, of*)*. **etw ~** to find out about sth; **darf man Ihre Absichten ~?** might one inquire as to your intentions? **(b)** *(erleben)* to experience; *(empfangen) Verständnis* to receive. **2** *vi irreg* to hear *(von* about, of*)*. **3** *adj* experienced.

Erfahrenheit *f* experience.

Erfahrung *f* experience. **aus (eigener) ~** from (one's own) experience; **nach meiner ~** in my experience; **~en sammeln** to gain experience; **die ~ hat gezeigt, daß ...** experience has shown that ...; **etw in ~ bringen** to learn *or* find out sth; **eine ~ machen** to have an experience; **ich habe die ~ gemacht, daß ...** I have found that ...; **mit dieser neuen Mitarbeiterin haben wir nur gute ~en gemacht** we have found this new employee (to be) completely satisfactory; **ich habe mit der Ehe nur schlechte ~en gemacht** I've had a very bad experience of marriage.

Erfahrungs-: ~austausch *m (Pol)* exchange of experiences; **e~gemäß** *adv* **e~gemäß ...** as experience shows ...

erfaßbar *adj* ascertainable.

erfassen* *vt* **(a)** *(mitreißen: Auto, Strömung)* to catch. **(b)** *(Furcht, Verlangen etc)* to seize. **Angst erfaßte sie** she was seized by fear. **(c)** *(begreifen)* to grasp. **(d)** *(registrieren)* to record, to register. **alle Fälle werden statistisch erfaßt** statistics of all cases are being recorded.

Erfassung *f* registration, recording.

erfinden* *vt irreg* to invent. **das hat sie glatt erfunden** she made it all up; **frei erfunden** completely fictitious.

Erfinder(in *f***)** *m* **-** inventor.

erfinderisch *adj* inventive; *(findig auch)* ingenious.

Erfindung *f* invention; *(Erdichtung, Lüge auch)* fabrication.

Erfolg *m* **-e** success; *(Ergebnis, Folge)* result, outcome. **mit/ohne ~** successfully/without success *or* unsuccessfully; **~/keinen ~ haben** to be successful/unsuccessful; **sie warnte mich mit dem ~, daß ...** the result of her warning me was that ...; **viel ~!** good luck.

erfolgen* *vi aux sein (form) (vollzogen werden)* to be effected *(form) or* carried out; *(stattfinden)* to take place. **nach erfolgter Zahlung** when payment has been made; **es erfolgte keine Antwort** no answer was forthcoming.

Erfolg-: e~los *adj* unsuccessful, without success; **~losigkeit** *f* lack of success, unsuccessfulness; **e~reich** *adj* successful.

Erfolgs-: ~erlebnis *nt* feeling of success, sense of achievement; **~leiter** *f (fig)* ladder to success; **~mensch** *m* success, successful person.

erfolgversprechend *adj* promising.

erforderlich *adj* necessary, requisite. **unbedingt ~** (absolutely) essential *or* imperative.

erfordern* *vt* to require, to call for.

Erfordernis *nt* requirement.

erforschen* *vt Land* to explore; *Probleme auch* to investigate; *Meinung, Wahrheit* to find out. **sein Gewissen ~** to examine one's conscience.

Erforscher *m (eines Landes)* explorer; *(in Wissenschaft)* investigator.

Erforschung *f siehe vt* exploration; investigation *(+gen* into*)*; finding out.

erfragen* *vt Weg* to ask; *Einzelheiten etc* to obtain.

erfreuen* **1** *vt* to please, to delight; *Herz* to gladden. **sehr erfreut!** *(form)* pleased to meet you!; **ja, sagte er erfreut** yes, he said delightedly. **2** *vr* **sich einer Sache** *(gen)* **~** *(geh)* to enjoy sth.

erfreulich *adj* pleasant; *Neuerung, Besserung etc* welcome; *(befriedigend)* gratifying. **es ist wenig ~, daß wir ...** it's not very satisfactory that we ...; **es wäre ~, wenn die Regierung ...** it would be good if the government ...; **sehr ~!** very nice!; **wir haben ~ viel geleistet** it's very encouraging how much we've done.

erfreulicherweise *adv* happily.

erfrieren* **1** *vi irreg aux sein* to freeze to death; *(Pflanzen)* to be killed by frost. **erfrorene Glieder** frostbitten limbs. **2** *vt* **sich** *(dat)* **die Füße ~** to suffer frostbite in one's feet.

erfrischen* **1** *vti* to refresh. **2** *vr* to refresh oneself; *(sich waschen)* to freshen up.

erfrischend *adj (lit, fig)* refreshing.

Erfrischung *f* refreshment.

erfüllen* **1** *vt* **(a)** *Raum etc* to fill. **Haß/Liebe** *etc* **erfüllte ihn** he was filled with hate/love *etc;* **es erfüllt mich mit Genugtuung, daß ...** it gives me great satisfaction to see that ...; **ein erfülltes Leben** a full life. **(b)** *(ausführen, einhalten)* to fulfil *(Brit)*, to fulfill *(US)*; *Bedingungen auch* to meet, to comply with; *Wunsch, Pflicht auch* to carry out; *Erwartungen auch* to come up to; *(Jur) Soll* to achieve; *Plan* to carry through; *Zweck* to serve. **ihr Wunsch wurde erfüllt** their wish came true. **2** *vr (Wunsch, Voraussagung)* to be fulfilled, to come true.

Erfüllung *f* fulfilment *(Brit)*, fulfillment *(US)*; *(einer Aufgabe auch)* performance; *(eines Solls)* achievement; *(eines Plans)* execution. **in ~ gehen** to be fulfilled.

ergänzen* *vt* to supplement; *(vervollständigen)* to complete; *Fehlendes* to supply; *Vorräte* to replenish; *Bericht auch* to add (sth) to; *Worte* to add; *Gesetz* to amend. **sich ~** to complement one another; **~d hinzufügen** to add *(zu* to*)*.

Ergänzung *f* **(a)** *(das Ergänzen)* supplementing; *(Vervollständigung)* completion; *(von Fehlendem)* supply(ing); *(eines Berichts)* addition *(+gen* to*)*; *(von Gesetz)* amendment; *(von Lager, Vorräten)* replenishment. **(b)** *(Zusatz, zu Buch etc)* supplement; *(Hinzugefügtes, Person)* addition; *(zu einem Gesetz)* amendment.

ergattern* *vt (col)* to get hold of.

ergeben* *irreg* **1** *vt* to yield, to produce; *(zum Ergebnis haben)* to result in; *Summe* to amount to. **2** *vr* **(a)** *(kapitulieren) (dat* to*)* to surrender, to capitulate. **sich in etw** *(acc)* **~** to submit to sth. **(b)** *(folgen)* to result, to arise *(aus* from*)*. **daraus können sich Nachteile ~** this could turn out to be disadvantageous. **(c)** *(sich herausstellen)* to come to light. **es ergab sich, daß unsere Befürchtungen ...** it turned out that our fears ... **3** *adj (hingebeben, treu)* devoted; *(demütig)* humble; *(unterwürfig)* submissive. **jdm treu ~ sein** to be loyally devoted to sb.

Ergebenheit *f (Hingabe, Treue)* devotion; *(Demut)* humility; *(Unterwürfigkeit)* submissiveness.

Ergebnis *nt* result; *(Sport auch)* score; *(Auswirkung auch)* consequence, outcome. **die Verhandlungen führten zu keinem ~** the negotiations were inconclusive; **zu einem ~ kommen** to come to *or* reach a conclusion.

ergebnislos *adj* unsuccessful, fruitless. **~ bleiben/verlaufen** to come to nothing.

ergehen* *irreg* **1** *vi aux sein* **(a)** *(form)* to go out *(an +acc* to*)*; *(Gesetz)* to be enacted. **~ lassen** to issue, to send; to enact. **(b) sie ließ alles über sich** *(acc)* **~** she submitted to everything. **2** *vi impers aux sein* **es ist ihm schlecht/gut ergangen** he fared badly/well; **es wird ihm schlecht ~** he will suffer. **3** *vr (fig)* **sich in etw** *(dat)* **~** to indulge in sth; **sich (in langen Reden) über ein Thema ~** to hold forth at length on sth.

Ergehen *nt no pl (geh)* (state of) health.

ergiebig *adj (lit, fig)* productive; *Geschäft* profitable, lucrative; *(fruchtbar)* fertile; *(sparsam im Verbrauch)* economic.

ergießen* *vr irreg (geh)* to pour forth *(liter) or* out *(auch fig)*.

ergo *conj* therefore, ergo *(liter, hum)*.

ergötzen* *(geh)* **1** *vt* to delight. **2** *vr* **sich an etw** *(dat)* **~** to take delight in sth.

ergrauen* *vi aux sein* to go grey *(Brit) or* gray *(US)*.

ergreifen* *vt irreg (lit, fig)* to seize; *(fassen auch)* to grasp, to grip; *Beruf* to take up; *Maßnahmen* to take; *(innerlich bewegen)* to move. **von Furcht** *etc* **ergriffen werden** to be seized with fear *etc*; **er ergriff das Wort** he began to speak; *(Parl, bei Versammlung etc)* he took the floor.

ergreifend *adj (fig)* moving.

ergriffen *adj (fig)* moved.

Ergriffenheit *f* emotion.

ergründen* *vt Sinn etc* to fathom; *Ursache, Motiv* to discover.

Ergründung *f siehe vt* fathoming; discovery.

Erguß *m* **¨sse** effusion; *(Samen~)* ejaculation; *(fig)* outpouring.

erhaben *adj* **(a)** *Gedanken, Stil* lofty, elevated; *Schönheit, Anblick* sublime; *Augenblick* solemn. **(b)** *(überlegen)* superior. **~ lächeln** to smile in a superior way; **über etw** *(acc)* **~ (sein)** (to be) above sth; **über jeden Verdacht ~ sein** to be above suspicion.

Erhalt *m no pl* receipt. **bei/nach ~** on receipt.

erhalten* *irreg* **1** *vt* **(a)** to get, to receive; *Resultat, Genehmigung* to obtain, to get. **das Wort ~** to receive permission to speak. **(b)** *(bewahren)* to preserve; *Gesundheit etc auch* to maintain. **jdn am Leben ~** to keep sb alive; **er hat sich** *(dat)* **seinen Optimismus ~** he retained his optimism; **gut ~** well preserved *(auch hum col)*. **2** *vr (Brauch etc)* to last.

erhältlich *adj* obtainable, available. **schwer ~** difficult to obtain, hard to come by.

Erhaltung *f (Bewahrung)* preservation.

erhängen* *vt* to hang. **Tod durch E~** death by hanging; **sich ~** to hang oneself.

erhärten* **1** *vt* to harden; *(fig) Behauptung etc* to corroborate. **2** *vr (fig: Verdacht)* to harden.

erheben* *irreg* **1** *vt* **(a)** to raise. **jdn in den Adelsstand ~** to raise *or* elevate sb to the peerage. **(b)** *Gebühren* to charge, to levy; *Steuern (auferlegen)* to impose. **2** *vr* **(a)** *(aufstehen)* to get up, to rise. **(b)** *(sich auflehnen)* to rise (up), to revolt. **(c)** *(aufragen)* to rise *(über +dat* above*)*.

erhebend *adj* elevating, uplifting; *(beeindruckend)* impressive.

erheblich *adj (beträchtlich)* considerable; *Verletzung* serious; *(relevant)* pertinent.

Erhebung *f* **(a)** *(Boden~)* elevation. **(b)** *(Aufstand)* uprising, revolt. **(c)** *(von Gebühren)* levying. **(d)** *(Umfrage etc)* investigation, inquiry.

erheitern* **1** *vt* to cheer (up); *(belustigen)* to amuse. **2** *vr* to be amused *(über +acc* by*)*.

Erheiterung *f* amusement.

erhellen* **1** *vt* to illuminate; *(fig: klären auch)* to elucidate. **2** *vr (lit, fig)* to brighten; *(plötzlich)* to light up.

erhitzen* **1** *vt* to heat *(auf +acc* to*).* **die Gemüter** ~ to whip up feeling. **2** *vr* to get hot, to heat up; *(fig: sich erregen)* to become heated *(an+dat* over*).* **die Gemüter erhitzten sich** feelings were running high.

Erhitzung *f* heating up; *(fig: Erregung)* excitement.

erhoffen* *vt* to hope for. **was erhoffst du dir davon?** what do you hope to gain from it?

erhöhen* **1** *vt* to raise; *Preise auch, Produktion, Wirkung, Spannung* to increase. **jdn im Rang** ~ to promote sb; **erhöhte Temperatur haben** to have a temperature. **2** *vr* to rise, to increase.

Erhöhung *f* **(a)** raising; *(von Produktion, Wirkung)* increase; *(von Spannung)* heightening. **(b)** *(Lohn~)* rise *(Brit)*, raise *(US)*; *(Preis~)* increase. **(c)** *(Hügel)* hill, elevation.

Erhöhungszeichen *nt (Mus)* sharp (sign).

erholen* *vr (von* from*)* to recover; *(sich entspannen auch)* to relax, to have a rest; *(fig: Preise, Aktien auch)* to rally, to pick up. **du siehst sehr erholt aus** you look very rested.

erholsam *adj* restful, refreshing.

Erholung *f siehe vr* recovery *(auch fig)*; relaxation, rest. **zur** ~ **in die Schweiz fahren** to go to Switzerland for a holiday *(esp Brit) or* a vacation *(US)* and a rest; **er braucht dringend** ~ he badly needs a rest.

Erholungs-: **e~bedürftig** *adj* in need of a rest, run-down; **~heim** *nt* rest home; *(Ferienheim)* holiday home; **~kur** *f* rest cure; **~ort** *m* spa, health resort; **~pause** *f* break; **~reise** *f* holiday *(Brit) or* vacation *(US)* trip.

erhören* *vt Gebet etc* to hear; *Bitte* to yield to.

Erika *f, pl* **Eriken** *(Bot)* heather.

er|innern* **1** *vt* **jdn an etw** *(acc)* ~ to remind sb of sth; **jdn daran** ~**, daß ...** to remind sb that ... **2** *vr* **sich an jdn/etw** ~ to remember *or* recall sb/sth; **soweit ich mich** ~ **kann** as far as I remember; **wenn ich mich recht erinnere** if I remember rightly. **3** *vi* ~ **an** *(+acc)* to be reminiscent of.

Er|innerung *f (an +acc* of*)* memory, recollection; *(euph: Mahnung)* reminder; *(Andenken)* memento. **~en** *pl (Lebens~)* reminiscences *pl*; *(Liter)* memoirs *pl*; **zur** ~ **an** *(+acc)* in memory of; *(an Ereignis)* in commemoration of; *(als Andenken)* as a memento of; **jdn/etw in guter** ~ **behalten** to have pleasant memories of sb/sth.

Er|innerungs-: **~schreiben** *nt (Comm)* reminder; **~stück** *nt* keepsake.

erkalten* *vi aux sein (lit, fig)* to cool (down).

erkälten* *vr* to catch (a) cold. **sich** *(dat)* **die Blase** ~ to catch a chill in one's bladder.

erkältet *adj* **wir sind alle** ~ we all have colds.

Erkältung *f* cold; *(leicht)* chill. **eine** ~ **bekommen** to catch a cold/chill.

erkämpfen* *vt* to win, to secure. **sich** *(dat)* **etw** ~ to win sth; **er hat sich** *(dat)* **seine Position hart erkämpft** he fought hard for his position.

erkaufen* *vt (fig)* to buy. **etw teuer** ~ to pay dearly for sth; **den Erfolg mit seiner Gesundheit** ~ to achieve success at the price of one's health.

erkennbar *adj (wieder~)* recognizable; *(sichtbar)* visible; *(ersichtlich)* discernible.

erkennen* *irreg* **1** *vt (wieder~, einsehen)* to recognize *(an+dat* by*)*; *(wahrnehmen)* to see, to make out; *Unterschied* to see. **er hat erkannt, daß das nicht stimmte** he realized that it wasn't right; **jdm zu** ~ **geben, daß ...** to give sb to understand that ...; **sich zu** ~ **geben** to reveal oneself *(als* to be*)*; ~ **lassen** to show, to reveal; **du bist erkannt!** I see what you're after, I know your game. **2** *vi* ~ **auf** *(+acc) (Jur) Freispruch* to grant; *Strafe* to impose; *(Sport) Freistoß* to give, to award.

erkenntlich *adj* **sich (für etw)** ~ **zeigen** to show one's gratitude *or* appreciation (for sth).

Erkenntnis *f (Wissen)* knowledge *no pl*; *(das Erkennen)* recognition, realization; *(Entdeckung)* discovery. **zu der** ~ **kommen, daß ...** to come to the realization that ..., to realize that ...

Erkennungs-: **~dienst** *m* police records department; **e~dienstlich** *adv* **jdn e~dienstlich behandeln** to fingerprint and photograph sb; ~ **marke** *f* identity disc; ~ **melodie** *f* signature tune; **~zeichen** *nt* identification; *(Mil: Abzeichen)* badge.

Erker *m* - bay; *(kleiner Vorbau)* oriel.

erklärbar *adj* explicable, explainable. **leicht** ~ easily explained; **schwer** ~ hard to explain.

erklären* **1** *vt* **(a)** *(erläutern)* to explain *(jdm etw* sth to sb*).* **ich kann mir nicht** ~**, warum ...** I can't understand why ... **(b)** *(bekanntgeben)* to declare *(als* to be*)*; *Rücktritt* to announce; *(Politiker, Pressesprecher etc)* to say. **einem Staat den Krieg** ~ to declare war on a country; **eine Ausstellung** *etc* **für eröffnet** ~ to declare an exhibition *etc* open; **jdn für schuldig** *etc* ~ to pronounce sb guilty *etc.* **2** *vr* **(a)** *(Sache)* to be explained. **das erklärt sich daraus, daß ...** it can be explained by the fact that ...; **das erklärt sich (von) selbst** that's self-explanatory. **(b)** *(Mensch)* to declare oneself. **er erklärte sich für gesund** he said that he was in good health.

erklärend *adj* explanatory. **einige ~e Worte** a few words of explanation.

erklärlich *adj* **(a)** = **erklärbar. (b)** *(verständlich)* understandable.

erklärt *adj attr Gegner etc* professed, avowed; *Favorit, Liebling* acknowledged.

Erklärung *f* **(a)** explanation. **(b)** *(Bekanntgabe)* declaration; *(eines Politikers etc)* statement.

erklingen* *vi irreg (geh) aux sein* to ring out. **ein Lied** ~ **lassen** to burst (forth) into song.

erkranken* *vi aux sein* to be taken ill *(an +dat* with*)*; *(Organ, Pflanze, Tier)* to become diseased *(an+dat* with*).* **er ist am Magen erkrankt** he has contracted a stomach illness.

Erkrankung *f* illness; *(von Organ, Pflanze, Tier)* disease.

erkunden* *vt (esp Mil) Gelände etc* to reconnoitre; *(feststellen)* to find out.

erkundigen* *vr* **sich nach etw/jdm** ~ to ask about sth/after sb; **ich werde mich** ~ I'll find out.

Erkundigung *f* inquiry; *(Nachforschung auch)* investigation. **~en einholen** to make inquiries.

Erkundung *f (Mil)* reconnaissance.

erlahmen* *vi aux sein (lit, fig)* to flag.

erlangen* *vt* to attain, to achieve.

Erlaß *m* **-sse (a)** decree, enactment. **(b)** *(Straf~ etc)* remission.

erlassen* *vt irreg* **(a)** *Verfügung* to pass; *Gesetz* to enact. **(b)** *Strafe etc* to remit; *Gebühren* to waive. **jdm etw** ~ *Schulden etc* to release sb from sth; *Gebühren* to waive sth for sb; **jdm die Strafarbeit** ~ to let sb off a punishment.

erlauben* **1** *vt* to allow, to permit. **jdm etw** ~ to allow *or* permit sb (to do) sth; **es ist mir nicht erlaubt, das zu tun** I am not allowed *or* permitted to do that; ~ **Sie?** may I?; ~ **Sie, daß ich das Fenster öffne?** do you mind if I open the window?; ~ **Sie, daß ich mich vorstelle** allow me *or* permit me to introduce myself; ~ **Sie mal!** do you mind!; **soweit es meine Zeit erlaubt** *(form)* time permitting. **2** *vr* **sich** *(dat)* **etw** ~ *(gestatten, sich gönnen)* to allow *or* permit oneself sth; *(wagen) Bemerkung* to venture sth; *(sich leisten)* to afford sth; **sich** *(dat)* ~**, etw zu tun** *(so frei sein)* to take the liberty of doing sth; *(sich leisten)* to afford to do sth; **was** ~ **Sie sich (eigentlich)!** how dare you!

Erlaubnis *f* permission; *(Schriftstück)* permit. **(jdn) um** ~ **bitten** to ask (sb) (for) permission.

erläutern* *vt* to explain, to elucidate; *Text* to comment on. **~d** explanatory; **~d fügte er hinzu** he added in explanation.
Erläuterung *f siehe vt* explanation, elucidation; commentary. **zur ~** in explanation.
Erle *f* **-n** alder.
erleben* *vt* to experience; *(noch lebend erreichen)* to live to see; *(durchmachen) schwere Zeiten* to go through; *Abenteuer, Enttäuschung, Erfolg* to have; *Jahrhundertwende* to see. **im Urlaub habe ich viel erlebt** I had an eventful time on holiday; **was haben Sie im Ausland erlebt?** what sort of experiences did you have abroad?; **er hat schon viel Schlimmes erlebt** he's had a lot of bad times *or* experiences; **ich habe es oft erlebt** I've often seen it happen; **so wütend habe ich ihn noch nie erlebt** I've never seen *or* known him so furious; **das werde ich nicht mehr ~** I shan't live to see that; **er möchte mal etwas ~** he wants to have a good time; **das muß man erlebt haben** you've got to have experienced it for yourself; **na, der kann was ~!** *(col)* he's going to be for it! *(col)*.
Erlebnis *nt* experience; *(Abenteuer)* adventure.
erledigen* **1** *vt* **(a)** to deal with; *Akte etc* to process; *(ausführen) Auftrag* to carry out; *Sache* to settle. **Einkäufe ~** to do the shopping; **ich habe noch einiges in der Stadt zu ~** I've still got a few things to do in town; **das ist erledigt** that's taken care of, that's been done. **(b)** *(col) (ermüden)* to wear out; *(ruinieren)* to finish, to ruin; *(töten)* to do in *(col)*; *(k.o. schlagen)* to finish off. **2** *vr* **das hat sich erledigt** that's all settled; **sich von selbst ~** to take care of itself.
erledigt *adj (col) (erschöpft)* shattered *(col)*, done in *pred (col)*; *(ruiniert)* finished, ruined.
Erledigung *f (Ausführung)* execution, carrying out; *(Durchführung, Beendung)* completion; *(einer Sache)* settlement. **die ~ meiner Korrespondenz** dealing with my correspondence; **einige ~en in der Stadt** a few things to do in town; **in ~ Ihrer Anfrage** *(form)* further to your inquiry *(form)*.
erlegen* *vt Wild* to shoot, to bag *(Hunt)*.
erleichtern* *vt (einfacher machen)* to make easier; *(fig) Last, Los* to lighten; *(lindern) Not, Schmerz etc* to relieve. **sein Herz/Gewissen ~** to unburden one's heart/conscience; **jdn um etw ~** *(hum)* to relieve sb of sth; **erleichtert aufatmen** to breathe a sigh of relief.
Erleichterung *f (von Last etc)* lightening; *(Linderung)* relief. **das trägt zur ~ meiner Aufgabe bei** it makes my work easier.
erleiden* *vt irreg* to suffer.
erlernen* *vt* to learn.
erlesen *adj* exquisite. **ein ~er Kreis** a select circle.
erleuchten* *vt* to light (up), to illuminate.
Erleuchtung *f (Eingebung)* inspiration.
erliegen* *vi irreg aux sein+dat (lit, fig)* to succumb to; *einem Irrtum* to be the victim of. **zum E~ kommen** to come to a standstill.
erlogen *adj* made-up.
Erlös *m* **-e** proceeds *pl (+gen* from*)*.
erlöschen* *vi irreg aux sein (Feuer)* to go out; *(Gefühle, Interesse)* to die; *(Anspruch etc)* to expire, to lapse; *(Firma)* to be dissolved. **ein erloschener Vulkan** an extinct volcano.
erlösen* *vt (retten)* to save, to rescue *(aus, von* from*)*; *(Rel)* to redeem, to save; *(von Sünden, Qualen)* to deliver *(esp Bibl)*, to release.
erlösend *adj* relieving, liberating. **sie sprach das ~e Wort** she spoke the word he/she/everybody *etc* was waiting for.
Erlöser(in *f***)** *m* **-** *(Rel)* Redeemer; *(Befreier)* saviour.
Erlösung *f* release, deliverance; *(Erleichterung)* relief; *(Rel)* redemption.
ermächtigen* *vt* to authorize, to empower *(zu etw* to do sth*)*.
Ermächtigung *f* authorization.
ermahnen* *vt* to exhort, to urge; *(warnend)* to warn; *(Jur)* to caution. **jdn zur Aufmerksamkeit ~** to urge sb to be attentive; **jdn im Guten ~** to give sb a friendly warning.
Ermahnung *f* exhortation, urging; *(warnend)* warning; *(Jur)* caution.
Ermang(e)lung *f*: **in ~** *+gen* because of the lack of.
ermäßigen **1** *vt* to reduce. **2** *vr* to be reduced.
Ermäßigung *f* reduction; *(Steuer~)* relief.
ermattet *adj (geh)* exhausted, weary.
ermessen* *vt irreg (einschätzen) Größe, Wert* to estimate; *(begreifen können)* to appreciate.
Ermessen *nt no pl (Urteil)* judgement; *(Gutdünken)* discretion. **nach meinem ~** in my judgement; **nach menschlichem ~** as far as anyone can judge; **nach eigenem ~ handeln** to act on one's own discretion; **in jds ~** *(dat)* **liegen** to be at sb's discretion.
Ermessens-: **~entscheidung** *f (Jur)* discretionary decision; **~frage** *f* matter of discretion.
ermitteln* **1** *vt* to determine *(auch Chem, Math)*, to ascertain; *Person* to trace; *Tatsache* to establish. **2** *vi* to investigate. **gegen jdn ~** to investigate sb.
Ermittlung *f* **(a)** *no pl siehe vt* determination, ascertaining; tracing; establishing. **(b)** *(esp Jur: Erkundigung)* investigation, inquiry. **~en anstellen** to make inquiries *(über+acc* about*)*.
Ermittlungs-: **~ausschuß** *m* committee of inquiry; **~richter** *m (Jur)* examining magistrate; **~verfahren** *nt (Jur)* preliminary proceedings *pl*.
ermöglichen* *vt* to facilitate, to make possible. **jdm das Studium ~** to make it possible for sb to study.
ermorden* *vt* to murder; *(Pol)* to assassinate.
Ermordung *f* murder; *(Pol)* assassination.
ermüden* **1** *vt* to tire. **2** *vi aux sein* to tire, to become tired; *(Tech)* to fatigue.
Ermüdung *f* fatigue *(auch Tech)*, tiredness.
Ermüdungs|erscheinung *f* sign of fatigue.
ermuntern* *vt (ermutigen)* to encourage *(jdn zu etw* sb to do sth*)*; *(aufmuntern)* to cheer up.
ermutigen* *vt (ermuntern)* to encourage; *(Mut geben)* to give courage.
Ermutigung *f* encouragement.
ernähren* **1** *vt* to feed; *(unterhalten)* to support, to keep. **schlecht/gut ernährt** undernourished/well-fed. **2** *vr* to eat. **sich von etw ~** to live on sth; **sich von Übersetzungen ~** to earn one's living by doing translations.
Ernährer(in *f***)** *m* **-** breadwinner, provider.
Ernährung *f* feeding; *(Nahrung)* food, nourishment, nutrition *(esp Med)*. **die ~ einer großen Familie** feeding a big family; **falsche/richtige/pflanzliche ~** the wrong/a proper/a vegetarian diet.
Ernährungs-: **~gewohnheiten** *pl* eating habits *pl*; **~weise** *f* diet.
ernennen* *vt irreg* to appoint *(jdn zu etw* sb sth*)*.
Ernennung *f* appointment *(zu* as*)*.
erneuern* *vt* to renew; *(renovieren)* to renovate; *(restaurieren)* to restore; *(auswechseln) Maschinenteile* to replace; *(wiederbeleben)* to revive.
Erneuerung *f siehe vt* renewal; renovation; restoration; replacement; revival.
erneut **1** *adj attr* renewed. **2** *adv* (once) again.
erniedrigen* **1** *vt (demütigen)* to humiliate; *(herabsetzen)* to degrade. **2** *vr* to humble oneself; *(pej)* to lower oneself.
Erniedrigung *f siehe vt* humiliation; degradation.
Erniedrigungszeichen *nt (Mus)* flat (sign).
Ernst *m no pl* seriousness. **im ~** seriously; **allen ~es** in all seriousness, quite seriously; **ist das Ihr ~?** are you (really) serious?; **das kann doch nicht dein ~ sein!** you can't be serious!; **es ist**

mir ~ **damit** I'm serious about it, I'm in earnest; **mit einer Drohung ~ machen** to carry out a threat; **der ~ des Lebens** the serious side of life; **mit ~ bei der Sache sein** to do sth seriously.

ernst *adj* serious. **es (mit jdm/etw) ~ meinen** to be serious (about sb/sth); **jdn/etw ~ nehmen** to take sb/sth seriously; **es steht ~ um ihn** things don't look too good for him.

Ernst-: ~fall *m* emergency; **im ~fall** in case of emergency; **e~gemeint** *adj attr* serious; **e~haft** *adj* serious; *(eindringlich, eifrig)* earnest; **~haftigkeit** *f siehe adj* seriousness; earnestness; **e~lich** *adj* serious.

Ernte *f* **-n (a)** harvest *(an+dat* of*)*; *(von Äpfeln, fig)* crop. **die ~ seines Fleißes** the fruits of his labour. **(b)** *(das Ernten) (von Getriede)* harvest(ing); *(von Kartoffeln)* digging; *(von Äpfeln etc)* picking.

Ernte-: ~arbeiter *m* harvester; *(von Kartoffeln, Obst)* picker; **~(dank)fest** *nt* harvest festival.

ernten *vt Getreide* to harvest, to reap; *Kartoffeln* to get in; *Äpfel, Erbsen* to pick; *(fig) Früchte, Unfrieden* to reap; *(Un)dank, Spott* to get.

ernüchtern* *vt* to sober up; *(fig)* to bring down to earth. **~d** sobering; **ich war sehr ernüchtert** my illusions were shattered.

Ernüchterung *f* sobering-up; *(fig)* disillusionment.

Er|oberer *m* **-, Er|oberin** *f* conqueror.

er|obern* *vt* to conquer; *Festung, Stadt* to capture; *(fig) Sympathie etc* to win; *(col: ergattern)* to get hold of.

Er|oberung *f (lit, fig)* conquest; *(einer Festung, Stadt)* capture.

er|öffnen* 1 *vt* to open; *Konkursverfahren* to institute. **jdm etw ~** *(hum, geh)* to disclose *or* reveal sth to sb. **2** *vr (Aussichten etc)* to open up.

Er|öffnung *f siehe vt* opening; institution; disclosure, revelation.

Er|öffnungs-: ~ansprache *f* inaugural *or* opening address; **~kurs** *m* opening price.

erogen *adj* erogenous.

er|örtern* *vt* to discuss (in detail).

Er|örterung *f* discussion.

Erosion *f (Geol, Med)* erosion.

Erotik *f* eroticism.

erotisch *adj* erotic.

Erpel *m* **-** drake.

erpicht *adj* **auf etw** *(acc)* **~ sein** to be keen on sth.

erpressen* *vt* to blackmail; *Geld etc* to extort.

Erpresser(in *f***)** *m* **-** blackmailer; *(bei Entführung)* kidnapper.

erpresserisch *adj Methode* blackmailing *attr*.

Erpressung *f* blackmail; *(von Geld etc)* extortion.

erproben* *vt (lit, fig)* to test. **erprobt** tried and tested.

erraten* *vt irreg* to guess.

errechnen* *vt* to calculate, to work out.

erregbar *adj* excitable; *(sexuell)* easily aroused; *(empfindlich)* sensitive.

Erregbarkeit *f siehe adj* excitability; ability to be aroused; sensitivity.

erregen* 1 *vt* **(a)** *(aufregen) jdn, Nerven etc* to excite; *(erzürnen)* to infuriate. **er war vor Wut ganz erregt** he was in a rage; **erregte Diskussionen** heated discussions; **freudig erregt** excited. **(b)** *(erzeugen)* to arouse; *Aufsehen, Heiterkeit* to cause, to create; *Aufmerksamkeit* to attract. **2** *vr* to get worked up *or* excited *(über +acc* about, over*)*; *(sich ärgern)* to get annoyed *(über+acc* at*)*.

Erreger *m* **-** *(Med)* cause.

Erregung *f* excitement; *(sexuell auch)* arousal; *(Beunruhigung)* agitation; *(Wut)* rage. **in ~ geraten** to get excited/aroused/agitated/into a rage.

erreichbar *adj* reachable; *(nicht weit)* within reach; *Ziel* attainable. **leicht ~** easily reached/within easy reach/easily attainable; **schwer ~ sein** *(Ort)* not to be very accessible; *(Mensch)* to be difficult to get hold of; **der Direktor ist nie ~** the director is never available.

erreichen* *vt* to reach; *Zug* to catch; *Zweck* to achieve; *(einholen)* to catch up with. **ein hohes Alter ~** to live to a great age; **vom Bahnhof leicht zu ~** within easy reach of the station; **wann kann ich Sie morgen ~?** when can I get in touch with you tomorrow?; **wir haben nichts erreicht** we achieved nothing.

errichten* *vt* to erect, to put up; *(fig: gründen)* to set up.

Errichtung *f no pl* erection, construction; *(fig: Gründung)* setting-up.

erringen* *vt irreg* to gain.

erröten* *vi aux sein* to blush.

Errungenschaft *f* achievement; *(col: Anschaffung)* acquisition.

Ersatz *m no pl* substitute *(auch Sport)*; *(für Altes, Mitarbeiter)* replacement; *(Mil: ~truppen)* replacements *pl; (das Ersetzen)* replacement, substitution; *(von Kosten)* reimbursement. **als** *or* **zum ~** as a substitute/replacement; **als ~ für jdn einspringen** to stand in for sb; **für etw ~ leisten** *(Jur)* to pay compensation for sth.

Ersatz-: ~dienst *m (Mil)* alternative service; **~kasse** *f* private health insurance; **~mann** *m, pl* **~männer** *or* **~leute** replacement; *(Sport)* substitute; **~spieler** *m (Sport)* substitute; **~teil** *nt* spare (part); **e~weise** *adv* as an alternative.

ersaufen* *vi irreg aux sein (col)* to drown; *(Aut)* to flood.

erschaffen *vt irreg* to create.

Erschaffung *f* creation.

erscheinen* *vi irreg aux sein* to appear; *(Buch auch)* to come out. **es erscheint (mir) wünschenswert** it seems *or* appears desirable (to me).

Erscheinen *nt no pl* appearance; *(von Buch auch)* publication. **um rechtzeitiges ~ wird gebeten** you are kindly requested to attend punctually.

Erscheinung *f* **(a)** *no pl (das Erscheinen)* appearance. **in ~ treten** *(Merkmale)* to appear; *(Gefühle)* to show themselves. **(b)** *(äußere ~)* appearance; *(Natur~, Vorkommnis)* phenomenon; *(Krankheits~, Alters~)* symptom; *(Zeichen)* sign. **(c)** *(Gestalt)* figure. **(d)** *(Geister~)* apparition; *(Traumbild)* vision.

Erscheinungs-: ~form *f* manifestation; **~jahr** *nt (von Buch)* year of publication.

erschießen* *irreg* **1** *vt* to shoot (dead). **2** *vr* to shoot oneself; *siehe* **erschossen.**

Erschießung *f* shooting; *(als Todesstrafe)* execution.

erschlaffen* *vi aux sein (ermüden)* to tire; *(schlaff werden)* to go limp; *(Interesse)* to flag.

Erschlaffung *f siehe vi* tiredness; limpness; flagging.

erschlagen* 1 *vt irreg* to kill. **2** *adj (col: todmüde)* worn out, dead beat *(col)*.

erschleichen* *vt irreg* **(sich** *dat***) etw ~** to obtain sth by devious means; **sich** *(dat)* **jds Vertrauen ~** to worm oneself into sb's confidence.

erschließen* *irreg* **1** *vt Gebiet, Absatzmarkt* to develop, to open up; *Bodenschätze* to tap. **2** *vr* **sich jdm ~** *(verständlich werden)* to disclose itself to sb.

erschlossen *adj Gebiet* developed.

erschöpfen* 1 *vt* to exhaust. **2** *vr* **(a)** *(körperlich)* to exhaust oneself. **(b)** *(fig)* **sich in etw** *(dat)* **~** to amount to nothing more than sth.

erschöpfend *adj* **(a)** *(ermüdend)* exhausting. **(b)** *(ausführlich)* exhaustive.

Erschöpfung *f* exhaustion. **bis zur ~ arbeiten** to work to the point of exhaustion.

erschossen *adj (col)* **(völlig) ~ sein** to be whacked *(col)*, to be dead (beat) *(col)*.

erschrecken* 1 *vt* to frighten, to scare;

(bestürzen) to startle. **2** *pret auch* **erschrak,** *ptp auch* **erschrocken** *vir (vi: aux sein)* to be frightened *(vor+dat* by*)*; *(bestürzt sein)* to be startled. **sie erschrak beim Gedanken, daß ...** the thought that ... gave her a start *or* a scare; **sie erschrak bei dem Knall** the bang made her jump; *siehe* **erschrocken.**

erschreckend *adj* alarming, frightening. **~ wenig Leute** alarmingly few people.

erschrocken *adj* frightened, scared; *(bestürzt)* startled.

erschüttern* *vt* to shake; *Glaubwürdigkeit* to cast doubt on; *Gesundheit* to upset. **über etw** *(acc)* **erschüttert sein** to be shaken *or* shattered by sth; **ihn kann nichts ~** he always keeps his cool *(col)*.

erschütternd *adj* shattering.

Erschütterung *f (des Bodens etc)* tremor, vibration; *(seelische Ergriffenheit)* emotion, shock. **die Krise kann zu einer ~ des Staates führen** this crisis could rock the state.

erschweren* *vt* to make more difficult. **~de Umstände** *(Jur)* aggravating circumstances; **es kommt noch ~d hinzu, daß ...** to compound matters ...

Erschwerung *f* obstruction *(gen* to*)*. **das bedeutet eine ~ meiner Arbeit** that will make my job more difficult.

erschwindeln* *vt* to obtain by fraud.

erschwinglich *adj Preise* affordable.

ersehen* *vt irreg* **etw aus etw ~** to see sth from sth.

ersehnt *adj* longed-for.

ersetzen* *vt* to replace.

Ersetzung *f no pl* replacing; *(von Unkosten)* reimbursement.

ersichtlicht *adj* obvious, clear.

ersinnen* *vt irreg* to devise, to think up.

ersparen* *vt Vermögen, Zeit, Kummer* to save. **jdm/sich etw ~** to spare *or* save sb/oneself sth; **ich kann mir jeglichen Kommentar ~** I don't think I need to comment; **ihr blieb auch nichts erspart** she was spared nothing; **das Ersparte** the savings *pl*.

Ersparnis *f* **(a)** *no pl (an Zeit etc)* saving *(an+dat* of*)*. **(b)** *usu pl* savings *pl*.

erst *adv* **(a)** first. **mach ~ (ein)mal die Arbeit fertig** finish your work first; **wenn du das ~ einmal hinter dir hast** once you've got that behind you. **(b)** *(nicht früher als, nicht mehr als, bloß)* only; *(nicht früher als auch)* not until. **gerade ~** just; **~ gestern** only yesterday; **~ jetzt verstehe ich** I have only just understood; **~ morgen** not until tomorrow; **wir fahren ~ später** we're not going until later; **~ als** only when, not until. **(c) da ging's ~ richtig los** then it really got going; **da fange ich ~ gar nicht an** I simply won't bother to begin; **jetzt ~ recht/recht nicht!** just for that I will/won't do it; **wäre er doch ~ zurück!** if only he were back!; **diese Gerüchte darf man gar nicht ~ aufkommen lassen** these rumours mustn't even be allowed to start.

erstarren* *vi aux sein (Finger)* to grow stiff; *(Flüssigkeit)* to solidify; *(Gips, Zement etc)* to set; *(fig: Blut)* to freeze, to run cold; *(Lächeln)* to freeze; *(vor Entsetzen)* to be paralyzed *(vor +dat* with*)*.

erstatten* *vt* **(a)** *Unkosten* to refund. **(b)** *(form)* **(Straf)anzeige gegen jdn ~** to report sb.

Erstattung *f no pl (von Unkosten)* reimbursement.

erstaunen* *vti* to astonish, to amaze; *siehe* **erstaunt.**

Erstaunen *nt no pl* astonishment, amazement. **jdn in ~ (ver)setzen** to astonish *or* amaze sb.

erstaunlich *adj* astonishing, amazing.

erstaunt *adj* astonished, amazed *(über +acc* about*)*. **er sah mich ~ an** he looked at me in astonishment *or* amazement.

Erst-: ~ausgabe *f* first edition; **e~beste(r, s)** *adj attr siehe* **erste(r, s) (b).**

erstechen* *vt irreg* to stab to death.

erstehen* *irreg* **1** *vt (col)* to get. **2** *vi aux sein (form)* to arise.

ersteigen* *vt irreg* to climb.

ersteigern* *vt* to buy at an auction.

Ersteigung *f* ascent.

erstellen* *vt* **(a)** *(bauen)* to construct. **(b)** *Liste etc* to draw up.

erstens *adv* first(ly), in the first place.

erste(r, s) *adj* **(a)** first; *Seite der Zeitung* front. **~ Etage** first floor *(Brit)*, second floor *(US)*; **der ~ Rang** *(Theat)* the dress-circle, the (first) balcony *(US)*; **~ Qualität** top quality; **E~ Hilfe** first aid; **der E~ in der Klasse** top of the class; **als ~s** first of all; **fürs ~** for the time being; **in ~r Linie** first and foremost; **zum ~n, zum zweiten, zum dritten** *(bei Auktionen)* going, going, gone!; *siehe* **vierte(r, s). (b) er hat den ~ n besten Kühlschrank gekauft** he bought the first fridge he saw, he bought any old fridge *(col)*.

erstere(r, s) *adj* the former.

erstgenannt *adj attr* first-mentioned.

ersticken* **1** *vt jdn* to suffocate, to smother; *Feuer* to smother; *(fig) Aufruhr* to suppress. **mit erstickter Stimme** in a choked voice. **2** *vi aux sein* to suffocate; *(Feuer)* to go out. **an etw** *(dat)* **~** to be suffocated by sth; **an einer Gräte ~** to choke (to death) on a bone; **vor Lachen ~** to choke with laughter; **in der Arbeit ~** *(col)* to be snowed under with work.

Erstickung *f* suffocation, asphyxiation.

Erstickungs-: ~gefahr *f* danger of suffocation; **~tod** *m* death by suffocation, asphyxia.

Erst-: e~klassig *adj* first-class, first-rate; **~kommunion** *f* first communion.

Erstling *m* first (child); *(Werk)* first work.

erst-: ~malig 1 *adj* first; **2** *adv* for the first time; **~mals** *adv* for the first time.

erstrangig ['eːɐstraŋɪç] *adj* first-rate.

erstreben* *vt* to strive for.

erstrebenswert *adj* worthwhile; *Beruf* desirable.

erstrecken* *vr* to extend *(auf, über+acc* over*)*; *(räumlich auch)* to stretch *(auf, über+acc* over*)*; *(zeitlich auch)* to last *(auf, über+acc* for*)*.

Erststimme *f* first vote.

erstunken *adj:* **das ist ~ und erlogen** *(col)* that's a pack of lies.

Erstwähler *m* first-time voter.

ersuchen* *vt (form)* to request *(jdn um etw* sth of sb*)*.

Ersuchen *nt - (form)* request.

ertappen* *vt* to catch. **ich habe ihn dabei ertappt** I caught him at it.

erteilen* *vt* to give; *Lizenz* to issue; *Auftrag auch* to place *(jdm* with sb*)*. **jdm einen Verweis ~** to reproach sb.

Erteilung *f siehe vt* giving; issue; placing.

ertönen* *vi aux sein (geh)* to sound, to ring out. **~ lassen** to sound.

Ertrag *m* **-ë** *(von Acker)* yield; *(Einnahmen)* return.

ertragen* *vt irreg* to bear; *(esp in Frage auch)* to stand. **wie erträgst du nur seine Launen?** how do you stand his moods?

erträglich *adj* bearable, endurable; *(leidlich)* tolerable.

ertragreich *adj Geschäft* profitable, lucrative.

ertränken* **1** *vt* to drown. **2** *vr* to drown oneself.

erträumen* *vt* to dream of, to imagine.

ertrinken* *vi irreg aux sein* to drown, to be drowned.

Ertrinken *nt no pl* drowning.

Ertüchtigung *f (geh)* getting in trim. **körperliche ~** physical training.

er|übrigen* **1** *vt Zeit, Geld* to spare. **2** *vr* to be unnecessary *or* superfluous.

erwachen* *vi aux sein* to awake, to wake (up);

(*aus Ohnmacht etc*) to come around (*aus* from); (*fig: Verdacht*) to be aroused. **ein böses E~** (*fig*) a rude awakening.

erwachsen* **1** *vi irreg aux sein* (*geh*) to arise, to develop; (*Vorteil, Kosten etc*) to result. **daraus erwuchsen ihm Unannehmlichkeiten** that caused him some trouble. **2** *adj* grown-up, adult. **~ sein** (*Mensch*) to be grown-up *or* an adult.

Erwachsenenbildung *f* adult education.

Erwachsene(r) *mf decl as adj* adult, grown-up.

erwägen* *vt irreg* to consider.

Erwägung *f* consideration. **etw in ~ ziehen** to take sth into consideration.

erwähnen* *vt* to mention, to refer to.

erwähnenswert *adj* worth mentioning.

Erwähnung *f* mention (*gen* of), reference (*gen* to).

erwärmen* **1** *vt* to warm. **2** *vr* to warm up. **sich für jdn/etw ~** (*fig*) to take to sb/sth; **ich kann mich für Goethe nicht ~** Goethe leaves me cold.

erwarten* *vt* to expect. **etw von jdm ~** to expect sth from *or* of sb; **ein Kind ~** to be expecting (a baby); **das war zu ~** that was to be expected; **er erwartet, daß wir sofort gehorchen** he expects us to obey immediately; **sie kann den Sommer kaum noch ~** she's really looking forward to the summer; **was mich da wohl erwartet?** I wonder what awaits me there.

Erwartung *f* expectation; (*Spannung, Ungeduld*) anticipation. **in ~ Ihrer baldigen Antwort** (*form*) in anticipation of your early reply.

erwartungs-: ~gemäß *adv* as expected; **~voll** *adj* expectant.

erwecken* *vt* **(a)** (*liter: aus Schlaf etc*) to rouse. **etw zu neuem Leben ~** to resurrect sth. **(b)** (*fig*) *Begeisterung etc* to arouse; *Hoffnungen, Zweifel* to raise; *Erinnerungen* to bring back.

erwehren* *vr* (*+gen*) (*geh*) to ward off. **er konnte sich kaum der Tränen ~** he could hardly hold back his tears.

erweichen* *vt* to soften; (*fig: überreden auch*) to move. **sich nicht ~ lassen** to be unmoved.

erweisen* *irreg* **1** *vt* **(a)** (*nachweisen*) to prove. **eine erwiesene Tatsache** a proven fact. **(b)** (*zuteil werden lassen*) to show. **jdm einen Dienst ~** to do sb a service. **2** *vr* **sich als etw ~** to prove to be sth, to turn out to be sth; **sich jdm gegenüber dankbar ~** to show one's gratitude to sb.

erweitern* *vtr* to widen, to enlarge; *Geschäft* to expand; *Kleid* to let out; (*Med*) to dilate; (*fig*) *Kenntnisse* to broaden; *Macht* to extend.

Erweiterung *f siehe vtr* widening, enlargement; expansion; letting out; dilation; broadening; extension.

Erwerb *m no pl* acquisition; (*Kauf*) purchase. **beim ~ eines Autos** when buying a car.

erwerben* *vt irreg* to acquire; *Ehre, Vertrauen,* (*Sport*) *Titel* to win, to gain; (*käuflich*) to purchase. **sich** (*dat*) **etw ~** to acquire *etc* sth; **er hat sich** (*dat*) **große Verdienste um die Firma erworben** he has done great service for the firm.

Erwerbs-: e~fähig *adj* (*form*) capable of gainful employment; **~fähigkeit** *f* (*form*) fitness for work; **e~los** *adj* = **arbeitslos**; **e~tätig** *adj* (gainfully) employed; **~tätigkeit** *f* gainful employment; **e~unfähig** *adj* unable to work; **~unfähigkeit** *f* inability to work.

Erwerbung *f* acquisition.

erwidern* *vt* **(a)** to reply (*auf +acc* to). **(b)** *Besuch, Grüße, Blick,* (*Mil*) *Feuer* to return; *Gefühle* to reciprocate.

Erwiderung *f* (*Antwort*) reply, answer. **in ~ Ihres Schreibens vom ...** (*form*) in reply to your letter of the ...

erwirtschaften* *vt Gewinn etc* to make by good management.

erwischen* *vt* (*col*) to catch. **jdn beim Stehlen ~** to catch sb stealing; **du darfst dich nicht ~ lassen** you mustn't get caught; **ihn hat's erwischt!** (*verliebt*) he's got it bad (*col*); (*krank*) he's got it; (*gestorben*) he's had it (*col*).

erwünscht *adj Wirkung etc* desired; *Eigenschaft, Kenntnisse* desirable; (*willkommen*) welcome.

erwürgen* *vt* to strangle, to throttle.

Erz *nt* **-e** ore.

erzählen* *vti* **(a)** to tell. **er hat den Vorfall erzählt** he told (us *etc*) about the incident; **jdm etw ~** to tell sth to sb; **man erzählt sich, daß ...** people say that ...; **wem ~ Sie das!** (*col*) you're telling me!; **das kannst du einem anderen ~** (*col*) pull the other one (*col*); **mir kannst du nichts ~** (*col*) don't give *or* tell me that! (*col*); **dem werd' ich was ~!** (*col*) I'll have something to say to him; **er kann gut ~** he's a good story-teller. **(b)** (*Liter*) to narrate. **~de Dichtung** narrative fiction.

Erzähler(in *f*) *m* **-** narrator (*auch Liter*); (*Geschichten~*) story-teller; (*Schriftsteller*) narrative writer.

erzählerisch *adj* narrative.

Erzählung *f* (*Liter*) story, tale; (*das Erzählen*) narration; (*Bericht*) account.

Erz-: ~bischof *m* archbishop; **~bistum** *nt* archbishopric; **~engel** *m* archangel.

erzeugen* *vt* to produce; *Strom auch* to generate; (*fig: bewirken*) to give rise to, to create.

Erzeuger(in *f*) *m* **-** (*Comm*) producer.

Erzeugerpreis *m* manufacturer's price.

Erzeugnis *nt* product; (*Agr*) produce *no indef art, no pl.*

Erzeugung *f no pl* production; (*von Strom auch*) generation; (*geistige, künstlerische*) creation.

Erz-: ~feind *m* arch-enemy; **~grube** *f* ore mine; **~hütte** *f* smelting works *sing or pl.*

erziehbar *adj Kind* educable; *Tier* trainable. **ein Heim für schwer ~e Kinder** a home for difficult children.

erziehen* *vt irreg Kind* to bring up; *Tier, Körper* to train; (*ausbilden*) to educate. **ein Kind zur Sauberkeit ~** to bring a child up to be clean; **gut/schlecht erzogen** well/badly brought-up.

Erzieher(in *f*) *m* **-** educator.

erzieherisch *adj* educational.

Erziehung *f no pl* upbringing; (*Ausbildung*) education; (*das Erziehen*) bringing up; (*von Tieren, Körper*) training.

Erziehungs-: ~anstalt *f* approved school, borstal (*Brit*), reformatory (*US*); **e~berechtigt** *adj* having parental authority; **~berechtigte(r)** *mf* parent or (legal) guardian.

erzielen* *vt Erfolg, Ergebnis* to achieve; *Kompromiß, Geschwindigkeit* to reach; *Gewinn* to make, to realize; (*Gegenstand*) *Preis* to fetch; (*Sport*) *Tor, Punkte* to score; *Rekord* to set.

erzittern* *vi aux sein* (*liter*) to tremble.

erzkonservativ *adj* ultraconservative.

erzürnen* *vt* (*geh*) to anger, to incense.

erzwingen* *vt irreg* to force. **etw von jdm ~** to force sth out of sb.

es *pers pron* it; (*auf männliches Wesen bezogen*) (*nom*) he; (*acc*) him; (*auf weibliches Wesen bezogen*) (*nom*) she; (*acc*) her. **wer ist da? — ich bin ~** who's there? — it's me; **sie ist klug, er ist ~ auch** she is clever, so is he; **wer ist die Dame? — ~ ist meine Frau** who's the lady? — it's *or* she's my wife; **alle dachten, daß das ungerecht war, aber niemand sagte ~** everyone thought it was unjust, but nobody said so; **ich hoffe ~** I hope so; **~ sitzt sich bequem hier** it's comfortable sitting here; **~ wurde getanzt** there was dancing; **~ kamen viele Leute** a lot of people came; **~ lebe der König!** long live the king!

Es *nt* **-** (*Mus: Dur*) E flat.

Esche *f* **-n** ash-tree.

Esel *m* **-** donkey; (*col: Dummkopf*) (silly) ass. **ich ~!** silly me!; **störrisch wie ein ~** as stubborn as a mule.

Eselin *f* she-ass.

Esels-: ~brücke *f (Gedächtnishilfe)* mnemonic, aide-mémoire; **~ohr** *nt (fig)* dog-ear; **ein Buch mit ~ohren** a dog-eared book.

Eskalation *f* escalation.

eskalieren* *vti (vi: aux sein)* to escalate.

Eskapade *f (fig)* escapade.

Eskimo *m* **-s** Eskimo.

Eskorte *f* **-n** *(Mil)* escort.

eskortieren* *vt* to escort.

esoterisch *adj* esoteric.

Espe *f* **-n** aspen.

Espenlaub *nt* aspen leaves *pl.* **zittern wie ~** to shake like a leaf.

Espresso *m* **-s** espresso.

Esprit [ɛs'pri:] *m no pl* wit.

Eß-: e~bar *adj* edible, eatable; *Pilz* edible; **habt ihr irgend etwas ~bares im Haus?** have you got anything to eat in the house?; **nicht e~bar** inedible, uneatable; **~besteck** *nt* set of cutlery.

essen *pret* **aß,** *ptp* **gegessen** *vti* to eat. **gut/schlecht ~** *(Appetit haben)* to have a good/poor appetite; **in dem Restaurant kann man gut ~** that's a good restaurant; **warm/kalt ~** to have a hot/cold meal; **etw zum Frühstück ~** to have *or* eat sth for breakfast; **~ Sie gern Äpfel?** do you like apples?; **beim E~ sein** to be in the middle of a meal; **~ gehen** *(auswärts)* to eat out; **nach dem Kino gingen wir noch ~** after the cinema we went for a meal.

Essen *nt* **-** *(Mahlzeit)* meal; *(Nahrung)* food; *(Küche)* cooking. **bleib doch zum ~** stay for lunch/supper, stay for a meal; **das ~ kochen** *or* **machen** *(col)* to get the meal; **jdn zum ~ einladen** to invite sb for a meal.

Essen(s)-: ~ausgabe *f* serving of meals; *(Stelle)* serving counter; **~marke** *f* meal voucher; **~zeit** *f* mealtime; **bei uns ist um 12 ~zeit** we have lunch at 12.

essentiell [ɛsɛn'tsiɛl] *adj (geh)* essential.

Essenz *f* essence.

Esser *m* **- ein guter/schlechter ~** a good/poor eater.

Eßgeschirr *nt* dinner service.

Essig *m* **-e** vinegar. **damit ist es ~** *(col)* it's all off.

Essig-: ~essenz *f* vinegar concentrate; **~gurke** *f* (pickled) gherkin; **~säure** *f* acetic acid.

Eß-: ~kastanie *f* sweet chestnut; **~löffel** *m* soup/dessert spoon; *(in Rezept)* tablespoon; **~tisch** *m* dining table; **~zimmer** *nt* dining room.

Estragon *m no pl* tarragon.

Estrich *m* **-e** stone/clay *etc* floor.

etablieren* **1** *vt (dated)* to establish. **2** *vr* to establish oneself; *(Comm)* to set up.

etabliert *adj* established. **die ~e Oberschicht** the upper echelons of the establishment.

Etablissement [etablɪsə'mã:] *nt* **-s** establishment.

Etage [e'ta:ʒə] *f* **-n** floor. **in** *or* **auf der 2. ~** on the 2nd *(Brit) or* 3rd *(US)* floor.

Etagen-: ~bett *nt* bunk bed; **~heizung** *f heating system which covers one floor of a building.*

Etappe *f* **-n (a)** stage; *(einer Strecke auch)* leg. **(b)** *(Mil)* communications zone.

Etappen-: ~sieg *m (Sport)* stage-win; **e~weise** *adv* step by step, stage by stage.

Etat [e'ta:] *m* **-s** budget.

Etat-: ~jahr *nt* financial year; **~posten** *m* item in the budget.

etc. = et cetera [ɛt'tse:tera] etc.

etepetete [e:tәpe'te:tә] *adj pred (col)* fussy, pernickety *(col).*

Ethik *f* ethics *pl (als Fach sing).*

ethisch *adj* ethical.

ethnisch *adj* ethnic.

Etikett *nt* **-e** *(lit, fig)* label.

Etikette *f* etiquette.

etikettieren* *vt (lit, fig)* to label.

etliche(r, s) *indef pron* **(a)** *sing attr* quite a lot of. **(b) etliche** *pl (substantivisch)* quite a few, several people/things; *(attr)* several, quite a few. **(c) ~s** *sing (substantivisch)* quite a lot.

Etüde *f* **-n** *(Mus)* étude.

Etui [ɛt'vi:, e'tyi:] *nt* **-s** case.

etwa *adv* **(a)** *(ungefähr, annähernd)* about, approximately. **so ~, ~ so** more or less like this. **(b)** *(zum Beispiel)* for instance. **(c)** *(entrüstet, erstaunt)* **hast du ~ schon wieder kein Geld dabei?** don't tell me you haven't got any money again!; **willst du ~ schon gehen?** (surely) you don't want to go already! **(d)** *(zur Bestätigung)* **Sie kommen doch, oder ~ nicht?** you are coming, aren't you?; **sind Sie ~ nicht einverstanden?** do you mean to say that you don't agree?; **ist das ~ wahr?** (surely) it's not true! **(e)** *(in Gegenüberstellung, einschränkend)* **nicht ~, daß ...** (it's) not that ...; **ich wollte dich nicht ~ beleidigen** I didn't intend to insult you.

etwaig ['ɛtva:ɪç] *adj attr* possible. **~e Unkosten** any costs which might arise.

etwas *indef pron* **(a)** *(substantivisch)* something; *(fragend, bedingend auch, verneinend)* anything; *(unbestimmter Teil einer Menge)* some; any. **kannst du mir ~ (davon) leihen?** can you lend me some (of it)?; **ohne ~ zu erwähnen** without saying anything; **~ sein** *(col)* to be somebody *(col)*; **aus ihm wird nie ~** *(col)* he'll never become anything; **er kann ~** he's good; **sein Wort gilt ~ beim Chef** what he says counts for something with the boss; **das ist sicher, wie nur ~** *(col)* that's as sure as (sure) can be *(col)*; **~ Kaltes** something cold. **(b)** *(adjektivisch)* some; *(fragend, bedingend auch)* any. **~ Salz?** some salt? **(c)** *(adverbial)* **~ besser** somewhat better, a little better.

Etwas *nt no pl* **das gewisse ~** that certain something.

Etymologie *f* etymology.

euch *pers pron dat, acc of* **ihr** *(in Briefen:* **E~***)* you; *(dat auch)* to/for you; *(refl)* yourselves. **ein Freund von ~** a friend of yours; **wascht ~!** wash yourselves; **setzt ~!** sit down!

euer 1 *poss pron (in Briefen:* **E~***)* your. **E~** *(Briefschluß)* yours. **2** *pers pron gen of* **ihr. ~ aller heimlicher Wunsch** the secret wish of all of you.

Eukalyptus *m, pl* **Eukalypten** eucalyptus *pl.*

Eule *f* **-n** owl. **~n nach Athen tragen** *(prov)* to carry coals to Newcastle *(prov).*

Euphemismus *m* euphemism.

Euphorie *f* euphoria.

euphorisch *adj* euphoric.

eure(r, s) *poss pron* yours. **der/die/das ~** *(geh)* yours.

eurerseits *adv (von eurer Seite)* on your part.

euresgleichen *pron inv* people like you.

euretwegen *adv (wegen euch)* because of you, on your account; *(euch zuliebe auch)* for your sake.

Euro- *in cpds* Euro-; **~cheque** *m* Eurocheque.

Europa *nt* Europe.

Europäer(in *f***)** *m* **-** European.

europäisch *adj* European. **das E~e Parlament** the European Parliament; **E~e (Wirtschafts)gemeinschaft** European (Economic) Community, Common Market.

Europa-: ~meister *m* European champion; *(Team, Land)* European champions *pl;* **~meisterschaft** *f* European championship; **~pokal** *m* *(Sport)* European cup; **~rat** *m* Council of Europe; **~straße** *f* Euroroute.

Euro-: ~scheck *m* Eurocheque; **~vision** *f* Eurovision.

Euter *nt* **-** udder.

Euthanasie *f* euthanasia.

ev. = evangelisch.

e.V. = eingetragener Verein.

evakuieren* [evaku'i:rәn] *vt* to evacuate.

Evakuierung [evaku'i:rʊŋ] *f* evacuation.
evangelisch [evaŋ'ge:lɪʃ] *adj* Protestant.
Evangelist [evaŋge'lɪst] *m* evangelist.
Evangelium [evaŋ'ge:liʊm] *nt* Gospel; *(fig)* gospel.
Eva(s)kostüm *nt (dated hum)* **im ~** in her birthday suit *(hum)*.
eventuell [evɛntu'ɛl] **1** *adj attr* possible. **2** *adv* possibly, perhaps. **~ rufe ich Sie später an** I may possibly call you later.
Evolution [evolu'tsio:n] *f* evolution.
Evolutionstheorie *f* theory of evolution.
evtl. = **eventuell.**
EWG [e:ve:'ge:] *f* = **Europäische Wirtschaftsgemeinschaft** EEC.
ewig 1 *adj* eternal; *Eis, Schnee* perpetual; *(col) Nörgelei etc auch* never-ending. **2** *adv* for ever, eternally. **auf ~** for ever; **das dauert ja ~, bis ...** it'll take ages until ...; **~ dankbar** eternally grateful; **ich habe Sie ~ lange nicht gesehen** *(col)* I haven't seen you for ages.
Ewigkeit *f* eternity; *(col)* ages. **in die ~ eingehen** to go to eternal rest; **bis in alle ~** for ever; **eine ~ dauern** *(col)* to take ages.
ex *adv (col)* **etw ~ trinken** to drink sth down in one.
Ex- *in cpds* ex.
exakt *adj* exact. **~ arbeiten** to work accurately.
exaltiert *adj* exaggerated, effusive.
Examen *nt, pl* **-** *or* **Examina** exam, examination; *(Univ)* finals *pl.* **~ machen** to do *or* take one's exams *or* finals.
Examens-: ~angst *f* exam nerves *pl;* **~arbeit** *f* dissertation; **~kandidat** *m* candidate (for an examination).
examinieren* *vt (geh)* to examine.
exekutieren* *vt (form)* to execute.
Exekution *f* execution.
Exekutionskommando *nt* firing squad.
Exekutive [-'ti:və] *f* executive.
Exempel *nt* **die Probe aufs ~ machen** to put it to the test.
Exemplar *nt* **-e** specimen; *(Buch~)* copy.
exemplarisch *adj* exemplary. **jdn ~ bestrafen** to punish sb as an example (to others).
exerzieren* *vti* to drill; *(fig)* to practise *(Brit)*, to practice *(US)*.
Exerzierplatz *m (Mil)* parade ground.
Exhibitionismus [ɛkshibɪtsio'nɪsmʊs] *m* exhibitionism.
Exhibitionist(in *f*) [ɛkshibɪtsio'nɪst(ɪn)] *m* exhibitionist.
exhumieren* *vt* to exhume.
Exil *nt* **-e** exile. **im (amerikanischen) ~ leben** to live in exile (in America); **ins ~ gehen** to go into exile.
Exilregierung *f* government in exile.
existent *adj (geh)* existing, existent.
Existentialismus [ɛksɪstɛntsia'lɪsmʊs] *m* existentialism.
existentialistisch [-tsia'lɪstɪʃ] *adj* existential(ist).
existentiell [ɛksɪstɛn'tsiɛl] *adj (geh)* existential. **von ~er Bedeutung** of vital significance.
Existenz *f* existence; *(Lebensgrundlage)* livelihood; *(pej col: Person)* character, customer *(col)*. **eine gescheiterte ~** *(col)* a failure; **sich eine ~ aufbauen** to make a life for oneself.
Existenz-: ~berechtigung *f* right to exist; **e~fähig** *adj* able to exist; *Firma* viable; **~grundlage** *f* basis of one's livelihood; **~kampf** *m* struggle for survival; **~minimum** *nt* subsistence level; *(Lohn)* minimal living wage; **das Gehalt liegt noch unter dem ~minimum** that is not even a living wage.
existieren* [ɛksɪs'ti:rən] *vi* to exist.
exklusiv *adj* exclusive.
Exklusivbericht *m (Press)* exclusive (report).
exklusive [-'zi:və] *prep+gen* exclusive of, excluding.
Exklusivität [-zivi'tɛ:t] *f* exclusiveness.
Exkommunikation *f (Eccl)* excommunication.
Exkrement *nt usu pl (geh)* excrement *no pl,* excreta *pl.*
Exkursion *f* (study) trip.
Exmatrikulation *f (Univ)* being taken off the university register. **bei seiner ~** when he left university.
exmatrikulieren* *vt (Univ)* to take off the university register.
Exorzismus *m* exorcism.
Exot(e) *m (wk)* **-en, -en, Exotin** *f* exotic *or* tropical animal/plant *etc; (Mensch)* exotic foreigner.
exotisch *adj* exotic.
Expander *m* **-** *(Sport)* chest-expander.
expandieren* *vi* to expand.
Expansion *f (Phys, Pol)* expansion.
expansiv *adj* expansionist; *Wirtschaftszweige* expanding.
Expedition *f (Forschungs~, Mil)* expedition.
Experiment *nt* experiment.
experimentell *adj* experimental.
experimentieren* *vi* to experiment.
Experte *m (wk)* **-n, -n, Expertin** *f* expert *(für* in*)*.
explizit *adj* explicit.
explodieren* *vi aux sein (lit, fig)* to explode.
Explosion *f* explosion. **etw zur ~ bringen** to detonate *or* explode sth.
Explosionsgefahr *f* danger of explosion.
explosiv *adj (lit, fig)* explosive.
Exponent *m (Math, fig)* exponent.
exponieren* *vt (herausheben)* to expose. **an exponierter Stelle stehen** to be in an exposed position.
Export *m* **-e** export *(an +dat* of*)*; *(~waren)* exports *pl.*
Export- *in cpds* export; **~abteilung** *f* export department; **~artikel** *m* export; **~geschäft** *nt* export trade.
exportieren* *vti* to export.
Exportkaufmann *m* exporter.
Exposé [ɛkspo'ze:] *nt* **-s** *(für Film etc)* outline.
Expreß-: ~brief *m* express letter; **~gut** *nt* express goods *pl.*
Expressionismus *m* expressionism.
Expressionist(in *f*) *m* expressionist.
expressionistisch *adj* expressionist *no adv.*
exquisit *adj* exquisite.
extensiv *adj* extensive.
extra *adv (besonders)* extra, (e)specially; *(eigens, ausschließlich)* (e)specially, just; *(gesondert)* separately; *(zusätzlich)* extra, in addition; *(col: absichtlich)* on purpose. **jetzt tu ich's ~!** *(col)* just for that I will do it!
Extra-: ~ausgabe *f,* **~blatt** *nt* special edition; **~tour** *f (fig col)* **sich** *(dat)* **~touren leisten** to do one's own thing *(col)*.
extravagant [-va'gant] *adj* extravagant; *Kleidung auch* flamboyant.
Extravaganz [-va'gants] *f siehe adj* extravagance; flamboyance.
Extrawurst *f (col: Sonderwunsch)* special favour *(Brit) or* favor *(US)*. **er will immer eine ~ (gebraten haben)** he always wants something different.
extrem *adj* extreme; *Belastung* excessive. **~ schlecht/gut** extremely badly/well; **die Lage hat sich ~ verschlechtert** the situation has deteriorated enormously; **ich habe mich ~ beeilt** I hurried as much as I could.
Extrem *nt* **-e** extreme. **von einem ~ ins andere fallen** to go from one extreme to the other.
Extremfall *m* extreme (case).
Extremist(in *f*) *m* extremist.
extremistisch *adj* extremist.
extrovertiert [-vɛr'ti:ɐt] *adj* extrovert.
Exzellenz *f* Excellency.
exzentrisch *adj (Math, fig)* eccentric.
Exzeß *m* **-sse** excess. **bis zum ~** to excess.

F

F, f [ɛf] *nt* **-, -** F, f. **nach Schema F** *(col)* in the usual old way.

Fa. = **Firma.**

Fabel *f* **-n (a)** fable. **(b)** *(col)* fantastic story.

Fabel-: f~haft *adj* splendid, magnificent; **~tier, ~wesen** *nt* mythical creature.

Fabrik *f* **-en** factory.

Fabrik|anlage *f* plant; *(~gelände)* factory site.

Fabrikant(in *f*) *m* **(a)** industrialist. **(b)** *(Hersteller)* manufacturer.

Fabrikat *nt* **(a)** *(Marke)* make; *(von Nahrungs- und Genußmitteln)* brand. **(b)** *(Produkt)* product; *(Ausführung)* model.

Fabrikation *f* manufacture, production.

Fabrik- *in cpds* factory; **~direktor** *m* managing director (of a factory); **~gelände** *nt* factory site.

fabrizieren* *vt* **(a)** *(dated: industriell)* to produce. **(b)** *(col) Möbelstück etc* to make; *geistiges Produkt* to produce; *Geschichte* to concoct, to fabricate.

fabulieren* *vi (geh)* **(a)** *(pej: schwätzen)* to romance. **(b)** *(erzählen)* to spin a yarn.

Facette [fa'sɛtə] *f* facet.

Fach *nt* **¨er (a)** compartment; *(in Handtasche etc auch)* pocket; *(in Schrank, Regal etc)* shelf; *(für Briefe etc)* pigeonhole. **(b)** *(Wissens-, Sachgebiet)* subject; *(Gebiet)* field; *(Handwerk)* trade. **ein Mann vom ~** an expert; **sein ~ verstehen** to know one's stuff *(col) or* one's subject/trade.

Fach-: ~arbeiter *m* skilled worker; **~arzt** *m* specialist *(für* in*)*; **~ausdruck** *m* technical *or* specialist term; **~bereich** *m* **(a)** (special) field; **(b)** *(Univ)* school, faculty; **~buch** *nt* reference book; **wasserbautechnische ~bücher** specialist books on hydraulic engineering.

fächeln *(geh) vt* to fan.

Fächer *m* **-** fan; *(fig)* range, array.

fächer-: ~artig, ~förmig 1 *adj* fan-shaped; **2** *adv* like a fan.

Fach-: ~gebiet *nt* (special) field; **f~gemäß, f~gerecht** *adj* expert; *Ausbildung* specialist *attr*; **~geschäft** *nt* specialist shop *(Brit) or* store *(US)*; **~geschäft für Lederwaren** leather shop; **~handel** *m* specialist shops *pl (Brit) or* stores *pl (US)*; **~hochschule** *f* technical/art college; **~idiot** *m (col)* narrow-minded specialist; **~jargon** *m* technical jargon; **~kenntnisse** *pl* specialized knowledge; **~kreise** *pl*: **in ~kreisen** among experts; **f~kundig** *adj* informed *no adv*; *(erfahren)* with a knowledge of the subject; *(fachmännisch)* proficient; **jdn f~kundig beraten** to give sb informed advice; **~lehrer** *m* specialist subject teacher.

fachlich *adj* technical; *Ausbildung* specialist *attr*; *(beruflich)* professional. **~ hochqualifiziert** highly qualified in one's field.

Fach-: ~literatur *f* specialist literature; **~mann** *m, pl* **~leute** expert; **f~männisch** *adj* expert; **f~männisch ausgeführt** professionally done; **~personal** *nt* specialist staff; **~richtung** *f* subject area; **~schule** *f* technical college; **~simpelei** *f (col)* shop-talk; **f~simpeln** *vi insep (col)* to talk shop; **f~spezifisch** *adj* technical, subject-specific; **~sprache** *f* technical terminology; **f~sprachlich 1** *adj* technical; **2** *adv* in technical terminology; **~welt** *f* profession; **~werk** *nt no pl* half-timbering; **~werkhaus** *nt* half-timbered house; **~wissen** *nt* (specialized) knowledge of the/one's subject; **~wörterbuch** *nt* specialist dictionary; *(technisches auch)* technical dictionary; **~zeitschrift** *f* specialist journal; *(für Berufe)* trade journal.

Fackel *f* **-n** *(lit, fig)* torch.

fackeln *vi (col)* **da wird nicht lange gefackelt** there won't be any shilly-shallying.

Fackel-: ~schein *m* torchlight; **~zug** *m* torchlight procession.

fad(e) *adj* **(a)** *Geschmack* insipid; *Essen auch* tasteless. **(b)** *(fig: langweilig)* dull.

Faden[1] *m* **¨** *(lit, fig)* thread; *(Bohnen~, an Marionetten)* string; *(Med)* stitch. **der rote ~** *(fig)* the central theme; **den ~ verlieren** *(fig)* to lose the thread; **alle ¨~ laufen hier zusammen** this is the nerve centre *(Brit) or* center *(US)* of the whole business; **er hält alle ¨~ in der Hand** he holds the reins; **sein Leben hing an einem ~** his life was hanging by a thread.

Faden[2] *m* **-** *(Naut)* fathom.

Faden-: ~kreuz *nt* crosshair; **~nudeln** *pl* vermicelli *pl*; **f~scheinig** *adj (fig)* flimsy; *Argument auch, Moral* threadbare *no adv.*

Fagott *nt* **-e** bassoon.

fähig *adj* capable, competent, able. **sie ist ein ~er Kopf** she has an able mind; **(dazu) ~ sein, etw zu tun** to be capable of doing sth; **zu allem ~ sein** to be capable of anything.

Fähigkeit *f* ability; *(praktisches Können)* skill. **die ~ haben, etw zu tun** to be capable of doing sth; **bei deinen ~en ...** with your talents ...

fahl *adj* pale.

fahnden *vi* to search *(nach* for*)*.

Fahndung *f* search.

Fahndungs-: ~aktion *f* search; **~buch** *nt*, **~liste** *f* wanted (persons) list.

Fahne *f* **-n (a)** flag; *(von Verein etc auch)* banner; *(Mil auch)* colours *pl (Brit)*, colors *pl (US)*. **die ~ hochhalten** *(fig)* to keep the flag flying; **etw auf seine ~ schreiben** *(fig)* to take up the cause of sth; **mit fliegenden ~n zu jdm/etw überlaufen** to go over to sb/sth. **(b)** *(col)* **eine ~ haben** to reek of alcohol. **(c)** *(Typ)* galley (proof).

Fahnen-: ~eid *m* oath of allegiance; **~flucht** *f (Mil, fig)* desertion; **f~flüchtig** *adj* **f~flüchtig sein** *(Mil, fig)* to be a deserter; **~flüchtige(r)** *mf (Mil, fig)* deserter; **~mast** *m*, **~stange** *f* flagpole.

Fähnrich *m (Mil)* officer cadet; *(Hist)* ensign. **~ zur See** midshipman.

Fahr-: ~ausweis *m (form)* ticket; **~bahn** road; *(Fahrspur)* lane; **f~bar** *adj* on castors; *Kran* mobile; **f~barer Untersatz** *(hum)* wheels *pl (hum)*; **f~bereit** *adj* in running order.

Fähre *f* **-n** ferry.

fahren *pret* **fuhr,** *ptp* **gefahren 1** *vi aux sein* **(a)** *(Fahrzeug, Fahrgast)* to go; *(reisen)* to travel; *(Fahrer)* to drive; *(Schiff)* to sail; *(Kran, Rolltreppe etc)* to move. **mit dem Zug/Motorrad/Taxi ~** to go by train/motorbike/taxi; **mit dem Aufzug ~** to take the lift, to ride the elevator *(US)*; **wollen wir ~ oder zu Fuß gehen?** shall we go by car/bus *etc* or walk?; **links/rechts ~** to drive on the left/right; **wie lange fährt man von hier nach Basel?** how long does it take to get to Basle from here?; **gegen einen Baum ~** to drive *or* go into a tree.

(b) *(losfahren)* to go, to leave.

(c) *(verkehren)* **es ~ täglich zwei Fähren** there are two ferries a day; **die U-Bahn fährt alle fünf Minuten** the underground goes *or* runs every five minutes.

(d) blitzartig fuhr es ihm durch den Kopf, daß ... the thought suddenly flashed through his mind that ...; **was ist (denn) in dich gefahren?** what's got *(Brit) or* gotten *(US)* into you?; **in seine Kleider ~** to fling on one's clothes; **der Blitz fuhr in die Eiche** the lightning struck the oak; **sich** *(dat)* **mit der Hand über die Stirn ~** to pass one's hand over one's brow; **einen ~ lassen** *(col)* to fart *(col)*.

(e) *(zurechtkommen)* **(mit jdm/etw) gut/schlecht ~** to get on all right/not very well (with sb/sth); **(bei etw) gut/schlecht ~** to do well/badly (with sth).

2 *vt* **(a)** *(lenken) Auto, Bus etc* to drive; *Fahrrad, Motorrad* to ride. **(b)** *aux sein Straße, Strecke, Buslinie etc* to take. **welche Strecke fährt der 59er?** which way does the 59 go?; **ich fahre lieber Autobahn als Landstraße** I prefer (driving on) motorways to ordinary roads. **(c)** *(benutzen) Kraftstoff etc* to use. **(d)** *(befördern)* to take; *(hierher~)* to bring; *(Lastwagen, Taxi: gewerbsmäßig)* to carry. **ich fahre dich nach Hause** I'll take *or* drive you home, I'll give you a lift home. **(e)** *aux sein Geschwindigkeit* to do. **(f)** *aux haben or sein (Sport) Rennen* to take part in; *Runde etc* to do; *Zeit, Rekord etc* to clock up. **(g)** *(Tech) (steuern, betreiben)* to run; *(durchführen) Sonderschicht* to put on.

3 *vr* **der neue Wagen fährt sich gut** the new car is nice to drive.

fahrend *adj* itinerant. **~es Volk** travelling people; **ein ~er Sänger** a wandering minstrel.

fahrenlassen* *vt sep irreg Hoffnung* to abandon.

Fahrer(in *f***)** *m* **- (a)** driver. **(b)** *(Sport col) (Rad~)* cyclist; *(Motorrad~)* motorcyclist.

Fahrerflucht *f* hit-and-run driving. **~begehen** to be involved in a hit-and-run.

Fahr-: ~erlaubnis *f (form)* driving licence *(Brit)*, driver's license *(US)*; **~gast** *m* passenger; **~gelegenheit** *f* transport *no indef art*; **~geschwindigkeit** *f (form)* speed; **~gestell** *nt (Aut)* chassis.

Fährhafen *m* ferry terminal.

fahrig *adj* nervous; *(unkonzentriert)* distracted.

Fahrkarte *f* ticket; *(fig)* passport *(nach* to*)*.

Fahrkarten-: ~ausgabe *f* ticket office; **~automat** *m* ticket machine; **~kontrolle** *f* ticket inspection; **~schalter** *m* ticket office.

Fahr-: f~lässig *adj* negligent *(auch Jur)*; **f~lässig handeln** to be guilty of negligence; **~lässigkeit** *f* negligence *(auch Jur)*; **~lehrer** *m* driving instructor.

Fährmann *m, pl* **-männer** *or* **-leute** ferryman.

Fahr-: ~plan *m* timetable, schedule *(US)*; *(fig)* schedule; **f~planmäßig 1** *adj* scheduled; **2** *adv* on schedule; *verlaufen* according to schedule; **~praxis** *f no pl* driving experience *no indef art*; **~preis** *m* fare; **~prüfung** *f* driving test.

Fahrrad *nt* bicycle, bike *(col)*.

Fahrrad-: ~fahrer *m* cyclist; **~händler** *m* bicycle dealer; *(Geschäft)* cycle shop *(Brit) or* store *(US)*; **~weg** *m* cycle path.

Fahr-: ~rinne *f (Naut)* shipping channel, fairway; **~schein** *m* ticket; **~schule** *f* driving school; **~schüler** *m* learner driver *(Brit)*, student driver *(US)*; **~spur** *f* lane; **~stil** *m* style of driving/riding/skiing *etc*; **~streifen** *m* lane; **~stuhl** *m* lift *(Brit)*, elevator *(US)*; **~stunde** *f* driving lesson.

Fahrt *f* **-en** journey; *(Aut auch)* drive; *(Ausflug)* trip; *(Naut)* voyage; *(Über~)* crossing. **nach zwei Stunden ~** after travelling for two hours; **was kostet eine ~ nach London?** how much is it to London?; **gute ~!** safe journey!; **volle ~ voraus!** *(Naut)* full speed ahead!; **jdn in ~ bringen** *(col)* to get sb going; **in ~ sein** *(col)* to have got going; *(wütend)* to be mad *(col)*.

Fahr-: f~tauglich *adj* fit to drive; **~tauglichkeit** *f* fitness to drive.

Fährte *f* **-n** tracks *pl*; *(Witterung)* scent; *(Spuren)* trail. **auf der richtigen/falschen ~ sein** *(fig)* to be on the right/wrong track; **jdn auf eine falsche ~ locken** *(fig)* to put sb off the scent.

Fahrtechnik *f* driving technique.

Fahrten-: ~buch *nt* driver's log; **~messer** *nt* sheath knife; **~schreiber** *m* tachograph.

Fahrtest *m* road test.

Fahrt-: ~kosten *pl* travelling *(Brit) or* traveling *(US)* expenses *pl*; **~richtung** *f* direction of travel; *(im Verkehr)* direction of the traffic; **entgegen der/in ~richtung** *(im Zug)* with one's back to the engine/facing the engine; *(im Bus etc)* facing backwards/the front; **die Autobahn ist in ~richtung Norden gesperrt** the northbound section of the motorway is closed; **~richtungsanzeiger** *m (Aut)* indicator.

Fahr-: f~tüchtig *adj* fit to drive; *Wagen etc* roadworthy; **~tüchtigkeit** *f* driving ability; roadworthiness.

Fahrtwind *m* airstream.

Fahr-: f~untauglich *adj* unfit to drive; *Wagen etc* unroadworthy; **~verbot** *nt* driving ban; **jdn mit ~verbot belegen** to ban sb from driving; **~verhalten** *nt (von Fahrer)* behaviour *(Brit) or* behavior *(US)* behind the wheel; *(von Wagen)* road performance; **~wasser** *nt* **(a)** *(Naut)* = **~rinne; (b)** *(fig)* **in jds ~wasser geraten** to get in with sb; **in ein gefährliches ~wasser geraten** to get on to dangerous ground; **~weise** *f* **seine ~weise** his driving; **~werk** *nt* **(a)** *(Aviat)* undercarriage, landing gear; **(b)** *(Aut)* chassis; **~zeit** *f* time for the journey; **bei einer ~zeit von fünf Stunden** on a five-hour journey.

Fahrzeug *nt* vehicle; *(Luft~)* aircraft; *(Wasser~)* vessel.

Fahrzeug-: ~führer *m (form)* driver of a vehicle; **~halter** *m* vehicle owner; **~papiere** *pl* vehicle documents *pl*.

Faible ['fɛːbl] *nt* **-s** *(geh)* liking; *(Schwäche auch)* weakness; *(Vorliebe auch)* penchant.

fair [fɛːɐ] **1** *adj* fair *(gegen* to*)*. **2** *adv* fairly **~ spielen** *(Sport)* to play fairly; *(fig)* to play fair.

Fäkalien [-iən] *pl* faeces *pl*.

Faksimile [fak'ziːmile] *nt* **-s** facsimile.

Faktor *m* factor *(auch Math)*.

Faktum *nt, pl* **Fakten** fact.

fakturieren* *vt (Comm)* to invoice.

Fakultät *f (Univ)* faculty.

Falke *m* **-n** falcon; *(fig)* hawk.

Falkner(in *f***)** *m* **-** falconer.

Fall *m* **¨-e (a)** *(Sturz)* fall; *(fig: von Menschen, Regierung auch)* downfall. **zu ~ kommen** *(lit, geh)* to fall; **über die Affäre ist er zu ~ gekommen** *(fig)* the affair was his downfall; **zu ~ bringen** *(lit geh)* to trip up; *(fig) Menschen, Regierung* to cause the downfall of; *Gesetz, Plan etc* to thwart.

(b) *(Umstand, Jur, Med, Gram)* case. **gesetzt den ~** assuming (that); **für den ~, daß ich ...** in case I ...; **für alle ¨~e** just in case; **auf jeden/keinen ~** at any rate/on no account; **das mache ich auf keinen ~** there's no way I'm going to do that; **im ~(e)** *+gen* in the event of; **auf alle ¨~e** in any case, anyway; **für solche ¨~e** for such occasions; **im äußersten ~(e)** if the worst comes to the worst; **im günstigsten/schlimmsten ~(e)** at best/worst; **in diesem ~** in this case *or* instance; **jds ~ sein** *(col)* to be sb's cup of tea *(col)*; **klarer ~!** *(col)* sure thing! *(col)*, you bet! *(col)*; **der erste/zweite/dritte/vierte ~** *(Gram)* the nominative/genitive/dative/accusative case.

Fallbeil *nt* guillotine.

Falle *f* **-n (a)** *(lit, fig)* trap. **in eine ~ geraten** *or* **gehen** *(lit)* to get caught in a trap; *(fig)* to fall into a trap; **jdm in die ~ gehen** to walk *or* fall into sb's trap; **in der ~ sitzen** to be trapped; **jdm eine ~ stellen** *(fig)* to set a trap for sb. **(b)** *(col: Bett)* bed. **in die ~ gehen** to hit the hay *(col)*.

fallen *pret* **fiel,** *ptp* **gefallen** *vi aux sein* **(a)** to fall. **etw ~ lassen** to drop sth; **über etw** *(acc)* ~ to fall over sth; **durch eine Prüfung ~** to fail an exam.

(b) *(abfallen, sinken)* to drop, to fall; *(Aktien, Barometer)* to fall; *(Nachfrage, Ansehen)* to fall off. **im Preis/Wert ~** to drop *or* fall in price/ value.

(c) *(im Krieg)* to fall, to be killed. **mein Mann ist gefallen** my husband was killed in the war.

(d) *(erobert werden: Festung, Stadt etc)* to fall.

(e) *(sich ereignen: Datum etc)* to fall *(auf+acc* on*)*; *(gehören)* to come *(unter+acc* under, *in+acc* within, under*)*. **in eine Zeit ~** to belong to an era.

(f) *(zufallen: Erbschaft etc)* to go *(an+acc* to*)*. **das Elsaß fiel an Frankreich** Alsace fell *or (nach Verhandlungen)* went to France.

(g) *(gemacht werden) (Entscheidung)* to be made; *(Urteil)* to be passed; *(Schuß)* to be fired; *(Sport: Tor)* to be scored; *(Wort)* to be uttered *or* spoken; *(Name)* to be mentioned; *(Bemerkung)* to be made.

fällen *vt* **(a)** *Baum* to fell. **(b)** *(fig) Entscheidung* to make; *Urteil* to pass.

fallenlassen* *vt sep irreg* to drop.

Fallensteller *m* - *(Hunt)* trapper.

fällig *adj* due *pred*; *Rechnung, Betrag auch* payable; *Wechsel* mature(d). **längst ~** long overdue; **die ~en Zinsen** the interest due; **~ werden** to become *or* fall due; *(Wechsel)* to mature.

Fälligkeit *f (Fin)* settlement date; *(von Wechseln)* maturity.

Fall|obst *nt* windfalls *pl*.

Fallout [fɔː'laut] *m* **-s** fall-out.

Fallrückzieher *m (Ftbl)* overhead kick, bicycle kick.

falls *conj (wenn)* if; *(für den Fall, daß)* in case.

Fallschirm *m* parachute. **mit dem ~ abspringen** to parachute; **etw mit dem ~ abwerfen** to drop sth by parachute.

Fallschirm-: ~absprung *m* parachute jump; **~jäger** *m (Mil)* paratrooper; **~springer** *m* parachutist; **~truppe** *f (Mil)* paratroops, paras *pl*.

Fall-: ~strick *m (fig)* trap, snare; **~studie** *f* case study; **~tür** *f* trapdoor.

Fällung *f no pl* **(a)** *(von Bäumen)* felling. **(b)** *(Jur: eines Urteils)* passing; *(einer Entscheidung)* reaching.

fallweise *adv* from case to case.

falsch *adj* **(a)** wrong. **richtig/wahr oder ~** right or wrong/true or false; **alles ~ machen** to do everything wrong; **wie man's macht, ist es ~** *(col)* whatever I/you *etc* do it's bound to be wrong; **~er Alarm** *(lit, fig)* false alarm; **etw ~ verstehen** to misunderstand sth, to get sth wrong; **etw ~ schreiben/aussprechen** to spell/pronounce sth wrongly, to misspell/mispronounce sth; **die Uhr geht ~** the clock is wrong; **~ spielen** *(Mus)* to play the wrong note/notes; *(unrein)* to play off key *or* out of tune; *(Cards)* to cheat; **~ singen** to sing out of tune *or* off key; **Sie sind hier ~** you're in the wrong place; **da sind Sie bei mir an den F~en geraten** you've picked the wrong person (in me); **~ liegen** *(col)* to be wrong *(bei, in+dat* about, *mit* in*)*.

(b) *(unecht) Zähne etc* false; *Geld* forged; *Paß* fake.

(c) *(unaufrichtig) Gefühl, Freund etc* false. **ein ~es Spiel (mit jdm) treiben** to play (sb) false.

fälschen *vt* to forge, to fake; *Tatsachen* to falsify; *siehe* **gefälscht.**

Fälscher(in *f)* *m* - forger.

Falsch-: ~fahrer *m* person/car driving in the wrong direction/on the wrong side of the road *etc*; **~geld** *nt* counterfeit *or* forged money.

fälschlich 1 *adj* false. **2** *adv* wrongly, falsely; *(versehentlich)* by mistake.

fälschlicherweise *adv* wrongly, falsely.

Falsch-: ~meldung *f (Press)* false report; **~münzer(in** *f)* *m* - forger, counterfeiter; **~münzerei** *f* forgery, counterfeiting; **f~spielen** *vi sep (Cards)* to cheat; **~spieler** *m (Cards)* cheat.

Fälschung *f* forgery.

fälschungssicher *adj* forgery-proof.

Falsett *nt* **-e** falsetto.

Falt-: ~blatt *nt* leaflet; *(in Zeitschrift etc)* insert; **~boot** *nt* collapsible boat.

Falte *f* **-n** fold; *(Knitter~)* crease; *(in Haut)* wrinkle. **die Stirn in ~n legen** to knit one's brow.

falten *vtr* to fold. **die Stirn ~** to knit one's brow.

Falten-: f~los *adj Haut* unlined; **f~reich** *adj Haut* wrinkled; **~rock** *m* pleated skirt.

Falter *m* - *(Tag~)* butterfly; *(Nacht~)* moth.

faltig *adj (zerknittert)* creased; *(in Falten gelegt)* hanging in folds; *Gesicht, Haut* wrinkled.

Falz *m* **-e** *(Kniff, Faltlinie)* fold.

falzen *vt Papierbogen* to fold.

Fam. = Familie.

familiär *adj* **(a)** family *attr*. **(b)** *(zwanglos)* informal; *(pej: plump-vertraulich)* familiar. **mit jdm ~ verkehren** to be on familiar terms with sb.

Familie [fa'miːliə] *f* family. **~ Müller** the Müller family; **~ Otto Francke** *(als Anschrift)* Mr. & Mrs. Otto Francke and family; **~ haben** *(col)* to have a family; **aus guter ~ sein** to come from a good family; **es liegt in der ~** it runs in the family; **zur ~ gehören** to be one of the family; **es bleibt in der ~** it'll stay in the family; **das kommt in den besten ~n vor** *(hum)* that can happen in the best of families.

Familien- [-iən-] *in cpds* family; **~angehörige(r)** *mf* dependant; **~anschluß** *m*: **Unterkunft mit ~anschluß** *accommodation where one is treated as one of the family;* **~anzeigen** *pl* personal announcements *pl*; **~kreis** *m* family circle; **~mitglied** *nt* member of the family; **~name** *m* surname, family name *(US)*; **~oberhaupt** *nt* head of the family; **~packung** *f* family(-size) pack; **~planung** *f* family planning; **~stand** *m* marital status; **~vater** *m* father of a family; **~verhältnisse** *pl* family circumstances; **~vorstand** *m (form)* head of the family.

famos *adj (dated col)* capital *(dated col)*, splendid.

Fan [fɛn] *m* **-s** fan.

Fanal *nt* **-e** *(liter)* signal *(gen* for*)*.

Fanatiker(in *f)* *m* - fanatic.

fanatisch *adj* fanatical.

Fanatismus *m* fanaticism.

fand *pret of* **finden.**

Fanfare *f* **-n** *(Mus)* fanfare.

Fang *m* **:-e** **(a)** *no pl (das Fangen)* hunting; *(Fischen)* fishing. **(b)** *no pl (Beute) (lit, fig)* catch; *(fig: von Gegenständen)* haul. **(c)** *usu pl (Hunt: Kralle)* talon. **in den ~en** *+gen (fig)* in the clutches of.

fangen *pret* **fing,** *ptp* **gefangen 1** *vti* to catch; *Verbrecher, Soldat etc auch* to capture; *siehe* **gefangen. 2** *vr* **(a)** *(in einer Falle etc)* to get caught. **(b)** *(das Gleichgewicht wiederfinden)* to steady oneself; *(beim Reden etc)* to compose oneself; *(seelisch)* to get on an even keel again.

Fänger *m* - *(Tier~)* hunter; *(Sport)* catcher.

Fang-: ~frage *f* catch *or* trick question; **~schiff** *nt* fishing boat; *(mit Netzen)* trawler.

Farb- *in cpds* colour *(Brit)*, color *(US)*; **~aufnahme** *f* colour *(Brit) or* color *(US)* photo(graph); **~bad** *nt* dye-bath; **~band** *nt (von Schreibmaschine)* (typewriter) ribbon.

Farbe *f* **-n** **(a)** colour *(Brit)*, color *(US)*. **~ bekommen** to get a bit of colour; **~ verlieren** to go pale. **(b)** *(Maler~)* paint; *(für Farbbad)* dye; *(Druck~)* ink. **(c)** *(Cards)* suit. **~ bekennen** *(fig)* to nail one's colours to the mast.

farb|echt *adj* colourfast *(Brit)*, colorfast *(US)*.
Färbemittel *nt* dye.
farb|empfindlich *adj (Phot)* colour-sensitive *(Brit)*, color-sensitive *(US)*.
färben 1 *vt* to colour *(Brit)*, to color *(US)*; *Stoff, Haar* to dye; *siehe* **gefärbt. 2** *vi (ab~)* to run. **3** *vr* to change colour. **sich grün/blau ~** to turn green/ blue.
Farben- *in cpds* colour *(Brit)*, color *(US)*; **f~blind** *adj* colour-blind *(Brit)*, color-blind *(US)*; **f~froh** *adj* colourful *(Brit)*, colorful *(US)*; **f~prächtig** *adj* gloriously colourful *(Brit) or* colorful *(US)*; **~reichtum** *m* wealth of colours *(Brit) or* colors *(US)*; **~sinn** *m* sense of colour *(Brit) or* color *(US) (auch Biol)*.
Farb-: ~fernsehen *nt* colour *(Brit) or* color *(US)* television; **~film** *m* colour *(Brit) or* color *(US)* film; **~gebung** *f* colouring *(Brit)*, coloring *(US)*.
farbig *adj* coloured *(Brit)*, colored *(US)*; *(fig) Schilderung* vivid, colourful *(Brit)*, colorful *(US)*.
Farbige(r) *mf decl as adj* coloured *(Brit) or* colored *(US)* man/woman/person *etc.* **die ~n** coloured people *pl.*
Farb-: ~kasten *m* paintbox; **f~los** *adj (lit, fig)* colourless *(Brit)*, colorless *(US)*; **~losigkeit** *f (lit, fig)* colourlessness *(Brit)*, colorlessness *(US)*; **~stift** *m* coloured *(Brit) or* colored *(US)* pen; *(Buntstift)* crayon; **~stoff** *m (Lebensmittel~)* (artificial) colouring *(Brit) or* coloring *(US)*; *(Haut~)* pigment; **~ton** *m* shade; *(Tönung)* tint.
Färbung *f* colouring *(Brit)*, coloring *(US)*; *(Tönung)* tinge; *(fig)* slant, bias.
Farce ['farsə] *f* **-n** *(Theat, fig)* farce.
Farm *f* **-en** farm.
Farmer *m* **-** farmer.
Farn *m* **-e, Farnkraut** *nt* fern.
Färöer *pl* Faeroes *pl*, Faeroe Islands *pl.*
Fasan *m* **-e** *or* **-en** pheasant.
Fasching *m* **-e** *or* **-s** Shrovetide carnival.
Faschismus *m* fascism.
Faschist(in *f*) *m* fascist.
faschistisch *adj* fascist.
faseln *(pej)* **1** *vi* to drivel *(col)*. **2** *vt* **Blödsinn ~** to talk drivel.
Faser *f* **-n** fibre *(Brit)*, fiber *(US)*.
fas(e)rig *adj* fibrous; *Fleisch, Spargel* stringy *(pej)*; *(zerfasert)* frayed.
Faser-: ~pflanze *f* fibre *(Brit) or* fiber *(US)* plant; **~platte** *f* fibreboard *(Brit)*, fiberboard *(US)*.
Faß *nt, pl* **Fässer** barrel; *(kleines Bier~)* keg; *(zum Gären, Einlegen)* vat; *(zum Buttern)* churn; *(für Öl, Benzin etc)* drum. **vom ~** on tap; *Bier* on draught *(Brit) or* draft *(US)*; **Bier vom ~** draught beer; **ein ~ ohne Boden** *(fig)* a bottomless pit; **das schlägt dem ~ den Boden aus** *(col)* that's too much!
Fassade *f (lit, fig)* façade.
Faß-: f~bar *adj* comprehensible; **das ist doch nicht f~bar!** that's incomprehensible!; **~bier** *nt* draught *(Brit) or* draft *(US)* beer.
Fäßchen *nt dim of* **Faß.**
fassen 1 *vt* **(a)** *(ergreifen)* to take hold of; *(hastig, kräftig)* to grab, to seize; *(festnehmen) Einbrecher etc* to apprehend, to seize. **jdn am Arm ~** to take/grab sb by the arm; **faß!** seize! **(b)** *(fig) Entschluß* to make, to take; *Mut* to take. **den Gedanken ~, etw zu tun** to form the idea of doing sth. **(c)** *(begreifen)* to grasp. **es ist nicht zu ~** it's unbelievable. **(d)** *(enthalten)* to hold. **(e)** *(fig: ausdrücken)* to express. **in Verse/Worte ~** to put into verse/words; **etw weit/eng ~** to interpret sth broadly/narrowly. **2** *vi (greifen)* **an/in etw** *(acc)* **~** to feel sth; *(berühren)* to touch sth; **faß mal unter den Tisch** feel under the table. **3** *vr (sich beherrschen)* to compose onself. **sich in Geduld ~** to possess one's soul in patience; **sich kurz ~** to be brief; *siehe* **gefaßt.**
Fasson [fa'sõ:] *f* **-s** style; *(Art und Weise)* way. **aus der ~ geraten** *(lit)* to lose its shape.
Fassonschnitt [fa'sõ:-] *m (für Herren)* short back and sides.
Fassung *f* **(a)** *(von Juwelen)* setting; *(von Bild)* frame; *(Elec)* holder. **(b)** *(Bearbeitung)* version. **ein Film in deutscher ~** a film with German dubbing. **(c)** *no pl (Ruhe, Besonnenheit)* composure. **etw mit ~ tragen** to take sth calmly; **völlig außer ~ geraten** to lose all self-control; **jdn aus der ~ bringen** to disconcert *or* throw *(col)* sb.
Fassungs-: f~los *adj* aghast, stunned; **~losigkeit** *f* complete bewilderment; **~vermögen** *nt* capacity; **das übersteigt mein ~vermögen** that is beyond me.
fast *adv* almost, nearly. **~ nie** hardly ever.
fasten *vi* to fast.
Fastenzeit *f (Eccl)* Lent.
Fastnacht *f no pl* Shrovetide carnival.
Fastnachtszeit *f* carnival period.
Faszination *f* fascination.
faszinieren* *vti* to fascinate *(an +dat* about*)*. **~d** fascinating.
fatal *adj (geh) (verhängnisvoll)* fatal, fateful; *(peinlich)* embarrassing, awkward.
Fata Morgana *f* **- -s** *(lit, fig)* Fata Morgana *(liter)*, mirage.
Fatzke *m* **-s** *(col)* stuck-up twit *(col)*.
fauchen *vti* to hiss.
faul *adj* **(a)** *(verfault)* bad; *Eier, Obst auch, Holz* rotten; *Geschmack, Geruch auch, Wasser* foul; *Laub* rotting. **(b)** *(träge)* lazy, idle. **(c)** *(verdächtig)* fishy *(col)*, suspicious; *Ausrede* feeble; *Kompromiß* uneasy; *(dumm) Witz* bad. **hier ist etwas ~** *(col)* there's something fishy here *(col)*.
faulen *vi aux sein or haben* to rot; *(Zahn)* to decay; *(Lebensmittel)* to go bad.
faulenzen *vi* to laze *or* loaf *(esp pej col)* about.
Faulenzer *m* **-** layabout.
Faulenzerei *f* lazing *or* loafing *(esp pej col)* about.
Faulheit *f* laziness, idleness.
faulig *adj* going bad; *Geruch, Geschmack* foul.
Fäulnis *f no pl* rot; *(von Zahn)* decay. **in ~ übergehen** to go rotten.
Faul-: ~pelz *m (col)* lazybones *sing (col)*; **~tier** *nt* sloth; *(col: Mensch)* lazybones *sing (col)*.
Fauna *f, pl* **Faunen** fauna.
Faust *f, pl* **Fäuste** fist. **jdm mit der ~ ins Gesicht schlagen** to punch sb in the face; **mit der ~ auf den Tisch schlagen** *(lit)* to thump the table (with one's fist); *(fig)* to take a hard line; **die ~ in der Tasche ballen** *(fig)* to choke back one's anger; **das paßt wie die ~ aufs Auge** *(paßt nicht)* it's all wrong; *(Farbe)* it clashes horribly; *(paßt gut)* it's just the job *(col)*; **auf eigene ~** *(fig)* on one's own initiative, off one's own bat *(col)*; *reisen, fahren* under one's own steam.
Faustball *m form of volleyball.*
Fäustchen *nt*: **sich** *(dat)* **ins ~ lachen** to laugh up one's sleeve.
faustdick *adj (col)* **eine ~e Lüge** a whopper *(col)*, a whopping (great) lie *(col)*; **er hat es ~ hinter den Ohren** he's a crafty one *(col)*.
fausten *vt Ball* to punch.
Faust-: f~groß *adj* as big as a fist; **~handschuh** *m* mitt(en).
Faustkampf *m* fist-fight.
Faust-: ~pfand *nt* security; **~recht** *nt no pl* law of the jungle; **~regel** *f* rule of thumb; **~schlag** *m* punch.
Favorit(in *f*) [favo'ri:t(ɪn)] *m (wk)* **-en, -en** favourite *(Brit)*, favorite *(US)*.
Faxen *pl* **~ machen** to fool around.
Fazit *nt* **-s** *or* **-e das ~ der Untersuchungen war ...** on balance the result of the investigations was ...; **wenn wir aus diesen vier Jahren das ~ ziehen** if we take stock of these four years.
FDP [ɛfde:'pe:] *f* = **Freie Demokratische Partei.**
Feature ['fi:tʃɐ] *nt* **-s** *(Rad, TV, Press)* feature.

Februar *m* **-e** February; *siehe* **März.**
fechten *pret* **focht,** *ptp* **gefochten** *vi (Sport)* to fence; *(geh: kämpfen)* to fight. **das F~** fencing.
Fechter(in *f*) *m* **-** fencer.
Fecht-: ~hieb *m* (fencing) cut; **~sport** *m* fencing.
Feder *f* **-n (a)** *(Vogel~)* feather. **~n lassen müssen** *(col)* not to escape unscathed; **in den ~n liegen** *(col)* to be/stay in one's bed *or* pit *(col)*. **(b)** *(Schreib~)* quill; *(an ~halter)* nib. **ich greife zur ~ ...** I take up my pen ... **(c)** *(Tech)* spring.
Feder-: ~ball *m (Spiel)* badminton; **~besen** *m* feather duster; **~bett** *nt* continental quilt *(Brit)*, comforter *(US)*; **f~führend** *adj* **(a)** *Behörde* in overall charge *(für* of); **(b) diese Firma ist bei Computern f~führend** this firm are the market-leaders in computers; **~führung** *f* **unter der ~führung** *+gen* under the overall control of; **die ~führung haben** to be in overall charge; **~gewicht** *nt (Sport)* featherweight; **~halter** *m* (dip) pen; *(Füll~)* (fountain) pen; **~kernmatratze** *f* interior sprung mattress; **~kiel** *m* quill; **~kissen** *nt* feather cushion; *(in Bett)* feather pillow; **~krieg** *m (fig)* war of words; **f~leicht** *adj* light as a feather; **~lesen** *nt*: **nicht viel ~lesens mit jdm/etw machen** to make short work of sb/sth; **ohne langes ~lesen** without any further ado; **~mäppchen** *nt* pencil case.
federn *vi* **(a)** *(als Eigenschaft)* to be springy. **(b)** *(zurück~ etc)* to spring back; *siehe* **gefedert.**
federnd *adj (Tech)* sprung. **einen ~en Gang haben** to have a springy step.
Federstrich *m* **mit einem ~** with a single stroke of the pen.
Federung *f* springs *pl*; *(Aut)* suspension.
Feder-: ~vieh *nt (col)* poultry; **~waage** *f* spring balance; **~weiße(r)** *m decl as adj (dial)* new wine; **~zeichnung** *f* pen-and-ink drawing.
Fee *f* **-n** ['fe:ən] fairy.
Fegefeuer *nt* **das ~** purgatory.
fegen 1 *vt* to sweep; *(auf~)* to sweep up. **2** *vi* **(a)** to sweep (up). **(b)** *aux sein (col: jagen)* to sweep.
Fehde *f* **-n** *(Hist)* feud. **mit jdm eine ~ ausfechten** to feud *or* carry on a feud with sb.
fehl *adj*: **~ am Platz(e)** out of place.
Fehl-: ~anzeige *f (col)* dead loss *(col)*; **~anzeige!** no go *(col)*; **f~bar** *adj* fallible; **~besetzung** *f* miscasting; **~betrag** *m* deficit; **~diagnose** *f* wrong diagnosis; **~einschätzung** *f* false estimation.
fehlen 1 *vi* **(a)** *(mangeln)* to be lacking; *(nicht vorhanden sein)* to be missing; *(in der Schule etc)* to be away or absent *(in+dat* from*)*. **jdm fehlt etw** sb lacks sth, sb doesn't have sth; *(wird schmerzlich vermißt)* sb misses sth; **mir fehlt Geld** I'm missing some money; **mir ~ 20 Pfennig am Fahrgeld** I'm 20 pfennigs short for my fare; **mir ~ die Worte** words fail me; **du fehlst mir sehr** I miss you a lot; **der/das hat mir gerade noch gefehlt!** *(col)* he/that was all I needed *(iro)*. **(b) was fehlt dir?** what's the matter (with you)?; **mir fehlt nichts** there's nothing the matter (with me); **weit gefehlt!** *(fig)* you're way out! *(col)*; *(ganz im Gegenteil)* far from it!

2 *vi impers* **es fehlt an etw** *(dat)* there is a lack of sth; *(völlig)* there is no sth, sth is missing; **es ~ drei Messer** there are three knives missing; **es fehlt jdm an etw** *(dat)* sb lacks sth; **wo fehlt es?** what's the trouble?, what's up? *(col)*; **es fehlte nicht viel, und ich hätte ihn verprügelt** I almost hit him.
Fehl|entscheidung *f* wrong decision.
Fehler *m* **- (a)** *(Irrtum)* mistake, error; *(Sport)* fault. **ihr ist ein ~ unterlaufen** she made a mistake. **(b)** *(Mangel)* fault, defect. **einen ~ aufweisen** to prove faulty; **einen ~ an sich** *(dat)* **haben** to have a fault; **in den ~ verfallen, etw zu tun** to make the mistake of doing sth.
Fehler-: f~frei *adj* perfect; *Arbeit, Aussprache etc auch* faultless, flawless; *Messung, Rechnung* correct; **f~freier Lauf/Sprung** *(Sport)* clear round/jump; **~grenze** *f* margin of error; **f~haft** *adj (Tech)* faulty, defective; *Ware* substandard, imperfect; *Messung, Rechnung* incorrect; *Arbeit, Aussprache* poor; **f~los** *adj* = **f~frei.**
Fehl-: ~farbe *f (Cards)* missing suit; *(Nicht-Trumpf)* plain *or* side suit; **~geburt** *f* miscarriage; **f~gehen** *vi sep irreg aux sein (geh: sich irren)* to be wrong *or* mistaken; **~griff** *m* mistake; **~information** *f* incorrect information *no pl*; **~leistung** *f* slip, mistake; **Freudsche ~leistung** Freudian slip; **~paß** *m (Ftbl)* bad pass; **~schlag** *m (fig)* failure; **f~schlagen** *vi sep irreg aux sein* to go wrong; *(Hoffnung)* to come to nothing; **~schluß** *m* false conclusion; **~start** *m* false start; *(Space)* faulty launch; **~tritt** *m (geh)* false step; *(fig) (Vergehen)* slip, lapse; *(Affäre)* indiscretion; **~urteil** *nt* miscarriage of justice; **~verhalten** *nt (Psych)* abnormal behaviour *(Brit) or* behavior *(US)*; **~versuch** *m* unsuccessful attempt; **~zündung** *f* misfiring *no pl*; **eine ~zündung** a backfire.
Feier *f* **-n** celebration; *(Party)* party; *(Zeremonie)* ceremony. **zur ~ von etw** to celebrate sth.
Feier|abend *m (Arbeitsschluß)* end of work; *(Geschäftsschluß)* closing time. **~ machen** to finish work, to knock off *(col)*; *(Geschäfte)* to close; **ich mache jetzt ~** I think I'll call it a day *(col)*; **nach ~** after work; **jetzt ist aber ~!** *(fig col)* enough is enough; **schönen ~!** have a nice evening!
feierlich *adj (ernsthaft, würdig)* solemn; *(festlich)* festive; *(förmlich)* ceremonial. **das ist ja nicht mehr ~** *(col)* that's beyond a joke *(col)*.
Feierlichkeit *f* **(a)** *siehe adj* solemnity; festiveness; ceremony. **(b)** *usu pl* celebrations *pl.*
feiern 1 *vt* **(a)** to celebrate; *Party, Orgie* to hold. **das muß gefeiert werden!** that calls for a celebration. **(b)** *(umjubeln)* to fête. **2** *vi* to celebrate.
Feier-: ~schicht *f* cancelled shift; **~stunde** *f* ceremony; **~tag** *m* holiday.
feig(e) 1 *adj* cowardly. **2** *adv* in a cowardly way. **er zog sich ~ zurück** he retreated like a coward.
Feige *f* **-n** fig.
Feigen-: ~blatt *nt* fig leaf; **ein ~blatt für etw** *(fig)* a front to hide sth; **als demokratisches ~blatt** *(fig)* to give a veneer of democracy.
Feigheit *f* cowardice.
Feigling *m* coward.
feilbieten *vt sep irreg (old)* to offer for sale.
Feile *f* **-n** file.
feilen *vti* to file. **an etw** *(dat)* **~** *(fig)* to perfect sth.
feilschen *vi (pej)* to haggle *(um* over*)*.
fein *adj* **(a)** fine; *Humor, Ironie* delicate. **(b)** *(erlesen)* excellent, choice; *Geruch, Geschmack* delicate; *(prima)* great *(col)*, fine. **ein ~er Kerl** a great guy *(col)*; **das ist etwas F~es** that's really something *(col)*; **~ (he)raussein** to be sitting pretty. **(c)** *Gehör etc* sensitive, keen. **(d)** *(vornehm)* refined, fine *(esp iro)*, posh *(col)*. **nicht ~ genug sein** not to be good enough; **sich ~ machen** to get all dressed up.
Feind(in *f*) *m* **-e** enemy. **jdn zum ~ haben** to have sb as an enemy; **sich** *(dat)* **jdn zum ~ machen** to make an enemy of sb.
Feind- *in cpds* enemy; **~berührung** *f* contact with the enemy; **~bild** *nt* concept of an/the enemy.
feindlich *adj (Mil)* enemy; *(feindselig)* hostile. **jdm/etw ~ gegenüberstehen** to be hostile to sb/sth.
Feindschaft *f* hostility. **sich** *(dat)* **jds ~ zuziehen** to make an enemy of sb.
feindselig *adj* hostile.
Feindseligkeit *f* hostility.
Fein-: f~fühlig *adj* sensitive; **~gefühl** *nt no pl* sensitivity; **~gold** *nt* refined gold.
Feinheit *f siehe adj* **(a)** fineness; delicacy. **(b)** excellence; delicateness. **(c)** keenness.
Fein-: ~kost *f* **„~kost"** "Delicatessen"; **~kost-**

handlung *f* delicatessen; **~mechaniker** *m* precision engineer; **~schmecker** *m* - gourmet; *(fig)* connoisseur; **~schnitt** *m (Tabak)* fine cut; **~silber** *nt* refined silver; **f~sinnig** *adj* sensitive; **~wäsche** *f* delicates *pl*; **~waschmittel** *nt* mild(-action) detergent.

fẹist *adj* fat; *Mensch auch* obese.

fẹixen *vi (col)* to smirk.

Fẹld *nt* **-er** field; *(Sport: Spiel~ auch)* pitch; *(auf Spielbrett)* square; *(offenes Gelände)* open country. **auf freiem ~** in the open country; **gegen jdn/etw zu ~e ziehen** *(fig)* to crusade against sb/sth; **Argumente ins ~ führen** to bring arguments to bear; **das ~ räumen** *(fig)* to bow out; **jdm das ~ überlassen** to give way to sb; *(freiwillig)* to hand over to sb.

Fẹld- *in cpds* field; **~arbeit** *f (Agr)* work in the fields; *(Sci, Sociol)* fieldwork; **~arbeiter** *m* fieldworker; **~besteck** *nt* eating irons *pl*; **~bett** *nt* campbed; **~blume** *f* wild flower; **~flasche** *f* canteen *(Mil)*, water bottle; **~herr** *m (old)* commander; **~jäger** *m (Mil)* military policeman; **die ~jäger** the military police; **~marschall** *m (old)* field marshal; **~maus** *f* field mouse; **~salat** *m* lamb's lettuce; **~spieler** *m (Sport)* player; **~stecher** *m* - (pair of) binoculars *or* field glasses; **~verweis** *m* sending-off.

Fẹld-Wald-und-Wi̱esen- *in cpds (col)* common-or-garden.

Fẹld-: **~webel** *m* sergeant; **~weg** *m* track across the fields; **~zug** *m (Mil, fig)* campaign.

Fẹlge *f* **-n** *(Tech)* (wheel) rim.

Fẹll *nt* **-e** fur; *(von Schaf)* fleece; *(von toten Tieren)* skin, fell. **einem Tier das ~ abziehen** to skin an animal; **ihm sind die ~e weggeschwommen** *(fig)* all his hopes were dashed; **ein dickes ~ haben** to be thickskinned, to have a thick skin; **jdm das ~ über die Ohren ziehen** to pull the wool over sb's eyes.

Fẹls-: **~block, ~brocken** *m* boulder.

fẹlsenfest *adj* firm. **~ überzeugt sein** to be firmly convinced; **sich ~ auf jdn verlassen** to put one's complete trust in sb.

fẹlsig *adj* rocky.

Fẹls-: **~massiv** *nt* rock massif; **~spalte** *f* crevice; **~vorsprung** *m* ledge; **~wand** *f* rock face.

feminịn *adj* feminine; *(pej)* effeminate.

Feminịnum *nt, pl* **Feminịna** *(Gram)* feminine noun.

Feminịsmus *m* feminism.

Feminịst(in *f***)** *m (wk)* **-en,-en** feminist.

feminịstisch *adj* feminist.

Fẹnchel *m no pl* fennel.

Fẹnster *nt* - window. **weg vom ~** *(col)* out of the game *(col)*, finished; **Geld zum ~ hinauswerfen** *(col)* to chuck money down the drain.

Fẹnster- *in cpds* window; **~bank** *f*, **~brett** *nt* windowsill, window ledge; **~flügel** *m side of a casement window*; **~glas** *nt* window glass; *(in Brille)* plain glass; **~kreuz** *nt* mullion and transom; **~laden** *m* shutter; **~leder** *nt* chamois, shammy (leather); **~platz** *m* window seat; **~putzer** *m* window cleaner; **~rahmen** *m* window frame; **~scheibe** *f* window pane; **~sims** *m* window ledge, windowsill.

Ferien ['fe:riən] *pl* holidays *pl (Brit)*, vacation *sing (US, Univ)*; *(Parlaments~, Jur)* recess *sing*. **die großen ~** the summer holidays *(Brit)*, the long vacation *(US, Univ)*; **~ machen** to take a holiday; **in die ~ fahren** to go on holiday.

Fẹrien- *in cpds* holiday *(Brit)*, vacation *(US)*; **~gast** *m* holidaymaker *(Brit)*, vacationist *(US)*; *(Besuch)* person staying on holiday *(Brit) or* vacation *(US)*; **~ort** *m* holiday *(Brit) or* vacation *(US)* resort; **~reise** *f* holiday *(Brit)*, vacation *(US)*.

Fẹrkel *nt* - piglet; *(fig)* pig.

Fermẹnt *nt* **-e** enzyme.

fẹrn *adj* **(a)** *(räumlich)* distant, faraway. **~ von hier** a long way (away) from here; **von ~(e) betrachtet** seen from a distance; **der F~e Osten** the Far East; **von ~(e) kennen** *(fig)* to know (only) slightly. **(b)** *(zeitlich)* far-off. **in nicht zu ~er Zeit** in the not-too-distant future; **der Tag ist nicht mehr ~, wo ...** the day is not far off when ...

Fern-: **f~ạb** *adv* far away; **~amt** *nt* (telephone) exchange; **~bedienung** *f* remote control; **f~bleiben** *vi sep irreg aux sein* to stay away *(dat, von* from*)*; **~bleiben** *nt* absence.

Fẹrne *f* **-n (a)** *(räumlich)* distance. **aus der ~** from a distance. **(b)** *(zeitlich)* **in weiter ~ liegen** to be in the distant future.

fẹrner *adj, adv* further. **für die ~e Zukunft** for the long term; **unter ~ liefen rangieren** *(col)* to be an also-ran.

Fẹrn-: **~fahrer** *m* long-distance lorry *(Brit) or* truck driver; **f~gelenkt** *adj* = **f~gesteuert;** **~gespräch** *nt* long-distance call; **f~gesteuert** *adj* remote-controlled; *Rakete* guided; *(fig)* manipulated *(von* by*)*; **~glas** *nt* (pair of) binoculars; **f~halten** *vtr sep irreg* to keep away; **~heizung** *f* district heating; **~kurs(us)** *m* correspondence course; **~lastverkehr** *m* long-distance goods traffic; **~lenkung** *f* remote control; **~licht** *nt (Aut)* full *or* high beam; **mit ~licht fahren** to drive on full beam; **f~liegen** *vi sep irreg (fig)* **(jdm) f~liegen** to be far from sb's thoughts *or* mind; **es liegt mir f~, das zu tun** far be it from me to do that; **nichts liegt mir f~er** nothing could be further from my mind.

Fẹrnmelde- *in cpds* telecommunications; *(Mil)* signals.

Fẹrnmelder *m (Mil col)* signaller *(Brit)*, signaler *(US)*.

Fẹrnmelde-: **~satellit** *m* communications satellite; **~technik** *f* telecommunications *sing*; **~wesen** *nt* telecommunications *sing*.

Fẹrn-: **~mündlich 1** *adj* telephone *attr*; **2** *adv* by telephone; **~ọst** *no art* **aus/in ~ost** from/in the Far East; **~ọ̈stlich** *adj* Far Eastern *attr;* **~rohr** *nt* telescope; **~ruf** *m (form)* telephone number; **~schreiben** *nt* telex; **~schreiber** *m* teleprinter; *(Comm)* telex; **f~schriftlich** *adj* by telex.

Fẹrnseh- *in cpds* television, TV; **~apparat** *m* television *or* TV (set).

fẹrnsehen *vi sep irreg* to watch television *or* TV.

Fẹrnsehen *nt no pl* television, TV. **vom ~ übertragen werden** to be televised; **im ~** on television *or* TV.

Fẹrnseher *m* - *(col) (Gerät)* television, TV, telly *(Brit col)*; *(Zuschauer)* (television) viewer.

Fẹrnseh-: **~gebühr** *f* television licence *(Brit) or* license *(US)* fee; **~gerät** *nt* television *or* TV set; **~programm** *nt* **(a)** *(Kanal)* channel, station *(US)*; **(b)** *(Sendung)* programme *(Brit)*, program *(US)*; *(Sendefolge)* programmes *pl (Brit)*, programs *pl (US)*; **(c)** *(~zeitschrift)* (television) programme *(Brit) or* program *(US)* guide; **~schirm** *m* television *or* TV screen; **~sendung** *f* television programme *(Brit) or* program *(US)*; **~spiel** *nt* television play; **~teilnehmer** *m (form)* television viewer; **~turm** *m* television tower; **~zuschauer** *m* (television) viewer.

Fẹrnsicht *f* **(eine) gute ~ haben** to be able to see a long way.

Fẹrnsprech- *in cpds (form) siehe auch* **Telefon-** telephone; **~apparat** *m* telephone; **~buch** *nt* telephone directory.

Fẹrnsprecher *m* - *(form)* (public) telephone.

Fẹrnsprech-: **~gebühr** *f* telephone charges *pl*; **~zelle** *f* (tele)phone box *or* booth *(US)*, callbox.

Fẹrn-: **f~stehen** *vi sep irreg*: **jdm/etw f~stehen** to have no connection with sb/sth; **ich stehe ihm ziemlich f~** I'm not on very close terms with him; **f~steuern** *vt sep* to operate by remote control; *siehe* **f~gesteuert;** **~steuerung** *f* remote control; **~straße** *f* major road, highway *(US)*;

~studium *nt* multi-media course, ≃ Open University course *(Brit)*; **~universität** *f* ≃ Open University *(Brit)*; **~unterricht** *m* = **~studium; ~verkehr** *m* long-distance traffic; **~wärme** *f* district heating; **~weh** *nt* wanderlust; **~ziel** *nt* long-term goal.

Fẹrse *f* **-n** heel. **jdm (dicht) auf den ~n bleiben** to stay hard on sb's heels.

Fẹrsengeld *nt*: **~ geben** to take to one's heels.

fẹrtig *adj* **(a)** *(zu Ende, vollendet)* finished; *(ausgebildet)* qualified; *(reif) Mensch, Charakter* mature. **etw ~ kaufen** to buy sth ready-made; *Essen* to buy sth ready-cooked; **~ ausgebildet** fully qualified; **mit etw ~ sein** to have finished sth; **~ essen/lesen** to finish eating/reading; **mit jdm ~ sein** *(fig)* to be finished with sb; **mit jdm/etw ~ werden** to cope with sb/sth; **ich werde damit nicht ~** I can't cope with it. **(b)** *(bereit)* ready. **~ zur Abfahrt** ready to leave. **(c)** *(col)* shattered *(col)*; *(ruiniert)* finished. **mit den Nerven ~ sein** to be at the end of one's tether.

Fẹrtig- *in cpds* finished; *(Build)* prefabricated; **~bau** *m* **-ten** prefabricated building; **f~bringen** *vt sep irreg* **(a)** *(vollenden)* to get done; **(b)** *(imstande sein)* to manage; *(iro)* to be capable of; **ich brachte es nicht f~, ihr die Wahrheit zu sagen** I couldn't bring myself to tell her the truth; **er bringt das f~** *(iro)* I wouldn't put it past him.

Fẹrtig-: ~gericht *nt* ready-to-serve meal; **~haus** *nt* prefabricated house, prefab.

Fẹrtigkeit *f* skill.

Fẹrtig-: f~machen *vt sep* **(a)** *(vollenden)* to finish; **(b)** *(bereit machen)* to get ready; **sich f~machen** to get ready; **(c)** *(col)* **jdn f~machen** *(erledigen)* to do for sb; *(ermüden)* to take it out of sb; *(deprimieren)* to get sb down; *(abkanzeln)* to lay into sb *(col)*; **f~stellen** *vt sep* to complete; **~stellung** *f* completion.

Fẹrtigung *f* production.

Fẹrtigungs- *in cpds* production; **~straße** *f* production line.

Fẹrtigware *f* finished product.

Fẹs, fẹs *nt* **-** *(Mus)* F flat.

fẹsch *adj (col) (modisch)* smart; *(hübsch)* attractive.

Fẹssel *f* **-n (a)** *(lit, fig)* bond, fetter; *(Kette)* chain. **jdm ~n anlegen** to fetter sb. **(b)** *(Anat) (von Huftieren)* pastern; *(von Menschen)* ankle.

fẹsseln *vt* **(a)** to tie (up), to bind; *(mit Handschellen)* to handcuff; *(mit Ketten)* to chain (up). **ans Bett gefesselt** *(fig)* confined to bed; **jdn an sich ~** *(fig)* to bind sb to oneself. **(b)** *(faszinieren)* to grip.

fẹsselnd *adj* gripping.

fẹst *adj* **(a)** *(hart)* solid. **~e Nahrung** solid food, solids *pl*. **(b)** *(stabil)* solid; *Gewebe, Schuhe* strong, sturdy; *(Comm, Fin)* stable. **(c)** *(sicher, entschlossen)* firm. **~ versprechen** to promise faithfully; **eine ~e Meinung von etw haben** to have definite views on sth; **etw ist ~** sth is definite; **~ entschlossen sein** to be absolutely determined. **(d)** *(kräftig)* firm; *Schlag* hard. **~ zuschlagen** to hit hard. **(e)** *(nicht locker)* tight; *Griff* firm; *(fig) Schlaf* sound. **~ packen** to grip firmly; **die Tür ~ schließen** to shut the door tight; **~ schlafen** to sleep soundly. **(f)** *(ständig)* regular; *Freund(in)* steady; *Stellung, Mitarbeiter* permanent; *Kosten, Einkommen* fixed. **~ befreundet sein** to be good friends; *(Freund und Freundin)* to be going steady.

Fẹst *nt* **-e (a)** *(Feier)* celebration; *(Party)* party. **man soll die ~e feiern, wie sie fallen** *(prov)* make hay while the sun shines *(Prov)*. **(b)** *(Weihnachts~)* Christmas.

Fẹst-: ~akt *m* ceremony; **f~angestellt** *adj* employed on a permanent basis; **f~beißen** *vr sep irreg (Hund etc)* to get a firm grip *(an+dat* on*)*; *(fig: nicht weiterkommen)* to get bogged down *(an +dat* in*)*; **~beleuchtung** *f* festive lights *pl*; *(col: im Haus)* blazing lights *pl*; **f~binden** *vt sep irreg* to tie up *(an+dat* to*)*; **~essen** *nt* banquet; **f~fahren** *vr sep irreg (lit, fig)* to get bogged down; **~geld** *nt (Fin)* time deposit; **~halle** *f* festival hall.

fẹsthalten *sep irreg* **1** *vt* **(a)** to keep hold of, to hold on to. **(b)** *(inhaftieren)* to hold, to detain. **(c)** *(speichern)* to record; *Atmosphäre etc* to capture. **etw schriftlich ~** to record sth. **2** *vi* **an etw** *(dat)* **~** to hold *or* stick *(col)* to sth. **3** *vr* to hold on *(an +dat* to*)*. **halt dich fest!** *(lit)* hold tight!; **halt dich fest, und hör dir das an!** *(col)* brace yourself and listen to this!

fẹstigen 1 *vt* to strengthen. **2** *vr* to become stronger.

Fẹstiger *m* **-** *(Haar~)* setting lotion.

Fẹstigkeit *f no pl* strength; *(fig)* steadfastness.

Fẹstigung *f* strengthening.

Festival ['fɛstivəl, 'fɛstival] *nt* **-s** festival.

Fẹst-: f~kleben *vti sep (vi: aux sein)* to stick (firmly) *(an+dat* (on)to*)*; **~kleid** *nt* formal dress; **f~klemmen** *sep* **1** *vt* to wedge fast; *(mit Klammer)* to clip; **2** *vir (vi: aux sein)* to jam; **~komma** *nt (Comp)* fixed point; **f~krallen** *vr sep (Tier)* to dig one's claws in *(an+dat* -to*)*; *(Mensch)* to dig one's nails in *(an+dat* -to*)*; *(fig)* to cling *(an +dat* to*)*.

Fẹstland *nt* mainland; *(nicht Meer)* dry land.

fẹstlegen *sep* **1** *vt* **(a)** *(festsetzen) Termin etc* to fix; *Regelung, Arbeitszeiten* to lay down. **etw schriftlich ~** to put sth down in writing. **(b) jdn auf etw** *(acc)* **~** *(festnageln)* to tie sb (down) to sth; *(verpflichten)* to commit sb to sth. **(c)** *Geld* to tie up. **2** *vr* **sich darauf ~, etw zu tun** to commit oneself to doing sth.

Fẹstlegung *f siehe vt (a, b)* **(a)** fixing; laying-down. **(b)** tying-down; commitment.

fẹstlich *adj* festive; *(feierlich)* solemn; *(prächtig)* magnificent. **etw ~ begehen** to celebrate sth.

Fẹst-: f~liegen *vi sep irreg* **(a)** *(f~gesetzt sein)* to have been fixed *or* definitely decided; **(b)** *(Fin: Geld)* to be tied up; **(c)** *(nicht weiterkönnen)* to be stuck; *(Naut)* to be aground; **f~machen** *sep* **1** *vt* **(a)** *(befestigen)* to fix on *(an+dat* -to*)*, to fasten *(an +dat* (on)to*)*; *(Naut)* to moor; **(b)** *(vereinbaren)* to arrange; **ein Geschäft f~machen** to clinch a deal; **2** *vi (Naut)* to moor; **~mahl** *nt (geh)* banquet, feast; **f~nageln** *vt sep (lit)* to nail (down/up/on); *(fig col) jdn* to nail down *(auf+acc* to*)*; **~nahme** *f* **-n** arrest; **f~nehmen** *vt sep irreg* to arrest; **vorläufig f~nehmen** to take into custody; **~platte** *f (Comp)* hard disk; **~preis** *m (Comm)* fixed price; **~rede** *f* speech; **die ~rede halten** to give the main speech; **~saal** *m* hall; *(Tanzsaal)* ballroom; **f~schrauben** *vt sep* to screw (on) tight; **f~schreiben** *vt sep irreg (fig)* to establish.

fẹstsetzen *sep* **1** *vt* **(a)** to fix *(bei, auf+acc* at*)*; *Ort, Termin auch* to arrange *(auf+acc, bei* for*)*. **(b)** *(inhaftieren)* to detain. **2** *vr (Staub, Schmutz)* to collect; *(fig: Gedanke)* to take root.

Fẹstsetzung *f* **(a)** *siehe vt (a)* fixing; arrangement. **(b)** *(Inhaftierung)* detention.

fẹstsitzen *vi sep irreg* to be stuck; *(Schmutz)* to cling.

Fẹstspiele *pl* festival *sing*.

fẹst-: ~stecken *sep* **1** *vt* to pin *(an+dat* (on)to, *in +dat* in*)*; *Haare* to pin up; **2** *vi aux sein (steckenbleiben)* to be stuck; **~stehen** *vi sep irreg (sicher sein)* to be certain; *(beschlossen sein)* to have been settled *or* fixed; **~stehend** *adj* **(a)** *(Mech)* fixed; **(b)** *attr (bestimmt)* definite; *Redewendung* set; **~stellbar** *adj (herauszufinden)* ascertainable.

fẹststellen *vt sep* **(a)** *(Mech)* to lock (fast). **(b)** *(ermitteln)* to ascertain, to find out; *Personalien, Ursache auch* to establish; *Schaden* to assess; *Krankheit* to diagnose. **der Arzt konnte nur noch seinen Tod ~** the doctor found him to be dead.

(c) *(erkennen)* to tell *(an+dat* from); *Fehler* to find, to detect; *(bemerken)* to discover; *(einsehen)* to realize. **ich mußte entsetzt/überrascht ~, daß...** I was horrified/surprised to find that... (d) *(aussprechen)* to stress, to emphasize.

Feststellung *f* **(a)** *siehe vt (b)* ascertainment; establishment; assessment; diagnosis. **(b)** *(Erkenntnis)* conclusion. **(c)** *(Wahrnehmung)* observation. **die ~ machen, daß ...** to realize that ...; **ist das eine Frage oder eine ~?** is that a question or a statement (of fact)? **(d)** *(Bemerkung)* remark, observation. **die ~ machen, daß...** to remark *or* observe that ...

Festtag *m* **(a)** *(Ehrentag)* special day. **(b)** *(Feiertag)* holiday, feast(day) *(Eccl)*.

fest-: **~treten** *sep irreg* **1** *vt* to tread down; *(in Teppich etc)* to tread in *(in+acc* -to); **2** *vr* to get trodden down/in; **~umrissen** *adj attr* clear-cut.

Festung *f* fortress; *(Burgfeste)* castle.

Fest-: **f~verwurzelt** *adj attr* deep-rooted; **f~verzinslich** *adj* fixed-interest *attr*; **~vortrag** *m* lecture, talk; **~woche** *f* festival week; **die ~wochen** the festival *sing*.

Fete, Fête ['fe:tə, 'fɛ:tə] *f* **-n** party.

Fetischist *m (wk)* fetishist.

fett *adj* **(a)** *(~haltig) Speisen* fatty. **~ essen** to eat fatty food; **ein ~er Brocken** *(fig)* a lucrative deal. **(b)** *(dick)* fat; *(Typ)* bold. **(c)** *(üppig) Boden, Weide)* rich; *Beute, Gewinn* fat; *Geschäft* lucrative. **~e Jahre** fat years.

Fett *nt* **-e** fat; *(zum Schmieren)* grease. **~ ansetzen** to put on weight; *(Tiere)* to fatten up; **sein ~ bekommen** *(col)* to get one's come-uppance *(col)*.

Fett-: **f~arm** *adj* low-fat; **f~arm essen** to eat low-fat foods; **~auge** *nt* globule of fat; **~creme** *f* skin cream with oil; **~druck** *m (Typ)* bold type.

fetten *vt* to grease.

Fett-: **~fleck(en)** *m* grease spot, greasy mark; **f~frei** *adj* fat-free; *Milch* low-fat; *Kost* non-fatty; *Creme* non-greasy; **f~gedruckt** *adj attr (Typ)* bold; **~gehalt** *m* fat content; **f~haltig** *adj* fatty.

fettig *adj* greasy; *Haut auch* oily.

Fettigkeit *f siehe adj* greasiness; oiliness.

Fett-: **~kloß** *m (pej)* fatty *(col)*; **f~leibig** *adj (geh)* obese, corpulent; **~leibigkeit** *f (geh)* obesity, corpulence; **f~los** *adj* fat-free; **~näpfchen** *nt (col)*: **ins ~näpfchen treten** to put one's foot in it *(bei jdm* with sb); **~polster** *nt (hum col)* flab *no pl*; **~polster haben** to be well-padded; **f~reich** *adj* high-fat; **f~reich essen** to eat foods with a high fat content; **~sack** *m (pej)* fatso *(col)*; **~schicht** *f* layer of fat; **~stift** *m* lip salve; **~sucht** *f no pl (Med)* obesity; **f~süchtig** *adj (Med)* obese; **~wanst** *m (pej)* potbelly; *(Mensch)* fatso *(col)*.

Fetzen *m* **-** shred; *(Papier~, Gesprächs~)* scrap; *(Kleidung)* rag. **das Kleid ist in ~ gegangen** the dress has fallen to pieces; **etw in ~/in tausend ~ (zer)reißen** to tear sth to shreds/into a thousand pieces; ..., **daß die ~ fliegen** *(col)* ... like mad *(col)*.

fetzen *vi aux sein (col: rasen)* to tear.

fetzig *adj (col)* lively.

feucht *adj* damp; *Lippen* moist; *(feuchtheiß) Klima* humid; *Hände* sweaty; *Tinte, Farbe* wet. **sie hatte ~e Augen** her eyes were moist; **ein ~er Abend** *(hum)* a boozy night; **eine ~e Aussprache haben** *(hum col)* to splutter when one speaks; **das geht dich einen ~en Kehricht** *or* **Dreck an** *(col!)* it's none of your damn business *(col)*.

feucht-: **~fröhlich** *adj (hum)* boozy; **~heiß** *adj* muggy.

Feuchtigkeit *f no pl* **(a)** *siehe adj* dampness; moistness; humidity; sweatiness; wetness. **(b)** *(Flüssigkeit)* moisture; *(Luft~)* humidity.

Feuchtigkeits-: **~creme** *f* moisturizer; **~gehalt, ~grad** *m* moisture content.

feuchtwarm *adj* muggy, humid.

feudal *adj (Pol, Hist)* feudal; *(col)* plush *(col)*.

Feudal- *in cpds* feudal; **~herrschaft** *f* feudalism.

Feudalismus *m* feudalism.

Feuer *nt* **- (a)** *(Flamme, Kamin~)* fire. **am ~** by the fire; **~ machen** to light a/the fire; **~ hinter etw** *(acc)* **machen** *(fig)* to chase sth up; **jdm ~ unter dem Hintern machen** *(col)* to put a bomb under sb *(col)*; **du spielst mit dem ~** *(fig)* you're playing with fire; **sie sind wie ~ und Wasser** they're as different as chalk and cheese; **~ legen** to start a fire; **~ fangen** to catch fire; **für jdn durchs ~ gehen** to go through fire and water for sb; **haben Sie ~?** do you have a light?; **jdm ~ geben** to give sb a light. **(b)** *(Naut, Funk~)* beacon; *(von Leuchtturm)* light. **(c) das/sie hat bei ihm ~ gefangen** he was really taken with it/her; **~ und Flamme sein** *(col)* to be dead keen *(col) (für* on). **(d)** *(Schießen)* fire. **~!** fire!; **~ frei!** open fire!; **das ~ eröffnen** to open fire; **das ~ einstellen** to cease fire; **etw unter ~** *(acc)* **nehmen** to open fire on sth.

Feuer- *in cpds* fire; **~alarm** *m* fire alarm; **~anzünder** *m* firelighter; **~befehl** *m (Mil)* order to fire; **~bekämpfung** *f* fire-fighting; **f~beständig** *adj* fire-resistant; **~bestattung** *f* cremation; **~eifer** *m* zeal; **~einstellung** *f* cessation of fire; *(Waffenstillstand)* cease-fire; **f~fest** *adj* fireproof; *Geschirr* heat-resistant; **~gefahr** *f* fire hazard *or* risk; **bei ~gefahr** in the event of fire; **f~gefährlich** *adj* inflammable; **~haken** *m* poker; **~leiter** *f (am Haus)* fire escape; **~löscher** *m* **-** fire extinguisher; **~meer** *nt (liter)* sea of flames; **~melder** *m* **-** fire alarm.

feuern 1 *vi* **(a)** *(heizen)* **mit Öl/Holz ~** to have oil heating/use wood for one's heating. **(b)** *(Mil)* to fire. **2** *vt* **(a)** *Ofen* to light. **(b)** *(col) (werfen)* to fling; *(Ftbl) Ball* to slam; *(ins Tor)* to slam in. **(c)** *(col: entlassen)* to fire *(col)*.

Feuer-: **~pause** *f* break in the firing; *(vereinbart)* ceasefire; **f~polizeilich** *adj Bestimmungen* laid down by the fire authorities; **~probe** *f* **die ~probe bestehen** *(fig)* to pass the (acid) test; **f~rot** *adj* fiery red.

Feuersbrunst *f (geh)* conflagration.

Feuer-: **~schein** *m* glow of the fire; **~schiff** *nt* lightship; **~schlucker** *m* **-** fire-eater; **~schutz** *m* **(a)** *(Vorbeugung)* fire prevention; **(b)** *(Mil: Deckung)* covering fire; **f~speiend** *adj attr Drache* fire-breathing; *Berg* belching flames; **~stein** *m* flint; **~stelle** *f* campfire site; *(Herd)* fireplace; **~taufe** *f* **die ~taufe bestehen/erhalten** to go through/have a baptism of fire; **~treppe** *f* fire escape; **~tür** *f* fire door.

Feuerung *f* heating; *(Brennstoff)* fuel.

Feuer-: **~versicherung** *f* fire insurance; **~wache** *f* fire station; **~waffe** *f* firearm; **~wechsel** *m* exchange of fire.

Feuerwehr *f* fire brigade *(Brit) or* department *(US)*. **fahren wie die ~** *(col)* to drive like the clappers *(Brit col)*, to drive flat out.

Feuerwehr-: **~auto** *nt* fire engine; **~mann** *m* fireman.

Feuer-: **~werk** *nt* fireworks *pl*; *(fig)* cavalcade; **~werkskörper** *m* firework; **~zangenbowle** *f red wine punch containing rum which has been flamed off*; **~zeug** *nt* (cigarette) lighter.

Feuilleton [fœjə'tõ, 'fœjətõ] *nt* **-s** *(Press)* feature section; *(Artikel)* feature (article).

feurig *adj* fiery.

Fez *m no pl (dated col: Spaß)* larking about *(col)*.

Fiaker *m* **-** *(Aus) (Kutsche)* (hackney) cab; *(Kutscher)* cab driver, cabby *(col)*.

Fiasko *nt* **-s** *(col)* fiasco.

Fibel *f* **-n** *(Sch)* primer.

Fiber *f* **-n** fibre *(Brit)*, fiber *(US)*.

Fiche [fi:ʃ] *m or nt* **-s** (micro)fiche.

Fichte *f* **-n** *(Bot)* spruce.

Fichten- *in cpds* spruce; **~zapfen** *m* spruce cone.

ficken *vti (col!!)* to fuck *(col!!)*.

fidel *adj (dated col)* jolly, merry.
Fidel *f* **-n** fiddle.
Fidschi|inseln *pl* Fiji Islands.
Fieber *nt* - temperature; *(Krankheit)* fever. **~ haben** to have a temperature; to be feverish; **40° ~ haben** to have a temperature of 40; **(jdm) das ~ messen** to take sb's temperature; **im ~ seiner Leidenschaft** in a fever of passion.
Fieber- *in cpds* feverish; **f~haft** *adj (lit, fig)* feverish.
fieb(e)rig *adj* feverish.
Fieberkurve *f* temperature curve.
fiebern *vi* to have a temperature; *(schwer)* to be feverish. **vor Ungeduld** *(dat)* **~** *(fig)* to be in a fever of impatience.
Fieberthermometer *nt* thermometer.
Fiedel *f* **-n** *(old, pej: Geige)* fiddle.
fiedeln *vti (hum, pej)* to fiddle.
fiel *pret of* **fallen.**
fies *adj (col)* nasty, horrible.
Figur *f* figure; *(Roman~, Film~ etc)* character; *(von Männern)* physique. **auf seine ~ achten** to watch one's figure; **eine gute/schlechte/traurige ~ abgeben** to cut a good/poor/sorry figure; **eine komische ~** *(col)* a strange character.
Fiktion *f* fiction.
fiktiv *adj* fictitious.
Filet [fi'leː] *nt* **-s** *(Cook)* fillet; *(Rinder~)* fillet steak; *(zum Braten)* piece of sirloin *or* tenderloin *(US)*.
filetieren* *vt* to fillet.
Filet- [fi'leː-]: **~steak** *nt* fillet steak; **~stück** *nt* piece of sirloin *or* tenderloin *(US)*.
Filiale *f* **-n** branch.
Filialleiter *m* branch manager.
Filius *m* **-se** *(hum)* son, offspring *(hum)*.
Film *m* **-e (a)** film; *(Spiel~ auch)* movie *(esp US)*. **in einen ~ gehen** to go and see a film *(Brit) or* movie *(US)*; **da ist bei mir der ~ gerissen** *(col)* I had a mental blackout *(col)*. **(b)** *(~branche)* films *pl*, the movies *pl (esp US)*. **zum ~ gehen** to go into films.
Film- *in cpds* film, movie *(esp US)*; **~atelier** *nt* film studio; **~bewertungsstelle** *f* ≃ board of film classification; **~diva** *f (dated)* screen goddess.
Filmemacher(in *f*) *m* film-maker.
Film-: ~festspiele *pl* film festival; **~geschäft** *nt* film *or* movie *(esp US)* industry; **~geschichte** *f* history of the cinema; **~geschichte machen** to make cinema history; **~gesellschaft** *f* film company; **~größe** *f* great star of the screen; **~held** *m* screen *or* movie *(esp US)* hero; **~hochschule** *f* film school.
filmisch *adj* cinematic.
Film-: ~kamera *f* film *or* movie *(esp US)* camera; *(Schmalfilmkamera)* cine-camera *(Brit)*; **~kritik** *f* film criticism; *(Artikel)* film review; *(Kritiker)* film critics *pl*; **~musik** *f* film music; **die originale ~musik** the original soundtrack; **~preis** *m* film *or* movie *(esp US)* award; **~produzent** *m* film *or* movie *(esp US)* producer; **~regie** *f* direction of a/the film; **~regisseur** *m* film *or* movie *(esp US)* director; **~riß** *m (lit)* tear in a film; *(col)* mental blackout *(col)*; **~rolle** *f (Spule)* spool of film; *(für Fotoapparat)* roll of film; *(Part)* film part; **~schaffende(r)** *mf decl as adj* film-maker; **~schauspieler(in** *f*) *m* film *or* movie *(esp US)* actor/actress; **~star** *m* filmstar, movie star *(esp US)*; **~sternchen** *nt* starlet; **~theater** *nt (form)* cinema *(Brit)*, movie theater *(US)*; **~trick** *m* film stunt; **~verleih** *m* film distributors *pl*; **~vorstellung** *f* film show.
Filou [fi'luː] *m* **-s** *(dated col)* devil *(col)*.
Filter *m or (esp Tech) nt* - filter. **eine Zigarette mit/ohne ~** a filter-tipped/plain cigarette.
Filterkaffee *m* filter *or* drip *(US)* coffee.
filtern *vti* to filter.
Filter-: ~papier *nt* filter paper; **~tüte** *f* filter bag.
Filterung *f* filtering.
Filterzigarette *f* filter-tipped cigarette.
filtrieren* *vt* to filter.
Filz *m* **-e** *(Tex)* felt.
filzen *vt (col) (durchsuchen) jdn* to frisk, to search; *Gepäck etc* to search; *(berauben)* to do over *(col)*.
Filzhut *m* felt hat.
Filzokratie *f (hum)* nepotism.
Filz-: ~pantoffel *m* (carpet) slipper; **~schreiber, ~stift** *m* felt-tip (pen).
Fimmel *m* - *(col)* obsession *(mit* about*)*. **du hast wohl einen ~!** you're crazy *(col)*.
Finale *nt* **-s** *or* - *(Mus)* finale; *(Sport)* final.
Finalist *m* finalist.
Finanz- *in cpds* financial; **~amt** *nt* tax office; **~beamte(r)** *mf* tax official; **~behörde** *f* tax authority.
Finanzen *pl* finances *pl*. **das übersteigt meine ~** that's beyond my means.
finanziell *adj* financial.
finanzieren* *vt* to finance. **frei ~** to finance privately; **ich kann meinen Urlaub nicht ~** I can't afford a holiday.
Finanzierung *f* financing. **zur ~ von etw** to finance sth.
Finanz-: ~jahr *nt* financial year; **f~kräftig** *adj* financially strong; **~minister** *m* minister of finance; **~politik** *f* financial policy; **f~schwach** *adj* financially weak; **f~stark** *adj* financially strong; **~wesen** *nt* financial system.
Findelkind *nt (old)* foundling *(old)*.
finden *pret* **fand,** *ptp* **gefunden 1** *vt* **(a)** to find; *Anklang, Zustimmung auch, Beifall* to meet with; *Berücksichtigung, Beachtung* to receive. **ich finde es nicht** I can't find it; **es war nicht/nirgends zu ~** it was not/nowhere to be found; **es ließ sich niemand ~** we/they *etc* couldn't find anybody; **etwas an jdm ~** to see something in sb; **nichts dabei ~** to think nothing of it. **(b)** *(ansehen, betrachten)* to think. **es kalt/warm/ganz erträglich ~** to find it cold/warm/quite tolerable; **etw gut/zu teuer/eine Frechheit ~** to think (that) sth is good/too expensive/a cheek; **jdn blöd/nett ~** to think (that) sb is stupid/nice; **wie findest du das?** what do you think?; **~ Sie?** do you think so?; **ich finde, wir sollten ...** I think we should ...; **ich fände es besser, wenn ...** I think it would be better if ....
2 *vi (lit, fig: den Weg ~)* to find one's way. **er findet nicht nach Hause** he can't find his way home; **ich finde schon allein hinaus** I can see myself out; **zu sich selbst ~** to sort oneself out.
3 *vr* **(a)** *(zum Vorschein kommen)* to be found; *(wiederauftauchen auch)* to turn up; *(sich befinden auch)* to be. **(b)** *(in Ordnung kommen: Angelegenheit etc)* to sort itself out; *(Mensch: zu sich ~)* to sort oneself out. **(c)** *(sich fügen)* **sich in etw** *(acc)* **~** to reconcile oneself to sth. **(d)** *(sich treffen) (lit, fig)* to find each other.
Finder(in *f*) *m* - finder.
Finderlohn *m* reward for the finder.
findig *adj* resourceful.
Findigkeit *f* resourcefulness.
Finesse *f* **(a)** *(Feinheit)* refinement; *(Kunstfertigkeit)* finesse *no pl*. **mit allen ~n** with all the refinements. **(b)** *(Trick)* trick.
fing *pret of* **fangen.**
Finger *m* - finger. **mit ~n auf jdn zeigen** *(fig)* to look askance at sb; **jdm mit dem ~ drohen** to wag one's finger at sb; **jdm auf die ~ hauen** *(lit)*/**klopfen** *(fig)* to give sb a rap on the knuckles; **sich** *(dat)* **nicht die ~ schmutzig machen** *(lit, fig)* not to get one's hands dirty; **das kann sich jeder an den (fünf) ~n abzählen** *(col)* it sticks out a mile *(col)*; **das läßt er nicht mehr aus den ~n** he won't let it out of his hands; **jdn/etw in die ~ bekommen** to get one's hands on sb/sth; **er hat überall seine ~ drin** *(col)* he has a finger in every

pie *(col)*; **wenn man ihm den kleinen ~ gibt, nimmt er (gleich) die ganze Hand** *(prov)* give him an inch and he'll take a mile *(col)*; **lange ~ machen** *(hum col)* to be light-fingered; **jdm in die ~ geraten** to fall into sb's hands *or* clutches; **die ~ von etw lassen** *(col)* to keep away from sth; **jdm (scharf) auf die ~ sehen** to keep an eye on sb; **sich** *(dat)* **etw aus den ~n saugen** to conjure sth up; **sich** *(dat)* **die ~ nach etw lecken** *(col)* to be dying for sth; **keinen ~ krumm machen** *(col)* not to lift a finger *(col)*; **mir juckt es in den ~n(, etw zu tun)** *(col)* I'm itching to (do sth); **jdn um den kleinen ~ wickeln** to twist sb around one's little finger; **etw im kleinen ~ haben** to have a natural feel for sth.

Fịnger-: ~abdruck *m* fingerprint; **f~breit** *adj* the width of a finger; **~farbe** *f* finger paint; **f~fertig** *adj* nimble-fingered, dexterous; **~fertigkeit** *f* dexterity; **~hakeln** *nt* finger-wrestling; **~handschuh** *m* glove; **~hut** *m* **(a)** *(Sew)* thimble; **(b)** *(Bot)* foxglove; **~knöchel** *m* knucklebone; **~kuppe** *f* fingertip; **~ling** *m* fingerstall.

fịngern *vi* **an etw** *(dat)* **~** to fiddle with sth; **nach etw ~** to fumble (around) for sth.

Fịnger-: ~nagel *m* fingernail; **~spitze** *f* fingertip; **das muß man in den ~spitzen haben** you have to have a feel for it; **~spitzengefühl** *nt no pl* sensitivity; **~zeig** *m* **-e** hint.

fingieren* [fɪŋ'giːrən] *vt (vortäuschen)* to fake; *(erdichten)* to fabricate. **fingiert** *(vorgetäuscht)* bogus; *(erfunden)* fictitious.

Finish ['fɪnɪʃ] *nt* **-s (a)** *(Endverarbeitung)* finish. **(b)** *(Sport: Endspurt)* final spurt.

Fịnk *m (wk)* **-en, -en** finch.

Fịnne *m (wk)* **-n, -n, Fịnnin** *f* Finn.

fịnnisch *adj* Finnish; *siehe* **deutsch.**

Fịnnisch(e) *nt* **-n** Finnish; *siehe* **Deutsch(e).**

Fịnnland *nt* Finland.

fịnster *adj* **(a)** *(lit, fig)* dark; *Zimmer, Wald, Nacht* dark (and gloomy). **im F~n** in the dark; **es sieht ~ aus** *(fig)* things look bleak. **(b)** *(dubios)* shady. **(c)** *(mürrisch, düster)* grim; *Wolken* dark, black. **~ entschlossen sein** to be grimly determined; **jdn ~ ansehen** to give sb a black look. **(d)** *(unheimlich) Gestalt, Blick, Gedanken* sinister.

Fịnsternis *f* **(a)** darkness. **(b)** *(Astron)* eclipse.

Fịnte *f* **-n (a)** *(Sport)* feint. **(b)** *(List)* ruse.

Fịrlefanz *m no pl (col)* **(a)** *(Kram)* frippery. **(b)** *(Albernheit)* **~ machen** to clown around.

fịrm *adj pred* **in etw** *(dat)* **~ sein** to have a sound knowledge of sth.

Fịrma *f, pl* **Fịrmen** company, firm. **die ~ Wahlster/Lexus** Wahlster(s)/Lexus; **die ~ dankt** *(hum)* much obliged (to you).

Firmamẹnt *nt no pl (poet)* firmament *(liter)*.

Fịrmen-: ~inhaber *m* owner of a/the company; **~name** *m* company name; **~register** *nt* register of companies; **~schild** *nt* company sign; **~verzeichnis** *nt* trade directory; **~wagen** *m* company car; **~zeichen** *nt* trademark.

firmieren* *vi*: **als ... ~** *(Comm, fig)* to trade under the name of ...

Fịrmung *f (Rel)* confirmation. **jdm die ~ erteilen** to confirm sb.

Fịrst *m* **-e** *(Dach~)* (roof) ridge.

Fịs *nt* **-** *(Mus)* F sharp. **in ~/f~** in F sharp major/minor.

Fịsch *m* **-e (a)** fish. **~e/drei ~e fangen** to catch fish/three fish(es); **das sind kleine ~e** *(fig col)* that's child's play *(col)*; **ein großer ~** *(fig col)* a big fish; **ein kleiner ~** one of the small fry; **sich wohl fühlen wie ein ~ im Wasser** to be in one's element; **stumm wie ein ~ sein** to be as silent as a post; **weder ~ noch Fleisch** neither fish nor fowl. **(b) ~e** *pl (Astrol)* Pisces.

Fịsch- *in cpds* fish; **~becken** *nt* fishpond; **~bestand** *m* fish population; **~dampfer** *m* trawler.

fịschen *vti (lit, fig)* to fish. **mit (dem) Netz ~** to trawl; **Heringe ~** to fish for herring.

Fịscher *m* **-** fisherman.

Fịscher-: ~boot *nt* fishing boat; **~dorf** *nt* fishing village.

Fischerei *f* **(a)** fishing. **(b)** *(~gewerbe)* fishing industry, fisheries *pl*.

Fischerei- *in cpds* fishing; **~grenze** *f* fishing limit.

Fịschernetz *nt* fishing net.

Fịschfang *m no pl* **vom ~ leben** to live by fishing; **zum ~ auslaufen** to set off for the fishing grounds.

Fịschfanggebiet *nt* fishing grounds *pl*.

Fịsch-: ~filet *nt* fish fillet; **~frikadelle** *f* fishcake; **~geruch** *m* smell of fish, fishy smell; **~geschäft** *nt* fishmonger; **~gräte** *f* fish bone; **~grätenmuster** *nt* herringbone (pattern); **~gründe** *pl* fishing grounds *pl*, fisheries *pl*; **~händler** *m* fishmonger; *(Großhändler)* fish merchant; **~konserve** *f* canned fish; **~kutter** *m* fishing cutter; **~laden** *m* fishmonger; **~markt** *m* fish market; **~mehl** *nt* fish meal; **~otter** *m* otter; **~schuppe** *f* (fish) scale; **~schwarm** *m* shoal of fish; **~stäbchen** *nt* fish finger *(Brit)*, fish stick *(US)*; **~sterben** *nt* death of fish; **~zucht** *f* fish-farming; **~zug** *m (fig: Beutezug)* raid, foray.

Fisimatẹnten *pl (col) (Ausflüchte)* excuses *pl*; *(Umstände)* fuss; *(Albernheiten)* nonsense.

Fịskus *m no pl (fig: Staatskasse)* Treasury.

Fịstelstimme *f* falsetto.

fịt *adj pred* fit. **sich ~ halten** to keep fit.

Fịtness, Fịtneß *f no pl* physical fitness.

Fịttich *m* **-e** *(liter)* wing. **jdn unter seine ~e nehmen** *(hum)* to take sb under one's wing.

Fịtzelchen *nt (col)* little bit.

fịx *adj* **(a)** *(col: flink)* quick. **mach ~!** look lively! **(b)** *(col)* **~ und fertig sein** to be all finished; *(bereit)* to be all ready; *(erschöpft, emotional)* to be shattered *(col)*; **jdn ~ und fertig machen** *(nervös machen)* to drive sb mad; *(erschöpfen, emotional)* to shatter sb *(col)*. **(c) ~e Idee** obsession.

fịxen *vi (col: Drogen spritzen)* to fix *(col)*.

Fịxer(in *f***)** *m* **-** *(col)* fixer *(col)*.

Fixierbad *nt (Phot)* fixer.

fixieren* *vt* **(a)** *(anstarren)* **jdn/etw ~** to stare at sb/sth. **(b)** *(festlegen)* to specify; *(schriftlich niederlegen)* to record. **er ist zu stark auf seine Mutter fixiert** *(Psych)* he has a mother fixation. **(c)** *(Phot)* to fix.

Fixierung *f (Festlegung) siehe vt (b)* specification; recording; *(Psych)* fixation.

Fịx-: ~kosten *pl* fixed costs *pl*; **~stern** *m* fixed star.

Fịxum *nt, pl* **Fịxa** basic salary.

Fjọrd *m* **-e** fiord.

FKK [ɛfkaː'kaː] *no art* = **Freikörperkultur.**

FKK-: ~-Anhänger *m* **~-Anhänger sein** to be a nudist; **~-Strand** *m* nudist beach.

flạch *adj* **(a)** flat; *Gebäude* low; *Abhang* gentle; *Gewässer* shallow. **~ liegen** to lie flat; **die ~e Hand** the flat of one's hand; **eine ~e Brust** a hollow chest; *(Busen)* a flat chest; **auf dem ~en Land** in the middle of the country. **(b)** *(fig)* flat; *Geschmack* insipid; *(oberflächlich)* shallow. **~ atmen** to take shallow breaths.

Flạchdach *nt* flat roof.

Fläche *f* **-n** *(auch Math)* area; *(Ober~)* surface; *(Gelände, Land~, Wasser~)* expanse.

Flạ̈chen-: ~brand *m* extensive fire; **sich zu einem ~brand ausweiten** *(fig)* to spread to epidemic proportions; **~inhalt** *m* area; **~maß** *nt* square measure.

Flạch-: f~fallen *vi sep irreg aux sein (col)* not to come off; *(Regelung)* to end; **~land** *nt* lowland; **f~liegen** *vi sep irreg (col)* to be laid up; **~mann** *m, pl* **~männer** *(col)* hipflask.

Flachs [flaks] *m no pl* **(a)** *(Bot, Tex)* flax. **(b)** *(col: Neckerei, Witzelei)* kidding *(col)*.

flachsen ['flaksn] *vi (col)* to kid around *(col)*.
Flachzange *f* flat-nosed pliers *pl*.
flackern *vi (lit, fig)* to flicker.
Fladen *m* - **(a)** *(Cook)* round flat dough-cake. **(b)** *(col: Kuh~)* cowpat.
Fladenbrot *nt* round flat loaf.
Flagge *f* **-n** flag. **die ~ streichen** *(fig)* to capitulate; **~ zeigen** to nail one's colours *(Brit) or* colors *(US)* to the mast.
flaggen *vi* **geflaggt haben** to fly flags/a flag.
Flaggenmast *m* flagpole.
Flagg-: ~offizier *m* flag officer; **~schiff** *nt (lit, fig)* flagship.
flagrant *adj* flagrant; *siehe* **in flagranti.**
Flair [flɛːɐ] *nt no pl (geh)* atmosphere; *(Nimbus)* aura.
Flak *f* - *or* **-s** = **Flug(zeug)abwehrkanone** anti-aircraft gun; *(Einheit)* anti-aircraft unit.
Flakon [fla'kõː] *nt or m* **-s** bottle, flacon.
flambieren* *vt (Cook)* to flambé.
Flame *m (wk)* **-n, -n, Flämin** *f* Fleming.
Flamingo [fla'mɪŋgo] *m* **-s** flamingo.
flämisch *adj* Flemish.
Flämisch(e) *nt* Flemish; *siehe* **Deutsch(e).**
Flamme *f* **-n** *(lit, fig)* flame. **in ~n stehen/ aufgehen** to be in flames/go up in flames.
flammend *adj* fiery. **mit ~em Gesicht** blazing.
flammendrot *adj (geh)* flame red, blazing red.
Flammen-: ~meer *nt* sea of flames; **~werfer** *m* flame-thrower.
Flandern *nt* Flanders *sing*.
Flanell *m* **-e** flannel.
flanieren* *vi* to stroll, to saunter.
Flanke *f* **-n** *(Anat, Mil)* flank; *(Sport) (Turnen)* flank-vault; *(Ftbl)* cross; *(Spielfeldseite)* wing.
flanken *vi (Ftbl)* to centre *(Brit)*, to center *(US)*.
Flanken-: ~angriff *m (Mil)* flank attack; **~ball** *m (Ftbl)* cross; **~deckung** *f (Mil)* flank defence *(Brit) or* defense *(US)*.
flankieren* *vt (Mil, fig)* to flank. **~de Maßnahmen** supporting measures.
Flansch *m* **-e** flange.
Flasche *f* **-n (a)** bottle. **mit der ~ aufziehen** to bottle-feed; **eine ~ Wein/Bier** a bottle of wine/ beer; **zur ~ greifen** *(fig)* to hit the bottle. **(b)** *(col: Versager)* dead loss *(col)*.
Flaschen-: ~bier *nt* bottled beer; **f~grün** *adj* bottle-green; **~hals** *m* neck of a bottle; *(fig)* bottleneck; **~kind** *nt* bottle-fed baby; **~milch** *f* bottled milk; **~öffner** *m* bottle-opener; **~pfand** *nt* deposit on a/the bottle; **~post** *f* message in a/the bottle; **per ~post** in a bottle; **~zug** *m* block and tackle.
Flatter-: f~haft *adj* fickle; **~haftigkeit** *f* fickleness.
flatt(e)rig *adj* fluttery; *Puls* fluttering.
flattern *vi (lit, fig)* to flutter; *(mit den Flügeln schlagen)* to flap its wings; *(Fahne, Segel)* to flap; *(Haar)* to fly; *(col: Mensch)* to be in a flap *(col)*. **ein Brief flatterte mir auf den Schreibtisch** a letter arrived on my desk.
flau *adj* **(a)** *Brise, Wind* slack. **(b)** *Stimmung* flat. **(c)** *(übel)* queasy; *(vor Hunger)* faint. **mir ist ~ (im Magen)** I feel queasy. **(d)** *(Comm)* slack. **in meiner Kasse sieht es ~ aus** *(col)* my finances aren't too healthy *(col)*.
Flaum *m no pl* fluff, down.
Flaum-: ~bart *m* downy beard, bum-fluff *(col) no indef art*; **~feder** *f* down feather.
flaumig *adj* downy.
flauschig *adj* fleecy; *(weich)* soft.
Flausen *pl (col)* **(a)** *(Unsinn)* nonsense; *(Illusionen)* fancy ideas *pl (col)*. **~ im Kopf haben** to have fancy ideas. **(b)** *(Ausflüchte)* excuses *pl*.
Flaute *f* **-n (a)** *(Naut)* calm. **das Schiff geriet in eine ~** the ship was becalmed. **(b)** *(fig)* slack period.
fläzen *vr (col)* to sprawl *(in+acc* in*)*.
Flechte *f* **-n** *(Bot, Med)* lichen.
flechten *pret* **flocht,** *ptp* **geflochten** *vt Haar* to plait; *Kranz, Korb* to weave.
Flechtwerk *nt* = **Geflecht.**
Fleck *m* **-e** *or* **-en (a)** *(Schmutz~)* mark. **dieses Zeug macht ~en** this stuff stains *(in/auf etw (acc)* sth*)*; **einen ~ auf der Weste haben** *(fig)* to have blotted one's copybook. **(b)** *(Farb~)* patch. **(c)** *(Stelle)* spot, place. **auf demselben ~** in the same place; **sich nicht vom ~ rühren** not to budge; **nicht vom ~ kommen** not to get any further; **vom ~ weg** on the spot.
Fleckchen *nt* **ein schönes ~ (Erde)** a lovely little spot.
Flecken *m* - **(a)** *(old: Markt~)* small town. **(b)** = **Fleck (a, b).**
fleckenlos *adj (lit, fig)* spotless.
Fleckenwasser *nt* stain-remover.
Fleckfieber *nt* typhus fever.
fleckig *adj* marked; *Obst* blemished; *Tierfell* speckled; *Gesichtshaut* blotchy.
Fledermaus *f* bat.
Flegel *m* - *(Lümmel)* lout, yob *(col)*; *(Kind)* brat *(col)*.
Flegel|alter *nt* awkward adolescent phase.
Flegelei *f* uncouthness *no pl*.
Flegel-: f~haft *adj* uncouth; **~haftigkeit** *f* uncouthness; **~jahre** *pl* = **~alter.**
flegeln *vr* to loll, to sprawl.
flehen *vi (geh)* to plead *(um+acc* for, *zu* with*)*.
flehentlich *adj* imploring, pleading. **jdn ~ bitten** to plead with sb.
Fleisch *nt no pl* **(a)** flesh. **vom ~ fallen** *(col)* to lose (a lot of) weight; **sich** *(dat or acc)* **ins eigene ~ schneiden** to cut off one's nose to spite one's face *(prov)*; **sein eigen ~ und Blut** *(liter)* his own flesh and blood; **jdm in ~ und Blut übergehen** to become second nature to sb. **(b)** *(Nahrungsmittel)* meat; *(Frucht~)* flesh.
Fleisch- *in cpds (Cook)* meat; *(Anat)* flesh; **~beschau** *f* **(a)** meat inspection; **(b)** *(hum col)* cattle market *(col)*; **~beschauer(in** *f***)** *m* meat inspector; **~brocken** *m* lump of meat; **~brühe** *f* meat stock; *(Gericht)* bouillon.
Fleischer *m* - butcher.
Fleischerei *f* butcher.
Fleischer-: ~haken *m* meat hook; **~handwerk** *nt* butcher's trade; **~hund** *m (lit)* butcher's dog; *(fig)* brute of a dog; **ein Gemüt wie ein ~hund haben** *(col)* to be a callous brute; **~laden** *m* butcher's (shop); **~messer** *nt* butcher's knife.
Fleisch-: f~farben, f~farbig *adj* flesh-coloured *(Brit)*, flesh-colored *(US)*; **f~fressend** *adj* carnivorous; **~fresser** *m (Zool)* carnivore.
fleischig *adj* fleshy.
Fleisch-: ~käse *m* meat loaf; **~klopfer** *m* steak hammer; **~kloß** *m*, **~klößchen** *nt* **(a)** meat ball; **(b)** *(pej col)* mountain of flesh; **f~lich** *adj attr Kost* meat; *(old liter: Begierden)* carnal; **f~los** *adj* **(a)** *(ohne Fleisch)* meatless; *Kost, Ernährung* vegetarian; **f~los essen/kochen** to eat no meat/to cook without meat; **(b)** *(mager)* thin, lean; **~saft** *m* meat juices *pl*; **~salat** *m* diced meat salad with mayonnaise; **f~verarbeitend** *adj attr* meat-processing; **~vergiftung** *f* food poisoning *(from meat)*; **~waren** *pl* meat products *pl*; **~wolf** *m* mincer, meat grinder *(esp US)*; **~wunde** *f* flesh wound; **~wurst** *f* pork sausage.
Fleiß *m no pl* industriousness. **~ aufwenden** to apply oneself; **mit ~ kann es jeder zu etwas bringen** anybody can succeed if he works hard; **mit ~ bei der Sache sein** to work hard; **ohne ~ kein Preis** *(Prov)* success never comes easily.
fleißig *adj* hard-working *no adv*, industrious; *Sammler* keen. **~ studieren/arbeiten** to study/ work hard; **~ wie die Bienen sein** to work like beavers; **ein ~er Arbeiter** a hard worker.
flennen *vi (pej col)* to blubb(er).

fletschen *vti*: **die Zähne ~** to bare one's teeth.
flexibel *adj (lit, fig)* flexible.
Flexibilität *f* flexibility.
flicken *vt* to mend; *(mit Flicken)* to patch.
Flicken *m* - patch. **eine Jacke mit ~** a patched jacket.
Flick-: ~schuster *m (old)* cobbler; *(fig pej)* bungler *(col)*; **~schusterei** *f* **das ist ~schusterei** *(fig pej)* that's a patch-up job; **~werk** *nt* **die Reform war reinstes ~werk** the reform had been carried out piecemeal; **~zeug** *nt (Nähzeug)* sewing kit; *(für Reifen)* (puncture) repair outfit.
Flieder *m* - lilac.
flieder-: ~farben, ~farbig *adj* lilac.
Fliege *f* **-n (a)** fly. **sie fielen um wie die ~n** they were dropping like flies; **sie starben wie die ~n** they fell like flies; **er tut keiner ~ etwas zuleide** *(fig)* he wouldn't hurt a fly; **zwei ~n mit einer Klappe schlagen** *(prov)* to kill two birds with one stone *(prov)*; **ihn stört die ~ an der Wand** every little thing irritates him; **die** *or* **'ne ~ machen** *(col)* to beat it *(col)*. **(b)** *(Schlips)* bow tie.
fliegen *pret* **flog,** *ptp* **geflogen 1** *vi aux sein* to fly. **nach Köln fliegt man zwei Stunden** it's a two-hour flight to Cologne; **ich kann doch nicht ~!** I haven't got wings *(col)*; **auf jdn/etw ~** *(col)* to be mad about sb/sth *(col)*; **von der Leiter ~** *(col)* to fall off the ladder; **durchs Examen ~** *(col)* to fail one's exam; **aus der Firma ~** *(col)* to get the sack *(col)*; **~der Puls** racing pulse; **geflogen kommen** to come flying; **in den Papierkorb ~** to go into the wastepaper basket; **ein Schuh flog ihm an den Kopf** he had a shoe flung at him; **aus der Kurve ~** to skid off the bend. **2** *vt* to fly.
fliegend *adj attr Fische, Untertasse, Start* flying. **in ~er Eile** in a tremendous hurry; **~e Hitze** hot flushes *pl*.
Fliegen-: ~draht *m* wire mesh; **~fänger** *m (Klebestreifen)* fly-paper; **~fenster** *nt* wire-mesh window; **~gewicht** *nt (Sport, fig)* flyweight; **~gewichtler** *m* - *(Sport)* flyweight; **~gitter** *nt* fly screen; **~klatsche** *f* fly-swat; **~pilz** *m* fly agaric.
Flieger *m* - airman; *(col: Flugzeug)* plane.
Flieger- *(Mil)*: **~alarm** *m* air-raid warning; **~angriff** *m* air-raid; **~horst** *m (Mil)* military airfield.
fliehen *pret* **floh,** *ptp* **geflohen** *vi* to flee; *(entkommen)* to escape *(aus* from*)*. **vor jdm/der Polizei ~** to flee from sb/the police; **aus dem Lande ~** to flee the country.
fliehend *adj Kinn* receding; *Stirn* sloping.
Fliehkraft *f* centrifugal force.
Fliese *f* **-n** tile. **etw mit ~n auslegen** to tile sth.
Fließ-: ~arbeit *f no pl* production-line work; **~band** *nt* conveyor-belt; **am ~band arbeiten** to work on the assembly *or* production line.
fließen *pret* **floß,** *ptp* **geflossen** *vi* to flow; *(Fluß auch, Tränen)* to run. **es ist genug Blut geflossen** enough blood has been shed.
fließend *adj* flowing; *Leitungswasser* running; *Verkehr* moving; *Übergang* fluid. **sie spricht ~ Französisch** she speaks fluent French.
Fließ-: ~heck *nt* fastback; **~komma** *nt (Comp)* floating point.
Flimmer-: ~kasten *m,* **~kiste** *f (col)* box *(col)*.
flimmern *vi* to shimmer; *(TV)* to flicker. **es flimmert mir vor den Augen** everything is swimming in front of my eyes.
flink *adj (geschickt)* nimble; *Zunge* quick. **ein bißchen ~** *(col)* get a move on!; **mit etw ~ bei der Hand sein** to be quick (off the mark) with sth.
Flinkheit *f siehe adj* nimbleness; quickness.
Flinte *f* **-n** *(Schrot~)* shotgun. **die ~ ins Korn werfen** *(fig)* to throw in the sponge.
Flipper *m* **-, Flipperautomat** *m* pinball machine.
flippern *vi* to play pinball.
Flirt [flœrt] *m* **-s** *(Flirten)* flirtation.
flirten ['flœrtn] *vi* to flirt.
Flittchen *nt* - *(pej col)* slut.
Flitter *m* - **(a)** *(~schmuck)* sequins *pl*. **(b)** *no pl (pej: Tand)* trumpery.
flittern *vi* to glitter, to sparkle.
Flitterwochen *pl* honeymoon *sing*. **in den ~ sein** to be on honeymoon.
flitzen *vi aux sein (col)* to whizz *(col)*, to dash.
Flitzer *m* - *(col) (Fahrzeug)* sporty little job *(col)*; *(Schnelläufer)* streak of lightning *(col)*.
floaten ['flo:tn] *vti (Fin)* to float. **~ (lassen)** to float.
Flocke *f* **-n (a)** flake; *(Schaum~)* blob (of foam). **(b) ~n** *pl (col: Geld)* dough *(col)*.
flockig *adj* fluffy.
flog *pret of* **fliegen.**
floh *pret of* **fliehen.**
Floh *m* **¨-e (a)** *(Zool)* flea. **es ist leichter, einen Sack ¨~e zu hüten, als ... ...** is absolutely impossible; **jdm einen ~ ins Ohr setzen** *(col)* to put an idea into sb's head. **(b)** *(col: Geld)* **¨~e** *pl* dough *(col)*.
Flohmarkt *m* flea market.
Flor *m* **-e (a)** *(dünnes Gewebe)* gauze; *(Trauer~)* crêpe. **(b)** *(Teppich~)* pile.
Flora *f pl* **Floren** flora.
Florett *nt* **-e** *(Waffe)* foil.
florieren* *vi* to flourish, to bloom.
Florist(in *f***)** *m (wk)* **-en, -en** florist.
Floskel *f* **-n** set phrase. **eine abgedroschene ~** a hackneyed phrase.
floskelhaft *adj* cliché-ridden, stereotyped.
floß *pret of* **fließen.**
Floß *nt* **¨-e** raft.
Flosse *f* **-n** *(Fisch~, Aviat)* fin; *(Wal~, Robben~, Taucher~)* flipper; *(col: Hand)* paw *(col)*.
Flöte *f* **-n (a)** pipe; *(Quer~)* flute; *(Block~)* recorder; *(Pikkolo~)* piccolo. **(b)** *(Kelchglas)* flute glass. **(c)** *(Cards)* flush.
flöten *vti (Vogel, hum)* to warble.
Flöten-: f~gehen *vi sep aux sein (col)* to go for a burton *(col)*; **~spieler** *m* piper; flautist; **~ton** *m* sound of flutes/a flute; **jdm die ~töne beibringen** *(col)* to teach sb what's what *(col)*.
Flötist(in *f***)** *m (wk)* **-en, -en** flautist; piccolo player.
flott *adj* **(a)** *(zügig) Fahrt* quick; *Tempo* brisk; *Bedienung* speedy *(col)*; *Tänzer* good; *(flüssig) Stil, Artikel* racy *(col)*; *(schwungvoll) Musik* lively; *Auto* sporty. **aber ein bißchen ~!** and look lively! **(b)** *(schick)* smart. **(c)** *(lebenslustig)* fun-loving, fast-living. **ein ~es Leben führen** to be a fast liver. **(d)** *pred* **wieder ~ werden** *(Schiff)* to be refloated; *(fig col) (Auto etc)* to get back on the road; *(Unternehmen)* to get back on its feet.
Flotte *f* **-n** *(Naut)* fleet.
Flotten-: ~basis *f,* **~stützpunkt** *m* naval base.
Fluch *m* **¨-e** curse. **ein ~ lastet auf diesem Haus** there is a curse on this house.
fluchen *vi* to curse *(auf or über jdn/etw (acc)* sb/sth*)*.
Flucht *f* **-en (a)** *(Fliehen)* flight; *(geglückt auch)* escape. **die ~ ergreifen** to take flight; **ihm glückte die ~** he succeeded in escaping; **auf der ~ sein** to be fleeing; *(Dieb)* to be on the run; **jdn/etw in die ~ schlagen** to put sb/sth to flight; **die ~ nach vorn antreten** to take the bull by the horns. **(b)** *(Häuser~)* row. **(c)** *(Zimmer~)* suite.
flucht|artig *adj* hasty. **in ~er Eile** in great haste.
flüchten *vi* **(a)** *aux sein (davonlaufen)* to flee; *(erfolgreich auch)* to escape. **vor der Wirklichkeit ~** to escape reality. **(b)** *auch vr (vi: aux sein) (Schutz suchen)* to take refuge.
Flucht-: ~fahrzeug *nt* escape vehicle; *(von Dieb)* getaway vehicle; **~gefahr** *f* risk of escape; **~hilfe** *f* **~hilfe leisten** to aid an escape.
flüchtig *adj* **(a)** *(geflüchtet)* **~ sein** to be at large. **(b)** *(kurz)* fleeting. **(c)** *(oberflächlich)* cursory. **etw ~ lesen** to skim through sth; **jdn ~ kennen**

to have met sb briefly. **(d)** *(Chem)* volatile.
Flüchtigkeit *f* **(a)** *(Kürze)* briefness. **(b)** *(Oberflächlichkeit)* cursoriness. **(c)** *(Chem)* volatility.
Flüchtigkeitsfehler *m* careless mistake.
Flüchtling *m* refugee.
Flüchtlings- *in cpds* refugee; **~hilfe** *f* aid to refugees; **~lager** *nt* refugee camp.
Flucht-: **~linie** *f* alignment; **~punkt** *m* vanishing point; **~verdacht** *m* **bei ~verdacht** if an attempt to abscond is thought likely; **~versuch** *m* escape attempt; **~weg** *m* escape route.
Flug *m* **¨-e** flight; *(Ski~)* jump. **im ~(e)** in the air; **einen ~ antreten** to take off *(nach* for); **wie im ~(e)** *(fig)* in a flash; **die letzte Woche verging wie im ~(e)** last week flew past.
Flug-: **~bahn** *f* flight path; *(von Rakete auch)* trajectory; *(Kreisbahn)* orbit; **~begleiter(in** *f*) *m* steward/stewardess; **f~bereit** *adj* ready for take-off; **~blatt** *nt* leaflet; **~dauer** *f* flying time.
Flügel *m* **-** **(a)** wing; *(von Hubschrauber)* blade; *(Windmühlen~)* sail, vane; *(Altar~)* sidepiece; *(Fenster~)* casement; *(Mil)* flank. **einem Vogel/jdm die ~ stutzen** to clip a bird's/sb's wings. **(b)** *(Konzert~)* grand piano.
Flügel-: **~schraube** *f* wing bolt; **~stürmer** *m* *(Sport)* wing forward; **~tür** *f* double door.
Flug-: **f~fähig** *adj* able to fly; *Flugzeug (in Ordnung)* airworthy; **~gast** *m* (airline) passenger.
flügge *adj* fully-fledged; *(fig) Jugendlicher* independent. **~ werden** *(lit)* to be able to fly; *(fig)* to leave the nest.
Flug-: **~gelände** *nt* airfield; **~gesellschaft** *f* airline; **~hafen** *m* airport; **~höhe** *f* flying height, altitude; **unsere ~höhe beträgt 10.000 Meter** we are flying at an altitude of 10,000 metres; **~kapitän** *m* captain; **~karte** *f (Ticket)* plane ticket; **~körper** *m* projectile; **~leitung** *f* air-traffic *or* flight control; **~linie** *f* **(a)** *(Strecke)* air route; **(b)** *(~gesellschaft)* airline; **~lotse** *m* air-traffic *or* flight controller; **~minute** *f* **30 ~minuten von hier** 30 minutes by air from here; **~netz** *nt* network of air routes; **~objekt** *nt*: **ein unbekanntes ~objekt** an unidentified flying object, a UFO; **~personal** *nt* flight personnel *pl*; **~plan** *m* flight schedule; **~platz** *m* airfield; *(größer)* airport; **~preis** *m* air fare; **~reise** *f* flight; **eine ~reise machen** to travel by air; **~reisende(r)** *mf* (airline) passenger; **~route** *f* air-route.
flugs [flʊks] *adv (dated)* without delay, speedily.
Flug-: **~sand** *m* drifting sand; **~schanze** *f (Sport)* ski-jump; **~schein** *m* **(a)** pilot's licence *(Brit) or* license *(US)*; **(b)** *(~karte)* air ticket; **~schreiber** *m* flight recorder; **~schrift** *f* pamphlet; **~sicherung** *f* air traffic control; **~steig** *m* gate; **~stunde** *f* **(a)** flying hour; **zehn ~stunden entfernt** ten hours away by air; **(b)** *(Unterricht)* flying lesson; **f~technisch** *adj* aeronautical; *Erfahrung, Fehler* flying *attr*; **f~tüchtig** *adj* airworthy; **~verbindung** *f* air connection; **~wesen** *nt no pl* aviation *no art*; **~zeit** *f* flying time.
Flugzeug *nt* **-e** plane, aircraft, aeroplane *(Brit)*, airplane *(US)*.
Flugzeug- *in cpds* aircraft; **~absturz** *m* plane *or* air crash; **~besatzung** *f* aircrew; **~entführer** *m* hijacker; **~entführung** *f* hijacking; **~führer** *m* (aircraft) pilot; **~halle** *f* (aircraft) hangar; **~katastrophe** *f* air disaster; **~träger** *m* aircraft carrier; **~unglück** *nt* plane *or* air crash.
fluktuieren* *vi* to fluctuate.
Flunder *f* **-n** flounder.
Flunkerei *f (col)* **(a)** *(no pl: Flunkern)* story-telling. **(b)** *(kleine Lüge)* story.
flunkern *(col)* **1** *vi* to tell stories. **2** *vt* to make up.
Flunsch *m* **-e** *(col)* pout. **einen ~ ziehen** to pout.
Fluor *nt no pl (Chem)* fluorine; *(~verbindung)* fluoride.
Flur[1] *m* **-e** corridor; *(in Privathaus)* hall; *(oben in Privathaus)* landing.
Flur[2] *f* **-en** *(geh)* open fields *pl*. **durch Wald/Feld und ~** through woods/fields and meadows; **allein auf weiter ~ stehen** *(fig)* to be out on a limb.
Fluß *m* **¨-sse** **(a)** river. **unten am ~** down by the river(side). **(b)** *(von Verkehr, Rede, Strom)* flow. **etw in ~** *(acc)* **bringen** to get sth moving; **im ~ sein** *(sich verändern)* to be in a state of flux; *(im Gange sein)* to be in progress.
Fluß- *in cpds* river; **f~ab(wärts)** *adv* downstream, downriver; **f~aufwärts** *adv* upstream, upriver; **~diagramm** *nt* flow chart.
flüssig *adj* **(a)** liquid; *Honig, Lack* runny; *Glas, Metall auch* molten. **(b)** *Stil, Spiel* flowing, fluid. **~ lesen** to read fluently; **den Verkehr ~ halten** to keep the traffic flowing. **(c)** *Geld* available. **~es Vermögen** liquid assets *pl*; **Wertpapiere ~ machen** to realize securities; **ich bin im Moment nicht ~** *(col)* I'm out of funds at the moment.
Flüssigkeit *f* **(a)** liquid; *(esp Anat)* fluid. **(b)** *no pl (von Metall)* liquidity; *(von Geldern)* availability; *(von Stil)* fluidity.
flüssigmachen *vt sep* to realize.
Fluß-: **~lauf** *m* course of a/the river; **~mündung** *f* estuary; **~pferd** *nt* hippopotamus.
flüstern *vti* to whisper. **das kann ich dir ~** *(col)* take it from me *(col)*; **dem werde ich was ~** *(col)* I'll tell him a thing or two *(col)*.
Flüster-: **~propaganda** *f* underground rumours *pl (Brit) or* rumors *pl (US)*; **~stimme** *f* whisper; **~ton** *m* whisper; **sich im ~ton unterhalten** to talk in whispers.
Flut *f* **-en** **(a)** incoming *or* flood tide; *(Zustand)* high tide. **die ~ kommt** the tide's coming in; **die ~ geht zurück** the tide has started to go out. **(b)** *usu pl (Wassermasse)* waters *pl*. **(c)** *(fig: Menge)* flood. **eine ~ von Tränen** floods of tears.
fluten *vi aux sein (geh: lit, fig)* to flood.
Flut-: **~licht** *nt* floodlight; **~mündung** *f* estuary.
flutschen *vi (col)* **(a)** *aux sein (rutschen)* to slide. **(b)** *(funktionieren)* to go well.
Flutwelle *f* tidal wave.
Föderation *f* federation.
föderativ *adj* federal.
Fohlen *nt* **-** foal; *(männlich auch)* colt; *(weiblich auch)* filly.
Föhn *m* **-e** *warm dry Alpine wind*, foehn.
Föhre *f* **-n** Scots pine (tree).
Folge *f* **-n** **(a)** sequence; *(Cards auch)* run; *(Fortsetzung)* instalment *(Brit)*, installment *(US)*; *(TV, Rad)* episode. **in rascher ~** in quick succession; **in der** *or* **für die ~** *(form)* in future. **(b)** *(Ergebnis)* consequence. **dies hatte seine Entlassung zur ~** this resulted in his dismissal; **die ~n werden nicht ausbleiben** there will be repercussions. **(c)** *(form)* **einem Befehl/einer Einladung ~ leisten** to obey an order/to accept an invitation.
Folge|erscheinung *f* result, consequence.
folgen *vi* **(a)** *aux sein* to follow *(jdm/einer Sache* sb/sth*)*. **auf jdn (im Rang) ~** to come after sb; **~ Sie mir (bitte)!** come with me please; **wie folgt** as follows; **daraus folgt, daß ...** it follows from this that ...; **können Sie mir ~?** do you follow (me)? **(b)** *(gehorchen)* to obey.
folgend *adj* following. **~es** the following; **im ~en** in the following; *(schriftlich auch)* below.
folgendermaßen *adv* like this, as follows.
folgen-: **~los** *adj* without consequences; **das konnte nicht ~los bleiben** that was bound to have serious consequences; **~schwer** *adj* serious; **die Maßnahme erwies sich als ~schwer** the measure had serious consequences.
Folge-: **f~richtig** *adj* (logically) consistent; **~richtigkeit** *f* logical consistency.
folgern *vti* to conclude. **daraus läßt sich ~, daß ...** we can conclude from this that ...
Folgerung *f* conclusion.
Folgezeit *f* following period.

folglich *adv, conj* consequently, therefore.
folgsam *adj* obedient.
Folgsamkeit *f* obedience.
Folie ['fo:liə] *f (Plastik~)* film; *(Metall~)* foil.
Folklore *f no pl* folklore; *(Volksmusik)* folk music.
folkloristisch *adj* folkloric; *Kleidung* ethnic.
Folter *f* **-n** *(lit, fig)* torture. **jdn auf die ~ spannen** *(fig)* to keep sb on tenterhooks.
Folterbank *f* rack.
Folterer *m* **-** torturer.
foltern 1 *vt* to torture; *(quälen auch)* to torment. **2** *vi* to use torture.
Folterung *f* torture.
Fön ® *m* **-e** hair-dryer.
Fond [fõ:] *m* **-s (a)** *(geh: Wagen~)* back. **(b)** *(Hintergrund)* background. **(c)** *(Cook: Fleischsaft)* meat juices *pl*.
Fonds [fõ:] *m* **- (a)** *(lit, fig)* fund. **(b)** *(Fin: Schuldverschreibung)* government bond.
fönen *vt* to dry (with a hair-dryer).
Fontäne *f* **-n** jet (of water).
foppen *vt (col)* **jdn ~** *(necken)* to pull sb's leg *(col)*.
forcieren* [fɔr'si:rən] *vt* to push; *Tempo* to force; *Konsum, Produktion* to push *or* force up.
forciert [fɔr'si:ɐt] *adj* forced.
Förder-: ~anlage *f* conveyor; **~band** *nt* conveyor belt.
Förderer *m* **-, Förderin** *f* sponsor; *(Gönner)* patron.
Förder-: ~korb *m (Min)* cage; **~leistung** *f (Min)* output.
förderlich *adj* beneficial *(dat* to*)*. **guten Beziehungen ~ sein** to be conducive to good relations.
fordern 1 *vt* **(a)** *(verlangen)* to demand; *Preis* to ask; *(in Aufrufen)* to call for; *(Anspruch erheben auf)* to claim. **viel von jdm ~** to ask *or* demand a lot of sb. **(b)** *(fig: kosten) Opfer* to claim. **(c)** *(fig: herausfordern)* to challenge. **(d)** *(Sport)* to make demands on. **2** *vi* to make demands.
fördern *vt* **(a)** *(unterstützen)* to support; *(propagieren)* to promote; *(finanziell) bestimmtes Projekt* to sponsor; *jds Talent, Neigung* to encourage, to foster; *Verdauung* to aid; *Appetit* to stimulate; *Untersuchung, Wahrheitsfindung, Wachstum* to further; *Verbrauch* to boost. **jdn beruflich ~** to help sb in his career. **(b)** *Bodenschätze* to extract.
Förderturm *m (Min)* winding tower; *(auf Bohrstelle)* derrick.
Forderung *f* **(a)** *(Verlangen)* demand *(nach* for*)*; *(Lohn~ etc)* claim; *(in Aufrufen etc)* call. **eine ~ nach etw erheben** to call for sth; **jds ~ erfüllen** to meet sb's demands/claim. **(b)** *(Comm: Anspruch)* claim *(an+acc* on*)*. **(c)** *(Herausforderung)* challenge.
Förderung *f* **(a)** *siehe* **fördern (a)** support; promotion; sponsorship; encouragement, fostering; aid; stimulation; furtherance; boosting. **(b)** *(Gewinnung)* extraction.
Forelle *f* trout.
Form *f* **-en (a)** form; *(Gestalt, Umriß)* shape. **in ~ von Dragees** in the form of pills; **seine ~ verlieren/aus der ~ geraten** to lose its shape; **einer Sache** *(dat)* **~ (und Gestalt) geben** *(lit, fig)* to give sth shape; **feste ~ annehmen** *(fig)* to take shape; **gewalttätige ~en annehmen** *(fig)* to become violent. **(b)** *(Umgangs~en)* **~en** *pl* manners *pl*; **die ~ wahren** to observe the proprieties; **der ~ wegen** for the sake of form; **in aller ~** formally. **(c)** *(Kondition)* form. **in ~ bleiben/kommen** to keep/get (oneself) in shape; **groß in ~** in great form. **(d)** *(Gieß~)* mould; *(Kuchen~)* baking tin *(Brit) or* pan *(US)*; *(Hut~, Schuh~)* block.
formal *adj* formal; *Besitzer, Grund* technical.
Form|aldehyd *m no pl* formaldehyde.
Formalität *f* formality. **alle ~en erledigen** to go through all the formalities.
Format *nt* **-e (a)** format. **(b)** *(Persönlichkeit)* stature. **(c)** *(fig: Niveau)* class *(col)*, quality.
Formation *f* formation; *(Gruppe)* group.
Form-: f~bar *adj (lit, fig)* malleable; **f~beständig** *adj* **f~beständig sein** to hold its shape; **~blatt** *nt* form.
Formel *f* **-n** formula; *(von Eid etc)* wording; *(Floskel)* set phrase. **etw auf eine ~ bringen** to reduce sth to a formula.
formelhaft *adj Sprache, Stil* stereotyped. **~ reden** to talk in set phrases.
formell *adj* formal.
formen *vt* to form, to shape; *Eisen* to mould; *Wörter* to articulate.
formenreich *adj* with a great variety of forms.
Form-: ~fehler *m* irregularity; *(gesellschaftlich)* breach of etiquette; **~gebung** *f (geh)* design.
formieren* **1** *vt Truppen* to draw up; *Kolonne, Zug* to form (into); *(bilden)* to form. **2** *vr* to form up.
Formierung *f* formation; *(von Truppen)* drawing-up.
förmlich *adj* **(a)** *(formell)* formal. **(b)** *(regelrecht)* positive.
Förmlichkeit *f* formality. **bitte keine ~en!** please don't stand on ceremony.
formlos *adj* **(a)** shapeless. **(b)** *(zwanglos)* informal, casual. **(c)** *(Admin) Antrag* unaccompanied by a form/any forms.
Form-: ~sache *f* formality; **f~schön** *adj* elegantly proportioned; **~schönheit** *f* elegant proportions *pl*; **~tief** *nt* loss of form; **sich in einem ~tief befinden** to be badly off form.
Formular *nt* **-e** form.
formulieren* *vt* to word, to phrase. **... wenn ich es mal so ~ darf** ... if I might put it like that.
Formulierung *f* wording. **eine bestimmte ~** a particular phrase.
Formung f **(a)** *no pl (das Formen)* forming, shaping; *(von Eisen)* moulding; *(von Wörtern)* articulation. **(b)** *(Form)* shape.
formvollendet *adj* perfect; *Vase etc* perfectly formed.
forsch *adj* dynamic.
forschen *vi* to search *(nach* for*)*; *(Forschung betreiben)* to research *(über+acc* on *or* into*)*.
forschend *adj* inquiring; *(musternd)* searching.
Forscher(in *f***)** *m* **- (a)** researcher; *(in Naturwissenschaften)* research scientist. **(b)** *(Forschungsreisender)* explorer.
Forschung *f* research *no pl*. **verschiedene ~en** various studies; **~ und Lehre** research and teaching.
Forschungs- *in cpds* research; **~auftrag** *m* research assignment; **~reise** *f* expedition; **~reisende(r)** *mf decl as adj* explorer.
Forst *m* **-e(n)** forest.
Forst|amt *nt* forestry office.
Förster(in *f***)** *m* **-** forest warden *or* ranger *(US)*.
Forstwirtschaft *f* forestry.
Fort [fo:ɐ] *nt* **-s** fort.
fort *adv* **(a)** *(weg)* away; *(verschwunden)* gone. **~ mit ihm/damit!** away with him/it!; **er ist ~** he has left *or* gone; **weit ~** far away. **(b)** *(weiter)* on. **und so ~** and so on; **in einem ~** incessantly.
fort- *pref in cpd vbs (weg)* away; *siehe* **weg-**.
Fort-: f~begeben* *vr sep irreg (geh)* to depart; **~bestand** *m no pl* continued existence; **f~bestehen*** *vi sep irreg* to continue to exist; **f~bewegen*** *vtr sep* to move; **~bewegung** *f no pl* locomotion; **f~bilden** *vt sep* **jdn/sich f~bilden** to continue sb's/one's education; **~bildung** *f no pl* further education; **berufliche ~bildung** further vocational training; **f~bleiben** *vi sep irreg* to stay away; **~bleiben** *nt no pl* absence; **f~bringen** *vt sep irreg* to take away; *(zur Reparatur, Reinigung etc)* to take in; *Brief, Paket etc* to post; **~dauer** *f* continuance, continuation; **f~dauern** *vi sep* to continue; **f~dauernd 1** *adj* continuing; *(in der Vergangenheit)* continued; **2** *adv* constantly, con-

tinuously; **f~entwickeln*** *vtr sep* to develop; **~entwicklung** *f no pl* development; **f~fahren** *sep* **1** *vi aux sein* **(a)** *(wegfahren)* to go away; *(Fahrer)* to drive off; *(abfahren)* to leave, to go; *(einen Ausflug machen)* to go out; **(b)** *(weitermachen)* to continue; **f~fahren, etw zu tun** to continue doing sth *or* to do sth; **2** *vt Wagen* to drive away; **~fall** *m* discontinuance; **f~fallen** *vi sep irreg aux sein (ausgelassen werden)* to be omitted; *(Bedenken etc)* to vanish; *(Zuschuß etc)* to be discontinued; **f~führen** *vt sep* **(a)** *(fortsetzen)* to continue, to carry on; **(b)** *(wegführen)* to take away; **~führung** *f* continuation; **~gang** *m no pl* **(a)** *(Weggang)* departure *(aus* from*)*; **(b)** *(Verlauf)* progress; **f~gehen** *vi sep aux sein* to go away, to leave; **f~geschritten** *adj* advanced; **er kam zu f~geschrittener Stunde** he came at a late hour; **~geschrittenenkurs(us)** *m* advanced course; **f~gesetzt** *adj* constant; **f~jagen** *sep* **1** *vt* to chase out *(aus, von* of*)*; *(hinauswerfen)* to throw out *(aus, von* of*)*; **2** *vi aux sein* to race off; **~kommen** *nt* **(a)** *(lit, fig)* progress; **(b)** *(Auskommen)* **sein ~kommen finden** to find a means of earning one's living; **f~lassen** *vt sep* **(a)** *(weggehen lassen)* **jdn f~lassen** to let sb go; **(b)** *(auslassen)* to leave out, to omit; **f~laufen** *vi sep irreg aux sein* to run away; **f~laufend** *adj Handlung* ongoing *no adv*; *Zahlungen* regular; *(andauernd)* continual; **f~laufend numeriert** consecutively numbered; **f~machen** *vr sep (col)* to clear out *(col)*; **f~nehmen** *vt sep irreg* to take away *(jdm* from sb*)*; **f~pflanzen** *vr sep (Mensch)* to reproduce; *(Schall, Licht)* to travel; **~pflanzung** *f no pl* reproduction; **f~räumen** *vt sep* to clear away; **f~reißen** *vt sep irreg* to tear away; *(Menge, Flut, Strom)* to sweep *or* carry away; *(fig)* to carry away; **jdn/etw mit sich f~reißen** *(lit)* to carry *or* sweep sb/sth along; *(fig)* to carry sb/sth away; **f~schaffen** *vt sep* to remove; **f~scheren** *vr sep (col)* to clear off *(aus* out of*)* *(col)*; **f~schreiten** *vi sep irreg aux sein* to progress, to advance; *(Zeit)* to march on; *siehe* **f~geschritten**; **f~schreitend** *adj* progressive; *Alter, Wissenschaft* advancing.

Fortschritt *m* advance, progress *no pl*. **gute ~e machen** to make good progress; **dem ~ dienen** to further progress.

fortschrittlich *adj* progressive *(auch Pol)*; *Mensch, Ideen auch* forward-looking.

Fort-: f~setzen *sep* **1** *vt* to continue; *(nach Unterbrechung auch)* to resume; **2** *vr (zeitlich)* to continue; *(räumlich)* to extend; **~setzung** *f* **(a)** continuation; *(nach Unterbrechung auch)* resumption; **(b)** *(Rad, TV)* episode; *(eines Romans)* instalment *(Brit)*, installment *(US)*; **„~setzung folgt"** "to be continued"; **~setzungsroman** *m* serialized novel; **f~stehlen** *vr sep irreg (geh)* to steal away; **f~währen** *vi sep (geh)* to continue, to persist; **f~während** *adj no pred* constant, continual; **f~wirken** *vi sep* to continue to have an effect; **f~ziehen** *sep irreg* **1** *vt* to pull away, to drag away; **2** *vi aux sein* **(a)** to move on; **(b)** *(von einem Ort)* to move away *(aus* from*)*.

Forum *nt, pl* **Foren** forum.

Forumsdiskussion *f* forum (discussion).

Fossil *nt* **-ien** [iən] fossil.

Foto *nt* **-s** photo(graph), snap(shot) *(col)*. **ein ~ machen** to take a photo(graph).

Foto- *in cpds* photo; **~album** *nt* photograph album; **~amateur** *m* amateur photographer; **~apparat** *m* camera; **~atelier** *nt* (photographic) studio.

fotogen *adj* photogenic.

Fotograf *m* photographer.

Fotografie *f* **(a)** photography. **(b)** *(Bild)* photo(graph).

fotografieren* **1** *vt* to photograph, to take a photo(graph) of. **sich ~ lassen** to have one's photo(graph) taken. **2** *vi* to take photo(graph)s.

Fotografin *f* photographer.

fotografisch *adj* photographic.

Foto-: ~kopie *f* photocopy; **~kopierer** *(col) m*, **~kopiergerät** *nt* photocopier; **f~kopieren*** *vt insep* to photocopy; **~labor** *nt* darkroom; **~modell** *nt* photographic model; **~reporter** *m* press photographer.

Foul [faul] *nt* **-s** *(Sport)* foul.

Foul|elfmeter ['faul-] *m (Ftbl)* penalty (kick).

foulen ['faulən] *vti (Sport)* to foul.

Foulspiel ['faul-] *nt (Sport)* foul play.

Fox *m* **-e (a)** fox-terrier. **(b)** *(auch* **~trott***)* foxtrot.

Foyer [foa'jeː] *nt* **-s** foyer; *(in Hotel auch)* lobby.

Fr. = **Frau** Mrs, Ms; *(unverheiratet)* Miss, Ms.

Fracht *f* **-en** freight *no pl*; *(von Flugzeug, Schiff auch)* cargo; *(~preis auch)* freightage *no pl*.

Frachtbrief *m* consignment note, waybill.

Frachter *m* **-** freighter.

Fracht-: f~frei *adj* carriage paid *or* free; **~gut** *nt* freight *no pl*; **~kosten** *pl* freight charges *pl*; **~raum** *m* hold; *(Ladefähigkeit)* cargo space; **~schiff** *nt* cargo ship, freighter.

Frack *m* **¨e** tails *pl*, tail coat. **im ~** in tails.

Frack-: ~hemd *nt* dress shirt; **~sausen** *nt*: **~sausen haben** *(col)* to be in a funk *(col)*; **~weste** *f* waistcoat *(Brit) or* vest *(US) worn with tails;* **~zwang** *m* requirement to wear tails; **„~zwang"** "tails".

Frage *f* **-n** question. **eine ~ zu etw** a question on sth; **jdm eine ~ stellen** to ask sb a question; **auf eine dumme ~ bekommt man eine dumme Antwort** *(prov)* ask a silly question (get a silly answer) *(prov)*; **das ist (doch sehr) die ~** that's (just) the question; **das ist die große ~** that's the sixty-four thousand dollar question *(col)*; **das ist gar keine ~, das steht außer ~** there's no question about it; **ohne ~** without question *or* doubt; **in ~ kommen** to be possible; **sollte er für diese Stelle in ~ kommen, ...** if he should be considered for this post ...; **für jdn/etw nicht in ~ kommen** to be out of the question for sb/sth; **in ~ kommend** possible; *Bewerber* worth considering.

Fragebogen *m* questionnaire; *(Formular)* form.

fragen 1 *vti* to ask. **nach** *or* **wegen** *(col)* **jdm ~** to ask for sb; *(nach jds Befinden)* to ask after sb; **ich fragte sie nach den Kindern** I asked her how the children were doing; **nach Arbeit/Post ~** to ask whether there is/was any work/mail; **nach den Ursachen ~** to inquire as to the causes; **nach den Folgen ~** to care about the consequences; **wegen etw ~** to ask about sth; **das frage ich *dich*!** I could ask you the same; **da fragst du noch?** you still have to ask?; **frag nicht so dumm!** don't ask silly questions; **da fragst du mich zuviel** *(col)* I really couldn't say; **man wird ja wohl noch ~ dürfen** *(col)* I only asked *(col)*; **wenn ich (mal) ~ darf?** if I might ask?; **ohne lange zu ~** without asking a lot of questions.

2 *vr* to wonder. **das/da frage ich mich** I wonder; **das frage ich mich auch** that's just what I was wondering; **es/man fragt sich, ob ...** it's questionable/one wonders whether ...; **da muß man sich ~, ob ...** you can't help wondering if ...

fragend *adj* questioning, inquiring.

Frager(in *f*) *m* **-** questioner.

Fragerei *f* questions *pl*.

Frage-: ~steller(in *f*) *m* **-** questioner; *(Interviewer)* interviewer; **~stellung** *f* **(a)** formulation of a/the question; **(b)** *(Frage)* question; **~stunde** *f (Parl)* question time; **~zeichen** *nt* question mark *(auch fig)*; **dastehen/dasitzen wie ein ~zeichen** *(col)* to slouch.

fraglich *adj* **(a)** doubtful, questionable. **(b)** *attr (betreffend)* in question.

fraglos *adv* undoubtedly, unquestionably.

Fragment *nt* fragment.

fragmentarisch *adj* fragmentary.
fragwürdig *adj* dubious.
Fragwürdigkeit *f* dubiousness.
Fraktion *f* **(a)** *(Pol)* ≈ parliamentary *or* congressional *(US)* party; *(Sondergruppe)* group, faction. **(b)** *(Chem)* fraction.
Fraktions- *in cpds (Pol)* party; **f~los** *adj* independent; **~mitglied** *nt* member of a parliamentary *etc* party; **~sitzung** *f* party meeting; **~vorsitzende(r)** *mf* party whip; **~zwang** *m* requirement to follow the party whip.
Fraktur *f* **(a)** *(Typ)* Gothic print. **~ reden** *(col)* to be blunt. **(b)** *(Med)* fracture.
frank *adv*: **~ und frei** frankly, openly.
Franken[1] *nt* Franconia.
Franken[2] *m* **- (Schweizer) ~** (Swiss) franc.
frankieren* *vt* to stamp; *(mit Maschine)* to frank.
Frankierung *f* franking.
franko *adj inv (Comm)* carriage paid; *(von Postsendungen)* post-free, postpaid.
Frankreich *nt* France.
Franse *f* **-n** (loose) thread; *(von Haar)* strand of hair. **~n** *(als Besatz)* fringe; *(Pony)* fringe *(Brit)*, bangs *pl (US)*.
Franzbranntwein *m* alcoholic liniment.
Franzose *m* **-n** Frenchman; French boy.
Französin *f* Frenchwoman; French girl.
französisch *adj* French. **die ~e Schweiz** French-speaking Switzerland; **~es Bett** divan bed; **sich (auf) ~ empfehlen** *(col)* to leave without saying good-bye/paying; *siehe* **deutsch.**
Französisch(e) *nt decl as adj* French; *siehe* **Deutsch(e).**
frappant *adj* striking.
frappieren* *vt (verblüffen)* to astound.
Fräse *f* **-n** *(Werkzeug)* milling cutter; *(für Holz)* moulding cutter; *(Boden~)* rotary hoe.
fräsen *vt* to mill; *Holz* to mould.
fraß *pret of* **fressen.**
Fraß *m* **-e (a) etw einem Tier zum ~ vorwerfen** to feed sth to an animal; **jdn den Kritikern zum ~ vorwerfen** to throw sb to the critics. **(b)** *(pej col: Essen)* muck *(col) no indef art.* **(c)** *(Abfressen)* **vom ~ befallen** eaten away.
Fratze *f* **-n** *(Grimasse)* grimace; *(col: Gesicht)* mug *(col)*; *(fig: Zerrbild)* caricature. **jdm eine ~ schneiden** to pull *or* make a face at sb.
Frau *f* **-en (a)** woman; *(Ehe~)* wife. **jdn zur ~ haben** to be married to sb. **(b)** *(Anrede, mit Namen)* Mrs, Ms; *(für eine unverheiratete ~)* Miss, Ms. **~ Doktor** doctor.
Frauchen *nt dim of* **Frau** *(col)* **(a)** *(Ehefrau)* little woman. **(b)** *(Herrin von Hund)* mistress.
Frauen- *in cpds* women's; *(einer bestimmten Frau)* woman's; *(Sport auch)* ladies'; **~arbeit** *f* female labour *(Brit) or* labor *(US)*; **~arzt** *m* gynaecologist *(Brit)*, gynecologist *(US)*; **~beruf** *m* career for women; **~bewegung** *f* feminist movement; **f~feindlich** *adj* anti-women *pred*; *Mensch, Verhalten auch* misogynous; **~heilkunde** *f* gynaecology *(Brit)*, gynecology *(US)*; **~held** *m* lady-killer; **~klinik** *f* gynaecological *(Brit) or* gynecological *(US)* clinic; **~kloster** *nt* convent; **~rechtlerin** *f* feminist; **f~rechtlerisch** *adj* feminist; **sich f~rechtlerisch betätigen** to be involved in women's rights *or (in der heutigen Zeit auch)* Women's Lib; **~zimmer** *nt (old)* woman; *(hum, pej)* female *(col)*, broad *(US col)*.
Fräulein *nt* **- *or* -s (a)** young lady. **ein altes *or* älteres ~** an elderly spinster. **(b)** *(Anrede)* Miss. **(c)** *(Verkäuferin)* assistant *(Brit)*, sales clerk *(US)*; *(Kellnerin)* waitress. **„~!"** "Miss!"; **das ~ vom Amt** *(dated)* the switchboard girl.
fraulich *adj* feminine; *(reif)* womanly *no adv.*
frech *adj* cheeky *(esp Brit)*, fresh *(esp US)*; *Lüge* bare-faced *no adv.* **~ wie Oskar sein** *(col)* to be a little monkey *(col)*.
Frechdachs *m (col)* cheeky monkey *(col)*.
Frechheit *f* **(a)** *no pl* impudence, cheek *(esp Brit)*. **die ~ besitzen, zu ...** to have the impudence to ... **(b)** *(Äußerung, Handlung)* piece of cheek *(esp Brit) or* impudence. **sich** *(dat)* **einige ~en erlauben** to be a bit cheeky *(esp Brit) or* fresh *(esp US)*.
Fregatte *f* frigate.
frei *adj* **(a)** free; *Blick* clear. **~e Hand haben** to have a free hand; **aus der ~en Hand zeichnen** to draw freehand; **jdm zur ~en Verfügung stehen** to be completely at sb's disposal; **aus ~en Stücken** *or* **~em Willen** of one's own free will; **~ nach ...** based on ...; **~ nach Goethe** *(Zitat)* to adapt a phrase of Goethe's; **ich bin so ~** *(form)* may I?; **von Kiel nach Hamburg hatten wir ~e Fahrt** we had a clear run from Kiel to Hamburg; **für etw ~e Fahrt geben** *(fig)* to give sth the go-ahead; **der Film ist ~ ab 16 (Jahren)** the film may be seen by people over (the age of) 16; **sich von etw ~ machen** to free onself from sth.
(b) *Schriftsteller etc* freelance; *(nicht staatlich)* private. **~er Beruf** independent profession; **als ~er Mitarbeiter arbeiten** to work freelance; **~er Markt** open market; **~e Marktwirtschaft** free market economy; **die ~e Wirtschaft** private enterprise.
(c) *(ohne Hilfsmittel) Rede* extemporary. **~ schwimmen** to swim unaided *or* on one's own; **~ in der Luft schweben** to hang in mid-air; **ein Vortrag in ~er Rede** a talk given without notes; **~ sprechen** to extemporize.
(d) *(verfügbar) Mittel, Geld* available; *Zeit, Mensch* free. **morgen/Mittwoch ist ~** tomorrow/Wednesday is a holiday; **einen Tag ~ nehmen/haben** to take/have a day off; **ist hier *or* ist dieser Platz noch ~?** is this seat free?; **„Zimmer ~"** "vacancies"; **eine Stelle wird ~** a position is becoming vacant; **einen Platz ~ machen** *(aufstehen)* to vacate a seat; **einen Platz für jdn ~ lassen** to leave a seat for sb.
(e) *(offen)* open. **unter ~em Himmel** in the open (air); **im ~en Raum** *(Astron)* in (outer) space; **eine Frage im ~en Raum stehenlassen** to leave a question hanging; **auf ~er Strecke** *(Rail)* between stations; *(Aut)* on the road.
(f) *(unbekleidet)* bare. **sich ~ machen** *(beim Arzt)* to take one's clothes off, to strip; **~ lassen** to leave bare.
Frei-: **~bad** *nt* open-air swimming pool, lido; **f~bekommen*** *vt sep irreg* **(a) jdn f~bekommen** to get sb freed *or* released; **(b) einen Tag f~bekommen** to get a day off; **~berufler(in *f*)** *m* **-** self-employed person; **f~beruflich** *adj* self-employed; **~betrag** *m* tax allowance; **~brief** *m (fig)* licence *(Brit)*, license *(US)*.
Freie *nt* **-n,** *no pl* **im ~n** in the open (air).
Freier *m* **- (a)** *(dated, hum)* suitor. **(b)** *(col: von Dirne)* (prostitute's) client, john *(US col)*.
Frei-: **~exemplar** *nt* free copy; **~flug** *m* free flight; **~frau** *f* baroness *(by marriage)*; **~gabe** *f siehe* **~geben** release; lifting of controls *(gen* on*)*; opening; passing; **f~geben** *sep irreg* **1** *vt* to release *(an+acc* to*)*; *Preise* to lift controls on; *Straße, Strecke* to open; *Film* to pass; **etw zum Verkauf f~geben** to allow sth to be sold on the open market; **jdm den Weg f~geben** to let sb past; **2** *vi* **jdm f~geben** to give sb a holiday; **f~gebig** *adj* generous; **~gebigkeit** *f* generosity; **~gehege** *nt* open-air enclosure; **f~haben** *vi sep irreg* to have a holiday; **eine Stunde f~haben** *(Sch)* to have a free period; **~hafen** *m* free port; **f~halten** *sep irreg* **1** *vt* **(a)** *(nicht besetzen)* to keep free *or* clear; **(b)** *(reservieren)* to keep, to save; **(c)** *(bezahlen)* to pay for; **sich von jdm f~halten lassen** to let sb pay for one; **2** *vr* **sich von etw f~halten** to avoid sth; *von Verpflichtungen* to keep oneself free of sth; **~handel** *m* free trade; **~handelszone** *f* free trade area; **f~händig** *adj Zeichnung* freehand; **f~händig radfahren** to ride

with no hands; **f~hängend** *adj attr* suspended.

Freiheit *f* freedom; *(Pol auch)* liberty; **in ~** *(dat)* **sein** to be free; **jdn in ~ setzen** to set sb free; **jdm die ~ schenken** to give sb his/her *etc* freedom; **dichterische ~** poetic licence *(Brit) or* license *(US)*; **alle ~en haben,** to have all the freedom possible; **die ~ haben, etw zu tun** to be free *or* at liberty to do sth; **sich** *(dat)* **die ~ nehmen, etw zu tun** to take the liberty of doing sth.

freiheitlich *adj* liberal; *Verfassung* based on the principle of liberty; *Demokratie* free.

Freiheits-: ~beraubung *f (Jur)* wrongful deprivation of personal liberty; **~bewegung** *f* liberation movement; **~entzug** *m* imprisonment; **~kampf** *m* fight for freedom; **~kämpfer** *m* freedom-fighter; **~rechte** *pl* civil rights and liberties *pl;* **~statue** *f* Statue of Liberty; **~strafe** *f* prison sentence.

Frei-: f~heraus *adv* candidly, frankly; **~herr** *m* baron; **~karte** *f* free *or* complimentary ticket; **f~kaufen** *vt sep* **jdn/sich f~kaufen** to buy sb's/one's freedom; **f~kommen** *vi sep irreg aux sein (entkommen)* to get out *(aus* of*)*; *(befreit werden)* to be released *or* freed *(aus, von* from*)*; **~körperkultur** *f no pl* nudism; **f~lassen** *vt sep irreg* to set free, to free; *(aus Haft auch)* to release; *Hund* to let off the lead; **~lassung** *f* release; *(von Sklaven)* setting free; **~lauf** *m (Aut)* neutral; *(bei Fahrrad)* freewheel; **f~laufen** *vr sep irreg (Sport)* to get free; **f~lebend** *adj* living free; **f~legen** *vt sep* to expose; *Ruinen, Trümmer* to uncover; **~legung** *f siehe vt* exposure; uncovering.

freilich *adv* **(a)** *(allerdings)* admittedly. **(b)** *(esp S Ger: natürlich)* of course.

Freilicht- *in cpds* open-air; **~bühne** *f* open-air theatre *(Brit) or* theater *(US)*.

Frei-: f~machen *sep* **1** *vt* to stamp; *(mit Frankiermaschine)* to frank; **2** *vi* to take time off; **ich habe eine Woche f~gemacht** I took a week off; **3** *vr* to take time off; **~maurer** *m* Mason, Freemason.

freimütig *adj* frank, honest.

Freimütigkeit *f* frankness, honesty.

Frei-: ~raum *m (fig)* freedom *no art (zu* for*)*; **die Universität ist kein gesellschaftlicher ~raum** university isn't a social vacuum; **f~schaffend** *adj attr* freelance; **~schaffende(r)** *mf decl as adj* freelance; **~schärler** *m* **-** guerrilla; **f~setzen** *vt sep* to release; *(euph) Arbeitskräfte* to make redundant; *(vorübergehend)* to lay off; **~setzung** *f* release; *(euph)* dismissal; *(vorübergehend)* laying off; **f~sprechen** *vt sep irreg* to acquit; **jdn von einem Verdacht f~sprechen** to clear sb of suspicion; **~spruch** *m* acquittal; **es ergeht ~spruch** the verdict is "not guilty"; **f~stehen** *vi sep irreg* **(a) es steht jdm f~, etw zu tun** sb is free to do sth; **das steht Ihnen völlig f~** that is completely up to you; **(b)** *(leerstehen)* to stand empty; **f~stellen** *vt sep* **(a)** *(anheimstellen)* **jdm etw f~stellen** to leave sth (up) to sb; **(b)** *(befreien)* to exempt.

Freistil- *in cpds* freestyle.

Frei-: ~stoß *m (Ftbl)* free kick; **~stunde** *f* free hour; *(Sch)* free period.

Freitag *m* Friday; *siehe* **Dienstag.**

freitags *adv* on Fridays.

Frei-: ~tod *m* suicide; **f~tragend** *adj* self-supporting; *Brücke* cantilever; **~übung** *f* exercise; **~umschlag** *m* stamped addressed envelope.

freiweg ['frai'vɛk] *adv* openly; *(freiheraus)* straight out, frankly.

Frei-: ~wild *nt (fig)* fair game; **f~willig** *adj* voluntary; *Versicherung, Unterricht* optional; **sich f~willig melden** to volunteer *(zu, für* for*)*; **~willige(r)** *mf decl as adj* volunteer; **~zeichen** *nt (Telec)* ringing tone.

Freizeit *f* **(a)** free *or* leisure time. **(b)** *(Zusammenkunft)* weekend/holiday course.

Freizeit-: ~gestaltung *f* organization of one's leisure time; **~kleidung** *f* casual clothes *pl;* *(Warengattung)* leisurewear *no pl.*

Frei-: f~zügig *adj* **(a)** *(reichlich) Gebrauch* liberal; **(b)** *(moralisch)* permissive; **~zügigkeit** *f siehe adj* **(a)** liberalness; **(b)** permissiveness; **(c)** *(Ortsungebundenheit)* freedom of movement.

fremd *adj* **(a)** *(unbekannt)* strange; *(ausländisch)* foreign; *Planeten* other; *Welt* different. **jdm ~ sein** to be foreign *or* alien to sb; **es ist mir ~, wie ...** I don't understand how ...; **ich bin hier ~** I'm a stranger here; **sich** *(dat)* **~ werden** to become strangers; **sich ~ fühlen** to feel like a stranger. **(b)** *(andern gehörig)* someone else's; *Bank, Firma* different; *(Comm, Pol)* outside *attr.* **unter ~em Namen** under an assumed name; **in ~e Hände übergehen** to come under outside control.

Fremde *f no pl (liter)* **die ~** foreign parts *pl*; **in die ~ gehen** to go to foreign parts.

Fremden-: ~führer *m* (tourist) guide; *(Buch)* guide(book); **~legion** *f* Foreign Legion; **~verkehr** *m* tourism *no def art*; **~zimmer** *nt* guest room; **„~zimmer"** "rooms to let" *(Brit)*, "rooms for rent" *(US)*.

Fremde(r) *mf decl as adj* stranger; *(Ausländer)* foreigner; *(Admin, Pol)* alien; *(Tourist)* visitor.

Fremd-: f~gehen *vi sep irreg aux sein (col)* to be unfaithful; **~körper** *m* foreign body; *(fig)* alien element; **f~ländisch** *adj* foreign *no adv; (exotisch)* exotic.

Fremdsprache *f* foreign language.

Fremdsprachen-: ~korrespondentin *f* bilingual secretary; **~unterricht** *m* language teaching.

Fremd-: f~sprachig *adj* in a foreign language; **f~sprachlich** *adj* **f~sprachlicher Unterricht** (foreign) language teaching; **~wort** *nt* foreign word; **Rücksichtnahme ist für ihn ein ~wort** *(fig)* he's never heard of the word consideration.

frenetisch *adj* frenetic, frenzied.

Frequenz *f* frequency; *(Stärke)* numbers *pl.*

Fressalien [-iən] *pl (col)* grub *sing (col).*

Fresse *f* **-n** *(col!) (Mund)* gob *(col!)*; *(Gesicht)* mug *(col).* **die ~ halten** to shut one's face *(col!).*

fressen *pret* **fraß,** *ptp* **gefressen 1** *vi* **(a)** to feed, to eat; *(col!: Menschen)* to eat; *(gierig)* to guzzle. **jdm aus der Hand ~** *(fig col)* to eat out of sb's hand. **(b)** *(zerstören)* to eat away *(an etw (dat)* sth*)*.

2 *vt (Tier, col!: Mensch)* to eat; *(sich ernähren von)* to feed on; *(col!: gierig essen)* to guzzle, to scoff; *(col: verbrauchen) Benzin, Ersparnisse* to eat up. **Kilometer ~** to burn up the kilometres; **ein Loch in den Geldbeutel ~** to make a big hole in one's pocket; **ich habe dich zum F~ gern** *(col)* you're good enough to eat *(col)*; **sie sah mich an, als ob sie mich ~ wollte** *(col)* she gave me a murderous look; **jdn/etw gefressen haben** *(col)* to have had one's fill of sb/sth; **jetzt hat er es endlich gefressen** *(col)* he's got it at last *(col)*; **einen Narren an jdm/etw gefressen haben** to dote on sb/sth.

3 *vr* **(a)** *(sich bohren)* to eat one's way *(in+acc* into*)*. **(b) sich voll/satt ~** to gorge oneself.

Fressen *nt* **- (a)** *no pl* food; *(col!)* grub *(col).* **(b)** *(Gelage)* blow-out *(col).*

Fresser *m* **-** *(Tier)* eater; *(col!: gieriger Mensch)* pig *(col)*, greedyguts *(col).*

Fresserei *f no pl (col) (übermäßiges Essen)* guzzling; *(Gefräßigkeit)* gluttony.

Freß-: ~gier *f* voraciousness; *(pej: von Menschen)* gluttony; **~napf** *m* feeding bowl; **~paket** *nt (col)* food parcel; **~sucht** *f (col)* gluttony; *(krankhaft)* craving for food.

Frettchen *nt* ferret.

Freude *f* **-n** pleasure; *(innig)* joy *(über+acc* at*)*. **~ an etw** *(dat)* **haben** to get *or* derive pleasure from sth; **~ am Leben haben** to enjoy life; **es ist mir eine ~, zu ...** it's a real pleasure for me to ...; **es macht ihnen keine/wenig ~** they don't enjoy it (at all)/much; **jdm eine ~ machen** *or* **bereiten** to make sb happy; **zu meiner großen ~** to my great delight; **aus Spaß an der ~** *(col)* for the fun *or* hell *(col)* of it; **mit ~n** with pleasure.

Freuden-: ~feuer *nt* bonfire; **~haus** *nt (dated, hum)* house of ill repute; **~mädchen** *nt (dated, hum)* lady of easy virtue *(euph)*, prostitute; **~tanz** *m* **einen ~tanz aufführen** to dance with joy; **~taumel** *m* ecstasy.

freudestrahlend *adj no pred* beaming with delight.

freudig *adj* joyful; *(begeistert)* enthusiastic. **jdn ~ stimmen** to raise sb's spirits; **etw ~ erwarten** to look forward to sth with great pleasure; **~ überrascht sein** to have a delightful surprise.

Freud-: f~los *adj* joyless, cheerless; **~losigkeit** *f no pl* joylessness, cheerlessness.

freuen 1 *vr* **(a)** to be glad *or* pleased *(über +acc* about*)*. **sich über ein Geschenk ~** to be pleased with a present; **er freut sich sehr an seinen Kindern** his children give him a lot of pleasure; **sich mit jdm ~** to share sb's happiness; **sich seines Lebens ~** to enjoy life. **(b) sich auf jdn/etw ~** to look forward to seeing sb/to sth; **sich zu früh ~** to get one's hopes up too soon. **2** *vt impers* to please. **es freut mich/ihn, daß ...** I'm/he's pleased *or* glad that ...; **es freut mich sehr, Ihre Bekanntschaft zu machen** *(form)* (I'm) pleased to meet you.

Freund *m* **-e** friend; *(Liebhaber)* boyfriend. **ein ~ der Kunst** an art-lover; **er ist kein ~ vieler Worte** he's a man of few words; **ich bin kein ~ von so etwas** I'm not one for that sort of thing.

Freundchen *nt (col)* my friend *(iro)*. **~! ~!** watch it, my friend!

Freundeskreis *m* circle of friends.

Freundin *f* friend; *(Liebhaberin)* girlfriend.

freundlich *adj* **(a)** friendly *no adv*; *Wetter etc* pleasant; *Zimmer, Farben* cheerful; *(Fin, Comm: günstig)* favourable *(Brit)*, favorable *(US)*. **jdn ~ behandeln** to be friendly towards sb; **bitte recht ~!** smile please! **(b)** *(liebenswürdig)* kind *(zu* to*)*. **würden Sie bitte so ~ sein und das tun?** would you be so kind as to do that?

freundlicherweise *adv* kindly.

Freundlichkeit *f* **(a)** *no pl siehe adj* friendliness; pleasantness; cheerfulness; favourableness. *(Brit)*, favorableness *(US)*. **würden Sie (wohl) die ~ haben, das zu tun?** would you be kind enough to do that? **(b)** *(Handlung, Gefälligkeit)* kindness. **jdm ein paar ~en sagen** to say a few kind words to sb.

Freundschaft *f* friendship. **in aller ~** in all friendliness; **da hört die ~ auf** *(col)* friendship doesn't go that far.

freundschaftlich *adj* friendly *no adv*. **jdm ~ gesinnt sein** to feel friendly towards sb; **jdm ~ auf die Schulter klopfen** to give sb a friendly slap on the back.

Freundschafts-: ~besuch *m (Pol)* goodwill visit; **~preis** *m* (special) price for a friend; **~spiel** *nt (Sport)* friendly match, friendly; **~vertrag** *m (Pol)* treaty of friendship.

Frevel *m* **-** *(geh)* sin *(gegen* against*)*; *(fig)* crime *(an+dat* against*)*.

frevelhaft *adj (geh)* sinful; *Leichtsinn* wanton.

Frevler(in *f***)** *m* **-** *(liter)* sinner.

Frieden *m* **-** peace. **im ~** in peacetime; **im ~ leben** to live in peace; **~ schließen** to make one's peace; *(Pol)* to make peace; **~ stiften** to make peace; **jdn in ~ lassen** to leave sb in peace; **um des lieben ~s willen** *(col)* for the sake of peace and quiet; **ich traue dem ~ nicht** *(col)* something (fishy) is going on *(col)*.

Friedens- *in cpds* peace; **~bemühung** *f usu pl* effort to achieve peace; **~bewegung** *f* peace movement; **~kämpfer** *m* peace campaigner; **~nobelpreis** *m* Nobel peace prize; **~pfeife** *f* peace-pipe; **~politik** *f* policy of peace; **~richter** *m* justice of the peace, JP; **~schluß** *m* peace agreement; **~sicherung** *f* maintenance of peace; **Maßnahmen zur ~sicherung** peacekeeping measures; **~stifter** *m* peacemaker; **~taube** *f* dove of peace; **~truppen** *pl* peacekeeping forces *pl*; **~vertrag** *m* peace treaty.

friedfertig *adj* peaceable.

Friedfertigkeit *f* peaceableness.

Friedhof *m* cemetery; *(Kirchhof)* graveyard.

friedlich *adj* peaceful; *(friedfertig) Mensch* peaceable; *Charakter, Art* placid. **etw auf ~em Wege lösen** to solve sth by peaceful means; **damit er endlich ~ ist** *(col)* to keep him happy; **nun sei doch endlich ~!** *(col)* give it a rest! *(col)*.

friedliebend *adj* peace-loving.

frieren *pret* **fror**, *ptp* **gefroren 1** *vi* **(a)** *auch vt impers (sich kalt fühlen)* to be/get cold. **ich friere, es friert mich** I'm cold; **ich friere an den Zehen** my toes are/get cold. **(b)** *aux sein (gefrieren)* to freeze. **2** *vi impers* to freeze. **heute nacht hat es gefroren** it was below freezing last night.

Friese *m (wk)* **-n, -n, Friesin** *f* Fri(e)sian.

frigid(e) *adj* frigid.

Frikadelle *f (Cook)* rissole.

Frikassee *nt* **-s** *(Cook)* fricassee.

frisch *adj* **(a)** fresh; *(feucht) Farbe, Fleck* wet. **~e Eier** new-laid eggs; **~ gestrichen** newly painted; *(auf Schild)* wet paint; **~ gewaschen** clean; **das Bett ~ beziehen** to change the bed; **sich ~ machen** to freshen up; **mit ~en Kräften** with renewed strength; **das ist mir noch ~ in Erinnerung** that is still fresh in my memory; **jdn auf ~er Tat ertappen** to catch sb red-handed *or* in the act. **(b)** *(munter) Wesen, Art* bright, cheery; *(gesund) Aussehen* fresh. **~ und munter sein** *(col)* to be bright and cheery; **~ gewagt ist halb gewonnen** *(Prov)* a good start is half the battle. **(c)** *(kühl)* cool, chilly; *Luft, Wind auch* fresh.

Frische *f no pl* **(a)** freshness. **in alter ~** *(col)* as always. **(b)** *(Kühle)* coolness, chilliness; *(von Luft, Wind auch)* freshness.

Frisch-: f~gebacken *(col) Ehepaar* newly wed; **~haltebeutel** *m* airtight bag; **~luft** *f* fresh air; **~milch** *f* fresh milk; **~wasser** *nt* fresh water; **f~weg** *adv (munter)* straight out *(col)*.

Friseur [fri'zøːɐ] *m* hairdresser.

Friseursalon *m* hairdresser's *(Brit)*, hairdressing salon.

Friseuse [fri'zøːzə] *f* hairdresser.

Frisiercreme *f* haircream.

frisieren* **1** *vt* **(a) jdn ~, jdm das Haar ~** to do sb's hair; **sie ist stets gut frisiert** her hair is always beautifully done. **(b)** *(col) Abrechnung* to fiddle; *Bericht* to doctor *(col)*. **die Bilanzen ~** to cook the books *(col)*. **(c)** *Auto* to soup up *(col)*. **2** *vr* to do one's hair.

Frisier-: ~spiegel *m* dressing (table) mirror; **~tisch** *m* dressing table.

Frisör *m* **-e, Frisöse** *f* **-n** hairdresser.

Frist *f* **-en** *(Zeitraum)* period; *(Zeitpunkt)* deadline *(zu* for*)*; *(bei Rechnung)* last date for payment. **eine ~ einhalten/verstreichen lassen** to meet a deadline/to let a deadline pass; *(bei Rechnung)* to pay/not to pay within the period stipulated; **innerhalb kürzester ~** without delay; **jdm eine ~ von vier Tagen geben** to give sb four days grace.

fristen *vt* **ein kümmerliches Dasein ~** to eke out a miserable existence; *(Partei, Institution)* to exist on the fringes.

Frist-: f~gerecht *adj* within the period stipulated; **f~los** *adj* without notice; **jdn f~los entlassen** to dismiss sb without notice; **~verlängerung** *f* extension.

Frisur *f* hairstyle.

Friteuse [fri'tøːzə] *f* chip pan *(Brit)*, deep fat fryer.

fritieren* *vt* to (deep-)fry.

frivol [fri'voːl] *adj* frivolous; *(anzüglich) Witz, Bemerkung* risqué.

Frivolität [frivoli'tɛːt] *f no pl* frivolity; *(von Witz etc)* suggestiveness.
Frl. = **Fräulein** Miss, Ms.
froh *adj* happy; *(dankbar auch)* glad; *(erfreut auch)* glad, pleased. **über etw** *(acc)* **~ sein** to be pleased with sth; **um etw ~ sein** to be grateful for sth; **seines Lebens nicht (mehr) ~ werden** not to enjoy life any more.
frohgestimmt *adj (geh)* happy, joyful *(liter)*.
fröhlich 1 *adj* cheerful, merry. **2** *adv (unbekümmert)* blithely, gaily.
Fröhlichkeit *f no pl* happiness; *(gesellige Stimmung)* merriment, gaiety.
Froh-: f~locken* *vi (geh)* to rejoice *(über +acc* over, at); **~sinn** *m no pl* cheerfulness; **f~sinnig** *adj* cheerful.
fromm *adj* **(a)** *(gläubig)* religious; *Christ, Leben* devout, pious; *(scheinheilig)* sanctimonious. **(b)** *(old: gehorsam)* docile. **~ wie ein Lamm sein** to be as gentle as a lamb.
Frömmelei *f (pej)* false piety.
Frömmigkeit *f siehe* **fromm (a)** religiousness; devoutness, piousness; sanctimoniousness.
frönen *vi+dat (geh)* to indulge in.
Fronleichnam *no art no pl* Corpus Christi.
Front *f* **-en** front. **die hintere/rückwärtige ~** the back/the rear; **auf breiter ~** along a wide front; **an der ~** at the front; **klare ~en schaffen** *(fig)* to clarify the position; **~ gegen jdn/etw machen** to make a stand against sb/sth; **in ~ liegen/gehen** *(Sport)* to be in/take the lead.
frontal 1 *adj no pred* frontal; *Zusammenstoß* head-on. **2** *adv* frontally; *zustammenstoßen* head-on.
Front-: ~antrieb *m (Aut)* front-wheel drive; **~motor** *m* front-mounted engine.
fror *pret of* **frieren.**
Frosch *m* **¨-e** frog. **einen ~ im Hals haben** *(col)* to have a frog in one's throat; **sei kein ~!** *(col)* be a sport!
Frosch-: ~hüpfen *nt* leapfrog; **~mann** *m* frogman; **~maul** *nt (fig col)* pout; **~perspektive** *f* **etw aus der ~perspektive sehen** to get a worm's-eye view of sth; **~schenkel** *m* frog's leg.
Frost *m* **¨-e (a)** frost. **bei eisigem ~** in heavy frost; **~ (ab)bekommen** *(Hände, Ohren)* to get frostbitten. **(b)** *(Med: Schüttel~)* fit of shivering.
Frost-: f~beständig *adj* frost-resistant; **~beule** *f* chilblain.
frösteln 1 *vi* to shiver. **2** *vt impers* **es fröstelte mich** I shivered.
Froster *m* **-** freezer.
frostig *adj (lit, fig)* frosty.
Frost-: ~schutz *m* protection against frost; **~schutzmittel** *nt (Aut)* antifreeze.
Frottee [frɔ'teː] *nt or m* **-s** terry towelling.
Frottee-: ~(hand)tuch *nt* (terry) towel; **~kleid** *nt* towelling dress.
frottieren* *vt Haut* to rub; *jdn, sich* to rub down.
Frottier(hand)tuch *nt* (terry) towel.
Frotzelei *f (col)* teasing.
frotzeln *vti (col)* to tease. **über jdn ~** to make fun of sb.
Frucht *f* **¨-e** *(Bot, fig)* fruit; *(Embryo)* foetus; *(no pl: Getreide)* crops *pl*. **¨~e** *(Obst)* fruit *sing*; **¨~e tragen** *(lit, fig)* to bear fruit.
fruchtbar *adj (lit, fig)* fruitful; *Boden* fertile. **etw für jdn ~ machen** to use sth to benefit sb.
Fruchtbarkeit *f siehe adj* fruitfulness; fertility.
Fruchtbarmachung *f (von Wüste)* reclamation.
Frucht-: ~becher *m* fruit sundae; **~bonbon** *m or nt* fruit drop; **f~bringend** *adj (geh)* fruitful.
Früchtchen *nt (col) (Tunichtgut)* good-for-nothing; *(Kind)* rascal *(col)*. **du bist mir ein sauberes** *or* **nettes ~** *(iro)* you're a right one *(col)*.
fruchten *vi* to bear fruit. **nichts ~** to be fruitless.
Fruchtfleisch *nt* flesh *(of a fruit)*.
fruchtig *adj* fruity.
Frucht-: f~los *adj (fig)* fruitless; **~losigkeit** *f* fruitlessness; **~saft** *m* fruit juice.
früh 1 *adj* early. **am ~en Morgen** in the early morning; **ein Werk des ~en Picasso** an early work by Picasso. **2** *adv* **(a)** early; *(in jungen Jahren)* at an early age; *(in Entwicklung)* early on. **es ist noch ~ am Tag** it is still early in the day; **von ~ bis spät** from morning till night. **(b) morgen ~** tomorrow morning; **heute ~** this morning.
Früh- *in cpds* early; **f~auf** *adv* **von f~auf** from an early age; **~aufsteher** *m* **-** early riser, early bird *(col)*; **~dienst** *m* early shift; **~dienst haben** to be on early shift.
Frühe *f no pl (Morgen)* **in der ~** early in the morning; **in aller ~** at the crack of dawn.
früher *comp of* **früh 1** *adj* **(a)** earlier. **in ~en Jahren/Zeiten** in the past; **in ~em Alter** when he/she *etc* was younger. **(b)** *(ehemalig)* former, previous. **der Kontakt zu seinen ~en Freunden ist abgebrochen** he lost contact with his old friends.
2 *adv* **(a)** earlier. **~ geht's nicht** that's the soonest possible; **das hättest du ~ sagen müssen** you should have said that before *or* sooner; **~ oder später** sooner or later. **(b)** *(in vergangenen Zeiten)* **Herr X, ~ Direktor eines ...** Herr X, formerly director of a ...; **ich habe ihn ~ mal gekannt** I used to know him; **~ habe ich so etwas nie gemacht** I never used to do that kind of thing; **~ stand hier eine Kirche** there used to be a church here; **Erzählungen von/Erinnerungen an ~** stories/memories of times gone by; **ich kannte/kenne ihn von ~** I knew him before/I've known him some time.
frühestens *adv* at the earliest. **wann kann das ~ fertig sein?** when's the earliest it can be ready?
frühestmöglich *adj attr* earliest possible.
Frühgeburt *f* premature birth; *(Kind)* premature baby.
Frühjahr *nt* spring.
Frühjahrs-: ~müdigkeit *f* springtime lethargy; **~putz** *m* spring-cleaning.
Frühling *m* spring. **es wird ~, der ~ kommt** spring is coming; **im ~** in spring; **einem neuen ~ entgegengehen** *(fig)* to start to flourish again; **seinen zweiten ~ erleben** to go through one's second adolescence.
Frühlings- *in cpds* spring; **~anfang** *m* first day of spring; **f~haft** *adj* springlike.
Früh-: ~messe *f* early mass; **f~morgens** *adv* early in the morning; **~nebel** *m* early morning mist; **f~reif** *adj* precocious; *(körperlich)* mature at an early age; **~rentner** *m* person who has retired early; **~schicht** *f* early shift; **~schoppen** *m* morning/lunchtime drink; **~sport** *m* early morning exercise.
Frühstück *nt* **-e** breakfast; *(~spause)* morning *or* coffee break. **zweites ~** ≈ elevenses *(Brit col)*, midmorning snack.
frühstücken *insep* **1** *vi* to have breakfast. **2** *vt* **etw ~** to have sth for breakfast.
Frühstücks-: ~fleisch *nt* luncheon meat; **~pause** *f* morning *or* coffee break.
Früh-: ~warnsystem *nt* early warning system; **~werk** *nt* early work; **~zeit** *f* early days *pl*; **f~zeitig 1** *adj* early; *(vorzeitig auch)* premature; **2** *adv* early; *(vorzeitig)* prematurely; *(ziemlich am Anfang)* early on.
Frust *m no pl (col)* frustration.
Frustration *f* frustration.
frustrieren* *vt* to frustrate; *(col: enttäuschen)* to upset.
Fuchs [fuks] *m* **¨-e (a)** *(Tier, Fell, fig)* fox. **er ist ein schlauer ~** *(col)* he's a cunning old devil *(col) or* fox *(col)*; **wo sich die ¨~e** *or* **wo sich Hase und ~ gute Nacht sagen** *(hum)* in the back of beyond. **(b)** *(Pferd)* chestnut; *(mit hellerem Schwanz und Mähne)* sorrel; *(col: Mensch)* redhead.
fuchsen ['fuksn] *vt (col)* to annoy.

fuchsig ['fʊksɪç] *adj (col: wütend)* mad *(col)*.
Füchsin ['fʏksɪn] *f* vixen.
Fuchs-: ~**jagd** *f* fox-hunt/-hunting; **f~rot** *adj Fell* red; *Pferd* chestnut; *Haar* ginger; ~**schwanz** *m* **(a)** fox's tail; **(b)** *(Säge)* handsaw; **f~teufelswild** *adj (col)* hopping mad *(col)*.
Fuchtel *f* **-n** *(fig col)* **unter jds** ~ under sb's control *or* thumb.
fuchteln *vi (col)* **(mit den Händen)** ~ to wave one's hands about *(col)*.
Fug *m*: **mit** ~ **und Recht** *(geh)* with complete justification.
Fuge *f* **-n (a)** joint; *(Ritze)* gap, crack. **in allen ~n krachen** to creak at the joints; **aus den ~n gehen** to come apart at the seams. **(b)** *(Mus)* fugue.
fügen 1 *vt* **(a)** *(setzen)* to put, to place; *(geh) Worte, Satz* to formulate. **(b)** *(geh: bewirken)* to ordain. **2** *vr* to obey. **sich jdm/einer Sache** *(geh)* ~ to bow to sb/sth; *einem Befehl etc* to comply with sth; **es fügte sich, daß ...** *(geh)* it so happened that ...
fügsam *adj Mensch* obedient.
Fügsamkeit *f* obedience.
Fügung *f* **eine glückliche** ~ a stroke of good fortune; **göttliche** ~ divine providence; **eine** ~ **des Schicksals** an act of fate.
fühlbar *adj (spürbar)* perceptible.
fühlen *vtir* to feel. **sich krank/verantwortlich** ~ to feel ill/responsible; **wie** ~ **Sie sich?** how do you feel?; **da hat er sich aber gefühlt** *(col)* he felt really great *(col)*.
Fühler *m* **-** *(Zool)* feeler; *(von Schnecke)* horn. **seine** ~ **ausstrecken** *(col)* to put out feelers.
Fühlung *f* contact. **mit jdm in** ~ **bleiben/stehen** to stay/be in contact *or* touch with sb.
fuhr *pret of* **fahren.**
Fuhre *f* **-n** *(Ladung)* load.
führen 1 *vt* **(a)** *(hin~, herum~)* to take. **eine alte Dame über die Straße** ~ to help an old lady over the road; ~ **Sie mich zum Geschäftsführer!** take me to the manager!; **eine Klasse zum Abitur** ~ to see a class through to A-levels; **der Hinweis führte die Polizei auf die Spur des Diebes** that tip put the police on the trail of the thief; **was führt Sie zu mir?** *(form)* what brings you to me?; **ein Land ins Chaos** ~ to reduce a country to chaos.
(b) *(an~)* to lead; *Firma etc* to run; *Armee etc* to command.
(c) *(handhaben) Pinsel, Kamera etc* to wield. **das Glas an die Lippen** ~ to raise one's glass to one's lips.
(d) *(haben, mit~)* to carry; *Autokennzeichen, Namen* to have, to bear. **Geld/seine Papiere bei sich** ~ *(form)* to carry money/one's papers on one's person; **der Fluß führt Hochwasser** the river is running high.
(e) *(Laden: im Angebot haben)* to stock.
2 *vi* **(a)** *(in Führung liegen)* to lead. **die Mannschaft führt mit 10 Punkten Vorsprung** the team has a lead of 10 points. **(b)** *(verlaufen) (Straße)* to go; *(Kabel, Pipeline etc)* to run; *(Spur)* to lead. **die Brücke führt über die Elbe** the bridge crosses the Elbe. **(c)** *(als Ergebnis haben)* **zu etw** ~ to lead to sth; **das führt zu nichts** that will come to nothing; **es führte zu dem Ergebnis, daß er entlassen wurde** it resulted in *or* led to his being dismissed; **wohin soll das alles nur** ~? where is it all leading (us)?
3 *vr (form: sich benehmen)* to conduct oneself.
führend *adj* leading *attr*; *Rolle, Persönlichkeit auch* prominent. **diese Firma ist im Stahlbau** ~ that is one of the leading firms in steel construction; **die Sowjets sind im Schach** ~ the Soviets lead the world in chess.
Führer(in *f***)** *m* **- (a)** *(Leiter)* leader; *(Oberhaupt)* head. **(b)** *(Fremden~, Berg~)* guide. **(c)** *(form: Lenker)* driver; *(von Flugzeug)* pilot; *(von Kran, Fahrstuhl)* operator. **(d)** *(Buch)* guide.
Führer-: ~**haus** *nt* cab; **f~los** *adj* leaderless *no adv*; *Wagen* driverless *no adv*; ~**schaft** *f* leadership; *(Oberhäupter)* heads *pl*; ~**schein** *m (für Auto)* driving licence *(Brit)*, driver's license *(US)*; **den ~schein machen** *(Aut)* to learn to drive; *(die Prüfung ablegen)* to take one's (driving) test; **ihm wurde der ~schein entzogen** he lost his licence; ~**scheinentzug** *m* disqualification from driving.
Führung *f* **(a)** *no pl* direction; *(von Partei, Expedition etc)* leadership; *(Mil)* command; *(eines Unternehmens etc)* management. **(b)** *no pl (die Führer)* leaders *pl*, leadership *sing*; *(Mil)* commanders *pl*; *(eines Unternehmens etc)* directors *pl*. **(c)** *(Besichtigung)* guided tour *(durch* of). **(d)** *no pl (Vorsprung)* lead. **in** ~ **gehen/liegen** to go into/be in the lead. **(e)** *no pl (Betragen)* conduct. **(f)** *(form: Lenken)* **zur** ~ **eines Kraftfahrzeugs berechtigt sein** to be licensed to drive a motor vehicle. **(g)** *no pl (Betreuung)* running. **die** ~ **der Akten/Bücher** keeping the files/books.
Führungs-: ~**anspruch** *m* claim to leadership; **seinen ~anspruch anmelden** to make a bid for the leadership; ~**kraft** *f* executive; ~**schicht** *f* ruling classes *pl*; ~**spitze** *f* highest echelon of the leadership; *(eines Unternehmens)* top management; ~**stab** *m (Mil)* command *no pl*; *(Comm)* top management.
Fuhr-: ~**unternehmen** *nt* haulage business; ~**unternehmer** *m* haulier, haulage contractor; ~**werk** *nt* wag(g)on; *(mit Pferden)* horse and cart; **f~werken** *vi insep (col)* **in der Küche f~werken** to bustle around in the kitchen.
Fülle *f no pl* **(a)** *(Körpermasse)* corpulence, portliness. **(b)** *(Stärke)* fullness. **(c)** *(Menge)* wealth.
füllen 1 *vt* to fill; *(Cook)* to stuff. **etw in Flaschen** ~ to bottle sth; **etw in Säcke** ~ to put sth into sacks. **2** *vr (Theater, Badewanne)* to fill up.
Füllen *nt* **-** foal.
Füller *m* **-**, **Füllfederhalter** *m* fountain pen.
Füllgewicht *nt (Comm)* weight at time of packing; *(auf Dosen)* net weight.
füllig *adj Mensch* corpulent, portly; *Figur* ample.
Füllung *f* filling; *(Fleisch~, Polster~)* stuffing; *(Tür~)* panel; *(von Pralinen)* centre *(Brit)*, center *(US)*.
Fummel *m* **-** *(col)* rag.
Fummelei *f (col)* fidgeting, fiddling; *(col: Petting)* petting, groping *(col)*.
fummeln *vi (col)* to fiddle; *(hantieren)* to fumble; *(bei Petting)* to pet, to grope *(col)*.
Fund *m* **-e** find; *(das Entdecken)* discovery, finding.
Fundament *nt (lit, fig)* foundation *(usu pl)*. **das** ~ **zu etw legen** to lay the foundations for sth.
fundamental *adj* fundamental.
Fund-: ~**büro** *nt* lost property office *(Brit)*, lost and found *(US)*; ~**grube** *f (fig)* treasure trove.
fundieren* *vt (fig)* to back up.
fundiert *adj* sound. **schlecht** ~ unsound.
fündig *adj (Min)* rich. ~ **werden** to make a strike; *(fig)* to strike it lucky.
Fund-: ~**ort** *m* **der ~ort von etw** (the place) where sth is/was found; ~**sachen** *pl* lost property *sing*; ~**stätte** = ~**ort.**
fünf *num* five. **seine** ~ **Sinne beisammen haben** to have all one's wits about one; ~**(e) gerade sein lassen** *(col)* to turn a blind eye; *siehe* **vier.**
Fünf- *in cpds* five; ~**eck** *nt* pentagon; **f~eckig** *adj* pentagonal, five-cornered.
Fünfer *m* **-** *(col)* five-pfennig piece; five-marks.
Fünf-: **f~fach** *adj* fivefold; ~**jahr(es)plan** *m* five-year plan; **f~jährig** *adj Frist, Plan* five-year; *Kind* five-year-old; ~**kampf** *m (Sport)* pentathlon; ~**ling** *m* quintuplet; **f~mal** *adv* five times; ~**prozentklausel** *f clause debarring parties with less than 5% of the vote from Parliament;* **f~tägig** *adj* five-day *attr*; **f~tausend** *num* five thousand.

Fünftel *nt* - fifth.
fünfte(r, s) *adj* fifth; *siehe* **vierte(r, s).**
fünfzehn *num* fifteen.
fünfzig *num* fifty.
Fünfziger *m* - *(col) (Mensch)* fifty-year-old; *(Geld)* fifty.
fungieren* [fʊŋ'giːrən] *vi* to function *(als* as a*)*.
Funk *m no pl* radio, wireless. **über ~** by radio.
Funk-: **~amateur** *m* radio ham; **~ausstellung** *f* radio and television exhibition.
Funke *m* **-ns, -n, Funken** *m* - **(a)** *(lit, fig)* spark. **~n sprühen** to spark; **arbeiten, daß die ~n fliegen** *(col)* to work like mad *(col)*; **zwischen den beiden sprang der ~ über** *(col)* something clicked between them *(col)*. **(b)** *(ein bißchen)* scrap; *(von Hoffnung auch)* glimmer; *(von Anstand auch)* spark.
funkeln *vi* to sparkle; *(Sterne)* to twinkle; *(Augen) (vor Freude)* to gleam; *(vor Zorn)* to flash; *(Edelmetall)* to gleam.
funkelnagelneu *adj (col)* brand-new.
funken 1 *vti* to radio. **SOS ~** to send out *or* radio an SOS. **2** *vi impers* **endlich hat es bei ihm gefunkt** *(col)* the light finally dawned (on him).
Funker *m* - radio *or* wireless operator.
Funk- *in cpds* radio; **~gerät** *nt* **(a)** *no pl* radio equipment; **(b)** *(Sprechfunkgerät)* radio set, walkie-talkie; **~haus** *nt* broadcasting studios *pl*; **~kolleg** *nt* educational radio broadcasts *pl*; **~meßgerät** *nt* radar (equipment) *no pl*; **~sprechverkehr** *m* radiotelephony; **~spruch** *m* radio signal; *(Mitteilung)* radio message; **~stille** *f* radio silence; **~streife** *f* police radio patrol.
Funktion *f (Zweck, Math)* function; *(no pl: Tätigkeit)* functioning; *(Amt)* office; *(Stellung)* position. **in ~ treten/sein** to come into/be in operation; **etw außer ~ setzen** to stop sth functioning.
Funktionär(in *f***)** *m* functionary, official.
funktionell *adj* functional.
funktionieren* *vi* to work; *(Maschine etc auch)* to function, to operate.
funktionsfähig *adj* able to function; *Maschine* working *pred.*
Funzel *f* **-n** *(col)* dim light, gloom.
Für *nt*: **das ~ und Wider** the pros and cons *pl.*
für *prep+acc* for. **~ was ist denn dieses Werkzeug?** *(col)* what is this tool for?; **~ zwei arbeiten** *(fig)* to do the work of two people; **~s erste** for the moment; **~s nächstemal** next time; **sich ~ etw entscheiden** to decide in favour *(Brit) or* in favor *(US)* of sth; **was Sie da sagen, hat etwas ~ sich** there's something in what you're saying; **er hat was ~ sich** he's not a bad person; **Tag ~ Tag** day after day; **Schritt ~ Schritt** step by step.
Fürbitte *f (Eccl, fig)* intercession.
Furche *f* **-n** furrow; *(Wagenspur)* rut.
furchen *vt* to furrow. **eine gefurchte Stirn** a furrowed brow.
Furcht *f no pl* fear. **aus ~ vor jdm/etw** for fear of sb/sth; **~ vor jdm/etw haben** to be afraid of sb/sth; **jdn in ~ versetzen, jdm ~ einflößen** to frighten *or* scare sb.
furchtbar *adj* terrible, awful. **ich habe einen ~en Hunger** I'm ever so hungry *(col)*.
furcht|einflößend *adj* terrifying, fearful.
fürchten 1 *vt* **jdn/etw ~** to be afraid of sb/sth, to fear sb/sth; **es war schlimmer, als ich gefürchtet hatte** it was worse than I had feared. **2** *vr* to be afraid *(vor+dat* of*)*. **3** *vi* **für** *or* **um etw ~** to fear for sth; **zum F~ aussehen** to look frightening; **da kannst du das F~ lernen** it will scare you stiff.
fürchterlich *adj* terrible, awful.
Furcht-: **f~erregend** *adj* terrifying, fearful. **f~los** *adj* fearless; **~losigkeit** *f* fearlessness; **f~sam** *adj* timorous; **~samkeit** *f* timorousness.
für|einander *adv* for each other, for one another.
Furie ['fuːriə] *f (Myth)* fury; *(fig)* hellcat.
Furnier *nt* **-e** veneer.
furnieren* *vt* to veneer.
Furore *f or nt no pl* sensation. **~ machen** *(col)* to cause a sensation.
Fürsorge *f no pl* **(a)** *(Betreuung)* care; *(Sozial~)* welfare. **(b)** *(col: Sozialamt)* welfare *(col)*. **der ~ zur Last fallen** to be a burden on the state. **(c)** *(col: Sozialunterstützung)* social security *(Brit)*, welfare *(US)*. **von der ~ leben** to live on social security *(Brit) or* the welfare *(US)*.
fürsorgend *adj* caring. **jdn ~ betreuen** to care for sb.
Fürsorger(in *f***)** *m* - (church) welfare worker.
fürsorglich *adj* caring. **jdn sehr ~ behandeln** to lavish care on sb.
Fürsprache *f* recommendation. **für jdn ~ einlegen** to put in a word of recommendation for sb *(bei* with*)*.
Fürsprecher(in *f***)** *m* advocate.
Fürst *m (wk)* **-en, -en** prince; *(Herrscher)* ruler. **wie ein ~ leben** to live like a lord.
Fürsten-: **~haus** *nt* royal house; **~tum** *nt* principality.
Fürstin *f* princess; *(Herrscherin)* ruler.
fürstlich *adj (lit, fig)* princely *no adv.* **jdn ~ bewirten** to entertain sb right royally; **~ leben** to live like a lord.
Furunkel *nt or m* - boil.
Fürwort *nt* **¨er** *(Gram)* pronoun.
Furz *m* **¨e** *(col!)* fart *(col)*.
furzen *vi (col!)* to fart *(col)*.
Fusel *m* - *(pej)* rotgut *(col)*, hooch *(US col)*.
Fusion *f* amalgamation; *(von Unternehmen)* merger; *(von Atomkernen, Zellen)* fusion.
fusionieren* *vti* to amalgamate; *(Unternehmen)* to merge.
Fuß *m* **¨e** **(a)** foot. **zu ~** on foot; **er ist gut/schlecht zu ~** he's good/not so good on his feet; **sich jdm zu ¨~en werfen** to prostrate oneself before sb; **jdm zu ¨~en fallen/liegen** to fall/lie at sb's feet; **das Publikum lag ihm zu ¨~en** he had the audience at his feet; **den ~ in die Tür stellen** to get one's foot in the door; **kalte ¨~e bekommen** *(lit, fig)* to get cold feet; **bei ~!** heel!; **jdm etw vor die ¨~e werfen** *(lit)* to throw sth at sb; *(fig)* to tell sb to keep sth; **jdn/etw mit ¨~en treten** *(lit)* to kick sb/sth about; *(fig)* to trample all over sb/sth; **(festen) ~ fassen** *(lit, fig)* to gain a foothold; *(sich niederlassen)* to settle down; **auf eigenen ¨~en stehen** *(fig)* to be able to stand on one's own two feet; **auf großem ~ leben** to live the high life; **mit jdm auf gutem ~ stehen** to be on good terms with sb.
(b) *(von Gegenstand)* base; *(Tisch-, Stuhlbein)* leg; *(von Schrank, Gebirge)* foot. **auf schwachen/tönernen ¨~en stehen** to be built on sand.
(c) *pl* - *(Längenmaß)* foot.
Fuß-: **~abdruck** *m* footprint; **~angel** *f (lit)* mantrap; *(fig)* catch, trap; **~bad** *nt* foot bath.
Fußball *m* football; *(Sportart auch)* soccer.
Fußballer *m* - *(col)* footballer.
Fußball-: **~mannschaft** *f* football team; **~platz** *m* football *or* soccer pitch; **~spiel** *nt* football *or* soccer match; *(Sportart)* football; **~spieler** *m* football *or* soccer player; **~toto** *m or nt* football pools *pl*; **~verein** *m* football club.
Fuß-: **~bank** *f* footstool; **~boden** *m* floor; **~bodenbelag** *m* floor covering; **~bremse** *f* footbrake; **~eisen** *nt* mantrap.
Fussel *f* **-n** fluff *no pl.* **eine ~** a bit of fluff.
fusselig *adj* fluffy. **sich** *(dat)* **den Mund ~ reden** *(col)* to talk till one is blue in the face.
fusseln *vi (Stoff, Kleid etc)* to go bobbly *(col)*.
fußen *vi* to rest, to be based *(auf +dat* on*)*.
Fuß|ende *nt (von Bett)* foot.
Fußgänger(in *f***)** *m* - pedestrian.
Fußgänger-: **~brücke** *f* footbridge; **~überweg** *m* pedestrian crossing *(Brit)*, crosswalk *(US)*;

(auch **~überführung***)* pedestrian bridge; **~unterführung** *f* pedestrian subway; **~zone** *f* pedestrian precinct.

Fuß-: **~gelenk** *nt* ankle; **~leiste** *f* skirting board *(Brit)*, baseboard *(US)*.

fußlig *adj* = **fusselig.**

Fuß-: **~marsch** *m* walk; *(Mil)* march; **~matte** *f* doormat; **~note** *f* footnote; **~pflege** *f* chiropody, podiatry *(US)*; **~pfleger** *m* chiropodist, podiatrist *(US)*; **~pilz** *m (Med)* athlete's foot *no art*; **~sohle** *f* sole of the foot; **~spitze** *f* toes *pl*; **sich auf die ~spitzen stellen** to stand on tiptoe; **~stapfen** *m* footprint; **in jds ~stapfen treten** *(fig)* to follow in sb's footsteps; **~stütze** *f* footrest; **~tritt** *m (Stoß)* kick; **jdm einen ~tritt geben** to kick sb, to give sb a kick; **einen ~tritt bekommen** *(fig)* to be kicked out; **~volk** *nt* **(a)** *(Mil old)* footmen *pl*; **(b)** *(fig)* **das ~volk** the rank and file; **~wanderung** *f* walk; **~weg** *m* **(a)** footpath; **(b) es sind nur 15 Minuten ~weg** it's only 15 minutes walk.

futsch *adj pred (col: weg)* gone, vanished.

Futter *nt* **- (a)** *no pl* food, feed; *(für Kühe, Pferde etc auch)* fodder. **gut im ~ sein** to be well-fed. **(b)** *(Kleider~, Briefumschlag~)* lining.

Futteral *nt* **-e** case.

Futter-: **~häuschen** *nt* bird box; **~krippe** *f* manger; **an der ~krippe sitzen** *(col)* to be well-placed.

futtern *(hum col)* **1** *vi* to stuff oneself *(col)*. **2** *vt* to scoff.

füttern *vt* **(a)** to feed. **„F~ verboten"** "do not feed the animals". **(b)** *Kleidungsstück* to line.

Futter-: **~napf** *m* bowl; **~neid** *m (fig)* material envy; **~pflanze** *f* forage plant; **~stoff** *m* lining (material); **~trog** *m* feeding trough.

Fütterung *f* feeding.

Futur *nt* **-e** *(Gram)* **(erstes) ~** future (tense); **zweites ~** future perfect.

futuristisch *adj* futuristic.

G

G, g [geː] *nt* **-, -** G, g.
g = **Gramm.**
gab *pret of* **geben.**
Gabe *f* **-n (a)** *(dated: Geschenk)* gift, present *(gen* of, from*)*. **(b)** *(Begabung)* gift. **die ~ haben, etw zu tun** to have a gift for doing sth.
Gabel *f* **-n** fork; *(Heu~, Mist~)* pitchfork; *(Telec)* rest, cradle.
Gabel-: g~förmig *adj* forked *no adv;* **~frühstück** *nt* buffet lunch.
gabeln *vtr* to fork.
Gabelstapler *m* **-** fork-lift truck.
Gabelung *f* fork.
Gabentisch *m table for Christmas or birthday presents.*
gackern *vi (lit, fig)* to cackle.
gaffen *vi* to gape, to stare *(nach* at*)*.
Gaffer(in *f)* *m* **- die neugierigen ~ bei einem Unfall** the nosy people standing gaping at an accident.
Gag [gɛk] *m* **-s** *(Film~)* gag; *(Werbe~)* gimmick.
Gage ['gaːʒə] *f* **-n** *(esp Theat)* fee.
gähnen *vi (lit, fig)* to yawn. **~de Leere** total emptiness; **ein ~der Abgrund** a yawning abyss; **ein G~** a yawn; **das G~ unterdrücken** to stop oneself (from) yawning.
Gala *f no pl* formal dress. **sich in ~ werfen** to get all dressed up.
Gala- *in cpds* formal; *(Mil)* full ceremonial; *(Theat)* gala; **~anzug** *m* formal dress; *(Mil)* full dress.
galaktisch *adj* galactic.
galant *adj (dated)* gallant.
Gala-: ~uniform *f (Mil)* (full) dress uniform; **~vorstellung** *f (Theat)* gala performance.
Galeere *f* **-n** galley.
Galerie *f* gallery. **auf der ~** in the gallery.
Galgen *m* **-** gallows *pl; (Film)* boom. **jdn an den ~ bringen** to bring sb to the gallows.
Galgen-: ~frist *f (col)* reprieve; **jdm eine ~frist geben** to give sb a reprieve, to reprieve sb; **~humor** *m* gallows humour *(Brit) or* humor *(US);* **~strick, ~vogel** *m (col)* gallows bird *(col).*
Galionsfigur *f* figurehead.
gälisch *adj* Gaelic.
Galle *f* **-n** gall; *(Organ)* gallbladder; *(Flüssigkeit auch)* bile. **seine ~ verspritzen** *(fig)* to pour out one's venom; **jdm kommt die ~ hoch** sb's blood begins to boil; **die ~ läuft ihm über** *(col)* he's livid.
galle(n)bitter *adj* bitter; *Bemerkung* caustic.
Gallen- *in cpds* gall; **~blase** *f* gall-bladder; **~stein** *m* gallstone.
gallig *adj* bitter; *(fig)* caustic.
gallisch *adj* Gallic.
Galopp *m* **-s** *or* **-e** gallop. **im ~** *(lit)* at a gallop; *(fig)* at top speed; **langsamer ~** canter.
galoppieren* *vi aux haben or sein* to gallop.
galt *pret of* **gelten.**
Gamasche *f* **-n** gaiter.
Gammastrahlen *pl* gamma rays *pl.*
Gammel *m no pl (col)* junk *(col)*, rubbish.
gamm(e)lig *adj (col) Lebensmittel* old, ancient; *Kleidung* tatty *(col).*
Gammler(in *f)* *m* **-** drop-out.
gang *adj:* **~ und gäbe sein** to be the usual thing.
Gang[1] *m* **⸗e (a)** *(no pl: ~art)* walk, way of walking, gait; *(eines Pferdes)* gait. **einen leichten/schnellen ~ haben** to be light on one's feet/to be a fast walker; **seinen ~ verlangsamen/beschleunigen** to slow down/to speed up.
(b) *(Besorgung)* errand; *(Spazier~)* walk. **einen ~ machen** to go on an errand/to go for a walk; **einen ~ zum Anwalt machen** to pay a visit to one's lawyer; **einen schweren ~ tun** to do something difficult; **das war für ihn immer ein schwerer ~** it was always hard for him; **den ~ nach Canossa antreten** *(fig)* to eat humble pie.
(c) *(Ablauf)* course; *(eines Dramas)* development. **der Motor hat einen leisen ~** the engine runs quietly; **seinen gewohnten ~ gehen** *(fig)* to run its usual course; **etw in ~ bringen** *or* **setzen** to get sth going; **etw in ~ halten** *(lit, fig)* to keep sth going; **in ~ kommen** to get going; **in ~ sein** to be going; *(fig)* to be off the ground; **in vollem ~** in full swing; **es ist etwas im ~(e)** *(col)* something's up *(col).*
(d) *(Arbeits~)* operation; *(Speisenfolge)* course. **ein Essen mit vier ⸗en** a four-course meal.
(e) *(Verbindungs~)* passage(way); *(Rail, in Gebäuden)* corridor; *(Hausflur) (offen)* passage(way); *(hinter Eingangstür)* hallway; *(im oberen Stock)* landing; *(Theat, Aviat, in Kirche)* aisle; *(Aviat, in Stadion)* gangway; *(in einem Bergwerk)* tunnel, gallery; *(Anat)* duct; *(Min: Erz~)* vein; *(Tech: eines Gewindes)* thread.
(f) *(Mech)* gear. **den ersten ~ einlegen** to engage first (gear); **auf** *or* **in den dritten ~ schalten** to change *or* shift *(US)* into third (gear).
Gang[2] [gɛŋ] *f* **-s** gang.
Gang|art *f* walk, way of walking, gait; *(von Pferd)* gait. **eine schnellere ~ vorlegen** to walk faster.
gangbar *adj (lit) Weg, Brücke* passable; *(fig)* practicable. **nicht ~** impassable/impracticable.
Gängelband *nt:* **jdn am ~ führen** *(fig) (Lehrer etc)* to spoon-feed sb; *(Mutter)* to keep sb tied to one's apron strings.
gängeln *vt (fig)* **jdn ~** to treat sb like a child; *(Mutter)* to keep sb tied to one's apron strings.
gängig *adj* **(a)** *(üblich)* common; *(aktuell)* current; *(vertretbar)* possible. **(b)** *(gut gehend) Waren* popular. **die ~ste Ausführung** the best-selling model.
Gangschaltung *f* gears *pl.*
Gangster ['gɛŋstɐ] *m* **-** gangster.
Gangster-: ~boß *m* gang boss; **~braut** *f* (gang) moll *(col);* **~methoden** *pl* strong-arm tactics *pl.*
Gangway ['gæŋweɪ] *f* **-s** *(Naut)* gangway; *(Aviat)* steps *pl.*
Ganove [ga'noːvə] *m* **-n** *(col)* crook.
Ganoven-: ~ehre *f* honour *(Brit) or* honor *(US)* among(st) thieves; **~sprache** *f* underworld slang.
Gans *f* **⸗e** goose.
Gänse- *in cpds* goose; **~blümchen** *nt* daisy; **~braten** *m* roast goose; **~füßchen** *pl (col)* inverted commas *pl;* **~haut** *f (fig)* goose-pimples *pl,* goose-flesh; **~marsch** *m:* **im ~marsch** in single *or* Indian file.
Gänserich *m* **-e** gander.
ganz 1 *adj* **(a)** whole, entire; *(vollständig)* complete; *Wahrheit* whole. **eine ~e Zahl** a whole

number; **eine ~e Note** *(Mus)* a semi-breve *(Brit)*, a whole note *(US)*; **~ England/London** the whole of England/London, all England/London; **die ~e Zeit** all the time, the whole time; **sein ~es Geld/Vermögen** all his money/fortune, his entire *or* whole fortune; **seine ~e Kraft** all his strength; **ein ~er Mann** a real *or* proper man; **etw im~en kaufen** to buy sth as a whole; **im (großen und) ~en (genommen)** on the whole, all in all. **(b)** *(col: unbeschädigt)* intact. **etw wieder ~ machen** to mend sth; **wieder ~ sein** to be mended. **(c)** *(col: nicht mehr als)* **~e 200 Mark im Monat** all of 200 marks a month.

2 *adv (völlig, ziemlich)* quite; *(ausnahmslos)* completely; *(sehr)* really; *(genau)* exactly, just. **~ hinten/vorn** right at the back/front; **nicht ~** not quite; **~ gewiß!** absolutely; **ein ~ gutes Buch** *(ziemlich)* quite a good book; *(sehr gut)* a very *or* really good book; **ein ~ billiger Trick** a really cheap trick; **er hat ~ recht** he's quite *or* absolutely right; **~ allein** all alone; **du bist ja ~ naß** you're all wet; **~ Aufmerksamkeit** *etc* **sein** to be all attention *etc;* **eine Zeitschrift ~ lesen** to read a magazine right through *or* from cover to cover; **~ und gar** completely, utterly; **~ und gar nicht** not at all, not in the least; **noch nicht ~ zwei Uhr** not quite two o'clock yet; **ein ~ klein wenig** just a tiny bit; **das mag ich ~ besonders gerne** I'm particularly fond of that; **sie ist ~ die Mutter** she's just *or* exactly like her mother; **etw ~ oder gar nicht machen** to do sth properly or not at all.

Gänze *f no pl (form)* entirety.

Ganze(s) *nt decl as adj* **das ~** the whole; *(alle Sachen zusammen)* the (whole) lot; *(ganzer Satz, ganze Ausrüstung)* the complete set. **etw als ~s sehen** to see sth as a whole; **das ~ kostet ...** altogether it costs ...; **das ~ gefällt mir gar nicht** I don't like it at all; **aufs ~ gehen** *(col)* to go all out; **es geht ums ~** everything's at stake.

Ganzheit *f (Einheit)* unity; *(Vollständigkeit)* entirety. **in seiner ~** in its entirety.

ganzheitlich *adj* integral.

Ganzheitsmethode *f* look-and-say method.

ganzjährig *adj* all-year *attr.*

gänzlich *adv* completely, totally.

ganztägig *adj* all-day *attr.*

ganztags *adv arbeiten* full-time.

Ganztags-: ~beschäftigung *f* full-time occupation; **~schule** *f* all-day schooling *no pl or* schools *pl;* **~stelle** *f* full-time job.

Ganzton *m (Mus)* (whole) tone.

gar 1 *adv* **(a)** *(überhaupt)* at all; *(ganz)* quite. **~ keines** not a single one, none whatsoever *or* at all; **~ kein Grund** no reason whatsoever *or* at all; **~ nichts** nothing at all; **~ nicht schlecht** not bad at all, not at all bad. **(b) er wäre ~ zu gern noch länger geblieben** he would really have liked to stay longer; **ein ~ feiner Mensch** *(old)* a really splendid person. **(c)** *(sogar)* even. **wie alt ist er? — 70, wenn nicht ~ 80** how old is he? — 70, if not 80. **2** *adj Speise* done *pred,* cooked.

Garage [ga'ra:ʒə] *f* **-n** garage; *(Hoch~, Tief~)* car-park *(Brit)*, parking garage *(US)*.

Garantie *f (lit, fig)* guarantee. **die Uhr hat ein Jahr ~** the watch is guaranteed for a year *or* has a year's guarantee; **das fällt noch unter die ~** that's covered by the guarantee.

Garantie-: ~frist *f* guarantee period; **~lohn** *m* guaranteed minimum wage.

garantieren* 1 *vt* to guarantee *(jdm etw* sb sth*)*. **er konnte mir nicht ~, daß ...** he couldn't guarantee that ... **2** *vi* to give a guarantee. **für etw ~** to guarantee sth.

garantiert *adv* guaranteed; *(col)* I bet *(col)*. **er kommt garantiert nicht** I bet he won't come *(col)*, he's bound not to come.

Garantieschein *m* guarantee.

Garaus *m: (col)* **jdm den ~ machen** to do sb in *(col)*, to bump sb off *(col)*.

Garbe *f* **-n** *(Korn~)* sheaf; *(Mil: Schuß~)* burst of fire. **zu ~n binden** to bind into sheaves.

Garde *f* **-n** guard. **bei der ~** in the Guards; **die alte ~** *(fig)* the old guard.

Gardemaß *nt:* **~ haben** *(hum)* to be as tall as a tree.

Garderobe *f* **-n (a)** *(Kleiderbestand)* wardrobe. **(b)** *(Kleiderablage)* hall-stand; *(im Theater, Kino etc)* cloakroom *(Brit)*, checkroom *(US)*. **(c)** *(Theat: Umkleideraum)* dressing-room.

Garderoben-: ~frau *f* cloakroom *(Brit) or* checkroom *(US)* attendant; **~haken** *m* coat hook; **~marke** *f* cloakroom *(Brit) or* checkroom *(US)* number; **~schein** *m* cloakroom *(Brit) or* checkroom *(US)* ticket; **~ständer** *m* hat-stand.

Gardine *f* curtain, drape *(US)*; *(Scheiben~)* net curtain.

Gardinen-: ~predigt *f (col)* **jdm eine ~predigt halten** to give sb a talking-to; **~stange** *f* curtain rail; *(zum Ziehen)* curtain rod.

garen *(Cook) vti* to cook.

gären 1 *vi aux haben or sein* to ferment; *(fig: Gefühle etc)* to seethe. **die Wut gärte in ihm** he was seething with anger. **2** *vt* to ferment.

Garn *nt* **-e** thread; *(Baumwoll~ auch)* cotton; *(Häkel~, fig: Seemanns~)* yarn. **ein ~ spinnen** *(fig)* to spin a yarn.

Garnele *f* **-n** *(Zool)* prawn, shrimp.

garnieren* *vt Kuchen, Kleid* to decorate; *Gericht, (fig) Reden etc* to garnish.

Garnierung *f siehe vt* decoration; garnishing.

Garnison *f (Mil)* garrison.

Garnison(s)- *in cpds* garrison.

Garnitur *f (Satz)* set; *(Unterwäsche)* set of underwear. **die erste ~** *(fig)* the pick of the bunch; **erste/zweite ~ sein** to be first-rate/second-rate.

Garnrolle *f* spool; *(von Baumwolle, Nähgarn)* cotton reel.

Garten *m* ̈ garden; *(Obst~)* orchard. **botanischer/zoologischer ~** botanic/zoological gardens *pl;* **im ~ arbeiten** to do some gardening; **das ist nicht in seinem ~ gewachsen** *(fig col: Ideen)* he didn't think of that himself.

Garten- *in cpds* garden; **~arbeit** *f* gardening *no pl;* **~bau** *m* horticulture; **~gerät** *nt* gardening tool; **~haus** *nt* summer house; **~laube** *f (~häuschen)* summer house; **~lokal** *nt* beer garden; *(Restaurant)* garden café; **~möbel** *pl* garden furniture; **~schere** *f* secateurs *pl (Brit)*, pruning-shears *pl;* **~schlauch** *m* garden hose; **~zwerg** *m* garden gnome; *(pej col)* squirt *(col)*.

Gärtner(in *f***)** *m* gardener.

Gärtnerei *f (Baumschule, für Setzlinge)* nursery; *(für Obst, Gemüse, Schnittblumen)* market-garden *(Brit)*, truck farm *(US)*.

gärtnerisch *adj attr* gardening. **wenn man sich ~ betätigt** if you do some gardening.

gärtnern *vi* to do gardening.

Gärung *f* fermentation; *(fig)* ferment, turmoil.

Gas *nt* **-e** gas; *(Aut: ~pedal)* accelerator, gas pedal *(esp US)*. **~ geben** *(Aut)* to accelerate, to step on the gas *(col)*; **~ wegnehmen** *(Aut)* to decelerate.

Gas- *in cpds* gas; **g~beheizt** *adj* gas-heated; **~flasche** *f* bottle of gas, gas canister; **g~förmig** *adj* gaseous; **~geruch** *m* smell of gas; **~hahn** *m* gas-tap; **~heizung** *f* gas central heating; **~herd** *m* gas cooker; **~kammer** *f* gas chamber; **~kocher** *m* camping stove; **~laterne** *f* gas (street) lamp; **~leitung** *f (Rohr)* gas pipe; **~licht** *nt* gaslight; *(Beleuchtung)* gaslighting; **~maske** *f* gasmask; **~ofen** *m (Heizofen)* gas fire *or* heater; **~pedal** *nt (Aut)* accelerator (pedal), gas pedal *(esp US)*.

Gasse *f* **-n** lane; *(Durchgang)* alley(way); *(S Ger, Aus: Straße)* street.

Gassen-: ~hauer *m (old, col)* popular melody; **~junge** *m (pej)* street urchin *or* arab.

Gassi *adv (col)* **mit einem Hund ~ gehen** to take a dog for walkies *(col)*.
Gast *m* **¨-e** guest; *(Besucher auch, Tourist)* visitor; *(in einer ~stätte)* customer; *(Theat)* guest (star); **vor geladenen ¨~en** before an invited audience; **wir haben heute abend ¨~e** we're having people around this evening; **bei jdm zu ~ sein** to be sb's guest(s); **in einem anderen Ort zu ~ sein** to visit another place.
Gast|arbeiter *m* immigrant *or* foreign worker.
Gäste-: ~bett *nt* spare *or* guest bed; **~buch** *nt* visitors' book; **~haus** *nt* guest house; **~zimmer** *nt* guest room.
Gast-: g~freundlich *adj* hospitable; **~freundlichkeit, ~freundschaft** *f* hospitality; **~geber** *m* host; **~geberin** *f* hostess; **~haus** *nt*, **~hof** *m* inn; **~hörer(in** *f*) *m (Univ)* observer, auditor *(US)*; **~land** *nt* host country; **g~lich** *adj* hospitable; **~lichkeit** *f* hospitality.
Gastritis *f, pl* **Gastritiden** gastritis.
Gastrolle *f (Theat)* **eine ~ spielen** *(lit)* to make a guest appearance; *(fig)* to put in a fleeting appearance.
Gastronomie *f (Kochkunst)* gastronomy; *(form: Gaststättengewerbe)* catering trade.
Gast-: ~spiel *nt (Theat)* guest performance; **ein ~spiel geben** *(lit)* to give a guest performance; *(fig col)* to put in a brief appearance; **~stätte** *f (Speise~)* restaurant; *(Trinklokal)* pub *(Brit)*, bar; **~wirt(in** *f*) *m (Besitzer)* restaurant owner; *(Pächter)* restaurant manager(ess *f*); *(von Trinklokal)* landlord/landlady; **~wirtschaft** *f* inn.
Gas-: ~uhr *f* gas meter; **~verbrauch** *m* gas consumption; **~vergiftung** *f* gas poisoning; **~versorgung** *f (System)* gas supply *(gen* to*)*; **~werk** *nt* gasworks *sing or pl*; *(Verwaltung)* gas board; **~zähler** *m* gas meter; **~zentralheizung** *f* gas central heating.
Gatte *m* **-n** *(form)* husband, spouse *(form)*.
Gatter *nt* **-** *(Tür)* gate; *(Zaun)* fence; *(Rost)* grating, grid.
Gattin *f (form)* wife, spouse *(form)*.
Gattung *f (Biol)* genus; *(Liter, Mus, Art)* genre, form; *(fig: Sorte)* type, kind.
Gattungsbegriff *m* generic concept.
GAU = **größter anzunehmender Unfall** maximum credible accident, MCA.
Gaudi *nt or (S Ger, Aus) f no pl (col)* fun.
Gaukler *m* **-** *(liter)* travelling *(Brit) or* traveling *(US)* entertainer.
Gaul *m, pl* **Gäule** *(pej)* nag, hack.
Gaumen *m* **-** palate *(auch fig)*, roof of the/one's mouth. **die Zunge klebte ihm vor Durst am ~** his tongue was hanging out (with thirst).
Gauner *m* **-** rogue, rascal; *(Betrüger)* crook; *(hum col: Schelm auch)* scamp.
Gaunerbande *f* bunch of rogues/crooks.
Gaunerei *f* swindling *no pl*, cheating *no pl*.
gaunerhaft *adj* rascally *no adv*.
gaunern *vi (col) (betrügen)* to swindle, to cheat; *(stehlen)* to thieve. **er hat sich durchs Leben gegaunert** he cheated his way through life.
Gaunersprache *f* underworld jargon.
Gaze ['ga:zə] *f* **-n** gauze.
Gazelle *f* gazelle.
ge|artet *adj* **gutmütig/freundlich ~ sein** to be good-natured/have a friendly nature; **sie ist ganz anders ~** she has a completely different nature.
Ge|äst *nt no pl* branches *pl*.
geb. = **geboren.**
Gebäck *nt* **-e** *(Kekse)* biscuits *pl (Brit)*, cookies *pl (US)*; *(Teilchen)* pastries *pl*.
gebacken *ptp of* **backen.**
Gebälk *nt* **-e** timberwork *no pl*, timbers *pl*.
geballt *adj (fig: konzentriert)* concentrated.
gebannt *adj* spellbound. **wie ~** as if spellbound.
gebar *pret of* **gebären.**
Gebärde *f* **-n** gesture; *(lebhafte auch)* gesticulation.
gebärden* *vr* to behave, to conduct oneself *(form)*.
Gebärdenspiel *nt no pl* gestures *pl*, gesticulation(s).
Gebaren *nt no pl* behaviour *(Brit)*, behavior *(US)*; *(Geschäfts~)* conduct.
gebären *pret* **gebar,** *ptp* **geboren 1** *vt* to give birth to; *(fig liter: erzeugen)* to breed. **geboren werden** to be born; **wo sind Sie geboren?** where were you born?; **aus der Not geborene Ideen** ideas springing from necessity; *siehe* **geboren. 2** *vi* to give birth.
Gebärmutter *f (Anat)* womb, uterus.
Gebäude *nt* **-** building; *(fig: Gefüge)* structure.
Gebäude-: ~komplex *m* (building) complex; **~reinigung** *f (das Reinigen)* commercial cleaning; *(Firma)* cleaning contractors *pl*.
gebaut *adj* built. **gut/stark ~ sein** to be well-built/sturdily built.
gebefreudig *adj* generous, open-handed.
Gebeine *pl (geh)* bones *pl*, mortal remains *pl (liter)*.
Gebell *nt no pl* barking.
geben *pret* **gab,** *ptp* **gegeben 1** *vt* **(a)** *(auch vi)* to give. **wer hat dir das gegeben?** who gave you that?; **gib's mir!** give it to me!, give me it!; **sich** *(dat)* **(von jdm) etw ~ lassen** to ask sb for sth; **was darf ich Ihnen ~?** what can I get you?; **~ Sie mir bitte zwei Flaschen Bier** I'd like two bottles of beer, please; **ich gebe dir das Auto für 100 Mark** I'll give you the car for 100 marks; **ein gutes Beispiel ~** to set a good example; **jdn/etw verloren ~** to give sb/sth up as lost; **~ Sie mir bitte Herrn Braun** *(Telec)* can I speak to Mr Braun please?; **Gott gebe, daß ...** God grant that ...; **es war ihm nicht gegeben, seine Eltern lebend wiederzusehen** he was not to see his parents alive again; **in die Post ~** to post; **ein Auto in Reparatur ~** to have a car repaired; **ein Kind in Pflege ~** to put *or* place a child in care; **2 + 2 gibt 4** 2 + 2 makes 4; **das gibt keinen Sinn** that doesn't make sense; **Rotwein gibt Flecken** red wine leaves stains; **was wird heute im Theater gegeben?** what's on at the theatre today?; **er gibt Englisch** he teaches English.
(b) viel/nicht viel auf etw *(acc)* **~** to set great store/not much store by sth; **ich gebe nicht viel auf seinen Rat** I don't think much of his advice; **etw von sich ~** *Laut, Worte, Flüche* to utter sth.
2 *vi (auch vt) (Cards)* to deal; *(Tennis: Aufschlag haben)* to serve. **wer gibt?** whose deal/serve is it?
3 *vt impers* **es gibt** *(+acc)* there is/are; **was gibt's?** what's the matter?, what's up?; **was gibt's zum Mittagessen?** what's for lunch?; **freitags gibt es bei uns immer Fisch** we always have fish on Fridays; **heute gibt's noch Regen** it's going to rain today; **dafür gibt es 10% Rabatt** you get 10% discount for it; **das gibt's doch nicht!** I don't believe it!; **da gibt's nichts** *(col)* there's no two ways about it *(col)*; **gleich gibt's was!** *(col)* there'll be trouble in a minute!
4 *vr* **(a)** *(nachlassen)* to ease off, to let up; *(sich erledigen)* to sort itself out; *(aufhören)* to stop. **sich gefangen/verloren ~** to give oneself up/to give oneself up for lost; **das wird sich schon ~** it'll all work out. **(b)** *(sich benehmen)* to behave.
Geber *m* **-** giver; *(Cards)* dealer.
Gebet *nt* **-e** prayer. **sein ~ verrichten** to say one's prayers; **jdn ins ~ nehmen** *(fig)* to take sb to task.
Gebetbuch *nt* prayer-book.
gebeten *ptp of* **bitten.**
gebeugt *adj Haltung* stooped; *Kopf* bowed; *Schultern* sloping. **~ sitzen/stehen** to sit/stand hunched up.
Gebiet *nt* **-e** area, region; *(Fläche)* area; *(Staats~)*

territory; *(fig: Fach)* field; *(Teil~)* branch. **auf diesem** ~ in this field.
gebieten* *irreg* **1** *vti (verlangen)* to demand; *(befehlen)* to command. **jdm etw** ~ to command sb to do sth. **2** *vi (liter: herrschen)* to have command *(über +acc* over). **über ein Land/Volk** ~ to have dominion over a country/nation.
Gebieter *m* - *(liter)* master.
Gebieterin *f (liter, old)* mistress.
gebieterisch *adj (geh)* imperious; *(herrisch)* domineering; *Ton* peremptory.
Gebiets-: ~**anspruch** *m* territorial claim; ~**hoheit** *f* territorial sovereignty.
Gebilde *nt* - thing, construction.
gebildet *adj* educated; *(gelehrt)* learned, erudite; *(kultiviert)* cultured.
Gebirge *nt* - mountains *pl*, mountain range. **im/ins** ~ in/into the mountains.
gebirgig *adj* mountainous.
Gebirgs- *in cpds* mountain; ~**bahn** *f* mountain railway *crossing a mountain range;* ~**rücken** *m* mountain ridge; ~**straße** *f* mountain road; ~**zug** *m* mountain range.
Gebiß *nt* **-sse** *(die Zähne)* (set of) teeth; *(künstliches* ~*)* dentures *pl.*
gebissen *ptp of* **beißen.**
Gebläse *nt* - blower.
geblasen *ptp of* **blasen.**
geblichen *ptp of* **bleichen.**
geblieben *ptp of* **bleiben.**
geblümt *adj* flowered.
Geblüt *nt no pl (geh: Abstammung)* descent, lineage. **von edlem** ~ of noble blood.
gebogen 1 *ptp of* **biegen. 2** *adj Nase* Roman.
geboren 1 *ptp of* **gebären. 2** *adj* born. **blind** ~ **sein** to have been born blind; **er ist blind** ~ he was born blind; ~**er Engländer sein** to be English by birth; **Hanna Schmidt** ~**e** *or* **geb. Müller** Hanna Schmidt, née Müller.
geborgen 1 *ptp of* **bergen. 2** *adj* **sich** ~ **fühlen/** ~ **sein** to feel/be secure *or* safe.
Geborgenheit *f* security.
geborsten *ptp of* **bersten.**
Gebot *nt* **-e (a)** *(Gesetz)* law; *(Regel, Vorschrift)* rule; *(Bibl)* commandment; *(moralisch)* precept; *(geh: Erfordernis)* requirement. **das** ~ **der Stunde** the needs of the moment; **das** ~ **der Vernunft** the dictates of reason. **(b)** *(Verfügung)* command. **jdm zu** ~**e stehen** to be at sb's command *or (Geld etc)* disposal. **(c)** *(Comm: bei Auktionen)* bid.
geboten 1 *ptp of* **bieten, gebieten. 2** *adj (geh) (ratsam)* advisable; *(notwendig)* necessary; *(dringend* ~*)* imperative. **bei aller** ~**en Achtung** with all due respect.
Gebr. = **Gebrüder** Bros.
gebracht *ptp of* **bringen.**
gebrannt 1 *ptp of* **brennen. 2** *adj* **ein** ~**es Kind scheut das Feuer** *(Prov)* once bitten twice shy *(Prov).*
gebraten *ptp of* **braten.**
Gebrauch *m, pl* **Gebräuche** *(Benutzung)* use; *(eines Wortes auch)* usage; *(Anwendung)* application; *(Brauch)* custom. **falscher** ~ misuse; misapplication; **von etw** ~ **machen** to make use of sth; **etw in** ~ *(dat)* **haben** to use sth; **allgemein in** ~ *(dat)* in general use; **zum äußerlichen/innerlichen** ~ to be taken externally/internally; **vor** ~ **(gut) schütteln** shake (well) before use.
gebrauchen* *vt (benutzen)* to use; *(anwenden)* to apply. **sich zu etw** ~ **lassen** to be useful for sth; *(ausnutzen)* to be used as sth; **nicht mehr zu** ~ **sein** to be no longer any use; **er/das ist zu nichts zu** ~ he's/that's (of) no use to anybody; **das kann ich gut** ~ I can really use that; **ich könnte ein neues Kleid** ~ I could use a new dress, I could do with a new dress.
gebräuchlich *adj (verbreitet)* common; *(gewöhnlich)* usual, customary. **nicht mehr** ~ *(Ausdruck etc)* no longer used.
Gebrauchs-: ~**anweisung** *f (für Arznei)* directions *pl; (für Geräte etc)* instructions *pl;* **etw g~fähig machen** to put sth into working order; **g~fertig** *adj* ready for use; *Nahrungsmittel* instant; ~**gegenstand** *m* basic commodity.
gebraucht *adj* second-hand, used. **etw** ~ **kaufen** to buy sth second-hand.
Gebrauchtwagen *m* used *or* second-hand car.
gebräunt *adj (braungebrannt)* (sun-)tanned.
Gebrechen *nt* - *(geh)* affliction.
gebrechlich *adj* frail.
gebrochen 1 *ptp of* **brechen. 2** *adj* broken. ~**en Herzens** broken-hearted; ~ **Deutsch sprechen** to speak broken German.
Gebrüder *pl (Comm)* ~ **Müller** Müller Brothers.
gebückt *adj* **eine** ~**e Haltung** a stoop; ~ **gehen** to stoop.
Gebühr *f* **-en (a)** charge; *(Post~)* postage *no pl; (Honorar)* fee; *(Studien~)* fees *pl; (Vermittlungs~)* commission; *(Rad, TV)* licence *(Brit)*, license *(US).* ~**en erheben** to make a charge, to charge postage/a fee *etc;* **zu ermäßigter** ~ at a reduced rate; ~ **(be)zahlt Empfänger** postage to be paid by addressee. **(b)** *(Angemessenheit)* **nach** ~ suitably, properly; **über** ~ excessively.
gebühren* *(geh)* **1** *vi* to be due *(dat* to). **ihm gebührt Anerkennung** he deserves *or* is due recognition. **2** *vr* to be proper *or* fitting. **wie es sich gebührt** as is proper.
gebührend *adj (verdient)* due; *(angemessen)* suitable; *(geziemend)* proper.
Gebühren-: ~**erhöhung** *f* increase in charges/fees; **g~frei** *adj* free of charge; *Brief, Paket* post-free; **g~pflichtig** *adj* chargeable; **g~pflichtige Verwarnung** *(Jur)* fine; **jdn g~pflichtig verwarnen** to fine sb.
gebunden 1 *ptp of* **binden. 2** *adj* tied *(an+acc* to sth*)*; *Kapital* tied up; *Preise* controlled; *(Ling, Phys, Buch)* bound; *Wärme* latent; *(Mus)* legato. **vertraglich** ~ **sein** to be bound by contract; **anderweitig** ~ **sein** to be otherwise engaged.
Geburt *f* **-en** *(lit, fig)* birth. **von** ~ by birth; **von** ~ **an** from birth; **das war eine schwere** ~**!** *(fig col)* that took some doing *(col).*
Geburten-: ~**kontrolle,** ~**regelung** *f* birth control; ~**rückgang** *m* drop in the birth rate; **g~schwach** *adj Jahrgang* with a low birth rate; **g~stark** *adj* with a high birth rate.
gebürtig *adj* ~**er Londoner sein** to have been born in London, to be a native Londoner.
Geburts-: ~**anzeige** *f* birth announcement; ~**datum** *nt* date of birth; ~**fehler** *m* congenital defect; ~**helfer(in** *f) m (Arzt)* obstetrician; ~**hilfe** *f (als Fach)* obstetrics *sing; (von Hebamme auch)* midwifery; ~**jahr** *nt* year of birth; ~**land** *nt* native country; ~**ort** *m* birth place.
Geburtstag *m* birthday. **herzlichen Glückwunsch zum** ~! happy birthday!, many happy returns (of the day)!; **jdm zum** ~ **gratulieren** to wish sb (a) happy birthday *or* many happy returns (of the day); **heute habe ich** ~ it's my birthday today; ~ **feiern** to celebrate one's/sb's birthday; **jdm etw zum** ~ **schenken** to give sb sth for his/her birthday.
Geburtstags- *in cpds* birthday.
Geburts-: ~**urkunde** *f* birth certificate; ~**wehen** *pl* labour *(Brit) or* labor *(US)* pains *pl.*
Gebüsch *nt* **-e** bushes *pl; (Unterholz)* undergrowth.
gedacht 1 *ptp of* **denken, gedenken. 2** *adj Linie, Fall* imaginary.
Gedächtnis *nt* memory; *(Andenken auch)* remembrance. **etw aus dem** ~ **hersagen** to recite sth from memory; **wenn mich mein** ~ **nicht trügt** if my memory serves me right; **zum** ~ **an die Toten** in memory *or* remembrance of the dead.

Gedächtnis-: ~**feier** *f* commemoration; ~**hilfe** *f* memory aid, mnemonic; ~**lücke** *f* gap in one's memory; ~**schwund** *m* amnesia, loss of memory; ~**verlust** *m* loss of memory.

gedämpft *adj Geräusch* muffled; *Farben, Instrument, Stimmung* muted; *Licht, Freude* subdued. **mit ~er Stimme** in a low voice.

Gedanke *m* **-n** thought *(über +acc* on, about*)*; *(Idee, Plan, Einfall)* idea; *(Konzept)* concept; *(Betrachtung)* reflection *(über+acc* on*)*. **der bloße ~ an ...** the mere thought of ...; **da kam mir ein ~** then I had an idea; **in ~n vertieft/verloren sein** to be deep/lost in thought; **jdn auf andere ~n bringen** to take sb's mind off things; **sich** *(dat)* **über etw** *(acc)* **~n machen** to think about sth; *(sich sorgen)* to worry about sth; **etw ganz in ~n** *(dat)* **tun** to do sth without thinking; **jds ~n lesen** to read sb's mind *or* thoughts; **auf einen ~n kommen** to have *or* get an idea; **auf dumme ~n kommen** *(col)* to get up to mischief; **jdn auf den ~n bringen, etw zu tun** to give sb the idea of doing sth.

Gedanken-: ~**freiheit** *f* freedom of thought; ~**lesen** *nt* mind-reading; **g~los** *adj (unüberlegt)* unthinking; *(zerstreut)* absent-minded; *(rücksichtslos)* thoughtless; **etw g~los tun** to do sth without thinking; ~**losigkeit** *f siehe adj* lack of thought; absentmindedness; thoughtlessness; ~**sprung** *m* mental leap; ~**strich** *m* dash; ~**übertragung** *f* telepathy *(auch fig)*, thought transference; **g~verloren** *adj* lost in thought.

gedanklich *adj* intellectual; *(vorgestellt)* imaginary.

Gedärme *pl* intestines *pl*.

Gedeck *nt* **-e** *(Tisch~)* cover; *(Menü)* set meal, table d'hôte; *(in Lokal)* cover charge; *set drink served with cover charge*. **ein ~ auflegen** to set a place.

gedeckt *adj Farben* muted; *Gang* covered.

Gedeih *m*: **auf ~ und Verderb** for better or (for) worse.

gedeihen *pret* **gedieh,** *ptp* **gediehen** *vi aux sein* to thrive, to flourish; *(geh: sich entwickeln)* to develop; *(fig: vorankommen)* to make progress. **die Sache ist so weit gediehen, daß...** the matter has reached the point *or* stage where ...

Gedeihen *nt no pl (Gelingen)* success.

Gedenken *nt no pl* memory. **zum ~ an jdn** in memory *or* remembrance of sb.

gedenken* *vi irreg +gen (geh: denken an)* to remember, to think of; *(feierlich)* to commemorate. **~, etw zu tun** to propose to do sth.

Gedenk-: ~**feier** *f* commemoration; ~**minute** *f* minute's silence; ~**stätte** *f* memorial; ~**stein** *m* memorial stone; ~**stunde** *f* hour of commemoration; ~**tag** *m* commemoration day.

Gedicht *nt* **-e** poem. **die ~e Enzensbergers** Enzensberger's poetry *or* poems; **dieses Kleid ist ein ~** *(fig col)* this dress is sheer poetry.

gediegen *adj* **(a)** *Metall* pure. **(b)** *(von Qualität)* high-quality; *(geschmackvoll)* tasteful; *(rechtschaffen)* upright; *Verarbeitung* solid; *Kenntnisse* sound.

gedieh *pret of* **gedeihen.**

gediehen *ptp of* **gedeihen.**

Gedränge *nt no pl (Menschenmenge)* crowd, crush; *(Drängeln)* jostling.

gedrängt *adj* packed; *(fig) Stil* terse. **~ voll** packed full, jam-packed *(col)*.

gedroschen *ptp of* **dreschen.**

gedruckt *adj* **lügen wie ~** *(col)* to lie through one's teeth.

gedrückt *adj* depressed, dejected. **~er Stimmung sein** to be in low spirits, to feel depressed.

gedrungen 1 *ptp of* **dringen. 2** *adj Gestalt* sturdy, stocky.

geduckt *adj Haltung, Mensch* crouching; *Kopf* lowered.

Geduld *f no pl* patience. **mit jdm/etw ~ haben** to be patient *or* have patience with sb/sth; **mir reißt die ~, ich verliere die ~** my patience is wearing thin, I'm losing my patience.

gedulden* *vr* to be patient.

geduldig *adj* patient. **~ wie ein Lamm** meek as a lamb.

Gedulds-: ~**faden** *m* **jetzt reißt mir aber der ~faden!** *(col)* I'm just about losing patience; ~**probe** *f* trial of (one's) patience; ~**spiel** *nt* puzzle.

gedungen *adj (pej geh) Mörder* hired.

gedurft *ptp of* **dürfen.**

ge|ehrt *adj* honoured *(Brit)*, honored *(US)*. **Sehr ~e Damen und Herren!** Ladies and Gentlemen!; *(in Briefen)* Dear Sirs; Dear Sir or Madam; **Sehr ~er Herr Kurz!** Dear Mr Kurz.

ge|eignet *adj (passend)* suitable; *(richtig)* right. **sie ist für diesen Posten nicht ~** she's not the right person for this job; **im ~en Augenblick** at the right moment; **er wäre zum Lehrer gut/schlecht ~** he would/wouldn't make a good teacher.

Gefahr *f* **-en (a)** danger *(für* to, for*)*; *(Bedrohung)* threat *(für* to, for*)*. **die ~en des Verkehrs/dieses Berufs** the dangers *or* perils *or* hazards of the traffic/this job; **in ~ sein/schweben** to be in danger *or* jeopardy; **außer ~** *(nicht gefährdet)* not in danger; *(nicht mehr gefährdet)* out of danger; *(Patient)* off the danger list; **sich einer ~ aussetzen** to put oneself in danger; **es besteht die ~, daß ...** there's a risk *or* the danger that ... **(b)** *(Wagnis, Risiko)* risk *(für* to, for*)*. **auf eigene ~** at one's own risk *or (stärker)* peril; **~ laufen, etw zu tun** to run the risk of doing sth.

gefährden* *vt* to endanger; *Chancen etc auch* to jeopardize; *(bedrohen)* to threaten.

Gefährdung *f no pl* **(a)** *siehe vt* endangering; jeopardizing. **(b)** *(Gefahr)* danger *(gen* to*)*.

gefahren *ptp of* **fahren.**

Gefahren-: ~**stelle** *f* danger spot; ~**zulage** *f* danger money.

gefährlich *adj* dangerous; *(gewagt auch)* risky.

Gefährlichkeit *f siehe adj* dangerousness; riskiness.

Gefahr-: g~los *adj* safe; ~**losigkeit** *f* safety.

Gefährte *m (wk)* **-n, -n, Gefährtin** *f (geh: lit, fig)* companion.

Gefälle *nt* **-** *(Neigung) (von Fluß)* drop, fall; *(von Land, Straße)* slope; *(Neigungsgrad)* gradient; *(fig: Unterschied)* difference. **das Gelände hat ein starkes ~** the land slopes down steeply; **starkes ~!** steep hill.

gefallen[1]* *vi irreg* to please *(jdm* sb*)*. **es gefällt mir (gut)** I like it (very much *or* a lot); **es gefällt ihm, wie sie spricht** he likes the way she talks; **das gefällt mir gar nicht** I don't like it at all; **sich** *(dat)* **etw ~ lassen** *(dulden)* to put up with sth.

gefallen[2] 1 *ptp of* **fallen, gefallen[1]. 2** *adj (Mil)* killed in action.

Gefallen[1] *nt no pl (geh)* pleasure. **an etw** *(dat)* **~ finden** to derive pleasure from sth; **an jdm ~ finden** to take to sb.

Gefallen[2] *m* **-** favour *(Brit)*, favor *(US)*. **jdn um einen ~ bitten** to ask a favour of sb; **tun Sie mir den ~ und schweigen Sie** would you do me a favour and be quiet; **ihm zu ~** to please him.

Gefallene(r) *mf decl as adj* soldier killed in action.

gefällig *adj* **(a)** *(hilfsbereit)* helpful, obliging. **(b)** *(ansprechend)* pleasing; *(freundlich)* pleasant. **(c) sonst noch etwas ~?** *(iro)* will there be anything else?

Gefälligkeit *f* **(a)** *(Gefallen)* favour *(Brit)*, favor *(US)*. **jdm eine ~ erweisen** to do sb a favour. **(b)** *no pl (gefälliges Wesen)* pleasantness. **etw aus ~ tun** to do sth out of the kindness of one's heart.

gefälligst *adv (col)* kindly. **sei ~ still!** will you kindly keep your mouth shut! *(col)*.

gefangen 1 *ptp of* **fangen. 2** *adj (~genommen)* captured; *(fig)* captivated. **sich ~ geben** to give oneself up, to surrender.

Gefangenen-: ~austausch *m* exchange of prisoners; **~lager** *nt* prison camp; **~wärter** *m* prison officer, (prison) warder.

Gefangene(r) *mf decl as adj* prisoner. **500 ~ machen** *(Mil)* to take 500 prisoners.

Gefangen-: g~halten *vt sep irreg* to hold prisoner; *Tiere* to keep in captivity; *(fig)* to captivate; **~nahme** *f* **-n** capture; *(Verhaftung)* arrest; **g~nehmen** *vt sep irreg Mensch* to take captive *or* prisoner; *(verhaften)* to arrest; *(fig)* to captivate; **~schaft** *f* captivity; **in ~schaft geraten** to be taken prisoner.

Gefängnis *nt* prison, jail; *(~strafe)* imprisonment. **im ~ sitzen** *(col)* to be in prison; **ins ~ kommen** to be sent to prison; **zwei Jahre ~ bekommen** to get two years' imprisonment.

Gefängnis- *in cpds* prison; **~aufseher** *m* warder *(Brit)*, guard *(US)*, prison officer; **~direktor** *m* prison governor, prison warden *(esp US)*; **~insasse** *m* inmate; **~strafe** *f* prison sentence; **er wurde zu einer ~strafe verurteilt** he was sent to prison, he was given a prison sentence; **~wärter** *m siehe* **~aufseher; ~zelle** *f* prison cell.

gefärbt *adj* coloured *(Brit)*, colored *(US)*; *Haar, Stoff* dyed; *Lebensmittel* artificially coloured *(Brit) or* colored *(US)*; *(fig) Bericht* biased.

Gefasel *nt no pl (pej)* drivel *(col)*.

Gefäß *nt* **-e** vessel *(auch Anat, Bot)*; *(Behälter)* receptacle.

gefaßt *adj (ruhig)* composed, calm. **auf etw** *(acc)* **~ sein** to be prepared *or* ready for sth; **er kann sich auf etwas ~ machen** *(col)* I'll give him something to think about *(col)*.

Gefecht *nt* **-e** *(lit, fig)* battle; *(Mil)* engagement; *(Scharmützel)* skirmish. **ein hartes ~** fierce fighting; **jdn/etw außer ~ setzen** *(lit, fig)* to put sb/sth out of action; **Argumente ins ~ führen** to advance arguments; **im Eifer des ~s** *(fig)* in the heat of the moment.

gefechtsbereit *adj* ready for action; *(einsatzfähig)* (fully) operational.

gefedert *adj (Matratze)* sprung.

gefeiert *adj* celebrated.

gefeit *adj* **gegen etw ~ sein** to be immune to sth.

gefestigt *adj Tradition* established; *Charakter* steadfast.

Gefieder *nt* - plumage, feathers *pl*.

gefiedert *adj* feathered.

Geflecht *nt* **-e** *(lit, fig)* network; *(Gewebe)* weave; *(Rohr~)* wickerwork.

gefleckt *adj* spotted; *Blume, Vogel* speckled; *Haut* blotchy.

Geflimmer *nt no pl* shimmering; *(Film, TV)* flicker(ing); *(heiße Luft)* heat-haze.

geflissentlich *adj (geh)* deliberate.

geflochten *ptp of* **flechten.**

geflogen *ptp of* **fliegen.**

geflohen *ptp of* **fliehen.**

geflossen *ptp of* **fließen.**

Geflügel *nt no pl (Zool, Cook)* poultry *no pl*.

Geflügel- *in cpds* poultry; **~händler** *m* poulterer, poultry dealer; **~schere** *f* poultry shears *pl*.

geflügelt *adj* winged. **~e Worte** familiar quotations.

Geflüster *nt no pl* whispering.

gefochten *ptp of* **fechten.**

Gefolge *nt* - retinue; *(Trauer~)* cortège. **im ~** in the wake *(+gen* of*)*; **etw im ~ haben** *(fig)* to bring sth in its wake.

Gefolgschaft *f (die Anhänger)* following; *(Hist: Gefolge)* retinue.

gefragt *adj* in demand *pred*.

gefräßig *adj* gluttonous; *(fig geh)* voracious.

Gefräßigkeit *f* gluttony.

Gefreite(r) *mf decl as adj (Mil)* lance corporal *(Brit)*, private first class *(US)*.

gefressen *ptp of* **fressen. jdn ~ haben** *(col)* to be sick of sb *(col)*.

gefrieren* *vi irreg aux sein (lit, fig)* to freeze.

Gefrier-: ~fach *nt* freezer compartment; **g~getrocknet** *adj* freeze-dried; **~punkt** *m* freezing point; **~truhe** *f* freezer, deep freeze.

gefroren *ptp of* **frieren, gefrieren.**

Gefüge *nt* - *(lit, fig)* structure.

gefügig *adj* submissive; *(gehorsam)* obedient. **jdn ~ machen** to make sb bend to one's will.

Gefühl *nt* **-e** feeling; *(~sregung auch)* emotion. **etw im ~ haben** to have a feel for sth; **ich habe ein ~, als ob ...** I feel as though ...; **ein ~ für Zahlen/Musik** a feeling for figures/music; **ein ~ für Gerechtigkeit/Anstand** a sense of justice/decency.

gefühllos *adj* insensitive, unfeeling; *Bein* numb.

Gefühllosigkeit *f siehe adj* insensitivity; numbness.

Gefühls-: ~ausbruch *m* emotional outburst; **g~betont** *adj* emotional; *Rede, Äußerung auch* emotive; **~duselei** *f (pej)* mawkishness; **g~ kalt** *adj* cold; **~kälte** *f* coldness; **~leben** *nt* emotional life; **g~mäßig** *adj* instinctive; **~mensch** *m* emotional person; **~regung** *f* stir of emotion; *(seelische Empfindung)* feeling.

gefühlvoll *adj (empfindsam)* sensitive; *(ausdrucksvoll)* expressive; *(liebevoll)* loving.

gefüllt *adj (Cook)* stuffed; *Pralinen* with soft centres *(Brit) or* centers *(US)*; *Brieftasche* full.

gefunden 1 *ptp of* **finden. 2** *adj* **das war ein ~es Fressen für ihn** that was handing it to him on a plate.

gefürchtet *adj* dreaded *usu attr*.

Gegacker *nt no pl (lit, fig)* cackle, cackling.

gegangen *ptp of* **gehen.**

gegeben 1 *ptp of* **geben. 2** *adj* given; *(Philos: real)* factual. **unter den ~en Umständen** given the circumstances; **bei den ~en Tatsachen** given these facts; **etw als ~ voraussetzen** to assume sth; **zu ~er Zeit** in due course.

gegebenenfalls *adv* should the situation arise.

Gegebenheit *f usu pl* (actual) fact; *(Zustand)* condition.

gegen *prep+acc* **(a)** *(wider)* against. **X ~ Y** *(Sport, Jur)* X versus Y; **~ seinen Befehl** contrary to *or* against his orders; **haben Sie ein Mittel ~ Schnupfen?** do you have anything for colds?; **nichts ~ jdn/etw haben** to have nothing against sb/sth. **(b)** *(in Richtung auf)* towards, toward; *(nach)* to; *(an)* against. **~ einen Baum fahren** to drive into a tree; **etw ~ das Licht halten** to hold sth to *or* against the light; **~ Osten fahren** to travel to(wards) the east; **es wird ~ Abend kühler** it grows cooler towards evening. **(c)** *(ungefähr)* round about, around. **ich komme ~ Abend vorbei** I'll come around early this evening. **(d)** *(gegenüber)* towards, toward, to. **gerecht ~ alle** fair to all. **(e)** *(im Austausch für)* for. **~ bar** for cash; **~ Quittung** against a receipt; **~ Bezahlung** in exchange for payment. **(f)** *(verglichen mit)* compared with.

Gegen-: ~angriff *m (Mil, fig)* counterattack; **~argument** *nt* counterargument; **~beispiel** *nt* counterexample; **~besuch** *m* return visit; **jdm einen ~besuch machen** to return sb's visit; **~beweis** *m* **den ~beweis zu etw erbringen** to produce evidence against sth.

Gegend *f* **-en** area; *(geographisches Gebiet, Körper~)* region. **die ~ von London** the London area; **hier in der ~** around here; **die ganze ~ spricht davon** the whole neighbourhood *(Brit) or* neighborhood *(US)* is talking about it.

Gegendarstellung *f (Press)* reply.

gegen|einander *adv* against each other; *(im Austausch)* for each other; *(zueinander)* to(wards) each other.

gegen|einander-: ~halten *vt sep irreg (lit)* to hold together; *(fig)* to compare; **~stehen** *vi sep irreg (fig)* to be on opposite sides; *(Aussagen)* to conflict; **~stoßen** *vi sep irreg aux sein* to bump into each other; *(kollidieren)* to collide.

Gegen-: ~erklärung *f* counterstatement; *(Dementi)* denial, disclaimer; **~fahrbahn** *f* oncoming lane; **~frage** *f* counterquestion; **jdm eine ~frage stellen** to ask sb a question in reply (to his); **~gerade** *f (Sport)* back straight; **~gewicht** *nt* counterbalance *(auch fig)*, counterweight; **~gift** *nt* antidote *(gegen* to*)*; **~kandidat** *m* rival candidate; **~kurs** *m (lit, fig)* opposite course; **einen ~kurs steuern** to take an opposing course of action; **~leistung** *f* service in return; **als ~leistung für etw** in return for sth; **~licht** *nt* **etw bei** *or* **im ~ aufnehmen** *(Phot)* to take a contre-jour photo(graph) of sth; **~liebe** *f* requited love; *(fig: Zustimmung)* approval; **der Vorschlag stieß auf wenig ~liebe** the suggestion was hardly welcomed with open arms; **~maßnahme** *f* countermeasure; **~maßnahmen zur Bekämpfung der Inflation** measures to counter inflation; **~meinung** *f* opposite opinion; **~mittel** *nt (Med)* antidote *(gegen* to*)*; **~partei** *f* other side; *(Sport)* opposing side; *(Jur)* opposing party; **~probe** *f* crosscheck; **~reaktion** *f* counter-reaction; **~rede** *f (Antwort)* reply; *(Widerrede)* contradiction; **~richtung** *f* opposite direction.

Gegensatz *m* **¨e** opposite; *(Kontrast)* contrast; *(Unvereinbarkeit)* conflict; *(Unterschied)* difference. **im ~ zu** unlike, in contrast to; **einen krassen ~ zu etw bilden** to contrast sharply with sth; **¨~e ausgleichen** to even out differences.

gegensätzlich *adj (konträr)* contrasting; *(widersprüchlich)* opposing; *(unterschiedlich)* different; *(unvereinbar)* conflicting. **eine ~e Meinung** a conflicting view.

Gegen-: ~schlag *m (Mil)* reprisal; *(fig)* retaliation *no pl*; **zum ~schlag ausholen** to prepare to retaliate; **~seite** *f (lit, fig)* other side; **g~seitig** *adj* mutual; **sie beschuldigten sich g~seitig** they (each) accused one another; **sich g~seitig ausschließen** to be mutually exclusive; **in g~seitigem Einverständnis** by mutual agreement; **~seitigkeit** *f* mutuality; **ein Vertrag auf ~seitigkeit** a reciprocal treaty; **~sinn** *m* **im ~sinn** in the opposite direction; **~spieler** *m* opponent; *(bei Mannschaftsspielen auch)* opposite number; **~sprechanlage** *f* (two-way) intercom.

Gegenstand *m* **¨e** *(Ding)* object, thing; *(Thema)* subject; *(der Neugier etc, Philos)* object. **~ des Gespötts** laughing stock.

gegenständlich *adj* concrete; *(Philos)* objective; *(Art)* representational.

gegenstandslos *adj (grundlos)* groundless; *(hinfällig)* irrelevant.

Gegen-: ~stimme *f (Parl)* vote against; **~stoß** *m (Mil, Sport)* counterattack; **~stück** *nt* opposite; *(passendes ~stück)* counterpart.

Gegenteil *nt* opposite *(von* of*)*; *(Umkehrung)* reverse *(von* of*)*. **im ~!** on the contrary!; **ganz im ~** quite the reverse; **das ~ bewirken** to have the opposite effect; *(Mensch)* to achieve the exact opposite; **ins ~ umschlagen** to swing to the other extreme.

gegenteilig *adj Ansicht, Wirkung* opposite, contrary. **eine ~e Meinung** a different opinion; **ich habe nichts G~es gehört** I've heard nothing to the contrary.

Gegentor *nt (esp Ftbl)* **ein ~ hinnehmen müssen** to concede a goal; **ein ~ erzielen** to score.

gegen|über 1 *prep+dat* **(a)** *(örtlich)* opposite. **er wohnt mir ~** he lives opposite me; **er saß mir schräg ~** he sat diagonally across from me. **(b)** *(zu)* to; *(in bezug auf)* with regard to, toward(s); *(angesichts, vor)* in the face of; *(im Vergleich zu)* in comparison with. **mir ~ hat er das nicht geäußert** he didn't say that to me; **er ist allem Neuen ~ wenig aufgeschlossen** he's not very open-minded about anything new. **2** *adv* opposite. **der Park ~** the park opposite; **die Leute von ~** *(col)* the people opposite.

Gegen|über *nt* **-** *(bei Kampf)* opponent; *(bei Diskussion)* opposite number. **mein ~ im Zug** the person opposite me in the train.

gegen|über-: ~liegen *sep irreg* **1** *vi+dat* to be opposite, to face; **2** *vr* **sich** *(dat)* **~liegen** to face each other; **~liegend** *adj attr* opposite; **~sehen** *vr sep irreg+dat* **sich einer Aufgabe ~sehen** to be faced *or* confronted with a task; **~sitzen** *vi sep irreg* to sit opposite *or* facing; **~stehen** *vi sep irreg +dat* to be opposite, to face; **jdm feindlich/freundlich ~stehen** to have a hostile/friendly attitude towards sb; **einer Gefahr ~stehen** to be faced with a danger; **~stellen** *vt sep (konfrontieren mit)* to confront *(dat* with*)*; *(fig: vergleichen)* to compare *(dat* with*)*; **G~stellung** *f* confrontation; *(fig: Vergleich)* comparison; **~treten** *vi sep irreg aux sein* **jdm ~treten** to face sb.

Gegen-: ~verkehr *m* oncoming traffic; **~vorschlag** *m* counter-proposal.

Gegenwart *f no pl* **(a)** present; *(Gram)* present (tense). **die Musik der ~** contemporary music; **die Probleme der ~** the problems of today. **(b)** *(Anwesenheit)* presence. **in ~ von** in the presence of.

gegenwärtig 1 *adj* **(a)** *attr (jetzig)* present; *(heutig auch)* current, present-day. **(b)** *(geh: anwesend)* present *pred*. **2** *adv (augenblicklich)* at present; *(heutzutage auch)* currently.

gegenwartsbezogen *adj Roman etc* relevant to present times.

Gegen-: ~wehr *f* resistance; **~wert** *m* equivalent; **~wind** *m* headwind; **g~zeichnen** *vt sep* to countersign; **~zeuge** *m* witness for the other side; **~zug** *m* **im ~zug zu etw** as a countermove to sth.

gegessen *ptp of* **essen.**

geglichen *ptp of* **gleichen.**

gegliedert *adj* jointed; *(fig)* structured.

geglitten *ptp of* **gleiten.**

geglommen *ptp of* **glimmen.**

geglückt *adj Feier* successful; *Überraschung* real.

Gegner(in *f***)** *m* **-** opponent *(auch Sport)*, adversary; *(Rivale)* rival; *(Feind)* enemy.

gegnerisch *adj attr* opposing; *(Mil: feindlich)* enemy *attr*, hostile; *Übermacht* of the enemy.

Gegnerschaft *f* opposition.

gegolten *ptp of* **gelten.**

gegoren *ptp of* **gären.**

gegossen *ptp of* **gießen.**

gegr. = **gegründet** established, est.

gegraben *ptp of* **graben.**

gegriffen *ptp of* **greifen.**

Gehabe *nt no pl (col)* affected behaviour *(Brit) or* behavior *(US)*.

gehabt *ptp of* **haben.**

Gehackte(s) *nt decl as adj* mince *(Brit)*, minced *or* ground *(US)* meat.

Gehalt[1] *m* **-e** content. **der ~ an Eiweiß** the protein content.

Gehalt[2] *nt* **¨er** salary.

gehalten 1 *ptp of* **halten. 2** *adj:* **~ sein, etw zu tun** *(form)* to be required to do sth.

gehaltlos *adj Nahrung* unnutritious; *(fig)* empty.

Gehalts-: ~abrechnung *f* salary statement; **~anspruch** *m* salary claim; **~empfänger** *m* **~empfänger sein** to receive a salary, to be salaried; **~erhöhung** *f* salary increase; *(regelmäßig)* increment; **~klasse** *f* salary bracket; **~konto** *nt* current *(Brit) or* checking *(US)* account; **~kürzung** *f* cut in salary; **~wunsch** *m* salary requirement; **~zulage** *f (~erhöhung)* salary increase; *(regelmäßig)* increment; *(Extrazulage)* bonus.

gehaltvoll *adj Speise* nutritious, nourishing; *(fig)* rich in content.
gehandikapt [gə'hɛndikɛpt] *adj* handicapped.
Gehänge *nt* - garland; *(Ohr~)* drop, pendant.
gehangen *ptp of* **hängen.**
geharnischt *adj (fig) Antwort etc* sharp, strong.
gehässig *adj* spiteful.
Gehässigkeit *f* spite, spitefulness.
gehäuft *adj Löffel* heaped.
Gehäuse *nt* - **(a)** case, casing; *(Lautsprecher~)* box. **(b)** *(Schnecken~)* shell. **(c)** *(Obst~)* core.
gehbehindert *adj* disabled.
Gehege *nt* - reserve; *(im Zoo)* enclosure, compound; *(Wild~)* preserve. **jdm ins ~ kommen** *(fig col)* to get under sb's feet *(col)*; *(ein Recht streitig machen)* to poach on sb's preserves.
geheiligt *adj Brauch, Recht* sacred.
geheim *adj* secret. **seine ~sten Gefühle/Wünsche** his innermost *or* most private feelings/wishes; **streng ~** top secret.
Geheim-: **~bund** *m* secret society; **~dienst** *m* secret service; **~fach** *nt* secret compartment; **g~halten** *vt sep irreg* **etw (vor jdm) g~halten** to keep sth a secret (from sb).
Geheimhaltung *f* secrecy. **zur ~ von etw verpflichtet sein** to be sworn to secrecy about sth.
Geheimnis *nt* secret; *(rätselhaftes ~)* mystery. **das ~ der Schönheit/des Erfolgs** the secret of beauty/success; **aus etw ein/kein ~ machen** to make a big secret about sth/no secret of sth.
Geheimnis-: **~krämer** *m (col)* mystery-monger *(col)*; **g~voll** *adj* mysterious; **g~voll tun** to be mysterious.
Geheim-: **~polizei** *f* secret police; **~rat** *m* privy councillor; **~ratsecken** *pl (col)* **er hat ~ratsecken** he is going bald at the temples; **~rezept** *nt* secret recipe; **~tip** *m* (personal) tip; **~waffe** *f* secret weapon.
Geheiß *nt no pl (geh)* **auf jds ~** *(acc)* at sb's behest.
geheißen *ptp of* **heißen.**
gehemmt *adj Mensch* inhibited.
gehen *pret* **ging,** *ptp* **gegangen** *aux sein* **1** *vi* **(a)** to go; *(zu Fuß)* to walk; *(abfahren, ausscheiden auch)* to leave; *(blicken: Fenster)* to look out *(auf +acc, nach* onto*)*. **über die Straße ~** to cross the road; **auf die andere Seite ~** to cross (over) to the other side; **zu jdm ~** to go to see sb; **er ging im Zimmer auf und ab** he walked *or* paced up and down the room; **wie lange geht man bis zum Bus?** how long a walk is it to the bus?; **wie geht man dorthin?** how do you get there?; **das Kind lernt ~** the baby is learning to walk; **wo er geht und steht** wherever he goes *or* is; **schwimmen/schlafen ~** to go swimming/to bed; **mit jdm ~** *(befreundet sein)* to go out with sb, to be with sb; **mit der Zeit/Mode ~** to move with the times/follow the fashion; **in sich** *(acc)* **~** to think things over; **nach einer Regel ~** to follow a *or* go by a rule; **das geht gegen meine Überzeugung** that goes *or* runs against my convictions; **er ging so weit, zu behaupten ...** *(fig)* he went so far as to claim ...; **das geht zu weit** *(fig)* that's going too far; **wie geht das Lied/Gedicht?** how does the song/poem go?; **heute geht ein scharfer Wind** there's a biting wind today; **die See geht hoch** there's a high sea, the sea is running high; **die Reise geht über Dresden** we/they *etc* are going via Dresden; **~ wir!** let's go; **das Schiff geht nach Harwich** the boat is going to *or* is bound for Harwich; **jdm aus dem Weg ~** to get *or* move out of sb's way.

(b) *(funktionieren)* to work; *(Auto, Uhr)* to go. **die Uhr geht falsch/richtig** the clock is wrong/right.

(c) *(dauern)* to go on. **wie lange geht das denn noch?** how much longer is it going to go on?

(d) *(reichen)* to go. **der Rock geht ihr bis zum Knie** her skirt goes down to her knees; **in die Tausende ~** to run into (the) thousands.

(e) *(Teig)* to rise; *(vor dem Backen auch)* to prove.

(f) *(urteilen)* **nach etw ~** to go by sth.

(g) *(sich kleiden)* **in etw** *(dat)* **~** to wear sth.

(h) *(ertönen: Klingel)* to go, to ring.

(i) wie ~ die Geschäfte? how's business?; **wieviele Leute ~ in deinen Wagen?** how many people can you get in your car?; **in diese Schachtel ~ 20 Stück** this packet holds 20; **das Buch ging um ...** the book was about ...; **mein Vorschlag geht dahin, daß ...** my suggestion is that ...; **diese Schublade geht schwer** this drawer is very stiff; **nichts geht über** *(+acc)* **...** there's nothing to beat ..., there's nothing better than ...; **in die Politik ~** to go into politics; **in die Gewerkschaft/Partei ~** to join the union/party; **unter die Künstler/Säufer ~** *(usu hum)* to join the ranks of artists/alcoholics; **das geht doch nicht** *(ist nicht möglich)* that's not on; **Dienstag geht auch nicht** *(col)* Tuesday is no good either; **was geht hier vor sich?** what's going on here?

2 *vi impers* **(a)** *(gesundheitlich)* **wie geht es Ihnen?** how are you?; *(zu Patient)* how are you feeling?; **(danke,) es geht** *(col)* all right *or* not too bad(, thanks) *(col)*; **es geht ihm gut/schlecht** he's quite well/not at all well; **sonst geht's dir gut?** *(iro)* are you sure you're feeling quite all right? *(iro)*.

(b) *(ergehen)* **wie geht's?** how are things?; *(bei Arbeit etc)* how's it going?; **es geht** not too bad, so-so; **mir ist es genauso gegangen** *(ich habe dasselbe erlebt)* it was just the same with me; *(ich habe dasselbe empfunden)* I felt the same way; **laß es dir gut ~** look after yourself, take care of yourself.

(c) es geht *(läßt sich machen)* it's all right *or* OK *(col)*; **solange es geht** as long as possible; **geht es?** *(ohne Hilfe)* can you manage?; **es geht nicht** *(ist nicht möglich)* it can't be done, it's impossible; *(kommt nicht in Frage)* it's not on; **so geht das, das geht so** that/this is how it's done; **so geht es** *or* **das (eben)** *(so ist das Leben)* that's how it goes; **morgen geht es nicht** tomorrow's no good.

(d) *(betreffen)* **ich weiß nicht, worum es geht** I don't know what this is about; **es geht um seinen Vertrag** it's about *or* it concerns his contract; **es geht um meine Ehre** my honour is at stake; **es geht ihm nur um eins** he's only interested in one thing; **darum geht es mir nicht** that's not the point; *(spielt keine Rolle)* that's not important to me; **wenn es nach mir ginge ...** if it were *or* was up to me ..., if I had my way ...

(e) *(führen)* **dann geht es immer geradeaus** *(Straßenrichtung)* then it's just straight on.

3 *vt* **er ging einen Kilometer** he walked a kilometre; **ich gehe immer diese Straße** I always walk *or* go along this road.
Gehen *nt no pl (Zu-Fuß-~, Sport)* walking; *(Abschied)* leaving.
gehenlassen* *sep irreg* **1** *vt (col: in Ruhe lassen)* to leave alone. **2** *vr* **(a)** to lose one's self-control. **(b)** *(nachlässig sein)* to let oneself go.
Geher(in *f)* *m* - *(Sport)* walker.
gehetzt *adj* harassed.
geheuer *adj* **nicht ~** *(beängstigend)* scary *(col)*; *(spukhaft)* creepy *(col)*; *(verdächtig)* fishy; *(unwohl)* uneasy; **es ist mir nicht ganz ~** it's scary *(col)*; it gives me the creeps *(col)*; it seems a bit fishy to me; I feel uneasy about it.
Gehilfe *m (wk)* **-n, -n, Gehilfin** *f (kaufmännischer ~)* trainee; *(Jur)* accomplice.
Gehirn *nt* **-e** brain; *(Geist)* mind.
Gehirn-: **~chirurg** *m* brain surgeon; **~erschütterung** *f* concussion; **~schlag** *m* stroke; **~wäsche** *f* brainwashing *no pl*; **jdn einer ~wäsche unterziehen** to brainwash sb.

gehoben 1 *ptp of* **heben. 2** *adj Ausdrucksweise* elevated, lofty; *(anspruchsvoll)* sophisticated; *Stellung* senior; *Stimmung* elated. **~er Dienst** *professional and executive levels of the civil service.*
Gehöft *nt* **-e** farm.
geholfen *ptp of* **helfen.**
Gehölz *nt* **-e** *(geh)* copse; *(Dickicht)* undergrowth.
Gehör *nt* **-e** hearing; *(Mus)* ear. **kein musikalisches ~ haben** to have no ear for music; **ein schlechtes ~ haben** to be hard of hearing; **nach dem ~ spielen** to play by ear; **absolutes ~** perfect pitch; **das ~ verlieren** to go deaf; **~ finden** to gain a hearing; **er fand kein ~** he was not given a hearing; **jdm ~/kein ~ schenken** to listen/not to listen to sb; **sich** *(dat)* **~ verschaffen** to gain attention; *(bei Behörde)* to obtain a hearing.
gehorchen* *vi* to obey *(jdm* sb*)*; *(Wagen, Maschine etc)* to respond *(jdm/einer Sache* to sb/sth*)*. **seine Stimme gehorchte ihm nicht mehr** he lost control over his voice.
gehören* 1 *vi* **(a) jdm ~** to belong to sb, to be sb's. **(b)** *(den richtigen Platz haben)* to belong; *(Gegenstand auch)* to go. **das gehört nicht hierher** *(Vorschlag)* that is irrelevant here; **das gehört nicht zur Sache** that's irrelevant; **er gehört ins Bett** he should be in bed. **(c) ~ zu** *(zählen zu)* to be one of; *(Bestandteil sein von)* to be part of; *(Mitglied sein von)* to belong to; **es gehört zu seinen Pflichten** it's one of his duties; **zur Familie ~** to be one of the family; **dazu gehört Mut** that takes courage; **dazu gehört (schon) einiges** *or* **etwas** that takes some doing *(col)*. **2** *vr* to be (right and) proper. **das gehört sich einfach nicht** that's just not done.
gehörig *adj* **(a)** *(geh)* **nicht zur Sache ~** irrelevant. **(b)** *attr, adv (gebührend)* proper. **mit dem ~en Respekt** with proper respect. **(c)** *(col: beträchtlich, groß)* good *attr,* well and truly *adv.* **eine ~e Achtung vor jdm haben** to have a healthy respect for sb.
gehörlos *adj (form)* deaf.
Gehörlose(r) *mf decl as adj (form)* deaf person.
gehorsam *adj* obedient.
Gehorsam *m no pl* obedience. **jdm den ~ verweigern** to refuse to obey sb.
Gehorsamkeit *f* obedience.
Gehörsinn *m* sense of hearing.
Gehsteig *m* pavement *(Brit)*, sidewalk *(US)*.
Gehweg *m* footpath.
Geier *m* **-** *(lit, fig)* vulture. **weiß der ~** *(col)* God knows *(col)*.
Geifer *m no pl* slaver; *(fig pej)* venom.
geifern *vi* to slaver; *(Schaum vor dem Mund haben)* to foam at the mouth. **gegen jdn/etw ~** to revile sb/sth.
Geige *f* **-n** violin. **die erste/zweite ~ spielen** *(lit)* to play first/second violin; *(fig)* to call the tune/play second fiddle.
geigen 1 *vi* to play the violin. **2** *vt Lied* to play on the violin.
Geigen-: ~bogen *m* violin bow; **~kasten** *m* violin-case.
Geiger(in *f)* *m* **-** violinist.
Geigerzähler *m* Geiger counter.
geil *adj* randy, horny; *(pej: lüstern)* lecherous.
Geilheit *f siehe adj* randiness, horniness; lecherousness.
Geisel *f* **-n** hostage. **jdn als ~ nehmen** to take sb hostage.
Geisel-: ~nahme *f* **-n** taking of hostages *no pl;* **~nehmer(in** *f)* *m* hostage-taker.
Geiß *f* **-en** *(Ziege)* (nanny-)goat.
Geißbock *m* billy-goat.
Geißel *f* **-n** *(lit, fig)* scourge; *(dial: Peitsche)* whip.
geißeln *vt (anprangern)* to castigate.
Geist *m* **-er (a)** *no pl (Denken, Vernunft)* mind. **~ und Materie** mind and matter; **etw im ~(e) vor sich sehen** to see sth in one's mind's eye; **sich im ~(e) als etw/an einem Ort sehen** to picture oneself as sth/in a place.
(b) *(Rel: Seele, außerirdisches Wesen)* spirit; *(Gespenst)* ghost. **~ und Körper** mind and body; **seinen ~ aufgeben** to give up the ghost; **der Heilige ~** the Holy Ghost *or* Spirit; **der ~ Gottes** the Spirit of God; **von allen guten ~ern verlassen sein** *(col)* to have taken leave of one's senses *(col)*.
(c) *(no pl: Intellekt)* intellect, mind; *(fig: Denker, Genie)* mind. **~ haben** to have a good mind *or* intellect; *(Witz)* to be witty; **hier scheiden sich die ~er** this is the parting of the ways; **sie sind verwandte ~er** they are kindred spirits.
(d) *no pl (Wesen, Gesinnung)* spirit. **in jds ~ handeln** to act in the spirit of sb.
Geister-: ~bahn *f* ghost train; **~fahrer** *m (col)* ghost-driver *(US col), person driving in the wrong direction;* **~hand** *f*: **wie von ~hand** as if by magic.
geistern *vi aux sein* to wander like a ghost. **der Gedanke geisterte durch sein Hirn** the thought haunted him.
Geister-: ~stadt *f* ghost town; **~stimme** *f* ghostly voice; **~stunde** *f* witching hour.
Geistes-: g~abwesend *adj* absent-minded; **~abwesenheit** *f* absent-mindedness; **~arbeiter** *m* brain-worker *(col)*; **~armut** intellectual poverty; **~blitz** *m* brainwave; **~gabe** *f* intellectual gift; **~gegenwart** *f* presence of mind; **g~gegenwärtig** *adj* quick-witted; **g~gegenwärtig duckte er sich unter das Steuer** with great presence of mind he ducked below the steering wheel; **g~gestört** *adj* mentally disturbed *or (stärker)* deranged; **~größe** *f* **(a)** *no pl (Genialität)* greatness of mind; **(b)** *(genialer Mensch)* great mind, genius; **~haltung** *f* mental attitude; **g~krank** *adj* mentally ill; **~kranke(r)** *mf* mentally ill person; **die ~kranken** the mentally ill; **~krankheit** *f* mental illness; *(Wahnsinn)* insanity; **~verfassung** *f* frame of mind; **g~verwandt** *adj* **die beiden sind g~verwandt** they are kindred spirits; **~wissenschaft** *f* arts subject; **die ~wissenschaften** the arts; *(als Studium)* the humanities; **~wissenschaftler** *m* arts scholar; *(Student)* arts student; **g~wissenschaftlich** *adj Fach* arts *attr;* **~zustand** *m* mental condition; **jdn auf seinen ~zustand untersuchen** to give sb a psychiatric examination.
geistig *adj* **(a)** *(unkörperlich)* spiritual. **~-seelisch** mental and spiritual. **(b)** *(intellektuell)* intellectual; *(Psych)* mental. **~e Arbeit** intellectual work; **~ anspruchsvoll/anspruchslos** intellectually demanding/undemanding, highbrow/lowbrow; **~er Diebstahl** plagiarism; **~es Eigentum** intellectual property; **~ behindert/zurückgeblieben** mentally handicapped/retarded; **etw vor seinem ~en Auge sehen** to see sth in one's mind's eye. **(c)** *attr (alkoholisch)* spirituous.
geistlich *adj* spiritual; *(religiös)* religious. **~es Amt/~er Orden** religious office/order; **~es Recht** canon law; **der ~e Stand** the clergy.
Geistliche *f (wk)* **-n, -n** woman priest; *(von Freikirchen)* woman minister.
Geistliche(r) *m decl as adj* clergyman; *(Priester)* priest; *(von Freikirchen)* minister; *(Gefängnis~, Militär~ etc)* chaplain.
Geistlichkeit *f siehe* **Geistliche(r)** clergy; priesthood; ministry.
Geist-: g~los *adj* stupid; *(langweilig)* dull; *(einfallslos)* unimaginative; **~losigkeit** *f* **(a)** *no pl siehe adj* stupidity; dullness; unimaginativeness; **(b)** *(Äußerung)* stupid remark; **g~reich** *adj (witzig)* witty; *(klug)* intelligent; *(einfallsreich)* ingenious; *Beschäftigung, Gespräch* intellectually stimulating; **g~tötend** *adj* soul-destroying; **g~voll** *adj Mensch, Äußerung* wise; *Buch, Beschäftigung* intellectual.
Geiz *m no pl* meanness.

geizen *vi* to be mean; *(mit Worten, Zeit)* to be sparing.

Geizhals *m* miser.

geizig *adj* mean.

Geizkragen *m (col)* skinflint *(col)*.

gekannt *ptp of* **kennen.**

Gekicher *nt no pl* giggling.

Gekläff *nt no pl* yapping.

gekleidet *adj* dressed. **weiß ~** dressed in white.

Geklimper *nt no pl (col) (Klavier~)* tinkling; *(stümperhaft)* plonking *(col)*; *(von Geld)* jingling.

Geklirr(e) *nt no pl* clinking; *(von Fensterscheiben)* rattling; *(von Ketten etc)* clanking; *(von Waffen)* clashing.

geklungen *ptp of* **klingen.**

Geknatter *nt no pl (von Motorrad)* roaring.

geknickt *adj (col)* glum, dejected.

gekniffen *ptp of* **kneifen.**

gekommen *ptp of* **kommen.**

gekonnt 1 *ptp of* **können. 2** *adj* neat; *(meisterhaft)* masterly.

Gekrakel *nt no pl (col)* scrawl.

gekräuselt *adj* ruffled.

Gekreisch(e) *nt no pl* screeching.

Gekritzel *nt no pl (Gekritzeltes)* scribble.

gekrochen *ptp of* **kriechen.**

gekühlt *adj* chilled.

gekünstelt *adj* artificial; *Sprache, Benehmen auch* affected.

Gel *nt* **-e** gel.

Gelächter *nt* **-** laughter. **in ~ ausbrechen** to burst out laughing; **jdn dem ~ preisgeben** *(geh)* to make sb a laughing stock.

geläckmeiert *adj (col)* conned *(col)*.

geladen 1 *ptp of* **laden. 2** *adj* loaded; *(Phys)* charged; *(col: wütend)* hopping mad *(col)*.

Gelage *nt* **-** feast, banquet.

gelagert *adj* **in anders/ähnlich ~en Fällen** in different/similar cases.

gelähmt *adj* paralyzed.

Gelände *nt* **- (a)** *(Land)* open country; *(Mil: Terrain)* ground. **offenes ~** open country; **schwieriges ~** difficult terrain *or* country. **(b)** *(Gebiet)* area. **(c)** *(Grundstück)* grounds *pl; (Bau~)* site.

Gelände-: ~fahrt *f* cross-country drive; **~fahrzeug** *nt* cross-country vehicle; **g~gängig** *adj Fahrzeug* suitable for cross-country work.

Geländer *nt* **-** railing(s *pl*); *(Treppen~)* bannister(s *pl*).

gelang *pret of* **gelingen.**

gelangen* *vi aux sein* **an/auf etw** *(acc)*/**zu etw ~** *(lit, fig)* to reach sth; *(fig: mit Mühe)* to attain sth; *(erwerben)* to acquire sth; **zum Ziel ~** to reach one's goal; **in jds Besitz ~** to come into sb's possession; **in die richtigen/falschen Hände ~** to fall into the right/wrong hands; **zu Ruhm ~** to achieve fame; **zu einer Überzeugung ~** to become convinced; **an die Macht ~** to come to power.

gelangweilt *adj* bored *no adv*.

gelassen 1 *ptp of* **lassen. 2** *adj* calm. **etw ~ hinnehmen** to take sth calmly.

Gelassenheit *f* calmness.

Gelatine [ʒela'tiːnə] *f no pl* gelatine.

gelaufen *ptp of* **laufen.**

geläufig *adj* common; *(vertraut)* familiar. **das ist mir nicht ~** I'm not familiar with that.

gelaunt *adj pred* **gut/schlecht ~** good-/bad-tempered; *(vorübergehend)* in a good/bad mood.

gelb *adj* yellow; *(bei Verkehrsampel)* amber *(Brit)*.

Gelb *nt* **-** *or (col)* **-s** yellow; *(von Verkehrsampel)* amber *(Brit)*.

Gelbe(s) *nt decl as adj (vom Ei)* yolk. **das war nicht gerade das ~ vom Ei** *(col)* that wasn't exactly brilliant.

gelbgrün *adj* yellowish-green.

gelblich *adj* yellowish; *Gesichtsfarbe* sallow.

Gelb-: ~sucht *f* jaundice; **g~süchtig** *adj* jaundiced.

Geld *nt* **-er (a)** money. **bares/großes/kleines ~** cash/notes *pl (Brit)*, bills *pl (US)*/change; **~ und Gut** wealth and possessions; **~ aufnehmen** to raise money; **zu ~ machen** to sell off; **(mit etw) ~ machen** *(col)* to make money (from sth); **etw für teures ~ kaufen** to pay a lot for sth; **er hat ~ wie Heu** *(col)* he's stinking rich *(col)*; **mit ~ um sich werfen** to chuck one's money around *(col)*; **jdm das ~ aus der Tasche ziehen** to squeeze money out of sb; **am ~ hängen** *or* **kleben** to be tight with money; **hinterm ~ hersein** *(col)* to be out for money; **das ist nicht für ~ zu haben** *(col)* that can't be bought; **sie/das ist nicht mit ~ zu bezahlen** *(col)* she/that is priceless; **nicht für ~ und gute Worte** *(col)* not for love nor money; **~ oder Leben!** your money or your life!; **~ stinkt nicht** *(Prov)* there's nothing wrong with money; **~ regiert die Welt** *(Prov)* money makes the world go round *(prov)*.
(b) *(~summen)* **~er** *pl* money, monies *pl;* **staatliche ~er** state funds *pl or* money.
(c) *(St Ex: ~kurs)* buying rate.

Geld-: ~angelegenheit *f* financial matter; **jds ~angelegenheiten** sb's financial affairs; **~anlage** *f* (financial) investment; **~automat** *m* cash dispenser; **~beutel** *m*, **~börse** *f* purse; **tief in den ~beutel greifen** *(col)* to dig deep (into one's pocket) *(col)*; **~dinge** *pl* financial *or* money matters *pl*; **~einwurf** *m* slot; **beim ~einwurf** when inserting the money; **~geber(in** *f***)** *m* financial backer; *(esp Rad, TV)* sponsor; *(hum: Arbeitgeber)* employer; **~geschäft** *nt* financial transaction; **~gier** *f* avarice; **g~gierig** *adj* avaricious; **~knappheit** *f* shortage of money; **~kurs** *m (St Ex)* buying rate.

geldlich *adj* financial.

Geld-: ~mangel *m* lack of money; **~markt** *m* money market; **~menge** *f* money supply; **~mittel** *pl* funds *pl;* **~quelle** *f* source of income; **~schein** *m* banknote *(Brit)*, bill *(US)*; **~schrank** *m* safe; **~schwierigkeiten** *pl* financial difficulties *pl;* **~sorgen** *pl* **in ~sorgen sein** to have financial worries; **~spende** *f* donation, gift of money; **~strafe** *f* fine; **jdn zu einer ~strafe verurteilen** to fine sb; **~stück** *nt* coin; **~umlauf** *m* circulation of money; **~verkehr** *m* transactions *pl;* **~verleiher** *m* moneylender; **~verschwendung** *f* waste of money; **~wechsel** *m* exchange of money; **„~wechsel“** “bureau de change”; **~wert** *m* cash value; *(Fin: Kaufkraft)* currency value.

geleckt *adj* **wie ~ aussehen** to be neat and tidy.

Gelee [ʒe'leː] *m or nt* **-s** jelly.

gelegen 1 *ptp of* **liegen. 2** *adj* **(a)** *(befindlich) Haus* situated. **(b)** *(passend)* **zu ~er Zeit** at a convenient time; **das kommt mir sehr ~** that's most convenient. **(c)** *pred (wichtig)* **mir ist viel/nichts daran ~** it matters a great deal/doesn't matter to me.

Gelegenheit *f* **(a)** *(günstiger Umstand)* opportunity. **bei ~** some time (or other); **bei passender/der ersten (besten) ~** when I get the opportunity/at the first opportunity. **(b)** *(Anlaß)* occasion. **bei dieser ~** on this occasion. **(c)** *(~skauf)* bargain.

Gelegenheits-: ~arbeit *f* **(a)** casual work *no pl;* **(b)** *(eines Autors)* minor work; **~arbeiter** *m* casual labourer *(Brit) or* laborer *(US)*; **~kauf** *m* bargain; **~raucher** *m* occasional smoker; **~trinker** *m* occasional drinker.

gelegentlich 1 *adj attr* occasional. **2** *adv (manchmal)* occasionally, now and again; *(bei Gelegenheit)* some time (or other). **lassen Sie ~ etwas von sich hören!** keep in touch.

gelehrig *adj* quick to learn. **sich bei etw ~ anstellen** to be quick to grasp sth.

Gelehrsamkeit *f (geh)* learning, erudition.
gelehrt *adj* learned, erudite; *(wissenschaftlich)* scholarly.
Gelehrte(r) *mf decl as adj* scholar.
Geleit *nt* **-e** *(Hist: Gefolge)* retinue; *(Begleitung, Mil)* escort; *(Leichenzug)* cortège. **freies** *or* **sicheres ~** safe conduct; **jdm das ~ geben** to escort *or* accompany sb.
geleiten* *vt (geh)* to escort.
Geleitschutz *m* escort. **jdm ~ gewähren** *or* **geben** to give sb an escort; *(persönlich)* to escort sb.
Gelenk *nt* **-e** joint; *(Hand~)* wrist; *(Fuß~)* ankle; *(Ketten~)* link; *(Scharnier~)* hinge.
gelenkig *adj* supple.
Gelenkigkeit *f* suppleness.
gelernt *adj* trained; *Arbeiter* skilled.
gelesen *ptp of* **lesen.**
geliebt *adj* dear, beloved *(liter, Eccl).*
Geliebte *f decl as adj* sweetheart; *(Mätresse)* mistress, lover.
Geliebte(r) *m decl as adj* sweetheart; *(Liebhaber)* lover.
geliefert *adj* **~ sein** *(col)* to have had it *(col).*
geliehen *ptp of* **leihen.**
gelind(e) *adj (geh)* gentle; *(mild) Urteil, Schmerz, Ausdruck* mild. **~ gesagt** to put it mildly.
gelingen *pret* **gelang,** *ptp* **gelungen** *vi aux sein* to succeed, to be successful. **es gelang ihm, das zu tun** he succeeded in doing it; **es gelang ihm nicht, das zu tun** he failed to do it, he didn't succeed in doing it; **dein Plan wird dir nicht ~** you won't succeed with your plan; **es will mir nicht ~** I can't seem to manage it.
Gelingen *nt no pl (geh) (Glück)* success; *(erfolgreiches Ergebnis)* successful outcome. **gutes ~ für Ihren Plan!** good luck with your plan!; **auf gutes ~!** to success!
gelitten *ptp of* **leiden.**
gellen *vi* to shrill; *(von lauten Tönen erfüllt sein)* to ring. **der Lärm gellt mir in den Ohren** the noise makes my ears ring.
gellend *adj* shrill, piercing.
geloben* *vt (geh)* to vow, to swear. **das Gelobte Land** *(Bibl)* the Promised Land.
Gelöbnis *nt (geh)* vow.
gelockt *adj Haar* curly; *Mensch* curly-haired.
gelogen *ptp of* **lügen.**
gelöst *adj* relaxed.
gelt *interj (S Ger)* right.
gelten *pret* **galt,** *ptp* **gegolten 1** *vi* **(a)** *(gültig sein)* to be valid; *(Gesetz)* to be in force; *(Preise)* to be effective; *(zählen)* to count. **die Wette gilt!** it's a bet!; **das gilt nicht!** that doesn't count!; *(nicht erlaubt)* that's not allowed!; **das Gesetz gilt für alle** the law applies to everyone. **(b)** *+dat (bestimmt sein für)* to be meant for *or* aimed at. **(c)** *(zutreffen)* **für jdn/etw ~** to hold (good) for sb/sth, to go for sb/sth; **das gleiche gilt auch für ihn** the same goes for him too. **(d) ~ als** to be regarded as; **es gilt als sicher, daß** ... it seems certain that ... **(e) ~ lassen** to accept; **das lasse ich ~!** I'll agree to that!, I accept that!; **für diesmal lasse ich es ~** I'll let it go this time.
2 *vti impers (geh)* **es gilt, ... zu ...** it is necessary to ...; **jetzt gilt es, zusammenzuhalten** it is now a question of sticking together.
3 *vt (wert sein)* to be worth. **was gilt die Wette?** what do you bet?
geltend *adj attr Preise* current; *Gesetz* in force; *Meinung etc* prevailing. **~ machen** *(form)* to assert; **einen Einwand ~ machen** to raise an objection.
Geltung *f (Gültigkeit)* validity; *(Ansehen)* prestige. **~ haben** to be valid; *(Gesetz)* to be in force; *(Preise)* to be effective; *(Einfluß haben)* to carry weight; *(angesehen sein)* to be recognized; **an ~ verlieren** to lose prestige; **einer Sache** *(dat)* **~ verschaffen** to enforce sth; **sich** *(dat)* **~ verschaffen** to establish one's position; **etw zur ~ bringen** to show sth off to advantage; *(durch Kontrast)* to set sth off; **zur ~ kommen** to show to advantage; *(durch Kontrast)* to be set off.
Geltungs-: ~bedürfnis *nt no pl* need for admiration; **g~bedürftig** *adj* needing admiration; **~dauer** *f no pl* period of validity; **~drang** *m no pl* need for admiration; **~sucht** *f no pl* craving for admiration; **g~süchtig** *adj* craving admiration.
Gelübde *nt* **-** *(Rel, geh)* vow. **ein/das ~ ablegen** to take a vow.
gelungen 1 *ptp of* **gelingen. 2** *adj attr* **(a)** *(geglückt)* successful. **eine nicht so recht ~e Überraschung** a surprise that didn't quite come off. **(b)** *(col: drollig)* funny, priceless.
Gelüst *nt* **-e** *(geh)* desire.
gelüsten* *vt impers (liter, iro)* **mich gelüstet nach** ... I have a craving for ...
Gemach *nt* **⸚er** *(geh)* chamber *(old, form).*
gemächlich *adj* leisurely *no adv; Mensch* unhurried. **ein ~ fließender Strom** a gently flowing river.
gemacht *adj* **(a) für etw ~ sein** to be made for sth; **das ist für ihn wie ~** it's made for him; **ein ~er Mann sein** to be made. **(b)** *(gewollt, gekünstelt)* false, contrived.
Gemahl *m* **-e** *(geh, form)* spouse *(old, form),* husband; *(Prinz~)* consort.
Gemahlin *f (geh, form)* spouse *(old, form),* wife; *(von König auch)* consort.
Gemälde *nt* **-** painting; *(fig: Schilderung)* portrayal.
Gemäldegalerie *f* picture gallery.
gemasert *adj Holz* grained.
gemäß 1 *prep+dat* in accordance with. **2** *adj* appropriate *(dat* to*).* **eine ihren Fähigkeiten ~e Arbeit** a job suited to her abilities.
gemäßigt *adj* moderate; *Klima, Zone* temperate; *Optimismus etc* qualified.
Gemäuer *nt* **-** *(geh)* masonry, walls *pl.*
Gemecker *nt no pl (von Ziegen)* bleating; *(col: Nörgelei)* moaning.
gemein *adj* **(a)** *(niederträchtig)* mean; *(roh, unverschämt auch)* nasty; *Verräter, Lüge* contemptible. **ein ~er Streich** a dirty *or* rotten trick. **(b)** *(ordinär)* vulgar; *Bemerkung, Witz auch* dirty, coarse. **(c)** *(col: unangenehm)* horrible, awful. **die Prüfung war ~ schwer** the exam was horribly difficult. **(d) etw ~ mit jdm/etw haben** to have sth in common with sb/sth; **das ist beiden ~** it is common to both of them. **(e) das ~e Volk** the common people; **der ~e Mann** the ordinary man.
Gemeinbesitz *m* common property.
Gemeinde *f* **-n (a)** *(Kommune)* municipality; *(~bewohner auch)* community. **(b)** *(Pfarr~)* parish; *(beim Gottesdienst)* congregation.
Gemeinde-: ~abgaben *pl* rates *pl (Brit),* local taxes *pl (US);* **~amt** *nt* local authority; *(Gebäude)* local administrative office; **~beamte(r)** *m* local government officer; **~ordnung** *f* bylaws *pl,* ordinances *pl (US);* **~rat** *m* district council; *(Mitglied)* district councillor *(Brit),* councilman *(US);* **~schwester** *f* district nurse; **~steuer** *f* rates *pl (Brit),* local taxes *pl (US);* **~wahl** *f* local election.
Gemein|eigentum *nt* common property.
Gemein-: g~gefährlich *adj Verbrecher* dangerous; **er/das ist g~gefährlich** he/it is a public menace; **~gefährlichkeit** *f* danger to the public; **~gut** *nt (lit, fig)* common property.
Gemeinheit *f* **(a)** *no pl (Niedertracht)* meanness. **(b)** *(Tat)* mean *or* dirty trick; *(Worte)* mean thing. **das war eine ~** that was a mean thing to do/say.
Gemein-: g~hin *adv* generally; **~kosten** *pl* overheads *pl (Brit),* overhead *(US);* **g~nützig** *adj* of benefit to the public; *(wohltätig)* charitable; **~nützigkeit** *f* **die ~nützigkeit einer Organisation** the charitable status of an organization;

~platz *m* platitude, commonplace.

gemeinsam 1 *adj* common; *Freund* mutual; *Konto, Aktion, Ausflug* joint. **ihnen ist vieles ~** they have a great deal in common; **die Firma ist ~es Eigentum der beiden Brüder** the two brothers are joint owners of the firm; **unser ~es Leben** our life together; **der G~e Markt** the Common Market; **mit jdm ~e Sache machen** *(pej)* to gang up with sb. **2** *adv* together. **etw ~ haben** to have sth in common; **es gehört den beiden ~** it belongs jointly to the two of them.

Gemeinsamkeit *f (gemeinsame Interessen, Eigenschaft etc)* common ground *no pl.* **die ~en zwischen ihnen sind sehr groß** they have a great deal in common.

Gemeinschaft *f* community; *(Gruppe)* group; *(Zusammensein)* company. **in ~ mit** jointly with; **die ~ mit jdm** sb's companionship; **eheliche ~** *(Jur)* matrimony.

Gemeinschafts-: ~antenne *f* party aerial *(Brit) or* antenna *(US)*; **~arbeit** *f* teamwork; **~aufgabe** *f* joint task; **~küche** *f* communal kitchen; *(Kantine)* canteen; **~kunde** *f* social studies *pl;* **~leistung** *f* collective achievement; **~raum** *m* common room; **g~schädigend** *adj Verhalten* anti-social; **~schule** *f* interdenominational school; **~wohnung** *f* shared house/apartment *etc.*

Gemein-: ~sinn *m* public spirit; **g~verständlich** *adj* generally comprehensible *no adv;* **sich g~verständlich ausdrücken** to make oneself generally understood; **~wesen** *nt* community; **~wohl** *nt* public welfare; **das dient dem ~wohl** it is in the public interest.

Gemenge *nt* **- (a)** *(Mischung)* mixture *(aus* of*)*; *(Durcheinander)* jumble *(aus* of*)*. **(b)** *(Gewühl)* bustle; *(Hand~)* scuffle.

gemessen 1 *ptp of* **messen. 2** *adj (würdevoll)* measured.

Gemetzel *nt* **-** bloodbath.

gemieden *ptp of* **meiden.**

Gemisch *nt* **-e (a)** *(auch Aut)* mixture *(aus* of*)*. **(b)** *no pl (Durcheinander)* jumble *(aus* of*)*.

gemischt *adj* mixed; *(col: nicht sehr gut auch)* patchy. **mit ~en Gefühlen** with mixed feelings.

Gemischt-: g~rassig *adj* of mixed race; *(mit mehreren Rassen)* multi-racial; **~warenhandlung** *f (dated)* general store.

gemocht *ptp of* **mögen.**

gemolken *ptp of* **melken.**

Gemse *f* **-n** chamois.

Gemurmel *nt no pl* murmuring.

Gemüse *nt* **-** vegetables *pl.* **frisches ~** fresh vegetables; **ein ~** a vegetable; **junges ~** *(hum col)* youngsters *pl.*

Gemüse-: ~beilage *f* vegetables *pl*; **~eintopf** *m* vegetable stew; **~händler** *m* greengrocer; **~handlung** *f*, **~laden** *m* greengrocer's *(Brit)*, greengrocer; **~markt** *m* vegetable market; **~platte** *f (Cook)* **eine ~platte** assorted vegetables *pl*; **~suppe** *f* vegetable soup.

gemußt *ptp of* **müssen.**

gemustert *adj* patterned.

Gemüt *nt* **-er (a)** *(Geist)* mind; *(Charakter)* nature, disposition; *(Seele)* soul; *(Gefühl)* feeling. **viel ~ haben** to be very warm-hearted; **etwas fürs ~** *(hum)* something for the soul; *(Film, Buch etc)* something sentimental; **sich** *(dat)* **etw zu ~e führen** *(beherzigen)* to take sth to heart; *(hum col) Speise, Buch etc* to indulge in sth. **(b)** *(fig: Mensch)* person; *(pl)* people. **die ~er erregen** to cause a stir; **wir müssen warten, bis sich die ~er beruhigt haben** we must wait until feelings have cooled down.

gemütlich *adj* **(a)** *(behaglich)* comfortable; *(freundlich)* friendly *no adv; (zwanglos)* informal; *(klein und intim)* cosy *(Brit)*, cozy *(US)*. **wir verbrachten einen ~en Abend** we spent a very pleasant evening; **es sich** *(dat)* **~ machen** to make oneself comfortable; **langsam wurde es ~** gradually the atmosphere became more relaxed. **(b)** *Mensch* good-natured, pleasant; *(gelassen)* easy-going *no adv*, relaxed *no adv.* **in ~em Tempo** at a leisurely speed.

Gemütlichkeit *f siehe adj* **(a)** comfortableness; friendliness; informality; cosiness. **(b)** good-naturedness, pleasantness; easy-going nature. **da hört doch die ~ auf!** *(col)* that's going too far; **in aller ~** *(gemächlich)* at one's leisure.

Gemüts-: ~art *f* disposition, nature; **~bewegung** *f* emotion; **g~krank** *adj* emotionally disturbed; **~krankheit** *f* emotional disorder; **~lage** *f* mood; **~mensch** *m* good-natured, phlegmatic person; **~ruhe** *f* calmness; *(Kaltblütigkeit)* composure; *(Phlegma)* placidness; **in aller ~ruhe** *(col)* (as) cool as a cucumber *(col)*; *(gemächlich)* at a leisurely pace; **~zustand** *m* frame of mind.

gemütvoll *adj* sentimental; *(warmherzig)* warm-hearted.

gen *prep+acc (old, liter)* toward.

Gen *nt* **-e** gene.

genannt *ptp of* **nennen.**

genas *pret of* **genesen.**

genau 1 *adj* exact, precise. **haben Sie die ~e Zeit?** have you got the right time?; **G~eres** further details *pl;* **man weiß nichts G~es über ihn** no-one knows anything definite about him. **2** *adv* **~!** *(col)* exactly!, precisely!, quite! **~ das Gegenteil** just *or* exactly the opposite; **~ in der Mitte** right in the middle; **ich kenne ihn ~** I know just what he's like; **etw ~ wissen** to know sth for certain; **er nimmt es sehr ~** he's very particular *(mit etw* about sth*)*; **einen Entschluß ~ überlegen** to think a decision over very carefully; **meine Uhr geht ~** my watch keeps accurate time; **~ auf die Minute** exactly on time; **so ~ wollte ich es gar nicht wissen!** *(iro)* you can spare me the details.

genaugenommen *adv* strictly speaking.

Genauigkeit *f* exactness, precision.

genauso *adv (vor Adjektiv)* just as; *(alleinstehend)* just *or* exactly the same.

genauso- = ebenso-.

genehmigen* *vt Baupläne etc* to approve; *(erlauben)* to sanction; *(Lizenz erteilen)* to license; *Aufenthalt* to authorize; *(zugestehen)* to grant. **sich** *(dat)* **einen ~** *(hum col)* to have a little drink.

Genehmigung *f siehe vt* approval; sanction; licence *(Brit)*, license *(US)*; authorization; *(Schein)* permit. **mit freundlicher ~ von** by kind permission of.

genehmigungspflichtig *adj (form)* requiring official approval; *(mit Visum, Stempel)* requiring official authorization.

geneigt *adj (geh) Aufmerksamkeit* kind. **~ sein, etw zu tun** to be inclined to do sth.

General *m* **-e** *or* **¨-e** *(Mil)* general. **Herr ~** General.

General-: ~angriff *m (Mil, fig)* general attack; **~direktor** *m* chairman *(Brit)*, president *(US)*; **~intendant** *m (Theat, Mus)* director; **~konsulat** *nt* consulate general; **~major** *m* major general; **~probe** *f (Theat, fig)* dress rehearsal; **~sekretär** *m* secretary general; **~stab** *m* general staff; **~streik** *m* general strike; **g~überholen*** *vt infin and ptp only* **etw g~überholen** to give sth a complete overhaul; **~überholung** *f* complete overhaul; **~versammlung** *f* general meeting; **~vertretung** *f* sole agency.

Generation *f* generation.

Generationskonflikt *m* generation gap.

Generator *m* generator.

generell *adj* general.

genesen *pret* **genas,** *ptp* **~** *vi aux sein (geh)* to convalesce; *(fig)* to recuperate.

Genesende(r) *mf decl as adj* convalescent.

Genesung *f* convalescence, recovery *(auch fig)*. **auf dem Wege der ~** on the road to recovery.

Genesungs-: ~prozeß *m* convalescence;

~**urlaub** *m* convalescent leave.
Genetik *f* genetics *sing.*
genetisch *adj* genetic.
Genf *nt* Geneva.
Genfer *adj attr* **der ~ See** Lake Geneva; **~ Konvention** *f* Geneva Convention.
genial *adj Entdeckung, Mensch* brilliant; *Künstler, Stil auch* inspired; *(erfinderisch)* ingenious. **ein ~er Mensch** a genius; **ein ~es Werk** a work of genius.
Genialität *f* genius; *(Erfindungsreichtum)* ingenuity.
Genick *nt* **-e** neck. **sich** *(dat)* **das ~ brechen** to break one's neck; **jdm/einer Sache das ~ brechen** *(fig)* to finish sb/sth.
Genick-: ~**schuß** *m* shot in the neck; ~**starre** *f* stiffness of the neck; *(Med)* (cerebral) meningitis; **~starre haben** *(col)* to have a stiff neck.
Genie [ʒe'niː] *nt* **-s** genius.
genieren* [ʒe'niːrən] *vr* to be embarrassed. **sich vor Fremden ~** to be shy with strangers; **ich geniere mich, das zu sagen** I don't like to say it; **er genierte sich (gar) nicht, das zu tun** it didn't bother him (at all) to do that.
genießbar *adj (eßbar)* edible; *(trinkbar)* drinkable. **er ist heute nicht ~** *(fig col)* he is unbearable today.
genießen *pret* **genoß,** *ptp* **genossen** *vt* **(a)** *(lit, fig)* to enjoy. **den Wein muß man ~** you must savour *(Brit)* or savor *(US)* the wine; **er ist heute nicht zu ~** *(col)* he is unbearable today. **(b)** *(essen)* to eat; *(trinken)* to drink. **das Essen ist kaum zu ~** the meal is scarcely edible.
Genießer(in *f*) *m* **-** connoisseur; *(des Lebens)* pleasure-lover; *(Feinschmecker)* gourmet.
genießerisch *adj* appreciative. **~ zog er an seiner Zigarre** he puffed at his cigar with relish.
Geniestreich [ʒe'niː-] *m* stroke of genius.
Genitalien [-iən] *pl* genitals *pl.*
Genitiv *m* genitive.
Genius *m, pl* **Genien** ['geːniən] genius.
genommen *ptp of* **nehmen.**
genoß *pret of* **genießen.**
Genosse *m (wk)* **-n, -n** comrade; *(pej: Kumpan)* mate *(Brit col)*, buddy *(US col)*.
genossen *ptp of* **genießen.**
Genossen-: ~**schaft** *f* co-operative; **g~schaftlich** *adj* co-operative; **g~schaftlich organisiert** organized as a co-operative.
Genossenschafts-: ~**bank** *f* co-operative bank; ~**betrieb** *m* co-operative.
Genossin *f siehe* **Genosse.**
genötigt *adj* **~ sein, etw zu tun** to be obliged to do sth; **sich ~ sehen, etw zu tun** to feel obliged to do sth.
Genre ['ʒɑ̃ːrə] *nt* **-s** genre.
genug *adj* enough. **das ist wenig ~** that's precious little; **und damit noch nicht ~** and that's not/that wasn't all; **sie sind jetzt ~, um ...** there are enough of them now to ...; **jetzt ist('s) aber ~!** that's enough!; **(von etw) ~ haben** to have enough (of sth); *(überdrüssig sein)* to have had enough (of sth).
Genüge *f no pl* **zur ~** enough; **etw zur ~ kennen** to know sth well enough; *(abwertender)* to know sth only too well; **jdm ~ tun** *(geh)* to satisfy sb.
genügen* *vi* **(a)** *(ausreichen)* to be enough *or* sufficient *(dat* for). **das genügt (mir)** that's enough (for me). **(b)** *Anforderungen* to satisfy; *Erwartungen* to fulfil *(Brit)*, to fulfill *(US)*.
genügend 1 *adj* **(a)** *inv (ausreichend)* enough, sufficient. **(b)** *(befriedigend)* satisfactory. **2** *adv (reichlich)* enough, sufficiently.
genügsam *adj (anspruchslos) Tier, Pflanze* undemanding; *Mensch auch* modest. **ein ~es Leben führen** to live modestly.
Genügsamkeit *f* simple needs *pl.*
Genugtuung *f* satisfaction *(über +acc* at). **ich hörte mit ~, daß ...** it gave me great satisfaction to hear that ....
Genus *nt, pl* **Genera** *(Gram)* gender.
Genuß *m* **⸗sse (a)** *no pl (das Zusichnehmen)* consumption; *(von Drogen)* taking, use; *(von Tabak)* smoking. **nach dem ~ der Pilze** after eating the mushrooms. **(b)** *(Vergnügen)* pleasure. **etw mit ~ essen** to eat sth with relish. **(c)** *no pl (Nutznießung)* **in den ~ von etw kommen** *(von Vergünstigungen)* to enjoy sth; *(von Rente, Prämie etc)* to be in receipt of sth.
genüßlich *adj* pleasurable. **er schmatzte ~** he smacked his lips with relish.
Genuß-: ~**mittel** *nt semi-luxury foods and tobacco;* **g~reich** *adj* enjoyable; **g~süchtig** *adj* hedonistic.
Geograph(in *f*) *m* geographer.
Geographie *f* geography.
geographisch *adj no pred* geographic(al).
Geologe *m,* **Geologin** *f* geologist.
Geologie *f* geology.
geologisch *adj no pred* geological.
Geometrie *f* geometry.
geometrisch *adj* geometric.
ge|ordnet *adj Leben, Zustände* well-ordered. **in ~en Verhältnissen leben** to live a well-ordered life; **~e Verhältnisse schaffen** to put things on an orderly basis.
Gepäck *nt no pl* luggage *no pl*, baggage *no pl; (Mil: Marsch~)* baggage; *(von Soldat, Pfadfinder etc)* kit; *(von Bergsteiger)* pack. **mit leichtem ~ reisen** to travel light.
Gepäck-: ~**abfertigung** *f (Stelle) (am Bahnhof)* luggage *or* baggage office; *(am Flughafen)* baggage check-in; ~**ablage** *f* luggage *or* baggage rack; ~**annahme** *f (am Bahnhof) (zur Beförderung)* (in-counter of the) luggage *or* baggage office; *(zur Aufbewahrung)* (in-counter of the) left-luggage office *(Brit)* or checkroom *(US)*; *(am Flughafen)* luggage *or* baggage check-in; ~**aufbewahrung** *f* left-luggage office *(Brit)*, baggage checkroom *(US)*; ~**kontrolle** *f* luggage *or* baggage control *or* check; ~**netz** *nt* luggage *or* baggage rack; ~**schein** *m* luggage *or* baggage ticket; ~**schließfach** *nt* luggage *or* baggage locker; ~**stück** *nt* piece of luggage *or* baggage; ~**träger** *m* **(a)** *(Person)* porter *(Brit)*, baggage handler; **(b)** *(am Fahrrad)* carrier; ~**wagen** *m* luggage van *(Brit)*, baggage car *(US)*.
Gepard *m* **-e** cheetah.
gepfeffert *adj (col) Preise* steep; *Fragen, Prüfung* tough; *Kritik* biting.
gepfiffen *ptp of* **pfeifen.**
gepflegt 1 *adj* **(a)** *(nicht vernachlässigt)* well looked after; *Mensch, Hund, Aussehen* well-groomed. **(b)** *(col: kultiviert)* civilized; *Atmosphäre* sophisticated; *Ausdrucksweise* cultured; *Sprache* cultured, refined. **(c)** *(erstklassig) Speisen* excellent. **2** *adv (kultiviert)* **sich ~ unterhalten** to have a civilized conversation; **sich ~ ausdrücken** to have a cultured way of speaking; **sehr ~ wohnen** to live in style.
Gepflogenheit *f (geh) (Gewohnheit)* habit; *(Verfahrensweise)* practice; *(Brauch)* custom, tradition.
Geplänkel *nt* **-** skirmish; *(fig)* squabble.
Geplapper *nt no pl* babbling; *(fig: Geschwätz auch)* chatter(ing).
Geplärr(e) *nt no pl* bawling; *(von Radio)* blaring.
geplättet *adj pred (col)* flabbergasted *(col)*.
Geplauder *nt no pl (geh)* chatting.
Gepolter *nt no pl (Krach)* din; *(an Tür etc)* banging.
Gepräge *nt no pl (fig: Eigentümlichkeit)* character; *(Aura)* aura. **das hat den 60er Jahren ihr ~ gegeben** it left its mark *or* stamp on the sixties.
gepriesen *ptp of* **preisen.**
gepunktet *adj Linie* dotted; *Stoff, Kleid* spotted.
gequält *adj Lächeln* forced; *Miene, Ausdruck*

pained; *Gesang, Stimme* strained.

Gequatsche *nt no pl (pej col)* gabbing *(col)*; *(Blödsinn)* twaddle *(col)*.

gequollen *ptp of* **quellen.**

gerade, grade *(col)* **1** *adj* straight; *Zahl* even; *(aufrecht) Haltung* upright. ~ **gewachsen sein** *(Mensch)* to be clean-limbed; *(Baum)* to be straight; **das ~ Gegenteil** the very opposite, just the opposite; **~sitzen/stehen** to sit up/stand up straight.

2 *adv* **(a)** *(im Augenblick, soeben)* just. **wenn Sie ~ Zeit haben** if you have time just now; **wo Sie ~ da sind** while you're here; **er wollte ~ aufstehen** he was just about to get up; ~ **erst** only just; **da wir ~ von Geld sprechen, ...** talking of money ...

(b) *(knapp)* just. **~ so viel, daß er davon leben kann** just enough for him to live on; ~ **noch** only just; **das hat ~ noch gefehlt!** *(iro)* that's all we wanted!

(c) *(genau)* just; *(direkt)* right. **~ zur rechten Zeit** at exactly the right time, just at the right time; ~ **deshalb** that's just *or* exactly why; **das ist es ja~!** that's just it!

(d) *(speziell, besonders)* especially. **~, weil ...** just because ...; ~ **du solltest dafür Verständnis haben** you especially should understand; **sie ist nicht ~ eine Schönheit** she's not exactly a beauty; **warum ~ das?** why that of all things?; **warum ~ heute/ich?** why today of all days/me of all people?; **warum hat er es ~ so gemacht?** why on earth did he do it like that?

(e) *(col: erst recht)* **nun ~!** you try and stop me now! *(col)*; **jetzt ~ nicht!** I'll be damned if I will! *(col)*.

Gerade *f (wk)* **-n, -n (a)** *(Math)* straight line. **(b)** *(Sport) (von Renn-, Laufbahn)* straight; *(beim Boxen)* straight left/right.

gerade-: **~aus** *adv* straight ahead; *gehen, fahren auch* straight on; **~biegen** *vt sep irreg (lit, fig)* to straighten out; **~halten** *sep irreg* **1** *vt* to hold straight; **2** *vr* to hold oneself (up) straight; **~heraus** *(col)* **1** *adj pred* forthright, frank; **2** *adv* frankly; **~heraus gesagt** quite frankly.

gerädert *adj (col)* **wie ~ sein, sich wie ~ fühlen** to be *or* feel (absolutely) whacked *(col)*.

gerade-: **~sogut** *adv* (just) as well; **~soviel** *adv* just as much; **~stehen** *vi sep irreg aux haben or sein* **(a)** *(aufrecht stehen)* to stand up straight; **(b) für jdn/etw ~stehen** *(fig)* to be answerable for sb/sth; **~wegs** *adv* straight; **~zu** *adv (beinahe)* virtually, almost; **das ist doch ~zu Selbstmord** that's nothing short of suicide; **das ist ja ~zu lächerlich!** that is absolutely ridiculous!

geradlinig *adj* straight; *Abstammung* direct; *Entwicklung etc* linear; *(fig: aufrichtig)* straight.

gerammelt *adv:* ~ **voll** *(col)* (jam-)packed *(col)*.

Gerangel *nt no pl (Balgerei)* scrapping; *(fig: zäher Kampf)* wrangling.

Geranie [-ɪə] *f* geranium.

gerannt *ptp of* **rennen.**

Geraschel *nt no pl* rustle, rustling.

Gerät *nt* **-e (a)** piece of equipment; *(Apparat)* gadget; *(elektrisches ~)* appliance; *(Radio~, Fernseh~)* set; *(Meß~)* instrument; *(Werkzeug, Garten~)* tool. **(b)** *no pl (Ausrüstung)* equipment *no pl*; *(von Handwerker)* tools *pl*.

geraten[1] **1** *vi irreg aux sein* **(a)** *(zufällig gelangen)* to get *(in+acc* into*)*. **an jdn ~** *(jdn kennenlernen)* to come across sb; **an etw** *(acc)* ~ to get sth, to come by sth; **an den Richtigen/Falschen ~** to come to the right/wrong person; **das Schiff ist in einen Sturm ~** the boat got caught in a storm; **unter schlechten Einfluß ~** to come under a bad influence. **(b)** *(sich entwickeln, ausfallen)* to turn out. **ihm gerät einfach alles** everything he does is a success. **2** *adj (geh: ratsam)* advisable.

geraten[2] *ptp of* **raten, geraten**[1].

Geräte-: **~schuppen** *m* toolshed; **~turnen** *nt* apparatus gymnastics *no pl*.

Geratewohl *nt:* **aufs ~** on the off-chance; *auswählen etc* at random.

Gerätschaften *pl (Ausrüstung)* equipment *sing*; *(Werkzeug)* tools *pl*.

Geratter *nt no pl* clatter(ing); *(von Maschinengewehr)* chatter(ing).

geraum *adj attr* **vor ~er Zeit** some time ago; **seit ~er Zeit** for some time.

geräumig *adj* spacious, roomy.

Geräumigkeit *f no pl* spaciousness, roominess.

Geräusch *nt* **-e** sound; *(esp unangenehm)* noise.

Geräusch-: **g~arm** *adj* quiet; **~kulisse** *f* background noise; *(Film, Rad, TV)* sound effects *pl*; **g~los** *adj* silent; **~losigkeit** *f no pl* silence; **~pegel** *m* sound level; **g~voll** *adj (laut)* loud; *(lärmend)* noisy.

gerben *vt* to tan.

Gerber *m* **-** tanner.

gerecht *adj* just; *(unparteiisch auch)* fair; *(rechtschaffen)* upright. ~ **gegen jdn sein** to be fair *or* just to sb; **~er Lohn für alle Arbeiter!** fair wages for all workers!; **den Schlaf des G~en schlafen** *(usu hum)* to sleep the sleep of the just; **~er Zorn** righteous anger; **jdm/einer Sache ~ werden** to do justice to sb/sth; **den Bedingungen ~ werden** to fulfil *(Brit) or* fulfill *(US)* the conditions.

gerechtfertigt *adj* justified.

Gerechtigkeit *f* justice; *(das Gerechtsein)* justness; *(Unparteilichkeit)* fairness; *(Rechtschaffenheit)* righteousness. **jdm ~ widerfahren lassen** to be just to sb; *(fig)* to do justice to sb.

Gerechtigkeits-: **~gefühl** *nt*, **~sinn** *m* sense of justice.

Gerede *nt no pl* talk; *(Klatsch)* gossip(ing). **jdn ins ~ bringen** to get sb talked about.

geregelt *adj Arbeit, Mahlzeiten* regular; *Leben* well-ordered.

gereichen* *vi (geh)* **jdm zur Ehre ~** to redound to sb's honour *(form)*; **zum Vorteil ~** to be an advantage to sb.

gereift *adj (fig)* mature.

gereizt *adj (verärgert)* irritated; *(reizbar)* irritable, touchy; *(nervös)* edgy. **im Zimmer herrschte ~e Stimmung** there was a strained atmosphere in the room.

Gereiztheit *f siehe adj* irritation; irritability; edginess; strainedness.

Gericht[1] *nt* **-e** *(Speise)* dish.

Gericht[2] *nt* **-e** *(Behörde)* court (of justice); *(Gebäude)* court(house), law courts *pl*; *(die Richter)* court, bench. **vor ~ erscheinen/aussagen** to appear/testify in court; **vor ~ stehen** to stand trial; **jdn/einen Fall vor ~ bringen** to take sb/sth to court; **das Jüngste ~** the Last Judgement; **über jdn zu ~ sitzen** *(fig)* to sit in judgement on sb; **mit jdm (scharf) ins ~ gehen** *(fig)* to judge sb harshly.

gerichtlich *adj attr* judicial; *Entscheidung etc* court; *Medizin* forensic; *Verhandlung* legal. **laut ~em Beschluß** according to the decision of a/the court; **ein ~es Nachspiel haben** to finish up in court; **~ gegen jdn vorgehen** to take legal proceedings against sb; **eine Sache ~ klären** to settle a matter in court.

Gerichts-: **~akten** *pl* court records *pl*; **~arzt** *m* court doctor; **~barkeit** *f* jurisdiction; **~beschluß** *m* court decision; **~diener** *m (old)* court usher; **~entscheid** *m*, **~entscheidung** *f* court decision; **~ferien** *pl* court vacation, recess; **~hof** *m* court (of justice), law court; **Oberster ~hof** Supreme Court (of Justice); **~kosten** *pl* court costs *pl*; **~medizin** *f* forensic medicine; **~mediziner** *m* forensic doctor; **g~medizinisch** *adj* forensic medical *attr*; **~reporter** *m* legal correspondent; **~saal** *m* courtroom; **~schreiber** *m* clerk of the court; **~termin** *m* date of a/the trial; *(für Zivilsachen)* date of a/the hearing; **~verfahren** *nt* court *or* legal proceedings *pl*; **ein ~verfahren gegen jdn einleiten** to institute legal proceedings against sb; **~verhandlung** *f* trial; *(zivil)* hearing; **~vollzieher** *m* bailiff; **~weg** *m* **auf dem ~weg** through the courts.

gerieben 1 *ptp of* **reiben. 2** *adj (fig col)* smart, sharp; *(verschlagen auch)* sly, fly *(col)*. **der ist verdammt ~** there are no flies on him *(col)*.

geriet *pret of* **geraten**[1].

gering *adj* **(a)** *(niedrig)* low; *Menge* small; *Wert* little *attr*; *(kurz) Zeit, Entfernung* short. **Berge von ~er Höhe** low hills; **seine Leistung erhielt eine zu ~e Bewertung** his performance wasn't rated highly enough. **(b)** *(unbedeutend, unerheblich)* slight; *Chance auch* small, slim; *Bedeutung, Rolle* minor. **das ist meine ~ste Sorge** that's the least of my worries; **die Kosten sind nicht ~** the costs are not inconsiderable; **nicht im ~sten** not in the least *or* slightest; **nichts G~eres als ...** nothing less than; **kein G~erer als Freud ...** no less a person than Freud. **(c)** *(unzulänglich) Qualität, Kenntnisse* poor; *(abschätzig) Meinung* low, poor.

geringelt *adj Muster* ringed; *Socken* hooped.

Gering-: g~fügig *adj (unwichtig)* insignificant; *Unterschied* slight; *Vergehen, Verletzung* minor; *Betrag* small; **sein Zustand hat sich g~fügig gebessert** his condition is marginally improved; **~fügigkeit** *f* **(a)** insignificance; slightness; **ein Verfahren wegen ~fügigkeit einstellen** *(Jur)* to dismiss a case because of the trifling nature of the offence; **(b)** *(Kleinigkeit)* small thing, trifle; **g~schätzen** *vt sep (verachten) Menschen, Leistung* to have a low opinion of; *(mißachten) Gefahr, Folgen* to disregard; **g~schätzig** *adj* contemptuous; **~schätzung** *f no pl (Ablehnung)* disdain; *(schlechte Meinung)* low opinion *(für, gen* of*)*; *(für menschliches Leben)* low regard *(für, gen* for*)*.

gerinnen* *vi irreg aux sein* to coagulate; *(Blut auch)* to clot; *(Milch auch)* to curdle. **mir gerann das Blut in den Adern** *(fig)* my blood ran cold.

Gerinnsel *nt (Blut~)* clot.

Gerinnung *f siehe vi* coagulation; clotting; curdling.

Gerippe *nt* - skeleton; *(von Schirm, Gebäude)* frame; *(fig: Grundplan)* framework. **er ist nur noch ein ~** he's nothing but skin and bones.

gerippt *adj* ribbed *no adv*.

gerissen 1 *ptp of* **reißen. 2** *adj* crafty, cunning.

Gerissenheit *f* cunning.

geritten *ptp of* **reiten.**

geritzt *adj pred (col)* **die Sache ist ~** everything's fixed up *or* settled.

Germane *n (wk)* **-n, -n, Germanin** *f* Teuton.

germanisch *adj* Germanic.

Germanist(in *f***)** *m* Germanist; *(Student auch)* German student; *(Wissenschaftler auch)* German specialist.

Germanistik *f* German (studies *pl*). **~ studieren** to study German.

gern(e) *adv, comp* **lieber,** *superl* **am liebsten (a)** *(freudig)* with pleasure; *(bereitwillig auch)* willingly, readily. **(aber) ~!** of course!; **kommst du mit? — ja, ~** are you coming too? — oh yes, I'd like to; **~ geschehen!** you're welcome!, not at all!; **von mir aus kann er ja ~ älter sein** I don't mind if he's older; **etw ~ tun** to like doing sth *or* to do sth *(esp US)*; **etw ~ essen/trinken** to like sth; **sie ißt am liebsten Spargel** asparagus is her favourite *(Brit) or* favorite *(US)* food; **er sieht** *or* **hat es nicht ~, wenn wir zu spät kommen** he doesn't like us coming too late; **ein ~ gesehener Gast** a welcome visitor; **das glaube ich ~** I can quite *or* well believe it; **jdn/etw ~ haben** *or* **mögen** to like sb/sth, to be fond of sb/sth; **jdn/etw am liebsten haben** *or* **mögen** to like sb/sth best *or* most; **ich hätte** *or* **möchte ~ ...** I would like ...; **du kannst mich mal ~ haben!** *(col)* (you can) go to hell! *(col)*; *siehe* **lieber.**
(b) *(gewöhnlich, oft)* **etw ~ tun** to tend to do sth; **morgens läßt er sich ~ viel Zeit** he likes to leave himself a lot of time in the mornings.

Gernegroß *m* **-, -e** *(hum)* **er war schon immer ein kleiner ~** he always did like to act big *(col)*.

gerochen *ptp of* **riechen.**

Geröll *nt* **-e** detritus *no pl*; *(größer)* boulders *pl*.

geronnen *ptp of* **rinnen, gerinnen.**

Gerste *f* **-n** barley.

Gersten-: ~korn *nt* **(a)** barleycorn; **(b)** *(Med)* stye; **~saft** *m (hum)* John Barleycorn *(hum)*, beer.

Gerte *f* **-n** switch; *(Reit~ auch)* crop.

gertenschlank *adj* slim and willowy.

Geruch *m* **¨-e (a)** smell *(nach* of*)*; *(Duft auch)* fragrance *(nach* of*)*; *(von Speise etc auch)* aroma *(nach* of*)*. **(b)** *no pl (~ssinn)* sense of smell. **(c)** *no pl (fig: Ruf)* reputation. **in den ~ von etw kommen** to get a reputation for sth.

geruchlos *adj* odourless *(Brit)*, odorless *(US)*; *(duftlos)* scentless.

Geruch(s)-: ~organ *nt* organ of smell, olfactory organ; **~sinn** *m* sense of smell.

Gerücht *nt* **-e** rumour *(Brit)*, rumor *(US)*. **das halte ich für ein ~** *(col)* I have my doubts about that.

gerüchtweise *adv* **etw ~ hören** to hear sth rumoured *(Brit) or* rumored *(US)*; **~ ist bekanntgeworden, daß ...** rumour *(Brit) or* rumor *(US)* has it that ...

gerufen *ptp of* **rufen.**

geruhsam *adj* peaceful; *Spaziergang etc* leisurely *no adv*. **~ essen** to eat in peace (and quiet).

Gerümpel *nt no pl* junk.

Gerundium *nt* gerund.

gerungen *ptp of* **ringen.**

Gerüst *nt* **-e** scaffolding *no pl*; *(Gestell)* trestle; *(fig: Gerippe)* framework *(zu* of*)*.

ges, Ges *nt* - *(Mus)* G flat.

gesalzen *adj (fig col) Preis, Rechnung* steep, stiff.

gesammelt *adj Aufmerksamkeit, Kraft* collective; *Werke* collected.

gesamt *adj attr* whole, entire. **die ~e Familie** the whole family; **die ~en Kosten** the total costs.

Gesamt-: ~auflage *f (von Zeitung etc)* total circulation; *(von Buch)* total edition; **~ausgabe** *f* complete edition; **~betrag** *m* total (amount); **g~deutsch** *adj* all-German; **~eindruck** *m* general impression; **~fläche** *f* total area; **~gewicht** *nt* total weight.

Gesamtheit *f* totality. **die ~ der ...** all the ...; *(die Summe)* the totality of ...; **die ~ (der Bevölkerung)** the population (as a whole); **in seiner ~** in its entirety; **das Volk in seiner ~** the nation as a whole.

Gesamt-: ~hochschule *f* polytechnic; **~kosten** *pl* total costs *pl*; **~lage** *f* general situation; **~masse** *f (Comm)* total assets *pl*; **~note** *f (Sch)* overall mark; **~schaden** *m* total damage; **ein ~schaden von 5.000 Mark** damage totalling *(Brit) or* totaling *(US)* 5,000 marks; **~schule** *f* comprehensive school; **~sieger** *m (Sport)* overall winner; **~summe** *f* total (amount); **~übersicht** *f* general survey *(über+acc* of*)*; **~umsatz** *m* total turnover; **~werk** *nt* complete works *pl*; **~wert** *m* total value; **im ~wert von ...** totalling *(Brit) or* totaling *(US)* ... in value; **~wertung** *f (Sport)* overall placings *pl*; **er liegt in der ~wertung vorn** he has the overall lead; **~zahl** *f* total number; **~zusammenhang** *m* general view.

gesandt *ptp of* **senden**[1].

Gesandte(r) *m decl as adj,* **Gesandtin** *f* envoy; *(col: Botschafter)* ambassador.

Gesandtschaft *f* legation; *(col: Botschaft)* embassy.

Gesang *m* **¨-e (a)** *(Lied, Vogel~)* song. **geistliche ¨~e** religious hymns and chants. **(b)** *no pl (das*

Singen) singing.
Gesang-: **~buch** *nt (Eccl)* hymnbook; **~lehrer** *m* singing teacher.
gesanglich *adj* vocal; *Begabung* for singing.
Gesangverein *m* choral society.
Gesäß *nt* **-e** seat, bottom, posterior *(hum).*
Gesäßtasche *f* back pocket.
gesättigt *adj (Chem)* saturated.
Geschädigte(r) *mf decl as adj* victim.
Geschäft *nt* **-e (a)** *(Gewerbe, Handel)* business *no pl; (~sabschluß)* (business) deal *or* transaction. **wie geht das ~?** how's business?; **mit jdm ins ~ kommen** to do business with sb; **im ~ sein** to be in business; **ein ~ tätigen** to carry out a transaction; **ein gutes/schlechtes ~ machen** to make a good/bad deal; **dabei hat er ein ~ gemacht** he made a profit out of it; **das war für mich ein/kein ~** that was a good/bad bit of business for me; **~e mit etw machen** to make money out of sth. **(b)** *(Aufgabe)* duty. **seinen ~en nachgehen** to go about one's business. **(c)** *(Firma)* business; *(Laden)* shop *(Brit)*, store *(US)*. **im ~** at work; *(im Laden)* in the shop. **(d)** *(baby-talk: Notdurft)* **ein ~ machen** to do a job *(baby-talk)*; **sein ~ verrichten** to do one's business *(euph).*
Geschäfte-: **g~halber** *adv verreist* on business; *verhindert* because of business; **~macher** *m (pej)* profiteer.
geschäftig *adj (betriebsam)* busy. **~es Treiben** hustle and bustle.
Geschäftigkeit *f (geschäftiges Treiben)* hustle and bustle.
geschäftlich 1 *adj (das Geschäft betreffend)* business *attr; (sachlich) Ton* businesslike. **2** *adv verreist* on business; *verhindert* because of business. **~ unterwegs** away on business; **ich habe mit ihm etwas G~es zu besprechen** I have some business to discuss with him.
Geschäfts-: **~abschluß** business deal *or* transaction; **~aufgabe, ~auflösung** *f* closure of a/the business; **~bank** *f* commercial bank; **~bedingungen** *pl* terms of business *pl*; **~bereich** *m (Parl)* responsibilities *pl*; **Minister ohne ~bereich** minister without portfolio; **~beziehungen** *pl* business connections *pl (zu* with); **~brief** *m* business letter; **~bücher** *pl* books *pl*, accounts *pl*; **~frau** *f* businesswoman; **g~führend** *adj attr* executive; *(stellvertretend)* acting; *Regierung* caretaker; **~führer** *m (von Laden)* manager; *(von GmbH)* managing director; *(von Verein)* secretary; *(von Partei)* whip; **~führung** *f* management; **~haus** *nt* **(a)** *(Gebäude)* business premises *pl; (von Büros)* office block; **(b)** *(Firma)* house, firm; **~inhaber(in** *f*) *m* owner; **~jahr** *nt* financial year; **~kapital** *nt* working capital; **~kosten** *pl* business expenses *pl;* **das geht alles auf ~kosten** it's all on expenses; **~leitung** *f* management; **~mann** *m, pl* **~leute** businessman; **g~mäßig** *adj* businesslike *no adv;* **~ordnung** *f* standing orders *pl*; **eine Frage zur ~ordnung** a question on a point of order; **~partner** *m* business partner; **~räume** *pl* (business) premises *pl*; *(Büroräume)* offices *pl*; **~reise** *f* business trip; **auf ~reise sein** to be on a business trip; **g~schädigend** *adj* bad for business; **g~schädigendes Verhalten** conduct *no art* injurious to the interests of the company *(form)*; **~schluß** *m* close of business; *(von Läden)* closing-time; **nach ~schluß** after working hours/closing-time; **~stelle** *f* offices *pl*; **~straße** *f* shopping street; **~tätigkeit** *f* business activity; **g~tüchtig** *adj* business-minded; **~welt** *f* business world; **~zimmer** *nt* office.
geschah *pret of* **geschehen.**
gescheckt *adj* spotted; *Pferd* skewbald, pinto *(US).*
geschehen *pret* **geschah,** *ptp* **~** *vi aux sein* to happen *(jdm* to sb); *(ausgeführt werden)* to be done; *(Verbrechen)* to be committed. **es ist nun einmal ~** what's done is done; **es wird ihm nichts ~** nothing will happen to him; **das geschieht ihm (ganz) recht** it serves him (jolly well *col*) right; **was soll mit ihm/damit ~?** what is to be done with him/it?; **als er sie sah, war es um ihn ~** he was lost the moment he set eyes on her; **da war es um meine Seelenruhe ~** that was an end to my peace of mind.
Geschehen *nt* - events *pl*, happenings *pl.*
gescheit *adj* clever; *Mensch, Idee auch* bright; *(vernünftig)* sensible. **du bist wohl nicht recht ~?** you must be out of your mind *or* off your head; **sei ~!** be sensible.
Geschenk *nt* **-e** present, gift; *(Schenkung)* gift. **jdm ein ~ machen** to give sb a present; **das war ein ~ des Himmels** it was a godsend.
Geschenk- *in cpds* gift; **~artikel** *m* gift; **~packung** *f* gift pack *or* box; *(von Pralinen)* gift box; **~papier** *nt* gift-wrapping paper; **~sendung** *f* gift parcel.
Geschichte *f* **-n (a)** *no pl (Historie)* history. **Alte/Neuere ~** ancient/modern history; **~ machen** to make history; **das ist längst ~** that's ancient history. **(b)** *(Erzählung, Lügen~)* story; *(Märchen, Fabel etc auch)* tale; *(Kurz~)* short story. **~n erzählen** to tell stories. **(c)** *(col: Angelegenheit, Sache)* affair, business *no pl.* **das sind alte ~n** that's old hat *(col)*; **alte ~n wieder aufwärmen** to rake up the past; **eine schöne ~!** *(iro)* a fine how-do-you-do! *(col)*; **die ~ mit seinem Magen** the business with his stomach; **mach keine ~n!** don't be silly! *(col)*; *(Dummheiten)* don't get up to anything silly!
Geschichten|erzähler *m (lit, fig)* storyteller.
geschichtlich *adj (historisch)* historical; *(bedeutungsvoll)* historic. **~ belegt** *or* **nachgewiesen sein** to be a historical fact.
Geschichts-: **~buch** *nt* history book; **~fälschung** *f* falsification of history; **~forscher** *m* historian; **~forschung** *f* historical research; **~kenntnis** *f* historical knowledge *no pl*; **~lehrer** *m* history teacher; **~schreiber** *m* historian; **~schreibung** *f* historiography.
Geschick[1] *nt* **-e** *(geh) (Schicksal)* fate; *(usu pl: politische etc Entwicklung)* fortune. **ein gütiges ~** good fortune, providence.
Geschick[2] *nt no pl (~lichkeit)* skill.
Geschicklichkeit *f siehe* **geschickt** skill; cleverness; agility. **für etw ~ haben** to be clever at sth.
Geschicklichkeitsspiel *nt* game of skill.
geschickt *adj* skilful *(Brit)*, skillful *(US)*; *(taktisch auch)* clever; *(beweglich)* agile.
Geschicktheit *f* = **Geschicklichkeit.**
geschieden *ptp of* **scheiden.**
Geschiedene(r) *mf decl as adj* divorcee.
geschienen *ptp of* **scheinen.**
Geschirr *nt* **-e (a)** *no pl (Teller etc)* crockery *(Brit)*, tableware; *(Küchen~)* pots and pans *pl*, kitchenware; *(Porzellan)* china. **(das) ~ spülen** to wash *or* do the dishes, to wash up *(Brit)*; **feuerfestes ~** ovenware. **(b)** *(Service)* (dinner/tea *etc*) service; *(Gläser)* set of glasses; *(feuerfestes ~)* set of ovenware. **(c)** *(von Zugtieren)* harness.
Geschirr-: **~schrank** *m* china cupboard; **~spülen** *nt* washing-up; **~spülmaschine** *f* dishwasher; **~tuch** *nt* tea towel *(Brit)*, dishtowel *(US).*
geschissen *ptp of* **scheißen.**
geschlafen *ptp of* **schlafen.**
geschlagen *ptp of* **schlagen.**
Geschlecht *nt* **-er (a)** sex; *(Gram)* gender. **Jugendliche beiderlei ~s** young people of both sexes; **das andere ~** the opposite sex. **(b)** *no pl (geh: Geschlechtsteil)* sex *(liter).* **(c)** *(liter) (Gattung)* race; *(Sippe)* house; *(Abstammung)* lineage. **das menschliche ~** the human race.
geschlechtlich *adj* sexual. **~e Erziehung** sex education; **mit jdm ~ verkehren** to have sexual

intercourse with sb.

Geschlechtlichkeit *f* sexuality.

Geschlechts-: ~**akt** *m* sex act; ~**erziehung** *f* sex education; **g~krank** *adj* suffering from VD; **g~krank sein** to have VD; ~**krankheit** *f* venereal disease; ~**leben** *nt* sex life; **g~los** *adj* asexual *(auch Biol)*, sexless; ~**losigkeit** *f* asexuality *(auch Biol)*, sexlessness; ~**merkmal** *nt* sex(ual) characteristic; ~**organ** *nt* sex organ; **g~reif** *adj* sexually mature; ~**reife** *f* sexual maturity; **g~spezifisch** *adj (Sociol)* sex-specific; ~**teil** *nt* genitals *pl*; ~**trieb** *m* sex drive; ~**umwandlung** *f* sex change; ~**verkehr** *m* sexual intercourse.

geschlichen *ptp of* **schleichen.**

geschliffen 1 *ptp of* **schleifen**[2]. **2** *adj Manieren* polished, refined; *Sätze* polished.

geschlossen 1 *ptp of* **schließen. 2** *adj* closed; *(vereint)* unified. **in sich** *(dat)* ~ self-contained; *Mensch, Charakter* well-rounded; *Handlung* well-knit; **ein ~es Ganzes** a unified whole; ~**e Gesellschaft** *(Fest)* private function; ~**e Ortschaft** built-up area. **3** *adv* ~ **für etw sein/stimmen** to be/vote unanimously in favour of sth; ~ **hinter jdm stehen** to stand solidly behind sb.

Geschlossenheit *f* unity.

geschlungen *ptp of* **schlingen.**

Geschmack *m* ⸚**e** *or (hum, col)* ⸚**er** *(lit, fig)* taste; *(Aroma)* flavour *(Brit)*, flavor *(US)*; *(no pl: ~ssinn)* sense of taste. **je nach** ~ to one's own taste; **Salz (je) nach** ~ **hinzufügen** add salt to taste; **an etw** *(dat)* ~ **finden** to acquire a taste for sth; **auf den** ~ **kommen** to acquire a taste for it; **er hat einen guten** ~ *(fig)* he has good taste; **das ist nicht nach meinem** ~ that's not to my taste; **die** ⸚**er sind verschieden** tastes differ; **über** ~ **läßt sich (nicht) streiten** *(Prov)* there's no accounting for taste(s) *(prov)*.

geschmacklich *adj (lit, fig)* as regards taste.

geschmacklos *adj (lit, fig)* tasteless.

Geschmacklosigkeit *f* **(a)** *no pl (lit, fig)* tastelessness, lack of taste; *(Taktlosigkeit auch)* bad taste. **(b)** *(Beispiel der ~)* example of bad taste; *(Bemerkung)* remark in bad taste.

Geschmacks-: ~**frage** *f* question of (good) taste; ~**richtung** *f* taste; *(von Speisen etc)* flavour *(Brit)*, flavor *(US)*; ~**sache** *f* matter of taste; **das ist ~sache** it's (all) a matter of taste; ~**sinn** *m* sense of taste; ~**verirrung** *f* **unter ~verirrung leiden** *(iro)* to have no taste.

geschmackvoll *adj* tasteful.

geschmeidig *adj* **(a)** *Haar, Leder, Haut* supple; *Fell* sleek; *(weich) Handtuch, Haar* soft; *Teig* workable. **(b)** *(fig) (anpassungfähig)* flexible; *(wendig)* adroit.

Geschmeidigkeit *f no pl siehe adj* **(a)** suppleness; sleekness; softness. **(b)** flexibility, adroitness.

Geschmier(e) *nt no pl (col)* mess; *(Geschriebenes)* scribble, scrawl.

geschmissen *ptp of* **schmeißen.**

geschmolzen *ptp of* **schmelzen.**

Geschmorte(s) *nt decl as adj (Cook)* braised meat.

Geschnatter *nt no pl (lit)* cackling; *(fig)* jabbering.

Geschnetzelte(s) *nt decl as adj (Cook) meat cut into strips stewed to produce a thick sauce.*

geschniegelt *adj (pej)* flashy.

geschnitten *ptp of* **schneiden.**

geschoben *ptp of* **schieben.**

gescholten *ptp of* **schelten.**

Geschöpf *nt* **-e** *(Geschaffenes)* creation; *(Lebewesen)* creature.

geschoren *ptp of* **scheren**[1].

Geschoß[1] *nt* **-sse** projectile *(form)*; *(Wurf~, Rakete etc auch)* missile; *(Kugel auch)* bullet.

Geschoß[2] *nt* **-sse** *(Stockwerk)* floor, storey *(Brit)*, story *(US)*.

Geschoßbahn *f* trajectory.

geschossen *ptp of* **schießen.**

geschraubt *adj (pej) Stil, Redeweise* pretentious.

Geschrei *nt no pl* shouts *pl*, shouting; *(von Verletzten, Babys, Popfans)* screams *pl*, screaming; *(fig: Aufhebens)* fuss, to-do *(col)*. **viel ~ um etw machen** to make a big fuss about sth.

geschrieben *ptp of* **schreiben.**

geschrie(e)n *ptp of* **schreien.**

geschritten *ptp of* **schreiten.**

geschunden *ptp of* **schinden.**

Geschütz *nt* **-e** gun. **schweres** ~ heavy artillery; **schweres ~ auffahren** *(fig)* to bring up one's big guns.

Geschütz-: ~**feuer** *nt* shell fire; ~**rohr** *nt* gun barrel.

geschützt *adj Winkel, Ecke* sheltered; *Pflanze, Tier* protected.

Geschwader *nt* - squadron.

Geschwafel *nt no pl (pej col)* waffle *(col)*.

Geschwätz *nt no pl (pej)* prattle; *(Klatsch)* tittle-tattle *(col)*, gossip.

geschwätzig *adj* talkative; *(klatschsüchtig)* gossipy.

Geschwätzigkeit *f no pl siehe adj* talkativeness; gossipy nature.

geschweift *adj* **(a)** curved. **(b)** *Stern* with a tail.

geschweige *conj* ~ **(denn)** let alone.

geschwiegen *ptp of* **schweigen.**

geschwind *adj* quick, fast *no adv*.

Geschwindigkeit *f* speed; *(Phys: von Masse)* velocity. **mit einer ~ von ...** at a speed of ...; **mit höchster** ~ at top speed.

Geschwindigkeits-: ~**begrenzung,** ~**beschränkung** *f* speed limit; **gegen die ~begrenzung verstoßen** to exceed the speed limit; ~**kontrolle** *f* speed check; ~**messer** *m* tachometer; *(Aut auch)* speedometer; ~**überschreitung** *f* exceeding the speed limit *no art*, speeding *no art*.

Geschwister *pl* brothers and sisters *pl*. **haben Sie noch ~?** do you have any brothers or sisters?

Geschwister-: ~**liebe** *f* brotherly/sisterly love; *(gegenseitig)* love between a brother and a sister; ~**paar** *nt* brother and sister *pl*.

geschwollen 1 *ptp of* **schwellen. 2** *adj (pej)* turgid.

geschwommen *ptp of* **schwimmen.**

geschworen *ptp of* **schwören.**

Geschworene(r) *mf decl as adj* juror. **die ~n** the jury *sing or pl*.

Geschwulst *f* ⸚**e** growth; *(Hirn~, Krebs~ etc auch)* tumour *(Brit)*, tumor *(US)*.

geschwunden *ptp of* **schwinden.**

geschwungen 1 *ptp of* **schwingen. 2** *adj* curved.

Geschwür *nt* **-e** ulcer; *(Furunkel)* boil; *(fig)* ulcer.

gesegnet *adj (geh)* **mit etw ~ sein** to be blessed with sth; **~es Neues Jahr!** Happy New Year; **einen ~en Schlaf haben** to be a sound sleeper.

gesehen *ptp of* **sehen.**

Geselle *m (wk)* **-n, -n (a)** *(Handwerks~)* journeyman. **(b)** *(dated col: Bursche)* fellow.

gesellen* *vr* **sich zu jdm** ~ to join sb.

Gesellen-: ~**brief** *m* articles *pl*; ~**prüfung** *f* examination to become a journeyman.

gesellig *adj* sociable, convivial; *Tier* gregarious; *Verkehr* social. **~es Beisammensein** social gathering.

Geselligkeit *f* **(a)** *no pl* sociability; *(geselliges Leben)* social intercourse. **die ~ lieben** to be sociable. **(b)** *(Veranstaltung)* social gathering.

Gesellschaft *f* **(a)** *(Sociol, Vereinigung)* society; *(Comm)* company. **die ~ verändern** to change society. **(b)** *(Abend~)* reception, party; *(Gäste)* guests *pl*, party. **geschlossene** ~ private party. **(c)** *(Umgang, Begleitung)* company. **in schlechte ~ geraten** to get into bad company; **jdm ~**

leisten to keep sb company; **darf ich Ihnen ~ leisten?** may I join you? **(d)** *(Kreis von Menschen)* group of people; *(pej)* crowd *(col)*. **wir waren eine bunte ~** we were a mixed bunch.

Gesellschafter(in *f*) *m* **- (a)** *(Unterhalter)* companion; *(euph: Prostituierte)* escort. **ein guter ~ sein** to be good company. **(b)** *(Comm) (Teilhaber)* shareholder; *(Partner)* partner. **stiller ~** sleeping *(Brit) or* silent *(US)* partner.

gesellschaftlich *adj* social. **er ist ~ erledigt** he's ruined socially.

Gesellschafts-: ~anzug *m* formal dress; **g~fähig** *adj Verhalten* socially acceptable; *Mensch, Aussehen auch* presentable; **~form** *f* social system; **~kapital** *nt (Comm)* authorized capital; **~klasse** *f (Sociol)* social class; **~klatsch** *m* society gossip; **~kleidung** *f* formal dress; **~kritik** *f* social criticism; **g~kritisch** *adj* critical of society; **g~kritisch denken** to have a critical attitude towards society; **~ordnung** *f* social system; **~reise** *f* group tour; **~roman** *m* social novel; **~schicht** *f* social stratum; **~spiel** *nt* party game; **~stück** *nt (Theat)* comedy of manners; *(Art)* genre painting; **~system** *nt* social system; **~tanz** *m* ballroom dance.

Gesenk *nt* **-e** *(Tech)* die.

gesessen *ptp of* **sitzen.**

Gesetz *nt* **-e** *(Jur, Natur~, Prinzip)* law; *(~buch)* statute book; *(Parl)* act; *(Vorlage)* bill; *(Satzung, Regel)* rule. **das Copyright-~** the Copyright Act; **nach dem ~** under the law *(über+acc* on*)*; **vor dem ~** in (the eyes of the) law; **im Sinne des ~es** within the meaning of the act; **steht etwas davon im ~?** is there any law about it?; **das ~ der Schwerkraft** the law of gravity; **das oberste ~ (der Wirtschaft** *etc***)** the golden rule (of industry *etc*); **ein ungeschriebenes ~** an unwritten rule.

Gesetz-: ~blatt *nt* law gazette; **~entwurf** *m* (draft) bill.

Gesetzes-: ~brecher(in *f*) *m* **-** law-breaker; **~hüter** *m (iro)* guardian of the law; **~novelle** *f* amendment; **~text** *m* wording of a/the law; **g~treu** *adj* law-abiding; **~treue** *f* law abidingness; **~übertretung** *f* infringement of a/the law.

Gesetz-: g~gebend *adj attr* legislative, law-making; **die g~gebende Gewalt** the legislature; **~geber** *m* legislator, lawmaker; **~gebung** *f* legislation *no pl*.

gesetzlich 1 *adj Bestimmungen, Vertreter, Zahlungsmittel* legal; *Feiertag, Reglungen* statutory; *(rechtmäßig)* lawful, legitimate. **2** *adv* legally; *(durch Gesetze auch)* by law; *(rechtmäßig)* lawfully, legitimately.

Gesetzlichkeit *f no pl (Gesetzmäßigkeit)* legality.

Gesetz-: g~los *adj* lawless; **~losigkeit** *f* lawlessness; **g~mäßig** *adj (gesetzlich)* legal; *(rechtmäßig)* lawful, legitimate; **~mäßigkeit** *f siehe adj* legality; lawfulness, legitimacy.

gesetzt 1 *adj (reif)* sedate, sober. **ein Herr im ~en Alter** a man of mature years. **2** *conj* **~ den Fall, ...** assuming (that) ...

Gesetz-: g~widrig *adj* illegal; *(unrechtmäßig)* unlawful; **~widrigkeit** *f siehe adj* illegality; unlawfulness *no pl*.

ges. gesch. = gesetzlich geschützt reg'd.

Gesicht *nt* **-er (a)** face. **ein trauriges/böses/wütendes ~ machen** to look sad/cross/angry; **ein langes ~ machen** to pull a long face; **was machst du denn heute für ein ~?** what's up with you today?; **jdm ins ~ sehen** to look sb in the face; **den Tatsachen ins ~ sehen** to face facts; **jdm etw ins ~ sagen** to tell sb sth to his face; **mir schien die Sonne ins ~** the sun was (shining) in my eyes; **es stand ihm im ~ geschrieben** it was written all over his face; **jdm ins ~ springen** *(fig col)* to go for sb; **sein wahres ~ zeigen** to show (oneself in) one's true colours *(Brit) or* colors *(US)*; **jdm wie aus dem ~ geschnitten sein** to be the spitting image of sb; **das/sein ~ verlieren** to lose face; **das ~ wahren** to save face.

(b) *(fig) (Aussehen)* look, appearance; *(geh: Charakter)* character. **die Sache bekommt ein anderes ~** the matter takes on a different complexion.

(c) *no pl* **das Zweite ~** second sight; **etw aus dem ~ verlieren** *(lit, fig)* to lose sight of sth; **jdn/etw zu ~ bekommen** to set eyes on sb/sth.

Gesichts-: ~ausdruck *m* (facial) expression; *(Mienenspiel auch)* face; **einen ängstlichen ~ausdruck haben** to look scared; **~creme** *f* face cream; **~farbe** *f* complexion; **~haut** *f* facial skin; **~kreis** *m* **(a)** *(dated: Umkreis)* field of vision; **jdn aus dem/seinem ~kreis verlieren** to lose sight of sb; **(b)** *(fig)* horizons *pl*, outlook; **g~los** *adj (fig)* faceless; **~packung** *f* face pack; **~pflege** *f* facial care; **~punkt** *m (Betrachtungsweise)* point of view; *(Einzelheit)* point; **unter diesem ~punkt betrachtet** looked at from this standpoint; **~verlust** *m* loss of face; **~wasser** *nt* face lotion; **~winkel** *m* visual angle; *(fig)* angle; **aus** *or* **unter diesem ~winkel betrachtet** looked at from this angle; **~züge** *pl* features *pl*.

Gesindel *nt no pl (pej)* riff-raff *pl*.

gesinnt *adj usu pred* **jdm gut/übel ~ sein** to be well/ill disposed to(wards) sb; **jdm freundlich/feindlich ~ sein** to be friendly/hostile to sb; **sozial ~ sein** to be socially minded; **er ist anders ~ als wir** his views are different from ours.

Gesinnung *f (Charakter)* cast of mind; *(Ansichten)* views *pl*, basic convictions *pl*; *(Einstellung)* fundamental attitude; *(Denkart)* way of thinking; *(einer Gruppe)* ethos. **seine wahre ~ zeigen** to show (oneself in) one's true colours *(Brit) or* colors *(US)*.

Gesinnungs-: ~genosse *m* like-minded person; **g~los** *adj (pej)* unprincipled; **sich g~los verhalten** to show a total lack of character; **~losigkeit** *f* lack of principle; **~schnüffelei** *f (pej)* **~schnüffelei betreiben** to pry into people's political convictions; **~täter** *m* person motivated by political/moral convictions; **g~treu** *adj* true to one's convictions; **~wandel** *m* conversion.

gesittet *adj* **(a)** *(wohlerzogen)* well-mannered, well-behaved. **(b)** *(zivilisiert)* civilized.

Gesocks *nt no pl (pej)* riff-raff *pl*.

Gesöff *nt* **-e** *(pej)* muck *(col)*; *(Bier)* piss *(col!)*.

gesoffen *ptp of* **saufen.**

gesogen *ptp of* **saugen.**

gesondert *adj* separate.

gesonnen 1 *ptp of* **sinnen. 2** *adj* **~ sein, etw zu tun** to be of a mind to do sth.

gespalten *adj Bewußtsein* split; *Lippe* cleft.

Gespann *nt* **-e** *(Pferde~)* horse and cart; *(zur Personenbeförderung)* horse and carriage; *(fig col: Paar)* pair. **ein gutes ~ abgeben** to make a good team.

gespannt *adj* **(a)** *Seil, Schnur* taut. **(b)** *(fig)* tense; *Beziehungen auch* strained. **seine Nerven waren aufs äußerste ~** his nerves were at breaking point. **(c)** *(neugierig)* curious; *(begierig)* eager; *Aufmerksamkeit* rapt. **in ~er Erwartung** in eager anticipation; **ich bin ~, wie er darauf reagiert** I wonder how he'll react to that; **ich bin auf seine Reaktion sehr ~** I'm dying to see how he'll react to that; **ich bin ~ wie ein Flitz(e)bogen** *(hum col)* I'm on tenterhooks; **da bin ich aber ~!** I'm looking forward to that; *(iro)* that I'd like to see!

Gespanntheit *f no pl siehe adj* **(a)** tension. **(b)** tension; strain. **(c)** curiosity; eagerness.

Gespenst *nt* **-er** ghost; *(fig: Gefahr)* spectre *(Brit)*, specter *(US)*. **~er sehen** *(fig col)* to imagine things.

Gespenster-: ~geschichte *f* ghost story; **g~haft** *adj* ghostly *no adv*; *(fig)* eerie, eery; **das Licht flackerte g~haft** the light flickered eerily; **~stunde** *f* witching hour.

gespenstisch *adj* = **gespensterhaft.**
gespie(e)n *ptp of* **speien.**
gespielt *adj* feigned. **mit ~em Interesse** with a pretence *(Brit) or* pretense *(US)* of being interested.
Gespinst *nt* **-e** *(fig geh)* web; *(der Phantasie)* product, fabrication.
gesponnen *ptp of* **spinnen.**
Gespött *nt no pl* mockery; *(Gegenstand des Spotts)* laughing stock. **sich zum ~ der Leute machen** to make oneself a laughing stock.
Gespräch *nt* **-e (a)** *(Unterhaltung)* conversation; *(Diskussion)* discussion; *(Dialog)* dialogue. **~e** *(Pol)* talks; **ein ~ unter vier Augen** a confidential *or* private talk; **im ~ sein** to be under discussion; **mit jdm ins ~ kommen** to get into conversation with sb; *(fig)* to establish a dialogue with sb. **(b)** *(~sstoff)* **das ~ des Tages** the topic of the hour; **das ~ der Stadt** the talk of the town; **zum ~ werden** to become a talking-point. **(c)** *(Telec: Anruf)* (telephone) call.
gesprächig *adj* talkative; *(mitteilsam)* communicative.
Gesprächs-: ~einheit *f (Telec)* unit; **~gegenstand** *m* topic; **~partner** *m* **~partner bei der Diskussion sind die Herren X, Y und Z** taking part in the discussion are Mr X, Mr Y and Mr Z; **mein ~partner bei den Verhandlungen** my opposite number at the talks; **wer war dein ~partner?** who did you talk with?; **~stoff** *m* topics *pl*; *(Diskussionsstoff)* topics to discuss; **~thema** *nt* topic.
gespreizt *adj (fig)* affected, unnatural.
gesprenkelt *adj* speckled.
gesprochen *ptp of* **sprechen.**
gesprossen *ptp of* **sprießen.**
gesprungen *ptp of* **springen.**
Gespür *nt no pl* feel(ing).
gest. = **gestorben.**
Gestalt *f* **-en (a)** *(lit, fig)* form; *(Umriß auch)* shape. **in ~ von** *(fig)* in the form of; **(feste) ~ annehmen** to take shape; **einer Sache** *(dat)* **~ geben** to shape sth; **sich in seiner wahren ~ zeigen** *(fig)* to show (oneself in) one's true colours *(Brit) or* colors *(US)*. **(b)** *(Wuchs)* build. **(c)** *(Persönlichkeit, Traum~)* figure; *(Liter auch, pej: Mensch)* character.
gestalten* **1** *vt* to shape, to form *(zu* into*)*; *Wohnung* to lay out; *Programm, Abend* to arrange; *Schaufenster* to dress; *Freizeit* to structure. **ich gestalte mein Leben so, wie ich will** I organize my life the way I want to; **etw interessanter** *etc* **~** to make sth more interesting *etc*; **schöpferisches G~** creative expression. **2** *vr (sich entwickeln)* to develop *(zu* into*)*.
Gestalter(in *f***)** *m* **-** creator.
gestalterisch *adj* formal, creative.
Gestaltung *f siehe vt* shaping, forming *(zu* into*)*; lay-out; arrangement; dressing; structuring.
gestanden 1 *ptp of* **stehen, gestehen. 2** *adj attr* **ein ~er Mann** a mature and experienced man.
geständig *adj* **~ sein** to have confessed.
Geständnis *nt* confession. **jdm ein ~ machen** to make a confession to sb.
Gestänge *nt* **-** *(von Gerüst)* bars *pl*, struts *pl*; *(von Zelt)* frame; *(von Maschine)* linkage.
Gestank *m no pl* stink, stench.
gestatten* *vti* to allow, to permit; *(einwilligen in)* to agree *or* consent to. **jdm ~, etw zu tun** to allow *or* permit sb to do sth; **~ Sie, daß ich ...?** may I ...?; **wenn Sie ~ ...** with your permission ...; **sich** *(dat)* **etw ~** to permit *or* allow oneself sth; **wenn ich mir eine Bemerkung ~ darf** *(geh)* if I might be permitted a comment.
Geste ['gɛstə, 'ge:stə] *f* **-n** *(lit, fig)* gesture.
Gesteck *nt* **-e** flower arrangement.
gestehen *vti irreg* to confess *(jdm etw* sth to sb*)*. **offen gestanden** quite frankly.
Gestein *nt* **-e** rock(s); *(Schicht)* rock stratum.
Gesteins-: ~brocken *m* rock; **~masse** *f* mass of rock.
Gestell *nt* **-e (a)** stand; *(Regal)* shelf; *(Ablage)* rack; *(Bett~, Brillen~)* frame; *(Fahr~)* chassis. **(b)** *(fig col: Beine)* pins *(col) pl*. **langes ~** beanpole *(col)*.
gestellt *adj (unecht)* posed.
gestelzt *adj* stilted.
gestern *adv* yesterday. **~ abend** *(früh)* yesterday evening; *(spät)* last night; **die Zeitung von ~** yesterday's paper; **Ansichten von ~** outdated views; **er ist nicht von ~** *(col)* he wasn't born yesterday.
gestiefelt *adj* **der G~e Kater** Puss-in-Boots; **~ und gespornt** *(fig col)* ready and waiting.
gestiegen *ptp of* **steigen.**
Gestik ['gɛstɪk] *f no pl* gestures *pl*.
gestikulieren* [gɛstiku'li:rən] *vi* to gesticulate.
gestimmt *adj* **froh/düster ~** in a cheerful/sombre mood.
Gestirn *nt* **-e** star, heavenly body.
gestoben *ptp of* **stieben.**
Gestöber *nt* **-** *(Schnee~)* snowstorm.
gestochen 1 *ptp of* **stechen. 2** *adj Handschrift* clear, neat. **~ scharfe Fotos** needle-sharp photographs.
gestohlen 1 *ptp of* **stehlen. 2** *adj* **der/das kann mir ~ bleiben** *(col)* he/it can go hang *(col)*.
gestorben *ptp of* **sterben.**
gestört *adj* disturbed; *Rundfunkempfang* poor, with a lot of interference. **~er Kreislauf** circulation problems; **Kinder aus ~en Familien** children from problem families.
gestoßen *ptp of* **stoßen.**
Gestotter *nt no pl* stuttering, stammering.
gestreift *adj* striped. **eine rot-grün ~e Bluse** a red and green striped blouse.
gestrichen 1 *ptp of* **streichen. 2** *adj* **(a) frisch ~!** wet paint. **(b)** *(genau voll)* **~ voll** level; *(sehr voll)* full to the brim; **ein ~er Teelöffel voll** a level teaspoon(ful); **er hat die Hosen ~ voll** *(col)* he's shitting himself *(col!)*; **ich habe die Nase ~ voll** *(col)* I'm fed up to the back teeth with it *(col)*.
gestrig *adj attr* yesterday's. **unser ~es Schreiben** our letter of yesterday; **die ewig G~en** the stick-in-the-muds.
gestritten *ptp of* **streiten.**
Gestrüpp *nt* **-e** undergrowth, brushwood; *(fig)* jungle.
gestunken *ptp of* **stinken.**
Gestüt *nt* **-e** stud; *(Anlage auch)* stud farm.
Gesuch *nt* **-e** petition *(auf, um+acc* for*)*; *(Antrag)* application *(auf, um+acc* for*)*. **ein ~ einreichen** to lodge a petition/an application.
gesucht *adj (begehrt)* sought after. **sehr ~** (very) much sought after.
gesund *adj, comp* **¨er** *superl* **¨este(r, s)** *or adv* **am ¨esten** healthy; *(leistungsfähig)* fit; *Unternehmen, Politik auch* sound. **~ und munter** hale and hearty; **ich fühle mich nicht ganz ~** I don't feel too well; **~ leben** to live a healthy life; **jdn ~ schreiben** to certify sb (as) fit; **sonst bist du ~?** *(iro col)* are you feeling all right? *(iro)*; **wieder ~ werden** to recover.
gesunden* *vi aux sein (geh)* to recover *(auch fig)*, to regain one's health.
Gesundheit *f no pl siehe adj* health; fitness; soundness; *(von Klima, Lebensweise etc)* healthiness. **bei guter ~** in good health; **~!** bless you; **auf Ihre ~!** your (very good) health.
gesundheitlich *adj* **~ geht es mir nicht besonders** my health is not particularly good; **aus ~en Gründen** for health reasons.
Gesundheits-: ~amt *nt* public health department; **~apostel** *m (iro)* health freak *(col)*; **~behörde** *f* health authorities *pl*; **g~fördernd** *adj* healthy, good for the health; **~fürsorge** *f* health

care; **~pflege** *f* hygiene; **öffentliche ~pflege** public health (care); **~schaden** *m* health defect; **~schäden** damage to one's health; **g~schädlich** *adj* unhealthy, damaging to (one's) health; **~wesen** *nt* health service; **~zeugnis** *nt* health certificate; **~zustand** *m no pl* state of health.

gesund-: ~schrumpfen *sep* **1** *vt (fig)* to trim down; **2** *vr* to streamline; **~stoßen** *vr sep irreg (col)* to line one's pockets *(col)*.

Gesundung *f no pl (lit, fig)* recovery; *(Genesung)* convalescence, recuperation.

gesungen *ptp of* **singen.**

gesunken *ptp of* **sinken.**

getan *ptp of* **tun. nach ~er Arbeit** when the day's work is done.

Getier *nt no pl* **(a)** *(Tiere, esp Insekten)* creatures *pl.* **(b)** *(einzelnes)* creature.

getigert *adj (mit Streifen)* striped; *(mit Flecken)* piebald.

Getöse *nt no pl* din, racket; *(von Auto, Beifall etc)* roar. **mit ~** with a din.

getragen *adj* **(a)** *Kleidung* secondhand. **(b)** *(fig) Melodie, Tempo etc* stately *no adv.*

Getränk *nt* **-e** drink, beverage *(form).*

Getränke-: ~automat *m* drinks machine *or* dispenser; **~karte** *f (in Café)* list of beverages; *(in Restaurant)* wine list; **~steuer** *f* alcohol tax.

getrauen* *vr* to dare. **getraust du dich das?** do you dare do that?

Getreide *nt* **-** grain, cereal.

Getreide-: ~(an)bau *m* cultivation of grain *or* cereals; **~ernte** *f* grain harvest; **~feld** *nt* grain field, cornfield *(Brit)*; **~pflanze** *f* cereal (plant); **~speicher** *m* silo.

getrennt *adj* separate. **~ leben** to be separated, to live apart; **~ schlafen** not to sleep together.

getreten *ptp of* **treten.**

getreu *adj* **(a)** *(genau, entsprechend)* faithful, true *no adv.* **(b)** *pred+dat* true to.

Getriebe *nt* **- (a)** *(Tech)* gears *pl*; *(~kasten)* gearbox; *(Antrieb)* drive; *(von Uhr)* movement, works *pl.* **(b)** *(lebhaftes Treiben)* bustle, hurly-burly.

getrieben *ptp of* **treiben.**

Getriebeschaden *m* gearbox trouble *no indef art.*

getroffen *ptp of* **treffen.**

getrogen *ptp of* **trügen.**

getrost *adv* **du kannst dich ~ auf ihn verlassen** you need have no fears about relying on him; **die Firma könnte ~ etwas mehr zahlen** the company could easily pay a little more.

getrunken *ptp of* **trinken.**

Getto *nt* **-s** ghetto.

Getue [gəˈtuːə] *nt no pl (pej)* to-do *(col)*, fuss. **ein ~ machen** to make a to-do *(col) or* fuss.

Getümmel *nt no pl* turmoil. **sich ins ~ stürzen** to plunge into the tumult *or* hurly-burly.

Getuschel *nt no pl* whispering.

ge|übt *adj Auge, Ohr, Griff* practised *(Brit)*, practiced *(US)*; *Fahrer, Segler etc* proficient. **im Reden ~ sein** to be a proficient talker.

Gewächs *nt* **-e (a)** *(Pflanze)* plant. **(b)** *(Med)* growth.

gewachsen 1 *ptp of* **wachsen**[1]. **2** *adj* **(a)** *(von allein entstanden)* evolved. **(b) einer Sache** *(dat)* **~ sein** to be up to sth; **er ist seinem Bruder (an Stärke/Intelligenz) durchaus ~** he is his brother's equal in strength/intelligence.

Gewächshaus *nt* greenhouse; *(Treibhaus)* hothouse.

gewagt *adj* **(a)** *(kühn)* daring; *(gefährlich)* risky. **(b)** *(moralisch bedenklich)* risqué.

gewählt *adj Sprache* refined *no adv*, elegant.

gewahr *adj pred* **eine(r) Sache ~ werden** to become aware of sth.

Gewähr *f no pl* guarantee. **dadurch ist die ~ gegeben, daß ...** that guarantees that ...; **die Angabe erfolgt ohne ~** we accept no liability for the accuracy of this information.

gewähren* *vt* to grant; *Rabatt, Vorteile* to give; *Sicherheit, Schutz* to afford, to give. **jdm Unterstützung ~** to provide sb with support; **jdn ~ lassen** *(geh)* not to stop sb.

gewährleisten* *vt insep* to ensure *(jdm etw* sb sth*)*; *(garantieren)* to guarantee *(jdm etw* sb sth*)*.

Gewährleistung *f* guarantee. **zur ~ der Sicherheit** to ensure safety.

Gewahrsam *m no pl* **(a)** *(Verwahrung)* safekeeping. **etw in ~ nehmen** to take sth into safekeeping. **(b)** *(Haft)* custody. **jdn in ~ nehmen** to take sb into custody.

Gewährsmann *m, pl* **-männer** *or* **-leute** source.

Gewährung *f no pl siehe vt* granting; giving; affording.

Gewalt *f* **-en (a)** *(Macht, Herrschaft)* power. **die ausübende/gesetzgebende/richterliche ~** the executive/legislature/judiciary; **elterliche ~** parental authority; **jdn/etw in seine ~ bringen** to gain control of sb/sth; **unter jds ~** *(dat)* **stehen** to be under sb's control. **(b)** *no pl (Zwang)* force; *(~tätigkeit)* violence. **~ anwenden** to use force; **höhere ~** acts/an act of God; **nackte ~** brute force; **mit ~** by force; **etw mit aller ~ wollen** *(col)* to want sth desperately; **jdm/einer Sache ~ antun** to do violence to sb/sth; **einer Frau ~ antun** to violate a woman. **(c)** *no pl (Heftigkeit, Wucht)* force; *(elementare Kraft auch)* power.

Gewalt-: ~akt *m* act of violence; **~anwendung** *f* use of force *or* violence.

Gewaltenteilung *f* separation of powers.

Gewalt-: ~herrschaft *f no pl* tyranny; **~herrscher** *m* tyrant.

gewaltig *adj* **(a)** *(heftig) Sturm etc* violent. **(b)** *(groß, riesig)* colossal, immense; *Anblick* tremendous; *Stimme* powerful; *(col: sehr groß) Unterschied, Hitze etc* tremendous, colossal *(col).* **sich ~ irren** to be very much mistaken.

Gewalt-: g~los 1 *adj* non-violent; **2** *adv* without force/violence; **~losigkeit** *f no pl* non-violence; **~marsch** *m* forced march; *(fig)* marathon; **~maßnahme** *f (fig)* drastic measure; **g~sam 1** *adj* forcible; *Tod* violent; **2** *adv* forcibly, by force; **~tat** *f* act of violence; **g~tätig** *adj* violent; **~tätigkeit** *f (no pl: Brutalität)* violence; *(Handlung)* act of violence; **~verbrechen** *nt* crime of violence; **~verbrecher** *m* violent criminal; **~verzicht** *m* non-aggression.

Gewand *nt* **¨er** *(geh: Kleidungsstück)* garment; *(weites, langes)* robe, gown; *(Eccl)* vestment, robe; *(fig: Äußeres)* look; *(fig: Maske)* guise.

gewandt 1 *ptp of* **wenden. 2** *adj* skilful *(Brit)*, skillful *(US)*; *(körperlich)* nimble; *Auftreten, Stil* elegant.

Gewandtheit *f no pl siehe adj* skilfulness; nimbleness; elegance.

gewann *pret of* **gewinnen.**

Gewäsch *nt no pl (pej col)* twaddle *(col).*

gewaschen *ptp of* **waschen.**

Gewässer *nt* **-** stretch of water. **~** *pl* inshore waters *pl*, lakes, rivers and canals *pl*; **ein fließendes/stehendes ~** a stretch of running/standing water.

Gewässerschutz *m* prevention of water pollution.

Gewebe *nt* **-** *(Stoff)* fabric, material; *(~art)* weave; *(Biol)* tissue; *(fig)* web.

Gewehr *nt* **-e** *(Flinte)* rifle; *(Schrotbüchse)* shotgun. **~ ab!** *(Mil)* order arms!; **das ~ über!** *(Mil)* shoulder arms!; **präsentiert das ~!** *(Mil)* present arms!; **~ bei Fuß stehen** *(Mil)* to stand at order arms; *(fig col)* to be at the ready; **ran an die ~e!** *(dated col)* let's get started.

Gewehr-: ~kolben *m* rifle butt/butt of a shotgun; **~kugel** *f* rifle bullet; **~lauf** *m* rifle barrel/barrel of a shotgun.

Geweih *nt* **-e** (set of *sing)* antlers *pl.*

Gewerbe *nt* **-** trade. **das älteste ~ der Welt** *(hum)* the oldest profession in the world *(hum)*; **ein ~ (be)treiben** to carry on a trade.

Gewerbe-: ~aufsichtsamt *nt* ≈ factory inspectorate; **~betrieb** *m* commercial enterprise; **~ordnung** *f* trading regulations *pl*; **~schein** *m* trading licence *(Brit) or* license *(US)*; **~steuer** *f* trade tax; **~treibende(r)** *mf decl as adj* trader.

gewerblich *adj* commercial; *(industriell)* industrial. **die ~e Wirtschaft** industry; **diese Räume dürfen nicht ~ genutzt werden** these rooms are not to be used for commercial purposes.

gewerbsmäßig 1 *adj* professional. **~e Unzucht** *(form)* prostitution. **2** *adv* professionally, for gain.

Gewerkschaft *f* (trade *or* labor *US*) union.

Gewerkschaft(l)er(in *f*) *m* - trade *or* labor *(US)* unionist.

gewerkschaftlich *adj* (trade *or* labor *US*) union *attr*. **wir haben uns ~ organisiert** we organized ourselves into a union.

Gewerkschafts- *in cpds* (trade *or* labor *US*) union; **~bewegung** *f* (trade *or* labor *US*) union movement; **~bund** *m* federation of trade *or* labor *(US)* unions, ≈ Trades Union Congress *(Brit)*, ≈ Federation of Labor *(US)*; **~mitglied** *nt* member of a/the (trade *or* labor *US*) union.

gewesen 1 *ptp of* **sein**[1]. **2** *adj attr* former.

gewichen *ptp of* **weichen.**

gewichst [gə'vɪkst] *adj (col)* fly *(col)*, crafty.

Gewicht *nt* **-e** *no pl (lit, fig)* weight. **dieser Stein hat ein ~ von 100 kg** this rock weighs 100 kg; **spezifisches ~** specific gravity; **~ haben** *(lit)* to be heavy; *(fig)* to carry weight; **ins ~ fallen** to be crucial; **nicht ins ~ fallen** to be of no consequence; **einer Sache** *(dat)* **~ beimessen** to set (great) store by sth.

Gewicht-: ~heben *nt no pl (Sport)* weight-lifting; **~heber** *m* - weight-lifter.

gewichtig *adj (fig) (wichtig)* weighty; *(einflußreich)* influential.

Gewichts-: ~klasse *f (Sport)* weight (category); **~kontrolle** *f* weight check; **g~los** *adj* weightless; *(fig)* lacking substance; **~verlust** *m* weight loss; **~zunahme** *f* increase in weight.

gewieft *adj (col)* fly *(col)*, crafty *(in+dat* at*)*.

gewiesen *ptp of* **weisen.**

gewillt *adj* **~ sein, etw zu tun** to be willing to do sth; *(entschlossen)* to be determined to do sth.

Gewimmel *nt no pl* swarm; *(Menge)* crush, throng.

Gewinde *nt* - *(Tech)* thread.

Gewinde- *(Tech)*: **~bohrer** *m* (screw) tap; **~bolzen** *m* threaded bolt.

Gewinn *m* **-e (a)** *(Ertrag)* profit. **~ abwerfen** to make a profit; **aus etw ~ schlagen** *(col)* to make a profit out of sth; **etw mit ~ verkaufen** to sell sth at a profit. **(b)** *(Preis, Treffer)* prize; *(bei Glücksspiel)* winnings *pl*. **jedes Los ist ein ~** every ticket a winner. **(c)** *no pl (fig: Vorteil)* gain. **das ist ein großer ~ (für mich)** that is of great benefit (to me).

Gewinn-: ~anteil *m* **(a)** *(Comm)* dividend; **(b)** *(beim Wetten etc)* share; **~ausschüttung** *f* prize draw; **~beteiligung** *f (Ind)* profit-sharing; **g~bringend** *adj (lit, fig)* profitable; **~chance** *f* chance of winning; **~chancen** *(beim Wetten)* odds.

gewinnen *pret* **gewann,** *ptp* **gewonnen 1** *vt* **(a)** to win. **jdn (für etw) ~** to win sb over (to sth); **jdn für sich ~** to win sb over (to one's side); **jdn zum Freund ~** to win sb as a friend; **den Eindruck ~, daß ...** to gain the impression that ...; **Zeit ~** to gain time; **was ist damit gewonnen?** what good is that?; **wie gewonnen, so zerronnen** *(prov)* easy come easy go *(prov)*. **(b)** *(als Profit)* to make (a profit of). **(c)** *(erzeugen)* to produce, to obtain; *Erze etc* to mine, to extract; *(aus Altmaterial)* to reclaim. **2** *vi* **(a)** to win *(bei, in+dat* at*)*. **(b)** *(profitieren)* to gain. **an Bedeutung ~** to gain (in) importance; **an Geschwindigkeit ~** to gain speed.

gewinnend *adj (fig)* winning, winsome.

Gewinner(in *f*) *m* - winner.

Gewinn-: ~spanne *f* profit margin; **~streben** *nt* pursuit of profit; **~sucht** *f* profit-seeking; **g~süchtig** *adj* profit-seeking *attr;* **g~trächtig** *adj* profitable.

Gewinnung *f no pl (von Kohle)* mining; *(von Zucker etc)* extraction.

Gewirr *nt no pl* tangle; *(fig: Durcheinander)* jumble; *(von Paragraphen, Straßen)* maze; *(von Stimmen)* confusion, babble.

gewiß 1 *adj* **(a)** *(sicher)* certain, sure *(+gen* of*)*. **(ja) ~!** certainly, sure *(esp US)*; **ich bin dessen ~** *(geh)* I'm certain *or* sure of it. **(b)** *attr* certain. **ein gewisser Herr Müller** a certain Herr Müller; **in gewissem Maße** to a certain extent. **2** *adv (geh)* certainly. **ich weiß es ganz ~** I'm certain of it.

Gewissen *nt no pl* conscience. **ein schlechtes ~** a guilty *or* bad conscience; **jdn/etw auf dem ~ haben** to have sb/sth on one's conscience; **jdm ins ~ reden** to have a serious talk with sb; **das mußt du vor deinem ~ verantworten** you'll have to answer to your own conscience for that.

Gewissen-: g~haft *adj* conscientious; **~haftigkeit** *f no pl* conscientiousness; **g~los** *adj* unprincipled; **~losigkeit** *f* lack of principle.

Gewissens-: ~bisse *pl* pangs of conscience *pl*; **mach dir deswegen keine ~bisse!** there's nothing for you to feel guilty about; **~bisse bekommen** to get a guilty conscience; **~entscheidung, ~frage** *f* matter of conscience; **~gründe** *pl* conscientious reasons *pl*; **~konflikt** *m* moral conflict; **~not** *f* moral dilemma.

gewissermaßen *adv (sozusagen)* so to speak, as it were; *(auf gewisse Weise)* in a way, to an extent.

Gewißheit *f* certainty. **mit ~** with certainty; *wissen* for certain *or* sure; **sich** *(dat)* **~ verschaffen** to find out for certain.

Gewitter *nt* - thunderstorm; *(fig)* storm.

Gewitterluft *f* thundery atmosphere.

gewittern* *vi impers* **es gewittert** it's thundering.

Gewitter-: ~regen, ~schauer *m* thundery shower; **~wolke** *f* thundercloud; *(fig col)* storm-cloud.

gewittrig *adj* thundery.

gewitzt *adj* crafty, cunning.

gewoben *ptp of* **weben.**

gewogen 1 *ptp of* **wiegen**[2]. **2** *adj (geh)* well-disposed *(+dat* towards*)*.

gewöhnen* 1 *vt* **jdn an etw** *(acc)* **~** to accustom sb to sth; **jdn an Höflichkeit ~** to teach sb to be polite; **jdn/etw gewöhnt sein** *(col)* to be used to sb/sth. **2** *vr* **sich an jdn/etw ~** to get used to sb/sth; **sich daran ~, etw zu tun** to get used *or* accustomed to doing sth.

Gewohnheit *f* habit. **aus (lauter) ~** from (sheer) force of habit; **die ~ haben, etw zu tun** to have a habit of doing sth; **sich** *(dat)* **etw zur ~ machen** to make a habit of sth.

Gewohnheits-: g~mäßig 1 *adj* habitual; **2** *adv (ohne nachzudenken)* automatically; **~mensch** *m* creature of habit; **~recht** *nt (Jur)* common law; **~trinker** *m* habitual drinker; **~verbrecher** *m* habitual criminal.

gewöhnlich 1 *adj* **(a)** *attr (allgemein, üblich)* usual; *(normal)* normal; *(alltäglich)* everyday. **ein ~er Sterblicher** an ordinary mortal. **(b)** *(pej: ordinär)* common. **2** *adv* normally, usually. **wie ~** as usual.

Gewöhnlichkeit *f (pej)* commonness.

gewohnt *adj* usual. **etw** *(acc)* **~ sein** to be used to sth.

gewohntermaßen *adv* usually.

Gewöhnung *f no pl (das Sich-Gewöhnen)* habituation *(an+acc* to*)*; *(das Angewöhnen)* training *(an +acc* in*)*; *(Sucht)* habit, addiction.

Gewölbe *nt* - *(Decken~)* vault; *(Keller~ auch)* vaults *pl.*
gewölbt *adj Stirn* domed; *Himmel, Decke* vaulted.
gewollt *adj* forced, artificial.
gewonnen *ptp of* **gewinnen.**
geworben *ptp of* **werben.**
geworden *ptp of* **werden.**
geworfen *ptp of* **werfen.**
gewrungen *ptp of* **wringen.**
Gewühl *nt no pl (Gedränge)* crowd, throng; *(Verkehrs~)* chaos, snarl-up *(col).*
gewunden 1 *ptp of* **winden. 2** *adj Weg, Fluß etc* winding; *Erklärung* roundabout *no adv,* tortuous.
gewunken *(dial) ptp of* **winken.**
gewürfelt *adj* check(ed).
Gewürz *nt* **-e** spice; *(Kräutersorte)* herb; *(Pfeffer, Salz)* seasoning.
Gewürz-: ~**bord** *nt* spice rack; ~**gurke** *f* pickled gherkin; ~**nelke** *f* clove; ~**ständer** *m* spice rack.
gewußt *ptp of* **wissen.**
Geysir ['gaizɪr] *m* **-e** geyser.
gez. = **gezeichnet.**
gezackt *adj Fels* jagged; *Blatt* serrated.
gezähnt *adj* serrated; *(Tech)* cogged; *Briefmarke* perforated.
gezeichnet *adj* marked; *(als Straffälliger auch)* branded. **vom Tode ~ sein** to have the mark of death on one.
Gezeiten *pl* tides *pl.*
Gezeiten-: ~**kraftwerk** *nt* tidal power station; ~**wechsel** *m* turn of the tide.
Gezeter *nt no pl (col: Schimpfen)* nagging.
gezielt *adj* purposeful; *Schuß* well-aimed; *Frage, Maßnahme etc* specific; *Hilfe* well-directed. ~ **schießen** to shoot to kill.
geziert *adj* affected.
Geziertheit *f* affectedness.
gezogen *ptp of* **ziehen.**
Gezwitscher *nt no pl* chirruping, twitter(ing).
gezwungen 1 *ptp of* **zwingen. 2** *adj (nicht entspannt)* forced; *Atmosphäre* strained; *Stil, Benehmen* stiff.
gezwungenermaßen *adv* of necessity. **etw ~ tun** to be forced to do sth, to do sth of necessity.
ggf. = **gegebenenfalls.**
Gicht *f no pl (Med)* gout.
Giebel *m* - gable; *(Tür~, Fenster~)* pediment.
Giebel-: ~**dach** *nt* gabled roof; ~**fenster** *nt* gable window; ~**haus** *nt* gabled house; ~**wand** *f* gable end *or* wall.
Gier *f no pl (nach* for) greed; *(Lüsternheit)* lust.
gierig *adj* greedy; *(nach Geld)* avaricious; *(lüstern)* lustful. ~ **nach etw sein** to be greedy for sth; *(nach Macht auch, sexuell)* to lust for sth.
gießen *pret* **goß,** *ptp* **gegossen 1** *vt* **(a)** to pour; *(verschütten)* to spill; *Pflanzen* to water. **(b)** *Metall* to cast *(zu* into). **2** *vi impers* to pour. **es gießt in Strömen** it's pouring down.
Gießer *m* - *(Metall)* caster, founder.
Gießerei *f (Werkstatt)* foundry.
Gieß-: ~**kanne** *f* watering can; ~**kannenprinzip** *nt no pl (col)* principle of indiscriminate all-round distribution.
Gift *nt* **-e** *(lit, fig)* poison; *(Schlangen~, fig: Bosheit)* venom. ~ **nehmen** to poison oneself; **das ist ~ für ihn** *(col)* that is very bad for him; **darauf kannst du ~ nehmen** *(col)* you can bet your life on it *(col)*; ~ **und Galle spucken** *(col)* to be fuming.
giften *vi (col)* to be vitriolic *(gegen* about).
Gift-: **g~frei** *adj* non-toxic; ~**gas** *nt* poison gas; **g~grün** *adj* bilious green; **g~haltig** *adj* poisonous, toxic.
giftig *adj* **(a)** *(Gift enthaltend)* poisonous; *Chemikalien etc auch* toxic. **(b)** *(fig) (boshaft)* venomous; *(zornig)* vitriolic. **(c)** *(grell)* bilious.
Gift-: ~**mischer(in** *f*) *m* - preparer of poison; *(fig)* trouble-maker; ~**müll** *m* toxic waste; ~**pfeil** *m* poisoned arrow; ~**pilz** *m* poisonous toadstool; ~**schlange** *f* poisonous snake; ~**zahn** *m* fang; ~**zwerg** *m (col)* spiteful little devil *(col).*
Gigant *m* giant.
gigantisch *adj* gigantic, colossal.
Gilde *f* **-n** guild.
Gin [dʒɪn] *m* **-s** gin. ~ **tonic** gin and tonic.
ging *pret of* **gehen.**
Ginster *m* - *(Bot)* broom; *(Stech~)* gorse.
Gipfel *m* - **(a)** *(Berg~)* summit; *(Spitze)* peak. **(b)** *(fig: Höhepunkt)* height; *(des Ruhms, der Karriere auch)* peak. **das ist der ~!** *(col)* that's the limit. **(c)** *(~konferenz)* summit.
Gipfel-: ~**konferenz** *f (Pol)* summit conference; ~**leistung** *f* crowning achievement.
gipfeln *vi* to culminate *(in +dat* in).
Gipfel-: ~**punkt** *m (lit)* zenith; *(fig)* high point; ~**stürmer** *m (liter)* conqueror of a/the peak; ~**treffen** *nt (Pol)* summit (meeting).
Gips *m* **-e** plaster. **einen Arm in ~ legen** to put an arm in plaster.
Gips- *in cpds* plaster; ~**abdruck** *m* plaster cast; ~**bein** *nt (col)* leg in plaster.
gipsen *vt* to plaster; *Arm, Bein* to put in plaster.
Gipser *m* - plasterer.
Gips-: ~**figur** *f* plaster (of Paris) figure; ~**verband** *m (Med)* plaster cast.
Giraffe *f* **-n** giraffe.
Girlande *f* **-n** garland *(aus* of).
Giro ['ʒiːro] *nt* **-s** *(Fin)* (bank) giro; *(Indossament)* endorsement. **durch ~** by giro.
Giro-: ~**bank** *f* giro bank; ~**konto** *nt* current *(Brit) or* checking *(US)* account; ~**verkehr** *m* giro system; *(~geschäft)* giro transfer (business).
girren *vi (lit, fig)* to coo.
Gis *nt* - *(Mus)* G sharp.
Gischt *m* **-e** *or f* **-en** spray.
Gitarre *f* **-n** guitar.
Gitarrespieler(in *f*) *m*, **Gitarrist(in** *f*) *m* guitarist, guitar-player.
Gitter *nt* - bars *pl*; *(vor Schaufenstern etc)* grille; *(in Fußboden, Straßendecke)* grid, grating; *(feines Draht~)* (wire-)mesh.
Gitter-: ~**fenster** *nt* barred window; ~**stab** *m* bar; ~**zaun** *m* paling; *(mit gekreuzten Stäben)* lattice fence.
Glacéhandschuh [gla'seː-] *m* kid glove. **jdn mit ~en anfassen** to handle sb with kid gloves.
Gladiator *m* gladiator.
Gladiole *f* **-n** *(Bot)* gladiolus.
Glanz *m no pl* gleam; *(von Oberfläche auch)* shine; *(Funkeln, von Augen)* sparkle; *(von Haaren, Seide)* sheen; *(von Farbe)* gloss; *(blendend: von Sonne)* glare; *(fig) (der Schönheit, Jugend)* radiance; *(von Ruhm)* glory; *(Pracht)* splendour *(Brit)*, splendor *(US)*. **mit ~ und Gloria** *(iro col)* in grand style; **eine Prüfung mit ~ bestehen** *(col)* to pass an exam with flying colours *(Brit) or* colors *(US).*
Glanz|abzug *m (Phot)* glossy *or* gloss print.
glänzen *vi (lit, fig)* to shine; *(glitzern)* to glisten; *(funkeln)* to sparkle; *(blenden)* to glare; *(Nase)* to be shiny. **vor jdm ~ wollen** to want to shine in front of sb.
glänzend *adj* shining; *(strahlend)* radiant; *(blendend)* dazzling; *(glitzernd)* glistening; *(funkelnd)* sparkling; *Papier* glossy, shiny; *Stoff, Nase* shiny; *(fig)* brilliant; *Aussehen, Fest* dazzling; *(erstklassig)* splendid. ~ **in Form** *(col)* in splendid form; **wir haben uns ~ amüsiert** we had a wonderful time; **mir geht es ~** I'm just fine.
Glanz-: ~**lack** *m* gloss (paint); ~**leistung** *f* brilliant achievement; **g~los** *adj (lit, fig)* dull; *Lack, Oberfläche* matt; ~**nummer** *f* big number, pièce de résistance; ~**papier** *nt* glossy paper; ~**punkt** *m (fig)* highlight, high spot; ~**stück** *nt* pièce de résistance; **g~voll** *adj (fig)* brilliant; *(prachtvoll)* glittering; ~**zeit** *f* heyday.
Glas *nt* **-̈er** *or (als Maßangabe)* **- (a)** *(Stoff, Gefäß)*

glass; *(Konserven~)* jar. **ein ~ Milch** a glass of milk; **ein ~ Marmelade** a jar of jam; **zwei ~ Wein** two glasses of wine; **zu tief ins ~ schauen** *(col)* to have one too many. **(b)** *(Brillen~)* lens *sing*; *(Fern~)* binoculars *pl*.

Glas- *in cpds* glass; **~bläser** *m* glassblower; **~bruch** *m* broken glass.

Gläschen ['glɛːsçən] *nt dim of* **Glas** *(Getränk)* little drink.

Glaser *m* - glazier.

Glaserei *f* **(a)** *no pl (Handwerk)* glasswork. **(b)** *(Werkstatt)* glazier's workshop.

Gläsertuch *nt* glasscloth.

Glas-: ~faser *f* fibreglass *(Brit)*, fiberglass *(US)*; **~fenster** *nt* glass window; **~fiberstab** *m (Sport)* fibreglass *(Brit) or* fiberglass *(US)* pole; **~form** *f* glass mould; *(Backform)* glass *or* Pyrex ® dish; **~geschirr** *nt* glassware; **~haus** *nt* greenhouse; *(in botanischen Gärten etc)* glasshouse; **wer (selbst) im ~haus sitzt, soll nicht mit Steinen werfen** *(Prov)* people who live in glass houses shouldn't throw stones *(Prov)*.

glasieren* *vt* to glaze; *Kuchen* to ice, to frost *(US)*.

glasig *adj Blick* glassy; *(Cook) Kartoffeln* waxy; *Speck, Zwiebeln* transparent.

Glas-: ~kasten *m* glass case; *(in Fabrik, Büro)* glass box; **g~klar** *adj (lit)* clear as glass; *(fig)* crystal-clear; **~kugel** *f* glass ball; *(Murmel)* marble; **~perle** *f* glass bead; **~platte** *f* glass top; **~scheibe** *f* sheet of glass; *(Fenster~)* pane of glass; **~scherbe** *f* piece of broken glass; **~scherben** broken glass; **~schneider** *m* glass cutter; **~schrank** *m* glass-fronted cupboard; **~splitter** *m* splinter of glass.

Glasur *f* glaze; *(Metall)* enamel; *(Zuckerguß)* icing, frosting *(US)*.

Glas-: ~waren *pl* glassware *sing*; **~watte, ~wolle** *f* glass wool.

glatt *comp* **-er** *or* **¨er,** *superl* **-este(r, s)** *or* **¨este(r, s)** *or (adv)* **am -esten** *or* **¨esten 1** *adj* **(a)** *(eben)* smooth; *Haar* straight; *(Med) Bruch* clean; *(faltenlos) Stoff* uncreased. **(b)** *(schlüpfrig)* slippery. **(c)** *(fig) Landung, Ablauf* smooth. **(d)** *attr (col: klar, eindeutig)* outright; *Lüge, Unsinn etc auch* downright. **(e)** *(pej: allzu gewandt)* smooth, slick. **2** *adv* **(a)** smoothly. **er hat sich ~ aus der Affäre gezogen** he wriggled neatly out of the whole affair. **(b)** *(ganz, völlig)* completely; *leugnen, ablehnen* flatly. **die Rechnung ist ~ aufgegangen** the sum works out exactly.

Glätte *f no pl* smoothness *(auch fig)*; *(von Haar)* sleekness; *(Schlüpfrigkeit)* slipperiness.

Glatt|eis *nt* ice. **„Vorsicht ~!"** "danger, black ice"; **sich auf ~ begeben** *(fig)* to be skating on thin ice; **jdn aufs ~ führen** *(fig)* to take sb for a ride *(col)*.

glätten 1 *vt (glattmachen)* to smooth out; *(glattstreichen) Haar, Tuch* to smooth. **2** *vr* to smooth out; *(Wellen, fig)* to subside.

Glatt-: g~gehen *vi sep irreg aux sein* to go smoothly; **g~hobeln** *vt sep* to plane smooth; **g~kämmen** *vt sep* to comb straight; **g~rasiert** *adj Mann, Kinn* clean-shaven; *Beine* shaved; **g~schleifen** *vt sep irreg* to rub smooth; *Diamanten etc* to grind smooth; **g~schneiden** *vt sep irreg* to cut straight; **g~streichen** *vt sep irreg* to smooth out; *Haare* to smooth (down); **g~weg** ['glatvɛk] *adv (col)* simply, just; **das ist g~weg erlogen** that's a blatant lie.

Glatze *f* **-n** bald head. **eine ~ bekommen/haben** to go/be bald.

Glatz-: ~kopf *m* bald head; *(col: Mann mit Glatze)* baldie *(col)*; **g~köpfig** *adj* bald(-headed).

Glaube(n) *m no pl (Vertrauen, Rel)* faith *(an+acc* in*)*; *(Überzeugung)* belief *(an+acc* in*)*. **in gutem ~n** in good faith; **(bei jdm) ~n finden** to be believed (by sb); **den ~n an jdn/etw verlieren** to lose faith in sb/sth; **jdm ~n schenken** to give credence to sb.

glauben *vti* to believe *(an +acc* in*)*; *(meinen, vermuten)* to think. **jdm ~** to believe sb; **das glaube ich dir nicht** I don't believe you; **glaube es mir** believe me; **jdm (etw) aufs Wort ~** to take sb's word (for sth); **d(a)ran ~ müssen** *(col)* to cop it *(col)*; *(sterben auch)* to buy it *(col)*; **das glaubst du doch selbst nicht!** you can't be serious; **ob du es glaubst oder nicht, ...** believe it or not ...; **wer's glaubt, wird selig** *(iro)* a likely story *(iro)*; **wer hätte das je geglaubt!** who would have thought it?; **er glaubte sich unbeobachtet** he thought nobody was watching him; **es ist nicht zu ~** it's incredible *or* unbelievable; **ich glaube, ja** I think so; **ich glaube, nein** I don't think so.

Glaubens-: ~bekenntnis *nt* creed; **~eifer** *m* religious zeal; **~frage** *f* question of faith; **~freiheit** *f* religious freedom; **~gemeinschaft** *f* religious sect; *(christliche auch)* denomination; **~kampf** *m* religious battle; **~satz** *m* dogma, doctrine; **~streit** *m* religious controversy.

glaubhaft *adj* credible, believable; *(einleuchtend)* plausible. **(jdm) etw ~ machen** to satisfy sb of sth.

Glaubhaftigkeit *f no pl* credibility; *(Evidenz)* plausibility.

gläubig *adj* religious; *(vertrauensvoll)* trusting.

Gläubige(r) *mf decl as adj* believer. **die ~n** the faithful.

Gläubiger(in *f***)** *m* - *(Comm)* creditor.

glaublich *adj*: **kaum ~** scarcely credible.

glaubwürdig *adj* credible. **~e Quellen** reliable sources.

Glaubwürdigkeit *f no pl* credibility.

gleich 1 *adj (identisch, ähnlich)* same; *(~wertig, ~berechtigt, Math)* equal. **die/das ~e ... wie** the same ... as; **in ~em Abstand** at an equal distance; **zu ~en Teilen** in equal parts; **in ~er Weise** in the same way; **mit ~er Post** with the same post; **das ~e, aber nicht dasselbe Auto** the same (type of) car, but not the identical one; **wir wollten alle das ~e** we all wanted the same thing; **es waren die ~en, die ...** it was the same ones who/which ...; **zwei mal zwei (ist) ~ vier** two times two equals *or* is four; **jdm (an etw** *dat***) ~ sein** to be sb's equal in sth; **ihr Männer seid doch alle ~!** you men are all the same!; **es ist mir (alles** *or* **ganz) ~** it's all the same to me; **ganz ~ wer/was** *etc* no matter who/what *etc*; **G~es mit G~em vergelten** to pay like with like; **~ und ~ gesellt sich gern** *(Prov)* birds of a feather flock together *(Prov)*.

2 *adv* **(a)** *(ebenso)* equally; *(auf ~e Weise)* alike, the same. **sie sind ~ groß/alt** they are the same size/age.

(b) *(räumlich)* immediately, just. **~ hinter dem Haus** just behind the house.

(c) *(sofort)* immediately, right away; *(bald)* in a minute. **~ am Anfang** at the very beginning; **~ danach** right after(wards); **ich komme ~** I'm just coming; **es ist ~ drei Uhr** it's very nearly three o'clock; **das habe ich mir ~ gedacht** I thought that straight away; **warum nicht ~ so?** why didn't you say/do that in the first place?; **wann machst du das? — ~!** when are you going to do it? — in just a moment; **so wirkt das Bild ~ ganz anders** suddenly, the picture has changed completely; **er ging ~ in die Küche** he went straight to the kitchen; **bis ~!** see you in a while.

(d) *(in Fragesätzen)* again. **wie war doch ~ Ihr Name?** what was your name again?

Gleich-: g~altrig *adj* (of) the same age; **g~artig 1** *adj* of the same kind *(+dat* as*)*; *(ähnlich)* similar *(+dat* to*)*; **2** *adv* in the same way; similarly; **~artigkeit** *f* similarity; **g~auf** *adv (esp Sport)* equal; **g~auf liegen** to be lying equal; **g~bedeutend** *adj* synonymous *(mit* with*)*; *(so gut wie)* tantamount *(mit* to*)*; **~behandlung** *f* equal treatment; **g~berechtigt** *adj* with equal rights; **g~berechtigt sein** to have equal rights; **~berechtigung** *f* equal rights *sing or pl*, equality *(+gen, von* for*)*; **g~bleiben** *sep irreg aux sein* **1** *vi* to remain the same; **2** *vr* **sich** *(dat)* **g~bleiben** *(Mensch)* to remain the same; **das bleibt sich g~** it doesn't matter; **g~bleibend** *adj* constant, steady; **bei g~bleibendem Gehalt** when one's salary stays the same.

gleichen *pret* **glich,** *ptp* **geglichen** *vi* **jdm/einer Sache ~** to be like sb/sth; **sich ~** to be alike; **jdm an Schönheit ~** to be sb's equal in beauty.

Gleich-: g~falls *adv (ebenfalls)* likewise; *(auch)* also; **danke g~falls!** thank you, (and) the same to you; **g~farbig** *adj* (of) the same colour *(Brit) or* color *(US)*; **g~förmig** *adj (einheitlich, fig: eintönig)* uniform *(auch Phys)*; **~förmigkeit** *f* uniformity; **g~geschlechtig** *adj (Biol, Zool)* of the same sex, same-sex *attr;* **g~geschlechtlich** *adj* **(a)** homosexual; **(b)** = **g~geschlechtig**; **g~gesinnt** *adj* like-minded; **g~gestellt** *adj* equal *(+dat* to, with*)*, on a par *(+dat* with*)*; **rechtlich g~gestellt** equal in law.

Gleichgewicht *nt no pl (lit, fig)* balance, equilibrium. **das ~ verlieren** to lose one's balance; *(fig)* to be thrown off balance; **das ~ (be)halten** *(lit)* to keep one's balance; *(fig)* to retain one's equilibrium; **jdn aus dem ~ bringen** to throw sb off balance.

gleichgewichtig *adj* balanced.

Gleichgewichts-: ~sinn *m* sense of balance; **~störung** *f* impaired balance.

gleichgültig *adj* indifferent *(gegenüber* to, towards*)*; *(uninteressiert)* apathetic *(gegenüber* towards*)*; *(unwesentlich)* trivial. **Politik ist ihm ~** he doesn't care about politics; **~, was er tut** no matter what he does; **bin ich dir gänzlich ~ geworden?** have I become a matter of complete indifference to you?

Gleichgültigkeit *f* indifference *(gegenüber* to, towards*)*; *(Desinteresse)* apathy *(gegenüber* towards*)*.

Gleichheit *f* **(a)** *no pl (gleiche Stellung)* equality; *(Identität)* identity; *(Übereinstimmung)* uniformity; *(Ind)* parity. **(b)** *(Ähnlichkeit)* similarity.

Gleichheits-: ~prinzip *nt* principle of equality; **~zeichen** *nt (Math)* equals sign.

Gleich-: ~klang *m (fig)* harmony, accord; **g~kommen** *vi sep irreg aux sein+dat* **(a) niemand kommt ihm an Dummheit g~** no-one can equal him for stupidity; **(b)** *(g~bedeutend sein mit)* to be tantamount *or* equivalent to; **~lauf** *m no pl (Tech)* synchronization; **g~laufend** *adj* parallel *(mit* to*)*; *(Tech)* synchronized; **g~lautend** *adj* identical; **~macherei** *f (pej)* levelling down *(pej)*, egalitarianism; **~maß** *nt no pl* **(a)** *(Ebenmaß)* evenness; *(von Proportionen)* symmetry; **(b)** *(Eintönigkeit)* monotony *(pej)*, regularity; **g~mäßig** *adj* even, regular; *Puls auch* steady; *Abstände* regular; **etw g~mäßig verteilen** to distribute sth equally; **die Farbe g~mäßig auftragen** to apply the paint evenly; **~mäßigkeit** *f siehe adj* evenness, regularity; steadiness; regularity; **~mut** *m* equanimity, serenity.

Gleichnis *nt* **(a)** *(Liter)* simile. **(b)** *(Allegorie)* allegory; *(Bibl)* parable.

Gleich-: g~rangig *adj Beamte etc* equal in rank *(mit* to*)*, at the same level *(mit* as*)*; *Probleme etc* equally important; **g~richten** *vt sep (Elec)* to rectify.

gleichsam *adv (geh)* as it were. **~, als ob** just as if.

Gleich-: g~schalten *vt sep (pej)* to bring into line; **~schaltung** *f (pej)* bringing into line; **g~schenk(e)lig** *adj Dreieck* isosceles; **~schritt** *m no pl (Mil)* marching in step; **im ~schritt** *(lit, fig)* in step; **im ~schritt, marsch!** forward march!; **g~seitig** *adj Dreieck* equilateral; **g~setzen** *vt sep (als dasselbe ansehen)* to equate *(mit* with*)*; *(als gleichwertig ansehen)* to treat as equivalent *(mit* to*)*; **~stand** *m no pl* **(a)** *(Sport)* **den ~stand erzielen** to draw level; **das Spiel wurde beim ~stand von 4:4 beendet** the game ended in a 4-all draw; **(b)** *(Pol)* equal stage of development; **g~stellen** *vt sep* **(a)** *(rechtlich etc)* to treat as equal; *siehe* **gleichgestellt**; **(b)** = **g~setzen; ~strom** *m (Elec)* direct current, DC; **g~tun** *vt impers sep irreg* **es jdm g~tun** to equal *or* match sb.

Gleichung *f* equation.

Gleich-: g~viel *adv (geh)* nonetheless; **g~viel ob** no matter whether; **g~wertig** *adj* of the same value; *(gleich zu bewerten) Leistung, Qualität* equal *(+dat* to*)*; *Gegner* evenly matched; **g~wohl** *(geh) adv* nevertheless, nonetheless; **g~zeitig** *adj* simultaneous; **ihr sollt nicht alle g~zeitig reden** you mustn't all speak at the same time; **~zeitigkeit** *f* simultaneity; **g~ziehen** *vi sep irreg (col)* to catch up *(mit* with*)*.

Gleis *nt* **-e** *(Rail)* line, track; *(einzelne Schiene)* rail; *(Bahnsteig)* platform; *(fig)* rut. **~ 6** platform *or* track *(US)* 6; **aus dem ~ springen** to jump the rails; **aus dem ~ kommen** *(fig)* to go off the rails *(col)*; **wieder ins richtige ~ kommen** *(fig)* to get back on the rails *(col)*.

Gleis-: ~arbeiten *pl* work on the line; **~bau** *m no pl* railway *(Brit) or* railroad *(US)* construction; **~kettenfahrzeug** *nt* caterpillar vehicle; **~körper** *m* railway *(Brit) or* railroad *(US)* track.

gleißen *vi (liter)* to gleam, to glisten.

gleiten *pret* **glitt,** *ptp* **geglitten** *vi aux sein* **(a)** to glide; *(Blick)* to pass; *(Hand auch)* to slide. **ein Lächeln glitt über ihr Gesicht** a smile flickered across her face. **(b)** *(rutschen)* to slide; *(Auto)* to skid; *(ent~: Gegenstand)* to slip. **ins G~ kommen** to start to slide *or* slip.

gleitend *adj* **~e Löhne** sliding wage scale; **~e Arbeitszeit** flexible working hours *pl*, flex(i)time.

Gleit-: ~flug *m* glide; **im ~flug niedergehen** to glide down; **~klausel** *f (Comm)* escalator clause; **~komma** *nt* floating point; **~zeit** *f* flex(i)time.

Gletscher *m* **-** glacier.

Gletscher-: ~bach *m* glacial stream; **~spalte** *f* crevasse; **~wasser** *nt* glacier water.

glich *pret of* **gleichen.**

Glied *nt* **-er (a)** *(Körperteil)* limb; *(Finger~, Zehen~)* joint. **seine ~er recken** to stretch (oneself); **das steckt ihr noch in den ~ern** she still hasn't got over it. **(b)** *(Penis)* penis. **(c)** *(Ketten~, fig)* link. **(d)** *(Teil)* section, part. **(e)** *(Mil)* rank. **ins ~ zurücktreten** to step back into the ranks.

gliedern 1 *vt* **(a)** *(ordnen)* to order, to organize. **(b)** *(unterteilen)* to (sub)divide *(in+acc* into*)*. **2** *vr* **sich ~ in** *(+acc)* to (sub)divide into.

Glieder-: ~puppe *f* jointed doll; *(Marionette)* (string) puppet, marionette; **~reißen** *nt*, **~schmerz** *m* rheumatic pains *pl*.

Gliederung *f* **(a)** *(das Gliedern)* organization; *(das Unterteilen)* subdivision. **(b)** *(Aufbau)* structure.

Glied-: ~maßen *pl* limbs *pl*; **~staat** *m* member state.

glimmen *pret* **glomm** *ptp* **geglommen** *vi* to glow.

Glimmstengel *m (hum col)* fag *(Brit col)*, cigarette, butt *(US col)*.

glimpflich *adj (mild)* mild, light. **~ davonkommen** to get off lightly; **~ ablaufen** *or* **verlaufen** to pass off without serious consequences.

glitschen *vi aux sein (col)* to slip *(aus* out of*)*.

glitschig *adj (col)* slippery, slippy *(col)*.

glitt *pret of* **gleiten.**

glitzern *vi* to glitter; *(Stern auch)* to twinkle.

global *adj* **(a)** *(weltweit)* global, worldwide. **(b)** *(ungefähr, pauschal)* general.

Globetrotter *m* **-** globetrotter.

Globus *m, pl* **Globen** *or* **-se** globe; *(col: Kopf)* nut *(col)*, bonze *(Brit col)*.

Glöckchen *nt* (little) bell.

Glocke *f* **-n** *(auch Blüte)* bell; *(Käse~ etc)* cover; *(Taucher~)* (diving) bell. **etw an die große ~ hängen** *(col)* to shout sth from the rooftops.

Glocken-: **~blume** *f* bellflower, campanula; **g~förmig** *adj* bell-shaped; **~geläut(e)** *nt* (peal of) bells; **~klöppel** *m* clapper; **~läuten** *nt* (peal of) bells; **~schlag** *m* stroke (of a/the bell); *(von Uhr auch)* chime; **~spiel** *nt (in Turm)* carillon; *(automatisch auch)* chimes *pl*; *(Instrument)* glockenspiel; **~strang** *m* bell rope; **~stuhl** *m* bell cage; **~ton** *m* sound of a/the bell; **~turm** *m* belfry.

Glöckner *m* **-** bellringer.

glomm *pret of* **glimmen.**

glorifizieren* *vt* to glorify.

Glorifizierung *f* glorification.

glorreich *adj* glorious. **seine Laufbahn ~ beenden** to bring one's career to a glorious conclusion.

Glossar *nt* **-e** glossary.

Glosse *f* **-n** **(a)** *(Press, Rad etc)* satirical commentary. **(b)** *(col)* **seine ~n über jdn/etw machen** *(col)* to make snide comments about sb/sth *(col)*.

glossieren* *vt (Press, Rad etc)* to do a satirical commentary on.

Glotzauge *nt (col)* **~n machen** to stare (goggle-eyed), to gawp.

Glotze *f* **-n** *(col)* goggle-box *(col)*.

glotzen *vi (pej col)* to gape *(auf, in+acc* at*)*.

Glück *nt no pl* **(a)** luck. **ein ~!** how lucky!, what a stroke of luck!; **~/kein ~ haben** to be lucky/unlucky; **er hat das ~ gehabt, zu ...** he was lucky enough to ...; **auf gut ~** *(aufs Geratewohl)* on the off-chance; *(unvorbereitet)* trusting to luck; *(wahllos)* at random; **du hast ~ im Unglück gehabt** it could have been a great deal worse (for you); **viel ~ (bei...)!** good luck *or* the best of luck (with ...)!; **~ bei Frauen haben** to be successful with women; **jdm zum Geburtstag ~ wünschen** to wish sb (a) happy birthday; **zum ~** luckily, fortunately; **das ist dein ~!** that's lucky for you!; **mehr ~ als Verstand haben** to have more luck than brains; **sie weiß noch nichts von ihrem ~** *(iro)* she doesn't know anything about it yet; **damit wirst du bei ihr kein ~ haben** you won't have any joy with her (with that) *(col)*; **sein ~ machen** to make one's fortune; **sein ~ probieren** to try one's luck; **er kann von ~ sagen, daß ...** he can count himself lucky that ...; **das hat mir gerade noch zu meinem ~ gefehlt!** *(iro)* that was all I wanted; **man kann niemanden zu seinem ~ zwingen** *(prov)* you can lead a horse to water but you can't make him drink *(prov)*.
(b) *(Freude)* happiness. **eheliches ~** wedded *or* marital bliss; **er ist ihr ganzes ~** he is her whole life.

Glück-: **~auf** *nt no pl* (cry of) "good luck"; **g~bringend** *adj* lucky, propitious *(form)*.

Glucke *f* **-n** *(Bruthenne)* broody hen; *(mit Jungen)* mother hen.

glucken *vi (brüten)* to brood; *(fig col)* to sit around.

glücken *vi aux sein* to be successful. **nicht ~** to be a failure; **es ist ihm geglückt zu fliehen** he succeeded in escaping; **es wollte nicht ~** it wouldn't go right.

gluckern *vi* to glug.

glücklich 1 *adj* **(a)** *(froh)* happy. **ein ~es Ende** a happy ending; **~ machen** to bring happiness. **(b)** *(erfolgreich, vom Glück begünstigt)* lucky, fortunate; *(vorteilhaft, erfreulich)* happy. **~e Reise!** have a pleasant journey! **2** *adv* **(a)** *(froh, selig)* happily. **(b)** *(mit Glück)* by luck; *(vorteilhaft, erfreulich)* happily. **(c)** *(col: endlich, zu guter Letzt)* finally, eventually.

glücklicherweise *adv* luckily, fortunately.

glücklos *adj* hapless, luckless.

Glücks-: **~bote** *m* bearer of (the) glad tidings; **~bringer** *m* **-** *(Talisman)* lucky charm.

glückselig *adj* blissful.

Glückseligkeit *f* bliss, rapture.

glucksen *vi* **(a)** *(Kleinkind)* to gurgle; *(Erwachsener)* to chortle. **(b)** *(gluckern)* to glug.

Glücks-: **~fall** *m* stroke of luck; **durch einen ~fall** by a lucky chance; **~gefühl** *nt* feeling of happiness; **~kind** *nt* child of Fortune; **~klee** *m* four-leaf(ed) clover; **~pilz** *m* lucky beggar *(col)*; **~rad** *nt* wheel of fortune; **~ritter** *m* adventurer; **~sache** *f* **das ist ~sache** it's a matter of luck; **das war reine ~sache** it was pure luck *or* a pure fluke *(col)*; **~spiel** *nt* game of chance; **~spieler** *m* gambler; **~strähne** *f* lucky streak; **~tag** *m* lucky day; **~treffer** *m* stroke of luck; *(beim Schießen, Ftbl)* lucky shot, fluke *(col)*; **~zahl** *f* lucky number.

Glückwunsch *m* **¨e** congratulations *pl (zu* on*)*. **herzlichen ~** congratulations; **herzlichen ~ zum Geburtstag!** happy birthday, many happy returns (of the day).

Glüh- *(Elec)*: **~birne** *f* (electric) light bulb; **~draht** *m* filament.

glühen 1 *vi* to glow. **vor Fieber ~** to be flushed with fever; **der Haß glühte in ihm** he was burning with hatred. **2** *vt* to heat until red-hot.

glühend *adj* glowing; *(heiß~) Metall* red-hot; *Hitze* blazing; *(fig: leidenschaftlich)* ardent; *Haß* burning; *Wangen* flushed, burning.

Glüh-: **~faden** *m (Elec)* filament; **~lampe** *f (form)* electric light bulb; **~wein** *m* glühwein, mulled wine, glogg *(US)*; **~würmchen** *nt* glow-worm; *(fliegend)* firefly.

Glut *f* **-en** **(a)** *(glühende Masse, Kohle)* embers *pl*; *(Tabaks~)* burning ash; *(Hitze)* heat. **(b)** *(fig liter) (glühende Farbe, Hitze)* glow; *(Leidenschaft)* ardour *(Brit)*, ardor *(US)*.

Glut-: **~hitze** *f* sweltering heat; **g~rot** *adj (liter)* fiery red.

Glyzerin *nt no pl (Chem)* glycerin(e).

GmbH [geːǀɛmbeːˈhaː] *f* **-s** = **Gesellschaft mit beschränkter Haftung** limited company, Ltd *(Brit)*, Inc *(US)*.

Gnade *f* **-n** *(Barmherzigkeit)* mercy; *(Rel)* grace; *(Gunst)* favour *(Brit)*, favor *(US)*; *(Verzeihung)* pardon. **um ~ bitten** to ask for mercy; **bei jdm ~ finden** to find favour with sb; **~ vor Recht ergehen lassen** to temper justice with mercy; **ohne ~** without mercy; **~!** mercy!; **Euer ~n!** *(Hist)* Your Grace; **die ~ haben, etw zu tun** *(iro)* to graciously consent to do sth.

gnaden *vi*: **(dann) gnade dir Gott!** (then) God help you *or* heaven have mercy on you.

Gnaden-: **~akt** *m* act of mercy; **~brot** *nt no pl* **jdm/einem Tier das ~brot geben** to keep sb/an animal in his/her/its old age; **einem Pferd das ~brot geben** to put a horse out to grass; **~frist** *f* (temporary) reprieve; **eine ~frist von 24 Stunden** 24 hours' grace; **~gesuch** *nt* plea for clemency; **g~los** *adj* merciless; **~losigkeit** *f* mercilessness; **~schuß** *m* **einem Tier den ~schuß geben** to put an animal out of its misery; **~stoß** *m* coup de grâce *(with sword etc, fig)*; **~tod** *m (geh)* mercy killing, euthanasia.

gnädig *adj (barmherzig)* merciful; *(herablassend)* gracious; *Strafe* lenient; *(freundlich)* kind. **~es Fräulein** *(form)* madam; *(jüngere Dame)* miss; **~e Frau** *(form)* madam, ma'am; **~er Gott!** *(col)* merciful heavens! *(col)*; **Gott sei uns ~!** *(geh)* Lord preserve us; **sei doch so ~, und mach mal Platz!** *(iro)* would you be so good as to make some room?; **es ~ machen** to show leniency.

Gnom *m (wk)* **-en, -en** gnome.

Gnu *nt* **-s** *(Zool)* gnu.

Gobelin [gobəˈlɛ̃ː] *m* **-s** tapestry, Gobelin.

Gockel *m* **-** *(esp SGer)* cock; *(fig)* old goat *(col)*.

Go-Kart *m* **-s** kart, go-cart.

Gold *nt no pl (lit, fig)* gold. **nicht mit ~ zu bezahlen** *or* **aufzuwiegen sein** to be worth one's weight in gold; **ein Herz aus ~** a heart of gold; **er hat ~ in der Kehle** he has a golden voice; **es ist nicht alles ~, was glänzt** *(Prov)* all that glitters is not gold *(Prov)*.

Gold- *in cpds* gold; *(von Farbe)* golden; **~ader** *f* vein of gold; **~barren** *m* gold ingot; **~barsch** *m (Rotbarsch)* redfish; **g~blond** golden blond.

golden *adj attr (lit, fig)* golden; *(aus Gold)* gold, golden *(liter)*. **~e Schallplatte** gold disc; **~er Humor** irrepressible sense of humour; **~e Worte** words of wisdom; **ein ~es Herz haben** to have a heart of gold; **die ~e Mitte wählen** to strike a happy medium; **~e Hochzeit** golden wedding (anniversary); **das G~e Zeitalter** *(Myth, fig)* the golden age; **der Tanz ums G~e Kalb** *(fig)* the worship of Mammon.

Gold-: g~farben, g~farbig *adj* golden, gold-coloured *(Brit)*, gold-colored *(US)*; **~fisch** *m* goldfish; **~gräber** *m* gold-digger; **~grube** *f (lit, fig)* goldmine; **~hamster** *m* (golden) hamster.

goldig *adj (fig col: allerliebst)* sweet, cute *(col)*. **du bist vielleicht ~!** *(iro)* the ideas you get!

Gold-: ~junge *m (col)* golden boy *(col)*; **~klumpen** *m* gold nugget.

Goldmedaille *f* gold medal.

Goldmedaillengewinner *m* gold medallist *(Brit) or* medalist *(US)*.

Gold-: ~mine *f* gold mine; **~rausch** *m* gold fever; **~regen** *m (Bot)* laburnum; *(Feuerwerkskörper)* Roman candle; *(fig)* riches *pl*; **~reserve** *f (Fin)* gold reserves *pl*; **g~richtig** *adj (col)* absolutely *or* dead *(col)* right; *Mensch* all right *(col)*; **~schatz** *m* golden treasure; *(von Geld)* hoard of gold; **~schmied** *m* goldsmith; **~schnitt** *m no pl* gilt edging; **~stück** *nt* piece of gold; *(fig col)* treasure; **~sucher** *m* gold-hunter; **~waage** *f* gold *or* bullion balance; **jedes Wort auf die ~waage legen** *(sich vorsichtig ausdrücken)* to weigh one's words; *(überempfindlich sein)* to be hypersensitive; **~währung** *f* gold standard; **~zahn** *m* gold tooth.

Golf[1] *m* **-e** *(Meerbusen)* gulf.

Golf[2] *nt no pl (Sport)* golf.

Golfer(in *f*) *m* **-** *(col)* golfer.

Golf- *in cpds (Sport)* golf; **~platz** *m* golf course; **~schläger** *m* golf club; **~spieler** *m* golfer; **~staaten** *pl* **die ~staaten** the Gulf States *pl*; **~strom** *m (Geog)* Gulf Stream.

Gondel *f* **-n** gondola.

gondeln *vi aux sein (col) (reisen)* to travel around; *(herumfahren)* to drive around. **durch die Welt ~** to go globetrotting *(col)*.

Gong *m* **-s** gong; *(bei Boxkampf etc)* bell.

Gongschlag *m* stroke of the gong.

gönnen *vt* **jdm etw ~** not to grudge sb sth; *(zuteil werden lassen)* to allow sb sth; **jdm etw nicht ~** to grudge sb sth; not to allow sb sth; **sich** *(dat)* **etw ~** to allow oneself sth; **er gönnte mir keinen Blick** he didn't spare me a single glance; **ich gönne ihm diesen Erfolg von ganzem Herzen** I'm delighted for him that he's had this success; **das sei ihm gegönnt** I don't grudge him that.

Gönner(in *f*) *m* **-** patron.

Gönner-: g~haft *adj (pej)* patronizing; **g~haft tun** to play the big benefactor; **~miene** *f (pej)* patronizing air.

gor *pret of* **gären.**

Gör *nt* **-en** *(NGer col)* **(a)** *(kleines Kind)* brat *(pej col)*, kid *(col)*. **(b)** *(auch* **Göre***: Mädchen)* (cheeky *or* saucy) little miss.

Gorilla *m* **-s** gorilla; *(col: Leibwächter)* heavy *(col)*.

Gosche *f* **-n** *(esp SGer pej)* gob *(col)*, mouth. **halt die ~!** shut your mouth *or* gob *(col)*.

goß *pret of* **gießen.**

Gosse *f* **-n** *(Rinnstein, fig)* gutter. **in der ~ enden** *or* **landen** to end up in the gutter.

Gossensprache *f* gutter language.

Gote *m (wk)* **-n, -n, Gotin** *f* Goth.

Gotik *f no pl (Art)* Gothic (style); *(Epoche)* Gothic period.

gotisch *adj* Gothic.

Gott *m* **⸚er (a)** god; *(als Name)* God. **~ der Herr** the Lord God; **~ der Allmächtige** Almighty God; **der liebe ~** the dear Lord; **er ist ihr ~** she worships him like a god; **bei ~ schwören** to swear by Almighty God.

(b) dein Schicksal liegt in ~es Hand your fate is in God's hands; **dem lieben ~ den Tag stehlen** to laze the day(s) away; **den lieben ~ einen guten Mann sein lassen** *(col)* to take things as they come; **wie ~ ihn geschaffen hat** *(hum col)* as naked as the day he was born; **ein Bild für die ⸚er** *(hum col)* a sight for sore eyes; **das wissen die ⸚er** *(col)* God (only) knows; **ich bin weiß ~ nicht prüde, aber ...** God knows I'm no prude but ...; **so ~ will** *(geh)* God willing, D.V.; **~ und die Welt** *(fig)* everybody; **über ~ und die Welt reden** *(fig)* to talk about everything under the sun; **leider ~es** alas; **wie ~ in Frankreich leben** *(col)* to be in clover.

(c) grüß ~! *(esp SGer, Aus)* hello, good morning/afternoon/evening; **~ hab' ihn selig!** God have mercy on his soul; **in ~es Namen!** for heaven's sake!; **ach (du lieber) ~!** *(col)* oh Lord! *(col)*; **großer ~!** good God!; **bei ~!** by God!; **~ behüte** *or* **bewahre!, da sei ~ vor!** God *or* Heaven forbid!; **um ~es willen!** for heaven's *or* God's sake!; **~ sei Dank!** thank God!

Gott|erbarmen *nt* **zum ~** *(col)* pitiful(ly), pathetic(ally) *(col)*.

Götter-: g~gleich *adj* godlike; **~speise** *f (Cook)* jelly *(Brit)*, jello *(US)*.

Gottes-: ~anbeterin *f (Zool)* praying mantis; **~beweis** *m* proof of the existence of God; **~dienst** *m* service; **zum ~dienst gehen** to go to church; **g~fürchtig** *adj* godfearing; **~gabe** *f* gift from God; **~haus** *nt* place of worship; **~lästerer** *m* blasphemer; **~lästerung** *f* blasphemy; **~lohn** *m no pl* **etw für einen ~lohn tun** to do sth for love; **~mutter** *f* Mother of God; **~sohn** *m* Son of God; **~urteil** *nt* trial by ordeal.

gott-: ~gegeben *adj* god-given; **~gewollt** *adj* willed by God.

Gottheit *f (Göttergestalt)* deity. **jdn wie eine ~ verehren** to worship sb like a god.

Göttin *f* goddess.

göttlich *adj (lit, fig)* divine.

Gott-: g~lob *interj* thank heavens; **g~los** *adj* godless; *(verwerflich)* ungodly; **~losigkeit** *f no pl* godlessness; **~vater** *m no pl* God the Father; **g~verdammt** *adj attr (col!)* goddamn(ed) *(col!)*, damn(ed) *(col!)*; **g~verlassen** *adj* godforsaken; **~vertrauen** *nt* trust in God.

Götze *m (wk)* **-n, -n** *(lit, fig)* idol.

Götzen-: ~bild *nt* idol, graven image *(Bibl)*; **~dienst** *m*, **~verehrung** *f* idolatry.

Gourmet [gʊr'meː] *m* **-s** gourmet.

Gouvernante [guvɛr'nantə] *f* **-n** *(dated)* governess.

Gouverneur [guvɛr'nøːɐ] *m* governor.

Grab *nt* **⸚er** grave; *(Gruft)* tomb; *(fig: Untergang)* end, ruination. **jdn zu ~e tragen** to bear sb to his grave; **ein Geheimnis mit ins ~ nehmen** to take a secret with one to the grave; **verschwiegen wie ein ~** (as) silent as the grave; **er würde sich im ~e umdrehen, wenn ...** he would turn in his grave if ...; **du bringst mich noch ins ~!** you'll send me to an early grave!; **sich** *(dat)* **sein eigenes ~ schaufeln** *(fig)* to dig one's own grave; **seine Hoffnungen** *etc* **zu ~e tragen** *(geh)* to abandon one's hopes *etc*.

graben *pret* **grub**, *ptp* **gegraben 1** *vti* to dig. **nach Gold/Erz ~** to dig for gold/ore. **2** *vr* **sich in etw** *(acc)* **~** *(Zähnen, Krallen)* to sink into sth;

das hat sich mir tief ins Gedächtnis gegraben (geh) it has imprinted itself firmly on my memory.
Graben *m* ¨ ditch; *(trockener ~, Mil)* trench; *(Sport)* ditch; *(Sport: Wasser~)* water-jump. **im ~ liegen** *(Mil)* to be in the trenches.
Grabenkrieg *m (Mil)* trench warfare.
Gräber *pl of* **Grab.**
Gräberfeld *nt* cemetery, burial ground.
Grabes- *(liter)*: **~stille** *f* deathly hush; **~stimme** *f* sepulchral voice.
Grab-: **~inschrift** *f* epitaph, inscription *(on gravestone etc)*; **~kammer** *f* burial chamber; **~legung** *f* burial; **~mal** *nt, pl* **-mäler** *or (geh)* **-e** monument; *(~stein)* gravestone; **~platte** *f* memorial slab; **~rede** *f* funeral oration; **~schänder(in** *f*) *m* - defiler of the grave(s)/of graves; **~schändung** *f* defilement of graves; **~stätte** *f* grave; *(Gruft)* tomb; **~stein** *m* gravestone, tombstone; **~stelle** *f* (burial) plot.
Gracht *f* **-en** canal.
Grad *m* **-e** *(Sci, Univ, fig)* degree; *(Mil)* rank. **ein Winkel von 45 ~** an angle of 45 degrees; **auf dem 32. ~ nördlicher Breite** latitude 32 degrees north; **null ~** zero; **es kocht bei 100 ~** boiling occurs at 100 degrees; **ein Verwandter zweiten/dritten ~es** a relative once/twice removed; **Verbrennungen ersten ~es** *(Med)* first-degree burns; **bis zu einem gewissen ~e** to a certain degree; **in hohem ~(e)** to a large extent; **im höchsten ~(e)** extremely.
Grad-, grad- = **Gerad-, gerade-.**
grad(e) *adj (col)* = **gerade.**
Grad-: **~einteilung** *f* calibration, graduation; **~messer** *m (fig)* gauge *(gen, für* of); **~netz** *nt (Geog)* latitude and longitude grid.
graduell *adj (allmählich)* gradual; *(gering)* slight.
graduieren* **1** *vi (Univ)* to graduate. **2** *vt (in Grade einteilen)* to calibrate, to graduate.
Graduierte(r) *mf decl as adj* graduate.
Graf *m (wk)* **-en, -en** count; *(als Titel)* Count; *(britischer ~)* earl; *(als Titel)* Earl.
Grafengeschlecht *nt* family of counts/earls.
Grafik = **Graphik.**
Gräfin *f* countess.
gräflich *adj* count's/earl's.
Grafschaft *f* land of a count; earldom; *(Admin)* county.
Grahambrot *nt* (type of) wholemeal *(Brit) or* wholewheat *(US)* bread.
Gralshüter *m (fig)* guardian.
Gram *m no pl (geh)* grief, sorrow. **vom ~ gebeugt** bowed down with grief *or* sorrow.
grämen 1 *vr* **sich über jdn/etw ~** to grieve over sb/sth; **sich zu Tode ~** to die of grief *or* sorrow. **2** *vt* to grieve.
grämlich *adj* morose.
Gramm *nt* **-e** *or (nach Zahlenangabe)* - gram. **100 ~ Mehl** 100 grams of flour.
Grammatik *f* grammar.
grammatikalisch *adj* grammatical.
grammatisch *adj* grammatical.
Grammophon ® [gramo'fo:n] *nt* **-e** gramophone.
Granatapfel pomegranate.
Granate *f* **-n** *(Mil) (Geschoß)* shell; *(Hand~)* grenade; *(Ftbl sl: Schuß aufs Tor)* cannonball *(col)*.
Granat-: **~feuer** *nt* shelling, shellfire; **~splitter** *m* shell/grenade splinter; **~trichter** *m* shell crater; **~werfer** *m* mortar.
grandios *adj* magnificent, superb.
Granit *m* **-e** granite. **auf ~ beißen (bei ...)** to bang one's head against a brick wall (with ...).
grantig *adj (col)* grumpy.
Grapefruit ['gre:pfru:t] *f* **-s** grapefruit.
Graphik *f* **(a)** *no pl (Art)* graphic arts *pl*; *(Technik, Comp)* graphics. **(b)** *(Art: Darstellung)* graphic; *(Druck)* print; *(Schaubild)* illustration; *(technisches Schaubild)* diagram.
Graphiker(in *f*) *m* - graphic artist; *(Illustrator)* illustrator.
graphisch *adj* graphic; *(schematisch)* diagrammatic, schematic.
Grapho-: **~loge** *m*, **~login** *f* graphologist; **~logie** *f* graphology.
grapschen *(col)* **1** *vt* **(sich** *dat***) etw ~** to grab sth. **2** *vi* **nach etw ~** to make a grab at sth.
Gras *nt* **¨er (a)** grass. **ins ~ beißen** *(col)* to bite the dust *(col)*; **das ~ wachsen hören** *(zuviel hineindeuten)* to read too much into things; **über etw** *(acc)* **~ wachsen lassen** *(fig)* to let the dust settle on sth; **wo er zuschlägt, wächst kein ~ mehr** *(col)* he really packs a punch. **(b)** *gen* **-,** *no pl (Drogen sl: Marihuana)* grass.
Gras- *in cpds* grass; **g~bewachsen** *adj* grassy, grass-covered; **~büschel** *nt* tuft of grass.
grasen *vi* to graze.
Gras-: **~fläche** *f* grassland; *(Rasen)* patch of grass; **g~grün** *adj* grass-green; **~halm** *m* blade of grass; **~hüpfer** *m* - *(col)* grasshopper; **~land** *nt no pl* grassland; **~mücke** *f (Orn)* warbler; **~narbe** *f* turf; **~samen** *m* grass seed.
grassieren* *vi* to be rife.
gräßlich *adj* **(a)** hideous. **(b)** *(intensiv, unangenehm)* dreadful; *Mensch* horrible.
Gräßlichkeit *f* **(a)** hideousness. **(b)** *(gräßliche Tat etc)* atrocity.
Grat *m* **-e** *(Berg~)* ridge; *(Archit)* hip *(of roof)*; *(fig)* (dividing) line, border.
Gräte *f* **-n** (fish-)bone. **ich brech' dir alle ~n einzeln!** *(col)* I'll break every bone in your body.
Gratifikation *f* bonus.
gratis *adv* free; *(Comm)* free (of charge).
Gratis- *in cpds* free; **~probe** *f* free sample.
Grätsche *f* **-n** *(Sport)* straddle.
grätschen 1 *vi aux sein* to do a straddle (vault). **2** *vt Beine* to straddle, to put apart.
Gratulant(in *f*) *m* well-wisher.
Gratulation *f* congratulations *pl*.
Gratulationscour [-ku:ɐ] *f* congratulatory reception.
gratulieren* *vi* **jdm (zu einer Sache) ~** to congratulate sb (on sth); **jdm zum Geburtstag ~** to wish sb many happy returns (of the day); **(ich) gratuliere!** congratulations!
Gratwanderung *f (fig)* tightrope walk.
grau *adj* grey *(Brit)*, gray *(US)*; *(trostlos)* bleak. **~e Haare bekommen, ~ werden** *(col)* to go grey; **er malte die Lage ~ in ~** *(fig)* he painted a bleak picture of the situation; **~e Eminenz** éminence grise; **die (kleinen) ~n Zellen** *(hum)* the little grey cells; **der ~e Alltag** drab reality; **in ~er Vorzeit** *(fig)* in the dim and distant past; **das ist bloß ~e Theorie** that's all very well in theory.
Grau *nt* **-(s)** grey *(Brit)*, gray *(US)*; *(fig)* dullness, drabness.
Grau-: **g~äugig** *adj* grey-eyed *(Brit)*, gray-eyed *(US)*; **g~blau** *adj* grey-blue *(Brit)*, gray-blue *(US)*; **g~braun** *adj* greyish *(Brit) or* grayish *(US)* brown; **~brot** *nt siehe* **Mischbrot.**
grauen *vi impers* **mir graut vor etw** *(dat)* I dread sth; **mir graut vor ihm** I'm terrified of him.
Grauen *nt no pl* **(a)** horror *(vor* of). **(b)** *(grauenhaftes Ereignis)* horror.
grauen-: **~haft, ~voll** *adj* terrible, atrocious.
Grau-: **~gans** *f* grey(lag) *(Brit) or* gray(lag) *(US)* goose; **g~grün** *adj* grey-green *(Brit)*, gray-green *(US)*; **g~haarig** *adj* grey-haired *(Brit)*, gray-haired *(US)*; **g~meliert** *adj attr* greying *(Brit)*, graying *(US)*.
Graupe *f* **-n** *usu pl* grain of pearl barley. **~n** pearl barley *sing*.
Graupel *f* **-n** (small) hailstone. **~n** soft hail *sing*.
Graupel-: **~regen** *m*, **~schauer** *m* sleet.
Graupensuppe *f* barley broth *or* soup.
Graus *m no pl (old)* horror. **es war ein ~ zu sehen, wie ...** it was terrible to see how ...

grausam *adj (gefühllos, roh)* cruel *(gegen, zu* to*).* **sich ~ für etw rächen** to take (a) cruel revenge for sth.

Grausamkeit *f* **(a)** *no pl* cruelty. **(b)** *(grausame Tat)* (act of) cruelty; *(stärker)* atrocity.

Grauschimmel *m (Pferd)* grey *(Brit) or* gray *(US)* (horse).

grausen *vi impers siehe* **grauen.**

Grausen *nt no pl* horror *(vor* of*).* **da kann man das kalte ~ kriegen** *(col)* it's enough to give you the creeps *(col).*

grausig *adj* terrible, atrocious.

Grau-: ~ton *m* grey colour *(Brit),* gray color *(US);* **~zone** *f (fig)* grey *(Brit) or* gray *(US)* area.

Graveur(in *f*) [gra'vøːɐ, -øːrɪn] *m* engraver.

gravieren* [gra'viːrən] *vt* to engrave.

gravierend [gra'viːrənt] *adj* serious, grave.

Gravitation [gravita'tsioːn] *f* gravitation.

gravitätisch [gravi'tɛːtɪʃ] *adj* grave, solemn.

Gravur [gra'vuːɐ] *f* engraving.

Grazie [-iə] *f no pl (Liebreiz)* grace(fulness).

grazil *adj* (delicately) slender, gracile *(liter).* **~ gebaut sein** to have a delicate figure.

graziös *adj* graceful; *(lieblich)* charming.

greifbar *adj (konkret)* tangible, concrete; *(erreichbar)* available; *Ware* available, in stock *pred.* **in g~barer Nähe** within reach.

greifen *pret* **griff,** *ptp* **gegriffen 1** *vt (nehmen, packen)* to take hold of, to grasp; *(grapschen)* to seize, to grab; *(fangen)* to catch; *Akkord* to strike. **diese Zahl ist zu niedrig gegriffen** *(fig)* this figure is too low; **zum G~ nahe sein** *(Sieg)* to be within reach; **die Gipfel waren zum G~ nahe** you could almost touch the peaks; **aus dem Leben gegriffen** taken from life.

2 *vi* **(a) um sich ~** *(fig)* to spread, to gain ground; **unter etw** *(acc)* **~** to reach under sth; **nach einer Sache ~** to reach for sth; *(um zu halten)* to clutch *or (hastig)* grab at sth; **an etw** *(acc)* **~** *(fassen)* to grasp sth; *(berühren)* to touch sth; **zu etw ~** to reach for sth; *zu Methoden, Mitteln* to resort to sth; **sich** *(dat)* **an den Kopf** *or* **an die Stirn ~** *(fig)* to shake one's head in disbelief; **in die Saiten/Tasten ~** to strike up a tune; **zu den Waffen ~** to take up arms; **zum Äußersten ~** to resort to extremes; **nach der Macht ~** to try to seize power. **(b)** *(nicht rutschen, einrasten)* to grip; *(fig: wirksam werden)* to be effective.

Greifer *m* **-** *(Tech)* grab.

Greifvogel *m* bird of prey.

Greis *m* **-e** old man.

greis *adj* aged; *(ehrwürdig)* venerable; *(altersgrau)* grey *(Brit),* gray *(US),* hoary *(liter, hum).* **sein ~es Haupt schütteln** *(usu iro)* to shake one's wise old head.

Greisen-: ~alter *nt* extreme old age; **g~haft** *adj* very old, aged *attr; (von jüngerem Menschen)* like an old man/woman.

Greisin *f* old lady.

grell *adj Stimme, Ton* shrill, piercing; *Licht* glaring; *Farbe* garish, loud; *Gegensatz* sharp; *(stärker)* glaring.

Gremium *nt* body; *(Ausschuß)* committee.

Grenadier *m* **-e** *(Mil: Infanterist)* infantryman.

Grenz- *in cpds* border, frontier; **~bereich** *m* frontier *or* border zone *or* area; *(fig)* limits *pl*; **im ~bereich liegen** *(fig)* to lie at the limits.

Grenze *f* **-n** border; *(Landes~ auch)* frontier; *(Stadt~, zwischen Grundstücken)* boundary; *(fig: zwischen Begriffen)* dividing line, boundary; *(fig: äußerstes Maß)* limits *pl,* bounds *pl.* **die ~ zwischen Spanien und Frankreich** the Spanish-French border *or* frontier; **die ~ zu Österreich** the Austrian border; **über die ~ gehen/fahren** to cross the border; **einer Sache** *(dat)* **~n setzen** to set a limit *or* limits to sth; **keine ~n kennen** *(fig)* to know no bounds; **seine ~n kennen** to know one's limitations; **seiner Großzügigkeit sind keine ~n gesetzt** there is no limit to his generosity; **hart an der ~ des Erlaubten** bordering on the limits of what is permitted; **sich in ~n halten** *(fig)* to be limited; **die oberste/unterste ~** *(fig)* the upper/lower limit; **alles hat seine ~n** there are limits to everything.

grenzen *vi* **an etw** *(acc)* **~** *(lit)* to border (on) sth; *(fig)* to border *or* verge on sth.

Grenzen-: g~los 1 *adj (lit, fig)* boundless; **2** *adv* boundlessly; *(fig)* immensely; **~losigkeit** *f* boundlessness; *(fig)* immensity.

Grenzer *m* **-** *(col) (Zöllner)* customs man; *(Grenzsoldat)* border *or* frontier guard.

Grenz- *in cpds* border, frontier; **~fall** *m* borderline case; **~gänger** *m* **-** *(Arbeiter)* international commuter *(across a local border)*; **~gebiet** *nt (lit, fig)* border area; **~konflikt** *m* border *or* frontier dispute; **~kontrolle** *f* frontier control; **~linie** *f* border; *(Sport)* line; **~situation** *f* borderline situation; **~stadt** *f* border town; **~streitigkeit** *f* boundary dispute; *(Pol)* border *or* frontier dispute; **~übergang** *m* **(a)** border *or* frontier crossing(-point); **(b)** = **~übertritt; ~übertritt** *m* crossing of the border; **~verkehr** *m* border *or* frontier traffic; **~verlauf** *m* boundary line *(between countries)*; **~zwischenfall** *m* border incident.

Gretchenfrage *f (fig)* crunch question *(col),* sixty-four-thousand-dollar-question *(col).*

Greuel *m* **-** *(no pl: Abscheu)* horror; *(~tat)* atrocity. **~ vor etw haben** to have a horror of sth; **er/es ist mir ein ~** I loathe *or* detest him/it; **die Prüfung ist mir ein ~** I'm really dreading the exam.

Greuel-: ~märchen *nt* horror story; **~propaganda** *f* atrocity propaganda; **~tat** *f* atrocity.

greulich *adj siehe* **gräßlich.**

Griebe *f* **-n** *usu pl* ≈ crackling *no indef art, no pl.*

Grieche *m (wk)* **-n, -n, Griechin** *f* Greek.

Griechenland *nt* Greece.

griechisch *adj* Greek; *Architektur, Vase, Stil auch* Grecian. **die ~e Tragödie** Greek tragedy; **das G~e** Greek; **~-römisch** Graeco-Roman.

Griesgram *m* **-e** grouch *(col),* misery.

griesgrämig *adj* grumpy, grouchy *(col).*

Grieß *m* **-e** *(Cook)* semolina.

Grieß-: ~brei *m* semolina; **~pudding** *m* semolina pudding.

Griff *m* **-e (a)** *(das Greifen)* **der ~ nach etw** reaching for sth; **einen tiefen ~ in den Geldbeutel tun** *(fig)* to dig deep in one's pocket; **der ~ nach der Flasche** taking to the bottle; **der ~ nach der Macht** the bid for power. **(b)** *(Handgriff)* grip, grasp; *(beim Ringen etc)* hold. **mit festem ~** firmly; **jdn/etw in den ~ bekommen** *(fig)* to gain control of sb/sth; *(geistig)* to get a grasp of sth; **(mit jdm/etw) einen guten** *or* **glücklichen ~ tun** to make a wise choice (with sb/sth). **(c)** *(Stiel, Knauf)* handle; *(Pistolen~)* butt; *(Schwert~)* hilt; *(an Saiteninstrumenten)* neck. **(d)** *usu pl (Hunt: Kralle)* talon.

griff *pret of* **greifen.**

griffbereit *adj* ready to hand, handy.

Griffel *m* **-** *(Schreibstift)* slate pencil.

griffig *adj Fahrbahn etc* that has a good grip; *(fig) Ausdruck* useful, handy.

Grill *m* **-s** grill; *(Aut: Kühler~)* grille.

Grille *f* **-n (a)** *(Zool)* cricket. **(b)** *(dated col: Laune)* silly notion *or* idea.

grillen 1 *vt* to grill. **2** *vt* **sich (in der Sonne) ~ (lassen)** *(col)* to soak up the sun.

Grimasse *f* **-n** grimace. **~n schneiden** to make faces.

grimmig *adj* **(a)** *(zornig)* furious. **~ lächeln** to smile grimly; **~er Humor** grim humour. **(b)** *(sehr groß, heftig) Kälte etc* severe.

Grind *m* **-e** *(Schorf)* scab.

grinsen *vi* to grin; *(höhnisch auch)* to smirk.

Grinsen *nt no pl siehe vi* grin; smirk.

Grippe *f* **-n** 'flu, influenza; *(Erkältung)* cold.
Grippe- *in cpds* 'flu, influenza; ~**welle** *f* wave of 'flu *or* influenza.
Grips *m* **-e** *(col)* nous *(Brit col)*, sense.
grob *adj comp* **⸗er,** *superl* **⸗ste(r, s)** *or (adv)* **am ⸗sten (a)** *(nicht fein)* coarse; *Arbeit* dirty *attr.* **(b)** *(ungefähr)* rough. ~ **geschätzt** at a rough estimate. **(c)** *(schlimm)* gross *(auch Jur).* **den ⸗sten Schmutz habe ich schon weggeputzt** I have already cleaned off the worst of the dirt; **ein** ~**er Fehler** a bad mistake; **wir sind aus dem G⸗sten heraus** we're out of the woods (now). **(d)** *(brutal, derb)* rough; *(fig: derb)* coarse; *(unhöflich)* ill-mannered. ~ **gegen jdn werden** to become offensive (towards sb).
Grob- *in cpds* coarse; **g**~**gemahlen** *adj attr* coarse-ground; ~**heit** *f* **(a)** *no pl (lit, fig)* coarseness; *(Brutalität)* roughness; *(fig: Unhöflichkeit)* ill-manneredness; **(b)** *(Beschimpfung)* foul language *no indef art.*
Grobian *m* **-e** boor, lout.
grobkörnig *adj* coarse-grained.
gröblich *adj (geh)* gross. **jdn** ~ **beleidigen** to insult sb grossly; **jdn** ~ **beschimpfen** to call sb rude names.
Grob-: g~**maschig** *adj* large-meshed; *(~gestrickt)* loose-knit *attr;* **g**~**schlächtig** *adj* coarse; *Mensch* heavily built; ~**schnitt** *m (Tabak)* coarse cut.
Grog *m* **-s** grog.
groggy ['grɔgi] *adj pred (Boxen)* groggy; *(col: erschöpft)* all-in *(col).*
grölen *vti (pej)* to bawl. ~**de Menge** raucous crowd.
Groll *m no pl (geh: Zorn)* anger, wrath *(liter)*; *(Erbitterung)* resentment. **einen** ~ **gegen jdn hegen** to harbour *(Brit) or* harbor *(US)* a grudge against sb.
grollen *vi (geh)* **(a)** *(Donner etc)* to rumble, to roll. **(b) (jdm)** ~ *(old)* to be filled with wrath (against sb) *(liter).*
Grönland *nt* Greenland.
Grönländer(in *f*) *m* **-** Greenlander.
Gros [gro:] *nt* **-** [gro:s] greater part, bulk.
Groschen *m (col)* 10-pfennig piece; *(Aus)* groschen; *(fig)* penny, cent *(US).* **der** ~ **ist gefallen** *(hum col)* the penny has dropped *(col).*
Groschen-: ~**grab** *nt (hum) (Spielautomat)* one-armed bandit; **diese Parkuhr ist ein richtiges** ~**grab** this parking meter just swallows up your money; ~**heft** *nt (pej)* pulp magazine; *(Krimi auch)* penny dreadful *(dated)*; ~**roman** *m (pej)* cheap *or* dime *(US)* novel.
groß *comp* **⸗er,** *superl* **⸗te(r, s)** *or (adv)* **am ⸗ten 1** *adj* big; *Fläche, Haus, Hände, Summe auch, Dose, Packung etc* large; *Erfolg, Interesse, Schreck, Hoffnung auch, Freude, Leid, Höhe, Breite* great; *Buchstabe auch* capital; *Pause, Rede auch* long; *(hoch, hochgewachsen)* tall; *(bedeutend) Werk, Persönlichkeit etc* great; *Lärm* a lot of; *Geschwindigkeit* high. **wie** ~ **bist du?** how tall are you?; **du bist** ~ **geworden** you've grown; **ein ganz** ~**es Haus/Buch** a great big house/book; **die Wiese ist 10.000 m²** ~ the field is 100 metres square; **die** ~**e Masse** *(fig)* the vast majority; **ich habe nur** ~**es Geld** I haven't any change on me; **im** ~**en und ganzen (gesehen)** (taken) by and large; **die** ~**en Ferien** the long holidays; **die G**~**en** *(Erwachsene)* the grown-ups; **mit etw** ~ **geworden sein** to have grown up with sth; ~ **und klein** young and old (alike); ~**e Worte machen** to use big words; ~**en Hunger haben** to be very hungry; **eine der ⸗eren Firmen** one of the major companies; **ich habe** ~**e Lust zu etw** I would really like sth; **ich habe keine** ~**e Lust** I don't particularly want to; ~**e Mode sein** to be all the fashion; **er ist kein** ~**er Esser** *(col)* he's not a big eater; **ich bin kein** ~**er Redner** *(col)* I'm no great speaker; **jds** ~**e Stunde** sb's big moment; **einen** ~**en Namen haben** to be a big name; **er hat G**~**es geleistet** he has achieved great things; **Friedrich der G**~**e** Frederick the Great; **G**~**-Paris** Greater Paris; **der G**~**e Ozean** the Pacific.
2 *adv* **jdn** ~ **anblicken** to give sb a hard stare; **was soll man da schon** ~ **machen/sagen?** *(col)* you can't really do/say anything, can you?; ~ **daherreden** *(col)* to talk big *(col)*; ~ **und breit** *(fig col)* at great *or* enormous length; ~ **machen** *(baby-talk)* to do number two *(baby-talk)*; **ein Wort** ~ **schreiben** to write a word with a capital; **ganz** ~ **rauskommen** *(col)* to make the big time *(col).*
Groß- *pref* Great; *(vor Städtenamen)* Greater.
Groß-: ⁓**abnehmer** *m (Comm)* bulk buyer; ⁓**aktionär** *m* major *or* principal shareholder; ⁓**alarm** *m* red alert; **g**⁓**angelegt** *adj attr* large-scale, on a large scale; ⁓**angriff** *m* large-scale attack; **g**⁓**artig** *adj* tremendous; *(prächtig) Bauwerk etc* magnificent; **er hat** ~**artiges geleistet** he has achieved great things; ⁓**artigkeit** *f (Pracht)* magnificence; ⁓**aufnahme** *f (Phot, Film)* close-up; ⁓**bank** *f* big bank; ⁓**betrieb** *m* large concern; *(Agr)* big farm; ⁓**brand** *m* major fire; ~**britannien** *nt* (Great) Britain; ⁓**buchstabe** *m* capital (letter), upper case letter *(Typ).*
Größe *f* **-n (a)** size. **nach der** ~ according to size. **(b)** *no pl (Höhe, Körper~)* height; *(Flächeninhalt)* area; *(Maße)* dimensions *pl*; *(Math, Phys)* quantity. **eine unbekannte** ~ *(lit, fig)* an unknown quantity. **(c)** *no pl (Ausmaß)* extent; *(Bedeutsamkeit)* significance. **(d)** *no pl (Erhabenheit)* greatness. **(e)** *(bedeutender Mensch)* important figure.
Groß-: ~**einkauf** *m* bulk purchase; ~**einsatz** *m* ~**einsatz der Polizei** *etc* large-scale operation by the police *etc*; ~**eltern** *pl* grandparents *pl*; ~**enkel** *m* great-grandchild; *(Junge)* great-grandson; ~**enkelin** *f* great-granddaughter.
Größen-: ~**klasse** *f (Comm)* (size) class; ~**ordnung** *f* scale; *(Größe)* magnitude; *(Math)* order (of magnitude).
großenteils *adv* for the most part.
Größen-: ~**unterschied** *m (im Format)* difference in size; *(in der Höhe)* difference in height; ~**verhältnis** *nt* proportions *pl (gen* between*)*; *(Maßstab)* scale; **im** ~**verhältnis 1:100** on the scale 1:100; ~**wahn(sinn)** *m* megalomania, delusions *pl* of grandeur; **g**~**wahnsinnig** *adj* megalomaniac; **g**~**wahnsinnig sein** to be a megalomaniac.
größer *comp of* **groß.**
Groß-: ~**fahndung** *f* large-scale manhunt; ~**familie** *f* extended family; ~**feuer** *nt* major fire; ~**format** *nt* large size; *(bei Büchern, Fotos auch)* large format; **g**~**formatig** *adj* large-size; *Bücher, Fotos auch* large-format; ~**grundbesitzer** *m* big landowner.
Großhandel *m* wholesale trade *no art.* **etw im** ~ **kaufen** to buy sth wholesale.
Großhandels- *in cpds* wholesale.
Groß-: ~**händler** *m* wholesaler; ~**handlung** *f* wholesale business; **g**~**herzig** *adj* generous, magnanimous; ~**herzigkeit** *f* generosity, magnanimity; ~**hirn** *nt* cerebrum; ~**industrielle(r)** *mf* major industrialist.
Grossist *m* wholesaler.
Groß-: g~**jährig** *adj (dated)* of age; **g**~**jährig werden** to come of age; ~**kapital** *nt* **das** ~**kapital** big business; ~**kapitalist** *m* big capitalist; ~**konzern** *m* large combine; **g**~**kotzig** *adj (pej col)* swanky *(col)*; ~**küche** *f* canteen kitchen; ~**kundgebung** *f* mass rally.
Großmacht *f (Pol)* big *or* great power.
Großmachtpolitik *f* power politics.
Groß-: ~**mannssucht** *f no pl (pej)* craving for status; ~**markt** *m* central market; **g**~**maschig** *adj* = **grobmaschig;** ~**maul** *nt (pej col)* big-mouth *(col)*; **g**~**mäulig** *adj (pej col)* big-mouthed *attr*

(col); **~mut** *f* magnanimity; **g~mütig** *adj* magnanimous; **~mutter** *f* grandmother; **das kannst du deiner ~mutter erzählen!** *(col)* who do you think you're kidding? *(col)*; **g~mütterlich** *adj attr* **(a)** *(von der ~ mutter)* of one's grandmother; **im g~mütterlichen Haus wohnen** to live in one's grandmother's house; **(b)** *(in der Art einer ~mutter)* grandmotherly; **~offensive** *f (Mil)* major offensive; **~onkel** *m* great-uncle; **~produktion** *f* large-scale production.

Großraum *m (einer Stadt)* **der ~ München** the Munich area *or* conurbation, Greater Munich.

Großraumbüro *nt* open-plan office.

Groß-: g~räumig *adj* **(a)** *(geräumig)* roomy, spacious; **(b)** *(über g~e Flächen)* extensive; **(c)** *(im g~en Umkreis)* **g~räumiges Umfahren eines Gebietes** making a large detour around an area; **~razzia** *f* large-scale raid; **~rechner** *m (Comp)* mainframe; **~reinemachen** *nt* thorough cleaning, ≃ spring-cleaning; **g~schnäuzig** *adj (pej col)* big-mouthed *attr (col)*; **g~schreiben** *vt sep irreg* **g~geschrieben werden** *(fig col)* to be stressed; **~schreibung** *f* capitalization; **g~sprecherisch** *adj (pej)* boastful; **g~spurig** *adj (pej)* flashy *(col)*.

Großstadt *f* city.

Großstädter *m* city-dweller.

großstädtisch *adj* big-city *attr.*

Großstadt- *in cpds* city; **~mensch** *m* city-dweller.

Groß-: ~tante *f* great-aunt; **~tat** *f* great feat; **~teil** *m* large part; **zum ~teil** for the most part.

größtenteils *adv* in the main, for the most part.

größte(r, s) *superl of* **groß.**

Größt-: ~maß *nt* maximum amount *(an+dat* of*)*; **g~möglich** *adj attr* greatest possible.

groß-: ~tuerisch [-tuːərɪʃ] *adj (pej)* boastful, bragging; **~tun** *sep irreg (pej) vi* to boast, to show off.

Großvater *m* grandfather.

großväterlich *adj* **(a)** *(vom Großvater)* of one's grandfather. **das ~e Erbe** one's inheritance from one's grandfather. **(b)** *(in der Art eines Großvaters)* grandfatherly.

Groß-: ~veranstaltung *f* big event; *(~kundgebung)* mass rally; **~verdiener** *m* big earner.

Großwild *nt* big game.

Großwild-: ~jagd *f* big-game hunting; **eine ~jagd** a big-game hunt; **~jäger** *m* big-game hunter.

Groß-: g~ziehen *vt sep irreg* to raise; *Tier* to rear; **g~zügig** *adj* generous; *(weiträumig)* spacious; *Plan* large-scale, ambitious; **~zügigkeit** *f siehe adj* generosity; spaciousness; (large) scale, ambitiousness.

grotesk *adj* grotesque.

Groteske *f* **-n** grotesque; grotesque play/novel.

Grotte *f* **-n** grotto.

grub *pret of* **graben.**

Grübchen *nt* dimple.

Grube *f* **-n** *(auch Min)* pit; *(kleine)* hole, hollow. **wer andern eine ~ gräbt(, fällt selbst hinein)** *(Prov)* you can easily fall into your own trap.

Grübelei *f* brooding *no pl.*

grübeln *vi* to brood *(über +acc* about, over*)*.

Grübler(in *f***)** *m* **-** brooder, brooding type.

grüblerisch *adj* pensive, brooding.

Gruft *f* **¨-e** tomb, vault; *(in Kirchen)* crypt.

grün *adj* green; *(Pol auch)* ecologist. **~e Heringe** fresh herrings; **~er Salat** lettuce; **die G~e Insel** the Emerald Isle; **ein ~er Junge** *(col)* a greenhorn *(col)*; **~es Licht (für etw) geben** *(fig)* to give the green light (for sth); **vom ~en Tisch aus** from a bureaucratic ivory tower; **~e Minna** *(col)* Black Maria *(Brit col)*, paddy wagon *(US col)*; **sich ~ und blau** *or* **gelb ärgern** *(col)* to be furious; **jdn ~ und blau schlagen** *(col)* to beat sb black and blue; **~e Welle** phased traffic lights; **~e Welle bei 60 km/h** traffic lights phased for 60 kmph; **auf keinen ~en Zweig kommen** *(fig col)* to get nowhere; **die beiden sind sich gar nicht ~** *(col)* there's no love lost between them; **das ist dasselbe in G~** *(col)* it's the same thing.

Grün- *in cpds* green; **~anlage** *f* green space *or* area; **g~äugig** *adj* green-eyed; **g~blau** *adj* greenish blue, greeny blue.

Grund *m* **¨-e (a)** *no pl (Erdboden, ~fläche)* ground. **~ und Boden** land; **in ~ und Boden** *(fig) sich blamieren, schämen* utterly; *verdammen* outright; **bis auf den ~ zerstören** to raze to the ground.
(b) *no pl (von Gefäßen, Becken etc)* bottom. **auf ~ laufen** *(Naut)* to run aground; **das Glas bis auf den ~ leeren** to drain the glass.
(c) *no pl (lit, fig: Fundament)* foundation(s *pl*); *(das Innerste)* depths *pl.* **von ~ auf** entirely, completely; **von ~ auf neu gebaut** rebuilt from scratch; **einer Sache** *(dat)* **auf den ~ gehen** *(fig)* to get to the bottom of sth; **im ~e (genommen)** basically, fundamentally.
(d) *(Ursache)* reason; *(Beweg~ auch)* grounds *pl.* **aus gesundheitlichen** *etc* **¨~en** for health *etc* reasons; **ohne ~** without reason; **auf ~ von** on the basis of; **auf ~ von Zeugenaussagen** on the strength of the witnesses' testimonies; **auf ~ einer Verwechslung** owing to a mistake; **ich habe ~ zu der Annahme, daß ...** I have reason to believe that ...; **einen ~ zum Feiern haben** to have good cause for (a) celebration; **du hast keinen ~ zum Klagen** you have no cause for complaint; **ich habe berechtigten ~ zu glauben, daß ...** I have good reason to believe that ...; **aus diesem ~** for this reason; **mit gutem ~** with good reason; **aus ¨~en** *(+gen)* for reasons (of).

Grund- *in cpds* basic; **~anstrich** *m* first coat; **~besitz** *m* land, property; *(das Besitzen)* ownership of land *or* property; **~besitzer** *m* landowner; **~buch** *nt* land register; **g~ehrlich** *adj* thoroughly honest; **~eigentum** *nt* = **~besitz.**

gründen 1 *vt* to found; *Argument etc* to base *(auf +acc* on*)*; *Geschäft* to set up. **2** *vi* to be based *or* founded *(in+dat* on*)*. **3** *vr* **sich auf etw** *(acc)* **~** to be based *or* founded on sth.

Gründer(in *f***)** *m* **-** founder.

Grund-: g~falsch *adj* utterly wrong; **~farbe** *f* primary colour *(Brit) or* color *(US)*; *(Grundierfarbe)* ground colour *(Brit) or* color *(US)*; **~festen** *pl (fig)* foundations *pl*; **etw bis in die ~festen erschüttern** to shake sth to its very foundations; **~fläche** *f (Math)* base; **~form** *f* basic form; *(Gram)* infinitive; **~gebühr** *f* basic charge.

Grundgesetz *nt (BRD Pol)* **das ~** the Constitution.

grundgesetzwidrig *adj* contrary to the Constitution, unconstitutional.

Grundhaltung *f* basic position.

grundieren* *vt* to undercoat.

Grundierung *f* **(a)** *no pl (das Grundieren)* undercoating. **(b)** *(Farbe, Fläche)* undercoat.

Grund-: ~kurs *m* basic course; **~lage** *f* basis; **als ~lage für etw dienen** to serve as a basis for sth; **auf der ~ lage** *+gen or* **von** on the basis of; **die ~lagen einer Wissenschaft** the fundamental principles of a science; **jeder ~lage entbehren** to be completely unfounded; **g~legend** *adj* fundamental, basic *(für* to*)*; *Werk* standard.

gründlich 1 *adj* thorough; *Arbeit auch* painstaking. **2** *adv* thoroughly. **jdm ~ die Meinung sagen** to give sb a piece of one's mind; **da haben Sie sich ~ getäuscht** you're completely mistaken there.

Gründlichkeit *f no pl* thoroughness.

Grund-: ~linie *f (Math, Sport)* baseline; **g~los 1** *adj* **(a)** *Tiefe etc* bottomless; **(b)** *(fig: unbegründet)* groundless, unfounded; **2** *adv (fig)* without reason; **~losigkeit** *f (fig)* groundlessness; **~mauer** *f* foundation wall; **bis auf die ~mauern niederbrennen** to be gutted; **~nahrungsmittel**

nt basic food(stuff).

Gründonnerstag [gry:n-] *m* Maundy Thursday.

Grund-: **~ordnung** *f* basic order; **~pfeiler** *m* *(Archit)* supporting pier; *(fig)* cornerstone, keystone; **~rechenart** *f* basic arithmetical operation; **~recht** *nt* basic *or* constitutional right; **~riß** *m (von Gebäude)* ground plan; *(Abriß)* outline, sketch.

Grundsatz *m* principle. **aus ~** on principle; **ein Mann mit Grundsätzen** a man of principle.

grundsätzlich 1 *adj* fundamental; *Frage* of principle. **2** *adv (allgemein, im Prinzip)* in principle; *(aus Prinzip)* on principle; *(immer)* always. **ihre Meinungen sind ~ verschieden** their views are fundamentally different; **das ist ~ verboten** it is absolutely forbidden.

Grundsatz|urteil *nt* judgement that establishes a principle.

Grund-: **~schuld** *f* mortgage; **~schule** *f* primary *(Brit) or* elementary school; **~schüler** *m* primary *(Brit) or* elementary(-school) pupil; **~schullehrer** *m* primary *(Brit) or* elementary(-school) teacher; **~stein** *m (lit, fig)* foundation stone; **den ~stein zu etw legen** *(lit)* to lay the foundation stone of sth; *(fig)* to lay the foundations for sth; **~stellung** *f(Turnen, Chess)* starting position; **~steuer** *f* (local) property tax, ≈ rates *pl (Brit)*; **~stimmung** *f* prevailing mood; **~stock** *m* basis, foundation; **~stoff** *m (Rohstoff)* raw material; *(Chem)* element.

Grundstück *nt* plot (of land); *(Anwesen)* estate; *(Bau~ auch)* site; *(bebaut)* property.

Grundstücksmakler *m* estate agent *(Brit)*, realtor *(US)*.

Grund-: **~studium** *nt (Univ)* basic course; **~stufe** *f* first stage; *(Sch)* ≈ junior *(Brit) or* grade *(US)* school; **~ton** *m (Mus) (eines Akkords)* root; *(einer Tonleiter)* tonic keynote; *(~farbe)* ground colour *(Brit) or* color *(US)*.

Gründung *f* founding, foundation; *(von Heim, Geschäft)* setting up. **die ~ einer Familie** getting married (and having a family).

Grund-: **g~verkehrt** *adj* completely wrong; **g~verschieden** *adj* totally *or* entirely different; **~wasser** *nt* ground water; **~wasserspiegel** *m* water table, ground-water level; **~wehrdienst** *m* national *(Brit) or* selective *(US)* service; **~zug** *m* essential feature *or* trait; **etw in seinen ~zügen darstellen** to outline (the essentials of) sth.

grünen *vi (geh)* to turn green; *(fig: Liebe, Hoffnung)* to blossom (forth).

Grüne(r) *m decl as adj* **(a)** *(Pol)* Ecologist, Green. **die ~n** *(als Partei)* the Greens. **(b)** *(dated col: Polizist)* cop *(col)*.

Grüne(s) *nt decl as adj (Gemüse)* greens *pl*, green vegetables *pl*. **ins ~ fahren** to go to the country.

Grün-: **~fläche** *f* green space *or* area; **~futter** *nt* green fodder, greenstuff; **g~gelb** *adj* greenish yellow, greeny-yellow; **~gürtel** *m* green belt; **~kohl** *m* (curly) kale; **g~lich** *adj* greenish; **~schnabel** *m (col)* (little) whippersnapper *(col)*; *(Neuling)* greenhorn *(col)*; **~span** *m no pl* verdigris; **~streifen** *m* central reservation *(Brit)*, median (strip) *(US)*; *(am Straßenrand)* grass verge.

grunzen *vti* to grunt.

Gruppe *f* **-n** group; *(von Mitarbeitern auch)* team; *(Mil)* ≈ squad; *(Klasse, Kategorie auch)* class.

Gruppen- *in cpds* group; **~arbeit** *f* teamwork; **~bild** *nt* group portrait; **~führer** *m* group leader; *(Mil)* squad leader; **~reise** *f* group travel *no pl*; **~sex** *m* group sex; **~sieg** *m (Sport)* **den ~sieg erringen** to win in one's group; **~sieger** *m (Sport)* group winnner; **g~spezifisch** *adj* group specific; **~therapie** *f* group therapy; **g~weise** *adv* in groups; *(Ind, Comm, Sport auch)* in teams; *(Mil)* in squads.

gruppieren* *vtr* to group.

Gruppierung *f* grouping; *(Gruppe)* group; *(Pol auch)* faction.

Gruselfilm *m* horror film.

grus(e)lig *adj* horrifying, gruesome.

gruseln 1 *vti impers* **mich** *or* **mir gruselt auf Friedhöfen** cemeteries give me the creeps. **2** *vr* **hier würde ich mich ~** a place like this would give me the creeps.

Gruß *m* **¨-e (a)** greeting; *(~geste, Mil)* salute. **er ging ohne ~ an mir vorbei** he walked past me without saying hello; **viele ¨~e** best wishes *(an +acc* to*)*; **sag ihm einen schönen ~** say hello to him (from me); **einen (schönen) ~ an Ihre Gattin!** my regards to your wife. **(b)** *(als Briefformel)* **mit bestem ~** *or* **besten ¨~en** yours; *(bei Anrede Mr/Mrs/Miss/Ms X)* yours sincerely, Yours truly *(esp US)*; *(bei Anrede Sir(s)/Madam)* Yours faithfully, Yours truly *(esp US)*.

Gruß-: **~adresse, ~botschaft** *f* message of greeting.

grüßen 1 *vt* **(a)** to greet; *(Mil)* to salute. **grüß dich!** *(col)* hello there!, hi! *(col)*. **(b)** *(Grüße übermitteln)* **Otto läßt dich (schön) ~** Otto sends his regards. **2** *vi* to say hello; *(Mil)* to salute. **Otto läßt ~** Otto sends his regards.

Gruß-: **~formel** *f* form of greeting; *(am Briefanfang)* salutation; *(am Briefende)* complimentary close, ending; **~telegramm** *nt* greetings telegram; *(Pol)* goodwill telegram; **~wort** *nt* greeting.

Grütze *f* **-n (a)** groats *pl*; *(Brei)* gruel. **rote ~** (type of) red fruit jelly. **(b)** *no pl (col: Verstand)* brains *(col)*.

gucken ['gʊkn, *(NGer)* 'kʊkn] **1** *vi (sehen)* to look *(zu* at*)*; *(heimlich auch)* to peep, to peek; *(hervorschauen)* to peep *(aus* out of*)*. **laß mal ~!** let's have a look. **2** *vt (col)* **Fernsehen ~** to watch television *or* telly *(Brit col)*.

Gucker *m* **-** *(col)* **(a)** *(Fernglas)* telescope; *(Opernglas)* opera glass(es). **(b)** *pl (Augen)* peepers *(col)*.

Guck-: **~kasten** *m (col: Fernseher)* telly *(Brit col)* tube *(US col)*; **~loch** *nt* peephole.

Guerilla[1] [ge'rɪlja] *f* **-s (a)** *(~krieg)* guerilla warfare. **(b)** *(~einheit)* guerilla unit.

Guerilla[2] [ge'rɪlja] *m* **-s** *(~kämpfer)* guerilla.

Gulasch *nt or m* **-e** *or* **-s** goulash.

Gulasch-: **~kanone** *f (Mil sl)* field kitchen; **~suppe** *f* goulash soup.

Gulden *m* **-** *(niederländisch)* g(u)ilder, gulden.

Gully ['gʊli] *m or nt* **-s** drain.

gültig *adj* valid. **nach den ~en Bestimmungen** according to current regulations; **ab wann ist der Fahrplan ~?** when does the timetable come into force?; **~ werden** to become valid; *(Gesetz, Vertrag)* to come into effect; *(Münze)* to become legal tender.

Gültigkeit *f no pl* validity; *(von Gesetz)* legal force. **das Fünfmarkstück verliert im Herbst seine ~** the five-mark piece ceases to be legal tender in the autumn.

Gummi *nt or m* **-s** *(Material)* rubber; *(Radier~)* rubber *(Brit)*, eraser; *(~band)* rubber *or* elastic *(Brit)* band; *(in Kleidung etc)* elastic; *(col: Kondom)* rubber *(col)*, Durex ®.

Gummi- *in cpds* rubber; **g~artig 1** *adj* rubbery; **2** *adv* like rubber; **~band** *nt* rubber *or* elastic *(Brit)* band; *(in Kleidung)* elastic; **~bärchen** *nt* jelly baby; **~baum** *m* rubber plant; **~boot** *nt* rubber dinghy.

gummieren* *vt* to gum.

Gummierung *f (gummierte Fläche)* gum.

Gummi-: **~knüppel** *m* rubber truncheon *(Brit) or* billy *(US)*; **~paragraph** *m (col)* ambiguous clause; **~reifen** *m* rubber tyre; **~schlauch** *m* rubber hose; *(bei Fahrrad etc)* inner tube; **~stiefel** *m* rubber boot, wellington (boot) *(Brit)*; **~zelle** *f* padded cell.

Gunst *f no pl* favour *(Brit)*, favor *(US)*; *(Wohlwollen auch)* goodwill; *(des Schicksals etc)* benevolence. **zu meinen/deinen ~en** in my/your favour; **jdm eine ~ erweisen** *(geh)* to do sb a kindness; **in jds ~** *(dat)* **stehen** to be in favour with sb.
günstig *adj* favourable *(Brit)*, favorable *(US)*; *(zeitlich, bei Reisen etc)* convenient; *Angebot, Preis etc* reasonable, good. **jdm/einer Sache ~ gesinnt sein** *(geh)* to be favourably disposed towards sb/sth; **bei ~er Witterung** weather permitting; **die Stadt liegt ~ (für)** the town is well situated (for); **wie komme ich am ~sten nach ...?** what's the best *or* easiest way to get to ...?; **im ~sten Fall(e)** with luck; **etw ~ kaufen/verkaufen** to buy/sell sth for a good price; **DM 30?, das war aber ~** 30 marks?, that's a bargain.
Günstling *m (pej)* favourite *(Brit)*, favorite *(US)*.
Gurgel *f* **-n** throat; *(Schlund)* gullet. **jdm die ~ zudrücken** *or* **abschnüren** *(lit, fig)* to strangle sb; **dann springt sie mir an die ~!** *(col)* she'll kill me *(col)*.
gurgeln *vi* **(a)** *(den Rachen spülen)* to gargle. **(b)** *(Wasser, Laut)* to gurgle.
Gurke *f* **-n (a)** cucumber; *(Essig~)* gherkin. **saure ~n** pickled gherkins. **(b)** *(hum col: Nase)* hooter *(col)*.
Gurken-: ~hobel *m* slicer; **~salat** *m* cucumber salad.
gurren *vi (lit, fig)* to coo.
Gurt *m* **-e** *(Gürtel, Patronen~)* belt; *(Sicherheits~)* safety belt; *(Riemen)* strap.
Gürtel *m* **-** belt. **den ~ enger schnallen** *(lit, fig)* to tighten one's belt.
Gürtel-: ~linie *f* waist; **ein Schlag unter die ~linie** *(lit)* a punch/blow *etc* below the belt; **das war ein Schlag unter die ~linie** *(fig)* that really was below the belt; **~reifen** *m* radial (tyre *(Brit) or* tire *US*); **~rose** *f (Med)* shingles *sing or pl*.
Guru *m* **-s** guru.
Guß *m, pl* **Güsse (a)** *(Metal) (no pl: das Gießen)* casting, founding; *(~stück)* cast. **(wie) aus einem ~** *(fig)* a unified whole. **(b)** *(Strahl)* stream, gush; *(col: Regen~)* cloudburst, downpour. **(c)** *(Zucker~)* icing, frosting *(US)*; *(durchsichtig)* glaze.
Guß-: ~eisen *nt* cast iron; **g~eisern** *adj* cast-iron; **~form** *f* mould *(Brit)*, mold *(US)*.
gut *comp* **besser,** *superl* **beste(r, s)** *or (adv)* **am besten 1** *adj* good. **probieren Sie unsere ~en Weine/Speisen!** try our fine wines/food; **er ist in der Schule/in Spanisch sehr ~** he's very good at school/Spanish; **das ist ~ gegen** *or* **für** *(col)* **Husten** it's good for coughs; **wozu ist das ~?** *(col)* what's that for?; **sei so ~ (und) gib mir das** would you mind giving me that; **dafür ist er sich zu ~** he wouldn't stoop to that sort of thing; **sind die Bilder ~ geworden?** did the pictures turn out all right?; **es wird alles wieder ~!** everything will be all right; **wie ~, daß ...** how fortunate that ...; **~, daß du das endlich einsiehst** it's a good thing you realize it at last; **ich will es damit ~ sein lassen** I'll leave it at that; **laß mal ~ sein!** that'll do; **jetzt ist aber ~!** *(col)* that's enough; **das ist ja alles ~ und schön, aber ...** that's all very well but ...; **ein ~es Pfund Reis** a good pound of rice; **~!** good; *(in Ordnung)* (all) right, OK; **also ~!** all right *or* OK then; **du bist ~!** *(col)* you're a fine one!

2 *adv* well. **~ schmecken/riechen** to taste/smell good; **sie spricht ~ Schwedisch** she speaks good Swedish; **er hat es in seiner Jugend nicht ~ gehabt** he had a hard time (of it) when he was young; **er hatte es immer ~ bei seinen Eltern** his parents were always good to him; **du hast es ~!** you've got it made; **das kann ~ sein** that may well be; **so ~ wie nichts** next to nothing; **so ~ wie nicht** hardly, scarcely; **so ~ wie verloren** as good as lost; **so ~ ich kann** as well as I can; **es dauert ~ drei Stunden** it lasts a good three hours; **~ und gern** easily; **paß ~ auf!** be very careful; **ich kann ihn jetzt nicht ~ im Stich lassen** I can't very well let him down now.
Gut *nt* **¨er (a)** *(Eigentum)* property; *(lit, fig: Besitztum)* possession. **irdische ¨~er** worldly goods. **(b)** *no pl (das Gute)* good, Good. **~ und Böse** good and evil. **(c)** *(Ware, Fracht~)* item. **¨~er** goods; *(Fracht~)* freight *sing*, goods *(esp Brit)*. **(d)** *(Land~)* estate.
Gut-: ~achten *nt* **-** report; **~achter(in** *f*) *m* **-** expert; *(Schätzer auch)* valuator; *(Jur: Prozeß)* expert witness; **g~artig** *adj Kind, Hund etc* good-natured; *Geschwür* benign; **g~aussehend** *adj* good-looking; **g~bezahlt** *adj attr* highly-paid; **g~bürgerlich** *adj* solid middle-class; *Küche* homely, good plain; **~dünken** *nt no pl* discretion; **nach (eigenem) ~dünken** at one's own discretion.
Güte *f no pl* **(a)** *(Herzens~, Freundlichkeit)* goodness, kindness. **würden Sie die ~ haben, zu ...** *(form, iro)* would you have the goodness *or* kindness to ...; **ein Vorschlag zur ~** a conciliatory proposal; **ach du liebe** *or* **meine ~!** *(col)* goodness me! **(b)** *(einer Ware)* quality.
Güteklasse *f (Comm)* grade.
Gute(r) *mf decl as adj* **der/die ~** the dear kind soul; *(mitleidig)* the poor soul; **die ~n und die Bösen** the good and the bad; *(col: in Filmen etc)* the goodies and the baddies *(col)*.
Güter-: ~abfertigung *f* **(a)** *no pl* dispatch of freight *or* goods *(esp Brit)*; **(b)** *(Abfertigungsstelle)* freight *or* goods *(esp Brit)* office; **~fernverkehr** *m* long-distance haulage; **~trennung** *f (Jur)* separation of property; **in ~trennung leben** to have separation of property; **~verkehr** *m* freight *or* goods *(esp Brit)* traffic; **~wagen** *m (Rail)* freight car *(US)*, goods truck *(Brit)*; **~zug** *m* freight *or* goods *(esp Brit)* train.
Gute(s) *nt decl as adj* **~s tun** to do good; **alles ~e!** all the best!; **das führt zu nichts ~m** it'll lead to no good; **das ist des ~n zuviel** that is too much of a good thing; **das ~ daran** the good thing about it; **das ~e im Menschen** the good in man; **ich sage es dir im g~n** I want to give you a friendly piece of advice.
Güte-: ~siegel *nt (Comm)* stamp of quality; **~zeichen** *nt* mark of quality; *(fig auch)* hallmark.
Gut-: g~gehen *sep irreg aux sein* **1** *vi impers* **es geht ihm g~** he is doing well *or* nicely; *(er ist gesund)* he is well; **sonst geht's dir g~!** *(iro)* are you in your right mind?; **2** *vi* to go (off) well; **das ist noch einmal g~gegangen** it turned out all right; **g~gehend** *adj attr* thriving; **g~gelaunt** *adj* cheerful, in a good mood; **g~gemeint** *adj attr* well-meant; **g~gläubig** *adj* trusting; *(vertrauensselig auch)* credulous; **~gläubigkeit** *f siehe adj* trusting nature; credulity; **g~haben** *vt sep irreg* **etw g~haben** to have sth coming (to one) *(col) (bei* from); **~haben** *nt* **-** *(Fin, Bank~)* credit; **auf meinem Konto ist ein ~haben von DM 500** my account is DM 500 in credit; **g~heißen** *vt sep irreg* to approve of; *(genehmigen)* to approve; **g~herzig** *adj* kind-hearted; **~herzigkeit** *f* kind-heartedness.
gütig *adj* kind; *(edelmütig)* gracious.
gütlich *adj* amicable. **sich an etw** *(dat)* **~ tun** to make free with sth.
Gut-: g~machen *vt sep* **(a)** *(in Ordnung bringen) Fehler* to put right, to correct; *Schaden* to make good; **(b)** *(gewinnen)* to make *(bei* out of, on); **g~mütig** *adj* good-natured; **~mütigkeit** *f* good-naturedness; **g~nachbarlich 1** *adj* neighbourly *(Brit)*, neighborly *(US)*; **2** *adv* as good neighbours *(Brit) or* neighbors *(US)*.
Gutsbesitzer(in *f*) *m* lord of the manor; *(als Klasse)* landowner.
Gut-: ~schein *m* voucher, coupon; *(für Umtausch)*

credit note; **g~schreiben** *vt sep irreg* to credit *(dat* to); **~schrift** *f (Bescheinigung)* credit note; *(Betrag)* credit (item).

Guts-: ~haus *nt* manor (house); **~hof** *m* estate.

gut-: ~situiert *adj attr* well-off; **~tun** *vi sep irreg* **jdm ~tun** to do sb good; **das tut ~** that's good; **~unterrichtet** *adj attr* well-informed; **~verdienend** *adj attr* with a good salary, high-income; **~willig** *adj* willing; *(nicht böswillig)* well-meaning.

Gymnasiallehrer ≃ grammar school teacher *(Brit)*, high school teacher *(US)*.

Gymnasiast(in *f***)** *m (wk)* **-en, -en** ≃ grammar school pupil *(Brit)*, high school student *(US)*.

Gymnasium *nt (Sch)* ≃ grammar school *(Brit)*, high school *(US)*.

Gymnastik *f* keep-fit exercises *pl*; *(Turnen)* gymnastics *sing*. **~ machen** to do keep-fit (exercises)/gymnastics.

gymnastisch *adj* gymnastic.

Gynäkologe *m*, **Gynäkologin** *f* gynaecologist *(Brit)*, gynecologist *(US)*.

Gynäkologie *f* gynaecology *(Brit)*, gynecology *(US)*.

gynäkologisch *adj* gynaecological *(Brit)*, gynecological *(US)*.

H

H, h [haː] *nt* **-, -** H, h; *(Mus)* B.

ha = **Hektar** hectare.

Haag *m:* **Den ~** The Hague.

Haar *nt* **-e** hair. **sie hat schönes ~** *or* **schöne ~e** she has nice hair; **~e auf den Zähnen haben** to be a tough customer; **~e lassen (müssen)** to come off badly; **jdm kein ~ krümmen** not to harm a hair of sb's head; **darüber laß dir keine grauen ~e wachsen** don't lose any sleep over it; **jdm aufs ~ gleichen** to be the spitting image of sb; **das ist an den ~en herbeigezogen** that's rather far-fetched; **an jdm kein gutes ~ lassen** to pull sb to pieces; **sich** *(dat)* **in die ~e kriegen** *(col)* to quarrel; **sich** *(dat)* **in den ~en liegen** to be at loggerheads; **jdm die ~e vom Kopf fressen** *(col)* to eat sb out of house and home.

Haar-: ~ansatz *m* hairline; **~ausfall** *m* hair loss; **~breit** *nt:* **um kein ~breit** not an inch; **~bürste** *f* hairbrush.

haaren *vi (auch vr: Tier)* to moult *(Brit)*, to molt *(US)*; *(Pelz, Teppich)* to shed.

Haarersatz *m (form)* hairpiece; *(Perücke)* wig.

Haaresbreite *f inv* **um ~** almost, very nearly; *verfehlen* by a hair's breadth; **er wich nicht um ~ von seiner Meinung ab** he did not change his opinion one iota.

Haar-: ~festiger *m* **-** (hair) setting lotion; **h~genau** *adj* exact; **jdm etw h~genau erklären** to explain sth to sb in great detail; **das trifft h~genau zu** that's absolutely right.

haarig *adj* hairy; *(col) (heikel, gefährlich)* hairy *(col)*; *(schwierig)* nasty.

Haar-: ~klammer *f* hairgrip *(Brit)*, barrette *(US)*; **h~klein** *adv* in minute detail; **~nadel** *f* hairpin; **~nadelkurve** *f* hairpin bend; **~netz** *nt* hairnet; **~pflege** *f* hair care; **h~scharf** *adj Beschreibung* exact; **das hat ihn h~scharf verfehlt** it only missed him by a hair's breadth; **~schleife** *f* hair ribbon; **~schnitt** *m* haircut; **~schopf** *m* mop *or* shock of hair; **~sieb** *nt* fine sieve; **~spalter(in** *f***)** *m* **-** pedant, hairsplitter; **~spalterei** *f* splitting hairs *no indef art, no pl;* **h~spalterisch** *adj* hairsplitting; **~spange** *f* hair slide, barrette *(US)*; **~spitze** *f* end (of a hair); **~strähne** *f* strand *or (dünner)* wisp of hair; **h~sträubend** *adj* hair-raising; *(unglaublich) Frechheit* incredible; **~töner** *m* **-** hair-tinting lotion; **~trockner** *m* **-** hair dryer; **~waschmittel** *nt* shampoo; **~ wasser** *nt* hair lotion; **~wuchs** *m* growth of hair; **einen kräftigen ~wuchs haben** to have a thick head of hair; **~wuchsmittel** *nt* hair restorer.

Hab *nt:* **~ und Gut** *sing vb* possessions, belongings, worldly goods *all pl.*

Habe *f no pl (geh)* possessions *pl*, belongings *pl.*

haben *pret* **hatte,** *ptp* **gehabt 1** *vt* to have, to have got *(esp Brit)*. **ich habe eine Idee** I have *or* I've got *(esp Brit)* an idea; **ein Meter hat 100 cm** there are 100 cm in a metre; **da hast du 10 Mark** there's 10 Marks; **die ~'s (ja)** *(col)* they can afford it; **wie hätten Sie es gern?** how would you like it?; **ich kann das nicht ~** *(col)* I can't stand it; **Ferien ~** to be on holiday; **er wollte sie zur Frau ~** he wanted to make her his wife; **Hunger/Angst/Sorgen ~** to be hungry/afraid/worried; **was hat er denn?** what's the matter with him?; **hast du was?** are you all right?, is (there) something the matter with you?; **was ~ wir heute für ein Wetter?** what's the weather like today?; **heute ~ wir 10°** it's 10° today; **es gut/schön ~** to have it good/nice; **sie hat es warm in ihrem Zimmer** it's warm in her room; **er hat es nicht leicht mit ihr** he has a hard time (of it) with her; **es am Herzen ~** *(col)* to have heart trouble; **es in den Beinen ~** *(col)* to have trouble with one's legs; **er hat es mit dem Malen** *(col)* he has a thing about painting *(col)*; **du hast zu gehorchen** *(müssen)* you must obey, you have to obey, you have got to obey *(esp Brit)*; **ich habe zu tun** I'm busy; **etw auf dem Boden liegen ~** to have sth lying on the floor; **etw ist zu ~** *(erhältlich)* sth is to be had; **jd ist zu ~** *(col) (nicht verheiratet)* sb is single; *(sexuell)* sb is available; **für etw zu ~ sein** to be keen on sth; **für ein gutes Essen ist er immer zu ~** he's always willing to have a good meal; **ich hab's** *(col)* I've got it, I know; **du kannst mich gern ~!** *(col)* get lost! *(col)*; **da hast du's/~ wir's!** *(col)* there you/we are; **woher hast du denn das?** where did you get that from?; **wie gehabt!** some things don't change; **jd hat eine nette Art an sich** *(dat)* there is something nice about sb; **sie werden schon merken, was sie an ihm ~** they'll see how valuable he is; **etwas mit jdm ~** *(col)* to have a thing with sb *(col)*; **etwas von etw ~** *(col)* to get something out of sth; **das hast du jetzt davon** now see what's happened; **nichts von etw ~** *(col)* to get nothing out of sth; **die blonden Haare hat sie von ihrem Vater** she gets her blond hair from her father; **er hat etwas von einem Erpresser (an sich** *dat***)** he's a bit of a blackmailer; **dieses Werk von Braque hat viel von Picasso** this work by Braque owes much to Picasso.

2 *vr (col: sich anstellen)* to make a fuss. **was hast du dich denn so?** what are you making such a fuss about?

3 *vr impers (col)* **und damit hat es sich** and that's that; **die Sache hat sich** *(ist erledigt)* that's done.

4 *aux* **ich habe/hatte gerufen** I have/had called, I've/I'd called; **ich habe gestern angerufen** I called yesterday; **du hättest den Brief früher schreiben können** you could have written the letter earlier; **etw getan ~** to have done sth.

Haben *nt no pl* credit. **im ~ stehen** to be on the credit side.

Habenichts *m* **-e** *(pej)* have-not.

Haben-: ~seite *f* credit side; **~zinsen** *pl* interest on credit *sing.*

Hab-: ~gier *f* greed, acquisitiveness; **h~gierig** *adj* greedy, acquisitive; **h~haft** *adj (geh)* **jds/einer Sache h~haft werden** to get hold of sb/sth.

Habicht *m* **-e** hawk.

Habilitation *f (Lehrberechtigung)* postdoctoral lecturing qualification.

habilitieren* *vr* to qualify as a university lecturer.

Hab-: ~schaft *f*, **~seligkeiten** *pl* belongings *pl;* **~sucht** *f* greed, acquisitiveness; **h~süchtig** *adj* greedy, acquisitive.

Hack-: ~beil *nt* chopper, cleaver; **~block** *m* chopping block; **~braten** *m* meat loaf; **~brett** *nt*

(a) chopping board; **(b)** *(Mus)* dulcimer.
Hacke[1] *f* **-n** *(Ferse, Absatz)* heel.
Hacke[2] *f* **-n** *(Pickel)* pickaxe *(Brit)*, pickax *(US)*; *(Garten~)* hoe.
hacken 1 *vt (zerkleinern)* to chop; *(im Fleischwolf)* to mince *(Brit)*, to grind *(US)*; *Garten* to hoe; *Loch* to hack; *(Vogel)* to peck. **2** *vi (nach* at*)* to hack; *(Vogel)* to peck *(nach* at*)*; *(im Garten)* to hoe.
Hacker *m* **-** *(Comp)* hacker.
Hack-: **~fleisch** *nt* mince *(Brit)*, minced *(Brit) or* ground *(US)* meat; **aus jdm ~fleisch machen** *(col)* to make mincemeat of sb *(col)*; **~klotz** *m* chopping block; **~ordnung** *f (lit, fig)* pecking order.
Häcksel *nt or m no pl* chaff.
hadern *vi (dated geh) (streiten)* to quarrel; *(unzufrieden sein)* to be at odds.
Hafen *m* **¨ (a)** harbour *(Brit)*, harbor *(US)*; *(Handels~)* port; *(~anlagen)* docks *pl*. **in den ~einlaufen** to put into harbour/port. **(b)** *(fig)* haven. **in den ~ der Ehe einlaufen** to enter the state of matrimony.
Hafen- *in cpds* harbour *(Brit)*, harbor *(US)*; port; **~anlagen** *pl* docks *pl*; **~arbeiter** *m* dockworker, docker; **~polizei** *f* harbour *(Brit) or* harbor *(US)* police; **~rundfahrt** *f* (boat-)trip round the harbour *(Brit) or* harbor *(US)*; **~stadt** *f* port; *(am Meer auch)* seaport; **~viertel** *nt* dock area.
Hafer *m* **-** oats *pl*. **ihn sticht der ~** *(col)* he's feeling his oats *(col)*.
Hafer-: **~ brei** *m* porridge; **~flocken** *pl* rolled oats *pl*; **~korn** *nt* (oat) grain; **~mehl** *nt* oatmeal; **~schleim** *m* gruel.
Haff *nt* **-s** *or* **-e** lagoon.
Haft *f no pl (vor dem Prozeß)* custody; *(~strafe)* imprisonment; *(~zeit)* prison sentence; *(politisch)* detention. **sich in ~ befinden** to be in custody/prison/detention; **eine schwere ~ verhängen** to impose a long term of imprisonment; **in ~ nehmen** to take into custody, to detain.
Haft-: **~anstalt** *f* detention centre *(Brit) or* center *(US)*; **h~bar** *adj (für jdn)* legally responsible; *(für etw)* (legally) liable; **~befehl** *m* warrant; **einen ~befehl gegen jdn austellen** to issue a warrant for sb's arrest; **~dauer** *f* term of imprisonment.
haften[1] *vi (Jur)* **für jdn ~** to be (legally) responsible for sb; **für etw ~** to be (legally) liable for sth; **die Versicherung hat für den Schaden nicht gehaftet** the insurance company did not accept liability (for the damage); **für Garderobe kann nicht gehaftet werden** all articles are left at owner's risk.
haften[2] *vi (lit, fig)* to stick *(an +dat* to*)*; *(Reifen, Phys)* to adhere; *(Rauch, Geruch)* to cling *(an +dat* to*)*; *(Blick)* to become fixed.
haftenbleiben *vi sep irreg aux sein (lit, fig)* to stick *(an or auf +dat* to*)*; *(Geruch)* to cling; *(Phys)* to adhere.
Häftling *m* prisoner; *(politisch auch)* detainee.
Haft-: **~pflicht** *f (Schadenersatzpflicht)* (legal) liability; **h~pflichtig** *adj* liable; **h~pflichtversichert** *adj* **h~pflichtversichert sein** to have personal liability insurance; *(Aut)* ≃ to have third-party insurance; **~pflichtversicherung** *f* personal *or* public *(US)* liability insurance *no indef art*; *(Aut)* ≃ third-party insurance; **~richter** *m* magistrate; **~schalen** *pl* contact lenses *pl*; **~strafe** *f* prison sentence.
Haftung *f* **(a)** *(Jur)* (legal) liability; *(für Personen)* (legal) responsibility. **(b)** *(Tech, Phys, von Reifen)* adhesion.
Hage-: **~butte** *f* **-n** rose hip; **~dorn** *m* hawthorn.
Hagel *m no pl (lit, fig)* hail.
Hagelkorn *nt* **(a)** hailstone. **(b)** *(Med)* eye cyst.
hageln 1 *vi impers* **es hagelt** it's hailing. **2** *vi* **etw hagelt auf jdn** *(lit, fig)* sth hails down on sb. **3** *vt impers (lit)* to hail (down). **es hagelte etw** *(fig)* sth hailed down.
Hagel-: **~schauer** *m* (short) hailstorm; **~schlag** *m (Met)* hail; **~sturm** *m* hailstorm.
hager *adj* gaunt, thin.
Häher *m* **-** jay.
Hahn *m* **¨e (a)** *(männlicher Vogel)* cock; *(jünger)* cockerel. **~ im Korb sein** *(col)* to be cock of the walk; **danach kräht kein ~ mehr** *(col)* no one cares two hoots about that any more *(col)*. **(b)** *pl auch* **-en** *(Tech)* tap, faucet *(US)*. **(c)** *(Abzug)* trigger.
Hähnchen *nt (Cook)* chicken.
Hahnenschrei *m* cockcrow. **beim ersten ~** *(fig)* at cockcrow.
Hai(fisch) *m* **-e** *(lit, fig)* shark.
Häkchen *nt* **(a)** *(Sew)* (small) hook. **(b)** *(Zeichen)* tick, check *(US)*.
häkeln *vti* to crochet.
Häkelnadel *f* crochet hook.
haken 1 *vi (klemmen)* to stick. **es hakt** *(fig col)* there's some delay; **es hakt (bei jdm)** *(col: nicht verstehen)* sb is stuck. **2** *vt (befestigen)* to hook *(an +acc* to*)*.
Haken *m* **- (a)** hook *(auch Boxen)*. **die Sache hat einen ~** *(col)* there's a snag *or* a catch; **einen ~ schlagen** to dart sideways. **(b)** *(Zeichen)* tick, check *(US)*.
Haken-: **~kreuz** *nt* swastika; **~nase** *f* hooked nose, hooknose.
halb 1 *adj* half. **ein ~er Meter** *etc* half a metre *etc*; **der ~e Tag** *etc* half the day *etc*; **eine ~e Stunde** half an hour; **alle ~e Stunde** every half hour; **ein ~es Jahr** six months *pl*; **auf ~em Wege** *or* **~er Strecke** halfway; **zum ~en Preis** (at) half price; **Kleid mit ~em Arm** dress with half-length sleeves; **eine ~e Note** a minim *(Brit)*, a half-note *(US)*; **ein ~er Ton** a semitone; **~e Pause** minim/half-note rest; **~ zehn** half past nine, half nine *(col)*; **fünf (Minuten) vor/nach ~ zwei** twenty-five (minutes) past one/to two; **~e Arbeit leisten** to do a bad job; **die ~e Wahrheit** half of the truth; **nichts H~es und nichts Ganzes** neither one thing nor the other; **mit ~em Ohr** with half an ear; **sich nur wie ein ~er Mensch fühlen** to feel only half a person; **keine ~en Sachen machen** not to do things by halves; **die ~e Stadt/Welt** half the town/world; **sie ist schon eine ~e Schottin** she is already half Scottish; **(noch) ein ~es Kind sein** to be scarcely more than a child.
2 *adv* half; *(beinahe)* almost. **die Zeit ist ~ vorbei** half the time has already gone; **~ so gut** half as good; **etw nur ~ verstehen** to only half understand something; **ich hörte nur ~ zu** I was only half listening; **das ist ~ so schlimm** it's not as bad as all that; *(Zukünftiges)* that won't be too bad; **etw nur ~ machen** to only half-do sth *(col)*; **wir haben uns ~ totgelacht** we almost died laughing; **mit jdm ~ und ~** *or* **~e-~e machen** *(col)* to go halves with sb; **gefällt es dir? — ~ und ~** do you like it? — sort of *(col)*.
Halb- *in cpds* half; **h~amtlich** *adj* semi-official; **~bildung** *f* smattering of knowledge *(pej)*; **h~bitter** *adj Schokolade* semi-sweet; **~blut** *nt no pl (Mensch)* half-breed; *(Tier)* crossbreed; **~bruder** *m* half-brother; **~dunkel** *nt* semi-darkness; *(Dämmerung)* dusk; **~edelstein** *m* semi-precious stone.
Halbe(r) *m or f decl as adj (col)* half a litre *(Brit) or* liter *(US)* (of beer).
Halb-: **h~fertig** *adj attr* half-finished; *(fig)* immature; **h~fest** *adj attr Zustand, Materie* semi-solid; *Gelee* half-set; **~finale** *nt* semi-final; **h~gar** *adj attr* half-cooked; **~gott** *m (Myth, fig)* demigod; **~götter in Weiß** *(iro)* doctors; **~heit** *f (pej)* half-measure; **er ist nicht für ~heiten** he is not one for half-measures; **h~herzig** *adj* half-hearted.
halbieren* *vt* to halve; *(schneiden)* to cut in half.
Halbierung *f* halving.
Halb-: **~insel** *f* peninsula; **~jahr** *nt* half-year

(auch Comm); six months; **h~jährig** *adj attr Kind* six-month-old; *Lehrgang etc* six-month; **h~jährlich 1** *adj* half-yearly *(auch Comm)*, six-monthly; **2** *adv* every six months, twice yearly; **~kreis** *m* semicircle; **~kugel** *f* hemisphere; **nördliche/südliche ~kugel** northern/southern hemisphere; **h~lang** *adj Rock* mid-calf length; *Haar* chin-length; **(nun) mach mal h~lang!** *(col)* now wait a minute!; **h~laut 1** *adj* low; **2** *adv* in a low voice; **h~leinen** *adj attr Stoff* fifty per cent linen; **~leiter** *m (Phys)* semiconductor; **h~links** *adv (Sport) spielen* (at) inside left; **h~links abbiegen** to fork left; **das Auto kam von h~links** the car approached from the left; **h~mast** *adv* at half-mast; **h~matt** *adj (Phot)* semimatt; **~messer** *m* radius; **~metall** *nt* semi-metal; **~mond** *m* half-moon; *(Symbol)* crescent; **wir haben ~mond** there's a half-moon; **h~nackt** *adj attr* half-naked; **h~offen** *adj attr* half-open; **~pension** *f* half-board *(Brit)*, European plan *(US)*; **h~rechts** *adv (Sport) spielen* (at) inside right; **h~rechts abbiegen** to fork right; **das Auto kam von h~rechts** the car approached from the right; **h~reif** *adj attr* half-ripe; **h~rund** *adj attr* semicircular; **~rund** *nt* semicircle, half circle; **im ~rund** in a semicircle; **~schatten** *m* half shadow; **~schlaf** *m* light sleep, doze; **im ~schlaf sein** to be half asleep; **~schuh** *m* shoe; **~schwergewichtler** *m* light-heavyweight; **~schwester** *f* half-sister; **~seide** *f* fifty per cent silk; **h~seiden** *adj (lit)* fifty per cent silk; *(fig) Dame* fast; *(homosexuell)* gay; **h~seidenes Milieu** the demimonde; **h~seitig** *adj Anzeige* half-page; **h~seitig gelähmt** hemiplegic; **~starke(r)** *m decl as adj* hooligan, rowdy; **h~tags** *adv* in the mornings/afternoons; **h~tags arbeiten** to work part-time.

Halbtags-: ~arbeit, ~beschäftigung *f* part-time job; **~kraft** *f* part-time employee.

Halb-: ~ton *m* half-tone; *(Mus)* semitone; **h~voll** *adj attr* half-filled; **h~wach** *adj attr* half awake; **in h~wachem Zustand** half awake; **~wahrheit** *f* half truth; **~waise** *f child/person who has lost one parent;* **h~wegs** *adv* partly; *gut* reasonably; *annehmbar* halfway; **wenn es dir wieder h~wegs besser geht** when you're feeling a bit better; **~welt** *f* demimonde; **~wertzeit** *f* half-life; **~wissen** *nt (pej)* superficial knowledge; **h~wüchsig** *adj* adolescent; **~wüchsige(r)** *mf decl as adj* adolescent; **~zeit** *f (Sport) (Hälfte)* half; *(Pause)* half-time.

Halde *f* **-n (a)** *(Abfall~)* mound, heap; *(Min: Abbau~)* slagheap. **(b)** *(geh: Abhang)* slope.

half *pret of* **helfen.**

Hälfte *f* **-n** half. **die ~ der Kinder war abwesend** half the children were absent; **die ~ von etw** half (of) sth; **die ~ ist gelogen** half of it is lies; **Rentner zahlen die ~** pensioners pay half price; **um die ~ steigen** to increase by half; **es ist zur ~ fertig** it is half finished; **das werde ich zur ~ bezahlen** I will pay half (of it); **meine bessere ~** *(hum col)* my better half *(hum col)*; **auf der ~ des Weges** halfway.

Halfter[1] *m or nt* **-** *(für Tiere)* halter.

Halfter[2] *f* **-n** *or nt* **-** *(Pistolen~)* holster.

Hall *m* **-e** echo.

Halle *f* **-n** hall; *(Hotel~)* lobby; *(Fabrik~)* shed; *(Sport~)* (sports) hall, gym(nasium). **Fußball in der ~** indoor football.

hallen *vi* to reverberate, to echo *(auch fig)*.

Hallen- *in cpds (Sport)* indoor; **~(schwimm)bad** *nt* indoor swimming pool.

hallo ['halo, ha'lo:] *interj* hello.

Halluzination *f* hallucination.

Halm *m* **-e** stalk, stem; *(Gras~)* blade of grass; *(Stroh~, zum Trinken)* straw.

Halogenscheinwerfer *m* halogen headlamp.

Hals *m* **¨-e (a)** neck. **sich** *(dat)* **nach jdm/etw den ~ verrenken** *(col)* to crane one's neck to see sb/sth; **jdm um den ~ fallen** to fling one's arms around sb's neck; **sich jdm an den ~ werfen** *(fig col)* to throw oneself at sb; **das wird ihm noch den ~ brechen** *(col)* it'll ruin him; **~ über Kopf abreisen** to leave in a rush; **ihm steht das Wasser bis zum ~** *(fig)* he is up to his neck in it *(col)*; **jdn auf dem** *or* **am ~ haben** *(col)* to be lumbered *or* saddled with sb *(col)*; **jdn jdm auf den ~ hetzen** *(col)* to put sb onto sb; **jdm mit etw vom ~(e) bleiben** *(col)* not to bother sb with sth *(col)*; **sich jdn/etw vom ~e schaffen** *(col)* to get sb/sth off one's back *(col)*.

(b) *(Kehle, Rachen)* throat. **sie hat es im ~** *(col)* she has a sore throat; **aus vollem ~(e)** at the top of one's voice; **es hängt mir zum ~ heraus** *(col)* I'm sick and tired of it; **sie hat es in den falschen ~ bekommen** *(col) (sich verschlucken)* it went down the wrong way; *(falsch verstehen)* she took it wrongly; **etw bleibt jdm im ~ stecken** *(lit, fig)* sth sticks in sb's throat; **er kann den ~ nicht voll (genug) kriegen** *(fig col)* he is never satisfied.

Hals-: ~abschneider *m* **-** *(pej col)* shark *(col)*; **h~abschneiderisch** *adj (pej col) Preise* extortionate; *Mensch* cutthroat *(col)*; **~ausschnitt** *m* neck(line); **~band** *nt (Hunde~)* collar; **h~brecherisch** *adj* dangerous; *Tempo* breakneck; *Fahrt* hair-raising; **~entzündung** *f* sore throat; **~kette** *f (Schmuck)* necklace; **~krause** *f* ruff.

Hals-Nasen-Ohren-Arzt *m* ear, nose and throat specialist.

Hals-: ~schlagader *f* carotid (artery); **~schmerzen** *pl* sore throat *sing;* **h~starrig** *adj* stubborn; **~starrigkeit** *f* stubbornness; **~tuch** *nt* scarf; **~- und Beinbruch** *interj* good luck; **~weh** *nt* sore throat; **~wirbel** *m* cervical vertebra.

Halt *m* **-e (a)** *(für Füße, Hände)* hold; *(lit, fig: Stütze)* support; *(fig: innerer ~)* security *no art.* **~ haben** *(Ding)* to hold; **keinen ~ haben** to have no hold/support; to be insecure; **ohne inneren ~** insecure. **(b)** *(geh: Anhalten)* stop.

halt[1] *interj* stop.

halt[2] *adv (dial) siehe* **eben 2 (b).**

haltbar *adj* **(a) ~ sein** to keep (well); **~e Lebensmittel** food which keeps (well); **etw ~ machen** to preserve sth; **~ bis 6.11.** use by 6 Nov. **(b)** *(widerstandsfähig)* durable; *Stoff, Kleider* hard-wearing. **(c)** *Theorie* tenable.

Haltbarkeit *f* **(a)** *(von Lebensmitteln)* **eine längere ~ haben** to keep longer; **Lebensmittel von kurzer ~** perishable food. **(b)** *siehe adj (b)* durability; hard-wearingness.

Haltbarkeitsdatum *nt* best-before date.

Haltegriff *m* handle; *(in Bus)* strap; *(an Badewanne)* handrail.

halten *pret* **hielt,** *ptp* **gehalten 1** *vt* **(a)** *(festhalten)* to hold; *(zurückhalten)* to stop; *(behalten, besitzen) Haustier, Vorsprung, Versprechen* to keep; *Rekord, Kurs, Position* to hold; *Auto* to run; *(beibehalten) Temperatur, Tempo* to keep up. **den Mund ~** *(col)* to keep one's mouth shut *(col)*; **ich konnte ihn/es gerade noch ~** I just managed to grab hold of him/it; **sie ist nicht zu ~** *(fig)* there's no holding her; **es hält mich hier nichts mehr** there's nothing to keep me here any more; **es hält dich niemand** nobody's stopping you; **die Wärme ~** to retain heat; **sich** *(dat)* **jdn/etw ~** to keep sb/sth; **den Ton ~** to stay in tune; **die These läßt sich nicht länger ~** this thesis is no longer tenable; **(mit jdm) Verbindung ~** to keep in touch (with sb).

(b) *(abhalten) Vorlesung* to give; *Rede auch* to make; *Gottesdienst* to hold; *Wache* to keep. **Mittagsschlaf ~** to have an afternoon nap.

(c) *(Sport) Ball* to save.

(d) einen Fuß ins Wasser ~ to put one's foot into the water; **er hält seine Kinder sehr streng**

he's very strict with his children; **es mit etw so/anders ~** to handle sth like this/differently; **das kannst du ~ wie du willst** that's completely up to you; **etw einfach ~** to keep sth simple; **der Film hält nicht, was er verspricht** the film doesn't live up to expectations; **jdn/etw für jdn/ etw ~** to take sb/sth for sb/sth; **jdn für ehrlich ~** to think *or* consider sb is honest; **wofür ~ Sie mich?** what do you take me for?; **etw von jdm/ etw ~** to think sth of sb/sth; **ich halte nichts davon, das zu tun** I don't think much of doing that; **nicht viel vom Sparen ~** not to be a great one for saving *(col)*.

2 *vi* **(a)** *(festhalten, zusammenhalten)* to hold. **kannst du mal 'n Moment ~?** can you just hold that (for) a moment? **(b)** *(bestehen bleiben, haltbar sein)* to last; *(Stoff)* to wear well. **(c)** *(stehenbleiben, anhalten)* to stop. **zum H~ bringen** to bring to a stop *or* standstill. **(d)** *(Sport)* to make a save. **(e) Sport hält jung** sport keeps you young; **auf etw** *(acc)* **~** *(zielen)* to aim at sth; *(steuern)* to head for sth; **etwas mehr nach links ~** to keep more to the left; *(zielen)* to aim more to the left; **zu jdm ~** to stand *or* stick by sb; **(sehr) auf etw** *(acc)* **~** *(Wert legen)* to attach (a lot of) importance to sth; **auf sich** *(acc)* **~** *(auf Äußeres achten)* to take a pride in oneself.

3 *vr* **(a)** *(sich festhalten)* to hold on *(an+dat -to)*. **(b)** *(sich nicht verändern)* to keep; *(Wetter)* to last; *(Preise)* to hold; *(nicht verschwinden)* to last; *(Geruch etc)* to stay; *(seine Position behaupten)* to hold on. **er hat sich gut gehalten** *(col)* he's well-preserved; **sich auf den Beinen ~** to stay on one's feet; **sich gut ~** *(in Prüfung, Spiel etc)* to make a good showing, to do well; **er hält sich sehr aufrecht** he holds *or* carries himself very erect; **der Autofahrer hielt sich ganz rechts** the driver kept to the right; **sich an ein Versprechen ~** to keep a promise; **sich an den Text ~** to keep *or* stick to the text; **sich an jdn ~** *(sich wenden an)* to ask sb; *(sich richten nach)* to follow sb; **sich nicht ~ können** to be unable to control oneself. **(c) er hält sich für besonders klug** he thinks he's very clever.

Halter *m* - **(a)** *(Halterung)* holder. **(b)** *(Jur: Kraftfahrzeug~, Tier~)* owner.

Halterung *f* mounting; *(für Regal etc)* support.

Halte-: ~schild *nt* stop *or* halt sign; **~signal** *nt (Rail)* stop signal; **~stelle** *f* stop; **~verbot** *nt* **(absolutes) ~verbot** no stopping; *(Bereich)* no stopping zone; **eingeschränktes ~verbot** no waiting; *(Bereich)* no waiting zone.

Halt-: h~los *adj (schwach)* insecure; *(hemmungslos)* unrestrained; *(unbegründet)* groundless; **~losigkeit** *f siehe adj* lack of security; uninhibitedness; groundlessness; **h~machen** *vi sep* to stop; **vor nichts h~machen** *(fig)* to stop at nothing; **vor niemandem h~machen** *(fig)* to spare no-one.

Haltung *f* **(a)** *(Körper~)* posture; *(Stellung)* position. **~ annehmen** *(esp Mil)* to stand to attention. **(b)** *(fig) (Auftreten)* manner; *(Einstellung)* attitude. **(c)** *no pl (Beherrschtheit)* composure. **~ bewahren** to keep one's composure. **(d)** *no pl (von Tieren, Fahrzeugen)* owning.

Halunke *m (wk)* **-n, -n** scoundrel.

Hamburger(in *f***)** *m* - native of Hamburg.

hämisch *adj* malicious, spiteful. **er hat sich ~ gefreut** he gloated.

Hammel-: ~beine *pl*: **jdm die ~beine langziehen** *(hum col)* to give sb a dressing-down; **~fleisch** *nt* mutton; **~keule** *f (Cook)* leg of mutton; **~sprung** *m (Parl)* division.

Hammer *m* ¨ hammer. **das ist ein ~!** *(col) (unerhört)* that's absurd!; *(prima)* that's fantastic! *(col)*.

hämmern 1 *vi (lit, fig)* to hammer; *(col: beim Klavierspielen etc)* to pound. **2** *vt* to hammer; *Metallgefäße, Schmuck etc* to beat. **jdm etw ins Bewußtsein ~** *(col)* to hammer sth into sb's head *(col)*.

Hammerwerfen *nt no pl* hammer(-throwing).

Hammond|orgel ['hæmənd-] *f* electric organ.

Hämorrhoiden [hɛmɔro'iːdən] *pl* piles *pl*, haemorrhoids *(Brit) pl*, hemorrhoids *(US) pl*.

Hampelmann *m, pl* **-männer (a)** jumping jack. **(b)** *(col: willenloser Mensch)* **er ist nur ein ~** he just lets people walk all over him.

hampeln *vi* to jump about; *(zappeln)* to fidget.

Hamster *m* - hamster.

Hamsterer(in *f***)** *m* - *(col)* squirrel *(col)*.

Hamsterkauf *m* panic-buying *no pl*. **Hamsterkäufe machen** to buy in order to hoard; *(bei Knappheit)* to panic-buy.

hamstern *vti (speichern)* to hoard; *(Hamsterkäufe machen)* to panic-buy.

Hand *f* ¨-e **(a)** hand. **jdm die ~ geben** to give sb one's hand; **jdn an die** *or* **bei der ~ nehmen** to take sb by the hand; **jdm etw aus der ~ nehmen** to take sth off sb *(auch fig)*; **mit der ~, von ~** by hand; **von ~ geschrieben/genäht** handwritten/ handsewn.

(b) *no pl (Sport: ~spiel)* hand-ball.

(c) *(Besitz, Obhut)* possession, hands. **aus privater ~** privately; **etw aus der ~ geben** to let sth out of one's sight; **etw geht in jds ¨~e über** sth passes into sb's hands; **zu ¨~en von jdm** for the attention of sb.

(d) ¨~e hoch! hands up!; **¨~e weg!** hands off!; **~ aufs Herz** cross your heart; **eine ~ wäscht die andere** *(Prov)* if you scratch my back I'll scratch yours; **ich wasche meine ¨~e in Unschuld** *(geh)* I wash my hands of it; **bei etw die** *or* **seine ~ im Spiel haben** to have a hand in sth; **er hat überall seine ~ im Spiel** he has a finger in every pie; **etw hat weder ~ noch Fuß** sth doesn't make sense; **sich mit ¨~en und Füßen gegen etw wehren** to fight sth tooth and nail; **rechter/linker ~** on the right-/left-hand side; **eine ruhige/sichere ~** a steady hand; **eine lockere ~ haben** *(hum col)* to let fly at the slightest provocation; **bei etw eine glückliche ~ haben** to have a lucky touch with sth; **in festen ¨~en sein** to be spoken for; **mit leeren/vollen ¨~en** empty-handed/open-handedly; **alle ¨~e voll zu tun haben** to have one's hands full; **sich die ~ fürs Leben reichen** *(geh)* to tie the knot; **die ~ für jdn ins Feuer legen** to vouch for sb; **jdn auf ¨~en tragen** to cherish sb; **(bei etw) mit ~ anlegen** to lend a hand (with sth); **~ an jdn legen** *(geh)* to lay a hand on sb; **die ~ auf etw** *(dat)* **halten** to keep a tight rein on sth; **das liegt auf der ~** *(col)* that's obvious; **an ~ eines Beispiels** by means of an example; **an ~ dieses Berichts** from this report; **aus erster/zweiter ~** first/ second hand; **zur ~ haben** to have sth to hand; *Ausrede, Erklärung* to have sth ready; **mit etw schnell bei der ~ sein** *(col)* to be ready with sth; **jdm in die ¨~e arbeiten** to play into sb's hands; **jdm in die ¨~e fallen** *or* **geraten** to fall into sb's hands; **jdn/etw in die ¨~e kriegen** *or* **bekommen** to get one's hands on sb/sth; **jdn (fest) in der ~ haben** to have sb (well) in hand; **von der ~ in den Mund leben** to live from hand to mouth; **ich habe diese Entscheidung nicht in der ~** it's not in my hands; **etw gegen jdn in der ~ haben** to have some hold on sb; **in jds ~ sein** to be in sb's hands; **etw in die ~ nehmen** to pick sth up; *(fig)* to take sth in hand; **jdm etw in die ¨~e spielen** to pass sth on to sb; **hinter vorgehaltener ~** on the quiet; **etw geht jdm flott/leicht von der ~** sb does sth quickly/finds sth easy; **es ist nicht von der ~ zu weisen** it cannot be denied; **zur ~ sein** to be at hand; **jdm zur ~ gehen** to lend sb a helping hand.

Hand|arbeit *f* work done by hand; *(Gegenstand)* handmade article; *(körperliche Arbeit)* manual work; *(Nähen, Sticken etc, als Schulfach)* needlework *no pl; (Stricken)* knitting *no pl; (Häkeln)* crochet(ing) *no pl.* **etw in ~ herstellen** to make sth by hand; **diese Tischdecke ist ~** this tablecloth is handmade.

Hand|arbeitsgeschäft *nt* needlework and wool shop *(Brit) or* store *(US).*

Hand-: ~auflegen *nt no pl* laying on of hands; **~ausgabe** *f (Buch)* concise edition; **~ball** *m or (col) nt (Spiel)* handball; **~bedienung** *f,* **~betrieb** *m* manual operation; **mit ~betrieb** hand-operated; **~bewegung** *f (Geste, Zeichen)* gesture; **~bibliothek** *f* reference library *(with open shelves)*; **~bohrer** *m* gimlet; **~bohrmaschine** *f* (hand) drill; **~breit** *f* - ≈ six inches; **~bremse** *f* brake; *(Aut)* handbrake *(Brit),* parking brake *(US)*; **~buch** *nt* handbook, reference book; *(technisch)* manual; **~creme** *f* hand cream.

Händedruck *m* handshake.

Handel *m no pl (das Handeln)* trade; *(esp illegal)* traffic; *(Wirtschaftszweig auch)* commerce; *(Warenmarkt)* market; *(Abmachung)* deal. **~ mit etw** trade in sth; **im ~ sein** to be on the market; **etw in den ~ bringen/aus dem ~ ziehen** to put sth on/take sth off the market; **(mit jdm) ~ treiben** to trade (with sb).

handeln 1 *vi* **(a)** to trade. **er handelt mit Gemüse** he trades *or* deals in vegetables; **er handelt mit Drogen** he traffics in drugs. **(b)** *(feilschen)* to bargain, to haggle *(um* about, over*)*; **ich lasse mit mir ~** I'm open to persuasion; *(in bezug auf Preis)* I'm open to offers. **(c)** *(tätig werden)* to act. **(d) von etw ~** to deal with sth. **2** *vr impers* **es handelt sich dabei um ein Versehen** this is an error; **sich um etw ~** to be about sth, to concern sth; **es handelt sich nur ums Überleben** it's simply a question of survival.

Handeln *nt no pl* **(a)** *(Feilschen)* bargaining, haggling. **(b)** *(das Handeltreiben)* trading. **(c)** *(Verhalten)* behaviour *(Brit),* behavior *(US).* **(d)** *(das Tätigwerden)* action.

handelnd *adj* **die ~en Personen in einem Drama** the characters in a drama.

Handels-: ~abkommen *nt* trade agreement; **~bank** *f* merchant bank *(Brit),* commercial bank; **~beziehungen** *pl* trade relations *pl;* **~bilanz** *f* balance of trade; **aktive/passive ~bilanz** balance of trade surplus/deficit; **~brauch** *m* commercial practice; **~defizit** *nt* trade deficit; **h~einig** *adj pred* **h~einig werden** to agree terms; **~gesellschaft** *f* commercial company; **~gesetz** *nt* commercial law; **~gewerbe** *nt* commerce *no art;* **~gut** *nt* commodity; **~kammer** *f* chamber of commerce; **~klasse** *f* grade; **~marine** *f* merchant navy; **~marke** *f* trade name; **~minister** *m* ≈ Trade Secretary *(Brit),* Secretary of Commerce *(US)*; **~organisation** *f* trading organization; **~politik** *f* trade *or* commercial policy; **~recht** *nt* commercial law *no def art;* **h~rechtlich 1** *adj* of/about commercial law; **2** *adv* according to commercial law; **~register** *nt* register of companies; **~reisende(r)** *mf decl as adj* commercial traveller *(Brit) or* traveler *(US)*; **~schiffahrt** *f* merchant shipping *no def art;* **~schranke** *f usu pl* trade barrier; **~schule** *f* commercial college; **~spanne** *f* profit margin; **~sperre** *f* trade embargo *(gegen* on*)*; **h~üblich** *adj* customary; **~unternehmen** *nt* commercial enterprise; **~verkehr** *m* trade; **~vertrag** *m* trade agreement; **~vertreter** *m* commercial traveller *(Brit) or* traveler *(US)*; **~vertretung** *f* trade mission; **~ware** *f* commodity; **~waren** *pl* commodities *pl,* merchandise *sing;* **~wert** *m* market value; **~zweig** *m* branch.

Hände-: h~ringend *adv* wringing one's hands; *(fig)* imploringly; **~trockner** *m* hand drier.

Hand-: ~feger *m* hand brush; **~fertigkeit** *f* dexterity; **h~fest** *adj* **(a)** *(kräftig) Mensch* sturdy, robust; *Essen* substantial; **(b)** *(fig) Schlägerei* violent; *Skandal* huge; *Beweis* solid, tangible; *Lüge, Betrug* flagrant, blatant; **~fläche** *f* palm *or* flat (of the/one's hand); **h~gearbeitet, h~gefertigt** *adj* handmade; *Stickerei etc* handworked; **~gelenk** *nt* wrist; **aus dem ~gelenk** *(col) (ohne Mühe)* effortlessly; *(improvisiert)* off the cuff; **h~gemacht** *adj* handmade; **h~gemalt** *adj* hand-painted; **~gemenge** *nt* scuffle, fight; **h~genäht** *adj* handsewn; **~gepäck** *nt* hand baggage *no pl;* **h~geschrieben** *adj* handwritten; **h~gesteuert** *adj (Tech)* hand-operated; **~granate** *f* hand grenade; **h~greiflich** *adj Streit* violent; **h~greiflich werden** to become violent; **~greiflichkeit** *f usu pl* violence *no pl;* **~griff** *m* **(a)** *(Bewegung)* movement; *(im Haushalt)* chore; **mit einem ~griff** *öffnen* with one flick of the wrist; *(schnell)* in no time; **(b)** *(an Gegenstand)* handle; **~habe** *f (fig)* **ich habe gegen ihn keine ~habe** I have no hold on him; **etw als ~habe (gegen jdn) benutzen** to use sth as a lever (against sb); **h~haben*** *vt insep* to handle; *Maschine auch* to operate; *Gesetz* to implement; **~habung** *f siehe vt* handling; operation; implementation.

Handikap ['hɛndikɛp] *nt* **-s** *(Sport, fig)* handicap.

Hand-: ~kante *f* side of the/one's hand; **~kantenschlag** *m* karate chop; **~käse** *m strong-smelling round German cheese;* **~koffer** *m* (small) suitcase; **~kuß** *m* kiss on the hand; **mit ~kuß** *(fig col)* with pleasure; **~langer** *m* - odd-job man, handyman; *(fig: Untergeordneter)* dogsbody *(col)*; *(fig pej: Gehilfe)* henchman; **~langerarbeit** *f (pej)* donkey work *no pl.*

Händler(in *f***)** *m* - trader, dealer; *(Ladenbesitzer)* shopkeeper, store owner *(US).* **fliegender ~** street trader.

handlich *adj Gerät, Form* handy; *Gepäckstück* manageable.

Handlichkeit *f no pl* handiness; manageability.

Handlung *f* action; *(Tat)* act; *(von Drama)* plot. **der Ort der ~** the scene of the action.

Handlungs-: ~ablauf *m* plot; **h~fähig** *adj Regierung* able to act; *(Jur)* empowered to act; **eine h~fähige Mehrheit** a working majority; **~fähigkeit** *f (von Regierung)* ability to act; *(Jur)* power to act; **~freiheit** *f* freedom of action; **h~unfähig** *adj Regierung* unable to act; *(Jur)* without power to act; **~unfähigkeit** *f (von Regierung)* inability to act; *(Jur)* lack of power to act; **~vollmacht** *f* proxy; **~weise** *f* way of behaving; **eine selbstlose ~weise** unselfish behaviour *(Brit) or* behavior *(US).*

Hand-: ~pflege *f* care of one's hands; **~puppe** *f* glove puppet; **~puppenspiel** *nt (Stück)* glove puppet show; **~rücken** *m* back of the/one's hand; **~schelle** *f usu pl* handcuff; **jdm ~schellen anlegen** to handcuff sb; **~schlag** *m* **(a)** *(Händedruck)* handshake; **ein Geschäft durch ~schlag abschließen** to shake on a deal; **(b) keinen ~schlag tun** not to do a stroke (of work); **~schrift** *f* **(a)** handwriting; *(fig)* (trade)mark; **etw trägt/verrät jds ~schrift** *(fig)* sth bears *or* has sb's (trade)mark; **(b)** *(Hist: Text)* manuscript; **h~schriftlich 1** *adj* handwritten; **2** *adv korrigieren, einfügen* by hand.

Handschuh *m (Finger~)* glove; *(Faust~)* mitten.

Handschuhfach *nt (Aut)* glove compartment.

Hand-: h~signiert *adj* signed; **~spiel** *nt no pl (Sport)* handball; **~stand** *m (Sport)* handstand; **~steuerung** *f* manual control; **~streich** *m* **im ~streich** in a surprise coup; **~tasche** *f* handbag, purse *(US)*; **~tuch** *nt* towel; **das ~tuch werfen** *(fig)* to throw in the towel; **~umdrehen** *nt (fig)*: **im ~umdrehen** in the twinkling of an eye; **~voll** *f* - *(lit, fig)* handful; **~wäsche** *f* washing by hand; *(Wäschestücke)* hand wash.

Handwerk *nt* trade; *(Kunst~)* craft; *(fig: Tätigkeit)* business. **sein ~ verstehen** *(fig)* to know one's job; **jdm ins ~ pfuschen** *(fig)* to interfere in sb's job; **jdm das ~ legen** *(fig)* to put a stop to sb's game *(col)*.

Hạndwerker(in *f*) *m* - (skilled) manual worker; *(Kunst~)* craftsman; craftswoman. **wir haben seit Wochen die ~ im Haus** we've had workmen in the house for weeks.

hạndwerklich *adj Ausbildung* as a manual worker/craftsman; *(fig)* technical. **~er Beruf** skilled trade; **~es Können** craftsmanship; **~e Fähigkeiten** manual skills.

Hạndwerks-: ~beruf *m* skilled trade; **~betrieb** *m* workshop; **~kammer** *f* trade corporation; **~zeug** *nt no pl* tools *pl*; *(fig)* tools of the trade *pl*.

Hạnd-: ~wörterbuch *nt* concise dictionary; **~zeichen** *nt* signal; *(Geste auch)* sign; *(bei Abstimmung)* show of hands; **durch ~zeichen** by a show of hands; **~zettel** *m* leaflet, handbill.

hạnebüchen *adj (dated, geh)* outrageous.

Hạnf *m no pl (Pflanze, Faser)* hemp.

Hạng *m* **¨e** **(a)** *(Abhang)* slope. **(b)** *no pl (Neigung)* tendency.

Hangar ['haŋgaːɐ] *m* **-s** hangar.

Hạ̈nge-: ~bauch *m* drooping belly *(col)*; **~brücke** *f* suspension bridge; **~gleiter** *m (Sport)* hang-glider; **~lampe** *f* drop-light.

hạngeln *vir* **er hangelte (sich) an einem Tau über den Fluß** he moved hand over hand along a rope over the river.

Hạ̈ngematte *f* hammock.

Hạ̈ngen *nt* **mit ~ und Würgen** *(col)* by the skin of one's teeth.

hängen 1 *vi pret* **hing,** *ptp* **gehangen (a)** to hang; *(sich festhalten)* to hang on *(an +dat* to); *(angeschlossen sein)* to be connected (up) *(an +dat* to); *(kleben)* to be stuck *(an +dat* on). **die Gardinen ~ schon** the curtains are already up; **mit ~den Schultern** with drooping shoulders; **die Blumen ließen die Köpfe ~** the flowers hung their heads; **den Kopf ~ lassen** *(fig)* to be downcast; **das Kleid hing ihr am Leib** *(col)* the dress hung on her; **das Bild hängt an der Wand** the picture is hanging on the wall; **sie hing ihm am Hals** she hung around his neck; **der Patient hängt an der künstlichen Niere/am Tropf** the patient is on the kidney machine/on the drip; **ihre Blicke hingen an dem Sänger** her eyes were fixed on the singer; **sie hängt dauernd am Telefon** *(col)* she's always on the phone; **er hängt den ganzen Tag vorm Fernseher** *(col)* he spends all day in front of the telly.

(b) *(lieben)* **an jdm/etw ~** to be very attached to sb/sth; **er hängt am Leben** he clings to life.

(c) daran hängt viel Arbeit there's a lot of work involved in that; **der Schrank hängt voller Kleider** the cupboard is full of clothes; **der Baum hängt voller Früchte** the tree is laden with fruit; **die ganze Sache hängt an ihm** it all depends on him.

2 *vt pret* **hạ̈ngte,** *ptp* **gehạ̈ngt** *(aufhängen, henken)* to hang; *(anschließen)* to connect *(an +acc* to); *(befestigen) Wohnwagen etc* to hitch up. **er hängte den Telefonhörer in die Gabel** he hung up.

3 *vr pret* **hạ̈ngte,** *ptp* **gehạ̈ngt sich an etw** *(acc)* **~** to hang on to sth; **er hängte sich ans Telefon** he got on the phone; **sich an jdn ~** *(sich anschließen)* to latch on to sb *(col)*; *(gefühlsmäßig binden)* to become attached to sb; *(verfolgen)* to set off in (hot) pursuit of sb.

hạ̈ngenbleiben *vi sep irreg aux sein* **(a)** to get caught *(an+dat* on). **(b)** *(Sport) (zurückbleiben)* to get left behind; *(nicht durch-, weiterkommen)* not to get through. **(c)** *(Sch col: nicht versetzt werden)* to stay down. **(d)** *(sich aufhalten)* to stay on. **bei einer Nebensächlichkeit ~** to get bogged down with a side issue. **(e)** *(haftenbleiben)* to get stuck *or* caught *(in, an+dat* on). **es bleibt ja doch alles an mir hängen** *(fig col)* in the end it's all down to me anyhow *(col)*; **der Verdacht ist an ihm hängengeblieben** suspicion rested on him; **vom Lateinunterricht ist bei ihm nicht viel hängengeblieben** *(fig col)* not much of his Latin stuck *(col)*.

hạ̈ngend *adj* hanging. **mit ~er Zunge kam er angelaufen** *(fig)* he came running up panting.

hạ̈ngenlassen *sep irreg, ptp* **hängen(ge)lassen 1** *vt* **(a)** *(vergessen)* to leave behind. **(b)** *(col: im Stich lassen)* to let down. **2** *vr* to let oneself go.

Hạ̈nge-: ~pflanze *f* trailing plant; **~schloß** *nt* padlock; **~schrank** *m* wall-cupboard.

Hạnglage *f* sloping site. **in ~** situated on a slope.

Hannover [ha'noːfɐ] *nt* Hanover.

Hannoverạner(in *f*) *m* - Hanoverian.

Hansdạmpf *m* **-e** Jack-of-all-trades (and master of none). **er ist ein ~ in allen Gassen** he knows everybody and everything.

Hänselei *f* teasing *no pl*.

hạ̈nseln *vt* to tease.

Hạnsestadt *f* Hanseatic *or* Hanse town.

Hanswụrst *m* **-e** *or (hum)* **¨e** clown.

Hạntel *f* **-n** *(Sport)* dumb-bell.

hantieren* *vi* **(a)** *(arbeiten)* to be busy. **(b)** *(umgehen mit)* **mit etw ~** to handle sth. **(c)** *(herum~)* to tinker about *(an+dat* with, on).

hapern *vi impers (col)* **es hapert an etw** *(dat) (fehlt)* there is a lack of sth; **es hapert bei jdm mit etw** *(fehlt)* sb is short of sth; **mit der Grammatik hapert es bei ihm** he's poor at grammar.

Hạ̈ppchen *nt dim of* **Happen** morsel; *(Appetithappen)* titbit.

hạ̈ppchenweise *adv (col: lit, fig)* bit by bit.

Hạppen *m* - *(col)* mouthful, morsel; *(kleine Mahlzeit)* bite. **ein fetter ~** *(fig)* a good catch; **ich habe heute noch keinen ~ gegessen** I haven't had a bite to eat all day.

hạppig *adj (col)* steep *(col)*.

Hardware ['haːdwɛə] *f (Comp)* hardware.

Harem *m* **-s** *(auch hum col)* harem.

Hạrfe *f* **-n** harp.

Hạrke *f* **-n** *(esp N Ger)* rake. **jdm zeigen, was eine ~ ist** *(fig col)* to show sb what's what *(col)*.

hạrmlos *adj* **(a)** *(ungefährlich)* harmless; *Berg, Piste* easy; *Schnupfen, Entzündung etc* slight. **(b)** *(arglos)* innocent; *(friedlich)* harmless. **er ist ein ~er Mensch** he's harmless (enough).

Hạrmlosigkeit *f no pl siehe adj* **(a)** harmlessness; easiness; slightness. **(b)** innocence; harmlessness. **in aller ~** in all innocence.

Harmonie *f (Mus, fig)* harmony.

harmonieren* *vi (Mus, fig)* to harmonize; *(farblich auch)* to match.

Harmonika *f* **-s** *or* **Harmoniken** harmonica; *(Mund~ auch)* mouth organ; *(Zieh~)* accordion.

harmonisch *adj* harmonious; *(Mus, Math)* harmonic.

harmonisieren* *vt (Mus)* to harmonize; *(fig)* to coordinate.

Hạrn *m* **-e** urine. **~ lassen** to pass water.

Hạrnblase *f* bladder.

Hạrnisch *m* **-e** armour *(Brit)*, armor *(US)*. **jdn in ~ bringen** *(fig)* to get sb up in arms; **wenn sie das sieht, gerät sie in ~** it gets her hackles up when she sees that.

Harpune *f* **-n** harpoon.

harpunieren* *vti* to harpoon.

hạrren *vi (geh)* **jds/einer Sache ~, auf jdn/etw ~** to await sb/sth, to wait for sb/sth.

Hạrsch *m no pl* frozen snow.

hạrsch *adj* **(a)** harsh. **(b)** *Schnee* frozen.

hart *comp* **¨er,** *superl* **¨este(r,s)** *or (adv)* **am ¨esten 1** *adj* **(a)** hard; *Winter auch, Strafe* severe; *Gesetze, Kurs* tough; *Auseinandersetzung* violent; *Wind* strong; *Ei* hard-boiled; *(stabil) Währung* stable; *(fig) Getränk, Droge* hard; *Verlust* cruel; *Wirklichkeit* harsh. **~ werden** to get hard, to harden; **Eier ~ kochen** to hard-boil eggs; **er hat einen ~en**

Schädel *or* **Kopf** *(fig)* he's obstinate; **ein ~es Herz haben** *(fig)* to have a hard heart, to be hard-hearted; **in ~en Dollars** in hard dollars; **~ bleiben** to stand firm; **~ mit jdm sein** to be hard on sb; **es geht ~ auf ~** it's a tough fight. **(b)** *(rauh) Spiel, Gegner* rough; *(robust)* tough. **kalte Duschen machen ~** cold showers make you tough; **er ist ~ im Nehmen** he's tough. **(c)** *(scharf) Konturen, (Phot) Negativ* sharp; *Klang, Akzent* harsh; *Gesichtszüge* hard.

2 *adv* **(a)** hard; *(scharf) konstrastiert* sharply; *(heftig, rauh)* roughly. **~ klingen** to sound harsh; **~ aneinandergeraten** to get into a fierce argument; **jdn ~ anfahren** to bite sb's head off *(col)*; **jdm ~ zusetzen** to press sb hard; **etw trifft jdn ~** *(lit, fig)* sth hits sb hard; **~ spielen** *(Sport)* to play rough; **~ durchgreifen** to take tough *or* rigorous action; **jdn ~ anfassen** to be hard on sb. **(b)** *(nahe)* close *(an+dat* to*)*. **das ist ~ an der Grenze** that's almost going too far; **wir fuhren ~ am Abgrund vorbei** *(fig)* we were on the brink of disaster.

Härte *f* **-n** *siehe adj* **(a)** hardness; severity; toughness; violence; strength; stability; cruelty; harshness. **soziale ~n** social hardships. **(b)** roughness; toughness. **(c)** sharpness; harshness; hardness.

Härte-: ~fall *m* case of hardship; *(col: Mensch)* hardship case; **~grad** *m* degree of hardness; **~klausel** *f* hardship clause.

härten *vtir* to harden.

Hart-: ~faserplatte *f* hardboard, fiberboard *(US)*; **h~gefroren** *adj attr* frozen hard *pred*; **h~gekocht** *adj attr* hard-boiled; **~geld** *nt* hard cash; **h~gesotten** *adj (fig)* hard-boiled; **h~herzig** *adj* hard-hearted; **~herzigkeit** *f* hard-heartedness; **~holz** *nt* hardwood; **~käse** *m* hard cheese; **h~-näckig** *adj* stubborn; **~näckigkeit** *f* stubbornness.

Härtung *f (Tech)* hardening.

Harz[1] *nt* **-e** resin; *(Mus)* rosin.

Harz[2] *m (Geog)* Harz Mountains *pl*.

Haschee *nt* **-s** *(Cook)* hash.

haschen *(dated, geh)* **1** *vt* to catch. **2** *vi* **nach Beifall/Lob** *etc* **~** to fish for applause/praise *etc*.

Häschen ['hɛsçən] *nt dim of* **Hase** young hare, leveret; *(col: Kaninchen)* bunny *(col)*.

Haschisch *nt or m no pl* hashish.

Hase *m (wk)* **-n, -n** hare; *(dial: Kaninchen, Oster~, in Märchen)* rabbit. **falscher ~** *(Cook)* meat loaf; **wissen, wie der ~ läuft** *(fig col)* to know which way the wind blows; **alter ~** *(fig col)* old hand; **da liegt der ~ im Pfeffer** *(col)* that's the crux of the matter; **mein Name ist ~(, ich weiß von nichts)** I don't know anything about anything.

Hasel-: ~maus *f* dormouse; **~nuß** *f* hazelnut; **~strauch** *m* hazel-bush.

Hasen-: h~füßig *adj (dated col)* chicken-hearted *(col)*; **~pfeffer** *m (Cook)* ≃ jugged hare; **~scharte** *f (Med)* hare-lip.

Haß *m no pl* **(a)** hatred, hate *(auf+acc, gegen* of*)*. **(b)** *(col: Wut)* **einen ~ (auf jdn) haben** *(col)* to be really mad (with sb) *(col)*.

hassen *vti* to hate. **etw ~ wie die Pest** *(col)* to detest sth.

hassenswert *adj* hateful, odious.

haß|erfüllt *adj* full of hate *or* hatred.

häßlich *adj* **(a)** *(auch Vorfall etc)* ugly. **~ wie die Nacht** (as) ugly as sin. **(b)** *(gemein)* nasty, mean. **~ über jdn sprechen** to be nasty *or* mean about sb.

Häßlichkeit *f siehe adj* **(a)** ugliness *no pl*. **(b)** nastiness *no pl*, meanness *no pl*; *(Bemerkung)* nasty remark.

Haßliebe *f* love-hate relationship *(für* with*)*.

Hast *f no pl* haste. **ohne ~** without haste, without rushing; **mit einer solchen ~** in such a hurry *or* rush.

haste *(col)* = **hast du. ~ was, biste was** *(prov)* money brings status.

hasten *vi aux sein (geh)* to hasten *(form)*, to hurry.

hastig *adj* hasty; *Essen auch, Worte* hurried. **nicht so ~!** not so fast!

hätscheln *vt (liebkosen)* to pet, to fondle; *(zu weich behandeln)* to mollycoddle; *(bevorzugen)* to pamper.

hatschi *interj* atishoo.

hatte *pret of* **haben.**

Haube *f* **-n (a)** bonnet; *(von Krankenschwester etc)* cap. **jdn unter die ~ bringen** *(hum)* to marry sb off; **unter der ~ sein/unter die ~ kommen** *(hum)* to be/get married. **(b)** *(bei Vögeln)* crest. **(c)** *(Bedeckung)* cover; *(Trocken~)* (hair) dryer, drying hood *(US)*; *(für Kaffee-, Teekanne)* cosy; *(Motor~)* bonnet *(Brit)*, hood *(US)*.

Hauch *m* **-e (a)** *(geh, poet) (Atem)* breath. **(b)** *(Luftzug)* breath of air, breeze. **(c)** *(Duft)* smell. **(d)** *(Andeutung)* hint, touch.

hauchdünn *adj* extremely thin; *Scheiben* wafer-thin; *(fig) Mehrheit* extremely narrow.

hauchen *vti* to breathe. **jdm etw** *(acc)* **ins Ohr ~** *(liter)* to whisper sth in sb's ear.

hauch-: ~fein *adj* extremely fine; **~zart** *adj* very delicate.

Haudegen *m (fig)* old campaigner.

Haue *f no pl (col: Prügel)* (good) hiding *(col)*.

hauen *pret* **haute,** *ptp* **gehauen 1** *vt* **(a)** *(col) (schlagen)* to hit, to clout *(col)*; *(verprügeln)* to hit, to thump *(col)*. **hau(t) ihn!** let him have it! *(col)*. **(b)** *(meißeln) Figur* to carve; *Stufen, Loch* to cut. **(c)** *(col: stoßen) jdn, Gegenstand* to shove *(col)*; *Körperteil* to bang, to knock *(an +acc* on, against*)*. **das haut einen vom Stuhl** it really knocks you sideways *(col)*. **(d)** *(col: werfen)* to chuck *(col)*, to fling. **(e)** *(dial) Baum* to chop (down); *Holz, Fleisch* to chop (up). **2** *vi (col: schlagen)* to hit. **jdm auf die Schulter ~** to slap sb on the shoulder. **3** *vr (col)* **(a)** *(sich prügeln)* to scrap, to fight. **(b)** *(sich setzen, legen)* to fling oneself.

Hauer *m* **- (a)** *(Min)* face-worker. **(b)** *(Zool)* tusk; *(hum: großer Zahn)* fang.

Häufchen *nt dim of* **Haufen** small pile. **ein ~ Unglück** *or* **Elend** a picture of misery.

Haufen *m* **- (a)** heap, pile. **jdn über den ~ rennen/fahren** *etc (col)* to knock sb down; **etw** *(acc)* **über den ~ werfen** *(col) (verwerfen)* to chuck sth out *(col)*; *(durchkreuzen)* to mess sth up *(col)*; **soviel Geld habe ich noch nie auf einem ~ gesehen** *(col)* I've never seen so much money altogether before. **(b)** *(col)* **ein ~ Arbeit/Geld** a load *or* heap of work/money, piles *or* loads of work/money *(all col)*; **ein ~ Unsinn** a load of nonsense *(col)*; **er hat einen ganzen ~ Freunde** he has loads of friends *(col)*. **(c)** *(Schar)* crowd. **dem ~ folgen** *(pej)* to follow the crowd; **der große ~** *(pej)* the common herd.

häufen 1 *vt* to pile up, to heap up. **ein gehäufter Teelöffel Salz** a heaped teaspoonful of salt. **2** *vr (lit, fig: sich ansammeln)* to mount up; *(zahlreicher werden: Unfälle, Fehler etc)* to occur increasingly often. **das kann schon mal vorkommen, es darf sich nur nicht ~** these things happen, just as long as they don't happen too often.

haufenweise *adv (col)* **etw ~ haben** to have piles *or* heaps *or* loads of sth *(all col)*.

häufig 1 *adj* frequent. **2** *adv* often, frequently.

Häufigkeit *f* frequency.

Häufung *f* **(a)** *(fig: das Anhäufen)* accumulation. **(b)** *(das Sich-Häufen)* increasing number.

Haupt *nt, pl* **Häupter (a)** *(geh: Kopf)* head. **entblößten ~es** bareheaded; **gesenkten/erhobenen ~es** with one's head bowed/raised. **(b)** *(zentrale Figur)* head.

Haupt- *in cpds* main, principal, chief; **~akteur** *m (lit, fig)* leading light; *(pej)* main figure; **~akzent** *m (fig)* **auf etw** *(acc)* **den ~akzent legen** to put the main emphasis on sth; **~anteil** *m* main part; **~bahnhof** *m* main *or* central station; **~beruf** *m* main occupation; **h~beruflich 1** *adj Lehrer, Gärtner etc* full-time; **2** *adv* full-time; **h~beruflich tätig sein** to be in full-time employment; **~beschäftigung** *f* main occupation; **~betrieb** *m* **(a)** headquarters *sing or pl*; **(b)** *(geschäftigste Zeit)* peak period; **~darsteller(in** *f***)** *m* principal actor/actress, leading man/lady; **~fach** *nt (Sch, Univ)* main subject, major *(US)*; **etw im ~fach studieren** to study sth as one's main subject, to major in sth *(US)*; **~figur** *f (Liter)* central character; *(fig)* central figure; **~film** *m* main film; **~gericht** *nt* main course.

Hauptgeschäft *nt* **(a)** *(Zentrale)* head office, headquarters *sing or pl.* **(b)** *(Hauptverdienst)* major part of one's business.

Hauptgeschäfts-: ~stelle *f* head office, headquarters *sing or pl*; **~straße** *f* main shopping street; **~zeit** *f* peak (shopping) period.

Haupt-: ~gewicht *nt (fig)* main emphasis; **~gewinn** *m* first prize; **~grund** *m* main reason; **~hahn** *m* mains cock; **~last** *f* main load; *(fig)* main burden; **~leitung** *f* mains *pl*.

Häuptling *m* chief(tain); *(esp von Dorf)* headman.

Haupt-: ~mahlzeit *f* main meal; **~mann** *m, pl* **-leute** *(Mil)* captain; **~merkmal** *nt* main feature; **~motiv** *nt* **(a)** *(Beweggrund)* primary *or* main motive; **(b)** *(Art, Liter, Mus)* main *or* principal motif; **~nahrungsmittel** *nt* staple food; **~niederlassung** *f* head office, headquarters *sing or pl*; **~person** *f (lit, fig)* central figure; **~post** *f (col)*, **~postamt** *nt* main post office; **~quartier** *nt (Mil, fig)* headquarters *sing or pl*; **~reisezeit** *f* peak travelling *(Brit) or* traveling *(US)* time(s *pl*); **~rolle** *f* main role, lead; **die ~rolle spielen** *(fig)* to be all-important; *(wichtigste Person sein)* to play the main role; **~sache** *f* main thing; *(in Brief, Rede etc)* main point; **in der ~sache** in the main, mainly; **~sache, es klappt** the main thing is that it works; **h~sächlich 1** *adv* mainly, principally; **2** *adj* main, principal; **~saison** *f* peak *or* high season; **~satz** *m (Gram)* main clause; **~schalter** *m (Elec)* master switch; **~schlagader** *f* aorta; **~schlüssel** *m* master key; **~schuld** *f* main blame, main guilt *(esp Jur)*; **~schuldige(r)** *mf* person mainly to blame, main offender *(esp Jur)*; **~schule** *f* ≈ secondary modern (school) *(Brit)*, junior high (school) *(US)*; **~sitz** *m* head office, headquarters *sing or pl*; **~stadt** *f* capital (city); **~straße** *f* main *or* major road; *(im Stadtzentrum etc)* main street; **~teil** *m* main part; *(größter Teil auch)* major part; **~thema** *nt* main topic; *(Mus, Liter)* main theme; **~tribüne** *f* main stand; *(Sport auch)* grandstand.

Hauptverkehrs-: ~straße *f (in Stadt)* main street; *(Durchgangsstraße)* main thoroughfare; *(zwischen Städten)* main highway, trunk road *(Brit)*; **~zeit** *f* peak traffic times *pl*; *(in Stadt, bei Pendlern auch)* rush hour.

Haupt-: ~wohnsitz *m* main place of residence; **~wort** *nt (Gram)* noun.

hau ruck *interj* heave-ho.

Haus *nt, pl* **Häuser (a)** *(Wohn~)* house; *(Firmengebäude)* building. **ins/im ~** indoors; **mit jdm ~ an ~ wohnen** to live next door to sb; **von ~ zu ~ gehen** to go from door to door *or* from house to house; **vor vollem ~ spielen** to play to a full house.

(b) *(Zuhause, Heim)* home. **~ und Hof** *(fig)* house and home; **etw ins/frei ~ liefern** *(Comm)* to deliver sth to the door/to deliver sth carriage paid; **wir liefern frei ~** we offer free delivery; **jdm das ~ verbieten** not to allow sb in the house; **aus dem ~ sein** to be away from home; **außer ~ essen** to eat out; **ins ~ stehen** *(fig)* to be coming up, to be forthcoming; **jdm steht etw ins ~** *(fig)* sb is facing sth; **nach ~e** *(lit, fig)* home; **zu ~e** at home *(auch Sport)*; **bei jdm zu ~e** at sb's (place), in sb's house *or* home; **bei uns zu ~e** at home; **für niemanden zu ~e sein** to be at home to nobody; **irgendwo zu ~e sein** *(Mensch, Tier)* to live somewhere; *(sich heimisch fühlen)* to be at home somewhere; **sich wie zu ~e fühlen** to feel at home; **fühl dich wie zu ~e!** make yourself at home!

(c) *(Bewohnerschaft eines ~es)* household. **ein Freund des ~es** a friend of the family; **der Herr des ~es** *(form)* the master of the house.

(d) *(geh: Herkunft)* **aus gutem/bürgerlichem ~(e)** from a good/middle-class family; **von ~e aus** *(ursprünglich)* originally; *(von Natur aus)* naturally.

(e) das ~ Windsor/Siemens the House of Windsor/Siemens; **das erste ~ am Platze** the best hotel in town; *(Kaufhaus)* the best store in town; **Hohes ~!** *(form)* ≈ honourable members (of the House)!; **dieses hohe ~** the *or* this House.

(f) *(von Schnecke)* shell, house *(col)*.

(g) grüß dich, altes ~! *(col)* hallo, old chap *(col)*.

Haus-: ~angestellte(r) *mf* domestic servant; **~anzug** *m* leisure suit; **~apotheke** *f* medicine chest; **~arbeit** *f* **(a)** housework *no pl*; **(b)** *(Sch)* homework *no indef art, no pl*; **~arrest** *m (im Internat)* detention; *(Jur)* house arrest; **~arzt** *m* family doctor, GP; **~aufgaben** *pl* homework *no indef art, no pl*; **h~backen** *adj (fig)* drab, homely *(US)*; **~bau** *m* house building; *(das Bauen)* building of a/the house; **~besetzer** *m* squatter; **~besetzung** *f* squat; **~besitzer(in** *f***)** *m* home-owner; *(Hauswirt)* landlord/landlady; **~besuch** *m* home visit; **~bewohner** *m* (house) occupant *or* occupier.

Häuschen ['hɔysçən] *nt* **(a)** *dim of* **Haus. (b)** *(fig col)* **ganz aus dem ~ sein** to be out of one's mind (with excitement/fear *etc*) *(col)*.

Haus-: h~eigen *adj* belonging to a/the hotel/firm *etc*; **~eigentümer** *m* home-owner; *(Hauswirt)* landlord/landlady.

hausen *vi* **(a)** *(pej: wohnen)* to live. **(b)** *(wüten)* **(übel** *or* **schlimm) ~** to wreak *or* create havoc; **wie die Wandalen ~** to act like vandals.

Häuser-: ~block *m* block (of houses); **~front** *f* front of a row of houses; **~makler** *m* estate agent *(Brit)*, realtor *(US)*; **~reihe, ~zeile** *f* row of houses; *(aneinandergebaut)* terrace.

Hausfrau *f* housewife.

Hausfrauenart *f* **Wurst** *etc* **nach ~** home-made-style sausage *etc*.

Haus-: ~friede(n) *m* domestic peace; **~friedensbruch** *m (Jur)* trespass *(in sb's house)*; **~gebrauch** *m* **für den ~gebrauch** *(Gerät)* for domestic *or* household use; **sein Französisch reicht für den ~gebrauch** *(col)* his French is good enough to get by; **~gehilfin** *f* home help; **h~gemacht** *adj* home-made; **~gemeinschaft** *f* household.

Haushalt *m* **-e (a)** household; *(~sführung)* housekeeping. **den ~ führen** to run the household; **jdm den ~ führen** to keep house for sb. **(b)** *(fig: Biol etc)* balance. **(c)** *(Etat)* budget.

haushalten *vi sep irreg* **(a) mit etw ~** to be economical with sth. **(b)** *(den Haushalt führen)* to keep house.

Haushälter(in *f***)** *m* - housekeeper.

Haushalts- *in cpds* household; *(Pol)* budget; **~artikel** *m* household article; **~buch** *nt* housekeeping book; **~debatte** *f (Parl)* budget debate; **~führung** *f* housekeeping; **~gerät** *nt* household appliance; **~hilfe** *f* domestic help; **~jahr** *nt (Pol, Econ)* financial *or* fiscal year; **~kasse** *f* household budget; **~mittel** *pl (Pol)* budgetary funds *pl*; **~plan** *m (Pol)* budget; **~politik** *f (Pol)* budgetary policy; **h~politisch** *adj* concerning budgetary policy.

Haus-: ~haltung *f (das Haushaltführen)* housekeeping; **~herr** *m* **(a)** head of the household; *(Gastgeber)* host; **(b)** *(Jur)* householder; **~her-**

rin *f* lady of the house; *(Gastgeberin)* hostess; **h~hoch 1** *adj* (as) high as a house/houses; *(fig) Sieg* crushing; **der h~hohe Favorit** the hot favourite *(col)*; **2** *adv* high (in the sky); **h~hoch gewinnen** to win hands down *or* by miles *(col)*; **jdm h~hoch überlegen sein** to be head and shoulders above sb; **h~hohe(r, s)** *adj siehe* **h~hoch.**

hausieren* *vi* to hawk, to peddle *(mit etw* sth*)*. **mit etw ~ gehen** *(fig) mit Plänen* to hawk sth about.

Hausierer(in *f*) *m* - hawker, peddler.

Haus-: h~intern *adj* internal company *attr*; **~kleid** *nt* hostess gown; **~lehrer(in *f*)** *m* (private) tutor.

häuslich *adj* domestic; *Mensch* domesticated; *(das Zuhause liebend)* home-loving. **der ~e Herd** the family home; **sich irgendwo ~ einrichten** *or* **niederlassen** to settle in somewhere.

Häuslichkeit *f* domesticity.

Hausmacherart *f* **Wurst** *etc* **nach ~** home-made-style sausage *etc.*

Haus-: ~mann *m, pl* **~männer** *(den Haushalt versorgender Mann)* man undertaking the role of housewife, house-husband *(hum)*; **~mannskost** *f* plain cooking; **~marke** *f (eigene Marke)* own brand; *(bevorzugte Marke)* favourite *(Brit) or* favorite *(US)* brand; **~meister** *m* caretaker, janitor; **~mitteilung** *f* internal memo; **~mittel** *nt* household remedy; **~ordnung** *f* house rules *pl*; **~rat** *m no pl* household equipment; **~ratsversicherung** *f* (household) contents insurance; **~recht** *nt* right(s *pl*) as a householder *(to forbid sb entrance)*; **~sammlung** *f* house-to-house *or* door-to-door collection; **~schlüssel** *m* front-door key, house key; **~schuh** *m* slipper; **~schwamm** *m* dry rot.

Hausse ['ho:s(ə)] *f* **-n** *(Econ)* boom *(an+dat* in*)*; *(St Ex)* bull market.

Haus-: ~segen *m* **bei ihnen hängt der ~segen schief** *(hum)* they're a bit short on domestic bliss *(col)*; **~stand** *m* household, home; **einen ~stand gründen** to set up house *or* home; **~suchung** *f* house search; **~suchungsbefehl** *m* search-warrant; **~tier** *nt* domestic animal; *(aus Liebhaberei gehalten)* pet; **~tür** *f* front door; **gleich vor der ~tür** *(fig col)* right on one's doorstep; **~verbot** *nt* **jdm ~verbot erteilen** to ban sb from the house; **in einem Lokal ~ verbot haben** to be barred *or* banned from a bar; **~verwalter** *m* (house) supervisor; **~verwaltung** *f* property management; **~wirt** *m* landlord; **~wirtin** *f* landlady.

Hauswirtschaft *f* **(a)** housekeeping. **(b)** *(Sch)* home economics *sing.*

hauswirtschaftlich *adj* domestic.

Haut *f, pl* **Häute** skin; *(dick, esp von größerem Tier)* hide. **naß bis auf die ~** soaked to the skin; **nur ~ und Knochen sein** to be nothing but skin and bones; **mit ~ und Haar(en)** *(col)* completely; **das geht unter die ~** *(col)* that gets under your skin; **in seiner ~ möchte ich nicht stecken** *(col)* I wouldn't like to be in his shoes; **ihm ist nicht wohl in seiner ~** *(col) (unzufrieden)* he's (feeling) rather unsettled; *(unbehaglich)* he feels uneasy; **er kann nicht aus seiner ~ heraus** *(col)* he can't change the way he is, a leopard can't change its spots *(prov)*; **aus der ~ fahren** *(col)* to go through the roof *(col)*; **sich auf die faule ~ legen** *(col)* to sit back and do nothing; **seine ~ zu Markte tragen** *(col)* to risk one's neck; **seine eigene ~ retten** *(col)* to save one's own skin; **sich seiner ~ wehren** *(col)* to defend oneself.

Haut- *in cpds* skin; **~abschürfung** *f* graze; **~arzt** *m* skin specialist, dermatologist; **~ausschlag** *m* (skin) rash.

Häutchen *nt - dim of* **Haut** *(auf Flüssigkeit)* skin; *(Anat, Bot)* membrane.

häuten 1 *vt Tiere* to skin. **2** *vr (Tier)* to shed its skin; *(hum: Mensch)* to peel.

Haut-: h~eng *adj* skintight; **~farbe** *f* skin colour *(Brit) or* color *(US)*; *(Teint)* complexion; **h~farben** *adj* flesh-coloured *(Brit)*, flesh-colored *(US)*; **h~nah** *adj* (very) close; *Schilderung, Szene* vivid, graphic; **~pflege** *f* skin care; **~wunde** *f* skin wound.

Havarie [hava'ri:] *f (Naut, Aviat) (Unfall)* accident; *(Schaden)* damage *no indef art, no pl.*

Haxe *f* **-n** *(Cook)* leg (joint); *(S Ger col) (Fuß)* foot; *(Bein)* leg.

Hbf = **Hauptbahnhof.**

h.c. [ha:'tse:] = **honoris causa. Dr. ~** honorary doctor.

Hebamme *f* **-n** midwife.

Hebe-: ~balken *m* lever; **~bühne** *f* hydraulic ramp.

Hebel *m* - lever. **den ~ ansetzen** to position the lever; *(fig col)* to tackle it; **alle ~ in Bewegung setzen** *(col)* to move heaven and earth; **am längeren ~ sitzen** *(col)* to have the whip hand.

Hebel-: ~kraft *f* leverage; **~wirkung** *f* leverage.

heben *pret* **hob,** *ptp* **gehoben 1** *vt* **(a)** to lift; *Arm, Fernglas auch, Augenbraue, Wrack* to raise; *Schatz* to dig up. **die Stimme ~** to raise one's voice; **einen ~ gehen** *(col)* to go for a drink; **er hebt gern einen** *(col)* he likes a drink; **heb deine Füße!** pick your feet up!; *siehe* **gehoben. (b)** *(steigern)* to increase; *Stimmung, Wohlstand* to improve; *Geschmack, jds Ansehen* to enhance. **das hebt den Mut** it's good for morale. **2** *vr* **(a)** to rise; *(Nebel, Deckel)* to lift. **(b)** *(verbessern, steigern)* to improve. **da hob sich seine Stimmung** that cheered him up. **3** *vi (Sport)* to do weight-lifting.

Hebräer(in *f*) *m* - Hebrew.

hebräisch *adj* Hebrew.

Hebung *f* **(a)** *(von Schatz, Wrack etc)* recovery, raising. **(b)** *(fig: Verbesserung)* improvement; *(von Effekt, Selbstbewußtsein)* heightening; *(von Lebensstandard, Niveau)* rise.

hecheln *vi* **(a)** *(col: lästern)* to gossip. **(b)** *(keuchen)* to pant.

Hecht *m* **-e** *(Zool)* pike; *(col: Bursche)* guy *(col)*. **er ist (wie) ein ~ im Karpfenteich** *(fig)* he certainly shakes people up.

hechten *vi aux sein (col)* to dive.

Hechtsprung *m (beim Schwimmen)* racing dive; *(beim Turnen)* forward dive; *(Ftbl col)* dive.

Heck *nt* **-e** *or* **-s** *(Naut)* stern; *(Aviat)* tail, rear; *(Aut)* rear, back.

Heck|antrieb *m (Aut)* rear-wheel drive.

Hecke *f* **-n** hedge; *(am Wegrand)* hedgerow.

Hecken-: ~rose *f* dogrose, wild rose; **~schere** *f* hedge-clippers *pl*; **~schütze** *m* sniper.

Heck-: ~fenster *nt (Aut)* rear window; **~klappe** *f (Aut)* hatchback *(Brit)*, tailgate *(US)*.

Heckmeck *m no pl (col) (dummes Gerede)* nonsense, rubbish; *(Umstände)* fuss, palaver *(col)*.

Heck-: ~motor *m (Aut)* rear engine; **~scheibe** *f (Aut)* rear window; **~tür** *f (Aut)* hatchback *(Brit)*, tailgate *(US)*; **~türmodell** *nt* hatchback.

Heer *nt* **-e** *(lit, fig)* army. **beim ~** in the army.

Heeresleitung *f* command.

Hefe *f* **-n** yeast.

Hefe-: ~gebäck *nt* yeast-risen pastry; **~pilz** *m* yeast plant; **~teig** *m* yeast dough.

Heft[1] *nt* **-e** *(von Werkzeug, Messer)* handle; *(von Dolch, Schwert)* hilt. **das ~ in der Hand haben** *(fig)* to hold the reins; **jdm das ~ aus der Hand nehmen** *(fig)* to seize control/power from sb.

Heft[2] *nt* **-e** *(Schreib~)* exercise book; *(Zeitschrift)* magazine; *(Comic~)* comic; *(Nummer)* number, issue; *(geheftetes Büchlein)* booklet.

Heftchen *nt* **(a)** *dim of* **Heft**[2]. **(b)** *(pej) (billiger Roman)* rubbishy *or* pulp novel *(pej)*; *(Comic~)* rag *(pej col)*. **(c)** *(Fahrkarten~, Briefmarken~)* book of tickets/stamps.

heften 1 *vt* **(a)** *(nähen) Saum* to tack (up); *Buch* to

sew, to stitch; *(klammern)* to clip *(an+acc* to); *(mit Heftmaschine auch)* to staple *(an +acc* to). **(b)** *(befestigen)* to pin, to fix. **den Blick auf jdn/etw ~** to stare at sb/sth. **2** *vr* **sich an jds Fersen** *or* **Sohlen ~** *(fig)* to dog sb's heels.
Hefter *m* - (loose-leaf) file.
heftig *adj* violent; *Schmerz, Liebe* intense; *Erkältung, Fieber* severe; *Weinen* bitter; *Kampf, Wind, Widerstand* fierce; *Regen, Frost* heavy. **ein ~er Regenguß** a downpour; **er hat sich ~ in sie verliebt** he has fallen violently in love with her; **~ nicken/rühren** to nod/stir vigorously.
Heftigkeit *f no pl siehe adj* violence; intensity; severity; bitterness; ferocity; heaviness.
Heft-: **~klammer** *f* staple; **~maschine** *f* stapler; **~pflaster** *nt* (sticking) plaster, adhesive tape *(US)*; **~zwecke** *f* drawing-pin *(Brit)*, thumb-tack *(US)*.
hegen *vt* **(a)** *Wild, Pflanzen* to care for, to tend. **jdn ~ und pflegen** to lavish care and attention on sb. **(b)** *Groll, Verdacht* to harbour *(Brit)*, to harbor *(US)*; *Mißtrauen, Abneigung* to feel; *Zweifel* to entertain; *Hoffnung, Wunsch* to cherish. **ich hege den starken Verdacht, daß ...** I have a strong suspicion that ...
Hehl *nt or m:* **kein** *or* **keinen ~ aus etw machen** to make no secret of sth.
Hehler(in *f***)** *m* - receiver (of stolen goods), fence *(col)*.
Hehlerei *f no pl* receiving (stolen goods).
Heia *f no pl (baby-talk)* **ab in die ~** off to bye-byes *(baby-talk)*.
Heide[1] *m (wk)* **-n, -n, Heidin** *f* heathen, pagan.
Heide[2] *f* **-n** moor, heath.
Heide-: **~kraut** *nt* heather; **~land** *nt* moorland, heathland.
Heidelbeere *f* bilberry, blueberry *(esp US)*.
Heiden- *(col)*: **~angst** *f*: **eine ~angst vor etw** *(dat)* **haben** to be scared stiff of sth *(col)*; **~arbeit** *f* real slog *(col)*; **~geld** *nt* packet *(col)*; **~krach, ~lärm** *m* unholy din *(col)*; **~respekt** *m* healthy respect; **~spaß** *m* terrific fun; **einen ~spaß haben** to have a whale of a time *(col)*; **~spektakel** *m* awful row; *(Schimpfen)* awful fuss.
Heidentum *nt no pl* paganism.
Heidin *f siehe* **Heide**[1].
heidnisch *adj* heathen, pagan.
heikel *adj* **(a)** *Situation, Thema* tricky, delicate. **(b)** *(dial) Mensch* particular, pernickety *(col) (in bezug auf +acc* about).
heil *adj* **(a)** *(unverletzt) Mensch* unhurt; *Glieder* unbroken; *Haut* undamaged. **wieder ~ sein/werden** *(wieder gesund)* to be/get better again; *(Wunde)* to have healed/to heal up; **~ nach Hause kommen** to get home safe and sound; **etw ~ überstehen** *Unfall* to come through sth without a scratch; *Prüfung* to get through sth; **mit ~er Haut davonkommen** to escape unscathed. **(b)** *(col: ganz)* intact; *Kleidungsstück* decent *(col)*. **die ~e Welt** an ideal world *(without problems etc)*.
Heil **1** *nt no pl* **(a)** *(Wohlergehen)* well-being, good. **(b)** *(Eccl, fig)* salvation. **sein ~ in der Flucht suchen** to flee for one's life. **2** *interj* **Ski/Petri ~!** good skiing/fishing!
Heiland *m* **-e** *(Rel)* Saviour, Redeemer.
Heil-: **~anstalt** *f* nursing home; *(für Sucht- oder Geisteskranke)* home; **~bad** *nt (Bad)* medicinal bath; *(Ort)* spa; **h~bar** *adj* curable; **h~bringend** *adj (Rel)* redeeming; *Wirkung* beneficial; *Kräuter* medicinal.
Heilbutt *m* **-e** halibut.
heilen **1** *vi aux sein* to heal (up). **2** *vt* to cure; *Wunde, (Rel)* to heal. **als geheilt entlassen werden** to be discharged with a clean bill of health; **jdn von etw ~** *(lit, fig)* to cure sb of sth; **von jdm/etw geheilt sein** *(fig)* to have got over sb/sth.
heilend *adj* healing.
heilfroh *adj pred (col)* jolly glad *(col)*.
heilig *adj* **(a)** holy; *(bei Namen von Heiligen)* Saint; **jdm ~ sein** *(lit, fig)* to be sacred to sb; **H~er Abend** Christmas Eve; **H~e Maria** Holy Mary; **der H~e Geist/Stuhl** the Holy Spirit *or* Ghost/See; **die H~en Drei Könige** the Three Wise Men; **die H~e Schrift** the Holy Scriptures *pl*. **(b)** *Pflicht* sacred; *Zorn* righteous; *Stille, Schauer* awed. **es ist mein ~er Ernst** I am deadly serious. **(c)** *(col: groß)* incredible *(col)*; *Respekt auch* healthy.
Heilig|abend *m* Christmas Eve.
heiligen *vt* to hallow; *Sonntag etc* to keep holy. **der Zweck heiligt die Mittel** the end justifies the means.
Heiligen-: **~bild** *nt* holy picture; **~schein** *m* halo; **jdn mit einem ~schein umgeben** *(fig)* to put sb on a pedestal.
Heilige(r) *mf decl as adj (lit, fig)* saint. **ein sonderbarer ~r** *(col)* a queer fish *(col)*.
Heilig-: **~keit** *f* holiness; **Seine ~keit** his Holiness; **h~sprechen** *vt sep irreg* to canonize; **~sprechung** *f* canonization; **~tum** *nt (Stätte)* shrine; *(Gegenstand)* (holy) relic; **jds ~tum sein** *(col) (Zimmer)* to be sb's sanctum; *(Gegenstand etc)* to be sacrosanct (to sb).
Heil-: **~kraft** *f* healing power; **h~kräftig** *adj Pflanze, Tee* medicinal; **~kraut** *nt usu pl* medicinal herb; **~kunde** *f* medicine; **~kundige(r)** *mf decl as adj* healer; **h~los** *adj* unholy *(col)*; *Schreck* terrible; **~methode** *f* cure; **~mittel** *nt (lit, fig)* remedy, cure; *(Medikament)* medicine; **~pflanze** *f* medicinal plant; **~praktiker** *m* non-medical practitioner; **~quelle** *f* medicinal spring; **h~sam** *adj Erfahrung, Strafe* salutary; *Wirkung* beneficial; *(dated: heilend)* healing.
Heils|armee *f* Salvation Army.
Heilung *f (von Wunde)* healing; *(von Krankheit, Kranken)* curing.
Heilungsprozeß *m* healing process.
heim *adv* home.
Heim *nt* **-e** home; *(Studentenwohn~)* hall of residence, hostel.
Heim- *in cpds* home; **~arbeit** *f (Ind)* homework, outwork *both no indef art*; **~arbeiter** *m (Ind)* homeworker.
Heimat *f* **-en** home. **die ~ verlassen** to leave one's home.
Heimat- *in cpds* home; **~dichter** *m* regional writer; **~film** *m sentimental film in idealized regional setting;* **~kunde** *f (Sch)* local history; **~land** *nt* native country; **h~lich** *adj* native; *Bräuche, Dialekt* local; *Gefühle* nostalgic; *Klänge* of home; **h~los** *adj* homeless; **~lose(r)** *mf decl as adj* homeless person; **~museum** *nt* local history museum; **~ort** *m* home town/village; **~vertriebene(r)** *mf decl as adj* displaced person.
heim-: **~begeben*** *vr sep irreg* to make one's way home; **~bringen** *vt sep irreg (nach Hause bringen)* to bring home; *(~begleiten)* to take home.
Heimchen *nt* **~ (am Herd)** *(pej: Frau)* housewife.
heimelig *adj* cosy, homely.
Heim-: **h~fahren** *vti sep irreg (vi: aux sein)* to drive home; **~fahrt** *f* journey home; *(Naut)* return voyage; **h~finden** *vi sep irreg* to find one's way home; **h~gehen** *vi sep irreg aux sein* to go home; **h~holen** *vt sep* to fetch home; **Gott hat ihn h~geholt** he has been called to his Maker.
heimisch *adj* **(a)** *(einheimisch)* indigenous, native *(in+dat* to); *(national)* home; *(ortsansässig)* local; *(regional)* regional. **(b)** *(vertraut)* familiar. **sich ~ fühlen** to feel at home; **~ werden** to become acclimatized *(an, in+dat* to).
Heim-: **~kehr** *f no pl* homecoming; **h~kehren** *vi sep aux sein* to return home *(aus* from); **~kehrer(in** *f***)** *m* homecomer; **~kind** *nt* child brought up in a home; **h~kommen** *vi sep irreg aux sein* to come home; **~leiter** *m* warden of a/the home/

hostel; **h~leuchten** *vi sep (fig col)* **jdm h~leuchten** to give sb a piece of one's mind.

heimlich 1 *adj* secret. **2** *adv* secretly; *lachen* inwardly. **er blickte sie ~ an** he stole a glance at her; **sich ~ entfernen** to sneak away; **~, still und leise** *(col)* quietly, on the quiet.

Heimlichkeit *f* secrecy; *(Geheimnis)* secret. **in aller ~** secretly, in secret.

Heimlich-: ~tuer(in *f***)** *m* - secretive person; **~tuerei** *f* secrecy; **h~tun** *vi sep irreg* to be secretive *(mit* about*)*.

Heim-: ~reise *f* homeward journey; *(Naut)* homeward voyage; **h~reisen** *vi sep aux sein* to travel home; **h~schicken** *vt sep* to send home; **~spiel** *nt (Sport)* home match; **~statt** *f* home.

heimsuchen *vt sep* to strike; *(für längere Zeit)* to plague; *(Gespenst)* to haunt; *(Krankheit, Alpträume)* to afflict; *(col: besuchen)* to descend on *(col)*. **von Dürre/Krieg heimgesucht** drought-stricken/war-torn.

heimtückisch *adj* insidious; *(boshaft)* malicious; *Glatteis, Maschine* treacherous.

Heim-: h~wärts *adv* homewards; **~weg** *m* way home; **sich auf den ~weg machen** to head for home; **~weh** *nt* homesickness *no art*; **~weh haben** to be homesick *(nach* for*)*; **~werker** *m* handyman; **h~zahlen** *vt sep* **jdm etw h~zahlen** to pay sb back for sth.

Heini *m* **-s** *(pej col)* guy *(col)*. **blöder ~** silly idiot.

Heinzelmännchen *nt* **die ~** the little people.

Heirat *f* **-en** marriage.

heiraten 1 *vt* to marry. **2** *vi* to get married, to marry. **in eine reiche Familie ~** to marry into a rich family.

Heirats-: ~antrag *m* proposal (of marriage); **jdm einen ~antrag machen** to propose to sb; **~anzeige** *(Annonce)* advertisement for a marriage partner; **h~fähig** *adj* marriageable; **~schwindler** *m person who makes a marriage proposal in order to obtain money*; **~vermittler** *m* marriage broker; **~vermittlung** *f* matchmaking *no pl*; *(Büro)* marriage bureau.

heiser *adj* hoarse.

Heiserkeit *f* hoarseness.

heiß *adj (lit, fig)* hot; *Zone* torrid; *Thema* hotly disputed; *Diskussion, Kampf* heated, fierce; *Begierde, Liebe, Wunsch* burning. **jdm wird ~** sb is getting hot; **sie hat einen ~en Kopf** she has a burning forehead; **etw ~ machen** to heat sth up; **es wird nichts so ~ gegessen wie es gekocht wird** *(prov)* things are never as bad as they seem; **es ging ~ her** things got heated; **die Stadt ist ~ umkämpft** the town is being fiercely fought over; **jdn/etw ~ und innig lieben** to love sb/sth madly; **~e Tränen weinen** to cry one's heart out; **sich die Köpfe ~ reden** to talk till one is blue in the face; **jdn ~ machen** *(col)* to turn sb on *(col)*; **ein ~es Eisen** a hot potato; **ein ~es Eisen anfassen** *(col)* to grasp the nettle; **~er Draht** hot line; **~e Spur** hot trail.

heißblütig *adj* hot-blooded.

heißen *pret* **hieß,** *ptp* **geheißen 1** *vi* **(a)** to be called *(Brit) or* named. **wie ~ Sie/heißt die Straße?** what's your name/the name of the street?; **ich heiße Müller** I'm called *or* my name is Müller; **sie heißt jetzt anders** she has changed her name; **eigentlich heißt es richtig X** actually the correct word is X; **... und wie sie alle ~** ... and the rest of them. **(b)** *(bestimmte Bedeutung haben)* to mean. **was heißt „gut" auf englisch?** what is the English for "gut"?; **was soll das ~?** what does that mean?; **das will schon etwas ~** that's quite something. **(c) das heißt** that is; *(in anderen Worten)* that is to say.

2 *vt (geh)* **(a)** *(nennen)* to call. **(b)** *(auffordern)* to tell. **jdn willkommen ~** to bid sb welcome.

3 *vi impers* **es heißt, daß ...** they say that ...; **in der Bibel/in seinem Brief heißt es, daß ...** the Bible/his letter says that ...; **es heißt hier ...** it says here ...; **nun heißt es handeln** now we must do something.

Heiß-: h~ersehnt *adj attr* much longed for; **h~geliebt** *adj* dearly beloved; **~hunger** *m* voracious appetite; **etw mit ~hunger verschlingen** *(lit, fig)* to devour sth; **h~hungrig** *adj* ravenous, voracious; **h~laufen** *vi sep irreg aux sein (Motor)* to overheat; **~luft** *f* hot air; **~mangel** *f (Gerät)* rotary iron; *(Geschäft) laundry specializing in ironing sheets etc*; **h~umstritten** *adj attr* hotly debated; **~wasserbereiter** *m* water-heater.

heiter *adj (fröhlich)* cheerful; *(ausgeglichen)* serene; *(amüsant) Geschichte* amusing; *(hell, klar) Farbe, Himmel, Tag* bright; *Wetter* fine; *(Met)* fair. **~ werden** to become cheerful; *(Wetter)* to clear up; **das kann ja ~ werden!** *(iro)* that sounds great *(iro)*; **aus ~em Himmel** *(fig)* out of the blue.

Heiterkeit *f no pl siehe adj* cheerfulness; serenity; amusingness; brightness, fineness; *(heitere Stimmung)* merriment.

Heiz-: h~bar *adj* heated; **schwer h~bar** difficult to heat; **~(bett)decke** *f* electric blanket.

heizen 1 *vi* to have the heating on. **der Ofen heizt gut** the stove gives off a good heat; **mit Holz/Strom ~** to use wood/electricity for heating. **2** *vt (warm machen)* to heat; *(verbrennen)* to burn.

Heizer *m* **-** *(von Hochofen)* boilerman.

Heiz-: ~gerät *nt* heater; **~kissen** *nt* electric heat pad; **~körper** *m (Gerät)* heater; *(von Zentralheizung)* radiator; **~lüfter** *m* fan heater; **~material** *nt* (heating) fuel; **~sonne** *f* electric fire.

Heizung *f* heating; *(Heizkörper)* heater.

Heizungs-: ~anlage *f* heating system; **~monteur** *m* heating engineer; **~rohr** *nt* heating pipe.

Hektar *nt or m* **-e** hectare.

Hektik *f no pl* hectic rush; *(von Leben etc)* hectic pace. **sie arbeitet mit einer solchen ~** she works at such a hectic pace; **nur keine ~** take it easy.

hektisch *adj* hectic.

Hektoliter *m or nt* hectolitre *(Brit)*, hectoliter *(US)*.

Held *m (wk)* **-en, -en** hero. **der ~ des Tages** the hero of the hour; **kein ~ in etw** *(dat)* **sein** not to be very brave about sth; *(in Schulfach etc)* to be no great shakes at sth *(col)*; **du bist mir ein schöner ~!** *(iro)* some hero you are!

Helden-: ~dichtung *f* heroic poetry; **h~haft, h~mütig** *adj* heroic; **~tat** *f* heroic deed; **~tum** *nt no pl* heroism.

Heldin *f* heroine.

helfen *pret* **half,** *ptp* **geholfen** *vi* to help *(jdm* sb*)*. **jdm bei etw ~** to help sb with sth, to lend sb a hand with sth; **ihm ist nicht zu ~** *(fig)* he is beyond help; **ich kann mir nicht ~, ich muß es tun** I can't help doing it; **ich werd' ihm (schon) ~!** I'll give him what for *(col)*; **ich werde dir ~, die Tapeten zu beschmieren** I'll teach you to mess up the wallpaper; **man muß sich** *(dat)* **nur zu ~ wissen** *(prov)* you just have to use your head; **er weiß sich** *(dat)* **nicht mehr zu ~** he is at his wits' end; **diese Arznei hilft gegen** *or* **bei Kopfweh** this medicine is good for headaches; **es hilft nichts** it's no use *or* no good; **da hilft alles nichts ...** there's nothing for it ...; **was hilft's?** what's the use?

Helfer(in *f***)** *m* **-** helper; *(Mitarbeiter)* assistant; *(von Verbrecher)* accomplice. **ein ~ in der Not** a friend in need.

Helfershelfer *m* accomplice.

hell *adj* **(a)** *(optisch)* light; *Licht, Himmel* bright; *Haar, Haut* fair. **es wird ~** it's getting light; **~ bleiben** to stay light; **am ~en Tage** in broad daylight; **in ~en Flammen** in flames, ablaze; **~es Bier** ≈ lager. **(b)** *Ton etc* high(-pitched). **(c)** *(col: klug)* bright; *Augenblicke* lucid. **er ist ein ~er Kopf** he has brains. **(d)** *attr (stark, groß)* great; *Verzweiflung, Unsinn* sheer, utter; *Neid* pure. **von etw ~ begeistert sein** to be very enthusiastic about sth; **in ~en Scharen** in great numbers.

hell- *in cpds (esp auf Farben bezüglich)* light; **~auf** *adv* completely, utterly; **~blond** *adj* very fair, blonde.

helle *adj pred (col)* bright, clever.

Heller *m* - **darauf geb ich keinen (roten) ~** I wouldn't give you tuppence *(Brit) or* a red cent *(US)* for it; **auf ~ und Pfennig** to the last penny.

Helle(s) *nt decl as adj* ≃ lager.

hell-: ~haarig *adj* fair-haired; **~häutig** *adj* fair-skinned; **~hörig** *adj (Archit)* poorly soundproofed; **~hörig sein** *(fig: Mensch)* to have sharp ears; **jdn ~hörig machen** to make sb prick up their ears.

hellicht *adj*: **am ~en Tage** in broad daylight.

Helligkeit *f no pl siehe* **hell (a)** lightness; brightness; fairness; *(helles Licht)* light; *(Phys, Astron)* luminosity.

hell-: ~sehen *vi infin only* **~sehen können** to be clairvoyant; **H~seher(in** *f***)** *m (lit, fig)* clairvoyant; **~seherisch** *adj attr* clairvoyant; **~wach** *adj (lit, fig)* wide-awake; **H~werden** *nt no pl* daybreak.

Helm *m* **-e** helmet.

Hemd *nt* **-en** shirt; *(Unter~)* vest *(Brit)*, undershirt *(US)*. **etw wie sein ~ wechseln** *(fig)* to change sth with monotonous regularity; **für dich gebe ich mein letztes ~ her** *(col)* I'd give you the shirt off my back *(col)*; **naß bis aufs ~** wet through; **jdn bis aufs ~ ausziehen** *(fig col)* to have the shirt off sb's back *(col)*.

Hemdbluse *f* shirt(-blouse), shirtwaist *(US)*.

Hemds-: ~ärmel *m* **in ~ärmeln** in one's shirt sleeves; **h~ärmelig** *adj* shirt-sleeved; *(fig col: salopp)* pally *(col)*; *Ausdrucksweise* casual.

Hemisphäre *f* **-n** hemisphere.

hemmen *vt Entwicklung* to hinder; *Lauf der Dinge, Maschine* to check; *(verlangsamen)* to slow down; *Wasserlauf* to stem; *(Psych)* to inhibit.

Hemmung *f* **(a)** *(Psych)* inhibition; *(Bedenken)* scruple. **da habe ich ~en** I've got scruples about that; **keine ~en kennen** to have no inhibitions; **nur keine ~en** don't feel inhibited. **(b)** *siehe vt* hindering; check *(gen* to*)*; slowing down; stemming.

Hemmungs-: h~los *adj (rückhaltlos)* unrestrained; *(skrupellos)* unscrupulous; **~losigkeit** *f siehe adj* lack of restraint; unscrupulousness.

Hengst *m* **-e** stallion; *(Kamel~, Esel~)* male.

Hengst-: ~fohlen, ~füllen *nt* (male) foal, colt.

Henkel *m* - handle.

Henkel- *in cpds* with a handle; **~mann** *m, pl* **~männer** *(col)* canteen.

henken *vt (dated)* to hang.

Henker *m* - hangman; *(Scharfrichter)* executioner. **was zum ~** *(col)* what the devil *(col)*; **scher dich zum ~!** *(col)* go to the devil! *(col)*.

Henne *f* **-n** hen.

her *adv* **(a) von Frankreich/dem Meer ~** from France/the sea; **~ zu mir!** *(col)* come here (to me); **um mich ~** (all) around me; **von weit ~** from a long way off; **~ damit!** *(col)* give me that; **immer ~ damit!** *(col)* let's have it/them (then). **(b) von der Idee/Form ~** as far as the idea/form goes; **vom finanziellen Standpunkt ~** from the financial point of view. **(c)** *(zeitlich)* **ich kenne ihn von früher ~** I know him from before; **von der Schule/meiner Kindheit ~** since school/my childhood; *siehe* **hersein (a)**.

herab *adv* down. **die Treppe ~** down the stairs; **von oben ~** from above.

herab- *pref* down; **~blicken** *vi sep (lit, fig)* to look down *(auf +acc* on*)*; **~hängen** *vi sep irreg* to hang down; **~lassen** *sep irreg* **1** *vt* to let down, to lower; **2** *vr (lit, fig)* to lower oneself; **sich zu etw ~ lassen** to condescend *or* deign to do sth; **~lassend** *adj* condescending; **~mindern** *vt sep (schlechtmachen) Leistung etc* to belittle; *(reduzieren) Geschwindigkeit, Niveau* to reduce; **~sehen** *vi sep irreg (lit, fig)* to look down *(auf +acc* on*)*; **~setzen** *vt sep Ware, Preise* to reduce; *Niveau* to lower; *(schlechtmachen) Leistungen, jdn* to belittle; **zu stark ~gesetzten Preisen** at greatly reduced prices; **~sinken** *vi sep irreg aux sein* to sink (down); *(Wasserstand)* to drop, to fall; **~stürzen** *sep* **1** *vt* to push off *(von etw* sth*)*; **2** *vi aux sein* to fall off *(von etw* sth*)*; *(Felsbrocken)* to fall down *(von* from*)*; **3** *vr* to jump off *(von etw* sth*)*; **~würdigen** *sep* **1** *vt* to disparage; **2** *vr* to lower oneself.

heran *adv* **bis an etw** *(acc)* **~** right beside sth; *(mit Bewegungsverb)* right up to sth.

heran-: ~bilden *vt sep* to train (up); *(in der Schule)* to educate; **~bringen** *vt sep irreg (herbringen)* to bring over; **die Schüler an diese Probleme ~bringen** to introduce the pupils to these problems; **~eilen** *vi sep aux sein* to hurry over; **~führen** *sep* **1** *vt jdn* to lead up; **jdn an etw** *(acc)* **~führen** to introduce sb to sth; **2** *vi* **an etw** *(acc)* **~führen** *(lit, fig)* to lead to sth; **~gehen** *vi sep irreg aux sein* to go up *(an +acc* to*)*; **ich würde nicht näher ~gehen** I wouldn't go any nearer; **an etw ~gehen** *an Problem, Aufgabe* to tackle sth; **~kommen** *vi sep irreg aux sein* **(a)** to draw near *(an +acc* to*)*, to approach *(an etw (acc)* sth*)*; **auf 1:3 ~kommen** to pull back to 1-3; **er läßt alle Probleme an sich ~kommen** he always adopts a wait-and-see attitude; **an den Chef/Motor kommt man nicht ~** you can't get hold of the boss/get at the engine; **(b)** *(sich messen können)* **an jdn/etw ~kommen** to be up to the standard of sb/sth; **~lassen** *vt sep irreg* **jdn an etw** *(acc)* **~lassen** to let sb near sth; **er läßt keinen an sich ~** he won't let anyone near him; **~machen** *vr sep (col)* **sich an etw** *(acc)* **~machen** to get down to sth; **sich an jdn ~machen** to approach sb; *an Frau* to chat sb up *(col)*; **~nahen** *vi sep aux sein (geh)* to approach; **~reichen** *vi sep* **an jdn/etw ~reichen** *(lit)* to reach sb/sth; *(fig: sich messen können)* to come near sb/sth; **~reifen** *vi sep aux sein (geh)* to ripen; *(fig)* to mature; **~rücken** *sep* **1** *vi aux sein (sich nähern)* to approach *(an etw (acc)* sth*)*; *(dicht aufrücken)* to come/go nearer *(an +acc* to*)*; **2** *vt* to pull/push up *(an +acc* to*)*; **~tragen** *vt sep irreg* to bring (over); **etw an jdn ~tragen** *(fig)* to take/bring sth to sb; **~treten** *vi sep irreg aux sein (lit)* to come/go up *(an +acc* to*)*; **näher ~treten** to come/go nearer; **mit etw an jdn ~treten** *(sich wenden an)* to approach sb with sth; **~wachsen** *vi sep irreg aux sein (geh)* to grow; *(Kind)* to grow up; **die ~wachsende Generation** the rising generation; **H~wachsende(r)** *mf decl as adj* adolescent; **~wagen** *vr sep* to venture near; **sich an etw** *(acc)* **~wagen** to venture to tackle sth; **~ziehen** *vt sep irreg* **(a)** to draw near *(an +acc* to*)*; **(b)** *(zu Hilfe holen)* to call in; *Literatur* to consult; **etw zum Vergleich ~ziehen** to use sth by way of comparison; **(c)** *Arbeitskräfte, Kapital* to bring in.

herauf 1 *adv* up. **vom Tal ~** up from the valley; **von unten ~** up from below. **2** *prep +acc* up. **den Berg/die Treppe ~** up the mountain/stairs.

herauf- *pref* up; **~arbeiten** *vr sep (lit, fig)* to work one's way up; **~beschwören*** *vt sep irreg Vergangenheit* to evoke; *Unglück, Krise* to cause; **~bringen** *vt sep irreg* to bring up; **~führen** *sep* **1** *vt Pferd etc* to lead up; *jdn* to show up; **2** *vi (Weg etc)* to lead up; **~kommen** *vi sep irreg aux sein* to come up; **~setzen** *vt sep Preise etc* to increase; **~steigen** *vi sep irreg aux sein* to climb up; *(Rauch)* to rise; *(Erinnerungen)* to well up *(in jdm* in sb*)*; **~ziehen** *sep irreg* **1** *vt* to pull up; **2** *vi aux sein (Gewitter, Unheil etc)* to approach.

heraus *adv* out. **~ damit!** *(col: gib her)* hand it over!; **~ mit der Sprache** out with it! *(col)*; **zum Fenster ~** out of the window; **nach vorn ~**

wohnen to live at the front; **aus dem Wunsch ~ ...** out of the desire to ...

heraus- *pref* out; **~arbeiten** *vt sep (aus Stein, Holz)* to carve *(aus* out of*)*; *(fig)* to bring out; **~bekommen** *vt sep irreg* **(a)** *Fleck, Nagel etc* to get out *(aus* of*)*; **(b)** *(ermitteln) Täter, Geheimnis* to find out *(aus jdm* from sb*)*; *Lösung, Aufgabe* to work out; **(c)** *Wechselgeld* to get back; **~boxen** *vt sep (aus* of*) Ball* to punch out; *(col) jdn* to bail out *(col)*; **~bringen** *vt sep irreg* **(a)** to bring out *(aus* of*)*; **(b)** *siehe* **~bekommen (a, b)**; **(c)** *(auf den Markt bringen)* to bring out; **jdn/etw ganz groß ~bringen** *(col)* to give sb/sth a big build-up; **(d)** *(col: hervorbringen) Worte* to say; **aus ihm war kein Wort ~zubringen** they couldn't get a single word out of him; **~drücken** *vt sep* to squeeze out *(aus* of*)*; **~fahren** *sep irreg* **1** *vi aux sein* to come out *(aus* of*)*; **2** *vt* **(a)** *Auto* to drive out *(aus* of*)*; **(b)** *(Sport)* **eine gute Zeit ~fahren** to make good time; **~finden** *sep irreg* **1** *vt Fehler, Täter etc* to find out; *(~lesen) Gesuchtes* to pick out *(aus* from*)*; **2** *vir* to find one's way out *(aus* of*)*.

Herausforderer *m* - challenger.

herausfordern *sep* **1** *vt* to challenge *(zu* to*)*; *(provozieren)* to provoke *(zu etw* to do sth*)*; *Kritik, Protest* to invite; *Gefahr, Unglück* to court. **das Schicksal ~** to tempt providence. **2** *vi* **zu etw ~** *(provozieren)* to invite sth.

herausfordernd *adj* provocative; *(Auseinandersetzung suchend) Haltung, Blick* challenging.

Herausforderung *f* challenge; *(Provokation)* provocation.

Herausgabe *f* **(a)** return; *(von Personen)* handing over. **(b)** *(von Buch etc)* publication.

herausgeben *sep irreg* **1** *vt* **(a)** *(zurückgeben)* to return, to give back; *Gefangene etc* to hand over. **(b)** *(veröffentlichen)* to issue; *Buch, Zeitung* to publish; *(bearbeiten)* to edit. **(c)** *(Wechselgeld geben) Betrag* to give as change. **wieviel hat er dir herausgegeben?** how much change did he give you? **(d)** *(herausreichen)* to hand out *(aus* of*)*. **2** *vi (Wechselgeld geben)* to give change *(auf +acc* for*)*. **können Sie (mir) ~?** can you give me change?; **falsch ~** to give the wrong change.

Herausgeber(in *f***)** *m (Verleger)* publisher; *(Redakteur)* editor.

heraus-: ~gehen *vi sep irreg aux sein (aus* of*)* to go out; *(Fleck, Korken etc)* to come out; **aus sich ~ gehen** *(fig)* to come out of one's shell; **~greifen** *vt sep irreg* to pick out *(aus* of*)*; *Beispiel* to take; **~haben** *vt sep irreg (col)* **(a) ich will ihn aus der Firma ~haben** I want him out of the firm; **(b)** *Rätsel, Aufgabe* to have solved; *Geheimnis* to have found out; **~halten** *sep irreg* **1** *vt* **(a)** *Hand, Gegenstand* to put out *(aus* of*)*; **(b)** *(fernhalten) Tiere, Eindringlinge* to keep out *(aus* of*)*; **2** *vr* to keep out of it; **~holen** *vt sep* **(a)** *(aus* of*)* to get out; *(~bringen)* to bring out; **(b)** *(fig col) Antwort, Geheimnis* to get out *(aus* of*)*; *Vorteil, Sieg* to gain *(aus* from*)*; *Zeit* to make up; *Ergebnis* to get; **~hören** *vt sep (wahrnehmen)* to hear; *(fühlen)* to detect *(aus* in*)*; **~kehren** *vt sep (lit)* to sweep out *(aus* of*)*; *(fig: betonen)* to parade; **den Vorgesetzten ~kehren** to act the boss.

herauskommen *vi sep irreg aux sein* **(a)** *(lit, fig)* to come out *(aus* of*)*; *(Schwindel etc)* to come to light. **er ist nie aus seinem Dorf herausgekommen** he has never been out of his village; **aus sich ~** to come out of one's shell; **er kam aus dem Staunen nicht heraus** he couldn't get over his astonishment; **aus einer schwierigen Lage ~** to get out of a difficult situation; **aus seinen Schwierigkeiten ~** to get over one's difficulties. **(b)** *(Resultat haben)* **bei etw ~** to come of sth; **und was soll dabei ~?** and what is that supposed to achieve?, and where is that supposed to get us?; **es kommt auf dasselbe heraus** it comes (down) to the same thing. **(c)** *(Cards)* to lead.

heraus-: ~kriegen *vt sep (col) siehe* **~bekommen; ~lesen** *vt sep irreg* **(a)** *(erkennen)* to gather *(aus* from*)*; **(b)** *(aussondern)* to pick out *(aus* from*)*; **~locken** *vt sep* to entice out *(aus* of*)*; **etw aus jdm ~locken** *(ablisten)* to get sth out of sb; **~machen** *sep (col)* **1** *vt (aus* of*)* to take out; *Fleck* to get out; **2** *vr (sich gut entwickeln)* to come on (well); *(nach Krankheit)* to pick up; **~nehmbar** *adj* removable; **~nehmen** *vt sep irreg* **(a)** to take out *(aus* of*)*; *Kind (aus der Schule etc)* to take away *(aus* from*)*; **sich** *(dat)* **die Mandeln ~nehmen lassen** to have one's tonsils out; **den Gang ~nehmen** *(Aut)* to put the car into neutral; **(b)** *(col: sich erlauben)* **sich** *(dat)* **Freiheiten ~nehmen** to take liberties; **Sie nehmen sich zuviel ~** you're going too far; **~platzen** *vi sep aux sein (col) (spontan sagen)* to blurt it out; *(lachen)* to burst out laughing; **~putzen** *vt sep jdn* to dress up; *Stadt, Wohnung etc* to deck out; **sich ~putzen** to get dressed up; **~ragen** *vi sep siehe* **hervorragen; ~reden** *vr sep* to talk one's way out of it *(col)*; **~reißen** *vt sep irreg* **(a)** *(lit) (aus* of*)* to tear out; *Zahn, Baum* to pull out; **(b) jdn aus etw ~reißen** *(aus Umgebung)* to tear sb away from sth; *(aus Schlaf)* to startle sb out of sth; *(col: aus Schwierigkeiten)* to get sb out of sth *(col)*; **~rücken** *sep* **1** *vt* to push out *(aus* of*)*; *(col: hergeben) Geld* to cough up *(col)*; *Beute, Gegenstand* to hand over; **2** *vi aux sein* **(a)** *(lit)* to move out; **(b)** *(col: hergeben)* **mit etw ~rücken** *(mit Geld)* to cough sth up *(col)*; *(mit Beute)* to hand sth over; *(col: aussprechen)* to come out with sth; **~rutschen** *vi sep aux sein (lit, fig)* to slip out *(aus* of*)*; **das ist mir nur so ~gerutscht** it just slipped out somehow; **~schauen** *vi sep (dial)* **(a)** *(Mensch)* to look out *(aus, zu* of*)*; **(b)** *(zu sehen sein)* to show; **(c) was schaut dabei (für mich) ~?** what's in it for me? *(col)*; **~schlagen** *sep irreg* **1** *vt* **(a)** *(lit)* to knock out *(aus* of*)*; **(b)** *(col) Geld* to make; *Gewinn, Vorteil* to get; *Zeit* to gain; **2** *vi aux sein (Flammen)* to shoot out; **~schleudern** *vt sep (werfen)* to hurl out *(aus* of*)*; *(fig) Fragen, Vorwürfe* to burst out with; **~schmecken** *vt sep* to taste; **~schmeißen** *vt sep irreg (col: lit, fig)* to chuck out *(aus* of*) (col)*.

heraussein *vi sep irreg aux sein (col)* to be out; *(bekannt sein)* to be known; *(entschieden sein)* to have been settled; *(Gesetz)* to be in force. **aus dem Gröbsten ~** to be over the worst.

heraus-: ~springen *vi sep irreg aux sein (aus* of*)* **(a)** *(lit)* to jump *or* leap out; **(b)** *(sich lösen)* to come out; **(c)** *(col) siehe* **~schauen (c)**; **~stellen** *sep* **1** *vt* **(a)** *(lit)* to put outside; **(b)** *(fig: hervorheben)* to emphasize, to underline; *jdn* to give prominence to; **2** *vr (Wahrheit)* to come to light; **sich als falsch/richtig ~stellen** to prove to be wrong/correct; **es stellte sich ~, daß ...** it turned out *or* emerged that ...; **das muß sich erst ~stellen** that remains to be seen; **~strecken** *vt sep* to stick out *(zu, aus* of*)*; **~streichen** *vt sep irreg* **(a)** *Fehler etc* to cross out, to delete *(aus* in*)*; **(b)** *(betonen) Verdienste etc* to stress; **~stürzen** *vi sep aux sein (eilen)* to rush out *(aus* of*)*; **~suchen** *vt sep* to pick out; **~treten** *vi sep irreg aux sein* to come out *(aus* of*)*, to emerge *(aus* from*)*; *(Adern etc)* to stand out; **~winden** *vr sep irreg (fig)* **sich aus etw ~winden** to wriggle out of sth; **~wollen** *vi sep* to want to get out *(aus* of*)*; **nicht mit etw ~wollen** *(col: sagen wollen)* not to want to come out with sth *(col)*; **~ziehen** *vt sep irreg* to pull out *(aus* of*)*; *(~schleppen)* to drag out *(aus* of*)*.

herb *adj Geruch* sharp; *Parfüm* tangy; *Wein* dry; *Enttäuschung, Verlust* bitter; *Worte, Kritik* harsh.

herbei-: ~eilen *vi sep aux sein* to hurry *or* rush over; **~führen** *vt sep* to bring about; **~holen** *vt sep* to bring; *Arzt, Polizisten* to fetch; **~laufen** *vi sep irreg aux sein* to come running up; **~rufen** *vt sep irreg* to call over; *Verstärkung* to call in; *Arzt, Polizei* to call; **~schaffen** *vt sep* to bring; *Geld* to get hold of; *Beweise* to produce; **~sehnen** *vt sep*

to long for; ~strömen *vi sep aux sein* to come flocking.
Herberge *f* **-n** *no pl* lodging *no indef art*; *(Jugend~)* (youth) hostel.
Herbergs-: ~**mutter** *f*/~**vater** *m* (youth hostel) warden.
her-: ~**bestellen*** *vt sep (col)* to send for; ~**bitten** *vt sep irreg* to ask to come; ~**bringen** *vt sep irreg* to bring (here).
Herbst *m* **-e** autumn, fall *(US)*. **im** ~ in autumn, in the fall *(US)*.
Herbst- *in cpds* autumn, fall *(US)*; ~**anfang** *m* beginning of autumn *or* fall *(US)*; ~**ferien** *pl* autumn *or* fall *(US)* holiday(s); *(Sch)* half-term holiday(s); **h~lich** *adj* autumn *attr*, fall *attr (US)*; **das Wetter ist h~lich kühl** the cooler days of autumn *or* fall *(US)* are upon us.
Herd *m* **-e (a)** *(Küchen~)* cooker, stove; *(Kohle~)* range. **(b)** *(Krankheits~)* focus; *(von Erdbeben)* epicentre *(Brit)*, epicenter *(US)*; *(fig: von Rebellion etc)* seat.
Herde *f* **-n** *(lit)* herd; *(von Schafen)* flock. **der ~ folgen** *(pej)* to follow the herd.
Herdentrieb *m (lit, fig pej)* herd instinct.
Herdplatte *f (von Elektroherd)* hotplate.
herein *adv* in. ~! come in!; **hier** ~! in here!; **von (dr)außen** ~ from outside.
herein- *pref* in; ~**bekommen** *vt sep irreg (col) Waren* to get in; *Radiosender* to get; *Unkosten etc* to recover; ~**bitten** *vt sep irreg* to ask (to come) in; ~**brechen** *vi sep irreg aux sein (Wasser, Flut)* to gush in; **das Unglück brach über ihn** ~ misfortune overtook him; ~**bringen** *vt sep irreg* **(a)** to bring in; **(b)** *(col) Geldverlust* to make good; *Zeit-, Produktionsverlust* to make up for; ~**drängen** *vir sep* to push one's way in; ~**dringen** *vi sep irreg aux sein (Licht, Wasser)* to come in *(in+acc* -to); **ein Geräusch drang ins Zimmer** ~ a sound was heard in the room; ~**fallen** *vi sep irreg aux sein* **(a)** to fall in *(in+acc* -to); **(b)** *(col)* to fall for it *(col)*; *(betrogen werden)* to be had *(col)*; **auf jdn/etw ~fallen** to be taken in by sb/sth; **mit jdm/etw ~fallen** to have a bad deal with sb/sth; ~**führen** *vt sep* to show in; ~**holen** *vt sep* to bring in *(in +acc* -to); ~**kommen** *vi sep irreg aux sein* to come in *(in+acc* -to); **wie ist er ~gekommen?** how did he get in?; ~**lassen** *vt sep irreg* to let in *(in+acc* -to); ~**legen** *vt sep (col)* **jdn ~legen** to take sb for a ride *(col)*; ~**platzen** *vi sep aux sein (col)* to burst in *(in+acc* -to); **bei jdm ~platzen** to burst in on sb; ~**regnen** *vi impers sep* **es regnet** ~ the rain is coming in; ~**schauen** *vi sep (dial)* to look in *(in +acc* -to); **(bei jdm) ~schauen** *(col)* to look sb up; ~**schneien** *sep* **1** *vi impers* **es schneit** ~ the snow's coming in; **2** *vi aux sein (col)* to drop in *(col)*; ~**spazieren*** *vi sep aux sein* to breeze in *(in +acc* -to); ~**spaziert!** come right in!; ~**strömen** *vi sep aux sein (in+acc* -to) to stream in; ~**stürmen** *vi sep aux sein* to storm in *(in +acc* -to); ~**stürzen** *vi sep aux sein* to rush in *(in+acc* -to).
Her-: **h~fahren** *sep irreg* **1** *vi aux sein* to come here; **hinter jdm h~fahren** to drive along behind sb; **2** *vt* to drive here; ~**fahrt** *f* journey here; **h~fallen** *vi sep irreg aux sein* **über jdn h~fallen** to attack sb; *(kritisieren)* to pull sb to pieces; **über etw** *(acc)* **h~fallen** to descend upon sth; *über Eßbares etc* to pounce upon sth; **h~finden** *vi sep irreg (col)* to find one's way here.
Hergang *m no pl (von Schlacht)* course. **der ~ des Unfalls** the way the accident happened.
her-: ~**geben** *sep irreg* **1** *vt (weggeben)* to give away; *(aushändigen)* to hand over; *(zurückgeben)* to give back; **gib das ~!** give me that; **viel/wenig ~geben** *(col: erbringen)* to be a lot of use/not to be much use; **das Thema gibt viel/nichts** ~ there's a lot/nothing to this topic; **was seine Beine ~gaben** as fast as his legs would carry him; **seinen Namen für etw ~geben** to lend one's name to sth; **2** *vr* **sich zu etw ~geben** to be a party to sth; ~**gebracht** *adj* **in ~gebrachter Weise** in the traditional way; ~**gehen** *sep irreg aux sein* **1** *vi* **(a) hinter/neben jdm ~gehen** to walk along behind/beside sb; **(b) ~gehen und etw tun** *(einfach tun)* just to go and do sth; **2** *vi impers (col: zugehen)* **es ging heiß** ~ things got heated; **hier geht es hoch** ~ there's plenty going on here; ~**gehören*** *vi sep* to belong here; ~**gelaufen** *adj attr (pej) siehe* **dahergelaufen;** ~**haben** *vt sep irreg (col)* **wo hat er das ~?** where did he get that from?; ~**halten** *vi sep irreg* **für etw ~halten** to pay for sth; **als Entschuldigung für etw ~halten** to be used as an excuse for sth; ~**holen** *vt sep (col)* to fetch; ~**holen lassen** to send for; **weit ~geholt sein** *(fig)* to be far-fetched; ~**hören** *vi sep (col)* to listen; **alle mal ~hören!** everybody listen.
Hering *m* **-e (a)** herring; *(col: Schwächling)* weakling. **wie die ~e zusammengedrängt** packed in like sardines. **(b)** *(Zeltpflock)* (tent) peg *(Brit) or* stake *(US)*.
her-: ~**kommen** *vi sep irreg aux sein* to come here; *(sich nähern)* to come, to approach; *(~stammen)* to come from; ~**kömmlich** *adj* conventional.
Herkunft *f no pl* origin; *(soziale)* background. **er ist britischer** *(gen)* ~ he is of British origin.
Herkunftsland *nt (Comm)* country of origin.
her-: ~**laufen** *vi sep irreg aux sein* to come running; **hinter jdm ~laufen** *(lit, fig)* to run after sb; ~**leiten** *sep* **1** *vt (folgern)* to derive *(aus* from); **2** *vr* **sich von etw ~leiten** to be derived from sth; ~**locken** *vt sep* to entice, to lure; ~**machen** *sep (col)* **1** *vr* **sich über etw** *(acc)* **~machen** *(in Angriff nehmen) Arbeit, Essen* to get stuck into sth *(col)*; *(Besitz ergreifen)* to pounce (up)on sth; **sich über jdn ~machen** to lay into sb *(col)*; **2** *vt* **viel ~machen** to look impressive.
Hermelin *m* **-e** *(Pelz)* ermine.
hermetisch *adj* hermetic. ~ **abgeriegelt** completely sealed off.
her-: ~**müssen** *vi sep irreg (col)* **(a) das muß** ~ I/we have to have it; **(b)** *(kommen müssen)* to have to come (here); **hinter jdm ~müssen** to have to go after sb; ~**nehmen** *vt sep irreg (beschaffen)* to get, to find. **wo soll ich das ~nehmen?** where am I supposed to get that from?
Heroin [hero'i:n] *nt no pl* heroin.
heroisch [he'ro:ɪʃ] *adj (geh)* heroic.
Herr *m (wk)* **-(e)n, -en (a)** *(Gebieter)* lord, master; *(Herrscher)* ruler *(über +acc* of); *(von Hund)* master. **die ~en der Schöpfung** *(hum: Männer)* the gentlemen; **sein eigener ~ sein** to be one's own master *or* boss; ~ **der Lage bleiben** to remain master of the situation; **über jdn/etw ~ werden** to master sb/sth; **niemand kann zwei ~en dienen** *(prov)* no man can serve two masters *(prov)*.
(b) *(Gott, Christus)* Lord. **Gott, der** ~ the Lord God.
(c) *(feiner ~, Mann)* gentleman. **„~en"** *(Toilette)* "gentlemen" *(Brit)*, "men's room" *(US)*.
(d) *(vor Eigennamen)* Mr. **mein ~!** sir!; **der ~ wünscht?** what can I do for you, sir?; **ja, ~ Doktor/Professor** yes, Doctor/Professor; ~ **Präsident/Vorsitzender** Mr President/Chairman; **der ~ Präsident/Vorsitzende** the President/Chairman; **lieber ~ A, sehr geehrter ~ A** *(in Brief)* Dear Mr A; **sehr geehrte ~en** *(in Brief)* Dear Sirs.
Herrchen *nt (col: von Hund)* master.
Herren- *in cpds* men's; *(auf einzelnes Exemplar bezüglich)* man's; ~**abend** *m* stag night; ~**ausstatter** *m* - men's outfitter; ~**begleitung** *f* **in ~begleitung** in the company of a gentleman; ~**bekleidung** *f* menswear; ~**besuch** *m* gentleman visitor/visitors; ~**friseur** *m* men's hairdresser, barber; ~**haus** *nt* manor house; **h~los** *adj* abandoned; *Hund etc* stray; ~**toilette** *f*

men's room *(US)*, gents *sing (Brit)*.

Herrgott *m (dated col) (Anrede)* God, Lord. **der ~** the Lord (God); **~ noch mal!** *(col)* damn it all! *(col)*.

Herrgottsfrühe *f*: **in aller ~** *(col)* at the crack of dawn.

herrichten *sep* **1** *vt* **(a)** *(vorbereiten)* to get ready *(dat, für* for*)*; *Bett* to make; *Tisch* to set. **(b)** *(instand setzen)* to do up *(col)*.**2** *vr (dial)* to get dressed up.

Herrin *f (Hist)* female ruler; *(von Hund)* mistress.

herrisch *adj* overbearing, imperious.

herrje, herrjemine *interj* goodness gracious.

herrlich *adj* marvellous *(Brit)*, marvelous *(US)*; *Kleid* gorgeous, lovely. **wir haben uns ~ amüsiert** we had marvellous fun.

Herrlichkeit *f* **(a)** *no pl (Pracht)* magnificence, splendour *(Brit)*, splendor *(US)*. **die ~ Gottes** the glory of God. **(b)** *usu pl (Gegenstand)* treasure.

Herrschaft *f* **(a)** *(Macht)* power; *(Staatsgewalt)* rule; *(Kontrolle)* control. **sich der ~ bemächtigen** to seize power; **unter der ~** under the rule *(gen, von* of*)*; **er verlor die ~ über sich** he lost his self-control; **er verlor die ~ über sein Auto** he lost control of his car. **(b) die ~en** *(Damen und Herren)* the ladies and gentlemen; **(meine) ~en!** ladies and gentlemen.

herrschaftlich *adj (vornehm)* grand.

Herrschafts-: ~anspruch *m* claim to power; **~bereich** *m* territory.

herrschen 1 *vi* **(a)** *(über etw (acc)* sth*)* to rule; *(König)* to reign; *(fig: Mensch)* to dominate. **(b)** *(vor~) (Angst, Ungewißheit)* to prevail; *(Krankheit)* to be rampant. **überall herrschte Freude** there was joy everywhere; **im Zimmer herrschte bedrückende Stille** it was oppressively quiet in the room; **hier ~ ja Zustände!** things are in a pretty state around here! **2** *vi impers* **es herrscht schlechtes Wetter** we're having bad weather; **es herrscht Ungewißheit darüber, ob** ... there is uncertainty about whether ...

herrschend *adj Partei, Klasse* ruling; *König* reigning; *Verhältnisse, Meinungen* prevailing; *Mode* current.

Herrscher(in *f***)** *m* - ruler *(über+acc* of*)*.

Herrscher-: ~geschlecht *nt* ruling dynasty; **~haus** *nt* ruling house.

Herrschsucht *f* domineeringness.

herrschsüchtig *adj* domineering.

her-: ~rufen *vt sep irreg* to call (over); **~rühren** *vi sep* **von etw ~rühren** to be due to sth, to stem from sth; **~sagen** *vt sep* to recite; **~sehen** *vi sep irreg* **(a)** to look this way; **(b) hinter jdm/etw ~sehen** to follow sb with one's eyes; **~sein** *vi sep irreg aux sein* **(a) das ist schon 5 Jahre ~** that was 5 years ago; **wie lange ist es ~?** how long ago was it?; **(b)** *(~stammen)* to come from; **mit jdm/etw ist es nicht weit ~** *(col)* sb/sth is not up to much *(col)*; **(c) hinter jdm/etw ~sein** to be after sb/sth; **~stammen** *vi sep* **(a) wo stammst du ~?** where do you come from?; **(b)** *(~rühren)* **von etw ~stammen** to stem from sth.

herstellen *vt sep* **(a)** *(erzeugen)* to produce; *(industriell auch)* to manufacture. **in Deutschland hergestellt** made in Germany. **(b)** *(zustande bringen)* to establish; *(Telec) Verbindung* to make; *Stromkreis* to complete. **(c)** *(gesundheitlich) jdn* to restore to health. **er ist wieder ganz hergestellt** he has quite recovered.

Hersteller(in *f***)** *m* - *(Produzent)* manufacturer.

Herstellung *f no pl siehe vt* **(a)** production; manufacture. **(b)** establishment; making; completion.

Herstellungs-: ~kosten *pl* manufacturing *or* production costs *pl*; **~land** *nt* country of manufacture.

hertragen *vt sep irreg (col) (an bestimmten Ort)* to carry here. **etw hinter jdm ~** to carry sth behind sb.

herüber *adv (hierher)* over here; *(über Straße, Grenze)* across.

herüber- *pref* over; *(über Straße, Grenze)* across; **~fahren** *sep irreg* **1** *vi aux sein* **er ist gestern ~gefahren** he came *or (mit Auto)* drove across yesterday; **2** *vt Fahrgast, Güter* to take over/across; **~holen** *vt sep* to fetch; **~kommen** *vi sep irreg aux sein* to come over/across *(über etw (acc)* sth*)*; *(col: zu Nachbarn)* to pop round *(col)*; **~reichen** *sep* **1** *vt* to pass *(über+acc* over*)*; **2** *vi* to reach across *(über etw (acc)* sth*)*; **~retten** *vt sep* **etw in die Gegenwart ~retten** to preserve sth; **~wechseln** *vi sep aux sein or haben* **in unsere Partei ~wechseln** to swap over to our party; **~ziehen** *sep irreg (über etw (acc)* sth*)* **1** *vt* to pull over/across; *(fig)* to win over; **2** *vi aux sein (Truppen, Wolken)* to move over/across.

herum *adv* **um Ulm ~** around Ulm; **um 50 ~** around 50; **links/rechts ~** around to the left/right; **hier/dort ~** around here/there; **oben ~** *(über Gegenstand, Berg)* over the top; *(in bezug auf Körper)* around the top; **unten ~** *(unter Gegenstand)* underneath; *(um Berg, in bezug auf Körper)* around the bottom.

herum- *pref* around; *siehe auch* **umher-; ~ärgern** *vr sep (col)* **sich mit jdm/etw ~ärgern** to keep struggling with sb/sth; **~basteln** *vi sep (col)* to tinker about *(an+dat* with*)*; **~bekommen** *vt sep irreg (col) jdn* to talk round; **~blättern** *vi sep* **(in einem Buch) ~blättern** to browse through a book; **~bummeln** *vi sep (col)* **(a)** *(trödeln)* to mess about *(col)*; **(b)** *aux sein (spazieren)* to stroll around *(in etw (dat)* sth); **~doktern** *vi sep (col)* **an jdm/einer Krankheit ~doktern** to try to cure sb/an illness; **~drehen** *sep* **1** *vt* to turn; **jdm das Wort im Mund ~drehen** to twist sb's words; **2** *vr* to turn around; *(im Liegen)* to turn over; **3** *vi (col)* **an etw** *(dat)* **~drehen** to fiddle about with sth; **~drücken** *vr sep* **(a)** *(sich aufhalten)* to hang around *(col) (um etw* sth*)*; **(b)** *(vermeiden)* **sich um etw ~drücken** to dodge sth; **~erzählen** *vt sep* **erzähl das nicht ~** don't spread it around; **~fahren** *sep irreg* **1** *vi aux sein* **(a)** to travel *or (mit Auto)* drive around; **(b)** *(sich rasch umdrehen)* to spin around; **2** *vt* to drive around; **~fragen** *vi sep (col)* to ask around *(bei* among*)*; **~fuchteln** *vi sep (col)* **(mit den Händen) ~fuchteln** to wave one's hands around; **~führen** *sep* **1** *vt* to lead around *(um etw* sth*)*; *(bei Besichtigung)* to take *or* show around; **2** *vi* **um etw ~führen** to go around sth; **~fuhrwerken** *vi sep (col)* to bustle about; **~fummeln** *vi sep (col) (an +dat* with*)* to fiddle about; *(basteln)* to tinker (about); **~gammeln** *vi sep (col)* to bum around *(col)*; **~gehen** *vi sep irreg aux sein (col)* **(a)** to go around *(um etw* sth*)*; **(b)** *(ziellos)* to wander around *(in etw (dat)* sth*)*; **es ging ihm im Kopf ~** it went round and round in his head; **(c)** *(~gereicht werden)* to be passed around; **etw ~gehen lassen** to circulate sth; **(d)** *Zeit* to pass; **~geistern** *vi sep aux sein (col) (Gespenster etc)* to haunt *(in etw (dat)* sth*)*; *(Mensch)* to wander around; **~hacken** *vi sep (col)* **auf jdm ~hacken** to pick on sb *(col)*; **~hängen** *vi sep irreg (col)* **(a)** to hang around; **(b)** *(sich lümmeln)* to loll about; **(c)** *(ständig zu finden sein)* to hang out *(col)*; **~kommen** *vi sep irreg aux sein (col)* **(a)** *(um eine Ecke etc)* to come around *(um etw* sth*)*; **(b)** *(~gehen können)* to get around *(um etw* sth*)*; **(c)** *(vermeiden können)* **um etw ~kommen** to get out of sth; **(d) er ist viel ~gekommen** he has been around a lot; **~kriegen** *vt sep (col) jdn* to talk around; **~laufen** *vi sep irreg aux sein (col)* to run *or (gehen)* walk around *(um etw* sth*)*; **~lungern** *vi sep (col)* to hang around; **~machen** *sep (col)* **1** *vi* **an etw** *(dat)* **~machen** *(sich beschäftigen)* to fuss about sth; *(~fingern)* to pick at sth; **2** *vt* to put around *(um etw* sth*)*; **~nörgeln** *vi sep* **an jdm/etw**

~nörgeln to find fault with sb/sth; ~quälen *vr sep (col)* to struggle; **sich mit Rheuma ~quälen** to be plagued by rheumatism; ~reden *vi sep (col)* to chat away; **um etw ~reden** *(ausweichend)* to talk around sth; ~reißen *vt sep irreg* to swing around (hard); **das Steuer ~reißen** *(fig)* to change course; ~reiten *vi sep irreg (fig col)* **auf jdm/etw ~reiten** to keep on at sb/about sth; **~schlagen** *sep irreg* **1** *vt Papier, Tuch* to wrap around *(um etw* sth*)*; **2** *vr (col)* **sich mit jdm/etw ~schlagen** *(fig)* to struggle with sb/sth; **~schleppen** *vt sep (col) Sachen* to lug around *(col)*; *jdn* to drag around; **etw mit sich ~schleppen** *Sorge, Problem* to be troubled by sth; *Krankheit* to have sth; **~schnüffeln** *vi sep (col)* to sniff around *(in etw (dat)* sth*)*; *(fig)* to snoop around *(in+dat* in*)*; **~schreien** *vi sep irreg (col)* to shout out loud; **~sein** *vi sep irreg aux sein (col)* **(a)** *(vorüber sein)* to be past *or* over; **(b)** *(in jds Nähe sein)* **um jdn ~sein** to be around sb; **~sprechen** *vr sep irreg* to get about; **~stehen** *vi sep irreg aux sein (Sachen)* to be lying around; *(Menschen)* to stand around *(um jdn/etw* sb/sth*)*; **~stochern** *vi sep (col)* to poke about; **im Essen ~stochern** to pick at one's food; **~streiten** *vr sep irreg (col)* to squabble; **~tragen** *vt sep irreg (col)* **(a)** to carry about; **Sorgen mit sich ~tragen** to have worries; **(b)** *(weitererzählen)* to spread around; **~treiben** *vr sep irreg (col) (sich aufhalten)* to hang around *(in +dat* in*) (col)*; *(liederlich leben)* to hang around in bad places/ company.

Herumtreiber(in *f*) *m* - *(pej)* tramp.

herum-: **~wälzen** *vr sep* to roll around; **sich (schlaflos) im Bett ~wälzen** to toss and turn; **~werfen** *sep irreg* **1** *vt* **(a)** *(col)* to throw around *(in etw (dat)* sth*)*; **(b)** *Kopf* to turn (quickly); *Steuer* to throw around; **2** *vr* **sich (im Bett) ~werfen** to toss and turn (in bed); **~wursteln** *vi sep (col)* to fiddle around *(an +dat* with*) (col)*; **~ziehen** *sep irreg* **1** *vi aux sein* to move around; **in der Welt ~ziehen** to roam the world; **2** *vt* **etw mit sich ~ziehen** to take sth around with one.

herunter 1 *adv* down. **~!** get down!; **~ mit ihm** get him down; **~ damit** get it down; *(in bezug auf Kleider)* get it off. **2** *prep +acc* **den Berg ~** down the mountain.

herunter- *pref* down; *siehe auch* **herab-;** **~bekommen** *vt sep irreg siehe* **~kriegen;** **~bringen** *vt sep irreg* **(a)** to bring down; **(b)** *(col) siehe* **~kriegen;** **~drücken** *vt sep* to press down; *Preise* to force down; *Niveau* to lower; **~fallen** *vi sep irreg aux sein* to fall down; **von etw ~fallen** to fall off sth; **~gehen** *vi sep irreg aux sein* to go down; *(Temperatur, Preise auch)* to drop; **mit den Preisen ~gehen** to lower one's prices; **~gekommen** *adj Haus* dilapidated; *Stadt* run-down; *Mensch* down-at-heel; **~handeln** *vt sep (col) Preis* to beat down; **etw um 20 Mark ~handeln** to get 20 marks knocked off sth; **~hauen** *vt sep irreg (col)* **jdm eine ~hauen** to give sb a clip around the ear *(col)*; **~holen** *vt sep* to fetch down; *(col) Vogel, Flugzeug* to bring down; **~klappen** *vt sep Kragen* to turn down; *Sitz* to fold down; *Deckel* to close; **~kommen** *vi sep irreg aux sein* **(a)** to come down; **(b)** *(fig col: verfallen) (Stadt, Firma)* to go downhill; *(gesundheitlich)* to become run-down; *siehe* **~gekommen;** **~können** *vi sep irreg* to be able to get down; **~kriegen** *vt sep (col) (~holen, schlucken können)* to get down; *(abmachen können)* to get off; **~lassen** *sep irreg vt Gegenstand* to let down; *Hose* to take down; **~leiern** *vt sep (col)* to reel off; **~machen** *vt sep (col)* **(a)** *(schlechtmachen)* to run down, to knock *(col)*; **(b)** *(zurechtweisen)* to tell off; **(c)** *(abmachen)* to take down; *Farbe, Dreck* to take off; **~nehmen** *vt sep irreg* to take down; *(col: von Schule)* to take away; **~putzen** *vt sep (col)* **jdn ~putzen** to tear sb off a strip *(col)*; **~rasseln** *vt sep (col)* to rattle off; **~reißen** *vt sep irreg (col)* **(a)** to pull down; **(b)** *(abreißen)* to pull off; **~schlucken** *vt sep* to swallow; **~schrauben** *vt sep (lit) Deckel* to screw off; *(fig) Ansprüche, Niveau* to lower; **~sehen** *vi sep irreg (lit, fig)* to look down *(auf +acc* on*)*; **~sein** *vi sep irreg aux sein (col)* **(a)** to be down; *(abgeschnitten sein)* to be (cut) off; **(b) mit den Nerven/der Gesundheit ~sein** to be at the end of one's tether/to be rundown; **~setzen** *vt sep (col) siehe* **herabsetzen;** **~spielen** *vt sep (col) Problem, Vorfall* to play down; **~wirtschaften** *vt sep (col)* to bring to the brink of ruin; **~wollen** *vi sep (col)* to want to get down; **~ziehen** *vt sep irreg* to pull down.

hervor *adv* **aus etw ~** out of sth; **hinter dem Tisch ~** out from behind the table.

hervor-: **~bringen** *vt sep irreg* **(a)** *Blüten* to produce; *Worte* to utter; **(b)** *(verursachen)* to create; **~gehen** *vi sep irreg aux sein* **(a)** *(geh: entstammen)* to come *(aus* from*)*; **(b) daraus geht ~, daß ...** from this it follows that ...; **(c) als Sieger ~gehen** to emerge victorious; **~heben** *vt sep irreg* to emphasize; **~ragen** *vi sep* to jut out, to project; *(fig: sich auszeichnen)* to stand out; **~ragend** *adj (ausgezeichnet)* outstanding; **er hat H~ragendes geleistet** his achievement was outstanding; **das hat ~ragend geklappt** it worked beautifully; **~rufen** *vt sep irreg* **(a) jdn ~rufen** to call sb out; *(Theat etc)* to call for sb; **(b)** *(bewirken) Bewunderung* to arouse; *Reaktion, Krankheit* to cause; *Eindruck* to create; **~stechen** *vi sep irreg aux sein (lit, fig)* to stand out; **~stechend** *adj* striking; **~stoßen** *vt sep irreg Worte* to gasp (out); **~treten** *vi sep irreg aux sein* **(a)** *(heraustreten)* to emerge *(hinter +dat* from behind*)*; *(Backenknochen)* to protrude; *(Adern)* to bulge; **(b)** *(sichtbar werden)* to stand out; **~tun** *vr sep irreg* to distinguish oneself; *(col: sich wichtig tun)* to show off *(mit etw* sth*)*; **~wagen** *vr sep* to dare to come out; **~zaubern** *vt sep (lit, fig)* to conjure up; **~ziehen** *vt sep irreg* to pull out *(unter +dat* from under*)*.

Herweg *m* way here.

Herz *nt* **-ens, -en (a)** *(lit, fig)* heart. **mir schlug das ~ bis zum Hals** my heart was pounding; **die ~en höher schlagen lassen** to make people's hearts beat faster; **ein goldenes ~** a heart of gold; **schweren ~ens** with a heavy heart; **es gab mir einen Stich ins ~** it hurt me; **seinem ~en Luft machen** to give vent to one's feelings; **sich** *(dat)* **etw vom ~en reden** to get sth off one's chest; **du sprichst mir aus dem ~en** that's just what I feel; **jdm das ~ schwer machen** to sadden sb; **im Grund seines ~ens** in his heart of hearts; **aus tiefstem ~en** from the bottom of one's heart; **mit ganzem ~en** wholeheartedly; **ich weiß, wie es dir ums ~ ist** I know how you feel; **jdm sein ~ schenken** to give sb one's heart; **dieser alte Hund ist mir ans ~ gewachsen** I have grown fond of this old dog; **er hat sie in sein ~ geschlossen** he has grown fond of her; **sein ~ an jdn/etw hängen** to commit oneself heart and soul to sb/sth; **sich** *(dat)* **ein ~ fassen** to take heart; **ihm rutschte das ~ in die Hose** *(col)* his heart sank; **ein ~ und eine Seele sein** to be the best of friends; **alles, was das ~ begehrt** everything one's heart desires; **er hat das ~ auf dem rechten Fleck** his heart is in the right place; **es liegt mir am ~en** I am very concerned about it; **jdm etw ans ~ legen** to entrust sth to sb; **etw auf dem ~en haben** to have sth on one's mind; **jdn/etw auf ~ und Nieren prüfen** to examine sb/sth very thoroughly; **eine schwere Last fiel ihr vom ~en** a heavy load was lifted from her mind; **von ~en** with all one's heart; **etw von ~en gern tun** to love doing sth; **von ~en kommend** heartfelt; **sich** *(dat)* **etw zu ~en nehmen** to take sth to heart.

(b) *pl* - *(Cards) (no pl: Farbe)* hearts *pl*; *(Karte)* heart.

Herz- *in cpds (Anat, Med)* cardiac; ~**anfall** *m* heart attack; ~**beschwerden** *pl* heart trouble *sing*; **h~bewegend** *adj* heart-rending.
Herzchen *nt (col: Kosewort)* darling.
herzeigen *vt sep* to show. **zeig (mal) her!** let's see; **das kann man** ~ that's worth showing off.
Herzens-: ~**bedürfnis** *nt (dated)* **es ist mir ein** ~**bedürfnis** it is a matter dear to my heart; ~**brecher** *m* - *(fig col)* heart-breaker; **h~gut** *adj* good-hearted; ~**lust** *f* **nach** ~**lust** to one's heart's content; ~**wunsch** *m* dearest wish.
Herz-: **h~erfrischend** *adj* refreshing; **h~ergreifend, h~erweichend** *adj* heart-rending; ~**fehler** *m* heart defect; **h~förmig** *adj* heart-shaped; **h~haft** *adj (kräftig)* hearty; *Händedruck, Griff* firm; *Geschmack* strong; **alle langten h~haft zu** everyone got stuck in *(col)*; **das schmeckt h~haft** that's tasty.
herziehen *sep irreg* **1** *vt* to pull closer. **jdn/etw hinter sich** *(dat)* ~ to pull sb/sth (along) behind one. **2** *vi aux sein* **(a) hinter jdm** ~ to march along behind sb. **(b) über jdn/etw** ~ *(col)* to pull sb/sth to pieces *(col)*.
Herz-: ~**infarkt** *m* heart attack; ~**kammer** *f* ventricle; ~**klappe** *f* (heart) valve; ~**klopfen** *nt no pl* **ich hatte/bekam** ~**klopfen** my heart was/started pounding; *(durch Kaffee etc)* I had/got palpitations; **mit** ~**klopfen** with a pounding heart; **h~krank** *adj* suffering from a heart condition; ~**kranzgefäß** *nt usu pl* coronary (blood) vessel; ~**leiden** *nt* heart condition.
herzlich **1** *adj Empfang, Mensch* warm; *Lachen* hearty; *Bitte* sincere. ~**e Grüße an ...** remember me to ...; **mit** ~**en Grüßen** kind regards; ~**en Dank!** thank you very much indeed; ~**es Beileid!** you have my deepest sympathy. **2** *adv (sehr)* ~ **gern!** with the greatest of pleasure!; ~ **schlecht** pretty awful; ~ **wenig** precious little; **ich habe es** ~ **satt** I'm sick and tired of it.
Herzlichkeit *f siehe adj* warmth; heartiness; sincerity.
Herz-: **h~los** *adj* heartless; ~**losigkeit** *f* heartlessness *no pl*; ~**mittel** *nt* cardiac drug.
Herzog ['hɛrtsoːk] *m* ¨**e** duke.
Herzogin ['hɛrtsoːgɪn] *f* duchess.
Herzogtum *nt* dukedom, duchy.
Herz-: ~**schlag** *m (einzelner)* heartbeat; *(~tätigkeit)* heart rate; *(~stillstand)* heart failure *no indef art*; ~**schrittmacher** *m* pacemaker; ~**schwäche** *f* **an** ~**schwäche leiden** to have a weak heart; **h~stärkend** *adj* **ein h~stärkendes Mittel** a cardiac stimulant; **h~zerreißend** *adj* heartbreaking.
Hessen *nt* Hesse.
hessisch *adj* Hessian.
hetero-: ~**gen** *adj (geh)* heterogeneous; ~**sexuell** *adj* heterosexual.
Hetze *f no pl* **(a)** *(Hast)* (mad) rush, hurry. **(b)** *(pej: ~kampagne)* smear campaign.
hetzen **1** *vt* **(a)** *(lit, fig: jagen)* to hound. **die Hunde auf jdn** ~ to set the dogs on sb. **(b)** *(col: antreiben)* to rush, to hurry. **2** *vr* to hurry oneself. **3** *vi* **(a)** *auch aux sein* to rush. **(b)** *(pej: Haß schüren)* to stir up hatred *(gegen* against); *(col: lästern)* to say malicious things. **bei jdm gegen jdn** ~ to try to set sb against sb.
Hetzer(in *f*) *m* - rabble-rouser, agitator.
Hetzerei *f* **(a)** *no pl (Hast)* (mad) rush. **(b)** *(das Haßschüren)* rabble-rousing, agitation.
Hetz-: ~**jagd** *f (lit, fig)* hounding *(auf +acc* of); ~**kampagne** *f* smear campaign.
Heu *nt no pl* hay. **Geld wie** ~ **haben** *(col)* to have pots of money *(col)*.
Heuboden *m* hayloft.
Heuchelei *f* hypocrisy.
heucheln **1** *vi* to be a hypocrite. **2** *vt Mitleid etc* to feign.
Heuchler(in *f*) *m* - hypocrite.
heuchlerisch *adj* hypocritical.
heuer *adv (S Ger, Aus, Sw)* this year.
Heuer *f* **-n** *(Naut)* pay.
heuern *vt* to sign on, to hire.
Heu-: ~**fieber** *nt* hay fever; ~**gabel** *f* pitchfork, hayfork; ~**haufen** *m* haystack.
heulen *vi* to howl; *(Motor)* to roar; *(Sirene)* to wail. **ich hätte** ~ **können** I could have wept; **es ist einfach zum H~** it's enough to make you weep.
Heulen *nt no pl siehe vi* howling; roaring; wailing.
Heul-: *(col)* ~**peter** *m*, ~**suse** *f* cry-baby *(col)*; ~**ton** *m (von Sirene)* wail.
Heu-: ~**schnupfen** *m* hay fever; ~**schrecke** *f* **-n** grasshopper; *(in heißen Ländern)* locust; ~**speicher** barn.
heute *adv* today. ~ **morgen** this morning; ~ **abend** this evening, tonight; ~ **früh** this morning; ~ **nacht** tonight; **bis** ~ *(bisher)* to this day; ~ **in einer Woche** a week today, today week; **lieber** ~ **als morgen** the sooner the better; **von** ~ **auf morgen** *(fig: plötzlich)* overnight, from one day to the next; **der Mensch von** ~ modern man.
heutig *adj attr* today's; *(gegenwärtig)* modern, contemporary. **am** ~**en Abend** this evening; **unser** ~**es Schreiben** *(Comm)* our letter of today('s date); **bis zum** ~**en Tage** to this day.
heutzutage *adv* nowadays.
Hexe *f* **-n** witch; *(col: altes Weib)* old hag.
hexen *vi* to do witchcraft. **ich kann doch nicht** ~ *(col)* I'm not a magician.
Hexen-: ~**häuschen** *nt* gingerbread house; ~**jagd** *f* witch hunt; ~**kessel** *m (fig)* pandemonium *no indef art*; ~**meister** *m* sorcerer; ~**schuß** *m (Med)* lumbago.
Hexerei *f* witchcraft *no pl*; *(Zaubertricks)* magic *no pl*.
HG = **Handelsgesellschaft.**
hg. = **herausgegeben** ed.
Hickhack *m or nt* **-s** *(col)* squabbling *no pl*.
Hieb *m* **-e** **(a)** *(Schlag)* stroke, blow; *(Peitschen~)* lash; *(Fechten)* cut. **(b)** *(~wunde)* gash, slash. **(c)** ~**e** *pl (col: Prügel)* ~**e bekommen** to get a hiding.
hieb- und stichfest *adj (fig)* watertight.
hielt *pret of* **halten.**
hier *adv* here. **dieser** ~ this one (here); ~ **draußen** out here; ~ **herum** hereabouts, around here; **er ist von** ~ he's a local (man); **Tag Klaus,** ~ **(spricht) Hans** *(Telec)* hello Klaus, it's Hans; ~ **spricht Dr. Müller** *(Telec)* this is Dr Müller (speaking); ~ **und da** (every) now and then.
hieran *adv* here. ~ **erkenne ich es** I recognize it by this.
Hierarchie *f* hierarchy.
hierarchisch *adj* hierarchical.
hier-: ~**auf** *adv* on this; *(daraufhin)* hereupon; ~**aufhin** *adv* hereupon; ~**aus** *adv* out of/from this, from here; ~**aus folgt daß ...** from this it follows that ...; ~**bei** *adv (bei dieser Gelegenheit)* on this occasion; *(in diesem Zusammenhang)* in this connection; ~**bleiben** *vi sep irreg aux sein* to stay here; ~**geblieben!** stop!; ~**durch** *adv (lit)* through here; *(fig)* through this; ~**durch teilen wir Ihnen mit, daß ...** we hereby inform you that ...; ~**für** *adv* for this; ~**her** *adv* here.
hierhergehören* *vi sep* to belong here; *(fig: relevant sein)* to be relevant. **nicht** ~**de Bemerkungen** irrelevant remarks.
hier-: ~**hin** *adv* here; **bis** ~**hin** up to here; ~**in** *adv (lit, fig)* in this; ~**mit** *adv* with this, herewith *(form)*; ~**mit ist der Fall erledigt** this settles the matter; ~**mit erkläre ich ...** *(form)* I hereby declare ... *(form)*; ~**nach** *adv* after this, afterwards; *(daraus folgend)* according to this; ~**sein** *vi sep irreg aux sein* to be here; **während meines H~seins** during my stay; ~**über** *adv (fig)* about this; ~**über ärgere ich mich** this makes me angry; ~**unter** *adv (lit)* under this *or* here; *(fig)* by

this *or* that; *(in dieser Kategorie)* among these; **~unter fallen auch die Sonntage** this includes Sundays; **~von** *adv* from this; **~von habe ich nichts gewußt** I knew nothing about this; **~von abgesehen** apart from this; **~vor** *adv* in front of this *or* here; **~vor ekele ich mich** it revolts me; **~vor hat er großen Respekt** he has a great respect for this; **~zu** *adv (dafür)* for this; *(dazu)* with this; *(außerdem)* in addition to this, moreover; *(zu diesem Punkt)* about this; **~zu gehören auch die Katzen** this also includes the cats; **~zulande** *adv* in these parts.

hiesig *adj attr* local. **meine ~en Verwandten** my relatives here; **er ist kein H~er** he is not a local (man).

hieß *pret of* **heißen.**

Hi-Fi-Anlage ['haifi-] *f* hi-fi set *or* system.

Hilfe *f* **-n (a)** *no pl* help; *(für Notleidende)* aid, relief. **(zu) ~!** help!; **jdm zu ~ kommen** to come to sb's aid *or* assistance; **jdm ~ leisten** to help sb; **bei jdm ~ suchen** to seek sb's help *or* assistance; **mit ~** with the help *or* aid *(gen* of*)*; **etw zu ~ nehmen** to use sth; **ohne fremde ~ gehen** to walk unaided. **(b)** *(Hilfsmittel)* aid. **du bist mir eine schöne ~!** *(iro)* a fine help *you* are!

Hilfe-: ~leistung *f* aid, assistance; **unterlassene ~leistung** *(Jur)* denial of assistance; **~ruf** *m* call for help; **~stellung** *f (Sport, fig)* support; **h~suchend** *adj* seeking help; *Blick* beseeching.

Hilf-: h~los *adj* helpless; **~losigkeit** *f* helplessness; **h~reich** *adj* helpful.

Hilfs-: ~aktion *f* relief action; **~arbeiter** *m* labourer *(Brit)*, laborer *(US)*; *(in Fabrik)* unskilled worker; **h~bedürftig** *adj* in need of help; *(notleidend)* needy, in need *pred*; **h~bereit** *adj* helpful, ready to help *pred*; **~bereitschaft** *f* helpfulness, readiness to help; **~dienst** *m* emergency service; *(bei Katastrophenfall)* (emergency) relief service; **~kraft** *f* assistant; *(Aushilfe)* temporary worker; **~maßnahme** *f* relief action *no pl*; *(zur Rettung)* rescue action *no pl*; **~mittel** *nt* aid; **~organisation** *f* relief organization; **~programm** *nt* relief programme *(Brit) or* program *(US)*; **~schule** *f (dated)* school for backward children; **~verb** *nt* auxiliary (verb); **~werk** *nt* relief organization.

Himalaja *m* **der ~** the Himalayas *pl.*

Himbeere *f* raspberry.

Himmel *m* **- (a)** sky. **am ~** in the sky; **zwischen ~ und Erde** in midair; **jdn/etw in den ~ heben** *or* **loben** to praise sb/sth to the skies; **ihr hängt der ~ voller Geigen** everything in the garden is lovely for her; **so was fällt nicht einfach vom ~** things like that don't grow on trees. **(b)** *(Rel)* heaven. **im ~** in heaven; **in den ~ kommen** to go to heaven; **das schreit zum ~** it's a scandal; **es stinkt zum ~** *(col)* it stinks to high heaven *(col)*; **(ach) du lieber ~!** *(col)* good Heavens! *(col)*; **um ~s willen** *(col)* for Heaven's sake *(col)*.

Himmel-: ~bett *nt* four-poster (bed); **h~blau** *adj* sky-blue.

Himmelfahrt *f* **(a) Christi ~** the Ascension of Christ; **Mariä ~** the Assumption of the Virgin Mary. **(b)** *(no art: Feiertag)* Ascension Day.

Himmelfahrts-: ~kommando *nt (Mil col)* suicide squad; *(Unternehmen)* suicide mission; **~tag** *m* Ascension Day.

Himmel-: h~hoch 1 *adj* sky-high; **2** *adv* high into the sky; **h~hoch jauchzend, zu Tode betrübt** up one minute and down the next; **~reich** *nt no pl (Rel)* Kingdom of Heaven; **h~schreiend** *adj* outrageous, appalling.

Himmels-: ~körper *m* heavenly *or* celestial body; **~richtung** *f* direction; **die vier ~richtungen** the four points of the compass.

himmelweit *adj* **ein ~er Unterschied** a world of difference; **wir sind noch ~ davon entfernt** we're still nowhere near it.

himmlisch *adj (lit, fig)* heavenly; *Geduld* infinite. **der ~e Vater** our Heavenly Father.

hin *adv* **(a)** *(räumlich)* **nach außen ~** *(fig)* outwardly; **~ fahre ich mit dem Zug, zurück ...** on the way out I'll take the train, coming back ...; **~ und her** *(räumlich)* to and fro, back and forth; **etw ~ und her überlegen** to think about sth a lot; **das H~ und Her** the comings and goings *pl*; **nach langem H~und Her** eventually; **Feiertag ~, Feiertag her** holiday or no holiday, whether it's a holiday or not; **~ und zurück** there and back; **einmal London ~ und zurück** a return to London *(Brit)*, a roundtrip ticket to London *(US)*; **~ und wieder** (every) now and again.

(b) *(zeitlich)* **es sind nur noch drei Tage ~** it's only three days from now; **gegen Mittag ~** towards midday; **über die Jahre ~** over the years.

(c) auf meine Bitte/meinen Vorschlag ~ at my request/suggestion; **auf meinen Brief ~** on account of my letter; **auf sein Versprechen/seinen Rat ~** on the basis of his promise/his advice; **etw auf etw** *(acc)* **~ untersuchen** to inspect sth for sth; **nichts wie ~** *(col)* let's go then!; **wo ist es/sie ~?** where has it/she gone?

hinab *adv, pref siehe* **hinunter.**

hin|arbeiten *vi sep*: **auf etw** *(acc)* **~** *auf Ziel* to work towards sth.

hinauf *adv* up. **den Berg ~** up the mountain.

hinauf- *pref* up; **~arbeiten** *vr sep (lit, fig)* to work one's way up; **~führen** *vti sep* to lead up; **~gehen** *vi sep irreg aux sein* to go up; **mit dem Preis ~gehen** to put up the price; **~reichen** *sep* **1** *vi* to reach up; **2** *vt* to pass up; **~ziehen** *vt sep irreg* to pull up.

hinaus *adv* **(a)** *(räumlich)* out. **~ (mit dir)!** (get) out!, out you go!; **über** *(+acc)* **~** beyond, over; **hier/dort ~** this/that way out; **hinten/vorn ~** at the back/front; **zur Straße ~** facing the street. **(b)** *(zeitlich)* **auf Jahre ~** for years to come; **bis weit über die Siebzig ~** until well over seventy; **über Mittwoch ~** until after Wednesday. **(c)** *(fig)* **über** *(+acc)* **... ~** over and above ...; **darüber ~** over and above this.

hinaus-: ~befördern* *vt sep (col) jdn* to kick out *(col) (aus* of*)*; **~drängen** *sep (aus* of*)* **1** *vt* to force out; *(eilig)* to hustle out; **2** *vi aux sein* to push one's way out; **~fahren** *sep irreg* **1** *vi aux sein* **(a) aus etw ~fahren** to go out of sth, to leave sth; **(b)** *(reisen)* to go out; **aufs Meer ~fahren** to put out to sea; **2** *vt Wagen* to drive out *(aus* of*)*; **~finden** *vi sep irreg* to find the way out *(aus* of*)*; **~fliegen** *vi sep irreg aux sein* **(a)** to fly out *(aus* of*)*; **(b)** *(col: ~geworfen werden)* to get kicked out *(col)*; **~führen** *sep* **1** *vi* **(a)** to lead out *(aus* of*)*; **(b) über etw** *(acc)* **~führen** *(lit, fig)* to go beyond sth; **2** *vt* to lead out *(aus* of*)*; *(Weg, Reise)* to take *(über +acc* beyond*)*; **~gehen** *sep irreg aux sein* **1** *vi* **(a)** to go out(side); **(b) auf etw** *(acc)* **~gehen** *(Tür)* to open onto sth; *(Fenster auch)* to look onto sth; **(c)** *(fig: überschreiten)* **über etw** *(acc)* **~gehen** to go beyond sth; **das geht über meine Kräfte ~** it's too much for me; **2** *vi impers* **wo geht es ~?** where's the way out?; **~kommen** *vi sep irreg aux sein* **(a)** to come out(side); **(b)** *(fig: ~laufen)* **das kommt auf dasselbe ~** it boils down to *or* comes to the same thing; **~komplimentieren*** *vt sep (hum)* to usher out *(aus* of*)*; **~laufen** *vi sep irreg aux sein (aus* of*)* **(a)** *(lit)* to run out; **(b)** *(fig)* **es läuft auf dasselbe ~** it amounts *or* comes to the same thing; **~lehnen** *vr sep* to lean out *(aus* of*)*; **~nehmen** *vt sep irreg* to take out *(aus* of*)*; **~ragen** *vi sep aux sein* to jut out *(über +acc* beyond*)*; **über jdn/etw ~ragen** *(fig)* to tower above sb/sth; **~schaffen** *vt sep* to take out *(aus* of*)*; **~schieben** *vt sep irreg* **(a)** *Gegenstand* to push out *(aus* of*)*; **(b)** *(fig)* to put off, to postpone; **~schießen** *vi sep irreg aux sein (~rennen)* to shoot out *(aus* of*)*;

über das Ziel ~schießen *(fig)* to overshoot the mark; **~schmeißen** *vt sep irreg (col)* to kick *or* chuck out *(col) (aus* of*)*; **~sehen** *vi sep irreg* to look out *(aus* of*)*; **~sein** *vi sep irreg aux sein* **über etw** *(acc)* **~sein** *über Kindereien, ein Alter* to be past sth; *über Enttäuschungen* to have got over sth; **~setzen** *vt sep* to put out(side); **jdn ~setzen** *(col)* to kick sb out *(col)*; **~stellen** *vt sep* to put out(side); *Sportler* to send off; **~strecken** *vt sep* to stick *or* put out *(aus* of*)*; **~stürzen** *vi sep aux sein (aus* of*)* **(a)** *(~fallen)* to fall out; **(b)** *(~eilen)* to rush out; **~tragen** *vt sep irreg* **(a)** to carry out *(aus* of*)*; **(b) etw in alle Welt ~tragen** to spread sth abroad; **~wachsen** *vi sep irreg aux sein* **über etw** *(acc)* **~wachsen** *(fig)* to outgrow sth; **er wuchs über sich selbst ~** he surpassed himself; **~weisen** *sep irreg* **1** *vt* **jdn ~weisen** to show sb the door; **2** *vi* to point out(wards); **~werfen** *vt sep irreg (aus* of*)* **(a)** to throw out; **einen Blick ~werfen** to take a look out(side); **(b)** *(col: entfernen)* to chuck *or* kick out *(col)*; **~wollen** *vi sep* to want to get out *(aus* of*)*; **worauf willst du ~?** *(fig)* what are you getting *or* driving at?; **hoch ~wollen** to aim high; **~ziehen** *sep irreg* **1** *vt* **(a)** *(nach draußen ziehen)* to pull out *(aus* of*)*; **(b)** *(fig) Verhandlungen etc* to protract, to drag out; *Urlaub etc* to prolong; **2** *vi aux sein* to go out *(aus* of*)*; **aufs Land ~ziehen** to move out into the country; **3** *vr (Verhandlungen etc)* to drag on; *(Abfahrt etc)* to be delayed; **~zögern** *sep* **1** *vt* to delay, to put off; **2** *vr* to be delayed, to be put off.

hin-: **~bekommen*** *vt sep irreg (col)* **das hast du gut ~bekommen** you've made a good job of it; **~blättern** *vt sep (col) Geld* to fork out *(col)*; **H~blick** *m*: **im** *or* **in H~blick auf** *(+acc) (angesichts)* in view of; *(mit Bezug auf)* with regard to; **~blicken** *vi sep* to look *(auf+acc, nach* at, towards*)*; **~bringen** *vt sep irreg* **(a)** to take there; **(b)** *(fig) Zeit* to spend; **(c)** *(fig col: zustande bringen)* to get done.

hinderlich *adj* **~ sein** to be in the way; **jds Karriere** *(dat)* **~ sein** to be a hindrance to sb's career; **jdm ~ sein** to get in sb's way.

hindern **1** *vt* **(a)** *Wachstum* to impede; *jdn* to hinder *(bei* in*)*. **(b)** *(abhalten von)* to prevent *(an +dat* from*)*, to stop. **ich will Sie nicht ~** I shan't stand in your way. **2** *vi* to be a hindrance *(bei* to*)*.

Hindernis *nt* **(a)** *(lit, fig)* obstacle; *(beim Sprechen)* impediment. **sie empfand das Kind als ~ für ihre Karriere** she saw the child as a hindrance to *or* an obstacle for her career. **(b)** *(beim ~ lauf)* jump.

Hindernis-: **~lauf** *m*, **~rennen** *nt* steeplechase.

Hinderungsgrund *m* obstacle.

hindeuten *vi sep* to point *(auf +acc, zu* at*)*. **es deutet alles darauf hin, daß ...** everything indicates that ...

hindrehen *vt sep (fig col)* to sort out.

hindurch *adv* through. **mitten ~** straight through; **das ganze Jahr ~** throughout the year; **die ganze Zeit ~** all the time; **Jahre ~** for years.

hindurchgehen *vi sep irreg aux sein (lit, fig)* to go through *(durch etw* sth*)*.

hindürfen *vi sep irreg* to be allowed to go *(zu* to*)*.

hinein *adv* in. **~ mit dir!** *(col)* in you go!; **in etw** *(acc)* **~** into sth; **bis tief in die Nacht ~** well into the night.

hinein- *pref* in; *siehe auch* **ein-, herein-;** **~bekommen*** *vt sep irreg (col)* to get in *(in+acc* to*)*; **~blicken** *vi sep* to look in *(in+acc* -to*)*; **~bringen** *vt sep irreg (~tragen)* to bring/take in *(in+acc* -to*)*; **~denken** *vr sep irreg* **sich in ein Problem ~denken** to think oneself into a problem; **sich in jdn ~denken** to put oneself in sb's position; **~fallen** *vi sep irreg aux sein* to fall in *(in+acc* -to*)*; **~finden** *vr sep irreg (fig) (sich vertraut machen)* to find one's feet; *(sich abfinden)* to come to terms with it; **~fressen** *vt sep irreg (col)* **etw in sich** *(acc)* **~fressen** *(lit)* to wolf sth (down) *(col)*; *(fig) Kummer etc* to suppress sth; **~gehen** *vi sep irreg aux sein* **(a)** to go in; **in etw** *(acc)* **~gehen** to go into sth; **(b)** *(~passen)* to go in *(in+acc* to*)*; **~geraten*** *vi sep irreg aux sein* **in etw** *(acc)* **~geraten** to get involved in sth; **~knien** *vr sep (fig col)* **sich in etw** *(acc)* **~knien** to get into sth *(col)*; **~kommen** *vi sep irreg aux sein (in+acc* -to*)* **(a)** to come in; **(b)** *(lit, fig: ~gelangen können)* to get in; **~kriegen** *vt sep (col)* to get in *(in+acc* -to*)*; **~legen** *vt sep (lit, fig)* to put in *(in +acc* -to*)*; **~lesen** *vt sep irreg* **etw in etw** *(acc)* **~lesen** to read sth into sth; **~passen** *vi sep* **in etw** *(acc)* **~passen** to fit into sth; *(fig)* to fit in with sth; **~platzen** *vi sep aux sein (fig col)* to burst in *(in +acc* -to*)*; **~reden** *vi sep (lit: unterbrechen)* to interrupt *(jdm* sb*)*; **jdm ~reden** *(fig: sich einmischen)* to interfere in sb's affairs; **~schlagen** *vt sep irreg (in+acc* -to*) Nagel* to knock in; **~schlingen** *vt sep irreg* **etw (gierig) in sich ~schlingen** to devour sth (greedily); **~schütten** *vt sep* to pour in *(in+acc* -to*)*; **etw in sich ~schütten** *(col)* to knock sth back *(col)*; **~setzen** *sep* **1** *vt* to put in *(in+acc* -to*)*; **2** *vr (in Fahrzeug)* to get into *(in etw (acc)* sth*)*; *(in Sessel)* to sit (oneself) down *(in +acc* in(to)*)*; **~spielen** *vi sep (beeinflussen)* to have a part to play *(in+acc* in*)*; **~stecken** *vt sep (in+acc* -to*)* to put in; **Geld/Arbeit in etw** *(acc)* **~stecken** to put money/some work into sth; **~steigern** *vr sep* to get worked up; **sich in seinen Ärger ~steigern** to work oneself up into a temper; **sie hat sich in die Vorstellung ~gesteigert, daß ...** she has managed to convince herself that ...; **~stopfen** *vt sep* to stuff *or* cram in *(in+acc* -to*)*; **Essen in sich** *(acc)* **~stopfen** to stuff oneself with food; **~stürzen** *sep* **1** *vi aux sein* to plunge in *(in+acc* -to*)*; *(~eilen)* to rush in *(in+ acc* -to*)*; **2** *vt* to throw *or* hurl in *(in +acc* -to*)*; **3** *vr* to plunge in *(in+acc* -to*)*; **sich in die Arbeit ~stürzen** to throw oneself into one's work; **sich ins Vergnügen ~stürzen** to plunge in and start enjoying oneself, to let it all hang out *(col)*; **~tun** *vt sep irreg* to put in *(in+acc* -to*)*; **einen Blick in etw** *(acc)* **~tun** to take a look in sth; *ins Buch etc* to take a look at sth; **~versetzen*** *vr sep* **sich in jdn** *or* **in jds Lage ~versetzen** to put oneself in sb's position; **sich in eine Rolle ~versetzen** to empathize with a part; **~wachsen** *vi sep irreg aux sein* **in etw** *(acc)* **~wachsen** *(lit, fig)* to grow into sth; **~wollen** *vi sep (col)* to want to get in *(in +acc* -to*)*; **~ziehen** *vt sep irreg* to pull *or* drag in *(in+acc* -to*)*; **jdn in eine Angelegenheit ~ziehen** to drag sb into an affair.

hin-: **~fahren** *sep irreg* **1** *vi aux sein* to go there; *(mit Fahrzeug auch)* to drive there; **2** *vt* to drive *or* take there; **H~fahrt** *f* outward journey; *(Naut)* voyage out; **~fallen** *vi sep irreg aux sein* to fall (down).

hinfällig *adj* **(a)** frail. **(b)** *(fig: ungültig)* invalid.

hin-: **~finden** *vir sep irreg (col)* to find one's way there; **~fliegen** *vi sep irreg aux sein* to fly there; *(col: ~fallen)* to fall over; **H~flug** *m* outward flight.

hinführen *vti sep* to lead there. **wo soll das ~?** *(fig)* where is this leading to?

hing *pret of* **hängen.**

Hingabe *f no pl (fig) (Begeisterung)* dedication; *(Selbstlosigkeit)* devotion. **mit ~ tanzen/singen** *etc* to dance/sing *etc* with abandon.

hingeben *sep irreg* **1** *vt* to give up. **2** *vr* **sich einer Sache** *(dat)* **~** *der Arbeit* to devote oneself to sth; *dem Laster, der Verzweiflung* to abandon oneself to sth; **sich Hoffnungen/einer Illusion ~** to cherish hopes/to labour *(Brit) or* labor *(US)* under an illusion; **sie gab sich ihm hin** she gave herself to him.

hingebungsvoll **1** *adj (selbstlos)* devoted. **2** *adv* devotedly; *(begeistert)* with abandon; *lauschen* raptly.

hingegen *conj* however.

hin-: ~**gehen** *vi sep irreg aux sein* **(a)** *(dorthin gehen)* to go (there); **gehst du auch** ~? are you going too?; **wo geht es hier** ~? where does this go?; **(b)** *(fig: tragbar sein)* **das geht gerade noch** ~ that will just about do; ~**gehören*** *vi sep* to belong; ~**gelangen*** *vi sep aux sein* to go there; ~**geraten*** *vi sep irreg aux sein* **irgendwo** ~**geraten** to get somewhere; **wo bin ich denn hier** ~**geraten?** *(col)* what kind of place is this then?; ~**gerissen** *adj* enraptured; ~**gerissen lauschen** to listen with rapt attention; **ich bin ganz** ~**- und hergerissen** *(iro)* that's absolutely great *(iro)*; ~**halten** *vt sep irreg* **(a)** *lit* to hold out *(jdm* to sb*)*; **(b)** *(fig) jdn* to put off, to stall.

hinhauen *sep irreg (col)* **1** *vt* **(a)** *(nachlässig machen)* to knock off *(col)*. **(b)** *(hinwerfen)* to slam down. **2** *vi* **(a)** *(zuschlagen)* to hit hard. **(b)** *aux sein (fallen)* to fall flat. **(c)** *(gutgehen)* **das wird schon** ~ it will be OK *(col) or* all right. **(d)** *(klappen)* to work. **(e)** *(ausreichen)* to do. **3** *vr (col) (sich schlafen legen)* to crash out *(col)*.

hinhören *vi sep* to listen.

hinken *vi* **(a)** to limp. **(b)** *(fig: Beispiel, Vergleich)* to be inappropriate.

hin-: ~**kommen** *vi sep irreg aux sein* **(a) (da)** ~**kommen** to get there; **wie komme ich zu dir** ~? how do I get to your place?; **(b)** *(gehören)* to go; **wo ist das Buch** ~**gekommen?** where has the book got to?; **wo kämen wir denn** ~**, wenn ...** *(col)* where would we be if ...; **(c)** *(col: auskommen)* to manage; **wir kommen (damit)** ~ we'll manage; **(d)** *(col: ausreichen, stimmen)* to be right; ~**kriegen** *vt sep (col)* **(a)** *(fertigbringen)* to do, to manage; **(b)** *(in Ordnung bringen)* to mend, to fix; *(gesundheitlich)* to cure; ~**langen** *vi sep (col) (zupacken)* to grab him/her *etc; (anfassen)* to touch; *(zuschlagen)* to take a (good) swipe *(col)*; ~**länglich 1** *adj* adequate; **2** *adv* adequately; *(zu Genüge)* sufficiently; ~**laufen** *vi sep irreg aux sein* **(a)** to run there; **(b)** *(col: nicht fahren)* to walk; ~**legen** *sep* **1** *vt* **(a)** to put down; *Zettel* to leave *(jdm* for sb*)*; *Verletzten etc* to lay down; *(col: bezahlen müssen)* to fork out *(col)*; **(b)** *(col: glänzend darbieten)* to give; **2** *vr* to lie down; **sich der Länge nach** ~**legen** *(col)* to fall flat; ~**nehmen** *vt sep irreg (ertragen)* to take; ~**neigen** *sep* **1** *vr (zu* towards*) (Mensch)* to lean; *(fig)* to incline; **2** *vi (fig)* **zu etw** ~**neigen** to incline towards sth; ~**passen** *vi sep* to fit (in); *(gut aussehen)* to go (well); ~**reichen** *vi sep* **(a)** *(ausreichen)* to be enough; **(b)** *(sich erstrecken)* **bis zu etw** ~**reichen** to stretch to sth; ~**reichend** *adj (ausreichend)* adequate; *(genug)* sufficient; *(reichlich)* ample; **H**~**reise** *f* journey out, outward journey; *(mit Schiff)* outward voyage; ~**reißen** *vt sep irreg (fig: begeistern)* to thrill; **sich** ~**reißen lassen** to let oneself get carried away; *siehe* ~**gerissen;** ~**reißend** *adj Landschaft, Anblick* enchanting; *Schönheit, Mensch* captivating; ~**richten** *vt sep* to execute; **H**~**richtung** *f* execution; ~**sagen** *vt sep* to say without thinking; ~**schaffen** *vt sep* **etw zu jdm** ~**schaffen** to get sth to sb; ~**schauen** *vi sep siehe* ~**sehen;** ~**schicken** *vt sep* to send; ~**schleppen** *sep* **1** *vt* to carry, to lug *(col)*; *(col: mitnehmen)* to drag along; **2** *vr (Mensch)* to drag oneself along; *(fig)* to drag on; ~**schmeißen** *vt sep irreg (col) (hinwerfen)* to fling down *(col)*; *(fig: aufgeben) Arbeit etc* to chuck in *(col)*, to pack in *(Brit col)*; ~**schreiben** *sep irreg* **1** *vt* to write; *(flüchtig)* to scribble down *(col)*; **2** *vi (col)* to write; ~**sehen** *vi sep irreg* to look; **ich kann (gar) nicht** ~**sehen** I can't bear to look; **bei genauerem H**~**sehen** on closer inspection.

hinsein *vi sep irreg aux sein (col)* **(a)** *(kaputt sein)* to have had it *(col)*. **(b)** *(verloren sein)* to be lost; *(Ruhe)* to be gone; *(ruiniert sein)* to be in ruins. **(c)** *(col: tot sein)* to have kicked the bucket *(col)*. **(d)** *(begeistert sein)* **(von etw)** ~ to be mad about sth *(col)*. **(e) bis dahin ist es noch lange hin** it's a long time till then.

hinsetzen *sep* **1** *vt* to put *or* set down. **2** *vr* to sit down.

Hinsicht *f no pl* **in dieser** ~ in this respect; **in mancher** *or* **gewisser** ~ in some *or* many respects *or* ways; **in finanzieller/wirtschaftlicher** ~ financially/economically; **in beruflicher** ~ with regard to my/his job.

hinsichtlich *prep+gen (bezüglich)* with regard to; *(in Anbetracht)* in view of.

hin-: ~**sollen** *vi sep (col)* **wo soll ich/das Buch** ~? where do I/does the book go?; **H**~**spiel** *nt (Sport)* first leg; ~**stellen** *sep* **1** *vt* **(a)** to put down; *(col) Gebäude* to put up; *(abstellen) Fahrzeug* to put; **(b) jdn/etw als jdn/etw** ~**stellen** to make sb/sth out to be sb/sth; **2** *vr* to stand; *(Fahrer)* to park; ~**strecken** *sep* **1** *vt Hand, Gegenstand* to hold out; **2** *vr* to stretch out.

hint|an-: ~**setzen,** ~**stellen** *vt sep (zurückstellen)* to put last; *(vernachlässigen)* to neglect.

hinten *adv* **(a)** behind; *(am rückwärtigen Ende)* at the back. **ein Blick nach** ~ a look behind; **von weit** ~ from the very back; ~ **im Buch/auf der Liste** at the back of the book/at the end of the list; **sich** ~ **anstellen** to join the end of the queue *(Brit) or* line *(US)*; ~ **im Bild** in the back of the picture; **etw** ~ **anfügen** to add sth at the end; **von** ~ from behind; ~ **im Auto** in the back of the car; **nach** ~ *fallen, ziehen* backwards; **ich sehe ihn am liebsten von** ~ *(col)* I'll be glad to see the back of him; **ein nach** ~ **gelegenes Zimmer** a room facing the back; **das Auto da** ~ the car back there; **sie waren ziemlich weit** ~ they were quite far back.

(b) *(fig)* ~ **und vorn** *betrügen* left, right and centre *(Brit) or* center *(US)*; *bedienen* hand and foot; **das stimmt** ~ **und vorn nicht** that is absolutely untrue; **das reicht** ~ **und vorn nicht** that's nowhere near enough; **ich weiß nicht mehr, wo** ~ **und vorn ist** I don't know whether I'm coming or going.

hinten-: ~**dran** *adv (col)* at the back; ~**herum** *adv* **(a)** from the back; **kommen Sie** ~**herum** come around the back; **(b)** *(fig col) (auf Umwegen)* in a roundabout way; *(illegal)* under the counter; ~**über** *adv* **er fiel** ~**über** he fell over backwards.

hinter *prep +dat or (mit Bewegungsverben) +acc* **(a)** behind. ~ **jdm/etw her** behind sb/sth; ~ **die Wahrheit kommen** to get to the truth; **sich** ~ **jdn stellen** *(fig)* to support sb; ~**jdm/etw stehen** *(lit, fig)* to be behind sb/sth; ~ **der Tür hervor** (out) from behind the door; **jdn weit** ~ **sich** *(dat)* **lassen** to leave sb a long way behind; **vier Kilometer** ~ **der Grenze** four kilometres beyond the border. **(b) etw** ~ **sich** *(dat)* **haben** *(zurückgelegt haben)* to have got through sth; *Strecke* to have covered sth; *(überstanden haben)* to have got sth over with; *anstrengende Tage* to have had sth; *Studium* to have completed sth; **sie hat viel** ~ **sich** she has been through a lot; **etw** ~ **sich** *(acc)* **bringen** to get sth over with; *Strecke* to cover sth; *Arbeit* to get sth done.

Hinter-: ~**achse** *f* rear axle; ~**ausgang** *m* back *or* rear exit; ~**backe** *f usu pl* buttock; **sich auf die** ~**backen setzen** *(fig col)* to get down to it; ~**bänkler** *m - (Pol pej)* backbencher; ~**bein** *nt* **sich auf die** ~**beine stellen** *or* **setzen** *(fig col: sich anstrengen)* to pull one's socks up *(col)*.

Hinterbliebene(r) *mf decl as adj* surviving dependent. **die** ~**n** the bereaved family.

hinter|einander *adv* one behind the other; *(nicht gleichzeitig)* one after the other. ~ **hereinkommen** to come in one by one; **zwei Tage** ~ two days running; **dreimal** ~ three times in a row.

hinter|einander-: **~her** *adv* behind one another; **~schalten** *vt sep (Elec)* to connect in series.

hintere(r, s) *adj* back; *(von Tier, Gebäude, Zug auch)* rear. **der/die/das H~** the one at the back.

Hinter-: **h~fragen*** *vt insep* to analyze; **~gedanke** *m* ulterior motive; **h~gehen*** *vt insep irreg (betrügen)* to deceive; *(umgehen) Gesetze* to circumvent.

Hintergrund *m (von Bild, fig)* background; *(von Saal)* back; *(Theat: Kulisse)* backcloth. **im ~** in the background; **im ~ der Bühne** at the back of the stage; **vor dem ~** *(lit, fig)* against the background; **in den ~ treten** *(fig)* to retreat into the background.

Hinter-: **h~gründig** *adj* cryptic, enigmatic; **~halt** *m* **(a)** ambush; **jdn aus dem ~halt überfallen** to ambush sb; **im ~halt lauern** to lie in wait; **(b)** *(col)* **etw im ~halt haben** to have sth in reserve; **h~hältig** *adj* underhand(ed), devious; **~hältigkeit** *f* underhandedness, deviousness.

hinterher *adv* behind; *(zeitlich)* afterwards.

hinterher-: **~kommen** *vi sep irreg aux sein* **(a)** *(räumlich)* to follow (behind); *(zeitlich)* to come after; **(b)** *(als letzter kommen)* to bring up the rear; **~laufen** *vi sep irreg aux sein* to run behind *(jdm* sb*)*; **jdm ~laufen** *(fig col: sich bemühen um)* to run around after sb; **~sein** *vi sep irreg aux sein (col)* to be after *(jdm* sb*)*; **~sein, daß ...** *(fig)* to see to it that ...

Hinter-: **~hof** *m* backyard; **~kopf** *m* back of one's head; **etw im ~kopf haben/behalten** *(col)* to have/keep sth in the back of one's mind; **~land** *nt* hinterland; **h~lassen*** *vt insep irreg* to leave; *(jdm etw* sb sth*)*; **h~lassene Werke/Schriften** posthumous works; **~lassenschaft** *f* estate; *(literarisch, fig)* legacy; **h~legen*** *vt insep* to deposit; *(als Pfand)* to leave; **~legung** *f* deposit.

Hinterlist *f no pl* **(a)** *siehe adj* craftiness, cunning; deceitfulness. **(b)** *(Trick, List)* ruse, trick.

hinterlistig *adj (tückisch)* crafty, cunning; *(betrügerisch)* deceitful.

Hintermann *m, pl* **¨er** **(a)** person/car behind (one). **mein ~** the person/car behind me. **(b)** *(Gewährsmann)* contact. **die ¨er des Skandals** the men behind the scandal.

Hintern *m* **-** *(col)* bottom, backside *(col)*. **jdm den ~ versohlen** to smack sb's bottom; **ein paar auf den ~ bekommen** to get one's bottom smacked; **sich auf den ~ setzen** *(eifrig arbeiten)* to buckle down to work; **jdm in den ~ kriechen** to suck up to sb.

Hinter-: **~rad** *nt* rear *or* back wheel; **h~rücks** *adv* from behind; *(fig: heimtückisch)* behind sb's back; **~seite** *f* back; **h~sinnig** *adj* cryptic.

hinterste(r, s) *adj superl of* **hintere(r, s)** very back; *(entlegenste)* remotest.

Hinter-: **~teil** *nt* **(a)** *(col)* backside *(col)*; *(von Tier)* hindquarters *pl;* **(b)** *auch m* back *or* rear part; **~treffen** *nt* **im ~treffen sein** to be at a disadvantage; **ins ~treffen geraten** to fall behind; **h~treiben*** *vt insep irreg (fig)* to foil, to thwart; *Gesetz* to block; **~treppe** *f* back stairs *pl;* **~tür** *f* back door; *(fig col)* loophole; **durch die ~tür** *(fig)* through the back door; **sich** *(dat)* **eine ~tür** *or* **ein ~türchen offenhalten** *(fig)* to leave oneself a loophole *or* a way out; **~wäldler** *m* **-** *(col)* backwoodsman, hillbilly *(esp US)*; **~wäldlerisch** *adj (col)* backwoods *attr;* **h~ziehen*** *vt insep irreg Steuern* to evade; *Material* to appropriate; **~ziehung** *f siehe vt* evasion; appropriation; **~zimmer** *nt* back room.

hintun *vt sep irreg (col)* to put. **ich weiß nicht, wo ich ihn ~ soll** *(fig)* I can't (quite) place him.

hinüber *adv* over; *(über Straße auch)* across.

hinüber-: **~fahren** *sep irreg* **1** *vt (über etw (acc)* sth*)* to take across; *Auto* to drive across; **2** *vi aux sein* to travel *or* go across; **über den Fluß ~fahren** to cross the river; **~führen** *sep* **1** *vt* **jdn (über die Straße) ~führen** to take sb across (the street); **2** *vi Straße, Brücke* to go across *(über etw (acc)* sth*)*; **~gehen** *vi sep irreg aux sein* to go across *or* over; **~kommen** *vi sep irreg aux sein (über etw (acc)* sth*)* to come across; *(über Hindernis, zu Besuch)* to come over; *(~können)* to get across/over; **~reichen** *sep* **1** *vt* to pass across; *(über Zaun etc)* to pass over *(jdm* to sb, *über etw (acc)* sth*)*; **2** *vi* to reach across *(über etw (acc)* sth*)*; *(fig)* to extend *(in +acc* into*)*; **~sein** *vi sep irreg aux sein (col) (verdorben sein)* to be off *(Brit) or* bad; *(unbrauchbar, tot sein)* to have had it *(col)*; **~wechseln** *vi sep aux haben or sein* to change over *(zu, in+acc* to*)*; **~ziehen** *sep irreg* **1** *vt* to pull across *(über etw (acc)* sth*)*; *(fig: umstimmen)* to win over *(auf+acc* to*)*; **2** *vi aux sein Wolken etc* to move across *(über etw (acc)* sth*)*.

hinunter **1** *adv* down. **bis ~ zu** down to. **2** *prep +acc* **den Berg ~** down the mountain.

hinunter- *pref* down; **~bringen** *vt sep irreg* to take down; **das bringe ich nicht ~** *(col) (trinken)* I can't drink that stuff; **~gehen** *vi sep irreg aux sein* to go down; *(Flugzeug)* to descend *(auf+acc* to*)*; **~gießen** *vt sep irreg,* **~kippen** *vt sep (col) Getränke* to knock back *(col)*; **~schlingen** *vt sep irreg (col)* to gulp down; *Essen* to gobble down; **~schlucken** *vt sep* to swallow (down); *(fig) Beleidigung* to swallow; *Kritik* to take; *Ärger, Tränen* to choke back; **~spülen** *vt sep* **(a)** to flush away; **(b)** *Essen, Tablette* to wash down; *(fig) Ärger* to soothe; **~stürzen** *sep* **1** *vi aux sein* **(a)** *(~fallen)* to tumble down; **(b)** *(eilig ~laufen)* to rush down; **2** *vt jdn* to throw *or* hurl down; *Getränk* to gulp down; **3** *vr* to throw *or* fling oneself down.

Hinweg *m* way there. **auf dem ~** on the way there.

hinweg *adv* **(a)** *(old: fort)* away. **(b)** **über jdn ~** *(fig)* over sb's head; **über eine Zeit/zwei Jahre ~** over a period of time/over (a period of) two years.

hinweg- *pref* away; **~bringen** *vt sep irreg (fig)* **jdn über etw** *(acc)* **~bringen** to help sb to get over sth; **~gehen** *vi sep irreg aux sein* **über etw** *(acc)* **~gehen** *(fig)* to pass over sth; **~helfen** *vi sep irreg (fig)* **jdm über etw** *(acc)* **~helfen** to help sb get over sth; **~kommen** *vi sep irreg aux sein (fig)* **über etw** *(acc)* **~kommen** to get over sth; **ich komme nicht darüber ~, daß ...** *(col)* I can't get over the fact that ...; **~sehen** *vi sep irreg* **über jdn/etw ~sehen** *(fig)* to ignore sb/sth; **darüber ~sehen, daß ...** to overlook the fact that ...; **~setzen** *vr sep (fig)* **sich über etw** *(acc)* **~setzen** to disregard sth; **~täuschen** *vt sep* **darüber ~täuschen, daß ...** to hide the fact that ...; **sich nicht darüber ~täuschen lassen, daß ...** not to blind oneself to the fact that ...; **~trösten** *vt sep* **jdn über etw** *(acc)* **~trösten** to console sb about sth.

Hinweis *m* **-e** **(a)** *(Rat)* tip, piece of advice; *(amtlich)* notice. **darf ich mir den ~ erlauben, daß ...?** may I point out that ...?; **~e für den Benutzer** notes for the user. **(b)** *(Verweis)* reference. **unter ~ auf** *(+acc)* with reference to. **(c)** *(Anhaltspunkt)* indication. **sachdienliche ~e** relevant information.

hinweisen *sep irreg* **1** *vt* **jdn auf etw** *(acc)* **~** to point sth out to sb. **2** *vi* **auf jdn/etw ~** to point to sb/sth; *(verweisen)* to refer to sb/sth; **darauf ~, daß ...** to point out that ...; *(nachdrücklich)* to stress that ...; *(anzeigen)* to indicate that ...

Hinweis-: **~schild** *nt,* **~tafel** *f* sign.

hin-: **~wenden** *vtr sep irreg* to turn *(zu, nach* towards*)*; **H~wendung** *f (fig)* turn *(zu* toward*)*; **~werfen** *sep irreg* **1** *vt* **(a)** to throw down; **jdm etw ~werfen** to throw sth to sb; **(b)** *Bemerkung* to drop casually; *Wort* to say casually; **eine ~geworfene Bemerkung** a casual remark; **(c)** *(col: aufgeben) Arbeit, Stelle* to chuck (in) *(col)*; **2** *vr* to throw *or* fling oneself down; **~wirken** *vi sep* **auf etw** *(acc)* **~wirken** to work towards sth.

Hinz *m:* **~ und Kunz** *(col)* every Tom, Dick and Harry *(col)*.

hin-: **~ziehen** *sep irreg* **1** *vt* **(a)** *(zu sich ziehen)* to draw *or* pull *(zu* towards*)*; *(fig: anziehen)* to attract *(zu* to*)*; **(b)** *(fig: in die Länge ziehen)* to drag out; **2** *vi aux sein* **(a)** to move *(über+acc* across, *zu* towards*)*; **(b)** *Wolken, Rauch* to drift, to move *(an +dat* across*)*; **3** *vr* **(a)** *(lange dauern)* to drag on; **(b)** *(sich erstrecken)* to stretch, to extend; **~zielen** *vi sep* **auf etw** *(acc)* **~zielen** to aim at sth.

hinzu *adv (obendrein)* besides, in addition.

hinzu-: **~fügen** *vt sep* to add *(dat* to*)*; *(beilegen)* to enclose; **H~fügung** *f* addition; **unter H~fügung von etw** *(form)* by adding sth; **~kommen** *vi sep irreg aux sein* **(a) sie kam gerade ~, als ...** she happened to come on the scene when ...; **es werden später noch mehrere ~kommen** more people will be joining us later; **(b)** *(zusätzlich eintreten)* to ensue; *(beigefügt werden)* to be added; **es kommt noch ~, daß ...** there is also the fact that ...; **kommt sonst noch etwas ~?** will there be anything else?; **~nehmen** *vt sep irreg* to include; **~treten** *vi sep irreg aux sein* **(a)** *(herantreten)* to come up; **zu den anderen ~treten** to join the others; **(b)** *(zusätzlich) siehe* **~kommen (b)**; **~tun** *vt sep irreg (col)* to add; **~zählen** *vt sep* to add; **~ziehen** *vt sep irreg* to consult.

Hiobsbotschaft *f* bad news *no pl*.

Hirn *nt* **-e (a)** *(Anat)* brain. **(b)** *(col) (Kopf)* head; *(Verstand)* brains *pl,* mind. **sich** *(dat)* **das ~ zermartern** to rack one's brain(s); **streng einmal dein ~ an** think hard. **(c)** *(Cook)* brains *pl*.

Hirn- *siehe auch* **Gehirn-;** **~gespinst** *nt* fantasy; **~hautentzündung** *f (Med)* meningitis; **h~rissig, h~verbrannt** *adj* hare-brained.

Hirsch *m* **-e** deer; *(Rot~)* red deer; *(männlicher Rot~)* stag; *(Cook)* venison.

Hirsch-: **~käfer** *m* stag-beetle; **~kuh** *f* hind; **~leder** *nt* buckskin, deerskin.

Hirse *f* **-n** millet.

Hirt *m (wk)* **-en, -en** herdsman; *(Schaf~)* shepherd.

Hirte *m* **-n** *(Eccl)* shepherd. **der Gute ~** the Good Shepherd.

Hirtenhund *m* sheepdog.

hissen *vt* to hoist.

Historiker(in *f***)** *m* **-** historian.

historisch *adj* historical; *(bedeutsam) Ereignis* historic. **das ist ~ belegt** there is historical evidence for this.

Hit *m* **-s** *(Mus, fig col)* hit.

Hit-: **~liste** *f* charts *pl;* **~parade** *f* hit parade.

Hitze *f* **-n (a)** heat; *(~zeit, ~welle)* hot spell. **vor ~ umkommen** to be sweltering; **bei starker/mäßiger ~ backen** *(Cook)* bake in a hot/moderate oven. **(b)** *(fig)* passion. **in ~/leicht in ~ geraten** to get heated/to get worked up easily; **sich in ~ reden** to get oneself all worked up; **in der ~ des Gefecht(e)s** *(fig)* in the heat of the moment.

Hitze-: **h~beständig** *adj* heat-resistant; **~beständigkeit** *f* heat resistance; **h~empfindlich** *adj* sensitive to heat; **h~frei** *adj* **h~frei haben** *to have time off from school on account of excessively hot weather;* **~welle** *f* heat wave.

hitzig *adj* **(a)** *Mensch* hot-headed; *Streit, Debatte* heated; *Temperament* passionate. **~ werden** *(Mensch)* to flare up; *(Debatte)* to grow heated; **nicht so ~!** don't get excited! **(b)** *(Zool)* on heat.

Hitz-: **~kopf** *m* hothead; **h~köpfig** *adj* hot-headed; **~schlag** *m (Med)* heat-stroke.

hl. = **heilig.**

Hl. = **Heilige(r)** St.

H-Milch ['haː-] *f* long-life milk.

HNO-Arzt [haː|ɛn'|oː-] *m* ENT specialist.

hob *pret of* **heben.**

Hobby *nt* **-s** hobby.

Hobel *m* **-** *(Tech)* plane; *(Cook)* slicer.

Hobel-: **~bank** *f* carpenter's bench; **~maschine** *f* planer, planing machine.

hobeln *vt* **(a)** *auch vi (Tech)* to plane *(an etw (dat)* sth*)*. **wo gehobelt wird, da fallen Späne** *(Prov)* you can't make an omelette *(Brit) or* omelet *(US)* without breaking eggs *(Prov)*. **(b)** *(Cook)* to slice.

Hoch *nt* **-s (a) ein ~ dem Brautpaar** a toast to the bride and groom. **(b)** *(Met, fig)* high.

hoch *attr* **hohe(r, s)** *comp* **höher,** *superl* **¨ste(r, s)** *or (adv)* **am ¨sten 1** *adj* high; *Baum, Leiter* tall; *Betrag* large; *Strafe, Gewicht* heavy; *Profit, Verlust auch, Lotteriegewinn* big; *Gut, Glück, Alter* great; *Schaden* extensive; *Persönlichkeit* distinguished; *Besuch, Feiertag* important; *Offizier* high-ranking. **das Hohe Haus** *(Parl)* the House; **ein hohes Tier** *(col)* a big fish *(col)*; **das Hohe C** top C; **ein hohes Alter erreichen** to live to a ripe old age; **das ist mir zu ~** *(col)* that's above my head; **hohe Flut** spring tide; **der hohe Norden** the far North.

2 *adv* **(a)** *(nach oben)* up; *(in einiger Höhe)* high. **er sah zu uns ~** he looked up to us; **~ emporragend** towering (up); **die Nase ~ tragen** *(col)* to go around with one's nose in the air *(col)*; **~ oben** high up; **die Sonne steht ~** the sun is high in the sky; **~ werfen/wachsen** to throw high/grow tall.

(b) *verehren, versichern, begabt* highly; *verlieren* heavily; *gewinnen* handsomely; *verschuldet* deeply; *erfreut* very. **das rechne ich ihm ~ an** (I think) that is very much to his credit; **~ hinauswollen** to aim high, to be ambitious; **zehn Mann ~** *(col)* ten of them; **wenn es ~ kommt** *(col)* at (the) most, at the outside; **~ setzen** *or* **spielen** *(im Spiel)* to play for high stakes.

(c) *(Math)* 7 **~ 3** 7 to the power of 3, 7 to the 3rd.

(d) *(col)* **es ging ~ her** there were lively goings-on *(col)*; **~ und heilig versprechen** to promise faithfully; **~ und heilig schwören** to swear blind *(col)*.

hoch- *pref (in Verbindung mit Bewegungsverb)* up; *versichert, begabt etc* highly; *zufrieden, erfreut, elegant etc* very; *besteuert* heavily; *verschuldet* deeply.

Hoch-: **~achtung** *f* deep respect; **bei aller ~achtung vor jdm/etw** with (the greatest) respect for sb/sth; **mit vorzüglicher ~achtung** *(form: Briefschluß)* yours faithfully; **h~achtungsvoll** *adv (Briefschluß)* yours faithfully; **~adel** *m* high nobility; **h~aktuell** *adj* highly topical; **~amt** *nt (Eccl)* High Mass; **h~angesehen** *adj attr* highly regarded; **h~arbeiten** *vr sep* to work one's way up; **~bau** *m no pl* structural engineering; **h~begabt** *adj attr* highly talented; **h~betagt** *adj* aged *attr,* advanced in years; **~betrieb** *m* peak period; *(im Verkehr)* rush hour; **~betrieb haben** to be at one's/its busiest; **h~bringen** *vt sep irreg (col)* **(a)** to bring *or* take up; **(b)** *(col: h~heben können)* to get up; **(c)** *(fig: leistungsfähig machen)* to get going; *Kranken* to get back on his *etc* feet; **~burg** *f (fig)* stronghold; **h~deutsch** *adj* High German; **h~dotiert** *adj attr Arbeit* highly paid.

Hochdruck *m* **(a)** *(Met, Phys)* high pressure. **mit ~ arbeiten** to work at full stretch. **(b)** *(Med)* high blood pressure. **(c)** *(Typ)* relief print.

Hoch-: **~ebene** *f* plateau; **h~empfindlich** *adj (Tech) Material, Instrumente* highly sensitive; *Film* fast; *Stoff* very delicate; **h~entwickelt** *adj attr Kultur, Land* highly developed; *Geräte, Methoden* sophisticated; **h~fahren** *sep irreg* **1** *vi aux sein* **(a)** to go up; *(in Auto auch)* to drive up; **(b)** *(erschreckt)* to jump; **2** *vt* to take up; *(in Auto auch)* to drive up; **~finanz** *f* high finance; **h~fliegen** *vi sep irreg aux sein* to fly up; *(hochgeschleudert werden)* to be thrown up; **h~fliegend** *adj* ambitious; *(übertrieben)* high-flown; **~form** *f* top form; **~frequenz** *f (Elec)* high frequency; **~ge-**

birge *nt* high mountains *pl;* **~gefühl** *nt* elation; **h~gehen** *vi sep irreg aux sein* **(a)** to rise; **(b)** *(col: hinaufgehen)* to go up; **(c)** *(col: explodieren)* to blow up; *(Bombe)* to go off; **etw h~gehen lassen** to blow sth up; **(d)** *(col: wütend werden)* to go through the roof *(col)*; **(e)** *(col: gefaßt werden)* to get caught; **jdn h~gehen lassen** to bust sb *(col)*; **h~geistig** *adj* highly intellectual, highbrow *no adv;* **h~gelegen** *adj attr* **ein h~gelegener Ort** a place situated high up; **~genuß** *m* great *or* special treat; *(großes Vergnügen)* great pleasure; **h~geschätzt** *adj attr Mensch* highly esteemed; *Sache* greatly valued; **h~geschlossen** *adj Kleid etc* high-necked; **~gesteckt** *adj (fig) Ziele* ambitious; **h~gestellt** *adj attr (fig) Persönlichkeit* high-ranking; **h~gestochen** *adj Reden* high-faluting; *Stil* pompous; *(eingebildet)* stuck-up; **h~gewachsen** *adj* tall; **h~gezüchtet** *adj Motor* souped-up *(col)*; *Geräte* fancy *(col)*; *Tiere, Pflanzen* overbred.

Hochglanz *m* high polish; *(Phot)* gloss. **etw auf ~ polieren** *or* **bringen** to polish sth until it shines.

hochglänzend *adj* very shiny; *Fotoabzug* very glossy; *Möbel* highly polished.

Hochglanz-: **~papier** *nt* high gloss paper; **~politur** *f* mirror polish *or* finish; *(Poliermittel)* (furniture) polish.

Hoch-: **h~gradig** *adj no pred* extreme; **h~hackig** *adj Schuhe* high-heeled; **h~halten** *vt sep irreg* to hold up; *(fig)* to uphold; **~haus** *nt* high-rise *or* multi-storey building; **h~heben** *vt sep irreg Hand* to hold up; *Last* to lift up; **h~intelligent** *adj* highly intelligent; **h~interessant** *adj* very interesting; **h~jagen** *vt sep (col)* **(a)** *(aufscheuchen) Menschen* to get up; **(b)** *(sprengen)* to blow up; **(c)** *Motor* to rev up; **h~kant** *adv* **(a)** **h~kant stellen** to put on end; **(b)** *(fig col)* **jdn h~kant hinauswerfen** to chuck sb out on his/her ear *(col)*; **h~klappen** *vt sep Tisch* to fold up; *Sitz* to tip up; *Deckel* to lift up; *Kragen* to turn up; **h~kommen** *vi sep irreg aux sein* **(a)** *(col)* to come up; **(b)** *(col)* **das Essen ist ihm h~gekommen** he threw up (his meal) *(col)*; **(c)** *(aufstehen können)* to (manage to) get up; *(fig: gesund werden)* to get back on one's feet; **(d)** *(col: gesellschaftlich)* to come up in the world; **~konjunktur** *f* boom; **h~rempeln** *vt sep* to roll up; **~kultur** *f* (very) advanced civilization; **~land** *nt* highland; **das schottische ~land** the Scottish Highlands *pl;* **h~leben** *vi sep* **jdn h~leben lassen** to give three cheers for sb; **er lebe h~!** three cheers (for him)!

Hochleistungs-: **~motor** *m* high-performance engine; **~sport** *m* competitive sport.

Hoch-: **h~modern** *adj* very modern, ultra-modern; **~mut** *m* arrogance; **h~mütig** *adj* arrogant; **h~näsig** *adj (col)* snooty *(col)*; **~nebel** *m* (low) stratus; **h~nehmen** *vt sep irreg* **(a)** to lift; *Kind* to pick *or* lift up; **(b)** **jdn h~nehmen** *(col) (necken)* to pull sb's leg; *(schröpfen)* to fleece sb *(col)*; *(verhaften)* to pick sb up; **~ofen** *m* blast furnace; **~parterre** *nt* raised ground floor; **h~prozentig** *adj Getränke* high-proof; *Lösung* highly concentrated; **~rad** *nt* penny-farthing; **h~rechnen** *vt sep* to project; **~rechnung** *f* projection; **h~rot** *adj* bright red; **mit h~rotem Gesicht** with one's face as red as a beetroot *(Brit)*, with a bright red face; **~ruf** *m* cheer; **~saison** *f* high season; **h~schlagen** *sep irreg* **1** *vt Kragen* to turn up; **2** *vi aux sein (Wellen)* to surge up; *(Flammen)* to leap up; **h~schrauben** *vt sep (fig) Preise* to force up; *Erwartungen* to raise; *Forderungen* to increase.

Hochschul-: **~abschluß** *m* degree; **~absolvent** *m* graduate; **~(aus)bildung** *f* university education.

Hochschule *f* college; *(Universität)* university.

Hochschul-: **~lehrer** *m* college/university teacher, lecturer *(Brit)*; **~reife** *f* **er hat (die) ~reife** ≈ he's got his A-levels *(Brit)*, he's graduated from high school *(US)*; **~studium** *nt* higher education.

hochschwanger *adj* pregnant, well advanced in pregnancy.

Hochsee-: **~fischerei** *f* deep-sea fishing; **~schiffahrt** *f* ocean-going shipping.

Hoch-: **~seil** *nt* high wire, tightrope; **~sitz** *m (Hunt)* (raised) hide; **~sommer** *m* height of the summer; **h~sommerlich** *adj* very summery.

Hochspannung *f (Elec, fig)* high tension.

Hochspannungs-: **~leitung** *f* high tension line, power line; **~mast** *m* pylon.

Hoch-: **h~spielen** *vt sep (fig)* to blow up; **~sprache** *f* standard language; **~sprung** *m* high jump.

höchst *adv (überaus)* highly, extremely.

Höchst- *in cpds (obere Grenze angebend) (mit n)* maximum; *(mit adj) siehe* **Hoch-;** *(mit adj: Intensität ausdrückend)* extremely, most; **~alter** *nt* maximum age.

Hoch-: **~stapelei** *f (Jur)* fraud; *(einzelner Fall)* confidence trick; **~stapler** *m* - confidence trickster, con man *(col)*; *(fig)* fraud.

Höchst-: **~betrag** *m* maximum amount; **~bietende(r)** *mf decl as adj* highest bidder.

hoch-: **~stecken** *vt sep* to pin up; *Haare auch* to put up; **~stehend** *adj (gesellschaftlich)* of high standing; *(geistig)* highly intellectual; *(entwicklungsmäßig)* superior; **~stellen** *vt sep* **(a)** *Stühle etc* to put up; **(b)** *Heizung etc, Kragen* to turn up.

höchstenfalls *adv* at (the) most.

höchstens *adv* **(a)** at the most. **(b)** *(außer)* except.

höchste(r, s) **1** *adj, superl of* **hoch** highest; *Wuchs, Baum* tallest; *Betrag, Summe* largest; *Strafe, Gewicht* heaviest; *Lotteriegewinn* biggest; *Schaden* most expensive; *(maximal) Verdienst, Temperatur, Geschwindigkeit etc* maximum *attr*; *Fest* most important; *Offizier* highest-ranking; *Genuß, Glück, Freude, Ehre, Gut* greatest; *Gefahr, Wichtigkeit* utmost, greatest; *Konzentration* extreme. **zu meiner ~n Zufriedenheit** to my great satisfaction; **im ~n Fall(e)** at the most; **die ~ Instanz** *(Jur)* the supreme court of appeal; **~ Zeit** high time; **aufs ~ erfreut** *etc* extremely *or* highly pleased *etc.*

2 *adv* **am ~n** highest; *schätzen, versichern* most; *besteuert, verlieren* (the) most heavily; *verschuldet* (the) most deeply; **in der Rangordnung am ~n stehen** to be the highest up in the hierarchy; **am ~n stehen** *(Kurse, Temperatur)* to be at its highest.

Höchste(s) *nt decl as adj (fig)* highest good. **nach dem ~n streben** to aspire to perfection.

Höchst-: **~fall** *m* **im ~fall** at the most; **~form** *f (Sport)* top form; **~geschwindigkeit** *f* top *or* maximum speed; **~grenze** *f* upper limit.

Hochstimmung *f* high spirits *pl.*

Höchst-: **~leistung** *f* best performance; *(bei Produktion)* maximum output; **~maß** *nt* maximum amount *(an+dat* of); **h~persönlich** *adv* personally; **es ist der Prinz h~persönlich** it's the prince in person; **~stand** *m* highest level; **h~wahrscheinlich** *adv* most probably.

Hoch-: **~tal** *nt* high-lying valley; **~tour** *f* **auf ~touren laufen/arbeiten** to be working flat out *(col)*; **h~tourig** *adj Motor* high-revving; **h~tourig laufen** to run at high revs; **h~trabend** *adj (pej)* pompous; **h~treiben** *vt sep irreg* to drive up; *(fig) Preise* to force up; **~- und Tiefbau** *m* structural and civil engineering; **h~verehrt** *adj attr* highly esteemed; **h~verehrter Herr Präsident!** Mr President, Sir!; **~verrat** *m* high treason; **~verräter** *m* traitor; **h~verschuldet** *adj attr* deep in debt; **~wald** *m* timber forest; **~wasser** *nt* high tide; *(in Flüssen)* high water; *(Überschwemmung)* flood; **~wasser haben** *(Fluß)* to be in flood; **h~wertig** *adj* high-quality; *Nahrungsmittel* highly nutritious; *Stahl* high-grade;

~**würden** *m no pl (Eccl: Anrede)* Reverend Father; ~**zahl** *f* exponent.
Hochzeit *f* **-en** wedding. ~ **feiern** to have a wedding; **man kann nicht auf zwei ~en tanzen** *(prov)* you can't have your cake and eat it *(prov)*.
Hochzeits- *in cpds* wedding; ~**fest** *nt* wedding celebration; ~**reise** f honeymoon; ~**tag** *m* wedding day; *(Jahrestag)* wedding anniversary.
hochziehen *sep irreg* **1** *vt* **(a)** to pull up; *Fahne* to run up; *Augenbrauen* to raise. **(b)** *(bauen) Wand* to put up *(col)*. **2** *vr* to pull oneself up.
Hocke *f* **-n** squatting position; *(Übung)* squat; *(beim Turnen)* squat vault; *(beim Skilaufen)* crouch.
hocken 1 *vi* **(a)** to squat, to crouch. **(b)** *(col: sitzen)* to sit; *(auf Hocker)* to perch. **2** *vr* **(a)** to squat. **(b)** *(col: sich setzen)* to sit down.
Hocker *m* **-** *(Stuhl)* stool.
Höcker *m* **-** *(von Kamel, col: Buckel)* hump.
Hockey ['hɔke] *nt no pl* hockey, field hockey *(US)*.
Hoden *m* **-** testicle.
Hodensack *m* scrotum.
Hof *m* **¨e (a)** *(Platz)* yard; *(Innen~)* courtyard. **(b)** *(Bauern~)* farm. **(c)** *(Fürsten~)* court. **bei ~e** at court; **am ~e Ludwigs XIV** at the court of Louis XIV. **(d) einem Mädchen den ~ machen** *(dated)* to court a girl *(dated)*. **(e)** *(um Sonne, Mond)* halo.
hoffen 1 *vi* to hope. **auf jdn ~** to set one's hopes on sb; **auf etw ~** *(acc)* to hope for sth; **da bleibt nur zu ~** one can only hope; **ich will nicht ~, daß er das macht** I hope he doesn't do that. **2** *vt* to hope for. **~ wir das Beste!** let's hope for the best!; **ich hoffe es** I hope so; **das will ich (doch wohl) ~** I should hope so; **ich will es nicht ~** I hope not.
hoffentlich *adv* hopefully. **~!** I hope so; **~ nicht** I/we hope not.
Hoffnung *f* hope; *(auf Gott)* trust *(auf+acc* in*)*. **sich** *(dat)* **~en machen** to have hopes; **sich** *(dat)* **keine ~en machen** not to hold out any hopes; **er macht sich ~en bei ihr** *(col)* he fancies his chances with her *(col)*; **mach dir keine ~(en)!** don't build up your hopes; **jdm ~en machen** to raise sb's hopes; **jdm auf etw** *(acc)* **~en machen** to lead sb to expect sth; **die ~ aufgeben/verlieren** to abandon/lose hope; **sich falschen ~en hingeben** to delude oneself; **guter ~ sein** *(euph: schwanger)* to be expecting.
Hoffnungs-: h~los *adj* hopeless; ~**losigkeit** *f no pl* hopelessness; *(Verzweiflung)* despair; ~**schimmer** *m* glimmer of hope; **h~voll 1** *adj* hopeful; *(vielversprechend)* promising; **2** *adv* full of hope.
hofieren* *vt* to court.
höflich *adj* polite.
Höflichkeit *f* **(a)** *no pl* politeness. **jdm etw mit aller ~ sagen** to tell sb sth very politely. **(b)** *(höfliche Bemerkung)* compliment.
Höflichkeits-: ~besuch *m* courtesy visit; ~**floskel** *f* polite phrase; **h~halber** *adv* out of courtesy.
hohe *adj siehe* **hoch.**
Höhe *f* **-n (a)** height; *(Flug~, Berg~ auch)* altitude; *(von Schnee, Wasser)* depth. **in die/der ~** (up) into/in the air; **in einer ~ von** at a height/an altitude of; **in die ~ gehen/treiben** *(fig: Preise etc)* to go up/force up; **er geht immer gleich in die Höhe** *(col)* he always flares up.
(b) *(An~)* hill; *(Gipfel)* top, summit; *(fig: ~punkt, Blütezeit etc)* height. **auf der ~ sein** *(fig col) (leistungsfähig)* to be at one's best; *(gesund)* to be fighting fit *(col)*; **nicht auf der ~ sein** *(fig col)* to feel below par; **die ~n und Tiefen des Lebens** the ups and downs of life; **das ist doch die ~!** *(fig col)* that's the limit!
(c) *(von Preisen, Temperatur, Geschwindigkeit, Strafe)* level; *(von Summe, Gewinn, Verlust, Geldstrafe)* size; *(von Wert, Druck)* amount; *(von Schaden)* extent. **ein Betrag in ~ von** an amount of; **ein Scheck in ~ von** a cheque *(Brit) or* check *(US)* for (the amount of); **Zinsen in ~ von** interest at the rate of; **bis zu einer ~ von** up to a maximum of.
(d) *(Mus)* pitch; *(Rad: Ton~)* treble *no pl.*
(e) *(Naut, Geog: Breitenlage)* latitude. **die beiden Schwimmer liegen auf gleicher ~** the two swimmers are level with each other.
Hoheit *f* **(a)** *no pl (Staats~)* sovereignty *(über +acc* over*)*. **(b)** member of a/the royal family; *(als Anrede)* Highness.
Hoheits-: ~bereich *m (Rechtsbereich)* jurisdiction; ~**gebiet** *nt* sovereign territory; ~**gewalt** *f* (national) jurisdiction; ~**gewässer** *pl* territorial waters *pl*; **h~voll** *adj* majestic; ~**zeichen** *nt* national emblem.
Höhen-: ~angst *f* fear of heights; ~**flug** *m* high-altitude flight; **geistiger ~flug** intellectual flight; ~**lage** *f* altitude; ~**luft** *f* mountain air; ~**messer** *m* **-** *(Aviat)* altimeter; ~**sonne** *f* mountain sun; *(Lampe)* sunray lamp; ~**unterschied** *m* difference in altitude.
Hohepriester *m (lit, fig)* high priest.
Höhepunkt *m* height, peak; *(des Tages, des Lebens, einer Veranstaltung)* high spot; *(eines Stücks, Orgasmus)* climax. **auf dem ~ ...** at the peak *(gen* of*)*; **den ~ erreichen** to reach a climax; *(Krankheit)* to reach a crisis; **den ~ überschreiten** to pass the peak.
hohe(r, s) *adj siehe* **hoch.**
höher *adj comp of* **hoch** *(lit, fig)* higher; *Macht* superior; *Klasse* upper; *Auflage* bigger. **~e Schule** secondary school, high school *(esp US)*; **~e Gewalt** an act of God; **in ~em Maße** to a greater extent; **sich ~ versichern** to increase one's insurance; **sich zu H~em berufen fühlen** to feel called to higher things.
höhergestellt *adj attr* higher, more senior.
hohl *adj (lit, fig)* hollow; *Geschwätz etc* empty, shallow; *Blick* empty, vacant. **ein ~es Kreuz** a hollow back; **in der ~en Hand** in the hollow of one's hand.
Höhle *f* **-n** cave; *(in Baum)* hole, hollow bit; *(Tierbehausung)* cave, den; *(fig: schlechte Wohnung)* hovel, hole *(col)*.
Höhlen- *in cpds* cave; ~**forschung, ~kunde** *f* speleology; ~**mensch** *m* caveman.
Hohl-: ~kopf *m (pej)* numskull *(col)*; ~**körper** *m* hollow body; ~**kreuz** *nt (Med)* hollow back; ~**maß** *nt* measure of capacity; ~**raum** *m* hollow space; *(Build auch)* cavity; ~**spiegel** *m* concave mirror.
Höhlung *f* hollow.
Hohn *m no pl* scorn. **nur ~ und Spott ernten** to get nothing but scorn and derision; **das ist der reine ~** it's sheer mockery.
Hohngelächter *nt* scornful laughter.
höhnisch *adj* scornful.
Hokuspokus *m no pl (Zauberformel)* hey presto; *(fig) (Täuschung)* hocus-pocus *(col)*, jiggery-pokery *(col)*; *(Drumherum)* palaver *(col)*, fuss.
hold *adj (poet, dated)* fair, sweet. **das Glück war ihm ~** fortune smiled upon him.
holen *vt* to get; *(abholen)* to fetch, to pick up; *Sieg, Preis auch* to win; *Krankheit auch* to catch. **gestern hat ihn die Polizei geholt** the police came to take him away yesterday; **jdn ~ lassen** to send for sb; **sich** *(dat)* **eine Erkältung ~** to catch a cold; **dabei ist nichts zu ~** *(col)* there's nothing in it; **bei ihm ist nichts zu ~** *(col)* you *etc* won't get anything out of him.
Holland *nt* Holland.
Holländer[1] *m* **-** Dutchman. **die ~** the Dutch (people).
Holländer[2] *m no pl* Dutch cheese.
Holländerin *f* Dutchwoman, Dutch girl.
holländisch *adj* Dutch.
Hölle *f* **-n** hell. **die ~ auf Erden** hell on earth; **in die ~ kommen** to go to hell; **ich werde ihm die ~**

heiß machen *(col)* I'll give him hell *(col)*; **es war die (reinste)** ~ *(col)* it was (pure) hell *(col)*.
Höllen- *in cpds* of hell, infernal; *(col: groß)* hellish *(col)*, infernal *(col)*; ~**angst** *f* terrible fear; **eine ~angst haben** to be scared stiff *(col)*; ~**lärm** *m* infernal noise; ~**qual** *f (fig col)* agony; ~**qualen ausstehen** to suffer agony.
höllisch *adj* **(a)** *attr* infernal, of hell. **(b)** *(col: groß)* dreadful, hellish *(col)*. **es tut ~ weh** it hurts like hell *(col)*; **die Prüfung war ~ schwer** the exam was hellish(ly) difficult *(col)*.
Holm *m* **-e (a)** *(von Barren)* bar; *(von Geländer)* rail; *(von Leiter)* side rail. **(b)** *(Griff)* shaft.
holp(e)rig *adj Weg* bumpy; *Rede* clumsy.
holpern *vi* to bump, to jolt.
holterdiepolter *adv* helter-skelter.
Holunder *m* - elder.
Holunder-: ~**beere** *f* elderberry; ~**busch,** ~**strauch** *m* elder bush.
Holz *nt* **¨er (a)** wood; *(zum Bauen, Schreinern auch)* timber, lumber *(US)*. **ein ~** a piece of wood *or* timber; *(~art)* a wood; **aus ~** made of wood, wooden; **~ fällen** to fell trees; **aus einem anderen/demselben ~ geschnitzt sein** *(fig)* to be cast in a different/the same mould *(Brit) or* mold *(US)*; **aus hartem ~ geschnitzt sein** *(fig)* to be made of sterner stuff. **(b)** *(Kegel)* skittle, ninepin. **gut ~!** have a good game!
Holz *in cpds* wood; *(aus ~ auch)* wooden; *(Build, Comm etc)* timber; ~**apfel** *m* crab apple; ~**bearbeitung** *f* woodworking; *(im Sägewerk)* timber processing; ~**bestand** *m* stock of wood *or* timber; ~**bläser** *m* woodwind player; ~**blasinstrument** *nt* woodwind instrument; ~**block** *m* block of wood; ~**bündel** *nt* bundle of wood.
Hölzchen *nt* small piece of wood; *(Streichholz)* match.
holzen *vi (esp Ftbl col)* to hack.
hölzern *adj (lit, fig)* wooden.
Holz-: ~**fällen** *nt no pl* tree-felling, lumbering; ~**fäller** *m* - woodcutter, lumberjack; ~**faserplatte** *f* (wood) fibreboard *(Brit) or* fiberboard *(US)*; **h~frei** *adj Papier* wood-free; ~**hacken** *nt no pl* chopping wood; **h~haltig** *adj Papier* woody; ~**hammer** *m* mallet; **jdm etw mit dem ~hammer beibringen** to hammer sth into sb *(col)*; ~**hammermethode** *f (col)* sledgehammer method *(col)*; ~**haufen** *m* pile of wood; ~**haus** *nt* wooden *or* timber house.
holzig *adj* woody; *Spargel auch* stringy, tough.
Holz-: ~**klotz** *m* block of wood; *(Spielzeug)* wooden brick; **er saß da wie ein ~klotz** *(col)* he sat there like a block *or* lump of wood; ~**kohle** *f* charcoal; ~**kopf** *m (fig col)* blockhead *(col)*; ~**scheit** *nt* piece of (fire)wood, log; ~**schuh** *m* wooden shoe, clog; ~**span** *m* wood chip; ~**stoß** *m* pile of wood; ~**verarbeitung** *f* wood-processing; ~**weg** *m* **auf dem ~weg sein** *(fig col)* to be on the wrong track *(col)*; ~**wirtschaft** *f* timber industry; ~**wolle** *f* wood-wool; ~**wurm** *m* woodworm.
homo- *in cpds* homo; ~**gen** *adj* homogeneous; ~**genisieren*** *vt* to homogenize.
Homöopath *m (wk)* **-en, -en** homoeopath *(Brit)*, homeopath *(US)*.
Homo-: ~**sexualität** *f* homosexuality; **h~sexuell** *adj* homosexual; ~**sexuelle(r)** *mf decl as adj* homosexual.
Honig *m no pl* honey. **sie schmierte ihm ~ ums Maul** *(col)* she buttered him up *(col)*.
Honig-: ~**biene** *f* honey bee; ~**kuchen** *m* honeycake; ~**kuchenpferd** *nt (col)* **grinsen wie ein ~kuchenpferd** to grin like a Cheshire cat; ~**lecken** *nt (fig)* **das ist kein ~lecken** it's no picnic; ~**melone** *f* honeydew melon; **h~süß** *adj* as sweet as honey; *(fig) Worte, Ton* honeyed; *Lächeln* sickly sweet; ~**wabe** *f* honeycomb.
Honorar *nt* **-e** fee; *(Autoren~)* royalty.
Honoratioren [honora'tsio:rən] *pl* dignitaries *pl*.
honorieren* *vt (Comm)* to honour *(Brit)*, to honor *(US)*, to meet; *(fig: anerkennen)* to reward. **meine Arbeit wird schlecht honoriert** my work is poorly remunerated.
Hopfen *m* - *(Bot)* hop; *(beim Brauen)* hops *pl*. **bei ihm ist ~ und Malz verloren** *(col)* he's a dead loss *(col)*.
hoppeln *vi aux sein (Hase)* to lollop.
hoppla *interj* whoops. **~, jetzt komm' ich!** look out, here I come!
hops *adj pred (col)* **~ gehen** *(verlorengehen)* to get lost; *(entzweigehen)* to get broken; *(verhaftet werden)* to get nabbed *(col)*; *(sterben)* to kick the bucket *(col)*; **jdn ~ nehmen** *(verhaften)* to nab sb *(col)*; **~ sein** *(verloren)* to be lost; *(Geld)* to be down the drain *(col)*; *(entzwei)* to be kaputt *(col)*.
hopsen *vi aux sein (col)* to hop, to skip.
Hopser *m (col: kleiner Sprung)* (little) jump.
hörbar *adj* audible. **sich ~ machen** to speak up.
horchen *vi* to listen *(dat, auf+acc* to*)*; *(heimlich)* to eavesdrop.
Horde *f* **-n** *(lit, fig)* horde.
hören *vti* **(a)** to hear. **ich höre dich nicht** I can't hear you; **ich hörte ihn kommen** I heard him coming; **gut/schlecht ~** to have good/bad hearing; **schwer ~** to be hard of hearing; **du hörst wohl schlecht!** *(col)* you must be deaf!; **das läßt sich ~** *(fig)* that doesn't sound bad; **ich habe es sagen ~** I've heard it said; **er hört sich gern reden** he likes the sound of his own voice; **na hör mal!, na ~ Sie mal!** wait a minute!, look here!; **von etw ~** to hear about *or* of sth; **von jdm gehört haben** to have heard of sb; **von jdm ~** *(Nachricht bekommen)* to hear from sb; **Sie werden noch von mir ~** *(Drohung)* you'll be hearing from me; **man hörte nie mehr etwas von ihm** he was never heard of again; **laß mal ~!** *(col)* tell us; **etwas/nichts von sich ~ lassen** to get/not to get in touch; **lassen Sie von sich ~** keep in touch; **ich lasse von mir ~** I'll be in touch; **er kommt, wie ich höre** I hear he's coming; **man höre und staune!** would you believe it!; **ich will davon nichts gehört haben** I don't want to know anything about it.
(b) *(anhören) Vortrag, Radio* to listen to; *Berichte, Sänger* to hear.
(c) auf jdn/etw ~ to listen to sb/sth; **er will nicht ~** he won't listen; **der Hund hört auf den Namen Joe** the dog answers to the name of Joe.
Hören *nt no pl* hearing; *(Radio~)* listening. **das ~ von Musik** listening to music; **es verging ihm ~ und Sehen** he didn't know whether he was coming or going *(col)*.
Hörensagen *nt*: **vom ~** from hearsay.
hörenswert *adj* worth listening to.
Hörer(in *f***)** *m* - *(Rad)* listener; *(Univ)* student/person (attending lectures); *(Telec)* receiver.
Hörerschaft *f (Rad)* listeners *pl*, audience.
Hör-: ~**fehler** *m (Med)* hearing defect; **das war ein ~fehler** I/he *etc* misheard it; ~**funk** *m* radio; ~**gerät** *nt* hearing aid.
hörig *adj* enslaved; *(Hist)* in bondage. **sie ist ihm (sexuell) ~** he has (sexual) power over her.
Horizont *m* **-e** *(lit, fig)* horizon. **am ~** on the horizon; **das geht über meinen ~** *(fig)* that is beyond me; **er hat einen beschränkten ~** he has limited horizons.
horizontal *adj* horizontal.
Horizontale *f* **-(n)** *(Math)* horizontal (line).
Hormon *nt* **-e** hormone.
hormonell *adj* hormone *attr*, hormonal. **jdn ~ behandeln** to give sb hormone treatment.
Hörmuschel *f* **-n** *(Telec)* earpiece.
Horn *nt* **¨er** *(von Tieren, Mus)* horn; *(fig col: Beule)* bump. **jdn mit den ~ern aufspießen** to gore sb; **sich** *(dat)* **die ~er abstoßen** *(col)* to sow one's wild oats; **den Stier bei den ~ern packen** *(fig)* to

take the bull by the horns; **jdm ~er aufsetzen** *(col)* to cuckold sb; **ins gleiche/in jds ~ blasen** to chime in.

Họrnbrille *f* horn-rimmed spectacles *pl*.

Hö̤rnchen *nt* - **(a)** little horn. **(b)** *(Gebäck)* croissant. **(c)** *(Zool)* squirrel.

Họrnhaut *f* callous; *(des Auges)* cornea.

Hornịsse *f* **-n** hornet.

Hornịst *m* horn player.

Họrnochs(e) *m (fig col)* blockhead *(col)*, idiot.

Horoskọp *nt* **-e** horoscope.

horrẹnd *adj* horrendous.

Hö̤rrohr *nt* ear trumpet; *(Med)* stethoscope.

Họrror *m no pl* horror *(vor +dat* of*)*.

Họrror- *in cpds* horror; **~film** *m* horror film.

Hö̤r-: ~saal *m (Univ)* lecture room *or* hall; **~spiel** *nt (Rad)* radio play.

Họrst *m* **-e** *(Nest)* nest; *(Adler~)* eyrie.

Họrt *m* **-e** **(a)** *(Kinder~) day-home for schoolchildren in the afternoon.* **(b)** *(old, poet: Schatz)* hoard, treasure. **(c)** *(geh: Zuflucht)* refuge, shelter.

họrten *vt Geld, Vorräte etc* to hoard; *Rohstoffe etc* to stockpile.

Hortẹnsie [-iə] *f* hydrangea.

Hö̤rweite *f* **in/außer ~** within/out of hearing *or* earshot.

Họse *f* **-n** trousers *pl*, pants *pl; (Damen~ auch)* slacks *pl; (Bade~)* swimming trunks *pl; (Unter~)* underpants *pl*, pants *pl (Brit)*; **ich brauche eine neue ~** I need a new pair of trousers *or* pants, I need some new trousers *or* pants; **die ~n anhaben** *(fig col)* to wear the trousers *or* pants *(col)*; **die ~n voll haben** to be wetting oneself *(col)*; **in die ~ gehen** *(col)* to be a complete flop *(col)*.

Họsen-: ~anzug *m* trouser suit *(Brit)*, pantsuit *(US)*; **~bein** *nt* trouser leg; **~boden** *m* seat (of trousers); **den ~boden vollkriegen** *(col)* to get a smacked bottom; **sich auf den ~boden setzen** *(col)* to get stuck in *(col)*; **~bund** *m* waistband; **~rock** *m* culottes *pl*, pantskirt; **~schlitz** *m* flies *pl*, fly; **~träger** *pl* (a pair of) braces *pl (Brit) or* suspenders *pl (US)*.

Hospitạl *nt* **-e** *or* **Hospitạ̈ler** *(dated: Krankenhaus)* hospital.

Hospịz *nt* **-e** hospice.

Hostẹss, Hostẹß *f, pl* **Hostẹssen** hostess.

Hostie ['hɔstiə] *f (Eccl)* host.

Hotẹl *nt* **-s** hotel.

Hotẹl- *in cpds* hotel; **~fach** *nt* hotel management.

Hotẹl gạrni *nt* bed and breakfast hotel.

Hr. = **Herr** Mr.

Hrsg. = **Herausgeber** ed.

Họb *m* **¨-e** **(a)** *(Kolben~)* (piston) stroke. **(b)** *(bei Kränen: Leistung)* hoisting capacity.

Hụb(b)el *m* - *(col)* bump.

hụbb(e)lig *adj (col)* bumpy.

hṳ̈ben *adv* over here, (on) this side. **~ und drüben** on both sides.

Hụb-: ~kraft *f* lifting *or* hoisting capacity; **~raum** *m (Aut)* cubic capacity.

hṳ̈bsch *adj* pretty; *Geschenk, Wohnung* nice. **sich ~ machen** to make oneself look pretty; **er macht das schon ganz ~** he's doing it very nicely; **das war ~/nicht ~ von dir** that was nice/not nice of you; **na, ihr beiden H~en** *(col)* well, you two; **eine ~e Geschichte/Bescherung** *(iro)* a pretty kettle of fish; **das kann ja ~ werden** *(col)* that'll be just great; **ein ~es Vermögen** a tidy sum; **es ist doch ganz ~ weit** it's pretty far, it's a fair old way *(col)*; **ganz ~ viel bezahlen** to pay quite a bit; **das wirst du ~ sein lassen** *(col)* you'll do nothing of the kind; **immer ~ langsam!** *(col)* nice and easy.

Hụbschrauber *m* - helicopter.

Hụcke *f* **-n** **jdm die ~ vollhauen** *(col)* to give sb a good hiding.

hụckepack *adv* piggy-back, pick-a-back.

Hụf *m* **-e** hoof. **einem Pferd die ~e beschlagen** to shoe a horse.

Hụf-: ~eisen *nt* horseshoe; **~schmied** *m* blacksmith.

Hṳ̈ft: ~bein *nt* hip-bone; **~bruch** *m* fractured hip.

Hṳ̈fte *f* **-n** hip; *(von Tieren)* haunch. **bis an die ~n reichen** to come up to the waist.

Hṳ̈ft-: ~gelenk *nt* hip joint; **~gürtel, ~halter** *m* girdle; **h~hoch** *adj Pflanzen etc* waist-high; *Wasser etc* waist-deep.

Hụftier *nt* hoofed animal.

Hṳ̈ft-: ~knochen *m* hip-bone; **~schmerz** *m* pain in the hip.

Hṳ̈gel *m* - hill; *(Erdhaufen)* mound.

hṳ̈g(e)lig *adj* hilly.

Hṳ̈gel-: ~kette *f* range *or* chain of hills; **~land** *nt* hilly country.

Hụhn *nt* **¨-er** chicken *(auch Cook)*; *(Henne auch)* hen; *(Gattung)* fowl. **da lachen ja die ¨~er** *(col)* it's enough to make a cat laugh *(col)*; **sie sah aus wie ein gerupftes ~** *(col)* she looked as though she'd been dragged through a hedge backwards *(col)*; **ein verrücktes ~** a queer fish *(col)*; **ein dummes** *(col)* **~** a silly goose.

Hṳ̈hnchen *nt* (young) chicken, pullet. **mit jdm ein ~ zu rupfen haben** *(col)* to have a bone to pick with sb *(col)*.

Hṳ̈hner-: ~auge *nt (Med)* corn; **~brühe** *f* (clear) chicken broth; **~ei** *nt* hen's egg; **~klein** *nt no pl (Cook)* chicken trimmings *pl;* **~stall** *m* henhouse, chicken-coop; **~stange** *f* perch, (chicken) roost.

hụldigen *vi+dat (geh) einem Künstler* to pay homage to; *einer Ansicht* to subscribe to; *einem Glauben* to embrace; *einem Laster* to indulge in.

Hṳ̈lle *f* **-n** cover; *(für Ausweiskarten etc auch)* holder; *(Cellophan~)* wrapping; *(liter, hum: Kleidung)* clothes *pl*, piece of clothing. **die ~ fallen lassen** to strip off; **die sterbliche ~** the mortal remains *pl;* **in ~ und Fülle** in abundance; **Whisky/Sorgen in ~ und Fülle** whisky/worries galore.

hụ̈llen *vt (geh)* to wrap. **in Nebel gehüllt** shrouded in mist; **sich in seinen Mantel ~** to wrap oneself up in one's coat; **sich (über etw** *acc*) **in Schweigen ~** to remain silent (about sth).

hụ̈llenlos *adj* unclothed.

Hụ̈lse *f* **-n** **(a)** *(Schale)* hull, husk; *(Schote)* pod. **(b)** *(Kapsel)* case; *(für Film)* cartridge.

Hụ̈lsenfrucht *f usu pl* pulse.

humạn *adj* humane; *(verständnisvoll auch)* considerate.

Humanịst(in *f*) *m* humanist; *(Altsprachler)* classicist.

humanịstisch *adj siehe n* humanist(ic); classical. **~ gebildet** educated in the classics *or* humanities; **~es Gymnasium** *secondary school with bias on Latin and Greek*; ≃ grammar school *(Brit)*.

humanitạ̈r *adj* humanitarian.

Humanitạ̈t *f no pl* humaneness, humanity.

Humạnmedizin *f* (human) medicine.

Hụmbug *m no pl (col)* humbug *(col)*.

Hụmmel *f* **-n** bumble-bee.

Hụmmer *m* - lobster.

Humọr *m* - humour *(Brit)*, humor *(US)*; *(Sinn für ~)* sense of humour. **er hat keinen (Sinn für) ~** he has no sense of humour; **er nahm die Bemerkung mit ~ auf** he took the remark in good humour; **er hat einen eigenartigen ~** he has a strange sense of humour; **er verliert nie den ~** he never loses his sense of humour.

Humorịst(in *f*) *m* humourist *(Brit)*, humorist *(US)*; *(Komiker)* comedian.

Humọr-: h~los *adj* humourless *(Brit)*, humorless *(US)*; **h~voll** *adj* humourous *(Brit)*, humorous *(US)*, amusing; **er kann sehr h~voll erzählen** he is a very amusing talker.

hụmpeln *vi* **(a)** *aux sein* to hobble. **(b)** *(ständig*

hinken) to have a limp.
Humpen *m* - tankard, mug; *(aus Ton)* stein.
Humus *m* -, *no pl* humus.
Hund *m* **-e** dog; *(Jagd~ auch)* hound; *(col!: Schurke)* bastard *(col!)*. **junger ~** puppy, pup; **~e, die bellen, beißen nicht** empty vessels make most noise *(Prov)*; **wie ~ und Katze leben** to live like cat and dog; **damit kann man keinen ~ hinterm Ofen hervorlocken** *(col)* that's not going to tempt anybody; **er ist bekannt wie ein bunter ~** *(col)* everybody knows him; **da liegt der ~ begraben** *(col)* that's the problem; **er ist ein armer ~** he's a poor devil *(col)*; **er ist völlig auf dem ~** *(col)* he's really gone to the dogs *(col)*; **auf den ~ kommen** *(col)* to go to the dogs *(col)*; **vor die ~e gehen** *(col)* to go to the dogs *(col)*.
Hunde-: ~arbeit *f (fig col)* **eine ~arbeit** an awful job; **h~elend** *adj (col)* **mir ist h~elend** I feel lousy *(col)*; **~futter** *nt* dog food; **~halsband** *nt* dog collar; **~halter(in *f*)** *m (form)* dog owner; **~hütte** *f (lit, fig)* (dog) kennel; **h~kalt** *adj (col)* freezing cold; **~kuchen** *m* dog-biscuit; **~leben** *nt (col)* dog's life *(col)*; **~leine** *f* dog lead *or* leash; **~marke** *f* dog licence disc *(Brit)*, dog tag *(US)*; **h~müde** *adj pred, adv (col)* dog-tired; **~narr** *m (col)* fanatical dog lover, dog freak *(col)*; **~rasse** *f* breed (of dog).
hundert *num* a *or* one hundred. **einige ~ Menschen** a few hundred people.
Hundert *nt* **-e** hundred. **es geht in die ~e** it runs into the hundreds; **einer unter ~en** one out of hundreds; **zu ~en** in (their) hundreds.
Hunderter *m* - hundred; *(col: Geldschein)* hundred.
Hundert-: h~fach 1 *adj* hundredfold; **die h~fache Menge** a hundred times the amount; **2** *adv* a hundred times; **h~fünfzigprozentig** *adj (iro)* fanatical; **~jahrfeier** *f* centenary, centennial *(US)*; **h~jährig** *adj attr* (one-)hundred-year-old; **h~mal** *adv* a hundred times; **~meterlauf** *m (Sport)* **der/ein ~meterlauf** the/a 100 metres *(Brit) or* meters *(US) sing;* **h~prozentig** *adj* (a *or* one) hundred per cent; *Alkohol* pure; **ein h~prozentiger Konservativer** *etc* an out-and-out conservative *etc;* **Sie haben h~prozentig recht** you're absolutely right.
Hundertsel *nt* - hundredth.
hundertste(r, s) *adj* hundredth. **vom H~n ins Tausendste kommen** *(fig)* to get carried away.
hunderttausend *num* a *or* one hundred thousand. **H~e von Menschen** hundreds of thousands of people.
Hunde-: ~salon *m* dog parlour *(Brit) or* parlor *(US)*; **~sohn** *m (pej liter)* cur; **~steuer** *f* dog licence *(Brit) or* license *(US)* fee; **~wetter** *nt (col)* filthy weather; **~zucht** *f* dog breeding.
Hündin *f* bitch.
Hunds-: h~gemein *adj (col)* mean; *(schwierig)* fiendishly difficult; **es tut h~gemein weh** it hurts like hell *(col)*; **h~miserabel** *adj (col)* lousy *(col)*; **~tage** *pl* dog days *pl*.
Hüne *m (wk)* **-n, -n ein ~ von Mensch** a giant of a man.
Hünen-: ~grab *nt* megalithic grave; **h~haft** *adj* gigantic.
Hunger *m no pl (lit, fig)* hunger *(nach* for*)*; *(Hungersnot auch)* famine; *(nach Sonne etc)* yearning. **~ bekommen/haben** to get/be hungry; **~ auf etw** *(acc)* **haben** to feel like (eating) sth; **ich habe ~ wie ein Wolf** *or* **Bär** *(col)* I could eat a horse *(col)*; **vor ~ sterben** to die of hunger *or* starvation, to starve to death; **ich sterbe vor ~** *(col)* I'm starving *(col)*.
Hunger-: ~gefühl *nt* hungry feeling; **~künstler** *m* **ich bin doch kein ~künstler** I'm not on a starvation diet.
hungern 1 *vi* **(a)** to go hungry, to starve. **jdn ~ lassen** to let sb go hungry. **(b)** *(fasten)* to go without food. **(c)** *(fig geh: verlangen)* to hunger *(nach* for*)*. **2** *vr* **sich zu Tode ~** to starve oneself to death; **sich schlank ~** to go on a starvation diet.
hungernd *adj, no comp* hungry, starving.
Hungersnot *f* famine.
Hunger-: ~streik *m* hunger strike; **~tuch** *nt* **am ~tuch nagen** *(fig)* to be starving.
hungrig *adj (lit, fig)* hungry *(nach* for*)*. **~ nach** *or* **auf** *(acc)* **etw sein** to feel like (eating) sth.
Hupe *f* **-n** horn. **auf die ~ drücken** to press/sound the horn.
hupen *vi* to sound the horn, to hoot.
hüpfen *vi aux sein* to hop; *(Ball)* to bounce. **vor Freude ~** to jump for joy; **das ist gehüpft wie gesprungen** *(col)* it's six of one and half a dozen of the other *(col)*; **H~ spielen** to play hopscotch.
Hup-: ~konzert *nt (col)* hooting (of car horns); **~signal, ~zeichen** *nt (Aut)* hoot.
Hürde *f* **-n (a)** *(Sport, fig)* hurdle. **eine ~ nehmen** to take a hurdle. **(b)** *(Viehzaun)* fold, pen.
Hürdenlauf *m (Sportart)* hurdling; *(Wettkampf)* hurdles *pl or sing*.
Hure *f* **-n** whore.
huren *vi (col)* to go whoring.
Hurensohn *m (pej)* bastard *(col!)*, son of a bitch *(US col!)*.
hurra [hʊ'ra:, 'hʊra] *interj* hurray, hurrah.
Hurra *nt* **-s** cheers *pl*.
Hurra-: ~geschrei *nt* cheering; **~patriotismus** *m* jingoism, chauvinism; **~ruf** *m* cheer.
Hurrikan *m* **-e** *or* **-s** hurricane.
hurtig *adj* nimble; *(schnell)* quick.
husch *interj (aufscheuchend)* shoo; *(schnell)* quick, quickly now. **und ~, weg war er** and whoosh! he was gone.
huschen *vi aux sein* to dart; *(Mäuse etc auch)* to scurry; *(Lächeln)* to flash.
hüsteln *vi* to give a little cough.
husten 1 *vi* to cough. **auf etw** *(acc)* **~** *(col)* not to give a damn for sth *(col)*. **2** *vt* to cough (up). **denen werde ich was ~** *(col)* I'll tell them where they can get off *(col)*.
Husten *m no pl* cough. **~ haben** to have a cough.
Husten-: ~anfall *m* coughing fit; **~bonbon** *m or nt* cough drop; **~mittel** *nt* cough medicine/drop; **~reiz** *m* irritation of the throat; **~saft** *m* cough mixture; **h~stillend** *adj* **das wirkt h~stillend** it relieves coughs; **~tropfen** *pl* cough drops *pl*.
Hut[1] *m* **¨-e** hat. **den ~ aufsetzen/abnehmen** *(geh)* to put on/take off one's hat; **vor jdm den ~ abnehmen** *(fig)* to take off one's hat to sb; **~ ab vor solcher Leistung!** I take my hat off to that; **das kannst du dir an den ~ stecken!** *(col)* you can keep it; **unter einen ~ bringen** *(col)* to reconcile; *Termine* to fit in; **da geht einem der ~ hoch** *(col)* it's enough to make you blow your top *(col)*; **seinen ~ nehmen (müssen)** *(col)* to (have to) go; **das ist doch ein alter ~!** *(col)* that's old hat! *(col)*.
Hut[2] *f no pl* **(a)** *(geh)* protection, keeping. **unter** *or* **in meiner ~** in my keeping; *(Kinder)* in my care. **(b) auf der ~ sein** to be on one's guard *(vor+dat* against*)*.
hüten 1 *vt* to look after, to mind; *Geheimnisse* to keep. **das Bett/Haus ~** to stay in bed/indoors; **hüte deine Zunge!** *(geh)* watch your tongue! **2** *vr* to guard *(vor+dat* against*)*, to beware *(vor+dat* of*)*. **ich werde mich ~!** not likely!; **ich werde mich ~, ihm das zu erzählen** there's no chance of me telling him that; **sich ~, etw zu tun** to take care not to do sth.
Hüter(in *f*) *m* - guardian, keeper.
Hut-: ~krempe *f* brim (of a hat); **~macher (in *f*)** *m* hatter; *(für Damen auch)* milliner; **~schachtel** *f* hatbox; **~schnur** *f* **das geht mir über die ~schnur** *(col)* that's going too far.
Hütte *f* **-n (a)** hut; *(schäbiges Häuschen auch)* shack; *(Holz~, Block~)* cabin. **(b)** *(Tech: Hüt-*

tenwerk) iron and steel works *pl or sing.*

Hütten-: ~**arbeiter** *m* worker in an iron and steel works; ~**industrie** *f* iron and steel industry; ~**käse** *m* cottage cheese; ~**werk** *nt siehe* **Hütte (b).**

hutz(e)lig *adj Obst* dried; *Mensch* wizened.

Hyäne *f* **-n** hyena; *(fig)* wildcat.

Hyazinthe [hya'tsɪntə] *f* **-n** hyacinth.

Hydrant *m* hydrant.

Hydraulik *f* hydraulics *sing; (Antrieb, Anlage)* hydraulics *pl.*

hydraulisch *adj* hydraulic.

Hygiene [hy'gieːnə] *f no pl* hygiene.

hygienisch [hy'gieːnɪʃ] *adj* hygienic.

Hymne ['hʏmnə] *f* **-n** hymn; *(National~)* (national) anthem.

hyper-: ~**modern** *adj (col)* ultramodern; ~**sensibel** *adj* hypersensitive.

Hypnose *f* **-n** hypnosis. **jdn in ~ versetzen** to put sb under hypnosis.

Hypnotiseur [hʏpnoti'zøːɐ] *m* hynotist.

hypnotisieren* *vt* to hypnotize.

Hypothek *f* **-en** mortgage; *(fig: Belastung)* burden of guilt. **eine ~ aufnehmen** to raise a mortgage; **etw mit einer ~ belasten** to mortgage sth.

Hypotheken-: ~**bank** *f bank specializing in mortgages;* ~**brief** *m* mortgage certificate; ~**darlehen** *nt* mortgage (loan); **h~frei** *adj* unmortgaged.

Hypothese *f* **-n** hypothesis.

hypothetisch *adj* hypothetical.

Hysterie *f* hysteria.

hysterisch *adj* hysterical. **einen ~en Anfall bekommen** *(fig)* to have hysterics.

I

I, i [iː] *nt* **-, -** I, i. **das Tüpfelchen auf dem ~** *(fig)* the final touch.
i [iː] *interj (col)* ugh *(col)*.
i.A. = **im Auftrag** pp.
iberisch *adj* Iberian. **die I~e Halbinsel** the Iberian Peninsula.
IC [iː'tseː] *m* **-s** = **Intercity-Zug.**
ich *pers pron* I. **immer ~!** it's always me!; **~ Idiot!** what an idiot I am!; **und ~ Idiot habe es gemacht** and idiot that I am, I did it; **~ nicht!** not me!; **~ selbst** I myself; **wer hat gerufen? — ~!** who called? — (it was) me, I did.
Ich *nt* **-(s)** self; *(Psych)* ego. **das eigene ~** one's (own) self/ego; **mein zweites ~** *(selbst)* my other self; *(andere Person)* my alter ego.
Ich-: i~bezogen *adj* egocentric; **~form** *f* first person; **~-Roman** *m* novel in the first person.
ideal *adj* ideal.
Ideal *nt* **-e** ideal. **sie ist mein ~ einer Frau** she's my ideal woman.
Ideal- *in cpds* ideal; **~fall** *m* ideal case; **im ~fall** ideally; **~gewicht** *nt* ideal weight.
idealisieren* *vt* to idealize.
Idealismus *m* idealism.
Idealist *m* idealist.
idealistisch *adj* idealistic.
Ideal-: ~typ(us) *m (Sociol)* ideal type; **~vorstellung** *f* ideal.
Idee *f* **-n** [i'deːən] **(a)** idea. **die ~ zu etw** the idea for sth; **wie kommst du denn auf *die* ~?** whatever gave you that idea?; **ich kam auf die ~, Andrea zu fragen** I hit on the idea of asking Andrea; **jdn auf die ~ bringen, etw zu tun** to give sb the idea of doing sth. **(b)** *(ein wenig)* shade, trifle. **eine ~ Salz** a touch of salt; **keine ~ besser** not a whit better.
ideell *adj, Wert, Ziele* non-material; *Bedürfnisse, Unterstützung* spiritual.
ideen- [i'deːən-]: **~arm** *adj* lacking in ideas; **~los** *adj* devoid of ideas; **~reich** *adj* full of ideas.
identifizieren* **1** *vt* to identify. **2** *vr* **sich ~ mit** to identify with.
Identifizierung *f* identification.
identisch *adj* identical *(mit* with*)*.
Identität *f* identity.
Ideologe *m*, **Ideologin** *f* ideologist.
Ideologie *f* ideology.
ideologisch *adj* ideological.
Idiom *nt* **-e** idiom.
idiomatisch *adj* idiomatic.
Idiot *m (wk)* **-en, -en** idiot.
Idioten-: ~hügel *m (hum col)* beginners' *or* nursery *(Brit)* slope; **i~sicher** *adj (col)* foolproof *no adv*.
Idiotie *f* idiocy.
Idiotin *f* idiot.
idiotisch *adj* idiotic.
Idol *nt* **-e** idol.
Idylle *f* **-n** idyll.
idyllisch *adj* idyllic.
IG [iː'geː] *f* **-s** = **Industriegewerkschaft.**
Igel *m* **-** *(Zool)* hedgehog.
igitt(igitt)! *interj* ugh! *(col)*.
Iglu ['iːglu] *m or nt* **-s** igloo.
Ignorant *m* ignoramus.
Ignoranz *f* ignorance.
ignorieren* *vt* to ignore.
ihm *pers pron dat of* **er, es** *(bei Personen)* to him; *(bei Tieren und Dingen)* to it; *(nach Präpositionen)* him/it. **ich gab es ~** I gave it (to) him/it; **es war ~, als ob er träumte** he felt as though he were dreaming; **es ist ~ nicht gut** he doesn't feel well; **sie schnitt ~ die Haare** she cut his hair (for him); **ein Freund von ~** a friend of his, one of his friends; **wir gingen zu ~ (nach Hause)** we went to his place; **sie hat ~ einen Pulli gestrickt** she knitted him a sweater.
ihn *pers pron acc of* **er** him; *(bei Tieren, Dingen)* it.
ihnen *pers pron dat of* **sie** *pl* to them; *(nach Präpositionen)* them; *siehe* **ihm.**
Ihnen *pers pron dat of* **Sie** to you; *(nach Präpositionen)* you; *siehe* **ihm.**
ihr 1 *pers pron* **(a)** *2. pers pl nom* you. **(b)** *dat of* **sie** *sing (bei Personen)* to her; *(bei Tieren und Dingen)* to it; *(nach Präpositionen)* her/it; *siehe* **ihm. 2** *poss pron* **(a)** *(einer Person)* her; *(eines Tiers, Dings)* its. **(b)** *(von mehreren)* their.
Ihr *poss pron* your. **~ Franz Müller** *(Briefschluß)* yours, Franz Müller.
ihrer *pers pron* **(a)** *gen of* **sie** *sing (bei Personen)* of her. **wir werden ~ gedenken** *(geh)* we will remember her. **(b)** *gen of* **sie** *pl* of them.
Ihrer *pers pron gen of* **Sie** of you.
ihre(r, s) *poss pron (substantivisch)* **(a)** *(einer Person)* hers; *(eines Tiers)* its. **I~ Majestät** Her Majesty; **sie und die I~n** *(geh: Familie)* she and her family. **(b)** *(von mehreren)* theirs. **sie taten das ~** *(geh)* they did their bit.
Ihre(r, s) *poss pron sing and pl (substantivisch)* yours. **tun Sie das ~** *(geh)* you do your bit.
ihrerseits *adv (bei einer Person)* for her part; *(bei mehreren)* for their part; *(von ihrer Seite)* on her/their part.
Ihrerseits *adv* for your part; *(von Ihrer Seite)* on your part.
ihresgleichen *pron inv (von einer Person)* people like her; *(von mehreren)* people like them; *(von Dingen)* others like it. **eine Frechheit, die ~ sucht!** an incredible cheek!
Ihresgleichen *pron inv* people like you.
ihret-: ~wegen, ~willen *adv (bei Personen) (wegen ihr/ihnen) (sing)* because of her; *(pl)* because of them; *(für sie)* on her/their behalf; *(bei Dingen und Tieren) (sing)* because of it; *(pl)* because of them; **sie sagte, ~wegen könnten wir gehen** she said that, as far as she was concerned, we could go.
Ihret-: ~wegen, ~willen *adv* because of you; *(für Sie)* on your behalf.
ihrige *poss pron (old, geh)* **der/die/das ~** *(von einer Person)* hers; *(von mehreren)* theirs.
Ihrige *poss pron* **der/die/das ~** yours.
i.J. = **im Jahre.**
Ikone *f* **-n** icon.
illegal *adj* illegal.
Illegalität *f* illegality.
illegitim *adj* illegitimate.
Illusion *f* illusion. **sich** *(dat)* **~en machen** to delude oneself; **darüber macht er sich keine ~en** he doesn't have any illusions about it.
illusionär *adj* illusionary.
illusorisch *adj* illusory. **es ist völlig ~, zu glau-**

ben ... it's a complete illusion to believe ...
Illustration *f* illustration. **zur ~ von etw** to illustrate sth.
illustrieren* *vt* to illustrate (*jdm etw* sth for sb).
Illustrierte *f (wk)* **-n, -n** magazine.
Iltis *m* **-se** polecat.
im *prep* = **in dem (a)** in the. **~ zweiten Stock** on the second floor; **~ Kino/Theater** at the cinema/theatre; **~ Bett** in bed; **~ „Faust"** in "Faust"; **~ Mai** in May; **~ Alter von 91 Jahren** at the age of 91; **~ nächsten Jahr** next year. **(b) nicht ~ geringsten** not in the slightest; **~ Kommen/Gehen sein** to be coming/going; **etw ~ Liegen/Stehen tun** to do sth lying down/standing up; **~ Trab/Laufschritt** at a trot/run.
Image ['ɪmɪtʃ] *nt* **-s** image.
Imagepflege *f (col)* image-building.
imaginär *adj* imaginary.
Imbiß *m* **-sse** snack.
Imbiß-: **~halle** *f* snack bar; **~stube** *f* cafe.
Imitation *f* imitation.
Imitator *m*, **Imitatorin** *f* imitator; *(von einem Bild)* copyist.
imitieren* *vt* to imitate.
Imker *m* **-** beekeeper.
immanent *adj* inherent, intrinsic. **einer Sache** *(dat)* **~ sein** to be inherent in sth.
Immatrikulation *f* matriculation.
immatrikulieren* *vr* to matriculate.
immens *adj* immense.
immer *adv* **(a)** always. **schon ~** always; **für ~** for ever, for always; **~ diese Probleme!** all these problems!; **~, wenn ...** whenever ...; **~ mal** *(col)* from time to time; **~ geradeaus gehen** to keep going straight on; **~ und ewig** *(liter)* for ever and ever; **~ noch** still; **~ noch nicht** still not; **~ wieder** again and again; **etw ~ wieder tun** to keep on doing sth; **wie ~** as always.
(b) *(+comp)* **~ besser** better and better; **~ häufiger** more and more often; **~ größer werdende Schulden** constantly increasing debts.
(c) wer/wie/wann/wo/was (auch) ~ whoever/however/whenever/wherever/whatever.
(d) *(col: jeweils)* **gib mir ~ drei Bücher auf einmal** give me three books at a time; **~ am dritten Tag** every third day.
immer-: **~fort** *adv* the whole time; **~grün** *adj attr (lit, fig)* evergreen; **~hin** *adv* anyhow, at any rate; *(wenigstens)* at least; *(schließlich)* after all; **~während** *adj attr* perpetual; **~zu** *adv* the whole time.
Immigrant(in *f***)** *m* immigrant.
Immigration *f* immigration.
immigrieren* *vi aux sein* to immigrate.
Immobilien [-'biːliən] *pl* real estate *sing*; *(in Zeitungsannoncen)* property *sing*.
Immobilienhändler *m* estate agent *(Brit)*, realtor *(US)*.
immun *adj* immune *(gegen* to*)*.
Immunität *f* immunity.
Imperativ *m (Gram)* imperative.
Imperfekt *nt* **-e** *(Gram)* imperfect (tense).
Imperialismus *m* imperialism.
imperialistisch *adj* imperialistic.
impfen *vt* to vaccinate, to inoculate.
Impf-: **~paß** *m* vaccination card; **~pistole** *f* vaccination gun; **~schein** *m* vaccination certificate; **~schutz** *m* protection given by vaccination; **~stoff** *m* vaccine, serum.
Impfung *f* vaccination, inoculation.
Impfzwang *m* compulsory vaccination.
implizieren* *vt* to imply.
implodieren* *vi aux sein* to implode.
imponieren* *vi* to impress *(jdm* sb*)*. **das imponiert mir** it's impressive.
imponierend *adj* impressive.
Import *m* **-e** import. **der ~ sollte den Export nicht übersteigen** imports should not exceed exports.
Importeur [ɪmpɔr'tøːɐ] *m* importer.
Import- *in cpds* import; **~geschäft** *nt (Handel)* import trade; *(Firma)* import business.
importieren* *vt* to import.
Importland *nt* importing country.
imposant *adj* imposing; *Leistung* impressive.
impotent *adj* impotent.
Impotenz *f* impotence.
imprägnieren* *vt* to impregnate; *(wasserdicht machen)* to waterproof.
Imprägnierung *f* impregnation; *(von Geweben)* waterproofing.
Impressionismus *m* impressionism.
Impressionist *m* impressionist.
impressionistisch *adj* impressionistic.
Impressum *nt, pl* **Impressen** imprint.
Improvisation [ɪmproviza'tsioːn] *f* improvization.
improvisieren* [-vi'ziːrən] *vti* to improvize.
Impuls *m* **-e** impulse. **etw aus einem ~ heraus tun** to do sth on impulse; **einer Sache** *(dat)* **neue ~e geben** to give sth new impetus.
impulsiv *adj* impulsive. **~ handeln** to act impulsively.
imstande *adj pred* **~ sein, etw zu tun** *(fähig)* to be capable of doing sth; *(in der Lage)* to be in a position to do sth; **er ist zu allem ~** he's capable of anything.
in 1 *prep siehe auch* **im, ins (a)** *(räumlich) (wo? +dat)* in; *(wohin?+acc)* in, into. **sind Sie schon ~ Deutschland gewesen?** have you ever been to Germany?; **~ die Schule gehen** to go to school; **er ist ~ der Schule** he's at *or* in school. **(b)** *(zeitlich) (wann? +dat)* in; *(bis +acc)* into. **~ diesem Jahr** *(laufendes Jahr)* this year; *(jenes Jahr)* in that year; **heute ~ zwei Wochen** two weeks today; **bis ~s 18. Jahrhundert** into *or* up to the 18th century. **(c) ~ Englisch steht er sehr schwach** he's very weak in *or* at English; **das ist ~ Englisch** it's in English; **~ die Hunderte gehen** to run into (the) hundreds; **es ~ sich haben** *(col) (Text)* to be tough; *(Whisky)* to have quite a kick; *(Torte)* to be heavy.
2 *adj pred (col)* **~ sein** to be in *(col)*.
in|aktiv *adj* inactive; *Mitglied* non-active.
In|angriffnahme *f no pl (form)* commencement.
In|anspruchnahme *f no pl (form) (eines Kredits)* taking out; *(von Rechten)* exertion. **im Falle einer ~ der Arbeitslosenunterstützung** where unemployment benefit has been sought.
Inbegriff *m* perfect example; *(der Schönheit, des Bösen etc)* epitome.
inbegriffen *adj pred* included.
Inbetriebnahme *f* **-n** *(form)* commissioning; *(von Gebäude, U-Bahn etc)* inauguration.
indem *conj* **(a)** *(während)* while; *(in dem Augenblick)* as. **(b)** *(dadurch, daß)* **~ man etw macht** by doing sth.
Inder(in *f***)** *m* **-** Indian.
indessen *adv* **(a)** *(inzwischen)* meanwhile, (in the) meantime. **(b)** *(jedoch)* however.
Index *m* **-e** *or* **Indizes** ['ɪnditseːs] index. **auf dem ~ stehen** *(fig)* to be banned.
Indianer(in *f***)** *m* **-** (Red *or* American) Indian.
indianisch *adj* (Red *or* American) Indian.
Indien ['ɪndiən] *nt* India.
indifferent *adj (geh)* indifferent *(gegenüber* to*)*.
indigniert *adj (geh)* indignant.
Indikation *f (Med)* indication *(Jur)*. **medizinische/soziale ~** *(Jur)* medical/social grounds for the termination of pregnancy.
Indikativ *m (Gram)* indicative.
Indikator *m* indicator.
indirekt *adj* indirect.
indisch *adj* Indian.
indiskret *adj* indiscreet.
Indiskretion *f* indiscretion.
indiskutabel *adj* out of the question.

indisponiert *adj (geh)* indisposed.
Individualist [ɪndividua'lɪst] *m* individualist.
individualistisch [ɪndividua'lɪstɪʃ] *adj* individualistic.
Individualität [ɪndividuali'tɛːt] *f no pl* individuality.
individuell [ɪndivi'duɛl] *adj* individual. **etw ~ gestalten** to give sth a personal note; **es ist ~ verschieden** it differs from person to person.
Individuum [ɪndi'viːduʊm] *nt, pl* **Individuen** [ɪndi'viːduən] individual.
Indiz *nt* **-ien** [-iən] **(a)** *(Jur)* clue; *(als Beweismittel)* piece of circumstantial evidence. **alles beruht nur auf ~ien** everything rests only on circumstantial evidence. **(b)** *(Anzeichen)* sign, indication *(für* of*)*.
Indizienbeweis *m* circumstantial evidence *no pl*; piece of circumstantial evidence.
indogermanisch *adj* Indo-Germanic.
indoktrinieren* *vt* to indoctrinate.
Indonesien [-iən] *nt* Indonesia.
indonesisch *adj* Indonesian.
Indossament *nt (Comm)* endorsement.
industrialisieren* *vt* to industrialize.
Industrialisierung *f* industrialization.
Industrie *f* industry. **in der ~ arbeiten** to be in industry.
Industrie- *in cpds* industrial; **~anlage** *f* industrial plant; **~betrieb** *m* industrial firm; **~erzeugnis** *nt* industrial product; **~gebiet** *nt* industrial area; **~gewerkschaft** *f* industrial trade union *or* labor union *(US)*; **~kaufmann** *m* industrial manager.
industriell *adj* industrial.
Industrielle(r) *mf decl as adj* industrialist.
Industrie-: ~roboter *m* industrial robot; **~staat** *m* industrial nation; **~- und Handelskammer** *f* chamber of industry and commerce; **~zweig** *m* branch of industry.
in|einander *adv sein, liegen etc* in each other; *legen, hängen etc* into each other. **~ übergehen** to merge (into each other); **sich ~ verlieben** to fall in love with each other.
in|einander-: ~fließen *vi sep irreg aux sein* to merge; **~greifen** *vi sep irreg (lit)* to interlock; *(Zahnräder)* to mesh; *(fig: Ereignisse etc)* to overlap; **~passen** *vi sep* to fit into each other.
infam *adj* infamous.
Infanterie *f* infantry.
Infanterist *m* infantryman.
infantil *adj* infantile.
Infarkt *m* **-e** *(Herz~)* coronary.
Infektion *f* infection.
Infektions-: ~herd *m* focus of infection; **~krankheit** *f* infectious disease.
Infiltration *f* infiltration.
Infinitiv *m* infinitive.
infizieren* **1** *vt* to infect. **2** *vr* to be infected *(bei* by*)*.
in flagranti *adv* in the act, red-handed.
Inflation *f* inflation.
inflationär [ɪnflatsio'nɛːɐ] *adj* inflationary. **sich ~ entwickeln** to become inflated.
Inflations-: i~hemmend *adj* anti-inflationary; **~rate** *f* rate of inflation.
infolge *prep +gen or von* as a result of.
infolgedessen *adv* consequently.
Informatik *f* information science.
Informatiker(in *f***)** *m* **-** information scientist.
Information *f* **(a)** information *no pl (über +acc* about, on*)*. **eine ~** (a piece of) information; **zu Ihrer ~** for your information. **(b)** *(~stelle)* information desk. **(c) ~en** *pl (Comp)* data.
informationell [ɪnfɔrmatsio'nɛl] *adj* informational.
Informations-: ~büro *n* information bureau; **~fluß** *m no pl* flow of information; **~material** *nt* informative material; **~quelle** *f* source of information; **~theorie** *f* information theory.
informativ *adj* informative.
informell *adj* informal.
informieren* **1** *vt* to inform *(über +acc, von* about*)*. **da bist du falsch informiert** you've been misinformed. **2** *vr* to find out.
Infra-: i~rot *adj* infra-red; **~rotstrahler** *m* **-** infra-red lamp; **~struktur** *f* infrastructure.
Infusion *f* infusion.
Ing. = Ingenieur.
Ingenieur(in *f***)** [ɪnʒe'niøːɐ, -iøːrɪn] *m* engineer.
Ingenieur-: ~büro *nt* engineer's office; **~schule** *f* school of engineering.
Ingwer *m no pl* ginger.
Inh. = Inhaber prop.; **Inhalt.**
Inhaber(in *f***)** *m* **-** *(von Geschäft)* owner; *(von Konto, Lizenz, Rekord)* holder; *(von Scheck, Paß)* bearer.
inhaftieren* *vt insep* to take into custody.
inhalieren* *vti insep (Med, col)* to inhale.
Inhalt *m* **-e (a)** contents *pl*; *(von Buch, Begriff auch)* content; *(des Lebens)* meaning. **was hatte das Gespräch zum ~?** what was the content of the discussion?; **ein Brief des ~s, daß ...** *(form)* a letter to the effect that ... **(b)** *(Math) (Flächen~)* area; *(Raum~)* volume.
inhaltlich *adj* as regards content.
Inhalts-: ~angabe *f* summary, précis *(esp Sch)*; **i~los** *adj* empty; *Buch, Vortrag* lacking in content; **i~reich** *adj* full; **~verzeichnis** *nt* list of contents.
inhuman *adj (unmenschlich, brutal)* inhuman.
Initiale [ini'tsiaːlə] *f* **-n** *(geh)* initial.
Initiative [initsia'tiːvə] *f* initiative. **aus eigener ~** on one's own initiative; **die ~ ergreifen** to take the initiative.
Initiator(in *f***)** [ini'tsiaːtɔr, -'toːrɪn] *m (geh)* initiator.
Injektion *f* injection.
injizieren* [ɪnji'tsiːrən] *vt (form)* to inject *(jdm etw* sb with sth*)*.
Inkaufnahme *f no pl (form)* acceptance. **unter ~ finanzieller Verluste** accepting the inevitable financial losses.
inkl. = inklusive incl.
inklusive [-ziːvə] **1** *prep +gen* inclusive of. **2** *adv* inclusive.
inkognito *adv* incognito.
inkompetent *adj* incompetent.
inkonsequent *adj* inconsistent.
Inkrafttreten *nt no pl* **bei ~ von etw** when sth comes/came *etc* into effect.
Inkubationszeit *f* incubation period.
Inland *nt no pl* **(a)** *(als Staatsgebiet)* home. **im ~ hergestellte Waren** home-produced goods; **im In- und Ausland** at home and abroad. **(b)** *(Inneres eines Landes)* inland. **im ~** inland.
Inland- *in cpds (Comm)* home, domestic; *(Geog)* inland; **~flug** *m* domestic *or* internal flight.
inländisch *adj* home *attr*, domestic; *(Geog)* inland.
Inlands-: ~gespräch *nt* inland call; **~markt** *m* home *or* domestic market; **~porto** *nt* inland postage.
inmitten 1 *prep +gen* in the middle of. **2** *adv* **~ von** amongst, surrounded by.
innehaben *vt sep irreg (form) Amt etc* to hold.
innehalten *vi sep irreg* to pause, to stop. **in der Rede ~** to pause.
innen *adv* inside. **~ und außen** inside and out(side); **nach ~** inwards; **tief ~ tut es doch weh** deep down inside it really hurts; **das Band befördert die Kohle nach ~** the conveyor-belt carries the coal inside; **von ~** from the inside.
Innen-: ~antenne *f* indoor aerial *(Brit) or* antenna *(US)*; **~architekt** *m* interior designer; **~aufnahme** *f* indoor photo(graph); *(Film)* indoor shot; **~ausstattung** *f* interior décor *no pl*; *(das Ausstat-*

ten) interior decoration and furnishing; *(von Auto)* interior fittings *pl*; ~**bahn** *f (Sport)* inside lane; ~**dienst** *m* office duty; **im** ~**dienst sein** to work in the office; ~**einrichtung** *f* interior furnishing; ~**hof** *m* inner courtyard; ~**kurve** *f* inside bend; ~**leben** *nt no pl (col)* **(a)** *(seelisch)* emotional life; **(b)** *(körperlich)* insides *pl*; ~**minister** *m* minister of the interior; *(in GB)* Home Secretary; *(in den USA)* Secretary of the Interior; ~**ministerium** *nt* ministry of the interior; *(in GB)* Home Office; *(in den USA)* Department of the Interior; ~**politik** *f* domestic policy/policies *pl*; **i**~**politisch** *adj* domestic, home *attr*; **auf i**~**politischem Gebiet** in the field of home affairs; ~**raum** *m* **(a)** inner room; **(b)** *no pl* room inside; *(von Wagen auch)* interior; *(von Stadion)* central area; **mit großem** ~**raum** with a lot of room inside; ~**seite** *f* inside; ~**stadt** *f* town/city centre *(Brit) or* center *(US)*; ~**tasche** *f* inside pocket; ~**temperatur** *f (in Gebäude)* indoor temperature; ~**welt** *f* inner world.

inner-: ~**betrieblich** *adj* internal company; **etw** ~**betrieblich regeln** to settle sth within the company; ~**deutsch** *adj* German domestic *attr*; ~**deutscher Handel** domestic trade in Germany.

Innereien *pl* innards *pl*.

innere(r, s) *adj* inner; *(im Körper befindlich, inländisch)* internal. **Facharzt für** ~ **Krankheiten** internist; **eine** ~ **Uhr** *(col)* an internal *or* a biological clock; **vor meinem** ~**n Auge** in my mind's eye; ~ **Führung** *(Mil)* moral leadership.

Innere(s) *nt decl as adj* **(a)** inside; *(von Wagen, Schloß auch)* interior; *(Mitte)* middle. **das** ~ **nach außen kehren** to turn something inside out; **die Organe im** ~**n des Körpers** the organs inside the body. **(b)** *(fig: Gemüt, Geist)* heart. **ich wußte, was in seinem** ~**n vorging** I knew what was going on inside him.

innerhalb 1 *prep +gen* inside, within. ~ **dieser Regelung** within this ruling. **2** *adv* inside.

innerlich *adj* **(a)** *(körperlich)* internal. **dieses Medikament ist** ~ **anzuwenden** this medicine is to be taken internally. **(b)** *(geistig, seelisch)* inward, inner *no adv*; *Mensch* inward; *Hemmung* inner. **ein** ~ **gefestigter Mensch** a person of inner strength.

Innerlichkeit *f (liter)* inwardness.

inner-: ~**örtlich** *adj* in built-up areas; ~**parteilich** *adj* within the party; ~**parteiliche Demokratie** democracy (with)in the party structure.

innerste(r, s) *adj superl of* **innere(r, s)** innermost.

Innerste(s) *nt decl as adj (lit, fig)* heart. **bis ins** ~ **getroffen** hurt to the quick.

innewohnen *vi sep +dat* to be inherent in.

innig *adj Grüße, Beileid* heartfelt; *Vergnügen* deep; *Freundschaft* intimate. **mein** ~**ster Wunsch** my dearest wish; **jdn** ~ **lieben** to love sb deeply.

Innigkeit *f (von Empfindung)* depth; *(von Liebe)* intensity; *(von Freundschaft)* intimacy.

Innung *f* (trade) guild. **du blamierst die ganze** ~ *(hum col)* you're letting the whole side down.

in|offiziell *adj* unofficial.

Input ['ɪnput] *m or nt* **-s** input.

Inquisition *f* Inquisition.

ins = **in das.** ~ **Rollen kommen** to start rolling.

Insasse *m (wk)* **-n, -n, Insassin** *f (eines Fahrzeuges)* passenger; *(einer Anstalt)* inmate.

Insassenversicherung *f* passenger insurance.

insbesondere *adv* particularly.

Inschrift *f* inscription.

Insekt *nt* **-en** insect.

Insekten-: ~**bekämpfung** *f* insect control; ~**gift** *nt* insecticide; ~**plage** *f* plague of insects; ~**pulver** *nt* insect powder; ~**stich** *m (von Mücken, Flöhen)* insect bite; *(von Bienen, Wespen)* (insect) sting; ~**vertilgungsmittel** *nt* insecticide.

Insel *f* **-n** *(lit, fig)* island.

Insel-: ~**bewohner** *m* islander; ~**gruppe** *f* archipelago, group of islands; ~**staat** *m* island state; ~**volk** *nt* island race; ~**welt** *f* island world; **die** ~**welt Mittelamerikas** the world of the Central American islands.

Inserat *nt* advert *(Brit col)*, ad *(col)*, advertisement.

Inserent *m* advertiser.

inserieren* *vti* to advertise.

insgeheim *adv* secretly, in secret.

insgesamt *adv (alles zusammen)* altogether; *(im großen und ganzen)* all in all. **die Kosten belaufen sich auf** ~ **1.000 DM** the costs amount to a total of DM 1,000.

Insider ['ɪnsaɪdə] *m* **-** insider. **der Witz war nur für** ~ **verständlich** that was an in-joke.

insofern 1 *adv* in this respect. ~ **... als** in so far as, inasmuch as. **2** [ɪnzo'fɛrn] *conj (wenn)* if.

Insolvenz ['ɪnzɔlvɛnts] *f (Comm)* insolvency.

insoweit [ɪn'zo:vait] *adv*, [ɪnzo'vait] *conj siehe* **insofern.**

in spe [ɪn'spe:] *adj (col)* **unser Schwiegersohn** ~ our son-in-law to be, our future son-in-law.

Inspekteur [ɪnspɛk'tø:ɐ] *m (Mil)* Chief of Staff.

Inspektion *f* inspection; *(Aut)* service. **ich habe mein Auto zur** ~ **gebracht** I've taken my car in for a service.

Inspektionsreise *f* tour of inspection.

Inspektor(in *f*) [ɪn'spɛktɔr, -'to:rɪn] *m* inspector.

Inspiration [ɪnspira'tsio:n] *f* inspiration.

inspirieren* [ɪnspi'ri:rən] *vt* to inspire. **sich von etw** ~ **lassen** to get one's inspiration from sth.

inspizieren* [ɪnspi'tsi:rən] *vt* to inspect.

Installateur [ɪnstala'tø:ɐ] *m* plumber; *(Elektro~)* electrician; *(Gas~)* gas-fitter.

Installation [ɪnstala'tsio:n] *f* installation.

installieren* [ɪnsta'li:rən] *vt* to install *(auch fig)*.

instand *adj* **etw** ~ **halten** to keep sth in good condition; **etw** ~ **setzen** to get sth into condition.

Instandhaltung *f* maintenance.

inständig *adj* urgent. ~ **bitten** to beg; ~ **hoffen** to hope fervently.

Instandsetzung *f (von Gerät)* overhaul; *(von Gebäude)* restoration.

Instanz [ɪn'stants] *f* **(a)** *(Behörde)* authority. **(b)** *(Jur)* court. **Verhandlung in erster/zweiter** ~ first/second court-case; **er ging von einer** ~ **zur anderen** he went through all the courts.

Instinkt [ɪn'stɪŋkt] *m* **-e** *(lit, fig)* instinct.

instinktiv [ɪnstɪŋk'ti:f] *adj* instinctive.

Institut [ɪnsti'tu:t] *nt* **-e** institute.

Institution [ɪnstitu'tsio:n] *f* institution.

instruieren* [ɪnstru'i:rən] *vt* to instruct; *(über Unternehmen, Plan etc)* to brief.

Instruktion [ɪnstrʊk'tsio:n] *f* instruction.

Instrument [ɪnstru'mɛnt] *nt* instrument.

instrumental [ɪnstrumɛn'ta:l] *adj (Mus)* instrumental.

Instrumental- *in cpds* instrumental.

Instrumentarium [ɪnstrumɛn'ta:rium] *nt* instruments *pl*; *(fig)* apparatus.

Insulaner(in *f*) *m* **-** *(usu hum)* islander.

Insulin *nt no pl* insulin.

inszenieren* *vt* **(a)** *(Theat)* to direct; *(TV)* to produce. **(b)** *(fig)* to stage-manage. **einen Streit** ~ to start an argument.

Inszenierung *f* production.

intakt *adj* intact.

integer *adj (geh)* **ein integrer Mensch** a person of integrity.

Integralrechnung *f* integral calculus.

Integration *f* integration.

integrieren* *vt* to integrate *(auch Math)*. **integrierte Gesamtschule** comprehensive (school) *(Brit)*.

Integrität *f* integrity.

Intellekt *m no pl* intellect.

intellektuell *adj* intellectual.
Intellektuelle(r) *mf decl as adj* intellectual.
intelligent *adj* intelligent.
Intelligenz *f* intelligence; *(Personengruppe)* intelligentsia *pl*.
Intelligenzbestie *f (pej col)* egghead *(col)*.
Intelligenz-: ~**quotient** *m* IQ; ~**test** *m* intelligence test; **einen ~test mit jdm machen** to test sb's IQ.
Intendant *m* director; theatre-manager *(Brit)*, theater-manager *(US)*.
intendieren* *vt (geh)* to intend.
Intensität *f* intensity.
intensiv *adj Arbeit, Forschung* intensive; *Farbe, Gefühl* intense; *Geruch* powerful.
intensivieren* [-'viːrən] *vt* to intensify.
Intensivierung *f* intensification.
Intensivstation *f* intensive care unit.
Intention *f (geh)* intention.
Inter- *in cpds* inter-; ~**city-Zug** *m* inter-city train.
interessant *adj* interesting. **zu diesem Preis ist das nicht ~ für uns** *(Comm)* we are not interested at that price; **sich ~ machen** to attract attention.
interessanterweise *adv* interestingly enough.
Interesse *nt* **-n** interest. **~ an jdm/etw** *or* **für jdn/etw haben** to be interested in sb/sth; **aus ~** out of interest; **es liegt in Ihrem eigenen ~** it's in your own interest(s); **sein ~ gilt ...** his interest lies in ...; **das ist für uns nicht von ~** that's of no interest to us.
Interesse-: **i~halber** *adv* out of interest; **i~los** *adj* indifferent; ~**losigkeit** *f* indifference.
Interessen-: ~**gebiet** *nt* field of interest; ~**gegensatz** *m* clash of interests.
Interessent(in *f***)** *m* interested party. **es haben sich mehrere ~en gemeldet** several people have shown interest.
Interessenvertretung *f* representation of interests; *(Personen)* group representing one's interests.
interessieren* **1** *vt* to interest *(für, an +dat* in*)*. **das interessiert mich nicht!** I'm not interested. **2** *vr* to be interested *(für* in*)*.
interessiert *adj* interested *(an +dat* in*)*. **~ zuhören** to listen with interest; **vielseitig ~ sein** to have a wide range of interests; **politisch ~** interested in politics.
Interims- *in cpds* interim; ~**regierung** *f* caretaker government.
Inter-: **i~konfessionell** *adj* interdenominational; ~**kontinentalrakete** *f* intercontinental missile.
Intermezzo [-'mɛtso] *nt* **-s** *or* **Intermezzi** *(Mus)* intermezzo; *(fig)* interlude.
intern *adj* internal. **diese Maßnahmen müssen ~ bleiben** these measures must be kept private.
Internat *nt* boarding school.
international [ɪntɐnatsio'naːl] *adj* international.
Internationale [ɪntɐnatsio'naːlə] *f* **-n** Internationale.
Internatsschüler *m* boarder.
internieren* *vt* to intern.
Internierung *f* internment.
Internist(in *f***)** *m* internist.
Interpol *f* Interpol.
Interpret *m (wk)* **-en, -en** interpreter *(of music, art etc)*. **Lieder verschiedener ~en** songs by various singers.
Interpretation *f* interpretation.
interpretieren* *vt* to interpret. **etw falsch ~** to misinterpret sth.
Interpretin *f siehe* **Interpret.**
Interpunktion *f* punctuation.
Intershop ['ɪntɐʃɔp] *m* **-s** *(DDR)* international shop.
Intervall [-'val] *nt* **-e** interval.
intervenieren* [-ve'niːrən] *vi* to intervene.
Intervention [-vɛn'tsioːn] *f* intervention.
Interview ['ɪntɐvjuː] *nt* **-s** interview.
interviewen* [-'vjuːən] *vt* to interview *(jdn zu etw* sb about sth*)*.
Interviewer(in *f***)** [-'vjuːɐ, -vjuːərɪn] *m* **-** interviewer.
intim *adj* intimate. **~e Beziehungen** *(euph: sexuell)* intimate relations; **ein ~er Kenner von etw sein** to have an intimate knowledge of sth.
Intim-: ~**bereich** *m (Anat)* genital area; ~**feind** *m* best enemy; ~**hygiene** *f* personal hygiene.
Intimität *f* intimacy. **zwischen den beiden kam es zu ~en** they became intimate with each other.
Intim-: ~**sphäre** *f* private life; **jds ~sphäre verletzen** to invade sb's privacy; ~**verkehr** *m* intimacy; **~verkehr mit jdm haben** to be intimate with sb.
intolerant *adj* intolerant *(jdm/einer Sache gegenüber* of sb/sth*)*.
Intoleranz *f* intolerance.
Intonation *f* intonation.
intonieren* *vt* **(a) einen Satz falsch ~** to give a sentence the wrong intonation. **(b)** *(Mus) Melodie* to sing; *(Kapelle)* to play; *Ton* to give.
intransitiv *adj* intransitive.
Intrigant(in *f***)** *m* schemer, intriguer.
Intrige *f* **-n** intrigue.
intrigieren* *vi* to intrigue, to scheme.
introvertiert [-vɛr'tiːɐt] *adj* introverted. **~ sein** to be an introvert.
Intuition [ɪntui'tsioːn] *f* intuition.
intuitiv [ɪntui'tiːf] *adj* intuitive.
intus *adj (col)* **etw ~ haben** *(wissen)* to have got sth into one's head *(col)*; *Essen, Alkohol* to have sth down one *(col)*.
Invalide [ɪnva'liːdə] *m (wk)* **-n, -n** disabled person, invalid.
Invalidenrente *f* disability pension.
Invalidität [ɪnvalidi'tɛːt] *f* disability.
Invasion [ɪnvaːzioːn] *f (lit, fig)* invasion.
Inventar [ɪnvɛntaːɐ] *nt* **-e (a)** *(Einrichtung)* fittings *pl*; *(Maschinen)* equipment *no pl*, plant *no pl*. **(b)** *(Verzeichnis)* inventory; *(Comm)* assets and liabilities *pl*. **er gehört schon zum ~** *(hum)* he's part of the furniture.
Inventur [ɪnvɛn'tuːɐ] *f* stocktaking. **~ machen** to stocktake.
investieren* [ɪnvɛs'tiːrən] *vti (Comm, fig)* to invest. **Gefühle in jdn ~** *(col)* to become emotionally involved with sb.
Investition [ɪnvɛst-] *f* investment.
Investment [ɪn'vɛstmənt] *nt* **-s** investment.
inwendig *adj* inside. **jdn/etw in- und auswendig kennen** *(col)* to know sb/sth inside out.
inwiefern, inwieweit *adv* to what extent. ~? in what way?
Inzest *m* **-e** incest *no pl*.
Inzucht *f* inbreeding.
inzwischen *adv* in the meantime, meanwhile. **er ist ~ 18 geworden** he's now 18.
Ion [ioːn] *nt* **-en** ion.
IOK [iː|oː'kaː] *nt* = **Internationales Olympisches Komitee** IOC.
IQ = **Intelligenzquotient** IQ.
i.R. [iː'|ɛr] = **im Ruhestand** retd.
Irak [i'raːk, 'iːrak] *m* **(der) ~** Iraq.
Iraker(in *f***)** *m* **-** Iraqi.
irakisch *adj* Iraqi.
Iran *m* **(der) ~** Iran.
Iraner(in *f***)** *m* **-** Iranian.
iranisch *adj* Iranian.
irden *adj* earthenware, earthen.
irdisch *adj* earthly *no adv*. **den Weg alles I~en gehen** to go the way of all flesh.
Ire *m (wk)* **-n, -n** Irishman; Irish boy. **die ~n** the Irish; **er ist ~** he is Irish.
irgend 1 *adv* **wenn ~ möglich** if it's at all possible; **wann du ~ kannst** whenever you can; **wer (es) ~ kann** whoever can; **so lange ich ~ kann** as long

as I possibly can; **wo es ~ geht** wherever possible. **2** *mit indef pron* **~ jemand** somebody; *(fragend, verneinend, bedingend)* anybody; **ich bin nicht ~ jemand** I'm not just anybody; **~ etwas** something; *(fragend, verneinend, bedingend)* anything; **was zieh' ich an? — ~ etwas** what shall I wear? — anything, any old thing *(col)*; **~ so ein Tier** some animal.

irgend|ein *indef pron* some; *(fragend, verneinend, bedingend)* any. **haben Sie noch ~en Wunsch?** is there anything else you would like?; **das kann ~ anderer machen** someone else can do it.

irgend|eine(r, s) *indef pron (nominal) (bei Personen)* somebody; *(bei Dingen)* something; *(fragend, verneinend, bedingend)* anybody/anything. **welchen wollen Sie? — ~n** which one do you want? — any one, any old one *(col)*.

irgend|einmal *adv* sometime; *(fragend, bedingend)* ever.

irgendwann *adv* sometime. **~ einmal** some time; *(fragend, bedingend)* ever.

irgendwas *indef pron (col) siehe* **irgend 2.**

irgendwelche(r, s) *indef pron* some; *(fragend, verneinend, bedingend, jede beliebige)* any.

irgendwer *indef pron (col) siehe* **irgend 2.**

irgendwie *adv* somehow (or other). **ist es ~ möglich?** is it at all possible?

irgendwo *adv* somewhere; *(fragend, verneinend, bedingend)* anywhere.

irgendwoher *adv* from somewhere; *(fragend, verneinend, bedingend)* from anywhere.

irgendwohin *adv* somewhere; *(fragend, verneinend, bedingend)* anywhere.

Irin *f* Irishwoman; Irish girl. **sie ist ~** she is Irish.

Iris *f* - iris.

irisch *adj* Irish.

Irland *nt* Ireland; *(Republik ~)* Eire.

Irländer(in *f*) *m* - *siehe* **Ire, Irin.**

Ironie *f* irony.

ironisch *adj* ironic, ironical.

ironisieren* *vt* to treat ironically.

irrational ['ɪratsiona:l] *adj* irrational.

irr(e) 1 *adj* **(a)** *(geistesgestört)* crazy, insane. **das macht mich ganz ~** it's driving me crazy; **wie ~** *(fig col)* like crazy *(col)*. **(b)** *pred (verwirrt, unsicher)* confused. **(c)** *(col) Party, Hut* wild *(col)*, crazy *(col)*. **2** *adv (verrückt)* insanely; *(col: sehr)* incredibly *(col)*. **~ gut** *(col)* way out *(col)*.

Irre *f*: **jdn in die ~ führen** *(lit, fig)* to lead sb astray.

irreal *adj* unreal.

Irre-: i~führen *vt sep* to mislead; **sich i~führen lassen** to be misled; **i~führend** *adj* misleading; **~führung** *f* misleading.

irregulär *adj* irregular.

irrelevant ['ɪrelevant) *adj* irrelevant *(für* for, to*)*.

irremachen *vt sep* to confuse, to muddle.

irren 1 *vi aux sein (umher~)* to wander. **2** *vir* to be mistaken *or* wrong. **I~ ist menschlich** *(Prov)* to err is human *(Prov)*; **jeder kann sich mal ~** anyone can make a mistake; **wenn ich mich nicht sehr irre ...** unless I'm very much mistaken ...

Irren-: ~anstalt *f (dated)*, **~haus** *nt (dated, pej)* lunatic asylum *(dated)*; **hier geht es zu wie im ~haus** *(col)* this place is an absolute madhouse.

irreparabel *adj* irreparable.

Irre(r) *mf decl as adj* lunatic; *(col auch)* madman. **ein armer ~r** *(hum col)* a poor fool.

Irr-: ~fahrt *f* wandering; **~glaube(n)** *m (Rel, fig)* heresy; *(irrige Ansicht)* mistaken belief.

irrig *adj* incorrect, wrong.

irritieren* *vt (verwirren)* to confuse, to muddle; *(ärgern)* to irritate.

Irr-: ~lehre *f* heresy; **~licht** *nt* will-o'-the-wisp.

Irrsinn *m no pl* madness, insanity. **so ein ~!** that's madness!

irrsinnig *adj* mad, crazy. **wie ein I~er** like a madman; **ein ~er Verkehr** *(col)* an incredible amount of traffic; **~ komisch** incredibly funny.

Irrtum *m* mistake, error. **ein ~ von ihm** a mistake on his part; **im ~ sein** to be wrong *or* mistaken; **~!** wrong!; **~ vorbehalten** errors excepted.

irrtümlich 1 *adj attr* mistaken, erroneous. **2** *adv* mistakenly; *(aus Versehen)* by mistake.

irrtümlicherweise *adv* mistakenly; *(aus Versehen)* by mistake.

Irrweg *m (fig)* **auf dem ~ sein** to be on the wrong track; **zu studieren erwies sich für ihn als ~** going to university proved to be a mistake for him.

Ischias *m or nt no pl* sciatica.

Ischiasnerv *m* sciatic nerve.

Islam *m no pl* Islam.

islamisch *adj* Islamic.

Island *nt* Iceland.

Isländer(in *f*) *m* - Icelander.

isländisch *adj* Icelandic.

Isolation *f* **(a)** isolation; *(von Häftlingen)* solitary confinement. **(b)** *(Elec, gegen Lärm, Kälte etc)* insulation.

Isolierband *nt* insulating tape *(Brit)*, friction tape *(US)*.

isolieren* 1 *vt* **(a)** to isolate. **völlig isoliert leben** to live in complete isolation. **(b)** *elektrische Leitungen, Häuser, Fenster* to insulate. **2** *vr* to isolate oneself (from the world).

Isolier-: ~haft *f* solitary confinement; **~station** *f* isolation ward.

Israel ['ɪsraɛl] *nt* Israel.

Israeli *m* **-(s)** Israeli.

israelisch *adj* Israeli.

iß *imper sing of* **essen.**

ist *3. pers sing pres of* **sein**[1] is.

Ist-: ~-Bestand *m (Geld)* cash in hand; *(Waren)* actual stock; **~-Stärke** *f (Mil)* effective strength.

Italien [-iən] *nt* Italy.

Italiener(in *f*) [-'lie:nɐ, -ərɪn] *m* - Italian.

italienisch [-'lie:nɪʃ] *adj* Italian. **die ~e Schweiz** Italian-speaking Switzerland.

i.V. = **in Vertretung** pp.

J

J, j [jɔt] *nt* **-, -** J, j.

ja *adv* **(a)** yes; *(bei Trauung)* I do. **kommst du morgen? — ~** are you coming tomorrow? — yes(, I am); **haben Sie das gesehen? — ~** did you see it? — yes(, I did); **ich glaube ~** (yes) I think so; **~ und amen zu allem sagen** *(col)* to accept everything without question.

(b) *(fragend, zweifelnd)* **~?** really?; **ich habe gekündigt — ~?** I've quit — have you?

(c) aber ~! yes, of course; **das ist also abgemacht, ~?** that's agreed then, OK?; **ach ~!** oh yes; **nun ~** oh well; **~ doch** yes, of course; **sei ~ vorsichtig!** do be careful; **vergessen Sie es** ***ja*** **nicht!** don't forget, whatever you do!; **sie ist ~ erst fünf** (after all) she's only five; **das ist ~ richtig, aber ...** that's (certainly) right, but ...; **das ist gut, ~ sogar sehr gut** it's good, in fact it's (even) very good; **da haben wir's ~** there you are (then); **da kommt er ~** here he comes; **das sag' ich ~!** that's just what I'm saying; **das wissen wir ~ alle** we know that (anyway); **Sie wissen ~, daß ...** as you know ...; **Sie wissen ~, wie das so ist** you know how it is, (don't you?); **das ist ~ fürchterlich** that's (really) terrible.

Ja *nt* **-(s)** yes. **mit ~ antworten/stimmen** to answer/vote yes.

Jacht *f* **-en** yacht.

Jacke *f* **-n** jacket, coat *(esp US)*; *(Woll~)* cardigan. **das ist ~ wie Hose** *(col)* it's six of one and half a dozen of the other *(col)*.

Jacken-: ~kleid *nt (Kleid und Jacke)* two-piece; **~tasche** *f* jacket *or* coat *(esp US)* pocket.

Jacketkrone ['dʒɛkɪt-] *f* jacket crown.

Jackett [ʒa'kɛt] *nt* **-s** jacket, coat *(esp US)*.

Jade *m or f no pl* jade.

Jagd *f* **-en** hunt; *(Ausführung der ~)* hunting; *(fig: Verfolgung)* hunt *(nach* for*)*, chase *(nach* after*)*; *(Wettlauf)* race. **die ~ auf Rotwild** deer-hunting; **auf die ~ (nach etw) gehen** *(lit, fig)* to go hunting (for sth); **auf jdn/etw ~ machen** *(lit, fig)* to hunt for sb/sth; **die ~ nach Geld** the pursuit of money.

Jagd-: j~bar *adj* ... **sind j~bar ...** may be hunted, ... are fair game; **~beute** *f* bag; **~bomber** *m (Mil)* fighter-bomber; **~flieger** *m (Mil)* fighter pilot; **~flugzeug** *nt (Mil)* fighter plane; **~gebiet** *nt* hunting ground; **~gesellschaft** *f* hunting party; **~gewehr** *nt* hunting rifle; **~hund** *m* hound; **~revier** *nt* shoot; **~schein** *m* hunting licence *(Brit) or* license *(US)*; **einen ~schein haben** *(hum col)* to be certified *(col)*; **~wild** *nt* game; **~wurst** *f* smoked sausage; **~zeit** *f* hunting season.

jagen 1 *vt* to hunt; *(hetzen)* to chase, to drive. **jdn in die Flucht ~** to put sb to flight; **ein Unglück jagte das andere** one misfortune followed on the other; **mit diesem Essen kannst du mich ~** *(col)* I wouldn't touch that food with a barge pole *(Brit col) or* a ten foot pole *(US col)*. **2** *vi* **(a)** *(auf die Jagd gehen)* to hunt, to go hunting. **(b)** *aux sein (rasen)* to race. **nach etw ~** to chase after sth.

Jäger *m* **- (a)** hunter, huntsman. **(b)** *(Mil: Flugzeug)* fighter (plane).

Jägerei *f no pl* hunting.

Jägerin *f* huntress, huntswoman.

Jäger-: ~latein *nt (col)* hunters' tales *pl*; **~schnitzel** *nt (Cook) cutlet served with mushroom sauce.*

Jaguar *m* **-e** jaguar.

jäh *adj (geh)* **(a)** *(plötzlich)* sudden. **(b)** *(steil)* sheer. **der Abhang fällt ~ herab** the slope falls sharply.

Jahr *nt* **-e** year. **ein halbes ~** six months *sing or pl*; **ein dreiviertel ~** nine months *sing or pl*; **anderthalb ~e** one and a half years *sing*, eighteen months *sing or pl*; **zwei ~e Garantie** a two-year guarantee; **im ~(e) 1066** in (the year) 1066; **die sechziger ~e** the sixties *sing or pl*; **alle zehn ~e** every ten years; **auf ~e hinaus** for years ahead; **auf ~ und Tag** to the very day; **einmal im ~(e)** once a year; **das Buch des ~es** the book of the year; **nach ~ und Tag** after (many) years; **mit den ~en** as the years go by; **zwischen den ~en** *(col)* between Christmas and New Year; **er ist zehn ~e (alt)** he is ten years old; **mit dreißig ~en** at the age of thirty; **in die ~e kommen** *(col)* to be getting on (in years); **in den besten ~en sein** to be in the prime of one's life.

jahr|aus *adv:* **~, jahrein** year in, year out.

Jahrbuch *nt* yearbook; *(Kalender)* almanac.

jahrelang 1 *adj attr* lasting for years. **~es Warten/~e Forschungen** years of waiting/research. **2** *adv* for years. **und dann dauerte es noch ~, bevor ...** and then it took years until ...

jähren *vr* **heute jährt sich der Tag, an dem ...** it's a year ago today that ...

Jahres- *in cpds* annual, yearly; **~abschluß** *m (Comm)* annual accounts *pl*; **~beginn** *m* beginning of a/the new year; **~beitrag** *m* annual subscription; **~bericht** *m* annual report; **~bestzeit** *f (Sport)* best time of the year; **~bilanz** *f (Comm)* annual balance sheet; **~einkommen** *nt* annual income; **~ende** *nt* end of the year; **~hauptversammlung** *f (Comm)* annual general meeting, AGM; **~karte** *f* annual season ticket; **~tag** *m* anniversary; **~umsatz** *m (Comm)* yearly turnover; **~urlaub** *m* annual holiday *or* leave; **~wechsel** *m*, **~wende** *f* new year; **~zeit** *f* season.

Jahr-: ~gang *m* **(a)** *(Sch, Univ)* year; **er ist ~gang 1950** he was born in 1950; **(b)** *(einer Zeitschrift)* year's issues *pl*; **(c)** *(von Wein)* vintage, year; **~hundert** *nt* **-e** century.

jahrhunderte-: ~alt *adj* centuries-old; **~lang 1** *adj* lasting for centuries; **2** *adv* for centuries.

Jahrhundertwende *f* turn of the century.

jährlich 1 *adj* annual, yearly. **2** *adv* annually, yearly; *(Comm)* per annum. **zweimal ~** twice a year.

Jahrmarkt *m* fair, funfair *(Brit)*.

Jahr-: ~tausend *nt* **-e** millennium, a thousand years; **~tausende** thousands of years; **~zehnt** *nt* **-e** decade; **j~zehntelang 1** *adj* lasting for decades; **2** *adv* for decades.

Jähzorn *m* violent temper.

jähzornig *adj* bad-tempered.

Jalousie [ʒalu'ziː] *f* venetian blind.

Jamaika *nt* Jamaica.

jamaikanisch *adj* Jamaican.

Jammer *m no pl (Elend)* misery, wretchedness; *(Klage)* wailing, lamentation. **es wäre ein ~, wenn ...** *(col)* it would be a crying shame if ... *(col)*.

Jammerlappen *m (pej col)* wet *(col)*.

jämmerlich 1 *adj* wretched; *Zustand auch* de-

plorable. **2** *adv (col: sehr)* terribly *(col)*.
jammern *vi* to wail *(über +acc* over*)*; *(sich beklagen auch)* to moan.
jammerschade *adj* **es ist ~** *(col)* it's a crying shame *(col)*.
Januar *m* **-e** January; *siehe* **März.**
Japan *nt* Japan.
Japaner(in *f***)** *m* **-** Japanese.
japanisch *adj* Japanese; *siehe* **deutsch.**
Japanisch(e) *nt decl as adj* Japanese; *siehe* **Deutsch(e).**
Jargon [ʒar'gõ:] *m* **-s** jargon.
Jasager *m* **-** *(pej)* yes-man.
Jasmin *m* **-e** jasmine.
Jastimme *f* vote in favour (of); *(Parl auch)* aye *(Brit)*, yea *(US)*.
jäten *vti* to weed. **Unkraut ~** to weed.
Jauche *f* **-n** liquid manure; *(pej col) (Getränk)* piss *(col!)*; *(Abwasser)* sewage.
Jauchegrube *f* cesspool, cesspit.
jauchzen *vi (geh)* to rejoice *(liter)*; *(Publikum)* to cheer.
jaulen *vi (lit, fig)* to howl.
jawohl, jawoll *(hum col) adv* yes; *(Mil)* yes, sir; *(Naut)* aye, aye, sir.
Jawort *nt* **jdm das ~ geben** to consent to marry sb; *(bei Trauung)* to say "I do".
Jazz [dʒæz, jats] *m no pl* jazz.
Jazzkeller *m* jazz club.
je 1 *adv* **(a)** *(jemals)* ever. **(b)** *(jeweils)* every, each. **für ~ drei Stück zahlst du eine Mark** you pay one mark for (every) three; **~ zwei Schüler aus jeder Klasse** two children from each class; **sie zahlten ~ eine Mark** they paid one mark each. **2** *prep +acc (pro)* per. **~ Person zwei Stück** two per person. **3** *conj* **(a) ~ eher, desto** *or* **um so besser** the sooner the better; **~ länger, ~ lieber** the longer the better. **(b) ~ nach** depending on; **~ nachdem** it all depends; **~ nachdem, wie/ob ...** depending on how/whether ...
Jeans [dʒi:nz] *pl* jeans.
Jeans-: ~anzug *m* denim suit; **~stoff** *m* denim.
jedenfalls *adv* anyhow, in any case; *(zumindest)* at least, at any rate. **er ist nicht reif zum Studieren, ~ jetzt noch nicht** he's not mature enough to go to university, at least not yet.
jede(r, s) *indef pron* **(a)** *(adjektivisch) (einzeln)* each; *(von zweien auch)* either; *(~ von allen)* every; *(~r beliebige)* any. **ohne ~ Anstrengung** without any effort; **es kann ~n Augenblick passieren** it might happen any minute; **fern von ~r Kultur** far from all civilization. **(b)** *(substantivisch) (einzeln)* each (one); *(~ von allen)* everyone, everybody; *(~ beliebige)* anyone, anybody. **~r von uns** each (one)/every one/any one of us; **~r zweite** every other one; **~r für sich** everyone for himself; **das kann nicht ~r** not everyone can do that; **er spricht nicht mit ~m** he doesn't speak to just anybody.
jedermann *indef pron* everyone, everybody; *(jeder beliebige auch)* anyone, anybody. **das ist nicht ~s Sache** it's not everyone's cup of tea *(col)*.
jederzeit *adv* at any time. **du kannst ~ kommen** you can come any time (you like).
jedesmal *adv* every *or* each time. **~, wenn sie ...** every time she ..., whenever she ...
jedoch *conj, adv* however. **er verlor ~ die Nerven** he lost his nerve however.
Jeep ® [dʒi:p] *m* **-s** jeep.
jegliche(r, s) *indef pron (adjektivisch)* any.
jeher ['je:he:ɐ] *adv:* **von** *or* **seit ~** always; **das ist schon seit ~ so** it has always been like that.
jein *adv (hum)* yes and no.
jemals *adv* ever.
jemand *indef pron* somebody, someone; *(bei Fragen, bedingenden Sätzen auch, Negation)* anybody, anyone. **ist da ~?** is anybody *or* somebody there?; **ohne ~en zu fragen** without asking anyone; **~ anders/Neues** somebody else/new.
Jenaer Glas ® ['je:naɐ-] *nt* Pyrex ®, heatproof glass.
jene(r, s) *dem pron (geh)* **(a)** *(adjektivisch)* that; *pl* those; *(der Vorherige, die Vorherigen)* the former. **in ~r Zeit** at that time. **(b)** *(substantivisch)* that one; *pl* those (ones); *(der Vorherige, die Vorherigen)* the former; *siehe* **diese(r, s).**
jenseitig *adj attr Ufer* opposite. **das ~e Leben** the life after death.
jenseits 1 *prep +gen* on the other side of. **2 km ~ der Grenze** 2 kms beyond the border. **2** *adv* **~ von** on the other side of; **~ von Gut und Böse** beyond good and evil; *(hum col)* past it *(col)*.
Jenseits *nt no pl* hereafter. **jdn ins ~ befördern** *(col)* to send sb to kingdom come *(col)*.
Jesuit *m (wk)* **-en, -en** Jesuit.
Jesus *m gen* **Jesu** Jesus. **~ Christus** Jesus Christ.
Jet [dʒɛt] *m* **-s** *(col)* jet.
Jeton [ʒə'tõ:] *m* **-s** chip.
jetzig *adj attr* present *attr*, current. **in der ~en Zeit** in our times.
jetzt *adv* now; *(heutzutage auch)* nowadays. **bis ~** so far; **ich bin ~ (schon) fünf Tage hier** I have been here five days now; **~ gleich** right now; **~ schon?** already?
jeweilig *adj attr* respective; *(vorherrschend) Verhältnisse* prevailing. **die ~e Regierung** the government of the day.
jeweils *adv* at any one time; *(jedesmal)* each time; *(jeder einzelne)* each. **~ am Monatsletzten** on the last day of each month; **die ~ größten aus einer Gruppe** the biggest from each group.
Jg. = Jahrgang.
Jh. = Jahrhundert.
jiddisch *adj* Yiddish.
Job [dʒɔp] *m* **-s** *(col)* job.
jobben ['dʒɔbn] *vi (col)* to work, to have a job.
Joch *nt* **-e** *(lit, fig)* yoke.
Jochbein *nt* cheek-bone.
Jockei ['jɔke], **Jockey** ['dʒɔki] *m* **-s** jockey.
Jod *nt no pl* iodine.
jodeln *vti* to yodel.
Jodler(in *f***)** *m* **-** yodeller *(Brit)*, yodeler *(US)*.
Joga *m or nt no pl* yoga.
joggen ['dʒɔgn] *vi* to jog.
Jogger(in *f***)** ['dzɔgɐ, -ərın] *m* **-** jogger.
Jogging ['dʒɔgiŋ] *nt no pl* jogging.
Joghurt *m or nt* **-(s)** yog(h)urt.
Johannis-: ~beere *f* **rote/schwarze ~beere** redcurrant/blackcurrant; **~nacht** *f* Midsummer's Eve.
johlen *vi* to howl.
Joint [dʒɔınt] *m* **-s** *(col)* joint *(col)*.
Jo-Jo *nt* **-s** yo-yo.
Joker ['jo:kɐ, 'dʒo:kɐ] *m* **-** *(Cards)* joker.
Jolle *f* **-n** *(Naut)* jolly-boat, dinghy.
Jongleur [ʒõ'glø:ɐ] *m* juggler.
jonglieren* [ʒõ'gli:rən] *vi (lit, fig)* to juggle.
Jordanien [-iən] *nt* Jordan.
Jordanier(in *f***)** [-iɐ, -iərın] *m* **-** Jordanian.
Jota *nt* **-s** iota. **kein ~** not a jot *or* one iota.
Journal [ʒʊr'na:l] *nt* **-e** journal; *(dated: Zeitschrift)* magazine.
Journalismus [ʒʊrna'lısmʊs] *m no pl* journalism.
Journalist(in *f***)** [ʒʊrna'lıst, -ıstın] *m* journalist.
journalistisch [ʒʊrna'lıstıʃ] *adj* journalistic.
jovial [jo'via:l] *adj* jovial.
jr. = junior jnr., jr.
Jubel *m no pl* jubilation; *(~rufe auch)* cheering. **~, Trubel, Heiterkeit** laughter and merriment.
Jubeljahr *nt* **alle ~e (einmal)** *(col)* once in a blue moon *(col)*.
jubeln *vi* to cheer. **vor Freude ~** to shout with joy.
Jubilar(in *f***)** *m person celebrating an anniversary.*
Jubiläum *nt, pl* **Jubiläen** jubilee; *(Jahrestag)* anniversary.

Jubiläums- *in cpds* jubilee.
jucken 1 *vti* to itch. **der Rücken juckt mir** my back itches; **der Stoff juckt mich** this material makes me itch; **es juckt mich, das zu tun** *(col)* I'm itching to do it *(col)*; **das juckt mich doch nicht** *(col)* I don't care; **ihm juckt das Fell** *(col)* he's asking for a good hiding. **2** *vt (kratzen)* to scratch.
Juck-: ~pulver *nt* itching powder; **~reiz** *m* itching.
Judas *m* **-, -se** *(fig liter)* Judas.
Judaslohn *m (liter)* blood money.
Jude *m (wk)* **-n, -n** Jew. **er ist ~** he is a Jew.
Juden-: j~feindlich *adj* anti-Semitic; **~stern** *m* star of David; **~verfolgung** *f* persecution of the Jews.
Jüdin *f* Jew(ess).
jüdisch *adj* Jewish.
Judo *nt no pl* judo.
Jugend *f no pl* **(a)** *(~zeit)* youth. **frühe ~** early youth, adolescence; **von ~ an** *or* **auf** from one's youth. **(b)** *(junge Menschen)* youth, young people *pl.* **die heutige ~** the youth of today.
Jugend-: ~alter *nt* adolescence; **~amt** *nt* youth welfare department; **~arbeit** *f no pl (~fürsorge)* youth work; **~bild** *nt* picture taken when one was young; **~bilder Churchills** photographs of the young Churchill; **~buch** *nt* book for the younger reader; **~erinnerung** *f* youthful memory; **j~frei** *adj* suitable for young people; *Film* U(-certificate), G *(US)*; **~freund** *m* friend of one's youth; **~fürsorge** *f* youth welfare; **j~gefährdend** *adj* liable to corrupt the young; **~gericht** *nt* juvenile court; **~gruppe** *f* youth group; **~herberge** *f* youth hostel; **~jahre** *pl* days of one's youth *pl*; **~kriminalität** *f* juvenile delinquency.
jugendlich *adj (jung)* young; *(jung wirkend)* youthful. **er kleidet sich immer sehr ~** he always wears very youthful clothes; **~e Banden** gangs of youths; **ein ~er Täter** a young offender.
Jugendliche(r) *mf decl as adj* young person; *(männlicher ~ auch)* youth.
Jugendlichkeit *f* youthfulness.
Jugend-: ~liebe *f (Geliebter)* love of one's youth; **~literatur** *f* literature for younger readers; **~mannschaft** *f* youth team; **~organisation** *f* youth organization; **~pflege** *f* youth welfare; **~pfleger** *m* youth (welfare) worker; **~recht** *nt* law relating to young persons; **~richter** *m (Jur)* magistrate *in a juvenile court*; **~schutz** *m* protection of children and young people; **~stil** *m (Art)* Art Nouveau; **~strafe** *f* detention *no art* in a reform school *etc*; **~sünde** *f* youthful misdeed; **~traum** *m* youthful dream; **~verband** *m* youth organization; **~verbot** *nt* **für einen Film ~verbot aussprechen** to ban a film for young people; **~zeit** *f* younger days *pl*; **~zentrum** *nt* youth centre *(Brit) or* center *(US)*.
Jugoslawe *m (wk)* **-n, -n, Jugoslawin** *f* Yugoslav.
Jugoslawien [-iən] *nt* Yugoslavia.
jugoslawisch *adj* Yugoslav(ian).
Juli *m* **-s** July; *siehe* **März.**
jun. = **junior** jun.
jung *adj, comp* **-̈er**, *superl* **-̈ste(r, s)** *or (adv)* **am -̈sten** *(lit, fig)* young. **~ und alt** (both) young and old; **von ~ auf** from one's youth; **sie ist 18 Jahre ~** *(hum)* she's 18 years young *(hum)*; **~ heiraten/sterben** to marry/die young.
Junge *m (wk)* **-n, -n** *or (col)* **Jungs** boy; *(Cards col)* jack, knave. **~, ~!** *(col)* boy oh boy *(col)*; **alter ~** *(col)* my old pal *(col)*; **unsere Jungs haben gewonnen** our lads won.
Jungen-: j~haft *adj* boyish; **sie ist ein j~haftes Mädchen** she's a bit of a tomboy; **~schule** *f* boys' school.
jünger *adj* **(a)** *comp of* **jung** younger. **sie ist eine ~e Frau** she's a fairly young woman; **Holbein der J~e** the younger Holbein. **(b)** *Geschichte etc* recent.
Jünger *m* **-** *(Bibl, fig)* disciple.
Jüngerin *f* disciple.
Junge(s) *nt decl as adj (Zool)* young one; *(von Hund)* pup(py); *(von Katze)* kitten; *(von Wolf, Löwe, Bär)* cub; *(von Vogel)* young bird. **die ~n** the young.
Jungfer *f* **-n** *(old, hum: ledige Frau)* spinster. **eine alte ~** an old maid.
Jungfern-: ~fahrt *f* maiden voyage; **~flug** *m* maiden flight; **~häutchen** *nt (Anat)* hymen, maidenhead; **~rede** *f (Parl)* maiden speech.
Jungfrau *f* virgin; *(Astrol)* Virgo *no art*. **ich bin ~** I am a virgin; I am (a) Virgo; **die ~ Maria** the Virgin Mary; **dazu bin ich gekommen wie die ~ zum Kind(e)** it just fell into my hands.
jungfräulich *adj* virgin; *(liter) Seele* pure.
Jungfräulichkeit *f siehe adj* virginity; purity.
Junggeselle *m* bachelor.
Junggesellen-: ~wohnung *f* bachelor flat *(Brit) or* apartment *(US)*; **~zeit** *f* bachelor days *pl.*
Junggesellin *f* bachelor girl; *(älter)* single woman.
Junglehrer *m* student teacher.
Jüngling *m (liter, hum)* youth.
Jungsozialist *m (BRD Pol)* Young Socialist.
jüngst *adv (geh)* recently, lately.
jüngste(r, s) *adj* **(a)** *superl of* **jung** youngest. **(b)** *Werk, Ereignis* latest, (most) recent; *Zeit, Vergangenheit* recent. **in der ~n Zeit** recently; **das J~ Gericht** the Last Judgement; **der J~ Tag** Doomsday, the Day of Judgement; **sie ist auch nicht mehr die J~** she's no chicken *(col)*.
Jung-: ~verheiratete(r) *mf decl as adj* newly-wed; **~wähler** *m* young voter.
Juni *m* **-s** June; *siehe* **März.**
junior *adj* **Franz Schulz ~** Franz Schulz, Junior.
Junior *m* **(a)** *(usu hum: Sohn)* junior. **(b)** *(Comm: auch* **~chef***)* son of the chairman/boss. **(c)** *usu pl (Sport)* junior.
Junta ['xʊnta, 'jʊnta] *f, pl* **Junten** *(Pol)* junta.
Jupiter *m* Jupiter.
Jura *no art (Univ)* law.
Jurastudium *nt* study of law.
Jurist(in *f***)** *m* jurist, legal eagle *(hum col)*; *(Student)* law student.
Juristen-: ~deutsch *nt*, **~sprache** *f no pl* legalese *(pej)*, legal jargon.
juristisch *adj* legal. **die J~e Fakultät** the Faculty of Law; **eine ~e Person** a legal entity.
Juror(in *f***)** ['juːrɔr, -'roːrɪn] *m* juror; *(bei Wettbewerb)* judge.
Jury [ʒy'riː, 'ʒyːriː] *f* **-s** jury *sing or pl*; *(bei Wettbewerb auch)* judges *pl.*
Juso *m* **-s** *(BRD Pol)* = **Jungsozialist** Young Socialist.
justieren* *vt Waage* to adjust; *(Typ)* to justify.
Justiz [jʊs'tiːts] *f no pl (als Prinzip)* justice; *(als Institution)* judiciary; *(die Gerichte)* courts *pl.*
Justiz-: ~beamte(r) *m* judicial officer; **~irrtum** *m* miscarriage of justice; **~minister** *m* minister of justice ≈ Attorney General *(US)*, ≈ Lord (High) Chancellor *(Brit)*; **~ministerium** *nt* ministry of justice, ≈ Department of Justice *(US)*; **~mord** *m* judicial murder.
Jute *f no pl* jute.
Juwel [ju'veːl] *nt* **-en** *or (fig)* **-e** jewel, gem.
Juwelier *m* **-e** jeweller *(Brit)*, jeweler *(US)*.
Jux *m* **-e** *(col)* **etw aus ~ tun/sagen** to do/say sth in fun; **sich** *(dat)* **einen ~ aus etw machen** to make a joke (out) of sth.
jwd [jɔtweː'deː] *adv (hum)* in the back of beyond.

K

K, k [ka:] *nt* -, - K, k.
Kabarett *nt* **-e** *or* **-s** cabaret. **ein politisches ~** a political satire.
Kabarettist(in *f***)** *m* cabaret artist.
kabarettistisch *adj Darbietung* cabaret; *Stil* revue *attr.*
Kabbelei *f (col)* bickering, squabbling.
Kabel *nt* - cable; *(Draht)* wire; *(Telefon~)* flex, cord.
Kabelfernsehen *nt* cable television.
Kabeljau *m* **-e** *or* **-s** cod.
kabeln *vti* to cable.
Kabine *f* cabin; *(Umkleide~, Dusch~)* cubicle; *(Telec)* booth; *(Seilbahn~)* car.
Kabinett[1] *nt* **-e** *(Pol)* cabinet.
Kabinett[2] *m* **-e** *m high quality German white wine.*
Kabinetts-: **~beschluß** *m* cabinet decision; **~mitglied** *nt* cabinet member.
Kabinettstück *nt (old: einer Sammlung)* pièce de résistance; *(fig)* masterstroke; **sich** *(dat)* **ein ~ leisten** *(iro)* to goof *(col).*
Kabrio *nt* **-s** *(col),* **Kabriolett** [kabrio'lɛt, *(Aus, S Ger)* kabrio'le:] *nt* **-s** *(Aut)* convertible.
Kachel *f* **-n** (glazed) tile.
kacheln *vt* to tile.
Kachel|ofen *m* tiled stove.
Kacke *f no pl (col!)* crap *(col!).*
kacken *vi (col!)* to crap *(col!).*
Kadaver [ka'da:vɐ] *m* - carcass.
Kadavergehorsam *m (pej)* blind obedience.
Kadenz *f* cadence; *(Improvisation)* cadenza.
Kader *m* - *(Mil, Pol)* cadre; *(Sport)* squad; *(DDR, Sw: Fachleute)* group of specialists.
Kadett *m (wk)* **-en, -en** *(Mil)* cadet.
Kadettenanstalt *f* cadet school.
Kadi *m* **-s** *(col)* beak *(col).* **jdn vor den ~ schleppen** to take sb to court.
Kadmium *nt* cadmium.
Käfer *m* - *(auch col: VW)* beetle.
Kaff *nt* **-s** *or* **-e** *(col)* dump *(col),* hole *(col).*
Kaffee [*or* ka'fe:] *m* **-s** **(a)** coffee. **zwei ~, bitte!** two coffees please; **~ mit Milch** white coffee *(Brit),* coffee with milk; **~ kochen** to make coffee; **das ist kalter ~** *(col)* that's old hat *(col).* **(b)** *no pl (Nachmittags~)* ≈ (afternoon) tea. **~ und Kuchen** coffee and cakes, ≈ afternoon tea.
Kaffee-: **~bohne** *f* coffee bean; **~-Extrakt** *m* coffee essence; **~filter** *m* coffee filter; *(col: Filterpapier)* filter (paper); **~geschirr** *nt* coffee set; **~haus** *nt* café; **~kanne** *f* coffeepot; **~klatsch** *(col) m no pl,* **~kränzchen** *nt* coffee klatsch *(US),* hen party *(col);* **~löffel** *m* coffee spoon; **~maschine** *f* coffee machine; **~mühle** *f* coffee grinder; **~pause** *f* coffee break; **~satz** *m* coffee grounds *pl;* **aus dem ~satz lesen** to read tea leaves; **~service** *nt* coffee set; **~strauch** *m* coffee tree; **~tante** *f (hum)* coffee addict; *(in Café)* old biddy; **~tasse** *f* coffee cup; **~tisch** *m (Frühstückstisch)* breakfast table; *(nachmittags)* (afternoon) tea table; **~wärmer** *m* - cosy (for coffee pot).
Käfig *m* **-e** cage.
kahl *adj Mensch, Kopf* bald; *(~geschoren)* shaved, shorn; *Wand, Raum, Baum* bare; *Landschaft* barren. **eine ~e Stelle** a bald patch; **~ werden** *(Mensch)* to go bald; *(Baum)* to lose its leaves.
Kahl-: **k~geschoren** *adj Kopf* shaven; **~heit** *f siehe adj* baldness; bareness; barrenness; **~kopf** *m* bald head; *(Mensch)* bald person; **k~köpfig** *adj* bald(-headed); **~schlag** *m (Forest)* clearing.
Kahn *m* **¨-e** **(a)** (small) boat. **~ fahren** to go boating. **(b)** *(Lastschiff)* barge. **ein alter ~** *(col)* an old tub *(col).*
Kahnfahrt *f* row.
Kai *m* **-e** *or* **-s** quay; *(Uferdamm auch)* waterfront.
Kaianlage *f* quayside.
Kaimauer *f* quay wall.
Kairo *nt* Cairo.
Kaiser *m* - emperor. **sich um des ~s Bart streiten** *(fig)* to split hairs.
Kaiserin *f* empress.
kaiserlich *adj* imperial.
Kaiser-: **~reich** *nt* empire; **~schmarr(e)n** *m* - *(Cook) sugared, cut-up pancake with raisins;* **~schnitt** *m* Caesarean (section).
Kajak *m or nt* **-s** kayak.
Kajüte *f* **-n** cabin; *(größer auch)* stateroom.
Kakadu *m* **-s** cockatoo.
Kakao [*auch* ka'kau] *m* **-s** cocoa. **jdn durch den ~ ziehen** *(col) (veralbern)* to make fun of sb; *(boshaft reden)* to run sb down.
Kakerlak *m* **-en** cockroach.
Kaktee *f* **-n** [-e:ən], **Kaktus** *m* **-**, **Kakteen** [-e:ən] *or (col)* **-se** cactus.
Kalauer *m* - corny joke; *(Wortspiel)* corny pun.
kalauern *vi (col)* to joke; to pun.
Kalb *nt* **¨-er** calf; *(von Rehwild auch)* fawn.
kalben *vi (Kuh)* to calve.
Kalbfleisch *nt* veal.
Kalbs-: **~braten** *m* roast veal; **~haxe** *f (Cook)* knuckle of veal; **~leber** *f* calves' liver; **~leder** *nt* calfskin; **~schnitzel** *nt* veal cutlet.
Kaleidoskop *nt* **-e** kaleidoscope.
Kalender *m* - calendar; *(Taschen~)* diary.
Kalender-: **~blatt** *nt* page of a/the calendar; **~jahr** *nt* calendar year; **~monat** *m* calendar month; **~spruch** *m* calendar motto.
Kali *nt* **-s** potash.
Kaliber *nt* - *(lit, fig)* calibre *(Brit),* caliber *(US).*
Kalifornien [-iən] *nt* **-s** California.
Kalium *nt no pl* potassium.
Kalk *m* **-e** lime; *(zum Tünchen)* whitewash; *(Anat)* calcium. **gebrannter/gelöschter ~** quicklime/slaked lime; **bei ihm rieselt schon der ~** *(col)* he's going a bit gaga *(col).*
kalken *vt (tünchen)* to whitewash; *(Agr)* to lime.
Kalk-: **~grube** *f* lime pit; **k~haltig** *adj Boden* chalky; *Wasser* hard; **~mangel** *m (Med)* calcium deficiency; *(von Boden)* lime deficiency; **~ofen** *m* lime kiln; **~stein** *m* limestone.
Kalkül *m or nt* **-e** *(geh)* calculation *usu pl.*
Kalkulation *f* calculation; *(Kostenrechnung)* costing.
kalkulieren* *vt* to calculate.
Kalorie *f* calorie.
Kalorien- [-iən]: **k~arm** *adj* low-calorie; **~gehalt** *m* calorie content; **k~reich** *adj* high-calorie.
kalt *adj comp* **¨-er**, *superl* **¨-este(r, s)** *or (adv)* **am ¨-esten** cold. **mir ist/wird ~** I am/I'm getting cold; **im K~en** in the cold; **~e Platte** cold meal; **abends essen wir ~** we have a cold meal in the evening; **etw ~ stellen** to put sth to chill; **die**

Wohnung kostet ~ **480 DM** the flat costs 480 DM without heating; **jdm die ~e Schulter zeigen** to give sb the cold shoulder, to cold-shoulder sb; **da kann ich nur ~ lächeln** *(col)* that makes me laugh; **es überlief ihn ~** cold shivers ran through him; **der ~e Krieg** the Cold War; **ein ~er Staatsstreich** a bloodless coup.

Kalt-: k~bleiben *vi sep irreg aux sein (fig)* to remain unmoved; **~blüter** *m - (Zool)* cold-blooded animal; **k~blütig** *adj (Zool, fig)* cold-blooded; *(gelassen)* cool; **~blütigkeit** *f siehe adj* cold-bloodedness; cool(ness).

Kälte *f no pl* coldness; *(Wetter)* cold; *(~periode)* cold spell. **fünf Grad ~** five degrees below freezing; **vor ~ zittern** to shiver with cold; **bei dieser ~** in this cold.

Kälte-: k~beständig *adj* cold-resistant; **~einbruch** *m* cold spell; **k~empfindlich** *adj* sensitive to cold; **~grad** *m* degree of frost; **~technik** *f* refrigeration technology; **~welle** *f* cold spell.

Kalt-: k~lächelnd *adv (iro)* cool as you please; **k~lassen** *vt sep irreg (fig)* **jdn k~lassen** to leave sb cold; **~luft** *f (Met)* cold air; **k~machen** *vt sep (col)* to do in *(col)*; **~miete** *f* rent exclusive of heating; **~schale** *f (Cook) cold sweet soup;* **k~schnäuzig** *adj (col) (gefühllos)* cold, callous; *(unverschämt)* insolent; **k~stellen** *vt sep (col) jdn* to put out of harm's way *(col)*.

Kalzium *nt no pl* calcium.

kam *pret of* **kommen.**

Kamel *nt* **-e (a)** camel. **(b)** *(col)* clown *(col)*. **ich ~!** silly me!

Kamel-: ~haar *nt (Tex)* camel hair; **~treiber** *m* camel driver; *(pej: Orientale)* wog *(pej)*.

Kamera *f* **-s** camera.

Kamerad *m (wk)* **-en, -en** *(Mil etc)* comrade; *(Freund)* friend.

Kameradschaft *f* comradeship, camaraderie.

kameradschaftlich *adj* comradely.

Kamera-: ~führung *f* camera work; **~mann** *m, pl* **~männer** cameraman.

Kamerun *nt* the Cameroons *pl.*

Kamille *f* **-n** camomile.

Kamillentee *m* camomile tea.

Kamin *m* **-e** *(Schornstein)* chimney; *(Abzugsschacht)* flue; *(offene Feuerstelle)* fireplace. **wir saßen am ~** we sat in front of the fire.

Kamin-: ~feger, ~kehrer *m - (dial)* chimney sweep; **~feuer** *nt* open fire; **~sims** *m or nt* mantelpiece.

Kamm *m* **⸚e (a)** comb. **alle/alles über einen ~ scheren** *(fig)* to lump everyone/everything together. **(b)** *(von Vogel)* comb. **(c)** *(Cook)* neck. **(d)** *(Gebirgs~, Wellen~)* crest.

kämmen 1 *vt* to comb. **2** *vr* to comb one's hair.

Kammer *f* **-n (a)** chamber; *(Parl auch)* house; *(Ärzte~, Anwalts~)* professional association; *(Herz~)* ventricle. **(b)** *(Zimmer)* small room.

Kammer-: ~diener *m* valet; **~gericht** *nt* ≃ Supreme Court; **~jäger** *m (Schädlingsbekämpfer)* pest controller; **~konzert** *nt* chamber concert.

Kämmerlein *nt* chamber. **im stillen ~** in private.

Kammer-: ~musik *f* chamber music; **~orchester** *nt* chamber orchestra; **~spiele** *pl* studio theatre *(Brit) or* theater *(US)*; **~ton** *m* concert pitch; **~zofe** *f* chambermaid.

Kamm-: ~garn *nt* worsted; **~stück** *nt (Cook)* shoulder.

Kampagne [kam'panjə] *f* **-n** campaign.

Kampf *m* **⸚e** fight, struggle *(um* for*)*; *(Gefecht)* battle; *(Box~)* fight, contest. **jdm/einer Sache den ~ ansagen** *(fig)* to declare war on sb/sth; **es kam zum ~** fighting broke out; **auf in den ~!** *(hum)* once more unto the breach! *(hum)*; **er ist im ~ gefallen** he fell in action *or* battle; **der ~ ums Dasein** the struggle for existence; **der ~ um die Macht** the battle *or* struggle for power; **ein ~ auf Leben und Tod** a fight to the death; **~ dem Atomtod!** fight the nuclear menace!; **innere ~e** inner conflicts.

Kampf-: ~ansage *f* declaration of war; *(Sport)* announcement; **~bahn** *f* sports stadium, arena; **k~bereit** *adj* ready for battle.

kämpfen 1 *vi* to fight, to struggle *(um, für* for*)*. **gegen etw ~** to fight (against) sth; **mit den Tränen ~** to fight back one's tears; **ich habe lange mit mir ~ müssen, ehe ...** I had a long battle with myself before ... **2** *vt (usu fig) Kampf* to fight.

Kampfer *m no pl* camphor.

Kämpfer(in *f*) *m* - fighter.

kämpferisch *adj* aggressive.

Kampf-: k~erprobt *adj* battle-tried; **k~fähig** *adj (Mil)* fit for action; *Boxer* fit to fight; **~flugzeug** *nt* fighter (plane); **~geist** *m* fighting spirit; **~handlung** *f usu pl* clash *usu pl*; **~kraft** *f* fighting strength; **k~los** *adj* **sich k~los ergeben** to surrender without a fight; **k~lustig** *adj* belligerent, pugnacious; **~platz** *m* battlefield; *(Sport)* arena, stadium; **~richter** *m (Sport)* referee; **~schrift** *f* broadsheet; **~stärke** *f (Mil)* combat strength; **~stoff** *m* weapon; **k~unfähig** *adj (Mil)* unfit for battle; *(Sport)* unfit; **ein Schiff k~unfähig machen** to put a ship out of action.

kampieren* *vi* to camp (out). **im Wohnzimmer ~** *(col)* to doss down in the sitting room *(col)*.

Kanada *nt* Canada.

Kanadier [-iɐ] *m* - Canadian; *(Sport)* Canadian canoe.

Kanadierin [-iərɪn] *f* Canadian (woman/girl).

kanadisch *adj* Canadian.

Kanal *m, pl* **Kanäle (a)** *(Schiffahrtsweg)* canal; *(Wasserlauf)* channel; *(zur Entwässerung)* drain; *(für Abwässer)* sewer. **der (Ärmel)~** the (English) Channel; **den ~ voll haben** *(col) (betrunken sein)* to be canned *(col)*; *(es satt haben)* to have had a bellyful *(col!)*. **(b)** *(Radio, TV, fig: Weg)* channel. **dunkle Kanäle** dubious channels.

Kanalisation *f (Abwasserkanäle)* sewerage system, sewers *pl.*

kanalisieren* 1 *vt (fig) Energie etc* to channel. **2** *vti* to lay sewers (in).

Kanaltunnel *m* channel tunnel.

Kanapee *nt* **-s** *(old, hum)* sofa, settee.

Kanarienvogel [-iən-] *m* canary.

Kandare *f* **-n** (curb) bit. **jdn an die ~ nehmen** *(fig)* to take sb in hand.

Kandidat(in *f*) *m (wk)* **-en, -en** candidate; *(bei Bewerbung auch)* applicant. **jdn als ~en aufstellen** to nominate sb.

Kandidatur *f* candidature, candidacy.

kandidieren* *vi (Pol)* to stand, to run *(für* for*)*.

kandiert *adj Frucht* candied.

Kandis(zucker) *m* rock candy.

Känguruh ['kɛŋguru] *nt* **-s** kangaroo.

Kaninchen *nt* rabbit.

Kaninchen-: ~bau *m* rabbit warren; **~stall** *m* rabbit hutch.

Kanister *m* - can.

Kännchen *nt* pot; *(für Milch)* jug.

Kanne *f* **-n** can; *(Tee~, Kaffee~)* pot; *(Milch~)* churn; *(Gieß~)* watering can.

Kannibale *m (wk)* **-n, -n, Kannibalin** *f* cannibal.

kannibalisch *adj* cannibalistic; *(brutal)* brutal.

kannte *pret of* **kennen.**

Kanon *m* **-s** canon.

Kanonade *f (Mil)* barrage; *(fig auch)* tirade.

Kanone *f* **-n (a)** gun; *(Hist)* cannon; *(col: Pistole)* shooter *(col)*. **mit ~n auf Spatzen schießen** *(col)* to take a sledgehammer to crack a nut. **(b)** *(fig col: Könner)* ace *(col)*. **(c)** *(col)* **das ist unter aller ~** that defies description.

Kanonen-: ~boot *nt* gunboat; **~donner** *m* rumbling of guns; **~futter** *nt (col)* cannon fodder; **~kugel** *f* cannon ball; **~rohr** *nt* gun barrel; **heiliges ~rohr!** *(col)* good grief *(col)*.

Kantate *f* **-n** *(Mus)* cantata.

Kante *f* **-n** *(Ecke)* edge; *(Rand, Borte)* border; *(Web~)* selvedge. **Geld auf die hohe ~ legen** *(col)* to put money by.
kantig *adj Holz* edged; *Gesicht* angular.
Kantine *f* canteen.
Kanu *nt* -s canoe.
Kanzel *f* **-n (a)** pulpit. **(b)** *(Aviat)* cockpit.
Kanzlei *f (Dienstelle)* office; *(Büro eines Notars etc)* chambers *pl.*
Kanzler *m* - chancellor.
Kap *nt* **-s** cape.
Kapazität *f* capacity; *(fig: Experte)* expert, authority.
Kapelle *f* **(a)** *(Kirche)* chapel. **(b)** *(Mus)* band, orchestra.
Kapellmeister *m* director of music; *(Mil, von Tanzkapelle etc)* bandmaster, bandleader.
Kaper *f* **-n** *(Bot, Cook)* caper.
kapern *vt (Naut)* to seize; *(fig col)* to grab.
kapieren* *vti (col)* to get *(col)*, to understand. **kapiert?** got it? *(col)*; **er hat schnell kapiert** he caught on quick *(col)*.
Kapital *nt* **-e** *or* **-ien** [-iən] **(a)** *(Fin)* capital *no pl*; *(pl: angelegtes ~)* capital investments *pl.* **(b)** *(fig)* asset. **aus etw ~ schlagen** *(pej: lit, fig)* to make capital out of sth.
Kapital-: ~anlage *f* capital investment; **~flucht** *f* flight of capital; **~gesellschaft** *f (Comm)* joint-stock company; **k~intensiv** *adj* capital-intensive.
Kapitalismus *m* capitalism.
Kapitalist *m* capitalist.
kapitalistisch *adj* capitalist.
Kapital-: ~markt *m* money market; **~verbrechen** *nt* serious crime; *(mit Todesstrafe)* capital crime.
Kapitän *m* **-e** captain. **~ zur See** captain.
Kapitel *nt* - **(a)** chapter; *(fig auch)* period; *(Angelegenheit)* chapter of events, story. **ein trauriges ~** a sad story; **das ist ein anderes ~** that's another story. **(b)** *(Eccl: Dom~)* chapter.
Kapitulation *f* surrender, capitulation *(auch fig) (vor +dat* to).
kapitulieren* *vi* to capitulate; *(Mil also)* to surrender. **ich kapituliere, das ist zu schwierig** I give up, it's too difficult.
Kappe *f* **-n** cap; *(von Flasche etc)* top. **das nehme ich auf meine ~** *(fig col)* I'll take the responsibility for that.
kappen *vt (Naut) Tau, Leine* to cut.
Käppi *nt* **-s** cap.
Kapriole *f* **-n** *(fig)* caper. **~n machen** to cut capers.
kapriziös *adj (geh)* capricious.
Kapsel *f* **-n** capsule; *(Etui)* container; *(an Flasche)* cap, top.
kaputt *adj (col)* broken; *esp Maschine, Glühbirne etc* kaput *(col)*; *(erschöpft) Mensch, Nerven* shattered *(col)*; *Beziehungen, Gesundheit* ruined; *Firma* bust *pred (col)*. **irgend etwas muß an deinem Auto ~ sein** something must be wrong with your car; **der Fernseher ist ~** the TV's not working; **meine Hose ist ~** my trousers have had it *(col)*; **ein ~er Typ** *(col)* a bum *(col)*.
kaputt-: ~fahren *vt sep irreg (col) Auto* to drive into the ground; *(durch Unfall)* to smash up; **~gehen** *vi sep irreg aux sein (col)* to break; *(esp Maschine)* to break down; *(Ehe)* to break up *(an +dat* because of*)*; *(Beziehungen, Nerven)* to be ruined; *(Firma)* to go bust *(col)*; *(Kleidung)* to come to pieces; *(zerrissen werden)* to tear; *(Blumen)* to die off; **er ist am Alkohol ~gegangen** alcohol was his downfall; **~kriegen** *vt sep (col)* **das Auto ist nicht ~zukriegen** this car just goes on for ever; **wie hast du denn das ~gekriegt?** how did you manage to break it?; **~lachen** *vr sep (col)* to die laughing *(col)*; **~machen** *sep (col)* **1** *vt* to ruin; *Zerbrechliches* to break; *Brücke, Sandburg* to knock down; *(erschöpfen) jdn* to wear out; **die Arbeit macht mich ~** this job will be the death of me *(col)*; **2** *vr (sich überanstrengen)* to wear oneself out; **~schlagen** *vt sep irreg (col)* to smash.
Kapuze *f* **-n** hood; *(Mönchs~)* cowl.
Kapuziner *m* - *(Bot)* nasturtium.
Karabiner *m* - *(Gewehr)* carbine.
Karacho *nt no pl*: **mit ~** *(col)* hell for leather *(col)*.
Karaffe *f* **-n** carafe; *(mit Stöpsel)* decanter.
Karambolage [karambo'la:ʒə] *f* **-n** *(Aut)* collision, crash; *(Billard)* cannon.
Karamel *m no pl* caramel *no pl.*
Karat *nt* **-e** *or (bei Zahlenangabe)* - carat.
Karate *nt no pl* karate. **~hieb** *m* karate chop.
Karawane *f* **-n** caravan.
Kardinal *m, pl* **Kardinäle** *(Eccl)* cardinal.
Kardinal-: ~fehler *m* cardinal error; **~zahl** *f* cardinal (number).
Karenzzeit *f* waiting period.
Karfiol *m no pl (Aus)* cauliflower.
Karfreitag *m* Good Friday.
karg *adj Vorrat, Gehalt* meagre *(Brit)*, meager *(US)*. **etw ~ bemessen** to be mean with sth.
Kargheit *f* meagreness *(Brit)*, meagerness *(US)*.
kärglich *adj* meagre *(Brit)*, meager *(US)*; *Mahl* frugal.
Kargo *m* **-s** cargo.
Karibik *f* **die ~** the Caribbean.
karibisch *adj* Caribbean. **das K~e Meer** the Caribbean Sea.
kariert *adj Stoff, Muster* checked, checkered *(esp US)*; *Papier* squared.
Karies ['ka:riɛs] *f no pl* caries.
Karikatur *f* caricature.
Karikaturist(in *f*) *m* cartoonist.
karikieren* *vt* to caricature.
Karitas *f no pl* charity.
karitativ *adj* charitable.
karmin(rot) *adj* carmine (red).
Karneval ['karnəval] *m* **-e** *or* **-s** carnival.
Karnevalszug *m* carnival procession.
Karnickel *nt* - *(col)* rabbit.
Karo *nt* **-s** *(Quadrat)* square; *(auf der Spitze stehend)* diamond, lozenge; *(Muster)* check; *(diagonal)* diamond; *(Cards) (Farbe)* diamonds *pl*; *(Karte)* diamond.
Karomuster *nt* checked *or* checkered *(esp US)* pattern.
Karosse *f* **-n** *(Prachtkutsche)* (state) coach.
Karosserie *f* bodywork.
Karosserie-: ~bauer *m* coachbuilder; **~schaden** *m* damage to the bodywork.
Karotte *f* **-n** (small) carrot.
Karpaten *pl* Carpathians *pl.*
Karpfen *m* - carp.
Karre *f* **-n (a)** *siehe* **Karren. (b)** *(col: Auto)* (old) crate *(col)*.
Karree *nt* **-s** square; *(Häuserblock)* block. **einmal ums ~ gehen** to walk around the block.
Karren *m* - **(a)** *(Wagen)* cart; *(esp für Garten, Baustelle)* (wheel)barrow; *(für Gepäck etc)* trolley *(Brit)*, cart *(US)*. **(b)** *(fig col)* **jdm an den ~ fahren** to take sb to task; **jdn vor seinen ~ spannen** to use sb; **den ~ in den Dreck fahren** to get things in a mess; **den ~ aus dem Dreck ziehen** to get things sorted out.
Karriere *f* **-n** *(Laufbahn)* career. **~ machen** to make a career for oneself.
Karsamstag m Easter Saturday.
Karst *m* **-e** *(Geog, Geol)* karst, *barren landscape.*
Karte *f* **-n (a)** card. **jdm die ~ lesen** to tell sb's fortune from the cards; **mit offenen ~n spielen** *(fig)* to put one's cards on the table; **er spielt mit verdeckten ~n** *(fig)* he's playing his cards very close to his chest; **alle ~n in der Hand halten** *(fig)* to hold all the cards; **es ist unmöglich, ihm in die ~n zu sehen** *(fig)* it's impossible to know what he's upto; **alles auf eine ~ setzen** to put all

one's eggs in one basket *(prov)*. **(b)** *(Fahr~, Eintritts~)* ticket; *(Einladungs~)* invitation (card). **die ~n, bitte!** tickets, please! **(c)** *(Land~)* map; *(See~)* chart. **(d)** *(Speise~)* menu; *(Wein~)* wine list.

Kartei *f* card index.

Kartei-: ~karte *f* file *or* record card; **~kasten** *m* file-card box; **~leiche** *f (hum)* non-active member; **~schrank** *m* filing cabinet.

Kartell *nt* **-e** cartel.

Kartellamt *nt* monopolies commission.

Karten-: ~haus *nt* **(a)** house of cards; **wie ein ~haus (in sich) zusammenfallen** to collapse like a house of cards; **(b)** *(Naut)* chart room; **~kunststück** *nt* card trick; **~legen** *nt* fortune-telling *(using cards)*; **~spiel** *nt* **(a)** card-playing; *(ein Spiel)* card game; **beim ~spiel** when playing cards; **(b)** *(Karten)* pack *or* deck (of cards).

Kartoffel *f* **-n** potato. **rein in die ~n, raus aus den ~n** *(col)* first it's one thing, then it's another; **jdn fallenlassen wie eine heiße ~** *(col)* to drop sb like a hot brick *(col)*.

Kartoffel- *in cpds* potato; **~brei** *m* mashed potatoes *pl*; **~chips** *pl* potato crisps *pl (Brit)*, potato chips *pl (US)*; **~käfer** *m* Colorado beetle; **~puffer** *m* potato fritter; **~püree** *nt* mashed potatoes *pl*; **~salat** *m* potato salad; **~schalen** *pl* potato peel(ings); **~schäler** *m* potato peeler.

Kartograph(in *f*) *m* cartographer.

Karton [kar'toŋ, kar'to:] *m* **-s (a)** *(Pappe)* card, cardboard. **(b)** *(Schachtel)* cardboard box.

kartoniert *adj Bücher* hardback, cased.

Karussell *nt* **-s** *or* **-e** merry-go-round, roundabout *(Brit)*.

Karwoche *f (Eccl)* Holy Week.

kaschieren* *vt* to conceal.

Kaschmir *m* **-e** *(Tex)* cashmere.

Käse *m* **- (a)** cheese. **(b)** *(col: Unsinn)* rubbish, twaddle *(col)*.

Käse- *in cpds* cheese; **~blatt** *nt (col)* rag *(col)*; **~brot** *nt* bread and cheese; **~gebäck** *nt* cheese savouries *(Brit) or* savories *(US) pl*; **~glocke** *f* cheese cover; **~kuchen** *m* cheesecake.

Kaserne *f* **-n** barracks *pl*.

Kasernenhof *m* barrack square.

kasernieren* *vt Truppen* to quarter in barracks.

käsig *adj* **(a)** *(fig col) Gesicht, Haut* pasty, pale; *(vor Schreck)* white. **(b)** *(lit)* cheesy.

Kasino *nt* **-s (a)** *(Spielbank)* casino. **(b)** *(Offiziers~)* (officers') mess; *(Speiseraum)* dining room.

Kaskade *f* cascade.

Kaskoversicherung *f (Aut) (Teil~)* ≃ third party, fire and theft insurance; *(Voll~)* fully comprehensive insurance.

Kasper *m* - *(im Puppenspiel)* Punch; *(col)* clown *(col)*.

Kasperl(e)-: ~figur *f* glove puppet; **~theater** *nt* Punch and Judy (show).

Kaspisches Meer *nt* Caspian Sea.

Kassandraruf *m* gloomy prediction.

Kasse *f* **-n (a)** cashdesk, cash point; *(in Supermarkt auch)* checkout; *(Zahlraum)* cashier's office; *(Theat etc)* box office. **an der ~** *(in Geschäft)* at the desk. **(b)** *(Geldkasten)* cashbox; *(in Läden)* cash register, till; *(bei Spielen)* kitty; *(in einer Spielbank)* bank. **die ~n klingeln** the money is really rolling in; **unsere ~ ist leer** the coffers are empty. **(c)** *(Bargeld)* cash. **bei ~ sein** *(col)* to be flush *(col)*; **wie bist du bei ~?** *(col)* how are you off for cash?; **knapp/gut/schlecht bei ~ sein** *(col)* to be short of cash/well-off/badly-off; **~ machen** to cash up; *(col: gut verdienen)* to make a bomb *(col)*; **die ~ führen** to be in charge of the money; **die ~ stimmt!** *(col)* the money's OK *(col)*; **zur ~ bitten** to ask for money; **jdn zur ~ bitten** to ask sb to pay up.

Kasseler *nt* - *lightly smoked pork loin.*

Kassen-: ~arzt *m* ≃ National Health doctor *(Brit)*, panel doctor *(US)*; **~bericht** *m* financial report; **~bestand** *m* cash in hand; **~bon** *m* sales slip; **~buch** *nt* cashbook; **~erfolg** *m (Theat etc)* box-office hit; **~magnet** *m (Theat etc)* big draw; **~patient** *m* ≃ National Health patient *(Brit)*; **~preis** *m* cash price; **~prüfung** *f* audit; **~schlager** *m (col) (Theat etc)* box-office hit; *(Ware)* big seller; **~stunden** *pl* hours of business; **~sturz** *m (Comm)* cashing-up; **~sturz machen** to check one's finances; *(Comm)* to cash up; **~wart** *m* **-e** treasurer; **~zettel** *m* sales slip.

Kasserolle *f* **-n** saucepan; *(mit Henkeln)* casserole.

Kassette *f* **(a)** cassette. **(b)** *(Kästchen)* case, box; *(Geschenk~)* gift set.

Kassetten-: ~deck *nt* cassette deck; **~recorder** *m* cassette recorder.

Kassiber *m* - secret message.

kassieren* 1 *vt* **(a)** *Gelder etc* to collect; *(col) Abfindung, Finderlohn* to pick up *(col)*; *Summe* to make. **(b)** *(col: wegnehmen)* to take away, to confiscate. **2** *vi* **bei jdm ~** to collect the money from sb; **darf ich ~, bitte?** would you like to pay now?; **bei diesem Geschäft hat er ganz schön kassiert** he made a packet on the deal *(col)*.

Kassierer(in *f*) *m* - cashier; *(Bank~)* clerk.

Kastagnette [kastan'jɛtə] *f* castanet.

Kastanie [-iə] *f* chestnut. **für jdn die ~n aus dem Feuer holen** *(fig)* to pull sb's chestnuts out of the fire.

Kastanien- [-iən]: **~baum** *m* chestnut tree; **k~braun** *adj* maroon; *Pferd, Haar* chestnut.

Kästchen *nt* **(a)** small box; *(für Schmuck)* case, casket. **(b)** *(auf kariertem Papier)* square.

Kaste *f* **-n** caste.

Kasten *m* ⸚ **(a)** box *(auch Sport)*; *(Kiste)* crate; *(Brief~)* postbox, letterbox; *(Brot~)* breadbin. **(b)** *(col) (Gebäude)* barn *(col)*; *(Auto)* crate *(col)*; *(Schiff)* tub *(col)*; *(Fernseher)* box *(Brit col)*, tube *(US col)*; *(Ftbl: Tor)* goal. **er hat was auf dem ~** *(col)* he's brainy *(col)*.

Kasten-: ~form *f (Cook)* (square) baking tin; **~wagen** *m (Aut)* van, panel truck *(US)*.

Kastrat *m (wk)* **-en, -en** eunuch; *(Mus)* castrato.

Kastration *f* castration.

kastrieren* *vt (lit, fig)* to castrate.

Katakombe *f* **-n** catacomb.

Katalog *m* **-e** catalogue.

katalogisieren* *vt* to catalogue.

Katalysator *m (lit, fig)* catalyst; *(Aut)* catalytic converter.

Katapult *nt or m* **-e** catapult.

katapultieren* 1 *vt* to catapult. **2** *vt* to catapult oneself; *(Pilot)* to eject.

Katapultsitz *m* ejector seat.

Katarrh *m* **-e** catarrh.

Kataster *m or nt* - land register.

Kataster|amt *nt* land registry.

katastrophal *adj* disastrous, catastrophic. **das sind ja ~e Zustände** it's a terrible state of affairs.

Katastrophe *f* **-n** disaster, catastrophe.

Katastrophen-: ~alarm *m* emergency alert; **~dienst** *m* emergency service; **~einsatz** *m* **im ~einsatz** on emergency duty; **~gebiet** *nt* disaster area; **~schutz** m disaster control; *(im voraus)* disaster prevention.

Katechismus *m* catechism.

Kategorie *f* category. **er gehört zur ~ derer, die ...** he's one of those who ...

kategorisch *adj* categorical, absolute; *Ablehnung auch* flat.

Kater *m* **- (a)** tom(cat). **wie ein verliebter ~** like an amorous tomcat. **(b)** *(col: Katzenjammer)* hangover.

Kater-: ~frühstück *nt breakfast (of pickled herring etc) to cure a hangover;* **~stimmung** *f* depression,

the blues *pl (col)*.
Kathedrale *f* **-n** cathedral.
Katheter *m* **-** *(Med)* catheter.
Kathode *f* **-n** *(Phys)* cathode.
Kathoden-: ~**strahlen** *pl (Phys)* cathode rays *pl*; ~**strahlröhre** *f (TV etc)* cathode ray tube.
Katholik(in *f***)** *m (wk)* **-en, -en** (Roman) Catholic.
katholisch *adj* (Roman) Catholic. **sie ist streng** ~ she's a strict Catholic.
Katholizismus *m* (Roman) Catholicism.
katzbuckeln *vi (pej col)* to bow and scrape.
Kätzchen *nt* **(a)** kitten. **(b)** *(Bot)* catkin.
Katze *f* **-n** cat. **sie ist eine falsche** ~ she's two-faced; **meine Arbeit war für die Katz** *(col)* my work was a waste of time; **Katz und Maus mit jdm spielen** *(col)* to play cat and mouse with sb; **die** ~ **aus dem Sack lassen** *(col)* to let the cat out of the bag; **die** ~ **im Sack kaufen** to buy a pig in a poke *(prov)*; **die** ~ **läßt das Mausen nicht** *(Prov)* the leopard cannot change its spots *(prov)*; **bei Nacht sind alle** ~**n grau** all cats are grey at night.
Katzen-: ~**auge** *nt (Rückstrahler)* reflector; **k**~**haft** *adj* cat-like, feline; ~**hai** *m* dogfish; ~**jammer** *m (col) (Kater)* hangover; *(jämmerliche Stimmung)* depression, the blues *pl (col)*; ~**musik** *f (fig)* caterwauling; ~**sprung** *m (col)* stone's throw; ~**tisch** *m (hum)* children's table; ~**wäsche** *f (hum col)* a lick and a promise *(col)*.
Kauderwelsch *nt no pl (pej)* double dutch.
kauen *vti* to chew; *Nägel* to bite. **an etw** *(dat)* ~ to chew (on) sth; **an den Nägeln** ~ to bite one's nails; **daran hatte ich lange zu** ~ *(fig)* it took me a long time to get over it.
kauern *vir (vi auch aux sein)* to crouch (down); *(ängstlich)* to cower.
Kauf *m, pl* **Käufe** purchase. **das war ein günstiger** ~ that was a good buy; **beim** ~ **eines Autos** when buying a car; **etw zum** ~ **anbieten** to offer sth for sale; **einen** ~ **tätigen** *(form)* to complete a purchase; **etw in** ~ **nehmen** *(fig)* to accept sth.
kaufen 1 *vt* **(a)** *(auch* **sich** *(dat)* ~*)* to buy, to purchase *(esp form)*. **ich habe (mir) einen neuen Anzug gekauft** I bought (myself) a new suit; **etw für teures Geld** ~ *(col)* to pay a lot (of money) for sth; **diese Zigaretten werden viel/nicht gekauft** a lot of people buy/nobody buys these cigarettes; **dafür kann ich mir nichts** ~ *(iro)* what use is that to me! **(b)** *(bestechen) jdn* to bribe, to buy off; *Stimmen* to buy. **der Sieg war gekauft** it was fixed. **(c) sich** *(dat)* **jdn** ~ *(col)* to give sb a piece of one's mind *(col)*; *(tätlich)* to fix sb *(col)*. **2** *vi* to buy; *(Einkäufe machen)* to shop.
Käufer(in *f***)** *m* **-** buyer, purchaser *(esp form)*; *(Kunde)* customer, shopper.
Kauf-: ~**haus** *nt* department store; ~**kraft** *f* purchasing power.
käuflich *adj* **(a)** for sale. **Glück ist nicht** ~ happiness cannot be bought; **etw** ~ **erwerben** *(form)* to purchase sth. **(b)** *(fig)* venal. ~ **sein** *(Mensch)* to be open to bribery; **ich bin nicht** ~ you can't buy me!; ~**e Liebe** *(geh)* prostitution.
Käuflichkeit *f (fig)* corruptibility.
Kauf-: ~**lust** *f* desire to buy things; *(St Ex)* buying; **k**~**lustig** *adj* in a buying mood; **in den Straßen drängten sich die** ~**lustigen** the streets were thronged with shoppers.
Kaufmann *m, pl* **-leute (a)** businessman; *(Händler)* trader. **(b)** *(Einzelhandels*~*)* small shopkeeper, grocer. **zum** ~ **gehen** to go to the grocer's *(Brit) or* grocer.
kaufmännisch *adj* commercial, business *attr*. ~**er Angestellter** office employee; ~**e Lehre** commercial training; **er wollte einen** ~**en Beruf ergreifen** he wanted to make a career in business; **er übt einen** ~**en Beruf aus** he is in business; ~ **denken** to think in business terms; **sie ist** ~ **veranlagt** she is commercially minded.
Kauf-: ~**preis** *m* purchase price; ~**vertrag** *m* bill of sale; ~**wert** *m* market value; ~**zwang** *m* obligation to buy; **kein/ohne** ~**zwang** no/without obligation.
Kaugummi *m* chewing gum.
Kaukasus *m* **der** ~ (the) Caucasus.
Kaulquappe *f* tadpole.
kaum 1 *adv* hardly, scarcely. ~ **jemand/jemals** hardly *or* scarcely anyone/ever; **wir hatten** ~ **noch Benzin** we had hardly any petrol left; **wohl** ~**/ich glaube** ~ I hardly think so; **das wird wohl** ~ **stimmen** surely that can't be right/true; **das wird** ~ **passieren** that's hardly likely to happen; **das wird wohl** ~ **noch was werden** *(col)* that's hardly likely to come to anything. **2** *conj* hardly, scarcely. ~ **hatte er das gesagt, da ...** hardly had he said that when ...
Kaumuskel *m* jaw muscle.
kausal *adj* causal.
Kausalzusammenhang *m* causal connection.
Kautabak *m* chewing tobacco.
Kaution *f* **(a)** *(Jur)* bail. **er stellte 1000 Mark** ~ he put up 1000 marks (as) bail; **gegen** ~ on bail; **jdn gegen** ~ **freibekommen** to bail sb out. **(b)** *(Comm)* security. **(c)** *(für Miete)* deposit.
Kautschuk *m* **-e** (india)rubber.
Kauz *m, pl* **Käuze (a)** screech owl. **(b)** *(Sonderling)* oddball *(col)*. **ein komischer** ~ an odd bird.
Käuzchen *nt dim of* **Kauz (a).**
kauzig *adj* odd, cranky.
Kavalier [kava'liːɐ] *m* **-e** gentleman. **er ist immer** ~ he's always a gentleman.
Kavaliersdelikt *nt* trivial offence.
Kavallerie [kavalə'riː] *f (Mil)* cavalry.
Kaviar ['kaːviar] *m* **-e** caviar.
keck *adj (dated)* **(a)** *(frech)* cheeky, saucy. **(b)** *(flott)* pert, saucy. **(c)** *(kühn)* bold.
Kegel *m* **- (a)** *(Spielfigur)* skittle; *(bei Bowling)* pin. **(b)** *(Geometrie)* cone; *(Berg*~*)* peak. **(c)** *(Licht*~*)* beam (of light).
Kegel-: ~**bahn** *f* (bowling) lane; *(Anlage)* skittle-alley; *(automatisch)* bowling alley; ~**bruder** *m (col) (eifriger Kegler)* skittle-player; bowling fanatic; **k**~**förmig** *adj* conical.
kegeln *vi* to play skittles; *(bei Bowling)* to play bowls. ~ **gehen** to play skittles; to go bowling.
Kegler(in *f***)** *m* **-** skittle-player; *(bei Bowling)* bowler.
Kehle *f* **-n** *(Gurgel)* throat. **er hat das in die falsche** ~ **bekommen** *(lit)* it went down the wrong way; *(fig)* he took it the wrong way; **eine trockene** ~ **haben** to be dry; **er hat Gold in der** ~ *(col)* his voice is/could be a real gold-mine; **aus voller** ~ at the top of one's voice.
Kehlkopf *m* larynx.
Kehlkopf|entzündung *f* laryngitis.
Kehllaut *m* guttural (sound).
Kehr-: ~**aus** *m* **-**, *no pl* last dance; *(fig: Abschiedsfeier)* farewell celebration; ~**besen** *m* broom; ~**blech** *nt* shovel.
Kehre *f* **-n** (sharp) bend.
kehren[1] *vt* to turn. **in sich** *(acc)* **gekehrt** *(versunken)* pensive; *(verschlossen)* introspective, introverted.
kehren[2] *vti (fegen)* to sweep. **jeder kehre vor seiner Tür!** *(Prov)* everyone should first put his own house in order.
Kehricht *m or nt no pl (old, form)* sweepings *pl*.
Kehr-: ~**maschine** *f (Straßen*~*)* road-sweeper; *(Teppich*~*)* carpet-sweeper; ~**reim** *m* chorus, refrain; ~**schaufel** *f* shovel; ~**seite** *f (von Münze)* reverse; *(col: Rücken)* back; *(hum: Gesäß)* backside *(col)*; *(fig: Nachteil)* drawback; *(fig: Schattenseite)* other side; **die** ~**seite der Medaille** the other side of the coin.
kehrt *interj (Mil)* about turn!
Kehrt-: **k**~**machen** *vi sep* to do an about-turn;

(zurückgehen) to turn back; **~wendung** *f* about-turn.

keifen *vi* to bicker.

Keil *m* **-e** *(lit, fig)* wedge.

Keile *pl (col)* thrashing, hiding.

Keil-: k~förmig *adj* wedge-shaped; **~hosen** *pl* ski pants *pl*; **~riemen** *m (Aut)* fan-belt.

Keim *m* **-e** shoot, sprout; *(Embryo, fig)* embryo; *(Krankheits~)* germ; *(fig: des Hasses etc)* seed *usu pl*. **etw im ~ ersticken** to nip sth in the bud; **den ~ zu etw legen** to sow the seeds of sth.

keimen *vi* to germinate; *(fig: Verdacht)* to be aroused.

Keim-: k~frei *adj* germ-free; *(Med auch, fig)* sterile; **k~frei machen** to sterilize; **k~tötend** *adj* germicidal; **~zelle** *f* germ cell.

kein, keine, kein *indef pron* **(a)** *(adjektivisch)* no. **~ Mann/~e Häuser/~ Whisky** no man/houses/whisky; **ich sehe da ~en Unterschied** I see no difference, I don't see any difference; **da sind ~e Häuser** there are no houses there, there aren't any houses there; **~e schlechte Idee** not a bad idea; **das ist ~e Antwort auf unsere Frage** that's not an answer to our question; **~ bißchen** not a bit; **ich habe ~ bißchen Lust** I've absolutely no desire to; **ich bin doch ~ Kind mehr!** I am not a child any longer; **in ~ster Weise** not in the least. **(b)** *(nicht einmal)* **~e Stunde/drei Monate** less than an hour/three months.

keine(r, s) *indef pron (niemand)* nobody, no-one; *(von Gegenstand)* not one, none. **es war ~r da** there was nobody there, there wasn't anybody there; *(Gegenstand)* there wasn't one there; **es waren ~ da** *(Gegenstände)* there weren't any there, there were none there; **ich habe ~s** I haven't got one; **~r von uns/von uns (beiden)** none/neither of us; *(betont)* not one of us; **~s der (beiden) Kinder** neither of the children; **~s der sechs Kinder** none of the six children; *(betont)* not one of the six children; **ist Bier da? — nein, ich habe ~s gekauft** is there any beer? — no, I didn't buy any; **Tee haben wir, aber Kaffee haben wir ~n** we've got tea but no coffee; **hast du schon ein Glas? — nein, ich habe ~s** have you a glass? — no, I haven't got one.

keinerlei *adj attr inv* no ... whatever.

keinesfalls *adv* under no circumstances.

keineswegs *adv* not at all.

keinmal *adv* never once, not once.

keins = keines *siehe* **keine(r, s).**

Keks *m* **-e** biscuit *(Brit)*, cookie *(US)*.

Kelch *m* **-e (a)** goblet; *(liter)* cup. **(b)** *(Bot)* calyx.

Kelle *f* **-n** *(Suppen~ etc)* ladle; *(Schaumlöffel)* strainer; *(Maurer~)* trowel; *(Signalstab)* signalling disc.

Keller *m* **-** cellar; *(Geschoß)* basement.

Kellerei *f* wine cellars *pl; (Firma)* wine producer.

Keller-: ~geschoß *nt* basement; **~gewölbe** *nt (Keller)* cellars *pl*; **~lokal** *nt* cellar bar; **~wohnung** *f* basement flat *(Brit) or* apartment.

Kellner *m* **-** waiter.

Kellnerin *f* waitress.

kellnern *vi (col)* to work as a waiter/waitress.

Kelte *m (wk)* **-n, -n, Keltin** *f* Celt.

Kelter *f* **-n** winepress; *(Obst~)* press.

keltern *vt Trauben, Wein* to press.

kennen *pret* **kannte,** *ptp* **gekannt** *vt* to know; *(geh: er~)* to recognize. **er kennt keine Müdigkeit** he doesn't know what tiredness is; **kein Erbarmen/Mitleid** *etc* **~** to know no mercy/pity *etc*; **so was ~ wir hier nicht!** we don't have that sort of thing here; **jdn als etw ~** to know sb to be sth; **~ Sie sich schon?** do you know each other (already)?; **~ Sie den (schon)?** *(Witz)* have you heard this one?; **kennst du mich noch?** do you remember me?; **wie ich ihn kenne ...** if I know him (at all) ...; **da kennst du mich aber schlecht** you don't know me.

kennenlernen *vt sep* to get to know; *(zum ersten Mal treffen)* to meet. **sich ~** to get to know each other; to meet each other; **ich freue mich, Sie kennenzulernen** *(form)* (I am) pleased to meet you *or* to make your acquaintance *(form)*; **der wird mich noch ~** *(col)* he'll have me to reckon with *(col)*; **bei näherem K~ erwies er sich als ...** on closer acquaintance he proved to be ...

Kenner(in *f***)** *m* **-** expert *(von or gen* on*)*, authority *(von or gen* on*)*; *(Wein~ etc)* connoisseur.

kennerhaft *adj* **mit ~em Blick/Griff** with an expert eye/touch.

Kennermiene *f* connoisseur's expression. **mit ~ betrachtete er ...** he looked at ... like a connoisseur.

kenntlich *adj (zu erkennen)* recognizable *(an +dat* by*)*; *(deutlich)* clear. **etw ~ machen** to identify sth (clearly).

Kenntnis *f* **(a)** *(Wissen)* knowledge *no pl*. **über ~se von etw verfügen** to be knowledgeable about sth; **gute ~se in Mathematik haben** to have a good knowledge of mathematics. **(b)** *no pl (form)* **etw zur ~ nehmen** to take note of sth; **jdn von etw in ~ setzen** to inform *or* advise *(Comm, form)* sb about sth.

Kenn-: ~wort *nt, pl* **~wörter** *(Chiffre)* code name; *(Losungswort)* password, code word; **~zeichen** *nt* **(a)** *(Aut)* **(amtliches/polizeiliches) ~zeichen** number plate *(Brit)*, license plate *(US)*; **(b)** *(Markierung, Erkennungszeichen)* mark, sign; *(Eigenart)* characteristic *(für, gen* of*)*; *(für Qualität)* hallmark; **unveränderliche ~zeichen** distinguishing marks; **k~zeichnen** *vt insep* **(a)** to mark; *(durch Etikett auch)* to label; **(b)** *(charakterisieren)* to characterize; **jdn als etw k~zeichnen** to show sb to be sth; **k~zeichnend** *adj* typical, characteristic *(für* of*)*; **~ziffer** *f* (code) number; *(Comm)* reference number.

kentern *vi aux sein (Schiff)* to capsize.

Keramik *f* **(a)** *no pl (Art)* ceramics *pl*; *(Gebrauchsgegenstände auch)* pottery. **(b)** *(Kunstgegenstand)* ceramic.

keramisch *adj* ceramic.

Kerbe *f* **-n** notch. **in die gleiche ~ hauen** *or* **schlagen** *(fig col)* to take the same line.

Kerbholz *nt*: **etwas auf dem ~ haben** *(col)* to have done something bad.

Kerker *m (Hist, geh)* dungeon; *(Strafe)* imprisonment.

Kerl *m* **-e** *or* **-s** *(col)* fellow *(col)*, guy *(col)*; *(pej)* character. **du gemeiner ~!** you swine *(col)*; **ein ganzer ~** a real man; **sie ist ein netter ~** she's a nice girl.

Kern *m* **-e** *(von Obst)* pip, seed; *(von Steinobst)* stone; *(Nuß~)* kernel; *(Phys, Biol)* nucleus; *(von Reaktor)* core; *(fig)* crux, core; *(von Stadt)* centre *(Brit)*, center *(US)*.

Kern- *in cpds (Nuklear-)* nuclear; **~fach** *nt (Sch)* core subject; **~frage** central question; **~gedanke** *m* central idea; **~gehäuse** *nt* core; **k~gesund** *adj* as fit as a fiddle.

kernig *adj (fig) Ausspruch* pithy; *(urwüchsig)* earthy; *(kraftvoll)* robust, powerful.

Kern-: ~kräfte *pl* nuclear forces *pl*; **~kraftwerk** *nt* nuclear power station; **~land** *nt* heartland; **k~los** *adj* seedless, pipless; **~obst** *nt fruit with core and pips such as apples*; **~problem** *nt* central problem; **~reaktor** *m* nuclear reactor; **~satz** *m* key sentence, key phrase; **~schmelze** *f* meltdown; **~seife** *f* washing soap; **~spaltung** *f* nuclear fission; **die erste ~spaltung** the first splitting of the atom; **~stück** *nt (fig)* main item; *(von Theorie etc)* central part, core; **~waffe** *f* nuclear weapon; **k~waffenfrei** *adj* nuclear-free; **~zeit** *f* core time.

Kerze *f* **-n** *(Wachs~)* candle; *(Aut)* plug; *(Turnen)* shoulder-stand.

Kerzen-: k~gerade *adj* (as) straight as a die;

~**halter** *m* candlestick; ~**licht** *nt*, ~**schein** *m* candlelight; ~**schlüssel** *m* (spark) plug spanner.
Kescher *m* - fishing-net.
keß *adj* saucy.
Kessel *m* - **(a)** *(Tee~)* kettle; *(für offenes Feuer)* cauldron; *(esp in Brauerei)* vat; *(Dampf~)* boiler; *(Behälter für Flüssigkeiten etc)* tank. **(b)** *(Mulde)* basin.
Kessel-: ~**haus** *nt* boiler house; ~**pauke** *f* kettle drum; ~**stein** *m* scale, fur.
Ketchup ['kɛtʃap] *m or nt* **-s** ketchup.
Kette *f* **-n** *(lit, fig)* chain; *(an Kettenfahrzeug)* chain track; *(von Truppen, Fahrzeugen)* line; *(Tex)* warp. **eine ~ aus Perlen** *etc* a string of pearls *etc*; **einen Hund an die ~ legen** to chain up a dog; **seine ~n sprengen** *(fig)* to throw off one's chains.
ketten *vt* to chain *(an +acc* to*)*. **jdn an sich ~** *(fig)* to bind sb to oneself.
Ketten-: ~**antrieb** *m* chain drive; ~**fahrzeug** *nt* tracked vehicle; ~**glied** *nt* (chain-)link; ~**hund** *m* guard-dog; ~**karussell** *nt* merry-go-round *(with gondolas suspended on chains)*; ~**rad** *nt* sprocket(-wheel); ~**raucher** *m* chainsmoker; ~**reaktion** *f* chain reaction; ~**schaltung** *f* dérailleur gear; ~**schutz** *m* chain guard; ~**stich** *m* *(Sew)* chain stitch.
Ketzer(in *f***)** *m* - *(Eccl, fig)* heretic.
keuchen *vi* to pant, to puff; *(Asthmatiker etc)* to wheeze.
Keuchhusten *m* whooping cough.
Keule *f* **-n** club; *(Sport)* (Indian) club; *(Cook)* leg.
Keulen-: ~**hieb**, ~**schlag** *m* blow with a club; **es traf ihn wie ein ~schlag** *(fig)* it hit him like a thunderbolt.
keusch *adj (lit, fig)* chaste.
Keuschheit *f* chastity.
kfm = **kaufmännisch.**
Kfz [ka|ɛf'tsɛt] *nt* **-(s)** *(form)* = **Kraftfahrzeug** motor vehicle.
kg = **Kilogramm** kg.
KG [ka'geː] *f* **-s** = **Kommanditgesellschaft** limited partnership.
khaki *adj pred* khaki.
Kibbuz *m, pl* **Kibbuzim** *or* **-e** kibbutz.
kichern *vi* to giggle.
kicken *(Ftbl)* **1** *vt* to kick. **2** *vi* to play football; *(den Ball ~)* to kick.
Kicker *m* - *(Ftbl sl)* player.
kidnappen ['kɪtnɛpn] *vt insep* to kidnap.
Kidnapper(in *f***)** ['kɪtnɛpɐ, -ərɪn] *m* - kidnapper.
Kidnapping ['kɪtnɛpɪŋ] *nt* **-s** kidnapping.
Kiebitz *m* **-e** *(Orn)* lapwing.
Kiefer[1] **-n** pine (tree); *(Holz)* pine(wood).
Kiefer[2] *n* - jaw; *(~knochen)* jawbone.
Kiefern-: ~**holz** *nt* pine(wood); ~**nadel** *f* pine needle; ~**zapfen** *m* pinecone.
Kieker *m* **jdn auf dem ~ haben** *(col)* to have it in for sb *(col)*.
Kiel *m* **-e** *(Schiffs~)* keel; *(Feder~)* quill. **ein Schiff auf ~ legen** to lay down a ship.
Kielwasser *nt* wake, wash. **in jds ~ segeln** *(fig)* to follow in sb's wake.
Kieme *f* **-n** gill.
Kies *m* **-e** gravel; *(am Strand)* shingle.
Kiesel -, Kieselstein *m* pebble.
Kies-: ~**grube** *f* gravel pit; ~**weg** *m* gravel path.
Killer(in *f***)** *m* - *(col)* killer, murderer; *(gedungener)* hit-man.
Kilo *nt* **-(s)** kilo.
Kilo- *in cpds* kilo-; ~**byte** [-'bait] *nt (Comp)* kilobyte; ~**gramm** *nt* kilogram(me); ~**hertz** *nt* kilohertz.
Kilometer *m* kilometre *(Brit)*, kilometer *(US)*; *(col: Stundenkilometer)* k *(col)*.
Kilometer-: ~**geld** *nt* mileage (allowance); **k~lang 1** *adj* miles long; **ein k~langer Stau** a hold-up several miles/kilometres long; **2** *adv* for miles (and miles), for miles on end; ~**stand** *m* mileage; ~**stein** *m* milestone; **k~weit 1** *adj* miles long; **2** *adv* for miles (and miles); ~**zähler** *m* mileometer *(Brit)*, odometer *(US)*.
Kilo-: ~**watt** *nt* kilowatt; ~**wattstunde** *f* kilowatt hour.
Kimme *f* **-n** *(von Gewehr)* back sight.
Kind *nt* **-er** child, kid *(col)*; *(Kleinkind)* baby; *(esp Psych, Med)* infant. **ein ~ erwarten/bekommen** to be expecting a baby/to have a baby *or* child; **von ~ auf** from childhood; **ein ~ seiner Zeit sein** to be a child of one's times; **sich freuen wie ein ~** to be as pleased as Punch; **das weiß doch jedes ~!** any five-year-old would tell you that!; **das ist nichts für kleine ~er** *(fig col)* that's not for your ears/eyes; **mit ~ und Kegel** *(hum col)* with the whole family; **das ~ mit dem Bade ausschütten** to throw out the baby with the bathwater *(prov)*; **~er, ~er!** good heavens!
Kindbett *nt* **im ~** in confinement.
Kinder-: ~**arbeit** *f* child labour *(Brit) or* labor *(US)*; ~**arzt** *m* paediatrician *(Brit)*, pediatrician *(US)*; ~**bekleidung** *f* children's wear; ~**besteck** *nt* child's cutlery; ~**bett** *nt* child's bed; ~**buch** *nt* children's book.
Kinderei *f* childishness *no pl*.
Kinder-: ~**erziehung** *f* bringing up of children; *(durch Schule)* education of children; **k~feindlich** *adj* hostile to children, anti-children; *Architektur, Planung* not catering for children; ~**feindlichkeit** *f* anti-children attitude; *(von Architektur)* failure to cater for children; ~**freibetrag** *m* child allowance; **k~freundlich 1** *adj Mensch* fond of children; *Gesellschaft* child-orientated; *Möbel, Architektur etc* catering for children; **2** *adv* with children in mind; ~**funk** *m* children's radio; ~**garten** *m* kindergarten; ~**gärtner(in** *f***)** *m* nursery-school teacher; ~**geld** *nt* child allowance; ~**heim** *nt* children's home; ~**hort** *m* day-nursery, crèche; ~**kleidung** *f* children's clothes *pl*; ~**klinik** *f* children's clinic; ~**krankenhaus** *nt* children's hospital; ~**krankheit** *f* children's disease; *(fig)* teething troubles *pl*; ~**krippe** *f* day-nursery, crèche; ~**laden** *m* (alternative) play-group; ~**lähmung** *f* poliomyelitis, polio; **k~leicht** *adj* childishly simple, dead easy *(col)*; **es ist k~leicht** it's child's play; **k~lieb** *adj* fond of children; ~**lied** *nt* nursery rhyme; **k~los** *adj* childless; ~**losigkeit** *f* childlessness; ~**mädchen** *f* nanny; ~**narr** *m* **er ist ein ~narr** he adores children; ~**pflegerin** *f* children's nurse; **k~reich** *adj* with many children; *Familie* large; ~**reichtum** *m* an abundance of children; ~**reim** *m* nursery rhyme; ~**sachen** *pl (Kleidung)* children's clothes *pl*; *(Spielsachen)* toys *pl*; ~**schreck** *m* bog(e)yman; ~**schuh** *m* child's shoe; **etw steckt noch in den ~schuhen** *(fig)* sth is still in its infancy; **den ~schuhen entwachsen sein** *(fig) (Mensch)* to have grown up; *(Technik etc)* to be no longer in its infancy; ~**schutz** *m* protection of children; ~**sitz** *m* child's seat; ~**spiel** *nt* children's game; *(fig)* child's play *no art*; ~**spielplatz** *m* children's playground; ~**spielzeug** *nt* (children's) toys *pl*; ~**sprache** *f* children's language; *(verniedlichend von Erwachsenen)* baby talk *no art*; ~**sterblichkeit** *f* infant mortality; ~**stube** *f (fig)* upbringing; ~**stuhl** *m* child's chair; *(Hochstuhl)* high chair; ~**wagen** *m* pram *(Brit)*, baby carriage *(US)*; *(Sportwagen)* pushchair *(Brit)*, babystroller *(US)*; ~**zimmer** *nt* child's/children's room; *(esp für Kleinkinder)* nursery; ~**zulage** *f*, ~**zuschlag** *m* child allowance.
Kindes-: ~**alter** *nt* childhood; **seit frühestem ~alter** from infancy; ~**annahme** *f* adoption; ~**beine** *pl*: **von ~beinen an** from childhood; ~**entführung** *f* kidnapping (of a child/children); ~**mißhandlung** *f* child abuse.
Kind-: **k~gemäß** *adj* suitable for a child/children;

~**heit** *f* childhood; *(früheste ~heit)* infancy; ~**heitserinnerung** *f* childhood memory.
kindisch *adj (pej)* childish. **sich ~ über etw** *(acc)* **freuen** to be as pleased as Punch about sth.
kindlich 1 *adj* childlike; *(pej)* childish. **2** *adv* like a child.
Kinds- *in cpds siehe* **Kindes-;** ~**kopf** *m (col)* big kid *(col)*.
Kinkerlitzchen *pl (col)* knicknacks *pl (col)*; *(dumme Streiche)* tomfoolery *sing (col)*.
Kinn *nt* **-e** chin.
Kinnhaken *m* hook to the chin.
Kino *nt* **-s** cinema *(Brit)*, movie theater *(US)*. **ins ~ gehen** to go to the cinema *or* pictures *(Brit) or* movies *(esp US)*; **das ~ der zwanziger Jahre** the cinema *(Brit) or* movies *(esp US)* in the twenties.
Kino- *in cpds* cinema *(Brit)*, movie *(esp US)*; ~**besucher** *m* cinemagoer *(Brit)*, movie-goer *(US)*; ~**karte** *f* cinema *(Brit) or* movie-theater *(US)* ticket; ~**kasse** *f* cinema *(Brit) or* movie theater *(US)* box office.
Kintopp *m or nt (dated)* cinema *(Brit)*, movie theater *(US)*.
Kiosk *m* **-e** kiosk.
Kippe *f* **-n (a) auf der ~ stehen** *(Gegenstand)* to be balanced precariously; **sie steht auf der ~** *(fig)* it's touch and go with her. **(b)** *(col: Zigarettenstummel)* cigarette stub, dog-end *(Brit col)*. **(c)** *(Müll~, Min)* tip.
kippen 1 *vt* **(a)** *Behälter, Fenster* to tilt; *Ladefläche, Tisch* to tip *or* tilt (up). **„bitte nicht ~“** “please do not tilt”. **(b)** *(schütten)* to tip. **2** *vi aux sein* to tip over, to topple over. **aus den Latschen ~** *(fig col) (überrascht sein)* to fall through the floor *(col)*; *(ohnmächtig werden)* to pass out.
Kipper *m* - *(Aut)* tipper, dump(er) truck.
Kipp-: ~**fenster** *nt* tilt window; ~**lore** *f* tipper wagon; ~**schalter** *m* rocker switch.
Kirche *f* **-n** church. **zur ~ gehen** to go to church.
Kirchen- *in cpds* church; ~**austritt** *m* leaving the Church *no art*; ~**bank** *f* pew; ~**besuch** *m* church-going; ~**buch** *nt* church register; ~**chor** *m* church choir; **k~feindlich** *adj* anticlerical; ~**fest** *nt* religious *or* church festival; ~**gemeinde** *f* parish; ~**jahr** *nt* church *or* ecclesiastical year; ~**licht** *nt*: **kein (großes) ~licht sein** *(fig col)* to be not very bright; ~**lied** *nt* hymn; ~**maus** *f*: **arm wie eine ~maus** poor as a church mouse; ~**recht** *nt* canon law; **k~rechtlich** *adj* canonical; ~**schiff** *nt (Längsschiff)* nave; *(Querschiff)* transept; ~**steuer** *f* church tax.
Kirch-: ~**gang** *m* going to church *no art*; ~**gänger(in** *f***)** *m* - churchgoer; ~**hof** *m* churchyard; *(Friedhof)* graveyard.
kirchlich *adj* church *attr*; *Zustimmung, Mißbilligung* by the church; *Gebot, Gericht* ecclesiastical. **sich ~ trauen lassen** to have a church wedding; **~ bestattet werden** to have a religious funeral.
Kirch-: ~**turm** *m* church steeple; ~**weih** *f* **-en** fair, kermis *(US)*.
Kirmes *f* **-sen** *(dial)* fair, kermis *(US)*.
Kirsch *m* - kirsch.
Kirsch- *in cpds* cherry; ~**baum** *m* cherry tree; *(Holz)* cherry (wood); ~**blüte** *f* cherry blossom.
Kirsche *f* **-n** cherry. **mit ihm ist nicht gut ~n essen** *(col)* it's best not to tangle with him.
Kirsch-: ~**kern** *m* cherry stone; ~**likör** *m* cherry brandy; ~**torte** *f*: **Schwarzwälder ~torte** Black Forest gateau; ~**wasser** *nt* kirsch.
Kissen *nt* - cushion; *(Kopf~)* pillow; *(Stempel~, an Heftpflaster)* pad.
Kissenbezug *m* cushion cover; *(Kopf~)* pillow case.
Kiste *f* **-n (a)** box; *(für Wein etc)* case; *(Latten~)* crate; *(Truhe)* chest; *(col: Fernsehen)* box *(Brit col)*, tube *(US col)*. **(b)** *(col: Angelegenheit)* affair.
kistenweise *adv* by the box/case *etc*.
Kitsch *m no pl* kitsch.
kitschig *adj* kitschy.
Kitt *m* **-e** *(Fenster~)* putty; *(für Porzellan, Stein etc)* cement; *(fig)* bond.
Kittel *m* - *(Arbeits~)* overall; *(von Arzt, Laborant etc)* (white) coat; *(blusenartig)* smock.
kitten *vt* to cement; *Fenster* to putty; *(füllen)* to fill; *(fig)* to patch up.
Kitz *nt* **-e** kid; *(Reh~)* fawn.
Kitzel *m* - tickle; *(fig)* thrill.
kitz(e)lig *adj (lit, fig)* ticklish.
kitzeln *vti (lit, fig)* to tickle.
Klacks *m* **-e** *(col) (von Kartoffelbrei, Sahne etc)* dollop *(col)*; *(von Senf, Farbe etc)* blob *(col)*. **das ist ein ~** that's nothing *(col)*.
klacksen *(col) vt Sahne etc* to dollop *(col)*; *Farbe* to splash.
Kladde *f* **-n** rough book; *(Block)* scribbling pad.
klaffen *vi* to gape. **da klafft eine Wunde** there is a gaping wound; **zwischen uns beiden klafft ein Abgrund** *(fig)* we are poles apart.
kläffen *vi (pej, fig)* to yap.
klaffend *adj* gaping; *(fig)* irreconcilable; *Widerspruch* blatant.
Kläffer *m* - *(lit, fig: pej)* yapper.
Klage *f* **-n (a)** *(Beschwerde)* complaint. **(bei jdm) über jdn/etw ~ führen** to lodge a complaint (with sb) about sb/sth; **~n (über jdn/etw) vorbringen** to make complaints (about sb/sth); **Grund zur ~** reason for complaint. **(b)** *(in Trauer)* lament(ation) *(um, über +acc* for*)*; *(~laut)* plaintive cry. **(c)** *(Jur)* action, suit; *(Scheidungs~ auch)* petition; *(~schrift)* charge. **eine ~ gegen jdn einreichen/erheben** to institute proceedings against sb.
Klage-: ~**erhebung** *f (Jur)* institution of proceedings; ~**frist** *f (Jur)* period for instituting proceedings; ~**laut** *m* plaintive cry; ~**lied** *nt* lament; **ein ~lied über jdn/etw anstimmen** *(fig)* to complain about sb/sth; ~**mauer** *f* **die ~mauer** The Wailing Wall.
klagen 1 *vi* **(a)** *(jammern)* to moan, to wail; *(Tiere)* to cry; *(Trauer äußern)* to lament *(um jdn/etw* sb/sth*)*. **(b)** *(sich beklagen)* to complain *(über +acc* about*)*. **über jdn nicht zu ~ haben** to have no complaints about sb. **(c)** *(Jur)* to sue *(auf +acc* for*)*. **2** *vt* **jdm sein Leid/seine Not ~** to pour out one's sorrow/distress to sb.
klagend *adj* lamenting; *Blick, Ton* plaintive; *Gesicht* sorrowful; *(jammernd)* complaining.
Kläger(in *f***)** *m* - *(Jur) (im Zivilrecht)* plaintiff; *(in Scheidung)* petitioner; *(im Strafrecht auch)* prosecuting party.
Klage-: ~**ruf** *m* plaintive cry; ~**schrift** *f (Jur)* charge; *(bei Scheidung)* petition; ~**weg** *m (Jur)* **auf dem ~weg(e)** by legal action; **den ~weg beschreiten** to take legal action.
kläglich 1 *adj* pitiful; *Rest* miserable; *Niederlage, Verhalten* despicable; *(pej: dürftig)* pathetic. **2** *adv (in beschämender Weise)* miserably.
klaglos *adv* uncomplainingly.
Klamauk *m no pl (col) (Alberei)* tomfoolery; *(Theater)* slapstick. **~ machen** to fool about.
klamm *adj (steif vor Kälte)* numb; *(naß und kalt)* clammy.
Klammer *f* **-n (a)** *(Wäsche~)* peg *(Brit)*, pin *(US)*; *(Hosen~, Med)* clip; *(Büro~)* paperclip; *(Heft~)* staple; *(Haar~)* (hair)grip *(Brit)*, barrette *(US)*; *(für Zähne)* brace; *(Bau~)* clamp. **(b)** *(in Text)* bracket. **~ auf/zu** open/close brackets; **in ~n** in brackets.
klammern 1 *vt (an +acc* to*) Papier etc* to staple; *(Tech)* to clamp; *(Med) Wunde* to clip; *Zähne* to brace. **2** *vr* **sich an jdn/etw ~** *(lit, fig)* to cling to sb/sth. **3** *vi (Sport)* to clinch.
klammheimlich *(col)* **1** *adj* secret. **2** *adv* on the quiet. **~ aus dem Haus gehen** to sneak out of the house.
Klamotte *f* **-n (a) ~n** *pl (col) (Kleider)* clothes *pl*;

(Zeug) stuff *no pl.* **(b)** *(pej: Film etc)* rubbishy old film *etc.* **das sind doch alte ~n** *(col)* that's old hat *(col).*

klang *pret of* **klingen.**

Klang *m* **⸚e** sound; *(Tonqualität)* tone. **⸚e** *(Musik)* sounds, tones.

Klang-: ~farbe *f* tone colour *(Brit) or* color *(US);* **k~lich 1** *adj* **k~liche Unterschiede** differences in sound; *(von Tonqualität)* tonal difference; **2** *adv* **k~lich gut sein** *(Musik, Stimme)* to sound good; *(Instrument, Gerät)* to have a good tone; **k~treu** *adj Wiedergabe* faithful; *Empfänger* high-fidelity; *Ton* true; **k~voll** *adj Stimme* sonorous; *(fig) Titel, Name* fine-sounding.

Klappbett *nt* folding bed.

Klappe *f* **-n (a)** flap; *(an Lastwagen)* tailgate; *(seitlich)* sidegate; *(an Kombiwagen)* back; *(von Tisch)* leaf; *(von Ofen)* shutter, flap; *(Klappdeckel)* (hinged) lid; *(an Oboe etc)* key; *(Falltür)* trapdoor; *(Film)* clapperboard; *(Herz~)* valve. **(b)** *(Schulter~)* strap; *(Hosen~, an Tasche)* flap; *(Augen~)* patch. **(c)** *(Fliegen~)* (fly) swat. **(d)** *(col: Mund)* **die ~ halten** to shut one's trap *(col);* **eine große ~ haben** to have a big mouth *(col).*

klappen 1 *vt* **etw nach oben/unten ~** *Sitz, Bett* to fold sth up/down; *Kragen* to turn sth up/down; *Deckel* to lift sth/to lower sth; **etw nach vorn/ hinten ~** *Sitz* to tip sth forward/back; *Deckel* to lift sth forward/back. **2** *vi* **(a)** to bang. **(b)** *(fig col)* to work; *(Aufführung, Abend)* to go smoothly. **hat es mit den Karten/dem Job geklappt?** did you get the tickets/job OK *(col)*?

Klapper *f* **-n** rattle.

klappern *vi* to clatter; *(Klapperschlange, Fenster)* to rattle. **er klapperte vor Kälte mit den Zähnen** his teeth were chattering with cold.

Klapper-: ~schlange *f (Zool)* rattlesnake; **~storch** *m* **er glaubt noch an den ~storch** he still thinks babies are found under the gooseberry bush.

Klapp(fahr)rad *nt* folding bicycle.

klapprig *adj* shaky.

Klapp-: ~sitz *m* folding seat; **~stuhl** *m* folding chair; **~tisch** *m* folding table.

Klaps *m* **-e** *(Schlag)* smack, slap. **einen ~ haben** *(col)* to have a screw loose *(col).*

klar *adj* clear; *(fertig)* ready. **~ zum Gefecht** *(Mil)* ready for action; **~ Schiff machen** *(lit, fig)* to clear the decks; **~er Fall!** *(col)* sure thing *(col);* **alles ~?** everything OK? *(col);* **jetzt ist mir alles ~!** now I understand; **bei ~em Verstand sein** to be in full possession of one's faculties; **etw ~ und deutlich sagen** to spell sth out; **jdm etw ~ und deutlich sagen** to tell sb sth straight *(col);* **etw ~ zum Ausdruck bringen** to make sth clear; **~ zutage treten** to become obvious; **sich** *(dat)* **über etw** *(acc)* **im ~en sein** to be aware of sth; **sich** *(dat)* **darüber im ~en sein, daß ...** to realize that ...; **ins ~e kommen** to get things straight.

Klär|anlage *f* sewage plant; *(von Fabrik)* purification plant.

klären 1 *vt* to clear; *Wasser, Luft* to purify; *Abwasser* to treat; *Fall* to clarify, to clear up; *Frage* to settle. **2** *vi (Sport)* to clear (the ball). **3** *vr (Wasser, Himmel)* to clear; *(Wetter)* to clear up; *(Meinungen, Sachlage)* to become clear; *(Streitpunkte)* to be clarified; *(Frage)* to be settled.

Klare(r) *m decl as adj (col)* schnapps.

Klarheit *f (lit: Reinheit)* clearness; *(fig: Deutlichkeit)* clarity; *(geistige ~)* lucidity. **sich** *(dat)* **~ über etw** *(acc)* **verschaffen** to get clear about sth.

Klarinette *f* clarinet.

Klar-: k~kommen *vi sep irreg aux sein (col)* to manage, to get by; **mit jdm/etw k~kommen** to be able to cope with sb/sth; **k~kriegen** *vt sep (col)* to sort out; **k~legen** *vt sep* to make clear; **k~machen** *sep* **1** *vt* to make clear; *Schiff* to make ready; *Flugzeug* to clear; **jdm etw k~machen** to make sth clear to sb; **sich** *(dat)* **etw k~machen** to get clear about sth; **2** *vi (Naut)* to make ready; **zum Gefecht k~machen** to clear the decks for action; **k~sehen** *vi sep irreg* to see clearly; **in etw** *(dat)* **k~sehen** to have understood sth; **~sichtfolie** *f* transparent film; **~sichtpackung** *f* transparent pack; **k~stellen** *vt sep (klären)* to clear up, to clarify; **ich möchte k~stellen, daß ...** I want to make it clear that ...; **~text** *m* **im ~text** in clear; *(fig col)* in plain English.

Klärung *f (lit)* purification; *(fig)* clarification.

klarwerden *sep irreg aux sein* **1** *vr* **sich** *(dat)* **(über etw** *acc***) ~** to get (sth) clear in one's mind. **2** *vi* **jetzt wird mir das klar** now it's clear, now I see.

klasse *adj inv (col)* great *(col).*

Klasse *f* **-n** class; *(Spiel~)* league; *(Steuer~ auch)* bracket; *(Güter~)* grade; *(Sch: ~nzimmer)* classroom. **ein Fahrschein erster/zweiter ~** a first-/second-class ticket; **das ist (große) ~!** *(col)* that's great *(col).*

Klasse- *in cpds (col)* top-class; **~frau** *f* fantastic woman.

Klassen- *in cpds* class; **~arbeit** *f* (written) class test; **~beste(r)** *mf* **er ist ~beste(r)** he is top of the class; **~bewußtsein** *nt* class consciousness; **~buch** *nt* (class-)register; **~feind** *m (Pol)* class enemy; **~gegensatz** *m usu pl (Sociol)* class difference; **~gesellschaft** *f* class society; **~haß** *m (Sociol)* class hatred; **~justiz** *f (Pol)* legal system with class bias; **~kamerad** *m* classmate; **~kampf** *m* class struggle; **~krieg** *m* class warfare; **~lehrer, ~leiter** *m* class *or* form teacher; **k~los** *adj Gesellschaft* classless; *Krankenhaus* one-class; **~sprecher(in** *f***)** *m (Sch)* class spokesperson; **~unterschied** *m* class difference; **~ziel** *nt (Sch)* **das ~ziel nicht erreichen** not to reach the required standard; *(fig)* not to make the grade; **~zimmer** *nt* classroom.

klassifizieren* *vt* to classify.

Klassifizierung *f* classification.

Klassik *f no pl* classical period.

Klassiker(in *f***)** *m* - classic. **ein ~ des Jazz** a jazz classic; **die antiken ~** the classics.

klassisch *adj* classical; *(typisch, zeitlos)* classic.

Klatsch *m* **-e (a)** splash; *(bei Schlag, Aufprall)* smack. **(b)** *no pl (pej col: Tratsch)* gossip.

Klatschbase *f (pej col)* gossip.

klatschen 1 *vi* **(a)** to clap. **in die Hände ~** to clap one's hands. **(b)** *(einen Klaps geben)* to slap. **jdm auf die Schenkel/sich** *(dat)* **gegen die Stirn ~** to slap sb's thighs/one's forehead. **(c)** *aux sein (aufschlagen) (harte Gegenstände)* to go smack; *(Flüssigkeiten)* to splash. **(d)** *(pej col: tratschen)* **über jdn/etw ~** to gossip about sb. **2** *vt* **(a)** to clap. **jdm Beifall ~** to applaud *or* clap sb. **(b)** *(knallen)* to smack, to slap; *(werfen)* to throw.

Klatschen *nt no pl (Beifall~)* applause; *(col: Tratschen)* gossiping.

Klatsch-: ~mohn *m* (corn) poppy; **k~naß** *adj (col)* sopping wet *(col);* **~spalte** *f (col)* gossip column; **~sucht** *f* passion for gossip; **k~süchtig** *adj* **ein k~süchtiger Mensch** a compulsive gossip; **~tante** *f (pej col)* gossip(monger).

Klaue *f* **-n** claw. **in den ~n der Verbrecher** *etc* in the clutches of the criminals *etc.*

klauen *(col)* **1** *vt* to pinch *(col) (jdm etw* sth from sb*).* **2** *vi* to steal, to pinch things *(col).*

Klausel *f* **-n** clause; *(Vorbehalt)* proviso.

Klausur *f* **(a)** *(Univ)* exam, paper. **(b)** *no pl (Abgeschlossenheit)* seclusion. **eine Arbeit in ~ schreiben** to write an essay *etc* under examination conditions.

Klaviatur [klavia'tuːɐ] *f* keyboard.

Klavier [-'viːɐ] *nt* **-e** piano.

Klavier- *in cpds* piano; **~auszug** *m* piano score; **~begleitung** *f* piano accompaniment; **~stimmer** *m* piano-tuner.

Klebeband *nt* adhesive tape *(Brit)*, sticky tape.
kleben 1 *vi* to stick. **an etw** *(dat)* ~ *(lit)* to stick to sth; **an seinen Händen klebt Blut** *(fig)* he has blood on his hands. **2** *vt* to stick; *(mit Klebstoff auch)* to glue; *Film, Tonband* to splice. **Marken** ~ *(col: Insur)* to pay stamps; **jdm eine** ~ *(col)* to belt sb one *(col)*.
klebenbleiben *vi sep irreg aux sein* to stick *(an +dat* to*)*; *(fig col: nicht wegkommen)* to get stuck.
Klebepflaster *nt* sticking plaster.
Kleber *m* - *(im Mehl)* gluten; *(col: Klebstoff)* glue.
Klebe-: ~**stelle** *f* join; *(an Film)* splice; ~**streifen** *m* adhesive tape; ~**zettel** *m* gummed label.
klebrig *adj* sticky; *(klebfähig)* adhesive.
Kleb-: ~**stoff** *m* adhesive; ~**streifen** *m* adhesive tape.
kleckern 1 *vt* to spill. **2** *vi* **(a)** to make a mess. **(b)** *(tropfen)* to spill.
Klecks *m* **-e** *(Tinten~)* (ink)blot; *(Farb~)* blob.
klecksen *vi (mit Tinte)* to make blots/a blob.
Klee *m no pl* clover. **jdn/etw über den grünen ~ loben** to praise sb/sth to the skies.
Kleeblatt *nt* cloverleaf; *(fig: Menschen)* threesome, trio. **vierblättriges** ~ four-leaf clover.
Kleid *nt* **-er (a)** *(Damen~)* dress. **ein zweiteiliges** ~ a two-piece (suit). **(b)** ~**er** *pl (Kleidung)* clothes *pl*. ~**er machen Leute** *(Prov)* fine feathers make fine birds *(Prov)*. **(c)** *(liter) (Feder~)* plumage; *(Pelz)* coat; *(fig: von Natur, Bäumen etc)* mantle *(liter)*.
kleiden 1 *vr* to dress. **2** *vt* **(a)** *(lit, fig)* to clothe. **etw in schöne Worte** ~ to dress sth up in fancy words. **(b) jdn** ~ *(jdm stehen)* to suit sb.
Kleider-: ~**bügel** *m* coathanger; ~**bürste** *f* clothes brush; ~**haken** *m* coat hook; ~**schrank** *m* wardrobe; ~**ständer** *m* coat-stand.
kleidsam *adj* flattering.
Kleidung *f no pl* clothes *pl*, clothing.
Kleidungsstück *nt* garment. ~**e** *pl* clothes *pl*.
Kleie *f no pl* bran.
klein *adj* **(a)** little, small; *Finger* little; *Format, Gehalt, Zahl, (Hand)schrift, Buchstabe* small; *Pause, Vortrag* short; *(Mus) Terz* minor. **der K~e Bär** the Little Bear, Ursa Minor; **haben Sie es nicht ~er?** haven't you got anything smaller?; **ein ~ bißchen** *or* **wenig** a little (bit); **ein ~ bißchen** *or* **wenig Salat** a little (bit of) salad; **ein ~es Bier, ein K~es** *(col)* ≃ half a pint, a half; **mein ~er Bruder** my little brother; **er ist ~er als sein Bruder** he's smaller than his brother; **er schreibt sehr** ~ his writing is very small; **sich ~ machen** to bend down low; to curl up tight; **macht euch ein bißchen ~er!** squeeze up closer; **~ aber oho!** *(col)* good things come in small packages; **ein Wort ~ schreiben** to write a word with small initial letters; **im ~en** in miniature; **bis ins ~ste** in minute detail; **von ~ an** *or* **auf** *(von Kindheit an)* from his childhood; *(von Anfang an)* from the very beginning; **~en Augenblick, bitte!** just one moment, please; **einen Kopf ~er als jd sein** to be a head shorter than sb; **beim ~sten Schreck** at the slightest *or* smallest shock; **das ~ere Übel** the lesser evil; **ein paar ~ere Fehler** a few minor mistakes.
(b) *(unbedeutend)* petty *(pej)*; *Leute* ordinary; *(armselig) Verhältnisse* humble. **er ist ein ~er Geist** he is small-minded; **der ~e Mann** the ordinary citizen, the man in the street; **ein ~er Ganove** a small-time crook; **sein Vater war (ein) ~er Beamter** his father was a minor civil servant; **~ anfangen** to start off in a small way.
Klein-: ~**anzeige** *f* small ad *(Brit)*, classified ad; ~**arbeit** *f* detailed work; **in zäher/mühseliger ~arbeit** with rigorous/painstaking attention to detail; ~**asien** *nt* Asia Minor; ~**bauer** *m* small farmer, smallholder; ~**betrieb** *m* small business; ~**bildkamera** *f* 35mm camera; ~**bürger** *m* petty bourgeois; **k~bürgerlich** *adj* lower middle-class, petty bourgeois *(pej)*; ~**bürgertum** *nt (Sociol)* lower middle class, petty bourgeoisie.
Kleine(r) *mf decl as adj* **(a)** little one; little boy/girl; baby. **unser ~r** *(Jüngster)* our youngest (child); **die lieben ~n** *(iro)* the dear little things. **(b)** *(col: auch* **~s:** *Liebling)* baby *(col)*.
Klein-: ~**familie** *f* small family, nuclear family *(Sociol)*; ~**format** *nt* small format; ~**garten** *m* allotment *(Brit)*; ~**gärtner** *m* allotment holder *(Brit)*; **k~gedruckt** *adj attr* in small print; ~**gedruckte(s)** *nt* small print; ~**geld** *nt* (small) change; **das nötige ~ geld haben** *(fig)* to have the necessary wherewithal *(col)*; **k~gemustert** *adj* small-patterned; **k~gewachsen** *adj* short, small; *Baum* small; **k~gläubig** *adj (zweiflerisch)* timid; **k~gläubig sein** to lack conviction; **k~hacken** *vt sep* to chop up small; ~**heit** *f* smallness, small size; ~**holz** *nt no pl* firewood; **aus etw ~holz machen** *(hum col)* to smash sth to pieces; **~holz aus jdm machen** *(col)* to make mincemeat out of sb *(col)*.
Kleinigkeit *f* **(a)** little *or* small thing; *(Bagatelle)* trivial matter, trifle; *(Einzelheit)* minor detail. **ich habe noch ein paar ~en in der Stadt zu erledigen** I still have a few little things to attend to in town; **es war nur eine ~ zu reparieren** there was only something minor to be repaired; **die Reparatur/Prüfung war eine ~** the repair job/exam was no trouble at all; **eine ~ essen** to have a bite to eat; **wegen** *or* **bei jeder ~** for the slightest reason; **großen Wert auf ~en legen** to be a stickler for detail(s). **(b)** *(ein bißchen)* **eine ~** a little (bit), a trifle; **eine ~ zu groß** a little (bit) *etc* too big.
Kleinigkeitskrämer *m (pej)* pedant.
Klein-: ~**kaliber** *nt* small bore; **k~kariert** *adj (fig)* small-time *(col)*; **k~kariert denken** to think small; ~**kind** *nt* small child, infant *(Psych)*; ~**kram** *m (col)* odds and ends *pl*; *(Trivialitäten)* trivia *pl*; ~**kredit** *m* personal loan; ~**krieg** *m (fig)* battle; **einen ~krieg mit jdm führen** to be fighting a running battle with sb.
kleinkriegen *vt sep* **(a)** *(lit) Holz* to chop (up); *Nuß* to break. **(b)** *(col: kaputtmachen)* to smash, to break. **(c)** *(col) (gefügig machen)* to bring into line *(col)*; *(unterkriegen)* to get down; *(körperlich)* to tire out. **er ist einfach nicht kleinzukriegen** he just won't be beaten.
Klein-: ~**kunst** cabaret; **k~laut** *adj* subdued; **dann wurde er ganz k~laut** that made him shut up; **k~laut um Verzeihung bitten** to apologize rather sheepishly.
kleinlich *adj* petty; *(knauserig)* mean, stingy *(col)*; *(engstirnig)* narrow-minded.
Kleinlichkeit *f siehe adj* pettiness; meanness, stinginess *(col)*; narrow-mindedness.
kleinmachen *vt sep* **(a)** to chop *or* cut up. **(b)** *(col) Geld* to change.
Klein-: **k~mütig** *adj* fainthearted, timid; **k~schneiden** *vt sep irreg* to cut up small; **k~schreiben** *vt sep irreg (fig)* **k~geschrieben werden** to count for (very) little; ~**schreibung** *f* use of small initial letters; ~**stadt** *f* small town; **k~städtisch** *adj* provincial, small-town *attr*.
kleinste(r, s) *superl of* **klein.**
kleinstmöglich *adj* smallest possible.
Klein-: ~**tier** *nt* small animal; ~**vieh** *nt*: **~vieh macht auch Mist** *(prov)* every little helps; ~**wagen** *m* small car.
Kleister *m* - *(Klebstoff)* paste.
kleistern *vti (zusammenkleben)* to paste.
Klemme *f* **-n (a)** *(Haar~, für Papiere etc)* clip; *(Elec)* crocodile clamp; *(Med)* clamp. **(b)** *(fig col)* **in der ~ sitzen** *or* **sein** to be in a fix *(col)*; **jdm aus der ~ helfen** to help sb out of a fix *(col)*.
klemmen 1 *vt Draht etc* to clamp, to clip; *(in Spalt)*

to wedge, to jam. **sich** *(dat)* **etw unter den Arm ~** to tuck sth under one's arm. **2** *vr* to catch oneself *(in +dat* in*)*. **sich hinter etw** *(acc)* **~** *(col)* to get stuck into sth *(col)*; **sich hinter jdn ~** *(col)* to get on to sb. **3** *vi (Tür, Schloß etc)* to stick, to jam.

Klempner *m* - plumber.

Klempnerei *f* **(a)** *no pl* plumbing. **(b)** *(Werkstatt)* plumber's workshop.

Klerus *m* -, *no pl* clergy.

Klette *f* **-n** *(Bot)* burdock; *(Blütenkopf)* bur(r); *(pej: lästiger Mensch)* nuisance. **sich wie eine ~ an jdn hängen** to cling to sb like a limpet.

Kletterer *m* - climber.

Klettergerüst *nt* climbing frame.

klettern *vi aux sein* to climb; *(mühsam)* to clamber. **auf Bäume ~** to climb trees.

Kletterpflanze *f* climbing plant.

klicken *vi* to click.

Klient(in *f***)** [kli'ɛnt(ɪn)] *m (wk)* **-en, -en** client.

Klima *nt* **-s** *or* **-te** [kli'maːtə] *(lit, fig)* climate.

Klima|anlage *f* air conditioning. **mit ~** air-conditioned.

klimatisch *adj no pred* climatic.

Klimazone *f* (climatic) zone.

Klimbim *m no pl (col)* odds and ends *pl*; *(Umstände)* fuss.

Klimmzug *m (Sport)* pull-up.

klimpern *vi* to tinkle; *(stümperhaft)* to plonk away *(col)*; *(auf Banjo)* to twang; *(Münzen)* to jingle.

Klinge *f* **-n** blade.

Klingel *f* **-n** bell.

Klingelknopf *m* bell push.

klingeln *vi* to ring *(nach* for*)*; *(Motor)* to pink, to knock. **es hat schon geklingelt** *(in Schule)* the bell has already gone; **es hat geklingelt** *(an Tür)* somebody just rang the doorbell; **immer wenn es an der Tür klingelt ...** whenever the doorbell rings *or* goes ...

klingen *pret* **klang,** *ptp* **geklungen** *vi* to sound; *(Glocke, Ohr)* to ring; *(Glas)* to clink; *(Metall)* to clang. **nach etw ~** to sound like sth.

Klinik *f* **-en** clinic; *(Universitäts~)* (university) hospital.

klinisch *adj* clinical. **~ tot** clinically dead.

Klinke *f* **-n** *(Tür~)* (door) handle.

Klinker *m* - *(Ziegelstein)* clinker (brick).

klipp *adv:* **~ und klar** clearly; *(offen)* frankly.

Klippe *f* **-n** *(Fels~)* cliff; *(im Meer)* rock; *(fig)* obstacle. **~n umschiffen** *(lit, fig)* to negotiate obstacles.

klirren *vi* to clink; *(Fensterscheiben)* to rattle; *(Lautsprecher, Mikrofon)* to crackle; *(Eis)* to crunch. **~de Kälte** *(liter)* crisp cold.

Klischee *nt* **-s** *(Typ)* plate; *(fig: Phrase)* cliché.

Klischeevorstellung *f* cliché, stereotype.

Klitoris *f* - clitoris.

Klo *nt* **-s** *(col)* loo *(Brit col)*, john *(US col)*.

Kloake *f* **-n** sewer.

klobig *adj* hefty *(col)*; *Mensch* hulking great *(col)*.

Klopapier *nt (col)* toilet *or* loo *(Brit col)* paper.

klopfen 1 *vt* to knock; *Fleisch, Teppich* to beat; *Steine* to knock down. **den Takt ~** to beat time. **2** *vi* to knock; *(Herz)* to beat; *(vor Aufregung, Anstrengung auch)* to pound; *(Puls)* to throb; *(Motor)* to knock, to pink *(Brit)*. **sie klopften wiederholt heftig an die Tür** they kept pounding away at the door; **es hat geklopft** there's someone knocking at the door; **jdm auf die Schulter/den Rücken ~** to tap sb on the shoulder/to pat sb on the back; *(heftig)* to slap sb on the shoulder/back; **mit ~dem Herzen** with beating *or* pounding heart.

Klopfer *m* - *(Tür~)* (door) knocker; *(Fleisch~)* (meat) mallet; *(Teppich~)* carpet beater.

Klöppel *m* - *(Glocken~)* clapper; *(Spitzen~)* bobbin; *(Trommel~)* stick.

klöppeln *vi* to make (pillow) lace.

Klöppelspitze *f* pillow lace.

Klops *m* **-e** *(Cook)* meatball.

Klosett *nt* **-e** *or* **-s** lavatory.

Klosett-: ~brille *f* toilet seat. **~bürste** *f* lavatory brush; **~deckel** *m* lavatory seat lid; **~frau** *f* lavatory attendant; **~papier** *nt* toilet paper.

Kloß *m* **¨-e** dumpling; *(Fleisch~)* meatball; *(Bulette)* rissole. **einen ~ im Hals haben** *(fig)* to have a lump in one's throat.

Kloßbrühe *f*: **klar wie ~** as clear as day; *(iro)* as clear as mud.

Kloster *nt* **¨** cloister; *(Mönchs~ auch)* monastery; *(Nonnen~ auch)* convent. **ins ~ gehen** to become a monk/nun.

Klosterschule *f* monastic/convent school.

Klotz *m* **¨-e** *(Holz~)* block (of wood); *(pej: Beton~)* concrete block; *(col: Person)* great lump *(col)*. **jdm ein ~ am Bein sein** to be a hindrance to sb.

Klub *m* **-s** club.

Klub-: ~abend *m* club night; **~garnitur** *f* (three-piece) suite; **~jacke** *f* blazer; **~sessel** *m* club chair.

Kluft *f* **¨-e (a)** *(Erdspalte)* cleft; *(in Bergen)* crevasse; *(Abgrund)* chasm. **(b)** *(fig)* gulf, gap. **in der Partei tat sich eine tiefe ~ auf** a deep rift opened up in the party. **(c)** *no pl (Uniform)* uniform; *(col: Kleidung)* gear *(col)*.

klug *adj, comp* **¨er,** *superl* **¨ste(r, s)** clever, intelligent; *(vernünftig) Entscheidung, Rat* sound; *Überlegung* prudent; *Geschäftsmann* shrewd. **es wird am ¨sten sein, wenn ...** it would be most sensible if ...; **es wäre politisch ~ ...** it would make good political sense ...; **ein ~er Kopf** a capable person; **in ~er Voraussicht** shrewdly; **ich werde daraus nicht ~** I can't make head or tail of it; **aus ihm werde ich nicht ~** I can't make him out; **~e Reden halten** *(iro)* to make fine-sounding speeches; **~e Bemerkungen/Ratschläge** *(iro)* clever *or* helpful remarks/advice *(iro)*; **nun bin ich genau so ~ wir vorher** I am still none the wiser.

klugerweise *adv* (very) cleverly, (very) wisely.

Klugheit *f siehe adj* cleverness, intelligence; soundness; prudence; shrewdness. **aus ~** (very) wisely; **menschliche ~** human understanding.

Klug-: ~redner *m* know-all, know-it-all *(US)*; **~scheißer** *m (col!)* smart-ass *(col!)*.

Klumpen *m* - lump; *(Gold~)* nugget; *(Blut~)* clot. **~ bilden** *(Mehl etc)* to go lumpy.

Klumpfuß *m* club-foot.

klumpig *adj* lumpy.

km = Kilometer km.

km/h = Kilometer pro Stunde kph.

knabbern *vti* to nibble. **nichts zu ~ haben** *(col)* to have nothing to eat.

Knabe *m (wk)* **-n, -n** *(liter)* boy, lad.

Knaben-: ~chor *m* boys' choir; **k~haft** *adj* boyish.

Knäckebrot *nt* crispbread.

knacken 1 *vt (lit, fig)* to crack; *(col) Auto* to break into. **2** *vi (brechen)* to crack; *(Dielen, Stuhl)* to creak; *(knistern: Holz)* to crackle. **daran wird er zu ~ haben** *(col)* that'll give him something to think about.

Knacker *m* **(a)** *type of frankfurter.* **(b)** *(pej col)* **alter ~** old fog(e)y *(col)*.

knackig *adj* crisp; *(col) Mädchen* juicy *(col)*.

Knacks *m* **-e** *(Sprung)* crack. **der Fernseher hat einen ~** *(col)* there is something wrong with the television.

Knackwurst *f type of frankfurter.*

Knall *m* **-e** bang; *(mit Peitsche)* crack; *(von Korken)* pop; *(col: Krach)* trouble. **~ auf Fall** *(col)* just like that *(col)*; **einen ~ haben** *(col)* to be crazy *(col) or* crackers *(Brit col)*.

knallen 1 *vi* **(a)** to bang, to explode; *(Schuß)* to ring out; *(Pfropfen)* to (go) pop; *(Peitsche)* to crack; *(Tür etc)* to bang, to slam; *(Auspuff)* to misfire; *(aux sein: auftreffen)* to bang. **mit der Tür ~** to bang *or* slam the door; **draußen knallte es**

there was a shot/were shots outside; **nicht so frech, sonst knallt's** *(col)* don't be so cheeky, or there'll be trouble. **(b)** *(col: Sonne)* to blaze down. **2** *vt* to bang; *Tür, Buch auch* to slam; *Schüsse* to fire (off); *Peitsche* to crack. **den Hörer auf die Gabel** ~ *(col)* to slam *or* bang down the receiver; **jdm eine** ~ *(col)* to clout sb *(col)*.

Knall-: ~frosch *m* jumping jack; **k~gelb** *adj (col)* bright yellow; **k~hart** *adj (col)* really hard; *Film* brutal; *Porno* hard-core; *Job, Truppen, Mensch* really tough; *Schuß, Schlag* really hard. **er sagte ihr k~hart ...** he said to her quite brutally ...

knallig *adj (col) Farben* loud, gaudy.

Knall-: ~körper *m* fire-cracker; **k~rot** *adj (col)* bright red.

knapp *adj* **(a)** *(nicht ausreichend)* scarce, in short supply; *Gehalt* low. **mein Geld ist** ~ I'm short of money; **mein Geld wird** ~ I am running short of money; **das Essen wird** ~ we/they *etc* are running short of food; **mein Geld/meine Zeit ist** ~ **bemessen** I am short of money/time. **(b)** *(gerade noch ausreichend) Zeit, Geld* just enough; *Mehrheit, Sieg* narrow; *Kleidungsstück etc (eng)* tight; *(kurz)* short; *Bikini* scanty. **wir haben** ~ **verloren/gewonnen** we only just lost/won. **(c)** *(nicht ganz)* almost. **ein ~es Pfund Mehl** just under a pound of flour. **(d)** *Stil, Worte* concise; *Geste* terse; *(lakonisch) Antwort* pithy. **(e)** *(gerade so eben)* just. **mit ~er Not** only just.

Knappheit *f* shortage; *(fig: des Ausdrucks)* conciseness.

Knarre *f* **-n** *(col: Gewehr)* shooter *(col)*.

knarren *vi* to creak. **eine ~de Stimme** a grating voice.

Knast *m no pl (col)* clink *(col)*, can *(US col)*.

Knatsch *m no pl (col)* trouble.

knattern *vi (Motorrad)* to roar; *(Preßlufthammer)* to hammer; *(Maschinengewehr)* to rattle; *(Schüsse)* to rattle out.

Knäuel *m or nt* **-** ball; *(wirres)* tangle; *(von Menschen)* group, knot.

Knauf *m, pl* **Knäufe** *(Tür~)* knob.

knauserig *adj (col)* mean, stingy *(col)*.

knausern *vi (col)* to be mean *or* stingy *(col) (mit* with*)*.

knautschen *vti (col)* to crumple (up).

Knautschzone *f (Aut)* crumple zone.

Knebel *m* **-** *(Mund~)* gag; *(Paket~)* (wooden) handle; *(an Mänteln)* toggle.

knebeln *vt jdn, Presse* to gag.

Kneb(e)lung *f no pl (lit, fig)* gagging.

Knecht *m* **-e** servant; *(beim Bauern)* (farm-) worker; *(Stall~)* stableboy; *(fig: Sklave)* slave *(gen* to*)*.

knechten *vt (geh)* to subjugate, to oppress.

Knechtschaft *f* slavery.

kneifen *pret* **kniff,** *ptp* **gekniffen 1** *vti* to pinch. **jdn** *or* **jdm in den Arm** ~ to pinch sb's arm. **2** *vi (col: ausweichen)* to back out *(vor +dat* of*)*.

Kneifer *m* **-** *(Brille)* pince-nez.

Kneifzange *f* pliers *pl*; *(kleine)* pincers *pl*. **eine** ~ (a pair of) pliers/(a pair of) pincers.

Kneipe *f* **-n** *(col: Lokal)* pub *(Brit)*, bar.

Kneipenwirt *m (col)* publican *(Brit)*, landlord *(Brit)*, barkeeper *(US)*.

Kneippkur *f* Kneipp cure, *type of hydropathic treatment combined with diet, rest etc.*

kneten *vt* to knead; *Ton* to work; *Figuren* to model.

Knet-: ~gummi *m or nt* plasticine ®; **~masse** *f* modelling *(Brit) or* modeling *(US)* clay.

Knick *m* **-e** *or* **-s** *(Falte)* crease; *(Biegung)* (sharp) bend; *(bei Draht)* kink. **einen** ~ **machen** to bend sharply.

knicken *vti (vi: aux sein)* to snap; *Papier* to fold. **„nicht ~!"** "do not bend".

knick(e)rig *adj (col)* stingy *(col)*, mean.

Knicks *m* **-e** bob; *(tiefer)* curts(e)y. **einen** ~ **machen** to curts(e)y *(vor +dat* to*)*.

knicksen *vi* to curts(e)y *(vor +dat* to*)*.

Knie *nt* **- (a)** knee. **auf ~n** on bended knee; **auf die** ~ **fallen** to drop to one's knees; **jdm auf ~n danken** to go down on one's knees and thank sb; **in die** ~ **gehen** to kneel; *(fig)* to be brought to one's knees; **jdn in** *or* **auf die** ~ **zwingen** to force sb to his knees; **jdn übers** ~ **legen** *(col)* to put sb across one's knee; **etw übers** ~ **brechen** *(fig)* to rush (at) sth. **(b)** *(Fluß~)* sharp bend; *(in Rohr)* elbow.

Knie-: ~beuge *f (Sport)* knee bend; **~fall** *m* **einen ~fall vor jdm machen** *(lit, fig)* to kneel before sb; **~gelenk** *nt* knee joint; **~hose** *f* knee breeches *pl*; **~kehle** *f* back of the knee; **k~lang** *adj* knee length.

knien [kniːn, 'kniːən] **1** *vi* to kneel. **im K~** kneeling. **2** *vr* to kneel (down). **sich in die Arbeit** ~ *(fig)* to get down to one's work.

Knie-: ~scheibe *f* kneecap; **~strumpf** *m* knee-length sock; **k~tief** *adj* knee-deep.

kniff *pret of* **kneifen.**

Kniff *m* **-e (a)** *(col)* trick. **den** ~ **bei etw heraushaben** to have the knack of sth *(col)*. **(b)** *(Falte)* crease, fold.

kniff(e)lig *adj (col)* fiddly; *(heikel)* tricky.

knipsen 1 *vt* **(a)** *(Phot col)* to snap *(col)*. **(b)** *Fahrschein* to punch, to clip. **2** *vi* **(a)** *(Phot col)* to take pictures. **(b) mit den Fingern** ~ to snap one's fingers.

Knirps *m* **-e (a)** *(Junge)* whippersnapper. **(b)** ® telescopic umbrella.

knirschen *vi (Sand, Schnee)* to crunch; *(Getriebe)* to grind. **mit den Zähnen** ~ to grind one's teeth.

knistern *vi (Feuer)* to crackle; *(Papier, Seide)* to rustle. **mit Papier** *etc* ~ to rustle paper *etc.*

knitterfrei *adj Stoff, Kleid* crease-resistant.

knittern *vti* to crease, to crush.

knobeln *vi (würfeln)* to play dice; *(um eine Entscheidung)* to toss for it *(col)*.

Knoblauch *m no pl* garlic.

Knoblauchzehe *f* clove of garlic.

Knöchel *m* **- (a)** *(Fuß~)* ankle. **bis über die** ~ up to the ankles. **(b)** *(Finger~)* knuckle.

knöcheltief *adj* ankle-deep.

Knochen *m* **-** bone. **Fleisch mit/ohne** ~ meat on/off the bone; **er ist bis auf die** ~ **abgemagert** he is just skin and bones; **ihm steckt die Grippe/Angst in den** ~ *(col)* he's got flu/he's scared stiff *(col)*; **naß bis auf die** ~ *(col)* soaked to the skin; **der Schreck fuhr ihm in die** ~ he was paralyzed with shock; **sich bis auf die** ~ **blamieren** *(col)* to make a proper fool of oneself *(col)*.

Knochen-: ~bau *m* bone structure; **~bruch** *m* fracture; **~gerüst** *nt* skeleton; **k~hart** *adj (col)* rock-hard; **~mark** *nt* bone marrow; **~mehl** *nt* bone meal; **~schinken** *m* ham on the bone; **k~trocken** *adj (col)* bone dry; *(fig) Humor etc* very dry.

knöchern *adj (aus Knochen)* bone.

knochig *adj* bony.

Knödel *m* **-** dumpling.

Knolle *f* **-n** *(Bot)* tubercule; *(von Kartoffel)* tuber.

knollig *adj Wurzel* tuberous; *Auswuchs* knobbly; *Nase* bulbous.

Knopf *m* **¨-e (a)** button. **etw an den ¨~en abzählen** to decide sth by tossing a coin. **(b)** *(an Tür, Stock)* knob; *(Sattel~, Degen~)* pommel. **(c)** *(col) (Kind)* little chap/little lass; *(Kerl)* chap, fellow.

knöpfen *vt* to button (up).

Knopfloch *nt* buttonhole.

Knorpel *m* **-** *(Anat)* cartilage; *(Cook)* gristle.

knorpelig *adj (Anat)* cartilaginous; *Fleisch* gristly.

knorrig *adj Baum* gnarled; *Holz* knotty; *(fig) alter Mann* rugged; *(eigenwillig) Mensch* surly, gruff.

Knospe *f* **-n** bud. **~n ansetzen** to bud.

knospen *vi* to bud. **~d** *(lit, fig liter)* budding.

Knoten *m* **-** knot *(auch Naut)*; *(Med: Geschwulst)* lump; *(Haar auch)* bun.

knoten *vt Seil etc* to tie a knot in.
Knotenpunkt *m (Mot)* (road) junction *(Brit)*, intersection; *(Rail)* junction; *(fig)* centre *(Brit)*, center *(US)*.
knotig *adj* knotted, full of knots; *Äste, Finger* gnarled.
knuffen *vti (col)* to poke *(col)*; *(mit Ellbogen)* to nudge.
knüllen *vti* to crumple, to crease (up).
Knüller *m* - *(col)* sensation; *(Press)* scoop.
knüpfen 1 *vt Knoten, Band* to tie; *Teppich* to knot; *Netz* to mesh; *Freundschaft* to form. **jdn an den Galgen ~** *(col)* to string sb up *(col)*; **große Erwartungen an etw** *(acc)* **~** to have great expectations of sth. **2** *vr* **sich an etw** *(acc)* **~** to be linked to sth.
Knüppel *m* - **(a)** stick; *(Waffe)* cudgel, club; *(Polizei~)* truncheon *(Brit)*, night stick *(US)*. **jdm ~ zwischen die Beine werfen** *(fig)* to put a spoke in sb's wheel. **(b)** *(Aviat)* joystick; *(Aut)* gear stick.
Knüppel-: k~dick *(col)* **1** *adj Steak, Schicht* very thick; **2** *adv* **wenn's kommt, kommt's immer gleich k~dick** it never rains but it pours *(prov)*; **~schaltung** *f (Aut)* floor-mounted gear shift; **k~voll** *adj (col)* jam-packed.
knurren 1 *vi (Hund etc)* to growl; *(Magen)* to rumble; *(fig: sich beklagen)* to groan *(über +acc* about*)*. **2** *vti (mürrisch sagen)* to growl.
Knurren *nt no pl siehe vi* growl(ing); rumbling; groaning.
knurrig *adj* grumpy; *Angestellte etc* disgruntled.
knusprig *adj Braten* crisp; *Gebäck auch* crunchy; *(fig) Mädchen* scrumptious *(col)*.
Knute *f* **-n unter jds ~** *(dat)* **stehen** to be completely dominated by sb.
knutschen *(col)* **1** *vt* to neck with *(col)*. **2** *vir* to neck *(col)*.
k. o. [kaː'|oː] *adj pred (Sport)* knocked out; *(fig col)* whacked *(col)*. **jdn ~ schlagen** to knock sb out.
koalieren* *vi (esp Pol)* to form a coalition.
Koalition *f (esp Pol)* coalition.
Koalitions- *in cpds* coalition; **~regierung** *f* coalition government.
Kobold *m* **-e** goblin, imp.
Koch *m* **¨-e** cook; *(von Restaurant auch)* chef. **viele ¨~e verderben den Brei** *(Prov)* too many cooks spoil the broth *(Prov)*.
Koch-: ~apfel *m* cooking apple; **~buch** *nt* cookery book, cookbook; **k~echt** *adj Farbe* fast; *Wäsche etc* that may be boiled.
kochen 1 *vi* **(a)** *(Flüssigkeit, Speise)* to boil. **etw zum K~ bringen** to bring sth to the boil; **jdn zum K~ bringen** *(fig col)* to make sb's blood boil; **das Auto kocht** *(col)* the car is overheating; **er kochte vor Wut** *(col)* he was seething. **(b)** *(Speisen zubereiten)* to cook; *(als Koch fungieren)* to do the cooking. **er kocht gut** he's a good cook; **er kocht scharf/pikant** his cooking is highly seasoned/spiced. **2** *vt* **(a)** *Nahrungsmittel, Wäsche* to boil. **etw auf kleiner Flamme ~** to simmer sth over a low heat. **(b)** *(zubereiten) Essen* to cook; *Kaffee, Tee* to make. **etw gar/weich ~** to cook sth through/until (it is) soft; **Eier weich/hart ~** to soft-boil/hard-boil eggs.
kochend *adj* boiling. **~ heiß sein** to be boiling hot; *(Suppe etc)* to be piping hot.
kochendheiß *adj attr* boiling hot; *Suppe etc* piping hot.
Kocher *m* - *(Herd)* cooker, stove.
Koch-: k~fertig *adj* ready-to-cook; **~gelegenheit** *f* cooking facilities *pl*; **~herd** *m* cooker.
Köchin *f* cook; *(von Restaurant auch)* chef.
Koch-: ~kunst *f* cooking; **~löffel** *m* cooking spoon; **~platte** *f (Herdplatte)* hotplate; **~rezept** *nt* recipe; **~salz** *nt* cooking salt; **~topf** *m* (cooking) pot; *(mit Stiel)* saucepan; **~wäsche** *f* washing that can be boiled; **~zeit** *f* cooking time.
Kode [koːt, 'koːdə] *m* **-s** code.
Köder *m* - bait; *(fig auch)* lure.
ködern *vt (lit)* to lure; *(fig)* to tempt. **jdn zu ~ versuchen** to woo sb; **jdn für etw ~** to rope sb into sth *(col)*; **sich von jdm/etw nicht ~ lassen** not to be tempted by sb/sth.
Kodewort *nt* code word.
Koffein *nt no pl* caffeine.
koffeinfrei *adj* decaffeinated.
Koffer *m* - (suit)case, bag; *(Schrank~)* trunk; *(Arzt~)* bag; *(für Schreibmaschine, Kosmetika etc)* case. **die ~** *pl (Gepäck)* the luggage *or* baggage *or* bags *pl*; **die ~ packen** *(lit, fig)* to pack one's bags.
Koffer-: ~gerät *nt* portable (set); **~kuli** *m* (luggage) trolley *(Brit)*, cart *(US)*; **~radio** *nt* portable radio; **~raum** *m (Aut)* boot *(Brit)*, trunk *(US)*; *(Volumen)* luggage space.
Kognak ['kɔnjak] *m* **-s** *or* **-e** brandy.
Kohl *m* **-e (a)** cabbage. **das macht den ~ auch nicht fett** *(col)* that's not much help. **(b)** *(col: Unsinn)* nonsense.
Kohldampf *m no pl (col)* **~ haben** to be famished.
Kohle *f* **-n (a)** coal; *(Stück ~)* (lump of) coal. **wir haben keine ~n mehr** we have no coal left; **zwei ~n** two lumps of coal; **(wie) auf glühenden** *or* **heißen ~n sitzen** to be like a cat on hot bricks. **(b)** *(Verkohltes, Holz~, Art)* charcoal. **(c)** *(Tech)* carbon. **(d)** *(col: Geld)* dough *(col)*, cash *(col)*. **die ~n stimmen** the money's right.
Kohle-: ~filter *m* charcoal filter; **~hydrat** *nt* carbohydrate.
Kohlen- *in cpds* coal; **~bergbau** *m* coal-mining; **~bergwerk** *nt* coalmine, pit, colliery; **~grube** *f* coalmine, pit; **~halde** *f* pile of coal; **~heizung** *f* coal heating; **~herd** *m* range; **~kasten** *m* coalbox; **~keller** *m* coal cellar; **~lager** *nt (Vorrat)* coal depot; *(im Stollen, Berg)* coal seam; **~monoxyd** *nt* carbon monoxide; **~ofen** *m* (coal-burning) stove; **~säure** *f (Chem)* carbonic acid; **ein Getränk ohne ~säure** a non-fizzy *or* still drink; **~schaufel** *f* coal shovel; **~stoff** *m* carbon; **~wasserstoff** *m* hydrocarbon.
Kohle-: ~papier *nt* carbon paper; **~tablette** *f (Med)* charcoal tablet; **~zeichnung** *f* charcoal drawing.
Kohl-: ~kopf *m* cabbage; **~meise** *f* great tit; **k~(pech)rabenschwarz** *adj Haar* jet black; *Nacht* pitch-black; **~rabi** *m* **-(s)** kohlrabi; **~rübe** *f* turnip; **k~schwarz** *adj Haare, Augen* jet black; *Gesicht, Hände* black as coal.
Koitus ['koːitʊs] *m* **-, -** *or* **-se** coitus.
Koje *f* **-n** *(esp Naut)* bunk; *(col: Bett)* bed.
Kokain *nt no pl* cocaine.
kokett *adj* coquettish, flirtatious.
kokettieren* *vi* to flirt. **mit seinem Alter ~** to play on one's age; **mit einem Gedanken ~** to toy with an idea.
Kokos- *in cpds* coconut; **~milch** *f* coconut milk; **~nuß** *f* coconut; **~palme** *f* coconut palm.
Koks *m* **-e** coke.
Koksheizung *f* coke heating.
Kolben *m* - *(Tech)* piston; *(Gewehr~)* butt; *(Chem: Destillier~)* retort; *(von Lötapparat)* bit.
Kolben-: k~förmig *adj* club-shaped; **~ring** *m* piston ring.
Kolibri *m* **-s** humming bird.
Kollaborateur(in *f***)** [-'tøːɐ, -'tøːrɪn] *m (Pol)* collaborator.
Kollage [kɔ'laːʒə] *f* **-n** *(Art, fig)* collage.
Kollaps *m* **-e** *(Med)* collapse.
Kolleg *nt* **-s** *or* **-ien** [-iən] *(Univ: Vorlesung)* lecture; *(Vorlesungsreihe)* (course of) lectures.
Kollege *m (wk)* **-n, -n, Kollegin** *f* colleague. **seine ~n vom Fach** his professional colleagues, his fellow doctors/teachers *etc*; **meine ~n** the people I work with; **Herr ~!** Mr X/Y.
kollegial *adj* cooperative. **sich ~ verhalten** to be cooperative.
Kollegialität *f* cooperativeness.

Kollegin *siehe* **Kollege.**
Kollegium *nt (Lehrer~ etc)* staff; *(Ausschuß)* working party.
Kollegmappe *f* document case.
Kollekte *f* **-n** *(Eccl)* collection.
Kollektion *f* collection; *(Sortiment)* range.
kollektiv *adj* collective.
Kollektiv *nt* collective.
Kollektiv-: **~schuld** *f* collective guilt; **~strafe** *f* collective punishment; **~wirtschaft** *f (Econ)* collective economy.
Koller *m* **-** *(col) (Anfall)* funny mood; *(Wutanfall)* rage; *(Tropen~, Gefängnis~)* tropical/prison madness. **seinen ~ bekommen/haben** to get into/to be one of one's silly *or* funny moods; **einen ~ haben/bekommen** to be in/fly into a rage.
kollidieren* *vi (geh)* **(a)** *aux sein (Fahrzeuge)* to collide. **(b)** *aux sein or haben (fig)* to clash.
Kollier [kɔ'lieː] **-s** necklet, necklace.
Kollision *f (geh) (Zusammenstoß)* collision; *(Streit)* conflict, clash.
Kollisionskurs *m* **auf ~ gehen** *(fig)* to be heading for trouble.
Kolloquium *nt* colloquium.
Köln *nt* Cologne.
Kölner *adj attr* Cologne.
Kölnischwasser, Kölnisch Wasser *nt* eau de Cologne, cologne.
Kolonial-: **~macht** *f* colonial power; **~warenhändler** *m (dated)* grocer.
Kolonie *f* colony; *(Ferien~)* camp.
Kolonne *f* **-n** column; *(Autoschlange)* queue *(Brit)*, line; *(Arbeits~)* gang. **„Achtung ~!"** "convoy"; **~ fahren** to drive in (a) convoy.
Koloß *m* **-sse** colossus.
kolossal 1 *adj* colossal, enormous. **2** *adv (col)* enormously.
Kolumbien [-iən] *nt* Colombia.
Kolumne *f* **-n** *(Typ, Press)* column.
Koma *nt* **-s** *or* **-ta** *(Med)* coma.
Kombi *m* **-s** *(Aut)* estate (car) *(Brit)*, station wagon *(esp US)*.
Kombination *f* **(a)** *(Verbindung, Zahlen~)* combination; *(Sport: Zusammenspiel)* (piece of) teamwork. **(b)** *(Schlußfolgerung)* deduction; *(Vermutung)* conjecture. **(c)** *(Kleidung)* suit, ensemble; *(Hemdhose)* combinations *pl*; *(Arbeitsanzug)* overalls *pl*, boilersuit; *(Flieger~)* flying suit.
Kombinationsschloß *nt* combination lock.
kombinieren* **1** *vt* to combine. **2** *vi (folgern)* to deduce; *(vermuten)* to suppose. **gut ~ können** to be good at deduction.
Kombi-: **~wagen** *m* estate (car) *(Brit)*, station wagon *(esp US)*; **~zange** *f* combination pliers *pl*.
Komet *m (wk)* **-en, -en** comet; *(fig)* meteor.
kometenhaft *adj (fig) Aufstieg* meteoric.
Komfort [kɔm'foːɐ] *m no pl (von Hotel etc)* luxury; *(von Möbel etc)* comfort; *(von Auto)* luxury features *pl*; *(von Gerät)* extras *pl*; *(von Wohnung)* amenities *pl*.
komfortabel *adj* luxurious, luxury *attr*; *(bequem) Sessel, Bett* comfortable.
Komik *f no pl (das Komische)* comic; *(komische Wirkung)* comic effect; *(lustiges Element: von Situation)* comic element.
Komiker *m* **-** *(lit, fig)* comedian, comic.
komisch *adj* **(a)** *(spaßig)* funny, comical; *(Theat)* comic. **(b)** *(seltsam)* funny, strange, odd. **das K~e daran ist ...** the funny *etc* thing about it is ...; **mir ist so ~** *(col)* I feel funny *or* strange *or* odd.
komischerweise *adv* funnily enough.
Komitee *nt* **-s** committee.
Komma *nt* **-s** *or* **-ta** comma; *(Math)* decimal point. **fünf ~ drei** five point three.
Kommandant *m (Mil)* commanding officer; *(Naut)* captain; *(von Stadt)* commandant.
kommandieren* **1** *vt* **(a)** *(befehligen)* to command, to be in command of. **(b)** *(befehlen)* **jdm etw ~** to command sb to do sth; **jdn an einen Ort ~** to order sb to a place. **2** *vi* **(a)** *(Befehlsgewalt haben)* to be in command. **~der General** commanding general. **(b)** *(Befehle geben)* to give orders.
Kommando *nt* **-s** **(a)** *(Befehl)* command, order. **das ~ zum Schießen geben** to give the command *or* order to fire; **auf ~ schreit ihr alle ...** on the command (you) all shout ...; **ich kann doch nicht auf ~ lustig sein** I can't be cheerful to order; **wie auf ~ stehenbleiben** to stand still as if by command. **(b)** *(Befehlsgewalt)* command. **das ~ haben** to be in command *(über +acc* of*)*. **(c)** *(Mil) (Behörde)* command; *(Abteilung)* commando.
Kommandobrücke *f (Naut)* bridge.
kommen *pret* **kam,** *ptp* **gekommen** *aux sein* **1** *vi* **(a)** to come; *(an~ auch)* to arrive; *(her~)* to come over; *(hervor~) (Blüten, Sonne)* to come out; *(Zähne auch)* to come through; *(sich entwickeln: Pflanzen)* to come on. **ich komme (schon)** I'm just coming; **er wird gleich ~** he'll be here right away; **der Nachtisch kommt gleich** dessert is coming straight away; **wann soll der Zug/das Baby ~?** when is the train/baby due?; **nach Hause ~** to come *or* get home; **der Wagen kommt in 16 sec. auf 100 km/h** the car does 0 to 100 km/h in 16 sec; **das Schlimmste kommt noch** the worst is yet to come; **ich komme zuerst an die Reihe** I'm first; **jetzt kommt's** here it comes, wait for it! *(col)*; **bohren, bis Öl/Grundwasser kommt** to bore until one strikes oil/finds water; **jetzt muß bald die Grenze/Hannover ~** we should soon be at the border/in Hanover; **wie sie (gerade) ~** just as they come; **bitte kommen!** *(Telec)* come in please; **daher kommt es, daß...** that's why ...; **das kommt davon, daß ...** that's because ...; **das kommt daher, daß es soviel geregnet hat** that comes from all the rain we've had; **das kommt davon!** see what happens?
(b) *(stattfinden, sich zutragen)* to happen; *(TV, Rad, etc)* to be on. **ich glaube, es kommt ein Unwetter** I think there's some bad weather on the way; **was kommt diese Woche im Kino?** what's on at the cinema this week?; **egal, was kommt, ich bleibe fröhlich** whatever happens, I shall remain cheerful; **komme, was da wolle** come what may; **so mußte es ja ~** it had to happen; **das hätte nicht ~ dürfen** that should never have happened.
(c) *(kosten, sich belaufen)* **wie hoch kommt das?** what does that come to?; **das kommt zusammen auf 20 DM** that makes DM 20.
(d) *(gelangen)* to get out of the house; *(mit Hand etc erreichen können)* to reach. **wie komme ich nach London?** how do I get to London?; **ich komme zur Zeit nicht aus dem Haus** at the moment I never get out of this house; **durch den Zoll/die Prüfung ~** to get through customs/the exam; **zu einem Entschluß/einer Einigung ~** to come to a conclusion/an agreement; **in das Alter ~, wo ...** to reach the age when ...
(e) *(hingehören, gebracht werden)* to go. **das Buch kommt ins oberste Fach** the book goes on the top shelf; **in die Ecke kommt noch ein Schrank** another cupboard is to go in that corner; **ins Gefängnis ~** to go to prison; **in die Schule ~** to go to school; **ins Krankenhaus ~** to go into hospital.
(f) **komm, wir gehen** come along, we're going; **ach komm!** come on!; **komm, fang bloß nicht wieder damit an** come on, don't start that again; **wenn mir die Lust kommt** when I feel like it; **ihm kamen Zweifel** he started to have doubts; **jdm kommen die Tränen** tears come to sb's eyes; **ihm kam das Grausen** terror seized him; **mir kommt eine Idee** I just had an idea; **du kommst mir**

gerade recht *(iro)* you're just what I need; **das kommt mir gerade recht** that's just fine; **jdm frech/dumm** ~ to be cheeky to sb/to act stupid; **angelaufen** ~ to come running along *or (auf einen zu)* up; **kommt essen!** come and eat!; **jdn besuchen** ~ to come and visit sb; **neben jdm zu sitzen** ~ to end up sitting next to sb; **jdn** ~ **sehen** to see sb coming; **ich habe es** ~ **sehen** I saw it coming; **die Zeit für gekommen halten** to think the time has come; **jdn** ~ **lassen** *Arzt, Polizei, Schüler, Sekretärin* to send for sb; **etw** ~ **lassen** *Mahlzeit, Taxi* to order; *Kupplung* to let in; *Seil* to let come; *Motor* to start up; **in Bewegung** ~ to start moving; **ins Erzählen** ~ to get talking; **zum Blühen/Wachsen** *etc* ~ to start flowering/growing; **zum Stehen/Stillsand** ~ to come to a halt/standstill; **kommt Zeit, kommt Rat** *(Prov)* things have a way of working themselves out; **wer zuerst kommt, mahlt zuerst** *(Prov)* first come first served.

(g) an etw *(acc)* ~ *(berühren)* to touch sth; *(sich verschaffen)* to get hold of sth; **auf etw** *(acc)* ~ *(sich erinnern)* to think of sth; *(sprechen über)* to get onto sth; **auf einen Gedanken** ~ to have a thought; **das kommt auf die Rechnung** that goes onto the bill; **auf ihn/darauf lasse ich nichts** ~ *(col)* I won't hear a word against him/it; **auf jeden** ~ **fünf Mark** there are five marks (for) each; **wie kommst du darauf?** what makes you think that?; **darauf bin ich nicht gekommen** I didn't think of that; **ich komme im Moment nicht auf seinen Namen** his name escapes me for the moment; **hinter etw** *(acc)* ~ *(herausfinden)* to find sth out; **mit einem Anliegen** ~ to have a request (to make); **um etw** ~ *(verlieren) um Besitz, Leben* to lose sth; *um Essen, Schlaf* to (have to) go without sth; **zu etw** ~ *(Zeit finden für)* to get around to sth; *(erhalten)* to come by sth; *(erben)* to come into sth; **wie komme ich zu der Ehre?** to what do I owe this honour?; **hierzu kommt noch seine Kurzsichtigkeit** then there's his shortsightedness on top of that; **zu sich** ~ to come to; *(sich fassen)* to recover; *(sich finden)* to sort oneself out.

2 *vi impers* **es** ~ **jetzt die Nachrichten** and now the news; **es werden viele Leute** ~ a lot of people will come; **es kommt noch einmal so weit** *or* **dahin, daß ...** it will get to the point where ...; **so weit kommt es (noch)** that'll be the day *(col)*; **wie kommt es, daß du ...?** how is it that you ...?; **ich wußte, daß es so** ~ **würde** I knew that would happen; **dazu kam es gar nicht mehr** it didn't come to that; **es kamzum Streit** there was a quarrel; **es kam eins zum anderen** one thing led to another; **und so kam es, daß ...** and that is how it happened that ...; **es kam, wie es** ~ **mußte** the inevitable happened; **es kommt immer anders, als man denkt** *(prov)* things never turn out the way you expect; **es mag** ~**, wie es** ~ **will** whatever happens.

3 *vt (col: kosten)* to cost.

Kommen *nt no pl* coming. **ein einziges** ~ **und Gehen** a constant coming and going; **jd ist im** ~ sb is on his/her way up.

kommend *adj Jahr, Woche, Generation* coming; *Ereignisse, Mode* future. **der** ~**e Meister** the future champion; **(am)** ~**en Montag** next Monday.

Kommentar *m (Bemerkung, Stellungnahme)* comment; *(Press, Jur, Liter)* commentary. **kein** ~**!** no comment; **einen** ~ **(zu etw) (ab)geben** to comment on sth.

Kommentator *m* commentator.

kommentieren* *vt (Press etc)* to comment on; **kommentierte Ausgabe** annotated edition.

kommerzialisieren* *vt* to commercialize.

kommerziell *adj* commercial.

Kommilitone *m (wk)* **-n, -n, Kommilitonin** *f* fellow student.

Kommissar *m (Polizei~)* inspector; *(ranghöher)* (police) superintendent.

Kommissariat *nt (Polizei) (Amt)* office of inspector; office of superintendent; *(Dienststelle)* superintendent's department.

kommissarisch 1 *adj* temporary. **2** *adv* on a temporary basis.

Kommission *f* **(a)** *(Ausschuß)* committee; *(zur Untersuchung)* commission. **(b)** *(Comm)* commission. **etw in** ~ **geben** to give (to a dealer) for sale on commission; **etw in** ~ **nehmen/haben** to take/have sth on commission.

Kommode *f* **-n** chest of drawers; *(hohe)* tallboy *(Brit)*, highboy *(US)*.

kommunal *adj* local; *(von Stadt auch)* municipal.

Kommunal-: ~**abgaben** *pl* rates *pl (Brit)*, local taxes *pl (US)*; ~**verwaltung** *f* local government; ~**wahlen** *pl* local (government) elections *pl*.

Kommune *f* **-n (a)** *(Gemeinde)* community. **(b)** *(Wohngemeinschaft)* commune.

Kommunikation *f* communication.

Kommunion *f (Eccl)* (Holy) Communion.

Kommuniqué [kɔmyniˈkeː] *nt* **-s** communiqué.

Kommunismus *m* communism.

Kommunist(in *f***)** *m* Communist.

kommunistisch *adj* communist.

kommunizieren* *vi* **(a)** to communicate. **(b)** *(Eccl)* to receive (Holy) Communion.

Komödie [-iə] *f* comedy; *(fig: heiteres Ereignis)* farce. ~ **spielen** *(fig)* to put on an act.

kompakt *adj* compact.

Kompakt|anlage *f (Rad)* audio system.

Kompanie *f (Mil)* company.

Komparativ *m (Gram)* comparative.

Komparse *m (wk)* **-n, -n, Komparsin** *f (Film)* extra; *(Theat)* supernumerary.

Kompaß *m* **-sse** compass. **nach dem** ~ by the compass.

Kompaßnadel *f* compass needle.

kompatibel *adj (Tech)* compatible.

Kompatibilität *f* compatibility.

Kompensation *f* compensation.

kompensieren* *vt* to compensate for, to offset.

kompetent *adj* competent; *(befugt)* authorized.

Kompetenz *f* (area of) authority *or* competence; *(eines Gerichts)* jurisdiction, competence. **da hat er ganz eindeutig seine** ~**en überschritten** he has clearly exceeded his authority here; **das fällt in die** ~ **dieses Amtes** that's the responsibility of this office; **seine mangelnde** ~ **in dieser Frage** his lack of competence in this issue.

Kompetenzstreitigkeiten *pl* dispute over respective areas of responsibility.

komplett 1 *adj* complete. **2** *adv* completely.

Komplex *m* **-e** complex.

komplex *adj* complex.

Komplikation *f* complication.

Kompliment *nt* compliment. **jdm** ~**e machen** to pay sb compliments *(wegen* on*)*.

Komplize *m (wk)* **-n, -n, Komplizin** *f* accomplice.

komplizieren* *vt* to complicate.

kompliziert *adj* complicated; *(Med) Bruch* compound.

Komplott *nt* **-e** plot, conspiracy. **ein** ~ **schmieden** to hatch a plot.

Komponente *f* **-n** component.

komponieren* *vti* to compose.

Komponist(in *f***)** *m* composer.

Komposition *f* composition.

Kompost *m* **-e** compost.

Komposthaufen *m* compost heap.

Kompott *nt* **-e** stewed fruit.

komprimieren* *vt* to compress; *(fig)* to condense.

Kompromiß *m* **-sse** compromise. **einen** ~ **schließen** to compromise.

Kompromiß-: **k**~**bereit** *adj* willing to compromise; ~**bereitschaft** *f* willingness to compromise; **k~los** *adj* uncompromising; **~lösung** *f* compromise solution.

kompromittieren* **1** *vt* to compromise. **2** *vr* to compromise oneself.

Kondensatiọn *f (Chem, Phys)* condensation.

Kondensạtor *m (Aut, Chem)* condenser; *(Elec auch)* capacitor.

kondensieren* *vti (lit, fig)* to condense; *(fig auch)* to distil *(Brit)*, to distill *(US)*.

Kondẹns-: **~milch** *f* evaporated milk; **~wasser** *nt* condensation.

Konditiọn *f* condition, shape; *(Durchhaltevermögen)* stamina. **wie ist seine ~?** what sort of condition is he in?; **~ haben, in ~ sein** to be in good condition; *(fig: beim Tanzen, Trinken etc)* to have stamina.

Konditiọnsschwäche *f* lack of fitness *no pl*.

Konditorei *f* cake shop; *(mit Café)* café.

Kondolẹnz- *in cpds* of condolence.

kondolieren* *vi* **(jdm) ~** to offer one's condolences (to sb).

Kondọm *m or nt* **-e** condom.

Konfẹkt *nt* **-e** confectionery.

Konfektiọn *f (Herstellung)* manufacture of ready-to-wear clothing; *(Bekleidung)* ready-to-wear clothes *pl or* clothing.

Konfektiọns- *in cpds* ready-to-wear.

Konferẹnz *f* conference; *(Besprechung)* meeting.

Konferẹnz- *in cpds* conference; **~schaltung** *f (Telec)* conference circuit; *(Rad, TV)* (television/radio) link-up.

Konfessiọn *f* (religious) denomination.

Konfessiọns-: **k~los** *adj* non-denominational; **~schule** *f* denominational school.

Konfẹtti *nt no pl* confetti.

Konfirmatiọn *f (Eccl)* confirmation.

konfiszieren* *vt* to confiscate.

Konfitụ̈re *f* **-n** jam.

Konflịkt *m* **-e** conflict. **bewaffneter ~** armed conflict; **er befindet sich in einem (inneren) ~** he is in a state of inner conflict.

Konflịkt-: **~fall** *m* **im ~fall** in case of conflict; **~herd** *m (esp Pol)* centre *(Brit) or* center *(US)* of conflict; **~situation** *f* conflict situation.

konfọrm *adj Ansichten etc* concurring. **mit jdm ~ gehen** to be in agreement with sb *(in + dat* about*)*.

Konformịst(in *f***)** *m (pej)* conformist.

konformịstisch *adj* conformist, conforming.

Konfrontatiọn *f* confrontation.

konfrontieren* *vt* to confront *(mit* with*)*.

konfụs *adj* confused, muddled.

Kongrẹß *m* **-sse** *(Pol)* congress; *(US Pol)* Congress; *(fachlich)* convention, conference.

Kongrẹß-: **~mitglied** *nt (US Pol)* congressman/-woman; **~teilnehmer** *m* person attending a congress/conference *or* convention.

kongruẹnt *adj (Math)* congruent.

Kọ̈nig *m* **-e** king.

Kọ̈nigin *f (auch Zool)* queen.

kọ̈niglich **1** *adj* royal. **2** *adv* **sich ~ amüsieren** *(col)* to have the time of one's life *(col)*.

Kọ̈nigreich *nt* kingdom, realm *(poet)*.

Kọ̈nigs-: **k~blau** *adj* royal blue; **~krone** *f* royal crown; **k~treu** *adj* royalist.

Konjugatiọn *f* conjugation.

konjugieren* *vt* to conjugate.

Konjunktiọn *f (Astron, Gram)* conjunction.

Kọnjunktiv *m (Gram)* subjunctive.

Konjunktụr *f* economic situation; *(Hoch~)* boom. **steigende/fallende ~** upward/downward economic trend.

konjunkturẹll *adj* economic. **~ bedingt** caused by economic factors.

Konjunktụrpolitik *f policies aimed at preventing economic fluctuation.*

konkạv *adj* concave.

konkrẹt *adj* concrete. **ich kann dir nichts K~es sagen** I can't tell you anything definite.

Konkurrẹnt *m* rival; *(Comm auch)* competitor.

Konkurrẹnz *f (Wettbewerb)* rivalry; *(~betrieb)* competitors *pl*; *(Gesamtheit der Konkurrenten)* competition, competitors *pl*. **die ~ auf diesem Gebiet ist größer geworden** the competition in this field has increased; **jdm ~ machen** *(Comm, fig)* to compete with sb; *(Comm)* to be in/enter into competition with sb.

Konkurrẹnz-: **k~fähig** *adj* competitive; **~kampf** *m* competition; *(zwischen zwei Menschen auch)* rivalry; **ein ~kampf, bei dem wir uns durchgesetzt haben** a competitive situation in which we won out; **k~los** *adj* without competition.

konkurrieren* *vi* to compete.

Konkụrs *m* **-e** bankruptcy. **in ~ gehen, ~ machen** *(col)* to go bankrupt.

Konkụrs-: **~verfahren** *nt* bankruptcy proceedings *pl*; **~verwalter** *m* receiver; *(von Gläubigern bevollmächtigt)* trustee.

kọ̈nnen *pret* **kọnnte,** *ptp* **gekọnnt** *or (bei modal aux)* **~** *vti, modal aux* **(a)** *(vermögen)* to be able to. **ich kann es machen** I can do it, I am able to do it; **ich kann es nicht machen** I can't do it; **man konnte ihn retten** they managed to save him; **man konnte ihn nicht retten** they couldn't save him; **ich konnte es nicht verstehen** I couldn't *or* was unable to understand it; **ich habe es sehen ~** I could see it; **er hat es gekonnt** he was able to do it; **morgen kann ich nicht** I can't (manage) tomorrow; **das hättest du gleich sagen ~** you could *or* might have said that straight away; **ich kann das nicht mehr sehen** I can't stand the sight of it any more; **ich kann nicht mehr** I can't go on; *(ertragen)* I can't take any more; *(essen)* I can't eat any more; **so schnell er konnte** as fast as he could.

(b) *(beherrschen) Sprache* to know, to be able to speak; *Schach* to be able to play; *Klavier spielen, lesen, schwimmen, Skilaufen etc* to be able to, to know how to. **sie kann keine Mathematik** she can't do mathematics; **was ~ Sie?** what can you do?; **was du alles kannst!** the things you can do!; **er kann was** he's very capable; **er kann gut Englisch** he speaks English well.

(c) *(dürfen)* to be allowed to. **kann ich jetzt gehen?** can I go now?; **könnte ich ...?** could I ...?; **er kann sich nicht beklagen** he can't complain; **man kann wohl sagen, daß ...** one could well say that ...; **du kannst mich (mal)!** *(col)* get lost! *(col)*; **kann ich mit?** *(col)* can I come with you?

(d) *(möglich sein)* **Sie könnten recht haben** you may be right; **er kann jeden Augenblick kommen** he might come any minute; **das kann nur er gewesen sein** it can only have been him; **wer könnte das gewesen sein?** who could it have been?; **das kann nicht sein** that can't be true; **es kann sein/es kann nicht sein, daß er dabei war** he may have been there/he couldn't have been there; **kann sein** maybe.

(e) **für etw ~** to be responsible for sth; **ich kann nichts dafür** it's not my fault.

Kọ̈nnen *nt no pl* ability, skill.

Kọ̈nner *m* **-** expert.

kọnnte *pret of* **können.**

Konsẹns *m* **-e** agreement, consent.

konsequẹnt *adj* consistent. **die Bestimmungen ~ einhalten** to observe the regulations strictly; **wir werden ~ durchgreifen** we will take rigorous action; **~e Weiterentwicklung eines Stils** logically consistent development of a style; **wenn du das ~ durchdenkst** if you follow it through to its logical conclusion; **ein Ziel ~ verfolgen** to pursue an objective single-mindedly.

Konsequẹnz *f* **(a)** *(Schlußfolgerung)* consequence. **die ~en tragen** to take the consequences; **(aus etw) die ~en ziehen** to take the appropriate step.

(b) *(Beharrlichkeit)* consistency; *(bei Maßnahmen)* rigorousness. **die ~, mit der er sein Ziel verfolgte** the single-mindedness with which he pursued his aim.

konservativ [-va-] *adj* conservative; *(Brit Pol)* Conservative, Tory.

Konservative(r) [-va-] *mf decl as adj* conservative; *(Brit Pol)* Conservative, Tory.

Konservatorium [-va-] *nt* conservatory.

Konserve [kɔn'zɛrvə] *f* **-n** preserved food; *(in Dosen)* tinned *(Brit)* *or* canned food; *(~ndose)* tin *(Brit)*, can; *(Med: Blut~ etc)* stored blood *etc*; blood bottle. **von ~n ernähren** to live out of cans.

Konserven-: **~büchse, ~dose** *f* tin *(Brit)*, can.

konservieren* [kɔnzɛr'vi:rən] *vt* to preserve.

Konservierung *f* preservation.

Konsolidierung *f* consolidation.

Konsonant *m* consonant.

Konsorten *pl (pej col)* gang *(col)*, mob *(col)*. **X und ~** X and his gang *etc.*

Konsortium [kɔn'zɔrtsiʊm] *nt* consortium.

Konspiration [kɔnspira'tsio:n] *f* conspiracy, plot.

konspirieren* [kɔnspi'ri:rən] *vi* to conspire, to plot.

konstant [kɔn'stant] *adj* constant.

Konstante [kɔn'stantə] *f* **-n** constant.

konstatieren* [kɔnsta'ti:rən] *vt (geh)* to see, to notice; *(sagen)* to state.

Konstellation [kɔnstɛla'tsio:n] *f* constellation; *(fig)* line-up; *(von Faktoren etc)* combination.

Konstitution [kɔnstitu'tsio:n] *f (Pol, Med)* constitution.

konstruieren* [kɔnstru'i:rən] *vt* to construct; *(Gram auch)* to construe. **ein konstruierter Fall** a hypothetical case.

Konstruktion [kɔnstrʊk'sio:n] *f* construction; *(Entwurf, Bauart auch)* design.

Konstruktionsfehler *m (im Entwurf)* design fault; *(im Aufbau)* structural defect.

konstruktiv [kɔnstrʊk'ti:f] *adj* constructive.

Konsul *m* **-n** consul.

Konsulat *nt* consulate.

Konsultation *f (form)* consultation.

konsultieren* *vt (form)* to consult.

Konsum *m* **-s (a)** [kɔn'zu:m] *no pl (Verbrauch)* consumption. **(b)** ['kɔnzu:m, 'kɔnzʊm] *(Genossenschaft)* cooperative society; *(Laden)* cooperative store, co-op *(col)*.

Konsum|artikel *m* consumer item. **~** *pl* consumer goods *pl.*

Konsument *m* consumer.

Konsum-: **~gesellschaft** *f* consumer society; **~güter** *pl* consumer goods *pl.*

konsumieren* *vt* to consume.

Kontakt *m* **-e** contact; *(pl: Aut)* contact points *pl.* **mit jdm in ~ kommen** to come into contact with sb; **zu jdm ~ finden** to get to know sb; **mit jdm ~ aufnehmen/in ~ stehen** to get/be in touch with sb; **~ herstellen** to make contact; **den ~ unterbrechen** to break contact; **keinen ~ mehr haben, den ~ verloren haben** to be out of touch.

Kontakt-: **~anzeigen** *pl* personal column; **k~arm** *adj* **er ist k~arm** he finds it difficult to make friends; **k~freudig** *adj* sociable; **~linse** *f* contact lens; **~mann** *m, pl* **~männer** *(Agent)* contact; **~schale** *f* contact lens.

Konten *pl of* **Konto.**

kontern *vti Schlag, Angriff* to counter.

Kontinent *m* **-e** continent.

kontinental *adj* continental.

Kontingent [kɔntɪŋ'gɛnt] *nt* **-e** *(Comm)* quota, share; *(Zuteilung)* allocation.

kontinuierlich *adj* continuous.

Kontinuität *f* continuity.

Konto *nt, pl* **-s** *or* **Konten** account. **auf meinem/mein ~** in my/into my account; **das geht auf mein ~** *(col) (ich bin schuldig)* I am to blame for this; *(ich zahle)* this is on me *(col)*.

Konto-: **~auszug** *m* (bank) statement; **~stand** *m* balance.

kontra *prep +acc* against; *(Jur)* versus.

Kontrabaß *m* double-bass.

Kontrahent [kɔntra'hɛnt] *m (bei Vertrag)* contracting party; *(Gegner)* opponent, adversary.

Kontrakt *m* **-e** contract.

konträr *adj (geh) Meinungen* contrary, opposite.

Kontrast *m* **-e** contrast.

Kontrastfarbe *f* contrasting colour *(Brit) or* color *(US)*.

kontrastieren* *vi* to contrast.

Kontroll|abschnitt *m (Comm)* counterfoil *(Brit)*, stub.

Kontrollampe *f* pilot lamp; *(Aut: für Ölstand etc)* warning light.

Kontrollbeamte(r) *m* inspector; *(an der Grenze)* frontier guard; *(zur Paßkontrolle)* passport officer; *(zur Zollkontrolle)* customs officer; *(zur Überwachung)* security officer.

Kontrolle *f* **-n (a)** *(Beherrschung, Regulierung)* control. **über jdn/etw die ~ verlieren** to lose control of sb/sth; **jdn/etw unter ~ haben/halten** to have/keep sb/sth under control. **(b)** *(Nachprüfung)* check *(gen* on*)*; *(Aufsicht)* supervision; *(Paß~)* passport control; *(Zoll~)* customs examination. **zur ~ haben wir noch einmal alles nachgerechnet** we went over all the figures again to check; **die ~ von Lebensmitteln** the inspection of foodstuffs. **(c)** *(Stelle) (für Nach-/Überprüfung, Verkehr)* checkpoint; *(Paß~/Zoll~)* passport control/customs; *(vor Fabrik)* gatehouse; *(an der Grenze)* border post.

Kontrolleur [kɔntrɔ'lø:ɐ] *m* inspector.

kontrollieren* *vt* **(a)** *(regulieren, beherrschen)* to control. **(b)** *(nachprüfen, überwachen)* to check; *(Aufsicht haben über)* to supervise; *Paß, Fahrkarte etc* to inspect, to check. **die Qualität der Waren muß streng kontrolliert werden** a strict check must be kept on the quality of the goods; **jdn/etw nach etw ~** to check sb/sth for sth.

Kontrolliste *f* check-list.

Kontroll-: **~kommission** *f* control commission; **~stelle** *f* checkpoint; **~turm** *m* control tower; **~uhr** *f* time clock; **~zentrum** *nt (Space)* control centre *(Brit) or* center *(US)*.

kontrovers [kɔntro'vɛrs] *adj* controversial.

Kontroverse [kɔntro'vɛrzə] *f* **-n** controversy.

Kontur *f* **-en** outline, contour.

Konvention [kɔnvɛn'tsio:n] *f* convention. **sich über die ~en hinwegsetzen** to ignore conventions.

Konventionalstrafe [kɔnvɛntsio'na:l-] *f* penalty *or* fine (for breach of contract).

konventionell [kɔnvɛntsio'nɛl] *adj* conventional.

Konversation [kɔnvɛrza'tsio:n] *f* conversation. **~ machen** to make conversation.

Konversationslexikon *nt* encyclopaedia *(Brit)*, encyclopedia *(US)*.

konvex [kɔn'vɛks] *adj* convex.

Konvoi ['kɔnvɔʏ, -'-] *m* **-s** convoy. **im ~ fahren** to drive in convoy.

Konzentrat *nt* concentrate.

Konzentration *f* concentration *(auf +acc* on*)*.

Konzentrations-: **~fähigkeit** *f* power of concentration *usu pl*; **~lager** *nt* concentration camp.

konzentrieren* **1** *vt* to concentrate *(auf +acc* on*)*; *Truppen auch* to mass. **2** *vr* to concentrate *(auf +acc* on*)*; *(Untersuchung, Arbeit etc)* to be concentrated *(auf +acc* on*)*.

konzentriert *adj* **(a)** *(Chem)* concentrated. **(b) mit ~er Aufmerksamkeit** with all one's concentration; **~ arbeiten/zuhören** to work/listen with concentration; **~ nachdenken** to concentrate.

Konzept *nt* **-e** *(Rohentwurf)* draft, notes *pl*; *(Plan, Programm)* plan; *(Begriff, Vorstellung)* concept. **jdn aus dem ~ bringen** to break sb's train of

thought; *(col: aus dem Gleichgewicht)* to upset sb; **das paßt mir nicht ins** ~ that doesn't fit in with my plans; *(gefällt mir nicht)* I don't like the idea.
Konzeption *f (geh)* conception.
konzeptionslos *adj* without a definite line.
Konzeptpapier *nt* rough paper.
Konzern *m* **-e** combine, group (of companies). **die ~e haben zuviel Macht** the big companies have too much power.
Konzert *nt* **-e** concert; *(Komposition)* concerto.
Konzert-: **~besucher** *m* concert-goer; **~flügel** *m* concert grand.
Konzertina *f, pl* **Konzertinen** concertina.
Konzert-: **~meister** *m* leader, concertmaster *(US)*; **~pianist** *m* concert pianist; **~saal** *m* concert hall.
Konzession *f* **(a)** *(Gewerbeerlaubnis)* concession, licence *(Brit)*, license *(US)*. **(b)** *(Zugeständnis)* concession *(an +acc* to*)*.
konzessionsbereit *adj* willing to make concessions.
Konzil *nt* **-e** *or* **-ien** [-iən] *(Eccl, Univ)* council.
konzipieren* *vt* to conceive; *(entwerfen auch)* to design.
Ko|operation *f* cooperation.
ko|operativ *adj* cooperative.
ko|operieren* *vi* to cooperate.
Ko|ordinate *f* **-en** *(Math)* coordinate.
Ko|ordination *f* coordination.
Ko|ordinator *m*, **Ko|ordinatorin** *f* coordinator.
ko|ordinieren* *vt* to coordinate.
Kopf *m* **⁼e** **(a)** head. **mit bloßem** ~ bareheaded; **~ an ~** shoulder to shoulder; *(Pferderennen, Sport)* neck and neck; **bis über den** ~ *(im Wasser)* up to one's neck; *(in Schulden)* up to one's ears; **~ hoch!** chin up!; **auf dem ~ stehen** to stand on one's head; **jdm den ~ waschen** *(col)* to give sb a piece of one's mind *(col)*; **den ~ oben behalten** to keep one's chin up; **jds ~ fordern** *(lit, fig)* to demand sb's head; **von ~ bis Fuß** from head to foot; **sich** *(dat)* **an den ~ fassen** *(fig)* to be speechless; **die ⁼e zusammenstecken** to put their heads together; *(heimlich)* to go into a huddle *(col)*; **einen schweren ~ haben** to have a thick head; **Geld** *etc* **auf den ~ hauen** *(col)* to blow one's money *etc (col)*; **jdm über den ~ wachsen** *(lit)* to outgrow sb; *(fig: Sorgen etc)* to be more than sb can cope with; **den ~ für jdn/etw hinhalten** *(col)* to take the blame for sb/sth; **etw auf den ~ stellen** *(lit, fig: durchsuchen)* to turn sth upside down; **Tatsachen auf den ~ stellen** to stand facts on their heads; **und wenn du dich auf den ~ stellst, ...** *(col)* no matter what you say/do ...; **jdn den ~ kosten** *(lit)* to cost sb his head; *(fig)* to cost sb his career *or* job; **~ und Kragen riskieren** *(col)* to risk one's neck; **auf jds ~** *(acc)* **eine Belohnung aussetzen** to put a reward on sb's head; **er ist nicht auf den ~ gefallen** he's no fool; **jdm Beleidigungen an den ~ werfen** *(col)* to hurl insults at sb; **jdm etw auf den ~ zusagen** to say sth straight out to sb; **den ~ hängenlassen** *(fig)* to be downcast *or* despondent; **jdn vor den ~ stoßen** to antagonize sb; **jdm den ~ zurechtrücken** to bring sb to his/her senses; **mit dem ~ durch die Wand wollen** *(col)* to be determined to get one's own way regardless; **(jdm) zu ~(e) steigen** to go to sb's head; **ich war wie vor den ~ geschlagen** I was dumbfounded; **über jds ~** *(acc)* **hinweg** over sb's head; **ein ~ Salat/Kohl** a head of lettuce/cabbage; **~ oder Zahl?** heads or tails?

(b) *(Einzelperson)* person. **pro ~** per person *or* head; **das Einkommen pro ~** the per capita income.

(c) *(fig) (Verstand)* head; *(Denker)* thinker; *(leitende Persönlichkeit)* leader; *(Bandenführer)* brains *sing*. **sich** *(dat)* **über etw** *(acc)* **den ~ zerbrechen** to rack one's brains over sth; **er ist nicht ganz richtig im ~** *(col)* he is not quite right in the head; **ein kluger ~** an intelligent person; **er ist ein fähiger ~** he has a good head on his shoulders; **die besten ⁼e** the best brains *or* minds.

(d) *(Sinn)* head, mind. **sich** *(dat)* **etw durch den ~ gehen lassen** to think about sth; **nichts als Tanzen/Fußball im ~ haben** to think of nothing but dancing/football; **andere Dinge im ~ haben** to have other things on one's mind; **ich weiß kaum, wo mir der ~ steht** I scarcely know whether I'm coming or going; **den ~ verlieren** to lose one's head; **sich** *(dat)* **etw aus dem ~ schlagen** to put sth out of one's mind; **jdm den ~ verdrehen** to turn sb's head; **der Gedanke will mir nicht aus dem ~** I can't get the thought out of my head *or* mind; **das will mir nicht in den ~ hinein** I just can't understand it; **im ~** in one's head; **etw im ~ rechnen** to work sth out in one's head; **aus dem ~** from memory; **sie hat es sich** *(dat)* **in den ~ gesetzt, das zu tun** she has taken it into her head to do that; **seinen ~ durchsetzen** to get one's own way.
Kopf-: **~-an-~-Rennen** *nt* neck-and-neck race; **~arbeit** *f* brain-work; **~bahnhof** *m* terminus (station); **~ball** *m (Ftbl)* header; **~bedeckung** *f* headgear; **ohne ~bedeckung** without a hat.
Köpfchen *nt dim of* **Kopf** little head; *(fig hum)* brains. **~ haben** to be brainy *(col)*.
köpfen *vti* **(a)** *jdn* to behead; *(hum) Flasche Wein* to crack (open). **(b)** *(Ftbl)* to head. **ins Tor ~** to head the ball in.
Kopf-: **~ende** *nt* head; **~geld** *nt* head money; **~haut** *f* scalp; **~hörer** *m* headphone.
Kopf-: **~jäger** *m* head-hunter; **~kissen** *nt* pillow; **~kissenbezug** *m* pillow case; **~lage** *f (Med)* head presentation; **~länge** *f* **um eine ~länge** by a head; **k~lastig** *adj (lit, fig)* top-heavy; *Flugzeug* nose-heavy; **k~los** *adj (fig)* in a panic; *(lit)* headless; **k~los werden** to get into a flap *(col)*; **~losigkeit** *f (fig)* panickiness; **~nicken** *nt no pl* nod (of the head); **~prämie** *f* reward; **~rechnen** *nt* mental arithmetic; **~salat** *m* lettuce; **k~scheu** *adj* **jdn k~scheu machen** to intimidate sb; **~schmerz** *m usu pl* headache; **~schmerzen haben** to have a headache; **sich** *(dat)* **wegen etw ~schmerzen machen** *(fig)* to worry about sth; **~schmerztablette** *f* aspirin, headache tablet; **~schuß** *m* shot in the head; **~schutz** *m* protection for the head; **~seite** *f (von Münze)* head, face side; **~sprung** *m* header, dive; **einen ~sprung machen** to dive (headfirst); **~stand** *m* headstand; **einen ~stand machen** to stand on one's head; **k~stehen** *vi sep irreg aux sein* **(a)** *(lit)* to stand on one's head; **(b)** *(fig) (vor Ausgelassenheit)* to go wild (with excitement); *(durcheinander sein)* to be all topsy-turvy *(col)*; **~steinpflaster** *nt* cobblestones *pl*; **eine Straße mit ~steinpflaster** a cobbled street; **~stütze** *f* headrest; **~tuch** *nt* (head)scarf; **k~über** *adv (lit, fig)* headfirst, headlong; **~verletzung** *f* head injury; **~wäsche** *f* shampoo, hair-wash; **~weh** *nt siehe* **~schmerz**; **~zerbrechen** *nt* **sich** *(dat)* **über etw** *(acc)* **~zerbrechen machen** to worry about sth.
Kopie *f* copy; *(fig)* carbon copy; *(Durchschlag auch)* carbon (copy); *(Ablichtung)* photocopy; *(Phot)* print.
kopieren* *vti (lit, fig)* to copy; *(nachahmen)* to imitate; *(ablichten)* to photocopy; *(durchpausen)* to trace; *(Phot, Film)* to print.
Kopierer *m* (photo)copier.
Kopier-: **~gerät** *nt* photocopier; **~papier** *nt* photocopy paper; **~stift** *m* indelible pencil.
Kopilot(in *f***)** *m* co-pilot.
Koppel *f* **-n** *(Weide)* paddock, enclosure. **auf der ~** in the paddock *etc*.
koppeln *vt* **(a)** *(zusammenbinden)* to tie together. **(b)** *(verbinden)* to couple, to join *(etw an etw (acc)*

sth to sth*)*; *zwei Dinge* to couple *or* join together; *(fig)* to link, to couple; *(als Bedingung)* to tie; *Ziele, Zwecke* to combine. **eine Dienstreise mit einem Urlaub ~** to combine a business trip with a holiday. **(c)** *(Elec)* to couple.

Kọpp(e)lung *f no pl* **(a)** *(Elec)* coupling. **(b)** *(Verbindung) (lit)* coupling, joining; *(fig, von Raumschiffen)* link-up.

Kọproduktion *f* co-production.

Kọproduzent *m* co-producer.

Kopulatiọn *f (Biol)* copulation, coupling.

kopulieren* *vi (koitieren)* to copulate.

Korạlle *f* **-n** coral.

Korạllen-: ~bank *f* coral-reef; **~kette** *f* coral necklace.

Korạn *m no pl* Koran.

Kọrb *m* **¨-e (a)** basket; *(Fisch~ auch)* creel; *(Bienen~)* hive; *(Förder~)* cage. **ein ~ Äpfel** a basket of apples. **(b)** *(~geflecht)* wicker. **ein Sessel aus ~** a wicker(work) chair. **(c)** *(col: Abweisung)* refusal, rebuff. **einen ~ bekommen, sich** *(dat)* **einen ~ holen** to be turned down; **jdm einen ~ geben** to turn sb down.

Kọrbball *m* basket-ball.

Kö̩rbchen *nt* **(a)** *dim of* **Korb. ins ~!** *(baby-talk)* off to bye-byes *(baby-talk)*. **(b)** *(von Büstenhalter)* cup.

Kọrb-: ~geflecht *nt* basketwork, wickerwork; **~sessel** *m* wicker(work) chair.

Kọrdel *f* **-n** cord.

Korẹa *nt* Korea.

Korịnthe *f* **-n** currant.

Kọrk *m* **-e** cork.

Kọrken *m* **-** cork; *(aus Plastik)* stopper.

Kọrkenzieher *m* **-** corkscrew.

Kọrn[1] *nt* **¨-er (a)** *(Samen~)* seed, grain; *(Pfeffer~)* corn; *(Salz~, Sand~, Phot)* grain; *(Hagel~)* stone. **(b)** *no pl (Getreide)* grain, corn *(Brit)*.

Kọrn[2] *m* **-** *or* **-s** *(Kornbranntwein)* corn schnapps.

Kọrn[3] *nt* **-e** *(am Gewehr)* front sight, bead. **jdn/etw aufs ~ nehmen** *(fig col)* to start keeping tabs on sb/to hit out at sth.

Kọrnblume *f* cornflower.

Kö̩rnchen *nt* **ein ~ Wahrheit** a grain of truth.

kö̩rnig *adj* granular, grainy.

Kö̩rnung *f (Tech)* grain size; *(Phot)* granularity.

Kö̩rper *m* **-** body; *(Schiffs~)* hull. **~ und Geist** mind and body. **am ganzen ~ zittern/frieren** to tremble/to be cold all over.

Kö̩rper-: ~bau *m* physique, build; **~beherrschung** *f* physical control; **k~behindert** *adj* physically handicapped, disabled; **~behinderte(r)** *mf* disabled person; **die ~behinderten** the disabled; **~geruch** *m* body odour *(Brit) or* odor *(US)*, BO *(col)*; **~gewicht** *nt* weight; **~größe** *f* height; **~kontakt** *m* physical contact; **~kraft** *f* physical strength.

kö̩rperlich *adj* physical; *(stofflich)* material, corporeal. **~e Arbeit** manual work; **~e Züchtigung** corporal punishment.

Kö̩rper-: k~los *adj* bodiless, incorporeal; **~maße** *pl* measurements *pl*; **~pflege** *f* personal hygiene; **~puder** *m or nt* body powder.

Kö̩rperschaft *f* corporation, (corporate) body. **gesetzgebende ~** legislative body; **~ des öffentlichen Rechts** public corporation *or* body.

Kö̩rper-: ~schwäche *f* physical weakness; **~teil** *m* part of the body; **~temperatur** *f* body temperature; **~verletzung** *f (Jur)* physical injury; **fahrlässige ~verletzung** physical injury resulting from negligence; **schwere ~verletzung** grievous bodily harm; **~wärme** *f* body heat.

Korporạl *m* **-e** *or* **Korporäle** corporal.

Korps [koːɐ] *nt* **-** [koːɐ(s)], **-** [koːɐs] *(Mil)* corps; *(Univ)* (duelling) corps.

korpulẹnt *adj* corpulent.

korrẹkt *adj* correct.

Korrektụr *f* correction; *(Typ) (Vorgang)* proof-reading; *(Verbesserung)* proof correction; **~ lesen** to proof-read *(bei etw* sth).

Korrespondẹnt(in *f***)** *m* correspondent.

Korrespondẹnz *f* correspondence. **mit jdm in ~ stehen** to be in correspondence with sb.

korrespondieren* *vi* to correspond.

Kọrridor *m* **-e** *(auch Luft~ etc)* corridor; *(Flur)* hall.

korrigieren* *vt (berichtigen)* to correct; *Aufsätze etc auch* to mark; *Meinung, Einstellung* to change.

Korrosiọn *f* corrosion.

Korrosiọnsschutz *m* corrosion prevention.

korrụpt *adj* corrupt.

Korruptiọn *f no pl* corruption.

Korsẹtt *nt* **-s** *or* **-e** corset(s *pl*).

Korvette [kɔrˈvɛtə] *f (Naut)* corvette.

Korvẹttenkapitän *m* lieutenant commander.

kọscher *adj (Rel, fig col)* kosher.

Kọse-: ~name *m* pet name; **~wort** *nt* term of endearment.

K.-o.-Sieg [kaːˈ|oː-] *m* knock-out victory.

Kosmẹtik *f no pl* beauty culture; *(Kosmetika, fig)* cosmetics *pl*.

Kosmẹtiker(in *f***)** *m* **-** beautician.

kosmẹtisch *adj* cosmetic. **ein ~es Mittel** a cosmetic.

kọsmisch *adj* cosmic. **~ beeinflußt werden** to be influenced by the stars.

Kosmo-: ~naut(in *f***)** *m (wk)* **-en, -en** cosmonaut; **k~polịtisch** *adj* cosmopolitan.

Kọsmos *m no pl* cosmos.

Kọst *f no pl (Nahrung, Essen)* food, fare. **vegetarische/fleischlose ~** vegetarian/meatless diet; **geistige ~** *(fig)* intellectual fare; **leichte/schwere ~** *(fig)* easy/heavy going *(col)*; **~ und Logis** board and lodging.

kọstbar *adj (wertvoll)* valuable, precious.

Kọstbarkeit *f* **(a)** value, preciousness. **(b)** *(Gegenstand)* treasure, precious object; *(Leckerbissen)* delicacy.

Kọsten *pl* cost(s); *(Jur)* costs *pl*; *(Un~)* expenses *pl*; *(Auslagen auch)* outlay. **die ~ tragen** to bear the cost(s); **auf ~ von** *or* *+gen (fig)* at the expense of; **auf meine ~** *(lit, fig)* at my expense; **auf seine ~ kommen** *(fig)* to get one's money's worth.

kọsten[1] *vti (lit, fig)* to cost; *Zeit, Geduld etc* to take. **was kostet das?** how much does it cost?, how much is it?; **koste es, was es wolle** whatever the cost; **das lasse ich mich etwas ~** I don't mind spending a bit of money on it; **jdn sein Leben/den Sieg ~** to cost sb his life/the victory.

kọsten[2] *vti (lit, fig: probieren)* to taste. **von etw ~** to taste sth.

Kọsten-: ~ersparnis *f* cost saving; **~erstattung** *f* reimbursement of expenses; **~frage** *f* question of cost(s); **k~los** *adj, adv* free (of charge); **k~pflichtig** *adj* **das ist k~pflichtig** there is a charge (on it); **ein Kfz k~pflichtig abschleppen** to tow away a car at the owner's expense; **~punkt** *m* cost question; **~punkt?** *(col)* what'll it cost? **~satz** *m* rate; **k~sparend** *adj* cost-saving; **~voranschlag** *m* (costs) estimate.

kö̩stlich *adj* **(a)** *Wein, Speise* exquisite. **(b)** *(amüsant)* priceless. **sich ~ amüsieren** to have a great time.

Kö̩stlichkeit *f* **(a)** *no pl* exquisiteness. **(b)** *(Leckerbissen etc)* (culinary) delicacy.

Kọst-: ~probe *f (von Wein, Käse)* taste; *(fig)* sample; **k~spielig** *adj* expensive.

Kostụ̈m *nt* **-e (a)** *(Theat: Tracht)* costume. **(b)** *(Schneider~)* costume *(dated)*, suit.

Kostụ̈m-: ~bildner(in *f***)** *m* costume designer; **~fest** *nt* fancydress ball.

kostümieren* *vr* to dress up.

Kostụ̈m-: ~probe *f (Theat)* dress rehearsal; **~verleih** *m* (theatrical*)* costume agency.

Kọt *m no pl (form)* excrement, faeces *(form) pl*.

Kotelett [ˈkɔtlɛt, kɔtˈlɛt] *nt* **-s** chop, cutlet.

Kotelẹtte *f usu pl* (side)whisker, sideburn *(US)*.
Kọ̈ter *m* - *(pej)* cur.
Kọtflügel *m (Aut)* wing *(Brit)*, fender *(US)*.
kọtzen *vi (col!)* to throw up *(col)*, to puke *(col!)*. **das ist zum K~** it makes you sick.
kọtzụ̈bel *adj (col!)* **mir ist ~** I feel like throwing up *(col)*.
KP [kaːˈpeː] *f* = **Kommunistische Partei.**
KPdSU [kaːpeːdeːǀɛsˈǀuː] *f* - = **Kommunistische Partei der Sowjetunion** Communist Party of the Soviet Union.
Krạbbe *f* **-n** *(Zool) (klein)* shrimp; *(größer)* prawn.
krạbbeln 1 *vi aux sein* to crawl. **2** *vt (kitzeln)* to tickle.
Krạch *m* **¨e (a)** *no pl (Lärm)* noise, din *(col)*; *(Schlag)* crash. **~ machen** to make a noise. **(b)** *(col: Streit)* row, quarrel. **mit jdm ~ haben** to (have a) row with sb; **mit jdm ~ kriegen** to get into trouble with sb; **~ schlagen** to make a fuss.
krạchen *vi* **(a)** *(Lärm machen)* to crash, to bang; *(Holz)* to creak; *(Schuß)* to ring out; *(Donner)* to crash. **~d fallen** *etc* to fall *etc* with a crash; **..., daß es nur so krachte** *(lit)* with a crash; *(fig)* with a vengeance. **(b)** *aux sein (col: aufplatzen)* to rip (open), to split.
Krạ̈chzen *nt no pl* croak(ing); *(von Vogel)* caw(ing).
krạ̈chzen *vi* to croak; *(Vogel)* to caw.
Krạcker *m* - *(Cook)* cracker.
Krạft *f* **¨e (a)** *(körperlich, sittlich)* strength *no pl*; *(geistig, schöpferisch)* powers *pl*; *(von Prosa, Stimme)* power, force; *(Energie)* energy, energies *pl*. **die ¨~e (mit jdm) messen** to pit one's strength (against sb); *(fig)* to pit oneself against sb; **seine ¨~e sammeln** to build up one's strength; **mit frischer ~** with renewed strength; **mit letzter ~** with one's last ounce of strength; **die ~ aufbringen, etw zu tun** to find the strength to do sth; **mit vereinten ¨~en werden wir ...** if we combine our efforts we will ...; **mit seinen ¨~en haushalten** to conserve one's energy; **das geht über meine ¨~e** it's more than I can take; **mit aller** *or* **voller ~** with all one's might; **er will mit aller ~ durchsetzen, daß ...** he will do his utmost to ensure that ...; **aus eigener ~** by himself/myself *etc*; **nach (besten) ¨~en** to the best of one's ability; **er tat, was in seinen ¨~en stand** he did everything (with)in his power; **nicht/wieder bei ¨~en sein** not to be in very good shape/to have (got) one's strength back; **wieder zu ¨~en kommen** to regain one's strength.

(b) *(Macht, der Sonne)* power; *(Phys)* force. **die treibende ~** *(fig)* the driving force; **das Gleichgewicht der ¨~e** *(Pol)* the balance of power; **halbe/volle ~ voraus!** half/full speed ahead.

(c) *(usu pl: in Wirtschaft, Politik etc)* force.

(d) *no pl (Jur: Geltung)* force. **in ~ sein/treten** to be in/come into force; **außer ~ sein** to be no longer in force; **außer ~ treten** to cease to be in force; **außer ~ setzen** to annul.

(e) *(Arbeits~)* employee, worker. **¨~e** staff, personnel *no pl*.
krạft *prep +gen (form)* by virtue of; *(mittels)* by use of. **~ meines Amtes** by virtue of my office.
Krạft-: **~aufwand** *m* effort; **~ausdruck** *m* swearword; **~brühe** *f* beef tea.
Krạ̈fteverhältnis *nt (Pol)* balance of power; *(von Mannschaften etc)* relative strength.
Krạftfahrer(in *f*) *m (form)* motorist, driver; *(als Beruf)* driver.
Krạftfahrzeug *nt* motor vehicle.
Krạftfahrzeug-: **~brief** *m* (vehicle) registration document, logbook *(Brit)*; **~mechaniker** *m* motor mechanic; **~schein** *m* (vehicle) registration document; **~steuer** *f* motor vehicle tax, road tax *(Brit)*.
krạ̈ftig 1 *adj* strong; *Muskel, Stimme auch* powerful; *Ausdrucksweise auch* forceful; *Haarwuchs, Pflanze auch* healthy; *Schlag* hard, powerful, hefty *(col)*; *Händedruck* firm; *Fluch* violent; *Suppe, Essen* nourishing; *(groß) Portion, Preiserhöhung* huge; *Beifall* loud. **einen ~en Schluck nehmen** to take a good swig.

2 *adv gebaut* powerfully; *zuschlagen, treten, pressen* hard; *klatschen* loudly; *lachen, mitsingen* heartily; *fluchen, niesen* violently. **etw ~ schütteln** to give sth a good shake; **jdn ~ verprügeln** to give sb a good beating; **er hat sich ~ dagegen gewehrt** he objected most strongly; *(körperlich)* he put up a strong resistance; **es hat ~ geregnet/geschneit** it rained/snowed heavily; **die Preise sind ~ gestiegen** prices have gone up a lot; **jdn ~ ausschimpfen** to give sb a good bawling out *(col)*.
krạ̈ftigen *vt (geh)* **jdn ~** to build up sb's strength; *(Luft, Bad etc)* to invigorate sb; *(Essen, Mittel etc)* to fortify sb; **ein ~des Mittel** a tonic.
krạftlos *adj (schwach)* feeble, weak; *(schlaff)* limp; *(machtlos)* powerless; *(Jur)* invalid.
Krạft-: **~-probe** *f* test of strength; *(zwischen zwei Gruppen etc)* trial of strength; **~rad** *nt* motorcycle, motorbike; **~stoff** *m* fuel; **k~strotzend** *adj* exuding vitality; *Pflanze* healthy-looking; *(muskulös)* with bulging muscles; **~übertragung** *f* power transmission; **k~voll** *adj Stimme* powerful; **~wagen** *m* motor vehicle; **~werk** *nt* power station.
Krạgen *m* - collar. **jdn am** *or* **beim ~ packen** to grab sb by the collar; *(fig col)* to collar sb; **mir platzte der ~** *(col)* I blew my top *(col)*; **jetzt platzt mir aber der ~!** this is the last straw!; **jdn** *or* **jdm den ~ kosten** *(fig)* to be sb's downfall; *(umbringen)* to be the end of sb; **es geht ihm jetzt an den ~** *(col)* he's in for it now *(col)*.
Krạgenweite *f (lit)* collar size. **das ist nicht meine ~** *(fig col)* that's not my cup of tea *(col)*.
Krạ̈he *f* **-n** crow. **eine ~ hackt der anderen kein Auge aus** *(Prov)* birds of a feather stick together *(Prov)*.
krạ̈hen *vi* to crow.
Krạke *m (wk)* **-n, -n** octopus.
krakẹẹlen* *vi (col)* to make a row *or* racket *(col)*.
krạkelig *adj* scrawly.
krạkeln *vti* to scrawl, to scribble.
Krạlle *f* **-n** claw; *(von Raubvogel auch)* talon; *(pej: Fingernagel)* claw. **jdn/etw in seinen ~n haben** *(fig col)* to have sb/sth in one's clutches.
krạllen 1 *vr* **sich an jdn/etw ~** *(lit, fig)* to cling to sb/sth; *(Katze)* to dig its claws into sb/sth; **sich in etw** *(acc)* **~** to sink its claws into sth; *(mit Fingern)* to dig one's fingers into sth; **sich jdn/etw ~** *(col)* to get a hold of sb/to pinch sth. **2** *vt* **die Finger in etw** *(acc)***/um etw ~** to dig one's fingers into sth. **3** *vi* to claw *(an +dat* at*)*.
Krạm *m no pl (col) (Gerümpel)* junk; *(Zeug)* things *pl*, stuff *(col)*; *(Angelegenheit)* business. **den ~ hinschmeißen** to chuck the whole thing *(col)*.
Krạmladen *m (pej col)* tatty little shop *(col)*.
Krạmpf *m* **¨e (a)** *(Zustand)* cramp; *(Verkrampfung)* spasm; *(wiederholt)* convulsion(s *pl*). **(b)** *no pl (col) (Getue)* palaver *(col)*; *(Unsinn)* rubbish.
Krạmpf-: **~ader** *f* varicose vein; **k~artig** *adj* convulsive.
krạmpfen 1 *vt Finger, Hand* to clench *(um etw* around sth*)*. **2** *vr* **sich um etw ~** to clench sth.
krạmpfhaft *adj Zuckung* convulsive; *(col: angestrengt, verzweifelt)* frantic, desperate; *Lachen* forced *no adv*; **sich ~ an etw** *(dat)* **festhalten** *(lit, fig col)* to cling desperately to sth.
Krạn *m* **¨e (a)** crane. **(b)** *(Hahn)* tap, faucet *(US)*.
Krạnführer *m* crane driver.
Krạnich *m* **-e** *(Orn)* crane.
krạnk *adj comp* **¨er,** *superl* **¨ste(r, s)** *or (adv)* **am ¨sten** ill *usu pred*, sick *(auch fig)*, not well; *(leidend)* invalid; *Pflanze, Organ* diseased; *Zahn, Bein* bad; *Wirtschaft* ailing. **~ werden** to fall ill;

schwer ~ seriously ill; **vor Aufregung/Angst** ~ sick with excitement/fear; **sich** ~ **melden** to let one's boss *etc* know that one is ill; *(telefonisch)* to phone in sick; *(esp Mil)* to report sick; **jdn** ~ **schreiben** to give sb a medical certificate; *(esp Mil)* to put sb on the sick-list; **er ist schon seit einem halben Jahr** ~ **geschrieben** he's been off sick for six months; **sich** ~ **stellen** to pretend to be ill, to malinger; **das macht mich** ~! *(col)* it gets on my nerves! *(col)*, it drives me round the bend! *(Brit col)*.

kränkeln *vi* to be ailing *(auch Wirtschaft)*, to be sickly, to be in poor health.

kranken *vi* to suffer *(an +dat* from*)*. **das krankt daran, daß** ... *(fig)* it suffers from the fact that ...

kränken *vt* **jdn** ~ to hurt sb('s feelings); **sie war sehr gekränkt** she was very hurt; **jdn in seiner Ehre** ~ to offend sb's pride; ~**d** hurtful.

Kranken-: ~**bericht** *m* medical report; ~**besuch** *m* visit (to a sick person); *(von Arzt)* (sick-)call; ~**bett** *nt* sick-bed; ~**geld** *nt* sickness benefit; *(von Firma)* sickpay; ~**geschichte** *f* medical history.

Krankenhaus *nt* hospital. **ins** ~ **gehen** *(als Patient)* to go into (the *US*) hospital; **im** ~ **liegen** to be in (the *US*) hospital.

Krankenhaus- *in cpds* hospital; ~**aufenthalt** *m* stay in hospital; ~**kosten** *pl* hospital charges *pl*.

Kranken-: ~**kasse** *f (Versicherung)* medical *or* health insurance; *(Gesellschaft)* medical *or* health insurance company; **er ist in keiner** ~**kasse** he has no medical insurance; ~**pflege** *f* nursing; ~**pfleger** *m* orderly; *(mit Schwesternausbildung)* male nurse; ~**pflegerin** *f* nurse; ~**schein** *m* medical insurance card; ~**schwester** *f* nurse; ~**versicherung** *f* medical *or* health insurance; **soziale/private** ~**versicherung** state *or* national/private health insurance; ~**wagen** *m* ambulance; ~**zimmer** *nt* sick-room; *(im Krankenhaus)* hospital room.

Kranke(r) *mf decl as adj* sick person, invalid; *(Patient)* patient. **die** ~**n** the sick.

krankfeiern *vi sep (col)* to be off sick; *(vortäuschend)* to skive *(Brit col)*.

krankhaft *adj* **(a)** *Stelle, Zelle* diseased; *Vergrößerung, Zustand* morbid; *Aussehen* sickly. ~**e Veränderung** affection. **(b)** *(seelisch)* pathological. **sein Geiz ist schon** ~ his meanness is almost pathological.

Krankheit *f (lit, fig)* illness, sickness; *(eine bestimmte* ~ *wie Krebs, Masern etc auch, von Pflanzen)* disease. **wegen** ~ due to illness; **sich** *(dat)* **eine** ~ **zuziehen** to contract an illness *(form)*; **nach langer schwerer** ~ after a long serious illness; **während meiner** ~ during my illness.

Krankheits|erreger *m* disease-causing agent.

kränklich *adj* sickly, in poor health.

Krankmeldung *f* notification of illness.

Kränkung *f* insult. **etw als** ~ **empfinden** to take offence *(Brit) or* offense *(US)* at sth; **das war eine** ~ **seiner Gefühle** that hurt his feelings.

Kranz *m* ¨**-e (a)** wreath; *(Sieger*~*, Braut*~ *auch)* garland; *(fig: von Geschichten etc)* cycle. **(b)** *(Tech: Rad*~*)* rim; *(von Glocke auch)* lip.

Kranzgefäß *nt (Anat)* coronary artery.

kraß *adj Gegensatz, Worte, Stil* stark; *Farben* garish; *Unterschied, Fall, Haltung* extreme; *Ungerechtigkeit, Lüge* blatant; *Materialist, Unkenntnis* crass; *Egoist* out-and-out; *Außenseiter* rank.

Krater *m* **-** crater.

Kratz-: ~**bürste** *f* wire brush; *(col)* prickly character; **k**~**bürstig** *adj (col)* prickly.

Krätze *f no pl (Med)* scabies.

kratzen 1 *vti* **(a)** to scratch; *(ab*~ *auch)* to scrape *(von* off*)*. **der Rauch kratzt (mich) im Hals** the smoke irritates my throat. **(b)** *(col: stören)* to bother. **das kratzt mich nicht** *(col)* I couldn't care less (about that). **2** *vr* to scratch oneself.

Kratzer *m* **-** *(Schramme)* scratch.

kratzig *adj (col)* scratchy *(col)*.

Kraul *nt no pl (Schwimmen)* crawl. **(im)** ~ **schwimmen** to do the crawl.

kraulen[1] *(Schwimmen) aux haben or sein* **1** *vi* to do the crawl. **2** *vt* **er hat** *or* **ist 100 m gekrault** he did a 100m's crawl.

kraulen[2] *vt* to fondle. **jdn am Kinn** ~ to chuck sb under the chin.

kraus *adj* crinkly; *Haar, Kopf* frizzy; *Stirn* furrowed; *(fig: verworren)* muddled, confused. **die Stirn** ~ **ziehen** to knit one's brow; *(mißbilligend)* to frown.

Krause *f* **-n (a)** *(Hals*~*)* ruff; *(an Ärmeln etc)* ruffle, frill. **(b)** *(col: Frisur)* frizzy hair.

kräuseln 1 *vt Haar* to make frizzy; *(Sew)* to gather *(in small folds)*; *(Tex)* to crimp; *Stirn* to knit; *Wasseroberfläche* to ripple. **2** *vr (Haare)* to go frizzy; *(Stoff)* to go crinkly; *(Stirn)* to wrinkle up; *(Wasser)* to ripple.

Kraus-: **k**~**haarig** *adj* frizzy-haired; ~**kopf** *m (Frisur)* frizzy hair; *(Mensch)* curly-head.

Kraut *nt, pl* **Kräuter (a)** herb. **dagegen ist kein** ~ **gewachsen** *(fig)* there's nothing anyone can do about that. **(b)** *no pl (grüne Teile von Pflanzen)* foliage, stems and leaves *pl*; *(von Gemüse)* tops *pl*. **wie** ~ **und Rüben durcheinanderliegen** *(col)* to lie (about) all over the place *(col)*; **ins** ~ **schießen** *(lit)* to run to seed; *(fig)* to get out of control. **(c)** *no pl (Rot*~*, Weiß*~*)* cabbage.

Kräuter-: ~**butter** *f* herb butter; ~**käse** *m* herb cheese; ~**likör** *m* herbal liqueur; ~**tee** *m* herb(al) tea.

Krautsalat *m* ≈ coleslaw.

Krawall *m* **-e** *(Aufruhr)* riot; *(col: Lärm)* racket *(col)*, din *(col)*. ~ **machen** *(col)* to kick up a row; *(randalieren)* to go on the rampage; *(sich beschweren)* to kick up a fuss.

Krawallmacher *m (col)* hooligan.

Krawatte *f* **-n** tie, necktie *(esp US)*.

Krawattennadel *f* tie-pin.

kraxeln *vi aux sein (S Ger)* to clamber (up).

Kreation *f (Fashion etc)* creation.

kreativ *adj* creative.

Kreativität [kreativi'tɛːt] *f* creativity.

Kreatur *f* **(a)** *(lit, fig, pej)* creature. **(b)** *no pl (alle Lebewesen)* creation. **die** ~ all creation.

Krebs *m* **-e (a)** crab; *(Fluß*~*)* crayfish, crawfish *(US)*. **rot wie ein** ~ red as a lobster. **(b)** *(Astrol)* Cancer. **(c)** *(Med)* cancer; *(Bot)* canker.

Krebs-: **k**~**erregend** *adj* carcinogenic; **k**~**erregend wirken** to cause cancer; ~**kranke(r)** *mf* cancer victim; *(Patient)* cancer patient; **k**~**rot** *adj* red as a lobster; ~**tiere** *pl* crustaceans *pl*.

Kredit *m* **-e** credit; *(Darlehen)* loan; *(fig auch)* standing. **auf** ~ on credit; **er hat bei der Bank** ~ his credit is good with the bank; ~ **haben** *(fig)* to have standing.

Kredit-: ~**anstalt** *f* credit institution; ~**aufnahme** *f* borrowing; ~**brief** *m* letter of credit; **k**~**fähig** *adj* credit-worthy; ~**hai** *m (col)* loanshark; ~**institut** *nt* credit institution; ~**karte** *f* credit card; **k**~**würdig** *adj* credit-worthy.

Kredo *nt* **-s** *(lit, fig)* creed.

Kreide *f* **-n** chalk. **eine** ~ a piece of chalk; **bei jdm (tief) in der** ~ **stehen** to be (deep) in debt to sb.

Kreide-: **k**~**bleich** *adj* (as) white as a sheet; ~**felsen** *m* chalk cliff; ~**zeichnung** *f* chalk drawing.

kreieren* [kre'iːrən] *vt* to create.

Kreis *m* **-e (a)** circle. **einen** ~ **ziehen** to describe a circle; **einen** ~ **um jdn bilden** to make a circle around sb; **im** ~ **(sitzen)** (to sit) in a circle; **(weite)** ~**e ziehen** *(fig)* to have (wide) repercussions; **sich im** ~ **drehen** *(lit)* to go around in a circle; *(fig)* to go around in circles; **der** ~ **schließt sich** *(fig)* the wheel turns full circle; **der** ~ **seiner Leser** his readers *pl*; **weite** ~**e der**

Bevölkerung wide sections of the population; **im ~e von Freunden** among friends; **eine Feier im kleinen ~e** a celebration for a few close friends and relatives; **das kommt auch in den besten ~en vor** that happens even in the best of circles. **(b)** *(Elec: Strom~)* circuit. **(c)** *(Bereich: von Interessen etc)* sphere. **(d)** *(Stadt~, Land~)* district. ~ **Bonn** Bonn District.

Kreis-: **~abschnitt** *m* segment; **~ausschnitt** *m* sector; **~bahn** *f (Astron, Space)* orbit.

kreischen *vi* to screech; *(Mensch auch)* to shriek.

Kreisel *m* - *(Tech)* gyroscope; *(Spielzeug)* (spinning) top.

kreisen *vi aux sein or haben* to circle *(um* around, *über +dat* over*)*; *(um eine Achse)* to revolve *(um* around*)*; *(Satellit, Planet auch)* to orbit *(um etw* sth*)*; *(fig: Gedanken, Gespräch)* to revolve *(um* around*)*. **die Arme ~ lassen** to swing one's arms around (in a circle).

kreisförmig *adj* circular.

Kreislauf *m (Blut~, Öl~, von Geld)* circulation; *(der Natur, des Wassers)* cycle.

Kreislauf-: **~mittel** *nt* cardiac stimulant; **~störungen** *pl* circulation trouble *sing*.

Kreissäge *f* circular saw.

Kreißsaal *m* delivery room.

Kreis-: **~stadt** *f* district town, ≃ county town *(Brit)*; **~tag** *m* district assembly, ≃ county council *(Brit)*; **~verkehr** *m* roundabout *(Brit)*, traffic circle *(US)*; **~wehrersatzamt** *nt* district recruiting office.

Krem *f* **-s** *or m* **-e** cream.

Krematorium *nt* crematorium.

kremig *adj* creamy.

Kreml *m* **der ~** the Kremlin.

Krempe *f* **-n** *(Hut~)* brim.

Krempel *m no pl (col) (Sachen)* stuff *(col)*; *(wertloses Zeug)* junk.

krepieren* *vi aux sein* **(a)** *(Mil sl: Bombe etc)* to explode. **(b)** *(col!: sterben)* to snuff it *(col)*; *(col: elend sterben)* to die a wretched death.

Krepp *m* **-e** *or* **-s** crepe.

Kreppapier *nt* crepe paper.

Kreppsohle *f* crepe sole.

Kresse *f no pl* cress.

Kreta *nt* Crete.

Kreuz *nt* **-e** **(a)** cross; *(als Anhänger etc)* crucifix. **ein ~ schlagen** *or* **machen** to make the sign of the cross; *(sich bekreuzigen auch)* to cross oneself; **mit jdm über ~ sein** *(fig)* to be on bad terms with sb; **sein ~ geduldig tragen** *(geh)* to bear one's cross with patience; **es ist ein ~ mit ihm/damit** he's/it's an awful problem; **ich mache drei ~e, wenn er geht** *(col)* it'll be such a relief when he has gone; **zu ~e kriechen** *(fig)* to eat humble pie, to eat crow *(US)*. **(b)** *(Anat)* small of the back; *(von Tier)* back. **ich hab's im ~** *(col)* I have back trouble; **aufs ~ fallen** to fall on one's back; *(fig col)* to be staggered *(col)*; **jdn aufs ~ legen** to throw sb on his back; *(fig col)* to take sb for a ride *(col)*. **(c)** *(Mus)* sharp. **(d)** *(Autobahn~)* intersection. **(e)** *(Cards) (Farbe)* clubs *pl*; *(Karte)* club. **die ~-Dame** the Queen of Clubs.

kreuz *adj*: **~ und quer** all over; **sie lagen ~ und quer durcheinander** they were lying all over the place.

Kreuz-: **~bein** *nt (Anat)* sacrum; **k~brav** *adj Kind* as good as gold.

kreuzen **1** *vt* to cross *(auch Biol)*. **die Arme ~** to fold one's arms. **2** *vr* to cross; *(Meinungen etc)* to clash. **3** *vi aux haben or sein (Naut)* to cruise.

Kreuzer *m* - *(Naut)* cruiser.

Kreuz-: **~fahrer** *m (Hist)* crusader; **~fahrt** *f (Naut)* cruise; **eine ~fahrt machen** to go on a cruise; **~feuer** *nt (Mil, fig)* crossfire; **ins ~feuer (der Kritik) geraten** *(fig)* to come under fire; **k~förmig** *adj* cross-shaped; **~gang** *m* cloister.

kreuzigen *vt* to crucify.

Kreuzigung *f* crucifixion.

Kreuz-: **~otter** *f (Zool)* adder, viper; **~ritter** *m (Hist)* crusader; **~schmerzen** *pl* backache *sing*; **~spinne** *f (Zool)* garden *or* cross spider.

Kreuzung *f* **(a)** *(Straßen~)* crossroads *sing or pl*, intersection *(esp US)*. **(b)** *(das Kreuzen)* crossing; *(von Tieren auch)* cross-breeding. **(c)** *(Rasse)* hybrid; *(Tiere auch)* cross(-breed).

Kreuz-: **~unglücklich** *adj* absolutely miserable; **~verhör** *nt* cross-examination; **jdn ins ~verhör nehmen** to cross-examine sb; **~weg** *m (fig)* crossroads *sing*; **k~weise** *adv* crosswise; **du kannst mich k~weise!** *(col!)* get stuffed! *(col!)*; **~worträtsel** *nt* crossword puzzle; **~zeichen** *nt* sign of the cross; **~zug** *m (lit, fig)* crusade.

Krevette [kre'vɛtə] *f* shrimp.

kribb(e)lig *adj (col)* fidgety *(col)*; *(kribbelnd)* tingly *(col)*.

kribbeln *vi* **(a)** *(jucken)* to itch; *(prickeln)* to tingle. **auf der Haut ~** to cause a prickling sensation; *(angenehm)* to make the skin tingle; **es kribbelt mir im Fuß** *(lit)* I have pins and needles in my foot; **es kribbelt mir in den Fingern, etw zu tun** *(col)* I'm itching to do sth. **(b)** *aux sein (Insekten)* **es kribbelt von Ameisen** the place is crawling with ants.

kriechen *pret* **kroch,** *ptp* **gekrochen** *vi aux sein* to creep, to crawl *(auch Schlange)*; *(fig: Zeit)* to creep by; *(fig: unterwürfig sein)* to grovel *(vor +dat* before*)*.

Kriecher *m* - crawler *(col)*.

kriecherisch *adj* grovelling *(Brit)*, groveling *(US)*, servile.

Kriech-: **~spur** *f* crawler lane; **~tier** *nt (Zool)* reptile.

Krieg *m* **-e** war; *(Art der Kriegsführung)* warfare. **~ anfangen mit** to start a war with; **einer Partei** *etc* **den ~ erklären** *(fig)* to declare war on a party *etc*; **~ führen (mit** *or* **gegen)** to wage war (on); **im ~ sein (mit)** to be at war (with); **im ~e fallen** to be killed in action; **in den ~ ziehen** to go to war.

kriegen *vt (col)* to get; *Bus, Schnupfen, Dieb etc auch* to catch; *Schlaganfall, eine Spritze, Besuch auch* to have; *Junge, ein Kind* to have. **sie kriegt ein Kind** she's going to have a baby; **graue Haare/eine Glatze ~** to go grey/bald; **sie** *or* **es ~** *(col: Prügel)* to get a hiding; **es mit der Angst/Wut ~** to get scared/angry; **es mit jdm zu tun ~** to be in trouble with sb; **sie ~ sich** *(in Kitschroman)* boy gets girl; **dann kriege ich zuviel** then it gets too much for me; **ich kriege ein Steak** I'll have a steak; **jdn dazu ~, etw zu tun** to get sb to do sth; **etw gemacht ~** to get sth done.

Krieger *m* - warrior.

Kriegerdenkmal *nt* war memorial.

kriegerisch *adj* warlike *no adv; Haltung auch* belligerent. **~e Auseinandersetzung** military conflict.

Krieg-: **k~führend** *adj* warring; **~führung** *f* warfare *no art; (eines Feldherrn)* conduct of the war.

Kriegs-: **~ausbruch** *m* outbreak of war; **k~bedingt** *adj* caused by war; **~beginn** *m* start of the war; **~beil** *nt* tomahawk; **das ~beil begraben** *(fig)* to bury the hatchet; **~bemalung** *f (lit, hum)* warpaint; **k~beschädigt** *adj* war-disabled; **~beschädigte(r)** *mf decl as adj* war-disabled (ex-serviceman); **~dienst** *m (old, form)* military service; **~dienstverweigerer** *m* - conscientious objector; **~ende** *nt* end of the war; **~erklärung** *f* declaration of war; **~erlebnis** *nt* war-time experience; **~fall** *m* **im ~fall** in the event of war; **~folge** *f* consequence of (a/the) war; **~fuß** *m (col)*: **mit jdm auf ~fuß stehen** to be at loggerheads with sb; **er steht mit der englischen Sprache auf ~fuß** his English is terrible; **~gebiet** *nt* war-zone; **~gefahr** *f* danger of war; **~gefangene(r)** *mf* prisoner of war, P.O.W.; **~gefangenschaft** *f* captivity; **in ~gefangenschaft**

sein to be a prisoner of war; ~**gericht** *nt* court-martial; **jdn vor ein ~gericht stellen** to court-martial sb; ~**herr** *m* **oberster ~herr** commander-in-chief; ~**hetze** *f* war-mongering; ~**hetzer** *m* - *(pej)* war-monger; ~**jahr** *nt* year of war; **die ~jahre** the war years; **im ~jahr 1945** (during the war) in 1945; ~**kamerad** *m* war-time comrade; ~**kosten** *pl* cost of the war *sing;* ~**list** *f (old, liter)* stratagem; ~**marine** *f* navy; **k~mäßig** *adj* for war; **k~müde** *adj* war-weary; ~**opfer** *nt* war victim; ~**pfad** *m (liter)*: **auf dem ~pfad** on the war-path; ~**rat** *m* council of war; ~**rat halten** *(fig)* to have a pow-wow *(col)*; ~**recht** *nt (Mil)* martial law; ~**schäden** *pl* war damage; ~**schauplatz** *m* theatre *(Brit) or* theater *(US)* of war; ~**schiff** *nt* warship; ~**spiel** *nt* war game; ~**teilnehmer** *m* combatant; *(ehemaliger Soldat)* ex-serviceman; ~**verbrechen** *nt* war crime; ~**verbrecher** *m* war criminal; ~**verletzung** *f* war wound; ~**zeit** *f* wartime; **in ~zeiten** in times of war; ~**zustand** *m* state of war; **im ~zustand** at war.

Krim *f* **die ~** the Crimea.

Krimi *m* **-s** *(col)* **(a)** (crime) thriller; *(mit Detektiv als Held)* detective novel; *(rätselhaft)* murder mystery. **(b)** *(TV)* detective series.

Kriminal-: ~**beamte(r)** *m* CID officer; ~**film** *m* crime film *or* movie *(esp US)*.

kriminalisieren* *vt* to criminalize.

Kriminalistik *f* criminology.

Kriminalität *f* crime; *(Ziffer)* crime rate.

Kriminal-: ~**kommissar** *m* detective superintendent; ~**komödie** *f* comedy thriller; ~**polizei** *f* criminal investigation department; ~**polizist** *m* detective, CID officer; ~**roman** *m siehe* **Krimi (a)**.

kriminell *adj (lit, fig col)* criminal. **~ werden** to turn to crime.

Kriminelle(r) *mf decl as adj* criminal.

Krimskrams *m no pl (col)* odds and ends *pl.*

Kringel *m* - *(der Schrift)* squiggle; *(Cook)* ring.

kringelig *adj* crinkly. **sich ~ lachen** *(col)* to kill oneself (laughing) *(col)*.

kringeln *vr* to go frizzy. **sich ~ vor Lachen** *(col)* to kill oneself (laughing) *(col)*.

Kripo *f* **-s** *(col)* = **Kriminalpolizei. die ~** the cops *(col) pl,* the CID.

Kripo- *in cpds (col)* police.

Krippe *f* **-n (a)** *(Futter~)* (hay)box. **(b)** *(Weihnachts~)* crib; *(Bibl auch)* manger. **(c)** *(Kinderhort)* crèche.

Krippenspiel *nt* nativity play.

Krise *f* **-n** crisis.

kriseln *vi impers (col)* **es kriselt** there is trouble brewing.

Krisen-: **k~fest** *adj* stable; ~**gebiet** *nt* crisis area; ~**herd** *m* flash point; ~**stab** *m* action *or* crisis committee.

Kristall[1] *m* **-e** crystal.

Kristall[2] *nt no pl* crystal.

Kristallglas *nt* crystal glass.

Kristallisation *f* crystallization.

kristallisieren* *vir (lit, fig)* to crystallize.

Kristall-: **k~klar** *adj* crystal-clear; ~**zucker** *m* refined sugar (in) crystals.

Kriterium *nt (Merkmal)* criterion.

Kritik *f* **-en (a)** *no pl* criticism *(an +dat* of*)*. **an jdm/etw ~ üben** to criticize sb/sth; **unter aller ~ sein** *(col)* to be beneath contempt. **(b)** *(Rezensieren)* criticism; *(Rezension auch)* review. **eine gute ~ haben** to get good reviews. **(c)** *no pl (die Kritiker)* critics *pl.* **(d)** *no pl (Urteilsfähigkeit)* discrimination. **ohne jede ~** uncritically.

kritiklos *adj* uncritical.

kritisch *adj* critical. **jdm/einer Sache ~ gegenüberstehen** to be critical of sb/sth.

kritisieren* *vti* to criticize.

kritteln *vi* to find fault *(an +dat, über +acc* with*)*.

Kritzelei *f* scribble; *(das Kritzeln)* scribbling; *(an Wänden)* graffiti.

kritzeln *vti* to scribble.

kroch *pret of* **kriechen.**

Krokant *m no pl (Cook)* cracknel.

Krokette *f (Cook)* croquette.

Krokodil *nt* **-e** crocodile.

Krokodilleder *nt* crocodile skin.

Krokodilstränen *pl* crocodile tears *pl.*

Krokus *m* - *or* **-se** crocus.

Krone *f* **-n (a)** crown. **die ~** *(fig)* the Crown. **(b)** *(Mauer~)* coping; *(Schaum~)* crest; *(Zahn~)* crown; *(Baum~)* top. **die ~ der Schöpfung** the pride of creation; **das setzt der Dummheit die ~ auf** *(col)* that beats everything for stupidity; **einen in der ~ haben** *(col)* to be tipsy; **dabei fällt dir kein Stein** *or* **Zacken aus der ~** *(col)* it won't hurt you. **(c)** *(Währungseinheit)* crown.

krönen *vt (lit, fig)* to crown. **jdn zum König ~** to crown sb king; **von Erfolg gekrönt sein/werden** to be crowned with success; **der ~de Abschluß** the culmination.

Kronenkorken *m* crown cap.

Kron-: ~**kolonie** *f* crown colony; ~**leuchter** *m* chandelier; ~**prinz** *m* crown prince; *(in Großbritannien auch)* Prince of Wales; *(fig)* heir apparent; ~**prinzessin** *f* crown princess.

Krönung *f* coronation; *(fig)* culmination.

Kronzeuge *m (Jur)* person who turns King's/Queen's evidence *or (US)* State's evidence; *(Hauptzeuge)* principal witness. **~ sein, als ~ auftreten** to turn King's/Queen's/State's evidence; to appear as principal witness

Kropf *m* **¨-e (a)** *(von Vogel)* crop. **(b)** *(Med)* goitre.

kroß *adj (N Ger)* crisp; *Brötchen auch* crusty.

Krösus *m* **-se ich bin doch kein ~** *(col)* I'm not made of money *(col)*.

Kröte *f* **-n (a)** *(Zool)* toad. **eine freche (kleine) ~** *(col)* a cheeky (little) minx *(col)*. **(b)** ~**n** *pl (col: Geld)* pennies *(col)*.

Krücke *f* **-n (a)** crutch; *(fig)* prop. **an ~n** *(dat)* **gehen** to walk on crutches. **(b)** *(Schirm~)* crook.

Krückstock *m* walking-stick.

Krug *m* **¨-e** jug; *(Bier~)* (beer-)mug.

Krume *f* **-n** *(geh)* **(a)** *(Brot ~)* crumb. **(b)** *(liter: Acker~)* (top)soil.

Krümel *m* - **(a)** *(Brot~ etc)* crumb. **(b)** *(col: Kind)* tiny tot *(col)*.

krümeln *vti* to crumble; *(beim Essen)* to make crumbs.

krumm *adj* **(a)** crooked; *(verbogen auch)* bent; *(hakenförmig)* hooked; *Beine auch* bandy; *Rücken* hunched. **~e Nase** hook(ed) nose; **~ gewachsen** crooked; **etw ~ biegen** to bend sth; **~ und schief** askew; **sich ~ und schief lachen** *(col)* to fall about laughing *(col)*; **keinen Finger ~ machen** *(col)* not to lift a finger; **steh/sitz nicht so ~ da!** stand/sit up straight. **(b)** *(col: unehrlich)* crooked *(col)*. **~er Hund** *(pej)* crooked swine; **ein ~es Ding drehen** *(col)* to do something crooked; **etw auf die ~e Tour versuchen** to try to wangle sth *(col)*.

krümmen 1 *vt* to bend. **die Katze krümmte den Buckel** the cat arched its back. **2** *vr* to bend; *(Fluß)* to wind; *(Straße)* to curve; *(Wurm)* to writhe. **sich ~ und winden** *(fig)* to squirm; **sich vor Lachen ~** to double up with laughter; **sich vor Schmerzen** *(dat)* **~** to writhe with pain.

krummnehmen *vt sep irreg (col)* **(jdm) etw ~** to take sth amiss.

Krümmung *f (von Weg, Fluß)* curve; *(Math, Med, Opt)* curvature.

Krüppel *m* - cripple. **zum ~ werden** to be crippled; **jdn zum ~ schlagen** to cripple sb.

Kruste *f* **-n** crust; *(von Schweinebraten)* crackling; *(von Braten)* crisped outside.

krustig *adj* crusty.

Kruzifix *nt* **-e** crucifix.

Kuba *nt* Cuba.
Kubaner(in *f***)** *m* - Cuban.
kubanisch *adj* Cuban.
Kübel *m* - bucket; *(für Jauche etc)* container; *(für Bäume)* tub. **es regnet (wie) aus ~n** it's bucketing down.
Kubik *nt* - *(Aut col: Hubraum)* cc.
Kubik-: **~meter** *m or nt* cubic metre *(Brit) or* meter *(US)*; **~zentimeter** *m or nt* cubic centimetre *(Brit) or* centimeter *(US)*, cc.
Kubismus *m (Art)* cubism.
Küche *f* **-n (a)** kitchen; *(klein)* kitchenette. **(b)** *(Kochkunst)* cooking, cuisine.
Kuchen *m* - cake; *(Torte auch)* gateau; *(mit Obst gedeckt)* (fruit) flan *(Brit)*, tart.
Küchen|abfälle *pl* kitchen scraps *pl*.
Kuchenblech *nt* baking sheet *or* tin.
Küchenchef *m* chef.
Kuchen-: **~form** *f* cake tin; **~gabel** *f* pastry fork.
Küchen-: **~gerät** *nt* kitchen utensil; *(kollektiv)* kitchen utensils *pl*; *(elektrisch)* kitchen appliance; **~geschirr** *nt* kitchenware *no pl*; **~herd** *m* (electric/gas) cooker; **~meister** *m* chef; **~messer** *nt* kitchen knife; **~schabe** *f (Zool)* cockroach; **~schrank** *m* (kitchen) cupboard.
Kuchenteig *m* cake mixture; *(Hefeteig)* dough.
Küchen-: **~tisch** *m* kitchen table; **~waage** *f* kitchen scales *pl*; **~zettel** *m* menu.
Kuckuck *m* **-e (a)** cuckoo. **(b)** *(col: Siegel des Gerichtsvollziehers)* bailiff's seal (for distraint of goods). **(c)** *(col)* **zum ~ (noch mal)!** hell's bells! *(col)*; **hol's der ~!** botheration! *(col)*; **geh zum ~** go to blazes *(col)*; **das weiß der ~** heaven (only) knows *(col)*.
Kuckucks-: **~ei** *nt* cuckoo's egg; **man hat uns ein ~ei untergeschoben** *(col)* we've been left holding the baby *(col)*; **~uhr** *f* cuckoo clock.
Kuddelmuddel *m or nt no pl (col)* mess.
Kufe *f* **-n** *(von Schlitten etc)* runner; *(von Flugzeug)* skid.
Kugel *f* **-n** ball; *(geometrische Figur)* sphere; *(Erd~)* sphere, globe; *(Kegel~)* bowl; *(Gewehr~)* bullet; *(für Luftgewehr)* pellet; *(Kanonen~)* (cannon)ball; *(beim ~stoßen)* shot; *(Murmel)* marble. **eine ruhige ~ schieben** *(col)* to have a cushy number *(col)*; *(aus Faulheit)* to swing the lead *(col)*; **rund wie eine ~** *(col)* like a barrel.
Kugel-: **~blitz** *m (Met)* ball-lightning; **k~förmig** *adj* spherical; **~gelenk** *nt (Anat, Tech)* ball-and-socket joint; **~hagel** *m* hail of bullets; **~kopf** *m* golf-ball; **~kopfschreibmaschine** *f* golf-ball typewriter; **~lager** *nt* ball-bearing.
kugeln 1 *vi aux sein (rollen, fallen)* to roll. **2** *vr* to roll (about). **sich (vor Lachen) ~** *(col)* to double up (laughing).
Kugel-: **k~rund** *adj* as round as a ball; *(col) Mensch* tubby *(col)*; **~schreiber** *m* ballpoint (pen), biro ®; **k~sicher** *adj* bullet-proof; **~stoßen** *nt no pl* shot-putting; **~stoßer(in** *f***)** *m* - shot-putter; **~wechsel** *m* exchange of shots.
Kuh *f* **⸚e** cow. **heilige ~** *(lit, fig)* sacred cow.
Kuh-: **~dorf** *nt (pej col)* one-horse town *(col)*; **~fladen** *m* cow-pat; **~glocke** *f* cowbell; **~handel** *m (pej col)* horse-trading *(col) no pl*; **~haut** *f* **das geht auf keine ~haut** *(col)* that's absolutely incredible; **~herde** *f* herd of cows.
kühl *adj (lit, fig)* cool; *(abweisend)* cold. **mir wird etwas ~** I'm getting rather chilly; **etw ~ lagern** to store sth in a cool place; **einen ~en Kopf bewahren** to keep a cool head, to keep one's cool *(col)*.
Kühle *f no pl (lit)* cool(ness); *(fig)* coolness; *(Abweisung)* coldness.
kühlen 1 *vt* to cool; *(auf Eis)* to chill. **2** *vi* to have a cooling effect.
Kühler *m* - *(Tech)* cooler; *(Aut)* radiator; *(col: ~haube)* bonnet *(Brit)*, hood *(US)*; *(Sekt~)* ice bucket.
Kühler-: **~figur** *f (Aut)* radiator mascot; **~haube** *f (Aut)* bonnet *(Brit)*, hood *(US)*.
Kühl-: **~fach** *nt* freezer compartment; **~haus** *nt* cold-storage depot; **~mittel** *nt (Tech)* coolant; **~raum** *m* cold storage room; **~schrank** *m* refrigerator, fridge *(Brit)*; **~tasche** *f* cold bag; **~truhe** *f* (chest) freezer, deep freeze *(Brit)*; **~turm** *m (Tech)* cooling tower.
Kühlung *f (das Kühlen)* cooling; *(Kühle)* coolness. **zur ~ des Motors** to cool the engine.
Kühlwasser *nt* radiator water, coolant.
Kuh-: **~milch** *f* cow's milk; **~mist** *m* cow dung.
kühn *adj (lit, fig)* bold. **das übertrifft meine ~sten Erwartungen** it's beyond my wildest dreams.
Kühnheit *f* boldness.
Kuh-: **~stall** *m* cow shed; **~weide** *f* pasture.
Küken *nt* - *(Huhn)* chick; *(col: Nesthäkchen)* baby of the family *(col)*.
kulant *adj* accommodating; *Bedingungen* generous.
Kulanz *f no pl siehe adj* accommodating attitude; generousness. **eine Reparatur auf ~** a free repair.
Kuli *m* **-s (a)** *(Lastträger)* coolie; *(fig)* slave. **(b)** *(col: Kugelschreiber)* ballpoint, biro ®.
kulinarisch *adj* culinary.
Kulisse *f* **-n** scenery *no pl*; *(fig: Hintergrund)* background, backdrop. **das ist alles nur ~** *(fig)* that is only a façade; **einen Blick hinter die ~n werfen** *(fig)* to have a glimpse behind the scenes.
Kulissenschieber(in *f***)** *m* - stagehand.
Kulleraugen *pl (col)* wide eyes *pl*.
kullern *vti (vi: aux sein) (col)* to roll.
Kult *m* **-e** cult; *(Verehrung)* worship. **einen ~ mit jdm/etw treiben** to make a cult out of sb/sth.
Kult-: **~figur** *f* cult figure; **~film** *m* cult film; **~handlung** *f* ritual(istic) act.
kultisch *adj* ritual(istic).
kultivieren* [kʊlti'viːrən] *vt (lit, fig)* to cultivate.
kultiviert *adj Mensch* cultured, refined; *Geschmack, Unterhaltung* cultivated. **wenn Sie ~ reisen wollen** if you want to travel in style; **Kerzen beim Essen, das ist sehr ~** meals by candlelight, very civilized.
Kultivierung [kʊlti'viːrʊŋ] *f (lit, fig)* cultivation.
Kultstätte *f* place of worship.
Kultur *f* **(a)** *(no pl: Kunst und Wissenschaft)* culture. **er hat keine ~** he is uncultured. **(b)** *(Lebensform)* civilization. **dort leben verschiedene ~en harmonisch zusammen** different cultures live harmoniously together there. **(c)** *(Bakterien~, Pilz~ etc)* culture; *(Bestand angebauter Pflanzen)* plantation.
Kultur-: **~austausch** *m* cultural exchange; **~banause** *m (col)* philistine; **~beutel** *m* toilet bag *(Brit)*, washbag.
kulturell *adj* cultural.
Kultur-: **~film** *m* documentary film; **~geschichte** *f* history of civilization; **~kreis** *m* culture group; **~leben** *nt* cultural life; **k~los** *adj* uncultured; **~losigkeit** *f* lack of culture; **~pessimismus** *m* despair of civilization; **~politik** *f* cultural and educational policy; **~revolution** *f* cultural revolution; **~stätte** *f* place of cultural interest; **~stufe** *f* level of civilization; **~teil** *m (von Zeitung)* arts section; **~volk** *nt* civilized nation.
Kultus-: **~minister** *m* minister of education and the arts; **~ministerium** *nt* ministry of education and the arts.
Kümmel *m* **- (a)** *no pl (Gewürz)* caraway (seed). **(b)** *(col: Schnaps)* kümmel.
Kummer *m no pl (Betrübtheit)* grief, sorrow; *(Unannehmlichkeit)* trouble. **hast du ~?** have you got problems?; **aus** *or* **vor ~ sterben** to die of grief; **vor ~ vergehen** to be pining away with sorrow; **er fand vor ~ keinen Schlaf mehr** he was so griefstricken that he could no longer sleep; **wir**

sind (an) ~ gewöhnt *(col)* we're used to that sort of thing.

kümmerlich *adj* **(a)** *(karg, armselig)* wretched, miserable; *Lohn, Rente auch* paltry; *Mahlzeit auch* meagre *(Brit)*, meager *(US)*. **(b)** *(schwächlich)* puny.

kümmern 1 *vt* to concern. **was kümmert Sie das?** what business is that of yours?; **was kümmert mich das?** what's that to me? **2** *vr* **sich um jdn/etw ~** to look after sb/sth; **sich darum ~, daß ...** to see to it that ...; **kümmere dich gefälligst um deine eigenen Angelegenheiten!** mind your own business!; **er kümmert sich nicht darum, was die Leute denken** he doesn't care what people think.

Kumpan(in *f***)** *m* **-e** *(dated col)* mate *(Brit col)*, buddy *(esp US col)*.

Kumpel *m* **-** *or (col)* **-s (a)** *(Min: Bergmann)* miner. **(b)** *(col: Kollege, Freund)* mate *(Brit col)*, buddy *(esp US col)*.

kündbar *adj Vertrag* terminable; *Anleihe* redeemable. **Beamte sind nicht ohne weiteres ~** civil servants cannot be dismissed without good cause.

Kündbarkeit *f (von Vertrag)* terminability; *(von Anleihe)* redeemability.

Kunde[1] *f no pl (geh)* news *sing*, tidings *pl (old)*.

Kunde[2] *m (wk)* **-n, -n** *(auch pej col)* customer.

künden *vi (geh)* **von etw ~** to tell of sth.

Kunden-: ~dienst *m* customer service; **~fang** *m (pej)* **auf ~fang sein** to be touting for customers; **ein Vertreter auf ~fang** a salesman chasing up some business; **~kreis** *m* customers *pl*, clientèle; **~werbung** *f* publicity (aimed at attracting custom *or* customers).

kundgeben *vt sep irreg (dated)* **etw ~** to announce sth *(jdm* to sb*)*; *Gefühle etc* to express sth.

Kundgebung *f (Versammlung)* rally.

kundig *adj (geh)* knowledgeable; *(sach~)* expert. **einer Sache** *(gen)* **~ sein** to have a knowledge of sth.

kündigen 1 *vt Stellung* to hand in one's notice for; *Abonnement, Mitgliedschaft* to cancel; *Vertrag* to terminate; *Tarife* to discontinue; *(col) jdn* to dismiss. **jdm die Wohnung ~** to give sb notice to quit his flat; **ich habe meine Wohnung gekündigt** I've given in notice that I'm leaving my flat; **die Stellung ~** to hand in one's notice; **jdm die Stellung ~** to give sb his/her notice; **sie hat ihm die Freundschaft gekündigt** she has broken off their friendship. **2** *vi (Arbeitnehmer)* to give in one's notice; *(Mieter)* to give notice. **jdm ~** *(Arbeitgeber)* to give sb his notice; *(Vermieter)* to give sb notice to quit; **zum 1. April ~** to give one's notice for April 1st; *(Mieter)* to give notice for April 1st; *(bei Mitgliedschaft)* to cancel one's membership as of April 1st.

Kündigung *f* **(a)** *(Mitteilung) (von Vermieter)* notice to quit; *(von Mieter, von Stellung)* notice; *(von Vertrag)* termination. **(b)** *(das Kündigen) (von Arbeitgeber)* dismissal; *(von Arbeitnehmer)* giving in one's notice; *(von Vertrag)* termination; *(von Mitgliedschaft, Abonnement)* cancellation.

Kündigungs-: ~frist *f* period of notice; **vierteljährliche ~frist haben** to have (to give) three months' notice; **~grund** *m* grounds *pl* for giving notice; *(von Arbeitgeber auch)* grounds *pl* for dismissal; **~schutz** *m* protection against wrongful dismissal.

Kundin *f* customer.

Kundschaft *f* customers *pl*.

Kundschafter *m* **-** spy; *(Mil)* scout.

kundtun *vt sep irreg (geh)* to make known.

künftig 1 *adj* future. **2** *adv* in future.

Kunst *f* **¨-e (a)** art. **die schönen ~̈e** fine art *sing*, the fine arts. **(b)** *(Können, Fertigkeit)* art, skill; *(Kunststück)* trick. **mit seiner ~ am Ende sein** to be at one's wits' end; **ärztliche ~** medical skill; **das ist keine ~!** it's like taking candy from a baby *(col)*; *(ein Kinderspiel)* it's a piece of cake *(col)*; **das ist eine brotlose ~** there's no money in that; **was macht die ~?** *(col)* how's tricks? *(col)*.

Kunst- *in cpds (Art)* art; *(künstlich)* artificial; **~akademie** *f* college of art; **~ausstellung** *f* art exhibition; **~banause** *m (pej)* philistine; **~druck** *m* art print; **~druckpapier** *nt* art paper; **~dünger** *m* artificial fertilizer; **~erzieher** *m* art teacher; **~erziehung** *f (Sch)* art; **~faser** *f* man-made fibre *(Brit) or* fiber *(US)*; **~fehler** *m* professional error; *(weniger ernst)* slip; **k~fertig** *adj (geh)* skilful *(Brit)*, skillful *(US)*; **~fertigkeit** *f* skill; **~flieger** *m* stunt flyer; **~flug** *m* aerobatics *sing*; **k~gerecht** *adj (fachmännisch)* skilful *(Brit)*, skillful *(US)*; **~geschichte** *f* history of art, art history; **~gewerbe** *nt* arts and crafts *pl*; **~gewerbler(in** *f***)** *m* **-** craftsman/-woman; **k~gewerblich** *adj* **k~gewerbliche Gegenstände** craft objects; **~griff** *m* trick, dodge *(col)*; **~handel** *m* art trade; **~händler** *m* art dealer; **~hochschule** *f* art college; **~kenner** *m* art connoisseur; **~kritik** *f no pl* art criticism; *(die Kritiker)* art critics *pl*; *(Rezension)* art review; **~kritiker** *m* art critic.

Künstler(in *f***)** *m* **- (a)** artist; *(Unterhaltungs~)* artiste. **bildender ~** visual artist. **(b)** *(Könner)* genius *(in +dat* at*)*.

künstlerisch *adj* artistic.

Künstler-: ~name *m* pseudonym; *(von Schriftsteller auch)* pen name; *(von Schauspieler auch)* stage name; **~pech** *nt (col)* hard luck.

künstlich *adj* artificial; *Zähne, Wimpern, Fingernägel* false; *Faserstoffe* synthetic; *Diamanten* imitation, fake *(col)*. **jdn ~ ernähren** *(Med)* to feed sb artificially; **sich ~ aufregen** *(col)* to get all worked up about nothing *(col)*; **sich ~ dumm stellen** to pretend to be stupid.

Kunst-: k~los *adj* unsophisticated; **~maler** *m* artist, painter; **~pause** *f* pause for effect; *(iro)* awkward pause; **~sammlung** *f* art collection; **~schätze** *pl* art treasures *pl*; **~seide** *f* artificial silk; **~springen** *nt* diving; **~stoff** *m* man-made material; **~stück** *nt* trick; **~stück!** *(iro)* no wonder!; **das ist kein ~stück** *(fig)* there's nothing to it; **~turnen** *nt* gymnastics *sing*; **~verstand** *m* appreciation of art; **k~voll** *adj* artistic; **~werk** *nt* work of art.

kunterbunt *adj Sammlung, Gruppe etc* motley *attr*; *(vielfarbig auch)* multi-coloured *(Brit)*, multicolored *(US)*; *Programm* varied. **~ durcheinander** higgledy-piggledy *(col)*.

Kupfer *nt no pl* copper.

Kupfergeld *nt* coppers *pl*, copper coins *pl*.

kupfern *adj* copper.

Kupfer-: k~rot *adj* copper-coloured *(Brit)*, copper-colored *(US)*; **~stecher** *m* **-** copper(plate) engraver; **~stich** *m* copperplate (engraving *or* etching).

kupieren* *vt Schwanz, Ohren* to dock.

Kupon [ku'põː] *m* **-s** coupon.

Kuppe *f* **-n** *(Berg~)* (rounded) hilltop; *(Finger~)* tip.

Kuppel *f* **-n** dome, cupola.

Kuppeldach *nt* dome-shaped roof.

Kuppelei *f (Jur)* procuring.

kuppeln 1 *vt (Tech)* to couple; *(fig auch)* to link. **2** *vi (Aut)* to operate the clutch.

Kuppler(in *f***)** *m* **-** *(Jur)* procurer/procuress.

Kupplung *f (Tech)* coupling; *(Aut etc)* clutch. **die ~ (durch)treten** to disengage the clutch; **die ~ kommen lassen** *(Aut)* to let the clutch in.

Kupplungs- *in cpds (Aut)* clutch; **~pedal** *nt* clutch pedal.

Kur *f* **-en** *(in Badeort)* (health) cure; *(Haar~ etc)* treatment *no pl*; *(Schlankheits~, Diät~)* diet. **zur ~ fahren** to go to a health resort; **eine ~ machen** to take a cure; *(Schlankheits~)* to diet; **jdn zur ~**

schicken to send sb to a health resort.
Kür *f* **-en (a)** *(Sport)* free section. **eine ~ laufen** to do the free skating. **(b)** *(old: Wahl)* election.
Kuratorium *nt (Vereinigung)* committee.
Kurbel *f* **-n** crank.
kurbeln *vti* to turn, to wind.
Kurbelwelle *f* crankshaft.
Kürbis *m* **-se** pumpkin; *(col: Kopf)* nut *(col)*.
küren *vt (old, geh)* to choose, to elect *(zu* as*)*.
Kurgast *m* patient at a health resort.
Kurier *m* **-e** courier, messenger.
kurieren* *vt (lit, fig)* to cure *(von* of*)*. **von ihm bin ich kuriert** I've gone right off him.
kurios *adj (merkwürdig)* curious, strange, odd.
Kuriosität *f* **(a)** *(Gegenstand)* curio(sity). **(b)** *(Eigenart)* peculiarity.
Kurkonzert *nt* concert (at a health resort).
Kürlauf(en *nt)* *m* free skating.
Kur-: ~ort *m* health resort, spa; **~pfuscher** *m (pej col)* quack (doctor); **~pfuscherei** *f (pej col)* quackery.
Kurs *m* **-e (a)** *(Naut, Aviat, fig)* course; *(Pol, Richtung auch)* line. **harter/weicher ~** *(Pol)* hard/soft line; **den ~ ändern/beibehalten** *(lit, fig)* to alter/hold (one's) course; **~ nehmen auf** *(+acc)* to set course for; **~ haben auf** *(+acc)* to be heading for. **(b)** *(Fin: Wechsel~)* exchange rate; *(Aktien~)* (going) rate; *(Marktpreis)* market value. **zum ~ von** at the rate of; **hoch im ~ stehen** *(Aktien)* to be high; *(fig)* to be popular *(bei* with*)*. **(c)** *(Lehrgang)* course *(in +dat, für* in*)*. **einen ~ besuchen** *or* **mitmachen** to attend a class.
Kurs-: ~änderung *f (lit, fig)* change of course; **~buch** *nt (Rail)* timetable *(Brit)*, schedule *(US)*.
Kürschner(in *f)* *m* **-** furrier.
kursieren* *vi aux haben or sein* to be in circulation; *(fig)* to circulate.
kursiv *adj* italic. **etw ~ drucken** to italicize sth.
Kursivschrift *f* italics *pl*.
Kurskorrektur *f (lit, fig)* course correction.
Kursus *m, pl* **Kurse** *(geh: Lehrgang)* course.
Kurs-: ~wagen *m (Rail)* through car; **~wert** *m (Fin)* market value.
Kurve ['kʊrvə] *f* **-n** *(Math, col: Körperrundung)* curve; *(Biegung, Straßen~ auch)* bend; *(an Kreuzung)* corner; *(statistisch, Fieber~ etc)* graph. **die Straße macht eine ~** the road bends; **die ~ kratzen** *(col: schnell weggehen)* to make tracks *(col)*; **die ~ nicht kriegen** *(col)* not to get around to it.
kurven ['kʊrvn] *vi aux sein (col) (Aviat)* to circle. **durch Italien ~** to drive around Italy.
kurvenreich *adj Straße* winding; *(col) Frau* curvaceous, shapely. **„~e Strecke"** "bends".
kurz *comp* **⸚er**, *superl* **⸚ste(r, s)** *or (adv)* **am ⸚esten 1** *adj* short; *Zeit, Aufenthalt, Bericht, Antwort etc auch* brief; *Blick, Folge* quick; *Gedächtnis auch* short-lived. **etw ⸚er machen** to shorten sth; **mach's ~!** make it quick; **den ⸚eren ziehen** *(fig col)* to get the worst of it; **mit ein paar ~en Worten** in a few brief words; **ein ⸚erer Weg** a quicker way; **in ⸚ester Frist** before very long.
2 *adv* **(a) ~ atmen** to take short breaths; **eine Sache ~ abtun** to dismiss sth out of hand; **zu ~ kommen** to get a raw deal *(col)*; **~ entschlossen** without a moment's hesitation; **~ gesagt** in a word; **sich ~ fassen** to be brief; **~ und bündig** concisely; **~ und gut** in short; **~ und schmerzlos** *(col)* short and sweet; **jdn/etw ~ und klein schagen** to beat sb up/to smash sth to pieces.
(b) *(für eine ~e Zeit)* briefly. **ich habe ihn nur ~ gesehen** I only saw him briefly; **ich bleibe nur ~** I'll only stay for a short while; **darf ich mal ~ stören?** could I just interrupt for a moment?
(c) *(zeitlich, räumlich: nicht lang)* shortly, just. **~ vor Köln/Ostern** shortly *or* just before Cologne/Easter; **er hat den Wagen erst seit ~em** he's only had the car for a short while; **seit ~em gibt es Bier in der Kantine** since recently there's been beer in the canteen; **über ~ oder lang** sooner or later; **(bis) vor ~em** (until) recently; **~ nacheinander** shortly after each other.
Kurz-: ~arbeit *f* short time; **k~arbeiten** *vi sep* to be on short time; **k~ärm(e)lig** *adj* short-sleeved; **k~atmig** *adj (fig)* feeble, lame; *(Med)* short-winded.
Kürze *f no pl* shortness; *(von Besuch, Bericht etc auch)* brevity; *(fig: Bündigkeit)* conciseness; **in ~** shortly; **in aller ~** very briefly; **in der ~ liegt die Würze** *(Prov)* brevity is the soul of wit *(prov)*.
kürzen *vt* to shorten; *(Math) Bruch* to cancel (down); *Gehalt, Etat, Produktion* to cut (back). **jdm das Gehalt** *etc* **~** to cut back sb's salary *etc*.
Kurze(r) *m decl as adj (col)* **(a)** *(Schnaps)* short. **(b)** *(Kurzschluß)* short(-circuit).
kurzerhand *adv* without further ado; *entlassen* on the spot.
Kurz-: ~fassung *f* abridged version; **k~fristig 1** *adj* short-term; *Wettervorhersage* short-range; **2** *adv (auf kurze Sicht)* for the short term; *(für kurze Zeit)* for a short time; **k~fristig seine Pläne ändern** to change one's plans at short notice; **k~gefaßt** *adj* concise; **~geschichte** *f* short story; **k~haarig** *adj* short-haired; **k~halten** *vt sep irreg* **jdn k~halten** to keep sb short; **k~lebig** *adj* short-lived, ephemeral.
kürzlich *adv* recently, lately. **erst ~** just recently.
Kurz-: ~meldung *f* news flash; **~nachrichten** *pl* news headlines *pl*; *(in Zeitung auch)* news in brief; **~schluß** *m* **(a)** short-circuit; **(b)** *(fig: auch* **~schlußhandlung***)* rash action; **~schrift** *f* shorthand; **k~sichtig** *adj (lit, fig)* short-sighted; **~sichtigkeit** *f (lit, fig)* short-sightedness; **~streckenläufer** *m (Sport)* sprinter; **k~treten** *vi sep irreg (fig col)* to go easy; **k~um** *adv* in a word.
Kürzung *f* shortening; *(eines Buchs)* abridgement; *(von Gehältern, der Produktion)* cut *(gen* in*)*.
Kurz-: ~urlaub *m* short holiday *(Brit) or* vacation *(US)*; *(Mil)* short leave; **~waren** *pl* haberdashery *(Brit)*, notions *pl (US)*; **k~weilig** *adj* entertaining; **~welle** *f (Rad)* short wave.
kuschelig *adj (col)* cosy, snug.
kuscheln *vr* **sich an jdn ~** to snuggle up to sb; **sich in etw** *(acc)* **~** to snuggle up in sth.
kuschen *vir (Hund etc)* to get down; *(fig)* to knuckle under.
Kusine *f* (female) cousin.
Kuß *m* **⸚sse** kiss.
Küßchen *nt* peck *(col)*. **gib ~** give us a kiss.
küssen 1 *vti* to kiss. **jdm die Hand ~** to kiss sb's hand. **2** *vr* to kiss (each other).
Kuß-: ~hand *f* **jdm eine ~hand zuwerfen** to blow sb a kiss; **jdn/etw mit ~hand nehmen** *(col)* to be only too glad to take sb/sth.
Küste *f* **-n** coast; *(Ufer)* shore.
Küsten- *in cpds* coastal; **~fischerei** *f* inshore fishing; **~gebiet** *nt* coastal area; **~gewässer** *pl* coastal waters *pl*; **~schiffahrt** *f* coastal shipping; **~wacht** *f* coastguard.
Küster *m* **-** verger, sexton.
Kutsche *f* **-n** coach, carriage; *(col: Auto)* jalopy *(col)*.
Kutscher *m* **-** coachman, driver.
kutschieren* **1** *vi aux sein* to drive, to ride. **durch die Gegend ~** *(col)* to drive around. **2** *vt* to drive.
Kutte *f* **-n** habit.
Kutter *m* **-** *(Naut)* cutter.
Kuvert [ku'veːɐ, ku'vɛːɐ] *nt* **-s** *(Brief~)* envelope.
Kuvertüre [kuvɛr'tyːrə] *f* **-n** *(Cook)* (chocolate) coating.
kW = Kilowatt.
Kybernetik *f* cybernetics *sing*.
kyrillisch *adj* Cyrillic.
KZ [kaː'tsɛt] *nt* **-s** concentration camp.

L

L, l [ɛl] *nt* **-, -** L, l.
l = Liter.
labb(e)rig *adj (col) Bier, Suppe* watery; *Kaffee, Tee auch* weak; *Essen* mushy.
laben *vr (liter)* to feast (oneself) *(an +dat* on*)*; *(an Quelle etc)* to refresh oneself *(mit, an +dat* with*)*.
labern *(col)* **1** *vi* to prattle (on) *(col)*. **2** *vt* to talk. **was laberst du denn da?** what are you prattling on about? *(col)*.
labil *adj (physisch) Gesundheit* delicate; *Kreislauf* poor; *Patient* frail; *(psychisch)* weak.
Labor *nt* **-s** *or* **-e** laboratory, lab *(col)*.
Laborant(in *f)* *m* lab(oratory) technician.
Laboratorium *nt* laboratory.
laborieren* *vi* to labour *(Brit)*, to labor *(US)* *(an +dat* at*)*; *(leiden)* to be plagued *(an +dat* by*)*.
Labyrinth *nt* **-e** labyrinth; *(fig auch)* maze.
Lach|anfall *m* laughing fit.
Lache[1] ['laxə, 'la:xə] *f* **-n** puddle; *(von Benzin, Blut auch)* pool.
Lache[2] *f* **-n** *(col)* laugh.
lächeln *vi* to smile. **verlegen/freundlich ~** to give an embarrassed/a friendly smile.
Lächeln *nt no pl* smile.
lachen 1 *vi* to laugh *(über +acc* at*)*. **jdn zum L~ bringen** to make sb laugh; **zum L~ sein** *(lustig)* to be hilarious; *(lächerlich)* to be laughable; **mir ist nicht zum L~ (zumute)** I'm in no laughing mood; **daß ich nicht lache!** *(col)* don't make me laugh! *(col)*; **da kann ich doch nur ~** I can't help laughing (at that); **du hast gut ~!** it's all right for you to laugh!; **gezwungen/verlegen ~** to give a forced/an embarrassed laugh; **wer zuletzt lacht, lacht am besten** *(Prov)* he who laughs last, laughs longest *(Prov)*; **die Sonne lacht** the sun is shining brightly; **ihm lachte das Glück** Fortune smiled on him.

2 *vt* **da gibt es gar nichts zu ~** that's nothing to laugh about; *(es ist etwas Ernstes auch)* that's not funny; **er hat bei seiner Frau nichts zu ~** *(col)* he has a hard time of it with his wife; **das wäre doch gelacht, wenn ...** it would be ridiculous if ...; **das wäre doch gelacht!** that's dead easy *(col)*; **sich schief ~** *(col)* to split one's sides (laughing) *(col)*.
Lachen *nt no pl* laughter, laughing; *(Art des ~s)* laugh. **dir wird das ~ schon noch vergehen!** you'll soon be laughing on the other side of your face.
Lacher *m* **- die ~ auf seiner Seite haben** to have the last laugh; *(einen Lacherfolg verbuchen)* to get a laugh.
Lach|erfolg *m* **ein ~ sein, einen ~ erzielen** to make everybody laugh.
lächerlich *adj* **(a)** ridiculous, absurd. **jdn/etw ~ machen** to make sb/sth look silly *(vor jdm* in front of sb*)*; **jdn/sich ~ machen** to make a fool of sb/oneself *(vor jdm* in front of sb*)*; **etw ins L~e ziehen** to make fun of sth. **(b)** *(geringfügig) Anlaß* trivial, petty.
Lächerlichkeit *f* **(a)** *no pl* ridiculousness; *(von Argument etc auch)* absurdity. **jdn der ~ preisgeben** to make a laughing stock of sb. **(b)** *(Geringfügigkeit)* triviality.
Lach-: ~gas *nt* laughing gas; **l~haft** *adj* ludicrous; *Argument auch* laughable; **~krampf** *m* **einen ~krampf bekommen** to go into fits of laughter.
Lachs [laks] *m* **-e** salmon.
Lachsalve *f* burst *or* roar of laughter.
Lachs-: l~farben *adj* salmon pink; **~forelle** *f* salmon *or* sea trout; **~schinken** *m smoked, rolled fillet of ham.*
Lack *m* **-e** *(Holz~, Nagel~)* varnish; *(Auto~)* paint.
Lack-: ~affe *m (pej col)* flash Harry *(col)*; **~farbe** *f* gloss paint.
lackieren* *vt Holz* to varnish; *Fingernägel auch* to paint; *Auto* to spray.
Lackierung *f* **(a)** *(das Lackieren) (von Autos)* spraying; *(von Möbeln)* varnishing. **(b)** *(der Lack) (von Auto)* paintwork; *(Holz~)* varnish.
Lackmuspapier *nt* litmus paper.
Lack-: ~schaden *m* damage to paintwork; **~schuh** *m* patent-leather shoe.
Lade *f* **-n** chest; *(col: Schub~)* drawer.
Lade-: ~bühne *f* loading ramp; **~fläche** *f* load area; **~hemmung** *f* **das Gewehr hat ~hemmung** the gun is jammed.
laden[1] *pret* **lud,** *ptp* **geladen** *vti* to load; *(Phys)* to charge. **das Schiff hat Autos geladen** the ship has a cargo of cars; **der Lkw hat zuviel geladen** the lorry is overloaded; **Verantwortung/Schulden auf sich** *(acc)* **~** to saddle oneself with responsibility/debts; **eine schwere Schuld auf sich** *(acc)* **~** to place oneself under a heavy burden of guilt; **er hatte schon ganz schön geladen** *(col)* he was already pretty tanked up *(col)*; **mit Spannung geladen** charged with tension; *siehe* **geladen.**
laden[2] *pret* **lud,** *ptp* **geladen** *vt (liter: einladen)* to invite; *(form: vor Gericht)* to summon. **nur für geladene Gäste** by invitation only.
Laden[1] *m* **¨** shop *(esp Brit)*, store *(US)*; *(col: Betrieb)* outfit *(col)*. **der ~ läuft** *(col)* business is good.
Laden[2] *m* **¨** *or* **-** *(Fenster~)* shutter.
Laden-: ~besitzer *m* shopowner *(esp Brit)*, shopkeeper *(esp Brit)*, storekeeper *(US)*; **~dieb** *m* shoplifter; **~diebstahl** *m* shoplifting; **~hüter** *m* non-seller; **~kasse** *f* till; **~kette** *f* chain of shops *or* stores; **~preis** *m* shop price; **~schluß** *m* **nach/vor ~schluß** after/before the shops *(esp Brit) or* stores *(US)* shut; **um fünf Uhr ist ~schluß** the shops/stores shut at five o'clock; **~tisch** *m* shop counter; **über den/unter dem ~tisch** over/under the counter.
Lade-: ~rampe *f* loading ramp; **~raum** *m* load room; *(Aviat, Naut)* hold.
lädieren* *vt* to damage. **lädiert sein** *(hum)***/aussehen** *(hum)* to be/look the worse for wear.
Ladung *f* **(a)** load; *(von Sprengstoff)* charge. **eine geballte ~ Schnee/Dreck** *(col)* a whole lot of snow/mud; **eine geballte ~ von Schimpfwörtern** a whole torrent of abuse. **(b)** *(Vorladung)* summons *sing*.
Lafette *f (Mil)* (gun)carriage.
lag *pret of* **liegen.**
Lage *f* **-n (a)** *(geographische ~)* situation, location. **in günstiger ~** well-situated; **eine gute/ruhige ~ haben** to be in a good/peaceful location. **(b)** *(Art des Liegens)* position. **(c)** *(Situation)* situation. **dazu bin ich nicht in der ~** I'm not in a position to

do that; **in der glücklichen ~ sein, etw zu tun** to be in the happy position of doing sth; **Herr der ~ sein** to be in control of the situation; **die ~ der Dinge erfordert es, daß ...** the situation requires that ... **(d)** *(Schicht)* layer. **(e)** *(Mus) (Stimm~)* register; *(Ton~)* pitch. **(f)** *(Runde)* round. **eine ~ schmeißen** *(col)* to stand a round.

Lage-: **~bericht** *m* report; *(Mil)* situation report; **~plan** *m* ground plan.

Lager *nt* - **(a)** *(Unterkunft)* camp; *(liter: Schlafstätte)* bed. **(b)** *(fig: Partei)* camp; *(von Staaten)* bloc. **ins andere ~ überwechseln** to change camps. **(c)** *pl auch* ¨ *(Vorratsraum)* store(room); *(von Laden)* stockroom; *(~halle)* warehouse; *(Vorrat)* stock. **etw auf ~ haben** to have sth in stock; *(fig) Witz etc* to have sth at the ready. **(d)** *(Tech)* bearing. **(e)** *(Geol)* bed.

Lager-: **~bestand** *m* stock; **~feuer** *nt* campfire; **~halle** *f*, **~haus** *nt* warehouse.

Lagerist(in *f*) *m* storeman/storewoman.

lagern **1** *vt* **(a)** *(aufbewahren)* to store. **kühl ~!** store in a cool place. **(b)** *(hinlegen) jdn* to lay down; *Bein etc* to rest. **einen Kranken weich ~** to lay an invalid on something soft; **das Bein hoch ~** to put one's leg up; *siehe* **gelagert. 2** *vi* **(a)** *(Lebensmittel etc)* to be stored. **(b)** *(liegen)* to lie. **(c)** *(von Truppen)* to camp, to be encamped.

Lager-: **~raum** *m* storeroom; *(in Geschäft)* stockroom; **~stätte** *f* **(a)** *(old liter)* bed, couch *(liter)*; **(b)** *(Geol)* deposit.

Lagerung *f* storage; *(das Lagern auch)* storing.

Lagune *f* **-n** lagoon.

lahm *adj* **(a)** *(gelähmt) Bein, Mensch* lame; *(col: steif)* stiff. **er hat ein ~es Bein** he is lame in one leg. **(b)** *(col: langsam, langweilig)* dreary, dull; *Geschäftsgang* slow, sluggish. **eine ~e Ente sein** *(col)* to have no zip *(col)*.

lähmen *vt* to paralyze; *(fig) Industrie auch* to cripple; *Verhandlungen, Verkehr* to hold up. **er ist an beiden Beinen gelähmt** he is paralyzed in both legs; **vor Angst wie gelähmt sein** to be petrified.

lahmlegen *vt sep Verkehr, Produktion* to bring to a standstill; *Industrie auch* to paralyze.

Lähmung *f (lit)* paralysis; *(fig)* immobilization.

Laib *m* **-e** loaf.

laichen *vi* to spawn.

Laie *m (wk)* **-n, -n** layman; *(fig also, Theat)* amateur. **die ~n** *(Eccl)* the laity.

Laien-: **l~haft** *adj Arbeit* amateurish; *Urteil, Meinung* lay *attr only;* **~prediger** *m* lay preacher; **~theater** *nt* amateur theatre *(Brit) or* theater *(US)*; *(Ensemble)* amateur theatre *(Brit) or* theater *(US)* group.

Lakai *m (wk)* **-en, -en** *(lit, fig)* lackey.

Lake *f* **-n** brine.

Laken *nt* - sheet.

lakonisch *adj* laconic.

Lakritz *m* **-e** *(dial)*, **Lakritze** *f* **-n** liquorice *(Brit)*, licorice *(US)*.

lala *adv (col)*: **so ~** so-so *(col)*, not too bad *(col)*.

lallen *vti* to babble; *(Betrunkener)* to mumble.

Lama *nt* **-s** llama.

Lamelle *f* **(a)** *(Biol)* lamella. **(b)** *(von Jalousien)* slat; *(von Heizkörper)* rib.

lamentieren* *vi* to moan, to complain.

Lametta *nt no pl* lametta.

Lamm *nt* ¨**er** lamb.

Lamm-: **~braten** *m* roast lamb; **~fell** *nt* lambskin; **~fleisch** *nt* lamb; **l~fromm** *adj Gesicht, Miene* innocent; **l~fromm sein** to be like a (little) lamb; **~wolle** *f* lambswool.

Lampe *f* **-n** light; *(Öl~, Steh~, Tisch~)* lamp; *(Glüh~)* bulb.

Lampen-: **~fieber** *nt* stage fright; **~schirm** *m* lampshade.

Lampion [lam'piõː, lam'piɔŋ] *m* **-s** Chinese lantern.

lancieren* [lã'siːrən] *vt Produkt, Künstler* to launch; *Nachricht* to put out.

Land *nt* ¨**er** **(a)** *(Gelände, Festland)* land. **ein Stück ~** a plot of land; **~ bestellen/bebauen** to till the soil/to cultivate the land; **an ~ gehen/schwimmen** to go/swim ashore; **~ sehen** *(lit)* to sight land; **endlich sehe ich ~** *(fig)* at last I can see the light at the end of the tunnel; **etw an ~ ziehen** to pull sth ashore; **einen Auftrag an ~ ziehen** *(col)* to land an order; **~ in Sicht!** land ahoy!; **~ unter!** land submerged!

(b) *(ländliches Gebiet)* country. **auf dem ~(e)** in the country.

(c) *(Staat)* country, land *(esp liter)*; *(Bundes~) (in BRD)* Land, state; *(in Österreich)* province. **das ~ Hessen/Tirol** the state of Hesse/the province of Tyrol; **außer ~es sein** to be out of the country; **~ und Leute kennenlernen** to get to know the country and its inhabitants; **aus aller Herren ~er** from all over the world.

Land-: **~adel** *m* landed gentry; **~arbeit** *f* agricultural work; **l~auf** *adv:* **l~auf, l~ab** the length and breadth of the country; **~besitzer** *m* landowner; **~bevölkerung** *f* rural population.

Lande-: **~bahn** *f* landing strip; **~erlaubnis** *f* landing permission; **~fähre** *f (Space)* landing module.

landeinwärts *adv* inland.

landen *vti (vi: aux sein)* to land. **weich ~** to make a soft landing; **im Gefängnis ~** to land (up) in prison; **mit deinen Komplimenten kannst du bei mir nicht ~** your compliments won't get you anywhere with me.

Ländereien *pl* estates *pl*.

Länderspiel *nt* international (match).

Landes-: **~grenze** *f (von Staat)* national boundary; *(von Bundesland)* state/provincial boundary; **~hauptstadt** *f* capital of the Land/province; **~innere(s)** *nt* interior; **~kunde** *f* regional studies *pl*; **l~kundig** *adj* **l~kundiger Reiseleiter** courier who knows the country; **l~kundlich** *adj Themen, Aspekte* regional; **~meister** *m (Sport)* regional champion; **~regierung** *f* government of a Land/ provincial government; **~sprache** *f* national language; **der ~sprache unkundig sein** not to know the language; **~teil** *m* region, area; **~tracht** *f* national dress *or* costume; **l~üblich** *adj* customary; **das ist dort l~üblich** that's the custom there; **~verrat** *m* treason; **~verteidigung** *f* national defence *(Brit) or* defense *(US)*.

Landeverbot *nt* refusal of landing permission; **~ erhalten** to be refused landing permission.

Land-: **~flucht** *f* emigration to the cities; **~friedensbruch** *m (Jur)* breach of the peace; **~funk** *m* farming (radio) programme *(Brit) or* program *(US)*; **~gericht** *nt* district court; **~gut** *nt* estate; **~haus** *nt* country house; **~heer** *nt* army; **~jäger** *m (Wurst) pressed smoked sausage;* **~karte** *f* map; **~klima** *nt* continental climate; **~kreis** *m* administrative district; **~krieg** *m* land warfare; **l~läufig** *adj* popular, common; **entgegen der l~läufigen Meinung** contrary to popular opinion; **~leben** *nt* country life.

ländlich *adj* rural; *Tracht* country *attr*; *Tanz* country *attr*, folk *attr*; *Idylle* pastoral.

Land-: **~luft** *f* country air; **~macht** *f* land power; **~plage** *f* plague; *(fig col)* pest; **~ratte** *f (hum)* landlubber; **~regen** *m* steady rain.

Landschaft *f* scenery *no pl*; *(einer bestimmten Gegend auch)* landscape; *(ländliche Gegend)* countryside. **eine öde ~** a barren landscape; **die ~ um London** the countryside around London; **die ~en Italiens** the types of countryside in Italy; **wir sahen eine reizvolle ~** we saw some delightful scenery; **in der ~ herumstehen** *(col)* to stand around; **die politische ~** the political scene.

landschaftlich *adj Schönheiten etc* scenic; *Besonderheiten* regional. **diese Gegend ist ~ ausgesprochen reizvoll** the scenery in this area is particularly delightful; **das ist ~ unterschiedlich** it differs from one part of the country to another.

Landsitz *m* country seat.

Lands-: ~mann *m*, **~männin** *f*, *pl* **~leute** fellow countryman/-woman.

Land-: ~straße *f* country road; *(Straße zweiter Ordnung)* secondary *or* B *(Brit)* road; **~streicher(in** *f*) *m* - *(pej)* tramp, hobo *(US)*; **~streitkräfte** *pl* land forces *pl*; **~strich** *m* area; **ein flacher ~strich** a flat belt of land; **~tag** *m* Landtag *(state parliament)*.

Landung *f (von Flugzeug, Truppen etc)* landing. **zur ~ gezwungen werden** to be forced down.

Landungs-: ~boot *nt* landing craft; **~brücke** *f* jetty, landing stage; **~steg** *m* landing stage *(Brit)*, jetty.

Land-: ~urlaub *m* shore leave; **~vermesser** *m* land surveyor; **~vermessung** *f* land surveying; **~wein** *m* table wine, vin ordinaire; **~wirt** *m* farmer.

Landwirtschaft *f* agriculture, farming; *(Betrieb)* farm. **~ betreiben** to farm.

landwirtschaftlich *adj* agricultural.

Landwirtschafts- *in cpds* agricultural; **~ministerium** *nt* ministry of agriculture.

Landzunge *f* spit (of land), promontory.

lang *comp* **¨er,** *superl* **¨ste(r, s)** *or (adv)* **am ¨sten 1** *adj* **(a)** long; *Film, Roman, Aufenthalt, Rede auch* lengthy. **das war seit ~em geplant** that was planned a long time ago; **ich habe seit ~em nichts von ihm gehört** I haven't heard from him for a long time; **vor ~er Zeit** a long time ago; **hier wird mir die Zeit nicht ~** I won't get bored here; **etw ¨er machen** to lengthen sth; **er machte ein ~es Gesicht** his face fell; **man sah überall nur ~e Gesichter** you saw nothing but long faces; **etw von ~er Hand vorbereiten** to prepare sth carefully; **einen ~en Hals machen** *(col)* to crane one's neck. **(b)** *(col: groß) Mensch* tall.

2 *adv* **der ~ erwartete Regen** the long-awaited rain; **der ~ ersehnte Urlaub** the longed-for holiday; **~ anhaltender Beifall** prolonged applause; **zwei Stunden ~** for two hours; **mein ganzes Leben ~** my whole life; **mein ganzes Leben ~ werde ich das nicht vergessen** I'll never forget that as long as I live; **~ und breit** at great length.

lang-: ~ärm(e)lig *adj* long-sleeved; **~atmig** *adj* long-winded; **~beinig** *adj* long-legged.

lang(e) *adv comp* **¨er,** *superl* **am längsten (a)** *(zeitlich)* a long time; *(in Fragen, Negativsätzen)* long. **die Sitzung hat heute ~ gedauert** the meeting went on (for) a long time today; **wie ~ lernst du schon Deutsch?** how long have you been learning German (for)?; **es ist noch gar nicht ~ her, daß wir diese Frage diskutiert haben** it's not long since we discussed this question; **bis Weihnachten ist es ja noch ~ hin** it's still a long time till Christmas, we're a long way from Christmas. **(b)** *(col: längst)* **noch ~ nicht** not by any means; **~ nicht so ...** not nearly as ...; **wenn der das schafft, kannst du das schon ~** if he can do it, you can do it easily.

Länge *f* **-n (a)** length; *(col: von Mensch)* height. **ein Seil von 10 Meter ~** a rope 10 metres long; **ein Vortrag/eine Fahrt von einer Stunde ~** an hour-long lecture/an hour's journey; **etw der ~ nach falten** to fold sth lengthways; **in die ~ gehen** *(Kleidungsstücke)* to stretch; **etw in die ~ ziehen** to drag sth out *(col)*; **sich in die ~ ziehen** to go on and on; **der ~ nach hinfallen** to fall flat (on one's face); **mit einer ~ gewinnen** *(Sport)* to win by a length. **(b)** *(Geog)* longitude. **der Ort liegt auf 20 Grad östlicher ~** the town has a longitude of 20 degrees east.

langen *(col)* **1** *vi* **(a)** *(sich erstrecken, greifen)* to reach *(nach* for, in *+acc* in, into*)*. **(b)** *(ausreichen)* to be enough; *(auskommen)* to get by, to manage. **jetzt langt's mir aber!** I've had just about enough! **2** *vt (reichen)* **jdm etw ~** to hand sb sth; **jdm eine ~** to give sb a clip on the ear *(col)*.

Längen-: ~grad *m* degree of longitude; **~maß** *nt* measure of length.

Langeweile *f no pl* boredom. **~ haben** to be bored.

Lang-: ~finger *m (hum)* pick-pocket; **l~fristig 1** *adj* long-term; **2** *adv* in the long term; *planen* for the long term; **l~haarig** *adj* long-haired; **l~jährig 1** *adj Freundschaft, Gewohnheit* long-standing; *Erfahrung, Verhandlungen* many years of; *Mitarbeiter* of many years' standing; **2** *adv* for many years; **~lauf** *m (Ski)* cross-country skiing; **~läufer** *m (Ski)* cross-country skier; **l~lebig** *adj* long-lasting; *Gerücht, Mensch, Tier* long-lived; **l~legen** *vr sep* to have a lie-down.

länglich *adj* long, elongated.

Lang-: ~mut *f no pl* patience, forbearance; **l~mütig** *adj* patient, forbearing.

längs 1 *adv* lengthways, lengthwise. **2** *prep +gen* along. **~ der Straße stehen Kastanien** chestnut trees line the road.

Längs|achse *f* longitudinal axis.

langsam 1 *adj* slow. **2** *adv* **(a)** slowly. **fahr/sprich ~er!** slow down!, drive/speak (a bit) more slowly!; **immer schön ~!** *(col)* easy does it!; **~ aber sicher** slowly but surely. **(b)** *(allmählich)* **es wird ~ Zeit, daß ...** it's getting about time that ...; **ich muß jetzt ~ gehen** I must be getting on my way; **~ (aber sicher) reicht es mir** I've just about had enough.

Langschläfer *m* late-riser.

Langspielplatte *f* long-playing record.

Längs-: ~schnitt *m* longitudinal section; **~seite** *f* long side; *(Naut)* broadside; **l~seit(s)** *adv, prep +gen* alongside.

längst *adv* **(a)** *(seit langem, schon lange)* for a long time. **das ist ~ nicht mehr so** it hasn't been like that for a long time; **als wir ankamen, war der Zug ~ weg** when we arrived the train had long since gone. **(b)** *siehe* **lange (b).**

Langstrecken-: ~flugzeug *nt* long-range aircraft; **~lauf** *m (Disziplin)* long-distance running; *(Wettkampf)* long-distance race; **~läufer** *m* long-distance runner.

Languste [laŋ'gustə] *f* **-n** crayfish, crawfish *(US)*.

langweilen *insep* **1** *vt* to bore. **2** *vi* to be boring. **3** *vr* to be/get bored.

Langweiler *m* - bore.

langweilig *adj* **(a)** boring. **(b)** *(col: langsam)* slow.

Lang-: ~welle *f* long wave; **l~wierig** *adj* long, lengthy; *Verhandlungen, Krankheit auch* prolonged; **~wierigkeit** *f* lengthiness; **~zeitprogramm** *nt* long-term programme *(Brit) or* program *(US)*.

Lanze *f* **-n** lance; *(zum Werfen)* spear. **für jdn eine ~ brechen** *(fig)* to take up the cudgels for sb, to go to bat for sb *(esp US)*.

lapidar *adj* succinct.

Lappalie [-iə] *f* trifle, petty little matter.

Lappe *m (wk)* **-n, -n, Lappin** *f* Lapp, Laplander.

Lappen *m* - **(a)** *(Stück Stoff)* cloth; *(Wasch~)* face cloth. **(b)** *(col: Geldschein)* note *(Brit)*, bill *(US)*. **(c)** *(col)* **jdm durch die ~ gehen** to slip through sb's fingers.

läppern *vr impers (col)* **es läppert sich** it (all) mounts up.

läppisch *adj* silly. **wegen ~en zwei Mark macht er so ein Theater** he makes such a fuss about a mere two marks.

Lappland *nt* Lapland.

Lapsus *m* **-, -** mistake, slip; *(gesellschaftlich, diplomatisch)* faux pas.

Lärche *f* **-n** larch.

Larifari *nt no pl (col)* nonsense.

Lärm *m no pl* noise; *(Geräuschbelästigung auch)* din, racket; *(Aufsehen)* fuss. **viel ~ um jdn/etw**

machen to make a big fuss about sb/sth.

Lärm-: ~**belästigung** *f* noise nuisance; **l~empfindlich** *adj* sensitive to noise.

lärmen *vi* to make a noise. ~**d** noisy.

Larve ['larfə] *f* **-n** *(Tier~)* larva.

las *pret of* **lesen.**

lasch *adj (col)* **(a)** *(schlaff) Bewegungen* feeble. **(b)** *Erziehung, Polizei* lax.

Lasche *f* **-n** *(Schlaufe)* loop; *(Schuh~)* tongue; *(als Verschluß)* tab, flap; *(Tech)* splicing plate.

Laserstrahl ['le:zɐ-] *m* laser beam.

lasieren* *vt Bild, Holz* to varnish; *Glas* to glaze.

lassen *pret* **ließ,** *ptp* **gelassen 1** *vt* **(a)** *(unter~)* to stop; *(momentan aufhören)* to leave. **laß das (sein)!** don't (do it)!; *(hör auf)* stop it!; **laß diese Bemerkungen!** that's enough of that kind of remark!; ~ **wir das!** let's leave it *or* that!; **er kann das Trinken nicht** ~ he can't stop drinking; **er kann es nicht** ~**!** he will keep on doing it!; **dann** ~ **wir es eben** let's drop the whole idea; **wenn du nicht willst, dann laß es doch** if you don't want to, then don't; **tu, was du nicht** ~ **kannst!** if you must, you must!

(b) *(zurück~, be~)* to leave. **jdn allein** ~ to leave sb alone; **etw** ~**, wie es ist** to leave sth (just) as it is.

(c) *(über~)* **jdm etw** ~ to let sb have sth; *(behalten ~)* to let sb keep sth; **das muß man ihr** ~ *(zugestehen)* you've got to grant her that.

(d) *(hinein~, hinaus~)* to let *(in +acc* into, *aus* out of*)*; *(col: los~)* to let go; *(in Ruhe ~)* to let be. **Wasser in die Badewanne (laufen)** ~ to run water into the bath.

2 *modal aux ptp* ~ **(a)** *(veranlassen)* **etw tun** ~ to have *or* get sth done; **sich** *(dat)* **etw schicken** ~ to have sth sent to one; **jdm ausrichten** ~**, daß ...** to leave a message for sb that ...; **jdn kommen** ~ to send for sb; **mein Vater wollte mich studieren** ~ my father wanted me to study.

(b) *(zu~)* **jdn etw wissen/sehen** ~ to let sb know/see sth; **sie hat mich nichts merken** ~ she didn't show it/anything; **sich** *(dat)* **einen Bart wachsen** ~ to grow a beard; **den Tee ziehen** ~ to let the tea draw; **das Licht brennen** ~ to leave the light on; **jdn warten** ~ to keep sb waiting; **er hat sich überreden** ~ he let himself be persuaded; **ich lasse mich nicht zwingen** I won't be coerced; **das Fenster läßt sich nicht öffnen** *(grundsätzlich nicht)* the window doesn't open; *(momentan nicht)* the window won't open; **das Wort läßt sich nicht übersetzen** the word is untranslatable; **das läßt sich machen** that can be done; **es ließ sich nicht ändern** it couldn't be changed; **daraus läßt sich schließen, daß ...** one can conclude from this that ...

(c) *(als Imperativ)* **laß uns gehen!** let's go!; **laß es dir gutgehen!** take care of yourself!; **laß dir das gesagt sein!** let me tell you this!

3 *vi* **(a) laß mal, ich mache das schon** leave it, I'll do it. **(b)** *(ab~)* **von jdm/etw** ~ to give sb/sth up.

lässig *adj (ungezwungen)* casual. **das hat er ganz** ~ **hingekriegt** *(col)* pretty cool, the way he did that *(col)*.

Lässigkeit *f* casualness.

läßlich *adj (Eccl) Sünde* venial, pardonable.

Lasso *m or nt* **-s** lasso.

Last *f* **-en (a)** load; *(Trag~ auch)* burden; *(lit, fig: Gewicht)* weight. **(b)** *(fig: Bürde)* burden. **jdm zur** ~ **fallen/werden** to be/become a burden on sb; **die** ~ **der Verantwortung/des Amtes** the burden of responsibility/the weight of office; **jdm eine** ~ **abnehmen** to take a load off sb's shoulders; **jdm etw zur** ~ **legen** to accuse sb of sth. **(c)** ~**en** *(Kosten)* costs; *(des Steuerzahlers)* charges; **soziale** ~**en** welfare costs *or* charges; **zu jds** ~**en gehen** to be chargeable to sb.

lasten *vi* to weigh heavily *(auf +dat* on*)*. **auf dem Haus lastet noch eine Hypothek** the house is still encumbered (with a mortgage) *(form)*; **auf ihm lastet die ganze Verantwortung** all the responsibility rests on him.

Lasten|aufzug *m* hoist, goods lift *(Brit) or* elevator *(US)*.

Laster[1] *m* - *(col)* lorry *(Brit)*, truck.

Laster[2] *nt* - vice.

Lästerei *f (col)* **(a)** *no pl (das Lästern)* running down *(über +acc* of*)*. **(b)** *(Lästerwort)* nasty remark.

lasterhaft *adj* depraved.

Lasterhöhle *f* den of vice *or* iniquity.

lästerlich *adj* malicious; *(gottes~)* blasphemous.

lästern 1 *vi* **über jdn/etw** ~ to make nasty remarks about sb/sth. **2** *vt Gott* to blaspheme against.

lästig *adj* tiresome; *(ärgerlich auch)* irksome, aggravating; *Husten etc* troublesome. **wie** ~**!** what a nuisance!; **jdm** ~ **sein** to bother sb; **dieser Verband ist mir** ~ this bandage is bothering me; **jdm** ~ **werden** to become a nuisance (to sb); *(zum Ärgernis werden)* to get annoying (to sb).

Last-: ~**kahn** *m* barge; ~**kraftwagen** *m (form)* heavy goods vehicle; ~**schiff** *nt* cargo ship; ~**schrift** *f* debit; *(Eintrag)* debit entry; ~**wagen** *m* lorry *(Brit)*, truck; ~**wagenfahrer** *m* lorry *(Brit) or* truck driver; ~**zug** *m* truck-trailer *(US)*, juggernaut *(Brit)*.

Lasur *f (auf Holz, Bild)* varnish; *(auf Glas, Email)* glaze.

Latein *nt* Latin. **mit seinem** ~ **am Ende sein** *(col)* to be stumped *(col)*.

Latein-: ~**amerika** *nt* Latin America; **l~amerikanisch** *adj* Latin-American.

lateinisch *adj* Latin.

latent *adj* latent; *Selbstmörder, Gefahr* potential. ~ **vorhanden sein** to be latent.

Laterne *f* **-n** lantern; *(Straßen~)* streetlamp.

Laternenpfahl *m* lamp post.

Latinum *nt no pl* **kleines/großes** ~ ≃ Latin O-/A-level (exam) *(Brit)*.

Latrine *f* latrine.

Latschen *m* - *(col) (Hausschuh)* slipper; *(pej: Schuh)* worn-out shoe.

latschen *vi aux sein (col)* to wander; *(durch die Stadt etc)* to traipse; *(schlurfend)* to slouch along.

Latte *f* **-n (a)** *(schmales Brett)* slat. **nicht alle auf der** ~ **haben** *(col)* to have a screw loose *(col)*. **(b)** *(Sport)* bar; *(Ftbl)* (cross)bar. **(c)** *(col: Liste)* **eine ganze** ~ **von Vorstrafen** a whole string of previous convictions.

Latten-: ~**kreuz** *nt* corner of the goalpost; ~**zaun** *m* wooden fence.

Latz *m* **¨e** *(Lätzchen, bei Kleidung)* bib; *(Hosen~)* (front) flap. **jdm eins vor den** ~ **knallen** *(col)* to sock sb one *(col)*.

Lätzchen *nt* bib.

Latzhose *f* (pair of) dungarees *pl*.

lau *adj* **(a)** *Wind, Abend* mild. **(b)** *Flüssigkeit* tepid, lukewarm; *(fig) Haltung* lukewarm.

Laub *nt no pl* leaves *pl*; *(an Bäumen etc auch)* foliage.

Laubbaum *m* deciduous tree.

Laube *f* **-n (a)** *(Gartenhäuschen)* summerhouse. **(b)** *(Gang)* pergola; *(Arkade)* arcade.

Laub-: ~**frosch** *m* (European) tree-frog; ~**säge** *f* fretsaw; ~**wald** *m* deciduous forest.

Lauch *m (esp S Ger: Porree)* leek.

Lauer *f no pl*: **auf der** ~ **sein** *or* **liegen** to lie in wait.

lauern *vi (lit, fig)* to lurk, to lie in wait *(auf +acc* for*)*; *(col)* to wait *(auf +acc* for*)*. **ein** ~**der Blick** a furtive glance.

Lauf *m, pl* **Läufe (a)** *(schneller Schritt)* run; *(Wett~)* race. **sein** ~ **wurde immer schneller** he ran faster and faster; **einen** ~ **machen** to go for a run. **(b)** *(Verlauf)* course. **im** ~**e der Jahre**

through the years; **im ~e des Gesprächs** in the course of the conversation; **sie ließ ihren Gefühlen freien ~** she gave way to her feelings; **den Dingen ihren ~ lassen** to let matters take their course. **(c)** *(Gang, Arbeit)* running, operation. **(d)** *(Fluß~, Astron)* course. **der obere/untere ~ der Donau** the upper/lower reaches of the Danube. **(e)** *(Gewehr~)* barrel. **(f)** *(Hunt: Bein)* leg.

Laufbahn *f* career. **eine ~ einschlagen** to embark on a career.

Laufbursche *m* errand-boy, messenger boy.

laufen *pret* **lief**, *ptp* **gelaufen 1** *vi aux sein* **(a)** to run. **die Erde läuft um die Sonne** the earth moves around the sun; **es lief mir eiskalt über den Rücken** a chill ran up my spine.

(b) *(col: gehen)* to go; *(zu Fuß gehen)* to walk. **das Kind läuft schon** the child is already walking; **das L~ lernen** to learn to walk; **es sind nur 10 Minuten zu ~** it's only 10 minutes' walk; **er läuft dauernd zur Polizei** he's always running to the police.

(c) *(fließen)* to run; *(schmelzen: Käse, Butter)* to melt; *(undicht sein) (Gefäß, Wasserhahn)* to leak; *(Nase, Wunde)* to run. **in Strömen ~** to stream *or* pour (in/out/down *etc*); **Wasser in die Badewanne ~ lassen** to run water into the bath; **ihm läuft die Nase** he's got a runny nose.

(d) *(in Betrieb sein)* to run, to go; *(Uhr)* to go; *(Elektrogerät) (eingeschaltet sein)* to be on; *(funktionieren)* to work.

(e) *(fig: im Gange sein) (Prozeß, Verhandlung)* to go on, to be in progress; *(Bewerbung, Antrag)* to be under consideration; *(gezeigt werden) (Film, Stück)* to be on. **der Film lief schon, als wir ankamen** the film had already started when we arrived; **der Film läuft über drei Stunden** the film goes on for three hours; **etw läuft gut/schlecht** sth is going well/badly; **mal sehen, wie die Sache läuft** let's see how things go; **die Dinge ~ lassen** to let things slide; **die Sache ist gelaufen** *(col)* it's in the bag *(col)*; **es ist zu spät, die Sache ist schon gelaufen** *(col)* it's too late now, it's all finished with.

(f) das Auto läuft auf meinen Namen the car is in my name; **das läuft unter „Sonderausgaben"** that comes under "special expenses".

2 *vt aux sein* **(a)** *auch aux haben (Sport) Rekordzeit* to run; *Rekord* to set. **Ski/Schlittschuh/Rollschuh** *etc* **~** to ski/skate/rollerskate *etc.* **(b)** *(fahren: Auto etc) Geschwindigkeit, Strecke* to do. **(c)** *(zu Fuß gehen)* to walk; *(schnell)* to run.

3 *vr* **sich müde ~** to tire oneself out; **in den Schuhen läuft es sich gut** these shoes are good for walking/running in.

laufend 1 *adj attr Arbeiten, Ausgaben* regular; *Monat, Jahr* current. **10 DM das ~e Meter** DM 10 per metre; **~e Nummer** serial number; *(von Konto)* number; **auf dem ~en bleiben/sein** to keep (oneself)/be up-to-date; **jdn auf dem ~en halten** to keep sb up-to-date. **2** *adv* continually, constantly.

laufenlassen *vt sep irreg (col)* **jdn ~** to let sb go.

Läufer *m* **- (a)** *(Sport)* runner; *(Hürden~)* hurdler; *(Ftbl)* halfback; *(Chess)* bishop. **rechter/linker ~** *(Ftbl)* right/left half. **(b)** *(Teppich)* rug; *(Treppen~, Tisch~)* runner.

Lauferei *f (col)* running about *no pl.*

Läuferin *f (Sport)* runner; *(Hürden~)* hurdler.

Lauf-: ~feuer *nt*: **sich wie ein ~feuer verbreiten** to spread like wildfire; **~gitter** *nt* playpen.

läufig *adj* on heat.

Lauf-: ~junge *m* errand-boy; **~kunde** *m* occasional customer; **~masche** *f* ladder *(Brit)*, run; **~paß** *m*: **jdm den ~paß geben** *(col)* to give sb his/her marching orders *(col)*; **~schritt** *m* trot; *(Mil)* double-quick; **im ~schritt** *(Mil)* at the double; **~stall** *m* playpen; **~steg** *m* catwalk; **~werk** *nt (Mech)* running gear; *(von Uhr)* movement; *(Comp)* drive; **~zeit** *f* **(a)** *(von Wechsel, Vertrag)* period of validity; **(b)** *(von Maschine)* life.

Lauge *f* **-n** *(Chem)* lye; *(Seifen~)* soapy water.

Laune *f* **-n (a)** *(Stimmung)* mood. **(je) nach (Lust und) ~** just as the mood takes one; **gute/schlechte ~ haben** to be in a good/bad mood. **(b)** *(Einfall)* whim. **etw aus einer ~ heraus tun** to do sth on a whim.

launenhaft, launisch *adj* moody; *(unberechenbar)* capricious.

Laus *f, pl* **Läuse** louse. **ihm ist (wohl) eine ~ über die Leber gelaufen** *(col)* something's biting him *(col)*.

Lausbub *m (hum)* rascal, scamp.

Lausch|angriff *m* bugging operation *(gegen* on*)*.

lauschen *vi* **(a)** *(geh)* to listen *(dat, auf +acc* to*)*. **(b)** *(heimlich)* to eavesdrop.

Lauscher(in *f*) *m* **-** eavesdropper.

Lausejunge *m (col)* little devil *(col)*; *(wohlwollend)* rascal.

lausen *vt* to delouse. **ich denk', mich laust der Affe!** *(col)* well blow me down! *(col)*.

lausig *(col)* **1** *adj* lousy *(col)*; *Kälte* perishing. **2** *adv* awfully.

laut[1] *adj* **(a)** loud. **~er sprechen** to speak up; **~ auflachen** to burst out laughing; **etw ~(er) stellen** to turn sth up (loud). **(b)** *(lärmend)* noisy; *(aufdringlich) Mensch* loudmouthed; *Farbe etc* loud. **(c)** *(hörbar)* aloud *pred, adv.* **etw ~ sagen** *(lit)* to say sth out loud; *(fig)* to shout sth from the rooftops; **das kannst du ~ sagen** you can say that again; **~ werden** *(bekannt)* to become known.

laut[2] *prep +gen or dat* according to.

Laut *m* **-e** sound. **keinen ~ von sich** *(dat)* **geben** not to make a sound.

Laute *f* **-n** lute.

lauten *vi* to be; *(Rede)* to go; *(Schriftstück)* to read. **auf den Namen ... ~** *(Paß)* to be in the name of ...; *(Scheck)* to be made out to ...

läuten *vti* to ring. **es hat geläutet** the bell rang; **er hat davon (etwas) ~ hören** *(col)* he has heard something about it.

lauter 1 *adj (geh) Absichten* honourable *(Brit)*, honorable *(US)*; *Wahrheit* honest. **2** *adv (nur)* nothing/nobody but. **~ Unsinn** sheer nonsense; **vor ~ Rauch kann man nichts sehen** you can't see anything for all the smoke.

läutern *vt (liter)* to purify; *(fig)* to reform.

lauthals *adv* at the top of one's voice.

Laut-: ~lehre *f* phonetics *sing*; **l~lich** *adj* phonetic; **l~los** *adj* noiseless; *(wortlos)* silent; **~losigkeit** *f siehe adj* noiselessness; silence; **l~malend** *adj* onomatopoeic; **~malerei** *f* onomatopoeia; **~schrift** *f* phonetics *pl.*

Lautsprecher *m* (loud)speaker.

Lautsprecher-: ~anlage *f* **öffentliche ~anlage** public address *or* PA system; **~wagen** *m* loudspeaker car/van.

Laut-: l~stark *adj* loud; *(Rad, TV etc)* high-volume; *Protest* vociferous; **~stärke** *f siehe adj* loudness; volume; vociferousness; **ein Radio in voller ~stärke spielen lassen** to have a radio on full volume.

lauwarm *adj (lit, fig)* lukewarm.

Lava ['la:va] *f, pl* **Laven** ['la:vn] lava.

Lavendel [la'vɛndl] *m* **-** lavender.

lavieren* [la'vi:rən] *vi* **(a)** *(Naut)* to tack. **(b)** *(fig)* to manoeuvre *(Brit)*, to maneuver *(US)*.

Lawine *f (lit, fig)* avalanche.

Lawinen-: l~artig *adj* like an avalanche; **l~artig anwachsen** to snowball; **~gefahr** *f* danger of avalanches.

Layout ['le:|aut] *nt* **-s** layout.

Lazarett *nt* **-e** *(Mil)* sick bay; *(Krankenhaus)* hospital.

leasen ['li:zn] *vt (Comm)* to lease.

Leasing ['li:zɪŋ] *nt* **-s** *(Comm)* leasing *no art, no pl.*

Leben *nt* - life. **das ~** life; **am ~ sein/bleiben** to be/stay alive; **solange ich am ~ bin** as long as I live; **jdm das ~ retten** to save sb's life; **ein glückliches** *etc* **~ führen** to live a happy *etc* life; **mit dem ~ davonkommen** to escape with one's life; **sein ~ aufs Spiel setzen** to take one's life in one's hands; **mit dem ~ abschließen** to prepare for death; **etw ins ~ rufen** to bring sth into being; **seines ~s nicht mehr sicher sein** to fear for one's life; **ums ~ kommen** to die; **sein ~ lassen (müssen)** to lose one's life; **jdn am ~ lassen** to spare sb's life; **sich** *(dat)* **das ~ nehmen** to take one's (own) life; **jdn wieder ins ~ zurückrufen** to bring sb back to life; *Bewußtlosen* to revive sb; **der Mann/die Frau meines ~s** my ideal man/woman; **etw für sein ~ gern tun** to love doing sth; **jdn künstlich am ~ erhalten** to keep sb alive artificially; **er hat es nie leicht gehabt im ~** he has never had an easy life; **ein ~ lang** one's whole life (long); **ich habe noch nie im ~ geraucht** I have never smoked in all my life; **nie im ~!** never!; **im ~ ist das ganz anders** in real life it's very different; **ein Film nach dem ~** a film from real life; **so ist das ~ (eben)** that's life; **~ in etw** *(acc)* **bringen** *(col)* to liven sth up.

leben *vi* to live; *(am Leben sein)* to be alive; *(weiter~)* to live on. **ich möchte nicht mehr ~** I don't want to go on living; **er wird nicht mehr lange zu ~ haben** he won't live much longer; **von etw ~** to live on sth; **lebst du noch?** *(hum col)* are you still in the land of the living? *(hum)*; **zum L~ zu wenig, zum Sterben zuviel** it's barely enough to keep body and soul together; **einsam ~** to lead a lonely life; **hier läßt es sich (gut) ~** it's a good life here.

lebend *adj* live *attr*, alive *pred*; *Wesen, Beispiel, Sprache* living. **ein Tier ~ fangen** to catch an animal alive; **~es Inventar** livestock.

Lebend-: **~geburt** *f* live-birth; **~gewicht** *nt* live weight.

lebendig *adj* **(a)** *(nicht tot)* live *attr*, alive *pred*; *Wesen* living. **jdn bei ~em Leibe verbrennen** to burn sb alive. **(b)** *(fig: lebhaft)* lively *no adv*; *Darstellung, Bild auch* vivid; *Glaube* fervent.

Lebens-: **~abend** *m* old age; **~abschnitt** *m* phase in one's life; **~alter** *nt* age; **ein hohes ~alter erreichen** to have a long life; **~angst** *f* fear of life; **~anschauung** *f* philosophy of life; **~art** *f no pl* **(a)** way of life; **(b)** *(Manieren)* manners *pl*; *(Stil)* style; **~auffassung** *f* attitude to life; **~bedingungen** *pl* living conditions *pl*; **l~bejahend** *adj* **eine l~bejahende Einstellung** a positive approach to life; **~bereich** *m* area of life; **~dauer** *f* life(span); *(von Maschine)* life; **l~echt** *adj* true-to-life; **~elixier** *nt* **das ist sein ~elixier** *(fig)* he thrives on it; **~ende** *nt* end of sb's/(one's) life; **~erfahrung** *f* experience of life; **~erwartung** *f* life expectancy; **l~fähig** *adj (lit, fig)* viable; **~form** *f (Biol)* life-form; *(Form des Zusammenlebens)* way of life; **~frage** *f* vital matter; **l~fremd** *adj* out of touch with life; **~freude** *f* joie de vivre; **l~froh** *adj* full of the joys of life; **~führung** *f* life-style; **~gefahr** *f* (mortal) danger; **„~gefahr!"** "danger"; **er schwebt in ~gefahr** his life is in danger; **außer ~gefahr sein** to be out of danger; **etw unter ~gefahr** *(dat)* **tun** to risk one's life doing sth; **l~gefährlich** *adj* highly dangerous; *Verletzung* critical; **~gefährte** *m*, **~gefährtin** *f* **ihr ~gefährte** the man she lives with; **~gemeinschaft** *f* long-term relationship; *(Biol, Zool)* symbiosis; **~geschichte** *f* life-story; **~gewohnheit** *f* habit; **l~groß** *adj* lifesize; **~größe** *f* **eine Figur in ~größe** a lifesize figure; **~haltungskosten** *pl* cost of living *sing*; **~hilfe** *f* counselling *(Brit)*, counseling *(US)*; **l~hungrig** *adj* thirsty for life; **~inhalt** *m* purpose in life; **etw zu seinem ~inhalt machen** to devote oneself to sth; **~jahr** *nt* year of (one's) life; **nach Vollendung des 18. ~jahres** on attaining the age of 18; **~kraft** *f* vitality; **~künstler** *m* master in the art of living; **~lage** *f* situation; **l~lang** *adj* lifelong; *Haft* life *attr*, for life; **l~länglich** *adj Rente, Strafe* for life; **sie hat ~länglich bekommen** *(col)* she got life *(col)*; **~lauf** *m* curriculum vitae, résumé *(US)*; **~lust** *f* zest for life; **l~lustig** *adj* in love with life.

Lebensmittel *pl* food *sing*, groceries *pl*.

Lebensmittel-: **~geschäft** *nt* grocer's (shop) *(Brit)*, grocer *(US)*; **~gesetz** *nt* food law; **~händler** *m* grocer.

Lebens-: **l~müde** *adj* tired of life; **ein ~müder** a potential suicide; **l~nah** *adj* true-to-life; **l~notwendig** *adj* essential; *Organ* vital (for life); **~qualität** *f* quality of life; **~raum** *m (Biol)* biosphere; **~regel** *f* rule (of life); **~retter** *m* rescuer; **~standard** *m* standard of living; **~stellung** *f* job for life; **~stil** *m* lifestyle; **l~tüchtig** *adj* able to cope with life; **~umstände** *pl* circumstances *pl*; **~unterhalt** *m* **seinen ~unterhalt verdienen** to earn one's living; **für jds ~unterhalt sorgen** to support sb; **~versicherung** *f* life insurance; **eine ~versicherung abschließen** to take out a life insurance; **~wandel** *m* way of life; **einen einwandfreien ~wandel führen** to lead an irreproachable life; **~weg** *m* journey through life; **alles Gute für den weiteren ~weg** every good wish for the future; **~weise** *f* way of life; **~weisheit** *f* maxim; *(~erfahrung)* wisdom; **~werk** *nt* life's work; **l~wert** *adj* worth living; **l~wichtig** *adj* vital; **~wille** *m* will to live; **~zeichen** *nt* sign of life; **kein ~zeichen mehr von sich geben** to show no sign(s) of life; **~zeit** *f* life(time); **auf ~zeit** for life; **Beamter auf ~zeit** permanent civil servant; **~ziel** *nt* aim in life.

Leber *f* **-n** liver. **ich habe es an der ~** *(col)* I've got liver trouble; **frei** *or* **frisch von der ~ weg reden** *(col)* to speak frankly.

Leber-: **~entzündung** *f* hepatitis; **~fleck** *m* liver spot; **~käse** *m no pl* ≈ meat loaf; **~knödel** *m* liver dumpling; **~krebs** *m* cancer of the liver; **~leiden** *nt* liver disorder; **~pastete** *f* liver pâté; **~tran** *m* cod-liver oil; **~wurst** *f* liver sausage.

Lebewesen *nt* living thing. **kleinste ~** micro-organisms.

Lebewohl *nt no pl (liter)* farewell *(liter)*.

Leb-: **l~haft** *adj* lively *no adv*; *Verkehr* brisk; *(deutlich) Erinnerung* vivid. **es geht l~haft zu** things are lively; **ich kann mir l~haft vorstellen, daß ...** I can (very) well imagine that ...; **etw in l~er Erinnerung haben** to remember sth vividly; **~kuchen** *m* gingerbread; **l~los** *adj Körper* lifeless; **l~loser Gegenstand** inanimate object; **~tag** *m (col)* **mein/dein** *etc* **~tag** all my/your *etc* life; **das werde ich mein ~tag nicht vergessen** I'll never forget that as long as I live; **~zeiten** *pl* **zu jds ~zeiten** *(Leben)* in sb's lifetime; *(Zeit)* in sb's day.

lechzen *vi (geh)* **nach etw ~** to thirst for sth.

leck *adj* leaky. **~ sein** to leak; **~ schlagen** to hole.

Leck *nt* **-s** leak.

lecken[1] *vi (undicht sein)* to leak.

lecken[2] *vti* to lick. **an jdm/etw ~** to lick sb/sth.

lecker *adj Speisen* delicious.

Leckerbissen *m (Speise)* delicacy; *(fig)* gem.

Leckerei *f* delicacy.

Leckermaul *nt (col)* sweet-toothed child/person *etc*. **ein ~ sein** to have a sweet tooth.

led. = **ledig.**

Leder *nt* - **(a)** leather; *(Wild~)* suede. **in ~ gebunden** leather-bound; **zäh wie ~** as tough as old boots *(col)*. **(b)** *(col: Fußball)* ball. **am ~ bleiben** to stick with the ball.

Leder- *in cpds* leather; **~hose** *f* leather trousers *pl*; *(von Tracht)* leather shorts *pl*; **~jacke** *f* leather jacket.

ledern *adj* leather; *(zäh) Fleisch* leathery.

Leder-: ~**waren** *pl* leather goods *pl*; ~**zeug** *nt* leather gear.

ledig *adj* **(a)** single; *Mutter* unmarried. **(b)** *(geh: frei)* free. **(los und)** ~ **sein** to be footloose and fancy free; **aller Pflichten** *(gen)* ~ **sein** to be free of all commitments.

lediglich *adv* merely, simply.

Lee *f no pl (Naut)* lee.

leer *adj* empty; *Blick* blank. **eine ~e Stelle** an empty space; **ins L~e greifen** toclutch at thin air; **mit ~en Händen** *(fig)* empty-handed; ~ **laufen** *(Motor)* to idle; **etw ~ machen** to empty sth; **den Teller ~ essen** to eat everything on the plate; ~ **stehen** to stand empty.

Leere *f no pl (lit, fig)* emptiness. **(eine) geistige ~** a mental vacuum; **(eine) gähnende ~** a gaping void.

leeren *vt* to empty.

Leer-: ~**gewicht** *nt* unladen weight; ~**gut** *nt* empties *pl*; ~**lauf** *m* **(a)** neutral; *(von Fahrrad)* freewheel; **im ~lauf fahren** to coast; **(b)** *(fig)* slack; **l~laufen** *vi sep irreg aux sein (Faß etc)* to run dry; **l~laufen lassen** to drain; **l~stehend** *adj* empty; ~**taste** *f* space-bar.

Leerung *f* emptying. **nächste ~: 18 Uhr** *(an Briefkasten)* next collection: 6 p.m.

Lefze *f* **-n** *usu pl* chaps *pl*; *(von Pferd)* lip.

legal *adj* legal, lawful.

legalisieren* *vt* to legalize.

Legalität *f* legality. **(etwas) außerhalb der ~** *(euph)* (slightly) outside the law.

Legasthenie *f* dyslexia.

Legastheniker(in *f*) *m* **-** dyslexic.

Leg(e)henne *f nt* layer, laying hen.

legen 1 *vt* **(a)** *(hin~)* to lay down; *(mit adv)* to lay; *(mit Raumangabe)* to put, to place; *(Sport sl)* to bring down. **etw an die Luft ~** to put sth out to air; **etw in Essig** *etc* ~ to preserve sth in vinegar *etc.* **(b)** *(verlegen) Fliesen, Leitungen, Schienen* to lay, to put down. **sich** *(dat)* **die Haare ~ lassen** to have one's hair set. **(c)** *auch vi Eier* to lay. **2** *vr* **(a)** *(hin~)* to lie down *(auf +acc* on). **sich ins Bett ~** to go to bed; **sich zu jdm ~** to lie down beside sb; **sich in die Sonne ~** to lie in the sun. **(b)** *(mit Ortsangabe) (nieder~: Nebel, Rauch)* to settle *(auf+acc* on). **sich auf die Seite ~** to lie on one's side; *(Boot)* to heel over; **sich in die Kurve ~** to lean into the corner. **(c)** *(nachlassen)* to die down; *(Rauch, Nebel)* to clear.

legendär *adj* legendary.

Legende *f* **-n** legend.

leger [le'ʒeːɐ] *adj* casual, informal.

Legierung *f* alloy.

Legion *f* legion.

legislativ *adj* legislative.

Legislative *f* legislature, legislative assembly.

Legislaturperiode *f* parliamentary term.

legitim *adj* legitimate.

Legitimation *f* identification; *(Berechtigung)* authorization; *(eines Kindes)* legitimation.

legitimieren* 1 *vt* to legitimize; *(berechtigen)* to entitle. **2** *vr* to show (proof of) authorization; *(sich ausweisen)* to identify oneself.

Legitimität *f no pl* legitimacy.

Lehm *m* **-e** clay; *(Boden)* loam.

Lehm-: ~**boden** *m* clay soil; ~**hütte** *f* mud hut.

lehmig *adj* loamy; *(tonartig)* clayey.

Lehm-: ~**packung** *f* mudpack; ~**ziegel** *m* clay brick.

Lehne *f* **-n** *(Arm~)* arm(-rest); *(Rücken~)* back(-rest).

lehnen 1 *vtr* to lean *(an +acc* against*)*. **2** *vi* to be leaning *(an +dat* against*)*.

Lehnstuhl *m* easy-chair.

Lehr-: ~**amt** *nt* **das ~amt** the teaching profession; ~**auftrag** *m (als Sonderlehrer)* special teaching post; **einen ~auftrag für etw haben** *(Univ)* to give lectures on sth; ~**beruf** *m* **(a)** *(als Lehrer)* teaching profession; **den ~beruf ergreifen** to go into teaching; **(b)** *(Beruf mit ~zeit)* trade requiring an apprenticeship; ~**brief** *m (Zeugnis)* apprenticeship certificate; ~**buch** *nt* textbook.

Lehre *f* **-n (a)** training; *(im Handwerk)* apprenticeship. **bei jdm in die ~ gehen** to serve one's apprenticeship with sb. **(b)** *(von Christus, Marx etc)* teachings *pl*; *(von Kant, Freud etc)* theory; *(von Schall, Leben etc)* science. **die christliche ~** Christian doctrine. **(c)** *(Erfahrung)* lesson; *(einer Geschichte)* moral. **seine ~(n) aus etw ziehen** to learn a lesson from sth; **laß dir das eine ~ sein!** let that be a lesson to you!

lehren *vti* to teach. **jdn lesen** *etc* ~ to teach sb to read *etc.*

Lehrer(in *f*) *m* **-** teacher; *(Flug~, Fahr~ etc)* instructor/instructress. **er ist ~** he's a teacher; ~ **für Naturwissenschaften** science teacher.

Lehrer-: ~**ausbildung** *f* teacher training; ~**kollegium** *nt* staff; ~**zimmer** *nt* staff *(esp Brit) or* teachers' room.

Lehr-: ~**gang** *m* course *(für* in*)*; ~**geld** *nt* ~**geld für etw zahlen müssen** *(fig)* to pay dearly for sth; **laß dir dein ~geld zurückgeben!** *(hum col)* go to the bottom of the class! *(hum col)*; **l~haft** *adj* didactic; ~**herr** *m* master (of an apprentice); ~**jahr** *nt* year as an apprentice; ~**kraft** *f (form)* teacher.

Lehrling *m* trainee; *(im Handwerk)* apprentice.

Lehrlings|ausbildung *f* training of trainees/apprentices.

Lehr-: ~**meister** *m* master; ~**methode** *f* teaching method; ~**mittel** *nt* teaching aid; ~**plan** *m* curriculum; ~**probe** *f* demonstration lesson, crit *(col)*; ~**programm** *nt* teaching programme *(Brit) or* program *(US)*; **l~reich** *adj (informativ)* instructive; ~**satz** *m (Math, Philos)* theorem; *(Eccl)* dogma; ~**stelle** *f* place; **dort sind noch zwei ~stellen frei** there are two vacancies for trainees/apprentices; ~**stuhl** *m (Univ)* chair *(für* of*)*; ~**werkstatt** *nt* training workshop; ~**zeit** *f* apprenticeship.

Leib *m* **-er** *(Körper)* body. **Gefahr für ~ und Leben** *(geh)* danger to life and limb; **mit ~ und Seele** heart and soul; **etw am eigenen ~(e) spüren** to experience sth for oneself; **kein Hemd mehr am ~ haben** to be completely destitute; **sich** *(dat)* **jdn/etw vom ~e halten** to keep sb/sth at bay; **halt ihn mir vom ~** keep him away from me.

Leib|eigenschaft *f* serfdom; *(fig)* bondage.

leiben *vi:* **wie er leibt und lebt** to a T *(col)*.

Leibes-: ~**erziehung** *f* physical education; ~**frucht** *f (geh)* unborn child; ~**kraft** *f*: **aus ~kräften schreien** *etc* to shout *etc* with all one's might; ~**übung** *f* (physical) exercise; ~**übungen** *(Schulfach)* physical education *no pl*; ~**visitation** *f* body check.

Leibgericht *nt* favourite *(Brit) or* favorite *(US)* meal.

leibhaftig *adj* personified. **die ~e Güte** *etc* goodness *etc* personified.

leiblich *adj Mutter, Vater* natural; *Kind* by birth; *Bruder, Schwester* full.

Leib-: ~**rente** *f* life annuity; ~**wächter** *m* bodyguard; ~**wäsche** *f* underwear.

Leiche *f* **-n** corpse. **eine wandelnde ~** *(col)* a corpse; **wie eine lebende ~ aussehen** to look like death (warmed up *col*); **er geht über ~n** *(col)* he'd stick at nothing; **nur über meine ~!** *(col)* over my dead body!

Leichen-: ~**beschauer** *m* **-** doctor conducting a post-mortem; **l~blaß** *adj* deathly pale; ~**halle** *f* mortuary; ~**hemd** *nt* shroud; ~**rede** *f* funeral address; ~**schändung** *f* desecration of corpses; ~**schau** *f* post-mortem (examination); ~**schmaus** *m* funeral meal; ~**tuch** *nt* shroud; ~**verbrennung** *f* cremation; ~**wagen** *m* hearse; ~**zug** *m* funeral procession.

leicht 1 *adj* **(a)** light; *(aus ~em Material) Kleidung* lightweight; *(schwach, gering)* slight; *(Jur) Diebstahl, Vergehen etc* minor, petty. **~e Musik/~es Essen** light music/food; **~ gewürzt** lightly seasoned; **er hat einen leichten Schlaf** he's a light sleeper; **~ bekleidet sein** to be scantily clad; **~es Mädchen** tart *(col)*; **mir ist so ~ ums Herz** my heart is so light; **nimm das nicht zu ~** don't take it too lightly. **(b)** *(ohne Schwierigkeiten, einfach)* easy. **mit dem werden wir (ein) ~es Spiel haben** he'll be no problem; **keinen ~en Stand haben** not to have an easy time (of it) *(bei, mit* with*)*; **nichts ~er als das!** nothing (could be) simpler; **die Aufgabe ist ~ zu lösen** the exercise is easy to do; **~ begreifen** to understand quickly; **das ist ~er gesagt als getan** that's easier said than done.

2 *adv* **(a)** *(schnell, unversehens)* easily. **er wird ~ böse** he gets angry easily; **~ zerbrechlich** very fragile; **man kann einen Fehler ~ übersehen** it's easy to miss a mistake; **das ist ~ möglich** that's quite possible; **das passiert mir so ~ nicht wieder** I won't let that happen again in a hurry *(col)*. **(b)** *(etwas)* **das ist ~ übertrieben** it's slightly exaggerated.

Leicht-: ~athlet *m* (track and field) athlete; **~athletik** *f* (track and field) athletics; **~bau(weise** *f)* *m* lightweight construction; **l~bewaffnet** *adj attr* lightly armed; **l~fallen** *vi sep irreg aux sein* to be easy *(jdm* for sb*)*; **Sprachen sind mir schon immer l~gefallen** I've always found languages easy; **l~fertig** *adj* thoughtless; **etw l~fertig aufs Spiel setzen** to risk sth heedlessly; **~fertigkeit** *f* thoughtlessness; **~gewicht** *nt (Sport, fig)* lightweight; **Weltmeister im ~gewicht** world lightweight champion; **l~gläubig** *adj* credulous; *(leicht zu täuschen)* gullible; **~gläubigkeit** *f siehe adj* credulity; gullibility.

Leichtigkeit *f* ease. **mit ~** with no trouble.

Leicht-: ~industrie *f* light industry; **l~lebig** *adj* easygoing; **l~machen** *vt sep* **jdm etw l~machen** to make sth easy for sb; **es sich** *(dat)* **l~machen** *(nicht gewissenhaft sein)* to make things too easy for oneself; **~matrose** *m* ordinary seaman; **~metall** *nt* light metal.

Leichtsinn *m* thoughtlessness. **sträflicher ~** criminal negligence.

leichtsinnig *adj* thoughtless. **~ mit etw umgehen** to be careless with sth.

Leicht-: l~verdaulich *adj attr* easily digestible; **l~verderblich** *adj attr* perishable; **l~verletzt** *adj attr* slightly injured; **~verletzte(r)** *mf decl as adj* slightly injured person; **l~verständlich** *adj attr* readily understandable.

leid *adj pred* **(a) es tut mir ~, daß ich so spät gekommen bin** I'm sorry for coming so late; **tut mir ~!** (I'm) sorry!; **er/sie tut mir ~** I'm sorry for him/her; **sie kann einem ~ tun** you can't help feeling sorry; **das wird dir noch ~ tun** you'll regret it, you'll be sorry. **(b)** *(überdrüssig)* **jdn/etw ~ sein** to be tired of sb/sth.

Leid *nt no pl* sorrow *no indef art; (Unglück)* misfortune; *(Böses, Schaden)* harm. **es soll dir kein ~ geschehen** you will come to no harm; **jdm sein ~ klagen** to tell sb one's troubles.

leiden *pret* **litt**, *ptp* **gelitten 1** *vt* **(a)** *Hunger, Schmerz etc* to suffer. **(b) ich kann** *or* **mag ihn/es (gut) ~** I like him/it (very much); **ich kann ihn/es nicht (gut) ~** I don't like him/it very much; **er kann es nicht ~, wenn man ihn kritisiert** he can't stand being criticized. **2** *vi* to suffer *(an +dat, unter +dat* from*)*.

Leiden *nt* **- (a)** suffering. **(b)** *(Krankheit)* complaint.

leidend *adj* ailing; *(col) Miene* long-suffering. **~ aussehen** to look ill.

Leidenschaft *f* passion. **ich koche mit großer ~** cooking is a great passion of mine.

leidenschaftlich *adj* passionate. **etw ~ gern tun** to absolutely love doing sth.

Leidens-: ~genosse *m*, **~genossin** *f* fellow-sufferer; **~geschichte** *f* tale of woe; **die ~geschichte (Christi)** *(Bibl)* Christ's Passion; **~miene** *f (hum col)* (long-)suffering expression.

leider *adv* unfortunately.

leidig *adj attr* tiresome.

leidlich 1 *adj* fair. **2** *adv* reasonably. **wie geht's — danke, ~!** how are you? — not too bad, thanks.

Leidtragende(r) *mf decl as adj (Benachteiligter)* **der/die ~** the sufferer.

Leidwesen *nt:* **zu jds ~** (much) to sb's disappointment.

Leier *f* **-n** *(Mus)* lyre; *(Dreh~)* hurdy-gurdy. **es ist immer die gleiche ~** *(col)* it's always the same old story.

Leierkasten *m* barrel-organ, hurdy-gurdy.

leiern *vti (col) Gedicht* to drone.

Leih-: ~auto *nt* hire(d) *(Brit) or* rental *(US)* car; **~bücherei** *f* lending library.

leihen *pret* **lieh**, *ptp* **geliehen** *vt (ver~)* to lend; *(ent~)* to borrow; *(mieten, aus~)* to hire *(esp Brit)*, to rent.

Leih-: ~gabe *f* loan; **~gebühr** *f* hire charge; *(für Buch)* lending charge; **~haus** *nt* pawnshop; **~mutter** *f* surrogate mother; **~wagen** *m* hire(d) *(Brit) or* rental *(US)* car.

Leim *m* **-e** glue. **jdm auf den ~ gehen** to be taken in by sb; **aus dem ~ gehen** *(col: Sache)* to fall apart.

leimen *vt* to glue. **jdn ~** *(col)* to take sb for a ride *(col)*; **der Geleimte** the mug *(col)*.

Leine *f* **-n** cord; *(Tau, Zelt~)* rope; *(Schnur)* string; *(Angel~, Wäsche~)* line; *(Hunde~)* leash. **Hunde bitte an der ~ führen!** dogs should be kept on a leash; **den Hund an die ~ nehmen** to put the dog on a lead; **~ ziehen** *(col)* to clear out *(col)*.

leinen *adj siehe* **Leinen** linen; canvas; cloth.

Leinen *nt* **-** linen; *(grob, segeltuchartig)* canvas; *(als Bucheinband)* cloth.

Leinen- *in cpds* linen; canvas; cloth; **~band** *m* cloth(-bound) volume; **~tuch** *nt* linen (cloth); *(grob)* canvas; **~zeug** *nt* linen.

Lein-: ~öl *nt* linseed oil; **~samen** *m* linseed.

Leinwand *f no pl* canvas; *(Film, für Dias)* screen.

leise *adj* **(a)** quiet; *Musik* soft; *Radio auch* low. **das Radio ~r stellen** to turn the radio down; **mit ~r Stimme** in a low voice; **sprich doch ~r!** keep your voice down a bit. **(b)** *(gering, schwach)* slight, faint; *Schlaf, Regen, Berührung* light; *Wind, Seegang* gentle. **nicht die ~ste Ahnung haben** not to have the slightest (idea).

Leisetreter *m* **-** *(pej col)* pussyfoot(er) *(pej col)*.

Leiste *f* **-n (a)** *(Holz~ etc)* strip (of wood/metal *etc*); *(Zier~)* trim; *(Umrandung)* border; *(zur Bilderaufhängung)* rail. **(b)** *(Anat)* groin.

leisten *vt* **(a)** to achieve; *Überstunden* to do; *(Maschine)* to manage. **etwas ~** *(arbeiten)* to do something; *(Motor etc)* to be quite powerful; **gute Arbeit ~** to do a good job. **(b) sich** *(dat)* **etw ~** to allow oneself sth; *(sich gönnen)* to treat oneself to sth; **sich** *(dat)* **etw ~ können** to be able to afford sth; **diese Frechheit würde er sich bei mir nicht ~** he wouldn't try that sort of cheek with me; **er hat sich tolle Sachen geleistet** he got up to the craziest things.

Leisten *m* **-** *(Schuh~)* last. **er schlägt alles über einen ~** he doesn't make distinctions.

Leistenbruch *m (Med)* hernia, rupture.

Leistung *f* **(a)** performance; *(großartige, gute, Sociol)* achievement; *(Ergebnis)* result(s); *(geleistete Arbeit)* work *no pl*; *(Produktion: von Fabrik)* output. **das ist eine ~!** that's quite an achievement; **das ist keine besondere ~** that's nothing special; **nach ~ bezahlt werden** to be paid on results; **seine schulischen ~en haben nachge-**

lassen his school work has deteriorated. **(b)** *(~sfähigkeit)* capacity; *(eines Motors)* power. **(c)** *(von Krankenkasse etc)* benefit; *(Zahlung)* payment.

Leistungs-: **~abfall** *m (in bezug auf Qualität)* drop in performance; *(in bezug auf Quantität)* drop in productivity; **~druck** *m* pressure (to do well); **l~fähig** *adj* efficient; *Motor* powerful; **~fähigkeit** *f* efficiency; *(von Motor)* power; **l~fördernd** *adj* conducive to efficiency; *(in Schule, Universität etc)* conducive to learning; **~gesellschaft** *f* meritocracy; **~klasse** *f (Sport)* class; **~kontrolle** *f (Sch, Univ)* assessment; *(in der Fabrik)* productivity check; **~kraft** *f* power; **~kurs** *m (Sch)* set; **~kurve** *f* productivity curve; **~prämie** *f* productivity bonus; **~prinzip** *nt* achievement principle; **~sport** *m* competitive sport; **~zulage** *f* productivity bonus.

Leit-: **~artikel** *m* leader; **~bild** *nt* model.

leiten 1 *vt* **(a)** to lead; *Verkehr* to route; *Gas, Wasser, (Phys)* to conduct. **etw an die zuständige Stelle ~** to pass sth on to the proper authority; **sich von jdm/etw ~ lassen** *(lit, fig)* to (let oneself) be guided by sb/sth. **(b)** *(verantwortlich sein für)* to be in charge of; *Orchester, Theatergruppe etc* to direct; *Expedition, Sitzung, Verhandlungen* to lead; *(als Vorsitzender)* to chair. **2** *vi (Phys)* to conduct. **gut ~** to be a good conductor.

leitend *adj* leading; *Gedanke, Idee* dominant; *Stellung, Position* managerial; *Ingenieur, Beamter* in charge; *(Phys)* conductive. **nicht ~** *(Phys)* non-conductive; **~e(r) Angestellte(r)** executive.

Leiter *f* **-n** *(lit, fig)* ladder; *(Steh~)* stepladder.

Leiter(in *f***)** *m* **- (a)** leader; *(von Hotel, Geschäft)* manager; *(Abteilungs~)* head; *(von Chor, Theatergruppe etc)* director. **kaufmännischer ~** sales director. **(b)** *(Phys)* conductor.

Leit-: **~faden** *m (Fachbuch)* introduction; **~gedanke** *m* central idea; **~hammel** *m* bellwether; *(fig col)* leader; **~linie** *f (fig)* broad outline; *(Bestimmung)* guideline; **~motiv** *nt (Mus, Liter, fig)* leitmotif; **~planke** *f* crash-barrier; **~satz** *m* basic principle; **~spruch** *m* motto; **~stelle** *f* regional headquarters *pl.*

Leitung *f* **(a)** *no pl siehe vt (a)* leading; routing; conducting. **(b)** *no pl (von Organisationen etc)* running; *(von Orchester etc)* direction; *(von Expedition)* leadership. **die ~ einer Abteilung haben** to be in charge of a department; **die ~ des Gesprächs hat Horst Bauer** Horst Bauer is leading *or (als Vorsitzender)* chairing the discussion. **(c)** *(die Leitenden)* leaders *pl*; *(eines Betriebes etc)* management *sing or pl*; *(einer Schule)* head teachers *pl.* **(d)** *(für Gas, Wasser)* main; *(im Haus)* pipe; *(Elec)* main; *(im Haus)* wire; *(dicker)* cable; *(Überlandleitung)* line; *(Telefon~) (Draht)* wire; *(Verbindung)* line. **da ist jemand in der ~** *(col)* there's somebody else on the line; **eine lange ~ haben** *(hum col)* to be slow on the uptake.

Leitungs-: **~draht** *m* wire; **~mast** *m (Elec)* (electricity) pylon; **~rohr** *nt* main; *(im Haus)* (supply) pipe; **~wasser** *nt* tapwater.

Leit-: **~werk** *nt (Aviat)* tail unit; **~wort** *nt* motto.

Lektion *f* lesson. **jdm eine ~ erteilen** *(fig)* to teach sb a lesson.

Lektor *m*, **Lektorin** *f (Univ)* foreign language assistant; *(Verlags~)* editor.

Lektorat *nt (im Verlag)* editorial office.

Lektüre *f* **-n** *(no pl: das Lesen)* reading; *(Lesestoff)* reading matter. **das wird zur ~ empfohlen** that is recommended reading; **das ist eine gute** *etc* **~** it makes good *etc* reading.

Lemming *m* lemming.

Lende *f* **-n** *(Anat, Cook)* loin.

Lenden-: **~schurz** *m* loincloth; **~stück** *nt* piece of loin.

Leninismus *m* Leninism.

lenkbar *adj (Tech)* steerable; *Kind* tractable; *Rakete* guided. **leicht/schwer ~ sein** to be easy/difficult to steer.

lenken *vt* **(a)** *(steuern)* to steer; *(führen, leiten)* to guide. **gelenkte Wirtschaft** planned economy. **(b)** *(fig) Schritte, Gedanken, Aufmerksamkeit, Blick* to direct *(auf +acc* to*)*; *Verdacht* to throw *(auf +acc* onto*)*; *Gespräch* to lead; *Schicksal* to guide.

Lenker *m* **- (a)** *(Fahrrad~ etc)* handlebars *pl.* **(b)** *(Tech, fig)* guide.

Lenk-: **~rad** *nt* (steering) wheel; **~stange** *f (von Fahrrad etc)* handlebars *pl.*

Lenkung *f* **(a)** *siehe vt* steering; guidance; *(fig)* direction. **(b)** *(Tech: Lenkeinrichtung)* steering.

Lenz *m* **-e** *(liter: Frühling)* spring(time). **einen ~ schieben** *(col)*, **sich** *(dat)* **einen (faulen) ~ machen** *(col)* to laze about, to swing the lead *(col)*.

Leopard *m (wk)* **-en, -en** leopard.

Lepra *f no pl* leprosy.

Lerche *f* **-n** lark.

Lern-: **l~bar** *adj* learnable; **l~behindert** *adj* educationally handicapped; **~eifer** *m* eagerness to learn; **l~eifrig** *adj* eager to learn.

lernen 1 *vt* to learn; *Bäcker, Schlosser etc* to train as. **lesen** *etc* **~** to learn to read *etc*; **Schreibmaschine ~** to learn typing; **etw von/bei jdm ~** to learn sth from sb; **er lernt's nie** he never learns. **2** *vi* to learn; *(arbeiten)* to study; *(als Berufsausbildung)* to train. **lerne fleißig in der Schule** work hard at school; **von ihm kannst du noch ~!** you could learn a thing or two from him; **er lernt bei der Firma Braun** he's training at Braun's.

Lern-: **~hilfe** *f* educational aid; **~mittel** *pl* school-books and equipment *pl*: **~schwester** *f* student nurse.

Les-: **~art** *f (lit, fig)* version; **l~bar** *adj* legible; *Buch* readable.

Lesbierin ['lɛsbiərɪn] *f* lesbian.

lesbisch *adj* lesbian.

Lese *f* **-n** *(Wein~)* vintage.

Lese-: **~brille** *f* reading glasses *pl*; **~buch** *nt* reader; **~lampe** *f* reading lamp.

lesen[1] *pret* **las**, *ptp* **gelesen 1** *vti* **(a)** to read; *(Eccl) Messe* to say. **(b)** *(deuten) Gedanken* to read. **jdm (sein Schicksal) aus der Hand ~** to read sb's palm. **2** *vi (Univ)* to lecture *(über +acc* on*)*.

lesen[2] *pret* **las**, *ptp* **gelesen** *vt* **(a)** *(sammeln) Trauben, Beeren* to pick. **(b)** *(ver~) Erbsen, Linsen etc* to sort; *Salat* to clean.

lesenswert *adj* worth reading.

Lese-: **~probe** *f* **(a)** *(Theat)* reading; **(b)** *(Ausschnitt aus Buch)* excerpt; **~pult** *nt* lectern.

Leser(in *f***)** *m* **-** reader.

Leseratte *f (col)* bookworm *(col)*.

Leser-: **~brief** *m* (reader's) letter; **„~briefe"** "letters to the editor"; **~kreis** *m* readership; **l~lich** *adj* legible; **~schaft** *f* readership.

Lese-: **~saal** *m* reading room; **~stoff** *m* reading material; **~zeichen** *nt* bookmark(er); **~zirkel** *m* magazine subscription club.

Lesung *f (auch Parl)* reading.

Lethargie *f (Med, fig)* lethargy.

lethargisch *adj (Med, fig)* lethargic.

Lettland *nt* Latvia.

Letzt *f*: **zu guter ~** finally, in the end.

letzte(r, s) *adj* **(a)** *(örtlich, zeitlich)* last; *(restlich)* last (remaining). **~(r) werden** to be last; **als ~(r) (an)kommen** to be the last to arrive, to arrive last; **auf dem ~n Platz liegen** to be last; **den ~n beißen die Hunde** *(Prov)* (the) devil take the hindmost *(prov)*; **er wäre der ~, den ich ...** he would be the last person I'd ...; **mein ~s Geld** the last of my money; **in ~r Zeit** recently; **zum ~n Mittel greifen** to resort to drastic methods; **der L~ Wille** the last will and testament; **zum ~en Mal** for the last time; **bis ins ~** (right) down to the last detail; **bis zum ~n** to the utmost. **(b)** *(neueste) Mode, Nachricht, Neuigkeit etc* latest. **(c)** *(schlechtester)* most terrible. **das ist der ~ Dreck** that's absolute trash; **jdn wie den ~n Dreck behandeln** to treat sb like dirt.

Letzte(r) *mf decl as adj* last; *(dem Rang nach)* lowest. **der ~ des Monats** the last (day) of the month; **der/die ~ in der Klasse sein** to be bottom of the class.

letztere(r, s) *adj* the latter.

Letzte(s) *nt decl as adj* last thing. **sein ~s geben** to do one's utmost; **das ist ja das ~!** *(col)* that really is the limit.

letzt-: ~lich *adv* in the end; **~möglich** *adj attr* last possible.

Leuchte *f* **-n** light; *(col: Mensch)* genius.

leuchten *vi* **(a)** to shine; *(Feuer, Zifferblatt)* to glow; *(auf~)* to flash. **(b)** *(Mensch)* **mit einer Lampe in/auf etw** *(acc)* **~** to shine a lamp into/onto sth; **leuchte mal hierher!** shine some light over here.

leuchtend *adj (lit, fig)* shining; *Farbe* bright. **etw in den ~sten Farben schildern** to paint sth in glowing colours *(Brit) or* colors *(US)*.

Leuchter *m* **-** *(Kerzen~)* candlestick; *(Kron~)* chandelier.

Leucht-: ~farbe *f* fluorescent paint/ink *etc*; **~feuer** *nt* navigational light; **~gas** *nt* town gas; **~geschoß** *nt* flare; **~käfer** *m* glow-worm; **~patrone** *f* flare; **~pistole** *f* flare pistol; **~rakete** *f* signal rocket; **~reklame** *f* neon sign; **~röhre** *f* fluorescent tube; **~schrift** *f* neon writing; **eine ~schrift** a neon sign; **~turm** *m* lighthouse.

leugnen 1 *vt* to deny. **~, etw getan zu haben** to deny having done sth; **es ist nicht zu ~, daß ...** it cannot be denied that ... **2** *vi* to deny everything.

Leukämie *f* leukaemia *(Brit)*, leukemia *(US)*.

Leukoplast ® *nt* **-e** sticking plaster, elastoplast ® *(Brit)*, Bandaid ® *(US)*.

Leumund *m no pl* reputation, name.

Leute *pl* **(a)** people *pl*. **alle ~** everybody; **kleine ~** *(fig)* ordinary people; **es ist nicht wie bei armen ~n** *(hum col)* we're not on the breadline yet *(hum col)*; **etw unter die ~ bringen** *(col) Gerücht etc* to spread sth around; **unter die ~ kommen** *(col) (Mensch)* to meet people; *(Gerüchte etc)* to go around. **(b)** *(Mannschaft, Arbeiter etc)* **der Offizier ließ seine ~ antreten** the officer ordered his men to fall in; **dafür brauchen wir mehr ~** we need more people/staff *etc* for that.

Leutnant *m* **-s** *or* **-e** (second) lieutenant. **~ zur See** sublieutenant *(Brit)*, lieutenant junior grade *(US)*.

leutselig *adj (umgänglich)* affable.

Leutseligkeit *f* affability.

Leviten [le'viːtən] *pl*: **jdm die ~ lesen** *(col)* to haul sb over the coals *(col)*.

Lexikon *nt, pl* **Lexika** encyclopedia; *(Wörterbuch)* dictionary.

Liane *f* **-n** liana.

Libanese *m (wk)* **-n, -n, Libanesin** *f* Lebanese.

Libanon *m* **-(s) der ~** *(Land)* the Lebanon.

Libelle *f (Zool)* dragonfly.

liberal *adj* liberal.

Liberale(r) *mf decl as adj (Pol)* Liberal.

liberalisieren* *vt* to liberalize.

Liberalisierung *f* liberalization.

Liberalismus *m* liberalism.

Libero *m* **-s** *(Ftbl)* sweeper.

Libretto *nt* **-s** *or* **Libretti** libretto.

Libyen ['lyːbiən] *nt* **-s** Libya.

Libyer(in *f***)** ['lyːbiɐ, -ərɪn] *m* **-** Libyan.

libysch ['lyːbɪʃ] *adj* Libyan.

Licht *nt* **-er (a)** light. **~ machen** *(anschalten)* to turn on the lights; *(anzünden)* to light a candle *etc*; **etw gegen das ~ halten** to hold sth up to the light; **gegen das ~ photographieren** to take a photograph into the light; **bei ~e besehen** *(fig)* in the cold light of day; **jdm im ~ stehen** *(lit)* to stand in sb's light; **das ~ der Welt erblicken** *(geh)* to see the light of day. **(b)** *(fig)* light; *(Könner)* genius. **~ in eine (dunkle) Sache bringen** to shed some light on a matter; **etw ans ~ bringen** to bring sth out into the open; **ans ~ kommen** to come to light; **jdn hinters ~ führen** to lead sb up the garden path; **mir geht ein ~ auf** it's dawned on me; **kein gutes ~ auf jdn/etw werfen** to show sb/sth in a bad light; **etw ins rechte ~ rücken** to show sth in its true light.

licht *adj* **(a)** *(hell)* light. **(b)** *Wald* sparse.

Licht-: ~anlage *f* lights *pl*; **l~beständig** *adj Farben, Stoff* non-fade; **~bild** *nt* photograph; *(Dia)* slide; **~bildervortrag** *m* illustrated, talk; **~blick** *m (fig)* ray of hope; **l~durchlässig** *adj* pervious to light; *(durchsichtig)* transparent; *(durchscheinend)* translucent; **l~echt** *adj* non-fade; **l~empfindlich** *adj* sensitive to light; **~empfindlichkeit** *f* sensitivity to light.

lichten[1] **1** *vt Wald* to thin (out). **2** *vr (Reihen, Wald, Haare)* to thin (out); *(Nebel)* to clear.

lichten[2] *vt Anker* to weigh.

Lichter-: l~loh *adv* **l~loh brennen** *(lit)* to be ablaze; *(fig: Herz)* to be aflame; **~meer** *nt (liter)* sea of light.

Licht-: ~geschwindigkeit *f* speed of light; **~hupe** *f (Aut)* flash (of the headlights); **die ~hupe benutzen** to flash one's lights; **~jahr** *nt* light year; **~kegel** *m (Phys)* cone of light; *(von Scheinwerfer)* beam (of light); **~leitung** *f* lighting wire; **l~los** *adj* dark; **~maschine** *f* dynamo; *(für Drehstrom)* alternator; **~mast** lamppost; **~pause** *f* photocopy; *(bei Blaupausverfahren)* blueprint; **~punkt** *m* point of light; **~quelle** *f* source of light; **~schacht** *m* air shaft; **~schalter** *m* light switch; **~schein** *m* gleam of light; **l~scheu** *adj* averse to light; *(fig) Gesindel* shady; **~schranke** *f* light barrier; **~signal** *nt* light signal; **~spielhaus** *nt* cinema; **~strahl** *m* beam of light; **l~undurch lässig** *adj* opaque.

Lichtung *f* clearing, glade.

Lichtverhältnisse *pl* lighting conditions *pl*.

Lid *nt* **-er** eyelid.

Lidschatten *m* eye-shadow.

lieb *adj* **(a)** kind; *(nett)* nice; *(artig) Kind* good; *Gast* pleasant. **(viele) ~e Grüße Deine Silvia** love Silvia; **sich ~ um jdn kümmern** to be very kind to sb; **würdest du (bitte) so ~ sein und das Fenster aufmachen** would you be so kind as to open the window; **sich bei jdm ~ Kind machen** *(pej)* to suck up to sb. **(b)** *(angenehm)* **es wäre mir ~, wenn ...** I'd be glad if ...; **es wäre ihm ~er** he would prefer it; **am ~sten hätte ich ...** what I'd like most would be (to have) ...; **am ~sten lese ich Kriminalromane** best of all I like detective novels; **am ~sten hätte ich ihm eine geklebt!** *(col)* I could have stuck one on him *(col)*. **(c)** *(in Anrede)* dear. **~ste (r, s)** favourite *(Brit)*, favorite *(US)*; **der ~e Gott** the Good Lord; **~er Gott** *(Anrede)* dear God; **L~e Anna, ~er Klaus! ...** Dear Anna and Klaus, ...; **den ~en langen Tag** *(col)* the whole livelong day; **(ach) du ~er Himmel/~er Gott/~e Zeit** good heavens *or* Lord!

Liebe *f no pl* love *(zu jdm, für jdn* for *or* of sb, *zu etw* of sth*)*. **die große ~** the love of one's life; **aus ~ zu jdm/einer Sache** for the love of sb/sth; **etw mit viel ~ tun** to do sth with loving care; **in ~** with love; **sie/er ist gut in der ~** *(col)* she/he is good at making love.

liebebedürftig *adj* **~ sein** to need a lot of affection.

Liebelei *f (col)* flirtation; affair.

lieben *vti* to love; *(als Liebesakt)* to make love *(jdn* to sb*)*. **etw nicht ~** not to like sth; **etw ~d gern tun** to love to do sth.

Liebende(r) *mf decl as adj* lover.

liebenswert *adj* lovable, endearing.

liebenswürdig *adj* kind. **würden Sie so ~ sein und die Tür schließen?** would you be so kind as to shut the door?
liebenswürdigerweise *adv* kindly.
Liebenswürdigkeit *f (Höflichkeit)* politeness; *(Freundlichkeit)* kindness.
lieber 1 *adj comp of* **lieb. 2** *adv comp of* **gern (a)** *(vorzugsweise)* rather. **das tue ich ~** *(im Augenblick)* I'd rather do that; *(grundsätzlich)* I prefer doing that; **das würde ich ~ tun** I would prefer to do that; **ich trinke ~ Wein als Bier** I prefer wine to beer; **(das möchte ich) ~ nicht!** I'd rather not. **(b)** *(besser)* better. **bleibe ~ im Bett** you'd better stay in bed; **ich hätte ~ nachgeben sollen** I'd have done better to have given in; **nichts ~ als das** there's nothing I'd rather do/have.
Liebes- *in cpds* love; **~abenteuer** *nt* amorous adventure; **~affäre** *f* (love-)affair; **~akt** *m* sex act; **~beziehung** *f* romantic attachment; (sexual) relationship; **~brief** *m* love letter; **~erklärung** *f* declaration of love; **~geschichte** *f* **(a)** *(Liter)* love story; **(b)** *(col: Liebschaft)* love-affair; **~heirat** *f* love-match; **~kummer** *m* lovesickness; **~kummer haben** to be lovesick; **~leben** *nt* love-life; **~lied** *nt* love song; **~müh(e)** *f*: **das ist vergebliche ~müh(e)** that is futile; **~paar** *nt* lovers *pl*; **~roman** *m* romantic novel; **~spiel** *nt* loveplay; **~szene** *f* love scene; **~verhältnis** *nt* (sexual) relationship.
liebevoll *adj* loving.
lieb-: **~gewinnen*** *vt sep irreg* to grow fond of; **~geworden** *adj attr* well-loved; *Brauch* favourite *(Brit)*, favorite *(US)*; **~haben** *vt sep irreg* to love; *(weniger stark)* to be (very) fond of.
Liebhaber(in *f*) *m* **- (a)** lover. **(b)** *(Interessent)* enthusiast; *(Sammler)* collector.
Liebhaberei *f (fig)* hobby. **etw aus ~ tun** to do sth as a hobby.
Liebhaberpreis *m* collector's price.
lieblich *adj* delightful; *Duft, Wein* sweet.
Liebling *m* darling; *(bevorzugter Mensch)* favourite *(Brit)*, favorite *(US)*.
Lieblings- *in cpds* favourite *(Brit)*, favorite *(US)*.
Lieb-: **l~los** *adj* unloving; *Bemerkung* unkind; *Benehmen* inconsiderate; **~schaft** *f* affair.
Liebste(r) *mf decl as adj* sweetheart.
Lied *nt* **-er** song; *(Kirchen~)* hymn. **das Ende vom ~** *(fig col)* the outcome (of all this); **davon kann ich ein ~ singen** I could tell you a thing or two about that *(col)*.
liederlich *adj (schlampig)* slovenly *attr, pred; (unmoralisch) Leben, Mann* dissolute; *Frau, Mädchen* loose. **ein ~es Frauenzimmer** *(pej)* a slut.
lief *pret of* **laufen.**
Lieferant *m* supplier; *(Auslieferer)* deliveryman.
Lieferanten|eingang *m* tradesmen's entrance; *(von Warenhaus etc)* goods entrance.
Liefer-: **l~bar** *adj (vorrätig)* available; **die Ware ist sofort l~bar** the article can be delivered at once; **~firma** *f* supplier; *(Zusteller)* delivery firm; **~frist** *f* delivery period; **die ~frist einhalten** to meet the delivery date.
liefern *vti* to supply; *Beweise, Informationen auch* to furnish; *Ertrag* to yield; *(col: stellen)* to provide; *(zustellen)* to deliver *(in +acc* to*)*. **jdm etw ~** to supply sb with sth/provide sb with sth/deliver sth to sb; **wir ~ nicht ins Ausland** we don't supply the foreign market; *siehe* **geliefert.**
Liefer-: **~schein** *m* delivery note; **~termin** *m* delivery date.
Lieferung *f* delivery; *(Versorgung)* supply. **bei ~ zu bezahlen** payable on delivery.
Liefer-: **~vertrag** *m* supply/delivery contract; **~wagen** *m* van, panel truck *(US)*; *(offen)* pick-up; **~zeit** *f* delivery period; **~zettel** *m* delivery order.
Liege *f* **-n** couch; *(Camping~)* camp bed *(Brit)*, cot *(US)*.
liegen *pret* **lag,** *ptp* **gelegen** *vi* **(a)** to lie. **hart/weich ~** to lie on a hard/soft bed *etc*; **unbequem ~** to lie uncomfortably; **auf den Knien ~** to be kneeling; **im Krankenhaus ~** to be in hospital; **der Kranke muß unbedingt ~** the patient must stay lying down; **der Schnee liegt 50 cm hoch** the snow is 50 cm deep; **der Schnee bleibt nicht ~** the snow isn't lying; **etw ~ lassen** to leave sth.
(b) *(sich befinden, sein)* to be; *(Haus, Stadt etc auch)* to be situated, to lie. **Paris liegt an der Seine** Paris is (situated) on the Seine; **nach Süden/der Straße ~** to face south/the road; **verstreut ~** to lie scattered; **das Haus liegt ganz ruhig** the house is in a very quiet location; **das liegt doch auf dem Weg/ganz in der Nähe** it's on the way; **das Schiff liegt am Kai** the ship is (tied up) alongside the quay; **die Betonung liegt auf der zweiten Silbe** the stress is on the second syllable; **so, wie die Dinge jetzt ~** as things stand at the moment; **damit liegst du (gold)richtig** *(col)* you're right there; **an der Spitze ~** to be right out in front; **der zweite Läufer liegt weit hinter dem ersten** the second runner is lying a long way behind the first; **die Preise ~ zwischen 60 und 80 Mark** the prices are between 60 and 80 marks.
(c) *(wichtig sein)* **es liegt mir wenig daran** that isn't very important to me; **mir liegt an guten Beziehungen** I am concerned that there should be good relations.
(d) *(begründet sein)* **an jdm/etw ~** to be because of sb/sth; **woran liegt es?** why is that?; **das liegt daran, daß ...** that is because ...; **an mir soll es nicht ~, wenn die Sache schiefgeht** it won't be my fault if things go wrong; **das liegt ganz bei dir** that is entirely up to you; **die Entscheidung liegt bei Ihnen** the decision rests with you.
(e) *(geeignet sein, passen)* **jdm liegt etw nicht** sth doesn't suit sb; *(Mathematik etc)* sb has no aptitude for sth; **Krankenschwester liegt mir nicht** *(col)* nursing doesn't appeal to me.
liegenbleiben *vi sep irreg aux sein* **(a)** *(nicht aufstehen)* to remain lying (down). **(im Bett) ~** to stay in bed; **bleib liegen!** don't get up! **(b)** *(vergessen werden)* to get left behind; *(nicht verkauft werden)* to be left unsold; *(nicht ausgeführt werden)* to be left (undone).
liegend *adj (Art)* reclining. **~ aufbewahren** to store flat.
liegenlassen *vt sep irreg, ptp* **~** *or* **liegengelassen** *(nicht erledigen)* to leave; *(vergessen)* to leave (behind); *(herum~)* to leave lying about.
Liege-: **~platz** *m* place to lie; *(Ankerplatz)* moorings *pl*; **~sitz** *m* reclining seat; *(auf Boot)* couchette; **~stuhl** *m (mit Holzgestell)* deck chair; *(mit Metallgestell)* lounger; **~stütz** *m (Sport)* press-up; **~wagen** *m (Rail)* couchette coach *or* car *(esp US)*; **~wiese** *f* lawn *(for sunbathing)*.
lieh *pret of* **leihen.**
ließ *pret of* **lassen.**
Lift *m* **-e** *or* **-s** *(Personen~)* lift *(Brit)*, elevator *(esp US)*.
Liga *f, pl* **Ligen** league.
liieren* *vt* to bring *or* get together. **liiert sein** to have joined forces; *(Firmen etc)* to be working together; *(Pol)* to be allied; *(ein Verhältnis haben)* to have a relationship.
Likör *m* **-e** liqueur.
lila *adj inv* purple.
Lilie [-iə] *f* lily.
Liliputaner(in *f*) *m* **-** midget.
Limit *nt* **-s** limit; *(Fin)* ceiling.
limitieren* *vt (form)* to limit; *(Fin)* to put a ceiling on.
Limonade *f* lemonade.
Limone *f* **-n** lime.
Limousine [limu'ziːnə] *f* saloon *(Brit)*, sedan *(US)*.
Linde *f* **-n** linden *or* lime (tree).

Lindenblütentee *m* lime blossom tea.
lindern *vt* to ease, to relieve.
Linderung *f* easing, relief.
Lineal *nt* **-e** ruler.
linear *adj* linear.
Linguistik *f* linguistics *sing*.
linguistisch *adj* linguistic.
Linie [-iə] *f* **(a)** line. **ein Schreibblock mit ~n** a ruled notepad; **in einer ~ stehen** to be in a line; **sich in einer ~ aufstellen** to line up; **einer Sache** *(dat)* **fehlt die klare ~** there's no clear line to sth; **eine ~ ziehen zwischen ...** *(+dat) (fig)* to draw a line between ...; **auf der ganzen ~** *(fig)* all along the line; **auf die ~ achten** to watch one's figure; **in erster ~** first and foremost. **(b)** *(Verkehrsverbindung)* route. **fahren Sie mit der ~ 2** take a *or* the 2; **die ~ Köln-Bonn** the Cologne-Bonn line.
Linien- [-iən]: **~bus** *m* regular bus; **~flug** *m* scheduled flight; **~papier** *nt* lined paper; **~richter** *m (Sport)* linesman; **~schiff** *nt* regular service ship; **l~treu** *adj* loyal to the party line; **l~treu sein** to toe the party line; **~verkehr** *m* regular traffic; *(Aviat)* scheduled traffic; **im ~verkehr fahren** to operate on regular services.
linieren* *vt* to rule, to draw lines on. **liniert** lined.
Linke *f (wk)* **-n, -n (a)** *(Hand)* left hand; *(Seite)* left side; *(Boxen)* left. **zu seiner ~n** to his left. **(b)** *(Pol)* Left.
Linke(r) *mf decl as adj (Pol)* left-winger, leftist *(pej)*.
linke(r, s) *adj attr* **(a)** left. **die ~ Seite** the left(-hand) side; *(von Stoff)* the wrong side; **das mache ich mit der ~n Hand** *(col)* I can do that with my eyes shut *(col)*; **er ist heute mit dem ~n Bein zuerst aufgestanden** *(col)* he got out of bed on the wrong side this morning *(col)*; **ein ganz ~r Hund** *(pej col)* a nasty piece of work *(pej col)*; **ein ganz ~s Ding drehen** *(col)* to get up to a bit of no good *(col)*. **(b)** *(Pol)* left-wing; *Flügel* left.
linkisch *adj* clumsy, awkward.
links 1 *adv* **(a)** on the left; *schauen, abbiegen* left. **nach ~** (to the) left; **von ~** from the left; **~ von etw** left of sth; **sich ~ halten** to keep to the left; **weiter ~** further to the left; **sich ~ einordnen** to move into the left-hand lane; **jdn ~ liegenlassen** *(fig col)* to ignore sb; **das mache ich mit ~** *(col)* I can do that with my eyes shut *(col)*. **(b)** *(Pol)* on the left. **nach ~** to the left; **~ von jdm** left of sb; **~ von der Mitte** left of centre; **~ stehen** *(col)* to be left-wing. **(c)** *(verkehrt) bügeln* on the reverse; *tragen* inside out; **~ stricken** to purl. **2** *prep +gen* on *or* to the left of.
Links-: **~abbieger** *m* motorist/vehicle turning left; **~außen** *m* **-** *(Ftbl)* outside left; *(Pol)* extreme left-winger; **~drall** *m (von Billardball)* spin to the left; *(von Auto, Pferd)* pull to the left; *(Pol col)* leaning to the left; **~extremist** *m* left-wing extremist; **l~gerichtet** *adj (Pol)* left-wing *no adv*; **~händer(in** *f*) *m* **-** left-hander; **~händer sein** to be left-handed; **l~herum** *adv* (around) to the left; **~kurve** *f (von Straße)* left-hand bend; **l~lastig** *adj* listing to the left; *(fig)* leftist *(pej)*, leaning to the left; **l~lastig sein** to list/lean to the left; **l~radikal** *adj (Pol)* radically left-wing; **die ~radikalen** the left-wing radicals; **~radikalismus** *m (Pol)* left-wing radicalism; **l~rheinisch** *adj* to *or* on the left of the Rhine; **~rutsch** *m (Pol)* swing to the left; **l~seitig** *adj* on the left(-hand) side; **l~seitig gelähmt** paralyzed in the left side; **~verkehr** *m no pl* driving on the left *no def art*; **in Großbritannien ist ~verkehr** they drive on the left in Britain.
Linoleum [li'no:leum] *nt no pl* linoleum, lino *(Brit)*.
Linse *f* **-n (a)** *(Bot, Cook)* lentil. **(b)** *(Opt)* lens.
linsen *vi (col)* to peek *(col)*.
Lippe *f* **-n** lip. **es soll kein Wort über meine ~n kommen** not a word shall pass my lips; **er brachte kein Wort über die ~n** he couldn't say *or* utter a word.
Lippen-: **~bekenntnis** *nt* lip-service; **~stift** *m* lipstick.
Liquidation *f (form)* liquidation. **in ~ treten** to go into liquidation.
liquid(e) *adj (Econ) Firma* solvent.
liquidieren* *vt* **(a)** *jdn* to liquidate. **(b)** *Geschäft* to wind up.
Liquidität *f (Econ)* liquidity.
lispeln *vti* to lisp.
List *f* **-en** *(Täuschung)* cunning; *(Plan)* trick. **mit ~ und Tücke** *(col)* with a lot of coaxing.
Liste *f* **-n** *(Aufstellung)* list; *(Wähler~)* register. **sich in eine ~ eintragen** to put one's name on a list.
Listen-: **~platz** *m (Pol)* place on the party list; **~preis** *m* list price.
listig *adj* cunning, wily *no adv*.
Litanei *f (Eccl, fig)* litany. **eine ~ von Klagen** a long list of complaints.
Litauen *nt* **-s** Lithuania.
litauisch *adj* Lithuanian.
Liter *m or nt* **-** litre *(Brit)*, liter *(US)*.
literarisch *adj* literary.
Literatur *f* literature.
Literatur-: **~angabe** *f* bibliographical reference; **~gattung** *f* literary genre; **~geschichte** *f* history of literature; **~kritiker** *m* literary critic; **~verzeichnis** *nt* bibliography; **~wissenschaft** *f* literary studies *pl*.
literweise *adv (lit)* by the litre *(Brit) or* liter *(US)*; *(fig)* by the gallon.
Litfaßsäule *f* advertising column.
Litho-: **~graph** *m* lithographer; **~graphie** *f* **(a)** *(Verfahren)* lithography; **(b)** *(Druck)* lithograph.
litt *ptp of* **leiden.**
Liturgie *f* liturgy.
Litze *f* **-n** braid; *(Elec)* flex.
live [laif] *adj pred, adv (Rad, TV)* live.
Live-Sendung [laif-] *f* live broadcast.
Lizenz *f* licence *(Brit)*, license *(US)*. **etw in ~ herstellen** to manufacture sth under licence.
Lizenz-: **~ausgabe** *f* licensed edition; **~geber** *m* licenser; *(Behörde)* licensing authority; **~gebühr** *f* licence fee *(Brit)*, license fee *(US)*; **~inhaber** *m* licensee; **er ist ~inhaber** he has a licence *(Brit) or* license *(US)*; **~spieler** *m (Ftbl)* professional player.
Lkw [ɛlka:'ve:] *m* **-(s) = Lastkraftwagen.**
Lob *nt no pl* praise. **(viel) ~ für etw bekommen** to come in for (a lot of) praise for sth; **jdm ~ spenden** *or* **zollen** to praise sb.
loben *vt* to praise. **jdn/etw ~d erwähnen** to commend sb/sth; **das lob ich mir** that's what I like (to see/hear *etc*).
lobenswert *adj* laudable.
Lob-: **~hudelei** *f (pej)* gushing; **~lied** *nt* song of praise; **ein ~ lied auf jdn/etw anstimmen** *(fig)* to sing sb's praises; **~rede** *f* eulogy; **eine ~rede auf jdn halten** *(lit)* to make a speech in sb's honour *(Brit) or* honor *(US)*; *(fig)* to eulogize sb.
Loch *nt* **⸗er** hole; *(Luft~)* gap; *(fig col: elende Wohnung)* dump *(col)*, hole *(col)*. **sich** *(dat)* **ein ~ in den Kopf schlagen** to gash one's head; **⸗er in die Luft gucken** to gaze into space; **ein großes ~ in jds Geldbeutel** *(acc)* **reißen** *(col)* to make a big hole in sb's pocket.
lochen *vt* to punch holes/a hole in; *Fahrkarte* to punch.
Locher *m* **- (a)** punch. **(b)** *(Mensch)* punch-card operator.
löcherig *adj* full of holes.
Loch-: **~karte** *f* punch card; **~streifen** *m* (punched) paper tape.
Lochung *f* punching; *(Stelle)* perforation.
Lochzange *f* punch.
Locke *f* **-n** *(Haar)* curl. **~n haben** to have curly

hair.

locken[1] *vtr Haar* to curl. **gelocktes Haar** curly hair.

locken[2] *vt* to lure. **jdn in einen Hinterhalt ~** to lure sb into a trap; **die Henne lockte ihre Küken** the hen called to its chicks.

lockend *adj* tempting.

Locken-: ~kopf *m* curly hairstyle; *(Mensch)* curlyhead; **~wickler** *m* - (hair-)curler.

locker *adj (lit, fig)* loose; *Kuchen, Schaum* light; *(nicht gespannt)* slack; *Haltung, Sitzweise* relaxed; *(col)* cool *(col)*. **~ werden** *(lit, fig)* to get loose; *(Muskeln, Mensch)* to loosen up; **etw ~ machen** to loosen sth/make sth light/slacken sth; **etw ~ lassen** to slacken sth off; *Bremse* to let sth off; **~ sitzen** *(Ziegel, Schraube etc)* to be loose; **bei ihr sitzt die Hand ziemlich ~** she's quick to lash out; **bei ihm sitzt der Revolver ~** he's trigger-happy; **das mache ich ganz ~** *(col)* I can do it just like that *(col)*.

locker-: ~lassen *vi sep irreg (col)* **nicht ~lassen** not to let up; **~machen** *vt sep (col) Geld* to shell out *(col)*.

lockern 1 *vt* **(a)** *(locker machen)* to loosen; *Seil, (lit, fig) Zügel* to slacken. **(b)** *(entspannen) Muskeln* to loosen up; *(fig) Vorschriften* to relax. **2** *vr* to work itself loose; *(Sport)* to loosen up; *(Verkrampfung)* to ease off; *(Atmosphäre)* to get more relaxed.

Lockerungsübung *f* loosening up exercise; *(zum Warmwerden)* limbering-up exercise.

lockig *adj Haar* curly; *Mensch* curlyheaded.

Lock-: ~mittel *nt* lure; **~ruf** *m* call.

Lockung *f* lure; *(Versuchung)* temptation.

Lockvogel *m (lit, fig)* decoy.

Lodenmantel *m* loden (coat).

lodern *vi (lit, fig)* to blaze.

Löffel *m* - spoon; *(als Maß)* spoonful; *(von Bagger)* bucket. **den ~ abgeben** *(col)* to kick the bucket *(col)*; **jdm ein paar hinter die ~ geben** to give sb a clout around the ear(s).

löffeln *vt* to spoon.

log *pret of* **lügen.**

Logarithmus *m* logarithm.

Logbuch *nt* log(book).

Loge ['lo:ʒə] *f* **-n (a)** *(Theat)* box; *(Pförtner~)* lodge. **(b)** *(Freimaurer~)* lodge.

Logenplatz ['lo:ʒən-] *m (Theat)* seat in a box.

Logik *f* logic.

Logiker(in *f*) *m* - logician.

Logis [lo'ʒi:] *nt* - **Kost und ~** board and lodging.

logisch *adj* logical; *(col: selbstverständlich)* natural. **gehst du auch hin? — ~** are you going too? — of course.

logischerweise *adv* logically.

Logistik *f* **(a)** *(Math)* logic. **(b)** *(Mil)* logistics *sing.*

logo *interj (col)* you bet *(col)*.

Logopäde *m (wk)* **-n, -n, Logopädin** *f* speech therapist.

Logopädie *f* speech therapy.

Lohn *m* **-e (a)** *(Arbeitsentgelt)* wage(s), pay *no pl, no indef art.* **bei jdm in ~ und Brot stehen** *(geh)* to be in sb's employ *(form)*. **(b)** *(fig: Belohnung)* reward; *(Strafe)* punishment. **zum ~ für ...** as a reward/punishment for ...; **das ist nun der ~ für meine Mühe!** *(iro)* that's what I get for my trouble.

Lohn-: l~abhängig *adj* on a payroll; **~abhängige(r)** *mf* worker; **~abrechnung** *f* wages slip; **~arbeit** *f* labour *(Brit)*, labor *(US)*; **~ausfall** *m* loss of earnings; **~büro** *nt* wages office; **~empfänger** *m* wage-earner.

lohnen 1 *vir* to be worth it. **es lohnt (sich), etw zu tun** it is worth doing sth; **die Mühe lohnt sich** it is worth the effort; **das lohnt sich nicht für mich** it's not worth my while. **2** *vt* **jdm etw ~** to reward sb for sth; **er hat mir meine Mühe schlecht gelohnt** he gave me poor thanks for my efforts.

löhnen *vti (col: bezahlen)* to shell out *(col)*.

lohnend *adj* rewarding; *(nutzbringend)* worthwhile; *(einträglich)* profitable.

lohnenswert *adj* worthwhile.

Lohn-: ~erhöhung *f* pay rise; **~forderung** *f* pay claim; **~fortzahlung** *f* continued payment of wages; **~gruppe** *f* wage group; **~kürzung** *f* wage cut; **~liste** *f* payroll; **~politik** *f* pay policy; **~skala** *f* pay scale; **~steuer** *f* income tax.

Lohnsteuer-: ~jahresausgleich *m* income tax return; **~karte** *f* (income) tax card.

Lohn-: ~stopp *m* pay freeze; **~streifen** pay slip; **~tarif** *m* wage rate; **~tüte** *f* pay packet; **~verhandlung** *f* pay negotiations *pl*; **~zahlung** *f* payment of wages.

Lok *f* **-s = Lokomotive** engine.

lokal *adj (örtlich)* local.

Lokal *nt* **-e** *(Gaststätte)* pub *(esp Brit)*, bar; *(Restaurant)* restaurant.

Lokal- *in cpds* local; **~anästhesie** *f (Med)* local anaesthetic *(Brit) or* anesthetic *(US)*.

lokalisieren* *vt* **(a)** *(Ort feststellen)* to locate. **(b)** *(Med)* to localize.

Lokalität *f* locality; *(innen)* premises *pl.*

Lokal-: ~kolorit *nt* local colour *(Brit) or* color *(US)*; **~nachrichten** *pl* local news *sing*; **~patriotismus** *m* local patriotism; **~teil** *m* local section; **~termin** *m (Jur)* visit to the scene of the crime; **~zeitung** *f* local newspaper.

Lokomotive *f* locomotive, (railway) engine.

Lokomotivführer *m* engine driver, engineer *(US)*.

Looping ['lu:pɪŋ] *m or nt* **-s** *(Aviat)* looping the loop. **einen ~ machen** to loop the loop.

Lorbeer *m* **-en** *(lit: Gewächs)* laurel; *(als Gewürz)* bayleaf; *(~kranz)* laurel wreath. **sich auf seinen ~en ausruhen** *(fig col)* to rest on one's laurels.

Lorbeer-: ~baum *m* laurel (tree); **~blatt** *nt* bayleaf; **~kranz** *m* laurel wreath.

Los *nt* **-e (a)** *(für Entscheidung)* lot; *(in der Lotterie)* ticket. **das Große ~ ziehen** *(lit, fig)* to hit the jackpot; **etw durch das ~ entscheiden** to decide sth by drawing lots; **jdn durch das ~ bestimmen** to pick sb by drawing lots; **das ~ fiel auf mich** it fell to my lot. **(b)** *no pl (Schicksal)* lot. **er hat ein hartes ~** his is a hard lot.

los 1 *adj pred* **(a)** *(nicht befestigt)* loose. **der Hund ist von der Leine ~** the dog is off the lead. **(b)** *(frei)* **jdn/etw ~ sein** *(col)* to be rid of sb/sth; **ich bin mein ganzes Geld ~** *(col)* I'm cleaned out *(col)*. **(c)** *(col)* **etwas ~ machen** *(col)* to make sth happen; **was ist denn hier ~?** what's going on here?; **was ist ~?** what's the matter?; **irgendwas ist mit ihm ~** there's something wrong with him; **mit dem ist doch nichts mehr ~** he isn't up to much any more; **da war was ~** there was plenty of action; *(Schlägerei etc)* all hell was let loose; **ist hier abends nichts ~?** isn't there anything to do here in the evenings?

2 *adv* **(a)** *(Aufforderung)* **~!** come on!; **nichts wie ~!** let's get going; **(na) ~, mach schon!** (come on,) get on with it; **~, fahr doch endlich** come on, start driving; **auf die Plätze, fertig, ~** on your marks, get set, go! **(b)** *(weg)* **wir wollen früh ~** we want to be off early.

los-: ~binden *vt sep irreg* to untie *(von* from*)*; **~brechen** *sep irreg* **1** *vt* to break off; **2** *vi aux sein (Gelächter etc)* to break out; *(Sturm, Gewitter)* to break.

Löschblatt *nt* sheet of blotting paper.

löschen *vt* **(a)** *Feuer, Kerze* to put out, to extinguish; *Durst* to quench; *Tonband* to erase; *Schuld* to pay off; *Eintragung, (Comp)* to delete; *Konto* to close; *(aufsaugen) Tinte* to blot. **(b)** *(Naut) Ladung* to unload.

Lösch-: ~fahrzeug *nt* fire engine; **~mittel** *nt* (fire-)extinguishing agent; **~papier** *nt* (piece of) blotting paper; **~zug** *m* set of fire-fighting appliances.

lose *adj (lit, fig)* loose; *(nicht gespannt) Seil* slack. **etw ~ verkaufen** to sell sth loose.

Lösegeld *nt* ransom (money).

losen *vi* to draw lots *(um* for*)*.

lösen 1 *vt* **(a)** *(losmachen)* to remove *(von* from*)*; *Boot* to cast off *(von* from*)*; *(aufbinden)* to undo; *Hände* to unclasp; *Handbremse* to release; *Husten, Krampf* to ease; *Muskeln* to loosen up; *(lit, fig: lockern)* to loosen; *siehe* **gelöst. (b)** *(klären)* to solve; *Konflikt* to resolve. **(c)** *(annullieren) Vertrag* to cancel; *Verlobung* to break off; *Verbindung* to sever; *Ehe* to dissolve. **(d)** *(kaufen) Karte* to buy, to get.

2 *vr* **(a)** *(sich losmachen)* to detach oneself *(von* from*)*; *(sich ab~)* to come off *(von etw* sth*)*; *(Knoten, Haare)* to come undone; *(Schuß)* to go off; *(Husten, Krampf)* to ease; *(Muskeln)* to loosen up; *(lit, fig: sich lockern)* to (be)come loose. **sich von jdm ~** to break away from sb; **sich von etw ~** *von Vorurteilen etc* to rid oneself of sth. **(b)** *(sich aufklären)* to be solved. **sich von selbst ~** *(Mordfall)* to solve itself. **(c)** *(in Flüssigkeit)* to dissolve *(in+dat* in*)*.

los-: ~fahren *vi sep irreg aux sein (abfahren)* to set off; *(Fahrzeug)* to move off; *(Auto)* to drive off; **~gehen** *vi sep irreg aux sein* **(a)** *(weggehen)* to set off; *(Schuß etc)* to go off; **(mit dem Messer) auf jdn ~gehen** to go for sb (with a knife); **(b)** *(col: anfangen)* to start; **gleich geht's ~** it's just about to start; **jetzt geht's ~!** here we go!; *(Reise, Bewegung)* we're/you're off!; **(c)** *(col: abgehen)* to come off; **~heulen** *vi sep (col: weinen)* to burst out crying; **~kommen** *vi sep irreg aux sein (Mensch)* to get away *(von* from*)*; *(sich befreien)* to free oneself *(von* from*)*; **~kriegen** *vt sep (col: ablösen)* to get off; **~lachen** *vi sep* to burst out laughing; **~lassen** *vt sep irreg* **(a)** to let go of; **der Gedanke läßt mich nicht mehr ~** the thought haunts me; **(b)** *(col: abfeuern) Feuerwerk* to let off; **(c) jdn (auf jdn) ~lassen** *(fig col)* to let sb loose (on sb); **die Hunde auf jdn ~lassen** to set the dogs on(to) sb; **~laufen** *vi sep irreg aux sein* to start to run; **~legen** *vi sep (col)* to get going; **nun leg mal ~ und erzähle ...** now come on and tell me/us ...

löslich *adj* soluble. **leicht/schwer ~** readily/not readily soluble.

los-: ~lösen *sep* **1** *vt* to remove *(von* from*)*; *(ablösen auch)* to take off *(von etw* sth*)*; *(lockern)* to loosen; **2** *vr* to detach oneself *(von* from*)*; *(sich ablösen auch)* to come off *(von etw* sth*)*; *(lockern)* to become loose; **sich von jdm ~lösen** to break away from sb; **~machen** *sep* **1** *vt* to free; *(~binden)* to untie; **2** *vi (col: sich beeilen)* to step on it *(col)*; **3** *vr* to get away *(von* from*)*.

Losnummer *f* ticket number.

los-: ~reißen *sep irreg* **1** *vt* to tear off *(von etw* sth*)*; **2** *vr* **sich (von etw) ~reißen** *(Hund etc)* to break free (from sth); *(fig)* to tear oneself away (from sth); **~rennen** *vi sep irreg aux sein (col)* to run off; *(anfangen zu laufen)* to start to run; **~sagen** *vr sep* **sich von etw ~sagen** to renounce sth; **~schicken** *vt sep* to send off; **~schießen** *vi sep irreg* **schieß ~!** *(fig col)* fire away! *(col)*; **~schlagen** *vi sep irreg* to hit out; **auf jdn ~schlagen** to go for sb; **~schnallen** *vt sep* to unbuckle; **~schrauben** *vt sep* to unscrew; *(lockern auch)* to loosen; **~stürzen** *vi sep aux sein* to rush off; **auf jdn/etw ~stürzen** to pounce on sb/sth.

Lostrommel *f* drum (for lottery draw).

Losung *f* **(a)** motto. **(b)** *(Kennwort)* password.

Lösung *f* **(a)** solution *(gen* to*)*; *(das Lösen)* solution *(gen* of*)*; *(eines Konfliktes)* resolving. **(b)** *(Chem)* solution.

Lösungsmittel *nt* solvent.

loswerden *vt sep irreg aux sein* to get rid of; *Gedanken* to get away from; *Geld (ausgeben)* to spend.

losziehen *vi sep irreg aux sein (aufbrechen)* to set out *(in+acc, nach* for*)*.

Lot *nt* **-e (a)** *(Senkblei)* plumbline. **im ~ sein** to be in plumb; **die Sache ist wieder im ~** things have been straightened out. **(b)** *(Math)* perpendicular. **das ~ fällen** to drop a perpendicular.

loten *vt* to plumb.

löten *vti* to solder.

Lothringen *nt* Lorraine.

lothringisch *adj* of Lorraine, Lorrainese.

Löt-: ~kolben *m* soldering iron; **~lampe** *f* blowlamp; **~metall** *nt* solder.

Lotosblume *f* lotus (flower).

lotrecht *adj (Math)* perpendicular.

Lotse *m (wk)* **-n, -n** *(Naut)* pilot; *(Flug~)* air-traffic controller.

lotsen *vt* to guide. **jdn irgendwohin ~** *(col)* to drag sb somewhere *(col)*.

Lotterie *f* lottery; *(Tombola)* raffle.

Lotterielos *nt* lottery/raffle ticket.

lott(e)rig *adj (col)* slovenly *no adv*.

Lotterleben *nt (col)* dissolute life.

Lotto *nt* **-s** national lottery. **(im) ~ spielen** to do the national lottery; **du hast wohl im ~ gewonnen** you must have won the pools *(Brit)*.

Lotto-: ~geschäft *nt*, **~laden** *m (col)* Lotto agency; **~gewinn** *m* Lotto win; *(Geld)* Lotto winnings *pl*; **~schein** *m* Lotto coupon; **~zahlen** *pl* winning Lotto numbers *pl*.

Löwe *m (wk)* **-n, -n** lion; *(Astron, Astrol)* Leo.

Löwen-: ~anteil *m (col)* lion's share; **~bändiger** *m* lion-tamer; **~jagd** *f* lion hunt; **~zahn** *m* dandelion.

Löwin *f* lioness.

loyal [loa'ja:l] *adj* loyal *(jdm gegenüber* to sb*)*.

Loyalität [loajali:'tɛ:t] *f* loyalty.

LP [ɛl'pe:] *f* **-s** = **Langspielplatte** LP.

Luchs [lʊks] *m* **-e** lynx.

Luchs|augen *pl (col)* eagle eyes *pl*.

Lücke *f* **-n** *(lit, fig)* gap; *(Gesetzes~)* loophole; *(in Versorgung)* break.

Lücken-: ~büßer, ~füller *m* stopgap; **l~haft** *adj* full of gaps; *Versorgung* deficient; *Gesetz, Alibi* full of holes; **sein Wissen ist sehr l~haft** there are great gaps in his knowledge; **l~los** *adj* complete; *Kenntnisse* perfect; *Versorgung, Überlieferung* unbroken; **~test** *m (Sch)* completion test.

lud *pret of* **laden**[1], **laden**[2].

Luder *nt* **-** *(col)* minx.

Luft *f* **(a)** air *no pl*. **im Zimmer ist schlechte ~** the air is stuffy in the room; **dicke ~** *(col)* a bad atmosphere; **(frische) ~ schnappen** *(col)* to get some fresh air; **die ~ ist rein** *(col)* the coast is clear; **aus der ~** from the air; **jdn an die (frische) ~ setzen** *(col)* to show sb the door; **in die ~ fliegen** *(col)* to explode; **etw in die ~ jagen** *(col)* to blow sth up; **leicht in die ~ gehen** *(fig)* to be quick to blow one's top *(col)*; **es liegt etwas in der ~** there's something in the air; **in die ~ gucken** to stare into space; **das kann sich doch nicht in ~ aufgelöst haben** it can't have vanished into thin air; **die Behauptung ist aus der ~ gegriffen** this statement is pure invention; **vor Freude in die ~ springen** to jump for joy; **von ~ und Liebe leben** to live on love; **er ist ~ für mich** I'm not speaking to him.

(b) *(Atem~)* breath. **der Kragen schnürt mir die ~ ab** this collar is choking me; **nach ~ schnappen** to gasp for breath; **die ~ anhalten** *(lit)* to hold one's breath; **nun halt mal die ~ an!** *(col) (rede nicht)* hold your tongue!; *(übertreibe nicht)* come off it! *(col)*; **keine ~ mehr kriegen** not to be able to breathe; **~ holen** to catch one's breath; **tief ~ holen** *(lit, fig)* to take a deep breath; **mir blieb vor Schreck die ~ weg** the shock took my breath away; **wieder ~ bekommen** *(nach Sport etc)* to get one's breath back;

(fig) to get a chance to catch one's breath; **seinem Herzen ~ machen** to get everything off one's chest; **seinem Zorn** *etc* **~ machen** to give vent to one's anger *etc*.
(c) *(fig: Spielraum)* space, room.

Luft: ~abwehr *f (Mil)* anti-aircraft defence *(Brit)* *or* defense *(US)*; **~angriff** *m* air-raid *(auf +acc* on*)*; **~aufnahme** *f* aerial photo; **~ballon** *m* balloon; **~blase** *f* air bubble; **~brücke** *f* airlift.

Lüftchen *nt* breeze.

Luft-: l~dicht *adj* airtight *no adv;* **die Ware ist l~dicht verpackt** the article is in airtight packaging; **~druck** *m* air pressure; **l~durchlässig** *adj* pervious to air.

lüften 1 *vt* **(a)** to air. **(b)** *Schleier* to raise. **2** *vi (Luft hereinlassen)* to let some air in.

Luft-: ~fahrt *f* aviation *no art;* **~fahrzeug** *nt* aircraft; **~feuchtigkeit** *f* humidity; **~fracht** *f* air freight; **l~gekühlt** *adj* air-cooled; **l~getrocknet** *adj* air-dried; **~gewehr** *nt* air-rifle, **~herrschaft** *f* air supremacy; **~hoheit** *f* air sovereignty.

luftig *adj Zimmer* airy; *Kleidung* light.

Luft-: ~kampf *m* air battle; *(Duell)* dogfight; **~kissen** *nt* air cushion; **~kissenboot** *nt* hovercraft; **~krieg** *m* aerial warfare; **~kühlung** *f* air-cooling; **~kurort** *m* health resort; **~landetruppe** *f* airborne troops *pl;* **l~leer** *adj* **(völlig) l~leer sein** to be a vacuum; **l~leerer Raum** vacuum; **~linie** *f* **200 km ~linie** 200 km as the crow flies; **~matratze** *f* airbed; **~pirat** *m* hijacker; **~post** *f* airmail; **mit ~post** by airmail; **~pumpe** *f (für Fahrrad)* (bicycle) pump; **~raum** *m* airspace; **~röhre** *f (Anat)* windpipe; **~schacht** *m* ventilation shaft; **~schicht** *f (Met)* layer of air; **~schiff** *nt* airship; **~schiffahrt** *f* aeronautics *sing*; **~schlacht** *f* air battle; **~schlange** *f* (paper) streamer; **~schloß** *nt (fig)* castle in the air; **~schneise** *f* air lane.

Luftschutz *m* anti-aircraft defence *(Brit)* *or* defense *(US)*.

Luftschutz-: ~bunker, ~keller *m* air-raid shelter; **~übung** *f* air-raid drill.

Luft-: ~spiegelung *f* mirage; **~sprung** *m* jump in the air; **~straße** *f* air route; **~streitkräfte** *pl* air force *sing*; **~strom** *m* stream of air; **~strömung** *f* current of air; **~stützpunkt** *m* airbase; **~temperatur** *f* air temperature.

Lüftung *f* airing.

Luft-: ~veränderung *f* change of air; **~verkehr** *m* air traffic; **~verschmutzung** *f* air pollution; **~versorgung** *f* air supplies *pl*; **~verteidigung** *f* air defence *(Brit)* *or* defense *(US)*; **~waffe** *f (Mil)* air force; **~weg** *m* **etw auf dem ~weg befördern** to transport sth by air; **~widerstand** *m* air resistance; **~zufuhr** *f* air supply; **~zug** *m* (mild) breeze; *(in Gebäude)* draught *(Brit)*, draft *(US)*.

Lug *m*: **~ und Trug** lies *pl* (and deception).

Lüge *f* **-n** lie. **das ist alles ~** that's all lies; **jdn/etw ~n strafen** to give the lie to sb/sth.

lügen *pret* **log,** *ptp* **gelogen** *vi* to lie. **ich müßte ~, wenn ...** I would be lying if ...; **das ist gelogen!** *(col)* that's a lie!

Lügen-: ~detektor *m* lie detector; **~geschichte** *f* pack of lies; **~märchen** *nt* tall story; **~maul** *nt (pej col)* liar; **~propaganda** *f* propagandist lies *pl*.

Lügner(in *f***)** *m* **-** liar.

lügnerisch *adj Mensch* lying *attr*, untruthful.

Luke *f* **-n** hatch; *(Dach~)* skylight.

lukrativ *adj* lucrative.

Lümmel *m* **-** *(pej)* lout, oaf.

lümmelhaft *adj (pej)* ill-mannered.

lümmeln *vr (col)* to sprawl; *(sich hin~)* to flop down.

Lump *m (wk)* **-en, -en** *(pej)* rogue.

lumpen *vt (col)* **er ließ sich nicht ~** he was very generous.

Lumpen *m* **-** rag.

Lumpen-: ~gesindel, ~pack *nt (pej)* rabble *pl* *(pej)*; **~kerl** *m (col)* bastard *(col)*; **~sammler** *m* **(a)** rag-and-bone man; **(b)** *(hum)* last bus/tram *etc*.

lumpig *adj* **(a)** *Gesinnung, Tat* shabby, mean. **(b) ~e 10 Mark** a measly 10 marks *(col)*.

Lunge *f* **-n** lung. **(auf) ~ rauchen** to inhale; **sich** *(dat)* **die ~ aus dem Hals schreien** *(col)* to yell till one is blue in the face *(col)*.

Lungen-: ~entzündung *f* pneumonia; **~flügel** *m* lung; **l~krank** *adj* tubercular; **l~krank sein** to have a lung disease; **~kranke(r)** *mf decl as adj* TB case; **~krankheit** *f* lung disease; **~krebs** *m* lung cancer.

Lunte *f* **-n ~ riechen** *(Verdacht schöpfen)* to smell a rat *(col)*; *(Gefahr wittern)* to sense danger.

Lupe *f* **-n** magnifying glass. **solche Leute kannst du mit der ~ suchen** people like that are few and far between; **jdn/etw unter die ~ nehmen** *(col)* to take a close look at sb/sth, to investigate sb/sth.

lupenrein *adj (lit) Edelstein* flawless; *(fig) Gentleman, Intellektueller* through and through *pred*.

Lurch *m* **-e** amphibian.

Lusche *f* **-n** *(Cards)* low card; *(fig col: Versager)* dead loss *(col)*.

Lust *f* **-ë (a)** *no pl (Freude)* pleasure, joy. **er hat die ~ daran verloren** he has lost all interest in it; **da kann einem alle ~ vergehen** it puts you off; **jdm die ~ an etw** *(dat)* **nehmen** to take all the fun out of sth for sb. **(b)** *no pl (Neigung)* inclination. **zu etw ~ haben** to feel like sth; **ich habe keine ~ zu arbeiten** I don't feel like working; **ich habe jetzt keine ~** I'm not in the mood just now; **ich hätte ~ dazu** I'd like to; **hast du ~?** how about it?; **auf etw** *(acc)* **~ haben** to fancy sth; **er kann bleiben, so lange er ~ hat** he can stay as long as he likes. **(c)** *(sinnliche Begierde)* desire; *(sexuell auch)* lust *(usu pej)*. **~ haben** to feel desire.

Lüster *m* **- (a)** *(Leuchter)* chandelier. **(b)** *(Stoff, Glanzüberzug)* lustre *(Brit)*, luster *(US)*.

lüstern *adj* lecherous.

Lust-: ~gefühl *nt* feeling of pleasure; **~gewinn** *m* pleasure.

lustig *adj Leute, Abend* cheerful. **die Party war ganz ~** the party was great fun; **er ist ein ganz ~er Typ** he's great fun; **so lange du ~ bist** *(col)* as long as you like; **es wurde ~** things got quite merry; **das kann ja ~ werden!** *(iro)* that's going to be fun *(iro)*; **sich über jdn/etw ~ machen** to make fun of sb/sth.

Lüstling *m* lecher.

Lust-: l~los *adj* unenthusiastic; *(Fin) Börse* slack; **~molch** *m (hum col)* sex maniac *(col)*; **~mord** *m* sex murder; **~prinzip** *nt (Psych)* pleasure principle; **~schloß** *nt* summer residence; **~spiel** *nt* comedy; **l~voll 1** *adj* full of relish; **2** *adv* with relish.

Lutheraner(in *f***)** *m* **-** Lutheran.

lutschen *vti* to suck *(an etw (dat)* sth*)*.

Lutscher *m* **-** lollipop *(Brit)*, popsicle ® *(US)*.

Luv [luːf] *f no pl (Naut)* windward.

Luxemburg *nt* Luxembourg.

luxemburgisch *adj* Luxembourgian.

luxuriös *adj* luxurious. **ein ~es Leben** a life of luxury.

Luxus *m no pl* luxury; *(pej: Verschwendung)* extravagance. **im ~ leben** to live in luxury.

Luxus- *in cpds* luxury; **~ausführung** *f* de luxe model; **~dampfer** *m* luxury cruise ship; **~limousine** *f* limousine; **~restaurant** *nt* first-class restaurant.

Lymphe ['lʏmfə] *f* **-n** lymph.

Lymphknoten *m* lymph(atic) gland.

lynchen ['lʏnçn 'linçn] *vt (lit)* to lynch; *(fig)* to kill.

Lynch- ['lʏnç-]**: ~justiz** *f* lynch-law; **~mord** *m* lynching.

Lyrik *f no pl* lyric poetry *or* verse.

Lyriker(in *f***)** *m* **-** lyric poet, lyricist.

lyrisch *adj (lit, fig)* lyrical; *Dichtung, Dichter* lyric.

M

M, m [ɛm] *nt* **-, -** M, m.
m = Meter.
Maat *m* **-e** *or* **-en** *(Naut)* (ship's) mate.
Mach|art *f* make; *(Muster)* design; *(lit, fig: Stil)* style.
machbar *adj* feasible, possible.
Mache *f no pl (col)* **reine ~ sein** to be (a) sham; **etw in der ~ haben** *(col)* to be working on sth; **jdn in der ~ haben** *(col)* to be having a go at sb *(col)*; *(verprügeln)* to be working sb over *(col)*.
machen 1 *vt* **(a)** to do; *(herstellen, bilden, formen, zubereiten)* to make. **was ~ Sie (beruflich)?** what do you do for a living?; **was habe ich nur falsch gemacht?** what have I done wrong?; **gut, wird gemacht** right, I'll get that done; **das ist zu/nicht zu ~** that can/can't be done; **(da ist) nichts zu ~** *(geht nicht)* (there's) nothing to be done; *(kommt nicht in Frage)* nothing doing; **wie man's macht, ist's verkehrt** whatever you do is wrong; **was machst du da?** what are you doing (there)?; **was machst du denn hier?** what (on earth) are you doing here?; **ich muß noch so viel ~** I still have so much to do; **ich kann da auch nichts ~** I can't do anything about it either; **so etwas macht man nicht** that sort of thing just isn't done; **wie ~ Sie das nur?** how do you do it; **sich/jdm etw ~ lassen** to have sth made for oneself/sb; **Bilder** *or* **Fotos ~** to take photos; **er ist für den Beruf wie gemacht** he's made for the job; **Bier wird aus Gerste gemacht** beer is made from barley; **aus Holz gemacht** made of wood; **das Essen ~** to get the meal; *siehe* **gemacht**.

(b) *(verursachen) Schwierigkeiten, Arbeit* to make *(jdm* for sb*)*; *Mühe, Schmerzen* to cause *(jdm* for sb*)*. **jdm Angst/Freude ~** to make sb afraid/happy; **jdm Kopfschmerzen ~** to give sb a headache; **das macht Hunger** that makes you hungry.

(c) *(bewirken)* to do; *(+infin)* to make. **das macht die Kälte** it's the cold that does that; **jdn lachen/etw vergessen ~** to make sb laugh/forget sth; **die Kälte macht, daß das Wasser gefriert** the cold makes the water freeze; **(viel) von sich reden ~** to be much talked about; **mach, daß du hier verschwindest!** (you just) get out of here!

(d) *(veranstalten) Party* to have, to give; *(teilnehmen an) Lehrgang* to do.

(e) *(ausmachen, schaden)* to matter. **macht nichts!** (it) doesn't matter; **macht das was?** does that matter?; **das macht sehr viel** it matters a lot; **das macht mir doch nichts!** that doesn't matter to me; **die Kälte macht mir nichts** I don't mind the cold; **die Kälte macht dem Motor nichts** the cold doesn't hurt the engine.

(f) *(erzielen) Punkte, Preis* to get, to win; *Doktor, Diplom etc* to do; *Gewinn, Verlust* to make.

(g) *(col: ergeben)* to make; *(kosten, Math)* to be. **drei und fünf macht acht** three and five is *or* are eight; **100 cm ~ einen Meter** 100 cm make a metre; **wieviel macht das (alles zusammen)?** how much is that *or* what does that make altogether?

(h) was macht die Arbeit? how's the work going?; **was macht dein Bruder?** how is your brother doing?; **mach's kurz!** make it brief; **mach's gut!** take care, all the best; **er wird's nicht mehr lange ~** *(col)* he won't last long; **mit mir kann man's ja ~!** *(col)* the things I put up with! *(col)*; **das läßt er nicht mit sich ~** he won't stand for that; **jdn unglücklich ~** to make sb unhappy; **etw sauber/schmutzig ~** to get sth clean/dirty; **jdn alt/jung ~** *(aussehen lassen)* to make sb look old/young; **mach es ihm nicht noch schwerer** don't make it harder for him; **er macht es sich** *(dat)* **nicht leicht** he doesn't make it easy for himself; **etw aus jdm/etw ~** *(darstellen, interpretieren als)* to make sth of sb/sth; *(verwandeln in)* to make sth (out) of sb/out of sth, to make sb/sth into sth; **jdn zu etw** *(dat)* **~** *(verwandeln in)* to turn sb into sth; *(Rolle, Image, Status geben)* to make sb sth; **jdm etw zur Hölle/Qual** *etc* **~** to make sth hell/a misery *etc* for sb; **jdn zu seiner Frau ~** to make sb one's wife; **Halt ~** to call a halt; **das Geschirr ~** to do the dishes; **eine Prüfung ~** to take an exam; **ein Spiel ~** to play a game; **das Auto/den Kühlschrank ~ lassen** to have the car/refrigerator seen to; **er macht mir die Haare/Zähne** *(col)* he does my hair/teeth; **das Bett ~** to make the bed; **jetzt macht er auf beleidigt** *(col)* now he's playing the injured innocent; **den Ghostwriter für jdn ~** *(col)* to act as sb's ghost writer; **groß/klein ~** *(col: Notdurft)* to do a big/little job *(baby-talk)*.

2 *vi* **(a) mach schon/schneller!** *(col)* get a move on! *(col)*, hurry up; **ich mach ja schon!** *(col)* I am hurrying; **sie machten, daß sie nach Hause kamen** they hurried home; **er macht in Politik/Malerei** *(col)* he's in politics/doing some painting; **jetzt macht sie auf große Dame** *(col)* she's playing the lady now; **sie macht auf gebildet** *(col)* she's doing her cultured bit *(col)*; **er macht auf Schau** *(col)* he's out for effect *(col)*; **laß ihn nur ~** *(verlaß dich auf ihn)* just leave it to him; **laß mich mal ~** let me do it; *(ich bringe das in Ordnung)* let me see to that; **gut, mache ich** right, I'll do that; **das macht müde** that makes you tired; **das Kleid macht schlank** that dress makes you look slim.

(b) *(col: Notdurft verrichten)* to go to the toilet; *(Hund etc)* to do its business *(euph)*. **(sich** *dat***) in die Hosen ~** *(lit, fig)* to wet oneself; **ins Bett ~** to wet the bed.

3 *vr* **wie macht sich der Garten?** how is the garden coming along?; **der Schal macht sich sehr hübsch zu dem Kleid** the scarf looks very pretty with that dress; **sich an etw** *(acc)* **~** to get down to sth/doing sth; **sich auf den Weg ~** to get going; **sich verständlich/wichtig ~** to make oneself understood/important; **sich bei jdm beliebt/verhaßt ~** to make oneself popular with/hated by sb; **sich** *(dat)* **viel aus jdm/etw ~** to like sb/sth; **sich** *(dat)* **wenig aus jdm/etw ~** not to be very keen on sb/sth; **mach dir nichts daraus** don't let it bother you; **sich** *(dat)* **einen schönen Abend ~** to have a nice evening; **sich** *(dat)* **jdn zum Freund ~** to make sb one's friend; **sich zum Fürsprecher ~** to make oneself spokesman.
Machenschaften *pl* wheelings and dealings *pl*.
Macher *m* **-** *(col)* doer, man of action.
Macht *f* **¨e (a)** *no pl* power; *(Stärke auch)* might. **die ~ der Gewohnheit/des Schicksals** the force of habit/destiny; **alles in unserer ~ Stehende** everything in our power; **mit aller ~** with all one's might; **die ~ ergreifen/erringen** to seize/

gain power; **an die ~ kommen** to come to power; **an der ~ sein** to be in power; **die ~ übernehmen** to assume power. **(b)** *(Staat)* power. **böse/himmlische ~e** evil forces/heavenly powers.
Macht-: ~befugnis *f* power, authority *no pl*; **~bereich** *m* sphere of influence; **~ergreifung** *f* seizure of power; **~haber** *m* - ruler; *(pej)* dictator.
mächtig 1 *adj* **(a)** *(einflußreich)* powerful. **(b)** *(sehr groß)* mighty; *Felsen auch, Körper* massive; *Stimme, Schlag auch* powerful; *Essen* heavy; *(col: enorm) Hunger, Durst* terrific *(col)*, tremendous. **~e Angst haben** *(col)* to be scared stiff. **(c)** *(liter)* **einer Sprache** *(gen)* **~ sein** to have a good command of a language. **2** *adv (col: sehr)* terrifically *(col)*, tremendously; *schneien, sich beeilen* like mad *(col)*. **sich ~ anstrengen** to make a tremendous effort.
Mächtigkeit *f (Größe)* mightiness.
Macht-: ~kampf power struggle; **m~los** *adj* powerless; *(hilflos)* helpless; **~losigkeit** *f no pl* powerlessness; helplessness; **~mißbrauch** *m* misuse of power; **~position** *f* position of power; **~probe** *f* trial of strength; **~übernahme** *f* takeover *(durch* by*)*; **m~voll** *adj* powerful; **~wort** *nt* **ein ~wort sprechen** to exercise one's authority.
Machwerk *nt (pej)* sorry effort. **ein elendes ~** a pathetic attempt; **das ist ein ~ des Teufels** that is the work of the devil.
Macke *f* **-n** *(col)* **(a)** *(Tick, Knall)* quirk. **eine ~ haben** *(col)* to have a screw loose *(col)*. **(b)** *(Fehler, Schadstelle)* fault.
Macker *m* - *(col)* fellow *(col)*, guy *(col)*. **spiel hier nicht den ~** don't come the tough guy here *(col)*.
Mädchen *nt* girl; *(Tochter auch)* daughter. **ein ~ für alles** *(col)* a dogsbody; *(im Haushalt auch)* a maid-of-all-work.
Mädchen-: m~haft *adj* girlish; *aussehen, sich kleiden* like a girl; **~klasse** *f* girls' class; **~kleidung** *f* girls' clothing; **~name** *m* **(a)** girl's name; **(b)** *(von verheirateter Frau)* maiden name; **~schule** *f* girls' school.
Made *f* **-n** maggot. **wie die ~ im Speck leben** *(col)* to live in luxury.
Mädel *nt* **-(s)** *(dial)* lass *(dial)*, girl.
madig *adj* maggoty; *Obst auch* worm-eaten. **jdm etw ~ machen** *(col)* to put sb off sth.
Magazin *nt* **-e (a)** *(Lager)* storeroom; *(Bibliotheks~)* stockroom. **(b)** *(am Gewehr)* magazine. **(c)** *(Zeitschrift)* magazine, journal; *(TV, Rad)* magazine programme *(Brit)* or program *(US)*.
Magd *f* **⸚e** *(old)* maid; *(Landarbeiterin)* farm lass.
Magen *m* **⸚** *or* - stomach. **auf nüchternen ~** on an empty stomach; **(die) Liebe geht durch den ~** *(Prov)* the way to a man's heart is through his stomach *(prov)*; **etw liegt jdm im ~** *(col)* sth lies heavily on sb's stomach; *(fig)* sth preys on sb's mind; **jdm auf den ~ schlagen** *(col)* to upset sb's stomach; *(fig)* to upset sb; **sich** *(dat)* **den ~ verderben** to upset one's stomach; **dabei dreht sich mir der ~ um** *(col)* it turns my stomach.
Magen-: ~beschwerden *pl* stomach trouble *sing*; **~bitter** *m* bitters *pl*; **~geschwür** *nt* stomach ulcer; **~knurren** *nt no pl* tummy rumbles *pl (col)*; **m~krank** *adj* **m~krank sein** to have stomach trouble; **~krebs** *m* cancer of the stomach; **~leiden** *nt* stomach disorder; **~schmerzen** *pl* stomach-ache *sing*, tummy-ache *sing (col)*; **~verstimmung** *f* stomach upset.
mager *adj* **(a)** *(fettarm) Fleisch* lean; *Kost* low-fat. **(b)** *(dünn)* thin, skinny *(col)*; *(abgemagert)* emaciated. **(c)** *Boden, Felder* poor, infertile. **(d)** *(dürftig)* meagre *(Brit)*, meager *(US)*; *Ergebnis* poor. **die sieben ~en Jahre** the seven lean years.
Mager-: ~milch *f* skimmed milk; **~quark** *m* low-fat curd cheese.
Magie *f no pl* magic.
Magier ['maːgiɐ] *m* - magician.
magisch *adj* magic(al); *Quadrat, (Tech) Auge* magic. **mit ~er Gewalt** with magical force; *(fig)* as if by magic.
Magister *m* - *(Univ)* M.A., Master of Arts.
Magistrat *m* **-e** municipal authorities *pl*.
Magnat *m (wk)* **-en, en** magnate *(auch Hist)*.
Magnet- *in cpds* magnetic; **~band** *nt* magnetic tape; **~feld** *nt* magnetic field.
magnetisch *adj (lit, fig)* magnetic.
Magnetismus *m no pl* magnetism.
Magnet-: ~nagel *f* magnetic needle; **~zündung** *f (Aut)* magneto ignition.
Mahagoni *nt no pl* mahogany.
Mähdrescher *m* combine (harvester).
mähen[1] **1** *vt Gras* to cut; *Getreide auch* to reap; *Rasen* to mow. **2** *vi* to reap; *(Rasen ~)* to mow.
mähen[2] *vi (Schaf)* to bleat.
Mahl *nt* **-e** *(geh)* meal, repast *(form)*; *(Gast~)* banquet.
mahlen *pret* **mahlte,** *ptp* **gemahlen** *vti* to grind.
Mahlzeit *f* meal. **~!** *(col) greeting used around mealtimes; (guten Appetit)* enjoy your meal; **(prost) ~!** *(iro col)* that's just great *(col) or* swell *(esp US col)*.
Mähmaschine *f* mower; *(Getreide~)* reaper.
Mahnbrief *m* reminder.
Mähne *f* **-n** *(lit, fig)* mane.
mahnen 1 *vt* **(a)** *(erinnern)* to remind *(wegen* of*)*; *(warnend)* to admonish *(wegen* on account of*)*. **gemahnt werden** *(Schuldner)* to receive a reminder. **(b)** *(auffordern)* **jdn zur Eile/Geduld** *etc* **~** to urge sb to hurry/be patient *etc*. **2** *vi* **(a)** *(wegen Schulden etc)* to send a reminder. **(b) zur Eile/Geduld ~** to urge haste/patience; **der Lehrer mahnte zur Ruhe** the teacher called for quiet.
Mahn-: ~mal *nt* memorial; **~schreiben** *nt* reminder.
Mahnung *f* **(a)** *(Ermahnung)* exhortation; *(warnend)* admonition. **(b)** *(Mahnbrief)* reminder.
Mai *m* **-e** May. **der Erste ~** May Day; *siehe* **März.**
Mai- *in cpds* May; *(Pol)* May Day; **~baum** *m* maypole; **~bowle** *f* white wine punch *(flavoured with woodruff)*; **~feier** *f* May Day celebrations *pl*; **~feiertag** *m (form)* May Day *no art*; **~glöckchen** *nt* lily of the valley; **~käfer** *m* cockchafer.
Mailand *nt* Milan.
Mais *m no pl* maize, (Indian) corn *(esp US)*.
Mais-: ~kolben *m* corn cob; *(Gericht)* corn on the cob; **~korn** *nt* grain of maize *or* corn *(esp US)*.
Majestät *f* **(a)** *(Titel)* Majesty. **Seine/Ihre/Eure ~** His/Her/Your Majesty. **(b)** *(liter)* majesty.
majestätisch *adj* majestic.
Majestätsbeleidigung *f* lèse-majesté.
Major *m* **-e** *(Mil)* major; *(in Luftwaffe)* squadron leader *(Brit)*, major *(US)*.
Majoran *m* **-e** marjoram.
majorisieren* *vt* to outvote.
Majorität *f* majority.
makaber *adj* macabre; *Witz, Geschichte* sick.
Makel *m* - **(a)** *(Schandfleck)* stigma. **ohne ~** without a stain on one's reputation; **mit einem ~ behaftet sein** *(liter)* to be stigmatized. **(b)** *(Fehler)* blemish; *(bei Waren)* defect. **ohne ~** flawless.
Mäkelei *f* carping *no pl*, fault-finding *no pl (an +dat, über +acc* about, over*)*.
makellos *adj Reinheit, Frische* spotless; *Charakter* unimpeachable; *Figur, Haut* flawless; *Kleidung* immaculate; *Alibi* watertight.
Makellosigkeit *f (Reinheit)* spotlessness; *(von Haut)* flawlessness; *(von Kleidung)* immaculateness.
mäkeln *vi (col: nörgeln)* to carp *(an +dat* at*)*.
Make-up [meːk'|ap] *nt* **-s** make-up; *(flüssig)* foundation.
Makkaroni *pl* macaroni *sing*.
Makler *m* - broker; *(Grundstücks~)* estate agent *(Brit)*, realtor *(US)*.

Maklergebühr *f* broker's commission, brokerage.
Makrele *f* **-n** mackerel.
Makro- *in cpds* macro-; ~**kosmos** *m* macrocosm.
Makrone *f* **-n** macaroon.
Mal[1] *nt* **-e (a)** *(lit, fig: Fleck)* mark. **(b)** *pl auch* **⸚er** *(liter: Ehren~)* memorial, monument.
Mal[2] *nt* **-e** time. **(nur) dieses eine** ~ (just) this once; **das eine oder andere** ~ now and then *or* again; **kein einziges** ~ not once; **wenn du bloß ein einziges** ~ **auf mich hören würdest** if you would only listen to me for once; **ein für alle** ~**e** once and for all; **das vorige** ~ the time before; **ein letztes** ~ *(liter)* one last time; **als ich das letzte** ~ **in London war** (the) last time I was in London; **beim ersten/letzten** ~ the first/last time; **zum ersten/letzten** ~ for the first/last time; **von** ~ **zu** ~ each *or* every time; **für dieses** ~ for the time being; **mit einem** ~**e** all of a sudden.
mal[1] *adv (Math)* times; *(bei Flächenangaben)* by.
mal[2] *adv (col) siehe* **einmal.**
Malaria *f no pl* malaria.
Malbuch *nt* colouring *(Brit) or* coloring *(US)* book.
malen *vti* to paint; *(col: zeichnen)* to draw. **sich** ~ **lassen** to have one's portrait painted; **etw rosig/schwarz** *etc* ~ *(fig)* to paint a rosy/black *etc* picture of sth.
Maler(in *f***)** *m* **-** painter; *(Kunst~ auch)* artist.
Malerei *f (no pl: Malkunst)* art; *(Bild)* painting; *(Zeichnung)* drawing.
malerisch *adj* **(a)** picturesque; *Landschaft auch* scenic. **(b)** *(bildnerisch)* in painting; *Talent* as a painter.
Malermeister *m* (master) painter.
Malheur [ma'løːɐ] *nt* **-s** *or* **-e** mishap. **das ist doch kein** ~! it's not serious.
Malkasten *m* paintbox.
Mallorca *nt* Majorca, Mallorca.
malnehmen *vti sep irreg* to multiply *(mit* by*)*.
Maloche *f no pl (col)* graft *(col)*. **du mußt zur** ~ you've got to go to work.
malochen* *vi (col)* to graft *(col)*, to sweat away *(col)*.
Mal-: ~**stift** *m* crayon; ~**technik** *f* painting technique.
Malteserkreuz *nt* Maltese cross.
maltesisch *adj* Maltese.
malträtieren* *vt* to ill-treat, to maltreat.
Malve ['malvə] *f* **-n** *(Bot)* mallow.
Malz *nt no pl* malt.
Malz-: ~**bier** *nt* malt beer; ~**bonbon** *nt or m* malt lozenge; ~**kaffee** *m coffee substitute made from barley malt.*
Mama, Mami *f* **-s** *(col)* mummy, mommy *(US)*.
Mammut- *in cpds (lit, fig)* mammoth; *(lange dauernd)* marathon; ~**baum** *m* sequoia, giant redwood.
mampfen *vti (col)* to munch, to chomp *(col)*.
man *indef pron* **(a)** you, one; *(ich)* one; *(wir)* we. ~ **kann nie wissen** you *or* one can never tell; **das tut** ~ **nicht** that's not done. **(b)** *(jemand)* somebody, someone. ~ **hat mir gesagt ...** I was told ...; ~ **hat festgestellt, daß ...** it has been established that ... **(c)** *(die Leute)* they *pl*, people *pl*. **früher glaubte** ~ people used to believe; ~ **will die alten Häuser niederreißen** they want to pull down the old houses. **(d)** ~ **nehme ...** take ...
Management ['mɛnɪdʒmənt] *nt* **-s** management.
managen ['mɛnɪdʒn] *vt* to manage. **ich manage das schon!** *(col)* I'll fix it somehow!
Manager ['mɛnɪdʒɐ] *m* **-** manager.
manch *indef pron* ~ **eine(r)** many a person; ~ **einem kann man nie Vernunft beibringen** some people never learn; ~ **anderer** many another; ~**er, der ...** many a person who ...; ~**es Schöne** quite a few beautiful things; **(so)** ~**es** a good many things; **in** ~**em hat er recht** he's right about some things.
mancherlei *adj inv (adjektivisch mit pl n)* various; *(substantivisch)* various things *pl*. ~ **Bier** various kinds of beer.
manchmal *adv* sometimes.
Mandant(in *f***)** *m (Jur)* client.
Mandarine *f* mandarin (orange), tangerine.
Mandat *nt (Auftrag, Vollmacht)* mandate *(auch Pol)*, authorization *(gen* from*)*; *(Parl: Abgeordnetensitz)* seat. **sein** ~ **niederlegen** *(Parl)* to resign one's seat.
Mandel *f* **-n (a)** almond. **(b)** *(Anat)* tonsil.
Mandel-: m~äugig *adj (poet)* almond-eyed; ~**baum** *m* almond tree; ~**entzündung** *f* tonsilitis.
Mandoline *f* mandolin.
Manege [ma'neːʒə] *f* **-n** ring, arena.
Mangel[1] *f* **-n** mangle; *(Heiß~)* rotary iron. **jdn durch die** ~ **drehen** *(fig col)* to put sb through it *(col)*; *Prüfling etc auch* to put sb through the mill.
Mangel[2] *m* **⸚ (a)** *(Fehler)* fault; *(bei Maschine auch)* defect; *(Charakter~)* flaw. **(b)** *no pl (das Fehlen)* lack *(an +dat* of*)*; *(Knappheit auch)* shortage *(an +dat* of*)*; *(Med auch)* deficiency *(an +dat* of*)*. **aus** ~ **an** *(+dat)* for lack of; **wegen** ~**s an Beweisen** for lack of evidence; **es herrscht** ~ **an etw** *(dat)* there is a shortage of sth.
Mängelbericht *m* list of faults.
Mangel-: ~**beruf** *m* understaffed profession; ~**erscheinung** *f (Med)* deficiency symptom.
mangelhaft *adj (unzulänglich)* poor; *Ausrüstung auch* inadequate; *Informationen, Interesse* insufficient; *(fehlerhaft) Ware* faulty; *(Schulnote auch)* unsatisfactory.
mangeln *vi impers* **es mangelt an etw** *(dat)* there is a lack of sth; *(unzureichend vorhanden auch)* there is a shortage of sth; **es mangelt jdm an etw** *(dat)* sb lacks sth; ~**des Verständnis** *etc* a lack of understanding *etc*; **wegen** ~**der Aufmerksamkeit** through not paying attention.
Mangelware *f* scarce commodity. ~ **sein** *(fig)* to be a rare thing; *(Ärzte, gute Lehrer etc)* not to grow on trees *(col)*.
Manie *f (Med, fig)* mania; *(fig auch)* obsession.
Manier *f* **-en (a)** *no pl (Art und Weise)* manner; *(eines Künstlers etc)* style. **in überzeugender** ~ in a most convincing manner. **(b)** ~**en** *pl (Umgangsformen)* manners; **das sind doch keine** ~**en** *(col)* that's no way to behave.
manieriert *adj* affected; *Benehmen auch* mannered.
manierlich 1 *adj Kind* well-mannered; *Benehmen* good; *Aussehen* respectable. **2** *adv essen* politely; *sich benehmen* properly; *sich kleiden* respectably.
Manifest *nt* **-e** *(Pol)* manifesto.
Maniküre *f* **-n (a)** *(Handpflege)* manicure. **(b)** *(Handpflegerin)* manicurist.
Manipulation *f* manipulation; *(Trick)* manoeuvre *(Brit)*, maneuver *(US)*.
manipulierbar *adj* manipulable. **leicht/schwer** ~ easily manipulated/difficult to manipulate.
manipulieren* *vt* to manipulate.
Manko *nt* **-s (a)** *(Comm: Fehlbetrag)* deficit. ~ **machen** *(col: bei Verkauf)* to make a loss. **(b)** *(fig: Nachteil)* shortcoming.
Mann *m* **⸚er (a)** man. **ein feiner** ~ a (perfect) gentleman; **ein** ~ **aus dem Volk(e)** a man of the people; **der** ~ **im Mond** the man in the moon; **ein** ~ **der Wissenschaft** a man of science; **ein** ~ **von Format** *etc* a man of stature *etc*; **er ist nicht der** ~ **dafür** he's not the man for that; *(nicht seine Art)* he's not the sort; **wie ein** ~ as one man; **etw an den** ~ **bringen** *(col)* to get rid of sth; **seinen** ~ **stehen** to hold one's own; **einen kleinen** ~ **im Ohr haben** *(hum col)* to be crazy *(col)*; **und ein** ~**, ein Wort, er hat's auch gemacht** and, as good as his word, he did it; ~ **für** ~ *(allesamt)* every single one; ~ **gegen** ~ man against man; **pro** ~ per

head; **ein Gespräch von ~ zu ~** a man-to-man talk.

(b) *(Ehe~)* husband. **~ und Frau werden** to become man and wife.

(c) *pl* **Leute** *(Besatzungsmitglied)* hand, man; *(Sport, Cards)* player, man. **20 ~** 20 hands *or* men; **mit ~ und Maus untergehen** to go down with all hands; *(Passagierschiff)* to go down with no survivors.

(d) *(col: als Interjektion)* (my) God *(col)*; *(bewundernd, erstaunt auch)* hey. **mach schnell, ~!** hurry up, man!; **~, oh ~!** oh boy! *(col)*.

Männchen *nt dim of* **Mann (a)** little man; *(Zwerg)* man(n)ikin. **~ malen** to draw (little) matchstick men, ≃ to doodle. **(b)** *(Biol)* male; *(Vogel~ auch)* cock. **(c) ~ machen** *(Hund)* to (sit up and) beg.

Mannequin ['manəkɛ̃] *nt* **-s** (fashion) model.

Männer *pl of* **Mann.**

Männer-: ~chor *m* male-voice choir; **~fang** *m (hum)* **auf ~fang ausgehen** to go looking for a man/for men; **~gesangverein** *m* male choral society; **m~mordend** *adj (hum)* man-eating; **~sache** *f (Angelegenheit)* man's business; *(Arbeit)* man's job; **Fußball war früher ~sache** football used to be a male preserve; **~stimme** *f* man's voice; *(Mus)* male voice.

Mannes-: ~alter *nt* manhood *no art*; **im besten ~alter sein** to be in the prime of (one's) life; **~kraft** *f (dated, hum)* virility.

mannhaft *adj* manly *no adv*; *(tapfer)* manful, valiant; *(entschlossen)* resolute; *Widerstand* stout.

mannigfach *adj attr* manifold, multifarious.

mannigfaltig *adj (geh)* diverse, varied.

Mannigfaltigkeit *f* diversity, variety.

männlich *adj* **(a)** male; *Wort* masculine. **(b)** *(fig: mannhaft) Mut, Entschluß* manly; *Frau* mannish.

Männlichkeit *f (fig)* manliness; *(von Frau)* mannishness.

Mannsbild *nt (dated pej)* fellow.

Mannschaft *f (Sport, fig)* team; *(Naut, Aviat)* crew. **~(en)** *(Mil)* men *pl*.

Mannschafts- *in cpds (Sport)* team; **~aufstellung** *f* team line-up; *(das Aufstellen)* selection of the team; **~geist** *m* team spirit; **~raum** *m (Sport)* team quarters *pl*; *(Naut)* crew's quarters *pl*.

manns-: ~hoch *adj* as high as a man; **der Schnee liegt ~hoch** the snow is six feet deep; **~toll** *adj* man-mad *(col)*.

Mannweib *nt (pej)* mannish woman.

Manometer *nt (Tech)* pressure gauge. **~!** *(col)* wow! *(col)*.

Manöver [ma'nø:vɐ] *nt* **-** *(lit, fig)* manoeuvre *(Brit)*, maneuver *(US)*.

manövrieren* [manø'vri:rən] *vti (lit, fig)* to manoeuvre *(Brit)*, to maneuver *(US)*.

Manövrier- [manø'vri:ɐ]: **m~fähig** *adj* manoeuvrable *(Brit)*, maneuverable *(US)*; **~fähigkeit** *f* manoeuvrability *(Brit)*, maneuverability *(US)*; **m~unfähig** *adj* disabled.

Mansarde *f* **-n** garret; *(Boden)* attic.

Manschette *f (Ärmelaufschlag)* cuff. **~n haben** *(col)* to be scared silly *(col)*.

Manschettenknopf *m* cufflink.

Mantel *m* **⸚ (a)** coat; *(fig)* cloak, mantle. **(b)** *(Tech)* casing; *(Rohr~)* jacket.

Mantel- *in cpds (Tex)* coat; **~stoff** *m* coat fabric; **~tarifvertrag** *m* general agreement on conditions of employment.

manuell *adj Arbeit* manual. **etw ~ bedienen** to operate sth manually.

Manuskript *nt* **-e** manuscript; *(Rad, Film, TV)* script.

maoistisch *adj* Maoist.

Mappe *f* **-n** *(Aktenhefter)* folder, file; *(Aktentasche)* briefcase; *(Schul~)* (school) bag; *(Feder~, Bleistift~)* pencil case.

Marathon- *in cpds* marathon; **~lauf** *m* marathon; **~läufer** *m* marathon runner.

Märchen *nt* **-** fairy story; *(col)* tall story.

Märchen- *in cpds* fairytale; **~buch** *nt* book of fairytales; **~erzähler** *m* teller of fairytales; *(fig)* storyteller; **m~haft** *adj* fairytale *attr*; *(fig)* fabulous; **~land** *nt* fairyland; **~prinz** *m* Prince Charming.

Marder *m* **-** marten.

Margarine *f* margarine.

Marge ['marʒə] *f* **-n** *(Comm)* margin.

Maria *f* **-** Mary. **die Mutter ~** the Virgin Mary.

Marien- [-i:ən]: **~bild** *nt* picture of the Virgin Mary; **~käfer** *m* ladybird.

Marihuana [mari'hua:na] *nt no pl* marijuana.

Marinade *f (Cook)* marinade; *(Soße)* mayonnaise-based sauce.

Marine *f* navy.

Marine- *in cpds* naval; **m~blau** *adj* navy blue; **~soldat** *m* marine.

marinieren* *vt Fisch, Fleisch* to marinate.

Marionette *f* marionette, puppet; *(fig)* puppet.

Marionetten- *in cpds* puppet; **~spieler** *m* puppeteer; **~theater** *nt* puppet theatre *(Brit) or* theater *(US)*.

Mark[1] *nt no pl (Knochen~)* marrow; *(Bot: Gewebe~)* medulla, pith. **bis ins ~** *(fig)* to the core; **jdn bis ins ~ treffen** *(fig)* to cut sb to the quick; **es geht mir durch ~ und Bein** *(col)* it goes right through me; **kein ~ in den Knochen haben** *(fig)* to have no backbone.

Mark[2] *f* **-** *or (hum)* **⸚er** mark. **Deutsche ~** German mark, deutschmark; **vier ~ zwanzig** four marks twenty (pfennigs); **mit jeder ~ rechnen müssen** to have to count every penny.

markant *adj (ausgeprägt)* clear-cut; *Schriftzüge* clearly defined.

Marke *f* **-n (a)** *(bei Lebens- und Genußmitteln)* brand; *(bei Industriegütern)* make. **du bist (vielleicht) eine ~!** *(col)* you're a fine one *(col)*. **(b)** *(Brief~)* stamp; *(Essen~)* voucher; *(Rabatt~)* (trading) stamp; *(Lebensmittel~)* coupon. **auf ~n** *(col)* on coupons. **(c)** *(Erkennungs~)* disc, tag; *(Garderoben~)* ticket, check *(US)*; *(Polizei~)* badge; *(Spiel~)* chip; *(Pfand~ etc)* token.

Marken-: ~artikel *m* proprietary article; **~butter** *f* best quality butter; **~erzeugnis, ~fabrikat** *nt* proprietary article; **~name** *m* brand name.

Marketing *nt no pl* marketing.

markieren* *vt (lit, fig, Sport)* to mark; *(col: vortäuschen)* to play. **den starken Mann ~** to come the strong man *(col)*.

Markierung *f* marking; *(Zeichen)* mark.

markig *adj (kraftvoll)* vigorous, pithy.

Markise *f* **-n** awning.

Mark-: ~knochen *(Cook)* marrowbone; **~stein** *m (lit, fig)* milestone; **~stück** *nt* (one-)mark piece.

Markt *m* **⸚e (a)** market; *(~platz)* marketplace; *(Jahr~)* fair. **~ abhalten** to hold a market; **dienstags ist ~** there is a market every Tuesday. **(b)** *(Comm)* market; *(Warenverkehr)* trade. **auf dem ~** on the market; **auf den ~ bringen** to put on the market.

Markt- *in cpds* market; **~anteil** *m* share of the market; **m~beherrschend** *adj* **m~beherrschend sein** to dominate the market; **~bude** *f* market stall; **~flecken** *m* small market town; **~forschung** *f* market research; **~frau** *f* market woman; **m~gerecht** *adj* geared to market requirements; **~halle** *f* covered market; **~lage** *f* state of the market; **~lücke** *f* gap in the market; **~platz** *m* marketplace; **am/auf dem ~platz** on/in the marketplace; **~schreier** *m* market crier; **m~schreierisch** *adj* loud and vociferous; *(fig)* blatant; **~stand** *m* market stall; **~weib** *nt (pej)* market woman; *(fig)* fish-wife; **~wert** *m* market value; **~wirtschaft** *f* market economy; **m~wirtschaftlich** *adj attr* free enterprise.

Marmelade *f* jam; *(Orangen~)* marmalade.

Marmeladenglas *nt* jam-jar.

Mạrmor *m* **-e** marble.
Mạrmorkuchen *m* marble cake.
marokkạnisch *adj* Moroccan.
Marọkko *nt* Morocco.
Marọne *f* **-n** (sweet *or* Spanish) chestnut.
Marọtte *f* **-n** quirk.
Mạrs *m no pl (Myth, Astron)* Mars.
mạrsch *interj* **(a)** *(Mil)* march. **vorwärts ~!** forward march! **(b)** *(col)* off with you. **~ ins Bett!** off to bed with you!
Mạrsch[1] *m* **⸚e (a)** *(das Marschieren)* march; *(Wanderung)* hike. **sich in ~ setzen** to move off. **(b)** *(~musik)* march. **jdm den ~ blasen** *(col)* to give sb a rocket *(col)*.
Mạrsch[2] *f* **-en** marsh, fen.
Mạrschall *m, pl* **Mạrschälle** (field) marshal.
Mạrsch-: ~befehl *m (Mil) (für Truppen)* marching orders *pl*; *(für einzelnen)* travel orders *pl*; **m~bereit** *adj* ready to move; **~flugkörper** *m* cruise missile; **~gepäck** *nt* pack.
marschieren* *vi aux sein* to march; *(fig)* to march off.
Mạrsch-: ~land *nt* marsh(land), fen; **~musik** *f* military marches *pl*; **~ordnung** *f* marching order; **~richtung** *f (lit)* route of march; *(fig)* line of approach; **~verpflegung** *f* rations *pl*; *(Mil)* field rations *pl*.
Mạrsmensch *m* Martian.
Mạrter *f* **-n** *(liter)* torment.
mạrtern *(liter) vt* to torture, to torment.
Mạrterpfahl *m* stake.
martialisch [mar'tsia:lɪʃ] *adj (geh)* martial, warlike.
Mạrtinshorn *nt* siren *(of police etc)*. **mit ~** with its siren blaring *or* going.
Mạ̈rtyrer(in *f*) *m* - *(Eccl, fig)* martyr.
Martyrium *nt (fig)* ordeal.
Marxịsmus *m* Marxism.
Marxịst(in *f*) *m* Marxist.
marxịstisch *adj* Marxist.
Mạ̈rz *m* **-e** March. **im ~** in March; **im Monat ~** in the month of March; **heute ist der zweite ~** today is the second of March *or* March second *(US)*; *(geschrieben)* today is 2nd March; **am ersten ~ fahren wir nach ...** on the first of March we are going to ...; **in diesem ~** this March; **im Laufe des ~** during March; **der ~ war sehr warm** March was very warm; **Anfang/Ende/Mitte ~** at the beginning/end/in the middle of March; **den 4. ~ 1987** 4th March 1987.
Mạsche *f* **-n (a)** *(Strick~, Häkel~)* stitch; *(von Netz)* hole. **die ~n eines Netzes** the mesh of a net; **durch die ~n schlüpfen** to slip through the net. **(b)** *(col: Trick)* trick, dodge *(col)*. **die ~ raushaben** to know how to do it; **das ist seine neueste ~** that's his latest (fad).
Mạschendraht *m* wire netting.
Maschịne *f* machine; *(Motor)* engine; *(col: Motorrad)* bike; *(Schreib~)* typewriter; *(Flugzeug)* plane. **etw mit der ~ schreiben** to type sth.
maschinẹll 1 *adj Herstellung* mechanical, machine *attr*. **2** *adv* mechanically, by machine.
Maschịnen-: ~bau *m* mechanical engineering; **~bauingenieur** *m* mechanical engineer; **~fabrik** *f* engineering works *sing or pl*; **m~geschrieben** *adj* typewritten; **~gewehr** *nt* machine-gun; **mit ~gewehr(en) beschießen** to machine-gun; **~haus** *nt* machine room; **~öl** *nt* lubricating oil; **~park** *m* plant; **~pistole** *f* submachine gun; **~raum** *m* plant room; *(Naut)* engine-room; **~schaden** *m* mechanical fault; *(Aviat etc)* engine fault; **~schlosser** *m* engine fitter; **~schrift** *f* typescript, typing; *(Schriftart)* typeface; **m~schriftlich** *adj* typewritten *no adv*; **~stürmer** *m* - machine wrecker; *(Hist)* Luddite; **~teil** *nt* machine part.
Maschinerịe *f (fig)* machinery.
maschịneschreiben *vi sep irreg* to type. **sie schreibt Maschine** she types.
Maschinịst(in *f*) *m* machine operator; *(Schiffs~)* engineer.
Mạser *f* **-n** *(von Holz)* vein.
Mạsern *pl* measles *sing*.
Mạserung *f* grain.
Mạske *f* **-n** *(lit, fig)* mask. **die ~ fallen lassen** *(fig)* to throw off one's mask; **jdm die ~ herunterreißen** *(fig)* to unmask sb; **ohne ~** *(fig)* undisguised; **unter der ~ von etw** *(fig)* under the guise of sth; **das ist alles nur ~** that's all just pretence *(Brit) or* pretense *(US)*.
Mạsken-: ~ball *m* masked ball; **~bildner(in** *f*) *m* make-up artist.
Maskerạde *f (Verkleidung)* costume; *(fig)* masquerade.
maskịeren* 1 *vt* **(a)** *(verkleiden)* to dress up; *(unkenntlich machen)* to disguise. **(b)** *(verbergen)* to mask. **2** *vr* to dress up; *(sich unkenntlich machen)* to disguise oneself.
maskịert *adj* masked.
Maskịerung *f (Verkleidung)* fancy-dress costume; *(von Spion etc)* disguise; *(Verhüllung)* masking.
Maskọttchen *nt* (lucky) mascot.
Maskulịnum *nt, pl* **Maskulịna** masculine noun.
Masochịsmus *m no pl* masochism.
Masochịst(in *f*) *m* masochist.
maß *pret of* **messen.**
Mạß[1] *nt* **-e (a)** *(~einheit)* measure *(für* of); *(Zollstock)* rule; *(Bandmaß)* tape measure. **~e und Gewichte** weights and measures; **das ~ aller Dinge** *(fig)* the measure of all things; **mit zweierlei ~ messen** *(fig)* to operate a double standard; **das ~ ist voll** *(fig)* that's enough (of that); **in reichem ~(e)** abundantly; **über das übliche ~ hinausgehen** to overstep the mark; **weder ~ noch Ziel kennen** to know no bounds.
(b) *(Meßgröße)* measurement; *(von Zimmer, Möbelstück auch)* dimension. **sich** *(dat)* **etw nach ~ anfertigen lassen** to have sth made to measure *or* order *(US)*; **~ nehmen** to measure up; **bei jdm ~ nehmen** to take sb's measurements.
(c) *(Ausmaß)* extent, degree. **ein gewisses ~ an ...** a certain degree of ...; **in hohem ~(e)** to a high degree; **in solchem ~(e), daß ...** to such an extent that ...; **in großem ~e** to a great extent; **in vollem ~e** fully; **in besonderem ~e** especially; **in höchstem ~e** extremely; **über alle ~en** *(liter)* extremely, beyond measure.
Maß[2] *f (S Ger, Aus)* litre *(Brit) or* liter *(US)* of beer.
Massage [ma'sa:ʒə] *f* **-n** massage.
Massagesalon *m (euph)* massage parlour *(Brit) or* parlor *(US)*.
Massạker *nt* - massacre.
massakrịeren* *vt* to massacre.
Mạß-: ~anzug *m* made-to-measure *or* made-to-order *(US)* suit; **~arbeit** *f (col)* **das war ~arbeit** that was a neat bit of work.
Mạsse *f* **-n (a)** *(Stoff, Phys)* mass; *(Cook)* mixture. **(b)** *(große Menge)* heaps *pl (col)*; *(von Besuchern etc)* host. **die (breite) ~ der Bevölkerung** *etc* the bulk of the population *etc*; **eine ganze ~** *(col)* a great deal; **die ~ muß es bringen** *(Comm)* the profit only comes with quantity. **(c)** *(Menschenmenge)* crowd. **(d)** *(Bevölkerungs~)* masses *pl (auch pej)*. **die breite ~** the masses *pl*.
Maßeinheit *f* unit of measurement.
Mạssel *m no pl (col)* **~ haben** to be dead lucky *(col)*.
Mạssen- *in cpds* mass; **~artikel** *m* mass-produced article; **~bedarfsgüter** *pl* basic consumer goods *pl*; **~grab** *nt* mass grave; **~güter** *pl* bulk goods *pl*; **m~haft** *adj* on a huge *or* massive scale; **m~haft Sekt** *etc (col)* masses of champagne *etc (col)*; **~medien** *pl* mass media *pl*; **~mord** *m* mass murder; **~mörder** *m* mass murderer; **~produktion** *f* mass production;

~**psychose** *f* mass hysteria; ~**szene** *f* crowd scene; ~**ware** *f* mass-produced article; **m~weise** *adj siehe* **m~haft.**
Masseur [ma'søːɐ] *m* masseur.
Masseuse [-'søːzə] *f* masseuse.
maßgebend, maßgeblich *adj (entscheidend) Einfluß* decisive; *Meinung* definitive; *Text* definitive, authoritative; *Fachmann* authoritative; *(wichtig) Persönlichkeit* leading; *Beteiligung* substantial; *(zuständig)* competent. ~**e Kreise** influential circles; **das war für mich nicht** ~ that didn't weigh with me.
maßgeschneidert *adj Anzug* made-to-measure, made-to-order *(US)*, custom *attr (US)*.
maßhalten *vi sep irreg* to practise *(Brit) or* practice *(US)* moderation.
Maßhalteparole *f* appeal for moderation.
massieren[1]* *vt* to massage.
massieren[2]* *vt Truppen* to mass.
massig 1 *adj* massive, huge. **2** *adv (col: sehr viel)* ~ **Geld** *etc* stacks of money *etc (col)*.
mäßig *adj* **(a)** moderate. ~ **essen** to eat with moderation; ~ **rauchen** to smoke in moderation; ~, **aber regelmäßig** in moderation but regularly. **(b)** *(schwach) Leistung etc* mediocre; *Begabung, Beifall* moderate.
mäßigen 1 *vt (mildern) Anforderungen* to moderate; *Sprache auch* to tone down; *Zorn, Ungeduld* to curb. **sein Tempo** ~ to slacken one's pace; *siehe* **gemäßigt. 2** *vr (im Essen, Trinken, Temperament)* to restrain oneself. ~ **Sie sich in Ihren Worten!** tone down your language!
Mäßigkeit *f (beim Essen, Trinken)* moderation; *(von Forderungen etc)* moderateness.
Mäßigung *f* restraint.
massiv *adj* **(a)** *(pur, stabil)* solid. **(b)** *(heftig) Beleidigung* gross; *Drohung, Kritik* heavy; *Anschuldigung* severe. ~ **werden** *(col)* to turn nasty.
Massiv *nt* **-e** *(Geol)* massif.
Maßkrug *m* litre *(Brit) or* liter *(US)* beer mug; *(Steinkrug)* stein.
maßlos 1 *adj* extreme; *Forderungen auch* excessive; *Freude, Ehrgeiz auch* boundless; *Mensch (in Essen etc)* immoderate. **er raucht/trinkt** ~ he smokes/drinks to excess. **2** *adv (äußerst)* extremely; *übertreiben* grossly, hugely.
Maßlosigkeit *f siehe adj* extremeness; excessiveness; boundlessness; lack of moderation.
Maßnahme *f* **-n** measure. ~**n treffen, um etw zu tun** to take steps to do sth.
maßregeln *vt insep (zurechtweisen)* to reprimand; *(bestrafen)* to discipline.
Maßreg(e)lung *f* **(a)** *no pl siehe vt* reprimanding; disciplining. **(b)** *(Rüge)* reprimand.
Maßstab *m* **(a)** *(Karten~)* scale. **im** ~ **1:1000** on a scale of 1:1000. **(b)** *(fig: Richtlinie, Kriterium)* standard. **einen strengen** ~ **anlegen** to apply a strict standard *(an +acc* to*)*; **als** ~ **dienen** to serve as a model; **sich** *(dat)* **etw zum** ~ **nehmen** to take sth as a yardstick.
maßstab(s)getreu *adj* (true) to scale. **eine** ~**e Karte** an accurate scale map.
maßvoll *adj* moderate.
Mast[1] *m* **-en** *or* **-e** *(Naut, Rad, TV)* mast; *(Stange)* pole; *(Elec)* pylon.
Mast[2] *f* **-en** *(das Mästen)* fattening.
Mastdarm *m* rectum.
mästen 1 *vt* to fatten. **2** *vr (col)* to gorge oneself.
Mast- *in cpds (zu mästen)* feeder; *(gemästet)* fattened; ~**futter** *nt* (fattening) feed; *(für Schweine)* mast; ~**schwein** *nt (zu mästen)* porker; *(gemästet)* fattened pig.
Masturbation *f* masturbation.
masturbieren* *vtir* to masturbate.
Matador *m* **-e** *(Stierkampf)* matador; *(fig)* kingpin.
Matchball *m (Tennis)* match point.
Material *nt* **-ien** [-iən] material; *(Bau~, Gerät)* materials *pl*; *(Beweis~)* evidence.
Materialfehler *m* defect in the material.
Materialismus *m* materialism.
Materialist(in *f***)** *m* materialist.
materialistisch *adj* materialist(ic); *(pej)* materialistic.
Materialkosten *pl* cost of materials *sing*.
Materie [-iə] *f* **(a)** *no pl (Phys, Philos)* matter *no art*. **(b)** *(Stoff, Thema)* subject-matter *no indef art*.
materiell *adj* **(a)** *(Philos)* material, physical. **(b)** *(wirtschaftlich)* financial; *Vorteile auch* material; *(gewinnsüchtig)* materialistic. ~ **eingestellt sein** to be materialistic.
Mathe *f no pl (Sch col)* maths *sing (Brit col)*, math *(US col)*.
Mathematik *f* mathematics *sing no art*.
Mathematiker(in *f***)** *m* mathematician.
mathematisch *adj* mathematical.
Matinee *f* **-n** [-eːən] matinée.
Matjeshering *m (col)* young herring.
Matratze *f* **-n** mattress.
Mätresse *f (dated pej)* mistress.
Matriarchat *nt* matriarchy.
Matrikel *f* **-n** *(Univ)* matriculation register.
Matrixdrucker *m* dot-matrix printer.
Matrize *f* **-n** *(Typ)* matrix, mould *(Brit)*, mold *(US)*; *(für Schreibmaschine)* stencil. **etw auf** ~ **schreiben** to stencil sth.
Matrose *m (wk)* **-n, -n** sailor; *(als Rang)* rating *(Brit)*, ordinary seaman.
Matrosenanzug *m* sailor suit.
Matsch *m no pl (col) (breiige Masse)* mush; *(Schlamm)* mud; *(Schnee~)* slush.
matschig *adj (col) (breiig)* gooey *(col)*, mushy; *(schlammig)* muddy; *Schnee* slushy.
matt *adj* **(a)** *(schwach) Kranker* weak. **sich** ~ **fühlen** to have no energy. **(b)** *Augen, Farbe* dull; *Farbe, Papier* mat(t); *Licht* dim; *Glühbirne* opal, pearl; *Spiegel* cloudy, dull. **(c)** *(fig) Ausdruck, Rede* lame, feeble. **(d)** *(Chess)* (check)mate. **jdn** ~ **setzen** to checkmate sb *(auch fig)*.
Matt *nt* **-s** *(Chess)* (check)mate.
Matte *f* **-n** mat. **auf der** ~ **stehen** *(col)* to be on the doorstep *(col)*; *(am Arbeitsplatz etc)* to be in.
Mattigkeit *f* weariness; *(von Kranken)* weakness.
Mattlack *m* mat(t) varnish.
Mattscheibe *f (Phot)* focus(s)ing screen; *(col: Fernseher)* telly *(Brit col)*, tube *(US col)*. **eine** ~ **haben** *(col: dumm sein)* to be soft in the head *(col)*; *(nicht klar denken können)* to have a mental block.
Mätzchen *nt (col)* antic. ~ **machen** to fool around *(col)*.
mau *adj pred (col)* poor, bad. **mir ist** ~ I feel poorly *(col)*.
Mauer *f* **-n** *(lit, fig)* wall. **etw mit einer** ~ **umgeben** to wall sth in; **die** ~**n einreißen** *(fig)* to tear down the barriers.
Mauerblümchen *nt (fig col)* wallflower.
mauern 1 *vi* **(a)** to build, to lay bricks. **(b)** *(Ftbl sl)* to stonewall *(Ftbl sl)*, to play defensively; *(fig)* to stonewall *(esp Parl)*. **2** *vt* to build.
Mauer-: ~**schwalbe** *f*, ~**segler** *m* swift; ~**vorsprung** *m* projection on a/the wall; ~**werk** *nt* **(a)** *(Steinmauer)* stonework, masonry; *(Ziegelmauer)* brickwork; **(b)** *(die Mauern)* walls *pl*.
Maul *nt, pl* **Mäuler** mouth; *(von Löwe etc)* jaws *pl*; *(pej: von Mensch)* gob *(col!)*. **ein loses** *or* **lockeres** ~ **haben** *(col) (frech sein)* to be an impudent so-and-so *(col)*; *(indiskret sein)* to be a blabbermouth *(col)*; **das** ~ **zu weit aufreißen** *(col!)* to be too cocksure *(col)*; **ein großes** ~ **haben** *(col!)* to be a big-mouth *(col)*; **darüber werden sich die Leute das** ~ **zerreißen** *(col)* that will start people's tongues wagging; **dem Volk** *or* **den Leuten aufs** ~ **schauen** *(col)* to listen to what people really say; **halt's** ~**!** *(col!)* shut your face *(col!)*; **jdm das** ~ **stopfen** *(col!)* to shut sb up *(col)*.
maulen *vi (col)* to moan.
Maul-: ~**esel** *m* mule; **m~faul** *adj (col)* uncommu-

nicative; ~**held** *m (pej)* loud-mouth *(col)*; ~**korb** *m (lit, fig)* muzzle; ~**tier** *nt* mule; ~**- und Klauenseuche** *f (Vet)* foot-and-mouth disease; ~**werk** *nt (col) siehe* **Mundwerk.**

Maulwurf *m, pl* **Maulwürfe** mole.

Maulwurfs-: ~**haufen,** ~**hügel** *m* mole-hill.

Maurer *m* - bricklayer. **pünktlich wie die** ~ *(hum)* super-punctual.

Maurer-: ~**arbeit** *f* bricklaying (work) *no pl*; ~**kelle** *f* (bricklayer's) trowel; ~**meister** *m* master builder.

Maus *f, pl* **Mäuse (a)** *(auch Comp)* mouse. **weiße** ~ *(fig col)* traffic cop *(col)*; **weiße Mäuse sehen** *(fig col)* to see pink elephants *(col)*; **eine graue** ~ *(col)* a mouse *(col)*. **(b) Mäuse** *pl (col: Geld)* bread *(col)*, dough *(col)*.

Mauschelei *f (col: Korruption)* fiddle *(col)*.

mauscheln *vti (manipulieren)* to fiddle *(col)*.

Mäuschen ['mɔysçən] *nt* **(a)** little mouse. **da möchte ich mal** ~ **sein** *(col)* I'd like to be a fly on the wall. **(b)** *(fig)* sweetheart *(col)*.

mäuschenstill ['mɔysçən-] *adj* dead quiet; *(reglos)* stock-still.

Mause-: ~**falle** *f* mouse-trap; ~**loch** *nt* mouse-hole; **sich in ein** ~**loch verkriechen** *(fig)* to crawl into a hole in the ground.

mausen *vt (dated col)* to pinch *(col)*.

Mauser *f no pl (Orn)* moult *(Brit)*, molt *(US)*. **in der** ~ **sein** to be moulting *(Brit) or* molting *(US)*.

mausern *vr (Orn)* to moult *(Brit)*, to molt *(US)*.

mausetot *adj (col)* stone-dead.

mausgrau *adj* **(a)** *(~farben)* mouse-grey *(Brit)*, mouse-gray *(US)*. **(b)** *(unauffällig)* mousy.

mausig *adj:* **sich** ~ **machen** *(col)* to get uppish *(col)*.

Mausoleum [-'le:ʊm] *nt, pl* **Mausoleen** [-'le:ən] mausoleum.

max. = **maximal.**

Maxi- *in cpds* maxi-.

maximal 1 *adj* maximum. **2** *adv (höchstens)* at most. **bis zu** ~ **$100** up to a maximum of $100.

Maximal- *in cpds* maximum.

Maxime *f* **-n** *(liter, Philos)* maxim.

maximieren* *vt (Econ)* to maximize.

Maximierung *f (Econ)* maximization.

Maximum *nt, pl* **Maxima** maximum *(an +dat* of*)*.

Maxi-Single [-'sɪŋgl] *f* twelve-inch single.

Mayonnaise [majɔ'nɛ:zə] *f* **-n** mayonnaise.

Mäzen *m* **-e** patron.

MdB [ɛm'de:'be:] *m* **-s** = **Mitglied des Bundestages** Member of the "Bundestag", ≈ MP.

m.E. = **meines Erachtens** in my opinion.

Mechanik *f* **(a)** *no pl (Phys)* mechanics *sing*. **(b)** *(Mechanismus)* mechanism.

Mechaniker(in *f*) *m* - mechanic.

mechanisch *adj* mechanical.

Mechanismus *m* mechanism.

Meckerei *f (col)* grumbling.

Meckerer *m* - *(col)* grumbler.

meckern *vi (Ziege)* to bleat; *(col: Mensch)* to moan, to bitch *(col)*.

Meckerziege *f (pej col)* sourpuss *(col)*.

Medaille [me'daljə] *f* **-n** *(bei Wettbewerben)* medal.

Medaillengewinner [me'daljən-] *m* medallist *(Brit)*, medalist *(US)*.

Medaillon [medal'jõ:] *nt* **-s** *(Bildchen)* medallion; *(Schmuckkapsel)* locket.

Medien ['me:diən] *pl* media *pl*.

Medikament *nt* medicine.

Meditation *f* meditation.

meditieren* *vi* to meditate.

Medium *nt* medium.

Medizin *f* **-en (a)** *no pl (Heilkunde)* medicine. **(b)** *(col: Heilmittel)* medicine.

Medizinball *m (Sport)* medicine ball.

Mediziner(in *f*) *m* - doctor; *(Univ)* medic *(col)*.

medizinisch *adj* **(a)** *(ärztlich)* medical. **M~e Fakultät** school *or* faculty of medicine; ~**-technische Assistentin** medical assistant. **(b)** *(heilend) Bäder* medicinal; *Shampoo* medicated.

Medizin-: ~**mann** *m, pl* **-männer** medicine man; *(hum: Arzt)* quack *(col)*, medico *(US col)*; ~**studium** *nt* study of medicine.

Meer *nt* **-e** sea; *(Welt~)* ocean. **am** ~**(e)** by the sea; **übers** ~ **fahren** to travel (across) the seas; **ans** ~ **fahren** to go to the sea(side); **über dem** ~ above sea-level.

Meer-: ~**busen** *m* gulf, bay; ~**enge** *f* straits *pl*, strait.

Meeres-: ~**arm** *m* arm of the sea, inlet; ~**boden,** ~**grund** *m* seabed; ~**klima** *nt* maritime climate; ~**kunde** *f* oceanography; ~**oberfläche** *f* surface of the sea; ~**spiegel** *m* sea-level; **über/unter dem** ~**spiegel** above/below sea-level; ~**tier** *nt* marine creature.

Meer-: ~**gott** *m (Myth)* sea-god; ~**göttin** *f* sea-goddess; ~**jungfrau** *f* mermaid; ~**rettich** *m* horseradish; ~**salz** *nt* sea salt; ~**schweinchen** *nt* guineapig; ~**wasser** *nt* sea water.

mega-, Mega- *in cpds* mega-.

Mega-: ~**phon** *nt* megaphone; ~**tonne** *f* megaton; ~**watt** *nt* megawatt.

Mehl *nt* **-e** flour; *(grober)* meal; *(Pulver)* powder.

mehlig *adj Äpfel, Kartoffeln* mealy.

Mehl-: ~**sack** *m* flour bag; ~**schwitze** *f (Cook)* roux.

mehr 1 *indef pron inv comp of* **viel, sehr** more. **was wollen Sie** ~? what more do you want?; ~ **will er nicht bezahlen** he doesn't want to pay (any) more; **ist das alles,** ~ **kostet das nicht?** is that all it costs?

2 *adv* **(a)** *(in höherem Maße)* more. **immer** ~ more and more; ~ **oder weniger** more or less; ~ **Geschäftsmann als Arzt** more (of) a businessman than a doctor; ~ **ein juristisches Problem** more (of) a legal problem. **(b)** *(+neg: sonst, länger)* **ich habe kein Geld** ~ I haven't any more money; **du bist doch kein Kind** ~! you're no longer a child!; **es besteht keine Hoffnung** ~ there's no hope left; **kein Wort** ~! not another word!; **es war niemand** ~ **da** there was no-one left; **wenn niemand** ~ **einsteigt, ...** if nobody else gets in ...; **das benutzt man nicht** ~ it's no longer used; **das darf nicht** ~ **vorkommen** that must not happen again; **nicht** ~ **lange** not much longer; **nichts** ~ nothing more; **nie** ~ never again, nevermore *(liter)*; **ich will dich nie** ~ **wiedersehen** I don't ever want to see you again.

Mehr *nt no pl (Zuwachs)* increase.

Mehr-: ~**arbeit** *f* extra time *or* work; ~**aufwand** *m* additional expenditure; ~**bedarf** *m* greater need *(an +dat* of, for*)*; *(Comm)* increased demand *(an +dat* for*)*; ~**belastung** *f* excess load; *(fig)* additional burden; **m~deutig** *adj* ambiguous; ~**einnahme** *f* additional revenue.

mehren 1 *vt (liter: vergrößern)* to augment. **2** *vr (geh: sich vermehren)* to multiply.

mehrere *indef pron* several; *(verschiedene auch)* various.

mehrfach 1 *adj* multiple; *(zahlreich)* numerous; *(wiederholt)* repeated. **ein** ~**er Millionär** a multi-millionaire; **der** ~**e Meister im 100-m-Lauf** the man who has several times been the 100 metres champion; **die Unterlagen in** ~**er Ausfertigung einsenden** to send in several copies of the documents. **2** *adv (öfter)* many *or* several times; *(wiederholt)* repeatedly.

Mehr-: ~**familienhaus** *nt* multiple dwelling *(form)*; **m~farbig** *adj* multicoloured *(Brit)*, multicolored *(US)*.

Mehrheit *f* majority. **die** ~ **besitzen/erringen** to have/gain a majority; **die** ~ **verlieren** to lose one's majority; **mit zwei Stimmen** ~ with a majority of two.

Mehrheits-: ~**beschluß** *m* majority decision; ~**prinzip** *nt* principle of majority rule; ~**wahl-**

recht *nt* majority vote system.

Mehr-: m~jährig *adj attr* of several years; **m~jährige Klinikerfahrung** several years of clinical experience; **~kosten** *pl* additional costs *pl*; **m~malig** *adj attr* repeated; **m~mals** *adv* several times; **~parteiensystem** *nt* multi-party system; **m~sprachig** *adj* multilingual; **m~sprachig aufwachsen** to grow up multilingual; **m~stimmig** *adj (Mus)* for several voices; **m~stimmiger Gesang** part-singing; **m~stimmig singen** to sing in harmony; **m~stöckig** *adj* multistorey *(Brit)*, multilevel *(US)*; **m~stündig** *adj attr* lasting several hours; **mit m~stündiger Verspätung eintreffen** to arrive several hours late; **m~tägig** *adj attr Konferenz* lasting several days; **m~teilig** *adj* in several parts; **~wegflasche** *f* returnable bottle; **~wert** *m (Econ)* added value; **~wertsteuer** *f* value added tax, VAT; **~zahl** *f no pl* **(a)** *(Gram)* plural; **(b)** *(Mehrheit)* majority.

Mehrzweck- *in cpds* multipurpose.

meiden *pret* **mied,** *ptp* **gemieden** *vt* to avoid.

Meile *f* **-n** mile. **das riecht man drei ~n gegen den Wind** *(col)* you can smell that a mile off *(col)*.

Meilen-: ~stein *m (lit, fig)* milestone; **m~weit** *adv* for miles; **m~weit entfernt** *(lit, fig)* miles away.

Meiler *m* **-** *(Kohlen~)* charcoal kiln; *(Atom~)* (atomic) pile.

mein *poss pron* **(a)** *(adjektivisch)* my. **(b)** *(old: substantivisch)* mine.

Mein|eid *m* perjury *no indef art.* **einen ~ leisten** to commit perjury.

meinen 1 *vi (denken, glauben)* to think. **ich meine, ...** I think ...; **~ Sie?** (do) you think so?; **wie Sie ~!** as you wish; *(drohend auch)* have it your own way; **wenn du meinst!** if you like; **man sollte ~** one would have thought. **2** *vt (der Ansicht sein)* to think; *(sagen wollen)* to mean; *(col: sagen)* to say. **was ~ Sie dazu?** what do you think *or* say?; **~ Sie das im Ernst?** are you serious about that?; **das will ich ~!** I quite agree!; **wie ~ Sie das?** how do you mean?; **damit bin ich gemeint** that refers to me; **sie meint es gut** she means well; **er meint es ehrlich mit dem Mädchen** his intentions towards the girl are honourable; **sie meint es nicht böse** she means no harm.

meiner *pers pron gen of* **ich** of me.

meine(r, s) *poss pron (substantivisch)* mine. **der/die/das ~** *(geh)* mine; **ich tue das M~** *(geh)* I'll do my bit.

meinerseits *adv* for my part. **Vorschläge ~** suggestions from me.

meines-: ~gleichen *pron inv (meiner Art)* people like myself; **~teils** *adv* for my part.

meinet-: ~halben *(dated)*, **~wegen** *adv* **(a)** *(wegen mir)* on my account; **(b)** *(von mir aus)* as far as I'm concerned; **~wegen!** if you like; **~willen** *adv:* **um ~willen** for my sake.

meins *poss pron* mine.

Meinung *f* opinion; *(Anschauung auch)* view. **meiner ~ nach** in my opinion; **ich bin der ~, daß ...** I take the view that ...; **seine ~ ändern** to change one's opinion *or* mind; **einer ~ sein** to think the same; **das ist auch meine ~!** that's just what I think; **jdm die ~ sagen** *(col)* to give sb a piece of one's mind *(col)*.

Meinungs-: ~äußerung *f* (expression of) opinion; **~austausch** *m* exchange of views *(über +acc* on, about*)*; **~forscher** *m* (opinion) pollster; **~forschung** *f* (public) opinion polling; **~forschungsinstitut** *nt* opinion research institute; **~freiheit** *f* freedom of speech; **~macher** *m (col)* opinion-maker; **~umfrage** *f* opinion poll; **~umschwung** *m* swing of opinion; **~verschiedenheit** *f* difference of opinion.

Meise *f* **-n** titmouse. **eine ~ haben** *(col)* to be crackers *(Brit col) or* crazy.

Meißel *m* **-** chisel.

meißeln *vti* to chisel.

meist *adv siehe* **meistens.**

meistbietend *adj* highest bidding; **~ versteigern** to auction to the highest bidder.

meisten: am ~ *adv superl of* **viel, sehr** the most, most of all.

meistens *adv* mostly; *(zum größten Teil)* for the most part.

meistenteils *adv siehe* **meistens.**

Meister *m* **- (a)** *(Handwerks~)* master (craftsman); *(Sport)* champion; *(Mannschaft)* champions *pl.* **seinen ~ machen** to take one's master craftsman's diploma. **(b)** *(Lehr~, Künstler)* master *(auch fig)*. **er hat seinen ~ gefunden** *(fig)* he's met his match; **es ist noch kein ~ vom Himmel gefallen** *(Prov)* no-one is born an expert.

meiste(r, s) *indef pron superl of* **viel (a)** *(adjektivisch)* **die ~n Leute** most people; **die ~n Gläser gingen kaputt** most of the glasses were broken; **meine ~ Zeit** most of my time. **(b)** *(substantivisch)* **die ~n (von ihnen)** most (of them).

Meister- *in cpds* master; **~brief** *m* master craftsman's diploma; **m~haft 1** *adj* masterly; **2** *adv* in a masterly manner; **er versteht es m~haft, zu lügen** he is brilliant at lying; **~hand** *f:* **von ~hand** by a master hand.

Meisterin *f (Handwerks~)* master craftswoman; *(Sport)* champion.

Meisterleistung *f* masterly performance; *(iro)* brilliant achievement.

meistern *vt* to master; *Schwierigkeiten* to overcome. **sein Leben ~** to come to grips with one's life.

Meisterschaft *f* **(a)** *(Sport)* championship; *(Veranstaltung)* championships *pl.* **(b)** *no pl (Können)* mastery.

Meisterschaftspiel *nt (Sport)* championship match.

Meister-: ~stück *nt (von Handwerker) work done to qualify as master craftsman; (fig)* masterpiece; *(geniale Tat)* master stroke; **~werk** *nt* masterpiece.

meist-: ~gekauft *adj attr* best-selling; **~genannt** *adj attr* most frequently mentioned.

Mekka *nt (Geog, fig)* Mecca.

Melancholie [melaŋko'li:] *f* melancholy.

melancholisch [melaŋ'ko:lɪʃ] *adj* melancholy.

Melasse *f* **-n** molasses.

Melde-: ~amt *nt* registration office; **~behörde** *f* registration authorities *pl.*

melden 1 *vt* to report; *(registrieren)* to register; *(ankündigen)* to announce. **Änderungen der Behörde** *(dat)* **~** to notify the authorities of changes; **wie soeben gemeldet wird** *(Rad, TV)* according to reports just coming in; **nichts zu ~ haben** *(col)* to have no say; **wen darf ich ~?** who(m) shall I say (is here)?

2 *vr* **(a)** to report *(zu* for*)*. **sich für etw ~** *(esp Mil)* to sign up for sth; *(für Lehrgang)* to enrol for sth; **sich krank/zum Dienst ~** to report sick/for work; **sich auf eine Anzeige ~** to answer an advertisement. **(b)** *(fig: sich ankündigen)* to announce one's presence; *(Sport, zur Prüfung)* to enter (one's name) *(zu* for*)*; *(durch Handaufheben)* to put one's hand up. **(c)** *(esp Telec: antworten)* to answer. **es meldet sich niemand** there's no answer. **(d)** *(von sich hören lassen)* to get in touch *(bei* with*)*. **seitdem hat er sich nicht mehr gemeldet** he hasn't been heard of since; **wenn du was brauchst, melde dich** if you need anything give a shout *(col)*.

Melde-: ~pflicht *f* obligation to register; **polizeiliche ~pflicht** obligation to register with the police; **m~pflichtig** *adj* **(a)** obliged to register; **(b)** *Krankheit* notifiable.

Meldung *f* **(a)** *(Mitteilung)* announcement; *(Press, Rad, TV)* report *(über +acc* on, about*)*. **~en vom Sport** sports news *sing.* **(b)** *(dienstlich, bei der Polizei)* report. **(eine) ~ machen** to make a

report. **(c)** *(Sport, Examens~)* entry.
meliert *adj Haar* streaked with grey *(Brit) or* gray *(US)*; *Wolle* flecked.
melken *pret* **melkte** *ptp* **gemolken** *vti* **(a)** to milk. **frisch gemolkene Milch** milk fresh from the cow. **(b)** *(fig col)* to milk *(col)*, to fleece *(col)*.
Melodie *f* melody; *(Weise auch)* tune.
melodiös *adj (geh)* melodious.
melodisch *adj* melodic, tuneful.
melodramatisch *adj* melodramatic *(auch fig)*.
Melone *f* **-n (a)** melon. **(b)** *(Hut)* bowler *(Brit)*, derby *(US)*.
Membran *f* **-en (a)** *(Anat)* membrane. **(b)** *(Phys, Tech)* diaphragm.
Memme *f* **-n** *(col)* cissy *(col)*, yellow-belly *(col)*.
Memoiren [me'moa:rən] *pl* memoirs *pl.*
Memorandum *nt, pl* **Memoranden** *or* **Memoranda** *(Pol)* memorandum.
Menge *f* **-n (a)** *(Quantum)* amount, quantity. **(b)** *(col) (große Anzahl)* lot, load *(col)*; *(Haufen auch)* pile *(col)*, heap *(col)*. **eine ~ Zeit/Häuser** lots *(col)* of time/houses; **jede ~** masses *pl (col)*, loads *pl (col)*; **wir haben jede ~ getrunken** we drank a hell of a lot *(col)*; **eine ganze ~** quite a lot. **(c)** *(Menschen~)* crowd; *(geh: Masse)* mass; *(pej: Pöbel)* mob.
mengen 1 *vt (geh)* to mix *(unter +acc* with*)*. **2** *vr* to mingle *(unter +acc* with*)*.
Mengen-: ~lehre *f (Math)* set theory; **~rabatt** *m* bulk discount.
Meniskus *m, pl* **Menisken** *(Anat, Phys)* meniscus.
Mensa *f, pl* **Mensen** *(Univ)* refectory *(Brit)*, commons *(US)*.
Mensch *m (wk)* **-en, -en (a)** *(Person)* person, man/woman. **von ~ zu ~** man to man/woman to woman; **es war kein ~ da** there was not a soul there; **als ~** as a person; **das konnte kein ~ ahnen!** no-one could have foreseen that! **(b)** *(als Gattung)* **der ~** man; **die ~en** man *sing*, human beings *pl*; **ein Tier, das keine ~en mag** an animal that doesn't like people; **ich bin auch nur ein ~!** I'm only human; **~ und Tier** man and beast. **(c)** *(die Menschheit)* **die ~en** mankind, man; **alle ~en** everyone. **(d)** *(col: als Interjektion)* hey. **~, das habe ich ganz vergessen** damn *(col)*, I completely forgot.
Mensch ärgere dich nicht *nt no pl (Spiel)* ludo.
Menschen- *in cpds* human; **~affe** *m* ape; **~alter** *nt* **(a)** *(30 Jahre)* generation; **(b)** *(Lebensdauer)* lifetime; **~ansammlung** *f* gathering (of people); **~auflauf** *m* crowd (of people); **~feind** *m* misanthropist; **m~feindlich** *adj Mensch* misanthropic; *Landschaft* hostile to man; **~fleisch** *nt* human flesh; **~fresser(in** *f)* *m* - *(col: Kannibale)* cannibal; **~freund** *m* philanthropist; **m~freundlich** *adj Mensch* philanthropic; *Gegend* hospitable; **~führung** *f* leadership; **~gedenken** *nt* **der kälteste Winter seit ~gedenken** the coldest winter in living memory; **~hai** *m* maneating shark; **~hand** *f* human hand; **von ~hand geschaffen** fashioned by the hand of man; **~handel** *m* slave trade; *(Jur)* trafficking in human beings; **~händler** *m* slave trader; *(Jur)* trafficker in human beings; **~kenner** *m* judge of character; **~kenntnis** *f no pl* knowledge of human nature; **~kenntnis haben** to know human nature; **~leben** *nt* human life; **ein ~leben lang** a whole lifetime; **~leben waren nicht zu beklagen** there was no loss of life; **das Unglück hat zwei ~leben gefordert** the accident claimed two lives; **m~leer** *adj* deserted; **~masse, ~ menge** *f* crowd (of people); **m~möglich** *adj* humanly possible; **das m~mögliche tun** to do all that is humanly possible; **~raub** *m (Jur)* kidnapping; **~recht** *nt* human right; **~rechtskonvention** *f* Human Rights Convention; **~scheu** *f* fear of people; **m~scheu** *adj* afraid of people; **~schlag** *m (col)* kind of people; **~seele** *f* human soul; **keine ~seele** *(fig)* not a soul.
Menschenskind *interj* good heavens.
Menschen-: m~unwürdig *adj* beneath human dignity; *Behandlung* inhumane; *Behausung* unfit for human habitation; **~verstand** *m* **gesunder ~verstand** common sense; **~würde** *f* human dignity *no art;* **m~würdig** *adj Behandlung* humane; *Unterkunft* fit for human habitation.
Menschheit *f* **die ~** mankind, humanity.
menschlich *adj* **(a)** human. **das ~e Leben** human life; **der ~e Körper/Geist** the human body/mind; **die ~e Gemeinschaft** human society; **er ist mir ~ sympathisch** I like him as a person; **(einigermaßen) ~ aussehen** *(col)* to look more or less human. **(b)** *(human) Behandlung etc* humane.
Menschlichkeit *f no pl* humanity *no art.* **aus reiner ~** on purely humanitarian grounds.
Menschwerdung *f (Bibl)* incarnation.
Mensen *pl of* **Mensa.**
Menstruation [menstrua'tsio:n] *f* menstruation.
Mensur *f (Univ)* (students') fencing bout.
Mentalität *f* mentality.
Menthol *nt* **-e** menthol.
Menü *nt* **-s** *(auch Comp)* menu.
Menuett *nt* **-e** *(Tanz, Mus)* minuet.
Merk-: m~bar *adj (wahrnehmbar)* noticeable; **~blatt** *nt* leaflet; *(mit Anweisungen auch)* instructions *pl.*
merken 1 *vt (entdecken)* to notice; *(spüren)* to feel; *(erkennen)* to realize. **davon habe ich nichts gemerkt** I didn't notice anything; **jdn etw ~ lassen** to make sb feel sth; **woran hast du das gemerkt?** how could you tell that?; **du merkst auch alles!** *(iro)* nothing escapes you, does it?; **das merkt keiner!** no-one will notice!; **ich merke keinen Unterschied** I can't tell the difference. **2** *vr* **sich** *(dat)* **jdn/etw ~** to remember sb/sth; **das werde ich mir ~!** I won't forget that; **merk dir das!** mark my words!; **sich** *(dat)* **eine Autonummer ~** to make a (mental) note of a licence number; **diesen Schriftsteller wird man sich** *(dat)* **~ müssen** this author is someone to take note of.
merklich *adj* noticeable. **kein ~er Unterschied** no noticeable difference.
Merkmal *nt* **-e** characteristic, feature.
Merksatz *m* mnemonic.
Merkur *m no pl (Myth, Astron)* Mercury.
Merk-: m~würdig *adj* strange, odd; **er hat sich ganz m~würdig verändert** he has undergone a curious change; **m~würdigerweise** *adv* strangely enough; **~würdigkeit** *f no pl* strangeness, oddness.
meschugge *adj (col)* nuts *(col)*.
Meß-: ~band *nt* tape measure; **m~bar** *adj* measurable; **~becher** *m (Cook)* measuring jug; **~diener** *m (Eccl)* server, acolyte *(form)*.
Messe *f* **-n (a)** *(Eccl, Mus)* mass. **zur ~ gehen** to go to mass. **(b)** *(Ausstellung)* (trade) fair. **auf der ~** at the fair. **(c)** *(Naut, Mil)* mess.
Messe- *in cpds* fair; **~gelände** *nt* exhibition centre *(Brit) or* center *(US)*; **~halle** *f* fair pavilion.
messen *pret* **maß,** *ptp* **gemessen 1** *vti* to measure; *(zeitlich)* to time; *(abschätzen) Entfernung etc* to judge. **jds Blutdruck ~** *(Arzt etc)* to take sb's blood pressure; **während ich lief, maß er die Zeit** I ran and he timed me; **seine Kräfte mit jdm ~** to match one's strength against sb's; **etw an etw** *(dat)* **~** *(ausprobieren)* to try sth out on sth; *(vergleichen)* to compare sth with sth. **2** *vr (geh: in Wettkampf etc)* to compete *(mit* against*)*. **sich mit jdm/etw nicht ~ können** to be no match for sb/sth.
Messer *nt* **-** knife; *(Tech auch)* cutter, blade; *(Rasier~)* (cutthroat) razor. **unter dem ~ sein** *(Med col)* to be under the knife; **jdm das ~ an die Kehle setzen** *(lit, fig)* to hold a knife to sb's

throat; **die ~ wetzen** *(fig)* to prepare for the kill; **damit würden wir ihn ans ~ liefern** *(fig)* that would be putting his head on the block; **ein Kampf bis aufs ~** *(fig)* a fight to the finish; **auf des ~s Schneide stehen** *(fig)* to hang in the balance.

Messer- *in cpds* knife; **m~scharf** *adj (lit, fig)* razor-sharp; **m~scharf schließen** *(iro)* to conclude with incredible logic *(iro)*; **~spitze** *f* knife point; **eine ~spitze (voll)** *(Cook)* a pinch; **~stecher(in** *f*) *m* - knifer *(col)*; **~stecherei** *f* knife fight; **~stich** *m* knife thrust; *(Wunde)* stab wound; **~werfer** *m* knife-thrower.

Messe-: **~stadt** *f* (town with an) exhibition centre *(Brit) or* center *(US)*; **~stand** *m* stand (at a fair).

Meßgerät *nt (für Öl, Druck etc)* measuring instrument, gauge.

Messias *m, gen - (Rel, fig)* Messiah.

Messing *nt no pl* brass.

Meß-: **~instrument** *nt* gauge; **~stab** *m (Aut: Ölmeßstab etc)* dipstick.

Messung *f* **(a)** *(das Messen)* measuring; *(das Ablesen)* reading; *(von Blutdruck)* taking. **(b)** *(Meßergebnis)* measurement; *(Ableseergebnis)* reading.

Meßwert *m* measurement; *(Ableseergebnis)* reading.

Metall *nt* **-e** metal.

Metall- *in cpds* metal-; **~arbeiter** *m* metalworker; **m~haltig** *adj* containing metal.

metallisch *adj* metal; *(metallartig), (fig) Stimme, Klang* metallic. **~ glänzen** to gleam like metal.

Metallurgie *f* metallurgy.

Metall-: **m~verarbeitend** *adj* **die m~verarbeitende Industrie** the metal-processing industry; **~verarbeitung** *f* metal processing.

Metapher [me'tafɐ] *f* **-n** *(Liter, Poet)* metaphor.

metaphorisch *adj (Liter, Poet)* metaphoric(al).

Metaphysik *f* metaphysics *sing.*

metaphysisch *adj* metaphysical.

Meteor *m* **-e** meteor.

Meteorit *m (wk)* **-en, -en** meteorite.

Meteorologe *m,* **Meteorologin** *f* meteorologist; *(im Wetterdienst)* weather forecaster.

Meteorologie *f* meteorology.

meteorologisch *adj* meteorological.

Meter *m or nt* - metre *(Brit)*, meter *(US)*. **in 500 ~ Höhe** at a height of 500 metres; **nach ~n** by the metre.

Meter-: **m~hoch** *adj Wellen etc* enormous; **~maß** *nt* **(a)** *(Bandmaß)* measuring tape; **(b)** *(Stab)* (metre *(Brit) or* meter *(US)*) rule; **~ware** *f (Tex)* piece goods; **m~weise** *adv* by the metre *(Brit) or* meter *(US)*.

Methode *f* **-n (a)** method. **etw mit ~ machen** to do sth methodically. **(b) ~n** *pl (Sitten)* behaviour *(Brit)*, behavior *(US)*; **was sind denn das für ~n?** what sort of way is that to behave?

Methodik *f* methodology.

methodisch *adj* methodical.

Methusalem *m* **alt wie ~** old as Methuselah.

Metier [me'tie:] *nt* **-s** *(hum)* job, profession.

Metrik *f (Poet, Mus)* metrics *sing.*

metrisch *adj (Sci)* metric; *(Poet, Mus auch)* metrical.

Metronom *nt* **-e** *(Mus)* metronome.

Metropole *f* **-n (a)** *(größte Stadt)* metropolis. **(b)** *(Zentrum)* capital.

Mett *nt no pl (Cook)* minced *(Brit) or* ground *(US)* pork.

Mette *f* **-n** *(Eccl)* matins *sing*; *(Abend~)* vespers *sing.*

Mettwurst *f* (smoked) pork/beef sausage.

Metzger *m* - butcher.

Metzger- *siehe* **Fleischer-.**

Metzgerei *f* butcher's (shop) *(Brit)*, butcher *(US)*.

Meuchel-: **~mord** *m* (treacherous) murder; **~mörder** *m* (treacherous) assassin.

Meute *f* **-n** pack (of hounds); *(fig pej)* mob.

Meuterei *f* mutiny; *(fig auch)* rebellion.

meutern *vi* to mutiny; *(col auch)* to rebel. **die ~den Soldaten** the mutinous soldiers.

Mexikaner(in *f*) *m* - Mexican.

mexikanisch *adj* Mexican.

Mexiko *nt* Mexico.

MEZ = **mitteleuropäische Zeit** CET.

MG [ɛm'ge:] *nt* **-(s)** = **Maschinengewehr.**

miau *interj* miaow.

miauen* *vi* to miaow.

mich 1 *pers pron acc of* **ich** me. **2** *reflexive pron* myself. **ich fühle ~ wohl** I feel fine.

mick(e)rig *adj (col)* pathetic; *Betrag auch* paltry; *altes Männchen* puny.

mied *pret of* **meiden.**

Mieder *nt* - *(Leibchen)* bodice.

Miederwaren *pl* corsetry *sing.*

Mief *m no pl (col)* fug; *(muffig)* stale air; *(Gestank)* stink, pong *(Brit col)*. **im Büro ist so ein ~** the air in the office is so stale.

miefen *vi (col)* to stink, to pong *(Brit col)*. **hier mieft es** there's a pong in here.

Miene *f* **-n** *(Gesichtsausdruck)* expression. **eine finstere ~ machen** to look grim; **gute ~ zum bösen Spiel machen** to grin and bear it.

Mienenspiel *nt* facial expressions *pl.*

mies *adj (col)* rotten *(col)*, lousy *(col)*. **jdn/etw ~ machen** to run sb/sth down.

Miesepeter *m* - *(col)* misery-guts *(col)*.

miesepet(e)rig *adj (col)* grouchy *(col)*.

Miesmacher *m (col)* kill-joy.

Miet|auto *nt* hire(d) car *(Brit)*, rental car *(US)*.

Miete *f* **-n** *(für Wohnung)* rent; *(für Gegenstände)* rental. **zur ~ wohnen** to live in rented accommodation *(Brit) or* accommodations *(US)*.

mieten *vt* to rent; *Boot, Auto auch* to hire *(Brit)*.

Mieter(in *f*) *m* - tenant; *(Untermieter)* lodger.

Miet|erhöhung *f* rent increase.

Mieterschutz *m* rent control.

Mietrecht *nt* rent law.

Miets-: **~haus** *nt* block of (rented) flats *(Brit)*, apartment house *(US)*; **~kaserne** *f (pej)* tenement house.

Miet-: **~verhältnis** *nt* tenancy; **~vertrag** *m* lease; **~wagen** *m* hire car *(Brit)*, rental car *(US)*; **~wohnung** *f* rented flat *(Brit) or* apartment; **~wucher** *m* **~wucher ist strafbar** charging exorbitant rent(s) is a punishable offence.

Mieze *f* **-n** *(col)* **(a)** *(Katze)* pussy *(col)*. **(b)** *(Mädchen)* chick *(col)*, bird *(Brit col)*.

Migräne *f no pl* migraine.

Mikado *nt* **-s** *(Spiel)* pick-a-stick.

Mikro- *in cpds* micro-.

Mikrofiche [-fi:ʃ] *m or nt* **-s** microfiche.

Mikrofon *nt* **-e** microphone.

Mikrokosmos *m* microcosm.

Mikroprozessor *m* microprocessor.

Mikroskop *nt* **-e** microscope.

mikroskopisch *adj* microscopic. **etw ~ untersuchen** to examine sth under the microscope.

Milbe *f* **-n** mite.

Milch *f no pl* milk; *(Fischsamen)* milt, soft roe. **~ geben** *(Kuh)* to yield milk.

Milch- *in cpds* milk; **~bart** *m (col)* fluffy beard; *(fig pej: Jüngling)* milksop; **~drüse** *f* mammary gland; **~flasche** *f* milk bottle; **~frau** *f (col)* dairywoman; **~gebiß** *nt* milk teeth *pl*; **~geschäft** *nt* dairy; **~gesicht** *nt (col)* baby face.

milchig *adj* milky.

Milch-: **~kaffee** *m* milky coffee; **~kanne** *f* milk can; *(größer)* (milk) churn; **~mädchenrechnung** *f (col)* naïve fallacy; **~mann** *m, pl* **-männer** milkman; **~pulver** *nt* dried milk; **~reis** *m* round-grain rice; *(gekocht)* rice pudding; **~straße** *f* Milky Way; **~tüte** *f* milk carton; plastic bag of milk; **~wirtschaft** *f* dairy farming; **~zahn** *m* milk tooth.

mild(e) *adj* mild; *Seife auch* gentle; *(nachsichtig) Behandlung, Richter, Urteil* lenient. **jdn ~ stimmen** to put sb in a good mood; **eine ~e Gabe** alms *pl*; **~ gesagt** to put it mildly.
Milde *f no pl siehe adj* **(a)** mildness. **(b)** leniency. **~ walten lassen** to be lenient.
mildern *vt (geh) Schmerz* to ease; *Furcht* to calm; *Urteil, Zorn, Worte* to moderate; *Gegensätze* to make less crass. **~de Umstände** *(Jur)* extenuating circumstances.
Milderung *f no pl (von Schmerz)* easing; *(von Ausdruck, Strafe, des Klimas)* moderation.
mildtätig *adj (geh)* charitable.
Milieu [mi'liøː] *nt* **-s** *(Umwelt)* environment, milieu.
militant *adj* militant.
Militär[1] *nt no pl* military, armed forces *pl*. **beim ~ sein** *(col)* to be in the forces; **zum ~ gehen** to join up.
Militär[2] *m* **-s** (army) officer.
Militär- *in cpds* military; **~dienst** *m* military service; **(seinen) ~dienst ableisten** to do one's military service; **~gericht** *nt* court martial.
militärisch *adj* military. **~ grüßen** to salute.
Militarismus *m no pl* militarism.
Militarist(in *f***)** *m* militarist.
Miliz *f* **-en** militia.
Milliardär(in *f***)** *m* multi-millionaire, billionaire.
Milliarde *f* **-n** thousand millions *(Brit)*, billion *(US)*.
Milli- *in cpds* milli-; **~bar** *nt* **-** millibar; **~gramm** *nt* milligramme *(Brit)*, milligram *(US)*; **~meter** *m or nt* millimetre *(Brit)*, millimeter *(US)*; **~meterpapier** *nt* graph paper.
Million *f* million. **zwei ~en Einwohner** two million inhabitants.
Millionär(in *f***)** *m* millionaire(ss). **es zum ~ bringen** to make a million.
Millionen-: **~auflage** *f* million copies *pl*; millions of copies; **~erbe** *m*, **~erbin** *f* inheritor of millions; **m~fach 1** *adj* millionfold; **2** *adv* a million times; **m~schwer** *adj (col)* worth a few million; **~stadt** *f* town with over a million inhabitants.
Millionstel *nt* millionth.
Milz *f* **-en** spleen.
Milzbrand *m (Med, Vet)* anthrax.
mimen *(old)* **1** *vt* to mime. **er mimt den Unschuldigen** *(col)* he's acting the innocent. **2** *vi* to play-act.
Mimik *f no pl* facial expression.
mimisch *adj* mimic.
Mimose *f* **-n** mimosa. **empfindlich wie eine ~ sein** to be oversensitive.
Min., min. = Minute(n).
minder *adv* less. **und das nicht ~** and no less so.
minder-: **~begabt** *adj* less gifted; **~bemittelt** *adj (dated)* less well-off; **geistig ~bemittelt** *(iro)* mentally less gifted.
mindere(r, s) *adj attr* lesser; *Qualität* inferior.
Minderheit *f* minority.
Minderheitsregierung *f* minority government.
Minder-: **m~jährig** *adj* who is (still) a minor; **jährige(r)** *mf decl as adj* minor; **~jährigkeit** *f* minority.
mindern 1 *vt (herabsetzen) Würde, Verdienste* to diminish; *(verringern) Wert, Qualität* to reduce. **2** *vr* to diminish.
Minderung *f siehe vb* diminishing *no indef art*; reduction *(gen* in*)*.
minderwertig *adj* inferior; *Waren, Material, Arbeit auch* poor-quality; *Qualität auch* low.
Minderwertigkeit *f* inferiority.
Minderwertigkeits-: **~gefühl** *nt* feeling of inferiority; **~komplex** *m* inferiority complex.
Minderzahl *f* minority. **in der ~** in the minority.
Mindest- *in cpds* minimum; **~alter** *nt* minimum age.
mindeste 1 *adj attr* least, slightest. **das ~** the (very) least; **ich verstehe nicht das ~ von (der) Kunst** I don't know the slightest thing about art. **2** *adv* **zum ~n** at the very least; **(nicht) im ~n** (not) in the least.
mindestens *adv* at least.
Mindest-: **~größe** *f* minimum size; *(von Menschen)* minimum height; **~maß** *nt* minimum amount *(an +dat* of*)*; **~umtausch** *m* minimum obligatory exchange.
Mine *f* **-n** **(a)** *(Min)* mine. **(b)** *(Mil)* mine. **auf eine ~ laufen** to hit a mine. **(c)** *(Bleistift~)* lead; *(Kugelschreiber~, Filzstift~)* refill.
Minen-: **~feld** *nt (Mil)* minefield; **~leger** *m* **-** *(Mil, Naut)* mine-layer; **~suchboot** *nt* minesweeper.
Mineral *nt* **-e** *or* **-ien** [-iən] mineral.
Mineral-: **~öl** *nt* (mineral) oil; **~ölsteuer** *f* tax on oil; **~quelle** *f* mineral spring; **~wasser** *nt* mineral water.
Mini- *in cpds* mini-.
Miniatur *f (Art)* miniature.
Miniatur- *in cpds* miniature; **~ausgabe** *f* miniature version; *(Buch)* miniature edition.
Minigolf *nt* crazy golf.
minimal *adj* minimal. **mit ~er Anstrengung** with a minimum of effort.
Minimal- *in cpds* minimum.
Minimum *nt, pl* **Minima** minimum *(an +dat* of*)*.
Minirock *m* mini-skirt.
Minister(in *f***)** *m* **-** *(Pol)* minister *(Brit) (für* of*)*, secretary *(für* for*)*.
Ministerialbeamte(r) *m* ministry official.
ministeriell *adj attr* ministerial.
Ministerium *nt* ministry *(Brit)*, department.
Ministerpräsident(in *f***)** *m* prime minister; *(eines Bundeslandes)* chief minister of a Federal German state.
Minna *f no pl* **jdn zur ~ machen** *(col)* to give sb a piece of one's mind.
Minne-: **~sang** *m* minnesong; **~sänger** *m* minnesinger.
minus 1 *prep +gen* minus, less; *(Math)* minus. **2** *adv* minus; *(Elec)* negative. **10 Grad ~ 10** degrees below zero; **~ machen** *(col)* to make a loss.
Minus *nt* **-, -** *(Fehlbetrag)* deficit; *(auf Konto)* overdraft; *(fig: Nachteil)* bad point; *(in Beruf etc)* disadvantage.
Minus-: **~pol** *m* negative pole; **~punkt** *m* penalty point; *(fig)* minus point; **~zeichen** *nt* minus sign.
Minute *f* **-n** minute. **auf die ~ (genau/pünktlich)** (right) on the dot; **in letzter ~** at the last minute; **es vergeht keine ~, ohne daß ...** not a moment goes by without ...
Minuten-: **m~lang 1** *adj attr* several minutes of; **2** *adv* for several minutes; **~zeiger** *m* minute-hand.
minuziös *adj (geh)* meticulous.
Minze *f* **-n** *(Bot)* mint.
Mio. = Million(en).
mir *pers pron dat of* **ich** to me; *(nach Präpositionen)* me. **ein Freund von ~** a friend of mine; **von ~ aus!** *(col)* I don't mind; **~ nichts, dir nichts** *(col)* without so much as a by-your-leave; **es war ~ nichts, dir nichts weg** the next thing I knew it had gone; **wie du ~, so ich dir** *(prov)* tit for tat *(col)*; *(als Drohung)* I'll get my own back.
Mirabelle *f* mirabelle, small yellow plum.
Misch-: **~batterie** *f* mixer tap; **~brot** *nt bread made from more than one kind of flour*; **~ehe** *f* mixed marriage.
mischen 1 *vtr* to mix. **sich unter die Menge ~** to mix with the crowd; **sich in etw** *(acc)* **~** to meddle in sth; **sich in das Gespräch ~** to butt into the conversation. **2** *vi (Cards)* to shuffle.
Misch-: **~farbe** *f* mixed *or* blended colour *(Brit) or* color *(US)*; *(Phys)* secondary colour; **~form** *f* mixture; *(von zwei Elementen auch)* hybrid

(form); ~**ling** *m (Mensch)* half-caste; *(Zool)* half-breed; ~**masch** *m* **-e** *(col)* hotchpotch; *(Essen auch)* concoction; ~**maschine** *f* cement-mixer; ~**pult** *nt (Rad, TV)* mixing panel.

Mischung *f* **(a)** *(das Mischen)* mixing. **(b)** *(lit, fig: Gemischtes)* mixture; *(von Tee etc auch)* blend.

Mischwald *m* mixed (deciduous and coniferous) woodland.

miserabel *adj (col)* lousy *(col)*; *Gesundheit* wretched; *Benehmen* dreadful.

Misere *f* **-n** *(von Leuten, Wirtschaft etc)* plight; *(von Hunger, Krieg etc)* misery, miseries *pl.* **in einer ~ stecken** to be in a dreadful state; *(Mensch)* to be in a mess.

miß|achten* *vt insep (ignorieren)* to disregard.

Miß|achtung *f* **(a)** disregard. **(b)** *(Geringschätzung)* disrespect *(gen* for*)*.

Mißbehagen *nt (geh) (Unbehagen)* uneasiness; *(Mißfallen)* discontent(ment).

mißbilden *ptp* **mißgebildet** *vt insep* to deform.

Mißbildung *f* deformity, malformation.

mißbilligen* *vt insep* to disapprove of.

Mißbilligung *f* disapproval.

Mißbrauch *m* abuse; *(falsche Anwendung)* misuse; *(von Notbremse, Feuerlöscher etc)* improper use. **unter ~ seines Amtes** in abuse of his office.

mißbrauchen* *vt insep* to abuse; *(geh: vergewaltigen)* to assault. **jdn zu etw ~** to use sb for sth *or* to do sth.

mißbräuchlich *adj (form)* improper.

mißdeuten* *vt insep* to misinterpret.

Mißdeutung *f* misinterpretation.

missen *vt (geh)* to do without. **das möchte ich nicht ~** I wouldn't do without it (for the world).

Miß|erfolg *m* failure; *(Theat, Buch etc auch)* flop *(col)*.

Miß|ernte *f* crop failure.

mißfallen* *vi insep irreg +dat* to displease. **es mißfällt mir, wie er ...** I dislike the way he ...

Mißfallen *nt no pl* displeasure *(über +acc* at*)*. **jds ~ erregen** to incur sb's displeasure.

Mißfallens-: ~**bekundung,** ~**kundgebung** *f* demonstration of displeasure.

mißfällig *adj Bemerkung* deprecatory.

Mißgeburt *f* deformed person/animal; *(fig col)* failure.

Mißgeschick *nt* mishap; *(Pech, Unglück)* misfortune.

mißglücken* *vi insep aux sein* to be unsuccessful. **der Versuch ist (ihm) mißglückt** the/his attempt was a failure.

mißgönnen* *vt insep* **jdm etw ~** to (be)grudge sb sth.

Mißgriff *m* mistake.

Mißgunst *f* resentment (at).

mißgünstig *adj* resentful *(auf +acc* towards*)*.

mißhandeln* *vt insep* to ill-treat, to maltreat.

Mißhandlung *f* ill-treatment, maltreatment.

Mission *f (Eccl, Pol, fig)* mission; *(diplomatische Vertretung)* legation, mission *(US)*; *(Gruppe)* delegation.

Missionar(in *f) m* missionary.

missionarisch *adj* missionary.

Mißklang *m* discord *(auch Mus)*, dissonance; *(Mißton, fig)* discordant note.

Mißkredit *m no pl* discredit. **jdn/etw in ~ bringen** to bring sb/sth into discredit.

mißlang *pret of* **mißlingen.**

mißlich *adj (geh)* awkward, difficult.

mißliebig *adj* unpopular.

Mißlingen *nt no pl* failure.

mißlingen *pret* **mißlang,** *ptp* **mißlungen** *vi aux sein* to be unsuccessful. **ein mißlungener Versuch** an unsuccessful attempt.

Mißmut *m* sullenness; *(Unzufriedenheit)* displeasure.

mißmutig *adj* sullen; *(unzufrieden)* discontented; *Äußerung, Aussehen* disgruntled.

mißraten* **1** *vi insep irreg aux sein* to go wrong. **der Kuchen ist mir ~** my cake was a failure. **2** *adj Kind* wayward.

Mißstand *m* anomaly; *(allgemeiner Zustand)* deplorable state of affairs *no pl*; *(Ungerechtigkeit)* abuse; *(Mangel)* defect.

Mißstimmung *f* **(a)** *(Uneinigkeit)* discord. **eine ~** a note of discord. **(b)** *(schlechte Laune)* bad mood; *(Unzufriedenheit)* discontent *no pl.*

Mißton *m (Mus, fig)* discordant note. **~e** *(Klang)* discordant sound; *(fig)* discord.

mißtrauen* *vi insep +dat* to mistrust.

Mißtrauen *nt no pl* mistrust *(gegenüber* of*)*. **~ gegen jdn/etw haben** to be suspicious of sb/sth.

Mißtrauensvotum *nt* vote of no confidence.

mißtrauisch *adj* distrustful; *(argwöhnisch)* suspicious.

Mißverhältnis *nt* discrepancy.

mißverständlich *adj* unclear.

Mißverständnis *nt* misunderstanding.

mißverstehen* *vt insep irreg* to misunderstand.

Mißwahl, Misswahl *f* beauty contest.

Mißwirtschaft *f* maladministration.

Mist *m no pl* **(a)** *(Tierkot)* droppings *pl*; *(Pferde~, Kuh~ etc)* dung; *(Dünger)* manure. **das ist nicht auf seinem ~ gewachsen** *(col)* he didn't think that up himself. **(b)** *(col) (Unsinn)* nonsense; *(Schund)* rubbish. **~!** blast! *(col)*; **da hat er ~ gemacht** *or* **gebaut** he really messed that up *(col)*; **mach keinen ~!** don't be a fool!

Mistel *f* **-n** mistletoe *no pl.*

Mist-: ~**fink** *m (col)* dirty-minded character; *(Journalist etc)* muck-raker *(col)*; ~**gabel** *f* pitchfork *(used for shifting manure)*; ~**haufen** *m* manure heap; ~**käfer** *m* dung beetle; ~**stück,** ~**vieh** *nt (col!) (Mann)* bastard *(col!)*; *(Frau auch)* bitch *(col!)*; ~**wetter** *nt (col)* lousy weather *(col)*.

mit **1** *prep +dat* with. **~ dem Hut in der Hand** (with) his hat in his hand; **ein Topf ~ Suppe** a pot of soup; **wie wär's ~ einem Bier?** *(col)* how about a beer?; **~ der Bahn/dem Bus/dem Auto** by train/bus/car; **~ Gewalt** by force; **~ Bleistift schreiben** to write in pencil; **~ dem nächsten Flugzeug/Bus kommen** to come on the next plane/bus; **~ einem Wort** in a word; **~ achtzehn Jahren** at (the age of) eighteen; **es wird ~ jedem Tag schlimmer** it's getting worse every day; **~ der Zeit** in time; **etw ~ DM 50.000 versichern** to insure sth for DM 50,000; **~ 80 km/h** at 80 km/h; **~ 4:2 gewinnen** to win 4-2; **~ mir waren es 5** there were 5 including me; **du ~ deinen dummen Ideen** *(col)* you and your stupid ideas; **~ lauter Stimme** in a loud voice; **~ Verlust** at a loss.

2 *adv* **er wollte ~** *(col)* he wanted to come too; **er war ~ dabei** he was there too; **er ist ~ der Beste der Gruppe** he is among the best in the group; **das gehört ~ dazu** that's part and parcel of it; **etw ~ in Betracht ziehen** to consider sth as well.

Mit|arbeit *f* collaboration; *(Hilfe auch)* assistance; *(Teilnahme)* participation *(auch Sch)*. **unter ~ von** in collaboration with.

mit|arbeiten *vi sep* to collaborate. **er hat beim Bau des Hauses mitgearbeitet** he helped build the house; **beim Unterricht ~** to take an active part in lessons; **seine Frau arbeitet mit** *(col)* his wife works too.

Mit|arbeiter(in *f) m (Betriebsangehöriger)* employee; *(Kollege)* colleague; *(an Projekt etc)* collaborator. **freier ~** freelance.

mitbekommen* *vt sep irreg* **(a)** to get *or* be given sth. **(b)** *(col: verstehen)* to get *(col)*.

Mitbesitzer *m* joint-owner.

mitbestimmen* *sep* **1** *vi* to have a say *(bei* in*)*; to participate *(bei* in*)*. **~d sein** to have an influence *(bei, für* on*)*. **2** *vt* to have an influence on.

Mitbestimmung *f* participation *(bei* in*)*. **~ am**

Arbeitsplatz worker participation.
Mitbewerber *m* (fellow) competitor. **meine ~** *(für Stelle)* the other applicants.
mitbringen *vt sep irreg* **(a)** to bring; *Freund, Begleiter* to bring along. **jdm etw von der Stadt/vom Bäcker ~** to bring sb sth back from town/fetch sb sth from the baker's; **was sollen wir der Gastgeberin ~?** what should we take to our hostess? **(b)** *Mitgift, Kinder* to bring with one. **etw in die Ehe ~** to have sth when one gets married. **(c)** *(fig) Befähigung etc* to have, to possess.
Mitbringsel *nt (Geschenk)* small present; *(Andenken)* souvenir.
Mitbürger *m* fellow citizen.
mitdürfen *vi sep irreg* **wir durften nicht mit** we weren't allowed to go along.
Mit|eigentümer *m* joint-owner.
mit|einander *adv* with one another; *(gemeinsam)* together. **wir haben lange ~ geredet** we had a long talk.
mit|empfinden* *sep irreg* **1** *vt* to share. **2** *vi* **mit jdm ~** to sympathize with sb.
mit|erleben* *vt sep Krieg* to live through; *(im Fernsehen)* to watch.
mit|essen *vt sep irreg Schale etc* to eat as well.
Mit|esser *m* - blackhead.
mitfahren *vi sep irreg aux sein* to go (with sb). **sie fährt mit** she is going too; **(mit jdm) ~** to go with sb; *(auf Reise auch)* to travel with sb; **kann ich (mit Ihnen) ~?** can you give me a lift?
Mitfahrer *m* passenger.
Mitfahrerzentrale *f* agency for arranging lifts.
Mitfahrgelegenheit *f* lift.
mitfühlen *vi sep siehe* **mitempfinden.**
mitfühlend *adj* compassionate.
mitführen *vt sep Papiere, Ware etc* to carry (with one); *(Fluß)* to carry along.
mitgeben *vt sep irreg* **jdm etw ~** to give sb sth to take with them; *Rat, Erziehung* to give sb sth.
Mitgefühl *nt* sympathy.
mitgehen *vi sep irreg aux sein* **(a)** to go too *or* along. **mit jdm ~** to go with sb. **(b)** *(fig: Publikum etc)* to respond (favourably) *(mit* to*)*. **(c)** *(col)* **etw ~ lassen** to pinch sth *(col)*.
Mitgift *f* **-en** dowry.
Mitgiftjäger *m (col)* dowry-hunter.
Mitglied *nt* member *(gen, bei, in +dat* of*)*.
Mitglieds-: ~ausweis *m* membership card; **~beitrag** *m* membership subscription.
Mitgliedschaft *f* membership.
Mitglied(s)staat *m* member state.
mithaben *vt sep irreg* **etw ~** to have sth (with one); **hast du alles mit?** have you got everything?
mithalten *vi sep irreg (bei Tempo etc)* to keep pace *(mit* with*)*. **bei einer Diskussion ~ können** to be able to hold one's own in a discussion.
mithelfen *vi sep irreg* to help. **beim Bau des Hauses ~** to help build the house.
Mithilfe *f* assistance, aid.
mithören *sep* **1** *vt* to listen to (too); *Gespräch* to overhear; *(heimlich)* to listen in on. **ich habe alles mitgehört** I heard everything. **2** *vi* to listen in *(bei* on*)*; *(zufällig)* to overhear.
Mit|inhaber *m* joint-owner.
mitklingen *vi sep irreg (Ton, Saite)* to sound, to resonate. **in ihrer Äußerung klang ein leichter Vorwurf mit** there was a slight note of reproach in her remark.
mitkommen *vi sep irreg aux sein* **(a)** to come along *(mit* with*)*. **ich kann nicht ~** I can't come; **komm doch mit!** why don't you come too? **(b)** *(col) (mithalten)* to keep up; *(verstehen)* to follow. **da komme ich nicht mit** that's beyond me; **sie kommt in der Schule gut mit** she is getting on well at school.
mitkriegen *vt sep (col)* = **mitbekommen.**
mitlaufen *vi sep irreg aux sein* to run *(mit* with*)*.
Mitläufer *m (Pol, pej)* fellow traveller *(Brit) or* traveler *(US)*.
Mitlaut *m* consonant.
Mitleid *nt no pl* pity, compassion *(mit* for*)*; *(Mitgefühl)* sympathy *(mit* with, for*)*.
Mitleidenschaft *f*: **jdn/etw in ~ ziehen** to affect sb/sth (detrimentally).
mitleidig *adj* pitying; *(mitfühlend)* sympathetic; *Mensch auch* compassionate. **~ lächeln** to smile pityingly.
mitleid(s)-: ~los *adj* heartless; **~voll** *adj* compassionate.
mitmachen *vti sep* **(a)** *(teilnehmen) Spiel, Singen etc* to join in; *Reise* to go on; *Kurs* to do; *Mode* to follow. **etw** *(acc) or* **bei etw** *(dat)* **~** to join in sth; **meine Beine machen nicht mehr mit** my legs are giving up. **(b)** *(col: einverstanden sein)* **da macht mein Chef nicht mit** my boss won't go along with that; **ich mache das nicht mehr lange mit** I won't take that much longer. **(c)** *(erleben)* to live through; *(erleiden)* to go through.
Mitmensch *m* fellow man.
mitmenschlich *adj Kontakte etc* human.
mitmischen *vi sep (col) (sich beteiligen)* to be involved *(in +dat, bei* in*)*; *(sich einmischen)* to interfere *(in +dat, bei* in sth*)*.
mitnehmen *vt sep irreg* **(a)** to take (with one); *(ausleihen)* to borrow; *(kaufen)* to take. **jdn (im Auto) ~** to give sb a lift; **einen Hamburger zum M~** a hamburger to take away *(Brit) or* to go *(US)*. **(b)** *(erschöpfen) jdn* to exhaust, to weaken; *(beschädigen)* to be bad for. **mitgenommen aussehen** to look the worse for wear. **(c)** *(stehlen)* to walk off with. **(d)** *(col) Sehenswürdigkeit etc* to take in.
mitrechnen *vt sep* to count; *Betrag* to count in.
mitreden *sep* **1** *vi (Meinung äußern)* to join in *(bei etw* sth*)*; *(mitbestimmen)* to have a say *(bei* in*)*. **da kann er nicht ~** he wouldn't know anything about that. **2** *vt* **Sie haben hier nichts mitzureden** this is none of your concern.
mitreisen *vi sep aux sein* to go/travel too. **mit jdm ~** to go/travel with sb.
Mitreisende(r) *mf* fellow traveller *(Brit) or* traveler *(US)*.
mitreißen *vt sep irreg (Fluß, Lawine)* to sweep away. **seine Rede hat alle mitgerissen** everyone was carried away by his speech.
mitreißend *adj Rhythmus* infectious; *Reden* rousing; *Film, Fußballspiel* thrilling, exciting.
mitsamt *prep +dat* together with.
mitschneiden *vt sep irreg* to record.
Mitschnitt *m* recording.
mitschreiben *sep irreg* **1** *vt* **etw ~** to write *or* take sth down. **2** *vi* to take notes.
Mitschrift *f* record; *(von Vorlesung etc)* notes *pl*.
Mitschuld *f* share of the blame *(an +dat* for*)*; *(an einem Verbrechen)* complicity *(an +dat* in*)*.
mitschuldig *adj (an Verbrechen)* implicated *(an +dat* in*)*; *(an Unfall)* partly responsible *(an +dat* for*)*.
Mitschuldige(r) *mf* accomplice.
Mitschüler *m* school-friend; *(in derselben Klasse)* class-mate.
mitsingen *sep irreg* **1** *vt* to join in (singing). **2** *vi* to sing along. **in einem Chor ~** to sing in a choir.
mitspielen *vi sep* **(a)** to play too; *(in Team etc)* to play *(bei* in*)*. **in einem Film ~** to be in a film. **(b)** *(Gründe, Motive)* to play a part *(bei* in*)*, to be involved *(bei* in*)*. **(c)** *(Schaden zufügen)* **er hat ihr übel/hart mitgespielt** he has treated her badly.
Mitspieler *m (Sport)* player; *(Theat)* member of the cast.
Mitsprache *f* a say.
Mitspracherecht *nt* right to a say in a matter. **jdm ein ~ einräumen** to allow sb a say *(bei* in*)*.
mitsprechen *sep irreg* **1** *vt Gebet* to join in (saying). **2** *vi (mitbestimmen)* to have a say in sth.
Mitstreiter *m (geh)* comrade-in-arms.

mittag *adv* **gestern/heute** ~ at midday yesterday/today, yesterday/today lunchtime.
Mittag *m* **-e (a)** midday. **jeden** ~ every day at midday, every lunchtime; **zu** ~ **essen** to have lunch. **(b)** *(col: ~spause)* lunch-hour, lunch-break. ~ **machen** to take one's lunch-hour.
Mittag|essen *nt* midday meal. **er kam zum** ~ he came to lunch.
mittäglich *adj attr* midday, lunchtime.
mittags *adv* at lunchtime. ~ **um 12 Uhr** at 12 noon; **sonnabends** ~ Saturday lunchtime.
Mittags-: ~**hitze** *f* midday heat; ~**pause** *f* lunch-hour, lunch-break; ~**pause machen/haben** to take/have one's lunch-hour *etc*; *(Geschäft etc)* to close at lunchtime; ~**ruhe** *f* period of quiet (after lunch); *(in Geschäft)* midday-closing; ~**schlaf** *m* afternoon nap; ~**stunde** *f* midday; **um die** ~**stunde** around midday; ~**zeit** *f* lunch time; **während** *or* **in der** ~**zeit** at lunch time.
Mittäter *m* accomplice.
Mitte *f* **-n** middle; *(fig auch, von Kreis, Kugel etc, Pol)* centre *(Brit)*, center *(US)*. **das Reich der** ~ *(liter)* the Middle Kingdom; **die** ~ **des Weges haben wir hinter uns** we have come more than halfway; ~**August** in the middle of August, in mid August; **er ist** ~ **vierzig** he's in his mid-forties; **die goldene** ~ the golden mean; **in der** ~ in the middle; *(zwischen zwei Menschen)* in between (them/us *etc*); *(zwischen Ortschaften)* halfway, midway; **einer aus unserer** ~ one of our number; **in unserer** ~ in our midst.
mitteilen *sep* **1** *vt* **jdm etw** ~ to tell sb sth; *(benachrichtigen)* to inform sb about sth; *(bekanntgeben)* to announce sth to sb; *(Comm, Admin)* to notify sb of sth. **2** *vr* to communicate *(jdm* with sb*)*. **er kann sich gut/schlecht** ~ he finds it easy/difficult to communicate.
mitteilsam *adj* communicative.
Mitteilung *f (Bekanntgabe)* announcement; *(Benachrichtigung)* notification; *(Comm, Admin)* communication; *(an Mitarbeiter etc)* memo. **jdm (eine)** ~ **(von etw) machen** *(form)* to inform sb (of sth); *(bekanntgeben)* to announce sth to sb; *(benachrichtigen)* to inform sb (of sth).
Mitteilungsbedürfnis *nt* need to talk to other people.
Mittel *nt* **- (a)** *(~ zum Zweck)* means *sing*; *(Maßnahme, Methode)* way, method. ~ **und Wege finden** to find ways and means; ~ **zum Zweck** a means to an end; **kein** ~ **unversucht lassen** to try everything; **als letztes** ~ as a last resort; **ihm ist jedes** ~ **recht** he will do anything (to achieve his ends); **etw mit allen** ~**n verhindern** to do one's utmost to prevent sth. **(b)** *pl (Geld~)* funds *pl*, means *pl*. **(c)** *(Medikament, kosmetisch)* preparation; *(Medizin)* medicine; *(Putz~)* cleaning agent; *(Wasch~)* detergent. **welches** ~ **nimmst du?** *(Med: einnehmen)* what do you take?; **das ist ein** ~ **gegen Schuppen** that is for dandruff; **sich** *(dat)* **ein** ~ **verschreiben lassen** to get the doctor to prescribe something; **das beste** ~ **gegen etw** the best cure for sth. **(d)** *(Math: Durchschnitt)* average. **arithmetisches** ~ arithmetical mean.
Mittel-: ~**alter** *nt* Middle Ages *pl*; **m**~**alterlich** *adj* medieval; ~**amerika** *nt* Central America (and the Caribbean); **m**~**amerikanisch** *adj* Central American; **m**~**bar** *adj* indirect *(auch Jur)*; **m**~**deutsch** *adj (Geog, Ling)* Central German; *(BRD Pol)* East German; ~**deutschland** *nt (BRD: als Land)* East Germany; ~**ding** *nt (Mischung)* cross; **ein** ~**ding** *(weder das eine noch das andere)* something in between; ~**europa** *nt* Central Europe; ~**europäer** *m* Central European; **m**~**europäisch** *adj* Central European; ~**feld** *nt (Sport)* midfield; ~**finger** *m* middle finger; **m**~**fristig** *adj Finanzplanung, Politik* medium-term; ~**gebirge** *nt* low mountain range; ~**gewicht** *nt* middleweight; **m**~**groß** *adj* medium-sized; ~**hochdeutsch** *nt* Middle High German; ~**klasse** *f* **(a)** *(Comm)* middle of the market; **(b)** *(Sociol)* middle classes *pl*; ~**klassewagen** *m* middle-market car; ~**linie** *f* centre *(Brit) or* center *(US)* line; **m**~**los** *adj* without means; *(arm)* impoverished; ~**losigkeit** *f* lack of means; *(Armut)* impoverishment; ~**maß** *nt* mediocrity *no art*; **das (gesunde)** ~**maß** the happy medium; **m**~**mäßig 1** *adj* mediocre; *Schriftsteller, Spieler etc auch* indifferent; **2** *adv* indifferently; **wie gefällt es dir hier? — so m**~**mäßig** how do you like it here? — so-so; ~**mäßigkeit** *f* mediocrity.
Mittelmeer *nt* Mediterranean (Sea), Med *(col)*.
Mittelmeer- *in cpds* Mediterranean.
Mittelmeerraum *m* Mediterranean (region).
Mittel-: **m**~**prächtig** *adj (hum col)* not bad *pred*, so-so *pred (col)*; ~**punkt** *m (Math, räumlich)* centre *(Brit)*, center *(US)*; *(fig: visuell)* focal point; **er steht im** ~**punkt des Interesses** he is the centre of attention; ~**scheitel** *m* centre parting *(Brit)*, center part *(US)*; ~**schicht** *f (Sociol)* middle class.
Mittelsmann *m*, *pl* **-männer** *or* **-leute** intermediary.
Mittel-: ~**stand** *m* middle classes *pl*; **m**~**ständisch** *adj* middle-class.
Mittelstrecken-: ~**flugzeug** *nt* medium-haul aircraft; ~**lauf** *m* middle-distance race; ~**rakete** *f* medium-range missile.
Mittel-: ~**streifen** *m* central reservation *(Brit)*, median (strip) *(US)*; ~**stück** *nt* middle part; ~**stufe** *f (Sch)* middle school *(Brit)*, junior high *(US)*; ~**stürmer** *m (Sport)* centre-forward; ~**weg** *m* middle course; **der goldene** ~**weg** the happy medium, the golden mean; ~**welle** *f (Rad)* medium wave(band); ~**wert** *m* mean.
mitten *adv* ~ **in/auf etw** (right) in the middle of sth; ~ **aus etw** (right) from the middle of sth; ~ **durch etw** (right) through the middle of sth; ~ **im Urwald** in the depths of the jungle; ~ **ins Gesicht** right in the face; ~ **unter uns** (right) in our midst.
mitten-: ~**drin** *adv* (right) in the middle of it; ~**durch** *adv* (right) through the middle.
Mitternacht *f* midnight *no art*.
mitternächtlich *adj attr* midnight. **zu** ~**er Stunde** *(geh)* at the midnight hour.
mittlere(r, s) *adj attr* **(a)** *(dazwischenliegend)* middle. **der/die/das** ~ the middle one; **der M**~ **Osten** the Middle East. **(b)** *(den Mittelwert bildend)* medium; *(mittelschwer) Kursus, Aufgabe* intermediate; *(durchschnittlich)* average; *(Math)* mean. ~**n Alters** middle-aged.
mittlerweile *adv* in the meantime.
Mitt-: ~**woch** *m* **-e** Wednesday; *siehe* **Dienstag**; **m**~**wochs** *adv* on Wednesdays.
mit|unter *adv* now and again, once in a while.
mitverantwortlich *adj* jointly responsible *pred*.
Mitverantwortung *f* share of the responsibility.
mitverdienen* *vi sep* to (go out to) work as well.
Mitverfasser *m* co-author.
Mitverschulden *nt* **ihn trifft ein** ~ **an diesem Vorfall** he was partly to blame for this incident.
mitwirken *vi sep (an +dat, bei* in*)* to play a part; *(beteiligt sein)* to be involved; *(Theat, in Diskussion)* to take part; *(in Film)* to appear.
Mitwirkende(r) *mf decl as adj* participant *(an +dat, bei* in*)*. **die** ~**n** *(Theat)* the cast *pl*.
Mitwirkung *f (Beteiligung)* involvement *(an +dat, bei* in*)*; *(an Buch, Film)* collaboration *(an +dat, bei* on*)*; *(Teilnahme) (an Diskussion, Projekt)* participation *(an +dat, bei* in*)*; *(von Schauspieler)* appearance *(an +dat, bei* in*)*. **unter** ~ **von** with the help of.
Mitwisser(in *f)* *m* **-** *(Jur)* accessory *(gen* to*)*. ~ **einer Sache** *(gen)* **sein** to know about sth.
mitzählen *vti sep* to count; *Betrag* to count in.
Mixbecher *m* (cocktail) shaker.

mixen *vt Getränke, (Rad, TV)* to mix.
Mixer *m* - **(a)** *(Bar~)* cocktail waiter. **(b)** *(Küchen~)* blender; *(Rührmaschine)* mixer. **(c)** *(Film, Rad, TV)* mixer.
Mixgetränk *nt* mixed drink; *(alkoholisch)* cocktail.
Mixtur *f (Pharm, Mus, fig)* mixture.
ml = **Milliliter** millilitre *(Brit)*, milliliter *(US)*.
mm = **Millimeter.**
Möbel *nt* - *(~stück)* piece of furniture. ~ *pl* furniture *sing.*
Möbel- *in cpds* furniture; **~lager** *nt* furniture showroom; **~packer** *m* removal man; **~spedition** *f* removal firm; **~stoff** *m* furnishing fabric; **~stück** *nt* piece of furniture; **~wagen** *m* removal van *(Brit)*, moving van *(US)*.
mobil *adj* **(a)** mobile. ~ **machen** *(Mil)* to mobilize. **(b)** *(col: flink, munter)* lively.
Mobile ['mo:bilə] *nt* **-s** mobile.
Mobiliar *nt no pl* furnishings *pl.*
mobilisieren* *vt (Mil, fig)* to mobilize.
Mobilmachung *f (Mil)* mobilization.
möblieren* *vt* to furnish. **ein möbliertes Zimmer** a furnished room; **möbliert wohnen** to live in furnished accommodation *(Brit) or* accommodations *(US)*.
mochte *pret of* **mögen.**
Möchtegern- *in cpds (iro)* would-be.
Modalität *f usu pl (von Plan, Vertrag etc)* arrangement; *(von Verfahren, Arbeit)* procedure.
Mode *f* **-n** fashion; *(Sitte)* custom. ~ **sein** to be the fashion; *(Sitte)* to be the custom; **in ~/aus der ~ kommen** to come into/go out of fashion.
Mode-: **~artikel** *m* fashion accessory; **m~bewußt** *adj* fashion-conscious; **~farbe** *f* in-colour *(Brit)*, in-color *(US)*; **~geschäft** *nt* fashion shop *(Brit) or* store *(US)*; **~heft, ~journal** *nt* fashion magazine.
Modell *nt* **-e** model. **zu etw ~ stehen** to be the model for sth.
Modell-: **~eisenbahn** *f* model railway; *(als Spielzeug)* train set; **~flugzeug** *nt* model aeroplane *or* airplane *(US)*.
modellieren* *vti* to model.
Modell-: **~kleid** *nt* model (dress); **~versuch** *m* *(esp Sch)* experiment.
Modem *m* **-s** modem.
Modenschau *f* fashion show.
Moder *m no pl* mustiness; *(Schimmel)* mildew. **es riecht nach ~** it smells musty.
Moderation *f (Rad, TV)* presentation.
Moderator(in *f*) *m* presenter.
Modergeruch *m* musty smell.
moderieren* *vti (Rad, TV)* to present.
mod(e)rig *adj Geruch* musty.
modern[1] *vi aux sein or haben* to rot.
modern[2] *adj* modern *no adv*; *(modisch)* fashionable; *Ansichten, Eltern, Lehrer* progressive.
Moderne *f no pl (geh)* modern age.
modernisieren* *vt Gebäude* to modernize; *Kleidung* to make more fashionable.
Mode-: **~schmuck** *m* costume jewellery *(Brit) or* jewelry *(US)*; **~schöpfer(in** *f*) *m* fashion designer; **~tanz** *m* popular dance; **~wort** *nt* trendy word; **~zeitschrift** *f* fashion magazine.
Modifikation *f* modification.
modifizieren* *vt* to modify.
modisch *adj* stylish, fashionable.
Modistin *f* milliner.
Modul -n *nt (Comp)* module.
modulieren* *vt* to modulate.
Modus *m* **-, Modi (a)** way. **(b)** *(Gram)* mood.
Mofa *nt* **-s** small moped.
mogeln *vi* to cheat.
mögen *pret* **mochte,** *ptp* **gemocht 1** *vt* to like. **~ Sie ihn?** do you like him?; **was möchten Sie, bitte?** what would you like?; *(Verkäufer)* what can I do for you?; **nein danke, ich möchte lieber Tee** no thank you, I would rather have tea.
2 *vi (etw tun ~)* to like to. **ich mag nicht mehr** I've had enough; *(bin am Ende)* I can't take any more; **kommen Sie mit? — ich möchte gern, aber ...** are you coming too? — I'd like to, but ...; **ich möchte lieber in die Stadt** I would prefer to go into town.
3 *ptp ~ modal aux* **(a)** to like to *+infin*; *(wollen)* to want. **möchten Sie etwas essen?** would you like something to eat?; **hier möchte ich nicht wohnen** *(würde nicht gern)* I wouldn't like to live here; *(will nicht)* I don't want to live here; **ich hätte gern dabeisein ~** I would like to have been there; **man möchte meinen, daß ...** you would think that ...; **sie mag nicht bleiben** she doesn't want to stay.
(b) es mag wohl sein, daß er recht hat, aber ... he may well be right, but ...; **wie dem auch sein mag** however that may be; **mag kommen was da will** come what may; **es mochten etwa fünf Stunden vergangen sein** about five hours must have passed; **wie alt mag sie sein?** how old is she, I wonder?; **was mag das wohl heißen?** what might that mean?
(c) *(Aufforderung, indirekte Rede)* **(sagen Sie ihm,) er möchte zu mir kommen** would you tell him to come and see me; **Sie möchten zu Hause anrufen** you should call home.
Mogler(in *f*) *m* - cheat.
möglich *adj* possible; *(attr: eventuell auch)* potential. **alles ~e** everything you can think of; **alles M~e tun** to do everything possible; **er hat allen ~en Blödsinn gemacht** he did all sorts of stupid things; **so viel/bald wie ~** as much/soon as possible; **es war mir nicht ~ mitzukommen** I couldn't manage to come; **nicht ~!** never!; **er tat sein ~stes** he did his utmost.
möglicherweise *adv* possibly. **~ kommt er morgen** he may (possibly) come tomorrow.
Möglichkeit *f* **(a)** possibility. **es besteht die ~, daß ...** there is a possibility that ...; **nach ~** if possible; **ist denn das die ~?** *(col)* I don't believe it! **(b)** *(Aussicht)* chance; *(Gelegenheit auch)* opportunity. **er hatte keine andere ~** he had no other choice.
möglichst *adv* **~ schnell/oft** as quickly/often as possible; **in ~ kurzer Zeit** as quickly as possible.
Mohammedaner(in *f*) [mohame'da:nɐ, -ərɪn] *m* - Mohammedan.
mohammedanisch [mohame'da:nɪʃ] *adj* Mohammedan.
Mohikaner [mohi'ka:nɐ] *m* - **der letzte ~** *(hum col)* the very last one.
Mohn *m* **-e (a)** poppy. **(b)** *(~samen)* poppy seed.
Mohn- *in cpds* poppy; *(Cook)* poppyseed; **~blume** *f* poppy.
Möhre *f* **-n** carrot.
Mohrenkopf *m small chocolate-covered cream cake.*
Mohrrübe *f* carrot.
mokieren* *vr* to sneer *(über +acc* at*)*.
Mokka *m* **-s** mocha, *strong coffee.*
Molch *m* **-e** salamander.
Mole *f* **-n** *(Naut)* mole.
Molekül *nt* **-e** molecule.
molekular *adj* molecular.
molk *pret of* **melken.**
Molke *f no pl* whey.
Molkerei *f* dairy.
Molkerei-: **~butter** *f* blended butter; **~produkt** *nt* dairy product.
Moll *nt* **-, -** *(Mus)* minor (key). **a-~** A minor.
mollig *adj (col)* **(a)** cosy *(Brit)*, cozy *(US)*. **(b)** *(rundlich)* plump.
Molltonleiter *f* minor scale.
Moment[1] *m* **-e** moment. **jeden ~** any moment; **~ mal!** just a minute!; **im ~** at the moment; **im ersten ~** for a moment.

Moment[2] *nt* **-e** *(Umstand)* fact; *(Faktor)* factor; *(Bestandteil)* element.
momentan **1** *adj (vorübergehend)* momentary; *(augenblicklich)* present *attr.* **2** *adv (vorübergehend)* momentarily; *(augenblicklich)* at present.
Monarch(in *f*) *m (wk)* **-en, -en** monarch.
Monarchie *f* monarchy.
Monarchist(in *f*) *m* monarchist.
Monat *m* **-e** month. **der ~ Mai** the month of May; **sie ist im sechsten ~ (schwanger)** she's five months pregnant; **was verdient er im ~?** how much does he earn a month; **am 12. dieses ~s** on the 12th (of this month).
monatelang **1** *adj attr Verhandlungen, Kämpfe* which go/went *etc* on for months. **nach ~em Warten** after months of waiting; **mit ~er Verspätung** months late. **2** *adv* for months.
monatlich *adj* monthly. **~ stattfinden** to take place every month.
Monats-: **~anfang** *m* beginning of the month; **~blutung** *f* menstrual period; **~ende** *nt* end of the month; **~erste(r)** *m decl as adj* first (day) of the month; **~gehalt** *nt* monthly salary; **ein ~gehalt** one month's salary; **~karte** *f* monthly season ticket; **~lohn** *m* monthly wage; **~lohn bekommen** to be paid monthly; **~rate** *f* monthly instalment *(Brit) or* installment *(US).*
Mönch *m* **-e** monk; *(Bettel~ auch)* friar.
Mond *m* **-e** moon. **auf** *or* **hinter dem ~ leben** *(col)* to be behind the times; **in den ~ gucken** *(col)* to go empty-handed; **deine Uhr geht nach dem ~** *(col)* your watch/clock is way out *(col).*
mondän *adj* chic.
Mond-: **~aufgang** *m* moonrise; **~bahn** *f* lunar orbit; **~finsternis** *f* lunar eclipse; **~gesicht** *nt* moonface; **~(lande)fähre** *f (Space)* lunar module; **~landschaft** *f* lunar landscape; **~landung** *f* lunar landing; **~licht** *nt* moonlight; **~nacht** *f (geh)* moonlit night; **~schein** *m* moonlight; **~sonde** *f (Space)* lunar probe; **m~süchtig** *adj* **m~süchtig sein** to sleepwalk; **~untergang** *m* moonset.
Monetarismus *m (Econ)* monetarism.
Moneten *pl (col)* bread *(col),* dough *(col).*
Mongole *m (wk)* **-n, -n, Mongolin** *f* Mongolian, Mongol.
Mongolei *f* **die ~** Mongolia.
Mongolismus *m (Med)* mongolism.
mongoloid *adj (Med)* mongoloid.
monieren* **1** *vt* to complain about. **2** *vi* to complain.
Monitor *m (TV, Phys)* monitor.
Mono-, mono- *in cpds* mono-.
Mono-: **m~chrom** [mono'kro:m] *adj* monochrome; **m~gam** *adj* monogamous; **~gamie** *f* monogamy; **~gramm** *nt* monogram.
Monokel *nt* **-** monocle.
Monolog *m* **-e** *(Liter, fig)* monologue; *(Selbstgespräch)* soliloquy. **einen ~ halten** *(fig)* to hold a monologue, to talk on and on.
Monopol *nt* **-e** monopoly *(auf +acc, für* on*).*
monopolisieren* *vt (lit, fig)* to monopolize.
Monopol-: **~kapital** *nt (Kapital)* monopoly capital; *(Kapitalisten)* monopoly capitalism; **~stellung** *f* monopoly.
monoton *adj* monotonous.
Monotonie *f* monotony.
Monster *nt* **-** *(col)* monster.
Monster- *in cpds (usu pej)* mammoth, monster; **~film** *m* mammoth (film) production.
Monstranz *f (Eccl)* monstrance.
monströs *adj* monstrous; *(riesig groß)* monster.
Monstrum *nt, pl* **Monstren** *(lit, fig)* monster.
Monsun *m* **-e** monsoon.
Montag *m* Monday; *siehe* **Dienstag.**
Montage [mɔn'ta:ʒə] *f* **-n** **(a)** *(Tech) (Aufstellung)* installation; *(von Gerüst)* erection; *(Zusammenbau)* assembly. **(b)** *(Art)* montage; *(Film)* editing.
Montagehalle *f* assembly shop.
montags *adv* on Mondays.
Montan|industrie *f* coal and steel industry.
Monteur(in *f*) [mɔn'tø:ɐ, -'tø:rɪn] *m (Tech)* fitter; *(Aut)* mechanic.
montieren* *vt (Tech)* to install; *(zusammenbauen)* to assemble; *(befestigen)* to fit *(auf or an +acc* to*)*; *(aufstellen) Gerüst* to erect.
Montur *f (col: Spezialkleidung)* gear *(col),* rig-out *(col).*
Monument *nt* monument.
monumental *adj* monumental.
Moor *nt* **-e** bog; *(Hoch~)* moor.
Moor-: **~bad** *nt* mud-bath; **~huhn** *nt* grouse.
moorig *adj* boggy.
Moos *nt* **-e** **(a)** moss. **~ ansetzen** to become covered with moss. **(b)** *no pl (col: Geld)* bread *(col),* dough *(col).*
moosig *adj* mossy.
Mop *m* **-s** mop.
Moped *nt* **-s** moped.
Mopedfahrer *m* moped rider.
Mops *m* **¨-e** **(a)** *(Hund)* pug (dog). **(b)** *(Dickwanst)* roly-poly *(col).* **(c)** **¨~e** *pl (col: Geld)* bread *sing (col),* dough *sing (col).*
mopsen *vt (col: stehlen)* to pinch *(col).*
mopsig *adj (col: frech)* **sich ~ machen, ~ werden** to get cheeky *(esp Brit) or* fresh *(esp US).*
Moral *f no pl* **(a)** *(Sittlichkeit)* morals *pl.* **die ~ sinkt/steigt** moral standards are declining/rising; **die bürgerliche ~** bourgeois morality; **eine doppelte ~** double standards *pl.* **(b)** *(Lehre)* moral. **und die ~ von der Geschicht'** and the moral of this story. **(c)** *(Disziplin: von Volk, Soldaten)* morale. **die ~ sinkt** morale is getting low.
Moral- *in cpds* moral; **~apostel** *m (pej)* upholder of moral standards.
moralisch *adj* moral. **das war eine ~e Ohrfeige für die Regierung** that was one in the eye for the government *(col)*; **einen M~en haben** *(col)* to have (a fit of) the blues *(col).*
Moralist(in *f*) *m* moralist.
Moralpredigt *f* homily, sermon. **~en halten** to moralize.
Morast *m* **-e** *(lit, fig)* mire; *(Sumpf auch)* morass.
morastig *adj* marshy; *(schlammig)* muddy.
Mord *m* **-e** murder, homicide *(US) (an +dat* of*)*; *(an Politiker etc)* assassination *(an +dat* of*).* **wegen ~es** for murder *or* homicide *(US)*; **politischer ~** political killing; **dann gibt es ~ und Totschlag** *(col)* there'll be hell to pay *(col).*
Mord-: **~anschlag** *m* assassination *(auf +acc* of*)*; *(erfolglos)* assassination attempt *(auf +acc* on*)*; **einen ~anschlag auf jdn verüben** to assassinate sb; **~drohung** *f* threat on one's life.
morden *vti (liter)* to murder, to slay *(liter).*
Mörder(in *f*) *m* **-** murderer *(auch Jur),* killer; *(Attentäter)* assassin.
Mörder-: **~bande** *f* gang of killers; **~grube** *f*: **aus seinem Herzen keine ~grube machen** to speak frankly.
mörderisch **1** *adj (fig) (schrecklich)* dreadful, terrible; *Preise* iniquitous; *Konkurrenzkampf* cut-throat. **2** *adv (col: entsetzlich)* dreadfully, terribly. **~ schreien** to scream blue murder *(col).*
Mord-: **~fall** *m* murder *or* homicide *(US)* (case); **~kommission** *f* murder squad, homicide squad *or* division *(US)*; **~prozeß** *m* murder trial.
Mords- *in cpds (col)* terrible, awful; *(toll, prima)* hell of a *(col)*; **~kerl** *m (col) (verwegen)* hell of a guy *(col)*; *(stark)* enormous fellow *(col)*; **m~mäßig** *(col)* **1** *adj* incredible; **2** *adv (+vb)* terribly, awfully.
Mord-: **~verdacht** *m* suspicion of murder; **unter ~verdacht** *(dat)* **stehen** to be suspected of murder; **~waffe** *f* murder weapon.
Morgen *m* **-** **(a)** *(Tagesanfang)* morning. **am ~** in

the morning; **bis in den ~ (hinein)** into the early hours; **eines ~s** one morning; **es wird ~** day is breaking; **guten ~!** good morning; **~!** *(col)* morning. **(b)** *(Measure)* ≈ acre. **drei ~ Land** three acres of land.

morgen *adv* **(a)** tomorrow. **~ früh** tomorrow morning; **~ in acht Tagen** a week (from) tomorrow; **~ um diese Zeit** this time tomorrow; **bis ~!** see you tomorrow; **~ ist auch (noch) ein Tag!** *(Prov)* there's always tomorrow; **die Technik von ~** the technology of tomorrow. **(b) gestern ~** yesterday morning; **heute ~** this morning.

Morgen- *in cpds* morning.

morgendlich *adj* morning *attr; (früh~)* early morning *attr.*

Morgen-: **~grauen** *nt* - dawn, daybreak; **~gymnastik** *f* morning exercises *pl*; **~land** *nt (old, liter)* Orient; **~luft** *f* early morning air; **~luft wittern** *(fig col)* to see one's chance; **~mantel** *m* dressing-gown; **~muffel** *m (col)* **er ist ein schrecklicher ~muffel** he's terribly grumpy in the mornings *(col)*; **~rock** *m* housecoat; **~rot** *nt no pl* sunrise; *(fig)* dawn(ing).

morgens *adv* in the morning. **(um) drei Uhr ~** at three a.m.; **von ~ bis abends** from morning to night; **Freitag ~** on Friday morning.

Morgen-: **~stunde** *f* morning hour; **bis in die frühen ~stunden** into the early hours (of the morning); **~stund(e) hat Gold im Mund(e)** *(Prov)* the early bird catches the worm *(Prov)*.

morgig *adj attr* tomorrow's.

Mormone *m (wk)* **-n, -n, Mormonin** *f* Mormon.

morsch *adj (lit, fig)* rotten; *Knochen* brittle; *Gebäude* ramshackle.

Morse|alphabet *nt* Morse (code).

morsen 1 *vi* to send a message in Morse (code). **2** *vt* to send in Morse (code).

Mörser *m* - mortar *(auch Mil)*.

Morsezeichen *nt* Morse signal.

Mörtel *m* - *(zum Mauern)* mortar; *(Putz)* stucco.

Mosaik *nt* **-e(n)** *(lit, fig)* mosaic.

Moschee *f* **-n** [-'e:ən] mosque.

Moschus *m no pl* musk.

Möse *f* **-n** *(col!!)* cunt *(col!!)*.

Mosel[1] *f (Geog)* Moselle.

Mosel[2] *m* **-, Moselwein** *m* Moselle (wine).

mosern *vi (col)* to gripe *(col)*, to belly-ache *(col)*.

Moskau *nt* Moscow.

Moskauer *adj attr* Moscow *attr.*

Moskito *m* **-s** mosquito.

Moslem *m* **-s** Moslem.

moslemisch *adj attr* Moslem.

Most *m no pl* **(a)** unfermented fruit juice; *(für Wein)* must. **(b)** *(S Ger, Sw: Obstwein)* fruit wine; *(Apfel~)* cider.

Motel *nt* **-s** motel.

Motiv *nt* **-e (a)** *(Psych, Jur, fig)* motive. **das ~ einer Tat** the motive for a deed. **(b)** *(Art, Liter)* subject; *(Leit~, Mus)* motif.

Motivation [-va'tsio:n] *f* motivation.

motivieren* [moti'vi:rən] *vt* **(a)** *(begründen)* **etw (jdm gegenüber) ~** to give (sb) reasons for sth. **(b)** *(anregen)* to motivate.

Motor *m* **-en** [mo'to:rən] motor; *(von Fahrzeug)* engine; *(fig)* driving force *(gen* in*)*.

Motor-: **~antrieb** *m* motor drive; **mit ~antrieb** motor-driven; **~boot** *nt* motorboat; **~haube** *f* bonnet *(Brit)*, hood *(US)*; *(Aviat)* engine cowling.

motorisch *adj (Physiol)* motor *attr.*

motorisiert* *adj* motorized.

Motor-: **~jacht** *f* motor yacht; **~leistung** *f* engine performance.

Motorrad *nt* motorbike, motorcycle.

Motorradfahrer *m* motorcyclist.

Motor-: **~raum** *m* engine compartment; **~säge** *f* power saw; **~schaden** *m* engine trouble *no pl*; **~sport** *m* motor sport.

Motte *f* **-n** moth. **von ~n zerfressen** moth-eaten; **du kriegst die ~n!** *(col)* blow me! *(col)*.

Motten-: **~kiste** *f (fig)* **etw aus der ~kiste hervorholen** to dig sth out; **~kugel** *f* mothball.

Motto *nt* **-s** *(Wahlspruch)* motto.

motzen *vi (col)* to beef *(col)*, to grouse *(col)*.

Möwe *f* **-n** seagull, gull.

MP [ɛm'pi:] = **Maschinenpistole.**

Mrd. = **Milliarde.**

Mücke *f* **-n** *(Insekt)* mosquito, midge. **aus einer ~ einen Elefanten machen** *(col)* to make a mountain out of a molehill.

Muckefuck *m no pl (col)* coffee substitute.

mucken 1 *vi (col)* to mutter. **ohne zu ~** without a murmur. **2** *vr* to make a sound.

Mucken *pl (col)* moods *pl.* **(seine) ~ haben** to be moody; *(Sache)* to be temperamental.

Mückenstich *m* mosquito *or* gnat bite.

Mucks *m* **-e** *(col)* sound. **keinen ~ sagen** not to make a sound; *(widersprechend)* not to say a word.

mucksen *vr (col)* **sich nicht ~** not to move (a muscle); *(sich nicht äußern)* not to make a sound.

mucksmäuschenstill [-'mɔysçən-] *adj (col)* (as) quiet as a mouse.

müde *adj* tired; *Haupt* weary. **sie wird nicht ~, das zu tun** she never wearies of doing that.

Müdigkeit *f (Schlafbedürfnis)* tiredness; *(Schläfrigkeit)* sleepiness. **vor ~** *(dat)* **umfallen** to drop from exhaustion; **nur keine ~ vorschützen!** *(col)* don't (you) tell me you're tired.

Muff[1] *m no pl (N Ger: Modergeruch)* musty smell.

Muff[2] *m* **-e** muff.

Muffel *m* - *(col: Murrkopf)* grouch, grouser.

muff(e)lig *adj (col)* grumpy.

Muffensausen *nt (col)*: **~ kriegen/haben** to be/get scared stiff *(col)*.

muffig *adj (dial) Geruch* musty.

muh *interj* moo.

Mühe *f* **-n** trouble; *(Anstrengung auch)* effort; *(Arbeitsaufwand auch)* bother. **ohne ~** without any bother; **nur mit ~** only just; **mit Müh und Not** *(col)* with great difficulty; **wenig/keine ~ haben** not to have much bother *(etw zu tun* doing sth*)*; **es ist der** *(gen)* **~ wert** it's worth the trouble *(etw zu tun* of doing sth*)*; **sich** *(dat)* **keine ~ geben** to take no trouble; **gib dir keine ~!** *(hör auf)* don't bother, save yourself the trouble; **sich** *(dat)* **die ~ machen, etw zu tun** to take the trouble to do sth; **jdm ~ machen** to give sb some bother; **verlorene ~** a waste of effort.

mühelos *adj* effortless; *Sieg, Aufstieg auch* easy.

Mühelosigkeit *f siehe adj* effortlessness; ease.

muhen *vi* to moo, to low.

mühevoll *adj* laborious, arduous; *Leben* arduous.

Mühle *f* **-n (a)** mill; *(Kaffee~)* grinder. **(b)** *(fig: Routine)* treadmill. **(c)** *(~spiel)* nine men's morris. **(d)** *(col) (Auto)* crate *(col)*, banger *(col)*, jalopy *(col)*; *(Fahrrad)* boneshaker *(col)*.

Mühsal ['my:za:l] *f* **-e** *(geh)* tribulation; *(Strapaze)* toil.

mühsam ['my:za:m] **1** *adj* arduous. **2** *adv* with difficulty. **~ verdientes Geld** hard-earned money.

mühselig ['my:ze:lɪç] *adj* arduous.

Mulatte *m (wk)* **-n, -n, Mulattin** *f* mulatto.

Mulde *f* **-n** *(Geländesenkung)* hollow.

Mull *m (Gewebe)* muslin; *(Med)* gauze.

Müll *m no pl (Haushalts~)* rubbish, garbage *(esp US)*, refuse *(form)*; *(Gerümpel)* rubbish; *(Industrie~)* waste.

Müllabfuhr *f* refuse *or* garbage *(US)* collection; *(Stadtreinigung)* refuse *etc* collection department.

Mullbinde *f* gauze bandage.

Müll-: **~deponie** *f* waste disposal site, sanitary (land)fill *(US form)*; **~eimer** *m* rubbish bin *(Brit)*, garbage can *(US)*; **~kippe** *f* rubbish *or* garbage *(US)* dump; **~mann** *m, pl* **~männer** *(col)* dustman *(Brit)*, trash collector *(US)*; ~**schlucker** *m* - refuse chute; ~**tonne** *f* dustbin *(Brit)*, trashcan *(US)*.

mulmig *adj* uncomfortable. **mir war ~ zumute** *(lit)* I felt queasy; *(fig)* I had butterflies *(col)*.

Multi *m* **-s** *(col)* multinational (organization).

Multi- *in cpds* multi-; **m~lateral** *adj* multilateral; ~**millionär** *m* multimillionaire.

multipel *adj* multiple. **multiple Sklerose** multiple sclerosis.

multiplizieren* **1** *vt (lit, fig)* to multiply *(mit* by*)*. **2** *vr (fig)* to multiply.

Mumie ['mu:miə] *f* mummy.

mumifizieren* *vt* to mummify.

Mumm *m no pl (col: Mut)* spunk *(dated col)*, guts *pl (col)*.

mümmeln *vi (col)* to nibble.

Mumpitz *m no pl (col)* balderdash *(dated col)*.

Mumps *m or (col) f* -, *no pl* (the) mumps *sing*.

München *nt* Munich.

Mund *m* **¨er** mouth; *(col: Mundwerk)* tongue. **etw in den ~ nehmen** to put sth in one's mouth; **dieses Wort nehme ich nicht in den ~** I never use that word; **den ~ aufmachen** *(fig: seine Meinung sagen)* to speak up; **einen großen ~ haben** *(fig) (aufschneiden)* to talk big *(col)*; *(frech sein)* to be cheeky *(esp Brit) or* fresh *(esp US)*; **jdm den ~ verbieten** to order sb to be quiet; **halt den ~!** shut up! *(col)*, hold your tongue!; **er kann den ~ einfach nicht halten** *(col)* he can't keep his big mouth shut *(col)*; **jdm über den ~ fahren** to cut sb short; **jdm den ~ stopfen** *(col)* to shut sb up *(col)*; **in aller ~e sein** to be on everyone's lips; **Sie nehmen mir das Wort aus dem ~** you've taken the (very) words out of my mouth; **jdm nach dem ~ reden** *(col)* to say what sb wants to hear; **sie ist nicht auf den ~ gefallen** *(col)* she's never at a loss for words; **den ~ (zu) voll nehmen** *(col)* to talk (too) big *(col)*.

Mund|art *f* dialect.

mund|artlich *adj* dialect(al).

Mündel *nt or (Jur) m* - ward.

munden *vi (liter)* **jdm köstlich ~** to taste delicious to sb; **sich** *(dat)* **etw ~ lassen** to savour *(Brit) or* savor *(US)* sth.

münden *vi aux sein or haben (Fluß)* to flow *(in +acc* into*)*; *(Straße)* to lead *(in +acc, auf +acc* into*)*.

Mund-: **m~faul** *adj (col)* uncommunicative; **sei doch nicht so m~faul!** make an effort and say something!; **m~gerecht** *adj* bite-sized; ~**geruch** *m* bad breath; ~**harmonika** *f* mouth organ.

mündig *adj* of age; *(fig)* mature.

Mündigkeit *f* majority; *(fig)* maturity.

mündlich *adj* verbal; *Prüfung, Leistung* oral. ~**e Verhandlung** *(Jur)* hearing; **das M~e** *(col: Sch, Univ)* the oral; **alles weitere ~!** let's talk about it more when I see you.

Mund-: ~**raub** *m (Jur)* theft of food for personal consumption; ~**stück** *nt (von Pfeife, Blasinstrument)* mouthpiece; *(von Zigarette)* (filter-)tip; **m~tot** *adj (col)* **jdn m~tot machen** to silence sb.

Mündung *f (von Fluß, Rohr etc)* mouth; *(Trichter~)* estuary; *(Gewehr~)* muzzle.

Mund-: ~**wasser** *nt* mouthwash; ~**werk** *nt (col)* **ein freches/großes ~werk haben** to be cheeky *(esp Brit) or* fresh *(esp US)*/talk big *(col)*; **ihr ~werk steht nie still** her tongue never stops wagging *(col)*; ~**winkel** *m* corner of one's mouth; **~-zu-~-Beatmung** *f* mouth-to-mouth resuscitation.

Munition *f* ammunition.

Munitions-: ~**depot** *nt* munitions dump; ~**fabrik** *f* munitions factory.

munkeln *vti* **man munkelt, daß ...** there's a rumour *(Brit) or* rumor *(US)* that ...

Münster *nt* - minster, cathedral.

munter *adj* **(a)** *(lebhaft)* lively *no adv; (fröhlich)* cheerful, merry. **~ und vergnügt** bright and cheery; **~ drauflos reden** to prattle away merrily. **(b)** *(wach)* awake; *(aufgestanden)* up and about.

Munterkeit *f (Lebhaftigkeit)* liveliness; *(Fröhlichkeit)* cheerfulness, merriness.

Münz|automat *m* slot machine.

Münze *f* **-n** coin. **jdm etw mit gleicher ~ heimzahlen** *(fig)* to pay sb back in his own coin for sth.

münzen *vt* to mint, to coin. **das war auf ihn gemünzt** *(fig)* that was aimed at him.

Münz-: ~**fernsprecher** *m (form)* pay phone; ~**tank** *m* coin operated petrol *(Brit) or* gas(oline) *(US)* pump.

mürb(e) *adj* crumbly; *(zerbröckelnd)* crumbling; *Fleisch* tender; *Obst* soft. **jdn ~ machen/ kriegen** *(fig: zermürbt)* to wear sb down/to break sb.

Mürbeteig *m* short(-crust) pastry.

Murks *m no pl (col)* **~ machen** to bungle things *(col)*; **das ist ~!** that's a botch-up *(col)*.

Murmel *f* **-n** marble.

murmeln *vti* to murmur; *(undeutlich)* to mumble; *(brummeln)* to mutter. **etw vor sich** *(acc)* **hin ~** to mutter sth to oneself.

Murmeltier *nt* marmot. **schlafen wie ein ~** to sleep like a log.

murren *vi* to grumble *(über +acc* about*)*.

mürrisch *adj (abweisend)* sullen, morose; *(schlechtgelaunt)* grumpy.

Mus *nt* **-e** mush. **jdn zu ~ schlagen** *(col)* to make mincemeat of sb.

Muschel *f* **-n** **(a)** mussel *(auch Cook)*, bivalve; *(Schale)* shell. **(b)** *(Ohr~)* external ear. **(c)** *(Telec) (Sprech~)* mouthpiece; *(Hör~)* earpiece.

Muse *f* **-n** *(Myth)* Muse. **die leichte ~** *(fig)* light entertainment; **von der ~ geküßt werden** *(fig)* to be inspired.

Museum [mu'ze:ʊm] *nt, pl* **Museen** [mu'ze:ən] museum.

Museums-: ~**führer** *m* museum guide; **m~reif** *adj (hum)* antique; **m~reif sein** to be almost a museum piece; ~**stück** *nt* museum piece.

Musical ['mju:zikl] *nt* **-s** musical

Musik *f* **-en** music. **das ist ~ in meinen Ohren** *(fig)* that's music to my ears.

musikalisch *adj* musical.

Musikant(in *f***)** *m* musician, minstrel *(old)*.

Musik-: ~**begleitung** *f* musical accompaniment; ~**box** *f* jukebox.

Musiker(in *f***)** *m* - musician.

Musik-: ~**hochschule** *f* college of music; ~**instrument** *nt* musical instrument; ~**kapelle** *f* band; ~**korps** *nt* music corps *sing*; ~**lehrer** *m* music teacher; ~**liebhaber** *m* music-lover; ~**saal** *m* music room; ~**sendung** *f* music programme *(Brit) or* program *(US)*; ~**stück** *nt* piece of music; ~**stunde** *f* music lesson.

musisch *adj Fächer* (fine) arts *attr*; *Begabung* for the arts; *Veranlagung, Mensch* artistic.

musizieren* *vi* to play. **sie saßen auf dem Marktplatz und musizierten** they sat in the market place playing their instruments.

Muskat *m* **-e, Muskatnuß** *f* nutmeg.

Muskel *m* **-n** muscle. **~n haben** to be muscular; **seine ~n spielen lassen** *(lit, fig)* to flex one's muscles.

Muskel-: ~**kater** *m* aching muscles *pl*; **~kater haben** to be stiff; ~**kraft** *f* physical strength; ~**krampf** *m* muscle cramp *no indef art*; ~**paket** *nt*, ~**protz** *m (col)* muscleman *(col)*; ~**riß** *m* torn muscle; ~**schwund** *m* muscular atrophy *or* wasting; ~**zerrung** *f* pulled muscle.

Muskulatur *f* muscular system.

muskulös *adj* muscular. **~ gebaut sein** to have a muscular build.

Müsli *nt* **-s** muesli.
Muß *nt no pl* **es ist ein/kein ~** it's/it's not a must.
Muße *f no pl* leisure. **dafür fehlt mir die ~** I don't have the leisure; **etw mit ~ tun** to do sth in a leisurely way.
müssen 1 *modal aux pret* **mußte,** *ptp* **~ (a)** *(Zwang)* to have to; *(Notwendigkeit auch)* to need to. **ich muß** *(Zwang)* I have to, I must *nur pres,* I've got to *(esp Brit)*; *(Notwendigkeit auch)* I need to; **ich muß nicht** *(Zwang)* I don't have to, I haven't got to *(esp Brit)*; *(Notwendigkeit auch)* I don't need to, I needn't; **muß er?** must he?, does he have to?, has he got to? *(esp Brit)*; **mußtest du?** did you have to?; **das muß irendwann mal gemacht werden** it will have to be done some time; **er sagte, er müsse bald gehen** he said he would have to go soon; **man mußte lachen/weinen** *etc* you couldn't help laughing/crying *etc*; **wenn es (unbedingt) sein muß** if it's absolutely necessary; **das muß man sich** *(dat)* **mal vorstellen!** (just) imagine that!; **was habe ich da hören ~?** what's this I hear?
(b) *(sollen)* **das müßtest du eigentlich wissen** you ought to *or* you should know that; **das mußt du nicht tun!** you oughtn't to *or* shouldn't do that.
(c) es muß geregnet haben it must have rained; **es muß wahr sein** it must be true; **es muß nicht wahr sein** it needn't be true; **es müssen zehntausend Zuschauer im Stadion gewesen sein** there must have been ten thousand spectators in the stadium; **er müßte schon da sein** he should be there by now; **so muß es gewesen sein** that's how it must have been; **man müßte noch mal von vorn anfangen können!** if only one could begin again!
2 *vi pret* **mußte,** *ptp* **gemußt wann müßt ihr zur Schule?** when do you have to go to school?; **der Brief muß heute noch zur Post** the letter must be mailed today; **ich muß mal** *(col)* I need to go to the loo *(Brit col) or* bathroom *(esp US)*.
Mußestunde *f* hour of leisure.
Mußheirat *f (col)* shotgun wedding *(col)*. **es war eine ~** they had to get married.
müßig *adj (untätig)* idle; *Leben, Stunden* of leisure; *(unnütz)* futile.
Müßig-: ~gang *m (liter)* idleness; **~gang ist aller Laster Anfang** *(Prov)* the devil finds work for idle hands *(Prov)*; **~gänger(in** *f*) *m* **-** idler.
mußte *pret of* **müssen.**
Muster *nt* **- (a)** *(Vorlage)* pattern; *(für Brief, Bewerbung etc)* specimen. **nach einem ~ stricken** *etc* to knit *etc* from a pattern. **(b)** *(Probestück)* sample; *(Buch etc)* specimen. **~ ohne Wert** sample of no commercial value. **(c)** *(fig: Vorbild)* model *(an +dat* of*)*. **als ~ dienen** to serve as a model; **ein ~ an Tugend** a paragon of virtue.
Muster- *in cpds* model; **~beispiel** *nt* classic example; **m~gültig, m~haft** *adj* exemplary; **er hat sich m~haft verhalten** his conduct was exemplary; **~knabe** *m (iro)* paragon.
mustern *vt* **(a)** *(betrachten)* to scrutinize. **(b)** *(Mil: inspizieren)* to inspect, to review. **(c)** *(Mil: für Wehrdienst)* **jdn ~** to give sb his/her medical. **(d)** *Stoff siehe* **gemustert.**
Muster-: ~prozeß *m* test case; **~schüler** *m* model pupil; *(fig)* star pupil.
Musterung *f* **(a)** pattern. **(b)** *(Mil) (von Truppen)* inspection, review; *(von Rekruten)* medical (examination). **(c)** *(durch Blicke)* scrutiny.
Mut *m no pl* courage, pluck *(col)*; *(Zuversicht)* heart. **~ fassen** to pluck up courage; **mit frischem ~** with new heart; **nur ~!** cheer up!, keep your pecker up! *(Brit col)*; **jdm den ~ nehmen** to discourage sb; **den ~ verlieren** to lose heart; **jdm ~ machen** to encourage sb; **das gab ihr wieder neuen ~** that gave her new heart; **mit dem ~ der Verzweiflung** with the courage born of desperation; **frohen/guten ~es sein** *(geh)* to be in good spirits.
Mütchen *nt:* **sein ~ an jdm kühlen** *(col)* to take it out on sb *(col)*.
mutig *adj (tapfer)* courageous, brave.
Mut-: m~los *adj* disheartened *no adv*; *(bedrückt)* despondent; **jdn m~los machen** to make sb lose heart; **~losigkeit** *f* despondency.
mutmaßen *vti insep* to conjecture.
mutmaßlich 1 *adj attr Vater, Täter* presumed. **2** *adv* **~ soll er der Vater sein** he is presumed to be the father.
Mutmaßung *f* conjecture.
Mutprobe *f* test of courage.
Mutter[1] *f* **¨** mother. **sie ist jetzt ~** she's a mother now; **sie ist ~ von drei Kindern** she's a mother of three; **~ Natur/Erde** *(liter)* Mother Nature/Earth; **wie bei ~n** *(col)* just like (at) home; *(Essen)* just like mother makes/used to make.
Mutter[2] *f* **-n** *(Tech)* nut.
Mutterboden *m* topsoil.
Mütterchen *nt* **(a)** *dim of* **Mutter**[1] mummy *(col)*, mommy *(US col)*. **(b)** *(alte Frau)* grandma.
Mutter-: ~erde *f* topsoil; **~freuden** *pl* the joys of motherhood *pl*; **~gesellschaft** *f (Comm)* parent company; **~instinkt** *m* maternal instinct; **~kuchen** *m (Anat)* placenta; **~land** *nt* mother country; **~leib** *m* womb.
mütterlich *adj* **(a)** maternal. **die ~en Pflichten** one's duties as a mother. **(b)** *(liebevoll besorgt)* motherly *no adv*. **jdn ~ umsorgen** to mother sb.
mütterlicherseits *adv* on his/her *etc* mother's side. **sein Großvater ~** his maternal grandfather.
Mütterlichkeit *f* motherliness.
Mutter-: ~liebe *f* motherly love; **m~los** *adj* motherless; **~mal** *nt* birthmark; **~milch** *f* mother's milk; **~mord** *m* matricide; **~mörder** *m* matricide; **~mund** *m (Anat)* cervix.
Mutterschaft *f* motherhood.
Mutterschafts-: ~geld *nt* maternity grant; **~urlaub** *m* maternity leave.
Mutter-: ~schutz *m* legal protection of expectant and nursing mothers; **m~seelenallein** *adj, adv* all on one's own; **~söhnchen** *nt (pej)* mummy's boy; **~sprache** *f* native language, mother tongue; **~stelle** *f* **bei jdm ~stelle vertreten** to take the place of sb's mother; **~tag** *m* Mother's Day; **~tier** *nt* mother (animal); *(Zuchttier)* brood animal; **~witz** *m (Schläue)* mother wit; *(Humor)* natural wit.
Mutti *f* **-s** *(col)* mummy, mum, mommy *(US)*.
Mutwille *m* **-ns,** *no pl (böse Absicht)* malice. **etw aus ~n tun** to do sth out of malice.
mutwillig 1 *adj (böswillig)* malicious; *Zerstörung auch* wilful. **2** *adv (absichtlich)* wilfully.
Mütze *f* **-n** cap.
MWSt. = Mehrwertsteuer VAT.
mysteriös *adj* mysterious.
Mysterium *nt* mystery.
Mystik *f* mysticism *no art.*
mystisch *adj* mystic(al); *(fig: geheimnisvoll)* mysterious.
mythisch *adj* mythical.
Mythologie *f* mythology.
mythologisch *adj* mythologic(al).
Mythos *m* **-, Mythen** *(lit, fig)* myth.

N

N, n [ɛn] *nt* **-, -** N, n. **n-te** nth.
N = **Norden.**
na *interj (col)* **(a)** well. ~**, kommst du mit?** are you coming then?; ~**, du?** well?; ~ **ja** well; ~ **gut,** ~ **schön** all right, OK *(col)*; ~ **also!,** ~ **eben!** (well,) there you are (then)!; ~ **und ob!** *(auf jeden Fall)* you bet! *(col)*; *(und wie)* and how! *(col)*. **(b)** *(Ermahnung)* now; *(Zurückweisung)* well. ~ **(**~**)!** now then!; ~ **warte!** just you wait!; ~ **so was!** well, I never!; ~ **und?** so what?
Nabe *f* **-n** hub.
Nabel *m* **-** *(Anat)* navel, umbilicus *(spec)*; *(Bot)* hilum. **der** ~ **der Welt** *(fig)* the hub of the universe.
Nabelschnur *f (Anat)* umbilical cord.
nach 1 *prep+dat* **(a)** *(örtlich)* to. **ich fuhr mit dem Zug** ~ **Mailand** I took the train to Milan; **er ist schon** ~ **London abgefahren** he has already left for London; ~ **Osten/Westen** eastward(s)/westward(s); ~ **links/rechts** (to the) left/right; ~ **hinten/vorn** to the back/front; ~ **Norden zu** *or* **hin** to *or* towards *(esp Brit) or* toward *(esp US)* the north.

(b) *(zeitlich, Reihenfolge)* after. **fünf (Minuten)** ~ **drei** five (minutes) past *or* after *(US)* three; **sie kam** ~ **zehn Minuten** she came ten minutes later; ~ **Empfang** *or* **Erhalt** on receipt; **drei Tage** ~ **Empfang** three days after receipt; **eine(r, s)** ~ **dem/der anderen** one after another; **(bitte)** ~ **Ihnen!** after you!; ~ **„mit" steht der Dativ** "mit" takes the dative.

(c) *(entsprechend)* according to; *(im Einklang mit)* in accordance with. ~ **dem Gesetz** according to the law; ~ **Artikel 142c** under article 142c; **etw** ~ **Gewicht kaufen** to buy sth by weight; ~ **Verfassern** in order of authors; **die Uhr** ~ **dem Radio stellen** to put a clock right by the radio; **ihrer Sprache** ~ **(zu urteilen)** judging by her language; ~ **dem, was er gesagt hat** according to what he's said; ~ **allem, was ich weiß** as far as I know; ~ **einem Gedicht von Schiller** after a poem by Schiller; **er wurde** ~ **seinem Großvater genannt** he was called after *or* for *(US)* his grandfather.

2 *adv* **(a)** *(räumlich)* **mir** ~**!** *(liter, hum)* follow me! **(b)** *(zeitlich)* ~ **und** ~ little by little; ~ **wie vor** still.
nach|äffen *vt sep (pej) Moden, Ideen* to ape; *jdn* to mimic.
nach|ahmen *vt sep* to imitate; *(karikieren)* to mimic; *(kopieren)* to copy.
nach|ahmenswert *adj* exemplary.
Nach|ahmer(in *f***)** *m* **-** imitator; *(pej: Art, Liter)* copyist.
Nach|ahmung *f siehe vt* **(a)** *(das Imitieren)* imitation; mimicking; copying. **etw zur** ~ **empfehlen** to recommend sth as an example. **(b)** *(die Imitation)* imitation; impression; copy.
nach|arbeiten *sep* **1** *vt* **(a)** *(aufholen)* to make up. **(b)** *(überarbeiten)* to work over. **(c)** *(nachbilden)* to copy, to reproduce. **2** *vi* **wir müssen morgen** ~ we'll have to make up the work tomorrow.
Nachbar(in *f***)** *m (wk)* **-n, -n** neighbour *(Brit)*, neighbor *(US)*. **Herr X war beim Konzert mein** ~ Mr X sat next to me at the concert; ~**s Garten** the next-door garden.
Nachbarhaus *nt* house next door.
nachbarlich *adj (freundlich)* neighbourly *no adv (Brit)*, neighborly *no adv (US)*; *(benachbart)* neighbouring *no adv (Brit)*, neighboring *no adv (US)*.
Nachbarschaft *f (Gegend)* neighbourhood *(Brit)*, neighborhood *(US)*; *(Nachbarn)* neighbours *pl (Brit)*, neighbors *pl (US)*; *(Nähe)* vicinity.
nachbehandeln* *vt sep (Med)* **jdn/etw** ~ to give sb after-care.
Nachbehandlung *f (Med)* follow-up treatment.
nachbessern *sep* **1** *vt* to put the finishing touches to. **2** *vi* to add the finishing touches.
nachbestellen* *vt sep* to order some more; *(Comm)* to reorder.
Nachbestellung *f (gen* for*)* repeat order.
nachbeten *vt sep (pej col)* to repeat parrot-fashion.
nachbezahlen* *sep* **1** *vt* to pay; *(später)* to pay later. **Steuern** ~ to pay back-tax. **2** *vi* to pay the rest.
nachbilden *vt sep* to copy; *(exakt)* to reproduce.
Nachbildung *f* copy; *(exakt)* reproduction.
nachdatieren* *vt sep* to postdate.
nachdem *conj (zeitlich)* after.
nachdenken *vi sep irreg* to think *(über +acc* about*)*. **darüber darf man gar nicht** ~ it doesn't bear thinking about; **denk doch mal nach!** think about it!
Nachdenken *nt* thought, reflection. **nach langem** ~ after (giving the matter) considerable thought; **gib mir ein bißchen Zeit zum** ~ give me a bit of time to think (about it).
nachdenklich *adj Mensch, Miene* thoughtful, pensive. **jdn** ~ **stimmen** to set sb thinking; ~ **gestimmt sein** to be in a thoughtful mood.
Nachdenklichkeit *f no pl* thoughtfulness, pensiveness.
Nachdichtung *f (Liter)* free rendering.
Nachdruck *m* **(a)** *no pl (Betonung)* stress, emphasis. **besondern** ~ **darauf legen, daß ...** to stress *or* emphasize particularly that ...; **etw mit** ~ **betreiben** to pursue sth energetically. **(b)** *(das Nachdrucken)* reprinting; *(das Nachgedruckte)* reprint.
nachdrucken *vt sep* to reprint.
nachdrücklich *adj* emphatic. ~ **auf etw** *(dat)* **bestehen** to insist firmly on sth; **jdm** ~ **raten, etw zu tun** to urge sb to do sth; **jdn** ~ **warnen** to give sb a firm warning.
nach|eifern *vi sep* **jdm/einer Sache** ~ to emulate sb/sth.
nach|einander *adv (räumlich)* one after the other; *(zeitlich auch)* in succession. **zweimal** ~ twice running; **kurz** ~ shortly after each other; **drei Tage** ~ three days running, three days on the trot *(col)*.
nach|empfinden *vt sep irreg* **(a)** *Stimmung* to feel. **das kann ich ihr** ~ I can understand her feelings. **(b)** *(nachgestalten)* to adapt *(dat* from*)*.
nach|erzählen* *vt sep* to retell.
Nach|erzählung *f* retelling; *(Sch)* (story) reproduction.
Nachf. = **Nachfolger.**
Nachfahr *m* **-en** *(liter)* descendant.
nachfahren *vi sep irreg aux sein* to follow (on).

jdm ~ to follow sb.

nachfassen *vi sep* **(a)** *(noch einmal zufassen)* to regain one's grip. **(b)** *(col: nachforschen)* to probe a bit deeper.

nachfeiern *vti sep (später feiern)* to celebrate later.

Nachfolge *f no pl* succession. **jds/die ~ antreten** to succeed sb/to succeed.

nachfolgen *vi sep aux sein (hinterherkommen)* to follow (on). **jdm** ~ to follow sb; **jdm im Amt** ~ to succeed sb in office.

nachfolgend *adj* following. **das N~e** the following.

Nachfolger(in *f***)** *m* - *(im Amt etc)* successor. **Friedrich Reißnagel** ~ successors to Friedrich Reißnagel.

nachforschen *vi sep* to try to find out; *(polizeilich etc)* to carry out an investigation *(dat* into*)*; *(amtlich etc)* to make inquiries *(dat* into*)*.

Nachforschung *f* inquiry; *(polizeilich etc)* investigation. **~en anstellen** to make inquiries.

Nachfrage *f* **(a)** *(Comm)* demand *(nach, in +dat* for*)*. **danach besteht eine rege** ~ there is a great demand for it. **(b)** *(Erkundigung)* inquiry. **danke der** ~ *(form)* thank you for your concern; *(col)* nice of you to ask.

nachfragen *vi sep* to ask, to inquire.

nachfüllen *vt sep leeres Glas etc* to refill; *halbleeres Glas, Batterie etc* to top up.

nachgeben *sep irreg* **1** *vi* **(a)** to give way *(dat* to*)*; *(federn)* to give; *(fig: Mensch)* to give in *(dat* to*)*. **(b)** *(Comm: Preise, Kurse)* to drop, to fall. **2** *vt (noch mehr geben)* **darf ich Ihnen noch etwas Gemüse ~?** may I give you a few more vegetables?

Nachgebühr *f* excess (postage).

Nachgeburt *f* afterbirth; *(Vorgang)* expulsion of the afterbirth.

nachgehen *vi sep irreg aux sein* **(a)** *+dat (hinterhergehen)* to follow; *jdm auch* to go after. **(b)** *(Uhr)* to be slow. **deine Uhr geht fünf Minuten nach** your clock is five minutes slow. **(c)** *+dat (ausüben) Beruf* to practise *(Brit)*, to practice *(US)*; *Studium, Vergnügungen etc* to pursue; *Geschäften* to go about. **einer geregelten Arbeit** ~ to have a steady job. **(d)** *+dat (erforschen)* to investigate, to look into.

nachgelassen *adj Werke, Papiere* posthumous.

nachgemacht *adj Gold, Leder etc* imitation; *Geld* counterfeit.

nachgerade *adv (geradezu)* practically, virtually.

Nachgeschmack *m (lit, fig)* aftertaste. **einen üblen ~ hinterlassen** *(fig)* to leave a bad taste in the mouth.

nachgiebig *adj* **(a)** *Material* pliable; *Boden etc* yielding, soft. ~ **sein** to give. **(b)** *(fig) Mensch, Haltung* soft; *(konziliant)* compliant. **sie behandelt die Kinder zu** ~ she's too soft with the children.

Nachgiebigkeit *f siehe adj* **(a)** pliability; softness. **(b)** softness; compliance.

nachgießen *vti sep irreg Wasser, Milch* to add. **darf ich Ihnen (noch etwas Wein) ~?** would you like some more (wine)?

nachgrübeln *vi sep* to think *(über +acc* about*)*; *(sich Gedanken machen)* to ponder *(über +acc* on*)*.

nachgucken *vti sep siehe* **nachsehen.**

nachhaken *vi sep (col)* to dig deeper.

Nachhall *m* reverberation; *(fig)* echo.

nachhallen *vi sep* to reverberate.

nachhaltig *adj* lasting *no adv*. **ihre Gesundheit hat sich ~ gebessert** there has been a lasting improvement in her health.

nachhängen *vi sep irreg+dat* to give oneself up to. **seinen Erinnerungen** ~ to lose oneself in one's memories.

Nachhauseweg *m* way home.

nachhelfen *vi sep irreg* to help. **er hat dem Glück ein bißchen nachgeholfen** he engineered himself a little luck.

nachher *adv* **(a)** *(danach)* afterwards; *(später auch)* later. **bis** ~ see you later! **(b)** *(col: womöglich)* ~ **stimmt das gar nicht** that might not be true at all.

Nachhilfe *f (Sch)* private tuition.

Nachhilfe-: **~lehrer** *m* private tutor; **~stunde** *f* private lesson; **~unterricht** *m* private tuition.

nachhinein *adv:* **im** ~ afterwards; *(rückblickend)* in retrospect.

nachhinken *vi sep aux sein (fig col)* to lag behind.

Nachholbedarf *m* **einen ~ an etw** *(dat)* **haben** to have a lot of sth to catch up on.

nachholen *vt sep* **(a)** *(aufholen)* to make up (for). **(b)** *(nachkommen lassen)* to get sb to join one.

Nachhut *f* **-en** *(Mil)* rearguard. **bei der** ~ in the rearguard.

Nach|impfung *f* booster.

nachjagen *vi sep aux sein+dat* to chase (after).

nachklingen *vi sep irreg aux sein (Ton, Echo)* to go on sounding; *(Worte, Erinnerung)* to linger on.

Nachkomme *m (wk)* **-n, -n** descendant.

nachkommen *vi sep irreg aux sein* **(a)** *(später kommen)* to follow later. **Sie können Ihr Gepäck ~ lassen** you can have your luggage sent on (after). **(b)** *(Schritt halten)* to keep up. **(c)**+*dat (erfüllen) einer Pflicht* to carry out; *einer Forderung, einem Wunsch* to comply with.

Nachkommenschaft *f* descendants *pl*.

Nachkriegs- *in cpds* post-war.

Nachlaß *m* **-lasse** *or* **-lässe** **(a)** *(Preis~)* discount *(auf +acc* on*)*. **(b)** *(Erbschaft)* estate. **literarischer** ~ unpublished works *pl*.

nachlassen *sep irreg* **1** *vt* **(a)** **die Hälfte des Preises** ~ to take 50% off the price; **10% vom Preis** ~ to give a 10% discount. **(b)** *(locker lassen) Seil* to slacken. **(c)** *siehe* **nachgelassen. 2** *vi* to decrease, to diminish; *(Interesse auch)* to flag, to wane; *(Regen, Nasenbluten)* to ease off; *(Leistung, Geschäfte)* to fall off; *(Preise)* to fall. **er hat in letzter Zeit sehr nachgelassen** he hasn't been nearly as good recently.

nachlässig *adj* careless; *(unachtsam)* thoughtless.

Nachlässigkeit *f siehe adj* carelessness; thoughtlessness.

Nachlaßverwalter *m* executor.

nachlaufen *vi sep irreg aux sein +dat* **jdm/einer Sache** ~ to run after sb/sth; **den Mädchen** ~ to chase girls.

nachlegen *vt sep* **noch Kohlen/Holz** ~ to put some more coal/wood on (the fire).

Nachlese *f* second harvest; *(Ertrag)* gleanings *pl*.

nachlesen *sep irreg* **1** *vt (in einem Buch)* to read; *(nachschlagen)* to look up. **man kann das in der Bibel** ~ it says so in the Bible. **2** *vi* to have a second harvest; *(Ähren ~)* to glean.

nachliefern *vt sep (später liefern)* to deliver at a later date; *(zuzüglich liefern)* to make a further delivery of.

nachlösen *vi sep* to pay on the train/when one gets off; *(zur Weiterfahrt)* to pay the extra.

nachmachen *vt sep* **(a)** to copy; *(nachäffen)* to mimic; *(fälschen)* to forge. **sie macht mir alles nach** she copies everything I do; **das soll erst mal einer ~!** I'd like to see anyone else do that!; *siehe* **nachgemacht. (b)** *(col: nachholen)* to make up.

nachmessen *vti sep irreg (prüfend messen)* to check.

Nachmieter *m* **unser** ~ the tenant after us; **wir müssen einen ~ finden** we have to find someone to take over the flat *etc*.

nachmittag *adv* **gestern/heute** ~ yesterday/this afternoon.

Nachmittag *m* afternoon. **am** ~ in the afternoon; **am heutigen** ~ this afternoon.

nachmittäglich *adj no pred* afternoon *attr*.
nachmittags *adv* in the afternoon. **dienstags ~** on Tuesday afternoons.
Nachmittags-: **~schlaf** *m* **~schlaf halten** to have a sleep after lunch; **~vorstellung** *f* matinée (performance).
Nachnahme *f* **-n** cash *or* collect *(US)* on delivery, COD; *(col: ~sendung)* COD parcel. **etw per ~ schicken** to send sth COD.
Nachnahme-: **~gebühr** *f* COD charge; **~sendung** *f* COD parcel.
Nachname *m* surname, family *or* last name.
nachplappern *vt sep* to repeat parrot-fashion.
Nachporto *nt* excess (postage).
nachprüfbar *adj* verifiable.
Nachprüfbarkeit *f* verifiability.
nachprüfen *vti sep* to verify, to check.
Nachprüfung *f (von Aussagen etc)* check *(gen* on*)*.
nachrechnen *vti sep* to check.
Nachrede *f* **(a)** *(Verunglimpfung)* **üble ~** *(Jur)* defamation of character; **üble ~n über jdn verbreiten** to cast aspersions on sb's character. **(b)** *(Epilog)* epilogue.
nachreden *vt sep* **(a)** *(wiederholen)* to repeat. **(b)** **jdm (etwas) Schlechtes ~** to speak badly of sb.
nachreichen *vt sep* to hand in later.
nachreisen *vi sep aux sein* **jdm ~** to follow sb.
Nachricht *f* **-en** (piece of) news; *(Botschaft)* message. **eine ~** a piece of news; a message; **die ~en** the news *sing (auch Rad, TV)*; **schlechte ~en** bad news; **~ erhalten, daß ...** to receive (the) news that ...; **wir geben Ihnen ~** we'll let you know.
Nachrichten-: **~agentur** *f* news agency; **~dienst** *m* **(a)** *(Rad, TV)* news service; **(b)** *(Pol, Mil)* intelligence (service); **~magazin** *nt* news magazine; **~satellit** *m* (tele)communications satellite; **~sperre** *f* news blackout; **~sprecher** *m* newsreader; **~technik** *f* telecommunications *sing*.
nachrücken *vi sep aux sein* to move up; *(Mil)* to advance.
Nachruf *m* obituary.
Nachruhm *m* fame after death.
nachsagen *vt sep* **(a)** *(wiederholen)* to repeat. **(b)** **jdm etw ~** to accuse sb of sth; **jdm Schlechtes ~** to speak ill of sb; **ihm wird nachgesagt, daß ...** it's said that he ...; **das lasse ich mir nicht ~!** I'm not having that said of me!
Nachsaison *f* off-season.
nachschauen *vti sep siehe* **nachsehen 1, 2 (a).**
nachschenken *vti sep* **darf ich Ihnen (etwas) ~?** may I top up your glass?
nachschicken *vt sep* to send on, to forward.
Nachschlag *m (col)* second helping.
nachschlagen *sep irreg* **1** *vt Stelle, Zitat* to look up. **2** *vi (in Lexikon etc)* to look.
Nachschlagewerk *nt* reference book *or* work.
nachschleichen *vi sep irreg aux sein+dat* to creep after.
Nachschlüssel *m* duplicate key; *(Dietrich)* skeleton key.
nachschmeißen *vt sep irreg (col)* **jdm etw ~** to fling sth after sb; **das ist ja nachgeschmissen!** it's a real bargain.
nachschnüffeln *vi sep (col)* **jdm ~** to spy on sb.
Nachschub ['na:xʃu:p] *m* supplies *pl (an+dat* of*)*.
Nachschub- *(Mil)*: **~linie** *f* supply line; **~weg** *m* supply route.
nachsehen *sep irreg* **1** *vi* to have a look; *(prüfen)* to check. **jdm/einer Sache ~** *(hinterherschauen)* to gaze after sb/sth. **2** *vt* **(a)** *(prüfen)* to check; *Schulaufgaben etc* to mark; *(nachschlagen)* to look up. **(b)** *(verzeihen)* **jdm etw ~** to forgive sb (for) sth.
Nachsehen *nt*: **das ~ haben** to be left standing; *(nichts bekommen)* to be left empty-handed.
nachsenden *vt sep irreg* to forward.
nachsetzen *sep* **1** *vi* **jdm ~** to pursue sb. **2** *vt Fuß* to drag.
Nachsicht *f no pl (Milde)* leniency; *(Geduld)* forbearance. **er kennt keine ~** he knows no mercy; **~ haben** to be lenient.
nachsichtig *adj (milde)* lenient; *(geduldig)* forbearing *(gegen, mit* with*)*.
Nachsilbe *f* suffix.
nachsinnen *vi sep irreg* to ponder *(über +acc* over, about*)*.
nachsitzen *vi sep irreg (Sch)* **~ (müssen)** to be kept in; **jdn ~ lassen** to keep sb in.
Nachsommer *m* Indian summer.
Nachspann *m* **-e** credits *pl*.
Nachspeise *f* dessert, sweet *(Brit)*.
Nachspiel *nt (Theat)* epilogue; *(Mus)* closing section; *(fig)* sequel. **das geht nicht ohne ~ ab** there are bound to be repercussions; **ein gerichtliches ~ haben** to have legal repercussions.
nachspielen *sep* **1** *vt* to play. **2** *vi (Sport)* to play extra time *(Brit) or* overtime *(US)*. **der Schiedsrichter ließ ~** the referee allowed extra time.
nachspionieren* *vi sep (col)* **jdm ~** to spy on sb.
nachsprechen *vt sep irreg* to repeat. **jdm etw ~** to repeat sth after sb.
nächstbeste *adj attr* **der/die/das ~ ...** the first ... I/you *etc* see; **der ~ Zug/Job** the first train/job that comes along.
nachstehen *vi sep irreg* **jdm ~** to take second place to sb; **jdm in nichts** *(dat)* **~** to be sb's equal in every way.
nachstehend *adj attr* following. **~es müssen Sie beachten** you must take note of the following.
nachsteigen *vi sep irreg aux sein* **jdm ~** *(fig col)* to run after sb.
nachstellen *sep* **1** *vt (Tech) (neu einstellen)* to adjust; *(zurückstellen)* to put back. **2** *vi* **jdm ~** to follow sb; *(aufdringlich umwerben)* to pester sb.
Nächstenliebe *f* brotherly love; *(Barmherzigkeit)* compassion.
nächstens *adv* **(a)** *(bald einmal)* some time soon. **(b)** *(col: am Ende)* next.
nächste(r, s) *adj superl of* **nah(e)** **(a)** *(räumlich)* nearest. **das ~ Telefon** the nearest telephone; **ist dies der ~ Weg zum Bahnhof?** is this the quickest way to the station?; **in ~r Nähe** in the immediate vicinity; **aus ~r Nähe** from close by; *betrachten* at close quarters; *schießen* at close range; **im ~n Haus** next door. **(b)** *(zeitlich)* next. **~s Mal** next time; **Ende ~n Monats** at the end of next month; **am ~n Tag** (the) next day; **in den ~n Tagen** in the next few days; **bei ~r Gelegenheit** at the earliest opportunity; **in ~r Zeit** some time soon. **(c)** **die ~n Verwandten** the immediate family; **der ~ Angehörige** the next of kin; **fürs ~** for the time being.
Nächste(r) *mf decl as adj* **(a)** next one. **der n~, bitte** next please, first please *(US, Scot)*. **(b)** *(Mitmensch)* neighbour *(Brit)*, neighbor *(US)*. **jeder ist sich selbst der ~** *(Prov)* it's every man for himself.
Nächste(s) *nt decl as adj* **das ~** the next thing; *(das erste)* the first thing; **als ~s** next/first.
nächst-: **~folgend** *adj attr* next; **~gelegen** *adj attr* nearest; **~höher** *adj attr* one higher; **die ~höhere Klasse** one class higher; **~jährig** *adj attr* next year's; **~liegend** *adj attr (lit)* nearest; *(fig)* most obvious; **das N~liegende** the most obvious thing (to do).
nachsuchen *vi sep* **(a)** to look. **(b)** *(form: beantragen)* **um etw ~** to request sth *(bei jdm* of sb*)*.
nacht *adv* **heute ~** tonight; *(letzte ~)* last night; **Dienstag ~** (on) Tuesday night.
Nacht *f* **¨-e** *(lit, fig)* night. **es wird/ist ~** it's getting/it is dark; **in der ~** at night; **in der ~ vom 12. zum 13. April** during the night of April 12th to 13th; **in der ~ auf Dienstag** during Monday night; **diese ~** tonight; **des ~s** *(geh)* at night; **bis tief in die ~ arbeiten** to work far into the night; **über ~** *(lit,*

fig) overnight; **sich** *(dat)* **die ~ um die Ohren schlagen** *(col)* to stay up all night (working *etc*); *(mit Feiern)* to make a night of it; **die ~ zum Tage machen** to stay up all night (working *etc*); **gute ~!** good night!; **na, dann gute ~!** *(col)* what a prospect!; **bei ~ und Nebel** *(col)* at dead of night.

Nacht- *in cpds* night; **~arbeit** *f* night-work; **~ausgabe** *f* late final (edition); **~blindheit** *f* night blindness; **~dienst** *m* night duty; **~dienst haben** to be on nights.

Nachteil *m* **-e** disadvantage. **~e durch etw haben** to lose by sth; **im ~ sein** to be at a disadvantage *(jdm gegenüber* with sb*)*; **der ~, allein zu leben** the disadvantage of living alone.

nachteilig *adj (ungünstig)* disadvantageous; *(schädlich)* detrimental. **er hat sich sehr ~ über mich geäußert** he spoke very unfavourably *(Brit) or* unfavorably *(US)* about me.

nächtelang *adv* for nights (on end).

Nacht-: ~eule *f (fig col)* night owl; **~falter** *m* moth; **~gebet** *nt* evening prayer; **~hemd** *nt (für Damen)* nightdress *(Brit)*, nightgown; *(für Herren)* nightshirt.

Nachtigall *f* **-en** nightingale.

nächtigen *vi (geh)* to spend the night.

Nachtisch *m* dessert, sweet *(Brit)*, pudding.

nächtlich *adj attr* night. **die ~e Stadt** the town at night; **zu ~er Stunde** at a late hour.

Nacht-: ~lokal *nt* night club; **~mensch** *m* night person; **~portier** *m* night porter; **~programm** *nt* late-night programme *(Brit) or* program *(US)*.

Nachtrag *m, pl* **Nachträge** postscript; *(zu einem Buch)* supplement.

nachtragen *vt sep irreg* **(a) jdm etw ~** *(lit)* to go after sb with sth. **(b)** *(fig)* to bear sb a grudge for sth. **(c)** *(hinzufügen)* to add.

nachtragend *adj* unforgiving.

nachträglich *adj (später)* later; *(verspätet)* belated; *(nach dem Tod)* posthumous.

nachtrauern *vi sep+dat* to mourn.

Nachtruhe *f* night's rest; *(in Anstalten)* lights-out.

nachts *adv* at night. **dienstags ~** (on) Tuesday nights.

Nacht-: ~schicht *f* night shift; **~schicht haben** to be on nights; **n~schlafend** *adj*: **zu n~schlafender Zeit** in the middle of the night; **~schwärmer** *m (fig hum)* night owl; **~schwester** *f* night nurse; **~speicherofen** *m* storage heater.

nachts|über *adv* by night.

Nacht-: ~tisch *m* bedside table; **~tischlampe** *f* bedside lamp; **~topf** *m* chamber pot.

nachtun *vt sep irreg* **es jdm ~** to copy sb.

Nacht-: ~vorstellung *f* late-night performance; **~wache** *f* night-watch; *(im Krankenhaus)* night duty; **~wache haben** to be on night duty; **~wächter** *m (in Betrieben etc)* night watchman; **~zeug** *nt* night things *pl*; **~zug** *m* night train; **~zuschlag** *m* night supplement.

Nach|untersuchung *f (weitere Untersuchung)* further examination; *(spätere Untersuchung)* check-up.

nachvollziehbar *adj* comprehensible.

nachvollziehen* *vt sep irreg* to understand, to comprehend.

Nachwahl *f (Pol)* ≈ by-election.

Nachwehen *pl* after-pains *pl*; *(fig)* painful aftermath *sing*.

nachweinen *vi sep+dat* to mourn. **dieser Sache weine ich keine Träne nach** I won't shed any tears over that.

Nachweis *m* **-e** *(Beweis)* proof *(gen, für, über+acc* of*)*; *(Zeugnis)* certificate. **den ~ für etw erbringen** *or* **liefern** to furnish proof of sth.

nachweisbar *adj (beweisbar)* provable; *Fehler* demonstrable; *(Tech)* detectable.

nachweisen *vt sep irreg (beweisen)* to prove; *(Tech)* to detect. **dem Angeklagten konnte seine Schuld nicht nachgewiesen werden** the accused's guilt could not be proved.

nachweislich *adj* provable; *Fehler* demonstrable. **er war ~ in London** it can be proved that he was in London.

Nachwelt *f* **die ~** posterity.

nachwerfen *vt sep irreg* **jdm etw ~** *(lit)* to throw sth after *or* at sb; **das ist nachgeworfen** *(col)* that's a gift.

Nachwirkung *f* after-effect; *(fig)* consequence.

Nachwort *nt* epilogue.

Nachwuchs *m* **(a)** *(fig: junge Kräfte)* young people *pl* (in the profession/sport *etc*). **der schauspielerische ~** the up and coming actors. **(b)** *(hum: Nachkommen)* offspring *pl*.

Nachwuchs-: ~kraft *f* junior member of the staff; **~sorgen** *pl* recruitment problems *pl*; **~spieler** *m (Sport)* junior.

nachzahlen *vti sep* to pay extra; *(später zahlen)* to pay later.

nachzählen *vti sep* to check.

Nachzahlung *f (nachträglich)* back-payment; *(zusätzlich)* additional payment.

nachziehen *sep irreg* **1** *vt* **(a)** *(hinterherziehen)* **etw ~** to drag sth behind one; **das rechte Bein ~** to drag one's right leg. **(b)** *Linie* to go over; *Lippen* to paint; *Augenbrauen* to pencil in. **(c)** *Schraube, Seil* to tighten (up). **2** *vi* **(a)** *aux sein+dat (folgen)* to follow. **(b)** *(col: gleichtun)* to follow suit.

Nachzügler(in *f***)** ['na:xtsy:klɐ, -ərin] *m* **-** latecomer *(auch fig)*.

Nackedei *m* **-e** *or* **-s** *(hum col)* naked person; *(Kind)* little bare monkey *(hum col)*.

Nacken *m* **-** (nape of the) neck. **jdn im ~ haben** *(col)* to have sb on one's tail; **jdm im ~ sitzen** *(col)* to breathe down sb's neck; **ihm sitzt die Furcht im ~** he's frightened out of his wits *(col)*.

nackt *adj (lit, fig)* naked; *Haut, Wand, Tatsachen* bare; *Wirklichkeit* stark. **~ baden/schlafen** to bathe/sleep in the nude; **das ~e Leben retten** to escape with one's bare life.

Nackt-: ~baden *nt* nude bathing; **~badestrand** *m* nudist beach; **~heit** *f* nakedness; *(von Mensch auch)* nudity; *(Kahlheit)* bareness; **~kultur** *f* nudism.

Nadel *m* **-n** needle; *(Steck~, Haar~)* pin; *(Häkel~)* hook.

Nadel-: ~baum *m* conifer; **~hölzer** *pl* conifers *pl*; **~kissen** *nt* pin-cushion; **~kopf** *m* pin-head.

nadeln *vi (Baum)* to shed (its needles).

Nadel-: ~öhr *nt* eye of a needle; **~stich** *m* prick; *(beim Nähen, Med)* stitch; **~streifen** *pl* pinstripes *pl*; **~streifenanzug** *m* pinstripe(d) suit; **~wald** *m* coniferous forest.

Nagel *m* ̈ nail *(auch Anat)*; *(Zwecke)* tack; *(an Schuhen)* hobnail, stud; *(Med)* pin. **sich** *(dat)* **etw unter den ~ reißen** *(col)* to pinch sth *(col)*; **etw an den ~ hängen** *(fig)* to chuck sth in *(col)*; **den ~ auf den Kopf treffen** *(fig)* to hit the nail on the head; **~̈ mit Köpfen machen** *(col)* to do the job properly.

Nagel-: ~bett *nt (Anat)* bed of the nail; *(von Fakir)* bed of nails; **~bürste** *f* nailbrush; **~feile** *f* nailfile; **~haut** *f* cuticle.

Nägelkauen *nt* nail-biting.

Nagel-: ~lack *m* nail varnish *(Brit) or* polish; **~lackentferner** *m* nail varnish *(Brit) or* polish remover.

nageln *vt* to nail *(an+acc* to*)*; *(Med)* to pin.

Nagel-: n~neu *adj (col)* brand-new; **~pflege** *f* nail care; **~probe** *f (fig)* acid test; **~schere** *f* (pair of) nail-scissors *pl*.

nagen 1 *vi (lit, fig)* to gnaw *(an+dat* at*)*; *(knabbern)* to nibble *(an+dat* at*)*; *(Rost)* to eat *(an+dat* into*)*. **2** *vt* to gnaw.

nagend *adj Hunger* gnawing; *Zweifel etc* nagging.

Nager *m* **-**, **Nagetier** *nt* rodent.

Nah|aufnahme *f (Phot)* close-up.

nah(e) *comp* **näher,** *superl* **nächte(r, s)** *or (adv)* **am nächsten 1** *adj* **(a)** *(örtlich)* near *pred*, nearby. **der N~e Osten** the Middle East; **von ~em** at close quarters; **jdm ~ sein** to be near (to) sb. **(b)** *(zeitlich)* near *pred*, approaching. **(c)** *(eng) Freund etc* close. **2** *adv* **(a)** *(örtlich)* near. **~e an** near *or* close to; **~e bei** close by, near; **~ vor** right in front of; **von ~ und fern** from near and far; **jdm zu ~(e) treten** *(fig)* to offend sb. **(b)** *(zeitlich)* **~ bevorstehend** approaching; **sie ist ~ an (die) achtzig** she's nearing eighty. **(c)** *(eng)* closely. **mit jdm ~ verwandt sein** to be closely related to sb. **3** *prep+dat* near (to). **dem Wahnsinn ~e sein** to be on the verge of madness.

Nähe *f no pl* **(a)** *(örtlich) (Nahesein)* nearness, proximity; *(Nachbarschaft)* vicinity. **in meiner ~** near me; **aus der ~** from close to. **(b)** *(zeitlich)* closeness.

nahebei *adv* nearby.

nahebringen *vt sep irreg+dat (fig)* **jdm etw ~** to bring sth home to sb.

nahegehen *vi sep irreg aux sein+dat (fig)* to upset.

nahekommen *vi sep irreg aux sein+dat (fig)* **jdm ~** *(vertraut werden)* to get on close terms with sb. **das kommt der Wahrheit schon eher nahe** that is getting nearer the truth.

nahelegen *vt sep (fig)* **jdm etw ~** to suggest sth to sb; **jdm ~, etw zu tun** to advise sb to do sth.

naheliegen *vi sep irreg (fig: Idee, Frage, Lösung)* to suggest itself. **der Verdacht liegt nahe, daß ...** it seems reasonable to suspect that ...

naheliegend *adj Gedanke* which suggests itself; *Vermutung* natural. **aus ~en Gründen** for obvious reasons.

nahen *vir aux sein (liter)* to approach *(jdm/einer Sache* sb/sth*)*, to draw near *or* nigh *(liter) (jdm/einer Sache* to sb/sth*)*.

nähen 1 *vt* to sew; *Kleid* to make; *Wunde* to stitch (up), to suture *(spec)*. **2** *vi* to sew.

näher *comp of* **nah(e) 1** *adj* **(a)** *(örtlich)* nearer. **dieser Weg ist ~** this road is quicker; **die ~e Umgebung** the immediate vicinity. **(b)** *(zeitlich)* closer, sooner *pred*. **(c)** *(genauer) Auskünfte* further *attr*, more detailed. **(d)** *(enger) Verwandter, Beziehungen* closer. **die ~e Verwandtschaft** the immediate family. **2** *adv* **(a)** *((örtlich, zeitlich)* nearer. **(b)** *(genauer)* more closely; *ausführen* in more detail. **jdn ~ kennenlernen** to get to know better; **ich kenne ihn nicht ~** I don't know him well.

näherbringen *vt sep irreg+dat* **jdm etw** to give sb an understanding of sth.

Nähere(s) *nt decl as adj* further details *pl*.

Näherin *f* seamstress.

näherkommen *vi sep irreg aux sein (fig)* **jdm ~** to get closer to sb.

näherliegen *vi sep irreg (fig)* to be more obvious.

nähern *vr* **sich (jdm/einer Sache) ~** to approach (sb/sth), to draw nearer (to sb/sth).

nahestehen *vi sep irreg+dat (fig)* to be close to; *(Pol)* to sympathize with. **sich ~** *(Menschen, Ideen)* to be close; **eine den Konservativen ~de Zeitung** a paper with Conservative sympathies.

nahezu *adv* nearly, almost, virtually.

Nahkampf *m (Mil)* hand-to-hand fighting.

Nähkästchen *nt* **aus dem ~ plaudern** *(col)* to give away private details.

nahm *pret of* **nehmen.**

Näh-: ~maschine *f* sewing machine; **~nadel** *f* needle.

Nah|ost *m* **in/aus ~** in/from the Middle East.

Nährboden *m (lit)* fertile soil; *(für Bakterien)* culture medium; *(fig)* breeding-ground.

nähren *vt (geh)* to feed; *(fig) (steigern)* to increase, to feed; *(haben) Hoffnungen* to nurse. **er sieht gut genährt aus** he looks well-fed.

nahrhaft *adj Kost* nourishing; *Boden* fertile.

Nähr-: ~mittel *pl* cereal products *pl*; **~stoff** *m usu pl* nutrient.

Nahrung *f no pl* food. **flüssige/feste ~** liquids/ solids *pl*; **geistige ~** intellectual stimulation; **einer Sache** *(dat)* **(neue) ~ geben** to reinforce sth.

Nahrungs-: ~aufnahme *f* ingestion (of food) *(form)*; **die ~aufnahme verweigern** to refuse food; **~mittel** *nt* food(stuff); **~suche** *f* search for food.

Nährwert *m* nutritional value.

Naht *f* ¨**-e** seam; *(Med)* stitches *pl*, suture *(spec)*; *(Anat)* suture. **aus allen ¨~en platzen** to be bursting at the seams.

nahtlos *adj (lit) Teil, Anzug* seamless; *(fig) Übergang* smooth.

Nahtstelle *f* **(a)** *(lit)* seam. **(b)** *(fig)* link.

Nahverkehr *m* local traffic. **der öffentliche ~** local public transport.

Nahverkehrszug *m* local train.

Nähzeug *nt* sewing kit, sewing things *pl*.

Nahziel *nt* immediate aim *or* objective.

naiv *adj* naive.

Naivität [naivi'tɛːt] *f* naivety.

Name *m* **-ns, -n** name; *(fig: Ruf auch)* reputation. **mit ~n** by the name of; **dem ~n nach** by name; **ich kenne das Stück nur dem ~n nach** I've heard of the play but that's all; **dem ~n nach müßte sie Jugoslawin sein** judging by her name she must be Yugoslavian; **auf jds ~n** *(acc)* in sb's name; **unter dem ~n** under the name of; **er nannte seinen ~n** he gave his name; **einen ~n haben** *(fig)* to have a name; **sich** *(dat)* **einen ~n machen** to make a name for oneself; **die Dinge beim ~n nennen** to call a spade a spade; **im ~n** *(+gen)* on *or* in *(US)* behalf of; **im ~n des Volkes** in the name of the people.

namenlos *adj* **(a)** nameless *(auch fig)*, unnamed; *Helfer* anonymous. **(b)** *(geh: unsäglich)* unspeakable.

namens 1 *adv (mit Namen)* by the name of. **2** *prep +gen (form: im Auftrag)* in the name of.

Namen(s)- *in cpds* name; **~änderung** *f* change of name; **~schild** *nt* nameplate; **~tag** *m* name day, Saint's day; **~vetter** *m* namesake; **~zeichen** *nt* initials *pl*; **~zug** *m* signature.

namentlich 1 *adj* by name. **~e Abstimmung** roll call vote; **~er Aufruf** roll call. **2** *adv* in particular.

namhaft *adj* **(a)** *(bekannt)* famous. **~ machen** *(form)* to identify. **(b)** *(beträchtlich)* considerable.

nämlich *adv* **(a)** namely. **(b)** *(denn)* **wir haben uns verspätet, wir haben ~ einen Umweg machen müssen** we were late since we had to make a detour.

nannte *pret of* **nennen.**

nanu *interj* well I never. **~, wer ist das denn?** hello (hello), who's this?

Napalm *nt no pl* napalm.

Napf *m* **-ë** bowl.

Napfkuchen *m* ≈ ring-shaped poundcake.

Narbe *f* **-n (a)** *(lit, fig)* scar. **(b)** *(Bot)* stigma. **(c)** *(Gras~)* turf.

narbig *adj* scarred.

Narkose *f* **-n jdm eine ~ geben** to give sb an anaesthetic *(Brit) or* anesthetic *(US)*; **aus der ~ aufwachen** to come to from an/the anaesthetic.

Narkose|arzt *m* anaesthetist *(Brit)*, anesthetist *(US)*.

Narkotikum *nt, pl* **Narkotika** *(Med)* narcotic.

narkotisch *adj* narcotic; *Düfte* overpowering.

Narr *m (wk)* **-en, -en** fool. **jdn zum ~en halten** to make a fool of sb.

narren *vt (geh)* **jdn ~** *(zum besten haben)* to make a fool of sb; *(täuschen)* to dupe sb.

Narren-: ~freiheit *f* **sie hat bei ihm ~freiheit** he gives her (a) free rein; **~kappe** *f* jester's cap; **n~sicher** *adj* foolproof.

Narrheit *f* **(a)** *no pl* folly. **(b)** *(Streich)* prank.
Närrin *f* fool.
närrisch *adj* foolish; *(verrückt)* mad; *(col: sehr)* madly. **die ~en Tage** *Fasching and the period leading up to it;* **ganz ~ auf etw sein** *(col)* to be crazy about sth *(col)*.
Narzisse *f* **-n** narcissus.
narzißtisch *adj* narcissistic.
Nasal *m* **-e** nasal.
nasal *adj* nasal. **~er Ton** nasal twang.
naschen 1 *vi* to eat sweet things; *(heimlich kosten)* to pinch a bit *(col)*. **darf ich mal ~?** can I try a bit?; **die Kinder haben den ganzen Tag nur genascht** the children have been nibbling all day. **2** *vt* to nibble. **hast du was zum N~?** have you something for my sweet tooth?
Nascherei *f no pl* nibbling; *(von Süßigkeiten)* eating sweets *(Brit) or* candy *(US)*.
Nasch-: n~haft *adj* fond of sweet things; **~katze** *f* *(col)* guzzler; **ich bin halt so eine alte ~katze** I've got such a sweet tooth.
Nase *f* **-n (a)** nose. **sich die ~ putzen** to wipe one's nose; *(sich schnäuzen)* to blow one's nose; **pro ~** *(hum)* per head; **(immer) der ~ nachgehen** *(col)* to follow one's nose; **die richtige ~ für etw haben** *(col)* to have a nose for sth; **faß dich an deine eigene ~!** *(col)* you can *or* can't talk!; **jdm etw unter die ~ reiben** *(col)* to rub sb's nose in sth *(col)*; **jdm auf der ~ herumtanzen** *(col)* to play sb up *(col)*; **seine ~ gefällt mir nicht** *(col)* I don't like his face; **es muß nicht immer nach deiner ~ gehen** *(col)* you can't always have it your way; **ich sah es ihm an der ~ an** *(col)* I could see it on his face *(col)*; **auf der ~ liegen** *(col) (krank sein)* to be laid up; *(hingefallen sein)* to be flat on one's face *(col)*; **steck deine ~ ins Buch!** *(col)* get on with your book; **auf die ~ fallen** *(lit, fig)* to fall flat on one's face; **jdm etw vor der ~ wegschnappen** *(col)* just to beat sb to sth; **jdm die Tür vor der ~ zuschlagen** *(col)* to slam the door in sb's face; **jdm etw unter die ~ halten** to shove sth right under sb's nose *(col)*; **jdm eins auf die ~ geben** *(lit)* to punch sb on the nose; *(fig)* to put sb in his/her place; **die ~ voll haben** *(col)* to have had enough; **jdn an der ~ herumführen** *(als Täuschung)* to lead sb by the nose; *(als Scherz)* to pull sb's leg; **jdm etw auf die ~ binden** *(col)* to tell sb all about sth; **er steckt seine ~ in alles (hinein)** *(col)* he pokes his nose into everything. **(b)** *(col: Farbtropfen)* run.
naselang *adv:* **alle ~** all the time, again and again.
näseln *vi* to talk *or* speak through one's nose.
Nasen-: ~bein *nt* nose bone; **~bluten** *nt* a nosebleed; **ein Mittel gegen ~bluten** something for nosebleeds; **ich habe ~bluten** my nose is bleeding; **~flügel** *m* side of the nose; **~höhle** *f* nasal cavity; **~länge** *f* *(fig)* **mit einer** *or* **um eine ~länge gewinnen** to win by a nose; **jdm eine ~länge voraus sein** to be a hair's breadth ahead of sb; **~loch** *nt* nostril; **~rücken** *m* bridge of the nose; **~spitze** *f* tip of the/sb's nose; **ich seh es dir an der ~spitze an** I can tell by your face; **~stüber** *m* - bump on the nose; **jdm einen ~stüber versetzen** *(lit)* to bop sb on the nose; *(fig)* to tick *or* tell sb off.
Nase-: n~rümpfend *adj* **er sagte n~rümpfend** wrinkling his nose, he said; **n~weis** *adj* cheeky; *(vorlaut)* precocious; **~weis** *m* **-e** *(Vorlauter)* cheeky *(esp Brit) or* precocious brat *(col)*; *(Überschlauer)* know-all *(col)*, wiseguy *(col)*.
Nashorn *nt* rhinoceros, rhino.
naß *adj* wet. **etw ~ machen** to make sth wet; *(für bestimmten Zweck)* to wet sth; **sich ~ machen** *(col)* to wet oneself; **mit nassen Augen** with moist eyes; **wie ein nasser Sack** *(col)* like a wet rag *(col)*.
Nassauer *m* - *(col)* scrounger.
Nässe *f no pl* wetness, moisture. **„vor ~ schützen"** "keep dry"; **vor ~ triefen** to be dripping wet.
nässen 1 *vi (Wunde)* to discharge. **2** *vt Bett* to wet.
Naß-: n~forsch *adj (col)* brash; **n~kalt** *adj* chilly and damp, raw; **~rasur** *f* **die ~rasur** wet shaving; **eine ~rasur** a wet shave.
Nation *f* nation.
national [natsio'naːl] *adj* national; *(patriotisch)* nationalist(ic).
National- *in cpds* national; **n~bewußt** *adj* nationally conscious; **~elf** *f* international (football) team; **~flagge** *f* national flag; **~garde** *f* National Guard; **~gefühl** *nt* national feeling; **~gericht** *nt* national dish; **~hymne** *f* national anthem.
Nationalismus *m* nationalism.
Nationalist(in *f***)** *m* nationalist.
nationalistisch *adj* nationalist(ic).
Nationalität *f* nationality.
National-: ~mannschaft *f* international team; **er spielt in der schottischen ~mannschaft** he plays for Scotland; **~ökonomie** *f* economics *sing*; **~sozialismus** *m* National Socialism; **~sozialist** *m* National Socialist; **~spieler** *m* international (footballer *etc*).
Natrium *nt no pl* sodium.
Natron *nt no pl sodium compound, esp bicarbonate of soda.*
Natter *f* **-n** adder, viper; *(fig)* snake.
Natur *f* **(a)** *no pl* nature. **gegen die ~** against nature; **ich bin von ~ aus schüchtern** I am shy by nature; **sein Haar ist von ~ aus blond** his hair is naturally blond. **(b)** *no pl (freies Land)* countryside. **(c)** *(Wesensart)* nature; *(Mensch)* type. **es liegt in der ~ der Sache** it is in the nature of things; **das geht gegen meine ~** it goes against the grain; **eine Frage allgemeiner ~** a question of a general nature; **das ist ihm zur zweiten ~ geworden** it's become second nature to him.
Naturalien [-iən] *pl* natural produce *sing.* **in ~ bezahlen** to pay in kind.
Naturalismus *m* nauralism.
Naturalist(in *f***)** *m* naturalist.
naturalistisch *adj* naturalistic.
Natur-: ~beschreibung *f* description of nature; **~bursche** *m* nature-boy *(col)*.
Naturell *nt* **-e** temperament, disposition.
Natur-: ~ereignis *nt*, **~erscheinung** *f* natural phenomenon; **~forscher** *m* natural scientist; **~freund** *m* nature-lover; **n~gegeben** *adj (lit, fig)* natural; **n~gemäß** *adj* natural; **~geschichte** *f* natural history; **~gesetz** *nt* law of nature; **n~getreu** *adj* true to life; *(in Lebensgröße)* life-size; **~heilkunde** *f* nature healing; **~heilverfahren** *nt* natural cure; **~katastrophe** *f* natural disaster; **~kunde** *f* natural history.
natürlich 1 *adj* natural. **in seiner ~en Größe** life-size; **eines ~en Todes sterben** to die of natural causes. **2** *adv* naturally. **die Krankheit verlief ganz ~** the illness took its natural course. **~!** naturally!, of course!, sure! *(esp US)*.
natürlicherweise *adv* naturally.
Natürlichkeit *f* naturalness.
Natur-: ~notwendigkeit *f* physical inevitability; **~produkt** *nt* natural product; **~produkte** natural produce *sing*; **n~rein** *adj* pure, unadulterated; **~schutz** *m* nature conservancy; **unter ~schutz stehen** to be legally protected; **~schutzgebiet** *nt* nature reserve; **~talent** *nt* natural prodigy; **~trieb** *m* (natural) instinct; **n~verbunden** *adj* nature-loving; **~wissenschaft** *f* natural sciences *pl*; *(Zweig)* natural science; **~wissenschaftler** *m* (natural) scientist; **n~wissenschaftlich** *adj* scientific; **~zustand** *m* natural state.
Nautik *f no pl* nautical science, navigation.
nautisch *adj* navigational. **~e Meile** nautical mile.
Navigation [naviga'tsioːn] *f* navigation.
Navigations-: ~fehler *m* navigational error; **~raum** *m* charthouse.

Nazi *m* **-s** *(pej)* Nazi.
Nazismus *m (pej: Nationalsozialismus)* Nazi(i)sm.
nazistisch *adj (pej)* Nazi.
Nazizeit *f* Nazi period.
n.Chr. = nach Christus AD.
NDR [ɛndeː'|ɛr] *m* = **Norddeutscher Rundfunk.**
Neandertaler *m* - Neanderthal man.
Neapel *nt* Naples.
Nebel *m* - mist; *(dichter)* fog; *(Mil: künstlich)* smoke; *(fig)* mist, haze. **bei ~** in mist/fog; **das fällt wegen ~(s) aus** *(hum col)* it's all off.
Nebel-: ~bank *f* fog bank; **n~haft** *adj (fig)* nebulous; **~horn** *nt (Naut)* foghorn.
neb(e)lig *adj* misty; *(bei dichterem Nebel)* foggy.
Nebel-: ~scheinwerfer *m (Aut)* fog light; **~schleier** *m (geh)* veil of mist; **~(schluß)leuchte** *f (Aut)* rear fog-light; **~wand** *f* wall of fog; *(Mil)* smokescreen.
neben *prep* **(a)** *(örtlich: +dat/acc)* beside, next to. **(b)** *(außer: +dat)* apart from, aside from *(esp US)*. **(c)** *(verglichen mit: +dat)* compared with.
nebenamtlich *adj Tätigkeit* secondary, additional. **das macht er nur ~** he does that just as a secondary occupation.
neben|an *adv* next door. **die Tür ~** the next door.
Neben|anschluß *m (Telec)* extension.
nebenbei *adv* **(a)** *(gleichzeitig)* at the same time. **etw ~ machen** to do sth on the side. **(b)** *(außerdem)* additionally, in addition. **(c)** *(beiläufig)* incidentally. **~ bemerkt** *or* **gesagt** by the way, incidentally.
Neben-: ~beruf *m* extra job; **er ist im ~beruf Nachtwächter** he has a second job as a night watchman; **n~beruflich 1** *adj* extra, supplementary; **2** *adv* as a second job, as a sideline *(col)*; **er verdient n~beruflich mehr als hauptberuflich** he earns more from his second job than he does from his main job; **~beschäftigung** *f (Zweitberuf)* extra job; **~buhler(in** *f*) *m* rival; **~darsteller(in** *f*) *m* supporting actor/actress.
neben|einander *adv* **(a)** *(räumlich)* side by side; *(bei Rennen)* neck and neck. **(b)** *(zeitlich)* at the same time.
neben|einanderher *adv* side by side. **sie leben nur noch ~** *(Ehepaar etc)* they're just two people living in the same house.
neben|einander-: ~legen *vt sep* to lay side by side; **~stellen** *vt sep* to place side by side; *(fig: vergleichen)* to compare.
Neben-: ~eingang *m* side entrance; **~einkünfte, ~einnahmen** *pl* supplementary income; **~fach** *nt (Sch, Univ)* subsidiary (subject), minor *(US)*; **~fluß** *m* tributary; **~frage** *f* side issue; **~gebäude** *nt* **(a)** *(Zusatzgebäude)* annex; **(b)** *(Nachbargebäude)* adjacent building; **~gedanke** *m* ulterior motive; **~geräusch** *nt (Rad, Telec)* interference; **~handlung** *f (Liter)* subplot; **~haus** *nt* house next door.
nebenher *adv* **(a)** *(zusätzlich)* in addition. **(b)** *(gleichzeitig)* at the same time.
nebenhin *adv (beiläufig)* in passing, casually.
Neben-: ~höhle *f (Physiol)* sinus (of the nose); **~kläger** *m (Jur)* joint plaintiff; **~kosten** *pl* additional costs *pl*; **~mann** *m, pl* **~männer Ihr ~mann** the person next to you; **~produkt** *nt* by-product; **~raum** *m (benachbart)* adjoining room; *(weniger wichtig)* side room; **~rolle** *f* supporting role; *(fig)* minor role; **das spielt für mich nur eine ~rolle** that's only of minor concern to me; **~sache** *f* trifle, triviality; **das ist ~sache** that's irrelevant; **n~sächlich** *adj* minor, peripheral; **~sächlichkeit** *f* triviality; **~satz** *m (Gram)* subordinate clause; **n~stehend** *adj* **n~stehende Erklärungen** explanations in the margin; **n~stehende Abbildung** illustration opposite; **~stelle** *f (Telec)* extension; *(Comm)* branch; **~straße** *f (in der Stadt)* side street; *(Landstraße)* minor road; **~strecke** *f (Rail)* branch *or* local line; **~tisch** *m* adjacent table; **am ~tisch** at the next table; **~verdienst** *m* secondary income; **~wirkung** *f* side effect; **~zimmer** *nt* adjoining room; **~zweck** *m* secondary aim.
neblig *adj* = **neb(e)lig.**
Necessaire [nesɛ'sɛːɐ] *nt* **-s** *(Kulturbeutel)* vanity bag; *(zur Nagelpflege)* manicure case; *(Nähzeug)* sewing bag.
necken *vt* to tease.
Neckerei *f* teasing *no pl*.
neckisch *adj (scherzhaft)* merry, teasing; *(col: kokett, keß) Kleid, Frisur* saucy; *Spielchen* mischievous.
nee *adv (col)* no, nope *(col)*.
Neffe *m (wk)* **-n, -n** nephew.
Negation *f* negation.
Negativ *nt (Phot)* negative.
negativ *adj* negative. **jdm auf eine Frage ~ antworten** to answer sb's question in the negative; **sich ~ zu etw äußern** to speak negatively about sth.
Neger *m* - negro.
Negerin *f* negress.
Negerkuß *m* chocolate marshmallow.
negieren* *vt (bestreiten) Tatsache* to deny.
Negligé [negli'ʒeː] *nt* **-s** negligee.
nehmen *pret* **nahm,** *ptp* **genommen** *vti* to take; *(verwenden)* to use. **etw an sich** *(acc)* **~** *(aufbewahren)* to take charge of sth; *(sich aneignen)* to take sth (for oneself); **jdm etw ~** to take sth (away) from sb; **jdm die Hoffnung ~** to deprive sb of his/her hope; **die Mauer nimmt einem die ganze Sicht** the wall blocks the whole view; **er ließ es sich** *(dat)* **nicht ~, mich persönlich hinauszubegleiten** he insisted on showing me out himself; **diesen Erfolg lasse ich mir nicht ~** I won't be robbed of this success; **sie ~ sich** *(dat)* **nichts** *(col)* there's nothing to choose between them; **man nehme ...** *(Cook)* take ...; **~ Sie sich doch bitte!** please help yourself; **jdn zu sich ~** to take sb in; **etw ~, wie es kommt** to take sth as it comes; **jdn ~, wie er ist** to take sb as he is; **etw auf sich** *(acc)* **~** to take sth upon oneself; **etw zu sich ~** to take sth, to partake of sth *(liter)*; **wie man's nimmt** *(col)* depending on your point of view; **sie weiß ihn zu ~** she knows how to take him.
Nehrung *f* spit (of land).
Neid *m no pl* envy. **aus ~** out of envy; **grün (und gelb) vor ~** *(col)* green with envy; **das muß ihm der ~ lassen** *(col)* give the devil his due.
neiden *vt* **jdm etw ~** to envy sb (for) sth.
Neider *m* - envious person. **reiche Leute haben viele ~** rich people are much envied.
Neidhammel *m (col)* envious person.
neidisch *adj* envious. **auf jdn/etw ~ sein** to be envious of sb/sth.
neidlos *adj* ungrudging, without envy.
Neige *f* **-n (a)** *(liter)* **das Glas bis zur ~ leeren** to drain the cup to the dregs. **(b)** *no pl (geh: Ende)* **zur ~ gehen** to draw to a close; **die Vorräte gehen zur ~** the provisions are fast becoming exhausted.
neigen 1 *vt Kopf, Körper* to bend; *Glas* to tip. **2** *vr (Ebene)* to slope; *(Mensch)* to bend; *(unter Last: Bäume etc)* to bow; *(Gebäude etc)* to lean; *(kippen)* to tip (up), to tilt (up). **3** *vi* **zu etw ~** to have a tendency to sth; *(für etw anfällig sein)* to be prone to sth; **zu der Ansicht ~, daß ...** to be inclined to take the view that ...; *siehe* **geneigt.**
Neigung *f* **(a)** *(das Neigen)* inclination; *(Gefälle auch)* incline, gradient *(esp Rail)*. **(b)** *(Tendenz)* tendency; *(Veranlagung)* leaning *usu pl*; *(Hang, Lust)* inclination. **künstlerische/politische ~en** artistic/political leanings; **etw aus ~ tun** to do sth by inclination; **keine ~ verspüren, etw zu tun** to have no inclination to do sth.

Neigungs-: ~**ehe** *f* love match; ~**winkel** *m* angle of inclination.
nein *adv* no. **kommt er? —** ~ is he coming? — no, (he isn't); **ich sage nicht** ~ I wouldn't say no; **Hunderte,** ~ **Tausende** hundreds, no *or* nay *(liter)* thousands; ~**, so was!** well I never!
Nein *nt no pl* no. **bei seinem** ~ **bleiben** to stick to one's refusal.
Nein-: ~**sager(in** *f*) *m* - **er ist ein ewiger** ~**sager** he always says no; ~**stimme** *f (Pol)* no(-vote), nay *(US)*.
Nektar *m no pl (Myth, Bot)* nectar.
Nektarine *f* nectarine.
Nelke *f* **-n (a)** carnation. **(b)** *(Gewürz)* clove.
nennen *pret* **nannte,** *ptp* **genannt 1** *vt* **(a)** *(bezeichnen)* to call. **jdn nach jdm** ~ to name sb after *or* for *(US)* sb; **das nenne ich Mut!** that's what I call courage!; **das nennst du schön?** you call that beautiful? **(b)** *(angeben, aufzählen)* to name; *(erwähnen)* to mention. **die genannten Namen** the names mentioned; **können Sie mir einen guten Anwalt** ~**?** could you give me the name of a good lawyer?; **das genannte Schloß** the castle referred to. **2** *vr* to call oneself; *(heißen)* to be called *(Brit) or* named. **und so was nennt sich Liebe** *(col)* and they call that love.
nennenswert *adj* considerable. **nicht** ~ not worth mentioning; **nichts N~es** nothing worth mentioning.
Nenner *m* - *(Math)* denominator. **etw auf einen** ~ **bringen** *(lit, fig)* to reduce sth to a common denominator.
Nennung *f (das Nennen)* naming; *(Sport)* entry.
Nennwert *m (Fin)* nominal *or* par value; **zum** ~ at par.
neo-, Neo- *in cpds* neo-.
Neon *nt no pl* neon.
Neon-: ~**licht** *nt* neon light; ~**reklame** *f* neon sign; ~**röhre** *f* neon tube.
Nepp *m no pl (col)* **der reinste** ~ daylight robbery *(col)*, a rip-off *(col)*.
neppen *vt (col)* to fleece *(col)*, to rip off *(col)*.
Nepplokal *nt (col)* clipjoint *(col)*.
Neptun *m* Neptune.
Nerv [nɛrf] *m* **-en** nerve. **leicht die** ~**en verlieren** to scare easily; **die** ~**en sind mit ihm durchgegangen** he lost control, he snapped *(col)*; **der hat (vielleicht)** ~**en!** *(col)* he's got a nerve! *(col)*; **es geht mir auf die** ~**en** *(col)* it gets on my nerves.
nerven [ˈnɛrfn] *(col)* **1** *vt* **jdn** ~ to get on sb's nerves. **2** *vi* **das nervt** it gets on your nerves.
Nerven- [ˈnɛrfn-]: ~**arzt** *m* neurologist; **n~aufreibend** *adj* nerve-racking; ~**belastung** *f* strain on the nerves; ~**bündel** *nt (fig col)* bundle of nerves *(col)*; ~**gas** *nt (Mil)* nerve gas; ~**gift** *nt* neurotoxin; ~**heilanstalt** *f* mental hospital; ~**heilkunde** *f* neurology; ~**kitzel** *m (fig)* thrill; ~**klinik** *f* psychiatric clinic; ~**kostüm** *nt (hum)* **ein starkes/schwaches** ~**kostüm haben** to have strong/weak nerves; **n~krank** *adj* suffering from a nervous disease; ~**krankheit** *f* nervous disorder; ~**krieg** *m (fig)* war of nerves; ~**leiden** *nt* nervous complaint; ~**probe** *f* trial; ~**sache** *f (col)* question of nerves; ~**säge** *f (col)* pain (in the neck) *(col)*; ~**system** *nt* nervous system; ~**zusammenbruch** *m* nervous breakdown.
nervlich [ˈnɛrflɪç] *adj* **der** ~**e Zustand des Patienten** the state of the patient's nerves; ~ **bedingt** nervous.
nervös [nɛrˈvøːs] *adj* nervous; *(aufgeregt auch)* jumpy *(col)*, on edge *pred*.
Nervosität [nɛrvoziˈtɛːt] *f* nervousness.
nervtötend [ˈnɛrf-] *adj (col)* nerve-racking; *Arbeit* soul-destroying.
Nerz *m* **-e** mink.
Nerzmantel *m* mink coat.
Nessel[1] *f* **-n** *(Bot)* nettle. **sich in die** ~**n setzen** *(col)* to put oneself in a spot *(col)*.
Nessel[2] *m* - *(Tex)* (untreated) cotton.
Nessel-: ~**fieber** *nt* nettle-rash fever; ~**sucht** *f* nettle rash.
Nest *nt* **-er (a)** *(Brutstätte)* nest. **(b)** *(fig: Schlupfwinkel)* hideout, lair. **(c)** *(fig: Heim)* nest, home. **sein eigenes** ~ **beschmutzen** to foul one's own nest; **da hat er sich ins warme** ~ **gesetzt** *(col)* he's got it made *(col)*. **(d)** *(fig: Bett)* bed. **(e)** *(pej col: Ort)* hole *(col)*, one-horse town *(col)*.
Nest-: ~**beschmutzer** *m (pej)* runner-down *(col)*, denigrator *(of one's family or country)*; ~**beschmutzung** *f (pej)* running-down *(col)*, denigration *(of one's family or country)*.
nesteln *vi* **an etw** *(dat)* ~ to fumble with sth.
Nest-: ~**häkchen** *nt* baby of the family; ~**wärme** *f (fig)* happy home life.
nett *adj* nice; *(hübsch auch)* pretty, cute. **das kann ja** ~ **werden!** *(iro)* that'll be nice (I don't think!) *(col)*; **sei so** ~ **und räum' auf!** would you mind clearing up?; ~**, daß Sie gekommen sind!** nice of you to come.
netterweise *adv* kindly.
Nettigkeit *f* **(a)** *no pl (nette Art)* kindness, goodness. **(b)** *(nette Worte)* ~**en** kind words.
netto *adv (Comm)* net.
Netto- *in cpds* net.
Netz *nt* **-e (a)** net; *(Spinnen~, fig: von Lügen etc)* web; *(Haar~)* (hair)net; *(Einkaufs~)* net bag; *(Gepäck~)* (luggage) rack. **ins** ~ **gehen** *(Ftbl)* to go into the net; **jdm ins** ~ **gehen** *(fig)* to fall into sb's trap; **jdm durchs** ~ **gehen** *(fig)* to give sb the slip. **(b)** *(System)* network; *(Strom~)* mains *sing or pl*. **(c)** *(Math)* net; *(Kartengitter)* grid.
Netz-: ~**anschluß** *m (Elec)* mains connection; ~**ball** *m (Tennis etc)* netball; ~**gerät** *nt* mains receiver; ~**haut** *f* retina; ~**hemd** *nt* string vest *(Brit) or* undershirt *(US)*; ~**karte** *f (Rail)* unlimited travel ticket; ~**spannung** *f* mains voltage; ~**teil** *nt* mains adapter; ~**werk** *nt (Elec, fig)* network; *(aus Draht)* netting.
neu *adj* new; *Kräfte, Hoffnung auch* fresh; *(kürzlich entstanden auch)* recent; *Wäsche* clean; *Wein* young. **das N~e Testament** the New Testament; **die N~e Welt** the New World; **ein** ~**er Anfang** a new *or* fresh start; ~**eren Datums** of (more) recent date; **die** ~**(e)ste Mode** the latest fashion; **die** ~**esten Nachrichten** the latest news; **ein ganz** ~**er Wagen** a brand-new car; **das ist mir** ~**!** that's new(s) to me; **in** ~**erer Zeit** in modern times; **erst in** ~**erer Zeit** only recently; **die** ~**eren Sprachen** modern languages; **seit** ~**(e)stem gibt es ...** since recently there has been ...; **aufs** ~**e** *(geh)* afresh; **auf ein** ~**es!** *(Aufmunterung)* let's try again; **der/die N~e** the newcomer, the new guy *(col)*; **was ist das N~e an dem Buch?** what's new about the book?; **weißt du schon das N~(e)ste?** have you heard the latest?; **was gibt's N~es?** *(col)* what's the latest?; **von** ~**em** *(von vorn)* from the beginning; *(wieder)* again, ~ **beginnen** to make a fresh start, to start again; **er ist** ~ **hinzugekommen** he's joined (him/them) recently; **ein Zimmer** ~ **einrichten** to refurnish a room.
Neu-: ~**ankömmling** *m* newcomer; ~**anschaffung** *f* new acquisition; **n~artig** *adj* new; **ein n~artiges Wörterbuch** a new type of dictionary; ~**auflage** *f* reprint; ~**ausgabe** *f* new edition.
Neubau *m* new house/building.
Neubau-: ~**siedlung** *f* new housing estate *(Brit) or* development; ~**wohnung** *f* newly-built flat.
Neu-: ~**bearbeitung** *f* revised edition; *(von Oper etc)* new version; *(das ~bearbeiten)* revision; reworking; ~**beginn** *m* new beginning(s); ~**druck** *m* reprint; ~**einstellung** *f* new appointment; ~**entdeckung** *f* rediscovery; *(Mensch)* new discovery; **n~entwickelt** *adj attr* newly developed; ~**entwicklung** *f* new development.

neuerdings *adv* recently. ~ **raucht er wieder** now he's started smoking again.
Neuerer *m* - innovator.
Neu-: n~eröffnet *adj attr* newly-opened; *(wiedereröffnet)* reopened; **~eröffnung** *f (Wiedereröffnung)* reopening; **die ~eröffnung der Fluglinie** the opening of the new airline; **~erscheinung** *f (Buch)* new publication; *(Schallplatte)* new release.
Neuerung *f* innovation; *(Reform)* reform.
Neu|erwerbung *f* new acquisition.
neu(e)stens *adv* lately, recently.
Neu-: ~fassung *f* revised version; **~fundland** *nt* Newfoundland; **~fundländer** *m* - *(Hund)* Newfoundland (dog); **n~geboren** *adj* newborn; **sich wie n~geboren fühlen** to feel (like) a new man/woman; **~geborene(s)** *nt decl as adj* new-born child; **n~gewählt** *adj attr* newly elected.
Neugier(de) *f no pl* curiosity, inquisitiveness; *(pej auch)* nosiness *(col)*. **aus** ~ out of curiosity.
neugierig *adj* inqisitive, curious *(auf +acc* about*)*; *(pej)* nos(e)y *(col)*; *(gespannt)* longing to know. **ein N~er** an inquisitive person; *(pej auch)* a nos(e)y parker *(col)*; **jdn ~ machen** to arouse sb's curiosity; **ich bin ~, ob** I wonder if; **da bin ich aber ~!** I can hardly wait *(col)*.
Neu-: n~griechisch *adj* modern Greek; **das ~griechische** modern Greek; **~gründung** *f (Wiederbegründung)* re-establishment; **die ~gründung von Universitäten** the founding of new universities.
Neuheit *f* **(a)** *no pl* novelty. **(b)** new thing/idea.
Neuigkeit *f* piece of news. **~en** news *sing*.
Neujahr *nt* New Year.
Neujahrs-: ~abend *m* New Year's Eve, Hogmanay *(Scot)*; **~tag** *m* New Year's Day.
Neuland *nt no pl* virgin land; *(fig)* new ground.
neulich *adv* recently, the other day. ~ **abend(s)** the other evening.
Neuling *m* newcomer.
neumodisch *adj* fashionable; *(pej)* new-fangled *(pej)*.
Neumond *m* new moon. **bei** ~ at new moon; **heute ist** ~ there's a new moon today.
Neun *f* **-en** nine. **ach du grüne ~e!** *(col)* well I'm blowed! *(col)*; *siehe* **Vier.**
neun *num* nine. **alle ~e!** *(beim Kegeln)* strike!; *siehe* **vier.**
Neun-: n~hundert *num* nine hundred; **n~mal** *adv* nine times; *siehe* **viermal; n~malklug** *adj (iro)* smart-aleck *attr (col)*.
Neuntel *nt* - ninth; *siehe* **Viertel**[1].
neuntens *adv* ninth(ly), in the ninth place.
neunte(r, s) *adj* ninth; *siehe* **vierte(r, s).**
neunzehn *num* nineteen; *siehe* **vierzehn.**
neunzig *num* ninety; *siehe* **vierzig.**
Neu-: ~ordnung *f* reorganization; *(Reform)* reform; **~philologe** *m* modern linguist.
Neuralgie *f* neuralgia.
Neu-: ~reg(e)lung *f* adjustment; **n~reich** *adj (pej)* nouveau riche; **~reiche(r)** *mf (pej)* nouveau riche.
Neuro- *in cpds* neuro; **~loge** *m*, **~login** *f* neurologist; **~logie** *f* neurology.
Neurose *f* **-n** neurosis.
Neurotiker(in *f*) *m* - neurotic.
neurotisch *adj* neurotic.
Neu-: ~schnee *m* fresh snow; **~seeland** *nt* New Zealand; **n~seeländisch** *adj* New Zealand; **~silber** *nt* German silver; **n~sprachlich** *adj* modern language; **n~sprachliches Gymnasium** ≃ grammar school *(Brit)*, high school *(esp US, Scot) stressing modern languages;* **~stadt** *f* new town.
neutral *adj* neutral.
neutralisieren* *vt* to neutralize.
Neutralität *f* neutrality.
Neutron *nt* **-en** [nɔy'troːnən] neutron.
Neutrum *nt, pl* **Neutra** *(Gram, fig)* neuter.
Neu-: ~wahl *f (Pol)* new election; **~wert** *m* value when new; **n~wertig** *adj* as new; **~zeit** *f* modern times *pl*; **Literatur der ~zeit** modern literature; **n~zeitlich** *adj* modern; **~zugang** *m* new entry; **~zulassung** *f (Aut)* ≃ registration of a new vehicle.
nicht *adv* **(a)** *(Verneinung)* not. **er raucht** ~ *(augenblicklich)* he isn't smoking; *(gewöhnlich)* he doesn't smoke; **kommst du? — nein, ich komme** ~ are you coming? — no, I'm not (coming); **ich kann das ~ — ich auch ~** I can't do it — neither *or* nor can I; ~ **mehr als** no more than; ~ **heute und ~ morgen** neither today nor tomorrow; **er ~!** not him. **(b)** *(Bitte, Verbot)* ~ **berühren!** do not touch; *(gesprochen)* don't touch; **~!** don't!, no!; **tu's ~!** don't do it!; ~ **doch!** stop it!; **bitte ~!** please don't. **(c)** *(rhetorisch)* **er kommt, ~ (wahr)?** he's coming, isn't he?; **er kommt ~, ~ wahr?** he isn't coming, is he?; **das ist schön, ~ (wahr)?** it's nice, isn't it?; **jetzt wollen wir Schluß machen, ~?** let's leave it now, OK?
Nicht-, nicht- *pref* non-.
Nicht-: ~achtung *f (+gen* for*)* disregard; **n~amtlich** *adj* unofficial; **~angriffspakt** *m* non-aggression pact; **~beachtung** *f* non-observance; **n~christlich** *adj* non-Christian.
Nichte *f* **-n** niece.
Nicht-: ~einhaltung *f* non-compliance *(+gen* with*)*; **~einmischung** *f (Pol)* non-intervention; **~erscheinen** *nt* non-appearance; **~gefallen** *nt*: **bei ~gefallen** if not satisfied.
nichtig *adj* **(a)** *(Jur: ungültig)* void. **(b)** *(unbedeutend)* trivial.
Nichtigkeit *f* **(a)** *(Jur: Ungültigkeit)* invalidity, nullity. **(b)** *no pl (Bedeutungslosigkeit)* vainness, emptiness. **(c)** *usu pl (Kleinigkeit)* triviality, trivia *pl*.
Nicht-: ~mitglied *nt* non-member; **n~öffentlich** *adj attr* not open to the public; **n~öffentliche Sitzung** meeting in camera *(Jur) or* behind closed doors; **~raucher** *m (auch Rail)* non-smoker; **ich bin ~raucher** I don't smoke; **~raucherabteil** *nt* no-smoking compartment; **n~rostend** *adj attr* rustproof.
Nichts *nt* **(a)** *no pl (Philos)* nothingness; *(Leere)* emptiness, void. **etw aus dem ~ aufbauen** to build sth up from nothing; **vor dem ~ stehen** to be left with nothing. **(b)** *pl* **-e** *(Mensch)* nonentity.
nichts *indef pron inv* nothing. **ich weiß** ~ I don't know anything, I know nothing; ~ **als** nothing but; ~ **(anderes) als** nothing but; ~ **von Bedeutung** nothing of (any) importance; ~ **Besseres/Neues** *etc* nothing better/new *etc*; ~ **da!** *(col) (weg da)* no you don't!; *(ausgeschlossen)* nothing doing *(col)*; **das ist ~ für mich** that's not my cup of tea *(col)*; **für ~ und wieder ~** *(col)* for nothing at all; **(es war) ~ mehr zu machen** there was nothing more that could be done; **ich weiß ~ Genaues** I don't know any details; ~ **wie raus/hin** *etc (col)* let's get out/over there *etc* (on the double).
nichts|ahnend *adj* unsuspecting.
Nicht-: ~schwimmer *m* non-swimmer; **sie ist ~schwimmer** she's a non-swimmer; **~schwimmerbecken** *nt* pool for non-swimmers.
nichts-: ~destotrotz *adv* notwithstanding *(form)*, nonetheless; **~destoweniger** *adv* nevertheless.
Nichtseßhafte(r) *mf decl as adj (form)* person of no fixed abode *(form)*.
Nichts-: ~könner *m* incompetent person; **~nutz** *m* **-e** good-for-nothing; **n~nutzig** *adj* useless; *(unartig)* good-for-nothing; **n~sagend** *adj Buch, Worte* meaningless; *Mensch* insignificant; *Gesichtsausdruck* blank; **~tuer(in** *f*) *m* - idler; **~tun** *nt* idleness; *(Muße)* leisure; **viel Zeit mit ~tun verbringen** to spend a lot of time doing nothing.

Nicht-: **~tänzer** *m* non-dancer; **ich bin ~tänzer** I don't dance; **~trinker** *m* non-drinker; **er ist ~trinker** he doesn't drink; **~vorhandensein** *nt* absence; **~wissen** *nt* ignorance; **~zutreffende(s)** *nt decl as adj* **(etwas) ~zutreffendes** something incorrect; **zutreffendes (bitte) streichen!** (please) delete as applicable.

Nickel *nt no pl* nickel.

Nickelbrille *f* metal-rimmed glasses *pl*.

nicken *vi* to nod. **mit dem Kopf ~** to nod one's head.

Nickerchen *nt (col)* forty winks *(col)*. **ein ~ machen** to have forty winks.

Nicki *m* **-s** velour pullover.

nie *adv* never. **~ im Leben, ~ und nimmer** never ever; **~ wieder** *or* **mehr** never again; **fast ~** hardly ever.

nieder 1 *adj attr* low; *(weniger bedeutend) Klasse, Stand* lower; *(geringer) Geburt, Herkunft* lowly; *Volk* common; *Arbeit* menial. **2** *adv* down.

Nieder- *pref (Geog)* lower; **n~beugen** *sep* **1** *vt (lit, fig)* to bow down; **2** *vr* to bend down; **n~brennen** *vti sep irreg (vi: aux sein)* to burn down; **n~brüllen** *vt sep Redner* to shout down; **n~deutsch** *adj (Ling)* Low German; **~druck** *m (Tech)* low pressure; **n~drücken** *vt sep (lit)* to press down; *(fig: bedrücken)* **jdn n~drücken** to depress sb, to get sb down *(col)*; **~gang** *m (fig: Verfall)* decline; **n~gehen** *vi sep irreg aux sein* to descend; *(Regen)* to fall; *(Gewitter)* to break *(auch fig)*; *(Boxer)* to go down; **n~geschlagen** *adj* dejected, despondent; **~geschlagenheit** *f* dejection, despondency; **n~halten** *vt sep irreg* to hold *or* keep down; *Volk* to oppress; *(Mil)* to pin down; **n~kämpfen** *vt sep Feuer* to fight down; *Feind* to overcome; *Tränen* to fight back; **n~knien** *vi sep aux sein* to kneel down; **n~kommen** *vi sep irreg aux sein (old)* to be delivered *(old) (mit of)*; **~kunft** *f* **¨-e** *(old)* delivery; **~lage** *f* defeat; **jdm eine ~lage beibringen** to inflict a defeat on sb.

Niederlande *pl* **die ~** the Netherlands *sing or pl*, the Low Countries *pl*.

Niederländer(in *f***)** *m* **-** Dutchman/Dutchwoman. **die ~** the Dutch.

niederländisch *adj* Dutch, Netherlands.

niederlassen *vr sep irreg* **(a)** *(geh)* to sit down; *(Vögel)* to alight. **(b)** *(Praxis, Geschäft eröffnen)* to establish oneself. **sich als Arzt/Rechtsanwalt ~** to set up as a doctor/lawyer.

Niederlassung *f* **(a)** *no pl (das Niederlassen)* settlement; *(eines Arztes etc)* setting-up. **(b)** *(Siedlung)* settlement. **(c)** *(Comm)* registered office; *(Zweigstelle)* branch.

niederlegen *sep* **1** *vt* **(a)** to lay *or* put down; *Waffen* to lay down. **(b)** *(aufgeben) Amt, Mandat* to resign (from), to give up; *Führung* to renounce, to give up. **die Arbeit ~** *(aufhören, streiken)* to stop work. **(c)** *(schriftlich festlegen)* to write down. **2** *vr* to lie down.

Niederlegung *f* **(a)** *(von Kranz)* laying. **(b)** *(von Amt, Mandat)* resignation (from). **~ der Arbeit** industrial action. **(c)** *(schriftlich)* setting-out.

Nieder-: **n~machen, n~metzeln** *vt sep* to massacre, to butcher; **n~prasseln** *vi sep aux sein (Regen etc)* to beat down; *(fig: Beschimpfungen)* to rain down; **n~reißen** *vt sep irreg* to pull down; *(fig) Schranken* to tear down; **~rhein** *m* Lower Rhine; **n~rheinisch** *adj* Lower Rhine; **n~rheinisch** *adj* Lower Rhine; **~sachsen** *nt* Lower Saxony; **n~schießen** *vt sep irreg* to shoot down.

Niederschlag *m* **(a)** *(Met)* precipitation *(form)*; *(Chem)* precipitate; *(Bodensatz)* sediment, dregs *pl*. **radioaktiver ~** (radioactive) fallout; **für morgen sind heftige ¨-e gemeldet** tomorrow there will be heavy rain/hail/snow. **(b)** *(Boxen)* knockdown blow.

niederschlagen *sep irreg* **1** *vt* **(a)** *jdn* to knock down; *Aufstand, Revolte* to put down; *Augen* to lower, to cast down *(liter)*; *siehe* **niedergeschlagen. (b)** *(Chem)* to precipitate. **2** *vr (Flüssigkeit)* to condense; *(Bodensatz)* to settle; *(Chem)* to precipitate. **sich in etw** *(dat)* **~** *(Erfahrungen etc)* to find expression in sth.

Niederschlags-: **n~frei** *adj* dry, without precipitation *(form)*; **~menge** *f* rainfall/snowfall, precipitation *(form)*.

Nieder-: **~schlagung** *f (eines Aufstands)* suppression; **n~schmettern** *vt sep* to batter down; *(fig)* to shatter; **n~schmetternd** *adj Nachricht, Ergebnis* shattering; **n~schreiben** *vt sep irreg* to write down; **~schrift** *f (das ~schreiben)* writing down, *(~geschriebenes)* notes *pl*; *(Protokoll) (einer Sitzung)* minutes *pl*; *(Jur)* record; **n~setzen** *sep* **1** *vt Kind, Glas* to put down; **2** *vr* to sit down; **~spannung** *f (Elec)* low voltage *or* tension; **n~stimmen** *vt sep* to vote down; **n~strecken** *vt sep (geh)* to lay low; **n~stürzen** *vi sep aux sein* to crash down; **n~tourig** [-tu:rɪç] *adj* low-revving; **n~tourig fahren** to drive with low revs.

Niedertracht *f* = **Niederträchtigkeit.**

niederträchtig *adj* malicious, spiteful. **jdn ~ verraten** to betray sb in a despicable way.

Niederträchtigkeit *f* **(a)** *no pl* **so viel ~ hätte ich ihm nicht zugetraut** I would not have suspected him of such a despicable act. **(b)** *(Tat)* malicious behaviour *no pl (Brit) or* behavior *no pl (US)*.

niedertreten *vt sep irreg* to trample down.

Niederung *f (Senke)* depression.

Nieder-: **n~werfen** *sep irreg* **1** *vt* to throw or cast *(liter)* down; *Aufstand* to suppress; *Gegner (lit)* to floor; *(fig)* to overcome; **er wurde von einer Krankheit n~geworfen** he was laid low by an illness; **2** *vr* to prostrate oneself; **~werfung** *f (von Aufstand)* suppression.

niedlich *adj* sweet, cute, pretty little *attr*.

Niedlichkeit *f* sweetness, cuteness.

niedrig *adj* low. **~ fliegen** to fly low; **~ste Preise** rock-bottom prices; **ich schätze seine Chancen sehr ~ ein** I don't think much of his chances.

Niedrig-: **n~stehend** *adj Volk, Kultur* primitive; **~wasser** *nt (Naut)* low water.

niemals *adv* never.

niemand *indef pron* nobody, no-one. **es war ~ zu Hause** there was nobody at home, there wasn't anyone at home; **~ anders kam** nobody else came; **ich habe ~ anders gesehen** I didn't see anybody else; **sag das ~(em)!** don't tell anybody.

Niemand *m no pl* **er ist ein ~** he's a nobody.

Niemandsland *nt* no man's land.

Niere *f* **-n** kidney. **künstliche ~** kidney machine; **es geht mir an die ~n** *(col)* it gets me down.

Nieren- *in cpds (Anat)* renal; **n~förmig** *adj* kidney-shaped; **~leiden** *nt* kidney disease; **~stein** *m* kidney stone, renal calculus *(spec)*; **~tisch** *m* kidney-shaped table.

nieseln *vi impers* to drizzle.

Nieselregen *m* drizzle.

niesen *vi* to sneeze.

Niespulver *nt* sneezing powder.

Niet *m* **-e** *(spec)*, **Niete**[1] *f* **-n** rivet; *(auf Kleidung)* stud.

Niete[2] *f* **-n** *(Los)* blank; *(col: Mensch)* dead loss *(col)*.

nieten *vt* to rivet.

Nietenhose *f* (pair of) studded jeans *pl*.

niet- und nagelfest *adj (col)* nailed down.

Nihilismus [nihi'lɪsmʊs] *m* nihilism.

Nihilist [nihi'lɪst] *m* nihilist.

nihilistisch [nihi'lɪstɪʃ] *adj* nihilistic.

Nikolaus *m* **-, -e** *or (hum col)* **Nikoläuse** St Nicholas; *(~tag)* St Nicholas' Day.

Nikotin *nt no pl* nicotine.

Nikotin-: **n~arm** *adj* low-nicotine; **n~frei** *adj* nicotine-free; **n~haltig** *adj* containing nicotine; **~vergiftung** *f* nicotine poisoning.

Nil *m* Nile.

Nilpferd *nt* hippopotamus, hippo.
Nimbus *m* **-, -se** *(Heiligenschein)* halo; *(fig)* aura.
Nimmer-: n~mehr *adv (liter)* nevermore *(liter)*, never again; **n~müde** *adj attr* tireless, untiring; **~satt** *m* **-e** glutton; **ein ~satt sein** to be insatiable; **n~satt** *adj* insatiable; **~wiedersehen** *nt (col)* **auf ~wiedersehen!** I never want to see you again; **auf ~wiedersehen verschwinden** to disappear never to be seen again.
nippen *vti* to nip *(an+dat* at). **am Wein ~** to sip (at) the wine.
Nippes *pl* knick-knacks *pl*, bric-à-brac *sing*.
nirgends, nirgendwo *adv* nowhere, not ... anywhere. **ihm gefällt es ~** he doesn't like it anywhere; **überall und ~** here, there and everywhere.
nirgendwohin *adv* nowhere, not ... anywhere.
Nische *f* **-n** alcove; *(Koch~ etc)* corner.
nisten *vi* to nest.
Nist-: ~kasten *m* nest(ing) box; **~platz** *m* nesting place; **~zeit** *f* (the) nesting season.
Nitrat *nt* nitrate.
Nitroglyzerin *nt* nitroglycerine.
Niveau [ni'vo:] *nt* **-s** *(lit, fig)* level. **auf gleichem ~ liegen** to be on the same level; **diese Schule hat ein hohes ~** this school has high standards; **unter ~** below par; **unter meinem ~** beneath me; **ein Hotel mit ~** a hotel with class.
niveau- [ni'vo:]: **~los** *adj* mediocre; **~voll** *adj* high-class.
Nivellierung [nivɛ'li:rʊŋ] *f (Ausgleichung)* levelling out.
nix *indef pron (col)* = **nichts.**
Nixe *f* **-n** water-sprite; *(mit Fischschwanz)* mermaid.
Nizza *nt* Nice.
NO = **Nordosten** NE.
nobel *adj (edelmütig)* noble; *(col) (großzügig)* generous; *(kostspielig)* extravagant; *(elegant)* posh *(col)*. **sich ~ zeigen** *(col)* to be generous.
Nobelpreis *m* Nobel prize.
Nobelpreisträger *m* Nobel prize winner.
noch 1 *adv* **(a)** *(weiterhin, bis jetzt)* still. **~ nicht** still not, not yet; **bist du fertig? — ~ nicht** are you ready? — not yet; **~ immer** still; **~ nie** never; **ich gehe kaum ~ aus** I hardly go out any more; **ich möchte gerne ~ bleiben** I'd like to stay on longer.
(b) *(irgendwann)* some time. **er wird sich (schon) ~ daran gewöhnen** he'll get used to it (one day); **das kann ~ passieren** that might still happen; **er wird ~ kommen** he'll come (yet).
(c) *(eben, nicht später als)* **ich habe ihn ~ vor zwei Tagen gesehen** I saw him only two days ago; **er ist ~ am selben Tag gestorben** he died the very same day; **~ im 18. Jahrhundert** as late as the 18th century; **können Sie das heute ~ erledigen?** can you do it (for) today?
(d) *(einschränkend)* (only) just. **(gerade) ~ gut genug** (only) just good enough.
(e) *(außerdem, zusätzlich)* **wer war ~ da?** who else was there?; **~ etwas Fleisch** some more meat; **~ einer** another (one); **~ einmal** once more; **und es regnete auch ~** and on top of that it was raining.
(f) *(bei Vergleichen)* even, still, yet. **~ größer** even bigger; **das ist ~ besser** that's better still; **seien sie auch ~ so klein** however small they might be.
(g) *(col)* **Geld ~ und ~** *or (hum col)* **~er** heaps and heaps of money *(col)*; **sie hat ~ und ~ versucht, ...** she tried again and again to ...
2 *conj* **weder X ~ Y** neither X nor Y.
nochmalig *adj attr* renewed. **eine ~e Überprüfung** a further check.
nochmals *adv* again.
NOK [ɛnlo:'ka] *nt* = **Nationales Olympisches Komitee.**
Nomade *m (wk)* **-n, -n** *(lit, fig)* nomad.
Nomaden- *in cpds* nomadic; **~tum** *nt* nomadism.
Nomadin *f (lit, fig)* nomad.
nominal *adj* nominal.
Nominal- *in cpds (Gram, Fin)* nominal; **~wert** *m (Fin)* nominal *or* par value.
Nominativ *m* nominative.
nominell *adj* nominal.
nominieren* *vt* to nominate.
nonchalant [nõʃa'lã:] *adj (geh)* nonchalant.
Nonkonformist(in *f*) *m* nonconformist.
nonkonformistisch *adj* nonconformist.
Nonne *f* **-n** nun.
Nonnenkloster *nt* convent, nunnery *(old, hum)*.
Nonplus|ultra *nt no pl (geh)* ultimate.
Nonsens *m no pl* nonsense.
nonstop [nɔn'ʃtɔp, nɔn'stɔp] *adv* non-stop.
Nonstop- *in cpds* non-stop.
Noppe *f* **-n** *(Knoten)* burl; *(Schlinge)* loop.
Nord *no art no pl (Naut, Met, liter)* north.
Nord- *in cpds (Geog)* North; **~amerika** *nt* North America; **n~deutsch** *adj* North German; **~deutschland** *nt* North(ern) Germany.
Norden *m no pl* north; *(von Land)* North. **von ~ her** from the north; **nach ~** north(wards), to the north; **der Balkon liegt nach ~** the balcony faces north(wards).
Nord-: ~england *nt* the North of England; **~irland** *nt* Northern Ireland, Ulster.
nördisch *adj Wälder* northern; *Völker, Sprache* nordic. **~e Kombination** *(Ski)* nordic combined.
Nord-: ~kap *nt* North Cape; **~küste** *f* north(ern) coast; **~länder(in** *f*) *m* **-** Scandinavian.
nördlich 1 *adj* northern; *Wind, Richtung* northerly. **der ~e Polarkreis** the Arctic Circle; **N~es Eismeer** Arctic Ocean; **52 Grad ~er Breite** 52 degrees north. **2** *adv* (to the) north. **~ von Köln (gelegen)** north of Cologne. **3** *prep +gen* (to the) north of.
Nordlicht *nt* northern lights *pl*, aurora borealis.
Nordost *m* north-east. **aus ~** from the north-east.
Nordosten *m* north-east; *(von Land)* North East.
nord|östlich 1 *adj Gegend* north-eastern; *Wind* north-east(erly). **2** *adv* (to the) north-east. **3** *prep +gen* (to the) north-east of.
Nord-Ostsee-Kanal *m* Kiel Canal.
Nordpol *m* North Pole.
Nordpolargebiet *nt* Arctic (Zone).
Nordrhein-Westfalen *nt* North Rhine-Westphalia.
Nordsee *f* North Sea.
Nord-: ~seite *f* north(ern) side; *(von Berg)* north(ern) face; **~stern** *m* North Star, Polar Star.
Nordwest *m* north-west. **aus ~** from the north-west.
Nordwesten *m* north-west; *(von Land)* North-West.
nordwestlich 1 *adj Gegend* north-western; *Wind* north-west(erly). **2** *adv* (to the) north-west. **3** *prep+gen* (to the) north-west of.
Nordwind *m* north wind.
Nörgelei *f* carping, niggling.
nörgeln *vi (an+dat* about) to carp, to niggle.
Nörgler(in *f*) *m* **-** carper, niggler.
Norm *f* **-en (a)** norm; *(Größenvorschrift)* standard (specification). **die ~ sein** to be (considered) normal. **(b)** *(Leistungssoll)* quota, norm. **die ~ erreichen** to achieve one's quota.
normal *adj* normal; *Format, Maß, Gewicht* standard. **bist du noch ~?** *(col)* have you gone mad?
Normal- *in cpds (üblich)* normal; *(genormt)* standard; **~benzin** *nt* two-star (petrol) *(Brit)*, regular (gas) *(US)*.
normalerweise *adv* normally, usually.
Normal-: ~fall *m* normal case; **im ~fall** normally; **~gewicht** *nt* normal weight; *(genormt)* standard weight.

normalisieren* **1** *vt* to normalize. **2** *vr* to return to normal.
Normalisierung *f* normalization.
Normalität *f* normality, normalcy.
Normal-: **~maß** *nt* standard (measure); **~verbraucher** *m* average consumer; **Otto ~verbraucher** *(col)* the average person *or* punter *(col)*, John Doe *(US)*.
Normandie *f* Normandy.
normen, normieren* *vt* to standardize.
Normierung, Normung *f* standardization.
Norwegen *nt* Norway.
Norweger(in *f*) *m* - Norwegian.
norwegisch *adj* Norwegian. **das N~e** Norwegian.
Nostalgie *f* nostalgia.
nostalgisch *adj* nostalgic.
Not *f* ¨-e **(a)** *no pl (Mangel, Elend)* need(iness), poverty. **eine Zeit der ~** a time of need; **aus ~** out of poverty; **~ leiden** to suffer deprivation; **in ~ leben** to live in poverty; **wenn ~ am Mann ist** if you/they *etc* are short *(col)*; *(im Notfall)* in an emergency; **~ macht erfinderisch** *(Prov)* necessity is the mother of invention *(Prov)*.
(b) *(Bedrängnis)* distress *no pl*; *(Problem)* problem. **in seiner ~** in his hour of need; **in unserer ~ blieb uns nichts anderes übrig** in this emergency we had no choice; **jdm seine~ klagen** to tell sb one's troubles; **in ~ sein** to be in distress; **in ~ geraten** to get into serious difficulties.
(c) *no pl (Sorge, Mühe)* difficulty, trouble. **er hat seine liebe ~ mit ihr/damit** he really has problems with her/it.
(d) *(Zwang, Notwendigkeit)* necessity. **etw ohne ~ tun** to do sth without having to; **zur ~** if need(s) be; *(gerade noch)* at a pinch; **aus der ~ eine Tugend machen** to make a virtue (out) of necessity.
not *adj (geh)* **~ tun** to be necessary.
Notar(in *f*) *m* notary.
Notariat *nt* notary's office.
notariell *adj* notarial. **~ beglaubigt** attested by a notary.
Not-: **~arzt** *m* emergency doctor; **~ausgang** *m* emergency exit; **~behelf** *m* stopgap (measure), makeshift; **~bremse** *f* emergency brake, communication cord *(Brit)*; **die ~bremse ziehen** *(Ftbl sl: foulen)* to hack sb down, to commit a blatant foul; **~bremsung** *f* emergency stop.
Notdurft *f no pl (euph geh)* call of nature *(euph)*. **seine ~ verrichten** to relieve oneself.
notdürftig *adj (kaum ausreichend)* meagre *(Brit)*, meager *(US)*; *Kleidung* scanty; *(behelfsmäßig)* makeshift *no adv*, rough and ready *no adv*. **damit Sie sich wenigstens ~ verständigen können** so that you can at least communicate to some extent; **nachdem wir den Reifen ~ geflickt hatten** when we had patched up the tyre in a rough-and-ready way.
Note *f* **-n (a)** *(Mus)* note. **~n** *pl* music; **~n lesen** to read music; **nach ~n spielen** to play from music. **(b)** *(Sch)* mark. **(c)** *(Pol)* note. **(d)** *(Bank~)* (bank)note *(Brit)*, bill *(US)*. **(e)** *no pl (Eigenart) (in bezug auf Gespräch, Brief etc)* note; *(in bezug auf Atmosphäre)* tone, character. **einer Sache** *(dat)* **eine persönliche ~ verleihen** to give sth a personal touch.
Noten-: **~bank** *f* issuing bank; **~blatt** *nt* sheet of music; **~papier** *nt* manuscript paper; **~presse** *f* money press; **~schlüssel** *m* clef; **~schrift** *f* musical notation; **~ständer** *m* music stand.
Notfall *m* emergency. **für den ~ nehme ich einen Schirm mit** I'll take an umbrella (just) in case; **im ~** if need be; **bei einem ~** in case of emergency.
notfalls *adv* if necessary, if need be.
notgedrungen *adv* of necessity. **ich muß mich ~ dazu bereit erklären** I've no choice but to agree.
Notgroschen *m* nest egg.
notieren* **1** *vt* **(a)** *(Notizen machen)* to make a note of; *(schnell)* to jot down. **(b)** *(vormerken) (Comm) Auftrag* to note, to book. **jdn ~** to put sb's name down. **(c)** *(St Ex: festlegen)* to quote *(mit* at*)*. **2** *vi (St Ex: wert sein)* to be quoted *(auf+acc* at*)*.
Notierung *f (Comm)* note; *(St Ex)* quotation.
nötig **1** *adj* necessary. **es ist nicht ~, daß er kommt** it's not necessary for him to come, there's no need for him to come; **wenn ~** if necessary, if need be; **etw ~ haben** to need sth; **er hat das natürlich nicht ~** *(iro)* but, of course, he's different; **ich habe es nicht ~, mich von dir anschreien zu lassen** I don't have to let you shout at me; **du hast es gerade ~, so zu reden** *(col)* you're a fine one to talk *(col)*; **das habe ich nicht ~!** I can do without that; **das N~ste** the (bare) necessities. **2** *adv (dringend)* **etw ~ brauchen** to need something urgently.
nötigen *vt (geh: zwingen)* to compel; *(Jur)* to coerce; *(auffordern)* to urge. **sich ~ lassen** to need urging; **lassen Sie sich nicht (erst) ~!** don't wait to be asked; *siehe* **genötigt.**
nötigenfalls *adv (form)* if necessary.
Nötigung *f (Zwang)* compulsion; *(Jur)* coercion.
Notiz *f* **-en (a)** *(Vermerk)* note; *(Zeitungs~)* item. **sich** *(dat)* **~en machen** to make notes. **(b) ~ nehmen von** to take notice of; **keine ~ nehmen von** to ignore.
Notiz-: **~block** *m* notepad; **~buch** *nt* notebook.
Notlage *f* crisis; *(Elend)* plight. **jds ~** *(acc)* **ausnützen** to exploit sb's situation; **in eine ~ geraten** to get into serious difficulties.
notlanden *pret* **notlandete,** *ptp* **notgelandet** *vi aux sein* to make an emergency landing.
Notlandung *f* emergency landing.
notleidend *adj* needy. **die N~en** the needy.
Not-: **~lösung** *f* compromise solution; *(provisorisch)* temporary solution; **~lüge** *f* white lie.
notorisch *adj* notorious.
Not-: **~ruf** *m (Telec) (Gespräch)* emergency call; *(Nummer)* emergency number; **~rufsäule** *f* emergency telephone; **n~schlachten** *pret* **n~schlachtete,** *ptp* **n~geschlachtet** *vt* to destroy, to put down; **~schlachtung** *f* putting down; **~signal** *nt* distress signal; **~situation** *f* emergency.
Notstand *m* crisis; *(Pol)* state of emergency; *(Jur)* emergency.
Notstands-: **~gebiet** *nt (wirtschaftlich)* depressed area; *(bei Katastrophen)* disaster area; **~gesetze** *pl (Pol)* emergency laws *pl*.
notwassern *pret* **notwasserte,** *ptp* **notgewassert** *vi* to ditch *(Aviat sl)*.
Notwehr *f no pl* self-defence *(Brit)*, self-defense *(US)*. **aus/in ~** in self-defence.
notwendig *adj* necessary. **~ brauchen** to need urgently; **das N~ste** the (bare) essentials.
notwendigerweise *adv* of necessity, inevitably.
Notwendigkeit *f* necessity. **die ~, etw zu tun** the necessity of doing sth.
Notzucht *f (Jur)* rape.
Nougat ['nu:gat] *m on nt* **-s** nougat.
Novelle [no'vɛlə] *f* **(a)** novella. **(b)** *(Pol)* amendment.
November [no'vɛmbɐ] *m* - November; *siehe* **März.**
Novize [no'vi:tsə] *m (wk)* **-n, -n, Novizin** *f* novice.
Novum ['no:vʊm] *nt, pl* **Nova** ['no:va] novelty.
NPD [ɛnpe:'de:] *f* = **Nationaldemokratische Partei Deutschlands.**
Nr. = **Nummer** No.
NS- [ɛn'|ɛs-] *in cpds* Nazi.
Nuance [ny'ã:sə] *f* **-n** nuance; *(Kleinigkeit)* shade. **um eine ~ zu laut** a shade too loud.
nüchtern *adj* **(a)** *(ohne Essen)* **eine Medizin ~ einnehmen** to take a medicine on an empty stomach; **mit ~em/auf ~en Magen** with/on an

empty stomach. **(b)** *(nicht betrunken)* sober. **wieder ~ werden** to sober up. **(c)** *(schmucklos)* sober; *(sachlich)* down-to-earth *no adv*, rational; *Zahlen, Tatsachen* bare, plain.

Nüchternheit *f* **(a)** *(Unbetrunkenheit)* soberness, sobriety. **(b)** *(Schmucklosigkeit)* soberness; *(Sachlichkeit)* rationality.

nuckeln *vi (col) (Mensch)* to suck *(an +dat* at*)*; *(Tier)* to suckle *(an +dat* from*)*. **am Daumen ~** to suck one's thumb.

Nudel *f* **-n** *usu pl* **(a)** *(als Beilage)* pasta *no pl*; *(als Suppeneinlage)* noodle. **(b)** *(col: Mensch) (dick)* dumpling *(col)*; *(komisch)* character.

Nudel-: **~brett** *nt* pastryboard; **~holz** *nt* rolling pin; **~suppe** *f* noodle soup.

Nudismus *m* nudism.

Nudist(in *f)* *m* nudist.

Nugat *m or nt* **-s** nougat.

nuklear *adj attr* nuclear.

Null *f* **-en** **(a)** *(Zahl)* nought, zero; *(Gefrierpunkt)* zero. **die ~** the figure nought, zero; **gleich ~ sein** to be absolutely nil; **in ~ Komma nichts** *(col)* in less than no time; **seine Stimmung sank auf ~** *(col)* his mood sank; **im Jahre ~** in the year nought; **die Stunde ~** the new starting point. **(b)** *(col: Mensch)* dead loss *(col)*.

Null *num* zero; *(Telec)* O [əʊ] *(Brit)*, zero *(US)*; *(Sport)* nil; *(Tennis)* love. **~ Komma eins** (nought) point one; **es ist ~ Uhr zehn** it's ten past midnight; **~ Grad** zero degrees; **~ Fehler** no *or* zero *(col)* mistakes; **es steht ~ zu ~** there's no score; **das Spiel wurde ~ zu ~ beendet** the game was a goalless draw; **~ und nichtig** *(Jur)* null and void.

null|achtfünfzehn *(col)* **1** *adj pred* run-of-the-mill *(col)*. **2** *adv* in a run-of-the-mill way.

Null|achtfünfzehn- *in cpds (col)* run-of-the-mill.

Nullpunkt *m* zero. **die Stimmung sank unter den ~** the atmosphere froze; **auf dem ~ angekommen sein** *(fig)* to have reached rock-bottom.

Null-: **~stellung** *f* zero position; **in der ~stellung sein** to be on zero; **~tarif** *m (für Verkehrsmittel)* free travel; **... gibt es nicht zum ~tarif** *(fig)* you can't have ... for nothing; **~wachstum** *nt (Econ)* zero growth.

numerieren* *vt* to number.

numerisch *adj* numeric(al).

Numerus *m, pl* **Numeri** *(Gram)* number. **~ clausus** *(Univ)* restricted entry.

Nummer *f* **-n** number; *(Größe)* size; *(col: Mensch)* character; *(col!: Koitus)* screw *(col!)*. **unser Haus hat die ~ 25** our house is number 25; **nur eine ~ unter vielen sein** *(fig)* to be a cog (in the machine); **auf ~ Sicher gehen** *(col)* to play (it) safe; **eine ~ abziehen** *(col)* to put on an act.

Nummern-: **~konto** *nt* numbered bank account; **~schild** *nt (Aut)* number plate, registration plate *(Brit)*, license plate *(US)*.

nun *adv* **(a)** *(jetzt)* now. **von ~ an** from now on, from here on in *(US)*; **~ erst** only now; **~ endlich** (now) at last; **was ~?** what now?; **was ~ (schon wieder)?** what (is it) now? **(b) er will ~ mal nicht** he simply doesn't want to; **~, wenn's unbedingt sein muß** well, if I/you *etc* really must; **das ist ~ (ein)mal so** that's just the way things are; **~ ja, aber ...** OK *(col)*, but ...; **~ ja** well yes; **~ gut** (well) all right, (well) OK *(col)*; **~ erst recht!** just for that (I'll do it)! **(c)** *(bei Fragen)* **~?** well?; **~, wird's bald?** *(col)* come on then.

nunmehr *adv (geh) (jetzt)* now, at this point; *(von jetzt an)* henceforth *(form)*, from now on.

nur *adv* **(a)** *(einschränkend)* only, just. **ich habe ~ ein Stück Brot gegessen** I've only eaten a piece of bread; **alle, ~ ich nicht** everyone but me; **~ schade, daß ...** it's just a pity that ...; **~ daß** it's just that, only; **~ noch zwei Minuten** just another two minutes; **nicht ~ ..., sondern auch** not only ... but also; **alles, ~ das nicht!** anything but that!; **warum möchtest du das denn wissen? — ach, ~ so!** why do you want to know? — oh no special reason; **ich hab' das ~ so gesagt** I was just talking.

(b) *(mit Fragepronomen)* -ever. **warum sie ~ dahin geht?** why ever does she go there?; **wie kannst du ~ (so etwas sagen)?** how could you (say such a thing)?; **sie bekommt alles, was sie ~ will** she gets whatever she wants.

(c) wenn (...) ~ if only; **wenn er ~ (erst) käme** if only he would come; **es wird klappen, wenn er ~ nicht die Nerven verliert** it will be all right as long as he doesn't lose his nerve.

(d) sagen Sie das ~ nicht Ihrer Frau! don't tell your wife (whatever you do); **geh ~!** go on; **~ zu!** go on; **sieh ~** just look; **~ her damit!** *(col)* let's have it; **Sie brauchen es ~ zu sagen** just say (the word); **er soll ~ lachen!** let him laugh.

Nürnberg *nt* Nuremberg.

nuscheln *vti (col)* to mutter, to mumble.

Nuß *f, pl* **Nüsse** **(a)** nut. **(b)** *(col: Mensch)* **eine taube ~** a dead loss *(col)*; **eine doofe ~** a stupid twit *(Brit col) or* clown *(col)*.

Nuß-: **~baum** *m (Baum)* walnut tree; *(Holz)* walnut; **~knacker** *m* nutcracker; **~schale** *f* nutshell; *(fig: Boot)* cockleshell.

Nüster *f* **-n** nostril.

Nut *f* **-en** *(spec)*, **Nute** *f* **-n** groove.

Nutte *f* **-n** *(pej, col!)* tart *(col)*, hooker *(esp US col)*.

nutzbar *adj* us(e)able; *Bodenschätze* exploitable. **~ machen** to make us(e)able; *Sonnenenergie* to harness; *Bodenschätze* to exploit.

Nutzbarmachung *f* utilization; *(von Bodenschätzen)* exploitation.

nutzbringend *adj* profitable. **etw ~ anwenden** to use sth to good effect, to put sth to good use.

nütze *adj pred* **zu etw/nichts ~ sein** to be useful for sth/to be no use for anything.

Nutzen *m* **-** **(a)** use; *(Nützlichkeit)* usefulness. **zum ~ der Öffentlichkeit** for the benefit of the public; **jdm von ~ sein** to be of use to sb. **(b)** *(Vorteil)* advantage, benefit; *(Gewinn)* profit. **jdm ~ bringen** *(Vorteil)* to be of advantage to sb; *(Gewinn)* to bring sb profit; **von etw ~ haben** to profit by sth.

nutzen, nützen **1** *vi* to be of use *(jdm zu etw* to sb for sth*)*. **die Ermahnungen haben genützt/nichts genützt** the warnings had the desired effect/didn't do any good; **da nützt alles nichts** there's nothing to be done; **das nützt (mir/dir) nichts** that won't help (me/you); **wozu soll das alles ~?** what's the point of that? **2** *vt* to make use of; *Gelegenheit* to take advantage of.

Nutz-: **~fahrzeug** *nt* farm vehicle; military vehicle *etc*; *(Comm)* commercial vehicle; **~fläche** *f* us(e)able floor space; *(Agr)* (agriculturally) productive land; **~last** *f* maximum load.

nützlich *adj* useful; *Hinweis, Buch auch* helpful. **~ für die Gesundheit** beneficial for the health; **sich ~ machen** to make oneself useful.

Nützlichkeit *f* usefulness, utility *(form)*.

nutzlos *adj* **(a)** useless; *(vergeblich)* futile, vain *attr*, in vain *pred*. **es ist völlig ~, das zu tun** it's absolutely pointless doing that. **(b)** *(unnötig)* needless. **sein Leben ~ aufs Spiel setzen** to risk one's life needlessly *or* unnecessarily.

Nutzlosigkeit *f* uselessness; *(Vergeblichkeit)* futility.

Nutznießer(in *f)* *m* **-** beneficiary.

Nutzung *f (Gebrauch)* use; *(das Ausnutzen)* exploitation. **ich habe ihm meinen Garten zur ~ überlassen** I gave him the use of my garden.

NW = Nordwesten NW.

Nylon ® ['nailɔn] *nt no pl* nylon.

Nylonstrumpf ['nailɔn-] *m* nylon (stocking).

Nymphe ['nʏmfə] *f* **-n** nymph.

Nymphomanin [nʏmfo-] *f* nymphomaniac, nympho *(col)*.

O

O, o [oː] *nt* **-, -** O, o.
O = Osten.
o *interj* oh.
O|ase *f* **-n, -n** oasis; *(fig)* haven, oasis.
ob *conj* **(a)** *(indirekte Frage)* if, whether. **Sie müssen kommen, ~ Sie (nun) wollen oder nicht** like it or not, you have to come; **~ er (wohl) morgen kommt?** I wonder if he'll come tomorrow; **~ wir jetzt Pause machen?** shall we have a break now?; **~ ich nicht lieber gehe?** maybe I'd better go; **~ Sie mir wohl mal helfen können?** I wonder if you could help me. **(b)** *(verstärkend)* **und ~** *(col)* you bet *(col)*; **und ~ ich das gesehen habe!** you bet I saw it! *(col)* **(c)** *(vergleichend)* **als ~** as if; **(so) tun als ~** *(col)* to pretend; **tu nicht so als ~!** stop pretending!
OB [oːˈbəː] *m* **-s = Oberbürgermeister.**
o.B. = ohne Befund.
Obacht *f no pl (esp S Ger)* **~!** watch out!, careful!; **~ geben auf** *(+acc) (aufmerken)* to pay attention to; *(bewachen)* to keep an eye on.
Obdach *nt no pl (geh)* shelter. **jdm ~ gewähren** to offer sb shelter; **kein ~ haben** to be homeless.
Obdach-: o~los *adj* homeless; **o~los werden** to be made homeless; **~lose(r)** *mf decl as adj* homeless person; **die ~losen** the homeless.
Obdachlosen-: ~asyl, ~heim *nt* hostel *or* shelter for the homeless; **~siedlung** *f* settlement for the homeless.
Obdachlosigkeit *f* homelessness.
Obduktion *f* post-mortem, autopsy.
obduzieren* *vt* to do a post-mortem *or* autopsy on.
O-Beine *pl (col)* bow *or* bandy legs *pl*.
oben *adv* **(a)** *(am oberen Ende)* at the top; *(an der Oberfläche)* on the surface; *(im Hause)* upstairs; *(in der Höhe)* up. **~ und unten (von etw) verwechseln** to get sth upside down; **wo ist ~ (bei dem Bild)?** which is the right way up (for the picture)?; **wir wohnen rechts ~** *or* **~ rechts** we live on the top floor to the right; **die Abbildung ~ links** *or* **links ~** the illustration in the top left-hand corner; **der ist ~ nicht ganz richtig** *(col)* he's not quite right up top *(col)*; **~ ohne gehen** *or* **tragen** *(col)* to be topless; **ganz ~** right at the top; **hier/dort ~** up here/there; **die ganze Sache steht mir bis hier ~** *(col)* I'm fed up to the back teeth with the whole thing *(col)*; **bis ~ (hin)** to the top; **hoch ~** high (up) above; **weiter ~** nearer the top; **~ auf dem Berg/der Leiter/dem Dach** on top of the mountain/ladder/roof; **~ am Himmel/im Norden** up in the sky/north; **nach ~** up, upwards; *(im Hause)* upstairs; **der Fahrstuhl fährt nach ~** the lift is going up; **der Weg nach ~** *(fig)* the road to the top; **endlich hat sie den Weg nach ~ geschafft** *(fig)* she finally made it (to the top); **nach ~ zu** *or* **hin** towards the top; **von ~ hat man eine schöne Aussicht** there's a nice view from the top; **von ~ bis unten** from top to bottom; *(von Mensch)* from top to toe; **jdn von ~ bis unten mustern** to look sb up and down; **jdn von ~ herab behandeln** to treat sb condescendingly; **weiter ~** further up.
(b) *(col: die Vorgesetzten)* **die da ~** the powers that be *(col)*; **das wird ~ entschieden** that's decided higher up; **etw nach ~ (weiter)melden** to report sth to a superior; **der Befehl kommt von ~** it's orders from above. **(c)** *(vorher)* above. **siehe ~** see above; **wie ~ erwähnt** as mentioned above; **der weiter ~ erwähnte Fall** the case referred to above.
oben-: ~an *adv* at the top *or* on (the) top; **~auf** *adv* on (the) top; **gestern war er krank, aber heute ist er wieder ~auf** *(col)* he wasn't well yesterday, but he's back on form today; **~drauf** *adv (col)* on top; **~drein** *adv (col)* on top of everything *(col)*; **~erwähnt, ~genannt** *adj attr* above-mentioned; **~hin** *adv* **etw nur so ~hin sagen** to say sth in an offhand way.
Ober *m* **-** *(Kellner)* waiter. **Herr ~!** waiter!
Ober-: ~arm *m* upper arm; **~arzt** *m* senior physician; **~aufseher** *m* (head) supervisor; *(im Gefängnis)* head warden *(Brit) or* guard *(US)*; **~aufsicht** *f* supervision; **die ~aufsicht haben** to have overall control *(über +acc* of*)*; **~befehl** *m (Mil)* **den ~befehl haben** to be in supreme command *(über +acc* of*)*; **~befehlshaber** *m (Mil)* commander-in-chief; **~begriff** *m* generic term; **~bekleidung** *f* outer clothing; **~bett** *nt* quilt; **~bürgermeister** *m* mayor; **~deck** *nt* upper *or* top deck.
obere(r, s) *adj attr Ende, Stockwerke, (Schul)klassen* upper, top. **die O~n** *(col)* the bosses; **die ~en Zehntausend** *(col)* high society.
Oberfläche *f* surface; *(Tech, Math)* surface area. **an die ~ kommen** *(lit)* to surface; *(fig)* to emerge; **an der ~ bleiben** *(lit)* to remain on the surface; **sein Referat blieb völlig an der ~** his paper only scratched the surface.
oberflächlich *adj* superficial. **~e Verletzung** surface wound; **bei ~er Betrachtung** at a quick glance; **seine Kenntnisse sind nur ~** his knowledge doesn't go beyond the surface; **~ arbeiten** to work superficially; **etw ~ lesen** to skim through sth; **jdn (nur) ~ kennen** to know sb (only) slightly; **nach ~er Schätzung** at a rough guess.
Oberflächlichkeit *f* superficiality.
Ober-: o~gärig *adj Bier* top fermented; **~geschoß** *nt* top floor; **im zweiten ~geschoß** on the second *(Brit) or* third *(US)* floor; **o~halb 1** *prep +gen* above; **2** *adv* above; **o~halb von Basel** above Basel; **weiter o~halb** further *or* higher up; **~hand** *f (fig)* upper hand; **die ~hand gewinnen** to get the upper hand *(über +acc* over*)*; **~haupt** *nt (Repräsentant)* head; *(Anführer)* leader; **~haus** *nt (Pol)* upper house; *(in GB)* House of Lords; **~hemd** *nt* shirt; **~herrschaft, ~hoheit** *f* sovereignty.
Oberin *f* **(a)** *(im Krankenhaus)* **= Oberschwester.** **(b)** *(Eccl)* Mother Superior.
Ober-: o~irdisch *adj* above ground; **~kellner** *m* head waiter; **~kiefer** *m* upper jaw; **~kommando** *nt (~befehl)* Supreme Command; *(Befehlsstab)* headquarters *pl*; **~körper** *m* upper part of the body; **mit bloßem** *or* **nacktem ~körper** stripped to the waist; **~lauf** *m* **am ~lauf des Rheins** in the upper reaches of the Rhine; **~leder** *nt* (leather) uppers *pl*: **~leitung** *f (Elec)* overhead cable; **~leutnant** *m* lieutenant *(Brit)*, first lieutenant *(US)*; *(Luftwaffe)* flying officer *(Brit)*, first lieutenant *(US)*; **~licht** *nt (hochgelegenes Fenster)*

small, high window; *(Lüftungsklappe, über einer Tür)* fanlight, transom (window); **~liga** *f (Sport)* top *or* first league; **~lippe** *f* upper lip; **~schenkel** *m* thigh; **~schicht** *f* top layer; *(Sociol)* upper strata (of society) *pl*; **~schwester** *f* senior nursing officer; *(von Station)* sister; **~seite** *f* top (side).

Oberst *m (wk)* **-en, -e(n)** **(a)** *(Heer)* colonel. **(b)** *(Luftwaffe)* group captain *(Brit)*, colonel *(US)*.

oberste(r, s) *adj* **(a)** *(ganz oben) Stockwerk, Schicht* uppermost, very top. **(b)** *Gesetz, Prinzip* supreme; *Dienstgrad* most senior. **O~er Gerichtshof** supreme court; *(in GB)* High Court (of Justice); *(in USA)* Supreme Court.

Ober-: **~stübchen** *nt (col)*: **er ist nicht ganz richtig im ~stübchen** he's not quite right up top *(col)*; **~studienrat** *m* senior teacher; **~stufe** *f* upper school; *(Univ)* advanced level; **~teil** *nt or m* upper part, top; **~trottel** *m (col)* prize idiot; **~verwaltungsgericht** *nt* Higher Administrative Court; **~wasser** *nt (fig col)* **sobald sein älterer Bruder dabei ist, hat er ~wasser** as soon as his elder brother is there he opens up; **~weite** *f* bust measurement.

obgleich *conj* although, (even) though.

Obhut *f no pl (geh)* care. **jdn/etw jds ~** *(dat)* **anvertrauen** to place sb/sth in sb's care.

obige(r, s) *adj attr* above. **der O~** *(form)* the above *(form)*.

Objekt *nt* **-e** *(auch Gram)* object. **das ~ der Untersuchung** the object under examination.

objektiv *adj* objective. **~ über etw** *(acc)* **urteilen** to judge sth objectively.

Objektiv *nt* (object) lens, objective.

Objektivität *f* objectivity. **sich um größte ~ bemühen** to try to be as objective as possible.

Objektsatz *m* object clause.

Oblate *f* **-n** wafer; *(Eccl)* host.

Obligation *f (auch Fin)* obligation.

obligatorisch *adj* obligatory; *Fächer, Vorlesung* compulsory; *Qualifikationen* necessary.

Oboe [o'boːə] *f* **-n** oboe.

Oboist [obo'ɪst] *m (wk)* oboist, oboe player.

Obolus *m* **-se** contribution.

Obrigkeit *f* **(a)** *(als Begriff)* authority. **(b)** *(Behörden)* **die ~** the authorities *pl*.

Obrigkeits-: **~denken** *nt* acceptance of authority; **~staat** *m* authoritarian state.

Obrist *m (wk)* colonel.

obschon *conj (liter)* although.

Observatorium [ɔpzɛrva'toːriʊm] *nt* observatory.

obskur *adj* obscure; *(fragwürdig)* suspect, dubious.

Obst *nt no pl* fruit.

Obst-: **~(an)bau** *m* fruit-growing; **~baum** *m* fruit-tree; **~garten** *m* orchard; **~händler** *m* fruit merchant; **~kuchen** *m* fruit flan.

Obstruktion *f (Pol)* obstruction, filibuster. **~ betreiben** to obstruct, to filibuster.

Obst-: **~saft** *m* fruit juice; **~torte** *f* fruit flan.

obszön *adj* obscene.

Obszönität *f* obscenity.

Obus *m* **-se** *(col)* trolley bus.

obwohl *conj* although, (even) though.

Ochse ['ɔksə] *m (wk)* **-n, -n** **(a)** ox, bullock. **~ am Spieß** roast ox; **er stand da wie der ~ vorm Berg** *(col)* he stood there utterly bewildered. **(b)** *(col: Dummkopf)* twit *(Brit col)*, clown *(col)*.

ochsen ['ɔksn] *(Sch sl) vti* to mug up *(col)*.

Ochsen- ['ɔksn-]: **~schwanzsuppe** *f* oxtail soup; **~tour** *f (col: Schinderei)* slog *(col)*.

Ocker *m or nt* **-** ochre *(Brit)*, ocher *(US)*.

ocker-: **~braun, ~gelb** *adj* ochre *(Brit)*, ocher *(US)*.

od. = oder.

Ode *f* **-n** ode.

öd(e) *adj* **(a)** *(verlassen) Stadt, Strand* deserted, empty; *(unbewohnt)* desolate, bleak; *(unbebaut)* waste. **öd und leer** dreary and desolate. **(b)** *(fig: fade)* dreary, tedious; *Dasein* barren.

Öde *f* **-n** *(liter)* **(a)** *(einsame Gegend)* waste(land). **(b)** *(Langeweile)* dreariness, monotony.

oder *conj* **(a)** or. **~ aber** or else; **~ auch** or even; **eins ~ das andere** one or the other; **entweder ... ~** either ... or. **(b)** *(in Fragen)* **so war's doch, ~ nicht?** that was what happened, wasn't it?; **du kommst doch, ~?** you're coming, aren't you?; **lassen wir es so, ~?** let's leave it at that, OK?

Ödipuskomplex *m* Oedipus complex.

Odyssee *f* **-n** [-eːən] *(Liter)* Odyssey; *(fig)* odyssey.

Ofen *m* **¨** **(a)** *(Heiz~)* heater; *(Elektro~, Gas~ auch)* fire; *(Kohle~)* stove. **hinter dem ~ hocken** to be a stay-at-home; **jetzt ist der ~ aus** *(col)* that does it *(col)*. **(b)** *(Herd)* oven, stove; *(Back~)* oven. **(c)** *(Tech)* furnace, oven; *(Brenn~)* kiln; *(Hoch~)* blast furnace.

Ofen-: **o~fertig** *adj Gericht* oven ready; **o~frisch** *adj Brot* oven fresh; **~heizung** *f* stove heating; **~rohr** *nt* stovepipe; **~schirm** *m* firescreen.

offen *adj (lit, fig)* open; *Bein* ulcerated; *Flamme* naked; *Stelle* vacant; *Rechnung* outstanding. **ein ~er Brief** an open letter; **die Haare ~ tragen** to wear one's hair loose; **der Laden hat bis 7 Uhr ~** the shop stays open until 7 o'clock; **~er Wein** wine by the carafe/glass; *(vom Faß)* wine on draught *(Brit) or* draft *(US)*; **auf ~er Strecke** *(Straße)* on the open road; *(Rail)* between stations; **auf ~er Straße** in the middle of the street; *(Landstraße)* on the open road; **auf ~er See** on the open sea; **Beifall auf ~er Szene** an outburst of applause; **mit ~em Munde dastehen** *(fig)* to stand gaping; **~e Türen einrennen** *(fig)* to kick at an open door; **Tag der ~en Tür** open day; **jdn mit ~en Armen empfangen** to welcome sb with open arms; **allem Neuen gegenüber ~ sein** to be receptive *or* open to (all) new ideas; **~e Handelsgesellschaft** general partnership; **~e Stellen** vacancies; **die Entscheidung ist noch ~** nothing has been decided yet; **~ gestanden** *or* **gesagt** quite honestly; **etw ~ zugeben** to admit sth frankly; **seine Meinung ~ sagen** to speak one's mind; **~ mit jdm reden** to be frank with sb.

offenbar 1 *adj* obvious. **sein Zögern machte ~, daß ...** it was obvious from the way he hesitated that ...; **~ werden** to become obvious. **2** *adv (vermutlich)* apparently. **er hat ~ den Zug verpaßt** he must have missed the train; **da haben Sie sich ~ geirrt** you seem to have made a mistake.

offenbaren* 1 *vt* to reveal. **2** *vr* to reveal itself/oneself. **sich als etw ~** to show oneself to be sth; **sich jdm ~** to reveal oneself to sb.

Offenbarung *f* revelation.

Offenbarungs|eid *m (Jur)* oath of disclosure, sworn statement in bankruptcy cases. **den ~ leisten** *(lit)* to swear an oath of disclosure.

offen-: **~bleiben** *vi sep irreg aux sein* to remain open; **alle ~gebliebenen Probleme** all unsolved problems; **~halten** *vt sep irreg* to keep open.

Offenheit *f* openness, frankness.

offen-: **~herzig** *adj* open, frank; *(hum col) Kleid* revealing; **O~herzigkeit** *f* openness, frankness; **~kundig** *adj* obvious; *Beweise* clear; **~lassen** *vt sep irreg* to leave open; **~sichtlich** *adj* obvious; *Irrtum, Lüge auch* blatant.

offensiv *adj* offensive.

Offensive *f* offensive. **in die ~ gehen** to take the offensive.

offenstehen *vi sep irreg* **(a)** *(Tür, Fenster)* to be open. **(b)** *(Comm: Rechnung, Betrag)* to be outstanding. **(c)** **jdm ~** *(fig: zugänglich sein)* to be open to sb; **die (ganze) Welt steht ihm offen** he has the (whole) world at his feet; **es steht ihr offen, sich uns anzuschließen** she's free to join us.

öffentlich *adj* public. **etw ~ bekanntmachen** to make sth public; **eine Persönlichkeit des ~en Lebens** a person in public life; **jdn ~ beschul-**

digen to accuse sb publicly; **die ~e Meinung/Moral** public opinion/morality; **die ~e Ordnung** law and order; **~es Recht** *(Jur)* public law; **Anstalt des ~en Rechts** public institution; **~e Schule** state school, public school *(US)*; **die ~e Hand** (central/local) government; **Ausgaben der ~en Hand** public spending.

Öffentlichkeit *f (Allgemeinheit)* the (general) public. **die ~ scheuen** to shun publicity; **in aller ~** in public; **unter Ausschluß der ~** in private; *(Jur)* in camera; **als er das erstemal vor die ~ trat** when he made his first public appearance; **etw vor die ~ bringen** to bring sth before the public; **an die ~ gelangen** to become known; **die ~ einer Versammlung herstellen** to make a meeting public.

Öffentlichkeits|arbeit *f* public relations work.

öffentlich-rechtlich *adj attr* (under) public law.

Offerte *f* **-n** *(Comm)* offer; *(für Auftrag)* tender.

offiziell *adj* official.**wie von ~er Seite verlautet** according to official sources.

Offizier *m* **-e** officer.

Offiziers-: ~anwärter *m* officer cadet; **~kasino** *nt* officers' mess; **~korps** *nt* officer corps; **~messe** *f* officers' mess.

öffnen 1 *vti* to open. **jdm den Blick für etw ~** to open sb's eyes to sth; **es hat geklingelt, könnten Sie mal ~?** that was the doorbell, would you answer it? **2** *vr (Tür, Blume, Augen)* to open; *(weiter werden)* to open out. **das Tal öffnet sich nach Süden** the valley opens to the south.

Öffner *m* **-** opener.

Öffnung *f* opening. **die ~ nach links** *(Pol)* the swing to the left.

Öffnungszeiten *pl* opening hours *pl*; *(von Geschäft)* hours of business *pl*.

Offsetdruck ['ɔfsɛt-] *m* offset (printing).

oft *adv comp* **¨er**, *superl* **am ¨esten** *(häufig)* often, frequently. **schon so ~, ~ genug** often enough; **wie ~ fährt der Bus?** how often does the bus go?; **wie ~ warst du schon in Deutschland?** how many times have you been to Germany?; **des ¨eren** quite frequently; **je ¨er ...** the more often ...

öfter(s) *adv* (every) now and then. **~ mal was Neues** *(col)* variety is the spice of life *(prov)*.

oftmals *adv (geh)* often, oft *(poet)*.

oh *interj* oh.

OHG = offene Handelsgesellschaft.

ohne 1 *prep +acc* **(a)** without. **~ Auto** without a car; **~ (die) Vororte hat die Stadt 100.000 Einwohner** the city has 100,000 inhabitants not counting the suburbs; **~ mich!** count me out!; **die Sache ist (gar) nicht (so) ~** *(col) (interessant)* it's not bad; *(schwierig)* it's not that easy *(col)*.
(b) ich hätte das ~ weiteres getan I'd have done it without a second thought; **ja, das kann man ~ weiteres sagen** yes, that's true enough; **ich würde ~ weiteres sagen, daß ...** I would not hesitate to say that ...; **das Darlehen ist ~ weiteres bewilligt worden** the loan was granted without any problem; **ihm können Sie ~ weiteres vertrauen** you can trust him implicitly; **das läßt sich ~ weiteres arrangieren** that can easily be arranged; **das kann man nicht ~ weiteres voraussetzen** you can't just assume that automatically.
2 *conj* **~ zu zögern** without hesitating; **~ daß ich ihn darum gebeten hätte** without my *or* me asking him.

ohne-: ~dies *adv siehe* **~hin; ~einander** *adv* without each other; **~gleichen** *adj inv* unparalleled; **ein Erfolg ~gleichen** an unparalleled success; **diese Frechheit ist ~gleichen!** I've never known such a cheek!; **~hin** *adv* anyway; **wir sind ~hin zu viel Leute** there are too many of us as it is; **es ist ~hin schon spät** it's late enough already.

Ohnmacht *f* **-en** *(Med)* faint; *(Machtlosigkeit)* helplessness. **in ~ fallen** to faint.

ohnmächtig *adj (bewußtlos)* unconscious; *(machtlos)* powerless, helpless. **~ werden** to faint, to pass out; **~e Wut, ~er Zorn** helpless rage; **einer Sache** *(dat)* **~ gegenüberstehen** to be helpless in the face of sth; **~ zusehen müssen** to look on helplessly.

Ohnmachts|anfall *m (lit, fig)* fainting fit. **als ich das hörte, habe ich fast einen ~ bekommen** *(col)* when I heard that I nearly passed out.

oho *interj* oho, hello.

Ohr *nt* **-en** ear. **seine ~en sind nicht mehr so gut** his hearing isn't too good any more; **auf einem ~ taub sein** to be deaf in one ear; **auf dem ~ bin ich taub** *(fig)* nothing doing *(col)*; **bei jdm ein offenes ~ finden** to find sb a sympathetic listener; **die ~en anlegen** *(Hund)* to put its ears back; *(fig col)* to brace oneself; **mach** *or* **sperr die ~en auf!** *(col)* clean your ears out *(col)*; **jdm die ~en volljammern** *(col)* to keep moaning at sb; **ganz ~ sein** *(hum)* to be all ears; **sich aufs ~ legen** *or* **hauen** *(col)* to kip down *(col)*; **sitzt er auf seinen ~en?** *(col)* is he deaf or something?; **jdm die ~en langziehen** *(col)* to tweak sb's ear(s); **jdm etw um die ~en hauen** *(col)* to hit sb over the head with sth; **schreib es dir hinter die ~en** *(col)* will you (finally) get that into your (thick) head *(col)*; **noch nicht trocken hinter den ~en sein** to be still wet behind the ears; **die Melodie geht ins ~** the tune is very catchy; **du hast wohl Watte in den ~en!** *(col)* are you deaf or something?; **ich habe seine Worte noch deutlich im ~** I can still hear his words clearly; **jdm in den ~en liegen** to keep on at sb *(col)*; **jdn übers ~ hauen** to pull a fast one on sb *(col)*; **bis über die** *or* **beide ~en verliebt sein** to be head over heels in love; **viel um die ~en haben** *(col)* to have a lot on (one's plate) *(col)*; **es ist mir zu ~en gekommen** it has come to my ears *(form)*; **das geht zum einen ~ hinein und zum anderen wieder hinaus** *(col)* it goes in one ear and out the other *(col)*; **halt die ~en steif!** take care.

Öhr *nt* **-e** eye.

Ohren-: ~arzt *m* ear specialist; **o~betäubend** *adj (fig)* earsplitting; **~sausen** *nt (Med)* buzzing in one's ears; **~schmalz** *nt* earwax; **~schmaus** *m* **das Konzert war ein richtiger ~schmaus** the concert was a feast for the ears; **~schmerzen** *pl* earache; **~schützer** *pl* earmuffs *pl*; **~sessel** *m* wing chair.

Ohrfeige *f* **-n** slap (on *or* around the face); *(als Strafe)* box on the ears. **jdm eine ~ geben** *or* **verabreichen** to slap sb's face; **eine ~ bekommen** to get a slap around the face.

ohrfeigen *vt insep* **jdn ~** to box sb's ears; **ich könnte mich selbst ~, daß ich das gemacht habe** I could kick myself for doing it.

Ohr-: ~läppchen *nt* (ear) lobe; **~muschel** *f* (outer) ear; **~ring** *m* earring; **~wurm** *m* earwig; **die Platte ist ein richtiger ~wurm** *(col)* that's a really catchy record *(col)*.

oje, ojemine *interj* oh dear.

Okkultismus *m* occultism.

Okkupation *f* occupation.

okkupieren* *vt* to occupy.

Öko- *in cpds* eco; **~bauer** *m (col)* ecologically-minded farmer.

Ökologe *m*, **Ökologin** *f* ecologist.

Ökologie *f* ecology.

ökologisch *adj* ecological, environmental.

Ökonomie *f* economy; *(als Wissenschaft)* economics *sing*. **politische ~ studieren** to study political economy.

ökonomisch *adj* economic; *(sparsam)* economical.

Ökosystem *nt* ecosystem.

Oktanzahl *f* octane rating. **Benzin mit einer hohen ~** high octane petrol.

Oktave [ɔk'ta:və] *f* **-n** octave.
Oktett *nt* **-e** octet.
Oktober *m* - October; *siehe* **März.**
ökumenisch *adj* ecumenical.
Öl *nt* **-e** oil. **auf ~ stoßen** to strike oil; **~ fördern** to extract oil; **in ~ malen** to paint in oils; **~ ins Feuer gießen** *(prov)* to add fuel to the fire *(prov)*.
Öl-: **~baum** *m* olive tree; **~bild** *nt* oil painting, oil; **~bohrung** *f* oil drilling.
Oldtimer ['ouldtaimɐ] *m* - *(Auto)* veteran car.
ölen *vt* to oil. **wie geölt** *(col)* like clockwork *(col)*; **wie ein geölter Blitz** *(col)* like greased lightning *(col)*.
Öl-: **~farbe** *f* oil-based paint; *(Art)* oil (paint); **mit ~farben malen** to paint in oils; **~feld** *nt* oil field; **~film** *m* film of oil; **~gemälde** *nt* oil painting; **~götze** *m (col)* **wie ein ~götze** like a tailor's dummy *(col)*; **~heizung** *f* oil-fired central heating.
ölig *adj* oily; *(fig auch)* greasy.
Oligarchie *f* oligarchy.
oliv *adj pred* olive(-green).
Olive [o'li:və] *f* **-n** olive.
Oliven-: **~baum** *m* olive tree; **~öl** *nt* olive oil.
olivgrün *adj* olive-green.
Öl-: **~jacke** *f* oilskin jacket; **~kännchen** *nt*, **~kanne** *f* oil can.
oll *adj (NGer col)* old. **das sind ~e Kamellen** *(col)* that's old hat *(col)*.
Öl-: **~malerei** *f* oil painting; **~meßstab** *m (Aut)* dip stick; **~ofen** *m* oil heater; **~plattform** *f* oil-rig; **ö~reich** *adj* oil-rich; **~sardine** *f* sardine; **wie die ~sardinen** *(col)* crammed in like sardines *(col)*; **~scheich** *m* oil sheik; **~spur** *f* patch of oil; **~stand** *m* oil level; **~standsanzeiger** *m* oil pressure gauge; **~teppich** *m* oil slick.
Ölung *f* oiling. **die Letzte ~** *(Eccl)* extreme unction.
Öl-: **~vorkommen** *nt* oil deposit; **~wanne** *f (Aut)* sump *(Brit)*, oil pan *(US)*; **~wechsel** *m* oil change; **den ~wechsel machen** to change the oil.
Olymp *m (Berg)* Mount Olympus.
Olympiade *f (Olympische Spiele)* Olympic Games *pl*, Olympics *pl*.
Olympia-: **~medaille** *f* Olympic medal; **~sieger** *m* Olympic gold-medallist *(Brit)* *or* gold-medalist *(US)*; **~stadion** *nt* Olympic stadium.
olympisch *adj (die Olympiade betreffend)* Olympic. **die O~en Spiele** the Olympic Games.
Öl-: **~zeug** *nt* oilskins *pl*; **~zweig** *m (lit, fig)* olive-branch.
Oma *f* **-s** *(col)* granny *(col)*, grandma *(col)*.
Omelett [ɔm(ə)'lɛt] *nt* **-e** *or* **-s** omelette *(Brit)*, omelet *(US)*.
Omen *nt* - omen.
ominös *adj (geh)* ominous, sinister.
Omnibus *m* bus.
Omnibuslinie *f* bus route.
Onanie *f* masturbation, onanism.
onanieren* *vi* to masturbate.
ondulieren* *vtr* to crimp.
Onkel *m* - uncle.
Onyx *m* **-e** onyx.
OP [o:'pe:] *m* **-s** = **Operationssaal.**
Opa *m* **-s** *(col)* grandpa *(col)*, grandad *(col)*.
Opal *m* **-e** opal.
Oper *f* **-n** opera; *(Ensemble)* Opera; *(Opernhaus)* Opera, Opera House. **in die ~ gehen** to go to the opera; **zur ~ gehen** to become an opera singer.
Operation *f* operation.
Operations-: **~saal** *m* operating theatre *(Brit)* *or* room *(US)*; **~schwester** *f* theatre sister *(Brit)*, operating room nurse *(US)*.
operativ *adj (Med)* surgical. **eine Geschwulst ~ entfernen** to remove a growth by surgery.
Operette *f* operetta.
operieren* **1** *vt Patienten, Krebs, Magen* to operate on. **jdn am Magen ~** to operate on sb's stomach. **2** *vi* to operate *(an jdm/etw* on sb/sth*)*. **sich ~ lassen** to have an operation.
Opern-: **~arie** *f* (operatic) aria; **~ball** *m* opera ball; **~glas** *nt* opera glasses *pl*; **~haus** *nt* opera house; **~sänger** *m* opera singer; **~text** *m* libretto.
Opfer *nt* - **(a)** *(~gabe)* sacrifice *(auch fig)*. **für ihre Kinder scheut sie keine ~** she sacrifices everything for her children; **wir müssen alle ~ bringen** we must all make sacrifices. **(b)** *(geschädigte Person)* victim. **jdm/einer Sache zum ~ fallen** to be (the) victim of sb/sth; **ein ~ einer Sache** *(gen)* **werden** to be a victim of sth, to fall victim to sth; **das Erdbeben forderte viele ~** the earthquake claimed many victims.
Opfer-: **o~bereit** *adj* willing to make sacrifices; **~bereitschaft** *f* readiness to make sacrifices; **~gabe** *f (liter)* sacrificial offering; *(Eccl)* offering; **~lamm** *nt (lit, fig)* sacrifical lamb; **~mut** *m* self-sacrifice.
opfern **1** *vt (lit, fig)* to sacrifice; *Feldfrüchte etc* to offer (up). **sein Leben ~** to sacrifice one's life. **2** *vr* **(a)** *(sein Leben hingeben)* to sacrifice one's life. **(b)** *(col: sich bereit erklären)* to be a martyr *(col)*. **wer opfert sich, die Reste aufzuessen?** who's going to volunteer to eat up the remains?
Opfer-: **~stätte** *f* sacrificial altar; **~stock** *m* offertory box; **~tier** *nt* sacrifical animal.
Opferung *f (das Opfern)* sacrifice; *(Eccl)* offertory.
Opiat *nt* opiate.
Opium *nt no pl* opium.
opponieren* *vi* to oppose *(gegen jdn/etw* sb/sth*)*, to offer opposition *(gegen* to*)*.
opportun *adj (geh)* opportune.
Opportunismus *m* opportunism.
Opportunist(in *f***)** *m* opportunist.
opportunistisch *adj* opportunistic, opportunist. **~ handeln** to act in an opportunist fashion.
Opposition *f* opposition. **etw aus lauter** *or* **reiner ~ tun** to do sth out of sheer contrariness.
oppositionell *adj Gruppen, Kräfte* opposition.
Oppositionsführer *m* leader of the opposition.
optieren* *vi (Pol form)* **~ für** to opt for.
Optik *f* **(a)** *(Phys)* optics. **(b)** *(Phot)* lens system. **du hast wohl einen Knick in der ~!** *(col)* can't you see straight? *(col)*; **das ist eine Frage der ~** *(fig)* it depends on your point of view; **das ist nur hier wegen der ~** *(fig)* it's just here for visual effect.
Optiker(in *f***)** *m* - optician.
optimal *adj* optimal, optimum *attr*.
Optimismus *m* optimism.
Optimist(in *f***)** *m (wk)* optimist.
optimistisch *adj* optimistic.
Option [ɔp'tsio:n] *f* option.
optisch *adj* visual; *Gesetze, Instrumente* optical. **~e Täuschung** optical illusion.
Orakel *nt* - oracle.
orakeln* *vi (col)* **(a)** *(rätseln)* **wir haben lange orakelt, was der Satz bedeuten sollte** we spent a long time trying to decipher the sentence. **(b)** *(weissagen)* to prognosticate *(hum)*.
oral *adj* oral.
Orange[1] [o'rã:ʒə] *f* **-n** *(Frucht)* orange.
Orange[2] [o'rã:ʒə] *nt* -, - *or (col)* **-s** orange.
orange(n) [o'rã:ʒə(n)] *adj* orange.
Orangeat [orã'ʒa:t] *nt* candied (orange) peel.
orange- [o'rã:ʒə-]: **~farben, ~farbig** *adj* orange.
Orangen- [o'rã:ʒən-]: **~marmelade** *f* orange marmalade; **~saft** *m* orange juice; **~schale** *f* orange peel.
Orang-Utan *m* **-s** orang-utan, orang-outang.
Oratorium *nt* **(a)** *(Mus)* oratorio. **(b)** *(Betraum)* oratory.
Orchester [ɔr'kɛstɐ] *nt* - orchestra.
Orchidee *f* **-n** [-'de:ən] orchid.
Orden *m* - **(a)** *(Ehrenzeichen)* decoration; *(Mil*

auch) medal. ~ **tragen** to wear one's decorations; **jdm einen ~ (für etw) verleihen** to decorate sb (for sth). **(b)** *(Gemeinschaft)* (holy) order. **in einem ~ eintreten, einem ~ beitreten** to become a monk/nun.

Ordens-: ~bruder *m (Eccl)* monk; **~gemeinschaft** *f* religious order; **~schwester** *f* nursing sister *or* nun.

ordentlich *adj* **(a)** *Mensch, Zimmer* tidy, neat. **stell den Stuhl wieder ~ hin** put the chair back neatly; ~ **arbeiten** to be a thorough and precise worker. **(b)** *(ordnungsgemäß)* **~es Gericht** law court; **~es Mitglied** full member; **~er Professor** (full) professor. **(c)** *(anständig)* respectable. **sich ~ benehmen** to behave properly. **(d)** *(col: tüchtig, richtig)* ~ **essen/trinken** to eat/drink (really) well; **ein ~es Frühstück** a proper breakfast; **wir haben ~ gearbeitet** we really got down to it; **jetzt hab' ich aber ~ Appetit** I'm really hungry now; **eine ~e Tracht Prügel** a proper hiding. **(e)** *(annehmbar, ganz gut) Preis, Leistung* reasonable.

Order *f* **-s** *or* **-n (a)** *(Comm: Auftrag)* order. **(b)** *(Anweisung)* order. **sich an eine ~ halten** to keep to one's orders.

ordinär *adj* **(a)** *(gemein, unfein)* vulgar, common. **(b)** *(alltäglich)* ordinary.

Ordinarius *m, pl* **Ordinarien** [-iən] *(Univ)* professor *(für* of*)*.

ordnen 1 *vt Gedanken, Material* to order, to organize; *Finanzen, Privatleben* to put in order, to straighten out; *siehe* **geordnet. 2** *vr* to get into order. **die Menge ordnete sich zu einem Festzug** the crowd formed itself into a procession.

Ordner *m* **- (a)** steward; *(bei Demonstration auch)* marshal. **(b)** *(Akten~)* file.

Ordnung *f* **(a)** *(geordneter Zustand)* order. ~ **halten** to keep things tidy; ~ **schaffen, für ~ sorgen** to put things in order, to tidy things up; **Sie müssen für mehr ~ in Ihrer Klasse sorgen** you'll have to keep your class in better order; **etw in ~ halten** to keep sth in order; *Garten, Haus etc auch* to keep sth tidy; **etw in ~ bringen** *(reparieren)* to fix sth; *(herrichten)* to put sth in order; *(bereinigen)* to sort sth out; **ich finde es (ganz) in ~, daß ...** I find it quite right that ...; **(das ist) in ~!** *(col)* (that's) OK *(col) or* all right!; **geht in ~** *(col)* that's all right *or* OK *(col)*; **Ihre Bestellung geht in ~** we'll put your order through; **der ist in ~** *(col)* he's OK *(col) or* all right *(col)*; **mit ihm/der Maschine ist etwas nicht in ~** there's something the matter with him/the machine; **es ist alles in bester ~** things couldn't be better; **jdn zur ~ rufen** to call sb to order; **bei ihm muß alles seine ~ haben** *(räumlich)* he has to have everything in its proper place; *(zeitlich)* he does everything according to a fixed schedule; **das Kind braucht seine ~** the child needs a routine.

(b) *(Vorschrift)* rules *pl.* **sich an eine ~ halten** to keep to the rules; **ich frage nur der ~ halber** it's only a routine question.

(c) *(Rang, Biol)* order. **Straße erster ~** first-class road; **das war ein Fauxpas erster ~** *(col)* that was a faux-pas of the first order.

Ordnungs-: ~amt *nt* ≈ town clerk's office; **~fanatiker** *m* fanatic for order; **o~gemäß** *adj* in accordance with the rules, proper; **o~halber** *adv* as a matter of form; **~hüter** *m (hum)* custodian of the law *(hum)*; **~liebe** *f* love of order; **o~liebend** *adj* tidy-minded, orderly; **~ruf** *m* call to order; **der Präsident mußte mehrere ~rufe erteilen** the chairman had to call the meeting to order several times; **~sinn** *m* sense of order; **~strafe** *f* fine; **jdn mit einer ~strafe belegen** to fine sb; **o~widrig** *adj* irregular; *Parken, Verhalten (im Straßenverkehr)* illegal; **o~widrig handeln** to infringe rules *or* regulations; **~widrigkeit** *f* infringement *(of law or rule)*.

Organ *nt* **-s, -e (a)** *(Med, Biol, fig)* organ. **(b)** *(col: Stimme)* voice.

Organisation *f* organization.

Organisationstalent *nt* talent for organization. **er ist ein ~** he has a talent for organization.

Organisator *m* organizer.

organisatorisch *adj* organizational. **eine ~e Höchstleistung** a masterpiece of organization.

organisch *adj Chemie, Verbindung, Salz* organic; *Erkrankung, Leiden* physical. **sich ~ einfügen** to merge, to blend *(in +acc* with, into*)*.

organisieren* 1 *vti* **(a)** to organize. **er kann ausgezeichnet ~** he's excellent at organizing. **(b)** *(col: stehlen)* to lift *(col)*, to get hold of. **2** *vr* to get organized; *(gewerkschaftlich auch)* to organize.

Organismus *m* organism.

Organist(in *f***)** *m (wk)* organist.

Organ-: ~spender *m* donor *(of an organ)*; **~spenderausweis** *m* donor's card; **~verpflanzung** *f* transplant(ation) *(of organs)*.

Orgasmus *m* orgasm.

Orgel *f* **-n** organ.

Orgel- *in cpds* organ; **~pfeife** *f* organ pipe; **die Kinder standen da wie die ~pfeifen** *(hum)* the children were standing in order of height.

Orgie [-iə] *f* orgy. **~n feiern** *(lit)* to have orgies/an orgy; *(fig)* to go wild.

Orient ['oːriɛnt, o'riɛnt] *m no pl (liter)* Orient. **der Vordere ~** the Near East.

Orientale [oriɛn'taːlə] *m (wk)* **-n, -n, Orientalin** *f* Oriental. **er ist ~** he is an Oriental.

orientalisch [oriɛn'taːlɪʃ] *adj* oriental.

orientieren* [oriɛn'tiːrən] **1** *vti* **(a)** *(unterrichten)* to put sb in the picture *(über +acc* about*)*. **gut/falsch orientiert** well/wrongly informed. **(b)** *(ausrichten) (lit, fig)* to orientate *(nach, auf* to, towards). **links orientiert sein** to tend to the left; **links orientierte Gruppen** left-wing groups. **2** *vr* **(a)** *(sich unterrichten)* to inform oneself *(über +acc* about *or* on*)*. **(b)** *(sich zurechtfinden)* to orientate oneself *(an +dat, nach* by*)*, to get one's bearings. **in einer fremden Stadt kann ich mich gar nicht ~** I just can't find my way around in a strange city. **(c)** *(sich ausrichten)* to adapt *or* orientate (oneself) *(an +dat* to*)*.

Orientierung [oriɛn'tiːrʊŋ] *f* orientation; *(Unterrichtung)* information. **die ~ verlieren** to lose one's bearings; **zu Ihrer ~** for your information.

Orientierungs-: ~punkt *m* point of reference; **~sinn** *m* sense of direction.

Original *nt* **-e (a)** original. **(b)** *(Mensch)* character.

original *adj* original. ~ **Meißener Porzellan** genuine Meissen porcelain.

Original-: ~ausgabe *f* first edition; **~fassung** *f* original (version); **o~getreu** *adj* true to the original.

Originalität *f no pl* **(a)** *(Echtheit)* authenticity, genuineness. **(b)** *(Urtümlichkeit)* originality.

originell *adj (selbständig) Idee, Argumentation* original; *(neu)* novel; *(geistreich)* witty. **das finde ich ~ (von ihm)** that's pretty original/witty.

Orkan *m* **-e** hurricane.

Orkan-: o~artig *adj Wind* gale-force; *Beifall* thunderous; **~stärke** *f* hurricane force.

Ornament *nt* decoration, ornament.

Ornat *m* **-e** regalia *pl*; *(Eccl)* vestments *pl*; *(Jur)* official robes *pl*. **in vollem ~** *(col)* dressed up to the nines *(col)*.

Ornithologe *m (wk)*, **Ornithologin** *f (form)* ornithologist.

Ort[1] *m* **-e** place. ~ **der Handlung** *(Theat)* scene of the action; **an den ~ der Tat** *or* **des Verbrechens zurückkehren** to return to the scene of the crime; **der Stuhl steht wieder an seinem ~** the chair is back in (its) place again; **am angegebenen ~** in the place quoted, loc cit *abbr*; **an ~ und Stelle** on the spot, there and then; **an ~**

und Stelle ankommen to arrive (at one's destination); **das ist höheren ~s entschieden worden** *(hum, form)* the decision came from above; **in einem kleinen ~ in Cornwall** in a little spot in Cornwall; **~e über 100.000 Einwohner** places with over 100,000 inhabitants; **am ~** in the place; **das beste Hotel am ~** the best hotel in town; **wir haben keinen Arzt am ~** we have no resident doctor; **am ~ wohnen** to live locally; **mitten im ~** in the centre (of the place/town); **der nächste ~** the next village/town *etc*; **von ~ zu ~** from place to place.

Ort[2] *m* **-̈er** *(Min)* coal face, (working) face. **vor ~** at the (coal) face; *(fig)* on the spot.

Örtchen *nt (col)* loo *(Brit col)*, john *(US col)*.

orten *vt* to locate, to get a fix on.

orthodox *adj (lit, fig)* orthodox.

Orthographie *f* orthography.

orthographisch *adj* orthographic(al). **ein ~er Fehler** a spelling mistake.

Orthopäde *m (wk)* **-n, -n, Orthopädin** *f* orthopaedic *(Brit) or* orthopedic *(US)* specialist.

orthopädisch *adj* orthopaedic *(Brit)*, orthopedic *(US)*.

örtlich *adj* local. **das ist ~ verschieden** it varies from place to place; **jdn/etw ~ betäuben** to give sb/sth a local anaesthetic.

Örtlichkeit *f* locality. **sich mit den ~en vertraut machen** to get to know the place; **die ~en** *(euph)* the cloakroom *(Brit euph)*, the comfort station *(US euph)*.

Orts-: ~angabe *f (bei Anschriften)* (name of the) town; **ohne ~angabe** *(von Buch)* no place of publication indicated; **o~ansässig** *adj* local; **die ~ansässigen** the local residents.

Ortschaft *f* **-en** village; town. **geschlossene ~** built-up area.

Orts-: o~fremd *adj* non-local; **ich bin hier o~fremd** I'm a stranger here; **~gespräch** *nt (Telec)* local call; **~gruppe** *f* local branch *or* group; **~kenntnis** *f* local knowledge; **(gute) ~kenntnisse haben** to know one's way around (well); **~krankenkasse** *f* **Allgemeine ~krankenkasse** *compulsory medical insurance scheme*; **o~kundig** *adj* **ein ~kundiger** somebody who knows the place; **~name** *m* place name; **~netz** *nt (Telec)* local (telephone) exchange area; *(Elec)* local grid; **~netzkennzahl** *f (Telec form)* dialling *(Brit) or* area code; **~schild** *nt* place name sign; **~sinn** *m* sense of direction; **~tarif** *m (Telec)* charge for local phone-calls; **o~üblich** *adj* local; **das ist hier o~üblich** it's a local custom here; **~verkehr** *m* local traffic; **Gebühren im ~verkehr** *(Telec)* charges for local (phone) calls; **~zeit** *f* local time; **~zuschlag** *m* (local) weighting allowance.

Öse *f* **-n** loop; *(an Kleidung)* eye.

Ost *m no pl (liter)* East.

Ost- *in cpds* East; *(geographisch auch)* Eastern, the East of ...; **~afrika** *nt* East Africa; **~asien** *nt* Eastern Asia; **~-Berlin** *nt* East Berlin; **~berliner** *adj attr* East Berlin; **~berliner** *m* East Berliner; **~block** Eastern bloc; **~blockland** *nt*, **~blockstaat** *m* Eastern bloc country; **o~deutsch** *adj* East German; **~deutschland** *nt (Pol)* East Germany; *(Geog)* Eastern Germany.

Osten *m no pl (auch Pol)* East. **der Ferne ~** the Far East; **der Nahe ~** the Middle East, the Near East; **im ~** in the East; **in den ~** to the East; **von ~** from the East.

ostentativ *adj (geh)* pointed.

Oster-: ~ei *nt* Easter egg; **~fest** *nt* Easter; **~glocke** *f* daffodil; **~hase** *m* Easter bunny.

österlich *adj* Easter.

Oster-: ~marsch *m* Easter demonstration; **~montag** *m* Easter Monday.

Ostern *nt* - Easter. **frohe** *or* **fröhliche ~!** Happy Easter!; **zu ~** at Easter.

Österreich *nt* Austria.

Österreicher(in *f***)** *m* - Austrian.

österreichisch *adj* Austrian. **das Ö~e** *(Ling)* Austrian.

Ostersonntag *m* Easter Sunday.

Ost-: ~europa *nt* East(ern) Europe; **o~europäisch** *adj* East European; **~friese** *m* East Friesian; **~geld** *nt (col)* East German money; **~küste** *f* East coast.

östlich 1 *adj Richtung, Winde* easterly; *Gebiete* eastern. **30° ~er Länge** 30° (longitude) east. **2** *adv* **~ von Hamburg/des Rheins** (to the) east of Hamburg/the Rhine. **3** *prep +gen* (to the) east of.

Ost-: ~mark *f (col)* East German Mark; **~politik** *f* Ostpolitik, *foreign policy regarding the Eastern bloc.*

Östrogen [œstro'geːn] *nt* **-e** oestrogen *(Brit)*, estrogen *(US)*.

Ostsee *f* **die ~** the Baltic (Sea).

Ost-: ~staaten *pl (in USA)* the Eastern *or* East coast states; **o~wärts** *adv* eastwards; **~-West-Verhandlungen** *pl* East-West negotiations; **~wind** *m* east *or* easterly wind.

Otter[1] *m* - otter.

Otter[2] *f* **-n** viper, adder.

Ottomotor *m* internal combustion engine, otto engine.

Ouvertüre [uvɛr'tyːrə] *f* **-n** overture.

oval [o'vaːl] *adj* oval.

Oval [o'vaːl] *nt* **-e** oval.

Ovation [ova'tsioːn] *f* ovation. **jdm eine ~** *or* **~en darbringen** to give sb an ovation.

Overall ['oʊvərɔːl] *m* **-s** *(Schutzanzug)* overalls *pl.*

Oxid, Oxyd *nt* **-e** oxide.

Oxidation, Oxydation *f* oxidation.

oxidieren*, oxydieren* *vti aux sein or haben* to oxidize.

Ozean *m* **-e** ocean.

Ozean-: ~dampfer *m* ocean steamer; **~riese** *m (col)* ocean liner.

ozeanisch *adj Flora* oceanic; *Sprachen* Oceanic.

Ozelot *m* **-e** ocelot.

Ozon *nt or (col) m no pl* ozone.

Ozonschicht *f* ozone layer.

P

P p [peː] *nt* **-, -** P, p.

Paar *nt* **-e** pair; *(Mann und Frau auch)* couple. **zwei ~ Socken** two pairs of socks; **ein ~ Würstchen** a couple of *or* two sausages.

paar *adj inv* **ein ~** a few; *(zwei oder drei auch)* a couple of; **alle ~ Minuten/Wochen** every few minutes/weeks.

paaren 1 *vt Tiere* to mate, to pair; *(Sport)* to match. **2** *vr (Tiere)* to mate; *(fig)* to be coupled.

Paar-: ~hufer *pl (Zool)* cloven-hoofed animals *pl*; **~lauf** *m*, **~laufen** *nt* pair-skating, pairs *pl*.

paarmal *adv* **ein ~** a few times; *(zwei- oder dreimal auch)* a couple of times.

Paarung *f* **(a)** *(Sport, fig liter)* combination; *(Sport: Begegnung)* draw, match. **(b)** *(Kopulation)* mating; *(Kreuzung)* crossing.

Paarungszeit *f* mating season.

paarweise *adv* in pairs, in twos.

Pacht *f* **-en** lease; *(Entgelt)* rent. **etw in ~ geben** to lease sth (out); **etw in ~ haben** to have sth on lease.

Pachtbrief *m* lease.

pachten *vt* to lease. **du hast das Sofa doch nicht für dich gepachtet** *(col)* don't hog the sofa *(col)*.

Pächter(in *f*) *m* leaseholder.

Pacht-: ~grundstück *nt* leasehold property; **~gut** *nt*, **~hof** *m* smallholding; **~vertrag** *m* lease; **~zins** *m* rent.

Pack[1] *m (von Büchern, Wäsche)* pile; *(zusammengeschnürt)* bundle.

Pack[2] *nt no pl (pej)* rabble *pl (pej)*.

Päckchen *nt* package; *(Post)* small parcel; *(Packung)* packet, pack. **ein ~ Zigaretten** a packet *or* pack *(esp US)* of cigarettes; **jeder hat sein ~ zu tragen** *(fig col)* we all have our cross to bear.

Pack|eis *nt* pack ice.

packen 1 *vti* **(a)** *Koffer* to pack; *(verstauen)* to pack (away). **etw in Watte ~** wrap sth (up) in cotton wool; **jdn ins Bett ~** *(col)* to tuck sb up (in bed). **(b)** *(fassen)* to grab (hold of); *(Gefühle)* to grip. **jdn am** *or* **beim Kragen ~** *(col)* to grab sb by the collar; **das Theaterstück hat mich gepackt** I was really gripped by the play. **(c)** *(col: schaffen)* to manage. **hast du die Prüfung gepackt?** did you (manage to) get through the exam? **(d)** *(col: aufhören)* **ich pack's jetzt!** I'm going to pack it in *(col)*. **(e)** *(col: gehen)* **~ wir's!** let's go. **(f)** *(col: kapieren)* **er packt es nie** he'll never get it *(col)*. **2** *vr (col)* to clear off.

Packen *m* **-** pile; *(Bündel)* bundle.

Packer(in *f*) *m* **-** packer.

Pack-: ~esel *m (fig)* packhorse; **~papier** *nt* wrapping paper.

Packung *f* **(a)** *(Schachtel)* packet, pack. **eine ~ Zigaretten** a packet *or* pack *(esp US)* of cigarettes. **(b)** *(Med)* pack; *(Kosmetik)* beauty pack. **(c)** *(col: Niederlage)* hammering *(col)*.

Packzettel *m* packing slip.

Pädagoge *m*, **Pädagogin** *f* educationalist.

Pädagogik *f* educational theory.

pädagogisch *adj* educational. **P~e Hochschule** college of education; **seine ~en Fähigkeiten** his teaching ability.

Paddel *nt* **-** paddle.

Paddelboot *nt* canoe.

paffen 1 *vi (col: rauchen)* to puff away; *(nicht inhalieren)* to puff. **2** *vt* to puff (away) at.

Page [ˈpaːʒə] *m (wk)* **-n, -n** *(Hotel~)* page(boy), bellhop *(US)*.

Pagen-: ~frisur *f*, **~kopf** *m* page-boy (hairstyle).

Paket *nt* **-e** *(Post)* parcel; *(Packung)* packet; *(fig)* package.

Paket-: ~adresse *f* stick-on address label; **~annahme/~ausgabe** *f* parcels office; **~karte** *f* dispatch form; **~schalter** *m* parcels counter.

Pakistan *nt* Pakistan.

Pakistaner(in *f*) *m* **-**, **Pakistani** *m* **-(s)** Pakistani.

Pakt *m* pact. **einem ~ beitreten** to enter into an agreement.

Palast *m, pl* **Paläste** *(lit, fig)* palace.

Palästina *nt* Palestine.

Palästinenser(in *f*) *m* **-** Palestinian.

Palaver [paˈlaːvɐ] *nt* **-** *(col)* unending discussion.

palavern* [paˈlaːvɐn] *vi (col)* to ramble on.

Palette *f* **(a)** *(Malerei)* palette; *(fig)* range. **(b)** *(Stapelplatte)* pallet.

Palisade *f* palisade.

Palisander(holz *nt*) *m* **-** jacaranda.

Palme *f* **-n** palm. **jdn auf die ~ bringen** *(col)* to make sb see red *(col)*.

Palm-: ~sonntag *m* Palm Sunday; **~wedel** *m* palm leaf.

Pampe *f no pl (col)* mush *(col)*.

Pampelmuse *f* **-n** grapefruit.

Pamphlet *nt* **-e** lampoon.

pampig *adj (col)* **(a)** *(breiig)* gooey *(col)*. **(b)** *(frech)* stroppy *(col)*.

pan- *pref* pan-; **~amerikanisch** pan-American.

Panama *nt* Panama.

Panamakanal *m* Panama Canal.

Paneel *nt* **-e** *(einzeln)* panel; *(Täfelung)* panelling *(Brit)*, paneling *(US)*, wainscoting.

Panflöte *f* panpipes *pl*, Pan's pipes *pl*.

panieren* *vt* to bread, to coat with breadcrumbs.

Paniermehl *nt* breadcrumbs *pl*.

Panik *f* **-en** panic. **in ~ ausbrechen** to panic; **von ~ ergriffen** panic-stricken; **nur keine ~!** don't panic!

Panikmache *f (col)* panicmongering.

panisch *adj no pred* panic-stricken. **er hatte eine ~e Angst zu ertrinken** he was terrified of drowning; **sich ~ fürchten (vor)** to be petrified (of); **sie rannten ~ durcheinander** they ran about in panic.

Panne *f* **-n** **(a)** *(Störung)* breakdown. **mein Auto hatte eine ~** my car broke down. **(b)** *(fig col)* boob *(Brit col)*, goof *(US col)*. **mit jdm/etw eine ~ erleben** to have (a bit of) trouble with sb/sth; **uns ist eine ~ passiert** we've boobed *(Brit col) or* goofed *(US col)*; **da ist eine ~ passiert mit dem Brief** something has gone wrong with the letter.

Pannen-: ~dienst *m*, **~hilfe** *f* breakdown service *(Brit)*, emergency road service *(US)*.

Panorama *nt, pl* **Panoramen** panorama.

panschen 1 *vt* to adulterate; *(verdünnen)* to water down. **2** *vi (col)* to splash (about).

Pantoffel *m* **-n** slipper. **unterm ~ stehen** *(col)* to be henpecked.

Pantoffelheld *m (col)* henpecked husband.

Pantomime[1] *f* **-n** mime.

Pantomime[2] *m (wk)* **-n, -n** mime.

pantschen *vti* = **panschen.**
Panzer *m* - **(a)** *(Mil)* tank. **(b)** *(Hist: Rüstung)* armour *(Brit)*, armor *(US) no indef art*, suit of armour *(Brit) or* armor *(US)*. **(c)** *(Panzerung)* armour *(Brit) or* armor *(US)* plate. **(d)** *(Zool)* shell; *(dicke Haut)* armour *(Brit)*, armor *(US)*. **(e)** *(fig)* shield.
Panzer-: **~abwehr** *f* anti-tank defence *(Brit) or* defense *(US)*; *(Truppe)* anti-tank unit; **~abwehrkanone** *f* anti-tank gun; **~faust** *f* bazooka; **~glas** *nt* bulletproof glass; **~grenadier** *m* armoured *(Brit) or* armored *(US)* infantryman; **~kampfwagen** *m* armoured *(Brit) or* armored *(US)* vehicle; **~kette** *f* tank-track.
panzern 1 *vt* to armour-plate *(Brit)*, to armor-plate *(US)*. **gepanzerte Fahrzeuge** armoured vehicles. **2** *vr (fig)* to arm oneself.
Panzer-: **~schrank** *m* safe; **~truppe** *f* tank division.
Panzerung *f* armour *(Brit) or* armor *(US)* plating; *(fig)* shield.
Panzerwagen *m* armoured *(Brit) or* armored *(US)* car.
Papa *m* **-s** *(col)* daddy *(col)*, pa *(US col)*.
Papagei *m* **-en** parrot. **er plappert alles wie ein ~ nach** he repeats everything parrot fashion.
Papi *m* **-s** *(col)* daddy *(col)*.
Papier *nt* **-e (a)** *no pl* paper. **ein Blatt ~** a sheet of paper; **das steht nur auf dem ~** that's only in theory. **(b)** *(Schriftstück)* paper. **~e** *pl* (identity) papers *pl*; *(Urkunden)* documents *pl*; **er hatte keine ~e bei sich** he had no means of identification with him; **seine ~e bekommen** *(entlassen werden)* to get one's cards. **(c)** *(Fin, Wert~)* security.
Papier-: **~deutsch** *nt* officialese; **~fabrik** *f* paper mill; **~korb** *m* wastepaper basket; **~kram** *m (col)* bumf *(Brit col)*, official document; **~krieg** *m (col)* **vor lauter ~krieg kommen wir nicht zur Forschung** there's so much paperwork we can't get on with our research; **erst nach einem langen ~krieg** after going through a lot of red tape; **~taschentuch** *nt* tissue, paper handkerchief; **~tiger** *m (fig)* paper tiger.
Pappdeckel *m* (thin) cardboard.
Pappe *f* **-n** *(Pappdeckel)* cardboard; *(Dach~)* roofing felt. **das ist nicht von ~** *(col)* that is really something.
Pappel *f* **-n** poplar.
pappen *(col)* **1** *vt* to stick *(an or auf +acc* on*)*. **2** *vi (col) (klebrig sein)* to be sticky; *(Schnee)* to pack.
Pappen-: **~deckel** *m* (thin) cardboard; **~heimer** *pl*: **ich kenne meine ~heimer** *(col)* I know you lot/that lot (inside out) *(col)*; **~stiel** *m (fig col)*: **5000 Mark sind kein ~stiel** 5000 marks isn't peanuts *(col)*; **das ist keinen ~stiel wert** that's not worth a penny.
papperlapapp *interj (col)* (stuff and) nonsense.
pappig *adj (col)* sticky.
Papp-: **~karton** *m (Schachtel)* cardboard box; *(Material)* cardboard; **~maché** [-maʃeː] *nt* **-s** papier-mâché; **~schnee** *m* wet snow.
Paprika *m* **-(s)** *(no pl: Gewürz)* paprika; *(~schote)* pepper.
Paprikaschote *f* pepper. **gefüllte ~n** stuffed peppers.
Papst *m* **⸚e** pope; *(fig)* high priest.
päpstlich *adj* papal; *(fig pej)* pontifical. **~er als der Papst sein** to be more Catholic than the Pope.
Parabel *f* **-n (a)** *(Liter)* parable. **(b)** *(Math)* parabola, parabolic curve.
Parabolspiegel *m* parabolic reflector.
Parade *f* **(a)** *(Mil)* review. **die ~abnehmen** to take the salute. **(b)** *(Sport: Fechten, Boxen)* parry; *(Ballspiele)* save; *(Reiten)* check. **jdm in die ~ fahren** *(fig)* to cut sb off short.
Parade-: **~beispiel** *nt* prime example; **~stück** *nt (fig)* showpiece; *(Gegenstand auch)* pièce de résistance.
Paradies *nt* **-e** *(lit, fig)* paradise. **das ~ auf Erden** heaven on earth.
paradiesisch *adj (fig)* heavenly. **hier ist es ~ schön** this is paradise; **~ leere Strände** blissfully empty beaches.
Paradiesvogel *m* bird of paradise.
paradox *adj* paradoxical.
Paradox *nt* **-e** paradox.
paradoxerweise *adv* paradoxically.
Paraffin *nt* **-e** *(Chem)* *(~öl)* paraffin *(Brit)*, kerosene *(US)*; *(~wachs)* paraffin wax.
Paragraph *m (Jur)* section; *(Abschnitt)* paragraph.
Paragraphenreiter *m (col)* pedant.
parallel *adj* parallel. **~ laufen** to run parallel; **~ schalten** *(Elec)* to connect in parallel.
Parallele *f* **-n** parallel (line); *(fig)* parallel. **eine ~ zu etw ziehen** *(fig)* to draw a parallel to sth.
Parallelogramm *nt* **-e** parallelogram.
Parallelschaltung *f* parallel connection.
paranoid [parano'iːt] *adj* paranoid, paranoiac.
Paranuß *f (Bot)* Brazil nut.
Paraphierung *f (Pol)* initialling *(Brit)*, initialing *(US)*.
Paraphrase *f* paraphrase; *(Mus)* variation.
Parapsychologie *f* parapsychology.
Parasit *m (wk)* **-en, -en** *(Biol, fig)* parasite.
parasitär *adj (Biol, fig)* parasitic(al).
parat *adj* prepared; *Werkzeug etc* handy. **er hatte immer eine Ausrede ~** he was always ready with an excuse.
Pärchen *nt* (courting) couple.
Parcours [par'kuːɐ] *m* **-, -** show-jumping course; *(Sportart)* show-jumping.
Pardon [par'dõː] *m or nt no pl* **(a)** *(dated)* pardon. **(b)** *(col)* **~!** *(Verzeihung)* sorry; **kein ~ kennen** to be ruthless; **das Zeug räumst du auf, da gibt's kein ~** you'll clear that stuff up and that's that! *(col)*.
Parfum [par'fœː] *nt* **-s, Parfüm** *nt* **-e** *or* **-s** perfume, scent.
Parfümerie *f* perfumery.
parfümieren* **1** *vt* to scent. **2** *vr* to put scent on.
parieren* **1** *vt* **(a)** *(Fechten, fig)* to parry; *(Ftbl)* to deflect. **(b)** *(Reiten)* to rein in. **2** *vi* to obey. **aufs Wort ~** to jump to it.
Pariser[1] *m* - **(a)** Parisian. **(b)** *(col: Kondom)* rubber *(col)*.
Pariser[2] *adj attr* Parisian.
Pariserin *f* Parisienne.
Parität *f* parity.
paritätisch *adj* equal. **~e Mitbestimmung** equal representation.
Park *m* **-s** park; *(von Schloß)* grounds *pl*.
Parka *m* **-s** parka.
Park|anlage *f* park.
parken *vti* to park.
Parkett *nt* **-e (a)** *(Fußboden)* parquet (flooring). **sich auf jedem ~ bewegen können** *(fig)* to be able to move in any society. **(b)** *(Tanzfläche)* (dance) floor. **eine tolle Nummer aufs ~ legen** *(col)* to put on a great show. **(c)** *(Theat)* stalls *pl*, parquet *(US)*. **wir sitzen ~** we sit in the stalls.
Parkett-: **~platz, ~sitz** *m (Theat)* seat in the stalls *or* parquet *(US)*.
Park-: **~gebühr** *f* parking fee; **~haus** *nt* multi-storey car park *(Brit)*, multilevel parking garage *(US)*; **~landschaft** *f* parkland; **~lücke** *f* parking space; **~platz** *m* car park *(Brit)*, parking lot *(US)*; *(für Einzelwagen)* (parking) space; **~scheibe** *f* parking disc; **~uhr** parking meter; **~verbot** *nt* parking ban; **hier ist ~verbot** there's no parking here.
Parlament *nt* parliament.
Parlamentarier(in *f***)** [-iɐ, -iərɪn] *m* - parliamentarian.
parlamentarisch *adj* parliamentary.

Parlaments-: ~**ausschuß** *m* parliamentary committee; ~**beschluß** *m* decision of parliament; ~**ferien** *pl* recess; ~**gebäude** *nt* parliamentary building(s); ~**mitglied** *nt* member of parliament, MP *(Brit); (in USA)* Congressman; ~**sitzung** *f* sitting (of parliament); ~**wahl** *f usu pl* parliamentary election(s).

Parodie *f* parody *(auf +acc* on, *zu* of*)*.

parodieren* *vt* to parody.

Parodontose *f* **-n** shrinking gums.

Parole *f* **-n (a)** *(Mil)* password. **(b)** *(fig: Wahlspruch)* motto; *(Pol)* slogan.

Paroli *nt*: **jdm ~ bieten** *(geh)* to defy sb.

Partei *f* **(a)** *(Pol, Jur)* party. **die ~ wechseln** to change parties; **die streitenden ~en** *(Jur)* the disputing parties; **für jdn ~ ergreifen** to side with sb; **gegen jdn ~ ergreifen** to take sides against sb; **ein Richter sollte über den ~en stehen** a judge should be impartial. **(b)** *(im Mietshaus)* tenant, party *(form)*.

Partei-: ~**anhänger** *m* party supporter; ~**buch** *nt* party membership book; ~**chef** *m* party leader; ~**führung** *f* leadership of a party; *(Vorstand)* party executive; ~**genosse** *m* party member; ~**intern** *adj* internal party; **etw p~intern lösen** to solve sth within the party.

parteiisch *adj* bias(s)ed, partial.

Parteilichkeit *f* bias, partiality.

Partei-: ~**linie** *f* party line; **auf die ~linie einschwenken** to toe the party line; **p~los** *adj* independent, non-party; ~**mitglied** *nt* party member; ~**nahme** *f* **-n** partisanship; ~**politik** *f* party politics *pl*; ~**politisch** *adj* party political; ~**programm** *nt* (party) manifesto; ~**tag** *m* party conference *or* convention; ~**versammlung** *f* party meeting; ~**vorsitzende(r)** *mf* party leader; ~**vorstand** *m* party executive; ~**zugehörigkeit** *f* party membership.

Parterre [par'tɛr(ə)] *nt* **-s** *(von Gebäude)* ground floor *(Brit)*, first floor *(US)*. **im ~ wohnen** to live on the ground floor.

Parterrewohnung *f* ground-floor flat *(Brit)*, first-floor apartment *(US)*.

Partie *f* **(a)** *(Teil, Theat, Mus)* part. **(b)** *(Sport)* game; *(Fechten)* round. **eine ~ Schach spielen** to play a game of chess. **(c)** *(Comm)* lot, batch. **(d)** *(col)* catch. **eine gute ~ (für jdn) sein** to be a good catch (for sb); **eine gute ~ (mit jdm) machen** to marry (into) money. **(e) mit von der ~ sein** to be in on it; **da bin ich mit von der ~** count me in.

partiell [par'tsiɛl] *adj* partial.

Partikel *f* **-n** *(Gram, Phys)* particle.

Partisan(in *f***)** *m* **-en** partisan.

Partisanenkrieg *m* partisan war; *(Art des Krieges)* guerrilla warfare.

Partitur *f (Mus)* score.

Partizip *nt* **-ien** [-iən] *(Gram)* participle. **~ Präsens/Perfekt** present/past participle.

Partner(in *f***)** *m* **-** partner; *(Film)* co-star. **als jds ~ spielen** *(in Film)* to play opposite sb; *(Sport)* to be partnered by sb.

Partnerschaft *f* partnership.

partnerschaftlich *adj* ~**es Verhältnis** (relationship based on) partnership; ~**e Zusammenarbeit** working together as partners.

Partnertausch *m (Tanz, Tennis)* change of partners; *(sexuell)* partner-swopping.

partout [par'tu:] *adv* **er will ~ ins Kino gehen** he insists on going to the cinema; **sie will ~ nicht nach Hause gehen** she just doesn't want to go home.

Party ['pa:ɐti] *f* **-s** party. **eine ~ veranstalten** to have a party; **bei** *or* **auf einer ~** at a party.

Pasch *m* **-e** *or* **¨e** *(beim Würfelspiel)* doublets *pl*.

Pascha *m* **-** pasha. **wie ein ~** like Lord Muck *(col)*.

Paß *m, pl* **Pässe (a)** passport. **(b)** *(im Gebirge etc)* pass. **(c)** *(Ballspiele)* pass.

passabel *adj* passable, reasonable.

Passage [pa'sa:ʒə] *f* **-n** passage; *(Ladenstraße)* arcade.

Passagier [pasa'ʒi:ɐ] *m* passenger.

Passagier-: ~**flugzeug** *nt* air-liner; ~**gut** *nt* passenger baggage.

Passah(fest) *nt* (Feast of the) Passover.

Paß|amt *nt* passport office.

Passant(in *f***)** *m (wk)* passer-by.

Passat(wind) *m* **-e** trade wind.

Paßbild *nt* passport photo(graph).

passé [pa'se:] *adj pred* **diese Mode ist längst ~** this fashion went out long ago; **die Sache ist längst ~** that's all in the past.

passen[1] *vi* **(a)** to fit. **die Schuhe ~ (mir) gut** the shoes fit (me) nicely *or* are a good fit (for me); **der Deckel paßt nicht** the lid won't fit (on).

(b) *(harmonieren)* **zu etw ~** to go with sth; **zu etw im Ton ~** to match sth; **zu jdm ~** *(Mensch)* to suit sb; **zueinander ~** to go together; *(Menschen auch)* to be well matched; **das paßt zu ihm, so etwas zu sagen** that's just like him to say that; **es paßt nicht zu dir, Bier zu trinken** you don't look right drinking beer; **das Rot paßt da nicht** the red is all wrong there; **er paßt nicht in dieses Team** he is out of place in this team.

(c) *(genehm sein)* to suit. **er paßt mir einfach nicht** I just don't like him; **Sonntag paßt uns nicht** Sunday is no good for us; **es paßt ihr gar nicht, daß sie jetzt schlafen gehen soll** she doesn't like the idea of having to go to bed now; **das könnte dir so ~!** *(col)* you'd like that, wouldn't you?

passen[2] *vi (Cards)* to pass. **(ich) passe!** (I) pass!; **bei dieser Frage muß ich ~** *(fig)* I'll have to pass on this question.

passend *adj* **(a)** *(in Größe, Form)* **gut/schlecht ~** well-/ill-fitting. **(b)** *(in Farbe, Stil)* matching. **etwas dazu P~es** something to match. **(c)** *(genehm) Zeit, Termin* convenient; *(angemessen) Bemerkung, Kleidung* suitable; *Wort* right. **er findet immer das ~e Wort** he always knows the right thing to say. **(d)** *Geld* exact. **haben Sie es ~?** have you got the right money?

Paß-: ~**form** *f* fit; **eine gute ~form haben** to be a good fit; ~**foto** *nt* passport photo(graph); ~**höhe** *f* top of the pass.

passierbar *adj* passable; *Fluß, Kanal* negotiable.

passieren* **1** *vt* **(a)** *auch vi* to pass. **die Grenze ~** to cross the border; **die Zensur ~** to be passed by the censor. **(b)** *(Cook)* to strain. **2** *vi aux sein (sich ereignen)* to happen *(mit* to*)*. **ist ihm etwas passiert?** has anything happened to him?; **beim Sturz ist ihm nichts passiert** he wasn't hurt in the fall; **es ist ein Unfall passiert** there has been an accident; **das kann auch nur mir ~!** just my luck!

Passierschein *m* pass, permit.

Passion *f* passion; *(religiös)* Passion. **etw aus ~ tun** to have a passion for doing sth.

passioniert *adj* enthusiastic, passionate.

Passions-: ~**blume** *f* passionflower; ~**zeit** *f* Lent.

passiv *adj* passive. **sich ~ verhalten** to be passive; ~**es Mitglied** non-active member; ~**e Handelsbilanz** *(Comm)* adverse trade balance.

Passiv *nt* **-e** *(Gram)* passive (voice).

Passiva [pa'si:va] *pl (Comm)* liabilities *pl*.

Passivität [pasivi'tɛ:t] *f* passivity.

Passiv- *(Comm)*: ~**posten** *m* debit entry; ~**saldo** *m* debit account; ~**seite** *f* debit side.

Paß-: ~**kontrolle** *f* passport control; ~**photo** *nt* passport photo; ~**straße** *f* (mountain) pass.

Paste *f* **-n** paste.

Pastell *nt* **-e** pastel (drawing).

Pastell-: ~**farbe** *f* pastel (crayon); *(Farbton)* pastel; **p~farben** *adj* pastel; ~**ton** *m* pastel shade.

Pastete *f* **-n (a)** *(Schüssel~)* pie; *(Pastetchen)* vol-au-vent; *(ungefüllt)* vol-au-vent case. **(b)**

(Leber~ etc) pâté.
pasteurisieren* [pastøri'zi:rən] *vt* to pasteurize.
Pastille *f* **-n** pastille.
Pastor *m*, **Pastorin** *f* = **Pfarrer(in).**
pastoral *adj* pastoral.
Pate *m* **-n** godfather, godparent. **bei einem Kind ~ stehen** to be a child's godparent; **bei etw ~ gestanden haben** *(fig)* to be the force behind sth.
Paten-: ~kind *nt* godchild; godson; goddaughter; **~onkel** *m* godfather; **~schaft** *f* duties *pl* as a godparent; **die ~schaft für jdn übernehmen** *(fig)* to adopt sb; **~stadt** *f* twin(ned) town *(Brit)*.
patent *adj (col)* ingenious, clever. **ein ~er Kerl** a great guy/girl *(col)*.
Patent *nt* **-e** *(Erfindung, Urkunde)* patent. **etw als** *or* **zum ~ anmelden** to apply for a patent on sth.
Patent|amt *nt* Patent Office.
Patentante *f* godmother.
Patent|anwalt *m* patent agent *or* attorney.
patentieren* *vt* to patent. **sich** *(dat)* **etw ~ lassen** to have sth patented.
Patent-: ~lösung *f (fig)* patent remedy; **~schrift** *f* patent specification.
Pater *m, pl* - *or* **Patres** *(Eccl)* Father.
Paternoster *m* - *(Aufzug)* paternoster.
pathetisch *adj* emotional; *Rede, Stil auch* emotive; *Gehabe auch* histrionic.
Pathologie *f* pathology.
pathologisch *adj* pathological.
Pathos *nt no pl* emotiveness, emotionalism.
Patience [pa'siã:s] *f* **-n** patience *no pl.* **~n legen** to play patience.
Patient(in *f***)** [pa'tsiɛnt(in)] *m (wk)* **-en, -en** patient.
Patin *f* godmother, godparent.
Patriarch *m (wk)* **-en, -en** *(lit, fig)* patriarch.
patriarchalisch *adj (lit, fig)* patriarchal.
Patriot(in *f***)** *m (wk)* **-en, -en** patriot.
patriotisch *adj* patriotic.
Patriotismus *m* patriotism.
Patron(in *f***)** *m* **-e** *(Eccl)* patron saint.
Patrone *f* **-n** *(Film, Mil, von Füller)* cartridge.
Patrouille [pa'trʊljə] *f* **-n** patrol. **~ gehen** to patrol.
patrouillieren* [patrʊl'ji:rən] *vi* to patrol. **an der Grenze ~** to patrol the border.
patsch *interj* splash, splat.
Patsche *f* **-n** *(col)* (tight) spot *(col)*. **in der ~ sitzen** to be in a jam *(col)*; **jdm aus der ~ helfen** to get sb out of a jam *(col)*.
patschen *vi (im Wasser)* to splash. **die Kinder ~ mit den Händen** *(col)* the children clap their hands (together).
Patsch-: ~händchen *nt (col)* paw *(col)*; **p~naß** *adj (col)* dripping wet.
Patt *nt* **-s** *(lit, fig)* stalemate.
patzen *vi (col)* to boob *(Brit col)*, to goof *(US col)*.
Patzer *m* - *(col: Fehler)* boob *(Brit col)*, goof *(US col)*.
patzig *adj (col)* snotty *(col)*, insolent.
Pauke *f* **-n** *(Mus)* timpani *pl.* **mit ~n und Trompeten durchfallen** *(col)* to fail dismally; **auf die ~ hauen** *(col) (angeben)* to brag; *(feiern)* to paint the town red *(col)*.
pauken 1 *vi (col: lernen)* to swot *(col)*. **2** *vt* to swot up *(col)*.
Paukenschlag *m* drum beat. **wie ein ~schlag** *(fig)* like a thunderbolt.
Pauker *m* - *(Sch col: Lehrer)* teacher.
Paukerei *f (Sch col)* swotting *(col)*.
Pausbacken *pl* chubby cheeks *pl.*
pausbäckig *adj* chubby-cheeked.
pauschal *adj (einheitlich)* flat-rate *attr only; (inklusiv)* inclusive. **die Werkstatt berechnet ~ pro Inspektion 250 DM** the garage has a flat rate of DM 250 per service; **die Gebühren werden ~ bezahlt** the charges are paid in a lump sum; **die Reisekosten verstehen sich ~** the travelling costs are inclusive; **so ~ kann man das nicht sagen** *(fig)* that's much too sweeping a statement.
Pauschale *f* **-n** *(Einheitspreis)* flat rate; *(vorläufig geschätzer Betrag)* estimated amount.
Pauschal-: ~ gebühr *f* flat rate (charge); **~preis** *m (Einheitspreis)* flat rate; *(Inklusivpreis)* all-in price; **~reise** *f* package tour; **~summe** *f* lump sum; **~urteil** *nt* sweeping statement; **~versicherung** *f* comprehensive insurance *no pl.*
Pauschbetrag *m* flat rate.
Pause *f* **-n (a)** break; *(das Innehalten)* pause; *(Theat)* interval, intermission; *(Sch)* break *(Brit)*, recess *(US)*. **(eine) ~ machen, eine ~ einlegen** *(sich entspannen)* to have a break; *(rasten)* to take a rest; *(innehalten)* to pause; **nach einer langen ~ sagte er ...** after a long silence he said ... **(b)** *(Mus)* rest. **(c)** *(Durchzeichnung)* tracing.
pausen *vt* to trace.
Pausen-: ~brot *nt* sandwich, something to eat at break *(Brit) or* in the recess *(US)*; **~hof** *m* playground, schoolyard; **p~los** *adj no pred* continuous; **er arbeitet p~los** he works non-stop; **~zeichen** *nt (Mus)* rest; *(Rad)* call sign.
pausieren* *vi* to (take a) break.
Pauspapier *nt* tracing paper; *(Kohlepapier)* carbon paper.
Pavian ['pa:via:n] *m* **-e** baboon.
Pavillon ['pavɪljõ:] *m* **-s** pavilion.
Pazifik *m* Pacific.
pazifisch *adj* Pacific. **der P~e Ozean** the Pacific (Ocean).
Pazifismus *m* pacifism.
Pazifist(in *f***)** *m* pacifist.
Pech *nt* **-e (a)** *(Stoff)* pitch. **die beiden halten zusammen wie ~ und Schwefel** *(col)* the two are inseparable. **(b)** *no pl (col: Mißgeschick)* hard luck. **bei etw ~ haben** to have bad luck with sth; **~ gehabt!** tough! *(col)*; **so ein ~!** just my/our *etc* luck!
Pech-: p~(raben)schwarz *adj (col)* pitch-black; *Haar* jet-black; **~strähne** *f (col)* unlucky patch; **~vogel** *m (col)* unlucky person; *(Frau auch)* Calamity Jane.
Pedal *nt* **-e** pedal. **(fest) in die ~e treten** to pedal (hard).
Pedant *m (wk)* pedant.
pedantisch *adj* pedantic.
Peddigrohr *nt* cane.
Pediküre *f* **-n (a)** *no pl (Fußpflege)* pedicure. **(b)** *(Fußpflegerin)* chiropodist *(Brit)*, podiatrist *(US)*.
Peep-Show ['pi:pʃo:] *f* peepshow.
Pegel *m* - water depth gauge; *(Elec)* level recorder.
Pegelstand *m* water level.
peilen *vt Wassertiefe* to sound; *Sender* to take the bearings of; *Richtung* to plot; *(entdecken)* to detect. **die Lage ~** *(col)* to see how the land lies; **über den Daumen ~** *(col)* to guess roughly; **über den Daumen gepeilt** *(col)* at a rough estimate.
Peilgerät *nt* direction finder.
Peilung *f (von Wassertiefe)* sounding; *(von Sender)* locating; *(von Richtung)* plotting.
Pein *f no pl (geh, liter)* agony, suffering.
peinigen *vt (geh)* to torture; *(fig)* to torment. **von Schmerzen/Zweifeln gepeinigt** tormented by pain/doubt.
peinlich *adj* **(a)** *(unangenehm)* (painfully) embarrassing; *Lage, Fragen auch* awkward. **es war ihm ~(, daß ...)** he felt embarrassed (because ...); **das ist mir ja so ~** I feel awful about it. **(b)** *(gewissenhaft)* painstaking. **in seinem Zimmer herrschte ~e Ordnung** his room was meticulously tidy; **der Koffer wurde ~ genau untersucht** the case was given a very thorough going-over *(col)*; **er vermied es ~st, davon zu sprechen** he was at pains not to talk about it.
Peinlichkeit *f (Unangenehmheit)* embarrassment.
Peitsche *f* **-n** whip.

peitschen *vti* to whip; *(fig)* to lash.
Peitschen-: ~**hieb** *m* lash; ~**knall** *m* crack of a whip.
Pekinese *m (wk)* **-n, -n** pekinese, peke *(col)*.
Pelikan *m* **-e** pelican.
Pelle *f* **-n** *(col)* skin. **der Chef sitzt mir auf der** ~ *(col)* I've got the boss on my back *(col)*; **er geht mir nicht von der** ~ *(col)* he won't stop pestering me.
pellen *vtr (col)* to peel.
Pellkartoffeln *pl* potatoes *pl* boiled in their jackets.
Pelz *m* **-e** fur; *(nicht gegerbt auch)* hide.
Pelz- *in cpds* fur; ~**besatz** *m* fur trimming; ~**händler** *m* furrier.
pelzig *adj* furry.
Pelz-: ~**mantel** *m* fur coat; ~**tier** *nt* animal prized for its fur; ~**waren** *pl* furs *pl*.
Pendant [pã'dã:] *nt* **-s** counterpart.
Pendel *nt* **-** pendulum.
pendeln *vi* **(a)** *(schwingen)* to swing (to and fro). **(b)** *aux sein (Zug, Fähre etc)* to shuttle; *(Mensch)* to commute; *(fig)* to fluctuate.
Pendel-: ~**tür** *f* swing door; ~**uhr** *f* pendulum clock; ~**verkehr** *m* shuttle service; *(Berufsverkehr)* commuter traffic.
Pendler(in *f***)** *m* **-** commuter.
penetrant *adj* **(a)** *Geruch* penetrating. **das schmeckt** ~ **nach Knoblauch** it has a very strong taste of garlic. **(b)** *(fig: aufdringlich)* insistent; *Selbstsicherheit* overpowering.
peng *interj* bang.
penibel *adj* pernickety *(col)*, precise.
Penis *m* **-, -se** *or* **Penes** penis.
Penizillin *nt* **-e** penicillin.
Pennbruder *m (col)* tramp, hobo *(US)*.
Penne *f* **-n** **(a)** *(Sch sl)* school. **(b)** *(col: Herberge)* doss house *(col)*.
pennen *vi (col)* to kip *(col)*.
Penner(in *f***)** *m* **-** *(col)* **(a)** tramp, hobo *(US)*. **(b)** *(verschlafener Mensch)* sleepyhead *(col)*.
Pension [*auch* pã'zio:n] *f* **-en** **(a)** *(Fremdenheim)* guest-house. **(b)** *no pl (Verpflegung)* board. **halbe/volle** ~ half/full board *(Brit)*, European/American plan *(US)*. **(c)** *(Ruhegehalt)* pension. **(d)** *no pl (Ruhestand)* retirement. **in** ~ **gehen** to retire; **in** ~ **sein** to be retired.
Pensionär(in *f***)** [*auch* pãzio'nɛ:ɐ, -ɛ:ərɪn] *m (Pension beziehend)* pensioner; *(im Ruhestand befindlich)* retired person.
pensionieren* [*auch* pãzio'ni:rən] *vt* to retire. **sich** ~ **lassen** to retire.
Pensionierung *f (Zustand)* retirement; *(Vorgang)* pensioning-off.
Pensions-: ~**alter** *nt* retiring age; ~**anspruch** *m* right to a pension; **p**~**berechtigt** *adj* entitled to a pension; ~**preis** *m* price for full board *(Brit) or* American plan *(US)*; **p**~**reif** *adj (col)* ready for retirement.
Pensum *nt, pl* **Pensa** *or* **Pensen** workload; *(Sch)* curriculum. **tägliches** ~ daily quota; **er hat sein** ~ **nicht geschafft** he didn't achieve his target.
Pep *m no pl (col)* pep *(col)*, life.
Peperoni *pl* chillies *pl*.
per *prep* **(a)** *(mittels)* by. **mit jdm** ~ **du sein** *(col)* to be on first-name terms with sb; ~ **pedes** *(hum)* on shanks's pony *(hum)*. **(b)** *(Comm) (bis)* by; *(pro)* per. ~ **Adresse** care of, c/o.
perfekt *adj* **(a)** *(vollkommen)* perfect. **(b)** *pred (abgemacht)* settled. **die Sache** ~ **machen** to clinch the deal; **der Vertrag ist** ~ the contract is all settled.
Perfekt *nt* **-e** perfect (tense).
Perfektion *f* perfection.
perfektionieren* [pɛrfɛktsio'ni:rən] *vt* to perfect.
Perfektionist(in *f***)** *m* perfectionist.
Perforation *f* perforation.
perforieren* *vt* to perforate.
Pergament *nt* parchment; *(Kalbs~ auch)* vellum.
Pergamentpapier *nt* greaseproof paper.
Pergola *f, pl* **Pergolen** bower.
Periode *f* **-n** period *(auch Physiol)*; *(von Wetter auch)* spell; *(Math)* repetend; *(Elec)* cycle. **0,33** ~ 0.33 recurring.
periodisch *adj* periodic(al); *(regelmäßig)* regular; *(Phys)* periodic.
peripher *adj* peripheral.
Peripherie *f* periphery; *(von Stadt)* outskirts *pl*. **an der** ~ **Bonns** on the outskirts of Bonn.
Peripheriegerät *nt (Comp)* peripheral.
Perle *f* **-n** **(a)** *(auch fig)* pearl. ~**n vor die Säue werfen** *(prov)* to cast pearls before swine *(prov)*. **(b)** *(Glas~, Holz~, von Schweiß)* bead; *(Luftbläschen)* bubble. **(c)** *(dated col: Hausgehilfin)* maid.
perlen *vi (sprudeln)* to bubble; *(fallen, rollen)* to trickle.
Perlen-: ~**kette** *f*, ~**kollier** *nt* pearl necklace.
Perl-: ~**huhn** *nt* guinea fowl; ~**muschel** *f* pearl oyster; ~**mutt** *nt no pl* mother-of-pearl.
Perlon ® *nt, no pl* ≈ nylon.
Perlwein *m* sparkling wine.
permanent *adj* permanent.
perplex *adj* dumbfounded, thunderstruck.
Perser(in *f***)** *m* **-** **(a)** Persian. **(b)** *(col: Teppich)* Persian carpet.
Perserteppich *m* Persian carpet.
Persianer *m* **-** **(a)** *(Pelz)* Persian lamb. **(b)** *(auch* ~**mantel***)* Persian lamb (coat).
Persien [-iən] *nt* Persia.
Persiflage [pɛrzi'fla:ʒə] *f* **-n** pastiche, satire *(gen, auf +acc* on, of*)*.
persisch *adj* Persian.
Person *f* **-en** **(a)** *(auch Gram)* person. ~**en** people, persons *(form)*; **eine aus 6** ~**en bestehende Familie** a family of 6; **die eigene** ~ oneself; **ich für meine** ~ **...** I myself ...; **ich hatte den Chef in** ~ **vor mir** I was talking to the boss himself; **er ist Finanz- und Außenminister in einer** ~ he's the Chancellor of the Exchequer and Foreign Secre tary rolled into one; **natürliche/juristische** ~ *(Jur)* natural/legal person; **sie ist die Geduld in** ~ she's patience personified; **lassen wir seine** ~ **aus dem Spiel** let's leave personalities out of it; **er ist klein von** ~ he's small in stature, he's a small person. **(b)** *(pej: Frau)* female. **(c)** *(Liter, Theat)* character.
Personal *nt no pl* personnel, staff. **ungenügend mit** ~ **versehen sein** to be understaffed.
Personal-: ~**abbau** *m* staff cuts *pl*; ~**abteilung** *f* personnel (department); ~**akte** *f* personal file; ~**angaben** *pl* particulars *pl*; ~**ausweis** *m* identity card; ~**büro** *nt* personnel (department); ~**chef** *m* personnel manager.
Personalien [-iən] *pl* particulars *pl*.
Personal-: ~**kartei** *f* personnel index; ~**leiter** *m* personnel manager; ~**pronomen** *nt* personal pronoun; ~**union** *f* **... in** ~**union** ... in one.
personell *adj* staff *attr*, personnel *attr*. **unsere Schwierigkeiten sind rein** ~ our difficulties are simply to do with staffing.
Personen-: ~**aufzug** *m* (passenger) lift *(Brit)*, elevator *(US)*; ~**beschreibung** *f* (personal) description; ~**gedächtnis** *nt* memory for faces; ~**kraftwagen** *m (form)* (private) car, automobile *(US)*; ~**kreis** *m* group of people; ~**kult** *m* personality cult; ~**schaden** *m* injury to persons; ~**stand** *m* marital status; ~**standsregister** *nt* register of births, marriages and deaths; ~**verkehr** *m* passenger services *pl*; ~**waage** *f* pair of scales; ~**wagen** *m (Rail)* carriage *(Brit)*, car; *(Aut)* (private) car, automobile *(US)*; ~**zug** *m* passenger train; *(Gegensatz: Schnellzug)* slow train.
Personifikation *f* personification.
personifizieren* *vt* to personify.

persönlich 1 *adj* personal; *Atmosphäre* friendly. ~ **werden** to get personal. **2** *adv* personally; *(auf Briefen)* private (and confidential). **etw ~ meinen/nehmen** to mean/take sth personally; **Sie müssen ~ erscheinen** you are required to appear in person; **~haften** *(Comm)* to be personally liable.

Persönlichkeit *f* personality. **er besitzt wenig ~** he hasn't got much personality; **er ist eine ~** he's quite a personality; **~en des öffentlichen Lebens** public figures.

Perspektive [-'ti:və] *f (Art, Opt)* perspective; *(Blickpunkt)* angle; *(fig: Zukunftsausblick)* prospects *pl*. **das eröffnet ganz neue ~n für uns** that opens new horizons for us.

perspektivisch [-'ti:vɪʃ] *adj* perspective *attr*, in perspective. **die Zeichnung ist nicht ~** the drawing is not in perspective.

Peru *nt* Peru.

Peruaner(in *f*) *m* - Peruvian.

Perücke *f* **-n** wig.

pervers [pɛr'vɛrs] *adj* perverted. **ein ~er Mensch** a pervert.

Perversion [pɛrvɛr'zio:n] *f* perversion.

Perversität [pɛrvɛrzi'tɛ:t] *f* perversion.

pervertieren* [pɛrvɛr'ti:rən] **1** *vt* to pervert. **2** *vi aux sein* to become perverted.

Pessar *nt* **-e** pessary; *(zur Empfängnisverhütung)* cap, diaphragm.

Pessimismus *m* pessimism.

Pessimist(in *f*) *m* pessimist.

pessimistisch *adj* pessimistic.

Pest *f no pl (Hist, Med)* plague. **jdn/etw wie die ~ hassen** *(col)* to loathe sb/sth; **jdn wie die ~ meiden** *(col)* to avoid sb like the plague; **wie die ~ stinken** *(col)* to stink to high heaven *(col)*.

Petersilie [-iə] *f* parsley.

Petition *f* petition.

Petro(l)chemie *f* petrochemistry.

Petroleum [pe'tro:leʊm] *nt no pl* paraffin (oil) *(Brit)*, kerosene *(US)*.

Petunie [-iə] *f* petunia.

Petze *f* **-n, Petzer** *m* - *(Sch sl)* sneak *(Sch sl)*.

petzen *(col)* **1** *vt* **der petzt alles** he always tells; **er hat's dem Lehrer gepetzt** he told sir *(Sch sl)*. **2** *vi* to tell (tales).

Pf = **Pfennig.**

Pfad *m* **-e** path, track.

Pfadfinder *m* - (boy) scout. **er ist bei den ~n** he's in the (Boy) Scouts.

Pfadfinderin *f* girl guide *(Brit)*, girl scout *(US)*.

Pfaffe *m (wk)* **-n, -n** *(pej)* cleric *(pej)*.

Pfahl *m* **⸚e** post; *(Zaun~ auch, Marter~)* stake; *(Brücken~)* pile.

Pfahlbau *m* **-ten (a)** *no pl (Bauweise)* building on stilts. **(b)** *(Haus)* pile dwelling.

Pfalz *f (Geog)* Palatinate.

Pfälzer(in *f*) *m* - **(a)** person from the Palatinate. **(b)** *(Wein)* wine from the Rhineland Palatinate.

pfälzisch *adj* Palatine.

Pfand *nt* **⸚er** security; *(beim Pfänderspiel)* forfeit; *(Flaschen~)* deposit; *(fig geh)* pledge. **etw als ~ geben** *(lit, fig)* to pledge sth; *(beim Pfänderspiel)* to pay sth as a forfeit; **auf der Flasche ist 10 Pf ~** there's 10 Pf (back) on the bottle *(col)*; **ein ~ einlösen** to redeem a pledge; **etw als ~ behalten** to keep sth as (a) security.

Pfandbrief *m* bond, debenture.

pfänden *vt (Jur)* to impound. **man hat ihm die Möbel gepfändet** they took away his furniture; **jdn ~ lassen** to get the bailiffs onto sb.

Pfand-: ~haus *nt*, **~leihe** *f* pawnshop; **~leiher** *m* - pawnbroker; **~schein** *m* pawn ticket.

Pfändung *f* seizure, distraint *(form)*.

Pfanne *f* **-n** *(Cook)* pan. **jdn in die ~ hauen** *(col)* to tear a strip off sb *(col)*.

Pfannkuchen *m* pancake. **Berliner ~** (jam) doughnut.

Pfarr|amt *nt* priest's office.

Pfarrei *f (Gemeinde)* parish; *(Amtsräume)* priest's office.

Pfarrer(in *f*) *m* - vicar; *(katholisch)* priest; *(von Freikirchen)* minister; *(Gefängnis~, Militär~ etc)* chaplain, padre.

Pfau *m* **-en** peacock. **aufgedonnert wie ein ~** *(col)* dressed up to the nines *(col)*.

Pfauen|auge *nt (Tag~)* peacock butterfly.

Pfeffer *m* - pepper. **er kann bleiben, wo der ~ wächst!** *(col)* he can take a running jump *(col)*.

pfeff(e)rig *adj* peppery.

Pfeffer-: ~korn *nt* peppercorn; **~kuchen** *m* gingerbread.

Pfefferminz(bonbon) *nt* **-(e)** peppermint.

Pfefferminze *f no pl* peppermint.

Pfeffermühle *f* pepper-mill.

pfeffern *vt* **(a)** *(Cook)* to pepper; *siehe* **gepfeffert. (b)** *(col) (heftig werfen)* to fling; *(hinauswerfen)* to sling out *(col)*. **jdm eine ~** to clout sb one *(col)*.

Pfeffernuß *f* gingerbread ball.

Pfeife *f* **-n (a)** whistle; *(Quer~)* fife *(esp Mil)*; *(Orgel~)* pipe. **nach jds ~ tanzen** to dance to sb's tune. **(b)** *(zum Rauchen)* pipe. **~ rauchen** to smoke a pipe.

pfeifen *pret* **pfiff,** *ptp* **gepfiffen** *vti* to whistle *(dat* for*)*; *(auf einer Trillerpfeife)* to blow one's whistle; *(Mus)* to pipe; *(col) Spiel* to ref *(col)*. **auf dem letzten Loch ~** *(col) (erschöpft sein)* to be on one's last legs *(col)*; *(finanziell)* to be on one's beam ends *(col)*; **ich pfeife darauf!** *(col)* I don't give a damn *(col)*; **das ~ ja schon die Spatzen von den Dächern** it's all over town.

Pfeifen-: ~kopf *m* bowl (of a pipe); **~stopfer** *m* tamper; **~tabak** *m* pipe tobacco.

Pfeifer *m* - piper.

Pfeiferei *f (col)* whistling.

Pfeifkonzert *nt* catcalls *pl*.

Pfeil *m* **-e** arrow; *(Wurf~)* dart. **~ und Bogen** bow and arrow; **er schoß wie ein ~ davon** he was off like a shot.

Pfeiler *m* - *(lit, fig)* pillar; *(Brücken~ auch)* pier; *(Stütz~)* buttress.

Pfeil-: p~gerade *adj Linie* dead straight; **sie kam p~gerade auf uns zu** she headed straight for us; **p~schnell** *adj* as swift as an arrow *(liter)*; **~spitze** *f* arrowhead; **~wurfspiel** *nt* darts *pl*.

Pfennig *m* **-e** *or (nach Zahlenangabe)* **-** pfennig *(one hundredth of a mark)*. **30 ~** 30 pfennigs; **er hat keinen ~ Geld** he hasn't got a penny to his name *or* doesn't have a dime *(US)*; **nicht für fünf ~** *(col)* not the slightest (bit of); **er hat nicht für fünf ~ Verstand** *(col)* he hasn't an ounce of intelligence; **mit jedem ~ rechnen müssen** *(fig)* to have to count every penny; **jeden ~ umdrehen** *(fig col)* to think twice about every penny one spends.

Pfennig-: ~absatz *m* stiletto heel; **~fuchser** *m* - *(col)* skinflint *(col)*; **~stück** *nt* pfennig (piece).

Pferch *m* **-e** fold, pen.

pferchen *vt* to cram, to pack.

Pferd *nt* **-e** *(Tier, Turngerät)* horse; *(beim Schachspiel)* knight, horse *(US col)*. **zu ~e** on horseback; **aufs falsche/richtige ~ setzen** *(lit, fig)* to back the wrong/right horse; **wie ein ~ arbeiten** *(col)* to work like a Trojan; **keine zehn ~e brächten mich dahin** *(col)* wild horses wouldn't drag me there; **mit ihm kann man ~e stehlen** *(col)* he's a great sport *(col)*; **er ist unser bestes ~ im Stall** he's our best man.

Pferde-: ~äpfel horse droppings *pl or* dung *no pl*; **~fuhrwerk** *nt* horse and cart; **~fuß** *m* **die Sache hat aber einen ~fuß** there's just one snag; **~gebiß** *nt* horsey teeth; **~haar** *nt* horsehair; **~knecht** *m* groom; **~koppel** *f* paddock; **~rennbahn** *f* race course; **~rennen** *nt (Sportart)* (horse-)racing; *(einzelnes Rennen)* (horse-)race; **~schwanz** *m* horse's tail; *(Frisur)* pony-tail; **~stall** *m* stable; **~stärke** *f* horse power *no pl*, hp *abbr;* **~wagen** *m (für Personen)* trap, horse-buggy *(US); (für Lasten)* horse and cart; **~zucht** *f* horse breeding; *(Gestüt)* stud-farm.

pfiff *pret of* **pfeifen.**

Pfiff *m* **-e (a)** whistle. **(b)** *(Reiz)* style. **der Soße fehlt noch der letzte ~** the sauce still needs that extra something.

Pfifferling *m* chanterelle. **er kümmert sich keinen ~ darum** *(col)* he doesn't give a damn about it *(col)*; **keinen ~ wert** *(col)* not worth a thing.

pfiffig *adj* smart, cute.

Pfingsten *nt* **-** Whitsun, Pentecost *(Eccl)*.

Pfingst-: ~montag *m* Whit Monday; **~ochse** *m*: **herausgeputzt wie ein ~ochse** *(col)* dressed up to the nines *(col)*; **~rose** *f* peony; **~sonntag** *m* Whit Sunday, Pentecost *(Eccl)*; **~zeit** *f* Whitsun(tide).

Pfirsich *m* **-e** peach.

Pflanze *f* **-n (a)** *(Gewächs)* plant. **(b)** *(col: Mensch)* **sie ist eine seltsame ~** she is an odd bird *(col)*.

pflanzen 1 *vt* to plant. **2** *vr (col)* to plonk oneself *(col)*.

Pflanzen-: ~fett *nt* vegetable fat; **~fresser** *m* herbivore; **~kunde, ~lehre** *f* botany; **~öl** *nt* vegetable oil; **~reich** *nt* vegetable kingdom; **~schädling** *m* pest; **~schutz** *m* protection of plants; *(gegen Ungeziefer)* pest control; **~schutzmittel** *nt* pesticide; **~welt** *f* **die ~welt des Mittelmeers** the flora of the Mediterranean.

pflanzlich *adj attr* vegetable.

Pflanzung *f (das Pflanzen)* planting; *(Plantage)* plantation.

Pflaster *nt* **- (a)** *(Heft~)* (sticking-)plaster. **(b)** *(Straßen~)* (road) surface; *(Kopfstein~)* cobbles *pl*. **ein teures ~** *(col)* a pricey place *(col)*.

pflastern *vt Straße* to surface; *(mit Kopfsteinpflaster)* to cobble; *(mit Steinplatten)* to pave.

Pflasterstein *m (Kopfstein)* cobble(stone); *(Steinplatte)* paving stone.

Pflaume *f* **-n (a)** plum. **getrocknete ~** prune. **(b)** *(col: Mensch)* twit *(Brit col)*, dope *(col)*.

Pflaumen-: ~kompott *nt* stewed plums *pl*; **~kuchen** *m* plum tart; **~mus** *nt* plum jam.

Pflege *f no pl* care; *(von Kranken auch)* nursing; *(von Garten auch)* attention; *(von Beziehungen, Künsten)* cultivation; *(von Maschinen, Gebäuden)* upkeep. **jdn/etw in ~ nehmen** to look after sb/sth; **ein Kind in ~ nehmen** *(dauernd)* to foster a child; **ein Kind in ~ geben** to have a child fostered; *(von Behörden)* to foster a child out *(zu jdm* with sb*)*.

Pflege-: p~bedürftig *adj* in need of care; **~eltern** *pl* foster parents *pl*; **~fall** *m* case for nursing; **~geld** *nt (für ~kinder)* boarding-out allowance; *(für Kranke)* attendance allowance; **~heim** *nt* nursing home; **~kind** *nt* foster child; **p~leicht** *adj* easy-care.

pflegen 1 *vt* to look after; *Kranke auch* to nurse; *Beziehungen, Kunst* to cultivate; *Maschinen, Gebäude* to maintain. **2** *vi (gewöhnlich tun)* to be in the habit *(zu* of*)*. **sie pflegte zu sagen** she used to say.

Pfleger *m* **-** *(im Krankenhaus)* orderly; *(voll qualifiziert)* (male) nurse.

Pflegerin *f* nurse.

Pflege-: ~satz *m* hospital and nursing charges *pl*; **~sohn** *m* foster son; **~station** *f* nursing ward; **~tochter** *f* foster daughter.

pfleglich *adj* careful.

Pflicht *f* **-en (a)** *(Verpflichtung)* duty. **als Abteilungsleiter hat er die ~, ...** it's his responsibility as head of department ...; **Rechte und ~en** rights and responsibilities; **seine ~ erfüllen** to do one's duty; **die ~ ruft** duty calls; **das/Schulbesuch ist ~** it's/going to school is compulsory; **es ist seine (verdammte** *col*) **~ und Schuldigkeit(, das zu tun)** he damn well ought to (do it) *(col)*. **(b)** *(Sport)* compulsory section.

Pflicht-: p~bewußt *adj* conscientious; **er ist sehr p~bewußt** he takes his duties very seriously; **~bewußtsein** *nt* sense of duty; **~fach** *nt* compulsory subject; **~gefühl** *nt* sense of duty; **p~gemäß** *adj* dutiful; **~lektüre** *f* compulsory reading; *(Sch auch)* set book(s); **~übung** *f* compulsory exercise; **p~vergessen** *adj* irresponsible; **~vergessenheit, ~versäumnis** *f* neglect of duty *no pl*; **p~versichert** *adj* compulsorily insured; **~versicherung** *f* compulsory insurance.

Pflock *m* **¨-e** peg; *(für Tiere)* stake.

pflücken *vt* to pick, to pluck.

Pflücker(in *f***)** *m* **-** picker.

Pflug *m* **¨-e** plough *(Brit)*, plow *(US)*.

Pflugschar *f* **-en** ploughshare *(Brit)*, plowshare *(US)*.

Pforte *f* **-n** *(Tor)* gate; *(Geog)* gap. **die ~ zum Himalaja** the gateway to the Himalayas.

Pförtner(in *f***)** *m* **-** porter; *(von Fabrik)* gateman; *(von Wohnhaus, Behörde)* doorman; *(von Schloß)* gatekeeper.

Pförtnerloge [-loːʒə] *f* porter's office; *(in Fabrik)* gatehouse; *(in Wohnhaus, Büro)* doorman's office.

Pfosten *m* **-** *(auch Ftbl)* post; *(senkrechter Balken)* upright; *(Fenster~, Tür~)* jamb; *(Stütze)* prop.

Pfote *f* **-n (a)** *(lit, fig col)* paw. **sich** *(dat)* **die ~n verbrennen** *(col)* to burn one's fingers. **(b)** *(col: schlechte Handschrift)* scribble, scrawl.

Pfropf *m* **-e** *or* **¨-e, Pfropfen** *m* **-** *(Stöpsel)* stopper; *(Kork, Sekt~)* cork; *(Watte~ etc)* plug; *(von Faß)* bung; *(Med: Blut~)* (blood) clot.

pfropfen *vt* **(a)** *Flasche* to put the stopper in. **(b)** *(col: hineinzwängen)* to cram. **gepfropft voll** crammed full.

pfui *interj (Ekel)* ugh, yuck; *(Mißbilligung)* tut tut; *(zu Hunden)* oy, hey; *(Buhruf)* boo. **~ Teufel!** *(col)* ugh, yuck; **~, schäm dich!** shame on you!

Pfund *nt* **-e** *or (nach Zahlenangabe)* **- (a)** *(Gewicht) (metrisches System)* 500 grams, half a kilo(gram); *(britisches System)* pound. **drei ~ Äpfel** three pounds of apples. **(b)** *(Währungseinheit)* pound. **zwanzig ~ Sterling** twenty pounds sterling; **das ~ sinkt** sterling *or* the pound is falling.

pfundig *adj (col)* fantastic, swell *no adv (US)*.

Pfundskerl *m (col)* great guy *(col)*.

pfundweise *adv* by the pound.

Pfusch *m no pl (col)* = **Pfuscherei.**

pfuschen *vi* to bungle; *(einen Fehler machen)* to slip up.

Pfuscher(in *f***)** *m* **-** *(col)* bungler.

Pfuscherei *f (das Pfuschen)* bungling *no pl*; *(gepfuschte Arbeit)* botched-up job.

Pfütze *f* **-n** puddle.

PH [peːˈhaː] *f* **-s** = **Pädagogische Hochschule.**

Phallussymbol *nt* phallic symbol.

Phänomen *nt* **-e** phenomenon.

phänomenal *adj* phenomenal.

Phantasie *f* **(a)** *no pl (Einbildung)* imagination. **in seiner ~** in his mind. **(b)** *usu pl (Trugbild)* fantasy.

Phantasie-: p~begabt *adj* imaginative; **~gebilde** *nt* **(a)** *(phantastische Form)* fantastic form; **(b)** *(Einbildung)* figment of the imagination; **p~los** *adj* unimaginative; **~losigkeit** *f* lack of imagination.

phantasieren* 1 *vi* to fantasize *(von* about*)*; *(von Schlimmem)* to have visions *(von* of*)*; *(Med)* to be delirious; *(Mus)* to improvise. **er phantasiert von einem großen Haus auf dem Lande** he has fantasies about a big house in the country. **2** *vt Geschichte* to dream up. **was phantasiert du denn da?** *(col)* what are you (going) on about? *(col)*.

Phantasie-: p~voll *adj* highly imaginative; **~vorstellung** *f* figment of the imagination.

Phantast *m (wk)* **-en, -en** dreamer, visionary.

phantastisch *adj* fantastic.

Phantom *nt* **-e** *(Trugbild)* phantom. **einem ~**

nachjagen *(fig)* to tilt at windmills.
Pharmakologie *f* pharmacology.
Pharmazeut(in *f*) *m (wk)* **-en, -en** pharmacist, druggist *(US)*.
pharmazeutisch *adj* pharmaceutical.
Pharmazie *f* pharmacy, pharmaceutics *sing.*
Phase *f* **-n** phase.
Philanthropie *f* philanthropy.
Philatelie *f* philately.
Philharmonie *f (Orchester)* philharmonic (orchestra); *(Konzertsaal)* philharmonic hall.
Philharmoniker *m* **- die ~** the philharmonic (orchestra).
Philippine *m (wk)* **-n, -n, Philippinin** *f* Filipino.
Philippinen *pl* Philippines *pl.*
Philologe *m*, **Philologin** *f* philologist.
Philologie *f* philology.
Philosoph(in *f*) *m (wk)* **-en, -en** philosopher.
Philosophie *f* philosophy.
philosophieren* *vi* to philosophize *(über +acc* about*)*.
philosophisch *adj* philosophical.
Phlegmatiker(in *f*) *m* **-** apathetic person.
phlegmatisch *adj* apathetic.
Phobie [fo'biː] *f* phobia *(vor* about*)*.
Phonetik *f* phonetics *sing.*
phonetisch *adj* phonetic.
Phonotypistin *f* audio-typist.
Phosphat [fɔs'faːt] *nt* phosphate.
Phosphor ['fɔsfɔr] *m no pl* phosphorus.
Photo *nt* **-s = Foto.**
Phrase *f* **-n** phrase; *(pej)* hollow phrase. **das sind alles nur ~n** that's just talk; **~n dreschen** *(col)* to churn out one cliché after another.
Phrasen-: ~drescher *m (pej)* windbag; **~drescherei** *f (pej)* phrase-mongering; *(Geschwafel)* hot air; **p~haft** *adj* empty.
Physik *f no pl* physics *sing.*
physikalisch *adj* physical; *Experimente* physics *attr*; **das ist ~ nicht erklärbar** that can't be explained by physics.
Physiker(in *f*) *m* **-** physicist.
Physikum *nt no pl (Univ) preliminary examination in medicine.*
Physiologe *m*, **Physiologin** *f* physiologist.
Physiologie *f* physiology.
physiologisch *adj* physiological.
physisch *adj* physical.
Pianist(in *f*) *m* pianist.
Pickel *m* **- (a)** spot, pimple. **(b)** *(Spitzhacke)* pick(axe *(Brit) or* ax *US*); *(Eis~)* ice axe *(Brit)*, ice ax *(US)*.
pick(e)lig *adj* spotty, pimply.
picken *vti* to peck *(nach* at*)*.
Picknick *nt* **-s** *or* **-e** picnic. **~ machen** to have a picnic.
picknicken *vi* to (have a) picnic.
piekfein *adj (col)* posh *(col)*.
pieksauber *adj (col)* spotless.
piep *interj* tweet(-tweet).
Piep *m* **-e** *(col)* **er sagt keinen ~** he doesn't say a (single) word; **keinen ~ mehr machen** to have had it *(col)*.
piepe, piep|egal *adj pred* **das ist mir ~!** *(col)* it's all one to me *(col)*.
piepen, pie|psen *vi (Vogel)* to cheep; *(Kinderstimme)* to pipe; *(Maus)* to squeak; *(Funkgerät etc)* to bleep. **bei dir piept's wohl!** *(col)* are you off your head?; **es war zum P~!** *(col)* it was a scream *(col)*.
Piepmatz *m (col: kleiner Vogel)* birdie *(col)*.
piepsig *adj (col)* squeaky.
Piepsstimme *f* squeaky voice.
Pier *m* **-s** *or* **-e** *or f* **-s** jetty, pier.
piesacken *vt (col) (quälen)* to torment; *(belästigen)* to pester.
Pietät [pie'tɛːt] *f* reverence *no pl*; *(Achtung)* respect.
pietätlos [pie'tɛːt-] *adj* irreverent.
Pigment *nt* pigment.
Pigmentfleck *m* pigmentation mark.
Pik[1] *m (col)* **einen ~ auf jdn haben** to have a grudge against sb.
Pik[2] *nt* **-s** *(Cards) (Farbe)* spades *pl*; *(Karte)* spade. **~-As** ace of spades.
pikant *adj* piquant; *Witz, Geschichte auch* racy.
Pikanterie *f* **(a)** *no pl siehe adj* piquancy; raciness. **(b)** *(Bemerkung)* racy remark.
Pike *f* **-n** pike. **etw von der ~ auf lernen** *(fig)* to learn sth starting from the bottom.
piken *vti (col)* to prick.
pikiert *adj (col)* peeved, piqued. **sie machte ein ~es Gesicht** she looked peeved.
Pikkolo *m* **-s (a)** *(Kellnerlehrling)* trainee waiter. **(b)** *(fig)* mini-version, baby; *(auch* **~flasche***) quarter bottle of champagne.* **(c)** *(Mus: auch* **~flöte***)* piccolo.
piksen *vti (col)* to prick.
Pilger(in *f*) *m* **-** pilgrim.
Pilgerfahrt *f* pilgrimage.
pilgern *vi aux sein* to make a pilgrimage; *(col: gehen)* to wend one's way.
Pille *f* **-n** pill. **sie nimmt die ~** she's on the pill.
Pilot(in *f*) *m (wk)* **-en, -en** pilot.
Pilotstudie *f* pilot study.
Pils -, -, Pils(e)ner *nt* **-** Pils.
Pilz *m* **-e (a)** fungus; *(giftig)* toadstool; *(eßbar)* mushroom; *(Atom~)* mushroom cloud. **wie ~e aus dem Boden schießen** to mushroom. **(b)** *(Haut~)* ringworm; *(Fuß~ auch)* athlete's foot.
Pilz-: ~krankheit *f* fungal disease; **~vergiftung** *f* fungus poisoning.
Pimmel *m* **-** *(col: Penis)* willie *(col)*.
pingelig *adj (col)* finicky *(col)*, fussy.
Pingpong *nt* **-s** *(col)* ping-pong.
Pinguin ['pɪŋguiːn] *m* **-e** penguin.
Pinie ['piːniə] *f* pine (tree).
Pinkel *m* **-** *(col)* **ein feiner** *or* **vornehmer ~** a swell, Lord Muck *(col)*.
pinkeln *vi (col)* to pee *(col)*, to piddle *(col)*.
Pinscher *m* **-** pinscher.
Pinsel *m* **- (a)** brush. **(b)** *(col)* **ein eingebildeter ~** a self-opinionated twerp *(col)*.
pinseln *vti (col)* to paint; *(pej: malen)* to daub.
Pinte *f* **-n** *(col: Lokal)* boozer *(Brit col)*, bar.
Pinzette *f* (pair of) tweezers *pl.*
Pionier *m* **-e (a)** *(Mil)* sapper. **(b)** *(fig)* pioneer.
Pionier|arbeit *f* pioneering work.
Pipi *nt or m* **-s** *(baby-talk)* wee-wee *(baby-talk)*. **~machen** to do a wee-wee.
Pirat *m (wk)* **-en, -en** pirate.
Piratensender *m* pirate radio station.
Piraterie *f (lit, fig)* piracy.
Pirsch *f no pl* stalk. **auf (die) ~ gehen** to go stalking.
pirschen *vi* to stalk, to go stalking.
Piß *m no pl*, **Pisse** *f no pl (col!)* piss *(col!)*.
pissen *vi (col!)* to (have a) piss *(col!)*; *(regnen)* to piss down *(col!)*.
Pistazie [pɪs'taːtsiə] *f* pistachio.
Piste *f* **-n** *(Ski)* piste, (ski-)run; *(Rennbahn)* track; *(Aviat)* runway; *(behelfsmäßig)* airstrip.
Pistole *f* **-n** pistol. **jdn mit vorgehaltener ~ zwingen** to force sb at gunpoint; **jdm die ~ auf die Brust setzen** *(fig)* to hold a pistol to sb's head; **wie aus der ~ geschossen** *(fig)* like a shot.
pitsch(e)naß *adj (col)* soaking (wet).
pittoresk *adj* picturesque.
Pkw ['peːkaːveː] *m* **-s = Personenkraftwagen.**
placken *vr (col)* to slave (away) *(col)*.
Plackerei *f (col)* grind *(col)*.
plädieren* *vi (Jur, fig)* to plead *(für, auf +acc* for*)*.
Plädoyer [plɛdoa'jeː] *nt* **-s** *(Jur)* summing up, summation *(US)*; *(fig)* plea.
Plage *f* **-n** *(fig)* nuisance. **man hat schon seine ~ mit dir** you are a nuisance.
Plagegeist *m* nuisance, pest.

plạgen 1 *vt* to torment; *(mit Bitten und Fragen auch)* to pester. **ein geplagter Mann** a harassed man. **2** *vr* **(a)** *(leiden)* to be bothered *(mit* by*)*. **(b)** *(arbeiten)* to slave away *(col)*.
Plagiạt *nt* plagiarism.
Plakạt *nt* **-e** poster; *(aus Pappe)* placard.
Plakạtfarbe *f* poster paint.
plakatiẹren* *vt* to placard; *(fig)* to broadcast.
Plakẹtte *f (Abzeichen)* badge; *(Münze)* commemorative coin; *(an Wänden)* plaque.
Plạn[1] *m* **¨e (a)** plan. **den ~ fassen, etw zu tun** to plan to do sth; **¨~e machen** *or* **schmieden** to make plans; **nach ~ verlaufen** to go according to plan. **(b)** *(Stadt~)* (street-)map; *(Grundriß, Bau~)* blueprint; *(Zeittafel)* timetable *(Brit)*, schedule *(US)*.
Plạn[2] *m* **¨e auf den ~ treten** *(fig)* to come on the scene; **jdn auf den ~ rufen** *(fig)* to bring sb into the arena.
Plạne *f* **-n** tarpaulin; *(von LKW)* hood; *(Schutzdach)* awning.
plạnen *vti* to plan.
Plạner(in *f***)** *m* **-** planner.
Planẹt *m (wk)* **-en, -en** planet.
Planetạrium *nt* planetarium.
Planẹtensystem *nt* planetary system.
plạngemäß *adj* = **planmäßig.**
planiẹren* *vt Boden* to level (off).
Planiẹrraupe *f* bulldozer.
Plạnke *f* **-n** plank, board; *(Leit~)* crash barrier.
plạnlos *adj* unsystematic; *(ziellos)* random.
Plạnlosigkeit *f* lack of planning.
plạnmäßig *adj (wie geplant)* as planned; *(pünktlich)* on schedule; *(methodisch)* methodical. **~e Ankunft/Abfahrt** scheduled time of arrival/departure.
Plạnschbecken *nt* paddling pool.
plạnschen *vi* to splash around.
Plạn-: **~soll** *nt* output target; **~stelle** *f* post.
Plantage [plan'taːʒə] *f* **-n** plantation.
Plạnung *f* planning. **in der ~** at the planning stage.
Plạn-: **~wagen** *m* covered wagon; **~wirtschaft** *f* planned economy.
Plạppermaul *nt (col)* chatterbox *(col)*; *(Schwätzer)* gossip *(col)*.
plạppern 1 *vi* to prattle; *(Geheimnis verraten)* to blab *(col)*. **2** *vt Blödsinn* to talk.
plạ̈rren *vti (col: weinen)* to bawl; *(Radio)* to blare (out).
Plạstik[1] *nt* **-s** *(Kunststoff)* plastic.
Plạstik[2] *f* **(a)** *(Bildhauerkunst)* plastic art *(form)*. **(b)** *(Skulptur)* sculpture.
plạstisch *adj* **(a)** *(knetbar)* malleable. **(b)** *(dreidimensional)* three-dimensional, 3-D; *(fig: anschaulich)* vivid. **~e Sprache** vivid language; **das kann ich mir ~ vorstellen** I can just picture it. **(c)** *(Art, Med)* plastic. **~e Chirurgie** plastic surgery.
Plastizitạ̈t *f no pl* **(a)** *(Formbarkeit)* malleability. **(b)** *(fig: Anschaulichkeit)* vividness.
Plateau [pla'toː] *nt* **-s** plateau.
Platin *nt no pl* platinum.
platọnisch *adj* platonic.
plạtsch *interj* splash, splosh.
plạtschen *vi (col)* to splash; *(regnen)* to pour.
plạ̈tschern *vi* to splash; *(Bach auch)* to babble. **eine ~de Unterhaltung** light conversation.
plạtschnaß *adj (col)* soaking (wet).
plạtt *adj* **(a)** *(flach)* flat. **etw ~ drücken** to flatten sth; **einen P~en** *(col) or* **einen ~en Reifen haben** to have a flat (tyre *(Brit) or* tire *US*). **(b)** *(fig: geistlos)* dull. **(c)** *(col: verblüfft)* **~sein** to be flabbergasted *(col)*.
Plạtt *nt no pl (col)* Low German, Plattdeutsch.
plạttdeutsch *adj* Low German.
Plạtte *f* **-n (a)** *(Holz~)* board; *(Glas~/Metall~/Plastik~)* sheet of glass/metal/plastic; *(Beton~, Stein~)* slab; *(zum Pflastern)* flagstone; *(Kachel, Fliese)* tile; *(Herd~)* hotplate; *(Tisch~)* (table-)top; *(Phot)* plate; *(Gedenktafel)* plaque. **(b)** *(Fleisch)* serving-dish; *(Torten~)* cake plate. **kalte ~** cold dish. **(c)** *(Schall~)* record, disc. **etw auf ~ aufnehmen** to record sth; **die ~ kenne ich schon** *(col)* I've heard all that before *(col)*; **leg doch mal eine neue ~ auf!** *(col)* change the record, can't you! **(d)** *(col: Glatze)* bald head; *(kahle Stelle)* bald patch.
plạ̈tten *vt (dial)* to iron, to press; *siehe* **geplättet.**
Plạtten-: **~leger** *m* **-** paver; **~sammlung** *f* record collection; **~spieler** *m* record-player; **~teller** *m* turntable; **~wechsler** *m* **-** record changer.
Plạtt-: **~fisch** *m* flatfish; **~form** *f* platform; *(fig: Grundlage)* basis; **~fuß** *m* flat foot; **p~füßig** *adj, adv* flat-footed; **~heit** *f* **(a)** *no pl (Geistlosigkeit)* dullness; **(b)** *usu pl (Redensart etc)* platitude.
Plạtz *m* **¨e (a)** *(freier Raum)* room, space. **~ für jdn/etw schaffen** to make room for sb/sth; **mehr als 10 Leute haben hier nicht ~** there's not room for more than 10 people here; **jdm den (ganzen) ~ wegnehmen** to take up all the room; **~ machen** to get out of the way *(col)*; **mach mal ein bißchen ~** make a bit of room; **~ für jdn/etw bieten** to have room for sb/sth; **~ da!** *(col)* (get) out of the way there! *(col)*.

(b) *(Sitzplatz)* seat. **~ nehmen** to take a seat; **behalten Sie doch bitte ~!** *(form)* please remain seated *(form)*; **der Saal hat 2.000 ~e** the hall seats 2,000; **mit jdm den ~ tauschen** to change places with sb; **~!** *(zum Hund)* sit!

(c) *(Stelle, Ort, Rang, Arbeits ~)* place. **etw (wieder) an seinen ~ stellen** to put sth (back) in (its) place; **fehl** *or* **nicht am ~e sein** to be out of place; **auf die ¨~e, fertig, los!** *(Sport)* on your marks, get set, go!; **seinen ~ behaupten** to stand one's ground; **das Buch hat einen festen ~ auf der Bestsellerliste** the book is firmly established on the bestseller list; **den ersten ~ einnehmen** *(fig)* to come first; **auf ~ zwei** in second place; **jdn auf die ¨~e verweisen** *(fig)* to beat sb; **auf ~ wetten** to make a place bet; **wir haben noch einen freien ~ im Büro** we've still got one vacancy in the office; **das erste Hotel am ~** the best hotel in town.

(d) *(umbaute Fläche)* square. **auf dem ~** in the square.

(e) *(Sport~)* playing field; *(Ftbl, Hockey)* pitch *(Brit)*, field; *(Handball~, Tennis~)* court; *(Golf~)* (golf) course. **einen Spieler vom ~ stellen** *or* **verweisen** to send a player off.
Plạtz-: **~angst** *(col)* claustrophobia; **~angst bekommen** to get claustrophobic; **~anweiser(in** *f***)** *m* **-** usher(ette).
Plạ̈tzchen *nt (Gebäck)* biscuit *(Brit)*, cookie *(US)*.
plạtzen *vi aux sein* **(a)** *(aufreißen)* to burst; *(Naht, Hose, Haut)* to split; *(explodieren)* to explode; *(einen Riß bekommen)* to crack. **wir sind vor Lachen fast geplatzt** we split our sides laughing; **ins Zimmer ~** *(col)* to burst into the room; **jdm ins Haus ~** *(col)* to descend on sb; **(vor Wut/Neid) ~** *(col)* to be bursting (with rage/envy). **(b)** *(col: scheitern) (Geschäft)* to fall through; *(Freundschaft)* to break up; *(Theorie, Verschwörung)* to collapse; *(Wechsel)* to bounce *(col)*. **die Verlobung ist geplatzt** the engagement is (all) off; **etw ~ lassen** *Plan* to make sth fall through; *Theorie* to explode sth; *Spionagering* to smash sth; *Wechsel* to make sth bounce *(col)*.
Plạtz-: **~hirsch** *m (lit)* stag; *(fig col: Mann)* macho type; **~karte** *f (Rail)* seat reservation (ticket); **~konzert** *nt* open-air concert; **~mangel** *m* lack of space; **~miete** *f (Theat)* season ticket; *(Sport)* ground rent; **~patrone** *f* blank (cartridge); **~regen** *m* cloudburst; **das ist nur ein ~regen** it's only a (passing) shower; **p~sparend** *adj* space-saving *attr*; **das ist p~sparender** that saves more space; **~verweis** *m* sending-off; **~wahl** *f*

toss-up; ~**wart** *m (Sport)* groundsman; ~**wechsel** *m* change of place; *(Sport)* change of position; ~**wette** *f* place bet; ~**wunde** *f* laceration.
Plauderei *f* chat, conversation.
Plauderer *m* **-, Plauderin** *f* conversationalist.
plaudern *vi* to chat *(über +acc, von* about); *(verraten)* to talk. **mit ihm läßt sich gut ~** he's easy to talk to.
Plausch *m* **-e** *(col)* chat.
plauschen *vi (col)* to have a chat.
plausibel *adj* plausible. **jdm etw ~ machen** to explain sth to sb.
Playback ['pleɪbæk] *nt* **-s (a)** *(Bandaufnahme)* backing track. **(b)** *no pl (Verfahren) (bei Schallplatte)* double-tracking *no pl*; *(TV)* miming *no pl.*
plazieren* **1** *vt* **(a)** *(Platz anweisen)* to put; *(Tennis)* to seed. **(b)** *(zielen) Ball* to position; *Schlag* to land. **gut plazierte Aufschläge** well-positioned services. **2** *vr* **(a)** *(col: sich setzen, stellen)* to plant oneself *(col)*. **(b)** *(Sport)* to be placed; *(Tennis)* to be seeded. **der Läufer konnte sich gut/nicht ~** the runner was well-placed/wasn't even placed.
Plazierung *f (Einlauf)* order; *(Tennis)* seeding; *(Platz)* place. **welche ~ hatte er?** where did he come in?
pleite *adj pred, adv (col) Mensch* broke *(col)*; *Firma auch* bust *(col)*. **~ gehen** to go bust.
Pleite *f* **-n** *(col)* bankruptcy; *(fig)* washout *(col)*. **~ machen** to go bust *(col)*; **damit/mit ihm haben wir eine ~ erlebt** it/he was a disaster.
Pleitegeier *m (col)* **(a)** *(drohende Pleite)* threat of bankruptcy. **(b)** *(Bankrotteur)* bankrupt.
plemplem *adj pred (col)* nuts *(col)*.
Plenar-: ~**saal** *m* assembly room; ~**sitzung** *f* plenary session.
Plenum *nt* plenum.
Pleuelstange *f* connecting rod.
Plissee-: ~**falte** *f* pleat; ~**rock** *m* pleated skirt.
Plombe *f* **-n (a)** *(Siegel)* lead seal. **(b)** *(Zahn~)* filling.
plombieren* *vt* **(a)** *(versiegeln)* to seal. **(b)** *Zahn* to fill. **er hat mir zwei Zähne plombiert** he did two fillings.
plötzlich 1 *adj* sudden. **2** *adv* all of a sudden. **aber etwas ~!** *(col)* look sharp! *(col)*; **das kommt alles so ~** *(col)* it all happens so suddenly.
Pluderhose *f* Turkish trousers *pl.*
Plumeau [ply'moː] *nt* **-s** eiderdown, quilt.
plump *adj Figur, Form* ungainly *no adv; Ausdruck* clumsy; *Bemerkung* crass; *Mittel, Lüge* crude. ~**e Annäherungsversuche** very obvious advances.
plumps *interj* bang; *(lauter)* crash.
Plumps *m* **-e** *(col) (Fall)* tumble; *(Geräusch)* thud. **einen ~ machen** *(baby-talk)* to fall; **mit einem ~ ins Wasser fallen** to fall into the water with a splash.
plumpsen *vi aux sein (col)* to tumble. **er plumpste ins Wasser** he fell into the water with a splash.
Plumpsklo(sett) *nt (col)* earth closet.
plump-vertraulich 1 *adj* hail-fellow-well-met. **2** *adv* in a hail-fellow-well-met sort of way.
Plunder *m no pl* junk, rubbish.
Plünd(e)rer *m* **-** looter, plunderer.
Plundergebäck *nt* flaky pastry.
plündern *vti* to loot; *(ausrauben)* to raid; *Obstbaum* to strip.
Plünderung *f* looting, pillage.
Plural *m* **-e** plural. **im ~ stehen** to be (in the) plural.
plus 1 *prep +gen* plus. **2** *adv* plus. **bei ~ 5 Grad** at 5 degrees (above freezing *or* zero).
Plus *nt* **- (a)** *(Phys col: ~pol)* positive (pole). **(b)** *(Comm) (Zuwachs)* increase; *(Gewinn)* profit; *(Überschuß)* surplus. **(c)** *(fig: Vorteil)* plus, advantage. **das ist ein ~ für dich** that's a point in your favour *(Brit) or* favor *(US)*.
Plüsch *m* **-e** plush.
Plüsch- *in cpds* plush; ~**tier** *nt* ≈ soft toy.
Plus-: ~**pol** *m (Elec)* positive pole; ~**punkt** *m (Sport)* point; *(Sch)* extra mark; *(fig)* plus point, advantage; ~**quamperfekt** *nt* pluperfect.
Plutonium *nt no pl* plutonium.
pneumatisch [pnɔy'maːtɪʃ] *adj* pneumatic.
Po *m* **-s** *(col)* = **Popo.**
Pöbel *m no pl* rabble, mob.
pöbelhaft *adj* uncouth, vulgar.
pochen *vi* to knock; *(Herz, Blut)* to pound. **auf etw** *(acc)* **~** *(fig)* to insist on sth.
pochieren* [pɔ'ʃiːrən] *vt Ei* to poach.
Pocken *pl* smallpox.
Pocken-: ~**narbe** *f* pockmark; ~**(schutz)impfung** *f* smallpox vaccination.
Podest *nt or m* **-e** *(Sockel)* pedestal *(auch fig)*; *(Podium)* platform; *(Treppenabsatz)* landing.
Podium *nt (lit, fig)* platform; *(des Dirigenten)* podium; *(bei Diskussion)* panel.
Podiumsdiskussion *f* panel discussion.
Poesie [poe'ziː] *f (lit, fig)* poetry.
Poet *m (wk)* **-en, -en** *(geh)* poet.
poetisch *adj* poetic.
Pointe ['poẽːtə] *f* **-n** *(eines Witzes)* punch-line; *(einer Geschichte)* point.
pointiert [poẽ'tiːɐt] *adj* trenchant, pithy.
Pokal *m* **-e** *(zum Trinken)* goblet; *(Sport)* cup.
Pokal-: ~**endspiel** *nt* cup final; ~**sieger** *m* cup-winners *pl*; ~**spiel** *nt* cup-tie.
Pökelfleisch *nt* salt meat.
pökeln *vt Fleisch, Fisch* to salt, to pickle.
Poker *nt no pl* poker.
pokern *vi* to play poker. **um etw ~** *(fig)* to haggle for sth.
Pol *m* **-e** pole. **der ruhende ~** *(fig)* the calming influence.
polar *adj* polar. ~**e Kälte** arctic coldness; **~ entgegengesetzt** diametrically opposed.
polarisieren* *vtr* to polarize.
Polarisierung *f* polarization.
Polar-: ~**kreis** *m* polar circle; **nördlicher/südlicher ~kreis** Arctic/Antarctic circle; ~**licht** *nt* polar lights *pl*; ~**stern** *m* pole Star.
Pole *m (wk)* **-n, -n** Pole.
Polemik *f* polemics *sing*; *(Streitschrift)* polemic.
polemisch *adj* polemic(al).
polemisieren* *vi* to polemicize. **~ gegen** to inveigh against.
Polen *nt* Poland.
Polente *f no pl (dated col)* cops *pl (col)*.
Police [po'liːsə] *f* **-n** (insurance) policy.
Polier *m* **-e** site foreman.
polieren* *vt (lit, fig)* to polish. **jdm die Fresse** *or* **Schnauze ~** *(col!)* to smash sb's face in *(col)*.
Polier-: ~**mittel** *nt* polish; ~**wachs** *nt* wax polish.
Poliklinik *f (Krankenhaus)* clinic *(for outpatients only)*; *(Abteilung)* outpatients' department.
Polin *f* Pole, Polish woman.
Politesse *f* (woman) traffic warden *(Brit)*.
Politik *f* **(a)** *no pl* politics *sing*; *(politischer Standpunkt)* politics *pl.* **welche ~ vertritt er?** what are his politics?; **in die ~ gehen** to go into politics. **(b)** *(bestimmte ~)* policy. **ihre gesamte ~** all their policies.
Politiker(in *f***)** *m* **-** politician.
politisch *adj* political.
politisieren* **1** *vi* to talk politics, to politicize. **2** *vt* to politicize; *jdn* to make politically aware.
Politisierung *f* politicization.
Politologe *m (wk)*, **Politologin** *f* political scientist.
Politologie *f* political science, politics *sing.*
Politur *f* polish. **die ~ ist runter** *(fig col)* the glamour *(Brit) or* glamor *(US)* has gone.
Polizei *f* police *pl*; *(Gebäude)* police station. **auf die** *or* **zur ~ gehen** to go to the police; **er ist bei der ~** he's in the police (force).
Polizei- *in cpds* police; ~**aufsicht** *f* **unter ~ aufsicht stehen** to be under police surveillance;

~**beamte(r)** *m* police official; *(Polizist)* police officer; ~**dienststelle** *f (form)* police station; ~**direktion** *f* police headquarters *pl*; ~**haft** *f* detention; ~**kommissar** *m* (police) inspector.
polizeilich *adj no pred* police *attr*. ~**es Führungszeugnis** *certificate issued by the police, stating that the holder has no criminal record*; **sich ~ melden** to register with the police.
Polizei-: ~**präsident** *m* chief constable, chief of police *(US)*; ~**präsidium** *nt* police headquarters *pl*; ~**revier** *nt (~wache)* police station; ~**staat** *m* police state; ~**streife** *f* police patrol; ~**stunde** *f* closing time; ~**wache** *f* police station.
Polizist(in *f*) *m* policeman/policewoman.
polnisch *adj* Polish.
Polnisch(e) *nt decl as adj* Polish; *siehe* **Deutsch(e)**.
Polohemd *nt* sports shirt; *(für Frau)* casual blouse.
Polster *nt* - **(a)** cushion; *(Polsterung)* upholstery *no pl*; *(bei Kleidung)* pad, padding *no pl*. **(b)** *(fig) (Fett~)* flab *no pl (col)*; *(Bauch)* spare tyre *(Brit) or* tire *(US)*; *(Geldreserve)* reserves *pl*.
Polster-: ~**garnitur** *f* three-piece suite; ~**möbel** *pl* upholstered furniture.
polstern *vt* to upholster; *Kleidung, Tür* to pad. **etw neu ~** to re-upholster sth; **sie ist gut gepolstert** *(col)* she's well-padded; *(finanziell)* she's not short of the odd penny.
Polsterung *f* upholstery.
Polter|abend *m party on the eve of a wedding with smashing of crockery*, ≃ shower *(US)*.
Poltergeist *m* poltergeist.
poltern *vi* **(a)** to crash about. **was hat da eben so gepoltert?** what was that crash?; **es poltert** there's a real din going on. **(b)** *aux sein (sich laut bewegen)* to crash, to bang. **(c)** *(col: schimpfen)* to rant (and rave).
Poly-: ~**ester** *m* - polyester; ~**gamie** *f* polygamy.
Polyp *m (wk)* **-en, -en (a)** *(Zool)* polyp. **(b)** *(Med)* ~**en** adenoids. **(c)** *(hum col: Polizist)* cop *(col)*.
Poly-: ~**technikum** *nt* polytechnic, poly *(col)*; **p~technisch** *adj* polytechnic.
Pomade *f* hair-cream.
Pommern *nt* Pomerania.
Pommes frites [pɔm'frit(s)] *pl* chips *pl (Brit)*, French fries *pl*.
Pomp *m no pl* pomp.
pompös *adj* grandiose.
Pontius ['pɔntsiʊs] *m*: **von ~ zu Pilatus** from pillar to post.
Pony[1] ['pɔni] *nt* **-s** pony.
Pony[2] ['pɔni] *m* **-s** fringe *(Brit)*, bangs *pl (US)*.
Ponyfrisur *f* **sie hat eine ~** she has a fringe *(Brit)*, she has bangs *(US)*.
Pool(billard) ['puːl(bɪljart)] *nt* pool.
Pop *m no pl (Mus)* pop; *(Art)* pop-art.
Popanz *m* **-e** *(Schreckgespenst)* bogey.
pop(e)lig *adj (col)* **(a)** *(knauserig)* stingy *(col)*. **(b)** *(dürftig)* crummy *(col)*.
Popelin *m* **-e, Popeline** *f* - poplin.
popeln *vi (col)* **(in der Nase) ~** to pick one's nose.
Pop-: ~**gruppe** *f* pop group; ~**konzert** *nt* pop concert; ~ **musik** *f* pop music.
Popo *m* **-s** *(col)* bottom, bum *(col)*.
poppig *adj (col) (Art, Mus)* pop *no adv*; *Kleidung* trendy.
Popper *m (col)* new romantic.
populär *adj* popular *(bei* with*)*.
popularisieren* *vt* to popularize.
Popularität *f* popularity.
populärwissenschaftlich *adj* popular science.
Pore *f* **-n** pore.
Porno *m* **-s** *(col)* porn *(col)*, porno *(US col)*.
Pornographie *f* pornography.
pornographisch *adj* pornographic.
porös *adj (durchlässig)* porous; *(brüchig)* perished.
Porree ['pɔre] *m* **-s** leek.
Portal *nt* **-e** portal.
Portemonnaie [pɔrtmɔ'neː] *nt* **-s** purse.
Portier [pɔr'tieː] *m* **-s** porter.
Portion *f* **(a)** *(beim Essen)* portion, helping. **eine halbe ~** *(fig col)* a half-pint *(col)*; **eine zweite ~** a second helping. **(b)** *(fig col: Anteil)* amount. **er besitzt eine ganze ~ Frechheit** he's got a fair bit of cheek *(col)*.
Porto *nt, pl* **-s** *or* **Porti** postage *no pl (für* on, for*)*; *(für Kisten etc)* carriage. **~ zahlt Empfänger** postage paid.
portofrei *adj* postage paid.
Porträt [*auch* pɔr'trɛː] *nt* **-s** *(lit, fig)* portrait.
porträtieren* *vt* **jdn ~** to paint sb's portrait; *(fig)* to portray sb.
Portugal *nt* Portugal.
Portugiese *m (wk)* **-n, -n, Portugiesin** *f* Portuguese.
portugiesisch *adj* Portuguese.
Portwein *m* port.
Porzellan *nt* **-e** *(Material)* porcelain; *(Geschirr)* china.
Porzellan- *in cpds* china; ~**erde** *f* china clay; ~**geschirr** *nt* china, crockery; ~**manufaktur** *f* china factory.
Posaune *f* **-n** trombone; *(fig)* trumpet.
posaunen* *(col)* **1** *vi* to play the trombone. **2** *vti (fig)* to bellow, to bawl. **etw in alle Welt ~** to tell sth to the whole world.
Posaunenbläser *m* trombonist.
Pose *f* **-n** pose.
posieren* *vi* to pose.
Position *f* position; *(Comm: auf Liste)* item.
Positionslicht *nt* navigation light.
positiv *adj* positive. **eine ~e Antwort** an affirmative (answer); **etw ~ wissen** to know sth for a fact; **~ zu etw stehen** to be in favour *(Brit) or* favor *(US)* of sth.
Positiv *nt (Phot)* positive.
Positur *f* posture. **sich in ~ setzen/stellen** to adopt a posture.
Posse *f* **-n** farce.
Possen *m* - *(dated)* prank, tomfoolery *no pl*. **~ reißen** to clown around.
Possessivpronomen *nt* possessive pronoun.
possierlich *adj* comical, funny.
Post *f* **-en** post *(Brit)*, mail; *(~amt, ~wesen)* post office. **war die ~ schon da?** has the post *or* mail come yet?; **ist ~ für mich da?** are there any letters for me?; **etw mit der ~ schicken** to send sth by post *or* mail; **etw auf die ~ geben** to post *or* mail sth; **auf die** *or* **zur ~ gehen** to go to the post office; **mit getrennter ~** under separate cover.
postalisch *adj* postal.
Post-: ~**amt** *nt* post office; ~**anweisung** *f* ≃ postal *(Brit) or* money order; ~**auto** *nt* post-office van; ~**beamte(r)** *m*, ~**beamtin** *f* post office official; ~**bote** *m* postman *(Brit)*, mailman *(US)*.
Posten *m* - **(a)** *(Anstellung)* post, job. **(b)** *(Mil: Wachmann)* guard; *(Stelle)* post. **~ stehen** to stand guard; **~ beziehen** to take up one's post. **(c) auf dem ~ sein** *(aufpassen)* to be awake; *(gesund sein)* to be fit; **nicht ganz auf dem ~ sein** to be off-colour *(Brit) or* off-color *(US)*. **(d)** *(Streik~)* picket. **(e)** *(Comm: Warenmenge)* quantity, lot. **(f)** *(Comm: im Etat)* item, entry.
Postenjäger *m (col)* go-getter *(col)*.
Poster *nt* **-(s)** poster.
Postfach *nt* post-office *or* PO box.
posthum *adj* posthumous.
postieren* **1** *vt* to position. **2** *vr* to position oneself.
Post-: ~**karte** *f* postcard; ~**kasten** *m* pillar box *(Brit)*, mailbox *(US)*; ~**kutsche** *f* mail coach, stagecoach; **p~lagernd 1** *adj* to be called for; **2** *adv* poste restante *(Brit)*, general delivery *(US)*; ~**leitzahl** *f* post(al) code, Zip code *(US)*; ~**minister** *m* ≃ postmaster general; ~**sache** *f*

post office mail *no pl*; **~scheck** *m* (Post Office *or* National) Giro cheque *(Brit)*; **~scheckamt** *nt* National Giro office *(Brit)*; **~scheckkonto** *nt* National *or* Post Office Giro account *(Brit)*; **~sparkasse** *f* Post Office savings bank; **~stempel** *m* postmark.
postulieren* *vt* to postulate.
Post-: p~wendend *adv* by return (of post) *(Brit)*, by return mail; **~wertzeichen** *nt (form)* postage stamp *(form)*; **~wurfsendung** *f* postal door to door delivery; **~zustellung** *f* mail delivery.
potent *adj* potent; *(fig) Phantasie* powerful.
Potential [potɛn'tsia:l] *nt* **-e** potential.
potentiell [potɛn'tsiɛl] *adj* potential.
Potenz *f* **(a)** *(Med)* potency; *(fig)* ability. **(b)** *(Math)* power. **zweite/dritte ~** square/cube.
potenzieren* *vt (Math)* to raise to the power of; *(col: steigern)* to multiply.
Potpourri ['pɔtpuri] *nt* **-s** *(Mus)* medley *(aus* of*)*; *(fig)* assortment.
Pott *m* **¨-e** *(col)* pot.
Pott-: ~asche *f* potash; **~wal** *m* sperm whale.
poussieren [pu'si:rən] *vi (dated col: flirten)* to flirt.
prä-, prae- *pref* pre-.
Präambel *f* preamble *(gen* to*)*.
Pracht *f no pl* splendour *(Brit)*, splendor *(US)*. **in seiner vollen** *or* **ganzen ~** in all its splendour; **es ist eine wahre ~** it's (really) superb.
Pracht-: ~entfaltung *f* magnificent display; **~exemplar** *nt* beauty *(col)*; *(fig: Mensch)* fine specimen.
prächtig *adj (prunkvoll, großartig)* splendid.
Pracht-: ~kerl *m (col)* great guy *(col)*; *(~exemplar)* beauty *(col)*; **~stück** *nt* = **~exemplar.**
prädestinieren* *vt* to predestine.
Prädikat *nt (Gram)* predicate; *(Bewertung)* rating; *(Rangbezeichnung)* title. **Wein mit ~** special quality wine.
Prag *nt* Prague.
prägen *vt* **(a)** to stamp; *Münzen* to mint; *Leder, Papier* to emboss; *(erfinden) Begriffe, Wörter* to coin. **(b)** *(fig: formen) Charakter* to form; *(Erlebnis, Kummer) jdn* to leave its/their mark on. **(c)** *(kennzeichnen) Stadtbild* to characterize.
Prägestempel *m* die, stamp.
Pragmatiker(in *f***)** *m* **-** pragmatist.
pragmatisch *adj* pragmatic.
prägnant *adj* concise, terse.
Prägnanz *f* conciseness, terseness.
Prägung *f* **(a)** *siehe vt (a, b)* stamping; minting; embossing; coining; forming. **(b)** *(auf Münzen)* imprint; *(auf Leder, Papier)* embossing; *(Eigenart)* character; *(von Charakter)* mould *(Brit)*, mold *(US)*.
prahlen *vi* to brag *(mit* about*)*.
Prahlerei *f* bragging *no pl.*
prahlerisch *adj* boastful, bragging *attr.*
Prahlhans *m, pl* **-hänse** *(col)* show-off.
Praktik *f* procedure, method; *(usu pl: Kniff)* practice, trick *(col)*.
praktikabel *adj* practicable, practical.
Praktikant(in *f***)** *m* trainee.
Praktiker(in *f***)** *m* **-** practical man/woman.
Praktikum *nt, pl* **Praktika** practical training.
praktisch 1 *adj* practical; *(nützlich auch)* handy. **~er Arzt** general practitioner; **~es Beispiel** concrete example. **2** *adv* practically; *(in der Praxis)* in practice.
praktizieren* 1 *vi* to practise *(Brit)*, to practice *(US)*. **2** *vt (ausführen)* to put into practice.
Praline *f* chocolate, chocolate candy *(US)*.
prall *adj Sack, Brieftasche* bulging; *Arme, Schenkel* big strong *attr*; *Sonne* blazing. **~ gefüllt** filled to bursting.
prallen *vi aux sein* **gegen etw ~** to crash into sth; *(Ball)* to bounce off sth.
prallvoll *adj* full to bursting; *Brieftasche* bulging.
Prämie [-iə] *f* premium; *(Belohnung)* bonus; *(Preis)* prize.
prämien- [-iən]: **~begünstigt** *adj* with benefit of premiums; **~sparen** *vi sep infin, ptp only* to save in a bonus scheme.
präm(i)ieren* *vt (auszeichnen)* to give an award; *(belohnen)* to give a bonus. **etw mit dem ersten Preis ~** to award sth first prize.
Präm(i)ierung *f* **(a)** *(das Prämieren)* **für diesen Film kommt eine ~ nicht in Frage** we can't possibly give this film an award. **(b)** *(Veranstaltung)* presentation.
Pranger *m* **-** stocks *pl*, pillory. **jdn/etw an den ~ stellen** *(fig)* to pillory sb/sth.
Pranke *f* **-n** *(auch col)* paw.
Präparat *nt* preparation.
präparieren* *vt* **(a)** *(konservieren)* to preserve. **(b)** *(Med: zerlegen)* to dissect.
Präposition *f* preposition.
Prärie *f* prairie.
Präsens *nt, pl* **Präsenzien** [-iən] present (tense).
präsent *adj* present. **etw ~ haben** to have sth at hand.
präsentieren* 1 *vt* to present. **jdm etw ~** to present sb with sth. **2** *vr* to present oneself.
Präsenzbibliothek *f* reference library.
Präservativ [prɛzɛrva'ti:f] *nt* contraceptive, condom.
Präsident(in *f***)** *m* president.
Präsidentschaft *f* presidency.
Präsidentschaftswahl *f* presidential election.
präsidieren* *vi* to preside.
Präsidium *nt (Vorsitz)* presidency; *(Führungsgruppe)* committee; *(Polizei~)* headquarters *pl.*
prasseln *vi* **(a)** *aux sein* to clatter; *(Regen)* to drum; *(fig)* to hail down. **(b)** *(Feuer)* to crackle.
prassen *vi (schlemmen)* to feast; *(in Luxus leben)* to live the high life.
Prasserei *f (Schlemmerei)* feasting; *(Luxusleben)* high life.
Präteritum *nt, pl* **Präterita** preterite.
präventiv [prɛvɛn'ti:f] *adj* prevent(at)ive.
Praxis *f, pl* **Praxen (a)** *no pl* practice; *(Erfahrung)* experience. **in der ~** in practice; **die ~ sieht anders aus** the facts are different; **ein Idee in die ~ umsetzen** to put an idea into practice; **ein Beispiel aus der ~** an example from real life. **(b)** *(eines Arztes, Rechtsanwalts)* practice. **(c)** *(Behandlungsräume)* surgery *(Brit)*, doctor's office *(US)*; *(Anwaltsbüro)* office.
Präzedenzfall *m* precedent.
präzis(e) *adj* precise.
präzisieren* *vt* to state more precisely.
Präzision *f* precision.
Präzisions- *in cpds* precision; **~arbeit** *f* precision work; **~arbeit leisten** to work with precision.
predigen *vti* to preach. **jdm etw ~** *(fig)* to lecture sb on sth.
Prediger(in *f***)** *m* **-** preacher/woman preacher.
Predigt *f* **-en** *(lit, fig)* sermon. **jdm eine ~ über etw** *(acc)* **halten** *(fig)* to give sb a sermon about sth.
Preis *m* **-e (a)** price *(für* of*)*. **zum halben ~** half-price; **um jeden ~** *(fig)* at all costs. **(b)** *(bei Wettbewerben)* prize; *(Auszeichnung)* award. **(c)** *(Belohnung)* reward. **(d)** *no pl (liter: Lob)* praise *(auf +acc* of*)*.
Preis-: ~angabe *f* **hier fehlt die ~angabe** there's no price given; **~anstieg** *m* rise in prices; **~ausschreiben** *nt* competition; **p~bewußt** *adj* price-conscious; **~bindung** *f* price fixing; **~brecher** *m (Firma)* undercutter; **~disziplin** *f* price restraint.
Preiselbeere *f* cranberry.
preisen *pret* **pries,** *ptp* **gepriesen** *vt (geh)* to praise. **sich glücklich ~** to count oneself lucky.
Preis-: ~entwicklung *f* price trend; **~erhöhung** *f* price increase; **~frage** *f* **(a)** question of price; **(b)** *(beim ~ausschreiben)* prize question *(in a*

competition); ~**gabe** *f (geh) (Aufgabe)* abandoning; *(von Geheimnis)* divulgence.

preisgeben *vt sep irreg (geh)* **(a)** *(ausliefern)* to leave to the mercy of. **(b)** *(aufgeben)* to abandon. **(c)** *(verraten)* to betray.

Preis-: ~**gefälle** *nt* price gap; **p~gekrönt** *adj* award-winning; ~**gericht** *nt* jury; **p~günstig** *adj* inexpensive; **etw p~günstig bekommen** to get sth at a good price; ~**lage** *f* price range.

preislich *adj no pred* price *attr*, in price.

Preis-: ~**nachlaß** *m* discount; **10% ~nachlaß bei Barbezahlung** 10% off cash sales; ~**politik** *f* prices policy; ~**rätsel** *nt* prize competition; ~**schild** *nt* price-tag; ~**schlager** *m* (all-time) bargain; ~**senkung** *f* price cut; **p~stabil** *adj* stable in price; ~**stopp** *m* price freeze; ~**träger(in** *f*) *m* prize-winner; *(Kultur~)* award-winner; ~**treiberei** *f* forcing up of prices; *(Wucher)* profiteering; ~**verleihung** *f* presentation (of prizes/awards); **p~wert** *adj* good value *pred*; **ein p~wertes Kleid** a dress which is good value (for money).

prekär *adj (peinlich)* awkward; *(schwierig)* precarious.

Prellbock *m (Rail)* buffers *pl*, buffer-stop; *(fig col)* scapegoat *(col)*, fallguy *(esp US col)*.

prellen 1 *vt* **(a)** to bruise; *(anschlagen)* to hit. **(b)** *(fig col: betrügen)* to swindle. **jdn um etw ~** to swindle sb out of sth; **die Zeche ~** to avoid paying the bill. **2** *vr* to bruise oneself.

Prellung *f* bruise, contusion.

Premiere [prə'mie:rə, pre-] *f* **-n** premiere.

Premierminister [prə'mie:-, pre-] *m* prime minister.

Presse *f* **-n** *(Mech, Zeitungen)* press. **eine gute ~ haben** to get a good press.

Presse-: ~**agentur** *f* news agency; ~**amt** *nt* press office; ~**erklärung** *f* press release; ~**freiheit** *f* freedom of the press; ~**konferenz** *f* press conference; ~**meldung** *f* press report.

pressen *vt* to press; *Obst auch* to squeeze; *(fig: zwingen)* to force *(in +acc* into*)*.

Presse-: ~**notiz** *f* paragraph in the press; ~**stelle** *f* press office.

pressieren* *vi (S Ger, Aus, Sw) (Sache)* to be urgent. **mir pressiert's** I am in a hurry.

Preß-: ~**luft** *f* compressed air; ~**lufthammer** *m* pneumatic hammer.

Prestige [prɛs'ti:ʒə] *nt no pl* prestige.

Preuße *m (wk)* **-n, -n, Preußin** *f* Prussian.

Preußen *nt* Prussia.

preußisch *adj* Prussian.

prickeln *vi (kribbeln)* to tingle; *(kitzeln)* to tickle; *(Bläschen bilden)* to sparkle, to bubble.

prickelnd *adj siehe vi* tingling; tickling; sparkling, bubbling. **der ~e Reiz der Neuheit** the thrill of novelty.

pries *pret of* **preisen.**

Priester *m* - priest.

Priesterin *f* priestess.

priesterlich *adj* priestly *no adv*.

Priester-: ~**seminar** *nt* seminary; ~**weihe** *f* ordination (to the priesthood).

prima *adj inv* **(a)** *(col)* fantastic *(col)*. **das hast du ~ gemacht** you did that beautifully. **(b)** *(Comm)* top-quality.

Prima *f, pl* **Primen** *(Sch) eighth and ninth year of German secondary school.*

Primaner(in *f*) *m* - *(Sch)* ≃ sixth-former.

primär *adj* primary.

Primas *m* **-, -se** *(Eccl)* primate.

Primat *m (wk)* **-en, -en** *(Zool)* primate.

Primel *f* **-n** *(Wald~)* (wild) primrose; *(farbige Garten~)* primula.

primitiv *adj* primitive.

Primzahl *f* prime (number).

Prinz *m (wk)* **-en, -en** prince.

Prinzessin *f* princess.

Prinzip *nt* **-ien** [-iən] principle. **aus ~** on principle; **im ~** in principle; **das funktioniert nach einem einfachen ~** it works on a simple principle; **ein Mann mit ~ien** a man of principle.

prinzipiell *adj (im Prinzip)* in principle; *(aus Prinzip)* on principle.

Priorität *f* priority. ~**en** *pl (Comm)* preference shares *pl*, preferred stock *(US)*; **~ vor etw** *(dat)* **haben** to take precedence over sth; **~en setzen** to establish one's priorities.

Prise *f* **-n** *(kleine Menge)* pinch.

Prisma *nt, pl* **Prismen** prism.

Pritsche *f* **-n (a)** *(Liegestatt)* plank bed. **(b)** *(von Lkw)* platform.

privat [pri'va:t] *adj* private. **~ ist er ganz anders** he's quite different socially; **jdn ~ sprechen** to speak to sb in private; **ich sagte es ihm ganz ~** I told him in absolute confidence; **etw an P~ verkaufen** *(Comm)* to sell sth to the public.

Privat- *in cpds* private; ~**adresse** *f* home address; ~**dozent** *m* outside lecturer; ~**gespräch** *nt* private conversation; *(am Telefon)* private call.

privatisieren* [privati'zi:rən] *vt* to privatize.

Privat-: ~**leben** *nt* private life; ~**person** *f* private individual; ~**recht** *nt* private *or* civil law; ~**sache** *f* private matter; **das ist meine ~sache** that's a private matter; ~**unterricht** *m* private tuition; ~**vermögen** *nt* private fortune; ~**wirtschaft** *f* private industry.

Privileg [privi'le:k] *nt* **-ien** [-'le:giən] privilege.

privilegieren* [privile'gi:rən] *vt* to favour *(Brit)*, to favor *(US)*. **privilegiert** privileged.

pro *prep* per. **~ Jahr** per annum *(form)*, a year; **~ Kopf** per capita *(form)*; **~ Stück** each, apiece.

Pro *nt* **(das) ~ und Kontra** the pros and cons *pl*.

Probe *f* **-n (a)** *(Prüfung)* test. **die ~ (auf eine Rechnung) machen** to check a calculation; **er ist auf ~ angestellt** he's employed for a probationary period; **jdn/etw auf ~ nehmen** to take sb/sth on trial; **jdn/etw auf die ~ stellen** to put sb/sth to the test; **zur ~** to try out. **(b)** *(Theat)* rehearsal. **(c)** *(Teststück, Beispiel)* sample.

Probe-: ~**abzug** *m* proof; ~**angebot** *nt* trial offer; ~**bohrung** *f* test drill; ~**exemplar** *nt* specimen (copy); **p~fahren** *sep irreg infin, ptp only* **1** *vt* to test-drive; **2** *vi aux sein* to go for a test drive; ~**fahrt** *f* test drive; ~**lauf** *m* trial run; *(Sport)* practice run.

proben *vti* to rehearse.

Probe-: ~**stück** *nt* specimen; **p~weise** *adv* on a trial basis; ~**zeit** *f* trial period.

probieren* 1 *vt* to have a try at; *(kosten) Speisen, Getränke* to sample; *(prüfen)* to test. **laß es mich mal ~!** let me have a go! **2** *vi (versuchen, kosten)* to try. **P~ geht über Studieren** *(Prov)* the proof of the pudding is in the eating *(Prov)*.

Problem *nt* **-e** problem.

Problematik *f* difficulty *(gen* with*)*; *(Problembereich)* problems *pl*.

problematisch *adj* problematic; *(fragwürdig)* questionable.

problemlos *adj* problem-free.

Produkt *nt* **-e** *(lit, fig)* product.

Produktion *f* production.

Produktions- *in cpds* production; ~**ausfall** *m* loss of production; ~**kosten** *pl* production costs *pl*; ~**menge** *f* output; ~**mittel** *pl* means of production *pl*; ~**rückgang** *m* drop in production.

produktiv *adj* productive.

Produktivität *f* productivity.

Produzent(in *f*) *m* producer.

produzieren* 1 *vt* **(a)** *auch vi* to produce. **(b)** *(col: hervorbringen) Lärm* to make; *Entschuldigung* to come up with *(col)*; *Romane* to churn out *(col)*. **2** *vr (pej)* to show off.

Prof. = **Professor.**

profan *adj (weltlich)* secular; *(gewöhnlich)* mundane.

professionell *adj* professional.
Professor *m*, **Professorin** *f* **(a)** *(Hochschul~)* professor. **(b)** *(Aus: Gymnasiallehrer)* grammar school teacher *(Brit)*, high school teacher *(US)*.
Professur *f* chair *(für* in, of*)*.
Profi *m* **-s** *(col)* pro *(col)*.
Profil *nt* **-e** **(a)** *(von Gesicht)* profile; *(fig: Ansehen)* image. **im ~** in profile; **die Partei hat mehr ~ bekommen** the party has sharpened its image. **(b)** *(von Reifen, Schuhsohle)* tread. **(c)** *(Querschnitt)* cross-section; *(Längsschnitt)* vertical section; *(fig: Skizze)* profile.
profilieren* **1** *vt (scharf umreißen)* to define. **2** *vr (sich ein Image geben)* to create a distinctive personal image for oneself. **er will sich akademisch/politisch ~** he wants to make his mark academically/in politics.
profiliert *adj (scharf umrissen)* clear-cut *no adv*; *(hervorstechend)* distinctive.
Profilsohle *f* sole with a tread.
Profit *m* **-e** profit. **~ aus etw ziehen** *(lit)* to make a profit from sth; *(fig)* to reap the benefits from sth; **den/keinen ~ von etw haben** to profit/not to profit from sth; **ohne/mit ~ arbeiten** to work unprofitably/profitably.
Profit-: p~bringend *adj* profitable; **~gier** *f* greed for profit.
profitieren* *vti* to profit; *(fig auch)* to gain. **und was profitierst du dabei** *or* **davon?** what do you stand to gain by it?
Profit-: ~jäger, ~macher *m (col)* profiteer; **~macherei** *f (col)* profiteering.
pro forma *adv* as a matter of form.
Pro-forma-Rechnung *f* pro forma invoice.
Prognose *f* **-n** prognosis; *(Wetter~)* forecast.
Programm *nt* **-e** programme *(Brit)*, program *(US, Comp)*; *(Tagesordnung)* agenda; *(TV: Sender)* channel; *(Sendefolge)* programmes *(Brit) pl*, programs *(US) pl*; *(gedrucktes Radio~, TV~)* programme *(Brit) or* program *(US)* guide; *(Verlags~)* list; *(Kollektion)* range. **nach ~** as planned; **auf dem ~ stehen** to be on the programme/agenda.
Programm-: ~heft *nt* programme *(Brit)*, program *(US)*; **~hinweis** *m (Rad, TV)* programme *(Brit) or* program *(US)* announcement.
programmieren* *vti* to programme *(Brit)*, to program *(US, Comp)*; *(fig auch)* to condition. **auf etw** *(acc)* **programmiert sein** *(fig)* to be geared to sth.
Programmierer(in *f)* *m* **-** programmer.
Programiersprache *f* programming language.
Programmierung *f* programming; *(fig auch)* conditioning.
Programm-: ~vorschau *f* preview *(für* of*)*; *(Film)* trailer; **~zeitschrift** *f* programme *(Brit) or* program *(US)* guide.
progressiv *adj* progressive.
Projekt *nt* **-e** project.
Projektion *f* projection.
Projektor *m* projector.
projizieren* *vt* to project.
proklamieren* *vt* to proclaim.
Pro-Kopf-Einkommen *nt* per capita income.
Prokura *f, pl* **Prokuren** *(form)* power of attorney.
Prokurist(in *f)* *m* attorney.
Prolet *m (wk)* **-en, -en** *(pej)* prole *(pej)*, pleb *(pej)*.
Proletariat *nt* proletariat.
Proletarier [-iɐ] *m* **-** proletarian.
proletarisch *adj* proletarian.
Prolog *m* **-e** prologue.
Promenaden-: ~deck *nt* promenade deck; **~mischung** *f (hum)* mongrel.
Promille *nt* **-** thousandth (part); *(col: Alkoholspiegel)* alcohol level. **0,8 ~** 80 millilitres *(Brit) or* milliliters *(US)* alcohol level.
Promillegrenze *f* legal (alcohol) limit.
prominent *adj* prominent.
Prominente(r) *mf decl as adj* VIP.
Prominenz *f* VIP's *pl*.
Promotion[1] *f (Univ)* doctorate, PhD. **während seiner ~** while he was doing his PhD.
Promotion[2] [prə'moʊʃən] *f (Comm)* promotion.
promovieren* [promo'viːrən] *vi* to do a PhD; *(Doktorwürde erhalten)* to receive a doctorate.
prompt 1 *adj* prompt. **2** *adv* promptly; *(wie erwartet)* of course.
Pronomen *nt* **-** pronoun.
Propaganda *f no pl* propaganda. **~ mit etw machen** to make propaganda out of sth.
Propagandist(in *f)* *m* **(a)** propagandist. **(b)** *(Comm)* demonstrator.
propagieren* *vt* to propagate.
Propangas *nt* propane gas.
Propeller *m* **-** propeller.
Propeller-: ~antrieb *m* propeller-drive; **~flugzeug** *nt* propeller-driven plane; **~turbine** *f* turboprop.
proper *adj (col)* neat, tidy.
Prophet(in *f)* *m (wk)* **-en, -en** prophet.
prophetisch *adj* prophetic.
prophezeien* *vt* to prophesy.
Prophezeiung *f* prophecy.
prophylaktisch *adj* prophylactic *(form)*, preventive.
Proportion *f* proportion.
proportional [proportsio'naːl] *adj* proportional.
Proporz *m* **-e** proportional representation *no art*.
proppe(n)voll *adj (col)* jam-packed *(col)*.
Prosa *f no pl* prose.
prosaisch [pro'zaːɪʃ] *adj* **(a)** *(nüchtern)* prosaic. **(b)** *(Liter)* prose *attr*.
prosit *interj* your health. **~ Neujahr!** happy New Year!
Prosit *nt* **-s** toast. **ein ~ der Köchin!** here's to the cook!
Prospekt [pro'spɛkt] *m* **-e** brochure; *(Werbezettel)* leaflet; *(Verzeichnis)* catalogue.
prost *interj* cheers, cheerio.
Prostata *f no pl* prostate gland.
Prostituierte [prostitu'iːɐtə] *f (wk)* **-n, -n** prostitute.
Prostitution [prostitu'tsioːn] *f* prostitution.
Protagonist *m (lit, fig)* protagonist.
protegieren* [prote'ʒiːrən] *vt Schriftsteller, Projekt* to sponsor; *Land, Regime* to support.
Protein *nt* **-e** protein.
Protektion *f (Schutz)* protection; *(Begünstigung)* patronage.
Protektorat *nt (Schirmherrschaft)* patronage; *(Schutzgebiet)* protectorate.
Protest *m* **-e** protest. **(scharfen) ~ gegen jdn/etw erheben** to make a (strong) protest against sb/sth; **aus ~** in protest; **unter ~** protesting; *(gezwungen)* under protest.
Protestant(in *f)* *m* Protestant.
protestantisch *adj* Protestant.
protestieren* *vi* to protest.
Protest-: ~marsch *m* protest march; **~schreiben** *nt* letter of protest. **~welle** *f* wave of protest.
Prothese *f* **-n** artificial limb, prosthesis *(Med, form)*; *(Gebiß)* dentures *pl*.
Protokoll *nt* **-e** **(a)** *(Niederschrift)* record; *(von Sitzung)* minutes *pl*; *(bei Polizei)* statement; *(bei Gericht)* transcript. **(das) ~ führen** *(bei Sitzung)* to take the minutes; *(bei Gericht)* to make a transcript of the proceedings; **etw zu ~ geben** to have sth put on record; *(bei Polizei)* to say sth in one's statement. **(b)** *(diplomatisch)* protocol. **(c)** *(Strafzettel)* ticket.
protokollarisch *adj* **(a)** *(protokolliert)* on record; *(in Sitzung)* minuted. **(b)** *(zeremoniell)* **~e Vorschriften** rules of protocol.
Protokollführer *m* secretary; *(Jur)* clerk (of the court).

protokollieren* **1** *vi (bei Sitzung)* to take the minutes (down); *(bei Polizei)* to take a/the statement down. **2** *vt* to take down; *Sitzung* to minute.
Proto-: ~**plasma** *nt* protoplasm; ~**typ** *m* prototype.
protzen *vi (col)* to show off. **mit etw** ~ to show sth off.
protzig *adj (col)* swanky *(col)*, showy *(col)*.
Proviant [pro'viant] *m* **-e** provisions *pl*, supplies *pl* *(esp Mil)*; *(Reise~)* food for the journey.
Provinz [pro'vɪnts] *f* **-en** province; *(im Gegensatz zur Stadt)* provinces *pl (auch pej)*, country. **das ist finsterste** ~ *(pej)* it's a cultural backwater.
provinziell [provɪn'tsiɛl] *adj* provincial *(auch pej)*.
Provision [provi'zio:n] *f* commission. **auf** ~ on commission.
provisorisch [provi'zo:rɪʃ] *adj* temporary. **Straßen mit ~em Belag** roads with a temporary surface; **ich habe den Stuhl ~ repariert** I've fixed the chair up for the time being.
Provokation [provoka'tsio:n] *f* provocation.
provokativ, provokatorisch [provoka-] *adj* provocative, provoking.
provozieren* [provo'tsi:rən] *vti* to provoke.
Prozedur *f* **(a)** *(Vorgang)* procedure. **(b)** *(pej)* carry-on *(col)*.
Prozent *nt* **-e** *or (nach Zahlenangaben)* **-** per cent *no pl*. **fünf** ~ five per cent; **wieviel ~?** what percentage?; **zu zehn** ~ at ten per cent; **zu hohen ~en** at a high percentage; **dieser Whisky hat 35** ~ this whisky contains 35 per cent alcohol; **~e bekommen** *(col)* to get a discount.
Prozentsatz *m* percentage; *(Zins)* interest rate.
prozentual *adj* percentage *attr*. **~er Anteil** percentage; **etw ~ ausdrücken** to express sth as a percentage; **~ gut abschneiden** to get a good percentage.
Prozeß *m* **-sse (a)** *(Straf~)* trial; *(Rechtsfall)* (court) case. **einen ~ gewinnen/verlieren** to win/lose a case; **gegen jdn einen ~ anstrengen** to bring an action against sb; **es zum ~ kommen lassen** to go to court; **jdm den ~ machen** *(col)* to take sb to court; **mit jdm/etw kurzen ~ machen** *(fig col)* to make short work of sb/sth *(col)*. **(b)** *(Vorgang)* process.
Prozeß-: **p~führend** *adj* **p~führende Partei** litigant; **~führung** *f* handling of a/the case.
prozessieren* *vi* to go to court. **er prozessiert mit fünf Firmen** he's got cases going on against five firms.
Prozession *f* procession.
Prozeßkosten *pl* legal costs *pl*.
Prozessor *m (Comp)* processor.
Prozeßordnung *f* legal procedure.
prüde *adj* prudish.
prüfen *vt* **(a)** *(auch vi) (Sch, Univ) jdn* to examine. **schriftlich geprüft werden** to have a written examination. **(b)** *(überprüfen)* to check *(auf +acc* for*)*; *(untersuchen)* to examine; *(durch Ausprobieren)* to test; *Geschäftsbücher* to audit, to examine; *Lebensmittel, Wein* to inspect, to test; *Beschwerde* to investigate, to look into. **(c)** *(erwägen)* to consider. **etw nochmals ~** to review sth. **(d)** *(mustern)* to scrutinize. **ein ~der Blick** a searching look. **(e)** *(heimsuchen)* to afflict. **er ist im Leben schwer geprüft worden** he's been much afflicted in his life.
Prüfer(in *f)* *m* **-** examiner; *(Wirtschafts~)* auditor.
Prüf-: **~stand** *m* test bed; **~stein** *m (fig)* touchstone *(für* of *or* for*)*, measure *(für* of*)*.
Prüfung *f siehe vt* **(a)** exam, examination. **eine ~ machen** to take an exam. **(b)** check; examination; test; audit; inspection; investigation. **nach der ~ wird das Auto ...** after being tested the car is ...; **bei nochmaliger ~ der Rechnung** on re-checking the account. **(c)** consideration. **(d)** *(Heimsuchung)* test, trial.
Prüfungs-: **~angst** *f* exam nerves *pl*; **~arbeit** *f* dissertation; **~ausschuß** *m* board of examiners; **~kandidat** *m* (examination) candidate; **~ordnung** *f* exam(ination) regulations *pl*.
Prügel *m* **- (a)** *(Stock)* club. **(b)** ~ *pl (col: Schläge)* thrashing; **~ bekommen** to get a thrashing.
Prügelei *f (col)* fight, punch-up *(Brit col)*.
Prügelknabe *m (fig)* whipping boy.
prügeln 1 *vti* to beat. **2** *vr* to fight. **sich mit jdm ~** to fight sb; **sich um etw** *(acc)* **~** to fight over sth.
Prügelstrafe *f* corporal punishment.
Prunk *m no pl (Pracht)* splendour *(Brit)*, splendor *(US)*. **großen ~ entfalten** to put on a show of great splendour.
Prunk-: **~saal** *m* palatial room; **~stück** *nt* showpiece; **p~voll** *adj* magnificent.
prusten *vi (col)* to snort. **vor Lachen ~** to snort with laughter.
PS [pe:'|ɛs] *nt* = **Pferdestärke** hp.
P.S., PS [pe:'|ɛs] *nt* **-, - Postskript(um)** PS.
Psalm *m* **-en** psalm.
Pseudo-, pseudo- *in cpds* pseudo.
Pseudonym *nt* **-e** pseudonym.
Psychiater *m* **-** psychiatrist.
Psychiatrie *f* psychiatry.
psychiatrisch *adj* psychiatric.
psychisch *adj Belastung etc* emotional, psychological; *Phänomen* psychic. **~e Erkrankung** mental illness; **~ gestört** emotionally *or* psychologically disturbed; **er ist ~ völlig am Ende** his nerves can't take any more.
Psycho- *in cpds* psycho-; **~analyse** *f* psychoanalysis; **~analytiker(in** *f)* *m* psychoanalyst; **p~analytisch** *adj* psychoanalytic(al); **~loge** *m*, **~login** *f* psychologist; **~logie** *f* psychology; **p~logisch** *adj* psychological; **~therapeut(in** *f)* *m* psychotherapist; **p~therapeutisch** *adj* psychotherapeutic; **~therapie** *f* psychotherapy.
pubertär *adj* of puberty, adolescent.
Pubertät *f* puberty.
Pubertäts-: **~alter** *nt* age of puberty; **~störungen** *pl* adolescent disturbances *pl*; **~zeit** *f* puberty (period).
publik *adj pred* public. **~ werden** to become public knowledge; **die Sache ist längst ~** that's long been common knowledge.
Publikation *f* publication.
Publikum *nt no pl* public; *(Zuschauer, Zuhörer)* audience; *(Sport)* crowd. **in diesem Lokal verkehrt ein schlechtes ~** this pub attracts a bad type of customer; **sein ~ finden** to find a public.
Publikums-: **~erfolg** *m* popular success; **~liebling** *m* darling of the public; **~verkehr** *m* **„heute kein ~verkehr"** "closed today for public business"; **p~wirksam** *adj* **p~wirksam sein** to have public appeal.
publizieren *vti* to publish.
Publizist(in *f)* *m* publicist; *(Journalist)* journalist.
Publizistik *f* journalism.
Pudding *m* **-s** ≃ blancmange.
Puddingpulver *nt* custard powder.
Pudel *m* poodle. **das ist des ~s Kern** *(fig)* that's what it's really all about.
Pudel-: **~mütze** *f* pom-pom hat *(col)*; **p~naß** *adj* dripping wet; **p~wohl** *adj (col)* **sich p~wohl fühlen** to feel on top of the world *(col)*.
Puder *m or (col) nt* **-** powder.
Puderdose *f* (powder) compact.
pudern *vt* to powder.
Puder-: **~quaste** *f* powder puff; **~zucker** *m* icing sugar.
Puff[1] *m* **¨e** *(Stoß)* blow; *(in die Seite)* dig.
Puff[2] *m or nt* **-s** *(col)* brothel, cathouse *(esp US col)*.
puffen 1 *vt* **(a)** *(schlagen)* to thump; *(in die Seite)* to prod. **(b)** *Rauch* to puff. **2** *vi (col: puff machen)* to go bang; *(Rauch, Abgase)* to puff.
Puffer *m* **- (a)** *(Rail, Comp)* buffer. **(b)** *(Cook)* potato fritter.

Pufferzone *f* buffer zone.
Puffreis *m* puffed rice.
puh *interj (Abscheu)* ugh; *(Erleichterung)* phew.
Pulk *m* **-s (a)** *(Mil)* group. **(b)** *(Menge) (von Menschen)* bunch; *(von Dingen)* pile.
Pulle *f* **-n** *(col)* bottle. **volle ~ fahren** *(col)* to drive flat out *(col)*.
Pulli *m* **-s** *(col)*, **Pullover** [pʊ'lo:vɐ] *m* **-** jumper *(Brit)*, sweater.
Pullunder *m* **-** slipover.
Puls *m* **-e** *(lit, fig)* pulse. **sein ~ geht regelmäßig** his pulse is regular; **jdm den ~ fühlen** to feel *or* take sb's pulse.
Puls|ader *f* artery. **sich** *(dat)* **die ~(n) aufschneiden** to slash one's wrists.
pulsieren* *vi (lit, fig)* to pulsate, to throb.
Puls-: ~schlag *m* pulse-beat; *(fig)* pulse; **den ~schlag der Zeit spüren** to feel life pulsing around one; **~wärmer** *m* **-** wrist warmer.
Pult *nt* **-e** desk.
Pulver ['pʊlfɐ, -lvɐ] *nt* **-** powder. **er hat das ~ nicht erfunden** *(fig)* he'll never set the Thames on fire *(prov)*; **sein ~ verschossen haben** *(fig)* to have shot one's bolt.
Pulver-: ~faß *nt (fig)* powder keg; **(wie) auf einem ~faß sitzen** *(fig)* to be sitting on a volcano.
pulv(e)rig ['pʊlv(ə)rɪç] *adj* powdery *no adv*.
pulverisieren * [pʊlveri'zi:rən] *vt* to pulverize.
Pulver-: ~kaffee *m (col)* instant coffee; **~schnee** *m* powder snow.
Puma *m* **-s** puma.
Pummelchen *nt (col)* roly-poly *(col)*.
pumm(e)lig *adj (col)* chubby, plump.
Pump *m no pl (col)* **auf ~ kaufen/leben** to buy/live on tick *(Brit col) or* credit.
Pumpe *f* **-n (a)** pump. **(b)** *(col) (Herz)* ticker *(col)*.
pumpen *vti* **(a)** to pump. **(b)** *(col) (entleihen)* to borrow; *(verleihen)* to loan.
Pumpernickel *m* **-** pumpernickel.
Pumphose *f* knickerbockers *pl*.
Pumps [pœmps] *m* **-, -** pump.
puncto *prep +gen*: **in ~ X** where X is concerned.
Punk [paŋk] *m* **-s (a)** *no pl* punk. **(b)** *(auch* **~er**: *Mensch)* punk.
Punkt *m* **-e (a)** *(Tupfen)* spot, dot. **(b)** *(Satzzeichen)* full stop, period *(esp US)*; *(Typ)* point; *(auf dem i, Mus, Auslassungszeichen, von ~linie)* dot. **nun mach aber mal einen ~!** *(col)* come off it! *(col)*; **ohne ~ und Komma reden** *(col)* to talk nineteen to the dozen *(col)*. **(c)** *(Stelle)* point. **~ 12 Uhr** at 12 o'clock on the dot; **wir sind auf** *or* **an dem ~ angelangt, wo ...** we have reached the point where ...; **in diesem ~** on this point. **(d)** *(Bewertungseinheit)* point, mark; *(bei Prüfung)* mark. **nach ~en führen** to lead on points.
Punkt-: p~gleich *adj (Sport)* level; **~gleichheit** *f (Sport)* level score; **bei ~gleichheit** if the scores are level.
punktieren* *vt* **(a)** *(Med)* to aspirate. **(b)** *(mit Punkten)* to dot. **punktierte Linie** dotted line.
pünktlich 1 *adj* punctual. **2** *adv* on time. **er kam ~ um 3 Uhr** he came at 3 o'clock sharp; **~ da sein** to be there on time.
Pünktlichkeit *f* punctuality.
Punkt-: ~richter *m* judge; **~sieg** *m* points win; **~sieger** *m* winner on points.
punktuell *adj* dealing with certain points. **~e Verkehrskontrollen** spot checks on traffic.
Punkt-: ~wertung *f* points system; **in der ~wertung liegt er vorne** he's leading on points; **~zahl** *f* score.
Punsch *m* **-e** (hot) punch.
Pupille *f* **-n** pupil.
Puppe *f* **-n (a)** *(Kinderspielzeug)* doll *(col)*; *(Marionette)* puppet; *(Schaufenster~, Mil: Übungs~)* dummy; *(col: Mädchen)* doll *(col)*, bird *(esp Brit col)*. **die ~n tanzen lassen** *(col)* to live it up *(col)*; **bis in die ~n schlafen** *(col)* to sleep to all hours. **(b)** *(Zool)* pupa.
Puppen- *in cpds* doll's; **p~haft** *adj* doll-like; **~haus** *nt* doll's house, dollhouse *(US)*; **~spiel** *nt* puppet show; **~spieler** *m* puppeteer; **~stube** *f* doll's house, dollhouse *(US)*; **~theater** *nt* puppet theatre *(Brit) or* theater *(US)*; **~wagen** *m* doll's pram *(Brit) or* baby carriage *(US)*.
Pups *m* **-e**, **Pupser** *m* **-** *(col: Furz)* rude noise/smell.
pupsen *vi (col)* to make a rude noise/smell.
pur *adj (rein)* pure; *(unverdünnt)* neat; *(völlig)* sheer. **~er Unsinn** absolute nonsense; **~er Zufall** sheer coincidence; **Whisky ~** neat whisky.
Püree *nt* **-s** puree; *(Kartoffel~)* creamed potatoes *pl*.
Purist(in *f***)** *m* purist.
puritanisch *adj (Hist)* Puritan; *(pej)* puritanical.
Purpur *m no pl* crimson.
Purpur-: p~farben *adj* crimson; **~mantel** *m* crimson *or* purple robe; **p~rot** *adj* crimson (red).
Purzelbaum *m* somersault. **einen ~ machen** *or* **schlagen** to turn a somersault.
purzeln *vi aux sein* to tumble.
Puste *f no pl (col)* puff *(col)*, breath. **außer ~ sein** to be out of puff *(col)*.
Pusteblume *f (col)* dandelion.
Pustel *f* **-n** *(Pickel)* pimple; *(Med)* pustule.
pusten *(col)* **1** *vi (blasen)* to puff; *(keuchen)* to puff (and pant). **2** *vt (blasen)* to puff, to blow.
Pute *f* **-n** turkey (hen). **dumme ~** *(col)* silly goose *(col)*.
Puter *m* **-** turkey (cock).
puterrot *adj* scarlet.
Putsch *m* **-e** coup (d'état), revolt.
putschen *vi* to rebel, to revolt.
Putschist(in *f***)** *m* rebel.
Putschversuch *m* attempted coup (d'état).
Pütt *m* **-s** *(dial)* pit, mine.
Putte *f* **-n** *(Art)* cherub.
Putz *m no pl* **(a)** *(Build)* plaster; *(Rauh~)* roughcast. **eine Mauer mit ~ verkleiden** to roughcast a wall; **unter ~** under the plaster. **(b) auf den ~ hauen** *(col) (angeben)* to show off; *(ausgelassen feiern)* to have a rave-up *(col)*; *(meckern)* to kick up a fuss *(col)*. **(c)** *(dated: Kleidung)* finery. **in vollem ~ erscheinen** to arrive all dressed up in one's Sunday best.
putzen 1 *vt* to clean; *(scheuern auch)* to scrub; *(polieren auch)* to polish; *(wischen auch)* to wipe. **die Schuhe ~** to clean *or* polish one's shoes; **Fenster ~** to clean the windows; **sich** *(dat)* **die Nase ~** to wipe one's nose; *(sich schneuzen)* to blow one's nose; **sich** *(dat)* **die Zähne ~** to brush one's teeth; **einem Baby den Hintern/die Nase ~** to wipe a baby's bottom/nose. **2** *vr* **(a)** *(sich säubern)* to wash oneself. **(b)** *(dated: sichschmücken)* to dress oneself up.
Putzfrau *f* cleaning lady, char(woman) *(Brit)*.
putzig *adj (col) (komisch)* comical; *(niedlich)* cute.
Putz-: ~lappen *m* cloth; *(Staubtuch)* duster; **~mittel** *nt (zum Scheuern)* cleansing agent; *(zum Polieren)* polish; **~mittel** *pl* cleaning things *pl*; **p~munter** *adj (col)* full of beans *(col)*; **~teufel** *m (col: Frau)* maniac for housework; **~tuch** *nt (Staubtuch)* duster; *(Wischlappen)* cloth; **~zeug** *nt* cleaning things *pl*.
Puzzle(spiel) ['pazl-] *nt* **-s** jigsaw (puzzle).
Pygmäe [pʏ'gmɛ:ə] *m (wk)* **-n, -n** pygmy.
Pyjama [py'dʒa:ma] *m* **-s** pyjamas *pl (Brit)*, pajamas *pl (US)*. **im ~** in his pyjamas.
Pyjamahose *f* pyjama *(Brit) or* pajama *(US)* trousers *pl*.
Pyramide *f* **-n** pyramid.
Pyrenäen [pyre'nɛ:ən] *pl* **die ~** the Pyrenees *pl*.
Pyro-: ~mane *m (wk)* **-n, -n**, **~manin** *f* pyromaniac; **~manie** *f* pyromania; **~technik** *f* pyrotechnics *sing*; **p~technisch** *adj* pyrotechnic.
Python(schlange *f***)** ['py:tɔn-] *m* **-s** python.

Q

Q, q [kuː] *nt* -, - Q, q.
qkm = **Quadratkilometer.**
qm = **Quadratmeter.**
quabbelig *adj Qualle* slimy; *Pudding* wobbly.
Quacksalber *m* - *(pej)* quack (doctor).
Quacksalberei *f* quack medicine.
Quaddel *f* **-n** hives *pl*, rash; *(durch Insekten)* bite.
Quader *m (Math)* rectangular solid; *(Archit)* ashlar, stone block.
Quadrat *nt* **-e** *(Fläche, Potenz)* square. **vier zum** ~ four squared; **drei Meter im** ~ three metres square.
Quadrat- *in cpds* square.
quadratisch *adj Form* square; *(Math) Gleichung* quadratic.
Quadrat-: **~latschen** *pl (hum) (Schuhe)* clodhoppers *(col)*; *(Füße)* plates of meat *(Brit col)*; **~meter** *m or nt* square metre *(Brit) or* meter *(US)*.
Quadratur *f* quadrature. **das käme der ~ des Kreises gleich** *(geh)* that's like trying to square the circle.
Quadrat-: **~wurzel** *f* square root; **~zahl** *f* square number.
quadrieren* *vt Zahl* to square.
quak *interj (von Frosch)* croak; *(von Ente)* quack.
quaken *vi (Frosch)* to croak; *(Ente)* to quack; *(col: Mensch)* to squawk *(col)*.
quäken *vti (col)* to screech, to squawk.
Quäker(in *f***)** *m* - Quaker.
Qual *f* **-en** *(Schmerz) (körperlich)* pain, agony; *(seelisch)* anguish. **jds ~(en) lindern** to lessen sb's suffering; **unter großen ~en sterben** to die in agony; **sein Leben war eine einzige ~** his life was a living death; **es ist eine ~, das mit ansehen zu müssen** it is agonizing to watch; **jeder Schritt wurde ihm zur ~** every step was agony for him; **er machte ihr das Leben zur ~** he made her life a misery; **die ~en, die sie um ihn ausgestanden hat** the suffering she has gone through because of him.
quälen 1 *vt* to torment; *Tiere auch* to tease; *(mit Bitten etc)* to pester. **jdn zu Tode ~** to torture sb to death; **~de Ungewißheit** agonizing uncertainty; **~der Durst** excruciating thirst; *siehe* **gequält. 2** *vr* **(a)** *(seelisch)* to torment oneself *(leiden)* to be in agony. **(b)** *(sich abmühen)* to struggle. **er mußte sich ~, damit er das schaffte** it was a struggle for him to do it; **sich durch ein Buch ~** to struggle through a book.
Quälerei *f* **(a)** *(Grausamkeit)* torture; *(seelische, nervliche Belastung)* torment. **das ist doch eine ~ für das Tier** that is cruel to the animal. **(b)** *(mühsame Arbeit)* struggle.
Quälgeist *m (col)* pest *(col)*.
Qualifikation *f* qualification. **er hat die ~ zu diesem Amt** he has the qualifications for this office; **zur ~ fehlten ihr nur wenige Sekunden** she only needed a few more seconds to qualify.
Qualifikationsspiel *nt* qualifying game.
qualifizieren* *vtr* to qualify *(für, zu* for).
qualifiziert *adj* **(a)** *Arbeiter, Nachwuchs* qualified; *Arbeit* professional. **(b)** *(Pol) Mehrheit* requisite.
Qualität *f* quality. **von ausgezeichneter ~** (of) top quality.
qualitativ *adj* qualitative.
Qualitäts- *in cpds* quality; **~arbeit** *f* quality work; **~kontrolle** *f* quality control; **~ware** *f* quality goods *pl*.
Qualle *f* **-n** jellyfish.
Qualm *m no pl* dense smoke; *(Tabaks~)* fug.
qualmen 1 *vi* **(a)** to smoke. **es qualmt aus dem Schornstein** clouds of smoke are coming from the chimney. **(b)** *(col: Mensch)* to smoke. **sie qualmt einem die ganze Bude voll** she fills the whole place with smoke. **2** *vt (col) Zigarette, Pfeife* to puff away at *(col)*.
qualmig *adj* smoky.
qualvoll *adj* painful; *Schmerzen* excruciating; *Gedanke* agonizing; *Anblick* harrowing.
Quant *nt* **-en** quantum.
Quanten *pl* **(a)** *pl of* **Quant, Quantum. (b)** *(col: Füße)* feet, plates of meat *(Brit col)*.
Quantentheorie *f* quantum theory.
Quantität *f* quantity.
quantitativ *adj* quantitative.
Quantum *nt, pl* **Quanten** *(Menge)* quantity; *(Anteil)* quota *(an+dat* of).
Quarantäne *f* **-n** quarantine. **unter ~ stellen** to put in quarantine; **über das Gebiet wurde ~ verhängt** the area was placed under quarantine.
Quarantänestation *f* isolation ward.
Quark *m no pl* **(a)** (soft) curd cheese. **(b)** *(col: Unsinn)* rubbish. **so ein ~!** stuff and nonsense!; **das geht ihn einen ~ an!** it's none of his business!
Quark-: **~kuchen** *m* cheesecake; **~tasche** *f*, **~teilchen** *nt curd cheese turnover*.
Quart[1] *f* **-en (a)** *(Mus: auch ~e)* fourth. **(b)** *(Fechten)* quarte.
Quart[2] *nt no pl (Typ)* quarto *(format)*.
Quarta *f, pl* **Quarten** *(Sch) third year of German secondary school.*
Quartal *nt* **-e** quarter (year). **Kündigung zum ~** quarterly notice date.
Quartal(s)-: **~abschluß** *m* end of the quarter; **~säufer** *m (col)* heavy drinker; **q~weise** *adj* quarterly.
Quartaner(in *f***)** *m* - *(Sch) pupil in third year of German secondary school.*
Quarte *f* **-n** *(Mus)* fourth.
Quartett *nt* **-e (a)** *(Mus)* quartet. **(b)** *(Cards) (Spiel)* ≃ happy familes; *(Karten)* set of four cards.
Quartier *nt* **-e (a)** *(Unterkunft)* accommodation *(Brit)*, accommodations *(US)*. **wir sollten uns ein ~ suchen** we should look for a place to stay; **wir hatten unser ~ in einem alten Bauernhof** we stayed in an old farmhouse. **(b)** *(Mil)* quarters *pl*, billet.
Quarz *m* **-e** quartz.
Quarz-: **~lampe** *f* quartz lamp; **~uhr** *f* quartz clock.
quasi 1 *adv* virtually. **2** *pref* quasi.
Quasselei *f (col)* gabbling *(col)*, blethering *(col)*.
quasseln *vti* to gabble *(col)*, to blether *(col)*.
Quaste *f* **-n** *(Troddel)* tassle; *(von Pinsel)* bristles *pl*; *(Schwanz~)* tuft.
Quästur *f (Univ)* bursary.
Quatsch *m no pl (col)* **(a)** *(Unsinn)* rubbish. **das ist der größte ~, den ich je gehört habe** that is the biggest load of rubbish I have ever heard; **red**

keinen ~! don't talk rubbish!; **so ein ~!** what rubbish. **(b)** *(Dummheiten)* nonsense. **hört doch endlich mit dem ~ auf!** stop being so stupid!; **laß den ~** cut it out! *(col)*; **~ machen** to mess about *(col)*; **mach keinen ~, sonst ...** don't try anything funny or ...

quatschen *(col)* **1** *vti (dummes Zeug reden)* to gab (away) *(col)*. **2** *vi* **(a)** *(plaudern)* to chatter, to natter *(Brit col)*. **ich hab' mit ihm am Telefon gequatscht** I had a good natter with him on the phone. **(b)** *(etw ausplaudern)* to squeal *(col)*, to talk.

Quatscherei *f (col)* blathering *(col)*, yacking *(col)*.

Quatschkopf *m (pej col) (Schwätzer)* windbag *(col)*; *(Dummkopf)* fool, twit *(Brit col)*.

Quecksilber *nt* mercury.

Quecksilber- *in cpds* mercury; **q~haltig** *adj* mercurial.

Quell *m* **-e** *(poet)* spring, source.

Quelle *f* **-n (a)** spring; *(von Fluß auch)* source; *(Erdöl~, Gas~)* well. **(b)** *(fig, für Waren)* source. **die ~ allen Übels** the root of all evil; **eine ~ der Freude** a source of pleasure; **aus zuverlässiger ~** from a reliable source; **an der ~ sitzen** *(fig)* to be well-placed.

quellen *vi pret* **quoll,** *ptp* **gequollen** *aux sein* **(a)** *(herausfließen)* to pour, to stream. **(b)** *(Reis, Erbsen)* to swell. **lassen Sie die Bohnen über Nacht ~** leave the beans to soak overnight.

Quellen-: ~angabe *f* reference; **~forschung** *f* source research.

Quell-: ~fluß *m* source (river); **~wasser** *nt* spring water.

Quengelei *f (col)* whining.

queng(e)lig *adj* whining. **die Kinder wurden ~** the children started to whine.

quengeln *vi (col)* to whine.

quer *adv (schräg)* crosswise; *(rechtwinklig)* at right angles. **er legte sich ~ aufs Bett** he lay down across the bed; **die Spur verläuft ~ zum Hang** the path runs across the slope; **die Straße/Linie verläuft ~** the road/line runs at right angles; **der Wagen stand ~ zur Fahrbahn** the car was at right angles to the road; **~ durch etw gehen/laufen** *etc* to go through sth; **~ über etw** *(acc)* **gehen/laufen** to go across sth.

Quer-: ~balken *m* crossbeam; *(von Türrahmen)* lintel; *(Sport)* crossbar; **q~beet** *adv (col) (wahllos)* at random; *(~feldein)* across country.

Quere *f no pl* **jdm in die ~ kommen** to cross sb's path; **der Lastwagen kam mir in die ~** the lorry got in my way.

Querele *f* **-n** *usu pl (geh)* dispute, quarrel.

querfeld|ein *adv* across country.

Querfeld|einrennen *nt* cross-country; *(Aut)* autocross; *(mit Motorrädern)* motocross; *(Radrennen)* cyclecross.

Quer-: ~flöte *f* (transverse) flute; **~format** *nt* oblong format; **q~gestreift** *adj attr* horizontally striped; **~kopf** *m (col)* awkward customer *(col)*; **q~köpfig** *adj* perverse; **~latte** *f* crossbar; **q~legen** *vr (fig col)* to be awkward; **~paß** *m* cross; **~schläger** *m* ricochet.

Querschnitt *m (lit, fig)* cross-section.

querschnittsgelähmt *adj* paraplegic. **seit dem Autounfall ist er ~** since the car accident he has been paralyzed from the waist down.

Quer-: q~stellen *vr sep (fig col)* to be awkward; **~straße** *f* **das ist eine ~straße zur Hauptstraße** it runs at right angles to the high street; **bei** *or* **an der zweiten ~straße fahren Sie links ab** turn left at the second junction *(Brit)* or crossroads; **die Kaiserallee hat viele ~ straßen** there are lots of streets (going) off the Kaiserallee; **~streifen** *m* horizontal stripe; **~strich** *m* (horizontal) stroke *or* line; **~summe** *f (Math)* sum of digits of a number; **~treiber** *m (col)* troublemaker.

Querulant(in *f***)** *m* grumbler.

Quer-: ~verbindung *f* conection, link; **~verweis** *m* cross-reference.

quetschen 1 *vt (drücken)* to squash, to crush; *(aus einer Tube)* to squeeze. **etw in etw** *(acc)* **~** to squeeze sth into sth; **sich den Finger ~** to squash one's finger. **2** *vr (sich klemmen)* to be caught; *(sich zwängen)* to squeeze (oneself).

Quetschkommode *f (hum col)* squeeze box *(col)*.

Quetschung, Quetschwunde *f (Med)* bruise, contusion *(form)*.

Queue [kø:] *nt* **-s** *(Billard)* cue.

quicklebendig *adj (col) Kind* lively, active; *ältere Person auch* spry.

quiek(s)en *vi* to squeal, to squeak.

quietschen *vi (Tür, Schloß)* to squeak; *(Reifen, Mensch)* to squeal.

quietschvergnügt *adj (col)* happy as a sandboy *(col)*.

Quint *f* **-en (a)** *(Mus: auch* **~e)** fifth. **(b)** *(Fechten)* quinte.

Quinta *f, pl* **Quinten** *(Sch) second year of German secondary school.*

Quintaner(in *f***)** *m* **-** *(Sch) pupil in second year of German secondary school.*

Quint|essenz *f (geh)* quintessence.

Quintett *nt* **-e** quintet.

Quirl *m* **-e (a)** *(Cook)* whisk, beater. **(b)** *(col: Mensch)* live wire *(col)*.

quirlen *vt* to whisk, to beat.

quirlig *adj* lively.

quitt *adj* **~ sein (mit jdm)** to be quits (with sb); **jdn/etw ~ sein** to be rid of sb/sth.

Quitte *f* **-n** quince.

quittieren* 1 *vt* **(a)** *(bestätigen) Betrag, Empfang* to give a receipt for. **lassen Sie sich** *(dat)* **die Rechnung ~** get a receipt for the bill. **(b)** *(beantworten)* to meet. **(c)** *(verlassen) Dienst* to quit, to resign. **2** *vi (bestätigen)* to sign.

Quittung *f* **(a)** receipt. **gegen ~** on production of a receipt; **eine ~ über 500 Mark** a receipt for 500 marks. **(b)** *(fig)* **das ist die ~ für Ihre Unverschämtheit** that is what you get for being so insolent; **er hat seine ~ bekommen** he's paid the penalty *or* price.

Quiz [kvɪz] *nt* **-, -** quiz.

Quizmaster ['kvɪsma:stɐ] *m* **-** quizmaster.

quoll *pret of* **quellen.**

Quorum *nt no pl* quorum.

Quote *f* **-n (a)** *(Statistik) (Anteilsziffer)* proportion; *(Rate)* rate. **(b)** *(Econ, Quantum)* quota.

Quotient [kvo'tsiɛnt] *m* quotient.

Quotierung *f (Comm)* quotation.

R

R, r [ɛr] *nt* **-, -** R, r.
Rabatt *m* **-e** discount. **mit 10% ~** at (a) 10% discount.
Rabatte *f (Beet)* border.
Rabattmarke *f (Comm)* (trading) stamp.
Rabatz *m no pl (col)* row, din.
Rabauke *m (wk)* **-n, -n** *(col)* hooligan, lout *(col)*.
Rabbi *m* **-s, Rabbiner** *m* **-** rabbi.
Rabe *m (wk)* **-n, -n** raven. **wie ein ~ stehlen** *(col)* to thieve like a magpie.
Raben-: ~eltern *pl (col)* bad parents *pl*; **~mutter** *f (col)* bad mother; **r~schwarz** *adj* pitch-black; *Haare* jet-black; **~vater** *m (col)* bad father.
rabiat *adj Kerl, Autofahrer, Umgangston* aggressive; *Geschäftsleute, Methoden* ruthless.
Rache *f no pl* revenge, vengeance. **das ist die ~ für deine Untat** this is the retribution for your misdeed; **(an jdm) ~ nehmen** *or* **üben** to take revenge (on sb); **etw aus ~ tun** to do sth in revenge; **~ ist süß** *(prov)* revenge is sweet *(prov)*.
Rache-: ~akt *m* act of revenge *or* vengeance; **r~durstig** *adj* thirsting for revenge; **~engel** *m* avenging angel.
Rachen *m* **-** throat, pharynx *(spec)*; *(von großen Tieren, fig)* jaws *pl*. **jdm etw in den ~ werfen** *(col)* to shove sth down sb's throat *(col)*.
rächen 1 *vt jdn, Untat* to avenge *(etw an jdm* sth on sb*)*. **2** *vr (Mensch)* to get one's revenge *(an jdm für etw* on sb for sth*)*; *(Sünde)* to be avenged. **deine Faulheit wird sich ~** you'll pay for being so lazy.
Rächer(in *f***)** *m* **-** avenger.
Rachitis *f no pl* rickets.
rachitisch *adj* rickety.
Rach-: ~sucht *f* vindictiveness; **r~süchtig** *adj* vindictive.
Racker *m* **-** *(col: Kind)* rascal *(col)*, monkey *(col)*.
rackern *vir (col)* to slave (away) *(col)*.
Rad *nt* **⸚er (a)** wheel; *(Rolle)* castor; *(Zahn~)* gearwheel. **ein ~ schlagen** *(Sport)* to do a cartwheel; **der Pfau schlägt ein ~** the peacock is fanning out its tail; **nur ein ~** *or* **Rädchen im Getriebe sein** *(fig)* to be only a cog in the works; **unter die ⸚er kommen** *(col)* to fall into bad ways; **das fünfte ~ am Wagen sein** *(col)* to be in the way. **(b)** *(Fahr~)* bicycle, bike *(col)*. **mit dem ~ fahren** to go by bicycle.
Radar *m or nt no pl* radar.
Radar-: ~anlage *f* radar (equipment) *no indef art*; **~falle** *f* speed trap; **~kontrolle** *f* radar speed check; **~schirm** *m* radar screen.
Radau *m no pl (col)* din, racket *(col)*. **~ machen** to kick up a row; *(Unruhe stiften)* to cause trouble.
Rad|aufhängung *f (Aut)* (wheel) suspension.
Rädchen *nt dim of* **Rad** small wheel; *siehe* **Rad.**
Raddampfer *m* paddle-steamer.
radebrechen *vti insep* to speak broken English/German *etc.*
radeln *vi aux sein (col)* to cycle.
Rädelsführer *m* ringleader.
rädern *vt (Hist)* to break on the wheel; *siehe* **gerädert.**
Räderwerk *nt (Mech)* works *pl*; *(fig)* machinery.
radfahren *vi sep irreg aux sein* **(a)** to cycle. **ich fahre Rad** I ride a bicycle; **kannst du ~?** can you ride a bike? **(b)** *(pej col: kriechen)* to crawl *(col)*.
Radfahrer *m* **(a)** cyclist. **(b)** *(pej col)* crawler *(col)*.
Radfahrweg *m* cycle track.
Radgabel *f* fork.
radial *adj* radial.
Radiator *m* radiator.
radieren* *vti* **(a)** to rub out. **(b)** *(Art)* to etch.
Radiergummi *m* rubber *(Brit)*, eraser *(esp US)*.
Radierung *f (Art)* etching.
Radieschen [ra'diːsçən] *nt* radish. **sich** *(dat)* **die ~ von unten ansehen** *(hum col)* to be pushing up the daisies *(col)*.
radikal *adj* radical; *Entfernen* total; *Ablehnung* flat. **~ gegen etw vorgehen** to take radical steps against sth.
Radikale(r) *mf decl as adj* radical.
Radikalisierung *f* radicalization.
Radikalismus *m (Pol)* radicalism.
Radikalkur *f (col)* drastic remedy.
Radio *nt* **-s** radio, wireless *(esp Brit)*. **~ hören** to listen to the radio; **im ~** on the radio.
Radio- *in cpds* radio; **r~aktiv** *adj* radioactive; **r~aktiver Niederschlag** (radioactive) fall-out; **~aktivität** *f* radioactivity; **~apparat** *m* radio (set); **~durchsage** *f* radio announcement; **~gerät** *nt* radio (set); **~loge** *m*, **~login** *f (Med)* radiologist; **~logie** *f (Med)* radiology; **~sender** *m (Rundfunkanstalt)* radio station; *(Sendeeinrichtung)* radio transmitter; **~sendung** *f* radio programme *(Brit) or* program *(US)*; **~station** *f* radio station; **~teleskop** *nt* radio telescope; **~wecker** *m* radio alarm (clock).
Radium *nt* radium.
Radius *m, pl* **Radien** [-iən] radius.
Rad-: ~kappe *f* hub cap; **~lager** *nt* wheel bearing.
Radler(in *f***)** *m* **-** *(col)* cyclist.
Rad-: ~mantel *m (Bereifung)* bicycle tyre *(Brit) or* tire *(US)*; **~nabe** *f* (wheel) hub; **~rennbahn** *f* cycle (racing) track; **~rennen** *nt* cycle race; *(Sportart)* cycle racing; **~rennfahrer** *m* racing cyclist; **~sport** *m* cycling; **~sportler** *m* cyclist; **~tour** *f* cycle tour; **~wechsel** *m* wheel change; **~weg** *m* cycle track.
raffen *vt* **(a)** *(anhäufen)* to pile, to heap. **(b)** *Stoff, Gardine* to gather; *langes Kleid, Rock* to gather up.
Raff-: ~gier *f* greed, avarice; **r~gierig** *adj* grasping.
Raffinade *f (Zucker)* refined sugar.
Raffinerie *f* refinery.
Raffinesse *f* **(a)** *(Feinheit)* refinement *no pl.* **(b)** *(Schlauheit)* cunning *no pl.*
raffiniert *adj* **(a)** *Zucker, Öl* refined. **(b)** *(col) Apparat* fancy *(col)*; *Kleidung* stylish. **(c)** *(schlau)* cunning; *(durchtrieben auch)* crafty.
Raffiniertheit *f siehe adj* fanciness *(col)*; stylishness; cunning; craftiness.
Rage ['raːʒə] *f no pl (Wut)* rage, fury. **jdn in ~ bringen** to infuriate sb.
ragen *vi* to tower, to loom; *(heraus~)* to jut.
Ragout [ra'guː] *nt* **-s** ragout.
Rahm *m no pl* cream.
rahmen *vt* to frame; *Dias* to mount.
Rahmen *m* **- (a)** frame. **(b)** *(fig)* framework; *(Atmosphäre)* setting; *(Größe)* scale. **im ~** within the framework *(gen* of*)*; **im ~ des Möglichen** within the bounds of possibility; **im ~ bleiben** not to go too far; **aus dem ~ fallen** to go too far;

mußt du den immer aus dem ~ fallen! do you always have to show yourself up?; **ein Geschenk, das aus dem ~ des Üblichen fällt** a present with a difference; **in den ~ von etw passen** to blend in with sth; **das würde den ~ sprengen** it would be beyond my/our *etc* scope; **einer Feier den richtigen ~ geben** to provide the appropriate setting for a celebration; **in größerem/kleinerem ~** on a large/small scale.

Rahmen-: ~handlung *f (Liter)* background story; **~plan** *m* outline plan; **~programm** *nt* framework; *(von Veranstaltung etc)* supporting acts *pl*; **~richtlinien** *pl* guidelines *pl*.

rahmig *adj* creamy.

Rahmkäse *m* cream cheese.

räkeln *vr* = **rekeln.**

Rakete *f* **-n** rocket *(auch Space)*; *(Mil auch)* missile.

Raketen- *in cpds* rocket; *(Mil auch)* missile; **~abwehr** *f* antimissile defence *(Brit) or* defense *(US)*; **~satz** *m* set of missiles; **~stufe** *f* stage (of a rocket/missile); **~stützpunkt** *m* missile base; **~werfer** *m* rocket launcher.

Rallye ['rali, 'rɛli] *f* **-s** rally.

Rallyefahrer *m* rally-driver.

rammdösig *adj (col)* giddy, dizzy.

Ramme *f* **-n** ram; *(für Pfähle)* pile-driver.

Rammelei *f (col: Gedränge)* crush *(col)*.

rammeln 1 *vt siehe* **gerammelt. 2** *vi (Hunt)* to mate; *(col!)* to have it off *(col!)*.

rammen *vt* to ram.

Rampe *f* **-n (a)** ramp. **(b)** *(Theat)* apron.

Rampenlicht *nt (Theat)* footlights *pl*. **sie möchte im ~ stehen** *(fig)* she wants to be in the limelight.

ramponieren* *vt (col)* to ruin; *Möbel* to bash about *(col)*. **er sah ziemlich ramponiert aus** he looked the worse for wear *(col)*.

Ramsch *m no pl (col)* junk, rubbish.

Ramsch-: ~händler *m (pej)* junk dealer; **~laden** *m (pej)* junk shop; **~ware** *f (pej)* trashy goods *pl*, rubbish.

Rand *m* **⸚er (a)** edge; *(von Brunnen, Tasse)* rim, brim; *(von Abgrund)* brink. **voll bis zum ~** full to the brim; **am ~e** *erwähnen* in passing; *interessieren, beteiligt sein* marginally; **am ~e des Waldes** at the edge of the forest; **am ~e der Stadt** on the outskirts of the town; **am ~e des Wahnsinns** on the verge of madness; **am ~e eines Krieges** on the brink of war; **etw am ~e miterleben** to experience sth from the sidelines; **am ~e der Gesellschaft** on the fringes of society.

(b) *(Umrandung)* border; *(Teller~)* edge, side; *(Brillen~)* rim; *(von Hut)* brim; *(Buch~, Heft~)* margin. **etw an den ~ schreiben** to write sth in the margin.

(c) *(Schmutz~)* ring. **rote ⸚er um die Augen haben** to have red rims around one's eyes.

(d) *(fig)* **sie waren außer ~ und Band** they were going wild; **allein komme ich damit nicht zu ~e** I can't manage (it) by myself; **halt den ~!** *(col)* shut your face *(col!)*.

randalieren* *vi* to rampage (about). **~de Jugendliche** (young) hooligans; **~de Studenten** rioting students; **die Gefangenen fingen an zu ~** the prisoners started to get violent.

Randalierer *m* **-** hooligan, trouble-maker.

Rand-: ~bemerkung *f* marginal note; *(fig)* (passing) comment; **~erscheinung** *f* matter of minor importance; *(Nebenwirkung)* side effect; **~figur** *f* minor figure; **~gebiet** *nt (Geog)* fringe; *(Pol)* border territory; *(fig)* subsidiary; **~gruppe** *f* fringe group; **r~los** *adj Brille* rimless; *Hut* brimless; **~zone** *f* peripheral zone; **in der ~zone** on the periphery.

rang *pret of* **ringen.**

Rang *m* **⸚e (a)** *(Mil)* rank; *(in Firma)* position; *(gesellschaftlich auch)* position. **im ~ eines Hauptmanns stehen** to have the rank of captain; **im ~ höher/tiefer stehen** to have a higher/lower rank/position, to rank higher/lower; **ein Mann ohne ~ und Namen** a man without any standing; **jdm den ~ ablaufen** *(fig)* to outstrip sb. **(b)** *(Qualität)* quality, class. **ein Künstler von ~** an artist of standing; **von hohem ~** high-class; **ein Essen ersten ~es** a first-rate meal. **(c)** *(Theat)* circle. **erster/zweiter ~** dress/upper circle; **vor leeren ⸚en spielen** to play to an empty house. **(d)** **⸚e** *pl (Sport)* stands *pl*. **(e)** *(Gewinnklasse)* prize category.

Rangälteste(r) *m (Mil)* senior officer.

rangehen *vi sep irreg aux sein (col)* to get stuck in *(col)*. **geh ran!** go on!; *siehe* **herangehen.**

Rangelei *f (col) siehe* **Gerangel.**

rangeln *vi (col)* to scrap; *(um Posten)* to wrangl *(um* for*)*.

Rang-: ~folge *f* order of rank *(esp Mil)*; **~höchste(r)** *mf* senior person; *(Mil)* highest-ranking officer.

Rangierbahnhof [rã'ʒiːɐ-] *m* marshalling yard.

rangieren* [rã'ʒiːrən] **1** *vt (Rail)* to shunt, to switch *(US)*. **2** *vi (Rang einnehmen)* to rank. **an erster/letzter Stelle ~** to come first/last.

Rangier- [rã'ʒiːɐ-]: **~gleis** *nt* siding, sidetrack *(US)*; **~lok(omotive)** *f* shunter, switcher *(US)*.

Rang-: ~liste *f (Mil)* active list; *(Sport)* **er steht auf der ~liste der weltbesten Boxer** he ranks among the world's top boxers; **r~mäßig** *adj* according to rank; **~ordnung** *f* hierarchy; *(Mil)* (order of) ranks; **~stufe** *f* rank; **~unterschied** *m* social distinction; *(Mil)* difference of rank.

ranhalten *vr sep irreg (col: sich beeilen)* to get a move on *(col)*.

rank *adj (liter)* **~ und schlank** slender and supple.

Ranke *f* **-n** tendril; *(von Weinrebe)* shoot.

Ränke *pl (liter)* intrigue, cabal *(liter)*. **~ schmieden** to intrigue, to cabal *(liter)*.

ranken 1 *vr* **sich um etw ~** *(lit, fig)* to have grown up around sth. **2** *vi aux haben or sein* **an etw** *(dat)* **~** to entwine itself around sth.

Ränkeschmied *m (liter)* intriguer.

ran:- ~kommen = **herankommen**; **~lassen** *vt irreg (col)* **jdn ~lassen** to let sb have a go; **sie läßt keinen (an sich** *acc***) ran** *(col)* she won't let anybody near her.

rann *pret of* **rinnen.**

rannte *pret of* **rennen.**

Ranzen *m* **- (a)** *(Schul~)* satchel. **(b)** *(col: Bauch)* belly *(col)*, gut *(col)*.

ranzig *adj* rancid.

rapid(e) *adj* rapid.

Rapier *nt* **-e** rapier.

Rappe *m (wk)* **-n, -n** black horse.

Rappel *m* **-** *(col)* **(a)** *(Fimmel)* craze. **seinen ~ kriegen** to get one of one's crazy moods. **(b)** *(Wutanfall)* **einen ~ kriegen** to throw a fit.

rapp(e)lig *adj (col)* **(a)** *(verrückt)* crazy *(col)* **(b)** *(nervös, unruhig)* jumpy *(col)*.

rappeln *vi (col) (lärmen)* to rattle. **bei dir rappelt's wohl!** are you crazy?

Rappen *m* **-** *(Sw)* centime, rappen.

Rapport *m* **-e** report. **sich zum ~ melden** to report.

Raps *m* **-e** *(Bot)* rape.

Rapunzel *f* **-n** *(Bot)* corn salad, lamb's lettuce.

rar *adj* rare. **sich ~ machen** *(col)* to stay away; *(sich zurückziehen)* to make oneself scarce.

Rarität *f* rarity.

rasant *adj (col)* **(a)** *Tempo, Spurt* lightning *attr (col)*; *Auto, Fahrer* fast; *Karriere* meteoric; *Entwicklung* rapid. **(b)** *(imponierend) Leistung* terrific.

Rasanz *f no pl (col: Geschwindigkeit)* speed.

rasch 1 *adj* **(a)** *(schnell)* quick; *Tempo* great. **(b)** *(übereilt)* hasty. **2** *adv* quickly.

rascheln *vi* to rustle. **es raschelt (im Laub)** there's something rustling (in the leaves); **mit**

etw ~ to rustle sth.

rasen *vi* **(a)** *(wüten, toben)* to rave; *(Sturm)* to rage. **er raste vor Schmerz/Wut** he was going wild with pain/he was mad with rage. **(b)** *aux sein (sich schnell bewegen)* to race, to tear; *(Puls)* to race. **das Auto raste in den Fluß** the car crashed into the river; **ras doch nicht so!** *(col)* don't go so fast!; **die Zeit rast** time flies.

Rasen *m* - grass *no indef art, no pl*; *(Zier~ auch)* lawn; *(von Sportplatz)* turf, grass; *(Sportplatz)* field, pitch *(Brit)*.

rasend 1 *adj* **(a)** *(enorm)* terrific; *Eile auch* tearing; *Hunger, Durst auch* raging; *Beifall auch* wild, rapturous; *Eifersucht* burning. **(b)** *(wütend)* furious. **er macht mich noch** ~ he'll drive me crazy. **2** *adv (col)* terrifically; *weh tun, sich beeilen* like mad *(col) or* crazy *(col)*; *verliebt, eifersüchtig sein* madly *(col)*. ~ **gern!** I'd simply love to!

Rasende(r) *mf decl as adj* maniac.

Rasen-: ~**fläche** *f* lawn; ~**mäher** *m* lawn-mower; ~**sprenger** *m* - (lawn) sprinkler.

Raser *m* - *(col)* speed merchant *(col)*.

Raserei *f* **(a)** *(Wut)* fury, frenzy. **(b)** *(col: schnelles Fahren, Gehen)* mad rush.

Rasier- *in cpds* shaving; ~**apparat** *m* razor; *(elektrisch auch)* shaver.

rasieren* *vtr* to shave. **sich naß/trocken** ~ to have a wet shave/to use an electric shaver.

Rasier-: ~**klinge** *f* razor blade; ~**messer** *nt* (open) razor; ~**pinsel** *m* shaving brush; ~**wasser** *nt* aftershave/pre-shave (lotion).

Räson [rɛ'zõː] *f no pl* **jdn zur** ~ **bringen** to make sb see sense.

Raspel *f* **-n (a)** *(Holzfeile)* rasp. **(b)** *(Cook)* grater.

raspeln *vt* to grate; *Holz* to rasp.

Rasse *f* **-n** *(Menschen~)* race; *(Tier~)* breed. **das Pferd/der Hund hat** ~ the horse/dog has spirit.

Rassehund *m* thoroughbred dog.

Rassel *f* **-n** rattle.

rasseln *vi* **(a)** to rattle. **mit etw** *(dat)* ~ to rattle sth. **(b)** *aux sein (col)* **durch eine Prüfung** ~ to flunk an exam *(col)*.

Rassen- *in cpds* racial; ~**diskriminierung** *f* racial discrimination; ~**haß** *m* race hatred; ~**krawall** *m* race riot; ~**trennung** *f* racial segregation.

Rassepferd *nt* thoroughbred (horse).

rassig *adj Pferd, Auto* sleek; *Frau* vivacious; *Wein* spirited, lively.

rassisch *adj* racial. **jdn** ~**verfolgen** to persecute sb because of his/her race.

Rassismus *m* racialism, racism.

rassistisch *adj* racialist, racist.

Rast *f no pl* rest, repose *(liter)*. ~ **machen** to stop (to eat); *(Mil)* to make a halt; **ohne** ~ **und Ruh** *(liter)* without respite.

Raste *f* **-n** notch.

rasten *vi* to rest; *(Mil)* to make a halt. **wer rastet, der rostet** *(Prov)* you have to keep active.

Raster *m* - *(Archit)* grid; *(Phot: Gitter)* screen; *(TV)* raster; *(fig)* framework.

rastern *vt (TV)* to scan.

Rast-: ~**haus** *nt* (travellers' *(Brit) or* travelers' *US*) inn; **r**~**los** *adj (unruhig)* restless; *(unermüdlich)* tireless; ~**losigkeit** *f* restlessness; ~**platz** *m* resting place; *(an Autostraßen)* picnic area; ~**stätte** *f* service area, services *pl*.

Rasur *f (Bart~)* shave; *(das Rasieren)* shaving.

Rat *m* **(a)** *pl* **Ratschläge** *(Empfehlung)* advice *no pl*. **ein** ~ a piece of advice; **jdm um** ~ **fragen** to ask sb's advice; **jdm mit** ~ **und Tat zur Seite stehen** to support sb in (both) word and deed; **da ist guter** ~ **teuer** it's hard to know what to do. **(b)** *no pl* **jdn/etw zu** ~**e ziehen** to consult sb/sth; ~ **(für etw) wissen** to know what to do (about sth); **sie wußte sich** *(dat)* **keinen** ~ **mehr** she was at her wits' end. **(c)** *pl* **¨e** *(Körperschaft)* council. **der** ~ **der Gemeinde/Stadt** ≃ the district council; **im** ~ **sitzen** to be on the council.

Rate *f* **-n** instalment *(Brit)*, installment *(US)*. **auf** ~**n kaufen** to buy on hire purchase *(Brit) or* on the installment plan *(US)*; **in** ~**n zahlen** to pay in instalments.

raten *pret* **riet,** *ptp* **geraten** *vti* **(a)** *(Ratschläge geben)* to advise. **jdm gut/schlecht** ~ to give sb good/bad advice; **jdm zu etw** ~ to recommend sth to sb; **jdm** ~**, etw nicht zu tun** to advise sb against doing sth; **das würde ich dir nicht** ~ I wouldn't advise it; **das möchte ich dir auch geraten haben!** you better had *(col)*; **was** *or* **wozu** ~ **Sie mir?** what do you advise? **(b)** *(erraten)* to guess; *Kreuzworträtsel etc* to solve, to do. **rate mal!** (have a) guess; **dreimal darfst du** ~ I'll give you three guesses *(auch iro)*; **das rätst du nie!** you'll never guess!; **(gut) geraten!** good guess!; **falsch geraten!** wrong!

Raten-: ~**kauf** *m (Kaufart)* hire purchase *(Brit)*, HP *(Brit col)*, the installment plan *(US)*; **r**~**weise** *adv* in instalments *(Brit) or* installments *(US)*; ~**zahlung** *f (Zahlung in Raten)* payment by instalments *(Brit) or* installments *(US)*.

Ratespiel *nt* guessing game; *(TV)* quiz; *(Berufe-raten etc auch)* panel game.

Rat-: ~**geber** *m* adviser, counsellor *(form)*; ~**haus** *nt* town hall; *(einer Großstadt)* city hall.

ratifizieren* *vt* to ratify.

Ratifizierung *f* ratification.

Ration [ra'tsioːn] *f* ration.

rational [ratsio'naːl] *adj* rational.

rationalisieren* [ratsionali'ziːrən] *vti* to rationalize.

Rationalisierung [ratsionali'ziːrʊŋ] *f* rationalization.

rationell [ratsio'nɛl] *adj* efficient.

rationieren* [ratsio'niːrən] *vt* to ration.

Rationierung [ratsio'niːrʊŋ] *f* rationing.

ratlos *adj* helpless. **ich bin völlig** ~**(, was ich tun soll)** I just don't know what to do; **sie machte ein** ~**es Gesicht** she looked helpless.

Ratlosigkeit *f* helplessness. **in meiner** ~ **...** being at a loss ...

ratsam *adj* advisable.

Ratschlag *m* piece of advice. **ein guter** ~ a good piece of advice; **Ratschläge** advice; **drei Ratschläge** three pieces of advice.

Rätsel *nt* **- (a)** riddle; *(Kreuzwort~)* crossword (puzzle); *(Silben~, Bilder~ etc)* puzzle. **jdm ein** ~ **aufgeben** to ask sb a riddle. **(b)** *(fig: Geheimnis)* mystery *(um* of*)*. **vor einem** ~ **stehen** to be baffled; **es ist mir ein** ~**, wie ...** it's a mystery to me how ...

Rätsel-: ~**ecke** *f* puzzle corner; **r**~**haft** *adj* mysterious; **es ist mir r**~**haft** it's a mystery to me; ~**heft** *nt* puzzle book.

rätseln *vi* to puzzle (over sth).

Rätselraten *nt* guessing game.

Rats-: ~**herr** *m* councillor *(esp Brit)*, councilman *(US)*; ~**sitzung** *f* council meeting.

ratsuchend *adj* seeking advice. **sich** ~ **an jdn wenden** to turn to sb for advice; **R**~**e** those seeking advice.

Ratte *f* **-n** rat.

Ratten-: ~**gift** *nt* rat poison; ~**schwanz** *m* **(a)** *(lit)* rat's tail; **(b)** *(fig col: Serie, Folge)* string.

rattern *vi* to clatter; *(Maschinengewehr)* to chatter.

Raub *m no pl* **(a)** *(das Rauben)* robbery. **(b)** *(Entführung)* abduction. **(c)** *(Beute)* booty, loot. **ein** ~ **der Flammen werden** *(liter)* to fall victim to the flames.

Raub-: ~**bau** *m no pl* overexploitation (of natural resources); ~**bau an etw** *(dat)* **treiben** to overexploit *etc* sth; **mit seiner Gesundheit** ~**bau treiben** to ruin one's health; ~**druck** *m* pirate(d) edition.

rauben 1 *vt* **(a)** *(wegnehmen)* to steal. **(b)** *(entführen)* to abduct, to carry off. **(c)** *(fig)* **jdm etw** ~ to rob sb of sth; **das hat uns viel Zeit geraubt** it cost us a lot of time. **2** *vi* to plunder, to pillage.

Räuber *m* - robber. **~ und Gendarm** cops and robbers.

Räuberbande *f (pej)* bunch of thieves.

räubern *vi (col)* to thieve. **in der Speisekammer ~** to raid the larder.

Räuberpistole *f (col)* far-fetched story.

Raub-: **~fisch** *m* predatory fish; **~gier** *f (liter)* rapacity; **r~gierig** *adj (liter)* rapacious; **~katze** *f* (predatory) big cat; **~kopie** *f* pirate copy; **~mord** *m* robbery with murder; **~mörder** *m* robber and murderer; **~tier** *nt* predator, beast of prey; **~überfall** *m* robbery; *(auf Bank etc auch)* raid; **einen ~überfall auf jdn verüben** to hold sb up; **~vogel** *m* bird of prey.

Rauch *m no pl* smoke; *(giftig auch)* fumes *pl*. **sich in ~ auflösen** *(lit, fig)* to go up in smoke.

Rauch-: **~abzug** *m* smoke outlet; **~bombe** *f* smoke bomb.

rauchen **1** *vi (Rauch abgeben)* to smoke. **sie sah, daß es in unserer Küche rauchte** she saw smoke coming from our kitchen; **mir raucht der Kopf** my head's spinning. **2** *vti* to smoke. **eine ~** to have a smoke; **hast du was zu ~?** have you got a smoke?; **„R~ verboten"** "no smoking"; **sich** *(dat)* **das R~ an-/abgewöhnen** to take up/give up smoking; **stark ~** to be a heavy smoker.

Raucher *m* - *(auch Rail)* smoker.

Räucher|aal *m* smoked eel.

Raucher|abteil *nt* smoking compartment.

Räucherhering *m* kipper.

Raucherhusten *m* smoker's cough.

Raucherin *f* smoker.

Räucher-: **~kerze** *f* incense cone; **~schinken** *m* smoked ham; **~speck** *m* ≈ smoked bacon; **~stäbchen** *nt* joss stick.

Rauch-: **~fang** *m (~abzug)* chimney hood; **~fleisch** *nt* smoked meat; **r~frei** *adj* smokeless; **~glocke** *f* pall of smoke.

rauchig *adj* smoky.

Rauch-: **~säule** *f* column of smoke; **~schleier** *m* veil of smoke; **~schwaden** *pl* drifts of smoke *pl*; **~signal** *nt* smoke signal; **~verbot** *nt* ban on smoking; **hier herrscht ~verbot** smoking is not allowed here; **~vergiftung** *f* fume poisoning; **~vorhang** *m*, **~wand** *f* smokescreen; **~waren**[1] *pl* tobacco (products *pl*); **~waren**[2] *pl (Pelze)* furs *pl*; **~wolke** *f* cloud of smoke.

Räude *f* **-n** *(Vet)* mange.

räudig *adj* mangy.

rauf *adv (col) siehe* **herauf, hinauf.**

Raufbold *m* **-e** *(dated)* ruffian.

raufen **1** *vt Unkraut* to pull up. **sich** *(dat)* **die Haare ~** to tear (at) one's hair. **2** *vir* to scrap.

Rauferei *f* scrap, rough-house *(col)*.

Rauf-: **~lust** *f* pugnacity; **r~lustig** *adj* ready for a fight.

rauh *adj* **(a)** rough; *Wind* raw; *Winter, Klima* harsh; *(unwirtlich) Gebiet* bleak; *(hart) Mann* tough. **im ~en Norden** in the rugged north; **(die) ~e Wirklichkeit** harsh reality, the hard facts *pl*; **~, aber herzlich** bluff; *Begrüßung, Ton* rough but jovial. **(b)** *Hals, Kehle* sore; *Stimme* husky; *(heiser)* hoarse. **(c)** *(col)* **in ~en Mengen** by the ton *(col)*, galore *(col)*; **Geld in ~en Mengen** tons of money.

Rauh-: **~bein** *nt (col)* rough diamond; **r~beinig** *adj (col)* rough-and-ready.

Rauheit *f no pl* roughness; *(von Klima etc)* harshness; *(von Hals)* soreness; *(von Stimme)* huskiness.

Rauh-: **~fasertapete** *f* woodchip paper; **~haardackel** *m* wire-haired dachshund; **r~haarig** *adj* coarse-haired; **~reif** *m* hoarfrost; *(gefrorener Nebel)* rime.

Raum *m, pl* **Räume** **(a)** room; *(no pl: Platz auch)* space; *(Gebiet, Bereich)* area; *(fig)* sphere. **auf engstem ~ leben** to live in a very confined space; **ein Frage im ~ stehen lassen** to leave a question unresolved; **der ~ Frankfurt** the Frankfurt area; **~ gewinnen** *(Mil, fig)* to gain ground. **(b)** *no pl (Phys, Space)* space *no art*. **der offene** *or* **leere ~** the void.

Raum-: **~anzug** *m* spacesuit; **~ausstatter(in** *f*) *m* - interior decorator.

Räumboot *nt* minesweeper.

räumen *vt* **(a)** *(verlassen) Gebäude, Gebiet* to evacuate; *(Mil: Truppen)* to withdraw from; *Wohnung* to move out of; *Sitzplatz* to vacate. **(b)** *(leeren) Gebäude, Lager* to clear *(von* of*)*. **(c)** *(weg~)* to shift; *Schnee, Schutt auch* to clear (away); *Minen* to clear. **räum deine Sachen in den Schrank** put your things away in the cupboard.

Raum-: **~fähre** *f* space shuttle; **~fahrer** *m* astronaut; *(sowjetisch)* cosmonaut.

Raumfahrt *f* space travel *no art or* flight *no art*. **das Zeitalter der ~** the space age.

Raumfahrt- *in cpds* space; **~behörde** *f* space authority; **~programm** *nt* space programme *(Brit) or* program *(US)*.

Raumfahrzeug *nt* spacecraft.

Räumfahrzeug *nt* bulldozer; *(für Schnee)* snow-clearer.

Raum-: **~flug** *m* space flight; **~gewinn** *m* extra space gained; **~inhalt** *m* volume, (cubic) capacity; **~kapsel** *f* space capsule.

räumlich *adj* **(a)** *(den Raum betreffend)* spatial. **~e Verhältnisse** physical conditions; **wir wohnen ~ sehr beengt** we live in very cramped conditions; **rein ~ ist das unmöglich** (just) from the point of view of space it's impossible. **(b)** *(dreidimensional)* three-dimensional. **ich kann mir das nicht ~ vorstellen** I can't really picture it.

Räumlichkeit *f* **(a)** *no pl* three-dimensionality. **(b)** **~en** *pl* premises *pl*.

Raum-: **~mangel** *m* lack of space; **~maß** *nt* unit of volume; **~not** *f* shortage of space; **~pflegerin** *f* cleaner, cleaning lady; **~schiff** *nt* spaceship; **~sonde** *f* space probe; **~station** *f* space station.

Räumung *f* clearing; *(von Wohnhaus)* vacation; *(wegen Gefahr etc)* evacuation; *(unter Zwang)* eviction; *(von Lager, Geschäft)* clearance.

Räumungs-: **~befehl** *m* eviction order; **~frist** *f* (period of) notice; **~klage** *f* action for eviction; **~verkauf** *m* clearance sale.

raunen *vti (liter)* to whisper. **es ging ein R~ durch die Menge** a murmur went through the crowd.

Raupe *f* **-n** **(a)** caterpillar. **(b)** *(Planier~)* bulldozer.

Raupen-: **~fahrzeug** *nt* caterpillar (vehicle); **~kette** *f* caterpillar track; **~schlepper** caterpillar (tractor).

raus *adv (col)* **~!** (get) out!; *siehe* **heraus, hinaus.**

Rausch *m, pl* **Räusche** **(a)** *(Trunkenheit)* intoxication; *(Drogen~)* high *(col)*. **einen ~ haben** to be drunk; **etw im ~ tun** to do sth while one is drunk; **seinen ~ ausschlafen** to sleep it off. **(b)** *(liter: Ekstase)* ecstasy, rapture; *(Blut~, Mord~ etc)* frenzy.

rauschen *vi* **(a)** *(Wasser, Meer, Brandung)* to roar; *(sanft, Wind)* to murmur; *(Baum, Wald)* to rustle; *(Seide)* to swish; *(Radio etc)* to hiss; *(Regen)* to pour down; *(Applaus)* to resound. **~de Feste** glittering parties. **(b)** *aux sein (sich bewegen) (Bach)* to rush; *(Geschoß)* to whizz. **(c)** *aux sein (col: Mensch)* to sweep. **sie rauschte aus dem Zimmer** she swept out of the room.

Rauschen *nt no pl siehe vi* roaring; murmuring; rustling; swishing; hissing. **das ~ des Regens** the sound of rain.

Rauschgift *nt* drug; *(Drogen)* drugs *pl*, narcotics *pl*.

Rauschgift-: **~handel** *m* drug traffic; **~händler** *m* drug trafficker; **~sucht** *f* drug addiction;

r~süchtig *adj* drug-addicted; **er ist r~süchtig** he's a drug addict; **~süchtige(r)** *mf* drug addict.
rausfliegen *vi sep irreg aux sein (col)* to be chucked out *(col)*.
rauskriegen *vt sep (col)* to get out; *(herausfinden)* to find out.
räuspern *vr* to clear one's throat.
rausreißen *vt sep irreg (col)* **jdn ~** to save sb's bacon *(col)*.
rausschmeißen *vt sep irreg (col)* to chuck out *(col)*. **das ist rausgeschmissenes Geld** that's money down the drain *(col)*.
Rausschmeißer(in *f*) *m* - *(col)* bouncer; *(letzter Tanz)* last dance.
Rausschmiß *m* **-sse** *(col)* booting out *(col)*. **man drohte uns mit dem ~** they threatened us with the push *(col)*.
Raute *f* **-n (a)** *(Bot)* rue. **(b)** *(Math)* rhombus.
rautenförmig *adj* rhomboid, diamond-shaped.
Razzia *f, pl* **Razzien** ['ratsiən] raid, swoop *(col)*.
Reagenzglas *nt (Chem)* test-tube.
reagieren* *vi* to react *(auf +acc* to*)*.
Reaktion *f* **(a)** reaction *(auf +acc* to*)*. **(b)** *(Pol pej)* reactionary forces *pl*.
reaktionär [reaktsio'nɛːɐ] *adj (Pol pej)* reactionary.
Reaktionär(in *f*) *m (pej)* reactionary.
Reaktions-: **~fähigkeit** *f* reactions *pl*; **r~schnell** *adj* with fast reactions; **r~schnell sein** to have fast reactions; **~zeit** *f* reaction time.
reaktivieren* [reakti'viːrən] *vt (Sci)* to reactivate; *(fig)* to revive; *Kenntnisse* to polish up.
Reaktor *m* reactor.
real *adj* real; *(wirklichkeitsbezogen)* realistic.
Real|einkommen *nt* real income.
Realization *f* realization; *(TV, Rad, Theat)* production.
realisierbar *adj* practicable, feasible.
realisieren* *vt* **(a)** *Pläne, Programm* to carry out; *(TV, Rad, Theat)* to produce. **(b)** *(Fin)* to realize.
Realisierung *f* realization.
Realismus *m* realism.
Realist(in *f*) *m* realist.
realistisch *adj* realistic.
Realität *f* reality. **~en** *pl (Gegebenheiten)* facts *pl*.
Realitäts-: **r~fremd** *adj* out of touch with reality; **~sinn** *m* sense of realism.
Real-: **~lexikon** *nt* specialist dictionary; **~lohn** *m* real wages *pl*; **~politik** *f* political realism; **~politiker** *m* political realist; **~schule** *f* ≃ secondary modern school *(Brit)*, high school *(US)*; **~wert** *m (Fin)* real value.
Rebe *f* **-n** *(Ranke)* shoot; *(Weinstock)* vine.
Rebell(in *f*) *m (wk)* **-en, -en** rebel.
rebellieren* *vi* to rebel, to revolt.
Rebellion *f* rebellion, revolt.
rebellisch *adj* rebellious.
Rebhuhn *nt* (common) partridge.
Reb-: **~laus** *f* vine pest; **~stock** *m* vine.
Rebus *m or nt* **-, -se** picture puzzle.
Rechaud [re'ʃoː] *m or nt* **-s** tea/coffee *etc* warmer; *(für Fondue)* spirit burner.
Rechen *m* - *(Harke)* rake.
Rechen-: **~aufgabe** *f* (arithmetical) problem; **~fehler** *m* (arithmetical) error; **~heft** *nt* arithmetic book; **~maschine** *f* adding machine; **~operation** *f* calculation.
Rechenschaft *f* account. **jdm über etw** *(acc)* **~ ablegen** to account to sb for sth; **jdm ~ schulden** to be accountable to sb; **jdn (für etw) zur ~ ziehen** to call sb to account (for *or* over sth).
Rechenschaftsbericht *m* report.
Rechen-: **~schieber** *m* slide-rule; **~zentrum** *nt* computer centre *(Brit) or* center *(US)*.
Recherche [re'ʃɛrʃə] *f* **-n** investigation.
recherchieren* [reʃɛr'ʃiːrən] *vti* to investigate.
rechnen 1 *vt* **(a)** *(addieren etc)* to calculate. **rund gerechnet** in round figures. **(b)** *(einstufen)* to count. **jdn/etw zu etw ~** to count sb among sth. **(c)** *(veranschlagen)* to estimate, to reckon. **wir hatten nur drei Tage gerechnet** we were only reckoning on three days; **das ist zu hoch/niedrig gerechnet** that's too high/low (an estimate). **(d)** *(einberechnen)* to take into account. **alles in allem gerechnet** taking everything into account.
2 *vi* **(a) falsch/richtig ~** to go wrong (in one's calculations), to calculate correctly; **gut/schlecht ~ können** to be good/bad at sums *(esp Sch) or* with figures; **~ lernen** to learn arithmetic. **(b)** *(eingestuft werden)* to count. **er rechnet noch als Kind** he still counts as a child. **(c)** *(sich verlassen)* **auf jdn/etw ~** to count on sb/sth. **(d) mit jdm/etw ~** to reckon with sb/sth; **damit ~ müssen, daß ...** to have to expect that ...; **du mußt damit ~, daß es regnet** you must reckon with it raining; **mit dieser Partei wird man ~ müssen** this party will have to be reckoned with; **damit hatte ich nicht gerechnet** I wasn't expecting that; **er rechnet mit einem Sieg** he reckons he'll win.
Rechnen *nt no pl* arithmetic; *(esp Sch)* sums *pl*.
Rechner *m* - **(a) ein guter ~ sein** to be good at arithmetic. **(b)** *(Elektronen~)* computer; *(Taschen~)* calculator.
rechnerisch *adj* arithmetical. **ich bin rein ~ überzeugt, aber ...** I'm convinced as far as the figures go but ...
Rechnung *f* **(a)** *(Berechnung)* calculation; *(als Aufgabe)* sum. **die ~ geht nicht auf** *(lit, fig)* it won't work (out). **(b)** *(Kostenforderung)* bill, check *(US)*; *(von Firma auch)* invoice. **das geht auf meine ~** I'm paying; **laut ~** as per invoice; **auf eigene ~** on one's own account; **(jdm) etw in ~ stellen** to charge (sb) for sth; **einer Sache** *(dat)* **~ tragen** to bear sth in mind.
Rechnungs-: **~betrag** *m* (total) amount of a bill *or* check *(US)*/invoice; **~hof** *m* ≃ Auditor-General's office *(Brit)*, audit division *(US)*; **~jahr** *nt* financial year; **~prüfer** *m* auditor; **~prüfung** *f* audit.
Recht *nt* **-e (a)** *(Rechtsordnung, sittliche Norm)* law; *(Gerechtigkeit auch)* justice. **~ sprechen** to administer justice; **nach englischem ~** under English law; **für das ~ kämpfen** to fight for justice; **von ~s wegen** as of right; *(col: eigentlich)* by rights *(col)*. **(b)** *(Anspruch, Berechtigung)* right *(auf +acc* to*)*. **sein ~ fordern** to demand one's rights; **sein ~ bekommen** to get one's rights; **zu seinem ~ kommen** *(lit)* to gain one's rights; *(fig)* to come into one's own; **gleiches ~ für alle!** equal rights for all!; **das ~ des Stärkeren** the law of the jungle; **mit** *or* **zu ~** rightly; **und (das) mit ~** and rightly so; **im ~ sein** to be in the right; **das ist mein gutes ~** it's my right; **mit welchem ~?** by what right?
recht 1 *adj* **(a)** *(richtig)* right. **es soll mir ~ sein** it's OK *(col)* by me; **ganz ~!** quite right; **ist schon ~!** *(col)* that's OK *(col)*; **alles, was ~ ist** *(empört)* fair's fair; *(anerkennend)* you can't deny it; **ich habe keine ~e Lust** I don't particularly feel like it; **nichts R~es** no good; **aus dem Jungen kann nichts R~es werden** that boy will come to no good; **er hat nichts R~es gelernt** he didn't learn any real trade; **nach dem R~en sehen** to see that everything's OK *(col)*; **es ist nicht mehr als ~ und billig** it's only right and proper. **(b) ~ haben** to be right; **~ behalten** to be right; **er will immer ~ behalten** he always has to be right; **jdm ~ geben** to admit that sb is right.
2 *adv* **(a)** *(richtig)* properly; *(wirklich)* really. **verstehen Sie mich ~** don't get me wrong *(col)*; **wenn ich Sie ~ verstehe** if I understand you rightly; **sehe/höre ich ~?** am I seeing/hearing things?; **das geschieht ihm ~** it serves him right; **du kommst gerade ~, um ...** you're just in time to

...; **das ist mir ~** that suits me fine; **gehe ich ~ in der Annahme, daß ...?** am I correct in assuming that ...?; **hat es dir gefallen? — nicht so ~** did you like it? — not really; **man kann ihm nichts ~ machen** you can't do anything right for him; **man kann es nicht allen ~ machen** you can't please all of the people all of the time. **(b)** *(ziemlich, ganz)* quite, fairly *(col)*. **~ viel** quite a lot. **(c)** *(sehr)* very, right *(dial)*. **~ herzlichen Dank** thank you very much indeed.

Rechte *f (wk)* **-n, -n (a)** *(Hand)* right hand; *(Seite)* right(-hand) side; *(Boxen)* right. **(b)** *(Pol)* Right.

Recht-: ~eck *nt* rectangle; **r~eckig** *adj* rectangular.

Rechtens *gen of* **Recht** *(form)* **die Sache war nicht ~** the matter was not right *or (Jur)* legal.

rechte(r, s) *adj attr* **(a)** right, right-hand. **jds ~ Hand sein** to be sb's right-hand man. **(b) ein ~r Winkel** a right angle. **(c)** *(konservativ)* right-wing. **der ~ Flügel** the right wing.

rechtfertigen *insep* **1** *vt* to justify. **2** *vr* to justify oneself.

Rechtfertigung *f* justification. **zu meiner ~** in my defence *(Brit) or* defense *(US)*.

Recht-: ~haber *m* **-** *(pej)* know-all *(col)*; **r~haberisch** *adj* know-all *attr (col)*, self-opinionated.

rechtlich *adj (gesetzlich)* legal. **~ zulässig** permissible in law, legal; **~ nicht zulässig** not permissible in law, illegal.

Recht-: r~los *adj* **(a)** without rights; **(b)** *Zustand* lawless; **~losigkeit** *f* **(a)** *(von Mensch)* lack of rights; **(b)** *(in Land)* lawlessness; **r~mäßig** *adj (legitim)* legitimate; *Erben, Besitzer auch* rightful; *(dem Gesetz entsprechend)* legal; **für r~mäßig erklären** to declare legal; **~mäßigkeit** *f (Legitimität)* legitimacy; *(Legalität)* legality.

rechts 1 *adv* on the right. **nach ~** (to the) right; **von ~** from the right; **sich ~ einordnen** to take the right-hand lane; **sich ~ halten** to keep (to the) right; **~ stehen** *or* **sein** *(Pol)* to be right-wing; **~ stricken** to knit (plain); **zwei ~, zwei links** *(beim Stricken)* knit two, purl two. **2** *prep +gen* **~ des Rheins** on the right of the Rhine.

Rechts- *in cpds (Jur)* legal; **~abbieger** *m* **-** motorist/cyclist/car *etc* turning right; **die Spur für ~abbieger** the right-hand turn-off lane; **~anspruch** *m* legal right; **einen ~anspruch auf etw** *(acc)* **haben** to be legally entitled to sth; **~anwalt** *m* lawyer, attorney *(US)*; *(als Berater auch)* solicitor *(Brit)*; *(vor Gericht auch)* barrister *(Brit)*; **~ausleger** *m (Boxen)* southpaw; **~außen** *m* **-, -** *(Ftbl)* outside-right; **~beistand, ~berater** *m* legal adviser; **~brecher** *m* **-** law-breaker.

rechtschaffen *adj (redlich)* honest, upright.

Rechtschaffenheit *f* honesty, uprightness.

Rechtschreibung *f* spelling.

Rechts-: ~drall *m (von Billardball)* spin to the right; *(von Auto, Pferd)* pull to the right; *(Pol col)* leaning to the right; **einen ~drall haben** to spin/pull/lean to the right; **~drehung** *f* turn to the right; **~empfinden** *nt* sense of justice; **~extremist** *m* right-wing extremist; **~fall** *m* court case; **r~gerichtet** *adj (Pol)* right-wing; **~geschäft** *nt* legal transaction; **~geschichte** *f* legal history; **~grundsatz** *m* legal maxim; **r~gültig** *adj* legally valid; **~gültigkeit** *f* legal validity; **~händer(in** *f***)** *m* **-** right-handed person, right-hander *(esp Sport)*; **~händer sein** to be right-handed; **r~händig** *adj* right-handed; **r~herum** *adv* (around) to the right; **r~kundig** *adj* versed in the law; **~kurve** *f* right-hand bend; **~lage** *f* legal position; **r~lastig** *adj* listing to the right; *(fig)* leaning to the right; **r~lastig sein** to lean to the right; **~ordnung** *f* **eine ~ordnung** a system of laws; **die ~ordnung** the law; **~partei** *f* right-wing party; **~pflege** *f* administration of justice; **~pfleger** *m official with certain judicial powers.*

Rechtsprechung *f* **(a)** *(Gerichtsbarkeit)* jurisdiction. **(b)** *(richterliche Tätigkeit)* dispensation of justice. **(c)** *(bisherige Urteile)* precedents *pl*.

Rechts-: r~radikal *adj* radical right-wing; **die ~radikalen** the right-wing radicals; **~radikalismus** *m* right-wing radicalism; **r~rheinisch** *adj* on the right of the Rhine; **~ruck, ~rutsch** *m (Pol)* swing to the right; **r~rum** *adv (col)* to the right; **~sache** *f* legal matter; *(Fall)* case; **~schutz** *m* legal protection; **~schutzversicherung** *f* legal costs insurance; **r~seitig** *adj* on the right(-hand) side; **r~seitig gelähmt** paralyzed in the right side; **~staat** *m* state under the rule of law; **r~staatlich** *adj* **r~staatliche Ordnung** law and order; **r~stehend** *adj attr* right-hand, on the right; *(Pol)* right-wing; **~steuerung** *f* right-hand drive; **~streit** *m* law-suit; **~verkehr** *m* driving on the right *no def art*; **in Deutschland ist ~verkehr** in Germany they drive on the right; **~verletzung** *f* infringement of the law; **~weg** *m* **den ~weg beschreiten** to go to law; **der ~weg ist ausgeschlossen** ≃ the judges' decision is final; **r~widrig** *adj* illegal.

recht-: ~winklig *adj* right-angled; **~zeitig 1** *adj (früh genug)* timely; *(pünktlich)* punctual; **um ~zeitige Anmeldung wird gebeten** you are requested to apply in good time; **2** *adv (früh genug)* in (good) time; *(pünktlich)* on time.

Reck *nt* **-e** *(Sport)* horizontal bar.

recken 1 *vt (aus-, emporstrecken)* to stretch. **den Kopf/Hals ~** to crane one's neck; **die Glieder ~** to stretch (oneself). **2** *vt* to stretch (oneself).

Reck-: ~stange *f* horizontal bar; **~turnen** *nt* bar exercises *pl*.

Redakteur(in *f***)** [-'tøːɐ, -'tøːrɪn] *m* editor.

Redaktion *f* **(a)** *no pl (das Redigieren)* editing. **(b)** *(Personal)* editorial staff. **(c)** *(~sbüro)* editorial office(s).

redaktionell [redaktsio'nɛl] *adj* editorial. **etw ~ bearbeiten** to edit sth.

Redaktionsschluß *m* time of going to press; *(Einsendeschluß)* copy deadline.

Rede *f* **-n (a)** speech; *(Ansprache)* address. **eine ~ halten** to make a speech; **direkte/indirekte ~** direct/indirect speech *or* discourse *(US)*; **in freier ~** without (consulting) notes; **der langen ~ kurzer Sinn** *(prov)* the long and the short of it.

(b) *(Äußerungen)* words *pl*, language *no pl*. **seine frechen ~n** his cheek; **große ~n führen** to talk big *(col)*; **das ist meine ~!** that's what I've always said; **das ist nicht der ~ wert** it's not worth mentioning.

(c) *(Gespräch)* conversation, talk. **die ~ kam auf** *(+acc)* the conversation turned to; **es war von einer Gehaltserhöhung die ~** there was talk of a salary increase; **von Ihnen war eben die ~** we were just talking about you; **aber davon war doch nie die ~** but no-one was ever talking about that; **davon kann keine ~ sein** it's out of the question.

(d) es geht die ~, daß rumour *(Brit)* or rumor *(US)* has it that; **(jdm) für etw ~ und Antwort stehen** to account (to sb) for sth; **jdn zur ~ stellen** to take sb to task.

Rede-: ~duell *nt* verbal exchange; **~fluß** *m* **er stockte plötzlich in seinem ~fluß** his flow of words suddenly stopped; **~freiheit** *f* freedom of speech; **r~gewandt** *adj* eloquent; **~gewandtheit** *f* eloquence; **~kunst** *f* **die ~kunst** rhetoric.

reden 1 *vi* to talk, to speak. **R~ während des Unterrichts** talking in class; **mit jdm ~** to talk to sb; **so lasse ich nicht mit mir ~!** I won't be spoken to like that!; **sie hat geredet und geredet** she talked and talked; **mit jdm über jdn/etw ~** to talk to sb about sb/sth; **~ Sie doch nicht!** *(col)* come off it! *(col)*; **(viel) von sich ~ machen** to become (very much) a talking point; **du hast gut ~!** it's all very well for you (to talk); **darüber läßt sich ~** that's a possibility; *(über Preis, Be-*

dingungen) I think we could discuss that; **er läßt mit sich ~** he could be persuaded; *(in bezug auf Preis)* he's open to offers; *(gesprächsbereit)* he's open to discussion; **R~ ist Silber, Schweigen ist Gold** *(Prov)* (speech is silver but) silence is golden *(Prov)*; **in so einem Dorf wird natürlich viel geredet** in a village like that naturally people talk a lot; **er kann gut ~** he is a good talker *or (als Redner)* speaker; **jdn zum R~ bringen** to get sb to talk.

2 *vt* to talk; *Worte* to say. **kein Wort ~** not to say a word; **einer Sache das Wort ~** to speak in favour *(Brit) or* favor *(US)* of sth; **Schlechtes über jdn ~** to say bad things about sb.

3 *vr* **sich heiser/in Wut ~** to talk oneself hoarse/into a fury.

Redens|art *f (Redewendung)* expression, idiom; *(Sprichwort)* saying; *(Phrase)* cliché. **bloße ~en** empty talk.

Rederei *f (Geschwätz)* chatter *no pl*, talk *no pl*; *(Klatsch)* gossip *no pl*.

Rede-: ~schwall *m* torrent of words; **~verbot** *nt* ban on speaking; **jdm ~verbot erteilen** to ban sb from speaking; **~weise** *f* manner (of speaking); **~wendung** *f* idiomatic expression.

redigieren* *vt* to edit.

redlich *adj* honest. **sich** *(dat)* **etw ~ verdient haben** to have really earned sth; **~ (mit jdm) teilen** to share (things) equally (with sb).

Redlichkeit *f* honesty.

Redner(in *f*) *m* **-** speaker.

rednerisch *adj* rhetorical, oratorical. **~ begabt sein** to be a gifted speaker.

Rednerpult *nt* lectern.

redselig *adj* talkative.

Redseligkeit *f* talkativeness.

reduzieren* **1** *vt* to reduce. **2** *vr* to decrease, to diminish.

Reduzierung *f* reduction.

Reeder *m* **-** ship owner.

Reederei *f* shipping company.

reell *adj* **(a)** *(ehrlich)* honest, straight; *(Comm) Geschäft* sound; *Preis* fair. **(b)** *(wirklich)* real.

Referat *nt* **(a)** *(Univ)* seminar paper. **ein ~ halten** to present a seminar paper. **(b)** *(Admin: Ressort)* department.

Referendar(in *f*) *m* trainee (in civil service); *(Studien~)* student teacher; *(Gerichts~)* articled clerk.

Referendarzeit *f* traineeship; *(Studien~)* teacher training.

Referendum *nt, pl* **Referenden** referendum.

Referent(in *f*) *m (Sachbearbeiter)* consultant, expert; *(Redner)* speaker; *(Univ: Gutachter)* examiner.

referieren* *vi* to (give a) report *(über +acc* on*)*.

reflektieren* **1** *vt* to reflect. **2** *vi* **(a)** *(nachdenken)* to reflect, to ponder *(über +acc* (up)on*)*. **(b)** **auf etw** *(acc)* **~** to be interested in sth.

Reflex *m* **-e** reflection; *(Physiol)* reflex.

Reflexbewegung *f* reflex action.

Reflexion *f (Phys, fig)* reflection.

Reflexionswinkel *m (Phys)* angle of reflection.

reflexiv *adj (Gram)* reflexive.

Reform *f* **-en** reform.

Reformation *f* Reformation.

reformbedürftig *adj* in need of reform.

Reformer *m* **-** reformer.

Reform-: r~freudig *adj* avid for reform; **~haus** *nt* health food shop *(Brit) or* store *(US)*.

reformieren* *vt* to reform.

Reformkost *f* health food.

Refrain [rəˈfrɛ̃ː, re-] *m* **-s** *(Mus)* chorus, refrain.

Regal *nt* **-e** *(Bord)* shelves *pl*.

Regatta *f, pl* **Regatten** regatta.

rege *adj (betriebsam)* lively. **ein ~s Treiben** a busy to-and-fro; **noch sehr ~ sein** to be very active still; **~ Beteiligung** lively participation; *(zahlreich)* good attendance.

Regel *f* **-n** **(a)** *(Vorschrift, Norm)* rule; *(Verordnung)* regulation. **nach allen ~n der Kunst** *(fig)* thoroughly; **sie überredete ihn nach allen ~n der Kunst, ...** she used every trick in the book to persuade him ... **(b)** *(Gewohnheit)* habit, rule. **sich** *(dat)* **etw zur ~ machen** to make a habit of sth; **in der ~** as a rule. **(c)** *(Monatsblutung)* period; *(Menstruation)* menstruation *no art*. **die ~ bekommen** to get one's period.

Regel-: r~bar *adj (steuerbar)* adjustable; **~fall** *m* rule; **im ~fall** as a rule; **r~los** *adj (ungeregelt)* irregular; *(unordentlich)* haphazard; **~losigkeit** *f siehe adj* irregularity; haphazardness; **r~mäßig** *adj* regular; **r~mäßig spazierengehen** to take regular walks; **er kommt r~mäßig zu spät** he's always late; **~mäßigkeit** *f* regularity.

regeln **1** *vt* **(a)** *(regulieren)* to control; *siehe* **geregelt.** **(b)** *(erledigen)* to see to; *(endgültig)* to settle; *Problem etc* to sort out; *(in Ordnung bringen)* to settle, to resolve. **wir haben die Sache so geregelt ...** we have arranged things like this ...; **gesetzlich geregelt sein** to be laid down by law. **2** *vr* to resolve itself.

regelrecht **1** *adj* real, proper; *Betrug, Beleidigung* downright; **das Spiel artete in eine ~e Schlägerei aus** the match degenerated into a regular brawl. **2** *adv* really; *beleidigend* downright.

Regelung *f* **(a)** *(Regulierung)* regulation, control. **(b)** *(Erledigung)* settling; *(von Unstimmigkeiten)* resolution. **(c)** *(Abmachung)* arrangement; *(Bestimmung)* ruling.

Regel-: r~widrig *adj* against the rules; *(gegen Verordnungen verstoßend)* against the regulations; **~widrigkeit** *f* irregularity; *(Verstoß auch)* breach of the rules.

regen **1** *vt (bewegen)* to move. **2** *vr (Mensch, Glied, Baum etc)* to move, to stir; *(Gefühl, Wind etc)* to stir. **unter den Zuhörern regte sich Widerspruch** there were mutterings of disapproval from the audience.

Regen *m* **-** rain; *(fig: von Schimpfwörtern, Blumen etc)* shower. **in den ~ kommen** to be caught in the rain; **ein warmer ~** *(fig)* a windfall; **jdn im ~ stehenlassen** *(fig)* to leave sb out in the cold; **vom ~ in die Traufe kommen** *(prov)* to fall out of the frying-pan into the fire *(prov)*.

regen|arm *adj* dry, rainless.

Regenbogen *m* rainbow.

Regenbogen-: ~farben *pl* colours *(Brit) or* colors *(US) pl* of the rainbow; **r~farben** *adj* rainbow-coloured *(Brit)*, rainbow-colored *(US)*; **~haut** *f (Anat)* iris; **~presse** *f* trashy magazines *pl*.

Regeneration *f* regeneration; *(fig auch)* revitalization.

regenerieren* **1** *vr (Biol)* to regenerate; *(fig)* to revitalize *or* regenerate oneself/itself; *(nach Anstrengung, Schock etc)* to recover. **2** *vt (Biol)* to regenerate; *(fig auch)* to revitalize.

Regen-: ~fall *m usu pl* (fall of) rain; **tropische ~fälle** tropical rains; **r~frei** *adj* rainless; **~guß** *m* downpour; **~mantel** *m* raincoat; **r~reich** *adj* rainy; **~rinne** *f* gutter; **~schauer** *m* shower (of rain); **~schirm** *m* umbrella.

Regent(in *f*) *m* sovereign, reigning monarch.

Regen-: ~tag *m* rainy day; **~tonne** *f* rain barrel; **~tropfen** *m* raindrop.

Regentschaft *f* reign.

Regen-: ~wald *m (Geog)* rain forest; **~wasser** *nt* rainwater; **~wetter** *nt* rainy weather; **er macht ein Gesicht wie drei** *or* **sieben Tage ~wetter** *(col)* he's got a face as long as a month of Sundays *(col)*; **~wolke** *f* rain cloud; **~wurm** *m* earthworm; **~zeit** *f* rainy season.

Regie [reˈʒiː] *f* **(a)** *(künstlerische Leitung)* direction; *(Theat, Rad, TV auch)* production *(Brit)*. **die ~ bei etw führen** to direct/produce sth; **unter der ~ von** directed/produced by. **(b)** *(Leitung,*

Verwaltung) management. **etw in eigener ~ tun** to do sth oneself.

Regie- [re'ʒiː-]: **~anweisung** *f* (stage) direction; **~assistent** *m* assistant producer/director.

regieren* **1** *vi (herrschen)* to rule; *(fig)* to reign. **2** *vt Staat* to rule (over), to govern; *Markt, Fahrzeug* to control; *(Gram)* to govern.

Regierung *f* government; *(von Monarch)* reign; *(Zeitabschnitt)* period of government. **die ~ Brandt** the Brandt government *or* administration; **an die ~ kommen** to come to power; *(durch Wahl auch)* to come into *or* take office; **die ~ antreten** to take power; *(nach Wahl auch)* to take office.

Regierungs-: **~antritt** *m* coming to power; **~bank** *f* government bench; **~bezirk** *m* ≈ region *(Brit)*, ≈ county *(US)*; **~bildung** *f* formation of a government; **~chef** *m* head of a/the government; **der belgische ~chef** the head of the Belgian government; **~erklärung** *f* inaugural speech; *(in GB)* King's/Queen's Speech; **r~feindlich** *adj* anti-government *no adv;* **~form** *f* form of government; **r~freundlich** *adj* pro-government *no adv;* **~kreise** *pl* government circles *pl*; **~krise** *f* government(al) crisis; **~rat** *m* senior civil servant; **~sitz** *m* seat of government; **~sprecher** *m* government spokesman; **~system** *nt* system of government; **r~treu** *adj* loyal to the government; **~umbildung** *f* cabinet reshuffle *or* shake-up *(US);* **~vorlage** *f* government bill; **~wechsel** *m* change of government.

Regime [re'ʒiːm] *nt* **-s** *(pej)* regime.

Regime-: **~gegner** *m* opponent of the regime; **~kritiker** *m* critic of the regime.

Regiment *nt* **-e** *or (Mil)* **-er** **(a)** *(Herrschaft)* rule. **das ~ führen** *(col)* to be the boss *(col)*; **ein strenges ~ führen** *(col)* to be strict. **(b)** *(Mil)* regiment.

Regiments- *in cpds* regimental.

Region *f* region.

regional *adj* regional. **~ verschieden sein** to vary from one region to another.

Regisseur(in *f***)** [reʒɪ'søːɐ, -'søːrɪn] *m* director; *(Theat, Rad, TV auch)* producer *(Brit)*.

Register *nt* **-** *(Liste, Mus)* register; *(Stichwortverzeichnis)* index. **alle ~ ziehen** *(fig)* to pull out all the stops.

Registertonne *f (Naut)* register ton.

Registratur *f* registration; *(Büro)* records office; *(Aktenschrank)* filing cabinet.

registrieren* *vti* to register; *(col: zur Kenntnis nehmen)* to note.

Registrierkasse *f* cash register.

Registrierung *f* registration.

reglementieren* *vt* to regulate; *jdn* to regiment.

Reglementierung *f siehe vt* regulation; regimentation.

Regler *m* **-** regulator, control.

reglos *adj* motionless.

regnen *vti impers* to rain. **es regnet in Strömen** it's pouring (with rain); **es regnet Proteste** protests are pouring in; **es regnete Vorwürfe** reproaches hailed down.

regnerisch *adj* rainy.

Regreß *m* **-sse** *(Jur)* recourse, redress.

Regreß-: **~anspruch** *m (Jur)* claim for compensation; **r~pflichtig** *adj* liable for compensation.

regsam *adj* active, alert, lively.

Regsamkeit *f* alertness, liveliness.

regulär *adj* normal; *(vorschriftsmäßig)* proper, regular. **~e Truppen** regular troops.

regulierbar *adj* adjustable.

regulieren* **1** *vt* **(a)** to regulate; *(nachstellen auch)* to adjust. **(b)** *Rechnung, Forderung* to settle. **2** *vr* to become more regular. **sich von selbst ~** to be self-regulating.

Regulierung *f* regulation.

Regung *f (Bewegung)* movement; *(des Gefühls, von Mitleid)* stirring. **ohne jede ~** without a flicker (of emotion).

regungslos *adj* motionless.

Regungslosigkeit *f* motionlessness.

Reh *nt* **-e** deer; *(weiblich)* roe deer. **~e** deer.

Rehabilitation *f* rehabilitation; *(von Ruf, Ehre)* vindication.

rehabilitieren* **1** *vt* to rehabilitate; *Ruf, Ehre* to vindicate. **2** *vr* to rehabilitate *(form) or* vindicate oneself.

Reh-: **~bock** *m* roebuck; **~braten** *m* roast venison; **r~braun** *adj* russet; *Augen* hazel; **~keule** *f (Cook)* haunch of venison; **~kitz** *nt* fawn; **~rücken** *m (Cook)* saddle of venison.

Reibach *m no pl (col)* killing *(col)*. **einen ~ machen** *(col)* to make a killing *(col)*.

Reibe *f* **-n** *(Cook)* grater.

Reib|eisen *nt* rasp; *(Cook)* grater; *(fig: zänkisches Weib)* shrew. **rauh wie ein ~** *(col)* like sandpaper.

Reibekuchen *m (Cook)* ≈ potato waffle.

reiben *pret* **rieb,** *ptp* **gerieben** **1** *vti* **(a)** to rub. **etw blank ~** to rub sth till it shines; **jdm den Rücken ~** to rub sb's back. **(b)** *(zerkleinern)* to grate. **2** *vr* to rub oneself *(an +dat* on, against*)*; *(sich verletzen)* to scrape oneself *(an +dat* on*)*.

Reiberei *f usu pl (col)* friction *no pl.*

Reibung *f* **(a)** *(das Reiben)* rubbing; *(Phys)* friction. **(b)** *(fig)* friction *no pl.*

Reibungs-: **~fläche** *f (fig)* source of friction; **r~los** *adj* frictionless; *(fig col)* trouble-free; **r~los verlaufen** to go off smoothly; **~wärme** *f (Phys)* frictional heat.

Reich *nt* **-e** **(a)** *(Herrschaft(sgebiet), Imperium)* empire; *(König~)* kingdom. **das Deutsche ~** the German Reich; **das Dritte ~** the Third Reich; **das ~ Gottes** the Kingdom of God. **(b)** *(Bereich, Gebiet)* realm. **das ~ der Tiere/Pflanzen** the animal/vegetable kingdom; **das ~ der Natur** the realm of nature; **das ist mein ~** *(fig)* that is my domain.

reich *adj* rich; *(wohlhabend auch)* wealthy; *(groß, vielfältig)* large, copious; *Auswahl, Erfahrung, Kenntnisse* wide; *Mahl* sumptuous; *Vegetation* rich. **~ heiraten** *(col)* to marry (into) money; **~ geschmückt** richly decorated; *Mensch* richly adorned; **eine ~ ausgestattete Bibliothek** a well stocked library; **~ mit Vorräten ausgestattet** amply stocked up with supplies; **jdn ~ belohnen** to give sb a rich reward; **jdn ~ beschenken** to shower sb with presents; **eine mit Kindern ~ beschenkte Familie** a family blessed with many children; **~ an etw** *(dat)* **sein** to be rich in sth; **in ~em Maße vorhanden sein** to abound; **~ illustriert** richly illustrated.

reichen **1** *vi* **(a)** *(sich erstrecken)* to stretch, to extend *(bis zu* to*)*; *(Stimme auch)* to carry *(bis zu* to*)*. **das Wasser reicht mir bis zum Hals** the water comes up to my neck; **jdm bis zur Schulter ~** to come up to sb's shoulder; **so weit ~ meine Beziehungen/Fähigkeiten nicht** my connections are not that extensive/my skills are not that wide-ranging; **so weit das Auge reicht** as far as the eye can see.

(b) *(langen)* to be enough, to suffice *(form)*. **der Saal reicht nicht für so viele Leute** the room isn't big enough for so many people; **reicht mein Geld noch bis zum Monatsende?** will my money last until the end of the month?; **reicht das Licht zum Lesen?** is there enough light to read by?; **dazu reicht meine Geduld nicht** I haven't got enough patience for that; **jetzt reicht's (mir aber)!** *(Schluß)* that's enough!

2 *vt (entgegenhalten, geben)* to hand; *(herüber~, hinüber~ auch)* to pass (over); *(anbieten)* to serve. **jdm etw ~** to hand/pass sb sth; **jdm die Hand ~** to hold out one's hand (to sb); **sich die Hände ~** to join hands; *(zur Begrüßung)* to shake hands.

Reiche(r) *mf decl as adj* rich *or* wealthy man/woman *etc.* **die ~n** the rich *or* wealthy.

Reich-: r~geschmückt *adj attr* richly adorned; **r~haltig** *adj* extensive; *Essen* rich; *Informationen* comprehensive; *Programm* varied; **~haltigkeit** *f siehe adj* extensiveness; comprehensiveness; variety.

reichlich 1 *adj* ample; *Zeit, Geld, Platz* ample, plenty of. **2** *adv* **(a)** *(sehr viel) belohnen, sich eindecken* amply; *verdienen* richly. **~ Trinkgeld geben** to tip generously; **~ Zeit/Geld haben** to have plenty of time/money; **~ vorhanden sein** to abound; **mehr als ~ belohnt** more than amply rewarded; **das ist ~ gerechnet** that's a generous estimate; **~ 1.000 Mark** a good 1,000 marks. **(b)** *(col: ziemlich)* pretty.

Reichtum *m (lit, fig)* wealth *no pl*; *(Besitz)* riches *pl.* **zu ~ kommen** to become rich; **~er erwerben** to gain riches; **damit kann man keine ~er gewinnen** you won't get rich that way; **der ~ an Fischen** the abundance of fish.

Reichweite *f (von Geschoß, Sender)* range; *(greifbare Nähe)* reach; *(fig: Einflußbereich)* scope. **in ~** within range/the reach *(gen* of*)*; **jd ist in ~** sb is nearby; **außer ~** out of range/reach *(gen* of*)*.

Reif *m siehe* **Rauhreif.**

reif *adj* ripe; *Ei, Mensch, Arbeit* mature. **in ~(er)em Alter** in one's mature(r) years; **im ~en Alter von ...** at the ripe old age of ...; **~ zur Veröffentlichung** ripe for publication; **die Zeit ist ~** the time is ripe; **eine ~e Leistung** *(col)* a brilliant achievement; **für etw ~ sein** *(col)* to be ready for sth.

Reife *f no pl (das Reifen)* ripening; *(das Reifsein)* ripeness; *(von Ei, Mensch, Arbeit)* maturity. **zur ~ kommen** to ripen; **ihm fehlt die ~** he lacks maturity; **mittlere ~** *(Sch) first public examination in secondary school,* ≈ O-Levels *pl (Brit).*

reifen 1 *vt Obst* to ripen; *jdn* to mature; *siehe* **gereift. 2** *vi aux sein* **(a)** *(Obst)* to ripen; *(Ei, Mensch)* to mature. **er reifte zum Manne** he became a man. **(b)** *(fig: Plan etc)* to mature. **zur Gewißheit ~** to harden into certainty.

Reifen *m* - tyre *(Brit)*, tire *(US)*; *(Spiel~, von Faß)* hoop; *(Arm~)* bangle.

Reifen-: ~druck *m* tyre *(Brit) or* tire *(US)* pressure; **~panne** *f* puncture, flat; **~profil** *nt* tyre *(Brit) or* tire *(US)* tread; **~wechsel** *m* tyre *(Brit) or* tire *(US)* change.

Reife-: ~prüfung *f (Sch) siehe* **Abitur; ~zeit** *f* ripening time; *(von Ei)* period of incubation; *(Pubertät)* puberty *no def art.*

reiflich *adj* thorough, careful. **sich** *(dat)* **etw ~ überlegen** to consider sth carefully.

Reifung *f* ripening; *(von Ei)* maturation.

Reigen *m* - round dance; *(fig)* round. **ein bunter ~ von Melodien** a varied selection of melodies.

Reihe *f* **-n (a)** *(geregelte Anordnung)* row, line; *(Sitz~, Sew)* row; *(Serie, Math, Mus, fig)* series *sing.* **in Reih und Glied antreten** to line up in formation; **aus der ~ tanzen** *(fig col)* to be different; *(gegen Konventionen verstoßen)* to step out of line; **die ~n schließen** *(Mil, fig)* to close ranks; **die ~n lichten sich** *(fig)* the ranks are thinning; **in den eigenen ~n** within our/their *etc* own ranks.

(b) *(Reihenfolge)* **er ist an der ~** it's his turn; **warte, bis du an die ~ kommst** wait till it's your turn; **der ~ nach** in order, in turn; **sie sollen der ~ nach hereinkommen** they are to come in one by one; **außer der ~** out of turn; *(ausnahmsweise)* out of the usual way of things; **er kommt immer außer der ~** he always comes just when he pleases.

(c) *(unbestimmte Anzahl)* number. **ein ganze ~ (von)** a whole lot (of).

(d) *(col: Ordnung)* **wieder in die ~ kommen** to get one's equilibrium back; *(gesundheitlich)* to get back on form; **in die ~ bringen** to put straight.

reihen 1 *vt* **(a) Perlen auf eine Schnur ~** to string beads (on a thread). **(b)** *(Sew)* to tack. **2** *vr* **etw reiht sich an etw** *(acc)* sth follows (after) sth.

Reihenfolge *f* order; *(notwendige Aufeinanderfolge)* sequence. **der ~ nach** in sequence; **zeitliche ~** chronological order.

Reihen-: ~haus *nt* terraced house; **~schaltung** *f (Elec)* series connection; **in ~schaltung** in series; **~untersuchung** *f* mass screening; **r~weise** *adv* **(a)** *(in Reihen)* in rows; **(b)** *(fig: in großer Anzahl)* by the dozen.

Reiher *m* - heron.

reihern *vi (col)* to puke (up) *(col!)*.

reih|um *adv* around. **es geht ~** everybody takes their turn; **etw ~ gehen lassen** to pass sth around.

Reim *m* **-e** rhyme. **ein ~ auf „Hut"** a rhyme for "hat"; **~e bilden** to make rhymes; **~e schmieden** *(hum)* to write verse; **sich** *(dat)* **einen ~ auf etw** *(acc)* **machen** *(col)* to make sense of sth; **ich kann mir keinen ~ darauf machen** *(col)* I can see no rhyme (n)or reason in it.

reimen *vtr* to rhyme *(auf +acc, mit* with*)*. **das reimt sich nicht** *(fig)* it doesn't make sense.

Reim-: r~los *adj* unrhymed, non-rhyming; **~schema** *nt* rhyme scheme; **~wort** *nt, pl* **-wörter** rhyme.

rein[1] *adv (col)* = **herein, hinein.**

rein[2] 1 *adj* pure; *Wahrheit* plain; *Gewinn* clear; *(sauber)* clean; *Haut auch, Gewissen* clear. **das ist die ~ste Freude/der ~ste Hohn** *etc* it's pure *or* sheer joy/mockery *etc*; **er ist der ~ste Künstler** he's a real artist; **die ~e Arbeit kostet ...** the work alone costs ...; **eine ~e Jungenklasse** an all boys' class; **eine ~e Industriestadt** a purely industrial town; **~en Tisch machen** *(fig)* to get things straight; **etw ins ~e schreiben** to write out a fair copy of sth; **etw ins ~e bringen** to clear sth up; **mit sich selbst ins ~e kommen** to sort things out with oneself. **2** *adv* **(a)** *(ausschließlich)* purely. **~ theoretisch gesprochen** speaking purely theoretically. **(b)** *(col: ganz, völlig)* absolutely. **~ alles/unmöglich** absolutely everything/impossible.

Rein(e)machefrau *f* cleaner, cleaning lady.

Reinemachen *nt no pl (col)* cleaning.

Rein-: ~erlös, ~ertrag *m* net profit(s).

rein(e)weg *adv (col)* completely, absolutely. **das ist ~ erlogen** it's a downright lie.

Reinfall *m (col)* disaster *(col)*; *(Pleite auch)* flop *(col)*.

reinfallen *vi sep irreg aux sein (col)* = **hereinfallen, hineinfallen.**

Rein-: ~gewicht *nt* net(t) weight; **~gewinn** *m* net(t) profit; **~haltung** *f* keeping clean; **die ~haltung des Spielplatzes** keeping the playground clean.

Reinheit *f* purity; *(Sauberkeit)* cleanness.

reinigen 1 *vt* to clean. **etw chemisch ~** to dry-clean sth; **ein ~des Gewitter** *(fig col)* a row which clears/cleared the air. **2** *vr* to clean itself; *(Mensch)* to cleanse oneself.

Reinigung *f* **(a)** cleaning. **(b)** *(chemische ~) (Vorgang)* dry cleaning; *(Anstalt)* (dry) cleaner's *(Brit) or* cleaner *(US)*.

Reinigungs-: ~creme *f* cleansing cream; **~mittel** *nt* cleansing agent.

reinkriegen *vt sep (col)* = **hereinbekommen, hineinbekommen.**

Reinkultur *f (Biol)* cultivation of pure cultures. **Kitsch in ~** *(col)* pure unadulterated rubbish.

reinlegen *vt sep (col)* = **hereinlegen, hineinlegen.**

reinlich *adj* cleanly; *(ordentlich)* neat, tidy; *(klar)* clear.

Reinlichkeit *f siehe adj* cleanliness; neatness, tidiness; clearness.

Rein-: **r~rassig** *adj* pure-blooded; *Tier* pure-bred, thoroughbred; **~rassigkeit** *f* racial purity; *(von Tier)* pure breeding; **r~reiten** *vt sep irreg* **jdn r~reiten** *(col)* to get sb into a mess *(col)*; **~schrift** *f (Geschriebenes)* fair copy; **r~seiden** *adj* pure silk; **~vermögen** *nt* net assets *pl*; **r~waschen** *sep irreg* **1** *vt (von* of*)* to clear; **2** *vr (fig)* to clear oneself; **r~weg** *adv* = **rein(e)weg.**

Reis *m* **-e** rice.

Reisbrei *m* ≈ creamed rice.

Reise *f* **-n** journey, trip; *(Schiffs~)* voyage; *(Geschäfts~)* trip. **seine ~n durch Europa** his travels through Europe; **eine ~ mit der Eisenbahn/dem Auto** a train/car journey; **eine ~ zu Schiff** a sea voyage; **eine ~ machen** to go on a journey; **auf ~n sein** to be away (travelling *(Brit) or* traveling *(US)*); **er ist viel auf ~n** he does a lot of travelling; **wann gehen Sie auf die ~?** when do you go (away) on your trip?; **wohin geht die ~?** where are you off to?; **gute ~!** bon voyage!, have a good journey!

Reise-: **~andenken** *nt* souvenir; **~apotheke** *f* first aid kit; **~begleiter** *m* travelling *(Brit) or* traveling *(US)* companion; *(~leiter)* courier; **~bericht** *m* account of one's journey; *(Buch)* travel story; *(Film)* travelogue; **~beschränkungen** *pl* travel restrictions *pl*; **~beschreibung** *f* description of one's travels; travel book *or* story; *(Film)* travelogue; **~büro** *nt* travel agency; **~erleichterungen** *pl* easing of travel restrictions; **r~fertig** *adj* ready to leave; **~fieber** *nt* **vom ~fieber gepackt** excited about going on a trip; **~führer** *m (Buch)* guidebook; *(Person)* courier; **~gefährte** *m* travelling *(Brit) or* traveling *(US)* companion; **~geld** *nt* fare; **~gepäck** *nt* luggage, baggage; **~gesellschaft** *f* (tourist) party; *(im Bus auch)* coach party *(Brit)*; *(Veranstalter)* travel company; **~koffer** *m* suitcase; **~leiter** *m* courier; **~leitung** *f (das Leiten)* organization of a/the tourist party; *(~leiter)* courier(s); **~lektüre** *f* reading matter (for a journey); **etw als ~lektüre mitnehmen** to take sth to read on the journey; **~lust** *f* wanderlust, travel bug *(col)*; **r~lustig** *adj* keen on travel.

reisen *vi aux sein* to travel. **in etw** *(dat)* **~** *(Comm)* to travel in sth.

Reisende(r) *mf decl as adj* traveller *(Brit)*, traveler *(US)*; *(Fahrgast)* passenger; *(Comm)* (commercial) traveller *(Brit)*, traveler *(US)*.

Reise-: **~paß** *m* passport; **~pläne** *pl* plans *pl* (for a/the journey); **~proviant** *m* food for the journey; **~route** *f* route, itinerary; **~scheck** *m* traveller's cheque *(Brit)*, traveler's check *(US)*; **~schreibmaschine** *f* portable typewriter; **~spesen** *pl* travelling *(Brit) or* traveling *(US)* expenses *pl*; **~tasche** *f* grip, travelling *(Brit) or* traveling *(US)* bag; **~verkehr** *m* holiday traffic; **~vorbereitungen** *pl* travel preparations *pl*; **~zeit** *f* time for travelling *(Brit) or* traveling *(US)*; **die beste ~zeit für Ägypten** the best time to go to Egypt; **~ziel** *nt* destination.

Reisfeld *nt* paddy-field.

Reisig *nt no pl* brushwood, twigs *pl*.

Reiskorn *nt* grain of rice.

Reiß|aus *m*: **~ nehmen** *(col)* to clear off *(col)*.

Reiß-: **~brett** *nt* drawing-board; **~brettstift** *m* drawing pin *(Brit)*, thumb tack *(US)*.

reißen *pret* **riß,** *ptp* **gerissen** **1** *vt* **(a)** *(zer~)* to tear, to rip. **(b)** *(ab~, ent~)* to tear, to pull, to rip *(etw von etw* sth off sth*)*; *(mit~, zerren)* to pull, to drag. **jdn zu Boden ~** to drag sb to the ground; **der Fluß hat die Brücke mit sich gerissen** the river swept the bridge away; **jdn aus seinen Träumen ~** to wake sb from his dreams; **hin und her gerissen sein** *(fig)* to be torn. **(c) etw an sich** *(acc)* **~** to seize sth; *Unterhaltung* to monopolize sth. **(d)** *(Sport) Latte, Hürde* to knock off. **(e)** *(töten)* to take, to kill. **(f)** *(col: machen) Witze* to crack *(col)*; *Possen* to play.

2 *vi* **(a)** *aux sein (zer~)* to tear, to rip; *(Seil)* to tear, to break, to snap; *(Risse bekommen)* to crack. **mir ist die Kette gerissen** my chain has broken *or* snapped; **wenn alle Stricke ~** *(fig col)* if the worst comes to the worst. **(b)** *(zerren) (an +dat* at*)* to tug; *(wütend)* to tear. **(c)** *(Sport) (Gewichtheben)* to snatch; *(Leichtathletik)* to knock the bar off.

3 *vr* **(a)** *(sich verletzen)* to cut oneself *(an +dat* on*)*. **(b)** *(sich los~)* to tear oneself/itself. **(c)** *(col)* **sich um jdn/etw ~** to scramble to get sb/sth.

Reißen *nt no pl* **(a)** *(Gewichtheben: Disziplin)* snatch. **(b)** *(col: Glieder~)* ache.

reißend *adj Fluß* torrential, raging; *Schmerzen* searing; *Verkauf, Absatz* massive. **~en Absatz finden** to sell like hot cakes *(col)*.

Reißer *m* **-** *(col) (Buch, Film)* thriller; *(Ware)* big seller.

reißerisch *adj* sensational.

Reiß-: **r~fest** *adj* tearproof; **~leine** *f* ripcord; **~verschluß** *m* zip(-fastener) *(Brit)*, zipper *(US)*; **~wolf** *m* shredder; **~zahn** *m* fang; **~zwecke** *f* drawing pin *(Brit)*, thumb tack *(US)*.

Reit-: **~anzug** *m* riding-habit; **~bahn** *f* arena.

reiten *pret* **ritt,** *ptp* **geritten** **1** *vi aux sein* to ride. **auf etw** *(dat)* **~** to ride (on) sth; **im Schritt/Galopp ~** to ride at a walk/gallop. **2** *vt* to ride. **ein schnelles Tempo ~** to ride at a fast pace.

Reiter *m* **- (a)** rider, horseman; *(Mil)* cavalryman. **(b)** *(Kartei~)* index-tab.

Reiterin *f* rider, horsewoman.

Reiterregiment *nt* cavalry regiment.

Reit-: **~gerte** *f* riding crop; **~hose** *f* riding-breeches *pl*; *(Sport)* jodhpurs *pl*; **~peitsche** *f* riding whip; **~pferd** *nt* saddle-horse, mount; **~sport** *m* (horse-)riding, equestrian sport *(form)*; **~stall** *m* riding-stable; **~stiefel** *m* riding-boot; **~turnier** *nt* horse show; *(Geländereiten)* point-to-point; **~weg** *m* bridle-path.

Reiz *m* **-e (a)** *(Physiol)* stimulus. **einen ~ auf etw** *(acc)* **ausüben** to act as a stimulus on sth. **(b)** *(Verlockung)* attraction, appeal; *(Zauber)* charm. **der ~ der Neuheit/des Verbotenen** the appeal of novelty/forbidden fruits; **(auf jdn) einen ~ ausüben** to hold great attraction(s) (for sb); **den ~ verlieren** to lose all one's/its charm; **weibliche ~e** feminine charms.

Reiz-: **r~bar** *adj (empfindlich)* sensitive, touchy *(col)*; *(erregbar, Med)* irritable; **leicht r~bar sein** to be very sensitive/irritable; **~barkeit** *f siehe adj* sensitivity, touchiness *(col)*; irritability.

reizen **1** *vt* **(a)** *(Physiol)* to irritate; *(stimulieren)* to stimulate. **(b)** *(verlocken)* to appeal to. **es würde mich ja sehr ~, ...** I'd love to ...; **Ihr Angebot reizt mich sehr** I find your offer very tempting. **(c)** *(ärgern)* to annoy; *(herausfordern)* to provoke. **jds Zorn ~** to arouse sb's anger; *siehe* **gereizt.** **(d)** *(Cards)* to bid. **2** *vi* **(a)** *(Med)* to irritate; *(stimulieren)* to stimulate. **zum Widerspruch ~** to invite contradiction. **(b)** *(Cards)* to bid.

reizend *adj* charming. **das ist ja ~** *(iro)* (that's) charming.

Reizhusten *m* chesty cough.

Reiz-: **r~los** *adj* dull, uninspiring; **~mittel** *nt (Med)* stimulant; **~stoff** *m* irritant.

Reizung *f* **(a)** *(Med)* stimulation; *(krankhaft)* irritation. **(b)** *(Herausforderung)* provocation.

Reiz-: **r~voll** *adj* charming, delightful; *Aufgabe, Beruf* attractive; **die Aussicht ist nicht gerade r~voll** the prospect is not particularly appealing; **~wäsche** *f (col)* sexy underwear; **~wort** *nt* emotive word.

rekapitulieren* *vt* to recapitulate.

rekeln *vr (col: sich strecken)* to stretch. **er rekelte sich im behaglichen Sessel** he snuggled down in the comfy chair.

Reklamation *f* complaint.

Reklame *f* **-n (a)** advertising. ~ **für jdn/etw machen** to advertise sb/sth; **mit etw ~ machen** *(pej)* to show off about sth. **(b)** *(Anzeige)* advertisement, advert *(Brit col)*, ad *(col)*; *(TV, Rad auch)* commercial.

Reklame-: **~schild** *nt* advertising sign; **~sendung** *f* commercial break; **~trommel** *f*: **die ~trommel für jdn/etw rühren** *(col)* to beat the (big) drum for sb/sth, to do a lot of promotion for sb/sth; **~zettel** *m* (advertising) leaflet.

reklamieren* **1** *vi (Einspruch erheben)* to complain, to make a complaint. **bei jdm wegen etw ~** to complain to sb about sth. **2** *vt* **(a)** *(bemängeln)* to complain about *(etw bei jdm* sth to sb*)*; *(in Frage stellen) Rechnung* to query *(etw bei jdm* sth with sb*)*. **(b)** *(beanspruchen)* **jdn/etw für sich ~** to lay claim to sb/sth.

rekonstruieren* *vt* to reconstruct.

Rekonstruktion *f* reconstruction.

Rekord *m* **-e** record.

Rekord- *in cpds* record; **~halter, ~inhaber** *m* record-holder; **~lauf** *m* record(-breaking) run; **~marke** *f (Sport, fig)* record; **~versuch** *m* attempt on the/a record; **~zeit** *f* record time.

Rekrut *m (wk)* **-en, -en** *(Mil)* recruit.

rekrutieren* **1** *vt (Mil, fig)* to recruit. **2** *vr (fig)* **sich ~ aus** to be drawn from.

Rekrutierung *f* recruitment, recruiting.

Rektor *m*, **Rektorin** *f (Sch)* headteacher, principal *(esp US)*; *(Univ)* vice-chancellor, rector *(US)*; *(von Fachhochschule)* principal.

Relais [rə'lɛː] *nt* **-** [rə'lɛː(s)], **-** [rə'lɛːs] *(Elec)* relay.

Relation *f* relation.

relativ **1** *adj* relative. **~e Mehrheit** *(Parl)* simple majority. **2** *adv* relatively.

relativieren* [relati'viːrən] *vt (geh)* to qualify.

Relativität [relativi'tɛːt] *f* relativity.

Relativ-: **~pronomen** *nt* relative pronoun; **~satz** *m* relative clause.

relevant [rele'vant] *adj* relevant.

Relevanz [rele'vants] *f* relevance.

Relief [reli'ɛf] *nt* **-s** *or* **-e** relief.

Religion *f* religion; *(Schulfach)* religious instruction *or* education, RI *(col)*.

Religions-: **~bekenntnis** *nt* denomination; **~freiheit** *f* freedom of worship; **~gemeinschaft** *f* religious community; **~lehrer** *m* teacher of religious education, RI teacher *(col)*; **r~los** *adj* not religious; **~stunde** *f* religious education *no indef art*, RI lesson *(col)*; **~unterricht** *m* religious education.

religiös *adj* religious. **~ erzogen werden** to receive a religious upbringing.

Religiosität *f* religiousness.

Relikt *nt* **-e** relic.

Reling *f* **-s** *or* **-e** *(Naut)* (deck) rail.

remis [rə'miː] *adj inv* drawn. **~ spielen** to draw; **die Partie ist ~** the game has ended in a draw.

Remis [rə'miː] *nt* **-** [rə'miː(s)], **-** [rə'miːs] *or* **-en** [rə'miːzn] *(Schach, Sport)* draw.

Remittende *f* **-n** *(Comm)* return.

Remittent *m (Fin)* payee.

remittieren* *vt (Comm) Waren* to return; *Geld* to remit.

Remmidemmi *nt no pl (col) (Krach)* row, rumpus *(col)*; *(Trubel)* rave-up *(col)*.

Rempelei *f (col)* jostling; *(Sport: Foul)* pushing.

rempeln *vti (col)* to jostle, to elbow; *(im Sport)* to barge *(jdn* into sb*)*; *(foulen)* to push.

Ren *nt* **-e** reindeer.

Renaissance [rənɛ'sãːs] *f* **-en (a)** *(Hist)* renaissance. **(b)** *(fig)* revival, rebirth.

Rendezvous [rãde'vuː] *nt* **-** [-'vuː(s)], **-** [-'vuːs] rendezvous *(liter, hum)*, date.

Rendite *f* **-n** *(Fin)* yield, return on capital.

renitent *adj* awkward, refractory.

Renitenz *f* awkwardness, refractoriness.

Renn- *in cpds* race; **~bahn** *f* (race)track.

rennen *pret* **rannte,** *ptp* **gerannt** **1** *vi aux sein* to run. **um die Wette ~** to have a race; **ins Unglück ~** to rush headlong into disaster; **er rennt zu jedem Fußballspiel** he goes to every football match; **gegen jdn/etw ~** to run into sb/sth; **er rannte mit dem Kopf gegen ...** he bumped his head against ... **2** *vt* **(a)** *aux haben or sein (Sport)* to run. **(b) jdn zu Boden** *or* **über den Haufen ~** to knock sb down. **(c)** *(stoßen) Messer etc* to run.

Rennen *nt* **-** running; *(Sport) (Vorgang)* racing; *(Veranstaltung)* race. **totes ~** dead heat; **gut im ~ liegen** *(lit, fig)* to be well placed; **das ~ ist gelaufen** *(lit)* the race is over; *(fig)* it's all over; **das ~ machen** *(lit, fig)* to win (the race).

Renner *m* **-** *(col)* winner, worldbeater.

Rennerei *f (col) (lit, fig: das Herumrennen)* running around; *(Hetze)* mad chase *(col)*.

Renn-: **~fahrer** *m (Rad~)* racing cyclist; *(Motorrad~)* racing motorcyclist; *(Auto~)* racing driver; **~pferd** *nt* racehorse; **~piste** *f* (race)track; **~platz** *m* racecourse; **~rad** *nt* racing bike *(col)*; **~saison** *f* racing season; **~schlitten** *m* bob(sleigh); **~schuhe** *pl (Sport)* spikes *pl*; **~sport** *m* racing; **~stall** *m (Tiere, Zucht)* stable; **~strecke** *f (~bahn)* (race)track; **~tag** *m* day of the race; **~wagen** *m* racing car.

Renommee *nt* **-s** reputation, name.

renommiert *adj* renowned, famous *(wegen* for*)*.

renovieren* [reno'viːrən] *vt* to renovate; *(esp tapezieren etc)* to redecorate, to do up *(col)*.

Renovierung [reno'viːrʊŋ] *f* renovation.

rentabel *adj* profitable. **es ist nicht ~, das reparieren zu lassen** it is not worth(while) having it repaired; **das ist eine rentable Sache** it will pay (off).

Rentabilität *f* profitability.

Rente *f* **-n** pension; *(aus Versicherung, Lebens~)* annuity; *(aus Vermögen)* income. **in ~ gehen** *(col)*/**sein** *(col)* to start drawing one's pension/to be on a pension.

Renten-: **~alter** *nt* retirement age; **~anspruch** *m* right to a pension; **~basis** *f* annuity basis; **~empfänger** *m* pensioner; **~erhöhung** *f* pension increase; **~papier** *nt (Fin)* fixed-interest security; **~versicherung** *f* pension scheme.

Rentier *nt (Zool)* reindeer.

rentieren* *vir* to be worthwhile; *(Geschäft etc auch, Maschine)* to pay. **das rentiert (sich) nicht** it's not worth it.

Rentner(in *f***)** *m* **-** pensioner; *(Alters~ auch)* senior citizen, old age pensioner *(Brit)*.

re|organisieren* *vt* to reorganize.

reparabel *adj* repairable.

Reparationen *pl* reparations *pl*.

Reparatur *f* repair. **~en am Auto** car repairs; **~en am Haus vornehmen** to do some repairs to the house; **in ~** being repaired; **etw in ~ geben** to have sth repaired.

Reparatur-: **r~anfällig** *adj* prone to break down; **r~bedürftig** *adj* in need of repair; **~kosten** *pl* repair costs *pl*; **~werkstatt** *f* workshop; *(Auto~)* garage.

reparieren* *vt* to mend; *Auto* to repair.

Repertoire [repɛr'toaːɐ] *nt* **-s** repertory, repertoire *(auch fig)*.

Replik *f* **-en** *(fig geh)* riposte, reply.

Report *m* **-e** report.

Reportage [repɔr'taːʒə] *f* **-n** report.

Reporter *m* **-** reporter.

Repräsentant(in *f***)** *m* representative.

Repräsentantenhaus *nt (US Pol)* House of Representatives.

repräsentativ *adj (stellvertretend, typisch)* representative *(für* of*)*; *Haus, Auto* prestigious. **zu ~en Zwecken** for purposes of prestige; **die ~en Pflichten eines Botschafters** the social duties of an ambassador.

repräsentieren* **1** *vt* to represent. **2** *vi* to per-

form official duties.
Repressalie [-iə] *f* reprisal.
Repression *f* repression.
repressiv *adj* repressive.
Reprise *f* **-n** *(Mus)* recapitulation; *(Film, Theat)* rerun; *(nach längerer Zeit)* revival.
Reproduktion *f* reproduction.
reproduktiv *adj* reproductive.
reproduzieren* *vt* to reproduce.
Reptil *nt* **-ien** [-iən] reptile.
Republik *f* **-en** republic.
Republikaner(in *f*) *m* **-** republican.
republikanisch *adj* republican.
Republik-: **~flucht** *f (DDR)* illegal crossing of the border; **~flüchtling** *m (DDR)* illegal emigrant.
Requiem ['re:kviɛm] *nt* **-s** requiem.
Requisit *nt* **-en** equipment *no pl*, requisite *(form)*. **~en** *(Theat)* props, properties *(form)*.
Requisiteur [-'tø:ɐ] *m (Theat)* props *or* property manager.
Reseda *f* **-s** *(Bot) (Gattung)* reseda; *(Garten~)* mignonette.
Reservat [resɛr'va:t] *nt* **(a)** *(Wildpark)* reserve. **(b)** *(für Volksstämme)* reservation.
Reserve [re'zɛrvə] *f* **-n** **(a)** *(Vorrat)* reserve(s) *(an +dat* of*)*; *(Geld)* savings *pl*; *(Mil, Sport)* reserves *pl*. **(b)** *(Zurückhaltung)* reserve. **jdn aus der ~ locken** to bring sb out of his/her shell *(col)*.
Reserve-: **~kanister** *m* spare can; **~rad** *nt* spare (wheel); **~reifen** *m* spare (tyre); **~tank** *m* reserve tank; **~truppen** *pl* reserves *pl*; **~übung** *f* (army) reserve training *no pl*.
reservieren* [rezɛr'vi:rən] *vt* to reserve.
reserviert *adj Platz, Mensch* reserved.
Reserviertheit *f* reserve.
Reservierung *f* reservation.
Reservist [rezɛr'vɪst] *m* reservist.
Reservoir [rezɛr'voa:ɐ] *nt* **-e** reservoir; *(fig auch)* pool.
Residenz *f (Wohnung)* residence.
residieren* *vi* to reside.
Resignation *f (geh)* resignation.
resignieren* *vi* to give up. **resigniert** resigned; ... **sagte er ~d ...** he said with resignation.
resolut *adj* determined.
Resolution *f (Pol) (Beschluß)* resolution; *(Bittschrift)* petition.
Resonanz *f* **(a)** *(Mus, Phys)* resonance. **(b)** *(fig)* response *(auf +acc* to*)*. **keine/große ~ finden** to meet with no/a good response.
resozialisieren* *vt* to rehabilitate.
Resozialisierung *f* rehabilitation.
Respekt *m no pl* respect; *(Angst)* fear. **bei allem ~ (vor jdm/etw)** with all due respect (to sb/for sth); **vor jdm/etw ~ haben** to have respect for sb/sth; *(Angst)* to be afraid of sb/sth.
respektabel *adj* respectable.
respektieren* *vt* to respect; *Wechsel* to honour *(Brit)*, to honor *(US)*.
respektive [respɛk'ti:və] *adv (geh, Comm)* **(a)** *siehe* **beziehungsweise. (b)** *(anders ausgedrückt)* or rather; *(genauer gesagt)* (or) more precisely.
Respekt-: **r~los** *adj* disrespectful, irreverent; **~losigkeit** *f* **(a)** *(no pl: Verhalten)* disrespect(fulness), irreverence; **(b)** *(Bemerkung)* disrespectful remark.
Respektsperson *f* person to be respected.
respektvoll *adj* respectful.
Ressentiment [rɛsãti'mã:, rə-] *nt* **-s** resentment *no pl (gegen* against*)*.
Ressort [rɛ'so:ɐ] *nt* **-s** department. **in das ~ von jdm fallen** *(lit, fig)* to be sb's department.
Rest *m* **-e** **(a)** rest; *(Stoff~)* remnant. **die ~e einer Stadt/Kultur** the remains of a city/civilization; **der letzte ~** the last bit; **dieser kleine ~** this little bit that's left (over); **jdm/einer Sache den ~ geben** *(col)* to finish sb/sth off. **(b)** **~e** *pl* *(Essens~)* left-overs *pl*.
Restaurant [rɛsto'rã:] *nt* **-s** restaurant.
Restaurator *m* restorer.
restaurieren* *vt* to restore.
Restaurierung *f* restoration.
Rest- *in cpds* remaining; **~bestand** *m* remaining stock; **~betrag** *m* balance; **r~lich** *adj* remaining, rest of the ...; **die r~lichen** the rest; **r~los 1** *adj* complete, total; **2** *adv* completely, totally; *begeistert* wildly; **~posten** *m (Comm)* remaining stock; **ein ~posten** remaining stock; **~summe** *f* balance, amount remaining.
Resultat *nt* result.
resultieren* *vi (geh)* to result *(in +dat* in*)*. **aus etw ~** to result from sth; **die daraus ~den ...** the resulting ...
Resümee *nt* **-s** *(geh)* summary, résumé.
resümieren* *vti (geh)* to summarize, to sum up.
Retorte *f* **-n** *(Chem)* retort. **aus der ~** *(col)* synthetic.
Retortenbaby *nt* test-tube baby.
retour [re'tu:ɐ] *adv (old, dial)* back.
Retourkutsche [re'tu:ɐ-] *f (col)* tit-for-tat answer.
retten 1 *vt* to save; *(befreien)* to rescue. **jdm das Leben ~** to save sb's life; **jdn vor jdm/etw ~** to save sb from sb/sth; **ein ~der Gedanke** a bright idea that saved the situation; **bist du noch zu ~?** *(col)* are you out of your mind? *(col)*. **2** *vr* to escape. **sich aus etw ~** to escape from sth; **sich vor jdm/etw ~** to escape (from) sb/sth; **sich vor etw nicht mehr ~ können** *(fig)* to be swamped with sth; **rette sich, wer kann!** (it's) every man for himself!
Retter(in *f*) *m* **-** rescuer; *(Rel)* Saviour *(Brit)*, Savior *(US)*.
Rettich *m* **-e** radish.
Rettung *f* rescue, deliverance *(liter)*; *(Rel)* salvation. **die ~ kam in letzter Minute** the situation was saved in the last minute; *(für Schiffbrüchige etc)* help came in the nick of time; **auf ~ hoffen** to hope to be saved; **für den Patienten gibt es keine ~ mehr** the patient is beyond saving; **das/er war meine ~** that/he was my salvation; **das war meine letzte ~** that was my last hope.
Rettungs-: **~aktion** *f* recue operation; **~anker** *m* sheet anchor; *(fig)* anchor; **~boot** *nt* lifeboat; **~dienst** *m* rescue service; **~kommando** *nt* rescue squad; **r~los 1** *adj* beyond saving; *Lage* hopeless; **2** *adv verloren* irretrievably; **~mannschaft** *f* rescue team; **~ring** *m* lifebelt; **~schwimmer** *m* lifesaver; *(am Strand)* lifeguard.
retuschieren* *vt (Phot)* to retouch, to touch up *(col, auch fig)*.
Reue *f no pl* remorse *(über +acc* at, about*)*, repentance *(auch Rel) (über +acc* of*)*; *(Bedauern)* regret *(über +acc* at, about*)*.
reuelos *adj* unrepentant.
reuen *vt (liter)* **etw reut jdn** sb regrets sth.
reuevoll, reuig *adj (liter) siehe* **reumütig.**
reumütig *adj* remorseful; *Sünder* contrite. **~ gestand er ...** full of remorse he confessed ...
Reuse *f* **-n** fish trap.
Revanche [re'vã:ʃ(ə)] *f* **-n** revenge; *(~partie)* return match. **du mußt ihm ~ geben!** you'll have to give him a return match.
revanchieren* [revã'ʃi:rən] *vr* **(a)** to get one's own back *(bei jdm für etw* on sb for sth*)*. **(b)** *(sich erkenntlich zeigen)* to reciprocate. **sich bei jdm für eine Einladung ~** to return sb's invitation.
Revanchismus [revã'ʃɪsmɪs] *m* revanchism.
revanchistisch [revã'ʃɪstɪʃ] *adj* revanchist.
Reverenz [reve'rɛnts] *f (old)* **jdm seine ~ erweisen** to show one's reverence for sb.
Revers [re've:ɐ] *nt or m* **-** [re've:ɐ(s)], **-** [reve:ɐs] *(an Kleidung)* lapel, revers *(esp US)*.
revidieren* [revi'di:rən] *vt* to revise; *(Comm)* to audit.

Revier [re'viːɐ] *nt* **-e (a)** *(Polizei~) (Dienststelle)* (police) station, station house *(US)*; *(Dienstbereich)* beat, precinct *(US)*, patch *(col)*. **(b)** *(Zool: Gebiet)* territory. **die Küche ist mein ~** the kitchen is my preserve. **(c)** *(Hunt: Jagd~)* hunting ground, shoot. **(d)** *(Min: Kohlen~)* (coal)mine. **im ~ an der Ruhr** in the mines of the Ruhr.
Revision [revi'zioːn] *f* **(a)** *(von Meinung, Politik etc)* revision. **(b)** *(Comm: Prüfung)* audit. **(c)** *(Jur: Urteilsanfechtung)* appeal *(an +acc* to*)*.
Revisionismus [revizio'nismus] *m (Pol)* revisionism.
revisionistisch [revizio'nɪstɪʃ] *adj (Pol)* revisionist.
Revisions-: **~frist** *f* time for appeal; **~verhandlung** *f* appeal hearing.
Revisor [re'viːzɔr] *m (Comm)* auditor.
Revolte [re'vɔltə] *f* **-n** revolt.
revoltieren* [revɔl'tiːrən] *vi* to revolt, to rebel.
Revolution [revolu'tsioːn] *f (lit, fig)* revolution.
revolutionär [revolutsio'nɛːɐ] *adj (lit, fig)* revolutionary.
Revolutionär(in *f*) [revolutsio'nɛːɐ, -'nɛːər(ɪn)] *m* revolutionary.
revolutionieren* [revolutsio'niːrən] *vt* to revolutionize.
Revolutions- *in cpds* revolutionary.
Revoluzzer [revo'lʊtsɐ] *m* **-** *(pej)* would-be revolutionary.
Revolver [re'vɔlvɐ] *m* **-** revolver, gun.
Revolver-: **~blatt** *nt (pej)* scandal sheet; **~held** *m (pej)* gunslinger.
Revue [rə'vyː] *f* **-n** [-yːən] *(Theat)* revue. **etw ~ passieren lassen** *(fig)* to pass sth in review.
Revuetänzerin [rə'vyː-] *f* chorus-girl.
rezensieren* *vt* to review.
Rezension *f* review, write-up *(col)*.
Rezept *nt* **-e (a)** *(Med)* prescription; *(fig)* remedy *(für, gegen* for*)*. **auf ~** on prescription. **(b)** *(Cook, fig)* recipe.
rezeptfrei 1 *adj* available without prescription. **2** *adv* over the counter.
Rezeption *f (von Hotel: Empfang)* reception.
Rezept-: **~pflicht** *f* prescription requirement; **r~pflichtig** *adj* available only on prescription.
Rezession *f (Econ)* recession.
rezitieren* *vti* to recite.
R-Gespräch ['ɛr-] *nt* reverse charge call *(Brit)*, collect call.
Rhabarber *m no pl (auch Gemurmel)* rhubarb.
Rhapsodie *f* rhapsody.
Rhein *m* Rhine.
Rhein-: **r~ab(wärts)** *adv* down the Rhine; **r~auf(wärts)** *adv* up the Rhine; **~fall** *m* Rhine Falls *pl*.
rheinisch *adj attr* Rhenish, Rhineland.
Rhein-: **~länder(in *f*)** *m* **-** Rhinelander; **r~ländisch** *adj* Rhineland; **~land-Pfalz** *nt* Rhineland-Palatinate; **~wein** *m* Rhine wine; *(weißer auch)* hock *(Brit)*.
Rhesus-: **~affe** *m* rhesus monkey; **~faktor** *m (Med)* rhesus *or* Rh factor.
Rhetorik *f* rhetoric.
rhetorisch *adj* rhetorical. **~e Frage** rhetorical question.
Rheuma *nt no pl* rheumatism.
Rheumatiker(in *f*) *m* **-** rheumatism sufferer.
rheumatisch *adj* rheumatic.
Rheumatismus *m* rheumatism.
Rhinozeros *nt* **-(ses), -se** rhinoceros, rhino *(col)*; *(col: Dummkopf)* fool.
Rhodesien [-iən] *nt* Rhodesia.
rhodesisch *adj* Rhodesian.
Rhododendron [rodo'dɛndrɔn] *m or nt, pl* **Rhododendren** rhododendron.
rhythmisch *adj* rhythmic(al).
Rhythmus *m (Mus, Poet, fig)* rhythm.
Richtantenne *f* directional aerial *(esp Brit) or* antenna.
richten 1 *vt* **(a)** *(lenken)* to direct *(auf +acc* towards*)*, to point *(auf +acc* at, towards*)*; *Augen, Aufmerksamkeit* to turn *(auf +acc* towards*)*, to focus *(auf +acc* on*)*. **(b)** *(aus~)* **etw nach jdm/etw ~** to suit sth to sb/sth; *Verhalten* to adapt sth to sb/sth. **(c)** *(adressieren) Briefe, Anfragen* to address *(an +acc* to*)*; *Bitten, Forderungen* to make *(an +acc* to*)*; *Kritik, Vorwurf* to direct *(gegen* at, against*)*. **(d)** *(esp SGer) (zurechtmachen)* to prepare, to get ready; *(in Ordnung bringen)* to do, to fix; *(reparieren)* to fix; *Haare* to do; *Tisch* to lay *(Brit)*, to set; *Betten* to make, to do. **(e)** *(instellen)* to set.
2 *vr* **(a)** *(sich hinwenden)* to focus, to be focussed *(auf +acc* on*)*, to be directed *(auf +acc* towards*)*. **(b)** *(sich wenden)* to consult *(an jdn* sb*)*; *(Maßnahme, Vorwurf etc)* to be aimed *(gegen* at*)*. **(c)** *(sich anpassen)* to follow *(nach jdm/etw* sb/sth*)*. **sich nach den Vorschriften/den Sternen ~** to go by the rules/the stars; **sich nach jds Wünschen ~** to comply with sb's wishes; **wir ~ uns ganz nach unseren Kunden** we are guided entirely by our customers' wishes; **und richte dich (gefälligst) danach!** *(col)* (kindly) do as you're told. **(d)** *(abhängen von)* to depend *(nach* on*)*. **(e)** *(esp SGer: sich zurechtmachen)* to get ready.
3 *vi (liter: urteilen)* to judge *(über jdn* sb*)*, to pass judgement *(über +acc* on*)*.
Richter(in *f*) *m* **-** judge. **jdn/etw vor den ~ bringen** to take sb/sth to court; **sich zum ~ machen** *(fig)* to set (oneself) up in judgement.
Richter-: **r~lich** *adj attr* judicial; **~schaft** *f* judiciary, Bench.
Richt-: **~fest** *nt* topping-out ceremony; **~geschwindigkeit** *f* recommended speed.
richtig 1 *adj* **(a)** right *no comp*; *(zutreffend auch)* correct. **eine ~e Erkenntnis** a correct realization; **ich halte es für ~/das ~ste, ...** I think it would be right/best ...; **bin ich hier ~ bei Müller?** *(col)* is this right for the Müllers? **(b)** *(wirklich, echt)* real, proper. **der ~e Vater/die ~e Mutter** the real father/mother; **ein ~er Idiot** *etc* a right idiot *etc (col)*.
2 *adv* **(a)** *(korrekt)* correctly, right. **die Uhr geht ~** the clock is right; **du kommst gerade ~!** you're just in time. **(b)** *(col: ganz und gar)* really, real *(esp US col)*. **(c)** *(wahrhaftig)* right, correct. **das ist doch Paul! — ach ja, ~** that's Paul — oh yes, so it is.
Richtige(r) *mf decl as adj* right person/man/woman *etc*. **sechs ~ im Lotto** six right in the lottery.
Richtige(s) *nt decl as adj* right thing. **das ist genau das ~** that's just the job *(col)*; **ich habe nichts ~s gegessen/gelernt** I haven't had a proper meal/I didn't really learn anything; **ich habe endlich was ~s gefunden** at last I've found something suitable.
richtiggehend 1 *adj attr Uhr, Waage* accurate; *(col: regelrecht)* real. **2** *adv (col)* **~ intelligent** really intelligent.
Richtigkeit *f* correctness, accuracy; *(von Verhalten, einer Entscheidung)* correctness. **an der ~ von etw zweifeln** to doubt whether sth is right; **das hat schon seine ~** it's right enough.
Richtig-: **r~stellen** *vt sep* to correct; **~stellung** *f* correction.
Richt-: **~kranz** *m wreath used in the topping-out ceremony;* **~linie** *f usu pl* guideline; **~mikrofon** *nt* directional microphone; **~platz** *m* place of execution; **~preis** *m* recommended price; **~schnur** *f (fig: Grundsatz)* guiding principle.
Richtung *f* **(a)** direction. **in ~ Hamburg** in the direction of Hamburg; **in nördliche ~** towards the north, in a northerly direction; **die Autobahn/der Zug ~ Hamburg** the Hamburg autobahn/train; **die ~ ändern** to change direction(s);

eine ~ **nehmen** *or* **einschlagen** to head in a direction; **seine Gedanken nahmen eine neue** ~ his thoughts took a new turn; **in jeder** ~ each way; *(fig: in jeder Hinsicht)* in every respect. **(b)** *(Tendenz)* trend; *(die Vertreter einer* ~*)* movement; *(Denk~, Lehrmeinung)* school of thought.

Richtungs-: ~**änderung** *f* change in direction; **r~los** *adj* lacking a sense of direction; ~**losigkeit** *f* lack of a sense of direction; ~**wechsel** *m* *(lit, fig)* change of direction.

richtungweisend *adj* pointing the way. ~ **sein** to point the way (ahead).

Richtzahl *f* approximate figure.

Ricke *f* **-n** doe.

rieb *pret of* **reiben.**

riechen *pret* **roch,** *ptp* **gerochen 1** *vti* to smell. **gut/schlecht** ~ to smell good/bad; **nach etw** ~ to smell of sth; **an jdm/etw** ~ to sniff (at) sb/sth; **ich rieche das Gewürz gern** I like the smell of this spice; **das riecht nach Betrug** *(fig col)* that smacks of deceit; **jdn nicht** ~ **können** *(col)* to hate sb's guts *(col)*; **das konnte ich doch nicht** ~**!** *(col)* how was I (supposed) to know? **2** *vi (Geruchssinn haben)* **nicht mehr** ~ **können** to have lost one's sense of smell. **3** *vi impers* to smell. **es riecht angebrannt** there's a smell of burning.

Riecher *m* - *(col)* **einen guten** *or* **den richtigen** ~ **(für etw) haben** *(col)* to have a nose (for sth) *(col)*.

Ried *nt* **-e** *(Schilf)* reeds *pl.*

Riedgras *nt* sedge.

rief *pret of* **rufen.**

Riege *f* **-n** *(Sport)* team, squad.

Riegel *m* - **(a)** *(Verschluß)* bolt. **einer Sache** *(dat)* **einen** ~ **vorschieben** *(fig)* to clamp down on sth. **(b)** *(Schokolade)* bar; *(Seife auch)* cake.

Riemen *m* - **(a)** *(Treib~, Gürtel)* belt; *(an Kleidung, Koffer~)* strap; *(Schnürsenkel)* shoelace. **den** ~ **enger schnallen** *(col)* to tighten one's belt; **sich am** ~ **reißen** *(fig col)* to get a grip on oneself. **(b)** *(Sport)* oar.

Riemenantrieb *m* belt-drive.

Riese[1]: **das macht nach Adam** ~ **DM 3,50** *(hum col)* the way I learned it at school that makes DM 3.50.

Riese[2] *m (wk)* **-n, -n** *(lit, fig)* giant; *(col: Tausendmarkschein)* 1000 mark note, big one *(esp US col)*.

rieseln *vi aux sein (Wasser, Sand)* to trickle; *(Regen)* to drizzle; *(Schnee)* to flutter down. **der Kalk rieselt von der Wand** lime is crumbling off the wall; **ein Schauder rieselte mir über den Rücken** a shiver went down my spine.

Riesen- *pref* gigantic; *(Zool, Bot etc auch)* giant; ~**chance** *f* tremendous chance; ~**erfolg** *m* gigantic success; *(Theat, Film)* smash hit; ~**gebirge** *nt (Geog)* Sudeten Mountains *pl*; **r~groß** *adj* gigantic; ~**hunger** *m (col)* enormous appetite; ~**rad** *nt* big *or* Ferris wheel; ~**schlange** *f* boa; ~**schritt** *m* giant stride; **sich mit** ~**schritten nähern** *(fig)* to be drawing on apace; ~**slalom** *m* giant slalom.

riesig 1 *adj* gigantic. **2** *adv (col: sehr)* enormously.

riet *pret of* **raten.**

Riff *nt* **-e** *(Felsklippe)* reef.

rigoros *adj* rigorous.

Rille *f* **-n** groove; *(in Säule)* flute.

Rimesse *f (Fin)* remittance.

Rind *nt* **-er (a)** *(Tier)* cow. ~**er** cattle *pl*; **10** ~**er** 10 head of cattle. **(b)** *(col: Rindfleisch)* beef. **vom** ~ beef.

Rinde *f* **-n** *(Baum~)* bark; *(Brot~)* crust; *(Käse~)* rind.

Rinder-: ~**braten** *m (roh)* joint of beef; *(gebraten)* roast beef *no indef art;* ~**filet** *nt* fillet of beef; ~**herde** *f* herd of cattle; ~**zucht** *f* cattle farming.

Rindfleisch *nt* beef.

Rindsleder *nt* leather.

Rindvieh *nt* **(a)** *no pl* cattle *pl.* **10 Stück** ~ 10 head of cattle. **(b)** *pl* **-viecher** *(col: Dummkopf)* ass *(col)*.

Ring *m* **-e (a)** ring; *(von Menschen auch)* circle; *(Ketten~)* link; *(Rettungs~)* lifebelt; *(~straße)* ring road. **die** ~**e tauschen** to exchange rings; ~**e** *(Turnen)* rings; ~ **frei!** *(Boxen)* seconds out! **(b)** *(Vereinigung)* circle, group; *(Bande)* ring. **(c)** *(liter: Kreislauf)* circle, cycle. **der** ~ **schließt sich** the wheel turns full circle.

Ringel-: ~**blume** *f* marigold; ~**locke** *f* ringlet.

ringeln 1 *vt (Pflanze)* to (en)twine; *Schwanz etc auch* to curl; *siehe* **geringelt. 2** *vr* to go curly, to curl; *(Rauch)* to curl up(wards). **die Schlange ringelte sich um den Baum** the snake coiled itself around the tree.

Ringel-: ~**natter** *f* grass snake; ~**reigen,** ~**reihen** ring-a-ring-o' roses; ~**taube** *f* wood-pigeon.

ringen *pret* **rang,** *ptp* **gerungen 1** *vt* **die Hände** ~ to wring one's hands; **er rang ihr das Messer aus der Hand** he wrested the knife from her hand. **2** *vi* **(a)** *(lit, fig; kämpfen)* to wrestle. **mit dem Tode** ~ to wrestle with death. **(b)** *(streben)* **nach** *or* **um etw** ~ to struggle for sth; **ums Überleben** ~ *(liter)* to struggle to survive.

Ringen *nt no pl (Sport)* wrestling; *(fig)* struggle.

Ringer *m* - wrestler.

Ring-: ~**finger** *m* ring finger; **r~förmig** *adj* ring-like; ~**kampf** *m* fight; *(Sport)* wrestling match; ~**kämpfer** *m* wrestler; ~**richter** *m* referee.

rings *adv* (all) around.

ringsherum *adv* all (the way) around.

Ringstraße *f* ring road.

ringsum *adv* (all) around.

Rinne *f* **-n** *(Rille)* groove; *(Furche, Abfluß~, Fahr~)* channel; *(Dach~, col: Rinnstein)* gutter.

rinnen *pret* **rann,** *ptp* **geronnen** *vi* **(a)** *aux sein (fließen)* to run. **das Geld rinnt ihm durch die Finger** *(fig)* money slips through his fingers. **(b)** *(undicht sein)* to leak.

Rinn-: ~**sal** *nt* **-e** rivulet; ~**stein** *m (Gosse)* gutter.

Rippchen *nt (Cook) slightly cured pork rib.*

Rippe *f* **-n** rib; *(von Apfelsine)* segment. **er hat nichts auf den** ~**n** *(col)* he's just skin and bones; **... damit du was auf die** ~**n kriegst** *(col)* ... to put a bit of flesh on you; **ich kann es mir nicht aus den** ~**n schneiden** *(col)* I can't just produce it from nowhere.

Rippen-: ~**bruch** *m* broken rib; ~**fell** *nt* pleura; ~**fellentzündung** *f* pleurisy; ~**speer** *m or nt* *(Cook)* spare rib; **Kasseler** ~**speer** *slightly cured pork spare rib;* ~**stoß** *m* dig in the ribs.

Risiko *nt, pl* **-s** *or* **Risiken** risk. **auf eigenes** ~ at one's own risk; **etw ohne** ~ **tun** to do sth without taking a risk.

riskant *adj* risky, chancy *(col)*.

riskieren* *vt (aufs Spiel setzen)* to risk; *(wagen)* to venture. **etwas/nichts** ~ to take chances/no chances; **seine Stellung** ~ to put one's job at risk; **in Gegenwart seiner Frau riskiert er kein Wort** when his wife is present he dare not say a word.

Rispe *f* **-n** *(Bot)* panicle.

riß *pret of* **reißen.**

Riß *m, pl* **Risse (a)** *(in Stoff, Papier etc)* tear, rip; *(in Erde, Gestein)* crevice, fissure; *(in Wand, Behälter etc)* crack; *(Haut~)* chap; *(fig: Kluft)* rift, split. **die Freundschaft hat einen** ~ **bekommen** a rift has developed in their friendship. **(b)** *(Tech etc: Zeichnung)* sketch, sketch plan.

rissig *adj Boden, Leder* cracked; *Haut* chapped.

Rist *m* **-e** *(am Fuß)* instep.

Riten *pl of* **Ritus.**

ritt *pret of* **reiten.**

Ritt *m* **-e** ride. **einen** ~ **machen** to go for a ride; **in einem** ~ *(col)* at one go *(col)*.

Ritter *m* - knight; *(Kavalier)* cavalier. **jdn zum** ~ **schlagen** to knight sb; **arme** ~ *pl (Cook) sweet French toast soaked in milk.*

Ritter-: ~**burg** *f* knight's castle; ~**kreuz** *nt (Mil)* Knight's Cross; ~**kreuzträger** *m* holder of the Knight's Cross; **r~lich** *adj (lit)* knightly; *(fig)* chivalrous; ~**lichkeit** *f* chivalry; ~**orden** *m* order of knights.
Rittersmann *m, pl* **-leute** *(poet)* knight.
Ritter-: ~**sporn** *m (Bot)* larkspur, delphinium; ~**stand** *m* knighthood.
Rittmeister *m (old Mil)* cavalry captain.
Ritual *nt* **-e** *or* **-ien** [-iən] *(lit, fig)* ritual.
rituell *adj* ritual.
Ritus *m* **-, Riten** rite; *(fig)* ritual.
Ritze *f* **-n** *(Riß)* crack; *(Fuge)* gap.
Ritzel *nt* **-** *(Tech)* pinion.
ritzen 1 *vt* to scratch; *(einritzen) Namen etc auch* to carve. **die Sache ist geritzt** *(col)* it's all fixed up. **2** *vr* to scratch oneself.
Rivale [ri'vaːlə] *m (wk)* **-n, -n, Rivalin** [ri'vaːlɪn] *f* rival.
rivalisieren* [rivali'ziːrən] *vi* **mit jdm** ~ to compete with sb; **34** ~**de Parteien** 34 rival parties.
Rivalität [rivali'tɛːt] *f* rivalry.
Rizinus(öl *nt*) *m* **-, -** *or* **-se** castor oil.
Roastbeef ['roːstbiːf] *nt* **-s** *(roh)* beef; *(gebraten)* roast beef.
Robbe *f* **-n** seal.
robben *vi aux sein (Mil)* to crawl.
Robben-: ~**fang** *m* seal hunting; ~**fänger** *m* seal hunter.
Robe *f* **-n (a)** *(Abendkleid)* evening gown. **(b)** *(Amtstracht)* (official) robe *or* robes *pl.*
Roboter *m* **-** robot.
Robotertechnik *f* robotics *sing.*
robust *adj Mensch, Gesundheit* robust; *Material* tough.
Robustheit *f siehe adj* robustness; toughness.
roch *pret of* **riechen.**
Rochade [rɔ'xaːdə, rɔ'ʃaːdə] *f (Chess)* castling. **die kleine/große** ~ castling king's side/queen's side.
Röcheln *nt no pl* groan; *(Todes~)* death rattle.
röcheln *vi* to groan; *(Sterbender)* to give the death rattle.
Rochen *m* **-** ray.
Rock[1] *m* **¨-e (a)** *(Damen~)* skirt; *(Schotten~)* kilt. **(b)** *(Jackett)* jacket.
Rock[2] *m no pl (Mus)* rock.
Rocker *m* **-** rocker.
Rock-: ~**falte** *f (von Damenrock)* inverted pleat; *(von Jackett)* vent; ~**futter** *nt* skirt lining.
Rockmusik *f* rock music.
Rock-: ~**saum** *m* hem of a/the skirt; ~**schoß** *m* coat-tail; **an jds** ~**schößen hängen** to cling to sb's coat-tails *(col)*; ~**zipfel** *m* **an Mutters** ~**zipfel hängen** *(col)* to cling to (one's) mother's apron-strings *(col)*.
Rodel *m* **-** sledge, toboggan, sleigh.
Rodelbahn *f* toboggan-run.
rodeln *vi aux sein or haben* to toboggan *(auch Sport)*, to sledge.
Rodelschlitten *m* toboggan, sledge.
roden *vt Wald, Land* to clear.
Rodung *f (das Roden, Fläche)* clearing.
Rogen *m* **-** roe.
Roggen *m no pl* rye.
Roggenbrot *nt* rye bread.
roh *adj* **(a)** *(ungekocht)* raw. **(b)** *(unbearbeitet)* rough; *Eisen, Metall* crude. **(c)** *(brutal)* rough. ~**e Gewalt** brute force.
Roh-: ~**bau** *m (Bauabschnitt)* shell (of a/the house); **das Haus ist im** ~**bau fertig(gestellt)** the house is structurally complete; ~**diamant** *m* rough *or* uncut diamond; ~**eisen** *nt* pig iron.
Roheit *f* **(a)** *no pl (Eigenschaft)* roughness; *(Brutalität auch)* brutality. **(b)** *(Tat)* brutality. **(c)** *(ungekochter Zustand)* rawness.
Roh-: ~**entwurf** *m* rough draft; ~**ertrag** *m* gross proceeds *pl*; ~**kost** *f* raw fruit and vegetables *pl*; ~**leder** *nt* rawhide; ~**ling** *m* **(a)** *(Grobian)* brute, ruffian; **(b)** *(Tech)* blank; ~**material** *nt* raw material; ~**öl** *nt* crude oil; ~**produkt** *nt* raw material.
Rohr *nt* **-e (a)** *(Tech, Mech)* pipe; *(Geschütz~)* (gun) barrel. **(b)** *(Schilf~)* reed; *(Zucker~)* cane; *(für Stühle etc)* cane, wicker *no pl.*
Rohrbruch *m* burst pipe.
Röhrchen *nt* tube; *(Chem)* test tube; *(col: zur Alkoholkontrolle)* breathalyzer. **ins** ~ **blasen (müssen)** *(col)* to be breathalyzed.
Röhre *f* **-n (a)** *(Hohlkörper)* tube; *(Neon~)* (neon) tube *or* strip; *(Elektronen~)* valve *(Brit)*, tube *(US)*; *(fig: Fernsehgerät)* telly *(Brit col)*, tube *(US col)*. **(b)** *(Ofen~)* warming oven; *(Back~)* oven. **in die** ~ **gucken** *(col)* to be left out.
Röhren-: **r~förmig** *adj* tubular; ~**hose** *f (col)* drainpipe trousers *pl.*
Rohr-: ~**geflecht** *nt* wickerwork, basketwork; ~**krepierer** *m* **-** *(Mil sl)* barrel burst; **ein** ~**krepierer sein** *(fig)* to backfire; ~**leitung** *f* pipe, conduit; ~**post** *f* pneumatic dispatch system; ~**spatz** *m* **schimpfen wie ein** ~**spatz** *(col)* to curse and swear; ~**stock** *m* cane; ~**zange** *f* pipe wrench; ~**zucker** *m* cane sugar.
Roh-: ~**seide** *f* wild silk; ~**stoff** *m* raw material; *(St Ex)* commodity; ~**zucker** *m* unrefined sugar; ~**zustand** *m* unprocessed state; **das Manuskript ist noch im** ~**zustand** the manuscript is still in a fairly rough state.
Rokoko *nt no pl* Rococo period; *(Stil)* Rococo, rococo.
Rolladen *m, pl* **Rolläden** *or* **-** *(an Fenster, Tür etc)* shutters *pl*; *(von Schreibtisch)* roll top.
Roll-: ~**bahn** *f* runway; ~**brett** *nt* skateboard.
Röllchen *nt* little roll; *(von Garn)* reel.
Rolle *f* **-n (a)** *(Zusammengerolltes)* roll; *(Garn~, Zwirn~)* reel; *(Urkunde)* scroll. **eine** ~ **Bindfaden** a ball of string. **(b)** *(walzenförmig)* roller; *(an Möbeln, Kisten)* castor; *(an Flaschenzug)* pulley. **(c)** *(Sport)* forward roll; *(Aviat)* roll. **die** ~ **rückwärts** the backward roll. **(d)** *(Theat, Film, fig)* role, part; *(Sociol)* role. **eine Ehe mit streng verteilten** ~**n** a marriage with strict allocation of roles; **jds** ~ **bei etw** *(fig)* sb's part in sth; **bei** *or* **in etw** *(dat)* **eine** ~ **spielen** to play a part in sth; *(Mensch auch)* to play a role in sth; **etw spielt eine große** ~ **(bei jdm)** sth is very important (to sb); **es spielt keine** ~, **(ob) ...** it doesn't matter (whether) ...; **bei ihm spielt Geld keine** ~ with him money is no object; **aus der** ~ **fallen** *(fig)* to forget oneself; **mußt du ständig aus der** ~ **fallen!** must you always show yourself up!
rollen 1 *vi* **(a)** *aux sein* to roll; *(Flugzeug)* to taxi. **etw/den Stein ins R~ bringen** *(fig)* to start sth/ the ball rolling; **es werden einige Köpfe** ~ heads will roll. **(b) mit den Augen** ~ to roll one's eyes. **2** *vt* to roll; *Teig* to roll out; *Teppich, Papier* to roll up. **3** *vr* to curl up.
Rollen-: ~**besetzung** *f (Theat, Film)* casting; ~**erwartung** *f (Sociol)* role expectation; ~**fach** *nt (Theat)* character; **r~förmig** *adj* cylindrical; **r~spezifisch** *adj* role-specific; ~**tausch** *m* exchange of roles; *(Sociol auch)* role reversal.
Roller *m* **- (a)** scooter. **(b)** *(Walze, Naut: Welle)* roller.
Roll-: ~**feld** *nt* runway; ~**film** *m* roll film; ~**kommando** *nt* raiding party; ~**kragen** *m* roll *or* polo neck; ~**mops** *m* rollmops, rolled pickled herring.
Rollo *nt* **-s** (roller) blind.
Roll-: ~**schinken** *m* smoked ham; ~**schrank** *m* roll-fronted cupboard.
Rollschuh *m* roller-skate. ~ **laufen** to roller-skate.
Rollschuh-: ~**bahn** *f* roller-skating rink; ~**laufen** *nt* rollerskating; ~**läufer** *m* roller-skater.
Roll-: ~**splitt** *m* grit; **„~splitt"** "loose chippings";

~**stuhl** *m* wheel-chair; ~**treppe** *f* escalator.
Rom *nt* Rome. **viele Wege führen nach** ~ *(Prov)* all roads lead to Rome *(Prov)*; **das sind Zustände wie im alten** ~ *(col) (unmoralisch)* it's disgraceful; *(primitiv)* it's medieval *(col)*.
Roman *m* **-e** novel. **(jdm) einen ganzen** ~ **erzählen** *(col)* to give sb a long rigmarole *(col)*.
Roman-: ~**autor** *m* novelist; **r**~**haft** *adj* like a novel; ~**heft** *nt* cheap pulp novel; ~**held** *m* hero of a/the novel.
Romanik *f (Archit, Art)* Romanesque period; *(Stil)* Romanesque (style).
romanisch *adj Volk, Sprache* Romance; *(Art)* Romanesque.
Romanist(in *f*) *m (Univ)* teacher/student/scholar of Romance languages and literature.
Romanistik *f (Univ)* Romance languages and literature.
Roman-: ~**leser** *m* novel reader; ~**schreiber** *m (col)* novelist; *(pej)* scribbler; ~**schriftsteller** *m* novelist.
Romantik *f* **(a)** *(Liter, Art, Mus)* Romanticism; *(Epoche)* Romantic period. **(b)** *(fig)* romance.
Romantiker(in *f*) *m* **-** *(Liter, Art, Mus)* Romantic; *(fig)* romantic.
romantisch *adj* romantic; *(Liter etc)* Romantic.
Romanze *f* **-n** *(Liter, Mus, fig)* romance.
Römer *m* **-** *(Weinglas) type of wineglass.*
Römer(in *f*) *m* **-** Roman. **die alten** ~ the (ancient) Romans.
Römer-: ~**reich** *nt* Roman Empire; ~**topf** ® *m (Cook)* ≃ (chicken) brick.
römisch *adj* Roman.
römisch-katholisch *adj* Roman Catholic.
Rommé [rɔ'meː, 'rɔme] *nt no pl* rummy.
Rondo *nt* **-s** *(Mus)* rondo.
röntgen *vt* to X-ray.
Röntgen *nt no pl* X-raying.
Röntgen-: ~**apparat** *m* X-ray equipment *no indef art, no pl*; ~**aufnahme** *f* X-ray (plate); ~**augen** *pl (hum)* X-ray eyes *pl (hum)*.
Röntgenologe *m*, **Röntgenologin** *f* radiologist.
Röntgenologie *f* radiology.
Röntgen-: ~**strahlen** *pl* X-rays *pl*; ~**untersuchung** *f* X-ray examination.
rosa *adj inv* pink. **ein** ~ *or* ~**nes** *(col)* **Kleid** a pink dress; **die Welt durch eine** ~**(rote) Brille sehen** to see the world through rose-coloured *(Brit) or* rose-colored *(US)* glasses; **in** ~**(rotem) Licht** in a rosy light.
rosa-: ~**farben,** ~**farbig,** ~**rot** *siehe* **rosa.**
Röschen ['røːsçən] *nt* (little) rose.
Rose *f* **-n** *(Blume)* rose. **er ist nicht auf** ~**n gebettet** *(fig)* life isn't a bed of roses for him.
Rosé *m* **-s** rosé (wine).
Rosen-: **r**~**farben, r**~**farbig** *adj* rose-coloured *(Brit) or* rose-colored *(US)*; ~**holz** *nt* rosewood; ~**knospe** *f* rosebud; ~**kohl** *m* Brussel(s) sprouts *pl*; ~**kranz** *m (Eccl)* rosary; **den** ~**kranz beten** to say a rosary; ~**montag** *m Monday preceding Ash Wednesday;* ~**montagszug** *m Carnival parade which takes place on the Monday preceding Ash Wednesday;* ~**öl** *nt* attar of roses; ~**strauch** *m* rosebush.
Rosette *f* rosette.
Roséwein *m* rosé wine.
rosig *adj (lit, fig)* rosy.
Rosine *f* raisin. **(große)** ~**n im Kopf haben** *(col)* to have big ideas; **sich** *(dat)* **die (besten)** ~**n herauspicken** *(col)* to take the pick of the bunch.
Rosmarin *m no pl* rosemary.
Roß *nt, pl* **-sse** *or* **¨sser** *(liter)* steed *(liter)*, horse. **hoch zu** ~ on horseback; **auf dem hohen** ~**sitzen** *(fig)* to be on one's high horse; ~ **und Reiter nennen** *(fig geh)* to name names.
Roß-: ~**haar** *nt* horsehair; ~**kastanie** *f* horse chestnut; ~**kur** *f (col)* kill-or-cure remedy; ~**täuscher** *m (fig)* horse-trader.

Rost[1] *m no pl (auch Bot)* rust. ~ **ansetzen** to start to rust.
Rost[2] *m* **-e** *(Ofen~)* grill. *(Gitter~)* grating, grille. **auf dem** ~ **braten** *(Cook)* to barbecue, to grill on charcoal.
Rost-: **r**~**beständig** *adj* rust-resistant; ~**bildung** *f* rust formation; ~**braten** *m (Cook)* ≃ roast; ~**bratwurst** *f* grilled *or* barbecued sausage; **r**~**braun** *adj* russet; *Haar* auburn.
Röstbrot *nt* toast.
rosten *vi aux sein or haben* to get rusty *(auch fig)*. **alte Liebe rostet nicht** *(Prov)* old love never dies.
rösten *vt* Kaffee to roast; *Brot* to toast. **sich in der Sonne** ~ **lassen** to lie in the sun and bake.
Rost-: **r**~**farben** *adj siehe* **r**~**braun;** ~**fleck** *m* patch of rust; **r**~**frei** *adj (Stahl)* stainless.
rostig *adj (lit, fig)* rusty.
Röstkartoffeln *pl* fried potatoes.
Rost-: ~**laube** *f (hum)* rust-heap *(hum)*; **r**~**rot** *adj* rust-coloured *(Brit)*, rust-colored *(US)*, russet; ~**schutz** *m* anti-rust protection; ~**schutzmittel** *nt* rust-proofer.
rot *adj* red *(auch Pol)*. ~**e Bete** beetroot; **das R**~**e Kreuz** the Red Cross; **der R**~**e Platz** Red Square; **das R**~**e Meer** the Red Sea; **die R**~**e Armee** the Red Army; **die R**~**en** *(pej)* the reds; **in den** ~**en Zahlen stecken** to be in the red; ~ **werden, einen** ~**en Kopf bekommen** to blush, to go red; **sich** *(dat)* **etw** ~ **(im Kalender) anstreichen** *(col)* to make sth a red-letter day.
Rot *nt* **-s** *or* **-** red; *(Wangen~)* rouge. **bei** ~ at red; **die Ampel stand auf** ~ the lights were (at) red.
Rot|armist *m* soldier in the Red Army.
Rotation *f* rotation.
Rotations-: ~**achse** *f* axis of rotation; ~**maschine,** ~**presse** *f (Typ)* rotary press.
Rot-: ~**barsch** *m* rosefish; **r**~**blond** *adj Haar* sandy; *Mann* sandy-haired; *Frau* strawberry blonde; **r**~**braun** *adj* reddish brown; ~**buche** *f* (common) beech; ~**dorn** *m* hawthorn.
Röte *f no pl* redness, red; *(Erröten)* blush. **die** ~ **stieg ihr ins Gesicht** her face reddened.
Röteln *pl* German measles *sing.*
röten 1 *vt (geh)* to redden, to make red; *Himmel* to turn red. **ein gerötetes Gesicht** a flushed face. **2** *vr* to turn red.
Rot-: ~**filter** *nt or m (Phot)* red filter; ~**fuchs** *m* red fox; *(Pferd)* sorrel *or* bay (horse); *(fig col)* carrot-top *(col)*; ~**gardist** *m* Red Guard; **r**~**glühend** *adj Metall* red-hot; **r**~**haarig** *adj* red-haired; ~**haut** *f (dated hum)* redskin; ~**hirsch** *m* red deer.
rotieren* *vi* to rotate.
Rot-: ~**käppchen** *nt (Liter)* Little Red Ridinghood; ~**kehlchen** *nt* robin; ~**kohl** *m*, ~**kraut** *nt* red cabbage.
Rotkreuz- *in cpds* Red Cross.
rötlich *adj* reddish.
Rotlicht *nt* red light.
Rotor *m* rotor.
Rotorflügel *m (Aviat)* rotor blade.
Rot-: **r**~**sehen** *vi sep irreg (col)* to see red *(col)*; ~**stift** *m* red pencil; **dem** ~**stift zum Opfer fallen** *(fig)* to be scrapped; ~**tanne** *f* Norway spruce.
Rotte *f* **-, -n** gang; *(Mil Aviat, Mil Naut)* pair *(of planes/ships operating together)*; *(von Hunden etc)* pack; *(Hunt)* herd.
Rottweiler *m* **-** *(Hund)* Rottweiler.
Rötung *f* reddening.
Rot-: **r**~**wangig** *adj* rosy-cheeked; ~**wein** *m* red wine; ~**wild** *nt* red deer.
Rotz *m no pl* **(a)** *(col)* snot *(col)*. ~ **und Wasser heulen** to blubber; **Graf** ~ Lord Muck *(col)*; **der ganze** ~ the whole bloody *(Brit) or* goddam *(US)* show *(col)*. **(b)** *(Vet)* glanders *sing.*
rotzfrech *adj (col)* cocky *(col)*.
rotzig *adj (col)* snotty *(col)*.

Rotz-: ~nase *f (col)* **(a)** snotty nose *(col)*; **(b)** *(Kind)* snotty-nosed brat *(col)*; **r~näsig** *adj (col)* **(a)** snotty-nosed *(col)*; **(b)** *(frech)* snotty *(col)*.
Rouge [ruːʒ] *nt* **-s** rouge.
Roulade [ru'laːdə] *f (Cook)* ≃ beef olive.
Roulett(e) [ru'lɛt(ə)] *nt* **-** *or* **-s** roulette.
Route ['ruːtə] *f* **-n** route.
Routine [ru'tiːnə] *f (Erfahrung)* experience; *(Gewohnheit, Trott)* routine.
Routine-: ~angelegenheit *f* routine matter; **r~mäßig 1** *adj* routine; **2** *adv* **ich gehe r~mäßig zum Zahnarzt** I make a routine visit to the dentist; **das wird r~mäßig überprüft** it's checked as a matter of routine; **~sache** *f* routine matter; **~untersuchung** *f* routine examination.
Routinier [ruti'nieː] *m* **-s** old hand.
routiniert [ruti'niːɐt] *adj* experienced.
Rowdy ['raudi] *m, pl* **-s** *or* **Rowdies** hooligan; *(zerstörerisch)* vandal; *(lärmend)* rowdy (type).
Rowdytum ['rauditu:m] *nt no pl* hooliganism.
rubbeln *vti (col)* to rub.
Rübe *f* **-n (a)** turnip. **rote ~** beetroot *(Brit)*, red beet *(US)*; **weiße ~** white turnip. **(b)** *(col: Kopf)* nut *(col)*. **eins auf die ~ kriegen** to get a bash on the nut *(col)*.
Rubel *m* **-** rouble. **der ~ rollt** *(col)* the money's rolling in *(col)*.
Rüben-: ~kraut *nt*, **~saft** *m* sugar beet syrup; **~zucker** *m* beet sugar.
rüber- *in cpds (col)* = **herüber-, hinüber-**.
Rubin *m* **-e** ruby.
rubinrot *adj* ruby-red, ruby.
Rubrik *f* **(a)** *(Kategorie)* category. **(b)** *(Zeitungs~)* section, column.
ruch-: ~bar *adj* **~bar werden** *(geh)* to become known; **~los** *adj (dated, geh)* dastardly *(liter)*.
Ruck *m* **-e** jerk, tug; *(von Fahrzeug)* jolt, jerk; *(Pol)* swing, shift. **er stand mit einem ~ auf** he sprang to his feet; **sich** *(dat)* **einen ~ geben** *(col)* to make an effort; **etw in einem ~ erledigen** to do sth at one fell swoop.
Rück-: ~ansicht *f* rear view; **~antwort** *f* reply; **um ~antwort wird gebeten** please reply.
ruck|artig *adj* jerky. **er stand ~ auf** he shot to his feet.
Rück-: ~besinnung *f* recollection; **~bildung** *f* *(Biol)* degeneration; **~blende** *f* flashback; **~blick** *m* look back *(auf +acc* at*)*; **im ~blick auf etw** *(acc)* looking back on sth; **r~blickend** *adj* retrospective; **r~blickend läßt sich sagen, daß ...** in retrospect we can say that ...; **r~datieren*** *vt sep infin, ptp only* to backdate.
rucken *vi* **(a)** *(Fahrzeug)* to jerk, to jolt. **(b)** *(Taube)* to coo.
Rücken *m* **-** back; *(Nasen~)* ridge; *(Fuß~)* instep; *(Hügel~, Berg~)* crest; *(Buch~)* spine. **auf dem/den ~** on one's back; **den Feind im ~ haben** to have the enemy in one's rear; **den Wind im ~ haben** to have a tail wind; **er hat doch die Firma des Vaters im ~** but he's got his father's firm behind him; **mit dem ~ zur Wand** *(lit, fig)* with one's back to the wall; **der verlängerte ~** *(hum col)* one's posterior *(hum col)*; **~ an ~** back to back; **hinter jds ~** *(dat) (fig)* behind sb's back; **jdm/einer Sache den ~ kehren** *(lit, fig) or* **zudrehen** *(lit)* to turn one's back on sb/sth; **jdm in den ~ fallen** *(fig)* to stab sb in the back; **sich** *(dat)* **den ~ freihalten** *(col)* to cover oneself; **jdm den ~ decken** *(fig col)* to back sb up *(col)*; **jdm den ~ stärken** *(fig)* to give sb encouragement.
rücken *vi aux sein* to move; *(Platz machen)* to move up *or (zur Seite auch)* over; *(weiter~: Zeiger)* to move on *(auf +acc* to*)*. **näher ~** to move closer; *(Zeit)* to get closer; **ins Manöver/an die Front ~** to go off on manoeuvres/to go up to the front; **an etw** *(dat)* **~** *an Uhrzeiger* to move sth; *an Krawatte* to pull sth (straight); *(schieben)* to push at sth; *(ziehen)* to pull at sth; **an jds Stelle** *(acc)* **~** to take sb's place; **jdm auf den Leib** *or* **Pelz** *(col) or* **die Pelle** *(col)* **~** *(zu nahe kommen)* to crowd sb; *(sich jdn vorknöpfen)* to get on at sb; *(hum: besuchen)* to move in on sb; **einer Sache** *(dat)* **zu Leibe ~** to have a go at sth.
Rücken-: ~deckung *f (fig)* backing; **jdm ~deckung geben** to back sb; **~lage** *f* supine position; **er schläft in ~lage** he sleeps on his back; **~lehne** *f* back, back-rest; **~mark** *nt* spinal cord; **~schmerz(en** *pl***)** *m* backache; **~schwimmen** *nt* backstroke; **~stärkung** *f (fig)* moral support.
Rück|entwicklung *f* fall-off *(gen* in*)*; *(Biol)* degeneration.
Rückenwind *m* tailwind.
Rück-: r~erstatten* *vt sep infin, ptp only* to refund; **~erstattung** *f* refund; **~fahrkarte** *f* return ticket *(Brit)*, round-trip ticket *(US)*; **~fahrscheinwerfer** *m (Aut)* reversing light; **~fahrt** *f* return journey; **~fall** *m (Med, fig)* relapse; *(Jur)* subsequent offence *(Brit) or* offense *(US)*; **r~fällig** *adj (Med, fig)* relapsed; *(Jur)* recidivistic *(form)*; **r~fällig werden** *(Med, fig)* to relapse; *(Jur)* to lapse back into crime; **~flug** *m* return flight; **~fluß** *m* reflux, flowing back; **~forderung** *f* **~forderung des Geldes** demand for the return of the money; **~frage** *f* question; **nach ~frage bei der Zentrale ...** after checking this with the exchange ...; **~führung** *f* **(a)** *(Deduktion)* tracing back; **die ~führung der Probleme auf** *(+acc)* tracing the problems back to; **(b)** *(von Menschen)* repatriation, return; **~gabe** *f* return; **~gaberecht** *nt* right of return; **~gang** *m* drop *(gen* in*)*; **r~gängig** *adj* **(a)** *(Comm: zurückgehend)* dropping; **(b)** **r~gängig machen** *(widerrufen)* to undo; *Bestellung, Termin* to cancel; *Verlobung, Hochzeit* to call off; **~gewinnung** *f* recovery; *(von Land, Gebiet)* reclaiming; *(aus verbrauchten Stoffen)* recycling.
Rückgrat *nt* **-e** spine, backbone. **er ist ein Mensch ohne ~** *(fig)* he's got no backbone; **jdm das ~ stärken** *(col)* to give sb enouragement; **jdm das ~ brechen** to ruin sb.
Rückgratverkrümmung *f* curvature of the spine.
Rück-: ~halt *m* **(a)** *(Unterstüzung)* support, backing; **(b)** *(Einschränkung)* **ohne ~halt** without reservation; **r~haltlos** *adj* complete; *Unterstützung auch* unqualified; **~hand** *f (Sport)* backhand; **~kauf** *m* repurchase; **~kehr** *f no pl* return; **bei seiner ~kehr** on his return; **jdn zur ~kehr bewegen** to persuade sb to return; **~lage** *f (Fin: Reserve)* reserve, reserves *pl*; *(Ersparnisse auch)* savings *pl*; **~lauf** *m no pl* reverse running; *(von Maschinenteil)* return travel; *(beim Tonband)* fast rewind; **r~läufig** *adj* dropping; *Tendenz* downward; **eine r~läufige Entwicklung** a decline; **~licht** *nt* rear light; **r~lings** *adv (von hinten)* from behind; *(auf dem Rücken)* on one's back; **~marsch** *m (Mil)* march back; *(~zug)* retreat; **~meldung** *f (Univ)* re-registration; **~nahme** *f* **-n** taking back; **ich bestehe auf der ~nahme des Gerätes** I must insist that you take this set back; **~paß** *m (Sport)* return pass; **~porto** *nt* return postage; **~reise** *f* return journey; **~ruf** *m (am Telefon)* **Herr X hat angerufen und bittet um ~ruf** Mr X called and asked you to call back.
Rucksack *m* rucksack.
Rück-: ~schau *f* reflection *(auf +acc* on*)*; *(in Medien)* review *(auf +acc* of*)*; **~schau halten** to reminisce; **auf etw** *(acc)* **~schau halten** to look back on sth; **~schein** *m* ≃ recorded delivery slip; **~schlag** *m (von Ball)* rebound; *(fig)* set-back; *(bei Patient)* relapse; **~schluß** *m* conclusion; **den ~schluß ziehen, daß ...** to conclude that ...; **~schritt** *m (fig)* retrograde step; **r~schrittlich** *adj* reactionary; *Entwicklung* retrograde; **~seite** *f* back; *(von Buchseite, Münze)* reverse;

siehe **~seite** see over(leaf); **~sendung** *f* return.

Rücksicht *f* **-en** *(Nachsicht)* consideration. **~en** *pl (Gründe, Interessen)* considerations *pl*; **aus** *or* **mit ~ auf jdn/etw** out of consideration for sb/sth; **ohne ~ auf jdn/etw** with no consideration for sb/sth; **ohne ~ auf Verluste** *(col)* regardless; **auf jdn/etw ~ nehmen** to show consideration for sb/sth; **er kennt keine ~** he's ruthless.

Rücksichtnahme *f no pl* consideration.

Rücksichts-: r~los *adj* thoughtless; *(im Verkehr)* reckless; *(unbarmherzig)* ruthless; **~losigkeit** *f siehe adj* thoughtlessness *no pl*; recklessness; ruthlessness; **r~voll** *adj* considerate *(gegenüber, gegen* towards*)*.

Rück-: ~sitz *m (von Motorrad)* pillion; *(von Auto)* back seat; **~spiegel** *m (Aut)* rear(-view) mirror; *(außen)* outside mirror; **~spiel** *nt (Sport)* return match; **~sprache** *f* consultation; **~sprache mit jdm nehmen** to confer with sb.

Rückstand *m* **(a)** *(Überrest)* remains *pl*; *(bei Verbrennung, Bodensatz)* residue. **(b)** *(Verzug)* delay; *(bei Aufträgen)* backlog. **im ~ sein/in ~ geraten** to be/fall behind; **mit 0:2 Toren im ~ sein** to be 2 goals down. **(c)** *usu pl (Außenstände)* arrears *pl*. **~e eintreiben** to collect arrears.

rückständig *adj* **(a)** *(überfällig) Betrag* overdue. **(b)** *(zurückgeblieben)* backward. **~ denken** to have antiquated ideas.

Rückständigkeit *f no pl* backwardness.

Rück-: ~stau *m (von Wasser)* backwater; *(von Autos)* tailback *(Brit)*, line of cars; **~stoß** *m* repulsion; *(bei Gewehr)* recoil; *(von Rakete)* thrust; **~strahler** *m* **-** reflector; **~strom** *m (von Menschen, Fahrzeugen)* return; **der ~strom der Urlauber aus Italien** the stream of holiday makers returning from Italy; **~taste** *f (an Schreibmaschine)* backspace key.

Rücktritt *m* **(a)** *(Amtsniederlegung)* resignation; *(von König)* abdication. **(b)** *(Jur: von Vertrag)* withdrawal *(von* from*)*.

Rücktrittbremse *f* backpedal brake.

Rücktritts-: ~drohung *f* threat to resign/abdicate; **~recht** *nt* right of withdrawal.

Rück-: r~vergüten* *vt sep infin, ptp only* to refund *(jdm etw* sb sth*)*; **~vergütung** *f* refund; **r~versichern*** *sep* **1** *vti* to reinsure; **2** *vr* to check (up *or* back); **~versicherung** *f* reinsurance; **~wand** *f* back wall; *(von Möbelstück etc)* back; **r~wärtig** *adj* back; *Tür auch, (Mil)* rear.

rückwärts *adv* **(a)** *(zurück)* backwards. **~ einparken** to back into a parking space. **(b)** *(esp SGer, Aus: hinten)* behind, at the back. **von ~** from behind.

Rückwärts-: ~drehung *f* reverse turn; **~gang** *m* reverse gear; **im ~gang fahren** to reverse.

Rückweg *m* way back. **sich auf den ~ machen** to head back.

ruckweise *adv* jerkily. **sich ~ bewegen** to move jerkily.

Rück-: r~wirkend *adj (Jur)* retrospective; *Lohn-, Gehaltserhöhung* backdated; **das Gesetz tritt r~wirkend vom 1. Januar in Kraft** the law is made retrospective to the 1st January; **~wirkung** *f* repercussion; **eine Zahlung mit ~wirkung vom ...** a payment backdated to ...; **r~zahlbar** *adj* repayable; **~zahlung** *f* repayment; **~zieher** *m* **- (a)** *(col)* **einen ~ zieher machen** to back out *(col)*; **(b)** *(Ftbl)* overhead kick.

ruck, zuck *adv* in a flash. **~!** jump to it!; **das geht ~** it won't take a second.

Rückzug *m (Mil)* retreat. **auf dem ~** in the retreat; **den ~ antreten** *(lit, fig)* to retreat.

Rückzugsgefecht *nt (Mil, fig)* rearguard action.

Rüde *m (wk)* **-n, -n** *(Männchen)* dog, male; *(Hetzhund)* hound.

rüde *adj* impolite; *Antwort* curt, brusque.

Rudel *nt* **-** *(von Hunden, Wölfen)* pack; *(von Wildschweinen, Hirschen)* herd; *(fig dated)* horde.

rudelweise *adv* in packs/herds/hordes.

Ruder *nt* **-** *(von ~boot etc)* oar; *(Naut, Aviat: Steuer~)* rudder; *(fig: Führung)* helm. **das ~ fest in der Hand haben** *(fig)* to be in control of the situation; **am ~ sein** *(lit, fig)*/**ans ~ kommen** *(fig)* to be at/to take over (at) the helm; **das ~ herumwerfen** *(fig)* to change tack.

Ruder-: ~bank *f* rowing seat; **~blatt** *nt* (oar) blade; **~boot** *nt* rowing boat *(Brit)*, rowboat *(US)*.

Ruderer *m* **-** oarsman.

Ruderin *f* oarswoman.

rudern 1 *vi* **(a)** *aux haben or sein* to row. **(b)** *(Schwimmvögel)* to paddle. **mit den Armen ~** *(fig)* to flail one's arms about. **2** *vt* to row.

Ruder-: ~regatta *f* rowing regatta; **~sport** *m* rowing *no def art*.

Rudiment *nt* rudiment.

rudimentär *adj* rudimentary.

Ruf *m* **-e (a)** *(Aus~, Vogel~, fig: Auf~)* call; *(lauter)* shout; *(Schrei)* cry. **dem ~ des Herzens folgen** *(fig)* to obey the voice of one's heart; **der ~ nach Freiheit** *(fig)* the call for freedom; **der ~ zur Ordnung** *(fig)* the call to order. **(b)** *(Ansehen, Leumund)* reputation. **einen guten ~ haben** to have a good reputation; **eine Firma von ~** a firm with a good name; **von üblem** *or* **zweifelhaftem ~ sein** to have a bad reputation; **jdn/etw in schlechten ~ bringen** to give sb/sth a bad name; **sie ist besser als ihr ~** she is better than she is made out to be. **(c)** *(Univ: Berufung)* offer of a chair. **(d)** *(~ nummer)* **„~: 27785"** "Tel: 27785".

rufen *pret* **rief**, *ptp* **gerufen 1** *vi* to call *(nach* for*)*; *(Mensch: laut ~)* to shout; *(Glocke etc)* to sound *(zu* for*)*. **um Hilfe ~** to call for help; **die Pflicht ruft** duty calls; **die Arbeit ruft** my/your *etc* work is waiting. **2** *vt* **(a)** to call; *(aus~)* to cry; *(Mensch: laut ~)* to shout. **bravo ~** to shout hooray. **(b)** *(kommen lassen)* to send for; *Arzt, Polizei auch, Taxi* to call. **~ Sie ihn bitte!** please send him to me; **jdn zu Hilfe ~** to call on sb to help; **du kommst wie gerufen** you're just the man/woman I wanted; **das kommt mir wie gerufen** that's just what I needed; *(kommt mir gelegen)* that suits me fine *(col)*.

Rüffel *m* **-** *(col)* telling-off, ticking-off *(col)*.

Ruf-: ~mord *m* character assassination; **~mordkampagne** *f* smear campaign; **~name** *m* Christian name (by which one is generally known); **~nummer** *f* telephone number; **~säule** *f (für Taxi)* telephone; *(an Autobahn)* emergency telephone; **~zeichen** *nt (von Telefon)* ringing tone.

Rugby ['ragbi] *nt no pl* rugby, rugger *(col)*.

Rüge *f* **-n** *(Verweis)* reprimand, rebuke; *(Kritik)* criticism *no indef art*. **jdm eine ~ erteilen** to reprimand sb *(für, wegen* for*)*.

rügen *vt (form) jdn* to reprimand *(wegen, für* for*)*; *etw* to reprehend.

Ruhe *f no pl* **(a)** *(Schweigen, Stille)* quiet, silence. **~!** quiet!, silence!; **gebt ~!** be quiet!; **sich** *(dat)* **~ verschaffen** to get silence; **es herrscht ~** all is silent; *(fig: Disziplin, Frieden)* all is quiet; **~ halten** *(lit, fig)* to keep quiet; **die ~ vor dem Sturm** *(fig)* the calm before the storm.

(b) *(Ungestörtheit, Frieden)* peace, quiet. **~ ausstrahlen** to radiate a sense of calm; **~ und Frieden** peace and quiet; **in ~ und Frieden leben** to live a quiet life; **~ und Ordnung** law and order; **ich brauche meine ~** I need a bit of peace; **laß mich in ~!** leave me in peace; **vor jdm ~ haben wollen** to want a rest from sb; *(endgültig)* to want to be rid of sb; **jdm keine ~ lassen** *(Mensch)* not to give sb any peace; **das läßt ihm keine ~** he can't stop thinking about it; **zur ~ kommen** to get some peace; *(solide werden)* to settle down; **jdn zur ~ kommen lassen** to give sb a chance to rest; **keine ~ finden (können)** to know no peace; **die letzte ~ finden** *(liter)* to be laid to rest *(liter)*.

(c) *(Erholung)* rest, repose *(liter)*; *(~stand)* retirement; *(Stillstand)* rest. **sich zur ~ begeben** *(form)* to retire (to bed) *(form)*; **angenehme ~!** sleep well!; **sich zur ~ setzen** to retire.

(d) *(Gelassenheit)* calm(ness); *(Disziplin)* quiet, order. **die ~ weghaben** *(col)* to be unflappable *(col)*; **~ bewahren** to keep calm; **die ~ selbst sein** to be calmness itself; **jdn aus der ~ bringen** to throw sb *(col)*; **sich nicht aus der ~ bringen lassen** not to (let oneself) get worked up; **sich** *(dat)* **etw in ~ ansehen** to look at sth in one's own time; **immer mit der ~** *(col)* don't panic.

Ruhe-: r~bedürftig *adj* in need of rest; **~gehalt** *nt (form)* superannuation; **~geld** *nt (form)* pension; **~lage** *f (von Mensch)* reclining position; *(Med: bei Bruch)* immobile position; **r~los** *adj* restless; **eine r~lose Zeit** a time of unrest; **~losigkeit** *f* restlessness.

ruhen *vi* **(a)** *(aus~, geh: liegen)* to rest; *(liter: schlafen)* to sleep. **nicht (eher) ~ bis ...** *(fig)* not to rest until ... **(b)** *(stillstehen)* to stop; *(Maschinen)* to stand idle; *(Arbeit auch, Verkehr)* to cease; *(Waffen)* to be laid down. **(c)** *(begraben sein)* to lie, to be buried. **„hier ruht ..."** "here lies ..."; **„ruhe sanft!"** "rest eternal".

Ruhe-: ~pause *f* break; **eine ~pause einlegen** to take a break; **~punkt** *m* place of rest; **~stand** *m* retirement; **im ~stand sein/leben** to be retired; **er ist Bankdirektor im ~stand** he is a retired bank director; **in den ~stand treten** to retire; **jdn in den ~stand versetzen** to retire sb; **~ständler** *m* - retired person; **~stätte** *f* resting place; **letzte ~stätte** last *or* final resting-place; **~stellung** *f (von Körper)* resting position; *(von Gegenstand)* resting point; *(von Maschinen)* off position; **r~störend** *adj* **r~störender Lärm** *(Jur)* disturbance of the peace; **~störer** *m* disturber of the peace; **~störung** *f (Jur)* disturbance of the peace; **~tag** *m* day off; *(von Geschäft etc)* closing day; **„Mittwoch ~tag"** "closed (on) Wednesdays".

ruhig 1 *adj* **(a)** *(still, geruhsam)* quiet; *Wetter, Meer* calm; *Überfahrt, Verlauf* smooth. **seid ~!** be quiet!; **sitz doch ~!** sit still!; **gegen 6 Uhr wird es ~er** it quietens down around 6 o'clock; **alles geht seinen ~en Gang** everything is going smoothly. **(b)** *(gelassen)* calm; *Gewissen* easy; *(sicher) Hand, Blick* steady. **nur ~ (Blut)!** take it easy *(col)*; **bei ~er Überlegung** on (mature) consideration; **du kannst/Sie können ganz ~ sein** I can assure you; **etw ~ mitansehen** *(gleichgültig)* to stand by and watch sth. **2** *adv* **du kannst ~ hierbleiben** feel free to stay here; **ihr könnt ~ gehen, ich passe schon auf** you just go and I'll look after things; **man kann ~ behaupten, daß ...** *(mit Recht)* one may well assert that ...; **du könntest ~ mal etwas für mich tun!** it's about time you did something for me!

Ruhm *m no pl* glory; *(Berühmtheit)* fame. **sich in seinem ~ sonnen** to rest on one's laurels.

rühmen 1 *vt (preisen, empfehlen)* to praise *(jdn wegen etw* sb for sth*)*. **2** *vr* **sich einer Sache** *(gen)* **~** *(prahlen)* to boast about sth; *(stolz sein)* to pride oneself on sth; **ohne mich zu ~** without wishing to boast.

Ruhmes-: ~blatt *nt (fig)* glorious chapter; **~tat** *f* glorious deed.

rühmlich *adj* praiseworthy; *Ausnahme* notable.

ruhm-: ~los *adj* inglorious; **r~reich** *adj (liter)*, **r~voll** *adj* glorious.

Ruhr *f no pl (Krankheit)* dysentery.

Rühr|ei *nt* scrambled eggs *pl*.

rühren 1 *vi* **(a)** *(um~)* to stir. **(b) an etw** *(acc)* **~** *(anfassen)* to touch sth; *(fig: erwähnen)* to touch on sth; **von etw ~** to stem from sth; **das rührt daher, daß ...** that is because ... **2** *vt* **(a)** *(um~) Teig, Farbe* to stir; *(schlagen) Eier* to beat. **(b)** *(lit, fig: bewegen)* to move; *Herz* to stir. **er rührte keinen Finger, um mir zu helfen** *(col)* he didn't lift a finger to help me *(col)*; **das kann mich nicht ~!** that leaves me cold; **jdn zu Tränen ~** to move sb to tears. **3** *vr* **(a)** to move; *(Blatt etc)* to stir; *(aktiv sein)* to buck up *(col)*; *(sich beeilen)* to get a move on *(col)*. **rührt euch!** *(Mil)* at ease!; **kein Lüftchen rührte sich** the air was still; **nichts hat sich gerührt** nothing happened. **(b)** *(Gewissen etc)* to be awakened.

rührend *adj* touching. **das ist ~ von Ihnen** that is sweet of you.

Ruhrgebiet *nt* Ruhr (area).

rührig *adj* active.

Rühr-: ~löffel *m* mixing spoon; **r~selig** *adj (pej)* tear-jerking *(pej col)*; **~seligkeit** *f no pl* sentimentality; **~stück** *nt (Theat)* melodrama; **~teig** *m* sponge mixture.

Rührung *f no pl* emotion. **vor ~ nicht sprechen können** to be choked with emotion.

Ruin *m no pl* ruin. **vor dem ~ stehen** to be on the verge of ruin; **du bist noch mein ~!** *(hum col)* you'll be the ruin of me.

Ruine *f* **-n** *(lit, fig)* ruin.

ruinieren* *vt* to ruin. **sich ~** to ruin oneself.

rülpsen *vi* to belch.

Rülpser *m* **-** *(col)* belch.

rum *adv (col)* = **herum.**

Rum *m* **-s** rum.

Rumäne *m (wk)* **-n, -n, Rumänin** *f* Romanian.

Rumänien [-iən] *nt* Romania.

rumänisch *adj* Romanian.

rumkriegen *vt sep (col)* **jdn ~** to talk sb around.

Rummel *m no pl* **(a)** *(col) (Betrieb)* (hustle and) bustle; *(Getöse)* racket *(col)*; *(Aufheben)* fuss *(col)*. **der ganze ~** the whole carry-on *(col)*. **(b)** *(Jahrmarkt)* fair.

Rummelplatz *m (col)* fairground.

rumoren* 1 *vi* to make a noise; *(Mensch)* to bang about; *(Bauch)* to rumble; *(Gewissen)* to play up. **2** *vi impers* **es rumort in meinem Bauch** my stomach's rumbling; **es rumort im Volk** *(fig)* there is growing unrest among the people.

Rumpelkammer *f (col)* junk room *(col)*.

rumpeln *vi aux sein (sich polternd bewegen)* to rumble; *(Mensch)* to clatter.

Rumpf *m* **¨e** trunk; *(Sport)* body; *(Statue)* torso; *(von Schiff)* hull; *(von Flugzeug)* fuselage.

rümpfen *vt* **die Nase ~** to turn up one's nose *(über +acc* at*)*.

Rumpsteak ['rʊmp-ste:k] *nt* rump steak.

rums *interj* bang.

Rum-: ~topf *m soft fruit in rum*; **~verschnitt** *m* blended rum.

rund 1 *adj* round; *Figur, Arme* plump; *Klang* full. **~e 50 Jahre/2000 Mark** a good 50 years/2,000 marks; **ein ~es Dutzend Leute** a dozen or more people; **Konferenz am ~en Tisch** round-table talks *pl*. **2** *adv* **(a)** *(herum)* (a)round. **~ um die Uhr** right (a)round the clock. **(b)** *(ungefähr)* (round) about, roughly. **(c)** *(fig: glattweg) ablehnen* flatly. **jetzt geht's ~** *(col)* this is where the fun starts *(col)*; **wenn der das erfährt, geht's ~** *(col)* there'll be a to-do when he finds out *(col)*.

Rund-: ~blick *m* panorama; **~brief** *m* circular.

Runde *f* **-n** **(a)** *(Gesellschaft)* company. **in der ~ herumgehen** to be passed around. **(b)** *(Rundgang)* walk, turn; *(von Wachmann)* rounds *pl*; *(von Briefträger etc)* round. **die ~ machen** to do the rounds; *(herumgegeben werden)* to be passed around; **eine ~ machen** to go for a walk; *(mit Fahrzeug)* to go for a ride *or* run. **(c)** *(Sport) (bei Rennen)* lap; *(Boxen etc, Gesprächs~)* round. **über die ~n kommen** *(Sport, fig)* to pull through. **(d)** *(von Getränken)* round. **eine ~ spendieren** *or* **schmeißen** *(col)* to stand a round.

runden 1 *vt Lippen* to round. **2** *vr (lit: rund werden)*

to become round; *(Lippen)* to grow round. **sich zu etw ~** *(fig)* to develop into sth.
Rund-: r~erneuern* *vt sep infin, ptp only* to remould *(Brit)*, to remold *(US)*; **~fahrt** *f* tour; **eine ~fahrt machen** to go on a tour; **~frage** *f* survey *(an +acc, unter +dat* of*)*.
Rundfunk *m* broadcasting; *(besonders Hörfunk)* radio. **im ~** on the radio; **~ hören** to listen to the radio; **beim ~ arbeiten** to be in broadcasting.
Rundfunk- *in cpds* radio; **~anstalt** *f* broadcasting corporation; **~gebühr** *f* radio licence *(Brit)* *or* license *(US)* fee; **~gerät** *nt* radio set; **~gesellschaft** *f* broadcasting company; *(Sendeanstalt)* radio station; **~sendung** *f* radio programme *(Brit)* *or* program *(US)*; **~techniker** *m* radio engineer; **~zeitschrift** *f* radio programme *(Brit)* *or* program *(US)* guide.
Rund-: ~gang *m (Spaziergang)* walk; *(zur Besichtigung)* tour *(durch* of*)*; *(von Wachmann)* rounds *pl*; *(von Briefträger etc)* round; **~heit** *f* roundness; **r~heraus** *adv* straight out; **r~heraus gesagt** frankly; **r~herum** *adv* all around; *(fig col: völlig)* totally; **r~lich** *adj* plump; **~reise** *f* tour *(durch* of*)*; **~schreiben** *nt* circular; **r~um** *adv* all around; *(fig)* completely; **r~weg** *adv* straight out.
Runkelrübe *f* mangel-wurzel.
runter *adv (col)* = **herunter, hinunter. ~!** down!
runter- *pref (col)* down; *siehe* **herunter-, hinunter-; ~holen** *vt sep* to get down; **sich einen ~holen** *(col!)* to jerk off *(col!)*.
Runzel *f* **-n** wrinkle.
runz(e)lig *adj* wrinkled.
runzeln 1 *vt Stirn* to wrinkle, to crease. **2** *vr* to become wrinkled.
Rüpel *m* **-** lout, yob(bo) *(Brit col)*.
rüpelhaft *adj* loutish.
rupfen *vt Gänse, Hühner* to pluck; *Gras, Unkraut* to pull up. **jdn ~** *(fig col)* to fleece sb *(col)*, to take sb to the cleaners *(col)*; **wie ein gerupftes Huhn aussehen** to look like a shorn sheep.
Rupie ['ruːpiə] *f* rupee.
ruppig *adj (grob)* rough; *Benehmen, Antwort* gruff; *Äußeres* scruffy.
Rüsche *f* **-n** ruche, frill.
Ruß *m no pl* soot; *(von Kerze)* smoke.
Russe *m (wk)* **-n, -n** Russian, Russian man/boy.
Rüssel *m* **-** snout *(auch col: Nase)*; *(Elefanten~)* trunk; *(von Insekt)* proboscis.
rußen *vi (Öllampe, Kerze)* to smoke; *(Ofen)* to produce soot.
rußig *adj* sooty.
Russin *f* Russian, Russian woman/girl.
russisch *adj* Russian. **~es Roulett** Russian roulette; **~e Eier** *(Cook)* egg(s) mayonnaise; *siehe* **deutsch.**
Russisch(e) *nt decl as adj* Russian; *siehe* **Deutsch(e).**
Rußland *nt* Russia.
rüsten 1 *vi (Mil)* to arm. **zum Kampf ~** to arm for battle; **gut/schlecht gerüstet sein** to be well/badly armed. **2** *vr* to prepare *(zu* for*)*; *(lit, fig: sich wappnen)* to arm oneself *(gegen* for*)*.
rüstig *adj* sprightly.
rustikal *adj* rustic. **sich ~ einrichten** to furnish one's home in a rustic style.
Rüstung *f* **(a)** *(das Rüsten)* armament; *(Waffen)* arms *pl*, weapons *pl*. **(b)** *(Ritter~)* armour *(Brit)*, armor *(US)*.
Rüstungs- *in cpds* arms; **~beschränkung** *f* arms limitation; **~industrie** *f* armaments industry; **~kontrolle** *f* arms control; **~wettlauf** *m* arms race.
Rüstzeug *nt no pl (fig)* qualifications *pl*.
Rute *f* **-n (a)** *(Gerte)* switch; *(esp Stock zum Züchtigen)* cane, rod; *(Birken~)* birch (rod). **(b)** *(Angel~)* (fishing) rod. **(c)** *(Hunt: Schwanz)* tail.
Rutsch *m* **-e** slip, slide; *(Erd~)* landslide; *(von Steinen)* rockfall; *(fig Pol)* shift, swing; *(col: Ausflug)* trip, outing. **guten ~!** *(col)* have a good new year; **in einem ~** in one go.
Rutschbahn *f (Kinder~)* slide.
rutschen *vi aux sein* **(a)** *(gleiten)* to slide; *(aus~, entgleiten)* to slip; *(Aut)* to skid; *(fig: Preise, Kurse)* to slip. **auf dem Stuhl hin und her ~** to fidget around on one's chair. **(b)** *(col: rücken)* to move up. **zur Seite ~** to move over. **(c)** *(~d kriechen)* to crawl.
rutschfest *adj* non-slip.
rutschig *adj* slippery, slippy *(col)*.
rütteln 1 *vt* to shake (about). **2** *vi* to shake; *(Fahrzeug)* to jolt. **an etw** *(dat)* **~** *an Tür, Fenster etc* to rattle (at) sth; *(fig) an Grundsätzen etc* to shake sth; **daran ist nicht zu ~** *(col)* there's no doubt about that.

S

S, s [ɛs] *nt*, -, - S, s.
S = **Süden** S; **Seite** p.
s. = **siehe.**
Saal *m, pl* **Säle** hall; *(für Sitzungen etc)* room; *(Tanz~)* ballroom; *(Theater~)* auditorium.
Saal|ordner *m* usher.
Saat *f* **-en (a)** *(das Säen)* sowing. **(b)** *(Samen, ~gut)* seed(s) *(auch fig)*. **wenn die ~ aufgeht** *(lit)* when the seed begins to grow; *(fig)* when the seeds bear fruit; **die ~ für etw legen** *(fig)* to sow the seed(s) of sth. **(c)** *(junges Getreide)* young crop(s), seedlings *pl*.
Saat-: **~gut** *nt no pl* seed(s); **~korn** *nt* seed corn; **~zeit** *f* sowing time.
Sabbat *m* **-e** Sabbath.
sabbeln *(dial)*, **sabbern** *(col)* **1** *vi* to slobber. **vor sich hin ~** *(fig)* to mutter away to oneself. **2** *vt* to blather *(col)*. **dummes Zeug ~** to talk drivel *(col)*.
Säbel *m* - sabre *(Brit)*, saber *(US)*. **mit dem ~ rasseln** *(fig)* to rattle the sabre.
Säbel-: **~fechten** *nt* sabre *(Brit)* or saber *(US)* fencing; **~hieb** *m* stroke of one's sabre *(Brit)* or saber *(US)*.
säbeln *(col)* **1** *vt* to saw away at. **2** *vi* to saw away *(an +dat* at*)*.
Säbel-: **~rasseln** *nt no pl* sabre-rattling, *(Brit)* saber rattling *(US)*; **s~rasselnd** *adj* sabre-rattling *(Brit)*, saber-rattling *(US)*.
Sabotage [zabo'taːʒə] *f* **-n** sabotage. **~ treiben** to perform acts of sabotage.
Sabotage|akt *m* act of sabotage.
Saboteur(in *f*) [-'tøːɐ, -'tøːrɪn] *m* saboteur.
sabotieren* *vt* to sabotage.
Sa(c)charin *nt no pl* saccharin.
Sach-: **~bearbeiter** *m* specialist; *(Beamter)* official in charge *(für* of*)*; **~bereich** *m* (specialist) area; **~beschädigung** *f* damage to property; **~buch** *nt* non-fiction book; **~dienlich** *adj* useful; **~dienliche Hinweise** helpful information.
Sache *f* **-n (a)** thing; *(Gegenstand auch)* object. **~n** *pl (col: Zeug)* things *pl*; *(Jur)* property; **das liegt in der Natur der ~** that's in the nature of things.
(b) *(Angelegenheit)* matter; *(Frage auch)* question; *(Thema)* subject; *(Jur)* case; *(Aufgabe)* job; *(Vorfall)* business, affair; *(no pl: Ideal)* cause. **eine ~ der Polizei** a matter for the police; **das ist eine ganz tolle ~** it's really fantastic; **ich habe mir die ~ anders vorgestellt** I had imagined things differently; **das ist eine andere ~** that's a different matter; **das ist meine/seine ~** that's my/his business; **in ~n A gegen B** *(Jur)* in the case (of) A versus B; **er versteht seine ~** he knows what he's doing; **er macht seine ~ gut** he's doing very well; *(beruflich)* he's doing a good job; **diese Frage können wir nicht hier mitbesprechen, das ist eine ~ für sich** we can't discuss this question now, it's a separate issue; **das ist so eine ~** *(col)* it's a bit tricky; **solche ~n liegen mir nicht** I don't like things like that; **wann ist die ~ passiert?** when did it (all) happen?; **was hat die Polizei zu der ~ gesagt?** what did the police say about it?; **das ist (eine) beschlossene ~** it's (all) settled; **mach keine ~n!** *(col)* don't be daft! *(col)*; **eine ~ des Geschmacks** a question of taste; **zur ~!** let's get on with it; *(Parl, Jur etc)* come to the point!; **das tut nichts zur ~** that doesn't matter; **bei der ~ sein** to be with it *(col)*; **bei der ~ bleiben** to keep one's mind on the job; *(bei Diskussion)* to keep to the point; **so steht die ~ also** so that's the way things are; **für eine gerechte ~ kämpfen** to fight for a just cause.
(c) *(Tempo)* **mit 60/100 ~n** *(col)* at 60/100.
Sachertorte *f a rich chocolate cake*, sachertorte.
Sach-: **~frage** *f* factual question; **~gebiet** *nt* area; **s~gemäß, s~gerecht** *adj* proper; **bei s~gemäßer Anwendung** if used properly; **~kenntnis** *f (in bezug auf Wissensgebiet)* knowledge of the/his *etc* subject; *(in bezug auf ~lage)* knowledge of the facts; **s~kundig** *adj* (well-)informed *no adv*; **s~kundig antworten** to give an informed answer; **~lage** *f* state of affairs.
sachlich *adj* **(a)** *(faktisch) Irrtum, Angaben* factual; *Grund, Einwand* practical; *(sachbezogen) Frage, Wissen* relevant. **rein ~ hast du recht** from a purely factual point of view you are right. **(b)** *(objektiv) Kritik etc* objective; *(unemotional)* matter-of-fact. **bleiben Sie mal ~** don't get carried away; *(nicht persönlich werden)* stay objective. **(c)** *(schmucklos)* functional, businesslike.
sächlich *adj (Gram)* neuter.
Sachlichkeit *f* **(a)** *siehe adj (b)* objectivity; matter-of-factness. **(b)** *(Schmucklosigkeit)* functionality.
Sach-: **~register** *nt* subject index; **~schaden** *m* damage (to property).
Sachse ['zaksə] *m (wk)* **-n, -n, Sächsin** ['zɛksɪn] *f* Saxon.
Sachsen ['zaksn] *nt* Saxony.
sächsisch ['zɛksɪʃ] *adj* Saxon.
sacht(e) *adj (leise)* soft; *(sanft)* gentle; *(vorsichtig)* cautious, careful; *(allmählich)* gentle, gradual. **~, ~!** *(col)* take it easy!
Sach-: **~verhalt** *m* **-e** facts *pl* (of the case); **~verständige(r)** *mf decl as adj* expert, specialist; *(Jur)* expert witness; **~wert** *m* real value; **~werte** *pl* material assets *pl*; **~wörterbuch** *nt* specialist dictionary.
Sack *m* **¨-e (a)** sack; *(aus Papier, Plastik)* bag. **drei ~ Kohlen** three bags of coal; **mit ~ und Pack** *(col)* with bag and baggage; **jdn in den ~ stecken** *(fig col)* to put sb in the shade. **(b)** *(Anat, Zool)* sac. **(c)** *(col!: Hoden)* balls *pl (col!)*. **(d)** *(col!: Kerl, Bursche)* bastard *(col!)*. **fauler ~** lazy bastard.
Sackbahnhof *m* terminus.
sacken *vi aux sein (lit, fig: sinken)* to sink. **in die Knie ~** to sag at the knees.
Sack-: **~gasse** *f* cul-de-sac *(esp Brit)*, dead end; *(fig)* dead end; **in eine ~gasse geraten** *(fig)* to finish up a blind alley; *(Verhandlungen)* to reach an impasse; **~hüpfen** *nt no pl* sack-race; **~karre** *f* hand-cart; **~leinen** *nt*, **~leinwand** *f* sacking, burlap *(US)*.
Sadismus *m no pl* sadism.
Sadist(in *f*) *m* sadist.
sadistisch *adj* sadistic.
säen *vti* to sow; *(fig)* to sow (the seeds of). **dünn gesät** *(fig)* thin on the ground, few and far between.
Safari *f* **-s** safari. **eine ~ machen** to go on safari.
Safe [zeːf] *m or nt* **-s** safe.
Saffian *m no pl*, **Saffianleder** *nt* morocco (leather).

Safran *m* **-e** saffron.
Saft **¨e** *(Obst~)* (fruit) juice; *(Pflanzen~)* sap; *(Fleisch~)* juice; *(Husten~ etc)* syrup; *(col: Strom, Benzin)* juice *(col)*. **ohne ~ und Kraft** *(fig)* wishy-washy *(col)*, effete.
saftig *adj* **(a)** *(voll Saft) Obst, Fleisch* juicy; *Wiese, Grün* lush. **(b)** *(col: kräftig) Witz* juicy *(col)*; *Rechnung, Ohrfeige* hefty *(col)*; *Brief, Antwort* potent.
Saftigkeit *f (von Obst, Witz)* juiciness; *(von Wiese etc)* lushness.
Saft-: **~laden** *m (pej col)* dump *(pej col)*; **s~los** *adj* not juicy; **~presse** *f* fruit-press; **~sack** *m (col!)* stupid bastard *(col!)*.
saft- und kraftlos *adj* wishy-washy *(col)*, effete.
Sage *f* **-n** legend; *(altnordische)* saga. **es geht die ~, daß ...** legend has it that ...; *(Gerücht)* rumour *(Brit) or* rumor *(US)* has it that ...
Säge *f* **-n** *(Werkzeug)* saw.
Säge-: **~blatt** *nt* saw blade; **~maschine** *f* mechanical saw; **~mehl** *nt* sawdust; **~messer** *nt* serrated knife; **~mühle** *f* sawmill.
sagen *vt* **(a)** to say. **jdm etw ~** to say sth to sb; *(mitteilen, ausrichten)* to tell sb sth; **sich** *(dat)* **etw ~** to say sth to oneself; **unter uns gesagt** between you and me (and the gatepost *hum col*); **genauer/deutlicher gesagt** to put it more precisely/clearly; **könnten Sie mir ~ ...?** could you tell me ...?; **ich sag's ihm** I'll tell him; **ich habe mir ~ lassen, ...** I've been told ...; **was ich mir von ihm nicht alles ~ lassen muß!** the things I have to take from him!; **das kann ich Ihnen nicht ~** I couldn't say; **so was sagt man doch nicht!** you mustn't say things like that; *(bei Schimpfen, Fluchen)* (mind your) language!; **das sage ich nicht!** I'm not telling; **was ich noch ~ wollte, ...** *(col)* there's something else I wanted to say ...; **dann will ich nichts gesagt haben** in that case forget I said anything; **ich sage, wie es ist** I'm just telling you the way it is; **um nicht zu ~** not to say; **jdm ~, er solle etw tun** to tell sb to do sth; **hat er im Betrieb etwas zu ~?** does he have a say in the firm?; **das S~ haben** to have the say; **laß dir das gesagt sein** take it from me; **er läßt sich** *(dat)* **nichts ~** he won't be told; **das laß ich mir von dem nicht ~** I won't take that from him; **sie ließen es sich** *(dat)* **nicht zweimal ~** they didn't need to be told twice; **ich möchte fast ~, ...** I'd almost say ...; **wenn ich so ~ darf** if I may say so; **da soll noch einer ~, ...** never let it be said ...
(b) *(bedeuten, meinen)* to mean. **was will er damit ~?** what does he mean (by that)?; **ich will damit nicht ~, daß ...** I don't mean to imply that ...; **damit ist nicht gesagt, daß ...** that doesn't mean (to say) that ...; **das hat nichts zu ~** that doesn't mean anything; **sagt dir der Name etwas?** does the name mean anything to you?
(c) ~ Sie mal/sag mal, ... tell me, ..., say, ...; **du, Veronika, sag mal, wollen wir ...** hey, Veronika, listen, shall we ...; **wem ~ Sie das!** you don't need to tell *me* that!; **sag bloß!** you don't say!; **was Sie nicht ~!** you don't say!; **das kann man wohl ~** you can say that again!; **ich muß schon ~** I must say; **das muß man ~** you must admit that; **das ist nicht gesagt** that's by no means certain; **leichter gesagt als getan** easier said than done; **gesagt, getan** no sooner said than done; **wie (schon) gesagt** as I/you *etc* said; **ich bin, ~ wir, in einer Stunde da** I'll be there in, let's say, an hour; **sage und schreibe 100 Mark** 100 marks, would you believe it.
sägen 1 *vti* to saw. **2** *vi (hum col: schnarchen)* to snore, to saw wood *(US col)*.
Sagen-: **~dichtung** *f* sagas *pl*; **s~haft** *adj* **(a)** *(nach Art einer Sage)* legendary; **(b)** *(col: hervorragend)* fantastic *(col)*, terrific *(col)*; **s~haft schnell** incredibly fast *(col)*; **s~umwoben** *adj* legendary; **~welt** *f* mythology, legend.
Säge-: **~späne** *pl* wood shavings *pl*; **~werk** *nt* sawmill.
Sago *m no pl* sago.
sah *pret of* **sehen.**
Sahara [za'ha:ra, 'za:hara] *f* Sahara (Desert).
Sahne *f no pl* cream.
Sahne-: **~bonbon** *m or nt* toffee; **~eis** *nt* ice-cream; **~torte** *f* cream gateau.
sahnig *adj* creamy.
Saison [zɛ'zõ:, zɛ'zɔŋ] *f* **-s** season. **außerhalb der ~** in the off-season.
saisonal [zɛzo'na:l] *adj* seasonal.
Saison- [zɛ'zõ:] *in cpds* seasonal; **~arbeit** *f* seasonal work; **~arbeiter** *m* seasonal worker; **s~bedingt** *adj* seasonal; **~beginn** *m* start of the season; **~betrieb** *m (Hochsaison)* high season; *(~geschäft)* seasonal business; **~eröffnung** *f* opening of the season; **~geschäft** *nt* seasonal business; **~schluß** *m* end of the season; **~zuschlag** *m* in-season supplement.
Saite *f* **-n** **(a)** *(Mus, Sport)* string. **(b)** *(fig liter)* **eine ~ in jdm berühren** to strike a chord in sb; **andere ~n aufziehen** *(col)* to get tough.
Saiten|instrument *nt* string(ed) instrument.
Sakko *m or nt* **-s** sports jacket *(Brit)*, sport coat *(US)*; *(aus Samt etc)* jacket.
sakral *adj* sacred, sacral.
Sakrament *nt* sacrament.
Sakrileg *nt* **-e** sacrilege.
Sakristei *f* sacristy.
Salamander *m* **-** salamander.
Salami *f* **-s** salami.
Salamitaktik *f (col)* policy of small steps.
Salat *m* **-e** **(a)** *(Pflanze, Kopf~)* lettuce. **(b)** *(Gericht)* salad. **da haben wir den ~!** *(col)* now we're in a fine mess.
Salat-: **~besteck** *nt* salad servers *pl*; **~gurke** *f* cucumber; **~kopf** *m* (head of) lettuce; **~öl** *nt* salad oil; **~platte** *f* salad; **~schüssel** *f* salad bowl; **~soße** *f* salad dressing.
Salbe *f* **-n** ointment.
Salbei *m or f no pl* sage.
salben *vt (liter)* to anoint.
salbungsvoll *adj (pej)* unctuous *(pej)*.
saldieren* *vt (Comm)* to balance.
Saldo *m, pl* **-s** *or* **Salden** *(Fin)* balance. **per ~** *(lit, fig)* on balance.
Säle *pl of* **Saal.**
Salmiak *m or nt no pl* sal ammoniac, ammonium chloride.
Salmiak-: **~geist** *m* (liquid) ammonia; **~pastille** *f bitter-tasting lozenge,* liquorice imp.
Salmonellen *pl* salmonellae.
salomonisch *adj Urteil* worthy of a Solomon.
Salon [za'lõ:, za'lɔŋ] *m* **-s** **(a)** *(Gesellschaftszimmer)* drawing room. **(b)** *(Friseur~, Mode~ etc)* salon.
Salon- [za'lõ:-]: **s~fähig** *adj (iro)* socially acceptable; *Leute, Aussehen* presentable; **ein nicht s~fähiger Witz** an objectionable joke; **~löwe** *m (pej col)* social lion.
salopp *adj* **(a)** *(nachlässig)* sloppy, slovenly; *Manieren* slovenly; *Sprache* slangy. **(b)** *(ungezwungen)* casual.
Salpeter *m no pl* saltpetre *(Brit)*, saltpeter *(US)*.
Salpetersäure *f* nitric acid.
Salto *m, pl* **-s** *or* **Salti** somersault. **ein anderthalbfacher ~** a one-and-a-half somersault *or* turn; **~ mortale** triple somersault.
Salut *m* **-e** *(Mil)* salute. **~ schießen** to fire a salute; **21 Schuß ~** 21-gun salute.
salutieren* *vti (Mil)* to salute.
Salve ['zalvə] *f* **-n** salvo, volley; *(Ehren~)* salute; *(fig: von Applaus)* volley, burst.
Salz *nt* **-e** salt. **das ist das ~ in der Suppe** *(fig)* that's what gives it that extra something; **wie eine Suppe ohne ~** *(fig)* like ham without eggs *(hum)*.
Salz-: **s~arm** *adj (Cook)* low-salt; **s~arm essen** to eat low-salt food; **~bergwerk** *nt* salt mine;

~**brezel** *f* pretzel.
salzen *pret* **salzte**, *ptp* **gesalzen** *vt* to salt; *siehe* **gesalzen.**
Salz-: s~frei *adj* salt-free; *Diät auch* no-salt *attr*; ~**gebäck** *nt* savoury biscuits *pl (Brit)*, savory cookies *pl (US)*; ~**gurke** *f* pickled gherkin; **s~haltig** *adj* salty, saline; ~**hering** *m* salted herring.
salzig *adj* salty, salt.
Salz-: ~**kartoffeln** *pl* boiled potatoes *pl*; ~**korn** *nt* grain of salt; **s~los** *adj* salt-free; **s~los essen** not to eat salt; ~**lösung** *f* saline solution; ~**säule** *f*: **zur** ~**säule erstarren** *(fig)* to stand as though rooted to the spot; ~**säure** *f* hydrochloric acid; ~**see** *m* salt lake; ~**stange** *f* pretzel stick; ~**streuer** *m* - salt shaker, salt cellar; ~**wasser** *nt* salt water; ~**wüste** *f* salt flat.
Samariter *m (Bibl, fig)* Samaritan. **der Barmherzige** ~ the good Samaritan.
Sambia *nt* Zambia.
sambisch *adj* Zambian.
Same *m* **-ns, -n** *(liter)*, **Samen** *m* - **(a)** *(Bot, fig)* seed; *(fig auch)* seeds *pl*. **(b)** *(Menschen~, Tier~)* sperm.
Samen-: ~**bank** *f* sperm bank; ~**erguß** *m* ejaculation; ~**flüssigkeit** *f* seminal fluid; ~**handlung** *f* seed shop *(Brit) or* store *(US)*; ~**kapsel** *f* seed capsule; ~**korn** *nt* seed; ~**leiter** *m* vas deferens, sperm duct; ~**zelle** *f* sperm cell.
sämig *adj* thick, creamy.
Sammel-: ~**album** *nt* (collector's) album; ~**anschluß** *m (Telec)* private (branch) exchange; *(von Privathäusern)* party line; ~**band** *m* anthology; ~**becken** *nt* collecting tank; *(fig)* melting pot *(von* for*)*; ~**begriff** *m* collective term; ~**bestellung** *f* joint order; ~**büchse** *f* collecting box; ~**karte** *f (für mehrere Fahrten)* multi-journey ticket; *(für mehrere Personen)* group ticket; ~**mappe** *f* file.
sammeln 1 *vt* to collect; *Holz, Material, Erfahrungen auch* to gather; *Blumen, Pilze etc* to pick, to gather; *Truppen, Anhänger* to gather, to assemble. **neue Kräfte** ~ to build up one's energy again. **2** *vr* **(a)** to gather, to collect; *(Wasser, Geld etc)* to collect, to accumulate; *(Lichtstrahlen)* to converge, to meet. **(b)** *(fig: sich konzentrieren)* to collect one's thoughts; *siehe* **gesammelt. 3** *vi* to collect *(für* for*)*.
Sammel-: ~**name** *m* collective term; ~ **nummer** *f (Telec)* private exchange number, switchboard number; ~**punkt** *m (Treffpunkt)* assembly point.
Sammelsurium *nt* conglomeration.
Sammler(in *f***)** *m* - collector.
Sammlung *f* **(a)** collection. **(b)** *(fig: Konzentration)* composure.
Samowar *m* **-e** samovar.
Samstag *m* **-e** Saturday; *siehe* **Dienstag.**
samstags *adj* on Saturdays.
samt 1 *prep +dat* together with. **sie kam** ~ **Katze** *(hum)* she came complete with cat. **2** *adv* **sie waren** ~ **und sonders ...** the whole lot of them were ... *(col)*.
Samt *m* **-e** velvet. **in** ~ **und Seide** *(liter)* in silks and satins.
Samt- *in cpds* velvet; ~**handschuh** *m* velvet glove; **jdn mit** ~**handschuhen anfassen** *(col)* to handle sb with kid gloves *(col)*.
sämtlich *adj (alle)* all; *(vollständig)* complete. **Schillers** ~**e Werke** the complete works of Schiller; ~**e Anwesenden** all those present.
samtweich *adj* velvety.
Sanatorium *nt* sanatorium *(Brit)*, sanitarium *(US)*.
Sand *m* **-e** sand; *(Scheuer~)* scouring powder; *(Streu~)* grit. **mit** ~ **bestreuen** to sand; **das/die gibt's wie** ~ **am Meer** *(col)* there are heaps of them *(col)*; **auf** ~ **laufen** to run aground; **auf** ~ **bauen** *(fig)* to build upon sandy ground; **jdm** ~ **in die Augen streuen** *(fig)* to throw dust in sb's eyes; ~ **ins Getriebe streuen** to throw a spanner in the works *(Brit)*, to cause problems; **im** ~**e verlaufen** *(col)* to peter out; **den Kopf in den** ~ **stecken** to bury one's head in the sand.
Sandale *f* **-n** sandal.
Sand- *in cpds* sand; ~**bank** *f* sandbank; ~**boden** *m* sandy soil.
Sandel-: ~**holz** *nt* sandalwood; ~**öl** *nt* sandalwood oil.
Sand-: s~farben, s~farbig *adj* sand-coloured *(Brit)*, sand-colored *(US)*; ~**haufen** *m* heap of sand.
sandig *adj* sandy.
Sand-: ~**kasten** *m* sandpit *(esp Brit)*, sandbox *(US)*; ~**kastenspiele** *pl (Mil)* sand-table exercises *pl*; *(fig)* tactical manoeuvrings *(Brit) or* maneuverings *(US) pl*; ~**korn** *nt* grain of sand; ~**kuchen** *m (Cook)* sand-cake *(a Madeira-type cake)*; ~**mann** *m*, ~**männchen** *nt (in Geschichten)* sandman; ~**papier** *nt* sandpaper; ~**sack** *m* sandbag; *(Boxen)* punchbag; ~**stein** *m* sandstone; **s~strahlen** *vti insep* to sandblast; ~**strahlgebläse** *nt* sandblasting equipment *no indef art, no pl*; ~**strand** *m* sandy beach; ~**sturm** *m* sandstorm.
sandte *pret of* **senden**[1].
Sand-: ~**uhr** *f* hour-glass; *(Eieruhr)* egg-timer; ~**wüste** *f* sandy waste; *(Geog)* (sandy) desert.
sanft *adj* gentle; *Haut* soft; *Schlaf, Tod* peaceful. **sich** ~ **anfühlen** to feel soft; **mit** ~**er Gewalt** gently but firmly; **er ist** ~ **entschlafen** he passed away peacefully.
Sänfte *f* **-n** litter; *(esp im 17., 18. Jh. Europas)* sedan-chair.
Sanftheit *f siehe adj* gentleness; softness.
Sanftmut *f no pl (liter)* gentleness.
sanftmütig *adj (liter)* gentle.
sang *pret of* **singen.**
Sang *m* **¨-e** *(old liter) (Gesang)* song; *(das Singen)* singing. **mit** ~ **und Klang** *(lit)* with drums drumming and pipes piping; *(fig iro) durchfallen etc* disastrously, catastrophically.
Sänger(in *f***)** *m* - singer; *(esp Jazz~, Pop~ auch)* vocalist.
sang- und klanglos *adv (col)* without any ado, quietly. **sie ist** ~ **verschwunden** she just simply disappeared.
sanieren* **1** *vt* **(a)** *Stadtteil* to redevelop; *Haus* to renovate; *Fluß* to clean up. **(b)** *(Econ) Unternehmen, Wirtschaft* to rehabilitate, to put (back) on its feet. **2** *vr* **(a)** *(Unternehmen, Industrie)* to get back in good shape. **(b)** *(col: sich bereichern)* to line one's own pocket *(col)*.
Sanierung *f* **(a)** *siehe vt (a)* redevelopment; renovation; cleaning up. **(b)** *(Econ)* rehabilitation.
Sanierungs-: ~**gebiet** *nt* redevelopment area; ~**maßnahme** *f (für Gebiete etc)* redevelopment measure; *(Econ)* rehabilitation measure.
sanitär *adj no pred* sanitary. ~**e Anlagen** sanitary facilities.
Sanitäter *m* - first-aid attendant; *(Mil)* (medical) orderly; *(in Krankenwagen)* ambulance man.
Sanitäts-: ~**auto** *nt* ambulance; ~**dienst** *m (Mil)* medical duty; *(Heeresabteilung)* medical corps; ~**kasten** *m* first-aid kit; ~**korps** *nt* medical corps; ~**offizier** *m (Mil)* Medical Officer, MO; ~**truppe** *f* medical corps; ~**wagen** *m* ambulance.
sank *pret of* **sinken.**
Sankt *adj inv* Saint.
Sanktion *f* sanction.
sanktionieren* *vt* to sanction.
sann *pret of* **sinnen.**
Saphir *m* **-e** sapphire.
Sardelle *f* anchovy.
Sardine *f* sardine.
Sardinenbüchse *f* sardine-can. **wie in einer** ~ *(fig col)* like sardines *(col)*.
Sardinien [-iən] *nt* Sardinia.

sardinisch, sardisch *adj* Sardinian.
Sarg *m* ¨-e coffin, casket *(US)*.
Sarg-: ~**deckel** *m* coffin lid, casket lid *(US)*; ~**nagel** *m* coffin nail; *(fig col: Zigarette)* cancer-stick *(col)*; ~**träger** *m* pall-bearer.
Sarkasmus *m* sarcasm.
sarkastisch *adj* sarcastic.
saß *pret of* **sitzen.**
Satan *m* **-e** *(Bibl, fig)* Satan.
satanisch *adj* satanic.
Satansbraten *m (hum col)* young devil.
Satellit *m (wk)* **-en, -en** satellite.
Satelliten- *in cpds* satellite; ~**bahn** *f* satellite orbit; ~**foto** *nt* satellite picture; ~**staat** *m* satellite state; ~**stadt** *f* satellite town; ~**station** *f* space station.
Satin [za'tɛ̃:] *m* **-s** satin.
Satire *f* **-n** satire *(auf +acc* on*)*.
Satiriker(in *f***)** *m* **-** satirist.
satirisch *adj* satirical.
satt *adj* **(a)** *(gesättigt) Mensch* full (up) *(col)*; *Magen, Gefühl* full. ~ **sein** to have had enough (to eat), to be full (up) *(col)*; ~ **werden** to have enough to eat; **von so was kann man doch nicht ~ werden** it's not enough to satisfy you; **das macht** ~ it's filling; **sich (an etw** *dat***)** ~ **essen** to eat one's fill (of sth); **wie soll sie ihre Kinder ~ kriegen?** *(col)* how is she supposed to feed her children?; **er ist kaum ~ zu kriegen** *(col: lit, fig)* he's insatiable; **er konnte sich an ihr nicht ~ sehen** he could not see enough of her; **jdn/etw ~ haben** *or* **sein** to be fed up with sb/sth *(col)*. **(b)** *(blasiert, übersättigt)* well-fed; *(selbstgefällig)* smug. **(c)** *(kräftig, voll) Farben* rich, full.
Sattel *m* ¨ saddle. **ohne** ~ bareback; **er ist in allen** ¨~**n gerecht** *or* **sicher** *(fig)* he can turn his hand to anything; **fest im ~ sitzen** *(fig)* to be firmly in the saddle.
Sattel-: ~**dach** *nt* saddle roof; ~**decke** *f* saddle-cloth; **s~fest** *adj* **s~fest sein** *(Reiter)* to have a good seat; **in etw** *(dat)* **s~fest sein** *(fig)* to have a firm grasp of sth.
satteln *vt Pferd* to saddle (up). **für etw gesattelt sein** *(fig)* to be ready for sth.
Sattel-: ~**schlepper** *m* articulated lorry *(Brit)*, semitrailer *(US)*, semi *(US col)*; ~**tasche** *f* saddlebag; *(Gepäcktasche am Fahrrad)* pannier.
Sattheit *f* **(a)** *(Gefühl)* feeling of being full. **(b)** *(Selbstgefälligkeit)* smugness, self-satisfaction. **(c)** *(von Farben)* richness, fullness.
sättigen 1 *vt* **(a)** *Hunger, Neugier* to satisfy, to satiate. **ich bin gesättigt** I am replete. **(b)** *(Comm, Chem)* to saturate. **2** *vi* to be filling. **3** *vr* **sich an etw** *(dat) or* **mit etw** ~ to eat one's fill of sth.
sättigend *adj Essen* filling.
Sättigung *f* **(a)** *(geh: Sattsein)* repletion. **die ~ der Hungrigen** the feeding of the hungry. **(b)** *(Chem, Comm)* saturation.
Sättigungs-: ~**grad** *m* degree of saturation; ~**punkt** *m* saturation point.
Sattler *m* **-** saddler; *(Polsterer)* upholsterer.
sattsam *adv* amply; *bekannt* sufficiently.
Saturn *m (Astron)* Saturn.
Satz *m* **-es,** ¨**-e (a)** sentence; *(Teilsatz)* clause; *(Jur: Gesetzabschnitt)* clause. **ich kann nur ein paar** ¨~**e Italienisch** I only know a few phrases of Italian. **(b)** *(Lehr~, Philos)* proposition; *(Math)* theorem. **(c)** *(Typ) (das Setzen)* setting; *(das Gesetzte)* type *no pl*. **das Buch ist im ~** the book is being set. **(d)** *(Mus)* movement. **(e)** *(Boden~)* dregs *pl*; *(Kaffee~)* grounds *pl*. **(f)** *(Zusammengehöriges)* set. **(g)** *(Sport)* set; *(Tischtennis)* game. **(h)** *(Tarif~)* charge; *(Spesen~)* allowance. **(i)** *(Sprung)* leap, jump. **einen ~ machen** to leap, to jump; **mit einem** ~ in one leap *or* bound.
Satz-: ~**ball** *m (Sport)* set point; *(Tischtennis)* game point; ~**bau** *m* sentence construction; ~**teil** *m* part of a/the sentence.
Satzung *f* constitution, statutes *pl*; *(Vereins~)* rules *pl*.
satzungsgemäß *adj* according to the statutes/rules.
Satzzeichen *nt* punctuation mark.
Sau *f, pl* **Säue** *or (Hunt)* **-en (a)** sow; *(col: Schwein)* pig; *(Hunt)* wild boar. **die ~ rauslassen** *(fig col)* to let it all hang out *(col)*; **wie eine gesengte** ~ *(col)* like a maniac *(col)*. **(b)** *(pej col: Schmutzfink)* dirty swine *(col)*; *(Frau auch)* bitch *(col)*. **(c)** *(fig col)* **jdn zur ~ machen** to bawl sb out *(col)*; **unter aller** ~ bloody *(Brit col) or* goddamn *(col)* awful.
sauber *adj* **(a)** *(rein, reinlich)* clean. ~ **sein** *(Hund etc)* to be house-trained; *(Kind)* to be (potty-)trained. **(b)** *(ordentlich)* neat, tidy; *(exact)* accurate. **(c)** *(anständig)* honest, upstanding. **(d)** *(col: großartig)* fantastic, great. **du bist mir ja ein ~er Freund!** *(iro)* a fine friend you are! *(iro)*.
sauberhalten *vt sep irreg* to keep clean.
Sauberkeit *f* **(a)** cleanness; *(Hygiene, Ordentlichkeit)* cleanliness. **(b)** *(Anständigkeit)* honesty.
säuberlich *adj* neat and tidy. **fein** ~ neatly and tidily.
saubermachen *vt sep* to clean.
säubern *vt* **(a)** to clean. **(b)** *(fig euph) Partei, Buch* to purge *(von* of*)*; *Saal, (Mil) Gegend* to clear *(von* of*)*.
Säuberung *f siehe vt* **(a)** cleaning. **(b)** purging; clearing; *(Pol: Aktion)* purge.
Säuberungs|aktion *f* cleaning-up operation; *(Pol)* purge.
Sau-: **s~blöd** *adj (col)* bloody *(Brit col) or* damn *(col)* stupid; ~**bohne** *f* broad bean.
Sauce ['zo:sə] *f* **-n** sauce; *(Braten~)* gravy.
Sauciere [zo'sie:rə, -'sie:rə] *f* **-n** sauce boat.
Saudi-: ~**-Arabien** *nt* Saudi Arabia; **s~arabisch** *adj* Saudi *attr*, Saudi-Arabian.
saudumm *adj (col)* damn stupid *(col)*. **sich ~ benehmen** to behave like a stupid idiot *(col)*.
sauer *adj* **(a)** *(nicht süß)* sour; *Wein, Bonbons* acid(ic), sharp. **saure Drops** acid drops. **(b)** *(verdorben)* off *pred (Brit)*, spoiled *(US)*. ~ **werden** *(Milch, Sahne)* to go sour, to turn. **(c)** *Gurke, Hering* pickled; *Sahne* soured. **(d)** *(Chem)* acid(ic). **Saurer Regen** acid rain. **(e)** *(col: schlecht gelaunt) (auf +acc* with*)* mad *(col)*, cross. ~ **reagieren** to get annoyed. **(f) das habe ich mir ~ verdient** I got that the hard way; **jdm das Leben ~ machen** to make sb's life a misery; **gib ihm Saures!** *(col)* let him have it! *(col)*.
Sauer-: ~**ampfer** *m* sorrel; ~**braten** *m* braised beef (marinaded in vinegar), sauerbraten *(US)*.
Sauerei *f (col)* **(a)** *(Unflätigkeit)* ~**en erzählen** to tell filthy stories. **(b) so eine ~!** it's a bloody *(esp Brit col) or* downright disgrace. **(c)** *(Dreck)* mess.
Sauer-: ~**kirsche** *f* sour cherry; ~**kraut** *nt* sauerkraut, pickled cabbage.
säuerlich *adj (lit, fig)* sour; *Wein auch* sharp.
Sauermilch *f* sour milk.
Sauerstoff *m no pl* oxygen.
Sauerstoff- *in cpds* oxygen; ~**flasche** *f* oxygen cylinder; ~**gerät** *nt* breathing apparatus; *(Med) (für künstliche Beatmung)* respirator; *(für Erste Hilfe)* resuscitator; **s~haltig** *adj* containing oxygen; ~**mangel** *m* lack of oxygen; *(akut)* oxygen deficiency; ~**zufuhr** *f* oxygen supply.
Sauer-: ~**teig** *m* sour dough; **s~töpfisch** *adj (pej col)* sour; *Mensch auch* sour-faced.
saufen *pret* **soff,** *ptp* **gesoffen** *vti* **(a)** *(Tiere)* to drink. **(b)** *(col: Mensch)* to booze *(col)*, to drink. **das S~** boozing; **wie ein Loch ~** to drink like a fish.
Säufer(in *f***)** *m* **-** *(col)* boozer *(col)*, drunkard.
Sauferei *f (col)* **(a)** *(Trinkgelage)* booze-up *(col)*. **(b)** *no pl (Trunksucht)* boozing *(col)*.

Säuferleber *f (col)* gin-drinker's liver *(col)*.
Sauf-: ~**gelage** *nt (pej col)* drinking bout, booze-up *(col)*; ~**kumpan** *m (pej col)* drinking pal.
saugen *pret* **sog** *or* **saugte,** *ptp* **gesogen** *or* **gesaugt** *vti* to suck; *(col: mit Staubsauger)* to vacuum. **an etw** *(dat)* ~ to suck sth; *an Pfeife* to draw on sth.
säugen *vt* to suckle.
Sauger *m* - **(a)** *(auf Flasche)* teat *(Brit)*, nipple *(US)*. **(b)** *(col: Staub~)* vacuum (cleaner).
Säugetier *nt* mammal.
Saug-: **s**~**fähig** *adj* absorbent; ~**fähigkeit** *f* absorbency.
Säugling *m* baby, infant *(form)*.
Säuglings- *in cpds* baby, infant *(form)*; ~**alter** *nt* babyhood; **das Kind ist noch im** ~**alter** the child is still a baby; ~**heim** *nt* home for babies; ~**pflege** *f* babycare; ~**schwester** *f* infant nurse; ~**sterblichkeit** *f* infant mortality.
Saug-: ~**napf** *m* sucker; ~**rohr** *nt* pipette.
Sau-: ~**haufen** *m (col)* bunch of layabouts *(col)*; **s**~**kalt** *adj (col)* bloody *(esp Brit col) or* damn *(col)* cold; ~**klaue** *f (col)* scrawl *(col)*.
Säule *f* **-n** column; *(col: Pfeiler, fig: Stütze)* pillar.
Saum *m, pl* **Säume** hem; *(Naht)* seam.
saumäßig *(col)* **1** *adj* lousy *(col)*; *(zur Verstärkung)* hell of a *(col)*. **2** *adv siehe adj* lousily; like hell.
säumen *vt (Sew)* to hem; *(fig geh)* to line.
säumig *adj (geh) Schuldner* defaulting; *Zahlung* outstanding, overdue.
saumselig *adj (geh)* dilatory.
Sauna *f, pl* **-s** *or* **Saunen** sauna.
Säure *f* **-n** **(a)** *(Chem, Magen~)* acid. **(b)** *siehe* **sauer (a)** sourness; acidity.
Säure-: **s**~**arm** *adj* low in acid; **s**~**frei** *adj* acid-free; ~**gehalt** *m* acid content.
Sauregurkenzeit *f (hum col)* bad time *or* period; *(in den Medien)* silly season.
säurehaltig *adj* acidic.
Saurier [-iɐ] *m* - dinosaur, saurian *(spec)*.
Saus *m*: **in** ~ **und Braus leben** to live like a lord.
säuseln **1** *vi (Wind)* to murmur, to sigh; *(Blätter)* to rustle; *(Mensch)* to purr. **2** *vt* to murmur, to purr.
sausen *vi* **(a)** *(Ohren, Kopf)* to buzz; *(Wind)* to whistle; *(Sturm)* to roar. **(b)** *aux sein (Geschoß, Peitsche)* to whistle. **(c)** *aux sein (col: Mensch)* to tear *(col)*, to charge *(col)*; *(Fahrzeug)* to roar. **in den Graben** ~ to fly into the ditch; **durch eine Prüfung** ~ to fail *or* flunk *(col)* an exam.
sausenlassen *vt sep irreg (col)* **jdn/etw** ~ to drop sb/sth; **das Kino heute abend laß ich sausen** I'll not bother going to the cinema tonight.
Sau-: ~**stall** *m (col)* pigsty *(col)*; ~**wetter** *nt (col)* bloody *(Brit col) or* damn *(col)* awful weather; **s**~**wohl** *adj pred (col)* **ich fühle mich s**~**wohl** I feel bloody *(Brit col) or* really good.
Saxophon *nt* **-e** saxophone, sax *(col)*.
Saxophonist(in *f*) *m* saxophone player, saxophonist.
S-Bahn ['ɛs-] *f* = **Schnellbahn, Stadtbahn.**
S-Bahnhof ['ɛs-] *m* suburban line station.
Schabe *f* **-n** cockroach.
schaben *vt* to scrape; *Fleisch* to chop finely; *Leder, Fell* to shave.
Schaber *m* - scraper.
Schabernack *m* **-e** prank, practical joke. **mit jdm einen** ~ **treiben** to play a prank on sb.
schäbig *adj* **(a)** *(abgetragen)* shabby. **(b)** *Kerl* mean; *Behandlung, Bezahlung* shabby.
Schäbigkeit *f siehe adj* **(a)** shabbiness. **(b)** meanness, shabbiness.
Schablone *f* **-n** **(a)** stencil; *(Muster)* template. **(b)** *(fig pej) (bei Arbeit, Arbeitsweise)* routine, pattern; *(beim Reden)* cliché. **in** ~**n denken** to think in a stereotyped way; **etw geht nach** ~ sth follows the same routine.
Schach *nt no pl* chess; *(Stellung im Spiel)* check. ~ **(dem König)!** check; ~ **und matt** checkmate; **im** ~ **stehen** to be in check; **jdn in** ~ **halten** *(fig)* to stall sb; *(mit Pistole etc)* to keep sb covered.
Schach-: ~**brett** *nt* chessboard; **s**~**brettartig** *adj* chequered *(Brit)*, checkered *(US)*; ~**brettmuster** *nt* chequered *(Brit) or* checkered *(US)* pattern.
schachern *vi (pej)* **um etw** ~ to haggle over sth.
Schach-: ~**feld** *nt* square (on a chessboard); ~**figur** *f* chess piece; *(fig)* pawn; **s**~**matt** *adj (lit)* (check)mated; *(fig: erschöpft)* exhausted; **s**~**matt!** (check)mate; **jdn s**~**matt setzen** *(lit)* to (check)mate sb; *(fig)* to snooker sb *(col)*; ~**partie** *f* game of chess; ~**spiel** *nt (Spiel)* game of chess; *(Spielart)* chess *no art; (Brett und Figuren)* chess set; ~**spieler** *m* chess player.
Schacht *m* **-e** shaft; *(Brunnen~)* well.
Schachtel *f* **-n** **(a)** box; *(Zigaretten~)* packet, pack. **eine** ~ **Pralinen** a box of chocolates. **(b)** *(pej: Frau)* bag *(col)*.
Schachtelsatz *m* complicated *or* multi-clause sentence.
Schach-: ~**turnier** *nt* chess tournament; ~**zug** *m* *(fig)* move.
schade *adj pred* **(das ist aber)** ~! what a pity *or* shame; **es ist** ~ **um jdn/etw** it's a pity *or* shame about sb/sth; **um sie ist es nicht** ~ she's no great loss; **für etw zu** ~ **sein** to be too good for sth; **sich** *(dat)* **für etw zu** ~ **sein** to consider oneself too good for sth.
Schädel *m* - skull. **mir brummt der** ~ *(col)* my head is spinning; *(vor Kopfschmerzen)* my head is throbbing; **einen dicken** ~ **haben** *(fig col)* to be stubborn.
Schädel-: ~**bruch** *m* fractured skull; ~**decke** *f* top of the skull.
schaden *vi +dat* to damage, to harm; *einem Menschen* to harm, to hurt. **Rauchen schadet Ihnen** smoking is bad for you; **das schadet nichts** it does no harm; *(macht nichts)* that doesn't matter; **es kann nichts** ~**, wenn ...** it wouldn't do any harm if ...; **das schadet dir gar nichts** it serves you right.
Schaden *m* ⸚ damage *no pl, no indef art (durch* caused by*)*; *(Personen~)* injury; *(Verlust)* loss; *(Unheil, Leid)* harm. **einen** ~ **verursachen** to cause damage; **ich habe einen** ~ **am Auto** my car has been damaged; ⸚ **an der Lunge** lung damage; ⸚ **aufweisen** to be defective; *(Organ)* to be damaged; **es soll sein** ~ **nicht sein** it will not be to his disadvantage; **den** ~ **von etw haben** to suffer for sth; **zu** ~ **kommen** to suffer; *(physisch)* to be injured; **an etw** *(dat)* ~ **nehmen** *(geh)* to damage sth; **jdm** ~ **zufügen** to harm sb; ~ **von etw abwenden** *(liter)* to preserve sth from harm; **durch** ~ **wird man klug** *(Prov)* you learn by your mistakes.
Schadenersatz *m* compensation. ~ **leisten** to pay compensation.
Schadenersatz-: ~**anspruch** *m* claim for compensation; **s**~**pflichtig** *adj* liable for compensation.
Schaden-: ~**freude** *f* malicious glee, gloating; ... **sagt er mit** ~**freude ...** he gloated; **s**~**froh** *adj* gloating.
schadhaft *adj no adv* faulty, defective; *(beschädigt)* damaged; *(abgenutzt) Kleidung* worn; *Zähne* decayed; *Gebäude* dilapidated.
schädigen *vt* to damage; *jdn* to hurt, to harm.
Schädigung *f siehe vt (gen* done to*)* damage; hurt, harm.
schädlich *adj* harmful; *Wirkung, Einflüsse* detrimental, damaging. ~ **für etw sein** to be damaging to sth.
Schädlichkeit *f* harmfulness.
Schädling *m* pest.
Schädlings-: ~**bekämpfung** *f* pest control *no art;* ~**bekämpfungsmittel** *nt* pesticide.
schadlos *adj* **sich an jdm** ~ **halten** to claim com-

pensation from sb.
Schadstoff *m* harmful substance.
Schaf *nt* **-e** sheep; *(col: Dummkopf)* twit *(Brit col)*, dope *(col)*. **das schwarze ~ sein** to be the black sheep *(in +dat, gen* of*)*.
Schafbock *m* ram.
Schäfchen *nt* lamb, little sheep. **~** *pl (hum col: Anvertraute)* flock *sing*; **sein ~ ins trockene bringen** *(prov)* to see oneself all right *(col)*.
Schäfer *m* **-** shepherd.
Schäferhund *m* alsatian (dog) *(Brit)*, German shepherd (dog).
Schäferin *f* shepherdess.
Schäferstündchen *nt (euph hum)* bit of hanky-panky *(hum col)*.
Schaffell *nt* sheepskin.
Schaffen *nt no pl* **die Freude am ~** the joy of creation; **sein künstlerisches ~** his artistic creations *pl*.
schaffen[1] *pret* **schuf**, *ptp* **geschaffen** *vt* to create; *(herstellen)* to make. **dafür ist er wie geschaffen** he's just made for it; **Platz ~** to make room; **Ruhe ~** to establish order.
schaffen[2] **1** *vt* **(a)** *(bewältigen)* to manage; *Prüfung* to pass. **schaffst du's noch?** *(col)* can you manage?; **so, das wäre geschafft!** there, that's done; **das ist nicht zu ~** that can't be done; **wir haben nicht viel geschafft** we haven't got much done. **(b)** *(col: überwältigen) jdn* to see off *(col)*. **das hat mich geschafft** it took it out of me; *(nervlich)* it got on top of me; **geschafft sein** to be shattered *(col)*. **(c)** *(bringen)* **wie sollen wir das auf den Berg ~?** how will we manage to get that up the mountain?; **einen Koffer zum Bahnhof ~** to take *or* get a case to the station. **(d)** *(verursachen) Ärger, Unruhe* to cause, to create.
2 *vi* **(a)** *(tun)* to do. **ich habe damit nichts zu ~** that has nothing to do with me; **was haben Sie dort zu ~?** what do you think you're doing (there)?; **sich** *(dat)* **an etw** *(dat)* **zu ~ machen** to fiddle about with sth. **(b)** *(zusetzen)* **(jdm schwer) zu ~ machen** to cause sb (a lot of) trouble; *(bekümmern)* to worry sb (a lot). **(c)** *(S Ger: arbeiten)* to work.
Schaffenskraft *f* creativity.
Schaffner(in *f***)** *m* **-** *(im Bus)* conductor/conductress; *(Rail)* guard *(Brit)*, conductor/conductress *(US)*.
Schaf-: ~herde *f* flock of sheep; **~hirt** *m* shepherd.
Schafott *nt* **-e** scaffold.
Schafs-: ~käse *m* sheep's milk cheese; **~milch** *f* sheep's milk.
Schaft *m* **¨-e** shaft *(auch Archit)*; *(von Gewehr)* stock; *(von Stiefel)* leg; *(von Schlüssel)* shank.
Schaftstiefel *pl* high boots *pl*; *(Mil)* jackboots *pl*.
Schaf-: ~wolle *f* sheep's wool; **~zucht** *f* sheep breeding *no art*.
Schakal *m* **-e** jackal.
Schal *m* **-s** *or* **-e** scarf; *(Umschlagtuch)* shawl.
schal *adj Getränk* flat; *Wasser, Geschmack* stale; *(fig: geistlos) Witz* stale, weak.
Schale *f* **-n (a)** *(Schüssel)* bowl; *(flach)* dish; *(von Waage)* pan. **(b)** *(von Obst, Gemüse)* skin; *(abgeschält)* peel *no pl*; *(von Nüssen, Eiern, Muscheln)* shell; *(von Getreide)* husk. **sich in ~ werfen** *(col)* to get dressed up; **in seiner rauhen ~ steckt ein guter Kern** beneath that rough exterior (there) beats a heart of gold *(prov)*.
schälen 1 *vti* to peel; *Tomate, Mandel* to skin; *Erbsen, Eier, Nüsse* to shell; *Getreide* to husk. **2** *vr* to peel. **sich aus den Kleidern ~** to peel off (one's clothes).
Schalk *m* **-e** *or* **¨-e** *(dated)* joker. **ihm sitzt der ~ im Nacken** he's in a devilish mood.
Schall *m* **-e** *or* **¨-e** sound. **Name ist ~ und Rauch** what's in a name?; **das ist alles ~ und Rauch** it's all hollow words.
Schall-: s~dämmend *adj* sound-deadening; **~dämpfer** *m* sound absorber; *(von Auto)* silencer *(Brit)*, muffler *(US)*; *(von Gewehr etc)* silencer; *(Mus)* mute; **~dämpfung** *f* sound absorption; *(Abdichtung gegen Schall)* soundproofing; **s~dicht** *adj* soundproof.
schallen *vi* to sound; *(Stimme, Glocke, Beifall)* to ring (out); *(widerhallen)* to resound, to echo.
schallend *adj Beifall, Ohrfeige* resounding; *Gelächter* ringing. **~ lachen** to roar with laughter.
Schall-: ~geschwindigkeit *f* speed of sound; **~grenze, ~mauer** *f* sound barrier.
Schallplatte *f* record.
Schallplatten- *in cpds* record; **~album** *nt* record case.
schalt *pret of* **schelten.**
Schalt-: ~anlage *f* switchgear; **~bild** *nt* circuit diagram; **~brett** *nt* switchboard.
schalten 1 *vt* to switch, to turn. **etw auf „2" ~** to switch sth to "2"; **in Reihe/parallel ~** *(Elec)* to connect in series/in parallel. **2** *vi* **(a)** *(Gerät)* to switch *(auf +acc* to*)*; *(Aut)* to change gear. **in den 2. Gang ~** to change *or* shift *(US)* (up/down) into 2nd gear. **(b) ~ und walten** to bustle around; **frei ~ (und walten) können** to have a free hand. **(c)** *(col: begreifen)* to latch on *(col)*, to get it *(col)*; *(reagieren)* to react.
Schalter *m* **- (a)** *(Elec etc)* switch. **(b)** *(in Post, Bank, Amt)* counter; *(im Bahnhof)* ticket window.
Schalter-: ~beamte(r) *m* counter clerk; *(im Bahnhof)* ticket clerk; **~halle** *f (in Post)* hall; *(in Bank)* (banking) hall; *(im Bahnhof)* booking hall; **~stunden** *pl* hours of business *pl*.
Schalt-: ~hebel *m* switch lever; *(Aut)* gear lever *(Brit)*, gearshift; **an den ~hebeln der Macht sitzen** to hold the reins of power; **~jahr** *nt* leap year; **~knüppel** *m (Aut)* gear lever *(Brit)*, gearshift; *(Aviat)* joystick; **~kreis** *m* **integrierter ~kreis** integrated circuit; **~plan** *m* circuit diagram; **~pult** *nt* control desk; **~stelle** *f (fig)* co-ordinating point; **~tag** *m* leap day.
Schaltung *f* switching; *(Elec)* wiring; *(Aut)* gear change, gearshift.
Scham *f no pl* **(a)** shame. **er wurde rot vor ~** he went red with shame; **er versteckte sich vor ~** he hid himself in shame; **nur keine falsche ~!** *(col)* no need to be embarrassed!; **ohne ~** unashamedly. **(b)** *(geh: Genitalien)* private parts *pl*; *(von Frau)* pudenda *pl*.
Schambein *nt* pubic bone.
schämen *vr* to be ashamed. **du solltest dich ~!** you ought to be ashamed of yourself!; **sich wegen jdn/etw ~** to be ashamed of sb/sth; **sich für jdn ~** to be ashamed for sb; **sich vor jdm ~** to feel ashamed in front of sb.
Scham-: ~gefühl *nt* sense of shame; **~gegend** *f* pubic region; **~haar** *nt* pubic hair; **s~haft** *adj* modest; *(verschämt)* bashful, coy; **~lippen** *pl* labia *pl*, lips *pl* of the vulva; **s~los** *adj* shameless; *(unanständig auch)* indecent; *Lüge* brazen, barefaced; **sich s~los kleiden** to dress indecently; **~losigkeit** *f siehe adj* shamelessness; indecency.
schamponieren* *vt* to shampoo.
Scham-: s~rot *adj* red (with shame); **~röte** *f* blush of shame; **die ~röte stieg ihr ins Gesicht** her face flushed with shame; **~teile** *pl* private parts *pl*, genitals *pl*.
Schande *f no pl* disgrace. **~ über jdn bringen** to disgrace sb; **jdm/einer Sache ~ machen** to be a disgrace to sb/sth; **zu meiner ~ muß ich gestehen, ...** to my shame I have to admit that ...
schänden *vt* to violate; *Ansehen, Namen* to dishonour *(Brit)*, to dishonor *(US)*, to discredit.
Schandfleck *m* blot *(in +dat* on*)*. **er war der ~ der Familie** he was the disgrace of his family.
schändlich *adj* disgraceful, shameful.
Schändlichkeit *f* disgracefulness, shamefulness.

Schand-: ~**mal** *nt* brand, stigma; ~**tat** *f* disgraceful deed; *(hum)* escapade; **zu jeder ~tat bereit sein** *(col)* to be always ready for mischief *(col)*.

Schändung *f siehe vt* violation; dishonouring, dishonoring.

Schank-: ~**betrieb** *m* bar service; ~**erlaubnis** *f* licence *(of publican) (Brit)*, excise license *(US)*; ~**tisch** *m* bar.

Schanze *f* **-n** *(Mil)* fieldwork, entrenchment; *(Sport)* (ski-)jump.

Schar *f* **-en** crowd, throng *(liter)*; *(von Vögeln)* flock; *(von Insekten etc)* swarm. **die Menschen kamen in (hellen) ~en nach Lourdes** people flocked to Lourdes.

scharen 1 *vt* **Menschen um sich ~** to gather people around one. **2** *vr* **sich um jdn ~** to gather around sb.

scharenweise *adv (in bezug auf Menschen)* in droves. **die Heuschrecken fielen ~ über die Saat her** swarms of locusts descended on the seedcrop.

scharf *adj comp* **¨er,** *superl* **¨ste(r, s)** *or (adv)* **am ¨sten (a)** sharp; *Verstand, Augen auch, Beobachter* keen; *Kälte, Wind* biting; *Auseinandersetzung, Konkurrenz, Protest* fierce; *Ton* piercing, shrill; *Brille* sharply focusing. **ein Messer ~ machen** to sharpen a knife; **etw aufs ¨ste verurteilen** to condemn sth in the strongest possible terms; **etw ~ einstellen** *Bild, Diaprojektor etc* to bring sth into focus; *Sender* to tune sth in (properly); ~ **aufpassen/zuhören** to pay close attention/to listen closely; **jdn ~ ansehen** to give sb a scrutinizing look; *(mißbilligend)* to look sharply at sb; ~ **nachdenken** to have a good *or* long think, to think long and hard; ~ **kalkulieren** to calculate exactly; **mit ~em Blick** *(fig)* with penetrating insight; ~ **bremsen** to brake sharply *or* hard.

(b) *(hart, streng) Maßnahmen* severe; *(col) Prüfung* strict, tough; *Lehrer, Polizist* tough; *Bewachung* close, tight; *Hund* fierce. **jdn ~ bewachen** to guard sb closely.

(c) *(stark gewürzt)* hot; *(mit Salz, Pfeffer)* highly seasoned; *Geruch, Geschmack* pungent, acrid; *Getränk (stark)* strong; *(brennend)* fiery; *Waschmittel, Lösung* caustic. ~ **würzen** to season highly; **Fleisch ~ anbraten** to sear meat; **~e Sachen** *(col)* hard stuff *(col)*.

(d) *(echt) Munition etc, Schuß* live. **etw ~ machen** to arm sth; **~e Schüsse abgeben** to fire live bullets; ~ **schießen** *(lit) (mit ~er Munition)* to shoot with live ammunition; *(auf den Mann)* to aim to hit.

(e) *(col) (geil)* randy *(Brit col)*, horny *(col)*; *(aufreizend)* sexy *(col)*; *Film* sexy *(col)*, blue *attr*; *(aufregend) Auto, Film* cool *(col)*, great *(col)*. **jdn ~ machen** to turn sb on *(col)*; **auf jdn/etw ~ sein** to be keen on sb/sth *(col)*, to fancy sb/sth *(col)*.

Scharfblick *m (fig)* perspicacity, keen insight.

Schärfe *f* **-n** *siehe adj* **(a)** sharpness; keenness; bite; ferocity; shrillness; *(an Kamera, Fernsehen)* focus. **(b)** severity; toughness; closeness, tightness. **(c)** hotness; pungency.

Scharf|einstellung *f* focusing.

schärfen *vt (lit, fig)* to sharpen.

Scharf-: **s~machen** *vt sep (col)* to stir up; ~**macher** *m (col)* agitator; ~**richter** *m* executioner; ~**schütze** *m* marksman; **s~sichtig** *adj* sharp-sighted; *(fig)* perspicacious; ~**sinn** *m* astuteness; **s~sinnig** *adj* astute.

Scharlach *m* **(a)** *no pl* scarlet. **(b)** *(auch* ~**fieber***)* scarlet fever.

scharlachrot *adj* scarlet (red).

Scharlatan *m* **-e** charlatan; *(Arzt auch)* quack.

Scharnier -e, Scharniergelenk *nt* hinge.

Schärpe *f* **-n** sash.

scharren *vti* to scrape; *(Pferd, Hund)* to paw; *(Huhn)* to scratch.

Scharte *f* **-n** nick; *(Schieß~)* embrasure. **eine ~ auswetzen** *(fig)* to make amends.

Schaschlik *nt* **-s** (shish-)kebab.

schassen *vt (col)* to boot out *(col)*.

Schatten *m* **-** *(lit, fig)* shadow; *(schattige Stelle)* shade. **im ~ sitzen** to sit in the shade; **40 Grad im ~** 40 degrees in the shade; **einen ~ auf etw** *(acc)* **werfen** *(lit, fig)* to cast a shadow on sth; **große Ereignisse werfen ihre ~ voraus** great events are often foreshadowed; **in jds ~** *(dat)* **stehen** *(fig)* to be in sb's shadow; **jdn/etw in den ~ stellen** *(fig)* to put sb/sth in the shade; **nur noch ein ~ (seiner selbst) sein** to be (only) a shadow of one's former self; ~ **unter den Augen** shadows under the eyes.

Schatten-: ~**dasein** *nt* shadowy existence; **s~haft** *adj (lit, fig)* shadowy; ~**kabinett** *nt (Pol)* shadow cabinet; **s~los** *adj* shadowless; ~**morelle** *f* morello cherry; ~**riß** *m* silhouette; ~**seite** *f* shady side; *(fig: Nachteil)* drawback; **die ~seite(n) des Lebens** the dark side of life.

Schattierung *f (lit, fig)* shade.

schattig *adj* shady.

Schatulle *f* **-n** casket; *(Geld~)* coffer.

Schatz *m* **¨e (a)** *(lit, fig)* treasure. **¨e** *pl (Boden~)* natural resources *pl*; *(Reichtum)* riches *pl*, wealth *sing*. **(b)** *(Liebling)* sweetheart.

schätzbar *adj* assessable. **schwer ~** difficult to assess.

Schätzchen *nt* darling.

schätzen 1 *vt* **(a)** *(veranschlagen)* to estimate *(auf +acc* at*)*; *Gemälde etc* to value; *(col: annehmen)* to reckon. **die Besucherzahl wurde auf 500.000 geschätzt** the number of visitors was estimated at 500,000; **ich hätte sie älter geschätzt** I'd have said she was older. **(b)** *(würdigen)* to regard highly. **jdn ~** to think highly of sb; **etw zu ~ wissen** to appreciate sth; **sich glücklich ~** to consider oneself lucky. **2** *vi (veranschlagen, raten)* to guess. **schätz mal** have a guess.

Schatz-: ~**gräber** *m* **-** treasure-hunter; ~**kammer** *f* treasure chamber *or* vault; ~**kanzler** *m (Brit Pol)* Chancellor of the Exchequer.

Schätzung *f* estimate; *(das Schätzen)* estimation; *(von Wertgegenstand)* valuation. **nach meiner ~ ...** I reckon that ...

schätzungsweise *adv (so vermutet man)* it is estimated; *(ungefähr)* roughly; *(so schätze ich)* I think. **wann wirst du ~ kommen?** when do you think you'll come?

Schätzwert *m* estimated value.

Schau *f* **-en (a)** *(Vorführung)* show; *(Ausstellung auch)* display, exhibition. **etw zur ~ stellen** *(ausstellen)* to put sth on show, to display sth; *(fig)* to make a show of sth; *(protzen mit)* to show off sth; **etw zur ~ tragen** to display sth. **(b)** *(col)* **eine ~ abziehen** to put on a show; **das ist nur ~** it's only show; **jdm die ~ stehlen** to steal the show from sb.

Schaubild *nt* diagram; *(Kurve)* graph.

Schauder *m* **-** shudder; *(vor Angst, Kälte auch)* shiver.

schauderhaft *adj (fig col)* dreadful, awful.

schaudern *vi (vor Grauen, Abscheu)* to shudder; *(vor Kälte, Angst auch)* to shiver. **ihr schaudert vor ihm** he makes her shudder.

schauen 1 *vi* to look. **traurig** *etc* ~ to look sad *etc*; **um sich ~** to look around (one); **nach jdm/etw ~** *(suchen)* to look for sb/sth; *(sich kümmern um)* to look after sb/sth; **da schau her!** *(S Ger)* well, well!; **schau, daß du ...** see (that) you ... **2** *vt (geh)* to see, to behold *(old, liter)*. **Gott ~** to see God.

Schauer *m* **- (a)** *(Regen~)* shower. **(b)** *(Schauder)* shudder.

Schauergeschichte *f (col)* horror story.

schauerlich *adj* **(a)** horrific, horrible; *(gruselig)* eerie, creepy *(col)*. **(b)** *(col: fürchterlich)* dreadful, awful.

Schauermärchen *nt (col)* horror story.

Schaufel *f* **-n** shovel; *(kleiner: für Zucker etc)* scoop; *(Kehricht~)* dustpan; *(von Bagger)* scoop; *(von Schaufelrad)* paddle; *(von Turbine)* vane.

schaufeln *vti* to shovel; *Grab, Grube* to dig.

Schaufenster *nt* shop *(Brit) or* store *(US)* window.

Schaufenster-: **~auslage** *f* window display; **~bummel** *m* **einen ~bummel machen** to go window-shopping; **~dekorateur** *m* window-dresser; **~gestaltung** *f* window-dressing; **~puppe** *f* display dummy.

Schau-: **~geschäft** *nt* show business; **~kampf** *m* exhibition bout; **~kasten** *m* showcase.

Schaukel *f* **-n** swing.

schaukeln 1 *vi* **(a)** *(mit Schaukel)* to swing; *(im Schaukelstuhl)* to rock. **(b)** *(Fahrzeug)* to bounce (up and down); *(Schiff)* to pitch and toss. **2** *vt* to rock. **wir werden das Kind** *or* **das schon ~** *(col)* we'll manage it.

Schaukel-: **~pferd** *nt* rocking horse; **~stuhl** *m* rocking chair.

Schau-: **s~lustig** *adj* curious; **~lustige** *pl decl as adj* (curious) onlookers *pl.*

Schaum *m, pl* **Schäume** foam, froth; *(Seifen~)* lather; *(auf Getränken)* froth; *(von Bier)* head. **etw zu ~ schlagen** *(Cook)* to beat sth until frothy; **~ schlagen** *(fig col)* to talk a lot of hot air *(col).*

Schaumbad *nt* bubble bath.

schäumen *vi* to foam, to froth; *(Shampoo, Waschmittel)* to lather (up). **vor Wut ~** to be foaming with rage.

Schaumgummi *nt or m* foam rubber.

schaumig *adj siehe* **Schaum** frothy; lathery. **etw ~ schlagen** *(Cook)* to beat sth until frothy.

Schaum-: **~krone** *f* white crest; **~löffel** *m* skimmer; **~schläger** *m (fig col)* hot-air merchant *(col)*; **~schlägerei** *f (fig col)* hot air *(col)*; **~stoff** *m* foam material; **~wein** *m* sparkling wine.

Schau-: **~platz** *m* scene; **vom ~platz berichten** to give an on-the-spot report; **~prozeß** *m* show trial.

schaurig *adj* gruesome; *(col: sehr schlecht)* abysmal *(col).*

schaurig-schön *adj* gruesomely beautiful.

Schauspiel *nt (Theat)* drama, play; *(fig)* spectacle.

Schauspieler *m* actor, player; *(fig)* (play-)actor.

Schauspielerei *f* acting.

Schauspielerin *f (lit, fig)* actress.

schauspielerisch 1 *adj* acting. **2** *adv* as regards acting.

schauspielern *vi insep* to act.

Schauspiel-: **~haus** *nt* playhouse, theatre *(Brit),* theater *(US)*; **~schule** *f* drama school; **~unterricht** *m* drama classes *pl.*

Scheck *m* **-s** cheque *(Brit),* check *(US).* **mit (einem)** *or* **per ~ bezahlen** to pay by cheque; **ein ~ über DM 200** a cheque for DM 200.

Scheck-: **~betrug** *m* cheque *(Brit) or* check *(US)* fraud; **~betrüger** *m* cheque *(Brit) or* check *(US)* fraud; **~buch, ~heft** *nt* chequebook *(Brit),* checkbook *(US).*

scheckig *adj* spotted; *Pferd* dappled; *(verfärbt)* blotchy, patchy.

Scheckkarte *f* cheque card *(Brit),* banker's card.

scheel *adj* **jdn ~ ansehen** to give sb a dirty look; *(abschätzig)* to look askance at sb.

scheffeln *vt Geld* to rake in *(col).*

Scheibe *f* **-n (a)** disc, disk; *(Schieß~)* target; *(Eishockey)* puck; *(Wähl~)* dial; *(Tech: Dichtungs~)* washer; *(Töpfer~)* wheel; *(col: Schallplatte)* disc *(col).* **(b)** *(abgeschnittene ~)* slice. **etw in ~n schneiden** to cut sth (up) into slices; **von ihm könntest du dir eine ~ abschneiden** *(fig col)* you could take a leaf out of his book *(col).* **(c)** *(Glas~)* (window)pane.

Scheiben-: **~bremse** *f* disc brake; **~honig, ~kleister** *interj (euph col)* sugar! *(euph col)*; **~schießen** *nt* target shooting; **~waschanlage** *f* windscreen *(Brit) or* windshield *(US)* washers *pl*; **~wischer** *m* windscreen *(Brit) or* windshield *(US)* wiper.

Scheich *m* **-e** sheik(h).

Scheide *f* **-n** sheath; *(Vagina)* vagina.

scheiden *pret* **schied,** *ptp* **geschieden 1** *vt* **(a)** *(geh: trennen)* to separate. **(b)** *Ehe* to dissolve; *Eheleute* to divorce. **eine geschiedene Frau/ein geschiedener Mann** a divorcee; **sich ~ lassen** to get a divorce, to get divorced; **von dem Moment an waren wir (zwei) geschiedene Leute** *(col)* after that it was the parting of the ways for us *(col).* **2** *vi aux sein (liter) (sich trennen)* to part; *(weggehen)* to depart. **aus dem Amt ~** to retire from one's office; **aus dem Leben ~** to depart this life. **3** *vr (Wege)* to divide; *(Meinungen)* to diverge.

Scheideweg *m (fig)* crossroads *sing.* **am ~ weg stehen** to be at a crossroads.

Scheidung *f* **(a)** *(das Scheiden)* separation. **(b)** *(Ehe~)* divorce. **in ~ leben** to be getting a divorce; **die ~ einreichen** to file a petition for divorce.

Scheidungs-: **~grund** *m* grounds *pl* for divorce; *(hum: Mensch)* reason for his/her *etc* divorce; **~prozeß** *m* divorce proceedings *pl.*

Schein[1] *m no pl* **(a)** *(Licht)* light; *(matt)* glow. **(b)** *(An~)* appearances *pl*; *(Vortäuschung)* pretence *(Brit),* pretense *(US),* sham. **~ und Sein** appearance and reality; **den ~ wahren** to keep up appearances; **etw nur zum ~ tun** only to pretend to do sth.

Schein[2] *m* **-e** *(Geld~)* note *(Brit),* bill *(US)*; *(Bescheinigung)* certificate; *(Fahr~)* ticket.

scheinbar *adj* apparent; *(vorgegeben)* ostensible. **er hörte s~bar interessiert zu** he seemed to be listening with interest.

scheinen *pre* **schien,** *ptp* **geschienen** *vi* **(a)** *(leuchten)* to shine. **(b)** *auch vi impers (den Anschein geben)* to seem, to appear. **mir scheint, (daß) ...** it seems to me that ...; **wie es scheint** apparently.

Schein-: **~gefecht** *nt* mock fight; **s~heilig** *adj* hypocritical; *(Arglosigkeit vortäuschend)* innocent; **tu nicht so s~heilig!** don't pretend to be so innocent; **~heilige(r)** *mf siehe adj* hypocrite; sham; **~heiligkeit** *f siehe adj* hypocrisy; feigned innocence; **~tod** *m* apparent death; **~werfer** *m (zum Beleuchten)* floodlight; *(im Theater)* spotlight; *(Such~)* searchlight; *(Aut)* (head)light, headlamp.

Scheiß *m no pl (col!)* shit *(col!),* crap *(col!).* **mach keinen ~!** don't be so damn *(col)* silly.

Scheiß- *in cpds (col!)* bloody *(Brit col),* fucking *(col!!).*

Scheißdreck *m (col!)* shit *(col!),* crap *(col!)*; *(unangenehme Sache)* effing thing *(col!),* bloody thing *(Brit col).* **das geht dich einen ~ an** it's got bugger-all to do with you *(col!)*; **einen ~ werd' ich tun!** like hell I will!

Scheiße *f no pl (col!)* shit *(col!),* crap *(col!).* **~ sein** to be bloody awful *(Brit col) or* goddamn *(col)* awful; **~!** bloody hell! *(Brit col),* shit! *(col!),* bugger *(col!)*; **in der ~ sitzen** to be in the shit *(col!).*

scheiß|egal *adj (col!)* **das ist mir doch ~!** I don't give a shit *(col!).*

scheißen *pret* **schiß,** *ptp* **geschissen** *vi (col!)* to shit *(col!),* to crap *(col!).* **auf etw** *(acc)* **~** *(fig)* not to give a shit about sth *(col!).*

Scheißer *m* **-** *(col!: Arschloch)* bugger *(col!).*

Scheiß-: **s~freundlich** *adj (pej col)* as nice as pie *(iro col)*; **~haus** *nt (col!)* shithouse *(col!)*; **~kerl** *m (col!)* bastard *(col!),* son-of-a-bitch *(US col!).*

Scheit *m* **-e** log, piece of wood.

Scheitel *m* **- (a)** *(Haar~)* parting *(Brit),* part *(US).* **vom ~ bis zur Sohle** from top to toe. **(b)** *(höch-*

ster Punkt) vertex.
scheiteln *vt* to part.
Scheitelpunkt *m* vertex.
Scheiterhaufen *m* (funeral) pyre; *(Hist: zur Hinrichtung)* stake.
scheitern *vi aux sein (an +dat* because of) *(Mensch, Plan)* to fail; *(Verhandlungen, Ehe)* to break down; *(Regierung)* to founder *(an +dat* on).
Scheitern *nt no pl siehe vi* failure; breakdown; foundering. **das war zum ~ verurteilt** that was doomed to failure.
Schelle *f* **-n (a)** bell. **(b)** *(Tech)* clamp.
schellen *vi* to ring *(nach jdm* for sb). **es hat geschellt** the bell has gone; *(an der Tür)* that was the doorbell.
Schellfisch *m* haddock.
Schelm *m* **-e** *(dated: Spaßvogel)* rogue.
Schelmen-: ~roman *m* picaresque novel; **~streich** *m (dated)* roguish prank.
schelmisch *adj* mischievous.
Schelte *f* **-n** scolding.
schelten *pret* **schalt,** *ptp* **gescholten** *(geh)* **1** *vt* to scold. **jdn einen Dummkopf ~** to call sb a blockhead. **2** *vi (schimpfen)* to curse.
Schema *nt, pl* **Schemen** *or* **-ta** scheme; *(Darstellung)* diagram; *(Muster)* pattern.
schematisch *adj* schematic; *(pej)* mechanical.
Schemel *m* **-** stool.
schemenhaft 1 *adj* shadowy. **2** *adv* **etw ~ sehen/zeichnen** to see the outlines of sth/to sketch sth in.
Schenke *f* **-n** tavern, inn.
Schenkel *m* **- (a)** *(Anat: Ober~)* thigh. **sich** *(dat)* **auf die ~ schlagen** to slap one's thighs. **(b)** *(Math: von Winkel)* side.
schenken 1 *vt* **(a) jdm etw ~** to give sb sth (as a present); **etw geschenkt bekommen** to get sth as a present; **etw zum Geburtstag geschenkt bekommen** to get sth for one's birthday; **ich möchte nichts geschenkt haben!** *(lit)* I don't want any presents!; *(fig: bevorzugt werden)* I don't want any special treatment!; **das ist geschenkt!** *(col: nicht der Rede wert)* that's no great shakes *(col)*; **das ist (fast) geschenkt!** *(col: billig)* that's dirt cheap *(col)*, that's just about giving it away; **einem Kind das Leben ~** *(geh)* to give birth to a child; **jdm seine Aufmerksamkeit ~** to give sb one's attention; **jdm Vertrauen ~** to put one's trust in sb; **einem geschenkten Gaul sieht man nicht ins Maul** *(Prov)* don't look a gift-horse in the mouth *(Prov)*. **(b)** *(erlassen)* **jdm etw ~** to let sb off sth; **ihm ist nie etwas geschenkt worden** *(fig)* he never had it easy.
2 *vr* **sich** *(dat)* **etw ~** to skip sth *(col)*; **deine Komplimente kannst du dir ~!** you can keep your compliments *(col)*; **er hat sich** *(dat)* **nichts geschenkt** he spared no pains.
Schenkung *f (Jur)* gift.
scheppern *vi (col)* to clatter. **es hat gescheppert** *(Autounfall)* there was a bang.
Scherbe *f* **-n** fragment, (broken) piece; *(Glas~ etc)* broken piece of glass *etc.* **etw in ~n schlagen** to shatter sth; **in ~n gehen** to shatter; *(fig)* to fall to pieces; **~n bringen Glück** *(Prov)* broken crockery brings you luck.
Schere *f* **-n (a)** *(klein)* scissors *pl*; *(groß)* shears *pl*. **eine ~** a pair of scissors/shears. **(b)** *(Zool)* pincer; *(von Hummer, Krebs etc auch)* claw. **(c)** *(Turnen, Ringen)* scissors *sing.*
scheren[1] *pret* **schor,** *ptp* **geschoren** *vt* to clip; *Schaf, (Tech)* to shear; *Haare* to crop; *Bart (rasieren)* to shave; *(stutzen)* to trim.
scheren[2] *vtr* **(a) sich nicht um jdn/etw ~** not to care about sb/sth. **(b)** *(col)* **scher dich (weg)!** beat it! *(col)*; **scher dich ins Bett!** get to bed!
Scherenschnitt *m* silhouette.
Schererei *f usu pl (col)* trouble *no pl.*
Scherflein *nt* **sein ~ (zu etw) beitragen** *(Geld)* to contribute one's mite (towards sth); *(fig)* to do one's bit (for sth).
Scher-: ~kopf *m* shaving head; **~messer** *nt* shearing knife.
Scherz *m* **-e** joke. **zum/im ~** as a joke/in fun; **einen ~ machen** to make a joke; *(Streich)* to play a joke; **mach keine ~e!** *(col)* you're joking!; **(ganz) ohne ~!** *(col)* no kidding! *(col)*.
Scherz|artikel *m usu pl* joke (article).
scherzen *vi (geh)* to joke; *(albern)* to banter. **mit etw ist nicht zu ~** one can't trifle with sth.
Scherz-: ~frage *f* riddle; **s~haft** *adj* jocular; *(spaßig) Einfall* playful; **etw s~haft sagen** to say sth as a joke *or* in fun.
scheu *adj* shy. **mach doch die Pferde nicht ~** *(fig col)* keep your hair on *(col)*.
Scheu *f no pl* fear *(vor +dat* of); *(Schüchternheit)* shyness; *(Hemmung)* inhibition; *(Ehrfurcht)* awe. **seine ~ verlieren** to lose one's inhibitions.
scheuchen *vt* to shoo (away).
scheuen 1 *vt Kosten, Arbeit* to shy away from; *Menschen, Licht* to shun. **weder Mühe noch Kosten ~** to spare neither trouble nor expense. **2** *vr* **sich vor etw** *(dat)* **~** *(Angst haben)* to be afraid of sth; *(zurückschrecken)* to shy away from sth. **3** *vi (Pferd etc)* to shy *(vor +dat* at).
Scheuer *f* **-n** barn.
Scheuer-: ~besen *m* scrubbing broom; **~bürste** *f* scrubbing brush; **~lappen** *m* floorcloth.
scheuern 1 *vti* **(a)** *(putzen)* to scour; *(mit Bürste)* to scrub. **(b)** *(reiben)* to chafe. **(c) jdm eine ~** *(col)* to clout sb one *(col)*. **2** *vt* **sich (an etw** *dat*) **~** to rub (against sth); **sich** *(acc)* **(wund) ~** to chafe oneself.
Scheuer-: ~sand *m* scouring powder; **~tuch** *nt* floorcloth.
Scheuklappe *f* blinker. **~n haben** *(lit, fig)* to be blinkered.
Scheune *f* **-n** barn.
Scheunen-: ~drescher *m*: **wie ein ~ drescher fressen** *(col)* to eat like a horse *(col)*; **~tor** *nt* barn door.
Scheusal *nt, pl* **-e** *or (col)* **Scheusäler** monster.
scheußlich *adj* dreadful; *(abstoßend häßlich)* hideous. **es hat ~ weh getan** *(col)* it was terribly painful.
Scheußlichkeit *f siehe adj* dreadfulness; hideousness.
Schi *m* **-er** *or* **- = Ski.**
Schicht *f* **-en (a)** *(Lage)* layer; *(dünne ~)* film; *(Farb~)* coat; *(der Gesellschaft)* level, stratum. **breite ~en der Bevölkerung** large sections of the population. **(b)** *(Ind)* shift. **er muß ~ arbeiten** he has to work shifts.
Schicht-: ~arbeit *f* shift-work; **~arbeiter** *m* shift-worker.
schichten *vt* to layer; *Holz, Bücher etc* to stack.
Schichtung *f* layering; *(von Holz, Büchern etc)* stacking.
Schicht-: ~wechsel *m* change of shifts; **s~weise** *adv* in layers; *(Farbe, Lack)* in coats.
schick *adj* elegant, smart; *Frauenmode* chic; *Wohnung auch, Möbel* stylish; *Auto* smart.
schicken 1 *vti* to send. **jdn einkaufen ~** to send sb to do the shopping. **2** *vr, vr impers (sich ziemen)* to be fitting *or* proper. **3** *vr (dated: sich abfinden)* **sich in etw** *(acc)* **~** to resign *or* reconcile oneself to sth.
Schickeria *f no pl (iro)* in-people *pl.*
schicklich *adj Kleidung etc* proper, fitting; *Verhalten* seemly, becoming.
Schicksal *nt* **-e** fate, destiny; *(Pech)* fate. **das ~ wollte es, (daß) ...** as fate would have it, ...; **das sind (schwere) ~e** those are tragic cases; **er hat ein schweres ~ gehabt** fate has been unkind to him; **(das ist) ~** *(col)* that's life; **jdn seinem ~ überlassen** to leave sb to his fate.
schicksalhaft *adj* fateful.

Schicksals-: ~**frage** *f* fateful question; ~**schlag** *m* great misfortune, stroke of fate.
Schiebe-: ~**dach** *nt (Aut)* sunroof; ~**fenster** *nt* sliding window.
schieben *pret* **schob,** *ptp* **geschoben 1** *vt* **(a)** to push, to shove; *(stecken)* to put. **etw von sich** *(dat)* ~ *(fig)* to put sth aside; *Schuld, Verantwortung* to reject sth; **etw vor sich** *(dat)* **her** ~ *(fig)* to put off sth; **etw auf jdn/etw** ~ to put the blame for sth onto sb/sth. **(b)** *(col: handeln mit)* to traffic in; *Drogen* to push *(col).* **(c)** *(col)* **Wache** ~ to do guard duty. **2** *vi* **(a)** to push, to shove. **(b)** *(col)* **mit etw/Drogen** ~ to traffic in sth/push *(col)* drugs. **(c)** *(col: betrügen)* to wangle *(col).* **3** *vr* **(a)** *(mit Anstrengung)* to push, to shove. **(b)** *(sich bewegen)* to move.
Schieber *m* - **(a)** slide; *(am Ofen etc)* damper. **(b)** *(Schwarzhändler)* black marketeer; *(Waffen~)* gun-runner; *(Drogen~)* pusher *(col).*
Schiebetür *f* sliding door.
Schiebung *f (Betrug)* string-pulling; *(im Sport)* rigging; *(Schiebergeschäfte)* shady deals *pl.* **das war doch** ~ that was rigged *or* a fix.
schied *pret of* **scheiden.**
Schieds-: ~**gericht** *nt* court of arbitration; ~**richter** *m (Sport)* referee; *(Hockey, Tennis)* umpire; *(Preisrichter)* judge; ~**spruch** *m* (arbitral) award.
schief *adj* crooked, not straight *pred; (nach einer Seite geneigt)* lopsided, tilted; *Winkel* oblique; *Blick* wry; *Absätze* worn(-down); *(fig: unzutreffend)* inappropriate; *Bild* distorted. ~**e Ebene** *(Phys)* inclined plane; **auf die** ~**e Bahn geraten** *(fig)* to leave the straight and narrow; **du siehst die Sache ganz** ~**!** *(fig)* you're looking at it all wrong!; **jdn** ~ **ansehen** *(fig)* to look askance at sb.
Schiefer *m* - *(Gesteinsart)* slate.
Schiefer-: ~**dach** *nt* slate roof; ~**tafel** *f* slate.
schief-: ~**gehen** *vi sep irreg aux sein* to go wrong; **es wird schon** ~**gehen!** *(hum)* it'll be OK *(col);* ~**lachen** *vr sep (col)* to kill oneself (laughing) *(col);* ~**laufen** *vi sep irreg aux sein (col)* to go wrong; ~**liegen** *vi sep irreg (col)* to be wrong.
schielen *vi* to squint, to be cross-eyed. **auf etw** *(acc)* ~ *(col)* to steal a glance at sth; **nach etw** ~ to have an eye on sth; **er schielte auf ihre Beine** *(col)* he was ogling her legs.
schien *pret of* **scheinen.**
Schienbein *nt* shin; *(~knochen)* shinbone.
Schiene *f* **-n** rail; *(Med)* splint. ~**n** *(Rail)* track *sing,* rails *pl;* **aus den** ~**n springen** to leave *or* jump the rails.
schienen *vt Arm, Bein* to splint.
Schienen-: ~**bus** *m* rail bus; ~**fahrzeug** *nt* track vehicle; ~**netz** *nt (Rail)* rail network; ~**strang** *m* (section of) track.
schier 1 *adj* pure; *(fig)* sheer. **2** *adv (beinahe)* nearly, almost.
Schieß-: ~**befehl** *m* order to fire *or* shoot; ~**bude** *f* shooting gallery; ~**budenfigur** *f (fig col)* clown; ~**eisen** *nt (col)* shooting iron *(col).*
schießen *pret* **schoß,** *ptp* **geschossen 1** *vt* to shoot; *Kugel, Rakete* to fire; *Tor auch* to score. **jdn in den Kopf/Bauch** ~ to shoot sb in the head/stomach; **ein paar Bilder** ~ *(Phot col)* to take a few shots. **2** *vi* **(a)** to shoot. **auf jdn/etw** ~ to shoot at sb/sth; **aufs Tor** ~ to shoot at goal; **das ist zum S**~ *(col)* that's a scream *(col).* **(b)** *aux sein* to shoot; *(in die Höhe ~)* to shoot up. **aus dem Boden** ~ *(lit, fig)* to spring *or* sprout up; **er kam um die Ecke geschossen** he shot around the corner; **jdm durch den Kopf** ~ *(fig: Gedanke)* to flash through sb's mind; **das Blut schoß ihm ins Gesicht** blood rushed *or* shot to his face; **die Tränen schossen ihr in die Augen** tears flooded her eyes.
Schießerei *f* gun battle; *(das Schießen)* shooting.
Schieß-: ~**gewehr** *nt (hum)* gun; ~**hund** *m:* **wie ein** ~**hund aufpassen** *(col)* to watch like a hawk; ~**pulver** *nt* gunpowder; ~**scharte** *f* embrasure; ~**scheibe** *f* target.
Schiff *nt* **-e (a)** ship. **(b)** *(Archit) (Mittel~)* nave; *(Seiten~)* aisle; *(Quer~)* transept.
Schiffahrt *f* shipping; *(~skunde)* navigation.
Schiffahrts-: ~**gesellschaft** *f* shipping company; ~**linie** *f* **(a)** *(Schiffsweg)* shipping route; **(b)** *(Unternehmen)* shipping line; ~**straße** *f,* ~**weg** *m (Kanal)* waterway; *(~linie)* shipping lane.
Schiff-: **s~bar** *adj* navigable; ~**barkeit** *f* navigability; ~**bau** *m* shipbuilding; ~**bauer** *m* shipwright; ~**bruch** *m* shipwreck; ~**bruch erleiden** *(lit)* to be shipwrecked; *(fig)* to fail; *(Unternehmen)* to founder; **s~brüchig** *adj* shipwrecked; ~**brüchige(r)** *mf decl as adj* shipwrecked person.
Schiffchen *nt* **(a)** *(zum Spielen)* little boat. **(b)** *(Mil, Fashion)* forage cap. **(c)** *(Tex, Sew)* shuttle.
schiffen *(col)* **1** *vi (urinieren)* to piss *(col!).* **2** *vi impers (regnen)* to piss down *(col!).*
Schiffer *m* - boatman, sailor; *(von Lastkahn)* bargee; *(Kapitän)* skipper.
Schiffer-: ~**klavier** *nt* accordion; ~**knoten** *m* sailor's knot; ~**mütze** *f* yachting cap.
Schiffschaukel *f* swing boat.
Schiffs- *in cpds* ship's; ~**eigner** *m* shipowner; ~**junge** *m* ship's boy; ~**ladung** *f* shipload; ~**mannschaft** *f* ship's crew; ~**rumpf** *m* hull; ~**schraube** *f* ship's propeller; ~**verkehr** *m* shipping; ~**werft** *f* shipyard.
Schikane *f* **-n (a)** harassment. **das hat er aus reiner** ~ **gemacht** he did it out of sheer bloody-mindedness. **(b) mit allen** ~**n** *(col)* with all the trimmings. **(c)** *(Sport)* chicane.
schikanieren* *vt* to harass; *Ehepartner, Freundin etc* to mess around; *Mitschüler* to bully.
schikanös *adj Mensch* bloody-minded; *Maßnahme etc* harassing.
Schild[1] *m* **-e** shield; *(von ~kröte)* shell. **etwas/nichts Gutes im** ~**e führen** *(fig)* to be up to something/to be up to no good.
Schild[2] *nt* **-er** *(Aushang, Verkehrs~)* sign; *(Wegweiser)* signpost; *(Namens~)* nameplate; *(Aut)* number plate *(Brit),* license plate *(US); (Preis~)* ticket; *(Etikett)* label; *(Plakat)* placard; *(an Monument, Haus, Grab)* plaque; *(von Mütze)* peak.
Schilddrüse *f* thyroid gland.
schildern *vt* to describe; *(skizzieren)* to outline; *Menschen, Landschaften* to portray. ~ **Sie den Verlauf des Unfalls** give an account of how the accident happened.
Schilderung *f (Beschreibung)* description; *(Bericht)* account; *(literarische ~)* portrayal.
Schild-: ~**kröte** *f* tortoise; *(Wasser~)* turtle; ~**krötensuppe** *f* turtle soup; ~**laus** *f* scale insect.
Schilf *nt* **-e** reed.
Schilf-: ~**dach** *nt* thatched roof; ~**gras** *nt* reed; ~**rohr** *nt* reed.
Schillerlocke *f* **(a)** *(Gebäck)* cream horn. **(b)** *(Räucherfisch)* strip of smoked rock-salmon.
schillern *vi* to shimmer.
schillernd *adj* shimmering; *(in Regenbogenfarben)* iridescent; *(fig) Charakter* enigmatic.
Schimmel[1] *m* - *(Pferd)* white horse, grey *(Brit),* gray *(US).*
Schimmel[2] *m no pl* mould *(Brit),* mold *(US).*
schimm(e)lig *adj* mouldy *(Brit),* moldy *(US).* ~ **werden** to go mouldy.
schimmeln *vi aux sein or haben (Nahrungsmittel)* to go mouldy *(Brit) or* moldy *(US).*
Schimmelpilz *m* mould *(Brit),* mold *(US).*
Schimmer *m no pl* glimmer, gleam; *(von Perlen, Seide)* shimmer; *(im Haar)* sheen. **beim** ~ **der Lampe** in the soft glow of the lamp; **keinen (blassen)** ~ **von etw haben** *(col)* not to have the slightest *or* faintest idea about sth.
schimmern *vi* to glimmer, to gleam; *(Perlen,*

Seide) to shimmer.
Schimpanse *m (wk)* **-n, -n** chimpanzee, chimp *(col).*
Schimpf *m no pl* **mit ~ und Schande** in disgrace.
schimpfen 1 *vi* to get angry; *(sich beklagen)* to grumble; *(fluchen)* to swear, to curse. **mit jdm ~** to tell sb off; **auf** *or* **über jdn/etw ~** to bitch about sb/sth *(col)*, to curse (about *or* at) sb/sth. **2** *vt (pej: nennen)* to call. **3** *vr* **sich etw ~** *(col)* to call oneself sth.
Schimpf-: ~kanonade *f* barrage of abuse; **~name** *m* nickname; **~wort** *nt* swearword.
Schindel *f* **-n** shingle.
schinden *pret* **schindete,** *ptp* **geschunden 1** *vt* **(a)** *Gefangene, Tiere* to maltreat. **(b)** *(col: herausschlagen) Zeilen* to pad (out); *Arbeitsstunden* to pile up. **Zeit ~** to play for time; **Mitleid ~** to get some sympathy. **2** *vr (hart arbeiten)* to struggle. **sich mit etw ~** to slave away at sth.
Schinderei *f (Plackerei)* struggle; *(Arbeit)* slavery *no indef art.*
Schindluder *nt (col)* **mit jdm ~ treiben** to make sb suffer; **mit etw ~ treiben** to abuse sth.
Schinken *m* **- (a)** ham; *(gekocht und geräuchert auch)* gammon. **(b)** *(pej col)* hackneyed and clichéed play/book/film; *(großes Buch)* tome; *(großes Bild)* great daub *(pej col).*
Schinken-: ~speck *m* bacon; **~wurst** *f* ham sausage.
Schippe *f* **-n** *(esp NGer: Schaufel)* shovel, spade. **jdn auf die ~ nehmen** *(fig col)* to pull sb's leg *(col).*
schippen *vt* to shovel. **Schnee ~** to clear the snow.
Schirm *m* **-e** *(Regen~)* umbrella; *(Sonnen~)* sunshade, parasol; *(Mützen~)* peak; *(Röntgen~, Wand~, Bild~)* screen; *(Lampen~)* shade.
Schirm-: ~bild *nt* x-ray (picture); **~herr(in** *f*) *m* patron; *(Frau auch)* patroness; **~herrschaft** *f* patronage; **~mütze** *f* peaked cap; **~ständer** *m* umbrella stand.
schiß *pret of* **scheißen.**
Schiß *m no pl (col)* **(fürchterlichen) ~ haben** to be terrified *(vor +dat* of*).*
schizophren *adj* **(a)** *(Med)* schizophrenic. **(b)** *(pej: widersinnig)* contradictory.
Schizophrenie *f* **(a)** *(Med)* schizophrenia. **(b)** *(pej: Widersinn)* contradictoriness.
schlabbern *(col) vti* to slurp.
Schlacht *f* **-en** battle. **die ~ bei** *or* **um X** the battle of X; **jdm eine ~ liefern** to battle with sb.
schlachten 1 *vt* to slaughter; *(hum) Sparschwein* to break into. **2** *vi* **heute wird geschlachtet** we're/they're *etc* slaughtering today.
Schlachtenbummler *m (col: Sport)* visiting *or* away supporter *or* fan.
Schlachter(in *f*) *m* **-** *(esp NGer)* butcher.
Schlächter *m* **-** *(dial, fig)* butcher.
Schlachterei *f (esp NGer)* butcher's (shop) *(Brit)*, butcher.
Schlacht-: ~feld *nt* battle-field; **~fest** *nt a country feast to eat up meat from freshly slaughtered pigs;* **~hof** *m* slaughter-house, abattoir; **~messer** *nt* butcher's knife; **~opfer** *nt* sacrifice; *(Mensch)* human sacrifice; **~ordnung** *f* battle formation; **~plan** *m* battle plan; *(für Feldzug)* campaign plan; *(fig auch)* plan of action; **s~reif** *adj (lit, fig)* ready for the slaughter; **~ruf** *m* battle cry; **~schiff** *nt* battleship; *(col: Auto)* tank *(col).*
Schlachtung *f* slaughter(ing).
Schlachtvieh *nt no pl* animals *pl* for slaughter.
Schlacke *f* **-n** clinker *no pl*; *(Aschenteile auch)* cinders *pl*; *(Metal, Geol)* slag *no pl*; *(Physiol)* waste products *pl.*
schlackern *vi (col)* to tremble, to shake; *(Kleidung)* to hang loosely, to be baggy. **mit den Ohren ~** *(fig)* to be (left) speechless.
Schlaf *m no pl* sleep. **einen leichten/tiefen ~ haben** to be a light/deep sleeper; **keinen ~ finden** to be unable to sleep; **um seinen ~ kommen/gebracht werden** to lose sleep; *(überhaupt nicht schlafen)* not to get any sleep; **jdn um seinen ~ bringen** to keep sb awake; **~ haben** to be sleepy; **in tiefstem ~ liegen** to be sound *or* fast asleep; **das macht** *or* **kann er im ~** *(fig col)* he can do that in his sleep.
Schlaf|anzug *m* pyjamas *pl (Brit)*, pajamas *pl (US).*
Schläfchen *nt* nap, snooze. **ein ~ machen** to have a nap *or* snooze.
Schläfe *f* **-n** temple. **graue ~n** greying *(Brit) or* graying *(US)* temples.
schlafen *pret* **schlief,** *ptp* **geschlafen** *vi* to sleep; *(col: nicht aufpassen) (bei bestimmter Gelegenheit)* to be asleep; *(immer)* not to pay attention. **er schläft immer noch** he's still asleep, he's still sleeping; **~ gehen** to go to bed; **sich ~ legen** to go to sleep; **schläfst du schon?** are you asleep?; **lange ~** to sleep for a long time; *(spät aufstehen)* to sleep late, to have a long lie (in); **schlaf gut** sleep well; **bei jdm ~** to stay overnight with sb; **das läßt ihn nicht ~** *(fig)* it preys on his mind; **darüber muß ich erst mal ~** *(fig: überdenken)* I'll have to sleep on it; **mit jdm ~** *(euph)* to sleep with sb.
Schlafengehen *nt* going to bed. **vor dem ~** before going to bed.
Schlafenszeit *f* bedtime.
Schläfer(in *f*) *m* **-** sleeper; *(fig)* dozy person *(col).*
schlaff *adj* limp; *(locker) Seil* slack; *Disziplin* lax; *Haut* loose; *Muskeln* flabby; *(erschöpft)* worn-out *(col)*, exhausted; *(energielos)* listless.
Schlaffheit *f siehe adj* limpness; slackness; laxity; looseness; flabbiness; exhaustion; listlessness.
Schlafgelegenheit *f* place to sleep.
Schlafittchen *nt*: **jdn am** *or* **beim ~ nehmen** *(col)* to take sb by the scruff of the neck; *(zurechtweisen)* to give sb a dressing down *(col).*
Schlaf-: ~krankheit *f* sleeping sickness; **~lied** *nt* lullaby; **s~los** *adj (lit, fig)* sleepless; **~losigkeit** *f* sleeplessness, insomnia *(Med)*; **~mittel** *nt* sleeping pill; *(fig iro)* soporific; **~mütze** *f (col)* dope *(col)*; **s~mützig** *adj (col)* dozy *(col)*, dopey *(col)*; **~raum** *m* dormitory *(Brit)*, dorm *(Brit col).*
schläfrig *adj* sleepy; *Mensch auch* drowsy.
Schläfrigkeit *f siehe adj* sleepiness; drowsiness.
Schlaf-: ~rock *m* dressing-gown; **Äpfel im ~rock** baked apples in puff pastry; **~saal** *m* dormitory; **~sack** *m* sleeping-bag; **~stelle** *f* place to sleep; **~tablette** *f* sleeping pill; **s~trunken** *adv* drowsily, half-asleep; **~wagen** *m* sleeping-car, sleeper *(Brit)*; **s~wandeln** *vi insep aux sein or haben* to sleepwalk; **~wandler(in** *f*) *m* **-** sleepwalker; **s~wandlerisch** *adj* **mit s~wandlerischer Sicherheit** intuitively, instinctively; **~zimmer** *nt* bedroom.
Schlag *m* **⸚e (a)** *(lit, fig)* blow; *(Faust~ auch)* punch; *(mit der Handfläche)* smack, slap; *(Handkanten~, Judo etc)* chop *(col)*; *(Ohrfeige)* cuff, clout; *(Tritt)* kick; *(mit Rohrstock etc)* stroke; *(Peitschen~)* stroke, lash; *(Glocken~)* chime; *(~anfall, Ruder~, Schwimmen, Tennis)* stroke; *(Herz~, Wellen~)* beat; *(Blitz~)* bolt; *(Donner~)* clap; *(Strom~)* shock. **⸚e kriegen** to get a hiding or beating; **zum entscheidenden ~ ausholen** *(fig)* to strike the decisive blow; **~ auf ~** *(fig)* in quick succession; **~ acht Uhr** *(col)* on the stroke of eight; **ein ~ ins Gesicht** *(lit, fig)* a slap in the face; **ein ~ ins Wasser** *(col)* a washout *(col)*; **auf einen ~** *(col)* all at once; **mit einem ~ berühmt werden** to become famous overnight; **die haben keinen ~ getan** *(col)* they haven't done a stroke (of work); **einen ~ weghaben** *(col: blöd sein)* to have a screw loose *(col)*; **ich dachte, mich trifft der ~**

(col) I was thunderstruck.

(b) *(col: Wesensart)* type (of person *etc*). **vom gleichen ~ sein** to be cast in the same mould *(Brit) or* mold *(US)*; *(pej)* to be tarred with the same brush; **vom alten ~** of the old school.

(c) *(col: Portion)* helping.

Schlag-: ~abtausch *m (Boxen)* exchange of blows; *(fig)* (verbal) exchange; **~ader** *f* artery; **~anfall** *m* stroke; **s~artig 1** *adj* sudden, abrupt; **2** *adv* suddenly; **~ball** *m* rounders *sing*; *(Ball)* rounders ball; **s~bar** *adj* beatable; **~baum** *m* barrier; **~bohrer** *m* percussion drill.

schlagen *pret* **schlug,** *ptp* **geschlagen 1** *vti* **(a)** to hit; *(hauen)* to beat; *(mit der flachen Hand)* to slap, to smack; *(mit der Faust)* to punch; *(treten)* to kick. **jdn bewußtlos ~** to knock sb out *or* unconscious; *(mit vielen Schlägen)* to beat sb unconscious; **um sich ~** to lash out; **mit der Faust auf den Tisch ~** to thump on the table with one's fist; **jdm etw aus der Hand ~** to knock sth out of sb's hand; **ihm schlug das Gewissen** his conscience pricked him; **einer Sache** *(dat)* **ins Gesicht ~** *(fig)* to be a slap in the face for sth. **(b)** *Teig, Eier* to beat; *(mit Schneebesen)* to whisk; *Sahne* to whip. **ein Ei in die Pfanne ~** to crack an egg into the pan. **(c)** *(läuten)* to chime; *Stunde* to strike. **die Uhr hat 12 geschlagen** the clock has struck 12; **eine geschlagene Stunde** a full hour. **(d)** *(flattern)* **mit den Flügeln ~** to flap its wings.

2 *vt* **(a)** *Gegner, Rekord* to beat. **jdn in etw** *(dat)* **~** to beat sb at sth; **na ja, ehe ich mich ~ lasse!** *(hum col)* yes, I don't mind if I do; **sich geschlagen geben** to admit defeat. **(b) das Schicksal schlug sie hart** fate dealt her a hard blow; **mit Blindheit geschlagen sein** to be blind. **(c)** *(fällen)* to fell. **(d)** *(Hunt: töten)* to kill. **(e)** *(spielen) Trommel* to beat; *(liter) Harfe, Laute* to pluck, to play. **(f)** *Kreis, Bogen* to describe; *Purzelbaum* to do; *Alarm* to raise; *Krach* to make. **Profit aus etw ~** to make profit from sth; **ein Schlacht ~** to fight a battle; **den Kragen nach oben ~** to turn up one's collar. **(g)** *(wickeln)* to wrap.

3 *vi* **(a)** *(Herz, Puls)* to beat; *(heftig)* to pound, to throb. **(b)** *(Regen)* to beat; *(Wellen auch)* to pound; *(Blitz)* to strike *(in etw (acc)* sth*)*. **(c)** *(singen: Nachtigall, Fink)* to sing. **(d)** *(betreffen)* **in jds Fach** *(acc)* **~** to be in sb's field. **(e)** *aux sein or haben (Flammen)* to shoot out *(aus* of*)*; *(Rauch)* to pour out *(aus* of*)*. **(f)** *aux sein* **mit dem Kopf auf etw** *(acc)* **~** to hit one's head on sth; **auf die Nieren** *etc* **~** to affect the kidneys *etc;* **er schlägt sehr nach seinem Vater** he takes after his father a lot.

4 *vr* **(a)** *(sich prügeln)* to fight; *(sich duellieren)* to duel. **als Schuljunge habe ich mich oft geschlagen** I often had fights when I was a schoolboy; **sich um etw ~** *(lit, fig)* to fight over sth. **(b)** *(sich bewähren)* to do, to fare. **sich tapfer** *or* **gut ~** to make a good showing. **(c)** *(sich begeben)* **sich nach links/Norden ~** to strike out to the left/for the North; **sich auf jds Seite ~** to side with sb; *(die Fronten wechseln)* to go over to sb.

schlagend *adj* **(a)** *Bemerkung, Vergleich* apt, appropriate; *Beweis* striking, convincing. **etw ~ beweisen/widerlegen** to prove/refute sth convincingly. **(b)** *Verbindung (Univ)* duelling.

Schlager *m* **- (a)** *(Mus)* pop-song; *(erfolgreich)* hit-song, hit. **(b)** *(col) (Erfolg)* hit; *(Verkaufs~)* bestseller.

Schläger *m* **- (a)** *(Tennis~, Federball~)* racket; *(Hockey~, Eishockey~)* stick; *(Golf~)* club; *(Kricket~, Baseball~, Tischtennis~)* bat; *(Polo~)* mallet. **(b)** *(Spieler) (Kricket)* batsman; *(Baseball)* batter. **(c)** *(Raufbold)* thug, ruffian.

Schlägerei *f* fight, brawl.

Schlager-: ~parade *f* hit-parade; **~sänger** *m* pop singer.

Schlägertyp *m (col)* thug.

Schlag-: s~fertig *adj* quick-witted; **~fertigkeit** *f* quick-wittedness; **~instrument** *nt* percussion instrument; **~kraft** *f (lit, fig)* power; *(Boxen)* punch(ing power); *(Mil)* strike power; **s~kräftig** *adj* powerful; *Beweise* clear-cut; **~licht** *nt* **ein ~licht auf etw** *(acc)* **werfen** *(fig)* to highlight *or* spotlight sth; **~loch** *nt* pothole; **~mann** *m, pl* **~männer** *(Rudern)* stroke; *(Kricket)* batsman; *(Baseball)* batter; **~sahne** *f* (whipping) cream; *(geschlagen)* whipped cream; **~seite** *f (Naut)* list; **~seite haben** *(Naut)* to have a list; *(hum col)* to be half-seas over *(col)*; **~stock** *m (form)* truncheon *(Brit)*, nightstick *(US)*; **~wort** *nt* **(a)** *pl* **~wörter** *(Stichwort)* headword; **(b)** *pl* **~worte** *(Parole)* catchword, slogan; **~zeile** *f* headline; **~zeilen machen** *(col)* to hit the headlines; **~zeug** *nt* drums *pl*; *(in Orchester)* percussion *no pl*; **~zeuger(in** *f***)** *m* **-** drummer.

schlaksig *(col)* **1** *adj* gangling, gawky. **2** *adv* gawkily.

Schlamassel *m or nt* **-** *(col) (Durcheinander)* mix-up; *(mißliche Lage)* mess. **der** *or* **das (ganze) ~** *(Zeug)* the whole caboodle *(col)*.

Schlamm *m* **-e** *or* **¨-e** mud; *(Schlick auch)* sludge.

Schlammbad *nt* mudbath.

schlammig *adj* muddy; *(schlickig auch)* sludgy.

Schlampe *f* **-n** *(pej col)* slut *(col)*.

schlampen *vi (col)* to be sloppy (in one's work).

Schlamperei *f (col)* sloppiness; *(schlechte Arbeit)* sloppy work. **das ist eine ~!** that's a disgrace.

schlampig *adj (col)* sloppy, careless.

schlang *pret of* **schlingen.**

Schlange *f* **-n (a)** snake, serpent *(liter)*; *(fig: Frau)* Jezebel. **eine falsche ~** a snake in the grass. **(b)** *(Menschen~, Auto~)* queue *(Brit)*, line *(US)*. **~ stehen** to queue (up) *(Brit)*, to stand in line *(US)*.

schlängeln *vr (Weg)* to wind (its way), to snake; *(Fluß auch)* to meander; *(Schlange)* to wriggle. **eine geschlängelte Linie** a wavy line.

Schlangen-: ~beschwörer *m* **-** snake-charmer; **~biß** *m* snakebite; **~gift** *nt* snake venom *or* poison; **~haut** *f* snake's skin; *(Leder)* snakeskin; **~linie** *f* wavy line; **(in) ~linien fahren** to swerve about; **~mensch** *m* contortionist.

Schlangestehen *nt* queuing *(Brit)*, standing in line *(US)*.

schlank *adj* slim. **ihr Kleid macht sie ~** her dress makes her look slim.

Schlankheit *f* slimness.

Schlankheitskur *f* diet. **eine ~ anfangen/machen** to go/be on a diet.

schlankweg *adv (col) ablehnen, sagen* point-blank, flatly.

schlapp *adj (col) (kraftlos)* shattered *(col)*; *(energielos)* listless; *(nach Krankheit etc)* run-down.

Schlappe *f* **-n** *(col)* set-back; *(esp Sport)* defeat. **jdm eine ~ beibringen** to defeat sb.

Schlappen *m* **-** *(col)* slipper.

Schlapp-: ~hut *m* floppy hat; **s~machen** *vi sep (col)* to wilt; *(zusammenbrechen)* to collapse; **die meisten Manager machen mit 40 s~** most managers are finished by the time they're 40; **~schwanz** *m (pej col)* weakling, softy *(col)*.

Schlaraffenland *nt* land of milk and honey.

schlau *adj* clever, smart; *(gerissen)* cunning; *Sprüche* clever. **ich werde nicht ~ aus ihm** I don't know what to make of him.

Schlauberger *m* **-** *(col)* clever-dick *(col)*.

Schlauch *m, pl* **Schläuche (a)** hose; *(Fahrrad~, Auto~)* (inner) tube. **sein Zimmer war eine Art ~** *(col)* his room was a sort of long, narrow corridor. **(b)** *(col: Strapaze)* slog *(col)*, grind.

Schlauchboot *nt* rubber dinghy.

schlauchen *(col)* **1** *vt (Arbeit etc) jdn* to wear out. **2** *vi* **diese Arbeit schlaucht** this job takes it out of you.

schlauchlos *adj Reifen* tubeless.

Schläue, Schlauheit *f no pl* cunning.

Schlaufe *f* **-n** loop; *(Aufhänger)* hanger.
Schlawiner *m* - *(hum col)* villain, rogue.
schlecht 1 *adj* **(a)** bad; *Geschmack, Leistung auch, Gesundheitszustand* poor. **das S~e in der Welt** the evil in the world; **nur S~es über jdn sagen** not to have a good word to say for sb; **jdm ist (es) ~** sb feels sick *or* ill; **~ aussehen** *(Mensch)* to look bad *or* sick *or* ill; *(Lage)* to look bad. **(b)** *pred (ungenießbar)* bad, off *(Brit)*. **die Milch ist ~** the milk has gone off *or* is off.
2 *adv* badly; *lernen, begreifen* with difficulty. **sich ~ vertragen** *(Menschen)* to get along badly; *(Dinge, Farben etc)* not to go well together; **~ über jdn sprechen/von jdm denken** to speak/think ill of sb; **er kann ~ nein sagen** he finds it hard to say no, he can't say no; **heute geht es ~** today is not very convenient; **das läßt sich ~ machen** that's not really possible *or* on *(col)*; **er ist ~ zu verstehen** he is hard to understand; **ich kann sie ~ sehen** I can't see her very well; **auf jdn ~ zu sprechen sein** not to have a good word to say for sb; **~ und recht, mehr ~ als recht** after a fashion; **er hat nicht ~ gestaunt** *(col)* he wasn't half surprised *(col)*.
schlechtbezahlt *adj attr* low-paid, badly paid.
schlechterdings *adv (völlig)* absolutely; *(nahezu)* virtually.
schlecht-: ~gehen *vi impers sep irreg aux sein* **es geht jdm ~** sb is in a bad way; *(finanziell)* sb is doing badly; **~gelaunt** *adj attr* bad-tempered; **~hin** *adv (vollkommen)* quite, absolutely; **Studenten ~hin** students as such *or* per se.
Schlechtigkeit *f* **(a)** *no pl* badness. **(b)** *(schlechte Tat)* misdeed.
schlechtmachen *vt sep* to denigrate, to run down.
schlecken 1 *vti* to lick *(an etw (dat)* sth*)*. **2** *vi (esp SGer: Süßigkeiten essen)* to eat sweets *(Brit) or* candies *(US)*.
Schleckermaul *nt (hum col)* **sie ist ein richtiges ~** she really has a sweet tooth.
Schlegel *m* - **(a)** stick. **(b)** *(Min)* miner's hammer.
Schlehe *f* **-n** sloe.
Schlei *m* **-e** tench.
schleichen *pret* **schlich,** *ptp* **geschlichen 1** *vi aux sein* to creep; *(heimlich auch)* to sneak; *(Fahrzeug)* to crawl. **2** *vr* to creep, to sneak.
schleichend *adj attr* creeping; *Krankheit, Gift* insidious; *Fieber* lingering.
Schleich-: ~handel *m* illicit trading *(mit* in*)*; **~weg** *m* secret path; **auf ~wegen** *(fig)* on the quiet; **~werbung** *f* a plug.
Schleier *m* - *(lit, fig)* veil; *(von Wolken, Nebel auch)* haze. **einen ~ vor den Augen haben** to have a mist in front of one's eyes; **einen ~ über etw** *(acc)* **breiten** *(fig)* to draw a veil over sth.
Schleier-: ~eule *f* barn owl; **s~haft** *adj (col)* mysterious.
Schleife *f* **-n (a)** loop *(auch Aviat)*; *(Straßen~)* twisty bend. **(b)** *(von Band)* bow; *(Schuh~)* bow(-knot); *(Fliege)* bow tie; *(Kranz~)* ribbon.
schleifen[1] **1** *vt (lit, fig)* to drag; *(ziehen auch)* to haul; *(Mus) Töne, Noten* to slur. **2** *vi* **(a)** *aux sein or haben* to trail, to drag. **(b)** *(reiben)* to rub. **die Kupplung ~ lassen** *(Aut)* to slip the clutch; **die Zügel ~ lassen** *(lit, fig)* to slacken the reins.
schleifen[2] *pret* **schliff,** *ptp* **geschliffen** *vt Messer etc* to sharpen, to whet; *Parkett* to sand; *Edelstein, Glas* to cut; *siehe* **geschliffen.**
Schleif-: ~lack *m* (coloured *(Brit) or* colored *US)* laquer *or* varnish; **~maschine** *f* grinding machine; **~papier** *nt* abrasive paper; **~stein** *m* grindstone; **er sitzt da wie ein Affe auf dem ~stein** *(col)* he looks a proper Charlie sitting there *(col)*.
Schleim *m* **-e (a)** slime; *(Med)* mucus. **(b)** *(Cook)* gruel.
Schleimhaut *f* mucous membrane.
schleimig *adj* **(a)** slimy; *(Med)* mucous. **(b)** *(pej: unterwürfig)* slimy *(col)*.
Schleim-: s~lösend *adj* expectorant; **~scheißer** *m (col!)* bootlicker *(col)*, arse-licker *(col!)*.
schlemmen 1 *vi (üppig essen)* to feast. **2** *vt* to feast on.
Schlemmer(in *f*) *m* - gourmet, bon vivant.
Schlemmerei *f* feasting; *(Mahl)* feast.
schlendern *vi aux sein* to stroll, to amble.
Schlendrian *m no pl (col)* casualness; *(Trott)* rut.
Schlenker *m* - swerve. **einen ~ machen** to swerve.
schlenkern *vti* to swing, to dangle.
schlenzen *vi (Sport)* to scoop.
Schlepp *m (Naut, fig)*: **jdn/etw in ~ nehmen** to take sb/sth in tow.
Schleppe *f* **-n** *(von Kleid)* train.
schleppen 1 *vt (tragen) Lasten* to lug, to schlepp *(US col)*; *(zerren)* to drag, to schlepp *(US col)*; *Auto, Schiff* to tow; *(fig)* to drag. **2** *vr* to drag oneself; *(Verhandlungen etc)* to drag on.
schleppend *adj Gang* dragging, shuffling; *Abfertigung, Nachfrage* sluggish. **die Unterhaltung kam nur ~ in Gang** conversation was very slow to start.
Schlepper *m* - **(a)** *(Aut)* tractor. **(b)** *(Naut)* tug. **(c)** *(col: Kundenfänger)* tout.
Schlepp-: ~kahn *m* (canal) barge; **~netz** *nt* trawl (net); **~tau** *nt (Naut)* tow rope; **jdn ins ~tau nehmen** *(col)* to take sb in tow.
Schlesien [-iən] *nt* Silesia.
Schlesier(in *f*) [-iɐ, -iərɪn] *m* - Silesian.
schlesisch *adj* Silesian.
Schleuder *f* **-n (a)** *(Waffe)* sling; *(Wurfmaschine)* catapult. **(b)** *(Zentrifuge)* centrifuge; *(Wäsche~)* spin-drier *(Brit)*, dryer *(US)*.
Schleuderhonig *m* extracted honey.
schleudern 1 *vti* **(a)** *(werfen)* to sling, to fling. **(b)** *(Tech)* to centrifuge, to spin; *Honig* to extract; *Wäsche* to spin-dry. **2** *vi aux sein or haben (Aut)* to skid. **ins S~ kommen** *or* **geraten** to go into a skid; *(fig col)* to run into trouble.
Schleuder-: ~preis *m* throwaway price; **~sitz** *m (Aviat)* ejector seat; *(fig)* hot seat; **~ware** *f* cut-price goods *pl*.
schleunigst *adv* at once. **aber ~!** and be quick about it!
Schleuse *f* **-n** *(für Schiffe)* lock; *(zur Regulierung des Wasserlaufs)* sluice.
schleusen *vt Schiffe* to pass through a lock, to lock; *Wasser* to channel; *Menschen* to filter; *(fig: heimlich)* to smuggle.
Schleusentor *nt (für Schiffe)* lock gate.
schlich *pret of* **schleichen.**
Schliche *pl* **jdm auf die ~ kommen** to get wise to sb.
schlicht *adj* simple. **die ~e Wahrheit** the plain *or* simple truth; **~ und einfach** plain and simple; **das ist ~ und einfach nicht wahr** that's just simply not true; **er sagte ~ und ergreifend nein** *(hum col)* he said quite simply no.
schlichten *vti Streit (vermitteln)* to mediate, to arbitrate *(esp Ind)*; *(beilegen)* to settle.
Schlichter(in *f*) *m* - mediator; *(Ind)* arbitrator.
Schlichtheit *f* simplicity.
Schlichtung *f siehe vti* arbitration; settlement.
Schlick *m* **-e** silt; *(Öl~)* slick.
schlief *pret of* **schlafen.**
Schließe *f* **-n** fastening, fastener.
schließen *pret* **schloß,** *ptp* **geschlossen 1** *vt* **(a)** *(zumachen)* to close, to shut; *(verriegeln)* to bolt; *(Betrieb einstellen)* to close *or* shut down; *Stromkreis* to close. **eine Lücke ~** *(lit)* to close a gap; *(fig auch)* to fill a gap. **(b)** *(beenden) Versammlung* to close, to wind up; *Brief* to close. **(c)** *(eingehen) Vertrag, Bündnis* to conclude; *Frieden auch* to make; *Freundschaft* to form. **die Ehe ~** to get married. **(d) etw in sich** *(dat)* **~** *(beinhalten: lit,*

fig) to include sth; *(indirekt)* to imply; **jdn in die Arme** ~ to embrace sb; **jdn/etw in sein Herz** ~ to take sb/sth to one's heart; **daran schloß er eine Bemerkung** he added a remark (to this).

2 *vr* to close, to shut. **sich um etw** ~ to close around sth.

3 *vi* **(a)** to close, to shut; *(Betrieb einstellen)* to close *or* shut down. **„geschlossen"** "closed". **(b)** *(enden)* to close, to conclude; *(St Ex)* to close. **(c)** *(schlußfolgern)* to infer. **auf etw** *(acc)* ~ **lassen** to suggest sth; **von sich auf andere** ~ to judge others by one's own standards; *siehe* **geschlossen.**

Schließfach *nt* left-luggage *(Brit) or* baggage *(US)* locker; *(Bank~)* safe-deposit box.

schließlich *adv (endlich)* in the end; *(immerhin)* after all. **er kam** ~ **doch** he came after all.

Schließung *f* closing; *(von Vertrag)* conclusion; *(Betriebseinstellung)* closure.

Schliff *m* **-e** *(das Schleifen)* cutting; *(Ergebnis)* cut; *(fig: Umgangsformen)* refinement, polish. **einer Sache den letzten** ~ **geben** *(fig)* to put the finishing touch(es) to sth.

schliff *pret of* **schleifen**[2].

schlimm *adj* bad. **sich** ~ **verletzen** to hurt oneself badly; **das war** ~ that was terrible; **mit der neuen Frisur siehst du** ~ **aus** you look awful with that new hairdo; **das finde ich nicht** ~ I don't find that so bad; **das ist halb so** ~! that's not so bad!; **er ist** ~ **dran** *(col)* he's in a bad way; **es steht** ~ **(um ihn)** things aren't looking too good (for him); **wenn es nichts S~eres ist!** if that's all it is!; **es gibt S~eres** it *or* things could be worse; **um so** ~**er** all the worse; **im** ~**sten Fall** if the worst comes to the worst.

schlimmstenfalls *adv* at (the) worst. ~ **müssen wir im Auto schlafen** if the worst comes to the worst we'll have to sleep in the car.

Schlinge *f* **-n** loop; *(an Galgen)* noose; *(Med: Armbinde)* sling; *(Falle)* snare. **den Kopf aus der** ~ **ziehen** *(fig)* to get out of a tight spot.

Schlingel *m* **-** rascal.

schlingen *pret* **schlang,** *ptp* **geschlungen 1** *vt (binden) Knoten* to tie; *(umbinden) Schal* to wrap. **2** *vr* **sich um etw** ~ to coil (itself) around sth. **3** *vi (hastig essen)* to bolt one's food.

schlingern *vi (Schiff)* to roll.

Schlips *m* **-e** *(col)* tie, necktie *(US)*. **mit** ~ **und Kragen** wearing a collar and tie; **jdm auf den** ~ **treten** to tread on sb's toes; **sich auf den** ~ **getreten fühlen** to feel offended.

Schlitten *m* **- (a)** sledge, sled; *(Pferde~)* sleigh; *(Rodel~)* toboggan. **mit jdm** ~ **fahren** *(col)* to give sb a rough time. **(b)** *(col: Auto)* car, motor *(col)*.

Schlitten-: ~**fahren** *nt* sledging; *(Rodeln)* tobogganing; ~**fahrt** *f* sledge ride; *(mit Rodel)* toboggan ride.

schlittern *vi aux sein* to slide; *(Wagen)* to skid.

Schlittschuh *m* (ice-)skate. ~ **laufen** to (ice-)skate.

Schlittschuh-: ~**laufen** *nt* (ice-)skating; ~**läufer(in** *f***)** *m* (ice-)skater.

Schlitz *m* **-e** slit; *(Einwurf~)* slot; *(Hosen~)* fly, flies *pl*.

Schlitz-: ~**auge** *nt* slant eye; *(pej: Chinese)* Chink *(pej)*; **s~äugig** *adj* slant-eyed; ~**ohr** *nt (fig)* crafty character, sly fox; **s~ohrig** *adj (fig)* crafty; ~**verschluß** *m (Phot)* focal-plane shutter.

schloß *pret of* **schließen.**

Schloß *nt* **¨sser (a)** castle; *(Palast)* palace; *(großes Herrschaftshaus)* mansion. **(b)** *(Tür~ etc)* lock; *(Vorhänge~)* padlock; *(an Handtasche etc)* fastener. **ins** ~ **fallen** to lock (itself); **jdn hinter** ~ **und Riegel bringen** to put sb behind bars.

Schlosser *m* **-** fitter, metalworker; *(für Schlösser)* locksmith.

Schlosserei *f (~werkstatt)* metalworking shop.

Schloß-: ~**herr** *m* owner of a castle *etc*; *(Adliger)* lord of the castle; ~**hof** *m* courtyard; ~**hund** *m* **heulen wie ein** ~**hund** *(col)* to howl one's head off *(col)*; ~**park** *m* castle *etc* grounds *pl*, estate.

Schlot *m* **-e** *(Schornstein)* chimney (stack), smokestack; *(von Vulkan)* chimney. **rauchen wie ein** ~ *(col)* to smoke like a chimney *(col)*.

schlottern *vi* **(a)** *(zittern)* to shiver; *(vor Angst)* to tremble. **er schlotterte mit den Knien** he was shaking at the knees. **(b)** *(Kleider)* to be baggy.

Schlucht *f* **-en** gorge, ravine.

schluchzen *vti (lit, fig)* to sob.

Schluck *m* **-e** drink; *(ein bißchen)* drop; *(das Schlucken)* swallow; *(großer)* gulp; *(kleiner)* sip. **etw** ~ **für** ~ **austrinken** to drink every drop; **einen (kräftigen)** ~ **nehmen** to take a (long) drink *or* swig *(col)*.

Schluck|auf *m no pl* hiccups *pl*. **einen** ~ **haben** to have (the) hiccups.

Schluckbeschwerden *pl* difficulties *pl* in swallowing.

Schlückchen *nt dim of* **Schluck** drop.

schlucken 1 *vt (lit, fig col)* to swallow; *(hastig)* to gulp down; *(col) Alkohol* to booze *(col)*; *(col: verschlingen)* to swallow up; *Benzin, Öl* to guzzle. **2** *vi* to swallow; *(hastig)* to gulp; *(col: Alkohol trinken)* to booze *(col)*.

Schlucker *m* **-** *(col)*: **armer** ~ poor devil.

Schluck-: ~**impfung** *f* oral vaccination; ~**specht** *m (col)* boozer *(col)*; **s~weise** *adv* in sips.

schlud(e)rig *adj (col) Arbeit* slipshod *no adv*. ~ **arbeiten** to work in a slipshod way.

schludern *vi (col)* to do sloppy work, to work sloppily.

schlug *pret of* **schlagen.**

Schlummer *m no pl (liter)* (light) slumber *(liter)*.

Schlummerlied *nt (geh)* lullaby.

schlummern *vi (liter)* to slumber *(liter)*.

Schlummerrolle *f* bolster.

Schlund *m* **¨e** *(Anat)* pharynx, gullet; *(fig liter)* maw *(liter)*.

schlüpfen *vi aux sein* to slip; *(Küken)* to hatch (out).

Schlüpfer *m* **-** panties *pl*, knickers *pl*.

Schlupfloch *nt* gap; *(Versteck)* hideout; *(fig)* loophole.

schlüpfrig *adj* **(a)** slippery. **(b)** *(fig) Bemerkung* risqué.

Schlupfwinkel *m* hiding place; *(fig)* quiet corner.

schlurfen *vi aux sein* to shuffle.

schlürfen *vti* to slurp.

Schluß *m* **¨sse (a)** *no pl (Ende)* end. ~**!** that'll do!, stop!; ~ **für heute!** that'll do for today; **... und damit** ~! ... and that's that!; ~ **jetzt!** that's enough now!; **dann ist** ~ that'll be it; ~ **folgt** to be concluded; **zum** ~ **sangen wir ...** at the end we sang ...; **zum** ~ **möchte ich noch darauf hinweisen, daß ...** in conclusion I would like to point out that ...; ~ **machen** to call it a day; *(Selbstmord begehen)* to end it all; **mit der Arbeit** ~ **machen** to stop work; **mit jdm** ~ **machen** to break with sb. **(b)** *(Folgerung)* conclusion. **aus etw den** ~ **ziehen, daß ...** to draw the conclusion from sth that ...

Schluß|akt *m (lit, fig)* final act.

Schlüssel *m* **-** *(lit, fig)* key; *(Tech)* spanner *(Brit)*, wrench; *(Verteilungs~)* ratio (of distribution); *(Mus)* clef.

Schlüssel-: ~**bein** *nt* collarbone, clavicle *(form)*; ~**blume** *f* cowslip; ~**brett** *nt* keyboard; ~**bund** *m or nt* bunch of keys; ~**erlebnis** *nt (Psych)* crucial experience; **s~fertig** *adj Neubau* ready for occupancy; ~**figur** *f* key figure; ~**industrie** *f* key industry; ~**kind** *nt (col)* latchkey child *(col)*; ~**loch** *nt* keyhole; ~**position** *f* key position; ~**ring** *m* key ring; ~**stellung** *f* key position.

schlußfolgern* *vi insep* to conclude, to infer.
Schluß-: **~folgerung** *f* conclusion, inference; **~formel** *f (in Brief)* complimentary close; *(bei Vertrag)* final clause.
schlüssig *adj* conclusive. **sich** *(dat)* **(über etw** *acc)* **~ sein** to have made up one's mind (about sth).
Schluß-: **~kapitel** *nt* concluding *or* final chapter; **~licht** *nt* tail lamp; *(col: bei Rennen etc)* back marker; **~licht in der Klasse sein** to be bottom of the class; **~pfiff** *m* final whistle; **~phase** *f* final stages *pl*; **~stand** *m* final result; *(von Spiel auch)* final score; **~stein** *m (Archit, fig)* keystone; **~strich** *m (fig)* final stroke; **einen ~strich unter etw** *(acc)* **ziehen** to consider sth finished; **~verkauf** *m* (end-of-season) sale; **~wort** *nt* closing words *pl*; *(~rede)* closing speech; *(Nachwort)* postscript.
Schmach *f no pl (geh)* ignominy *no indef art*.
schmachten *vi (geh: leiden)* to languish. **nach jdm/etw ~** to pine for sb/sth; **jdn ~ lassen** to torment sb.
Schmachtfetzen *m (hum)* tear-jerker *(col)*.
schmächtig *adj* frail, weedy *(pej)*.
schmachvoll *adj (geh) Niederlage* ignominious.
schmackhaft *adj (wohlschmeckend)* tasty. **jdm etw ~ machen** *(fig)* to make sth palatable to sb.
schmähen *vti (geh)* to abuse, to vituperate against *(liter)*.
schmählich *adj (geh)* ignominious; *(demütigend)* humiliating.
Schmäh-: **~rede** *f (geh)* diatribe; **~schrift** *f* defamatory piece of writing; *(Satire)* lampoon.
Schmähung *f (geh)* abuse, vituperation *(liter)*.
schmal *adj comp* **-er** *or* **¨er**, *superl* **-ste(r, s)** *or* **¨ste(r, s)** *or (adv)* **am -sten** *or* **¨sten (a)** narrow; *Hüfte auch, Mensch, Buch* slim; *Lippen* thin. **er ist sehr ~ geworden** he has got very thin. **(b)** *(fig: karg)* meagre *(Brit)*, meager *(US)*, slender.
schmalbrüstig *adj* narrow-chested; *(fig)* limited.
schmälern *vt* to diminish.
Schmälerung *f* diminishing.
Schmal-: **~film** *m* cine-film; **~filmkamera** *f* cine-camera *(Brit)*, movie camera *(US)*; **~seite** *f* narrow side; **~spur** *f (Rail)* narrow gauge; **~spur-** *in cpds (pej)* small-time; **s~spurig** *adj (Rail) Strecke* narrow-gauge.
Schmalz[1] *nt* **-e** fat; *(Schweine~)* lard; *(Braten~)* dripping.
Schmalz[2] *m no pl (pej col)* schmaltz *(col)*.
schmalzig *adj (pej col)* schmaltzy *(col)*, slushy *(col)*.
schmarotzen* *vi* to sponge, to freeload *(esp US) (bei* on, off*)*; *(Biol)* to be parasitic *(bei* on*)*.
Schmarotzer(in *f*) *m* - *(Biol)* parasite; *(fig auch)* sponger, freeloader *(esp US)*.
Schmarr(e)n *m* - **(a)** *(S Ger, Aus) (Cook) pancake cut up into small pieces.* **(b)** *(col: Quatsch)* rubbish *(col)*.
schmatzen *vi* to eat noisily. **schmatz nicht so!** don't make so much noise when you eat!
Schmaus *m, pl* **Schmäuse** *(dated)* feast.
schmausen *(geh)* **1** *vi* to feast. **2** *vt* to feast on.
schmecken 1 *vi (Geschmack haben)* to taste *(nach* of*)*; *(gut ~)* to taste good. **ihm schmeckt es** *(gut finden)* he likes it; *(Appetit haben)* he likes his food; **das schmeckt ihm nicht** *(lit, fig)* he doesn't like it; **nach etw ~** *(fig)* to smack of sth; **das schmeckt nach mehr!** *(col)* it tastes more-ish *(hum col)*; **schmeckt es (Ihnen)?** is it good?; are you enjoying your food *or* meal? *(esp form)*; **das hat geschmeckt** that was good; **das schmeckt nicht (gut)** it doesn't taste nice; **es sich ~ lassen** to tuck in. **2** *vt* to taste.
Schmeichelei *f* flattery.
schmeichelhaft *adj* flattering.
schmeicheln *vi* to flatter *(jdm* sb*)*. **es schmeichelt mir, daß ...** it flatters me that ...
Schmeichler(in *f*) *m* - flatterer; *(Kriecher)* sycophant.
schmeichlerisch *adj* flattering.
schmeißen *pret* **schmiß**, *ptp* **geschmissen** *(col)* **1** *vt* **(a)** *(werfen)* to sling *(col)*, to chuck *(col)*; *Tür* to slam. **sich jdm an den Hals ~** *(fig)* to throw oneself at sb. **(b)** *(spendieren)* **eine Runde** *or* **Lage ~** to stand a round. **(c)** *(managen)* **den Laden ~** to run the (whole) show; **die Sache ~** to handle it. **2** *vi (werfen)* to throw, to chuck *(col)*. **mit Steinen ~** to throw stones; **mit etw um sich ~** to chuck sth around *(col)*.
Schmeißfliege *f* bluebottle.
Schmelz *m* **-e** *(Glasur)* glaze; *(Zahn~)* enamel.
schmelzen *pret* **schmolz**, *ptp* **geschmolzen 1** *vi aux sein (lit, fig)* to melt. **2** *vt Metall, Fett* to melt; *Erz* to smelt.
Schmelz-: **~hütte** *f* smelting plant *or* works *sing or pl*; **~käse** *m* cheese spread; *(in Scheiben)* processed cheese; **~ofen** *m* melting furnace; *(für Erze)* smelting furnace; **~punkt** *m* melting point; **~tiegel** *m (lit, fig)* melting pot; **~wasser** *nt* melted snow and ice; *(Geog, Phys)* meltwater.
Schmerbauch *m (col)* paunch, potbelly.
Schmerz *m* **-en** pain; *(Kummer auch)* grief *no pl*. **ihre ~en** her pain; **sie schrie vor ~en** she cried out in pain; **~en haben** to be in pain; **~en in den Ohren/im Hals haben** to have ear-ache/to have a sore throat; **jdm ~en bereiten** to cause sb pain; **jdn/etw mit ~en erwarten** to wait impatiently for sb/sth.
schmerz|empfindlich *adj Mensch* sensitive to pain; *Körperteil* tender.
schmerzen *(geh) vti* to hurt; *(Wunde etc)* to be sore; *(Kopf, Bauch auch)* to ache. **es schmerzt** *(lit, fig)* it hurts; **eine ~de Stelle** a painful spot *or* area.
Schmerzens-: **~geld** *nt (Jur)* damages *pl*; **~schrei** *m* scream of pain.
Schmerz-: **s~frei** *adj* free of pain; *Operation* painless; **s~haft** *adj (lit, fig)* painful; **s~lich** *adj (geh)* painful; *Lächeln* sad; **s~lindernd** *adj* pain-relieving; **s~los** *adj (lit, fig)* painless; **~losigkeit** *f (lit, fig)* painlessness; **~mittel** *nt* pain-killer; **s~stillend** *adj* pain-killing, analgesic *(Med)*; **s~stillendes Mittel** pain-killing drug, analgesic *(Med)*; **~tablette** *f* pain-killer, ≃ aspirin *(col)*; **s~voll** *adj (fig)* painful.
Schmetterling *m (auch Schwimmart)* butterfly.
Schmetterlings-: **~netz** *nt* butterfly net; **~stil** *m* butterfly stroke.
schmettern 1 *vt (schleudern)* to smash; *Tür* to slam; *(Sport) Ball* to smash. **2** *vi* **(a)** *(Sport)* to smash, to hit a smash. **(b)** *(Trompete etc)* to blare (out); *(Sänger)* to bellow; *(Vogel)* to sing, to warble.
Schmied *m* **-e** (black)smith.
Schmiede *f* **-n** smithy, forge.
Schmiede-: **~arbeit** *f (das Schmieden)* forging; *(Gegenstand)* piece of wrought-iron work; **~eisen** *nt* wrought iron; **s~eisern** *adj* wrought-iron; **~hammer** *m* blacksmith's hammer.
schmieden *vt* to forge *(zu* into*)*; *(ersinnen) Plan* to hatch, to concoct; *(hum) Verse* to concoct. **geschmiedet sein** *(Gartentür etc)* to be made of wrought-iron.
schmiegen *vr* **sich an jdn ~** to cuddle *or* snuggle up to sb; **sich um etw ~** to hang gracefully on sth.
schmiegsam *adj* supple; *Stoff* soft; *(fig: anpassungsfähig)* adaptable, flexible.
Schmiere *f* **-n (a)** *(col)* grease; *(Salbe)* ointment. **(b)** *(pej) (schlechtes Theater)* flea-pit. **(c)** *(col)* **~ stehen** to be the look-out.
schmieren 1 *vt* **(a)** *(streichen)* to smear; *Butter, Aufstrich* to spread; *Brot* to butter; *Salbe, Make-up* to rub in *(in +acc* -to*)*; *(einfetten, ölen)* to grease.

es läuft wie geschmiert it's going like clockwork; **jdm eine ~** *(col)* to clout sb one *(col)*. **(b)** *(pej: schreiben)* to scrawl. **(c)** *(col: bestechen)* **jdn ~** to grease sb's palm *(col)*. **2** *vi* **(a)** *(pej) (schreiben)* to scrawl; *(malen)* to daub. **(b)** *(col: bestechen)* to give a bribe/bribes.

Schmieren-: ~komödiant *m (pej)* ham (actor); **~theater** *nt (pej: schlechtes Theater)* flea-pit.

Schmiererei *f (pej col) (Geschriebenes)* scrawl, scribble; *(Parolen etc)* graffiti *pl*; *(Malerei)* daubing; *(Schriftstellerei)* scribbling; *(das Schmieren)* scrawling, scribbling.

Schmier-: ~fink *m (pej)* **(a)** *(Autor, Journalist)* hack, scribbler; **(b)** *(Schüler)* messy writer; **~geld** *nt (col)* bribe-money; **~heft** *nt* jotter.

schmierig *adj* greasy; *(fig: unanständig)* dirty, filthy.

Schmier-: ~mittel *nt* lubricant; **~seife** *f* soft soap.

Schmierung *f* lubrication.

Schminke *f* **-n** make-up.

schminken 1 *vt* to make up. **sich** *(dat)* **die Lippen ~** to put on lipstick. **2** *vr* to put on make-up.

Schmirgel *m no pl* emery.

schmirgeln 1 *vt* to sand, to rub down. **2** *vi* to sand.

Schmirgelpapier *nt* sandpaper.

Schmiß *m* **-sse (a)** *(Narbe)* duelling scar. **(b)** *(dated: Schwung)* dash, élan.

schmiß *pret of* **schmeißen.**

schmissig *adj (dated)* dashing; *Musik auch* spirited.

Schmock *m* **⸚e** *or* **-s** *(pej)* hack *(col)*.

Schmöker *m* **-** book *(usu of light literature)*; *(dick)* tome.

schmökern *(col)* **1** *vi* to bury oneself in a book; *(in Büchern blättern)* to browse. **2** *vt* to bury oneself in.

schmollen *vi* to pout; *(gekränkt sein)* to sulk.

Schmoll-: ~mund *m* pout; **~winkel** *m (col)* **im ~winkel sitzen** to have the sulks *(col)*.

schmolz *pret of* **schmelzen.**

Schmorbraten *m* pot-roast.

schmoren 1 *vt* to braise. **2** *vi (Cook)* to braise; *(col: schwitzen)* to roast, to swelter. **jdn ~ lassen** to leave sb to stew.

Schmu *m no pl (col)* cheating. **~ machen** to cheat.

schmuck *adj (dated) Haus etc* neat, tidy; *Bursche, Mädel* smart, spruce.

Schmuck *m* **(a)** *(~stücke)* jewellery *(Brit) no pl*, jewelry *(US) no pl*. **(b)** *(Verzierung)* decoration; *(fig)* embellishment.

schmücken 1 *vt* to decorate, to adorn; *Rede* to embellish. **~des Beiwerk** embellishment. **2** *vr (zum Fest etc) (Mensch)* to adorn oneself; *(Stadt)* to be decorated.

Schmuck-: ~kasten *m* jewellery *(Brit) or* jewelry *(US)* box; **s~los** *adj* plain; *(fig) Stil, Prosa etc* simple; **~losigkeit** *f siehe adj* plainness; simplicity; **~sachen** *pl* jewellery *(Brit) sing*, jewelry *(US) sing*; **~stück** *nt (Ring etc)* piece of jewellery *(Brit) or* jewelry *(US)*; *(fig: Prachtstück)* gem.

schmudd(e)lig *adj* messy; *(schmutzig auch)* dirty; *(schmierig, unsauber)* filthy.

Schmuggel *m no pl* smuggling.

Schmuggelei *f* smuggling *no pl*.

schmuggeln *vti (lit, fig)* to smuggle.

Schmuggeln *nt no pl* smuggling.

Schmuggelware *f* contraband *no pl*.

Schmuggler(in *f*) *m* **-** smuggler.

schmunzeln *vi* to smile.

Schmunzeln *nt no pl* smile.

schmusen *vi (col: zärtlich sein)* to cuddle. **mit jdm ~** to cuddle sb, to canoodle with sb *(col)*.

Schmutz *m no pl* dirt; *(fig auch)* filth, smut. **jdn/etw in den ~ ziehen** *(fig)* to drag sb/sth through the mud.

schmutzen *vi* to get dirty.

Schmutz-: ~fink *m (col) (unsauberer Mensch)* dirty slob *(col)*; *(Kind)* mucky pup *(col)*; *(fig: Mann)* dirty old man; **~fleck** *m* dirty mark.

schmutzig *adj* dirty. **sich ~ machen** to get oneself dirty; **~e Wäsche waschen** to wash one's dirty linen in public.

Schmutzigkeit *f* dirtiness.

Schmutzwasser *nt* dirty water.

Schnabel *m* **⸚ (a)** *(Vogel~)* beak, bill. **(b)** *(von Kanne)* spout. **(c)** *(col: Mund)* mouth. **halt den ~!** shut your mouth *(col)*; **reden, wie einem der ~ gewachsen ist** to say exactly what comes into one's head; *(unaffektiert)* to talk naturally.

Schnabeltasse *f* feeding cup.

Schnack *m* **-s** *(N Ger col) (Unterhaltung)* chat; *(pej: Geschwätz)* silly talk.

schnacken *vi (N Ger col)* to chat.

Schnake *f* **-n (a)** *(col: Stechmücke)* gnat, midge. **(b)** *(Weberknecht)* daddy-long-legs.

Schnalle *f* **-n** *(Schuh~, Gürtel~)* buckle; *(an Handtasche, Buch)* clasp.

schnallen *vt* **(a)** to strap; *Gürtel* to buckle, to fasten. **(b)** *(col: begreifen)* **hast du das immer noch nicht geschnallt?** have you still not got the message?

Schnallenschuh *m* buckled shoe.

schnalzen *vi* **mit den Fingern ~** to snap *or* click one's fingers; **mit der Zunge ~** to click one's tongue.

schnappen 1 *vi* **(a) nach jdm/etw ~** to snap at sb/sth; *(greifen)* to snatch at sb/sth. **(b)** *aux sein* **die Tür schnappt ins Schloß** the door clicks shut. **2** *vt (col)* **(a)** *(ergreifen)* to snatch, to grab. **(b)** *(fangen)* to nab *(col)*.

Schnapp-: ~schloß *nt (an Tür)* springlock; *(an Schmuck)* spring clasp; **~schuß** *m (Foto)* snap(shot).

Schnaps *m* **⸚e** *(klarer ~)* schnapps; *(col: Branntwein)* spirits *pl*; *(col: Alkohol)* booze *(col)*, liquor *(esp US col)*.

Schnäpschen [ˈʃnɛpsçən] *nt (col)* little drink, wee dram *(esp Scot)*.

Schnaps-: ~flasche *f* bottle of booze *(col) or* liquor *(esp US col)*; **~glas** *nt* small glass for spirits; **~idee** *f (col)* crackpot idea *(col)*; **~leiche** *f (col)* drunk.

schnarchen *vi* to snore.

schnarren *vi (Wecker etc)* to buzz; *(Maschine, Klingel)* to clatter. **mit ~der Stimme** in a rasping *or* grating voice.

Schnatter-: ~gans *f (col)*, **~maul** *nt (col)* chatterbox.

schnattern *vi (Gans)* to gabble; *(Ente)* to quack; *(col: schwatzen)* to natter *(col)*.

schnauben *vi* to snort. **vor Wut ~** to snort with rage.

schnaufen *vi* **(a)** *(schwer atmen)* to wheeze; *(keuchen)* to puff, to pant. **(b)** *aux sein (sich keuchend bewegen: Auto)* to struggle.

Schnaufer *m* **-** *(col)* breath. **den letzten ~ tun** to breathe one's last.

Schnauferl *nt* **-** *(hum: Oldtimer)* veteran car.

Schnauzbart *m* walrus moustache *(Brit) or* mustache *(US)*.

Schnauze *f* **-n (a)** *(von Tier)* muzzle. **mit einer Maus in der ~** with a mouse in its mouth. **(b)** *(col) (von Fahrzeugen)* front; *(von Flugzeug, Schiff)* nose. **(c)** *(col!: Mund)* gob *(col)*, trap *(col)*. **~!** shut your trap *(col!)*; **auf die ~ fallen** to fall flat on one's face; *(fig)* to come a cropper *(col)*; **die ~ (gestrichen) voll haben** to be fed up to the back teeth *(col) (von etw* with sth*)*; **eine große ~ haben** to have a big mouth *(col)*; **die ~ halten** to hold one's tongue; **etw frei nach ~ machen** to do sth any old how *(col)*.

schnauzen *vi (col)* to shout; *(jdn anfahren)* to snap.

Schnauzer *m* **- (a)** *(Hund)* schnauzer. **(b)** *(col: Bart)* walrus moustache *(Brit) or* mustache *(US)*.

Schnecke *f* **-n (a)** *(Zool, fig)* snail; *(Nackt~)* slug;

(*Cook auch*) escargot. **jdn zur ~machen** (*col*) to give sb a real bawling-out (*col*). **(b)** (*Cook: Gebäck*) ≃ Chelsea bun.

Schnecken-: s~förmig *adj* spiral; (*Archit*) *ornament* scroll-shaped; **~haus** *nt* snail-shell; **sich in sein ~haus zurückziehen** (*fig col*) to retreat into one's shell; **~tempo** *nt* (*col*) **im ~tempo** at a snail's pace.

Schnee *m no pl* **(a)** (*auch TV*) snow. **vom ~ eingeschlossen sein** to be snowbound. **(b)** (*Ei~*) whisked (*Brit*) *or* whipped (*US*) egg-white. **Eiweiß zu ~ schlagen** to whisk (*Brit*) *or* whip (*US*) the egg-white(s) till stiff.

Schnee-: ~ball *m* snowball; **~ballschlacht** *f* snowball fight; **s~bedeckt** *adj* snow-covered; *Berg auch* snow-capped; **~besen** *m* (*Cook*) whisk; **s~blind** *adj* snowblind; **~decke** *f* blanket *or* covering of snow; **~fall** *m* snowfall, fall of snow; **~flocke** *f* snowflake; **s~frei** *adj* free of snow; **~gestöber** *nt* (*leicht*) snow flurry; (*stark*) snowstorm; **~glöckchen** *nt* snowdrop; **~grenze** *f* snow-line; **~kette** *f* (*Aut*) snow chain; **~könig** *m*: **sich freuen wie ein ~könig** to be as pleased as Punch; **~mann** *m*, *pl* **~männer** snowman; **~matsch** *m* slush; **~pflug** *m* (*Tech, Ski*) snowplough (*Brit*), snowplow (*US*); **~regen** *m* sleet; **~schaufel** *f* snow-shovel, snow-pusher (*US*); **~schmelze** *f* thaw; **~schuh** *m* snow-shoe; **~sturm** *m* snowstorm; (*stärker*) blizzard; **~treiben** *nt* driving snow; **~verwehung, ~wehe** *f* snowdrift; **s~weiß** *adj* snow-white, as white as snow; *Haare* snowy-white; **~wittchen** *nt* Snow White.

Schneid *m no pl* (*col*) nerve, courage.

Schneidbrenner *m* (*Tech*) oxyacetylene cutter.

Schneide *f* **-n** (sharp *or* cutting) edge; (*von Messer, Schwert*) blade.

schneiden *pret* **schnitt**, *ptp* **geschnitten 1** *vi* to cut. **der Wind schneidet** the wind is biting.

2 *vt* **(a)** (*auch fig: meiden*) to cut; (*in Scheiben*) to slice; (*klein~*) *Gemüse etc* to chop; (*Sport*) *Ball* to slice; (*schnitzen*) *Namen, Figuren* to carve; (*Weg*) to cross. **sein schön/scharf geschnittenes Gesicht** his clean-cut/sharp features; **die Luft ist zum S~** (*fig col*) the air is very bad; **die Atmosphäre ist zum S~** (*fig col*) you could cut the atmosphere with a knife; **jdn ~** (*beim Überholen*) to cut in on sb; **weit/eng geschnitten sein** (*Sew*) to be cut wide/narrow. **(b)** *Film, Tonband* to edit. **(c)** (*col: operieren*) to operate on.

3 *vr* **(a)** (*Mensch*) to cut oneself. **sich in den Finger** *etc* **~** to cut one's finger *etc*. **(b)** (*col: sich täuschen*) **da hat er sich aber geschnitten!** he's very mistaken. **(c)** (*Linien, Straßen etc*) to intersect.

schneidend *adj* biting; *Kälte auch* bitter; *Schmerz* sharp; *Stimme* piercing.

Schneider *m* **-** **(a)** (*Beruf*) tailor; (*Damen~*) dressmaker. **(b)** (*col*) **frieren wie ein ~** to be/get frozen to the marrow (*col*); **aus dem ~ sein** (*fig*) to be out of the woods. **(c)** (*Gerät*) cutter; (*col: für Brot etc*) slicer. **(d)** (*Schnake*) daddy-long-legs.

Schneiderei *f* **(a)** *no pl* (*Handwerk*) tailoring; (*für Damen*) dressmaking. **(b)** (*Werkstatt*) tailor's/dressmaker's workshop.

Schneiderin *f* tailor; (*Damen~*) dressmaker.

Schneidermeister *m* master tailor/dressmaker.

schneidern 1 *vi* (*beruflich*) to be a tailor/dressmaker; (*als Hobby*) to do dressmaking. **2** *vt* to make, to sew; *Herrenanzug* to tailor, to make.

Schneider-: ~sitz *m* **im ~sitz sitzen** to sit cross-legged; **~werkstatt** *f* tailor's/dressmaker's workshop.

Schneidezahn *m* incisor.

schneidig *adj* dashing; *Tempo* fast.

schneien 1 *vi impers* to snow. **2** *vt impers* **es schneite Konfetti** confetti rained down. **3** *vi aux sein* (*fig*) to rain down. **jdm ins Haus ~** (*col*) (*Besuch*) to drop in on sb; (*Rechnung, Brief*) to arrive through one's letterbox *or* in the mail.

Schneise *f* **-n** (*Wald~*) firebreak; (*Flug~*) flight path.

schnell *adj* quick; *Bedienung, Tempo auch, Auto, Zug, Strecke* fast; *Abreise, Hilfe* speedy. **~ gehen/fahren** to walk/drive quickly/fast; **sie wird ~ böse** she loses her temper quickly; **diese dünnen Gläser gehen ~ kaputt** these thin glasses break easily; **er ist sehr ~ mit seinem Urteil** he's very quick to judge; **nicht so ~!** not so fast!; **ich muß mir nur noch ~ die Haare kämmen** I must just give my hair a quick comb; **sein Puls ging ~** his pulse was very fast; **das geht ~** (*grundsätzlich*) it doesn't take long; **das ging ~** that was quick; **in unserem Büro muß alles ~ gehen** in our office things must be done quickly *or* fast; **das werden wir ~ erledigt haben** we'll soon have that finished.

Schnelläufer *m* (*Sport*) sprinter.

Schnell-: ~bahn *f* high-speed railway (*Brit*) *or* railroad (*US*); **~boot** *nt* speedboat; **~dienst** *m* express service.

Schnelle *f* **-n** **(a)** *no pl* (*Schnelligkeit*) quickness, speed. **(b)** (*Strom~*) rapids *pl*. **(c) etw auf die ~ machen** to do sth in a rush.

schnellebig *adj* *Zeit* fast-moving.

schnellen *vi aux sein* (*lit, fig*) to shoot. **in die Höhe ~** to shoot up.

Schnell-: ~feuer *nt* (*Mil*) rapid fire; **~feuergewehr** *nt* automatic pistol; **~gaststätte** *f* cafeteria, fast-food restaurant (*US*); **~gericht** *nt* **(a)** (*Jur*) summary court; **(b)** (*Cook*) instant meal, convenience food (*esp pej*), TV dinner (*US col*); **~hefter** *m* spring folder.

Schnelligkeit *f* (*von Auto, Verkehr*) speed; (*von Tempo auch*) quickness; (*von Schritten auch, von Puls*) rapidity; (*von Bote, Hilfe*) speediness.

Schnell-: ~imbiß *m* **(a)** (*Essen*) (quick) snack; **(b)** (*Raum*) snack-bar; **~kochtopf** *m* (*Dampfkochtopf*) pressure cooker; **~kurs** *m* crash course; **~paket** *nt* express parcel.

schnellstens *adv* as quickly as possible.

Schnell-: ~straße *f* expressway; **~zug** *m* fast train; (*Fern~zug*) express (train).

Schnepfe *f* **-n** (*Orn*) snipe.

schneuzen 1 *vr* to blow one's nose. **2** *vt* **einem Kind/sich die Nase ~** to blow a child's/one's nose.

Schnickschnack *m no pl* (*col: Unsinn*) twaddle (*col*) *no indef art*, poppycock (*col*) *no indef art*.

schniefen *vi* (*dial*) to sniffle.

schniegeln *vtr* (*col*) *siehe* **geschniegelt**.

Schnippchen *nt* **jdm ein ~ schlagen** (*col*) to play a trick on sb.

schnippeln *vti* (*col*) to snip (*an +dat* at); (*mit Messer*) to hack (*an +dat* at).

schnippen 1 *vi* **mit den Fingern ~** to snap one's fingers. **2** *vt* **etw von etw ~** to flick sth off *or* from sth.

schnippisch *adj* saucy, pert.

Schnipsel *m or nt* **-** (*col*) scrap; (*Papier~*) scrap of paper.

schnitt *pret of* **schneiden.**

Schnitt *m* **-e** **(a)** cut; (*Haar~ auch*) haircut; (*von Gesicht, Augen*) shape; (*Sew: ~muster*) pattern. **(b)** (*Film*) editing *no pl*. **~: L. Schwarz** editor-L. Schwarz. **(c)** (*Math*) (*~punkt*) (point of) intersection; (*Längs~, Quer~*) section; (*col: Durch~*) average. **im ~** on average.

Schnitt-: ~blumen *pl* cut flowers *pl*; **~bohnen** *pl* French *or* green beans *pl*.

Schnitte *f* **-n** slice; (*belegt*) open sandwich; (*zusammengeklappt*) sandwich.

Schnitt-: s~fest *adj* *Tomaten* firm; **~fläche** *f* (*Math*) section.

schnittig *adj* smart; *Auto, Formen auch* stylish; *Tempo auch* snappy (*col*).

Schnitt-: **~lauch** *m no pl* chives *pl*; **~muster** *nt (Sew)* (paper) pattern; **~punkt** *m* intersection; **~stelle** *f (Comp)* interface; **~wunde** *f* cut; *(tief)* gash.

Schnitzel[1] *nt or m* - *(Papier~)* scrap of paper; *(Holz~)* shaving; *(Karotten~)* shred.

Schnitzel[2] *nt* - *(Cook)* veal/port cutlet, schnitzel.

Schnitzeljagd *f* paper-chase.

schnitzen *vti* to carve.

Schnitzer *m* - **(a)** wood carver. **(b)** *(col) (in Benehmen)* boob *(Brit col)*, goof *(US col)*; *(Fehler)* howler *(col)*.

Schnitzerei *f* (wood-)carving.

schnodd(e)rig *adj (col)* offhand, brash.

Schnodd(e)rigkeit *f (col)* brashness.

schnöd(e) *adj (niederträchtig)* despicable; *Behandlung, Antwort* contemptuous. **~r Mammon/~s Geld** filthy lucre.

Schnorchel *m* - *(von U-Boot, Taucher)* snorkel.

Schnörkel *m* - flourish; *(an Möbeln, Säulen)* scroll; *(fig: Unterschrift)* squiggle *(hum)*, signature.

schnörkelig *adj* ornate; *Rede auch* flowery.

schnorren *vti (col)* to cadge *(col) (bei* from*)*.

Schnorrer *m* - *(col)* cadger *(col)*.

Schnösel *m* - *(col)* snotty(-nosed) little upstart *(col)*.

schnuckelig *adj (col: gemütlich)* snug.

Schnüffelei *f (fig col: das Spionieren)* snooping *no pl (col)*.

schnüffeln *vi* **(a)** *(schnuppern)* to sniff. **an etw** *(dat)* **~** to sniff (at) sth. **(b)** *(fig col: spionieren)* to snoop around *(col)*.

Schnüffler(in *f***)** *m* - *(col) (fig)* snooper *(col)*, Nosey Parker *(col)*; *(Detektiv)* sleuth *(col)*.

Schnuller *m* - *(col)* dummy *(Brit)*, pacifier *(US)*; *(auf Flasche)* teat *(Brit)*, nipple *(US)*.

Schnulze *f* **-n** *(col)* schmaltzy film/song *(col)*.

schnupfen *vti* **(Tabak) ~** to take snuff.

Schnupfen *m* - cold. **(einen) ~ bekommen** to catch (a) cold; **(einen) ~ haben** to have a cold.

Schnupftabak *m* snuff.

schnuppe *adj pred (col)* **jdm ~ sein** to be all the same to sb; **das Wohl seiner Angestellten ist ihm völlig ~** he couldn't care less about the welfare of his employees.

schnuppern *vti* to sniff. **an etw** *(dat)* **~** to sniff (at) sth.

Schnur *f* **¨-e** *(Bindfaden)* string; *(Kordel)* cord; *(Kabel)* flex, lead.

Schnürchen *nt* **es läuft** *or* **klappt alles wie am ~** everything's going like clockwork.

schnüren 1 *vt Paket etc* to tie up; *Mieder* to lace (up). **Schuhe zum S~** lace-up shoes. **2** *vi (col: eng sein)* to be too tight.

schnurgerade *adj* (dead) straight.

Schnurrbart *m* moustache *(Brit)*, mustache *(US)*.

schnurren *vi (Katze)* to purr; *(Spinnrad etc)* to hum, to whirr.

Schnurrhaare *pl* whiskers *pl*.

Schnür-: **~schuh** *m* laced shoe, lace-up; **~senkel** *m* shoelace; *(für Stiefel)* bootlace.

schnurstracks *adv* straight, directly. **~ auf jdn/etw zugehen** to make a bee-line for sb/sth *(col)*.

schnurz *adj (col)* = **schnuppe.**

schob *pret of* **schieben.**

Schober *m* - *(Scheune)* barn.

Schock *m* **-s** shock. **unter ~ stehen** to be in (a state of) shock.

Schockeinwirkung *f* state of shock; **unter ~ stehen** to be in (a state of) shock.

schocken *vt (col)* to shock.

schockieren* *vti* to shock; *(stärker)* to scandalize. **schockiert sein** to be shocked *(über +acc* at*)*.

Schocktherapie *f* shock therapy.

Schöffe *m (wk)* **-n, -n, Schöffin** *f* ≃ juror.

Schöffengericht *nt* court *(with jury)*.

Schokolade *f* chocolate.

Schokoladen- *in cpds* chocolate; **s~braun** *adj* chocolate-coloured *(Brit)*, chocolate-colored *(US)*.

Scholle[1] *f* **-n** *(Fisch)* plaice.

Scholle[2] *f* **-n** *(Eis~)* (ice) floe; *(Erd~)* clod (of earth).

Scholli *m*: **mein lieber ~!** *(col) (drohend)* now look here!; *(erstaunt)* my oh my!

schon *adv* **(a)** *(bereits)* already; *(in Fragen: überhaupt ~)* ever. **er ist ~ da** he's there already, he's already there; **ist er ~ da?** is he there yet?; **warst du ~ dort?** have you been there yet?; *(je)* have you ever been there?; **mußt du ~ gehen?** must you go already, must you go so soon?; **er wollte ~ die Hoffnung aufgeben, als ...** he was just about to give up hope when ...; **ich warte nun ~ seit drei Wochen** I've already been waiting (for) three weeks; **~ damals** even then; **~ vor 100 Jahren** as far back as 100 years ago; **~ am nächsten Tag** the very next day; **der Briefträger kommt ~ um 6 Uhr** the postman comes as early as 6 o'clock; **ich habe das ~ mal gehört** I've heard that before; **das habe ich dir doch ~ hundertmal gesagt** I've told you that a hundred times (before); **das habe ich ~ oft gehört** I've heard that often; **ich bin ~ lange fertig** I've been ready for ages; **wartest du ~ lange?** have you been waiting (for) long?; **wie ~ so oft** as so often (before); **~ immer** always; **was, ~ wieder?** what - *again?*

(b) *(allein bloß)* just; *(ohnehin)* anyway. **allein ~ das Gefühl ...** just the very feeling ...; **~ die Tatsache, daß ...** the very fact that ...; **wenn ich das ~ sehe/höre!** I can't bear to see/hear it; **~ weil** if only because.

(c) *(bestimmt)* all right. **du wirst ~ sehen** you'll see (all right); **das wirst du ~ noch lernen** you'll learn that one day.

(d) *(tatsächlich, allerdings)* really. **das ist ~ eine Frechheit!** that's a real cheek!; **da gehört ~ Mut** *etc* **dazu** that takes real courage *etc*; **das ist ~ möglich** that's quite possible; **das mußt du ~ machen!** you really ought to do that.

(e) *(einschränkend)* **ja ~, aber ...** *(col)* yes (well), but ...; **da haben Sie ~ recht, aber ...** yes, you're right (there), but ...

(f) **hör ~ auf damit!** will you stop that!; **so antworte ~!** come on, answer; **nun sag ~!** come on, tell me/us *etc*; **ich komme ja ~!** I'm just coming!; **was macht das ~, wenn ...** what does it matter if ...; **3 Seiten schreiben, was ist das ~?** write 3 pages? that's nothing; **und wenn ~!** *(col)* so what? *(col)*; **~ gut** *(col)* all right, okay *(col)*; **ich verstehe ~** I understand; **danke, es geht ~** thank you, I/we *etc* will manage.

schön 1 *adj* **(a)** *(hübsch anzusehen)* beautiful, lovely; *Mann* handsome.

(b) *(nett, angenehm)* good; *Stimme, Musik, Wetter auch* lovely; *Gelegenheit* great, splendid. **die ~en Künste** the fine arts; **die ~e Literatur** belletristic literature; **eines ~en Tages** one fine day; **das S~e beim Skilaufen ist ...** the nice *or* beautiful thing about skiing is ...; **~en Urlaub!** have a good *or* nice holiday; **~, daß du gekommen bist** (how) nice of you to come; **ein ~er frischer Wind** a nice cool wind.

(c) *(iro) Unordnung* fine, nice; *Überraschung* lovely; *Unsinn* absolute. **da hast du etwas S~es angerichtet** you've made a fine *or* nice mess; **du bist mir ein ~er Freund/Held** *etc* a fine friend/hero *etc* you are; **das wäre ja noch ~er** *(col)* that's (just) too much!

(d) **das war nicht ~ von dir** *(col)* that wasn't very nice of you; **zu ~, um wahr zu sein** *(col)* too good to be true; **(also) ~, na ~** okay, all right; **~ und gut, aber ...** that's all very well but ...; **ein ~es Stück weiterkommen** to make good progress; **eine ganz ~e Menge** quite a lot.

2 *adv* **(a)** *(bei Verben)* well; *scheinen* brightly; *schreiben* beautifully. **sich ~ anziehen** to get dressed up; **es ~ haben** to be well off; *(im Urlaub etc)* to have a good time (of it); **schlaf ~** sleep well; **erhole dich ~** have a good rest. **(b)** *(col: sehr, ziemlich)* really. **~ weich/warm** nice and soft/warm; **sich** *(dat)* **~ weh tun** to hurt oneself a lot; **sich ~ ärgern** to be very angry; **ganz ~ teuer/kalt** pretty expensive/cold; **ganz ~ lange** quite a while. **(c) iß mal ~ deinen Teller leer** eat it all up nicely (now); **sei ~ still/ordentlich** *etc (als Aufforderung)* be nice and quiet/tidy *etc*; **fahr ~ langsam** drive nice and slowly.

schonen 1 *vt Gesundheit, Herz, Kleider* to look after, to take care of; *eigene Nerven, Bremsen* to go easy on; *jds Nerven* to spare; *Gegner, Kind* to be easy on; *Teppich, Füße* to save; *(schützen)* to protect. **ein Waschmittel, das die Wäsche schont** a detergent that is kind to your washing; **vernünftiges Schalten schont das Getriebe** careful gearchanging saves the gears. **2** *vr* to look after *or* take care of oneself.

schonend *adj* gentle; *(rücksichtsvoll)* considerate. **jdm etw ~ beibringen** to break sth to sb gently; **etw ~ behandeln** to treat sth with care.

Schoner[1] *m* - *(Naut)* schooner.

Schoner[2] *m* - cover; *(für Rückenlehnen)* antimacassar, chairback.

Schön-: s~färben *sep* **1** *vt (fig)* to gloss over; **2** *vi* to gloss things over; **~färberei** *f (fig)* glossing things over.

Schonfrist *f* period of grace.

schöngeistig *adj* aesthetic *(Brit)*, esthetic *(US)*.

Schönheit *f* beauty.

Schönheits-: ~chirurgie *f* cosmetic surgery; **~fehler** *m* blemish; *(von Gegenstand)* flaw; **~ideal** *nt* ideal of beauty; **~königin** *f* beauty queen; **~operation** *f* cosmetic operation; **~pflege** *f* beauty care; **~wettbewerb** *m* beauty contest.

Schonkost *f* light diet.

Schönling *m (pej)* pansy *(col)*, pretty boy *(col)*.

Schön-: s~machen *sep* **1** *vt Kind* to dress up; *Wohnung* to decorate; **2** *vr* to get dressed up; *(sich schminken)* to make (oneself) up; **~schrift** *f* **in ~schrift** in one's best (hand)writing; **s~tun** *vi sep irreg* **jdm s~tun** *(schmeicheln)* to flatter *or* soft-soap *(col)* sb; *(sich lieb Kind machen)* to pay court to sb, to play up to sb.

Schonung *f* **(a)** *(Forest)* (protected) forest plantation area. **(b)** *(das Schonen) (von Gefühlen)* sparing; *(von Teppich, Kleidern)* saving; *(das Schützen)* protection. **der Patient braucht noch ein paar Wochen ~** the patient still needs looking after for a few weeks; **zur ~ meiner Gefühle** to spare my feelings; **zur ~ Ihrer Augen** to look after your eyes; **zur ~ des Getriebes** to give your gears a longer life. **(c)** *(Nachsicht, Milde)* mercy.

Schonungs-: s~los *adj* ruthless; *Wahrheit* blunt; *Kritik* savage; **~losigkeit** *f* ruthlessness; *(von Kritik)* savageness; **s~voll** *adj* gentle.

Schönwetterperiode *f* period of fine weather.

Schonzeit *f* close season; *(fig)* honeymoon period.

Schopf *m* ¨-e (shock of) hair. **eine Gelegenheit beim ~ ergreifen** *or* **fassen** to seize *or* grasp an opportunity with both hands.

schöpfen *vt* **(a)** *auch vi (aus* from*) Wasser* to scoop; *Suppe* to ladle. **(b)** *Atem* to draw, to take; *Mut, Kraft* to summon up; *Hoffnung* to find.

Schöpfer(in *f***)** *m* - **(a)** creator; *(Gott)* Creator. **(b)** *(col: Schöpflöffel)* ladle.

schöpferisch *adj* creative.

Schöpf-: ~kelle *f*, **~löffel** *m* ladle.

Schöpfung *f* creation. **die ~** *(Rel)* the Creation.

Schoppen *m* - *(Glas Wein)* glass of wine.

schor *pret of* **scheren**[1].

Schorf *m* **-e** crust, scaly skin; *(Wund~)* scab.

Schorle *f* **-n** wine and soda water mix.

Schornstein *m* chimney; *(von Schiff)* funnel, (smoke)stack.

Schornsteinfeger(in *f***)** *m* - chimney-sweep.

schoß *pret of* **schießen.**

Schoß *m* ¨-e **(a)** lap. **die Hände in den ~ legen** *(fig)* to sit back (and take it easy); **das ist ihm nicht in den ~ gefallen** *(fig)* it didn't just fall into his lap. **(b)** *(liter: Mutterleib)* womb. **im ~e der Familie** in the bosom of one's family. **(c)** *(an Kleidungsstück)* tail.

Schoßhund *m* lap-dog.

Schößling *m (Bot)* shoot.

Schote *f* **-n** *(Bot)* pod.

Schotte *m (wk)* **-n, -n** Scot, Scotsman.

Schotten-: ~muster *nt* tartan; **~rock** *m* kilt; *(für Frauen)* tartan skirt.

Schotter *m* - gravel; *(im Straßenbau)* (road) metal; *(Rail)* ballast.

Schotter-: ~decke *f* gravel surface; **~straße** *f* gravel road.

Schottin *f* Scot, Scotswoman.

schottisch *adj* Scottish, Scots.

Schottland *nt* Scotland.

schraffieren* *vt* to hatch.

Schraffierung *f* hatching.

schräg 1 *adj* **(a)** *(geneigt)* sloping; *Augen* slanted, slanting; *Kante* bevelled *(Brit)*, beveled *(US)*. **(b)** *(nicht gerade, nicht parallel)* oblique. **(c)** *(col: verdächtig)* suspicious, fishy *(col)*. **ein ~er Vogel** a queer fish *(col)*. **2** *adv* **(a)** *(geneigt)* at an angle; *halten* on the slant, slanting. **~ stehende Augen** slanting *or* slanted eyes. **(b)** *(nicht gerade, nicht parallel)* obliquely; *überqueren, gestreift* diagonally; *(Sew)* on the bias. **~ gegenüber/hinter** diagonally opposite/behind; **~ rechts/links** diagonally to the right/left; **die Straße biegt ~ ab** the road forks off; **~ gedruckt** in italics.

Schräge *f* **-n** **(a)** *(schräge Fläche)* slope, sloping surface; *(schräge Kante)* bevel. **(b)** *(Schrägheit)* slant, angle; *(im Zimmer)* sloping ceiling.

Schräg-: ~kante *f* bevelled *(Brit) or* beveled *(US)* edge; **~lage** *f* angle, slant; *(von Flugzeug)* bank(ing); **~schrift** *f (Handschrift)* slanting hand(writing) *or* writing; *(Typ)* italics *pl*; **~streifen** *m* **(a)** *(Muster)* diagonal stripe; **(b)** *(Sew)* bias binding; **~strich** *m* oblique.

Schramme *f* **-n** scratch.

schrammen *vt* to scratch.

Schrank *m* ¨-e cupboard, closet *(US)*; *(Kleider~)* wardrobe.

Schränkchen *nt dim of* **Schrank** small cupboard; *(Arznei~)* cabinet.

Schranke *f* **-n** barrier; *(Rail: Gatter)* gate; *(fig) (Grenze)* limit; *(Hindernis)* barrier. **meine Geduld hat ~n** there are limits to my patience; **keine ~n kennen** to know no bounds; *(Mensch)* not to know when to stop; **einer Sache** *(dat)* **(enge) ~n setzen** to put a limit on sth; **jdn in seine ~n (ver)weisen** *(fig)* to put sb in his place.

Schranken-: s~los *adj (fig) Weiten* boundless, unlimited; *Forderungen* unrestrained; **~wärter** *m* gatekeeper *(at rail crossing)*.

Schrank-: ~fach *nt* shelf; **~koffer** *m* wardrobe trunk; **~wand** *f* wall unit.

Schraube *f* **-n** **(a)** screw; *(ohne Spitze)* bolt. **bei ihr ist eine ~ locker** *(col)* she's got a screw loose *(col)*. **(b)** *(Naut, Aviat)* propeller, prop *(col)*. **(c)** *(Sport)* twist. **(d) alte ~** *(pej col)* old bag *(col)*.

schrauben *vti* to screw. **etw in die Höhe ~** *(fig) Preise, Rekorde* to push sth up; *Ansprüche* to raise; *siehe* **geschraubt.**

Schrauben-: ~schlüssel *m* spanner *(Brit)*, wrench; **~zieher** *m* - screwdriver.

Schraub-: ~stock *m* vice; **~verschluß** *m* screw top *or* cap.

Schrebergarten *m* allotment *(Brit)*.

Schreck *m* **-e** fright, scare. **vor ~** in fright; *zittern* with fright; **zu meinem großen ~(en)** to my great horror *or* dismay; **einen ~(en) bekommen** to get a fright *or* scare; **auf den ~ (hin)** to get over the fright; **sich vom ersten ~ erholen** to recover from the initial shock; **freudiger ~** pleasant surprise; **ach du ~** *(col)* (oh) crumbs! *(col)*; **o ~ laß nach** *(hum col)* for goodness sake! *(col)*.

schrecken 1 *vt (ängstigen)* to frighten, to scare; *(stärker)* to terrify. **jdn aus dem Schlaf ~** to startle sb out of his sleep. **2** *vi aux sein* **aus dem Schlaf ~** to be startled out of one's sleep.

Schrecken *m* - **(a)** = **Schreck. (b)** *(Furcht, Entsetzen)* terror, horror. **seinen ~ vor etw** *(dat)* **verlieren** to loose one's fear *or* terror of sth; **er war der ~ der ganzen Lehrerschaft** he was the terror of all the teachers.

schrecken|erregend *adj* terrifying, horrifying.

Schreckens-: s~bleich *adj* as white as a sheet *or* ghost; **~herrschaft** *f* (reign of) terror; **~kammer** *f* chamber of horrors; **~nachricht** *f* terrible news *no pl or* piece of news.

Schreck-: ~gespenst *nt* nightmare; **das ~gespenst der Inflation** the bogey of inflation; **s~haft** *adj* easily startled.

schrecklich *adj* terrible, dreadful; *(col: sehr, groß auch)* awful. **sich ~ freuen** *(col)* to be terribly *or* awfully pleased; **~ gerne!** *(col)* I'd absolutely love to.

Schrecklichkeit *f* terribleness, dreadfulness.

Schreck-: ~schraube *f (pej col)* (old) battle-axe *(col)*; *(in bezug auf Äußeres)* dolled-up old bag *(col)*; **~schuß** *m* warning shot; **~sekunde** *f* moment of shock.

Schrei *m* **-e** cry, shout; *(gellend)* scream; *(kreischend)* shriek; *(von Eule etc)* screech; *(von Hahn)* crow. **der ~ nach Freiheit/Rache** the call for freedom/revenge; **ein ~ der Entrüstung** an (indignant) outcry; **der letzte ~** *(col)* the latest thing, all the rage *(col)*.

Schreib-: ~bedarf *m* writing materials *pl*, stationery; **~block** *m* (writing) pad.

schreiben *pret* **schrieb,** *ptp* **geschrieben 1** *vt* **(a)** to write; *Scheck auch, Rechnung* to make out, to write out; *(mit Schreibmaschine)* to type (out); *Klassenarbeit, Übersetzung* to do; *(berichten: Zeitung etc)* to say. **jdm einen Brief ~** to write a letter to sb, to write sb a letter; **seinen Namen unter etw** *(acc)* **~** to put one's signature to sth, to sign sth; **wo steht das geschrieben?** where does it say that?; **es steht geschrieben** *(Rel)* it is written; **es steht Ihnen im Gesicht geschrieben** it's written all over your face. **(b)** *(orthographisch)* to spell. **ein Wort falsch ~** to misspell a word, to spell a word wrong(ly). **(c)** *(Datum)* **wir ~ heute den 10. Mai** today is the 10th May; **man schrieb das Jahr 1939** the year was 1939, it was (in) 1939.

2 *vi* to write; *(tippen)* to type; *(berichten)* to say. **jdm ~** to write to sb, to write sb *(US)*; **ich schrieb ihm, daß ...** I wrote and told him that ...; **an einem Roman** *etc* **~** to be working on *or* writing a novel *etc*; **wieviel Silben schreibt sie pro Minute?** what is her (typing) speed?; **mit Bleistift ~** to write in pencil.

3 *vr* **(a)** *(korrespondieren)* to write (to each other), to correspond. **(b)** *(geschrieben werden)* to be spelt. **wie schreibt sich das?** how is that spelt?

Schreiben *nt* - **(a)** *no pl* writing. **(b)** *(Mitteilung)* communication *(form)*; *(Comm: Brief)* letter.

Schreiber(in *f***)** *m* - writer, author; *(Gerichts~)* clerk; *(pej: Schriftsteller)* scribbler.

Schreiberei *f (col)* writing *no indef art; (pej: von Schriftsteller)* scribbling.

Schreiberling *m (pej: Schriftsteller)* scribbler.

Schreib-: s~faul *adj* lazy (about letter-writing); **er ist s~faul** he's a poor correspondent; **~faulheit** *f* laziness (about letter-writing); **~fehler** *m* (spelling) mistake; *(aus Flüchtigkeit)* slip of the pen; *(Tippfehler)* (typing) mistake *or* error; **~heft** *nt* exercise book; **~kraft** *f* typist; **~maschine** *f* typewriter; **mit der ~maschine schreiben** to type; **mit der ~maschine geschrieben** typewritten, typed; **~maschinenpapier** *nt* typing paper; **~stube** *f (Mil)* orderly room; **~tisch** *m* desk; **~tischtäter** *m* mastermind behind the scenes (of a/the crime); **~übung** *f* writing exercise; **~unterlage** *f* pad; *(auf ~tisch)* desk pad; **~waren** *pl* stationery *sing*, writing materials *pl*; **~warenhändler** *m* stationer; **~weise** *f (Stil)* style; *(Rechtschreibung)* spelling.

schreien *pret* **schrie,** *ptp* **geschrie(e)n 1** *vti* to shout, to cry out; *(gellend)* to scream; *(vor Angst, vor Schmerzen)* to cry out/to scream; *(kreischend)* to shriek; *(heulen: Kind)* to howl; *(jammern)* to moan; *(Eule etc)* to screech; *(Hahn)* to crow. **es war zum S~** *(col)* it was a scream *(col) or* a hoot *(col)*; **nach etw ~** *(fig)* to cry out for sth; **jdm etw ins Gesicht ~** to shout sth in sb's face. **2** *vr* **sich heiser ~** to shout oneself hoarse; *(Baby)* to cry itself hoarse.

schreiend *adj Farben* loud, garish; *Unrecht* glaring, flagrant.

Schrei-: ~hals *m (col) (Baby)* bawler *(col)*; *(Unruhestifter)* noisy troublemaker; **~krampf** *m* screaming fit.

Schrein *m* **-e** *(old)* shrine.

Schreiner *m* - carpenter, joiner; *(Möbel~)* cabinet-maker.

schreiten *pret* **schritt,** *ptp* **geschritten** *vi aux sein (geh) (schnell gehen)* to stride; *(feierlich gehen)* to walk; *(stolzieren)* to strut. **zu etw ~** *(fig)* to proceed with sth; **zum Äußersten ~** to take extreme measures; **zur Abstimmung ~** to go to a vote.

schrie *pret of* **schreien.**

schrieb *pret of* **schreiben.**

Schrieb *m* **-e** *(col)* missive *(hum)*.

Schrift *f* **-en (a)** writing; *(~system)* script; *(Typ)* type, typeface. **gotische ~** Gothic script; **er hat eine schlechte ~** he has bad handwriting. **(b)** *(~stück)* document; *(Broschüre)* leaflet; *(Buch)* work; *(kürzere Abhandlung)* paper. **seine früheren ~en** his early writings.

Schrift-: ~art *f (Hand~)* script; *(Typ)* type, typeface; **~bild** *nt* script; **~deutsch** *nt* written German; **~form** *f (Jur)* **dieser Vertrag erfordert die ~form** this contract must be drawn up in writing; **~führer** *m* secretary; **~gelehrte(r)** *m (Bibl)* scribe.

schriftlich 1 *adj* written. **in ~er Form** in writing; **die ~e Prüfung** the written exam. **2** *adv* in writing. **ich bin ~ eingeladen worden** I have had a written invitation; **das kann ich Ihnen ~ geben** *(fig col)* I can tell you that for free *(col)*.

Schrift-: ~probe *f (Hand~)* specimen of one's handwriting; **~satz** *m (Jur)* legal document; **~setzer** *m* typesetter, compositor; **~sprache** *f* written language.

Schriftsteller *m* - author, writer.

Schriftstellerin *f* author(ess), writer.

schriftstellerisch *adj* literary. **er ist ~ begabt** he has literary talent *or* talent as a writer.

Schrift-: ~stück *nt* paper; *(Jur)* document; **~tum** *nt no pl* literature; **~verkehr, ~wechsel** *m* correspondence; **~zeichen** *nt* character; **~zug** *m usu pl* stroke; *(Handschrift)* hand.

schrill *adj* shrill; *(fig) Mißklang* jarring.

schritt *pret of* **schreiten.**

Schritt *m* **-e (a)** *(lit, fig)* step; *(hörbar)* footstep. **einen ~ zurücktreten** to step back; **ein paar ~e spazierengehen** to go for *or* take a short walk *or* stroll; **einen ~ machen** to take a step; **kurze/große ~e machen** to take small steps/long strides; **den ersten ~ tun** *(fig)* to make the first move; *(etw beginnen)* to take the first step; **~e**

gegen jdn/etw unternehmen to take steps against sb/sth; **auf ~ und Tritt** *(lit, fig)* wherever *or* everywhere one goes; **~ für ~** step by step. **(b)** *(Gang)* walk, gait; *(Tempo)* pace. **~ halten** *(lit, fig)* to keep pace; **mit der Zeit ~ halten** to keep abreast of the times; **langsamen ~es** *(geh)* with slow steps. **(c)** *(~geschwindigkeit)* walking pace. **„~fahren"** "dead slow". **(d)** *(Maßangabe)* **mit zehn ~en Abstand** at a distance of ten paces. **(e)** *(Hosen~)* crotch.

Schrittempo *nt* walking speed.

Schritt-: ~macher *m (Sport, Med)* pacemaker; *(fig auch)* pacesetter; **s~weise 1** *adv* gradually, little by little; **2** *adj* gradual.

schroff *adj (rauh, barsch)* curt; *(kraß, abrupt)* abrupt; *(steil) Fels, Klippe* precipitous. **~e Gegensätze** stark *or* sharp contrasts.

Schroffheit *f siehe adj* curtness; abruptness; precipitousness; *(schroffes Wort)* curt remark.

schröpfen *vt* **jdn ~** *(fig)* to fleece sb *(col)*.

Schrot *m or nt* **-e (a)** whole-corn/-rye *etc* meal; *(Weizen)* wholemeal *(Brit)*, wholewheat *(US)*. **ein Schotte von echtem ~ und Korn** a true Scot; **vom alten ~ und Korn** *(fig)* of the old school. **(b)** *(Hunt)* shot.

Schrot-: ~büchse, ~flinte *f* shotgun; **~kugel** *f* pellet; **~ladung** *f* round of shot.

Schrott *m no pl* scrap metal. **ein Auto zu ~ fahren** to write off a car.

Schrott-: ~händler *m* scrap dealer *or* merchant; **~haufen** *m (lit)* scrap heap; **~platz** *m* scrap yard; **s~reif** *adj* ready for the scrap heap; **~wert** *m* scrap value.

schrubben *vti* to scrub.

Schrubber *m* - (long-handled) scrubbing brush.

Schrulle *f* **-n (a)** *(Marotte)* quirk. **(b)** *(pej: alte Frau)* old crone.

schrullig *adj* odd, cranky.

schrump(e)lig *adj (col)* wrinkled.

schrumpfen *vi aux sein (lit, fig)* to shrink; *(Leber, Niere)* to atrophy; *(runzlig werden)* to get wrinkled; *(Exporte, Interesse)* to dwindle.

Schrumpf-: ~kopf *m* shrunken head; **~leber** *f* cirrhosis of the liver.

Schrumpfung *f* shrinking; *(Raumverlust)* shrinkage; *(Med)* atrophy(ing); *(von Exporten)* dwindling.

Schub *m* **¨-e (a)** *(Stoß)* push, shove. **(b)** *(Phys)* thrust. **(c)** *(Gruppe, Anzahl)* batch.

Schuber *m* - slipcase.

Schub-: ~fach *nt* drawer; **~karre** *f*, **~karren** *m* wheelbarrow; **~kasten** *m* drawer; **~kraft** *f (Phys)* thrust; **~lade** *f* **-n** drawer.

Schubs *m* **-e** *(col)* shove, push; *(Aufmerksamkeit erregend)* nudge.

schubsen *vti (col)* to shove, to push; *(Aufmerksamkeit erregend)* to nudge.

schubweise *adv* in batches.

schüchtern *adj* shy.

Schüchternheit *f* shyness.

schuf *pret of* **schaffen**[1].

Schuft *m* **-e** heel *(col)*, cad *(dated col)*.

schuften *vi (col)* to graft (away) *(col)*, to slave away.

Schufterei *f (col)* graft *(col)*, hard work.

schuftig *adj* mean, shabby.

Schuh *m* **-e** shoe. **jdm etw in die ~e schieben** *(col)* to put the blame for sth on sb; **wissen, wo jdn der ~ drückt** to know what is troubling sb; **umgekehrt wird ein ~ draus!** *(col)* quite the reverse is true.

Schuh- *in cpds* shoe; **~anzieher** *m* shoehorn; **~creme** *f* shoe polish *or* cream; **~macher** *m* shoemaker; **~nummer** *f (col)* shoe size; **~plattler** *m* - *Bavarian folk dance;* **~putzer** *m* bootblack, shoe-shine boy *(US)*; **ich bin doch nicht dein ~putzer!** I'm not your slave!; **~riemen** *m* strap (of a/one's shoe); *(Schnürsenkel)* shoelace; **~sohle** *f* sole (of a/one's shoe); **~werk** *nt no pl* footwear; **~wichse** *f (col)* shoe polish.

Schuko- ®: **~steckdose** *f* safety socket *(Brit) or* outlet *(US)*; **~stecker** *m* safety plug.

Schul-: ~abgänger(in *f***)** *m* - school-leaver; **~anfang** *m* beginning of term; *(~eintritt)* first day at school; **~anfänger** *m* child just starting school; **~arbeit** *f usu pl* homework *no pl;* **~aufgaben** *pl* homework *sing*; **~bank** *f* school desk; **die ~bank drücken** *(col)* to go to school; **~beginn** *m (~jahrsbeginn)* beginning of the school year; *(nach Ferien)* beginning of term; **(der) ~beginn ist um neun** school starts at nine; **~behörde** *f* education authority; **~beispiel** *nt (fig)* classic example *(für* of*)*; **~besuch** *m* school attendance; **~bildung** *f* (school) education; **~buch** *nt* schoolbook, textbook; **~bus** *m* school bus.

schuld *adj pred* **~ sein** *or* **haben** to be to blame *(an +dat* for*)*; **er war** *or* **hatte ~ an dem Streit** the argument was his fault, he was to blame for the argument; **du hast** *or* **bist selbst ~** that's your own fault.

Schuld *f* **-en (a)** *no pl (Ursache, Verantwortlichkeit)* **die ~ an etw** *(dat)* **haben** to be to blame for sth; **die ~ auf sich** *(acc)* **nehmen** to take the blame; **jdm die ~ geben** *or* **zuschieben** to blame sb; **die ~ auf jdn schieben** to put the blame on sb; **die ~ bei anderen suchen** to try to blame somebody else; **das ist meine eigene ~** it's my own fault, I've only myself to blame; **durch meine/deine ~** because of me/you.

(b) *no pl (~gefühl)* guilt; *(Unrecht)* wrong; *(Rel: Sünde)* sin. **ich bin mir keiner ~ bewußt** I'm not aware of having done anything wrong; **~ auf sich** *(acc)* **laden** to burden oneself with a deep sense of guilt; **für seine ~ büßen** to pay for one's sin/sins; **~ und Sühne** crime and punishment.

(c) *(Zahlungsverpflichtung)* debt. **~en machen** to run up debts; **~en haben** to be in debt; **DM 10.000 ~en haben** to have debts of DM 10,000; **ich stehe tief in seiner ~** *(fig)* I'm deeply indebted to him.

Schuld-: ~bekenntnis *nt* confession; **s~beladen** *adj* burdened with guilt; **s~bewußt** *adj Mensch* feeling guilty; *Miene* guilty; **~bewußtsein** *nt* feelings of guilt *pl*.

schulden *vt* to owe. **das schulde ich ihm** I owe it to him; **jdm Dank ~** to owe sb a debt of gratitude.

Schulden-: s~frei *adj* free of debt(s); *Grundstück etc* unmortgaged; **~last** *f* debts *pl*.

Schuld-: ~forderung *f* claim; **~frage** *f* question of guilt; **s~frei** *adj* blameless; **~gefühl** *nt* feeling of guilt; **s~haft** *adj (Jur)* culpable.

Schuldienst *m* (school-)teaching *no art;* **im ~ sein** to be a teacher.

schuldig *adj* **(a)** *(schuldhaft, straffällig)* guilty; *(verantwortlich)* to blame *pred (an +dat* for*)*; *(Rel)* sinful. **einer Sache** *(gen)* **~ sein, sich einer Sache** *(gen)* **~ machen** to be guilty of sth; **jdn ~ sprechen** to find sb guilty; **sich ~ bekennen** to admit one's guilt; *(Jur)* to plead guilty; **~ geschieden sein** to be the guilty party in a/the divorce. **(b)** *(geh: gebührend)* due. **jdm den ~en Respekt zollen** to give sb the respect due to him/her. **(c)** *(verpflichtet)* **jdm etw** *(acc)* **~ sein** *(lit, fig)* to owe sb sth; **was bin ich Ihnen ~?** how much do I owe you?; **jdm Dank ~ sein** to owe sb a debt of gratitude; **sie blieb mir die Antwort ~** she didn't have an answer.

Schuldigkeit *f no pl* duty. **seine ~ tun** to do one's duty.

Schul-: ~direktor *m* head teacher, headmaster *(esp Brit)*, principal; **~direktorin** *f* head teacher, headmistress *(esp Brit)*, principal.

Schuld-: ~komplex *m* guilt complex; **s~los** *adj (an Verbrechen)* innocent *(an +dat* of*)*; *(an Fehler, Unglück etc)* blameless, free from blame; **s~los**

geschieden sein to be the innocent party in a/the divorce; **~losigkeit** *f siehe adj* innocence; blamelessness.

Schuldner(in *f***)** *m* - debtor.

Schuld-: **~prinzip** *nt (Jur)* principle of the guilty party; **~schein** *m* IOU, promissory note; **~spruch** *m* verdict of guilty.

Schule *f* **-n** school. **in die ~ kommen/gehen** to start school/go to school; **in der ~** at school; **die ~ wechseln** to change schools; **von der ~ abgehen** to leave school; **durch eine harte ~ gegangen sein** *(fig)* to have learned in a hard school; **~ machen** to become the accepted thing; **aus der ~ plaudern** to tell tales out of school *(col)*.

schulen *vt* to train.

Schüler(in *f***)** *m* - schoolboy/schoolgirl; *(einer bestimmten Schule)* pupil; *(Jünger)* follower, disciple. **als ~ habe ich ...** when I was at school I ...; **alle ~ und ~innen dieser Stadt** all the schoolchildren of this town.

Schüler-: **~austausch** *m* school *or* student exchange; **~ausweis** *m* (school) student card; **~lotse** *m pupil acting as a road-crossing warden;* **~mitverwaltung** *f* school *or* student council; **~schaft** *f* pupils *pl*.

Schul-: **~fach** *nt* school subject; **~ferien** *pl* school holidays *pl (Brit) or* vacation; **~fernsehen** *nt* schools' *or* educational television; **~fest** *nt* school function; **s~frei** *adj* **die Kinder haben morgen s~frei** the children don't have to go to school tomorrow; **~funk** *m* schools' broadcast; **~gebäude** *nt* school building; **~gelände** *nt* school grounds *pl*; **~geld** *nt* school fees *pl*; **~heft** *nt* exercise book; **~hof** *m* school playground *(Brit)*, schoolyard.

schulisch *adj Leistungen, Probleme* at school; *Angelegenheiten* school *attr*. **aus ~er Sicht** from the school angle.

Schul-: **~jahr** *nt* school year; *(Klasse)* year; **ihre ~jahre** her schooldays; **~junge** *m* schoolboy; **~kamerad** *m* schoolmate, schoolfriend; **~kenntnisse** *pl* knowledge *sing* acquired at school; **~klasse** *f* (school) class; **~leiter** *m* head teacher, headmaster *(esp Brit)*, principal; **~leiterin** *f* head teacher, headmistress *(esp Brit)*, principal; **~mädchen** *nt* schoolgirl; **~medizin** *f* orthodox medicine; **~meinung** *f* received opinion; **~meister** *m (old, hum, pej)* schoolmaster; **s~meisterlich** *adj (pej)* schoolmasterish; **s~meistern** *insep* **1** *vt* to lecture (at *or* to); **2** *vi* to lecture; **~ordnung** *f* school rules *pl*; **~pflicht** *f* compulsory school attendance *no art;* **es besteht ~pflicht** school attendance is compulsory; **s~pflichtig** *adj Kind* required to attend school; **~politik** *f* education policy; **~reife** *f* **die ~reife haben** to be ready to go to school; **~schiff** *nt* training ship; **~schluß** *m* end of school; **~schluß ist um 13[10]** school finishes at 13.10; **~sprecher(in** *f***)** *m* head boy/girl *(Brit)*; **~stunde** *f* (school) period *or* lesson; **~tag** *m* schoolday; **der erste ~tag** the/one's first day at school.

Schulter *f* **-n** shoulder. **breite ~n haben** *(lit)* to be broad-shouldered, to have broad shoulders; *(fig)* to have a broad back; **er ließ die ~n hängen** he was slouching; *(niedergeschlagen)* he hung his head; **jdm auf die ~ klopfen** to give sb a slap on the back; *(lobend)* to pat sb on the back; **die** *or* **mit den ~n zucken** to shrug one's shoulders; **etw auf die leichte ~ nehmen** to take sth lightly.

Schulter-: **~blatt** *nt* shoulder blade; **~höhe** *f* shoulder height; **in ~höhe** at shoulder level *or* height; **~klappe** *f (Mil)* epaulette; **s~lang** *adj* shoulder-length.

schultern *vt* to shoulder.

Schulter-: **~riemen** *m* shoulder strap; **~stück** *nt* **(a)** *(Mil)* epaulette; **(b)** *(Cook)* piece of shoulder.

Schultüte *f large conical bag of sweets/candy given to children on their first day at school.*

Schulung *f (Ausbildung)* training; *(Pol)* political instruction.

Schul-: **~unterricht** *m* school lessons *pl*; **~weg** *m* way to/from school; *(Entfernung)* distance to/from school; **~weisheit** *f (pej)* booklearning; **~wesen** *nt* school system; **~zeit** *f (~jahre)* schooldays *pl*; **nach 13jähriger ~zeit** after 13 years at school; **~zeugnis** *nt* school report.

schummeln *vi (col)* to cheat *(bei etw* at sth*)*.

schumm(e)rig *adj Beleuchtung* dim; *Raum* dimly-lit. **bei ~em Licht** in the half-light.

Schund *m no pl (pej)* trash, rubbish.

Schundroman *m* trashy novel.

schunkeln *vi* to link arms and sway from side to side in time to the music.

Schupo *m* **-s** *(dated col)* = **Schutzpolizist** cop *(col)*, copper *(Brit col)*.

Schuppe *f* **-n (a)** *(Bot, Zool)* scale. **es fiel mir wie ~n von den Augen** my eyes were opened, all was clear. **(b)** *(Kopf~)* **~n** *pl* dandruff *sing*.

Schuppen *m* **- (a)** shed. **(b)** *(col) (Haus etc)* hole *(pej col)*; *(übles Lokal)* dive *(col)*.

schuppen 1 *vt Fische* to scale. **2** *vr* to flake.

Schuppen-: **s~artig** *adj* scale-like; **~flechte** *f (Med)* psoriasis *(spec)*.

schuppig *adj* scaly; *(abblätternd auch)* flaking.

Schur *f* **-en** *(das Scheren)* shearing.

schüren *vt* **(a)** *Feuer, Glut* to rake, to poke. **(b)** *(fig)* to stir up; *Zorn etc* to fan the flames of.

schürfen 1 *vi (Min)* to prospect *(nach* for*)*. **tief ~** *(fig)* to dig deep. **2** *vt Bodenschätze* to mine. **3** *vtr* to graze oneself. **sich am Knie ~** to graze one's knee.

Schürf-: **~recht** *nt* mining rights *pl*; **~wunde** *f* graze, abrasion.

Schürhaken *m* poker.

Schurke *m (wk)* **-n, -n** *(dated)* villain, scoundrel.

Schurwolle *f* virgin wool. **„reine ~"** "pure new wool".

Schurz *m* **-e** apron; *(Lenden~)* loincloth.

Schürze *f* **-n** apron.

Schürzen-: **~jäger** *m (col)* philanderer, one for the girls *(col);* **~zipfel** *m* apron-string; **er hängt der Mutter noch am ~zipfel** he's still tied to his mother's apron strings.

Schuß *m* **¨sse (a)** shot; *(~ Munition)* round. **sechs ~** *or* **Schüsse** six shots/rounds; *(lit)* **ein ~ ins Schwarze** *(lit, fig)* a bull's-eye; **weit vom ~ sein** *(fig col)* to be miles from where the action is *(col)*; **er ist keinen ~ Pulver wert** *(fig)* he is not worth tuppence *(Brit col) or* a red cent *(US col)*; **das war ein ~ vor den Bug** *(fig)* that was a warning shot across the bows; **ein ~ in den Ofen** *(col)* a complete waste of time. **(b)** *(Ftbl)* kick; *(zum Tor auch)* shot. **(c)** *(Spritzer) (von Wein, Essig etc)* dash; *(von Whisky)* shot; *(von Humor etc auch)* touch. **2** *(col)* **(gut) in ~ sein** to be in good shape *or* nick *(col)*; *(Mensch)* to be on form; **etw in ~ halten** to keep sth in good shape.

Schuß-: **~bereich** *m* (firing) range; **im ~bereich** within range; **s~bereit** *adj* ready to fire; *Gewehr auch* cocked.

Schussel *m* **-** *(col)* dolt *(col)*; *(zerstreut)* scatterbrain *(col)*.

Schüssel *f* **-n** bowl; *(Servier~ auch)* dish; *(Wasch~)* basin.

schusselig *adj (col)* daft; *(zerstreut)* scatterbrained *(col)*, muddle-headed *(col)*.

Schuß-: **~fahrt** *f (Ski)* schuss; *(das ~fahren)* schussing; **~feld** *nt* field of fire; *(Übungsplatz)* firing range; **s~fest** *adj* bulletproof; **~linie** *f* line of fire; *(fig auch)* firing line; **~verletzung** *f* bullet wound; **~waffe** *f* firearm; **~waffengebrauch** *m (form)* use of firearms; **~wechsel** *m* exchange of shots *or* fire; **~weite** *f* range (of fire); **in/außer ~weite** within/out of range; **~wunde** *f* bullet wound.

Schuster *m* - shoemaker. **auf ~s Rappen** *(hum)* by Shanks's pony; **~, bleib bei deinem Leisten!** *(Prov)* cobbler, stick to your last *(Prov)*.

Schutt *m no pl (Trümmer, Bau~)* rubble; *(Geol)* debris, detritus *(spec)*. **„~abladen verboten"** "no tipping"; **in ~ und Asche liegen** to be in ruins.

Schutt|abladeplatz *m* tip, dump.

Schüttelfrost *m (Med)* shivering fit.

schütteln 1 *vt* to shake; *(rütteln)* to shake about, to jolt (about). **den** *or* **mit dem Kopf ~** to shake one's head; **von Fieber geschüttelt werden** to be racked with fever. **2** *vr* to shake oneself; *(vor Kälte)* to shiver *(vor* with*)*; *(vor Ekel)* to shudder *(vor* with, in*)*. **sich vor Lachen ~** to shake with laughter.

schütten 1 *vt* to tip; *Flüssigkeiten* to pour; *(ver~)* to spill. **2** *vi impers (col)* **es schüttet** it's pouring (with rain), it's bucketing (down) *(col)*.

schütter *adj Haar* thin.

Schutt-: ~haufen *m* pile *or* heap of rubble; **~platz** *m* tip.

Schutz *m no pl* protection *(vor +dat, gegen* against, from*)*; *(Zuflucht auch)* shelter, refuge *(vor +dat, gegen* from*)*; *(der Natur, Umwelt etc)* conservation; *(esp Mil: Deckung)* cover. **bei jdm ~ suchen** to look to sb for protection; to seek refuge with sb; **im ~ der Dunkelheit** under cover of darkness; **zum ~ der Augen** to protect the eyes; **jdn in ~ nehmen** *(fig)* to take sb's part.

Schutz-: ~anstrich *m* protective coat; **~anzug** *m* protective clothing *no indef art, no pl*; **s~bedürftig** *adj* in need of protection; **~behauptung** *f* lie to cover oneself; **~blech** *nt* mudguard; **~brief** *m (Insur)* (international) motoring cover; **~brille** *f* protective goggles *pl*; **~dach** *nt* porch; *(an Haltestelle)* shelter.

Schütze *m (wk)* **-n, -n (a)** marksman; *(Schießsportler)* rifleman; *(Bogen~)* archer; *(Ftbl: Tor~)* scorer. **(b)** *(Astrol)* Sagittarius *no art*. **sie ist ~** she's Sagittarius *or* a Sagittarian.

schützen 1 *vt* to protect *(vor +dat, gegen* from, against*)*; *(esp Mil: Deckung geben)* to cover. **gesetzlich geschützt/urheberrechtlich geschützt** registered/protected by copyright; **ein geschützter Platz** a sheltered spot *or* place; **vor Sonnenlicht ~!** keep away from sunlight; **vor Nässe ~!** keep dry. **2** *vi* to give *or* offer protection *(vor +dat, gegen* against, from*)*; *(esp Mil: Deckung geben)* to give cover. **3** *vr* to protect oneself *(vor +dat, gegen* from, against*)*.

schützend *adj* protective. **ein ~es Dach** *(gegen Wetter)* a shelter.

Schützenfest *nt fair featuring shooting matches.*

Schutz|engel *m* guardian angel.

Schützen-: ~graben *m* trench; **~hilfe** *f (fig)* support; **jdm ~hilfe geben** to back sb up; **~loch** *nt (Mil)* foxhole; **~panzer** *m* armoured *(Brit) or* armored *(US)* personnel carrier; **~verein** *m* rifle *or* shooting club.

Schutz-: ~farbe *f (Biol)* protective *or* adaptive colouring *(Brit) or* coloring *(US)*; **~gebiet** *nt (Pol)* protectorate; **~gebühr** *f* (token) fee; **~haft** *f (Jur)* protective custody; **~haut** *f* protective covering; **~heilige(r)** *mf* patron saint; **~helm** *m* safety helmet; **~herrschaft** *f (Pol)* protection, protectorate; **~hülle** *f* protective cover; *(Buchumschlag)* dust cover *or* jacket; **s~impfen** *ptp* **s~geimpft** *vt* to vaccinate, to inoculate; **~impfung** *f* vaccination, inoculation; **~kleidung** *f* protective clothing.

Schützling *m* protégé; *(esp Kind)* charge.

Schutz-: s~los *adj (wehrlos)* defenceless *(Brit)*, defenseless *(US)*; *(gegen Kälte etc)* unprotected; **~macht** *f (Pol)* protecting power, protector; **~mann** *m, pl* **~leute** *(dated)* policeman, constable *(Brit)*; **~marke** *f* trademark; **~maßnahme** *f* precautionary measure; *(~vorbeugend)* preventive measure; **~schicht** *f* protective layer; *(Überzug)* protective coating; **~schild** *m* shield; *(an Geschützen)* gun shield; **~schirm** *m (Tech)* protective screen; **s~suchend** *adj* seeking protection; *(nach Obdach)* seeking refuge *or* shelter; **~umschlag** *m* dust cover *or* jacket; **~verband** *m (Med)* protective bandage *or* dressing; **~zoll** *m* protective duty *or* tariff.

schwabbelig *adj (col) Körperteil* flabby; *Gelee* wobbly.

schwabbeln *vi (col)* to wobble (about).

Schwabe *m (wk)* **-n, -n, Schwäbin** *f* Swabian.

Schwaben *nt* Swabia.

schwäbisch *adj* Swabian.

schwach *adj comp* **¨er,** *superl* **¨ste(r, s)** *or (adv)* **am ¨sten** weak *(auch Gram)*; *Gesundheit, Beteiligung, Gedächtnis* poor; *Ton, Anzeichen, Hoffnung* faint, slight; *Gehör* poor, dull; *Licht* poor, dim; *Wind* light; *(Comm) Nachfrage, Geschäft* slack, poor. **~e Augen** weak *or* poor (eye)sight; **das ist ein ~es Bild** *(col) or* **eine ~e Leistung** *(col)* that's a poor show *(col)*; **trotz des ~en Erfolges des Buchs** in spite of the book's lack of success; **jds ~e Seite** sb's weak point; **ein ~er Trost** cold *or* small comfort; **mach mich nicht ~!** *(col)* don't say that! *(col)*; **auf ~en Beinen** *or* **Füßen stehen** *(fig)* to be on shaky ground; *(Theorie)* to be shaky; **¨er werden** to grow weaker, to weaken; *(Augen)* to fail, to grow worse; *(Stimme)* to grow fainter; *(Licht)* to (grow) dim; *(Ton)* to fade; *(Nachfrage)* to fall off, to slacken; **~ besiedelt** *or* **bevölkert** sparsely populated; **~ besucht** poorly attended; **die S~en** the weak.

Schwäche *f* **-n** weakness; *(von Gesundheit)* poorness; *(von Licht)* dimness; *(von Nachfrage)* slackness. **eine ~ überkam sie** a feeling of weakness came over her; **menschliche ~n** human failings *or* frailties; **eine ~ für etw haben** to have a weakness for sth.

schwächen *vt (lit, fig)* to weaken.

Schwachheit *f no pl (fig)* weakness, frailty.

Schwachkopf *m (col)* dimwit *(col)*, idiot.

schwächlich *adj* weakly; *(zart auch)* puny.

Schwächling *m* weakling.

Schwach-: s~sichtig *adj (Med)* poor- or weak-sighted; **~sichtigkeit** *f (Med)* dimness of vision; **~sinn** *m (Med)* mental deficiency; *(fig col) (unsinnige Tat)* idiocy *no indef art*; *(Quatsch)* rubbish *(col)*; **s~sinnig** *adj (Med)* mentally deficient; *(fig col)* daft *(col)*, idiotic; **~sinnige(r)** *mf decl as adj* mental defective; *(fig col)* moron *(col)*, imbecile *(col)*; **~stelle** *f* weak point; **~strom** *m (Elec)* low-voltage *or* weak current.

Schwächung *f* weakening.

Schwaden *m* - *usu pl* cloud.

Schwadron *f* **-en** *(Mil Hist)* squadron.

schwadronieren* *vi* to bluster.

Schwafelei *f (pej col)* drivel *no pl (col)*, twaddle *no pl (col)*.

schwafeln *(pej col)* **1** *vi* to drivel (on) *(col)*; *(in einer Prüfung)* to waffle *(col)*. **2** *vt* **dummes Zeug ~** to talk drivel *(col)*.

Schwager *m* **¨** brother-in-law.

Schwägerin *f* sister-in-law.

Schwalbe *f* **-n** swallow. **eine ~ macht noch keinen Sommer** *(Prov)* one swallow doesn't make a summer *(Prov)*.

Schwall *m* **-e** flood, torrent.

schwamm *pret of* **schwimmen.**

Schwamm *m* **¨e (a)** sponge. **etw mit dem ~ abwischen** to sponge sth (down); **~ drüber!** *(col)* (let's) forget it! **(b)** *(Haus~)* dry rot.

schwammig *adj* **(a)** *(lit)* spongy. **(b)** *(fig) Gesicht* puffy, bloated; *(vage) Begriff* woolly.

Schwan *m* **¨e** swan. **mein lieber ~!** *(col) (überrascht)* my goodness!; *(drohend)* my lad/girl.

schwand *pret of* **schwinden.**

schwanen *vi impers* **ihm schwante etwas** he

sensed something might happen; **mir schwant nichts Gutes** I've a feeling something nasty is going to happen.
Schwanen-: **~gesang** *m (fig)* swansong; **~hals** *m* swan's neck; *(fig)* swanlike neck; *(Tech)* gooseneck, swan-neck.
schwang *pret of* **schwingen.**
schwanger *adj* pregnant.
Schwangere *f decl as adj* pregnant woman.
schwängern *vt* to make pregnant, to impregnate *(form)*. **mit etw geschwängert sein** *(fig)* to be impregnated with sth.
Schwangerschaft *f* pregnancy.
Schwangerschafts|abbruch *m* termination of pregnancy, abortion.
Schwank *m* **¨e** *(Liter)* merry *or* comical tale; *(Theat)* farce.
schwanken *vi* **(a)** *(wanken, sich wiegen)* to sway; *(Schiff) (auf und ab)* to pitch; *(seitwärts)* to roll; *(beben)* to rock. **(b)** *aux sein (gehen)* to stagger, to totter. **(c)** *(variieren)* to vary; *(Preise, Stimmung etc auch)* to fluctuate; *(Kompaßnadel etc)* to swing. **(d)** *(unschlüssig sein)* to waver; *(zögern)* to hesitate. **(e) ins S~ kommen** *(Baum, Gebäude etc)* to start to sway; *(Preise, Kurs etc)* to start to fluctuate *or* vary; *(Überzeugung etc)* to begin to waver.
schwankend *adj* **(a)** *siehe vi (a)* swaying; pitching; rolling; rocking. **(b)** *Mensch* staggering; *Gang* rolling; *Schritt* unsteady. **(c)** *siehe vi (c)* varying; fluctuating *esp attr*; oscillating; *Kurs, Gesundheit auch* unstable. **(d)** *(unschlüssig)* uncertain, wavering *attr*; *(zögernd)* hesitant. **~ werden** to waver.
Schwankung *f* **(a)** *(hin und her)* swaying *no pl*; *(auf und ab)* shaking *no pl*, rocking *no pl*. **um die ~en des Turms zu messen** to measure the extent to which the tower sways. **(b)** *siehe vi (c)* variation *(gen* in*)*; fluctuation.
Schwanz *m* **¨e (a)** *(lit, fig)* tail. **den ~ hängen lassen** *(lit)* to let its tail droop; *(fig col)* to be down in the dumps *(col)*; **kein ~** *(col)* not a (blessed) soul *(col)*. **(b)** *(col!!: Penis)* prick *(col!!)*.
schwänzen *(col)* **1** *vt Stunde, Vorlesung* to skip *(col)*, to cut *(col)*; *Schule* to play truant *or* hooky *(esp US col)* from, to skive off *(Brit col)*. **2** *vi* to play truant, to play hooky *(esp US col)*, to skive *(Brit col)*.
Schwanz-: **~feder** *f* tail feather; **~flosse** *f (auch Aviat)* tail fin; **s~los** *adj* tailless.
schwappen *vi* **(a)** *(Wasser)* to slosh around. **(b)** *aux sein (über~)* to splash, to slosh.
Schwarm *m* **¨e (a)** swarm; *(Flugzeugformation)* flight. **(b)** *(col: Angebeteter)* idol. **der neue Englischlehrer ist ihr ~** she's got a crush on the new English teacher *(col)*.
schwärmen *vi* **(a)** *aux sein* to swarm. **(b)** *(begeistert reden)* to enthuse *(von* about*)*, to go into raptures *(von* about*)*. **für jdn/etw ~** to be mad *or* crazy about sb/sth *(col)*; **ins S~ kommen** *or* **geraten** to go into raptures.
Schwärmer *m* **-** *(Begeisterter)* enthusiast, zealot; *(Phantast)* dreamer, visionary; *(sentimentaler ~)* sentimentalist.
Schwärmerei *f (Begeisterung)* enthusiasm; *(in Worten ausgedrückt)* effusion *no pl*; *(Verzückung)* rapture.
schwärmerisch *adj (begeistert)* enthusiastic; *Worte, Übertreibung* effusive; *(verliebt)* infatuated; *(verzückt)* enraptured.
Schwarte *f* **-n (a)** *(Speck~)* rind. **(b)** *(col: Buch)* old book, tome *(hum)*.
Schwartenmagen *m (Cook)* brawn.
schwarz *adj comp* **¨er**, *superl* **¨este(r, s)** *or (adv)* **am ¨esten (a)** *(lit, fig)* black. **das S~e Brett** the notice-board *(Brit)*, the bulletin board *(US)*; **~er Humor** black humour *(Brit) or* humor *(US)*; **~er Kaffee/Tee** black coffee/tea; **die S~e Kunst** *(Buchdruckerkunst)* (the art of) printing; *(Magie)* the Black Art; **~e Liste** blacklist; **jdn auf die ~e Liste setzen** to blacklist sb, to put sb on the blacklist; **das S~e Meer** the Black Sea; **S~er Peter** *(Cards) children's card game;* **jdm den S~en Peter zuschieben** *(fig: die Verantwortung abschieben)* to pass the buck to sb *(col)*; **ein ~er Tag** a black day; **etw ~ auf weiß haben** to have sth in black and white; **~ wie die Nacht/wie Ebenholz** jet-black; **in den ~en Zahlen** in the black; **sich ~ ärgern** to get extremely annoyed; **er wurde ~ vor Ärger** his face went black; **mit wurde ~ vor den Augen** I blacked out; **da kannst du schreien, bis du ~ wirst** *(col)* you can shout until you're blue in the face *(col)*; **ins S~e treffen** *(lit, fig)* to score a bull's-eye.
(b) *(col: ungesetzlich)* illicit. **der ~e Markt** the black market; **sich** *(dat)* **etw ~ besorgen** to get sth illicitly/on the black market; **~ über die Grenze gehen** to cross the border illegally.
(c) *(col: katholisch)* Catholic, Papist *(pej)*; *(Pol col: konservativ)* conservative. **dort wählen alle ~** they all vote conservative there.
Schwarz-: **~afrika** *nt* Black Africa; **~arbeit** *f* illicit work; *(nach Feierabend)* moonlighting *(col)*; **s~arbeiten** *vi sep* to do illicit work; to moonlight *(col)*; **~arbeiter** *m* person doing illicit work; moonlighter *(col)*; **s~braun** *adj* dark brown; **~brenner** *m* illicit distiller, moonshine distiller *(col)*; **~brennerei** *f* illicit still, moonshine still *(col)*; **~brot** *nt (braun)* brown rye bread; *(Pumpernickel)* black bread, pumpernickel; **~drossel** *f* blackbird.
Schwarze *f (wk)* **-n, -n** *(Negerin)* black woman; *(Schwarzhaarige)* brunette.
Schwärze *f no pl (Dunkelheit)* blackness.
schwärzen *vtr* to blacken.
Schwarze(r) *m decl as adj (Neger)* black; *(Schwarzhaariger)* dark man/boy; *(col: Katholik)* Catholic, Papist *(pej)*. **die ~n** *(Pol col)* the Conservatives.
Schwarz-: **s~fahren** *vi sep irreg aux sein (ohne zu zahlen)* to travel without paying, to dodge paying the fare *(col)*; **~fahrer** *m* fare-dodger *(col)*; **s~haarig** *adj* black-haired; **eine ~haarige** a brunette; **~handel** *m no pl* black market; *(Tätigkeit)* black-marketeering; **im ~handel** on the black market; **~händler** *m* black marketeer; **s~hören** *vi sep (Rad)* to use a radio without having a licence *(Brit) or* license *(US)*; **~hörer** *m (Rad)* radio-owner without a licence *(Brit) or* license *(US)*; **s~malen** *sep* **1** *vi* to be pessimistic; **2** *vt* to be pessimistic about; **~maler** *m* pessimist; **~malerei** *f* pessimism; **~markt** *m* black-market; **~marketpreis** *m* black-market price; **s~sehen** *sep irreg* **1** *vt* to be pessimistic about; **2** *vi* **(a)** to be pessimistic; **für jdn/etw s~sehen** to be pessimistic about sb/sth; **(b)** *(TV)* to watch TV without a licence *(Brit) or* license *(US)*; **~seher** *m* **(a)** pessimist; **(b)** *(TV)* (TV) licence-dodger *(Brit) or* license-dodger *(US) (col)*; **~seherei** *f* pessimism; **~sender** *m* pirate (radio) station; **~wald** *m* Black Forest; **~wälder** *adj attr* Black Forest; **~wälder Kirschtorte** Black Forest gateau.
schwarzweiß *adj* black and white.
Schwarzweiß-: **~aufnahme** *f* black and white (shot); **~fernseher** *m* black and white *or* monochrome television (set); **~film** *m* black and white film; **~foto** *nt* black and white (photo).
Schwarz-: **~wild** *nt* wild boars *pl*; **~wurzel** *f (Cook)* salsify.
Schwatz *m* **-e** *(col)* chat, chinwag *(col)*. **auf einen ~ kommen** to come for a chat.
schwatzen, schwätzen *vti* to talk; *(pej) (unaufhörlich)* to chatter; *(über belanglose Dinge)* to prattle; *(Unsinn reden)* to blather *(col)*; *(klatschen)* to gossip. **dummes Zeug ~** to talk a lot of rubbish *(col)*.

Schwätzer(in *f*) *m* - *(pej)* chatterer; *(Kind, Schüler)* chatterbox; *(Schwafler)* wind-bag *(col)*; *(Klatschmaul)* gossip.

Schwätzerei *f (pej) (Gerede, im Unterricht)* talk, chatter; *(über Belanglosigkeiten, kindisch)* prattle; *(Unsinn)* drivel *(col)*; *(Klatsch)* gossip.

schwatzhaft *adj* talkative, garrulous; *(klatschsüchtig)* gossipy.

Schwebe *f no pl* **in der ~ sein** *(fig)* to be in the balance; *(Jur, Comm)* to be pending.

Schwebe-: ~bahn *f* suspension railway *(Brit) or* railroad *(US)*; **~balken** *m (Sport)* beam.

schweben *vi* **(a)** to hang; *(in der Luft auch)* to float; *(Vogel etc)* to hover. **ihr war, als ob sie schwebte** she felt as if she was walking *or* floating on air; **etw schwebt jdm vor Augen** *(fig)* sb has sth in mind; *(Bild)* sb sees sth in his mind's eye. **(b)** *aux sein (durch die Luft gleiten)* to float, to sail; *(sich leichtfüßig bewegen)* to glide, to float. **(c)** *(schwanken)* to hover, to waver; *(Angelegenheit)* to hang *or* be in the balance. **~des Verfahren** *(Jur)* pending case.

Schwebezustand *m (fig)* state of suspense; *(zwischen zwei Stadien)* in-between state.

Schwede *m (wk)* **-n, -n, Schwedin** *f* Swede.

Schweden *nt* Sweden.

schwedisch *adj* Swedish. **hinter ~en Gardinen** *(col)* behind bars.

Schwedisch(e) *nt decl as adj* Swedish; *siehe* **Deutsch(e).**

Schwefel *m no pl* sulphur *(Brit)*, sulfur *(US)*.

Schwefel- *in cpds* sulphur *(Brit)*, sulfur *(US)*; **s~haltig** *adj* containing sulphur *(Brit) or* sulfur *(US)*; **~säure** *f* suphuric *(Brit) or* sulfuric *(US)* acid.

schweflig *adj* sulphurous *(Brit)*, sulfurous *(US)*.

Schweif *m* **-e** *(auch Astron)* tail.

schweifen *vi aux sein (lit geh, fig)* to roam. **warum in die Ferne ~ ...?** why roam so far afield ...?

Schweige-: ~geld *nt* hush-money; **~marsch** *m* silent march (of protest); **~minute** *f* one minute('s) silence.

schweigen *pret* **schwieg,** *ptp* **geschwiegen** *vi* to be silent; *(still sein auch)* to keep quiet. **~ Sie!** be silent *or* quiet!; **kannst du ~?** can you keep a secret?; **seit gestern ~ die Waffen** yesterday the guns fell silent; **plötzlich schweig er** suddenly he fell *or* went silent; **zu etw ~** to make no reply to sth; **ganz zu ~ von ...** to say nothing of ...

Schweigen *nt no pl* silence. **jdn zum ~ bringen** to silence sb *(auch euph)*.

schweigend *adj* silent. **die ~e Mehrheit** the silent majority; **~ über etw** *(acc)* **hinweggehen** to pass over sth in silence.

Schweigepflicht *f* pledge of secrecy; *(von Anwalt)* requirement of confidentiality. **die ärztliche ~** medical confidentiality *or* secrecy; **unter ~ stehen** to be bound to observe confidentiality.

schweigsam *adj* silent; *(als Charaktereigenschaft)* reticent; *(verschwiegen)* discreet.

Schweigsamkeit *f siehe adj* silence; reticence; discretion.

Schwein *nt* **-e (a)** pig, hog *(US)*. **sich wie die ~e benehmen** *(col)* to behave like pigs *(col)*. **(b)** *(col: Mensch)* pig *(col)*; *(gemein)* swine *(col)*, bastard *(col!)*. **ein armes/faules ~** a poor/lazy sod *(col)*; **kein ~** nobody, not one single person. **(c)** *no pl (col: Glück)* **~ haben** to be lucky.

Schweinchen *nt dim of* **Schwein** little pig; *(fig col: Schmutzfink)* mucky pup *(col)*.

Schweine-: ~bauch *m (Cook)* belly of pork; **~braten** *m* joint of pork; *(gekocht)* roast pork; **~filet** *nt* fillet of pork; **~fleisch** *nt* pork; **~geld** *nt (col)* **ein ~geld** a packet *(col)*; **~hund** *m (pej col)* bastard *(col!)*, swine *(col)*; **den inneren ~hund überwinden** *(col)* to conquer one's weaker self; **~kotelett** *nt* pork chop.

Schweinerei *f (col)* **(a)** *no pl* mess. **es ist eine ~, wenn ...** it's disgusting if ...; **so eine ~!** how disgusting! **(b)** *(Gemeinheit)* dirty *or* mean trick *(col)*; *(Zote)* smutty *or* dirty joke; *(unzüchtige Handlung)* indecent act. **~en machen** to do dirty *or* filthy things; **das Buch besteht nur aus ~en** the book is just a lot of dirt *or* filth.

Schweine-: ~schmalz *nt* dripping; *(als Kochfett)* lard; **~schnitzel** *nt* pork cutlet; **~stall** *m (lit, fig)* pigsty, pig pen *(esp US)*.

Schweinigel *m (col)* dirty pig *(col)*.

schweinisch *adj (col) Benehmen* piggish *(col)*, swinish *(col)*; *Witz* dirty.

Schweinkram *m (col)* dirt, filth.

Schweins-: ~galopp *m*: **im ~galopp davonlaufen** *(hum col)* to go galumphing off *(col)*; **~haxe** *f (Cook)* knuckle of pork; **~leder** *nt* pigskin; **s~ledern** *adj* pigskin; **~ohr** *nt* pig's ear; *(Gebäck) (kidney-shaped)* pastry.

Schweiß *m no pl* sweat; *(von Mensch auch)* perspiration. **in ~ geraten** *or* **kommen** to break into a sweat; **der ~ brach ihm aus** he broke out in a sweat; **das hat viel ~ gekostet** it was a sweat *(col)*; **im ~e seines Angesichts** *(Bibl, liter)* in the sweat of his brow *(Bibl, liter)*.

Schweiß-: ~ausbruch *m* sweating *no indef art, no pl*; **~band** *nt* sweatband; **s~bedeckt** *adj* covered in sweat; **~brenner** *m (Tech)* welding torch; **~drüse** *f (Anat)* sweat gland.

schweißen *vti (Tech)* to weld.

Schweißer(in *f*) *m* - *(Tech)* welder.

Schweiß-: ~fuß *m* sweaty foot; **s~gebadet** *adj* bathed in sweat; **~naht** *f (Tech)* weld, welded joint; **s~naß** *adj* sweaty; **~perle** *f* bead of perspiration *or* sweat; **~stelle** *f* weld; **s~triefend** *adj* dripping with perspiration *or* sweat; **~tropfen** *m* drop of sweat *or* perspiration.

Schweiz *f* **die ~** Switzerland.

Schweizer *adj attr* Swiss.

Schweizer(in *f*) *m* - Swiss.

Schweizer-: ~deutsch *nt* Swiss German; **~garde** *f* Swiss Guard.

schweizerisch *adj* Swiss.

Schwelbrand *m* smouldering *(Brit) or* smoldering *(US)* fire.

schwelen *vi* to smoulder *(Brit)*, to smolder *(US)*.

schwelgen *vi* to indulge oneself *(in +dat* in*)*. **wir schwelgten in Kaviar und Sekt** we feasted on caviar and champagne; **in Farben/Worten ~** to revel in colour/in the sound of words; **in Gefühlen ~** to revel in one's emotions; **in Erinnerungen ~** to indulge in reminiscences.

Schwelle *f* **-n** *(Tür~, fig, Psych)* threshold. **an der ~ einer neuen Zeit** on the threshold of a new era; **an der ~ des Todes** at death's door.

schwellen 1 *vi pret* **schwoll,** *ptp* **geschwollen** *aux sein* to swell. **der Wind schwoll zum Sturm** the wind grew into a storm; *siehe* **geschwollen. 2** *vt (geh) Segel, Brust* to swell.

Schwellenangst *f (Psych)* fear of entering a place.

Schwemme *f* **-n (a)** *(für Tiere)* watering place. **(b)** *(Überfluß)* glut *(an +dat* of*)*.

schwemmen *vt (treiben) Sand etc* to wash.

Schwengel *m* - *(Glocken~)* clapper; *(Pumpen~)* handle.

Schwenk *m* **-s** *(Drehung)* wheel; *(Film)* pan, panning shot. **einen ~ machen** *(Kolonne)* to swing *or* wheel around.

Schwenk-: ~arm *m* swivel arm; **s~bar** *adj* swivelling; *Geschütz* traversable.

schwenken 1 *vt (schwingen)* to wave; *Lampe etc* to swivel; *Kran, Geschütz* to swing; *Kamera* to pan; *Kartoffeln* to toss; *Tanzpartnerin* to swing around, to spin (around). **2** *vi aux sein* to swing; *(Kolonne)* to wheel; *(Kamera)* to pan; *(fig)* to swing over, to switch. **links schwenkt!** *(Mil)* left wheel!

Schwenker *m* - *(Kognak~)* balloon glass.

Schwenkung *f* swing; *(Mil)* wheel; *(von Geschütz)* traverse; *(von Kamera)* pan(ning).

schwer 1 *adj* **(a)** *(lit, fig)* heavy. **ein 10 kg ~er Sack** a sack weighing 10 kgs *or* 10kgs in weight; **~ beladen/bewaffnet sein** to be heavily laden/ armed.

(b) *(ernst) Sorge, Unrecht, Unfall, Verlust, Krankheit* serious, grave; *Fehler, Enttäuschung auch* big; *Strafe* severe. **~ erkältet sein** to have a heavy cold; **~ geprüft sein** to be sorely tried; **~ verletzt/krank sein** to be seriously wounded/ill; **~ verunglücken** to have a serious accident; **~ betroffen sein** to be hard hit.

(c) *(hart, anstrengend) Arbeit, Tag, Schicksal* hard; *Frage, Entscheidung auch* difficult, tough. **es ~ haben** to have a hard time (of it); **~ schuften müssen** to have to work hard; **er lernt ~** he's a slow learner; **~ hören** to be hard of hearing; **~ zu sehen/sagen** hard *or* difficult to see/say; **sich ~ entschließen können** to find it hard *or* difficult to decide.

(d) *(col)* **~es Geld machen** to make a packet *(col)*; **ein ~er Junge** a (big-time) crook.

2 *adv (col: sehr)* really; *gekränkt, verletzt* deeply. **da mußte ich ~ aufpassen** I really had to watch out; **~ betrunken** rolling drunk *(col)*; **~ verdienen** to earn a packet *(col)*; **~ im Irrtum sein** to be badly *or* seriously mistaken; **er ist ~ in Ordnung** he's a good bloke *(Brit col) or* guy *(col)*.

Schwer-: ~arbeit *f* heavy labour *(Brit) or* labor *(US)*; **~arbeiter** *m* labourer *(Brit)*, laborer *(US)*; **~athlet** *m* weight-lifter; boxer; wrestler; **~athletik** *f weight-lifting sports, boxing, wrestling etc*; **s~beladen** *adj attr* heavily-laden; **s~bepackt** *adj attr* heavily-loaded *or* -laden; **s~beschädigt** *adj attr* (seriously) disabled; **~beschädigte(r)** *mf* disabled person; **s~bewaffnet** *adj attr* heavily armed.

Schwere *f no pl siehe adj* **(a)** heaviness. **(b)** seriousness, gravity; severity. **(c)** hardness; difficulty.

Schwere-: s~los *adj* weightless; **~losigkeit** *f* weightlessness.

schwer|erziehbar *adj attr* maladjusted.

schwerfallen *vi sep irreg aux sein* to be difficult *or* hard *(jdm* for sb*)*.

schwerfällig *adj Gang* clumsy, awkward; *Verstand* slow; *Stil* ponderous.

Schwerfälligkeit *f siehe adj* clumsiness, awkwardness; slowness; ponderousness.

Schwer-: ~gewicht *nt* **(a)** *(Sport, fig)* heavyweight; **(b)** *(Nachdruck)* emphasis; **das ~gewicht auf etw** *(acc)* **legen** to put the emphasis on sth; **s~gewichtig** *adj* heavyweight; **~gewichtler(in** *f***)** *m* **-** *(Sport)* heavyweight; **s~hörig** *adj* hard of hearing; **~hörigkeit** *f* hardness of hearing; **~industrie** *f* heavy industry; **~kraft** *f* gravity; **s~krank** *adj attr* seriously *or* critically ill; **~kranke(r)** *mf* seriously *or* critically ill patient; **s~lich** *adv* hardly, scarcely; **s~machen** *vt sep* **es jdm/jdm das Leben s~machen** to make it/life difficult for sb; **~metall** *nt* heavy metal; **~mut** *f no pl* melancholy; **s~mütig** *adj* melancholy; **s~nehmen** *vt sep irreg* **etw s~nehmen** to take sth hard.

Schwerpunkt *m (Phys)* centre *(Brit) or* center *(US)* of gravity; *(fig) (Zentrum)* centre *(Brit)*, center *(US)*, main focus; *(Hauptgewicht)* main emphasis. **den ~ auf etw** *(acc)* **legen** to put the main emphasis *or* stress on sth.

Schwerpunkt-: ~streik *m* pinpoint strike; **~verlagerung** *f* shift of emphasis.

schwerreich *adj attr (col)* stinking rich *(col)*.

Schwert *nt* **-er** sword. **das ~ ziehen** to draw one's sword.

Schwert-: ~fisch *m* swordfish; **~hieb** *m* sword stroke; **~lilie** *f (Bot)* iris.

schwertun *vr sep irreg (col)* **sich** *(dat)* **mit etw ~** to make heavy weather of sth *(col)*.

Schwertwal *m* killer whale.

Schwer-: ~verbrecher *m* criminal, felon *(esp Jur)*; **s~verdaulich** *adj attr Speisen* indigestible; *(fig auch)* difficult; **s~verdient** *adj attr Geld* hard-earned; **s~verletzt** *adj attr* seriously injured; **~verletzte(r)** *mf* serious casualty; *(bei Unfall etc auch)* seriously injured person; **s~verständlich** *adj attr* difficult to understand, incomprehensible; **s~wiegend** *adj (fig)* serious.

Schwester *f* **-n** sister; *(Kranken~)* nurse; *(Stations~)* sister; *(Ordens~)* nun, sister; *(Gemeinde~)* district nurse.

Schwester- *in cpds* sister; **~firma** *f* sister *or* associate(d) company; **~lich** *adj* sisterly.

Schwestern-: ~heim *nt* nurses' home; **~helferin** *f* nursing auxiliary *(Brit) or* assistant *(US)*.

schwieg *pret of* **schweigen.**

Schwieger-: ~eltern *pl* parents-in-law *pl*; **~mutter** *f* mother-in-law; **~sohn** *m* son-in-law; **~tochter** *f* daughter-in-law; **~vater** *m* father-in-law.

Schwiele *f* **-n** callus; *(Vernarbung)* welt.

schwielig *adj Hände* callused.

schwierig *adj* difficult; *(schwer zu lernen etc auch)* hard.

Schwierigkeit *f* difficulty. **in ~en geraten** to get into difficulties *or* trouble; **jdm ~en machen** to make difficulties *or* trouble for sb; **es macht mir überhaupt keine ~en** it won't be at all difficult for me; **mach keine ~en!** *(col)* don't be difficult, don't make any trouble; **ohne ~en** without any difficulty.

Schwierigkeitsgrad *m* degree of difficulty.

Schwimm-: ~bad *nt* swimming pool; *(Hallenbad auch)* swimming baths *pl (Brit)*; **~becken** *nt* (swimming) pool.

schwimmen *pret* **schwamm,** *ptp* **geschwommen** *aux sein* **1** *vi* **(a)** *auch aux haben* to swim. **~ gehen** to go swimming *or* for a swim. **(b)** *(auf dem Wasser treiben)* to float. **(c)** *(col: überschwemmt sein: Boden)* to be swimming *(col)*, to be awash. **in Fett** *(dat)* **~** to be swimming in fat; **in seinem Blut ~** to be soaked in blood; **im Geld ~** to be rolling in money *(col)*. **(d)** *(fig: unsicher sein)* to be at sea, to flounder. **ins S~ geraten** *(fig)* to begin to flounder. **(e) es schwimmt mir vor den Augen** I feel dizzy. **2** *vt auch aux haben (Sport)* to swim.

Schwimmer *m* **- (a)** swimmer. **(b)** *(Tech)* float.

Schwimmerbecken *nt* swimmers' pool.

Schwimmerin *f* swimmer.

Schwimm-: ~flosse *f (von Taucher)* flipper; **~halle** *f* swimming bath(s *pl*) *(Brit)*, (indoor) swimming pool; **~haut** *f (Orn)* web; **~lehrer** *m* swimming instructor; **~stil** *m* stroke; *(Technik)* (swimming) style; **~unterricht** *m* swimming lessons *pl*; **~verein** *m* swimming club; **~vogel** *m* waterfowl; **~weste** *f* life jacket.

Schwindel *m no pl* **(a)** *(Gleichgewichtsstörung)* dizziness. **(b)** *(Lüge)* lie; *(Betrug)* swindle, fraud, con *(col)*. **das ist alles ~, was er da sagt** what he says is all a pack of lies *or* a big con *(col)*.

Schwindel|anfall *m* dizzy turn, attack of dizziness.

Schwindelei *f (col) (leichte Lüge)* fib *(col)*; *(leichter Betrug)* swindle.

Schwindel-: s~erregend *adj* **(a) in s~erregender Höhe** at a dizzy height; **(b)** *Preise* astronomical; **~firma** *f* bogus firm *or* company; **s~frei** *adj* **s~frei sein** to have no fear of heights; **Linsey ist nicht s~frei** Linsey can't stand heights, Linsey suffers from vertigo; **~gefühl** *nt* feeling of dizziness.

schwind(e)lig *adj* dizzy. **mir ist ~** I feel dizzy.

schwindeln 1 *vi* **(a) mir schwindelt** I feel dizzy; **mir schwindelte der Kopf** my head was reeling; **in ~der Höhe** at a dizzy height. **(b)** *(col: lügen)* to fib *(col)*, to tell fibs *(col)*. **2** *vt (col)* **das ist alles**

geschwindelt it's all lies. **3** *vr* **sich durch die Kontrollen ~** to con *or* wangle one's way through the checkpoint *(col)*.

schwinden *pret* **schwand,** *ptp* **geschwunden** *vi aux sein (abnehmen)* to dwindle; *(Schönheit)* to fade, to wane; *(Erinnerung, Angst, Zeit, Dunkelheit)* to fade away; *(Kräfte)* to fade, to fail. **sein Mut schwand** his courage failed him; **ihm schwanden die Sinne** *(liter)* he grew faint.

Schwindler *m* - swindler; *(Hochstapler)* con-man *(col)*; *(Lügner)* liar, fraud.

schwindlig *adj* = **schwind(e)lig.**

Schwindsucht *f (dated)* consumption.

schwindsüchtig *adj (dated)* consumptive.

Schwinge *f* **-n** *(liter, Flügel)* wing.

schwingen *pret* **schwang,** *ptp* **geschwungen 1** *vt* to swing; *(drohend) Schwert, Stock etc* to brandish; *Hut, Fahne* to wave; *siehe* **geschwungen. 2** *vr* **sich auf etw** *(acc)* **~** to leap *or* jump onto sth, to swing oneself onto sth; **sich in etw** *(acc)* **~** to vault into sth, to swing oneself into sth. **3** *vi* **(a)** to swing. **(b)** *(vibrieren: Brücke, Saite)* to vibrate.

Schwinger *m* - *(Boxen)* swing.

Schwing-: ~flügel *m* casement window; **~tür** *f* swing door.

Schwingung *f (Phys, fig)* vibration; *(von Wellen)* oscillation. **etw in ~(en) versetzen** to start sth vibrating; to start sth oscillating.

Schwips *m* **-e** *(col)* **einen (kleinen) ~ haben** to be tiddly *(Brit col) or* (slightly) tipsy.

schwirren *vi aux sein* to whizz; *(Bienen, Fliegen etc)* to buzz. **Gerüchte ~ durch die Presse** the press is buzzing with rumours; **mir schwirrt der Kopf** my head is buzzing.

Schwitzbad *nt* Turkish bath; *(Dampfbad)* steam bath.

Schwitze *f* **-n** *(Cook)* roux.

schwitzen 1 *vi (lit, fig)* to sweat; *(Fenster)* to steam up. **2** *vt (Cook) Mehl* to brown in fat. **3** *vr* **sich naß ~** to get drenched in sweat.

Schwitzkasten *m (Ringen)* headlock. **jdn in den ~ nehmen** to put a headlock on sb.

Schwof *m* **-e** *(col)* hop *(col)*, dance.

schwofen *vi (col)* to dance.

schwoll *pret of* **schwellen.**

schwören *pret* **schwor,** *ptp* **geschworen** *vti* to swear. **ich kann darauf ~, daß ...** I could swear to it that ...; **jdm/sich etw ~** to swear sth to sb/oneself; **auf jdn/etw ~** *(fig)* to swear by sb/sth.

schwul *adj (col)* gay, queer *(pej col)*.

schwül *adj (lit, fig) Tag, Stimmung* sultry; *Wetter auch* close, muggy.

Schwüle *f no pl siehe adj* sultriness; closeness, mugginess.

Schwulen- *(col)*: **~bar** *f*, **~lokal** *nt* gay bar.

Schwule(r) *mf decl as adj (col)* gay, queer *(pej col)*, fag *(US pej col)*.

Schwulität *f usu pl (col)* trouble *no indef art*, difficulty. **in ~en kommen** to get into a fix *(col)*; **jdn in ~en bringen** to get sb into trouble *or* hot water *(col)*.

Schwulst *m no pl (pej) (in der Sprache)* bombast, pompousness; *(in der Kunst)* ornateness.

schwülstig *adj (pej) Stil, Redeweise* bombastic, pompous.

Schwund *m no pl* **(a)** *(Abnahme)* decrease *(gen* in*)*, decline *(gen* in*)*, dwindling *(gen* of*)*. **(b)** *(von Material)* shrinkage. **(c)** *(Med)* atrophy.

Schwung *m* **¨-e (a)** swing. **jdm/etw einen ~ geben** to give sb/sth a push. **(b)** *no pl (fig: Elan)* verve, zest; *(von Mensch auch)* go *(col)*; *(lit: Antrieb)* momentum. **in ~ kommen** *(lit: Schlitten etc)* to gather *or* gain momentum; *(fig auch)* to get going; **jdn/etw in ~ bringen** *(lit, fig)* to get sb/sth going; **~ in die Sache bringen** *(col)* to liven things up; **in ~ sein** *(lit: Schlitten etc)* to be going full speed; *(fig)* to be in full swing; **voller/ohne ~** full of/lacking verve *or* zest. **(c)** *no pl (col: Menge) (Sachen)* stack, pile *(col)*; *(Leute)* bunch *(col)*.

Schwung-: s~haft *adj Handel* flourishing, roaring; **sich s~haft entwickeln** to grow hand over fist; **~kraft** *f* centrifugal force; **~rad** *nt* flywheel; **~voll** *adj Linie, Bewegung* sweeping; *Rede, Aufführung* lively.

Schwur *m* **¨-e** *(Eid)* oath; *(Gelübde)* vow.

Schwurgericht *nt court with a jury*. **vor das ~ kommen** to be tried by jury.

sechs [zɛks] *num* six; *siehe* **vier.**

Sechs- [zɛks-]: **~eck** *nt* hexagon; **s~eckig** *adj* hexagonal; **s~fach 1** *adj* sixfold; **2** *adv* sixfold, six times; *siehe* **vierfach; s~hundert** *num* six hundred; **s~mal** *adv* six times; **~tagerennen** *nt* six-day (bicycle) race; **s~tägig** *adj* six-day.

Sechstel ['zɛkstl] *nt* - sixth.

sechstens ['zɛkstns] *adv* sixth(ly), in the sixth place.

sechste(r, s) ['zɛkstə] *adj* sixth. **einen ~n Sinn für etw haben** to have a sixth sense (for sth); *siehe* **vierte(r, s).**

sechzehn ['zɛçtseːn] *num* sixteen.

Sechzehntel(note *f)* *nt* - *(Mus)* semiquaver *(Brit)*, sixteenth note *(US)*.

sechzig ['zɛçtsɪç] *num* sixty; *siehe* **vierzig.**

SED [ɛs|eː'deː] *f* = **Sozialistische Einheitspartei Deutschlands.**

Sediment *nt (Geol)* sediment.

Sedimentgestein *nt (Geol)* sedimentary rock.

See[1] *f* **-n** [zeːən] sea. **an der ~** by the sea, at the seaside; **an die ~ fahren** to go to the sea(side); **auf hoher ~** on the high seas; **auf ~** at sea; **in ~ stechen** to put to sea.

See[2] *m* **-n** [zeːən] lake; *(in Schottland)* loch.

See-: ~aal *m* **(a)** *(Zool)* conger (eel); **(b)** *(Comm)* dogfish; **~bad** *nt (Kurort)* seaside resort; **~bär** *m* **(a)** *(hum col)* seadog *(col)*; **(b)** *(Zool)* fur seal; **~beben** *nt* seaquake; **s~fahrend** *adj attr Volk* seafaring; **~fahrer** *m* seafarer; **~fahrt** *f* **(a)** *(Fahrt)* (sea) voyage; *(Vergnügungs~)* cruise; **(b)** *(Schiffahrt)* seafaring *no art;* **s~fest** *adj* **s~fest sein** to be a good sailor; **~gang** *m* swell; **hoher ~gang** heavy seas *or* swell; **~gras** *nt (Bot)* eelgrass, sea grass *or* hay; **~hafen** *m* seaport; **~handel** *m* maritime trade; **~herrschaft** *f* naval *or* maritime supremacy; **~höhe** *f* sea level; **~hund** *m* seal; **~jungfrau** *f (Myth)* mermaid; **~karte** *f* sea *or* nautical chart; **~klima** *nt* maritime climate; **s~krank** *adj* seasick; **Paul wird leicht s~krank** Paul is a bad sailor; **~krankheit** *f* seasickness; **~lachs** *m (Cook)* pollack.

Seele *f* **-n** *(Rel, fig, Mensch)* soul; *(Herzstück, Mittelpunkt)* life and soul. **in tiefster ~** *(geh)* in one's heart of hearts; **mit ganzer ~** with all one's soul; **jdm aus der ~ sprechen** to express exactly what sb feels; **das liegt mir auf der ~** it weighs heavily on my mind; **sich** *(dat)* **etw von der ~ reden** to get sth off one's chest; **sich** *(dat)* **die ~ aus dem Leib reden** *(col)* to talk until one is blue in the face *(col)*; **das tut mir in der ~ weh** I am deeply distressed; **zwei ~n und ein Gedanke** *(prov)* two minds with but a single thought; **dann/nun hat die liebe** *or* **arme ~ Ruh** that'll put him/us *etc* out of his/our *etc* misery; **eine ~ von Mensch** an absolute dear.

Seelen-: ~amt *nt (Eccl)* requiem; **~friede(n)** *m (geh)* peace of mind; **~heil** *nt* salvation of one's soul; *(fig)* spiritual welfare; **~leben** *nt* inner life; **~ruhe** *f* calmness, coolness; **in aller ~ruhe** calmly; *(kaltblütig)* as cool as you please; **s~ruhig** *adv* calmly; *(kaltblütig)* as cool as you please, as cool as a cucumber *(col)*; **~tröster** *m (hum: Schnaps)* pick-me-up *(col)*; **s~verwandt** *adj* congenial *(liter)*; **sie waren s~verwandt** they were kindred spirits; **~verwandtschaft** *f* affinity; **~wanderung** *f (Rel)* transmigration of souls, metempsychosis; **~zustand** *m* psychological *or* mental state.

See-: **~leute** *pl of* **~mann**; **~lilie** *f* sea lily.
seelisch *adj (Rel)* spiritual; *(geistig)* mental, psychological; *Belastung* emotional; *Grausamkeit* mental. **~ bedingt sein** to be psychologically conditioned.
Seelöwe *m* sea lion.
Seelsorge *f no pl* spiritual welfare.
Seelsorger(in *f*) *m* - pastor.
See-: **~luft** *f* sea air; **~macht** *f* sea *or* maritime power.
Seemann *m, pl* **-leute** sailor, seaman.
seemännisch *adj* nautical.
Seemanns-: **~garn** *nt no pl (col)* sailor's yarn; **~garn spinnen** to spin a yarn; **~heim** *nt* sailors' home; **~lied** *nt* sea shanty.
Seemeile *f* nautical *or* sea mile.
Seengebiet ['ze:ən-] *nt* lakeland district.
Seenot *f no pl* distress. **in ~ geraten** to get into distress.
Seenot-: **~(rettungs)dienst** *m* sea rescue service; **~zeichen** *nt* nautical distress signal.
See-: **~otter** *m* sea otter; **~pferd(chen)** *nt* seahorse; **~räuber** *m* pirate; **~räuberei** *f* piracy; **~recht** *nt* maritime law; **~reise** *f* (sea) voyage; *(Kreuzfahrt)* cruise; **~rose** *f* waterlily; **~schaden** *m* damage at sea, average *(spec)*; **~schiffahrt** *f* maritime *or* ocean shipping; **~schlacht** *f* naval *or* sea battle; **~stern** *m (Zool)* starfish; **~streitkräfte** *pl* naval forces *pl*, navy; **~tang** *m* seaweed; **s~tüchtig** *adj* seaworthy; **~ufer** *nt* lakeside; **~vogel** *m* sea bird; **~volk** *nt (Nation)* seafaring nation *or* people; **~weg** *m* sea route; **auf dem ~weg reisen** to go *or* travel by sea; **~zeichen** *nt* navigational aid; **~zunge** *f* sole.
Segel *nt* - sail. **mit vollen ~n** under full sail *or* canvas; *(fig)* with gusto; **die ~ streichen** *(Naut)* to strike sail; *(fig)* to give in.
Segel-: **~boot** *nt* sailing boat *(Brit)*, sailboat *(US)*; **s~fliegen** *vi infin only* to glide; **~fliegen** *nt* gliding; **~flieger** *m* glider pilot; **~flugzeug** *nt* glider; **~jacht** *f* (sailing) yacht, sailboat *(US)*; **~klub** *m* sailing club.
segeln *vti* **(a)** *aux haben or sein* to sail. **eine Strecke ~** to sail a course; **~ gehen** to go for a sail. **(b)** *aux sein (col)* **durch eine Prüfung ~** to flop in an exam *(col)*, to fail (in) an exam.
Segeln *nt no pl* sailing.
Segel-: **~regatta** *f* sailing *or* yachting regatta; **~schiff** *nt* sailing ship *or* vessel; **~sport** *m* sailing *no art*; **~tuch** *nt* canvas.
Segen *m* - **(a)** *(lit, fig)* blessing. **es ist ein ~, daß ...** it is a blessing that ...; **jdm den ~ erteilen** to give sb one's blessing *or* benediction; **meinen ~ hat er** he has my blessing. **(b)** *(col)* **der ganze ~** the whole lot.
segensreich *adj* beneficial; *Tätigkeit* beneficent.
Segler *m* - **(a)** *(Segelsportler)* yachtsman, sailor. **(b)** *(Schiff)* sailing vessel. **(c)** *(Orn)* swift.
Seglerin *f* yachtswoman.
Segment *nt* segment.
segnen *vt (Rel)* to bless; *siehe* **gesegnet**.
Segnung *f (Rel)* blessing, benediction.
sehbehindert *adj* partially sighted.
sehen *pret* **sah**, *ptp* **gesehen** **1** *vt* **(a)** to see; *(an~ auch)* to look at; *Fernsehsendung auch* to watch. **sieht man das?** does it show?; **das kann man ~** you can tell that (just by looking); **siehst du irgendwo mein Buch?** can you see my book anywhere?; **von ihm war nichts mehr zu ~** he was no longer to be seen; **darf ich das mal ~?** can I have a look at that? **ich kann diesen Kerl nicht mehr ~** I can't stand the sight of that guy any more; **jdn kommen ~** to see sb coming; **jdn/etw zu ~ bekommen** to get to see sb/sth; **den möchte ich ~, der ...** I'd like to meet the man who ...; **da sieht man es mal wieder!** that's typical; **also, wir ~ uns morgen** right, I'll see you tomorrow; **das müssen wir erst mal ~** that remains to be seen; **das sehe ich noch nicht** *(col)* I still don't see that happening; **das wollen wir (doch) erst mal ~!** we'll see about that!
(b) *(beurteilen)* to see; *(deuten auch)* to look at. **wie siehst du das?** how do you see it?; **das darf man nicht so ~** that's not the way to look at it; **du siehst das nicht richtig** you've got it wrong; **das sehe ich anders** that's not how I see it; **rein menschlich gesehen** from a purely personal point of view; **so gesehen** looked at in this way; **du hast wohl keine Lust, oder wie sehe ich das?** *(col)* you don't feel like it, do you?
(c) sich ~ lassen to put in an appearance, to appear; **er läßt sich kaum noch bei uns ~** he hardly comes to see us any more; **er kann sich in der Nachbarschaft nicht mehr ~ lassen** he can't show his face in the neighbourhood any more; **kann ich mich in diesem Anzug ~ lassen?** do I look all right in this suit?; **das neue Rathaus kann sich ~ lassen** the new town hall is certainly something to be proud of.
2 *vr* **sich betrogen/getäuscht ~** to see oneself cheated/deceived; **sich gezwungen ~, zu ...** to see *or* find oneself obliged to ...
3 *vi* to see. **siehe oben/unten** see above/below; **siehst du (wohl)!, siehste!** *(col)* you see!; **sieh doch!** look (here)!; **~ Sie mal!** look!; **er sieht gut/schlecht** he can/cannot see very well; **laß mal ~** let me see *or* look *or* have a look, give us a look *(col)*; **na siehst du** (there you are,) you see?; **wie ich sehe ...** I (can) see ...; **ich sehe schon, du willst nicht** I can see you don't want to; **da kann man mal ~** that just shows (you), that just goes to show; **mal ~, ob ...** *(col)* let's see if ...; **mal ~!** *(col)* we'll see; **sieh, daß du ...** see (that) you ...; **das Boot sah kaum aus dem Wasser** the boat hardly showed above the water; **das Fenster sieht auf den Garten** the window looks onto the garden; **nach jdm ~** *(jdn betreuen)* to look after sb; *(jdn besuchen)* to go/come to see sb; **nach etw ~** to look after sth; **darauf ~, daß ...** to make sure (that) ...
Sehen *nt no pl* seeing; *(Sehkraft)* sight, vision. **ich kenne ihn nur vom ~** I only know him by sight.
sehenswert *adj* worth seeing.
Sehenswürdigkeit *f* sight. **die Kneipe ist wirklich eine ~!** that pub is really (a sight) worth seeing!
seherisch ['ze:ərɪʃ] *adj attr* prophetic.
Seh-: **~fehler** *m* visual *or* sight defect; **~kraft** *f* (eye)sight.
Sehne *f* **-n** **(a)** *(Anat)* tendon, sinew. **(b)** *(Bogen~)* string.
sehnen *vr* **sich nach jdm/etw ~** to long *or* yearn *(liter)* for sb/sth.
Sehnenzerrung *f* pulled tendon.
Sehnerv *m* optic nerve.
sehnig *adj Mensch* sinewy, wiry; *Fleisch* stringy.
sehnlich *adj* ardent; *Erwartung* eager. **sein ~ster Wunsch** his fondest *or* most ardent *(liter)* wish.
Sehnsucht *f* **⸚e** longing, yearning *(nach* for). **~ haben** to have a longing *or* yearning.
sehnsüchtig *adj* longing, yearning; *Wunsch etc* ardent; *Erwartung* eager.
sehnsuchtsvoll *adj* longing, yearning; *Blick, Brief, Schilderung* wistful.
sehr *adv* **(a)** *(mit adj, adv)* very. **er ist ~ dafür/dagegen** he is all for it/he is very much against it; **~ zu meiner Überraschung** very much to my surprise; **es geht ihm ~ viel besser** he is very much better; **wir haben ~ viel Zeit** we have plenty of time *or* lots of time; **wir haben nicht ~ viel Zeit** we don't have very much time.
(b) *(mit vb)* very much, a lot. **so ~** so much; **jdn so ~ schlagen, daß ...** to hit sb so hard that ...; **sich über etw** *(acc)* **so ~ ärgern/freuen, daß ...** to be so (very) annoyed/pleased about sth that ...; **wie ~** how much; **wie ~ er sich auch**

bemühte, ... however much he tried ...; **sich** *(dat)* **etw ~ überlegen** to consider sth very carefully; **sich ~ anstrengen** to try very hard; **hat sie ~ geweint?** did she cry very much *or* a lot?; **freust du dich darauf? — ja, ~** are you looking forward to it? — yes, very much; **tut es weh? — ja, ~** does it hurt? — yes, a lot; **zu ~** too much.

Seh-: ~schwäche *f* poor eyesight; **~test** *m* eye test; **~vermögen** *nt* powers of vision *pl.*

sei *imper sing, 1. and 3. pers sing subjunc of* **sein** *(imper)* be; *(subjunc)* am; is.

seicht *adj (lit, fig)* shallow.

Seichtheit *f (lit, fig)* shallowness.

seid *2. pers pl pres, imper pl of* **sein** are; *(imper)* be.

Seide *f* **-n** silk.

Seidel *nt* **-** *(Gefäß)* stein, (beer) mug.

seiden *adj attr (aus Seide)* silk, silken *(liter).*

Seiden- *in cpds* silk; **~band** *nt* silk ribbon; **~gewebe** *nt* silk fabric; **~glanz** *m* silky *or* silken sheen; **~papier** *nt* tissue paper; **~raupe** *f* silkworm; **~stoff** *m* silk cloth *or* fabric.

seidig *adj (wie Seide)* silky, silken.

Seife *f* **-n** soap.

Seifen-: ~blase *f* soap-bubble; *(fig)* bubble; **~blasen machen** to blow (soap-)bubbles; **~kistenrennen** *nt* soap-box derby; **~lauge** *f* (soap)suds *pl*; **~pulver** *nt* soap powder; **~schale** *f* soap dish; **~schaum** *m* lather.

seifig *adj* soapy.

Seihe *f* **-n** strainer, colander.

seihen *vt (Flüssigkeit abgießen von)* to strain.

Seil *nt* **-e** rope; *(Hoch~)* tightrope, highwire. **auf dem ~ tanzen** *(fig)* to be walking a tightrope.

Seil-: ~bahn *f* cable railway; *(Berg~ auch)* funicular; **s~hüpfen** *vi sep aux sein* to skip; **~schaft** *f (Bergsteigen)* rope, roped party; **s~springen** *vi sep irreg aux sein* to skip; **~tanz** *m* tightrope *or* high-wire act; **s~tanzen** *vi sep* to walk the tightrope *or* high-wire; **~tänzer** *m* tightrope walker, high-wire performer.

Sein *nt no pl* being *no art.* **~ und Schein** appearance and reality; **~ oder Nichtsein** to be or not to be.

sein[1] *pret* **war,** *ptp* **gewesen** *aux sein* **1** *vi* **(a)** to be. **wir waren** we were; **wir sind gewesen** we have been, we've been; **seien Sie nicht böse, aber ...** don't be angry but ...; **sei so nett und ...** be so kind as to ...; **das wäre gut** that would *or* that'd be a good thing; **es wäre schön gewesen** it would *or* it'd have been nice; **er ist Lehrer/ein Verwandter** he is a teacher/a relative; **was sind Sie (beruflich)?** what do you do?; **in der Küche sind noch viele** there's *or* there are still plenty in the kitchen; **wenn ich Sie wäre** if I were *or* was you; **er war es nicht** it wasn't him; **das bist natürlich wieder du gewesen** of course it was you again; **das kann schon ~** that may well be; **das wär's!** that's all, that's it; **wie war das noch?** what was that again?; **bist du's/ist er's?** is that you/him?; **morgen bin ich in Rom** I'll *or* I will *or* I shall be in Rome tomorrow; **waren Sie mal in Rom?** have you ever been to Rome?; **wir waren essen** we went out for a meal; **wo warst du so lange?** what kept you?

(b) *(mit infin +zu)* **du bist nicht zu sehen** you cannot be seen; **das war ja vorauszusehen** that was to be expected; **wie ist das zu verstehen?** how is that to be understood?; **er ist nicht zu ersetzen** he cannot be replaced; **mit ihr ist ja nicht zu sprechen** you can't talk to her.

(c) was ist? what's the matter?, what is it?; **ist was?** what is it?; *(paßt dir was nicht)* is something the matter?; **das kann nicht ~** that can't be (true); **..., es sei denn, daß ...** ... unless ...; **wie dem auch sei** be that as it may; **wie wäre es mit ...?** how about ...?, what about ...?; **wie wäre es, wenn wir ihn besuchen würden?** what about *or* how about going to see him?; **wenn du nicht gewesen wärest ...** if it hadn't been for you ...; **er ist nicht mehr** *(euph)* he is no more *(euph liter)*; **mir ist kalt** I'm cold; **was ist Ihnen?** what's the matter with you?; **mir ist, als hätte ich ihn früher schon einmal gesehen** I have a feeling I've seen him before.

2 *aux* to have. **er war jahrelang krank gewesen** he had been *or* he'd been ill for years; **er ist verschwunden** he has *or* he's disappeared; **er ist gestern verschwunden** he disappeared yesterday; **er ist geschlagen worden** he has been beaten.

sein[2] *poss pron (adjektivisch) (bei Männern)* his; *(bei Dingen)* its; *(bei Mädchen)* her; *(bei Tieren)* its, his/her; *(bei Ländern, Städten)* its, her; *(auf „man" bezüglich)* one's *(Brit)*, his *(US)*, your. **wenn man ~ Leben betrachtet** when one looks at one's *or* his *(US)* life, when you look at your life; **jeder hat ~e Probleme** everybody has his *or* their *(col)* problems; **er ist gut ~e zwei Meter** *(col)* he's a good two metres.

seiner *pers pron gen of* **er, es** *(geh)* **gedenke ~** remember him; **er war ~ nicht mächtig** he was not in command of himself.

seine(r, s) *poss pron (substantivisch)* his. **der/die/das ~** *(geh)* his; **er hat das S~ getan** *(geh)* he did his bit; **jedem das S~** to each his own; **die S~n** *(geh)* his family, his people; *(auf „man" bezüglich)* one's *(Brit) or* his *(US)* family *or* people.

seiner-: ~seits *adv (von ihm)* on his part; *(er selbst)* for his part; **~zeit** *adv* at that time.

seines *poss pron siehe* **seine(r, s).**

seinesgleichen *pron inv (gleichartig)* his kind *pl*; *(auf „man" bezüglich)* of one's own kind; *(pej)* the likes of him *pl.* **jdn wie ~ behandeln** to treat sb as an equal *or* on equal terms; **das sucht ~** it is unparalleled.

seinet-: ~wegen *adv* **(a)** *(wegen ihm)* because of him, on his account; *(um ihn)* about him; **(b)** *(von ihm aus)* as far as he is concerned; **~ willen** *adv:* **um ~willen** for his sake.

seinlassen *vt sep irreg* **etw ~** *(aufhören)* to stop sth/doing sth; *(nicht tun)* to drop sth, to leave sth; **laß es sein!** stop that!

seins *poss pron* his.

seit 1 *prep +dat (Zeitpunkt)* since; *(Zeitdauer)* for, in. **~ wann?** since when?; **~ Jahren** for years; **schon ~ zwei Jahren nicht mehr** not since two years ago; **~ etwa einer Woche** since about a week ago, for about a week. **2** *conj* since.

seitdem 1 *adv* since then. **2** *conj* since.

Seite *f* **-n** side; *(Buch~, Zeitungs~)* page. **die hintere/vordere ~** the back/front; **auf beiden ~n des Hauses** on both sides of the house; **~ an ~** side by side; **an jds ~** *(dat)* **gehen** to walk at *or* by sb's side; **jdn von der ~ ansehen** to give sb a sidelong glance; **zur ~ treten** to step aside; **die ~n wechseln** *(Sport)* to change ends *or* over; *(fig)* to change sides; **die Hände in die ~n gestemmt** with arms akimbo, with one's hands on one's hips; **jdm zur ~ stehen** *(fig)* to stand by sb's side; **das Recht ist auf ihrer ~** she has right on her side; **sich jdm an die ~ stellen** *(fig)* to put *or* set oneself beside sb; **jdn zur ~ nehmen** to take sb aside *or* on one side; **auf der einen ~ ..., auf der anderen (~) ...** on the one hand ..., on the other (hand) ...; **jds starke ~** sb's forte, sb's strong point; **jds schwache ~** sb's weakness, sb's weak spot; **sich von seiner besten ~ zeigen** to show oneself at one's best; **von dieser ~ kenne ich ihn gar nicht** I didn't know that side of him; **einer Sache** *(dat)* **die beste ~ abgewinnen** to make the best *or* most of sth; **von allen ~n** *(lit, fig)* from all sides; **nach allen ~n auseinandergehen** to scatter in all directions; **das habe ich von einer anderen ~ erfahren** *(fig)* I heard it from another source; **von meiner ~ aus** *(fig)* on my part.

seiten *prep +gen* **auf/von ~** on the part of.

Seiten- *in cpds* side; *(esp Tech, Sci etc)* lateral; **~angabe** *f* page reference; **~ansicht** *f* side view; *(Tech)* side elevation; **~blick** *m* sidelong glance; **mit einem ~blick auf** *(+acc) (fig)* with one eye on; **~fläche** *f (Tech)* lateral face *or* surface; **~hieb** *m (Fechten)* side cut; *(fig)* side-swipe; **~lage** *f* side position; **in ~lage schlafen** to sleep on one's side; **s~lang** *adj* several pages long, going on for pages; **~linie** *f (Tennis)* sideline; *(Ftbl etc)* touchline.

seitens *prep +gen (form)* on the part of.

Seiten-: ~scheitel *m* side parting *(Brit)*, side part *(US)*; **~schiff** *nt (Archit)* (side) aisle; **~sprung** *m (fig)* bit on the side *(esp hum col) no pl*, infidelity; **~stechen** *nt* stitch; **~stechen haben** to have a stitch; **~straße** *f* side-street, side road; **~streifen** *m* verge; *(der Autobahn)* hard shoulder, berm *(US)*; **„~streifen nicht befahrbar"** "soft verges" *(Brit)*, "soft shoulder"; **s~verkehrt** *adj* the wrong way around; **~wechsel** *m (Sport)* changeover; **~weg** *m* side road, byway; **~wind** *m* crosswind; **~zahl** *f* page number.

seither [zait'heːɐ] *adv* since then.

seitlich 1 *adj* lateral *(esp Sci, Tech)*, side *attr.* **2** *adv* at the side; *(von der Seite)* from the side. **~ von** at the side of; **die Kisten sind ~ grün bemalt** the sides of the boxes are painted green. **3** *prep +gen* to *or* at the side of.

seitwärts *adv* sideways.

Sek., sek. = Sekunde sec.

Sekretär *m* **(a)** secretary. **(b)** *(Schreibschrank)* bureau, secretaire.

Sekretariat *nt* office.

Sekretärin *f* secretary.

Sekretion *f (Physiol)* secretion.

Sekt *m* **-e** sparkling wine, champagne.

Sekte *f* **-n** sect.

Sektierer(in *f***)** *m* **-** sectarian.

sektiererisch *adj* sectarian.

Sektion *f* **(a)** section. **(b)** *(Obduktion)* post-mortem (examination), autopsy.

Sektor *m* sector; *(Sachgebiet)* field.

Sektorengrenze *f* sector boundary.

Sektschale *f* champagne glass.

Sekunda *f, pl* **Sekunden** *(Sch) sixth and seventh year of German secondary school.*

Sekundaner(in *f***)** *m* **-** *(Sch) pupil in sixth and seventh year of German secondary school.*

Sekundant *m* second.

sekundär *adj* secondary.

Sekundärliteratur *f* secondary literature.

Sekunde *f* **-n** *(auch Mus, Math)* second. **eine ~, bitte!** just a second, please; **auf die ~ genau** to the second.

Sekunden-: ~bruchteil *m* split second, fraction of a second; **~schnelle** *f*: **in ~schnelle** in a matter of seconds; **~zeiger** *m* second hand.

sekundieren* *vi +dat* to second; *(unterstützen auch)* to back up.

selber *dem pron siehe* **selbst 1.**

Selbermachen *nt* do-it-yourself, DIY; *(von Kleidern etc)* making one's own. **Möbel zum ~** do-it-yourself furniture.

selbst 1 *dem pron* **(a) ich/er/das Haus ~** I myself/he himself/the house itself; **wir/sie/die Häuser ~** we ourselves/they themselves/the houses themselves; **sie ist die Tugend ~** she's virtue itself; **~ ist der Mann/die Frau!** self-reliance is the name of the game *(col)*; **er braut sein Bier ~** he brews his own beer; **zu sich ~ kommen** to collect one's thoughts; **eine Sache um ihrer ~ willen tun** to do sth for its own sake; **wie geht's? — gut, und ~?** how are things? — fine, (and) yourself? **(b)** *(ohne Hilfe)* alone, on one's/his/your *etc* own. **das muß er ~ wissen** it's up to him; **das funktioniert von ~** it works by itself *or* automatically; **er kam ganz von ~** he came of his own accord. **2** *adv* even. **~ Gott** even God (himself); **~ wenn** even if.

Selbst *nt no pl* self.

Selbst|achtung *f* self-respect, self-esteem.

selbständig *adj* independent; *(steuerlich)* self-employed. **~ denken** to think for oneself; **~ arbeiten/handeln** to work/act independently *or* on one's own; **sich ~ machen** *(beruflich)* to set up on one's own, to start one's own business; *(hum: verschwinden)* to grow legs *(hum)*.

Selbständige(r) *mf decl as adj* independent businessman/-woman; *(steuerlich)* self-employed person.

Selbständigkeit *f* independence.

Selbst- *in cpds* self; **~anzeige** *f* **~anzeige erstatten** to come forward oneself; **~auslöser** *m (Phot)* delayed-action shutter release, delay timer; **~bedienung** *f* self-service; **~bedienungsladen** *m* self-service shop *(Brit) or* store *(US)*; **~befriedigung** *f* masturbation; *(fig)* self-gratification; **~beherrschung** *f* self-control; **die ~beherrschung verlieren** to lose one's self-control *or* temper; **~bekenntnis** *nt* confession; **~bestätigung** *f* self-affirmation; **das empfand er als ~bestätigung** it boosted his ego; **~bestimmung** *f* self-determination; **~beteiligung** *f (Insur)* excess; **~betrug** *m* self-deception.

selbstbewußt *adj (s~sicher)* self-assured, self-confident.

Selbstbewußtsein *nt* self-assurance, self-confidence.

Selbst-: ~bildnis *nt* self-portrait; **~darstellung** *f* self-portrayal; **~disziplin** *f* self-discipline; **~einschätzung** *f* self-assessment; **~erhaltung** *f* self-preservation, survival; **~erhaltungstrieb** *m* survival instinct; **~erkenntnis** *f* self-knowledge; **s~ernannt** *adj* self-appointed; *(in bezug auf Titel)* self-styled; **~fahrer** *m (Aut)* **Autovermietung für ~fahrer** self-drive car hire *(Brit) or* rental; **s~gebacken** *adj* home-baked, home-made; **s~gebaut** *adj* home-made, self-made; *Haus* self-built; **~gedrehte** *f decl as adj* roll-up *(col)*; **~gedrehte rauchen** to roll one's own; **s~gefällig** *adj* smug, complacent; **~gefälligkeit** *f* smugness, complacency; **s~gemacht** *adj Möbel etc* home-made; **s~gerecht** *adj* self-righteous; **~gerechtigkeit** *f* self-righteousness; **~gespräch** *nt* **~gespräche führen** to talk to oneself; **s~gestrickt** *adj* **(a)** *Pulli* hand-knitted; **ist das s~gestrickt?** did you knit it yourself?; **(b)** *(col) Methode* homespun, amateurish; **s~herrlich** *adj (pej)* **(a)** *(eigenwillig)* high-handed; **(b)** *(s~gerecht)* self-satisfied; **~hilfe** *f* self-help; **zur ~hilfe greifen** to take matters into one's own hands; **~justiz** *f* arbitrary law; **~justiz üben** to take the law into one's own hands; **s~klebend** *adj* self-adhesive; **~kosten** *pl (Econ)* prime costs *pl*; **~kostenpreis** *m* cost price *(Brit)*; **zum ~kostenpreis** at cost; **~kritik** *f* self-criticism; **s~kritisch** *adj* self-critical; **~laut** *m* vowel; **s~los** *adj* selfless; **~losigkeit** *f* selflessness; **~mord** *m (lit, fig)* suicide; **~mörder** *m* suicide; **s~mörderisch** *adj (lit, fig)* suicidal; **~mordversuch** *m* suicide attempt, attempted suicide; **s~sicher** *adj* self-assured; **~sicherheit** *f* self-assurance; **~studium** *nt* private study; **etw im ~studium lernen** to learn sth by studying on one's own; **~sucht** *f* egoism; **s~süchtig** *adj* egoistic; **s~tätig** *adj* **(a)** *(automatisch)* automatic, self-acting; **(b)** *(eigenständig)* independent; **~tor** *nt (Sport, fig)* own goal; **~tötung** *f* suicide; **~überwindung** *f* will-power; **s~verdient** *adj* **s~verdientes Geld** money one has earned oneself; **s~vergessen** *adj* absent-minded; *Blick* faraway; **~vergessenheit** *f* absent-mindedness; **~verleugnung** *f* self-denial; **~verschulden** *nt* one's own fault; **wenn ~verschulden vorliegt ...** if you yourself *etc* are at fault ...; **s~verschuldet** *adj* wenn der Unfall s~verschuldet ist if there is personal responsibility for the accident; ~versorger *m* ~versorger sein to be self-sufficient *or* self-reliant; Urlaub für ~versorger self-catering holiday.

selbstverständlich 1 *adj Freundlichkeit* natural; *Wahrheit* self-evident. **das ist doch ~!** that goes without saying; **kann ich mitkommen? — ~** can I come too? — of course; **das ist keineswegs ~** it cannot be taken for granted; **etw für ~ halten, etw als ~ hinnehmen** to take sth for granted. **2** *adv* of course.

Selbstverständlichkeit *f* naturalness; *(Unbefangenheit)* casualness *no indef art; (von Wahrheit)* self-evidence; *(selbstverständliche Wahrheit etc)* self-evident truth *etc.* **etw für eine ~ halten** to take sth as a matter of course.

Selbst-: ~verständnis *nt* **nach seinem eigenen ~verständnis** as he sees himself; **~versuch** *m* experiment on oneself; **~verteidigung** *f* self-defence *(Brit)*, self-defense *(US)*; **~vertrauen** *nt* self-confidence; **~wählferndienst** *m (Telec)* automatic dialling *(Brit) or* dial *(US)* service, subscriber trunk dialling *(Brit)*, STD *(Brit)*; **~wertgefühl** *nt* feeling of one's own worth *or* value, self-esteem; **s~zufrieden** *adj* self-satisfied; **~zufriedenheit** *f* self-satisfaction; **~zweck** *m* end in itself; **als ~zweck** as an end in itself.

selektiv *adj* selective.

selig *adj* **(a)** *(Rel)* blessed; *(old: verstorben)* late. **bis an mein ~es Ende** *(old, hum)* until the day I die. **(b)** *(überglücklich)* overjoyed; *Stunden* blissful.

Seligkeit *f* **(a)** *(Rel)* salvation. **(b)** *(Glück)* (supreme) happiness, bliss.

Selig-: s~sprechen *vt sep irreg (Eccl)* to beatify; **~sprechung** *f (Eccl)* beatification.

Sellerie *m* **-(s)** celeriac; *(Stangen~)* celery.

selten 1 *adj* rare. **2** *adv (nicht oft)* rarely, seldom; *(besonders)* exceptionally. **~ so gelacht!** *(col)* what a laugh! *(col).*

Seltenheit *f* rarity. **das ist keine ~ bei ihr** it's nothing unusual with her.

Seltenheitswert *m* rarity value.

Selters *nt* **-, -** *(col)*, **Selter(s)wasser** *nt* soda (water).

seltsam *adj* strange; *(komisch auch)* odd.

seltsamerweise *adv* strangely enough.

Seltsamkeit *f* **(a)** *no pl* strangeness, oddness. **(b)** *(seltsame Sache)* oddity.

Semester *nt* **-** *(Univ)* semester *(US)*, term *(of a half-year's duration)*. **im 7./8. ~ sein** to be in one's 4th year; **ein älteres ~** a senior student; *(hum)* an old boy/girl.

Semester- *(Univ)*: **~ferien** *pl* vacation *sing;* **~schluß** *m* end of term, end of the semester *(US).*

Semi- *in cpds* semi-; **~finale** ['ze:mi-] *nt (Sport)* semifinal(s); **~kolon** [zemi'ko:lɔn] *nt, pl* **-s** *or* **~kola** semicolon.

Seminar *nt* **-e (a)** *(Univ)* department; *(~übung)* seminar. **(b)** *(Priester~)* seminary. **(c)** *(Lehrer~, Studien~)* teacher training college, college of education.

Semit(in *f*) *m (wk)* **-en, -en** Semite.

semitisch *adj* Semitic.

Semmel *f* **-n** *(dial)* roll. **sie gehen weg wie warme ~n** *(col)* they're selling like hot cakes *(col).*

Semmel-: ~brösel(n) *pl* breadcrumbs *pl;* **~knödel** *(SGer, Aus) m* bread dumpling.

sen. = senior sen.

Senat *m* **-e** *(Pol, Univ)* senate.

Senator *m*, **Senatorin** *f* senator.

Sende-: ~bereich *m* transmission range; **~gebiet** *nt* area; **~leiter** *m* producer.

senden[1] *pret* **sandte,** *ptp* **gesandt 1** *vt* to send *(an +acc* to*)*. **jdm etw ~** to send sb sth, to send sth to sb. **2** *vi* **nach jdm ~** to send for sb.

senden[2] *vti (Rad, TV)* to broadcast; *Signal etc* to transmit.

Sendepause *f (Rad, TV)* interval.

Sender *m* **-** transmitter; *(~kanal) (Rad)* station; *(TV)* channel *(Brit)*, station *(esp US).*

Sende-: ~raum *m* studio; **~reihe** *f* (radio/television) series; **~schluß** *m (Rad, TV)* closedown; **bis zum ~schluß** until we close down; **~turm** *m* radio tower; **~zeichen** *nt* call sign; **~zeit** *f* broadcasting time.

Sendung *f* **(a)** *no pl (das Senden)* sending. **(b)** *(Brief~)* letter; *(Päckchen)* packet; *(Paket)* parcel; *(Comm)* consignment. **(c)** *(Rad, TV)* programme *(Brit)*, program *(US)*; *(Rad auch)* broadcast; *(das Senden)* broadcasting.

Senf *m* **-e** mustard. **seinen ~ dazugeben** *(col)* to put one's oar in *(col).*

Senf-: ~früchte *pl (Cook)* pickles *pl;* **~gas** *nt (Chem)* mustard gas; **~korn** *nt* mustard seed; **~packung** *f (Med)* mustard poultice.

sengen 1 *vt* to singe. **2** *vi* to scorch.

senil *adj (pej)* senile.

senior *adj* senior.

Senior *m* **(a)** *(auch* **~chef***)* boss. **kann ich mal den ~ sprechen?** can I speak to Mr X senior? **(b)** *(Sport)* senior player. **die ~en** the seniors. **(c)** **~en** *pl* senior citizens *pl; (hum)* old folk *pl.*

Senioren-: ~karte *f* senior citizen's ticket; **~mannschaft** *f* senior team; **~paß** *m* senior citizen's travel pass.

Senke *f* **-n** valley.

senken 1 *vt* to lower; *Lanze, Fahne* to dip; *Kopf* to bow; *(Tech) Schraube, Schacht* to sink. **2** *vr* to sink; *(Decke)* to sag; *(Stimme)* to drop.

Senk-: ~fuß *m (Med)* fallen arches *pl;* **~grube** *f* cesspit; **~lot** *nt* plumbline; *(Gewicht)* plummet.

senkrecht *adj* vertical; *(Math)* perpendicular.

Senkrechte *f decl as adj* vertical; *(Math)* perpendicular.

Senkrechtstarter *m (Aviat)* vertical take-off aircraft; *(fig col)* whizz kid *(col).*

Senkung *f* **(a)** sinking; *(von Boden, Straße)* subsidence; *(von Wasserspiegel)* drop *(gen* in*)*; *(als Maßnahme)* lowering. **(b)** *(Vertiefung)* hollow, valley.

Senner(in *f*) *m* **-** (Alpine) dairyman/dairymaid.

Sennerei *f (Gebäude)* Alpine dairy.

Sensation *f* sensation.

sensationell [zɛnzatsio'nɛl] *adj* sensational.

Sensations-: ~blatt *nt* sensational paper; **~lust** *f* desire for sensation; **~nachricht** *f* scoop; **~presse** *f* yellow press.

Sense *f* **-n** scythe. **dann ist ~!** *(col)* that's the end!

sensibel *adj* sensitive.

sensibilisieren* *vt* to sensitize.

Sensibilisierung *f* sensitization.

Sensibilität *f* sensitivity.

sensitiv *adj (geh)* sensitive.

Sensitivität *f (geh)* sensitivity.

Sensor *m* sensor.

sentimental *adj* sentimental.

Sentimentalität *f* sentimentality.

separat *adj* separate; *Wohnung, Zimmer* self-contained.

Separatismus *m (Pol)* separatism.

separatistisch *adj (Pol)* separatist.

September *m* **-** September; *siehe* **März.**

Septime *f* **-n** *(Mus)* seventh.

septisch *adj* septic.

Sequenz *f* sequence.

Serbe *m (wk)* **-n, -n** Serbian.

Serbien ['zɛrbiən] *nt* Serbia.

Serbin *f* Serbian (woman/girl).

serbisch *adj* Serbian.

Serenade *f* serenade.

Serie ['ze:riə] *f* series *sing.* **in ~ gehen** to go into production; **in ~ hergestellt werden** to be mass-produced.

Serien- ['ze:riən-]: **s~mäßig 1** *adj Ausstattung* standard; *Herstellung* series *attr*; **2** *adv herstellen* in series; **das wird s~mäßig eingebaut** it's a standard fitting; **~nummer** *f* serial number; **~produktion** *f* mass production; **s~weise** *adv produzieren etc* in series; *(col: in Mengen)* wholesale.

seriös *adj (anständig)* respectable; *Firma* sound.

Seriosität *f siehe adj* respectability; soundness.

Sermon *m* **-e** *(pej)* sermon, lecture.

Serpentine *f* winding road; *(Kurve)* double bend. **die Straße führt in ~n den Berg hinauf** the road winds *or* snakes its way up the mountain.

Serum *nt, pl* **Seren** serum.

Service[1] [zɛr'vi:s] *nt* **-** [zɛr'vi:sə] *(Geschirr)* dinner/ coffee *etc* service; *(Gläser~)* set.

Service[2] ['sə:vɪs] *m or nt* **-s** *(Comm, Sport)* service.

servieren* [zɛr'vi:rən] *vti* to serve *(jdm etw* sb sth, sth to sb*)*.

Serviererin [zɛr'vi:rərɪn] *f* waitress.

Servier- [zɛr'vi:ɐ-]: **~tisch** *m* serving table; **~wagen** *m* trolley *(Brit)*, tea cart *(US)*.

Serviette [zɛr'viɛtə] *f* serviette.

Servo- ['zɛrvo-] *(Tech)*: **~bremse** *f* servo brake; **~lenkung** *f* servo steering.

Servus ['zɛrvʊs] *interj (Aus, S Ger) (beim Treffen)* hello; *(beim Abschied)* goodbye, so long *(col)*.

Sesam *m* **-s** sesame. **~, öffne dich!** open Sesame!

Sessel *m* **-** (easy) chair; *(Polstersessel)* armchair.

Sessel-: **~lehne** *f* (chair) arm; **~lift** *m* chairlift.

seßhaft *adj* settled; *(ansässig)* resident. **~ werden** to settle down.

Seßhaftigkeit *f no pl* settled form of existence; *(von Lebensweise)* settledness.

Set *m or nt* **-s (a)** set. **(b)** *(Deckchen)* tablemat.

Setter *m* **-** setter.

setzen 1 *vt* **(a)** to put, to place; *(bei Spielen) Stein, Figur* to move; *(bestimmen) Ziel, Grenze, Termin, Norm* to set. **etw auf die Rechnung ~** to put sth on the bill; **etw an den Mund ~** to put sth to one's mouth; **jdn an Land ~** to put sb ashore; **jdn über den Fluß ~** to take sb across the river; **Geld auf ein Pferd ~** to put money on a horse; **auf seinen Kopf sind 100.000 Dollar gesetzt** there's 100,000 dollars on his head; **jdm ein Denkmal ~** to build a monument to sb; **seinen Namen unter etw** *(acc)* **~** to put one's signature to sth; **seine Hoffnung in jdn/etw setzen** to put *or* place one's hopes in sb/sth; **dann setzt es was** *(col)* there'll be trouble. **(b)** *(Hort: pflanzen)* to plant.

2 *vr* **(a)** *(Platz nehmen)* to sit down; *(Vogel)* to alight. **sich auf einen Stuhl ~** to sit down on a chair; **sich ins Auto ~** to get into the car; **sich zu jdm ~** to sit with sb. **(b)** *(Kaffee, Tee, Lösung)* to settle.

3 *vi* **(a)** *(bei Glücksspiel, Wetten)* to bet. **auf ein Pferd ~** to bet on a horse; **auf jdn/etw ~** *(lit, fig)* to back sb/sth. **(b)** *(Typ)* to set. **(c)** *(springen) (Pferd, Läufer)* to jump. **über einen Fluß ~** to cross a river.

Setzer *m* **-** *(Typ)* typesetter.

Setz-: **~kasten** *m (Typ)* case; *(an Wand)* ornament shelf; **~ling** *m (Hort)* seedling.

Seuche *f* **-n** epidemic; *(fig pej)* scourge.

Seuchen-: **s~artig** *adj* epidemic; **sich s~artig ausbreiten** to reach epidemic proportions, to spread like the plague; **~bekämpfung** *f* epidemic control; **~gebiet** *nt* epidemic area.

seufzen *vti* to sigh.

Seufzer *m* **-** sigh.

Sex *m no pl* sex.

Sex-: **~-Appeal** [-ə'pi:l] *m no pl* sex appeal; **~bombe** *f (col)* sex bomb *(col)*; **~film** *m* sex film; **~foto** *nt* sexy photo.

Sexismus *m* sexism.

sexistisch *adj* sexist.

Sexta *f, pl* **Sexten** *(Sch) first year in a German secondary school.*

Sextaner(in *f***)** *m* **-** *pupil in the first year of a German secondary school.*

Sextant *m (Naut)* sextant.

Sexte *f* **-n** *(Mus)* sixth.

Sextett *nt* **-e** *(Mus)* sextet(te).

Sexual|erziehung *f* sex education.

Sexualität *f no pl* sexuality.

Sexual-: **~leben** *nt* sex life; **~mörder** *m* sex murderer; **~trieb** *m* sex(ual) drive; **~wissenschaft** *f* sexology.

sexuell *adj* sexual.

sexy ['zɛksi] *adj pred (col)* sexy *(col)*.

sezieren* *vti (lit, fig)* to dissect.

Shampoo(n) [ʃam'pu:(n)] *nt* **-s** shampoo.

Shorts [ʃɔrts] *pl* (pair of) shorts.

Show [ʃo:] *f* **-s** show. **eine ~ abziehen** *(col)* to put on a show *(col)*.

Show-: **~geschäft** *nt* show business; **~master** ['ʃoʊma:stə] *m* **-** compère, emcee *(US)*.

siamesisch *adj* **~e Zwillinge** Siamese twins.

Siamkatze *f* Siamese (cat).

Sibirien [zi'bi:riən] *nt* Siberia.

sibirisch *adj* Siberian.

sich *refl pron* **(a)** *(acc) (+infin, bei „man")* oneself; *(3. pers sing)* himself; herself; itself; *(Höflichkeitsform)* yourself; yourselves; *(3. pers pl)* themselves. **~ wiederholen** to repeat oneself/itself. **(b)** *(dat) (+infin, bei „man")* to oneself; *(3. pers sing)* to himself; to herself; to itself; *(Höflichkeitsform)* to yourself/yourselves; *(3. pers pl)* to themselves. **~ die Haare waschen** to wash one's hair; **sie hat ~ einen Pullover gekauft** she bought herself a pullover. **(c)** *acc, dat (mit prep) (+infin, bei „man")* one; *(3. pers sing)* him; her; it; *(Höflichkeitsform)* you; *(3. pers pl)* them. **haben Sie Ihren Ausweis bei ~?** do you have your pass on you? **(d)** *(einander)* each other, one another. **(e)** *(impers)* **hier sitzt es ~ gut** it's good to sit here; **dieses Auto fährt ~ gut** this car drives well.

Sichel *f* **-n** sickle; *(Mond~)* crescent.

sicher 1 *adj* **(a)** *(gewiß)* certain, sure. **der ~e Tod** certain death; **(sich** *dat***) einer Sache/jds ~ sein** to be sure of sth/sb; **soviel ist ~** that much is certain. **(b)** *(geschützt)* safe; *(geborgen)* secure. **vor jdm/etw ~ sein** to be safe from sb/sth; **~ leben** to lead a secure life; **~ ist ~** you can't be too sure. **(c)** *(zuverlässig)* reliable; *(fest) Gefühl, Zusage* definite; *Hand, Job* steady; *Stellung* secure. **(d)** *(selbstbewußt)* confident. **~ wirken/ auftreten** to give an impression of confidence. **2** *adv* **(a)** *fahren etc* safely. **(b)** *(natürlich)* of course. **du hast dich ~ verrechnet** you must have counted wrongly; **das weiß ich ganz ~** I know that for certain; **aber er kommt ~ noch** I'm sure he'll come.

sichergehen *vi sep irreg aux sein* to be sure.

Sicherheit *f* **(a)** *no pl (Gewißheit)* certainty. **das ist mit ~ richtig** that is definitely right. **(b)** *no pl (Schutz, das Sichersein)* safety; *(als Aufgabe von Sicherheitsbeamten etc)* security. **~ und Ordnung** law and order; **die öffentliche ~** public security; **jdn/etw in ~ bringen** to get sb/sth to safety; **~ im Straßenverkehr** road safety; **zu Ihrer eigenen ~** for your own safety; **in ~ sein** to be safe. **(c)** *no pl (Zuverlässigkeit)* reliability; *(von Hand, Einkommen)* steadiness; *(von Stellung)* security. **(d)** *no pl (Selbstbewußtsein)* (self-)confidence. **(e)** *(Comm)* security; *(Pfand)* surety. **~ leisten** *(Comm)* to offer security.

Sicherheits-: **~abstand** *m* safe distance; **~beamte(r)** *m* security officer; **~bestimmungen** *pl* safety regulations *pl*; *(betrieblich, Pol etc)* security controls *pl*; **~gurt** *m* seat belt; **s~halber** *adv* to be on the safe side; **~kontrolle** *f* security check; **~maßnahme** *f* safety precaution; *(betrieblich, Pol etc)* security measure; **~nadel** *f* safety pin; **~risiko** *nt* security risk;

~**schloß** *nt* safety lock; ~**truppen** *pl* security troops *pl*; ~**verschluß** *m* safety catch; ~**vorkehrung** *f* safety precaution; *(betrieblich, Pol etc)* security precaution.

sichern 1 *vt* **(a)** *(gegen, vor +dat against)* to safeguard; *(absichern)* to protect; *(sicher machen) Tür, Fahrrad etc* to secure; *Bergsteiger etc* to belay. **(b) jdm/sich etw** ~ to secure sth for sb/oneself. **2** *vr* to protect oneself *(vor +dat, gegen against)*.

sicherstellen *vt sep* **(a)** *Waffen, Heroin* to take possession of. **(b)** *(garantieren)* to guarantee.

Sicherung *f* **(a)** *siehe vt (a)* safeguarding; protection; securing; belaying. **(b)** *(Schutz)* safeguard. **(c)** *(Elec)* fuse; *(von Waffe)* safety catch. **da ist (bei) ihm die** ~ **durchgebrannt** *(fig col)* he blew a fuse *(col)*.

Sicht *f no pl* **(a)** *(Sehweite)* visibility. **eine** ~ **von 30 Metern** 30 metres' visibility; **in** ~ **sein/kommen** to be in/come into sight; **auf lange/kurze** ~ *(fig)* in the long/short term; *planen* for the long/short term. **(b)** *(Ausblick, Gesichtspunkt)* view. **aus meiner/seiner** ~ from my/his point of view. **(c)** *(Comm)* **auf** *or* **bei** ~ at sight.

sichtbar *adj (lit, fig)* visible. ~ **werden** *(fig)* to become apparent.

sichten *vt* **(a)** *(durchsehen)* to look through; *(ordnen)* to sift through. **(b)** *(erblicken)* to sight.

Sicht-: ~**gerät** *nt* monitor; *(Comp auch)* VDU, visual display unit; ~**grenze** *f* visibility limit.

sichtlich 1 *adj* obvious. **2** *adv* obviously, visibly.

Sicht-: ~**verhältnisse** *pl* visibility *sing;* ~**vermerk** *m* visa; ~**weite** *f* visibility *no art*; **außer** ~**weite** out of sight

Sickergrube *f* soakaway.

sickern *vi aux sein* to seep; *(in Tropfen)* to drip. **in die Presse** ~ to be leaked to the press.

sie *pers pron 3. pers* **(a)** *sing (von Frau, weiblichem Tier) (nom)* she; *(acc)* her; *(von Dingen)* it; *(acc)* them *pl*. ~ **ist es** it's her. **(b)** *pl (nom)* they; *(acc)* them. ~ **sind es** it's them.

Sie *pers pron 2. pers sing or pl* you. **jdn mit** ~ **anreden** to call sb "Sie".

Sieb *nt* **-e** sieve; *(Tee~)* strainer; *(Gemüse~)* colander.

sieben[1] **1** *vt* to pass through a sieve; *(Cook)* to sift, to sieve. **2** *vi (fig col)* **bei der Prüfung wird stark gesiebt** the exam will weed a lot of people out.

sieben[2] *num* seven.

Sieben *f* - *or* **-en** seven; *siehe* **Vier.**

Sieben- *in cpds siehe auch* **Vier-; s~hundert** *num* seven hundred; **s~mal** *adv* seven times; ~**meter** *m (Sport)* penalty; ~**sachen** *pl (col)* belongings *pl*; ~**schläfer** *m (Zool)* dormouse; **s~tausend** *num* seven thousand.

Siebtel *nt* - seventh.

siebtens *adv* seventh(ly), in the seventh place.

siebte(r, s) *adj* seventh; *siehe* **vierte(r, s).**

siebzehn *num* seventeen.

siebzig *num* seventy; *siehe* **vierzig.**

siedeln *vi* to settle.

sieden 1 *vi (Wasser, Zucker etc)* to boil. **2** *vt Seife, Leim* to produce by boiling. ~**d heiß** boiling hot.

Siedepunkt *m (Phys, fig)* boiling-point.

Siedler *m* - settler; *(Bauer)* smallholder.

Siedlung *f* **(a)** *(Ansiedlung)* settlement. **(b)** *(Wohn~)* housing estate *(Brit)*, development.

Sieg *m* **-e** victory *(über +acc over)*. **einen** ~ **erringen** to win a victory; **einer Sache** *(dat)* **zum** ~ **verhelfen** to help sth to triumph.

Siegel *nt* - seal.

Siegellack *m* sealing wax.

siegeln *vt Urkunde* to affix a/one's seal to; *(ver~) Brief* to seal.

Siegelring *m* signet ring.

siegen *vi (Mil)* to be victorious; *(in Wettkampf)* to win. **über jdn/etw** ~ *(fig)* to triumph over sb/sth; *(in Wettkampf)* to beat sb/sth.

Sieger(in *f***)** *m* - victor; *(in Wettkampf)* winner. **zweiter** ~ runner-up; ~ **werden** to win.

Sieger|ehrung *f (Sport)* presentation ceremony.

Sieger-: ~**macht** *f usu pl (Pol)* victorious power; ~**urkunde** *f (Sport)* winner's certificate.

Sieges-: **s~bewußt** *adj* confident of victory; ~**denkmal** *nt* victory monument; ~**feier** *f* victory celebration; ~**preis** *m* winner's prize; *(Boxen)* winner's purse; **s~sicher** *adj* certain of victory; ~**zug** *m* triumphal march.

siegreich *adj* victorious, triumphant; *(in Wettkampf)* winning *attr*.

siehe *imper sing of* **sehen** see.

Siel *nt or m* **-e** *(Schleuse)* sluice; *(Abwasserkanal)* sewer.

siezen *vt* **sich** ~ to address each other as "Sie".

Signal *nt* **-e** signal. **(ein)** ~ **geben** to give a signal.

Signal|anlage *f* signals *pl*, set of signals.

signalisieren* *vt (lit, fig)* to signal.

Signal-: ~**lampe** *f* signal lamp; ~**mast** *m* signal mast.

Signatur *f* **(a)** *(Bibliotheks~)* shelf mark. **(b)** *(auf Landkarten)* symbol.

Silbe *f* **-n** syllable. **er hat es mit keiner** ~ **erwähnt** he didn't say a word about it.

Silber *nt no pl* silver. **aus** ~ made of silver.

Silber- *in cpds* silver; ~**arbeit** *f* silverwork *no pl*; ~**besteck** *nt* silver(ware); **s~farben** *adj* silver; ~**fischchen** *nt* silverfish; ~**folie** *f* silver foil; ~**fuchs** *m* silver fox; ~**geld** *nt* silver; ~**hochzeit** *f* silver wedding (anniversary); ~**löwe** *m* puma; ~**möwe** *f* herring gull.

silbern *adj* silver. ~**e Hochzeit** silver wedding (anniversary).

Silber-: ~**pappel** *f* white poplar; ~**schmied** *m* silversmith; ~**stickerei** *f (Kunst)* silver embroidery; ~**streif(en)** *m (fig)* **es zeichnete sich ein** ~**streif(en) am Horizont ab** there was light at the end of the tunnel; ~**stück** *nt* silver coin; ~**waren** *pl* silver *sing;* **s~weiß** *adj* silvery white.

silbrig *adj* silvery.

Silhouette [zi'luɛtə] *f* silhouette.

Silikon *nt* **-e** silicone.

Silikon-: ~**chip** *m*, ~**plättchen** *nt* silicon chip.

Silikose *f* **-n** *(Med)* silicosis.

Silizium *nt no pl* silicon.

Silo *m* **-s** silo.

Silvester [zɪl'vɛstɐ] *m or nt* - New Year's Eve.

simpel *adj* simple; *(vereinfacht)* simplistic.

Simpel *m* - *(col)* simpleton.

Sims *m or nt* **-e** *(Fenster~)* sill; *(Gesims)* ledge.

Simulant(in *f***)** *m* malingerer.

Simulator *m (Sci)* simulator.

simulieren* **1** *vi* **er simuliert nur** he's shamming. **2** *vt* **(a)** *Krankheit* to feign. **(b)** *(Sci)* to simulate.

simultan *adj* simultaneous.

Simultandolmetscher *m* simultaneous interpreter.

sind *1., 3. pers pl, bei Sie sing/pl pres of* **sein** are.

Sinfonie *f* symphony.

Sinfonie-: ~**konzert** *nt* symphony concert; ~**orchester** *nt* symphony orchestra.

Sinfoniker(in *f***)** *m* - member of a symphony orchestra. **die Münchner** ~ the Munich Symphony Orchestra.

sinfonisch *adj* symphonic.

Singapur ['zɪŋgapuːɐ] *nt* Singapore.

singen *pret* **sang,** *ptp* **gesungen 1** *vti* **(a)** *(lit, fig)* to sing; *(esp Eccl: eintönig, feierlich)* to chant. **zur Gitarre** ~ to sing to the guitar; **ein** ~**der Tonfall** a lilt; **jdn in den Schlaf** ~ to sing sb to sleep. **(b)** *(col: gestehen)* to squeal *(col)*. **2** *vr* **sich heiser** ~ to sing oneself hoarse.

Single[1] ['sɪŋgl] *f* **-s** *(Schallplatte)* single.

Single[2] ['sɪŋgl] *m* **-s** *(Alleinlebender)* single.

Sing-: ~**sang** *m* **-s** *(Gesang)* monotonous singing; ~**stimme** *f* vocal part.

Singular *m* singular.

Sing-: ~**vogel** *m* song-bird; ~**weise** *f* way of singing.

sinken *pret* **sank,** *ptp* **gesunken** *vi aux sein* **(a)** to sink; *(Ballon)* to descend; *(Nebel)* to come down. **ins Bett** ~ to fall into bed; **in jds Meinung/Achtung** *(dat)* ~ to go down in sb's estimation. **(b)** *(Boden, Gebäude)* to subside; *(Fundament)* to settle. **in Schutt und Asche** ~ *(geh)* to fall in ruins. **(c)** *(niedriger, geringer werden: Temperatur, Preise etc)* to drop; *(Ansehen)* to diminish; *(Hoffnung, Stimmung)* to sink. **den Mut/die Hoffnung** ~ **lassen** to lose courage/hope.

Sinn *m* **-e (a)** sense; *(Bedeutung)* meaning. **er war von** ~**en** he was out of his senses *or* mind; **im übertragenen** ~ in the figurative sense; **der Satz (er)gibt keinen** ~ the sentence doesn't make sense.

(b) *(Gedanken, Denkweise)* mind. **sich** *(dat)* **jdn/etw aus dem** ~ **schlagen** to put sb/sth out of one's mind; **es kam ihm gar nicht in den** ~**, ihr zu helfen** it did not occur to him to help her; **das will mir einfach nicht in den** ~ I just can't understand it; **das geht mir nicht aus dem** ~ I can't get it out of my mind; **etw im** ~ **haben** to have sth in mind.

(c) *(Verständnis)* feeling. ~ **für Humor haben** to have a sense of humour; **er hat keinen** ~ **für Kunst** he has no appreciation of art.

(d) *(Geist)* spirit. **im** ~**e des Gesetzes** according to the spirit of the law; **im** ~**e des Verstorbenen** in accordance with the wishes of the deceased.

(e) *(Zweck)* point. **das ist nicht der** ~ **der Sache** that is not the point; **der** ~ **des Lebens** the meaning of life; **ohne** ~ **und Verstand sein** to make no sense at all; **das hat keinen** ~ there is no point in that; **es hat keinen** ~**, jetzt noch loszugehen** there's no point (in) starting out now.

Sinn-: ~**bild** *nt* symbol; **s**~**bildlich** *adj* symbolic(al).

sinnen *pret* **sann,** *ptp* **gesonnen** *vi (geh)* to ponder, to muse; *(grübeln)* to brood. **über etw** *(acc)* ~ to reflect on/brood over sth; **auf Verrat/Rache** ~ to plot treason/revenge.

Sinnes-: ~**eindruck** *m* sensory impression; ~**nerv** *m* sensory nerve; ~**organ** *nt* sense organ; ~**reiz** *m* sensory stimulus; ~**täuschung** *f* hallucination; ~**wandel** *m* change of mind.

sinngemäß *adj* **(a)** *(inhaltlich)* **etw** ~ **wiedergeben** to give the gist of sth. **(b)** *(esp Jur: analog)* corresponding, analogous. **etw** ~ **anwenden** to apply sth by analogy.

sinnig *adj* apt; *Vorrichtung* practical; *(iro: wenig sinnvoll)* clever.

sinnlich *adj* **(a)** *(vital, sinnenfroh)* sensuous; *(erotisch)* sensual. ~**e Liebe** sensual love. **(b)** ~ **wahrnehmbar** perceptible by the senses.

Sinnlichkeit *f (Vitalität)* sensuousness; *(Erotik)* sensuality.

sinnlos *adj* **(a)** *(unsinnig) Redensarten, Geschwätz* meaningless; *Verhalten, Töten* senseless. **(b)** *(zwecklos)* pointless; *Wut* blind. ~ **betrunken** blind drunk.

Sinnlosigkeit *f siehe adj* meaninglessness; senselessness; pointlessness.

sinn-: ~**verwandt** *adj* synonymous; ~**voll** *adj Satz* meaningful; *(fig)* sensible; *(nützlich)* useful.

Sintflut *f (Bibl)* Flood. **nach uns die** ~ *(col)* it doesn't matter what happens after we've gone.

sintflut|artig *adj* ~**e Regenfälle** torrential rain.

Sinus *m* - *(Math)* sine.

Siphon ['zi:fõ] *m* **-s** siphon.

Sippe *f* **-n** (extended) family; *(col: Verwandtschaft)* clan *(col)*.

Sippschaft *f (pej col)* tribe *(col)*.

Sirene *f* **-n** *(Tech, fig)* siren.

Sirup *m* **-e** syrup.

Sisal(hanf) *m no pl* sisal (hemp).

Sit-in [sɪt'|ɪn] *nt* **-s** sit-in. **ein** ~ **machen** to stage a sit-in.

Sitte *f* **-n (a)** *(Brauch)* custom; *(Mode)* practice. ~ **sein** to be the custom/the practice. **(b)** *usu pl (gutes Benehmen)* manners *pl*; *(Sittlichkeit)* morals *pl*. **gegen die (guten)** ~**n verstoßen** to offend common decency; **was sind denn das für** ~**n?** what sort of a way is that to behave!

Sitten-: ~**gesetz** *nt* moral law; ~**kodex** *m* moral code; **s**~**los** *adj* immoral; ~**losigkeit** *f* immorality; ~**polizei** *f* vice squad; ~**richter** *m* judge of public morals; **s**~**streng** *adj* highly moral; ~**strolch** *m (col)* sex fiend *(col)*; ~**verfall** *m* decline in moral standards; ~**wächter** *m (iro)* guardian of public morals; **s**~**widrig** *adj (form)* immoral.

Sittich *m* **-e** parakeet.

sittlich *adj* moral.

Sittlichkeit *f no pl* morality.

Sittlichkeits-: ~**delikt** *nt* sexual offence *(Brit) or* offense *(US)*; ~**verbrechen** *nt* sex crime; ~**verbrecher** *m* sex offender.

sittsam *adj* demure.

Sittsamkeit *f* demureness.

Situation *f* situation.

situiert *adj* **gut/schlecht** ~ **sein** to be well/poorly situated financially.

Sitz *m* **-e (a)** *(~platz, Parl)* seat. **(b)** *(von Regierung, Universität, fig)* seat; *(Wohn~)* residence; *(von Firma, Verwaltung)* headquarters *pl*. **(c)** *no pl (Tech, von Kleidungsstück)* sit; *(von der Größe her)* fit. **einen guten/schlechten** ~ **haben** to sit/fit well/badly.

sitzen *vi pret* **saß,** *ptp* **gesessen** *aux haben or (Aus, S Ger, Sw) sein* **(a)** to sit; *(Vogel)* to perch. **er saß bei uns am Tisch** he was sitting at our table; **bleiben Sie bitte** ~**!** please don't get up; ~ **Sie bequem?** are you comfortable?; **etw im S**~ **tun** to do sth sitting down; **an einer Aufgabe** ~ to sit over a task; **einen** ~ **haben** *(col)* to have had one too many. **(b)** *(col: im Gefängnis ~)* to be inside *(col)*. **(c)** *(sein)* to be. **er sitzt im Kultusministerium** *(col)* he's in the ministry of culture. **(d)** *(angebracht sein)* to sit. **der Deckel sitzt fest** the lid is on tightly; **locker** ~ to be loose; **fest** ~ to be stuck tight(ly); **deine Krawatte sitzt nicht richtig** your tie isn't straight; **das hat gesessen!** *(col)* that hit home. **(e)** *(im Gedächtnis ~)* to have sunk in.

sitzenbleiben *vi sep irreg aux sein (col)* **(a)** *(Sch)* to stay down. **(b) auf einer Ware** ~ to be left with a product. **(c)** *(unverheiratete Frau)* to be left on the shelf *(col)*.

sitzenlassen *vt sep irreg ptp* ~ *or* **sitzengelassen** *(col)* **(a)** *(Sch: nicht versetzen)* to keep down (a year). **(b) eine Beleidigung auf sich** *(dat)* ~ to take an insult. **(c) jdn** ~ *(im Stich lassen)* to leave sb in the lurch; *Freund(in)* to stand sb up; *(nicht heiraten)* to jilt.

Sitz-: ~**fleisch** *nt (col)* ~**fleisch haben** to be able to sit still; ~**gelegenheit** *f* seats *pl*; ~**kissen** *nt* (floor) cushion; ~**ordnung** *f* seating plan; ~**platz** *m* seat; ~**reihe** *f* row of seats; ~**streik** *m* = **Sit-in.**

Sitzung *f* meeting; *(Jur)* session; *(Parlaments~)* sitting.

Sitzungssaal *m* conference hall.

Sizilianer(in *f***)** *m* - Sicilian.

sizilianisch *adj* Sicilian.

Sizilien [zi'tsi:liən] *nt* Sicily.

Skai ® *nt no pl* imitation leather.

Skala *f, pl* **Skalen** scale; *(fig)* range.

Skalp *m* **-e** scalp.

Skalpell *nt* **-e** scalpel.

skalpieren* *vt* to scalp.

Skandal *m* **-e** scandal; *(col: Krach)* fuss. **einen** ~ **machen** to cause a scandal; to make a fuss.

Skandal-: ~**blatt** *nt (pej)* scandal sheet; ~**ge-**

schichte *f* (bit *or* piece of) scandal.
skandalös *adj* scandalous.
Skandalpresse *f (pej)* gutter press.
Skandinavien [skandiˈnaːviən] *nt* Scandinavia.
Skandinavier(in *f*) *m* - Scandinavian.
skandinavisch *adj* Scandinavian.
Skat *m* **-e** *(Cards)* skat.
Skelett *nt* **-e** *(lit, fig)* skeleton.
Skepsis *f no pl* scepticism. **mit/voller ~** sceptically.
Skeptiker(in *f*) *m* - sceptic.
skeptisch *adj* sceptical.
Sketch [skɛtʃ] *m* **-e(s)** *(Art, Theat)* sketch.
Ski [ʃiː] *m* **-er** [ˈʃiːɐ] ski. **~ laufen** to ski.
Ski- *in cpds* ski; **~fahrer(in *f*)** *m* skier; **~gebiet** *nt* ski(ing) area; **~hütte** *f* ski hut *or* lodge *(US)*; **~kurs** *m* skiing course; **~lauf** *m* skiing; **~läufer(in *f*)** *m* skier; **~lehrer** *m* ski instructor; **~lift** *m* ski-lift; **~piste** *f* ski-run; **~sport** *m* skiing; **~springen** *nt* ski jumping; **~stock** *m* ski stick.
Skizze [ˈskɪtsə] *f* **-n** sketch; *(fig: Grundriß)* plan.
Skizzen- [ˈskɪtsn-]: **~buch** *nt* sketchbook; **s~haft 1** *adj Zeichnung etc* roughly sketched; *Beschreibung etc* (given) in broad outline; **2** *adv* **etw s~haft zeichnen** to sketch sth roughly.
skizzieren* [skɪˈtsiːrən] *vt* to sketch; *(fig) Plan etc* to outline.
Sklave [ˈsklaːvə] *m (wk)* **-n, -n** slave. **~ einer Sache** *(gen)* **sein** *(fig)* to be a slave to sth.
Sklaven- [ˈsklaːvn]: **~arbeit** *f* slavery; **~handel** *m* slave trade; **~treiber** *m* slave-driver.
Sklaverei [sklaːvəˈrai] *f no pl (lit, fig)* slavery *no art.*
Sklavin [ˈsklaːvɪn] *f* slave.
sklavisch [ˈsklaːvɪʃ] *adj* slavish.
Sklerose *f* **-n** sclerosis.
Skonto *nt or m, pl* **-s** *or* **Skonti** cash discount.
Skorbut *m no pl* scurvy.
Skorpion *m* **-e** *(Zool)* scorpion; *(Astrol)* Scorpio.
Skrupel *m* - *usu pl* scruple. **er hatte keine ~, das zu tun** he had no scruples about doing it; **ohne ~** without scruples.
Skrupel-: s~los *adj* unscrupulous; **~losigkeit** *f* unscrupulousness.
Skulptur *f* sculpture.
Skunk *m* **-s** skunk.
skurril *adj (geh)* droll, comical.
S-Kurve [ˈɛs-] *f* S-bend.
Slalom *m* **-s** slalom.
Slang [slæŋ] *m no pl* slang.
Slawe *m (wk)* **-n, -n, Slawin** *f* Slav.
slawisch *adj* Slavonic, Slavic.
Slip *m* **-s** (pair of) briefs *pl.*
Slipper *m* - slip-on (shoe).
Slogan [ˈsloːgn] *m* **-s** slogan.
Slum [slam] *m* **-s** slum.
Smaragd *m* **-e** emerald.
Smog *m* **-s** smog.
Smoking [ˈsmoːkɪŋ] *m* **-s** dinner-jacket, tuxedo *(US).*
Snob *m* **-s** snob.
snobistisch *adj* snobbish.
SO = Südosten SE.
s.o. = siehe oben.
so 1 *adv* **(a)** *(mit adj, adv)* so; *(mit vb: ~ sehr)* so much, **~ groß** *etc* so big *etc*; **eine ~ große Frau** such a big woman; **~ groß wie ...** as big as ...; **~ gut es geht** as best as I/he *etc* can; **er ist nicht ~ dumm, das zu glauben** he's not so stupid as to believe that; **das hat ihn ~ geärgert, daß ...** that annoyed him so much that ...; **~ ein Fehler** such a mistake; **~ ein Idiot!** what an idiot!; **hast du ~ etwas schon einmal gesehen?** have you ever seen anything like it?; **na ~ was!** well I never!; **~ etwas Schönes** such a beautiful thing; **~ einer wie ich** somebody like me.
(b) *(auf diese Weise)* like this/that. **mach es nicht ~** don't do it like that; **mach es ~, wie er es vorgeschlagen hat** do it the way he suggested; **~ ist sie nun einmal** that's the way she is; **(ach) ~ ist das!** I see!; **~ oder/und ~** in one way or the other; **und ~ weiter** and so on; **gut ~!** fine!; **das ist gut ~** that's fine; **mir ist (es) ~, als ob ...** it seems to me as if ...; **das kam ~: ...** this is what happened ...; **es verhält sich ~: ...** the facts are as follows ...; **das habe ich nur ~ gesagt** I didn't really mean it.
(c) *(etwa)* about, or so. **ich komme ~ um 8 Uhr** I'll come at 8 or so.
(d) *(col: umsonst)* for nothing.
(e) *(als Füllwort) nicht übersetzt.* **~ beeil dich doch!** do hurry up!; **~ mancher** a number of people *pl.*
2 *conj* **(a) ~ daß** so that. **(b) ~ wie es jetzt ist** as things are at the moment. **(c) ~ klein er auch sein mag** however small he may be.
3 *interj* so; *(wirklich)* oh, really; *(abschließend)* well, right. **er ist schon da — ~** he's here already — is he?; **~, ~!** well well.
sobald *conj* as soon as.
Socke *f* **-n** sock. **sich auf die ~n machen** *(col)* to get going *(col).*
Sockel *m* - base; *(von Denkmal, Statue)* pedestal.
Soda *nt no pl* soda.
Sodawasser *nt* soda water.
Sodbrennen *nt* heartburn.
Sodomie *f* buggery, bestiality.
so|eben *adv* just (this moment).
Sofa *nt* **-s** sofa, settee *(esp Brit).*
sofern *conj* provided (that). **~ ... nicht** if ... not.
soff *pret of* **saufen.**
sofort *adv* immediately. **komm hierher, und zwar ~!** come here this instant!; **(ich) komme ~!** (I'm) just coming!
Soforthilfe *f* emergency relief *or* aid.
sofortig *adj* immediate, instant.
Sofortmaßnahme *f* immediate measure.
Soft|eis [ˈsɔft-] *nt* soft ice-cream.
Software [ˈsɔftwɛːɐ] *f* **-s** *(Comp)* software.
sog *pret of* **saugen.**
sog. = sogenannt.
Sog *m* **-e** *(saugende Kraft)* suction; *(von Strudel)* vortex; *(fig)* maelstrom.
sogar *adv* even. **schön, ~ sehr schön** beautiful, in fact very beautiful.
sogenannt *adj attr* so-called.
sogleich *adv* = **sofort.**
Sohle *f* **-n (a)** *(Fuß~ etc)* sole; *(Einlage)* insole. **auf leisen ~n** softly. **(b)** *(Boden)* bottom.
Sohn *m* **¨-e** *(lit, fig)* son.
Soja *f, pl* **Sojen** soy.
Soja-: ~bohne *f* soybean; **~soße** *f* soya sauce.
solang(e) *conj* as long as, so long as.
Solar- *in cpds* solar.
solch *adj inv,* **solche(r, s)** *adj* such. **ein ~er Mensch** such a person; **wir haben ~en Durst** we're so thirsty; **~ ein langer Weg** such a long way; **~es** that kind of thing; **Rechtsanwälte gibt es ~e und ~e** there are lawyers and lawyers.
solcherlei *adj attr inv* such.
Sold *m no pl (Mil)* pay.
Soldat *m (wk)* **-en, -en** soldier. **~ spielen** to play soldiers.
Soldaten-: ~friedhof *m* military cemetery; **~sprache** *f* military slang; **~tum** *nt* soldiery *no art; (Tradition)* military tradition; **~verband** *m* ex-servicemen's association.
soldatisch *adj (militärisch)* military; *(soldatengemäß)* soldierly.
Söldner *m* - mercenary.
Söldnertruppe *f* mercenary force.
Sole *f* **-n** brine, salt water.
Solei [ˈzoːl|ai] *nt* pickled egg.
solidarisch *adj* **sich mit jdm ~ erklären** to declare one's solidarity with sb; **~ mit jdm handeln** to act in solidarity with sb.

solidarisieren* *vr* **sich ~ mit** to show (one's) solidarity with.
Solidarität *f* solidarity.
Solidaritätsstreik *m* sympathy strike.
solid(e) *adj Haus, Möbel etc* solid, sturdy; *Arbeit, Wissen, Handwerker* sound; *Mensch, Lokal* respectable; *Firma* solid; *Preise* reasonable.
Solist(in *f*) *m (Mus)* soloist.
Soll *nt* **-(s)** *(Schuld)* debit; *(Schuldseite)* debit side. **~ und Haben** debit and credit; **sein ~ erfüllen** to meet one's target.
sollen 1 *modal aux pret* **sollte,** *ptp* **~ (a)** *(bei Befehl, Anordnung, Absicht)* to be (supposed) to. **was soll ich/er tun?** what shall *or* should I/should he do?; **er weiß nicht, was er tun soll** he doesn't know what to do; **sie sagte ihm, er solle draußen warten** she told him to wait outside; **was ich (nicht) alles tun/wissen soll!** the things I'm supposed to do/know!; **es soll nicht wieder vorkommen** it won't happen again; **er soll reinkommen** tell him to come in; **niemand soll sagen, daß ...** let no-one say that ...; **das Haus soll nächste Woche gestrichen werden** the house is to be painted next week; **was sollte ich/er deiner Meinung nach tun?** what do you think I/he should do *or* ought to do?; **das hättest du nicht tun ~** you shouldn't have *or* oughtn't to have done that.
(b) *(bei Gerücht, Vermutung)* to be supposed *or* meant to. **sie soll verheiratet sein** I've heard she's married; **Xanthippe soll zänkisch gewesen sein** Xanthippe is said to have been quarrelsome; **das soll gar nicht so einfach sein** they say it's not that easy; **was soll das heißen?** what's that supposed to mean?; **mir soll es gleich sein** it's all the same to me; **so etwas soll es geben** these things happen; **man sollte glauben, daß ...** you would think that ...; **sollte das möglich sein?** can that be possible?
(c) sollte das passieren, ... if that should happen ...; **er sollte sie nie wiedersehen** he was never to see her again.
2 *vti pret* **sollte,** *ptp* **gesollt was soll das?** what's all this?; *(warum denn das)* what's that for?; **was soll's?** what the hell! *(col)*; **das sollst du nicht** you shouldn't do that; **was man nicht alles soll!** *(col)* the things you're meant to do!
Söller *m* **-** balcony.
Soll-: **~seite** *f (Fin)* debit side; **~stärke** *f* required strength.
solo *adv (Mus)* solo; *(fig col)* on one's own, alone.
Solo *nt, pl* **Soli** solo.
solvent [zɔl'vɛnt] *adj (Fin)* solvent.
somit *adv* consequently, therefore.
Sommer *m* **-** summer. **im ~** in (the) summer; **im nächsten ~** next summer; **~ wie Winter** all year round.
Sommer- *in cpds* summer; **~abend** *m* summer('s) evening; **~anfang** *m* beginning of summer; **~ferien** *pl* summer holidays *pl (Brit) or* vacation *(US)*; *(Jur, Parl)* summer recess; **~gast** *m* summer guest; **~haus** *nt* holiday home; **~kleidung** *f* summer clothing.
sommerlich *adj* summer *attr; (sommerartig)* summery.
Sommer-: **~mantel** *m* summer coat; **~monat** *m* summer month; **~nacht** *f* summer('s) night; **~pause** *f* summer break; *(Jur, Parl)* summer recess; **~reifen** *m* normal tyre *(Brit) or* tire *(US)*; **~saison** *f* summer season; **~schlußverkauf** *m* summer sale; **~semester** *nt (Univ)* summer semester, ≃ summer term *(Brit)*; **~sitz** *m* summer residence; **~spiele** *pl* **die Olympischen ~spiele** the Summer Olympics; **~sprosse** *f* freckle; **~tag** *m* summer's day; **~weizen** *m* spring wheat; **~wetter** *nt* summer weather; **~zeit** *f* summer time *no art.*
Sonate *f* **-n** sonata.
Sonde *f* **-n** *(Space, Med)* probe.
Sonder- *in cpds* special; **~anfertigung** *f* special model; **~angebot** *nt* special offer; **~ausgabe** *f* **(a)** special edition; **(b) ~ausgaben** *pl (Fin)* additional *or* extra expenses *pl.*
sonderbar *adj* strange, peculiar, odd.
sonderbarerweise *adv* strange to say.
Sonder-: **~beauftragte(r)** *mf (Pol)* special emissary; **~fahrt** *f* special excursion; **~fall** *m* special case; *(Ausnahme)* exception; **~genehmigung** *f* special permission; *(Schein)* special permit; **s~gleichen** *adv inv* **eine Frechheit s~gleichen** an incredible cheek; **~konto** *nt* special account.
sonderlich 1 *adj attr* particular. **ohne ~e Begeisterung** without any particular enthusiasm. **2** *adv* particularly.
Sonderling *m* eccentric.
Sonder-: **~marke** *f* special issue (stamp); **~maschine** *f* special plane; **~meldung** *f (Rad, TV)* special announcement.
sondern[1] *conj* but.
sondern[2] *vt (geh)* to separate; *siehe* **gesondert.**
Sonder-: **~preis** *m* special reduced price; **~recht** *nt* (special) privilege; **~regelung** *f* special provision; **~schicht** *f* special shift; *(zusätzlich)* extra shift; **~schule** *f* special school; **~stellung** *f* special position; **~stempel** *m (bei der Post)* special postmark; **~wünsche** *pl* special requests *pl*; **~zug** *m* special train.
sondieren* *vti* to sound out. **das Terrain ~** to spy out the land; **die Lage ~** to find out how the land lies.
Sondierungsgespräch *nt* exploratory talk.
Sonett *nt* **-e** sonnet.
Sonn|abend *m* Saturday; *siehe* **Dienstag.**
sonn|abends *adv* on Saturdays, on a Saturday.
Sonne *f* **-n** sun. **an die ~ gehen** to go out in the sun; **geh mir aus der ~!** *(col)* get out of the way!; *(aus dem Licht)* get out of the light!
sonnen *vr* to sun oneself. **sich in etw** *(dat)* **~** *(fig)* to bask in sth.
Sonnen-: **~anbeter** *m (lit, fig)* sun-worshipper; **~aufgang** *m* sunrise; **~bad** *nt* sunbathing *no pl*; **ein ~bad nehmen** to sunbathe; **~batterie** *f* solar battery.
Sonnenblume *f* sunflower.
Sonnenblumen-: **~kern** *m* sunflower seed; **~öl** *nt* sunflower oil.
Sonnen-: **~brand** *m* sunburn *no art;* **~bräune** *f* suntan; **~brille** *f* (pair of) sunglasses *pl;* **~deck** *nt (Naut)* sundeck; **~energie** *f* solar energy; **~finsternis** *f* solar eclipse; **~fleck** *m (Astron)* sunspot; **s~gebräunt** *adj* suntanned; **~gott** *m* sungod; **~hut** *m* sunhat; **~jahr** *nt (Astron)* solar year; **s~klar** *adj (col)* crystal clear; **~kollektor** *m* solar panel; **~kult** *m* sun cult; **~licht** *nt* sunlight; **~öl** *nt* suntan oil; **~schein** *m* sunshine; **bei strahlendem ~schein** in brilliant sunshine; **~schirm** *m* sunshade; **~schutz** *m* protection against the sun; **~seite** *f (lit, fig)* sunny side; **~stand** *m* position of the sun; **~stich** *m* sunstroke *no art;* **du hast wohl einen ~stich!** *(col)* you must have been out in the sun too long!; **~strahl** *m* sunbeam; **~system** *nt* solar system; **~uhr** *f* sundial; **~untergang** *m* sunset; **~wende** *f* solstice.
sonnig *adj* sunny.
Sonntag *m* Sunday; *siehe* **Dienstag.**
sonntäglich *adj* Sunday *attr.* **~ gekleidet** dressed in one's Sunday best.
sonntags *adv* on Sundays, on a Sunday.
Sonntags- *in cpds* Sunday; **~arbeit** *f* Sunday working; **~ausflug** *m* Sunday trip; **~beilage** *f* Sunday supplement; **~dienst** *m (von Polizist etc)* Sunday duty; **~dienst haben** *(Apotheke)* to be open on Sundays; **~fahrer** *m (pej)* Sunday driver; **~maler** *m* Sunday painter; **~zeitung** *f* Sunday paper.
sonor *adj* sonorous.

sonst 1 *adv* **(a)** *(außerdem) (mit pron, adv)* else; *(mit n)* other. ~ **noch Fragen?** any other questions?; **wer/wie** *etc* **(denn) ~?** who/how *etc* else?; **er denkt, er ist ~ wer** *(col)* he thinks he's somebody special; ~ **noch etwas?** is that all?, anything else?; **wo warst du ~ noch?** where else did you go?; ~ **geht's dir gut?** *(iro col)* are you feeling okay? *(col)*. **(b)** *(andernfalls)* otherwise. **(c)** *(in anderen Beziehungen)* in other ways. **wenn ich Ihnen ~ noch behilflich sein kann** if I can help you in any other way. **(d)** *(gewöhnlich)* usually. **genau wie es ~ ist** just as it usually is; **genau wie/anders als ~** the same as/different from usual; **alles war wie ~** everything was as it always used to be. **2** *conj* otherwise, or (else).

sonstig *adj attr* other; *Fragen, Auskünfte etc* further. **„S~es"** "other".

sonst-: **~wann** *adv (col)* some other time; **~was** *indef pron (col)* **da kann ja ~was passieren** anything could happen; **ich habe ~was versucht** I've tried everything; **~wie** *adv (col)* (in) some other way; *(sehr)* like mad *(col)*; **~wo** *adv (col)* somewhere else; **~wohin** *adv (col)* somewhere else.

so|oft *conj* whenever.

Sopran *m* **-e** soprano; *(von Jungen)* treble.

Sopranistin *f* soprano.

Sorge *f* **-n (a)** worry. **keine ~!** *(col)* don't worry!; **wir betrachten diese Entwicklung mit ~** we view this development with concern; **~n haben** to have problems; **ich habe solche ~** I'm so worried; **du hast ~n!** *(iro)* you think you've got troubles! *(col)*; **jdm ~n machen** *(Kummer bereiten)* to cause sb a lot of worry; **machen Sie sich** *(dat)* **deshalb keine ~n** don't worry about that; **lassen Sie das meine ~ sein** let me worry about that; **das ist nicht meine ~** that's not my problem; **dafür ~ tragen, daß ...** *(geh)* to see to it that ... **(b)** *(Für~, Jur)* care.

sorgen 1 *vi* ~ **für** *(sich kümmern um)* to look after; *(vorsorgen für)* to provide for; *(herbeischaffen) Proviant, Musik* to provide; *(bewirken)* to ensure; **dafür ~, daß ...** to see to it that ...; **dafür ist gesorgt** that's taken care of. **2** *vr* to worry. **sich ~ um** to worry about.

Sorgen-: **s~frei** *adj* free of care; *(heiter)* carefree; **~kind** *nt (col)* problem child; **s~voll** *adj* worried; *Leben* full of worries.

Sorgerecht *nt (Jur)* custody.

Sorgfalt *f no pl* care. **ohne ~ arbeiten** to work carelessly; **viel ~ auf etw** *(acc)* **verwenden** to take a lot of care over sth.

sorgfältig *adj* careful.

sorglos *adj* carefree; *(leichtfertig)* careless.

Sorglosigkeit *f siehe adj* carefreeness; carelessness.

sorgsam *adj* careful.

Sorte *f* **-n (a)** type, kind; *(Qualität, Klasse)* grade; *(Marke)* brand. **beste ~** top quality. **(b)** *(Fin) usu pl* foreign currency.

sortieren* *vt* to sort. **etw in einen Schrank ~** to tidy sth away into a cupboard.

Sortierer(in *f***)** *m* **-** sorter.

Sortiermaschine *f* sorting machine.

Sortiment *nt* **(a)** assortment. **(b)** *(Buchhandel)* retail book trade.

Sortimentsbuchhandlung *f* retail bookshop *(Brit)* or bookstore *(US)*.

SOS [ɛs|oː'|ɛs] *nt* **-, -** SOS.

sosehr *conj* however much, no matter how much.

soso *interj* **~!** I see!; *(erstaunt)* well well!; *(drohend)* well!

Soße *f* **-n** sauce; *(Braten~)* gravy; *(pej col)* gunge *(col)*.

Souffleur [zu'fløːɐ] *m*, **Souffleuse** [zu'fløːzə] *f* *(Theat)* prompter.

soufflieren* [zu'fliːrən] *vti (Theat)* to prompt *(jdm* sb*)*.

so|undso *adv* ~ **lange** for such and such a time; ~ **viele** so and so many; **Paragraph ~** article such-and-such; **er sagte, mach das ~** he said, do it in such and such a way.

so|undsovielte(r, s) *adj* umpteenth. **am S~n** *(Datum)* on such and such a date.

Souterrain ['zuːtɛrɛ̃] *nt* **-s** basement.

Souvenir [zuvə'niːɐ] *nt* **-s** souvenir.

souverän [zuvə'rɛːn] *adj* sovereign *no adv*; *(fig)* supremely good; *(überlegen)* (most) superior *no adv*. **sein Gebiet ~ beherrschen** to have a commanding knowledge of one's field.

Souveränität [zuvərɛni'tɛːt] *f* sovereignty.

soviel 1 *adv* so much. **halb ~** half as much; ~ **wie ...** as much as ...; **noch einmal ~** *(doppelt ~)* twice as much; ~ **für heute!** that's all for today. **2** *conj* as far as. ~ **ich weiß, nicht!** not as far as I know.

sovielmal *adv* so many times.

soweit 1 *adv* **(a)** on the whole; *(bis jetzt)* up to now; *(bis zu diesem Punkt)* thus far. ~ **wie möglich** as far as possible. **(b)** ~ **sein** to be finished *or (bereit)* ready; **es ist bald ~** it's nearly time. **2** *conj* as far as; *(insofern)* in so far as.

sowenig *adv* no more, not any more *(wie* than*)*. ~ **wie möglich** as little as possible.

sowie *conj* **(a)** *(sobald)* as soon as. **(b)** *(und auch)* as well as.

sowieso *adv* anyway. **das ~!** obviously!

sowjetisch *adj* Soviet.

Sowjet- *in cpds* Soviet; **~republik** *f* Soviet Republic; **~russe** *m* Soviet Russian; **~union** *f* Soviet Union.

sowohl *conj* ~ **X als** *or* **wie (auch) Y** both X and Y, X as well as Y.

Sozi *m* **-s** *(esp pej col)* Socialist.

sozial *adj* social; *(~ eingestellt)* public-spirited. **~er Wohnungsbau** ≈ council housing *(Brit)*, state-subsidized housing.

Sozial-: **~abgaben** *pl* (social) welfare contributions *pl*; **~amt** *nt* (social) welfare office; **~arbeit** *f* social work; **~arbeiter** *m* social worker; **~beruf** *m* caring profession; **~demokrat** *m* social democrat; **~demokratie** *f* social democracy; **s~demokratisch** *adj* social-democratic; **~einrichtungen** *pl* social facilities *pl*; **~fall** *m* hardship case; **~gericht** *nt* (social) welfare tribunal; **~hilfe** *f* welfare (aid).

Sozialisation *f (Psych, Sociol)* socialization.

Sozialismus *m* socialism.

Sozialist(in *f***)** *m* socialist.

sozialistisch *adj* socialist.

Sozial-: **~politik** *f* social policy; **~versicherung** *f* social security; **~wohnung** *f* ≈ council flat *(Brit)*, state-subsidized apartment.

Sozio-: **~loge** *m (wk)*, **~login** *f* sociologist; **~logie** *f* sociology; **s~logisch** *adj* sociological.

Sozius *m* **-se (a)** *(Beifahrer)* pillion rider. **(b)** *(Partner)* partner.

Soziussitz *m* pillion (seat).

sozusagen *adv* so to speak, as it were.

Spachtel *m (Werkzeug)* spatula.

Spachtelmasse *f* filler.

spachteln 1 *vt Mauerfugen, Ritzen* to fill (in). **2** *vi (col: essen)* to tuck in.

Spagat *m or nt* **-e** splits *pl*. ~ **machen** to do the splits.

Spaghetti [ʃpa'gɛti] *pl* spaghetti *sing*.

spähen *vi* to peer.

Spähtrupp *m (Mil)* reconnaissance party.

Spalier *nt* **-e** *(von Menschen)* row, line; *(zur Ehrenbezeigung)* guard of honour *(Brit)* or honor *(US)*. ~ **stehen/ein ~ bilden** to form a guard of honour.

Spalt *m* **-e (a)** *(Öffnung)* gap, opening; *(Riß)* crack; *(Fels~)* crevice. **das Fenster einen ~ öffnen** to open the window slightly. **(b)** *(fig: Kluft)* split.

spaltbar *adj (Phys) Atomkerne* fissionable.

Spaltbreit *m*: **etw einen ~ öffnen** to open sth

slightly.

Spalte *f* **-n (a)** *(esp Geol)* fissure; *(in Wand)* crack. **(b)** *(Typ, Press)* column.

spalten *ptp auch* **gespalten** *vt (lit, fig)* to split; *Holz* to chop. **bei dieser Frage sind die Meinungen gespalten** opinions are divided on this question; *siehe* **gespalten.**

Spaltung *f (lit, fig)* splitting; *(in Partei etc)* split.

Span *m* **¨-e** *(Hobel~)* shaving; *(Metall~)* filing.

Spanferkel *nt* sucking pig.

Spange *f* **-n** clasp; *(Haar~)* hair slide *(Brit)*, barrette *(US)*; *(Schuh~)* strap; *(Arm~)* bangle; *(Zahn~)* brace.

Spanien ['ʃpaːniən] *nt* Spain.

Spanier(in *f***)** ['ʃpaːniɐ, -iərɪn] *m* **-** Spaniard. **die ~** the Spanish, the Spaniards.

spanisch *adj* Spanish. **~e Wand** (folding) screen; **das kommt mir ~ vor** *(col)* that seems odd to me; siehe **deutsch.**

Spanisch(e) *nt decl as adj* Spanish.

Spankorb *m* chip basket.

Spann *m* **-e** instep.

spann *pret of* **spinnen.**

spannen 1 *vt* **(a)** *Saite, Seil* to tighten; *Bogen* to draw; *Muskeln* to flex. **(b)** *(straff befestigen) Werkstück* to clamp; *Wäscheleine* to put up; *Netz, Plane* to stretch. **(c)** *(anschirren)* to hitch (up) *(vor +acc* to*)*. **2** *vr* **(a)** *(Haut, Muskeln)* to go *or* become taut. **(b) sich über etw** *(acc)* **~** *(Brücke)* to span sth. **3** *vi (Kleidung)* to be (too) tight.

spannend *adj* exciting; *(stärker)* thrilling. **mach's nicht so ~!** *(col)* don't keep me/us in suspense.

Spanner *m* **- (a)** *(Hosen~)* hanger; *(Schuh~)* shoetree. **(b)** *(col: Voyeur)* peeping Tom.

Spannkraft *f (von Feder)* tension; *(von Muskel)* tone; *(fig)* vigour *(Brit)*, vigor *(US)*.

Spannung *f (lit, fig)* tension; *(Elec auch)* voltage; *(Mech)* stress. **mit großer/atemloser ~** with great/breathless excitement; **etw mit ~ erwarten** to await sth full of suspense.

Spannungs-: ~feld *nt (lit)* electric field; *(fig)* area of conflict; **~gebiet** *nt (Pol)* flashpoint, area of tension; **~prüfer** *m* voltage detector.

Spannweite *f (von Flügeln, Aviat)* (wing)span.

Spanplatte *f* chipboard.

Spar-: ~buch *nt* savings book; **~büchse** *f* moneybox.

sparen 1 *vt* to save. **keine Kosten/Mühe ~** to spare no expense/effort; **spar' dir deine guten Ratschläge!** *(col)* you can keep your advice!; **diese Mühe/diese Kosten hätten Sie sich** *(dat)* **~ können** you could have saved *or* spared yourself the trouble/this expense. **2** *vi* to save; *(haushalten)* to economize. **an etw** *(dat)* **~** to be sparing with sth; *(mit etw haushalten)* to save *or* economize on sth; **er hatte nicht mit Lob gespart** he was lavish in his praise; **für** *or* **auf etw** *(acc)* **~** to save up for sth.

Sparer(in *f***)** *m* **-** *(bei Bank etc)* saver.

Sparflamme *f* low flame. **auf ~** *(fig col)* just ticking over *(col)*.

Spargel *m* **-** asparagus.

Spar-: ~groschen *m* nest egg; **~guthaben** *nt* savings account; **~kasse** *f* savings bank; **~konto** *nt* savings account, deposit account *(Brit)*.

spärlich *adj* sparse; *Ausbeute, Reste, Kleidung, Kenntnisse* scanty; *Beleuchtung* poor. **~ bevölkert** sparsely populated.

Spar-: ~maßnahme *f* economy measure; **~packung** *f* economy size; **~prämie** *f* savings premium.

sparsam *adj* thrifty; *(haushälterisch)* economical. **~ im Verbrauch** economical; **~ verwenden** to use sparingly.

Sparsamkeit *f* thrift; *(das Haushalten)* economizing.

Sparschwein *nt* piggy bank.

spartanisch *adj* Spartan. **~ leben** to lead a Spartan life.

Sparte *f* **-n (a)** *(Comm) (Branche)* line of business; *(Teilgebiet)* area. **(b)** *(Rubrik)* column.

Spar-: ~vertrag *m* savings agreement; **~zinsen** *pl* interest *no pl.*

Spaß *m* **¨-e** *(no pl: Vergnügen)* fun; *(Scherz)* joke; *(Streich)* prank. **~ beiseite** joking apart; **viel ~!** have fun! *(auch iro)*; **an etw** *(dat)* **~ haben** to enjoy sth; **es macht mir ~/keinen ~** it's fun/no fun; **Hauptsache, es macht ~** the main thing is to have fun; **(nur so,) zum ~** for fun; **etw im ~ sagen** to say sth in fun; **da hört der ~ auf** that's going beyond a joke; **ein teurer ~** an expensive business; **~ muß sein** there's no harm in a joke; **es war ein ~, ihm bei der Arbeit zuzusehen** it was a joy to see him at work; **sich** *(dat)* **einen ~ daraus machen, etw zu tun** to get enjoyment out of doing sth; **seinen ~ mit jdm treiben** to make fun of sb; **er versteht keinen ~!** he has no sense of humour *(Brit) or* humor *(US)*; **da verstehe ich keinen ~!** I won't stand for any nonsense.

spaßen *vi* **mit Blutvergiftung ist nicht zu ~** blood poisoning is no joke; **mit ihm ist nicht zu ~** he doesn't stand for any nonsense.

spaßeshalber *adv* for the fun of it, for fun.

spaßig *adj* funny, droll.

Spaß-: ~macher *m* joker; **~verderber** *m* **-** spoilsport; **~vogel** *m* joker.

Spastiker(in *f***)** *m* **-** spastic.

spastisch *adj* spastic. **~ gelähmt** suffering from spastic paralysis.

spät *adj* late; *Reue, Ruhm, Glück* belated. **am ~en Nachmittag** in the late afternoon; **~ in der Nacht/am Tage** late at night/in the day; **heute abend wird es ~** it'll be a late night tonight; *(nach Hause kommen)* I/he *etc* will be late this evening; **von früh bis ~** from morning till night; **wie ~ ist es?** what's the time?; **zu ~** too late; **er kommt morgens regelmäßig fünf Minuten zu ~** he's always five minutes late in the mornings; **wir sind ~ dran** we're late.

Spaten *m* **-** spade.

Spatenstich *m* **den ersten ~ tun** to turn the first sod.

Spät|entwickler *m* late developer.

später *comp of* **spät** *adj* later; *(zukünftig)* future. **was will er denn ~ (einmal) werden?** what does he want to do later (on)?; **an ~ denken** to think of the future; **bis ~!** see you later!

spätestens *adv* at the latest. **~ morgen** tomorrow at the latest; **~ um 8** by 8 at the latest; **bis ~ in einer Woche** in one week at the latest.

Spät-: ~geburt *f* late birth; **~herbst** *m* late autumn, late fall *(US)*; **~lese** *f* late vintage; **~nachmittag** *m* late afternoon; **~schicht** *f* late shift; **~sommer** *m* late summer.

Spatz *m (wk)* **-en, -en (a)** sparrow. **wie ein ~ essen** to peck at one's food. **(b)** *(col: Kind)* tot *(col)*.

Spätzle *pl (Cook)* home-made pasta.

Spätzünder *m (hum col)* **~ sein** to be slow on the uptake.

spazieren* *vi aux sein* to stroll. **wir waren ~** we went for a walk *or* stroll.

spazieren-: ~fahren *sep irreg* **1** *vi aux sein* to go for a drive; **2** *vt* **jdn ~fahren** to take sb for a drive; **das Baby (im Kinderwagen) ~fahren** to take the baby for a walk (in the pram); **~gehen** *vi sep irreg aux sein* to go for a walk.

Spazier-: ~fahrt *f* drive; **eine ~fahrt machen** to go for a run; **~gang** *m* walk; **einen ~gang machen** to go for a walk; **~gänger** *m* **-** stroller; **~stock** *m* walking stick.

SPD [ɛspeː'deː] *f* **- = Sozialdemokratische Partei Deutschlands.**

Specht *m* **-e** woodpecker.

Speck *m* **-e** *(Schweine~)* bacon fat; *(Schinken~, durchwachsener ~)* bacon. **~ ansetzen** *(col)* to get fat; **mit ~ fängt man Mäuse** *(Prov)* you need a sprat to catch a mackerel *(prov)*; **ran an den ~** *(col)* let's get stuck in *(col)*.

speckig *adj* greasy.

Speckschwarte *f* bacon rind.

Spediteur [ʃpedi'tøːɐ] *m* haulage contractor; *(Umzugsfirma)* furniture remover *(Brit) or* mover.

Spedition *f (auch* **~sfirma***)* haulage contractor; *(Umzugsfirma)* removal firm *(Brit)*, furniture movers *pl (US)*.

Speer *m* **-e** spear; *(Sport)* javelin.

Speer-: **~spitze** *f (lit, fig)* spearhead; **~werfen** *nt (Sport)* **das ~werfen** throwing the javelin.

Speiche *f* **-n (a)** spoke. **(b)** *(Anat)* radius.

Speichel *m no pl* saliva, spittle.

Speichel-: **~drüse** *f* salivary gland; **~lecker** *m* - *(pej col)* bootlicker *(col)*.

Speicher *m* - *(Lagerhaus)* storehouse; *(im Haus)* loft; *(Wasser~)* tank; *(Comp)* memory. **auf dem ~** in the loft.

Speicherkapazität *f* storage capacity; *(Comp)* memory capacity.

speichern 1 *vt Vorräte, Energie, Daten* to store. **2** *vr* to accumulate.

Speicherung *f* storing, storage.

speien *pret* **spie,** *ptp* **gespie(e)n** *vti* to spit; *Lava, Feuer* to spew (forth); *Wasser* to spout.

Speise *f* **-n** *(geh: Nahrung)* food; *(Gericht)* dish. **kalte und warme ~n** hot and cold meals.

Speise-: **~eis** *nt* icecream; **~fett** *nt* cooking fat; **~kammer** *f* larder; **~karte** *f* menu.

speisen 1 *vti (geh)* to eat, to dine *(form)*. **2** *vt (liter, Tech)* to feed.

Speise-: **~öl** *nt* salad oil; *(zum Braten)* cooking oil; **~reste** *pl* left-overs *pl*; **~röhre** *f (Anat)* gullet; **~saal** *m* dining hall; *(in Hotel etc)* dining room; **~schrank** *m* larder; **~wagen** *m (Rail)* dining car.

Spektakel *m* - *(col: Lärm)* row; *(Aufregung)* fuss.

spektakulär *adj* spectacular.

Spektralfarbe *f* colour *(Brit) or* color *(US)* of the spectrum.

Spektrum *nt, pl* **Spektren** spectrum.

Spekulant(in *f***)** *m* speculator.

Spekulation *f* *(auch Fin)* speculation *(mit* in*)*. **~ mit Grundstücken** property speculation; **~en anstellen** to make speculations.

Spekulatius [ʃpeku'laːtsiʊs] *m* **-, -** spiced biscuit *(Brit) or* cookie *(US)*.

spekulativ *adj* speculative.

spekulieren* *vi* *(auch Fin)* to speculate *(mit* in*)*. **auf etw** *(acc)* **~** *(col)* to have hopes of sth.

Spelze *f* **-n** *(Bot)* husk.

spendabel *adj (col)* generous, open-handed.

Spende *f* **-n** donation; *(Beitrag)* contribution.

spenden *vti Lebensmittel, Blut, Geld* to donate; *(beitragen) Geld* to contribute; *Trost* to give.

Spendenkonto *nt* donations account.

Spender(in *f***)** *m* - donator; *(Beitragleistender)* contributor; *(Med)* donor.

spendieren* *vt* to buy, to get *(jdm etw* sb sth, sth for sb*)*. **spendierst du mir einen?** *(col)* are you going to buy me a drink?

Sperling *m* sparrow.

Sperma *nt, pl* **Spermen** *or* **-ta** sperm.

sperr|angelweit *adv (col)* **~ offen** wide open.

Sperrbezirk *m* no-go area.

Sperre *f* **-n (a)** *(Schlagbaum, Bahnsteig~ etc)* barrier; *(Polizei~)* roadblock; *(Tech)* locking device. **(b)** *(Verbot, Sport)* ban; *(Comm)* embargo; *(Nachrichten~)* (news) blackout.

sperren 1 *vt* **(a)** *(schließen) Grenze, Straße etc* to close; *(Comm) Konto* to freeze; *Einfuhr, Ausfuhr, (Sport)* to ban; *(Tech)* to lock. **etw für jdn/etw ~** to close sth to sb/sth; **jdm das Gehalt ~** to stop sb's salary; **jdm den Strom/das Telefon ~** to cut off sb's electricity/telephone. **(b)** *(einschließen)* **jdn in etw** *(acc)* **~** to lock sb in sth. **(c)** *(Typ)* to space out. **2** *vr* **sich (gegen etw) ~** to ba(u)lk (at sth). **3** *vi (Sport)* to obstruct.

Sperr-: **~feuer** *nt (Mil, fig)* barrage; **~frist** *f* waiting period *(auch Jur)*; *(Sport)* (period of) suspension; **~gebiet** *nt* no-go area; **~gut** *nt* bulky freight; **~holz** *nt* plywood.

sperrig *adj* bulky; *(unhandlich)* unwieldy.

Sperr-: **~kette** *f* chain; *(an Haustür)* safety chain; **~konto** *nt* blocked account; **~müll** *m* bulky refuse; **~sitz** *m (im Kino)* back seats *pl*; *(im Zirkus)* front seats *pl*; **~stunde** *f* closing time.

Sperrung *f* **(a)** *siehe vt (a)* closing; freezing; banning; locking. **(b)** *(Verbot, Sport)* ban.

Spesen *pl* expenses *pl*. **auf ~ reisen/essen** to travel/eat on expenses; **außer ~ nichts gewesen** *(col)* there was nothing doing *(col)*.

Spesen-: **s~frei** *adj* free of charge; **~konto** *nt* expense account.

Spezial-: **~ausbildung** *f* specialized training; **~ausführung** *f* special model; **~fall** *m* special case; **~gebiet** *nt* special field; **~geschäft** *nt* specialist shop *(Brit) or* store *(US)*; **ein ~geschäft für Sportkleidung** a sportswear specialist.

spezialisieren* *vr* **sich** *(auf etw acc)* **~** to specialize (in sth).

Spezialisierung *f* specialization.

Spezialist(in *f***)** *m* specialist *(für* in*)*.

Spezialität *f* speciality *(Brit)*, specialty *(US)*.

speziell 1 *adj* special. **2** *adv* (e)specially.

spezifisch *adj* specific.

spezifizieren* *vt* to specify.

Sphäre *f* **-n** *(lit, fig)* sphere.

sphärisch *adj* spherical; *Klänge, Musik* celestial.

Sphinx *f* **-e** sphinx.

spicken *vt (Cook) Braten* to lard. **mit Fehlern gespickt** peppered with mistakes.

Spickzettel *m* crib.

spie *pret of* **speien.**

Spiegel *m* - **(a)** *(lit, fig)* mirror. **jdm den ~ vorhalten** *(fig)* to hold up a mirror to sb. **(b)** *(Wasser~, Alkohol~, Zucker~)* level.

Spiegel-: **~bild** *nt (lit, fig)* reflection; *(seitenverkehrtes Bild)* mirror image; **s~bildlich** *adj Zeichnung etc* mirror-image; **s~blank** *adj* shining.

Spiegel|ei *nt* fried egg.

Spiegel-: **~fechterei** *f (fig)* shadow-boxing; *(Vortäuschung)* bluff; **s~glatt** *adj* like glass.

spiegeln 1 *vi* to reflect; *(glitzern)* to gleam. **2** *vt* to reflect. **3** *vr* to be reflected *or* mirrored.

Spiegel-: **~reflexkamera** *f* reflex camera; **~schrift** *f* mirror writing; **etw in ~schrift schreiben** to write sth backwards.

Spiegelung *f* reflection; *(Luft~)* mirage.

Spiel *nt* **-e (a)** game; *(Wettkampfs~ auch)* match; *(Theat: Stück)* play. **im ~ sein** *(fig)* to be at work; **das ~ verloren geben** *(fig)* to throw in the towel; **sein Geld beim ~ verlieren** to lose one's money gambling. **(b)** *(Bewegung, Zusammenspiel)* play. **das (freie) ~ der Kräfte** the (free) (inter)play of forces. **(c)** *(Spielzubehör)* game; *(Karten)* deck, pack; *(Satz)* set. **(d)** *(fig)* **leichtes ~ (mit** *or* **bei jdm) haben** to have an easy job of it (with sb); **jdm das ~ verderben** to spoil sb's little game; **das ~ ist aus** the game's up; **die Finger im ~ haben** to have a hand in affairs; **jdn/etw aus dem ~ lassen** to leave sb/sth out of it; **etw aufs ~ setzen** to put sth at stake; **auf dem ~(e) stehen** to be at stake; **sein ~ mit jdm treiben** to play games with sb.

Spiel-: **~automat** *m* gambling machine; *(zum Geldgewinnen)* fruit machine *(Brit)*; **~ball** *m (fig)* plaything; **ein ~ball der Wellen sein** *(geh)* to be at the mercy of the waves; **~bank** *f* casino; **~dose** *f* musical box *(Brit)*, music box *(US)*.

spielen 1 *vt* to play. **jdm einen Streich ~** to play a trick on sb; **Klavier ~** to play the piano; **was wird heute im Theater/Kino gespielt?** what's on at the theatre/cinema today?; **den Beleidigten ~**

to act all offended; **was wird hier gespielt?** *(col)* what's going on here? **2** *vi* to play; *(Theaterstück, Film)* to be on; *(beim Glücksspiel)* to gamble. **seine Beziehungen ~ lassen** to bring one's connections to bear; **das Stück spielt im 18. Jahrhundert** the play is set in the 18th century; **mit dem Gedanken ~, etw zu tun** to toy with the idea of doing sth.

spielend 1 *adj* playing. **2** *adv* easily. **das ist ~ leicht** that's very easy.

Spieler(in *f***)** *m* **-** player; *(Glücks~)* gambler.

Spielerei *f no pl (Kinderspiel)* child's play *no art.* **das ist nur ~** I am/he is *etc* just playing about.

spielerisch 1 *adj (verspielt) Geste, Katze etc* playful. **(b)** *(Sport)* playing; *(Theat)* acting. **~es Können** playing/acting ability. **2** *adv* **(a)** *(verspielt)* playfully. **(b)** *(Sport)* in playing terms; *(Theat)* in acting terms.

Spiel-: ~feld *nt* field, pitch *(Brit)*; *(Tennis, Basketball)* court; **~figur** *f* piece; **~film** *m* feature film; **~folge** *f (Sport)* order of play; *(Theat)* programme *(Brit)*, program *(US)*; **~gefährte** *m* playmate; **~geld** *nt* **(a)** *(Einsatz)* stake; **(b)** *(unechtes Geld)* toy money; **~hölle** *f* gambling den; **~kamerad** *m* playmate; **~karte** *f* playing-card; **~kasino** *nt* (gambling) casino; **~klasse** *f* division; **~leidenschaft** *f* gambling mania; **~macher** *m* key player; **~mannszug** *m* (brass) band; **~minute** *f* minute (of play); **~plan** *m (Theat, Film)* programme *(Brit)*, program *(US)*; **ein Stück vom ~plan absetzen** to drop a play; **~platz** *m (für Kinder)* playground; **~raum** *m* room to move; *(fig)* scope; *(zeitlich)* time; *(bei Planung etc)* leeway; *(Tech)* clearance, (free) play; **~regel** *f (lit, fig)* rule of the game; **sich an die ~regeln halten** *(lit, fig)* to play the game; **gegen die ~regeln verstoßen** *(lit, fig)* not to play the game; **~sachen** *pl* toys *pl*; **~saison** *f (Theat, Sport)* season; **~schuld** *f* gambling debt; **~stand** *m* score; **bei einem ~stand von ...** with the score at ...; **~tag** *m* day; **~tisch** *m (beim Glückspiel)* gaming table; **~trieb** *m* play instinct; **~uhr** *f* musical box *(Brit)*, music box *(US)*; **~verbot** *nt (Sport)* ban; **~verbot haben** to be banned; **~verderber(in** *f***)** *m* **-** spoilsport; **~verlängerung** *f* extra time *(Brit)*, overtime *(US)*; **~verlauf** *m* action; **~warengeschäft** *nt* toy shop *(Brit) or* store *(US)*; **~weise** *f* way of playing; **~werk** *nt* musical mechanism; **~wiese** *f* playing field; *(fig)* playground; **~zeit** *f* **(a)** *(Saison)* season; **(b)** *(~dauer)* playing time.

Spielzeug *nt* toy; toys *pl*; *(fig auch)* plaything.

Spielzeug- *in cpds* toy; **~eisenbahn** *f* toy train set.

Spielzimmer *nt* playroom.

Spieß *m* **-e (a)** spear; *(Brat~)* spit; *(kleiner)* skewer. **am ~ gebraten** spitroast(ed); **wie am ~(e) schreien** *(col)* to squeal like a stuck pig; **den ~ umdrehen** *(fig)* to turn the tables. **(b)** *(Mil col)* sarge *(col)*.

Spießbraten *m* joint roasted on a spit.

Spießbürger *m* (petit) bourgeois.

spießbürgerlich *adj* (petit) bourgeois.

spießen *vt* **etw auf etw** *(acc)* **~** *(auf Pfahl)* to impale sth on sth; *(auf Gabel)* to skewer sth on sth.

Spießer *m* **-** *(col)* (petit) bourgeois.

Spießgeselle *m (hum: Komplize)* crony *(col)*.

spießig *adj (col)* (petit) bourgeois.

Spießrute *f* **~n laufen** *(fig)* to run the gauntlet.

Spikes [ʃpaiks, sp-] *pl (Sportschuhe)* spikes *pl*; *(Autoreifen)* studded tyres *pl (Brit) or* tires *pl (US)*; *(Stifte an Reifen)* studs *pl.*

Spinat *m no pl* spinach.

Spind *m or nt* **-e** locker.

Spindel *f* **-n** spindle; *(Treppen~)* newel.

spindeldürr *adj (pej)* spindly, thin as a rake.

Spinett *nt* **-e** *(Mus)* spinet.

Spinne *f* **-n** spider.

spinnefeind *adj pred (col)* **sich** *or* **einander** *(dat)* **~ sein** to be deadly enemies.

spinnen *pret* **spann,** *ptp* **gesponnen 1** *vti* to spin; *Lügen* to concoct, to invent. **2** *vi (col) (leicht verrückt sein)* to be crazy; *(Unsinn reden)* to talk rubbish. **ich denk' ich spinne** I don't believe it; **du spinnst wohl!, spinnst du?** you must be crazy!

Spinnen-: ~faden *m* spider's thread; **~netz** *nt* cobweb.

Spinner(in *f***)** *m* **- (a)** *(col)* nutcase *(col)*, screwball *(esp US col)*. **(b)** spinner.

Spinnerei *f* **(a)** *(Spinnwerkstatt)* spinning mill. **(b)** *(col)* crazy behaviour *(Brit) or* behavior *(US) no pl*; crazy thing; *(Unsinn)* rubbish.

Spinn-: ~faser *f* spinning fibre *(Brit) or* fiber *(US)*; **~gewebe** *nt* cobweb; **~rad** *nt* spinning-wheel; **~webe** *f* **-n** spider's web.

Spion *m* **-e** spy; *(col: Guckloch)* peephole.

Spionage [ʃpio'naːʒə] *f no pl* espionage. **~ treiben** to spy.

Spionage-: ~abwehr *f* counter-intelligence; **~ring** *m* spy-ring.

spionieren* *vi* to spy; *(col: nachforschen)* to snoop about *(col)*.

Spionin *f* (woman) spy.

Spirale *f* **-n** spiral; *(Med)* coil.

Spiralfeder *f* coil spring.

Spiritismus *m* spiritualism.

spiritistisch *adj* spiritualist.

spirituell *adj* spiritual.

Spirituosen *pl* spirits *pl.*

Spiritus *m* **-,** *no pl (Alkohol)* spirit. **mit ~kochen** to cook with a spirit stove; **etw in ~ legen** to put sth in alcohol.

Spiritus-: ~kocher *m* spirit stove; **~lampe** *f* spirit lamp.

spitz *adj* **(a)** *(mit einer Spitze)* pointed; *Bleistift, Nadel etc* sharp; *(Math) Winkel* acute. **~ zulaufen** to taper; **etw mit ~en Fingern anfassen** *(col)* to pick sth up gingerly. **(b)** *(gehässig) Bemerkung* pointed, barbed; *Zunge* sharp.

Spitz *m* **-e** *(Hund)* spitz.

Spitz-: ~bart *m* goatee; **s~bekommen*** *vt sep irreg (col)* **etw s~bekommen** to get wise to sth *(col)*; **~bub(e)** *m* villain, rogue; *(col: Schlingel)* scamp *(col)*; **s~bübisch** *adj* mischievous.

Spitze *f* **-n (a)** point; *(Finger~, Nasen~, Bart~, Schuh~)* tip; *(Berg~, Fels~, Baum~, Turm~)* top. **auf der ~ stehen** to be upside-down; **etw auf die ~ treiben** to carry sth too far; **einer Sache** *(dat)* **die ~ nehmen** *(fig)* to take the sting out of sth. **(b)** *(Führung)* head; *(vorderes Ende)* front; *(Tabellen~)* top; *(fig: Höchstwert)* peak. **an der ~ stehen** to be at the head; **an der ~ liegen** *(Sport, fig)* to be in the lead; **sich an die ~ setzen** to put oneself at the head; *(in Wettbewerb etc, Sport)* to take the lead. **(c)** *(fig: Stichelei)* dig. **das ist eine ~ gegen Sie** that's a dig at you. **(d)** *(Gewebe)* lace. **(e)** *(col: prima)* great *(col)*.

Spitzel *m* **-** informer; *(Spion)* spy; *(Schnüffler)* snooper; *(Polizei~)* police informer.

spitzen *vt (spitz machen) Bleistift* to sharpen; *Lippen, Mund* to purse; *(zum Küssen)* to pucker; *Ohren (lit, fig)* to prick up.

Spitzen- *in cpds* top; *(aus Spitze)* lace; **~belastung** *f* peak load; **~bluse** *f* lace blouse; **~erzeugnis** *nt* top(-quality) product; **~feld** *nt (Sport)* leading group; **~funktionär** *m* top official; **~gehalt** *nt* top salary; **~geschwindigkeit** *f* top speed; **~hös chen** *nt* lace panties *pl*; **~kandidat** *m* top candidate; **~klasse** *f* top class; **Sekt der ~klasse** top-class champagne; **~leistung** *f* top performance; *(von Maschine, Auto)* peak performance; *(bei der Herstellung von Produkten, Energie)* peak output; **~lohn** *m* top wage(s *pl*); **~position** *f* leading position; **~qualität** *f* top quality; **~reiter** *m (Sport)* leader; *(fig) (Kandidat)* frontrunner; *(Ware)* top seller; *(Schlager)* number one; **~sportler** *m* top(-class) sportsman; **~stellung** *f* leading position; ~**verband** *m* leading organization; ~**verdiener** *m* top earner; ~**verkehrszeit** *f* peak period; ~**wein** *m* top-quality wine; ~**wert** *m* peak; ~**zeit** *f (Sport)* record time.

Spitzer *m* sharpener.

Spitz-: **s~findig** *adj* over-subtle; ~**findigkeit** *f* over-subtletly; ~**hacke** *f* pick-axe *(Brit)*, pickax *(US)*; **s~kriegen** *vt sep (col)* = **s~bekommen;** ~**maus** *f* shrew; ~**name** *m* nickname; **mit dem ~namen** ... nicknamed ...; **s~züngig** *adj* sharp-tongued.

Spleen [ʃpliːn] *m* **-s** *(col) (Angewohnheit)* crazy habit; *(Idee)* crazy idea; *(Fimmel)* obsession. **du hast ja einen ~!** you're off your head *(col)*.

spleenig [ˈʃpiːnɪç] *adj (col)* crazy, nutty *(col)*.

Splint *n* **-e** cotter (pin), split pin.

Splitt *m* **-e** stone chippings *pl*; *(Streumittel)* grit.

Splitter *m* **-** splinter; *(Granat~)* fragment.

Splitter-: ~**bombe** *f (Mil)* fragmentation bomb; ~**gruppe** *f (Pol)* splinter group.

splittern *vi aux sein or haben (Holz, Glas)* to splinter.

splitternackt *adj* stark naked.

Splitterpartei *f (Pol)* splinter party.

sponsern [ʃp-, sp-] *vti* to sponsor.

Sponsor [ʃp-, sp-] *m* **-en** sponsor.

spontan *adj* spontaneous.

Spontaneität [ʃpɔntaneiˈtɛːt] *f* spontaneity.

sporadisch *adj* sporadic.

Spore *f* **-n** *(Biol)* spore.

Sporen *pl (auch Zool, Bot)* spurs. **einem Pferd die ~ geben** to spur a horse; **sich** *(dat)* **die (ersten) ~ verdienen** *(fig)* to win one's spurs.

Sport *m no pl* sport. **treiben Sie ~?** do you do any sport?; **etw zum ~ betreiben** *(als Hobby)* to do sth as a hobby.

Sport-: ~**abzeichen** *nt* sports certificate; ~**angler** *m* angler; ~**art** *f* (kind of) sport; ~**artikel** *m* ~**artikel** *pl* sports equipment *with sing vb;* ~**arzt** *m* sports physician; **s~begeistert** *adj* keen on sport; ~**bericht** *m* sports report; ~**ereignis** *nt* sporting event; ~**fest** *nt* sports festival; ~**flieger** *m* amateur pilot; ~**flugzeug** *nt* sporting aircraft; ~**freund** *m* sport(s)-fan; ~**geschäft** *nt* sports shop *(Brit) or* store *(US)*; ~**halle** *f* sports hall; ~**hemd** *nt* sports *or* sport *(US)* shirt; ~**hochschule** *f* college of physical education; ~**kleidung** *f* sportswear; ~**klub** *m* sports club; ~**lehrer(in** *f*) *m* sports instructor; *(Sch)* PE *or* physical education teacher.

Sportler *m* **-** sportsman, athlete.

Sportlerin *f* sportswoman, (woman) athlete.

sportlich *adj* **(a)** *Mensch, Auto* sporty; *Veranstaltung, Wettkampf* sporting; *(durchtrainiert)* athletic. **(b)** *(fair)* sportsmanlike *no adv.* **(c)** *Kleidung* smart but casual; *(wie Sportkleidung aussehend)* sporty.

Sportlichkeit *f* **(a)** *(von Menschen)* sportiness; *(Durchtrainiertheit)* athleticism. **(b)** *(Fairneß)* sportsmanship.

Sport-: ~**medizin** *f* sports medicine; ~**nachrichten** *pl* sports news *with sing vb or* reports *pl*; ~**platz** *m* sports field; ~**rad** *nt* sports bike *(col)*; ~**reportage** *f* sports report.

Sports-: ~**freund** *m (fig col)* buddy *(col)*; ~**kanone** *f (col)* sporting ace *(col)*.

Sport-: ~**veranstaltung** *f* sporting event; ~**verein** *m* sports club; ~**wagen** *m* sports *(Brit) or* sport *(US)* car; *(für Kind)* push-chair *(Brit)*, (baby-)stroller *(US)*; ~**zeitung** *f* sports paper.

Spot [spɔt] *m* **-s** commercial, advertisement.

Spott *m no pl* mockery, ridicule. **seinen ~ mit jdm treiben** to make fun of sb.

Spott-: ~**bild** *nt (fig)* travesty; **s~billig** *adj* dirt-cheap *(col)*.

spötteln *vi* to mock *(über jdn/etw* sb/sth*)*.

spotten *vi* to mock. **über jdn/etw ~** to mock sb/sth; **das spottet jeder Beschreibung** that simply defies description.

Spötter(in *f*) *m* **-** mocker.

Spott-: ~**figur** *f* joke figure; **eine ~figur sein** to be an object of ridicule; ~**gedicht** *nt* satirical poem.

spöttisch *adj* mocking.

Spott-: ~**lied** *nt* satirical song; ~**name** *m* derisive nickname; ~**preis** *m* ridiculously low price; ~**rede** *f* satirical speech; ~**vers** *m* satirical verse.

sprach *pret of* **sprechen.**

Sprach-: ~**barriere** *f* language barrier; **s~begabt** *adj* good at languages; ~**begabung** *f* talent for languages.

Sprache *f* **-n** language; *(das Sprechen, Sprechweise)* speech; *(Fähigkeit zu sprechen)* faculty of speech. **eine ~ sprechen** to speak a language; **in französischer** *etc* **~** in French *etc*; **heraus mit der ~!** *(col)* come on, out with it!; **zur ~ kommen** to be mentioned; **etw zur ~ bringen** to bring sth up; **hast du die ~ verloren?** have you lost your tongue?; **es verschlägt einem die ~** it takes your breath away.

Sprachenschule *f* language school.

Sprach-: ~**fehler** *m* speech defect; ~**forscher** *m* linguist; ~**forschung** *f* linguistic research; ~**führer** *m* phrase-book; ~**gebiet** *nt* language area; **ein französisches** *etc* **~gebiet** a French-speaking *etc* area; ~**gebrauch** *m* usage; **moderner deutscher ~gebrauch** modern German usage; ~**gefühl** *nt* feeling for language; ~**gemeinschaft** *f* speech community; ~**genie** *nt* linguistic genius; ~**geschichte** *f* linguistic history; **s~gewandt** *adj* articulate; ~**kenntnisse** *pl* linguistic proficiency *sing;* **mit englischen ~kenntnissen** with a knowledge of English; **haben Sie irgendwelche ~kenntnisse?** do you know any languages?; ~**kurs(us)** *m* language course; ~**labor** *nt* language laboratory; ~**lehrer** *m* language teacher.

sprachlich *adj* linguistic; *Unterricht, Schwierigkeiten* language *attr; Fehler* grammatical. **~ falsch/richtig** grammatically incorrect/correct.

sprachlos *adj* speechless. **ich bin ~!** I'm speechless.

Sprachlosigkeit *f* speechlessness.

Sprach-: ~**rohr** *nt (Megaphon)* megaphone; *(fig)* mouthpiece; ~**schöpfung** *f* linguistic innovation; ~**schule** *f* language school; ~**störung** *f* speech disorder; ~**studium** *nt* study of language; ~**übung** *f* language exercise; ~**unterricht** *m* language teaching; ~**wissenschaft** *f* linguistics *sing*; ~**wissenschaftler** *m* linguist; **s~wissenschaftlich** *adj* linguistic.

sprang *pret of* **springen.**

Spray [ʃpreː, spreː] *m or nt* **-s** spray.

Spraydose [ˈʃpreː-, ˈspreː-] *f* aerosol (can), spray.

sprayen [ˈʃpreːən, sp-] *vti* to spray.

Sprech-: ~**anlage** *f* intercom; ~**chor** *m* chorus; *(fig)* chorus of voices; ~**einheit** *f (Telec)* unit.

sprechen *pret* **sprach,** *ptp* **gesprochen 1** *vi* to speak *(über +acc, von* about, of*)*; *(reden, sich unterhalten auch)* to talk *(über +acc, von* about*)*. **viel ~** to talk a lot; **frei ~** to extemporize; **er spricht wenig** he doesn't say very much; **im Schlaf ~** to talk in one's sleep; **es spricht/es ~ ...** the speaker is/the speakers are ...; **nicht gut auf jdn zu ~ sein** to be on bad terms with sb; **wie sprichst du mit mir?** who do you think you're talking to?; **wir ~ nicht mehr miteinander** we are no longer on speaking terms; **mit wem spreche ich?** to whom am I speaking, please?; **darüber spricht man nicht** one doesn't talk about such things; **wovon ~ Sie eigentlich?** what are you talking about?; **~ wir von etwas anderem** let's change the subject; **es wird kaum noch von ihm gesprochen** he's hardly mentioned now; **es spricht für jdn/etw(, daß ...)** it says something for sb/sth (that ...); **das**

spricht für ihn that's a point in his favour *(Brit)* or favour *(US)*; **das spricht für sich (selbst)** that speaks for itself; **es spricht vieles dafür** there's a lot to be said for it; **es spricht vieles dafür, daß ...** there is every reason to believe that ...; **was spricht dafür/dagegen?** what is there to be said for/against it?; **er sprach vor den Studenten** he spoke to the students; **ganz allgemein gesprochen** generally speaking.

2 *vt* **(a)** *(sagen)* to say, to speak; *eine Sprache* to speak; *Gebet, Gedicht* to say. **~ Sie Japanisch?** do you speak Japanese?; **hier spricht man Spanisch** Spanish spoken. **(b)** *(mit jdm reden)* to speak to. **kann ich bitte Herrn Kurz ~?** may I speak to Mr Kurz, please?; **er ist nicht zu ~** he can't see anybody; **wir ~ uns noch!** you haven't heard the last of this! **(c)** *Urteil* to pronounce.

Sprecher(in *f*) *m* - speaker; *(Nachrichten~)* newsreader; *(für Dokumentarfilme etc)* narrator; *(Ansager)* announcer; *(Wortführer)* spokesman.

Sprech-: s~faul *adj* taciturn; **~funk** *m* radiotelephone system; **~funkgerät** *nt* radiotelephone; **~gebühr** *f (Telec)* call charge; **~muschel** *f (Telec)* mouthpiece; **~organ** *nt* speech organ; **~probe** *f* voice trial; **~rolle** *f* speaking part; **~schulung** *f* voice training; **~stunde** *f* consultation (hour); *(von Arzt)* surgery *(Brit)*, doctor's office *(US)*; **~stunden** consultation hours; *(von Arzt)* surgery *(Brit)*; **~stundenhilfe** *f* receptionist; **~übung** *f* speech exercise; **~weise** *f* way of speaking; **~werkzeuge** *pl* organs of speech; **~zeit** *f (Telec)* call time; **~zimmer** *nt* consulting room.

spreizen 1 *vt* to spread. **2** *vr (sich sträuben)* to kick up *(col)*.

Spreng|arbeiten *pl* blasting operations *pl*.

sprengen *vt* **(a)** to blow up; *Fels* to blast. **(b)** *Tür* to force (open); *Tresor* to break open; *Bande, Fesseln, (Spiel)bank* to break; *Versammlung* to break up. **(c)** *(bespritzen)* to sprinkle.

Spreng-: ~kapsel *f* detonator; **~kopf** *m* warhead; **~körper** *m* explosive device; **~kraft** *f* explosive force; **~ladung** *f* explosive charge; **~satz** *m* explosive device.

Sprengstoff *m* explosive.

Sprengstoff|anschlag *m* bomb attack. **auf ihn wurde ein ~ verübt** he was the subject of a bomb attack.

Sprengung *f* blowing-up; *(von Fels)* blasting; *(von Versammlung)* breaking-up.

Sprenkel *m* - *(Tupfen)* spot, speckle.

sprenkeln *vt Farbe* to sprinkle spots of; *siehe* **gesprenkelt.**

Spreu *f no pl* chaff. **die ~ vom Weizen trennen** *(fig)* to separate the wheat from the chaff.

Sprichwort *nt* **¨er** proverb.

sprichwörtlich *adj (lit, fig)* proverbial.

sprießen *pret* **sproß** *or* **sprießte,** *ptp* **gesprossen** *vi aux sein (aus der Erde)* to spring up; *(Knospen)* to shoot.

Springbrunnen *m* fountain.

springen *pret* **sprang,** *ptp* **gesprungen** *vi aux sein* **(a)** *(lit, fig, Sport, bei Brettspielen)* to jump; *(mit Schwung auch)* to leap; *(beim Stabhochsprung)* to vault; *(Raubtier)* to pounce; *(sich springend fortbewegen)* to bound; *(hüpfen, seilhüpfen)* to skip; *(Ball etc)* to bounce; *(Wassersport)* to dive. **die Kinder kamen gesprungen** the children came running. **(b) etw ~ lassen** *(col)* to fork out for sth *(col)*; *Geld* to fork out sth *(col)*; **für jdn etw ~ lassen** *(col)* to treat sb to sth. **(c)** *(Saite, Glas)* to break; *(Risse bekommen)* to crack.

Springen *nt* - *(Sport)* jumping; *(Stabhoch~)* vaulting.

springend *adj* **der ~e Punkt** the crucial point.

Springer(in *f*) *m* - **(a)** jumper; *(Stabhoch~)* vaulter. **(b)** *(Chess)* knight. **(c)** *(Ind)* stand-in.

Spring-: ~flut *f* spring tide; **~form** *f (Cook)* springform; **~pferd** *nt* jumper; **~reiten** *nt* show jumping; **~turnier** *nt* show jumping competition.

Sprinkler *m* - sprinkler.

Sprint *m* - sprint.

sprinten *vti aux sein* to sprint.

Sprit *m* **-e** *(col: Benzin)* gas *(col)*, juice *(col)*.

Spritz-: ~beutel *m* icing bag; **~düse** *f* nozzle.

Spritze *f* **-n** syringe; *(Feuer~, Garten~)* hose; *(Injektion)* injection. **eine ~ bekommen** to have an injection.

spritzen 1 *vti* **(a)** to spray; *(verspritzen) Wasser, Schmutz etc* to splash; *(aus Wasserpistole etc)* to squirt. **(b)** *Wein* to dilute with soda water/mineral water. **(c)** *(injizieren) Serum etc* to inject; *Heroin etc auch* to shoot *(col)*. **wir müssen (dem Kranken) Morphium ~** we have to give (the patient) a morphine injection. **2** *vi aux haben or sein (heißes Fett)* to spit; *(in einem Strahl)* to spurt; *(aus einer Tube etc)* to squirt.

Spritzer *m* - *(Farb~, Wasser~)* splash.

spritzig *adj Wein* tangy; *Aufführung, Dialog etc* sparkling; *(witzig)* witty.

Spritz-: ~lack *m* spray paint; **~pistole** *f* spray-gun; **~tour** *f (col)* spin *(col)*; **~tülle** *f* nozzle.

spröd(e) *adj Glas, Haar* brittle; *Haut* rough; *Stimme* thin; *(abweisend)* aloof.

sproß *pret of* **sprießen.**

Sproß *m* **-sse** shoot.

Sprosse *f* **-n** *(lit, fig)* rung.

Sprossenwand *f (Sport)* wall bars *pl*.

Sprößling *m* shoot; *(fig hum)* offspring.

Spruch *m* **¨e** **(a)** saying; *(Wahl~)* motto; *(Bibel~)* quotation. **¨e** *(col: Gerede)* patter *no pl (col)*; **¨e klopfen** *(col)* to talk fancy *(col)*; **das sind doch nur ¨e!** that's just talk. **(b)** *(Richter~)* judgement; *(Urteils~)* verdict; *(Schieds~)* ruling.

Spruchband *nt* banner.

Sprücheklopfer *m (col)* patter-merchant *(col)*.

spruchreif *adj (col)* **die Sache ist noch nicht ~** it's not definite yet.

Sprudel *m* - mineral water.

sprudeln *vi* **(a)** *(lit, fig)* to bubble; *(Sekt, Limonade)* to fizz. **(b)** *aux sein (hervor~) (Wasser etc)* to bubble; *(fig: Worte)* to pour out.

sprudelnd *adj Getränke* fizzy; *(fig)* effervescent.

Sprühdose *f* spray (can).

sprühen 1 *vi* **(a)** *aux haben or sein* to spray; *(Funken)* to fly. **(b)** *(fig) (vor Witz etc)* to bubble over; *(Augen: vor Freude etc)* to sparkle. **2** *vt* to spray.

sprühend *adj Laune, Temperament etc* bubbling, effervescent; *Witz* sparkling, bubbling.

Sprühregen *m* drizzle.

Sprung *m* **¨e** **(a)** jump; *(schwungvoll, fig: Gedanken~ auch)* leap; *(Hüpfer)* skip; *(von Raubtier)* pounce; *(Stabhoch~)* vault; *(Wassersport)* dive. **ein großer ~ nach vorn** *(fig)* a great leap forward; **damit kann man keine großen ¨e machen** *(col)* you can't exactly live it up on that *(col)*; **immer auf dem ~ sein** *(col)* to be always on the go *(col)*; *(aufmerksam)* to be always on the ball *(col)*; **jdm auf die ¨e helfen** *(wohlwollend)* to give sb a (helping) hand; *(drohend)* to show sb what's what. **(b)** *(col: kurze Strecke)* **auf einen ~ bei jdm vorbeikommen** to drop in to see sb *(col)*. **(c)** *(Riß)* crack. **einen ~ haben/bekommen** to be cracked/to crack.

Sprung-: ~brett *nt (lit, fig)* springboard; **~feder** *f* spring; **s~haft 1** *adj* **(a)** *Charakter* volatile; *Denken* disjointed; **(b)** *(rapide)* rapid; **2** *adv ansteigen, sich entwickeln* by leaps and bounds; **~schanze** *f (Ski)* ski-jump; **~turm** *m* diving platform.

Spucke *f no pl (col)* spittle, spit. **da bleibt einem die ~ weg!** it's flabbergasting *(col)*; **mit Geduld und ~** *(col)* with blood, sweat and tears *(col)*.

spucken *vti* to spit; *(fig col) Lava, Flammen* to spew (out). **in die Hände ~** *(fig)* to roll up one's sleeves.

Spucknapf *m* spittoon.
Spuk *m* **-e** *(Geistererscheinung)* apparition. **dem ~ ein Ende bereiten** *(fig)* to put an end to the nightmare.
spuken *vi* to haunt. **es spukt auf dem Friedhof** the cemetery is haunted; **das spukt noch immer in den Köpfen** that still has a hold on people's minds.
Spuk-: **~geschichte** *f* ghost story; **s~haft** *adj* eerie.
Spül|automat *m* (automatic) dishwasher.
Spule *f* **-n** spool, reel; *(Nähmaschinen~, Ind)* bobbin; *(Elec)* coil.
Spüle *f* **-n** sink.
spulen *vt* to spool, to reel.
spülen *vti* **(a)** *(aus~, ab~)* to rinse; *(Med)* to irrigate; *(abwaschen) Geschirr* to wash up *(Brit)*, to wash the dishes; *(auf der Toilette)* to flush. **(b) etw an Land ~** to wash sth ashore.
Spül-: **~maschine** *f* dishwasher; **~mittel** *nt* washing-up liquid *(Brit)*, dish-washing liquid; **~schüssel** *f* washing-up bowl; **~tisch** *m* sink (unit).
Spülung *f* rinsing; *(Wasser~)* flush; *(Med)* irrigation.
Spülwasser *nt (beim Abwaschen)* dishwater.
Spund *m* **-e (a)** bung, spigot. **(b) junger ~** *(dated col)* young pup *(dated col)*.
Spundloch *nt* bunghole.
Spur *f* **-en (a)** track; *(Anzeichen, Beweisstück)* trace, sign. **von den Tätern fehlt jede ~** the criminals left no trace; **jds ~ aufnehmen** to take up sb's trail; **jdm auf der ~ sein** to be on sb's trail; **auf der richtigen ~ sein** *(lit, fig)* to be on the right track; **jdm auf die ~ kommen** to get onto sb; **(seine) ~en hinterlassen** *(fig)* to leave its mark. **(b)** *(fig: kleine Menge, Überrest)* trace; *(von Vernunft, Anstand etc)* scrap. **von Anstand/Takt keine ~** *(col)* no decency/tact at all; **keine ~** *(col)* not at all/nothing at all; **eine ~ zu laut/grell** a shade too loud/garish. **(c)** *(Fahrbahn)* lane. **auf der linken ~ fahren** to drive in the left-hand lane; **in der ~ bleiben** to keep in lane.
spürbar *adj* noticeable, perceptible.
spuren *vi (col)* to obey; *(sich fügen)* to toe the line.
spüren 1 *vt* to feel; *(ahnen auch)* to sense. **sie spürte, daß der Erdboden leicht bebte** she felt the earth trembling underfoot; **sie ließ mich ihr Mißfallen ~** she let me know that she was displeased; **etw zu ~ bekommen** *(lit)* to feel sth; *(fig)* to feel the (full) force of sth. **2** *vti (Hunt)* **(nach) etw ~** to track sth.
Spuren-: **~element** *nt* trace element; **~sicherung** *f* securing of evidence.
Spürhund *m* tracker dog; *(col: Mensch)* sleuth.
spurlos *adj* without trace. **~ an jdm vorübergehen** to have no effect on sb.
Spür-: **~nase** *f (Hunt)* nose; **~sinn** *m (Hunt, fig)* nose; *(fig: Gefühl)* feel.
Spurt *m* **-s** spurt.
spurten *vi aux sein (Sport)* to spurt; *(col: rennen)* to sprint.
sputen *vr (dated col)* to hurry.
St. = **Stück; Sankt** St.
Staat *m* **-en (a)** state; *(Land)* country. **beim ~ arbeiten** to be employed by the government. **(b)** *(von Insekten)* colony. **(c)** *(fig) (Pracht)* pomp; *(Kleidung, Schmuck)* finery. **damit ist kein ~ zu machen** that's nothing to write home about *(col)*.
Staaten-: **~bund** *m* confederation; **s~los** *adj* stateless.
staatlich 1 *adj* state *attr*. **2** *adv* by the state. **~ geprüft** state-certified.
Staats-: **~affäre** *f* **(a)** *(lit)* affair of state; **(b)** *(fig)* major operation; **~akt** *m (lit)* state occasion; **~aktion** *f* major operation; **~amt** *nt* public office; **~angehörige(r)** *mf decl as adj* national; **~angehörigkeit** *f* nationality; **~anleihe** *f* government bond; **~anwalt** *m* prosecuting attorney *(US)*, public prosecutor; **~apparat** *m* apparatus of state; **~archiv** *nt* state archives *pl*; **~aufsicht** *f* state control; **~ausgaben** *pl* public spending *sing*; **~bank** *f* national bank; **~bankrott** *m* national bankruptcy; **~beamte(r)** *m* public servant; **~begräbnis** *nt* state funeral; **~besitz** *m* state property; **(in) ~besitz sein** to be state-owned; **~besuch** *m* state visit; **~betrieb** *m* state-owned enterprise; **~bibliothek** *f* national library; **~bürger** *m* citizen; **~chef** *m* head of state; **~dienst** *m* civil service; **s~eigen** *adj* state-owned; **~eigentum** *nt* state property *no art*; **~empfang** *m* state reception; **~examen** *nt* ≈ university degree; **~feiertag** *m* national holiday; **~feind** *m* enemy of the state; **~finanzen** *pl* public finances *pl*; **~flagge** *f* national flag; **~form** *f* type of state; **~gebiet** *nt* national territory *no art*; **~geheimnis** *nt (lit, fig hum)* state secret; **~gelder** *pl* public funds *pl*; **~gewalt** *f* authority of the state; **~grenze** *f* state frontier; **~haushalt** *m* national budget; **~hoheit** *f* sovereignty; **~interesse** *nt* interests *pl* of (the) state; **~kasse** *f* treasury; **~kirche** *f* state church; **~kosten** *pl* public expenses *pl*; **auf ~kosten** at the public expense; **~mann** *m* statesman; **s~männisch** *adj* statesmanlike; **~oberhaupt** *nt* head of state; **~präsident** *m* president; **~recht** *nt* **(a)** national law; **(b)** *(Verfassungsrecht)* constitutional law; **~regierung** *f* state government; **~religion** *f* state religion; **~rente** *f* state pension; **~schuld** *f (Fin)* national debt; **~sekretär** *m (BRD: Beamter)* ≈ permanent secretary *(Brit)*, senior official in government department; **~sicherheit** *f* national security; **~streich** *m* coup (d'état).
Stab *m* **¨-e (a)** rod; *(Gitter~)* bar; *(Bischofs~)* crosier; *(Hirten~)* crook; *(Dirigenten~, für Staffellauf)* baton; *(als Amtzeichen)* mace; *(für ~hochsprung)* pole; *(Meß~)* (measuring) rod; *(Zauber~)* wand. **(b)** *(Mitarbeiter~, Mil)* staff; *(von Experten)* panel.
Stäbchen *nt dim of* **Stab** *(Eß~)* chopstick.
Stab-: **~hochspringer** *m* pole-vaulter; **~hochsprung** *m* pole vault.
stabil *adj Möbel, Schuhe* sturdy, robust; *Währung, Beziehung, Charakter* stable; *Gesundheit* sound.
Stabilisator [ʃtabili'zaːtɔr, st-] *m* stabilizer.
stabilisieren* *vtr* to stabilize.
Stabilität *f* stability.
Stabreim *m* alliteration.
Stabs-: **~arzt** *m (Mil)* captain in the medical corps; **~chef** *m (Mil col)* chief of staff; **~offizier** *m (Mil)* staff officer; *(Rang)* field officer.
stach *pret of* **stechen.**
Stachel *m* **-n** *(von Rosen etc)* thorn; *(von Kakteen, Igel)* spine; *(von ~schwein)* quill, spine; *(auf ~draht)* barb; *(zum Viehantrieb)* goad; *(Gift~: von Bienen etc)* sting. **einer Sache** *(dat)* **den ~ nehmen** *(geh)* to take the sting out of sth.
Stachel-: **~beere** *f* gooseberry; **~draht** *m* barbed wire.
stach(e)lig *adj Rosen* thorny; *Kaktus, Igel* spiny;- *(sich ~ anfühlend)* prickly; *Kinn, Bart* bristly.
Stachelschwein *nt* porcupine.
Stadion *nt, pl* **Stadien** [-iən] stadium.
Stadium *nt, pl* **Stadien** [-iən] stage. **im vorgerückten/letzten ~** *(Med)* at an advanced/terminal stage.
Stadt *f* **¨-e (a)** town; *(Groß~)* city. **die ~ Paris** the city of Paris; **~ und Land** town and country; **in die ~ gehen** to go into town. **(b)** *(~verwaltung)* (town) council; *(von Groß~)* corporation. **die ~ Ulm** Ulm Corporation.
Stadt-: **s~auswärts** *adv* out of town; **~autobahn** *f* urban motorway *(Brit) or* freeway *(US)*; **~bad** *nt* municipal swimming pool; **~bahn** *f* suburban railway *(Brit)*, city railroad *(US)*; **s~be-**

kannt *adj* known all over town; **~bewohner** *m* town-dweller; *(von Groß~)* city-dweller; **~bezirk** *m* municipal district; **~bücherei** *f* town/city library.

Städtebau *m* urban development.

stadt|einwärts *adv* into town.

Städteplanung *f* town planning.

Städter(in *f***)** *m* **-** town-dweller; *(Groß~)* city-dweller.

Stadt-: **~flucht** *f* exodus from the cities; **~gebiet** *nt* municipal area; **~gespräch** *nt* **(das) ~gespräch sein** to be the talk of the town; **~grenze** *f* town/city boundary; **~gue(r)rilla** *f* urban guerrilla.

städtisch *adj* municipal, town/city *attr*; *(nach Art einer Stadt)* urban.

Stadt-: **~kämmerer** *m* town/city treasurer; **~kasse** *f* town/city treasury; **~kern** *m* town/city centre *(Brit) or* center *(US)*; **~kreis** *m* town/city borough; **~mauer** *f* city wall; **~mitte** *f* town/city centre *(Brit) or* center *(US)*; **~park** *m* municipal park; **~parlament** *nt* city council; **~plan** *m* (street) map; **~planung** *f* town planning; **~rand** *m* outskirts *pl* (of a/the town/city); **am ~rand** on the outskirts (of the town/city); **~rat** *m (Behörde)* (town/city) council; **~rundfahrt** *f* (sightseeing) tour of a/the town/city; **~staat** *m* city state; **~streicher(in** *f***)** *m* **-** (town/city) tramp; **~teil** *m* district, part of town; **~theater** *nt* municipal theatre *(Brit) or* theater *(US)*; **~tor** *nt* town/city gate; **~verwaltung** *f (Behörde)* municipal authority; **~viertel** *nt* part of town; **~zentrum** *nt* town/city centre *(Brit) or* center *(US)*.

Staffel *f* **-n (a)** echelon; *(Aviat: Einheit)* squadron. **(b)** *(Sport)* relay (race); *(Mannschaft)* relay team. **~ laufen/schwimmen** to run/swim in a relay (race).

Staffelei *f* easel.

Staffellauf *m* relay (race).

staffeln *vt Gehälter, Fahrpreise* to grade; *Anfangszeiten, Startplätze* to stagger.

Staff(e)lung *f siehe vt* grading; staggering.

Stagnation *f* stagnation.

stagnieren* *vi* to stagnate.

stahl *pret of* **stehlen.**

Stahl *m* **-e** *or* **⸚e** steel. **Nerven wie ~** nerves of steel.

Stahl- *in cpds* steel; **~bau** *m* steel-girder construction; **~beton** *m* reinforced concrete; **~blech** *nt* sheet-steel.

stählen *vt* to harden, to toughen.

stählern *adj* steel; *(fig) Muskeln, Wille* of iron, iron *attr*; *Nerven* of steel.

Stahl-: **~feder** *f* steel nib; **~gerüst** *nt* tubular steel scaffolding; *(Gerippe)* steel-girder frame; **s~hart** *adj* (as) hard as steel; **~rohr** *nt* tubular steel; *(Stück)* steel tube; **~roß** *nt (hum)* bike *(col)*; **~träger** *m* steel girder; **~werk** *nt* steelworks *sing or pl*; **~wolle** *f* steel wool.

stak *(geh) pret of* **stecken 1.**

Stalinismus *m* Stalinism.

Stalin|orgel *f* multiple rocket launcher.

Stall *m* **⸚e (a)** *(Pferde~, Gestüt, Aut: Renn~)* stable; *(Kuh~)* cowshed, (cow) barn *(US)*; *(Hühner~)* hen-house; *(Kaninchen~)* hutch; *(Schweine~)* (pig)sty, (pig)pen *(US)*. **(b)** *(col: Hosenschlitz)* flies *pl*.

Stallung(en *pl***)** *f* stables *pl*.

Stamm *m* **⸚e (a)** *(Baum~)* trunk. **(b)** *(Ling)* stem. **(c)** *(Volks~)* tribe; *(Abstammung)* line; *(Bakterien~)* strain. **(d)** *(Personal, Kunden)* regulars *pl*; *(Arbeiter)* regular workforce; *(Angestellte)* permanent staff *pl*. **zum ~ gehören** to be one of the regulars *etc*.

Stamm-: **~baum** *m* family tree; *(von Zuchttieren)* pedigree; **~buch** *nt book of family events with some legal documents,* ≈ family bible; **jdm etw ins ~buch schreiben** *(fig)* to make sb take note of sth.

stammeln *vti* to stammer.

stammen *vi* to come *(von, aus* from*)*; *(zeitlich)* to date *(von, aus* from*)*. **die Uhr stammt von seinem Großvater** the watch was handed down from his grandfather.

Stamm-: **~form** *f* base form; **~gast** *m* regular; **~gericht** *nt* standard meal.

stämmig *adj* stocky, thickset *no adv; (kräftig)* sturdy.

Stamm-: **~kapital** *nt (Fin)* ordinary share *or* common stock *(US)* capital; **~kneipe** *f (col)* local *(Brit col)*; **~kunde** *m* regular (customer); **~lokal** *nt* favourite *(Brit) or* favorite *(US)* café/restaurant *etc*; *(Kneipe)* local *(Brit)*, favorite bar *(US)*; **~personal** *nt* permanent staff *pl*; **~platz** *m* usual seat; **~tisch** *m (Tisch in Gasthaus)* table reserved for the regulars; *(~tischrunde)* group of regulars.

stampfen 1 *vi* **(a)** *(laut auftreten)* to stamp. **mit dem Fuß ~** to stamp one's foot. **(b)** *aux sein (gehen)* to tramp; *(wütend)* to stamp; *(stapfen)* to trudge. **2** *vt* **(a)** *(festtrampeln) Lehm, Sand* to stamp; *Trauben* to press; *(mit den Füßen)* to tread. **(b)** *(mit Stampfer)* to mash.

Stampfer *m* **-** *(Stampfgerät)* pounder.

stand *pret of* **stehen.**

Stand *m* **⸚e (a)** *no pl (das Stehen)* standing position. **aus dem ~** from a standing position; **bei jdm** *or* **gegen jdn einen schweren ~ haben** *(fig)* to have a hard time of it with sb. **(b)** *(Markt~ etc)* stand; *(Taxi~)* rank *(Brit)*, stand *(US)*. **(c)** *no pl (Lage)* state; *(Niveau)* level; *(Zähler~ etc)* reading, level; *(Konto~)* balance; *(Spiel~)* score. **beim jetzigen ~ der Dinge** the way things stand at the moment; **etw auf den neuesten ~ bringen** to bring sth up to date. **(d)** *(soziale Stellung)* station, status; *(Klasse)* rank, class; *(Beruf, Gewerbe)* profession.

Standard- *in cpds* standard.

standardisieren* *vt* to standardize.

Standardisierung *f* standardization.

Standarte *f* **-n** *(Mil, Pol)* standard.

Standbild *nt* statue.

Ständchen *nt* serenade. **jdm ein ~ bringen** to serenade sb.

Ständer *m* **-** stand; *(Pfeiler)* upright.

Standes-: **~amt** *nt* registry office *(Brit)*; **s~amtlich** *adj* **s~amtliche Trauung** registry office *(Brit)* wedding; **sich s~amtlich trauen lassen** to get married in a registry office *(Brit)*, to have a civil marriage *(US)*; **~beamte(r)** *m* registrar; **~bewußtsein** *nt* status consciousness; **~dünkel** *m* snobbery; **s~gemäß 1** *adj* befitting one's rank; **2** *adv* in a manner befitting one's rank; **~organisation** *f* professional association; **~unterschied** *m* class difference.

Stand-: **s~fest** *adj Tisch, Leiter* stable, steady; *(fig)* steadfast; **~festigkeit** *f* stability *(auch Sci)*; *(fig auch)* steadfastness; **~foto** *nt* still (photograph); **~gericht** *nt (Mil)* drumhead court martial; **vor ein ~gericht kommen** to be summarily court-martialled *(Brit) or* court-martialed *(US)*; **s~haft** *adj* steadfast; **sie blieb s~haft im Glauben** her faith did not falter; **er weigerte sich s~haft** he steadfastly refused; **s~halten** *vi sep irreg (Mensch)* to stand firm; *(Gebäude, Brücke etc)* to hold; *(+dat)* to stand up to; **Versuchungen** *(dat)* **s~halten** to resist temptation; **einer Prüfung s~halten** to stand up to close examination.

ständig *adj* **(a)** *(dauernd)* permanent; *Mitglied* full. **~er Ausschuß** standing committee. **(b)** *(unaufhörlich)* constant. **sie kommt ~ zu spät** she's always late; **müssen Sie mich ~ unterbrechen?** do you have to keep on interrupting me?

Standlicht *nt* sidelights *pl*. **mit ~ fahren** to drive on sidelights.

Stand|ort *m* location; *(von Schütze, Schiff, fig)* position; *(Mil)* garrison; *(Bot)* habitat.

Stand-: ~**pauke** *f (col)* lecture *(col)*; **jdm eine ~pauke halten** to give sb a lecture *(col)*; ~**platz** *m* stand; ~**punkt** *m (Meinung)* point of view; **auf dem ~punkt stehen, daß ...** to take the view that ...; **von seinem ~punkt aus** from his point of view; **s~rechtlich** *adj* **s~rechtlich erschießen** to put before a firing squad; **s~sicher** *adj* stable; *Mensch* steady (on one's feet/skis *etc*); ~**spur** *f (Aut)* hard shoulder; ~**uhr** *f* grandfather clock.

Stange *f* **-n (a)** *(langer, Stab)* pole; *(Querstab, Ballett~)* bar; *(Kleider~, Teppich~)* rail; *(Gardinen~)* rod; *(Vogel~)* perch. **(b)** *(länglicher Gegenstand)* stick. **eine ~ Zigaretten** a carton of 200 cigarettes. **(c) ein Anzug von der ~** a suit off the peg; **jdm die ~ halten** *(col)* to stick up for sb *(col)*; **eine schöne ~ Geld** *(col)* a tidy sum *(col)*.

Stangen-: ~**bohne** *f* runner bean; ~**brot** *nt* French bread; *(Laib)* French loaf; ~**spargel** *m* asparagus spears *pl*.

stank *pret of* **stinken.**

stänkern *vi (col)* to stir things up *(col)*.

Stanniol *nt* **-e** silver foil.

Stanniolpapier *nt* silver paper.

Stanze *f* **-n** die, stamp; *(Loch~)* punch.

stanzen *vt* to press; *(prägen)* to stamp; *Löcher* to punch.

Stapel *m* **- (a)** stack, pile. **(b)** *(Naut: Schiffs~)* stocks *pl*. **vom ~ laufen** to be launched.

Stapellauf *m (Naut)* launching.

stapeln 1 *vt* to stack; *(lagern)* to store. **2** *vr* to pile up.

stapfen *vi aux sein* to trudge, to plod.

Star[1] *m* **-e** *(Orn)* starling.

Star[2] *m* **-e** *(Med)* **grauer/grüner ~** cataract/glaucoma.

Star[3] *m* **-s** *(Film etc)* star.

starb *pret of* **sterben.**

Star-: ~**besetzung** *f* star cast; ~**gast** *m* star guest.

stark *comp* **¨er,** *superl* **¨ste(r, s)** *or (adv)* **am ¨sten 1** *adj* **(a)** *(kräftig, konzentriert)* strong. **sich für etw ~ machen** *(col)* to stand up for sth; **das ist ein ~es Stück** *(col)* that's a bit much!

(b) *(dick)* thick; *(euph: korpulent) Dame, Herr* large.

(c) *(heftig) Schmerzen, Kälte* severe; *Regen, Verkehr, Raucher, Druck* heavy; *Sturm, Abneigung* violent; *Erkältung* bad, heavy; *Wind, Strömung, Eindruck* strong; *Beifall* hearty, loud; *Übertreibung* great.

(d) *(leistungsfähig) Motor* powerful; *Sportler* able; *Mannschaft, Brille, Arznei* strong.

(e) *(zahlreich) Nachfrage* great, big. **zehn Mann ~** ten strong; **das Buch ist 300 Seiten ~** the book is 300 pages long.

(f) *(col: hervorragend) Leistung, Werk* great *(col)*.

2 *adv (mit vb)* a lot; *(mit adj, ptp)* very; *beschädigt etc* badly; *vergrößert, verkleinert* greatly. **~ wirken** to have a strong effect; **~ gesalzen/gewürzt** very salty/highly spiced; **¨er befahrene Straßen** busier roads; **er ist ~ erkältet** he has a bad cold.

Starkbier *nt* strong beer.

Stärke[1] *f* **-n (a)** strength *(auch fig)*. **(b)** *(Dicke)* thickness; *(Macht)* power. **(c)** *(von Leid)* intensity; *(von Sturm, Abneigung)* violence. **(d)** *(Anzahl) (von Mannschaft)* size; *(von Nachfrage)* amount; *(Auflage)* size.

Stärke[2] *f* **-n** *(Chem)* starch.

Stärkemehl *nt (Cook)* thickening agent.

stärken 1 *vt* **(a)** *(lit, fig)* to strengthen; *Selbstbewußtsein* to boost; *Gesundheit* to improve. **(b)** *(erfrischen)* to fortify. **(c)** *Wäsche* to starch. **2** *vi* to be fortifying. **~des Mittel** tonic. **3** *vr* to fortify oneself.

Starkstrom *m (Elec)* heavy current.

Starkstrom- *in cpds* power; ~**leitung** *f* power line.

Stärkung *f* **(a)** strengthening *(auch fig)*; *(des Selbstbewußtseins)* boosting. **(b)** *(Erfrischung)* refreshment. **eine ~ zu sich nehmen** to take some refreshment.

Stärkungsmittel *nt (Med)* tonic.

starr *adj* **(a)** stiff; *(unbeweglich)* rigid. **~ vor Frost** stiff with frost. **(b)** *(unbewegt) Augen* glassy; *Blick auch* fixed. **(c)** *(regungslos)* paralyzed. **(d)** *(nicht flexibel) Regelung, Prinzip* inflexible, rigid.

Starre *f no pl* stiffness, rigidity.

starren *vi* **(a)** *(starr blicken)* to stare *(auf +acc* at*)*. **ins Leere ~** to stare into space; **vor sich** *(acc)* **hin ~** to stare straight ahead. **(b)** *(steif sein)* to be stiff *(von, vor +dat* with*)*. **vor Dreck ~** to be filthy.

Starrheit *f siehe adj (a)* stiffness; rigidity.

Starr-: ~**kopf** *m (Mensch)* stubborn mule; **s~köpfig** *adj* stubborn; ~**köpfigkeit** *f* stubbornness; ~**krampf** *m (Med)* tetanus, lockjaw; **s~sinnig** *adj* stubborn, mulish.

Start *m* **-s (a)** *(Sport)* start. **einen guten/schlechten ~ haben** *(lit, fig)* to get (off to) a good/bad start. **(b)** *(Aviat)* take-off; *(Raketen~)* launch.

Start-: ~**automatik** *f (Aut)* automatic choke; ~**bahn** *f (Aviat)* runway; **s~bereit** *adj (Sport, fig)* ready to go; *(Aviat)* ready for take-off; ~**block** *m (Sport)* starting block.

starten 1 *vi aux sein* to start; *(Aviat)* to take off; *(zum Start antreten)* to take part. **2** *vt Satelliten, Rakete* to launch; *Motor* to start.

Starter *m* **-** *(Aut, Sport)* starter.

Start-: ~**erlaubnis** *f (Sport)* permission to take part; *(Aviat)* clearance for take-off; ~**hilfe** *f (Aviat)* rocket-assisted take-off; *(fig)* initial aid; **jdm ~hilfe geben** to help sb get off the ground; ~**hilfekabel** *nt* jump leads *pl (Brit)*, jumper cables *pl (US)*; **s~klar** *adj (Aviat)* clear for take-off; *(Sport)* ready to start; ~**kommando** *nt (Sport)* starting signal; ~**linie** *f (Sport)* starting line; ~**loch** *nt (Sport)* **in den ~löchern** on their marks; ~**rampe** *f (Space)* launching pad; ~**schuß** *m (Sport)* starting signal; *(fig)* signal *(zu* for*)*; **den ~schuß geben** to fire the pistol; *(fig: Erlaubnis geben)* to give the go-ahead; ~**verbot** *nt (Aviat)* ban on take-off; *(Sport)* ban; **~verbot bekommen** to be banned.

Statik ['ʃta:tɪk, st-] *f* **(a)** *(Sci)* statics *sing*. **(b)** *(Build)* structural engineering.

Statiker(in *f***)** *m* **-** *(Tech)* structural engineer.

Station *f* **(a)** station; *(Haltestelle)* stop; *(fig: Abschnitt: von Reise)* stage. **~ machen** to stop off. **(b)** *(Kranken~)* ward.

stationär [ʃtatsio'nɛ:ɐ] *adj (Astron, Sociol)* stationary; *(Med)* in-patient *attr*. **~er Patient** in-patient; **~ behandeln** to treat in hospital.

stationieren* [ʃtatsio'ni:rən] *vt Truppen* to station; *Atomwaffen etc* to deploy.

Stationierung [ʃtatsio'ni:rʊŋ] *f siehe vt* stationing; deployment.

Stations-: ~**arzt** *m* ward doctor; ~**schwester** *f* ward sister; ~**vorsteher** *m (Rail)* station-master.

statisch ['ʃta:tɪʃ, st-] *adj (lit, fig)* static.

Statist *m (Film)* extra; *(Theat)* supernumerary; *(fig)* cipher.

Statistenrolle *f (lit, fig)* minor role.

Statistik statistics *sing*. **eine ~** a set of statistics.

Statistiker(in *f***)** *m* **-** statistician

statistisch *adj* statistical.

Stativ *nt* tripod.

statt 1 *prep +gen* instead of. **~dessen** instead; **~ meiner/seiner** in my/his place. **2** *conj* instead of. **~ zu bleiben** instead of staying.

Statt *f no pl (form)* stead *(form)*, place. **an Kindes ~ annehmen** *(Jur)* to adopt.

Stätte *f* **-n** *(liter)* place.

Statt-: **s~finden** *vi sep irreg* to take place; **s~haft** *adj pred* permitted; ~**halter** *m* governor.

stattlich *adj (hochgewachsen, groß) Tier* magnificent; *Bursche* strapping; *Erscheinung* imposing; *Gebäude, Park* splendid; *Sammlung* impressive; *Familie* large; *Summe* handsome.
Statue *f* **-n** statue.
statuieren* *vt* **ein Exempel (an jdm) ~** to make an example (of sb); **ein Exempel mit etw ~** to use sth as a warning.
Statur *f* build.
Status *m* - status. **~ quo** status quo.
Statussymbol *nt* status symbol.
Statut *nt* **-en** statute.
Stau *m* **-s** *(Wasserstauung)* build-up; *(Verkehrsstauung)* tailback *(Brit)*, line of cars.
Staub *m, pl* **-e** *or* **Stäube** dust; *(Bot)* pollen. **~ saugen** to vacuum; **~ wischen** to dust; **sich vor jdm in den ~ werfen** to throw oneself at sb's feet; **sich aus dem ~e machen** *(col)* to clear off *(col.*
Staubecken *nt* reservoir.
stauben *vi* to be dusty; *(Staub machen)* to make a lot of dust.
stäuben *vt* **Mehl auf etw** *(acc)* **~** to sprinkle flour on sth.
Staub-: **~fänger** *m (col)* dust collector; **~flocke** *f* piece of fluff.
staubig *adj* dusty.
Staub-: **~korn** *nt* speck of dust; **~lappen** *m* duster; **~lunge** *f (Med)* dust on the lung; *(von Kohlenstaub)* black lung; **s~saugen** *vi insep, ptp* **s~gesaugt** to vacuum; **~sauger** *m* vacuum cleaner; **~tuch** *nt* duster.
stauchen *vt* to compress *(auch Tech)*.
Staudamm *m* dam.
Staude *f* **-n** *(Busch)* shrub; *(Bananen~, Tabak~)* plant.
stauen 1 *vt Wasser* to dam; *Blut* to stop the flow of. **2** *vr (sich anhäufen)* to pile up; *(ins Stocken geraten)* to get jammed; *(Wasser, Blut, fig)* to build up. **der Verkehr staute sich über eine Strecke von 2 km** there was a 2 km tailback *(Brit) or* a 2 km line of cars.
Staumauer *m* dam wall.
staunen *vi* to be astonished *(über +acc* at*)*. **~d** in astonishment; **da kann man nur noch ~** it's just amazing; **da staunst du, was?** *(col)* you didn't expect that, did you!
Staunen *nt no pl* astonishment, amazement *(über +acc* at*)*. **jdn in ~ versetzen** to amaze sb.
Stausee *m* reservoir, artificial lake.
Stauung *f* **(a)** *(Stockung)* pile-up; *(von Verkehr)* tailback *(Brit)*, line of cars. **(b)** *(von Wasser)* build-up (of water). **(c)** *(Blut~)* congestion *no pl*.
Std. = **Stunde** hr.
Steak [steːk] *nt* **-s** steak.
stechen *pret* **stach,** *ptp* **gestochen 1** *vti (Dorn, Stachel etc)* to prick; *(Insekt)* to sting; *(Mücken)* to bite; *(mit Messer etc)* to stab *(nach* at*)*. **2** *vi* **(a)** *(Sonne)* to beat down. **(b)** *(Cards)* to play a trump. **Karo sticht** diamonds are trumps. **3** *vt* **(a)** *(Cards)* to trump. **(b)** *Spargel, Torf* to cut. **4** *vr* to prick oneself *(an +dat* on, *mit* with*)*. **sich** *(acc or dat)* **in den Finger ~** to prick one's finger. **5** *vti impers* **es sticht** it is prickly.
Stechen *nt* **- (a)** *(Sport)* play-off/jump-off *etc.* **(b)** *(Schmerz)* sharp pain.
stechend *adj* piercing; *Schmerz* sharp; *(durchdringend) Augen auch* penetrating; *(beißend) Geruch* pungent.
Stech-: **~karte** *f* clocking-in card; **~mücke** *f* gnat; **~uhr** *f* time-clock.
Steck-: **~brief** *m* "wanted" poster; *(fig)* personal description; **s~brieflich** *adv* **s~brieflich gesucht werden** to be wanted; **~dose** *f (Elec)* socket *(Brit)*, outlet *(US)*.
stecken 1 *vi pret* **steckte** *or* **stak** *(geh), ptp* **gesteckt (a)** *(festsitzen)* to be stuck; *(an- or eingesteckt sein)* to be; *(Nadel, Splitter etc)* to be (sticking); *(Brosche etc)* to be (pinned). **der Schlüssel steckt** the key is in the lock. **(b) wo steckt er?** where has he got to?; **darin steckt viel Mühe** a lot of work has gone into that; **da steckt etwas dahinter** *(col)* there's something behind it; **zeigen, was in einem steckt** to show what one is made of; **in einer Krise ~** to be in the throes of a crisis.
2 *vt pret* **steckte,** *ptp* **gesteckt (a)** to put; *Haare* to put up; *Brosche* to pin *(an +acc* onto*)*. **die Hände in die Taschen ~** to put one's hands in one's pockets; **das Hemd in die Hose ~** to tuck one's shirt in (one's trousers); **jdn ins Gefängnis ~** *(col)* to stick sb in prison *(col)*. **(b)** *(Sew)* to pin. **(c)** *(col: investieren) Geld, Mühe* to put *(in +acc* into*)*; *Zeit* to devote *(in +acc* to*)*. **(d)** *(pflanzen)* to set.
Stecken-: **s~bleiben** *vi sep irreg aux sein* to get stuck; *(in Rede)* to falter; **etw bleibt jdm im Halse s~** *(lit, fig)* sth sticks in sb's throat; **s~lassen** *vt sep irreg* **den Schlüssel s~lassen** to leave the key in the lock; **~pferd** *nt (lit, fig)* hobby-horse.
Stecker *m* - *(Elec)* plug.
Steckling *m (Hort)* cutting.
Stecknadel *f* pin. **man hätte eine ~ fallen hören können** you could have heard a pin drop; **eine ~ im Heuhaufen suchen** *(fig)* to look for a needle in a hay-stack.
Steck-: **~nadelkissen** *nt* pincushion; **~rübe** *f* swede, rutabaga *(US)*; turnip; **~schloß** *nt* bicycle lock; **~schlüssel** *m* box spanner *(Brit) or* wrench *(US)*; **~zwiebel** *f* bulb.
Steg *m* **-e (a)** *(Brücke)* footbridge; *(Landungs~)* landing stage *(Brit)*, jetty. **(b)** *(Mus, Brillen~)* bridge.
Stegreif *m* **eine Rede aus dem ~ halten** to make an impromptu speech *or* a speech off the cuff.
Stegreif-: **~rede** *f* impromptu speech; **~spiel** *nt (Theat)* improvisation.
Steh- *in cpds* stand-up.
Steh|aufmännchen *nt (Spielzeug)* tumbler. **er ist ein richtiges ~** *(fig)* he always bounces back.
stehen *pret* **stand,** *ptp* **gestanden** *aux haben or (SGer, Aus Sw) sein* **1** *vi* **(a)** to stand; *(col: fertig sein)* to be finished; *(col: geregelt sein)* to be settled. **gebückt/krumm ~** to slouch; **so wahr ich hier stehe** as sure as I'm standing here; **mit jdm/etw ~ und fallen** to depend on sb/sth; *(wesentlich sein für)* to stand or fall by sb/sth.
(b) *(sich befinden)* to be. **meine alte Schule steht noch** my old school is still there; **die Sonne steht abends im Westen** the sun in the evening is in the West; **unter Schock ~** to be in a state of shock; **unter Drogeneinwirkung ~** to be under the influence of drugs; **vor einer Entscheidung ~** to be faced with a decision; **ich tue, was in meinen Kräften steht** I'll do everything I can.
(c) *(geschrieben, angezeigt sein)* to be. **wo steht das?** *(lit)* where does it say that?; **was steht da?** what does it say?; **das steht im Gesetz** the law says so; **es stand im „Kurier“** it was in the "Courier"; **das steht in der Bibel** it says that in the Bible; **der Zeiger steht auf 4 Uhr** the clock says 4 (o'clock); **es steht 2:1 für München** the score is 2-1 to Munich; **wie steht das Pfund?** how does the pound stand?; **die Sache steht mir bis hier** *(col)* I'm sick and tired of it *(col)*.
(d) *(angehalten haben)* to have stopped. **meine Uhr steht** my watch has stopped; **der ganze Verkehr steht** all traffic is at a complete standstill.
(e) *(Gram) (bei Satzstellung)* to come; *(bei Zeit, Fall, Modus)* to be. **mit dem Dativ ~** to take the dative.
(f) *(passen zu)* **jdm ~** to suit sb.
(g) *(Belohnung, Strafe etc)* **auf Betrug steht eine Gefängnisstrafe** the penalty for fraud is imprisonment.

(h) *(Redewendungen)* **zu seinem Versprechen** ~ to stand by one's promise; **zu dem, was man gesagt hat,** ~ to stick to what one has said; **zu jdm** ~ to stand by sb; **wie** ~ **Sie dazu?** what are your views on that?; **für etw** ~ to stand for sth; **auf jdn/etw** ~ *(col)* to be mad about sb/sth *(col)*, to be into sb/sth *(col)*; **hinter jdm/etw** ~ to be behind sb/sth.

2 *vr* **sich gut/schlecht** ~ to be well-off/badly off; **sich mit jdm/etw gut/schlecht** ~ to be well-off/badly off with sb/sth.

3 *vi impers* **es steht schlecht/gut um jdn** *(bei Aussichten)* things look bad/good for sb; *(gesundheitlich, finanziell)* sb is doing badly/well; **wie steht's?** how are things?; **wie steht es damit?** how about it?

4 *vt Posten, Wache* to stand. **sich** *(acc)* **müde** ~, **sich** *(dat)* **die Beine in den Bauch** *(col)* ~ to stand until one is ready to drop.

Stehen *nt no pl* standing. **zum** ~ **bringen** to stop; **zum** ~ **kommen** to stop.

stehenbleiben *vi sep irreg aux sein (anhalten)* to stop; *(nicht weitergehen) (Mensch, Tier)* to stay; *(Zeit)* to stand still; *(Auto, Zug)* to stand.

stehend *adj attr Fahrzeug* stationary; *Gewässer* stagnant; *(ständig) Heer* regular. ~**e Redensart** stock phrase.

stehenlassen *ptp* ~ *or* **stehengelassen** *vt sep irreg* to leave; *(Cook)* to let stand. **alles stehen- und liegenlassen** to drop everything; **jdn einfach** ~ to leave sb standing (there); **sich** *(dat)* **einen Bart** ~ to grow a beard.

Steh-: ~**imbiß** *m* stand-up snack-bar; ~**kneipe** *f* stand-up bar; ~**lampe** *f* standard lamp *(Brit)*, floor lamp *(US)*; ~**leiter** *f* stepladder.

stehlen *pret* **stahl,** *ptp* **gestohlen 1** *vti* to steal. **jdm die Zeit** ~ to waste sb's time. **2** *vr* to steal. **sich aus dem Haus** ~ to steal out of the house.

Steh-: ~**platz** *m* **ich bekam nur noch einen** ~**platz** I had to stand; **ein** ~**platz kostet 10 Mark** a standing ticket costs 10 marks; ~**pult** *nt* high desk; ~**vermögen** *nt* staying power, stamina.

steif *adj (lit, fig)* stiff; *Penis* erect; *Empfang* formal; *(gestärkt)* starched. ~ **und fest auf etw** *(dat)* **beharren** to insist stubbornly on sth.

steifen *vt* to stiffen; *Wäsche* to starch.

Steifftier ® *nt* soft toy (animal).

steigen *pret* **stieg,** *ptp* **gestiegen** *aux sein* **1** *vi* **(a)** *(klettern)* to climb. **auf einen Berg** ~ to climb (up) a mountain; **aufs Fahrrad** ~ to get on(to) one's bicycle; **vom Fahrrad** ~ to get off one's bicycle; **aus dem Zug** ~ to get off the train. **(b)** *(sich aufwärts bewegen)* to rise; *(Flugzeug, Straße)* to climb; *(Nebel)* to lift; *(Fieber)* to go up. **Drachen** ~ **lassen** to fly kites; **das Blut stieg ihm in den Kopf** the blood rushed to his head; **in jds Achtung** *(dat)* ~ to rise in sb's estimation. **2** *vt Treppen, Stufen* to climb (up).

Steiger *m* - *(Min)* pit foreman.

steigern 1 *vt* **(a)** to increase; *(verschlimmern) Übel, Zorn* to aggravate. **(b)** *(Gram)* to form the comparative and superlative of. **2** *vi* to bid *(um* for*)*. **3** *vr* **(a)** *(sich erhöhen)* to increase; *(Farben)* to be intensified; *(Zorn, Übel)* to be aggravated. **(b)** *(sich verbessern)* to improve.

Steigerung *f* **(a)** *siehe vt (a) (das Steigern)* increase *(gen* in*)*; aggravation. **(b)** *(Verbesserung)* improvement. **(c)** *(Gram)* comparison.

Steigung *f (Hang)* slope; *(von Hang, Straße, Math)* gradient.

Steigungsgrad *m* gradient.

steil *adj* **(a)** steep. **eine** ~**e Karriere** *(fig)* a rapid rise. **(b)** *(senkrecht)* upright. **sich** ~ **aufrichten** to sit/stand up straight. **(c)** *(Sport)* ~**er Paß** through ball.

Steil-: ~**hang** *m* steep slope; ~**küste** *f* steep coast; ~**paß** *m (Sport)* through ball.

Stein *m* **-e (a)** stone; *(Ziegel~)* brick; *(in Uhr)* jewel; *(Spiel~)* piece. **der** ~ **der Weisen** *(lit, fig)* the philosophers' stone; **es blieb kein** ~ **auf dem anderen** not a stone was left standing; **mir fällt ein** ~ **vom Herzen!** *(fig)* that's a load off my mind!; **bei jdm einen** ~ **im Brett haben** *(fig col)* to be well in with sb *(col)*; **den ersten** ~ **(auf jdn) werfen** to cast the first stone (at sb); **es friert** ~ **und Bein** *(fig col)* it's freezing cold outside; ~ **und Bein schwören** *(fig col)* to swear blind *(col)*.

Stein-: ~**adler** *m* golden eagle; **s**~**alt** *adj* as old as the hills; ~**bock** *m* **(a)** *(Zool)* ibex; **(b)** *(Astrol)* Capricorn; ~**bohrer** *m* masonry drill; *(Gesteinsbohrer)* rock drill; ~**bruch** *m* quarry.

steinern *adj* stone; *(fig)* stony.

Stein-: ~**erweichen** *nt* **zum** ~**erweichen weinen** to cry heartbreakingly; ~**frucht** *f* stone fruit; ~**fußboden** *m* stone floor; ~**garten** *m* rockery; ~**gut** *nt* stoneware; **s**~**hart** *adj* rock hard.

steinig *adj* stony.

steinigen *vt* to stone.

Steinkohle *f* hard coal.

Steinkohlenbergbau *m* coal mining.

Stein-: ~**krug** *m (Kanne)* stoneware jug; *(Becher)* stoneware mug; ~**meißel** *m* stone chisel; ~**metz** *m (wk)* **-en, -en** stonemason; ~**obst** *nt* stone fruit; ~**pilz** *m type of mushroom*; ~**platte** *f* stone slab; *(zum Pflastern)* flagstone; **s**~**reich** *adj (col)* stinking rich *(col)*; ~**salz** *nt* rock salt; ~**schlag** *m* rockfall; **„Achtung** ~**schlag"** "danger falling stones"; ~**tafel** *f* stone tablet; ~**topf** *m* stoneware pot; ~**wurf** *m (fig)* stone's throw; ~**wüste** *f* stony desert; *(fig)* concrete jungle; ~**zeit** *f* Stone Age.

Steißbein *nt (Anat)* coccyx.

Stellage [ʃtɛ'la:ʒə] *f* **-n** *(col: Gestell)* rack, frame.

Stelldichein *nt* **-(s)** *(dated)* rendezvous.

Stelle *f* **-n (a)** place; *(Fleck: rostend, naß, faul etc)* patch. **an dieser** ~ in this place; **eine kahle** ~ **am Kopf** a bald patch on one's head; **eine empfindliche** ~ *(lit)* a sensitive spot *or* place; *(fig)* a sensitive point; **eine schwache** ~ a weak spot; **auf der** ~ **treten** *(lit)* to mark time; *(fig)* not to make any headway; **auf der** ~ *(fig: sofort)* on the spot; *kommen, gehen* straight away; **nicht von der** ~ **kommen** not to make any progress; **sich nicht von der** ~ **rühren** to refuse to move; **zur** ~ **sein** to be on the spot; *(bereit, etw zu tun)* to be at hand.

(b) *(in Buch etc)* place; *(Abschnitt)* passage; *(Text~, esp beim Zitieren)* reference; *(Bibel~)* verse; *(Mus)* passage. **an dieser** ~ here; **an anderer** ~ elsewhere.

(c) an erster ~ in the first place; **(bei jdm) an erster/letzter** ~ **kommen** to come first/last (for sb); **an führender** ~ **stehen** to be in a leading position; **an** ~ **von** *or (+gen)* in place of; **an jds** ~ *(acc)*/**an die** ~ **einer Sache** *(gen)* **treten** to take sb's place; **ich möchte jetzt nicht an seiner** ~ **sein** I wouldn't like to be in his position; **an deiner** ~ **würde ich ...** if I were you I would ...

(d) *(Math)* digit; *(hinter Komma)* place. **drei** ~**n hinter dem Komma** three decimal places.

(e) *(Posten)* job; *(Ausbildungs~)* place; *(Dienst~)* office; *(Behörde)* authority. **eine freie** *or* **offene** ~ a vacancy; **ohne** ~ without a job.

stellen 1 *vt* **(a)** *(hin~)* to put. **jdm etw auf den Tisch** ~ to put sth on the table for sb; **auf sich** *(acc)* **selbst gestellt sein** *(fig)* to have to fend for oneself. **(b)** *(arrangieren) Szene* to arrange; *Aufnahme* to pose. **eine gestellte Pose** a pose. **(c)** *(zur Verfügung* ~*)* to provide. **(d)** *(ein~)* to set *(auf +acc* at*)*; *Uhr etc* to set *(auf +acc* for*)*. **das Radio lauter/leiser** ~ to turn the radio up/down. **(e)** *(finanziell)* **gut/besser gestellt** well/better off. **(f)** *Verbrecher* to catch; *(fig col)* to corner. **(g)** *Aufgabe, Bedingung* to set *(jdm* sb*)*; *Frage* to put *(jdm, an jdn* to sb*)*; *Antrag, Forderung* to make. **jdn vor ein Problem** ~ to confront sb with a problem.

2 *vr* **(a)** to (go and) stand *(an +acc* at, by*)*; *(sich auf~, sich einordnen)* to position oneself; *(sich aufrecht hin~)* to stand up. **sich gegen jdn/etw ~** *(fig)* to oppose sb/sth; **sich hinter jdn/etw ~** *(fig)* to support sb/sth.

(b) *(fig: sich verhalten)* **sich anders zu etw ~** to have a different attitude towards sth; **wie stellst du dich zu ...?** how do you regard ...?; **sich gut mit jdm ~** to put oneself on good terms with sb.

(c) *(sich ein~: Gerät etc)* to set itself *(auf +acc* at*)*.

(d) *(sich ausliefern, antreten)* to give oneself up *(jdm* to sb*)*. **sich den Journalisten ~** to make oneself available to the reporters; **sich einer Herausforderung ~** to take up a challenge.

(e) *(sich ver~)* **sich krank/schlafend** *etc* **~** to pretend to be ill/asleep *etc*.

Stellen-: **~angebot** *nt* offer of employment; **„~angebote"** "situations vacant"; **~anzeige** *f* job advertisement *or* ad *(col)*; **~gesuch** *nt* advertisement seeking employment; **„~gesuche"** "situations wanted"; **~markt** *m* job market; *(in Zeitung)* appointments section; **~vermittlung** *f* employment bureau; **s~weise** *adv* in places; **s~weise Schauer** showers in places; **~wert** *m* *(fig)* status.

Stellung *f* *(lit, fig, Mil)* position; *(Posten auch)* post. **in ~ bringen/gehen** to bring/get into position; **die ~ halten** *(Mil)* to hold one's position; *(hum)* to hold the fort; **~ beziehen** *(Mil)* to move into position; *(fig)* to make it clear where one stands; **zu etw ~ nehmen** to give one's opinion on sth; **für/gegen jdn/etw ~ nehmen** *or* **beziehen** to come out in favour *(Brit) or* favor *(US)* of/to come out against sb/sth; **in führender ~** in a leading position; **die rechtliche ~ des Mieters** the legal status of the tenant; **ohne ~ sein** *(arbeitslos)* to be unemployed.

Stellungnahme *f* **-n** statement *(zu* on*)*. **eine ~ zu etw abgeben** to make a statement on sth.

Stellungs-: **~krieg** *m* positional warfare *no indef art;* **s~los** *adj* unemployed; **~suche** *f* search for employment; **auf ~suche sein** to be looking for employment.

Stell-: **s~vertretend** *adj (von Amts wegen)* deputy *attr*; *(vorübergehend)* acting *attr*; **s~vertretend für jdn** acting for sb; **s~vertretend für jdn handeln** to act for sb; **~vertreter** *m* (acting) representative; *(von Amts wegen)* deputy; **~werk** *nt (Rail)* signal box *(Brit) or* tower *(US)*.

Stelze *f* **-n** stilt.

stelzen *vi aux sein (col)* to stalk.

Stemm|eisen *nt* crowbar.

stemmen 1 *vt* **(a)** *(stützen)* to press; *Ellenbogen* to prop. **die Arme in die Seiten** *or* **Hüften gestemmt** with arms akimbo. **(b)** *(hoch~)* to lift (above one's head). **(c)** *(meißeln)* to chisel. **2** *vr* **sich gegen etw ~** to brace oneself against sth; *(fig)* to set oneself against sth.

Stempel *m* **-** **(a)** *(Gummi~)* (rubber-)stamp. **(b)** *(Abdruck)* stamp; *(Post~)* postmark. **jdm/einer Sache einen/seinen ~ aufdrücken** *(fig)* to make a/one's mark on sb/sth. **(c)** *(Tech) (Präge~)* die; *(stangenförmig, Loch~)* punch. **(d)** *(Bot)* pistil.

Stempel-: **~farbe** *f* stamping ink; **~geld** *nt (col)* dole (money) *(col)*; **~kissen** *nt* ink pad.

stempeln 1 *vt* to stamp; *Brief* to postmark; *Briefmarke* to frank. **jdn zum Lügner ~** *(fig)* to brand sb as a liar. **2** *vi (col)* **(a) ~ gehen** to be/go on the dole *(col)*. **(b)** *(Stempeluhr betätigen)* to clock in; *(beim Hinausgehen)* to clock out.

Stempeluhr *f* time-clock.

Stengel *m* **-** stem, stalk. **vom ~ fallen** *(col) (Schwächeanfall haben)* to collapse; *(überrascht sein)* to be staggered *(col)*.

Steno *f no pl (col)* shorthand.

Steno-: **~gramm** *nt* text in shorthand; *(Diktat)* shorthand dictation; **~grammblock** *m* shorthand pad; **~graph(in** *f***)** *m (im Büro)* shorthand secretary; *(esp in Gericht, bei Konferenz etc)* stenographer; **~graphie** *f* shorthand; **s~graphieren*** **1** *vt* to take down in shorthand; **2** *vi* to do shorthand; **s~graphisch** *adj* shorthand *attr*; **~typist(in** *f***)** *m* shorthand typist.

Steppdecke *f* quilt.

Steppe *f* **-n** steppe.

steppen *vti (Sew)* to quilt.

Steppjacke *f* quilted jacket.

Step-: **~tanz** *m* tap-dance; **~tänzer** *m* tap dancer.

Sterbe-: **~bett** *nt* death-bed; **~fall** *m* death; **~hilfe** *f* euthanasia; **~kasse** *f* death benefit fund.

sterben *pret* **starb,** *ptp* **gestorben** *vti aux sein* to die. **einen schnellen Tod/eines natürlichen Todes ~** to die quickly/to die a natural death; **an einer Krankheit/Verletzung ~** to die of an illness/from an injury; **er stirbt vor Angst** *(fig)* he's frightened to death; **er ist für mich gestorben** *(fig col)* he might as well be dead.

Sterben *nt no pl* death. **Angst vor dem ~** fear of death; **im ~ liegen** to be dying.

Sterbens-: **~angst** *f (col)* mortal fear; **s~elend** *adj (col)* wretched; **s~krank** *adj* mortally ill; **s~langweilig** *adj (col)* deadly boring; **~wörtchen** *nt (col)* **er hat kein ~wörtchen gesagt** he didn't say a word.

Sterbe-: **~stunde** *f* dying hour; **~urkunde** *f* death certificate; **~ziffer** *f* death rate.

sterblich *adj* mortal.

Sterbliche(r) *mf decl as adj* mortal.

Sterblichkeit *f* mortality; *(Zahl)* death-rate.

Stereo *nt* **in ~** in stereo.

stereo *adj pred* (in) stereo.

Stereo- *in cpds* stereo; *(s~skopisch)* stereoscopic; **~anlage** *f* stereo unit; **~aufnahme** *f* stereo recording; **~gerät** *nt* stereo unit; **~kamera** *f* stereoscopic camera; **s~phon 1** *adj* stereophonic; **2** *adv* stereophonically; **~skop** *nt* **-e** stereoscope; **s~typ** *adj (fig)* stereotyped.

steril *adj (lit, fig)* sterile.

Sterilisation *f* sterilization.

sterilisieren* *vt* to sterilize.

Sterilisierung *f* sterilization.

Sterilität *f (lit, fig)* sterility.

Stern *m* **-e** star. **das steht (noch) in den ~en** *(fig)* it's in the lap of the gods; **nach den ~en greifen** *(fig)* to reach for the stars; **sein ~ ist im Sinken** his star is on the decline; **mein guter ~** my lucky star; **unter einem glücklichen ~ geboren sein** to be born under a lucky star; **unter einem guten ~ stehen** to be blessed with good fortune.

Sternbild *nt (Astron)* constellation; *(Astrol)* sign.

Sternchen *nt dim of* **Stern (a)** little star. **(b)** *(Typ)* asterisk.

Sterndeuter *m* astrologer.

Sternen-: **~banner** *nt* Stars and Stripes *sing*; **~himmel** *m* starry sky.

Stern-: **~fahrt** *f (Mot, Pol)* rally; **s~förmig** *adj* star-shaped; **s~hagelvoll** *adj (col)* rolling drunk *(col)*; **~kunde** *f* astronomy; **~marsch** *m (Pol)* protest march; **~schnuppe** *f* shooting star; **~stunde** *f* great moment; **~system** *nt* galaxy; **~warte** *f* observatory; **~zeichen** *nt (Astrol)* sign of the zodiac; **im ~zeichen der Jungfrau** under the sign of Virgo.

stet *adj attr* constant.

Stethoskop *nt* **-e** stethoscope.

stetig *adj* steady; *(Math) Funktion* continuous.

stets *adv* always.

Steuer[1] *nt* **-** *(Naut)* helm, tiller; *(Aut)* (steering-)wheel; *(Aviat)* controls *pl*. **am ~ stehen** *(Naut) or* **sein** *(Naut, fig)* to be at the helm; **am ~ sitzen** *(col) (Aut)* to be at the wheel; *(Aviat)* to be at the controls; **das ~ übernehmen** *(lit, fig)* to take over; **das ~ fest in der Hand haben** *(fig)* to be firmly in control; **das ~ herumrei-**

ßen *(fig)* to turn the tide of events.
Steuer² *f* **-n** *(Abgabe)* tax; *(Gemeinde~)* rates *pl (Brit)*, local tax *(US)*. **~n** tax; *(Arten von ~n)* taxes; **~n zahlen** to pay tax.
Steuer-: ~beamte(r) *m* tax officer; **s~begünstigt** *adj Investitionen, Hypothek* tax-deductible; *Waren* taxed at a lower rate; **~behörde** *f* tax authorities *pl*, inland *(Brit) or* internal *(US)* revenue authorities *pl*; **~berater** *m* tax consultant; **~bescheid** *m* tax assessment; **~betrug** *m* tax evasion; **~bord** *nt no pl (Naut)* starboard; **s~bord(s)** *adv (Naut)* to starboard; **~einnahmen** *pl* revenue from taxation; **~erklärung** *f* tax return; **~erlaß** *m* tax exemption; **~erstattung** *f* tax rebate; **~flucht** *f* tax evasion; **s~frei** *adj* tax-free; **~freiheit** *f* tax exemption; **~gelder** *pl* tax money; **~gerät** *nt* tuner-amplifier; **~hinterziehung** *f* tax evasion; **~inspektor** *m* tax inspector; **~jahr** *nt* tax year; **~karte** *f* tax notice; **~klasse** *f* tax bracket; **~knüppel** *m* control column.
steuerlich *adj* tax *attr*. **~e Belastung** tax burden.
steuerlos *adj* out of control; *(fig)* leaderless.
Steuer-: ~mann *m pl* **~männer** *or* **~leute** helmsman; *(als Rang)* (first) mate; **~marke** *f* revenue stamp; *(für Hunde)* dog licence disc *(Brit)*, dog tag *(US)*; **~moral** *f* tax-payer honesty.
steuern 1 *vt* to steer; *Schiff auch* to navigate; *Flugzeug* to pilot; *(fig) Wirtschaft, Politik, (Comp)* to control. **staatlich gesteuert** state-controlled; **einen Kurs ~** *(lit, fig)* to steer a course. **2** *vi* **(a)** *aux sein* to head. **(b)** *(am Steuer sein) (Naut)* to be at the helm; *(Aut)* to be at the wheel; *(Aviat)* to be at the controls.
Steuer-: ~oase *f* tax haven; **~pflicht** *f* liability to tax; **s~pflichtig** *adj Einkommen* taxable, liable to tax; **~politik** *f* tax policy; **~progression** *f* progressive taxation; **~prüfer** *m* tax inspector; **~prüfung** *f* tax inspector's investigation; **~rad** *nt (Aviat)* control wheel; *(Aut)* (steering-)wheel; **~recht** *nt* tax law; **~reform** *f* tax reform; **~ruder** *nt* rudder; **~satz** *m* rate of taxation; **~schuld** *f* tax liability.
Steuerung *f* **(a)** *no pl (das Steuern) (von Schiff)* navigation; *(von Flugzeug)* piloting. **(b)** *(Steuervorrichtung) (Aviat)* controls *pl*; *(Tech)* steering apparatus. **automatische ~** *(Aviat)* autopilot; *(Tech)* automatic steering (device).
Steuer-: ~vorteil *m* tax advantage; **~zahler** *m* taxpayer.
Steven ['ste:vn] *m* - *(Naut) (Vorder~)* prow; *(Achter~)* stern.
Stewardeß ['stju:ɐdɛs] *f* **-ssen** stewardess.
StGB [ɛste:ge:'be:] *nt* = **Strafgesetzbuch.**
stibitzen* *vt (hum)* to swipe *(col)*, to pinch *(col)*.
Stich *m* **-e (a)** *(Insekten~)* sting; *(Mücken~)* bite; *(Nadel~)* prick; *(Messer~)* stab. **(b)** *(Schmerz)* stabbing pain; *(Seiten~)* stitch; *(fig)* pang. **(c)** *(Sew)* stitch. **(d)** *(Kupfer~, Stahl~)* engraving. **(e)** *(Schattierung)* shade *(in +acc* of*)*; *(Tendenz)* suggestion *(in +acc* of*)*. **ein ~ ins Rote** a tinge of red. **(f)** *(Cards)* trick. **einen ~ machen** to get a trick. **(g) jdn im ~ lassen** to let sb down; *(verlassen)* to desert sb. **(h) einen ~ haben** *(Eßwaren)* to be bad *or* off *(Brit)*; *(Milch)* to be sour; *(col: Mensch: verrückt sein)* to be nuts *(col)*.
Stichel *m* - *(Art)* gouge.
Stichelei *f (pej col: boshafte Bemerkung)* dig. **deine ständigen ~en kannst du dir sparen** stop getting at me.
sticheln *vi (pej col)* to make snide remarks *(col)*.
Stich-: ~flamme *f* tongue of flame; **s~haltig** *adj* valid; *Beweis* conclusive; **~haltigkeit** *f no pl* validity; conclusiveness.
Stichling *m (Zool)* stickleback.
Stich-: ~probe *f* spot check; **~tag** *m* qualifying date; **~waffe** *f* stabbing weapon; **~wahl** *f (Pol)* final ballot, run-off *(US)*.
Stichwort *nt* **(a)** *pl* **-wörter** *(in Lexikon)* headword. **(b)** *pl* **-worte** *(Theat, fig)* cue. **(c)** *pl* **-worte** *usu pl* notes *pl*.
Stichwort-: s~artig *adj* abbreviated; **etw s~artig zusammenfassen** to summarize the main points of sth; **~katalog** *m* classified catalogue; **~verzeichnis** *nt* index.
Stichwunde *f* stab wound.
Stick|arbeit *f* embroidery.
sticken *vti* to embroider.
Stickerei *f* embroidery.
stickig *adj Luft, Zimmer* stuffy; *Klima* humid.
Stickstoff *m* nitrogen.
stieben *pret* **stob** *or* **stiebte,** *ptp* **gestoben** *or* **gestiebt** *vi (geh) aux haben or sein (sprühen) (Funken, Staub, Schnee)* to fly; *(Wasser)* to spray.
Stiefbruder *m* stepbrother.
Stiefel *m* - **(a)** boot. **(b)** *(Trinkgefäß) large, boot-shaped beer glass.*
Stiefel-: ~absatz *m* (boot-)heel; **~knecht** *m* boot-jack.
stiefeln *vi aux sein (col)* to hoof it *(col)*; *siehe* **gestiefelt.**
Stief-: ~eltern *pl* step-parents *pl*; **~kind** *nt* stepchild; *(fig)* poor cousin; **~mutter** *f* stepmother; **~mütterchen** *nt (Bot)* pansy; **s~mütterlich** *adj (fig)* **jdn/etw s~mütterlich behandeln** to pay little attention to sb/sth; **~schwester** *f* stepsister; **~sohn** *m* stepson; **~tochter** *f* stepdaughter; **~vater** *m* stepfather.
stieg *pret of* **steigen.**
Stiege *f* **-n** *(Treppe)* (narrow) flight of stairs.
Stieglitz *m* **-e** goldfinch.
Stiel *m* **-e (a)** *(Griff)* handle; *(Pfeifen~, Glas~)* stem. **(b)** *(Stengel)* stalk.
Stiel|augen *pl (fig col)* **er machte ~** his eyes (nearly) popped out of his head.
stier *adj (stumpfsinnig) Blick* vacant, blank.
Stier *m* **-e (a)** bull; *(junger ~)* bullock. **wütend wie ein ~** beside oneself with rage. **(b)** *(Astrol)* Taurus.
stieren *vi* to stare *(auf +acc* at*)*.
Stier-: ~kampf *m* bull-fight; **~kampfarena** *f* bull-ring; **~kämpfer** *m* bull-fighter.
stieß *pret of* **stoßen.**
Stift *m* **-e (a)** *(Metall~)* pin; *(Nagel)* tack. **(b)** *(Blei~)* pencil. **(c)** *(col: Lehrling)* apprentice (boy).
stiften *vt* **(a)** *(spenden)* to donate; *(gründen) Kirche* to found. **(b)** *Verwirrung* to cause; *Unfrieden, Frieden* to bring about; *Ehe* to arrange.
stiftengehen *vi sep irreg aux sein (col)* to hop it *(col)*.
Stifter(in *f***)** *m* - *(Gründer)* founder; *(Spender)* donator.
Stiftung *f* **(a)** *(Gründung)* foundation; *(Schenkung)* donation. **(b)** *(Organisation)* foundation.
Stiftzahn *m* post crown.
Stigma *nt* **-men** *or* **-ta** *(Bio, Rel, fig)* stigma.
Stil *m* **-e** style; *(Eigenart)* way, manner. **im großen ~** in a big way; **schlechter ~** bad style; **das ist schlechter ~** *(fig)* that is bad form.
Stil-: ~blüte *f (hum)* stylistic howler; **~bruch** *m* stylistic incongruity.
Stilett *nt* **-e** stiletto.
Stil-: ~fehler *m* stylistic lapse; **~gefühl** *nt* feeling for style.
stilisieren* *vt* to stylize.
Stilistik *f (Liter)* stylistics *sing*.
stilistisch *adj* stylistic.
still *adj* **(a)** *(ruhig)* quiet, silent; *Seufzer, Plätzchen* quiet; *Gebet, Vorwurf, Beobachter* silent. **~ werden** to go quiet; **im Saal wurde es ~** the room fell silent; **um ihn ist es ~ geworden** you don't hear anything about him any more; **~ weinen/leiden** to cry quietly/to suffer in silence; **in ~er Trauer** in silent grief; **im ~en** quietly; **ich dachte mir im ~en** I thought to myself; **sich** *(dat)* **~**

gegenübersitzen to sit opposite one another in silence; **die S~en im Lande** the quiet ones; **sei doch ~!** be quiet; **~e Messe** silent mass. **(b)** *(unbewegt) Luft* still. **der S~e Ozean** the Pacific (Ocean); **~ sitzen** to sit still; **die Füße ~ halten** to keep one's feet still; **er ist ein ~es Wasser** he's a deep one. **(c)** *(heimlich)* secret. **im ~en** in secret. **(d)** *(Comm) Teilhaber* sleeping *(Brit)*, silent *(US)*; *Reserven, Rücklagen* hidden. **~e Beteiligung** sleeping partnership *(Brit)*, non-active interest.

Stille *f no pl* **(a)** *(Ruhe)* quiet(ness), peace(fulness); *(Schweigen)* silence. **die Beerdigung fand in aller ~ statt** it was a quiet funeral. **(b)** *(Unbewegtheit)* calm(ness); *(der Luft)* stillness. **(c)** *(Heimlichkeit)* secrecy. **in aller ~** secretly.

Stilleben ['ʃtɪlleːbn] *nt* still life.

stillegen *vt sep* to close down.

Stillegung *f* closure.

Stillehre *f* stylistics *sing*.

stillen 1 *vt* **(a)** *(zum Stillstand bringen) Tränen* to stop; *Schmerzen* to ease. **(b)** *(befriedigen) Neugier, Hunger* to satisfy; *Durst auch* to quench. **(c)** *Säugling* to breast-feed. **2** *vi* to breast-feed.

Stillhalte|abkommen *nt (Fin, fig)* moratorium.

stillhalten *vi sep irreg* to keep still; *(fig)* to keep quiet.

stilliegen *vi sep irreg aux sein or haben* **(a)** *(außer Betrieb sein)* to be shut down. **(b)** *(lahmliegen)* to be at a standstill.

Stillschweigen *nt* silence. **über etw** *(acc)* **~ bewahren** to observe silence about sth; **etw mit ~ übergehen** to pass over sth in silence.

stillschweigend *adj* silent; *Einverständnis* tacit. **über etw** *(acc)* **~ hinweggehen** to pass over sth in silence.

stillsitzen *vi sep irreg aux sein or haben* to sit still.

Stillstand *m* standstill; *(in Entwicklung)* halt. **zum ~ kommen** *(Verkehr)* to come to a standstill; **etw zum ~ bringen** to stop sth.

stillstehen *vi sep irreg aux sein or haben* **(a)** *(Produktion, Handel etc)* to be at a standstill; *(Herz)* to have stopped. **(b)** *(stehenbleiben)* to stop; *(Maschine)* to stop working.

stillvergnügt *adj* contented.

Stil-: **~mittel** *nt* stylistic device; **~möbel** *pl* period furniture *sing*; **s~voll** *adj* stylish; **~wörterbuch** *nt* dictionary of correct usage.

Stimm-: **~abgabe** *f* voting; **~band** *nt usu pl* vocal chord; **s~berechtigt** *adj* entitled to vote; **~berechtigte(r)** *mf decl as adj* person entitled to vote; **~bezirk** *m* constituency; **~bruch** *m* **er ist im ~bruch** his voice is breaking.

Stimme *f* **-n (a)** *(lit, fig)* voice; *(Mus: Part)* part; *(Orgel~)* register. **mit leiser/lauter ~** in a soft/loud voice; **zweite ~** *(in Chor)* second part; **bei einem Lied die erste/zweite ~ singen** to sing the top part of/descant to a song; **die ~n mehren sich, die ...** there is a growing body of opinion that ...; **der ~ des Gewissens folgen** to follow one's conscience. **(b)** *(Wahl~)* vote. **eine/keine ~ haben** to have the vote/not to be entitled to vote; *(Mitspracherecht)* to have a/no say; **seine ~ abgeben** to vote; **jdm seine ~ geben** to vote for sb.

stimmen 1 *vi* **(a)** *(richtig sein)* to be right. **stimmt es, daß ...?** is it true that ...?; **hier stimmt was nicht!** there's something wrong here; **stimmt so!** that's all right. **(b)** *(zusammenpassen)* to go (together). **(c)** *(wählen, sich entscheiden)* to vote. **für/gegen jdn/etw ~** to vote for/against sb/sth. **2** *vt Instrument* to tune. **jdn froh/traurig ~** to make sb (feel) cheerful/sad.

Stimmen-: **~gewirr** *nt* babble of voices; **~gleichheit** *f* tied vote; **bei ~gleichheit** in the event of a tie; **~mehrheit** *f* majority of votes.

Stimm-: **~enthaltung** *f* abstention; **~gabel** *f* tuning fork; **s~haft** *adj (Ling)* voiced; **s~haft ausgesprochen werden** to be voiced.

stimmlich *adj* vocal. **ihre ~en Qualitäten** the quality of her voice.

Stimm-: **s~los** *adj (Ling)* unvoiced; **s~los ausgesprochen werden** not to be voiced; **~recht** *nt* right to vote.

Stimmung *f* **(a)** *(auch St Ex)* mood; *(Moral)* morale. **in (guter)/gehobener ~** in a good mood/in high spirits; **in ~ kommen** to liven up; **ich bin nicht in der ~ dazu** I'm not in the mood for that. **(b)** *(Meinung)* opinion. **~ gegen/für jdn/etw machen** to stir up (public) opinion against/in favour *(Brit) or* favor *(US)* of sb/sth.

Stimmungs-: **~kanone** *f (col)* life and soul of the party; **~mache** *f no pl (pej)* cheap propaganda; **~musik** *f* light music; **~umschwung** *m* change of atmosphere; *(Pol)* swing (in public opinion); **s~voll** *adj Bild* idyllic; *Atmosphäre* tremendous; *Gedicht* full of atmosphere.

Stimm-: **~vieh** *nt (pej)* gullible voters *pl*; **~volk** *nt* voters *pl*, electorate; **~zettel** *m* ballot paper.

stimulieren* *vt (Med, fig)* to stimulate.

Stinkbombe *f* stink bomb.

stinken *pret* **stank,** *ptp* **gestunken** *vi* to stink *(nach* of*)*. **er stinkt nach Kneipe** he smells of drink; **er stinkt vor Faulheit** he's bone-idle; **das stinkt zum Himmel** it's an absolute scandal; **die Sache stinkt mir** *(col)* I'm fed up to the back teeth (with it) *(col)*.

Stink-: **s~faul** *adj (col)* bone-lazy; **s~langweilig** *adj (col)* deadly boring; **s~reich** *adj (col)* stinking rich *(col)*; **~tier** *nt* skunk; **~wut** *f (col)* raging temper; **eine ~wut (auf jdn) haben** to be livid (with sb).

Stipendium *nt* grant; *(als Auszeichnung etc erhalten)* scholarship.

Stirn *f* **-en** forehead. **es steht ihm auf der ~ geschrieben** *(geh)* it is written in his face; **die ~ haben zu ...** to have the nerve to ...; **jdm/einer Sache die ~ bieten** *(geh)* to stand up to sb.

Stirn-: **~band** *nt* headband; **~falte** *f* wrinkle (on one's forehead); **~glatze** *f* receding hair-line; **~runzeln** *nt no pl* frown.

stob *pret of* **stieben.**

stöbern *vi* to rummage *(in +dat* in, *durch* through*)*.

stochern *vi* to poke *(in +dat* at*)*; *(im Essen)* to pick *(in +dat* at*)*. **sich** *(dat)* **in den Zähnen ~** to pick one's teeth.

Stock *m* **⸗e (a)** stick; *(Rohr~)* cane; *(Takt~)* baton; *(Zeige~)* pointer; *(Billard~)* cue. **am ~ gehen** *(lit)* to walk with a stick; **da gehst du am ~** *(col)* you'll be flabbergasted *(col)*. **(b)** *(Pflanze) (Reb~)* vine; *(Rosen~)* rose-bush; *(Blumen~)* pot-plant. **über ~ und Stein** up hill and down dale. **(c)** *pl* **-** *(~werk)* floor, storey *(Brit)*, story *(US)*. **im ersten ~** on the first floor *(Brit)*, on the second floor *(US)*.

Stock-: **s~betrunken** *(col) adj* blind drunk; **s~blind** *adj (col)* as blind as a bat; **s~dunkel** *adj (col)* pitch-dark.

Stöckelschuh *m* stiletto-heeled shoe.

stocken *vi* **(a)** *(Herz, Puls)* to miss a beat; *(nicht vorangehen) (Arbeit, Entwicklung)* to make no progress; *(Unterhaltung)* to flag; *(innehalten) (in der Rede)* to falter; *(im Satz)* to break off; *(Verkehr)* to be held up. **ihm stockte das Herz/der Puls** his heart/pulse missed a beat; **ihm stockte der Atem** he caught his breath; **ins S~ geraten** *(Gespräch)* to begin to flag. **(b)** *(stagnieren) (Verhandlungen)* to break off; *(Geschäfte, Handel)* to drop off. **(c)** *(gerinnen: Blut)* to thicken. **das Blut stockte ihm in den Adern** *(geh)* the blood froze in his veins.

stockend *adj* faltering, hesitant.

Stock-: **s~finster** *adj (col)* pitch-black; **~fisch** *m* dried cod; **s~konservativ** *adj (col)* arch-conservative; **s~nüchtern** *adj (col)* stone-cold sober *(col)*; **s~sauer** *adj (col)* pissed-off *(col)*; **~schlag** *m* blow (from a stick); *(mit Rohr~)* stroke of the cane; **s~steif** *adj (col)* as stiff as a poker.

Stockung *f* **(a)** hold-up *(gen, in +dat* in); *(Verkehrs~)* traffic-jam. **(b)** *(Pause) (im Gespräch)* lull; *(in der Rede)* hesitation.

Stockwerk *nt* floor, storey *(Brit)*, story *(US)*. **im 5. ~** on the 5th *(Brit) or* 6th *(US)* floor; **ein Haus mit vier ~en** a four-storeyed *(Brit) or* four-storied *(US)* building.

Stoff *m* **-e (a)** material, fabric; *(als Materialart)* cloth. **(b)** *(no pl: Materie)* matter. **(c)** *(Substanz, Chem)* substance; *(Papier~)* pulp. **(d)** *(Thema)* subject (matter); *(Unterhaltungs~, Diskussions~)* topic; *(Material)* material. **~ zum Lesen** reading matter. **(e)** *(col: Rauschgift)* dope *(col)*.

Stoff-: **~bahn** *f* length of material; **~ballen** *m* roll of cloth.

Stoffel *m* **-** *(pej col)* lout *(col)*, boor.

stoff(e)lig *adj (pej col)* uncouth, boorish.

Stoffhandschuh *m* fabric glove.

stofflich *adj (Philos)* material; *(den Inhalt betreffend)* as regards subject matter.

Stoff-: **~puppe** *f* rag doll; **~rest** *m* remnant.

Stoffwechsel *m* metabolism.

Stoffwechselstörung *f* metabolic disturbance.

stöhnen *vi* to groan. **~d** with a groan.

stoisch *adj* stoic(al); *(Philos)* Stoic.

Stola ['ʃtoːla, st-] *f, pl* **Stolen** stole.

Stollen *m* **- (a)** *(Min, Mil)* gallery, tunnel. **(b)** *(Cook)* fruit loaf *(eaten at Christmas)*, stollen *(US)*.

stolpern *vi aux sein* to stumble, to trip *(über +acc* over); *(fig: zu Fall kommen)* to come a cropper *(col)*. **über einen Hinweis ~** *(fig)* to stumble upon a clue.

stolz *adj* **(a)** proud *(auf +acc* of). **darauf kannst du ~ sein** that's something to be proud of. **(b)** *(imposant) Bauwerk* majestic; *(iro: stattlich) Preis* princely.

Stolz *m no pl* pride. **sein Garten ist sein ganzer ~** his garden is his pride and joy.

stolzieren* *vi aux sein* to strut; *(hochmütig)* to stalk.

stopfen 1 *vt* **(a)** *(füllen)* to stuff; *Pfeife, Loch* to fill. **jdm das Maul** *(col)* **~** to silence sb; **gierig stopfte er alles in sich hinein** he greedily stuffed down everything. **(b)** *(ausbessern, flicken) Loch, Strümpfe etc* to darn. **2** *vi* **(a)** *(Speisen) (ver~)* to cause constipation. **(b)** *(flicken)* to darn.

Stopf-: **~garn** *nt* darning thread; **~nadel** *f* darning needle.

Stopp *m* **-s** stop, halt; *(Lohn~)* freeze.

Stoppball *m* dropshot.

Stoppel *f* **-n** *(Getreide~, Bart~)* stubble.

Stoppel-: **~bart** *m* stubbly beard; **~feld** *nt* stubble-field.

stopp(e)lig *adj Bart* stubbly; *Kinn auch* bristly.

stoppen 1 *vt* to stop; *Zeit, Läufer* to time. **er hat die Zeit genau gestoppt** he timed exactly how long it took. **2** *vi* to stop.

Stopper *m* **-** *(Ftbl)* centre half.

Stopp-: **~licht** *nt* stop-light, red light; **~schild** *nt* stop sign; **~uhr** *f* stop-watch.

Stöpsel *m* **-** plug; *(Pfropfen)* stopper.

stöpseln *vti (Telec)* to connect.

Stör *m* **-e** *(Zool)* sturgeon.

Stör-: **~aktion** *f* disruptive action *no pl*; **s~anfällig** *adj* susceptible to interference.

Storch *m* **¨-e** stork.

Store [ʃtoːɐ] *m* **-s** *usu pl* net curtain.

stören 1 *vt* **(a)** *Schlaf, öffentliche Ordnung, Frieden etc* to disturb; *Verhältnis, Harmonie etc* to spoil; *Rundfunkempfang* to interfere with; *(absichtlich)* to jam. **jds Pläne ~** to upset sb's plans. **(b)** *Prozeß, Vorlesung* to disrupt. **(c)** *(unangenehm berühren)* to disturb, to bother. **was mich an ihm/daran stört** what I don't like about him/it; **lassen Sie sich nicht ~!** don't let me disturb you; **stört es Sie, wenn ich rauche?** do you mind if I smoke?; **sie läßt sich durch nichts ~** she doesn't let anything bother her.

2 *vr* **sich an etw** *(dat)* **~** to be bothered about sth; **ich störe mich an seiner Unpünktlichkeit** I take exception to his unpunctuality.

3 *vi* **(a)** *(lästig, im Weg sein)* to get in the way; *(unterbrechen)* to interrupt; *(Belästigung darstellen: Musik, Lärm etc)* to be disturbing. **bitte nicht ~!** please do not disturb!; **ich möchte nicht ~** I don't want to be in the way; **etw als ~d empfinden** to find sth bothersome. **(b)** *(unangenehm auffallen)* to spoil the effect.

Störenfried *m* **-e, Störer** *m* **-** trouble-maker.

Störmanöver *nt* disruptive action.

stornieren* *vti (Comm) Auftrag* to cancel; *Buchungsfehler* to reverse.

Storno *m or nt, pl* **Storni** *(Comm) (von Buchungsfehler)* reversal; *(von Auftrag)* cancellation.

störrisch *adj* stubborn, obstinate; *Kind* unmanageable; *Pferd* restive.

Störsender *m (Rad)* jamming transmitter.

Störung *f* **(a)** disturbance; *(von Ablauf, Verhandlungen etc)* disruption; *(Verkehrs~)* hold-up. **(b)** *(Tech)* fault. **(c)** *(Rad)* interference; *(absichtlich)* jamming. **(d)** *(Med)* disorder. **nervöse ~en** nervous trouble.

Störungs-: **s~frei** *adj* trouble-free; *(Rad)* free from interference; **~stelle** *f (Telec)* faults service.

Stoß *m* **¨-e (a)** push, shove; *(leicht)* poke; *(mit Faust)* punch; *(mit Fuß)* kick; *(mit Ellbogen)* nudge; *(mit Kopf, Hörnern)* butt; *(Dolch~ etc)* stab; *(Fechten)* thrust; *(Atem~)* gasp. **seinem Herzen einen ~ geben** to pluck up courage. **(b)** *(Anprall)* impact; *(Erd~)* tremor; *(eines Wagens)* jolt. **(c)** *(Stapel)* pile, stack. **(d)** *(Trompeten~ etc)* blast *(in +acc* on).

Stoßdämpfer *m (Aut)* shock absorber.

Stößel *m* **-** pestle; *(Aut: Ventil~)* tappet.

stoß|empfindlich *adj* susceptible to shock.

stoßen *pret* **stieß,** *ptp* **gestoßen 1** *vt* **(a)** to push, to shove; *(leicht)* to poke; *(mit Faust)* to punch; *(mit Fuß)* to kick; *(mit Ellbogen)* to nudge; *(mit Kopf, Hörnern)* to butt; *(stechen) Dolch* to plunge; *(Sport) Kugel* to put. **sich** *(dat)* **den Kopf** *etc* **~** to hit one's head *etc*; **jdn von sich ~** to push sb away; *(fig)* to cast sb aside; **er stieß den Ball mit dem Kopf ins Tor** he headed the ball into the goal. **(b)** *(zerkleinern) Zimt, Pfeffer* to pound.

2 *vr* to bump oneself. **sich an etw** *(dat)* **~** *(lit)* to bump oneself on sth; *(fig)* to take exception to sth.

3 *vi* **(a)** *(mit den Hörnern)* to butt *(nach* at). **(b)** *(Tech)* to butt *(an +acc* against). **(c)** *(Gewichtheben)* to jerk. **(d)** *aux sein* **an etw** *(acc)* **~** to bump into sth; *(grenzen)* to border on sth; **gegen etw ~** to run into sth; **zu jdm ~** to meet up with sb; **auf jdn ~** to bump into sb; **auf etw** *(acc)* **~** *(Schiff)* to hit sth; *(fig: entdecken)* to come across sth; **auf Erdöl ~** to strike oil; **auf Widerstand ~** to meet with resistance.

Stoß-: **~gebet** *nt* quick prayer; **ein ~gebet zum Himmel schicken** to say a quick prayer; **~seufzer** *m* deep sigh; **s~sicher** *adj* shock-proof; **~stange** *f (Aut)* bumper; **~trupp** *m (Mil)* raiding party; **~verkehr** *m* rush-hour (traffic); **~waffe** *f* thrust weapon; **s~weise** *adv* **(a)** *(ruckartig)* by fits and starts; **(b)** *(stapelweise)* by the pile; **~zahn** *m* tusk; **~zeit** *f (im Verkehr)* rush-hour; *(in Geschäft etc)* peak period.

stottern *vti* to stutter; *(Motor)* to splutter. **leicht/stark ~** to stutter slightly/badly; **ins S~ kommen** to start stuttering.

Stövchen *nt* (teapot- *etc*)warmer.

Str. = **Straße** St.

Straf-: **~anstalt** *f* penal institution, prison; **~antrag** *m* legal proceedings *pl*; **~antrag stellen** to institute legal proceedings; **~anzeige** *f* **~anzeige gegen jdn erstatten** to bring a charge against sb; ~**arbeit** *f (Sch)* lines *pl*, imposition; ~**bank** *f (Sport)* penalty bench.

strafbar *adj Vergehen* punishable. ~**e Handlung** punishable offence; **sich ~ machen** to commit an offence *(Brit) or* offense *(US)*.

Strafe *f* **-n** punishment; *(Jur, Sport)* penalty; *(Geld~)* fine; *(Gefängnis~)* sentence. **... bei ~ verboten ...** forbidden; **etw unter ~ stellen** to make sth a punishable offence *(Brit) or* offense *(US)*; **unter ~ stehen** to be a punishable offence *(Brit) or* offense *(US)*; **seine ~ absitzen** to serve one's sentence; **~ zahlen** to pay a fine; **100 Dollar ~ zahlen** to pay a $100 fine; **zur ~** as a punishment; **~ muß sein!** discipline is necessary; **seine gerechte ~ bekommen** to get one's just deserts; **er hat seine ~ weg** *(col)* he's had his punishment.

strafen *vti* to punish. **mit etw gestraft sein** to be cursed with sth; **sie ist vom Schicksal gestraft** she is cursed by fate; **er ist gestraft genug** he has been punished enough.

strafend *adj attr* punitive; *Blick* reproachful.

Straf-: ~**entlassene(r)** *mf decl as adj* ex-convict; ~**erlaß** *m* remission (of sentence); ~**expedition** *f* punitive expedition.

straff *adj Seil* tight, taut; *Haut* smooth; *(fig: streng) Disziplin, Organisation* strict. **~ sitzen** to fit tightly; **etw ~ spannen** to tighten sth; **das Haar ~ zurückkämmen** to comb one's hair back severely.

straffällig *adj* **~ werden** to commit a criminal offence *(Brit) or* offense *(US)*.

Straffällige(r) *mf decl as adj* offender.

straffen 1 *vt* to tighten; *(raffen) Darstellung* to tighten up. **2** *vr* to tighten; *(Haut)* to become smooth.

Straf-: **s~frei** *adj* **s~frei ausgehen** to go unpunished; ~**freiheit** *f* impunity; ~**gebühr** *f* surcharge; ~**gefangene(r)** *mf decl as adj* prisoner; ~**gericht** *nt* criminal court; **ein ~gericht abhalten** to hold a trial; **das göttliche ~gericht** divine judgement; ~**gesetz** *nt* penal law; ~**gesetzbuch** *nt* Criminal Code; ~**justiz** *f* criminal justice *no art;* ~**kolonie** *f* penal colony; ~**kompanie** *f (Mil)* punishment batallion.

sträflich 1 *adj (lit, fig)* criminal. **2** *adv vernachlässigen etc* criminally.

Sträfling *m* prisoner.

Sträflingskleidung *f* prison clothing.

Straf-: ~**mandat** *nt* ticket; ~**maß** *nt* sentence; **das höchste ~maß** the maximum penalty; **s~mildernd** *adj* mitigating; ~**minute** *f (Sport)* penalty minute; ~**porto** *nt* excess postage; ~**predigt** *f* dressing-down *(col)*; **jdm eine ~predigt halten** to give sb a dressing-down; ~**prozeß** *m* criminal proceedings *pl*; ~**punkt** *m (Sport)* penalty point; ~**raum** *m (Sport)* penalty area; ~**recht** *nt* criminal law; **s~rechtlich** *adj* criminal; **jdn/etw s~rechtlich verfolgen** to prosecute sb/sth; ~**richter** *m* criminal judge; ~**sache** *f* criminal matter; ~**stoß** *m (Ftbl etc)* penalty (kick); *(Hockey etc)* penalty (shot); ~**tat** *f* criminal offence *(Brit) or* offense *(US)*; ~**täter** *m* offender; ~**verfahren** *nt* criminal proceedings *pl*; ~**verfolgung** *f* criminal prosecution; **s~versetzen*** *vt insep Beamte* to transfer for disciplinary reasons; ~**verteidiger** *m* counsel for the defence *(Brit) or* defense *(US)*; ~**vollzug** *m* penal system; ~**vollzugsanstalt** *f (form)* penal institution; **s~würdig** *adj (form)* criminal; ~**wurf** *m (Sport)* penalty throw; ~**zettel** *m (col)* ticket.

Strahl *m* **-en** *(lit, fig)* ray; *(Radio~, Laser~ etc)* beam; *(Wasser~, Luft~)* jet.

strahlen *vi (Sonne, Licht etc)* to shine; *(Sender, fig: Gesicht)* to beam; *(Kernreaktor etc)* to radiate. **er strahlte (übers ganze Gesicht)** he was beaming all over his face.

strahlend *adj* radiant; *Wetter, Tag* bright. ~**es Lachen** beaming smile; **mit ~em Gesicht** with a beaming face.

Strahlen-: **s~förmig** *adj* radial; **s~geschädigt** *adj* suffering from radiation damage; ~**krankheit** *f* radiation sickness; ~**schäden** *pl* radiation injuries *pl*; ~**schutz** *m* radiation protection; ~**therapie** *f* radiotherapy.

Strahltriebwerk *nt* jet engine.

Strahlung *f* radiation.

Strähne *f* **-n** *(Haar~)* strand. **ich habe schon eine weiße ~** I already have a white streak.

strähnig *adj Haar* straggly.

stramm *adj (straff) Seil, Hose* tight; *(schneidig) Haltung, Soldat* erect; *(kräftig, drall) Mädchen, Junge* strapping; *Junge, Beine* sturdy; *Brust* firm; *(col) (tüchtig) Marsch, Arbeit* hard; *(überzeugt)* staunch. **~ sitzen** *(Kleidung)* to be tight; **~e Haltung annehmen** to stand to attention; **~ marschieren** *(col)* to march hard.

stramm-: ~**stehen** *vi sep irreg (Mil col)* to stand to attention; ~**ziehen** *vt sep irreg Seil, Hose* to pull tight; **jdm den Hosenboden ~ziehen** *(col)* to give sb a good hiding.

Strampelhöschen [-'hø:sçən] *nt* rompers *pl*.

strampeln *vi* **(a)** to thrash about. **(b)** *aux sein (col: radfahren)* to pedal.

Strand *m* **⸗e** *(Meeres~)* beach; *(Seeufer)* shore. **am ~** on the beach.

Strand-: ~**anzug** *m* beach suit; ~**bad** *nt* (seawater) swimming pool; *(Badeort)* bathing resort.

stranden *vi aux sein* to run aground; *(fig)* to fail; *(Mädchen)* to go astray.

Strand-: ~**gut** *nt (lit, fig)* flotsam and jetsam; ~**hafer** *m* marram (grass); ~**hotel** *nt* seaside hotel; ~**kleidung** *f* beachwear; ~**korb** *m* wicker beach chair with a hood; ~**promenade** *f* promenade; ~**räuber** *m* beachcomber.

Strang *m* **⸗e** *(Nerven~, Muskel~)* cord; *(Rail: Schienen~)* track. **der Tod durch den ~** death by hanging; **am gleichen ~ ziehen** *(fig)* to be in the same boat; **über die ⸗e schlagen** to run riot.

strangulieren* *vt* to strangle.

Strapaze *f* **-n** strain.

strapazieren* 1 *vt* to be a strain on; *Kleidung* to be hard on; *(fig col) Begriff* to flog *(col)*; *Nerven* to strain. **2** *vr* to tax oneself.

strapazierfähig *adj Schuhe, Kleidung* hard-wearing; *(fig col) Nerven* tough.

strapaziös *adj (lit, fig)* wearing, exhausting.

Straße *f* **-n** **(a)** road; *(in Stadt, Dorf)* street, road *(Brit)*; *(kleine Land~)* lane. **an der ~** by the roadside; **auf der ~** in the street; **auf die ~ gehen** *(lit)* to go out on the street; *(als Demonstrant)* to take to the streets; **auf der ~ liegen** *(fig col)* to be out of the work; **auf die ~ gesetzt werden** *(col)* to be turned out (onto the streets); **über die ~ gehen** to cross (the road/street); **er wohnt drei ~n weiter** he lives three blocks further on; **dem Druck der ~ nachgeben** *(fig)* to give in to the demands of demonstrators. **(b)** *(Meerenge)* strait(s *pl*). **(c)** *(Tech) (Fertigungs~)* (production) line.

Straßenarbeiten *pl* roadworks *(Brit) pl*, roadwork *(US)*.

Straßenbahn *f (Wagen)* tram *(Brit)*, streetcar *(US)*.

Straßenbahn-: ~**fahrer** *m* tram *(Brit) or* streetcar *(US)* driver; ~**haltestelle** *f* tram *(Brit) or* streetcar *(US)* stop; ~**linie** *f* tramline *(Brit)*, streetcar line *(US)*.

Straßen-: ~**bau** *m* road construction; ~**bauarbeiten** *pl* roadworks *(Brit) pl*, roadwork *(US)*; ~**benutzungsgebühr** *f* (road) toll; ~**decke** *f* road surface; ~**ecke** *f* street corner; ~**gabelung** *f* fork (in a/the road); ~**glätte** *f* slippery road surface; ~**graben** *m* ditch; ~**händler** *m* street trader; ~**junge** *m (pej)* street urchin; ~**kampf** *m* street fighting *no pl*; ~**karte** *f* road map; ~**kehrer** *m* - road sweeper; ~**kreuzer** *m* - *(col)* limousine; ~**kreuzung** *f* crossroads *sing or pl*, intersection *(US)*; ~**laterne** *f* street lamp; ~**mädchen** *nt* streetwalker; ~**netz** *nt* road network; ~**rand** *m* roadside; ~**raub** *m* mugging; ~**räuber** *m* mugger; ~**reinigung** *f* street cleaning; ~**rennen** *nt* road race; ~**sammlung** *f* street collection; ~**schild** *nt* street sign; ~**schuh** *m* walking shoe; ~**seite** *f* side of a/the road; ~**sperre** *f* road block; ~**strich** *m (col)* street-walking; **auf den ~strich gehen** to walk the streets; ~**theater** *nt* street theatre *(Brit) or* theatre *(US)*; ~**überführung** *f* footbridge; ~**unterführung** *f* underpass; ~**verhältnisse** *pl* road conditions *pl*; ~**verkauf** *m* street-trading; take-away *(Brit) or* take-out *(US)* sales *pl*; ~**verkäufer** *m* street vendor; ~**verkehr** *m* traffic; ~**verkehrsordnung** *f (Jur)* Road Traffic Act; ~**verzeichnis** *nt* index of street names; ~**wacht** *f* road patrol; ~**zustand** *m* road conditions *pl*; ~**zustandsbericht** *m* road report.

Stratege *m (wk)* **-n, -n** strategist.

Strategie *f* strategy.

strategisch *adj* strategic.

Stratosphäre *f no pl* stratosphere.

sträuben 1 *vr* **(a)** *(Haare, Fell)* to stand on end; *(Gefieder)* to become ruffled. **da ~ sich einem die Haare** it's enough to make your hair stand on end. **(b)** *(fig)* to struggle *(gegen* against*)*. **es sträubt sich alles in mir, das zu tun** I am most reluctant to do it. **2** *vt Gefieder* to ruffle.

Strauch *m, pl* **Sträucher** bush, shrub.

straucheln *vi aux sein* **(a)** *(geh: stolpern)* to stumble. **(b)** *(fig)* to transgress; *(Mädchen)* to go astray.

Strauchwerk *nt no pl (Gebüsch)* bushes *pl*, shrubs *pl*; *(Gestrüpp)* undergrowth.

Strauß[1] *m* **-e** *(Orn)* ostrich.

Strauß[2] *m, pl* **Sträuße** bunch; *(Blumen~)* bunch of flowers; *(als Geschenk)* bouquet, bunch of flowers.

Strebe *f* **-n** brace, strut; *(Decken~)* joist.

Strebebalken *m* diagonal brace.

streben *vi (geh)* **(a)** *(sich bemühen)* to strive *(nach* for*)*; *(Sch pej)* to swot *(col)*. **danach ~, etw zu tun** to strive to do sth. **(b)** *aux sein (sich bewegen)* **nach** *or* **zu etw ~** to make one's way to sth.

Streben *nt no pl (Drängen)* striving *(nach* for*)*; *(nach Ruhm, Geld)* aspiration *(nach* to*)*; *(Bemühen)* efforts *pl*.

Strebepfeiler *m* buttress.

Streber *m* **-** *(pej col)* pushy person; *(Sch)* swot *(col)*.

strebsam *adj* assiduous, industrious.

Strebsamkeit *f no pl* assiduity, industriousness.

Strecke *f* **-n** **(a)** *(Entfernung)* distance; *(Math)* line. **eine ~ zurücklegen** to cover a distance. **(b)** *(Abschnitt) (von Straße, Fluß)* stretch; *(von Bahnlinie)* section. **(c)** *(Weg, Route)* route; *(Straße)* road; *(Bahnlinie, Sport: Bahn)* track; *(fig: Passage)* passage. **für die ~ London-Glasgow brauchen wir 5 Stunden** the journey from London to Glasgow will take us 5 hours; **auf der ~ Paris-Brüssel** on the way from Paris to Brussels; **auf der ~ bleiben** *(fig)* to fall by the wayside. **(d)** *(Hunt)* **zur ~ bringen** to bag.

strecken 1 *vt* **(a)** *Arme, Beine* to stretch; *Hals* to crane. **die Zunge aus dem Mund ~** to stick out one's tongue; **die Beine von sich ~** to stretch out one's legs; **den Kopf aus dem Fenster ~** to stick one's head out of the window. **(b)** *(Med) Bein, Arm* to straighten. **(c)** *(col: absichtlich verlängern) Vorräte, Geld* to eke out; *Arbeit* to drag out *(col)*; *Essen* to make go further. **2** *vr* **(a)** *(sich recken)* to stretch. **sich ins Gras ~** to stretch out on the grass. **(b)** *(sich hinziehen)* to drag on.

Strecken-: ~**abschnitt** *m (Rail)* track section; ~**netz** *nt* rail network; **s~weise** *adv* in parts.

Streich *m* **-e** *(Schabernack)* prank, trick. **jdm einen ~ spielen** *(lit)* to play a trick on sb; *(fig: Gedächtnis etc)* to play tricks on sb.

streicheln *vti* to stroke. **jdm die Wange ~** to stroke sb's cheek.

streichen *pret* **strich,** *ptp* **gestrichen 1** *vt* **(a)** to stroke. **etw glatt~** to smooth sth (out); **sich** *(dat)* **die Haare aus der Stirn ~** to push one's hair back from one's forehead; *siehe* **gestrichen. (b)** *(auftragen) Butter, Brot etc* to spread; *Salbe, Farbe etc* to apply, to put on. **(c)** *(an~: mit Farbe)* to paint. **frisch gestrichen!** wet paint. **(d)** *(tilgen) Zeile, Satz* to delete; *Auftrag, Zug etc* to cancel; *Schulden* to write off; *Zuschuß etc* to cut. **jdn/etw von der Liste ~** to take sb/sth off the list.

2 *vi* **(a)** *(über etw hinfahren)* to stroke. **mit der Hand über etw** *(acc)* **~** to stroke sth; **sie strich ihm über das Haar** she stroked his hair. **(b)** *aux sein (streifen)* to brush past *(an etw (dat)* sth*)*. **um/durch etw ~** *(herum~)* to prowl around/through sth; **die Katze strich mir um die Beine** the cat rubbed against my legs. **(c)** *(malen)* to paint.

Streicher *pl (Mus)* strings *pl*.

Streich-: **s~fähig** *adj* easy to spread; ~**holz** *nt* match; ~**holzschachtel** *f* matchbox; ~**instrument** *nt* string(ed) instrument; ~**käse** *m* cheese spread; ~**orchester** *nt* string orchestra.

Streichung *f (Tilgung) (von Zeile, Satz)* deletion; *(Kürzung)* cut; *(von Auftrag, Zug)* cancellation.

Streifband *nt* wrapper.

Streifbandzeitung *f newspaper sent at printed paper rate.*

Streife *f* **-n** *(Patrouille)* patrol. **auf ~ gehen/sein** to go/be on patrol; **ein Polizist auf ~** a policeman on his beat.

streifen 1 *vt* **(a)** to touch, to brush (against); *(Kugel)* to graze; *(Auto)* to scrape. **jdn mit einem Blick ~** to glance fleetingly at sb. **(b)** *(flüchtig erwähnen)* to touch (up)on. **(c)** *(ab~, überziehen)* **die Schuhe von den Füßen ~** to slip one's shoes off; **sich** *(dat)* **die Handschuhe über die Finger ~** to pull on one's gloves. **2** *vi (geh)* **(a)** *aux sein (wandern)* to roam; *(Fuchs)* to prowl. **(b)** *aux sein (Blick etc)* **sie ließ ihren Blick über die Menge ~** she scanned the crowd.

Streifen *m* **-** **(a)** *(Stück, Band)* strip; *(Loch~, Klebe~ etc)* tape. **ein ~ Land** a strip of land. **(b)** *(Strich)* stripe. **ein goldener ~ am Horizont** a streak of gold on the horizon. **(c)** *(Tresse)* braid; *(Mil)* stripe. **(d)** *(Film)* film *(Brit)*, movie *(esp US)*.

Streifen-: ~**dienst** *m* patrol duty; ~**wagen** *m* patrol car.

Streif-: ~**licht** *nt (fig)* highlight; **ein ~licht auf etw** *(acc)* **werfen** to highlight sth; ~**schuß** *m* graze; ~**zug** *m (Bummel)* expedition; *(fig: kurzer Überblick)* brief survey *(durch* of*)*.

Streik *m* **-s** strike. **zum ~ aufrufen** to call a strike; **in den ~ treten** to come out on strike, to strike.

Streik-: ~**aufruf** *m* strike call; ~**brecher** *m* **-** strikebreaker, scab *(pej)*.

streiken *vi* to be on strike; *(in den Streik treten)* to strike; *(hum col) (nicht funktionieren)* to pack up *(col)*; *(Gedächtnis)* to fail. **der Computer streikt** the computer's packed up *(col)*, the computer's on the blink *(col)*; **da streike ich** *(col)* I refuse!

Streikende(r) *mf decl as adj* striker.

Streik-: ~**geld** *nt* strike pay; ~**kasse** *f* strike fund; ~**posten** *m* picket; ~**posten aufstellen** to put up pickets; ~**recht** *nt* right to strike; ~**welle** *f* wave of strikes.

Streit *m* **-e** argument *(über +acc* about*)*; *(leichter)* quarrel; *(Auseinandersetzung)* dispute. **wegen etw mit jdm (einen) ~ haben** to argue with sb about sth; **~ anfangen** to start an argument; **mit jdm in ~ liegen** to be at loggerheads with sb.

Streit|axt *f (Hist)* battleaxe *(Brit)*, battleax *(US)*.

streiten *pret* **stritt,** *ptp* **gestritten 1** *vi* *(über +acc* about, over*)* to argue; *(leichter)* to quarrel.

darüber läßt sich ~ that's debatable; **die** ~**den Parteien** *(Jur)* the litigants. **2** *vr* to argue, to quarrel. **wir wollen uns deswegen nicht** ~! don't let's fall out over that!

Streit-: ~**fall** *m* dispute, conflict; *(Jur)* case; **im** ~**fall** in case of dispute; **im** ~**fall Müller gegen Braun** in the case of Müller versus Braun; ~**frage** *f* dispute; ~**gespräch** *nt* debate; ~**hahn** *m (col)* squabbler.

streitig *adj* **jdm das Recht auf etw** *(acc)* ~ **machen** to dispute sb's right to sth.

Streitigkeiten *pl* quarrels *pl*, squabbles *pl*.

Streit-: ~**kräfte** *pl* armed forces *pl*; **s**~**lustig** *adj (aggressiv)* aggressive; ~**macht** *f* armed forces *pl*; ~**punkt** *m* contentious issue; ~**sache** *f* dispute; *(Jur)* case; ~**sucht** *f* quarrelsomeness; **s**~**süchtig** *adj* quarrelsome.

streng *adj* strict; *Blick, Bestrafung, Anforderung, Winter* severe; *Geruch, Geschmack* pungent. ~ **gegen jdn/etw vorgehen** to deal severely with sb/sth; ~ **aber gerecht** severe but just; **etw** ~ **befolgen** to keep strictly to sth; ~ **geheim** top secret; ~ **vertraulich** strictly confidential; ~ **nach Vorschrift** strictly according to regulations; ~ **verboten!** strictly prohibited.

Strenge *f no pl siehe adj* strictness; severity; pungency.

streng-: ~**genommen** *adv* strictly speaking; *(eigentlich)* actually; ~**gläubig** *adj* strict.

Streß *m* **-sse** stress. **im** ~ **sein** to be under stress.

stressen *vt* to put under stress. **gestreßt sein** to be under stress.

Streu *f no pl* straw; *(aus Sägespänen)* sawdust.

streuen 1 *vt Futter, Samen* to scatter; *Dünger, Sand* to spread; *Gewürze, Zucker etc* to sprinkle; *Straße* to grit; to salt. **2** *vi (mit Streumittel)* to grit; to put down salt.

Streuer *m* - shaker; *(Salz~)* cellar; *(Pfeffer~)* pot.

Streufahrzeug *nt* gritter, sander.

streunen *vi* **(a)** to roam about; *(Hund, Katze)* to stray. ~**de Katzen** stray cats. **(b)** *aux sein* **durch etw** ~ to roam through sth.

Streusand *m* sand; *(für Straße)* grit.

Streusel *nt* - *(Cook)* crumble (mixture).

Streuselkuchen *m thin sponge cake with crumble topping*.

Streuung *f (Statistik)* mean variation; *(Phys)* scattering.

strich *pret of* **streichen.**

Strich *m* **-e (a)** line; *(Quer~)* dash; *(Schräg~)* oblique, slash *(esp US)*; *(Feder~, Pinsel~)* stroke; *(von Land)* stretch. **jdm einen** ~ **durch die Rechnung machen** to thwart sb's plans; **einen** ~ **(unter etw** *acc***) machen** *(fig)* to forget sth; **unterm** ~ **sein** *(col)* not to be up to scratch; **sie ist nur noch ein** ~ *(col)* she's as thin as a rake now. **(b)** *(von Teppich)* pile; *(von Gewebe)* nap; *(von Fell, Haar)* direction of growth. **gegen den** ~ **bürsten** *(lit)* to brush the wrong way; **es geht (mir) gegen den** ~ *(col)* it goes against the grain; **nach** ~ **und Faden** *(col)* good and proper *(col)*. **(c)** *(Mus: Bogen~)* stroke, bow. **(d)** *(col) (Prostitution)* prostitution *no art; (Bordellgegend)* red-light district. **auf den** ~ **gehen** to be/go on the game *(col)*.

stricheln *vti (schraffieren)* to hatch. **eine gestrichelte Linie** a broken line.

Strich-: ~**junge** *m (col)* male prostitute; ~**mädchen** *nt (col)* tart *(col)*; **s**~**weise** *adv (Met)* **s**~**weise Regen** rain in places.

Strick *m* **-e** rope. **jdm aus etw einen** ~ **drehen** to use sth against sb.

stricken *vti* to knit.

Strickerei *f* knitting *no indef art, no pl*.

Strick-: ~**jacke** *f* cardigan; ~**leiter** *f* rope ladder; ~**maschine** *f* knitting machine; ~**nadel** *f* knitting needle; ~**waren** *pl* knitwear *sing*; ~**wolle** *f* knitting wool; ~**zeug** *nt* knitting.

Striegel *m* - currycomb.

striegeln 1 *vt* to curry(comb); *(fig col: kämmen)* to comb. **2** *vr (col)* to spruce oneself up.

Strieme *f* **-n** weal.

strikt *adj* strict.

Strippe *f* **-n** *(col)* **(a)** *(Bindfaden)* string. **(b)** *(Telefonleitung)* phone. **an der** ~ **hängen** to be on the phone.

stritt *pret of* **streiten.**

strittig *adj* controversial. **noch** ~ still in dispute.

Stroh *nt no pl* straw; *(Dach~)* thatch.

Stroh-: ~**ballen** *m* bale of straw; **s**~**blond** *adj Mensch* flaxen-haired; *Haare* flaxen; ~**blume** *f* strawflower; ~**dach** *nt* thatched roof; **s**~**dumm** *adj* thick *(col)*; ~**feuer** *nt*: **ein** ~ **feuer sein** *(fig)* to be a passing fancy; ~**halm** *m* straw; **sich an einen** ~**halm klammern** to clutch at a straw; ~**hut** *m* straw hat; ~**kopf** *m (col)* blockhead *(col)*; ~**mann** *m, pl* ~**männer** *(fig)* front man; ~**sack** *m* **heiliger** ~**sack!** *(col)* good(ness) gracious (me)!; ~**witwe** *f* grass widow; ~**witwer** *m* grass widower.

Strolch *m* **-e** *(pej)* rogue, rascal.

Strom *m* **¨-e (a)** (large) river; *(Strömung)* current; *(von Besuchern)* stream. **ein reißender** ~ a raging torrent; **in** ¨~**en regnen** to be pouring with rain; **der Wein floß in** ¨~**en** the wine flowed like water; **mit dem/gegen den** ~ **schwimmen** *(lit, fig)* to swim with/against the current. **(b)** *(Elec)* current; *(Elektrizität)* electricity. ~ **führen** to be live; **unter** ~ **stehen** *(lit)* to be live; **der** ~ **ist ausgefallen** the power is off.

Strom-: **s**~**ab** *adv* downstream; **s**~**abwärts** *adv* downstream; ~**anschluß** *m* ~**anschluß haben** to be connected to the electricity mains; **s**~**auf(wärts)** *adv* upstream; ~**ausfall** *m* power failure.

strömen *vi aux sein* to stream; *(heraus~)* to pour *(aus* from*)*. **bei** ~**dem Regen** in (the) pouring rain.

Strom-: ~**kabel** *nt* electric cable; ~**kreis** *m* (electrical) circuit; ~**leitung** *f* electric cables *pl*; ~**linienform** [-liːniən-] *f* streamlined design; **s**~**linienförmig** [-liːniən-] *adj* streamlined; ~**netz** *nt* power supply system; ~**quelle** *f* source of power; ~**schnelle** *f* rapids *pl*; ~**speicher** *m* (storage) battery; ~**sperre** *f* power cut.

Strömung *f* current.

Strom-: ~**verbrauch** *m* power consumption; ~**versorgung** *f* power supply; ~**zähler** *m* electricity meter.

Strophe *f* **-n** verse.

strotzen *vi* to abound *(von, vor +dat* with*)*; *(von Kraft, Gesundheit)* to be bursting *(von* with*)*. **von Schmutz** ~ to be thick with dirt.

strubb(e)lig *adj (col) Haar, Fell* tousled.

Strudel *m* - **(a)** *(lit, fig)* whirlpool. **(b)** *(Cook)* strudel.

strudeln *vi* to whirl, to swirl.

Struktur *f* structure; *(von Stoff etc)* texture.

strukturell *adj* structural.

strukturieren* *vt* to structure.

Strumpf *m* **¨-e** sock; *(Damen~)* stocking. **ein Paar** ¨~**e** a pair of socks/stockings.

Strumpf-: ~**band** *nt* garter; ~**geschäft** *nt* hosiery shop *(Brit) or* store *(US)*; ~**halter** *m* - suspender *(Brit)*, garter *(US)*; ~**hose** *f* tights *pl (Brit)*, panty-hose; **eine** ~**hose** a pair of tights *(Brit) or* panty-hose; ~**waren** *pl* hosiery *sing*.

struppig *adj* unkempt; *Tier* shaggy.

Stube *f* **-n** room. **die gute** ~ the parlour *(Brit) or* parlor *(US) (dated)*.

Stuben-: ~**arrest** *m* confinement to one's room *or (Mil)* quarters; ~**arrest haben** to be confined to one's room/quarters; ~**fliege** *f* (common) housefly; ~**hocker** *m* - *(pej col)* stay-at-home *(col)*; **s**~**rein** *adj Katze, Hund* house-trained; *(hum) Witz* clean.

Stuck *m no pl* stucco.
Stück *nt* **-e** *or (nach Zahlenangaben)* **- (a)** piece; *(von Vieh, Wild)* head; *(von Zucker)* lump; *(Seife)* bar; *(von Land)* plot. **ich nehme fünf ~** I'll take five; **20 ~ Vieh** 20 head of cattle; **sechs ~ von diesen Apfelsinen** six of these oranges; **10 Pfennig das ~** 10 pfennigs each; **am ~** in one piece; **aus einem ~** in one piece; **~ für ~** *(ein Exemplar nach dem andern)* one by one; **ein ~ Garten** a patch of garden; **das ist unser bestes ~** *(hum)* that is our pride and joy.
(b) *(Teil, Abschnitt)* piece, bit; *(von Buch, Rede)* part. **~ für ~** *(einen Teil um den andern)* bit by bit; **in ~e gehen** to be broken to pieces; **etw in ~e schlagen** to smash sth to pieces; **ich komme ein ~ (des Weges) mit** I'll come part of the way with you; **ein ~ spazierengehen** to go for a walk; **das ist ein starkes ~!** *(col)* that's a bit much *(col)*; **große ~e auf jdn halten** to think highly of sb; **aus freien ~en** of one's own free will.
(c) *(Bühnen~)* play; *(Musik~)* piece.
Stückeschreiber *m* dramatist, playwright.
Stück-: ~gut *nt (Rail)* parcel service; **etw als ~gut schicken** to send sth as a parcel; **~lohn** *m* piece(work) rate; **~preis** *m* unit price; **s~weise** *adv* bit by bit; **s~weise verkaufen** to sell individually; **~werk** *nt no pl* incomplete work; **~werk sein/bleiben** to be/remain incomplete; **~zahl** *f* number of pieces.
Student *m* student.
Studenten-: ~ausweis *m* student card; **~bewegung** *f* student movement; **~bude** *f (col)* student digs *pl*; **~futter** *nt* nuts and raisins; **~gemeinde** *f* student religious society; **~schaft** *f* student body; **~verbindung** *f* students' society; **~werk** *nt* student administration; **~wohnheim** *nt* hall of residence.
Studentin *f* student.
studentisch *adj attr* student *attr*.
Studie [ˈʃtuːdiə] *f* study *(über +acc* of*)*.
Studien- [ˈʃtuːdiən-]: **~abschluß** *m* completion of a course of study; **~aufenthalt** *m* study visit; **~beratung** *f* course guidance service; **~fach** *nt* subject; **~fahrt** *f* study trip; *(Sch)* educational trip; **~förderung** *f* study grant; *(an Universität)* university grant; **~gang** *m* course of studies; **~gebühren** *pl* tuition fees *pl*; **~jahr** *nt* academic year; **~jahre** *pl* university/college years *pl*; **~platz** *m* university place; **ein ~platz in Medizin** a place to study medicine; **~rat** *m*, **~rätin** *f* teacher at a secondary school; **~referendar** *m* student teacher; **~reform** *f* university/college reform; **~zeit** *f* **(a)** student days *pl*; **(b)** *(Dauer)* duration of a/one's course of studies.
studieren* **1** *vi* to study. **ich studiere an der Universität Bonn** I am at Bonn University; **wo haben Sie studiert?** what university/college did you go to?; **bei jdm ~e** to study under sb. **2** *vt* to study; *(genau betrachten)* to scrutinize.
Studio *nt* **-s** studio.
Studiobühne *f* studio theatre *(Brit) or* theater *(US)*.
Studium *nt* study; *(Hochschul~)* studies *pl*. **das ~ hat fünf Jahre gedauert** the course of study lasted five years; **während seines ~s** while he is/was *etc* a student.
Stufe *f* **-n (a)** step; *(Mus: Ton~)* degree; *(im Haar)* layer. **(b)** *(fig)* stage; *(Niveau)* level; *(Rang)* grade. **sich mit jdm/etw auf eine ~ stellen** to put oneself on a level with sb/sth.
stufen *vt Schüler, Preise* to grade.
Stufen-: s~förmig 1 *adj (lit)* stepped; *Landschaft* terraced; *(fig)* gradual; **2** *adv (lit)* in steps; *angelegt* in terraces; *(fig)* in stages; **~leiter** *f (fig)* ladder *(gen* to*)*; **s~los** *adj Übergang* direct; *(fig: gleitend)* smooth; *(Tech)* infinitely variable; **~plan** *m* graduated plan *(zu* for*)*; **s~weise 1** *adv* step by step; **2** *adj attr* gradual.
Stufung *f* gradation.
Stuhl *m* **¨-e (a)** chair. **zwischen zwei ¨~en sitzen** *(fig)* to fall between two stools; **das haut einen vom ~** *(col)* it knocks you sideways *(col)*; **jdm den ~ vor die Tür setzen** *(fig)* to kick sb out *(col)*. **(b)** *(Königs~)* throne. **der Heilige ~** the Holy See. **(c)** *(~gang)* bowel movement; *(Kot)* stool.
Stuhl-: ~bein *nt* chair leg; **~gang** *m no pl* bowel movement; **~lehne** *f* back of a chair.
Stuka *m* **-s = Sturzkampfflugzeug.**
Stukkateur [ʃtʊkaˈtøːɐ] *m* plasterer.
Stukkatur *f* stucco, ornamental plasterwork.
stülpen *vt* **den Kragen nach oben ~** to turn up one's collar; **etw auf/über etw** *(acc)* **~** to put sth on/over sth.
stumm *adj* **(a)** *(lit, fig)* dumb; *(schweigend)* mute. **die ~e Kreatur** *(geh)* the dumb creatures *pl*; **~ vor Schmerz** in silent agony; **sie sah mich ~ an** she looked at me without speaking; **~ bleiben** to stay silent. **(b)** *Rolle* non-speaking; *Film, Szene* silent.
Stummel *m* **- (a)** *(Zigaretten~, Kerzen~)* stub; *(von Gliedmaßen, Zahn)* stump. **(b)** *(Stummelschwanz)* dock.
Stummfilm *m* silent film *(Brit) or* movie *(esp US)*.
Stümper(in *f*) *m* **-** *(pej)* amateur; *(Pfuscher)* bungler.
Stümperei *f (pej)* amateur work; *(Pfuscherei)* bungling; *(stümperhafte Arbeit)* botched job.
stümperhaft *adj (pej)* amateurish.
stümpern *vi* **bei einer Arbeit ~** to do a job in an amateur way.
stumpf *adj* **(a)** blunt; *Nase* snub, turned-up. **(b)** *(fig) Haar, Farbe, Mensch* dull. **~ vor sich hin brüten** to sit brooding impassively. **(c)** *(Math) Winkel* obtuse.
Stumpf *m* **¨-e** stump; *(Bleistift~)* stub. **etw mit ~ und Stiel ausrotten** to eradicate sth root and branch.
Stumpf-: ~sinn *m* mindlessness; *(Langweiligkeit)* tedium; **s~sinnig** *adj* mindless; *(langweilig)* tedious.
Stunde *f* **-n (a)** hour. **eine viertel/halbe/dreiviertel ~** a quarter of an hour/half an hour/three-quarters of an hour; **eine halbe ~ Pause** a half-hour break; **~ um ~** hour after hour; **von ~ zu ~** by the hour; **90 Meilen in der ~** 90 miles per hour. **(b)** *(Augenblick, Zeitpunkt)* time. **zu dieser ~** at this/that time; **zu später ~** at a late hour; **bis zur ~** up to the present moment; **eine schwere ~** a time of difficulty; **seine ~ hat geschlagen** *(fig)* his hour has come; **die ~ der Entscheidung** the moment of decision. **(c)** *(Unterricht, Sch)* lesson.
stunden *vt* **jdm etw ~** to give sb time to pay sth.
Stunden-: ~geschwindigkeit *f* speed per hour; **eine ~geschwindigkeit von 90 km** a speed of 90 km per hour; **~glas** *nt* hour-glass; **~kilometer** *pl* kilometres *(Brit) or* kilometers *(US)* per hour *pl*.
stundenlang 1 *adj* lasting several hours. **nach ~em Warten** after hours of waiting. **2** *adv* for hours.
Stunden-: ~lohn m hourly wage; **~lohn bekommen** to be paid by the hour; **~plan** *m (Sch)* timetable; **s~weise** *adv (pro Stunde)* by the hour; *(stündlich)* every hour; **Kellner s~weise gesucht** part-time waiters required; **~zeiger** *m* hour-hand.
stündlich 1 *adj* hourly. **2** *adv* hourly, every hour.
Stunk *m no pl* **~ machen** *(col)* to kick up a stink *(col)*.
stupid(e) *adj (geh)* mindless.
Stups *m* **-e** nudge.
stupsen *vt* to nudge.
Stupsnase *f* snub nose.
stur *adj* stolid; *Nein, Arbeiten* dogged; *(hartnäckig)* stubborn; *(querköpfig)* cussed. **~ weitermachen** *etc* to carry on regardless; **er fuhr ~ geradeaus** he just carried straight on; **sich ~ stellen, auf ~**

stellen *(col)* to dig one's heels in; **ein ~er Bock** *(col)* a pig-headed fellow.

Sturheit *f siehe adj* stolidness; doggedness; stubbornness; cussedness.

Sturm *m* **¨-e (a)** *(lit, fig)* storm. **die Zeichen stehen auf ~** *(fig)* there's a storm brewing; **die Ruhe vor dem ~** the calm before the storm; **ein ~ im Wasserglas** *(fig)* a storm in a teacup; **~ läuten** to keep one's finger on the doorbell; **ein ~ der Begeisterung** a wave of enthusiasm. **(b)** *(Angriff)* attack. **etw im ~ nehmen** *(Mil, fig)* to take sth by storm; **zum ~ blasen** *(Mil, fig)* to sound the attack; **gegen etw ~ laufen** *(fig)* to be up in arms against sth; **ein ~ auf die Banken** a run on the banks.

Sturm-: ~angriff *m (Mil)* assault *(auf +acc* on*)*; **~bö** *f* squall.

stürmen 1 *vi* **(a)** *(Meer)* to rage; *(Sport, Mil)* to attack. **(b)** *aux sein (rennen)* to storm. **2** *vi impers* to be blowing a gale. **3** *vt (Mil, fig)* to storm; *Bank etc* to make a run on.

Stürmer *m* **-** *(Sport)* forward.

Sturm-: ~flut *f* storm tide; **s~frei** *adj (Mil)* unassailable; **eine s~freie Bude** *(col)* a room free from disturbance.

stürmisch *adj* **(a)** *Meer* rough; *Wetter* blustery; *(mit Regen)* stormy. **(b)** *(fig)* tempestuous; *Entwicklung* rapid; *Liebhaber* passionate; *Beifall* tumultuous. **nicht so ~** take it easy.

Sturm-: ~schritt *m (Mil, fig)* double-quick pace; **im ~schritt** at the double; **~warnung** *f* gale warning; **~wind** *m* whirlwind.

Sturz *m* **¨-e** fall; *(in Temperatur, Preis auch)* drop; *(Pol: durch Coup)* overthrow.

Sturzbach *m (lit)* fast-flowing stream.

stürzen 1 *vi aux sein* **(a)** to fall *(auch Pol)*. **ins Wasser ~** to plunge into the water; **vom Pferd ~** to fall off a/one's horse; **er ist schwer gestürzt** he had a bad fall. **(b)** *(rennen)* to dash. **sie kam ins Zimmer gestürzt** she burst into the room. **2** *vt* **(a)** *(werfen)* to fling, to hurl. **jdn ins Unglück ~** to bring disaster upon sb. **(b)** *(kippen)* to turn upside down. **„nicht ~!"** "this side up". **(c)** *(Pol) Regierung etc* to bring down; *(durch Coup)* to overthrow; *König* to dispose. **3** *vr* **sich zu Tode ~** to fall to one's death; *(absichtlich)* to jump to one's death; **sich aus dem Fenster ~** to fling *or* hurl oneself out of the window; **sich auf jdn/etw ~** to pounce on sb/sth; *auf Essen* to fall on sth; **sich in Schulden ~** to plunge into debt; **sich ins Unglück ~** to plunge headlong into disaster; **sich in Unkosten ~** to go to great expense.

Sturz-: ~flug *m* (nose)dive; **~helm** *m* crash helmet; **~kampfflugzeug** *nt* dive bomber.

Stuß *m no pl (col)* nonsense, rubbish *(col)*.

Stute *f* **-n** mare.

Stütze *f* **-n (a)** support; *(Pfeiler)* pillar; *(Buch~)* rest. **(b)** *(Halt)* support; *(Fuß~)* foot-rest. **(c)** *(fig) (Hilfe)* help, aid *(für* to*)*; *(Beistand)* support; *(wichtiger Mensch)* mainstay. **die ~n der Gesellschaft** the pillars of society.

stutzen[1] *vi* to stop short; *(zögern)* to hesitate.

stutzen[2] *vt* to trim; *Flügel, Hecke* to clip; *Schwanz* to dock.

Stutzen *m* **- (a)** *(Gewehr)* carbine. **(b)** *(Rohrstück)* connecting piece; *(Endstück)* nozzle.

stützen 1 *vt (Halt geben)* to support; *Gebäude, Mauer* to shore up. **einen Verdacht auf etw** *(acc)* **~** to base a suspicion on sth; **die Ellbogen auf den Tisch ~** to prop one's elbows on the table. **2** *vr* **sich auf jdn/etw ~** *(lit)* to lean on sb/sth; *(fig)* to count on sb/sth; *(Beweise, Theorie)* to be based on sb/sth.

Stutzer *m* **-** *(pej)* fop, dandy.

stutzig *adj pred* **~ werden** *(argwöhnisch)* to become suspicious; **jdn ~ machen** to make sb suspicious.

Stütz-: ~mauer *f* retaining wall; **~pfeiler** *m* supporting pillar; **~punkt** *m (Mil, fig)* base.

Stützung *f* support.

s.u. = **siehe unten.**

sub|altern *adj (pej) Stellung* subordinate.

Subjekt *nt* **-e (a)** subject. **(b)** *(pej: Mensch)* character *(col)*.

subjektiv *adj* subjective.

Subjektivität [-vɪ'tɛːt] *f* subjectivity.

Sub-: ~kontinent *m* subcontinent; **~kultur** *f* subculture.

sublimieren* *vt (Psych, Chem)* to sublimate.

substantiell [zupstan'tsiɛl] *adj (fig geh: bedeutsam)* fundamental.

Substantiv ['zupstantiːf] *nt* **-e** noun.

Substanz [zup'stants] *f* **(a)** substance. **(b)** *(Fin)* capital assets *pl*. **von der ~ zehren** to live on one's capital.

subtil *adj (geh)* subtle.

subtrahieren* [zuptra'hiːrən] *vti* to subtract.

Subtraktion *f* subtraction.

subtropisch ['zuptroːpɪʃ] *adj* subtropical.

Subvention [zupvɛn'tsioːn] *f* subsidy.

subventionieren* [zupvɛntsio'niːrən] *vt* to subsidize.

subversiv [zupvɛr'ziːf] *adj* subversive. **sich ~ betätigen** to engage in subversive activities.

Such-: ~aktion *f* search operation; **~dienst** *m* missing persons tracing service.

Suche *f no pl* search *(nach* for*)*. **auf die ~ nach jdm/etw gehen** to go in search of sb/sth.

suchen 1 *vt* **(a)** to look for; *(stärker, intensiv)* to search for. **Verkäufer(in) gesucht** sales person wanted; **was suchst du hier?** what are you doing here?; **du hast hier nichts zu ~** you have no business being here; **seinesgleichen ~** to be unparalleled. **(b)** *(streben nach)* to seek. **ein Gespräch ~** to try to have a talk. **2** *vi* to search, to hunt. **nach etw ~** to look for sth; *(stärker)* to search for sth; **nach Worten ~** to search for words; *(sprachlos sein)* to be at a loss for words; **such!** *(zu Hund)* seek!, find!; **gesucht!** wanted *(wegen* for*)*.

Sucher *m* **-** *(Phot)* viewfinder.

Such-: ~mannschaft *f* search party; **~meldung** *f* SOS message; **~scheinwerfer** *m* searchlight.

Sucht *f* **¨-e** addiction *(nach* to*)*; *(fig)* obsession *(nach* with*)*. **eine krankhafte ~ haben, etw zu tun** *(fig)* to be obsessed with doing sth; **an einer ~ leiden** to be an addict.

süchtig *adj* addicted *(nach* to*)*. **~ machen** *(Droge)* to be addictive.

Süchtige(r) *mf decl as adj* addict.

Sud *m* **-e** liquid; *(esp von Fleisch, für Suppe)* stock.

Süd *m no pl (Naut, Met, liter)* south.

Süd- *in cpds* South; **~afrika** *nt* South Africa; **~amerika** *nt* South America.

Sudan [zu'daːn, 'zuːdan] *m* **der ~** the Sudan.

Sudanese *m (wk)* **-n, -n, Sudanesin** *f* Sudanese.

Süd-: s~deutsch *adj* South German; **~deutschland** *nt* South(ern) Germany.

Süden *m no pl* south; *(von Land)* South. **aus dem ~, vom ~ her** from the south; **nach ~ hin** to the south; **weiter im ~** further south.

Süd-: ~europa *nt* Southern Europe; **~früchte** *pl* citrus and tropical fruit(s *pl*); **~küste** *f* south(ern) coast; **~lage** *f* southern aspect; **~länder** *m* **-** southerner; Mediterranean *or* Latin type; **s~ländisch** *adj* southern; *(italienisch, spanisch etc)* Latin.

südlich 1 *adj* **(a)** southern; *Kurs, Richtung* southerly. **(b)** *(mediterran)* Mediterranean, Latin; *Temperament* Latin. **2** *adv* (to the) south. **~ von Wien (gelegen)** (to the) south of Vienna; **es liegt weiter ~** it is further (to the) south. **3** *prep +gen* (to the) south of.

Süd|ost *m (Met, Naut)* south-east.

Süd|osten *m* south-east; *(von Land)* South East. **aus** *or* **von ~** from the south-east; **nach ~** to the south-east.

süd|östlich 1 *adj Gegend* south-eastern; *Wind* south-east(erly). **2** *adv* south-east. **3** *prep +gen* (to the) south-east of.

Süd-: ~pol *m* South Pole; **~polarmeer** *nt* Antarctic Ocean; **~see** *f* South Seas *pl*; **~seite** *f* south side; *(von Berg)* south(ern) face.

südwärts *adv* south(wards).

Südwest *m (Naut, Met)* south-west.

Südwesten *m* south-west; *(von Land)* South West. **aus** *or* **von ~** from the south-west; **nach ~** to the south-west.

südwestlich 1 *adj Gegend* south-western; *Wind* south-west(erly). **2** *adv* (to the) south-west. **3** *prep +gen* (to the) south-west of.

Südwind *m* south wind.

Suezkanal *m* Suez Canal.

Suff *m no pl (col)* **dem ~ verfallen sein** to be on the bottle *(col)*; **etw im ~ sagen** to say sth when one is tight *(col)*.

süffeln *vi (col)* to tipple *(col)*.

süffig *adj* light and sweet.

süffisant *adj* smug, complacent.

Suffix *nt* **-e** suffix.

suggerieren* *vt* to suggest. **jdm etw ~** to influence sb by suggesting sth; **jdm ~, daß ...** to get sb to believe that ...

Suggestion *f* suggestion.

Suggestivfrage *f* suggestive question.

suhlen *vr (lit, fig)* to wallow.

Sühne *f* **-n** *(Rel, geh)* atonement; *(von Schuld)* expiation. **~ leisten** to atone *(für* for*)*.

sühnen 1 *vt Unrecht, Verbrechen* to atone for; *Schuld* to expiate. **2** *vi* to atone.

Sühnetermin *m (Jur)* conciliatory hearing.

Sulfat *nt* sulphate *(Brit)*, sulfate *(US)*.

Sultan *m* **-e** sultan.

Sultanat *nt* sultanate.

Sultanine *f (Rosine)* sultana.

Sülze *f* **-n** brawn.

summarisch *adj (auch Jur)* summary. **etw ~ zusammenfassen** to summarize sth.

Sümmchen *nt dim of* **Summe. ein schönes ~** *(hum)* a tidy sum, a pretty penny *(col)*.

Summe *f* **-n** sum; *(fig)* sum total.

summen 1 *vt Melodie etc* to hum. **2** *vi* to buzz; *(Mensch, Motor)* to hum.

Summer *m* **-** buzzer.

summieren* 1 *vt* to sum up. **2** *vr* to mount up. **das summiert sich** it (all) adds up.

Summton *m* buzz, buzzing sound.

Sumpf *m* **¨e** marsh; *(Morast)* mud; *(in tropischen Ländern)* swamp.

Sumpf-: ~boden *m* marshy ground; **~fieber** *nt* malaria.

sumpfig *adj* marshy, swampy.

Sumpf-: ~land *nt* marshland; *(in tropischen Ländern)* swampland; **~pflanze** *f* marsh plant; **~vogel** *m* wader.

Sund *m* **-e** sound, straits *pl*.

Sünde *f* **-n** sin. **eine ~ begehen** to sin, to commit a sin.

Sünden-: ~bekenntnis *nt* confession of one's sins; *(Gebet)* confession (of sins); **~bock** *m (col)* scapegoat; **~fall** *m (Rel)* Fall; **~register** *nt (fig)* list of sins; **jds ~register** the list of sb's sins.

Sünder(in *f***)** *m* **-s, -** sinner. **armer ~** *(fig)* poor wretch.

sündhaft *adj (lit)* sinful; *(fig col) Preise* wicked. **~ teuer** *(col)* wickedly expensive.

sündig *adj* sinful.

sündigen *vi* to sin *(an +dat* against*)*; *(hum)* to indulge.

Super *nt no pl (Benzin)* four-star (petrol) *(Brit)*, premium *(US)*, super.

super *(col)* **1** *adj inv* super *(col)*. **2** *adv (mit vb)* incredibly well *(col)*.

Super- *in cpds* super-; *(sehr)* ultra-; **~-8-Film** *m* super-8 film.

superklug *adj (iro col)* brilliant. **du bist ein S~er** *(Besserwisser)* you are a (real) know-all *(col)*.

Superlativ *m (Gram, fig)* superlative.

Super-: ~macht *f* superpower; **~mann** *m, pl* **~männer** superman; **~markt** *m* supermarket; **s~modern** *adj (col)* ultramodern; **~star** *m (col)* superstar.

Suppe *f* **-n** soup; *(sämig mit Einlage)* broth; *(klare Brühe)* bouillon; *(fig col: Nebel)* pea-souper *(col)*. **du mußt die ~ auslöffeln, die du dir eingebrockt hast** *(col)* you've made your bed, now you must lie on it *(prov)*; **jdm die ~ versalzen** *(col)* to put a spoke in sb's wheel *(col)*.

Suppen- *in cpds* soup; **~fleisch** *nt* meat for making soup; **~gemüse** *nt* vegetables *pl* for making soup; **~grün** *nt* herbs and vegetables *pl* for making soup; **~huhn** *nt* boiling fowl; **~kasper** *m (col)* poor eater; **~kelle** *f* soup ladle; **~löffel** *m* soup spoon; **~schüssel** *f* tureen; **~tasse** *f* soup bowl; **~teller** *m* soup plate; **~würfel** *m* stock cube; **~würze** *f* soup seasoning.

surfen ['sœrfn] *vi* to surf.

Surfing ['sœrfɪŋ] *nt no pl (Sport)* surfing.

Surrealismus *m no pl* surrealism.

surrealistisch *adj* surrealist(ic).

surren *vi* to hum; *(Insektenflügel)* to whirr.

suspekt [zʊs'pɛkt] *adj* suspicious. **jdm ~ sein** to seem suspicious to sb.

suspendieren* [zʊspɛn'di:rən] *vt* to suspend *(von* from*)*.

süß *adj (lit, fig)* sweet. **gern ~ essen** to have a sweet tooth; **das ~e Leben** the good life; **(mein) S~er/meine S~e** *(col)* my sweetheart.

süßen 1 *vt* to sweeten; *(mit Zucker) Tee, Kaffee* to sugar. **2** *vi* **mit Honig** *etc* **~** to use honey *etc* as a sweetener.

Süßholz *nt* liquorice *(Brit)*, licorice *(US)*. **~ raspeln** *(fig)* to turn on the blarney.

Süßigkeit *f* **(a)** *no pl (lit, fig)* sweetness. **(b) ~en** *pl* sweets *pl (Brit)*, candy *(US)*.

Süßkirsche *f* sweet cherry.

süßlich *adj* sweetish; *(unangenehm süß)*, *(fig) Töne, Miene* sickly sweet; *(kitschig)* mawkish.

Süß-: ~most *m* unfermented fruit juice; **s~sauer** *adj* sweet-and-sour; *Gurken etc* pickled; *(fig: gezwungen) Lächeln* forced; *Miene* artificially friendly; **~speise** *f* sweet dish; **~stoff** *m* sweetener; **~waren** *pl* confectionery *sing*; **~warengeschäft** *nt* sweetshop *(Brit)*, candy store *(US)*; **~wasser** *nt* freshwater; **~wasserfisch** *m* freshwater fish.

SW = **Südwesten** SW.

Swimming-pool ['swɪmɪŋpu:l] *m* **-s** swimming pool.

Symbol *nt* **-e** symbol.

Symbolik *f* symbolism.

symbolisch *adj* symbolic(al) *(für* of*)*.

symbolisieren* *vt* to symbolize.

Symbolismus *m* symbolism.

Symmetrie *f* symmetry.

symmetrisch *adj* symmetric(al).

Sympathie [zʏmpa'ti:] *f (Zuneigung)* liking; *(Mitgefühl, Solidaritätsgefühl)* sympathy. **für jdn/etw ~ haben** to have a liking for/a certain amount of sympathy with sb/sth; **durch seine Unverschämtheit hat er sich** *(dat)* **alle ~(n) verscherzt** he has turned everyone against him with his rudeness.

Sympathie-: ~kundgebung *f* demonstration of support; **~streik** *m* sympathy strike.

Sympathisant(in *f***)** *m* sympathizer.

sympathisch *adj* pleasant, nice. **er ist mir ~** I like him.

sympathisieren* *vi* to sympathize *(mit* with*)*.

Symphonie [zʏmfo'ni:] *f* symphony.

symphonisch *adj* symphonic.

Symposium [zʏm'po:ziʊm] *nt, pl* **Symposien**

[zʏm'po:ziən] symposium.
Symptom *nt* **-e** symptom.
symptomatisch *adj* symptomatic *(für* of*)*.
Synagoge *f* **-n** synagogue.
synchron [zʏn'kro:n] *adj* synchronous.
Synchrongetriebe [zʏn'kro:n-] *nt (Aut)* synchromesh gearbox.
Synchronisation [zʏnkroniza'tsio:n] *f (Film, TV)* dubbing; *(Tech)* synchronization.
synchronisieren* [zʏnkroni'zi:rən] *vt Film* to dub; *(Tech)* to synchronize.
Syndikat *nt (Kartell)* syndicate.
Syndrom *nt* **-e** syndrome.
Synkope [zʏn'ko:pə] *f* **-n** *(Mus)* syncopation.
Synode *f* **-n** *(Eccl)* synod.
Synonym [zyno'ny:m] *nt* **-e** synonym.
synonym [zyno'ny:m] *adj* synonymous.
Synonymwörterbuch *nt* dictionary of synonyms, thesaurus.
syntaktisch *adj* syntactic(al).
Sytnax *f no pl* syntax.
Synthese *f* **-n** synthesis.
Synthetics *pl* synthetics *pl*.
synthetisch *adj* synthetic.
Syphilis ['zy:filɪs] *f no pl* syphilis.
Syrer(in *f*) *m* - Syrian.
Syrien ['zy:riən] *nt* Syria.
syrisch *adj* Syrian.
System [zʏs'te:m] *nt* **-e** system. **etw mit ~ machen** to do sth systematically; **hinter dieser Sache steckt ~** there's method behind it; **~ in etw** *(acc)* **bringen** to get some system into sth; **ein ~ von Straßen/Kanälen** a road/canal system.
System-: **~analyse** *f* systems analysis; **~analytiker** *m* systems analyst.
Systematik *f no pl* system.
systematisch *adj* systematic.
System-: **~kritiker** *m* critic of the system; **s~kritisch** *adj* critical of the system.
Szene *f* **-n** *(Theat, fig)* scene; *(Theat: Bühnenausstattung)* set. **hinter der ~** backstage; *(fig)* behind the scenes; **etw in ~ setzen** *(lit, fig)* to stage sth; **sich in ~ setzen** to play to the gallery; **die ~ beherrschen** *(fig)* to dominate the scene *(gen* in*)*; *(meistern)* to control things; **sich in der ~ auskennen** *(col)* to know the scene; **(jdm) eine ~ machen** to make a scene (in front of sb).
Szenenwechsel *m* scene change.
Szenerie *f (Theat, fig)* scenery.
Szepter ['stseptɐ] *nt* - sceptre *(Brit)*, scepter *(US)*.

T

T, t [teː] *nt* -, - T, t.
t = **Tonne.**
Tabak ['taːbak, 'tabak] *m* **-e** tobacco; *(Schnupf~)* snuff.
Tabak- *in cpds* tobacco; **~händler** *m* tobacconist; **~laden** *m* tobacconist's *(Brit)*, tobacco store *(US)*.
Tabaks-: ~beutel *m* tobacco pouch; **~dose** *f* tobacco tin; **~pfeife** *f* pipe.
Tabak-: ~steuer *f* duty on tobacco; **~waren** *pl* tobacco goods.
tabellarisch 1 *adj* tabular; *Lebenslauf* in tabular form. **2** *adv* in tables/a table.
Tabelle *f* table; *(Diagramm)* chart.
Tabellen-: ~form *f*: **in ~form** in tabular form; as a chart; **~führer** *m (Sport)* league leaders *pl*; **~platz** *m (Sport)* position in the league.
Tablett *nt* **-s** *or* **-e** tray. **jdm etw auf einem silbernen ~ servieren** *(fig: einfach machen)* to hand sb sth on a plate.
Tablette *f* tablet, pill.
Tabu *nt* **-s** taboo.
tabu *adj pred* taboo.
tabuisieren* *vt* to make taboo.
Tabulator *m* tabulator, tab *(col)*.
Tach(e)les *no art (col)* **(mit jdm) ~ reden** to have a talk with sb.
Tacho *m* **-s** *(col)* speedo *(Brit col)*, speedometer.
Tachometer *m or nt* - speedometer.
Tadel *m* - *(Verweis)* reprimand; *(Vorwurf)* reproach; *(Kritik)* criticism; *(geh: Makel)* blemish; *(Sch: Eintrag)* black mark. **ein Leben ohne jeden ~** *(geh)* a spotless life.
tadellos 1 *adj* perfect; *(col)* splendid. **2** *adv* perfectly; *gekleidet* immaculately.
tadeln *vt jdn* to reprimand; *jds Benehmen* to criticize.
tadelnd *adj attr* reproachful.
tadelnswert *adj (geh)* reprehensible.
Tadels|antrag *m (Parl)* motion of censure.
Tafel *f* **-n (a)** *(Platte)* slab; *(Holz~)* panel; *(Wand~)* (black)board; *(Schreib~)* slate; *(Schokoladen~)* bar; *(Gedenk~)* plaque; *(Elec: Schalt~)* control panel, console; *(Anzeige~)* board. **(b)** *(Bildseite)* plate. **(c)** *(form: festlicher Speisetisch)* table; *(Festmahl)* meal; *(mittags)* luncheon *(form)*; *(abends)* dinner. **die ~ aufheben** to officially end the meal.
Tafel-: ~apfel *m* eating apple; **~besteck** *nt* (best) silver; **t~fertig** *adj* ready to serve; **~freuden** *pl* culinary delights *pl*; **~geschirr** *nt* tableware; **~lappen** *m* (blackboard) duster.
tafeln *vi (geh)* to feast.
täfeln *vt Wand* to wainscot; *Decke* to panel.
Tafel-: ~obst *nt* (dessert) fruit; **~öl** *nt* cooking/salad oil; **~salz** *nt* table salt; **~silber** *nt* silver.
Täf(e)lung *f siehe* **täfeln** wainscoting; (wooden) panelling *(Brit) or* paneling *(US)*.
Tafel-: ~wasser *nt* mineral water; **~wein** *m* table wine.
Taft *m* **-e** taffeta.
Tag *m* **-e (a)** day. **an dem/diesem ~** on that/this day; **am ~(e) des/der ...** (on) the day of ...; **am ~** during the day; **alle ~e** *(col)*, **jeden ~** every day; **am vorigen ~(e)** the day before; **auf den ~ (genau)** to the day; **auf ein paar ~e** for a few days; **auf seine alten ~e** at his age; **den ganzen ~ (lang)** *(lit, fig)* all day long; **eines ~es** one day; **sich** *(dat)* **einen schönen/faulen ~ machen** to have a nice/lazy day; **~ für ~** day by day; **von ~ zu ~** from day to day; **welcher ~ ist heute?** what day is it today?; **guten ~!** hello; *(esp bei Vorstellung)* how do you do; *(vormittags auch)* good morning; *(nachmittags auch)* good afternoon; **~!** *(col)* hello, hi *(col)*; **zweimal am ~(e)** *or* **pro ~** twice a day; **von einem ~ auf den anderen** overnight; **seinen guten/schlechten ~ haben** to have a good/bad day; **in den ~ hinein leben** to take each day as it comes; **~ und Nacht** night and day; **bei ~(e)** *ankommen* while it's light; *arbeiten, reisen* during the day; **es wird schon ~** it's getting light already; **an den ~ kommen** *(fig)* to come to light; **er legte großes Interesse an den ~** he showed great interest.
(b) *(col: Menstruation)* **ihre ~e** her period.
(c) *(Min)* **über/unter ~e arbeiten** to work above/below ground.
tag|aus *adv* **~, tagein** day in, day out.
Tagdienst *m* day duty.
Tage-: ~bau *m* **-e** *(Min)* open-cast mining; **~blatt** *nt* daily (news)paper; **~buch** *nt* diary; **(über etw** *acc*) **~buch führen** to keep a diary (of sth); **~geld** *nt* daily allowance; **t~lang** *adj* lasting for days; **t~lange Regenfälle** several days' rain; **er war t~lang verschwunden** he disappeared for days; **~löhner(in** *f*) *m* - day labourer *(Brit)*, day laborer *(US)*.
tagen 1 *vi impers (geh)* **es tagt** day is breaking. **2** *vi (konferieren)* to sit.
Tages-: ~anbruch *m* daybreak, dawn; **~arbeit** *f* day's work; **~ausflug** *m* day trip; **~creme** *f* day cream; **~decke** *f* bedspread; **~fragen** *pl* issues of the day; **~gespräch** *nt* talk of the town; **~karte** *f* **(a)** *(Speisekarte)* menu of the day; **(b)** *(Fahr-, Eintrittskarte)* day ticket; **~kasse** *f* **(a)** *(Theat)* box-office; **(b)** *(Econ)* day's takings *pl*; **~klinik** *f* day clinic; **~lauf** *m* day; **~leistung** *f* daily workload; *(von Maschine, Schriftsteller etc)* daily output; **~licht** *nt no pl* daylight; **ans ~licht kommen** *(fig)* to come to light; **~lohn** *m* day's wages; **~marsch** *m* day's march; **~mutter** *f* child minder; **~nachrichten** *pl* (today's) news; **~ordnung** *f* agenda; **etw auf die ~ordnung setzen** to put sth on the agenda; **auf der ~ordnung stehen** to be on the agenda; **zur ~ordnung übergehen** to proceed to the agenda; *(wie üblich weitermachen)* to carry on as usual; **an der ~ordnung sein** *(fig)* to be the order of the day; **~ordnungspunkt** *m* item on the agenda; **~presse** *f* daily newspapers; **~reise** *f* **(a)** *(Entfernung)* day's journey; **(b)** *(Ausflug)* day trip; **~satz** *m* daily rate; **~zeit** *f* time (of day); **zu jeder ~- und Nachtzeit** at all hours of the day and night; **~zeitung** *f* daily (paper).
Tage-: t~weise *adv* on a daily basis; **~werk** *nt* *(geh)* day's work.
taghell *adj* (as) bright as day. **es war schon ~** it was already broad daylight.
täglich 1 *adj* daily; *(attr: gewöhnlich)* everyday. **das reicht gerade fürs ~e Leben** it's just about enough to get by on; **sein ~(es) Brot verdienen** to earn a living. **2** *adv* every day. **einmal ~** once a day.

tags *adv* ~ **zuvor** the day before, the previous day; ~ **darauf** *or* **danach** the next *or* following day.

Tagschicht *f* day shift. ~ **haben** to be on day shift.

tags|über *adv* during the day.

Tag-: **t~täglich 1** *adj* daily; **2** *adv* every (single) day; **~traum** *m* daydream; **~undnachtgleiche** *f* equinox.

Tagung *f* conference; *(von Ausschuß)* sitting, session.

Tagungsort *m* venue (of a/the conference).

Taifun *m* **-e** typhoon.

Taille ['taljə] *f* **-n** waist. **auf seine ~ achten** to watch one's waistline.

Takel *nt* **-** *(Naut)* tackle.

Takelage [takə'la:ʒə] *f* **-n** *(Naut)* rigging, tackle.

Takt *m* **-e (a)** *(Mus)* bar; *(Phon, Poet)* foot. **(b)** *(Rhythmus)* time. **den ~ schlagen** to beat time; **gegen den ~** out of time; **den ~ angeben** to give the beat. **(c)** *(Aut)* stroke. **(d)** *(Ind)* phase. **(e)** *no pl (Taktgefühl)* tact.

Taktgefühl *nt* **(a)** sense of tact. **(b)** *(Mus)* sense of rhythm.

taktieren* *vi* to manoeuvre *(Brit)*, to maneuver *(US)*. **so kann man nicht ~** you can't use those tactics.

Taktik *f* tactics *pl.* **eine ~** tactics *pl.*

Taktiker(in *f*) *m* **-** tactician.

taktisch *adj* tactical. **~ klug vorgehen** to use good tactics.

Takt-: **t~los** *adj* tactless; **~losigkeit** *f* tactlessness; **~stock** *m* baton; **~strich** *m (Mus)* bar (line); **t~voll** *adj* tactful.

Tal *nt* **-̈er** valley.

tal|ab(wärts) *adv* down into the valley.

Talar *m* **-e** *(Univ)* gown; *(Jur, Eccl)* robe(s).

tal|aufwärts *adv* up the valley.

Tal-: **~brücke** *f* bridge over a valley; **~enge** *f* gorge.

Talent *nt* **-e (a)** *(Begabung)* talent *(zu* for*)*. **ein großes ~ haben** to be very talented; **sie hat viel ~ zum Singen/zur Schauspielerin** she has a great talent for singing/acting. **(b)** *(Mensch)* talented person. **junge ~e** young talent.

talentiert *adj* talented, gifted.

Talfahrt *f* descent; *(fig)* decline.

Talg *m* **-e** tallow; *(Cook)* suet; *(Haut~)* sebum.

Talisman *m* **-e** talisman, (lucky) charm; *(Maskottchen)* mascot.

Talk *m no pl* talc(um).

Talkessel *m* basin, hollow.

Talkpuder *m or nt* talcum powder.

Tal-: **~senke** *f* hollow (of a/the valley); **~sohle** *f* bottom of a/the valley; *(fig)* rock bottom; **in der ~sohle** *(fig)* at rock bottom; **~sperre** *f* dam; **t~wärts** *adv* down to the valley.

Tambour ['tambu:ɐ] *m* **-e** drummer.

Tamburin *nt* **-e** tambourine.

Tampon [tam'pɔ:n] *m* **-s** tampon.

tamponieren* *vt* to plug, to tampon.

Tamtam *nt* **-s (a)** *(Mus)* tomtom. **(b)** *(col: Wirbel)* fuss, ballyhoo *(col)*; *(Lärm)* din *(col)*.

Tand *m no pl (liter)* knick-knacks *pl*; *(fig)* dross.

tändeln *vi (liter) (flirten)* to flirt; *(herumspielen)* to play around; *(trödeln)* to dilly-dally.

Tandem *nt* **-s** tandem.

Tang *m* **-e** seaweed.

Tangens ['taŋgɛns] *m* **-** *(Math)* tan(gent).

Tangente [taŋ'gɛntə] *f* **-n** *(Math)* tangent; *(Straße)* ring-road, expressway.

tangieren* [taŋ'gi:rən] *vt Problem* to touch on; *(betreffen)* to affect; *(col: kümmern)* to bother.

Tango ['taŋgo] *m* **-s** tango.

Tank *m* **-s** *or* **-e** tank.

tanken *vti* **(a)** *(bei Auto)* to fill up; *(bei Rennwagen, Flugzeug)* to refuel. **wo kann man hier ~?** where can I get petrol *(Brit) or* gas *(US)* around here?; **wir hielten an, um zu ~** we stopped for petrol/gas; **was tankst du? — ich tanke nur Super** what grade (of petrol/gas) do you use? — I only use 4 star; **ich tanke nur für 10 Mark** I'll just put 10 marks' worth in. **(b)** *(col) frische Luft, neue Kräfte* to get. **er hat ganz schön getankt** he's had a few.

Tanker *m* **-** *(Naut)* tanker.

Tank-: **~fahrzeug** *nt (Aut)* tanker; **~lager** *nt* oil *or* petrol depot; **~laster** *m* tanker; **~säule** *f* petrol pump *(Brit)*, gas(oline) pump *(US)*; **~schiff** *nt* tanker; **~stelle** *f* petrol *(Brit) or* gas(oline) *(US)* station; **~uhr** *f* fuel gauge; **~verschluß** *m* petrol *(Brit) or* gas *(US)* cap; **~wagen** *m* tanker; *(Rail)* tank wagon *or* car; **~wart** *m* petrol pump *(Brit) or* gas station *(US)* attendant.

Tanne *f* **-n** fir, pine; *(Holz)* pine.

Tannen-: **~baum** *m* fir-tree, pine-tree; *(Weihnachtsbaum)* Christmas tree; **~zapfen** *m* fir cone, pine cone.

Tante *f* **-n (a)** *(Verwandte)* aunt, aunty. **(b)** *(pej col: Frau)* old girl *(col)*. **(c)** *(baby-talk: Frau)* lady.

Tante-Emma-Laden *m (col)* corner shop.

tantenhaft *adj* **(a)** *(col)* old-maidish. **(b)** *(pej: betulich)* twee.

Tantieme [tã'tie:mə] *f* **-n** fee; *(für Künstler)* royalty.

Tanz *m* **-̈e** dance. **dort ist heute abend ~** there's a dance there this evening; **jdn zum ~ auffordern** to ask sb to dance.

Tanz-: **~abend** *m* dance; **~bar** *f* bar with dancing; **~bär** *m* dancing bear; **~bein** *nt*: **das ~bein schwingen** *(hum)* to trip the light fantastic *(hum)*; **~boden** *m (~fläche)* dance floor; *(Saal)* dance hall; **~café** *nt* restaurant with dancing.

tänzeln *vi aux haben or (bei Richtungsangabe) sein* to mince; *(Boxer)* to skip; *(Pferd)* to step delicately.

tanzen *vti aux haben or (bei Richtungsangabe) sein* to dance; *(Boot auch)* to bob; *(Kreisel)* to spin; *(hüpfen)* to hop. **~ gehen** to go dancing.

Tänzer(in *f*) *m* **-** dancer; *(Partner)* (dancing) partner.

tänzerisch *adj* dance-like. **~ veranlagt sein** to have a talent for dancing; **sein ~es Können** his dancing ability.

Tanz-: **~fläche** *f* dance floor; **~gruppe** *f* dance group; **~kapelle** *f* dance band; **~kurs(us)** *m* dancing course; **~lehrer** *m* dancing teacher; **~lokal** *nt* café with dancing; **~musik** *f* dance music; **~saal** *m* dance hall; *(in Hotel etc)* ballroom; **~schritt** *m* (dance) step; **~schule** *f* dancing school; **~stunde** *f* dancing class; **~turnier** *nt* dancing competition.

Tapet *nt*: **etw aufs ~ bringen** *(col)* to bring sth up.

Tapete *f* **-n** wallpaper *no pl.* **die ~n wechseln** *(fig col)* to have a change of surroundings.

Tapeten-: **~bahn** *f* strip of wallpaper; **~rolle** *f* roll of wallpaper; **~wechsel** *m (col)* change of surroundings.

Tapezierer *m* **-** paperhanger, decorator.

tapezieren* *vt* to (wall)paper. **neu ~** to repaper.

tapfer *adj* brave, courageous; *(wacker)* steadfast. **sich ~ schlagen** *(col)* to put on a brave show.

Tapferkeit *f siehe adj* bravery, courage; steadfastness.

tappen *vi* **(a)** *aux sein (tapsen)* to go/come falteringly; *(Bär)* to lumber; *(dial: gehen)* to wander. **er ist in eine Pfütze getappt** *(col)* he walked smack into a puddle *(col)*. **(b)** *(tasten)* **nach etw ~** to grope for sth; **im dunkeln ~** *(fig)* to grope in the dark.

tapsen *vi aux sein (col) (Kind)* to toddle; *(Bär)* to lumber; *(Kleintier)* to waddle.

tapsig *adj (col)* awkward, clumsy.

Tara *f, pl* **Taren** *(Comm)* tare.

Tarantel *f* **-n** tarantula. **wie von der ~ gestochen** as if stung by a bee.

Tarif *m* **-e** rate; *(Wasser~, Gas~, Verkehrs~ etc auch)* tariff. **die Gewerkschaft hat die ~e gekün-**

digt the union has put in a new wage claim; **nach/über/unter ~ bezahlen** to pay according to/above/below the (union) rate(s).
Tarif-: ~autonomie *f* free collective bargaining; **~gruppe** *f* grade; **~kommission** *f* joint working party on pay.
tariflich *adj* agreed, union. **der ~e Mindestlohn** the agreed minimum wage.
Tarif-: ~lohn *m* standard wage; **~partner** m **die ~partner** union and management; **~verhandlungen** *pl* pay negotiations *pl*; **~vertrag** *m* pay agreement.
tarnen 1 *vti* to camouflage; *(fig) Absichten, Identität etc* to disguise. **2** *vr (Tier)* to camouflage itself; *(Mensch)* to disguise oneself.
Tarnfarbe *f* camouflage colour *(Brit) or* color *(US)*/paint.
Tarnung *f* camouflage; *(von Agent etc)* disguise.
Tarock *m or nt* **-s** tarot.
Tasche *f* **-n (a)** *(Hand~)* bag *(Brit)*, purse *(US)*; *(Reise~, Schul~ etc)* bag; *(Akten~)* (brief)case; *(Backen~)* pouch. **(b)** *(bei Kleidungsstücken)* pocket. **in die eigene ~ wirtschaften** to line one's own pockets; **etw in der ~ haben** *(col)* to have sth in the bag *(col)*; **jdm das Geld aus der ~ ziehen** to get sb to part with his money; **etw aus der eigenen ~ bezahlen** to pay for sth out of one's own pocket; **jdm auf der ~ liegen** *(col)* to live off sb; **die Hände in die ~n stecken** *(lit)* to put one's hands in one's pockets; *(fig)* to stand idly by; **jdn in die ~ stecken** *(col)* to put sb in the shade *(col)*.
Taschen-: ~ausgabe *f* pocket edition; **~buch** *nt* paperback (book); **~dieb** *m* pickpocket; **~diebstahl** *m* pickpocketing; **~format** *nt* pocket size; **~geld** *nt* pocket-money; **~lampe** *f* torch *(Brit)*, flashlight *(US)*; **~messer** *nt* pocket-knife, penknife; **~rechner** *m* pocket calculator; **~schirm** *m* collapsible umbrella; **~spieler** *m* conjurer; **~spielertrick** *m (fig)* sleight of hand *no indef art, no pl*; **~tuch** *nt* handkerchief; *(aus Papier)* tissue; **~uhr** *f* pocket watch.
Tasse *f* **-n** cup; *(Suppen~)* bowl. **eine ~ Kaffee** a cup of coffee; **er hat nicht alle ~n im Schrank** *(col)* he's not all there.
Tastatur *f* keyboard.
Taste *f* **-n** key; *(Knopf an Gerät auch)* button. **auf die ~n hauen** *(col)* to hammer away at the keyboard.
tasten 1 *vi* to feel. **nach etw ~** *(lit, fig)* to feel *or* grope for sth; **~de Schritte** *(lit, fig)* tentative steps. **2** *vr* to feel *or* grope one's way. **3** *vti (drücken)* to press; *Telex, (Typ: setzen)* to key.
Tasten-: ~instrument *nt (Mus)* keyboard instrument; **~telefon** *nt* pushbutton telephone.
Tast-: ~organ *nt* organ of touch; **~sinn** *m* sense of touch.
Tat *f* **-en** *(das Handeln)* action; *(Einzel~auch)* act; *(Helden~, Un~)* deed; *(Leistung)* feat; *(Verbrechen)* crime. **eine gute/böse ~** a good/wicked deed; **etw in die ~ umsetzen** to put sth into action; **zur ~ schreiten** to act; **in der ~** indeed; *(wider Erwarten)* actually.
tat *pret of* **tun.**
Tatbestand *m (Jur)* facts (of the case) *pl*.
Taten-: ~drang *m* energy; **t~los** *adj* idle; **t~los herumstehen** to stand idly by; **wir mußten t~los zusehen** we could only stand and watch.
Täter(in *f***)** *m* **-** culprit; *(Jur)* perpetrator *(form)*. **als ~ verdächtigt werden** to be a suspect; **wer war der ~?** who did it?
Täterschaft *f* guilt. **die ~ leugnen/zugeben** to deny/admit one's guilt.
tätig *adj* **(a)** *attr* active. **~e Nächstenliebe** practical charity. **(b)** *(arbeitend)* **~ sein** to work; **er ist im Bankwesen ~** he's in banking.
tätigen *vt (Comm)* to conclude; *(geh) Einkäufe* to carry out; *(geh) Anruf* to make.
Tätigkeit *f* activity; *(Beschäftigung)* occupation; *(Arbeit)* work; *(Beruf)* job. **in/außer ~ setzen** *Maschine* to start up/to stop.
Tätigkeits-: ~bereich *m* field of activity; **~bericht** *m* progress report.
Tat-: ~kraft *f no pl* energy, drive; **t~kräftig** *adj* energetic; *Hilfe* active.
tätlich *adj* violent. **gegen jdn ~ werden** to assault sb.
Tat|ort *m* scene of the crime.
tätowieren* *vt* to tattoo.
Tätowierung *f* tattooing; *(Darstellung)* tattoo.
Tatsache *f* fact. **~?** *(col)* really?, no!; **das ist ~** *(col)* that's a fact; **jdn vor vollendete ~n stellen** to present sb with a fait accompli.
Tatsachenbericht *m* documentary (report).
tatsächlich 1 *adj attr* real, actual. **2** *adv* actually, really, in fact. **willst du das ~ tun?** are you really *or* actually going to do it?; **da kommt er! — ~!** he's coming! — so he is!
tätscheln *vt* to pat.
Tattergreis *m (pej col)* old dodderer *(pej)*.
tatt(e)rig *adj (col) Mensch* doddery; *Hände, Schriftzüge* shaky.
Tat-: ~verdacht *m* suspicion *(of having committed a crime)*; **unter ~verdacht stehen** to be under suspicion; **t~verdächtig** *adj* suspected.
Tatze *f* **-n** *(lit, fig)* paw.
Tau[1] *m no pl* dew.
Tau[2] *nt* **-e** *(Seil)* rope; *(Naut auch)* hawser.
taub *adj* deaf; *Glieder* numb; *Ähre* unfruitful; *Nuß* empty. **sich ~ stellen** to pretend not to hear; **gegen** *or* **für etw ~ sein** *(fig)* to be deaf to sth.
Taube *f* **-n (a)** *(Zool)* pigeon; *(Turtel~, fig)* dove.
Taubenschlag *m* dovecot(e). **hier geht es zu wie im ~** *(fig)* it's like Waterloo Station here *(Brit col)*, it's like Grand Central Station here *(US col)*.
Taube(r) *mf decl as adj* deaf person. **die ~n** the deaf.
Taubheit *f* deafness; *(von Körperteil)* numbness.
Taub-: t~stumm *adj* deaf and dumb, deaf-mute *attr*; **~stumme(r)** *mf* deaf-mute.
tauchen 1 *vi aux haben or sein* to dive *(nach* for*)*; *(als Sport auch)* to skin-dive; *(kurz ~)* to duck under; *(unter Wasser sein)* to stay under water; *(U-Boot auch)* to submerge; *(aux sein: auf ~)* to emerge *(aus* out of, from*)*. **2** *vt (kurz ~)* to dip; *Menschen, Kopf* to duck; *(ein~)* to immerse.
Taucher(in *f***)** *m* **-** diver.
Taucher-: ~anzug *m* diving suit; **~brille** *f* diving goggles *pl*; **~glocke** *f* diving bell.
Tauch-: ~sieder *m* **-** immersion coil *(for boiling water)*; **~sport** *m* (skin-)diving; **~station** *f* **auf ~station gehen** *(U-Boot)* to dive; *(fig: sich verstecken)* to make oneself scarce; **auf ~station sein** *(U-Boot)* to be submerged.
tauen *vti (vi: aux haben or sein) (Schnee)* to melt, to thaw. **es taut** it is thawing.
Taufbecken *nt* font.
Taufe *f* **-n** baptism; *(Kindes~ auch)* christening; *(Schiffs~)* launching (ceremony).
taufen *vt* to baptize; *(nennen) Kind, Schiff etc* to christen. **sich ~ lassen** to be baptized; **jdn auf den Namen Rufus ~** to christen sb Rufus.
Täufer *m* **-: Johannes der ~** John the Baptist.
Tauf-: ~pate *m* godfather; **~patin** *f* godmother; **~schein** *m* certificate of baptism; **~zeuge** *m* godparent.
taugen *vi* **(a)** *(geeignet sein)* to be suitable *(zu, für* for*)*. **er taugt zu gar nichts** he is useless; **er taugt nicht zum Arzt** he wouldn't make a good doctor. **(b)** *(wert sein)* **etwas/nichts ~** to be all right/to be no good.
Taugenichts *m* **-e** good-for-nothing.
tauglich *adj (zu* for*)* suitable; *(Mil)* fit.
Tauglichkeit *f* suitability; *(Mil)* fitness (for service).

Taumel *m no pl (geh: Schwindel)* (attack of) dizziness; *(liter: Rausch)* frenzy. **wie im ~** in a daze.
taumeln *vi aux sein* to stagger; *(zur Seite)* to sway.
Tausch *m* **-e** exchange, swap; *(~handel)* barter. **im ~ gegen etw** in exchange for sth; **einen guten/schlechten ~ machen** to get a good/bad deal.
tauschen 1 *vt (gegen* for*)* to exchange, to swap; *Güter* to barter; *(aus~) Briefmarken etc* to swap; *Geld* to change *(in+acc* into*)*. **2** *vi* to swap; *(in Handel)* to barter. **ich möchte nicht mit ihm ~** I wouldn't like to be in his place.
täuschen 1 *vt* to deceive; *Vertrauen* to betray. **wenn mich mein Gedächtnis nicht täuscht** if my memory serves me right; **wenn mich nicht alles täuscht** unless I'm completely wrong. **2** *vr* to be wrong *or* mistaken *(in+dat, über+acc* about*)*. **3** *vi (irreführen: Aussehen etc)* to be deceptive.
täuschend 1 *adj Nachahmung* remarkable; *Ähnlichkeit auch* striking. **2** *adv* **sich** *(dat)* **~ ähnlich sehen/sein** to look/be remarkably alike *or* almost identical.
Tauschgeschäft *nt* exchange; *(Handel)* barter.
Täuschung *f* **(a)** *(das Täuschen)* deception. **(b)** *(Irrtum)* mistake, error; *(falsche Wahrnehmung)* illusion; *(Selbst~)* delusion. **er gab sich einer ~** *(dat)* **hin** he was deluding himself.
Täuschungsmanöver *nt (Sport)* feint; *(col)* ploy.
tausend *num* a *or* one thousand; *siehe* **hundert**.
Tausender *m* **- (a)** *(Zahl)* **ein ~** a figure in the thousands; **die ~** the thousands. **(b)** *(Geldschein)* thousand.
tausenderlei *adj inv* a thousand kinds of.
Tausend-: ~füßler *m* **-** centipede; **~jahrfeier** *f* millenary; **t~jährig** *adj attr* thousand year old; *(t~ Jahre lang)* thousand year (long); **t~mal** *adv* a thousand times; **~sas(s)a** *m* **-s** *(col)* hell of a guy *(col)*.
tausendste(r, s) *adj* thousandth.
Tau-: ~werk *nt no pl (Naut)* rigging; **~wetter** *nt* thaw; *(fig auch)* relaxation; **es ist ~wetter** it is thawing; **~ziehen** *nt no pl (lit, fig)* tug-of-war.
Taxi *nt* **-s** taxi, cab. **~ fahren** to drive a taxi; *(als Fahrgast)* to go by taxi.
Taxi-: ~fahrer *m* taxi *or* cab driver, cabby *(col)*; **~fahrt** *f* taxi ride; **~stand** *m* taxi rank *(Brit) or* stand *(US)*.
Tb [teːˈbeː] **-s = Tuberkulose** TB.
Teak(holz) [ˈtiːk-] *nt* teak. **ein Tisch aus ~** a teak table.
Team|arbeit [ˈtiːm-] *f* teamwork.
Technik *f* **(a)** *(no pl: Technologie)* technology. **(b)** *(Arbeitsweise, Verfahren)* technique. **(c)** *(no pl: Funktionsweise)* mechanics *pl*.
Techniker(in *f***)** *m* **-** engineer; *(Beleuchtungs~, Labor~, fig: Fußballspieler, Künstler)* technician.
Technikum *nt, pl* **Technika** college of technology.
technisch *adj* technical; *(technologisch)* technological. **er ist ~ begabt** he is technically minded; **T~e Hochschule** polytechnic.
Technokrat *m (wk)* **-en, -en** technocrat.
Technologie *f* technology.
technologisch *adj* technological.
Techtelmechtel *nt* **-** *(col)* affair, carry-on *(col)*.
Teddy [ˈtɛdi] *m* **-s** *(auch* **~bär***)* teddy (bear).
Tee *m* **-s** tea. **einen im ~ haben** *(col)* to be tipsy *(col)*.
Tee-: ~beutel *m* tea bag; **~gebäck** *nt no pl* sweet biscuits *pl*; **~glas** *nt* tea-glass; **~kanne** *f* teapot; **~kessel** *m* kettle; **~licht** *nt* night-light; **~löffel** *m* teaspoon; *(Menge)* teaspoonful; **~mischung** *f* blend of tea.
Teen [tiːn] *m* **-s** *(col)* teenager.
Teepause *f* tea break.
Teer *m* **-e** tar.
Teerdecke *f* tarred (road) surface.
teeren *vt* to tar.
Teer-: ~gehalt *m* tar content; **t~haltig** *adj* **eine wenig/stark t~haltige Zigarette** a low/high tar cigarette; **~pappe** *f* roofing felt.
Tee-: ~service *nt* tea-set; **~sieb** *nt* tea-strainer; **~stube** *f* tea-room; **~tasse** *f* teacup.
Teich *m* **-e** pond.
Teig *m* **-e** dough; *(Blätter~ etc)* pastry.
teigig *adj* doughy.
Teigwaren *pl (Nudeln)* pasta *sing*.
Teil[1] *m* **-e (a)** part. **zum ~** partly; **zum größten ~** for the most part, mostly; **er hat die Bücher darüber zum großen/größten ~ gelesen** he has read many/most of the books about that. **(b)** *(auch nt: An~)* share. **zu gleichen ~en erben** to get an equal share of an inheritance; **er hat seinen ~ dazu beigetragen** he did his bit *or* share; **sich** *(dat)* **sein(en) ~ denken** *(col)* to draw one's own conclusions. **(c)** *(auch nt)* **ich für mein(en) ~ ...** I, for my part ...
Teil[2] *nt* **-e (a)** part; *(Bestand~ auch)* component; *(Ersatz~)* spare, (spare) part. **etw in seine ~e zerlegen** to take sth apart *or* to pieces. **(b) = Teil**[1] **(b,c)**.
Teil-: t~bar *adj* divisible; **~bereich** *m* part; **~betrag** *m* part (of an amount); *(auf Rechnung)* item; *(Rate)* instalment *(Brit)*, installment *(US)*; *(Zwischensumme)* subtotal.
Teilchen *nt* particle; *(dial: Gebäckstück)* cake.
teilen 1 *vt* **(a)** to divide *(durch* by*)*. **geteilter Meinung sein** to have different opinions; **darüber sind die Meinungen geteilt** opinions differ on that. **(b)** *(auf~)* to share (out) *(unter +dat* amongst). **etw mit jdm ~** to share sth with sb. **(c)** *(an etw teilhaben)* to share. **sie haben Freud und Leid miteinander geteilt** they shared the rough and the smooth; **sie teilten unser Schicksal** they shared the same fate as us. **2** *vr* **(a)** *(in Gruppen)* to split up. **(b)** *(Straße, Fluß)* to fork, to divide. **(c) sich** *(dat)* **etw ~** to share sth; **teilt euch das!** share that between you. **3** *vi* to share. **er teilt nicht gern** he doesn't like sharing.
Teil-: ~erfolg *m* partial success; **~gebiet** *nt (Bereich)* branch; *(räumlich)* area; **t~haben** *vi sep irreg (geh)* **an etw** *(dat)* **t~haben** to have a part in sth; **~haber(in** *f***)** *m* **-** *(Comm)* partner.
Teilkaskoversicherung *f insurance covering more than third party liability but giving less than fully comprehensive coverage.*
Teilnahme *f no pl* **(a)** *(Anwesenheit)* attendance *(an+dat* at*)*; *(Beteiligung)* participation *(an +dat* in*)*. **(b)** *(Interesse)* interest *(an+dat* in*)*; *(Mitgefühl)* sympathy. **jdm seine herzliche ~ aussprechen** to offer sb one's heartfelt condolences.
teilnahmeberechtigt *adj* eligible.
teilnahms-: ~los *adj (gleichgültig)* indifferent, apathetic; *(stumm leidend)* listless; **~voll** *adj* compassionate, sympathetic.
teilnehmen *vi sep irreg* **an etw** *(dat)* **~** *(sich beteiligen)* to take part in sth; **an einem Ausflug ~** to go on an outing; **am Unterricht ~** to attend school.
Teilnehmer(in *f***)** *m* **-** participant; *(bei Wettbewerb)* competitor, contestant; *(Kurs~)* student.
teils *adv* partly. **bist du zufrieden? — ~, ~** are you happy? — sort of *(col)*.
Teil-: ~strecke *f* stage; *(von Straße)* stretch; *(bei Bus etc)* fare-stage; **~stück** *nt* part.
Teilung *f* division.
teilweise 1 *adv* partly; *(manchmal)* sometimes. **~ sind sie interessiert** to a certain extent they are interested. **2** *adj attr* partial.
Teil-: ~zahlung *f* hire-purchase *(Brit)*, installment plan *(US)*; *(Rate)* instalment *(Brit)*, installment *(US)*; **auf ~zahlung** on hire purchase/the installment plan; **~zeitarbeit** *f* part-time job/work.
Teint [tɛ̃ː] *m* **-s** complexion.
Tel. = Telefon.

Telebrief *m* facsimile, fax.
Telefon *nt* **-e** (tele)phone. **am** ~ on the phone; **ans** ~ **gehen** to answer the phone.
Telefon- *in cpds* (tele)phone; ~**anruf** *m* (tele)phone call; ~**apparat** *m* telephone.
Telefonat *nt* (tele)phone call.
Telefon-: ~**buch** *nt* (tele)phone book; ~**gebühr** *f* call charge; *(Grundgebühr)* telephone rental; ~**gespräch** *nt* (tele)phone call.
telefonieren* *vi* to make a (tele)phone call. **er telefoniert gerade** he's on the phone; **bei jdm** ~ to use sb's phone; **mit jdm** ~ to speak to sb on the phone.
telefonisch *adj* ~**e Auskunft/Beratung** telephone information/advice service; **eine** ~**e Mitteilung** a (tele)phone message; **jdm etw** ~ **mitteilen** to tell sb sth over the phone; **etw** ~ **bestellen** to order sth on the phone *or* by phone; **ich bin** ~ **zu erreichen** I can be contacted by phone.
Telefonist(in *f***)** *m* telephone operator; *(in Betrieb auch)* switchboard operator.
Telefon-: ~**leitung** *f* telephone line; ~**netz** *nt* telephone network; ~**nummer** *f* (tele)phone number; ~**rechnung** *f* (tele)phone bill; ~**verbindung** *f* telephone line; *(zwischen Orten)* telephone link; ~**zelle** *f* (tele)phone box *(Brit)* *or* booth; ~**zentrale** *f* (telephone) switchboard.
Telegraf *m (wk)* **-en, -en** telegraph.
Telegrafie *f* telegraphy.
telegrafieren* *vti* to telegram, to cable.
telegrafisch *adj* telegraphic. **jdm** ~ **Geld überweisen** to wire sb money.
Telegramm *nt* **-e** telegram.
Tele- ['tele-]: ~**kolleg** *nt* ≃ Open University *(Brit)*; ~**objektiv** *nt (Phot)* telephoto lens; ~**pathie** *f* telepathy; ~**pathisch** *adj* telepathic.
Teleskop *nt* **-e** telescope.
Telex *nt* **-e** telex.
Teller *m* **-** plate. **ein** ~ **Suppe** a plate of soup.
Tellerwäscher *m* dishwasher.
Tempel *m* **-** temple *(auch fig)*.
Temperament *nt* **(a)** *(Wesensart)* temperament. **ein hitziges** ~ **haben** to be hot-tempered. **(b)** *no pl (Lebhaftigkeit)* vitality, vivacity. **viel/kein** ~ **haben** to be very/not to be lively; **sein** ~ **ist mit ihm durchgegangen** he went over the top.
temperament-: ~**los** *adj* lifeless; ~**voll** *adj* vivacious, lively; *Aufführung auch* spirited.
Temperatur *f* temperature. **erhöhte** ~ **haben** to have a temperature; **die** ~**en sind angestiegen/gesunken** the temperature has risen/fallen.
Temperatur-: ~**anstieg** *m* rise in temperature; ~**regler** *m* thermostat; ~**rückgang** *m* fall in temperature; ~**schwankung** *f* variation in temperature.
temperieren* *vt* **etw** ~ *(anwärmen)* to warm sth up; **der Raum ist angenehm temperiert** the room is at a pleasant temperature.
Tempo *nt* **-s** speed; *(Arbeits~, Schritt~ auch)* pace. ~**!** *(col)* hurry up!; **nun mach mal ein bißchen** ~**!** *(col)* get a move on! *(col)*; ~ **100 fahren** to be doing 100; **das** ~ **angeben** *(fig)* to set the pace.
Tendenz *f* trend; *(Neigung)* tendency; *(Absicht)* intention; *(no pl: Parteilichkeit)* bias, slant. **die** ~ **haben, zu ...** to have a tendency to ...; **er hat nationalistische** ~**en** he has nationalist leanings.
tendenziell *adj* **eine** ~**e Veränderung** a change in direction; **nur** ~**e Unterschiede** merely differences in emphasis.
tendenziös *adj* tendentious.
tendieren* *vi* **dazu** ~**, etw zu tun** to tend to do sth; **zum Kommunismus** ~ to have communist leanings *or* tendencies.
Tennis *nt* **-,** *no pl* tennis.
Tennis- *in cpds* ~**platz** *m* tennis court; ~**schläger** *m* tennis racket.
Tenor *m* **⸗e** *(Mus)* tenor.
Teppich *m* **-e** carpet; *(Wand~)* tapestry. **etw unter den** ~ **kehren** *(lit, fig)* to sweep sth under the carpet.
Teppich-: ~**boden** *m* fitted carpet(s); ~**kehrmaschine** *f* carpet-sweeper; ~**klopfer** *m* carpet-beater.
Termin *m* **-e** date; *(für Fertigstellung)* deadline; *(Comm: Liefertag)* delivery date; *(bei Arzt, Besprechung etc)* appointment; *(Jur: Verhandlung)* hearing. **die** ~**e besprechen** to discuss the schedule; **der letzte** ~ the deadline; *(bei Bewerbung etc)* the closing date; **sich** *(dat)* **einen** ~ **geben lassen** to make an appointment; **schon einen anderen** ~ **haben** to have a prior engagement.
Terminal ['tœrminəl] *nt or m* **-s** terminal.
Termin-: **t**~**gerecht** *adj* on schedule; ~**geschäfte** *pl* futures; ~**kalender** *m* (appointments *or* engagements) diary.
terminlich *adj* **etw** ~ **einrichten** to fit sth in (to one's schedule); ~**e Verpflichtungen** commitments.
Terminologie *f* terminology.
Termite *f* **-n** termite.
Terpentin *nt* **-e** turpentine; *(col: ~öl)* turps *(col)*.
Terrain [tɛ|rɛ̃ː] *nt* **-s** land, terrain; *(fig)* territory. **das** ~ **sondieren** *(Mil)* to reconnoitre the terrain; *(fig)* to see how the land lies.
Terrasse **-n** terrace; *(Dach~)* roof garden.
terrassenförmig **1** *adj* terraced. **2** *adv* in terraces.
Territorium *nt* territory.
Terror *m no pl* terror; *(Terrorismus)* terrorism; *(~herrschaft)* reign of terror; *(Einschüchterung)* intimidation. **blutiger** ~ terrorism and bloodshed; ~ **machen** *(col)* to raise hell *(col)*.
Terror-: ~**anschlag** *m* terrorist attack; ~**herrschaft** *f* reign of terror.
terrorisieren* *vt* to terrorize.
Terrorismus *m* terrorism.
Terrorist(in *f***)** *m* terrorist.
Terror|organisation *f* terrorist organization.
Tertia ['tɛrtsia] *f, pl* **Tertien** ['tɛrtsiən] *(Sch) (Unter-/Ober~) fourth/fifth year of German secondary school.*
Tertianer(in *f***)** [tɛrtsi'aːnɐ, -ərɪn] *m* **-** *(Sch) pupil in fourth/fifth year of German secondary school.*
Terz *f* **-en** *(Mus)* third; *(Fechten)* tierce.
Tesafilm ® *m* Sellotape ® *(Brit)*, Scotch tape ® *(esp US)*.
Test *m* **-s** *or* **-e** test.
Testament *nt* **(a)** *(Jur)* will; *(fig)* legacy. **sein** ~ **machen** to make one's will. **(b)** *(Bibl)* **Altes/Neues** ~ Old/New Testament.
testamentarisch *adj* testamentary. **etw** ~ **festlegen** to write sth in one's will.
Testbild *nt (TV)* testcard.
testen *vt* to test *(auf+acc* for*)*. **jdn auf seine Intelligenz** ~ to test sb's intelligence.
Test-: ~**fahrer** *m* test driver; ~**fall** *m* test case; ~**person** *f* subject (of a test); ~**pilot** *m* test-pilot.
teuer *adj* expensive, dear *usu pred*; *(fig)* dear. **etw** ~ **kaufen/verkaufen** to buy/sell sth for a high price; **etw für teures Geld kaufen** to pay good money for sth; **in Tokio lebt man** ~ life is expensive in Tokyo; **das wird ihn** ~ **zu stehen kommen** *(fig)* that will cost him dear; **einen Sieg** ~ **erkaufen** to pay dearly for a victory.
Teuerung *f* rise in prices.
Teufel *m* **-** **(a)** *(lit, fig)* devil. **(b)** *(col)* **scher dich zum** ~ go to hell *(col!)*; **jdn zum** ~ **jagen** to send sb packing *(col)*; **wer zum** ~**?** who the devil *(col)* *or* the hell *(col!)*?; **zum** ~ **mit dem Ding!** damn *(col)* *or* blast *(col)* the thing!; **den** ~ **an die Wand malen** *(schwarzmalen)* to imagine the worst; *(Unheil heraufbeschwören)* to tempt fate *or* providence; **wenn man vom** ~ **spricht** *(prov)* talk of the devil; **das müßte schon mit dem** ~ **zugehen**

that really would be a stroke of bad luck; **in ~s Küche kommen** to get into a mess; **sich den ~ um etw kümmern** not to give a damn about sth *(col)*.

Teufels-: ~**arbeit** *f (col)* hell of a job *(col)*; ~**austreibung** *f* casting out of devils *no pl*, exorcism; ~**kerl** *m (dated)* devil of a fellow *(dated)*; ~**kreis** *m* vicious circle.

teuflisch *adj* fiendish, devilish, diabolical.

Text *m* **-e** text; *(einer Urkunde auch, eines Gesetzes)* wording; *(von Lied)* words *pl*; *(von Schlager)* lyrics *pl*; *(von Film, Rede etc)* script; *(Bild~)* caption; *(auf Plakat)* words *pl*.

Text-: ~**buch** *nt* script; *(für Lieder)* songbook; ~**dichter** *m* songwriter; *(bei Oper)* librettist.

texten 1 *vt* to write. **2** *vi siehe* **Texter(in)** to write songs/copy.

Texter(in *f*) *m* **-** *(für Schlager)* songwriter; *(für Werbesprüche)* copywriter.

Textil- *in cpds* textile; ~**arbeiter** *m* textile worker; ~**branche** *f* textile trade.

Textilien [-iən] *pl* textiles *pl*.

Textilindustrie *f* textile industry.

Text-: ~**kritik** *f* textual criticism; ~**stelle** *f* passage; ~**system** *nt* word-processor; ~**verarbeitung** *f* word-processing; ~**verarbeitungssystem** *nt* word-processor.

TH [teːˈhaː] *f* **-s** = **Technische Hochschule.**

Thailand *nt* Thailand.

Thailänder(in *f*) *m* **-** Thai.

Theater *nt* **- (a)** theatre *(Brit)*, theater *(US)*; *(~kunst auch)* drama; *(Schauspielbühne)* theatre *(Brit) or* theater *(US)* company. **beim/im ~ arbeiten** to be on the stage/work in the theatre; **zum ~ gehen** to go on the stage; **ins ~ gehen** to go to the theatre. **(b)** *(fig)* carry-on *(col)*, fuss. **(ein) ~ machen** to make a (big) fuss *(mit jdm* of sb*)*.

Theater- *in cpds* theatre *(Brit)*, theater *(US)*; ~**aufführung** *f* stage production; *(Vorstellung, Darbietung)* performance; ~**besucher** *m* theatregoer *(Brit)*, theatergoer *(US)*; ~**kritiker** *m* drama critic; ~**stück** *nt* (stage) play.

theatralisch *adj* theatrical, histrionic.

Theke *f* **-n** *(Schanktisch)* bar; *(Ladentisch)* counter. **etw unter der ~ verkaufen** to sell sth under the counter.

Thema *nt, pl* **Themen** *or* **-ta** subject, topic; *(Leitgedanke, Mus)* theme. **beim ~ bleiben/vom ~ abschweifen** to stick to/wander off the subject; **das ~ wechseln** to change the subject.

Thematik *f* topic.

thematisch *adj* thematic.

Themenkreis *m* topic.

Theologe *m*, **Theologin** *f* theologian.

Theologie *f* theology.

theologisch *adj* theological.

Theoretiker(in *f*) *m* **-** theorist, theoretician.

theoretisch *adj* theoretical. ~ **gesehen** in theory, theoretically.

Theorie *f* theory.

Therapeut(in *f*) *m (wk)* **-en, -en** therapist.

therapeutisch *adj* therapeutic(al).

Therapie *f* therapy.

Thermal-: ~**bad** *nt (Badeort)* spa; ~**quelle** *f* thermal spring.

thermisch *adj attr (Phys)* thermal.

Thermo- *in cpds* thermo-.

Thermometer *nt* **-** thermometer.

Thermosflasche *f* thermos (flask) ®.

Thermostat *m* **-e** thermostat.

These *f* **-n** hypothesis, thesis.

Thron *m* **-e** throne. **von seinem ~ herabsteigen** *(fig)* to come down off one's high horse.

thronen *vi* to sit enthroned; *(fig: in exponierter Stellung sitzen)* to sit in state.

Thron-: ~**erbe** *m*, ~**erbin** *f* heir to the throne; ~**folge** *f* line of succession; ~**folger(in** *f*) *m* **-** heir to the throne, heir apparent.

Thunfisch *m* tuna (fish).

Thymian *m* **-e** thyme.

tick *interj* tick. ~ **tack** tick-tock.

Tick *m* **-s** tic; *(col: Schrulle)* quirk. **Uhren sind sein ~** he has a thing about clocks *(col)*; **einen ~ haben** *(col)* to be crazy.

ticken *vi* to tick (away). **du tickst ja nicht richtig** you're off your rocker! *(col)*.

tief 1 *adj* deep; *(niedrig) Ton, Ausschnitt* low; *(tiefgründig auch)* profound; *Schmerz* intense; *Not* dire; *Elend* utter. ~**er Teller** soup plate; **die ~eren Ursachen** the underlying causes; **aus ~stem Herzen/~ster Seele** from the bottom of one's heart/the depths of one's soul; **bis ~ in die Nacht hinein** late into the night; ~ **im Wald** deep in the forest; **im ~en Winter** in the depths of winter; ~ **in der Nacht** at dead of night.

2 *adv* **(a)** *(weit nach unten, innen etc)* deep; *untersuchen* in depth; *sich bücken* low. ~ **in etw** *(acc)* **einsinken** to sink deep into sth; **3 m ~ fallen** to fall 3 metres; ~ **sinken** *(fig)* to sink low; **(ganz) ~ unter uns** a long way below us, far below us; ~ **verschneit** deep with snow; ~ **in Gedanken (versunken)** deep in thought; ~ **in Schulden stecken** to be deep in debt; ~ **in die Tasche greifen müssen** *(col)* to have to dig deep in one's pocket. **(b)** *(schwer, stark)* deeply; *erschrecken* terribly. ~ **atmen** to breathe deeply; **im Winter steht die Sonne ~er** the sun is lower (in the sky) in winter.

Tief *nt* **-e** *(Met)* depression; *(fig)* low. **ein moralisches ~** *(fig)* a low.

Tief-: ~**bau** *m* civil engineering *(excluding the construction of buildings)*; **t~betrübt** *adj attr* deeply distressed.

Tiefdruck *m* **(a)** *(Met)* low pressure. **(b)** *(Typ)* gravure.

Tiefe *f* **-n** *siehe* **tief** depth; lowness; profundity. **unten in der ~** far below.

Tief|ebene *f* lowland plain.

Tiefen-: ~**psychologie** *f* depth psychology; psychoanalysis; ~**wirkung** *f* deep action.

Tief-: ~**flug** *m* low-level *or* low-altitude flight; ~**gang** *m (Naut)* draught *(Brit)*, draft *(US)*; *(fig col)* depth; ~**garage** *f* underground car park *(Brit) or* parking lot *(US)*; **t~gekühlt** *adj (gefroren)* frozen; **t~gründig** *adj* profound, deep; *(durchdacht)* well-grounded.

Tiefkühl-: ~**fach** *nt* freezer compartment; ~**kost** *f* frozen food; ~**truhe** *f* deep-freeze.

Tief-: ~**lader** *m* **-** low-loader; ~**land** *nt* lowlands *pl*; **t~liegend** *adj attr Gegend, Häuser* low-lying; *Augen* deep-set; *(nach Krankheit)* sunken; ~**parterre** *nt* basement; ~**punkt** *m* low; ~**schlag** *m (Boxen, fig)* hit below the belt; ~**see** *f* deep sea; ~**sinn** *m* profundity; **t~sinnig** *adj* profound; ~**stand** *m* low; **t~stapeln** *vi sep* to understate the case; *(in bezug auf eigene Leistung)* to be modest.

Tiegel *m* **-** (sauce)pan; *(Chem)* crucible.

Tier *nt* **-e** animal; *(Haus~ auch)* pet; *(col: grausamer Mensch)* brute. **hohes ~** *(col)* big shot *(col)*.

Tier- *in cpds* animal; *(Med)* veterinary; ~**arzt** *m* vet, veterinary surgeon *(form)*, veterinarian *(US)*; ~**freund** *m* animal lover; ~**garten** *m* zoo; ~**halter** *m (von Haustieren)* pet-owner; *(von Nutztieren)* livestock owner; ~**handlung** *f* pet shop *(Brit) or* store *(US)*; ~**heim** *nt* animal home.

tierisch *adj* animal *attr*; *(fig) Roheit* bestial. ~**er Ernst** *(col)* deadly seriousness.

Tier-: ~**kreis** *m* zodiac; ~**kreiszeichen** *nt* sign of the zodiac; ~**kunde** *f* zoology; ~**liebe** *f* love of animals; **t~liebend** *adj* fond of animals, animal-loving *attr*; ~**medizin** *f* veterinary medicine; ~**park** *m* zoo; ~**pfleger** *m* zoo-keeper; ~**quälerei** *f* cruelty to animals; ~**reich** *nt* animal kingdom; ~**schutz** *m* protection of animals; ~**schutzverein** *m* society for the prevention of cruelty to animals; ~**versuch** *m* animal experiment.

Tiger *m* - tiger.

Tigerin *f* tigress.

tilgen *vt (geh) Schulden* to pay off.

Tilgung *f (von Schulden)* repayment.

Tinnef *m no pl (col)* rubbish, trash *(col)*.

Tinte *f* **-n** ink. **in der ~ sitzen** *(col)* to be in the soup *(col)*.

Tinten-: ~**faß** *nt* inkpot; ~**fisch** *m* cuttlefish; *(Kalmar)* squid; *(achtarmig)* octopus; ~**fleck** *m* ink stain; ~**klecks** *m* ink blot.

Tip *m* **-s** *(Sport, St Ex)* tip; *(Andeutung)* hint; *(an Polizei)* tip-off. **kannst du mir einen ~ geben, wo ich ...?** can you give me an idea where I ...?

Tippelbruder *m (col)* tramp, gentleman of the road *(hum)*.

tippeln *vi aux sein (col) (gehen)* to foot it *(col)*; *(auf Zehenspitzen)* to tiptoe.

tippen *vti* **(a)** to tap *(an/auf/gegen etw (acc)* sth*)*; *(zeigen)* to touch *(auf or an etw (acc)* sth*)*. **jdm auf die Schulter ~** to tap sb on the shoulder; **sich** *(dat)* **an die Stirn ~** to tap one's forehead. **(b)** *(col: auf der Schreibmaschine)* to type *(an etw (dat)* sth*)*. **(c)** *(wetten)* to fill in one's coupon; *(im Toto auch)* to do the pools. **im Lotto ~** to do the lottery; **ich tippe auf Kohl** *(col)* I'll put my money on Kohl.

Tippfehler *m* typing error.

Tippse *f* **-n** *(pej)* typist.

tipptopp *(col)* **1** *adj* immaculate; *(prima)* first-class. **2** *adv* immaculately; *(prima)* really well.

Tippzettel *m (im Toto)* football pools coupon; *(im Lotto)* lottery coupon.

Tirol *nt* the Tyrol.

Tiroler(in *f***)** *m* - Tyrolese, Tyrolean.

Tisch *m* **-e** table; *(Schreib~)* desk. **bei ~** at table; **bitte zu ~!** lunch/dinner is served!; **vor/nach ~** before/after the meal; **unter den ~ fallen** *(col)* to go by the board; **jdn unter den ~ trinken** to drink sb under the table; **es wird gegessen, was auf den ~ kommt!** you'll eat what you're given; **vom ~ sein** *(fig)* to be cleared out of the way.

Tisch- *in cpds* table; ~**dame** *f* dinner partner; ~**decke** *f* tablecloth; ~**herr** *m* dinner partner; ~**karte** *f* place card; ~**kasten** *m* drawer in the table.

Tischler *m* - joiner, carpenter; *(Möbel~)* cabinet-maker.

Tischlerei *f (Werkstatt)* joiner's *or* carpenter's/ cabinet-maker's workshop.

Tischlerhandwerk *nt* joinery, carpentry; cabinetmaking.

tischlern *vi (col)* to do woodwork.

Tisch-: ~**nachbar** *m* neighbour *(Brit) or* neighbor *(US)* (at table); ~**ordnung** *f* seating plan; ~**rechner** *m* desk calculator; ~**rede** *f* after-dinner speech; ~**tennis** *nt* table tennis; ~**tuch** *nt* tablecloth; ~**wein** *m* table wine.

Titel *m* - title. **jdn mit ~ ansprechen** to address sb by his/her title; **unter dem ~** under the title.

Titel-: ~**bild** *nt* cover (picture); ~**blatt** *nt* title page; ~**kampf** *m (Sport)* finals *pl*; *(Boxen)* title fight; ~**rolle** *f* title role; ~**schutz** *m* copyright *(of a title)*; ~**seite** *f (von Zeitschrift)* cover; *(von Zeitung)* front page; ~ **verteidiger** *m* title holder.

titulieren* *vt jdn* to address *(mit* as*)*.

tja *interj* well.

Toast [to:st] *m* **-e (a)** *(Brot)* toast. **ein ~** some toast. **(b)** *(Trinkspruch)* toast.

toasten ['to:stn] **1** *vi* to drink a toast *(auf+acc* to*)*. **2** *vt Brot* to toast.

toben *vi* **(a)** *(wüten)* to rage; *(Mensch)* to throw a fit; *(vor Begeisterung etc)* to go wild *(vor* with*)*. **(b)** *(ausgelassen spielen)* to rollick (about).

Tobsucht *f (bei Tieren)* madness; *(bei Menschen)* maniacal rage. **er hat wieder mal die ~** *(col)* he's gone raving mad again *(col)*.

Tochter *f* ⸚ daughter; *(~firma)* subsidiary.

Tochtergesellschaft *f* subsidiary (company).

Tod *m* **-e** death. **~ durch Ersticken** death by suffocation; **eines natürlichen/gewaltsamen ~es sterben** to die of natural causes/to die a violent death; **sich zu ~e trinken** to drink oneself to death; **sich** *(dat)* **den ~ holen** to catch one's death (of cold); **sich zu ~(e) langweilen** to be bored to death; **zu ~e betrübt sein** to be in the depths of despair.

tod|ernst *adj (col)* deadly serious.

Todes-: ~**angst** *f* fear of death; ~**ängste ausstehen** *(col)* to be scared to death *(col)*; ~**anzeige** *f* obituary (notice); ~**fall** *m* death; *(in der Familie auch)* bereavement; ~**jahr** *nt* year of sb's death; ~**kampf** *m* death throes *pl*; **t~mutig** *adj* absolutely fearless; ~**opfer** *nt* death, casualty, fatality; ~**qualen** *pl* final agony; ~**qualen ausstehen** *(fig)* to suffer agonies; ~**stoß** *m* deathblow; **jdm/einer Sache den ~stoß versetzen** *(lit, fig)* to deal sb/sth the deathblow; ~**strafe** *f* death penalty; ~**tag** *m* day of sb's death; *(Jahrestag)* anniversary of sb's death; ~**ursache** *f* cause of death; ~**urteil** *nt* death sentence; ~**verachtung** *f (col)* **mit ~verachtung** with utter disgust.

Tod-: ~**feind** *m* deadly *or* mortal enemy; **t~krank** *adj* dangerously *or* critically ill.

tödlich *adj* fatal; *Gefahr* mortal; *Gift* deadly, lethal; *(col) Langeweile* deadly. **~ verunglücken** to be killed in an accident.

Tod-: **t~müde** *adj (col)* dead tired *(col)*; **t~schick** *adj (col)* dead smart *(col)*; **t~sicher** *(col)* **1** *adj* dead certain *(col)*; *Methode, Tip* sure-fire *(col)*; **2** *adv* for sure; ~**sünde** *f* mortal *or* deadly sin.

Toilette [toa'lɛtə] *f* **(a)** *(Abort)* toilet. **öffentliche ~** public conveniences *pl (Brit)*, comfort station *(US)*. **auf die ~ gehen/auf der ~ sein** to go to/be in the toilet. **(b)** *no pl (geh: Körperpflege)* toilet.

Toiletten- [toa'lɛtn-] *in cpds* toilet; ~**artikel** *m usu pl* toiletry; ~**beutel** *m* toilet bag; ~**papier** *nt* toilet paper; ~**schrank** *m* bathroom cabinet; ~**wasser** *nt* toilet water.

tolerant *adj* tolerant *(gegen* of*)*.

Toleranz *f* tolerance *(gegen* of*)*.

tolerieren* *vt* to tolerate.

toll *adj* **(a)** *(wild, ausgelassen)* wild, mad. **(b)** *(col: verrückt)* mad, crazy. **(c)** *(col: schlimm)* terrible. **(d)** *(col: großartig)* fantastic *(col)*, great *(col) no adv*.

tollen *vi* to romp about; *(aux sein: laufen)* to rush about.

Toll-: **t~kühn** *adj* daredevil *attr*, daring; ~**wut** *f* rabies; **t~wütig** *adj* rabid.

Tolpatsch *m* **-e** *(col)* clumsy creature.

Tölpel *m* - *(col)* fool.

Tomate *f* **-n** tomato. **du treulose ~!** *(col)* you're a fine friend!

Tomaten- *in cpds* tomato; ~**mark,** ~**püree** *nt* tomato puree.

Ton[1] *m* **-e** *(Erdart)* clay.

Ton[2] *m* ⸚**e (a)** *(Laut)* sound; *(von Zeitzeichen, im Telefon, Klangfarbe)* tone; *(Mus: note)* note. **den ~ angeben** *(Mus)* to give an A; *(fig: Mensch)* to set the tone; **keinen ~ herausbringen** not to be able to say a word; **keinen ~ sagen** not to make a sound; **hast du ⸚e!** *(col)* did you ever! *(col)*; **dicke** *or* **große ⸚e spucken** *(col)* to talk big. **(b)** *(Betonung)* stress; *(Tonfall)* intonation. **(c)** *(Redeweise, Umgangston)* tone. **den richtigen ~ finden** to strike the right note; **ich verbitte mir diesen ~** I will not be spoken to like that; **einen anderen ~ anschlagen** to change one's tune; **der gute ~** good form. **(d)** *(Farb~)* tone; *(Nuance)* shade.

Ton-: ~**abnehmer** *m* pick-up; ~**arm** *m* pick-up arm; ~**art** *f (Mus)* key; *(fig: Tonfall)* tone.

Tonband *nt* tape; *(col: Gerät)* tape recorder.

Tonband-: ~**aufnahme** *f* tape recording; ~**gerät**

nt tape recorder.
tönen[1] *vi (lit, fig: klingen)* to sound; *(schallen auch)* to resound; *(großspurig reden)* to sound off.
tönen[2] *vt* to tint. **etw leicht rot** *etc* ~ to tinge sth (with) red *etc.*
Ton|erde *f* aluminium oxide.
tönern *adj attr* clay. **auf ~en Füßen stehen** *(fig)* to be shaky.
Ton-: **~fall** *m* tone of voice; *(Intonation)* intonation; **~film** *m* sound film, talkie *(col)*; **~folge** *f* sequence of notes/sounds; **~geschirr** *nt* earthenware; **~höhe** *f* pitch; **~ingenieur** *m* sound engineer; **~kopf** *m* recording head; **~lage** *f* pitch (level); *(~umfang)* register; **~leiter** *f* scale; **t~los** *adj* toneless.
Tonne *f* **-n (a)** *(Behälter)* barrel; *(aus Metall)* drum; *(Müll~)* bin *(Brit)*, trash can *(US)*; *(col: Mensch)* fatso *(col)*. **(b)** *(Gewicht)* metric tonne. **(c)** *(Register~)* (register) ton.
Ton-: **~störung** *f* sound interference; **~taube** *f* clay pigeon; **~waren** *pl* earthenware *sing.*
Top- *in cpds* top.
Topas *m* **-e** topaz.
Topf *m* **¨-e** pot; *(Koch~ auch)* (sauce)pan; *(Nacht~)* potty *(col)*; *(col: Toilette)* loo *(Brit col)*, john *(US col)*. **alles in einen ~ werfen** *(fig)* to lump everything together.
Topfblume *f* potted flower.
Töpfer(in *f*) *m* **-** potter.
Töpferei *f* pottery.
töpfern 1 *vi* to do pottery. **2** *vt* to make (in clay).
Töpfer-: **~scheibe** *f* potter's wheel; **~waren** *pl* pottery *sing*; *(irden)* earthenware *sing.*
Topfhandschuh *m* ovenglove.
topfit ['tɔp'fɪt] *adj pred* in top form.
Topf-: **~lappen** *m* ovencloth; **~pflanze** *f* potted plant.
Tor *nt* **-e (a)** *(lit, fig, Ski)* gate; *(Durchfahrt etc)* gateway; *(von Garage, Scheune)* door. **(b)** *(Sport)* goal. **im ~ stehen** to be in goal.
Tor-: **~bogen** *m* arch, archway; **~einfahrt** *f* entrance gate.
Toresschluß *m*: **(kurz) vor ~** right at the last minute.
Torf *m no pl* peat.
Torf-: **~boden** *m* peat; **~erde** *f* peat.
torfig *adj* peaty.
Torf-: **~moor** *nt* peat bog *or (trocken)* moor; **~stecher** *m* **-** peat-cutter.
Torheit *f* foolishness; *(Handlung)* foolish action.
töricht *adj* foolish; *Wunsch, Hoffnung* idle.
torkeln *vi aux sein* to stagger, to reel.
Tor-: **~latte** *f* crossbar; **~lauf** *m* slalom; **~linie** *f* goal-line; **~mann** *m, pl* **~männer** goalkeeper, goalie *(col)*.
Tornister *m* **-** *(Mil)* knapsack; *(dated: Schulranzen)* satchel.
torpedieren* *vt (Naut, fig)* to torpedo.
Torpedo *m* **-s** torpedo.
Tor-: **~pfosten** *m* gatepost; *(Sport)* goalpost; **~schluß** *m (fig) siehe* **~esschluß; ~schlußpanik** *f (col)* last minute panic; *(von Unverheirateten)* fear of being left on the shelf; **~schütze** *m* (goal) scorer.
Torte *f* **-n** cake, gâteau; *(Obst~)* flan *(Brit)*, tart.
Torten-: **~boden** *m* flan *(Brit) or* tart *(US)* base; **~guß** *m* glaze; **~heber** *m* **-** cake slice; **~platte** *f* cake plate; **~schaufel** *f* cake slice.
Tortur *f* torture; *(fig auch)* ordeal.
Tor-: **~verhältnis** *nt* score; **~wart** *m* goalkeeper.
tosen *vi* to roar, to thunder; *(Wind, Sturm)* to rage. **~der Beifall** thunderous applause.
tot *adj (lit, fig)* dead; *Augen* sightless; *Haus, Stadt* deserted; *Gegend, Landschaft etc* bleak; *Wissen* useless; *Vulkan* extinct; *Farbe* lifeless; *(Rail) Gleis* disused. **mehr ~ als lebendig** *(fig col)* more dead than alive; **~ geboren werden** to be stillborn; **~ umfallen** to drop dead; **er war auf der Stelle ~** he died instantly; **ein ~er Briefkasten** a dead-letter box; **der ~e Winkel** the blind spot; **ein ~er Punkt** *(Stillstand)* a standstill; *(in Verhandlungen)* deadlock; *(körperliche Ermüdung)* low point; **ein ~es Rennen** *(lit, fig)* a dead heat; **ein ~er Mann** *(fig col)* a goner *(col)*.
total 1 *adj* total. **2** *adv* totally.
Totalausverkauf *m* clearance sale.
totalitär *adj* totalitarian.
Totalität *f* totality, entirety.
Total-: **~operation** *f* extirpation; *(von Gebärmutter)* hysterectomy; **~schaden** *m* write-off.
tot-: **~arbeiten** *vr sep (col)* to work oneself to death; **~ärgern** *vr sep (col)* to be/become livid.
töten *vti (lit, fig)* to kill. **das kann einem den Nerv ~** *(fig col)* he/that really gets on my/one's *etc* nerves.
Toten-: **~bett** *nt* deathbed; **t~blaß** *adj* deathly pale; **~glocke** *f* death knell; **~gräber** *m* gravedigger; **~hemd** *nt* shroud; **~klage** *f* lamentation of the dead; *(Liter)* dirge, lament; **~kopf** *m* skull; *(als Zeichen)* death's-head; *(auf Piratenfahne, Arzneiflasche etc)* skull and crossbones; **~messe** *f* requiem mass; **~reich** *nt (Myth)* kingdom of the dead; **~schein** *m* death certificate; **t~still** *adj* deathly silent; **~starre** *f* rigor mortis; **~wache** *f* wake.
Tote(r) *mf decl as adj* dead person, dead man/woman; *(bei Unfall etc)* fatality, casualty. **die ~n** the dead; **es gab 3 ~** 3 people were killed.
Tot-: **t~geboren** *adj attr* stillborn; **ein t~geborenes Kind sein** *(fig)* to be doomed to failure; **~geburt** *f* stillbirth; *(Kind)* stillborn baby; **~gesagte(r)** *mf decl as adj* person *or* man/woman *etc* who has been declared dead; **t~kriegen** *vt sep (col)* **nicht t~ zukriegen sein** to go on for ever; **t~lachen** *vr sep (col)* to die laughing *(col)*.
Toto *m or nt* **-s** (football) pools. **(im) ~ spielen** to do the pools.
Toto- *in cpds* pools; **~zettel** *m* pools coupon.
Tot-: **~schlag** *m (Jur)* manslaughter; *(US)* homicide; **t~schlagen** *vt sep irreg (lit, fig)* to kill; *(col) Menschen auch* to beat to death; **~schläger** *m* cudgel, club; **t~schweigen** *vt sep irreg* to hush up *(col)*; **t~stellen** *vr sep* to pretend to be dead.
toupieren* [tu'piːrən] *vt* to backcomb.
Tour [tuːɐ] *f* **-en (a)** *(Fahrt)* trip, outing; *(Ausflugs~)* tour; *(Spritz~) (mit Auto)* drive; *(mit Rad)* ride; *(Wanderung)* walk; *(Berg~)* climb. **eine ~ machen** to go on a trip *or* outing/tour; to go for a drive/ride/walk/climb. **(b)** *(Umdrehung)* revolution, rev *(col)*. **auf ~en kommen** *(Auto)* to reach top speed; *(fig col)* to get into top gear; *(sich aufregen)* to get worked up *(col)*; **auf vollen ~en laufen** *(lit)* to run at full speed; *(fig)* to be in full swing; **in einer ~** *(col)* the whole time. **(c)** *(col: Art und Weise)* ploy. **mit der ~ brauchst du mir gar nicht zu kommen** don't try that one on me; **auf die krumme ~** by dishonest means.
Touren- ['tuːrən-]: **~rad** *nt* tourer; **~zähler** *m* rev counter.
Tourismus [tu'rɪsmʊs] *m* tourism.
Touristik [tu'rɪstɪk] *f* tourism, tourist industry.
Tournee [tʊr'neː] *f* **-n** [-eːən] *or* **-s** tour.
Trab *m no pl* trot. **im ~** at a trot; **(im) ~ reiten** to trot; **auf ~ sein** *(col)* to be on the go *(col)*; **jdn auf ~ bringen** *(col)* to make sb get a move on *(col)*.
Trabant *m (Astron, fig)* satellite.
Trabantenstadt *f* satellite town.
traben *vi* **(a)** *aux haben or sein* to trot. **(b)** *aux sein (col: laufen)* to trot.
Tracht *f* **-en** *(Kleidung)* dress; *(Volks~ etc)* costume; *(Schwestern~)* uniform. **eine ~ Prügel** a good thrashing.
trachten *vi (geh)* to strive *(nach* for, after*)*. **jdm nach dem Leben ~** to be after sb's blood.
trächtig *adj Tier* pregnant; *(fig geh)* laden *(von* with*)*.

Tradition [tradi'tsio:n] *f* tradition.
traditionell [traditsio'nɛl] *adj usu attr* traditional.
traf *pret of* **treffen.**
Trafo *m* **-s** *(col)* transformer.
tragbar *adj* **(a)** *Apparat, Gerät* portable; *Kleid* wearable. **(b)** *(annehmbar)* acceptable *(für* to); *(erträglich)* bearable.
Trage -n *(Bahre)* litter; *(Tragkorb)* pannier.
träge *adj* **(a)** sluggish; *Mensch, Bewegung auch* lethargic. **(b)** *(Phys) Masse* inert.
tragen *pret* **trug,** *ptp* **getragen 1** *vt* **(a)** to carry; *(an einen Ort bringen)* to take. **etw mit sich** ~ to carry sth with one. **(b)** *Kleid, Brille etc* to wear; *(im Moment auch)* to have on; *Bart, Gebiß* to have; *Waffen* to carry. **getragene Kleider** second-hand clothes; *(abgelegt)* cast-offs. **(c)** *(stützen, halten, fig)* to support; *Schicksal, Leid etc* to bear, to endure. **(d)** *Zinsen* to yield; *Ernte auch* to produce; *(lit, fig) Früchte* to bear. **(e)** *(trächtig sein)* to be carrying. **(f)** *Verluste* to absorb; *Kosten* to bear, to carry; *Risiko, Folgen* to take; *(unterhalten) Verein* to support, to back. **(g)** *Titel, Aufschrift etc* to bear, to have; *Vermerk* to contain.
2 *vi* **(a)** *(Baum, Acker etc)* to produce a crop. **(b)** *(reichen: Geschütz, Stimme)* to carry. **(c)** *(Eis)* to take weight. **(d) schwer an etw** *(dat)* ~ to have a job carrying sth; *(fig)* to find sth hard to bear. **(e) zum T~ kommen** to come to fruition; *(nützlich werden)* to come in useful.
3 *vr* **(a) sich leicht** ~ to be easy to carry; **der Anzug trägt sich gut** this suit feels comfortable (on). **(b)** *(finanziell)* to be self-supporting.
tragend *adj Säule, Bauteil* load-bearing; *Idee, Motiv* fundamental.
Träger *m* **- (a)** *(an Kleidung)* strap; *(Hosen~)* braces *pl (Brit)*, suspenders *pl (US)*. **(b)** *(Holz~, Beton~)* (supporting) beam; *(Stahl~, Eisen~)* girder. **(c)** *(Tech: Stütze von Brücken etc)* support. **(d)** *(Mensch) (von Lasten)* bearer, porter; *(von Namen)* bearer. **(e)** *(fig) (der Kultur, Staatsgewalt etc)* representative; *(einer Veranstaltung)* sponsor.
Träger-: ~kleid *nt* pinafore dress *(Brit)*, jumper *(US)*; **~rakete** *f* carrier rocket.
Tragetasche *f* carrier bag *(Brit)*, carry-all *(US)*.
Trag-: t~fähig *adj (Brücke, Balken)* able to take a load; *(Kompromiß, Beschluß)* acceptable; **~fläche** *f* wing; *(von Boot)* hydrofoil; **~flächenboot** *nt* hydrofoil.
Trägheit *f siehe adj* sluggishness; lethargy; *(Faulheit)* laziness; *(Phys)* inertia.
Tragik *f* tragedy.
Tragiker *m* - tragedian.
Tragikomödie *f* tragicomedy.
tragisch *adj* tragic. **etw ~ nehmen** *(col)* to take sth to heart; **das ist nicht so** ~ *(col)* it's not the end of the world.
Trag-: ~korb *m* pannier; **~last** *f* load.
Tragödie [-iə] *f (Liter, fig)* tragedy.
Trag-: ~pfeiler *m* load-bearing pillar; *(von Brücke)* support; **~riemen** *m* strap; **~weite** *f (von Geschütz)* range; *(fig)* consequences *pl: (von Gesetz)* scope; **von großer ~weite sein** to have far-reaching consequences.
Trainer(in *f*) ['trɛːnɐ, 'treː-] *m* - coach, trainer; *(bei Fußball)* manager.
trainieren* [trɛ'niːrən, treː'n-] **1** *vt* to train; *Mannschaft, Sportler auch* to coach; *Sprung, Übung* to practise *(Brit)*, to practice *(US)*. **ein (gut) trainierter Sportler** an athlete who is in training; **jdn auf** *or* **für etw** *(acc)* ~ to train *or* coach sb for sth. **2** *vi (Sportler)* to train; *(Übungen machen)* to exercise; *(üben)* to practise *(Brit)*, to practice *(US)*. **auf** *or* **für etw** *(acc)* ~ to train/practise for sth. **3** *vr* to train *(auf+acc* for); *(üben)* to practise *(Brit)*, to practice *(US)*.
Training ['trɛːnɪŋ, 'treːn-] *nt* **-s** training *no pl*; *(Fitneß~)* exercise *no pl*; *(fig: Übung)* practice.
Trainings-: ~anzug *m* track-suit; **~hose** *f* track-suit trousers *pl*; **~jacke** *f* track-suit top; **~schuh** *m* trainer; **~zeit** *f* practice time.
Trakt *m* **-e** *(Gebäudeteil)* section; *(Flügel)* wing.
Traktat *m or nt* **-e** *(Abhandlung)* treatise; *(Flugschrift, religiöse Schrift)* tract.
traktieren* *vt (col) (schlecht behandeln)* to maltreat; *(quälen) Geschwister, Tiere* to torment.
Traktor *m* **-en** tractor.
Trampel *m or nt* - clumsy clot *(col)*.
trampeln 1 *vi* **(a)** to stamp. **(b)** *aux sein (schwerfällig gehen)* to stamp along. **über die Wiese** ~ to tramp across the meadow. **2** *vt Weg* to trample. **jdn zu Tode** ~ to trample sb to death.
Trampel-: ~pfad *m* track, path; **~tier** *nt (Zool)* (Bactrian) camel; *(col)* clumsy oaf *(col)*.
trampen ['trɛmpn] *vi* to hitch-hike, to hitch *(col)*.
Tramper(in *f*) ['trɛmpɐ, -ərɪn] *m* - hitch-hiker.
Trampolin *nt* **-e** trampoline.
Tran *m* **-e (a)** *(von Fischen)* train oil. **(b)** *(col)* **im** ~ dop(e)y *(col)*; *(leicht betrunken)* merry *(col)*. **das habe ich im ~ ganz vergessen** it completely slipped my mind.
tranchieren [trã'ʃiːrən] *vt* to carve.
Tranchier-: ~gabel *f* carving-fork; **~messer** *nt* carving-knife.
Träne *f* **-n** tear; *(einzelne ~)* tear(drop). **den ~n nahe sein** to be on the verge of tears; **~n lachen** to laugh till one cries; **deswegen vergieße ich keine ~n** *(fig)* I'm not going to shed any tears over that; **bittere ~n weinen** to weep bitterly.
tränen *vi* to water.
Tränen-: ~drüse *f* lachrymal gland; **der Film drückt sehr auf die ~drüsen** the film is a real tear-jerker; **~gas** *nt* tear gas.
Tranfunzel *f (col)* slowcoach *(Brit col)*, slowpoke *(US col)*.
tranig *adj (col)* slow, sluggish.
Trank *m* **¨-e** *(liter)* drink, draught *(liter)*.
trank *pret of* **trinken.**
Tränke *f* **-n** drinking trough.
tränken *vt Tiere* to water; *(durchnässen)* to soak.
Trans|aktion *f* transaction.
trans|atlantisch *adj* transatlantic.
Transformation *f* transformation.
Transformator *m* transformer.
transformieren* *vt* to transform.
Transfusion *f* transfusion
Transistorradio *nt* transistor (radio).
Transit *m* **-e** transit.
transitiv *adj (Gram)* transitive.
Transitverkehr *m* transit traffic.
transparent [transpa'rɛnt] *adj* transparent; *(fig geh) Argument* lucid, clear. **eine Entscheidung ~ machen** to make a decision-making process open.
Transparent [transpa'rɛnt] *nt* **-e** *(Reklameschild etc)* neon sign; *(Durchscheinbild)* transparency; *(Spruchband)* banner.
Transparentpapier *nt* waxed tissue paper; *(zum Pausen)* tracing paper.
Transparenz [transpa'rɛnts] *f siehe adj* transparency; lucidity, clarity.
Transplantation [transplanta'tsioːn] *f (Med)* transplant; *(von Haut)* graft; *(Bot)* grafting.
Transport [trans'pɔrt] *m* **-e (a)** transport. **ein ~ auf dem Landweg** road transport; **ein ~ des Kranken ist ausgeschlossen** moving the patient is out of the question. **(b)** *(Fracht)* consignment, shipment; *(Menschen)* transport.
transportabel [transpɔr'taːbl] *adj* transportable.
Transport|arbeiter *m* transport worker.
Transporter [trans'pɔrtɐ] *m* - *(Schiff)* cargo ship; *(Flugzeug)* transport plane; *(Auto)* van.
Transporteur [transpɔr'tøːɐ] *m* removal man *(Brit)*, furniture mover.
transportfähig *adj* moveable.
transportieren* [transpɔr'tiːrən] **1** *vt* to trans-

port; *Patienten* to move; *Film* to wind on. **2** *vi* *(Förderband)* to move; *(Kamera)* to wind on.
Transport- [trans'pɔrt-]: **~kosten** *pl* freight costs *pl*; **~schiff** *nt* cargo ship; *(Mil)* transport ship; **~unternehmen** *nt* haulier, haulage firm.
Transuse *f* **-n** *(col)* slowcoach *(Brit col)*, slowpoke *(US col)*.
Transvestit [transvɛs'tiːt] *m (wk)* **-en, -en** transvestite.
transzendent(al) *adj* transcendent(al).
Trapez *nt* **-e** *(von Artisten)* trapeze.
trappeln *vi aux sein* to clatter; *(Pony)* to clip-clop.
Trara *nt* **-s** *(fig col)* hullabaloo *(col)* *(um* about*)*.
trat *pret of* **treten.**
Tratsch *m no pl (col)* gossip, scandal.
tratschen *vi (col)* to gossip.
Tratsch-: **~maul** *nt*, **~tante** *f (pej col)* scandal-monger, gossip.
Tratte *f* **-n** *(Fin)* draft.
Traube *f* **-n** *(Beere)* grape; *(ganze Frucht)* bunch of grapes; *(Menschen~)* bunch. **~n** *(Fruchtart)* grapes.
Trauben-: **~lese** *f* grape harvest; **~saft** *m* grape juice; **~zucker** *m* glucose, dextrose.
trauen 1 *vi+dat* to trust. **ich traute meinen Augen nicht** I couldn't believe my eyes. **2** *vr* to dare. **sich** *(acc)* **~, etw zu tun** to dare (to) do sth; **ich trau' mich nicht** I daren't, I dare not; **sich auf die Straße ~** to dare to go out (of doors). **3** *vt* to marry. **sich ~ lassen** to get married.
Trauer *f no pl (das Trauern, ~zeit, ~kleidung)* mourning; *(Schmerz, Leid)* sorrow, grief.
Trauer-: **~anzeige** *f* obituary, death notice; **~fall** *m* bereavement, death; **~feier** *f* funeral service; **~flor** *m* black ribbon; **~gemeinde** *f* mourners *pl*; **~kleidung** *f* mourning; **~kloß** *m (col)* wet blanket *(col)*; **~marsch** *m* funeral march; **~miene** *f (col)* long face.
trauern *vi* to mourn *(um jdn/etw* sb/sth*)*.
Trauer-: **~schleier** *m* black veil; **~spiel** *nt* tragedy; *(fig col)* fiasco; **~weide** *f* weeping willow; **~zug** *m* funeral procession.
Traufe *f* **-n** eaves *pl*.
träufeln *vt* to dribble.
traulich *adj* cosy *(Brit)*, cozy *(US)*.
Traum *m, pl* **Träume** *(lit, fig)* dream. **aus der ~!** it's all over; **das fällt mir nicht im ~ ein** I wouldn't dream of it.
Trauma *nt, pl* **Traumen** *or* **-ta** *(lit, fig)* trauma.
traumatisch *adj (lit, fig)* traumatic.
Traum-: **~beruf** *m* dream job; **~deutung** *f* interpretation of dreams.
träumen *vti (lit, fig)* to dream. **von jdm/etw ~** to dream about sb/sth; **das hätte ich mir nicht ~ lassen** I'd never have thought it possible.
Träumer(in *f***)** *m* **-** dreamer.
träumerisch *adj* dreamy.
traumhaft *adj (phantastisch)* fantastic; *(wie im Traum)* dreamlike.
traurig *adj* sad; *Leben auch* unhappy; *Leistung, Rekord* pathetic, sorry; *Wetter* miserable.
Traurigkeit *f* sadness.
Trau-: **~ring** *m* wedding ring; **~schein** *m* marriage certificate.
Trauung *f* wedding.
Trauzeuge *m* witness *(at marriage ceremony)*.
Treck *m* **-s** trek, trail; *(Leute)* train.
Treff *m* **-s** *(col) (Treffen)* meeting, get-together *(col)*; *(~punkt)* haunt, rendezvous.
treffen *pret* **traf,** *ptp* **getroffen 1** *vt* **(a)** *(durch Schlag etc)* to hit *(an/in+dat* on, *in+acc* in*)*; *(Blitz, Faust auch, Unglück)* to strike. **auf dem Photo bist du gut getroffen** *(col)* that's a good photo of you. **(b)** *(betreffen)* to hit, to affect. **er fühlte sich getroffen** he took it personally. **(c)** *(jdm begegnen)* to meet; *(an~)* to find. **(d)** *(finden)* to hit upon, to find; *(lit, fig) Ton* to hit. **(e) es mit dem Wetter gut/schlecht ~** to be lucky/unlucky with the weather. **(f)** *Vereinbarung* to reach; *Entscheidung* to make, to take; Maßnahmen to take. **2** *vi* **(a)** *(Schlag, Schuß etc)* to hit. **nicht ~** to miss. **(b)** *aux sein (stoßen)* **auf jdn/etw ~** to meet sb/sth. **(c)** *(verletzen)* to hurt. **3** *vr (zusammen~)* to meet. **4** *vr impers* **es trifft sich, daß ...** it (just) happens that ...; **das trifft sich gut/schlecht, daß ...** it is convenient/inconvenient that ...
Treffen *nt* **-** meeting; *(Sport, Mil)* encounter.
treffend *adj* apt; *Ähnlichkeit* striking.
Treffer *m* **-** hit; *(Tor)* goal; *(fig: Erfolg)* hit; *(Gewinnlos)* winner.
Treff-: **~punkt** *m* meeting place; **t~sicher** *adj* accurate; *Urteil* sound.
Treib|eis *nt* drift ice.
treiben *pret* **trieb,** *ptp* **getrieben 1** *vt* **(a)** *(lit, fig)* to drive; *(auf Treibjagd) Wild* to beat; *Teig* to make rise; *(fig: drängen)* to rush; *(an~)* to push. **jdn zum Wahnsinn ~** to drive sb mad; **jdn zur Eile/Arbeit ~** to make sb hurry up/work; **die ~de Kraft** the driving force; **jdm den Schweiß/das Blut ins Gesicht ~** to make sb sweat/blush. **(b)** *Geschäfte, Sport* to do; *Studien, Politik* to pursue; *Gewerbe* to carry on; *Unsinn* to be up to; *Aufwand* to create. **was treibst du?** what are you up to?; **Handel mit etw/jdm ~** to trade in sth/with sb. **(c)** *(col)* **wenn du es weiter so treibst ...** if you carry on like that ...; **es toll ~** to have a wild time; **es zu weit ~** to go too far; **es mit jdm ~** to have sex with sb. **(d)** *Blüten etc* to sprout; *(im Treibhaus)* to force. **2** *vi* **(a)** *aux sein (sich fortbewegen)* to drift. **sich ~ lassen** *(lit, fig)* to drift. **(b)** *(wachsen)* to sprout. **(c)** *(Hefe)* to make dough *etc* rise. **~de Medikamente** diuretics.
Treiben *nt* **-** *(Getriebe)* hustle and bustle; *(von Schneeflocken)* swirling.
Treiber *m* **-** *(Hunt)* beater; *(Vieh~)* drover.
Treib-: **~gas** *nt* propellant; **~haus** *nt* hothouse; **~holz** *nt* driftwood; **~jagd** *f* shoot *(in which game is sent up by beaters)*; *(fig)* witchhunt; **~mittel** *nt* *(in Sprühdosen)* propellant; *(Cook)* raising agent; **~sand** *m* quicksand; **~stoff** *m* fuel.
Trend *m* **-s** trend.
trennbar *adj* separable.
trennen 1 *vt* **(a)** to separate *(von* from*)*; *Kopf, Glied etc* to sever; *(abmachen)* to detach *(von* from*)*; *Aufgenähtes* to take off, to remove; *Saum, Naht* to undo; *Begriffe* to distinguish (between); *(nach Rasse, Geschlecht)* to segregate. **jetzt kann uns nichts mehr ~** now nothing can ever come between us. **(b)** *(in Bestandteile zerlegen) Kleid* to take to pieces; *Wort* to split; *(Chem) Gemisch* to separate (out). **2** *vr (auseinandergehen)* to separate; *(Partner, Eheleute etc auch)* to split up; *(Abschied nehmen)* to part; *(Wege, Flüsse)* to divide. **sich von jdm/der Firma ~** to leave sb/the firm; **die zwei Mannschaften trennten sich 2:2** the final score was 2:2; **sich von etw ~** to part with sth; **hier ~ sich unsere Wege** *(fig)* now we must go our separate ways.
Trennschärfe *f* selectivity.
Trennung *f* separation; *(Abschied)* parting; *(in Teile)* division; *(von Wort)* division; *(Rassen~, Geschlechter~)* segregation.
Trenn(ungs)-: **~strich** *m* hyphen; **~wand** *f* partition (wall); **~zeichen** *nt* hyphen.
trepp|auf *adv*: **~, treppab** up and down stairs.
Treppe *f* **-n** stairs *pl*, staircase; *(im Freien)* steps *pl*. **eine ~** a staircase, a flight of stairs/steps; **sie wohnt zwei ~n höher** she lives two flights up.
Treppen-: **~absatz** *m* half-landing; **~geländer** *nt* banister; **~haus** *nt* stairwell; **im ~haus** on the stairs; **~stufe** *f* step, stair.
Tresen *m* **-** *(Theke)* bar; *(Ladentisch)* counter.
Tresor *m* **-e** safe; *(Raum)* strongroom, vault.
Tret-: **~auto** *nt* pedal car; **~boot** *nt* pedal boat, pedalo.
treten *pret* **trat,** *ptp* **getreten 1** *vi* **(a) gegen etw**

~ to kick sth. **(b)** *aux sein* to step. **näher an etw** *(acc)* ~ to move *or* step closer to sth; **jdm auf den Fuß** ~ to step *or* tread on sb's foot; **jdm auf die Füße** ~ *(fig)* to tread on sb's toes; **aufs Gas(pedal)** ~ to press the accelerator; *(col: schnell fahren)* to step on it *(col)*. **(c) der Schweiß trat ihm auf die Stirn** sweat appeared on his forehead; **der Fluß trat über die Ufer** the river overflowed its banks. **(d)** *aux sein* **in den Streik** ~ to go on strike; **in den Stand der Ehe** ~ to enter into the state of matrimony. **2** *vt* to kick; *(Sport) Ecke, Freistoß* to take. **jdn ans Bein** ~ to kick sb on the leg; **jdn mit dem Fuß** ~ to kick sb.

Tret-: **~mine** *f (Mil)* (anti-personnel) mine; **~mühle** *f (lit, fig)* treadmill; **in der ~mühle sein** to be in a rut *(col)*; **~roller** *m* scooter.

treu **1** *adj Freund, Sohn, Kunde etc* loyal; *Hund, Gatte etc* faithful; *Abbild* true; *(~herzig)* trusting; *Miene* innocent. ~ **sein/bleiben** to be/ remain faithful to sb; **seinen Grundsätzen** ~ **bleiben** to stay true to one's principles. **2** *adv* faithfully; *sorgen* devotedly; *(~herzig)* trustingly; *ansehen* innocently.

Treu-: **~bruch** *m* breach of faith; **t~brüchig** *adj* faithless, false; **t~doof** *adj (col)* naive.

Treue *f no pl siehe* **treu** loyalty; faithfulness; *(eheliche ~)* faithfulness, fidelity.

Treu|eid *m* oath of allegiance.

Treueprämie *f* long-service bonus.

Treu-: **~händer(in** *f)* *m* trustee; **~handgesellschaft** *f* trust company; **t~herzig** *adj* trusting; **t~los** *adj* disloyal, faithless; **t~los an jdm handeln** to fail sb; **~losigkeit** *f* disloyalty, faithlessness.

Triangel *m* - triangle.

Tribunal *nt* **-e** tribunal.

Tribüne *f* **-n** *(Redner~)* platform; *(Zuschauer~, Zuschauer)* stand; *(Haupt~)* grandstand.

Tribut *m* **-e** *(lit, fig)* tribute; *(Opfer)* toll.

Trichine *f* trichina.

Trichter *m* - funnel; *(Bomben~)* crater; *(von Trompete etc)* bell; *(von Hörgerät)* trumpet; *(von Lautsprecher)* cone; *(Einfüll~)* hopper. **auf den ~ kommen** *(col)* to catch on *(col)*.

Trick *m* **-s** trick. **keine faulen ~s!** no funny business! *(col)*; **das ist der ganze ~** that's all there is to it; **der ~ dabei ist, ...** the trick is to ...; **jdm einen ~ verraten** to give sb a tip.

Trick-: **~betrug** *m* confidence trick; **~film** *m* trick film; *(Zeichen~)* cartoon (film); **t~reich** *adj (col)* tricky; *(raffiniert)* clever.

trieb *pret of* **treiben.**

Trieb *m* **-e** **(a)** *(Psych, Natur~)* drive; *(Drang, Verlangen)* urge; *(Neigung, Hang)* inclination; *(Selbsterhaltungs~)* instinct. **(b)** *(Bot)* shoot.

Trieb-: **~feder** *f (fig)* motivating force *(gen* behind*)*; **t~haft** *adj Handlungen* compulsive; **sie ist ein t~hafter Mensch** she is ruled by her physical desires; **~kraft** *f (Mech)* motive power; *(fig)* driving force; **~leben** *nt (Geschlechtsleben)* sex life; **~rad** *nt* driving wheel; **~täter** *m* sexual offender; **~wagen** *m (Rail)* railcar; **~werk** *nt* power plant; *(in Uhr)* mechanism.

triefen *vi* to be dripping wet; *(Nase)* to run; *(Auge)* to water. ~ **vor** to be dripping with; *(fig pej)* to gush with; **~d** soaking (wet).

triezen *vt (col)* **jdn** ~ to pester sb; *(schuften lassen)* to drive sb hard.

triftig *adj* cogent.

Trigonometrie *adj* trigonometry.

Trikolore *f* **-n** tricolour *(Brit)*, tricolor *(US)*.

Trikot [tri'ko:, 'trɪko] *nt* **-s** *(Hemd)* shirt, jersey.

Triller *m* - *(Mus)* trill.

trillern *vti* to warble, to trill.

Trillerpfeife *f* (pea-)whistle.

Trillion *f* **-en** trillion *(Brit)*, quintillion *(US)*.

Trilogie *f* trilogy.

Trimester *nt* - term.

Trimm-: **~-Aktion** *f* keep-fit campaign; **~-dich-Gerät** *nt* keep-fit apparatus; **~-dich-Pfad** *m* keep-fit trail.

trimmen **1** *vt Hund, Schiff, Flugzeug* to trim; *(col) Mensch, Tier* to teach, to train. **2** *vr* to do keep-fit (exercises). **trimm dich durch Sport** keep fit with sport.

trinkbar *adj* drinkable.

trinken *pret* **trank,** *ptp* **getrunken** *vti* to drink; *ein Bier, Tasse Tee, Flasche Wein auch* to have. **er trinkt gern einen** *(col)* he likes his drink; **jdm zu ~ geben** to give sb something to drink; **auf jdn/etw ~** to drink to sb/to sth.

Trinker(in *f)* *m* - drinker.

Trinkerheil|anstalt *f* detoxification centre *(Brit) or* center *(US)*.

Trink-: **t~fest** *adj* **ich bin nicht sehr t~fest** I can't hold my drink very well; **~geld** *nt* tip; **jdm ~geld geben** to tip sb, to give sb a tip; **~halle** *f (Kiosk)* refreshment kiosk; **~halm** *m* drinking straw; **~milch** *f* milk; **~schokolade** *f* drinking chocolate; **~spruch** *m* toast; **~wasser** *nt* drinking water.

Triole *f* **-n** *(Mus)* triplet.

trippeln *vi aux haben or (bei Richtungsangabe) sein* to trip; *(Kind, alte Dame)* to toddle.

Tripper *m* - gonorrhoea *no art (Brit)*, gonorrhea *no art (US)*.

trist *adj* dreary, dismal; *Farbe* dull.

Tritt *m* **-e** **(a)** *(Schritt)* step. **im ~ marschieren/~ halten** to march/keep in step. **(b)** *(Fuß~)* kick. **jdm einen ~ geben** to give sb a kick, to kick sb; *(fig) (entlassen etc)* to kick sb out *(col)*; *(col: anstacheln)* to give sb a kick up the backside *(col)*. **(c)** *(bei ~leiter, Stufe)* step; *(Gestell)* steps *pl*.

Tritt-: **~brett** *nt* step; *(an Auto)* running board; **~brettfahrer** *m (fig col)* free-rider *(col)*; **er ist ein politischer ~brettfahrer** he has jumped on the political bandwagon; **~leiter** *f* stepladder.

Triumphbogen *m* triumphal arch.

triumphieren* *vi (frohlocken)* to rejoice, to exult. **über jdn/etw ~** *(geh)* to triumph over sb/sth.

Triumphzug *m* triumphal procession.

trivial [tri'via:l] *adj* trivial.

Trivialliteratur [tri'via:l-] *f* light fiction.

trocken *adj (lit, fig)* dry. **da bleibt kein Auge ~** everyone is moved to tears; **~ aufbewahren/ lagern** to keep/store in a dry place; **sich ~ rasieren** to use an electric razor; **auf dem ~en sitzen** *(col)* to be in a tight spot *(col)*.

Trocken-: **~automat** *m* tumble dryer; **~boden** *m* drying room *(in attic)*; **~dock** *nt* dry dock; **~futter** *nt* dried food; **~haube** *f* (salon) hairdryer.

Trockenheit *f (lit, fig)* dryness; *(Dürre)* drought.

Trocken-: **~kurs** *m (Ski)* ski training course using dry slopes; **t~legen** *vt sep* **(a)** *Baby* to change; **(b)** *Sumpf* to drain; **~milch** *f* dried milk; **~zeit** *f (Jahreszeit)* dry season.

trocknen **1** *vt* to dry. **2** *vi aux sein* to dry.

Troddel *f* **-n** tassel.

Trödel *m no pl (col)* junk.

Trödelmarkt *m (col)* flea market.

trödeln *vi* to dawdle.

Trödler *m* - **(a)** *(Händler)* junk dealer. **(b)** *(col: langsamer Mensch)* dawdler.

Trog *m* **¨e** trough; *(Wasch~)* tub.

trog *pret of* **trügen.**

trollen *vr (col)* to push off *(col)*.

Trommel *f* **-n** *(Mus, Tech)* drum. **die ~ rühren** *(fig col)* to drum up support.

Trommel-: **~bremse** *f* drum brake; **~fell** *nt* eardrum; **~feuer** *nt* drumfire, heavy barrage.

trommeln **1** *vi* to drum; *(Regen)* to beat (down). **mit den Fingern ~** to drum one's fingers. **2** *vt Marsch, Lied* to play on the drum/drums.

Trommel-: **~schlag** *m* drum beat; *(das Trommeln)* drumming; **~stöcke** *pl* drumsticks *pl*.

Trommler(in *f)* *m* - drummer.

Trompete *f* **-n** trumpet.
trompeten* **1** *vi* to trumpet. **2** *vt Marsch* to play on the trumpet.
Trompeter(in *f*) *m* - trumpeter.
Tropen *pl* tropics *pl.*
Tropen- *in cpds* tropical; **~helm** *m* pith-helmet, topee.
Tropf *m* **¨-e** *(col)* **(a)** *(Schelm)* rogue, rascal. **armer ~** poor devil. **(b)** *no pl (Infusion)* drip *(col).*
tröpfeln 1 *vi (Leitung, aux sein: Flüssigkeit)* to drip; *(Nase)* to run. **2** *vt* to drip.
tropfen *vi* to drip; *(Nase)* to run.
Tropfen *m* - drop; *(Schweiß~ auch)* bead; *(fallender ~)* drip; *(col: kleine Menge)* drop. **~** *pl (Medizin)* drops; **ein guter** *or* **edler ~** *(col)* a good wine; **bis auf den letzten ~** to the last drop; **ein ~ auf den heißen Stein** *(fig col)* a drop in the ocean.
Tropf-: t~naß *adj* dripping wet; **~steinhöhle** *f* cave with stalactites/stalagmites.
Trophäe [tro'fɛːə] *f* **-n** trophy.
tropisch *adj* tropical.
Trost *m no pl* consolation, comfort. **ein ~, daß jetzt alles vorbei ist** it is a relief that everything is over; **das ist ein schwacher** *(iro)* **~** some comfort that is!
trösten *vt* to comfort. **sich/jdn über etw** *(acc)* **~** to get over sth/to help sb to get over sth.
tröstlich *adj* cheering, comforting.
trostlos *adj* hopeless; *Jugend, Verhältnisse* miserable, wretched; *(öde, trist)* dreary.
Trost-: ~pflaster *nt* consolation; **~preis** *m* consolation prize.
Trott *m no pl* (slow) trot; *(fig)* routine. **im ~** at a (slow) trot.
Trottel *m* - *(col)* idiot, dope *(col).*
trotten *vi aux sein* to trot along.
trotz *prep+gen (geh) or +dat (col)* in spite of, despite.
Trotz *m no pl* defiance; *(trotziges Verhalten)* contrariness. **jdm/einer Sache zum ~** in defiance of sb/sth.
Trotz|alter *nt* defiant age.
trotzdem *adv* nevertheless. **(und) ich mache das ~!** I'll do it all the same.
trotzen *vi* **(a)**+*dat* to defy; *der Kälte, Klima etc* to withstand; *der Gefahr* to brave. **(b)** *(trotzig sein)* to be awkward.
trotzig *adj* defiant; *Kind etc* difficult, awkward.
Trotz-: ~kopf *m (col)* contrary so-and-so *(col);* **~reaktion** *f* act of defiance.
trüb(e) *adj* **(a)** dull; *Flüssigkeit* cloudy; *Sonne, Licht* dim. **im ~en fischen** *(col)* to fish in troubled waters. **(b)** *(fig: bedrückend, unerfreulich) Zeiten* bleak; *Erfahrung* grim. **~e Tasse** *(col)* drip *(col).*
Trubel *m no pl* hurly-burly.
trüben 1 *vt* **(a)** *Flüssigkeit* to make cloudy; *Glas, Metall* to dull; *Blick* to cloud. **sie sieht aus, als könnte sie kein Wässerlein ~** *(col)* she looks as if butter wouldn't melt in her mouth. **(b)** *(fig) Glück, Verhältnis* to spoil; *Bewußtsein, Verstand* to dull. **2** *vr (Flüssigkeit)* to go cloudy; *(Spiegel, Metall)* to become dull; *(geh) (Verstand)* to become dulled; *(Augen)* to dim; *(Himmel)* to cloud over; *(Glück, Freude)* to be marred.
Trüb-: ~sal *f* gloom; **~sal blasen** *(col)* to mope; **t~selig** *adj* gloomy; *Behausung, Wetter* miserable; **~sinn** *m no pl* gloom, melancholy.
trudeln *vi aux sein or haben (Aviat)* to spin.
Trüffel[1] *f* **-n** *(Pilz)* truffle.
Trüffel[2] *m* - truffle.
Trug *m no pl (liter)* deception; *(der Sinne)* illusion.
trug *pret of* **tragen.**
trügen *pret* **trog,** *ptp* **getrogen 1** *vt* to deceive. **wenn mich nicht alles trügt** unless I am very much mistaken. **2** *vi* to be deceptive.
trügerisch *adj (irreführend)* deceptive.
Trugschluß *m* fallacy.
Truhe *f* **-n** chest.
Trümmer *pl* rubble *sing; (Ruinen, fig: von Glück etc)* ruins *pl; (von Schiff, Flugzeug etc)* wreckage *sing; (Überreste)* remnants *pl.* **etw in ~ schlagen** to smash sth to pieces.
Trümmerfeld *nt* expanse of rubble/ruins; *(fig)* scene of devastation.
Trumpf *m* **¨-e** *(Cards) (~karte, auch fig)* trump card; *(Farbe)* trumps *pl.* **~ sein** to be trumps; *(fig col: modisch sein)* to be in *(col);* **den ~ in der Hand haben/aus der Hand geben** *(fig)* to hold the/throw away one's trump card.
trumpfen 1 *vt* to trump. **2** *vi* to play a trump (card).
Trumpf-: ~farbe *f* trumps *pl;* **~karte** *f* trump (card).
Trunk *m* **¨-e (a)** *(old, liter)* draught *(old, liter).* **(b) dem ~ verfallen sein** to have taken to drink.
Trunken-: ~bold *m* **-e** *(pej)* drunkard; **~heit** *f* drunkenness; **~heit am Steuer** drunken driving.
Trunksucht *f* alcoholism.
Trupp *m* **-s** *(Einheit)* group; *(Mil)* squad.
Truppe *f* **-n (a)** *(Mil)* army, troops *pl; (Panzer~ etc)* corps *sing.* **~n** *pl* troops. **nicht von der schnellen ~ sein** *(col)* to be slow. **(b)** *(Künstler~)* troupe, company.
Truppen-: ~gattung *f* corps *sing;* **~übung** *f* field exercise; **~übungsplatz** *m* military training area.
Trut-: ~hahn *m* turkey(cock); **~henne** *f* turkey(hen); **~huhn** *nt usu pl* turkey.
Tscheche *m (wk)* **-n, -n, Tschechin** *f* Czech.
tschechisch *adj* Czech.
Tschechoslowake *m (wk)* **-n, -n, Tschechoslowakin** *f* Czechoslovak.
Tschechoslowakei *f* **die ~** Czechoslovakia.
tschüs *interj (col)* cheerio *(Brit col),* so long *(col).*
Tsetsefliege *f* tsetse fly.
TU [teː'|uː] *f* - = **Technische Universität.**
Tube *f* **-n** tube. **auf die ~ drücken** *(col)* to get a move on *(col).*
Tuberkulose *f* **-n** tuberculosis.
tuberkulosekrank *adj* tubercular.
Tuch *nt* **¨-er (a)** cloth; *(Hals~, Kopf~)* scarf. **das wirkt wie ein rotes ~ auf ihn** it's like a red rag to a bull. **(b)** *pl* **-e** *(old: Stoff)* cloth.
Tuch-: ~fabrik *f* textile factory; **~fühlung** *f* physical contact; **~händler** *m* cloth merchant; **~macher** *m* clothworker.
tüchtig 1 *adj* **(a)** *(fähig)* competent *(in+dat* at); *(fleißig)* efficient. **etwas T~es lernen/werden** *(col)* to get a proper training/job; **~, ~!** not bad! **(b)** *(col: groß) Portion* big. **2** *adv* **(a)** *(fleißig, fest)* hard; *essen* heartily. **hilf ~ mit** give us a hand. **(b)** *(col: sehr)* good and proper *(col).* **~ regnen** to pelt down *(col);* **~ zulangen** to tuck in *(col).*
Tüchtigkeit *f (Fähigkeit)* competence; *(von Arbeiter etc)* efficiency.
Tücke *f* **-n (a)** *(no pl: Bosheit)* malice, spite. **(b)** *(Gefahr)* danger, peril; *(von Krankheit)* perniciousness. **voller ~n stecken** to be difficult; *(gefährlich)* to be treacherous; **seine ~n haben** *(Maschine etc)* to be temperamental. **(c)** *(des Schicksals)* vagary *usu pl.*
tückisch *adj Mensch* malicious, spiteful;*Berge, Strom* treacherous; *Krankheit* pernicious.
tüfteln *vi (col)* to puzzle; *(basteln)* to fiddle about *(col).* **an etw** *(dat)* **~** to fiddle about with sth; *(geistig)* to puzzle over sth.
Tüftler(in *f*) *m* - *(col) person who likes doing fiddly or finicky things.*
Tugend *f* **-en** virtue.
Tugend-: ~bold *m* **-e** *(pej)* paragon of virtue; **t~haft** *adj* virtuous.
Tüll *m* **-e** tulle; *(für Gardinen)* net.
Tulpe *f* **-n** *(Bot)* tulip; *(Glas)* tulip glass.
tummeln *vr* **(a)** to romp (about). **(b)** *(sich beeilen)* to hurry.
Tummelplatz *m* play area; *(fig)* hotbed.

Tümmler *m* - (bottle-nosed) dolphin.
Tumor *m* **-en** [tu'moːrən] tumour *(Brit)*, tumor *(US)*.
Tümpel *m* - pond.
Tumult *m* **-e** commotion.
tun *pret* **tat,** *ptp* **getan 1** *vt* **(a)** to do; *Blick, Schritt* to take. **was ~?** what shall we do?; **du kannst ~ und lassen, was du willst** you can do as you please; **tu, was du nicht lassen kannst** well, if you must; **damit ist es noch nicht getan** and that's not all; **etwas gegen etw ~** to do something about sth; **Sie müssen etwas für sich ~** you should treat yourself; *(sich schonen)* you should take care of yourself; **so etwas tut man nicht!** that's just not done; **es tat einen Knall** there was a bang; **das hat nichts mit ihm zu ~** that is nothing to do with him; **ich habe mit mir (selbst) genug zu ~** I have enough problems of my own; **es mit jdm zu ~ bekommen** *(col)* to get into trouble with sb; **er hat es mit der Leber zu ~** *(col)* he has liver trouble; **was tut's?** what difference does it make?; **jdm etwas ~** to do something to sb; *(stärker)* to harm *or* hurt sb.
(b) *(col: an bestimmten Ort legen)* to put. **etw in die Tasche ~** to put sth in one's pocket.
(c) *(col: funktionieren)* **die Uhr tut es nicht mehr** this watch has had it *(col)*; **das Radio tut es wieder** the radio is going again.
2 *vr (geschehen)* **es tut sich etwas** there is something happening; **hat sich in dieser Hinsicht schon etwas getan?** has anything been done about this?
3 *vi* **(a) zu ~ haben** *(beschäftigt sein)* to be busy, to have work to do; **in der Stadt zu ~ haben** to have things to do in town; **mit jdm zu ~ haben** to deal with sb. **(b)** *(sich benehmen)* to act. **so ~, als ob ...** to pretend that ...; **tust du nur so dumm?** are you just acting stupid?; **sie tut nur so** she's only pretending. **(c) Sie täten gut daran, früh zu kommen** you would do well to come early.
Tünche *f* **-n** whitewash; *(fig)* veneer.
tünchen *vt* to whitewash.
Tunesien [-iən] *nt* Tunisia.
Tunichtgut *m* **-e** good-for-nothing.
Tunke *f* **-n** sauce; *(Braten~)* gravy.
tunken *vt* to dip; *(stippen)* to dunk *(col)*; *jdn* to duck.
tunlichst *adv* if possible. **ich werde es ~ vermeiden, ihm meine Meinung zu sagen** I'll do my best to avoid telling him what I think.
Tunnel *m* - *or* **-s** tunnel.
Tunte *f* **-n** *(col)* fairy *(pej col)*.
Tüpfel *m or nt* **-, Tüpfelchen** *nt* dot.
tupfen *vt* to dab. **getupft** spotted.
Tupfen *m* - spot; *(klein)* dot.
Tupfer *m* - swab.
Tür *f* **-en** door; *(Garten~)* gate. **in der ~** in the doorway; **an die ~ gehen** to answer the door; **Weihnachten steht vor der ~** Christmas is just around the corner; **jdn vor die ~ setzen** *(col)* to throw sb out; **jdm die ~ weisen** to show sb the door; **ein jeder kehre vor seiner ~** *(prov)* everyone should set his own house in order; **mit der ~ ins Haus fallen** *(col)* to blurt it/things out; **zwischen ~ und Angel** in passing.
Tür|angel *f* (door) hinge.
Turban *m* **-e** turban.
Turbine *f* turbine.
Turbinenflugzeug *nt* turbo-jet.
Turbomotor *m* turbocharged engine.
turbulent *adj* turbulent.
Turbulenz *f* turbulence *no pl*.
Tür-: ~drücker *m* doorknob; *(col: Öffner)* buzzer; **~flügel** *m* door *(of a pair of doors)*.
Türke *m (wk)* **-n, -n, Türkin** *f* Turk.
Türkei *f* **die ~** Turkey.
türken *vt (col) Papiere, Zahlen* to fiddle.
Türkis *m* **-e** *(Edelstein)* turquoise.
türkis *adj* turquoise.
türkisch *adj* Turkish.
Tür-: ~klinke *f* door handle; **~klopfer** *m* door-knocker.
Turm *m* **¨-e (a)** tower; *(spitzer Kirch~)* spire. **(b)** *(Chess)* castle, rook.
türmen 1 *vt* to pile up. **2** *vr* to pile up; *(Wolken)* to build up; *(Wellen)* to tower up. **3** *vi aux sein (col: davonlaufen)* to run off.
Turm-: ~falke *m* kestrel; **~schwalbe** *f* swift; **~uhr** *f* clock (on a/the tower); *(Kirch~)* church clock.
Turnanzug *m* gym costume.
turnen *vi* **(a)** to do gymnastics; *(Sch)* to do gym. **am Reck ~** to do exercises on the horizontal bar. **(b)** *aux sein (herumklettern)* to climb about; *(Kind)* to romp.
Turnen *nt no pl* gymnastics *sing*.
Turner(in *f***)** *m* - gymnast.
Turn-: ~fest *nt* gymnastics display; *(von Schule)* sports day; **~gerät** *nt* (piece of) gymnastic equipment; **~halle** *f* gym(nasium); **~hemd** *nt* gym shirt; **~hose** *f* gym shorts *pl*.
Turnier *nt* **-e** tournament; *(Tanz~)* competition; *(Reit~)* show.
Turnierpferd *nt* show horse.
Turn-: ~lehrer *m* gym teacher; **~schuh** *m* gym shoe; **~stunde** *f* gym lesson; **~übung** *f* gymnastic exercise.
Turnus *m* **-se** rota. **im (regelmäßigen) ~** in rotation.
Turn-: ~verein *m* gymnastics club; **~zeug** *nt* gym kit.
Tür-: ~öffner *m* buzzer; **~pfosten** *m* doorpost; **~rahmen** *m* doorframe; **~schild** *nt* doorplate; **~schloß** *nt* door lock; **~schwelle** *f* threshold.
Turteltaube *f (lit, fig col)* turtle-dove.
Türvorleger *m* doormat.
Tusch *m* **-e** *(Mus)* flourish.
Tusche *f* **-n** *(Auszieh~)* Indian ink; *(~farbe)* water colour *(Brit) or* color *(US)*.
tuscheln *vti* to whisper. **hinter seinem Rücken über jdn ~** to talk about sb behind his/her back.
tuschen *vt* to draw in Indian ink. **sich** *(dat)* **die Wimpern ~** to put one's mascara on.
Tusch-: ~farbe *f* water colour *(Brit) or* color *(US)*; **~zeichnung** *f* pen-and-ink drawing.
Tüte *f* **-n** bag; *(Eis~)* cornet, cone; *(col: für Alkoholtest)* breathalyzer. **in die ~ blasen** *(col)* to be breathalyzed; **~n kleben** *(col)* to be in clink *(col)*; **das kommt nicht in die ~!** *(col)* no way! *(col)*.
tuten *vti* to toot; *(Schiff)* to sound its horn. **von T~ und Blasen keine Ahnung haben** *(col)* not to have a clue *(col)*.
TÜV [tyf] *m* **-s = Technischer Überwachungs-Verein** ≃ MOT *(Brit)* **das Auto ist durch den ~ gekommen** the car passed its MOT.
Twen *m* **-s** *person in his/her twenties.*
Typ *n* **-en** type; *(von Auto auch)* model; *(col: Mensch)* person, character; *(col: Mann, Freund)* guy *(col)*. **er ist nicht mein ~** *(col)* he's not my type *(col)*; **dein ~ wird verlangt** *(col)* you're wanted; **dein ~ ist nicht gefragt** *(col)* you're not wanted around here.
Type *f* **-n (a)** *(Druckbuchstabe)* character. **~n** *(Schrift)* type *sing*; **~n gießen** to set type. **(b)** *(col: Mensch)* character.
Typhus *m no pl* typhoid (fever).
Typhuskranke(r) *mf* typhoid case.
typisch *adj* typical *(für* of*)*. **~ deutsch** typically German.
Typographie *f* typography.
Tyrann(in *f***)** *m (wk)* **-en, -en** tyrant.
Tyrannei *f* tyranny.
tyrannisch *adj* tyrannical.
tyrannisieren* *vt* to tyrannize.

U

U, u [uː] *nt* -, - U, u.
u. = **und.**
u.a. = **und andere(s); unter anderem/ anderen.**
U-Bahn ['uː-] *f* underground *(Brit)*, subway *(US)*; *(in London)* tube.
U-Bahnhof ['uː-] *m* underground *etc* station.
übel 1 *adj* bad; *Erkältung etc auch* nasty; *(moralisch auch)* wicked, evil. **er war übler Laune** he was in a bad mood; **das ist eine üble Sache!** it's a bad business; **in übler** *or* **~ster Weise** in a most unpleasant way; **mir wird ~** I feel ill *or* sick. **2** *adv* badly. **etw ~ aufnehmen** to take sth badly; **das schmeckt gar nicht so ~** it doesn't taste so bad; **ich hätte nicht ~ Lust, jetzt nach Paris zu fahren** I wouldn't mind going to Paris now.
Übel *nt* - evil. **ein notwendiges/das kleinere ~** a necessary/the lesser evil; **das alte ~** the old trouble; **von ~ sein** to be a bad thing, to be bad; **zu allem ~ ...** to make matters worse ...
übelgelaunt *adj attr* sullen, morose.
Übelkeit *f (lit, fig)* nausea.
Übel-: ü~launig *adj* ill-tempered; **ü~nehmen** *vt sep irreg* **(jdm) etw ü~nehmen** to take sth amiss; **ü~riechend** *adj* foul-smelling, evil-smelling; **~täter** *m (geh)* wrongdoer.
üben *vtir* to practise *(Brit)*, to practice *(US)*; *(Mil)* to drill; *Gedächtnis, Muskeln etc* to exercise. **mit geübtem Auge** with a practised eye; **Kritik an etw** *(dat)* **~** to criticize sth; **sich in etw** *(dat)* **~** to practise sth.
über 1 *prep* **(a)**+*acc (räumlich)* over; *(quer ~ auch)* across; *(weiter als)* beyond. **er lachte ~ das ganze Gesicht** he was beaming all over his face.
(b)+*dat (räumlich) (Lage, Standort)* over, above; *(jenseits)* over, across. **zwei Grad ~ Null** two degrees above zero; **~ jdm stehen** *(fig)* to be over *or* above sb.
(c)+*dat (zeitlich: bei, während)* over. **~ der Arbeit einschlafen** to fall asleep over one's work.
(d)+*acc* **Macht ~ jdn haben** to have power over sb; **sie liebt ihn ~ alles** she loves him more than anything; **das geht mir ~ den Verstand** that's beyond my understanding.
(e)+*acc (vermittels, auf dem Wege ~)* via. **die Nummer erfährt man ~ die Auskunft** you'll get the number from *or* through *or* via directory enquiries; **nach Köln ~ Aachen** to Cologne via Aachen.
(f)+*acc (zeitlich)* over. **~ Weihnachten** over Christmas; **den ganzen Sommer ~** all summer long; **~ Wochen** for weeks on end; **die ganze Zeit ~** all the time; **~ kurz oder lang** sooner or later.
(g)+*acc (bei Zahlenangaben)* **ein Scheck ~ DM 20** a cheque for 20 DM; **Kinder ~ 14 Jahre** children over 14 years *or* of 14 and over.
(h)+*acc (betreffend)* about. **ein Buch ~ ...** a book about *or* on ...; **~ jdn/etw lachen** to laugh about *or* at sb/sth; **sich ~ etw freuen/ärgern** to be pleased/angry about *or* at sth.
(i)+*acc (steigernd)* **Fehler ~ Fehler** mistake upon *or* after mistake.
2 *adv* **~ und ~** all over; **er wurde ~ und ~ rot** he went red all over.
über|all *adv* everywhere. **~ wo** wherever; **~ Bescheid wissen** *(wissensmäßig)* to have a wide-ranging knowledge; **es ist ~ dasselbe** it's the same wherever you go.
über|all-: ~her *adv* from all over; **~hin** *adv* everywhere.
Über-: ~angebot *nt* surplus *(an+dat* of*)*; **ü~ängstlich** *adj* overanxious; **ü~anstrengen*** *insep* **1** *vt* to overstrain; *Kräfte* to overtax; *Augen* to strain; **2** *vr* to overstrain oneself; **~anstrengung** *f* overexertion; **eine ~anstrengung der Nerven/Augen** a strain on the nerves/eyes; **ü~arbeiten*** *insep* **1** *vt* to rework; **in einer ü~arbeiteten Fassung** published in a revised edition; **2** *vr* to overwork; **~arbeitung** *f no pl* **(a)** revision; **(b)** *(~anstrengung)* overwork; **ü~aus** *adv* extremely; **ü~backen*** *vt insep irreg* to put in the oven/under the grill; **ü~backene Käseschnitten** cheese on toast.
Überbau *m* **-e** *(Build, Philos)* superstructure.
überbauen* *vt insep* to build over; *(mit einem Dach)* to build a roof over.
Über-: ü~beanspruchen* *vt insep* **(a)** *Menschen, Körper, Maschine* to overtax; **(arbeitsmäßig) ü~beansprucht sein** to be overworked; **(b)** *Einrichtungen, Dienste* to overburden; **ü~belegen*** *vt insep usu ptp* to overcrowd; *Kursus, Fach etc* to oversubscribe; **ü~belichten*** *vt insep (Phot)* to overexpose; **~beschäftigung** *f* overemployment; **ü~besetzt** *adj Abteilung* overstaffed; **ü~betonen*** *vt insep (fig)* to overemphasize; **ü~betrieblich** *adj* industry-wide; **~bevölkerung** *f* overpopulation; **ü~bewerten*** *vt insep (lit)* to overvalue; *(fig auch)* to overrate; *Schulleistung etc* to mark too high; *Äußerungen* to attach too much importance to; **~bezahlung** *f* overpayment; **ü~bieten*** *insep irreg* **1** *vt (bei Auktion)* to outbid *(um* by*)*; *(fig)* to outdo; *Leistung, Rekord* to beat; **das ist kaum noch zu ü~bieten** *(Frechheit etc)* it's outrageous; **2** *vr* **sich in etw** *(dat)* **(gegenseitig) ü~bieten** to vie with each other in sth; **~bleibsel** *nt* - remnant; *(Speiserest)* leftovers *pl*; *(Brauch, Angewohnheit etc)* survival, hangover.
Überblick *m (über+acc* of*)* **(a)** *(freie Sicht)* view. **(b)** *(Einblick)* overview. **er hat keinen ~** he has no overall picture; **den ~ verlieren** to lose track (of things). **(c)** *(Abriß)* survey; *(Übersicht)* synopsis, summary. **sich** *(dat)* **einen ~ verschaffen** to get a general idea.
überblicken* *vt insep* **(a)** *(lit) Platz, Stadt* to overlook. **(b)** *(fig)* to see; *Lage etc auch* to grasp.
überbraten* *vt insep irreg (Cook)* to fry lightly.
überbringen* *vt insep irreg* **jdm etw ~** to bring sb sth.
Überbringer(in *f***)** *m* - bringer; *(von Scheck)* bearer.
überbrücken* *vt insep Kluft, Zeitraum* to bridge; *Krisenzeiten* to get over; *Gegensätze* to reconcile.
Überbrückung *f* **100 Mark zur ~** 100 marks to tide me/him *etc* over.
Überbrückungskredit *m* bridging loan.
Über-: ü~dachen* *vt insep* to cover; **ü~dauern*** *vt insep* to survive; **~decke** *f* bedspread; **ü~decken**[1] *vt sep* to cover up *or* over; *(col) Tischtuch* to put on; **ü~decken**[2]* *vt insep Riß, Geschmack* to cover up; **ü~dehnen*** *vt insep Muskel*

etc to strain; *Gummi, (fig) Begriff* to overstretch; **ü~denken*** *vt insep irreg* to think over.

überdies *adv (geh) (außerdem)* moreover; *(ohnehin)* anyway.

Über-: ü~dimensional *adj* colossal, oversize; **~dosis** *f* overdose, OD *(col); (zu große Zumessung)* excessive amount; **ü~drehen*** *vt insep Uhr etc* to overwind; *Gewinde* to strip; **~druck** *m, pl* **~drücke** *(Tech)* excess pressure *no pl.*

Überdruß *m no pl (Übersättigung)* surfeit *(an+dat* of*); (Widerwille)* aversion *(an +dat* to*).* **bis zum ~** ad nauseam.

überdrüssig *adj* **jds/einer Sache** *(gen)* **~ sein/ werden** to be/grow weary of sb/sth.

über-: ~durchschnittlich 1 *adj* above-average; **2** *adv* exceptionally; **~eifrig** *adj* overzealous; **~eignen*** *vt insep (geh)* **jdm etw ~eignen** to make sth over to sb; **~eilen*** *vtr insep* to rush; **~eilen Sie nichts!** don't rush things!; **~eilt** *adj* hasty.

über|einander *adv* **(a)** *(räumlich)* on top of each other; *hängen* one above the other. **(b)** *reden etc* about each other.

über|einander-: ~legen *vt sep* to put one on top of the other; **~liegen** *vi sep irreg* to lie on top of each other; **~schlagen** *vt sep irreg* **die Beine ~schlagen** to cross one's legs.

über|einkommen *vi sep irreg aux sein* to agree.

Über|einkunft *f* **-̈e** agreement. **eine ~ treffen/ erzielen** to make/reach an agreement.

über|einstimmen *vi sep* to agree; *(Angaben, Meßwerte etc)* to tally; *(Farben, Stile etc)* to match; *(mit Tatsachen)* to fit. **mit jdm in etw** *(dat)* **~** to agree with sb on sth.

über|einstimmend 1 *adj* corresponding; *Meinungen* concurring; *Farben* matching. **nach ~en Meldungen** according to all reports. **2** *adv* **alle erklärten ~, daß ...** everybody agreed that ...

Über|einstimmung *f* correspondence, agreement; *(von Meinung)* agreement. **zwei Dinge in ~ bringen** to bring two things into line; **darin besteht bei allen Beteiligten ~** all parties involved are agreed on that; **in ~ mit jdm/etw** in agreement with sb/in accordance with sth.

über-: ~empfindlich *adj (gegen* to*)* oversensitive, hypersensitive *(auch Med)*; **~erfüllen*** *vt insep Norm, Soll* to exceed *(um* by*)*; **~ernähren*** *vt insep* to overfeed; **~essen¹** *vt sep irreg* **sich** *(dat)* **etw ~essen** to grow sick of sth; **~essen²** *pret* **~aß,** *ptp* **~gessen** *vr insep* to overeat; **sich an Käse ~essen** to eat too much cheese.

überfahren¹ *sep irreg* **1** *vt (mit Boot etc)* to take *or* ferry across. **2** *vi aux sein* to cross over.

überfahren²* *vt insep irreg* **(a)** *jdn, Tier* to run over, to knock down. **(b)** *(hinwegfahren über)* to go *or* drive over. **(c)** *Ampel* to jump.

Überfahrt *f* crossing.

Überfall *m* attack *(auf+acc* on*)*; *(auf offener Straße auch)* mugging *(auf+acc* of*)*; *(auf Bank etc)* raid *(auf+acc* on*)*.

überfallen* *vt insep irreg* **(a)** to attack; *(auf offener Straße auch)* to mug; *Bank, Lager* to raid. **(b)** *(fig geh: Gefühle, Müdigkeit)* to come over.

Über-: ü~fällig *adj* overdue *usu pred;* **~fallkommando** *nt* flying squad; **ü~fliegen*** *vt insep irreg* **(a)** to fly over, to overfly; **(b)** *(flüchtig ansehen) Buch etc* to take a quick look at; **ü~fließen** *vi sep irreg aux sein (Gefäß)* to overflow; *(fig: vor Dank etc auch)* to gush *(vor+dat* with*)*; **ü~flügeln*** *vt insep* to outdo.

Überfluß *m no pl* abundance *(an +dat* of*)*; *(Luxus)* affluence. **Arbeit im ~** plenty of work; **zu allem** *or* **zum ~** *(unnötigerweise)* superfluously; *(obendrein)* to crown it all *(col)*.

überflüssig *adj* superfluous; *(frei, entbehrlich)* spare; *(unnötig)* unnecessary; *(zwecklos)* useless.

überflüssigerweise *adv* superfluously.

Über-: ü~fluten* *vt insep (lit, fig)* to flood; *(fig auch)* to inundate; **ü~fordern*** *vt insep* to overtax; *jdn auch* to ask too much of; **ü~fragt** *adj pred* stumped; **da bin ich ü~fragt** there you've got me; **ü~führen¹** *vt sep* to transfer; *Wagen* to drive; **ü~führen²*** *vt insep* **(a)** *siehe* **ü~führen¹**; **(b)** *Täter* to convict *(gen* of*)*, to find guilty *(gen* of*)*; **(c) einen Fluß mit einer Brücke ü~führen** to build a bridge over a river; **~führung** *f* **(a)** transportation; **(b)** *no pl (Jur)* conviction; **(c)** *(Brücke über Straße etc)* bridge *(auch Rail)*, overpass; *(Fußgänger~)* footbridge; **ü~füllt** *adj* overcrowded; *Kurs* oversubscribed; *(Comm) Lager* overstocked; **ü~füttern*** *vt insep* to overfeed.

Übergabe *f no pl* handing over *no pl*; *(von Neubau)* opening; *(Mil)* surrender.

Übergang *m* **(a)** *(das Überqueren)* crossing. **(b)** *(Fußgänger~)* crossing, crosswalk *(US)*; *(Brücke)* footbridge; *(Rail)* level *(Brit) or* grade *(US)* crossing. **(c)** *(fig: Wechsel)* transition.

Übergangs-: ü~los *adj* without a transition; **~zeit** *f* transitional period.

übergeben* *insep irreg* **1** *vt* to hand over *(jdm* to sb*)*; *(Mil auch)* to surrender. **eine Straße dem Verkehr ~** to open a road to traffic. **2** *vr (sich erbrechen)* to vomit, to be sick *(Brit)*.

übergehen¹ *vi sep irreg aux sein* **(a) in etw** *(acc)* **~** to turn *or* change into sth; *(Farben)* to merge into sth; **in jds Besitz** *(acc)* **~** to become sb's property. **(b) auf jdn ~** *(geerbt, übernommen werden)* to pass to sb. **(c) zu jdm ~** *(überwechseln)* to go over to sb.

übergehen²* *vt insep irreg jdn* to pass over; *Einwände etc auch* to ignore.

Über-: ü~geordnet *adj Behörde* higher; **ü~geschnappt** *adj (col)* crazy; **~gewicht** *nt* overweight; *(fig)* predominance; **~gewicht haben** to be overweight; **ü~gießen*** *vt insep irreg* to pour over; *jdn* to douse; *Braten* to baste; **jdn/sich mit etw ü~gießen** to pour sth over sb/oneself; **ü~glücklich** *adj* overjoyed; **ü~greifen** *vi sep irreg (auf Rechte etc)* to encroach *(auf+acc* on*)*; *(Feuer, Streik, Krankheit etc)* to spread *(auf +acc* to*)*; **ineinander ü~greifen** to overlap; **ü~greifend** *adj (fig) Überlegungen* general; **~griff** *m (Einmischung)* encroachment *(auf +acc* on*)*; *(Mil)* incursion *(auf+acc* into*)*; **~größe** *f (bei Kleidung)* outsize; **ü~haben** *vt sep irreg (col)* **(a)** *(satt haben)* to be sick of *(col)*; **(b)** *(übrig haben)* to have left (over); **für etw nichts ü~haben** not to like sth.

überhandnehmen *vi sep irreg* to get out of hand.

Über-: ~hang *m* **(a)** *(Fels~)* overhang; **(b)** *(Comm: Überschuß)* surplus *(an+dat* of*)*; **ü~hängen** *sep* **1** *vi irreg aux haben or sein* to overhang; **2** *vt* **sich** *(dat)* **einen Mantel ü~hängen** to put a coat over one's shoulders; **ü~hastet** *adj* overhasty; **ü~hastet sprechen** to speak too fast; **ü~häufen*** *vt insep jdn* to overwhelm; **jdn mit Geschenken/Vorwürfen ü~häufen** to heap presents/reproaches on sb.

überhaupt *adv* **(a)** *(in Fragen, Verneinungen)* at all. **~ nicht** not at all; **~ kein Grund** no reason at all *or* whatsoever; **hast du denn ~ keinen Anstand?** have you no decency at all?; **das habe ich ja ~ nicht gewußt** I had no idea at all. **(b)** *(sowieso, im allgemeinen)* in general; *(überdies, außerdem)* anyway, anyhow. **er ist ~ sehr schüchtern** he's very shy in general; **er sagt ~ immer sehr wenig** he never says very much anyway *or* anyhow. **(c)** *(erst, eigentlich)* **waren Sie ~ schon in dem neuen Film?** have you actually been to the latest film?; **wenn ~** if at all; **wie ist das ~ möglich?** how is that (even) possible?; **wer sind Sie ~?** who do you think you are?

über-: ~heblich *adj* arrogant; **~hitzen*** *vt insep* to overheat; **~hitzt** *adj (fig) Diskussion* very heated; **~höht** *adj Forderungen, Preise* exorbitant.

überholen* *vti insep* **(a)** *Fahrzeug* to overtake

(Brit), to pass; *(fig: übertreffen)* to overtake. **(b)** *Motor etc* to overhaul.

Überhol-: ~spur *f* fast lane; **~verbot** *nt* restriction on overtaking *(Brit)* *or* passing; *(als Schild etc)* no overtaking *(Brit)*, no passing.

überhören* *vt insep* not to hear; *(nicht hören wollen)* to ignore. **das möchte ich überhört haben!** (I'll pretend) I didn't hear that!

Über-Ich *nt* superego.

über-: ~irdisch *adj* celestial, heavenly; **~kandidelt** *adj (col)* eccentric; **~kippen** *vi sep aux sein* to topple over; **~kleben*** *vt insep* **die Kiste ü~kleben** to stick something over the box; **~kochen** *vi sep aux sein (lit, fig)* to boil over; **~kommen*** *vt insep irreg (geh: ergreifen)* to come over; **Furcht** *etc* **~kam ihn** he was overcome with fear *etc*; **~kriegen** *vt sep (col)* **(a)** *(ü~drüssig werden)* to get fed up with *(col)*; **(b) eins ~kriegen** to get landed one *(col)*; **~laden*** **1** *vt insep irreg* to overload; *(reichlich geben)* to shower; *(zu stark verzieren auch)* to clutter; **sich** *(dat)* **den Magen ~laden** to overeat; **2** *adj Wagen* overloaded; *(fig) Stil* over-ornate; *Bild* cluttered; **~lagern*** *insep* **1** *vt* **(a)** *Schichten* to overlie; *Sender* to blot out; **(b)** *Konflikt etc* to eclipse; **2** *vr (sich überschneiden)* to overlap; **~lang** *adj* too long; **~lappen*** *vir insep* to overlap.

überlassen* *vt insep irreg* **jdm etw ~** *(haben lassen)* to let sb have sth; *(in Obhut geben)* to leave sth in sb's care; **es jdm ~, etw zu tun** to leave it up to sb to do sth; **das bleibt Ihnen ~** that's up to you; **jdn sich** *(dat)* **selbst ~** to leave sb to his/her own devices; **jdn seinem Schicksal ~** to leave *or* abandon sb to his fate.

überlasten* *vt insep* to put too great a strain on; *jdn* to overtax; *(Elec) Telefonnetz, (durch Gewicht)* to overload. **überlastet sein** to be under too great a strain; *(überfordert sein)* to be overtaxed; *(Elec etc)* to be overloaded.

überlaufen[1]* *vt insep irreg (Angst etc)* to seize. **es überlief ihn kalt** a cold shiver ran down his spine.

überlaufen[2] *vi sep irreg aux sein* **(a)** *(Wasser)* to overflow; *(überkochen)* to boil over. **(b)** *(Mil: überwechseln)* to desert *(zu* to*)*.

überlaufen[3] *adj* overcrowded; *Stadt (mit Touristen)* overrun.

Überläufer *m (Mil)* deserter.

überleben* *insep* **1** *vti* **(a)** to survive; *die Nacht auch* to last, to live through. **(b)** *(länger leben als)* to outlive. **2** *vr* **das hat sich überlebt** that's had its day.

Überlebende(r) *mf decl as adj* survivor.

überlebensgroß *adj* larger-than-life.

überlebt *adj* outmoded, out-of-date.

überlegen[1] *insep* **1** *vi (nachdenken)* to think. **hin und her ~** to deliberate; **ohne zu ~** without thinking; *(ohne zu zögern)* without thinking twice. **2** *vt* to think over *or* about, to consider. **das werde ich mir ~** I'll think it over, I'll think about it; **ich habe es mir anders/noch mal überlegt** I've changed my mind; **wenn man es sich** *(dat)* **recht überlegt** when you think about it; **das hätten Sie sich** *(dat)* **vorher ~ müssen** you should have thought of that sooner.

überlegen[2] **1** *adj* superior; *Sieg* convincing. **jdm ~ sein** to be superior to sb. **2** *adv* in a superior manner.

Überlegenheit *f no pl* superiority.

überlegt 1 *adj* considered. **2** *adv* in a considered way.

Überlegung *f* consideration, thought; *(Bemerkung)* observation. **~en anstellen** to make observations *(zu* about *or* on*)*.

Über-: ü~leiten *sep* **1** *vt Abschnitt etc* to link up *(in +acc* with*)*; **2** *vi* **zu etw ü~leiten** to lead up to sth; **~leitung** *f* connection; *(zur nächsten Frage, Mus)* transition; **ü~lesen*** *vt insep irreg* **(a)** *(flüchtig lesen)* to glance through; **(b)** *(übersehen)* to overlook, to miss; **ü~liefern*** *vt insep Brauch* to hand down; **~lieferung** *f* tradition; **schriftliche ~lieferungen** (written) records; **ü~listen*** *vt insep* to outwit.

überm = über dem.

Über-: ~macht *f no pl* superior strength; **ü~mächtig** *adj Gewalt* superior; *Feind* powerful; *Wunsch* overpowering; **ü~malen*** *vt insep* to paint over; **~maß** *nt no pl* excess *(an+acc* of*)*; **im ~maß** to excess; **er hat Zeit im ~maß** he has more than enough time; **ü~mäßig 1** *adj* excessive; *Schmerz, Sehnsucht* violent; *Freude* intense; **das war nicht ü~mäßig** that was not too brilliant; **2** *adv* excessively; *essen, trinken auch* to excess; **~mensch** *m* superman; **ü~menschlich** *adj* superhuman; **ü~mitteln*** *vt insep* to convey *(jdm* to sb*)*; *(telefonisch etc)* to transmit; **ü~morgen** *adv* the day after tomorrow; **ü~müden*** *vt insep usu ptp* to overtire; **~mut** *m* high spirits *pl*; **ü~mütig** *adj (ausgelassen)* high-spirited; *(zu mutig)* cocky *(col)*.

übern = über den.

übernächste(r, s) *adj attr* **das ~ Haus** the next house but one; **die ~ Woche** the week after next; **er kommt ~en Freitag** he's coming Friday week.

Über-: ü~nachten* *vi insep* to sleep; *(in Hotel)* to stay; *(eine Nacht)* to stay the night; **ü~nächtigt** *adj* bleary-eyed; **~nachtung** *f* overnight stay; **~nachtung mit Frühstück** bed and breakfast; **~nahme** *f* **-n** takeover; *(von Ausdruck, Ansicht)* adoption; *(von Zitat, Wort)* borrowing; *(von Amt)* assumption; **durch ~nahme dieser Aufgabe** by taking on this task; **ü~natürlich** *adj* supernatural; **ü~nehmen*** *insep irreg* **1** *vt* **(a)** *Aufgabe, Verantwortung, (Jur) Fall* to take on; *Amt* to assume; *Klasse* to take charge of; **lassen Sie mal, das ü~nehme ich!** let me take care of that; **den Befehl ü~nehmen** to take (over) command; **(b)** *(stellvertretend, ablösend)* to take over *(von* from*)*; *Zitat, Wort* to take; **2** *vr* to take on too much; *(sich überanstrengen)* to overdo it; *(beim Essen)* to overeat; **ü~ordnen** *vt sep* **jdn jdm ü~ordnen** to put sb over sb; **etw einer Sache** *(dat)* **ü~ordnen** to give sth precedence over sth; **ü~parteilich** *adj Zeitung* independent; *(Parl) Problem* all-party *attr*; *Amt, Präsident etc* above party politics; **~produktion** *f* overproduction; **ü~prüfen*** *vt insep (auf+acc* for*)* to check; *Entcheidung, Lage, Frage* to examine; *Ergebnisse, Teilnehmer etc* to scrutinize; *(Pol) jdn* to screen.

Überprüfung *f* **(a)** *no pl siehe vt* checking; examination; scrutiny; *(Pol)* screening. **(b)** *(Kontrolle)* check.

über-: ~quellen *vi sep irreg aux sein* to overflow *(von, mit* with*)*; *(Reis)* to boil over; **~queren*** *vt insep* to cross; **~ragen*** *vt insep* to tower above; *(fig: übertreffen)* to outshine *(an +dat, in +dat* in*)*; **~ragend** *adj* outstanding; *Bedeutung* paramount; **~raschen*** *vt insep* to surprise; *(überrumpeln auch)* to take by surprise; **jdn bei etw ~raschen** to surprise *or* catch sb doing sth; **~raschend** *adj* surprising; *Besuch* surprise *attr*; *Tod, Weggang* unexpected; **~rascht** *adj* surprised *(über+acc* at*)*; **jdn ~rascht ansehen** to look at sb in surprise.

Überraschung *f* surprise. **zu meiner ~** to my surprise.

Überraschungs|angriff *m* surprise attack.

überreden* *vt insep* to persuade. **jdn ~, etw zu tun** to persuade sb to do sth, to talk sb into doing sth; **jdn zu etw ~** to talk sb into sth.

Überredung *f* persuasion.

Überredungskunst *f* powers of persuasion *pl*.

Über-: ü~regional *adj* national; *Zeitung, Sender auch* nationwide; **ü~reich** *adj* lavish, abundant; *(zu reich)* overabundant; **ü~reich an etw** *(dat)* overflowing with sth; **ü~reichen*** *vt insep* **(jdm) etw ~** to hand sth over (to sb); **ü~reichlich** *adj* ample, abundant; *(zu reichlich)* overabundant; **in ü~reichlichem Maße** in abundance; **ü~reif** *adj* overripe; **ü~reizen*** *insep* **1** *vt Nerven, Augen* to overstrain; **2** *vtr (Cards)* to overbid; **ü~reizt** *adj Augen* overstrained; *(nervlich)* overwrought; *(zu erregt)* overexcited; **ü~rennen*** *vt insep irreg* to run down; *(Mil)* to overrun; **~rest** *m* remnant, remains *pl*; **ü~rollen*** *vt insep* to run down; *(Mil, fig)* to overrun; **ü~rumpeln*** *vt insep (col)* to take by surprise, to catch unawares; *(überwältigen)* to overpower; **ü~runden*** *vt insep (Sport)* to lap; *(fig)* to outstrip.

übers = über das.

Über-: ü~säen* *vt insep* to strew; **ü~sät** strewn; *(mit Abfall etc)* littered; *(mit Sternen) Himmel* studded; **ü~sättigen*** *vt insep* to satiate; *Markt* to oversaturate; **~schall-** *in cpds* supersonic; **ü~schatten*** *vt insep (geh) (lit, fig)* to overshadow; *(fig: trüben)* to cast a shadow over; **ü~schätzen*** *vt insep* to overestimate; **ü~schaubar** *adj Plan* easily comprehensible, clear; **damit die Abteilung ü~schaubar bleibt** so that one can keep track of the department; **ü~schäumen** *vi sep aux sein* to froth over; *(fig)* to bubble over *(vor +dat* with*)*; *(vor Wut)* to seethe; **~schicht** *f (Ind)* extra shift; **ü~schlafen*** *vt insep irreg Problem* to sleep on.

Überschlag *m* **(a)** *(Berechnung)* (rough) estimate. **(b)** *(Drehung)* somersault.

überschlagen[1]* *insep irreg* **1** *vt* **(a)** *(auslassen)* to skip (over). **(b)** *Kosten etc* to estimate (roughly). **2** *vr* **(a)** to somersault; *(Mensch: versehentlich)* to go head over heels; *(fig: Ereignisse)* to come thick and fast. **(b)** *(Stimme)* to crack.

überschlagen[2] *sep irreg* **1** *vt Beine* to cross; *Arme* to fold; *Decke* to fold back. **2** *vi aux sein* **(a)** *(Wellen)* to break. **(b)** *(Stimmung etc)* **in etw** *(acc)* **~** to turn into sth.

Über-: ü~schnappen *vi sep aux sein (Stimme)* to break; *(col: Mensch)* to crack up *(col)*; **ü~schneiden*** *vr insep irreg (unerwünscht)* to clash; *(Linien)* to intersect; **ü~schreiben*** *vt insep irreg* **(a)** *(betiteln)* to head; **(b) etw auf jdn ü~schreiben** to make sth over to sb; **ü~schreiten*** *vt insep irreg* to cross; *(fig)* to exceed; *Höhepunkt, Alter* to pass; **~schrift** *f* heading; *(Schlagzeile)* headline; **~schuh** *m* overshoe; **ü~schuldet** *adj* heavily in debt; *Grundstück* heavily mortgaged; **Ü~schuß** *m* surplus *(an +dat* of*)*; **ü~schüssig** *adj* surplus; **ü~schütten*** *vt insep* **jdn/etw mit etw ü~schütten** to cover sb/sth with sth; *(mit Flüssigkeit)* to pour sth onto sb/sth; **jdn mit etw ü~schütten** *(fig: überhäufen)* to heap sth on sb; **~schwang** *m no pl* exuberance; **ü~schwappen** *vi sep aux sein* to splash over; **ü~schwemmen*** *vt insep (lit, fig)* to flood; *(Touristen) Land etc auch* to overrun; *(mit Aufträgen)* to swamp, to inundate; **~schwemmung** *f* flood; **ü~schwenglich** *adj* effusive, gushing *(pej)*.

Übersee *no art* **in/nach ~** overseas; **aus/von ~** from overseas.

Übersee-: ~dampfer *m* ocean liner; **~hafen** *m* international port; **~handel** *m* overseas trade.

überseeisch ['y:bɐze:ɪʃ] *adj* overseas.

Überseeverkehr *m* overseas traffic.

übersehbar *adj (fig) Folgen, Zusammenhänge etc* clear; *Kosten, Dauer etc* assessable.

übersehen* *vt insep irreg* **(a)** *Folgen, Zusammenhänge, Sachlage* to see clearly; *Fachgebiet* to have an overall view of; *(abschätzen) Schaden, Kosten, Dauer* to assess. **(b)** *(ignorieren, nicht erkennen)* to overlook; *(nicht bemerken)* to miss.

übersein *vi sep irreg aux sein (col)* **jdm ist etw über** sb is fed-up with sth *(col)*.

übersenden* *vt insep irreg* to send.

übersetzen[1]* *vti insep* **(a)** to translate. **aus dem** *or* **vom Englischen ins Deutsche ~** to translate from English into German; **etw falsch ~** to mistranslate sth; **sich leicht/schwer ~ lassen** to be easy/hard to translate. **(b)** *(Tech: übertragen)* to transmit.

übersetzen[2] *sep* **1** *vi aux sein* to cross (over). **2** *vt (mit Fähre)* to take *or* ferry across.

Übersetzer(in *f***)** *m* - translator.

Übersetzung *f* **(a)** translation. **(b)** *(Tech: Übertragung)* transmission.

Übersetzungsbüro *nt* translation bureau *or* agency.

Übersicht *f* **(a)** *no pl (Überblick)* overall view. **die ~ verlieren** to lose track. **(b)** *(Abriß, Resümee)* survey; *(Tabelle)* table.

übersichtlich *adj Gelände etc* open; *Darstellung etc* clear.

Übersichtskarte *f* general map.

übersiedeln *sep*, **übersiedeln*** *insep vi aux sein* to move *(von* from, *nach, in+acc* to*)*.

über-: ~sinnlich *adv* supersensory; *(übernatürlich)* supernatural; **~spannen*** *vt insep* **(a)** *(Brücke etc)* to span; **(b)** *(zu stark spannen)* to put too much strain on; **~spannt** *adj Ideen, Forderungen* wild, extravagant; *(exaltiert)* eccentric; *(hysterisch)* hysterical; *Nerven* overexcited; **~spielen*** *vt insep* **(a)** *(verbergen)* to cover (up); **(b)** *(übertragen) Aufnahme* to transfer; **~spitzt 1** *adj (zu spitzfindig)* oversubtle; *(übertrieben)* exaggerated; **2** *adv* oversubtly; in an exaggerated fashion.

überspringen[1]* *vt insep irreg* **(a)** *Hindernis, Höhe* to jump, to clear. **(b)** *(auslassen)* to skip.

überspringen[2] *vi sep irreg aux sein (Begeisterung)* to spread quickly *(auf+acc* to*)*.

über-: ~sprudeln *vi sep aux sein (lit, fig)* to bubble over *(vor* with*)*; **~stehen*** *vt insep irreg (durchstehen)* to come *or* get through; *(überleben)* to survive; *Gewitter* to weather, to ride out; *Krankheit* to get over; **~steigen*** *vt insep irreg* **(a)** to climb over; **(b)** *(hinausgehen über)* to exceed, to go beyond; **~steigert** *adj* excessive; **~steuern*** *vi insep (Aut)* to oversteer; **~stimmen*** *vt insep* to outvote; *Antrag* to vote down; **~strapazieren*** *insep* **1** *vt* to wear out; **2** *vr* to wear oneself out; **~streichen*** *vt insep irreg* to paint/varnish over; **~streifen** *vt sep* **(sich** *dat***) etw ~streifen** to slip sth on.

überströmen[1]* *vt insep (überfluten)* to flood. **von Blut überströmt sein** to be streaming with blood.

überströmen[2] *vi sep aux sein (lit, fig)* to overflow *(vor+dat* with*)*.

überstülpen *vt sep* **sich** *(dat)* **etw ~** to put on sth; **jdm/einer Sache etw ~** to put sth on sb/sth.

Überstunde *f* hour of overtime. **~n** overtime *sing*; **~n machen** to do overtime.

über-: ~stürzen* *insep* **1** *vt* to rush into; **2** *vr (Ereignisse etc)* to happen in a rush; *(Nachrichten)* to come fast and furious; **~stürzt** *adj* overhasty; **~tariflich** *adj, adv* above the agreed *or* union rate; **~tippen*** *vt insep* to type over; **~tölpeln*** *vt insep* to take in; **~tönen*** *vt insep* to drown.

Übertrag *m* **-̈e** amount carried forward.

übertragbar *adj* transferable; *Methode, Maßstab* applicable *(auf+acc* to*)*; *Krankheit* infectious; *(durch Berührung)* contagious.

übertragen[1]* *insep irreg* **1** *vt* **(a)** to transfer; *Krankheit, (Tech) Bewegung* to transmit; *Daten* to communicate. **(b)** *(übersetzen) Text* to render *(in +acc* into*)*. **(c)** *(anwenden) Methode* to apply *(auf +acc* to*)*. **(d)** *Verantwortung etc* to give *(jdm* sb*)*; *(auftragen) Aufgabe* to assign *(jdm* to sb*)*. **(e)** *(TV, Rad)* to broadcast; *(TV auch)* to televise. **2** *vr (Eigenschaft, Krankheit etc, Tech)* to be transmitted *(auf+acc* to*)*; *(Heiterkeit etc)* to spread *(auf+acc* to*)*.

übertragen[2] *adj Bedeutung etc* figurative.

Überträger *m (Med)* carrier.

Übertragung *f siehe vt* **(a)** transference; transmission. **(b)** rendering. **(c)** application. **(d)** *(Aufgabe)* assignment. **(e)** *(TV, Rad)* transmission.

übertreffen* *insep irreg* **1** *vt* to surpass *(an+dat* in*)*; *(mehr leisten als auch)* to outdo; *(übersteigen auch)* to exceed. **2** *vr* **sich selbst** ~ to surpass *or* excel oneself.

übertreiben* *vti insep irreg* to exaggerate. **es mit der Sauberkeit** ~ to carry cleanliness too far; **man kann es auch** ~ you can overdo things.

Übertreibung *f* exaggeration.

übertreten[1] *vi sep irreg aux sein* **(a)** *(Fluß)* to break its banks. **(b)** *(zu anderer Partei etc)* to go over *(zu* to*)*.

übertreten[2]* *vt insep irreg Gesetz* to break.

Übertretung *f (von Gesetz etc)* violation; *(Jur: strafbare Handlung)* misdemeanour *(Brit)*, misdemeanor *(US)*.

Über-: ü~trieben *adj* exaggerated; *(übermäßig) Vorsicht, Training* excessive; **~tritt** *m (über Grenze)* crossing *(über+acc* of*)*; *(zu anderem Glauben)* conversion; *(von Abtrünnigen, esp zu anderer Partei)* defection; **ü~trumpfen*** *vt insep (Cards)* to overtrump; *(fig)* to outdo; **ü~tünchen*** *vt insep* to whitewash; *(mit Farbton)* to distemper; *(fig)* to cover up; **~völkerung** *f* overpopulation; **ü~voll** *adj* overfull *(von* with*)*; **ü~vorteilen*** *vt insep* to cheat; **ü~wachen*** *vt insep (kontrollieren)* to supervise; *(beobachten)* to keep a watch on; *Verdächtigen* to keep under surveillance; *(auf Monitor, mit Radar, fig)* to monitor; **ü~wältigen*** *vt insep (lit)* to overpower; *(zahlenmäßig)* to overwhelm; *(bezwingen, fig: Schlaf, Angst)* to overcome; **ü~wältigend** *adj* overwhelming; *Schönheit* stunning; *Gestank, Gefühl auch* overpowering; **ü~wechseln** *vi sep* to move *(in+acc* to*)*; *(zu Partei etc)* to go over *(zu* to*)*; *(Wild)* to cross over; **~weg** *m* **~weg für Fußgänger** pedestrian crossing; **ü~weisen*** *vt insep irreg (an +acc* to*) Geld* to transfer; *Patienten* to refer; **~weisung** *f (Geld~)* (credit) transfer; **~weite** *f* large size.

überwerfen[1]* *vr insep irreg* **sich (mit jdm)** ~ to fall out (with sb).

überwerfen[2] *vt sep irreg* to put over; *Kleidungsstück* to put on; *(sehr rasch)* to throw on.

Über-: ü~wiegen* *insep irreg* **1** *vt* to outweigh; **2** *vi (das Übergewicht haben)* to predominate; **ü~wiegend 1** *adj* predominant; *Mehrheit* vast; **2** *adv* predominantly, mainly; **ü~winden*** *insep irreg* **1** *vt* to overcome; **2** *vr* to overcome one's inclinations; **sich ü~winden, etw zu tun** to force oneself to do sth; **~windung** *f* overcoming; *(Selbstüberwindung)* will power; **das hat mich viel ~windung gekostet** that was a real effort of will for me; **ü~wintern*** *vi insep* to (spend the) winter; *(col: Winterschlaf halten)* to hibernate; **ü~wuchern*** *vt insep* to overgrow; *(fig)* to obscure; **ü~wunden** *adj Standpunkt, Haltung etc* of the past; *Angst* conquered; **~wurf** *m (Kleidungsstück)* wrap; **~zahl** *f no pl* **in der ~zahl sein** to be in the majority; *(Feind)* to be superior in number; **ü~zählig** *adj (überschüssig)* surplus; *(überflüssig)* superfluous; *(übrig)* spare.

überzeugen* *insep* **1** *vt* to convince; *(Jur)* to satisfy. **ich bin davon überzeugt, daß ...** I am convinced that ...; **er ist sehr von sich überzeugt** he is very sure of himself. **2** *vi* to be convincing. **3** *vr* **sich (selbst)** ~ to convince oneself *(von* of*)*; *(mit eigenen Augen)* to see for oneself.

überzeugt *adj attr Anhänger, Vegetarier etc* dedicated; *Christ, Moslem* devout.

Überzeugung *f* **(a)** *(das Überzeugen)* convincing. **(b)** *(Überzeugtsein)* conviction; *(Prinzipien)* convictions *pl*. **meiner ~ nach ...** I am convinced (that) ...; **zu der ~ gelangen, daß ...** to become convinced that ...

überziehen[1]* *insep irreg* **1** *vt* **(a)** *(bedecken)* to cover; *(mit Schicht, Belag)* to coat; *(mit Metall)* to plate; *(mit Zuckerguß)* to ice, to frost *(esp US)*. **ein Bett frisch ~** to change the sheets; **Polstermöbel neu ~ lassen** to have furniture re-covered. **(b)** *Konto* to overdraw *(um +acc* by*)*. **(c)** *Redezeit etc* to overrun. **2** *vi (Fin)* to overdraw one's account. **3** *vr (Himmel)* to cloud over.

überziehen[2] *vt sep irreg* **(a) (sich** *dat***) etw** ~ to put sth on. **(b) jdm eins** ~ *(col)* to give sb a clout *(col)*.

Über-: ü~züchten* *vt insep* to overbreed; **ü~zuckern*** *vt insep* to sugar; *(zu stark zuckern)* to put too much sugar in/on; **~zug** *m* **(a)** *(Beschichtung)* coat(ing); *(aus Metall)* plating; *(für Kuchen, esp aus Zuckerguß)* icing, frosting *(esp US)*; **(b)** *(von Bett, Sessel etc)* cover; *(von Kopfkissen auch)* (pillow)slip.

üblich *adj* usual; *(herkömmlich)* customary; *(typisch, normal)* normal. **wie ~** as usual; **das ist bei ihm so ~** that's usual for him; **allgemein ~ sein** to be common practice.

üblicherweise *adv* usually, normally.

U-Boot *nt* submarine, sub *(col)*.

übrig *adj* **(a)** *attr (verbleibend)* remaining; *(andere auch)* other. **meine ~en Sachen** the rest of my things. **(b)** *pred* left (over); *(zu entbehren)* spare. **etw ~ haben** to have sth left/to spare. **(c)** *(mögen)* **für jdn/nichts ~ haben** to have no time for sb; **für jdn/etw etwas ~ haben** to be fond of sb/sth. **(d)** *(substantivisch)* **das ~e** the rest, the remainder; **im ~en** moreover, also.

übrig-: ~behalten* *vt sep irreg* to have left over; **~bleiben** *vi sep irreg aux sein* to be left over, to remain; **wieviel ist ~ geblieben?** how much is left?; **was blieb mir anderes ~ als ...?** what choice did I have but ...?

übrigens *adv* incidentally, by the way.

übriglassen *vt sep irreg* to leave *(jdm* for sb*)*. **(einiges)/viel zu wünschen ~** *(col)* to leave something/a lot to be desired.

Übung *f* practice; *(Mil, Sport, Sch)* exercise; *(Feuerwehr~)* exercise, drill; *(Univ: Kursus)* seminar. **aus der ~ kommen/außer ~ sein** to get/be out of practice; **zur ~** as practice; **~ macht den Meister** *(Prov)* practice makes perfect *(Prov)*.

Übungs-: ~arbeit *f (Sch)* mock test; **~aufgabe** *f (Sch)* exercise; **~heft** *nt (Sch)* exercise book; **~platz** *m* training ground; *(Mil)* drill ground.

UdSSR [u:de:|ɛs|ɛs'|ɛr] *f* = **Union der Sozialistischen Sowjetrepubliken. die ~** the USSR.

Ufer *nt* - *(Fluß~)* bank; *(See~)* shore. **direkt am ~ gelegen** right on the waterfront; **etw ans ~ spülen** to wash sth ashore; **das sichere ~ erreichen** to reach dry land.

Ufer-: ~befestigung *f* bank reinforcement; **~böschung** *f* embankment; **u~los** *adj* endless; *(grenzenlos)* boundless; **ins u~lose gehen** *(Debatte etc)* to go on forever; *(Kosten)* to go up and up; **~mauer** *f* sea wall; **~straße** *f* lakeside/riverside road.

Ugander(in *f***)** *m* - Ugandan.

U-Haft *f (col)* custody.

Uhr *f* **-en** clock; *(Armband~, Taschen~)* watch; *(Anzeiger)* gauge, dial. **nach meiner ~** by my watch; **um drei (~)** at three (o'clock); **ein ~ dreißig** half past one, one-thirty; **wieviel ~ ist es?** what time is it?, what's the time?; **um wieviel ~?** at what time?

Uhr(arm)band *nt* watch strap; *(aus Metall)* watch bracelet.

Uhr-: ~feder *f* watch spring; **~kette** *f* watch chain; **~macher(in** *f***)** *m* watchmaker; clockmaker; **~werk** *nt* clockwork mechanism *(auch fig)*, movements *pl*; **~zeiger** *m* (clock/watch) hand; **~zeigersinn** *m* **im ~zeigersinn** clockwise; **entgegen dem ~zeigersinn** anticlockwise *(Brit)*,

counterclockwise *(US)*; ~**zeit** *f* time (of day).
Uhu ['u:hu] *m* **-s** eagle-owl.
Ukrainer(in *f*) *m* **-** Ukrainian.
UKW [u:ka:'ve:] = **Ultrakurzwelle** ≈ FM.
Ulk *m* **-e** *(col)* lark *(col)*; *(Streich)* practical joke; *(Spaß)* fun *no pl, no indef art.* **mit jdm seinen ~ treiben** *(Streiche spielen)* to play tricks on sb.
ulkig *adj (col)* funny.
Ulme *f* **-n** elm.
ultimativ *adj Forderung etc* given as an ultimatum. **jdn ~ zu etw auffordern** to give sb an ultimatum to do sth.
Ultimatum *nt, pl* **-s** *or* **Ultimaten** ultimatum. **jdm ein ~ stellen** to give sb an ultimatum.
Ultra *m* **-s** *(pej)* extremist.
Ultra- *in cpds* ultra; **u~kurz** *adj (Phys)* ultra-short.
Ultrakurzwelle *f (Phys)* ultra-short wave; *(Rad)* ≈ very high frequency, ≈ frequency modulation.
Ultra-: u~modern *adj* ultramodern; **~schall** *m (Phys)* ultrasound.
um 1 *prep+acc* **(a) ~ ... (herum)** around; **~ sich schauen** to look around (one) *or* about one; **~ Weihnachten/Ostern** around Christmas/Easter; **~ acht** at eight. **(b)** *(betreffend, über)* about. **es geht ~ das Prinzip** it's a question of principles; **der Kampf ~ den Titel** the battle for the title; **~ Geld spielen** to play for money; **die Sorge ~ die Zukunft** concern for *or* about the future. **(c)** *(bei Differenzangaben)* by. **~ 10% teurer** 10% more expensive; **~ einiges besser** quite a bit better; **etw ~ 4 cm verkürzen** to shorten sth by 4cm. **(d)** *(bei Verlust)* **jdn ~ etw bringen** to deprive sb of sth. **(e)** *(nach)* after, upon. **Stunde ~ Stunde** hour after *or* upon hour.

2 *prep+gen* **~ ... willen** for the sake of; **~ Gottes willen!** for goodness *or (stärker)* God's sake!

3 *conj* **(a) ~ ... zu** (in order) to; **intelligent genug/zu intelligent, ~ ... zu** intelligent enough/ too intelligent to ...; **er studierte jahrelang Jura, ~ dann Taxifahrer zu werden** he studied law for several years only to become a taxi-driver. **(b)** *(desto)* **~ so besser/schlimmer!** so much the better/worse!; **je mehr, ~ so besser** the more the better; **~ so mehr, als ...** all the more considering ...

4 *adv* **(a)** *(ungefähr)* **~ (die) 30 Schüler** about *or* around 30 pupils. **(b) die zwei Stunden sind jetzt ~** the two hours are now up.
um|adressieren* *vt sep* to readdress.
um|ändern *vt sep* to alter.
um|arbeiten *vt sep* to alter; *Buch etc* to rewrite; *Metall etc* to rework.
um|armen* *vt insep* to embrace; *(fester)* to hug.
Umbau *m siehe vt* rebuilding, renovation; conversion; alterations *pl (+gen, von* to); modification; reorganization; changing.
umbauen[1] *sep* **1** *vt Gebäude (gründlich renovieren)* to rebuild, to renovate; *(zu etw anderem)* to convert *(zu* into); *(umändern)* to alter; *Maschine etc* to modify; *(fig: Organisation)* to reorganize; *(Theat) Kulissen* to change. **2** *vi* to rebuild.
umbauen[2]* *vt insep* to enclose.
umbenennen* *vt sep irreg* to rename *(in etw* sth).
umbesetzen* *vt sep (Theat)* to recast; *Mannschaft* to change; *Posten, Stelle* to find someone else for.
umbestellen* *vi sep* to change one's order.
umbetten *vt sep Kranken* to move (to another bed).
umbilden *vt sep (fig)* to reorganize; *(Pol) Kabinett* to reshuffle *(Brit)*, to shake up *(US)*.
umbinden *vt sep irreg* to put on; *(mit Knoten)* to tie on. **sich** *(dat)* **einen Schal ~** to put a scarf on.
umblättern *vti sep* to turn over.
umblicken *vr sep* to look around *(nach* at).
umbringen *sep irreg* **1** *vt* to kill *(auch fig col)*, to murder. **2** *vr* to kill oneself.
Umbruch *m* **(a)** radical change. **(b)** *(Typ)* makeup.
umbuchen *sep* **1** *vi* to change one's reservation. **2** *vt* to change.
umdenken *vi sep irreg* to change one's ideas.
umdirigieren* *vt sep* to redirect.
umdisponieren* *vi sep* to change one's plans.
umdrängen* *vt insep* to crowd around; *(stärker)* to mob.
umdrehen *sep* **1** *vt* to turn over; *(auf den Kopf)* to turn up (the other way); *(mit der Vorderseite nach hinten)* to turn around; *(von innen nach außen) Tasche etc* to turn inside out; *(um die Achse)* to turn around; *Schlüssel* to turn. **einem Vogel/jdm den Hals ~** to wring a bird's/sb's neck; **jdm den Arm ~** to twist sb's arm. **2** *vr* to turn around *(nach* to look at); *(im Bett etc)* to turn over. **3** *vi* to turn around.
Umdrehung *f* turn; *(Phys, Mot)* revolution.
um|einander *adv* about each other; *(räumlich)* around each other.
um|erziehen* *vt sep irreg (Pol euph)* to re-educate *(zu* to become).
umfahren[1] *vt sep irreg* to run over, to knock down.
umfahren[2]* *vt insep irreg* to travel around; *(mit dem Auto)* to drive around; *(auf Umgehungsstraße)* to bypass; *(um etw zu vermeiden)* to make a detour around.
umfallen *vi sep irreg aux sein* to fall over *or* down; *(fig col: nachgeben)* to give in. **zum U~ müde sein** to be fit to drop.
Umfang *m, pl* **Umfänge (a)** *(von Kreis etc)* perimeter, circumference *(auch Geom)*; *(von Baum auch, Bauch~)* girth. **(b)** *(Fläche)* area; *(Rauminhalt)* capacity; *(Größe)* size; *(von Gepäck etc)* amount. **das Buch hat einen ~ von 800 Seiten** the book extends to 800 pages. **(c)** *(fig) (Ausmaß)* extent; *(Reichweite)* range; *(von Untersuchung etc)* scope; *(von Verkehr, Verkauf etc)* volume. **in großem ~** on a large scale; **in vollem ~** fully.
umfangen* *vt insep irreg* **(a)** *(geh: umarmen)* to embrace. **(b)** *(fig: umgeben)* to envelop.
umfangreich *adj* extensive; *(geräumig)* spacious; *Buch* thick.
umfassen* *vt insep* **(a)** to grasp, to clasp; *(umarmen)* to embrace. **(b)** *(einschließen) Zeitperiode* to cover; *(enthalten)* to contain.
umfassend *adj* extensive; *(vieles enthaltend)* comprehensive; *Vorbereitung* thorough; *Geständnis* full, complete.
Umfeld *nt* **zum ~ von etw gehören** to be associated with sth.
umfliegen* *vt insep irreg* to fly around.
umformen *vt sep* **(a)** to reshape *(in+acc* into). **(b)** *(Elec)* to convert.
Umfrage *f (Social)* survey; *(esp Pol)* (opinion) poll. **eine ~ halten** to carry out a survey/an opinion poll; **~ halten** to ask around.
umfüllen *vt sep* to transfer into another bottle/ container *etc.*
umfunktionieren* *vt sep* **etw in** *(+acc) or* **zu etw ~** to change *or* turn sth into sth.
Umgang *m no pl* **(a)** contact; *(Bekanntenkreis)* acquaintances *pl,* friends *pl.* **schlechten ~ haben** to keep bad company; **keinen ~ mit jdm haben** to have nothing to do with sb; **er ist kein ~ für dich** he's not fit company for you. **(b) im ~ mit Jugendlichen** in dealing with young people; **an den ~ mit Kindern gewöhnt sein** to be used to children.
umgänglich *adj (entgegenkommend)* obliging; *(gesellig)* friendly.
Umgangs-: ~formen *pl* manners *pl*; **~sprache** *f* colloquial language; **u~sprachlich** *adj* colloquial.
umgeben* *vt insep irreg* to surround *(auch fig)*. **mit einer Mauer/einem Zaun ~ sein** to be walled/

fenced in, to be surrounded by a wall/fence.

Umgebung *f (Umwelt)* surroundings *pl*; *(Nachbarschaft)* vicinity; *(gesellschaftlicher Hintergrund)* background; *(Freunde etc)* people *pl* about one. **in der näheren/weiteren ~ Münchens** on the outskirts/in the environs of Munich.

umgehen[1] *vi sep irreg aux sein* **(a)** *(Gerücht, Grippe etc)* to go around *or* about; *(Gespenst)* to walk. **(b) mit jdm/etw ~ können** to know how to handle sb/sth; **sorgsam/verschwenderisch mit etw ~** to be careful/lavish with sth.

umgehen[2]* *vt insep irreg* to go around; *(vermeiden)* to avoid; *(Straße)* to bypass; *(Mil)* to outflank; *(fig)* to avoid; *Gesetz* to get around.

umgehend 1 *adj* immediate. **2** *adv* immediately.

Umgehungsstraße *f* by-pass.

umgekehrt 1 *adj* reversed; *Reihenfolge* reverse; *(gegenteilig)* opposite; *(anders herum)* the other way around. **nein, ~!** no, the other way around; **genau ~!** just the opposite!; **im ~en Verhältnis zu etw stehen** *or* **sein** to be in inverse proportion to sth. **2** *adv (anders herum)* the other way around; *(dagegen)* conversely; *proportional* inversely. **... und ~** ... and vice versa; **~ als** *or* **wie** *(col)* ... the other way around to what ...

umgestalten* *vt sep* to alter; *(reorganisieren)* to reorganize; *(umbilden)* to remodel; *(umordnen)* to rearrange.

umgewöhnen* *vr sep* to re-adapt.

umgraben *vt sep irreg* to dig over; *Erde* to turn.

umgrenzen* *vt insep* to surround; *(umfassen auch)* to enclose; *(fig)* to delimit.

umgruppieren* *vt sep Möbel etc* to rearrange; *Mitarbeiter* to regroup.

umgucken *vr sep* = **umsehen.**

umhaben *vt sep irreg (col)* to have on.

Umhang *m, pl* **Umhänge** cape; *(länger)* cloak; *(Umhängetuch)* shawl, wrap.

umhängen *vt sep Rucksack etc* to put on; *Jacke, Schal etc* to drape around. **sich** *(dat)* **etw ~** to put sth on; to drape sth around one.

Umhängetasche *f* shoulder bag.

umhauen *vt sep irreg* **(a)** to cut down. **(b)** *(col: umwerfen)* to knock flying *(col) or* over. **(c)** *(col: erstaunen)* to bowl over *(col)*.

umhegen* *vt insep (geh)* to care for lovingly.

umher *adv* around, about. **weit ~** all around.

umher- *pref siehe auch* **herum-** around, about; **~fahren** *vi sep irreg aux sein* to travel around; *(mit Auto)* to drive around; **~gehen** *vi sep irreg aux sein* to walk around; **~irren** *vi sep aux sein (in etw (dat)* sth*)* to wander around; *(Blick, Augen)* to roam about; **~laufen** *vi sep irreg aux sein* to walk around; *(rennen)* to run around; **im Garten ~laufen** to walk/run around the garden; **~wandern** *vi sep aux sein* to wander about *(in etw (dat)* sth*)*; **~ziehen** *vi sep irreg aux sein* to travel around *(in etw (dat)* sth*)*.

umhinkönnen *vi sep irreg* **er kann nicht umhin, das zu tun** he can't avoid doing it; *(einem Zwang folgend)* he can't help doing it.

umhören *vr sep* to ask around.

umhüllen* *vt insep* to wrap (up) *(mit* in*)*.

umkämpfen* *vt insep Entscheidung* to dispute; *Wahlkreis, Sieg* to contest. **die Stadt wurde wochenlang umkämpft** the battle for the city lasted weeks.

Umkehr *f no pl* **(a)** *(lit)* turning back. **jdn zur ~ zwingen** to force sb to turn back. **(b)** *(fig geh: Änderung)* change.

umkehren *sep* **1** *vi aux sein* to turn back; *(fig)* to change one's ways. **2** *vt Kleidungsstück* to turn inside out; *Reihenfolge* to reverse, to invert *(auch Gram, Mus)*. **das ganze Zimmer ~** *(col)* to turn the whole room upside down *(col)*. **3** *vr (Verhältnisse)* to become reversed.

umkippen *sep* **1** *vt* to tip over, to upset; *Auto, Boot* to overturn; *Leuchter, Vase* to knock over. **2** *vi aux sein* **(a)** to tip *or* fall over; *(Auto, Boot)* to overturn; *(volles Gefäß, Bier)* to be upset. **(b)** *(es sich anders überlegen)* to come around. **(c)** *(Fluß, See)* to become polluted.

umklammern* *vt insep* to wrap one's arms/legs around; *(mit Händen)* to clasp; *(festhalten)* to cling to; *(Ringen)* to hold.

umklappen *sep* **1** *vt* to fold down. **2** *vi aux sein (col)* to pass out.

Umkleidekabine *f* changing cubicle *(Brit)*, dressing room *(US)*.

umkleiden *vr sep* to change (one's clothes).

Umkleideraum *m* changing room.

umknicken *sep* **1** *vt Ast* to snap; *Papier* to fold (over). **2** *vi aux sein (Ast)* to snap; *(Halm)* to get bent over. **mit dem Fuß ~** to twist one's ankle.

umkommen *vi sep irreg aux sein* to die, to be killed. **ich komme um vor Hitze** *(col)* the heat is killing me *(col)*.

Umkreis *m* **im ~ das Flughafens** in the airport area; **im näheren/weiteren ~** in the immediate/general vicinity; **im ~ von 20 km** within a radius of 20 km.

umkreisen* *vt insep* to circle; *(Space)* to orbit.

umkrempeln *vt sep* **(a)** to turn up; *(mehrmals)* to roll up. **(b)** *(umwenden)* to turn inside out; *Betrieb* to shake up *(col)*. **jdn ~** *(fig col)* to change sb's ways.

umladen *vt sep irreg* to transfer; *(Naut)* to transship.

Umlage *f* **eine ~ machen** to split the cost.

umlagern[1]* *vt insep* to besiege.

umlagern[2] *vt sep* to transfer *(in+acc* into*)*.

Umland *nt no pl* surrounding countryside.

Umlauf *m, pl* **Umläufe (a)** *(von Erde etc)* revolution; *(das Kursieren)* circulation *(auch fig)*. **im ~ sein** to be in circulation; **in ~ bringen** to circulate; *Geld* to put in circulation. **(b)** *(Rundschreiben)* circular.

Umlaufbahn *f* orbit.

umlaufen *vi sep irreg aux sein* to circulate.

Umlaut *m* umlaut.

umlegen *vt sep* **(a)** *(umhängen)* to put around; *Verband* to put on. **(b)** *Mauer, Baum* to bring down. **(c)** *(umklappen)* to tilt (over); *Kragen* to turn down. **(d)** *(verlegen) Kranke* to transfer; *Leitung* to re-lay. **(e)** *Termin* to change *(auf+acc* to*)*. **(f)** *(verteilen)* **die 20 Mark wurden auf uns fünf umgelegt** the five of us each had to pay a contribution towards the 20 marks. **(g)** *(col: ermorden)* to do in *(col)*.

umleiten *vt sep* to divert *(Brit)*, to detour.

Umleitung *f* diversion *(Brit)*, detour.

umlernen *vi sep* to retrain; *(fig)* to change one's ideas.

umliegend *adj* surrounding.

ummelden *vtr sep* **jdn/sich ~** to notify (the police of) a change in sb's/one's address.

Umnachtung *f* **geistige ~** mental derangement.

um|ordnen *vt sep* to rearrange.

um|organisieren* *vt sep* to reorganize.

um|orientieren* *vr sep (fig)* to reorientate oneself.

umpflanzen *vt sep* to transplant.

umpflügen *vt sep* to plough up.

umquartieren* *vt sep* to move; *Truppen* to requarter.

umrahmen* *vt insep* to frame.

umranden* *vt insep* to edge, to border.

umräumen *sep* **1** *vt (anders anordnen)* to rearrange; *(an anderen Platz bringen)* to move. **2** *vi* to rearrange the furniture.

umrechnen *vt sep* to convert *(in +acc* into*)*.

Umrechnung *f* conversion.

Umrechnungskurs *m* exchange rate.

umreißen[1] *vt sep irreg* to tear down; *(umwerfen)* to knock over.

umreißen[2]* *vt insep irreg* to outline.

ụmrennen *vt sep irreg* to (run into and) knock down.
umrịngen* *vt insep* to surround.
Ụmriß *m* outline; *(Kontur)* contour(s *pl*).
ụmrühren *vt sep* to stir.
ụmrüsten *vt sep* **(a)** *(Tech)* to adapt *(auf+acc* to*)*. **(b)** *(Mil)* to re-equip.
ụms = um das.
ụmsatteln *sep* **1** *vt Pferd* to resaddle. **2** *vi (col: beruflich)* to change jobs.
Ụmsatz *m (Comm)* sales *pl*, turnover. **500 Mark ~ machen** *(col)* to do 500 marks' worth of business.
Ụmsatz-: ~beteiligung *f* commission; **~steuer** *f* sales tax.
umsäumen* *vt insep* to line; *(Sew)* to edge. **von Bäumen umsäumt** tree-lined.
ụmschalten *sep* **1** *vt (auf+acc* to*) Schalter* to flick; *Hebel* to throw; *Strom* to convert; *Gerät* to switch over. **2** *vi* to flick the/a switch; to push/pull a/the lever; *(auf anderen Sender)* to change over *(auf +acc* to*)*; *(Aut)* to change *(Brit)*, to shift *(in +acc* to*)*. **„wir schalten jetzt um nach Hamburg"** "and now we go over to Hamburg".
Ụmschalttaste *f* shift-key.
Ụmschau *f no pl (fig)* review. **~ halten** to look around *(nach* for*)*.
ụmschauen *vr sep* = **umsehen.**
ụmschichten *vt sep* to restack.
ụmschichtig *adv* on a shift basis.
umschịffen* *vt insep* to sail around; *Erde auch* to circumnavigate.
Ụmschlag *m* **(a)** *(Veränderung)* (sudden) change *(+gen* in, *in +acc* into*)*. **(b)** *(Hülle)* cover; *(Brief~)* envelope; *(als Verpackung)* wrapping; *(Buch~)* jacket. **(c)** *(Med)* compress; *(Packung)* poultice. **(d)** *(Ärmel~)* cuff; *(Hosen~)* turn-up *(Brit)*, cuff *(US)*. **(e)** *(umgeschlagene Gütermenge)* volume of traffic.
ụmschlagen *sep irreg* **1** *vt* **(a)** *Seite etc* to turn over; *Ärmel, Hosenbein, Saum* to turn up; *Teppich, Decke* to turn back; *Kragen* to turn down. **(b)** *(um die Schultern) Schal* to put on. **(c)** *(absetzen) Güter* to handle. **2** *vi aux sein (sich ändern)* to change (suddenly); *(Wind auch)* to veer; *(Stimme)* to break. **in etw** *(acc)* **~** to change *or* turn into sth.
Ụmschlag-: ~entwurf *m* jacket design; **~hafen** *m* port of transshipment; **~platz** *m* trade centre *(Brit) or* center *(US)*.
umschlịngen* *vt insep irreg (Pflanze)* to twine around. **jdn (mit den Armen) ~** to embrace sb.
ụmschmeißen *vt sep irreg (col)* **(a)** *siehe* **umhauen (b, c). (b)** *(col) Pläne* to screw up *(col)*.
ụmschreiben[1] *vt sep irreg* **(a)** *Text etc* to rewrite; *(bearbeiten) Theaterstück etc* to adapt *(für* for*)*. **(b)** *Hypothek etc* to transfer *(auf +acc* to*)*.
umschreiben[2]* *vt insep irreg (mit anderen Worten)* to paraphrase; *(darlegen)* to outline; *(verhüllen) Sachverhalt* to refer to obliquely.
Ụmschuldung *f* rescheduling (of debts).
ụmschulen *vt sep* **(a)** to retrain; *(Pol euph)* to re-educate. **(b)** *(auf andere Schule)* to transfer (to another school).
ụmschütten *vt sep (verschütten)* to spill, to upset.
Ụmschweife *pl* **ohne ~** straight out, plainly; **mach keine ~!** come (straight) to the point.
ụmschwenken *vi sep* **(a)** *aux sein or haben (Anhänger, Kran)* to swing out; *(fig)* to do an about-turn. **(b)** *(Wind)* to veer.
Ụmschwung *m* **(a)** *(Gymnastik)* circle. **(b)** *(fig) (Veränderung)* drastic change; *(ins Gegenteil)* about-turn.
umsẹgeln* *vt insep* to sail around; *Erde auch* to circumnavigate.
ụmsehen *vr sep irreg* to look around *(nach* for*)*; *(rückwärts)* to look back. **sich in der Stadt ~** to have a look around town; **sich in der Welt ~** to see something of the world; **ich möchte mich nur mal ~** *(in Geschäft)* I'm just looking; **ohne mich wird er sich noch ~** *(col)* he's not going to find it easy without me.
ụmsein *vi sep irreg aux sein (Zeit)* to be up.
ụmseitig *adj* overleaf *pred.*
ụmsetzen *sep* **1** *vt* **(a)** *Pflanzen* to transplant; *Schüler* to move. **(b)** *Waren* to turn over. **(c) etw in etw** *(acc)* **~** to convert sth into sth; **etw in die Tat ~** to translate sth into action. **2** *vr (Schüler)* to change places.
Ụmsicht *f* circumspection.
ụmsichtig *adj* circumspect.
ụmsiedeln *vti sep (vi: aux sein)* to resettle. **von einem Ort an einen anderen ~** to move from one place and settle in another.
Ụmsiedler *m* resettler.
ụmso *siehe* **um 3.**
umsọnst *adv* **(a)** *(unentgeltlich)* free. **(b)** *(vergebens)* in vain, to no avail. **(c)** *(ohne Grund)* for nothing.
umsọrgen* *vt insep* to care for.
ụmspringen *vi sep irreg aux sein* to change; *(Wind)* to veer around *(nach* to*)*. **so kannst du nicht mit ihr ~!** *(col)* you can't treat her like that!
Ụmstand *m, pl* **Ụmstände (a)** circumstance; *(Tatsache)* fact. **den Umständen entsprechend** much as one would expect (under the circumstances); **die näheren Umstände** further details; **in anderen Umständen sein** to be expecting; **unter diesen/keinen Umständen** under these/no circumstances; **unter Umständen** possibly. **(b) Umstände** *pl (Mühe, Schwierigkeiten)* bother *sing;* trouble *sing; (Förmlichkeit)* fuss *sing;* **jdm Umstände machen** to cause sb bother; **machen Sie bloß keine Umstände!** please don't go to any bother.
ụmständehalber *adv* owing to circumstances. **„~ zu verkaufen"** "forced to sell".
ụmständlich *adj Arbeitsweise, Methode* (awkward and) involved; *(langsam und ungeschickt)* ponderous; *Vorbereitung* elaborate; *Erklärung, Übersetzung, Anleitung* long-winded; *Abfertigung* laborious; *Arbeit, Reise* awkward. **er ist fürchterlich ~** he always makes such heavy weather of everything; **etw ~ machen** to make heavy weather of doing sth; **etw ~ beschreiben** to describe sth in a roundabout way.
Ụmstands-: ~kleid *nt* maternity dress; **~krämer** *m (col)* fusspot *(col)*, fussbudget *(US col)*; **~wort** *nt* adverb.
ụmstehend *adj attr* **(a)** standing round about. **die U~en** the bystanders. **(b)** *(umseitig)* overleaf.
ụmsteigen *vi sep irreg aux sein* **(a)** to change *(nach* for*)*. **(b)** *(fig col)* to change over, to switch (over) *(auf+acc* to*)*.
ụmstellen[1] *sep* **1** *vti* **(a)** *Möbel* to rearrange. **(b)** *Hebel* to throw; *Fernsehgerät* to switch over; *Radio* to switch to another station; *Uhr* to alter, to put back/forward. **auf etw** *(acc)* **~** *(Betrieb)* to go *or* switch over to sth; *auf Erdgas etc* to convert to sth. **2** *vr* to move about; *(fig)* to get used to a different lifestyle. **sich auf etw** *(acc)* **~** to adjust to sth.
umstẹllen[2]* *vt insep* to surround.
Ụmstellung *f* **(a)** *(von Möbeln etc)* rearrangement. **(b)** *(von Hebel)* throwing; *(von Uhr)* putting back/forward. **(c)** *(fig: das Sichumstellen)* adjustment *(auf+acc* to*)*.
ụmstimmen *vt sep* **(a)** *Instrument* to retune. **(b) jdn ~** to change sb's mind.
ụmstoßen *vt sep irreg Gegenstand* to knock over; *(fig) Plan etc* to change; *(Umstände)* to upset.
umstrịtten *adj (fraglich)* controversial; *(wird noch debattiert)* disputed.
ụmstrukturieren* *vt sep* to restructure.
ụmstülpen *vt sep* to turn upside down; *Tasche* to turn out.
Ụmsturz *m* coup (d'état).

umstürzen *sep* **1** *vt* to overturn; *(fig) Staat* to overthrow; *Demokratie* to destroy. **2** *vi aux sein* to fall; *(Möbelstück, Wagen etc)* to overturn.
Umtausch *m* exchange. **diese Waren sind vom ~ ausgeschlossen** these goods cannot be exchanged.
umtauschen *vt sep* to exchange; *Geld* to change *(in+acc* into*)*.
umtopfen *vt sep Blumen etc* to repot.
umtreten *vt sep irreg* to tread down.
Umtriebe *pl* machinations *pl*. **subversive ~** subversive activities.
umverteilen* *vt sep or insep* to redistribute.
umwälzend *adj (fig)* radical; *Veränderungen auch* sweeping; *Ereignisse* revolutionary.
Umwälzung *f (fig)* radical change.
umwandeln *vt sep* to transform *(in +acc* into*)*; *(Comm, Fin, Sci)* to convert *(in +acc* to*)*; *(Jur) Strafe* to commute *(in+acc* to*)*.
umwechseln *vt sep Geld* to change *(in +acc* to, into*)*.
Umweg ['ʊmveːk] *m* detour; *(fig)* roundabout way. **einen ~ machen/fahren** to go a long way around; *(absichtlich auch)* to make a detour.
Umwelt *f no pl* environment.
Umwelt- *in cpds* environmental; **~belastung** *f* ecological damage; **u~feindlich** *adj* damaging to the environment; **u~freundlich** *adj* pollution-free; **~freundlich hergestellt** manufactured without harm to the environment; **u~gestört** *adj (Psych)* maladjusted; **~politik** *f* ecological policy; **u~schädlich** *adj* harmful to the environment; **~schutz** *m* conservation *no art;* **~schützer** *m* environmentalist; **~sünder** *m (col)* polluter of the environment; **~verschmutzung** *f* pollution (of the environment).
umwenden *sep irreg* **1** *vt* to turn over. **2** *vr* to turn (around) *(nach* to*)*.
umwerben* *vi insep irreg* to court.
umwerfen *vt sep irreg* **(a)** *Gegenstand* to knock over. **(b)** *(fig: ändern)* to upset. **(c)** *jdn (körperlich)* to knock down; *(Ringen)* to throw down; *(fig col)* to bowl over. **(d) sich** *(dat)* **etw ~** to put sth around one's shoulders.
umwerfend *adj* fantastic. **von ~er Komik** hilarious.
umwickeln* *vt insep* to wrap around; *(mit Schnur)* to wind around.
umzäunen* *vt insep* to fence around.
Umzäunung *f* fencing.
umziehen *sep irreg* **1** *vi aux sein* to move *(nach* to*)*. **2** *vr* to change.
umzingeln* *vt insep* to surround, to encircle.
Umzug ['ʊmtsuːk] *m* **(a)** *(Wohnungs~)* move. **(b)** *(Festzug)* procession; *(Demonstration)* parade.
un|ab|änderlich *adj* **(a)** unalterable; *Entschluß, Urteil auch* irrevocable. **~ feststehen** to be absolutely certain. **(b)** *(ewig) Gesetze* immutable.
un|abdingbar *adj* indispensable; *Recht* inalienable.
un|abhängig *adj* independent *(von* of*)*. **~ davon, was Sie meinen** irrespective of what you think; **sich ~ machen** to go one's own way; **sich von jdm/etw ~ machen** to become independent of sb/sth.
Un|abhängigkeit *f* independence.
un|abkömmlich *adj (geh)* busy.
un|ablässig *adj* continual; *Versuche, Bemühungen* unremitting.
un|absehbar *adj* **(a)** *(fig) Folgen etc* unforeseeable; *Schaden* incalculable. **auf ~e Zeit** for an indefinite period. **(b)** *(lit)* interminable.
un-: **~abweisbar** *adj* irrefutable; **~abwendbar** *adj* inevitable; **~achtsam** *adj (unaufmerksam)* inattentive; *(nicht sorgsam)* careless; *(unbedacht)* thoughtless; **~ähnlich** *adj* dissimilar; **einer Sache/jdm ~ähnlich sein** to be unlike sth/sb; **~anfechtbar** *adj Urteil* incontestable; *Argument etc* unassailable; *Beweis* irrefutable; **~angebracht** *adj Bemerkung* uncalled-for; *Sparsamkeit auch* misplaced; *(unzweckmäßig) Maßnahmen* inappropriate; **~angefochten** *adj* unchallenged *no adv; Testament, Wahlkandidat, Urteil* uncontested; **~angemeldet** *adj* unannounced *no adv; Besucher* unexpected; *Patient etc* without an appointment.
un|angemessen *adj (zu hoch)* unreasonable; *(unzulänglich)* inadequate. **einer Sache** *(dat)* **~ sein** to be inappropriate to sth.
un|angenehm *adj* unpleasant; *(peinlich) Zwischenfall, Begegnung* embarrassing. **das ist mir immer so ~** I don't like that at all.
un-: **~angetastet** *adj* untouched; **~angetastet bleiben** *(Rechte)* not to be violated; **~angreifbar** *adj* unassailable; *Festung, Land* impregnable; **~annehmbar** *adj* unacceptable.
Un|annehmlichkeit *f usu pl* trouble *no pl*. **~en haben/bekommen** to be in/to get into trouble.
un|ansehnlich *adj* unsightly; *Frau etc* plain; *Tapete, Möbel* shabby.
un|anständig *adj* **(a)** *(unerzogen)* ill-mannered; *(unverschämt)* rude. **(b)** *(anstößig)* dirty; *Kleidung* indecent.
un-: **~antastbar** *adj* inviolable, sacrosanct; **~appetitlich** *adj (lit, fig)* unappetizing.
Un|art *f* bad habit.
un|artig *adj* naughty.
Un-: **u~ästhetisch** *adj Anblick* not aesthetically *(Brit) or* esthetically *(US)* pleasing; **u~aufdringlich** *adj* unobtrusive; *Parfüm auch* discreet; *Mensch* unassuming; **u~auffällig 1** *adj* inconspicuous; *(unscheinbar, schlicht)* unobtrusive; **2** *adv* unobtrusively, discreetly; **u~auffindbar** *adj* nowhere to be found; **u~aufgefordert 1** *adj* unsolicited *(esp Comm)*; **2** *adv* without being asked; **u~aufgefordert zugesandte Manuskripte** unsolicited manuscripts; **u~aufhaltbar** *adj* unstoppable; **u~aufhaltsam** *adj* **(a)** *(unaufhaltbar)* unstoppable; **(b)** *(unerbittlich)* inexorable; **u~aufhörlich** *adj* continual, incessant; **u~auflösbar** *adj Ehe* indissoluble; **u~aufmerksam** *adj* inattentive; **u~aufrichtig** *adj* insincere; **~aufrichtigkeit** *f* insincerity; **u~aufschiebbar** *adj* urgent; **u~ausbleiblich** *adj* inevitable, unavoidable; **u~ausgeglichen** *adj* unbalanced; **u~ausgegoren** *adj* immature; *Idee, Plan* half-baked *(col)*; **u~ausgeschlafen** *adj* tired; **u~ausgesetzt** *adj* incessant, constant; **u~ausgesprochen** *adj* unspoken; **u~ausgewogen** *adj* unbalanced; **u~ausrottbar** *adj Unkraut* indestructible; *(fig) Vorurteile etc* ineradicable; **u~aussprechlich** *adj* **(a)** *Wort* unpronounceable; **(b)** *Schönheit,Leid etc* inexpressible; **u~ausstehlich** *adj* intolerable; **u~ausweichlich** *adj* inevitable; *Folgen auch* inescapable.
unbändig *adj* **(a)** *Kind* boisterous. **(b)** *(ungezügelt)* unrestrained *no adv; Haß, Zorn etc auch* unbridled *no adv; Hunger* enormous.
un-: **~bar** *adj (Comm)* **etw ~bar bezahlen** not to pay sth in cash; **~barmherzig** *adj* merciless; **~beabsichtigt** *adj* unintentional.
unbe|achtet *adj* unnoticed; *Warnung, Vorschläge* unheeded. **wir wollen die weniger wichtigen Punkte zunächst ~ lassen** let's leave aside the less important points for the time being.
un-: **~bebaut** *adj Land* undeveloped; *Feld* uncultivated; **~bedacht** *adj* rash; **~bedarft** *adj (col)* clueless *(col)*; **~bedeckt** *adj* bare; **~bedenklich** *adj (ungefährlich)* completely harmless; **~bedeutend** *adj* insignificant; *(geringfügig) Änderung etc* minor.
unbedingt 1 *adj attr* absolute. **2** *adv (auf jeden Fall)* really; *nötig, erforderlich* absolutely. **müßt ihr denn ~ in meinem Arbeitszimmer spielen?** do you *have* to play in my study?; **~!** absolutely!; **nicht ~** not necessarily.

Un-: ụ~beeindruckt *adj* unimpressed; **ụ~beeinflußt** *adj* uninfluenced *(von* by*)*; **u~befạhrbar** *adj Straße* impassable; *Gewässer* unnavigable; **ụ~befahren** *adj Straße, Seeweg* unused; **ụ~befangen** *adj* **(a)** *(unparteiisch)* impartial; **(b)** *(natürlich)* natural; *(ungehemmt)* uninhibited; **~befangenheit** *f siehe adj* impartiality; naturalness; uninhibitedness; **ụ~befriedigend** *adj* unsatisfactory; **ụ~befriedigt** *adj (frustriert)* unsatisfied; *(unerfüllt auch)* unfulfilled; *(unzufrieden)* dissatisfied; **ụ~befristet** *adj* permanent; **ụ~befugt** *adj* unauthorized; **Eintritt für ~befugte verboten** no admittance to unauthorized persons; **ụ~beglichen** *adj* unpaid, unsettled.

unbegreiflich *adj* incomprehensible. **es wird mir immer ~ bleiben, wie/daß ...** I shall never understand how/why ...

ụnbegreiflicherweise *adv* inexplicably.

ụnbegrenzt *adj* unlimited; *Möglichkeiten, Energie etc auch* limitless; *Land, Meer etc* boundless; *Zeitspanne, Frist* indefinite. **zeitlich ~** indefinite; **~, auf ~e Zeit** indefinitely; **„~ haltbar"** "will keep indefinitely".

ụnbegründet *adj* unwarranted.

ụnbehaart *adj* hairless; *(auf dem Kopf)* bald.

Ụnbehagen *nt* uneasiness; *(Unzufriedenheit)* discontent *(an+dat* with*)*; *(körperlich)* discomfort.

ụnbehaglich *adj* uncomfortable; *Gefühl* uneasy.

un-: ~behẹlligt *adj (unbelästigt)* unmolested; *(unkontrolliert)* unchecked; **jdn ~behelligt lassen** to leave sb alone; **~beherrscht** *adj* uncontrolled; *(Mensch)* lacking self-control; *(gierig)* greedy; **~behịndert** *adj* unimpeded; **~beholfen** *adj* clumsy, awkward; *(hilflos)* helpless; **~beịrrbar** *adj* unwavering; **~beịrrt** *adj* unflustered.

ụnbekannt *adj* unknown; *Gesicht auch* unfamiliar. **das war mir ~** I was unaware of that; **Angst ist ihm ~** he doesn't know what fear is; **~e Größe** *(Math, fig)* unknown quantity; **nach ~ verzogen** moved - address unknown; **~e Täter** person or persons unknown.

Ụnbekannte *f (wk)* **-n, -n** *(Math)* unknown.

Ụnbekannte(r) *mf decl as adj* stranger.

ụnbekannterweise *adv* **grüße sie ~ von mir** give her my regards although I don't know her.

ụnbekleidet *adj* bare. **sie war ~** she had nothing on.

unbekụmmert *adj* **(a)** *(unbesorgt)* unconcerned. **sei ganz ~** don't worry. **(b)** *(sorgenfrei)* carefree.

ụnbelastet *adj* **(a)** *(ohne Last)* unloaded, unladen. **(b)** *(ohne Schulden)* unencumbered. **(c)** *(Pol: ohne Schuld)* guiltless. **(d)** *(ohne Sorgen)* free from worries.

un-: ~belebt *adj Straße* quiet; *Natur* inanimate; **~belẹhrbar** *adj* fixed in one's views; *Rassist etc* dyed-in-the-wool *attr;* **~beleuchtet** *adj* unlit; *Fahrzeug* without lights; **~beliebt** *adj* unpopular *(bei* with*)*; **~bemannt** *adj Raumflug* unmanned; *Fahrzeug* driverless; **~bemẹrkbar** *adj* imperceptible; **~bemerkt** *adj* unnoticed; **~bemittelt** *adj* without means; **~benọmmen** *adj pred (form)* **es bleibt** *or* **ist Ihnen ~benommen, zu ...** you are at liberty to ...; **~beobachtet** *adj* unobserved, unnoticed; **wenn er sich ~beobachtet fühlt ...** when he thinks nobody is looking ...; **~bequem** *adj (ungemütlich)* uncomfortable; *(lästig) Situation* awkward; *Aufgabe* unpleasant; *(mühevoll)* difficult; **der Regierung ~bequem sein** to be an embarrassment to the government; **~berẹchenbar** *adj* unpredictable; **ụ~berechtigt** *adj* unwarranted; *Sorge, Kritik etc* unfounded; *(unbefugt)* unauthorized.

unberụcksichtigt *adj* unconsidered. **etw ~ lassen** not to consider sth.

unberụhrbar *adj* untouchable.

ụnberührt *adj* **(a)** untouched; *Wald etc* virgin; *Natur* unspoiled. **~ sein** *(Mädchen)* to be a virgin. **(b)** *(mitleidlos)* unmoved. **(c)** *(unbetroffen)* unaffected.

unbeschạdet *prep+gen (form)* regardless of.

ụnbeschädigt *adj* undamaged; *Siegel* unbroken. **~ bleiben** not to be damaged/broken; *(seelisch etc)* to come off unscathed

ụnbeschäftigt *adj (müßig)* idle; *(arbeitslos)* not working.

ụnbescheiden *adj* presumptuous.

ụn-: ~bescholten *adj (geh)* respectable; *Ruf* spotless; **~beschrankt** *adj (Rail)* without gates.

unbeschrạ̈nkt *adj* unlimited; *Macht* absolute.

unbeschreiblich *adj* indescribable.

ụn-: ~beschrieben *adj* blank; **~beschwert** *adj* **(a)** *(sorgenfrei)* carefree; *Melodien* light; **(b)** *(ohne Gewicht)* unweighted.

unbesẹhen *adv* indiscriminately; *(ohne es anzusehen)* without looking at it/them.

un-: ~besetzt *adj* vacant; *Stuhl, Platz auch* unoccupied; *Bus, Zug* empty; *Schalter* closed; **~besiegbar** *adj Armee etc* invincible; *(Sport auch)* unbeatable; **~besonnen** *adj* rash.

ụnbesorgt 1 *adj* unconcerned. **Sie können ganz ~ sein** you can set your mind at rest. **2** *adv* without worrying.

un-: ~beständig *adj Wetter* changeable; *Mensch* erratic; *(launisch)* moody; *Liebhaber* inconstant; **~bestẹchlich** *adj* **(a)** *Mensch* incorruptible; **(b)** *Urteil, Blick* unerring; **~bestịmmbar** *adj* indeterminable; **~bestimmt** *adj (ungewiß)* uncertain; *Gefühl, Erinnerung* vague; *(Gram)* indefinite; **auf ~bestimmte Zeit** indefinitely.

unbestreitbar *adj Tatsache* indisputable; *Verdienste, Fähigkeiten* unquestionable.

ụnbestritten *adj* undisputed, indisputable.

ụnbeteiligt *adj* **(a)** *(uninteressiert)* indifferent. **(b)** *(nicht teilnehmend)* uninvolved *no adv (an +dat, bei* in*)*; *(Jur, Comm)* disinterested.

un-: ~betont *adj* unstressed; **~beugsam** *adj* uncompromising; *Wille* unshakeable; **~bewacht** *adj (lit, fig)* unguarded; *Parkplatz* unattended; **~bewaffnet** *adj* unarmed; **~beweglich** *adj* immovable; *(steif)* stiff; *(geistig)* rigid, inflexible; *(bewegungslos)* motionless; **~bewegt** *adj* motionless; *(fig: unberührt)* unmoved; **~bewiesen** *adj* unproven; **~bewọhnbar** *adj* uninhabitable; **~bewohnt** *adj Gegend* uninhabited; *Haus* unoccupied; **~bewußt** *adj* unconscious; *Reflex* involuntary; **~bezạhlbar** *adj* **(a)** *(zu teuer)* prohibitively expensive; **(b)** *(fig) (komisch)* priceless; *(nützlich)* invaluable; **~bezahlt** *adj* unpaid; **~bezạ̈hmbar** *adj Optimismus etc* irrepressible; *Verlangen* uncontrollable; **~bezwịnglich** *adj* unconquerable; *Gegner* invincible; *Festung* impregnable; *Drang* uncontrollable; **~blutig 1** *adj* bloodless; **2** *adv* without bloodshed; **~brauchbar** *adj (nutzlos)* useless; *(nicht zu verwenden)* unusable; **~bürokratisch** *adj* without any red tape.

ụnd *conj* and. **~?** well?; **~ dann?** then what?; **ich ~ ihm Geld leihen?** *(col)* me, lend him money?; **er konnte ~ konnte nicht aufhören** he simply couldn't stop; **... ~ wenn ich selbst bezahlen muß** ... even if I have to pay myself.

Ụndank *m* ingratitude. **~ ernten** to get little thanks; **~ ist der Welt Lohn** *(Prov)* never expect thanks for anything.

ụndankbar *adj* ungrateful; *Arbeit* thankless.

Ụndankbarkeit *f* ingratitude.

un-: ~definierbar *adj* indefinable; **~dẹnkbar** *adj* unthinkable, inconceivable.

ụndeutlich *adj* indistinct; *Erinnerung* vague; *Schrift* illegible; *Ausdrucksweise* unclear. **~ sprechen** to speak indistinctly, to mumble.

ụndicht *adj Dose, Gefäß* not air-/water-tight. **das Rohr ist ~** the pipe leaks; **das Fenster ist ~** the window lets in a draught *(Brit) or* draft *(US)*; **eine ~e Stelle haben** *(Rohr etc)* to leak; *(Reifen)* to have a hole.

undifferenziert *adj* simplistic.

Unding *nt no pl* **es ist ein ~, ...** it is absurd ...

Un-: u~diplomatisch *adj* undiplomatic; **u~diszipliniert** *adj* undisciplined; **u~duldsam** *adj* intolerant *(gegen* of*)*; **~duldsamkeit** *f no pl* intolerance *(gegen* of*)*; **u~durchdringlich** *adj Urwald* impenetrable; *Gesicht* inscrutable; **u~durchführbar** *adj* impracticable, unworkable; **u~durchlässig** *adj* impermeable *(gegen* to*)*; **u~durchschaubar** *adj* unfathomable; *Mensch* inscrutable; **u~durchsichtig** *adj Fenster* opaque; *Papier Stoff* non-transparent; *(fig pej) Mensch, Methoden* devious; *Motive* obscure.

un|eben *adj* uneven; *Straße auch* bumpy.

Un|ebenheit *f siehe adj* unevenness; bumpiness. **kleine ~en** uneven patches.

un-: ~echt *adj* false; *Schmuck, Edelstein, Blumen etc* artifical, fake *(usu pej)*; **~edel** *adj Metalle* base; **~ehelich** *adj* illegitimate; **~ehelich geboren sein** to be illegitimate; **~ehrenhaft** *adj* dishonourable *(Brit)*, dishonorable *(US)*; **~ehrlich** *adj* dishonest; **~ehrlich spielen** to cheat; **~eigennützig** *adj* unselfish, selfless.

un|eingeschränkt *adj* absolute, total; *Rechte, Handel* unrestricted; *Zustimmung* unqualified.

Un-: u~einheitlich *adj* non-uniform; *Preise* unsteady; **u~einheitlich sein** to vary; **u~einig** *adj* in disagreement; *Familie* divided; **über etw** *(acc)* **u~einig sein** to disagree about sth; **~einigkeit** *f* disagreement *(gen* between*)*; **u~einnehmbar** *adj* impregnable.

un|eins *adj pred* divided. **(mit jdm) ~ sein/werden** to disagree with sb.

un-: ~empfänglich *adj (für* to*)* not susceptible; *(für Eindrücke, Atmosphäre)* insensitive; **~empfindlich** *adj (gegen* to*)* insensitive; *Bazillen etc* immune; *Pflanzen* hardy; *Textilien* practical.

un|endlich 1 *adj* infinite; *(zeitlich)* endless. **2** *adv* endlessly; *(fig: sehr)* terribly. **~ lange diskutieren** to argue endlessly.

Un|endlichkeit *f* infinity; *(zeitlich)* endlessness.

un-: ~entbehrlich *adj* indispensable; **~entgeltlich** *adj* free of charge.

un|entschieden *adj* undecided; *(entschlußlos)* indecisive; *(Sport)* drawn. **~ enden** to end in a draw; **ein ~es Rennen** a dead heat.

Un|entschieden *nt - (Sport)* draw.

un|entschlossen *adj* undecided; *(entschlußlos) Mensch* indecisive.

un|entschuldbar *adj* inexcusable.

un|entschuldigt 1 *adj* unexcused. **~es Fernbleiben von der Arbeit/Schule** absenteeism/truancy. **2** *adv* without an excuse.

un|entwegt 1 *adj* constant, untiring. **einige U~e** a few stalwarts. **2** *adv* constantly, without tiring; *weiterarbeiten* unceasingly.

un|erbittlich *adj* relentless.

Un-: u~erfahren *adj* inexperienced; **u~erfindlich** *adj* incomprehensible; **u~erforschlich** *adj* impenetrable; *Wille* unfathomable; **u~erfreulich** *adj* unpleasant; **~erfreuliches** *(schlechte Nachrichten)* bad news *sing*; *(Übles)* bad things *pl*; **~erfüllbar** *adj* unrealizable; **u~erfüllt** *adj* unfulfilled; **u~ergiebig** *adj Quelle, Thema* unproductive; *Boden, Ernte, Nachschlagewerk* poor; **u~ergründlich** *adj* unfathomable; **u~erheblich** *adj* insignificant; **u~erhofft** *adj* unexpected.

un|erhört[1] **1** *adj attr (ungeheuer)* enormous; *(empörend)* outrageous; *Frechheit* incredible. **2** *adv* incredibly. **~ viel** a tremendous amount (of).

un|erhört[2] *adj Bitte* unanswered.

un-: ~erkannt *adj* unrecognized; **~erklärlich** *adj* inexplicable; **~erklärt** *adj Phänomen* unexplained; *Krieg, Liebe* undeclared; **~erläßlich** *adj* imperative.

un|erlaubt *adj* forbidden; *Betreten, Parken* unauthorized; *(ungesetzlich)* illegal.

un|erledigt *adj* unfinished; *Post* unanswered; *Rechnung* outstanding; *(schwebend)* pending.

un-: u~ermeßlich *adj* immense, vast; **~ermüdlich** *adj* untiring; **u~erprobt** *adj* untested, untried; **u~erreichbar** *adj Ziel* unattainable; *Ort* inaccessible; *(telefonisch)* unobtainable; **~erreicht** *adj* unequalled; *Ziel* unattained; **~ersättlich** *adj* insatiable; **~erschlossen** *adj Land* undeveloped; *Boden* unexploited; *Vorkommen, Markt* untapped; **~erschöpflich** *adj* inexhaustible; **~erschrocken** *adj* intrepid, courageous; **~erschütterlich** *adj* unshakeable; *Ruhe* imperturbable; **~erschwinglich** *adj* exorbitant, prohibitive; **für jdn ~erschwinglich sein** to be beyond sb's means; **~ersetzlich** *adj* irreplaceable; **~erträglich** *adj* unbearable; **~erwartet** *adj* unexpected; **~erwünscht** *adj Kind* unwanted; *Besuch, Effekt* unwelcome; **~erzogen** *adj* ill-mannered; *Kind auch* badly brought up.

unfachmännisch *adj* unprofessional.

unfähig *adj* **(a)** *attr* incompetent. **(b) ~ sein, etw zu tun** to be incapable of doing sth.

Unfähigkeit *f* **(a)** *(Untüchtigkeit)* incompetence. **(b)** *(Nichtkönnen)* inability.

Unfall *m, pl* **Unfälle** accident.

Unfall-: ~arzt *m* specialist for accident injuries; **~flucht** *f* failure to stop after an accident; **~flucht begehen** to commit a hit-and-run offence *(Brit) or* offense *(US)*; **~folge** *f* result of an/the accident; **u~frei 1** *adj* accident-free; *Auto* with no accident damage; **2** *adv* without an accident; **~klinik** *f* accident hospital; **~opfer** *nt* casualty; **~ort** *m* scene of an/the accident; **~station** *f* accident *or* emergency ward; **~wagen** *m* car involved in an/the accident; *(col: Rettungswagen)* ambulance; **~zahl, ~ziffer** *f* number of accidents.

unfaßbar, unfaßlich *adj* incomprehensible.

un-: ~fehlbar 1 *adj* infallible; **2** *adv* without fail; **~fein** *adj* unrefined; **das ist ~fein** that's bad manners; **~fertig** *adj* unfinished, incomplete; *Mensch* immature; **~folgsam** *adj* disobedient; **~förmig** *adj (formlos)* shapeless; *(groß)* cumbersome; *Füße, Gesicht* unshapely; **~frankiert** *adj* unstamped.

unfrei *adj* **(a)** not free. **(b)** *(befangen)* constrained, uneasy. **(c)** *Brief* unfranked.

unfreiwillig *adj* compulsory; *Witz, Fehler* unintentional. **ich war ~er Zeuge** I was an unwilling witness.

unfreundlich *adj* unfriendly *(zu, gegen* to*)*; *Landschaft, Zimmer, Farbe* cheerless; *Akt* hostile.

Unfriede(n) *m* strife.

un-: ~frisiert *adj Haare* uncombed; *Mensch* with one's hair all over the place; **~fruchtbar** *adj* infertile; *(fig) Debatte etc* fruitless; **die ~fruchtbaren Tage** *(Med)* the days of infertility.

Unfug ['unfu:k] *m no pl* nonsense. **~ treiben** to get up to mischief.

Ungar(in *f***)** ['ʊŋgar(ɪn)] *m (wk)* **-n, -n** Hungarian.

ungarisch ['ʊŋgarɪʃ] *adj* Hungarian.

Ungarn ['ʊŋgarn] *nt* Hungary.

ungastlich *adj* inhospitable.

unge|achtet *prep+gen* in spite of, despite.

un-: ~geahndet *adj (Jur)* unpunished; **~geahnt** *adj* undreamt-of; **~gebärdig** *adj* unruly; **~gebeten** *adj* uninvited; **~gebildet** *adj* uncultured; *(ohne Bildung)* uneducated; **~geboren** *adj* unborn; **~gebräuchlich** *adj* uncommon; **~gebrochen** *adj* unbroken.

ungebührlich *adj* improper. **sich ~ aufregen** to get unduly excited.

ungebunden *adj* **(a)** *Buch* unbound; *Blumen* loose. **(b) in ~er Rede** in prose. **(c)** *Leben* (fancy-)free; *(unverheiratet)* unattached; *(Pol)* independent. **frei und ~** footloose and fancy-free.

ungedeckt *adj* **(a)** *(schutzlos)* unprotected; *(Sport) Tor* undefended; *Spieler* unmarked;

Scheck uncovered. **(b)** *Tisch* unlaid *(Brit)*, not set *pred.*
Ungeduld *f* impatience. **vor ~** with impatience; **voller ~** impatiently.
ungeduldig *adj* impatient.
unge|eignet *adj* unsuitable.
ungefähr 1 *adj attr* approximate, rough. **2** *adv* roughly, approximately. **(so) ~ dreißig** about *or* approximately thirty; **das kommt nicht von ~** it's no accident; **wo ~?** whereabouts?; **so ~!** more or less!; **damit ich ~ weiß, ...** so that I have a rough idea ...; **~ (so) wie** a bit like.
un-: ~gefährdet *adj* safe; **~gefährlich** *adj* safe; *Tier, Krankheit, Arzneimittel etc* harmless; **~gefällig** *adj Mensch* unobliging; **~gefärbt** *adj Haare, Stoff* undyed; *Lebensmittel* without colouring *(Brit) or* coloring *(US)*; **~gefedert** *adj* without springs; **~gegliedert** *adj Körper* unjointed; *(fig)* disjointed; *Satz, Aufsatz etc* unstructured; **~gehalten** *adj* indignant *(über +acc* about*)*.
Ungeheuer *nt* - monster.
ungeheuer 1 *adj* **(a)** *(riesig)* enormous, immense. **(b) = ungeheuerlich. 2** *adv (sehr)* enormously, tremendously; *(negativ)* terribly.
ungeheuerlich *adj* monstrous; *Verdacht, Dummheit* dreadful; *Leichtsinn* outrageous, appalling.
un-: ~gehindert *adj* unhindered; **~gehobelt** *adj Mensch* boorish; **~gehörig** *adj* impertinent; **~gehorsam** *adj* disobedient; **~gekämmt** *adj Haar* uncombed; **~gekämmt aussehen** to look unkempt; **~geklärt** *adj Abwasser* untreated; *Frage, Verbrechen* unsolved; *Ursache* unknown; **~gekocht** *adj* raw; *Flüssigkeit* unboiled; *Obst etc* uncooked; **~gekünstelt** *adj* natural; **~gekürzt** *adj* not shortened; *Buch* unabridged; *Film* uncut; *Ausgaben* not cut back.
ungelegen *adj* inconvenient. **komme ich (Ihnen) ~?** is this an inconvenient time for you?
Ungelegenheiten *pl* inconvenience *sing.* **jdm ~ bereiten** to inconvenience sb.
un-: ~gelehrig *adj* unteachable; **~gelenkig** *adj* stiff; *(fig col: nicht flexibel)* inflexible; **~gelernt** *adj attr* unskilled; **~gelogen** *adv* honestly.
ungemein *adj* immense, tremendous.
ungemustert *adj* plain.
un-: ~gemütlich *adj* uncomfortable; *Mensch* awkward; *Land, Wetter, Wochenende* unpleasant; **mir wird es hier ~gemütlich** I'm getting a bit uncomfortable; **er kann ~gemütlich werden** he can get nasty; **~genannt** *adj* anonymous; **~genau** *adj* inaccurate; *(vage)* vague; *(ungefähr)* approximate.
ungeniert ['ʊnʒeniːɐt] **1** *adj* free and easy; *(bedenkenlos, taktlos)* uninhibited. **2** *adv* openly; *(bedenkenlos, taktlos)* without any inhibition.
ungenießbar *adj (nicht zu essen)* inedible; *(nicht zu trinken)* undrinkable; *(unschmackhaft)* unpalatable; *(col) Mensch* unbearable.
ungenügend *adj* inadequate, insufficient; *(Sch)* unsatisfactory.
Un-: u~genutzt *adj* unused; **eine Chance u~genutzt lassen** to miss an opportunity; **u~geordnet** *adj* disordered; **u~gepflegt** *adj Mensch* untidy; *Park, Hände etc* neglected; **sich u~gepflegt ausdrücken** to talk in a common way; **u~gerade** *adj* odd; **u~geraten** *adj Kind* ill-bred; **u~gerecht** *adj* unjust; **u~geregelt** *adj* irregular; **u~gereimt** *adj Verse* unrhymed; *(fig)* inconsistent; **~gereimtheit** *f (fig)* inconsistency.
ungern *adv* reluctantly. **(höchst) ~!** if I/we really have to!
un-: ~gerufen *adj* without being called; **~gerührt** *adj* unmoved; **~gesagt** *adj* unsaid; **etw ~gesagt machen** to pretend sth has never been said; **~geschehen** *adj* undone; **etw ~geschehen machen** to undo sth; **~geschickt** *adj* clumsy, awkward; *(unbedacht)* careless; **~geschlechtlich** *adj* asexual; **~geschliffen** *adj Edelstein* uncut; *Messer* blunt; *(fig) Benehmen* uncouth; **~geschmälert** *adj* undiminished; **~geschmeidig** *adj Stoff, Leder* rough; *Haar* coarse; **~geschminkt** *adj* without make-up; *(fig) Wahrheit* unvarnished.
ungeschoren *adj* unshorn; *(fig)* spared. **jdn ~ lassen** *(col)* to spare sb; *(ungestraft)* to let sb off.
un-: ~geschult *adj* untrained; **~geschützt** *adj* unprotected; *(Mil) Einheit* exposed; **~gesetzlich** *adj* illegal; **~gesichert** *adj* unsecured, not secured; *Schußwaffe* with the safety catch off; **~gesittet** *adj* uncivilized; **~gestört** *adj* undisturbed; *(Rad, TV etc)* without interference; **~gestraft** *adv* with impunity.
ungestüm ['ʊngəʃtyːm] *adj* impetuous.
un-: ~gesund *adj* unhealthy; **~getan** *adj* undone; **~getrübt** *adj* clear; *Glück* perfect.
Ungetüm *nt* **-e** monster.
un-: ~geübt *adj* unpractised *(Brit)*, unpracticed *(US)*; *Mensch* out of practice; **~gewandt** *adj* awkward.
ungewiß *adj* uncertain; *(vage)* vague. **jdn (über etw *acc*) im ungewissen lassen** to leave sb in the dark (about sth).
Ungewißheit *f* uncertainty.
ungewöhnlich 1 *adj* unusual. **2** *adv* unusually.
ungewohnt *adj* unusual; *(fremdartig)* strange, unfamiliar. **das ist mir ~** I am not used to it.
ungewollt *adj* unintentional.
Ungeziefer *nt no pl* vermin.
ungezogen *adj* ill-mannered.
Ungezogenheit *f* bad manners *no indef art.*
un-: ~gezügelt 1 *adj (unbeherrscht)* unbridled; *(ausschweifend)* dissipated; **2** *adv* without restraint; **~gezwungen** *adj* casual, informal; **sich ~gezwungen bewegen** to feel quite free; **~giftig** *adj* non-poisonous.
unglaubhaft *adj* incredible, unbelievable.
ungläubig 1 *adj* unbelieving; *(zweifelnd)* doubting. **~er Thomas** doubting Thomas. **2** *adv* doubtingly, in disbelief.
Ungläubige(r) *mf* unbeliever.
unglaublich *adj* unbelievable, incredible.
unglaubwürdig *adj* implausible; *Dokument* dubious; *Mensch* unreliable. **sich ~ machen** to lose credibility.
ungleich 1 *adj Charaktere* dissimilar; *Größe, Farbe* different; *(nicht gleichwertig, nicht vergleichbar) Mittel, Waffen* unequal; *(Math)* not equal. **2** *adv* much, incomparably.
ungleichartig *adj* dissimilar.
Ungleich-: u~mäßig *adj* uneven; *Atemzüge, Gesichtszüge, Puls* irregular; **~mäßigkeit** *f siehe adj* unevenness; irregularity.
Unglück *nt* **-e** *(Unfall, Vorfall)* accident; *(Schicksalsschlag)* disaster, tragedy; *(Unheil)* misfortune; *(Pech, im Aberglauben, bei Glücksspiel)* bad luck; *(Unglücklichsein)* unhappiness. **das ist auch kein ~** that's not a disaster; **das ~ wollte es, daß ...** as (bad) luck would have it, ...; **zu allem ~** to make matters worse; **ein ~ kommt selten allein** *(Prov)* it never rains but it pours *(Prov)*.
unglücklich *adj* **(a)** *(traurig)* unhappy; *Liebe* unrequited. **ich U~(r)!** poor me! **(b)** *(bedauerlich)* sad, unfortunate. **~ enden** to turn out badly.
unglücklicherweise *adv* unfortunately.
unglückselig *adj (liter)* unfortunate; *(armselig)* miserable; *(unglückbringend)* disastrous.
Unglücks-: ~fall *m* accident; **~rabe** *m (col)* unlucky thing *(col)*; **~zahl** *f* unlucky number.
Ungnade *f* **bei jdm in ~ fallen** to fall out of favour *(Brit) or* favor *(US)* with sb.
ungnädig *adj* ungracious.
ungültig *adj* invalid; *(Sport) Tor* disallowed. **etw für ~ erklären** to declare sth null and void; **eine Ehe für ~ erklären** to annul a marriage.
ungünstig *adj* unfavourable *(Brit)*, unfavorable *(US)*, disadvantageous; *Termin* inconvenient; *Augenblick, Wetter* bad; *(nicht preiswert)*

expensive.

ungut *adj* bad. **ein ~es Gefühl haben** to have an uneasy *or* bad feeling; **nichts für ~!** no offence *(Brit) or* offense *(US)*!

un-: ~haltbar *adj Zustand* intolerable; *Vorwurf, Behauptung etc* untenable; *Torschuß* unstoppable; **~handlich** *adj* unwieldy.

Unheil *nt no pl* disaster. **~ stiften** to do damage.

unheilbar *adj* incurable.

Unheil-: u~bringend *adj* fateful, ominous; **~stifter** *m* mischief-maker; **u~voll** *adj* disastrous.

unheimlich 1 *adj* **(a)** *(angsterregend)* frightening, sinister. **das/er ist mir ~** it/he gives me the creeps *(col)*. **(b)** *(col)* tremendous *(col)*. **2** *adv (col: sehr)* incredibly *(col)*. **~ viele Menschen** an incredible number of people.

un-: ~höflich *adj* impolite; **~hörbar** *adj* silent; *Frequenzen* inaudible.

Uni *f* **-s** *(col)* university.

uni [y'niː] *adj pred* self-coloured *(Brit)*, self-colored *(US)*, plain.

Uniform *f* **-en** uniform.

uniformieren* *vt (einheitlich machen)* to make uniform.

un-: ~interessant *adj* uninteresting; **sein Angebot ist für uns ~interessant** we're not interested in his offer; **~interessiert** *adj (neutral)* disinterested; *(nicht interessiert)* uninterested.

Union *f* **-en** union. **die ~** *(BRD Pol)* the CDU and CSU.

Unionsparteien *pl (BRD Pol)* CDU and CSU parties *pl*.

universal, universell [univɛr-] *adj* universal.

Universal- [univɛr'zaːl-] *in cpds* universal; *Bildung etc* general; **~genie** *nt* universal genius.

Universität [univɛrzi'tɛːt] *f* university. **die ~ Freiburg, die Freiburger ~** the University of Freiburg, Freiburg University; **auf die ~ gehen, die ~ besuchen** to go to university.

Universitäts- *in cpds* university; **~klinik** *f* university clinic *or* hospital.

Universum [uni'vɛrzʊm] *nt no pl* universe.

Unkenruf *m (fig)* prophecy of doom.

unkenntlich *adj* unrecognizable; *Inschrift etc* indecipherable.

Unkenntlichkeit *f siehe adj* unrecognizableness; indecipherability. **bis zur ~** beyond recognition.

Unkenntnis *f no pl* ignorance. **in ~ über etw** *(acc)* **sein** to be ignorant about sth.

unklar *adj* unclear; *Wetter* hazy. **ich bin mir darüber noch im ~en** I'm not quite clear about that yet; **jdn über etw** *(acc)* **im ~en lassen** to leave sb in the dark about sth; **nur ~ zu erkennen sein** not to be easily discernible.

Unklarheit *f* lack of clarity; *(über Tatsachen)* uncertainty. **darüber herrscht noch ~** it is still unclear.

un-: ~klug *adj* unwise; **~kollegial** *adj* uncooperative; **~kompliziert** *adj* straightforward, uncomplicated; **~kontrollierbar** *adj* uncontrollable; **~kontrollierbar werden** *(Mißbrauch etc)* to get out of hand; **~kontrolliert** *adj* unchecked; **~korrekt** *adj* **(a)** improper; **(b)** *(unrichtig)* incorrect.

Unkosten *pl* costs *pl*; *(Ausgaben)* expenses *pl*. **sich in ~ stürzen** *(col)* to go to a lot of expense.

Unkraut *nt* weed. **von ~ übersät** overgrown with weeds; **~ vergeht nicht** *(Prov)* it would take more than that to finish *me/him etc* off!

Unkraut-: ~bekämpfung *f* weed control; **~vertilgungsmittel** *nt* weed killer.

unkündbar *adj* permanent; *Vertrag* binding. **in ~er Stellung** in a permanent position.

unkundig *adj (geh)* ignorant *(+gen* of*)*. **des Lesens/Schreibens ~ sein** to be illiterate.

un-: ~längst *adv (geh)* recently; **~lauter** *adj* dishonest; *Wettbewerb* unfair; **~leserlich** *adj* unreadable; *Handschrift etc auch* illegible; **~leugbar** *adj* undeniable; indisputable; **~lieb** *adj*: **es ist mir nicht ~lieb, daß ...** I am quite glad that ...; **~liebsam** *adj* unpleasant; **~lösbar** *adj Problem, (Chem)* insoluble; *(untrennbar)* indissoluble; *Widerspruch* irreconcilable.

Unlust *f no pl* **(a)** *(Widerwille)* reluctance. **(b)** *(Lustlosigkeit)* listlessness.

unlustig *adj (gelangweilt)* bored; *(widerwillig)* reluctant.

unmännlich *adj* unmanly.

Unmasse *f (col)* load *(col)*. **eine ~ Leute** loads of people.

unmaßgeblich *adj* inconsequential. **nach meiner ~en Meinung** *(hum)* in my humble opinion *(hum)*.

unmäßig *adj* excessive, immoderate.

Unmenge *f* vast number; *(bei unzählbaren Begriffen)* vast amount. **~n von Leuten** vast numbers of people.

Unmensch *m* monster.

unmenschlich *adj* inhuman.

un-: ~merklich *adj* imperceptible; **~mißverständlich** *adj* unequivocal.

unmittelbar 1 *adj* direct; *Nähe etc* immediate. **2** *adv* immediately; *(direkt)* directly. **~ vor** *(+dat) (zeitlich)* immediately before; *(räumlich)* right *or* directly in front of.

un-: ~möbliert *adj* unfurnished; **~modern** *adj* old-fashioned.

unmöglich 1 *adj* impossible. **das ist mir ~** that is impossible for me; **U~es/das U~e** the impossible; **~ aussehen** *(col)* to look ridiculous. **2** *adv (keinesfalls)* not possibly; *(pej col: unpassend)* impossibly. **ich kann es ~ tun** I cannot possibly do it.

Un-: ~moral *f* immorality; **u~moralisch** *adj* immoral; **u~mündig** *adj (minderjährig)* underage; **wir wollen nicht länger wie ~mündige behandelt werden** we don't want to go on being treat ed as though we were incapable of thinking for ourselves.

Unmut *m* ill-humour *(Brit)*, ill-humor *(US)*; *(Unzufriedenheit)* displeasure *(über+acc* at*)*.

un-: ~nachahmlich *adj* inimitable; **~nachgiebig** *adj* inflexible; *(fig) Mensch auch* intransigent; **~nachsichtig 1** *adj* severe; *Strenge* unrelenting; **2** *adv hinrichten* mercilessly; *bestrafen* severely; **~nahbar** *adj* unapproachable; **~natürlich** *adj* unnatural; **~normal** *adj* abnormal; **~nötig** *adj* unnecessary; **~nötigerweise** *adv* unnecessarily, needlessly.

unnütz *adj* useless; *Geschwätz* idle.

UNO ['uːno] *f no pl* **die ~** the UN *sing*.

unordentlich *adj* untidy; *Lebenswandel* disorderly.

Un|ordnung *f* disorder *no indef art; (in Zimmer etc auch)* untidiness *no indef art; (Durcheinander)* mess. **mach nicht so eine ~!** don't make such a mess!

un-: ~organisch *adj* inorganic; **~organisiert** *adj* disorganized; **~orthodox** *adj* unorthodox; **~pädagogisch** *adj* educationally unsound; *Lehrer etc* bad (as a teacher).

unparteiisch *adj* impartial.

Unparteiische(r) *mf decl as adj* neutral person. **der ~** *(Sport)* the referee.

Un-: u~passend *adj* unsuitable; *Zeit auch* inconvenient; **u~päßlich** *adj (geh)* indisposed *(form)*; **~person** *f* persona non grata; **u~persönlich** *adj* impersonal *(auch Ling)*; *Mensch* aloof; **u~praktisch** *adj Mensch* unpractical; *Maschine, Lösung* impractical; **u~problematisch** *adj* unproblematic; *(einfach)* uncomplicated; **u~produktiv** *adj* unproductive; **u~pünktlich** *adj Mensch* unpunctual; *Zug* not on time; **~pünktlich kommen/abfahren** to come/leave late; **u~qualifiziert** *adj* unqualified; *Äußerung* incompetent.

Unrast *f no pl (geh)* restlessness.

Unrat ['ʊnraːt] *m no pl (geh)* refuse; *(fig)* filth.
un-: ~**rationell** *adj* inefficient; ~**ratsam** *adj* inadvisable; ~**recht** *adj* wrong; **das ist mir gar nicht so ~recht** I don't really mind.
Unrecht *nt no pl* wrong, injustice. **zu ~** *verdächtigt* wrongly, unjustly; **nicht zu ~** not without good reason; **im ~ sein** to be wrong; **u~ haben** to be wrong; **jdm u~ tun** to do sb an injustice.
unrechtmäßig *adj* unlawful, illegal.
un-: ~**redlich** *adj* dishonest; ~**reell** *adj* unfair; *(unredlich)* dishonest; *Preis* unreasonable.
unregelmäßig *adj* irregular.
Unregelmäßigkeit *f* irregularity.
Un-: **u~reif** *adj* immature; *Obst* unripe; ~**reife** *f siehe adj* immaturity; unripeness.
unrein *adj* not clean; *Ton* impure; *Atem, Haut* bad; *Gedanken, Taten* impure. **etw ins ~e schreiben** to write sth out in rough.
unrentabel *adj* unprofitable.
unrichtig *adj* incorrect.
Unruhe *f* **-n (a)** *no pl* restlessness; *(Nervosität)* agitation; *(Besorgnis)* disquiet. **(b)** *no pl (Lärm)* noise, disturbance; *(Geschäftigkeit)* bustle. **(c)** *no pl (Unfrieden)* unrest *no pl*, trouble. **~ stiften** to create unrest; *(in Familie, Schule)* to make trouble.
Unruhestifter(in *f***)** *m* - troublemaker.
unruhig *adj* restless; *(nervös auch)* fidgety *no adv; (laut, belebt)* noisy; *Schlaf* fitful; *Zeit etc, Meer* troubled.
unrühmlich *adj* inglorious.
uns 1 *pers pron acc, dat of* **wir** us; *(dat auch)* to/for us. **bei ~** *(zu Hause, im Betrieb etc)* at our place; *(in unserer Beziehung)* between us; *(in unserem Land)* in our country; **ein Freund von ~** a friend of ours. **2** *refl pron acc, dat* ourselves; *(einander)* each other, one another. **~ selbst** ourselves; **unter ~ gesagt** between you and me; **mitten unter ~** in our midst; **hier sind wir unter ~** we are alone here; **das bleibt unter ~** it won't go any further.
unsachgemäß *adj* improper.
unsachlich *adj* unobjective; *(fehl am Platz)* uncalled-for. **~ werden** to become personal.
unsanft *adj* rough; *(unhöflich)* rude.
unsauber *adj* **(a)** *(schmutzig)* dirty. **(b)** *Handschrift, Arbeit* untidy; *(nicht exakt) Schuß, Schnitt* inaccurate; *Klang* impure. **(c)** *(unmoralisch)* shady; *Spielweise* dirty.
unschädlich *adj* harmless; *Bombe auch* safe. **jdn ~ machen** *(col)* to take care of sb *(col)*.
unscharf *adj* blurred, fuzzy; *Foto auch* out of focus; *(Rad)* unclear.
unschätzbar *adj* incalculable; *Hilfe* invaluable. **von ~em Wert** invaluable; *Schmuck* priceless.
unscheinbar *adj* inconspicuous; *(unattraktiv) Mensch* unprepossessing.
unschicklich *adj* unseemly, improper.
unschlagbar *adj* unbeatable.
unschlüssig *adj* undecided. **er ist sich** *(dat)* **noch ~** he's still undecided, he hasn't made up his mind yet.
unschön *adj (häßlich)* unsightly; *(stärker)* ugly; *Gesicht* plain; *(unangenehm)* unpleasant. **~e Szenen** ugly scenes.
Unschuld *f no pl* innocence; *(Jungfräulichkeit)* virginity; *(fig: Mädchen)* innocent.
unschuldig *adj* innocent *(an +dat* of*)*. **schuldig oder ~** guilty or not guilty; **sie ist noch ~** she is still a virgin.
Unschulds-: ~**engel** *m (col)* little innocent; ~**miene** *f* innocent expression.
unschwer *adv* easily, without difficulty.
unselbständig 1 *adj Denken, Handeln* lacking in independence; *Mensch auch* dependent, unable to stand on one's own two feet. **Einkünfte aus ~er Arbeit** income from (salaried) employment. **2** *adv (mit fremder Hilfe)* not independently.
Unselbständige(r) *mf decl as adj (Fin)* employed person.
unselig *adj* unfortunate; *(verhängnisvoll)* ill-fated.
unser *poss pron* our.
unser|einer, unser|eins *indef pron (col)* the likes of us *(col)*.
uns(e)re(r, s) *poss pron (substantivisch)* ours. **der/die/das ~** *(geh)* ours; **wir tun das U~** *(geh)* we are doing our bit; **die U~n** *(geh)* our family.
unser(er)seits *adv (auf unserer Seite)* for our part; *(von unserer Seite)* on our part.
uns(e)resgleichen *indef pron* people like us.
uns(e)rige(r, s) *poss pron (old,geh)* **der/die/das ~** ours; *siehe* **uns(e)re(r, s)**.
unseriös *adj* **(a)** not serious. **(b)** *(unehrlich)* not straight, untrustworthy.
unsert-: ~**halben,** ~**wegen** *adv* on our behalf; ~**willen** *adv:* **um ~willen** for our sake.
unsicher *adj* **(a)** *(gefährlich)* dangerous, unsafe. **die Gegend ~ machen** *(fig col)* to knock about the district *(col)*. **(b)** *(nicht selbstbewußt)* insecure. **(c)** *(ungewiß, zweifelhaft)* unsure, uncertain; *Verhältnisse* unstable. **(d)** *(ungeübt, ungefestigt)* unsure; *Hand* unsteady; *Kenntnisse* shaky. **~ auf den Beinen** unsteady on one's feet.
Unsicherheit *f siehe adj* **(a)** danger. **(b)** insecurity. **(c)** uncertainty; instability.
unsichtbar *adj (lit, fig)* invisible.
Unsinn *m no pl* nonsense *no indef art*, rubbish *no indef art*. **~ machen** to do silly things; **~ reden** to talk nonsense; **laß den ~!** stop fooling about!
unsinnig *adj (sinnlos)* nonsensical; *(ungerechtfertigt)* unreasonable.
Unsitte *f (schlechte Gewohnheit)* bad habit.
unsittlich *adj* immoral.
unsolid(e) *adj Mensch* free-living; *(unredlich) Firma* unreliable.
un-: ~**sozial** *adj Verhalten* antisocial; *Politik* unsocial; ~**spezifisch** *adj* non-specific; ~**sportlich** *adj* unathletic; *(unfair)* unsporting; ~**statthaft** *adj (form)* inadmissible; *(~gesetzlich)* illegal; *(Sport)* not allowed.
unsterblich 1 *adj* immortal; *Liebe* undying. **jdn ~ machen** to immortalize sb. **2** *adv (col)* utterly.
Unsterblichkeit *f* immortality.
unstet *adj Glück, Liebe* fickle; *Mensch* restless; *(wankelmütig)* changeable; *Entwicklung* unsteady; *Leben* unsettled.
Un-: **u~stillbar** *adj Durst* unquenchable; *Sehnsucht, Hunger* insatiable; ~**stimmigkeit** *f (Streit)* difference; **u~streitig** *adv* indisputably; ~**summe** *f* vast sum.
unsympathisch *adj* unpleasant, disagreeable. **das/er ist mir ~** I don't like that/him.
untad(e)lig *adj* impeccable; *Mensch* beyond reproach.
Untat *f* atrocity.
untätig *adj (müßig)* idle; *(nicht handelnd)* passive; *Vulkan* inactive, dormant.
un-: ~**tauglich** *adj (zu, für* for*)* unsuitable *(für Wehrdienst)* unfit; ~**teilbar** *adj* indivisible.
unten *adv* at the bottom; *(tiefer, drunten)* (down) below; *(an der Unterseite)* underneath; *(in Gebäude)* downstairs. **~ am Berg/im Glas** at the bottom of the mountain/glass; **nach ~** down; **bis ~** to the bottom; **dort** *or* **da/hier ~** down there/here; **weiter ~** further down; **~ bleiben** to stay down; **rechts/links ~** down on the right/left; **siehe ~** see below; **er ist bei mir ~ durch** *(col)* I'm through with him *(col)*.
unten-: ~**an** *adv (am unteren Ende)* at the far end; *(in Reihenfolge: lit, fig)* at the bottom; **(bei jdm) ~an stehen** *(fig)* to be at the bottom of sb's list; ~**drunter** *adv (col)* underneath.
unter *prep* **(a)** *+dat* under; *(drunter)* underneath, below; *(zwischen, innerhalb)* among(st). **~ 18 Jahren** under 18 years (of age); **Temperaturen**

~ **25 Grad** temperatures below 25 degrees; **sie waren ~ sich** *(dat)* they were by themselves; **jdn ~ sich haben** to have sb under one; ~ **anderem** among other things. **(b)**+*acc* under. **bis ~ das Dach voll mit ...** full to the rafters with...

Unter-: ~abteilung *f* subdivision; **~arm** *m* forearm; **~art** *f (esp Biol)* subspecies; **~bau** *m, pl* **-ten** *(von Gebäude)* foundations *pl*; *(bei Straßen)* (road)bed; **u~belegt** *adj Hotel etc* not full; *Kurs* under-subscribed; **u~belichten*** *vti insep (Phot)* to underexpose; **u~besetzt** *adj* understaffed; **u~bewerten*** *vt insep* to underrate; **u~bewußt** *adj* subconscious; **~bewußtsein** *nt* subconscious; **im ~bewußtsein** subconsciously; **u~bezahlen*** *vt insep* to underpay; **u~bieten*** *vt insep irreg Konkurrenten* to undercut; *(fig)* to surpass; **u~binden*** *vt insep irreg* to stop, to prevent; **u~bleiben*** *vi insep irreg aux sein* **(a)** *(aufhören)* to stop; **in Zukunft muß das u~bleiben** that must not happen again in the future; **(b)** *(versäumt werden)* to be omitted; **u~brechen*** *vt insep irreg* to interrupt; *Reise, Eintönigkeit* to break; *(langfristig)* to break off; *Telefonverbindung* to disconnect; *Spiel* to suspend, to stop; **wir sind u~brochen worden** *(am Telefon)* we've been cut off; **~brecherkontakte** *pl* points *pl*; **~brechung** *f* interruption; break *(+gen* in); *(von Telefonverbindung)* disconnection; *(von Spiel)* stoppage; **ohne ~brechung** without a break; **u~breiten*** *vt insep Plan* to present; **(jdm) einen Vorschlag u~breiten** to make a proposal (to sb).

unterbringen *vt sep irreg* **(a)** to put; *Arbeitslose etc* to fix up *(bei* with). **ich kann nicht alles im Schrank ~** I can't put *or* get everything in the cupboard; **ich kenne ihn, aber ich kann ihn nirgends ~** *(col)* I know him, but I just can't place him. **(b)** *(Unterkunft geben) Menschen* to accommodate; *(in Haus, Hotel etc auch)* to put up. **gut/schlecht untergebracht sein** to have good/bad accommodation *(Brit) or* accommodations *(US)*; *(versorgt werden)* to be well/badly looked after.

Unterbringung *f* accommodation *(Brit)*, accommodations *pl (US)*.

unterbuttern *vt sep (col)* **(a)** *(zuschießen)* to throw in. **(b)** *(unterdrücken)* to ride roughshod over.

unterderhand *adv* secretly; *verkaufen* privately.

unterdessen *adv* (in the) meantime, meanwhile.

unterdrücken* *vt insep* **(a)** *Neugier, Lachen* to suppress; *Gähnen* to stifle; *Tränen, Bemerkung* to hold back. **(b)** *(beherrschen) Menschen* to oppress; *Freiheit, Revolution* to suppress.

Unterdrücker(in *f*) *m* - oppressor.

unterdurchschnittlich *adj* below average.

unter|einander *adv* **(a)** *(gegenseitig)* each other; *(miteinander)* among ourselves/themselves *etc*. **(b)** *(räumlich)* one below the other.

unter|einander- *pref* **(a)** *(durcheinander-)* together. **(b)** *(örtlich)* one below the other.

unter|entwickelt *adj* underdeveloped.

untere(r, s) *adj, superl* **unterste(r, s)** lower.

Unter-: u~ernährt *adj* undernourished; **~ernährung** *f* malnutrition.

Unterfangen *nt* - *(geh)* venture, undertaking.

Unterführung *f* underpass.

Untergang *m* **(a)** *(von Schiff)* sinking. **(b)** *(von Gestirn)* setting. **(c)** *(das Zugrundegehen) (allmählich)* decline; *(völlig)* destruction; *(der Welt)* end; *(von Individuum)* downfall, ruin. **dem ~ geweiht sein** to be doomed.

Untergebene(r) *mf decl as adj* subordinate.

untergegangen *adj Volk etc* extinct.

untergehen *vi sep irreg aux sein* **(a)** *(versinken)* to sink; *(Schiff auch)* to go down; *(fig: im Lärm etc)* to be drowned. **(b)** *(Gestirn)* to set. **(c)** *(Kultur, Welt)* to come to an end; *(Individuum)* to perish; *(im Existenzkampf)* to go under.

Unter-: u~geordnet *adj Dienststelle* subordinate; *Bedeutung* secondary; **~geschoß** *nt* basement; **~gewicht** *nt* **~gewicht haben** to be underweight; **u~gliedern*** *vt insep* to subdivide; **u~graben*** *vt insep irreg* to undermine.

Untergrund *m no pl* **(a)** *(Geol)* subsoil. **(b)** *(farblicher Hintergrund)* background. **(c)** *(Pol etc)* underground. **in den ~ gehen** to go underground.

Untergrund- *in cpds (Pol etc)* underground; **~bahn** *f* underground *(Brit)*, subway *(US)*.

Unter-: ~gruppe *f* subgroup; **u~haken** *vr sep* **sich bei jdm u~haken** to link arms with sb.

unterhalb 1 *prep+gen* below. **2** *adv* below.

Unterhalt *m no pl* **(a)** *(Lebens~)* keep, maintenance *(esp Jur)*. **seinen ~ verdienen** to earn one's living; **seinen ~ haben** to earn enough. **(b)** *(Instandhaltung)* upkeep.

unterhalten* *insep irreg* **1** *vt* **(a)** *(versorgen)* to support. **(b)** *Geschäft, Kfz,* to run; *Konto* to have. **(c)** *(pflegen) Kontakte* to maintain. **(d)** *Gäste, Publikum* to entertain. **2** *vr* **(a)** *(sprechen)* to talk *(mit* to, with). **sich mit jdm (über etw** *acc*) **~** to (have a) talk with sb (about sth). **(b)** *(sich vergnügen)* to enjoy oneself.

Unterhalter(in *f*) *m* - **(a)** entertainer. **(b)** *(Verdiener)* breadwinner.

unterhaltsam *adj* entertaining.

Unterhaltskosten *pl* maintenance costs *pl*.

Unterhaltung *f* **(a)** *(Gespräch)* talk, conversation. **(b)** *(Amüsement)* entertainment. **(c)** *no pl (Instandhaltung)* upkeep; *(von Gebäuden auch, von Kfz, Maschinen)* maintenance.

Unterhaltungs-: ~elektronik *f (Industrie)* entertainment electronics *sing*; *(Geräte)* audio systems *pl*; **~literatur** *f* light fiction; **~programm** *nt* light entertainment programme *(Brit) or* program *(US)*.

Unterhändler *m* negotiator.

Unterhaus *nt* House of Commons *(Brit)*, Lower House.

Unterhemd *nt* vest *(Brit)*, undershirt *(US)*.

unterhöhlen* *vt insep* to hollow out; *(fig)* to undermine.

Unterholz *nt no pl* undergrowth.

Unterhose *f (Herren~)* (pair of) underpants *pl*; *(Damen~)* (pair of) pants *pl*. **lange ~n** long johns *pl*.

unter|irdisch *adj* underground.

unterjochen* *vt insep* to subjugate.

unterjubeln *vt sep (col)* **jdm etw ~** *(andrehen)* to palm sth off on sb *(col)*; *(anlasten)* to pin sth on sb *(col)*.

unterkellern* *vt insep* to build with a cellar.

Unter-: ~kiefer *m* lower jaw; **~klasse** *f* **(a)** subclass; **(b)** *(Sociol)* lower class; **~kleidung** *f* underwear, underclothes *pl*.

unterkommen *vi sep irreg aux sein* **(a)** *(Unterkunft finden)* to find accommodation *(Brit) or* accommodations *(US)*; *(col: Stelle finden)* to find a job *(als* as, *bei* with, at). **bei jdm ~** to stay at sb's (place). **(b) so etwas ist mir noch nie untergekommen!** *(col)* I've never come across anything like it!

Unterkommen *nt* - *(Obdach)* accommodation *(Brit)*, accommodations *(US)*. **bei jdm ein ~ finden** to be put up at sb's (place).

Unter-: ~körper *m* lower part of the body; **u~kriegen** *vt sep (col)* **sich nicht u~kriegen lassen** not to let things get one down; **u~kühlen*** *vt insep Körper* to expose to subnormal temperatures; **u~kühlt** *adj Körper* affected by hypothermia; *(fig) Atmosphäre, Mensch* cool; **~kühlung** *f (Med)* hypothermia.

Unterkunft *f, pl* **Unterkünfte (a)** accommodation *(Brit)*, accommodations *(US)*. **~ und Verpflegung** board and lodging. **(b)** *(von Soldaten etc)* quarters *pl*; *(esp in Privathaus)* billet.

Unterlage *f* **(a)** base; *(für Teppich)* underlay; *(im*

Bett) drawsheet. **(b)** *usu pl (Papiere)* document, paper.

unterlassen* *vt insep irreg (nicht tun)* to refrain from; *(nicht durchführen)* not to carry out; *(auslassen)* to omit; *etwas Dummes etc* to refrain from doing. **er hat es ~, mich zu benachrichtigen** he failed *or* omitted to notify me.

Unterlassung *f (Versäumnis)* omission (of sth), failure (to do sth).

Unterlauf *m* lower reaches (of a river).

unterlaufen[1]* *insep irreg* **1** *vi+dat aux sein* **mir ist ein Fehler ~** I made a mistake. **2** *vt Bestimmungen* to get around.

unterlaufen[2] *adj* **mit Blut ~** bloodshot.

unterlegen *adj* inferior; *(besiegt)* defeated. **jdm ~ sein** to be inferior to sb.

Unterlegene(r) *mf decl as adj* underdog.

Unterleib *m* abdomen.

Unterleibs- *in cpds* abdominal; **~krebs** *m* cancer of the abdomen; cancer of the womb.

unterliegen* *vi insep irreg aux sein* **(a)** *(besiegt werden)* to be defeated *(+dat* by*)*. **(b)** *+dat (unterworfen sein)* to be subject to; *einer Gebühr, Steuer* to be liable to. **es unterliegt keinem Zweifel, daß ...** it's not open to any doubt that ...

Unterlippe *f* bottom *or* lower lip.

unterm = unter dem.

untermalen* *vt insep (mit Musik)* to provide with background music.

untermauern* *vt insep (Build, fig)* to underpin.

Untermensch *m* subhuman creature.

Untermiete *f* subtenancy. **bei jdm zur ~ wohnen** to rent a room from sb.

Untermieter(in *f***)** *m* lodger, subtenant *(Jur)*.

unterminieren* *vt insep (lit, fig)* to undermine.

untern = unter den.

unternehmen* *vt insep irreg* to do; *(durchführen auch)* to undertake; *Versuch, Vorstoß, Reise* to make. **etwas/nichts gegen jdn/etw ~** to do something/nothing about sb/sth.

Unternehmen *nt* **-** **(a)** *(Firma)* business, enterprise. **(b)** *(Aktion, Vorhaben)* undertaking, enterprise; *(Mil)* operation.

Unternehmens-: ~berater *m* management consultant; **~leitung** *f* management.

Unternehmer(in *f***)** *m* **-** (business) employer; *(alten Stils)* entrepreneur. **die ~** the employers.

unternehmerisch *adj* entrepreneurial.

Unternehmer-: ~kreise *pl* **in/aus ~kreisen** in/from business circles; **~verband** *m* employers' association.

Unternehmung *f* **(a)** *siehe* **Unternehmen. (b)** *(Transaktion)* undertaking.

Unternehmungs-: ~geist *m no pl* enterprise; **~lust** *f no pl* enterprise; **u~lustig** *adj* enterprising.

Unter-: ~offizier *m* non-commissioned officer, NCO; **u~ordnen** *sep* **1** *vt* to subordinate *(+dat* to*)*; **2** *vr* to subordinate oneself *(+dat* to*)*; **~ordnung** *f* **(a)** *no pl* subordination; **(b)** *(Biol)* sub-order; **~organisation** *f* subsidiary organization; **u~privilegiert** *adj* underprivileged.

unterreden* *vr insep* **sich (mit jdm) ~** to confer (with sb).

Unterredung *f* discussion; *(Pol auch)* talks *pl*.

Unterricht *m no pl* lessons *pl*, classes *pl*. **~ in Mathematik/Englisch** maths/English lessons *or* classes; **seine Art des ~s** his way of teaching; **(jdm) ~ geben** to teach (sb) *(in etw (dat)* sth*)*; **am ~ teilnehmen** to attend classes; **zu spät zum ~ kommen** to be late for class.

unterrichten* *insep* **1** *vt* **(a)** *Schüler, Fach* to teach. **jdn in etw** *(dat)* **~** to teach sb sth. **(b)** *(informieren)* to inform *(von, über+acc* about*)*. **gut ~e Kreise** well-informed circles. **2** *vi* to teach. **3** *vr* **sich über etw** *(acc)* **~** to inform oneself about sth.

Unterrichts-: ~einheit *f* teaching unit; **~fach** *nt* subject; **u~frei** *adj Stunde, Tag* free; **der Montag ist u~frei** there are no classes on Monday; **~gegenstand** *m* topic, subject; **~methode** *f* teaching method; **~mittel** *nt* teaching aid; **~stoff** *m* subject matter; **~zwecke** *pl* **zu ~zwecken** for teaching purposes.

Unterrock *m* underskirt, slip.

unters = unter das.

untersagen* *vt insep* to forbid, to prohibit. **jdm etw ~** to forbid sb sth.

Untersatz *m* mat; *(für Blumentöpfe etc)* base.

unterschätzen* *vt insep* to underestimate.

unterscheiden* *insep irreg* **1** *vt* to distinguish. **A nicht von B ~ können** to be unable to tell the difference between A and B, to be unable to tell A from B. **2** *vi* to differentiate, to distinguish. **3** *vr* **sich von etw ~** to differ (from) sth.

Unterscheidung *f* differentiation; *(Unterschied)* difference, distinction. **eine ~ treffen** to make a distinction.

Unterschenkel *m* lower leg.

Unterschicht *f (Sociol)* lower class.

unterschieben[1]* *vt insep irreg (col: unterstellen)* **jdm etw ~** to attribute sth to sb; **du unterschiebst mir immer, daß ich schwindle** you're always accusing me of cheating.

unterschieben[2] *vt sep irreg* **(a)** *(lit)* **etw unter etw** *(acc)* **~** to push sth under(neath) sth. **(b)** *(fig)* **jdm etw ~** to foist sth on sb.

Unterschied *m* **-e** difference; *(Unterscheidung auch)* distinction. **einen ~ (zwischen zwei Dingen) machen** to make a distinction (between two things); **das macht keinen ~** that makes no difference; **im ~ zu jdm/etw** in contrast to sb/sth; **alle ohne ~ halfen mit** everyone without exception lent a hand; **es wurden alle ohne ~ getötet** everyone was killed indiscriminately.

unterschiedlich *adj* different; *(veränderlich)* variable; *(gemischt)* varied, patchy. **das ist sehr ~** it varies a lot; **~ gut/lang** of varying quality/length.

unterschiedslos *adv* indiscriminately; *(gleichmäßig)* on an equal basis.

unterschlagen* *vt insep irreg Geld* to embezzle; *Brief, Beweise* to withhold; *(col) Nachricht etc* to keep quiet about.

Unterschlagung *f (von Geld)* embezzlement.

Unterschlupf *m, pl* **Unterschlüpfe** *(Obdach)* shelter; *(Versteck)* hiding place.

unterschlüpfen *vi sep aux sein (col)* to take cover *or* shelter; *(Versteck finden)* to hide out *(col) (bei jdm* at sb's*)*.

unterschreiben* *vti insep irreg* to sign. **das kann ich ~!** *(fig)* I'll subscribe to that!

unterschreiten* *vt insep irreg* to fall short of; *Temperatur, Zahlenwert* to fall below.

Unterschrift *f* **(a)** signature. **seine ~ leisten** to give one's signature; **jdm etw zur ~ vorlegen** to give sb sth to sign; **eigenhändige ~** personal signature. **(b)** *(Bild~)* caption.

unterschrifts-: ~berechtigt *adj* authorized to sign; **~reif** *adj Vertrag* ready to be signed.

unterschwellig *adj* subliminal.

Unterseeboot *nt* submarine.

unterseeisch [-zeːɪʃ] *adj* undersea, submarine.

Unter-: ~seite *f* underside; **~setzer** *m* **-** *siehe* **~satz; u~setzt** *adj* stocky; **~stadt** *f* lower part of a/the town; **~stand** *m* shelter; *(Mil)* dugout.

unterstehen* *insep irreg* **1** *vi+dat* to be under; *jdm* to be subordinate to; *(in Firma)* to report to; *dem Gesetz* to be subject to. **2** *vr* to dare. **untersteh dich (ja nicht)!** (don't) you dare!

unterstellen[1]* *vt insep* **(a)** *(unterordnen)* to subordinate *(dat* to*)*. **jdm/etw unterstellt sein** to be under sb/sth; *(in Firma)* to report to sb/sth; **jdm etw ~** to put sb in charge of sth. **(b)** *(annehmen)* to assume, to suppose. **(c)** *(pej: unterschieben)* **jdm etw ~** to insinuate that sb has done/said sth.

unterstellen[2] *sep* **1** *vt (abstellen, unterbringen)* to keep; *Möbel auch* to store. **2** *vr* to take shelter.
Unterstellung *f (falsche Behauptung)* misrepresentation; *(Andeutung)* insinuation. **das ist eine ~!** what are you insinuating!
unterste(r, s) *adj superl of* **untere(r, s)** lowest; *(tiefste auch)* bottom; *(letzte)* last. **das U~ zuoberst kehren** to turn everything upside down.
untersteuern* *vi insep* to understeer.
Unter-: u~streichen* *vt insep irreg (lit, fig)* to underline; **~strömung** *f (lit, fig)* undercurrent; **~stufe** *f (Sch)* lower school, lower grade *(US)*.
unterstützen* *vt insep* to support.
Unterstützung *f* **(a)** *no pl* support *(zu, für* for). **(b)** *(Zuschuß)* assistance, aid; *(col: Arbeitslosen~)* unemployment benefit *(Brit)*, welfare *(US)*.
unterstützungsbedürftig *adj* needy.
untersuchen* *vt insep* **(a)** to examine *(auf+acc* for); *(erforschen)* to look into, to investigate; *(chemisch, technisch etc)* to test *(auf +acc* for). **sich ärztlich ~ lassen** to have a medical *or* a check-up; **etw gerichtlich ~** to try sth (in court). **(b)** *(nachprüfen)* to check, to verify.
Untersuchung *f siehe vt* **(a)** examination; investigation *(gen, über+acc* into); test; *(ärztlich)* examination, check-up. **(b)** check, verification.
Untersuchungs-: ~ausschuß *m* fact-finding committee; *(nach Unfall etc)* committee of inquiry; **~ergebnis** *nt (Jur)* findings *pl*; *(Med)* result of an/the examination; *(Sci)* test result; **~gefangene(r)** *mf* prisoner awaiting trial; **~haft** *f* custody; **~richter** *m* examining magistrate.
Untertage- *in cpds* underground; **~arbeiter** *m* (coal)face worker; **~bau** *m no pl* underground mining.
Untertan *m (wk)* **-en, -en** *(old: Staatsbürger)* subject; *(pej)* underling *(pej)*.
untertan *adj pred* subject *(+dat* to).
untertänig *adj* subservient, submissive. **jdn ~st bitten** to ask sb most humbly.
Unter-: u~tariflich *adj Bezahlung* below the agreed *or* union rate; **~tasse** *f* saucer; **~tauchen** *sep* **1** *vi aux sein* to dive (under); *(fig)* to disappear; **2** *vt* to immerse; *jdn* to duck; **~teil** *nt or m* bottom *or* lower part; **~teilen*** *vt insep* to subdivide *(in+acc* into); **~teller** *m* saucer; **~titel** *m* subtitle; *(für Bild)* caption; **~ton** *m (Mus, fig)* undertone; **u~treiben*** *insep irreg* **1** *vt* to understate; **2** *vi* to play things down; **~treibung** *f* understatement; **u~tunneln*** *vt insep* to tunnel under; **u~vermieten*** *vti insep* to sublet, to sublease; **u~wandern*** *vt insep* to infiltrate.
Unterwäsche *f no pl* underwear *no pl*.
Unterwasser- *in cpds* underwater.
unterwegs *adv* on the way *(nach, zu* to); *(auf Reisen)* away. **bei denen ist wieder ein Kind ~** they've got another child on the way.
unterweisen* *vt insep irreg (geh)* to instruct *(in +dat* in).
Unterwelt *f (lit, fig)* underworld.
unterwerfen* *insep irreg* **1** *vt* **(a)** *Volk* to subjugate. **(b)** *(unterziehen)* to subject *(dat* to). **einer Sache** *(dat)* **unterworfen sein** to be subject to sth. **2** *vr (lit, fig)* **sich jdm/einer Sache ~** to submit to sb/sth.
unterworfen *adj* **der Mode ~ sein** to be subject to fashion.
unterwürfig *adj (pej)* obsequious.
unterzeichnen* *vt insep (form)* to sign.
Unterzeichner *m* - signatory.
unterziehen[1]* *insep irreg* **1** *vr* **sich einer Sache** *(dat)* **~** to undergo sth; **sich einer Prüfung** *(dat)* **~** to take an examination. **2** *vt* to subject *(dat* to).
unterziehen[2] *vt sep irreg Kleidung* to put on underneath.
Untiefe *f (seichte Stelle)* shallow.
Untier *nt* monster.
untragbar *adj* intolerable, unbearable.
untreu *adj Liebhaber etc* unfaithful; *(einer Sache)* disloyal *(dat* to). **sich** *(dat)* **selbst ~ werden** to be untrue to oneself.
Untreue *f siehe adj* unfaithfulness; disloyalty.
untröstlich *adj* inconsolable *(über +acc* about).
untrüglich *adj Gedächtnis* infallible; *Zeichen* unmistakable
Untugend *f* vice; *(Angewohnheit)* bad habit.
un-: ~überbietbar *adj Preis, Rekord etc* unbeatable; *Frechheit, Eifer* unparalleled; **~überbrückbar** *adj (fig) Gegensätze etc* irreconcilable; *Kluft* unbridgeable; **~überlegt** *adj* rash; **~übersehbar** *adj Schaden etc* incalculable; *Menge* vast, immense; *(auffällig) Fehler etc* obvious; **~übersichtlich** *adj Gelände* broken; *Kurve* blind; *System, Plan* confused; **~übertrefflich 1** *adj* matchless; *Rekord* unbeatable; **2** *adv* superbly, magnificently; **~übertroffen** *adj* unsurpassed; **~überwindlich** *adj* insurmountable; *Gegner, Heer* invincible; *Festung* impregnable.
un|umgänglich *adj* essential; *(unvermeidlich)* inevitable.
un|umschränkt *adj* unlimited. **~ herrschen** to have absolute rule.
un|umstößlich *adj Tatsache* incontrovertible; *Entschluß* irrevocable. **~ feststehen** to be absolutely definite.
un-: ~umstritten *adj* indisputable, undisputed; **~umwunden** *adv* frankly; **~unterbrochen** *adj* uninterrupted; *(unaufhörlich)* incessant; **~veränderlich** *adj* unchanging; *(unwandelbar)* unchangeable; **~verändert** *adj* unchanged; **du siehst ~verändert jung aus** you look just as young as ever; **~verantwortlich** *adj* irresponsible; **~verarbeitet** *adj (lit, fig)* raw; **~veräußerlich** *adj Rechte* inalienable; **~verbesserlich** *adj* incorrigible; **~verbindlich** *adj* **(a)** *(nicht bindend)* not binding; *Besichtigung* free; **sich** *(dat)* **etw ~verbindlich schicken lassen** to have sth sent without obligation; **(b)** *(vage, allgemein)* non-committal; *(nicht entgegenkommend)* abrupt; **~verbleit** *adj Benzin* unleaded; **~verblümt** *adj* blunt; **~verbraucht** *adj (fig)* unspent; **~verbürgt** *adj* unconfirmed; **~verdächtig** *adj* unsuspicious; *(nicht unter Verdacht stehend)* unsuspected, above suspicion; **~verdaulich** *adj (lit, fig)* indigestible; **~verdient** *adj* undeserved; **~verdorben** *adj (lit, fig)* unspoilt, pure; **~verdrossen** *adj* undeterred; *(unermüdlich)* untiring; **~verdünnt** *adj* undiluted; **~vereinbar** *adj* incompatible; **~verfälscht** *adj (lit, fig)* unadulterated; *Dialekt* pure; *Natürlichkeit* unaffected; *Natur* unspoilt; **~verfänglich** *adj* harmless.
unverfroren *adj* insolent.
unvergänglich *adj* immortal; *Eindruck, Erinnerung* everlasting.
unvergessen *adj* unforgotten.
unvergeßlich *adj* unforgettable. **das wird mir ~ bleiben** I'll never forget that.
un-: u~vergleichlich *adj* unique, incomparable; **~verhältnismäßig** *adv* disproportionately; *(übermäßig)* excessively; **~verheiratet** *adj* unmarried; **~verhofft** *adj* unexpected; **~verhohlen** *adj* open, unconcealed; **~verhüllt** *adj* **(a)** *Tatsachen* undisguised; **(b)** *siehe* **~verhohlen; ~verkäuflich** *adj* unsaleable; **„~verkäuflich"** "not for sale"; **~verkennbar** *adj* unmistakable; **~verlangt** *adj* unsolicited; **~verletzlich** *adj (fig) Rechte* inviolable; *(lit)* invulnerable; **~vermeidlich** *adj* inevitable; *(nicht zu umgehen)* unavoidable; **~vermindert** *adj* undiminished; **~vermischt** *adj* unmixed; *(rein)* pure; **~vermittelt** *adj (plötzlich)* sudden, unexpected.
Unvermögen *nt no pl* inability.
unvermögend *adj (arm)* without means.
unvermutet *adj* unexpected.

Unvernunft *f (Torheit)* stupidity; *(mangelnder Verstand)* irrationality; *(Uneinsichtigkeit)* unreasonableness.

unvernünftig *adj siehe n* stupid; irrational; unreasonable.

unverrichtet *adj:* **~er Dinge** empty-handed.

unverrückbar *adj (fig)* unshakeable. **~ feststehen** to be absolutely definite.

unverschämt *adj* outrageous; *Mensch, Frage, Benehmen etc* impudent, impertinent; *Lüge auch* blatant, barefaced.

Unverschämtheit *f* **(a)** *no pl* outrageousness. **(b)** *(Bemerkung)* impertinence; *(Tat)* outrageous thing. **das ist eine ~!** it's outrageous!

unverschuldet *adj* occurring through no fault of one's own.

unversehens *adv* suddenly; *(überraschend)* unexpectedly.

un-: **~versehrt** *adj Mensch (lit, fig)* unscathed; **~versöhnlich** *adj* irreconcilable.

Unverstand *m* lack of judgement; *(Torheit)* folly.

unverstanden *adj* not understood; *(mißverstanden)* misunderstood.

unverständlich *adj* incomprehensible.

Unverständnis *nt no pl* lack of understanding; *(für Kunst etc)* lack of appreciation.

un-: **~versucht** *adj:* **nichts ~versucht lassen** to try everything; **~verträglich** *adj* **(a)** *(streitsüchtig)* quarrelsome; **(b)** *(unverdaulich)* indigestible; *(Med: mit anderer Substanz etc)* incompatible; **~verwandt** *adv* fixedly, steadfastly; **~verwechselbar** *adj* ummistakable, distinctive; **~verwüstlich** *adj* indestructible; *Gesundheit* robust; *Mensch* irrepressible; **~verzagt** *adj* undaunted; **~verzeihlich** *adj* unforgivable; **~verzichtbar** *adj attr Recht* inalienable; *Anspruch* indisputable; *Bedingung* indispensible; **~verzinslich** *adj* interest-free; **~verzollt** *adj* duty-free; **~verzüglich 1** *adj* immediate; **2** *adv* immediately; **~vollendet** *adj* unfinished; **~vollkommen** *adj (unvollständig)* incomplete; *(fehlerhaft, mangelhaft)* imperfect.

unvollständig *adj* incomplete. **er hat das Formular ~ ausgefüllt** he didn't fill the form out properly.

un-: **~vorbereitet** *adj* unprepared *(auf +acc* for*)*; **eine ~vorbereitete Rede halten** to make an impromptu speech; **~voreingenommen** *adj* unbiased, unprejudiced; **~vorhergesehen** *adj* unforeseen; *Besuch* unexpected; **~vorschriftsmäßig** *adj* not in keeping with the regulations; **~vorsichtig** *adj* careless; *(voreilig)* rash; **~vorstellbar** *adj* inconceivable; **~vorteilhaft** *adj* disadvantageous; *Kleid, Frisur etc* unbecoming; **~vorteilhaft aussehen** not to look one's best.

Un-: **u~wahr** *adj* untrue; **u~wahrhaftig** *adj* untruthful; *Gefühle* insincere; **~wahrheit** *f* untruth.

unwahrscheinlich 1 *adj* improbable; *(col: groß)* incredible *(col)*. **2** *adv (col)* incredibly *(col)*.

unwandelbar *adj (geh)* unalterable; *Treue* unwavering.

unwegsam *adj Gelände etc* rough.

unweiblich *adj* unfeminine.

unweigerlich 1 *adj attr Folge* inevitable. **2** *adv* inevitably.

unweit *prep+gen, adv* not far from.

Unwesen *nt no pl (übler Zustand)* terrible state of affairs. **sein ~ treiben** *(Mörder etc)* to be at large.

unwesentlich *adj* irrelevant; *(unwichtig)* unimportant, insignificant.

Unwetter *nt* (thunder)storm. **ein ~ brach los** a storm broke.

un-: **~wichtig** *adj* unimportant; *(belanglos)* irrelevant; *(verzichtbar)* non-essential; **~widerleglich** *adj* irrefutable; **~widerruflich** *adj* irrevocable; **es steht ~widerruflich fest, daß ...** it is absolutely definite that ...; **~widersprochen** *adj Behauptung* unchallenged; **~widerstehlich** *adj* irresistible; **~wiederbringlich** *adj (geh)* irretrievable.

Unwille(n) *m no pl* displeasure *(über +acc* at*)*; *(Ungeduld)* irritation. **jds ~n erregen** to incur sb's displeasure.

unwillig *adj* indignant *(über +acc* about*)*; *(widerwillig)* unwilling, reluctant.

unwillkommen *adj* unwelcome.

unwillkürlich *adj* spontaneous; *(instinktiv)* instinctive.

Un-: **u~wirklich** *adj* unreal; **u~wirksam** *adj* ineffective; *Vertrag etc* void; **u~wirsch** *adj* surly, gruff; *Bewegung* brusque; **u~wirtlich** *adj* inhospitable; **u~wissend** *adj* ignorant; *(ahnungslos)* unsuspecting; *(unerfahren)* inexperienced; **~wissenheit** *f no pl siehe adj* ignorance; unsuspectingness; inexperience; **u~wissenschaftlich** *adj* unscientific; *Ausdrucksweise* unacademic; **u~wissentlich** *adv* unwittingly, unknowingly.

unwohl *adj (unpäßlich)* unwell; *(unbehaglich)* uneasy. **mir ist ~** I don't feel well.

Unwohlsein *nt* indisposition; *(unangenehmes Gefühl)* unease.

un-: **~wohnlich** *adj Zimmer etc* uncomfortable; **~würdig** *adj* unworthy *(+gen* of*)*; *Verhalten* undignified; *Situation* degrading.

Unzahl *f* **eine ~ von** a host of.

unzählbar *adj* innumerable, countless.

unzählig 1 *adj* innumerable, countless. **~e Male** countless times, time and again. **2** *adv* **~ viele** huge numbers.

unzähmbar *adj* untameable; *(fig auch)* indomitable.

Unze *f* **-n** ounce.

un-: **~zeitgemäß** *adj (altmodisch)* old-fashioned; **~zerstörbar** *adj* indestructible; **~zertrennlich** *adj* inseparable.

Unzucht *f no pl (esp Jur)* sexual offence *(Brit) or* offense *(US)*. **~ mit jdm treiben** to fornicate with sb.

unzüchtig *adj (esp Jur)* indecent; *Reden* obscene.

Un-: **u~zufrieden** *adj* discontent; **~zufriedenheit** *f no pl* discontent; **u~zugänglich** *adj Gegend* inaccessible; *Mensch* inapproachable; *(unaufgeschlossen gegen)* deaf *(+dat* to*)*; **u~zulänglich** *adj* insufficient, inadequate; **~zulänglichkeit** *f* **(a)** insufficiency, inadequacy; **(b)** *usu pl* shortcomings *pl*; **u~zulässig** *adj (auch Jur)* inadmissible; *Gebrauch* improper; *Belastung, Geschwindigkeit* excessive; **u~zumutbar** *adj* unreasonable; **u~zurechnungsfähig** *adj* not responsible for one's actions; **jdn für u~zurechnungsfähig erklären lassen** *(Jur)* to have sb certified (insane); **u~zureichend** *adj* insufficient, inadequate; **u~zustellbar** *adj* undeliverable; **u~zuträglich** *adj* **jds Gesundheit u~zuträglich sein** to be bad for sb's health; **u~zutreffend** *adj* inapplicable; *(unwahr)* incorrect; **~zutreffendes bitte streichen** delete as applicable; **u~zuverlässig** *adj* unreliable; **~zuverlässigkeit** *f* unreliability; **u~zweckmäßig** *adj (nicht ratsam)* unadvisable; *(unpraktisch)* impractical; *(ungeeignet)* unsuitable; **u~zweideutig** *adj* unambiguous, unequivocal; *(fig: unanständig)* explicit; **er sagte mir u~zweideutig, daß ...** he told me in no uncertain terms that ...; **u~zweifelhaft 1** *adj* indubitable, unquestionable; **2** *adv* without doubt.

üppig *adj Wachstum* luxuriant; *Vegetation auch* lush; *Haar* thick; *Mahl, Ausstattung* sumptuous; *Gehalt* lavish; *Figur, Frau* voluptuous; *Leben* luxurious; *Phantasie* rich. **~ leben** to live in style.

Ur- *in cpds (erste)* first; *(ursprünglich)* original; **~abstimmung** *f* ballot; **~ahn(e)** *m (Vorfahr)* forefather; *(~großvater)* great-grandfather; **~ahne** *f (Vorfahr)* forebear; *(~großmutter)* great-grandmother; **u~alt** *adj* ancient.

Uran *nt no pl* uranium.
ur|aufführen *vt ptp* **uraufgeführt** to give the first performance of; *Film* to premiere.
Ur|aufführung *f* premiere; *(von Theaterstück etc auch)* first night *or* performance.
urbar *adj* **die Wüste/Land ~ machen** to to reclaim the desert/to cultivate land.
Ur-: ~bevölkerung *f* original inhabitants *pl*; **~christentum** *nt* early Christianity; **u~eigen** *adj* very own; **~einwohner** *m* original inhabitant; *(in Australien und Neuseeland)* Aborigine; **~enkel** *m* great-grandchild, great-grandson; **~enkelin** *f* great-granddaughter; **~fassung** *f* original version; **~geschichte** *f* prehistory; **~gewalt** *f* elemental force.
Urgroß-: ~eltern *pl* great-grandparents *pl*; **~mutter** *f* great-grandmother; **~vater** *m* great-grandfather.
Urheber(in *f***)** *m* - originator; *(Jur: Verfasser)* author.
Urheber-: ~recht *nt* copyright *(an+dat* on*)*; **u~rechtlich** *adj* **u~rechtlich geschützt** copyright.
urig *adj (col) Mensch* earthy.
Urin *m* **-e** urine.
urinieren* *vi* to urinate.
Ur-: ~knall *m (Astron)* big bang; **u~komisch** *adj (col)* screamingly funny *(col)*.
Urkunde *f* **-n** document; *(Kauf~)* deed; *(Gründungs~ etc)* charter; *(Sieger~, Diplom, Bescheinigung etc)* certificate.
urkundlich *adj* documentary. **~ verbürgt** authenticated; **~ erwähnt** mentioned in a document, documented.
Urlaub *m* **-e** *(Ferien)* holiday(s) *(Brit)*, vacation *(US)*; *(esp Mil)* leave. **~ haben** to have a holiday *or* vacation/to have leave; **in ~ fahren** to go on holiday *or* vacation/on leave; **(sich** *dat***) einen Tag ~ nehmen** to take a day off.
Urlauber(in *f***)** *m* - holiday-maker *(Brit)*, vacationist *(US)*.
Urlaubs-: ~geld *nt* holiday *(Brit) or* vacation *(US)* money; **u~reif** *adj (col)* ready for a holiday *(Brit) or* vacation *(US)*; **~reise** *f* holiday *(Brit) or* vacation *(US)* trip; **~tag** *m* (one day of) holiday *(Brit) or* vacation *(US)*; **ich habe noch drei ~tage gut** I've still got three days' holiday to come; **~zeit** *f* holiday *(Brit) or* vacation *(US)* period.
Urmensch *m* primeval man; *(col)* caveman *(col)*.
Urne *f* **-n** urn; *(Los~)* box; *(Wahl~)* ballot-box. **zur ~ gehen** to go to the polls.
Ur-: ~oma *f (col)* great-granny *(col)*; **~opa** *m (col)* great-grandpa *(col)*, **~pflanze** *f* primordial plant; **u~plötzlich** *adv (col)* all of a sudden.
Ursache *f* **-n** cause; *(Grund)* reason; *(Beweggrund)* motive. **~ und Wirkung** cause and effect; **keine ~!** *(auf Dank)* don't mention it, you're welcome; *(auf Entschuldigung)* that's all right; **ohne (jede) ~** for no reason (at all); **jdm ~ geben, etw zu tun** to give sb cause to do sth; **alle/keine ~ haben, etw zu tun** to have every/no reason to do sth.
Ur-: ~schrei *m (Psych)* primal scream; **~schrift** *f* original (text).
Ursprung *m, pl* **Ursprünge** origin.
ursprünglich 1 *adj* **(a)** *attr* original; *(anfänglich)* initial, first. **(b)** *(urwüchsig)* natural; *Natur* unspoilt. **2** *adv* originally; *(anfänglich)* initially.
Ursprungsland *nt (Comm)* country of origin.
Urteil *nt* **-e (a)** judgement; *(Entscheidung)* decision; *(Meinung)* opinion. **nach meinem ~** in my judgement/opinion; **ich kann darüber kein ~ abgeben** I am no judge of this; **sich** *(dat)* **ein ~ über etw** *(acc)* **erlauben/ein ~ über etw fällen** to pass judgement on sth; **sich** *(dat)* **kein ~ über etw** *(acc)* **erlauben können** to be in no position to judge sth; **zu dem ~ kommen, daß ...** to come to the conclusion that ...; **sich** *(dat)* **ein ~ über jdn/etw bilden** to form an opinion about sb/sth. **(b)** *(Jur: Gerichts~)* verdict; *(Richterspruch)* judgement; *(Strafmaß)* sentence; *(Schiedsspruch)* award; *(Scheidungsspruch)* decree. **das ~ über jdn sprechen** *(Jur)* to pass judgement on *or* upon sb.
urteilen *vi* to judge *(nach* by*)*. **über etw** *(acc)* **~** to judge sth; *(seine Meinung äußern)* to give one's opinion on sth.
Urteils-: ~begründung *f (Jur)* opinion; **u~fähig** *adj* competent to judge; *(umsichtig)* discriminating; **~findung** *f (Jur)* reaching a verdict *no art;* **~kraft** *f no pl* power of judgement; *(Umsichtigkeit)* discrimination; **~spruch** *m (Jur)* judgement; *(von Geschworenen)* verdict; *(von Strafgericht)* sentence; *(von Schiedsgericht)* award; **~verkündung** *f (Jur)* pronouncement of judgement; **~vermögen** *nt siehe* **~kraft.**
Ur-: ~text *m* original (text); **~trieb** *m* basic drive; **u~tümlich** *adj siehe* **u~wüchsig;** **~typ(us)** *m, pl* **~typen** prototype.
Ur|ur- *in cpds* great-great-.
Ur-: ~vater *m* forefather; **u~verwandt** *adj Wörter* cognate; **~viech, ~vieh** *nt (col)* real character; **~wald** *m* primeval forest; *(in den Tropen)* jungle; **~welt** *f* primeval world; **u~weltlich** *adj* primeval, primordial; **u~wüchsig** *adj* natural; *Natur* unspoilt; *(urweltlich) Flora* primeval; *(ursprünglich)* original; *(bodenständig)* rooted to the soil; *(unberührt) Land etc* untouched; *(urgewaltig) Kraft* elemental; *(derb, kräftig)* sturdy; *Mensch* rugged; *Humor, Sprache* earthy; **~zeit** *f* primeval times *pl*; **seit ~zeiten** since primeval times; *(col)* for donkey's years *(col)*; **u~zeitlich** *adj* primeval; **~zustand** *m* primordial state.
USA [uːǀɛsˈǀaː] *pl* **die ~** the USA *sing*.
usf. = und so fort.
Usurpator *m (liter)* usurper.
usurpieren* *vt (liter)* to usurp.
usw. = und so weiter etc.
Utensil *nt* **-ien** [-iən] utensil, implement.
utilitaristisch *adj* utilitarian.
Utopie *f* utopia.
utopistisch *adj (pej)* utopian.
u.U. = unter Umständen.
Ü-Wagen *m (Rad, TV)* outside broadcast vehicle.
uzen *vti (col)* to tease, to kid *(col)*.
Uzname *m (col)* nickname.

V

V, v [fau] *nt* **-, -** V, v.
V = **Volt; Volumen.**
Vagabund [vaga'bʊnt] *m (wk)* **-en, -en** vagabond.
vag(e) [va:k,'va:gə] *adj* vague.
Vagheit ['va:khait] *f* vagueness.
Vakuum ['va:kuʊm] *nt, pl* **Vakuen** ['va:kuən] *(lit, fig)* vacuum. **unter/im** ~ in a vacuum.
Vakuum- ['va:kuʊm-] *in cpds* vacuum; **~pumpe** *f* vacuum pump; **v~verpackt** *adj* vacuum-packed.
Valentinstag ['va:lɛnti:ns-] *m* (St) Valentine's Day.
Vampir [vam'pi:ɐ] *m* **-e** vampire.
Vandalismus [vanda'lɪsmʊs] *m no pl* vandalism.
Vanille [va'nɪljə, va'nɪlə] *f no pl* vanilla.
Vanille-: **~eis** *nt* vanilla ice-cream; **~geschmack** *m* vanilla flavour *(Brit) or* flavor *(US)*; **mit ~geschmack** vanilla-flavoured *(Brit) or* -flavored *(US)*; **~zucker, Vanillinzucker** *m* vanilla sugar.
variabel [va'ria:bl] *adj* variable.
Variable [va'ria:blə] *f (wk)* **-n, -n** variable.
Variante [va'riantə] *f* **-n** variant *(zu* on*)*.
Variation [varia'tsio:n] *f* variation. **~en zu einem Thema** variations on a theme.
Varieté [varie'te:] *nt* **-s (a)** variety, vaudeville *(US)*. **(b)** *(Theater)* variety theatre *(Brit)*, music hall *(Brit)*, vaudeville theater *(US)*.
variieren* [vari'i:rən] *vti* to vary.
Vasall [va'zal] *m (wk)* **-en, -en** *(Hist, fig)* vassal.
Vase ['va:zə] *f* **-n** vase.
Vater *m* **¨** *(lit, fig)* father. ~ **unser** *(Rel)* Our Father; **unsere** **~̈** *pl (geh: Vorfahren)* our (fore)fathers; **wie der ~, so der Sohn** *(prov)* like father, like son *(prov)*; ~ **Staat** *(hum)* the State.
Vater-: **~figur** *f* father figure; **~freuden** *pl* joys of fatherhood *pl*; **~haus** *nt* parental home.
Vaterland *nt* native country; *(esp Deutschland auch)* Fatherland. **unser** ~ our country.
vaterländisch *adj* national; *(patriotisch)* patriotic.
Vaterlands-: **~liebe** *f* patriotism; **v~liebend** *adj* patriotic; **~verräter** *m* traitor.
väterlich *adj* paternal, fatherly.
väterlicherseits *adv* on one's father's side. **meine Großeltern** ~ my paternal grandparents.
Vater-: **~liebe** *f* fatherly love; **v~los** *adj* fatherless; **~recht** *nt* patriarchy.
Vaterschaft *f* fatherhood *no art; (esp Jur)* paternity.
Vaterschaftsklage *f* paternity suit.
Vater-: **~stelle** *f* **bei jdm ~stelle vertreten** to take the place of sb's father; **~tag** *m* Father's Day; **~unser** *nt* **-** **das ~unser** the Lord's Prayer.
Vati *m* **-s** *(col)* dad(dy) *(col)*.
Vatikan [vati'ka:n] *m* Vatican.
Vatikanstadt [vati'ka:n-] *f* Vatican City.
V-Ausschnitt ['fau-] *m* V-neck.
v. Chr. = **vor Christus** BC.
Vegetarier(in *f***)** [vege'ta:riɐ, -iərɪn] *m* **-** vegetarian.
vegetarisch [vege'ta:rɪʃ] *adj* vegetarian. ~ **leben** to be a vegetarian.
Vegetation [vegeta'tsio:n] *f* vegetation.
vegetieren* [vege'ti:rən] *vi* to vegetate; *(kärglich leben)* to eke out a bare existence.
Vehikel [ve'hi:kl] *nt* **-** *(pej col)* boneshaker *(col)*.
Veilchen *nt* violet; *(col: blaues Auge)* shiner *(col)*, black eye. **blau wie ein** ~ *(col)* roaring drunk *(col)*.
Velours [və'lu:ɐ, ve'lu:ɐ] *m* **-** *(Tex)* velour(s).
Velours(leder) *nt* **-** [və'lu:ɐ-, ve'lu:ɐ-] suede.
Vene ['ve:nə] *f* **-n** vein.
Venedig [ve'ne:dɪç] *nt* Venice.
Venezolaner(in *f***)** [venetso'la:nɐ, -ərɪn] *m* **-** Venezuelan.
venezolanisch [venetso'la:nɪʃ] *adj* Venezuelan.
Venezuela [vene'tsue:la] *nt* Venezuela.
Ventil [vɛn'ti:l] *nt* **-e** valve; *(fig)* outlet.
Ventilation [vɛntila'tsio:n] *f* ventilation.
Ventilator [vɛnti'la:tɔr] *m* ventilator.
Venus ['ve:nʊs] *f no pl (Myth, Astron)* Venus.
ver|abreden* **1** *vt* to arrange; *Termin auch* to agree; *Straftat* to collude in; *Hochverrat* to conspire in. **es war eine verabredete Sache** it was arranged beforehand; **wir haben verabredet, daß wir uns um 5 Uhr treffen** we have arranged to meet at 5 o'clock; **schon verabredet sein** *(für* on*)* to have a prior engagement *(esp form)*, to have something else on; **mit jdm verabredet sein** to have arranged to meet sb. **2** *vr* **sich mit jdm/miteinander** ~ to arrange to meet sb/to meet.
Ver|abredung *f (Vereinbarung)* arrangement, agreement; *(Treffen)* appointment; *(esp mit Freund)* date. **ich habe eine** ~ I'm meeting somebody.
ver|abreichen* *vt Tracht Prügel etc* to give; *Arznei auch* to administer *(form) (jdm* to sb*)*.
ver|abscheuen* *vt* to detest, to abhor, to loathe.
ver|abscheuungswürdig *adj* detestable.
ver|abschieden* **1** *vt* to say goodbye to; *(entlassen)* to discharge; *(Pol) Haushaltsplan* to adopt; *Gesetz* to pass. **2** *vr* **sich (von jdm)** ~ to say goodbye (to sb), to take one's leave (of sb).
ver|achten* *vt* to despise; *(liter) Tod, Gefahr* to scorn. **nicht zu** ~ *(col)* not to be scoffed at.
ver|achtenswert *adj* despicable, contemptible.
ver|ächtlich *adj* contemptuous; *(verachtenswert)* despicable, contemptible.
Ver|achtung *f no pl* contempt *(von* for*)*. **jdn mit ~ strafen** to treat sb with contempt.
ver|albern* *vt (col)* to make fun of.
ver|allgemeinern* *vti* to generalize.
Ver|allgemeinerung *f* generalization.
ver|alten* *vi aux sein* to become obsolete; *(Mode)* to go out of date.
ver|altet *adj* obsolete; *Mode* out-of-date.
Veranda [ve'randa] *f, pl* **Veranden** veranda, porch.
ver|änderlich *adj* variable; *Wetter, Mensch* changeable.
ver|ändern* **1** *vt* to change. **2** *vr* to change; *(Stellung wechseln)* to change one's job; *(Wohnung wechseln)* to move. **verändert aussehen** to look different.
Ver|änderung *f* change. **eine berufliche** ~ a change of job.
ver|ängstigen* *vt (erschrecken)* to frighten; *(einschüchtern)* to intimidate.
ver|ankern* *vt (Naut, Tech)* to anchor; *(fig)* to embed *(in+dat* in*)*.
ver|anlagen* *vt* to assess *(mit* at*)*.
ver|anlagt *adj* **melancholisch** ~ **sein** to have a

ngen* **1** *vr* to narrow; *(Gefäße, Pupille)* to tract; *(Kleid, Taille)* to go in. **2** *vt* to make rower; *Kleid* to take in.
rben* **1** *vt* **(a)** *Besitz* to leave, to bequeath , *an +acc* to). **(b)** *Anlagen* to pass on *(dat,* +*acc* to); *Krankheit* to transmit. **2** *vr* to be sed on/transmitted *(auf +acc* to).
wigen* **1** *vt* to immortalize; *Zustand, Ver-nisse* to perpetuate. **2** *vr (lit, fig)* to immorta- oneself.
ahren¹* *vi irreg aux sein (vorgehen)* to act, to ceed.
ahren²* *irreg* **1** *vt Geld, Zeit* to spend in velling *(Brit) or* traveling *(US)*; *Benzin* to use **2** *vr* to lose one's way; *(fig)* to get muddled.
ahren³ *adj Angelegenheit* muddled.
ahren *nt* - *(Vorgehen)* actions *pl*; *(~sweise)* cedure; *(Tech)* process; *(Methode)* method;) proceedings *pl*. **ein ~ gegen jdn einleiten** to e legal proceedings against sb.
all *m no pl* **(a)** *(Zerfall)* decay; *(von Gebäu-* dilapidation; *(gesundheitlich, geistig, sittlich, Kultur)* decline. **(b)** *(von Anspruch, Rechnung* lapsing; *(von Scheck, Fahrkarte)* expiry.
allen¹* *vi irreg aux sein* **(a)** *(zerfallen)* to de- ; *(Bauwerk)* to fall into disrepair; *(Zellen)* to , *(körperlich und geistig)* to deteriorate; *(Sitten, ch)* to decline. **(b)** *(Geldscheine)* to become alid; *(Scheck, Fahrkarte)* to expire; *(Termin, pruch)* to lapse. **(c)** *(abhängig werden)* **jdm/ er Sache ~/~ sein** to become/be a slave to sth; **jdm völlig ~ sein** to be completely under s spell. **(d) auf etw** *(acc)* **~** to think of sth; *(aus zweiflung)* to resort to sth. **(e) in etw** *(acc)* **~** ink into sth; **in einen tiefen Schlaf ~** to fall a deep sleep; **in einen Fehler ~** to make a take.
allen² *adj Gebäude* dilapidated, ruined; sch *(körperlich)* emaciated; *(geistig)* senile; *gelaufen) Fahrkarten, Briefmarken* invalid; *fe* lapsed; *Scheck* expired.
alls-: **~datum** *nt* expiry date; *(der Haltbar-)* best before date; **~tag** *m* expiry date.
älschen* *vt* to falsify; *Lebensmittel, Wein* to lterate.
angen* *irreg* **1** *vr* to get caught. **sich in lersprüchen ~** to contradict oneself. **2** *vi* to accepted. **bei jdm nicht ~** not to cut any ice h sb *(col)*.
änglich *adj Situation* awkward, embarrass- ; *Aussage, Beweismaterial, Blicke* incriminat- ; *(gefährlich)* dangerous; *Angewohnheit* dious; *Frage* tricky.
ärben* *vr* to change colour *(Brit) or* color); *(Metall, Stoff)* to discolour *(Brit)*, to discolor). **sich grün/rot ~** to turn green/red.
assen* *vt* to write; *Gesetz, Urkunde* to draw

asser(in *f*) *m* - writer, author.
assung *f* **(a)** *(Pol)* constitution. **(b)** *(Zustand)* e; *(körperlich)* state of health; *(seelisch)* state nind. **sie ist in guter/schlechter ~** she is in d/bad shape.
assungs-: **~änderung** *f* constitutional endment; **v~feindlich** *adj* anticonstitutional; hutz *m* defence *(Brit) or* defense *(US)* he constitution; *(Amt) office responsible for nding the constitution;* **v~treu** *adj* loyal to constitution; **v~widrig** *adj* unconstitutional.
ulen* *vi aux sein* to decay, to rot; *(fig)* to enerate.
ult *adj* decayed; *Fleisch, Obst etc* rotten; per decomposed.
echten* *vt irreg* to defend; *Lehre* to advocate.
echter(in *f*) *m* - advocate, champion.
ehlen* *vt (nicht treffen)* to miss. **den Zweck ~** to achieve its purpose; **das Thema ~** to be pletely off the subject.

verfehlt *adj* unsuccessful; *(unangebracht)* appropriate.
Verfehlung *f* **(a)** *(des Ziels)* missing. *(Vergehen)* misdemeanour *(Brit)*, misdemean *(US)*; *(Sünde)* transgression.
verfeinden* *vr* to quarrel. **sich mit jdm ~** make an enemy of sb; **verfeindet sein** to on bad terms.
verfeinern* **1** *vt* to improve; *Methode auch* refine. **2** *vr* to improve; *(Methoden auch)* to b come refined.
verfeinert *adj Methode, Geräte* sophisticated.
Verfeinerung *f* refinement.
verfestigen* **1** *vt* to harden; *Flüssigkeit* to soli fy; *(verstärken)* to strengthen. **2** *vr* to harde *(Flüssigkeit)* to solidify; *(Kenntnisse)* to be r inforced; *(Ideen, Gewohnheiten)* to become set
Verfettung *f (von Organ, Muskeln)* fatty degene ation.
verfeuern* *vt* to burn; *Munition* to fire; *(restlos)* use up.
verfilmen* *vt* to film, to make a film of.
Verfilmung *f* film (version).
verfilzen* *vi aux sein (Wolle)* to become felte *(Haare)* to become matted. **verfilzt** felte matted.
verfinstern* **1** *vt* to darken; *Sonne, Mond* eclipse. **2** *vr (lit, fig)* to darken.
verflachen* **1** *vi aux sein* to flatten out; *(fig: D kussion)* to become superficial. **2** *vr (Gelände)* flatten out.
verflechten* *irreg* **1** *vt* to interweave; *Method* to combine; *Firmen* to interlink. **eng mit e verflochten sein** *(fig)* to be closely linked wi sth. **2** *vr* to interweave; *(sich verwirren)* to b come entangled *(mit* in); *(Methoden)* to combin
verfliegen* *irreg* **1** *vi aux sein* to vanish; *(Zeit)* fly (past). **2** *vr* to stray; *(Pilot, Flugzeug)* to lo one's/its bearings.
verfließen* *vi irreg aux sein (geh)* to go by, to pas
verflixt *(col)* **1** *adj* darned *(col)*; *(komplizie* tricky. **2** *adv* darned *(col)*. **3** *interj* **~!** blow! *(co*
verfluchen* *vt* to curse.
verflucht *(col)* **1** *adj* damn *(col)*. **~ (noch mal** damn (it) *(col)*. **2** *adv* damned *(col)*.
verflüchtigen* **1** *vt* to evaporate. **2** *vr (Alkoh etc)* to evaporate; *(Duft)* to disappear; *(Gase)* volatilize.
verflüssigen* *vtr* to liquefy.
verfolgen* *vt jdn, Ziel, Karriere etc* to pursu *Idee, Gedanken* to follow up; *(politisch, religiös)* persecute. **jdn politisch ~** to persecute sb fo political reasons; **jdn gerichtlich ~** to prosecut sb; **jdn mit den Augen ~** to follow sb with one eyes.
Verfolger(in *f*) *m* - pursuer; *(politisch)* pe secutor.
Verfolgte(r) *mf decl as adj (politisch)* victim o persecution.
Verfolgung *f* pursuit; *(politische)* persecution *n pl.* **die ~ aufnehmen** to take up the chase **strafrechtliche ~** prosecution.
Verfolgungs-: **~jagd** *f* chase, pursuit; **~renne** *nt (Sport)* pursuit race; **~wahn** *m* persecutio mania.
verformen* **1** *vt* to distort *(zu* into); *(umformen* to work. **verformt sein** to be out of shape *(Mensch, Gliedmaßen)* to be deformed. **2** *vr* to g out of shape.
verfrachten* *vt* to ship. **etw in eine Kiste ~** *(col* to dump sth in a crate.
verfremden* *vt* to make unfamiliar.
verfressen* *(col!)* **1** *vt irreg* to blow on food *(col)* **2** *adj* greedy, piggish *(col)*.
verfroren *adj* sensitive to cold; *(durchge froren)* frozen.
verfrüht *adj (zu früh)* premature; *(früh)* early.
verfügbar *adj* available.

melancholy disposition; **praktisch ~ sein** to be practically minded; **künstlerisch ~ sein** to be artistic; **zu** *or* **für etw ~ sein** to be cut out for sth.
Ver|anlagung *f* **(a)** *(körperlich, esp Med)* predisposition; *(charakterlich)* nature, disposition; *(Hang)* tendency; *(allgemeine Fähigkeiten)* natural abilities *pl*; *(künstlerisches, praktisches etc Talent)* bent. **(b)** *(von Steuern)* assessment.
ver|anlassen* *vt* **(a) etw ~** to arrange for sth; *(befehlen)* to order sth. **(b)** *auch vi (bewirken)* to give rise *(zu* to). **jdn zu etw ~, jdn (dazu) ~, etw zu tun** to cause sb to do sth.
Ver|anlassung *f* cause, reason. **auf ~ von** *or* +*gen* at the instigation of; **keine ~ zu etw haben/ keine ~ haben, etw zu tun** to have no cause *or* reason for sth/to do sth.
ver|anschaulichen* *vt* to illustrate *(an +dat, mit* with). **sich** *(dat)* **etw ~** to visualize sth.
ver|anschlagen* *vt* to estimate *(auf +acc* at). **etw zu hoch/niedrig ~** to overestimate/underestimate sth.
ver|anstalten* *vt* to organize, to arrange; *(kommerziell) Konzerte etc* to promote; *Party* to hold.
Ver|anstalter(in *f*) *m* - organizer; *(Comm: von Konzerten etc)* promoter.
Ver|anstaltung *f* **(a)** event *(von* organized by); *(feierlich, öffentlich)* function. **(b)** *no pl (das Veranstalten)* organization.
ver|antworten* **1** *vt* to accept responsibility for; *die Folgen auch, sein Tun* to answer for *(vor +dat* to). **wie könnte ich es denn ~, ...?** it would be most irresponsible of me ...; **eine nicht zu ~de Fahrlässigkeit** inexcusable negligence. **2** *vr* **sich für** *or* **wegen etw ~** to justify sth *(vor+dat* to).
ver|antwortlich *adj* responsible; *(haftbar)* liable. **jdm (gegenüber) ~ sein** to be responsible to sb; **jdn für etw ~ machen** to hold sb responsible for sth.
Ver|antwortung *f* responsibility *(für* for). **auf eigene ~** on one's own responsibility; **auf deine ~!** you take the responsibility!; **jdn zur ~ ziehen** to call sb to account.
Ver|antwortungs-: **v~bewußt** *adj* responsible; **~bewußtsein** *nt* sense of responsibility; **v~los** *adj* irresponsible; **v~voll** *adj* responsible.
ver|arbeiten* *vt* to use *(zu etw* to make sth); *(Tech, Biol, Comp)* to process; *Ton, Gold etc* to work; *(verbrauchen)* to consume; *Erlebnis etc* to assimilate, to digest. **~de Industrie** processing industries *pl*; **etw geistig ~** to assimilate *or* digest sth.
ver|arbeitet *adj* **gut ~** *Rock etc* well finished.
Ver|arbeitung *f* **(a)** *(von Rohstoffen etc)* processing. **(b)** *(Ausführung)* finish.
ver|ärgern* *vt* to annoy.
ver|armen* *vi aux sein (lit, fig)* to become impoverished. **verarmt** impoverished.
ver|arschen* *vt (col!)* to take the piss out of *(col!)*; *(für dumm verkaufen)* to mess around *(col)*.
ver|arzten* *vt (col)* to fix up *(col)*.
ver|ästeln* *vr* to branch out; *(fig)* to ramify.
ver|ausgaben* *vr* to overexert oneself; *(finanziell)* to overspend. **ich habe mich total verausgabt** *(finanziell)* I'm completely spent out.
ver|äußern* *vt (form: verkaufen)* to dispose of.
Verb [vɛrp] *nt* **-en** verb.
verbal [vɛr'ba:l] *adj* verbal.
verballhornen* *vt* to parody; *(unabsichtlich)* to get wrong.
Verband *m* ⸗**e (a)** *(Med)* dressing; *(mit Binden)* bandage. **(b)** *(Bund)* association. **(c)** *(Mil)* unit.
Verband(s)-: **~kasten** *m* first-aid box; **~päckchen** *nt* gauze bandage; **~stoff** *m* dressing; **~zeug** *nt* dressing.
verbannen* *vt* to banish *(auch fig)*, to exile *(aus* from, *auf* to).

Verbannte(r) *mf decl as adj* exile.
verbarrikadieren* **1** *vt* to barricade. **2** *vr* to barricade oneself in *(in etw (dat)* sth).
verbauen* *vt* **(a)** *(versperren)* to obstruct, to block. **sich** *(dat)* **alle Chancen ~** to spoil one's chances. **(b)** *(verbrauchen) Holz, Geld* to use in building. **(c)** *(schlecht bauen)* to construct badly.
verbeißen* *irreg* **1** *vt (fig col)* **sich** *(dat)* **etw ~** *Schmerz* to hide sth; **sich** *(dat)* **das Lachen ~** to keep a straight face. **2** *vr* **sich in etw** *(acc)* **~** *(fig)* to become obsessed with sth; *siehe* **verbissen.**
verbergen* *vtr irreg (lit, fig)* to hide *(vor +dat* from).
verbessern* **1** *vt* **(a)** to improve; *Leistung, Bestzeit* to improve on; *die Welt* to reform. **eine neue, verbesserte Auflage** a new revised edition. **(b)** *(korrigieren)* to correct. **2** *vr* to improve, to get better; *(beruflich, finanziell)* to better oneself; *(sich korrigieren)* to correct oneself.
Verbesserung *f* **(a)** improvement *(von* in); *(beruflich, finanziell)* betterment. **(b)** *(Berichtigung)* correction.
verbeugen* *vr* to bow *(vor +dat* to).
Verbeugung *f* bow.
verbeulen* *vt* to dent.
verbiegen* *vtr irreg* to bend; *(Holz)* to warp; *siehe* **verbogen.**
verbieten *vt irreg* to forbid; *(amtlich auch)* to prohibit; *Zeitung, Partei* to ban. **jdm ~, etw zu tun** to forbid sb to do sth; *(amtlich auch)* to prohibit sb from doing sth; *siehe* **verboten.**
verbilden* *vt (fig) jdn* to bring up badly; *Geschmack, Charakter* to spoil.
verbilligen* **1** *vt* to reduce the cost of; *Kosten, Preis* to reduce. **verbilligte Waren** reduced goods. **2** *vr* to become cheaper.
verbinden* *irreg* **1** *vt* **(a)** to connect. **jdn (mit jdm) ~** *(Telec)* to put sb through (to sb); **falsch verbunden!** wrong number; **die damit verbundenen Kosten** the costs involved; **uns verbindet nichts** we have nothing in common; *siehe* **verbunden. (b) ich verbinde die Geschäftsreise mit einem Kurzurlaub** I'll combine the business trip with a short holiday; **was ~ Sie mit diesem Begriff?** what do you associate with this concept? **(c)** *(Med)* to dress; *(mit Binden)* to bandage. **jdm die Augen ~** to blindfold sb. **2** *vr* **(a)** to combine *(zu* to form). **(b)** *(assoziiert werden)* to be associated; *(hervorgerufen werden)* to be evoked *(mit* by). **3** *vi* **(a) ich verbinde!** I'll put you through. **(b)** *(emotional)* to form a bond.
verbindlich *adj* **(a)** obliging. **(b)** *(verpflichtend)* obligatory, compulsory; *Regelung, Zusage* binding; *(verläßlich) Auskunft* reliable. **~ zusagen** to accept definitely.
Verbindlichkeit *f siehe adj* **(a)** obligingness. **~en** polite words *pl*. **(b)** *no pl* obligatory nature; binding nature; reliability. **(c) ~en** *pl (Comm, Jur)* obligations *pl*; *(finanziell auch)* liabilities *pl*.
Verbindung *f* **(a)** connection; *(einflußreiche Beziehung auch, Kontakt)* contact *(zu, mit* with). **in ~ mit** *(zusammen mit)* in conjunction with; *(im Zusammenhang mit)* in connection with; **jdn/etw mit etw in ~ bringen** to connect sb/sth with sth; *(assoziieren)* to associate sb/sth with sth; **~ mit jdm aufnehmen** to contact sb; **(mit jdm) in ~ treten** to get in touch *or* contact (with sb), to contact sb; **mit jdm in ~ stehen** to be in touch *or* contact with sb.
(b) *(Telec: Anschluß)* line. **telefonische ~** telephone link; **eine ~ (zu einem Ort) bekommen** to get through (to a place).
(c) *(Kombination)* combination.
(d) *(Vereinigung, Bündnis)* association; *(eheliche)* union; *(Univ: Burschenschaft)* fraternity.
(e) *(Chem) (Prozeß)* combination; *(Ergebnis)* compound *(aus* of).
Verbindungs- *in cpds (esp Tech, Archit)* con-

necting; ~**mann** *m, pl* ~**leute** *or* ~**männer** intermediary; *(Agent)* contact; ~**stelle** *f* join; *(von Gleisen)* junction; *(Amt)* liaison office.

verbissen *adj* grim; *Arbeiter, Gesicht* determined. **das darfst du nicht so ~ sehen** *(col)* you shouldn't be so rigid about it.

verbitten* *vr irreg* **das verbitte ich mir!** I won't have it!

verbittern* **1** *vt* to embitter, to make bitter. **2** *vi aux sein* to become embittered *or* bitter. **verbittert** embittered, bitter.

Verbitterung *f* bitterness.

verblassen* *vi aux sein (lit, fig)* to fade; *(Mond)* to pale.

verbleiben* *vi irreg aux sein* to remain. **verbleibe ich Ihr ...** *(form)* ... I remain, Yours sincerely ...; **wir sind so verblieben, daß wir ...** we agreed to ...

verbleien* *vt Benzin* to lead.

verblüffen* *vt (erstaunen)* to amaze; *(verwirren)* to baffle. **sich durch** *or* **von etw ~ lassen** to be taken in by sth.

verblühen* *vi aux sein (lit, fig)* to fade.

verbluten* *vi aux sein* to bleed to death.

verbogen *adj* bent; *Rückgrat* curved.

verbohren* *vr (col)* **sich in etw** *(acc)* ~ to become obsessed with sth.

verbohrt *adj Haltung* stubborn, obstinate.

verborgen[1]* *vt* to lend out *(an+acc* to*)*.

verborgen[2] *adj* hidden. **etw/sich ~ halten** to hide sth/to hide; **im V~en leben** to live hidden away; **im ~en liegen** to be not yet known.

Verbot *nt* **-e** ban *(etw zu tun* on doing sth*)*. **er ging trotz meines ~s** he went even though I had forbidden him to do so.

verboten *adj* forbidden; *(amtlich auch)* prohibited; *(gesetzeswidrig) Handel* illegal; *Zeitung, Partei, Buch etc* banned. **Rauchen/Parken ~** no smoking/parking; **er sah ~ aus** *(col)* he looked a real sight *(col)*.

Verbots-: ~**schild** *nt*, ~**tafel** *f* sign (prohibiting something); *(im Verkehr)* prohibition sign.

verbrämen* *vt (geh) Kleidungsstück* to trim; *(fig) Rede* to pad; *Wahrheit* to gloss over; *Kritik* to veil *(mit* in*)*.

verbrannt *adj* burnt; *(fig) Erde* scorched.

Verbrauch *m no pl* consumption *(von, an +dat* of*)*; *(von Geld)* expenditure; *(von Kräften)* drain *(von, an+dat* on*)*.

verbrauchen* *vt* **(a)** to use; *Vorräte* to use up; *Nahrungsmittel etc auch* to consume. **der Wagen verbraucht 10 Liter Benzin auf 100 km** the car does 10 kms to the litre. **(b)** *(abnützen) Kräfte etc* to exhaust; *Kleidung etc* to wear out. **sich ~** to wear oneself out; **verbrauchte Luft** stale air.

Verbraucher *m* - consumer.

Verbraucher- *in cpds* consumer; **v~gerecht** *adj Verpackung* handy; ~**schutz** *f* consumer protection; ~**verband** *m* consumer council.

Verbrauchsgüter *pl* consumer goods *pl*.

Verbrechen *nt* - *(lit, fig)* crime *(an +dat* against*)*.

verbrechen *vt irreg* **etwas ~** to commit a crime; *(col: anstellen)* to be up to something *(col)*.

Verbrecher(in *f***)** *m* - criminal.

Verbrecherbande *f* gang of criminals.

verbrecherisch *adj* criminal.

Verbrecherkartei *f* criminal records *pl*.

verbreiten* **1** *vt* to spread; *Zeitung* to circulate; *Wärme, Ruhe* to radiate; *Licht* to shed. **eine (weit) verbreitete Ansicht** a widely held opinion. **2** *vr* to spread. **sich über ein Thema ~** to expound on a subject.

verbreitern* *vtr* to widen.

verbrennen* *irreg* **1** *vt* to burn; *(einäschern) Tote* to cremate; *(versengen)* to scorch; *Haar* to singe; *(verbrühen)* to scald. **sich** *(dat)* **den Mund ~** *(lit)* to burn one's mouth; *(fig)* to say too much. **2** *vr* to burn oneself; *(sich verbrühen)* to scald oneself. **3** *vi aux sein* to burn; *(Mensch, Tier)* to burn to death; *(Haus etc)* to burn down; *(durch Sonne, Hitze)* to be scorched. **alles verbrannte** everything was destroyed in the fire.

Verbrennung *f* **(a)** *no pl* burning; *(von Treibstoff)* combustion; *(von Leiche)* cremation. **(b)** *(Brandwunde)* burn; *(Verbrühung)* scald.

Verbrennungs-: ~**anlage** *f* incineration plant; ~**motor** *m* internal combustion engine.

verbriefen* *vt* to document. **verbriefte Rechte** attested rights.

verbringen *vt irreg* to spend.

verbrühen* **1** *vt* to scald. **2** *vr* to scald oneself.

Verbrühung *f* scalding; *(Wunde)* scald.

verbuchen* *vt* to enter. **Erfolge (für sich) ~** to notch up successes *(col)*.

verbummeln* *(col)* **1** *vt (verlieren)* to lose; *Zeit* to waste, to fritter away; *Verabredung* to miss. **2** *vi aux sein (herunterkommen)* to go to seed.

verbunden *adj (form: dankbar)* **jdm (für etw) ~ sein** to be obliged to sb (for sth).

verbünden* *vr* to form an alliance.

Verbundenheit *f no pl (von Völkern)* solidarity; *(mit Menschen, Natur)* closeness *(mit* to*)*; *(mit Land, Tradition)* attachment *(mit* to*)*.

Verbündete(r) *mf decl as adj* ally.

verbürgen* *vtr* to guarantee. **sich für jdn/etw ~** to vouch for sb/sth; **verbürgte Nachricht** confirmed report; **ein verbürgtes Recht** an established right.

verbüßen* *vt* to serve.

verchromt* [fɛɐ'kro:mt] *adj* chromium-plated.

Verdacht *m no pl* suspicion. **jdn in ~ haben** to suspect sb; **im ~ stehen, etw getan zu haben** to be suspected of having done sth; **jdn wegen ~s einer Sache** *(gen)* **festnehmen** to arrest sb on suspicion of sth; **(gegen jdn) ~ schöpfen** to become suspicious (of sb); **es besteht ~ auf Krebs** *(acc)* cancer is suspected.

verdächtig *adj* suspicious. **sich ~ machen** to arouse suspicion; **einer Sache** *(gen)* **~ sein** to be suspected of sth.

verdächtigen* *vt* to suspect *(gen* of*)*.

Verdächtige(r) *mf decl as adj* suspect.

verdammen* *vt* to damn; *(verurteilen)* to condemn.

verdammt *(col)* **1** *adj, adv* damned *(col)*. **das tut ~ weh** that hurts like hell *(col)*; **mir geht's ~ schlecht** I'm in a pretty bad way *(col)*. **2** *interj* **~!** damn (it) *(col)*; **~ noch mal!** *(col!)* bloody hell *(Brit col!)*, damn *(col)*.

verdampfen* *vti (vi: aux sein)* to vaporize; *(Cook)* to boil away.

verdanken* *vt* **jdm etw ~** to owe sth to sb; **das haben wir ihm zu ~** that's thanks to him.

verdarb *pret of* **verderben.**

verdauen* *vti (lit, fig)* to digest.

verdaulich *adj* digestible. **leicht ~** easy to digest.

Verdauung *f* digestion *no indef art*.

Verdauungs- *in cpds* digestive; ~**spaziergang** *m* constitutional; ~**störung** *f usu pl* indigestion *no pl*.

Verdeck *nt* **-e** *(von Kinderwagen)* canopy; *(von Auto)* soft top; *(von Schiff)* sundeck.

verdecken* *vt* to hide, to conceal; *(zudecken)* to cover (up); *Sicht* to block.

verdenken* *vt irreg* **ich kann es ihm nicht ~(, daß er es getan hat)** I can't blame him (for doing it).

verderben *pret* **verdarb**, *ptp* **verdorben** **1** *vt* to spoil; *(stärker)* to ruin; *Luft* to pollute; *(moralisch)* to corrupt; *(verwöhnen)* to spoil. **jdm etw ~** to ruin sth for sb; **sich** *(dat)* **den Magen ~** to give oneself an upset stomach; **sich** *(dat)* **die Augen ~** to ruin one's eyes; **die Preise ~** to force prices down/up; **jdm die Freude an etw** *(dat)* **~** to spoil sb's enjoyment of sth; **es (sich dat) mit jdm ~** to fall out with sb. **2** *vi aux sein (Material)* to become spoiled/ruined; *(Nahrungsmittel)* to go bad; *(Ernte)* to be ruined; *(Mensch)* to become depraved.

Verderben *nt no pl* **(a)** ruin. **in sein ~ rennen** to be heading for disaster. **(b)** *(von Material)* spoiling, ruining; *(von Nahrungsmittel)* going off.

verderblich *adj* pernicious; *Lebensmittel* perishable.

verdeutlichen* *vt (deutlicher machen)* to clarify; *(erklären)* to explain. **sich** *(dat)* **etw ~** to think sth out for oneself.

verdeutschen* *vt* to translate into German; *(eindeutschen)* to Germanize.

verdichten* **1** *vt (Phys, fig)* to compress; *Gefühle* to intensify, to heighten. **2** *vr* to thicken; *(Gas)* to become compressed; *(fig: häufen)* to increase; *(Verdacht, Eindruck)* to deepen.

Verdichter *m* - compressor.

verdicken* **1** *vt* to thicken. **2** *vr* to thicken; *(anschwellen)* to swell.

verdienen* **1** *vt* **(a)** *(einnehmen)* to earn; *(Gewinn machen)* to make *(an+dat* on*)*. **sich** *(dat)* **etw ~** to earn the money for sth. **(b)** *(fig) Lob, Strafe* to deserve. **er verdient es nicht anders** he doesn't deserve anything else. **2** *vi* to earn; *(Gewinn machen)* to make (a profit) *(an +dat* on*)*. **er verdient gut** he earns a lot; **am Krieg ~** to profit from war.

Verdiener *m* - wage-earner.

Verdienst[1] *m* **-e** income; *(Profit)* profit.

Verdienst[2] *nt* **-e** **(a)** merit; *(Dank)* credit. **es ist sein ~/das ~ der Wissenschaftler (, daß...)** it is thanks to him/the scientists (that ...); **nach ~** on merit. **(b)** *usu pl (um* to*) (Leistung)* contribution; *(um Wissenschaft, Staat)* service.

Verdienst-: ~**ausfall** *m* loss of earnings; ~**orden** *m* order of merit; **v~voll** *adj* commendable.

verdient *adj* **(a)** *Lohn, Strafe* rightful; *Ruhe, Lob* well-deserved. **(b)** *Wissenschaftler, Politiker, Sportler* of outstanding merit. **sich um etw ~ machen** to render outstanding services to sth.

verdonnern* *vt (col: zu Haft etc)* to sentence *(zu* to*)*. **jdn zu etw ~, jdn dazu ~, etw zu tun** to order sb to do sth as a punishment.

verdoppeln* *vtr* to double.

verdorben **1** *ptp of* **verderben. 2** *adj Lebensmittel* bad; *Magen* upset; *Stimmung, Urlaub, Freude* spoiled, ruined; *(moralisch)* corrupt; *(verzogen) Kind* spoiled.

verdorren* *vi aux sein* to wither.

verdrängen* *vt jdn* to drive out; *Gegner auch* to oust; *(ersetzen)* to replace; *(Phys) Wasser* to displace; *(Met)* to drive; *(fig) Sorgen* to dispel; *(Psych)* to repress, to suppress.

verdrecken* *vti (vi: aux sein) (col)* to get filthy.

verdrehen* *vt (lit, fig)* to twist; *(verknacksen)* to sprain; *Hals* to crick; *Augen* to roll. **das Recht ~** to pervert the course of justice; **sich** *(dat)* **den Hals ~** *(fig col)* to crane one's neck.

verdreht *adj (col)* crazy *(col)*; *Bericht* confused.

verdreifachen* *vtr* to treble, to triple.

verdrießen *pret* **verdroß**, *ptp* **verdrossen** *vt jdn* to annoy. **sich** *(dat)* **den Abend durch etw ~ lassen** to let sth spoil one's evening.

verdrießlich *adj* morose; *Arbeit* irksome.

verdroß *pret of* **verdrießen.**

verdrossen **1** *ptp of* **verdrießen. 2** *adj (schlechtgelaunt)* morose; *(unlustig) Mensch, Gesicht* unwilling, reluctant.

Verdrossenheit *f (schlechte Laune)* moroseness; *(Lustlosigkeit)* unwillingness, reluctance.

verdrucken* *vr (col)* to make a misprint.

verdrücken* **1** *vt Kleider* to crumple; *(col) Essen* to polish off *(col)*. **2** *vr (col)* to beat it *(col)*. **sich heimlich ~** to slip away.

Verdruß *m* **-sse** frustration. **~ mit jdm haben** to get frustrated with sb; **zu jds ~** to sb's annoyance.

verduften* *vi aux sein (col)* to beat it *(col)*.

verdummen* **1** *vt* **jdn ~** *(für dumm verkaufen)* to make sb out to be stupid; *(dumm machen)* to dull sb's mind. **2** *vi aux sein* to become stul

verdunkeln* **1** *vt* to darken; *Bühne* *Krieg)* to black out; *(fig) Zusammenhä* obscure. **die Sonne ~** *(Mond)* to eclips *(Wolken)* to obscure the sun. **2** *vr* to da

verdünnen* **1** *vt* to thin (down); *(mit* water down; *Lösung* to dilute. **den Teig ser ~** to add water to the dough. **2** *vr (* become diluted; *(schmaler werden)* t thinner.

Verdünner *m* - thinner.

verdunsten* *vi aux sein* to evaporate.

Verdunster *m* - humidifier.

verdursten* *vi aux sein* to die of thirs

verdüstern* *vtr* to darken.

verdutzt *adj, adv (col)* taken aback; baffled.

ver|ebben* *vi aux sein* to subside.

ver|edeln* *vt Metalle, Erdöl* to refine finish; *Boden, Geschmack* to improve

ver|ehren* *vt* to admire; *(anbeten)* to

Ver|ehrer(in *f***)** *m* - admirer.

ver|ehrt *adj* **(sehr) ~e Anwesende Publikum** Ladies and Gentlemen.

Ver|ehrung *f* admiration; *(von Heilige* *(Liebe)* adoration.

ver|eidigen* *vt* to swear in. **jdn auf et** make sb swear on sth; **vereidigter** sworn translator.

Ver|ein *m* **-e** organization, society; *(S* *(col)* crowd. **ein wohltätiger ~** a ch **mit** in conjunction with.

ver|einbar *adj* compatible; *Aussagen*

ver|einbaren* *vt* **(a)** to agree; *Zeit* to arrange. **(es) ~, daß ...** to agree/a ... **(b) etw mit etw ~** to reconcile s **mit etw zu ~ sein** to be compatible

Ver|einbarung *f siehe vt (a) (das* agreeing; arranging; *(Abmachung)* arrangement. **laut ~** as agreed; arrangement.

ver|einen* **1** *vt* to unite; *Ideen,* reconcile. **vereint handeln** to act to **einte Nationen** United Nations *sing.*

ver|einfachen* *vt* to simplify.

Ver|einfachung *f* simplification.

ver|einheitlichen* *vt* to standardiz

ver|einigen* **1** *vt* to unite; *Kräfte, Eig* combine; *Firmen* to merge *(zu* into pool. **etw mit etw ~** to combine s *(vereinbaren)* to reconcile sth with **Hand vereinigt sein** to be held b person; **alle Stimmen auf sich** *(acc)* all the votes; **Vereinigtes Königr** Kingdom; **Vereinigte Staaten** Unite to unite; *(sich verbünden auch)* to *(Firmen)* to merge; *(zusammenkom* bine; *(Flüsse)* to meet; *(sich versam* semble.

Ver|einigung *f* **(a)** *siehe vt* uniting merging; pooling; *(körperliche,* union. **(b)** *(Organisation)* organizati

ver|einnahmen* *vt (geh)* to take. **j** make demands on sb; *(Beruf)* to occ

ver|einsamen* *vi aux sein* to becom

Ver|einsmeier *m* - *(col)* **er ist ein ri** he thinks about is his club.

ver|einzelt **1** *adj* occasional; *Regen* lated. **2** *adv* occasionally.

ver|eisen* *vi aux sein* to freeze; *(St* *scheibe)* to ice over.

ver|eist *adj Straßen, Fenster* icy; *B* *Türschloß* iced-up; *Land* covered in

ver|eiteln* *vt* to thwart, to foil.

ver|eitern* *vi aux sein* to go septic.

ver|elenden* *vi aux sein* to becor ished.

ver|enden* *vi aux sein* to perish, to

verfugen* *vt* to fit flush.
verfügen* **1** *vi* **über etw** *(acc)* ~ to have sth at one's disposal; *(besitzen)* to have sth; **über jdn/etw** ~ *(bestimmen über)* to be in charge of sb/sth; **du kannst doch nicht über mich** ~ you can't tell me what to do; **über etw** *(acc)* **frei** ~ **können** to be able to do as one wants with sth; **ich kann im Moment über meine Zeit nicht frei** ~ I am not master of my own time just now; ~ **Sie über mich** I am at your disposal. **2** *vt* to order; *(gesetzlich)* to decree.
Verfügung *f* **(a)** *no pl* **jdm etw zur** ~ **stellen** to put sth at sb's disposal; **jdm zur** ~ **stehen** to be at sb's disposal; **(jdm) zur** ~ **stehen** *(verfügbar sein)* to be available (to sb); **etw zur** ~ **haben** to have sth at one's disposal. **(b)** *(behördlich)* order; *(von Gesetzgeber)* decree; *(testamentarisch)* provision; *(Anweisung)* instruction.
Verfügungsgewalt *f (Jur)* right of disposal.
verführen* *vt* to tempt; *(esp sexuell)* to seduce; *die Jugend, das Volk etc* to lead astray.
Verführer *m* **-** seducer.
Verführerin *f* seductress, temptress.
verführerisch *adj* seductive; *(verlockend)* tempting.
Verführung *f* seduction; *(von Jugend, Volk)* tempting; *(Verlockung)* enticement.
verfüttern* *vt* **etw an die Vögel** ~ to feed sth to the birds.
Vergabe *f* **-n** *(von Arbeiten)* allocation; *(von Stipendium, Auftrag etc)* award.
vergällen* *vt (geh)* **jdm die Freude/das Leben** ~ to spoil sb's fun/to sour sb's life.
vergaloppieren* *vr (col: sich irren)* to be on the wrong track.
vergammeln* *(col)* **1** *vi aux sein (Speisen)* to go bad; *(verlottern)* to go to the dogs *(col)*. **vergammelt aussehen** to look scruffy. **2** *vt Zeit* to waste.
vergangen *adj* **(a)** *(letzte)* last. **(b)** *Jahre* past; *Zeiten, Bräuche* bygone. **das V~e** the past.
Vergangenheit *f* past; *(Gram)* past (tense). **der** ~ **angehören** to be a thing of the past.
Vergangenheitsbewältigung *f* coming to terms with the past.
vergänglich *adj* transitory.
vergasen* *vt (töten)* to gas.
Vergaser *m* **-** *(Aut)* carburettor *(Brit)*, carburetor *(US)*.
vergaß *pret of* **vergessen.**
vergeben* *irreg* **1** *vt* **(a)** *Auftrag, Preis* to award *(an+acc* to*)*; *Studienplätze, Stellen* to allocate; *(fig) Chance, Möglichkeit* to throw away. **ein Amt an jdn** ~ to appoint sb to an office; **zu** ~ **sein** to be available; ~ **sein** *(Wohnung, Plätze)* to have been taken; *(Stelle)* to have been filled. **(b)** *(verzeihen)* to forgive. **jdm etw** ~ to forgive sb (for) sth. **2** *vr* **sich** *(dat)* **etwas/nichts** ~ to lose/not to lose face.
vergebens *adj pred, adv* in vain.
vergeblich **1** *adj* futile; *Bitten, Mühe auch* vain *attr*, in vain. **2** *adv* in vain.
Vergebung *f no pl* forgiveness.
vergegenwärtigen* *vr* **sich** *(dat)* **etw** ~ to imagine sth.
Vergehen *nt* **-** *(Verstoß)* offence *(Brit)*, offense *(US)*. **das ist doch kein** ~**, oder?** that's not a crime, is it?
vergehen* *irreg* **1** *vi aux sein* **(a)** to pass; *(Liebe, Leidenschaft auch)* to die; *(Zeit, Jahre etc auch)* to go by; *(Schönheit, Glück)* to fade. **wie doch die Zeit vergeht** how time flies; **mir ist der Appetit vergangen** I have lost my appetite. **(b) vor etw** *(dat)* ~ to be dying of sth; **vor Angst** ~ to be scared to death; **vor Sehnsucht** ~ to pine away. **2** *vr* **sich an jdm** ~ to do sb wrong; *(unsittlich)* to assault sb indecently; **sich gegen das Gesetz** ~ to violate the law.
vergeistigt *adj* cerebral, spiritual.
vergelten *vt* to repay. **jdm etw** ~ to repay sb for sth.
Vergeltung *f (Rache)* retaliation.
Vergeltungsmaßnahme *f* retaliatory measure.
vergesellschaften* *vt (Pol)* to nationalize.
vergessen *pret* **vergaß,** *ptp* ~ **1** *vti* to forget; *(liegenlassen auch)* to leave (behind). **... und nicht zu** ~ **seine Ehrlichkeit** ... and not forgetting his honesty; **das werde ich dir nie** ~ I will never forget that. **2** *vr (Mensch)* to forget oneself.
Vergessenheit *f no pl* oblivion. **in** ~ **geraten** to fall into oblivion.
vergeßlich *adj* forgetful.
vergeuden* *vt* to waste, to squander.
vergewaltigen* *vt* to rape.
Vergewaltigung *f* rape.
vergewissern* *vr* to make sure. **sich einer Sache** *(gen) or* **über etw** *(acc)* ~ to make sure of sth.
vergießen* *vt irreg Kaffee, Wasser* to spill; *Blut auch, Tränen* to shed.
vergiften* *vt (lit, fig)* to poison.
vergilben* *vi aux sein* to go yellow. **vergilbt** yellowed.
Vergißmeinnicht *nt* **-(e)** forget-me-not.
vergittert *adj Fenster* barred.
verglasen* *vt* to glaze.
Vergleich *m* **-e** **(a)** comparison. **~e ziehen** to make comparisons; **im** ~ **zu** *or* **mit** in comparison with; **in keinem** ~ **zu etw stehen** to be out of all proportion to sth; *(Leistungen)* not to compare with sth; **dem** ~ **mit jdm standhalten, den** ~ **mit jdm aushalten** to bear comparison with sb. **(b)** *(Jur)* settlement.
vergleichbar *adj* comparable.
vergleichen* *irreg* **1** *vt* to compare. **etw mit etw** ~ to compare sth to sth; *(prüfend)* to compare sth with sth; **vergleiche oben** compare above. **2** *vr* **(a) sich mit jdm** ~ to compare oneself with sb. **(b)** *(Jur)* to reach a settlement, to settle.
vergleichsweise *adv* comparatively.
verglimmen* *vi irreg aux sein (Zigarette)* to go out; *(Licht, Feuer auch)* to die away.
verglühen* *vi aux sein (Feuer)* to die away; *(Draht)* to burn out; *(Raumkapsel, Meteor etc)* to burn up.
vergnügen* *vr* to enjoy oneself. **sich mit jdm/etw** ~ to amuse oneself with sb/sth; **sich mit Lesen** ~ to amuse oneself by reading.
Vergnügen *nt* **-** *(Freude, Genuß)* pleasure; *(Spaß)* fun *no indef art*; *(Erheiterung)* amusement. **das macht** *or* **bereitet mir** ~ I enjoy it, it gives me pleasure; **nur zum** ~ just for pleasure *or* for the fun of it; **das war ein teures** ~ *(col)* that was an expensive bit of fun; **viel ~!** enjoy yourself/yourselves *(auch iro)*.
vergnüglich *adj* enjoyable; *(erheiternd)* amusing.
vergnügt *adj Stunden* enjoyable; *Mensch, Stimmung* cheerful.
Vergnügung *f* pleasure; *(Veranstaltung)* entertainment.
Vergnügungs-: **~industrie** *f* entertainment industry; **~park** *m* amusement park; **~reise** *f* pleasure trip; **~steuer** *f* entertainment tax; **~sucht** *f* craving for pleasure; **~viertel** *nt* entertainments district.
vergolden* *vt (mit Blattgold)* to gild; *(mit Gold)* to gold-plate; *(fig: verschönern)* to enhance.
vergönnen* *vt (geh)* **es war ihr noch vergönnt, das zu sehen** she was granted the privilege of seeing it.
vergöttern* *vt* to idolize.
vergraben* *irreg* **1** *vt* to bury. **2** *vr (lit, fig)* to bury oneself.
vergrämt *adj (kummervoll) Gesicht* troubled.
vergreifen* *vr irreg* **(a)** to make a mistake. **sich im Ton/Ausdruck** ~ *(fig)* to adopt the wrong tone/use the wrong expression. **(b) sich an etw** *(dat)* ~ *(stehlen)* to misappropriate sth; **sich an**

jdm ~ *(angreifen)* to lay hands on sb.
vergreisen* *vi aux sein (Bevölkerung)* to age; *(Mensch)* to become senile.
vergriffen *adj* unavailable; *Buch* out of print.
vergröbern* *vtr* to coarsen.
vergrößern 1 *vt* to enlarge; *Gelände auch* to extend; *Firma, Absatzmarkt* to expand; *Anzahl, Probleme, Einfluß* to increase; *(Lupe, Brille)* to magnify. **2** *vr* to increase; *(räumlich)* to be extended; *(Firma, Absatzmarkt)* to expand; *(Organ)* to become enlarged.
Vergrößerung *f siehe vb* enlargement; extension; expansion; increase; magnification. **in 1.000facher ~** magnified 1,000 times.
Vergrößerungsglas *nt* magnifying glass.
vergucken* *vr* **da hab ich mich verguckt** *(col)* I didn't see it properly.
vergünstigt *adj Lage* improved; *Preis* reduced.
Vergünstigung *f (Vorteil)* privilege; *(Preisermäßigung)* reduction.
vergüten* *vt* **jdm etw ~** *Unkosten* to reimburse sb for sth; *Arbeit, Leistung* to pay sb for sth.
Vergütung *f* reimbursement.
verh. = verheiratet.
verhaften* *vt* to arrest. **Sie sind verhaftet!** you are under arrest!
Verhaftete(r) *mf decl as adj* person under arrest.
Verhaftung *f* arrest.
verhallen* *vi aux sein (Geräusch etc)* to die away.
verhalten[1]* *vr irreg* **1 (a)** to behave; *(handeln)* to act. **sich ruhig ~** to keep quiet; *(sich nicht bewegen)* to keep still. **(b)** *(Sachen, Marktlage)* to be; *(Chem)* to react. **wie verhält sich die Sache?** how do things stand? **2** *vr impers* **wie verhält es sich damit?** *(wie ist die Lage?)* how do things stand?; *(wie wird das gehandhabt?)* how do you go about it?; **damit verhält es sich anders** the situation is different; **wenn sich das so verhält, ...** if that is the case ...
verhalten[2] 1 *adj* restrained; *Stimme* muted; *Atem* bated; *Wut* suppressed; *Tempo, Rhythmus* measured. **2** *adv* with restraint; *laufen* at a measured pace.
Verhalten *nt no pl (Benehmen)* behaviour *(Brit)*, behavior *(US)*; *(Vorgehen)* conduct; *(Chem)* reaction.
Verhaltens-: ~forschung *f* behaviourism *(Brit)*, behaviorism *(US)*; **v~gestört** *adj* disturbed; **~maßregel** *f* rule of conduct; **~weise** *f* behaviour *(Brit)*, behavior *(US)*.
Verhältnis *nt* **(a)** *(Proportion)* proportion; *(Math, Mischungs~)* ratio. **im ~ zu** in relation *or* proportion to; **im ~ zu früher** in comparison with earlier times; **in keinem ~ zu etw stehen** to be out of all proportion to sth. **(b)** *(Beziehung)* relationship; *(zwischen Ländern, innerhalb einer Gruppe)* relations *pl (zu* with*)*; *(Einstellung)* attitude *(zu* to*)*. **(c)** *(Liebes~)* affair. **(d) ~se** *pl* conditions *pl*; *(finanzielle)* circumstances *pl*; **so wie die ~se liegen** as things stand; **aus welchen ~sen kommt er?** what sort of background does he come from?; **über seine ~se leben** to live beyond one's means; **für klare ~se sorgen, klare ~se schaffen** to get things straight.
Verhältnis-: v~mäßig relatively; **~wahl(recht** *nt) f* proportional representation *no art*.
verhandeln* 1 *vi* **(a)** to negotiate *(über+acc* about*)*; *(col: diskutieren)* to argue. **über den Preis läßt sich ~** *(col)* we can discuss the price. **(b)** *(Jur)* **gegen jdn/in einem Fall ~** to hear sb's/a case. **2** *vt* **(a)** to negotiate. **(b)** *(Jur) Fall* to hear.
Verhandlung *f* **(a)** negotiations *pl*; *(das Verhandeln)* negotiation. **~en führen** to negotiate. **(b)** *(Jur)* hearing; *(Straf~)* trial.
Verhandlungs-: ~basis *f* basis for negotiation(s); **~basis DM 2.500** DM 2,500 or near offer; **v~bereit** *adj* ready to negotiate; **~partner** *m* negotiating party; **wer war Ihr ~partner?** who were you negotiating with?; **~tisch** *m* negotiating table.
verhangen *adv* overcast.
verhängen* *vt* **(a)** *Embargo, Strafe* to impose *(über+acc* on*)*; *Ausnahmezustand* to declare *(über +acc* in*)*. **(b)** *(zuhängen)* to cover *(mit* with*)*.
Verhängnis *nt* fate. **jdm zum ~ werden** to be sb's undoing.
verhängnisvoll *adj* disastrous, fatal; *Tag* fateful.
verharmlosen* *vt* to play down.
verharren* *vi aux haben or sein* to pause; *(in einer bestimmten Stellung)* to remain. **auf einem Standpunkt ~** to adhere to a viewpoint.
verharschen* *vi aux sein (Schnee, Piste)* to crust.
verhaßt *adj* hated; *Arbeit, Pflicht* hateful. **sich ~ machen** to make oneself hated *(bei* by*)*.
verhätscheln* *vt* to spoil, to pamper.
Verhau *m or nt* **-e** *(zur Absperrung)* barrier; *(Käfig)* coop.
verhauen* *irreg (col)* **1** *vt* **(a)** *(verprügeln)* to beat up; *(zur Strafe)* to beat. **(b)** *Prüfung etc* to muff *(col)*. **2** *vr* **(a)** *(sich verprügeln)* to have a fight. **(b)** *(beim Schreiben etc)* to make a mistake. **(c)** *(sich irren)* to slip up *(col)*.
verheben* *vr irreg* to hurt oneself lifting something.
verheddern* *vr (col: lit, fig)* to get into a tangle.
verheerend *adj Sturm, Folgen* devastating, disastrous; *Anblick* ghastly.
verhehlen* *vt* to conceal *(jdm* from sb*)*.
verheilen* *vi aux sein (lit, fig)* to heal.
verheimlichen* *vt* to keep secret, to conceal *(jdm* from sb*)*. **ich habe nichts zu ~** I have nothing to hide.
verheiraten* 1 *vt* to marry *(mit* to*)*. **2** *vr* to get married, to marry. **sich mit jdm ~** to marry sb, to get married to sb.
verheiratet *adj* married.
verheißen* *vt irreg (geh)* to promise.
verheißungsvoll *adj* promising; *Blicke* alluring.
verheizen* *vt* to burn, to use as fuel. **Soldaten ~** *(col)* to send soldiers to the slaughter.
verhelfen* *vi irreg* **jdm zu etw ~** to help sb to get sth.
verherrlichen* *vt* to glorify.
verheult *adj Augen, Gesicht* puffy. **du siehst ~ aus** you look as though you've been crying.
verhexen* *vt* to bewitch; *(col) Maschine etc* to put a jinx on *(col)*. **das ist doch wie verhext** *(col)* it's maddening *(col)*.
verhindern* *vt* to prevent; *Versuch, Plan* to foil. **ich konnte es nicht ~, daß er die Wahrheit erfuhr** I couldn't prevent him from finding out the truth; **das läßt sich leider nicht ~** it can't be helped, unfortunately; **er war an diesem Abend (dienstlich) verhindert** he was unable to come that evening (for reasons of work); **ein verhinderter Politiker** *(col)* a would-be politician.
verhöhnen* *vt* to mock, to deride.
verhökern* *vt (col)* to get rid of *(col)*.
Verhör *nt* **-e** questioning, interrogation.
verhören* 1 *vt* to question, to interrogate. **2** *vr* to mishear.
verhüllen* 1 *vt* to veil; *Haupt, Körperteil* to cover. **2** *vr* to disguise oneself; *(Frau)* to veil oneself.
verhüllend *adj Ausdruck* euphemistic.
verhungern* *vi aux sein (lit, fig)* to starve, to die of starvation.
verhunzen* *vt (col)* to ruin.
verhüten* *vt* to prevent.
verhütten *vt* to smelt.
Verhütung *f* prevention; *(Empfängnis~)* contraception.
Verhütungsmittel *nt* contraceptive.
verhutzelt *adj Gesicht, Männlein* wizened; *Haut* wrinkled; *Obst* shrivelled *(Brit)*, shriveled *(US)*.
verifizieren* [verifi'tsiːrən] *vt* to verify.
ver|innerlichen* *vt* to internalize.

ver|irren* *vr* to get lost, to lose one's way; *(fig)* to go astray; *(Tier, Kugel)* to stray.
Ver|irrung *f* losing one's way *no art; (fig)* aberration.
verjagen* *vt (lit, fig)* to chase away.
verjähren* *vi aux sein* to come under the statute of limitations; *(Anspruch)* to lapse.
Verjährung *f* limitation; *(von Anspruch)* lapse.
verjubeln* *vt (col) Geld* to blow *(col)*.
verjüngen* **1** *vt* to rejuvenate; *(jünger aussehen lassen)* to make look younger; *Baumbestand* to regenerate. **eine Mannschaft ~** to build up a younger team. **2** *vr* **(a)** to become younger; *(Haut, Erscheinung)* to become rejuvenated; *(jünger aussehen)* to look younger. **(b)** *(dünner werden)* to taper.
verkabeln *vt Leitung* to lay; *Haus* to wire; *(col) Stadtteil* to wire up for cable television.
verkalken* *vi aux sein (Arterien)* to become hardened; *(Gewebe)* to calcify; *(Wasserleitung etc)* to fur up; *(col: Mensch)* to become senile.
verkalkt *adj (col)* senile.
verkalkulieren* *vr* to miscalculate.
verkannt *adj* unrecognized.
verkappt *adj attr* hidden; *(Med)* undiagnosed.
verkatert *adj (col)* hung-over *(col)*.
Verkauf *m, pl* **Verkäufe** sale. **zum ~ stehen** to be up for sale.
verkaufen* **1** *vti (lit, fig)* to sell *(für, um* for*)*. **„zu ~"** "for sale"; **jdm etw** *or* **etw an jdn ~** to sell sb sth, to sell sth to sb. **2** *vr (Ware)* to sell; *(Mensch)* to sell oneself.
Verkäufer(in *f***)** *m* - seller; *(in Geschäft)* sales assistant *(Brit)*, sales clerk *(US)*; *(im Außendienst)* salesman/saleswoman, salesperson.
verkäuflich *adj* sal(e)able, marketable; *(zu verkaufen)* for sale. **leicht/schwer ~** easy/hard to sell.
Verkaufs- *in cpds* sales; **~abteilung** *f* sales department; **~förderung** *f* sales promotion; **~leiter** *m* sales manager; **v~offen** *adj* open for business; **~personal** *nt* sales personnel; **~preis** *m* retail price; **~schlager** *m* big seller.
Verkehr *m no pl* **(a)** traffic; *(Beförderung, Verkehrsmittel)* transport. **für den ~ freigeben** *Straße etc* to open to traffic; *Transportmittel* to bring into service; **aus dem ~ ziehen** to withdraw from service. **(b)** *(Verbindung)* contact, communication; *(Umgang)* company; *(Geschlechts~)* intercourse. **(c)** *(Umlauf)* circulation. **etw in (den) ~ bringen/aus dem ~ ziehen** to put sth into/withdraw sth from circulation.
verkehren* **1** *vi* **(a)** *aux haben or sein (fahren)* to run; *(Flugzeug)* to fly. **(b)** *(Gast sein, Kontakt pflegen)* **bei jdm ~** to frequent sb's house; **mit jdm ~** to associate with sb; **in Künstlerkreisen ~** to move in artistic circles; **mit jdm brieflich/schriftlich ~** *(form)* to correspond with sb; **mit jdm (geschlechtlich) ~** to have (sexual) intercourse with sb. **2** *vtr* to turn *(in+acc* into*)*. **etw ins Gegenteil ~** to reverse sth.
Verkehrs- *in cpds* traffic; **~ampel** *f* traffic lights *pl (Brit)*, traffic light *(US)*; **v~arm** *adj Zeit, Straße* quiet; **ein v~armes Gebiet** an area with little traffic; **~aufkommen** *nt* volume of traffic; **~behinderung** *f (Jur)* obstruction (of traffic); **~betriebe** *pl* transport services *pl*; **~büro** *nt* tourist information office; **~delikt** *nt* traffic offence *(Brit) or* offense *(US)*; **~erziehung** *f* road safety training; **~flugzeug** *nt* commercial aircraft; **~funk** *m* radio traffic service; **~gefährdung** *f (durch Fahrer)* dangerous driving; **v~günstig** *adj* convenient; **~hindernis** *nt* (traffic) obstruction; **~insel** *f* traffic island; **~knotenpunkt** *m* traffic junction; **~kontrolle** *f* traffic check; **~minister** *m* minister of transport; **~mittel** *nt* means of transport *sing*; **öffentliche/private ~mittel** public/private transport; **~netz** *nt* traffic network; **~opfer** *nt* road casualty; **~polizei** *f* traffic police *pl*; **~regel** *f* traffic regulation; **v~reich** *adj Straße* busy; **v~reiche Zeit** peak (traffic) time; **~schild** *nt* road sign; **v~schwach** *adj Zeit* off-peak; **v~sicher** *adj Fahrzeug* roadworthy; *Brücke* safe (for traffic); **~stau** *m* traffic jam; **~stockung** *f* traffic hold-up; **~sünder** *m (col)* traffic offender; **~teilnehmer** *m* road-user; **~tote(r)** *mf* road casualty; **v~tüchtig** *adj Fahrzeug* roadworthy; *Mensch* fit to drive; **~unfall** *m* road accident; **~unternehmen** *nt* transport company; **~unterricht** *m* road safety instruction; **~verbindung** *f* public transport facilities *pl*; *(Anschluß)* connection; **~verbund** *m* transport association; **~verein** *m* tourist information office; **~verhältnisse** *pl* traffic situation *sing*; *(Straßenzustand)* road conditions *pl*; **~wesen** *nt* transport and communications *no art*; **v~widrig** *adj* contrary to road traffic regulations; **~zeichen** *nt* road sign.
verkehrt **1** *adj* wrong; *Welt* topsy-turvy. **2** *adv* wrongly. **etw ~ (herum) anhaben** to have sth on the wrong way around; **das V~este, was du tun könntest** the worst thing you could do.
verkeilen* *vr* to become wedged together.
verkennen* *vt irreg* to misjudge. **es ist nicht zu ~, daß ...** it is undeniable that ...; *siehe* **verkannt.**
verketten* *vt Tür, Kiste* to put a chain on; *(fig)* to link.
Verkettung *f* **eine ~ unglücklicher Umstände** an unfortunate chain of events.
verkitten* *vt* to cement; *Fenster* to putty around.
verklagen* *vt* to sue *(wegen* for*)* **jdn auf etw** *(acc)* **~** to take sb to court for sth.
verklammern* *vt* to staple together; *(fig)* to link.
verklärt *adj* transfigured.
verklausulieren* *vt Vertrag* to hedge in with (restrictive) clauses.
verkleben* **1** *vt (zusammenkleben)* to stick together; *(zukleben)* to cover *(mit* with*)*. **2** *vi aux sein (Wunde)* to close; *(Augen)* to get gummed up; *(Briefmarken, Bonbons)* to stick together; *(Haare)* to become matted. **mit etw ~** to stick to sth.
verklebt *adj* sticky; *Augen* gummed up; *Haare* matted.
verkleckern* *vr (col)* to spill.
verkleiden* **1** *vt* **(a)** to disguise; *(kostümieren)* to dress up. **(b)** *Schacht, Tunnel* to line; *(vertäfeln)* to panel; *Heizkörper* to cover in. **2** *vr* to disguise oneself; *(sich kostümieren)* to dress (oneself) up.
Verkleidung *f* **(a)** *(Kleidung)* disguise; *(Kostüm)* fancy dress. **(b)** *siehe vt (b)* lining; panelling *(Brit)*, paneling *(US)*; covering.
verkleinern* **1** *vt* to reduce; *Raum, Gebiet, Firma* to make smaller. **2** *vr* to be reduced; *(Raum, Gebiet, Firma)* to become smaller.
Verkleinerung *f* reduction.
verklemmen* *vr* to get stuck.
verklemmt *adj (col) Mensch* inhibited; *Beine* crossed.
verklingen* *vi irreg aux sein* to die away.
verklumpen* *vi aux sein* to get lumpy.
verknacksen* *vt (col)* **(sich** *dat***) den Fuß ~** to twist one's ankle.
verknallen* *vr (col)* **sich (in jdn) ~** to fall for sb.
verknappen* *vt* to cut back.
verkneifen* *vr irreg (col)* **sich** *(dat)* **etw ~** to stop oneself (from) saying/doing *etc* sth; **ich konnte mir das Lachen nicht ~** I couldn't help laughing.
verkniffen *adj Gesicht (angestrengt)* strained; *(verbittert)* pinched.
verknöchert* *adj (fig)* fossilized.
verknoten* **1** *vt* to tie, to knot; *(col) Paket* to tie up. **2** *vr* to become knotted.
verknüpfen* *vt* **(a)** to tie (together). **(b)** *(fig)* to combine; *(in Zusammenhang bringen)* to link, to connect; *Gedanken* to associate. **so ein Umzug ist immer mit großen Ausgaben verknüpft** moving

house always involves a lot of expense.

verkochen* *vti (vi: aux sein) (Flüssigkeit)* to boil away; *(Kartoffeln, Gemüse)* to overboil.

verkohlen* **1** *vi aux sein* to become charred. **2** *vt* **(a)** *Holz* to char. **(b)** *(col)* **jdn** ~ to have sb on *(col)*.

verkommen[1]* *vi irreg aux sein* **(a)** *(Mensch)* to go to the dogs; *(moralisch)* to become dissolute; *(Kind)* to run wild. **zu etw** ~ to degenerate into sth. **(b)** *(Gebäude, Auto)* to fall to pieces; *(Stadt)* to become run-down; *(Gelände)* to run wild; *(Begabung)* to go to waste; *(Lebensmittel)* to go bad.

verkommen[2] *adj Mensch* depraved; *Auto, Gebäude* dilapidated; *Garten* wild.

verkoppeln* *vt* to connect, to couple; *(Space)* to link (up).

verkorken* *vt* to cork (up).

verkorkst *adj (col)* ruined; *Magen* upset. **eine ~e Sache** a mess.

verkörpern* *vt* to embody; *(Theat)* to play.

Verkörperung *f* embodiment.

verköstigen* *vt* to feed.

verkrachen* *vr (col)* **sich (mit jdm)** ~ to fall out (with sb).

verkracht *adj (col) Leben* ruined; *Typ* dead-beat *(col)*. **sie sind** ~ *(zerstritten)* they have fallen out with each other.

verkraften* *vt* to cope with; *(seelisch)* to come to terms with; *(finanziell, col: essen, trinken können)* to manage.

verkrampfen* *vr* to become cramped; *(Hände)* to clench up; *(Mensch)* to go tense. **verkrampft** *(fig)* tense.

verkriechen* *vr irreg* to creep away; *(fig)* to hide (oneself away). **sich unter den** *or* **dem Tisch** ~ to crawl *or* creep under the table.

verkrümeln* **1** *vr (col)* to disappear. **2** *vt* to crumble.

verkrümmen* *vtr* to bend; *(Rückgrat)* to become curved; *(Holz)* to warp; *(Baum)* to grow crooked.

Verkrümmung *f* bend *(gen* in*)*; *(von Fingern, Knochen, Bäumen)* crookedness *no pl*. ~ **der Wirbelsäule** curvature of the spine.

verkrüppeln* **1** *vt* to cripple. **2** *vi aux sein* to become crippled; *(Zehen, Füße)* to become deformed; *(Baum etc)* to grow stunted.

verkrusten* *vir (vi: aux sein)* to become encrusted.

verkümmern* *vi aux sein (Glied, Organ)* to atrophy; *(Pflanze)* to die; *(Talent)* to go to waste; *(Mensch)* to waste away. **emotionell/geistig** ~ to become emotionally/intellectually stunted.

verkünden* *vt* to announce; *Urteil* to pronounce; *Evangelium* to preach; *Gesetz* to promulgate.

Verkünder(in *f***)** *m* **- ein** ~ **des Evangeliums** a preacher of the gospel.

verkündigen* *vt* to proclaim; *(iro)* to announce; *Evangelium auch* to preach.

verkupfert *adj* copper-plated.

verkuppeln* *vt (pej)* to pair off. **jdn an jdn** ~ *(Zuhälter)* to procure sb for sb.

verkürzen* **1** *vt* to shorten; *Strecke, Wege etc auch* to cut; *Aufenthalt* to cut short; *Haltbarkeit* to reduce; *Leiden* to end. **sich** *(dat)* **die Zeit** ~ to pass the time; **verkürzte Arbeitszeit** shorter working hours. **2** *vr* to be shortened; *(Strecke, Zeit auch)* to be cut; *(Haltbarkeit)* to be reduced; *(Leiden)* to be ended; *(Urlaub, Aufenthalt)* to be cut short.

verladen* *vt irreg* to load.

Verlag *m* **-e** publisher. **in** *or* **bei welchem** ~ **ist das erschienen?** who published it?

verlagern* *vtr (lit, fig)* to shift.

Verlagerung *f* shift.

Verlags-: **~anstalt** *f* publishing firm; **~buchhandel** *m* publishing trade; **~wesen** *nt* publishing *no art*.

verlangen* **1** *vt* **(a)** *(fordern)* to demand; *(wollen)* to want; *Preis* to ask; *Qualifikationen, Erfahrung* to require. **(b)** *(erwarten)* to ask *(von* of*)*. **es wird von jdm verlangt, daß ...** it is required *or* expected of sb that ...; **das ist nicht zuviel verlangt** it's not asking too much. **(c)** *(fragen nach)* to ask for. **Sie werden am Telefon verlangt** you are wanted on the phone; **ich verlange den Geschäftsführer (zu sprechen)** I want to see the manager. **2** *vi* ~ **nach** to ask for; *(sich sehnen nach)* to long for.

Verlangen *nt* **-** *(nach* for*)* desire; *(Sehnsucht)* yearning, longing; *(Begierde)* craving; *(Forderung)* request. **auf** ~ on demand; **auf** ~ **der Eltern** at the parents' request.

verlängern* **1** *vt* to extend; *(zeitlich) Wartezeit, Schmerzen etc* to prolong; *Hosenbein, Ärmel etc* to lengthen; *Paß, Abonnement etc* to renew. **ein verlängertes Wochenende** a long weekend. **2** *vr* to be extended; *(zeitlich auch, Leiden etc)* to be prolonged.

Verlängerung *f* **(a)** *siehe vt* extension; prolongation; lengthening; renewal. **(b)** *(von Spielzeit)* extra time *(Brit)*, overtime *(US)*.

Verlängerungs-: **~kabel** *nt*, **~schnur** *f (Elec)* extension lead.

verlangsamen* *vtr* to slow down *or* up. **das Tempo** ~ to slow down.

Verlaß *m no pl* **auf ihn ist kein** ~ there's no relying on him.

verlassen[1]* *irreg* **1** *vt* to leave; *(fig: Mut etc)* to desert; *(im Stich lassen)* to desert, to abandon. **2** *vr* **sich auf jdn/etw** ~ to rely *or* depend on sb/sth; **darauf können Sie sich** ~ you can depend on that.

verlassen[2] *adj* deserted; *Auto* abandoned; *(öd)* desolate; *(einsam)* lonely. **einsam und** ~ so all alone.

verläßlich *adj* reliable.

Verlauf *m, pl* **Verläufe** course; *(Ausgang)* end. **im ~(e) des Tages** *etc* during the course of the day *etc*. **einen guten/schlechten** ~ **nehmen** to go well/badly.

verlaufen* *irreg* **1** *vi aux sein* **(a)** *(Tag, Prüfung)* to go; *(Kindheit)* to pass; *(Untersuchung)* to proceed. **(b)** *(sich erstrecken)* to run. **(c)** *(auseinanderfließen)* to run. **die Spur verlief im Sand** the track disappeared in the sand. **2** *vr* **(a)** *(sich verirren)* to get lost, to lose one's way. **(b)** *(Menschenmenge)* to disperse; *(Spur, Weg)* to disappear.

verlautbaren* *vti (form)* to announce.

Verlautbarung *f* announcement.

verlauten* **1** *vi* **etwas** ~ **lassen** to give an indication. **2** *vi impers* **es verlautet, daß ...** it is reported that ...; **wie aus Bonn verlautet** according to reports from Bonn.

verleben* *vt* to spend. **eine schöne Zeit** ~ to have a nice time.

verlegen[1]* **1** *vt* **(a)** *(an anderen Ort)* to transfer, to move. **(b)** *(verschieben)* to postpone *(auf +acc* until*)*; *(vorverlegen)* to bring forward *(auf +acc* to*)*. **(c)** *(an falschen Platz legen)* to mislay. **(d)** *Kabel, Fliesen etc* to lay. **(e)** *(drucken lassen)* to publish. **2** *vr* **sich auf etw** *(acc)* ~ to resort to sth; **sich aufs Unterrichten** ~ to take up teaching.

verlegen[2] *adj* embarrassed *no adv*. **um Worte** ~ **sein** to be at a loss for words.

Verlegenheit *f* **(a)** *no pl* embarrassment. **jdn in** ~ **bringen** to embarrass sb; **in** ~ **kommen** *or* **geraten** to get embarrassed. **(b)** *(unangenehme Lage)* embarrassing situation.

Verleger *m* **-** publisher.

verleiden* *vt* **jdm etw** ~ to put sb off sth.

Verleih *m* **-e** **(a)** *(Unternehmen)* rental *or* hire *(Brit)* company; *(Auto~)* car rental *or* hire *(Brit)*; *(Film~)* distributor(s). **(b)** *(das Verleihen)* renting (out), hiring (out) *(Brit)*; *(Film~)* distribution. **der** ~ **von Büchern** the lending of books.

verleihen* *vt irreg* **(a)** *(verborgen)* to lend *(an jdn* to sb*)*; *(gegen Gebühr)* to rent, to hire *(Brit)*. **(b)**

(zuerkennen) to award *(jdm* (to) sb*)*; *Titel, Ehrenbürgerrechte* to confer *(jdm* on sb*)*. **(c)** *(geben, verschaffen)* to give.
Verleiher *m* **-** hire *(Brit) or* rental firm; *(von Filmen)* distributor; *(von Büchern)* lender.
Verleihung *f siehe vt (a, b)* **(a)** lending; renting, hiring *(Brit)*. **(b)** award(ing), conferment.
verleimen* *vt* to glue.
verleiten* *vt* **(a)** *(verlocken)* to tempt; *(verführen)* to lead astray. **jdn dazu ~, die Schule zu schwänzen** to encourage sb to play truant. **(b)** *(veranlassen)* **jdn zu etw ~** to lead sb to sth.
verlernen* *vt* to forget. **das Tanzen ~** to forget how to dance.
verlesen* *irreg* **1** *vt* **(a)** *(vorlesen)* to read (out). **(b)** *Gemüse etc* to sort. **2** *vr* **ich habe mich wohl ~** I must have misread it.
verletzen* **1** *vt* **(a)** to injure; *(in Kampf etc, mit Kugel, Messer)* to wound; *(fig) jdn* to hurt, to offend; *jds Schönheitssinn etc* to offend. **(b)** *Gesetz* to break; *Pflicht, Rechte, Intimsphäre* to violate. **2** *vr* to injure oneself.
verletzend *adj Bemerkung* hurtful.
verletzlich *adj* vulnerable.
Verletzte(r) *mf decl as adj* injured person; *(Unfall~ auch)* casualty; *(bei Kampf)* wounded man. **die ~n** the injured/the wounded.
Verletzung *f siehe vt* **(a)** injuring; wounding; *(fig)* hurting, offending. **(b)** breaking; violation. **(c)** *(Wunde)* injury.
verleugnen* *vt* to deny; *Kind* to disown. **er läßt sich immer ~** he always pretends not to be there; **sich (selbst) ~** to deny one's own self.
verleumden* *vt* to slander; *(schriftlich)* to libel.
verleumderisch *adj siehe vt* slanderous; libellous *(Brit)*, libelous *(US)*.
Verleumdung *f (Bemerkung)* slander; *(Bericht)* libel.
verlieben* *vr* to fall in love *(in +acc* with*)*.
verliebt *adj Benehmen, Blicke, Worte* amorous. **(in jdn) ~ sein** to be in love (with sb).
verlieren *pret* **verlor,** *ptp* **verloren 1** *vti* to lose. **kein Wort über jdn/etw ~** not to say a word about sb/sth; **das/er hat hier nichts verloren** *(col)* that/he has no business to be here; **sie hat an Schönheit verloren** she has lost some of her beauty; **sie/die Altstadt** *etc* **hat sehr verloren** she/the old town *etc* is not what she/it *etc* used to be; **durch etw ~** to lose (something) by sth. **2** *vr (Menschen)* to lose each other; *(verschwinden)* to disappear; *(verhallen)* to fade away. **sich in etw** *(dat)* **~** to get lost in sth; *(fig)* to become absorbed in sth; *siehe* **verloren.**
Verlierer(in *f***)** *m* **-** loser
Verlies *nt* **-e** dungeon.
verloben* *vr* to get engaged *(mit* to*)*. **verlobt sein** to be engaged.
Verlobte(r) *mf decl as adj* **mein ~r** my fiancé; **meine ~** my fiancée; **die ~n** the engaged couple.
Verlobung *f* engagement.
Verlobungs- *in cpds* engagement.
verlocken* *vti* to entice, to tempt.
Verlockung *f* enticement.
verlogen *adj Mensch* lying; *Komplimente, Versprechungen* false; *Moral, Gesellschaft* hypocritical.
verlor *pret of* **verlieren.**
verloren 1 *ptp of* **verlieren. 2** *adj* lost; *(Cook) Eier* poached. **jdn/etw ~ geben** to give sb/sth up for lost; **auf ~em Posten kämpfen** *or* **stehen** to be fighting a losing battle.
verlorengehen *vi sep irreg aux sein* to be lost. **an ihm ist ein Sänger verlorengegangen** he would have made a good singer.
verlöschen* *vi aux sein* to go out; *(Inschrift, Farbe, Erinnerung)* to fade.
verlosen* *vt* to raffle (off).
Verlosung *f (das Verlosen)* raffling; *(Lotterie)* raffle.
verlöten* *vt* to solder.
verlottern* *vi aux sein (col) (Stadt, Restaurant)* to become run down; *(Garten)* to run wild; *(Mensch)* to go to the dogs; *(moralisch)* to go to the bad.
verlottert *adj (col) Stadt* run-down; *Garten* wild; *Mensch, Aussehen* scruffy; *(moralisch)* dissolute.
Verlust *m* **-e** loss. **mit ~ verkaufen** to sell at a loss.
Verlust-: **~anzeige** *f* "lost" notice; **~betrieb** *m* loss-maker; **v~bringend** *adj* loss-making; **v~bringend arbeiten** to work at a loss; **~geschäft** *nt* **das war ein ~geschäft** I/he *etc* made a loss; **~liste** *f (Mil)* casualty list; **v~reich** *adj* with heavy losses.
vermachen* *vt* **jdm etw ~** to leave *or* bequeath sth to sb.
Vermächtnis *nt* bequest, legacy; *(fig)* legacy.
vermählen* *(form)* **1** *vt* to marry. **frisch vermählt sein** to be newly married. **2** *vr* **sich (mit jdm) ~** to marry (sb).
Vermählte(r) *mf decl as adj* **die beiden ~n** the newly-weds; **die/der soeben ~** the bride/groom.
vermasseln* *vt (col)* to mess up *(col)*.
vermauern* *vt* to wall *or* brick up.
vermehren* **1** *vt* to increase; *(fortpflanzen)* to breed. **diese Fälle treten vermehrt auf** these cases are happening increasingly often. **2** *vr* to increase; *(sich fortpflanzen)* to reproduce, to breed; *(Bakterien)* to multiply; *(Pflanzen)* to propagate.
vermeidbar *adj* avoidable.
vermeiden* *vt irreg* to avoid. **~, daß etw passiert** to avoid letting sth happen; **es läßt sich nicht ~, daß ...** it is inevitable *or* unavoidable that ...
vermeidlich *adj* avoidable.
vermeintlich *adj attr* putative.
vermengen* *vt* to mix; *(fig col: durcheinanderbringen)* to mix up.
vermenschlichen* *vt* to humanize.
Vermerk *m* **-e** note, remark; *(im Kalender)* entry; *(in Paß)* observation; *(Stempel)* stamp.
vermerken* *vt* to make a note of; *(in Paß, Karte)* to record. **sich** *(dat)* **etw ~** to make a note of sth; **jdm etw übel ~** to take sth amiss.
vermessen[1]* *vt irreg* to measure; *Land, Gelände* to survey.
vermessen[2] *adj (anmaßend)* presumptuous; *(kühn) Unterfangen* bold.
Vermessung *f* measurement; *(von Land, Gelände)* survey.
Vermessungs-: **~amt** *nt* land survey(ing) office; **~ingenieur** *m* land surveyor.
vermiesen* *vt (col)* **jdm etw ~** to spoil sth for sb.
vermietbar *adj* rentable. **schlecht ~** difficult to rent.
vermieten* *vti* to rent (out), to let (out) *(Brit)*; *Boot, Auto* to rent (out), to hire (out) *(Brit)*. **Zimmer zu ~** room to let *(Brit) or* for rent.
Vermieter *m* **-** lessor; *(von Wohnung)* landlord.
Vermieterin *f* landlady.
vermindern* **1** *vt* to reduce, to decrease; *Ärger* to lessen; *Schmerzen* to ease. **2** *vr siehe vt* to decrease; to lessen; to ease.
Verminderung *f siehe vb* reduction *(gen* of*)*; lessening; easing.
verminen* *vt* to mine.
vermischen* **1** *vt* to mix; *Teesorten etc* to blend. **vermischte Schriften** miscellaneous writings. **2** *vr* to mix; *(Elemente, Klänge, Farben)* to blend.
vermissen* *vt* to miss. **vermißt werden** to be missing; **vermißt sein, als vermißt gemeldet sein** to be reported missing; **etw an jdm ~** to find sb lacking in sth; **wir haben dich bei der Party vermißt** we didn't see you at the party; **etw ~ lassen** to be lacking in sth.
Vermißten|anzeige *f* missing persons report.
Vermißte(r) *mf decl as adj* missing person.

vermitteln* **1** *vt* to arrange (*jdm* for sb); *Stelle, Privatschüler* to find (*jdm* for sb); *Aushilfskräfte, Lehrer etc* to place; *(Telec) Gespräch* to connect; *Lösung etc* to negotiate; *Gefühl, Bild, Idee* to convey, to give (*jdm* to sb); *Wissen* to impart (*jdm* to sb). **jdm etw ~** to get sth for sb. **2** *vi* to mediate. **~de Worte** conciliatory words.

Vermittler(in *f*) *m* **-** **(a)** mediator. **(b)** *(Comm)* agent; *(Fin, Heirats~)* broker; *(von Anleihe)* negotiator; *(Stellen~)* clerk in an employment agency.

Vermittlung *f* **(a)** *siehe vt* arranging; finding; placing; connection; negotiation; conveying; imparting. **durch seine freundliche ~** with his kind help. **(b)** *(Schlichtung)* mediation. **(c)** *(Stelle, Agentur)* agency; *(Heirats~)* marriage bureau; *(Wohnungs~)* estate agent's *(Brit)*, realtor *(US)*; *(Arbeits~)* employment agency. **(d)** *(Telec)* exchange; *(in Firma etc)* switchboard.

Vermittlungs-: **~gebühr** *f* commission; **~stelle** *f* agency; *(Telec)* (telephone) exchange; *(in Firma etc)* switchboard.

vermodern* *vi aux sein* to moulder, to decay.

vermögen *vt aux (geh)* **etw zu tun ~, (es) ~, etw zu tun** to be able to do sth; **Geduld vermag viel bei ihm** patience works wonders with him.

Vermögen *nt* **-** **(a)** *(Reichtum, viel Geld)* fortune. **~ haben** to have money. **(b)** *(Besitz)* property. **mein ganzes ~ besteht aus ...** my entire assets consist of ... **(c)** *(Können)* ability, capacity.

vermögend *adj (reich)* wealthy, well-off.

Vermögens-: **~abgabe** *f* property levy; **~bildung** *f* wealth creation; **~steuer** *f* wealth tax; **~verhältnisse** *pl* financial circumstances *pl*; **~werte** *pl* assets *pl*; **v~wirksam** *adj* profitable; **sein Geld v~wirksam anlegen** to invest one's money profitably; **v~wirksame Leistungen** employers' contributions to tax-deductible savings scheme.

vermummen* *vr* **(a)** to wrap up (warm). **(b)** *(sich verkleiden)* to disguise.

Vermummung *f* disguise.

vermurksen* *vt (col)* **etw ~** to make a mess of sth.

vermuten* *vt* to suspect. **ich vermute es nur** that's only an assumption; **wir haben ihn dort nicht vermutet** we didn't expect to find/see *etc* him there; **es ist zu ~, daß ...** it may be supposed that ...

vermutlich **1** *adj attr* presumable; *Täter* suspected. **2** *adv* presumably.

Vermutung *f (Annahme)* supposition, assumption; *(Verdacht)* suspicion. **die ~ liegt nahe, daß ...** there are grounds for assuming that ...; **meine ~en waren doch richtig** my guess was right.

vernachlässigen* **1** *vt* to neglect; *(Schicksal) jdn* to be unkind to. **das können wir ~** *(nicht berücksichtigen)* we can ignore that. **2** *vr* to neglect one's appearance.

Vernachlässigung *f* neglect.

vernageln* *vt* to nail up. **etw mit Brettern ~** to board sth up.

vernähen* *vt Wunde, Saum* to stitch (up).

vernarben* *vi aux sein* to heal *or* close (up).

vernarren* *vr (col)* **sich in jdn/etw ~** to fall for sb/sth; **in jdn/etw vernarrt sein** to be crazy about sb/sth *(col)*.

vernaschen* *vt Süßigkeiten* to eat up; *Geld* to spend on sweets *(Brit) or* candy *(US)*; *(col) Mädchen, Mann* to make it with *(col)*.

vernebeln* *vt (Mil)* to cover with a smoke screen; *(fig) Tatsachen* to obscure; *(col) Zimmer* to fug up.

vernehmbar *adj (hörbar)* audible.

vernehmen* *vt irreg* **(a)** *(hören, erfahren)* to hear. **(b)** *(Jur) Zeugen, Angeklagte* to examine; *(Polizei)* to question.

Vernehmen *nt*: **dem ~ nach** from what I/we *etc* hear.

vernehmlich *adj* clear, audible.

Vernehmung *f (Jur: von Zeugen, Angeklagten)* examination; *(durch Polizei)* questioning.

verneigen* *vr* to bow. **sich vor jdm/etw ~** *(lit)* to bow to sb/sth; *(fig)* to bow down before sb/sth.

verneinen* *vti Frage* to answer in the negative; *(leugnen) Tatsache, Existenz Gottes etc* to deny; *These* to dispute; *(Gram, Logik)* to negate. **die verneinte Form** the negative (form).

verneinend *adj (auch Gram)* negative.

Verneinung *f (Leugnung)* denial; *(von These etc)* disputing; *(Gram, Philos)* negation; *(verneinte Form)* negative.

vernichten* *vt (lit, fig)* to destroy.

vernichtend *adj* devastating; *Niederlage* crushing. **jdn ~ schlagen** *(Mil, Sport)* to annihilate sb.

Vernichtung *f* destruction.

Vernichtungs-: **~krieg** *m* war of extermination; **~lager** *nt* extermination camp; **~schlag** *m* devastating blow; **~waffe** *f* doomsday weapon.

verniedlichen* *vt* to trivialize.

vernieten* *vt* to rivet.

Vernunft *f no pl* reason. **zur ~ kommen** to come to one's senses; **~ annehmen** to see reason; **etw mit/ohne ~ tun** to do sth sensibly/foolishly.

Vernunft-: **v~begabt** *adj* rational; **v~gemäß** *adv* rationally; **~glaube(n)** *m* rationalism; **~gründe** *pl* rational grounds *pl*; **~heirat** *f* marriage of convenience.

vernünftig **1** *adj* sensible; *(logisch denkend)* rational; *(col: ordentlich, anständig)* decent; *Vorschlag* reasonable. **2** *adv siehe adj* sensibly; rationally; decently; reasonably; *(tüchtig)* properly *(col)*.

Vernunft-: **v~los** *adj* irrational; **~mensch** *m* rational person; **v~widrig** *adj* irrational.

ver\|öffentlichen* *vti* to publish.

Ver\|öffentlichung *f* publication.

ver\|ordnen* *vt* to prescribe (*jdm etw* sth for sb).

Ver\|ordnung *f* **(a)** *(Med)* prescription. **(b)** *(Verfügung)* decree.

verpachten* *vt* to lease, to rent out (*an +acc* to).

Verpachtung *f* lease.

verpacken* *vt* to pack; *(verbrauchergerecht)* to package; *(einwickeln)* to wrap.

Verpackung *f siehe vt* packing; packaging; wrapping.

verpassen* *vt* **(a)** *(versäumen)* to miss. **(b)** *(col: zuteilen)* **jdm etw ~** to give sb sth; *(aufzwingen)* to make sb have sth; **jdm eine Ohrfeige ~** to clout sb one *(col)*.

verpatzen* *vt (col)* to spoil; *Examen* to make a mess of. **sich** *(dat)* **etw ~** to spoil sth/mess sth up *(col)*.

verpennen* *(col)* **1** *vt (verpassen)* to miss by oversleeping; *(schlafend verbringen) Tag, Morgen etc* to sleep through. **2** *vir* to oversleep.

verpesten* *vt* to pollute.

verpetzen* *vt (col)* to tell on (*bei* to).

verpfänden* *vt* to pawn; *(Jur)* to mortgage.

verpfeifen* *vt irreg (col)* to grass on (*bei* to) *(col)*.

verpflanzen* *vt (lit, fig)* to transplant; *Haut* to graft.

verpflegen* **1** *vt* to feed. **2** *vr* **sich (selbst) ~** to feed oneself; *(selbst kochen)* to cook for oneself.

Verpflegung *f* **(a)** *(das Verpflegen)* catering; *(Mil)* rationing. **(b)** *(Essen)* food; *(Mil)* rations *pl*.

verpflichten* **1** *vt* **(a)** to oblige; *(vertraglich)* to commit. **verpflichtet sein, etw zu tun, zu etw verpflichtet sein** to be obliged/committed to do sth; **jdm verpflichtet sein** to be under an obligation to sb; **~d** *Zusage* binding. **(b)** *(einstellen)* to engage; *Sportler* to sign on. **2** *vi* to involve a commitment. **das verpflichtet zu nichts** there's no obligation involved. **3** *vr* to commit oneself. **sich zu etw ~** to commit oneself to doing sth.

Verpflichtung *f* **(a)** obligation (*zu etw* to do sth); *(Pflicht auch, finanzielle ~)* commitment (*zu etw*

to do sth); *(Aufgabe)* duty. **(b)** *(Einstellung)* engaging; *(von Sportlern)* signing on.
verpfuschen* *vt (col)* to make a mess of.
verplanen* **1** *vt Zeit* to book up; *Geld* to budget. **jdn** ~ *(col)* to fill up all sb's spare time (for him/her). **2** *vr* to plan badly; *(falsch berechnen)* to miscalculate.
verplappern* *vr (col)* to open one's big mouth *(col)*.
verplempern* *vt (col)* to waste, to fritter away.
verpönt *adj* frowned upon *(bei* by*)*.
verprassen* *vt* to blow *(col) (für* on*)*.
verprellen* *vt* to put off, to intimidate.
verprügeln* *vt* to thrash, to beat up.
verpuffen* *vi aux sein* to (go) pop; *(fig)* to fall flat.
Verputz *m no pl* plaster; *(Rauhputz)* roughcast.
verputzen* *vt* **(a)** to plaster; *(mit Rauhputz)* to roughcast. **(b)** *(col: aufessen)* to polish off *(col)*.
verqualmen* *vt Zimmer* to fill with smoke.
verrammeln* *vt* to barricade.
verramschen* *vt (col)* to sell off cheap.
Verrat *m no pl* betrayal *(an +dat* of*)*; *(Jur)* treason *(an +dat* against*)*. ~ **an jdm üben** to betray sb.
verraten* *irreg* **1** *vt* to betray; *(bekanntgeben, ausplaudern)* to tell; *(fig: erkennen lassen)* to show. **nichts** ~! don't say a word!; **er hat es** ~ he let it out. **2** *vr* to give oneself away.
Verräter(in *f*) *m* - traitor *(+gen* to*)*.
verräterisch *adj* treacherous; *(Jur)* treasonable; *Blick etc* telltale *attr*.
verrauchen* **1** *vi aux sein (fig: Zorn)* to blow over. **2** *vt Zimmer* to fill with smoke; *Geld* to spend on smoking.
verräuchern* *vt* to fill with smoke.
verrechnen* **1** *vt (begleichen)* to settle; *Scheck* to clear; *Gutschein* to redeem. **etw mit etw** ~ *(gegeneinander aufrechnen)* to balance sth with sth. **2** *vr* to miscalculate; *(col: sich täuschen)* to be mistaken. **sich um eine Mark** ~ to be out by one mark.
Verrechnungsscheck *m* crossed *(Brit) or* non negotiable cheque *(Brit) or* check *(US)*.
verrecken* *vi aux sein (col!)* to die; *(elend sterben)* to die a wretched death. **er ist elend verreckt** he died like a dog *(col)*.
verregnet *adj* rainy, wet.
verreiben* *vt irreg* to rub *(auf +dat* into*)*.
verreisen* *vi aux sein* to go away (on a trip). **er ist geschäftlich verreist** he's away on business.
verreißen* *vt irreg (kritisieren)* to tear to pieces.
verrenken* **1** *vt* to dislocate; *Hals* to crick. **2** *vr* to contort oneself.
verrennen* *vr irreg* **sich in etw** *(acc)* ~ to get stuck on sth.
verrichten* *vt Arbeit* to carry out.
verriegeln* *vt* to bolt.
verringern* **1** *vt* to reduce. **2** *vr* to decrease; *(Qualität, Leistungen)* to deteriorate.
Verringerung *f siehe vb* reduction; decrease; deterioration.
verrinnen* *vi irreg aux sein (Wasser)* to trickle away *(in +dat* into*)*; *(Zeit)* to elapse.
Verriß *m* **-sse** slating review.
verrohen* *vi aux sein* to become brutalized.
Verrohung *f* brutalization.
verrosten* *vi aux sein* to rust. **verrostet** rusty.
verrotten* *vi aux sein* to rot; *(organisch)* to decompose.
verrucht *adj* despicable; *(verrufen)* disreputable.
verrücken* *vt* to move.
verrückt *adj* mad. ~ **auf** *(+acc) or* **nach** *(col)* crazy *or* mad about *(col)*; **wie** ~ like mad *or* crazy *(col)*; **die Leute kamen wie** ~ *(col)* loads of people came *(col)*; **jdn** ~ **machen** *(col)* to drive sb crazy *or* mad; ~ **werden** *(col)* to go crazy; ~ **spielen** *(col)* to play up *(col)*.
Verrückte(r) *mf decl as adj (col)* lunatic.
Verruf *m no pl* **in** ~ **kommen** to fall into disrepute.
verrufen *adj* disreputable.
verrühren* *vt* to mix, to stir.
verrußen* *vi aux sein* to get sooty.
verrutschen* *vi aux sein* to slip.
Vers [fɛrs] *m* **-e** verse *(auch Bibl)*; *(Zeile)* line.
versachlichen* *vt* to objectify.
versacken* *vi aux sein* **(a)** *(lit)* to sink. **(b)** *(fig col) (herunterkommen)* to go downhill; *(lange zechen)* to get involved in a booze-up *(col)*.
versagen* **1** *vt* **jdm/sich etw** ~ to deny sb/oneself sth; *(verweigern)* to refuse sb sth. **2** *vi* to fail. **die Beine/Nerven** *etc* **versagten ihm** his legs/nerves *etc* gave way.
Versagen *nt no pl* failure; *(von Maschine)* breakdown. **menschliches** ~ human error.
Versager *m* - failure, flop *(col)*.
versalzen[1]* *vt irreg* to put too much salt in/on; *(col: verderben)* to spoil.
versalzen[2] *adj Essen* too salty.
versammeln* **1** *vt* to assemble. **2** *vr* to assemble; *(Parliament)* to sit; *(Ausschuß, Verein)* to meet.
Versammlung *f* meeting, assembly.
Versammlungs-: ~**freiheit** *f* freedom of assembly; ~**lokal** *nt* meeting place.
Versand *m no pl* dispatch; *(das Vertreiben)* distribution.
Versand-: ~**abteilung** *f* dispatch department; ~**artikel** *m* article for dispatch; ~**bahnhof** *m* dispatch station; **v~bereit** *adj* ready for dispatch.
versanden* *vi aux sein* to silt (up); *(fig)* to peter out.
Versand-: ~**gut** *nt* goods *pl* for dispatch; ~**handel** *m* mail order business; ~**haus** *nt* mail order firm; ~**kosten** *pl* transport(ation) costs *pl*.
Versandweg *m* **auf dem** ~ by mail order.
versauen* *vt (col)* to mess up *(col)*.
versaufen* *irreg (col)* **1** *vt Geld* to spend on booze *(col)*. **2** *vi aux sein (ertrinken)* to drown.
versäumen* *vt* to miss; *Zeit* to lose; *Pflicht* to neglect. **(es)** ~**, etw zu tun** to fail to do sth; **das Versäumte** what one has missed; **die versäumte Zeit aufholen** to make up for lost time.
Versäumnis *nt (Fehler)* failing; *(Unterlassung)* omission.
verschachern* *vt* to sell off.
verschachtelt *adj Satz* encapsulated, complex.
verschaffen 1 *vt* **jdm etw** ~ to provide sb with sth; *Erleichterung, Genugtuung* to give sb sth; *Respekt* to earn sb sth. **2** *vr* **sich** *(dat)* **etw** ~ to obtain sth; *Ansehen, Vorteil* to gain sth; *Ruhe, Respekt* to get sth; **sich mit Gewalt Zutritt** ~ to force an entry.
verschalen* *vt Wand* to panel; *Heizung etc* to box in.
verschämt *adj* coy.
verschandeln* *vt* to ruin.
verschanzen* **1** *vt (Mil)* to fortify. **2** *vr (Mil, fig)* to entrench oneself *(hinter+dat* behind*)*; *(sich verbarrikadieren)* to barricade oneself in *(in etw (dat)* sth*)*.
verschärfen* **1** *vt (erhöhen) Tempo* to increase; *Gegensätze* to intensify; *(verschlimmern) Lage* to aggravate; *(strenger machen) Kontrollen, Gesetze* to tighten up. **2** *vr siehe vt* to increase; to intensify; to become aggravated; to become tighter.
verscharren* *vt* to bury.
verschätzen* *vr* to miscalculate *(in etw (dat)* sth*)*.
verschenken* *vt (lit, fig)* to give away.
verscherzen* *vt* **sich** *(dat)* **etw** ~ to forfeit sth; **es sich** *(dat)* **mit jdm** ~ to spoil things with sb.
verscheuchen* *vt* to scare off; *(fig) Sorgen etc* to drive away.
verschicken* *vt (versenden)* to send out; *(zur Kur etc)* to send away; *(deportieren)* to deport.
verschieben* *irreg* **1** *vt* **(a)** *(verrücken)* to move, to shift; *(Rail)* to shunt. **(b)** *(auf später)* to postpone *(um* for, *auf +acc* until*)*. **(c)** *(col) Waren,*

Devisen to traffic in. **2** *vr* to shift; *(zeitlich)* to be postponed.
Verschiebung *f (zeitlich)* postponement.
verschieden 1 *adj* **(a)** *(unterschiedlich)* different. **die ~sten Sorten** many different kinds; **das ist ganz ~** *(wird ~ gehandhabt)* that varies, that just depends. **(b)** *attr (mehrere, einige)* various, several. **(c)** *(substantivisch)* **~e** *pl* various *or* several people; **~es** several things; **V~es** *(in Zeitung, Liste)* miscellaneous. **2** *adv* differently. **die Häuser sind ~ hoch** the houses vary in height.
veschieden|artig *adj* different; *(mannigfaltig)* various, diverse. **die ~sten Dinge** all sorts of things.
Verschiedenheit *f* difference *(gen* of, in*)*; *(Unähnlichkeit)* dissimilarity.
verschießen* *vt irreg Munition* to use up.
verschiffen* *vt* to ship; *Sträfling* to transport.
verschimmeln* *vi aux sein (Nahrungsmittel)* to go mouldy *(Brit) or* moldy *(US)*; *(Leder, Papier etc)* to go mildewy. **verschimmelt** *(lit)* mouldy *(Brit)*, moldy *(US)*; mildewy.
verschlafen* *irreg* **1** *vir* to oversleep. **2** *vt Termin* to miss by oversleeping; *Tag* to sleep through. **3** *adj* sleepy; *(trottelig)* dozy *(col)*.
Verschlag *m* **¨-e** *(Schuppen)* shed; *(für Kaninchen)* hutch.
verschlagen[1]* *vt irreg* **(a) etw mit Brettern ~** to board sth up; **etw mit Nägeln ~** to nail sth up. **(b)** *Atem* to take away. **das hat mir die Sprache ~** it left me speechless. **(c)** *(geraten lassen)* to bring. **an einen Ort ~ werden** to end up somewhere. **(d)** *(Sport) Ball* to mishit. **(e)** *(verblättern) Seite, Stelle* to lose.
verschlagen[2] *adj Mensch, Blick etc* sly.
Verschlagenheit *f* slyness.
verschlammen* *vi aux sein* to silt up.
verschlampen* *(col)* **1** *vt (verlieren)* to lose *(col)*. **2** *vi aux sein (Mensch)* to go to seed *(col)*.
verschlechtern* **1** *vt* to make worse. **2** *vr* to get worse; *(gehaltlich)* to take a lower-paid job. **sich beruflich ~** to take a worse job.
Verschlechterung *f* worsening.
verschleiern* **1** *vt* to veil; *(fig)* to disguise; *Blick* to blur. **2** *vr (Frau)* to veil oneself; *(Himmel)* to become hazy; *(Blick)* to become blurred.
Verschleiß *m* **-e** *(lit, fig)* wear and tear; *(Verbrauch)* consumption. **ein ~ deiner Kräfte** a drain on your strength.
verschleißen *pret* **verschliß,** *ptp* **verschlissen 1** *vt* to wear out; *(verbrauchen)* to use up. **2** *vi aux sein* to wear out. **3** *vr* to wear out; *(Menschen)* to wear oneself out.
verschleppen* *vt* **(a)** *(entführen) jdn* to abduct; *Kunstschätze etc* to carry off. **(b)** *(verbreiten) Seuche* to spread. **(c)** *(hinauszögern)* to protract; *(Pol) Gesetzesänderung etc* to delay.
verschleudern* *vt (Comm)* to dump; *(vergeuden)* to squander.
verschließen* *irreg* **1** *vt* **(a)** *(abschließen)* to lock up; *(fig)* to close, to shut; *(versperren)* to bar; *(mit Riegel)* to bolt. **(b)** *(zumachen)* to close; *(mit Pfropfen) Flasche* to cork. **die Augen (vor etw** *dat***) ~** to shut one's eyes (to sth). **2** *vr (Reize, Sprache, Möglichkeit)* to be closed *(dat* to*)*; *(Mensch: reserviert sein)* to shut oneself off *(dat* from*)*. **sich einer Sache** *(dat) or* **gegen etw ~** to close one's mind to sth.
verschlimmbessern *vt insep (hum)* to make worse.
verschlimmern* *vtr* to worsen.
verschlingen* *irreg* **1** *vt* **(a)** *(lit, fig)* to devour; *(Wellen etc, verbrauchen)* to swallow up. **(b)** *(verknoten)* to entwine; *Arme* to fold. **ein verschlungener Pfad** a winding path. **2** *vr* to become entwined.
verschliß *pret of* **verschleißen.**
verschlissen 1 *ptp of* **verschleißen. 2** *adj* worn (out).
verschlossen *adj* closed; *(fig: unzugänglich)* reserved. **etw bleibt jdm ~** sth is a closed book to sb; **wir standen vor ~er Tür** we were left standing on the doorstep.
Verschlossenheit *f (von Mensch)* reserve.
verschlucken* **1** *vt* to swallow; *Geld* to swallow up; *Schall* to deaden. **2** *vr* to swallow the wrong way; *(fig)* to splutter.
Verschluß *m* **¨-sse (a)** *(Schloß)* lock; *(luft-, wasserdicht, für Zoll)* seal; *(Deckel, Klappe)* top, lid; *(Pfropfen, Stöpsel)* stopper; *(an Kleidung)* fastener. **etw unter ~ halten** to keep sth under lock and key. **(b)** *(Phot)* shutter.
verschlüsseln* *vt* to (put into) code, to encode.
verschmachten* *vi aux sein* to languish *(vor +dat* for*)*. **(vor Durst/Hitze) ~** *(col)* to be dying of thirst/heat *(col)*.
verschmähen* *vt* to spurn.
verschmälern* *vtr* to narrow.
verschmelzen* *irreg* **1** *vi aux sein* to melt together; *(Metalle)* to fuse; *(Farben)* to blend; *(fig)* to blend *(zu* into*)*. **2** *vt Metalle* to fuse; *Farben* to blend; *(fig)* to unify *(zu* into*)*.
verschmerzen* *vt* to get over.
verschmieren* **1** *vt* **(a)** *Salbe, Schmiere* to spread *(in +dat* over*)*. **(b)** *(verputzen) Löcher* to fill in. **(c)** *(verwischen) Fenster, Gesicht* to smear; *Geschriebenes, Schminke* to smudge. **2** *vi* to smudge.
verschmiert *adj Hände* smeary; *Schminke* smudged.
verschmitzt *adj* mischievous.
verschmutzen* **1** *vt* to dirty; *Umwelt* to pollute; *Gewehr, Zündkerze* to foul; *Fahrbahn* to make muddy; *(Hund) Bürgersteig* to foul. **2** *vi aux sein* to get dirty; *(Umwelt)* to become polluted.
verschmutzt *adj* dirty, soiled; *Luft etc* polluted.
verschnaufen* *vir (col)* to have a breather.
verschneiden* *vt irreg* **(a)** *Rum etc* to blend. **(b)** *Flügel, Hecke* to clip. **(c)** *(falsch schneiden)* to cut wrongly. **(d)** *Tiere* to castrate.
verschneit *adj* snow-covered. **tief ~** thick with snow.
Verschnitt *m* **(a)** *(von Rum etc)* blend. **(b)** *(Abfall)* clippings *pl*.
verschnörkelt *adj* ornate.
verschnupft *adj (col)* **~ sein** to have a cold; *(beleidigt)* to be peeved *(col)*.
verschnüren* *vt* to tie up.
verschollen *adj* missing; *Literaturwerk* forgotten.
verschonen* *vt* to spare *(jdn von etw* sb sth*)*. **von etw verschont bleiben** to escape sth.
verschöne(r)n* *vt* to improve (the appearance of); *Wohnung* to brighten up.
Verschönerung *f siehe vt* improvement; brightening up.
verschränken* *vt* to cross over; *Arme* to fold; *Beine* to cross; *Hände* to clasp.
verschrauben* *vt* to screw together.
verschreckt *adj* frightened, scared.
verschreiben* *irreg* **1** *vt* **(a)** *(verordnen)* to prescribe. **(b)** *Papier* to use up. **2** *vr* **(a)** *(falsch schreiben)* to make a slip (of the pen). **(b) sich einer Sache** *(dat)* **~** to devote oneself to sth.
verschrie(e)n *adj* notorious.
verschroben *adj* eccentric, odd.
verschrotten* *vt* to scrap.
verschrumpeln* *vi aux sein* to shrivel.
verschüchtern* *vt* intimidate.
verschulden* **1** *vt* to be to blame for. **2** *vi aux sein (in Schulden geraten)* to get into debt. **verschuldet sein** to be in debt.
Verschulden *nt no pl* fault. **ohne sein/mein ~** through no fault of his/my own.
verschütten* *vt* **(a)** *Flüssigkeit* to spill. **(b)** *(zuschütten) Brunnen* to fill in. **(c) verschüttet wer-**

den *(Mensch)* to be buried (alive); *(fig)* to be submerged.
verschwägert *adj* related (by marriage) *(mit* to*)*.
verschweigen* *vt irreg Tatsachen, Wahrheit etc* to conceal *(jdm etw* sth from sb*)*.
verschweißen* *vt* to weld together.
verschwenden* *vt* to waste *(auf or an +acc* on*)*.
Verschwender(in *f*) *m* - spendthrift.
verschwenderisch *adj* wasteful; *Leben* extravagant; *(üppig)* lavish.
Verschwendung *f* waste.
Verschwendungs-: **~sucht** *f no pl* extravagance; **v~süchtig** *adj* extravagant.
verschwiegen *adj Mensch* discreet; *Ort* secluded.
Verschwiegenheit *f no pl (von Mensch)* discretion. **zur ~ verpflichtet** bound to secrecy.
verschwimmen* *vi irreg aux sein* to become blurred. **ineinander ~** to merge into one another; *siehe* **verschwommen.**
verschwinden* *vi irreg aux sein* to disappear, to vanish. **verschwinde!** clear off! *(col)*; **neben jdm/etw ~** *(in bezug auf Größe)* to look minute beside sb/sth.
Verschwinden *nt no pl* disappearance.
verschwindend *adj Anzahl, Menge* insignificant. **~ wenig** very, very few; **~ klein** minute.
verschwistert *adj* **(miteinander) ~ sein** to be brother and sister; *(Brüder)* to be brothers; *(Schwestern)* to be sisters; *(Städte)* to be twinned.
verschwitzen* *vt* **(a)** *Kleidung* to make sweaty. **(b)** *(fig col)* to forget.
verschwitzt *adj* sweat-stained; *Mensch* sweaty.
verschwommen *adj Foto, Umrisse* blurred; *Berge* hazy; *Begriffe, Erinnerung* vague.
verschworen *adj Gesellschaft* sworn.
verschwören* *vr irreg* **(a)** to conspire, to plot *(mit* with, *gegen* against*)*. **sich zu etw ~** to plot sth; **alles hat sich gegen mich verschworen** *(fig)* there's a conspiracy against me. **(b) sich einer Sache** *(dat)* **~** to give oneself over to sth.
Verschwörer(in *f*) *m* - conspirator.
Verschwörung *f* conspiracy, plot.
verschwunden *adj* missing.
versehen* *irreg* **1** *vt* **(a)** *Amt, Stelle* to hold; *Dienst* to perform; *(sich kümmern um)* to look after. **(b)** *(ausstatten)* **jdn mit etw ~** to provide *or* supply sb with sth; **etw mit etw ~** to put sth on/in sth; *(montieren)* to fit sth with sth; **mit etw ~ sein** to have sth; **jdn mit einer Vollmacht ~** to invest sb with full powers. **2** *vr* **(a)** *(sich irren)* to make a mistake. **(b) sich mit etw ~** *(sich versorgen)* to provide oneself with sth; *(sich ausstatten)* to equip oneself with sth. **(c) ehe man sich's versieht** before you know what's happening.
Versehen *nt* - mistake, error; *(Unachtsamkeit)* oversight. **aus ~** by mistake, inadvertently.
versehentlich 1 *adj attr* inadvertent; *(irrtümlich)* erroneous. **2** *adv* inadvertently, by mistake.
Versehrte(r) *mf decl as adj* disabled person.
verselbständigen* *vr* to become independent.
versenden* *vt irreg or reg* to send.
versengen* *vt* **(a)** to scorch; *(Feuer)* to singe. **(b)** *(col: verprügeln)* to wallop *(col)*.
versenken* **1** *vt* **(a)** *Schiff etc* to sink; *Leiche, Sarg* to lower; *das eigene Schiff* to scuttle. **(b)** *Schraube* to countersink; *Tischplatte* to fold away. **2** *vr* **sich in etw** *(acc)* **~** to become immersed in sth.
Versenkung *f* **(a)** *siehe vt (a)* sinking; lowering; scuttling. **(b)** *(das Sichversenken)* immersion. **innere/mystische ~** inner/mystic contemplation. **(c) in der ~ verschwinden** *(col)* to vanish; **aus der ~ auftauchen** to re-appear.
versessen *adj* **auf etw** *(acc)* **~ sein** to be very keen on sth.
versetzen* **1** *vt* **(a)** to move, to shift; *(nicht geradlinig anordnen)* to stagger; *(beruflich)* to transfer, to move. **(b)** *(Sch: in höhere Klasse)* to move up. **(c)** *(col) (verkaufen)* to flog *(Brit col)*, to sell; *(verpfänden)* to pawn. **(d)** *(col: nicht erscheinen)* **jdn ~** to stand sb up *(col)*. **(e) etw in Bewegung ~** to set sth in motion; **jdn in Wut/in fröhliche Stimmung ~** to send sb into a rage/to put sb in a cheerful mood; **jdn in Angst ~** to frighten sb; **jdn in die Lage ~, etw zu tun** to put sb in a position to do sth; **jdn in seine Jugend ~** to take sb back to his/her youth. **(f)** *Stoß, Schlag, Tritt etc* to give. **jdm einen Stich ~** *(fig)* to cut sb to the quick, to wound sb (deeply).
2 *vr (sich an andere Stelle setzen)* to move (to another place). **sich in jdn/in jds Lage ~** to put oneself in sb's place; **sich in eine frühere Zeit** *etc* **~** to imagine oneself back in an earlier period.
Versetzung *f* **(a)** *(beruflich)* transfer. **(b)** *(Sch)* moving up. **seine ~ ist gefährdet** he's in danger of having to stay down. **(c)** *(nicht geradlinige Anordnung)* staggering. **(d)** *(Vermischung)* mixing.
verseuchen* *vt* to contaminate.
Versfuß *m (Poet)* (metrical) foot.
Versicherer *m* - insurer; *(bei Schiffen)* underwriter.
versichern* **1** *vt* **(a)** *(beteuern)* **jdm ~, daß ...** to assure sb that ...; **jdm etw ~, jdn einer Sache** *(gen)* **~** to assure sb of sth; **seien Sie versichert, daß ...** rest assured that ... **(b)** *(gegen Diebstahl etc)* to insure. **2** *vr* **(a)** to insure oneself *(mit* for*)*. **(b)** *(sich vergewissern)* to make sure *or* certain.
Versicherung *f siehe vt* **(a)** assurance. **(b)** insurance; *(~sgesellschaft)* insurance company.
Versicherungs-: **~beitrag** *m* insurance premium; *(bei staatlicher Versicherung etc)* insurance contribution; **~betrug** *m* insurance fraud; **~dauer** *f* period of insurance; **~gesellschaft** *f* insurance company; **~nehmer** *m (form)* policy holder; **~pflicht** *f* compulsory insurance; **~police** *f* insurance policy; **~prämie** *f* insurance premium; **~schutz** *m* insurance cover; **~summe** *f* sum insured; **~vertreter** *m* insurance agent; **~wert** *m* insurance value; **~wesen** *nt* insurance (business).
versickern* *vi aux sein* to seep away; *(fig: Interesse etc)* to peter out.
versiegeln* *vt* to seal.
versiegen* *vi aux sein (lit, fig)* to dry up; *(Interesse)* to peter out; *(Humor, Kräfte)* to fail.
versiert [vɛr-] *adj* **in etw** *(dat)* **~ sein** to be experienced *or (in bezug auf Wissen)* well versed in sth.
versilbern* *vt* to silver(-plate).
versinken* *vi irreg aux sein* to sink. **ich hätte im Boden/vor Scham ~ mögen** I wished the ground would swallow me up; **in etw** *(acc)* **~** *(fig) in Trauer, Melancholie* to sink into sth; *in Anblick, Gedanken, Musik* to lose oneself in sth.
versinnbildlichen* *vt* to symbolize.
Version [vɛr'zioːn] *f* version.
versklaven* [fɛɐ'sklaːvn] *vt (lit, fig)* to enslave.
Vers-: **~lehre** *f* study of verse; **~maß** *nt* metre *(Brit)*, meter *(US)*.
versohlen* *vt (col)* to belt *(col)*.
versöhnen* **1** *vt* to reconcile; *(besänftigen) jdn, Götter* to placate. **~de Worte** conciliatory words. **2** *vr* to be(come) reconciled; *(Streitende)* to make it up. **sich mit etw ~** to reconcile oneself to sth.
versöhnlich *adj Mensch* conciliatory; *(nichts nachtragend)* forgiving.
Versöhnung *f* reconciliation; *(Beschwichtigung)* appeasement.
versonnen *adj Gesichtsausdruck* pensive, thoughtful; *(träumerisch) Blick* dreamy.
versorgen* **1** *vt* **(a)** *(sich kümmern um)* to look after. **(b)** *(beliefern)* to supply. **(c)** *(unterhalten) Familie* to provide for, to support. **2** *vr* **sich mit etw ~** to provide oneself with sth; **sich selbst ~** to look after oneself.

Versorger(in *f*) *m* - **(a)** *(Ernährer)* provider, breadwinner. **(b)** *(Belieferer)* supplier.

Versorgung *f* **(a)** *(Pflege)* care. **(b) die ~ dieses Gebiets mit Bussen** the bus service for this district. **(c)** *(Unterhalt)* **die ~ im Alter** providing for one's old age.

Versorgungs-: v~berechtigt *adj* entitled to maintenance; *(durch Staat)* entitled to benefit; **~betrieb** *m* public utility; **~güter** *pl* supplies *pl*; **~netz** *nt (Wasser~, Gas~ etc)* (supply) grid; *(von Waren)* supply network.

verspachteln* *vt Risse* to fill in.

verspannen* **1** *vt* to brace. **2** *vr (Muskeln)* to tense up.

verspäten* *vr (zu spät kommen)* to be late.

verspätet *adj Zug, Flugzeug* delayed, late *pred; Ankunft, Frühling, Entwicklung* late; *Glückwunsch* belated.

Verspätung *f (von Verkehrsmitteln)* delay; *(von Mensch)* late arrival; *(von Glückwunsch etc)* belatedness. **(10 Minuten) ~ haben** to be (10 minutes) late; **eine zweistündige ~** a delay of two hours; **die ~ aufholen** to catch up lost time; **mit zwanzig Minuten ~** twenty minutes late.

verspeisen* *vt (geh)* to consume.

versperren* *vt* to block.

verspielen* **1** *vt (lit, fig) Geld, Chancen* to gamble away; *Vorteile* to bargain away. **2** *vi (fig)* **jetzt hast du (bei ihr) verspielt** you've had it now (with her) *(col)*.

verspielt *adj Kind, Katze* playful; *Frisur, Muster* pretty.

versponnen *adj* airy-fairy.

verspotten* *vt* to mock.

versprechen* *irreg* **1** *vt* to promise *(jdm etw* sb sth). **nichts Gutes ~** to be ominous. **2** *vr* **(a) sich** *(dat)* **viel/wenig von jdm/etw ~** to have high hopes/no great hopes of sb/sth. **(b)** *(etwas Nicht-Gemeintes sagen)* to make a slip of the tongue.

Versprechen *nt* - promise.

Versprecher *m* - *(col)* slip (of the tongue).

Versprechung *f* promise.

verspritzen* *vt* **(a)** to spray; *(versprengen)* to sprinkle; *(zuspritzen) Fugen* to seal by injection moulding *(Brit) or* molding *(US)*. **(b)** *(verkleckern) Farbe, Kleidung* to sp(l)atter. **(c)** *(verbrauchen) Wasser, Farbe etc* to use.

versprühen* *vt* to spray; *Funken* to send out; *(verbrauchen)* to use. **Witz/Geist ~** *(fig)* to scintillate.

verspüren* *vt* to feel, to be conscious of.

verstaatlichen* *vt* to nationalize.

Verstaatlichung *f* nationalization.

verstädtern* **1** *vt* to urbanize. **2** *vi aux sein* to become urbanized.

Verstand *m no pl (Fähigkeit zu denken)* reason; *(Intellekt)* mind, intellect; *(Vernunft)* (common) sense; *(Urteilskraft)* (powers *pl* of) judgement. **den ~ verlieren** to lose one's mind; **nicht recht** *or* **ganz bei ~ sein** not to be in one's right mind; **das geht über meinen ~** it's beyond me; **etw ohne ~ tun** to do sth mindlessly.

verstandesmäßig *adj* rational.

verständig *adj (vernünftig)* sensible; *(einsichtig)* understanding.

verständigen* **1** *vt* to notify. **2** *vr* to communicate; *(sich einigen)* to come to an understanding.

Verständigung *f no pl* **(a)** *(Benachrichtigung)* notification. **(b)** *(das Sichverständigen)* communication *no indef art*. **(c)** *(Einigung)* understanding.

verständlich *adj (begreiflich)* understandable; *(intellektuell erfaßbar)* comprehensible; *(hörbar)* audible. **schwer ~** hard to understand; **jdm etw ~ machen** to make sb understand sth; *(erklären)* to explain sth to sb; **sich ~ machen** to make oneself understood; *(sich klar ausdrücken)* to make oneself clear.

verständlicherweise *adv* understandably (enough).

Verständnis *nt no pl* understanding *(für* of); *(Mitgefühl)* sympathy *(für* for). **für etw kein ~ haben** to have no understanding of/sympathy for sth; *für Kunst etc* to have no appreciation of sth; *für Unordnung etc* to have no time for sth; **dafür hast du mein vollstes ~** you have my fullest sympathy.

verständnis-: ~los *adj* uncomprehending; *(ohne Mitgefühl)* unsympathetic *(für* towards); *(für Kunst)* unappreciative *(für* of); **~voll** *adj* understanding; *Blick* knowing *no pred*.

verstärken* **1** *vt* to strengthen, to reinforce; *Truppen* to reinforce; *Spannung, Zweifel* to increase; *(Elec, Mus)* to amplify. **2** *vr (fig)* to intensify; *(sich vermehren)* to increase.

Verstärker *m* - *(Rad, Elec)* amplifier.

Verstärkung *f siehe vt* strengthening; reinforcement; increase; amplification.

verstauben* *vi aux sein* to get dusty; *(fig)* to gather dust. **verstaubt** dusty; *(fig) Ansichten* fuddy-duddy *(col)*.

verstauchen* *vt* **sich** *(dat)* **die Hand/den Fuß ~** to sprain one's hand/foot.

verstauen* *vt Gepäck* to load *(in +dat* in).

Versteck *nt* **-e** hiding-place; *(von Verbrechern)* hide-out. **~ spielen** to play hide-and-seek.

verstecken* **1** *vt* to hide, to conceal *(vor* from). **2** *vr* to hide. **sich vor jdm ~** to hide from sb; **sich vor jdm nicht zu ~ brauchen** *(fig)* not to need to fear comparison with sb.

Versteckspiel *nt (lit, fig)* hide-and-seek.

versteckt *adj* **(a)** hidden; *(nicht leicht sichtbar) Eingang, Tür* concealed; *(abgelegen auch) Ort* secret. **(b)** *(fig) Lächeln, Blick* furtive; *Andeutung* veiled; *Bedeutung* hidden.

verstehen 1 *vti* **(a)** to understand. **etw unter etw** *(dat)* **~** to understand sth by sth; **wie soll ich das ~?** how am I supposed to take that?; **das ist nicht wörtlich zu ~** that isn't to be taken literally; **jdn/etw falsch ~** to misunderstand sb/sth; **jdm zu ~ geben, daß ...** to give sb to understand that ... **(b)** *(können, beherrschen)* to know. **es ~, etw zu tun** to know how to do sth; **es mit Kindern ~** to be good with children; **etwas von etw ~** to know something about sth. **2** *vr* **(a)** to understand each other; *(auskommen)* to get on. **(b)** *(klar sein)* to go without saying. **das versteht sich von selbst** that goes without saying; **die Preise ~ sich einschließlich Lieferung** prices are inclusive of delivery. **(c)** *(auffassen)* **sich als etw ~** to see oneself as sth. **(d) sich auf etw** *(acc)* **~** to be an expert at sth.

versteifen* **1** *vt* to strengthen, to reinforce. **2** *vr* to stiffen up; *(fig: Haltung, Gegensätze)* to harden. **sich auf etw** *(acc)* **~** *(fig)* to become set on sth.

versteigen* *vr irreg* **er hat sich zu der Behauptung verstiegen, daß ...** he presumed to claim that ...

versteigern* *vt* to auction (off). **etw ~ lassen** to put sth up for auction.

Versteigerung *f* auction.

versteinern* **1** *vi aux sein (Pflanzen, Tiere)* to fossilize; *(Holz)* to petrify. **2** *vr (fig) Miene* to harden.

verstellbar *adj* adjustable.

verstellen* **1** *vt* **(a)** *(anders einstellen)* to adjust; *Möbel* to move; *(in Unordnung bringen)* to put in the wrong place; *(falsch einstellen)* to adjust wrongly; *Radio* to alter the tuning of; *Uhr* to set wrong. **(b)** *Stimme* to disguise. **(c)** *(versperren)* to block, to obstruct. **2** *vr* to move (out of position); *(fig)* to act a part.

versteuern* *vt* to pay tax on. **versteuert** taxed; **zu ~n** taxable.

verstiegen *adj (fig: überspannt)* extravagant, fantastic.

verstimmen* *vt* to put out of tune; *(fig)* to put out.

verstimmt *adj Klavier etc* out of tune; *(fig) Magen* upset; *(verärgert)* put out, disgruntled.
Verstimmung *f* disgruntlement; *(zwischen Parteien)* ill-feeling, ill-will.
verstockt *adj* obstinate, stubborn; *Sünder* unrepentant.
verstohlen *adj* furtive, surreptitious.
verstopfen* *vt* to stop up; *Straße* to block, to jam.
verstopft *adj* blocked; *Straßen auch* jammed; *Mensch* constipated.
Verstopfung *f* blockage; *(Med)* constipation.
Verstorbene(r) *mf decl as adj* deceased.
verstört *adj* disturbed; *(vor Angst)* distraught.
Verstoß *m* **-̈e** violation *(gegen* of*)*.
verstoßen* *irreg* **1** *vt jdn* to disown, to repudiate; *(ausschließen)* to expel *(aus* from*)*. **2** *vi* **gegen etw** ~ to offend against sth.
Verstoßene(r) *mf decl as adj* outcast.
verstrahlt *adj* radioactively contaminated, irradiated.
Verstrebung *f (Strebebalken)* support(ing beam).
verstreichen* *irreg* **1** *vt Salbe, Farbe* to put on; *Butter* to spread *(auf +dat* on*)*; *Riß* to fill in; *(verbrauchen)* to use. **2** *vi aux sein (Zeit)* to pass (by); *(Frist)* to expire.
verstreuen* *vt* to scatter; *(versehentlich)* to spill.
verstricken* **1** *vt* **(a)** *Wolle* to use. **(b)** *(fig)* to involve. **2** *vr (fig)* to become entangled.
verströmen* *vt (lit, fig)* to exude.
verstümmeln* *vt* to mutilate, to maim; *(fig) Nachricht* to distort.
verstummen* *vi aux sein (Mensch)* to go silent; *(Geräusch, Beifall)* to stop; *(langsam verklingen)* to die away; *(fig: sich legen)* to subside. **jdn/etw zum V~ bringen** to silence sb/sth.
Versuch *m* **-e** attempt *(zu tun* at doing, to do*)*; *(wissenschaftlich)* experiment, test. **einen ~ machen** to make an attempt; to do an experiment *or* a test; **das käme auf einen ~ an** we'll have to have a try.
versuchen* **1** *vt* **(a)** *(auch vi)* to try. **es mit jdm/etw ~** to give sb/sth a try; **versuchter Mord** attempted murder; **das Unmögliche ~** to attempt the impossible. **(b)** *(in Versuchung führen)* to tempt. **2** *vr* **sich an** *or* **in etw** *(dat)* ~ to try one's hand at sth.
Versucher(in *f***)** *m* **-** tempter/temptress.
Versuchs-: **~anstalt** *f* research institute; **~ballon** *m* sounding balloon; **einen ~ballon steigen lassen** *(fig)* to fly a kite; **~bohrung** *f* experimental drilling; **~kaninchen** *nt (fig)* guinea-pig; **~objekt** *nt* test object; *(fig: Mensch)* guinea-pig; **~person** *f* experimental subject; **~reihe** *f* series of experiments; **~stadium** *nt* experimental stage; **~strecke** *f* test track; **~tier** *nt* laboratory animal; **v~weise** *adv* as a trial, on a trial basis.
Versuchung *f* temptation. **jdn in ~ führen** to lead sb into temptation.
versumpfen* *vi aux sein* **(a)** *(Gebiet)* to become marshy. **(b)** *(fig col) (verwahrlosen)* to go to pot *(col)*; *(zechen)* to get involved in a booze-up *(col)*.
versündigen* *vr (geh)* **sich an jdm/etw ~** to sin against sb/sth.
versunken *adj* sunken, submerged; *Kultur* submerged; *(fig)* engrossed. **in Gedanken ~** lost in thought.
versüßen* *vt (fig)* to sweeten *(jdm etw* sth for sb*)*.
vertagen* **1** *vti* to adjourn; *(verschieben)* to postpone *(auf+acc* until*)*. **2** *vr* to adjourn.
vertauschbar *adj* exchangeable *(gegen* for*)*; *(miteinander)* interchangeable.
vertauschen* *vt* **(a)** to exchange *(gegen or mit* for*)*; *(miteinander)* to interchange. **vertauschte Rollen** reversed roles. **(b)** *(verwechseln) Mäntel etc* to mix up.
Vertauschung *f (Austausch)* exchange.
verteidigen* **1** *vti* to defend. **2** *vr* to defend oneself; *(vor Gericht)* to conduct one's own defence *(Brit) or* defense *(US)*.
Verteidiger(in *f***)** *m* **-** defender; *(Anwalt)* defence *(Brit) or* defense *(US)* lawyer. **der ~ des Angeklagten** the counsel for the defence.
Verteidigung *f* defence *(Brit)*, defense *(US)*. **zur ~ von** *or +gen* in defence of.
Verteidigungs- *in cpds* defence *(Brit)*, defense *(US)*; **~krieg** *m* defensive war; **~minister** *m* Minister of Defence *(Brit)*, Defense Secretary *(US)*; **~ministerium** *nt* Ministry of Defence *(Brit)*, Defense Department *(US)*; **~schlacht** *f* defensive battle; **~spieler** *m* defence *(Brit) or* defense *(US)* player; **~stellung** *f* defensive position; **~system** *nt* defence *(Brit) or* defense *(US)* system; **~waffe** *f* defensive weapon.
verteilen* **1** *vt (an+acc* to, *unter +acc* among*)* to distribute; *Essen* to dish out; *(Theat) Rollen* to cast; *Investitionen, Lehrstoff* to spread *(über +acc* over*)*; *(Mil)* to deploy; *(verstreuen)* to spread out; *(streichen) Farbe etc* to spread; *(streuen) Sand* to sprinkle. **2** *vr (Menschen, Flüssigkeiten)* to spread out; *(Reichtum etc)* to be spread *or* distributed; *(zeitlich)* to be spread *(über +acc* over*)*.
Verteiler *m* **-** *(Comm, Aut)* distributor.
Verteilung *f* distribution.
verteuern* **1** *vt* to make more expensive. **2** *vr* to become more expensive.
Verteuerung *f* increase in price.
verteufeln* *vt* to condemn.
verteufelt *(col)* **1** *adj Lage* devilish *(col)*, tricky. **2** *adv (mit adj)* damned *(col)*.
vertiefen* **1** *vt (lit, fig)* to deepen; *(Sch) Lehrstoff* to consolidate. **2** *vr (lit, fig)* to deepen; *(fig: Lehrstoff)* to be consolidated. **sich in etw** *(acc)* ~ *(fig)* to become engrossed in sth.
Vertiefung *f* **(a)** *siehe vt* deepening; consolidation. **(b)** *(in Oberfläche)* depression. **(c)** *(in Arbeit etc)* absorption.
Vertikale [vɛrti'ka:lə] *f* **-n** vertical line.
vertilgen* *vt* **(a)** *Unkraut etc* to eradicate. **(b)** *(col: aufessen)* to demolish *(col)*.
Vertilgungsmittel *nt* weed-killer; *(Insekten~)* pesticide.
vertippen* *vr (col)* to make a typing error.
vertonen* *vt* to set to music; *Film etc* to add a sound-track to.
Vertrag *m* **-̈e** contract; *(Abkommen)* agreement; *(Pol: Friedens~)* treaty. **unter ~ stehen** to be under contract.
vertragen* *irreg* **1** *vt* to take; *(aushalten auch)* to stand. **Eier vertrage ich nicht** eggs don't agree with me; **synthetische Stoffe vertrage ich nicht** I can't wear synthetics; **viel ~ können** *(col: Alkohol)* to be able to hold one's drink. **2** *vr* **sich (mit jdm) ~** to get along (with sb); **sich wieder ~** to be friends again; **sich mit etw ~** *(Nahrungsmittel, Farbe)* to go with sth; *(Aussage, Verhalten)* to be consistent with sth.
vertraglich **1** *adj* contractual. **2** *adv* by contract; *festgelegt* in the/a contract.
verträglich *adj (friedlich, umgänglich)* peaceable, easy-going; *Speise* digestible; *(bekömmlich)* wholesome; *Medikament* well tolerated *(für* by*)*. **gut ~** easily digestible.
Verträglichkeit *f no pl siehe adj* easy-going nature; digestibility; wholesomeness.
Vertrags-: **~bruch** *m* breach of contract; breaking of an/the agreement; breaking of a/the treaty; **v~gemäß** *adj, adv* as stipulated in the contract/agreement/treaty; **~händler** *m* concessionary; **v~schließend** *adj* contracting; **~werkstätte** *f* authorized repair shop; **v~widrig** **1** *adj* contrary to the contract/agreement/treaty; **2** *adv* in breach of contract/the agreement/the treaty.
vertrauen* *vi* **jdm/einer Sache ~** to trust sb/sth; **auf jdn/etw ~** to trust in sb/sth.
Vertrauen *nt no pl* trust, confidence *(zu, in +acc,*

auf +acc in); *(Pol)* confidence. **im ~ (gesagt)** strictly in confidence; **im ~ darauf, daß ...** confident that ...; **~ zu jdm fassen** to gain confidence in sb; **jdn ins ~ ziehen** to take sb into one's confidence.

Vertrauens-: **~bruch** *m* breach of confidence; **~mann** *m, pl* **~leute** *or* **~männer** intermediary; **~person** *f* someone to confide in, confidant(e); **~sache** *f (vertrauliche Angelegenheit)* confidential matter; *(Frage des Vertrauens)* question of trust; **v~selig** *adj* trusting; **v~voll** *adj* trusting; **~votum** *nt (Parl)* vote of confidence; **v~würdig** *adj* trustworthy.

vertraulich **1** *adj* **(a)** *(geheim)* confidential. **(b)** *(freundschaftlich)* friendly; *(plump ~)* familiar. **~ werden** to take liberties. **2** *adv* **(a)** confidentially. **(b)** in a friendly way.

Vertraulichkeit *f* confidentiality.

verträumt *adj* dreamy; *Städtchen etc* sleepy.

vertraut *adj* intimate; *(bekannt) Gesicht, Umgebung* familiar. **sich mit etw ~ machen** to familiarize oneself with sth; **sich mit dem Gedanken ~ machen, daß ...** to get used to the idea that ...; **mit jdm ~ werden** to become friendly with sb.

Vertraute(r) *mf decl as adj* close friend.

Vertrautheit *f no pl siehe adj* intimacy; familiarity.

vertreiben* *vt irreg Tiere, Menschen, Sorgen* to drive away; *(aus Haus, Land)* to drive out *(aus* of); *(aus Amt, von Stellung)* to oust *(aus* from); *Feind* to drive off; *(Comm) Waren* to sell. **jdm/sich die Zeit mit etw ~** to help sb pass the time/to pass the time with sth.

Vertreibung *f (aus* from) expulsion; *(aus Amt etc)* ousting; *(von Feind)* repelling.

vertretbar *adj* justifiable; *Theorie* tenable.

vertreten* *vt irreg* **(a)** *(ersetzen)* to replace; *Kollegen auch* to stand in for. **(b)** *jds Interessen, Firma, Wahlkreis* to represent; *Sache* to look after; *(Jur) Fall* to plead. **~ sein** to be represented. **(c)** *(Comm)* to be the agent for; *(Angestellter)* to represent. **(d)** *(verfechten) Standpunkt* to support; *Meinung* to hold; *Kunstrichtung* to represent; *(rechtfertigen)* to justify *(vor* to). **(e)** **sich** *(dat)* **den Fuß ~** to twist one's ankle; **sich** *(dat)* **die Beine** *or* **Füße ~** *(col)* to stretch one's legs.

Vertreter(in *f*) *m* **- (a)** representative; *(Comm) (Firma)* agent; *(Angestellter)* (sales) representative, rep *(col)*. **(b)** *(Ersatz)* replacement; *(im Amt)* deputy. **(c)** *(Verfechter) (von Doktrin)* supporter, advocate; *(von Meinung)* holder.

Vertretung *f siehe vt (a-d)* **(a)** replacement. **die ~ (für jdn) übernehmen** to stand in (for sb); **in ~** *+gen* on behalf of; *(in Briefen)* pp. **(b)** representation. **X übernimmt die ~ des Falles** X is pleading the case. **(c)** *(Comm)* agency. **(d)** supporting; holding; representation.

Vertretungs-: **~stunde** *f (Sch)* stand-in class; **v~weise** *adv* as a replacement; *(bei Amtsperson)* as a deputy.

Vertrieb *m* **-e** *no pl* sales *pl.* **der ~ eines Produktes** the sale of a product; **den ~ für eine Firma haben** to have the (selling) agency for a firm.

Vertriebene(r) *mf decl as adj* exile.

Vertriebs-: **~abteilung** *f* sales department; **~gesellschaft** *f* marketing company; **~kosten** *pl* marketing costs *pl.*

vertrinken* *vt irreg* to spend on drink.

vertrocknen* *vi aux sein* to dry out; *(Eßwaren)* to go dry; *(Pflanzen)* to shrivel; *(Quelle)* to dry up.

vertrödeln* *vt (col)* to fritter away.

vertrösten* *vt* to put off *(auf +acc* until). **jdn auf ein andermal/auf später ~** to put sb off.

vertun* *irreg* **1** *vt Zeit etc* to waste. **2** *vr (col)* to make a mistake.

vertuschen* *vt* to hush up. **etw vor jdm ~** to keep sth from sb.

ver|übeln* *vt* **jdm etw ~** not to be at all pleased with sb for doing sth; **das kann ich dir nicht ~** I can't blame you for that.

ver|üben* *vt* to commit.

ver|ulken* *vt (col)* to make fun of.

ver|unglimpfen* *vt jdn* to disparage.

ver|unglücken* *vi aux sein (Mensch)* to have an accident; *(Fahrzeug)* to crash; *(fig col: mißlingen)* to go wrong. **mit dem Flugzeug ~** to be in a plane crash.

ver|unglückt *adj (fig) Versuch etc* unsuccessful.

Ver|unglückte(r) *mf decl as adj* casualty, victim.

ver|unreinigen* *vt Fluß etc* to pollute; *(beschmutzen)* to dirty; *(Hund etc)* to foul.

Ver|unreinigung *f siehe vt* pollution; dirtying; fouling.

ver|unsichern* *vt* to make unsure *(in +dat* of). **sie versuchten, ihn zu ~** they tried to throw him.

ver|unstalten* *vt* to disfigure.

ver|untreuen* *vt* to embezzle.

Ver|untreuung *f* embezzlement.

ver|ursachen* *vt* to cause.

Ver|ursacher(in *f*) *m* **-** person responsible *(gen* for), perpetrator *(gen* of).

ver|urteilen* *vt* to condemn *(Jur)*; *(für schuldig befinden)* to convict *(für* of); *(zu Strafe)* to sentence *(zu* to). **jdn zu einer Geldstrafe von 1.000 DM ~** to fine sb DM 1,000.

Ver|urteilte(r) *mf decl as adj* convicted man/woman. **der zum Tode ~** the condemned man.

Ver|urteilung *f* condemnation; *(Jur)* conviction.

vervielfachen* *vtr* to multiply.

vervielfältigen* *vt* to duplicate.

Vervielfältigung *f* duplication; *(Abzug)* copy.

vervierfachen* *vtr* to quadruple.

vervollkommnen* **1** *vt* to perfect. **2** *vr* to make oneself perfect.

vervollständigen* **1** *vt* to complete. **2** *vr* to be completed.

Vervollständigung *f* completion.

verwachsen[1]* *vi irreg aux sein* **(a)** *(zusammenwachsen)* to grow together; *(Narbe, Wunde)* to heal; *(Knochen)* to knit. **mit etw ~** to grow into sth. **(b)** *(fig: Menschen)* to grow closer (together). **zu etw ~** to grow into sth; **mit etw ~** *mit Aufgabe, Traditionen* to become caught up in sth; **mit etw ~ sein** to have very close ties with sth.

verwachsen[2] *adj* **(a)** *Mensch* deformed; *(verkümmert)* stunted. **(b)** *(überwuchert)* overgrown.

verwackeln* *vt* to blur.

verwählen* *vr* to dial the wrong number.

verwahren* **1** *vt (aufbewahren)* to keep safe. **2** *vr* **sich gegen etw ~** to protest against sth.

verwahrlosen* *vi aux sein* to go to pot *(col)*; *(Gebäude auch)* to fall into disrepair; *(Mensch)* to let oneself go; *(verwildern)* to run wild.

verwahrlost *adj* neglected. **sittlich ~** decadent.

Verwahrung *f* **(a)** *no pl (von Geld etc)* keeping; *(von Täter)* custody, detention. **jdm etw in ~ geben** to give sth to sb for safekeeping; **etw in ~ nehmen** to take sth into safekeeping; *(Behörde)* to take possession of sth; **jdn in ~ nehmen** to take sb into custody. **(b)** *(Einspruch)* protest.

verwaist *adj* orphaned; *(fig)* deserted.

verwalten* *vt* to manage; *Amt* to hold; *(Pol) Provinz etc* to govern; *(Beamte)* to administer; *(Rel)* to administer. **sich selbst ~** *(Pol)* to be self-governing.

Verwalter(in *f*) *m* **-** administrator.

Verwaltung *f* **(a)** *siehe vt* management; holding; government; administration. **(b)** *(Behörde, Abteilung)* administration; *(Haus~)* management. **städtische ~** municipal authorities *pl.*

Verwaltungs-: **~angestellte(r)** *mf* administrative employee; **~apparat** *m* administrative machinery; **~beamte(r)** *m* government official; **~bezirk** *m* administrative district; **~gericht** *nt* Administrative Court; **~weg** *m* **auf dem ~weg**

through administrative channels.
verwandeln* 1 *vt* to change, to transform. **jdn/etw in etw** *(acc)* ~ to turn sb/sth into sth; **ein Gebäude in einen Trümmerhaufen** ~ to reduce a building to a pile of rubble; **er ist wie verwandelt** he's a changed man. **2** *vi (Sport sl)* **zum 1:0** ~ to make it 1-0. **3** *vr* to change. **sich in etw** *(acc) or* **zu etw** ~ to change *or* turn into sth.
Verwandlung *f* change, transformation. **eine ~ durchmachen** to undergo a transformation.
verwandt *adj (lit, fig)* related *(mit* to*)*. **geistig ~ sein** *(fig)* to be kindred spirits.
Verwandte(r) *mf decl as adj* relation, relative.
Verwandtschaft *f* relationship; *(die Verwandten)* relations *pl*, relatives *pl*; *(fig)* affinity.
verwandtschaftlich *adj* family *attr*.
verwarnen* *vt* to caution, to warn.
Verwarnung *f* caution, warning.
verwaschen *adj* faded; *(verwässert) Farbe* watery.
verwässern* *vt (lit, fig)* to water down.
verwechseln* *vt* to confuse, to mix up. **jdn (mit jdm)** ~ to confuse sb with sb; *(für jdn halten auch)* to mistake sb for sb; **sie sind sich zum V~ ähnlich** it's impossible to tell the difference between them.
Verwechslung *f* confusion; *(Irrtum)* mistake. **das muß eine ~ sein** there must be some mistake.
verwegen *adj* daring, bold; *(tollkühn)* foolhardy; *(keck)* saucy.
verwehen* 1 *vt Rauch* to blow away; *Spur* to cover over. **2** *vi aux sein (Spur)* to be covered over.
verwehren* *vt (geh)* **jdm etw** ~ to refuse *or* deny sb sth; **jdm ~, etw zu tun** to bar sb from doing sth.
Verwehung *f* drift.
verweichlichen* 1 *vt* **jdn** ~ to make sb soft; **ein verweichlichter Mensch** a weakling. **2** *vi aux sein* to get soft.
verweigern* *vt* to refuse; *Befehl* to refuse to obey; *Kriegsdienst* to refuse to do. **jdm etw** ~ to refuse *or* deny sb sth.
Verweigerung *f* refusal. ~ **des Kriegsdienstes** refusal to do (one's) military service; ~ **des Gehorsams** disobedience.
verweilen* *vi (geh) (Mensch)* to stay; *(Blick, Gedanken)* to dwell. **bei einer Sache** ~ to dwell on sth.
verweint *adj Augen* tear-swollen; *Gesicht* tear-stained.
Verweis *m* **-e (a)** *(Rüge)* reprimand. **jdm einen ~ erteilen** to reprimand sb. **(b)** *(Hinweis)* reference *(auf +acc* to*)*.
verweisen* *irreg* **1** *vt* **(a)** *(hinweisen)* **jdn auf etw** *(acc)***/an jdn** ~ to refer sb to sth/sb. **(b)** *(von der Schule)* to expel. **jdn des Landes** ~ to expel sb (from the country); **jdm vom Platz** *or* **des Spielfeldes** ~ to send sb off; **jdn auf den zweiten Platz** ~ *(Sport)* to relegate sb to second place. **(c)** *(Jur)* to refer *(an +acc* to*)*. **2** *vi* **auf etw** *(acc)* ~ to refer to sth.
verwelken* *vi aux sein (Blumen)* to wilt; *(fig)* to fade. **ein verwelktes Gesicht** a worn face.
verweltlichen* *vt* to secularize.
verwendbar *adj* usable *(zu* for*)*. **das ist nur einmal** ~ it can be used once only.
Verwendbarkeit *f no pl* usability.
verwenden 1 *vt* to use. **Mühe auf etw** *(acc)* ~ to put effort into sth; **Zeit auf etw** *(acc)* ~ to spend time on sth. **2** *vr* **sich (bei jdm) für jdn** ~ to approach sb on sb's behalf.
Verwendung *f* use; *(von Zeit, Geld)* expenditure *(auf +acc* on*)*.
Verwendungs-: ~möglichkeit *f* (possible) use; **~weise** *f* manner of use; **~zweck** *m* use, purpose.
verwerfen* *irreg vt (ablehnen)* to reject; *(Jur) Klage, Antrag* to dismiss; *Urteil* to quash; *(kritisieren) Handlungsweise* to condemn.
verwerflich *adj* reprehensible.
verwertbar *adj* usable.
verwerten* *vt (verwenden)* to utilize; *Erfindung, Material etc* to exploit.
Verwertung *f siehe vt* utilization; exploitation.
verwesen* *vi aux sein* to decay; *(Fleisch)* to rot.
Verweser *m* - *(old, liter)* administrator.
Verwesung *f no pl* decay.
verwickeln* 1 *vt Fäden etc* to tangle (up). **jdn in etw** *(acc)* ~ to involve sb in sth. **2** *vr (Fäden etc)* to get tangled up. **sich in etw** *(acc)* ~ *(lit, fig)* to become entangled in sth.
verwickelt *adj (fig col: schwierig)* involved, complicated.
Verwicklung *f* involvement *(in +acc* in*)*; *(Komplikation)* complication; *(Verwirrung)* confusion.
verwildern* *vi aux sein (Garten)* to become overgrown; *(Pflanzen)* to grow wild; *(Haustier)* to become wild.
verwildert *adj* wild; *Garten* overgrown; *Aussehen* unkempt.
verwirken *vt (geh)* to forfeit.
verwirklichen* 1 *vt* to realize. **2** *vr* to be realized; *(Mensch)* to fulfil *(Brit) or* fulfill *(US)* oneself.
Verwirklichung *f no pl* realization.
verwirren* 1 *vt* **(a)** *Haar* to tousle; *Fäden etc* to get tangled up. **(b)** *(durcheinanderbringen)* to confuse; *(konfus machen)* to bewilder. **2** *vr (Fäden etc)* to become tangled up; *(Haare)* to become tousled; *(fig)* to become confused.
Verwirrung *f (Durcheinander)* confusion.
verwirtschaften* *vt* to squander away.
verwischen* 1 *vt (verschmieren)* to smudge; *(lit, fig) Spuren* to cover over; *(fig) Erinnerungen* to blur. **2** *vr (lit, fig)* to become blurred.
verwittern* *vi aux sein* to weather.
verwitwet *adj* widowed.
verwöhnen* 1 *vt* to spoil; *(Schicksal)* to be good to. **2** *vr* to spoil oneself.
verwöhnt *adj* spoilt; *Kunde, Geschmack* discriminating.
verworfen *adj (geh)* depraved.
verworren *adj* confused, muddled; *(verwickelt)* intricate.
verwundbar *adj (lit, fig)* vulnerable.
verwunden* *vt* to wound.
verwunderlich *adj* surprising; *(sonderbar)* strange, odd.
verwundern* 1 *vt* to astonish. **2** *vr* to be astonished *(über +acc* at*)*.
Verwunderung *f no pl* astonishment.
Verwundete(r) *mf decl as adj* casualty. **die ~n** *(Mil)* the wounded.
Verwundung *f* wound.
verwünschen* *vt* **(a)** *(verfluchen)* to curse. **(b)** *(in Märchen: verzaubern)* to enchant.
verwurzelt *adj* ~ **sein** *(Pflanze)* to be rooted; **(fest) in** *or* **mit etw** ~ *(fig)* deeply rooted in sth.
verwüsten* *vt* to devastate, to ravage.
Verwüstung *f* devastation *no pl*, ravaging *no pl*.
verzagen* *vi (geh)* to lose heart.
verzagt *adj* disheartened.
verzählen* *vr* to miscount.
verzahnen* *vt* to dovetail; *Zahnräder* to cut teeth in. **ineinander verzahnt sein** *(lit, fig)* to mesh.
verzapfen* *vt (col) Unsinn* to come out with.
verzärteln* *vt (pej)* to mollycoddle, to pamper.
verzaubern* *vt* to cast a spell on; *(bezaubern)* to enchant. **jdn in etw** *(acc)* ~ to turn sb into sth.
verzehnfachen* *vtr* to increase ten-fold.
Verzehr *m no pl* consumption.
verzehren* *vt (form: lit, fig)* to consume.
verzeichnen* *vt* to record; *(in einer Liste auch)* to enter. **einen Erfolg zu ~ haben** to have scored a success.

Verzeichnis *nt* index; *(Tabelle)* table; *(Namens~, esp amtlich)* register; *(Aufstellung)* list.
verzeihen *pret* **verzieh,** *ptp* **verziehen** *vti (vergeben)* to forgive; *(entschuldigen)* to excuse, to pardon. **jdm (etw)** ~ to forgive sb (for sth); ~ **Sie!** excuse me!
verzeihlich *adj* forgivable; *(zu entschuldigen)* excusable.
Verzeihung *f no pl* forgiveness; *(Entschuldigung)* pardon. ~! excuse me!; **(jdn) um ~ bitten** *(sich entschuldigen)* to apologize (to sb).
verzerren* **1** *vti (lit, fig)* to distort; *Gesicht* to contort; *Sehne, Muskel* to strain, to pull. **etw verzerrt darstellen** *(fig)* to present a distorted picture of sth. **2** *vr* to become distorted; *(Gesicht etc)* to become contorted *(zu* in*)*.
Verzerrung *f (lit, fig)* distortion; *(von Gesicht)* contortion.
verzetteln* **1** *vt* to waste. **2** *vr* to waste a lot of time; *(bei Aufgabe)* to get bogged down.
Verzicht *m* **-e** renunciation *(auf +acc* of*)*; *(auf Anspruch)* abandonment *(auf +acc* of*)*; *(Opfer)* sacrifice; *(auf Thron)* abdication *(auf +acc* of*)*. **ein ~, der mir nicht schwerfällt** that's something I can easily do without.
verzichten* *vi* to do without; *(Opfer bringen)* to make sacrifices. **der Kandidat hat zugunsten eines Jüngeren verzichtet** the candidate stepped down in favour of a younger man; **auf jdn/etw** ~ *(ohne auskommen müssen)* to do without sb/sth; *(aufgeben)* to give up sb/sth; *auf Erbschaft* to renounce sth; *(von etw absehen) auf Kommentar, Anzeige etc* to abstain from sth; *auf Amt* to refuse sth; **auf den Thron** ~ to abdicate.
verzieh *pret of* **verzeihen.**
verziehen[1]* *irreg* **1** *vt* **(a)** *Mund, Züge etc* to twist *(zu* into*)*. **das Gesicht** ~ to pull a face; **den Mund** ~ to turn up one's mouth; **keine Miene** ~ not to turn a hair. **(b)** *Stoff* to pull out of shape; *Holz* to warp. **(c)** *(verwöhnen)* to spoil. **2** *vr* **(a)** *(Stoff)* to go out of shape; *(Holz)* to warp. **(b)** *(Mund, Gesicht etc)* to twist *(zu* into*)*. **(c)** *(verschwinden)* to disappear; *(Gewitter)* to pass; *(Nebel, Wolken)* to disperse. **3** *vi aux sein* to move *(nach* to*)*. **verzogen** *(Vermerk)* no longer at this address.
verziehen[2] *ptp of* **verzeihen.**
verzieren* *vt* to decorate; *(verschönern)* to embellish.
Verzierung *f siehe vt* decoration; embellishment.
verzinsen* **1** *vt* to pay interest on. **das Geld wird mit 3% verzinst** 3% interest is paid on the money. **2** *vr* **sich (mit 6%)** ~ to yield (6%) interest.
verzinslich *adj* interest-bearing *attr.* **~/fest ~ sein** to yield interest/a fixed rate of interest; **nicht** ~ interest-free.
verzogen *adj Kind* spoilt.
verzögern* **1** *vt* to delay; *(verlangsamen)* to slow down. **2** *vr* to be delayed.
Verzögerung *f* **(a)** delay, hold-up. **(b)** *no pl (das Verzögern)* delaying; *(Verlangsamung)* slowing down.
verzollen* *vt* to pay duty on. **haben Sie etwas zu ~?** have you anything to declare?; **verzollt** duty-paid.
verzuckern* **1** *vi aux sein (Honig etc)* to crystallize. **2** *vt* to put too much sugar on.
verzückt *adj* enraptured, ecstatic.
Verzückung *f no pl* rapture, ecstasy. **in ~ geraten** to go into ecstasies *(wegen* over*)*.
Verzug *m* delay; *(Fin)* arrears *pl.* **bei ~ (der Zahlungen)** on default of payment; **mit etw in ~ geraten** to fall behind with sth; *mit Zahlungen auch* to fall into arrears with sth.
verzweifeln* *vi aux sein* to despair *(an +dat* of*)*. **es ist zum V~!** it drives you to despair!
verzweifelt *adj* desperate; *Blick, Stimme etc auch* despairing.
Verzweiflung *f (Gemütszustand)* despair; *(Ratlosigkeit)* desperation. **jdn zur ~ treiben** to drive sb to despair.
verzweigen* *vr* to branch.
verzweigt *adj Baum, Firma* with a lot of branches; *Verkehrsnetz* complex.
verzwickt *adj (col)* tricky.
Vesper *f* **-n** *(Eccl)* vespers *pl.*
Veteran [vete'raːn] *m (wk)* **-en, -en** *(Mil, fig)* veteran.
Veto ['veːto] *vt* **-s** veto.
Vetorecht ['veːto-] *nt* right of veto.
Vetter *m* **-n** cousin.
Vetternwirtschaft *f (col)* nepotism.
vgl. = **vergleiche** cf.
v.H. = **vom Hundert** per cent.
via ['viːa] *adv* via.
Viadukt [via'dʊkt] *m* **-e** viaduct.
Vibration [vibra'tsioːn] *f* vibration.
vibrieren* [vi'briːrən] *vi* to vibrate; *(Stimme)* to tremble.
Video ['viːdeo] *nt* **-s** video. **auf ~ aufnehmen** to video.
Video-: ['viːdeo-] *in cpds* video; **~aufnahme** *f* video (recording); **~band** *nt* video-tape; **~gerät** *nt* video; **~kassette** *f* video (cassette); **~recorder** *m* video recorder; **~technik** *f* video technology; **~text** *m* viewdata *sing.*
Vieh *nt no pl* **(a)** *(Nutztiere)* livestock; *(Rinder auch)* cattle *pl.* **(b)** *(col: Tier)* animal.
Vieh-: **~bestand** *m* livestock; **~futter** *nt* animal fodder; **~handel** *m* livestock/cattle trade.
viehisch *adj* brutish; *Schmerzen* beastly.
Vieh-: **~markt** *m* livestock/cattle market; **~seuche** *f* livestock disease; **~zeug** *nt (col)* animals *pl;* **~zucht** *f* (live)stock/cattle breeding.
viel *indef pron, adj, comp* **mehr,** *superl* **meiste(r, s)** *or (adv)* **am meisten (a)** *sing (adjektivisch)* a lot of; *(fragend, verneint auch)* much; *(substantivisch)* a lot; *(fragend, verneint auch)* much. **~es** a lot of things; **sehr ~ Geld** a lot of money, a very large sum of money; **in ~em** in many respects; **mit ~em** with a lot of things; **noch (ein)mal so ~ (Zeit** *etc***)** as much (time *etc*) again; **gleich ~ (Gewinn** *etc***)** the same amount (of profit *etc*); **einer zu ~** one too many; **~ Neues/Schönes** *etc* a lot of *or* many new/beautiful *etc* things; **das ~e/sein ~es Geld** all that/all his money.
(b) **~e** *pl (adjektivisch)* many, a lot of; *(substantivisch)* many, a lot; **gleich ~e (Angestellte/Anteile** *etc***)** the same number (of employees/shares *etc*); **so/zu ~e (Menschen/Fehler** *etc***)** so/too many (people/mistakes *etc*); **aufgrund der ~en Fehler** because of all the mistakes; **~e hundert Menschen** many hundreds of people.
(c) *(adverbial: mit vb)* a lot, a great deal; *(fragend, verneint auch)* much. **er arbeitet ~/nicht ~** he works a lot/doesn't work much; **er arbeitet zu/so ~** he works too/so much *or* such a lot; **die Straße wird (sehr/nicht) ~ befahren** this street is (very/not very) busy; **sich ~ einbilden** to think a lot of oneself.
(d) *(adverbial: mit adj, adv)* much, a lot. **~ größer** much *or* a lot bigger; **~ zu ...** much too ...; **~ zu ~e** far too many.
Viel-: **v~beschäftigt** *adj attr* very busy; **v~deutig** *adj* ambiguous; **v~diskutiert** *adj attr* much discussed; **~eck** *nt* polygon.
vielerlei *adj inv* **(a)** all sorts of. **(b)** *(substantivisch)* all sorts of things.
vieler|orts *adv* in many places.
vielfach **1** *adj* multiple *attr.* **ein ~er Millionär** a multimillionaire; **auf ~e Weise** in many various ways; **um ein ~es besser** many times better. **2** *adv* many times; *(in vielen Fällen)* in many cases; *(auf ~e Weise)* in many ways; *(col: häufig)* frequently. **~ bewährt** tried and tested many times.
Vielfache(s) *nt decl as adj (Math)* multiple. **um**

ein ~s many times over; **er verdient ein ~s von dem, was ich verdiene** his salary is many times larger than mine.

Vielfalt *f* (great) variety.

vielfältig *adj* varied, diverse.

Viel-: v~farbig *adj* multicoloured *(Brit)*, multicolored *(US)*; **~fraß** *m* **-e** glutton; **v~gehaßt** *adj attr* much-hated; **v~geliebt** *adj attr* much-loved; **v~geprüft** *adj attr (hum)* sorely tried; **v~gereist** *adj attr* much-travelled *(Brit)*, much-traveled *(US)*; **~götterei** *f* polytheism; **v~köpfig** *adj (col) Familie, Schar* large.

vielleicht *adv* **(a)** perhaps; *(in Bitten auch)* by any chance. **ja, ~** yes, perhaps *or* maybe; **~ sagst du mir mal, warum** you'd better tell me why; **hat er sich ~ verirrt/weh getan?** maybe he has got lost/hurt himself; **hast du ihm das ~ erzählt?** did you perhaps tell him that?; *(entsetzt: denn etwa)* you didn't tell him that, did you?; **~, daß ...** it could be that ... **(b)** *(col)* **soll ich ~ 24 Stunden arbeiten?!** am I supposed to work 24 hours then?; **du bist ~ ein Idiot!** you really are an idiot!; **ich war ~ nervös!** I wasn't half nervous! *(col)*, was I nervous!

vielmalig *adj attr* repeated.

vielmals *adv* **danke ~!** many thanks!; **ich bitte ~ um Entschuldigung!** I do apologize!; **er läßt ~ grüßen** he sends his best regards.

vielmehr *adv* rather; *(sondern, nur)* just.

Viel-: v~sagend *adj* meaningful, significant; **jdn v~sagend ansehen** to give sb a meaningful look; **v~schichtig** *adj (fig)* complex; **~schreiber** *m* **er ist ein richtiger ~schreiber** *(pej)* he really churns out the stuff *(col)*; **v~seitig** *adj (lit)* many-sided; *Mensch, Gerät* versatile; *Interessen* varied; *Ausbildung* all-round *attr*; **auf v~seitigen Wunsch** by popular request; **v~sprachig** *adj* multilingual, polyglot; **v~stimmig** *adj* many-voiced; **v~versprechend** *adj* promising; **~völkerstaat** *m* multinational state; **~weiberei** *f* polygamy; **~zahl** *f* multitude.

Vielzweck- *in cpds* multipurpose.

vier *num* four. **sie ist ~ (Jahre)** she's four (years old); **mit ~ (Jahren)** at the age of four; **es ist ~ (Uhr)** it's four (o'clock); **~ Uhr ~** four minutes past four; **für** *or* **auf ~ Tage** for four days; **in ~ Tagen** in four days, in four days' time; **wir waren ~** there were four of us; **jdn unter ~ Augen sprechen** to speak to sb in private; **~ Augen sehen mehr als zwei** *(prov)* two heads are better than one *(prov)*; **alle ~e von sich strecken** *(col: ausgestreckt liegen)* to stretch out; **auf allen ~en** *(col)* on all fours.

Vier *f* **-en** four. **die Herz ~** the four of hearts.

Vier-: ~beiner *m* **-** *(hum)* four-legged friend *(hum)*; **v~beinig** *adj* four-legged; **v~blätt(e)rig** *adj* four-leaved; **~eck** *nt* four-sided figure; *(Rechteck)* rectangle; **v~eckig** *adj* square; **v~einhalb** *num* four and a half.

Vierer *m* **-** *(Rudern, Sch)* four; *(Golf)* foursome.

Vierer-: ~bande *f* gang of four; **~bob** *m* four-man bob; **v~lei** *adj inv* **(a)** *attr Brot, Käse, Wein* four kinds *or* sorts of; *Möglichkeiten, Größen* four different; **(b)** *(substantivisch)* four different things; *(vier Sorten)* four different kinds.

vierfach 1 *adj* fourfold, quadruple. **die ~e Größe** four times the size; **in ~er Ausfertigung** in quadruplicate. **2** *adv* four times, fourfold. **das Papier ~ legen** to fold the paper in four.

Vierfache(s) *nt decl as adj* four times the amount, quadruple. **um das ~ zunehmen** to quadruple.

Vier-: ~farbendruck *m (Verfahren)* four-colour *(Brit) or* four-color *(US)* printing; *(Erzeugnis)* four-colour *(Brit) or* four-color *(US)* print; **~farb(en)stift** *m* four-colour *(Brit) or* four-color *(US)* pen; **v~füßig** *adj* four-legged; **~ganggetriebe** *nt* four-speed gearbox; **v~geschossig** *adj* four-storey *attr (Brit)*, four-story *attr (US)*; **v~händig** *adv* for four hands.

vierhundert *num* four hundred.

vierhundertste(r, s) *adj* four hundredth.

Vier-: v~kant *adj, adv (Naut)* square; **~kant** *m or nt* **-e** *(Tech)* square; **v~kantig** *adj* square(-headed); **v~köpfig** *adj Ungeheuer* four-headed; **eine v~köpfige Familie** a family of four.

Vierling *m* quadruplet, quad.

Viermächte|abkommen *nt* four-power agreement.

Vier-: v~mal *adj* four times; **v~malig** *adj* **nach v~maligem Versuch** after the fourth attempt; **~master** *m* **-** *(Naut)* four-master; **v~motorig** *adj* four-engined; **v~räd(e)rig** *adj* four-wheel *attr*, four-wheeled; **v~seitig** *adj* four-sided; *Abkommen, Verhandlungen* quadripartite; *Broschüre* four-page *attr*; **~sitzer** *m* **-** four-seater; **v~sitzig** *adj* four-seater *attr*; **v~spurig** *adj* four-lane *attr*; **v~stellig** *adj* four-figure *attr*; **v~stimmig** *adj* four-part *attr*, for four voices.

viert *adj* **wir gingen zu ~** four of us went.

Vier-: ~tagewoche *f* four-day week; **v~tausend** *num* four thousand; **~tausender** *m* **-** *(Berg)* four-thousand-metre *(Brit) or* -meter *(US)* mountain.

vierte *adj siehe* **vierte(r, s).**

vierteilig *adj* four-piece *attr*; *Roman* four-part *attr*.

Viertel[1] ['fırtl] *nt* **-** quarter. **ein ~ Leberwurst/Wein** a quarter of liver sausage/wine; **(ein) ~ nach/vor sechs** (a) quarter past/to six; **(ein) ~ sechs** (a) quarter past five; **drei ~ sechs** (a) quarter to six.

Viertel[2] ['firtl] *nt* **-** *(Stadtbezirk)* quarter, district.

viertel ['firtl] *adj inv* quarter. **ein ~ Liter/Pfund** a quarter (of a) litre/pound; **drei ~ Liter** three quarters of a litre.

Viertelfinale *nt* quarter-finals *pl*.

Vierteljahr *nt* three months *pl*, quarter *(Comm, Fin)*.

Vierteljahres- *in cpds* quarterly; **~schrift** *f* quarterly.

Viertel- [fırtl-]: **~jahrhundert** *nt* quarter of a century; **v~jährig** *adj attr Kind etc* three-month-old; *Aufenthalt, Frist* three months; **v~jährlich 1** *adj* quarterly; *Kündigung* three months' *attr*; **2** *adv* quarterly, every three months.

vierteln ['firtln] *vt (in vier Teile teilen)* to divide into four; *Summe, Gewinn* to divide by four.

Viertel- ['fırtl-]: **~note** *f* crotchet *(Brit)*, quarter note *(US)*; **~pfund** *nt* ≈ quarter (of a pound); **~stunde** *f* quarter of an hour; **v~stündig** *adj attr Abstand* quarter-hour; **v~stündlich** *adv* every quarter of an hour; **~ton** *m* quarter tone.

viertens *adv* fourth(ly), in the fourth place.

Vierte(r) *mf decl as adj* fourth. **Karl IV** *or* **der ~** Charles IV *or* the Fourth.

vierte(r, s) *adj* fourth. **der ~ Oktober** the fourth of October; **der ~ Stock** the fourth *(Brit) or* fifth *(US)* floor; **er war ~r im Rennen** he was *or* came fourth in the race; **du bist der ~, der mich das fragt** you're the fourth person to ask me that.

vier-: ~türig *adj* four-door *attr*; **~undzwanzig** *num* twenty-four.

Viervierteltakt [-'fırtl-] *m* four-four *or* common time.

Vierwaldstätter See *m* Lake Lucerne.

vier-: ~wöchentlich *adj, adv* every four weeks; **~wöchig** *adj* four-week *attr*.

vierzehn ['fırtse:n] *num* fourteen. **~ Uhr** 2 p.m.; *(auf Fahrplan, Mil)* fourteen hundred hours, 14.00; **~ Tage** two weeks, a fortnight *sing (Brit)*.

vierzehn- ['fırtse:n-]: **~tägig** *adj* two-week *attr*, lasting two weeks; **~täglich** *adj, adv* fortnightly *(Brit)*, every two weeks.

Vierzehntel ['fırtse:ntl] *nt* **-** fourteenth.

vierzehnte(r, s) ['fırtse:ntə(r, s)] *adj* fourteenth.

vierzig ['fɪrtsɪç] *num* forty. **mit ~ (km/h) fahren** to drive at forty (kilometres an hour); **Mitte (der) V~** in one's mid-forties.
vierziger ['fɪrtsɪgɐ] *adj attr inv* **die ~ Jahre** the forties.
Vierziger(in *f*) ['fɪrtsɪgɐ, -ərɪn] *m* - *(Mensch)* forty-year-old; *(Wein)* wine of vintage forty. **er ist Mitte der ~** he is in his mid-forties; **er ist in den ~n** he is in his forties.
vierzigmal *adv* forty times.
Vierzigstel ['fɪrtsɪçstl] *nt* - fortieth.
vierzigstel ['fɪrtsɪçstl] *adj inv* fortieth.
vierzigste(r, s) ['fɪrtsɪçstə(r, s)] *adj* fortieth.
Vierzigstundenwoche [fɪrtsɪç-] *f* forty-hour week.
Vierzimmerwohnung *f* four-room flat *(Brit) or* apartment.
Vietnam [viɛt'nam] *nt* Vietnam.
Vietnamese [viɛtna'me:zə] *m (wk)* **-n, -n, Vietnamesin** *f* Vietnamese.
Vikar [vi'ka:ɐ] *m* curate.
Villa ['vɪla] *f, pl* **Villen** villa.
Villenviertel ['vɪlən-] *nt* exclusive residential area.
violett [vio'lɛt] *adj* violet.
Violine [vio'li:nə] *f* violin.
Violinist(in *f*) [violi'nɪst(ɪn)] *m* violinist.
Violin- [vio'li:n-]: **~konzert** *nt* violin concerto; *(Darbietung)* violin concert; **~schlüssel** *m* treble clef.
Viper ['vi:pɐ] *f* **-n** viper, adder.
Viren ['vi:rən] *pl of* **Virus.**
virtuos [vɪr'tuo:s] *adj* virtuoso *attr.* **~ spielen** to give a virtuoso performance.
Virtuose [vɪr'tuo:zə] *m (wk)* **-n, -n, Virtuosin** *f* virtuoso.
Virus ['vi:rʊs] *nt or m, pl* **Viren** virus.
Virus|infektion *f* virus infection.
Visage [vi'za:ʒə] *f* **-n** *(pej)* face, (ugly) mug *(col).*
vis-à-vis [viza'vi:] *(dated)* **1** *adv* opposite *(von* to*).* **2** *prep +dat* opposite (to).
Visier [vi'zi:ɐ] *nt* **-e (a)** *(am Helm)* visor. **(b)** *(an Gewehren)* sight.
Vision [vi'zio:n] *f* vision.
Visite [vi'zi:tə] *f* **-n** *(Med)* round. **um 9 Uhr ist ~** the doctors do their rounds at 9 o'clock.
Visitenkarte [vi'zi:tn-] *f (lit, fig)* visiting *or* calling *(US)* card.
visuell [vi'zuɛl] *adj* visual.
Visum ['vi:zʊm] *nt, pl* **Visa** *or* **Visen** visa.
Visumzwang ['vi:zʊm-] *m* obligation to hold a visa.
vital [vi'ta:l] *adj* energetic; *(lebenswichtig)* vital.
Vitalität [vitali'tɛ:t] *f* vitality, vigour *(Brit),* vigor *(US).*
Vitamin [vita'mi:n] *nt* **-e** vitamin.
Vitamin- [vita'mi:n-]: **v~arm** *adj* low in vitamins; **~bedarf** *m* vitamin requirement; **v~haltig** *adj* containing vitamins; **v~haltig sein** to contain vitamins; **~mangel** *m* vitamin deficiency; **v~reich** *adj* rich in vitamins.
Vitrine [vi'tri:nə] *f (Schrank)* glass cabinet; *(Schaukasten)* showcase, display case.
Vivisektion [vivizɛk'tsio:n] *f* vivisection.
Vize ['fi:tsə] *m* - *(col)* number two *(col)*; *(~meister)* runner-up.
Vize- ['fi:tsə-] *in cpds* vice-; **~kanzler** *m* vice-chancellor; **~könig** *m* viceroy; **~meister** *m* runner-up; **~präsident** *m* vice-president.
Vlies [fli:s] *nt* **-e** fleece.
V-Mann ['fau-] *m* = **Verbindungsmann.**
Vogel *m* **¨** *(lit, fig)* bird. **ein seltsamer** *etc* **~** *(col)* a queer bird *(col);* **ein lustiger ~** *(col)* a lively character *(col)*; **den ~ abschießen** *(col)* to surpass everyone *(iro)*; **einen ~ haben** *(col)* to have a screw loose *(col)*; **jdm den ~ zeigen** *(col)* ≈ to give sb the V sign *(Brit) or* the finger *(US).*
Vogel-: **~bauer** *nt* bird-cage; **~beere** *f (auch* **~beerbaum***)* rowan(-tree), mountain ash; *(Frucht)* rowan(-berry); **~dreck** *m* bird droppings *pl*; **~ei** *nt* bird's egg; **v~frei** *adj (Hist)* outlawed; **~futter** *nt* bird food; *(Samen)* birdseed; **~käfig** *m* bird-cage; **~kirsche** *f (wilde Süßkirsche)* wild cherry; **~kunde** *f* ornithology. **~nest** *nt* bird's nest; **~perspektive** *f* bird's-eye view; **~scheuche** *f (lit, fig col)* scarecrow; **~schutz** *m* protection of birds; **~-Strauß-Politik** *f* head-in-the-sand policy; **~warte** *f* ornithological station; **~zug** *m* bird migration.
Vokabel [vo'ka:bl] *f* **-n** word. **~n** *pl* vocabulary *sing.*
Vokabular [vokabu'la:ɐ] *nt* **-e** vocabulary.
Vokal [vo'ka:l] *m* **-e** vowel.
Vokalmusik [vo'ka:l-] *f* vocal music.
Volk *nt* **¨er** people *pl*; *(~sstamm)* people *sing*; *(Zool)* colony; *(col: Gruppe)* crowd *pl*; *(pej: Pack)* rabble *pl.* **das ~ verlangt, daß ...** the people demand that ...; **viel ~** lots of people *pl*; **etw unters ~ bringen** *Nachricht* to spread sth; *Geld* to spend sth; **da verkehrt vielleicht ein ~!** there's a really strange crowd there!
Völkchen *nt (col: Gruppe)* lot *(col),* crowd. **ein ~ für sich sein** to be a race apart.
Völker-: **~bund** *m (Hist)* League of Nations; **~kunde** *f* ethnology; **~mord** *m* genocide; **~recht** *nt* international law; **v~rechtlich 1** *adj Vertrag, Anerkennung* under international law; *Frage, Thema, Standpunkt* of international law; **2** *adv* according to international law; **~verständigung** *f* international understanding.
volkreich *adj* populous.
Volks- *in cpds* popular; *(auf ein Land bezogen)* national; *(Pol, esp DDR)* people's; **~abstimmung** *f* plebiscite; **~armee** *f (DDR)* People's Army; **~ausgabe** *f* popular edition; **~befragung** *f* public opinion poll; **~belustigung** *f* public entertainment; **~bibliothek** *f* public library; **~bildung** *f* national education; *(Erwachsenenbildung)* adult education; **~deutsche(r)** *mf* ethnic German; **~dichter** *m* poet of the people; **v~eigen** *adj (DDR)* nationally-owned; *(in Namen)* People's Own; **~einkommen** *nt* national income; **~empfinden** *nt* public feeling; **das gesunde ~empfinden** popular sentiment; **~entscheid** *m* referendum; **~erhebung** *f* national uprising; **~feind** *m* enemy of the people; **v~feindlich** *adj* hostile to the people; **~fest** *nt* public festival; *(Jahrmarkt)* fair; **~front** *f (Pol)* popular front; **~gemeinschaft** *f (NS)* national community; **~gerichtshof** *m (NS)* People's Court; **~gesundheit** *f* public health; **~glaube(n)** *m* popular belief; **~gruppe** *f* ethnic group; **~held** *m* popular hero; *(Held des Landes)* national hero; **~hochschule** *f* adult education centre *(Brit) or* center *(US)*; **~kunde** *f* folklore; **~lied** *nt* folk song; **~märchen** *nt* folktale; **~meinung** *f* public *or* popular opinion; **~menge** *f* crowd, mob *(pej)*; **~mund** *m* vernacular; **~musik** *f* folk music; **~partei** *f* people's party; **~polizei** *f (DDR)* People's Police; **~republik** *f* people's republic; **~sage** *f* folk legend; **~schicht** *f* level of society; **~schule** *f (dated)* ≈ elementary school; **~seuche** *f* epidemic; **~stamm** *m* tribe; **~stimme** *f* voice of the people; **~stück** *nt* dialect folk play; **~tanz** *m* folk dance; **~theater** *nt* folk theatre *(Brit) or* theater *(US)*; **~tracht** *f* traditional costume; **~tum** *nt* national traditions *pl*, folklore; **v~tümlich** *adj* folk *attr,* folksy *(col)*; *(traditionell, überliefert)* traditional; *(beliebt)* popular; **~vermögen** *nt* national wealth; **~versammlung** *f* people's assembly; *(Kundgebung)* public gathering; **~vertreter** *m* representative of the people; **~wahl** *f* direct election(s *pl*); **~wirt** *m* economist; **~wirtschaft** *f* national economy; *(Fach)* economics *sing,* political economy; **~wirtschaftler** *m* economist; **~zählung** *f* (national) census;

~**zugehörigkeit** *f* ethnic origin.

voll 1 *adj* full; *Haar* thick; *Satz, Service, Erfolg* complete; *Wahrheit* whole. ~ **von** *or* **mit etw** full of sth; *(bedeckt mit)* covered with sth; **mit ~em Mund** with one's mouth full; **aus dem ~en schöpfen** to draw on unlimited resources; **die Uhr schlägt nur alle ~en Stunden** the clock only strikes the full hour; **die Zahl ist ~** the numbers are complete; **in ~er Fahrt** at full speed; **in ~er Größe** *(Bild)* life-size; *(bei plötzlicher Erscheinung etc)* large as life; **~e Gewißheit über etw** *(acc)* **haben** to be fully certain about sth; **jdn nicht für ~ nehmen** not to take sb seriously; ~ **sein** *(col) (satt)* to be full (up); *(betrunken)* to be plastered *(col)*. **2** *adv* fully. ~ **und ganz** completely, wholly; **eine Rechnung ~ bezahlen** to pay a bill in full.

volladen *vt sep irreg* to load up. **vollgeladen** fully-laden.

voll|auf *adv* fully, completely. **das genügt ~** that's quite enough; ~ **zu tun haben** to have quite enough to do.

vollaufen *vi sep irreg aux sein* to fill up. **etw ~ lassen** to fill sth (up); **sich ~ lassen** *(col)* to get tanked up *(col)*.

Voll-: v~automatisch *adj* fully automatic; **~bad** *nt* (proper) bath; **~bart** *m* (full) beard; **v~bekommen*** *vt sep irreg* to (manage to) fill; **v~berechtigt** *adj attr* with full rights; **~beschäftigung** *f* full employment; **~besitz** *m*: **im ~besitz+***gen* in full possession of.

Vollblut *nt no pl* thoroughbred.

Vollblut- *in cpds (lit: Tier)* thoroughbred; *(fig)* full-blooded.

Voll-: ~blüter *m* - thoroughbred; **v~blütig** *adj* thoroughbred; *(fig)* full-blooded; **~bremsung** *f* emergency stop; **eine ~bremsung machen** to slam on the brakes *(col)*; **v~bringen*** *vt insep irreg (ausführen)* to accomplish, to achieve; *Wunder* to perform; **v~busig** *adj* full-bosomed; **~dampf** *m (Naut)* **mit ~dampf** at full steam.

voll|enden* *insep* **1** *vt* to complete. **2** *vr (zum Abschluß kommen)* to come to an end; *(vollkommen werden)* to be completed.

voll|endet *adj (vollkommen)* completed; *Tugend, Schönheit* perfect; *Mensch* accomplished. **nach ~em 18. Lebensjahr** upon completion of one's 18th year.

vollends *adv* **(a)** *(völlig)* completely. **(b)** *(besonders)* especially.

Voll|endung *f no pl* completion; *(Vollkommenheit)* perfection.

voller *adj* full *(gen* of*)*.

Völlerei *f* gluttony.

voll-: ~essen *vr sep irreg (col)* to gorge oneself; **~fett** *adj* full-fat.

vollführen* *vt insep* to execute, to perform.

Voll-: ~gas *nt no pl* full speed *or* throttle; **~gas geben** to go flat out *(col)*; **~gefühl** *nt*: **im ~gefühl** *+gen* fully aware of; **~genuß** *m*: **im ~genuß** *+gen* in full enjoyment of; **v~gießen** *vt sep irreg* to fill (up); **v~gültig** *adj attr Paß* fully valid; *Ersatz* completely satisfactory; **~gummi** *nt or m* solid rubber; **~idiot** *m (col)* complete idiot.

völlig 1 *adj* complete. **2** *adv* completely. **es genügt ~** that's quite enough; **er hat ~ recht** he's absolutely right.

Voll-: v~jährig *adj* of age; **v~jährig werden/sein** to come/be of age; **~jährige(r)** *mf decl as adj* major; **~jährigkeit** *f* majority *no art;* **v~kaskoversichert** *adj* comprehensively insured; **~kasko(versicherung** *f) nt* fully comprehensive insurance; **v~klimatisiert** *adj* fully air-conditioned.

vollkommen 1 *adj* perfect; *(völlig)* complete, absolute. **sein Glück war ~** his happiness was complete. **2** *adv* completely.

Vollkommenheit *f no pl siehe adj* perfection; completeness.

Voll-: ~kornbrot *nt* wholemeal *(Brit) or* wholewheat *(US)* bread; **v~machen** *vt sep* **(a)** *Gefäß* to fill (up); *Zahl, Dutzend* to make up; **(b)** *(col) Hosen, Windeln* to fill; **~macht** *f* **-en** power, authority *no pl, no indef art; (Urkunde)* power of attorney; **~matrose** *m* able-bodied seaman; **~milch** *f* full-cream milk; **~mond** *m* full moon; **heute ist ~mond** there's a full moon today; **v~mundig** *adj Wein* full-bodied; **~narkose** *f* general anaesthetic *(Brit) or* anesthetic *(US)*; **v~packen** *vt sep (lit, fig)* to pack full; *jdn* to load up; **~pension** *f* full board *(Brit)*, American plan *(US)*; **v~pumpen** *vt sep* to fill (up); **~rausch** *m* drunken stupor; **einen ~rausch haben** to be in a drunken stupor; **v~reif** *adj* fully ripe; **v~saugen** *vr sep irreg* to become saturated; **v~schlank** *adj* plump, stout; **v~schmieren** *sep* **1** *vt* to mess up; **2** *vr* to make oneself all messy; **v~schreiben** *vt sep irreg Heft, Seite* to fill; *Tafel* to cover (with writing).

vollständig 1 *adj* complete; *Adresse* full *attr.* **etw ~ machen** to complete sth. **2** *adv* completely, entirely.

Vollständigkeit *f no pl* completeness.

vollstopfen *vt sep* to cram full.

vollstrecken* *vt insep* to execute.

Voll-: v~tanken *vti sep* to fill up; **v~tönend** *adj* resonant, sonorous; **~treffer** *m (lit, fig)* bull's eye; **v~trunken** *adj* completely drunk; **~versammlung** *f* general meeting; **~waise** *f* orphan; **v~wertig** *adj* full *attr*; *Stellung* equal; *Ersatz* fully adequate; **v~zählig** *adj usu pred* complete; **v~zählig anwesend** all present.

vollziehen* *insep irreg* **1** *vt* to carry out, to execute; *Trauung* to perform; *Bruch* to make. **die ~de Gewalt** the executive (power). **2** *vr* to take place; *(jds Schicksal)* to be fulfilled.

Vollziehung *f*, **Vollzug** *m no pl siehe vt* carrying out, execution; performance; making.

Volontär(in *f)* [volɔn'tɛːɐ, -'tɛːərɪn] *m* trainee.

Volt [vɔlt] *nt* - volt.

Volt- [vɔlt-]: **~meter** *nt* voltmeter; **~zahl** *f* voltage.

Volumen [vo'luːmən] *nt, pl* - *(lit, fig)* volume.

vom = von dem. ~ 10. September an from the 10th September.

von *prep +dat* **(a)** *(Ausgangspunkt)* from. **nördlich ~** to the north of; **~ ... an** from ...; **Waren ~ 5 Mark an** *or* **ab** goods from 5 marks; **~ heute ab** from today (on); **~ ... aus** from ...; **~ dort aus** from there; **etw ~ sich aus tun** to do sth of one's own accord; **~ ... bis** from ... to; **~ morgens bis abends** from morning till night; **~ ... zu** from ... to; **etw ~ etw nehmen/abreißen** to take/tear sth off sth; **~ einem Bus abspringen** to jump off a bus; **~ wo/wann ...?** where/when ... from?

(b) *(Ursache, Urheberschaft, im Passiv)* by. **das Gedicht ist ~ Schiller** the poem is by Schiller; **ein Kind ~ jdm kriegen** to have a child by sb; **~ etw müde** tired from sth.

(c) *(als Genitiv)* of. **jeweils zwei ~ zehn** two out of every ten; **ein Riese ~ einem Mann** *(col)* a giant of a man; **nett ~ dir** nice of you; **die Königin ~ England** the queen of England; **der Geburtstag ~ meinem Vater** my father's birthday; **ein „~ (und zu)" sein** to have a handle to one's name.

(d) *(über)* about. **er erzählte vom Urlaub** he talked about his holiday; **da weiß ich nichts ~** *(col)* I don't know anything about it.

(e) *(col)* **~ wegen** no way! *(col)*.

von|einander *adv* from each other; *wissen* of each other.

vonnöten *adj:* **~ sein** to be necessary.

vonstatten *adv:* **~ gehen** *(stattfinden)* to take place; **alles ging gut ~** everything went well.

vor 1 *prep+acc or dat* **(a)***+dat (räumlich)* in front of; *(außerhalb von)* outside; *(~ Hintergrund)* against; *(in jds Achtung)* in the eyes of; *(bei Reihenfolge)* before. **~ der Kirche rechts abbiegen**

turn right before the church; ~ **allen Dingen,** ~ **allem** above all. **(b)**+*acc (Richtung)* in front of; *(außerhalb von)* outside. **(c)** +*dat (zeitlich)* before. **zwanzig (Minuten) ~ drei** twenty (minutes) to three; **das liegt noch ~ uns** this is still to come; ~ **fünf Jahren** five years ago. **(d)** +*acc* ~ **sich hin summen** to hum to oneself; ~ **sich hin schreiben/arbeiten** to write/work away. **(e)** +*dat* ~ **sich her** before one, in front of one. **(f)**+*dat (Ursache angebend)* with. ~ **Kälte zittern** to shiver with cold; ~ **Hunger sterben** to die of hunger; ~ **lauter Arbeit** because of work. **(g)** **sich ~ jdm verstecken** to hide from sb. **2** *adv* ~ **und zurück** backwards and forwards; **alle kleinen Kinder ~!** all small children to the front!

vor|ab *adv* to begin with.

Vor-: ~**abdruck** *m* preprint; ~**abend** *m* evening before; **am ~abend der Revolution** *(fig)* on the eve of revolution; ~**ahnung** *f* premonition.

voran *adv* **(a)** *(vorn, an der Spitze)* first. **ihm/ihr** ~ in front of him/her; **mit dem Kopf ~ fallen** to fall head first. **(b)** *(vorwärts)* forwards. **nur** *or* **immer** ~ keep going.

voran- *pref siehe auch* **voraus-;** ~**bringen** *vt sep irreg* to make progress with; ~**gehen** *vi sep irreg aux sein* **(a)** *(an der Spitze gehen)* to go first *or* in front; *(fig: Einleitung etc)* to precede *(dat* sth*)*; **jdm ~gehen** to go ahead of sb; **(b)** *(zeitlich vor jdm gehen)* to go on ahead; **einer Sache** *(dat)* ~**gehen** to precede sth; **(c)** *auch vi impers (Fortschritte machen)* to make progress *or* headway; ~**kommen** *vi sep irreg aux sein* to get on.

Vor|anschlag *m* estimate.

voran-: ~**stellen** *vt sep* to put in front *(dat* of*)*; *(fig)* to give precedence *(dat* over*)*; ~**treiben** *vt sep irreg* to drive forward.

Vor-: ~**arbeit** *f* preliminary work, groundwork; **v~arbeiten** *sep* **1** *vi* to work in advance; **2** *vr* to work one's way forward; ~**arbeiter(in** *f***)** *m* foreman; forewoman.

voraus *adv* **(a)** *(voran)* in front *(+dat* of*)*. **er ist den anderen/seiner Zeit** ~ he is ahead of the others/ his time. **(b)** *(vorher)* **im** ~ in advance.

Voraus-: **v~blicken** *vi sep* to look ahead; **v~blickend 1** *adj* foresighted; **2** *adv* with regard to the future; **v~eilen** *vi sep aux sein (lit, fig)* to hurry on ahead; **v~fahren** *vi sep irreg aux sein (an der Spitze)* to drive/go in front *(dat* of*)*; *(früher)* to drive/go on ahead; **v~gehen** *vi sep irreg aux sein siehe* **vorangehen (a, b); v~gesetzt** *adj* **v~gesetzt, (daß) ...** provided (that) ...; **v~ haben** *vt sep irreg* **jdm viel v~haben** to have a great advantage over sb; **v~laufen** *vi sep irreg aux sein (an der Spitze)* to run in front *(dat* of*)*; *(früher)* to run on ahead; **v~planen** *vti sep* to plan ahead; **v~sagen** *vt sep* to predict *(jdm* for sb*)*; *Wetter* to forecast; **jdm die Zukunft v~sagen** to foretell sb's future; **v~schicken** *vt sep* to send on ahead *(dat* of*)*; *(fig: vorher sagen)* to say in advance *(dat* of*)*; **v~sehen** *vt sep irreg* to foresee.

voraussetzen *vt sep* to presuppose; *(als selbstverständlich, sicher annehmen)* to take for granted; *(erfordern)* to require, to demand. **etw als bekannt** ~ to assume that everyone knows sth.

Voraussetzung *f* prerequisite; *(Qualifikation)* qualification; *(Erfordernis)* requirement; *(Annahme)* assumption. **unter der ~, daß ...** on condition that ...

Voraus-: ~**sicht** *f* foresight; *(Erwartung)* anticipation; **aller ~sicht nach** in all probability; **v~sichtlich 1** *adj* expected; **2** *adv* probably; **er wird v~sichtlich gewinnen** he is expected to win; ~**zahlung** *f* advance payment.

Vorbau *m* porch; *(Balkon)* balcony.

vorbauen *sep* **1** *vt (anbauen)* to build on (in front). **2** *vi (Vorkehrungen treffen)* to take precautions.

Vorbedacht *m*: **mit/ohne ~** *(Überlegung)* with/without due consideration; *(Absicht)* intentionally/unintentionally.

Vorbedingung *f* precondition.

Vorbehalt *m* -e reservation. **unter dem ~, daß ...** with the reservation that ...

vorbehalten* *vt sep irreg* **sich** *(dat)* **etw** ~ to reserve sth (for oneself); *Recht* to reserve sth; **diese Entscheidung bleibt ihm** ~ this decision is left up to him; **alle Rechte** ~ all rights reserved; **Änderungen (sind)** ~ subject to alterations.

vorbehaltlich *prep+gen (form)* subject to.

vorbehaltlos *adj* unconditional, unreserved.

vorbei *adv* **(a)** *(räumlich)* past, by. ~ **an** *(+dat)* past. **(b)** *(zeitlich)* ~ **sein** to be past; *(Sorgen)* to be over; *(Schmerzen)* to be gone; **damit ist es nun** ~ that's all over now; **aus und** ~ over and done.

vorbei- *pref (vorüber)* past; *(zu Besuch)* over; ~**bringen** *vt sep irreg (col)* to drop off; ~**dürfen** *vi sep irreg (col)* to be allowed past; **dürfte ich bitte ~?** could I get past *or* by, please?; ~**fahren** *vi sep irreg aux sein* to pass *(an jdm/etw* sb/sth*)*; **bei jdm ~fahren** to call in on sb; ~**gehen** *vi sep irreg aux sein* **(a)** *(lit, fig) (an jdm/etw* sb/sth*)* to go past, to pass; **an etw** *(dat)* ~**gehen** *(fig: nicht beachten)* to overlook sth; **bei jdm ~gehen** *(col)* to drop in on sb; **(b)** *(vergehen)* to pass; **(c)** *(verfehlen)* to miss *(an etw (dat)* sth*)*; ~**kommen** *vi sep irreg aux sein* **(a)** *(an jdm/etw* sb/sth*)* to pass, to go past; *(an einem Hindernis)* to get past *or* by; **an einer Aufgabe nicht ~kommen** to be unable to avoid a task; **(b) bei jdm ~kommen** *(col)* to drop *or* call in on sb; ~**können** *vi sep irreg* to be able to get past *or* by *(an etw (dat)* sth*)*; ~**lassen** *vt sep irreg* to let past *(an jdm/etw* sb/sth*)*; ~**laufen** *vi sep irreg aux sein (an jdm/etw* sb/sth*)* to run past; *(col: ~gehen)* to go *or* walk past; ~**marschieren*** *vi sep aux sein* to march past; ~**müssen** *vi sep irreg (an jdm/etw* sb/sth*)* to have to go past; **bei jdm ~müssen** *(col)* to have to call in at sb's; ~**reden** *vi sep* **an etw** *(dat)* ~**reden** to talk around sth; **aneinander ~reden** to talk at cross purposes; ~**ziehen** *vi sep irreg aux sein* to file past *(an jdm/etw* sb/sth*)*.

vorbelastet *adj* handicapped; *(voreingenommen)* biased *(von* because of*)*.

Vorbemerkung *f* introductory remark.

vorbereiten* *vtr sep* to prepare *(auf +acc* for*)*.

vorbereitend *adj attr* preparatory, preliminary.

Vorbereitung *f* preparation. ~**en (für** *or* **zu etw) treffen** to make preparations (for sth).

Vorbereitungs- *in cpds* preparatory.

Vor-: ~**besprechung** *f* preliminary meeting; **v~bestellen*** *vt sep* to book (in advance), to reserve; **v~bestraft** *adj* previously convicted; **er ist schon einmal v~bestraft** he has a previous conviction; **v~beten** *sep* **1** *vi* to lead the prayer/ prayers; **2** *vt* **jdm etw v~beten** *(fig col)* to keep spelling sth out for sb *(col)*.

Vorbeugehaft *f* preventive custody.

vorbeugen *sep* **1** *vi* to prevent *(einer Sache (dat)* sth*)*. **2** *vtr* to bend forward.

vorbeugend *adj* preventive.

Vorbeugung *f* prevention *(gegen, von* of*)*.

Vorbeugungs- *in cpds* preventive.

Vorbild *nt* model; *(Beispiel)* example *(für jdn* to sb*)*. **er/sein Verhalten kann uns zum ~ dienen** he/his behaviour is an example to us; **sich** *(dat)* **jdn zum ~ nehmen** to model oneself on sb.

vorbildlich *adj* exemplary; *sich benehmen* in an exemplary fashion.

Vor-: ~**bildung** *f* educational background; ~**bote** *m (fig)* herald.

vorbringen *vt sep irreg Plan* to propose; *Meinung, Wunsch, Forderung* to express, to state; *Einwand, Beschwerde* to make; *Entschuldigung* to offer.

Vor-: **v~christlich** *adj* pre-Christian; ~**dach** *nt* canopy; **v~datieren*** *vt sep* to postdate.

Vorder-: ~**achse** *f* front axle; ~**ansicht** *f* front view; ~**asien** *nt* Near East; ~**bein** *nt* foreleg.

Vordere(r) *mf decl as adj* person in front.

vordere(r, s) *adj* front.

Vorder-: ~front *f* frontage; **~fuß** *m* forefoot; **~grund** *m* foreground; *(fig)* fore(front); **sich in den ~grund drängen** to push oneself to the fore; **im ~grund stehen** *(fig)* to be to the fore; **v~gründig** *adj (oberflächlich)* superficial; **~mann** *m, pl* **~männer** person in front; **etw auf ~mann bringen** *(fig col)* to get sth into shape; **~pfote** *f* front paw; **~rad** *nt* front wheel; **~seite** *f* front; *(von Münze)* head; **~sitz** *m* front seat.

vorderste(r, s) *adj superl of* **vordere(r, s)** front(most). **der/die V~ in der Schlange** the first person in the queue *(Brit) or* line *(US)*.

Vorder-: ~teil *m or nt* front; **~tür** *f* front door; **~zahn** *m* front tooth; **~zimmer** *nt* front room.

vordrängen *vr sep* to push to the front. **sich in der Schlange ~** to jump the queue *(Brit)*, to push to the front of the line *(US)*.

vordringen *vi sep irreg aux sein* to advance. **bis zu jdm/etw ~** to get as far as sb/sth.

vordringlich *adj* urgent, pressing.

Vordruck *m* form.

vor|ehelich *adj attr* premarital.

vor|eilig *adj* rash. **~e Schlüsse ziehen** to jump to conclusions.

vor|einander *adv (räumlich)* in front of each other; *(einander gegenüber)* face to face.

vor|eingenommen *adj* prejudiced, biased.

Vor|eingenommenheit *f no pl* prejudice, bias.

vor|enthalten* *vt sep irreg* **jdm etw ~** to withhold sth from sb.

Vor|entscheidung *f* preliminary decision.

vor|erst *adv* for the time being.

Vorfahr *m (wk)* **-en, -en** forefather, ancestor.

vorfahren *sep irreg* **1** *vi aux sein* **(a)** to go *or* move forward. **(b)** *(ankommen)* to drive up. **(c)** *(früher fahren)* to go on ahead. **(d)** *(an der Spitze fahren)* to drive in front. **2** *vt* **(a)** *(weiter nach vorn fahren)* to move up *or* forward. **(b)** *(vor den Eingang fahren)* to drive up.

Vorfahrt *f no pl* right of way. **„~ (be)achten"** "give way" *(Brit)*, "yield" *(US)*; **jdm die ~ nehmen** to ignore sb's right of way.

Vorfahrts-: v~berechtigt *adj* **v~berechtigt sein** to have (the) right of way; **~regel** *f* rule on (the) right of way; **~schild** *nt* give way *(Brit) or* yield *(US)* sign; **~straße** *f* major road.

Vorfall *m* incident, occurrence.

vorfallen *vi sep irreg aux sein* to occur, to happen.

Vor-: ~feld *nt (fig)* run-up *(+gen* to*)*; **v~fertigen** *vt sep* to prefabricate; **~film** *m* short; **v~finden** *vt sep irreg* to find, to discover; **~freude** *f* anticipation; **~frühling** *m* early spring.

vorfühlen *vi sep (fig)* to put out feelers. **bei jdm ~** to sound sb out.

vorführen *vt sep* **(a)** *(zeigen)* to present; *Film* to show; *Mode* to model; *Übung, (Vertreter) Gerät* to demonstrate *(dat* to*)*; *Theaterstück auch, Kunststücke* to perform *(dat* to, in front of*)*. **(b)** *Angeklagten* to bring forward.

Vorführung *f* presentation; *(von Filmen)* showing; *(von Mode)* modelling *(Brit)*, modeling *(US)*; *(von Geräten, Modellen, Übungen)* demonstration; *(von Theaterstück, Kunststücken)* performance.

Vorgang *m* **(a)** *(Ereignis)* event, occurrence; *(Ablauf, Hergang)* series of events. **(b)** *(Sci)* process.

Vorgänger(in *f***)** *m* **-** predecessor.

Vorgarten *m* front garden.

vorgaukeln *vt sep* **jdm etw ~** to lead sb to believe in sth; **jdm ~, daß ...** to lead sb to believe that ...

vorgeben *vt sep irreg (vortäuschen)* to pretend; *(fälschlich beteuern)* to profess.

Vorgebirge *nt* foothills *pl*.

vorgefaßt *adj Meinung* preconceived.

Vorgefühl *nt* anticipation; *(böse Ahnung)* presentiment.

vorgehen *vi sep irreg aux sein* **(a)** *(handeln)* to act, to proceed. **gerichtlich gegen jdn ~** to take legal action against sb. **(b)** *(geschehen, vor sich gehen)* to go on, to happen. **(c)** *(Uhr) (spätere Zeit anzeigen)* to be fast; *(zu schnell gehen)* to gain. **(d)** *(nach vorn gehen)* to go forward. **(e)** *(vorangehen)* to go first; *(früher gehen)* to go on ahead. **(f)** *(den Vorrang haben)* to come first, to have priority.

Vorgehen *nt no pl* action.

Vor-: v~gerückt *adj Stunde* late; *Alter* advanced; **~geschichte** *f* **(a)** *(eines Falles)* past history; **(b)** *(Urgeschichte)* prehistory, prehistoric times *pl*; **~geschmack** *m (fig)* foretaste.

Vorgesetzte(r) *mf decl as adj* superior.

vorgestern *adv* the day before yesterday. **von ~** *(fig)* antiquated.

vorgreifen *vi sep irreg* to anticipate; *(verfrüht handeln)* to act prematurely. **jdm ~** to forestall sb; **einer Sache** *(dat)* **~** to anticipate sth.

vorhaben *vt sep irreg* to intend; *(planen)* to have planned. **was haben Sie heute vor?** what are your plans for today?, what do you have on today?

Vorhaben *nt* plan; *(Absicht)* intention.

Vorhalle *f (Diele)* entrance hall; *(von Parlament)* lobby.

vorhalten *sep irreg* **1** *vt* **(a) jdm etw ~** *(vorwerfen)* to reproach sb for sth; *(als Beispiel)* to hold sth up to sb. **(b)** *(vor den Körper halten)* to hold up; *(beim Niesen etc)* to put in front of one's mouth. **mit vorgehaltener Pistole** at gunpoint. **2** *vi (anhalten)* to last.

vorhanden *adj (verfügbar)* available; *(existierend)* existing.

Vorhang *m, pl* **Vorhänge** curtain.

Vorhängeschloß *nt* padlock.

Vorhaut *f* foreskin.

vorher *adv* before(hand); *(früher)* before. **am Tage ~** the day before, the previous day.

vorher-: ~bestimmen* *vt sep* to determine in advance; *Schicksal* to predetermine; *(Gott)* to preordain; **es war ihm ~bestimmt ...** he was predestined ...; **~gehen** *vi sep irreg aux sein* to go first *or* in front; *(fig)* to precede; **~gehend** *adj Tag, Ereignisse* preceding.

vorherig [foːɐ'heːrɪç] *adj attr* prior, previous; *(ehemalig)* former.

Vorherrschaft *f* predominance, supremacy.

vorherrschen *vi sep* to predominate, to prevail.

vorherrschend *adj* predominant; *(weitverbreitet)* prevalent.

Vorher-: ~sage *f* forecast; **v~sagen** *vt sep* = **voraussagen; v~sehen** *vt sep irreg* to foresee.

vorhin *adv* a little while ago.

vorhinein *adv:* **im ~** in advance.

Vor-: ~hof *m* forecourt; **~hut** *f* **-en** *(Mil)* advance guard.

vorig *adj attr* previous; *Jahr, Woche etc* last.

Vor-: ~jahr *nt* previous year, year before; **v~jährig** *adj* of the previous year; **v~jammern** *vti sep* **jdm (etwas) v~jammern** to moan to sb *(von* about*)*; **~kämpfer(in** *f***)** *m* pioneer *(für* of*)*; **v~kauen** *vt sep Nahrung* to chew; **jdm etw v~kauen** *(fig col)* to spoonfeed sth to sb *(col)*.

Vorkehrung *f* **~en treffen** to take precautions.

Vorkenntnis *f* previous knowledge *no pl*.

vorknöpfen *vt sep (fig col)* **sich** *(dat)* **jdn ~** to take sb to task.

vorkommen *vi sep irreg aux sein* **(a)** *auch vi impers (sich ereignen)* to happen. **das soll nicht wieder ~** it won't happen again; **so was soll ~!** that's life! **(b)** *(vorhanden sein, auftreten)* to occur; *(Pflanzen, Tiere)* to be found. **(c)** *(erscheinen)* to seem *(jdm* to sb*)*. **sich** *(dat)* **überflüssig ~** to feel superfluous; **sich** *(dat)* **klug ~** to think one is clever. **(d)** *(nach vorn kommen)* to come forward.

Vorkommen *nt* **-** *(no pl: das Auftreten)* occurrence; *(Min)* deposit.

Vorkriegs- *in cpds* pre-war; **~zeit** *f* pre-war

period.
vorladen *vt sep irreg (bei Gericht)* to summons.
Vorlage *f* **-n** **(a)** *no pl (von Dokument, Scheck etc)* presentation; *(von Beweismaterial)* submission. **(b)** *(Muster) (zum Stricken, Nähen)* pattern; *(Liter)* model. **etw nach einer ~ machen** to model sth on sth. **(c)** *(Entwurf)* draft; *(Parl: Gesetzes~)* bill.
vorlassen *vt sep irreg* **(a)** *(col)* **jdn ~** *(nach vorn gehen lassen)* to let sb go in front; *(überholen lassen)* to let sb pass. **(b)** *(Empfang gewähren)* to allow in.
Vorlauf *m (Sport)* preliminary heat/round.
vorlaufen *vi sep irreg aux sein (col) (vorauslaufen)* to run on ahead; *(nach vorne laufen)* to run to the front.
Vorläufer *m* forerunner *(auch Ski)*, precursor.
vorläufig **1** *adj* temporary; *(provisorisch)* provisional. **2** *adv (einstweilig)* temporarily; *(fürs erste)* for the time being.
vorlaut *adj* cheeky, impertinent.
Vorleben *nt* past (life).
Vorlegebesteck *nt* serving cutlery; *(Tranchierbesteck)* carvers *pl*.
vorlegen *sep vt* **(a)** to present; *Paß, Zeugnisse* to produce; *Beweismaterial* to submit; *(Pol) Entwurf* to table *(Brit)*, to introduce. **(b)** *Speisen* to serve; *(hinlegen) Futter* to put down *(dat* for*)*. **(c)** *Riegel* to put across.
Vorleger *m* **-** mat; *(Bett~ auch)* (bedside) rug.
vorlehnen *vr sep* to lean forward.
Vorleistung *f (Econ) (Vorausbezahlung)* advance (payment); *(Vorarbeit)* preliminary work; *(Pol)* prior concession.
vorlesen *vti sep irreg* to read aloud. **jdm (etw) ~** to read (sth) to sb.
Vorlesung *f (Univ)* lecture; *(Vorlesungsreihe)* course (of lectures). **über etw** *(acc)* **~en halten** to give (a course of) lectures on sth; **~en hören** to go to lectures.
Vorlesungsverzeichnis *nt* lecture timetable.
vorletzte(r, s) *adj* last but one, penultimate. **im ~n Jahr** the year before last.
Vorliebe *f* predilection. **etw mit ~ tun** to particularly like doing sth.
vorliebnehmen *vi sep irreg* **mit jdm/etw ~** to make do with sb/sth.
vorliegen *vi sep irreg (zur Verfügung stehen)* to be available; *(Urteil)* to be known; *(eingereicht, vorgelegt sein)* to have come in. **jdm ~** *(Unterlagen, Akten etc)* to be with sb; **etw liegt gegen jdn vor** sb is charged with sth; **hier liegt ein Irrtum vor** there is an error here.
vorliegend *adj attr Gründe* existing; *Akten, Unterlagen* on hand; *Frage* at issue; *Ergebnisse* available.
vorlügen *vt sep irreg* **jdm etwas ~** to lie to sb.
vormachen *vt sep* **(a) jdm etw ~** *(zeigen)* to show sb how to do sth. **(b)** *(fig)* **jdm etwas ~** *(täuschen)* to fool sb; **er läßt sich** *(dat)* **von niemandem etwas ~** nobody can fool him; **mach mir doch nichts vor** don't try and fool me.
Vormacht(stellung) *f* supremacy *(gegenüber* over*)*.
Vormarsch *m (Mil)* advance. **im ~ sein** to be on the advance.
vormerken *vt sep* to make a note of; *(bei Bestellung auch)* to take an order for; *Plätze* to book. **sich für einen Kursus ~ lassen** to put oneself down for a course.
Vormittag *m* morning. **am ~** in the morning.
vormittag *adv* **heute/gestern/morgen ~** this/yesterday/tomorrow morning.
vormittags *adv* in the morning; *(jeden Morgen)* in the morning(s).
Vormund *m* **-e** guardian. **ich brauche keinen ~** *(fig)* I don't need anyone to tell me what to do.
Vormundschaft *f* guardianship. **jdn unter ~ stellen** to place sb under the care of a guardian.
vorn *adv* **(a)** in front; *(am vorderen Ende, auf der Vorderseite)* at the front. **von ~** from the front; **nach ~** *(ganz nach ~)* to the front; *(weiter nach ~)* forwards; **von weit ~** from the very front; **~ im Buch/in der Schlange/auf der Liste** at the front of the book/queue/at the top of the list; **sich ~ anstellen** to join the front of the queue *(Brit) or* line *(US)*; **~ im Bild** in the front of the picture; **von ~** from the front; **jdn von ~ sehen** to see sb's face; **~ im Auto/Bus** in the front of the car/bus; **das Buch ist ~ schmutzig** the front of the book is dirty; **das Auto da ~** the car in front *or* ahead there; **sie waren ziemlich weit ~** they were quite far ahead.
(b) *(am Anfang)* **von ~** from the beginning; **von ~ anfangen** to start from the beginning; *(von neuem)* to start (all) over again; *(neues Leben)* to make a fresh start; **er betrügt sie von ~ bis hinten** he deceives her right, left and centre *(Brit) or* center *(US)*.
Vorname *m* Christian name, first name.
vornehm *adj* **(a)** *(von hohem Rang) Familie, Kreise* distinguished; *(von adliger Herkunft)* aristocratic; *(kultiviert) Herr, Dame* posh *(col)*; *Manieren, Art, Benehmen* refined; *(edel) Gesinnung, Charakter, Handeln* noble. **die ~e Gesellschaft** high society; **in ~en Kreisen** in polite society. **(b)** *(elegant, luxuriös)* smart, posh *(col)*; *Geschäft* exclusive, posh *(col)*; *Kleid, Äußeres* elegant, stylish.
vornehmen *vt sep irreg* **(a)** *(ausführen)* to carry out. **(b) sich** *(dat)* **etw ~** *(in Angriff nehmen)* to get to work on sth; *(planen, vorhaben)* to intend to do sth; *(Vorsatz fassen)* to have resolved to do sth; **sich** *(dat)* **zuviel ~** to take on too much. **(c) sich** *(dat)* **jdn ~** *(col)* to have a word with sb.
vornehmlich *adv (hauptsächlich, vor allem)* principally; *(vorzugsweise)* first and foremost.
vorneigen *vtr sep* to lean forward.
vorn(e)weg *adv* in front; *(als erstes)* first.
vorn-: ~herein *adv*: **von ~herein** from the outset; **~über** *adv* forwards.
Vor|ort *m (Vorstadt)* suburb.
Vor|ortzug *m* suburban train; *(im Berufsverkehr)* commuter train.
Vor-: ~platz *m* forecourt; **~posten** *m (Mil)* outpost; **v~programmieren*** *vt sep (lit, fig)* to preprogramme *(Brit)*, to preprogram *(US)*; **v~programmiert** *adj Erfolg, Antwort* automatic.
Vorrang *m no pl* **~ haben** to have priority; *(vor +dat* over*)*; **jdm/einer Sache (den) ~ geben** *or* **einräumen** to give sb/a matter priority.
vorrangig **1** *adj* of prime importance, priority *attr*. **2** *adv* as a matter of priority.
Vorrangstellung *f* pre-eminence *no indef art*.
Vorrat *m, pl* **Vorräte** *(an +dat* of*)* stock; *(von Waren)* stocks *pl*. **etw auf ~ kaufen** to stock up with sth; **Vorräte anlegen** to lay in a stock; **solange der ~ reicht** *(Comm)* while stocks last.
vorrätig *adj* in stock; *(verfügbar)* available. **etw nicht mehr ~ haben** to be out of sth.
Vorrats-: ~kammer *f* store cupboard; *(für Lebensmittel)* larder; **~raum** *m* store room; *(in Geschäft)* stock room.
Vorraum *m* anteroom; *(Büro)* outer office.
vorrechnen *vt sep* **jdm etw ~** to calculate sth for sb; *(als Kritik)* to point sth out to sb.
Vorrecht *nt* prerogative; *(Vergünstigung)* privilege.
Vorrede *f* introductory speech; *(Theat)* prologue.
Vorredner *m (vorheriger Redner)* previous speaker.
Vorreiter *m (fig)* precursor.
vorrennen *vi sep irreg aux sein (col) (voraus)* to race ahead; *(nach vorn)* to run forward.
Vorrichtung *f* device, gadget.
vorrücken *sep* **1** *vt* to move forward. **2** *vi aux sein*

to move forward; *(Mil)* to advance; *(Uhrzeiger)* to move on. **mit dem Stuhl ~** to move one's chair forward; *siehe* **vorgerückt.**

Vọrrunde *f (Sport)* preliminary round.

vọrsagen *sep (Sch)* **1** *vt Lösung* to tell. **2** *vi* **jdm ~** to tell sb the answer.

Vọrsaison *f* low season, early season.

Vọrsatz *m* (firm) intention. **den ~ haben, etw zu tun** to intend to do sth.

vọrsätzlich *adj* deliberate; *(Jur)* wilful; *Mord* premeditated. **jdn ~ töten** to kill sb intentionally.

Vọrschau *f* preview; *(Film)* trailer; *(Wetter~)* forecast.

Vọrschein *m* **zum ~ bringen** *(lit: zeigen)* to produce; *(fig: deutlich machen)* to bring to light; **zum ~ kommen** *(lit: sichtbar werden)* to appear; *(fig: entdeckt werden)* to come to light.

vọrschieben *vt sep irreg* **(a)** *(davorschieben)* to push in front; *Riegel* to put across; *(nach vorn schieben)* to push forward. **(b)** *(Mil)* **vorgeschobener Posten** advance party. **(c)** *(fig: vorschützen)* to put forward as an excuse. **(d) jdn ~** to put sb forward as a front man.

vọrschießen *sep irreg* **1** *vt* **jdm Geld ~** to advance sb money. **2** *vi aux sein* to shoot forward.

Vọrschlag *m* suggestion; *(Rat)* advice; *(Pol: von Kandidaten)* proposal. **auf ~ von** *or* *+gen* at *or* on the suggestion of.

vọrschlagen *vt sep irreg* to suggest. **jdn für ein Amt ~** to propose sb for a post; **jdm ~, daß er etw tut** to suggest to sb that he do(es) sth.

Vọrschlaghammer *m* sledgehammer.

vọrschreiben *vt sep irreg (befehlen)* to stipulate. **ich lasse mir nichts ~** I won't be dictated to.

vọrschreiten *vi sep irreg aux sein* to progress. **im vorgeschrittenen Alter** at an advanced age; **zu vorgeschrittener Stunde** at a late hour.

Vọrschrift *f* **-en** rule, regulation; *(Anweisung)* instruction. **nach ~ des Arztes** according to doctor's orders; **jdm ~en machen** to give sb orders.

vọrschrifts-: ~gemäß, ~mäßig 1 *adj Signal, Verhalten* correct, proper *attr*; **2** *adv* according to (the) regulations; *(laut Anordnung)* as instructed; **~widrig** *adj, adv* contrary to regulations.

Vọrschub *m*: **jdm/einer Sache ~ leisten** to encourage sb/sth.

vọrschulisch *adj* pre-school *attr.*

Vọrschuß *m* advance.

vọrschützen *vt sep* to put forward as a pretext; *Unwissenheit* to plead. **er schützte vor, daß ...** he pretended that ...

vọrschwärmen *vti sep* **jdm von jdm/etw ~** to go into raptures over sb/sth.

vọrschweben *vi sep* **jdm schwebt etw vor** sb has sth in mind.

vọrschwindeln *vt sep* **jdm etwas ~** to lie to sb.

vọrsehen *sep irreg* **1** *vt* to provide for; *(planen)* to plan; *Zeit* to allow. **etw für etw ~** *(bestimmen)* to intend sth for sth; *Geld* to earmark sth for sth; **jdn für etw ~** *(bestimmen)* to designate sb for sth; **er ist für dieses Amt vorgesehen** we have him in mind for this post. **2** *vr (sich in acht nehmen)* to take care. **sich vor jdm/etw ~** to beware of sb/sth.

Vọrsehung *f no pl* **die ~** Providence.

vọrsetzen *vt sep* **(a)** to move forward; *Fuß* to put forward; *Schüler* to move (up) to the front. **(b)** *(davorsetzen)* to put in front *(vor +acc* of*)*. **(c) jdm etw ~** *(anbieten)* to serve sth up for sb.

Vọrsicht *f no pl* care; *(bei Gefahr)* caution; *(Behutsamkeit)* wariness. **(jdn) zur ~ (er)mahnen** to advise sb to be careful/cautious/wary; **„~ Stufe"** "mind the step"; **mit ~** carefully; cautiously; warily; **was er sagt ist mit ~ zu genießen** *(hum col)* you have to take what he says with a pinch of salt *(col)*; **dieser Wein ist mit ~ zu genießen** *(col)* I should be a bit wary of this wine; **~ ist besser als Nachsicht** *(Prov)* better safe than sorry.

vọrsichtig *adj* careful; *(besonnen)* cautious; *(mißtrauisch)* wary; *Schätzung* conservative.

Vọrsichts-: v~halber *adv* as a precaution; **~maßnahme** *f* precaution; **~maßnahmen treffen** to take precautions.

Vọr-: ~silbe *f* prefix; **v~singen** *sep irreg* **1** *vti* **jdm (etw) v~singen** to sing (sth) to sb. **2** *vi (zur Prüfung)* to have a singing test; **v~sintflutlich** *adj (col)* antiquated.

Vọrsitz *m* chairmanship; *(Amt eines Präsidenten)* presidency. **den ~ haben** *or* **führen (bei etw)** to be chairman *or* chairperson (of sth); *(bei Sitzung)* to chair sth.

Vọrsitzende(r) *mf decl as adj* chairman/chairwoman, chairperson; *(von Verein)* president.

Vọrsorge *f no pl (Vorsichtsmaßnahme)* precaution; *(vorherplanende Fürsorge)* provision(s *pl*) *no def art.* **zur ~** as a precaution; **~ treffen** to take precautions; *(fürs Alter)* to make provisions.

vọrsorgen *vi sep* to make provisions *(daß* so that*)*. **für etw ~** to make provisions for sth.

vọrsorglich 1 *adj* precautionary; *Mensch* cautious. **2** *adv* as a precaution.

Vọrspann *m* **-e** *(Film, TV)* opening credits *pl.*

vọrspannen *vt sep Pferde* to harness.

Vọrspeise *f* starter.

vọrspiegeln *vt sep* to sham. **jdm ~(, daß ...)** to pretend to sb (that...).

Vọrspiegelung *f* pretence *(Brit)*, pretense *(US)*. **das ist ~ falscher Tatsachen** it's false pretences.

Vọrspiel *nt (Einleitung)* prelude; *(Ouvertüre)* overture; *(Theat)* prologue; *(Sport)* preliminary match; *(bei Geschlechtsverkehr)* foreplay.

vọrspielen *sep* **1** *vt* **jdm etw ~** *(Mus)* to play sth to sb; *(Theat)* to act sth to sb; *(fig)* to act out a sham of sth in front of sb. **2** *vi (vor Zuhörern)* to play; *(Mus, Theat) (zur Prüfung)* to do one's practical (exam). **jdm ~** *(Mus)* to play for sb; *(Theat)* to act (a role) in front of sb.

vọrsprechen *sep irreg* **1** *vt (vortragen)* to recite. **jdm etw ~** to pronounce sth for sb. **2** *vi* **(a)** *(form: jdn aufsuchen)* to call *(bei jdm* on sb*)*. **(b)** *(Theat)* to audition. **jdn ~ lassen** to audition sb.

vọrspringen *vi sep irreg aux sein* to leap out; *(vorwärts)* to jump forward; *(herausragen)* to jut out; *(Nase, Kinn)* to be prominent.

vọrspringend *adj* projecting; *Nase, Kinn* prominent.

Vọrsprung *m* **(a)** *(Archit)* projection; *(Fels~)* ledge. **(b)** *(Sport, fig: Abstand)* lead *(vor +dat* over*)*; *(Vorgabe)* start. **einen ~ vor jdm haben** to be ahead of sb.

Vọr-: ~stadt *f* suburb; **v~städtisch** *adj* suburban.

Vọrstand *m (leitendes Gremium)* board; *(von Verein)* committee; *(von Partei)* executive.

Vọrstandssitzung *f (von Firma)* board meeting.

vọrstecken *vt sep* to put forward; *Kopf* to stick out.

vọrstehen *vi sep irreg aux haben or sein* **(a)** *(hervorragen)* to project; *(Zähne)* to protrude; *(Knochen, Kinn, Nase)* to be prominent. **(b)** *dem Haushalt* to preside over; *einer Firma, einer Partei* to be the chairman of; *einem Geschäft* to manage; *einer Abteilung* to head (up); *einem Amt* to hold.

Vọrsteher(in *f***)** *m* **-** *(von Abteilung)* head; *(von Gefängnis)* governor *(Brit)*, warden *(US)*; *(Bahnhofs~)* station-master.

vọrstellbar *adj* conceivable. **das ist nicht ~** it's inconceivable.

vọrstellen *sep* **1** *vt* **(a)** *Tisch, Stuhl, Auto* to move forward; *Bein* to put out; *Uhr* to put forward *(um* by*)*. **(b)** *(col: davorstellen)* **etw ~** to put sth in front. **(c)** *(darstellen)* to represent; *(bedeuten)* to mean. **etwas ~** *(fig: Ansehen haben)* to count for something. **(d)** *(bekannt machen)* **jdn jdm ~** to introduce sb to sb. **(e)** *(bekanntmachen, vorführen)* to present. **jdm etw ~** to show sb sth.

2 *vr* **(a) sich** *(dat)* **etw ~** to imagine sth; **sich** *(dat)* **etw unter etw** *(dat)* **~** *Begriff, Wort* to understand sth by sth; **darunter kann ich mir nichts ~** it doesn't mean anything to me; **stell dir das nicht so einfach vor** don't think it's so easy; **so stelle ich mir einen gelungenen Urlaub vor** that's my idea of a successful holiday. **(b)** *(sich nach vorn stellen)* to move forward. **(c)** *(sich bekannt machen)* to introduce oneself *(jdm* to sb*)*; *(bei Bewerbung)* to go for an interview.

Vorstellung *f* **(a)** *(Gedanke)* idea; *(bildlich)* picture; *(Einbildung)* illusion; *(~skraft)* imagination. **sich** *(dat)* **eine ~ von etw machen** to form an idea *or (Bild)* picture of sth; **du machst dir keine ~, wie schwierig das ist** you have no idea how difficult that is. **(b)** *(Theat etc)* performance. **(c)** *(das Bekanntmachen) (zwischen Leuten)* introduction; *(Vorführung)* presentation; *(bei Bewerbung)* interview *(bei* with*)*.

Vorstellungs-: ~gespräch *nt* interview; **~kraft** *f* imagination; **~vermögen** *nt* powers of imagination *pl*.

Vorstoß *m (Vordringen)* venture; *(Mil)* advance; *(fig: Versuch)* attempt.

vorstoßen *sep irreg* **1** *vt* to push forward. **2** *vi aux sein* to venture; *(Sport)* to attack; *(Mil)* to advance.

Vorstrafe *f* previous conviction.

vorstrecken *vt sep* to stretch forward; *Hände* to stretch out; *(fig) Geld* to advance *(jdm* sb*)*.

Vorstufe *f* preliminary stage; *(von Entwicklung)* early stage.

vorstürmen *vi sep aux sein* to rush forward.

Vortag *m* day before.

vortäuschen *vt sep Krankheit* to feign; *Schlag* to fake.

Vortäuschung *f* pretence *(Brit)*, pretense *(US)*, fake. **unter ~ falscher Tatsachen** under false pretences.

Vorteil *m* **-e** advantage *(auch Sport)*. **die Vor- und Nachteile** the pros and cons; **auf seinen ~ bedacht sein** to have an eye to one's own interests; **jdm gegenüber im ~ sein** to have an advantage over sb; **sich zu seinem ~ ändern** to change for the better; **von ~ sein** to be advantageous.

vorteilhaft *adj* advantageous; *Kleider* flattering; *Geschäft* lucrative. **~ aussehen** to look one's best; **etw ~ verkaufen** to sell sth for a profit.

Vortrag *m, pl* **Vorträge (a)** talk. **einen ~ halten** to give a talk. **(b)** *(Darbietung)* performance; *(von Gedicht)* reading.

vortragen *vt sep irreg (berichten)* to report; *(förmlich mitteilen) Fall, Forderung* to present; *Beschwerde* to lodge; *Meinung, Wunsch* to express; *(einen Vortrag halten über)* to give a talk on; *(vorsprechen) Gedicht* to recite; *(Mus)* to perform.

Vortrags-: ~abend *m* lecture evening; *(mit Gedichten)* poetry evening; *(mit Musik)* recital; **~reihe** *f* series of lectures.

vortrefflich *adj* splendid, superb.

vortreten *vi sep irreg aux sein* **(a)** *(lit)* to step forward. **(b)** *(hervorragen)* to project; *(Augen)* to protrude.

Vortritt *m no pl* priority. **jdm den ~ lassen** *(lit, fig)* to let sb go first.

vorüber *adv* **~ sein** *(räumlich, Jugend)* to be past; *(Gewitter etc)* to be over; *(Schmerz)* to have gone.

vorüber- *pref siehe auch* **vorbei-; ~gehen** *vi sep irreg aux sein* to pass *(an etw (dat)* sth*)*; *(Gewitter)* to blow over; **~gehend** *adj (flüchtig)* momentary; *Krankheit* short; *(zeitweilig)* temporary.

Vor|urteil *nt* prejudice *(gegenüber* against*)*. **~e haben** to be prejudiced.

vor|urteils-: ~frei, ~los 1 *adj* unprejudiced; **2** *adv* without prejudice.

Vor-: ~väter *pl* forefathers *pl;* **~verkauf** *m* advance booking; **sich** *(dat)* **Karten im ~verkauf besorgen** to buy tickets in advance.

vorverlegen* *vt sep* **(a)** *Termin* to bring forward. **(b)** *(Mil) Front, Gefechtslinie* to push forward.

vorwagen *vr sep* to venture forward.

Vorwahl *f* **(a)** preliminary election; *(US)* primary. **(b)** *(Telec)* area code.

Vorwahlnummer *f* area code.

Vorwand *m, pl* **Vorwände** pretext.

vorwärmen *vt sep* to pre-heat; *Teller* to heat.

Vorwarnung *f* (advance) warning.

vorwärts *adv* forwards, forward. **~!** *(col)* let's go *(col)*; *(Mil)* forward march!; **weiter ~** further on.

Vorwärts-: ~bewegung *f* forward movement; **~gang** *m* forward gear; **v~gehen** *sep irreg aux sein (fig)* **1** *vi* to progress; **2** *vi impers* **mit etw geht es v~** sth is going well; **v~kommen** *vi sep irreg aux sein (fig)* to get on *(in, mit* with*)*.

Vorwäsche *f*, **Vorwaschgang** *m* prewash.

vorweg *adv (an der Spitze)* at the front; *(vorher)* before(hand); *(von vornherein)* at the outset.

Vorweg-: ~nahme *f* **-n** anticipation; **v~nehmen** *vt sep irreg* to anticipate.

Vorweihnachtszeit *f* pre-Christmas period.

vorweisen *vt sep irreg* to show; *Zeugnisse* to produce. **etw ~ können** *(fig)* to possess sth.

vorwerfen *vt sep irreg* **(a)** *(fig)* **jdm etw/Unpünktlichkeit ~** to reproach sb for sth/for being unpunctual; *(beschuldigen)* to accuse sb of sth/of being unpunctual; **das wirft er mir heute noch vor** he still holds it against me; **ich habe mir nichts vorzuwerfen** my conscience is clear. **(b)** *(lit)* **Tieren/Gefangenen etw ~** to throw sth down for the animals/prisoners.

vorwiegend 1 *adj attr* predominant. **2** *adv* predominantly.

Vorwissen *nt* previous knowledge.

vorwitzig *adj (keck)* cheeky; *(vorlaut)* forward.

Vorwort *nt* **-e** foreword, preface.

Vorwurf *m, pl* **Vorwürfe** reproach; *(Beschuldigung)* accusation. **jdm/sich große Vorwürfe machen** to reproach sb/oneself; **ich habe mir keine Vorwürfe zu machen** my conscience is clear; **jdm etw zum ~ machen** to reproach sb with sth.

vorwurfsvoll *adj* reproachful.

Vorzeichen *nt (Omen)* omen; *(Med)* early symptom; *(Math)* sign. **positives/negatives ~** *(Math)* plus/minus (sign); **mit umgekehrtem ~** *(fig)* the other way around.

vorzeichnen *vt sep Linien etc* to sketch (out). **jdm etw ~** *(fig)* to map sth out for sb.

vorzeigen *vt sep* to show, to produce.

Vorzeit *f* prehistoric times *pl*.

vorzeitig *adj* early; *Geburt, Altern etc* premature.

vorzeitlich *adj* prehistoric; *(fig)* archaic.

vorziehen *vt sep irreg* **(a)** *(hervorziehen)* to pull out; *(nach vorne ziehen) Stuhl etc* to pull up; *(zuziehen) Vorhänge* to draw. **etw hinter/unter etw** *(dat)* **~** to pull sth out from behind/under sth. **(b)** *(fig) (lieber mögen)* to prefer; *(bevorzugen) jdn* to favour *(Brit)*, to favor *(US)*. **etw einer anderen Sache ~** to prefer sth to sth else; **es ~, etw zu tun** to prefer to do sth. **(c)** *(zuerst behandeln, abfertigen)* to give priority to.

Vorzimmer *nt* anteroom; *(Büro)* outer office.

Vorzug *m, pl* **Vorzüge** preference; *(Vorteil)* advantage; *(gute Eigenschaft)* asset. **einer Sache** *(dat)* **den ~ geben** *(form)* to prefer sth.

vorzüglich *adj* excellent.

vorzugsweise *adv* preferably; *(hauptsächlich)* chiefly. **etw ~ trinken** to prefer to drink sth.

Votum ['vo:tʊm] *nt, pl* **Voten** vote.

vulgär [vʊl'gɛ:ɐ] *adj* vulgar.

Vulkan [vʊl'ka:n] *m* **-e** volcano. **ein Tanz auf dem ~** playing with fire.

Vulkan|ausbruch [vʊl'ka:n-] *m* volcanic eruption.

vulkanisch [vʊl'ka:nɪʃ] *adj* volcanic.

W

W, w [veː] *nt* **-, -** W, w.
W = **Westen.**
Waage *f* **-n (a)** *(Gerät)* scales *pl*; *(Feder~, Apotheker~)* balance. **eine ~** a pair of scales; **sich** *(dat)* **die ~ halten** *(fig)* to balance one another. **(b)** *(Astrol)* Libra.
Waag(e)-: w~recht *adj* horizontal; **~rechte** *f* horizontal.
Waagschale *f* (scale) pan. **(schwer) in die ~fallen** *(fig)* to carry weight; **seine Autorität in die ~ werfen** *(fig)* to bring one's authority to bear.
wạbb(e)lig *adj Pudding* wobbly; *Mensch* flabby.
Wạbe *f* **-n** honeycomb.
wạch *adj* awake *pred; (fig: aufgeweckt)* alert. **in ~em Zustand** in the waking state; **~ werden** to wake up.
Wạch-: ~ablösung *f* changing of the guard; *(fig: Regierungswechsel)* change of government; *(Mensch)* relief guard; **~boot** *nt* patrol boat; **~dienst** *m* look-out; *(Mil)* guard (duty); *(Naut)* watch; **~dienst haben/machen** to be on guard (duty); *(Naut)* to have the watch.
Wạche *f* **-n (a)** *no pl (Wachdienst)* guard (duty). **(bei jdm) ~ halten** to keep watch (over sb); *(Kranken~)* to keep watch (at sb's bedside); **~ stehen** *or* **schieben** *(col)* to be on guard (duty); *(Dieb, Schüler etc)* to keep a look-out. **(b)** *(Mil) (Wachposten)* guard; *(Gebäude)* guardhouse. **(c)** *(Naut: Personen, Dauer)* watch. **~ haben** to be on watch. **(d)** *(Polizei~)* (police) station.
wạchen *vi* **(a)** *(wach sein)* to be awake. **(b)** *(Wache halten)* to keep watch. **bei jdm ~** to sit up with sb; **über etw** *(acc)* **~** to (keep) watch over sth; *über Verkehr* to supervise sth.
Wạch-: w~habend *adj attr* duty; **w~halten** *vt sep irreg (fig) Interesse etc* to keep alive; **~hund** *m (lit, fig)* watchdog; *(lit auch)* guard-dog; **~mannschaft** *f* guards *pl*; *(Naut)* watch.
Wachọlder *m* **-** *(Bot)* juniper (tree).
Wachọlder-: ~beere *f* juniper berry; **~schnaps** *m* spirit made from juniper berries, ≈ gin.
wạch-: ~rufen *vt sep irreg (fig) Erinnerung etc* to evoke; **~rütteln** *vt sep (fig)* to (a)rouse.
Wachs [vaks] *nt* **-e** wax. **weich wie ~** as soft as butter.
wạchsam *adj* vigilant; *(vorsichtig)* on one's guard.
Wạchsamkeit *f no pl* vigilance; *(Vorsichtigkeit)* guardedness.
Wạchschiff *nt* patrol ship.
wachsen[1] ['vaksn] *pret* **wuchs** [vuːks], *ptp* **gewạchsen** *vi aux sein* to grow. **in die Breite/Länge ~** to broaden (out)/to lengthen; **sich** *(dat)* **einen Bart ~ lassen** to grow a beard; **gut gewachsen** *Baum* well-grown; *Mensch* having a good figure.
wachsen[2] ['vaksn] *vt* to wax.
Wachs- ['vaks-]: **~farbe** *f* **(a)** *(Farbstift)* wax crayon; **(b)** *(Farbstoff)* wax dye; **~figur** *f* wax figure; **~kerze** *f* wax candle; **~malstift** *m*, **~malkreide** *f* wax crayon; **~papier** *nt* waxed paper; **~stift** *m* wax crayon.
Wachstube ['vaxʃtuːbə] *f* guard-room; *(von Polizei)* duty room.
Wachstum ['vakstuːm] *nt no pl* growth. **im ~ zurückgeblieben** stunted.
Wạchstums-: w~hemmend *adj* growth-inhibiting; **~störung** *f* disturbance of growth.
Wạchtel *f* **-n** quail.
Wächter *m* **-** guardian; *(Nacht~)* watchman.
Wạchtposten *m* sentry; *(Schüler, Dieb etc)* look-out.
Wạch(t)turm *m* watch-tower.
Wạch- und Schließgesellschaft *f* security corps.
wạck(e)lig *adj* wobbly; *(fig) Firma* shaky. **~ auf den Beinen sein** *(col: Patient)* to be wobbly on one's legs; **~ stehen** *(lit)* to be unsteady; *(fig: Unternehmen, Schüler)* to be shaky.
Wạckelkontakt *m* loose connection.
wạckeln *vi* **(a)** to wobble; *(zittern)* to shake; *(Zahn, Schraube)* to be loose; *(beim Fotografieren)* to move. **mit den Ohren/Hüften/dem Kopf/Schwanz ~** to waggle one's ears/wiggle one's hips/wag one's head/its tail. **(b)** *aux sein (langsam, unsicher gehen)* to totter.
wạcker *adj (tapfer)* brave, valiant. **sich ~ schlagen** *(col)* to put up a brave fight.
Wạde *f* **-n** calf.
Wạden-: ~bein *nt* fibula; **~krampf** *m* cramp in one's calf; **~strumpf** *m* half stocking; **~wickel** *m (Med)* compress around the leg.
Wạffe *f* **-n** *(lit, fig)* weapon; *(Schuß~)* gun; *(Mil: Waffengattung)* arm. **~n** *(Mil)* arms; **~n tragen** to carry arms; **die ~n strecken** *(lit, fig)* to surrender; **jdn mit seinen eigenen ~n schlagen** *(fig)* to beat sb at his own game.
Wạffel *f* **-n** waffle; *(Keks, Eis~)* wafer; *(Eistüte)* cornet.
Wạffel|eisen *nt* waffle iron.
Wạffen- *in cpds* arms; **~arsenal** *nt* arsenal; *(von Staat)* stockpile; **~gattung** *f (Mil)* arm of the service; **~gewalt** *f* force of arms; **mit ~gewalt** by force of arms; **~hilfe** *f* military assistance; **~lager** *nt (von Armee)* ordnance depot; *(von Terroristen)* cache; **w~los** *adj* unarmed; **~ruhe** *f* ceasefire; **~schein** *m* firearms *or* gun licence *(Brit) or* license *(US)*; **~schmuggel** *m* gunrunning, arms smuggling; **~stillstand** *m* armistice.
wagemutig *adj* daring, bold.
wagen 1 *vt* to venture; *(sich getrauen)* to dare. **es ~, etw zu tun** to venture to do sth; to dare (to) do sth; **wage nicht, mir zu widersprechen!** don't you dare (to) contradict me! **2** *vr* to dare. **sich an etw** *(acc)* **~** to venture to do sth; **sich auf ein Gebiet ~** to venture into an area.
Wagen *m* **-** *(Personen~)* car; *(Liefer~)* van; *(von Pferden gezogen)* wag(g)on, cart; *(Kutsche)* coach; *(Kinder~)* pram *(Brit)*, baby carriage *(US)*; *(Hand~)* (hand)cart; *(Kofferkuli, Einkaufs~)* trolley *(Brit)*, cart *(US)*; *(Schreibmaschinen~)* carriage; *(Eisenbahn~)* car, carriage *(Brit)*.
wägen *pret* **wọg,** *ptp* **gewọgen** *vt (old)* to weigh.
Wagen-: ~abteil *nt (Rail)* compartment; **~führer** *m* driver; **~heber** *m* jack; **~ladung** *f (von Lastwagen)* lorryload *(Brit)*, truckload; *(von Eisenbahn)* wag(g)onload; **~park** *m* fleet of cars; **~rad** *nt* cartwheel; **~wäsche** *f* carwash.
Waggon [va'gɔŋ] *m* **-s** (goods) wag(g)on *(Brit)*, freight car *(US)*; *(Ladung)* wag(g)onload/carload.
Wag-: ~hals *m* daredevil; **w~halsig** *adj* fool-

hardy, daredevil *attr.*

Wagnis *nt* hazardous business; *(Risiko)* risk.

Wahl *f* **-en (a)** *(Auswahl)* choice. **die ~ fiel auf ihn** he was chosen; **aus freier ~** of one's own free choice; **wir hatten keine (andere) ~(, als)** we had no alternative *or* choice (but); **jdm die ~ lassen** to leave (it up to) sb to choose; **jdm etw zur ~ stellen** to give sb a choice of sth; **seine ~ treffen** to make one's selection; **wer die ~ hat, hat die Qual** *(Prov)* he is/you are *etc* spoilt for choice.

(b) *(Pol etc)* election; *(Abstimmung)* vote; *(geheim)* ballot. **seine ~ in den Vorstand/zum Präsidenten** his election to the board/as president; **zur ~ gehen** to go to the polls; **jdn zur ~ aufstellen** to put sb up as a candidate; **sich zur ~ stellen** to stand, to run (for parliament *etc*); **die ~ annehmen** to accept the vote.

(c) *(Qualität)* **erste ~** top quality; *(Gemüse, Eier)* grade one; **Waren erster ~** top-quality goods; **Gemüse zweiter ~** grade-two vegetables.

wählbar *adj* eligible (for office).

Wahl-: ~benachrichtigung *f* polling card; **w~berechtigt** *adj* entitled to vote; **~beteiligung** *f* poll, turnout; **~bezirk** *m* ward.

wählen 1 *vt* **(a)** to choose *(von* from, out of*)*; *siehe* **gewählt. (b)** *(Telec) Nummer* to dial. **(c)** *(Pol)* to elect; *(sich entscheiden für) Partei* to vote for. **jdn ins Parlament ~** to elect sb to Parliament; **jdn zum Präsidenten ~** to elect sb president. **2** *vi* **(a)** *(auswählen)* to choose. **(b)** *(Telec)* to dial. **(c)** *(Stimme abgeben)* to vote.

Wähler(in *f*) *m* **-** *(Pol)* elector, voter.

Wahl|ergebnis *nt* election result.

wählerisch *adj* particular; *Geschmack, Kunde* discriminating. **sei nicht so ~!** don't be so choosy *(col)*.

Wähler-: ~stimme *f* vote; **~verzeichnis** *nt* electoral roll.

Wahl-: ~fach *nt (Sch)* optional subject; **~gang** *m* ballot; **~geheimnis** *nt* secrecy of the ballot; **~geschenk** *nt* pre-election vote-catching gimmick; **~gesetz** *nt* electoral law; **~heimat** *f* country of adoption; **~helfer** *m (im ~kampf)* election assistant; *(bei der Wahl)* polling officer; **~kabine** *f* polling booth; **~kampf** *m* election(eering) campaign; **~kreis** *m* constituency; **~lokal** *nt* polling station; **w~los 1** *adj* indiscriminate; **2** *adv* at random, haphazardly; *(nicht wählerisch)* indiscriminately; **~mann** *m, pl* **~männer** delegate; **~möglichkeit** *f* option; **~ordnung** *f* election regulations *pl*; **~periode** *f* lifetime of a/the parliament; **~pflicht** *f* electoral duty; **~recht** *nt* (right to) vote; **allgemeines ~recht** universal franchise; **das aktive ~recht** the right to vote; **das passive ~recht** eligibility (for political office); **~rede** *f* election speech; **~reform** *f* electoral reform.

Wählscheibe *f* dial.

Wahl-: ~schein *m* polling card; **~spruch** *m* motto; **~system** *nt* electoral system; **~tag** *m* election day; **~urne** *f* ballot box; **~verfahren** *nt* electoral procedure; **~versammlung** *f* election meeting; **~versprechungen** *pl* election promises *pl*; **~vorschlag** *m* election proposal; **w~weise** *adv* alternatively; **w~weise Kartoffeln oder Reis** a choice of potatoes or rice.

Wählzeichen *nt (Telec)* dialling tone.

Wahn *m no pl* illusion, delusion; *(Manie)* mania. **in dem ~ leben, daß ...** to labour *(Brit) or* labor *(US)* under the delusion that ...

Wahnsinn *m no pl* madness. **das ist doch (heller) ~, so ein ~!** that's sheer madness.

wahnsinnig 1 *adj (col) (verrückt)* mad, crazy; *(attr: sehr groß, viel)* awful, dreadful. **eine ~e Arbeit** a crazy amount of work; **das macht mich ~** *(col)* it's driving me crazy; **~ werden** to go mad *(col)*; **ich werde ~!** it's mind-blowing! *(col)*. **2** *adv (col)* incredibly *(col)*. **~ verliebt** madly in love; **~ viele/viel** an incredible number/amount *(col)*.

Wahnsinnige(r) *mf decl as adj* lunatic.

Wahnsinns- *in cpds (col: verrückt)* crazy; *(col: prima)* incredible *(col)*.

Wahn-: ~vorstellung *f* delusion; **w~witzig 1** *adj* crazy *attr*; **2** *adv* terribly.

wahr *adj Geschichte, Liebe, Glaube etc* true; *(echt) Kunst, (attr: wirklich)* real, veritable. **im ~sten Sinne des Wortes** in the true sense of the word; **daran ist kein Wort ~** *or* **kein ~es Wort** there's not a word of truth in it; **da ist etwas W~es daran** there's some truth in that; **da hast du ein ~es Wort gesprochen** *(col)* there's a lot of truth in that; **etw ~ machen** *Pläne* to make sth a reality; *Versprechung, Drohung* to carry sth out; **~ werden** to come true; **so ~ mir Gott helfe!** so help me God!; **das darf** *or* **kann doch nicht ~ sein!** *(col)* it can't be true!; **das ist nicht das W~e** *(col)* it's no great shakes *(col)*.

wahren *vt Interessen, Rechte* to look after; *Autorität, Ruf, Würde* to preserve, to keep; *Geheimnis* to keep; *gute Manieren* to adhere to, to observe.

währen *vi (geh)* to last.

während 1 *prep +gen or dat* during. **~ eines Zeitraums** over a period of time. **2** *conj* while.

währenddessen *adv* meanwhile.

Wahr-: w~haben *vt sep irreg* **etw nicht w~haben wollen** not to want to admit sth; **w~haft 1** *adj* real; **2** *adv* really, truly; **w~haftig** *adv* really; *(tatsächlich)* actually.

Wahrheit *f* truth. **in ~** in reality; **die ~ sagen** to tell the truth.

wahrheits-: ~getreu *adj Bericht* truthful; *Darstellung* faithful; **~liebend** *adj* truth-loving; *(ehrlich)* truthful.

Wahr-: w~nehmbar *adj* perceptible; **mit bloßem Auge w~nehmbar** visible to the naked eye; **w~nehmen** *vt sep irreg* **(a)** *(sinnlich)* to perceive; *Veränderungen etc* to be aware of; **nichts mehr um sich herum w~nehmen** to be no longer aware of anything around one; **(b)** *Frist, Termin* to observe; *Gelegenheit* to take; *Interessen, Rechte* to look after; **~nehmung** *f siehe vt* **(a)** perception; awareness; **(b)** *(von Frist)* observing; *(von Interessen)* looking after; **w~sagen** *vi sep or insep* to tell fortunes; **aus den Karten w~sagen** to read cards; **~sager(in** *f*) *m* **-** fortuneteller.

wahrscheinlich 1 *adj* probable, likely; *(glaubhaft)* plausible. **2** *adv* probably.

Wahrscheinlichkeit *f* probability; *(Glaubhaftigkeit)* plausibility. **mit großer ~, aller ~ nach, in aller ~** in all probability.

Währung *f* currency.

Währungs- *in cpds* currency; **~einheit** *f* monetary unit; **~fonds** *m* Monetary Fund; **~krise** *f* monetary crisis; **~reform** *f* currency reform.

Wahrzeichen *nt (von Stadt, Verein)* emblem; *(Gebäude, Turm etc)* symbol.

Waid- *in cpds* = **Weid-.**

Waise *f* **-n** orphan.

Waisen-: ~haus *nt* orphanage; **~kind** *nt* orphan; **~knabe** *m* **gegen dich ist er ein ~knabe** *(col)* he's no match for you; **~rente** *f* orphan's allowance.

Wal *m* **-e** whale.

Wald *m* **¨er** wood(s *pl*); *(großer)* forest; *(no pl: ~land)* woodland(s *pl*). **er sieht den ~ vor lauter Bäumen nicht** he can't see the wood for the trees.

Wald-: ~ameise *f* red ant; **~arbeiter** *m* forestry worker; **~blume** *f* woodland flower; **~brand** *m* forest fire; **~erdbeere** *f* wild strawberry.

waldig *adj* wooded, woody.

Wald-: ~land *nt* woodland(s *pl*); **~lauf** *m* cross-country running; *(einzelner Lauf)* cross-country run; **~lehrpfad** *m* nature trail; **~meister** *m (Bot)* woodruff; **w~reich** *adj* densely wooded; **~sterben** *nt no pl* loss of trees due to pollution.

Wald- und Wiesen- *in cpds (col)* common-or-garden *(col)*.
Wald-: ~**weg** *m* woodland/forest path; ~**wiese** *f* glade.
Wal-: ~**fang** *m* whaling; ~**fänger** *m* whaler.
Waliser(in *f*) *m* - Welshman; Welsh woman.
walisisch *adj* Welsh.
Wall *m* ¨**e** embankment; *(Mil)* rampart; *(fig)* bulwark.
Wallach *m* **-e** gelding.
Wallfahrer(in *f*) *m* - pilgrim.
Wallfahrt *f* pilgrimage.
Wallone *m (wk)* **-n, -n, Wallonin** *f* Walloon.
Walnuß *f* walnut.
Walroß *nt* **-sse** walrus.
walten *vi (geh)* to reign *(in +dat* over*)*; *(wirken: Mensch, Naturkräfte)* to be at work. **über jdm/etw** ~ to rule (over) sb/sth; **Vernunft** ~ **lassen** to let reason prevail; **Vorsicht** ~ **lassen** to exercise caution.
Walzblech *nt* sheet metal.
Walze *f* **-n** roller.
walzen *vt* to roll.
wälzen 1 *vt* **(a)** *(rollen)* to roll. **(b)** *(col) Akten, Bücher* to pore over; *Probleme, Gedanken, Pläne* to turn over in one's mind. **die Verantwortung auf jdn** ~ to shift the responsibility onto sb. **2** *vr* to roll; *(schlaflos im Bett)* to toss and turn; *(fig: Menschenmenge, Wassermassen)* to surge.
walzenförmig *adj* cylindrical.
Walzer *m* - waltz.
Wälzer *m* - *(col)* heavy *or* weighty tome *(hum)*.
Walz-: ~**straße** *f* rolling train; ~**werk** *nt* rolling mill.
wand *pret of* **winden.**
Wand *f* ¨**e** wall; *(nicht gemauerte Trenn~)* partition (wall); *(von Gefäß, Behälter, Schiff)* side; *(Fels~)* (rock) face; *(fig)* barrier, wall. **spanische** ~ (folding) screen; ~ **an** ~ wall to wall; **in seinen vier** ~̈**en** *(fig)* within one's own four walls; **weiß wie die** ~ as white as a sheet; **jdn an die** ~ **spielen** to put sb in the shade; *(Sport auch)* to outplay sb; **jdn an die** ~ **drücken** *(fig)* to push sb to the wall; **jdn an die** ~ **stellen** *(fig)* to send sb before the firing squad; **er lachte, daß die** ~̈**e wackelten** *(col)* he raised the roof (with his laughter) *(col)*; **das ist, um die** ~̈**e hochzugehen** *(col)* it's enough to drive you up the wall *(col)*.
Wand-: ~**behang** *m* wall hanging; ~**bekleidung** *f* wall covering; *(aus Holz)* panelling *(Brit)*, paneling *(US)*; ~**bord,** ~**brett** *nt* (wall) shelf.
Wandel *m no pl* change. **im** ~ **der Zeiten** throughout the ages.
Wandel-: **w~bar** *adj* changeable; ~**halle** *f* foyer; *(im Parlament)* lobby.
wandeln[1] *vtr (ändern)* to change.
wandeln[2] *vi aux sein (geh: gehen)* to walk, to stroll. **ein** ~**des Wörterbuch** *(hum)* a walking dictionary.
Wander-: ~**ameise** *f* army ant; ~**ausstellung** *f* touring exhibition; ~**bühne** *f* touring company; ~**düne** *f* shifting dune.
Wanderer *m* - hiker; *(esp in Verein)* rambler.
Wander-: ~**falke** *m* peregrine (falcon); ~**freund(in** *f*) *m* hiker; ~**karte** *f* map of walks; ~**kleidung** *f* hiking outfit; ~**leben** *nt* roving *or* wandering life; *(fig)* unsettled life; ~**lied** *nt* hiking song; ~**lust** *f* wanderlust.
wandern *vi aux sein* to hike; *(in Verein)* to ramble; *(umherschweifen)* to roam; *(Wanderbühne)* to travel; *(Tiere, Völker)* to migrate; *(Wolken)* to drift; *(weitergegeben werden)* to be passed on; *(col: in den Papierkorb)* to land.
Wander-: ~**niere** *f* floating kidney; ~**pokal** *m* challenge cup; ~**prediger** *m* itinerant preacher; ~**preis** *m* challenge trophy; ~**ratte** *f* brown rat.
Wanderschaft *f no pl* travels *pl.* **auf (der)** ~ **sein** to be on one's travels; **auf** ~ **gehen** to go off on one's travels.
Wander-: ~**schauspieler** *m* travelling *(Brit) or* traveling *(US)* actor; ~**schuhe** *pl* walking shoes *pl*; ~**truppe** f touring company.
Wanderung *f* **(a)** *(Ausflug)* walk. **eine** ~ **machen** to go on a ramble. **(b)** *(von Tieren, Völkern)* migration.
Wander-: ~**verein** *m* rambling club; ~**weg** *m* trail, (foot)path; ~**zirkus** *m* travelling *(Brit) or* traveling *(US)* circus.
Wand-: ~**gemälde** *nt* mural, wall-painting; ~**kalender** *m* wall calendar; ~**karte** *f* wall map; ~**lampe** *f* wall lamp; ~**leuchter** *m* wall bracket.
Wandlung *f (Wechsel, Wandel)* change; *(völlige Um~)* transformation. **eine** ~ **durchmachen** to undergo a change.
Wand-: ~**malerei** *f* mural painting; ~**schirm** *m* screen; ~**schrank** *m* wall cupboard; ~**tafel** *f* (black)board.
wandte *pret of* **wenden.**
Wand-: ~**teller** *m* wall plate; ~**teppich** *m* tapestry, wall hanging; ~**uhr** *f* wall clock; ~**verkleidung** *f* wall covering; *(aus Holz)* panelling *(Brit)*, paneling *(US)*; ~**zeitung** *f* (wall) news-sheet.
Wange *f* **-n** *(geh)* cheek.
wankelmütig *adj* fickle, inconstant.
wanken *vi* **(a)** *(Mensch, Gebäude)* to sway; *(Knie)* to shake, to wobble; *(unsicher sein/werden)* to waver. **(b)** *aux sein (gehen)* to stagger; *(alter Mensch)* to totter.
wann *interrog adv* when. ~ **(auch) immer** whenever; **seit** ~ **bist/hast du ...?** how long have you been/have you had ...?; *(entrüstet etc)* since when are you/do you have ...?
Wanne *f* **-n** bath; *(Öl~)* reservoir.
Wanze *f* **-n** *(Zool, col: Abhörgerät)* bug.
Wappen *nt* - coat of arms.
Wappen-: ~**kunde** *f* heraldry; ~**tier** *nt* heraldic animal.
wappnen *vr (fig)* **sich (gegen etw)** ~ to prepare (oneself) (for sth); **gewappnet sein** to be forearmed.
war *pret of* **sein**[1] was.
warb *pret of* **werben.**
Ware *f* **-n** product; *(einzelne ~)* article; *(als Sammelbegriff)* goods *pl.* ~**n** *pl* goods *pl.*
Waren-: ~**angebot** *nt* range of goods for sale; ~**aufzug** *m* goods hoist; ~**haus** *nt* (department) store; ~**lager** *nt* warehouse; *(Bestand)* stocks *pl*; ~**probe** *f* trade sample; ~**sendung** *f* trade sample *(sent by post)*; ~**zeichen** *nt* trademark.
warf *pret of* **werfen.**
warm *adj comp* ¨**er,** *superl* ¨**ste(r, s)** *or (adv)* **am** ¨**sten** *(lit, fig)* warm; *(col: homosexuell)* queer *(col)*. **mir ist** ~ I'm warm; **das Essen** ~ **machen** to heat up the food; **das Essen** ~ **stellen** to keep the food hot; **sich** ~ **anziehen** to dress up warmly; **sich** ~ **laufen** to warm up; **jdn/etw** ~̈**stens empfehlen** to recommend sb/sth warmly; **mit jdm** ~ **werden** *(col)* to get close to sb.
Warm-: ~**blüter** *m* warm-blooded animal; **w~blütig** *adj* warm-blooded.
Wärme *f no pl (lit, fig)* warmth; *(von Wetter etc, Phys)* heat. **10 Grad** ~ 10 degrees above zero; **ist das eine** ~! isn't it warm!
wärmen 1 *vt* to warm; *Essen* to heat up. **2** *vi (Kleidung, Sonne)* to be warm. **3** *vr* to warm up. **sich gegenseitig** ~ to keep each other warm.
Wärme-: ~**regler** *m* thermostat; ~**technik** *f* heat technology; ~**verlust** *m* heat loss.
Wärmflasche *f* hot-water bottle.
Warm-: ~**front** *f (Met)* warm front; **w~herzig** *adj* warm-hearted; **w~laufen** *vi sep irreg aux sein* **den Motor w~laufen lassen** to warm up the engine; ~**luft** *f* warm air.
Warmwasser-: ~**heizung** *f* hot-water central heating; ~**leitung** *f* hot-water pipe; ~**speicher** *m*

hot-water tank.

Warn-: **~anlage** *f* warning system; **~blinkanlage** *f (Aut)* hazard warning lights *pl*; **~dreieck** *nt* warning triangle.

warnen *vti* to warn *(vor +dat* of*)*. **jdn (davor) ~, etw zu tun** to warn sb not to do sth.

Warn-: **~kreuz** *nt* warning cross; **~schild** *nt* warning sign; **~schuß** *m* warning shot; **~streik** *m* token strike.

Warnung *f* warning *(vor +dat* of*)*.

Warn-: **~vorrichtung** *f* warning system; **~zeichen** *nt* warning sign; *(hörbar)* warning signal.

Warschau *nt* Warsaw. **~er Pakt** Warsaw Pact.

Warte *f* **-n** observation point; *(fig)* viewpoint. **von jds ~ (aus)** *(fig)* from sb's standpoint.

Warte-: **~frist** *f* waiting period; *(für Lieferung)* delivery time; **~halle** *f* waiting room; **~liste** *f* waiting list.

warten[1] *vi* to wait *(auf+acc* for*)*. **warte mal!** wait a minute; *(überlegend)* let me see; **na warte!** *(col)* just you wait!; **mit dem Essen auf jdn ~** to wait for sb before eating; **lange auf sich ~ lassen** to be a long time (in) coming.

warten[2] *vt Auto, Maschine* to service.

Wärter(in *f***)** *m* **-** attendant; *(Tier~)* keeper; *(Gefängnis~)* warder/wardress *(Brit)*, guard.

Warte-: **~saal** *m* waiting room; **~zeit** *f* waiting period; **~zimmer** *nt* waiting room.

Wartung *f (von Auto, Maschine)* servicing. **das Auto muß zur ~** the car has to go in for a service.

warum *interrog adv* why. **~ nicht gleich so!** that's better.

Warze *f* **-n** wart; *(Brust~)* nipple.

was 1 *interrog pron* **(a)** what. **~ ist, kommst du mit?** well, are you coming?; **~ denn?** what is it?; *(ungläubig)* what?; **wenn nicht das, ~ denn?** if not that, what then?; **wenn ein Unfall passiert, ~ dann?** what if there's an accident?; **~ haben wir gelacht!** *(col)* how we laughed! **(b)** *(col: warum)* what ... for. **(c) ~ für ...** what sort *or* kind of ...; **~ für ein schönes Haus!** what a lovely house! **2** *rel pron (auf Satz bezogen)* which. **das, ~ ...** that which ..., what ...; **ich weiß, ~ ich/er tun soll** I know what to do/what he should do; **~ auch (immer)** whatever; **alles, ~ ...** everything *or* all (that)...; **lauf, ~ du kannst!** *(col)* run as fast as you can! **3** *(col) indef pron abbr of* **etwas** something; *(fragend, verneint)* anything; *(Teil einer Menge)* some; any. **(na,) so ~!** well I never!; *siehe* **etwas.**

Wasch-: **~anlage** *f (für Autos)* carwash; **w~bar** *adj* washable; **~bär** *m* rac(c)oon; **~becken** *nt* wash-basin *(Brit)*, washbowl *(US)*; **~beutel** *m* sponge bag; **~brett** *nt* wash-board; **~creme** *f* cream detergent.

Wäsche *f no pl* **(a)** washing; *(Schmutz~)* laundry. **große ~ haben** to have a large amount of washing (to do); **in der ~** in the wash. **(b)** *(Bett~, Küchen~)* linen; *(Unter~)* underwear. **dumm aus der ~ gucken** *(col)* to look stupid.

Wäschebeutel *m* dirty clothes bag.

wasch|echt *adj Farbe* fast; *(fig)* genuine.

Wäsche-: **~klammer** *f* clothespeg *(Brit)*, clothespin *(US)*; **~korb** *m* dirty clothes basket; **~leine** *f* (clothes-)line.

waschen *pret* **wusch,** *ptp* **gewaschen 1** *vt* to wash; *Gold etc* to pan. **(Wäsche) ~** to do the washing; **etw** *(acc)* **warm/kalt ~** to wash sth in hot/cold water; **sich** *(dat)* **die Hände ~** to wash one's hands. **2** *vr* to wash (oneself/itself); *(Stoff)* to wash. **eine Geldbuße, die sich gewaschen hat** *(col)* a really heavy fine.

Wäscherei *f* laundry.

Wäsche-: **~sack** *m* laundry bag; **~schleuder** *f* spin-drier *(Brit)*, dryer; **~schrank** *m* linen cupboard; **~ständer** *m* clothes-horse; **~stärke** *f* starch; **~trockner** *m (Ständer)* clothes-horse; *(Trockenautomat)* drier.

Wasch-: **~gang** *m* stage of the washing programme *(Brit) or* program *(US)*; **~gelegenheit** *f* washing facilities *pl*; **~haus** *nt* wash-house, laundry; **~kessel** *m* (wash-)boiler; **~küche** *f* washroom; **~lappen** *m* flannel *(Brit)*, washcloth *(US)*; *(col: Feigling)* softy *(col)*; **~lauge** *f* suds *pl*; **~maschine** *f* washing-machine; **w~maschinenfest** *adj* machine-washable; **~mittel** *nt* detergent; **~pulver** *nt* washing-powder *(Brit)*, soap powder; **~salon** *m* launderette *(Brit)*, laundromat *(US)*; **~schüssel** *f* wash-basin *(Brit)*, washbowl *(US)*; **~wasser** *nt* washing water; **~zettel** *m (Typ)* blurb; **~zeug** *nt* toilet *or* washing things *pl*; **~zuber** *m* wash-tub.

Wasser *nt* **- (a)** *no pl* water. **das ist ~ auf seine Mühle** *(fig)* this is all grist to his mill; **dort wird auch nur mit ~ gekocht** *(fig)* they're no different from anybody else (there); **ihr kann er nicht das ~ reichen** *(fig)* he can't hold a candle to her; **unter ~ stehen** to be flooded; **ins ~ fallen** *(fig)* to fall through; **sich über ~ halten** *(fig)* to keep one's head above water; **mit allen ~n gewaschen sein** *(col)* to be a shrewd customer; **ein Boot zu ~ lassen** to launch a boat; **nahe am ~ gebaut haben** *(col)* to be a cry-baby *(col)*; **~ lassen** *(euph)* to pass water. **(b)** *pl* ¨ *(Flüssigkeit) (Abwasch~ etc)* water; *(medizinisch)* lotion; *(Parfüm)* cologne; *(Mineral~)* mineral water. **das ~ läuft mir im Mund zusammen** my mouth is watering.

Wasser-: **w~abstoßend** *adj* water-repellent; **w~arm** *adj* arid; **~ball** *m* **(a)** *(no pl: Spiel)* water polo; **(b)** *(Ball)* beach-ball; *(fürs ~ballspiel)* water-polo ball; **~bett** *nt* water-bed.

Wässerchen *nt* **er sieht aus, als ob er kein ~ trüben könnte** he looks as if butter wouldn't melt in his mouth.

Wasser-: **~dampf** *m* steam; **w~dicht** *adj (lit, fig)* watertight; *Uhr, Stoff etc* waterproof; **~enthärter** *m* water-softener; **~fahrzeug** *nt* water-craft; **~fall** *m* waterfall; **~farbe** *f* watercolour *(Brit)*, watercolor *(US)*; **w~fest** *adj* waterproof; **~floh** *m* water-flea; **~flugzeug** *nt* seaplane; **w~gekühlt** *adj* water-cooled; **~glas** *nt (Trinkglas)* tumbler; **~glätte** *f* aquaplaning; **~graben** *m (Sport)* water-jump; *(um Burg)* moat; **~hahn** *m* tap, faucet *(US)*; **~härte** *f* hardness of water.

wässerig *adj (lit, fig)* watery. **jdm den Mund ~ machen** *(col)* to make sb's mouth water.

Wasser-: **~kessel** *m* kettle; *(Tech)* boiler; **~klosett** *nt* water-closet; **~kraft** *f* water-power; **~kraftwerk** *nt* hydroelectric power station; **~kreislauf** *m* water cycle; **~kühlung** *f* water-cooling; **mit ~kühlung** water-cooled; **~lassen** *nt* passing water; **~lauf** *m* watercourse; **~leiche** *f* drowned body; **~leitung** *f (Rohr)* water pipe; *(Anlagen)* plumbing *no pl*; **~lilie** *f* water-lily; **w~löslich** *adj* water-soluble; **~mann** *m, pl* **~männer** *(Astrol)* Aquarius *no art;* **~melone** *f* water-melon; **~mühle** *f* water-mill.

wassern *vi (Aviat)* to land on water.

wässern *vti* to water; *Erbsen etc* to soak. **mir ~ die Augen** my eyes are watering.

Wasser-: **~pfeife** *f* hookah; **~pflanze** *f* aquatic plant; **~pistole** *f* water-pistol; **~rad** *nt* water-wheel; **~ratte** *f* water-rat *or* -vole; *(col: Schwimmer)* water-baby; **w~reich** *adj Gebiet* abounding in water; *Fluß* containing a lot of water; **~rohr** *nt* water-pipe; **~scheide** *f* watershed; **w~scheu** *adj* scared of water; **~schildkröte** *f* turtle; **~schutz polizei** *f (auf Flüssen, ~wegen)* river police; *(im Hafen)* harbour *(Brit) or* harbor *(US)* police; *(auf der See)* coastguard service; **~ski** *nt* water-skiing; **~spiegel** *m (Oberfläche)* surface of the water; *(~stand)* water-level; **~sport** *m* **der ~sport** water sports *pl*; **~spülung** *f* flush; **~stand** *m* water-level; **niedriger/hoher ~stand** low/high water.

Wasserstoff *m* hydrogen.

Wasserstoffbombe *f* H-bomb.

Wasser-: ~**straße** *f* waterway; ~**sucht** *f* dropsy; ~**tank** *m* water-tank; ~**tier** *nt* aquatic animal; ~**träger** *m* water-carrier; ~**treten** *nt (Med)* paddling *(in cold water as therapy)*; ~**tropfen** *m* drop of water; ~**turm** *m* water-tower; ~**uhr** *f* water-meter; ~**verbrauch** *m* water consumption *no def art;* ~**versorgung** *f* water-supply; ~**vogel** *m* waterfowl; ~**waage** *f* spirit-level; ~**weg** *m* waterway; **auf dem** ~**weg** by water *or (Meer)* sea; ~**werfer** *m* water-cannon; ~**werk** *nt* waterworks *sing or pl*; ~**wirtschaft** *f* water-supply (and distribution); ~**zähler** *m* water-meter; ~**zeichen** *nt* watermark.

wäßrig *adj* = **wässerig**.

waten *vi aux sein* to wade.

watscheln *vi aux sein* to waddle.

Watt[1] *nt* - *(Elec)* watt.

Watt[2] *nt* **-en** *(Geog)* mud-flats *pl.*

Watte *f* **-n** cotton wool *(Brit)*, absorbent cotton *(US)*; *(zur Polsterung)* wadding.

Wattebausch *m* cotton ball.

Wattenmeer *nt* mud-flats *pl.*

Wattestäbchen *nt* cotton swab.

wattieren* *vt* to pad; *(füttern)* to line with padding; *(und absteppen) Stoff* to quilt.

Wattzahl *f* wattage.

WC [veː'tseː] *nt* **-s** WC.

weben *pret* **webte** *or (liter, fig)* **wob,** *ptp* **gewebt** *or (liter, fig)* **gewoben** *vti (lit, fig)* to weave; *Spinnennetz* to spin.

Weber(in *f***)** *m* - weaver.

Weberei *f* **(a)** *(Betrieb)* weaving mill. **(b)** *(Zeug)* woven article.

Web-: ~**stuhl** *m* loom; ~**waren** *pl* woven goods *pl.*

Wechsel ['vɛksl] *m* - **(a)** change; *(abwechselnd)* alternation; *(Geld~)* exchange. **(b)** *(Staffel~)* change-over; *(Ftbl etc)* substitution. **(c)** *(Fin)* bill (of exchange).

Wechsel- ['vɛksl-]: ~**bäder** *pl (lit)* alternating hot and cold baths *pl*; ~**beziehung** *f* correlation, interrelation; ~**fälle** *pl* vicissitudes *pl*; ~**geld** *nt* change; **w**~**haft** *adj* changeable; ~**jahre** *pl* menopause *sing*; **in die** ~**jahre kommen** to start the menopause; ~**kurs** *m* exchange rate.

wechseln ['vɛksln] **1** *vt* to change *(in +acc* into*)*; *(austauschen)* to exchange. **die Schule/das Hemd** ~ to change schools/one's shirt; **die Farbe** ~ to change colour; **Briefe** ~ to correspond *(mit* with*)*; **können Sie (mir) 10 Mark** ~? can you change 10 marks (for me)? **2** *vi* **(a)** to change; *(einander ablösen)* to alternate. **ich kann leider nicht** ~ I'm sorry, I don't have any change. **(b) über die Straße** ~ to cross the road.

wechselnd ['vɛkslnt] *adj* changing; *(einander ablösend)* alternating; *Stimmungen* changeable; *Winde, Bewölkung* variable. **mit** ~**em Erfolg** with varying (degrees of) success.

Wechsel ['vɛksl-]: ~**rahmen** *m* clip-on picture frame; **w**~**seitig** *adj* reciprocal; ~**strom** *m* alternating current, A.C.; ~**stube** *f* currency exchange, bureau de change; **w**~**voll** *adj* varied; ~**wirkung** *f* interaction.

Wechsler ['vɛkslɐ] *m* - *(Automat)* change dispenser.

wecken *vt* to wake (up); *(fig)* to arouse; *Bedarf* to create; *Erinnerungen* to revive.

Wecker *m* - alarm clock. **jdm auf den** ~ **fallen** *(col)* to get on sb's nerves.

Weck-: ~**glas** ® *nt* preserving jar; ~**radio** *nt* radio-alarm clock; ~**ruf** *m (Telec)* alarm call.

Wedel *m* - *(Staub~)* feather duster.

wedeln *vi* **(mit dem Schwanz)** ~ to wag its tail; **mit etw** ~ *(winken)* to wave sth.

weder *conj* ~ ... **noch** ... neither ... nor ...

weg *adv* away. ~ **sein** to have *or* be gone; *(nicht hier, entfernt)* to be away; *(col: eingeschlafen)* to be out like a light *(col)*; *(col: begeistert)* to be taken *(von* with*)*; **über etw** *(acc)* ~ **sein** *(emotional)* to have got over sth; **über den Tisch** ~ across the table; **nichts wie** *or* **nur** ~ **von hier!** let's get out of here; ~ **da!** (get) out of the way!; ~ **damit!** *(mit Schere etc)* put it away!; **Hände** ~**!** hands off!; **in einem** ~ *(col)* non-stop.

Weg *m* **-e (a)** *(Pfad, fig)* path. **am** ~**e** by the wayside; **jdm den** ~ **versperren** to block sb's way; **jdm/einer Sache im** ~ **stehen** *(fig)* to stand in the way of sb/sth; **jdm Steine in den** ~ **legen** *(fig)* to put obstructions in sb's way; **jdm nicht über den** ~ **trauen** *(fig)* not to trust sb an inch; **etw aus dem** ~ **räumen** *(fig)* to get sth out of the way; **den** ~ **des geringsten Widerstandes gehen** to follow the line of least resistance.

(b) *(lit, fig: Route)* way; *(Entfernung)* distance; *(Reise)* journey; *(zu Fuß)* walk. **ich muß diesen** ~ **jeden Tag zweimal gehen** I have to walk this stretch twice a day; **den richtigen** ~ **einschlagen** *(lit)* to follow the right road; **jdm einen guten Rat mit auf den** ~ **geben** to give sb good advice to follow in life; **jdm/einer Sache aus dem** ~ **gehen** *(lit)* to get out of sb's way/the way of sth; **jdm über den** ~ **laufen** *(fig)* to run into sb; **etw in die** ~**e leiten** to arrange sth; **auf dem besten** ~ **sein, etw zu tun** to be well on the way to doing sth.

(c) *(Mittel, Art und Weise)* way. **auf diesem** ~**e** this way; **auf diplomatischem** ~**e** through diplomatic channels; **auf legalem** ~**e** legally.

wegbekommen* *vt sep irreg* to get rid of *(von* from*)*; *Fleck* to get off; *(von bestimmtem Ort) jdn* to get away *(von* from*)*.

Weg-: ~**bereiter** *m* precursor, forerunner; ~**bereiter einer Sache** *(gen) or* **für etw sein** to pave the way for sth; ~**biegung** *f* turn, bend.

weg-: ~**blasen** *vt sep irreg* to blow away; **wie** ~**geblasen sein** *(fig)* to have vanished; ~**bleiben** *vi sep irreg aux sein* to stay away; **mir bleibt die Spucke** ~**!** *(col)* I'm absolutely flabbergasted!; ~**bringen** *vt sep irreg* to take away; *(zur Reparatur)* to take in; ~**denken** *vt sep irreg*: **das Auto ist aus unserem Leben nicht mehr** ~**zudenken** life today without the car is something that cannot be imagined; ~**dürfen** *vi sep irreg* to be allowed to leave; *(col: ausgehen dürfen)* to be allowed to go out.

Wegelagerer *m* - highwayman; *(zu Fuß)* footpad.

wegen *prep +gen* because of. **von** ~**!** *(col)* you must be joking!

Wegerich *m* **-e** *(Bot)* plantain.

wegfahren *vi sep irreg aux sein (abfahren)* to leave; *(Auto, Fahrer)* to drive off; *(im Boot)* to sail away; *(zum Einkaufen, als Ausflug)* to go out; *(verreisen)* to go away.

wegfallen *vi sep irreg aux sein* to be discontinued; *(Bestimmung)* to cease to apply; *(unterbleiben)* to be lost; *(überflüssig werden)* to become unnecessary; *(ausgelassen werden)* to be omitted. ~ **lassen** to discontinue; *(auslassen)* to omit.

weg-: ~**fegen** *vt sep (lit, fig)* to sweep away; ~**fliegen** *vi sep irreg aux sein* to fly away; *(Hut)* to fly off; *(mit Flugzeug)* to leave; ~**führen** *vt sep* to lead away.

Weggabelung *f* fork (in the road).

weggeben *vt sep irreg (verschenken)* to give away. **seine Wäsche (zum Waschen)** ~ to have one's washing done.

weggehen *vi sep irreg aux sein* to go, to leave; *(verreisen, umziehen etc)* to go away; *(ausgehen)* to go out; *(col: Fleck)* to come off; *(col: Ware)* to sell.

weggucken *vi sep* to look away.

weghaben *vt sep irreg (col) (erledigt haben)* to have got done; *(bekommen, verstanden haben)* to have got. **du hast deinen Denkzettel weg** you have had your punishment; **einen** ~ *(col: verrückt sein)* to have a screw loose *(col)*.

weg-: ~**helfen** *vi sep irreg* **jdm von irgendwo** ~**helfen** to help sb get away from a place;

~holen *vt sep* to take away; *(abholen)* to fetch; **~hören** *vi sep* not to listen; **~jagen** *vt sep* to chase away.

wegkommen *vi sep irreg aux sein (col)* **(a)** *(abhanden kommen)* to disappear; *(weggehen können)* to get away; *(aus dem Haus)* to get out. **mach, daß du wegkommst!** hop it! *(col)*; **gut/schlecht (bei etw) ~** to come off well/badly (with sth). **(b)** = **hinwegkommen**.

Weg-: **~kreuzung** *f* crossroads; **~krümmung** *f* bend in the road.

weg-: **~lassen** *vt sep irreg (auslassen)* to leave out; *(col: gehen lassen)* to let go; **~laufen** *vi sep irreg aux sein* to run away *(vor +dat* from*)*; **das läuft (dir) nicht ~!** *(fig hum)* that can wait; **~legen** *vt sep* to put away; *(zum späteren Verbrauch)* to put aside.

wegmachen *vt sep (col)* to get rid of.

wegmüssen *vi sep irreg* to have to go; *(entfernt werden)* to have to be removed. **ich muß eine Zeitlang aus New York weg** I must get out of New York for a while.

wegnehmen *vt sep irreg* to take; *(fortnehmen, entziehen)* to take away; *Platz* to take up. **Gas ~** *(Aut)* to ease off the accelerator *or* gas *(US)*; **jdm die Frau ~** to steal sb's wife.

weg-: **~packen** *vt sep* to pack away; **~putzen** *vt sep* to wipe away; *(col: essen)* to polish off.

Wegrand *m* wayside.

weg-: **~räumen** *vt sep* to clear away; *(in Schrank)* to put away; **~reißen** *vt sep irreg* to tear away *(jdm* from sb*)*; **~rennen** *vi sep irreg aux sein (col)* to run away; **~rücken** *vti sep (vi: aux sein)* to move away; **~rufen** *vt sep irreg* to call away; **~rutschen** *vi sep aux sein (aus der Hand etc)* to slip away; *(auf Eis etc)* to slide away; **~schaffen** *vt sep (beseitigen)* to get rid of; *(~räumen)* to clear away; *(~tragen)* to remove; **~schicken** *vt sep Brief, jdn* to send away; *(um etwas zu holen etc)* to send off; **~schleichen** *vir sep irreg (vi: aux sein)* to creep *or* steal away; **~schleppen** *vt sep* to drag away *or* off; *(tragen)* to carry off; **~schließen** *vt sep irreg* to lock away; **~schmeißen** *vt sep irreg (col)* to chuck away *(col)*; **~schnappen** *vt sep (col)* **jdm etw ~schnappen** to snatch sth (away) from sb; **jdm die Freundin ~schnappen** to pinch sb's girl-friend *(col)*; **~schütten** *vt sep* to tip away; **~schwemmen** *vt sep* to wash away; **~sehen** *vi sep irreg* to look away; **~setzen** *vt sep* to move (away); *(wegstellen)* to put away; **~sollen** *vi sep irreg (col)* **das soll ~** that is to go; **ich soll von London ~** I am (supposed) to leave London; **~spülen** *vt sep* to wash away; **~stecken** *vt sep* to put away; *(col: verkraften)* to cope with; **~stehlen** *vr sep irreg* to steal away; **~stellen** *vt sep* to put away; **~sterben** *vi sep irreg aux sein (col)* to die off; **~stoßen** *vt sep irreg* to push away; *(mit Fuß)* to kick away; **~tragen** *vt sep irreg* to carry away; **~treiben** *sep irreg* **1** *vt Tier etc* to drive away; **2** *vi aux sein* to drift away; **~treten** *vi sep irreg aux sein (Mil)* to fall out; **~treten!** dismiss!; **geistig ~getreten sein** *(col: geistesabwesend)* to be away with the fairies *(col)*; **~tun** *vt sep irreg* to put away; **~wehen** *vti sep (vi: aux sein)* to blow away.

Weg-: **w~weisend** *adj* pioneering *attr*, revolutionary; **~weiser** *m* - sign; *(an einem Pfosten)* signpost; *(fig: Buch etc)* guide.

Wegwerf- *in cpds* disposable.

weg-: **~werfen** *vt sep irreg* to throw away; **das ist ~geworfenes Geld** that's throwing money away; **~werfend** *adj* disdainful; **~wischen** *vt sep* to wipe off; **~wollen** *vi sep irreg (verreisen)* to want to go away; *(~gehen: von Party etc)* to want to leave; *(hinausgehen)* to want to go out; **~zaubern** *vt sep* to make disappear; **~ziehen** *sep irreg* **1** *vt* to pull away *(jdm* from sb*)*; **2** *vi aux sein* to move away.

weh *adj (wund)* sore. **~ tun** *(lit, fig)* to hurt; **mir tut der Rücken ~** my back hurts; **sich/jdm ~ tun** *(lit, fig)* to hurt oneself/sb.

wehe *interj* **~ (dir), wenn du das tust** you'll regret it if you do that; **darf ich das anfassen? — ~ (dir)!** can I touch? — you dare!

Wehe *f* **-n (a)** *(Schnee~ etc)* drift. **(b)** *(Geburts~)* **~n** *pl (lit)* contractions; **in den ~n liegen** to be in labour *(Brit) or* labor *(US)*.

wehen 1 *vi (Wind)* to blow; *(Fahne)* to flutter; *(Haare)* to blow about. **2** *vt* to blow *(von* off*)*; *(sanft)* to waft.

Weh-: **w~leidig** *adj* oversensitive to pain; *(jammernd)* whining *attr*; *(voller Selbstmitleid)* self-pitying; **sei nicht so w~leidig!** stop feeling sorry for yourself; **~mut** *f no pl (geh)* melancholy; *(Sehnsucht)* wistfulness; **w~mütig** *adj siehe n* melancholy; wistful.

Wehr[1] *f* **-en (a)** *(Feuer~)* fire brigade *(Brit) or* department *(US)*. **(b) sich zur ~setzen** to defend oneself.

Wehr[2] *nt* **-e** weir.

Wehr- *in cpds* defence *(Brit)*, defense *(US)*; **~dienst** *m* military service; **jdn zum ~dienst einberufen** to call sb up, to draft sb *(US)*; **~dienstverweigerer** *m* conscientious objector.

wehren 1 *vr* to defend oneself; *(aktiv kämpfen)* to (put up a) fight. **2** *vi +dat (geh)* **wehret den Anfängen!** these things must be nipped in the bud.

Wehr-: **~etat** *m* defence *(Brit) or* defense *(US)* budget; **w~fähig** *adj* fit for military service; **w~haft** *adj (geh)* able to put up a fight; *Stadt etc* well-fortified; **w~los** *adj* defenceless *(Brit)*, defenseless *(US)*; *(fig: hilflos)* helpless; **jdm w~los ausgeliefert sein** to be at sb's mercy; **~pflicht** *f* **(allgemeine) ~pflicht** (universal) conscription; **w~pflichtig** *adj* liable for military service; **~pflichtige(r)** *mf decl as adj* person liable for military service; **~sold** *m* (military) pay; **~übung** *f* reserve duty training exercise.

Wehwehchen *nt (col)* (minor) complaint.

Weib *nt* **-er** woman, female *(pej)*, broad *(US col)*.

Weibchen *nt* little woman; *(Zool)* female.

Weiber-: **~feind** *m* woman-hater, misogynist; **~geschichten** *pl* sexploits *pl (hum)*; **~geschwätz** *nt (pej)* women's talk; **~held** *m (pej)* womanizer.

weibisch *adj* effeminate.

weiblich *adj* female; *(Gram, fraulich)* feminine.

Weiblichkeit *f* femininity; *(Frauen)* women.

weich *adj* soft *(auch fig, Ling, Phot)*; *Ei* soft-boiled; *Fleisch, Gemüse* tender. **~ werden** *(lit, fig)* to soften; **die Knie wurden mir ~** my knees turned to jelly; **~ machen** to soften.

Weiche[1] *f* **-n** *(Seite)* side; *(von Tier auch)* flank.

Weiche[2] *f* **-n** *(Rail)* points *pl (Brit)*, switch *(US)*. **die ~n stellen** *(lit)* to switch the points; *(fig)* to set the course.

weichen[1] *vti (vi: aux haben or sein) (ein~)* to soak.

weichen[2] *pret* **wich**, *ptp* **gewichen** *vi aux sein* **(a)** to give way *(dat* to*)*; *(zurück~)* to retreat *(dat, vor +dat* from*)*; **(nicht) von jdm** *or* **jds Seite ~** (not) to leave sb's side. **(b)** *(Schmerz)* to go.

Weich-: **w~gekocht** *adj attr Ei* soft-boiled; *Fleisch, Gemüse* boiled until tender; **w~herzig** *adj* soft-hearted; **~käse** *m* soft cheese.

weichlich *adj (lit, fig)* soft; *Charakter* weak.

Weichling *m (pej)* softy *(col)*.

Weich-: **w~machen** *vt sep (fig)* to soften up; **~macher** *m (Chem)* softener; **w~spülen** *vt sep* to condition; *Wäsche* to use softener on; **~spüler** *m* conditioner; **~teile** *pl* soft parts *pl*; **~tier** *nt* mollusc.

Weide[1] *f* **-n** *(Bot)* willow.

Weide[2] *f* **-n** *(Agr)* pasture; *(Wiese)* meadow. **auf der ~ sein** to be grazing.

weiden 1 *vi* to graze. **2** *vt* to (put out to) graze. **3** *vr* **sich an etw** *(dat)* **~** *(fig)* to gloat over sth.

Weiden-: **~baum** *m* willow tree; **~busch** *m* wil-

low bush; ~**kätzchen** *nt* willow catkin; ~**korb** *m* wicker basket; ~**rost** *m* cattle grid.
Weideplatz *m* pasture.
weidlich *adv (mit adj)* pretty. **etw ~ ausnutzen** to make full use of sth.
Weid-: ~**mann** *m, pl* ~**männer** *(liter)* huntsman, hunter; **w~männisch 1** *adj* huntsman's *attr*; **das ist nicht w~männisch** that's not done in hunting; **2** *adv* like a professional hunter.
weigern *vr* to refuse.
Weigerung *f* refusal.
Weihe *f* **-n** *(Eccl)* consecration; *(Priester~)* ordination.
weihen *vt* **(a)** *(Eccl)* to consecrate. **jdn zum Bischof/Priester ~** to consecrate sb bishop/ ordain sb priest. **(b)** *(widmen)* **etw jdm/einer Sache ~** to dedicate sth to sb/sth; **dem Untergang geweiht** *(liter)* doomed.
Weiher *m* **-** pond.
Weihnachten *nt* **-** Christmas. **fröhliche ~!** happy *or* merry Christmas!; **(an) ~** at Christmas; **~ nach Hause fahren** to go home for Christmas; **etw zu ~ bekommen/schenken** to get sth for Christmas/to give sth as a Christmas present; **weiße/grüne ~** (a) white Christmas/(a) Christmas without snow.
weihnachten *vi impers (poet, iro)* **es weihnachtet sehr** Christmas is very much in evidence.
weihnachtlich *adj* Christmassy *(col)*.
Weihnachts- *in cpds* Christmas; ~**baum** *m* Christmas tree; ~**einkauf** *m* Christmas shopping *no pl*; ~**feier** *f* Christmas celebration(s *pl*); ~**(feier)tag** *m (erster)* Christmas Day; *(zweiter)* Boxing Day *(Brit)*; ~**fest** *nt* Christmas; ~**gans** *f* Christmas goose; **jdn ausnehmen wie eine ~gans** *(col)* to fleece sb *(col)*, to take sb to the cleaners *(col)*; ~**geld** *nt* Christmas bonus; ~**geschenk** *nt* Christmas present; ~**karte** *f* Christmas card; ~**lied** *nt* carol; ~**mann** *m, pl* ~**männer** Father Christmas, Santa Claus; *(pej col)* clown *(pej col)*; ~**markt** *m* Christmas fair; ~**zeit** *f* Christmas time.
Weih-: ~**rauch** *m* incense; ~**wasser** *nt* holy water.
weil *conj* because.
Weilchen *nt* **ein ~** a while.
Weile *f no pl* while. **eine ~** for a while.
Weiler *m* **-** hamlet.
Weimarer Republik *f* Weimar Republic.
Wein *m* **-e** wine. **jdm reinen ~ einschenken** to tell sb the truth.
Wein- *in cpds (auf Getränk bezogen)* wine; *(auf Pflanze bezogen)* vine; ~**bau** *m* wine-growing; ~**bauer** *m* wine-grower; ~**berg** *m* vineyard; ~**bergschnecke** *f* snail; ~**brand** *m* brandy; ~**brennerei** *f* brandy distillery.
weinen *vti* to cry; *(aus Trauer auch)* to weep *(um* for, *über +acc* over*)*. **sich** *(dat)* **die Augen rot ~** to cry one's eyes out; **es ist zum W~!** it's enough to make you weep!
weinerlich *adj* whining, whiny *(col)*.
Wein-: ~**ernte** *f* grape harvest; ~**essig** *m* wine vinegar; ~**faß** *nt* wine cask; ~**garten** *m* vineyard; ~**gegend** *f* wine-growing area; ~**geist** *m* (ethyl)alcohol; ~**gut** *nt* wine-growing estate; ~**händler** *m* wine dealer; ~**handlung** *f* wine shop *(Brit) or* store; ~**karte** *f* wine list; ~**keller** *m* wine-cellar; *(Lokal)* wine bar; ~**kelter** *f* wine press; ~**kenner** *m* wine connoisseur.
Weinkrampf *m* crying fit.
Wein-: ~**küfer** *m* cellarman; ~**land** *nt* wine-growing country; ~**laub** *nt* vine leaves *pl*; ~**lese** *f* grape harvest; ~**lokal** *nt* wine bar; ~**panscherei** *f* wine-adulterating; ~**probe** *f* wine-tasting; ~**rebe** *f* vine; **w~rot** *adj* wine-red; ~**säure** *f (Chem)* tartaric acid; **w~selig** *adj* merry with wine; ~**stock** *m* vine; ~**traube** *f* grape.
weise *adj* wise.
Weise *f* **-n (a)** *(Verfahren etc)* manner. **auf diese ~** in this way; **auf geheimnisvolle** *etc* **~** in a mysterious way; **in gewisser/keiner ~** in a/no way; **in der ~, daß ...** in such a way that ... **(b)** *(liter: Melodie)* melody.
weisen *pret* **wies**, *ptp* **gewiesen** *(geh)* **1** *vt* **jdm etw ~** *(lit, fig)* to show sb sth; **jdn aus dem Lande ~** to expel sb; **jdn vom Platz ~** *(Sport)* to order sb off (the field); **jdn von der Schule ~** to expel sb (from school); **etw (weit) von sich ~** *(fig)* to reject sth (emphatically). **2** *vi* to point *(nach* to(wards), *auf +acc* at*)*.
Weise(r) *m decl as adj* wise man.
Weisheit *f* **(a)** *no pl* wisdom. **das ist auch nicht der ~ letzter Schluß** that's not exactly the ideal solution; **er hat die ~ nicht mit Löffeln gefressen** he's not so bright. **(b)** *(weiser Spruch)* wise saying; *(iro)* pearl of wisdom.
Weisheitszahn *m* wisdom tooth.
weismachen *vt sep* **er wollte uns ~, daß ...** he would have us believe that ...; **das kannst du mir nicht ~!** you can't expect me to believe that.
weiß *adj* white. **ein ~es (Blatt) Papier** a blank sheet of paper; **ein ~er Fleck (auf der Landkarte)** a blank area (on the map); **das W~e Haus** the White House; **das W~e im Auge** the whites of one's eyes; **das W~e vom Ei** the white of an egg.
Weiß *nt* **-** white.
weissagen *vt insep* to foretell.
Weiß-: ~**blech** *nt* tinplate; **w~blond** *adj* ash-blond(e); ~**brot** *nt* white bread; *(Laib)* white loaf; ~**buch** *nt (Pol)* white paper.
weißen *vt* to whiten; *(tünchen)* to whitewash.
Weiße(r) *mf decl as adj* white, white man/woman.
Weiß-: ~**glut** *f* **jdn zur ~glut bringen** to make sb see red; **w~haarig** *adj* white-haired; ~**herbst** *m* ≃ rosé; ~**kohl** *m* white cabbage; **w~lich** *adj* whitish; ~**metall** *nt* white metal; ~**wal** *m* white whale; ~**waren** *pl* linen *sing*; ~**wein** *m* white wine; ~**wurst** *f* veal sausage.
Weisung *f* directive; *(Jur)* ruling. **auf ~** on instructions.
weit *siehe auch* **weiter 1** *adv* **(a)** far. **es ist noch ~ bis Bremen** there's still a long way to go till Bremen; **~ zurückliegen** to be far behind; *(zeitlich)* to be a long time ago; **~ nach Mitternacht** well after midnight; **~ und breit** for miles around; **ziemlich ~ am Ende** fairly near the end; **von ~em** from a long way off; **~ entfernt** a long way away; **~er entfernt** farther away; **ich bin ~ davon entfernt, das zu tun** I have no intention of doing that; **~ gefehlt!** far from it; **~ offen** wide open; **~ herumkommen** to get around a lot; **~ verbreitet** widespread.

(b) *(in Entwicklung)* **~ fortgeschritten** well advanced; **wie ~ bist du?** how far have you got?; **er hat es ~ gebracht** he has come a long way; **es so ~ bringen, daß ...** to bring it about that ...

(c) *(fig: erheblich) (mit adj, adv)* far; *(mit vb)* by far. **~ besser** far better; **bei ~em nicht so gut** *etc* **(wie...)** not nearly as good *etc* (as ...); **~ über 60** well over 60.

(d) das ist nicht ~ her *(col)* that's not up to much *(col)*; **das würde zu ~ führen** that would be taking things too far; **zu ~ gehen** to go too far; **das geht zu ~** that's going too far; **etw zu ~ treiben** to carry sth too far.

2 *adj* **(a)** wide; *(fig) Begriff, Horizont etc* broad; *Meer* open; *Herz* big. **im ~eren Sinne** in the broader *or* wider sense; **das ist ein ~es Feld** *(fig)* that is a big subject. **(b)** *(lang) Reise, Wurf etc* long. **in ~en Abständen** at long intervals; **man hat hier einen ~en Blick** you can see a long way from here; **in ~er Ferne** in the far distance; **das liegt in ~er Ferne** it's still a long way away.
Weit-: **w~ab** *adv* **w~ab von** far (away) from; **w~aus** *adv* far; **w~aus besser** far better; **w~ausholend** *adj Geste etc* expansive; *(fig)*

Erzählung etc long-drawn-out; **~blick** *m (fig)* far-sightedness; **w~blickend** *adj (fig)* far-sighted.

Weite *f* **-n** *(Ferne)* distance; *(Länge)* length; *(Größe)* expanse; *(Durchmesser)* width. **etw in der ~ ändern** to alter the width of sth.

weiten *vtr* to widen; *(Pupille)* to dilate.

weiter 1 *adj* further; *(andere)* other. **2** *adv (noch hinzu)* further; *(außerdem)* furthermore; *(sonst)* otherwise; *(nachher)* afterwards. **nichts ~** *(darüber hinaus nichts)* nothing further; **~ nichts?** is that all?; **~ nichts als ...** nothing but ...; **ich brauche ~ nichts** that's all I need; **wenn es ~ nichts ist, ...** well, if that's all (it is), ...; **außer uns war ~ niemand da** there was nobody else there besides us; **das hat ~ nichts zu sagen** that doesn't really matter; **etw ~ tun** to continue to do sth; **immer ~** on and on; *(Anweisung)* keep on (going); **was geschah (dann) ~?** what happened then?

weiter-: ~arbeiten *vi sep* to work on; **an einer Sache** *(dat)* **~arbeiten** to do some more work on sth; **~bewegen*** *vtr sep* to move further; **~bilden** *vr sep* to continue one's education; **~bringen** *vt sep irreg* to take further; **das bringt uns auch nicht ~** that doesn't get us any further; **~denken** *vi sep irreg* to think it out; *(an Zukünftiges)* to think ahead; **~empfehlen*** *vt sep irreg* to recommend (to one's friends *etc*); **~erzählen*** *vt sep Geheimnis etc* to pass on.

Weitere(s) *nt decl as adj* further details *pl*. **das ~** the rest; **alles ~** all the rest; **bis auf w~s** for the time being.

Weiter-: w~fahren *vi sep irreg aux sein (Fahrt fortsetzen)* to travel on; **w~fliegen** *vi sep irreg aux sein* to fly on; **die Maschine fliegt in 10 Minuten w~** the plane will take off again in 10 minutes; **w~führen** *vti sep* to continue; **das führt nicht w~** *(fig)* that doesn't get us anywhere; **w~führend** *adj Schule* secondary; **w~geben** *vt sep irreg* to pass on; **w~gehen** *vi sep irreg aux sein* to go on; **so kann es nicht w~gehen** *(fig)* things can't go on like this; **wie soll es nun w~gehen?** what's going to happen now?; **w~helfen** *vi sep irreg* to help (along) *(jdm* sb*)*; **w~kommen** *vi sep irreg aux sein* to advance; **nicht w~kommen** *(fig)* to be stuck down; **w~können** *vi sep irreg* to be able to carry on; **ich kann nicht w~** I can't go on; **w~laufen** *vi sep irreg aux sein* to run/walk on; *(Film, Produktion)* to go on; *(Gehalt)* to continue to be paid; **w~leben** *vi sep* to live on; **w~leiten** *vt sep* to pass on *(an +acc* to*)*; *(senden)* to forward; **w~machen** *vti sep* to carry on *(etw* with sth*)*; **w~reichen** *vt sep* to pass on; **~reise** *f* continuation of the/one's journey; **auf der ~reise nach ...** when I *etc* was travelling *(Brit) or* traveling *(US)* on to ...; **w~sagen** *vt sep* to pass on; **nicht w~sagen!** don't tell anyone!; **w~senden** *vt sep irreg* to forward; **w~verarbeiten*** *vt sep* to process; **w~verfolgen*** *vt sep Idee* to follow up; **~verkauf** *m* resale; **w~verkaufen*** *vti sep* to resell; **w~vermieten*** *vt sep* to sublet; **w~wissen** *vi sep irreg* **nicht (mehr) w~wissen** *(verzweifelt sein)* to be at one's wits' end; **w~wollen** *vi sep irreg* to want to go on; **w~wursteln** *vi sep (col)* to muddle on.

Weit-: w~gehend 1 *adj Vollmachten etc* far-reaching, extensive; *Übereinstimmung etc* a large degree of; **2** *adv* to a large extent; **w~gereist** *adj attr* widely travelled *(Brit) or* traveled *(US)*; **w~her** *adv (auch* **von w~her***)* from far away; **w~hergeholt** *adj attr* far-fetched; **w~herzig** *adj* charitable; **w~hin** *adv* widely; *(weitgehend)* to a large extent; **w~hin unbekannt** largely unknown; **w~läufig** *adj* **(a)** *Park, Gebäude* spacious; *Dorf* sprawling *attr*; *(fig) Erzählung* long-drawn-out; **(b)** *Verwandte* distant; **w~maschig** *adj Netz* wide-meshed; **w~reichend** *adj (fig)* far-reaching; **w~schweifig** *adj* long-winded; **~sicht** *f (fig)* far-sightedness; **w~sichtig** *adj (lit, fig)* far-sighted; **~sichtigkeit** *f* far-sightedness; **~sprung** *m (Sport)* the long jump *or* broad jump *(US)*; **w~verbreitet** *adj attr* widespread; *Zeitung* with a wide circulation; **w~verzweigt** *adj attr Straßensystem* extensive.

Weizen *m no pl* wheat.

Weizen-: ~brot *nt* wheat bread; **~keime** *pl (Cook)* wheatgerm *sing*; **~mehl** *nt* wheat flour; **~schrot** *m or nt* wheatmeal.

welch *interrog pron inv (geh)* **(a) ~ friedliches Bild!** what a peaceful scene! **(b)** *(in indirekten Fragesätzen)* **~ ein(e)** what.

welche(r, s) 1 *interrog pron* **(a)** *(adjektivisch)* what; *(bei Auswahl)* which. **~r Mensch könnte behaupten ...?** what person could claim ...?; **~s Kleid soll ich anziehen?** which dress shall I wear? **(b)** *(substantivisch)* which (one). **~r von den beiden?** which (one) of the two?; **~s sind die Symptome dieser Krankheit?** what are the symptoms of this illness? **(c)** *(in Ausrufen)* **~ Freude!** what joy! **2** *indef pron* some; *(in Fragen)* any. **ich habe keine Äpfel, haben Sie ~?** I don't have any apples, do you have any? **3** *rel pron (Mensch)* who; *(Sache)* which, that. **~(r, s) auch immer** whoever/whichever/whatever.

welcher|art *interrog adj inv (geh) (attributiv)* what kind of; *(substantivisch)* of what kind.

welk *adj Pflanze* wilted, faded; *Blatt* dead; *Gesicht* tired-looking.

welken *vi aux sein (lit, fig)* to fade, to wilt.

Wellblech *nt* corrugated iron.

Welle *f* **-n (a)** wave; *(Rad: Frequenz)* wavelength. **weiche ~** *(col)* soft line; **(hohe) ~n schlagen** *(fig)* to create (quite) a stir. **(b)** *(Tech)* shaft.

wellen *vt* to wave. **gewelltes Haar** wavy hair.

Wellen-: ~bad *nt* wave pool; **~bereich** *m (Phys, Telec)* frequency range; *(Rad)* waveband; **~brecher** *m* breakwater; **w~förmig 1** *adj* wave-like; *Linie* wavy; **2** *adv* in the form of waves; **~gang** *m no pl* waves *pl*, swell; **starker ~gang** heavy sea(s) *or* swell; **~länge** *f (Phys, Telec)* wavelength; **die gleiche ~länge haben** *(col)* to be on the same wavelength *(col)*; **~linie** *f* wavy line; **~reiten** *nt (Sport)* surfing; **~sittich** *m* budgerigar, budgie *(col)*.

Wellfleisch *nt* boiled pork.

wellig *adj Haar etc* wavy; *Oberfläche* uneven; *Hügelland* rolling.

Wellpappe *f* corrugated cardboard.

Welpe *m (wk)* **-n, -n** pup, whelp; *(von Wolf etc)* cub.

Wels *m* **-e** catfish.

Welt *f* **-en** *(lit, fig)* world. **die (große) weite ~** the big wide world; **der höchste Berg der ~** the highest mountain in the world; **die Alte/Neue/Freie/Dritte ~** the Old/New/Free/Third World; **die ~ der Oper** the world of opera; **eine ~ brach für ihn zusammen** his whole world collapsed about him; **das ist doch nicht die ~** it isn't as important as all that; **deswegen geht die ~ nicht unter** *(col)* it isn't the end of the world; **das kostet doch nicht die ~** it won't cost the earth; **zwischen ihnen liegen ~en** they are worlds apart; **auf der ~** in the world; **aus aller ~** from all over the world; **aus der ~ schaffen** to eliminate; **in aller ~** all over the world; **warum in aller ~ ...?** why on earth ...?; **um nichts in der ~** not for anything on earth; **ein Kind in die ~ setzen** to bring a child into the world; **ein Mann/eine Dame von ~** a man/woman of the world; **vor aller ~** in front of everybody; **zur ~ bringen** to give birth to; **auf die ~ kommen** to be born.

Welt- *in cpds* world; **~all** *nt no pl* universe; **w~anschaulich** *adj* ideological; **~anschauung** *f (Philos, Pol)* world view; **~ausstellung** *f* world exhibition; **~bank** *f* World Bank; **w~berühmt** *adj* world-famous; **w~beste(r, s)** *adj attr* world's best; **w~bewegend** *adj* world-shattering; **~bild** *nt* conception of the world; *(jds Ansichten)* philosophy; ~**bürger** *m* citizen of the world.

Weltenbummler *m* globetrotter.

Weltergewicht *nt (Boxen)* welterweight.

Welt-: w~fremd *adj* unworldly; ~**frieden** *m* world peace; ~**geschichte** *f* world history; **w~geschichtlich** *adj* **von w~geschichtlicher Bedeutung** of great significance in world history; ~**gesundheitsorganisation** *f* World Health Organization; ~**handel** *m* world trade; ~**herrschaft** *f* world domination; ~**karte** *f* map of the world; ~**kirchenrat** *m* World Council of Churches; ~**klasse** *f* ~**klasse sein** to be world-class; ~**krieg** *m* world war; **der Erste/Zweite ~krieg** World War One/Two, the First/Second World War; ~**kugel** *f* globe; **w~lich** *adj* worldly; *(säkular)* secular; ~**literatur** *f* world literature; ~**macht** *f* world power; **w~männisch** *adj* urbane; ~**markt** *m* world market; ~**meer** *nt* ocean; ~**meister** *m* world *or* world's *(US)* champion; ~**meisterschaft** *f* world *or* world's *(US)* championship; *(Ftbl)* World Cup; **w~offen** *adj* liberal-minded; ~**ordnung** *f* world order; ~**politik** *f* world politics *pl*; **w~politisch** *adj* **die w~politische Entwicklung** the development of world politics; **von w~politischer Bedeutung** of importance in world politics.

Weltraum *m* (outer) space.

Weltraum- *in cpds* space; ~**fahrer** *m* space traveller *(Brit) or* traveler *(US)*; ~**forschung** *f* space research; ~**station** *f* space station; ~**waffen** *pl* space weapons *pl*.

Welt-: ~**reich** *nt* empire; ~**reise** *f* world tour; **eine ~reise machen** to go around the world; ~**rekord** *m* world record; ~**religion** *f* world religion; ~**revolution** *f* world revolution; ~**ruf** *m* world-wide reputation; ~**ruhm** *m* world fame; ~**sicherheitsrat** *m (Pol)* (United Nations) Security Council; ~**sprache** *f* world language; ~**stadt** *f* cosmopolitan city; **w~städtisch** *adj* cosmopolitan; ~**umseglung** *f* circumnavigation of the globe; ~**untergang** *m (lit, fig)* end of the world; ~**verbesserer** *m* starry-eyed idealist; **w~weit** *adj* world-wide; ~**wirtschaft** *f* world economy; ~**wirtschaftskrise** *f* world economic crisis; ~**wunder** *nt* **die sieben ~wunder** the Seven Wonders of the World.

wem *dat of* **wer** *interrog pron* who ... to, to whom. **mit ~ ...** who ... with, with whom; **~ von euch soll ich den Schlüssel geben?** which (one) of you should I give the key to?

wen *acc of* **wer 1** *interrog pron* who, whom. **an ~ hast du geschrieben?** who did you write to?; **~ von den Schülern kennst du?** which (one) of these pupils do you know?

Wende *f* **-n** turn; *(Veränderung)* change.

Wendekreis *m* **(a)** tropic. **(b)** *(Aut)* turning circle.

wenden *pret* **wendete** *or* **wandte,** *ptp* **gewendet** *or* **gewandt 1** *vt* to turn; *(auf die andere Seite)* to turn (over); *(Cook)* to toss. **bitte ~!** please turn over; **wie man es auch wendet ...** whichever way you look at it ... **2** *vr* to turn (around); *(Wetter, Glück)* to change. **sich nach links ~** to turn to the left; **sich zu jdm/etw ~** to turn towards sb/sth; **sich zum Besseren/Schlimmeren ~** to take a turn for the better/worse; **sich an jdn ~** *(um Auskunft)* to consult sb; *(um Hilfe)* to turn to sb; *(Buch etc)* to be directed at sb; **sich gegen jdn/etw ~** to come out against sb/sth. **3** *vi* to turn *(auch Sport)*; *(umkehren)* to turn around.

Wende-: ~platz *m* turning place; ~**punkt** *m* turning point.

wendig *adj (lit, fig)* agile; *Auto etc* manoeuvrable *(Brit)*, maneuverable *(US)*.

Wendigkeit *f siehe adj* agility; manoeuvrability *(Brit)*, maneuverability *(US)*.

Wendung *f* **(a)** turn; *(Veränderung)* change. **eine ~ zum Besseren nehmen** to take a turn for the better. **(b)** *(Rede~)* expression, phrase.

wenig 1 *adj, indef pron* **(a)** *sing* (a) little. **ich habe ~** I have only a little; **hast du Zeit? — ~!** have you got time? — not much; **das ~e, was er übrig hatte** the little he had left; **es fehlte (nur) ~, und er wäre überfahren worden** he was very nearly run over; **er gibt sich mit ~ zufrieden** *(verlangt nicht viel)* he is satisfied with a little; *(ist selten zufrieden)* not much satisfies him; **sie hat zu ~ Geld** *etc* she doesn't have enough money *etc*; **ein Exemplar zu ~** one copy too few; **£ 20 zu ~** £20 too little. **(b) ~e** *pl (ein paar)* a few; *(nicht viele)* few; **in ~en Tagen** in (just) a few days; **einige ~e Leute** a few people. **(c)** *(auch adv)* **ein ~** a little; **ein ~ Salz** a little salt.

2 *adv* little. **~ besser** little better; **~ bekannt** little-known *attr*, little known *pred*; **sie kommt (nur) ~ raus** she doesn't get out very often.

weniger *comp of* **wenig 1** *adj, indef pron* less; *pl* fewer. **~ werden** to get less and less. **2** *adv* less. **das finde ich ~ schön!** that's not so nice!; **je mehr ... desto ~ ...** the more ... the less ...; **sieben ~ drei ist vier** seven less three is four.

wenigstens *adv* at least.

wenigste(r, s) *superl of* **wenig** *adj, indef pron*, **am ~n** *adv* least; *pl* fewest. **er hat von uns allen am ~n Geld/Sorgen** he has the least money/the fewest worries of any of us; **diese Farbe ist am ~n schön** this colour is the least attractive one; **die ~n glauben das** very few believe that.

wenn *conj* **(a)** *(konditional, bei Wünschen)* if. **selbst** *or* **und ~** even if; **~ ... auch ...** even though *or* if ...; **~ er auch noch so dumm sein mag, ...** however stupid he may be, ...; **~ schon!** so what? *(col)*; **~ es schon sein muß** well, if that's the way it's got to be; **~ wir erst die neue Wohnung haben** once we get the new flat; **~ ich doch ...** if only I ...; **außer ~** except if, unless. **(b)** *(zeitlich)* when. **immer ~** whenever; **außer ~** except when.

Wenn *nt*: **das ~ und Aber** (the) ifs and buts; **ohne ~ und Aber** unequivocally.

wennschon *adv (col)* **(na,) ~!** what of it?; **~, dennschon!** in for a penny, in for a pound!

wer 1 *interrog pron* who. **~ von ...** which (one) of ... **2** *rel pron (derjenige, der)* the person who; *(jeder, der)* anyone *or* anybody who. **~ ... auch (immer)** whoever ... **3** *indef pron (col: jemand)* somebody, someone. **ist da ~?** is somebody there?; **~ sein** to be somebody *(col)*.

Werbe- *in cpds* advertising; ~**abteilung** *f* publicity department; ~**agentur** *f* advertising agency; ~**aktion** *f* advertising campaign; ~**antwort** *f* business reply card; ~**etat** *m* advertising budget; ~**fernsehen** *nt* commercial television; ~**film** *m* promotional film; *(Spot)* (filmed) commercial; ~**funk** *m* radio commercials *pl*; ~**gag** *m* publicity stunt *or* gimmick; ~**geschenk** *nt* gift *(from company)*, freebie *(col)*; *(zu Gekauftem)* free gift; ~**kampagne** *f* publicity campaign; ~**muster** *nt* advertising sample.

werben *pret* **warb,** *ptp* **geworben 1** *vt Mitglieder, Soldaten* to recruit; *Kunden, Stimmen* to attract, to win. **2** *vi* to advertise. **für etw ~** to advertise sth; **für eine Partei ~** to try to get support for a party; **um Unterstützung ~** to try to enlist support; **um junge Wähler ~** to try to attract young voters; **um ein Mädchen ~** to court a girl.

Werbe-: ~**schrift** *f* publicity leaflet; ~**schriften** promotional literature *sing*; ~**slogan** *m* publicity slogan; ~**spot** *m* commercial; ~**text** *m* advertising copy *no pl*; ~**texter** *m* copywriter; ~**träger** *m* carrier of advertising; ~**trommel** *f*: **die ~trommel (für etw) rühren** *(col)* to beat the big drum (for sth) *(col)*; **w~wirksam** *adj* **w~wirksam sein** to be good publicity; ~**wirksamkeit** *f* publicity value.

Werbung *f (esp Comm)* advertising; *(für Produkt auch)* publicity, promotion; *(Werbeabteilung)* publicity department. ~ **für etw machen** to advertise sth.

Werbungskosten *pl (von Mensch)* professional outlay *sing or* expenses *pl*; *(von Firma)* business expenses *pl*.

werden *pret* **wurde,** *ptp* **geworden** *aux sein* **1** *vi* to become; *(mit adj auch)* to get. **blind** ~ to go blind; **krank** ~ to fall ill; **rot** ~ to turn red; **es wird kalt** it's getting cold; **mir wird warm** I'm getting warm; **mir wird schlecht** I feel bad; **anders** ~ to change; **die Fotos sind gut geworden** the photos have come out nicely; **aus ihm ist ein großer Komponist geworden** he has become a great composer; **ich will Lehrer** ~ I want to be a teacher; **Erster** ~ to come *or* be first; **was soll das ~? — das wird ein Pullover** what's that going to be? — it's going to be a pullover; **daraus ist nichts geworden** it came to nothing; **es wird bald ein Jahr, daß ...** it's almost a year since ...; **es wird Zeit, daß er kommt** it's time (that) he came; **es wird Nacht/Tag** it's getting dark/light; **es wird Winter** winter is coming; **er wird am 8. Mai 36** he is 36 on the 8th of May; **er ist gerade 40 geworden** he has just turned 40; **was soll nun ~?** so what's going to happen now?; **es wird schon** ~ *(col)* it'll come all right in the end; **er wird mal wie sein Vater** he's going to be like his father; **wie soll der Pullover ~?** what's the pullover going to be like?

2 *aux* **(a)** *(bei Futur und Konjunktiv)* **er wird es tun** he will do it, he'll do it; **er wird das nicht tun** he will not *or* won't do that; **es wird gleich regnen** it's going to rain; **wer wird denn gleich!** *(col)* come on, now!; **das würde ich gerne tun** I would *or* I'd gladly do that. **(b)** *(bei Vermutung)* **sie wird wohl in der Küche sein** she will be in the kitchen; **er wird (wohl) ausgegangen sein** he will have gone out. **(c)** *(bei Passiv) ptp* **worden gebraucht** ~ to be used; **er ist erschossen worden** he was shot/he has been shot; **hier wird nicht geraucht!** there's no smoking here; **mir wurde gesagt, daß ...** I was told ...

werdend *adj* **~e Mutter** expectant mother.

werfen *pret* **warf,** *ptp* **geworfen 1** *vt* to throw *(nach* at*)*; *Tor, Korb* to score. **Bomben** ~ *(von Flugzeug)* to drop bombs; **eine Münze** ~ to toss a coin; **„nicht ~"** "handle with care"; **Bilder an die Wand** ~ to project pictures onto the wall; **etw auf jdn/etw** ~ to throw sth at sb/sth; **etw auf den Boden** ~ to throw sth to the ground; **billige Waren auf den Markt** ~ to dump cheap goods on the market; **jdn aus der Firma** ~ to throw sb out (of the firm); **jdn ins Gefängnis** *etc* ~ to throw sb into prison *etc*; **etw in den Briefkasten** ~ to put sth in the letter box. **2** *vi* **(a)** to throw. **mit etw (auf jdn/etw)** ~ to throw sth (at sb/sth); **mit Geld um sich** ~ to throw one's money about; **mit Fremdwörtern um sich** ~ to bandy foreign words about. **(b)** *(Tier)* to have its young. **3** *vr* to throw oneself *(auf +acc* (up)on, at*)*.

Werft *f* **-en** shipyard; *(für Flugzeuge)* hangar.

Werft|arbeiter *m* shipyard worker.

Werg *nt no pl* tow.

Werk *nt* **-e (a)** *(Arbeit)* work *no indef art; (geh: Tat)* deed, act; *(Kunst~, Buch)* work; *(Gesamt~)* works *pl*. **das ~ eines Augenblicks** the work of a moment; **das ist sein** ~ this is his doing; **das ~ jahrelanger Arbeit** the product of many years of work; **gute ~e tun** to do good works; **ein ~ der Nächstenliebe** an act of charity; **ans ~ gehen** to set to work. **(b)** *(Betrieb, Fabrik)* works *sing or pl*, plant. **ab** ~ *(Comm)* ex works. **(c)** *(Trieb~)* works *pl*.

Werk- *in cpds* works, factory; *siehe auch* **Werk(s)-**; **~bank** *f* workbench.

werkeln *vi (col)* to potter about.

werken *vi* to be busy. **W~** *(Sch)* handicrafts.

Werk-: ~halle *f* factory building; **~meister** *m* foreman.

Werk(s)-: ~angehörige(r) *mf* factory employee; **~arzt** *m* works *or* company doctor.

Werkschutz *m* works security service.

Werks-: w~eigen *adj* company *attr*; **~fahrer** *m* company *or* factory driver; **~feuerwehr** *f* factory fire service; **~gelände** *nt* factory premises *pl*; **~kantine** *f* works canteen; **~küche** *f* works kitchen; **~leiter** *m* works director *or* manager; **~leitung** *f* factory management; **~spionage** *f* industrial espionage.

Werk-: ~statt *f* workshop *(auch fig)*; *(für Autoreparaturen)* garage; *(von Künstler)* studio; **~stoff** *m* material; **~stück** *nt* workpiece; **~student** *m* working student.

Werk(s)-: ~verkehr *m* company transport; **~wohnung** *f* company flat *(Brit) or* apartment.

Werktag *m* working day, workday.

werktags *adv* on working days.

Werk-: ~tisch *m* work-table; **~unterricht** *m* woodwork/metalwork *etc* instruction.

Werkzeug *nt (lit, fig)* tool.

Werkzeug-: ~kasten *m* toolbox; **~macher** *m* toolmaker; **~maschine** *f* machine tool.

Wermut *m no pl (~wein)* vermouth.

Wermutstropfen *m (fig geh)* drop of bitterness.

wert *adj* **(a) etw ~ sein** to be worth sth; **nichts ~ sein** to be worthless; **Glasgow ist eine Reise** ~ Glasgow is worth a visit; **es ist der Mühe** ~ it's worth the trouble; **es ist nicht der Rede** ~ it's not worth mentioning; **er ist es nicht ~, daß man ihm vertraut** he doesn't deserve to be trusted. **(b)** *(nützlich)* useful. **ein Auto ist viel** ~ a car is very useful; **das ist schon viel** ~ *(erfreulich)* that's very encouraging.

Wert *m* **-e** value; *(esp menschlicher)* worth; *(von Banknoten, Briefmarken)* denomination. **~e** *pl (Ergebnisse)* results *pl*; **im ~e von** to the value of; **an ~ verlieren** to decrease in value; **etw unter ~ verkaufen** to sell sth for less than its true value; **sie hat innere ~e** she has certain inner qualities; **~ auf etw** *(acc)* **legen** *(fig)* to attach importance to sth.

Wert-: ~angabe *f* declaration of value; **~arbeit** *f* craftsmanship; **w~beständig** *adj* stable in value.

werten *vti (einstufen)* to rate *(als* as*)*; *Klassenarbeit etc* to grade; *(beurteilen)* to judge *(als* to be*)*; *(Sport) (als gültig ~)* to allow; *(Punkte geben)* to give a score. **ein Tor nicht** ~ *(Ftbl etc)* to disallow a goal.

Wert-: ~gegenstand *m* object of value; **~gegenstände** *pl* valuables *pl*; **w~frei** value-free; **w~los** *adj* worthless; **~losigkeit** *f* worthlessness; **~marke** *f* stamp; *(Gutschein)* voucher; **~maßstab** *m* standard; **~papier** *nt* bond; **~papiere** *pl* stocks and shares *pl*; **~papierbörse** *f* stock market.

Wertung *f* evaluation; *(von Jury etc)* judging; *(Punkte)* score.

Wert-: ~urteil *nt* value judgement; **w~voll** *adj* valuable; **~vorstellung** *f* moral concept.

Wesen *nt* **- (a)** *no pl* nature; *(Wesentliches)* essence. **es liegt im ~ einer Sache ...** it's in the nature of a thing ... **(b)** *(Geschöpf)* being. **ein weibliches/männliches** ~ a female/male.

Wesens-: ~art *f* nature; **w~gleich** *adj* essentially alike; **w~verwandt** *adj* related in character; **~zug** *m* trait.

wesentlich 1 *adj (hauptsächlich)* essential; *(grundlegend)* fundamental; *(wichtig)* important. **das W~e** the essential thing; *(von Text, Rede)* the gist; **im ~en** essentially; *(im großen)* in the main. **2** *adv* fundamentally; *(erheblich)* considerably. **es ist mir ~ lieber, wenn wir ...** I would much rather we ...

weshalb 1 *interrog adv* why. **2** *rel adv* **der Grund, ~ ...** the reason why ...

Wespe *f* **-n** wasp.

Wespen-: ~nest *nt* wasps' nest; **in ein ~nest stechen** *(fig)* to stir up a hornets' nest; **~stich** *m* wasp sting.

wessen *pron* **1** *gen of* **wer** *interrog* whose. **2** *gen of* **was** *(liter)* **~ hat man dich angeklagt?** of what have you been accused?

West *m no pl (Naut, Met, liter)* west.

West- *in cpds (in Ländernamen) (politisch)* West; *(geographisch auch)* the West of ..., Western; **~-Berlin, ~berlin** *nt* West Berlin; **~berliner** *adj attr* West Berlin; **~berliner(in** *f***)** *m* West Berliner; **w~deutsch** *adj* West German; **~deutsche(r)** *mf* West German; **~deutschland** *nt* West Germany.

Weste *f* **-n** waistcoat *(Brit)*, vest *(US)*. **eine reine ~ haben** *(fig)* to have a clean slate.

Westen *m no pl* west; *(von Land)* West. **der ~** *(Pol)* the West.

Westentasche *f* waistcoat *(Brit) or* vest *(US)* pocket. **etw wie seine ~ kennen** *(col)* to know sth like the back of one's hand *(col)*.

Western *m* **-** western.

west|europäisch *adj* West(ern) European. **~e Zeit** Greenwich Mean Time.

Westfale *m (wk)* **-n, -n, Westfälin** *f* Westphalian.

Westfalen *nt* Westphalia.

westfälisch *adj* Westphalian.

westlich 1 *adj* western; *Wind, Richtung* westerly; *(Pol)* Western. **der ~ste Ort** the westernmost place. **2** *adv* (to the) west *(von* of*)*. **3** *prep +gen* (to the) west of.

West-: ~mächte *pl (Pol)* **die ~mächte** the western powers *pl*; **~mark** *f (col)* West German mark; **w~östlich** *adj* west-to-east; **in w~östlicher Richtung** from west to east; **~politik** *f* western policy; **~sektor** *m* western sector; **w~wärts** *adv* westward(s); **~wind** *m* west wind.

weswegen *interrog adv* why.

wett *adj pred* **~ sein** to be quits.

Wettbewerb *m* competition. **mit jdm in ~ stehen/treten** to be in/enter into competition with sb.

Wettbewerbs-: ~beschränkung *f* restraint of trade; **w~fähig** *adj* competitive; **~teilnehmer** *m* competitor.

Wettbüro *nt* betting office.

Wette *f* **-n** bet *(auch Sport)*, wager. **eine ~ abschließen** to make a bet; **darauf gehe ich jede ~ ein** I'll bet you anything you like; **was gilt die ~?** what are you betting?; **die ~ gilt!** done!, you're on! *(col)*; **um die ~ laufen** to run a race (with each other); **sie schreien um die ~** they're having a screaming competition.

wett|eifern *vi insep* **mit jdm um etw ~** to compete with sb for sth.

wetten *vti* to bet. **(wollen wir) ~?** (do you) want to bet?; **~, daß ich recht habe?** (I) bet you I'm right!; **so haben wir nicht gewettet!** that's not part of the bargain!; **auf etw** *(acc)* **~** to bet on sth; **mit jdm ~** to bet with sb; **(mit jdm) um 5 Mark ~** to bet (sb) 5 marks; **ich wette 100 gegen 1(, daß ...)** I'll bet 100 to 1 (that ...).

Wetter[1] *m* **-** better.

Wetter[2] *nt* **- (a)** weather *no indef art*. **bei jedem ~** in all weathers; **das ist vielleicht ein ~!** *(col)* what weather!; **was haben wir heute für ~?** what's the weather like today?; **wir haben herrliches ~** the weather's marvellous. **(b)** *usu pl (Min)* air. **schlagende ~** *pl* firedamp *sing*.

Wetter-: ~amt *nt* met office; **~aussichten** *pl* weather outlook; **~beobachtung** *f* meteorological observation; **~bericht** *m* weather report; **~besserung** *f* improvement in the weather; **w~beständig** *adj* weatherproof; **~dienst** *m* meteorological service; **w~empfindlich** *adj* sensitive to the weather; **~fahne** *f* weather vane; **w~fest** *adj* weatherproof; **w~fühlig** *adj* sensitive to the weather; **~häuschen** *nt* weather house; **~karte** *f* weather chart; **~lage** *f* weather situation; **~leuchten** *nt no pl* sheet lightning; **~meldung** *f* meteorological report.

wettern *vi* to curse and swear. **gegen etw ~** to rail against sth.

Wetter-: ~regel *f* weather saying; **~satellit** *m* weather satellite; **~schaden** *m* weather damage; **~seite** *f* windward side; **~station** *f* weather station; **~störung** *f* meteorological disturbance; **~umschlag** *m* sudden change in the weather; **~verhältnisse** *pl* weather conditions *pl*; **~vorhersage** *f* weather forecast; **~warte** *f* weather station; **w~wendisch** *adj (fig)* moody; **~wolke** *f* storm cloud.

Wett-: ~fahrt *f* race; **~kampf** *m* competition; **~kämpfer** *m* competitor; **~lauf** *m* race; **einen ~lauf machen** to run a race; **ein ~lauf mit der Zeit** a race against time; **~läufer** *m* runner (in a/the race).

wettmachen *vt sep* to make up for; *Verlust etc* to make good.

Wett-: ~rennen *nt (lit, fig)* race; **~rüsten** *nt* arms race; **~schein** *m* betting slip; **~schuld** *f* betting debt; **~streit** *m* competition.

wetzen 1 *vt* to whet. **2** *vi aux sein (col)* to scoot *(col)*.

Wetzstein *m* whetstone.

Whisky ['vɪski] *m* **-s** whisky, whiskey *(US)*.

wich *pret of* **weichen**[2].

wichsen ['vɪksn] **1** *vti Schuhe* to polish; *Boden etc* to wax. **2** *vi (col!: onanieren)* to jerk *or* toss off *(col!)*.

Wicht *m* **-e** *(Kobold)* goblin; *(kleiner Mensch)* titch *(col)*; *(fig: verachtenswerter Mensch)* scoundrel.

wichtig *adj* important. **eine ~e Miene machen** to try to look important; **er will sich nur ~ machen** he just wants to get attention; **sich selbst/etw (zu) ~ nehmen** to take oneself/sth (too) seriously; **sich** *(dat)* **~ vorkommen** to be full of oneself; **alles W~e** everything of importance; **W~eres zu tun haben** to have more important things to do; **nichts W~eres zu tun haben** to have nothing better to do.

Wichtigkeit *f* importance.

Wichtigtuer(in *f***)** *m* **-** *(pej)* pompous ass *(col)*.

wichtigtuerisch *adj* pompous.

Wicke *f* **-n** *(Bot)* vetch; *(Garten~)* sweet pea.

Wickel *m* **- (a)** *(Med)* compress. **(b)** *(Rolle)* reel; *(Locken~)* curler. **(c)** *(col)* **jdn am ~ kriegen/haben** to grab/have sb by the scruff of the neck; *(fig)* to give sb a good talking to *(col)*.

Wickel-: ~bluse *f* wrap-around blouse; **~kind** *nt* babe-in-arms; **~kleid** *nt* wrap-around dress.

wickeln 1 *vt* **(a)** *(schlingen)* to wind *(um* around*)*; *Verband etc* to bind; *Haare* to put in curlers. **sich** *(dat)* **eine Decke um die Beine ~** to wrap a blanket around one's legs; **da bist du schief gewickelt!** *(fig col)* you're very much mistaken. **(b)** *(einwickeln)* to wrap *(in +acc* in*)*; *(mit Verband)* to dress. **einen Säugling ~** to put on a baby's nappy *(Brit) or* diaper *(US)*. **2** *vr* to wrap oneself *(in +acc* in*)*. **sich um etw ~** to wrap itself around sth; *(Schlange, Pflanze)* to wind itself around sth.

Wickeltisch *m* baby's changing table.

Widder *m* **-** ram; *(Astrol)* Aries.

wider *prep +acc (geh)* against. **~ Erwarten** contrary to expectations.

widerfahren* *vi, vi impers insep irreg aux sein +dat (geh)* to happen *(jdm* to sb*)*.

Wider-: ~haken *m* barb; **~hall** *m* echo; **(bei jdm) keinen ~hall finden** *(Interesse)* to meet with no response (from sb).

widerlegbar *adj* refutable. **nicht ~** irrefutable.

widerlegen* *vt insep* to refute; *jdn* to prove wrong.

Wider-: w~lich *adj* revolting; **~ling** *m (pej col)*

repulsive creep *(col)*; **w~natürlich** *adj* unnatural; **w~rechtlich** *adj* unlawful; **sich** *(dat)* **etw w~rechtlich aneignen** to misappropriate sth; **~rede** *f* contradiction; **keine ~rede!** don't argue!

Widerruf *m siehe vb* withdrawal; retraction; cancellation; withdrawal. **bis auf ~** until revoked.

widerrufen* *insep irreg* **1** *vt Erlaubnis etc* to withdraw; *Aussage* to retract; *Befehl* to cancel. **2** *vi (bei Verleumdung etc)* to withdraw.

Wider-: ~sacher(in *f*) *m* - adversary; **w~setzen** *vr insep* **sich jdm/einer Sache w~setzen** to oppose sb/sth; *der Polizei, Festnahme* to resist sb/sth; *einem Befehl* to refuse to comply with sth; **w~sinnig** *adj* absurd; **w~spenstig** *adj* unruly; *(störrisch)* stubborn; *Haar* unmanageable; **~spenstigkeit** *f siehe adj* unruliness; stubbornness; **w~spiegeln** *sep* **1** *vt (lit, fig)* to reflect; **2** *vr (lit, fig)* to be reflected; **~spieg(e)lung** *f* reflection.

widersprechen* *insep irreg* **1** *vi* **jdm/einer Sache ~** to contradict sb/sth; **das widerspricht meinen Grundsätzen** that goes against my principles. **2** *vr (einander)* to contradict one another. **sich (selbst) ~** to contradict oneself.

Widerspruch *m* **(a)** *(Gegensätzlichkeit)* contradiction. **ein ~ in sich** a contradiction in terms; **im ~ zu** contrary to; **in ~ zu etw geraten** to come into conflict with sth; **in** *or* **im ~ zu etw stehen** to conflict with sth. **(b)** *(Widerrede)* contradiction; *(Ablehnung)* opposition. **kein ~!** don't argue!; **er duldet keinen ~** he won't have any argument; **es erhob sich ~** there was opposition *(gegen* to); **~ erheben** to protest.

widersprüchlich *adj* contradictory, inconsistent.

widerspruchs-: ~frei *adj Theorie* consistent; **~los 1** *adj Zustimmung* unopposed; **2** *adv* without opposition; **etw ~los hinnehmen** to accept sth unquestioningly; **~voll** *adj* full of inconsistencies.

Widerstand *m* ⸚**e** resistance; *(Ablehnung)* opposition. **jdm/einer Sache ~ leisten** to resist sb/sth.

Widerstands-: ~bewegung *f* resistance movement; **w~fähig** *adj* robust; *Pflanze* hardy; *(Med, Tech etc)* resistant *(gegen* to); **~fähigkeit** *f siehe adj* robustness; hardiness; resistance *(gegen* to); **~kämpfer** *m* resistance fighter; **w~los** *adj, adv* without resistance; **~nest** *nt (Mil)* pocket of resistance.

widerstehen* *vi insep irreg +dat* **einer Sache ~** to resist sth; *einem Erdbeben etc* to withstand sth.

widerstreben* *vi insep +dat* **jds sittlichem Empfinden ~** to go against sb's moral sense; **es widerstrebt mir, so etwas zu tun** I am reluctant to do anything like that.

Widerstreben *nt no pl* reluctance.

widerstrebend *adj (gegensätzlich) Interessen* conflicting; *(widerwillig)* reluctant.

widerwärtig *adj* disgusting. **er ist mir ~** he disgusts me.

Widerwille *m (Abscheu, Ekel)* disgust *(gegen* for), revulsion; *(Abneigung)* distaste *(gegen* for); *(Widerstreben)* reluctance.

widerwillig *adj* reluctant, unwilling.

Widerworte *pl* answering back *sing*. **er tat es ohne ~** he did it without protest.

widmen 1 *vt* **jdm etw ~** to dedicate sth to sb. **2** *vr +dat* to devote oneself to; *den Gästen, einer Aufgabe* to attend to.

Widmung *f (in Buch etc)* dedication *(an +acc* to).

widrig *adj* adverse.

wie 1 *interrog adv* how. **~ anders ...?** how else ...?; **~ wär's (mit uns beiden** *etc*) *(col)* how about it? *(col)*; **~ wär's mit einem Whisky?** *(col)* how about a whisky?; **~ ist er (denn)?** what's he like?; **Sie wissen ja, ~ das so ist** well, you know how it is; **~ nennt man das?** what is that called?; **~ bitte?** pardon?; **~ bitte?!** *(entrüstet)* I beg your pardon!; **das macht dir Spaß, ~?** you like that, don't you?; **und ~!, aber ~!** and how! *(col)*; **~ groß er ist!** isn't he big!

2 *adv* **(a)** *(relativ)* **die Art, ~ sie geht** the way she walks. **(b)** *(in Verbindung mit auch)* **~ stark du auch sein magst** however strong you may be.

3 *conj* **(a)** *(vergleichend)* **so ... ~** as ... as; **weiß ~ Schnee** (as) white as snow; **ein Mann ~ er** a man like him; **in einer Lage ~ diese(r)** in a situation like this; **ich fühlte mich ~ im Traum** I felt as if I was dreaming; **~ du weißt** as you know; **~ noch nie** as never before. **(b)** *(zum Beispiel)* **~ (zum Beispiel)** such as (for example). **(c)** *(bei Verben der Wahrnehmung)* **er sah, ~ es geschah** he saw it happen; **er hörte, ~ der Regen fiel** he heard the rain falling. **(d)** *(zeitlich: als)* **~ ich mich umdrehte, sah ich ...** as I turned around I saw ...

Wie *nt no pl* **das ~ und Wann werden wir später besprechen** we'll talk about how and when later.

Wiedehopf *m* **-e** hoopoe.

wieder *adv* again. **~ nüchtern** sober again; **immer ~** again and again; **~ ist ein Jahr vorbei** another year has passed; **wie, schon ~?** what, again?; **das ist auch ~ wahr** that's true; **da sieht man mal ~, ...** it just shows ...; **das fällt mir schon ~ ein** I'll remember it again.

Wieder- *pref* re; *(bei Verben) (erneut)* again; *(zurück)* back; **~aufbau** *m (lit, fig)* reconstruction; **w~aufbauen** *vti sep* to reconstruct; **w~aufbereiten*** *vt sep* to recycle; *Atommüll* to reprocess; **~aufbereitungsanlage** reprocessing plant; **w~aufforsten** *vti sep* to reforest; **w~aufführen** *vt sep Theaterstück* to revive; *Film* to rerun; **w~aufladen** *vt sep irreg* to recharge; **w~aufleben** *vi sep aux sein* to revive; **~aufleben** *nt* revival; **~aufnahme** *f* **(a)** *(von Tätigkeit etc)* resumption; **(b)** *(in Verein etc)* readmittance; *(von Patienten)* readmission; **w~aufnehmen** *vt sep irreg* **(a)** to resume; *Gedanken, Hobby* to take up again; *Thema* to revert to; *(Jur) Verfahren* to reopen; **(b)** *Menschen* to take back; *(in Verein, Klinik)* to readmit; **w~aufrüsten** *vti sep* to rearm; **~aufrüstung** *f* rearmament; **w~bekommen*** *vt sep irreg* to get back; **w~beleben*** *vt sep* to revive; **~belebung** *f* revival; **w~beschaffen*** *vt sep* to recover; **~beschaffung** *f* recovery; **w~bewaffnen*** *vr sep* to rearm; **~bewaffnung** *f* rearmament; **w~bringen** *vt sep irreg* to bring back; **w~einführen** *vt sep* to reintroduce; **~einführung** *f* reintroduction; **~einnahme** *f (Mil)* recapture; **w~einnehmen** *vt sep irreg (Mil)* to recapture; **w~einsetzen** *sep* **1** *vt* to reinstate *(in +acc* in); **2** *vi (Regen)* to start up again; *(Med: Fieber, Schmerzen)* to recur; **~einsetzung** *f* reinstatement; **w~einstellen** *vt sep* to re-engage; **~einstellung** *f* re-engagement; **w~entdecken*** *vt sep (lit, fig)* to rediscover; **~entdeckung** *f* rediscovery; **w~ergreifen*** *vt sep irreg* to recapture; **~ergreifung** *f* recapture; **w~erkennen*** *vt sep irreg* to recognize; **er war nicht w~zuerkennen** he was unrecognizable; **w~eröffnen*** *vti sep* to reopen; **w~erscheinen*** *vi sep irreg aux sein* to reappear; *(Buch etc)* to be republished; **w~erstatten*** *vt sep Unkosten etc* to refund *(jdm etw* sb for sth); **~erstattung** *f* reimbursement; **w~finden** *sep irreg* **1** *vt* to find again; *(fig) Selbstachtung etc* to regain; **2** *vr (nach Schock)* to recover; **sich irgendwo w~finden** to find oneself somewhere.

Wiedergabe *f* **(a)** *(von Rede, Ereignis)* account, report; *(Wiederholung)* repetition. **(b)** *(Darbietung: von Stück, Konzert)* performance; *(Interpretation)* interpretation. **(c)** *(Reproduktion)* reproduction.

Wiedergabegerät *nt* playback unit.

wiedergeben *vt sep irreg* **(a)** *Gegenstand, Geld* to give back. **jdm ein Buch** ~ to give a book back to sb. **(b)** *(erzählen)* to give an account of; *(wiederholen)* to repeat. **(c)** *Gedicht* to recite; *Musikstück etc* to perform. **(d)** *(reproduzieren)* to reproduce.

Wieder-: ~**geburt** *f* rebirth; **w~gewinnen*** *vt sep irreg (lit, fig)* to regain; *Land, Rohstoffe etc* to reclaim; *Geld, Selbstvertrauen* to recover; **w~gutmachen** *vt sep* to make good; *Schaden* to compensate for; *(Pol)* to make reparations for; *(Jur)* to redress; ~**gutmachung** *f* compensation; *(Pol)* reparations *pl*; *(Jur)* redress; **w~haben** *vt sep irreg (col)* to have (got) back; **w~herstellen** *vt sep Gebäude, Frieden, jds Gesundheit* to restore; ~**herstellung** *f* restoration.

wiederholbar *adj* repeatable. **schwer** ~ hard to repeat.

wiederholen[1]* *insep* **1** *vti* to repeat; *(mehrmals) Forderung etc* to reiterate; *Lernstoff* to revise; *Spiel* to replay. **eine Klasse** ~ *(Sch)* to repeat a year. **2** *vr (Mensch)* to repeat oneself; *(Thema, Ereignis)* to recur.

wiederholen[2] *vt sep* to get back.

wiederholt *adj* repeated. **zum ~en Male** once again.

Wiederholung *f* repetition; *(von Aufführung)* repeat performance; *(von Sendung)* repeat; *(in Zeitlupe)* replay; *(von Lernstoff)* revision; *(von Spiel)* replay.

Wiederholungs-: ~**kurs** *m* refresher course; ~**spiel** *nt (Sport)* replay; ~**täter** *m (Jur)* second-time offender; *(mehrmalig)* persistent offender; ~**zeichen** *nt (Mus)* repeat (mark).

Wieder-: ~**hören** *nt* **(auf)** ~**hören!** goodbye!; **w~käuen** *vti sep* to ruminate; *(fig col)* to go over again and again; ~**käuer** *m* - ruminant.

Wiederkehr *f no pl (geh) (Rückkehr)* return; *(wiederholtes Vorkommen)* recurrence; *(von Ereignis)* anniversary.

wiederkehren *vi sep aux sein* to return; *(sich wiederholen)* to recur.

wiederkehrend *adj* recurrent.

Wieder-: **w~kennen** *vt sep irreg (col)* to recognize; **w~kommen** *vi sep irreg aux sein* to come back; **komm doch mal w~!** you must come again!; **w~sehen** *vt sep irreg* to see again; ~**sehen** *nt* (another) meeting; *(nach längerer Zeit)* reunion; **sie hofften auf ein baldiges ~sehen** they hoped to meet again soon; **(auf) ~sehen!** goodbye!; **w~tun** *vt sep irreg* to do again.

wiederum *adv* **(a)** *(andrerseits)* on the other hand; *(allerdings)* though. **(b)** *(seinerseits etc)* in turn. **er ~ wollte ...** he, for his part, wanted ...

Wieder-: **w~vereinigen*** *sep* **1** *vt Menschen* to reunite; *Land* to reunify; **2** *vr* to reunite; ~**vereinigung** *f* reunification; **w~verheiraten*** *vr sep* to remarry; ~**verheiratung** *f* remarriage; ~**verkauf** *m* resale; **w~verkaufen*** *vt sep* to resell; **w~verwendbar** *adj* reusable; **w~verwenden*** *vt sep* to reuse; ~**verwendung** *f* re-use; **w~verwerten*** *vt sep* to reutilize; ~**verwertung** *f* reutilization; ~**wahl** *f* re-election; **w~wählen** *vt sep* to re-elect.

Wiege *f* **-n** cradle. **es ist ihm auch nicht an der ~ gesungen worden, daß ...** no-one could have foreseen that ...

wiegen[1] **1** *vt* to rock; *Kopf* to shake (slowly); *Hüften* to sway. **2** *vr* **sich in trügerischen Hoffnungen** ~ to nurture false hopes.

wiegen[2] *pret* **wog,** *ptp* **gewogen** *vti* to weigh. **schwer** ~ *(fig)* to carry a lot of weight; *(Irrtum)* to be serious; *siehe* **gewogen.**

Wiegenlied *nt* lullaby.

wiehern *vi* to neigh. **(vor Lachen)** ~ to bray with laughter.

Wien *nt* Vienna.

Wiener *adj attr* Viennese. ~ **Würstchen** frankfurter, wiener (sausage) *(esp US)*; ~ **Schnitzel** Wiener schnitzel.

Wiener(in *f*) *m* - Viennese.

wies *pret of* **weisen.**

Wiese *f* **-n** meadow; *(col: Rasen)* lawn. **auf der grünen** ~ *(fig)* in the open countryside.

Wiesel *nt* - weasel. **schnell** *or* **flink wie ein** ~ quick as a flash.

Wiesenblume *f* meadow flower.

wieso *interrog adv* why. ~ **gehst du nicht?** how come you're not going? *(col)*; ~ **weißt du das?** how do you know that?

wieviel *interrog adv* how much; *(bei Mehrzahl)* how many.

wievielmal *interrog adv* how many times.

wievielte(r, s) *interrog adj* **das ~ Kind ist das jetzt?** how many children is that now?; **den ~n Platz hat er im Wettkampf belegt?** where did he come in the competition?; **das ~ Mal bist du schon in England?** how often have you been to England?; **ich habe morgen Geburtstag! — der ~ ist es denn?** it's my birthday tomorrow! — how old will you be?; **den W~n haben wir heute?** what's the date today?

wieweit *conj* to what extent.

Wikinger *m* - Viking.

wild *adj* wild; *Stamm* savage; *(ausgelassen)* boisterous; *(heftig) Kampf, (zornig) Blick* fierce; *(ungesetzlich) Parken etc* illegal; *Streik* wildcat *attr*, unofficial. **den ~en Mann spielen** *(col)* to come the heavy *(col)*; **der W~e Westen** the Wild West; **in ~er Ehe leben** *(dated, hum)* to live in sin; ~ **durcheinanderliegen** to be strewn all over the place; **dann ging alles ~ durcheinander** there was chaos then; **wie ~ rennen** to run like mad; ~ **drauflosreden** to talk nineteen to the dozen; **seid nicht so ~!** calm down a bit!; **einen Hund ~ machen** to drive a dog wild; ~ **werden** to go wild *(auch col)*; **ich könnte ~ werden** *(col)* I could scream *(col)*; ~ **entschlossen** *(col)* dead set *(col)*.

Wild *nt no pl* game; *(Rot~)* deer; *(Fleisch von Rot~)* venison.

Wild-: ~**bach** *m* torrent; ~**bahn** *f* **in freier ~bahn** in the wild; ~**bestand** *m* game population; ~**braten** *m* roast venison; ~**bret** *nt no pl* game; *(von Rotwild)* venison; ~**dieb** *m* poacher; ~**diebstahl** *m* poaching; ~**ente** *f* wild duck.

Wilde(r) *mf decl as adj* savage; *(fig)* maniac.

Wilderer *m* - poacher.

wildern *vi (Mensch)* to poach; *(Hund etc)* to kill game.

Wild-: ~**esel** *m* wild ass; ~**fang** *m* little rascal; **w~fremd** *adj (col)* **w~fremde Leute** complete strangers; ~**gans** *f* wild goose; ~**hüter** *m* gamekeeper; ~**katze** *f* wildcat; **w~lebend** *adj attr* living in the wild; ~**leder** *nt* suede.

Wildnis *f (lit, fig)* wilderness. **in der ~ leben** to live in the wild.

Wild-: ~**park** *m* game park; *(für Rotwild)* deer park; ~**reservat** *nt* game reserve; ~**schaden** *m* damage caused by game; ~**schutzgebiet** *nt* game preserve; ~**schwein** *nt* wild boar; **w~wachsend** *adj attr* wild(-growing); ~**wasser** *nt* white water; ~**wechsel** *m* **„~wechsel"** "wild animals"; ~**west** *no art* the wild west; ~**westfilm** *m* western; ~**westroman** *m* western; ~**wuchs** *m (geh)* rank growth; *(fig)* proliferation.

Wille *m* **-ns,** *no pl* will; *(Absicht)* intention. **nach jds ~n** as sb wanted/wants; **wenn es nach ihrem ~n ginge** if she had her way; **das geschah gegen meinen ~n** that was done against my will; **jds ~n tun** to do sb's will; **seinen ~n durchsetzen** to get one's (own) way; **jdm seinen ~n lassen** to let sb have his own way; **seinen eigenen ~n haben** to be self-willed; **beim besten ~n nicht** not with the best will in the world; **es war kein böser ~** there was no ill-will intended; **der gute ~** good will.

willen *prep siehe* **um 2.**

willenlos *adj* weak-willed. **völlig ~ sein** to have no will of one's own; **jds ~es Werkzeug sein** to be the mere tool of sb.

willens *adj (geh)* **~ sein** to be willing.

Willens-: **~äußerung** *f* expression of will; **~freiheit** *f* freedom of will; **~kraft** *f* willpower; **w~schwach** *adj* weak-willed; **~schwäche** *f* weakness of will; **w~stark** *adj* strong-willed; **~stärke** *f* willpower.

willentlich *adj* wilful *(Brit)*, willful *(US)*, deliberate.

willig *adj* willing.

willkommen *adj* welcome. **du bist (mir) immer ~** you are always welcome; **jdn ~ heißen** to welcome sb; **herzlich ~** welcome *(in +dat* to*)*; **es ist mir ganz ~, daß ...** I quite welcome the fact that ...

Willkommen *nt* - welcome.

Willkommensgruß *m* greeting, welcome.

Willkür *f no pl* capriciousness; *(politisch)* despotism; *(bei Handlungen)* arbitrariness. **das ist reinste ~** that is purely arbitrary.

Willkür-: **~akt** *m* despotic act; **~herrschaft** *f* tyranny.

willkürlich *adj* arbitrary; *Herrscher* autocratic.

wimmeln *vi auch vi impers* **der See wimmelt von Fischen** the lake is teeming with fish; **hier wimmelt es von Mücken/Menschen** this place is swarming with midges/people.

wimmern *vi* to whimper.

Wimpel *m* - pennant.

Wimper *f* **-n** (eye)lash. **ohne mit der ~ zu zucken** *(fig)* without batting an eyelid.

Wimperntusche *f* mascara.

Wind *m* **-e (a)** wind. **bei ~ und Wetter** in all weathers; **der ~ dreht sich** the wind is changing direction; **merken, woher der ~ weht** *(fig)* to see the way the wind is blowing; **daher weht der ~!** *(fig)* so that's the way the wind is blowing; **seither weht ein anderer/frischer ~** *(fig)* things have changed since then; **viel ~ um etw machen** *(col)* to make a lot of fuss about sth; **den Mantel** *or* **das Fähnchen nach dem ~ hängen** to trim one's sails to the wind; **jdm den ~ aus den Segeln nehmen** *(fig)* to take the wind out of sb's sails; **sich** *(dat)* **den ~ um die Ohren wehen lassen** to see a bit of the world; **etw in den ~ schlagen** to turn a deaf ear to sth; **in alle (vier) ~e** to the four winds; **von etw ~ bekommen** *(fig col)* to get wind of sth. **(b)** *(Med: Blähung)* wind.

Wind-: **~beutel** *m* **(a)** cream puff; **(b)** *(col: Mensch)* rake; **~bö(e)** *f* gust of wind.

Winde[1] *f* **-n** *(Tech)* winch, windlass.

Winde[2] *f* **-n** *(Bot)* bindweed, convulvulus.

Windel *f* **-n** nappy *(Brit)*, diaper *(US)*.

windelweich *adj* **jdn ~ schlagen** *(col)* to beat the living daylights out of sb *(col)*.

winden *pret* **wand,** *ptp* **gewunden 1** *vt* to wind; *Kranz* to bind. **2** *vr (Bach, Schlange, Pflanze)* to wind; *(Mensch) (durch Menge etc)* to wind (one's way); *(vor Schmerzen)* to writhe *(vor* with, in*)*; *(fig: ausweichen)* to try to wriggle out.

Windes|eile *f* **etw in ~ tun** to do sth in no time (at all); **sich in** *or* **mit ~ verbreiten** to spread like wildfire.

Wind-: **w~geschützt 1** *adj* sheltered (from the wind); **2** *adv* in a sheltered place; **~geschwindigkeit** *f* wind speed; **~hauch** *m* breath of wind; **~hose** *f* vortex; **~hund** *m* **(a)** *(Hund)* greyhound; **(b)** *(fig pej)* rake.

windig *adj* windy; *(fig) Sache* dodgy *(col)*.

Wind-: **~jacke** *f* windcheater *(Brit)*, windbreaker ® *(US)*; **~jammer** *m* - *(Naut)* windjammer; **~mühle** *f* windmill; **gegen ~mühlen (an)kämpfen** *(fig)* to tilt at windmills; **~mühlenflügel** *m* windmill sail; **~pocken** *pl* chickenpox *sing;* **~richtung** *f* wind direction; **~rose** *f (Naut)* compass card; *(Met)* wind rose; **~schatten** *m* lee; *(von Autos)* slipstream; **w~schief** *adj* crooked; **~schirm** *m* windbreak; **~schutzscheibe** *f* windscreen *(Brit)*, windshield *(US)*; **~seite** *f* windward side; **~skala** *f* wind scale; **~stärke** *f (Met)* wind-force; **w~still** *adj* windless; *Ecke etc* sheltered; **wenn es völlig w~still ist** when there is no wind at all; **~stille** *f* calm; **~stoß** *m* gust of wind.

Windung *f (von Weg, Fluß etc)* meander; *(von Schlange, Spule)* coil; *(von Schraube)* thread.

Wink *m* **-e** *(Zeichen)* sign; *(mit der Hand)* wave *(mit* of*)*; *(mit dem Kopf)* nod *(mit* of*)*; *(Hinweis, Tip)* hint, tip.

Winkel *m* **- (a)** angle. **(b)** *(fig: Ecke)* corner; *(Plätzchen)* place, spot. **jdn/etw in allen (Ecken und) ~n suchen** to look high and low for sb/sth.

Winkel-: **~advokat** *m (pej)* incompetent lawyer; **~eisen** *nt* angle iron.

wink(e)lig *adj Haus, Altstadt* full of nooks and crannies; *Gasse* twisty, windy.

Winkelmesser *m* - protractor.

winken *ptp* **gewinkt** *or (col)* **gewunken 1** *vi* to wave *(jdm* to *sb)*. **sie winkte mit einem Fähnchen** she waved a flag; **einem Taxi ~** to hail a taxi; **dem Sieger winkt eine Reise nach Italien** the winner will receive (the attractive prize of) a trip to Italy. **2** *vt* to wave; *Abseits* to signal; *Taxi* to hail; *Kellner* to call. **jdn zu sich ~** to beckon sb over to one.

winseln *vti* to whimper; *(pej)* to grovel.

Winter *m* - winter. **es ist/wird ~** winter is here/is coming; **im/über den ~** in (the)/over the winter; **über den ~ kommen** to get through the winter.

Winter- *in cpds* winter; **~anfang** *m* beginning of winter; **~einbruch** *m* onset of winter; **w~fest** *adj* winterproof; *(Bot)* hardy; **~garten** *m* winter garden; **~getreide** *nt* winter crop; **~halbjahr** *nt* winter; **~kleid** *nt* winter dress; *(Zool)* winter coat; **~kleidung** *f* winter clothing; **w~lich** *adj* wintry; *Kleidung* winter *attr*; **w~lich gekleidet** dressed for winter; **~obst** *nt* winter fruit; **~pause** *f* winter break; **~quartier** *nt* winter quarters *pl*; **~reifen** *m* winter tyre *(Brit) or* tire *(US)*; **~saat** *f* winter seed; **~sachen** *pl* winter clothes *pl*; **~schlaf** *m* hibernation; **~schlaf halten** to hibernate; **~schlußverkauf** *m* winter sale; **~semester** *nt* winter semester; **~spiele** *pl* **(Olympische) ~spiele** Winter Olympics *pl*; **~sport** *m* winter sports *pl*; *(Sportart)* winter sport; **~zeit** *f* winter time; *(Jahreszeit)* winter.

Winzer(in *f***)** *m* - wine-grower; *(Weinleser)* grape-picker.

winzig *adj* tiny. **~ klein** minute, tiny little *attr.*

Wipfel *m* - treetop.

Wippe *f* **-n** seesaw.

wippen *vi (auf und ab)* to bob up and down; *(hin und her)* to teeter. **~der Gang** bouncing gait.

wir *pers pron* we. **~ alle/beide/drei** all/both/the three of us; **~ Armen** we poor people; **wer ist da? — ~ (sind's)** who's there? — (it's) us; **trinken ~ erst mal einen** let's have a drink first.

Wirbel *m* **- (a)** *(lit, fig)* whirl; *(in Fluß etc)* whirlpool, eddy; *(der Ereignisse)* turmoil. **einen ~ um jdn/etw machen** to make a fuss about sb/sth. **(b)** *(Haar~)* crown. **(c)** *(Anat)* vertebra. **(d)** *(Trommel~)* (drum) roll.

wirbellos *adj (Zool)* invertebrate. **die W~en** the invertebrates.

wirbeln 1 *vi* **(a)** *aux sein* to whirl. **(b) mir wirbelt der Kopf** *(col)* my head is reeling. **(c)** *(Trommeln etc)* to roll. **2** *vt* to whirl.

Wirbel-: **~säule** *f (Anat)* spinal column; **~sturm** *m* whirlwind; **~tier** *nt* vertebrate; **~wind** *m* whirlwind.

wirken[1] **1** *vi* **(a)** *(Wirkung haben)* to have an effect. **die Arznei hat nicht gewirkt** the medicine did not work; **schalldämpfend ~** to have a sound-proofing effect; **das Bild wirkt hier nicht richtig** the picture doesn't fit in here; **etw auf sich** *(acc)*

~ **lassen** to take sth in. **(b)** *(erscheinen)* to seem, to appear. **nervös (auf jdn)** ~ to give (sb) the impression of being nervous; **sie wirkt abstoßend auf mich** I find her repulsive. **(c)** *(geh: tätig sein) (Mensch)* to work; *(Einflüsse, Kräfte etc)* to be at work. **2** *vt (geh: tun) Gutes* to do; *Wunder* to work.

wirken[2] *vt Teppiche, Stoffe* to weave.

wirklich *adj* real. **im ~en Leben** in real life. **2** *adv* really. **~?** really?

Wirklichkeit *f* reality. ~ **werden** to come true; **in** ~ in reality.

wirklichkeits-: **~fremd** *adj* unrealistic; **~getreu** *adj* realistic; **etw ~getreu abbilden** to paint a realistic picture of sth.

wirksam *adj* effective. **mit (dem)/am 1. Januar ~ werden** *(form: Gesetz)* to take effect on *or* from January 1st.

Wirksamkeit *f* effectiveness.

Wirkstoff *m (esp Physiol)* active substance.

Wirkung *f* effect *(bei* on*)*; *(von Tabletten etc)* effects *pl*. **seine ~ tun** to have an effect; *(Droge)* to take effect; **ohne ~ bleiben** to have no effect; **seine ~ verfehlen** not to have the desired effect; **mit ~ vom 1. Januar** *(form)* with effect from January 1st.

Wirkungs-: **~bereich** *m* field (of activity/interest *etc*); *(Domäne)* domain; **w~los** *adj* ineffective; **~losigkeit** *f* ineffectiveness; **w~voll** *adj* effective; **~weise** *f (von Medikament)* action; **die ~weise eines Kondensators** the way a condenser works.

Wirkwaren *pl* knitwear *sing*.

wirr *adj* confused; *Blick* crazed; *(unordentlich) Haare* tangled; *Gedanken* weird. **er ist ~ im Kopf** he is confused in his mind; **mach mich nicht ~** don't confuse me; **alles lag ~ durcheinander** everything was in chaos.

Wirren *pl* confusion *sing*, turmoil *sing*.

Wirrkopf *m (pej)* muddle-head.

Wirrwarr *m no pl* confusion; *(von Stimmen)* hubbub; *(von Fäden, Haaren etc)* tangle.

Wirsing *m no pl* savoy cabbage.

Wirt *m* **-e** *(Gastwirt, Vermieter)* landlord.

Wirtin *f* landlady; *(Gastgeberin)* hostess.

Wirtschaft *f* **(a)** *(Volks~)* economy; *(Geschäftsleben)* industry and commerce; *(Finanzwelt)* business world. **freie ~** free market economy. **(b)** *(Gast~)* ≃ pub *(Brit)*, saloon *(US)*. **(c)** *(col: Zustände)* **eine schöne/saubere ~** *(iro)* a fine state of affairs.

wirtschaften 1 *vi* **(a)** *(sparsam sein)* to economize. **gut ~ können** to be economical. **(b)** *(col: sich betätigen)* to busy oneself. **2** *vt* **jdn/etw zugrunde ~** to ruin sb/sth financially.

Wirtschafter(in *f***)** *m* **- (a)** *(Verwalter)* manager. **(b)** *(im Haushalt, Heim etc)* housekeeper.

wirtschaftlich *adj* economic; *(sparsam)* economical.

Wirtschaftlichkeit *f* economy.

Wirtschafts- *in cpds* economic; **~berater** *m* economic advisor; **~form** *f* economic system; **~gebäude** *nt* working quarters *pl*; **~geld** *nt* housekeeping (money); **~gemeinschaft** *f* economic community; **~güter** *pl* economic goods *pl*; **~hilfe** *f* economic aid; **~krieg** *m* economic war/warfare; **~kriminalität** *f* white-collar crime; **~krise** *f* economic crisis; **~lage** *f* economic situation; **~minister** *m* minister of economic affairs; **~ministerium** *nt* ministry of economic affairs; **~ordnung** *f* economic order; **~politik** *f* economic policy; **~prüfer** *m* accountant; *(zum Überprüfen der Bücher)* auditor; **~recht** *nt* commercial *or* business law; **~spionage** *f* industrial espionage; **~system** *nt* economic system; **~verband** *m* business association; **~wissenschaft** *f* economics *sing*; **~wissenschaftler** *m* economist; **~wunder** *nt* economic miracle; **~zeitung** *f* financial paper; **~zweig** *m* branch of industry.

Wirts-: **~haus** *nt* ≃ pub *(Brit)*, saloon *(US)*; *(esp auf dem Land)* inn; **~leute** *pl* landlord and landlady; **~stube** *f* lounge.

Wisch *m* **-e** *(pej col)* piece of paper; *(mit Gedrucktem)* piece of bumph *(Brit col)*.

wischen 1 *vti* to wipe. **Staub ~** to dust; **mit einem Tuch über eine Schallplatte ~** to wipe a record with a cloth; **sie wischte sich** *(dat)* **den Schweiß von der Stirn** she wiped the sweat from her brow; **Bedenken (einfach) vom Tisch ~** *(fig)* to brush aside misgivings; **jdm eine ~** *(col)* to clout sb one *(col)*; **eine gewischt bekommen** *(col: elektrischen Schlag)* to get a shock. **2** *vi aux sein (sich schnell bewegen)* to whisk.

Wischer *m* **-** *(Aut)* wiper.

Wischerblatt *nt (Aut)* wiper blade.

Wischiwaschi *nt no pl (pej col)* drivel *(col)*.

Wischlappen *m* cloth; *(für Fußboden)* floorcloth.

Wisent *m* **-e** bison.

wispern *vti* to whisper.

Wißbegier(de) *f* thirst for knowledge.

wißbegierig *adj Kind* eager to learn.

wissen *pret* **wußte,** *ptp* **gewußt** *vti* **(a)** to know *(von* about*)*. **ich weiß (es)** I know; **er weiß von nichts** he doesn't know anything about it; **weißt du schon das Neuste?** have you heard the latest?; **als ob ich das wüßte!** how should I know?; **von jdm/etw nichts ~ wollen** not to be interested in sb/sth; **er weiß es nicht anders/besser** he doesn't know any different/better; **das mußt du (selbst) ~** it's your decision; **das hättest du ja ~ müssen!** you ought to have realized that; **man kann nie ~** you never know; **weiß Gott** *(col)* God knows *(col)*; **sie hält sich für wer weiß wie klug** *(col)* she doesn't half think she's clever *(col)*; **... oder was weiß ich** *(col)* ... or something; **er ist wieder wer weiß wo** *(col)* goodness knows where he's got to again *(col)*; **nicht, daß ich wüßte** not as far as I know; **gewußt wie/wo** *etc*! sheer brilliance!; **ich weiß sie in Sicherheit** I know that she is safe.

(b) *(sich erinnern)* to remember; *(sich vor Augen führen)* to realize. **ich weiß seine Adresse nicht mehr** I can't remember his address; **du mußt ~, daß ...** you must realize that ...

Wissen *nt no pl* knowledge. **meines ~s** to my knowledge; **etw gegen (sein) besseres ~ tun** to do sth against one's better judgement; **nach bestem ~ und Gewissen** to the best of one's knowledge and belief.

Wissenschaft *f* science.

Wissenschaftler(in *f***)** *m* **-** scientist; *(Geistes~)* academic.

wissenschaftlich *adj* scientific; *(geistes~)* academic. **W~er Assistent** assistant lecturer.

Wissens-: **~durst** *m (geh)* thirst for knowledge; **~gebiet** *nt* field (of knowledge); **~stoff** *m* material; **w~wert** *adj* worth knowing.

wissentlich 1 *adv* knowingly, deliberately. **2** *adj* deliberate.

wittern 1 *vi (Wild)* to sniff the air. **2** *vt* to scent.

Witterung *f* **(a)** *(Wetter)* weather. **bei günstiger ~** if the weather is good. **(b)** *(Hunt) (Geruch)* scent *(von* of*)*; *(Geruchssinn)* sense of smell.

Witterungs- *in cpds* weather; **~einflüsse** *pl* effects *pl* of the weather; **~umschlag** *m* change in the weather.

Witwe *f* **-n** widow. **~ werden** to be widowed.

Witwen-: **~geld** *nt* widow's allowance; **~rente** *f* widow's pension; **~stand** *m* widowhood.

Witwer *m* **-** widower.

Witz *m* **-e (a)** *(Äußerung)* joke *(über +acc* about*)*. **einen ~ machen** to make a joke; **mach keine ~e!** don't be funny; **das ist doch wohl ein ~** he/you *etc* must be joking; **die Prüfung war ein ~** *(col)* the exam was a joke. **(b)** *(Geist)* wit. **der ~ an der Sache ist, daß ...** the great thing about it is that ...

Witz-: ~**blatt** *nt* joke book; ~**bold** *m* **-e** joker; **du bist vielleicht ein** ~**bold!** *(iro)* you're a great one! *(iro).*

witzeln *vi* to joke *(über +acc* about*).*

Witzfigur *f (fig col)* figure of fun.

witzig *adj* funny.

witzlos *adj (col: unsinnig)* pointless, futile.

wo 1 *interrog, rel adv* where; *(irgendwo)* somewhere. **überall,** ~ wherever; ~ **immer ...** wherever ...; **ach** ~! *(col)* nonsense! **2** *conj* ~ **nicht/möglich** if not/possible; ~ **er doch wußte, daß ich nicht kommen konnte** when he knew I couldn't come.

wo-: ~**anders** *adv* somewhere else; ~**andersher** *adv* from somewhere else; ~**andershin** *adv* somewhere else.

wob *pret of* **weben.**

wobei *adv* **(a)** *interrog* ~ **ist das passiert?** how did that happen?; ~ **hast du ihn erwischt?** what did you catch him at *or* doing? **(b)** *rel* **... sagte er,** ~ **er mich scharf ansah ...,** he said with a penetrating look; **...,** ~ **er das Buch aufschlug ...** opening the book; ~ **mir gerade einfällt** which reminds me.

Woche *f* **-n** week. **zweimal in der** ~ twice a week; **in dieser** ~ this week.

Wochenbett *nt* **im** ~ **sterben** to die after childbirth; **während sie im** ~ **lag** during the period after the birth of her child.

Wochen|end- *in cpds* weekend.

Wochen|ende *nt* weekend. **schönes** ~! have a nice weekend; **verlängertes** ~ long weekend.

Wochen-: ~**karte** *f* weekly ticket; **w**~**lang** *adj, adv* for weeks; ~**lohn** *m* weekly wage; ~**markt** *m* weekly market; ~**schau** *f* newsreel; ~**tag** *m* weekday *(including Saturday);* **was ist heute für ein** ~**tag?** what day is it today?; **w**~**tags** *adv* on weekdays.

wöchentlich 1 *adj* weekly. **2** *adv* weekly; *(einmal pro Woche)* once a week. **sich** ~ **abwechseln** to take turns every week.

Wochen-: **w**~**weise** *adv* by the week; ~**zeitschrift** *f* weekly; ~**zeitung** *f* weekly (paper).

Wöchnerin *f woman who has recently given birth.*

Wodka *m* **-s** vodka.

wodurch *adv* **(a)** *interrog* how. **(b)** *rel* as a result of which.

wofür *adv* **(a)** *interrog* for what, what ... for. **(b)** *rel* for which, which ... for.

wog *pret of* **wiegen**[2].

Woge *f* **-n** wave; *(fig auch)* surge.

wogegen *adv* **(a)** *interrog* against what, what ... against. **(b)** *rel* against which, which ... against.

woher *adv* **(a)** *interrog* where ... from. ~ **weißt du das?** how do you (come to) know that?; ~ **kommt es eigentlich, daß ...** how is it that ...? **(b)** *rel* from which, where ... from.

wohin *adv* **(a)** *interrog* where. **(b)** *rel* where. ~ **man auch schaut** wherever you look.

wohingegen *conj* whereas, while.

wohinter *adv* **(a)** *interrog* what *or* where ... behind. **(b)** *rel* behind which.

wohl 1 *adv* **(a)** *(angenehm zumute)* happy; *(gesund)* well. **sich** ~/~**er fühlen** to feel happy/happier; *(gesundheitlich)* to feel well/better; **bei dem Gedanken ist mir nicht** ~ I'm not very happy at the thought; ~ **oder übel** whether one likes it or not; ~ **dem, der ...** happy the man who ... **(b)** *(wahrscheinlich)* probably; *(iro: bestimmt)* surely. **er ist** ~ **schon zu Hause** he's probably at home by now; **das ist doch** ~ **nicht dein Ernst!** surely you're not serious! **(c)** *(vielleicht)* perhaps; *(etwa)* about. **das mag** ~ **sein** that may well be; **ob das** ~ **stimmt?** I wonder if that's true; **willst du das** ~ **lassen!** I wish you'd stop (doing) that. **(d)** *(durchaus)* well. **ich denke, ich verstehe dich sehr** ~! I think I understand you very well.
2 *conj (zwar)* **er hat es** ~ **versprochen, aber ...** he may have promised, but ....

Wohl *nt no pl* welfare, well-being. **das öffentliche** ~ the public good; **zu eurem** ~ for your benefit *or* good; **zum** ~! cheers!; **auf dein** ~! your health!; **auf jds** ~ **trinken** to drink sb's health.

Wohl-: **w**~**auf** *adj pred* in good health; ~**befinden** *nt* well-being; **w**~**begründet** *adj* well-founded; *Maßnahme, Strafe* well-justified; ~**behagen** *nt* feeling of well-being; **w**~**behalten** *adj Mensch* safe and sound; *Gegenstand* intact; **w**~**bekannt** *adj* well-known; **w**~**beleibt** *adj (hum)* stout, portly; **w**~**durchdacht** *adj* well thought out; ~**ergehen** *nt no pl* welfare; **w**~**erzogen** *adj (geh)* well-mannered.

Wohlfahrt *f no pl* welfare.

Wohlfahrts-: ~**einrichtung** *f* social service; ~**marke** *f* charity stamp; ~**organisation** *f* charity; ~**pflege** *f* welfare work; **freie** ~**pflege** voluntary welfare work; ~**staat** *m* welfare state.

Wohl-: ~**gefallen** *nt no pl* pleasure; **sich in** ~**gefallen auflösen** *(hum) (Gegenstände, Probleme)* to vanish into thin air; *(zerfallen)* to fall apart; **w**~**gefällig** *adj (gefallend)* pleasing; **w**~**geformt** *adj* well-shaped; *Körperteil* shapely; *Satz* well-formed; ~**gefühl** *nt* sense of well-being; **w**~**gemeint** *adj* well-intentioned; **w**~**gemerkt** *adv* mark you; **w**~**genährt** *adj* well-fed; **w**~**geraten** *adj (geh) Kind* fine; *Werk* successful; ~**geruch** *m (geh)* pleasant smell ~**geschmack** *m (geh)* pleasant taste; **w**~**gesinnt** *adj (geh)* well-disposed *(dat* towards*)*; **w**~**habend** *adj* well-to-do.

wohlig *adj* pleasant; *(gemütlich)* cosy *(Brit),* cozy *(US).* ~ **warm** nice and warm.

Wohl-: ~**klang** *m (geh)* melodious sound; **w**~**klingend** *adj* melodious; ~**leben** *nt (geh)* life of luxury; **w**~**meinend** *adj* well-meaning; **w**~**riechend** *adj* fragrant.

Wohlstand *m no pl* affluence, prosperity.

Wohlstandsgesellschaft *f* affluent society.

Wohltat *f* **(a)** *(Genuß)* relief. **(b)** *(Gefallen)* favour *(Brit),* favor *(US)*; *(gute Tat)* good deed. **jdm eine** ~ **erweisen** to do sb a favour.

Wohltäter(in *f***)** *m* benefactor; benefactress.

wohltätig *adj* charitable. **für** ~**e Zwecke** for charity.

Wohltätigkeits-: ~**basar** *m* charity bazaar; ~**verein** *m* charity.

Wohl-: **w**~**tuend** *adj* pleasant; **w**~**tun** *vi sep irreg (angenehm sein)* to do good *(jdm* sb*)*; **das tut w**~ that's good; **w**~**überlegt** *adj* **etw w**~**überlegt machen** to do sth after careful consideration; **w**~**verdient** *adj* well-deserved; ~**verhalten** *nt* good conduct; ~**wollen** *nt no pl* goodwill; **w**~**wollend** *adj* benevolent.

Wohn-: ~**anhänger** *m* caravan *(Brit),* trailer *(US)*; ~**bau** *m, pl* **-ten** residential building; ~**block** *m, pl* **-s** block of flats *(Brit),* apartment house *(US).*

wohnen *vi* to live; *(vorübergehend)* to stay. **er wohnt (in der) Friedrichstraße 11** he lives at (number) 11 Friedrichstraße; **wir** ~ **da sehr schön** it's very nice where we live.

Wohn-: ~**fläche** *f* living space; ~**gebiet** *nt* residential area; ~**geld** *nt* a rent allowance; ~**gemeinschaft** *f (Menschen)* people sharing a/the flat *(Brit) or* apartment/house; **in einer** ~**gemeinschaft leben** to share a flat *etc*; ~**haus** *nt* residential building; ~**heim** *nt (esp für Arbeiter)* hostel; *(für Studenten)* hall (of residence), dormitory *(US)*; *(für Senioren)* home; ~**komfort** *m* **mit sämtlichem** ~**komfort** with all mod cons; ~**komplex** *m* housing estate; ~**küche** *f* kitchen-cum-livingroom; ~**kultur** *f* style of home décor; **w**~**lich** *adj* cosy *(Brit),* cozy *(US)*; **es sich** *(dat)* **w**~**lich machen** to make oneself comfortable; ~**mobil** *nt* motor caravan *(Brit) or* trailer *(US)*; ~**ort** *m* place of residence; ~**siedlung** *f* housing estate *(Brit),* development; ~**sitz**

m domicile; **ohne festen ~sitz** of no fixed abode; **~stadt** *f* residential town.

Wọhnung *f* flat *(Brit)*, apartment. **1.000 neue ~en** 1,000 new homes.

Wọhnungs-: ~amt *nt* housing office; **~bau** *m no pl* house building *no def art;* **~besetzer(in** *f***)** *m* - squatter; **~inhaber** *m* householder; *(Eigentümer auch)* owner-occupier; **w~los** *adj* homeless; **~makler** *m* estate agent *(Brit)*, realtor *(US)*; **~mangel** *m* housing shortage; **~markt** *m* housing market; **~not** *f* serious housing shortage; **~suche** *f* flat-hunting *(Brit)*; **auf ~suche sein** to be looking for a flat *(Brit) or* an apartment; **~tür** *f* door (to the flat *(Brit) or* apartment); **~wechsel** *m* change of address.

Wọhn-: ~viertel *nt* residential area; **~wagen** *m* caravan *(Brit)*, trailer *(US)*; **~zimmer** *nt* living-room.

wọ̈lben 1 *vt* to curve; *Dach* to vault. **2** *vr* to curve; *(Tapete)* to bulge out; *(Decke, Brücke)* to arch.

Wọ̈lbung *f* curvature; *(kuppelförmig)* dome; *(bogenförmig)* arch; *(von Körperteil)* curve.

Wọlf *m* **⸚e (a)** wolf. **ein ~ im Schafspelz** a wolf in sheep's clothing; **mit den ⸚en heulen** *(fig)* to run with the pack. **(b)** *(Tech)* shredder; *(Fleisch~)* mincer *(Brit)*, grinder *(US)*.

Wọlfram *nt no pl (Chem)* tungsten.

Wọlfs-: ~hund *m* Alsatian *(Brit)*, German shepherd; **irischer ~hund** Irish wolfhound; **~milch** *f (Bot)* spurge; **~rachen** *m (Med)* cleft palate; **~rudel** *nt* pack of wolves.

Wọlke *f* **-n** *(lit, fig)* cloud. **aus allen ~n fallen** *(fig)* to be flabbergasted *(col)*.

Wolken-: ~bank *f* cloudbank; **~bruch** *m* cloudburst; **w~bruchartig** *adj* torrential; **~decke** *f* cloud cover; **~kratzer** *m* skyscraper; **~kụckucksheim** *nt* cloud-cuckoo-land; **w~los** *adj* cloudless; **w~verhangen** *adj* overcast.

wọlkig *adj* cloudy.

Wọlldecke *f* (woollen *(Brit) or* woolen *US*) blanket.

Wọlle *f* **-n** wool. **sich mit jdm in die ~kriegen** *(fig col)* to start squabbling with sb.

wọllen[1] *adj attr* woollen *(Brit)*, woolen *(US)*.

wọllen[2] **1** *modal aux ptp* ~ to want to. **er will ein Haus kaufen** he wants to buy a house; **etw gerade tun** ~ to be going to do sth; **wolltest du gerade weggehen?** were you just leaving?; **es sieht aus, als wollte es regnen** it looks as if it's going to rain; **es will einfach nicht klappen** it just won't work; **keiner will es gewesen sein** nobody will admit to it; **er will ihn gesehen haben** he claims to have seen him; **und so jemand** *or* **etwas** *(col)* **will Lehrer sein!** and he calls himself a teacher; **ich wollte, ich wäre ...** I wish I were ...; **darauf ~ wir mal anstoßen!** let's drink to that; **das will alles gut überlegt sein** that needs a lot of thought.

2 *vti* to want. **kommt er nun? — nein, er will nicht** is he coming? — no, he doesn't want to; **ich will nach Hause** I want to go home; **oh, das hab ich nicht gewollt** oh, I didn't mean to do that; **ich will, daß du genau zuhörst** I want you to listen carefully; **ob du willst oder nicht** whether you like it or not; **er hat nichts zu ~** he has no say; **ich weiß nicht, was er will** *(verstehe ihn nicht)* I don't know what he's on about; *siehe* **gewollt**.

Wọll-: ~faser *f* wool fibre *(Brit) or* fiber *(US)*; **~garn** *nt* woollen *(Brit) or* woolen *(US)* yarn.

wọllig *adj* woolly.

Wọll-: ~jacke *f* cardigan; **~knäuel** *nt* ball of wool; **~sachen** *pl* woollens *pl (Brit)*, woolens *pl (US)*; **~stoff** *m* woollen *(Brit) or* woolen *(US)* material.

Wọllust *f no pl (geh) (Sinnlichkeit)* sensuality; *(Lüsternheit)* lust.

wọllüstig *adj (geh) (sinnlich)* sensual; *(lüstern)* lascivious.

Wọllwaren *pl* woollens *pl (Brit)*, woolens *pl (US)*.

womịt *adv* **(a)** *interrog* with what, what ... with. **~ kann ich dienen?** what can I do for you? **(b)** *rel* with which; *(auf ganzen Satz bezüglich)* by which. **das ist es, ~ ich nicht einverstanden bin** that's what I don't agree with; **~ ich nicht sagen will, daß ...** by which I don't mean that ...

womọ̈glich *adv* possibly.

wonạch *adv* **(a)** *interrog* after what, what ... after. **~ sollen wir uns richten?** what should we go by? **(b)** *rel* **das war es, ~ ich mich erkundigen wollte** that was what I wanted to ask about.

Wọnne *f* **-n** *(geh) (Glückseligkeit)* bliss *no pl*; *(Vergnügen)* joy, delight. **die ~n der Liebe** the joys of love; **es ist eine wahre ~** it's a sheer delight.

wọnnevoll *adj Gefühl* blissful; *Kind, Anblick* delightful. **~ lächeln** to smile with delight.

wọnnig *adj* delightful; *Gefühl* blissful.

worạn *adv* **(a)** *interrog* **~ liegt das?** what's the reason for it? **(b)** *rel* by which. **das, ~ ich mich gerne erinnere** what I like to recall; **~ ich merkte, daß ...** which made me realize that ...

worauf *adv* **(a)** *interrog (räumlich)* on what, what ... on. **~ wartest du?** what are you waiting for? **(b)** *rel (zeitlich)* whereupon. **~ er einen Wutanfall bekam** whereupon he flew into a rage; **~ du dich verlassen kannst** of that you can be sure.

woraus *adv* **(a)** *interrog* out of what, what ... out of. **(b)** *rel* out of which, which ... out of. **~ ich schließe, daß ...** from which I conclude that ...

wọrden *ptp of* **werden 2 (c)**.

worịn *adv siehe auch* **in (a)** *interrog* in what, what ... in. **~ war das eingewickelt?** what was it wrapped in? **(b)** *rel* in which, which ... in. **das ist etwas, ~ wir nicht übereinstimmen** that's something we don't agree on.

Wọrt *nt* **-e (a)** *pl usu* **⸚er** *(Vokabel)* word. **~ für ~** word for word.

(b) *(Äußerung)* word. **genug der ~e!** enough talk!; **~en Taten folgen lassen** to suit the action to the word(s); **mit einem ~** in a word; **mit anderen ~en** in other words; **hast du (da noch) ~e!** it leaves you speechless; **mir fehlen die ~e** words fail me; **kein ~ von etw sagen** not to say one word about sth; **ich verstehe kein ~!** I don't understand a word (of it); *(hören)* I can't hear a word (that's being said); **ein ~ mit jdm sprechen** to have a word with sb; **ein ernstes ~ mit jdm reden** to have a serious talk with sb; **davon hat man mir kein ~ gesagt** they didn't tell me anything about it; **man kann sein eigenes ~ nicht (mehr) verstehen** you can't hear yourself speak; **um nicht viel(e) ~e zu machen** to make it brief; **jdm das ~ im Mund (her)umdrehen** to twist sb's words; **die passenden ~e für etw finden** to find the right words for sth; **jdm aufs ~ glauben** to believe sb implicitly; **jdm aufs ~ gehorchen** to obey sb's every word; **dabei habe ich auch (noch) ein ~ mitzureden** I (still) have something to say about that too; **jdn beim ~ nehmen** to take sb at his word; **ich gebe Ihnen mein ~ darauf** I give you my word on it; **sein ~ halten** to keep one's word.

(c) *no pl* **das große ~ führen** *(col)* to shoot one's mouth off *(col)*; **das ~ an jdn richten** to address (oneself to) sb; **jdm ins ~ fallen** to interrupt sb; **zu ~ kommen** to get a chance to speak; **sich zu ~ melden** to ask to speak; **jdm das ~ erteilen** to allow sb to speak.

(d) *(Ausspruch)* saying; *(Zitat)* quotation; *(Rel)* Word. **ein ~ Goethes** a quotation from Goethe.

(e) *(Text)* words *pl*. **in ~en** in words; **in ~ und Bild** in words and pictures; **in ~ und Schrift** in speech and writing; **etw in ~e fassen** to put sth into words.

Wọrt-: ~art *f (Gram)* part of speech; **~bruch** *m* **das wäre ein ~bruch** that would be breaking your/my *etc* word; **w~brüchig** *adj* false; **w~brü-**

chig werden to break one's word.
Wörtchen *nt dim of* **Wort da habe ich wohl ein ~ mitzureden** *(col)* I think I have some say in that.
Wörter-: **~buch** *nt* dictionary; **~verzeichnis** *nt* vocabulary; *(von Spezialbegriffen)* glossary.
Wort-: **~führer** *m* spokesman; **~gebühr** *f (Telec)* rate per word; **~gefecht** *nt* battle of words; **w~getreu** *adj, adv* verbatim; **w~gewandt** *adj* eloquent; **w~karg** *adj* taciturn; **~klauberei** *f* quibbling; **~laut** *m* wording; **im ~laut** verbatim.
wörtlich *adj Bedeutung* literal; *Rede* direct. **etw ~ wiedergeben** to repeat sth word for word; **das hat er ~ gesagt** those were his very words.
Wort-: **w~los 1** *adj* silent; **2** *adv* without saying a word; **~meldung** *f* **wenn es keine weiteren ~meldungen gibt** if nobody else wishes to speak; **w~reich** *adj Rede, Erklärung etc* wordy; *Sprache* rich in vocabulary; **~schatz** *m* vocabulary; **~spiel** *nt* pun; **~stellung** *f (Gram)* word order; **~wahl** *f* choice of words; **~wechsel** *m* verbal exchange; **w~wörtlich 1** *adj* word-for-word; **2** *adv* quite literally.
worüber *adv* **(a)** *interrog* about what, what ... about; *(örtlich)* over what, what ... over. **(b)** *rel* about which, which ... about; *(örtlich)* over which, which ... over.
worum *adv* **(a)** *interrog* about what, what ... about. **~ handelt es sich?** what's it about? **(b)** *rel* about which, which ... about.
worunter *adv* **(a)** *interrog* under what, what ... under. **(b)** *rel* under which, which ... under.
wovon *adv* **(a)** *interrog* from what, what ... from. **(b)** *rel* from which, which ... from. **das ist ein Gebiet, ~ er viel versteht** that is a subject he knows a lot about.
wovor *adv* **(a)** *interrog (örtlich)* before what, what ... before. **~ fürchtest du dich?** what are you afraid of? **(b)** *rel* before which, which ... before.
wozu *adv* **(a)** *interrog* to what, what ... to; *(warum)* why. **~ soll das gut sein?** what's the point of that? **(b)** *rel* to which, which ... to. **das, ~ ich am meisten neige** what I'm most inclined to do.
Wrack *nt* **-s** wreck.
wringen *pret* **wrang,** *ptp* **gewrungen** *vti* to wring.
Wucher *m no pl* profiteering. **das ist der reinste ~!** that's daylight robbery! *(col)*.
Wucherer(in *f***)** *m* **-** profiteer.
Wuchergeschäft *nt* profiteering *no pl*.
wucherisch *adj* profiteering; *Zinsen etc* extortionate.
wuchern *vi* **(a)** *aux sein or haben (Pflanzen)* to grow rampant. **(b)** *(Kaufmann etc)* to profiteer.
wuchernd *adj Pflanzen* rampant.
Wucherpreis *m* exorbitant price.
Wucherung *f* rank growth; *(Med)* growth.
Wucherzins *m* exorbitant interest *no pl*.
wuchs [vu:ks] *pret of* **wachsen**[1].
Wuchs [vu:ks] *m no pl (Wachstum)* growth; *(von Mensch)* stature.
Wucht *f no pl* force. **mit voller ~** with full force; **er ist eine ~!** *(col)* he's smashing! *(col)*.
wuchten *vti* to heave.
wuchtig *adj* massive; *Schlag* powerful.
wühlen 1 *vi* **(a)** *(nach* for*)* to dig; *(Maulwurf etc)* to burrow; *(Schwein, Vogel)* to root. **in den Haaren ~** to run one's fingers through one's hair. **(b)** *(suchen)* to rummage *(nach etw* for sth*)*. **in den Schubladen ~** to rummage through the drawers. **(c)** *(Untergrundarbeit leisten)* to stir things up. **2** *vr* **sich durch etw ~** to burrow one's way through sth.
Wühlmaus *f* vole.
Wulst *m or f* **¨-e** bulge.
wulstig *adj* bulging; *Rand, Lippen* thick.
wund *adj* sore. **sich** *(dat)* **die Füße ~ laufen** *(lit)* to get sore feet from walking; *(fig)* to walk one's legs off; **ein ~er Punkt** a sore point.
Wundbrand *m* gangrene.
Wunde *f* **-n** *(lit, fig)* wound. **alte ~n wieder aufreißen** *(fig)* to open up old sores; **an eine alte ~ rühren** *(fig geh)* to touch on a sore point; **Salz in eine/jds ~ streuen** *(fig)* to turn the knife in the wound.
Wunder *nt* **-** miracle *(auch Rel)*, wonder. **~ wirken** to work miracles; **das grenzt an ein ~** it verges on the miraculous; **die ~ der Natur** the wonders of nature; **es ist ein/kein ~, daß ...** it's a wonder/small wonder that ...; **ist es ein ~, daß er dick ist?** is it any wonder that he's fat?
wunder *adv inv* **meine Eltern denken ~ was passiert ist** my parents think goodness knows what has happened; **er glaubt, ~ wer er ist** he thinks he's so fantastic.
wunderbar *adj* **(a)** wonderful. **(b)** *(übernatürlich)* miraculous.
wunderbarerweise *adv* miraculously.
Wunder-: **~droge** *f* wonder drug; **w~gläubig** *adj* **w~gläubig sein** to believe in miracles; **~heiler** *m* faith-healer; **~kerze** *f* sparkler; **~kind** *nt* child prodigy; **~land** *nt* wonderland; **w~lich** *adj* **(a)** *(merkwürdig)* strange, odd; **(b)** *(w~sam)* wondrous; **~mittel** *nt* miracle cure.
wundern 1 *vr* to be surprised *(über +acc* at*)*. **du wirst dich ~!** you'll be amazed!; **ich wundere mich über gar nichts mehr** nothing surprises me any more; **dann darfst du dich nicht ~, wenn ...** then don't be surprised if ... **2** *vt, vt impers* to surprise. **es wundert mich, daß er noch nicht hier ist** I'm surprised that he is not here yet; **das würde mich nicht ~** I shouldn't be surprised.
Wunder-: **w~schön** *adj* beautiful; **~täter** *m* miracle worker; **w~tätig** *adj* miraculous; *Leben, Heilige* miracle-working; **~tüte** *f* surprise packet; **w~voll** *adj* marvellous *(Brit)*, marvelous *(US)*; **~waffe** *f* wonder weapon; **~werk** *nt* miracle.
Wund-: **~fieber** *nt* traumatic fever; **~infektion** *f* wound infection; **w~liegen** *vr sep irreg* to get bedsores; **~pflaster** *nt* adhesive plaster; **~salbe** *f* ointment; **~starrkrampf** *m* tetanus.
Wunsch *m* **¨-e** **(a)** wish; *(sehnliches Verlangen)* desire; *(Bitte)* request. **ein Pferd war schon immer mein ~** I've always wanted a horse; **haben Sie (sonst) noch einen ~?** *(beim Einkauf etc)* is there anything else you'd like?; **alles geht nach ~** everything is going smoothly; **auf ~** on request; **auf jds (besonderen/ausdrücklichen) ~ hin** at sb's (special/express) request. **(b)** *usu pl (Glückwunsch)* wish.
Wunsch-: **~bild** *nt* ideal; **~denken** *nt* wishful thinking.
Wünschelrute *f* divining rod.
wünschen 1 *vt* **(a)** **sich** *(dat)* **etw ~** to want sth; *(den Wunsch äußern)* to ask for sth; **ich wünsche mir das** I would like that; **ich wünsche mir, daß du ...** I would like you to ...; **das habe ich mir von meinen Eltern zu Weihnachten gewünscht** I asked my parents to give me that for Christmas; **er wünscht sich** *(dat)* **diesen Mann als Lehrer** he wishes that this man was his teacher; **was wünschst du dir?** what would you like?; **du darfst dir etwas ~** you may make a wish; **sie haben alles, was man sich** *(dat)* **nur ~ kann** they have everything you could possibly wish for.
(b) **jdm etw ~** to wish sb sth; **jdm einen guten Morgen ~** to wish sb good morning; **wir ~ dir gute Besserung/eine gute Reise** we hope you get well soon/have a pleasant journey; **ich wünschte, ich hätte dich nie gesehen** I wish I'd never seen you.
(c) *(begehren, verlangen)* to want. **was ~ Sie?** *(in Geschäft)* what can I do for you?; *(in Restaurant)* what would you like?; **wen ~ Sie zu sprechen?** to whom would you like to speak?
2 *vi* to wish. **Sie ~?** what can I do for you?;

ganz wie Sie ~ (just) as you wish; **zu ~/viel zu ~ übrig lassen** to leave something/a great deal to be desired.
wünschenswert *adj* desirable.
Wunsch-: w~gemäß *adv* as requested; **~kind** *nt* planned child; **~konzert** *nt (Rad)* musical request programme *(Brit) or* program *(US)*; **w~los** *adj Mensch* content(ed); **w~los glücklich** perfectly happy; **~sendung** *f (Rad)* request programme *(Brit) or* program *(US)*; **~traum** *m* dream; **das ist doch bloß ein ~traum** that's just a pipe-dream; **~zettel** *m* list of things one would like.
wurde *pret of* **werden.**
Würde *f* **-n (a)** *no pl* dignity. **unter aller ~ sein** to be beneath contempt; **unter jds ~ sein** to be beneath sb *or* sb's dignity. **(b)** *(Auszeichnung)* honour *(Brit)*, honor *(US)*; *(Titel)* title; *(Amt)* rank.
würdelos *adj* undignified.
Würdenträger(in *f*) *m* - dignitary.
würdevoll *adj* = **würdig (a).**
würdig *adj* **(a)** dignified. **sich ~ verhalten** to behave with dignity. **(b)** *(wert)* worthy. **jds/einer Sache** *(gen)* **~/nicht ~ sein** to be worthy/unworthy of sb/sth.
würdigen *vt* **(a)** to appreciate; *(lobend erwähnen)* to acknowledge. **etw zu ~ wissen** to appreciate sth. **(b)** *(geh)* **jdn einer Sache** *(gen)* **~** to deem sb worthy of sth; **jdn keines Blickes ~** not to deign to look at sb.
Würdigung *f* **(a)** *siehe vt* appreciation; acknowledgement; *(Ehrung)* honour *(Brit)*, honor *(US)*. **(b)** *(Rede, Artikel)* appreciation.
Wurf *m* **⸚e (a)** throw; *(beim Kegeln etc)* bowl. **mit dem Film ist ihm ein großer ~ gelungen** this film is a big hit for him *(col)*. **(b)** *no pl (das Werfen)* throwing. **(c)** *(Zool)* litter.
Würfel *m* **- (a)** dice. **~ spielen** to play at dice; **die ~ sind gefallen** the die is cast. **(b)** *(Math)* cube; *(Zucker~)* lump.
Würfel-: ~becher *m* shaker; **w~förmig** *adj* cube-shaped.
würfeln *vti* to throw; *(Würfel spielen)* to play at dice. **um etw ~** to throw dice for sth.
Würfel-: ~spiel *nt (Partie)* game of dice; *(Spielart)* dice; **~zucker** *m* cube sugar.
Wurf-: ~geschoß *nt* projectile; **~messer** *nt* throwing knife; **~pfeil** *m* dart; **~ring** *m* quoit; **~sendung** *f* circular; **~speer** *m* javelin; **~waffe** *f* missile.
Würgegriff *m (lit, fig)* stranglehold.
würgen 1 *vt jdn* to throttle; *(fig: Angst)* to choke. **2** *vi* **(a)** to choke. **an etw** *(dat)* **~** to choke on sth, to gag. **(b)** *(beim Erbrechen)* to retch. **mit Hängen und W~** by the skin of one's teeth.
Wurm *m* **⸚er** worm; *(Made)* maggot; *(col: Kind)* (little) mite. **da steckt der ~ drin** *(fig col)* there's something wrong somewhere; *(verdächtig)* there's something fishy about it *(col)*.
wurmen *vt, vt impers (col)* to rankle with.
wurmig *adj Obst* maggoty.
Wurm-: ~mittel *nt* vermifuge; **w~stichig** *adj Holz* full of worm-holes; *(madig auch) Obst* maggoty.
Wurst *f* **⸚e** sausage; *(col: Kot)* turd *(col!)*. **jetzt geht es um die ~** *(fig col)* the moment of truth has come; **das ist mir ~** *(col)* I don't give a damn *(col)*.
Wurst-: ~aufschnitt *m* assortment of sliced sausage; **~brot** *nt* open sausage sandwich; *(zusammengeklappt)* sausage sandwich.
Würstchen *nt* **(a)** *dim of* **Wurst** small sausage. **heiße** *or* **warme ~** hot sausages. **(b)** *(pej: Mensch)* squirt *(col)*, nobody. **ein armes ~** *(fig)* a poor soul.
Würstchen-: ~bude *f*, **~stand** *m* sausage stand; hot-dog stand.
wursteln *vi (col)* to muddle along. **sich durchs Leben ~** to muddle through life.
Wurst-: ~finger *pl (pej col)* podgy fingers *pl*; **~salat** *m* sausage salad; **~waren** *pl* sausages *pl;* **~zipfel** *m* sausage end.
Würze *f* **-n** *(Gewürz)* seasoning, spice; *(Aroma)* aroma; *(fig: Reiz)* spice.
Wurzel *f* **-n (a)** *(lit, fig)* root. **etw mit der ~ ausrotten** *(fig)* to eradicate sth; **~n schlagen** *(lit)* to root; *(fig)* to put down roots. **(b)** *(Math)* root. **~n ziehen** to find the roots; **(die) ~ aus 4 ist 2** the square root of 4 is 2.
Wurzel-: ~gemüse *nt* root vegetables *pl*; **w~los** *adj (lit, fig)* rootless.
wurzeln *vi (lit, fig)* to be rooted.
Wurzel-: ~werk *nt no pl* root system; **~zeichen** *nt (Math)* radical sign.
würzen *vt (lit, fig)* to season.
würzig *adj Speise* tasty; *(scharf)* spicy; *Luft* tangy; *Wein, Bier* full-bodied.
wusch *pret of* **waschen.**
Wuschelhaar *nt (col)* mop of curly hair.
wusch(e)lig *adj (col) Tier* shaggy; *Haare* fuzzy.
Wuschelkopf *m (Mensch)* fuzzy-head *(col)*.
wußte *pret of* **wissen.**
Wust *m no pl (col) (Durcheinander)* jumble; *(Menge)* pile.
wüst *adj* **(a)** *(öde)* desert *attr*, desolate. **(b)** *(unordentlich)* wild. **~ aussehen** to look a real mess. **(c)** *(ausschweifend)* wild. **~ feiern** to have a wild party. **(d)** *(rüde) Beschimpfung* vile. **jdn ~ beschimpfen** to use vile language to sb.
Wüste *f* **-n** *(lit, fig)* desert; *(Ödland)* waste. **die ~ Gobi** the Gobi Desert; **jdn in die ~ schicken** *(fig)* to send sb packing *(col)*.
Wüsten-: ~fuchs *m* desert fox; **~könig** *m (poet)* king of the desert *(poet)*; **~schiff** *nt (poet)* ship of the desert *(poet)*.
Wüstling *m* lecher.
Wut *f no pl* **(a)** *(Zorn, Raserei)* rage. **(auf jdn/etw) eine ~ haben** to be furious (with sb/sth); **eine ~ im Bauch haben** *(col)* to be seething; **eine ~ haben** to be in a rage; **in ~ geraten** to fly into a rage; **jdn in ~ versetzen** to infuriate sb. **(b)** *(Verbissenheit)* frenzy. **mit einer wahren ~** like crazy *(col)*.
Wut-: ~anfall *m* fit of rage; *(esp von Kind)* tantrum; **~ausbruch** *m* outburst of fury.
wüten *vi (lit, fig) (toben)* to rage; *(zerstörerisch hausen)* to cause havoc.
wütend *adj* furious, enraged; *Menge* angry. **auf jdn/etw** *(acc)* **~ sein** to be mad at sb/sth.
wut|entbrannt *adj* furious, enraged. **~ hinauslaufen** to leave in a rage.
Wüterich *m* brute.
wutverzerrt *adj* distorted with rage.
Wwe. = **Witwe.**

X

X, x [ɪks] *nt* **-, -** X, x. **Herr X** Mr X; **jdm ein X für ein U vormachen** to put one over on sb *(col)*.
Xanthippe [ksan'tɪpə] *f* **-n** *(fig col)* shrew.
X-Beine ['ɪks-] *pl* knock-knees *pl*.
x-beinig ['ɪks-] *adj* knock-kneed.
x-beliebig [ɪks-] *adj* any old *(col)*. **wir können uns an einem ~en Ort treffen** we can meet anywhere you like *or* any old place you like *(col)*.
xerographieren* *vti insep* to Xerox.
xerokopieren* *vti insep* to Xerox.
x-fach ['ɪks-] *adj* **die ~e Menge** *(Math)* n times the amount.
x-mal ['ɪks-] *adv (col)* n (number of) times *(col)*.
x-te ['ɪkstə] *adj (Math, col)* nth. **zum ~n Male** for the nth *or* umpteenth time *(col)*.
Xylophon *nt* **-e** xylophone.

Y

Y, y ['ʏpsilɔn] *nt* **-, -** Y, y.
Yen [jɛn] *m* **-(s)** yen.
Yoga ['jo:ga] *m or nt no pl* yoga.
Yogi ['jo:gi] *m* **-s** yogi.
Ypsilon ['ʏpsilɔn] *nt* **-s** y.
Yucca ['jʊka] *f* **-s** yucca.

Z

Z, z [tsɛt] *nt* **-, -** Z, z.
Zack *m no pl (col)* **auf ~ sein** to be on the ball *(col)*.
zack *interj (col)* pow, zap *(col)*. **~ ~!** chop-chop! *(col)*; **bei uns muß alles ~, ~ gehen** we have to do everything chop-chop *(col)*.
Zacke *f* **-n** point; *(von Gabel)* prong; *(von Kamm)* tooth; *(Berg~)* jagged peak.
zackig *adj* **(a)** *(gezackt)* jagged. **(b)** *(col) Soldat* smart; *Tempo, Musik* brisk. **... aber ein bißchen ~!** ... and make it snappy *(col)*!
zaghaft *adj* timid.
Zaghaftigkeit *f* timidity.
zäh *adj* tough; *(dickflüssig)* glutinous; *Verkehr etc* slow-moving; *(ausdauernd)* dogged. **ein ~es Leben haben** to have a tenacious hold on life; *(fig: Idee etc)* to die hard.
zähflüssig *adj* viscous; *Verkehr* slow-moving.
Zähigkeit *f* toughness; *(Ausdauer)* doggedness.
Zahl *f* **-en** number; *(in Statistik, als Größe auch)* figure. **~en nennen** to give figures; **eine fünfstellige ~** a five-figure number; **in großer ~** in great numbers.
zahlbar *adj* payable *(an +acc* to*)*.
zählbar *adj* countable.
zählebig *adj* hardy; *Vorurteil* persistent.
zahlen *vti* to pay. **Herr Ober, (bitte) ~!** waiter, the bill *or* check *(US)* please; **dort zahlt man gut/schlecht** they pay well/badly; **wenn er nicht bald zahlt, dann ...** if he doesn't pay up soon, then ...; **laß mal, ich zahl's** no no, I'll pay; **ich zahle dir ein Bier** I'll buy you a beer.
zählen 1 *vi* **(a)** to count. **(b)** *(gehören)* **er zählt zu den besten Schriftstellern unserer Zeit** he ranks as one of the best authors of our time; **zählt Aids zu den unheilbaren Krankheiten?** is AIDS an incurable disease? **(c)** *(sich verlassen)* **auf jdn/etw ~** to count on sb/sth. **(d)** *(gelten)* to count. **2** *vt* to count. **seine Tage sind gezählt** his days are numbered; **der König zählt 5 Punkte** *(Cards)* the King counts as 5 points.
Zahlen-: ~angabe *f* figure; **ich kann keine genauen ~angaben machen** I can't quote any precise figures; **~folge** *f* order of numbers; **~gedächtnis** *nt* memory for numbers; **~material** *nt* figures *pl*; **~schloß** *nt* combination lock; **~verhältnis** *nt* (numerical) ratio.
Zähler *m* **- (a)** *(Math)* numerator. **(b)** *(Meßgerät)* meter.
Zählerstand *m* meter reading.
Zahl-: ~grenze *f* fare stage; **~karte** *f* transfer form; **z~los** *adj* countless, innumerable; **~meister** *m (Naut)* purser; **z~reich** *adj* numerous; **~stelle** *f* payments office; **~tag** *m* payday.
Zahlung *f* payment. **in ~ geben/nehmen** to give/take in part-exchange; **gegen eine ~ von $ 500 erhalten Sie ...** on payment of $500 you will receive ...
Zählung *f* count.
Zahlungs-: ~anweisung *f* transfer order; **~aufforderung** *f* request for payment; **~aufschub** *m* extension (of credit); **~bedingungen** *pl* terms (of payment) *pl*; **~befehl** *m* order to pay; **~bi-**

lanz *f* balance of payments; **~empfänger** *m* payee; **z~fähig** *adj* able to pay; *Firma* solvent; **~fähigkeit** *f* ability to pay; solvency; **~frist** *f* period allowed for payment; **z~kräftig** *adj* wealthy; **~mittel** *nt* means *sing* of payment; *(Münzen, Banknoten)* currency; **gesetzliches ~mittel** legal tender; **z~pflichtig** *adj* obliged to pay; **~schwierigkeiten** *pl* financial difficulties *pl*; **z~unfähig** *adj* unable to pay; *Firma* insolvent; **~unfähigkeit** *f* inability to pay; insolvency; **z~unwillig** *adj* unwilling to pay; **~verkehr** *m* payments *pl*; **~verpflichtung** *f* obligation to pay; **~verzug** *m* default; **~weise** *f* method of payment; **z~willig** *adj* willing to pay.

Zählwerk *nt* counter.

Zahlwort *nt* numeral.

zahm *adj* tame.

zähmen *vt* to tame; *(fig) Leidenschaft* to control.

Zahn *m* **¨-e** tooth; *(von Briefmarke)* perforation; *(Rad~)* cog. **künstliche ¨~e** false teeth *pl*; **¨~e bekommen** to cut one's teeth; **die ersten/zweiten ¨~e** one's milk teeth/second set of teeth; **die dritten ¨~e** *(hum)* false teeth; **diese Portion reicht** *or* **ist für den hohlen ~** *(col)* that's hardly enough to satisfy a mouse *(col)*; **der ~ der Zeit** the ravages *pl* of time; **die ¨~e zeigen** to bare one's teeth; *(fig col)* to show one's teeth; **jdm einen ~ ziehen** *(lit)* to pull a tooth out; *(fig)* to put an idea out of sb's head; **jdm auf den ~ fühlen** *(aushorchen)* to sound sb out; *(streng befragen)* to give sb a grilling; **einen ~ draufhaben** *(col: Geschwindigkeit)* to be going like the clappers *(col)*.

Zahn-: **~arzt** *m* dentist; **z~ärztlich** *adj* dental; **~belag** *m* plaque; **~bürste** *f* tooth brush; **~creme** *f* toothpaste.

zähne-: **~fletschend** *adj attr, adv* snarling; **~knirschend** *adj attr, adv (fig)* gnashing one's teeth.

zahnen *vi* to teethe.

Zahn-: **~ersatz** *m* dentures *pl*; **~fleisch** *nt* gum(s *pl*); **auf dem ~fleisch gehen** *(col)* to be all in *(col)*, to be on one's last legs *(col)*; **~fleischbluten** *nt* bleeding of the gums; **~füllung** *f* filling; **~heilkunde** *f* dentistry; **~höhle** *f* pulp cavity; **~klinik** *f* dental hospital; **~krone** *f* crown; **z~los** *adj* toothless; **~lücke** *f* gap between one's teeth; **~medizin** *f* dentistry; **~pasta** *f* toothpaste; **~pflege** *f* dental hygiene; **~rad** *nt* cogwheel; **~radbahn** *f* rack-railway *(Brit)*, rack-railroad *(US)*; **~radgetriebe** *nt* gear mechanism; **~schmelz** *m* (tooth) enamel; **~schmerz** *m usu pl* toothache *no pl*; **~spange** *f* brace; **~stein** *m* tartar; **~stocher** *m* - toothpick; **~techniker** *m* dental technician; **~weh** *nt* toothache; **~wurzel** *f* root (of a/the tooth).

Zange *f* **-n** *(Flach~, Rund~)* (pair of) pliers *pl*; *(Beiß~)* (pair of) pincers *pl*; *(Greif~, Zucker~)* (pair of) tongs *pl*; *(von Tier)* pincers *pl*. **jdn in die ~ nehmen** *(fig)* to put the screws on sb *(col)*.

Zank *m no pl* squabble. **~ und Streit** trouble and strife.

Zank|apfel *m (fig)* bone of contention.

zanken *vr* to squabble.

zänkisch *adj* quarrelsome; *Weib* nagging *attr*.

Zäpfchen *nt (Gaumen~)* uvula.

Zapfen *m* - *(Spund)* bung; *(Tannen~ etc)* cone; *(Holzverbindung)* tenon.

zapfen *vt* to tap, to draw.

Zapfenstreich *m (Mil)* tattoo.

Zapf-: **~hahn** *m* tap; **~säule** *f* petrol pump *(Brit)*, gas pump *(US)*.

zapp(e)lig *adj* wriggly; *(unruhig)* fidgety.

zappeln *vi* to wriggle; *(unruhig sein)* to fidget. **jdn ~ lassen** *(fig col)* to keep sb in suspense.

Zar *m (wk)* **-en, -en** Tzar, Czar.

Zarin *f* Tzarina, Czarina.

zart *adj Haut, Töne* soft; *Braten, Gemüse* tender; *Gebäck, Teint, Kind, Gefühle* delicate; *Berührung* gentle. **im ~en Alter von ...** at the tender age of ...; **~ besaitet sein** to be very sensitive.

Zart-: **z~besaitet** *adj attr* highly sensitive; **z~bitter** *adj Schokolade* plain; **z~fühlend** *adj* sensitive; **~gefühl** *nt* delicacy of feeling, sensitivity.

Zartheit *f siehe adj* softness; tenderness; delicacy; gentleness.

zärtlich *adj* tender, affectionate.

Zärtlichkeit *f* **(a)** *no pl* affection, tenderness. **(b)** *(Liebkosung)* caress. **~en** *(Worte)* loving words.

Zaster *m no pl (col)* lolly *(col)*.

Zäsur *f* caesura; *(fig)* break.

Zauber *m* - *(lit, fig)* magic. **fauler ~** *(col)* humbug *no indef art*.

Zauberei *f no pl* magic.

Zauberer *m*, **Zauberin** *f* - magician.

Zauber-: **z~haft** *adj* enchanting; **~künstler** *m* conjurer; **~kunststück** *nt* conjuring trick; **~mittel** *nt* magical cure; *(Trank)* magic potion.

zaubern **1** *vi* to do magic; *(Kunststücke vorführen)* to do conjuring tricks. **ich kann doch nicht ~!** *(col)* I'm not a magician! **2** *vt* **etw aus etw ~** to conjure sth out of sth.

Zauber-: **~spruch** *m* spell; **~stab** *m* wand; **~trank** *m* magic potion; **~trick** *m* conjuring trick; **~wort** *nt* magic word.

Zauderer *m* - vacillator.

zaudern *vi* to vacillate. **etw ohne zu ~ tun** to do sth without hesitating.

Zaum *m*, *pl* **Zäume** bridle. **jdn/etw im ~ halten** *(fig)* to keep a tight rein on sb/sth; **seine Ungeduld im ~e halten** *(fig)* to control one's impatience.

zäumen *vt* to bridle.

Zaun *m*, *pl* **Zäune** fence. **einen Streit vom ~ brechen** to pick a quarrel.

Zaun-: **~gast** *m* mere onlooker; **~könig** *m (Orn)* wren; **~pfahl** *m* (fencing) post; **jdm einen Wink mit dem ~pfahl geben** to drop sb a broad hint.

zausen *vt* to ruffle; *Haare* to tousle.

z.B. = **zum Beispiel** eg.

ZDF [tsɛtde:ǀɛf] = **Zweites Deutsches Fernsehen.**

Zebra *nt* **-s** zebra.

Zebrastreifen *m* zebra crossing *(Brit)*, crosswalk *(US)*.

Zeche *f* **-n** **(a)** *(Rechnung)* bill, check *(US)*. **die (ganze) ~ (be)zahlen** *(lit, fig)* to foot the bill. **(b)** *(Bergwerk)* (coal-)mine.

zechen *vi* to booze *(col)*, to drink.

Zecher(in *f*) *m* - boozer *(col)*, drinker.

Zech-: **~kumpan** *m* drinking-pal *(col)*; **~preller** *m* - *person who leaves a bar/restaurant without paying the bill*; **~prellerei** *f* skipping payment in restaurants *etc*; **~tour** *f (col)* pub-crawl *(esp Brit col)*, bar hop *(US col)*.

Zeder *f* **-n** cedar.

Zeh *m* **-en**, **Zehe** *f* **-n** toe; *(Knoblauch~)* clove. **jdm auf die ~en treten** *(lit, fig)* to tread on sb's toes.

Zehen-: **~nagel** *m* toenail; **~spitze** *f* tip of the toe; **auf (den) ~spitzen** on tiptoe; **auf (den) ~spitzen gehen** to tiptoe.

zehn *num* ten; *siehe* **vier**.

Zehn *f* **-en** ten; *siehe* **Vier**.

Zehner *m* - **(a)** *(Math)* ten. **(b)** *(col) (Groschen)* ten-pfennig piece; *(Schein)* tenner *(col)*.

Zehner-: **~packung** *f* packet of ten; **~system** *nt* decimal system.

Zehn-: **~fingersystem** *nt* touch-typing method; **~kampf** *m (Sport)* decathlon; **~markschein** *m* ten mark note *(Brit) or* bill *(US)*.

zehntausend *num* ten thousand. **Z~e von Menschen** tens of thousands of people.

Zehntel *nt* - tenth.

zehnte(r, s) *adj* tenth; *siehe* **vierte(r, s)**.

zehren *vi* **(a)** **von etw ~** *(lit)* to live off sth; *(fig)* to feed on sth. **(b)** **an jdm/etw ~** *an Menschen, Kraft etc* to wear sb/sth out; *an Gesundheit* to undermine sth.

Zeichen *nt* - sign; *(Sci, auf Landkarte)* symbol; *(Schrift~)* character; *(Hinweis, Signal)* signal; *(Erkennungs~)* identification; *(Vermerk)* mark. **es ist ein ~ unserer Zeit, daß ...** it is a sign of the times that ...; **als ~ von etw** as a sign of sth; **als ~ der Verehrung** as a token of respect; **jdm ein ~ geben** to give sb a signal; **unser/Ihr ~** *(form)* our/your reference; **unter dem ~ von etw stehen** *(fig: Konferenz etc)* to take place against a background of sth.

Zeichen-: **~block** *m* sketch pad; **~brett** *nt* drawing-board; **~erklärung** *f (auf Fahrplänen etc)* key (to the symbols); *(auf Landkarte)* legend; **~lehrer** *m* art teacher; **~papier** *nt* drawing paper; **~saal** *m* art-room; **~setzung** *f* punctuation; **~sprache** *f* sign language; **~stift** *m* drawing pencil; **~stunde** *f* art lesson; **~system** *nt* notation; **~tisch** *m* drawing table; **~trickfilm** *m* (animated) cartoon; **~unterricht** *m* art; *(Unterrichtsstunde)* art lesson.

zeichnen 1 *vt* **(a)** to draw; *(entwerfen) Plan* to draft. **(b)** *(kennzeichnen)* to mark. **2** *vi* to draw. **gezeichnet: XY** signed, XY.

Zeichner(in *f***)** *m* - draughtsman/-woman *(Brit)*, draftsman/-woman *(US)*; *(Art auch)* artist.

zeichnerisch 1 *adj Darstellung* graphic(al). **sein ~es Können** his drawing ability. **2** *adv* **~ begabt sein** to have a talent for drawing.

Zeichnung *f* **(a)** drawing. **(b)** *(Muster)* pattern; *(von Gefieder, Fell)* markings *pl*.

zeichnungsberechtigt *adj* authorized to sign.

Zeigefinger *m* index finger, forefinger.

zeigen 1 *vi* to point *(auf +acc* to*)*. **2** *vt* to show. **jdm etw ~** to show sb sth *or* sth to sb; **dem werd' ich's (aber) ~!** *(col)* I'll show him!; **zeig mal, was du kannst!** let's see what you can do! **3** *vr* to appear; *(Gefühle)* to show. **in dem Kleid kann ich mich doch nicht ~** I can't be seen in a dress like that; **er zeigte sich befriedigt** he was satisfied; **es zeigt sich, daß ...** it turns out that ...; **es wird sich ~, wer recht hat** we shall see who's right.

Zeiger *m* - pointer; *(Uhr~)* hand.

Zeigestock *m* pointer.

Zeile *f* **-n** line. **vielen Dank für Deine ~n** many thanks for your letter; **zwischen den ~n** between the lines.

Zeilen-: **~abstand** *m* line spacing; **~schalter** *m* line spacer.

Zeisig *m* **-e** *(Orn)* siskin.

Zeit *f* **-en (a)** time; *(Epoche)* age. **die gute alte ~** the good old days; **das waren noch ~en!** those were the days; **die ~ Goethes** the age of Goethe; **für alle ~en** for ever; **mit der ~ gehen** to move with the times; **die ~ wird knapp** time is running out, it's getting tight; **die ~ wurde mir lang** time hung heavy on my hands; **eine Stunde ~ haben** to have an hour (to spare); **haben Sie vielleicht einen Augenblick ~?** do you have a moment?; **sich** *(dat)* **für jdn/etw ~ nehmen** to devote time to sb/sth; **damit hat es noch ~** there's no hurry; **das hat ~ bis morgen** that can wait until tomorrow; **laß dir ~** take your time; **auf unbestimmte ~** for an indefinite period; **in letzter ~** recently; **die ganze ~ über** the whole time; **mit der ~** *(allmählich)* in time; **nach ~ bezahlt werden** to be paid by the hour; **auf ~ spielen** *(Sport)* to play for time; **es wird ~, daß wir gehen** it's about time we left; **Soldat auf ~** soldier serving for a set time; **seit dieser ~** since then; **zur ~ Königin Viktorias** in Queen Victoria's times; **zu der ~, als ...** (at the time) when ...; **von ~ zu ~** from time to time; **zur ~** at the moment. **(b)** *(Ling)* tense.

zeit *prep +gen* **~ meines Lebens** in my lifetime.

Zeit-: **~abschnitt** *m* period (of time); **~alter** *nt* age; **~angabe** *f* time; *(Datum)* date; **~ansage** *f (Rad)* time check; *(Telec)* speaking clock; **~arbeit** *f* temporary work/job; **~aufwand** *m* time *(needed for a task)*; **~bombe** *f* time bomb; **~druck** *m* pressure of time; **unter ~druck** under pressure; **~frage** *f* question of time; **~geist** *m* spirit of the times; **z~gemäß** *adj* up-to-date; **z~gemäß sein** to be in keeping with the times; **~genosse** *m* contemporary; **z~genössisch** *adj* contemporary.

zeitig *adj, adv* early.

zeitigen *vt (geh) Ergebnis* to bring about.

Zeit-: **~karte** *f* season ticket; **z~kritisch** *adj Aufsatz* full of comment on contemporary issues; **~lang** *f* **eine ~lang** a while, a time; **eine ~lang ist das ganz schön** for a while it's quite nice; **z~lebens** *adv* all one's life.

zeitlich 1 *adj* temporal; *Reihenfolge* chronological. **in kurzem ~em Abstand** at short intervals (of time); **das Z~e segnen** *(euph)* to depart this life. **2** *adv* timewise *(col)*. **das kann sie ~ nicht einrichten** she can't find (the) time for that; **das ist ~ ungünstig** that's bad timing; **~ unmöglich** not possible timewise; **ist das ~ begrenzt?** is there a time limit?

Zeit-: **z~los** *adj* timeless; **~lupe** *f* slow motion *no art;* **Wiederholung in ~lupe** slow-motion replay; **~lupentempo** *nt* **im ~lupentempo** *(fig)* at a snail's pace; **~mangel** *m* **aus ~mangel** for lack of time; **~not** *f* shortage of time; **in ~not sein** to be pressed for time; **~plan** *m* schedule; **~punkt** *m* time; **zu diesem ~punkt** at that time; **~raffer** *m no pl* time-lapse photography; **z~raubend** *adj* time-consuming; **~raum** *m* period of time; **in einem ~raum von ...** over a period of ...; **~rechnung** *f* calendar; **~schrift** *f* magazine; *(wissenschaftlich)* journal; **~spanne** *f* period of time; **z~sparend** *adj* timesaving; **~tafel** *f* chronological table.

Zeitung *f* (news)paper.

Zeitungs- *in cpds* newspaper; **~anzeige** *f* newspaper advertisement; *(Familienanzeige)* announcement in the paper; **~ausschnitt** *m* newspaper cutting; **~austräger** *m* paperboy/-girl; **~beilage** *f* newspaper supplement; **~händler** *m* newsagent *(Brit)*, news vendor *(US)*; **~junge** *m* paperboy; **~korrespondent** *m* newspaper correspondent; **~leser** *m* newspaper reader; **~papier** *nt* newsprint; *(als Altpapier)* newspaper; **~redakteur** *m* newspaper editor; **~ständer** *m* newspaper rack; **~verleger** *m* newspaper publisher.

Zeit-: **~unterschied** *m* time difference; **~verlust** *m* loss of time; **ohne ~verlust** without losing any time; **~verschwendung** *f* waste of time; **~vertreib** *m* way of passing the time; *(Hobby)* pastime; **z~weilig** *adj* temporary; **z~weise** *adv* at times; **~wort** *nt* verb; **~zeichen** *nt* time signal; **~zünder** *m* time fuse.

zelebrieren* *vt* to celebrate.

Zelle *f* **-n** cell *(auch Sci, Pol)*; *(Kabine)* cabin; *(Telefon~)* box *(Brit)*, booth.

Zell-: **~gewebe** *nt* cell tissue; **~kern** *m* nucleus (of a/the cell).

Zellophan *nt no pl* cellophane.

Zellstoff *m* cellulose.

Zelluloid [*auch* -'lɔyt] *nt no pl* celluloid.

Zellulose *f* **-n** cellulose.

Zelt *nt* **-e** tent; *(Zirkus~)* big top. **seine ~e aufschlagen/abbrechen** *(fig)* to settle down/to pack one's bags.

Zelt-: **~bahn** *f* strip of canvas; **~dach** *nt* tent-roof.

zelten *vi* to camp.

Zelt-: **~lager** *nt* camp; **~mast** *m* tent pole; **~pflock** *m* tent peg *(Brit) or* stake *(US)*; **~plane** *f* tarpaulin; **~platz** *m* camp site; **~stange** *f* tent pole.

Zement *m* **-e** cement.

zementieren* *vt* to cement; *(fig)* to reinforce.

Zementmaschine *f* cement mixer.

Zenit *m no pl (lit, fig)* zenith. **die Sonne steht im ~**

the sun is at its zenith.
zensieren* *vt* **(a)** *auch vi (benoten)* to mark. **(b)** *(Bücher etc)* to censor.
Zensor *m* censor.
Zensur *f* **(a)** *(no pl)* censorship *no indef art; (Prüfstelle)* censors *pl.* **einer ~ unterliegen** to be censored. **(b)** *(Note)* mark.
Zenti-: ~meter *m or nt* centimetre *(Brit)*, centimeter *(US)*; **~metermaß** *nt* (metric) tape measure.
Zentner *m* **-** (metric) hundredweight; *(Aus, Sw)* 100kg.
zentral *adj (lit, fig)* central.
Zentral- *in cpds* central; **~bank** *f* central bank.
Zentrale *f* **-n** head office; *(für Taxis etc)* headquarters *sing or pl; (Telefon~)* exchange
Zentralheizung *f* central heating.
Zentralisation *f* centralization.
zentralisieren* *vt* to centralize.
zentralistisch *adj* centralist.
Zentralkomitee *nt* central committee.
zentrieren* *vti (Typ)* to centre *(Brit)*, to center *(US)*.
zentrifugal *adj* centrifugal.
Zentrifuge *f* **-n** centrifuge.
Zentrum *nt, pl* **Zentren** *(lit, fig)* centre *(Brit)*, center *(US)*.
Zeppelin *m* **-e** zeppelin.
Zepter *nt* **-** sceptre *(Brit)*, scepter *(US)*. **das ~ führen** to wield the sceptre.
zerbeißen* *vt irreg* to chew; *Bonbon, Keks etc* to crunch; *(beschädigen)* to chew to pieces.
zerbersten* *vi irreg aux sein* to burst.
zerbeulen* *vt* to dent. **zerbeult** battered.
zerbomben* *vt* to flatten with bombs. **zerbombt** *Stadt* bombed.
zerbrechen* *irreg* **1** *vt (lit)* to break into pieces; *Glas, Porzellan etc* to smash; *Ketten (lit, fig)* to break. **2** *vi aux sein* to break into pieces; *(Glas, Porzellan etc)* to smash; *(fig)* to be destroyed *(an +dat* by*)*.
zerbrechlich *adj* fragile.
Zerbrechlichkeit *f* fragility.
zerbröckeln* *vti* to crumble.
zerdrücken* *vt* to squash; *Gemüse* to mash; *(zerknittern)* to crush.
Zeremonie *f* ceremony.
zeremoniell *adj* ceremonial.
Zeremonienmeister [-'mo:niən-] *m* master of ceremonies.
zerfahren *adj* scatty; *(unkonzentriert)* distracted.
Zerfahrenheit *f siehe adj* scattiness; distraction.
Zerfall *m no pl* disintegration; *(von Gebäude auch, von Atom)* decay; *(von Leiche, Holz etc)* decomposition; *(von Kultur, Gesundheit)* decline.
zerfallen* **1** *vi irreg aux sein* **(a)** to disintegrate; *(Atomkern)* to decay; *(Leiche, Holz etc)* to decompose; *(Reich, Moral, Gesundheit)* to decline. **(b)** *(sich gliedern)* to fall *(in +acc* into*)*. **2** *adj Haus* tumble-down.
zerfetzen* *vt* to tear to pieces.
zerfetzt *adj Hose* tattered; *Arm* lacerated.
zerfleddert *adj (col)* tattered.
zerfleischen* *vt* to tear to pieces.
zerfließen* *vi irreg aux sein (Tinte, Makeup etc)* to run.
zerfranst *adj* frayed.
zerfressen* *vt irreg* to eat away; *(Motten, Mäuse etc)* to eat. **(von Motten/Würmern) ~ sein** to be moth-/worm-eaten.
zerfurchen* *vt* to furrow.
zergehen* *vi irreg aux sein* to dissolve; *(schmelzen)* to melt. **auf der Zunge ~** *(Gebäck etc)* to melt in the mouth.
zergliedern* *vt (Biol)* to dissect; *(fig)* to analyse.
zerhauen* *vt irreg* to chop in two; *(in viele Stücke)* to chop up.
zerkauen* *vt* to chew.
zerkleinern* *vt* to cut up.
zerklüftet *adj Küste* jagged. **tief ~es Gestein** deeply fissured rock.
zerknirscht *adj* overcome with remorse.
zerknittern* *vt* to crease, to crumple.
zerknüllen* *vt* to crumple up.
zerkratzen* *vt* to scratch.
zerkrümeln* *vt* to crumble.
zerlaufen* *vi irreg aux sein* to melt.
zerlegbar *adj* **die Möbel waren leicht ~** the furniture could easily be taken apart.
zerlegen* *vt* to take apart; *(zerschneiden)* to cut up; *(Fleisch)* to carve up; *(Biol)* to dissect. **etw in seine Einzelteile ~** to take sth to pieces.
zerlumpt *adj* ragged.
zermahlen* *vt* to grind.
zermalmen* *vt* to crush.
zermartern* *vt* **sich** *(dat)* **das Hirn ~** to rack one's brains.
zermürben* *vt (fig)* **jdn ~** to wear sb down; **~d** wearing.
zernagen* *vt* to gnaw to pieces.
zerpflücken* *vt* to pick to pieces.
zerplatzen* *vi aux sein* to burst.
zerquetschen* *vt* to crush; *Kartoffeln* to mash. **10 Mark und ein paar Zerquetschte** *(col)* 10 marks something (or other), 10 marks odd.
Zerrbild *nt (fig)* caricature.
zerreden* *vt* to flog to death *(col)*.
zerreiben* *vt irreg (lit, fig)* to crush.
zerreißen* *irreg* **1** *vt* to tear up; *(aus Versehen)* to tear; *Faden, Seil etc* to break; *(zerfleischen)* to tear apart. **2** *vi aux sein (Stoff)* to tear; *(Band, Seil etc)* to break.
Zerreißprobe *f (lit)* pull test; *(fig)* real test.
zerren 1 *vt* to drag; *Sehne* to pull. **2** *vi* **an etw** *(dat)* **~** to tug at sth.
zerrinnen* *vi irreg aux sein (lit, fig)* to melt away; *(Geld)* to disappear.
zerrissen *adj (fig) Volk, Partei* strife-torn; *Mensch* torn.
Zerrissenheit *f (von Volk, Partei)* disunity *no pl; (innere ~)* (inner) conflict.
Zerrspiegel *m (lit)* distorting mirror; *(fig)* travesty.
Zerrung *f* **eine ~** a pulled ligament/muscle.
zerrütten* *vt (lit, fig)* to destroy; *Nerven* to shatter. **eine zerrüttete Ehe** a broken marriage.
Zerrüttung *f* destruction; *(von Nerven)* shattering; *(von Ehe)* breakdown.
Zerrüttungsprinzip *nt* principle of irretrievable breakdown.
zersägen* *vt* to saw up.
zerschellen* *vi aux sein (Schiff, Flugzeug)* to be smashed to pieces.
zerschlagen* *irreg* **1** *vt* **(a)** *(Mensch)* to smash (to pieces). **(b)** *(fig) Opposition* to crush; *Vereinigung* to break up. **2** *vr (Plan etc)* to fall through; *(Hoffnung)* to be shattered. **3** *adj pred* washed out *(col)*; *(nach Anstrengung)* shattered *(col)*, worn out.
Zerschlagung *f (fig) (von Bewegung, Opposition)* crushing; *(von Plänen etc)* failure.
zerschlissen *adj Kleider* tattered.
zerschmelzen* *vi irreg aux sein* to melt.
zerschmettern* **1** *vt* to shatter; *Feind* to crush. **2** *vi aux sein* to shatter.
zerschneiden* *vt irreg* to cut; *(in Stücke)* to cut up.
zersetzen* **1** *vt* to decompose; *(Säure)* to corrode; *(fig)* to subvert. **2** *vr* to decompose; *(durch Säure)* to corrode.
zersetzend *adj (fig)* subversive.
Zersetzung *f (Chem)* decomposition; *(durch Säure)* corrosion; *(fig: Untergrabung)* subversion.
zerspalten* *vt* to split; *Gemeinschaft* to split up.
zersplittern* **1** *vt* to shatter; *Holz* to splinter; *(fig) Kräfte, Zeit* to dissipate. **2** *vi aux sein* to shatter; *(Holz)* to splinter; *(fig)* to split up. **3** *vr*

(fig) to dissipate one's energies; *(Gruppe, Partei)* to become fragmented.
zerspringen* *vi irreg aux sein* to shatter; *(einen Sprung bekommen)* to crack.
zerstampfen* *vt (zertreten)* to stamp on; *(zerkleinern)* to crush.
zerstäuben* *vt* to spray.
Zerstäuber *m* - spray; *(Parfüm~ auch)* atomizer.
zerstechen* *vt irreg* **(a)** *(Mücken)* to bite (all over). **(b)** *Material, Haut* to puncture; *Finger* to prick.
zerstieben* *vi irreg aux sein* to scatter; *(Wasser)* to spray.
zerstören* *vt* to destroy; *(Rowdys)* to vandalize; *Gesundheit* to ruin.
Zerstörer *m* - *(Naut)* destroyer.
zerstörerisch *adj* destructive.
Zerstörung *f no pl* destruction *no pl.*
Zerstörungswut *f* destructive mania.
zerstoßen* *vt irreg* to crush.
zerstreiten* *vt irreg* to quarrel, to fall out.
zerstreuen* **1** *vt* **(a)** to scatter *(in +dat* over*)*; *(fig)* to dispel. **(b) jdn ~** to take sb's mind off things. **2** *vr* **(a)** *(sich verteilen)* to scatter; *(fig)* to be dispelled. **(b)** *(sich ablenken)* to take one's mind off things.
zerstreut *adj (fig) Mensch* absent-minded.
Zerstreutheit *f no pl* absent-mindedness.
Zerstreuung *f* **(a)** *no pl siehe vt* scattering. **(b)** *(Ablenkung)* diversion. **zur ~** as a diversion.
zerstritten *adj* estranged. **mit jdm ~ sein** to be on very bad terms with sb.
zerstückeln* *vt (lit)* to cut up; *Leiche* to dismember; *Land* to carve up.
zerteilen* *vt* to split up.
Zertifikat *nt* certificate.
zertrampeln* *vt* to trample on.
zertrennen* *vt* to sever; *(auftrennen) Nähte* to undo.
zertreten* *vt irreg* to crush (underfoot); *Rasen* to ruin.
zertrümmern* *vt* to smash; *Einrichtung* to smash up; *Ordnung* to wreck.
Zervelatwurst [tsɛrvəˈlaːt-] *f* German salami, cervelat.
zerwühlen* *vt* to ruffle up, to tousle; *Bett* to rumple (up); *(aufwühlen) Erdboden* to churn up.
zerzaust *adj* dishevelled *(Brit)*, disheveled *(US)*.
Zeter *nt*: **~ und Mordio schreien** to scream blue murder.
zetern *vi (pej)* to clamour *(Brit)*, to clamor *(US)*; *(keifen)* to scold.
Zettel *m* - piece of paper; *(Notiz~)* note; *(Kartei~)* card; *(Kassen~)* receipt; *(Formular)* form.
Zettel-: ~kartei *f* card index; **~kasten** *m* file-card box; **~wirtschaft** *f (pej)* **eine ~wirtschaft haben** to have bits of paper everywhere.
Zeug *nt no pl (col)* stuff *no indef art, no pl*; *(Unsinn)* nonsense, rubbish *(col)*; *(Kleidung)* things *pl (col)*. **altes ~** junk, trash; **das ~ zu etw haben** to have (got) what it takes to be sth; **jdm etwas am ~ flicken** *(col)* to find fault with sb; **was das ~ hält** for all one is worth; *laufen* like mad; *fahren* like the blazes *(col)*; **sich ins ~ legen** to go flat out *(col)*; **dummes ~ reden** to talk a lot of nonsense.
Zeuge *m (wk)* **-n, -n** *(Jur, fig)* witness *(gen* to*)*. **~ eines Unfalls sein** to be a witness to an accident.
zeugen[1] *vt Kind* to father.
zeugen[2] *vi* **(a) von etw ~** to show sth. **(b)** *(aussagen)* to testify *(vor +dat* to*)*.
Zeugen-: ~aussage *f* testimony; **~bank** *f*, **~stand** *m* witness box *(Brit)*, witness stand *(US)*.
Zeugin *f* witness.
Zeugnis *nt* **(a)** *(Bescheinigung)* certificate; *(Schul~)* report; *(von Arbeitgeber)* reference. **jdm ein ~ ausstellen** to give sb a reference. **(b)** *(esp liter: Zeugenaussage)* evidence. **für/gegen jdn ~ ablegen** to testify for/against sb.
Zeugnis-: ~konferenz *f (Sch) staff meeting to decide on marks etc*; **~papiere** *pl* certificates *pl*; *(von Arbeitgeber)* references *pl.*
Zeugungs-: z~fähig *adj* fertile; **~fähigkeit** *f* fertility; **z~unfähig** *adj* sterile; **~unfähigkeit** *f* sterility.
z.H(d). = **zu Händen** att, attn.
Zicke *f* **-n** **(a)** nanny goat. **(b)** *(pej col: Frau)* old bag *(col)*.
Zicken *pl (col)* nonsense *no pl.* **mach bloß keine ~!** no nonsense now!; **~ machen** to make trouble.
zickig *adj (albern)* silly; *(prüde)* prudish.
Zickzack *m* **-e** zigzag. **z~** *or* **im ~ laufen** to zigzag.
Zickzack-: ~kurs *m* zigzag course; **~linie** *f* zigzag.
Ziege *f* **-n** **(a)** goat. **(b)** *(pej col: Frau)* cow *(col!)*.
Ziegel *m* - *(Backstein)* brick; *(Dach~)* tile. **ein Dach mit ~n decken** to tile a roof.
Ziegel-: ~bau *m, pl* **-ten** brick building; **~brenner** *m* brickmaker; *(von Dachziegeln)* tilemaker; **~dach** *nt* tiled roof.
Ziegelei *f* brickworks *sing or pl*; *(für Dachziegel)* tile-making works *sing or pl.*
Ziegelstein *m* brick.
Ziegen-: ~bart *m (hum: Bart)* goatee (beard); **~bock** *m* billy goat; **~fell** *nt* goatskin; **~käse** *m* goat's milk cheese; **~leder** *nt* kid(-leather), kidskin; **~milch** *f* goat's milk; **~peter** *m* - mumps *sing.*
Zieh-: ~brücke *f* drawbridge; **~brunnen** *m* well; **~eltern** *pl* foster parents *pl.*
ziehen *pret* **zog,** *ptp* **gezogen** **1** *vt* **(a)** to pull; *(schleppen)* to drag; *Hut* to raise; *Handbremse* to put on; *(heraus~)* to pull out *(aus* of*)*; *Fäden* to take out. **den Ring vom Finger ~** to pull one's ring off (one's finger); **die Mütze tiefer ins Gesicht ~** to pull one's hat further down over one's face; **er zog noch einen Pullover übers Hemd** he put on a pullover over his shirt; **unangenehme Folgen nach sich ~** to have unpleasant consequences. **(b)** *(zeichnen, anlegen) Kreis, Linie* to draw; *Graben, Furchen* to dig; *Mauer* to build; *Grenze* to set up. **(c)** *(herstellen) Draht, Kerzen* to make; *(züchten) Blumen* to grow; *Tiere* to breed.
2 *vi* **(a)** to pull. **an etw** *(dat)* **~** to pull (on *or* at) sth. **(b)** *aux sein (um~)* to move. **nach Bayern/in eine größere Wohnung ~** to move to Bavaria/into a bigger flat; **zu jdm ~** to move in with sb. **(c)** *aux sein (sich bewegen)* to move, to go; *(Soldaten)* to march; *(durchstreifen)* to roam. **in den Krieg ~** to go to war. **(d)** *(mit Spielfigur)* to move. **mit dem Turm ~** to move the rook; **wer zieht?** whose move is it? **(e)** *(Cook) (Tee, Kaffee)* to draw; *(in Kochwasser)* to simmer. **(f)** *(col: Eindruck machen)* **so was zieht bei mir nicht** I don't like that sort of thing.
3 *vi impers* **es zieht** there's a draught *(Brit) or* draft *(US)*; **wenn es dir zieht** if you're in a draught; *(von Schmerzen)* **mir zieht's im Rücken** my back hurts.
4 *vt impers* **es zog ihn in die weite Welt** he felt drawn towards the big wide world.
5 *vr* **(a)** *(sich erstrecken, verlaufen)* to stretch. **dieses Thema zieht sich durch das ganze Buch** this theme runs throughout the whole book. **(b)** *(sich dehnen)* to stretch; *(Holz)* to warp; *(Metall)* to bend.
Ziehen *nt no pl (Schmerz)* ache.
Ziehharmonika *f* concertina.
Ziehung *f* draw.
Ziel *nt* **-e** **(a)** *(Reise~)* destination; *(Absicht, Zweck)* goal, aim; *(von Wünschen, Spott)* object. **mit dem ~ zu gewinnen** with the aim of winning; **jdm/sich ein ~ stecken** to set sb/oneself a goal; **sich** *(dat)* **etw zum ~ setzen** to set sth as one's goal; **zum ~ kommen** *(fig)* to reach one's goal; **am ~ sein** to be at one's destination; *(fig)* to have reached one's goal. **(b)** *(Sport)* finish. **durchs ~**

gehen to cross the finishing line. **(c)** *(Mil etc)* target. **ins ~ treffen** to hit the target; **über das ~ hinausschießen** *(fig)* to overshoot the mark.

Ziel-: ~band *nt* finishing-tape; **z~bewußt** *adj* purposeful.

zielen *vi* to aim *(auf +acc, nach* at*)*; *(fig)* to be aimed *(auf +acc* at*)*. **ich weiß, worauf deine Bemerkungen ~** I know what you're driving at.

Ziel-: ~fernrohr *nt* telescopic sight; **~gruppe** *f* target group; **~hafen** *m* port of destination; **~linie** *f (Sport)* finishing-line; **z~los** *adj* aimless; **~losigkeit** *f* lack of purpose; **~ort** *m* destination; **~scheibe** *f* target; **z~sicher** *adj* unerring; *Handeln* purposeful; **z~strebig 1** *adj* single-minded; **2** *adv* single-mindedly, full of determination; **~strebigkeit** *f* single-mindedness; **~vorstellung** *f* objective.

ziemen *vr, vr impers (geh)* **das/es ziemt sich nicht (für dich)** it is not proper (for you).

ziemlich 1 *adv* **(a)** quite, pretty *(col)*; *sicher, genau* reasonably. **wir haben uns ~ beeilt** we've hurried quite a bit; **~ lange** quite a long time; **~ viel** quite a lot. **(b)** *(col: beinahe)* almost, nearly. **so ~** more or less; **so ~ alles** just about everything; **so ~ dasselbe** pretty much the same. **2** *adj attr Anzahl, Strecke* fair; *Vermögen* sizeable. **eine ~e Anstrengung** quite an effort.

Zierat *m* **-e** *(geh)* decoration.

Zierde *f* **-n** ornament, decoration; *(Schmuckstück)* adornment. **zur ~** for decoration; **das alte Haus ist eine ~ der Stadt** the old house is one of the beauties of the town.

zieren 1 *vt* to adorn; *(fig: auszeichnen)* to grace. **2** *vr (sich bitten lassen)* to need a lot of pressing; *(sich gekünstelt benehmen)* to be affected. **zier dich nicht!** don't be shy *or* silly *(col)*.

Zier-: ~fisch *m* ornamental fish; **~garten** *m* ornamental garden; **~leiste** *f* border; *(an Auto)* trim; *(an Wand, Möbeln)* moulding *(Brit)*, molding *(US)*.

zierlich *adj* dainty; *Frau auch* petite.

Zierlichkeit *f siehe adj* daintiness; petiteness.

Zierpflanze *f* ornamental plant.

Ziffer *f* **-n (a)** digit; *(Zahl)* figure, number. **römische/arabische ~n** roman/arabic numerals; **eine Zahl mit drei ~n** a three-figure number. **(b)** *(eines Paragraphs)* clause.

Zifferblatt *nt (an Uhr)* dial; *(hum: Gesicht)* face.

zig *adj inv (col)* umpteen *(col)*.

Zigarette *f* cigarette.

Zigaretten- *in cpds* cigarette; **~automat** *m* cigarette machine; **~dose** *f* cigarette box; **~etui** *nt* cigarette case; **~kippe** *f* cigarette end; **~pause** *f* break for a cigarette; **~schachtel** *f* cigarette packet *or* pack; **~spitze** *f* cigarette-holder.

Zigarillo *m or nt* **-s** cigarillo.

Zigarre *f* **-n (a)** cigar. **(b)** *(col: Verweis)* **jdm eine ~ verpassen** to give sb a dressing-down.

Zigarren- *in cpds* cigar; **~kiste** *f* cigar-box; **~spitze** *f* cigar-holder; **~stummel** *m* cigar butt.

Zigeuner(in *f***)** *m* **-** gipsy.

Zigeunerschnitzel *nt (Cook) cutlet served in a spicy sauce with green and red peppers.*

zigmal *adv (col)* umpteen times *(col)*.

Zimmer *nt* **-** room. **~ frei** vacancies.

Zimmer-: ~antenne *f* indoor aerial *(Brit) or* antenna *(US)*; **~arbeit** *f* carpentry job; **~brand** *m* fire in a/the room; **~flucht** *f* suite of rooms; **~handwerk** *nt* carpentry; **~kellner** *m* room-waiter; **~lautstärke** *f* **bitte auf ~lautstärke stellen** please keep volume down; **~mädchen** *nt* chambermaid *(Brit)*, maid *(US)*; **~mann** *m, pl* **~leute** carpenter.

zimmern 1 *vt* to make from wood. **2** *vi* to do woodwork.

Zimmer-: ~pflanze *f* house plant; **~suche** *f* room hunting; **auf ~suche sein** to be looking for rooms/a room; **~temperatur** *f* room temperature; **~vermittlung** *f* accommodation *(Brit) or* accommodations *(US)* agency.

zimperlich *adj* squeamish; *(prüde)* prissy; *(wehleidig)* soft. **sei doch nicht so ~** don't be so silly; **da darf man nicht so ~ sein** you can't afford to be soft.

Zimt *m* **-e** *(Gewürz)* cinnamon.

Zimt-: ~stange *f* stick of cinnamon; **~ziege** *f (col)* stupid cow *(col!)*.

Zink *nt no pl* zinc.

Zinke *f* **-n** *(von Gabel)* prong; *(von Kamm, Harke)* tooth.

Zinken *m* **- (a)** *(col: Nase)* hooter *(col)*. **(b) = Zinke.**

zinken *vt Karten* to mark.

Zinn *nt no pl* **(a)** tin. **(b)** *(Legierung)* pewter. **(c)** *(~produkte)* pewter, pewterware.

Zinnbecher *m* pewter tankard.

zinnoberrot *adj* vermilion.

Zinnsoldat *m* tin soldier.

Zins *m* **-en** *usu pl (Geld~)* interest *no pl*. **~en bringen** to earn interest; *(fig)* to pay dividends; **Darlehen zu 10% ~en** loan at 10% interest; **jdm etw mit ~en heimzahlen** *(fig)* to pay sb back for sth with interest.

Zinseszins *m* compound interest.

Zins-: z~frei *adj* interest-free; **~fuß** *m* interest rate; **z~los** *adj* interest-free; **~rechnung** *f* calculation of interest; **~satz** *m* interest rate; **~senkung** *f* reduction in the interest rate.

Zionismus *m* Zionism.

zionistisch *adj* Zionist.

Zipfel *m* **-** *(von Tuch)* corner; *(von Mütze)* point; *(von Jacke)* tail; *(von Wurst)* end; *(von Land)* tip.

Zipfelmütze *f* pointed cap *or* hat.

zirka *adv* about.

Zirkel *m* **-** *(Gerät)* pair of compasses, compasses *pl*; *(Stech~)* pair of dividers, dividers *pl*.

zirkulieren* *vi* to circulate.

Zirkus *m* **-se (a)** circus. **(b)** *(col: Getue)* fuss, to-do *(col)*.

Zirkus- *in cpds* circus; **~zelt** *nt* big top.

zirpen *vi* to chirp, to cheep.

Zirrhose [tsi'roːzə] *f* **-n** cirrhosis.

zischeln *vi* to whisper.

zischen 1 *vi* to hiss; *(Limonade)* to fizz; *(Fett)* to sizzle. **2** *vt* **(a)** *(~d sagen)* to hiss. **(b)** *(col: ohrfeigen)* **jdm eine ~** to belt *or* clout sb one *(col)*.

Zischlaut *m (Ling)* sibilant.

ziselieren* *vt* to engrave.

Zitadelle *f* citadel.

Zitat *nt* **-e** quotation, quote. **ein falsches ~** a misquotation; **~ ... Ende des ~s** quote ... unquote.

Zither *f* **-n** zither.

zitieren* *vt* **(a)** to quote. **(b)** *(vorladen, rufen)* to summon *(vor +acc* before, *an +acc, zu* to*)*.

Zitronat *nt* candied lemon peel.

Zitrone *f* **-n** lemon; *(Getränk)* lemon drink. **jdn wie eine ~ auspressen** to squeeze sb dry.

Zitronen-: z~gelb *adj* lemon yellow; **~limonade** *f* lemonade; **~melisse** *f* (lemon) balm; **~saft** *f* lemon juice; **~säure** *f* citric acid; **~schale** *f* lemon peel.

Zitrusfrucht *f* citrus fruit.

Zitter-: ~aal *m* electric eel; **~greis** *m (col)* old dodderer *(col)*.

zitt(e)rig *adj* shaky.

zittern *vi* to tremble *(vor +dat* with*)*. **am ganzen Körper ~** to shake all over; **mir ~ die Knie** my knees are trembling; **vor jdm ~** to be terrified of sb.

Zittern *nt no pl* shaking, trembling. **mit ~ und Zagen** in fear and trembling.

Zitze *f* **-n** teat.

zivil [tsi'viːl] *adj* **(a)** civilian; *Schaden* non-military. **~er Bevölkerungsschutz** civil defence *(Brit) or* defense *(US)*. **(b)** *(col: anständig)* civil; *Preise* reasonable.

Zivil [tsi'viːl] *nt no pl* **in ~** *Soldat* in civilian clothes,

in civvies; **Polizist in ~** plain-clothes policeman.
Zivil-: ~beruf *m* civilian profession/trade; **~bevölkerung** *f* civilian population; **~courage** *f* courage *(to stand up for one's beliefs)*; **~dienst** *m* alternative service *(for conscientious objectors)*; **~ehe** *f* civil marriage; **~flughafen** *m* civil airport; **~gericht** *nt* civil court.
Zivilisation [tsiviliza'tsio:n] *f* civilization.
Zivilisationskrankheit [tsiviliza'tsio:ns-] *f* illness caused by civilization.
zivilisatorisch [tsiviliza'to:rɪʃ] *adj* of civilization.
zivilisiert [tsivili'zi:ɐt] *adj* civilized.
Zivilist [tsivi'lɪst] *m* civilian.
Zivil-: ~kleidung *f* = **Zivil; ~leben** *nt* civilian life, civvy street *(col)*; **~person** *f* civilian; **~prozeß** *m* civil action; **~recht** *nt* civil law; **~richter** *m* civil court judge; **~sache** *f* matter for a civil court; **~schutz** *m* civil defence *(Brit) or* defense *(US)*.
ZK [tsɛt'ka:] *nt* **-s** = **Zentralkomitee.**
Zobel *m* - *(Zool, Pelz)* sable.
Zofe *f* **-n** lady's maid; *(von Königin)* lady-in-waiting.
zog *pret of* **ziehen.**
zögern *vi* to hesitate. **er zögerte lange mit der Antwort** he hesitated a long time before replying.
Zögern *nt no pl* hesitation. **nach langem ~** after hesitating a long time.
Zölibat *nt or m no pl* celibacy. **im ~ leben** to lead a life of celibacy.
Zoll[1] *m* - *(Measure)* inch.
Zoll[2] *m* **¨-e (a)** *(Waren~)* customs duty; *(Brücken~, Straßen~)* toll. **darauf wird ~ erhoben** there is duty to pay on that. **(b)** *(Stelle)* **der ~** customs *pl*.
Zoll-: ~amt *nt* customs house *or* office; **~beamte(r)** *m* customs officer *or* official; **~behörde** *f* customs authorities *pl*, customs *pl*; **~bestimmung** *f usu pl* customs regulation.
zollen *vt* **jdm Anerkennung/Achtung ~** to acknowledge/respect sb.
Zoll-: ~erklärung *f* customs declaration; **~fahndung** *f* customs investigation department; **z~frei** *adj* duty-free; **etw z~frei einführen** to import sth free of duty; **~gebiet** *nt* customs area *or* territory; **~grenze** *f* customs border; **~kontrolle** *f* customs check; **~papiere** *pl* customs documents *pl*; **z~pflichtig** *adj* dutiable; **~schranke** *f* customs barrier; **~stock** *m* inch rule; **~tarif** *m* customs tariff; **~union** *f* customs union.
Zone *f* **-n** zone; *(von Fahrkarte)* fare stage.
Zonen-: ~grenze *f* zonal border; **die ~grenze** *(col)* the border (with East Germany); **~randgebiet** *nt* border area (with East Germany).
Zoo [tso:] *m* **-s** zoo.
Zoologe [tsoo'lo:gə] *m (wk)* **-n, -n, Zoologin** *f* zoologist.
Zoologie [tsoolo'gi:] *f* zoology.
zoologisch [tsoo'lo:gɪʃ] *adj* zoological.
Zoom [zu:m] *nt* **-s** zoom shot; *(Objektiv)* zoom lens.
Zoowärter *m* zoo keeper.
Zopf *m* **¨-e** pigtail. **das Haar in ¨-e flechten** to plait one's hair; **ein alter ~** *(fig)* an antiquated custom.
Zopf-: ~band *nt* hair ribbon; **~spange** *f* clip.
Zorn *m no pl* anger. **der ~ Gottes** the wrath of God; **jds ~ heraufbeschwören** to incur sb's wrath; **in ~ geraten** to fly into a rage; **im ~** in a rage; **in gerechtem ~** in righteous indignation; **einen ~ auf jdn haben** to be furious with sb.
Zorn(es)ausbruch *m* fit of anger *or* rage.
zornig *adj* angry, furious. **(leicht) ~ werden** to lose one's temper (easily); **auf jdn ~ sein** to be angry with sb.
Zote *f* **-n** dirty joke.
Zotte *f* **-n, Zottel** *f* **-n** *(col)* rat's tail *(col)*.
Zottelhaar *nt (col)* shaggy hair.
zottelig *adj (col) Haar* shaggy.
zottig *adj Fell* shaggy.
z.T. = **zum Teil.**
zu 1 *prep +dat* **(a)** *(örtlich)* to. **~m Bahnhof** to the station; **~m Arzt gehen** to go to the doctor's *(Brit) or* doctor; **bis ~** as far as; **(bis) ~m Bahnhof sind es 5 km** it's 5 kms to the station; **~r Schule/Kirche gehen** to go to school/church; **~m Film/Ballett gehen** to go into films/to join the ballet; **~m Fenster herein/hinaus** in (at)/out of the window; **~r Decke sehen** to look (up) at the ceiling; **~jdm/etw hinaufsehen** to look up at sb/sth; **sie sah ~ ihm hin** she looked towards him; **das Zimmer liegt ~r Straße hin** the room looks out onto the street; **ein Zimmer mit Blick ~m Meer** a room with a view of the sea; **die Tür ~m Keller** the door to the cellar; **~r Stadtmitte hin** towards the town/city centre; **~ meiner Linken** to *or* on my left; **~ Lande und ~ Wasser** on land and sea; **der Dom ~ Köln** Cologne Cathedral.
(b) *(zeitlich)* at. **~ später Stunde** at a late hour; **~ Mittag** *(am Mittag)* at noon; *(bis Mittag)* by midday; **~ Ostern** at Easter; **rechtzeitig ~m Essen kommen** to be in time for dinner; **bis ~m 15. April** until 15th April; *(nicht später als)* by 15th April; **der Wechsel ist ~m 15. April fällig** the bill is due on 15th April; **~m 31. Mai kündigen** to give in one's notice for May 31st.
(c) *(Zusatz, Zusammengehörigkeit)* with. **Wein ~m Essen trinken** to drink wine with one's meal; **~r Gitarre singen** to sing to a/the guitar; **die Melodie ~ dem Lied** the tune of the song; **Vorwort/Anmerkungen ~ etw** preface/notes to sth; **~ dem kommt noch, daß ich ...** on top of that I ...; **etw ~ etw legen** to put sth with sth; **sich ~ jdm setzen** to sit down beside sb; **setz dich doch ~ uns** (come and) sit with us; **Liebe ~ jdm** love for sb; **sein Verhältnis ~ ihr** his relationship with her.
(d) *(Zweck)* for. **Wasser ~m Waschen** water for washing; **Papier ~m Schreiben** paper to write on; **er sagte das nur ~ ihrer Beruhigung** he said that just to set her mind at rest; **etw ~m Geburtstag/~ Weihnachten bekommen** to get sth for one's birthday/for Christmas; **jdm ~ etw gratulieren** to congratulate sb on sth; **Ausstellung ~m Jahrestag der Revolution** exhibition to mark the anniversary of the revolution; **~ dieser Frage möchte ich folgendes sagen** I should like to say the following to this question.
(e) *(Folge, Umstand, Art und Weise)* **~ seinem Besten** for his own good; **~m Glück** luckily; **~ meiner Freude** *etc* to my joy *etc*; **~/~m Tode** to death; **es ist ~m Weinen** it's enough to make you (want to) weep; **~ Fuß/Pferd** on foot/horseback; **~ Schiff** by ship *or* sea.
(f) *(Veränderung)* into. **~ etw werden** to turn into sth; **Leder ~ Handtaschen verarbeiten** to make handbags out of leather; **jdn/etw ~ etw machen** to make sb/sth (into) sth; **~ Asche verbrennen** to burn to ashes; **jdn ~m König wählen** to choose sb as king; **jdn ~ etw ernennen** to nominate sb sth.
(g) *(bei Zahlen)* **drei ~ zwei** *(Sport)* three-two; **drei Sätze ~ zwei** *(Tennis)* three sets to two; **Äpfel das Stück ~ 30 Pfennig** apples at 30 pfennigs each; **~m halben Preis** at half price; **~m ersten Male** for the first time.
2 *adv* **(a)** *(allzu)* too. **~ sehr** too much; **das war einfach ~ dumm!** *(col)* it was so stupid! **(b)** *(geschlossen)* shut, closed. **auf, ~** *(an Hähnen etc)* on, off; **Tür ~!** *(col)* shut the door; **die Geschäfte haben jetzt ~** the shops are closed now. **(c)** *(col: los, weiter)* **dann mal ~!** right, off we go!; **nur ~!** just keep on!; **mach ~!** hurry up! **(d)** *(örtlich)* toward(s). **auf den Wald ~** towards the forest.
3 *conj* **(a)** *(mit Infinitiv)* to. **etw ~ essen** sth to

eat; **der Fußboden ist noch ~ fegen** the floor still has to be swept; **er hat ~ gehorchen** he has to obey; **ohne es ~ wissen** without knowing it; **um besser sehen ~ können** in order to see better; **ich komme, um mich ~ verabschieden** I've come to say goodbye. **(b)** *(mit Partizip)* **noch ~ bezahlende Rechnungen** bills that are still to be paid; **nur winzige, leicht ~ übersehende Punkte** only very small points (that are) easily overlooked.

4 *adj (col: geschlossen)* **eine ~e Tür** a closed door; *siehe* **zusein.**

zu|aller-: ~erst *adv* first of all; **~letzt** *adv* last of all.

zubauen *vt sep Lücke* to fill in; *Platz, Gelände* to build up.

Zubehör *nt* **-e** equipment *no pl*; *(Zusatzgeräte, ~teile)* accessories *pl*. **Küche mit allem ~** fully equipped kitchen.

Zubehörteil *nt* accessory.

zubeißen *vi sep irreg* to bite.

zubekommen* *vt sep irreg (col) Tür, Fenster* to get shut *or* closed. **ich bekomm' den Reißverschluß nicht zu** I can't get my zip done up.

Zuber *m* **-** (wash)tub.

zubereiten* *vt sep* to prepare.

Zubereitung *f* preparation.

zubilligen *vt sep* **jdm etw ~** to allow sb sth.

zubinden *vt sep irreg* to tie up. **jdm die Augen ~** to blindfold sb.

zubringen *vt sep irreg* **(a)** *(verbringen)* to spend. **(b)** *(herbeibringen)* to bring to, to take to.

Zubringer *m* **- (a)** *(Tech)* conveyor. **(b)** *(Straße)* feeder road. **(c) ~(bus)** shuttle (bus); *(zum Flughafen)* airport bus.

Zubrot *nt (hum)* extra income. **ein kleines ~ verdienen** to earn a bit on the side *(col)*.

Zucchini [tsu'ki:ni] *f* **-** courgette *(Brit)*, zucchini *(US)*.

Zucht *f* **(a)** *(Disziplin)* discipline. **~ und Ordnung** discipline. **(b)** *(Aufzucht) (von Tieren)* breeding; *(von Pflanzen)* cultivation. **(c)** *(~generation)* stock.

Zuchtbulle *m* breeding bull.

züchten *vt* to breed; *Bienen* to keep; *Pflanzen* to grow; *Perlen, Bakterien* to cultivate.

Züchter(in *f*) *m* **-** *(von Tieren)* breeder; *(von Pflanzen)* cultivator; *(von Bienen)* keeper.

Zuchthaus *nt (Gebäude)* prison *(for capital offenders)*, penitentiary *(US)*.

Zuchthäusler *m* **-** *(col)* convict.

Zuchthengst *m* breeding stallion.

züchtig *adj (liter)* chaste; *(tugendhaft)* virtuous.

züchtigen *vt (geh)* to beat.

Züchtigung *f* beating. **körperliche ~** corporal punishment.

Zucht-: ~perle *f* cultured pearl; **~stute** *f* broodmare; **~tier** *nt* breeding animal; **~vieh** *nt* breeding cattle.

zucken 1 *vi* **(a)** *(nervös)* to twitch; *(vor Schreck)* to start; *(vor Schmerzen)* to flinch; *(verwundetes Tier)* to thrash about. **er zuckte ständig mit dem Mund** his mouth kept twitching; **mit den Schultern ~** to shrug (one's shoulders). **(b)** *(aufleuchten) (Blitz)* to flash; *(Flammen)* to flare up. **2** *vt* **die Schultern ~** to shrug (one's shoulders).

zücken *vt Schwert* to draw; *(col) Notizbuch, Brieftasche* to take out.

Zucker *m no pl* **(a)** sugar. **ein Stück ~** a lump of sugar. **(b)** *(Med) (~gehalt)* sugar; *(Krankheit)* diabetes *sing*. **~ haben** *(col)* to be a diabetic.

Zucker-: ~dose *f* sugar bowl; **~erbse** *f* mangetout (pea); **~gehalt** *m* sugar content, **~guß** *m* icing, frosting *(esp US)*; **mit ~guß überziehen** to ice, to frost *(esp US)*; **~hut** *m* sugarloaf.

zuck(e)rig *adj* sugary.

Zucker-: z~krank *adj* diabetic; **~lecken** *nt*: **das ist kein ~lecken** *(col)* it's no picnic *(col)*.

zuckern *vt* to sugar. **zu stark gezuckert** too sweet.

Zucker-: ~rohr *nt* sugar-cane; **~rübe** *f* sugar beet; **~spiegel** *m (Med)* (blood) sugar level; **~stange** *f* stick of rock *(Brit) or* candy *(US)*; **z~süß** *adj (lit, fig)* sugar-sweet, sugary; **~watte** *f* candy floss; **~zange** *f* sugar tongs *pl*.

Zuckung *f* twitch; *(krampfhaft)* convulsion.

zudecken *vt sep* to cover; *(im Bett)* to tuck up *or* in. **jdn/sich (mit etw) ~** to cover sb/oneself up (with sth); to tuck sb/oneself up (in sth).

zudem *adv (geh)* moreover.

zudrehen *sep* **1** *vt Wasserhahn etc* to turn off; *(zuwenden)* to turn *(dat* to*)*. **2** *vr* to turn *(dat* to*)*.

zudringlich *adj Mensch* pushy *(col)*; *Nachbarn* intrusive. **~ werden** *(zu einer Frau)* to make advances *(zu* to*)*.

Zudringlichkeit *f siehe adj* pushiness *(col)*; intrusiveness; *(einer Frau gegenüber)* advances *pl*.

zudrücken *vt sep* to press shut. **jdm die Kehle ~** to throttle sb.

zu|eilen *vi sep aux sein* **auf jdn/etw ~** to rush towards sb/sth.

zu|einander *adv (gegenseitig)* to each other; *Vertrauen* in each other; *(zusammen)* together. **~ passen** to go together; *(Menschen)* to suit each other.

zu|erkennen* *vt sep irreg Preis* to award *(jdm* to sb*)*; *Recht* to grant; *(vor Gericht) Entschädigung* to award *(jdm etw* sb sth*)*.

zu|erst *adv* first; *(anfangs)* at first. **~ an die Reihe kommen** to be first.

zufahren *vi sep irreg aux sein* **(a) auf jdn/etw ~** to drive/ride towards sb/sth. **(b) fahren Sie doch zu!** go on then!

Zufahrt *f* approach (road); *(zu einem Haus)* drive(way). **„keine ~ zum Krankenhaus"** "no access to hospital".

Zufahrtsstraße *f* access road; *(zur Autobahn)* approach road.

Zufall *m* chance; *(Zusammentreffen)* coincidence. **das ist ~** it's pure chance; **durch ~** (quite) by chance; **es ist kein ~, daß ...** it's no accident that ...; **es war ein glücklicher ~, daß ...** it was lucky that ...; **welch ein ~!** what a coincidence!; **etw dem ~ überlassen** to leave sth to chance.

zufallen *vi sep irreg aux sein* **(a)** *(sich schließen: Fenster etc)* to close. **die Tür fiel laut zu** the door slammed shut; **die Augen fielen ihm zu** he fell asleep. **(b) jdm ~** *(Preis etc)* to go to sb; *(Aufgabe)* to fall to sb.

zufällig 1 *adj* chance *attr*; *Zusammentreffen auch* coincidental. **das war rein ~** it was pure chance. **2** *adv* **(a)** by chance. **er ging ~ vorüber** he happened to be passing; **wenn Sie das ~ wissen sollten** if you (should) happen to know. **(b)** *(in Fragen)* by any chance.

Zufalls- *in cpds* chance; **~bekanntschaft** *f* chance acquaintance; **~treffer** *m* fluke; **einen ~treffer machen** to make a lucky choice.

zufassen *vi sep* **(a)** *(zugreifen)* to take hold of it/them; *(fig: schnell handeln)* to seize an/the opportunity. **(b)** *(helfen)* to lend a hand.

zufliegen *vi sep irreg aux sein* **(a) auf etw** *(acc)* **~** to fly towards sth. **(b)** *+dat* to fly to. **der Vogel ist uns zugeflogen** the bird flew into our house/flat *etc*; **ihm fliegt alles nur so zu** *(fig)* everything comes so easily to him. **(c)** *(col: Fenster, Tür)* to slam shut.

zufließen *vi sep irreg aux sein +dat* to flow to(wards); *(fig: Geld)* to flow into.

Zuflucht *f* refuge *(vor +dat* from*)*. **du bist meine letzte ~** *(fig)* you are my last hope; **zu etw ~ nehmen** *(fig)* to resort to sth.

Zufluchtsstätte *f* place of refuge.

Zufluß *m* **(a)** *no pl* influx; *(Mech: Zufuhr)* supply. **(b)** *(Nebenfluß)* tributary; *(zu Binnensee)* inlet.

zuflüstern *vti sep* **jdm (etw) ~** to whisper (sth) to sb.

zufolge *prep +dat (gemäß)* according to; *(auf Grund)* as a result of. **dem Bericht ~** according to the report.

zufrieden *adj* contented, content. **ein ~es Gesicht machen** to look pleased; **~ lächeln** to smile contentedly; **mit jdm/etw ~ sein** to be satisfied *or* happy with sb/sth; **er ist mit nichts ~** nothing pleases him.

Zufrieden-: z~geben *vr sep irreg* **sich mit etw z~geben** to be satisfied with sth; **~heit** *f* contentment, contentedness; *(Befriedigtsein)* satisfaction; **zur allgemeinen ~heit** to everyone's satisfaction; **z~lassen** *vt sep irreg* to leave alone; **laß mich damit z~!** *(col)* shut up about it! *(col)*; **z~stellen** *vt sep* to satisfy; **schwer z~zustellen sein** to be hard to please.

zufrieren *vi sep irreg aux sein* to freeze (over).

zufügen *vt sep* **(a)** *Leid* to cause. **jdm Schaden ~** to harm sb; **jdm etw ~** to cause sb sth. **(b)** *(col)* = **hinzufügen.**

Zufuhr *f* **-en** *(Versorgung)* supply *(in +acc, nach* to*)*; *(Mil)* supplies *pl*; *(Met)* influx.

zuführen *sep* **1** *vt +dat* **(a)** *(versorgen mit)* to supply. **jdm etw ~** to supply sb with sth. **(b)** *(bringen)* to bring. **jdn der gerechten Strafe ~** to give sb the punishment he/she deserves. **2** *vi* **auf etw** *(acc)* **~** to lead to sth.

Zug[1] *m* **¨-e (a)** *(Luft~)* draught *(Brit)*, draft *(US)*; *(Atem~)* breath; *(an Zigarette etc)* puff, drag; *(Schluck)* mouthful. **einen ~ machen** *(an Zigarette etc)* to take a drag; **das Glas in einem ~ leeren** to empty the glass with one gulp; **etw in vollen ¨~en genießen** to enjoy sth to the full; **in den letzten ¨~en liegen** *(col)* to be at one's last gasp.

(b) *no pl (von Vögeln, Menschen)* migration; *(der Wolken)* drifting. **im ~e** *(im Verlauf)* in the course *(gen* of*)*; **das liegt im ~ der Zeit** it's a sign of the times.

(c) *(beim Schwimmen)* stroke; *(beim Rudern)* pull *(mit* at*)*; *(bei Brettspiel)* move. **einen ~ machen** *(beim Schwimmen)* to do a stroke; **~ um ~** *(fig)* step by step; **zum ~e kommen** *(col)* to get a look-in *(col)*; **du bist am ~** *(bei Brettspiel, fig)* it's your move; **etw in groben ¨~en darstellen/umreißen** to outline sth.

(d) *no pl (Ziehen)* pull, tug *(an +dat* on, at*)*.

(e) *(Gruppe) (von Menschen)* procession; *(Mil)* platoon; *(Abteilung)* section.

Zug[2] *m* **¨-e** *(Eisenbahn~)* train; *(Last~)* truck and trailer. **mit dem ~ fahren** to go/travel by train.

Zug[3] *m* **¨-e** *(Gesichts~, Charakter~)* feature; *(brutal etc)* streak; *(Anflug)* touch. **das war kein schöner ~ von dir** that wasn't nice of you.

Zugabe *f* extra, bonus; *(Comm)* free gift; *(Theat)* encore. **~!** encore!

Zugang *m* **(a)** *(Eingang, Einfahrt)* entrance; *(Zutritt)* access *(zu* to*)*. **er hat keinen ~ zur Musik** music doesn't mean anything to him. **(b)** *(von Patienten)* admission; *(von Schülern)* intake; *(von Büchern)* acquisition.

zugange *adj pred*: **mit jdm/etw ~ sein** *(col)* to be busy with sb/sth; *(euph: sexuell)* to be carrying on with sb *(col)*.

zugänglich *adj (dat, für* to*) (erreichbar) Gelände, Ort* accessible; *öffentliche Einrichtungen* open; *(umgänglich) Mensch, Vorgesetzter* approachable. **etw der Allgemeinheit ~ machen** to open sth to the public; **für etw leicht/nicht ~ sein** to respond/not to respond to sth.

Zugänglichkeit *f (Erreichbarkeit)* accessibility; *(Verfügbarkeit)* availability; *(Umgänglichkeit)* approachability.

Zug-: ~begleiter *m (Rail)* guard *(Brit)*, conductor *(US)*; **~brücke** *f* drawbridge.

zugeben *vt sep irreg* **(a)** *(zugestehen, einräumen)* to admit. **er gab zu, es getan zu haben** he admitted (to) having done it; **jdm gegenüber etw ~** to confess sth to sb; **zugegeben** granted. **(b)** *(hinzufügen)* to add. **(c)** *(zusätzlich geben)* to give as an extra. **jdm etw ~** to give sb sth extra.

zugegebenermaßen *adv* admittedly.

zugegen *adv (geh)* **~ sein** to be present.

zugehen *sep irreg aux sein* **1** *vi* **(a)** *(Tür, Deckel)* to shut. **der Koffer geht nicht zu** the case won't shut. **(b) auf jdn/etw ~** to go towards sb/sth; **direkt auf jdn/etw ~** to go straight up to sb/sth; **es geht auf den Winter zu** winter is drawing in; **er geht schon auf die Siebzig zu** he's getting on for seventy; **dem Ende ~** to draw to a close. **(c)** *+dat (Nachricht etc)* to reach. **der Brief ist uns noch nicht zugegangen** the letter hasn't reached us yet. **2** *vi impers* **dort geht es ... zu** things are ... there; **hier geht es nicht mit rechten Dingen zu** there's something odd going on here.

zugehörig *adj attr (geh)* accompanying; *(verbunden)* affiliated *(dat* to*)*.

Zugehörigkeit *f* **(a)** *(zu Land, Glauben)* affiliation; *(Mitgliedschaft)* membership *(zu* of*)*. **(b)** *(Zugehörigkeitsgefühl)* sense of belonging.

zugeknöpft *adj (fig col) Mensch* reserved.

Zügel *m* **-** rein *(auch fig)*. **die ~ anziehen** *(lit)* to draw in the reins; *(fig)* to keep a tighter rein *(bei* on*)*; **die ~ fest in der Hand behalten** *(fig)* to keep things firmly in hand; **die ~ locker lassen** *(fig)* to give free rein *(bei* to*)*; **die ~ an sich** *(acc)* **reißen** *(fig)* to seize the reins.

zugelassen *adj* authorized; *Arzt* registered; *Kfz* licensed. **amtlich/staatlich ~ sein** to be authorized/to be state-registered; **eine nicht ~e Partei** an illegal party; **als Kassenarzt ~ sein** ≈ to be registered as a GP.

Zügel-: z~los *adj (fig)* unbridled *no adv*, unrestrained; **~losigkeit** *f (fig)* lack of restraint; *(in sexueller Hinsicht)* promiscuity.

zügeln 1 *vt Pferd* to rein in; *(fig)* to curb, to check. **2** *vr* to restrain oneself.

Zugeständnis *nt* concession *(dat, an +acc* to*)*. **~se machen** to make allowances.

zugestehen* *vt sep irreg (einräumen) Recht* to concede, to grant; *(zugeben)* to admit. **jdm etw ~** *(einräumen)* to grant sb sth.

zugetan *adj* **jdm/einer Sache ~ sein** to be fond of sb/sth.

Zugezogene(r) *mf decl as adj* newcomer.

Zug-: ~folge *f (Rail)* order of incoming trains; **z~frei** *adj Raum* draught-free *(Brit)*, draft-free *(US)*; **~führer** *m (Rail)* chief guard *(Brit) or* conductor *(US)*.

zugig *adj* draughty *(Brit)*, drafty *(US)*.

zügig *adj* swift, speedy; *Handschrift* smooth.

zugkräftig *adj (fig) Werbetext, Titel* eye-catching; *Stück* crowd-pulling *attr*, popular.

zugleich *adv (auch ebenso)* at the same time.

Zug-: ~luft *f* draught *(Brit)*, draft *(US)*; **~maschine** *f* towing vehicle; *(von Sattelschlepper)* traction engine; **~personal** *nt (Rail)* train personnel; **~pferd** *nt* draught *(Brit) or* draft *(US)* horse; *(fig)* crowd puller.

zugreifen *vi sep irreg* **(a)** to grab it/them; *(fig)* to act fast *or* quickly; *(bei Tisch)* to help oneself. **(b)** *(Polizei)* to step in quickly.

Zugriff *m* **(a) durch raschen ~** by acting fast; **sich dem ~ der Polizei entziehen** to evade justice. **(b)** *(Comp)* access.

Zugriffszeit *f (Comp)* access time.

zugrunde *adv* **(a) ~ gehen** to perish; **jdn/etw ~ richten** to destroy sb/sth; *(finanziell)* to ruin sb/sth; **er wird daran nicht ~ gehen** he'll survive; *(finanziell)* it won't ruin him. **(b) einer Sache** *(dat)* **~ liegen** to form the basis of sth; **etw einer Sache** *(dat)* **~ legen** to base sth on sth.

Zugtier *nt* draught *(Brit) or* draft *(US)* animal.

zugucken *vi sep* = **zusehen.**

Zug|unglück *nt* train accident.

zugunsten *prep* **~ von** *or +gen* in favour of *(Brit)*, in favor of *(US)*.

zugute *adv* **jdm etw ~ halten** to grant sb sth; *(Verständnis haben)* to make allowances for sth; **einer Sache/jdm ~ kommen** to come in useful for sth/to sb; *(Geld, Erlös)* to benefit sth/sb.

Zug-: **~verbindung** *f* train connection; **~verkehr** *m (Rail)* rail services *pl*; **starker ~verkehr** heavy rail traffic; **~vieh** *nt no pl* draught *(Brit) or* draft *(US)* cattle; **~vogel** *m* migratory bird; **~zwang** *m (Chess)* zugzwang; **unter ~zwang stehen** *(fig)* to be in a tight spot.

zuhaben *vi sep irreg (col: Geschäft)* to be closed.

zuhalten *sep irreg* **1** *vt* to hold shut. **sich** *(dat)* **die Nase ~** to hold one's nose; **sich** *(dat)* **die Augen/Ohren ~** to put one's hands over one's eyes/ears. **2** *vi* **auf etw** *(acc)* **~** to head straight for sth.

Zuhälter(in *f)* *m* - pimp, procurer.

zuhängen *vt sep* to cover up *or* over.

zuhauen *sep irreg* **1** *vt Baumstamm* to hew; *Stein* to trim. **2** *vi* to strike out.

zuhause *adv* at home.

Zuhause *nt no pl* home.

zuheilen *vi sep aux sein* to heal up.

Zuhilfenahme *f*: **unter ~ von** *or +gen* with the aid of.

zuhinterst *adv* right at the back.

zuhören *vi sep* to listen *(dat* to*)*. **hör mal zu!** *(drohend)* now (just) listen (to me)!

Zuhörer *m* listener. **die ~** *(das Publikum)* the audience *sing.*

zujubeln *vi sep* **jdm ~** to cheer sb.

zukehren *vt sep (zuwenden)* to turn. **jdm das Gesicht ~** to turn to face sb; **jdm den Rücken ~** *(lit, fig)* to turn one's back on sb.

zuklappen *sep* **1** *vt Buch, Deckel* to close. **2** *vi aux sein (Tür etc)* to click shut.

zukleben *vt sep Briefumschlag* to stick down.

zuknallen *vti sep (vi: aux sein) (col)* to slam *or* bang (shut).

zukneifen *vti sep irreg* to pinch; *Augen* to screw up; *Mund* to shut tight(ly).

zuknöpfen *vt sep* to button (up); *siehe* **zugeknöpft.**

zukommen *vi sep irreg aux sein* **(a) auf jdn/etw ~** to come toward(s) *or (direkt)* up to sb/sth; **die Aufgabe, die nun auf uns zukommt** the task which now confronts us; **die Dinge auf sich** *(acc)* **~ lassen** to take things as they come. **(b) jdm etw ~ lassen** *Brief etc* to send sb sth; *(schenken auch), Hilfe* to give sb sth. **(c)** *+dat (geziemen)* to befit, to become. **diesem Treffen kommt große Bedeutung zu** this meeting is of the utmost importance.

zukriegen *vt sep (col)* = **zubekommen.**

Zukunft *f no pl (auch Gram)* future. **in ferner/naher ~** in the distant/near future; **unsere gemeinsame ~** our future together.

zukünftig **1** *adj* future. **meine Z~e** *(col)*/**mein Z~er** *(col)* my future wife/husband. **2** *adv* in future.

Zukunfts-: **~aussichten** *pl* future prospects *pl*; **~glaube** *m* belief in the future; **z~gläubig** *adj* believing in the future; **~musik** *f (fig col)* pie in the sky *(col)*; **~pläne** *pl* plans *pl* for the future; **~roman** *m* novel dealing with the future; *(Science-fiction)* science fiction novel; **z~weisend** *adj* forward-looking.

zulächeln *vi sep* **jdm ~** to smile at sb.

Zulage *f* **(a)** *(Geld~)* extra pay *no indef art.* **eine ~ von 100 Mark** an extra 100 marks pay. **(b)** *(Gehaltserhöhung)* rise *(Brit)*, raise *(US)*.

zulande *adv* **bei uns ~** in our country.

zulangen *vi sep (col: Dieb, beim Essen)* to help oneself.

zulassen *vt sep irreg* **(a)** *(Zugang gewähren)* to admit; *(amtlich)* to authorize; *Arzt* to register; *Kraftfahrzeug* to license; *Rechtsanwalt, Prüfling* to admit. **(b)** *(dulden, gestatten)* to allow, to permit. **~, daß etw passiert** to allow sth to happen. **(c)** *(geschlossen lassen)* to leave closed.

zulässig *adj* permissible, permitted. **~es Gesamtgewicht** *(Mot)* maximum laden weight; **~e Höchstgeschwindigkeit** (upper) speed limit.

Zulassung *f* **(a)** *no pl (Erlaubnis, Gewährung von Zugang)* admission; *(amtlich)* authorization; *(von Kfz)* licensing; *(als Arzt)* registration. **(b)** *(Dokument)* papers *pl*; *(Lizenz)* licence *(Brit)*, license *(US)*.

Zulauf *m no pl* **großen ~ haben** *(Geschäft)* to be very popular.

zulaufen *vi sep irreg aux sein* **(a) auf jdn/etw ~** to run towards sb/sth. **(b)** *(auslaufen)* **spitz ~** to taper. **(c)** *(Wasser etc)* **laß noch etwas kaltes Wasser ~** run in some more cold water. **(d)** *(Tier)* **jdm ~** to stray into sb's house/place; **eine zugelaufene Katze** a stray (cat).

zulegen *sep* **1** *vt* **(a)** *(dazulegen)* to put on. **(b)** *Geld* to add; *(bei Verlustgeschäft)* to lose. **die fehlenden 20 DM legte meine Mutter zu** my mother made up the remaining DM 20. **(c) etwas Tempo ~** *(col)* to get a move on *(col)*. **2** *vi (col)* **(a)** *(an Gewicht)* to put on (weight). **(b)** *(sich mehr anstrengen) (col)* to pull one's finger out *(col)*; *(Sport)* to step up the pace *(col)*. **3** *vr* **sich** *(dat)* **etw/jdn ~** *(col)* to get oneself sth/sb.

zuleide *adv* **jdm etwas ~ tun** to harm sb.

zuleiten *vt sep Wasser etc* to supply; *Post, Waren* to send on.

Zuleitung *f (Tech)* supply.

zuletzt *adv* **(a)** in the end. **~ kam sie doch** she came in the end; **wir blieben bis ~** we stayed to the very end; **ganz ~** at the very last moment. **(b)** *(als letzte(r, s), an letzter Stelle)* last. **ich kam ~** I came last; **ganz ~** last of all; **nicht ~ wegen** not least because of.

zuliebe *adv* **etw jdm ~ tun** to do sth for sb's sake.

Zulieferbetrieb *m (Econ)* supplier.

Zulu ['tsu:lu] *mf* **-(s)** Zulu.

zum = zu dem.

zumachen *sep* **1** *vt (schließen)* to close; *(col: auflösen) Laden etc* to close (down). **2** *vi (col)* **(a)** *(den Laden ~)* to close (down); *(fig)* to call it a day. **(b)** *(sich beeilen)* to hurry up.

zumal **1** *conj* **~ (da)** especially as. **2** *adv (besonders)* especially.

zumauern *vt sep* to brick up, to wall up.

zumeist *adv* mostly.

zumessen *vt sep irreg Zeit* to allocate *(dat* for*)*; *Schuld* to attribute *(jdm* to sb*)*; *Bedeutung* to attach *(dat* to*)*.

zumindest *adv* at least.

zumutbar *adj* reasonable. **es ist mir nicht ~, das zu tun** I can't be expected to do that.

zumute *adv* **mir ist traurig ~** I feel sad; **mir ist gar nicht lächerlich ~** I'm not in a laughing mood.

zumuten *vt sep* **jdm etw ~** to expect sth of sb; **Sie wollen mir doch wohl nicht ~, diesen Unsinn zu lesen** you surely don't expect me to read this nonsense; **sich** *(dat)* **zuviel ~** to take on too much.

Zumutung *f* unreasonable demand; *(Unverschämtheit)* nerve *(col)*. **das ist eine ~!** that's a bit much!

zunächst *adv* **(a)** *(zuerst)* first (of all). **~ einmal** first of all. **(b)** *(vorläufig)* for the time being.

zunageln *vt sep Fenster etc* to nail up; *(mit Brettern, Pappe etc)* to board up; *Kiste etc* to nail down.

zunähen *vt sep* to sew up.

Zunahme *f* **-n** increase *(gen, an +dat* in*)*.

Zuname *m* surname, last name.

zünden **1** *vi* to ignite; *(Streichholz)* to light; *(Motor)* to fire; *(Sprengkörper)* to go off; *(fig)* to kindle enthusiasm. **2** *vt* to ignite; *Rakete* to fire; *Sprengkörper* to detonate; *Feuerwerkskörper* to let off.

zündend *adj (fig)* stirring.

Zunder *m* - tinder. **~ kriegen/jdm ~ geben** *(col)* to get/to give sb a good hiding *(col)*.

Zünder *m* - igniter; *(für Sprengstoff, Bombe etc)* fuse; *(für Mine)* detonator.

Zünd-: **~flamme** *f* pilot light; **~holz** *nt* match; **~hütchen** *nt* percussion cap; **~kabel** *nt (Aut)* plug lead; **~kapsel** *f* detonator; **~kerze** *f (Aut)* spark plug; **~plättchen** *nt* cap; **~schloß** *nt (Aut)* ignition lock; **~schlüssel** *m (Aut)* ignition key; **~schnur** *f* fuse; **~spule** *f* ignition coil; **~stoff** *m* inflammable matter; *(Sprengstoff)* explosives *pl*; *(fig)* inflammatory stuff.

Zündung *f* ignition. **die ~ einstellen** *(Aut)* to adjust the timing.

zunehmen *vi sep irreg* **1** *vi* to increase; *(an Weisheit etc)* to gain *(an +dat* in*)*; *(an Gewicht)* to put on weight; *(Mond)* to wax. **2** *vt (Mensch: an Gewicht)* to gain.

zunehmend 1 *adj* increasing, growing. **bei ~em Alter** with advancing age; **wir haben ~en Mond** there is a crescent moon; **in ~em Maße** to an increasing degree. **2** *adv* increasingly.

zuneigen *sep +dat* **1** *vi* to be inclined towards. **jdm zugeneigt sein** *(geh)* to be well disposed towards sb. **2** *vr* to lean towards. **sich dem Ende ~** *(geh)* to be drawing to a close; *(Vorräte etc)* to be running out.

Zuneigung *f* affection *(zu* for*)*.

Zunft *f* **¨-e** *(Hist)* guild; *(hum col)* brotherhood.

zünftig *adj Kleidung* professional; *(col: ordentlich)* proper. **eine ~e Ohrfeige** a hefty box on the ears.

Zunge *f* **-n** tongue; *(von Waage)* pointer. **das brennt auf der ~** that burns the tongue; **jdm die ~ herausstrecken** to stick one's tongue out at sb; **eine spitze/lose ~ haben** to have a sharp/loose tongue; **böse ~n behaupten, ...** malicious gossip has it ...; **mir liegt das Wort auf der ~** the word is on the tip of my tongue; **mir hängt die ~ zum Hals heraus** *(col)* my tongue is hanging out; *(erschöpft)* I'm exhausted.

züngeln *vi (Flammen)* to lick.

Zungen-: **~brecher** *m* tongue-twister; **z~fertig** *adj (geh)* fluent; *(pej)* glib; **~kuß** *m* French kiss; **~spitze** *f* tip of the tongue; **~wurst** *f* tongue sausage.

Zünglein *nt*: **das ~ an der Waage sein** *(fig)* to tip the scales.

zunichte *adv* **~ machen/werden** *(geh)* to ruin/to be ruined.

zunicken *vi sep* **jdm ~** to nod to sb; **jdm freundlich ~** to give sb a friendly nod.

zunutze *adv* **sich** *(dat)* **etw ~ machen** *(verwenden)* to make use of sth; *(ausnutzen)* to take advantage of sth.

zu|oberst *adv* right at the top.

zu|ordnen *vt sep +dat* to assign to.

zupacken *vi sep (col)* **(a)** *(zugreifen)* to make a grab for it *etc*. **(b)** *(bei der Arbeit)* to get down to it. **(c)** *(helfen)* **mit ~** to give me/them *etc* a hand.

zupfen *vti* to pick; *Unkraut, Fäden* to pull. **jdn am Ärmel** *etc* **~** to tug at sb's sleeve *etc*; **sich** *(dat or acc)* **am Bart ~** to pull at one's beard.

Zupf|instrument *nt (Mus)* plucked string instrument.

zuprosten *vi sep* **jdm ~** to drink sb's health.

zur = zu der.

zuraten *vi sep irreg* **jdm ~, etw zu tun** to advise sb to do sth.

zurechnen *vt sep* **(a)** *(col: dazurechnen)* to add to. **(b)** *(fig: zuordnen)* to class *(dat* with*)*; *Kunstwerk etc* to ascribe *(dat* to*)*.

Zurechnungs-: **z~fähig** *adj* of sound mind; *(esp Jur, fig col)* compos mentis *pred*; **~fähigkeit** *f* soundness of mind; **verminderte ~fähigkeit** diminished responsibility.

zurecht-: **~biegen** *vt sep irreg* to bend into shape; *(fig)* to twist; **er hat alles wieder ~gebogen** *(col)* he has straightened everything out again; **~finden** *vr sep irreg* to find one's way *(in +dat* around*)*; **sich in der Welt nicht mehr ~finden** not to be able to cope with the world any longer; **~kommen** *vi sep irreg aux sein* **(a)** *(fig)* to get on; *(schaffen)* to cope; *(genug haben)* to have enough; **(b)** *(rechtzeitig kommen)* to come in time; **(c)** *(finanziell)* to manage; **~legen** *vt sep irreg* to lay out ready; **sich** *(dat)* **etw ~legen** to get sth out ready; *(fig)* to work sth out; **~machen** *vt sep (col)* **(a)** *Zimmer, Essen etc* to prepare; *Bett* to make up; **(b)** *(anziehen)* to dress; *(schminken)* to make up; **sich ~machen** to get ready; to put on one's make-up; **~rücken** *vt sep (lit, fig)* to put straight; *Brille, Hut etc* to adjust; **~stutzen** *vt sep* to trim; *(fig)* to lick into shape; **~weisen** *vt sep irreg (form)* to rebuke; *Schüler etc* to reprimand; **Z~weisung** *f siehe vt* rebuke; reprimand.

zureden *vi sep* **jdm ~** to encourage sb; *(überreden)* to persuade sb; **wenn du ihm gut zuredest, hilft er dir** if you talk to him nicely, he'll help you.

zureiten *sep irreg* **1** *vt Pferd* to break in. **2** *vi aux sein* **auf jdn/etw ~** to ride toward(s) sb/sth.

zurichten *vt sep* **(a)** *Essen etc* to prepare. **(b)** *(verunstalten)* to make a mess of; *(verletzen)* to injure. **jdn übel ~** to knock sb about.

zürnen *vi (geh)* **jdm ~** to be angry with sb.

zurück *adv* back; *(mit Zahlungen)* behind; *(fig: zurückgeblieben: von Kind)* backward. **in Mathematik (sehr) ~ sein** *(fig)* to be (really) behind in maths; **~!** get back!; **~ an Absender** return to sender; **hinter jdm ~ sein** *(fig)* to lie behind sb; **es gibt kein Z~ (mehr)** there's no going back.

zurück-: **~behalten*** *vt sep irreg* to keep (back); **er hat Schäden ~behalten** he suffered lasting damage; **~bekommen*** *vt sep irreg* to get back; **~berufen*** *vt sep irreg* to recall; **~bewegen*** *vtr sep* to move back; **~bilden** *vr sep (Geschwür)* to recede; *(Muskel)* to become wasted; *(Biol)* to regress.

zurückbleiben *vi sep irreg aux sein* **(a)** to stay behind. **(b)** *(übrigbleiben)* to be left, to remain. **ihm ist eine Narbe zurückgeblieben** he has been left with a scar. **(c)** *(nicht Schritt halten)* to fall behind; *(in Entwicklung)* to be retarded; *(Sport)* to be behind. **ihre Leistung blieb hinter meinen Erwartungen zurück** her performance did not come up to my expectations; *siehe* **zurückgeblieben.**

zurück-: **~blicken** *vi sep* to look back *(auf +acc* at*)*; *(fig)* to look back *(auf +acc* on*)*; **~bringen** *vt sep irreg* to bring back; *(wieder wegbringen)* to take back; **~denken** *vi sep irreg* to think back *(an +acc* to*)*; **so weit ich ~denken kann** as far as I can recall; **~drängen** *vt sep* to force back; *(Mil)* to drive back; **~drehen** *vt sep* to turn back; **~dürfen** *vi sep irreg (col)* to be allowed back; **~erhalten*** *vt sep irreg* to get back; **~erinnern*** *vr sep* to remember; **~erobern*** *vt sep (Mil)* to recapture; **~erstatten*** *vt sep* to reimburse; **~fahren** *sep irreg* **1** *vi aux sein* to return; **2** *vt* to drive back; **~fallen** *vi sep irreg aux sein* to fall back; *(Sport)* to drop back; *(in Leistungen)* to fall behind; *(fig) (an Besitzer)* to revert *(an +acc* to*)*; *(Schande, Vorwurf etc)* to reflect *(auf +acc* on*)*; **~finden** *vi sep irreg* to find the way back; **~fliegen** *vti sep irreg (vi aux sein)* to fly back; **~fließen** *vi sep irreg aux sein (lit, fig)* to flow back; **~fordern** *vt sep* **etw ~fordern** to ask for sth back; **~fragen** *vi sep* to ask a question back; *(wegen Auskunft)* to check back *(bei* with*)*.

zurückführen *sep* **1** *vt* **(a)** *(zurückbringen)* to lead back. **(b)** *(ableiten aus)* to put down to. **2** *vi* to lead back. **es führt kein Weg zurück** *(fig)* there's no going back.

zurückgeben *vt sep irreg* to give back; *Ball, Beleidigung* to return.

zurückgeblieben *adj* **geistig/körperlich ~**

mentally/physically retarded.

zurückgehen *vi sep irreg aux sein* **(a)** to go back *(nach, in +acc* to, *fig: auf +acc* to*)*. **er ging zwei Schritte zurück** he took two steps back; **Waren/ Essen ~ lassen** to send back goods/food. **(b)** *(zurückweichen)* to retreat, to fall back; *(fig: abnehmen)* to go down; *(Geschäft, Umsatz)* to fall off; *(Schmerz, Blutung)* to ease

zurück-: ~gezogen *adj Mensch* retiring; *Lebensweise* secluded; **er lebt sehr ~gezogen** he lives a very secluded life; **~greifen** *vi sep irreg (fig)* to fall back *(auf +acc* on*)*; *(zeitlich)* to go back *(auf +acc* to*)*; **~haben** *vt sep irreg (col)* to have back; **ich will mein Geld ~haben** I want my money back.

zurückhalten *sep irreg* **1** *vt* to hold back; *(aufhalten) jdn* to hold up; *(nicht freigeben) Informationen* to withhold; *(unterdrücken) Tränen* to keep back. **jdn von etw** *(dat)* **~** to keep sb from sth. **2** *vr (sich beherrschen)* to restrain oneself; *(im Hintergrund bleiben)* to keep in the background; *(bei Verhandlung etc)* to keep a low profile. **Sie müssen sich beim Essen sehr ~** you must cut down a lot on what you eat. **3** *vi* **mit etw ~** *(verheimlichen)* to hold sth back.

zurückhaltend *adj* restrained; *(reserviert)* reserved; *Empfang, Nachfrage* low-key. **sich ~ über etw** *(acc)* **äußern** to be restrained in one's comments about sth.

Zurück-: ~haltung *f siehe adj* restraint; reserve; **z~holen** *vt sep* to fetch back; **z~kaufen** *vt sep* to buy back; **z~kehren** *vi sep aux sein* to return *(von, aus* from; *nach, zu* to*)*; **z~kommen** *vi sep irreg aux sein* to come back; **z~können** *vi sep irreg (col)* to be able to go back; **ich kann nicht mehr z~** *(fig)* there's no going back!; **z~kriegen** *vt sep (col)* to get back; **z~lassen** *vt sep irreg* **(a)** to leave; *(liegenlassen, fig: übertreffen)* to leave behind; **(b)** *(col: z~kehren lassen)* to allow back; **z~laufen** *vi sep irreg aux sein* to run back; *(z~gehen)* to walk back.

zurücklegen *sep* **1** *vt* **(a)** to put back. **(b)** *Kopf* to lay *or* lean back. **(c)** *(aufbewahren)* to put aside; *(sparen)* to lay aside. **jdm etw ~** to keep sth for sb. **(d)** *Strecke* to cover, to do. **2** *vr* to lie back.

Zurück-: z~lehnen *vtr sep* to lean back; **z~liegen** *vi sep irreg* **der Unfall liegt etwa eine Woche z~** the accident was about a week ago; **z~melden** *vtr sep* to report back; **z~müssen** *vi sep irreg (col)* to have to go back; **~nahme** *f* **-n** *siehe* **z~nehmen** taking back; revoking; reversal; withdrawal; **z~nehmen** *vt sep irreg* to take back; *Verordnung* to revoke; *Entscheidung* to reverse; *Angebot* to withdraw; **sein Wort z~nehmen** to go back on one's word; **z~prallen** *vi sep aux sein* to bounce back; **z~reichen** *vi sep (Tradition etc)* to go back *(in +acc* to*)*; **z~reißen** *vt sep irreg* to pull back; **z~rollen** *vti sep (vi: aux sein)* to roll back; **z~rufen** *vti sep irreg* to call back; *Botschafter, fehlerhafte Autos* to recall; **jdn ins Leben z~rufen** to bring sb back to life; **jdm/sich etw ins Gedächtnis z~rufen** to remind sb of sth/to recall sth; **z~schalten** *vi sep* to change back; **z~schauen** *vi sep* to look back *(auf +acc (lit)* at, *(fig)* on*)*; **z~schicken** *vt sep* to send back; **z~schieben** *vt sep irreg* to push back.

zurückschlagen *sep irreg* **1** *vt* **(a)** *Ball* to return; *Angriff etc* to repulse. **(b)** *Decke* to fold back; *Kragen* to turn down. **2** *vi* to hit back.

zurück-: ~schrauben *vt sep* **seine Ansprüche ~schrauben** to lower one's sights; **~schrecken** *vi sep irreg aux sein or haben (fig)* to shy away *(vor +dat* from*)*; **vor nichts ~schrecken** to stop at nothing; **~sehen** *vi sep irreg* to look back *(auf +acc (lit)* at, *(fig)* on*)*; **~sehnen** *vr sep* to long to return *(nach* to*)*; **sich nach der guten alten Zeit ~sehnen** to long for the good old days; **~senden** *vt sep irreg* to send back.

zurücksetzen *sep* **1** *vt (nach hinten)* to move back; *(an früheren Platz)* to put back. **2** *vr* to sit back. **3** *vi (mit Fahrzeug)* to reverse, to back.

Zurück-: ~setzung *f (fig: Benachteiligung)* neglect; **z~sinken** *vi sep irreg aux sein* to sink back *(in +acc* into*)*; **z~spielen** *vti sep (Sport)* to play back; **z~stecken** *sep* **1** *vt* to put back; **2** *vi* **(a)** *(weniger Ansprüche stellen)* to lower one's expectations; **(b)** *(nachgeben)* to backtrack.

zurückstehen *vi sep irreg* **(a)** *(Haus etc)* to stand back. **(b)** *(hintangesetzt werden)* to take second place *(hinter +dat* to*)*.

zurückstellen *vt sep* **(a)** *(an seinen Platz, Uhr)* to put back; *(nach hinten)* to move back. **(b)** *Waren* to put aside *or* by. **(c)** *(fig) Schüler* to keep down. **jdn vom Wehrdienst ~** to defer sb's military service. **(d)** *(fig: verschieben)* to defer; *Bedenken etc* to put aside. **persönliche Interessen hinter etw** *(dat)* **~** to put one's personal interests after sth.

Zurück-: ~stellung *f (Aufschub, Mil)* deferment; **z~stoßen** *vt sep irreg* to push back; *(fig)* to reject; **z~stufen** *vt sep* to downgrade; **z~tragen** *vt sep irreg* to carry back; **z~treiben** *vt sep irreg* to drive back.

zurücktreten *sep irreg* **1** *vi aux sein* **(a)** to step back; *(fig: Hochwasser)* to go down. **bitte ~!** stand back, please!; **einen Schritt ~** to take a step back. **(b)** *(Regierung)* to resign; *(von einem Amt)* to step down. **(c)** *(von einem Vertrag etc)* to withdraw *(von* from*)*. **(d)** *(fig: geringer werden)* to decrease; *(Wald)* to recede. **hinter jdm/etw ~** to come second to sb/sth. **2** *vti (mit Fuß)* to kick back.

Zurück-: z~verfolgen* *vt sep (fig)* to trace back; **z~verlangen*** *vt sep* to demand back; **z~verlegen*** *vt sep* **(a)** *(zeitlich)* to set back; **(b)** *Front etc, Wohnsitz* to move back; **z~versetzen*** *sep* **1** *vt* **(a)** *(in alten Zustand)* to restore *(in +acc* to*)*; *(in andere Zeit)* to take back *(in +acc* to*)*; **(b)** *Beamte etc* to transfer back; **2** *vr* to think oneself back *(in +acc* to*)*; **z~verweisen*** *vt sep irreg* to refer back; *(Parl) Gesetzentwurf* to recommit; **z~weichen** *vi sep irreg aux sein* to shrink back *(vor +dat* from*)*; **z~weisen** *vt sep irreg* to reject; *Bittsteller* to turn away; *(an der Grenze)* to turn back; **~weisung** *f siehe vt* rejection; turning away; turning back; **z~werfen** *vt sep irreg Ball, Kopf* to throw back; *Feind auch* to repel; *Strahlen, Schall* to reflect; *(fig: wirtschaftlich)* to set back *(um* by*)*; **z~wollen** *vi sep (col)* to want to go back; **z~zahlen** *vt sep* to pay back.

zurückziehen *sep irreg* **1** *vt* to pull back; *Antrag, Klage etc* to withdraw. **2** *vr* to withdraw *(von* from*)*; *(von Tätigkeit)* to retire; *siehe* **zurückgezogen. 3** *vi aux sein* to move back.

Zuruf *m* shout; *(aufmunternd)* cheer.

zurufen *vi sep irreg* **jdm etw ~** to shout sth to sb.

Zusage *f* **-n** **(a)** *(Verpflichtung)* commitment. **(b)** *(Annahme)* acceptance. **(c)** *(Versprechen)* promise.

zusagen *vi sep* **(a)** *(annehmen)* **(jdm) ~** to accept. **(b)** *(gefallen)* **jdm ~** to appeal to sb.

zusammen *adv* together. **wir hatten ~ 100 Mark zum Ausgeben** between us we had 100 marks to spend; **er verdient mehr als wir alle ~** he earns more than the rest of us put together; **das macht ~ 50 Mark** that makes 50 marks altogether.

Zusammen-: ~arbeit *f* co-operation; **z~arbeiten** *vi sep* to co-operate; **~ballung** *f* accumulation; **~bau** *m no pl* assembly; **z~bauen** *vt sep* to assemble; **etw wieder z~bauen** to reassemble sth; **z~beißen** *vt sep irreg* **die Zähne z~beißen** *(lit)* to clench one's teeth; *(fig)* to grit one's teeth; **z~bekommen*** *vt sep irreg* to get together; *Wortlaut etc* to remember; **z~binden** *vt sep irreg* to tie together; **z~bleiben** *vi sep irreg aux sein* to stay together; **z~brauen** *sep* **1** *vt (col)* to concoct; **2** *vr (Gewitter, Unheil etc)* to be brewing.

zusammenbrechen *vi sep irreg aux sein* to collapse; *(Mensch auch, Verhandlungen, Telefonverbindungen)* to break down; *(Verkehr etc)* to come to a standstill.

zusammenbringen *vt sep irreg* to collect; *Geld* to raise; *(ins Gedächtnis zurückrufen)* to remember; *(bekannt machen) Menschen* to bring together.

Zusammenbruch *m (von Beziehungen, Kommunikation, Nerven~)* breakdown; *(fig)* collapse.

zusammen-: **~drängen** *vtr* to crowd together; **~drücken** *vt sep* to press together; **z~fahren** *sep irreg* **1** *vi aux sein* **(a)** *(~stoßen)* to collide; **(b)** *(erschrecken)* to start; **2** *vt (col) Fahrzeug* to wreck; **~fallen** *vi sep irreg aux sein* **(a)** *(einstürzen)* to collapse; **(b)** *(Ereignisse)* to coincide; **~falten** *vt sep* to fold up.

zusammenfassen *sep* **1** *vt* to combine *(zu* in*)*. **2** *vti (das Fazit ziehen)* to summarize. **~d kann man sagen, ...** to sum up, one can say ...

Zusammen-: **~fassung** *f* **(a)** combination; **(b)** *(Überblick)* summary; **z~fegen** *vt sep* to sweep together; **z~fließen** *vi sep irreg aux sein* to meet; *(Farben)* to run together; **~fluß** *m* confluence; **z~fügen** *sep* **1** *vt* to join together; *(Tech)* to fit together; **etw zu etw z~fügen** to join/fit sth together to make sth; **2** *vr* to fit together; **z~führen** *vt sep* to bring together; *Familie* to reunite; **z~gehen** *vi sep irreg aux sein (sich vereinen)* to unite; *(Linien etc)* to meet; **z~gehören*** *vi sep* to belong together; *(Gegenstände)* to go together, to match; **z~gehörig** *adj Kleidungsstücke etc* matching; **~gehörigkeit** *f (Einheit)* unity; **~gehörigkeitsgefühl** *nt* sense of belonging; *(in Familie)* sense of a common bond; **z~gesetzt** *adj* **aus etw ~gesetzt sein** to be composed of sth; **z~gewürfelt** *adj* motley; **z~haben** *vt sep irreg (col)* **etw z~haben** to have got sth together; **~halt** *m no pl* cohesion; *(Tech)* (cohesive) strength.

zusammenhalten *sep irreg* **1** *vt* to hold together; *(col) Geld etc* to hold on to. **2** *vi* to hold together; *(fig: Freunde, Gruppe etc)* to stick together.

Zusammenhang *m* connection *(von, zwischen +dat* between*)*; *(im Text)* context. **etw mit etw in ~ bringen** to connect sth with sth; **im** *or* **in ~ mit etw stehen** to be connected with sth; **etw aus dem ~ reißen** to take sth out of its context.

zusammenhängen *vi sep irreg* to be joined (together); *(fig)* to be connected. **~d** *Erzählung* coherent.

zusammenhang(s)los **1** *adj* disjointed. **2** *adv* incoherently.

Zusammen-: **z~hauen** *vt sep irreg (col) (zerstören)* to smash to pieces; **jdn z~hauen** to beat sb up; **z~heften** *vt sep* to staple together; **z~heilen** *vi sep aux sein* to heal (up); *(Knochen)* to knit (together); **z~kehren** *vt sep* to sweep together; **z~klappbar** *adj* folding; **z~klappen** *sep* **1** *vt* to fold up; *Schirm* to shut; **2** *vi aux sein* **(a)** *(Stuhl etc)* to collapse; **(b)** *(fig col: vor Erschöpfung)* to flake out *(col)*; **z~kleben** *vti sep (vi: aux haben or sein)* to stick together; **z~kneifen** *vt sep irreg Lippen etc* to press together; *Augen* to screw up; **z~knüllen** *vt sep* to crumple up; **z~kommen** *vi sep irreg aux sein* to meet; *(Umstände)* to combine; *(Geld)* to be collected; **er kommt viel mit Menschen zusammen** he meets a lot of people; **z~kratzen** *vt sep* to scrape together; **z~kriegen** *vt sep (col)* = **z~bekommen**; **~kunft** *f, pl* **~künfte** meeting; *(zwanglos)* get-together; **z~lassen** *vt sep irreg* to leave together.

zusammenlaufen *vi sep irreg aux sein* **(a)** *(an eine Stelle laufen)* to gather; *(Flüssigkeit)* to collect. **(b)** *(Farben)* to run together; *(Linien)* to intersect. **(c)** *(Stoff)* to shrink.

zusammenleben *vi sep* to live together.

Zusammenleben *nt* living together *no art.* **das ~ der Menschen** the social life of man; **das menschliche ~** social existence.

zusammen-: **~legen** *vt sep* **(a)** to fold (up); **(b)** *(stapeln)* to pile together; **(c)** *(vereinigen)* to put together, to combine; *Grundstücke* to join; *Termine* to hold together; **sie legten ihr Geld ~** they pooled their money; **~nähen** *vt sep* to sew *or* stitch together.

zusammennehmen *sep irreg* **1** *vt* to gather up; *Mut* to summon up; *Gedanken* to collect. **alles zusammengenommen** all in all. **2** *vr* to pull oneself together.

Zusammen-: **z~packen** *vt sep* to pack up together; **pack (deine Sachen) z~!** get packed!; **z~passen** *vi sep* to be suited to each other; *(Farben, Stile)* to go together; **z~pferchen** *vt sep* to herd together; **~prall** *m* collision; *(fig)* clash; **z~prallen** *vi sep aux sein* to collide; *(fig)* to clash; **z~pressen** *vt sep* to press together; **z~raffen** *sep* **1** *vt* **(a)** *(fig) Mut* to summon up; **(b)** *(fig pej: anhäufen)* to amass, to pile up; **2** *vr* to pull oneself together; **z~rechnen** *vt sep* to add up; **z~reimen** *vt sep (col)* **das kann ich mir nicht z~reimen** I can't make head or tail of this; **z~reißen** *vr sep irreg* to pull oneself together; **z~rollen** *sep* **1** *vt* to roll up; **2** *vr* to curl up; *(Schlange)* to coil up; **z~rotten** *vr sep (pej)* to gang up *(gegen* against*)*; *(in aufrührerischer Absicht)* to form a mob; **z~rücken** *sep* **1** *vt Möbel etc* to move closer together; **2** *vi aux sein* to move up closer; **z~rufen** *vt sep irreg* to call together; **z~scharen** *vr sep* to gather; **z~schießen** *vt sep irreg* to shoot up; **z~schlagen** *sep irreg* **1** *vt* **(a)** *(aneinanderschlagen)* to knock together; *Hacken* to click; **die Hände überm Kopf z~schlagen** to throw up one's hands in horror; **(b)** *(verprügeln)* to beat up; *(zerschlagen)* to smash up; **2** *vi aux sein* **über jdm/etw z~schlagen** *(Wellen etc)* to close over sb/sth; **z~schließen** *vr sep irreg* to combine; *(Comm, Pol)* to merge; **~schluß** *m siehe vr* combining; merger; **z~schmelzen** *vi sep irreg aux sein* **(a)** *(verschmelzen)* to fuse; **(b)** *(zerschmelzen)* to melt (away); *(Anzahl)* to dwindle; **z~schreiben** *vt sep irreg* **(a)** *Wörter* to write together; **(b)** *(pej: verfassen)* **was der für einen Mist zusammenschreibt** what a load of rubbish he writes; **z~schrumpfen** *vi sep aux sein* to shrivel up; *(fig)* to dwindle *(auf +acc* to*)*.

zusammensein *vi sep irreg aux sein* **mit jdm ~** to be with sb; *(col: befreundet)* to be going out with sb; *(euph: mit jdm schlafen)* to sleep with sb.

Zusammensein *nt* **(a)** being together. **(b)** *(Zusammenkunft)* get-together.

zusammensetzen *sep* **1** *vt* to put together. **2** *vr* **(a)** to sit together; *(um etwas zu tun)* to get together. **(b)** **sich ~ aus** to consist of.

Zusammen-: **~setzung** *f (Struktur)* composition; *(Mischung)* mixture; **das Team in dieser ~setzung** the team in this line-up; **z~sinken** *vi sep irreg aux sein* **(in sich) z~sinken** to slump; *(Gebäude)* to cave in; **z~sparen** *vt sep* to save up; **~spiel** *nt* teamwork; *(von Kräften etc)* interaction; **z~stauchen** *vt sep (col)* to give a dressing-down *(col)*; **z~stecken** *sep* **1** *vt Einzelteile* to fit together; *(mit Nadeln etc)* to pin together; **die Köpfe z~stecken** *(col)* to put their/our *etc* heads together; *(flüstern)* to whisper to each other; **2** *vi (col)* to be together; **z~stehen** *vi sep irreg* to stand together; *(Gegenstände)* to be together; *(fig)* to stand by each other.

zusammenstellen *vt sep* to put together; *(nach System)* to arrange; *Liste* to draw up.

Zusammenstellung *f* **(a)** *siehe vt* putting together; arranging; drawing up. **(b)** *(nach System)* arrangement; *(Liste)* list; *(Zusammensetzung)* composition; *(Übersicht)* survey.

Zusammenstoß *m* collision, crash; *(Mil, fig:*

Streit) clash.

zusammenstoßen *sep irreg* **1** *vi aux sein (z~prallen)* to collide; *(Mil, fig: sich streiten)* to clash. **mit jdm ~** to collide with sb; *(fig)* to clash with sb; **sie stießen mit den Köpfen zusammen** they banged their heads together. **2** *vt* to knock together.

Zusammen-: z~streichen *vt sep irreg* to cut (down) *(auf +acc* to*)*; **z~strömen** *vi sep aux sein (Menschen)* to flock together; **z~stürzen** *vi sep aux sein (einstürzen)* to collapse; **z~suchen** *vt sep* to collect (together*)*; **sich** *(dat)* **etw z~suchen** to find sth; **z~tragen** *vt sep irreg* to collect; **z~treffen** *vi sep irreg aux sein (Menschen)* to meet; *(Ereignisse)* to coincide; **mit jdm z~treffen** to meet sb; **z~treten** *vi sep irreg aux sein (Vorstand etc)* to meet; **z~trommeln** *vt sep (col)* to round up *(col)*; **z~tun** *sep irreg* **1** *vt (col)* to put together; *(vermischen)* to mix; **2** *vr* to get together; **z~wachsen** *vi sep irreg aux sein* to grow together; *(Wunde)* to close; *(Knochen)* to knit; **z~wirken** *vi sep* to combine; **z~zählen** *vt sep* to add up.

zusammenziehen *sep irreg* **1** *vt* **(a)** to draw together; *(verengen)* to narrow; *Augenbrauen* to knit. **(b)** *(fig) Truppen, Polizei* to assemble. **(c)** *(kürzen) Wörter etc* to contract; *Zahlen* to add together. **2** *vr (esp Biol, Sci)* to contract; *(Gewitter)* to be brewing. **3** *vi aux sein* to move in together.

zusammenzucken *vi sep aux sein* to start.

Zusatz *m* addition; *(zu Gesetz)* rider; *(Beimischung)* additive.

Zusatz- *in cpds* supplementary; **~bestimmung** *f* supplementary provision; **~gerät** *nt* attachment.

zusätzlich 1 *adj* additional. **2** *adv* in addition.

Zusatz-: ~mittel *nt*, **~stoff** *m* additive.

zuschanzen *vt sep (col)* **jdm etw ~** to make sure sb gets sth.

zuschauen *vi sep* = **zusehen.**

Zuschauer *m* - spectator; *(TV)* viewer; *(Theat)* member of the audience; *(Beistehender)* onlooker. **die ~** *pl* the spectators *pl*; *(TV)* the viewers *pl; (Theat)* the audience *sing.*

Zuschauer-: ~raum *m* auditorium; **~tribüne** *f (esp Sport)* stand.

zuschicken *vt sep* **jdm etw ~** to send sth to sb *or* sb sth; **sich** *(dat)* **etw ~ lassen** to send for sth.

zuschieben *vt sep irreg* **(a) jdm etw ~** to push sth over to sb; **jdm die Schuld ~** to put the blame on sb. **(b)** *(schließen)* to push shut.

zuschießen *sep irreg* **1** *vt* **(a) jdm den Ball ~** to kick the ball (over) to sb. **(b)** *Geld etc* to contribute. **Geld für etw ~** to put money towards sth. **2** *vi aux sein (col)* **auf jdn ~** to shoot up to sb.

Zuschlag *m* **(a)** *(Erhöhung)* surcharge *(esp Comm, Econ)*; *(Rail)* supplement *(für +acc* on*)*. **(b) er erhielt den ~** *(bei Auktion)* it went to him; *(bei Auftragsvergabe)* he won the order.

zuschlagen *sep irreg* **1** *vt* **(a)** *Tür, Fenster* to slam (shut). **(b)** *Gebiet* to annex *(dat* to*)*. **2** *vi* **(a)** *(kräftig schlagen)* to strike *(auch fig)*. **schlag zu!** hit me/him/it *etc!* **(b)** *aux sein (Tür)* to slam (shut).

Zuschlag(s)- *(Rail)*: **~karte** *f* supplementary ticket; **z~pflichtig** *adj Zug* subject to a supplement.

zuschließen *vt sep irreg* to lock; *Laden* to lock up.

zuschmieren *vt sep (col)* to smear over; *Löcher* to fill in.

zuschnappen *vi sep* **(a) der Hund schnappte zu** the dog snapped at me/him *etc.* **(b)** *aux sein (Schloß)* to snap shut.

zuschneiden *vt sep irreg* to cut to size; *(Sew)* to cut out. **auf etw** *(acc)* **zugeschnitten sein** *(fig)* to be geared to sth.

Zuschneider *m* cutter.

zuschneien *vi sep aux sein* to snow in.

Zuschnitt *m* **(a)** *no pl* cutting. **(b)** *(Form)* cut; *(fig)* calibre *(Brit)*, caliber *(US)*.

zuschnüren *vt sep* to tie up; *Schuhe, Mieder* to lace up. **die Angst schnürte ihm die Kehle zu** he was choked with fear.

zuschrauben *vt sep Hahn etc* to screw shut; *Deckel etc* to screw on.

zuschreiben *vt sep irreg (fig)* to ascribe *(dat* to*)*. **das hast du dir selbst zuzuschreiben** you've only got yourself to blame for that; **das ist nur seiner Dummheit zuzuschreiben** that can only be put down to his stupidity.

Zuschrift *f* letter; *(auf Anzeige)* reply.

zuschulden *adv:* **sich** *(dat)* **etwas ~ kommen lassen** to do something wrong.

Zuschuß *m* contribution; *(staatlich)* subsidy, grant.

Zuschußbetrieb *m* loss-making concern.

zuschütten *vt sep* to fill in; *(hin~)* to add.

zusehen *vi sep irreg* **(a)** to watch; *(unbeteiligter Zuschauer sein)* to look on; *(etw dulden)* to sit back (and watch). **jdm/(bei) einer Sache ~** to watch sb/sth; *(etw dulden)* to sit back and watch sth; **jdm bei der Arbeit ~** to watch sb working; **ich kann doch nicht ~, wie er ...** *(dulden)* I can't sit back and watch him ... **(b)** *(dafür sorgen)* **~, daß ...** to see to it that ...

zusehends *adv* visibly; *(rasch)* rapidly.

zusein *vi sep irreg aux sein (col)* to be shut.

zusenden *vt sep irreg* to send, to forward.

zusetzen *sep* **1** *vt (hinzufügen)* to add. **2** *vi* **jdm ~** *(unter Druck setzen)* to lean on sb *(col)*; *dem Gegner* to harass sb; *(schwer treffen)* to hit sb hard; *(Kälte, Krankheit etc)* to take a lot out of sb.

zusichern *vt sep* **jdm etw ~** to assure sb of sth; **mir wurde zugesichert, daß ...** I was assured that ...

Zusicherung *f* assurance.

zuspielen *vt sep Ball* to pass *(dat* to*)*. **jdm etw ~** *(fig)* to pass sth on to sb; *(der Presse)* to leak sth to sb.

zuspitzen *sep* **1** *vt Stock etc* to sharpen. **2** *vr* to be pointed; *(fig: Lage)* to become acute.

zusprechen *sep irreg* **1** *vt (Jur), Preis, Gewinn etc* to award; *Kind* to grant custody of. **jdm Mut/Trost ~** *(fig)* to encourage/comfort sb. **2** *vi* **dem Essen tüchtig ~** to tuck into the food.

zuspringen *vi sep irreg aux sein* **(a)** *(Schloß, Tür)* to snap shut. **(b) auf jdn ~** to leap towards sb.

Zuspruch *m no pl* **(a)** *(Worte)* words *pl*; *(Aufmunterung)* encouragement; *(tröstlich)* comfort. **(b) (großen) ~ finden** to be (very) popular.

Zustand *m* state; *(von Haus, Ware, Med)* condition; *(Lage)* state of affairs. **Zustände** *pl* conditions; **in gutem/schlechtem ~** in good/poor condition; *(Haus)* in good/bad repair; **in ungepflegtem/baufälligem ~** in a state of neglect/disrepair; **Zustände bekommen** *or* **kriegen** *(col)* to have a fit *(col)*; **das sind ja schöne Zustände!** *(iro)* that's a fine state of affairs! *(iro)*.

zustande *adv* **(a) ~ bringen** to manage; *Arbeit* to get done; *Ereignis, Frieden etc* to bring about. **(b) ~ kommen** *(erreicht werden)* to be achieved; *(geschehen)* to come about.

zuständig *adj* responsible; *Behörde etc* appropriate. **dafür ist er ~** that's his responsibility.

Zuständigkeit *f (Kompetenz)* competence; *(Verantwortlichkeit)* responsibility.

Zuständigkeitsbereich *m* area of responsibility.

zustatten *adj* **jdm ~ kommen** *(geh)* to come in useful for sb.

zustecken *vt sep* **(a)** *Kleid etc* to pin up. **(b) jdm etw ~** to slip sb sth.

zustehen *vi sep irreg* **ihm stehen 6 Wochen Urlaub zu** he is entitled to 6 weeks' holiday.

zusteigen *vi sep irreg aux sein* to get on, to board. **noch jemand zugestiegen?** *(in Zug)* tickets please!

zustellen *vt sep* **(a)** *Brief* to deliver. **(b)** *Tür etc* to block.
Zusteller(in *f***)** *m* - deliverer; *(Briefträger)* postman *(Brit)*, mailman *(US)*.
Zustellung *f* delivery.
zusteuern *sep* **1** *vi aux sein* **auf etw** *(acc)* ~ *(geh)* to head for sth; *(beim Gespräch)* to steer toward(s) sth. **2** *vt (beitragen)* to contribute *(zu* to*)*.
zustimmen *vi sep* **(einer Sache** *dat***)** ~ to agree (to sth); *(einwilligen)* to consent (to sth); **jdm (in einem Punkt)** ~ to agree with sb (on a point).
Zustimmung *f (Einverständnis)* agreement, assent; *(Einwilligung)* consent; *(Beifall)* approval. **allgemeine ~ finden** to meet with general approval.
zustopfen *vt sep* to stop up.
zustöpseln *vt sep Flasche* to stopper; *(mit Korken)* to cork.
zustoßen *sep irreg* **1** *vt Tür etc* to push shut. **2** *vi* **(a)** to plunge a/the knife/sword *etc* in; *(Stier etc)* to strike. **(b)** *(passieren) aux sein* **jdm** ~ to happen to sb.
Zustrom *m no pl (fig: Menschenmenge)* stream (of visitors *etc*); *(hineinströmend)* influx; *(Met)* inflow.
zuströmen *vi sep aux sein +dat (Fluß)* to flow toward(s); *(fig: Menschen)* to stream toward(s).
zustürzen *vi sep aux sein* **auf jdn/etw** ~ to rush up to sb/sth
zutage *adj* **etw ~ fördern** to unearth sth; **~ kommen** to come to light.
Zutaten *pl (Cook)* ingredients *pl*; *(fig)* accessories *pl*.
zuteil *adv (geh)* **jdm wird etw** ~ sb is granted sth, sth is granted to sb.
zuteilen *vt sep (jdm* to sb*)* to allocate; *Arbeitskraft* to assign.
Zuteilung *f siehe vt* allocation; assignment.
zutiefst *adv* deeply.
zutragen *sep irreg* **1** *vt (fig: weitersagen)* to report *(jdm* to sb*)*. **2** *vr (liter)* to take place.
zuträglich *adj* good *(dat* for*)*, beneficial *(dat* to*)*.
zutrauen *vt sep* **jdm etw** ~ *(Aufgabe, Tat)* to believe sb (is) capable of (doing) sth; **sich** *(dat)* **zuviel** ~ to overrate one's own abilities; **sich** *(dat)* **nichts** ~ to have no confidence in oneself; **das hätte ich ihm nie zugetraut!** I would never have thought him capable of it!; **jdm viel/wenig** ~ to think/not to think a lot of sb.
Zutrauen *nt no pl* confidence *(zu* in*)*. **zu jdm ~ fassen** to begin to trust sb.
zutraulich *adj Kind* trusting; *Tier* friendly.
zutreffen *vi sep irreg (gelten)* to apply *(auf +acc, für* to*)*; *(stimmen)* to be correct, to be true. **das trifft zu** that is so.
zutreffend *adj* accurate. **Z~es bitte unterstreichen** underline where applicable.
zutreten *vi sep irreg* **(a)** to kick him/it *etc*. **(b)** *aux sein* **auf jdn/etw** ~ to step up to sb/sth.
zutrinken *vi sep irreg* **jdm** ~ to drink to sb; *(mit Trinkspruch)* to toast sb.
Zutritt *m no pl (Einlaß)* admittance; *(Zugang)* access. **kein ~, ~ verboten** no admittance; **sich ~ verschaffen** to gain admission; *(Dieb)* to gain access.
Zutun *nt no pl* **es geschah ohne mein** ~ I did not have a hand in the matter.
zu|ungunsten *prep +gen* to the disadvantage of.
zu|unterst *adv* right at the bottom.
zuverlässig *adj* reliable.
Zuverlässigkeit *f* reliability.
Zuversicht *f no pl* confidence; *(religiös)* faith.
zuversichtlich *adj* confident.
zuviel *adj, adv* too much; *(col: zu viele)* too many. **viel** ~ far too much; **da krieg' ich** ~ *(col)* I blow my top *(col)*; **einer/zwei** *etc* ~ one/two *etc* too many; **was ~ ist, ist** ~ that's just too much.
zuvor *adv* before. **im Jahr** ~ the year before.
zuvorderst *adv* right at the front.
zuvorkommen *vi sep irreg aux sein +dat* to anticipate; *(verhindern) einer Gefahr etc* to forestall. **jemand ist uns zuvorgekommen** somebody beat us to it.
zuvorkommend *adj* obliging; *(hilfsbereit)* helpful.
Zuwachs ['tsu:vaks] *m, pl* **Zuwächse (a)** *no pl (Wachstum)* growth *(an +dat* of*)*. **(b)** *(Ansteigen)* increase *(an +dat* in*)*. **~ bekommen** *(col: ein Baby)* to have an addition to the family.
zuwachsen ['tsu:vaksən] *vi sep irreg aux sein* **(a)** *(Loch)* to grow over; *(Garten)* to become overgrown. **(b)** *(Wunde)* to heal (over).
Zuwachsrate ['tsu:vaks-] *f* rate of increase.
Zuwanderer *m* immigrant.
zuwandern *vi sep aux sein* to immigrate.
Zuwanderung *f* immigration.
zuwege *adv* **etw ~ bringen** to manage sth; *(erreichen)* to achieve sth; **mit etw ~ kommen** to (be able to) cope with sth.
zuweilen *adv (geh)* (every) now and then.
zuweisen *vt sep irreg* to allocate *(jdm etw* sth to sb*)*.
zuwenden *sep irreg* **1** *vt (lit, fig)* to turn *(dat* to, towards*)*; **2** *vr* **sich jdm/einer Sache** ~ *(lit, fig)* to turn to sb/sth; *(sich widmen, liebevoll)* to devote oneself to sb/sth.
Zuwendung *f* **(a)** *(Liebe)* care. **(b)** *(Geldsumme)* sum (of money).
zuwenig *adj* too little; *(col: zu wenige)* too few. **du schläfst** ~ you don't get enough sleep; **zwei** ~ two too few.
zuwerfen *vt sep irreg* **(a)** *(hinwerfen)* **jdm etw** ~ to throw sth to sb; **jdm einen Blick** ~ to cast a glance at sb; **jdm einen bösen Blick** ~ to look daggers at sb. **(b)** *(schließen) Tür* to slam (shut).
zuwider *adj* **er/das ist mir** ~ I detest *or* loathe him/that.
Zuwider-: z~handeln *vi sep +dat (geh)* to go against; *einem Verbot, Befehl* to defy; *dem Gesetz* to contravene; **~handlung** *f (form)* contravention; **z~laufen** *vi sep irreg aux sein +dat* to run counter to.
zuwinken *vi sep* **jdm** ~ to wave to sb.
zuzahlen *sep* **1** *vt* **10 Mark** ~ to pay another 10 marks. **2** *vi* to pay extra.
zuzählen *vt sep (col)* to add; *(einbeziehen)* to include *(zu* in*)*.
zuziehen *sep irreg* **1** *vt* **(a)** *Vorhang* to draw; *Tür* to pull shut; *Knoten* to tighten; *Arzt etc* to consult. **(b) sich** *(dat)* **jds Zorn** ~ to incur sb's anger; **sich** *(dat)* **eine Verletzung** ~ *(form)* to sustain an injury. **2** *vr (Schlinge etc)* to tighten. **3** *vi aux sein* to move into the area.
Zuzug *m (Zustrom)* influx; *(von Familie etc)* move *(nach* to*)*.
zuzüglich *prep +gen* plus.
zuzwinkern *vi sep* **jdm** ~ to wink at sb.
zwang *pret of* **zwingen.**
Zwang *m* **⸚e** compulsion; *(Gewalt)* force; *(Verpflichtung)* obligation. **gesellschaftliche ⸚e** social constraints; **unter ~** *(dat)* **stehen** to be under duress; **etw ohne ~ tun** to do sth without being forced to; **auf jdn ~ ausüben** to exert pressure on sb; **darf ich rauchen? — tu dir keinen ~ an** may I smoke? — feel free; **der ~ der Verhältnisse** the force of circumstances.
zwängen *vt* to force; *(hinein~)* to cram. **sich in/durch etw** *(acc)* ~ to squeeze into/through sth.
zwang-: ~haft *adj (Psych)* compulsive; **~los** *adj (ohne Förmlichkeit)* informal; *(locker)* casual; *(frei)* free; **da geht es recht ~los zu** things are very informal there.
Zwangs-: ~abgabe *f (Econ)* compulsory levy; **~ernährung** *f* force feeding; **~jacke** *f (lit, fig)* straitjacket; **~lage** *f* predicament; **z~läufig** *adj* inevitable; **das mußte ja z~läufig so kommen**

that had to happen; ~**läufigkeit** *f* inevitability; ~**maßnahme** *f* compulsory measure; *(Pol)* sanction; ~**räumung** *f* compulsory evacuation; ~**verkauf** *m* forced sale; ~**versteigerung** *f* compulsory auction; ~**vollstreckung** *f* execution; ~**vorstellung** *f (Psych)* obsession.

zwanzig *num* twenty; *siehe* **vierzig.**

Zwanziger(in *f*) *m* - **(a)** man/woman in his/her twenties. **(b)** *(col: Geldschein)* twenty (mark note *(Brit) or* bill *US*).

Zwanzigmarkschein *m* twenty mark note *(Brit) or* bill *(US).*

zwanzigste(r, s) *adj* twentieth.

zwar *adv* **(a)** *(wohl)* **sie ist ~ sehr schön, aber ...** it's true she's very beautiful but ... **(b) und ~** in fact, actually; **er ist tatsächlich gekommen, und ~ um 4 Uhr** he really did come, at 4 o'clock actually; **er hat mir das anders erklärt, und ~ so: ...** he explained it differently to me(, like this) ...; **mach deine Hausaufgaben, und ~ sofort** get on with your homework, now!

Zweck *m* **-e (a)** purpose. **einem ~ dienen** to serve a purpose; **Spenden für wohltätige ~e** donations to charity; **seinen ~ erfüllen** to serve its/one's purpose; **zu welchem ~?** for what purpose?; **einen ~ verfolgen** to have a specific aim. **(b)** *(Sinn)* point. **was soll das für einen ~ haben?** what's the point of that?; **es hat keinen ~, darüber zu reden** there is no point (in) talking about it.

Zweck-: ~**bau** *m* **-ten** functional building; **z~dienlich** *adj* appropriate; *(nützlich)* useful; **z~dienliche Hinweise** (any) relevant information.

Zweck-: **z~entfremden*** *vt insep* to use sth for another purpose; **etw als etw z~entfremden** to use sth as sth else; ~**entfremdung** *f* misuse; **z~entsprechend** *adj* appropriate; **z~frei** *adj Forschung etc* pure; **z~gebunden** *adj* for a specific purpose; **z~los** *adj* pointless; **es ist z~los, hier zu bleiben** it's pointless staying here; ~**losigkeit** *f no pl* pointlessness; **z~mäßig** *adj (nützlich)* useful; *(wirksam)* effective; *(ratsam)* advisable; *(z~entsprechend) Arbeitskleider etc* suitable; ~**mäßigkeit** *f (Nützlichkeit)* usefulness.

zwecks *prep +gen (form)* for (the purpose of).

zwei *num* two. **dazu gehören ~** *(col)* it takes two; *siehe* **vier.**

Zwei *f* **-en** two; *siehe* **Vier.**

Zwei-: **z~beinig** *adj* two-legged; ~**bettzimmer** *nt* twin room; **z~deutig** *adj* ambiguous; *(schlüpfrig)* suggestive; **z~dimensional** *adj* two-dimensional; ~**drittelmehrheit** *f (Parl)* two-thirds majority; **z~eiig** *adj Zwillinge* non-identical.

Zweier *m* - two; *(Zweipfennigstück)* two pfennig piece; *siehe* **Vierer.**

Zweier- *(Sport)*: ~**bob** *m* two-man bob; ~**kajak** *m or nt (Kanu)* double kayak; *(Disziplin)* kayak pairs.

zweierlei *adj inv attr Brot, Käse* two kinds *or* sorts of; *Möglichkeiten, Größen* two different. **auf ~ Art** in two different ways; **~ Handschuhe/Strümpfe** *etc* odd gloves/socks *etc.*

zweifach *adj* double; *(zweimal)* twice; *siehe* **vierfach.**

Zwei-: ~**familienhaus** *nt* two-family house; **z~farbig** *adj* two-colour *(Brit)*, two-color *(US).*

Zweifel *m* - doubt. **außer ~** beyond doubt; **im ~** in doubt; **ohne ~** without doubt; **über allen ~ erhaben** beyond all doubt; **es besteht kein ~, daß ...** there is no doubt that ...; **da habe ich meine ~** I have my doubts; **etw in ~ ziehen** to call sth into question; **ich bin mir im ~, ob ich das tun soll** I'm in two minds whether I should do that.

zweifelhaft *adj* doubtful.

zweifellos *adv* undoubtedly.

zweifeln *vi* to doubt. **an etw/jdm ~** to doubt sth/sb.

Zweifelsfall *m* difficult case. **im ~** in case of doubt.

Zweifler(in *f*) *m* - sceptic.

Zweifrontenkrieg *m* war/warfare on two fronts.

Zweig *m* **-e (a)** *(Ast)* branch; *(dünner, kleiner)* twig. **(b)** *(fig)* branch; *(Abteilung)* department.

Zweig-: ~**betrieb** *m* branch; ~**gesellschaft** *f* subsidiary (company).

zweigleisig *adj* double-track *attr.* **~ argumentieren** to argue along two different lines.

Zweig-: ~**linie** *f* branch line; ~**niederlassung** *f* subsidiary; ~**stelle** *f* branch (office); ~**werk** *nt (Fabrik)* branch.

zwei-: ~**händig** *adj* two-handed; *(Mus)* for two hands; ~**höck(e)rig** *adj Kamel* two-humped.

zweihundert *num* two hundred.

zweijährig *adj attr Kind etc* two-year-old *attr*, two years old; *(Dauer)* two-year *attr*, of two years.

Zweikampf *m* single combat; *(Duell)* duel.

zweimal *adv* twice. **sich** *(dat)* **etw ~ überlegen** to think twice about sth; **das lasse ich mir nicht ~ sagen** I don't have to be told twice.

zweimalig *adj attr* **nach ~er Aufforderung** after being told twice.

Zwei-: ~**markstück** *nt* two-mark piece; **z~motorig** *adj* twin-engined; ~**parteiensystem** *nt* two-party system; ~**pfennigstück** *nt* two-pfennig piece; ~**rad** *nt* two-wheeler; **z~räd(e)rig** *adj* two-wheeled; **z~reihig 1** *adj* double-row *attr*, in two rows; *Anzug* double-breasted; **2** *adv* in two rows; ~**samkeit** *f (liter, hum)* togetherness; **z~schneidig** *adj (lit, fig)* double-edged; **das ist ein z~schneidiges Schwert** *(fig)* it cuts both ways; **z~seitig 1** *adj Vertrag etc* bilateral; *Kleidungsstück* reversible; **2** *adv* on two sides; ~**sitzer** *m* - *(Aut, Aviat)* two-seater; **z~sprachig** *adj* bilingual; **z~spurig** *adj* double-tracked, double-track *attr*; *Autobahn* two-lane *attr*; ~**spur(tonband)gerät** *nt* twin-track (tape) recorder; **z~stellig** *adj Zahl* two-digit *attr*, with two digits; **z~stimmig** *adj (Mus)* for two voices; **z~stimmig singen** to sing in two parts; **z~stöckig** *adj* two-storey *attr (Brit)*, two-story *attr (US)*; **z~stündig** *adj* two-hour *attr.*

zweit *adv*: **zu ~** *(in Paaren)* in twos; **wir gingen zu ~ spazieren** the two of us went for a walk; **das Leben zu ~** living with someone; *siehe* **vier.**

Zwei-: **z~tägig** *adj* two-day *attr*, of two days; ~**taktmotor** *m* two-stroke engine.

Zweit-: **z~älteste(r, s)** *adj* second eldest; ~**ausfertigung** *f (form)* copy; **z~beste(r, s)** *adj* second best.

zwei-: ~**teilen** *vt sep, infin, ptp only* to divide (into two); ~**teilig** *adj Roman* two-part *attr*, in two parts; *Kleidungsstück* two-piece.

zweitens *adv* secondly.

zweite(r, s) *adj* second. **~ Klasse** *(Rail etc)* second class; **Bürger ~r Klasse** second-class citizen(s); **jeder ~** *(lit, col: sehr viele)* every other; **zum ~n** secondly; **ein ~r Caruso** another Caruso; *siehe* **vierte(r, s).**

Zweite(r) *mf decl as adj* second; *(Sport etc)* runner-up. **wie kein z~r** like nobody else.

Zweit-: ~**gerät** *nt (Rad, TV)* second set; **z~größte(r, s)** *adj* second biggest/largest; **z~klassig** *adj (fig)* second-class, second-rate *(pej)*; **z~letzte(r, s)** *adj* last but one; ~**schlüssel** *m* duplicate key; ~**stimme** second vote.

zweitürig *adj* two-door.

Zweit-: ~**wagen** *m* second car; ~**wohnung** *f* second home.

Zwei-: ~**vierteltakt** *m (Mus)* two-four time; **z~wöchig** *adj* two-week *attr*, of two weeks, fortnightly *(Brit)*; ~**zeiler** *m (Liter)* couplet; **z~zeilig** *adj* two-lined; *(Typ) Abstand* double-spaced; **z~zeilig schreiben** to double-space; ~**zimmerwohnung** *f* two-room(ed) flat *(Brit) or* apartment; **z~zylindrig** *adj* two cylinder *attr.*

Zwerchfell *nt (Anat)* diaphragm.
Zwerg(in *f*) *m* **-e** dwarf; *(fig: Knirps)* midget; *(pej: unbedeutender Mensch)* squirt *(col)*.
zwergenhaft *adj* dwarfish; *(fig)* diminutive.
Zwerg-: ~**huhn** *nt* bantam; ~**pinscher** *m* pet terrier; ~**schule** *f (Sch col)* village school; ~**staat** *m* miniature state; ~**wuchs** *m* dwarfism; **z~wüchsig** *adj attr* dwarfish.
Zwetsch(g)e *f* **-n** plum.
Zwetsch(g)enschnaps *m* plum brandy.
zwicken 1 *vt (col)* to pinch; *(leicht schmerzen)* to hurt. **2** *vt impers* **es zwickt mich in der Schulter** I've a twinge in my shoulder.
Zwicker *m* - pince-nez.
Zwickmühle *f* **in der ~ sitzen** *(fig)* to be in a dilemma.
Zwieback *m* **-e** *or* **-̈e** ≃ rusk.
Zwiebel *f* **-n** onion; *(Blumen~)* bulb; *(hum col: Uhr)* watch.
Zwiebel-: **z~förmig** *adj* onion-shaped; ~**kuchen** *m* onion tart; ~**ring** *m* onion ring; ~**suppe** *f* onion soup; ~**turm** *m* onion tower.
Zwie-: ~**gespräch** *nt* dialogue; ~**licht** *nt no pl* twilight; *(morgens)* half-light; **ins ~licht geraten sein** *(fig)* to appear in an unfavourable *(Brit) or* unfavorable *(US)* light; **z~lichtig** *adj (fig)* shady; ~**spalt** *m (der Gefühle etc)* conflict; *(zwischen Menschen)* rift, gulf; **z~spältig** *adj Gefühle* mixed, conflicting *attr*; **ein z~spältiger Mensch** a man/woman of contradictions; ~**sprache** *f (geh)* ~**sprache mit jdm halten** to commune with sb; ~**tracht** *f no pl* discord; ~**tracht säen** to sow discord.
Zwilling *m* **-e** twin; *(Gewehr)* double-barrelled *(Brit) or* double-barreled *(US)* gun. ~**e** *(Astrol)* Gemini.
Zwillings-: ~**bruder** *m* twin brother; ~**geburt** *f* twin birth; ~**paar** *nt* twins *pl*; ~**schwester** *f* twin sister.
Zwinge *f* **-n** *(Tech)* (screw) clamp; *(an Stock, Schirm)* tip; *(an Werkzeuggriff)* ferrule.
zwingen *pret* **zwang,** *ptp* **gezwungen 1** *vt* to force. **jdn ~, etw zu tun** to force sb to do sth; **jdn zu etw ~** to force sb to do sth; **jdn zum Handeln ~** to force sb to act; **die Regierung wurde zum Rücktritt gezwungen** the government was forced to step down; *siehe* **gezwungen. 2** *vr* to force oneself. **3** *vi* **zum Handeln/Umdenken ~** to force *or* compel us/them *etc* to act/re-think.
zwingend *adj Notwendigkeit* urgent; *(logisch notwendig)* necessary; *Schluß, Beweis* conclusive; *Argument, Gründe* cogent.
Zwinger *m* - *(Käfig)* cage; *(Hunde~)* kennels *pl*.
zwinkern *vi* to blink; *(als Zeichen)* to wink; *(lustig)* to twinkle. **mit den Augen ~** to blink (one's eyes).
zwirbeln *vt Bart* to twirl; *Schnur* to twist.
Zwirn *m* **-e** (strong) thread, yarn.
Zwirnsfaden *m* thread.
zwischen *prep +dat or (mit Bewegungsverben) +acc* between; *(bei mehreren auch)* among. **mitten ~** right in the midst of.
Zwischen-: ~**akt** *m (Theat)* intermission; ~**aufenthalt** *m* stopover; ~**bemerkung** *f* interjection; **wenn Sie mir eine kurze ~bemerkung erlauben** if I may just interrupt; ~**bericht** *m* interim report; ~**bescheid** *m* provisional notification *no indef art;* ~**bilanz** *f (Comm)* interim balance; ~**deck** *nt (Naut)* 'tween deck; **im ~deck** 'tween decks; ~**ding** *nt* cross (between the two); **z~durch** *adv* **(a)** *(zeitlich)* in between times; *(inzwischen)* meantime; *(nebenbei)* on the side; **(b)** *(örtlich)* here and there; ~**ergebnis** *nt* interim result; *(Sport)* latest score; ~**fall** *m* incident; ~**frage** *f* question; ~**gericht** *nt (Cook)* entrée; ~**größe** *f* in-between size; ~**handel** *m* wholesaling; ~**händler** *m* middleman; **z~landen** *vi sep (Aviat)* to stop over; ~**landung** *f (Aviat)* stopover; ~**lösung** *f* temporary solution; ~**mahlzeit** *f* snack (between meals); **z~menschlich** *adj attr* interpersonal; ~**musik** *f* interlude; ~**produkt** *nt* intermediate product; ~**prüfung** *f* intermediate examination; ~**raum** *m* gap, space; *(zeitlich)* interval; ~**ruf** *m* interruption; ~**rufe** heckling; ~**rufer(in *f*)** *m* - heckler; ~**runde** *f* intermediate round; **z~schalten** *vt sep (Elec)* to insert; *(fig)* to interpose; ~**schalter** *m (Elec)* circuit breaker; ~**spiel** *nt (Mus)* intermezzo; *(Theat, fig)* interlude; ~**spurt** *m (Sport)* short burst (of speed); **z~staatlich** *adj attr* international; ~**stadium** *nt* intermediate stage; ~**station** *f* (intermediate) stop; **in London machten wir ~station** we stopped off in London; ~**stecker** *m (Elec)* adapter; ~**stück** *nt* connecting piece; ~**summe** *f* subtotal; ~**text** *m* inserted text; ~**ton** *m (Farbe)* shade; ~**töne** *(fig)* nuances; ~**wand** *f* dividing wall; *(Stellwand)* partition; ~**zeit** *f* **(a)** *(Zeitraum)* interval; **in der ~zeit** (in the) meantime; **(b)** *(Sport)* intermediate time; **z~zeitlich** *adv* in between; *(inzwischen)* (in the) meantime; ~**zeugnis** *nt (Sch)* interim report.
Zwist *m (rare)* **-e** *(geh)* discord; *(Fehde, Streit)* strife *no indef art*. **mit jdm in ~ (acc) geraten** to become involved in a dispute with sb.
Zwistigkeit *f usu pl* dispute.
zwitschern *vti* to twitter. **einen ~** *(col)* to have a drink.
Zwitter *m* - hermaphrodite; *(fig)* cross *(aus* between*)*.
zwo *num (Telec, col)* two.
zwölf *num* twelve. **~ Uhr mittags/nachts** (12 o'clock) midday/midnight; **fünf Minuten vor ~** *(fig)* at the eleventh hour; *siehe* **vier.**
Zwölf-: **z~fach** *adj* twelve-fold; *siehe* **vierfach;** ~**fingerdarm** *m* duodenum; ~**kampf** *m (Sport)* twelve-exercise event.
zwölftens *adv* twelfth(ly), in the twelfth place.
zwölfte(r, s) *adj* twelfth; *siehe* **vierte(r, s).**
Zyankali [tsya:n'ka:li] *nt no pl (Chem)* potassium cyanide.
zyklisch 1 *adj* cyclic(al). **2** *adv* cyclically.
Zyklon *m* **-e** cyclone.
Zyklus ['tsy:klʊs] *m* **-, Zyklen** ['tsy:klən] cycle.
Zylinder *m* **- (a)** *(Math, Tech)* cylinder. **(b)** *(Hut)* top-hat.
zylindrisch *adj* cylindrical.
Zyniker(in *f*) ['tsy:nikɐ, -ərɪn] *m* - cynic.
zynisch ['tsy:nɪʃ] *adj* cynical.
Zynismus *m* cynicism.
Zypern ['tsy:pɐn] *nt* Cyprus.
Zypresse *f (Bot)* cypress.
Zypriot(in *f*) *m (wk)* **-en, en** Cypriot.
zypriotisch, zyprisch ['tsy:prɪʃ] *adj* Cyprian, Cypriot.
Zyste ['tsʏstə] *f* **-n** cyst.
z.Z(t). = **zur Zeit.**

ENGLISH–GERMAN DICTIONARY
ENGLISCH–DEUTSCH

A

A, a [eɪ] *n* A, a *nt*; *(Sch: as a mark)* sehr gut; *(Mus)* A, a *nt*. **to get from A to B** von A nach B kommen; **A sharp/flat** *(Mus)* Ais, ais *nt*/As, as *nt*.

a [eɪ, ə] *indef art, before vowel* **an (a)** ein; *(before feminine noun)* eine. **so large ~ country** ein so großes Land; **an unusual feeling** ein merkwürdiges Gefühl. **(b)** *(in negative constructions)* **not ~** kein(e); **he didn't want ~ present** er wollte kein Geschenk. **(c)** *(with profession, nationality etc)* **he's ~ doctor/Frenchman** er ist Arzt/Franzose; **he's ~ famous doctor/Frenchman** er ist ein berühmter Arzt/Franzose. **(d)** *(per)* pro. **£4 ~ head** £4 pro Person; **50p ~ kilo** 50 Pence das *or* pro Kilo; **twice ~ month** zweimal im *or* pro Monat.

aback [ə'bæk] *adv*: **to be taken ~** erstaunt sein; *(upset)* betroffen sein.

abandon [ə'bændən] **1** *vt* **(a)** *(leave, forsake)* verlassen; *wife, family also* im Stich lassen; *baby* aussetzen; *car* (einfach) stehenlassen. **to ~ ship** das Schiff verlassen. **(b)** *(give up)* aufgeben. **to ~ play** das Spiel abbrechen. **(c)** *(fig)* **to ~ oneself to sth** sich einer Sache *(dat)* hingeben. **2** *n* **with ~** mit ganzer Seele.

abandoned [ə'bændənd] *adj* **(a)** *(dissolute)* verkommen. **(b)** *(unrestrained)* hingebungsvoll.

abashed [ə'bæʃd] *adj* beschämt.

abate [ə'beɪt] *vi* nachlassen.

abatement [ə'beɪtmənt] Nachlassen *nt*. **the noise ~ society** die Gesellschaft zur Bekämpfung von Lärm.

abattoir ['æbətwɑːʳ] *n* Schlachthof *m*.

abbey ['æbɪ] *n* Abtei *f*; *(church)* Klosterkirche *f*.

abbot ['æbət] *n* Abt *m*.

abbreviate [ə'briːvɪeɪt] *vt* abkürzen *(to* mit*)*.

abbreviation [ə,briːvɪ'eɪʃən] *n* Abkürzung *f*.

abdicate ['æbdɪkeɪt] **1** *vt* verzichten auf *(+acc)*. **2** *vi (monarch)* abdanken.

abdication [,æbdɪ'keɪʃən] *n* Abdankung *f*. **his ~ of the throne** sein Verzicht auf den Thron.

abdomen ['æbdəmen] *n* Unterleib *m*; *(of insects)* Hinterleib *m*.

abdominal [æb'dɒmɪnl] *adj* Unterleibs-.

abduct [æb'dʌkt] *vt* entführen.

abduction [æb'dʌkʃən] *n* Entführung *f*.

abductor [æb'dʌktəʳ] *n* Entführer(in *f*) *m*.

aberration [,æbə'reɪʃən] *n* Anomalie *f*; *(in statistics)* Abweichung *f*; *(mistake)* Irrtum *m*; *(moral)* Verirrung *f*. **in a moment of (mental) ~** *(col)* in einem Augenblick geistiger Verwirrung.

abet [ə'bet] *vt see* **aid 2.**

abeyance [ə'beɪəns] *n no pl* **to be in ~** *(law, rule, issue)* ruhen; *(custom, office)* nicht mehr ausgeübt werden.

abhor [əb'hɔːʳ] *vt* verabscheuen.

abhorrence [əb'hɒrəns] *n* Abscheu *f (of* vor *+dat)*.

abhorrent [əb'hɒrənt] *adj* abscheulich.

abide [ə'baɪd] *vt (usu neg, interrog) person* ausstehen; *(endure)* aushalten. **I cannot ~ living here** ich kann es nicht ertragen, hier zu leben.

♦ **abide by** *vi +prep obj decision, law etc* sich halten an *(+acc)*. **I ~ ~ what I said** ich bleibe bei dem, was ich gesagt habe.

ability [ə'bɪlɪtɪ] *n* Fähigkeit *f*. **to the best of my ~** nach (besten) Kräften; *(with mental activities)* so gut ich kann; **a man of many abilities** ein sehr vielseitiger Mensch.

abject ['æbdʒekt] *adj state, liar, thief* elend, erbärmlich; *poverty* bitter; *apology* demütig.

ablaze [ə'bleɪz] *adv, adj pred* in Flammen. **to be ~** in Flammen stehen; **to be ~ with light** hell erleuchtet sein.

able [eɪbl] *adj* **(a)** *person* fähig, kompetent; *piece of work, exam paper, speech* gekonnt. **(b) to be ~ to do sth** etw tun können; *(be in a position to)* in der Lage sein, etw zu tun.

able-bodied [,eɪbl'bɒdɪd] *adj* (gesund und) kräftig; *(Mil)* tauglich.

able(-bodied) seaman *n* Vollmatrose *m*.

ablutions [ə'bluːʃənz] *npl (lavatory)* sanitäre Einrichtungen *pl*.

ably ['eɪblɪ] *adv* gekonnt, fähig.

abnormal [æb'nɔːməl] *adj* anormal; *(deviant, Med)* abnorm.

abnormality [,æbnɔː'mælɪtɪ] *n* Anormale(s) *nt*; *(deviancy, Med)* Abnormität *f*.

abnormally [æb'nɔːməlɪ] *adv* **(a)** *see adj*. **(b)** *(exceptionally)* außergewöhnlich.

aboard [ə'bɔːd] **1** *adv (on plane, ship)* an Bord. **all ~!** alle an Bord!; *(on train, bus)* alles einsteigen!; **to go ~** an Bord gehen. **2** *prep* **~ the ship** an Bord des Schiffes.

abode [ə'bəʊd] *n (liter: dwelling)* Aufenthalt *m*. **a humble ~** *(iro)* eine bescheidene Hütte *(iro)*; **of no fixed ~** ohne festen Wohnsitz.

abolish [ə'bɒlɪʃ] *vt* abschaffen; *law also* aufheben.

abolition [,æbəʊ'lɪʃən] *n* Abschaffung *f*.

abominable [ə'bɒmɪnəbl] *adj* gräßlich, abscheulich. **A~ Snowman** Schneemensch *m*.

abominably [ə'bɒmɪnəblɪ] *adv* gräßlich, abscheulich. **~ rude** furchtbar unhöflich.

abomination [ə,bɒmɪ'neɪʃən] *n* **(a)** *no pl* Verabscheuung *f*. **to be held in ~ by sb** von jdm verabscheut werden. **(b)** *(thing)* Scheußlichkeit *f*.

aborigine [,æbə'rɪdʒɪnɪ] *n* Ureinwohner(in *f*) *m* (Australiens).

abort [ə'bɔːt] **1** *vi (Med: mother)* eine Fehlgeburt haben. **2** *vt (Med) foetus* abtreiben; *(break off) mission etc* abbrechen.

abortion [ə'bɔːʃən] *n* Abtreibung *f*. **to have an ~** abtreiben lassen.

abortive [ə'bɔːtɪv] *adj (unsuccessful) attempt* gescheitert. **to be ~** scheitern, fehlschlagen.

abound [ə'baʊnd] *vi* im Überfluß vorhanden sein; *(persons)* sehr zahlreich sein. **to ~ in** reich sein an *(+dat)*.

about [ə'baʊt] **1** *adv* **(a)** herum, umher; *(present)* in der Nähe. **to walk ~** herum- *or* umhergehen; **with flowers all ~** mit Blumen ringsumher; **to be (up and) ~ again** wieder auf den Beinen sein; **there's a lot of measles ~** die Masern gehen um; **there's nobody ~** es ist keiner da; **he's/it's ~ somewhere** er/es ist irgendwo in der Nähe; **it's the other way ~** es ist gerade umgekehrt.

(b) to be ~ to im Begriff sein zu; *(esp US col: intending)* vorhaben, zu ...; **I was ~ to go out** ich wollte gerade ausgehen; **it's ~ to rain** es regnet gleich; **we are ~ to run out of petrol** uns geht gleich das Benzin aus; **are you ~ to tell me ...?** willst du mir etwa erzählen ...?

(c) *(approximately)* ungefähr. **he's ~ 40** er ist ungefähr 40 *or* um die 40; **he is ~ the same,**

doctor sein Zustand hat sich kaum geändert, Herr Doktor; **that's ~ it** das ist so ziemlich alles, das wär's *(col)*; **I've had ~ enough of this** jetzt reicht es mir aber allmählich *(col)*.

2 *prep* **(a)** um (... herum); *(in)* in *(+dat)* (... herum). **the fields ~ the house** die Felder ums Haus; **scattered ~ the room** über das ganze Zimmer verstreut; **somewhere ~ here** hier irgendwo; **to do jobs ~ the house** sich im Haus nützlich machen; **he looked ~ him** er schaute sich um; **there's something ~ him** er hat so etwas an sich *(dat)*; **while you're ~ it** wenn du schon dabei bist; **you've been a long time ~ it** du hast lange dazu gebraucht.

(b) *(concerning)* über *(+acc)*. **what's the film ~?** wovon handelt der Film?; **what's it all ~?** worum geht es eigentlich?; **he's promised to do something ~ it** er hat versprochen, (in der Sache) etwas zu unternehmen; **they fell out ~ money** sie haben sich wegen Geld zerstritten; **how** *or* **what ~ me?** und ich?, und was ist mit mir? *(col)*; **how** *or* **what ~ going to the pictures?** wollen wir ins Kino gehen?; **(yes,) what ~ it/him?** ja *or* na und(, was ist damit/mit ihm)?

about-face [əˌbaʊt'feɪs], **about-turn** [əˌbaʊt'tɜːn] *n (Mil)* Kehrtwendung *f*; *(fig also)* Wendung *f* um hundertachtzig Grad. **to do an ~** kehrtmachen; *(fig)* sich um hundertachtzig Grad drehen.

above [ə'bʌv] **1** *adv* oben; *(in a higher position)* darüber. **from ~** von oben; **the flat ~** die Wohnung oben *or* (*~ that one*) darüber.

2 *prep* über *(+dat)*; *(with motion)* über *(+acc)*; *(upstream of)* oberhalb *(+gen)*. **~ all** vor allem; **I couldn't hear ~ the din** ich konnte bei dem Lärm nichts hören; **to be ~ sb/sth** über jdm/etw stehen; **~ criticism/praise** über jede Kritik/jedes Lob erhaben; **he's ~ that sort of thing** er ist über so etwas erhaben; **he's not ~ a bit of blackmail** er ist sich *(dat)* nicht zu gut *or* zu schade für eine kleine Erpressung; **it's ~ my head** *or* **me** das ist mir zu hoch; **to be/get ~ oneself** *(col)* größenwahnsinnig werden.

3 *adj attr* **the ~ figures** die obengenannten Zahlen; **the ~ paragraph** der obige Abschnitt.

above: ~ board *adj pred* korrekt; **~-mentioned** *adj* obenerwähnt.

abrasion [ə'breɪʒən] *n (Med)* (Haut)abschürfung *f*.

abrasive [ə'breɪsɪv] **1** *adj surface* rauh; *(fig) personality, person* aggressiv; *tongue, voice* scharf. **2** *n (cleanser)* Scheuermittel *nt*; (*~ substance*) Schleifmittel *nt*.

abrasiveness [ə'breɪsɪvnɪs] *n (of personality)* Aggressivität *f*.

abreast [ə'brest] *adv* Seite an Seite. **to march four ~** im Viererglied *(Mil) or* zu viert nebeneinander marschieren; **to keep ~ of the news** mit den Nachrichten auf dem laufenden bleiben.

abridged [ə'brɪdʒd] *adj* gekürzt.

abroad [ə'brɔːd] *adv* **(a)** im Ausland. **to go ~** ins Ausland gehen; **from ~** aus dem Ausland. **(b) there is a rumour ~ that ...** es geht das Gerücht, daß ...; **to get ~** an die Öffentlichkeit dringen.

abrupt [ə'brʌpt] *adj* abrupt; *descent, drop* jäh; *manner, reply* schroff.

abruptness [ə'brʌptnɪs] *n* abrupte Art; *(of person)* schroffe Art; *(of descent, drop)* Steilheit *f*; *(of reply)* Schroffheit *f*.

abscess ['æbses] *n* Abszeß *m*.

abscond [əb'skɒnd] *vi* sich (heimlich) davonmachen; *(schoolboys also)* durchbrennen.

absence ['æbsəns] *n* **(a)** Abwesenheit *f*; *(from school, work etc also)* Fehlen *nt*. **in the ~ of the chairman** in Abwesenheit des Vorsitzenden; **in his ~** in seiner Abwesenheit. **(b)** *(lack)* Fehlen *nt*. **~ of enthusiasm** Mangel *m* an Enthusiasmus; **in the ~ of further evidence** in Ermangelung weiterer Beweise.

absent ['æbsənt] **1** *adj* **(a)** abwesend, nicht da. **to be ~ from school/work** in der Schule/am Arbeitsplatz fehlen. **(b)** *expression, look* (geistes) abwesend. **2** [æb'sent] *vr* **to ~ oneself (from)** *(not go, not appear)* fernbleiben *(+dat*, von*)*; *(leave temporarily)* sich zurückziehen.

absentee [ˌæbsən'tiː] *n* Abwesende(r) *mf*. **there were a lot of ~s** es fehlten viele.

absenteeism [ˌæbsən'tiːɪzəm] *n* häufige Abwesenheit; *(of workers also)* Nichterscheinen *nt* am Arbeitsplatz; *(pej)* Krankfeiern *nt*; *(Sch)* Schwänzen *nt*.

absently ['æbsəntlɪ] *adv* (geistes)abwesend.

absent-minded [ˌæbsənt'maɪndɪd] *adj (lost in thought)* geistesabwesend; *(forgetful)* zerstreut.

absent-mindedness [ˌæbsənt'maɪndɪdnɪs] *n see adj* Geistesabwesenheit *f*; Zerstreutheit *f*.

absolute ['æbsəluːt] *adj* absolut; *idiot* ausgemacht.

absolutely ['æbsəluːtlɪ] *adv* absolut; *prove* eindeutig; *agree, trust also, true, correct* vollkommen, völlig; *deny, refuse* strikt; *forbidden* streng; *stupid also* völlig. **~!** genau!; **do you agree? — ~** sind Sie einverstanden? — vollkommen; **do you ~ insist?** muß das unbedingt sein? **~ amazing** wirklich erstaunlich.

absolution [ˌæbsə'luːʃən] *n (Eccl)* Absolution *f*.

absolve [əb'zɒlv] *vt (from sins)* lossprechen *(from* von*)*; *(from blame)* freisprechen *(from* von*)*.

absorb [əb'sɔːb] *vt* absorbieren; *liquid also* aufsaugen; *knowledge, news also* in sich *(acc)* aufnehmen; *shock* dämpfen; *costs etc* tragen. **to be/get ~ed in a book** in ein Buch vertieft sein/sich in ein Buch vertiefen; **she was completely ~ed in her family/job** sie ging völlig in ihrer Familie/Arbeit auf.

absorbency [əb'sɔːbənsɪ] *n* Saugfähigkeit *f*.

absorbent [əb'sɔːbənt] *adj* saugfähig, absorbierend.

absorbent cotton *n (US)* Watte *f*.

absorbing [əb'sɔːbɪŋ] *adj* fesselnd.

absorption [əb'sɔːpʃən] *n see vt* Absorption *f*; Aufsaugen *f*; Aufnahme *f*; Dämpfung *f*.

abstain [əb'steɪn] *vi* **(a)** sich enthalten *(from gen)*. **(b)** *(in voting)* sich der Stimme enthalten.

abstemious [əb'stiːmɪəs] *adj person, life* enthaltsam; *meal, diet* bescheiden.

abstention [əb'stenʃən] *n* **(a)** *no pl* Enthaltung *f*; *(from alcohol also)* Abstinenz *f*. **(b)** *(in voting)* (Stimm)enthaltung *f*.

abstinence ['æbstɪnəns] *n* Abstinenz, Enthaltung *f (from* von*)*.

abstract[1] ['æbstrækt] **1** *adj* abstrakt. **in the ~** abstrakt. **2** *n* (kurze) Zusammenfassung *f*.

abstract[2] [æb'strækt] *vt* abstrahieren; *information* entnehmen *(from* aus*)*; *metal etc* trennen.

abstruse [æb'struːs] *adj* abstrus.

absurd [əb'sɜːd] *adj* absurd. **don't be ~!** sei nicht albern; **you're just being ~** du bist ja nicht recht bei Trost!

absurdity [əb'sɜːdɪtɪ] *n* Absurde(s) *nt no pl (of* an *+dat)*; *(thing etc also)* Absurdität *f*.

abundance [ə'bʌndəns] *n* Fülle *f (of* von, *gen)*. **in ~** in Hülle und Fülle; **an ~ of raw materials** großer Reichtum an Rohstoffen.

abundant [ə'bʌndənt] *adj* reich; *time, proof* reichlich; *energy, self-confidence etc* ungeheuer.

abundantly [ə'bʌndəntlɪ] *adv* reichlich. **to make it ~ clear that ...** überdeutlich zu verstehen geben, daß ...

abuse [ə'bjuːs] **1** *n* **(a)** *no pl (insults)* Beschimpfungen *pl*. **a term of ~** ein Schimpfwort *nt*. **(b)** *(misuse)* Mißbrauch *m*; *(unjust practice)* Mißstand *m*. **the system is open to ~** das System kann leicht mißbraucht werden. **2** [ə'bjuːz] *vt* **(a)** *(revile)* beschimpfen. **(b)** *(misuse)* mißbrauchen; *one's health* Raubbau treiben mit.

abusive [əb'juːsɪv] *adj* beleidigend. **~ language** Beschimpfungen *pl*; **to become ~ (with sb)** (jdm gegenüber) beleidigend *or* ausfallend werden.

abysmal [ə'bɪzməl] *adj (fig)* entsetzlich; *performance, work etc* miserabel.

abyss [ə'bɪs] *n (lit, fig)* Abgrund *m*.

academic [ˌækə'demɪk] **1** *adj* **(a)** akademisch, wissenschaftlich. ~ **year** Studienjahr. **(b)** *(theoretical)* **out of** ~ **interest** aus rein akademischem Interesse; **it's purely** ~ **now** das ist jetzt nur noch eine rein theoretische Frage. **2** *n* Akademiker(in *f*) *m*; *(Univ)* Hochschullehrer *m*.

academy [ə'kædəmɪ] *n* Akademie *f*.

accede [æk'siːd] *vi* **(a) to** ~ **to the throne** den Thron besteigen. **(b)** *(agree)* zustimmen *(to dat)*. **(c) to** ~ **to a treaty** einem Pakt beitreten.

accelerate [æk'seləreɪt] **1** *vt* beschleunigen. **2** *vi* beschleunigen; *(driver also)* Gas geben; *(speed, change, growth, inflation etc)* zunehmen.

acceleration [ækˌselə'reɪʃən] *n* Beschleunigung *f*.

accelerator [æk'seləreɪtə[r]] *n* **(a)** *(Aut)* Gaspedal, Gas *(col) nt*. **(b)** *(Phys)* Beschleuniger *m*.

accent ['æksənt] *n* Akzent *m*; *(stress also)* Betonung *f*. **to speak without/with an** ~ akzentfrei *or* ohne/mit Akzent sprechen; **to put the** ~ **on sth** *(fig)* den Akzent auf etw *(acc)* legen.

accentuate [æk'sentjʊeɪt] *vt* betonen; *(in speaking, Mus)* akzentuieren.

accept [ək'sept] **1** *vt* annehmen; *suggestion, work also, report, findings, person* akzeptieren; *responsibility* übernehmen; *(recognize) need* einsehen, anerkennen; *(allow, put up with) behaviour, fate, conditions* hinnehmen. **it is generally ~ed that ...** es ist allgemein anerkannt, daß ...; **we must** ~ **the fact that ...** wir müssen uns damit abfinden, daß ...; **it's the ~ed thing** es ist allgemein *or* so üblich. **2** *vi* annehmen; *(with offers also)* akzeptieren; *(with invitations)* zusagen.

acceptable [ək'septəbl] *adj* annehmbar *(to* für*)*, akzeptabel *(to* für*)*; *behaviour* zulässig; *(suitable) gift* passend.

acceptance [ək'septəns] *n see vt* Annahme *f*; Akzeptierung *f*; Übernahme *f*. **to meet with general** ~ allgemeine Anerkennung finden.

access ['ækses] **1** *n* Zugang *m (to* zu*)*; *(to room, private grounds etc also)* Zutritt *m (to* zu*)*. **this location offers easy** ~ **to shops and transport facilities** von hier sind Läden und Verkehrsmittel leicht zu erreichen; **the thieves gained** ~ **through the window** die Diebe gelangten durch das Fenster hinein; ~ **road** Zufahrt(sstraße) *f*. **2** *vt (Comp) file, data* Zugriff haben auf *(+acc)*.

accessible [æk'sesəbl] *adj information, person* zugänglich *(to dat)*; *place also* (leicht) zu erreichen *(to* für*)*.

accession [æk'seʃən] *n* **(a)** *(to an office)* Antritt *m (to gen)*; *(also* ~ **to the throne***)* Thronbesteigung *f*. **(b)** *(consent: to treaty, demand)* Zustimmung *(to* zu*)*, Annahme *(to gen) f*.

accessory [æk'sesərɪ] *n* **(a)** Extra *nt*; *(in fashion)* Accessoire *nt*. **accessories** *pl* Zubehör *nt*. **(b)** *(Jur)* Mitschuldige(r) *mf (to* an *+dat)*.

accident ['æksɪdənt] *n (Mot, in home, at work)* Unfall *m*; *(Rail, Aviat, disaster)* Unglück *nt*; *(mishap)* Mißgeschick *nt*; *(chance occurrence)* Zufall *m*. **she has had an** ~ sie hat einen Unfall gehabt *or (caused it)* gebaut *(col)*; *(by car, train etc also)* sie ist verunglückt; **by** ~ *(by chance)* durch Zufall, zufällig; *(unintentionally)* aus Versehen.

accidental [ˌæksɪ'dentl] *adj (unplanned)* zufällig, Zufalls-; *(unintentional)* versehentlich. ~ **death** Tod durch Unfall.

accidentally [ˌæksɪ'dentəlɪ] *adv (by chance)* zufällig; *(unintentionally)* versehentlich.

accident-prone ['æksɪdəntˌprəʊn] *adj* vom Pech verfolgt.

acclaim [ə'kleɪm] **1** *vt (applaud)* feiern *(as* als*)*. **to** ~ **sb the winner** jdn zum Sieger erklären. **2** *n* Beifall *m*.

acclamation [ˌæklə'meɪʃən] *n* Beifall *m no pl*; *(of critics also)* Anerkennung *f*.

acclimatization [əˌklaɪmətaɪ'zeɪʃən], *(US)* **acclimation** [ˌæklaɪ'meɪʃən] *n* Akklimatisierung *f (to* an *+acc)*.

acclimatize [ə'klaɪmətaɪz], *(US)* **acclimate** [ə'klaɪmət] *vt* gewöhnen *(to* an *+acc)*. **to become ~d** sich akklimatisieren.

accommodate [ə'kɒmədeɪt] *vt* **(a)** *(provide lodging for)* unterbringen. **(b)** *(hold, have room for)* Platz haben für. **(c)** *theory, plan, forecasts* Rechnung *f* tragen *(+dat)*. **(d)** *(form: oblige)* dienen *(+dat)*; *wishes* entgegenkommen *(+dat)*.

accommodating [ə'kɒmədeɪtɪŋ] *adj* entgegenkommend.

accommodation [əˌkɒmə'deɪʃən] *n (US* **~s** *pl)* Unterkunft *f*; *(room also)* Zimmer *nt*; *(flat also)* Wohnung *f*. **"~"** „Fremdenzimmer“; **they found** ~ **in a youth hostel** sie kamen in einer Jugendherberge unter; ~ **bureau** Wohnungsvermittlung *f*; **seating** ~ Sitzplätze.

accompaniment [ə'kʌmpənɪmənt] *n* Begleitung *f (also Mus)*.

accompanist [ə'kʌmpənɪst] *n* Begleiter(in *f*) *m*.

accompany [ə'kʌmpənɪ] *vt* begleiten *(also Mus)*.

accomplice [ə'kʌmplɪs] *n* Komplize *m*, Komplizin *f*.

accomplish [ə'kʌmplɪʃ] *vt* schaffen. **he ~ed a great deal in his short career** er hat in der kurzen Zeit seines Wirkens Großes geleistet; **that didn't** ~ **anything** damit war nichts erreicht.

accomplished [ə'kʌmplɪʃt] *adj (skilled) player* fähig; *performance* vollendet.

accomplishment [ə'kʌmplɪʃmənt] *n (skill)* Fertigkeit *f*; *(achievement)* Leistung *f*.

accord [ə'kɔːd] **1** *n* Übereinstimmung, Einigkeit *f*. **of one's/its own** ~ von selbst; **with one** ~ geschlossen; *sing, cheer, say etc* wie aus einem Mund(e); **to be in** ~ **with sth** mit etw in Einklang sein. **2** *vt* gewähren *(sb sth* jdm etw*)*. **3** *vi* **to** ~ **with sth** einer Sache *(dat)* entsprechen.

accordance [ə'kɔːdəns] *n* **in** ~ **with** entsprechend *(+dat)*, gemäß *(+dat)*; **to be in** ~ **with sth** einer Sache *(dat)* entsprechen.

accordingly [ə'kɔːdɪŋlɪ] *adv (correspondingly)* (dem)entsprechend; *(so, therefore also)* folglich.

according to [ə'kɔːdɪŋ'tuː] *prep* entsprechend *(+dat)*, nach. ~ **this** danach; ~ **the map** der Karte zufolge; ~ **Peter** laut Peter, Peter zufolge; ~ **what he says** seiner Aussage nach; **we did it** ~ **the rules** wir haben uns an die Regeln gehalten.

accordion [ə'kɔːdɪən] *n* Akkordeon *nt*.

accost [ə'kɒst] *vt* ansprechen, anpöbeln *(pej)*.

account [ə'kaʊnt] *n* **(a)** *(description)* Darstellung *f*; *(report also)* Bericht *m*. **to keep an** ~ **of one's expenses** über seine Ausgaben Buch führen; **by all ~s** nach allem, was man hört; **to give an** ~ **of sth** über etw *(acc)* Bericht erstatten; **to give an** ~ **of oneself** Rede und Antwort stehen; **to give a good** ~ **of oneself** sich bewähren.

(b) *(consideration)* **to take** ~ **of sb/sth, to take sb/sth into** ~ jdn/etw in Betracht ziehen; **to take no** ~ **of sb/sth, to leave sb/sth out of** ~ jdn/etw außer Betracht lassen; **on no** ~**, not on any** ~ auf (gar) keinen Fall; **on this/that** ~ deshalb; **on** ~ **of him/the weather** seinetwegen/wegen des Wetters; **on my/his/their** ~ meinet-/seinet-/ihretwegen; **on one's own** ~ für sich (selbst).

(c) *(benefit)* **to turn sth to (good)** ~ (guten) Gebrauch von etw machen, etw (gut) nützen.

(d) *(importance)* **of no** ~ ohne Bedeutung.

(e) *(Fin, Comm) (at bank, shop)* Konto *nt (with* bei*)*; *(bill)* Rechnung *f*. **to buy sth on** ~ etw auf (Kunden)kredit kaufen; **please charge it to my** ~ stellen Sie es mir bitte in Rechnung; **£50 on** ~ £50 als Anzahlung; ~ **number** Kontonummer *f*; **~s department** Buchhaltung *f*; *(of shop)* Kreditbüro *nt*.

(f) **~s** *pl (of company, club)* (Geschäfts)bücher *pl.* **to keep the ~s** die Bücher führen.

♦**account for** *vi +prep obj* **(a)** *(explain)* erklären; *(give account of) actions, expenditure* Rechenschaft ablegen über *(+acc)*. **all the children were ~ed ~** man wußte, wo alle Kinder waren; **there's no ~ing ~ taste** über Geschmack läßt sich (nicht) streiten. **(b) this area alone ~s ~ some 25% of the population** allein in diesem Gebiet leben etwa 25% der Bevölkerung. **(c)** *(be cause of death, downfall)* zur Strecke bringen; *(illness)* fertigmachen, den Rest geben *(+dat)*.

accountability [əˌkaʊntəˈbɪlətɪ] *n* Verantwortlichkeit *f (to sb* jdm gegenüber*)*.

accountable [əˈkaʊntəbl] *adj* verantwortlich *(to sb* jdm*)*. **to hold sb ~ (for sth)** jdn (für etw) verantwortlich machen.

accountancy [əˈkaʊntənsɪ] *n* Buchhaltung *f*.

accountant [əˈkaʊntənt] *n* Buchhalter(in *f*) *m*; *(external financial adviser)* Wirtschaftsprüfer(in *f*) *m*; *(tax ~)* Steuerberater(in *f*) *m*.

accredited [əˈkredɪtɪd] *adj* (offiziell) zugelassen.

accrue [əˈkruː] *vi* **(a)** *(accumulate)* sich ansammeln; *(Fin: interest)* auflaufen. **(b) to ~ to sb** *(honour, costs etc)* jdm erwachsen *(geh)* *(from* aus*)*.

accumulate [əˈkjuːmjʊleɪt] **1** *vt* ansammeln, anhäufen; *evidence* sammeln. **2** *vi* sich ansammeln; *(possessions, wealth also)* sich anhäufen; *(evidence)* sich häufen.

accumulation [əˌkjuːmjʊˈleɪʃən] *n see vi* Ansammlung *f*; Anhäufung *f*; Häufung *f*.

accuracy [ˈækjʊrəsɪ] *n* Genauigkeit *f*.

accurate [ˈækjʊrɪt] *adj* genau. **his aim was ~** er hat genau gezielt.

accusation [ˌækjʊˈzeɪʃən] *n* Anschuldigung *f*; *(Jur)* Anklage *f*; *(reproach)* Vorwurf *m*.

accusative [əˈkjuːzətɪv] *n* Akkusativ *m*.

accuse [əˈkjuːz] *vt* **(a)** *(Jur)* anklagen *(of* wegen, *gen)*. **(b) to ~ sb of doing sth** jdn beschuldigen *or* bezichtigen, etw getan zu haben; **are you accusing me of lying?** willst du (damit) vielleicht sagen, daß ich lüge?; **to ~ sb of being untidy** jdm vorwerfen, unordentlich zu sein.

accused [əˈkjuːzd] *n* **the ~** der/die Angeklagte; die Angeklagten *pl*.

accusing [əˈkjuːzɪŋ] *adj* anklagend.

accustom [əˈkʌstəm] *vt* **to be ~ed to sth/to doing sth** an etw *(acc)* gewöhnt sein/gewöhnt sein, etw zu tun; **to become ~ed to sth/to doing sth** sich an etw *(acc)* gewöhnen/sich daran gewöhnen, etw zu tun.

ace [eɪs] *n (Cards, Tennis, col: expert)* As *nt*. **the ~ of clubs** das Kreuzas; **he came within an ~ of winning** er hätte um ein Haar gesiegt.

ache [eɪk] **1** *n* Schmerz *m*. **I have an ~ in my side** ich habe Schmerzen in der Seite; **just a few little ~s and pains** nur ein paar Wehwehchen *(col)*. **2** *vi* **(a)** weh tun, schmerzen. **my head/stomach ~s** mir tut der Kopf/Magen weh; **it makes my heart ~ to see him** *(fig)* es tut mir in der Seele weh, wenn ich ihn sehe. **(b)** *(fig: yearn)* **to ~ to do sth** sich danach sehnen, etw zu tun.

achieve [əˈtʃiːv] *vt* erreichen, schaffen; *success* erzielen; *victory* erringen; *rank also, title* erlangen. **she ~d a great deal** *(did a lot of work)* sie hat eine Menge geleistet; *(was quite successful)* sie hat viel erreicht.

achievement [əˈtʃiːvmənt] *n* **(a)** *(act) see vt* Erreichen *nt*; Erzielen *nt*; Erringen *nt*; Erlangen *nt*. **(b)** *(thing achieved)* Leistung *f*; *(of civilization, technology)* Errungenschaft *f*. **that's quite an ~!** das ist wirklich eine Leistung! *(also iro)*.

acid [ˈæsɪd] **1** *adj (sour, Chem)* sauer; *(fig)* ätzend. **~ rain** Saurer Regen; **~ test** *(fig)* Feuerprobe *f*. **2** *n (Chem)* Säure *f*.

acidity [əˈsɪdɪtɪ] *n* Säure *f*; *(Chem)* Säuregehalt *m*.

acknowledge [əkˈnɒlɪdʒ] *vt* anerkennen; *truth, fault, defeat etc* eingestehen, zugeben; *(note receipt of) letter etc* bestätigen; *(respond to) greetings, cheers etc* erwidern. **to ~ oneself beaten** sich geschlagen geben; **to ~ sb's presence** jds Anwesenheit zur Kenntnis nehmen.

acknowledged [əkˈnɒlɪdʒd] *adj attr* anerkannt.

acknowledgement [əkˈnɒlɪdʒmənt] *n see vt* Anerkennung *f*; Eingeständnis *nt*; Bestätigung *f*; Erwiderung *f*. **in ~ of** in Anerkennung *(+gen)*.

acme [ˈækmɪ] *n* Höhepunkt, Gipfel *m*.

acne [ˈæknɪ] *n* Akne *f*.

acorn [ˈeɪkɔːn] *n* Eichel *f*.

acoustic [əˈkuːstɪk] *adj* akustisch.

acoustics [əˈkuːstɪks] *n sing or pl* Akustik *f*.

acquaint [əˈkweɪnt] *vt* **(a)** *(make familiar)* bekannt machen. **to be ~ed/thoroughly ~ed with sth** mit etw bekannt/vertraut sein; **to become ~ed with sth** etw kennenlernen; **to ~ oneself with sth** sich mit etw vertraut machen. **(b)** *(with person)* **to be ~ed with sb** mit jdm bekannt sein; **to become** *or* **get ~ed** sich (näher) kennenlernen.

acquaintance [əˈkweɪntəns] *n* **(a)** *(person)* Bekannte(r) *mf*. **(b)** *(with person)* Bekanntschaft *f*; *(with subject etc)* Kenntnis *f (with gen)*. **to make sb's ~** jds Bekanntschaft machen; **it improves on ~** man kommt mit der Zeit auf den Geschmack.

acquiesce [ˌækwɪˈes] *vi* einwilligen *(in* in *+acc)*; *(submissively)* sich fügen *(in dat)*.

acquiescence [ˌækwɪˈesns] *n see vi* Einwilligung *f (in* in *+acc)*; Fügung *f (in* in *+acc)*.

acquiescent [ˌækwɪˈesnt] *adj* fügsam.

acquire [əˈkwaɪəʳ] *vt* erwerben; *habit* annehmen. **to ~ a taste for sth** Geschmack an etw *(dat)* finden; **it's an ~d taste** das ist (nur) was für Kenner.

acquisition [ˌækwɪˈzɪʃən] *n* **(a)** *(act)* Erwerb *m*. **(b)** *(thing acquired)* Anschaffung *f*.

acquisitive [əˈkwɪzɪtɪv] *adj* auf Erwerb aus, habgierig *(pej)*.

acquit [əˈkwɪt] **1** *vt* freisprechen. **2** *vr* **he ~ted himself well** er hat seine Sache gut gemacht.

acquittal [əˈkwɪtl] *n* Freispruch *m*.

acre [ˈeɪkəʳ] *n* ≈ Morgen *m*.

acrid [ˈækrɪd] *adj taste* bitter; *(of wine)* sauer; *comment, smoke* beißend.

acrimonious [ˌækrɪˈməʊnɪəs] *adj discussion, argument* erbittert; *person, words* bissig.

acrimony [ˈækrɪmənɪ] *n see* **acrimonious** erbitterte Schärfe; Bissigkeit *f*.

acrobat [ˈækrəbæt] *n* Akrobat(in *f*) *m*.

acrobatic [ˌækrəʊˈbætɪk] *adj* akrobatisch.

acrobatics [ˌækrəʊˈbætɪks] *npl* Akrobatik *f*.

across [əˈkrɒs] **1** *adv* **(a)** *(direction) (to the other side)* hinüber; *(from the other side)* herüber; *(crosswise)* (quer)durch. **to cut sth ~** etw (quer) durchschneiden; **he was already ~** er war schon drüben; **~ from your house** gegenüber von eurem Haus; **the stripes go ~** es ist quer gestreift. **(b)** *(measurement)* breit; *(of round object)* im Durchmesser. **how far is it ~?** wie groß ist der Durchmesser? **(c)** *(in crosswords)* waagerecht.

2 *prep* **(a)** *(direction)* über *(+acc)*; *(diagonally ~)* quer durch *(+acc)*. **to run ~ the road** über die Straße laufen; **a tree fell ~ the path** ein Baum fiel quer über den Weg. **(b)** *(position)* über *(+dat)*. **a tree lay ~ the path** ein Baum lag quer über dem Weg; **from ~ the sea** von jenseits des Meeres *(geh)*, von der anderen Seite des Meeres; **he lives ~ the street from us** er wohnt uns gegenüber; **from ~ the hall** von der anderen Seite der Halle.

across-the-board [əˈkrɒsðəˈbɔːd] *adj attr* allgemein.

act [ækt] **1** *n* **(a)** *(deed, thing done)* Tat *f*; *(official, ceremonial)* Akt *m*. **an ~ of mercy** ein Gnadenakt *m*; **an ~ of God** höhere Gewalt *no pl*; **an ~ of folly/madness** reine Dummheit/reiner Wahnsinn. **(b) to be in the ~ of doing sth** (gerade) dabei sein, etw zu tun; **to catch sb in the ~** jdn auf frischer Tat ertappen. **(c) ~ (of Parliament)** Gesetz *nt.* **(d)** *(Theat) (of play, opera)* Akt *m; (turn)* Nummer *f.* **to get in on the ~** *(fig col)* mit von der Partie sein. **(e)** *(fig: pretence)* **it's all an ~** das ist alles nur Theater *or* Schau *(col).*

2 *vt part* spielen; *play* aufführen. **to ~ the fool** herumalbern, den Clown spielen.

3 *vi* **(a)** *(Theat) (perform)* spielen; *(to be an actor, fig)* schauspielern, Theater spielen. **he's only ~ing** er tut (doch) nur so; **to ~ stupid/innocent** den Dummen/Unschuldigen spielen *or* markieren *(col).* **(b)** *(function) (brakes etc)* funktionieren; *(drug)* wirken. **to ~ as ...** wirken als ...; *(have function)* fungieren als ...; **it ~s as a deterrent** das wirkt abschreckend; **to ~ for sb** jdn vertreten. **(c)** *(behave)* sich verhalten. **~ like a man!** sei ein Mann!; **she ~ed as though she was surprised** sie tat so, als ob sie überrascht wäre. **(d)** *(take action)* handeln. **he ~ed to stop it** er unternahm etwas dagegen.

♦**act on** *or* **upon** *vi +prep obj* **(a)** *(affect)* wirken auf *(+acc).* **(b)** *(take action on) warning, report* handeln auf *(+acc)* ... hin; *suggestion, advice* folgen *(+dat).*

♦**act out** *vt sep fantasies etc* durchspielen. **the affair was ~ed ~ at ...** die Affäre spielte sich in ... ab.

♦**act up** *vi (col) (bad knee etc)* Ärger machen; *(person also)* Theater machen *(col); (to attract attention)* sich aufspielen; *(machine also)* verrückt spielen *(col).*

acting ['æktɪŋ] **1** *adj* **(a)** stellvertretend *attr.* **(b)** *attr (Theat)* schauspielerisch. **2** *n (Theat: profession)* Schauspielerei *f.* **what was the/his ~ like?** wie waren die Schauspieler/wie hat er gespielt?; **I didn't like his ~** ich mochte seine Art zu spielen nicht.

action ['ækʃən] *n* **(a)** *no pl (activity)* Handeln *nt; (of play, novel etc)* Handlung *f.* **now is the time for ~** die Zeit zum Handeln ist gekommen; **a man of ~** ein Mann der Tat; **to take ~** etwas *or* Schritte unternehmen; **course of ~** Vorgehen *nt.*

(b) *(deed)* Tat *f.*

(c) *(motion, operation)* **in/out of ~** *(machine)* in/außer Betrieb; *(operational)* einsatzfähig/nicht einsatzfähig; **to go into ~** in Aktion treten; **to put a plan into ~** einen Plan in die Tat umsetzen; **to put out of ~** außer Gefecht setzen.

(d) *(exciting events)* Action *f (col).* **a novel full of ~** ein handlungsgeladener Roman.

(e) *(Mil) (fighting)* Aktionen *pl; (battle)* Kampf *m,* Gefecht *nt.* **enemy ~** feindliche Handlungen *or* Aktionen *pl;* **killed in ~** gefallen; **he saw ~ in the desert** er war in der Wüste im Einsatz; **they never went into ~** sie kamen nie zum Einsatz.

(f) *(way of operating) (of machine)* Arbeitsweise *f; (of piano etc)* Mechanik *f; (of watch, gun)* Mechanismus *m; (way of moving: of athlete etc)* Bewegung *f.*

(g) *(esp Chem, Phys: effect)* Wirkung *f (on* auf *+acc).*

(h) *(Jur)* Klage *f.* **to bring an ~ (against sb)** eine Klage (gegen jdn) anstrengen.

actionable ['ækʃnəbl] *adj* verfolgbar; *statement* klagbar.

action: ~ group *n* Initiative *f;* **~-packed** *adj film, book* aktions- *or* handlungsgeladen; **~ replay** *n* Wiederholung *f.*

activate ['æktɪveɪt] *vt* betätigen; *(automatically) alarm etc* auslösen; *(lever)* in Gang setzen.

active ['æktɪv] *adj* aktiv *(also Gram); mind, social life* rege; *volcano also* tätig; *dislike* offen. **to be ~ in politics** politisch aktiv *or* tätig sein; **to be under ~ consideration** ernsthaft erwogen werden; **on ~ service** *(Mil)* im Einsatz; **he played an ~ part in it** er war aktiv daran beteiligt.

actively ['æktɪvlɪ] *adv* aktiv.

activist ['æktɪvɪst] *n* Aktivist(in *f*) *m.*

activity [æk'tɪvɪtɪ] *n* **(a)** *no pl* Aktivität *f; (in classroom, station, on beach etc also)* reges Leben; *(in market, town, office)* Geschäftigkeit *f.* **(b)** *(pastime)* Betätigung *f.* **the church organizes many activities** die Kirche organisiert viele Veranstaltungen; **business/social activities** geschäftliche/gesellschaftliche Unternehmungen *pl.*

actor ['æktə^r] *n (lit, fig)* Schauspieler *m.*

actress ['æktrɪs] *n (lit, fig)* Schauspielerin *f.*

actual ['æktjʊəl] *adj* eigentlich; *reason, price also, result* tatsächlich; *case, example* konkret. **in ~ fact** eigentlich; **what were his ~ words?** was hat er genau gesagt?; **this is the ~ house** das ist hier das Haus.

actuality [,æktjʊ'ælɪtɪ] *n (reality)* Wirklichkeit *f.*

actually ['æktjʊəlɪ] *adv* **(a)** *(to tell the truth, in actual fact)* eigentlich; *(by the way)* übrigens. **you don't know him, do you? — ~ I do** Sie kennen ihn (doch) nicht, oder? — doch, ich kenne ihn (tatsächlich); **I'm going soon, tomorrow ~** ich gehe bald, genauer gesagt morgen; **you're never home — ~ I was home last night** du bist nie zu Hause — doch, gestern abend war ich da. **(b)** *(truly, in reality, showing surprise)* tatsächlich. **don't tell me you're ~ going now!** sag bloß, du gehst jetzt tatsächlich *or* wirklich!; **oh, you're ~ in!** oh, du bist sogar da!; **I wasn't ~ there, but ...** ich war zwar selbst nicht dabei aber ...; **as for ~ working ...** was die Arbeit selbst betrifft ...

actuary ['æktjʊərɪ] *n (Insur)* Aktuar *m.*

actuate ['æktjʊeɪt] *vt (lit)* auslösen; *(fig)* treiben.

acumen ['ækjʊmen] *n* Scharfsinn *m.* **business/political ~** Geschäftssinn *m*/politische Klugheit.

acupuncture ['ækjʊ,pʌŋktʃə^r] *n* Akupunktur *f.*

acute [ə'kjuːt] *adj* **(a)** *(intense, serious, Med)* akut; *pleasure* intensiv. **(b)** *eyesight* scharf; *hearing also, sense of smell* fein. **(c)** *(shrewd)* scharf; *person* scharfsinnig; *child* aufgeweckt. **(d)** *(Math) angle* spitz.

acutely [ə'kjuːtlɪ] *adv* **(a)** *(intensely)* akut; *feel* intensiv; *embarrassed, uncomfortable* äußerst. **(b)** *(shrewdly)* scharfsinnig; *observe* scharf.

acuteness [ə'kjuːtnɪs] *n* **(a)** *(of problem)* Dringlichkeit *f.* **(b)** *see adj (b)* Schärfe *f;* Feinheit *f.* **(c)** *see adj (c)* Schärfe *f;* Scharfsinn *m;* Aufgewecktheit *f.*

AD = Anno Domini A.D., a.D.

ad [æd] = **advertisement** Anzeige *f,* Inserat *nt.* **small ~s** Kleinanzeigen *pl.*

Adam ['ædəm] *n* **~'s apple** Adamsapfel *m;* **I don't know him from ~** *(col)* ich habe keine Ahnung, wer er ist *(col).*

adamant ['ædəmənt] *adj* hart. **since you're ~** da Sie darauf bestehen; **he was ~ about going** er bestand hartnäckig darauf zu gehen.

adapt [ə'dæpt] **1** *vt* anpassen *(to dat); machine* umstellen *(to, for* auf *+acc); vehicle, building* umbauen *(to, for* für*); text, book etc* adaptieren, bearbeiten *(for* für*).* **2** *vi* sich anpassen *(to dat).*

adaptability [ə,dæptə'bɪlɪtɪ] *n see adj* Anpassungsfähigkeit *f;* Vielseitigkeit *f;* Flexibilität *f.*

adaptable [ə'dæptəbl] *adj person* anpassungsfähig; *vehicle* vielseitig; *schedule* flexibel.

adaptation [,ædæp'teɪʃən] *n (process)* Adaptation *f (to* an *+acc); (of person, plant, animal)* Anpassung *f (to* an *+acc); (of machine)* Umstellung *f (to* auf *+acc); (of vehicle, building)* Umbau *m; (of text)* Bearbeitung *f.*

adapter, adaptor [ə'dæptə^r] *n (Elec)* Adapter *m; (for several plugs)* Doppel-/Dreifachstecker, Mehrfachstecker *m.*

add [æd] **1** *vt* **(a)** *(Math)* addieren; *(~ up) several numbers also* zusammenzählen. **(b)** hinzufügen *(to* zu*)*; *ingredients, money also* dazutun *(to* zu*)*; *(say in addition also)* dazusagen; *(build on)* anbauen. **~ed to which ...** hinzu kommt, daß ... **2** *vi (Math)* addieren.

♦ **add to** *vi +prep obj (expand) collection* erweitern; *(increase) problems* vergrößern; *(improve) flavour* steigern, verfeinern.

♦ **add up 1** *vt sep* zusammenzählen. **2** *vi* **(a)** *(figures etc)* stimmen; *(fig: make sense)* sich reimen. **it's beginning to ~ ~** jetzt wird so manches klar. **(b) to ~ ~ to** *(column, figures, fig)* ergeben; *(expenses also)* sich belaufen auf *(+acc)*; **it doesn't ~ ~ to much** *(fig)* das ist nicht berühmt *(col)*.

adder ['ædə^r] *n* Otter *f*.

addict ['ædɪkt] *n (lit, fig)* Süchtige(r) *mf*. **he's a TV/heroin ~** er ist fernseh-/heroinsüchtig.

addicted [ə'dɪktɪd] *adj* süchtig. **to be/become ~ to heroin** heroinsüchtig sein/werden; **he's ~ to it** *(fig)* das ist bei ihm schon zur Sucht geworden.

addiction [ə'dɪkʃən] *n* Sucht *f (to* nach*)*; *(no pl: state of dependence also)* Süchtigkeit *f*. **~ to alcohol** Trunksucht *f*.

addictive [ə'dɪktɪv] *adj* **to be ~** *(lit)* süchtig machen; *(fig)* zu einer Sucht werden können.

addition [ə'dɪʃən] *n* **(a)** *(Math)* Addition *f*. **the ~ of Greece to the EEC** die Erweiterung der EG durch Griechenland. **(b)** *(thing added)* Zusatz *m (to* zu*)*; *(to list)* Ergänzung *f (to* zu*)*. **they are expecting an ~ to their family** *(col)* sie erwarten (Familien)zuwachs. **(c) in ~** außerdem, obendrein; **in ~ to sth** zusätzlich zu etw.

additional [ə'dɪʃənl] *adj* zusätzlich. **~ charge** Aufpreis *m*; **an ~ chapter** ein weiteres Kapitel.

additive ['ædɪtɪv] *n* Zusatz *m*.

address [ə'dres] **1** *n* **(a)** Adresse *f*. **home ~** Privatadresse *f*; *(when travelling)* Heimatanschrift *f*. **(b)** *(speech)* Ansprache *f*. **(c) form of ~** (Form *f* der) Anrede *f*. **2** *vt* **(a)** *letter, parcel* adressieren *(to* an *+acc)*. **(b)** *(direct) complaints, speech, remarks* richten *(to* an *+acc)*. **(c)** *(speak to) meeting* sprechen zu; *jury* sich wenden an *(+acc)*; *person* anreden. **3** *vr* **to ~ oneself to sb** *(speak to)* jdn ansprechen; **to ~ oneself to a task** *(form)* sich einer Aufgabe widmen.

address book *n* Adreßbuch *nt*.

addressee [ˌædre'siː] *n* Empfänger(in *f*) *m*.

adenoids ['ædɪnɔɪdz] *npl* Rachenmandeln *pl*.

adept ['ædept] **1** *n* Meister(in *f*) *m (in, at* in *+dat)*. **2** *adj* **~ at sewing** geschickt im Nähen.

adequate ['ædɪkwɪt] *adj* adäquat, angemessen; *(sufficient) supply, heating system* ausreichend; *time* genügend *inv*. **to be ~** *(sufficient)* (aus)reichen; *(good enough)* angemessen sein; **this is just not ~** das ist einfach unzureichend.

adhere [əd'hɪə^r] *vi* haften *(to* an *+dat)*.

♦ **adhere to** *vi +prep obj* festhalten an *(+dat)*.

adherence [əd'hɪərəns] *n* Festhalten *nt (to* an *+dat)*.

adherent [əd'hɪərənt] *n* Anhänger(in *f*) *m (of gen)*.

adhesive [əd'hiːzɪv] **1** *n* Klebstoff *m*. **2** *adj* haftend; *(more firmly)* klebend. **~ plaster** Heftpflaster *nt*; **~ tape** Klebstreifen *m*.

ad hoc [ˌæd'hɒk] *adj, adv* ad hoc *inv*.

adjacent [ə'dʒeɪsənt] *adj* angrenzend; *room also, angles* Neben-. **to be ~ to sth** an etw *(acc)* angrenzen, neben etw *(dat)* liegen.

adjective ['ædʒektɪv] *n* Adjektiv, Eigenschaftswort *nt*.

adjoin [ə'dʒɔɪn] **1** *vt* grenzen an *(+acc)*. **2** *vi* aneinander grenzen.

adjoining [ə'dʒɔɪnɪŋ] *adj room* Neben-, Nachbar-; *field* angrenzend; *(of two things)* nebeneinanderliegend. **in the ~ office** im Büro nebenan.

adjourn [ə'dʒɜːn] **1** *vt* **(a)** vertagen *(until* auf *+acc)*. **he ~ed the meeting for three hours** er unterbrach die Konferenz für drei Stunden. **(b)** *(US: end)* beenden. **2** *vi* **(a)** sich vertagen *(until* auf *+acc)*. **to ~ for lunch/one hour** für die Mittagspause/für eine Stunde unterbrechen. **(b) to ~ to the lounge** sich ins Wohnzimmer begeben.

adjournment [ə'dʒɜːnmənt] *n* Vertagung *f (until* auf *+acc)*; *(within a day)* Unterbrechung *f*.

adjudicate [ə'dʒuːdɪkeɪt] **1** *vt claim* entscheiden; *competition* Preisrichter sein bei. **2** *vi* entscheiden, urteilen *(on, in* bei*)*; *(in dispute)* Schiedsrichter sein *(on* bei, in *+dat)*; *(in competition, dog-show etc)* als Preisrichter fungieren.

adjudicator [ə'dʒuːdɪkeɪtə^r] *n (in competition)* Preisrichter(in *f*) *m*; *(in dispute)* Schiedsrichter(in *f*) *m*.

adjust [ə'dʒʌst] **1** *vt (set) machine, carburettor, brakes, knob etc* einstellen; *(alter) plan, terms* ändern; *height, speed* verstellen; *(correct, readjust)* nachstellen; *height, speed, flow* regulieren; *hat, tie* zurechtrücken. **to ~ sth to new requirements/conditions** etw neuen Erfordernissen/Bedingungen anpassen. **2** *vi (to new circumstances)* sich anpassen *(to dat)*; *(to new requirements, demands)* sich einstellen *(to* auf *+acc)*.

adjustable [ə'dʒʌstəbl] *adj tool, angle* verstellbar; *shape* veränderlich, variabel; *speed, temperature* regulierbar; *tax, rate of production* beweglich, flexibel; *person, animal, plant* anpassungsfähig. **~ spanner** Engländer *m*.

adjustment [ə'dʒʌstmənt] *n* **(a)** *see vt* Einstellung *f*; Änderung *f*; Verstellen *nt*; Nachstellen *nt*; Regulierung *f*. **to make an ~ to sth** etw einstellen/verstellen/nachstellen *etc*; **to make ~s** Änderungen vornehmen. **(b)** *(socially etc)* Anpassung *f*.

ad-lib [æd'lɪb] **1** *adv* aus dem Stegreif. **2** *adj* improvisiert, Stegreif-. **3** *vti* improvisieren.

administer [əd'mɪnɪstə^r] *vt* **(a)** *institution, funds* verwalten; *business, affairs* führen; *(run) company, department* die Verwaltungsangelegenheiten regeln *(+gen)*. **(b)** *(to sb* jdm*) medicine* verabreichen; *sacraments* spenden. **to ~ an oath to sb** jdm einen Eid abnehmen.

administration [ədˌmɪnɪs'treɪʃən] *n* **(a)** *no pl* Verwaltung *f*; *(of a project etc)* Organisation *f*. **(b) the Schmidt ~** die Regierung Schmidt. **(c)** *no pl (of remedy)* Verabreichung *f*; *(of sacrament)* Spenden *nt*. **the ~ of an oath** die Vereidigung; **the ~ of justice** die Rechtsprechung.

administrative [əd'mɪnɪstrətɪv] *adj* administrativ.

administrator [əd'mɪnɪstreɪtə^r] *n* Verwalter *m*.

admirable ['ædmərəbl] *adj* bewundernswert, erstaunlich; *(excellent)* ausgezeichnet.

admiral ['ædmərel] *n* Admiral *m*.

Admiralty ['ædmərəltɪ] *n (Brit)* britisches Marineministerium.

admiration [ˌædmə'reɪʃən] *n* Bewunderung *f*.

admire [əd'maɪə^r] *vt* bewundern.

admissible [əd'mɪsəbl] *adj* zulässig.

admission [əd'mɪʃən] *n* **(a)** *(entry)* Zutritt *m*; *(to club also, university)* Zulassung *f*; *(price)* Eintritt *m*; *(to hospital)* Einlieferung *f*. **(b)** *(confession)* Eingeständnis *nt*. **by his own ~** nach eigenem Eingeständnis; **that would be an ~ of failure** das hieße, sein Versagen einzugestehen.

admit [əd'mɪt] *vt* **(a)** *(let in)* hinein-/hereinlassen; *(permit to join)* zulassen *(to* zu*)*, aufnehmen *(to* in *+acc)*. **to be ~ted to hospital** ins Krankenhaus eingeliefert werden; **children not ~ted** kein Zutritt für Kinder. **(b)** *(acknowledge)* zugeben. **he ~ted himself beaten** er gab sich geschlagen.

admittance [əd'mɪtəns] *n (to building)* Zutritt *(to* zu*)*.

admittedly [əd'mɪtɪdlɪ] *adv* zugegebenermaßen.

ad nauseam [ˌæd'nɔːsɪæm] *adv* bis zum Überdruß, bis zum Gehtnichtmehr *(col)*.

ado [ə'duː] *n* **without further ~** ohne weiteres.

adolescence [ˌædəʊ'lesns] *n* Jugend *f*; *(puberty)* Pubertät *f*.
adolescent [ˌædəʊ'lesnt] **1** *n* Jugendliche(r) *mf*. **2** *adj* Jugend-; *(in puberty)* Pubertäts-; *(immature)* unreif. **he is so ~** er steckt noch in der Pubertät.
adopt [ə'dɒpt] *vt* **(a)** *child* adoptieren; *family, city* die Patenschaft übernehmen für. **(b)** *suggestion, method* übernehmen; *mannerisms* annehmen. **(c)** *(Pol) motion* annehmen; *candidate* nominieren.
adopted [ə'dɒptɪd] *adj son, daughter* Adoptiv-, adoptiert; *country* Wahl-.
adoption [ə'dɒpʃən] *n* **(a)** *(of child)* Adoption *f*; *(into the family)* Aufnahme *f*. **(b)** *(of method, idea)* Übernahme *f*; *(of mannerisms: law, candidate)* Annahme *f*.
adorable [ə'dɔːrəbl] *adj* bezaubernd, hinreißend.
adoration [ˌædə'reɪʃən] *n* (grenzenlose) Liebe *(of* für*)*; *(of God)* Anbetung *f*.
adore [ə'dɔːʳ] *vt* über alles lieben.
adorn [ə'dɔːn] *vt* schmücken.
adrenalin(e) [ə'drenəlɪn] *n* Adrenalin *nt*. **when the ~'s going he ...** wenn er richtig aufgedreht ist, ... er ...
Adriatic (Sea) [ˌeɪdrɪ'ætɪk('siː)] *n* Adria *f*.
adrift [ə'drɪft] *adv, adj pred* **to be ~** *(Naut)* treiben; **to come ~** *(wire, hair etc)* sich lösen; *(plans)* fehlschlagen; *(theory)* zusammenbrechen.
adroit [ə'drɔɪt] *adj* gewandt; *mind* scharf.
adulation [ˌædjʊ'leɪʃən] *n* Verherrlichung *f*.
adult ['ædʌlt] **1** *n* Erwachsene(r) *mf*. **2** *adj person* erwachsen; *film* für Erwachsene; *(mature) decision* reif. **~ education** Erwachsenenbildung *f*.
adulterate [ə'dʌltəreɪt] *vt drink* panschen; *food, (fig) text* verhunzen *(col)*.
adultery [ə'dʌltərɪ] *n* Ehebruch *m*. **to commit ~** Ehebruch begehen.
advance [əd'vɑːns] **1** *n* **(a)** *(progress)* Fortschritt *m*. **(b)** *(of science)* Weiterentwicklung *f*; *(of ideas, sea)* Vordringen *nt*. **recent ~s** jüngste Entwicklungen; **with the ~ of old age** mit fortschreitendem Alter. **(c)** *(Mil)* Vorrücken *nt*. **(d)** *(money)* Vorschuß *m (on* auf *+acc)*. **(e)** *(amorous, fig)* **~s** *pl* Annäherungsversuche *pl*. **(f) in ~** im voraus; *(temporal also)* vorher; **to send sb on in ~** jdn vorausschicken; **to arrive in ~ of the others** vor den anderen ankommen.
2 *vt* **(a)** *(move forward) date, time* vorverlegen. **(b)** *(further) work, project* voranbringen; *cause, interests* fördern; *growth* vorantreiben. **(c)** *suggestion, opinion* vorbringen. **(d)** *(pay beforehand) (sb* jdm) (als) Vorschuß geben, vorschießen *(col)*; *(lend)* als Kredit geben.
3 *vi* **(a)** *(Mil)* vorrücken. **(b)** *(move forward)* vorankommen. **to ~ towards sb/sth** auf jdn/etw zugehen/-kommen; **to ~ upon sb** drohend auf jdn zukommen. **(c)** *(fig: progress)* Fortschritte machen.
advance booking *n* Reservierung *f*; *(Theat)* Vorverkauf *m*.
advanced [əd'vɑːnst] *adj student, level, age* fortgeschritten; *studies, mathematics etc* höher; *technology also, ideas* fortschrittlich; *version, model* verbessert, neu(er); *level of civilization* hoch; *position, observation post etc* vorgeschoben. **~ in years** in fortgeschrittenem Alter.
advancement [əd'vɑːnsmənt] *n (furtherance)* Förderung *f*.
advance: ~ notice *or* **warning** *n* frühzeitiger Bescheid; *(of sth bad)* Vorwarnung *f*; **~ party** *n (Mil, fig)* Vorhut *f*; **~ payment** *n* Vorauszahlung *f*.
advantage [əd'vɑːntɪdʒ] *n* Vorteil *m (also Tennis)*. **to have an ~ (over sb)** (jdm gegenüber) im Vorteil sein; **he had the ~ of greater experience** er war durch seine größere Erfahrung im Vorteil; **that gives you an ~ over me** damit sind Sie mir gegenüber im Vorteil; **to take ~ of sb/sth** jdn/etw ausnutzen; **he took ~ of her** *(euph)* er hat sie mißbraucht; **to turn sth to (good) ~** Nutzen aus etw ziehen; **it would be to our ~** es wäre vorteilhaft für uns.
advantageous [ˌædvən'teɪdʒəs] *adj* vorteilhaft.
advent ['ædvənt] *n* **(a)** *(of era)* Beginn, Anbruch *m*; *(of jet plane etc)* Aufkommen *nt*. **(b)** *(Eccl)* **A~** Advent *m*.
adventure [əd'ventʃəʳ] *n* Abenteuer *nt*. **an ~ into the unknown** ein Vorstoß ins Unbekannte.
adventurer [əd'ventʃərəʳ] *n* Abenteurer(in *f*) *m*.
adventurous [əd'ventʃərəs] *adj person* abenteuerlustig; *journey* abenteuerlich; *scheme* gewagt.
adverb ['ædvɜːb] *n* Adverb, Umstandswort *nt*.
adversary ['ædvəsərɪ] *n* Widersacher(in *f*) *m*; *(in contest)* Gegner(in *f*) *m*.
adverse ['ædvɜːs] *adj* ungünstig; *criticism, comment, reaction* negativ; *effect* nachteilig.
adversity [əd'vɜːsɪtɪ] *n no pl* Not *f*. **in ~** im Unglück, in der Not.
advert ['ædvɜːt] *n (Brit)* = **advertisement.**
advertise ['ædvətaɪz] *vti* **(a)** *(publicize)* Werbung *or* Reklame machen (für), werben (für). **(b)** *(in paper etc) flat, table etc* inserieren; *job, post also* ausschreiben. **to ~ for sb** jdn (per Anzeige) suchen.
advertisement [əd'vɜːtɪsmənt] *n* **(a)** *(Comm)* Werbung, Reklame *f no pl*; *(in paper also)* Anzeige *f*. **(b)** *(announcement)* Anzeige *f*; *(in paper also)* Inserat *nt*. **to put an ~ in the paper (for sb/sth)** eine Anzeige (für jdn/etw) in die Zeitung setzen.
advertiser ['ædvətaɪzəʳ] *n (in paper)* Inserent(in *f*) *m*.
advertising ['ædvətaɪzɪŋ] *n* Werbung, Reklame *f*. **he is in ~** er ist in der Werbung (tätig).
advertising *in cpds* Werbe-; **~ agency** *n* Werbeagentur *f*; **~ campaign** *n* Werbekampagne *f*.
advice [əd'vaɪs] *n* **(a)** *no pl* Rat *m no pl*. **a piece of ~, some ~** ein Rat(schlag) *m*; **to take sb's ~** jds Rat (be)folgen; **take my ~** hör auf mich. **(b)** *(Comm)* Bescheid *m*. **~ note** *(Brit)* Benachrichtigung *f*.
advisable [əd'vaɪzəbl] *adj* ratsam.
advise [əd'vaɪz] *vti* **(a)** *(give advice to)* raten *(+dat)*; *(professionally)* beraten. **to ~ caution** zur Vorsicht raten; **I would ~ you to do it/not to do it** ich würde dir zuraten/abraten; **to ~ sb against sth/doing sth** jdm von etw abraten/jdm abraten, etw zu tun. **(b)** *(Comm)* unterrichten.
advisedly [əd'vaɪzɪdlɪ] *adv* richtig. **and I use the word ~** ich verwende bewußt dieses Wort.
adviser [əd'vaɪzəʳ] *n* Ratgeber(in *f*) *m*; *(professional)* Berater(in *f*) *m*.
advisory [əd'vaɪzərɪ] *adj* beratend. **to act in a purely ~ capacity** rein beratende Funktion haben.
advocate ['ædvəkɪt] **1** *n* **(a)** *(of cause etc)* Verfechter, Befürworter *m*. **(b)** *(esp Scot: Jur)* (Rechts)anwalt *m*/-anwältin *f*. **2** ['ædvəkeɪt] *vt* eintreten für; *plan etc* befürworten.
Aegean [iː'dʒiːən] *n* **the ~ (Sea)** das Ägäische Meer.
aerial ['ɛərɪəl] **1** *n (esp Brit)* Antenne *f*. **2** *adj* Luft-.
aerial: ~ photograph *n* Luftbild *nt*, Luftaufnahme *f*; **~ photography** *n* Luftaufnahmen *pl*.
aero- ['ɛərəʊ] *pref* aero- *(form)*, Luft-.
aerobatics ['ɛərəʊ'bætɪks] *npl* Kunstfliegen *nt*.
aerobics [ɛər'əʊbɪks] *n sing* Aerobic *nt*.
aerodrome ['ɛərədreʊm] *n (Brit)* Flugplatz *m*.
aerodynamic ['ɛərəʊdaɪ'næmɪk] *adj* aerodynamisch.
aerodynamics ['ɛərəʊdaɪ'næmɪks] *n sing* Aerodynamik *f*.
aerofoil ['ɛərəʊfɔɪl] *n* Tragflügel *m*; *(on racing cars)* Spoiler *m*.
aeronautic(al) [ˌɛərə'nɔːtɪk(əl)] *adj* Luftfahrt-. **~ engineering** Flugzeugbau *m*.
aeronautics [ˌɛərə'nɔːtɪks] *n sing* Luftfahrt *f*.
aeroplane ['ɛərəpleɪn] *n (Brit)* Flugzeug *nt*.
aerosol ['ɛərəsɒl] *n (can)* Spraydose *f*; *(mixture)*

Aerosol *nt.*

aerospace *in cpds* Raumfahrt-.

aesthete, *(US)* **esthete** ['iːsθiːt] *n* Ästhet(in *f*) *m.*

aesthetic(al), *(US)* **esthetic(al)** [iːs'θetɪk(əl)] *adj* ästhetisch.

aesthetics, *(US)* **esthetics** [iːs'θetɪks] *n sing* Ästhetik *f.*

afar [ə'fɑːʳ] *adv (liter)* weit. **from ~** aus der Ferne.

affable ['æfəbl] *adj* umgänglich, freundlich.

affair [ə'fɛəʳ] *n* **(a)** Sache, Angelegenheit *f.* **the Watergate ~** die Watergate-Affäre; **the state of ~s with the economy** die Lage der Wirtschaft; **in the present state of ~s** beim gegenwärtigen Stand der Dinge; **there's a fine state of ~s!** das sind ja schöne Zustände!; **~s of state** Staatsangelegenheiten *pl*; **it's not your ~ what I do in the evenings** was ich abends tue, geht dich nichts an; **that's my/his ~!** das ist meine/seine Sache! **(b)** *(love ~)* Verhältnis *nt*, Affäre *f.*

affect[1] [ə'fekt] *vt* **(a)** *(have effect on)* sich auswirken auf *(+acc)*; *decision, sb's life also* beeinflussen; *health, person* schaden *(+dat).* **(b)** *(concern)* betreffen. **(c)** *(emotionally)* berühren.

affect[2] *vt (feign)* vortäuschen, vorgeben.

affectation [ˌæfek'teɪʃən] *n (pretence)* Vortäuschung *f*; *(artificiality)* Affektiertheit *f no pl.*

affected [ə'fektɪd] *adj person, clothes* affektiert; *behaviour, style, accent also* gekünstelt.

affection [ə'fekʃən] *n (fondness)* Zuneigung *f no pl (for, towards* zu*).* **I have a great ~ for her** ich mag sie sehr gerne; **you could show a little more ~ towards me** du könntest etwas liebevoller (zu mir) sein; **children who lacked ~** Kinder, denen die Liebe fehlte.

affectionate [ə'fekʃənɪt] *adj* liebevoll, zärtlich.

affidavit [ˌæfɪ'deɪvɪt] *n (Jur)* eidesstattliche Versicherung.

affiliated [ə'fɪlɪeɪtɪd] *adj* angeschlossen, Schwester-.

affiliation [əˌfɪlɪ'eɪʃən] *n* Angliederung *f (to, with* an *+acc).* **what are his political ~s?** wie steht es mit seiner politischen Zugehörigkeit?

affinity [ə'fɪnɪtɪ] *n* **(a)** *(liking)* Neigung *f (for, to* zu*)*; *(for person)* Verbundenheit *f (for, to* mit*).* **(b)** *(resemblance, connection)* Verwandtschaft *f.*

affirm [ə'fɜːm] *vt* versichern; *(very forcefully)* beteuern.

affirmation [ˌæfə'meɪʃən] *n see vt* Versicherung *f*; Beteuerung *f.*

affirmative [ə'fɜːmətɪv] *adj* bejahend, positiv. **to answer in the ~** bejahend *or* mit „ja" antworten.

afflict [ə'flɪkt] *vt* plagen, zusetzen *(+dat)*; *(emotionally, mentally also)* belasten; *(troubles, inflation, injuries)* heimsuchen. **the ~ed** die Leidenden *pl.*

affliction [ə'flɪkʃən] *n (distress)* Not *f*; *(pain)* Leiden *pl*; *(illness)* Beschwerde *f.*

affluence ['æfluəns] *n* Reichtum, Wohlstand *m.*

affluent ['æfluənt] *adj* reich, wohlhabend. **the ~ society** die Wohlstandsgesellschaft.

afford [ə'fɔːd] *vt* **(a)** *(also non-financially)* sich *(dat)* leisten. **I can't ~ to buy both of them** ich kann es mir nicht leisten, beide zu kaufen. **(b)** *(liter: provide) (sb sth* jdm etw*)* gewähren, bieten; *pleasure* bereiten.

affray [ə'freɪ] *n (esp Jur)* Schlägerei *f.*

affront [ə'frʌnt] **1** *vt* beleidigen. **2** *n* Beleidigung *f (to sb* jds, *to sth* für etw*)*, Affront *m (to* gegen*).*

Afghanistan [æf'gænɪstæn] *n* Afghanistan *nt.*

afield [ə'fiːld] *adv* **further ~** weiter entfernt.

afloat [ə'fləʊt] *adj pred, adv (Naut)* **to be ~** schwimmen; **the largest navy ~** die größte Flotte auf See; **to get a business ~** *(fig)* ein Geschäft auf die Beine stellen.

afoot [ə'fʊt] *adv* im Gange. **what's ~?** was geht hier vor?

aforementioned [əˌfɔː'menʃənd], **aforesaid** [əˌfɔː'sed] *adj attr (form)* obengenannt.

afraid [ə'freɪd] *adj pred* **(a)** *(frightened)* **to be ~ (of sb/sth)** (vor jdm/etw) Angst haben, sich (vor jdm/etw) fürchten; **don't be ~!** keine Angst!; **I am ~ of hurting him** *or* **that I might hurt him** ich fürchte, ihm weh zu tun *or* ich könnte ihm weh tun; **I was ~ of waking the children** ich wollte die Kinder nicht wecken; **he's not ~ to say what he thinks** er scheut sich nicht, zu sagen, was er denkt; **that's what I was ~ of, I was ~ that would happen** das habe ich befürchtet. **(b)** *(expressing polite regret)* **I'm ~ I can't do it** leider kann ich es nicht machen; **I'm ~ you'll have to wait** Sie müssen leider warten; **I'm ~ not/I'm ~ so** leider nicht/ja, leider.

afresh [ə'freʃ] *adv* noch einmal von vorn.

Africa ['æfrɪkə] *n* Afrika *nt.*

African ['æfrɪkən] **1** *n* Afrikaner(in *f*) *m.* **2** *adj* afrikanisch.

aft [ɑːft] *(Naut) adv sit* achtern; *go* nach achtern.

after 1 *prep* nach *(+dat).* **~ that** danach; **the week ~ next** übernächste Woche; **to run ~ sb** hinter jdm herlaufen; **he shut the door ~ her** er machte die Tür hinter ihr zu; **~ what has happened** nach allem, was geschehen ist; **to do sth ~ all** etw schließlich doch tun; **~ all our efforts!** und das, nachdem wir uns soviel Mühe gegeben haben!; **you tell me lie ~ lie** du erzählst mir eine Lüge nach der anderen; **~ El Greco** in der Art von El Greco; **to be ~ sb/sth** hinter jdm/etw hersein; **what are you ~?** was willst du?; *(looking for)* was suchst du?

2 *adv (time, order)* danach. **the year/week ~** das Jahr/die Woche danach *or* darauf.

3 *conj* nachdem. **~ finishing it I will/I went ...** wenn ich das fertig habe, werde ich .../als ich das fertig hatte, ging ich ...; **~ arriving they went ...** nachdem sie angekommen waren, gingen sie ...

4 *n* **~s** *pl (Brit col)* Nachtisch *m.*

after: ~birth *n* Nachgeburt *f*; **~-care** *n (of convalescent)* Nachbehandlung *f*; **~-dinner** *adj speech, speaker* Tisch-; **~-effect** *n* Nachwirkung *f*; **~-life** *n* Leben *nt* nach dem Tode; **~math** *n* Nachwirkungen *pl*; **in the ~math of sth** nach etw.

afternoon ['ɑːftə'nuːn] *n* Nachmittag *m.* **in the ~** am Nachmittag, nachmittags; **at three o'clock in the ~** (um) drei Uhr nachmittags; **on Sunday ~** (am) Sonntag nachmittag; **this/tomorrow ~** heute/morgen nachmittag; **good ~!** Guten Tag!

after: ~-pains *npl* Nachwehen *pl*; **~-sales service** *n (Brit)* Kundendienst *m*; **~ shave (lotion)** *n* After-shave, Rasierwasser *nt*; **~thought** *n* nachträgliche Idee.

afterwards ['ɑːftəwədz] *adv* nachher; *(after that, after some event etc)* danach, anschließend.

again [ə'gen] *adv* **(a)** wieder. **~ and ~** immer wieder; **to do sth ~** etw noch (ein)mal tun; **not to do sth ~** etw nicht wieder tun; **I'll ring ~ tomorrow** ich rufe morgen noch einmal an; **never ~** nie wieder; **if that happens ~** wenn das noch einmal passiert; **all over ~** noch (ein)mal von vorn; **not ~!** schon wieder! **(b)** *(in quantity)* **as much ~** doppelt soviel, noch (ein)mal soviel. **(c)** *(on the other hand)* wiederum; *(besides, moreover)* außerdem. **but then ~, it may not be true** vielleicht ist es auch gar nicht wahr.

against [ə'genst] *prep* gegen *(+acc).* **he's ~ her going** er ist dagegen, daß sie geht; **to have something ~ sb/sth** etwas gegen jdn/etw haben; **~ their wish** entgegen ihrem Wunsch; **the advantages of flying (as) ~ going by boat** die Vorteile von Flugreisen gegenüber Schiffsreisen.

age [eɪdʒ] **1** *n* **(a)** Alter *nt.* **what is her ~, what ~ is she?** wie alt ist sie?; **he is ten years of ~** er ist zehn Jahre alt; **at the ~ of 15** im Alter von 15 Jahren, mit 15 Jahren; **when I was your ~** als ich

in deinem Alter war; **but he's twice your ~** aber er ist doppelt so alt wie du; **over ~** zu alt; **be** *or* **act your ~!** sei nicht kindisch! **(b)** *(length of life)* Lebensdauer *f*. **(c)** *(Jur)* **to come of ~** volljährig *or* mündig werden, die Volljährigkeit erlangen; **under ~** minderjährig, unmündig. **(d)** *(period, epoch)* Zeit(alter *nt*) *f*. **the ~ of technology** das technologische Zeitalter; **down the ~s** durch alle Zeiten. **(e)** *(col: long time)* **I haven't seen him for ~s, it's been ~s since I saw him** ich habe ihn eine Ewigkeit *or* ewig nicht gesehen *(col)*; **it/he takes ~s** das dauert ewig/er braucht ewig *(col)*.
2 *vi* alt werden, altern.
3 *vt (worry, experience etc)* altern lassen; *(dress, hairstyle etc)* älter machen.

aged [eɪdʒd] **1** *adj* **(a)** im Alter von, ... Jahre alt, -jährig. **a boy ~ ten** ein zehnjähriger Junge. **(b)** ['eidʒɪd] *person* bejahrt, betagt. **2** ['eidʒɪd] *npl* **the ~** die alten Menschen, die Alten *pl*.

age: ~ difference *or* **gap** *n* Altersunterschied *m*; **~-group** *n* Altersgruppe *f*; **~ limit** *n* Altersgrenze *f*.

agency ['eɪdʒənsɪ] *n* **(a)** *(Comm)* Agentur *f*. **typing/tourist ~** Schreib-/Reisebüro *nt*; **they have the Citroën ~** sie haben die Citroën-Vertretung. **(b) through the ~ of friends** durch die Vermittlung *or* mit Hilfe von Freunden.

agenda [ə'dʒendə] *n* Tagesordnung *f*. **on the ~** auf dem Programm.

agent ['eɪdʒənt] *n* **(a)** *(Comm) (person)* Vertreter(in *f*) *m*; *(organization)* Vertretung *f*. **(b)** *(literary, press, secret ~ etc)* Agent(in *f*) *m*; *(Pol)* Wahlkampfleiter(in *f*) *m*. **you're a free ~** du bist dein eigener Herr. **(c)** *(Chem, means)* Mittel *nt*.

age-old ['eidʒəuld] *adj* uralt.

aggravate ['ægrəveɪt] *vt* **(a)** *(worsen)* verschlimmern. **(b)** *(annoy)* aufregen; *(deliberately)* reizen.

aggravating ['ægrəveɪtɪŋ] *adj* ärgerlich; *noise, child* lästig.

aggravation [ˌægrə'veɪʃən] *n* **(a)** Verschlimmerung *f*. **(b)** *(annoyance)* Ärger *m*. **her constant ~ made him ...** sie reizte ihn so, daß er ...

aggregate ['ægrɪgɪt] **1** *n* **(a)** Summe, Gesamtheit *f*. **they won on ~** sie wurden Gesamtsieger. **(b)** *(Build)* Zuschlagstoffe *pl*. **2** *adj* gesamt, Gesamt-.

aggression [ə'greʃən] *n* Aggression *f*; *(of person: aggressiveness)* Aggressivität *f*. **an act of ~** eine aggressive Handlung.

aggressive [ə'gresɪv] *adj* aggressiv; *salesman, businessman etc* dynamisch, aufdringlich *(pej)*.

aggressiveness [ə'gresɪvnɪs] *n see adj* Aggressivität *f*; Dynamik, Aufdringlichkeit *(pej) f*.

aggressor [ə'gresə^r] *n* Angreifer(in *f*) *m*.

aggrieved [ə'griːvd] *adj (offended)* verletzt *(at, by* durch*)*.

aghast [ə'gɑːst] *adj pred* entgeistert *(at* über *+acc)*.

agile ['ædʒaɪl] *adj person, thinker* beweglich; *body movements* geschmeidig; *animal* flink. **she has an ~ mind** sie ist geistig sehr rege.

agility [ə'dʒɪlɪtɪ] *n see adj* Beweglichkeit *f*; Geschmeidigkeit *f*; Flinkheit *f*.

agitate ['ædʒɪteɪt] **1** *vt* **(a)** *(excite, upset)* aufregen, aus der Fassung bringen. **(b)** *(lit: shake) liquid* schütteln. **2** *vi* agitieren. **to ~ for sth** sich für etw stark machen.

agitated ['ædʒɪteɪtɪd] *adj* aufgeregt, erregt. **to get ~** sich aufregen.

agitation [ˌædʒɪ'teɪʃən] *n* **(a)** *(anxiety, worry)* Erregung *f*, Aufruhr *m*. **(b)** *(incitement)* Agitation *f*.

agitator ['ædʒɪteɪtə^r] *n (person)* Agitator(in *f*) *m*.

AGM = annual general meeting.

agnostic [æg'nɒstɪk] **1** *adj* agnostisch. **2** *n* Agnostiker(in *f*) *m*.

agnosticism [æg'nɒstɪsɪzəm] *n* Agnostizismus *m*.

ago [ə'gəʊ] *adv* vor. **years/a week/a little while ~** vor Jahren/einer Woche/kurzem; **that was years/a week ~** das ist schon Jahre/eine Woche her; **how long ~ is it since you last saw him?** wann haben Sie ihn das letzte Mal gesehen?; **how long ~?** wie lange ist das her?; **that was long ~** das ist schon lange her; **as long ~ as 1950** schon 1950; **no longer ~ than yesterday** erst gestern (noch).

agog [ə'gɒg] *adj pred* gespannt.

agonize ['ægənaɪz] *vi* sich *(dat)* den Kopf zermartern *(over* über *+acc)*.

agonizing ['ægənaɪzɪŋ] *adj* qualvoll.

agony ['ægənɪ] *n* **(a)** Qual *f*; *(mental also)* Leid *nt*. **that's ~** das ist eine Qual; **to be in ~** schreckliche Schmerzen haben; **put him out of his ~** *(lit)* mach seiner Qual ein Ende; *(fig)* nun spann ihn doch nicht länger auf die Folter.

agony column *n (Brit col)* Kummerkasten *m*.

agree [ə'griː] *pret, ptp* **~d 1** *vt* **(a)** *price, date etc* vereinbaren, abmachen. **we all ~ that ...** wir sind alle der Meinung, daß ...; **it was ~d that ...** man einigte sich darauf *or* es wurde beschlossen, daß ...; **to ~ to differ** sich *(dat)* verschiedene Meinungen zugestehen. **(b)** *(consent)* **to ~ to do sth** sich bereit erklären, etw zu tun. **(c)** *(admit)* zugeben. **I ~ (that) I was wrong** ich gebe zu, daß ich mich geirrt habe.
2 *vi* **(a)** *(hold same opinion) (two or more people)* übereinstimmen; *(one person)* der gleichen Meinung sein. **to ~ with sb** jdm zustimmen; **I quite ~** ganz meine Meinung!; **it's too late now, don't you ~?** meinen Sie nicht auch, daß es jetzt zu spät ist?; **to ~ with the figures** *(accept)* die Zahlen akzeptieren. **(b)** *(come to an agreement)* sich einigen, Einigkeit erzielen *(about* über *+acc)*. **(c)** *(people: get on together)* miteinander auskommen. **(d)** *(statements, figures, Gram)* übereinstimmen. **(e) I don't ~ with children drinking wine** ich bin nicht damit einverstanden, daß Kinder Wein trinken. **(f)** *(food, climate etc)* **whisky doesn't ~ with me** Whisky bekommt mir nicht.

agreeable [ə'griːəbl] *adj* **(a)** *(pleasant)* angenehm. **(b)** *pred* **are you ~ to that?** sind Sie damit einverstanden?

agreed [ə'griːd] *adj* **(a)** *pred* **are we all ~?** sind wir uns da einig?; *(on course of action)* sind alle einverstanden? **(b)** *(arranged)* vereinbart; *price also* festgesetzt; *time also* verabredet. **it's all ~** es ist alles abgesprochen; **~?** einverstanden?

agreement [ə'griːmənt] *n* **(a)** *(understanding, arrangement)* Abmachung, Übereinkunft *f*; *(treaty, contract)* Abkommen *nt*, Vertrag *m*. **to reach an ~ (with sb)** (mit jdm) zu einer Einigung kommen. **(b)** *(sharing of opinion)* Einigkeit *f*. **by mutual ~** in gegenseitigem Einvernehmen; **to be in ~ with sb** mit jdm einer Meinung sein; **to be in ~ with/about sth** mit etw übereinstimmen/über etw *(acc)* einig sein. **(c)** *(consent)* Zustimmung *f (to* zu*)*. **(d)** *(between figures, Gram etc)* Übereinstimmung *f*.

agricultural [ˌægrɪ'kʌltʃərəl] *adj produce, tool etc* landwirtschaftlich; *studies* Landwirtschafts-. **~ worker** Landarbeiter(in *f*) *m*.

agriculture ['ægrɪkʌltʃə^r] *n* Landwirtschaft *f*.

aground [ə'graʊnd] *adv* **to go** *or* **run ~** auflaufen, auf Grund laufen.

ahead [ə'hed] *adv* **(a) there's some thick cloud ~** da vorne ist eine große Wolke; **the German runner was/drew ~** der deutsche Läufer lag vorn/zog nach vorne; **he is ~ by about two minutes** er hat etwa zwei Minuten Vorsprung; **we sent him on ~** wir schickten ihn voraus; **in the months ~** in den bevorstehenden Monaten; **I can see problems ~** ich sehe Probleme auf mich/uns *etc* zukommen. **(b) ~ of sb/sth** vor jdm/etw; **walk ~ of me** geh voran; **we arrived ten minutes ~ of time** wir kamen zehn Minuten vorher an; **to be ~ of one's time** *(fig)* seiner Zeit voraus sein.

ahoy [ə'hɔɪ] *interj (Naut)* ahoi. **ship ~!** Schiff ahoi!

aid [eɪd] **1** *n* **(a)** *no pl (help)* Hilfe *f*. **(foreign) ~** Entwicklungshilfe *f*; **with the ~ of** mit Hilfe; *(+gen)* **to come to sb's ~** jdm zu Hilfe kommen; **a sale in ~ of the blind** ein Verkauf zugunsten der Blinden; **what's all this wiring in ~ of?** *(col)* wozu sind all diese Drähte da *or* gut? **(b)** *(useful person, thing)* Hilfe *f (to* für*)*; *(piece of equipment)* Hilfsmittel *nt*; *(teaching ~)* Lehrmittel *nt*. **2** *vt* unterstützen, helfen *(+dat)*. **to ~ sb's recovery** jds Heilung fördern; **to ~ and abet sb** *(Jur)* jdm Beihilfe leisten; *(after crime)* jdn begünstigen.

aide [eɪd] *n* Helfer(in *f*) *m*; *(adviser)* Berater(in *f*) *m*.

AIDS [eidz] *n* Aids *nt*.

ailing ['eɪlɪŋ] *adj (lit)* kränklich; *(fig) industry, economy etc* krankend, krank.

ailment ['eɪlmənt] *n* Gebrechen, Leiden *nt*. **minor ~s** leichte Beschwerden *pl*.

aim [eɪm] **1** *n* **(a)** Zielen *nt*. **to take ~** zielen *(at* auf *+acc)*; **his ~ was good** er zielte gut. **(b)** *(purpose)* Ziel *nt*, Absicht *f*. **what is your ~ in life?** was ist Ihr Lebensziel?; **what is your ~ in doing that?** was wollen Sie damit bezwecken?

2 *vt* **(a)** *guided missile, camera* richten *(at* auf *+acc)*; *stone etc* zielen mit *(at* auf *+acc)*. **to ~ a pistol at sb/sth** eine Pistole auf jdn/etw richten, mit einer Pistole auf jdn/etw zielen. **(b)** *(fig) remark, insult, criticism* richten *(at* gegen*)*. **this programme is ~ed at the general public** dieses Programm ist für die breite Öffentlichkeit gedacht; **to be ~ed at sth** *(cuts, measure, new law etc)* auf etw *(acc)* abzielen.

3 *vi* **(a)** *(with gun, punch etc)* zielen *(at, for* auf *+acc)*. **(b)** *(try, strive for)* **to ~ high** sich *(dat)* hohe Ziele setzen; **isn't that ~ing a bit high?** wollen Sie nicht etwas zu hoch hinaus?; **to ~ at** *or* **for sth** etw anstreben, auf etw *(acc)* abzielen; **he ~s at only spending £10 per week** er hat es sich zum Ziel gesetzt, mit £10 pro Woche auszukommen. **(c)** *(col: intend)* **to ~ to do sth** vorhaben, etw zu tun.

aimless ['eɪmlɪs] *adj* ziellos.

ain't [eɪnt] *(incorrect)* = **am not; is not; are not; has not; have not.**

air [ɛəʳ] **1** *n* **(a)** Luft *f*. **to go for a breath of (fresh) ~** frische Luft schnappen (gehen); **by ~** per *or* mit dem Flugzeug; *(transport)* auf dem Luftweg.

(b) *(fig phrases)* **there's something in the ~** es liegt etwas in der Luft; **it's still all up in the ~** *(col)* es ist noch alles offen; **to clear the ~** die Atmosphäre reinigen; **to be walking on ~** wie auf Wolken gehen.

(c) *(Rad, TV)* **to be on the ~** *(programme)* gesendet werden; *(station)* senden; **he's on the ~ every day** er ist jeden Tag im Radio zu hören; **to go off the ~** das Programm beenden.

(d) *(facial expression)* Miene *f*; *(appearance)* Aussehen *nt*; *(atmosphere)* Atmosphäre *f*. **there was an ~ of mystery about her** sie hatte etwas Geheimnisvolles an sich *(dat)*.

(e) ~s *pl* Getue, Gehabe *nt*; **to give oneself ~s** vornehm tun; **~s and graces** Allüren *pl*.

(f) *(Mus)* Weise *f (old)*; *(tune also)* Melodie *f*.

2 *vt* **(a)** *clothes, bed, room* (aus)lüften. **(b)** *anger, grievance* Luft machen *(+dat)*; *opinion* darlegen.

3 *vi (clothes etc) (after washing)* nachtrocknen; *(after storage)* (aus)lüften.

air *in cpds* Luft-; **~ base** *n* Luftwaffenstützpunkt *m*; **~borne** *adj troops* Luftlande-; **to be ~borne** sich in der Luft befinden; **~ brake** *n (on truck)* Druckluftbremse *f*; **~bus** *n* Airbus *m*; **~-conditioned** *adj* klimatisiert; **~-conditioning** *n (plant)* Klimaanlage *f*; **~-cooled** *adj* luftgekühlt; **~craft** *n, pl* **~craft** Flugzeug *nt*, Maschine *f*; **~craft carrier** *n* Flugzeugträger *m*; **~drome** *n (US)* Flugplatz *m*; **~field** *n* Flugplatz *m*; **~ force** *n* Luftwaffe *f*; **~-freight 1** *n* Luftfracht *f*; **2** *vt* per Luftfracht senden; **~ hostess** *n* Stewardeß *f*.

airing ['ɛərɪŋ] *n* **to give sth an ~** etw gut durch- *or* auslüften lassen; *(fig col) idea* etw darlegen.

airing cupboard *n (Brit)* (Wäsche)trockenschrank *m*.

air: ~ intake *n* Lufteinlaß *m*; *(for engine)* Luftansaugstutzen *m*; *(quantity)* Luftmenge *f*; **~lane** *n* Flugroute *f*; **~less** *adj (lit) space* luftleer; *(stuffy) room* stickig; *(with no wind) day* windstill; **~ letter** *n* Luftpostbrief *m*; **~lift** *n* Luftbrücke *f*; **~line** *n* Fluggesellschaft, Fluglinie *f*; **~lock** *n (in spacecraft etc)* Luftschleuse *f*; *(in pipe)* Luftsack *m*; **~mail** *n* Luftpost *f*; **to send sth (by) ~** etw per *or* mit Luftpost schicken; **~plane** *n (US)* Flugzeug *nt*; **~ pocket** *n* Luftloch *nt*; **~port** *n* Flughafen *m*; **~ raid** *n* Luftangriff *m*; **~ rifle** *n* Luftgewehr *nt*; **~-sea rescue service** *n* Seenotrettungsdienst *m*; **~ship** *n* Luftschiff *nt*; **~sick** *adj* luftkrank; **~space** *n* Luftraum *m*; **~strip** *n* Start- und Landebahn *f*; **~ terminal** *n* Terminal *m*; **~tight** *adj* luftdicht; **~-to-~** *adj (Mil)* Luft-Luft-; **~-to-ground** *adj (Mil)* Luft-Boden-; **~-traffic controller** *n* Fluglotse *m*; **~ waybill** *n* Luftfrachtbrief *m*; **~worthy** *adj* flugtüchtig.

airy ['ɛərɪ] *adj (+er)* **(a)** *room* luftig. **(b)** *(casual) manner, gesture* lässig, nonchalant; *(vague) promise* vage; *theory* versponnen.

airy-fairy ['ɛərɪ'fɛərɪ] *adj (col)* versponnen; *excuse* windig; *talk also* larifari *inv (col)*.

aisle [aɪl] *n* Gang *m*; *(in church)* Seitenschiff *nt*; *(central ~)* Mittelgang *m*. **he had them rolling in the ~s** die Leute kugelten sich vor Lachen.

ajar [ə'dʒɑːʳ] *adj, adv* angelehnt.

akimbo [ə'kɪmbəʊ] *adv*: **with arms ~** die Arme in die Hüften gestemmt.

akin [ə'kɪn] *adj pred* verwandt *(to* mit*)*.

à la carte [ɑːlɑː'kɑːt] *adj, adv* à la carte.

alacrity [ə'lækrɪtɪ] *n* **to accept with ~** ohne zu zögern annehmen.

alarm [ə'lɑːm] **1** *n* **(a)** *(warning)* Alarm *m*. **to give/sound the ~** Alarm geben *or (fig)* schlagen. **(b)** *(device)* Alarmanlage *f*. **(c) to cause a good deal of ~** große Unruhe auslösen. **2** *vt* **(a)** *(worry)* beunruhigen; *(frighten)* erschrecken. **don't be ~ed** erschrecken Sie nicht. **(b)** *(warn)* warnen; *fire brigade etc* alarmieren.

alarm *in cpds* Alarm-; **~ call** *n (Telec)* Weckruf *m*; **~ clock** *n* Wecker *m*.

alarming [ə'lɑːmɪŋ] *adj (worrying)* beunruhigend; *(frightening)* erschreckend; *news* alarmierend.

alarmist [ə'lɑːmɪst] *n* Unheilsprophet *m*.

alas [ə'læs] *interj* leider.

Albania [æl'beɪnɪə] *n* Albanien *nt*.

Albanian [æl'beɪnɪən] **1** *adj* albanisch. **2** *n* **(a)** Albaner(in *f*) *m*. **(b)** *(language)* Albanisch *nt*.

albatross ['ælbətrɒs] *n* Albatros *m*.

albeit [ɔːl'biːɪt] *conj (liter)* obgleich, wenn auch.

albino [æl'biːnəʊ] **1** *n* Albino *m*. **2** *adj* Albino-.

album ['ælbəm] *n* Album *nt*.

alchemy ['ælkɪmɪ] *n* Alchemie, Alchimie *f*.

alcohol ['ælkəhɒl] *n* Alkohol *m*.

alcoholic [ˌælkə'hɒlɪk] **1** *adj drink* alkoholisch. **2** *n* **to be an ~** Alkoholiker(in) sein.

alcoholism ['ælkəhɒlɪzəm] *n* Alkoholismus *m*.

alcove ['ælkəʊv] *n* Nische *f*.

ale [eɪl] *n (old)* Ale, Bier *nt*.

alert [ə'lɜːt] **1** *adj* aufmerksam; *(as character trait)* aufgeweckt; *mind* scharf, hell. **2** *vt* warnen *(to* vor *+dat)*. **3** *n* Alarm *m*. **to put troops on the ~** Truppen in Alarmbereitschaft versetzen; **to be on (the) ~** einsatzbereit sein; *(be on lookout)* auf der Hut sein *(for* vor *+dat)*.

A level ['eɪˌlevl] *n (Brit)* ≃ Abitur *nt no pl*.

alfresco [æl'freskəʊ] *adj, adv* im Freien.

algebra ['ældʒɪbrə] *n* Algebra *f*.

Algeria [æl'dʒɪərɪə] *n* Algerien *nt*.

Algerian [æl'dʒɪərɪən] **1** *n* Algerier(in *f*) *m*. **2** *adj*

algerisch.
alias ['eɪlıæs] 1 *adv* alias. 2 *n* Deckname *m*.
alibi ['ælıbaı] *n* Alibi *nt*.
alien ['eɪlıən] 1 *n (esp Pol)* Ausländer(in *f*) *m*; *(Sci-Fi)* außerirdisches Wesen. 2 *adj (foreign)* ausländisch; *(Sci-Fi)* außerirdisch; *(different)* fremd. **to be ~ to sb's nature** jdm fremd sein.
alienate ['eɪlıəneɪt] *vt people* befremden. **to be ~d from sb** jdm entfremdet sein.
alienation [ˌeɪlıə'neɪʃən] *n* Entfremdung *f*.
alight[1] [ə'laɪt] *vi* **(a)** *(form: person)* aussteigen *(from* aus*)*. **(b)** *(bird)* sich niederlassen *(on* auf *+dat)*.
alight[2] *adj pred* **to be ~** brennen; **to keep the fire ~** das Feuer in Gang halten; **to set sth ~** etw in Brand setzen *or* stecken.
align [ə'laɪn] *vt* **(a)** *wheels of car, gun sights etc* ausrichten; *(bring into line also)* in eine Linie bringen. **(b)** *(Fin, Pol) currencies, policies* aufeinander abstimmen. **to ~ oneself with a party** sich einer Partei anschließen.
alignment [ə'laɪnmənt] *n* Ausrichtung *f*; *(of policies etc also)* Orientierung *f (with* nach*)*. **to be out of ~** *(wheels etc)* nicht richtig ausgerichtet sein; *(views, policies)* nicht übereinstimmen; **the new ~ of world powers** die Neugruppierung der Weltmächte.
alike [ə'laɪk] *adj pred, adv* gleich; *(similar)* ähnlich. **you men are all ~!** ihr Männer seid doch alle gleich!; **winter and summer ~** Sommer wie Winter.
alimentary [ˌælı'mentərı] *adj (Anat)* Verdauungs-. **~ canal** Verdauungskanal *m*.
alimony ['ælımənı] *n* Unterhaltszahlung *f*. **to pay ~** Unterhalt zahlen.
alive [ə'laɪv] *adj* **(a)** *pred (living)* lebendig, lebend *attr*. **dead or ~** tot oder lebendig; **to be ~** leben; **the greatest violinist ~** der größte lebende Geiger; **it's good to be ~** das Leben ist schön; **to stay ~** am Leben bleiben; **to keep sb/sth ~** *(lit, fig)* jdn/etw am Leben erhalten. **(b)** *(lively)* lebendig. **(c)** *pred (aware)* **to be ~ to sth** sich *(dat)* einer Sache *(gen)* bewußt sein. **(d) to be ~ with tourists/fish/insects** *etc* von Touristen/Fischen/Insekten *etc* wimmeln.
alkali ['ælkəlaɪ] *n, pl* **-(e)s** Base, Lauge *f*.
all [ɔːl] 1 *adj (with pl n)* alle *no art*; *(with sing n)* ganze(r, s), alle(r, s) *no art*. **~ the books/people** alle Bücher/Leute, die ganzen Bücher; **~ the tobacco/milk/fruit** der ganze Tabak/die ganze Milch/das ganze Obst; **~ my books/friends/strength** all(e) meine Bücher/Freunde/meine ganze Kraft; **~ my life** mein ganzes Leben (lang); **~ Spain** ganz Spanien; **we ~ sat down** wir setzten uns alle; **~ day (long)** den ganzen Tag (lang); **I don't understand ~ that** ich verstehe das alles nicht; **in ~ respects** in jeder Hinsicht; **why me of ~ people?** warum ausgerechnet ich?; **of ~ the idiots!** so ein Idiot!; **with ~ possible speed** so schnell wie möglich.
2 *pron* **(a)** *(everything)* alles; *(everybody)* alle *pl*. **~ of them/of it** (sie) alle/alles; **~ of Paris/of the house** ganz Paris/das ganze Haus; **the score was two ~** es stand zwei zu zwei. **(b)** *(phrases)* **at ~** überhaupt; **nothing at ~** überhaupt *or* gar nichts; **it's not bad at ~** das ist gar nicht schlecht; **for ~ I know she could be ill** was weiß ich, vielleicht ist sie krank; **in ~** insgesamt; **~ in ~** alles in allem; **happiest of ~** am glücklichsten; **the best car of ~** das allerbeste Auto.
3 *adv* **(a)** *(quite, entirely)* ganz. **dressed ~ in white** ganz in Weiß (gekleidet); **an ~ wool carpet** ein reinwollener Teppich; **~ along the road** die ganze Straße entlang; **I'll tell you ~ about it** ich erzähl dir alles; **that's ~ very well** das ist alles ganz schön und gut; **it's not as bad as ~ that** so schlimm ist es nun auch wieder nicht; **if at ~ possible** wenn irgend möglich; **to be ~ in** *(col)* total erledigt sein *(col)*; **he's ~/not ~ there** *(col)* er ist voll da/er ist nicht ganz da *(col)*.
(b) ~ but fast; **he ~ but died** er wäre fast gestorben.
(c) *(with comp)* **~ the happier** noch glücklicher; **~ the sadder because ...** um so trauriger, weil ...; **~ the more so since ...** besonders weil ..., zumal ...
4 *n* **one's ~** alles.
allay [ə'leɪ] *vt* verringern; *doubt, fears, suspicion* (weitgehend) zerstreuen.
all-clear *n* Entwarnung *f*.
allegation [ˌælı'geɪʃən] *n* Behauptung *f*.
allege [ə'ledʒ] *vt* behaupten. **he is ~d to have said that ...** er soll angeblich gesagt haben, daß ...
alleged *adj*, **~ly** *adv* [ə'ledʒd, ə'ledʒıdlı] angeblich.
allegiance [ə'liːdʒəns] *n* Treue *f (to dat)*.
allegory ['ælıgərı] *n* Allegorie *f*.
all-embracing [ˌɔːlım'breısıŋ] *adj* (all)umfassend.
allergic [ə'lɜːdʒık] *adj (lit, fig)* allergisch *(to* gegen*)*.
allergy ['ælədʒı] *n* Allergie *f (to* gegen*)*.
alleviate [ə'liːvıeɪt] *vt* lindern.
alley ['ælı] *n (between buildings)* (enge) Gasse.
alliance [ə'laɪəns] *n* Verbindung *f*; *(of institutions also, of states)* Bündnis *nt*; *(in historical contexts)* Allianz *f*.
Allied ['ælaɪd] *adj* **the ~ forces** die Alliierten.
alligator ['ælıgeıtə[r]] *n* Alligator *m*.
all: ~-important *adj* außerordentlich wichtig; **the ~-important question** die Frage, auf die es ankommt; **~-in** *adj* **(a)** *(inclusive)* Inklusiv-; **(b)** *(Sport)* **~-in wrestling** Freistilringen *nt*.
alliteration [əˌlıtə'reıʃən] *n* Alliteration *f*.
all-night [ˌɔːl'naıt] *adj attr café* durchgehend geöffnet. **to have an ~ party** die ganze Nacht durchfeiern.
allocate ['æləʊkeıt] *vt (allot)* zuteilen, zuweisen *(to sb* jdm*)*; *(apportion)* verteilen *(to* auf *+acc)*; *tasks* vergeben *(to* an *+acc)*. **to ~ money to** *or* **for a project** Geld für ein Projekt bestimmen.
allocation [ˌæləʊ'keıʃən] *n (sum)* Zuwendung *f*.
allot [ə'lɒt] *vt* zuteilen *(to sb/sth* jdm/etw*)*; *time* vorsehen *(to* für*)*; *money* bestimmen *(to* für*)*.
allotment [ə'lɒtmənt] *n (Brit: land)* Schrebergarten *m*.
all-out [ˌɔːl'aʊt] 1 *adj strike* total; *attack* massiv; *effort* äußerste(r, s). **to make an ~ attempt** alles daransetzen. 2 *adv* mit aller Kraft. **to go ~ to do sth** alles daransetzen, etw zu tun.
allow [ə'laʊ] 1 *vt* **(a)** *(permit) sth* erlauben, gestatten. **to ~ sb sth/to do sth** jdm etw erlauben/jdm erlauben, etw zu tun; **to be ~ed to do sth** etw tun dürfen; **smoking is not ~ed** Rauchen ist nicht gestattet; **to ~ oneself sth** sich *(dat)* etw erlauben; *(treat oneself)* sich *(dat)* etw gönnen; **~ me!** gestatten Sie *(form)*; **to ~ sth to happen** zulassen, daß etw geschieht; **to ~ sb in/out** jdn hinein-/hinauslassen; **to be ~ed in/out/past** hinein-/hinaus-/vorbeidürfen. **(b)** *(recognize, accept) claim* anerkennen; *goal also* geben. **(c)** *(allocate, grant) discount* geben; *space* lassen; *time* einplanen, einberechnen; *(in tax, Jur)* zugestehen. **~ (yourself) an hour** rechnen Sie mit einer Stunde; **~ 5 cms extra** geben Sie 5 cm zu.
2 *vi* **if time ~s** falls es zeitlich möglich ist.
♦ **allow for** *vi +prep obj* berücksichtigen.
allowance [ə'laʊəns] *n* **(a)** finanzielle Unterstützung; *(paid by state)* Beihilfe *f*; *(father to child)* Unterhaltsgeld *nt*; *(for unsociable hours, overseas ~ etc)* Zulage *f*; *(on business trip)* Spesen *pl*; *(spending money)* Taschengeld *nt*. **clothing ~** Kleidungsgeld *nt*. **(b)** *(Fin: tax ~)* Freibetrag *m*. **(c)** *(Fin, Comm: discount)* (Preis)nachlaß *m (on* für*)*. **(d) to make ~(s) for sth** etw berücksichtigen; **you have to make ~s** Sie müssen (gewisse) Zugeständnisse machen.
alloy ['ælɔı] *n* Legierung *f*.

all: ~**-powerful** *adj* allmächtig; ~**-purpose** *adj* Allzweck-.

all right ['ɔːl'raɪt] **1** *adj pred* in Ordnung, okay *(col)*. **it's** ~ *(not too bad)* es geht; *(working properly)* es ist in Ordnung; **that's** *or* **it's** ~ *(after thanks, apology)* schon gut; **to taste** ~ ganz gut schmecken; **is it** ~ **for me to leave early?** kann ich früher gehen?; **it's** ~ **for you** du hast's gut; **are you** ~? *(healthy)* geht es Ihnen gut?; *(unharmed)* ist Ihnen etwas passiert?; **are you feeling** ~? fehlt Ihnen was?; *(iro)* sag mal, fehlt dir was?
2 *adv* **(a)** *(satisfactory)* ganz gut, ganz ordentlich; *(safely)* gut. **did I do it** ~? habe ich es richtig gemacht?; **did you get home** ~? bist du gut nach Hause gekommen?; **did you get/find it** ~? haben Sie es denn bekommen/gefunden? **(b)** *(certainly)* schon. **he'll come** ~ er wird schon kommen; **that's the boy** ~ das ist der Junge; **he's a clever man** ~ er ist schon intelligent; **oh yes, we heard you** ~ o ja, und ob wir dich gehört haben.
3 *interj* okay *(col)*; *(in agreement also)* in Ordnung. ~, ~! **I'm coming** schon gut, schon gut, ich komme ja!

all: ~**-round** *adj athlete* Allround-; *improvement* in jeder Beziehung; ~**-rounder** *n* Allroundmann *m*; *(Sport)* Allroundsportler(in *f*) *m*; **A**~ **Saints' Day** *n* Allerheiligen *nt*; ~**-time** *adj record* ungebrochen; **an** ~**-time high/low** der höchste/niedrigste Stand aller Zeiten.

allude to [ə'luːd] *vi +prep obj* anspielen auf *(+acc)*.

allure [ə'ljʊəʳ] *n* Reiz *m*.

alluring [ə'ljʊərɪŋ] *adj* verführerisch.

allusion [ə'luːʒən] *n* Anspielung *f (to* auf *+acc)*.

ally ['ælaɪ] **1** *n* Verbündete(r) *mf*, Bundesgenosse *m*; *(Hist)* Alliierte(r) *m*. **2** [ə'laɪ] *vr* **to** ~ **o.s. with sb** sich mit jdm verbünden.

almanac ['ɔːlmənæk] *n* Almanach *m*.

almighty [ɔːl'maɪtɪ] **1** *adj* allmächtig; *(col)* Mords-, gewaltig. **2** *n* **the A**~ der Allmächtige.

almond ['ɑːmənd] *n* Mandel *f*; *(tree)* Mandelbaum *m*.

almost ['ɔːlməʊst] *adv* beinahe, fast. **he** ~ **fell** er wäre fast gefallen.

alms [ɑːmz] *npl* Almosen *pl*.

aloft [ə'lɒft] *adv (into the air)* empor; *(in the air)* hoch droben.

alone [ə'ləʊn] **1** *adj pred* allein(e). **we're not** ~ **in thinking that** wir stehen mit dieser Meinung nicht allein. **2** *adv* allein(e). **to live on bread** ~ von Brot allein leben; **the hotel** ~ **cost £35** das Hotel allein kostete (schon) £35, schon das Hotel kostete £35.

along [ə'lɒŋ] **1** *prep (direction)* entlang *(+acc)*, lang *(+acc) (col)*; *(position)* entlang *(+dat)*. **he walked** ~ **the river** er ging den Fluß entlang; **somewhere** ~ **here/there** irgendwo hier/dort (herum); *(in this/that direction)* irgendwo in dieser Richtung/der Richtung. **2** *adv* **to move** ~ weitergehen; **he was just strolling** ~ er ist bloß so dahingeschlendert; **run** ~ nun lauf!; **he'll be** ~ **soon** er muß gleich da sein; **I'll be** ~ **about eight** ich komme ungefähr um acht; ~ **with** zusammen mit; **to come/sing** ~ **with sb** mit jdm mitkommen/mitsingen; **take an umbrella** ~ nimm einen Schirm mit.

alongside [ə'lɒŋ'saɪd] **1** *prep* neben *(+dat)*. **we were moored** ~ **the pier** wir lagen am Pier vor Anker; **the houses** ~ **the river** die Häuser am Fluß; **he works** ~ **me** *(with)* er ist ein Kollege von mir; *(next to)* er arbeitet neben mir. **2** *adv* daneben; *(Naut)* längsseits. **a police car drew up** ~ ein Polizeiauto fuhr neben mich/ihn *etc* heran; **they brought their dinghy** ~ sie brachten ihr Dingi heran.

aloof [ə'luːf] **1** *adv (lit, fig)* abseits. **to remain** ~ sich abseits halten. **2** *adj* unnahbar.

aloud [ə'laʊd] *adv* laut.

alphabet ['ælfəbet] *n* Alphabet *nt*.

alphabetic(al) [ˌælfə'betɪk(əl)] *adj* alphabetisch. **in** ~ **order** in alphabetischer Reihenfolge.

alpine ['ælpaɪn] *adj* alpin; *flowers, scenery* Alpen-, Gebirgs-.

Alps [ælps] *npl* Alpen *pl*.

already [ɔːl'redɪ] *adv* schon, bereits.

alright ['ɔːlˌraɪt] *adj, adv* = **all right.**

Alsace ['ælsæs] *n* Elsaß *nt*.

Alsace-Lorraine ['ælsæslə'reɪn] *n* Elsaß-Lothringen *nt*.

alsatian [æl'seɪʃən] *n (Brit: dog)* Schäferhund *m*.

Alsatian [æl'seɪʃən] *adj* elsässisch.

also ['ɔːlsəʊ] *adv* **(a)** auch. **(b)** *(moreover)* ~, **I must explain that ...** außerdem muß ich erklären, daß ...

also-ran [ˌɔːlsəʊ'ræn] *n* **to be an** ~ *(Sport, fig)* unter „ferner liefen" kommen.

altar ['ɒltəʳ] *n* Altar *m*.

alter ['ɒltəʳ] **1** *vt* ändern; *(modify also)* abändern. **to** ~ **sth completely** etw vollkommen verändern. **2** *vi* sich (ver)ändern.

alteration [ˌɒltə'reɪʃən] *n* Änderung *f*; *(modification also)* Abänderung *f*; *(of appearance)* Veränderung *f*; *(to building)* Umbau *m*. **to make** ~**s in** *or* **to sth** Änderungen an etw *(dat)* vornehmen.

alternate [ɒl'tɜːnɪt] **1** *adj* **(a)** **on** ~ **days** jeden zweiten Tag; **they put down** ~ **layers of brick and mortar** sie schichteten abwechselnd Ziegel und Mörtel aufeinander. **(b)** *(alternative)* Alternativ-. ~ **route** Ausweichstrecke *f*. **2** ['ɔːltəneɪt] *vi* (sich) abwechseln.

alternating ['ɒltɜːneɪtɪŋ] *adj* wechselnd. ~ **current** Wechselstrom *m*.

alternative [ɒl'tɜːnətɪv] **1** *adj* Alternativ-; *route* Ausweich-. **2** *n* Alternative *f*.

alternatively [ɒl'tɜːnətɪvlɪ] *adv* **or** ~ oder aber.

alternator ['ɒltɜːneɪtəʳ] *n (Elec)* Wechselstromgenerator *m*; *(Aut)* Lichtmaschine *f*.

although [ɔːl'ðəʊ] *conj* obwohl, obgleich.

altitude ['æltɪtjuːd] *n* Höhe *f*. **at this** ~ in dieser Höhe.

alto ['æltəʊ] *n* Alt *m*, Altstimme *f*; *(person)* Alt *m*; *(also* ~ **saxophone***)* Altsaxophon *nt*.

altogether [ˌɔːltə'geðəʳ] **1** *adv* **(a)** im ganzen, insgesamt. **taken** ~, *or* ~ **it was very pleasant** alles in allem war es sehr nett. **(b)** *(wholly)* vollkommen, ganz und gar. **he wasn't** ~ **wrong/pleased** er hatte nicht ganz unrecht/war nicht besonders zufrieden. **2** *n* **in the** ~ *(hum col)* hüllenlos, im Adams-/Evaskostüm.

altruism ['æltruɪzəm] *n* Altruismus *m*.

altruistic [ˌæltru'ɪstɪk] *adj* altruistisch.

aluminium [ˌælju'mɪnɪəm], *(US)* **aluminum** [ə'luːmɪnəm] *n* Aluminium *nt*. ~ **foil** Alufolie *f*.

always ['ɔːlweɪz] *adv* **(a)** immer. **(b) we could** ~ **go by train** wir könnten doch auch den Zug nehmen.

am [æm] *1st pers sing pres of* **be.**

amalgam [ə'mælgəm] *n* Amalgam *nt*; *(fig also)* Gemisch *nt*, Mischung *f*.

amalgamate [ə'mælgəmeɪt] **1** *vt companies* fusionieren; *departments* zusammenlegen. **2** *vi (companies)* fusionieren; *(metals)* amalgamieren.

amass [ə'mæs] *vt* anhäufen; *money also* scheffeln.

amateur ['æmətəʳ] **1** *n* Amateur *m*; *(pej)* Dilettant(in *f*) *m*. **2** *adj attr* Amateur-; *photographer also, painter* Hobby-; *dramatics also* Laien-.

amateurish ['æmətərɪʃ] *adj (pej)* dilettantisch; *performance, work also* laienhaft.

amaze [ə'meɪz] *vt* erstaunen. **to be** ~**d at sth** über etw *(acc)* erstaunt sein.

amazement [ə'meɪzmənt] *n* Erstaunen *nt*. **much to my** ~ zu meinem großen Erstaunen.

amazing [ə'meɪzɪŋ] *adj* erstaunlich; *(col) holiday etc* toll *(col)*.

amazingly [ə'meɪzɪŋlɪ] *adv* erstaunlich; *simple,*

obvious also verblüffend. ~ **enough** erstaunlicherweise.
Amazon ['æməzən] *n* Amazonas *m*; *(Myth, fig)* Amazone *f*.
ambassador [æm'bæsədəʳ] *n* Botschafter(in *f*) *m*; *(fig)* Repräsentant(in *f*), Vertreter(in *f*) *m*.
amber ['æmbəʳ] **1** *n (substance)* Bernstein *m*; *(colour)* Bernsteingelb *nt*; *(Brit: in traffic lights)* Gelb *nt*. **2** *adj (~-coloured)* bernsteinfarben.
ambidextrous [ˌæmbɪ'dekstrəs] *adj* mit beiden Händen gleich geschickt, beidhändig.
ambiguity [ˌæmbɪ'gjʊɪtɪ] *n* Zweideutigkeit *f*.
ambiguous [æm'bɪgjʊəs] *adj* zweideutig.
ambition [æm'bɪʃən] *n* **(a)** *(desire)* Ambition *f*. **she has ~s in that direction/for her son** sie hat Ambitionen in dieser Richtung/ehrgeizige Pläne für ihren Sohn. **(b)** *(ambitious nature)* Ehrgeiz *m*.
ambitious [æm'bɪʃəs] *adj* ehrgeizig, ambitiös *(pej)*. **she is ~ for her husband** sie hat ehrgeizige Pläne für ihren Mann.
ambivalent [æm'bɪvələnt] *adj* ambivalent.
amble ['æmbl] *vi* schlendern.
ambulance ['æmbjʊləns] *n* Krankenwagen *m*.
ambulance: ~ driver *n* Krankenwagenfahrer *m*; **~man** *n* Sanitäter *m*.
ambush ['æmbʊʃ] **1** *n* Überfall *m* (aus dem Hinterhalt). **to lie in ~ for sb** *(Mil, fig)* jdm im Hinterhalt auflauern. **2** *vt* (aus dem Hinterhalt) überfallen.
ameba *n (US)* = **amoeba.**
amelioration [əˌmiːlɪə'reɪʃən] *n (form)* Verbesserung *f*.
amen [ˌɑː'men] **1** *interj* amen. **2** *n* Amen *nt*.
amenable [ə'miːnəbl] *adj* zugänglich *(to dat)*.
amend [ə'mend] *vt* ändern.
amendment [ə'mendmənt] *n* Änderung *f (to gen)*. **the First/Second** *etc* **A~** *(US Pol)* das Erste/ Zweite *etc* Amendement, Zusatz 1/2 *etc*.
amends [ə'mendz] *npl* **to make ~ (for sth)** etw wiedergutmachen.
amenity [ə'miːnɪtɪ] *n* **(public) ~** öffentliche Einrichtung; **the lack of amenities in many parts of the city** der Mangel an Einkaufs-, Unterhaltungs- und Transportmöglichkeiten in vielen Teilen der Stadt; **close to all amenities** in günstiger (Einkaufs- und Verkehrs)lage.
America [ə'merɪkə] *n* Amerika *nt*.
American [ə'merɪkən] **1** *adj* amerikanisch. **~ plan** *(US)* Vollpension *f*. **2** *n* Amerikaner(in *f*) *m*.
americanize [ə'merɪkənaɪz] *vt* amerikanisieren.
amethyst ['æmɪθɪst] *n* Amethyst *m*; *(colour)* Amethystblau *nt*.
amiable ['eɪmɪəbl] *adj* liebenswürdig.
amicable ['æmɪkəbl] *adj* freundlich; *relations* freundschaftlich; *(Jur) settlement* gütlich.
amid(st) [ə'mɪd(st)] *prep* inmitten *(+gen)*.
amiss [ə'mɪs] **1** *adj pred* **there's something ~** da stimmt irgend etwas nicht. **2** *adv* **to take sth ~** (jdm) etw übelnehmen; **a drink would not go ~** etwas zu trinken wäre gar nicht verkehrt.
ammonia [ə'məʊnɪə] *n* Ammoniak *nt*.
ammunition [ˌæmjʊ'nɪʃən] *n (lit, fig)* Munition *f*. **~ dump** *n* Munitionslager *nt*.
amnesia [æm'niːzɪə] *n* Amnesie *f (form)*, Gedächtnisschwund *m*.
amnesty ['æmnɪstɪ] *n* Amnestie *f*.
amoeba, *(US)* **ameba** [ə'miːbə] *n* Amöbe *f*.
amok [ə'mɒk] *adv* = **amuck.**
among(st) [ə'mʌŋ(st)] *prep* unter *(+acc or dat)*. **~ other things** unter anderem; **this habit is widespread ~ the French** diese Sitte ist bei den Franzosen weitverbreitet; **there were ferns ~ the trees** zwischen den Bäumen wuchs Farnkraut.
amoral [æ'mɒrəl] *adj* amoralisch.
amorous ['æmərəs] *adj* amourös; *look also* verliebt.
amorphous [ə'mɔːfəs] *adj* amorph, formlos; *style, ideas, play, novel* strukturlos.
amount [ə'maʊnt] **1** *vi* **(a)** *(total)* sich belaufen *(to* auf *+acc)*. **(b)** *(be equivalent)* gleichkommen *(to +dat)*. **it ~s to the same thing** das läuft *or* kommt aufs gleiche hinaus; **he will never ~ to much** aus ihm wird nie etwas werden. **2** *n* **(a)** *(of money)* Betrag *m*. **total ~** Gesamtsumme *f*, Endbetrag *m*; **a large/small ~ of money** eine große/geringe Summe. **(b)** *(quantity)* Menge *f*; *(of luck, intelligence, skill etc)* Maß *nt (of* an *+dat)*. **an enormous ~ of work** sehr viel Arbeit; **any ~ of food** jede Menge Essen.
amp(ère) ['æmp(ɛəʳ)] *n* Ampere *nt*.
amphetamine [æm'fetəmiːn] *n* Amphetamin *nt*.
amphibian [æm'fɪbɪən] *n* Amphibie *f*; *(vehicle)* Amphibienfahrzeug *nt*.
amphibious [æm'fɪbɪəs] *adj animal, (Mil)* amphibisch; *vehicle, aircraft* Amphibien-.
amphitheatre, *(US)* **amphitheater** ['æmfɪˌθɪətəʳ] *n* Amphitheater *nt*.
ample ['æmpl] *adj (+er)* **(a)** *(plentiful)* reichlich. **more than ~** überreichlich; **~ time** genügend Zeit. **(b)** *(large) figure, proportions* üppig; *boot of car etc* geräumig; *garden* weitläufig, ausgedehnt.
amplifier ['æmplɪfaɪəʳ] *n (Rad)* Verstärker *m*.
amplify ['æmplɪfaɪ] **(a)** *(Rad)* verstärken. **(b)** *(expand) statement, idea* näher ausführen.
amply ['æmplɪ] *adv* reichlich.
amputate ['æmpjʊteɪt] *vti* amputieren.
amputation [ˌæmpjʊ'teɪʃən] *n* Amputation *f*.
amuck [ə'mʌk] *adv*: **to run ~** Amok laufen.
amuse [ə'mjuːz] **1** *vt* **(a)** *(cause mirth)* amüsieren, belustigen. **I was ~d to hear ...** es hat mich amüsiert *or* belustigt zu hören ...; **he was not ~d** er fand es überhaupt nicht komisch. **(b)** *(entertain)* unterhalten. **let the children do it if it ~s them** laß die Kinder doch, wenn es ihnen Spaß macht; **I have no problem keeping myself ~d** ich habe keinerlei Schwierigkeiten, mir die Zeit zu vertreiben. **2** *vr* **the children can ~ themselves for a while** die Kinder können sich eine Zeitlang selbst beschäftigen.
amusement [ə'mjuːzmənt] *n* **(a)** *(enjoyment, fun)* Vergnügen *nt*; *(pastime)* Zeitvertreib *m*. **the toys were a great source of ~** das Spielzeug bereitete großen Spaß; **I see no cause for ~** ich sehe keinen Grund zur Heiterkeit; **to my great ~/to everyone's ~** zu meiner großen/zur allgemeinen Belustigung. **(b)** *(entertainment: of guests)* Belustigung, Unterhaltung *f*. **(c) ~s** *pl (place of entertainment)* Vergnügungsstätte *f usu pl*; *(at fair)* Attraktionen *pl*.
amusement: ~ arcade *n* Spielhalle *f*; **~ park** *n* Vergnügungspark *m*.
amusing [ə'mjuːzɪŋ] *adj* amüsant. **I don't find that very ~** das finde ich gar nicht lustig.
an [æn, ən, n] *indef art see* **a.**
anachronism [ə'nækrənɪzəm] *n* Anachronismus *m*.
anaemia, *(US)* **anemia** [ə'niːmɪə] *n* Anämie, Blutarmut *f*.
anaemic, *(US)* **anemic** [ə'niːmɪk] *adj* **(a)** anämisch, blutarm. **(b)** *(fig)* saft- und kraftlos.
anaesthetic, *(US)* **anesthetic** [ˌænɪs'θetɪk] *n* Narkose, Anästhesie *(spec) f*; *(substance)* Narkosemittel *nt*. **general ~** Vollnarkose *f*; **local ~** örtliche Betäubung, Lokalanästhesie *(spec) f*; **under the ~** in der Narkose.
anaesthetist, *(US)* **anesthetist** [æ'niːsθɪtɪst] *n* Anästhesist(in *f*) *m*.
anagram ['ænəgræm] *n* Anagramm *nt*.
analog computer ['ænəlɒgkəm'pjuːtəʳ] *n* Analogrechner *m*.
analogous [ə'næləgəs] *adj* analog *(to, with* zu*)*.
analogue ['ænəlɒg] *n* Gegenstück *nt*, Parallele *f*.
analogy [ə'nælədʒɪ] *n* Analogie *f*. **to draw an ~** eine Analogie herstellen; **on the ~ of** analog zu.
analyse, *(US)* **analyze** ['ænəlaɪz] *vt* analysieren.
analysis [ə'næləsɪs] *n, pl* **analyses** [ə'næləsiːz] **(a)**

Analyse *f*; **in the final** ~ letzten Endes; **on (closer)** ~ bei genauerer Untersuchung. **(b)** *(psycho~)* Psychoanalyse, Analyse *(col) f.*
analyst ['ænəlɪst] *n* Analytiker *m.*
analytic(al) [ˌænə'lɪtɪk(əl)] *adj* analytisch.
analyze ['ænəlaɪz] *vt (US)* = **analyse.**
anarchist ['ænəkɪst] *n* Anarchist(in *f*) *m.*
anarchy ['ænəkɪ] *n* Anarchie *f.*
anathema [ə'næθɪmə] *n no art (fig)* **it is ~ to me** das ist mir ein Greuel.
anatomical [ˌænə'tɒmɪkəl] *adj* anatomisch.
anatomy [ə'nætəmɪ] *n* Anatomie *f.*
ancestor ['ænsestə[r]] *n* Vorfahr, Ahne *m.*
ancestral [æn'sestrəl] *adj* Ahnen-, seiner/ihrer Vorfahren. ~ **home** Stammsitz *m.*
ancestry ['ænsɪstrɪ] *n (descent)* Abstammung, Herkunft *f*; *(ancestors)* Ahnenreihe, Familie *f.*
anchor ['æŋkə[r]] **1** *n (Naut)* Anker *m.* **to drop** ~ vor Anker gehen; **to weigh** ~ den Anker lichten; **to be** *or* **lie at** ~ vor Anker liegen. **2** *vt (Naut, fig)* verankern. **3** *vi (Naut)* ankern.
anchorage ['æŋkərɪdʒ] *n (Naut)* Ankerplatz *m.*
anchorman ['æŋkə[r]ˌmæn] *n (TV etc)* Koordinator(in *f*) *m*; *(in team)* Zentralfigur *f*; *(last person in relay race)* Letzte(r) *mf.*
anchovy ['æntʃəvɪ] *n* Sardelle, An(s)chovis *f.*
ancient ['eɪnʃənt] *adj* alt; *(col) person, clothes etc* uralt. **in ~ times** im Altertum; *(Greek, Roman also)* in der Antike; ~ **Rome** das alte Rom; ~ **monument** *(Brit)* historisches Denkmal, historische Stätte.
ancillary [æn'sɪlərɪ] *adj (secondary)* Neben-; *(auxiliary) service, troops* Hilfs-.
and [ænd, ənd, nd, ən] *conj* und. **nice ~ early/warm** schön früh/warm; **try ~ come** versuch zu kommen; **~/or** und/oder; ~ **so on** und so weiter; **better ~ better** immer besser; **I tried ~ tried** ich habe es immer wieder versucht; **three hundred ~ ten** dreihundert(und)zehn.
Andes ['ændiːz] *npl* **the ~** die Anden *pl.*
anecdote ['ænɪkdəʊt] *n* Anekdote *f.*
anemia *etc (US)* = **anaemia** *etc.*
anemone [ə'nemənɪ] *n (Bot)* Anemone *f,* Buschwindröschen *nt*; *(sea ~)* Seeanemone *f.*
anesthetic *etc (US)* = **anaesthetic** *etc.*
anew [ə'njuː] *adv* aufs neue. **to start ~** noch einmal *or* wieder von vorn anfangen.
angel ['eɪndʒəl] *n (lit, fig)* Engel *m.* **be an ~ and ...** sei so lieb und ...
angelic [æn'dʒelɪk] *adj* **(a)** *(of angel)* Engels-; *hosts* himmlisch. **(b)** *(like an angel)* engelhaft.
anger ['æŋgə[r]] **1** *n* Ärger *m*; *(wrath: of gods etc)* Zorn *m.* **a fit of ~** ein Wutanfall *m*; **red with ~** rot vor Wut; **public ~** öffentliche Entrüstung. **2** *vt* verärgern.
angina [æn'dʒaɪnə] *n* Angina, Halsentzündung *f.* ~ **pectoris** Angina pectoris *f.*
angle[1] ['æŋgl] *n* **(a)** Winkel *m.* **at an ~ of 40°** in einem Winkel von 40°; **at an ~** schräg; *(hat)* schief. **(b)** *(projecting corner)* Ecke *f.* **(c)** *(of problem etc: aspect)* Seite *f.* **(d)** *(point of view)* Standpunkt *m,* Position *f.*
angle[2] *vi (Fishing)* angeln.
♦**angle for** *vi +prep obj (fig)* **to ~ ~ sth** auf etw *(acc)* aus sein.
angler ['æŋglə[r]] *n* Angler(in *f*) *m.*
Anglican ['æŋglɪkən] **1** *n* Anglikaner(in *f*) *m.* **2** *adj* anglikanisch.
anglicism ['æŋglɪsɪzəm] *n* Anglizismus *m.*
anglicize ['æŋglɪsaɪz] *vt* anglisieren.
angling ['æŋglɪŋ] *n* Angeln *nt.*
Anglo- ['æŋgləʊ] *pref* Anglo-; *(between two countries)* Englisch-; **~-German** *adj* deutsch-englisch.
angora [æŋ'gɔːrə] *n* Angora(wolle *f*) *nt.*
angrily ['æŋgrɪlɪ] *adv* wütend.
angry ['æŋgrɪ] *adj (+er)* **(a)** böse; *letter, look also, animal* wütend. **to be ~ with** *or* **at sb** jdm *or* auf jdn böse sein; **to be/get ~ at** *or* **about sth** sich über etw *(acc)* ärgern; **don't get ~!** reg dich nicht auf!; **to make sb ~** jdn verärgern; **it makes me so ~** es ärgert mich furchtbar. **(b)** *(fig) sea* aufgewühlt; *sky, clouds* bedrohlich, finster; *(inflamed) wound* entzündet, böse.
anguish ['æŋgwɪʃ] *n* Qual *f.*
anguished ['æŋgwɪʃt] *adj* qualvoll; *look* gequält.
angular ['æŋgjʊlə[r]] *adj shape* eckig; *face, features* kantig.
animal ['ænɪməl] **1** *n* Tier *nt*; *(brutal person also)* Bestie *f.* **man is a social ~** der Mensch ist ein soziales Wesen. **2** *adj attr story, picture* Tier-; *products, fat, lust* tierisch. ~ **kingdom** Tierreich *nt*, Tierwelt *f*; ~ **magnetism** körperliche Anziehungskraft.
animate ['ænɪmeɪt] *vt (enliven)* beleben.
animated ['ænɪmeɪtɪd] *adj* lebhaft, rege; *discussion also* angeregt. ~ **cartoon** Zeichentrickfilm *m.*
animation [ˌænɪ'meɪʃən] *n* Lebhaftigkeit *f*; *(Film)* Animation *f.*
animosity [ˌænɪ'mɒsɪtɪ] *n* Animosität *(geh),* Feindseligkeit *f (towards* gegenüber, gegen*).*
aniseed ['ænɪsiːd] *n* Anis *m.*
ankle ['æŋkl] *n* Knöchel *m.*
annals ['ænəlz] *npl* Annalen *pl.*
annex [ə'neks] **1** *vt* annektieren. **2** ['æneks] *n* **(a)** *(to document etc)* Anhang *m.* **(b)** *(building)* Nebengebäude *nt*; *(extension)* Anbau *m.*
annexation [ˌænek'seɪʃən] *n* Annexion *f.*
annexe ['æneks] *n* = **annex 2 (b).**
annihilate [ə'naɪəleɪt] *vt (lit, fig)* vernichten; *(col) person, team* fertigmachen *(col).*
annihilation [əˌnaɪə'leɪʃən] *n (lit, fig)* Vernichtung *f.* **our team's ~** die vollständige Niederlage unserer Mannschaft.
anniversary [ˌænɪ'vɜːsərɪ] *n* Jahrestag *m*; *(wedding ~)* Hochzeitstag *m.* **the ~ of his death** sein Todestag *m.*
announce [ə'naʊns] *vt (lit, fig: person)* bekanntgeben, verkünden; *arrival, departure, radio programme* ansagen; *(over intercom)* durchsagen; *(formally) birth, marriage etc* anzeigen; *coming of spring etc* ankündigen. **to ~ sb** jdn melden.
announcement [ə'naʊnsmənt] *n (public declaration)* Bekanntgabe, Bekanntmachung *f*; *(of impending event, speaker)* Ankündigung *f*; *(over intercom etc)* Durchsage *f*; *(on radio etc)* Ansage *f*; *(written: of birth, marriage etc)* Anzeige *f.*
announcer [ə'naʊnsə[r]] *n (Rad, TV)* Ansager(in *f*), Radio-/Fernsehsprecher(in *f*) *m.*
annoy [ə'nɔɪ] *vt* ärgern; *(noise, questions etc)* aufregen; *(pester)* belästigen. **to be ~ed that ...** ärgerlich *or* verärgert sein, weil ...; **to be ~ed with sb/about sth** sich über jdn/etw ärgern, (mit) jdm/über etw *(acc)* böse sein.
annoyance [ə'nɔɪəns] *n* **(a)** *no pl (irritation)* Ärger *m.* **to his ~** zu seinem Ärger. **(b)** *(nuisance)* Plage, Belästigung *f,* Ärgernis *nt.*
annoying [ə'nɔɪɪŋ] *adj* ärgerlich; *habit* lästig.
annual ['ænjʊəl] **1** *n* **(a)** *(Bot)* einjährige Pflanze. **(b)** *(book)* Jahrbuch *nt.* **2** *adj (happening once a year)* jährlich; *salary etc* Jahres-. ~ **general meeting** *(Brit)* Jahreshauptversammlung *f*; ~ **report** Geschäftsbericht *m.*
annually ['ænjʊəlɪ] *adv* jährlich.
annuity [ə'njuːɪtɪ] *n* (Leib)rente *f.*
annul [ə'nʌl] *vt* annullieren; *law, decree, judgement* aufheben; *contract, marriage also* auflösen.
annulment [ə'nʌlmənt] *n see vt* Annullierung *f*; Aufhebung *f*; Auflösung *f.*
Annunciation [əˌnʌnsɪ'eɪʃən] *n (Bibl)* Mariä Verkündigung *f.*
anode ['ænəʊd] *n* Anode *f.*
anoint [ə'nɔɪnt] *vt* salben.
anomalous [ə'nɒmələs] *adj* ano(r)mal, ungewöhnlich.

anomaly [ə'nɒməlɪ] *n* Anomalie *f*; *(in law etc)* Besonderheit *f*.

anonymity [ˌænə'nɪmɪtɪ] *n* Anonymität *f*.

anonymous [ə'nɒnɪməs] *adj* anonym.

anorak ['ænəræk] *n (Brit)* Anorak *m*.

anorexia (nervosa) [ænə'reksiə(nɜː'vəʊsə)] *n* Magersucht *f*.

another [ə'nʌðə^r] **1** *adj* **(a)** *(additional)* noch eine(r, s). ~ **one** noch eine(r, s); **take** ~ **ten** nehmen Sie noch (weitere) zehn; **I don't want** ~ **drink!** ich möchte nichts mehr trinken; ~ **20 years and he ...** noch 20 Jahre, und er ...; **without** ~ **word** ohne ein weiteres Wort; **and (there's)** ~ **thing** und noch eins, und (da ist) noch etwas; ~ **Shakespeare** ein zweiter Shakespeare. **(b)** *(different)* ein anderer, eine andere, ein anderes. **that's quite** ~ **matter** das ist etwas ganz anderes. **2** *pron* ein anderer, eine andere, ein anderes. **have** ~**!** nehmen Sie (doch) noch einen/eins *etc*; **tell me** ~**!** *(col)* das glaubst du doch wohl selbst nicht!; **what with one thing and** ~ bei all dem Trubel; **is this** ~ **of your brilliant ideas!** ist das wieder so eine deiner Glanzideen!

answer ['ɑːnsə^r] **1** *n* **(a)** Antwort *f (to* auf *+acc)*. **there was no** ~ *(to telephone, doorbell)* es hat sich niemand gemeldet; **the** ~ **to our prayers** ein Geschenk des Himmels; **there's no** ~ **to that** *(col)* was soll man da groß machen/sagen! *(col)*; **in** ~ **to your letter/my question** in Beantwortung Ihres Briefes *(form)*/auf meine Frage hin. **(b)** *(solution)* Lösung *f (to gen)*. **his** ~ **to any difficulty is ...** seine Reaktion auf jede Schwierigkeit ist ...

2 *vt* **(a)** antworten auf *(+acc)*, erwidern auf *(+acc) (geh)*; *person* antworten *(+dat)*; *exam questions* beantworten, antworten auf *(+acc)*; *objections, criticism also* beantworten. **will you** ~ **that?** *(phone/door)* gehst du ran/hin?; **to** ~ **the telephone/bell** *or* **door** das Telefon abnehmen, ans Telefon gehen/die Tür aufmachen. **(b)** *(fulfil) description* entsprechen *(+dat)*; *prayer (God)* erhören; *need* befriedigen. **(c)** *(Jur) charge* sich verantworten wegen *(+gen)*.

3 *vi (also react)* antworten. **if the phone rings, don't** ~ wenn das Telefon läutet, geh nicht ran *or* nimm nicht ab.

♦**answer back** *vi* widersprechen; *(children also)* freche Antworten geben. **don't** ~ ~**!** keine Widerrede!

♦**answer for** *vi +prep obj* **(a)** *(be responsible for)* verantwortlich sein für; *(person also)* verantworten; *mistakes also* einstehen für. **he has a lot to** ~ ~ er hat eine Menge auf dem Gewissen. **(b)** *(guarantee)* sich verbürgen für; *(speak for also)* sprechen für.

♦**answer to** *vi +prep obj* **(a)** *(be accountable to)* **to** ~ ~ **sb for sth** jdm für etw Rechenschaft schuldig sein. **(b) to** ~ ~ **a description** einer Beschreibung entsprechen. **(c) to** ~ ~ **the name of ...** auf den Namen ... hören.

answerable ['ɑːnsərəbl] *adj* **(a)** *(responsible)* **to be** ~ **to sb (for sth)** jdm gegenüber für etw verantwortlich sein. **(b)** *question* zu beantworten.

answering machine ['ɑːnsərɪŋmə'ʃiːn] *n* (automatischer) Anrufbeantworter.

ant [ænt] *n* Ameise *f*.

antagonism [æn'tægənɪzəm] *n* Antagonismus *m*; *(towards sb, ideas)* Feindseligkeit *f (to(wards)* gegenüber*)*.

antagonist [æn'tægənɪst] *n* Gegner, Antagonist *m*.

antagonistic [ænˌtægə'nɪstɪk] *adj* feindselig. **to be** ~ **towards sb/sth** jdm/gegen etw feindselig gesinnt sein.

antagonize [æn'tægənaɪz] *vt* gegen sich aufbringen.

antarctic [ænt'ɑːktɪk] **1** *adj* antarktisch. **A**~ **Circle** südlicher Polarkreis; **A**~ **Ocean** Südpolarmeer *nt*. **2** *n* **the A**~ die Antarktis.

Antarctica [ænt'ɑːktɪkə] *n* die Antarktis.

ante- *pref* vor-.

anteater ['æntˌiːtə^r] *n* Ameisenbär *m*.

antecedent [ˌæntɪ'siːdənt] *n* ~**s** *(of person) (past history)* Vorleben *nt*; *(ancestry)* Abstammung *f*; *(of event)* Vorgeschichte *f*.

ante: ~**date** *vt document, cheque* vordatieren *(to* auf *+acc)*; *event* vorausgehen *(+dat) (by* um*)*; ~**diluvian** *adj (lit, fig col)* vorsintflutlich.

antelope ['æntɪləʊp] *n* Antilope *f*.

antenatal ['æntɪ'neɪtl] *adj* vor der Geburt, pränatal *(form)*. ~ **care/excercises** Schwangerschaftsfürsorge/-gymnastik *f*; ~ **clinic** Klinik *f* für werdende Mütter.

antenna [æn'tenə] *n* **(a)** *pl* **-e** [æn'teniː] *(Zool)* Fühler *m*. **(b)** *pl* **-e** *or* **-s** *(Rad, TV)* Antenne *f*.

anteroom ['æntɪruːm] *n* Vorzimmer *nt*.

anthem ['ænθəm] *n* Hymne *f*; *(by choir)* Chorgesang *m*.

anthology [æn'θɒlədʒɪ] *n* Anthologie *f*.

anthracite ['ænθrəsaɪt] *n* Anthrazit *m*.

anthropoid ['ænθrəʊpɔɪd] *n* Anthropoid *m (spec)*; *(ape)* Menschenaffe *m*.

anthropologist [ˌænθrə'pɒlədʒɪst] *n* Anthropologe *m*, Anthropologin *f*.

anthropology [ˌænθrə'pɒlədʒɪ] *n* Anthropologie *f*.

anti ['æntɪ] *prep (col)* gegen *(+acc)*. ~ **everything** grundsätzlich gegen alles.

anti- *in cpds* anti-, gegen-; ~**-aircraft** *adj gun, rocket* Flugabwehr-; ~**ballistic missile** *n* Anti(-Raketen)-Rakete *f*; ~**biotic** *n* Antibiotikum *nt*; ~**body** *n* Antikörper *m*.

anticipate [æn'tɪsɪpeɪt] **1** *vt* **(a)** *(expect)* erwarten. **(b)** *(see in advance)* vorhersehen; *(see in advance and cater for) objection, need etc* zuvorkommen *(+dat)*. **(c)** *(do before sb else)* zuvorkommen *(+dat)*. **2** *vi (chess-player etc)* vorauskalkulieren.

anticipation [ænˌtɪsɪ'peɪʃən] *n* **(a)** *(expectation)* Erwartung *f*. **thanking you in** ~ herzlichen Dank im voraus; **to wait in** ~ gespannt warten. **(b) his uncanny** ~ **of every objection** die verblüffende Art, in der er jedem Einwand zuvorkam; **the driver showed good** ~ der Fahrer zeigte ein gutes Reaktionsvermögen. **(c)** *(of discovery, discoverer)* Vorwegnahme *f*.

anti: ~**climax** *n* Enttäuschung *f*; ~**clockwise** *adv* nach links, gegen den Uhrzeigersinn.

antics ['æntɪks] *npl* Eskapaden *pl*; *(tricks)* Streiche *pl*.

anti: ~**cyclone** *n* Hoch(druckgebiet) *nt*; ~**depressant** *n* Mittel *nt* gegen Depressionen; ~**dote** *n* *(Med, fig)* Gegenmittel *nt (for* gegen*)*; ~**freeze** *n* Frostschutz *m*; ~**histamine** *n* Antihistamin *nt*; ~**missile** *adj* Raketenabwehr-.

antipathy [æn'tɪpəθɪ] *n* Antipathie, Abneigung *f (towards* gegen*)*.

antipodes [æn'tɪpədiːz] *npl* die entgegengesetzten Teile der Erde. **A**~ *(Brit)* Australien und Neuseeland.

antiquated ['æntɪkweɪtɪd] *adj* antiquiert; *machines, ideas also* überholt; *institutions also* veraltet.

antique [æn'tiːk] **1** *adj* antik. **2** *n* Antiquität *f*.

antique dealer *n* Antiquitätenhändler(in *f*) *m*.

antiquity [æn'tɪkwɪtɪ] *n* das Altertum; *(Roman, Greek* ~*)* die Antike; *(great age)* großes Alter.

anti: ~**-rust** *adj* Rostschutz-; ~**-Semitic** *adj* antisemitisch; ~**-Semitism** *n* Antisemitismus *m*; ~**septic 1** *n* Antiseptikum *nt*; **2** *adj* antiseptisch; ~**social** *adj* unsozial; *(Psych)* asozial; **in an** ~**social mood** nicht in Gesellschaftslaune.

antithesis [æn'tɪθɪsɪs] *n*, *pl* **antitheses** [æn'tɪθɪsiːz] *(direct opposite)* genaues Gegenteil *(to, of gen)*; *(contrast)* Gegensatz *m*.

antler ['æntlə^r] *n* Geweihsprosse *f*. **(set** *or* **pair of)** ~**s** Geweih *nt*.

antonym ['æntənɪm] *n* Antonym *nt*.

anus ['eɪnəs] *n* After *m*.
anvil ['ænvɪl] *n* Amboß *m*.
anxiety [æŋg'zaɪətɪ] *n* **(a)** Sorge *f*. **to suffer from ~** unter Angst leiden. **(b)** *(keen desire)* **in his ~ to get away** weil er unbedingt wegkommen wollte.
anxious ['æŋkʃəs] *adj* **(a)** *(worried)* besorgt; *person (as character trait)* ängstlich. **to be ~ about sb/sth** sich *(dat)* um jdn/etw Sorgen machen, um jdn/etw besorgt sein. **(b)** *(worrying) moment, minutes* der Angst, bang *(geh)*. **it's been an ~ time for us all** wir alle haben uns (in dieser Zeit) große Sorgen gemacht. **(c) to be ~ to do sth** etw unbedingt wollen; **they were ~ for news** sie warteten auf Nachricht; **we are ~ for a settlement** uns ist an einer Klärung sehr gelegen; **I am ~ for him to do it** mir liegt viel daran, daß er es tut.
anxiously ['æŋkʃəslɪ] *adv* **(a)** besorgt. **(b)** *(keenly)* begierig.
any ['enɪ] **1** *adj* **(a)** *(in interrog, conditional, neg sentences) not translated*; *(emph: ~ at all) (with sing n)* irgendein(e); *(with pl n)* irgendwelche; *(with uncountable n)* etwas. **do you have ~ wine/cigarettes?** haben Sie Wein/Zigaretten?; **not ~** kein/keine; **not *any* ... at all** überhaupt kein/keine ...; **if I had *any* plan/ideas/money (at all)** wenn ich irgendeinen Plan/irgendwelche Ideen/(auch nur) etwas Geld hätte; **without ~ difficulty (at all)** ohne jede Schwierigkeit; **hardly ~ difference at all** kaum ein Unterschied.
(b) *(no matter which)* jede(r, s) (beliebige); *(with pl or uncountable n)* alle. **~ one will do** es ist jede(r, s) recht; **you can have ~ book/books you find** du kannst jedes Buch/alle Bücher haben, das/die du findest; **take ~ two points** wähle zwei beliebige Punkte; **~ one you like** was du willst; **~ one of us** jeder von uns.
2 *pron* **(a)** *(in interrog, conditional, neg sentences) (replacing sing n)* ein(e), welche(r, s); *(replacing pl n)* einige, welche; *(replacing uncountable n)* etwas, welche. **I need some butter/stamps, do you have ~?** ich brauche Butter/Briefmarken, haben Sie welche?; **have you seen ~ of my ties?** haben Sie eine von meinen Krawatten gesehen?; **haven't you ~ (at all)?** haben Sie (gar) keinen/keine/keines?; **the profits, if ~** die eventuellen Gewinne; **if ~ of you can sing** wenn (irgend) jemand *or* (irgend)einer/-eine von euch singen kann; **few, if ~, will come** wenn überhaupt, werden nur wenige kommen. **(b)** *(no matter which)* alle. **~ I have ...** alle, die ich habe ...
3 *adv* **if it gets ~ colder** wenn es (noch) kälter wird; **not ~ colder/bigger** nicht kälter/größer; **it won't get ~ colder** es wird nicht mehr kälter; **we can't go ~ further** wir können nicht mehr weitergehen; **are you feeling ~ better?** geht es dir etwas besser?; **do you want ~ more soup?** willst du noch etwas Suppe?; **I don't want ~ more** ich möchte nichts mehr.
anybody ['enɪ,bɒdɪ] **1** *pron* **(a)** (irgend) jemand, (irgend)eine(r). **not ... ~** niemand, keine(r); **don't tell ~** erzähl das niemand(em) *or* keinem. **(b)** *(no matter who)* jede(r). **~ will tell you the same** jeder wird dir dasselbe sagen. **2** *n* **she'll never be ~** sie wird es nie zu etwas bringen; **he's not just ~** er ist nicht einfach irgend jemand.
anyhow ['enɪhaʊ] *adv* **(a) ~, that's what I think** das ist jedenfalls meine Meinung; **it's no trouble, I'm going there ~** es ist keine Mühe, ich gehe sowieso hin; **I told him not to, but he did it ~** ich habe es ihm verboten, aber er hat es trotzdem gemacht; **who cares, ~?** überhaupt, wen kümmert es denn schon? **(b)** *(carelessly)* irgendwie; *(at random also)* aufs Geratewohl.
anyone ['enɪwʌn] *pron, n* = **anybody.**
anyplace ['enɪpleɪs] *adv (US col)* = **anywhere.**
anything ['enɪθɪŋ] **1** *pron* **(a)** (irgend) etwas. **not ~** nichts; *(euph)* gar *or* überhaupt nichts. **(b)** *(no matter what)* alles. **~ you like** (alles,) was du willst; **they eat ~** sie essen alles; **not just ~** nicht bloß irgend etwas; **I wouldn't do it for ~** ich würde es um keinen Preis tun. **2** *adv (col)* **it isn't ~ like him** das sieht ihm überhaupt nicht ähnlich; **it didn't cost ~ like £100** es kostete bei, weitem keine £ 100; **not ~ like as wet as ...** nicht annähernd so naß wie ...; **she's been working like ~** *(col)* sie hat wie verrückt gearbeitet.
anyway ['enɪweɪ] *adv* = **anyhow (a).**
anywhere ['enɪwɛəʳ] *adv* **(a)** *be, stay, live* irgendwo; *go, travel* irgendwohin. **not ~** nirgends/nirgendwohin; **I haven't found ~ to live yet** ich habe noch nichts gefunden, wo ich wohnen kann; **he'll never get ~** er wird es zu nichts bringen; **I wasn't getting ~** ich kam (einfach) nicht weiter. **(b)** *(no matter where) be, stay, live* überall; *go, travel* überallhin. **they could be ~** sie könnten überall sein; **~ you like** wo/wohin du willst.
aorta [eɪ'ɔːtə] *n* Aorta *f*.
apart [ə'pɑːt] *adv* **(a)** auseinander. **to sit with one's legs ~** mit gespreizten Beinen dasitzen; **I can't tell them ~** ich kann sie nicht auseinanderhalten; **to live ~** getrennt leben; **to come** *or* **fall ~** entzweigehen, auseinanderfallen; **to take sth ~** etw auseinandernehmen. **(b)** *(to one side)* zur Seite, beiseite; *(on one side)* abseits *(from gen)*. **a class/thing ~** eine Klasse/Sache für sich. **(c)** *(excepted)* abgesehen von, bis auf *(+acc)*. **these problems ~** abgesehen von diesen Problemen; **~ from that** abgesehen davon.
apartheid [ə'pɑːteɪt] *n* Apartheid *f*.
apartment [ə'pɑːtmənt] *n* **(a)** *(Brit: room)* Raum *m*. **(b) ~s** *pl (Brit: suite of rooms)* Appartement *nt*. **(c)** *(esp US: flat)* Wohnung *f*. **~ house** Wohnblock *m*.
apathetic [,æpə'θetɪk] *adj* apathisch, teilnahmslos.
apathy ['æpəθɪ] *n* Apathie, Teilnahmslosigkeit *f*.
ape [eɪp] **1** *n (lit, fig)* Affe *m*. **2** *vt* nachäffen *(pej)*, nachmachen.
aperitif [ə,perɪ'tiːf] *n* Aperitif *m*.
aperture ['æpətʃjʊəʳ] *n* Öffnung *f*; *(Phot)* Blende *f*.
apex ['eɪpeks] *n* Spitze *f*; *(fig)* Höhepunkt *m*.
aphorism ['æfərɪzəm] *n* Aphorismus *m*.
aphrodisiac [,æfrəʊ'dɪzɪæk] *n* Aphrodisiakum *nt*.
apiary ['eɪpɪərɪ] *n* Bienenhaus *nt*.
apiece [ə'piːs] *adv* pro Stück; *(per person)* pro Person. **I gave them two ~** ich gab ihnen je zwei; **they had two ~** sie hatten jeder zwei.
aplomb [ə'plɒm] *n* Gelassenheit *f*.
Apocalypse [ə'pɒkəlɪps] n Apokalypse *f*.
apocryphal [ə'pɒkrɪfəl] *adj (untrue)* erfunden.
apologetic [ə,pɒlə'dʒetɪk] *adj gesture, look* entschuldigend *attr*. **he was most ~ (about it)** er entschuldigte sich vielmals (dafür).
apologize [ə'pɒlədʒaɪz] *vi* sich entschuldigen *(to bei)*.
apology [ə'pɒlədʒɪ] *n* Entschuldigung *f*. **to make** *or* **offer sb an ~** jdn um Verzeihung bitten; **to make one's apologies** sich entschuldigen; **Mr Jones sends his apologies** Herr Jones läßt sich entschuldigen; **an ~ for a breakfast** ein erbärmliches Frühstück.
apoplexy ['æpəpleksɪ] *n* Schlaganfall *m*.
apostle [ə'pɒsl] *n (lit, fig)* Apostel *m*.
apostrophe [ə'pɒstrəfɪ] *n (Gram)* Apostroph *m*.
appal, *(US also)* **appall** [ə'pɔːl] *vt* entsetzen. **to be ~led (at** *or* **by sth)** (über etw *acc*) entsetzt sein.
appalling [ə'pɔːlɪŋ] *adj* entsetzlich.
apparatus [,æpə'reɪtəs] *n (lit, fig)* Apparat *m*; *(equipment also)* Ausrüstung *f*; *(in gym)* Geräte *pl*. **a piece of ~** ein Gerät *nt*.
apparent [ə'pærənt] *adj* **(a)** *(obvious)* offensichtlich. **to be ~ to sb** jdm klar sein; **to become ~** sich (deutlich) zeigen. **(b)** *(seeming)* scheinbar.

apparently [ə'pærəntlɪ] *adv* anscheinend.

apparition [ˌæpə'rɪʃən] *n* **(a)** *(ghost, hum: person)* Erscheinung *f.* **(b)** *(appearance)* Erscheinen *nt.*

appeal [ə'piːl] **1** *n* **(a)** *(request: for help, money etc)* Appell *m*, Bitte *f (for* um*)*; *(for mercy)* Gesuch *nt (for* um*)*. **~ for funds** Spendenaufruf *m or* -aktion *f*; **to make an ~ to sb (to do sth)/to sb for sth** an jdn appellieren(, etw zu tun)/jdn um etw bitten. **(b)** *(against decision)* Einspruch *m*; *(Jur: against sentence)* Berufung *f*; *(actual trial)* Berufungsverhandlung *f.* **he lost his ~** er verlor in der Berufung; **right of ~** Einspruchsrecht *nt*; *(Jur)* Berufungsrecht *nt*; **Court of A~** Berufungsgericht *nt.* **(c)** *(attraction)* Reiz *m (to* für*)*. **his music has a wide ~** seine Musik findet großen Anklang.

2 *vi* **(a)** *(make request)* **to ~ to sb for sth** jdn um etw bitten; **to ~ to the public to do sth** die Öffentlichkeit (dazu) aufrufen, etw zu tun. **(b)** *(against decision: to authority etc)* Einspruch erheben *(to* bei*)*; *(Jur)* Berufung einlegen *(to* bei*)*. **(c)** *(apply: for support, decision)* appellieren *(to* an *+acc)*; *(Sport)* Einspruch erheben *(to* bei*)*. **to ~ to sb's better nature** an jds besseres Ich appellieren. **(d)** *(be attractive)* reizen *(to sb* jdn*)*, zusagen *(to sb* jdm*)*; *(plan, candidate, idea)* zusagen *(to sb* jdm*)*; *(book, magazine)* ansprechen *(to sb* jdn*)*. **how does that ~?** wie gefällt dir/Ihnen das?; **the story ~ed to his sense of humour** die Geschichte sprach seinen Sinn für Humor an.

appealing [ə'piːlɪŋ] *adj (attractive)* attraktiv, reizvoll; *character, smile* ansprechend, gewinnend.

appear [ə'pɪəʳ] *vi* **(a)** erscheinen; *(unexpectedly)* auftauchen; *(personality, ghost also)* sich zeigen; *(Theat)* auftreten. **to ~ in court** vor Gericht erscheinen; **to ~ for sb** jdn vertreten. **(b)** *(seem)* scheinen. **he ~ed (to be) tired** er schien müde zu sein; **it ~s that ...** anscheinend ...; **so it ~s, so it would ~** so scheint es; **it ~s not** anscheinend nicht, es sieht nicht so aus; **it ~s from his statement that ...** aus seiner Bemerkung geht hervor, daß ...

appearance [ə'pɪərəns] *n* **(a)** Erscheinen *nt*; *(unexpected)* Auftauchen *nt no pl*; *(Theat)* Auftritt *m.* **many successful court ~s** viele erfolgreiche Auftritte vor Gericht; **to put in** *or* **make an ~** sich sehen lassen. **(b)** *(look)* Aussehen *nt*; *(of person also)* Äußere(s) *nt*, äußere Erscheinung. **~s** *(outward signs)* der äußere (An)schein; **in ~** dem Aussehen nach; **at first ~** auf den ersten Blick; **for the sake of ~s** um den Schein zu wahren; *(as good manners)* der Form halber; **to keep up ~s** den (äußeren) Schein wahren; **~s are often deceptive** der Schein trügt oft; **to all ~s** allem Anschein nach.

appease [ə'piːz] *vt person, anger* beschwichtigen, besänftigen; *hunger, curiosity* stillen.

appeasement [ə'piːzmənt] *n (esp Pol)* Beschwichtigung *f.*

append [ə'pend] *vt notes etc* anhängen *(to* an *+acc)*, hinzufügen; *signature* setzen *(to* under *+acc)*.

appendage [ə'pendɪdʒ] *n (fig)* Anhängsel *nt.*

appendicitis [əˌpendɪ'saɪtɪs] *n* Blinddarmentzündung *f.*

appendix [ə'pendɪks] *n, pl* **appendices (a)** *(Anat)* Blinddarm *m.* **to have one's ~ out** sich *(dat)* den Blinddarm herausnehmen lassen. **(b)** *(to book etc)* Anhang, Appendix *m.*

appetite ['æpɪtaɪt] *n (for* auf etw *+acc)* Appetit *m*; *(fig: desire)* Lust *f.* **to have a good ~** einen guten *or* gesunden Appetit haben.

appetizer ['æpɪtaɪzəʳ] *n (food)* Appetitanreger *m*; *(drink)* appetitanregendes Getränk.

appetizing ['æpɪtaɪzɪŋ] *adj* appetitlich *(also fig)*; *smell* lecker.

applaud [ə'plɔːd] *vti (lit, fig)* applaudieren *(+dat)*; *(fig) efforts, courage* loben; *decision* begrüßen.

applause [ə'plɔːz] *n no pl (lit fig)* Beifall *m.*

apple ['æpl] *n* Apfel *m.* **to be the ~ of sb's eye** jds Liebling sein.

apple *in cpds* Apfel-; **~-pie** *n* ≃ gedeckter Apfelkuchen; **~-tree** *n* Apfelbaum *m*; **~ turnover** *n* Apfeltasche *f.*

appliance [ə'plaɪəns] *n* Vorrichtung *f*; *(household ~)* Gerät *nt.*

applicable [ə'plɪkəbl] *adj* anwendbar *(to* auf *+acc)*; *(on forms)* zutreffend *(to* für*)*. **that isn't ~ to you** das trifft auf Sie nicht zu.

applicant ['æplɪkənt] *n (for job)* Bewerber(in *f*) *m (for* um, für*)*; *(for loan etc)* Antragsteller(in *f*) *m (for* für*)*.

application [ˌæplɪ'keɪʃən] *n* **(a)** *(for job etc)* Bewerbung *f (for* um, für*)*; *(for grant, loan etc)* Antrag *m (for* auf *+acc)*. **~ form** Bewerbung(sformular *nt*) *f*; Antrag(sformular *nt*) *m*; *(for course, exhibition etc)* Anmeldeformular *nt.* **(b)** *(act of applying)* see **apply 1** Anwendung *f*; Auftragen *nt*; Anlegen *nt*; *Betätigung f*; Verwertung *f.* **(c)** *(diligence, effort)* Fleiß, Eifer *m.*

applied [ə'plaɪd] *adj attr maths etc* angewandt.

apply [ə'plaɪ] **1** *vt* anwenden *(to* auf *+acc)*; *paint etc* auftragen *(to* auf *+acc)*; *dressing* anlegen; *brakes* betätigen; *results, findings* verwerten *(to* für*)*. **to ~ oneself** *or* **one's mind (to sth)** sich (bei etw) anstrengen. **2** *vi* **(a)** sich bewerben *(for* um, für*)*. **to ~ for a loan** einen Kredit beantragen. **(b)** *(be applicable)* gelten *(to* für*)*.

appoint [ə'pɔɪnt] *vt* **(a)** *(to a job)* einstellen; *(to a post)* ernennen. **to ~ sb sth** jdn zu etw ernennen. **(b)** *(designate, ordain)* bestimmen. **at the ~ed time** zur vereinbarten Zeit.

-appointed [-ə'pɔɪntɪd] *adj suf* **well-~** gut ausgestattet.

appointment [ə'pɔɪntmənt] *n* **(a)** Verabredung *f*; *(business ~, with doctor, lawyer etc)* Termin *m (with* bei*)*. **to make an ~ with sb** mit jdm eine Verabredung treffen; einen Termin mit jdm vereinbaren; **do you have an ~?** sind Sie angemeldet?; **by ~** auf Verabredung; *(on business, to see doctor, lawyer etc)* mit (Vor)anmeldung, nach Vereinbarung. **(b)** *(act of appointing) see vt (a)* Einstellung *f*; Ernennung *f.* **(c)** *(post)* Stelle *f.* **~s (vacant)** Stellenangebote *pl.*

apportion [ə'pɔːʃən] *vt* aufteilen. **to ~ sth to sb** jdm etw zuteilen.

apposite ['æpəzɪt] *adj* treffend, passend.

appraisal [ə'preɪzəl] *n see vt* Schätzung *f*; Beurteilung *f.*

appraise [ə'preɪz] *vt* schätzen; *character, ability* beurteilen.

appreciable [ə'priːʃəbl] *adj* beträchtlich, deutlich; *difference, change also* merklich.

appreciate [ə'priːʃɪeɪt] **1** *vt* **(a)** *(be aware of)* sich *(dat)* bewußt sein *(+gen)*; *(understand) sb's wishes, reluctance etc also* Verständnis haben für. **I ~ that you can't come** ich habe Verständnis dafür, daß ihr nicht kommen könnt. **(b)** *(value, be grateful for)* zu schätzen wissen. **thank you, I ~ it** vielen Dank, sehr nett von Ihnen; **I would really ~ that** das wäre mir wirklich sehr lieb. **(c)** *(enjoy) art, music, poetry* schätzen. **2** *vi (Fin)* im Wert steigen, an Wert gewinnen.

appreciation [əˌpriːʃɪ'eɪʃən] *n* **(a)** *(awareness)* Erkennen *nt.* **(b)** *(esteem, respect)* Anerkennung *f*; *(of abilities, efforts also)* Würdigung *f*; *(of person also)* Wertschätzung *f*; *(gratitude)* Dankbarkeit *f.* **in ~ of sth** in Anerkennung *(+gen)*, zum Dank für etw. **(c)** *(enjoyment, understanding)* Verständnis *nt*; *(of art)* Sinn *m (of* für*)*. **(d)** *(Fin: increase)* (Wert)steigerung *f.*

appreciative [ə'priːʃɪətɪv] *adj* anerkennend; *audience* dankbar; *(grateful)* dankbar. **to be ~ of sth** etw zu schätzen wissen; *of music, art etc* Sinn für etw haben.

apprehend [ˌæprɪ'hend] *vt (arrest)* festnehmen.
apprehension [ˌæprɪ'henʃən] *n* **(a)** *(fear)* Besorgnis, Befürchtung *f*. **a feeling of ~** eine dunkle Ahnung. **(b)** *(arrest)* Festnahme *f*.
apprehensive [ˌæprɪ'hensɪv] *adj* ängstlich. **to be ~ of sth/that ...** etw befürchten/fürchten, daß ...
apprentice [ə'prentɪs] *n* Lehrling *m*, Auszubildende(r) *mf*.
apprenticeship [ə'prentɪʃɪp] *n* Lehre *f*.
approach [ə'prəʊtʃ] **1** *vi (physically)* sich nähern, näherkommen; *(date, summer etc)* nahen.
2 *vt* **(a)** *(come near)* sich nähern *(+dat)*; *(Aviat also)* anfliegen; *(in quality, stature)* herankommen an *(+acc)*. **to ~ thirty** auf die Dreißig zugehen. **(b)** *person, committee* herantreten an *(+acc) (about* wegen*)*. **he is easy/difficult to ~** er ist leicht/nicht leicht ansprechbar. **(c)** *(tackle) problem* angehen.
3 *n* **(a)** *(drawing near)* (Heran)nahen *nt*; *(of troops, in time also)* Heranrücken *nt*; *(of night)* Einbruch *m*; *(Aviat)* Anflug *m (to* auf *+acc)*. **(b) to make ~es/an ~ to sb** *(with request)* an jdn herantreten; *(man to woman)* Annäherungsversuche machen. **(c)** *(way of tackling, attitude)* Ansatz *m (to* zu*)*. **an easy ~ to maths** ein einfacher Weg, Mathematik zu lernen; **his ~ to the problem** sein Problemansatz *m*; **you've got the wrong ~** du machst das verkehrt; **try a different ~** versuch's doch mal anders. **(d)** *(access)* Zugang, Weg *m*; *(road also)* Zufahrt(sstraße) *f*.
approachable [ə'prəʊtʃəbl] *adj* **(a)** *person* umgänglich, zugänglich. **(b)** *place* zugänglich.
approach road *n (to city etc)* Zufahrtsstraße *f*; *(to motorway)* Zubringer *m*.
approbation [ˌæprə'beɪʃən] *n* Billigung *f*; *(from critics)* Beifall *m*.
appropriate[1] [ə'prəʊprɪɪt] *adj* **(a)** *(suitable, fitting)* passend, geeignet *(for, to* für*)*; *name, remark also* treffend. **(b)** *(relevant)* entsprechend; *body, authority also* zuständig. **where ~** wo es angebracht ist/war, an gegebener Stelle; **delete as ~** Nichtzutreffendes streichen.
appropriate[2] [ə'prəʊprɪeɪt] *vt (authorities)* beschlagnahmen; *(take for oneself)* sich *(dat)* aneignen, mit Beschlag belegen.
appropriately [ə'prəʊprɪɪtlɪ] *adv* treffend; *dressed* passend *(for, to* für*)*; *(to fit particular needs) designed, equipped* zweckmäßig *(for, to* für*)*.
approval [ə'pruːvəl] *n* Zustimmung *(of* zu*)*, Billigung *f*. **to meet with sb's ~** jds Zustimmung *or* Beifall finden; **to show one's ~ of sth** zeigen, daß man einer Sache *(dat)* zustimmt *or* etw billigt; **on ~** *(Comm)* auf Probe; *(to look at)* zur Ansicht.
approve [ə'pruːv] **1** *vt decision* billigen, gutheißen; *minutes, motion* annehmen; *project* genehmigen. **an ~d campsite** ein empfohlener Campingplatz. **2** *vi* **I don't ~ of him/it** ich halte nichts von ihm/davon; **I don't ~ of children smoking** ich finde es nicht richtig, daß Kinder rauchen; **do you ~?** findest du das richtig *or* in Ordnung?
approved school [ə'pruːvd'skuːl] *n (Brit)* Erziehungsheim *nt*.
approximate [ə'prɒksɪmɪt] **1** *adj* ungefähr. **2** [ə'prɒksəmeɪt] *vti* **to ~ (to) sth** einer Sache *(dat)* in etwa entsprechen.
approximately [ə'prɒksɪmətlɪ] *adv* ungefähr.
approximation [əˌprɒksɪ'meɪʃən] *n* Annäherung *f (of, to* an *+acc)*; *(figure, sum etc)* (An)näherungswert *m*.
apricot ['eɪprɪkɒt] *n* Aprikose *f*.
April ['eɪprəl] *n* April *m*. **~ fool!** ≃ April, April!; **~ Fool's Day** der erste April; *see* **September.**
apron ['eɪprən] *n* Schürze *f*; *(Aviat)* Vorfeld *nt*. **to be tied to one's mother's ~-strings** seiner Mutter *(dat)* am Schürzenzipfel hängen *(col)*.
apse [æps] *n* Apsis *f*.
apt [æpt] *adj (+er)* **(a)** *(suitable, fitting)* passend; *comparison, remark also* treffend. **(b)** *(able, intelligent)* begabt *(at* für*)*. **(c)** *(liable)* **to be ~ to do sth** dazu neigen, etw zu tun.
aptitude ['æptɪtjuːd] *n* Begabung *f*. **~ test** Eignungsprüfung *f*.
aptly ['æptlɪ] *adv* passend.
aqualung ['ækwəlʌŋ] *n* Tauchgerät *nt*.
aquarium [ə'kweərɪəm] *n* Aquarium *nt*.
Aquarius [ə'kweərɪəs] *n* Wassermann *m*.
aquatic [ə'kwætɪk] *adj* Wasser-.
aqueduct ['ækwɪdʌkt] *n* Aquädukt *m or nt*.
aquiline ['ækwɪlaɪn] *adj nose* Adler-, gebogen.
Arab ['ærəb] **1** *n* Araber *m (also horse)*, Araberin *f*. **2** *adj attr* arabisch; *policies, ideas also* der Araber.
arabesque [ˌærə'besk] *n* Arabeske *f*.
Arabia [ə'reɪbɪə] *n* Arabien *nt*.
Arabian [ə'reɪbɪən] *adj* arabisch. **tales of the ~ Nights** Märchen aus Tausendundeiner Nacht.
Arabic ['ærəbɪk] **1** *n* Arabisch *nt*. **2** *adj* arabisch.
arable ['ærəbl] *adj land* bebaubar; *(being used)* Acker-.
arbitrary ['ɑːbɪtrərɪ] *adj* willkürlich.
arbitrate ['ɑːbɪtreɪt] **1** *vt dispute* schlichten. **2** *vi* vermitteln.
arbitration [ˌɑːbɪ'treɪʃən] *n* Schlichtung *f*. **to go to ~** vor eine Schlichtungskommission gehen; *(dispute)* vor eine Schlichtungskommission gebracht werden.
arbitrator ['ɑːbɪtreɪtə^r] *n* Vermittler *m*; *(esp Ind)* Schlichter *m*.
arc [ɑːk] *n* Bogen *m*.
arcade [ɑː'keɪd] *n (Archit)* Arkade *f*; *(shopping ~)* Passage *f*.
arcane [ɑː'keɪn] *adj* obskur.
arch[1] [ɑːtʃ] **1** *n* **(a)** Bogen *m*. **(b)** *(Anat)* **fallen ~es** Senkfuß *m*. **2** *vi* sich wölben; *(arrow etc)* einen Bogen beschreiben. **3** *vt back* krümmen. **the cat ~ed his back** die Katze machte einen Buckel.
arch[2] *adj attr* Erz-. **~ traitor** Hochverräter *m*.
archaeological, *(US)* **archeological** [ˌɑːkɪə'lɒdʒɪkəl] *adj* archäologisch.
archaeologist, *(US)* **archeologist** [ˌɑːkɪ'ɒlədʒɪst] *n* Archäologe *m*, Archäologin *f*.
archaeology, *(US)* **archeology** [ˌɑːkɪ'ɒlədʒɪ] *n* Archäologie *f*.
archaic [ɑː'keɪɪk] *adj word etc* veraltet, archaisch *(spec)*; *(col)* vorsintflutlich.
arch: ~angel ['ɑːkˌeɪndʒəl] *n* Erzengel *m*; **~bishop** *n* Erzbischof *m*; **~duke** *n* Erzherzog *m*.
arched [ɑːtʃt] *adj* gewölbt; *window* (Rund)bogen-.
arch-enemy [ˌɑːtʃ'enɪmɪ] *n* Erzfeind *m*.
archeological *etc (US)* = **archaeological** *etc*.
archer ['ɑːtʃə^r] *n* Bogenschütze *m*.
archery ['ɑːtʃərɪ] *n* Bogenschießen *nt*.
archetypal ['ɑːkɪtaɪpəl] *adj* archetypisch *(geh)*; *(typical)* typisch.
archetype ['ɑːkɪtaɪp] *n* Urbild *nt*, Urtyp *m*.
archipelago [ˌɑːkɪ'pelɪgəʊ] *n, pl* **-(e)s** Archipel *m*.
architect ['ɑːkɪtekt] *n (lit, fig)* Architekt(in *f*) *m*.
architectural [ˌɑːkɪ'tektʃərəl] *adj* architektonisch.
architecture ['ɑːkɪtektʃə^r] *n* Architektur *f*; *(of building also)* Baustil *m*.
archives ['ɑːkaɪvz] *npl* Archiv *nt*.
archway ['ɑːtʃˌweɪ] *n* Torbogen *m*.
arc lamp ['ɑːkˌlæmp] *n* Bogenlampe *f*.
arctic ['ɑːktɪk] **1** *adj (lit, fig)* arktisch. **A~ Circle** nördlicher Polarkreis; **A~ Ocean** Nordpolarmeer *nt*. **2** *n* **the A~** die Arktis.
ardent ['ɑːdənt] *adj* leidenschaftlich; *supporter also* begeistert; *admirer also* glühend.
ardour, *(US)* **ardor** ['ɑːdə^r] *n (of person)* Leidenschaft *f*; *(of feelings also)* Heftigkeit *f*; *(passion)* Leidenschaftlichkeit *f*.
arduous ['ɑːdjʊəs] *adj* beschwerlich, mühsam; *course, work* anstrengend; *task* mühselig.
are [ɑː^r] *2nd pers sing, 1st, 2nd, 3rd pers pl pres of* **be.**
area ['eərɪə] *n* **(a)** *(measure)* Fläche *f*.
(b) *(region, district)* Gebiet *nt*; *(neighbourhood,*

vicinity) Gegend *f*; *(separated off, piece of ground etc)* Gelände *nt*; *(on plan, diagram etc)* Bereich *m*; *(slum ~, residential ~, commercial ~ also)* Viertel *nt*. **in the** ~ in der Nähe; **dining/sleeping** ~ Eß-/Schlafbereich *m*; **no smoking/reception** ~ Nichtraucherzone *f*/Empfangsbereich *m*; **this ~ is for directors' cars** dieser Platz ist für die Direktorenwagen vorgesehen; **the infected ~s of the lungs** die befallenen Lungenpartien; **in the ~ of the station** in der Bahnhofsgegend; **in the London** ~ im Raum London, im Londoner Raum; ~ **code** *(Telec)* Vorwahl(nummer) *f*; ~ **office** Bezirksbüro *nt*.

(c) *(fig)* Bereich *m*. **his ~ of responsibility** sein Verantwortungsbereich *m*; **the ~s in which we agree** die Bereiche, in denen wir übereinstimmen; ~ **of interest/study** Interessen-/Studiengebiet *nt*; **in the ~ of £100** um die hundert Pfund.

arena [ə'ri:nə] *n (lit, fig)* Arena *f*.

aren't [ɑ:nt] = **are not; am not**; *see* **be.**

Argentina [ˌɑ:dʒən'ti:nə] *n* Argentinien *nt*.

Argentinian [ˌɑ:dʒən'tɪnɪən] **1** *n (person)* Argentinier(in *f*) *m*. **2** *adj* argentinisch.

arguable ['ɑ:gjʊəbl] *adj* **(a)** *(capable of being maintained)* vertretbar. **it is ~ that ...** es läßt sich der Standpunkt vertreten, daß ... **(b)** *(doubtful)* **it is ~ whether ...** es ist (noch) die Frage, ob ...

arguably ['ɑ:gjʊəblɪ] *adj* **this is ~ his best book** dies dürfte (wohl) sein bestes Buch sein.

argue ['ɑ:gju:] **1** *vi* **(a)** *(dispute)* streiten; *(quarrel)* sich streiten. **don't ~ (with me)!** keine Widerrede! **(b)** *(present reasons)* **he ~s that ...** er vertritt den Standpunkt, daß ..., er behauptet, daß ...; **to ~ for** *or* **in favour of sth** für etw sprechen; *(in book)* sich für etw aussprechen; **to ~ against sth** gegen etw sprechen; *(in book)* sich gegen etw aussprechen; **to ~ from a position of ...** von einem Standpunkt *(+gen)* aus argumentieren. **2** *vt (debate) issue* diskutieren, erörtern; *(Jur, present) case* vertreten. **a well ~d case** ein gut dargelegter Fall.

argument ['ɑ:gjʊmənt] *n* **(a)** *(discussion)* Diskussion *f*. **for the sake of** ~ rein theoretisch; **this is open to** ~ darüber läßt sich streiten. **(b)** *(quarrel)* Auseinandersetzung *f*. **to have an** ~ sich streiten. **(c)** *(reason)* Argument *nt*; *(line of reasoning)* Argumentation, Beweisführung *f*; *(statement of proof)* Beweis *m*. **(d)** *(theme: of play, book etc)* Aussage *f*; *(claim)* These *f*.

argumentative [ˌɑ:gjʊ'mentətɪv] *adj* streitsüchtig.

aria ['ɑ:rɪə] *n* Arie *f*.

arid ['ærɪd] *adj* dürr; *(fig) subject* trocken.

Aries ['ɛəri:z] *n (Astrol)* Widder *m*.

arise [ə'raɪz] *pret* **arose** [ə'rəʊz], *ptp* **arisen** [ə'rɪzn] *vi* **(a)** *(occur)* entstehen; *(misunderstanding, problem also)* aufkommen; *(protest, cry)* sich erheben; *(question)* sich stellen. **(b)** *(result)* **to ~ from sth** sich aus etw ergeben. **(c)** *(old, liter: get up)* sich erheben *(liter)*.

aristocracy [ˌærɪs'tɒkrəsɪ] *n* Aristokratie *f*.

aristocrat ['ærɪstəkræt] *n* Aristokrat(in *f*) *m*, Adlige(r) *mf*.

aristocratic [ˌærɪstə'krætɪk] *adj (lit, fig)* aristokratisch, adlig; *(fig also)* vornehm.

arithmetic [ə'rɪθmətɪk] *n* Rechnen *nt*. **could you check my ~?** kannst du das mal nachrechnen?

ark [ɑ:k] *n* Arche *f*. **Noah's** ~ die Arche Noah.

arm[1] [ɑ:m] *n* **(a)** Arm *m*. **under one's** ~ unter dem *or* unterm Arm; **to take sb in one's ~s** jdn in die Arme nehmen; **to put one's ~s around sb** jdn umarmen; ~ **in** ~ Arm in Arm; *(~s linked)* eingehakt, untergehakt; **to keep sb at ~'s length** *(fig)* jdn auf Distanz halten; **with open ~s** mit offenen Armen; **within ~'s reach** in Reichweite. **(b)** *(sleeve)* Arm, Ärmel *m*; *(of river)* (Fluß)arm *m*; *(of armchair)* (Arm)lehne *f*; *(of record player)* Tonarm *m*.

arm[2] **1** *vt person, nation etc* bewaffnen. **to ~ sth with sth** etw mit etw ausrüsten; **to ~ oneself with sth** *(lit, fig)* sich mit etw bewaffnen; *(fig: non-aggressively)* sich mit etw wappnen; **he came ~ed with an excuse** er hatte eine Ausrede parat. **2** *vi* aufrüsten. **to ~ for war** zum Krieg rüsten.

armament ['ɑ:məmənt] *n* **(a)** **~s** *pl (weapons)* Ausrüstung *f*. **(b)** *(preparation)* Aufrüstung *f no pl*.

armchair [ˌɑ:m'tʃɛəʳ] *n* Sessel, Lehnstuhl *m*.

armed [ɑ:md] *adj* bewaffnet.

armed: ~ **forces** *pl* Streitkräfte *pl*; ~ **robbery** *n* bewaffneter Raubüberfall.

armful ['ɑ:mfʊl] *n* Armvoll *m no pl*, Ladung *f (col)*.

armistice ['ɑ:mɪstɪs] *n* Waffenstillstand *m*.

armour, *(US)* **armor** ['ɑ:məʳ] *n* **(a)** Rüstung *f*; *(of animal)* Panzer *m*. **suit of** ~ Rüstung *f*. **(b)** *(no pl: steel plates)* Panzerplatte(n *pl*) *f*. **(c)** *(vehicles)* Panzerfahrzeuge *pl*.

armoured ['ɑ:məd] *adj division* Panzer-. ~ **car** Panzerwagen.

armour: **~-piercing** *adj* panzerbrechend; **~-plated** *adj* gepanzert.

armoury, *(US)* **armory** ['ɑ:mərɪ] *n* Arsenal, Waffenlager *nt*; *(US: factory)* Munitionsfabrik *f*.

arm: **~pit** *n* Achselhöhle *f*; **~rest** *n* Armlehne *f*.

arms [ɑ:mz] *npl* **(a)** *(weapons)* Waffen *pl*. **to be up in ~ (about sth)** *(fig col)* (über *etw acc*) empört sein; ~ **race** Wettrüsten *nt*. **(b)** *(Her)* Wappen *nt*.

army ['ɑ:mɪ] **1** *n* **(a)** Armee *f*, Heer *nt*. **to join the** ~ zum Militär gehen. **(b)** *(fig)* Heer *nt*. **(c)** *(division)* Armee(korps *nt*) *f*. **2** *attr* Militär-; *discipline* militärisch; *life, slang* Soldaten-. ~ **officer** Offizier *m* (in der Armee).

aroma [ə'rəʊmə] *n* Duft *m*, Aroma *nt*.

aromatic [ˌærəʊ'mætɪk] *adj* aromatisch.

arose [ə'rəʊz] *pret of* **arise.**

around [ə'raʊnd] **1** *adv* herum, rum *(col)*. **with gardens all** ~ mit Gärten ringsherum; **I looked all** ~ ich sah mich nach allen Seiten um; **books were lying all** ~ überall lagen Bücher herum; **for miles** ~ meilenweit im Umkreis; **is he ~?** ist er da?; **he's been ~!** der kennt sich aus!; **it's been ~ for ages** das ist schon uralt; **see you ~!** *(col)* bis bald! **2** *prep* **(a)** *(movement, position)* um *(+acc)*; *(in a circle)* um *(+acc)* ... herum. **(b)** *(in, through)* **to wander ~ the city** durch die Stadt spazieren; **to talk ~ a subject** um ein Thema herumreden. **(c)** *(approximately) (with date)* um *(+acc)*; *(with time of day)* gegen *(+acc)*; *(with weight, price)* etwa, um die *(col)*; *see also* **round.**

arousal [ə'raʊzəl] *n (sexual)* Erregung *f*.

arouse [ə'raʊz] *vt* **(a)** *(lit liter)* wecken. **(b)** *(excite)* erregen; *interest, suspicion etc also* (er)wecken.

arrange [ə'reɪndʒ] *vt* **(a)** *(order)* ordnen; *furniture, objects* aufstellen, hinstellen; *flowers* arrangieren; *room* einrichten. **(b)** *(fix)* vereinbaren, ausmachen; *details* regeln; *party* arrangieren, organisieren. **I have ~d for a car to pick you up** ich habe Ihnen einen Wagen bestellt, der Sie abholt; **if you could ~ to be there at five** wenn du es einrichten kannst, um fünf Uhr da zu sein; **that's easily ~d** das läßt sich leicht einrichten *or* arrangieren; **a meeting has been ~d for next month** nächsten Monat ist ein Treffen angesetzt; **good, that's ~d then** gut, das ist abgemacht!; **but you ~d to meet me!** aber du wolltest dich doch mit mir treffen! **(c)** *(Mus)* bearbeiten; *light music* arrangieren.

arrangement [ə'reɪndʒmənt] *n* **(a)** Anordnung *f*; *(of room)* Einrichtung *f*. **a floral** ~ ein Blumenarrangement *nt*. **(b)** *(agreement)* Vereinbarung *f*; *(to meet)* Verabredung *f*; *(esp shifty)* Arrangement *nt*. **a special** ~ eine Sonderregelung; **to have an ~ with sb** eine Regelung mit jdm getroffen haben; **to make an ~ with sb** eine

Vereinbarung *or* Absprache mit jdm treffen; **to come to an ~ with sb** eine Regelung mit jdm treffen; *(settle dispute)* sich mit jdm einigen. **(c)** **~s** *pl (plans)* Pläne *pl*; *(preparations)* Vorbereitungen *pl*. **to make ~s for sth** für etw Vorbereitungen treffen; **to make ~s for sth to be done** veranlassen, daß etw getan wird. **(d)** *(Mus)* Bearbeitung *f*; *(light music)* Arrangement *nt*.

arrant ['ærənt] *adj* **~ nonsense** barer Unsinn.

array [ə'reɪ] *n (collection)* Ansammlung *f*, Aufgebot *nt*. **in battle ~** in Kampfaufstellung.

arrears [ə'rɪəz] *npl* Rückstände *pl*. **to be in ~ with sth** mit etw im Rückstand sein.

arrest [ə'rest] **1** *vt* **(a)** festnehmen, verhaften. **(b)** *(check)* hemmen; *sth unwanted* (Ein)halt gebieten *(+dat)*. **2** *n* Festnahme, Verhaftung *f*. **you are under ~** Sie sind festgenommen/verhaftet; **to put sb under ~** jdn festnehmen/verhaften.

arresting [ə'restɪŋ] *adj (striking)* atemberaubend; *features* markant.

arrival [ə'raɪvəl] *n* **(a)** *(coming)* Ankunft *f no pl*; *(of person also)* Kommen, Eintreffen *nt no pl*; *(of train also, of goods, news)* Eintreffen *nt no pl*. **on ~** bei Ankunft. **(b)** *(person)* **new ~** Neuankömmling *m*; *(at school also)* Neue(r) *mf*.

arrive [ə'raɪv] *vi* ankommen, eintreffen *(geh)*. **to ~ home** nach Hause kommen; **the great day ~d** der große Tag kam.

♦ **arrive at** *vi +prep obj decision* gelangen zu; *price* sich einigen auf *(+acc)*.

arrogance ['ærəgəns] *n* Arroganz, Überheblichkeit *f*.

arrogant ['ærəgənt] *adj* arrogant, überheblich.

arrow ['ærəʊ] *n (weapon, sign)* Pfeil *m*.

arse [ɑːs] *(col!)* Arsch *m (col!)*.

♦ **arse about** *vi (col)* rumblödeln *(col)*.

arsenal ['ɑːsɪnl] *n (Mil) (store)* Arsenal *nt*; *(factory)* Waffen-/Munitionsfabrik *f*.

arsenic ['ɑːsnɪk] *n* Arsen *nt*.

arson ['ɑːsn] *n* Brandstiftung *f*.

arsonist ['ɑːsənɪst] *n* Brandstifter(in *f*) *m*.

art [ɑːt] *n* **(a)** Kunst *f*. **there's an ~ to it** das ist eine Kunst; **~s and crafts** Kunsthandwerk, Kunstgewerbe *nt*. **(b)** **~s** *(Univ)* Geisteswissenschaften *pl*; **Faculty of A~s** Philosophische Fakultät.

art college *n* Kunsthochschule *f*.

artefact *(Brit)*, **artifact** ['ɑːtɪfækt] *n* Artefakt *nt*.

arteriosclerosis [ɑː'tɪərɪəʊsklɪ'rəʊsɪs] *n (Med)* Arteriosklerose, Arterienverkalkung *f*.

artery ['ɑːtərɪ] *n* **(a)** *(Anat)* Arterie *f*, Schlagader *f*. **(b)** *(also* **traffic ~***)* Verkehrsader *f*.

artful ['ɑːtfʊl] *adj person, trick* raffiniert, schlau.

art gallery *n* Kunstgalerie *f*.

arthritic [ɑː'θrɪtɪk] *adj* arthritisch. **she is ~** sie hat Arthritis.

arthritis [ɑː'θraɪtɪs] *n* Arthritis, Gelenkentzündung *f*.

artichoke ['ɑːtɪtʃəʊk] *n* Artischocke *f*.

article ['ɑːtɪkl] *n* **(a)** *(item)* Gegenstand *m*; *(in list)* Posten *m*; *(Comm)* Ware *f*, Artikel *m*. **~s of clothing** Kleidungsstücke *pl*; **toilet ~s** Toilettenartikel *pl*. **(b)** *(in newspaper)* Artikel, Beitrag *m*; *(encyclopedia entry)* Eintrag *m*. **(c)** *(of constitution)* Artikel *m*; *(of treaty, contract)* Paragraph *m*. **~s of association** Gesellschaftsvertrag *m*. **(d)** *(Gram)* Artikel *m*. **(e)** *(of articled clerk)* **to be under ~s** (Rechts)referendar sein.

articulate [ɑː'tɪkjʊlɪt] **1** *adj* **(a)** *sentence, book* leicht verständlich. **to be ~** sich gut *or* klar ausdrücken können; **clear and ~** klar und deutlich. **2** [ɑː'tɪkjʊleɪt] *vt* **(a)** *(pronounce)* artikulieren. **(b)** *(state) reasons, views etc* darlegen. **(c)** **~d lorry** *(Brit) or* **truck** Sattelschlepper *m*.

articulation [ɑːˌtɪkjʊ'leɪʃən] *n (of speech)* Artikulation *f*.

artifact *n* = **artefact.**

artifice ['ɑːtɪfɪs] *n (guile)* List *f no pl*.

artificial [ˌɑːtɪ'fɪʃəl] *adj (lit, fig)* künstlich; *(pej) smile* gekünstelt, unecht. **~ insemination** *n* künstliche Befruchtung; **~ limb** Prothese *f*.

artificiality [ˌɑːtɪfɪʃɪ'ælɪtɪ] *n* **(a)** Künstlichkeit *f*. **(b)** *(insincerity, unnaturalness)* Gekünsteltheit *f*.

artillery [ɑː'tɪlərɪ] *n (weapons, troops)* Artillerie *f*.

artisan ['ɑːtɪzæn] *n* Handwerker *m*.

artist ['ɑːtɪst] *n* Künstler(in *f*) *m*.

artiste [ɑː'tiːst] *n* Künstler(in *f*) *m*; *(circus ~)* Artist(in *f*) *m*.

artistic [ɑː'tɪstɪk] *adj* künstlerisch; *(tasteful) arrangements* kunstvoll; *(appreciative of art)* kunstverständig. **~ temperament** Künstlertemperament *nt*; **she's very ~** sie ist künstlerisch veranlagt.

artistry ['ɑːtɪstrɪ] *n (lit, fig)* Kunst *f*.

artless ['ɑːtlɪs] *adj* unschuldig.

Art Nouveau ['ɑːnuː'vəʊ] *n* Jugendstil *m*.

art school *n* Kunsthochschule *f*.

arty ['ɑːtɪ] *adj (+er) (col)* Künstler-; *type also, tie, clothes* verrückt *(col)*; *person* künstlerisch angehaucht *(col)*; *decoration, style* auf Kunst getrimmt *(col)*; *film, novel* geschmäcklerisch.

arty-farty ['ɑːtɪ'fɑːtɪ] *adj (hum col) see* **arty.**

as [æz, əz] **1** *conj* **(a)** *(when, while)* als; *(two parallel actions)* während, als, indem. **~ he got older** mit zunehmendem Alter; **~ a child** als Kind. **(b)** *(since)* da. **~ it's late** da es spät ist. **(c)** *(although)* **rich/big ~ he is** und wenn er noch so reich/groß ist; **much ~ I admire her, ...** so sehr ich sie auch bewundere, ...; **try ~ he might** so sehr er sich auch bemüht/bemühte. **(d)** *(manner)* wie. **~ I said** wie gesagt; **do ~ you like** machen Sie, was Sie wollen; **leave it ~ it is** lassen Sie es so; **he drinks enough ~ it is** er trinkt sowieso schon genug; **~ it were** sozusagen. **(e)** *(phrases)* **~ if** *or* **though** als ob; **he rose ~ if to go** er erhob sich, als wollte er gehen; **it isn't ~ if he didn't see me** schließlich hat er mich ja gesehen; **~ for him/you** (und) was ihn/dich angeht; **~ from** *or* **of the 5th/now** vom Fünften an/von jetzt an.

2 *adv* **~ ... ~** so ... wie; **not ~ ... ~** nicht so ... wie; **twice ~ old** doppelt so alt; **just ~ nice** genauso nett; **late ~ usual!** wie immer zu spät!; **is it ~ difficult ~ that?** ist das denn so schwierig?; **~ many/much ~ I could** so viele/soviel ich (nur) konnte.

3 *prep (in the capacity of)* als. **to be employed as a ...** als ... angestellt sein.

asap = **as soon as possible.**

asbestos [æz'bestəs] *n* Asbest *m*.

ascend [ə'send] **1** *vi (rise)* aufsteigen. **in ~ing order** in aufsteigender Reihenfolge. **2** *vt stairs* hinaufsteigen; *mountain, throne* besteigen.

ascendancy [ə'sendənsɪ] *n* **to gain the ~ over sb** die Vorherrschaft über jdn gewinnen.

ascendant [ə'sendənt] *n* **to be in the ~** *(Astrol)* im Aszendenten stehen; *(fig)* im Aufstieg begriffen sein.

Ascension [ə'senʃən] *n* **the ~** (Christi) Himmelfahrt *f*; **~ Day** Himmelfahrt(stag *m*) *nt*.

ascent [ə'sent] *n* Besteigung *f*, Aufstieg *m (of* auf *+acc)*.

ascertain [ˌæsə'teɪn] *vt* ermitteln, feststellen.

ascetic [ə'setɪk] **1** *adj* asketisch. **2** *n* Asket *m*.

asceticism [ə'setɪsɪzəm] *n* Askese *f*.

ascribe [ə'skraɪb] *vt* zuschreiben *(sth to sb* jdm etw*)*.

ash[1] [æʃ] *n (also* **~ tree***)* Esche *f*.

ash[2] *n* **(a)** Asche *f*. **~es** Asche *f*; **to reduce sth to ~es** etw total *or* völlig niederbrennen; *(in war)* etw in Schutt und Asche legen. **(b)** *(Cricket)* **the A~es** *Testmatch nt zwischen Australien und England.*

ashamed [ə'ʃeɪmd] *adj* beschämt. **to be** *or* **feel ~ (of sb/sth)** sich schämen (für jdn/für *or* wegen etw); **it's nothing to be ~ of** deswegen braucht man sich nicht zu schämen; **... I'm ~ to say ...,**

muß ich leider zugeben; **you ought to be ~ (of yourself)** du solltest dich (was) schämen!
ashore [ə'ʃɔːʳ] *adv* an Land. **to go ~** an Land gehen.
ash: ~tray *n* Aschenbecher *m*; **A~ Wednesday** *n* Aschermittwoch *m*.
Asia ['eɪʃə] *n* Asien *nt*.
Asian ['eɪʃn] **1** *adj* asiatisch. **2** *n* Asiat(in *f*) *m*.
aside [ə'saɪd] **1** *adv* **(a)** *(with verb)* zur Seite, beiseite. **to turn ~** sich zur Seite drehen, sich abwenden *(esp fig)*. **(b)** *(Theat etc)* beiseite. **(c) ~ from** außer; **this criticism, ~ from being wrong, is ...** diese Kritik ist nicht nur falsch, sondern auch ... **2** *n (Theat)* **to say sth in an ~** etw beiseite sprechen.
asinine ['æsɪnaɪn] *adj* idiotisch.
ask [ɑːsk] **1** *vt* **(a)** *(inquire)* fragen; *question* stellen. **to ~ sb the way/the time/his opinion** jdn nach dem Weg/der Uhrzeit/seiner Meinung fragen; **to ~ if ...** (nach)fragen, ob ...; **he ~ed me where I'd been** er fragte mich, wo ich gewesen sei; **if you ~ me** wenn du mich fragst; **don't ~ me!** *(col)* was weiß ich! *(col)*, da bin ich überfragt!; **I ~ you!** *(col)* ich muß schon sagen! **(b)** *(invite)* einladen; *(in dancing)* auffordern. **to ~ sb to lunch** jdn zum (Mittag)essen einladen; **to ~ sb in/up** jdn hereinbitten/heraufbitten. **(c)** *(request)* bitten *(sb for sth* jdn um etw*)*; *(require, demand)* verlangen *(sth of sb* etw von jdm*)*. **to ~ sb to do sth** jdn darum bitten, etw zu tun; **you don't ~ for much, do you?** *(iro)* sonst noch was? *(iro)*; **it's not ~ing much** das ist nicht (zu)viel verlangt. **(d)** *(Comm) price* verlangen, fordern. **~ing price** Verkaufspreis *m*.
2 *vi* **(a)** *(inquire)* fragen. **to ~ about sb/sth** sich nach jdm/etw erkundigen; **~ away!** frag nur!; **well may you ~** das fragt man sich mit Recht. **(b)** *(request)* bitten *(for sth* um etw*)*. **I'm not ~ing for sympathy** ich will kein Mitleid; **it's yours for the ~ing** du kannst es haben; **that's ~ing for trouble** das kann ja nicht gutgehen; **you ~ed for it** *(col)* du hast es ja so gewollt; **to ~ for Mr X** Herrn X verlangen.
♦ **ask after** *vi +prep obj* sich erkundigen nach. **tell her I was ~ing ~ her** grüß sie schön von mir.
♦ **ask out** *vt sep* einladen.
askance [ə'skɑːns] *adv* **to look ~ at sb** jdn entsetzt ansehen.
askew [ə'skjuː] *adv* schief.
asleep [ə'sliːp] *adj pred* **to be (fast) ~** (fest) schlafen; **to fall ~** einschlafen *(also euph)*.
asparagus [əs'pærəgəs] *n no pl* Spargel *m*.
aspect ['æspekt] *n* **(a)** *(of question etc)* Aspekt *m*, Seite *f*. **(b)** *(of building)* **to have a southerly ~** Südlage haben.
aspersion [əs'pɜːʃən] *n*: **to cast ~s upon sb/sth** abfällige Bemerkungen über jdn/etw machen.
asphalt ['æsfælt] *n* Asphalt *m*.
asphyxia [æs'fɪksɪə] *n* Erstickung *f*.
asphyxiate [æs'fɪksɪeɪt] *vti* ersticken. **to be ~d** ersticken.
aspic ['æspɪk] *n (Cook)* Aspik, Gelee *m or nt*.
aspiration [ˌæspə'reɪʃən] *n* Ziel, Bestreben *nt*.
aspire [ə'spaɪəʳ] *vi* **to ~ to sth** nach etw streben; **to ~ to do sth** danach streben, etw zu tun.
aspirin ['æsprɪn] *n* Kopfschmerztablette *f*.
aspiring [ə'spaɪərɪŋ] *adj* aufstrebend.
ass[1] [æs] *(lit, fig col)* Esel *m*.
ass[2] *n (US col!)* = **arse**.
assail [ə'seɪl] *vt (lit, fig)* angreifen; *(fig: with questions etc)* überschütten, bombardieren.
assailant [ə'seɪlənt] *n* Angreifer(in *f*) *m*.
assassin [ə'sæsɪn] *n* Attentäter(in *f*), Mörder(in *f*) *m*.
assassinate [ə'sæsɪneɪt] *vt* ein Attentat *or* einen Mordanschlag verüben auf *(+acc)*. **JFK was ~d in Dallas** JFK wurde in Dallas ermordet.
assassination [əˌsæsɪ'neɪʃən] *n* (geglücktes) Attentat, (geglückter) Mordanschlag *(of* auf *+acc)*. **~ attempt** Attentat *nt*; **to plan an ~** ein Attentat planen.
assault [ə'sɔːlt] **1** *n* **(a)** *(Mil)* Sturm(angriff) *m (on* auf *+acc)*; *(fig)* Angriff *m (on* gegen*)*. **(b)** *(Jur)* Körperverletzung *f*. **~ and battery** Körperverletzung *f*; **indecent/sexual ~** Notzucht *f*. **2** *vt* angreifen; *(Jur)* tätlich werden gegen; *(sexually)* herfallen über *(+acc)*; *(rape)* sich vergehen an *(+dat)*.
assemble [ə'sembl] **1** *vt* zusammenbauen; *car, machine etc also* montieren. **2** *vi* sich versammeln.
assembly [ə'semblɪ] *n* **(a)** *(gathering)* Versammlung *f*. **(b)** *(Sch)* Morgenandacht *f*; Versammlung *f*. **(c)** *(putting together)* Zusammenbau *m*; *(of machine, cars also)* Montage *f*.
assembly: ~ hall *n (Sch)* Aula *f*; **~ line** *n* Montageband *nt*.
assent [ə'sent] **1** *n* Zustimmung *f*. **2** *vi* **to ~ to sth** einer Sache *(dat)* zustimmen.
assert [ə'sɜːt] *vt* **(a)** *(declare)* behaupten; *one's innocence* beteuern. **(b) to ~ one's authority** seine Autorität geltend machen; **to ~ one's rights** sein Recht behaupten; **to ~ oneself** sich behaupten *or* durchsetzen *(over* gegenüber*)*.
assertion [ə'sɜːʃən] *n* Behauptung *f*.
assertive [ə'sɜːtɪv] *adj* bestimmt.
assess [ə'ses] *vt* **(a)** einschätzen; *proposal, advantages* abwägen. **(b)** *property* schätzen; *person (for tax purposes)* veranlagen *(at* mit*)*; *tax* festsetzen *(at* auf *+acc)*; *damages* schätzen *(at* auf *+acc)*.
assessment [ə'sesmənt] *n see vt* **(a)** Einschätzung *f*; Abwägen *nt*. **what's your ~ of the situation?** wie beurteilen Sie die Lage? **(b)** Schätzung *f*; Veranlagung *f*. **(c)** Festsetzung *f*; Schätzung *f*.
assessor [ə'sesəʳ] *n* Schätzer *m*.
asset ['æset] *n* **(a)** *usu pl* Vermögenswert *m*; *(on balance sheet)* Aktivposten *m*. **~s** Vermögen *nt*; *(on balance sheet)* Aktiva *pl*; **~ stripping** *Aufkauf von finanziell gefährdeten Firmen und anschließender Verkauf ihrer Vermögenswerte.* **(b)** *(fig)* **to be an ~ to** vorteilhaft sein für; **the new man is an ~ to the company** der neue Mann ist ein Gewinn für die Firma.
assiduous [ə'sɪdjuəs] *adj* gewissenhaft.
assign [ə'saɪn] *vt (allot)* zuweisen, zuteilen *(to sb* jdm*)*; *(Jur)* übertragen *(to sb* jdm*)*; *room* bestimmen *(to* für*)*; *meaning* zuordnen *(to dat)*; *(attribute) novel, play, music* zuschreiben *(to dat)*. **she was ~ed to this school** sie wurde an diese Schule berufen.
assignation [ˌæsɪg'neɪʃən] *n (lovers')* Rendezvous *nt*.
assignment [ə'saɪnmənt] *n* **(a)** *(task)* Aufgabe *f*. **(b)** *(to post etc)* Berufung *f*. **(c)** *(Jur)* Übertragung *f*.
assimilate [ə'sɪmɪleɪt] *vt food, knowledge* aufnehmen; *(fig: into society etc also)* integrieren.
assimilation [əˌsɪmɪ'leɪʃən] *n see vt* Aufnahme *f*; Integration *f*. **his powers of ~** seine geistige Aufnahmefähigkeit.
assist [ə'sɪst] **1** *vt* helfen *(+dat)*; *(act as an assistant to)* assistieren *(+dat)*. **to ~ sb in doing** *or* **to do sth** jdm helfen, etw zu tun. **2** *vi* helfen. **to ~ with sth** bei etw helfen.
assistance [ə'sɪstəns] *n* Hilfe *f*. **to come to sb's ~** jdm zu Hilfe kommen; **can I be of any ~?** kann ich irgendwie behilflich sein?
assistant [ə'sɪstənt] **1** *n* Assistent(in *f*) *m*; *(Brit: shop ~)* Verkäufer(in *f*) *m*. **2** *adj attr manager etc* stellvertretend.
associate [ə'səʊʃɪɪt] **1** *n (colleague)* Kollege *m*, Kollegin *f*; *(Comm)* Partner *m*; *(accomplice)* Komplize *m*, Komplizin *f*; *(of a society)* außerordentliches Mitglied. **~ professor** *n (US)* außerordentlicher Professor. **2** [ə'səʊʃɪeɪt] *vt* assoziieren *(also Psych)*. **to ~ oneself with sb/sth** sich jdm/

einer Sache anschließen; **to be ~d with sb/sth** mit jdm/einer Sache in Verbindung gebracht *or* assoziiert werden; **I don't ~ ... with sport** bei ... denke ich nicht an Sport. **3** [ə'səʊʃɪeɪt] *vi* **to ~ with** verkehren mit.

association [ə,səʊsɪ'eɪʃən] *n* **(a)** *no pl (with people)* Verkehr, Umgang *m*; *(co-operation)* Zusammenarbeit *f*. **he has had a long ~ with the party** er hat seit langem Verbindung zur Partei. **(b)** *(organization)* Verband *m*. **(c)** *(mental)* Assoziation *f (with* an *+acc) (also Psych)*. **~ of ideas** Gedankenassoziation *f*.

assorted [ə'sɔːtɪd] *adj (mixed)* gemischt.

assortment [ə'sɔːtmənt] *n* Mischung *f*; *(of goods)* Auswahl *f (of* an *+dat)*, Sortiment *nt (of* von*)*.

assuage [ə'sweɪdʒ] *vt hunger etc* stillen, befriedigen; *anger etc* beschwichtigen; *grief* lindern.

assume [ə'sjuːm] *vt* **(a)** annehmen; *(presuppose)* voraussetzen. **let us ~ that you are right** nehmen wir an *or* gehen wir davon aus, Sie hätten recht; **assuming (that) ...** angenommen(, daß) ... **(b)** *power, control* übernehmen; *(forcefully)* ergreifen. **(c)** *(take on) title, guise, shape* annehmen. **under an ~d name** unter anderem Namen.

assumption [ə'sʌmpʃən] *n* **(a)** Annahme *f*; *(presupposition)* Voraussetzung *f*. **to go on the ~ that ...** von der Voraussetzung ausgehen, daß ...; **that's just an ~** das ist nur eine Vermutung. **(b)** *(of power, role etc)* Übernahme *f*; *(forcefully)* Ergreifen *nt*. **(c)** *(of guise, false name etc)* Annahme *f*. **(d)** *(Eccl)* **the A~** Mariä Himmelfahrt *f*.

assurance [ə'ʃʊərəns] *n* **(a)** Versicherung *f*; *(promise also)* Zusicherung *f*. **he gave me his ~ that it would be done** er versicherte mir, daß es erledigt würde; **you have my ~ that ...** Sie können versichert sein, daß ... **(b)** *(self-confidence)* Sicherheit *f*. **(c)** *(confidence)* Zuversicht *f*. **(d)** *(esp Brit: life ~)* (Lebens)versicherung *f*.

assure [ə'ʃʊəʳ] *vt* **(a)** versichern *(+dat)*; *(promise)* zusichern *(+dat)*. **to ~ sb of sth** *(of love, willingness etc)* jdn einer Sache *(gen)* versichern; *(of service, support, help)* jdm etw zusichern; **... I ~ you ...** das versichere ich Ihnen. **(b)** *(make certain of) success, happiness, future* sichern. **(c)** *(esp Brit: insure) life* versichern.

assured [ə'ʃʊəd] *adj* sicher; *income, future also* gesichert. **to rest ~ that ...** sicher sein, daß ...

asterisk ['æstərɪsk] *n* Sternchen *nt*.

astern [ə'stɜːn] *(Naut) adv* achtern; *(towards the stern)* nach achtern; *(backwards)* achteraus.

asteroid ['æstərɔɪd] *n* Asteroid *m*.

asthma ['æsmə] *n* Asthma *nt*.

asthmatic [æs'mætɪk] *n* Asthmatiker(in *f*) *m*.

astigmatism [æs'tɪgmətɪzəm] *n* Astigmatismus *m*.

astonish [ə'stɒnɪʃ] *vt* erstaunen, überraschen. **I was ~ed to learn that ...** ich war sehr erstaunt, als ich hörte, daß ...

astonishing [ə'stɒnɪʃɪŋ] *adj* erstaunlich.

astonishingly [ə'stɒnɪʃɪŋlɪ] *adv* erstaunlich. **~ (enough)** erstaunlicherweise.

astonishment [ə'stɒnɪʃmənt] *n* Erstaunen *nt (at* über *+acc)*. **look of ~** erstaunter Blick; **she looked at me in ~** sie sah mich erstaunt an; **to my ~** zu meinem Erstaunen.

astound [ə'staʊnd] *vt* in Erstaunen versetzen. **to be ~ed (at)** höchst erstaunt sein *(über +acc)*.

astounding [ə'staʊndɪŋ] *adj* erstaunlich.

astray [ə'streɪ] *adj* verloren. **to go ~** *(person) (lit)* vom Weg abkommen; *(fig: morally)* auf Abwege geraten; *(letter, object)* verlorengehen; **to lead sb ~** *(fig)* jdn vom rechten Weg abbringen; *(mislead)* jdn irreführen.

astride [ə'straɪd] *prep* rittlings auf.

astrologer [əs'trɒlədʒəʳ] *n* Astrologe *m*, Astrologin *f*.

astrology [əs'trɒlədʒɪ] *n* Astrologie *f*.

astronaut ['æstrənɔːt] *n* Astronaut(in *f*) *m*.

astronomer [əs'trɒnəməʳ] *n* Astronom(in *f*) *m*.

astronomical [,æstrə'nɒmɪkəl] *adj (fig also* **astronomic***)* astronomisch.

astronomy [əs'trɒnəmɪ] *n* Astronomie *f*.

astrophysics [,æstrəʊ'fɪzɪks] *n sing* Astrophysik *f*.

astute [ə'stjuːt] *adj* schlau; *remark also* scharfsinnig; *mind* scharf.

astuteness [əs'tjuːtnɪs] *n see adj* Schlauheit *f*; Scharfsinnigkeit *f*; Schärfe *f*.

asylum [ə'saɪləm] *n* **(a) to ask for (political) ~** um (politisches) Asyl bitten. **(b)** *(lunatic ~)* (Irren)anstalt *f*.

asymmetric(al) [,eɪsɪ'metrɪk(əl)] *adj* asymmetrisch.

at [æt] *prep* **(a)** *(position)* an *(+dat)*, bei *(+dat)*; *(with place)* in *(+dat)*. **~ the window/corner** am *or* beim Fenster/an der Ecke; **~ university/school/the hotel/the zoo** an *or* auf der Universität/in der Schule/im Hotel/im Zoo; **~ my brother's** bei meinem Bruder; **~ a party** auf *or* bei einer Party; **~ the station** am Bahnhof.

(b) *(direction)* **to aim/point** *etc* **~ sb/sth** auf jdn/etw zielen/zeigen *etc*; **to look/growl** *etc* **~ sb** jdn ansehen/anknurren *etc*.

(c) *(time, frequency, order)* **~ ten o'clock** um zehn Uhr; **~ night** bei Nacht; **~ Christmas/Easter** zu Weihnachten/Ostern; **~ your age/16** in deinem Alter/mit 16; **three ~ a time** drei auf einmal; **~ the start/end of sth** am Anfang/am Ende einer Sache.

(d) *(activity)* **~ play/work** beim Spiel/bei der Arbeit; **good/bad/an expert ~ sth** gut/schlecht/ein Experte in etw *(dat)*; **while we are ~ it** *(col)* wenn wir schon mal dabei sind.

(e) *(as a result of, upon)* auf *(+acc)* ... (hin). **~ his request** auf seine Bitte (hin); **~ her death** bei ihrem Tod; **~ that/this he left the room** daraufhin verließ er das Zimmer.

(f) *(cause: with) delighted etc* über *(+acc)*.

(g) *(rate, value, degree)* **~ 50 km/h** mit 50 km/h; **~ 50p a pound** für 50 Pence pro Pfund; **~ 5% interest** zu 5% Zinsen; **when the temperature is ~ 90** wenn die Temperatur auf 90° ist.

ate [et, eit] *pret of* **eat.**

atheism ['eɪθɪɪzəm] *n* Atheismus *m*.

atheist ['eɪθɪɪst] *n* Atheist(in *f*) *m*.

Athens ['æθɪnz] *n* Athen *nt*.

athlete ['æθliːt] *n* Athlet(in *f*) *m*; *(in track and field events)* Leichtathlet(in *f*) *m*. **he is a natural ~** er ist der geborene Sportler; **~'s foot** Fußpilz *m*.

athletic [æθ'letɪk] *adj* sportlich; *build* athletisch.

athletics [æθ'letɪks] *n sing or pl* Leichtathletik *f*. **~ meeting** Leichtathletikwettkampf *m*.

Atlantic [ət'læntɪk] *n (also* **~ Ocean***)* Atlantik *m*, Atlantischer Ozean.

atlas ['ætləs] *n* Atlas *m*.

atmosphere ['ætməsfɪəʳ] *n (lit, fig)* Atmosphäre *f*; *(fig: of novel also)* Stimmung *f*.

atmospheric [,ætməs'ferɪk] *adj* atmosphärisch; *(full of atmosphere) description* stimmungsvoll.

atmospherics [,ætməs'ferɪks] *npl (Rad)* atmosphärische Störungen *pl*.

atom ['ætəm] *n* Atom *nt*. **~ bomb** Atombombe *f*.

atomic [ə'tɒmɪk] *adj* atomar.

atomic *in cpds* Atom-; **~ age** *n* Atomzeitalter *nt*; **~ bomb** *n* Atombombe *f*.

atomizer ['ætəmaɪzəʳ] *n* Zerstäuber *m*.

atone [ə'təʊn] *vi* **to ~ for sth** für etw sühnen *or* büßen.

atonement [ə'təʊnmənt] *n* Sühne, Buße *f*. **to make ~ for sth** für etw Sühne *or* Buße tun; **the A~** *(Eccl)* das Sühneopfer (Christi).

atrocious [ə'trəʊʃəs] *adj* grauenhaft.

atrocity [ə'trɒsɪtɪ] *n* Grausamkeit *f*; *(act also)* Greueltat *f*.

atrophy ['ætrəfɪ] **1** *n* Atrophie *f*; *(Med)* Schwund *m*. **2** *vi* verkümmern, schwinden.

attach [ə'tætʃ] *vt* **(a)** *(join)* festmachen, befestigen (*to* an +*dat*). **please find ~ed ...** beiliegend finden Sie ...; **is he/she ~ed?** ist er/sie schon vergeben? (*col*) **(b) to be ~ed to sb/sth** (*be fond of*) an jdm/etw hängen. **(c)** (*attribute*) *value, importance* beimessen, zuschreiben (*to dat*).

attaché [ə'tæʃeɪ] *n* Attaché *m*. **~ case** Aktenkoffer *m*.

attachment [ə'tætʃmənt] *n* **(a)** (*accessory*) Zusatzteil, Zubehörteil *nt*. **(b)** (*fig: affection*) Zuneigung *f* (*to* zu). **(c) he's (working) here on ~** er ist (vorübergehend) hierher versetzt worden.

attack [ə'tæk] **1** *n* **(a)** (*Mil, Sport, fig*) Angriff *m* (*on* auf +*acc*). **to be under ~** angegriffen werden; (*fig also*) unter Beschuß stehen; **to leave oneself open to ~** Angriffsflächen bieten. **(b)** (*Med etc*) Anfall *m*. **2** *vt* **(a)** (*Mil, Sport, fig*) angreifen; (*from ambush, in robbery etc*) überfallen. **(b)** (*tackle*) *task, problem* in Angriff nehmen.

attacker [ə'tækə[r]] *n* Angreifer *m*.

attain [ə'teɪn] *vt rank, age* erreichen; *knowledge* erlangen; *happiness, power* gelangen zu.

attainment [ə'teɪnmənt] *n* **(a)** (*act*) Erreichen *nt*; (*of knowledge, happiness, prosperity, power*) Erlangen *nt*. **(b)** (*usu pl: accomplishment*) Fertigkeit *f*.

attempt [ə'tempt] **1** *vt* versuchen; *task* sich versuchen an (+*dat*). **~ed murder** Mordversuch *m*. **2** *n* Versuch *m*. **an ~ on the record** ein Versuch, den Rekord zu brechen; **to make an ~ on sb's life** einen Anschlag auf jdn *or* jds Leben verüben; **he made no ~ to help us** er unternahm keinen Versuch, uns zu helfen; **at the first ~** auf Anhieb, beim ersten Versuch.

attend [ə'tend] **1** *vt* **(a)** *classes, church, meeting* besuchen; *wedding, funeral* anwesend sein bei (+*dat*). **(b)** (*wait on*) *queen etc* bedienen. **2** *vi* **(a)** (*be present*) anwesend sein. **are you going to ~?** gehen Sie hin? **(b)** (*pay attention*) aufpassen.

♦ **attend to** *vi* +*prep obj* (*see to*) sich kümmern um; (*pay attention to*) *work etc* Aufmerksamkeit schenken (+*dat*); *customers* bedienen. **are you being ~ed ~?** werden Sie schon bedient?; **that's being ~ed ~** das wird (bereits) erledigt.

attendance [ə'tendəns] *n* **(a)** Anwesenheit *f* (*at* bei). **regular ~ at school** regelmäßiger Schulbesuch. **(b)** (*number present*) Teilnehmerzahl *f*.

attendant [ə'tendənt] *n* (*in art galleries, museums*) Aufseher(in *f*), Wärter(in *f*) *m*; (*in public toilets*) Toilettenwart *m*, Toilettenfrau *f*; (*in swimming baths*) Bademeister(in *f*) *m*.

attention [ə'tenʃən] *n* **(a)** *no pl* Aufmerksamkeit *f*. **to call** *or* **draw sb's ~ to sth** jdn auf etw (*acc*) aufmerksam machen; **to attract sb's ~** jdm auffallen; (*by waving etc*) jdn auf sich (*acc*) aufmerksam machen; **to turn one's ~ to sb/sth** jdm/einer Sache seine Aufmerksamkeit zuwenden; **to pay ~/no ~ to sb/sth** jdn/etw beachten/nicht beachten; **to pay ~ to the teacher** dem Lehrer zuhören; **to hold sb's ~** jdn fesseln; **your ~, please** ich bitte um Aufmerksamkeit; (*over tannoy*) Achtung, Achtung!; **it has come to my ~ that ...** ich habe feststellen müssen, daß ...; **it has been brought to my ~ that ...** es ist mir zu Ohren gekommen, daß ...; **the bodywork needs a little ~** an der Karosserie muß etwas getan werden. **(b) ~s** *pl* (*kindnesses*) Aufmerksamkeiten *pl*. **(c)** (*Mil*) **to stand at ~** stillstehen; **~!** stillgestanden! **(d)** (*Comm*) **for the ~ of ...** zu Händen von ...

attentive [ə'tentɪv] *adj* aufmerksam.

attenuating [ə'tenjʊeɪtɪŋ] *adj*: **~ circumstances** mildernde Umstände.

attest [ə'test] *vt* (*certify*) bestätigen, bescheinigen; *signature also* beglaubigen.

♦ **attest to** *vi* +*prep obj* bezeugen.

attic [ætɪk] *n* Dachboden, Speicher *m*; (*lived-in*) Mansarde *f*. **in the ~** auf dem (Dach)boden.

attire [ə'taɪə[r]] *n no pl* Kleidung *f*. **ceremonial ~** Festtracht *f*; (*of priest*) Ornat *nt*.

attitude [ætɪtju:d] *n* (*way of thinking*) Einstellung *f* (*to, towards* zu); (*way of acting, posture, manner*) Haltung *f* (*to, towards* gegenüber). **well, if that's your ~** ja, wenn du *so* denkst.

attorney [ə'tɜ:nɪ] *n* (*US: lawyer*) (Rechts)anwalt *m*, (Rechts)anwältin *f*. **~ general** (*US*) (*of state government*) ≃ Generalstaatsanwalt *m*; (*of federal government*) ≃ Generalbundesanwalt *m*; (*Brit*) ≃ Justizminister *m*.

attract [ə'trækt] *vt* (*also Phys*) anziehen; *sb's attention* auf sich (*acc*) ziehen *or* lenken; (*idea, music, place etc*) ansprechen. **she feels ~ed to him/to the idea** sie fühlt sich zu ihm hingezogen/die Idee reizt sie.

attraction [ə'trækʃən] *n* **(a)** (*Phys, fig*) Anziehungskraft *f*. **to lose its ~** seinen Reiz verlieren; **to have an ~ for sb** eine Anziehungskraft *or* einen Reiz auf jdn ausüben; **the ~ of the city** der Reiz der Großstadt. **(b)** (*attractive thing*) Attraktion *f*.

attractive [ə'træktɪv] *adj* attraktiv, reizvoll.

attractiveness [ə'træktɪvnɪs] *n* Attraktivität *f*; (*of house, furnishing, view etc*) Reiz *m*.

attributable [ə'trɪbjʊtəbl] *adj* **to be ~ to sb/sth** jdm/einer Sache zuzuschreiben sein.

attribute [ə'trɪbju:t] **1** *vt* **to ~ sth to sb** *play, remark etc* jdm etw zuschreiben; *intelligence, feelings etc* jdm etw zusprechen; **to ~ sth to sth** *success, accident etc* etw auf etw (*acc*) zurückführen. **2** ['ætrɪbju:t] *n* (*quality*) Merkmal *nt*, Eigenschaft *f*.

attributive [ə'trɪbjʊtɪv] (*Gram*) *adj* attributiv.

attrition [ə'trɪʃən] *n* Zermürbung *f*. **war of ~** (*Mil*) Zermürbungskrieg *m*.

aubergine ['əʊbəʒi:n] *n* (*Brit*) Aubergine *f*.

auburn ['ɔ:bən] *adj hair* rotbraun, rostrot.

auction ['ɔ:kʃən] **1** n Auktion, Versteigerung *f*. **2** *vt* (*also* **~ off**) versteigern.

auctioneer [,ɔ:kʃə'nɪə[r]] *n* Auktionator *m*.

audacious [ɔ:'deɪʃəs] *adj* **(a)** (*impudent*) dreist, unverfroren. **(b)** (*bold*) kühn.

audacity [ɔ:'dæsɪtɪ] *n* **(a)** (*impudence*) **to have the ~ to do sth** die Dreistigkeit *or* Unverfrorenheit besitzen, etw zu tun. **(b)** (*boldness*) Kühnheit *f*.

audible ['ɔ:dɪbl] *adj* hörbar, (deutlich) vernehmbar. **she was hardly ~** man konnte sie kaum hören.

audience ['ɔ:dɪəns] *n* **(a)** Publikum *nt no pl*; (*Theat, TV also*) Zuschauer *pl*; (*of speaker also*) Zuhörer *pl*; (*Rad, Mus also*) Zuhörerschaft *f*. **(b)** (*formal interview*) Audienz *f*.

audio ['ɔ:dɪəʊ] *adj attr* Audio-.

audio: ~ typist *n* Phonotypistin *f*; **~-visual** *adj* audiovisuell.

audit ['ɔ:dɪt] **1** *n* Buchprüfung *f*. **2** *vt* prüfen.

audition [ɔ:'dɪʃən] **1** *n* Vorsprechprobe *f*; (*Mus*) Probespiel *nt*; (*of singer*) Vorsingen *nt*. **2** *vt* vorsprechen/vorspielen/vorsingen lassen.

auditor ['ɔ:dɪtə[r]] *n* Wirtschaftsprüfer *m*.

auditorium [,ɔ:dɪ'tɔ:rɪəm] *n* Auditorium *nt*; (*in theatre, cinema*) Zuschauerraum *m*.

au fait [,əʊ'feɪ] *adj* vertraut.

augment [ɔ:g'ment] **1** *vt* vermehren; *income also* vergrößern. **2** *vi* zunehmen.

augur ['ɔ:gə[r]] *vi* **to ~ well/ill** etwas Gutes/nichts Gutes verheißen.

august [ɔ:'gʌst] *adj* illuster; *occasion* erhaben.

August ['ɔ:gəst] *n* August *m*; *see* **September.**

aunt [ɑ:nt] *n* Tante *f*.

auntie, aunty ['ɑ:ntɪ] *n* (*col*) Tante *f*.

au pair ['əʊ'pɛə] *n, pl* **- -s** (*also* **~ girl**) Au-pair(-Mädchen) *nt*.

aura ['ɔ:rə] *n* Aura *f* (*geh*), Ausstrahlung *f*. **she has an ~ of ...** sie strahlt ... aus.

auspices ['ɔ:spɪsɪz] *npl* **under the ~ of** unter der Schirmherrschaft (+*gen*).

auspicious [ɔ:s'pɪʃəs] *adj* günstig; *start* vielversprechend. **an ~ occasion** ein feierlicher Anlaß.

Aussie ['ɒzɪ] *(col)* Australier(in *f*) *m*.

austere [ɒs'tɪəʳ] *adj* streng; *way of life also* asketisch; *room* schmucklos.

austerity [ɒs'terɪtɪ] *n* **(a)** *(severity)* Strenge *f*; *(simplicity)* strenge Einfachheit, Schmucklosigkeit *f*. **(b)** *(hardship)* **after the ~ of the war years** nach den Entbehrungen der Kriegsjahre; **a life of ~** ein Leben der Entsagung; **~ measures** Sparmaßnahmen *pl*.

Australasia [ˌɔːstrə'leɪsjə] *n* Australien und Ozeanien *nt*.

Australia [ɒs'treɪlɪə] *n* Australien *nt*.

Australian [ɒs'treɪlɪən] **1** *n* Australier(in *f*) *m*. **2** *adj* australisch.

Austria ['ɒstrɪə] *n* Österreich *nt*.

Austrian ['ɒstrɪən] **1** *n* Österreicher(in *f*) *m*; *(dialect)* Österreichisch *nt*. **2** *adj* österreichisch.

authentic [ɔː'θentɪk] *adj* echt; *document etc* authentisch; *claim* berechtigt.

authenticate [ɔː'θentɪkeɪt] *vt* bestätigen; *signature, document* beglaubigen; *manuscript, work of art* für echt befinden.

authenticity [ˌɔːθen'tɪsɪtɪ] *n* Echtheit, Authentizität *(geh) f*; *(of claim to title)* Berechtigung *f*.

author ['ɔːθəʳ] *n* Autor(in *f*), Schriftsteller(in *f*) *m*; *(of report, pamphlet)* Verfasser(in *f*) *m*; *(fig)* Urheber(in *f*) *m*.

authoritarian [ˌɔːθɒrɪ'teərɪən] *adj* autoritär.

authoritative [ɔː'θɒrɪtətɪv] *adj* **(a)** *(commanding)* bestimmt, entschieden. **(b)** *(definitive)* maßgeblich, maßgebend.

authority [ɔː'θɒrɪtɪ] *n* **(a)** *(power)* Autorität *f*; *(right, entitlement)* Befugnis *f*; *(specifically delegated power)* Vollmacht *f*; *(permission)* Erlaubnis *f*. **people who are in ~** Menschen, die Autorität haben; **the person in ~** der Zuständige *or* Verantwortliche; **to be in** *or* **have ~ over sb** jdm übergeordnet sein; **on one's own ~** auf eigene Verantwortung; **by what ~ do you claim the right to ...?** mit welcher Berechtigung verlangen Sie, daß ...?; **to have the ~ to do sth** berechtigt *or* befugt sein, etw zu tun; **to do sth on sb's ~** etw in jds Auftrag *(dat)* tun; **to have** *or* **carry (great) ~** viel gelten *(with* bei*)*; **to speak/write with ~** mit Sachkenntnis sprechen/schreiben.

(b) *(also pl: ruling body)* Behörde *f*; *(body of people)* Verwaltung *f*; **the authorities** die Behörden *pl*; **the university authorities** die Universitätsverwaltung; **the local ~** die Gemeinde-/Stadtverwaltung.

(c) *(expert)* Autorität *f*, Fachmann *m (on* auf dem Gebiet *+gen)*; *(definitive book etc)* (anerkannte) Autorität; *(source)* Quelle *f*. **to have sth on good ~** etw aus zuverlässiger Quelle wissen; **this book is the ~ on spelling** dieses Buch ist maßgebend für die Rechtschreibung.

authorization [ˌɔːθəraɪ'zeɪʃən] *n* Genehmigung *f*; *(delegated authority)* Vollmacht *f*; *(right)* Recht *nt*.

authorize ['ɔːθəraɪz] *vt* **(a)** *(empower)* berechtigen, ermächtigen. **to be ~d to do sth** *(have right)* das Recht haben, etw zu tun; **he was specially ~d to ...** er hatte eine Sondervollmacht, zu ... **(b)** *(permit)* genehmigen; *money, claim etc* bewilligen; *translation, biography etc* autorisieren. **the A~d Version** *englische Bibelfassung von 1611*.

autistic [ɔː'tɪstɪk] *adj* autistisch.

auto ['ɔːtəʊ] *n (US)* Auto *nt*, Pkw *m*.

auto- ['ɔːtəʊ] *pref* auto-, Auto-.

autobiography [ˌɔːtəʊbaɪ'ɒgrəfɪ] *n* Autobiographie *f*.

autocratic [ˌɔːtəʊ'krætɪk] *adj* autokratisch.

autocue ['ɔːtəʊkjuː] *n (Brit TV)* Neger *m*.

autograph ['ɔːtəgrɒːf] **1** *n* Autogramm *nt*. **2** *vt* signieren.

automat ['ɔːtəmæt] *n (US)* Automatenrestaurant *nt*.

automate ['ɔːtəmeɪt] *vt* automatisieren.

automatic [ˌɔːtə'mætɪk] **1** *adj (lit, fig)* automatisch; **~ choke** Startautomatik *f*; **the ~ model** das Modell mit Automatik; **~ pilot** Autopilot *m*. **2** *n (car)* Automatikwagen *m*.

automatically [ˌɔːtə'mætɪkəlɪ] *adv* automatisch.

automation [ˌɔːtə'meɪʃən] *n* Automatisierung *f*.

automaton [ɔː'tɒmətən] *n, pl* **-s** *or* **automata** [-etə] *(robot)* Roboter *m*; *(fig also)* Automat *m*.

automobile ['ɔːtəməbiːl] *n* Auto(mobil), Kraftfahrzeug *nt*.

autonomous [ɔː'tɒnəməs] *adj* autonom.

autonomy [ɔː'tɒnəmɪ] *n* Autonomie *f*.

autopilot [ˌɔːtəʊ'paɪlət] *n* Autopilot *m*.

autopsy ['ɔːtɒpsɪ] *n* Autopsie, Obduktion *f*.

autumn ['ɔːtəm] *(esp Brit)* **1** *n (lit, fig)* Herbst *m*. **in (the) ~** im Herbst. **2** *adj attr* Herbst-, herbstlich.

autumnal [ɔː'tʌmnəl] *adj* herbstlich, Herbst-.

auxiliary [ɔːg'zɪlɪərɪ] **1** *adj* Hilfs-; *(emergency also)* Not-; *(additional) engine, generator etc* Zusatz-. **~ nurse** Schwesternhelferin *f*. **2** *n* **(a)** *(Mil)* **auxiliaries** *pl* Hilfstruppe(n *pl*) *f*. **(b)** *(general: assistant)* Hilfskraft *f*, Helfer(in *f*) *m*. **(c)** *(~ verb)* Hilfsverb *nt*.

avail [ə'veɪl] **1** *vr* **to ~ oneself of sth** von etw Gebrauch machen. **2** *n* **of no ~** erfolglos, ohne Erfolg; **to no ~** vergebens, vergeblich.

availability [əˌveɪlə'bɪlɪtɪ] *n see adj* Erhältlichkeit *f*; Lieferbarkeit *f*; Verfügbarkeit *f*; *(presence: of secretarial staff, mineral ore etc)* Vorhandensein *nt*. **the market price is determined by ~** der Marktpreis richtet sich nach dem vorhandenen Angebot; **the ~ of jobs** *etc* das Angebot an Stellen *etc*.

available [ə'veɪləbl] *adj object* erhältlich; *(Comm) (from supplier also)* lieferbar; *(free) time, seats etc* frei; *(at one's disposal) means, resources etc* verfügbar. **to be ~** *(at one's disposal)* zur Verfügung stehen; *(can be reached)* erreichbar sein; *(for discussion)* zu sprechen sein; **to make sth ~ to sb** jdm etw zur Verfügung stellen; *(accessible) knowledge etc* jdm etw zugänglich machen; **the best dictionary ~, the best ~ dictionary** das beste Wörterbuch, das es gibt; **to try every ~ means (to achieve sth)** nichts unversucht lassen(, um etw zu erreichen).

avalanche ['ævəlɑːnʃ] *n (lit, fig)* Lawine *f*.

avant-garde ['ævɑ̃ŋ'gɑːd] **1** *n* Avantgarde *f*. **2** *adj* avantgardistisch.

avarice ['ævərɪs] *n* Habgier *f*.

avaricious [ˌævə'rɪʃəs] *adj* habgierig.

avenge [ə'vendʒ] *vt* rächen. **to ~ oneself on sb (for sth)** sich an jdm (für etw) rächen.

avenue ['ævənjuː] *n* **(a)** *(tree-lined)* Allee *f*; *(broad street)* Boulevard *m*. **(b)** *(fig)* **~s of approach** Verfahrensweisen; **to explore every ~** alle sich bietenden Wege prüfen.

average ['ævərɪdʒ] **1** *n* (Durch)schnitt *m*. **to do an ~ of 50 miles a day** durchschnittlich *or* im (Durch)schnitt 50 Meilen pro Tag fahren; **on ~** durchschnittlich, im (Durch)schnitt; *(normally)* normalerweise; **above/below ~** überdurchschnittlich, unter dem Durchschnitt. **2** *adj* durchschnittlich; *(ordinary)* Durchschnitts-; *(not good or bad)* mittelmäßig. **the ~ man, Mr A~** der Durchschnittsbürger; **he's a man of ~ height** er ist von mittlerer Größe. **3** *vt* **we ~d 80 km/h** wir sind durchschnittlich 80 km/h gefahren; **the factory ~s 500 cars a week** die Fabrik produziert im (Durch)schnitt 500 Autos pro Woche.

♦ **average out** *vi* durchschnittlich ausmachen *(at acc)*; *(balance out)* sich ausgleichen. **how does it ~ ~ on a weekly basis?** wieviel ist das durchschnittlich pro Woche?

averse [ə'vɜːs] *adj pred* **I am not ~ to a glass of wine** einem Glas Wein bin ich nicht abgeneigt.

aversion [ə'vɜːʃən] *n* Abneigung, Aversion *f (to*

gegen). ~ **therapy** Schocktherapie *f*.

avert [ə'vɜːt] *vt* **(a)** *eyes* abwenden. **(b)** *(prevent)* verhindern; *suspicion* ablenken.

aviary ['eɪvɪərɪ] *n* Vogelhaus *nt*.

aviation [ˌeɪvɪ'eɪʃən] *n* Luftfahrt *f*. **the art of** ~ die Kunst des Fliegens.

avid ['ævɪd] *adj* **(a)** *(desirous)* gierig *(for* nach*)*. **(b)** *(keen)* begeistert, passioniert. **I am an** ~ **reader** ich lese leidenschaftlich gern.

avionics [ˌeɪvɪ'ɒnɪks] *n sing* Avionik *f*.

avocado [ˌævə'kɑːdəʊ] *n, pl* **-s** Avocado *f*.

avoid [ə'vɔɪd] *vt* vermeiden; *damage, accident also* verhüten; *person, danger* meiden, aus dem Weg gehen *(+dat)*; *obstacle* ausweichen *(+dat)*; *difficulty, duty, truth* umgehen. **in order to** ~ **being seen** um nicht gesehen zu werden; **I'm not going if I can possibly** ~ **it** wenn es sich irgendwie vermeiden läßt, gehe ich nicht hin.

avoidable [ə'vɔɪdəbl] *adj* vermeidbar. **if it's (at all)** ~ wenn es sich (irgend) vermeiden läßt.

avoidance [ə'vɔɪdəns] *n* Vermeidung *f*.

avowed [ə'vaʊd] *adj* erklärt.

avuncular [ə'vʌŋkjʊlə[r]] *adj* onkelhaft.

await [ə'weɪt] *vt* erwarten; *future events, decision etc* entgegensehen *(+dat)*. **the long** ~**ed day** der langersehnte Tag.

awake [ə'weɪk] *pret* **awoke,** *ptp* **awoken** *or* **awaked** [ə'weɪkt] **1** *vi (lit, fig)* erwachen. **to** ~ **to sth** *(fig) (realize)* sich *(dat)* einer Sache *(gen)* bewußt werden. **2** *vt* wecken; *(fig) suspicion, interest etc also* erwecken. **3** *adj pred (lit, fig)* wach. **to be/stay** ~ wach sein/bleiben; **to keep sb** ~ jdn wachhalten; **wide** ~ *(lit, fig)* hellwach; **to be** ~ **to sth** *(fig)* sich *(dat)* einer Sache *(gen)* bewußt sein.

awaken [ə'weɪkən] *vti* = **awake 1, 2.**

awakening [ə'weɪknɪŋ] *n (lit, fig)* Erwachen *nt*. **a rude** ~ *(lit, fig)* ein böses Erwachen.

award [ə'wɔːd] **1** *vt prize etc* zusprechen *(to sb* jdm*)*; *(present) prize, degree, medal etc* verleihen *(to sb* jdm*)*; *penalty, free kick* geben. **to be** ~**ed damages** Schadenersatz zugesprochen bekommen. **2** *n* **(a)** *(prize)* Preis *m*; *(for bravery)* Auszeichnung *f*. **(b)** *(Univ)* Stipendium *nt*.

aware [ə'wɛə[r]] *adj esp pred* bewußt. **to be/become** ~ **of sb/sth** sich *(dat)* jds/einer Sache bewußt sein/werden; *(notice)* jdn bemerken/etw merken; **I was not** ~ **(of the fact) that ...** es war mir nicht klar *or* bewußt, daß ...; **are you** ~ **that ...?** ist dir eigentlich klar, daß ...?; **not that I am** ~ **(of)** nicht daß ich wüßte; **as far as I am** ~ soviel ich weiß; **to make sb more** ~**/**~ **of sth** jds Bewußtsein wecken/jdm etw bewußt machen; **she's very** ~ **of language** sie ist sehr sprachbewußt.

awareness [ə'wɛənɪs] *n* Bewußtsein *nt*.

awash [ə'wɒʃ] *adj pred decks, rocks etc* überspült; *cellar* unter Wasser.

away [ə'weɪ] *adv* **1 (a)** weg. **three miles** ~ **(from here)** drei Meilen (entfernt) von hier; **to look** ~ wegsehen; ~ **we go!** los (geht's)! **(b)** *(absent)* fort, weg. **he's** ~ **from work (with a cold)** er fehlt (wegen einer Erkältung); **he's** ~ **in London** er ist in London; **when I have to be** ~ wenn ich nicht da sein kann. **(c)** *(Sport)* **to play** ~ auswärts spielen. **(d) to put/give** ~ weglegen/weggeben; **to gamble/die** ~ verspielen/verhallen; **to work/knit** *etc* ~ vor sich hin arbeiten/stricken *etc*; **ask** ~! frag nur!, schieß los *(col)*. **(e)** *(col)* **he's** ~ **again** *(talking, giggling, drunk etc)* es geht wieder los; ~ **with you!** ach wo! **2** *adj attr (Sport) team* auswärtig, Gast-; *match, win* Auswärts-.

awe [ɔː] **1** *n* Ehrfurcht *f*. **to be** *or* **stand in** ~ **of sb** Ehrfurcht vor jdm haben; *(feel fear)* große Furcht vor jdm haben. **2** *vt* ~**d by the beauty/silence** von der Schönheit/der Stille ergriffen.

awe-inspiring ['ɔːɪnˌspaɪərɪŋ], **awesome** ['ɔːsəm] *adj* ehrfurchtgebietend.

awful ['ɔːfəl] *adj (col)* schrecklich, furchtbar. **you are** ~! du bist wirklich schrecklich!; **it's not an** ~ **lot better** das ist nicht viel besser.

awfully ['ɔːflɪ] *adv (col)* furchtbar *(col)*, schrecklich *(col)*.

awkward ['ɔːkwəd] *adj* **(a)** *(difficult)* schwierig; *time, moment, angle, shape* ungünstig. **(b)** *(embarrassing)* peinlich. **(c)** *(embarrassed)* verlegen; *silence* betreten. **the** ~ **age** das schwierige Alter; **to feel** ~ **in sb's company** sich in jds Gesellschaft *(dat)* nicht wohl fühlen. **(d)** *(clumsy)* unbeholfen.

awning ['ɔːnɪŋ] *n (on window, of shop)* Markise *f*.

awoke [ə'wəʊk] *pret of* **awake.**

awoken [ə'wəʊkən] *ptp of* **awake.**

awry [ə'raɪ] *adj pred, adv* schief. **to go** ~ *(plans etc)* schiefgehen.

axe, *(US)* **ax** [æks] **1** *n* Axt *f*, Beil *nt*. **to have an/no** ~ **to grind** *(fig)* ein/kein persönliches Interesse haben. **2** *vt plans, jobs* streichen; *person* entlassen.

axiom ['æksɪəm] *n* Axiom *nt*.

axiomatic [ˌæksɪəʊ'mætɪk] *adj* axiomatisch.

axis ['æksɪs] *n, pl* **axes** ['æksiːz] Achse *f*. **the A**~ **(powers)** *(Hist)* die Achsenmächte *pl*.

axle ['æksl] *n* Achse *f*.

aye [aɪ] *interj (esp Scot, dial)* ja. ~**,** ~ **Sir** jawohl, Herr Kapitän *etc*.

azalea [ə'zeɪlɪə] *n* Azalee *f*.

azure ['æʒə[r]] **1** *n* Azur(blau *nt*) *m*. **2** *adj* azurblau.

B

B, b [biː] *n* **(a)** B, b *nt.* **(b)** *(Mus)* H, h *nt.* ~ **flat/sharp** B, b *nt*/His, his *nt.*
BA = **Bachelor of Arts.**
babble ['bæbl] **1** *n* **(a)** Gemurmel *nt*; *(of baby, excited person etc)* Geplapper *nt.* ~ **(of voices)** Stimmengewirr *nt.* **(b)** *(of stream)* Murmeln *nt no pl (liter).* **2** *vi* **(a)** *(person)* plappern. **(b)** *(stream)* murmeln *(liter).*
baboon [bə'buːn] *n* Pavian *m.*
baby ['beɪbɪ] *n* **(a)** Kind, Baby *nt*; *(of animal)* Junge(s) *nt.* **to have a** ~ ein Kind *or* Baby bekommen; **I've known him since he was a** ~ ich kenne ihn von Kindesbeinen an; **the** ~ **of the family** das Nesthäkchen; **don't be such a** ~! stell dich nicht so an! *(col)*; **he's a big** ~ er ist ein großes Kind; **to be left holding the** ~ der Dumme sein *(col)*, die Sache ausbaden müssen *(col)*; **to throw out the** ~ **with the bathwater** das Kind mit dem Bade ausschütten. **(b)** *(col: girlfriend, boyfriend)* Schatz *m.* **(c)** *(esp US col: as address)* Schätzchen *nt (col)*; *(man to man)* Junge *m.*
baby *in cpds* **(a)** *(for baby)* Baby-, Säuglings-. **(b)** *(little)* Klein-. **(c)** *(of animal)* ~ **crocodile** Krokodiljunge(s) *nt.*
baby: ~ **boy** *n* Junge *m*; ~ **carriage** *n (US)* Kinderwagen *m*; ~ **clothes** *npl* Babywäsche *f*; ~ **face** *n* Kindergesicht *nt*; *(of adult male)* Milchgesicht *nt*; ~ **girl** *nt* Töchterchen *nt*; ~ **grand (piano)** *n* Stutzflügel *m.*
babyhood ['beɪbɪhʊd] *n* Säuglingsalter *nt.*
babyish ['beɪbɪɪʃ] *adj* kindisch.
baby: ~**-minder** *n* Tagesmutter *f*; ~**-sit** *pret, ptp* ~**-sat** *vi* babysitten; **she** ~**-sits for her** sie geht bei ihr babysitten; ~**-sitter** *n* Babysitter(in *f*) *m.*
bachelor ['bætʃələʳ] *n* **(a)** Junggeselle *m.* **(b)** *(Univ)* **B~ of Arts/Science** ≃ Magister *m* der Geisteswissenschaften/Naturwissenschaften.
bachelor: ~ **flat** *n* Junggesellenwohnung *f*; ~ **girl** *n* Junggesellin *f.*
bacillus [bə'sɪləs] *n, pl* **bacilli** [bə'sɪlaɪ] Bazillus *m.*
back [bæk] **1** *n* **(a)** *(of person, animal, book)* Rücken *m*; *(of chair also)* (Rücken)lehne *f.* **with one's** ~ **to the engine** entgegen der Fahrtrichtung; **to break one's** ~ *(fig)* sich abrackern; **we've broken the** ~ **of the job** wir sind mit der Arbeit übern Berg *(col)*; **behind sb's** ~ *(fig)* hinter jds Rücken *(dat)*; **to put one's** ~ **into sth** *(fig)* bei etw Einsatz zeigen; **to put** *or* **get sb's** ~ **up** jdn gegen sich aufbringen; **to turn one's** ~ **on sb** *(lit, fig)* sich von jdm abwenden; **he's at the** ~ **of all the trouble** er steckt hinter dem ganzen Ärger; **get these people off my** ~ *(col)* schaff mir diese Leute vom Hals! *(col)*; **to have one's** ~ **to the wall** *(fig)* in die Enge getrieben sein; **I was pleased to see the** ~ **of them** *(col)* ich war froh, sie endlich los zu sein *(col).*

(b) *(as opposed to front)* Rück- *or* Hinterseite *f*; *(of hand, dress)* Rücken *m*; *(of house, page, cheque)* Rückseite *f*; *(of material)* linke Seite. **I know London like the** ~ **of my hand** ich kenne London wie meine Westentasche; **at the** ~ **of the book** hinten im Buch; **he drove into the** ~ **of me** er ist mir hinten reingefahren *(col)*; **in the** ~ **(of a car)** hinten (im Auto); **one consideration was at the** ~ **of my mind** ich hatte dabei eine Überlegung im Hinterkopf; **there's one other worry at the** ~ **of my mind** da ist noch etwas, das mich beschäftigt; **at the** ~ **of beyond** am Ende der Welt, j.w.d. *(hum).*

(c) *(Ftbl)* Verteidiger *m.*

2 *adj wheel, yard* Hinter-; *rent* ausstehend.

3 *adv* zurück. ~ **and forth** hin und her; **to pay sth** ~ etw zurückzahlen; **to come/go** ~ zurückkommen/-gehen; **there and** ~ hin und zurück; **I'll never go** ~ da gehe ich nie wieder hin; **a week** ~ vor einer Woche; **as far** ~ **as the 18th century** *(dating back)* bis zurück ins 18. Jahrhundert.

4 *prep (US)* ~ **of** hinter.

5 *vt* **(a)** *(support)* unterstützen. **I will** ~ **you whatever you do** egal, was du tust, ich stehe hinter dir. **(b)** *(Betting)* setzen auf *(+acc).* **(c)** *(cause to move) car* zurücksetzen. **he** ~**ed his car into the tree/garage** er fuhr rückwärts gegen den Baum/in die Garage.

6 *vi (car, train)* zurücksetzen. **the car** ~**ed into the garage** das Auto fuhr rückwärts in die Garage; **she** ~**ed into me** sie fuhr rückwärts in mein Auto.

♦ **back away** *vi* zurückweichen *(from* vor *+dat).*
♦ **back down** *vi (fig)* nachgeben, klein beigeben.
♦ **back on to** *vi +prep obj* hinten angrenzen an *(+acc).*
♦ **back out 1** *vi* **(a)** *(car etc)* rückwärts herausfahren. **(b)** *(fig: of contract, deal etc)* aussteigen *(of, from* aus) *(col).* **2** *vt sep vehicle* rückwärts herausfahren *or* -setzen.
♦ **back up 1** *vi* **(a)** *(car etc)* zurücksetzen. **to** ~ ~ **to sth** rückwärts an etw *(acc)* heranfahren. **(b)** *(US: drains)* **to have** ~**ed** ~ verstopft sein. **2** *vt sep (support)* unterstützen; *(confirm) story* bestätigen; *(in discussion etc also)* den Rücken stärken *(+dat)*; *claim, theory* untermauern. **he can** ~ **me** ~ **in this** er kann das bestätigen.
back: ~**ache** *n* Rückenschmerzen *pl*; ~**bencher** *n (esp Brit)* Abgeordnete(r) *mf (auf den hinteren Reihen im britischen Parlament)*; ~**bone** *n (lit, fig)* Rückgrat *nt*; ~**-breaking** *adj* äußerst anstrengend; ~**chat** *n no pl* Widerrede *f*; ~**-cloth** *n* Hintergrund *m*; ~**comb** *vt hair* toupieren; ~ **copy** *n* alte Ausgabe; ~**date** *vt* (zu)rückdatieren; ~**dated to May** rückwirkend ab Mai; ~ **door** *n (lit, fig)* Hintertür *f*; ~**drop** *n* = ~**-cloth.**
backer ['bækəʳ] *n* **(a)** *(supporter)* **his** ~**s** (die,) die ihn unterstützen. **(b)** *(Comm)* Geldgeber *m.*
back: ~**fire 1** *n (Aut)* Fehlzündung *f*; **2** *vi* **(a)** *(Aut)* Fehlzündungen haben; **(b)** *(col: plan etc)* ins Auge gehen *(col)*; **it** ~**fired on us** der Schuß ging nach hinten los *(col)*; ~**gammon** *n* Backgammon *nt*; ~ **garden** *n* Garten *m* (hinterm Haus).
background ['bækgraʊnd] **1** *n* **(a)** *(of painting etc, fig)* Hintergrund *m.* **to stay in the** ~ sich im Hintergrund halten. **(b)** *(educational etc)* Werdegang *m*; *(social)* Verhältnisse *pl*; *(family* ~*)* Herkunft *f no pl.* **he comes from a** ~ **of poverty** er kommt aus ärmlichen Verhältnissen. **(c)** *(of case, event, problem etc)* Zusammenhänge, Hintergründe *pl.* **the** ~ **to the crisis** die Hintergründe der Krise. **2** *cpds:* ~ **information** Hintergrundinformationen *pl*; ~ **music** Musikuntermalung *f*; ~ **reading** Sekundärliteratur *f.*

back: ~hand 1 *n (Sport)* Rückhand *f no pl*; *(one stroke)* Rückhandschlag *m*; **2** *adj stroke* Rückhand-; **3** *adv* mit der Rückhand; **~handed** *adj compliment* zweifelhaft; *shot* Rückhand-; **~hander** *n (col: bribe)* Schmiergeld *nt*; **to give sb a ~hander** jdn schmieren *(col)*.

backing ['bækıŋ] *n* **(a)** *(support)* Unterstützung *f*. **(b)** *(Mus)* Begleitung *f*. **(c)** *(for picture frame, for strengthening)* Rücken(verstärkung *f*) *m*.

back: ~lash *n (fig)* Gegenreaktion *f*; **~log** *n* Rückstände *pl*; **I have a ~log of work** ich bin mit der Arbeit im Rückstand; **~ number** *n (of paper)* alte Ausgabe *or* Nummer; **~pack** *n* Rucksack *m*; **~ pay** *n* Nachzahlung *f*; **~-pedal** *vi (lit)* rückwärts treten; *(fig col)* einen Rückzieher machen; **~ room** *n* Hinterzimmer *nt*; **~ seat** *n* Rücksitz *m*; **to take a ~ seat** *(col)* sich zurückhalten; **~seat driver** *n* **she is a terrible ~seat driver** sie redet beim Fahren immer rein; **~side** *n (col)* Hinterteil *nt (col)*; **~-space** *vi (Typing)* zurücksetzen; **~stage** *adv, adj* hinter den Kulissen; *(in dressing-room area)* in der Garderobe; **~ street** *n* Seitensträßchen *nt*; **he comes from the ~ streets of Liverpool** er kommt aus dem ärmeren Teil von Liverpool; **~-street abortionist** *n* Engelmacher(in *f*) *m (col)*; **~stroke** *n (Swimming)* Rückenschwimmen *nt*; **~ to ~** *adv* Rücken an Rücken; *(things)* mit den Rückenseiten aneinander; **~ to front** *adv* verkehrt herum; *read* von hinten nach vorne; **~-up 1** *n* Unterstützung *f*; **2** *adj troops* Hilfs-.

backward ['bækwəd] **1** *adj* **(a) ~ and forward movement** Vor- und Zurückbewegung *f*; **a ~ glance** ein Blick zurück. **(b)** *(fig)* **a ~ step/move** ein Schritt *m* zurück/eine (Zu)rückentwicklung. **(c)** *(retarded) child* zurückgeblieben; *region, country* rückständig. **2** *adv* = **backwards.**

backwards ['bækwədz] *adv* rückwärts. **to fall ~** nach hinten fallen; **to walk ~ and forwards** hin und her gehen; **to bend over ~ to do sth** *(col)* sich *(dat)* ein Bein ausreißen, um etw zu tun *(col)*; **I know it ~** das kenne ich in- und auswendig.

back: ~water *n (lit)* Stauwasser *nt*; *(fig)* rückständiges Nest; **this town is a cultural ~water** kulturell gesehen ist diese Stadt tiefste Provinz; **~yard** *n* **(a)** Hinterhof *m*; **(b)** *(US)* = **~ garden.**

bacon ['beıkən] *n* Speck *m*. **~ and eggs** Eier mit Speck; **to save sb's ~** *(col)* jds Rettung sein.

bacteria [bæk'tıərıə] *npl* Bakterien *pl*.

bacterial [bæk'tıərıəl] *adj* Bakterien-, bakteriell.

bacteriology [bæk,tıərı'ɒlədʒı] *n* Bakteriologie *f*.

bad [bæd] *adj, comp* **worse,** *superl* **worst (a)** schlecht; *risk* hoch; *word* unanständig; *(immoral, wicked also)* böse; *(naughty, misbehaved)* unartig, ungezogen; *dog* böse. **you ~ boy!** du Lümmel!; **I didn't mean that word in a ~ sense** ich habe mir bei dem Wort nichts Böses gedacht; **to go ~** schlecht werden; **to be ~ for sb/sth** schlecht für jdn/etw sein; **he's ~ at tennis** er spielt schlecht Tennis; **it would not be a ~ thing** das wäre nicht schlecht; **(that's) too ~!** *(indignant)* so was!; *(~ luck)* Pech!; **too ~ you couldn't make it** wirklich schade, daß Sie nicht kommen konnten.

(b) *(serious) wound, situation* schlimm. **to have it ~ for sb** *(col)* schwer in jdn verknallt sein *(col)*; **things are going from ~ to worse** es wird immer schlimmer.

(c) *(in poor health, sick) stomach* krank; *leg, knee, hand* schlimm. **he/the economy is in a ~ way** es geht ihm schlecht/es steht schlecht mit der Wirtschaft; **to feel ~** sich nicht wohl fühlen; **I feel ~** mir geht es nicht gut; **how is he? — he's not so ~** wie geht es ihm? — nicht schlecht.

(d) *(regretful)* **I feel really ~ about not having told him** ich habe ein schlechtes Gewissen, daß ich ihm das nicht gesagt habe; **don't feel ~ about it** mach dir keine Gedanken (darüber).

baddie ['bædı] *n (col)* Schurke, Bösewicht *m*.

bade [beıd] *pret of* **bid.**

badge [bædʒ] *n* Abzeichen *nt*; *(made of metal: women's lib, joke ~ etc)* Button *m*, Plakette *f*. **~ of office** Dienstmarke *f*.

badger ['bædʒə[r]] **1** *n* Dachs *m*. **2** *vt* zusetzen *(+dat)*.

badly ['bædlı] *adv* **(a)** schlecht. **the party went ~** die Party war ein Reinfall *(col)*. **(b)** *wounded, mistaken* schwer. **~ beaten** *(Sport)* vernichtend geschlagen; *person* schwer verprügelt. **(c)** *(very much)* äußerst, sehr; *in debt, overdrawn* hoch. **to want sth ~** etw unbedingt wollen; **he ~ needs** *or* **wants a haircut** er muß dringend zum Friseur.

bad-mannered [,bæd'mænəd] *adj* unhöflich; *child also* ungezogen.

badminton ['bædmıntən] *n* Federball *nt*; *(on court)* Badminton *nt*.

bad-tempered [,bæd'tempəd] *adj* schlechtgelaunt *attr*. **to be ~** schlechte Laune haben; *(as characteristic)* ein reizbarer Mensch sein.

baffle ['bæfl] *vt (confound, amaze)* verblüffen; *(cause incomprehension)* vor ein Rätsel [illegible] **~d look** ein verdutzter Blick; **it really** [illegible] **how ...** es ist mir wirklich ein Rätsel, w[illegible]

baffling ['bæflıŋ] *adj case* rätselhaft; *c*[illegible] verwirrend; *mystery* unergründlich.

bag [bæg] *n* Tasche *f*; *(with drawstrings, po*[illegible] tel *m*; *(for school)* Schultasche *f*; *(made* [illegible] *plastic)* Tüte *f*; *(sack)* Sack *m*; Reisetasche *f*. **~s** (Reise)gepäck *nt*; **to be a ~ o**[illegible] **bones** *(fig col)* nur Haut und Knochen sein *(col)*; **it's in the ~** *(fig col)* das ist gelaufen *(col)*; **~s under the eyes** *(black)* Ringe *pl* unter den Augen; *(of skin)* Tränensäcke *pl*; **~s of** *(col: a lot)* jede Menge *(col)*; **(old) ~** *(pej col: woman)* (alte) Ziege *(pej col)*.

baggage ['bægıdʒ] *n (luggage)* (Reise)gepäck *nt*.

baggage: ~ car *n* Gepäckwagen *m*; **~ check-room** *n (US)* Gepäckaufbewahrung *f*; **~ claim** *n* Gepäckausgabe *f*.

baggy ['bægı] *adj (+er) (ill-fitting)* (zu) weit; *skin* schlaff; *(out of shape) trousers, suit* ausgebeult; *jumper* ausgeleiert.

bagpipe(s *pl***)** ['bægpaıp(s)] *n* Dudelsack *m*.

bag-snatcher ['bæg,snætʃə[r]] *n* Handtaschendieb *m*.

Bahamas [bə'hɑːməz] *npl* **the ~** die Bahamas.

bail[1] [beıl] *n (Jur)* Kaution *f*. **to stand ~ for sb** für jdn (die) Kaution stellen; **to grant ~** die Freilassung gegen Kaution bewilligen; **to let sb out on ~** jdn gegen Kaution freilassen.

♦**bail out** *vt sep* **(a)** *(Jur)* gegen Kaution freibekommen. **(b)** *(fig)* aus der Patsche helfen *(+dat) (col)*.

bail[2] *vti* = **bale**[2].

bailiff ['beılıf] *n* **(sheriff's) ~** Amtsdiener *m*; *(for property)* Gerichtsvollzieher *m*; *(in court)* Gerichtsdiener *m*; *(on estate)* (Guts)verwalter *m*.

bait [beit] **1** *n (lit, fig)* Köder *m*. **to swallow the** *or* **rise to the ~** *(lit, fig)* anbeißen. **2** *vt* **(a)** *hook, trap* mit einem Köder versehen. **(b)** *(torment) animal* (mit Hunden) hetzen; *person* quälen.

baize [beız] *n* Fries *m*. **green ~** Billardtuch *nt*.

bake [beık] *vt* **(a)** *(Cook)* backen. **~d beans** *pl* gebackene Bohnen *pl*; **~d potatoes** *pl* in der Schale gebackene Kartoffeln *pl*. **(b)** *pottery, bricks* brennen; *(sun) earth* ausdörren.

baker ['beıkə[r]] *n* Bäcker(in *f*) *m*. **~'s (shop)** *(Brit)* Bäckerei *f*; **~'s dozen** 13 (Stück).

bakery ['beıkərı] *n* Bäckerei *f*.

baking ['beıkıŋ] *n (act) (Cook)* Backen *nt*; *(of earthenware)* Brennen *nt*.

baking: ~ day *n* Backtag *m*; **~ dish** *n* Backform *f*; **~ powder, ~ soda** *n* Backpulver *nt*; **~ tin** *n* Backform *f*.

Balaclava [,bælə'klɑːvə] *n* Kapuzenmütze *f*.

balance ['bæləns] **1** *n* **(a)** *(apparatus)* Waage *f*. **to be** *or* **hang in the ~** *(fig)* in der Schwebe sein. **(b)**

(counterpoise) Gegengewicht *nt (to* zu); *(fig also)* Ausgleich *m (to* für). **(c)** *(lit, fig: equilibrium)* Gleichgewicht *nt.* **to keep/lose one's ~** das Gleichgewicht halten/verlieren; **to throw sb off (his) ~** jdn aus dem Gleichgewicht bringen; **the ~ of power** das Gleichgewicht der Kräfte; **to strike the right ~** den goldenen Mittelweg finden; **on ~** *(fig)* alles in allem. **(d)** *(Comm, Fin: state of account)* Saldo *m; (with bank also)* Kontostand *m; (of company)* Bilanz *f.* **~ carried forward** Saldoübertrag *m;* **~ due** *(banking)* Soll *nt; (Comm)* Rechnungsbetrag *m;* **~ of payments/trade** Zahlungs-/Handelsbilanz *f.* **(e)** *(fig: remainder)* Rest *m.*

2 *vt* **(a)** *(keep level, in equilibrium)* im Gleichgewicht halten; *(as trick) ball etc* balancieren; *(bring into equilibrium)* ins Gleichgewicht bringen. **(b)** *(weigh in the mind) two solutions* (gegeneinander) abwägen. **to ~ sth against sth** etw einer Sache *(dat)* gegenüberstellen. **(c)** *(equal, make up for)* ausgleichen. **(d)** *(Comm, Fin) account (add up)* abschließen; *(make equal)* ausgleichen. **to ~ the books** die Bilanz ziehen.

3 *vi* **(a)** *(be in equilibrium)* Gleichgewicht halten; *(scales)* sich ausbalancieren. **he ~d on one foot** er balancierte auf einem Bein. **(b)** *(Comm, Fin: of accounts)* ausgeglichen sein. **the books don't ~** die Abrechnung stimmt nicht.

♦ **balance out 1** *vt sep* ausgleichen. **they ~ each other ~** sie halten sich die Waage; *(personalities)* sie gleichen sich aus. **2** *vi* sich ausgleichen.

balanced ['bælənst] *adj* ausgewogen; *personality* ausgeglichen.

balance sheet *n (Fin)* Bilanz *f.*

balancing trick ['bælənsɪŋ,trɪk] *n* Balancekunststück *nt.*

balcony ['bælkənɪ] *n* **(a)** Balkon *m.* **(b)** *(Theat)* oberster Rang.

bald [bɔːld] *adj (+er)* **(a)** *person* kahl, glatzköpfig; *type* abgefahren. **he is ~** er hat eine Glatze; **to go ~** eine Glatze bekommen; **~ patch** kahle Stelle. **(b)** *style, statement* knapp.

baldly ['bɔːldlɪ] *adv (fig: bluntly)* unverblümt.

baldness ['bɔːldnɪs] *n* **(a)** Kahlheit *f.* **(b)** *(of style, statement)* Knappheit *f.*

bale[1] [beɪl] *n (of hay)* Ballen *m.*

bale[2] *vti (Naut)* schöpfen.

♦ **bale out 1** *vi* **(a)** *(Aviat)* abspringen, aussteigen *(col) (of* aus). **(b)** *(Naut)* schöpfen. **2** *vt sep (Naut) water* schöpfen; *ship* ausschöpfen.

Balearic [,bælɪ'ærɪk] *adj* **the ~ Islands** die Balearen *pl.*

baleful ['beɪlfʊl] *adj (evil)* böse; *(sad)* traurig.

balk, baulk [bɔːk] *vi (person)* zurückschrecken *(at* vor *+dat); (horse)* scheuen *(at* bei).

Balkan ['bɔːlkən] **1** *adj* Balkan-. **2** *n* **the ~s** der Balkan, die Balkanländer *pl.*

ball[1] [bɔːl] *n* **(a)** Ball *m; (Billiards)* Kugel *f; (of wool, string)* Knäuel *m; (US: baseball)* Baseball *nt.* **to keep the ~ rolling** *(fig)* das Ganze in Gang halten; **to start** *or* **set the ~ rolling** *(fig)* den Stein ins Rollen bringen; **the ~ is with you** *or* **in your court** *(fig)* Sie sind am Ball *(col);* **to be on the ~** *(fig col)* auf Zack *or* Draht sein *(col);* **~ of the foot/thumb** Fuß-/Handballen *m.* **(b)** *(col!: testicle)* Ei *nt usu pl (col!).* **~s!** *(nonsense)* red keinen Scheiß! *(col!).*

ball[2] *n (dance)* Ball *m.* **to have a ~** *(col)* sich prima amüsieren *(col).*

ballad ['bæləd] *n (Mus, Liter)* Ballade *f.*

ballast ['bæləst] *n (Naut, Aviat, fig)* Ballast *m.*

ball: ~-bearing *n* Kugellager *nt;* **~-cock** *n* Schwimmerhahn *m.*

ballerina [,bælə'riːnə] *n* Ballerina *f.*

ballet ['bæleɪ] *n* Ballett *nt.*

ballet: ~-dancer *n* Ballettänzer(in *f*) *m;* **~shoe** *n* Ballettschuh *m.*

ballistic [bə'lɪstɪk] *adj* ballistisch. **~ missile** Raketengeschoß *nt.*

ballistics [bə'lɪstɪks] *n sing* Ballistik *f.*

balloon [bə'luːn] *n* Ballon *m; (toy also)* Luftballon *m; (in cartoon)* Sprechblase *f.*

balloonist [bə'luːnɪst] *n* Ballonfahrer(in *f*) *m.*

ballot ['bælət] **1** *n* (geheime) Abstimmung. **to decide sth by ~** über etw *(acc)* (geheim) abstimmen; **to take** *or* **hold a ~** abstimmen. **2** *vt members* abstimmen lassen.

ballot: ~-box *n* Wahlurne *f;* **~-paper** *n* Stimmzettel *m.*

ball: ~park *n (US)* Baseballstadion *nt;* **~-point (pen)** *n* Kugelschreiber *m;* **~room** *n* Ballsaal *m;* **~room dancing** *n* Gesellschaftstänze *pl.*

balm [bɑːm] *n (lit, fig)* Balsam *m.*

balmy ['bɑːmɪ] *adj (+er) (fragrant)* wohlriechend; *(mild)* sanft. **~ breezes** linde Lüfte *(geh).*

balsa ['bɔːlsə] *n (also* **~ wood***)* Balsa(holz) *nt.*

Baltic ['bɔːltɪk] *adj* Ostsee-. **~ (Sea)** Ostsee *f;* **the ~ States** *(Hist)* das Baltikum.

balustrade [,bælə'streɪd] *n* Balustrade *f.*

bamboo [bæm'buː] *n* Bambus *m.*

bamboozle [bæm'buːzl] *vt (col) (baffle)* verblüffen; *(trick)* hereinlegen *(col).*

ban [bæn] **1** *n* Verbot *nt.* **to put a ~ on sth** etw verbieten; **a ~ on smoking** Rauchverbot *nt.* **2** *vt (prohibit)* verbieten; *footballer etc* sperren. **she was ~ned from driving** ihr wurde Fahrverbot erteilt.

banal [bə'nɑːl] *adj* banal.

banality [bə'nælɪtɪ] *n* Banalität *f.*

banana [bə'nɑːnə] *n* Banane *f.* **~ republic** Bananenrepublik *f.*

bananas [bə'nɑːnəz] *adj pred (col: crazy)* bescheuert *(col).* **this is driving me ~** dabei dreh' ich noch durch *(col).*

banana skin *n* Bananenschale *f.*

band[1] [bænd] *n* **(a)** *(of cloth, iron)* Band *nt; (of leather)* Band *nt,* Riemen *m; (waist ~)* Bund *m; (on machine)* Riemen *m.* **(b)** *(stripe)* Streifen *m.*

band[2] *n* **(a)** Schar *f; (of robbers etc)* Bande *f; (of workers)* Trupp *m* Kolonne *f.* **(b)** *(Mus)* Band *f; (dance ~)* Tanzkapelle *f; (brass ~, Mil etc)* (Musik)kapelle *f.*

♦ **band together** *vi* sich zusammenschließen.

bandage ['bændɪdʒ] **1** *n* Verband *m; (strip of cloth)* Binde *f.* **2** *vt (also* **~ up***) cut* verbinden; *broken limb* bandagieren.

B & B [,biːənd'biː] *n* = **bed and breakfast.**

bandit ['bændɪt] *n* Bandit, Räuber *m.*

bandsman ['bandzmən] *n, pl* **-men** [-mən] Musiker *m.* **military ~** Mitglied *nt* eines Musikkorps.

band: ~stand *n* Musikpavillon *m;* **~wagon** *n:* **to jump** *or* **climb on the ~wagon** auf den fahrenden Zug aufspringen; **~width** *n (Rad)* Bandbreite *f.*

bandy ['bændɪ] *adj* krumm. **~ legs** *(of people)* O-Beine.

♦ **bandy about** *or* **around** *vt sep story* herumerzählen; *words, technical expressions* um sich werfen mit; *sb's name* immer wieder nennen.

bandy-legged [,bændɪ'legd] *adj* mit krummen Beinen; *person* O-beinig.

bane [beɪn] *n (cause of distress)* Fluch *m.* **he's the ~ of my life** mit ihm bin ich geschlagen.

bang [bæŋ] **1** *n (noise)* Knall *m; (of sth falling)* Plumps *m.* **there was a ~ outside** draußen hat es geknallt; **to go off with a ~** mit lautem Knall losgehen; *(col: be a success)* ein Bombenerfolg sein *(col).* **2** *adv* **(a) to go ~** knallen; *(gun also, balloon)* peng machen *(col); (balloon)* zerplatzen. **(b)** *(col)* **his answer was ~ on** seine Antwort war genau richtig; **she came ~ on time** sie war auf die Sekunde pünktlich. **3** *interj* peng. **~ went a £10 note** *(col)* und schon war ein 10-Pfund-Schein futsch *(col).* **4** *vt* **(a)** *(thump)* schlagen, knallen *(col).* **he ~ed his fist on the table** er schlug mit der Faust auf den Tisch. **(b)** *(shut noisily) door* zuknallen *(col).* **(c) to ~ one's head** *etc* **on sth** sich *(dat)* den Kopf *etc* an etw *(dat)* anschlagen. **5** *vi*

(a) *(door: shut)* zuknallen *(col)*; *(fireworks, gun)* knallen. **(b) to ~ on** *or* **at sth** gegen *or* an etw *(acc)* schlagen.

♦ **bang down** *vt sep* (hin)knallen *(col)*. **to ~ ~ the receiver** den Hörer aufknallen *(col)*.

banger ['bæŋəʳ] *n* **(a)** *(col: sausage)* Wurst *f*. **(b)** *(col: old car)* Kiste *f (col)*. **(c)** *(Brit: firework)* Knallkörper *m*.

bangle ['bæŋgl] *n* Armreif *m*; *(for ankle)* Fußreif *m*.

bangs [bæŋz] *n pl (US: in hair)* Franse *f*.

banish ['bænɪʃ] *vt person* verbannen; *cares, fear* vertreiben.

banisters ['bænɪstəz] *npl* Geländer *nt*.

banjo ['bændʒəʊ] *n, pl* **-es,** *(US)* **-s** Banjo *nt*.

bank[1] [bæŋk] **1** *n* **(a)** *(of earth, sand)* Wall, Damm *m*; *(slope)* Böschung *f*, Abhang *m*; *(on racetrack)* Kurvenüberhöhung *f*. **(b)** *(of river, lake)* Ufer *nt*. **(c)** *(of clouds)* Wand, Bank *f*. **2** *vi (Aviat)* eine Kurve fliegen.

bank[2] **1** *n (Fin, Med)* Bank *f*. **2** *vt money* einzahlen. **3** *vi* **where do you ~?** bei welcher Bank sind Sie?

♦ **bank (up)on** *vi +prep obj* sich verlassen auf *(+acc)*.

bank: ~ account *n* Bankkonto *nt*; **~book** *n* Sparbuch *nt*; **~ charges** *pl (Brit)* Bankgebühren *pl*; **~ clerk** *n* Bankangestellte(r) *mf*.

banker ['bæŋkəʳ] *n (Fin)* Bankier *m*; *(gambling)* Bankhalter *m*.

banker's card ['bæŋkəz,kɑːd] *n* Scheckkarte *f*.

bank holiday *n (Brit)* öffentlicher Feiertag; *(US)* Bankfeiertag *m*.

banking ['bæŋkɪŋ] *n* **he wants to go into ~** er will ins Bankfach gehen.

banking hours *npl* Schalterstunden *pl*.

bank: ~loan *n* Darlehen *nt*; **~ manager** *n* Filialleiter(in *f*) *m*; **~note** *n (Brit)* Banknote *f*, Geldschein *m*; **~ rate** *n* Diskontsatz *m*.

bankrupt ['bæŋkrʌpt] *adj (Jur)* bankrott. **to go ~** Bankrott machen; **to be ~** bankrott *or* pleite *(col)* sein.

bankruptcy ['bæŋkrəptsɪ] *n (lit, fig)* Bankrott *m*.

bank statement *n* Kontoauszug *m*.

banner ['bænəʳ] *n* Banner *(also fig) nt*; *(in processions)* Transparent *nt*.

bannisters ['bænɪstəz] *n* = **banisters.**

banns [bænz] *npl (Eccl)* Aufgebot *nt*. **to read the ~** das Aufgebot verlesen.

banquet ['bæŋkwɪt] *n (lavish feast)* Festessen *nt*; *(ceremonial dinner)* Bankett *nt*.

bantam ['bæntəm] *n* Bantamhuhn *nt*.

bantamweight ['bæntəm,weɪt] *n* Bantamgewicht *nt*.

banter ['bæntəʳ] *n* Geplänkel *nt*. **enough of this foolish ~** lassen wir das alberne Gerede!

baptism ['bæptɪzəm] *n* Taufe *f*. **~ of fire** *(fig)* Feuertaufe *f*.

Baptist ['bæptɪst] *n* Baptist(in *f*) *m*. **John the ~** Johannes der Täufer.

baptize [bæp'taɪz] *vt* taufen.

bar[1] [bɑːʳ] **1** *n* **(a)** *(of metal, wood)* Stange *f*; *(of toffee etc)* Riegel *m*; *(of electric fire)* Element *nt*. **~ of gold/silver** Gold-/Silberbarren *m*; **a ~ of chocolate, a chocolate ~** *(slab)* eine Tafel Schokolade; *(smaller)* ein Schokoladenriegel *m*; **a ~ of soap** ein Stück *nt* Seife. **(b)** *(of window, cage)* (Gitter)stab *m*; *(of door)* Stange *f*. **behind ~s** hinter Gittern. **(c)** *(fig: obstacle)* Hindernis *(to* für*) nt*. **to be a ~ to sth** einer Sache *(dat)* im Wege stehen. **(d)** *(for drinks)* Bar *f*; *(counter)* Theke *f*, Tresen *m*. **(e)** *(Jur)* **the B~** die Anwaltschaft; **to be called** *or* **admitted** *(US)* **to the B~** als Anwalt zugelassen werden; **"prisoner at the ~"** „Angeklagter!" **(f)** *(Mus)* Takt *m*.

2 *vt* **(a)** *(obstruct) road* versperren. **(b)** *(fasten) door* verriegeln. **(c)** *(exclude, prohibit) person* ausschließen; *action, thing* verbieten. **to ~ sb from a competition** jdn von (der Teilnahme an) einem Wettbewerb ausschließen.

bar[2], **barring** *prep* **barring accidents** falls nichts passiert; **bar none** ohne Ausnahme.

barb [bɑːb] *n (of fish-hook, arrow)* Widerhaken *m*.

Barbados [bɑː'beɪdɒs] *n* Barbados *nt*.

barbarian [bɑː'bɛərɪən] **1** *n (Hist, fig)* Barbar(in *f*) *m*. **2** *adj (Hist, fig)* barbarisch.

barbaric [bɑː'bærɪk] *adj* barbarisch; *guard etc* grausam, roh; *(fig col) conditions* grauenhaft.

barbarous ['bɑːbərəs] *adj (Hist, fig)* barbarisch; *(cruel)* grausam.

barbecue ['bɑːbɪkjuː] **1** *n (Cook: grid)* Grill *m*; *(occasion)* Grillparty *f*; *(meat)* Grillfleisch *nt*/-wurst *f etc*. **2** *vt* grillen.

barbed wire ['bɑːbd'waɪəʳ] *n* Stacheldraht *m*.

barber ['bɑːbəʳ] *n* (Herren)friseur *m*. **at/to the ~'s** *(Brit)* beim/zum Friseur.

barbiturate [bɑː'bɪtjʊrɪt] *n* Barbiturat *nt*.

bard [bɑːd] *n (old)* Barde *m*.

bare [bɛəʳ] **1** *adj (+er)* **(a)** *skin, floor* nackt, bloß; *countryside, room* kahl. **~ patch** kahle Stelle; **to lay ~ one's heart** sein Innerstes bloßlegen; **with his ~ hands** mit bloßen Händen; **a ~ statement of the facts** eine reine Tatsachenfeststellung. **(b)** *(scanty, mere)* knapp. **a ~ majority** eine knappe Mehrheit; **with just the ~st hint of garlic** nur mit einer winzigen Spur Knoblauch. **2** *vt parts of the body* entblößen; *(at doctor's)* freimachen; *end of a wire* freilegen.

bare: ~back *adv, adj* ohne Sattel; **~faced** *adj liar* unverfroren, schamlos; **~foot** *adv* barfuß; **~headed** *adj* ohne Kopfbedeckung.

barely ['bɛəlɪ] *adv (scarcely)* kaum. **we ~ know him** wir kennen ihn kaum.

bargain ['bɑːgɪn] **1** *n* **(a)** *(transaction)* Handel *m*, Geschäft *nt*. **to make** *or* **strike a ~** sich einigen; **I'll make a ~ with you, if you ...** ich mache Ihnen ein Angebot, wenn Sie ...; **it's a ~!** abgemacht!; **you drive a hard ~** Sie stellen ja harte Forderungen!; **then it started raining into the ~** dann hat es (obendrein) auch noch angefangen zu regnen. **(b)** *(cheap offer)* Sonderangebot *nt*; *(thing bought)* Gelegenheitskauf *m*. **what a ~!** das ist aber günstig! **2** *vi* handeln *(for* um*)*; *(in negotiations)* verhandeln.

♦ **bargain for** *vi +prep obj (col: expect)* erwarten. **I hadn't ~ed ~ that** damit hatte ich nicht gerechnet; **I got more than I ~ed ~** ich habe vielleicht mein blaues Wunder erlebt! *(col)*.

barge [bɑːdʒ] **1** *n (for freight)* Last- *or* Frachtkahn *m*; *(unpowered)* Schleppkahn *m*; *(ceremonial)* Barkasse *f*. **2** *vt* **he ~d me out of the way** er hat mich weggestoßen.

♦ **barge in** *vi (col)* hinein-/hereinplatzen *(col)*; *(interrupt)* dazwischenplatzen *(col) (on* bei*)*.

♦ **barge into** *vi +prep obj* **(a)** *(knock against) person* (hinein)rennen in *(+acc) (col)*; *(shove)* (an)rempeln; *thing* rennen gegen *(col)*. **(b)** *(col) room, party, conversation* (hinein-/herein)platzen in *(+acc) (col)*.

barge pole *n*: **I wouldn't touch it/him with a ~** *(Brit col)* von so etwas/so jemandem lasse ich die Finger *(col)*; *(because disgusting, unpleasant)* das/den würde ich noch nicht mal mit der Kneifzange anfassen *(col)*.

baritone ['bærɪtəʊn] *n (voice, singer)* Bariton *m*.

barium ['bɛərɪəm] *n* Barium *nt*. **~ meal** Bariumbrei, Kontrastbrei *m*.

bark[1] [bɑːk] *n (of tree)* Rinde, Borke *f*.

bark[2] **1** *n (dog)* Bellen *nt*. **his ~ is worse than his bite** *(Prov)* Hunde, die bellen, beißen nicht *(Prov)*. **2** *vi* bellen. **to ~ at sb** jdn anbellen; *(person)* jdn anfahren; **to be ~ing up the wrong tree** *(fig col)* auf dem Holzweg sein *(col)*.

♦ **bark out** *vt sep orders* bellen.

barley ['bɑːlɪ] *n* Gerste *f*. **~ sugar** *n* Malzzucker *m*; *(sweet)* Malzbonbon *nt*.

bar: ~maid *n* Bardame *f*; **~man** *n* Barkeeper *m*.

barmy ['bɑːmɪ] *adj (Brit col)* bekloppt *(col).*
barn [bɑːn] *n* Scheune *f.*
barn: ~ **owl** *n* Schleiereule *f;* ~**yard** *n* (Bauern)hof *m.*
barometer [bə'rɒmɪtə^r] *n (lit, fig)* Barometer *nt.*
baron ['bærən] *n (lit, fig)* Baron *m.*
baroque [bə'rɒk] **1** *adj* barock, Barock-. **2** *n (style)* Barock *m or nt.*
barracks ['bærəks] *npl (often with sing vb) (Mil)* Kaserne *f; (fig pej also)* Mietskaserne *f.*
barrage ['bærɑːʒ] *n* **(a)** *(across river)* Wehr *nt; (larger)* Staustufe *f.* **(b)** *(Mil)* Sperrfeuer *nt.* **under this** ~ **of stones ...** unter diesem Steinhagel ... **(c)** *(fig: of questions etc)* Hagel *m.*
barrel ['bærəl] *n* **(a)** Faß *nt; (for rainwater etc)* Tonne *f; (measure: of oil)* Barrel *nt.* **they've got us over a** ~ *(col)* sie haben uns in der Zange *(col).* **(b)** *(of handgun)* Lauf *m; (of cannon etc)* Rohr *nt.*
barrel organ *n* Drehorgel *f,* Leierkasten *m.*
barren ['bærən] *adj (lit, fig)* unfruchtbar; *land also* karg; *landscape* kahl, öde.
barricade [,bærɪ'keɪd] **1** *n* Barrikade *f.* **2** *vt* verbarrikadieren.
barrier ['bærɪə^r] *n (lit, fig)* Barriere *f; (railing etc)* Schranke *f; (crash* ~*)* Leitplanke *f.* **ticket** ~ Sperre *f.*
barrier cream *n* (Haut)schutzcreme *f.*
barring ['bɑːrɪŋ] *prep* = **bar**².
barrister ['bærɪstə^r] *n (Brit)* Rechtsanwalt *m*/-anwältin *f* (bei Gericht).
barrow ['bærəʊ] *n* Karre(n *m*) *f.*
bartender ['bɑːtendə^r] *n (US)* Barkeeper *m.*
barter ['bɑːtə^r] **1** *vt* tauschen *(for* gegen*).* **2** *vi* tauschen; *(as general practice also)* Tauschhandel treiben. **to** ~ **for sth** um etw handeln. **3** *n* (Tausch)handel *m.*
♦ **barter away** *vt sep one's rights* verspielen.
base¹ [beɪs] **1** *n* **(a)** *(lowest part)* Basis *f; (support for statue etc)* Sockel *m; (of lamp, mountain)* Fuß *m.* **(b)** *(main ingredient)* Hauptbestandteil *m.* **(c)** *(Mil)* Stützpunkt *m; (for holidays)* Standort *m.* **(d)** *(Chem)* Lauge, Base *f.* **2** *vt* **(a)** stellen. **to be** ~**d on** ruhen auf *(+dat); (statue)* stehen auf *(+dat);* **something to** ~ **it on** eine Unterlage dafür. **(b)** *(fig) opinion, theory* basieren *(on* auf *+acc); hopes* setzen *(on* auf *+acc); relationship* bauen *(on* auf *+acc).* **to be** ~**d on sb/sth** auf jdm/etw basieren. **(c)** *(Mil)* stationieren. **the company/my job is** ~**d in London** die Firma hat ihren Sitz in London/ich arbeite in London.
base² *adj (+er)* **(a)** *motive* niedrig; *person, action* gemein, niederträchtig. **(b)** *metal* unedel.
baseball ['beɪsbɔːl] *n* Baseball *m or nt.*
base camp *n* Basislager *nt.*
-based [beɪst] *adj suf* **London-**~ mit Sitz in London.
base line *n (Tennis)* Grundlinie *f.*
basement ['beɪsmənt] *n (in building)* Untergeschoß *nt; (in house also)* Keller *m.* ~ **flat** Kellerwohnung *f.*
bash [bæʃ] *(col)* **1** *n* **(a)** Schlag *m.* **the bumper has had a** ~ die Stoßstange hat 'ne Delle abgekriegt *(col).* **(b)** *(fig)* **I'll have a** ~ **(at it)** ich probier's mal *(col).* **2** *vt person* (ver)hauen *(col); ball* knallen *(col); car, wing* eindellen *(col).* **to** ~ **one's head/shin (against** *or* **on sth)** sich *(dat)* den Kopf/das Schienbein (an etw *dat*) anschlagen; **to** ~ **sb on the head with sth** jdm etw auf den Kopf hauen *(col).*
♦ **bash in** *vt sep (col) door* einschlagen. **to** ~ **sb's head** ~ jdm den Schädel einschlagen *(col).*
♦ **bash up** *vt sep (Brit col) person* vermöbeln *(col).*
bashful ['bæʃfʊl] *adj* schüchtern; *(on particular occasion)* verlegen.
basic ['beɪsɪk] **1** *adj* **(a)** *(fundamental)* Grund-; *problem also, reason, issue* Haupt-; *points, issues* wesentlich. **there's no** ~ **difference** es besteht kein grundlegender Unterschied; **must you be so** ~! müssen Sie sich denn so direkt ausdrücken?; ~ **salary** Grundgehalt *nt;* ~ **English** englischer Grundwortschatz. **(b)** *(original)* zu Grunde liegend. **(c)** *(essential)* notwendig. **2** *npl* **the** ~**s** das Wesentliche.
basically ['beɪsɪkəlɪ] *adv* im Grunde; *(mainly)* im wesentlichen.
basil ['bæzl] *n (Bot)* Basilikum *nt.*
basin ['beɪsn] *n* **(a)** *(vessel)* Schüssel *f; (wash*~*)* (Wasch)becken *nt.* **(b)** *(Geog)* Becken *nt.*
basis ['beɪsɪs] *n (foundation)* Basis *f; (for assumption)* Grund *m.* **we're working on the** ~ **that ...** wir gehen von der Annahme aus, daß ...; **on the** ~ **of this evidence** aufgrund dieses Beweismaterials.
bask [bɑːsk] *vi (in sun)* sich aalen *(in* in *+dat).*
basket ['bɑːskɪt] *n* Korb *m; (for rolls, fruit etc)* Körbchen *nt.*
basket: ~**ball** *n* Basketball *m;* ~**work chair** *n* Korbstuhl *m.*
Basle [bɑːl] *n* Basel *nt.*
bass [beɪs] *(Mus)* **1** *n* Baß *m.* **2** *adj* Baß-. ~ **clef** Baßschlüssel *m;* ~ **drum** große Trommel.
bassoon [bə'suːn] *n* Fagott *nt.*
bastard ['bɑːstəd] *n* **(a)** *(lit)* uneheliches Kind; *(fig: hybrid)* Kreuzung *f.* **(b)** *(col!: person)* Scheißkerl *m (col!).* **poor** ~ armes Schwein *(col).*
baste¹ [beɪst] *vt (Sew)* heften.
baste² *vt (Cook)* (mit Fett) beträufeln.
bat¹ [bæt] *n (Zool)* Fledermaus *f.* **(as) blind as a** ~ blind wie ein Maulwurf.
bat² *(Sport)* **1** *n (Baseball, Cricket)* Schlagholz *nt; (Table-tennis)* Schläger *m.* **off one's own** ~ *(fig)* auf eigene Faust *(col).* **2** *vi (Baseball, Cricket)* Schlagmann sein.
bat³ *vt* **without** ~**ting an eyelid** ohne mit der Wimper zu zucken; **he didn't** ~ **an eyelid** er blieb seelenruhig.
batch [bætʃ] *n (of loaves)* Schub *m; (of prisoners, recruits also)* Trupp *m; (of things dispatched)* Sendung *f; (of letters, work)* Stoß, Stapel *m.*
bated ['beɪtɪd] *adj*: **with** ~ **breath** mit angehaltenem Atem.
bath [bɑːθ] **1** *n* **(a)** Bad *nt.* **to have** *or* **take a** ~ baden; **a room with** ~ ein Zimmer mit Bad. **(b)** *(bathtub)* (Bade)wanne *f.* **(c) (swimming)** ~**s** *pl* (Schwimm)bad *nt;* **(public)** ~**s** *pl* Badeanstalt *f; (Hist)* Bäder *pl.* **2** *vt (Brit)* baden. **3** *vi (Brit)* (sich) baden.
bath: ~**chair** *n* Rollstuhl *m;* ~**cube** *n* Würfel *m* Badesalz.
bathe [beɪð] **1** *vt* baden; *(with cottonwool etc)* waschen. **to be** ~**d in light/sweat** in Licht/Schweiß gebadet sein. **2** *vi (US)* (sich) baden.
bather ['beɪðə^r] *n* Badende(r) *mf.*
bathing: ~**-cap** *n* Badekappe *f;* ~**-costume** *n (Brit)* Badeanzug *m;* ~**-trunks** *npl (Brit)* Badehose *f.*
bath: ~**mat** *n* Badematte *f;* ~**robe** *n* Bademantel *m;* ~**room** *n* Bad(ezimmer) *nt; (euph: lavatory)* Toilette *f;* ~**salts** *npl* Badesalz *nt;* ~**towel** *n* Badetuch *nt;* ~**tub** *n* Badewanne *f.*
baton ['bætən] *n* **(a)** *(Mus)* Taktstock *m; (Mil)* (Kommando)stab *m.* **(b)** *(of policeman)* Schlagstock *m; (for directing traffic)* Stab *m.* **(c)** *(in relay race)* Staffelholz *nt,* Stab *m.*
battalion [bə'tælɪən] *n (Mil, fig)* Bataillon *nt.*
batter¹ ['bætə^r] *n (Cook)* Teig *m.*
batter² **1** *vt* **(a)** einschlagen auf *(+acc); wife, baby* (ver)prügeln. **the house was** ~**ed by the wind** der Wind rüttelte unentwegt am Haus. **(b)** *(damage)* übel zurichten; *car also, metal* zer- *or* verbeulen. **(c)** *(col) opponent* eins draufgeben *(+dat) (col).* **2** *vi* **to** ~ **at the door** an die Tür hämmern *(col).*
♦ **batter down** *vt sep door* einschlagen.
battered ['bætəd] *adj* übel zugerichtet; *wife, baby* mißhandelt; *object* verbeult; *furniture* ramponiert *(col); nerves* zerrüttet.

battering ram ['bætərɪŋ,ræm] *n* Rammbock *m*.

battery ['bætərɪ] *n* Batterie *f*; *(fig: of arguments etc)* Reihe *f*.

battery: **~-charger** *n* Ladesatz *m*; **~ farming** *n* (Hühner- *etc*) batterien *pl*; **~ hen** *n (Agr)* Batteriehenne *f*.

battle ['bætl] **1** *n (lit)* Schlacht *f*; *(fig)* Kampf *m*. **to give ~** sich zum Kampf stellen; **to fight a ~** eine Schlacht schlagen; **killed in ~** (im Kampf) gefallen; **~ of words/wits** Wortgefecht *nt*/geistiger Wettstreit; **that's half the ~** damit ist schon viel gewonnen. **2** *vi* kämpfen *(for* um*)*.

battle: **~-axe, ~-ax** *(US) (col: woman)* Drachen *m (col)*; **~field, ~ground** *n* Schlachtfeld *nt*.

battlements ['bætlmənts] *npl* Zinnen *pl*.

battleship ['bætl,ʃɪp] *n* Schlachtschiff *nt*.

batty ['bætɪ] *adj (+er) (col)* verrückt.

bauble ['bɔːbl] *n* Flitter *m no pl*. **~s** Flitterzeug *nt*.

baulk [bɔːk] *vi* = **balk.**

bauxite ['bɔːksaɪt] *n* Bauxit *m*.

Bavaria [bə'vɛərɪə] *n* Bayern *nt*.

Bavarian [bə'vɛərɪən] **1** *n* **(a)** *(person)* Bayer(in *f*) *m*. **(b)** *(dialect)* Bayrisch *nt*. **2** *adj* bay(e)risch.

bawdy ['bɔːdɪ] *adj (+er)* derb.

bawl [bɔːl] *vi* **(a)** *(shout)* brüllen, schreien; *(sing)* grölen *(col)*. **(b)** *(col: weep)* heulen *(col)*.

♦ **bawl out** *vt sep* **(a)** *order* brüllen; *song* grölen *(pej col)*. **(b)** *(col: scold)* ausschimpfen.

bay[1] [beɪ] *n* Bucht *f*; *(of sea also)* Bai *f*.

bay[2] *n* **(a)** *(Archit)* Erker *m*. **(b)** *(loading ~)* Ladeplatz *m*.

bay[3] **1** *n (of dogs)* Bellen *nt no pl*; *(Hunt)* Melden *nt no pl*. **to keep** *or* **hold sb/sth at ~** jdn/etw in Schach halten. **2** *vi* bellen; *(Hunt also)* melden.

bay[4] *adj horse* (kastanien)braun.

bayleaf ['beɪliːf] *n* Lorbeerblatt *nt*.

bayonet ['beɪənɪt] **1** *n* Bajonett, Seitengewehr *nt*. **2** *vt* mit dem Bajonett aufspießen.

bay window *n* Erkerfenster *nt*.

bazaar [bə'zɑːʳ] *n* Basar *m*.

BBC = **British Broadcasting Corporation** BBC *f*.

BC = **before Christ** v. Chr.

be [biː] *pres* **am, is, are,** *pret* **was, were,** *ptp* **been 1 (a)** *(with adj, n)* sein. **he is a soldier/a German** er ist Soldat/Deutscher; **who is that? — it's me/that's Mary** wer ist das? — ich bin's/das ist Mary; **if I were you** wenn ich Sie wäre; **~ sensible!** sei vernünftig! **(b) how are you?** wie geht's?; **I'm better now** es geht mir jetzt besser; **to ~ hungry/thirsty** Hunger/Durst haben; **I am hot/cold** mir ist heiß/kalt. **(c)** *(age)* sein. **he'll ~ three** er wird drei (Jahre alt). **(d)** *(cost)* kosten. **how much is that?** wieviel *or* was kostet das?; *(altogether)* wieviel macht das? **(e)** *(Math)* sein. **two times two is** *or* **are four** zwei mal zwei ist *or* sind vier. **(f)** *(with poss)* gehören *(+dat)*. **that book is your brother's** das Buch gehört Ihrem Bruder. **(g)** *(in exclamations)* **was he pleased to hear it!** er war vielleicht froh, das zu hören!

2 *aux* **(a)** *(+prp: continuous tenses)* **what are you doing?** was machst du da?; **she is always complaining** sie beklagt sich dauernd; **they're coming tomorrow** sie kommen morgen; **will you ~ seeing her tomorrow?** treffen Sie sie morgen?; **I'll ~ starting soon** ich fange gleich an; **I have been waiting for you for half an hour** ich warte schon seit einer halben Stunde auf Sie.

(b) *(+ptp: passive)* werden. **the box had been opened** die Schachtel war geöffnet worden; **the car is to ~ sold** das Auto soll verkauft werden.

(c) he is to ~ pitied/not to ~ envied er ist zu bedauern/nicht zu beneiden; **not to ~ confused with** nicht zu verwechseln mit.

(d) *(intention, obligation, command)* sollen. **I am to look after my mother** ich soll mich um meine Mutter kümmern; **he is not to open it** er soll es nicht öffnen.

(e) *(~ destined)* sollen. **she was never to return** sie sollte nie zurückkehren.

(f) *(suppositions, wishes)* **if it were** *or* **was to snow** falls *or* wenn es schneien sollte; **I would ~ surprised if ...** ich wäre überrascht, wenn ...

(g) *(in tag questions, short answers)* **he's always late, isn't he? — yes he is** er kommt doch immer zu spät, nicht? — ja, das stimmt; **he's never late, is he? — yes he is** er kommt nie zu spät, oder? — o, doch.

3 *vi* **(a)** sein; *(remain)* bleiben. **to ~ or not to ~** Sein oder Nichtsein; **the powers that ~** die zuständigen Stellen; **let me/him ~** laß mich/ihn (in Ruhe); **~ that as it may** wie dem auch sei. **(b)** *(be situated)* sein; *(town, country, carpet etc also)* liegen; *(car, bottle, chair also)* stehen. **(c)** *(visit, call)* **I've been to Paris** ich war schon (ein)mal in Paris; **the postman has already been** der Briefträger war schon da. **(d) now you've been and done it** *(col)* jetzt hast du aber was angerichtet! *(col)*.

4 *vb impers* **(a)** sein. **it is dark/morning** es ist dunkel/Morgen; **it's 5 km to the nearest town** es sind 5 km bis zur nächsten Stadt. **(b)** *(emphatic)* **it was us** *or* **we** *(form)* **who found it** *wir* haben das gefunden. **(c)** *(wishes etc)* **were it not for him, if it weren't** *or* **wasn't for him** wenn er nicht wäre.

beach [biːtʃ] *n* Strand *m*. **on the ~** am Strand.

beach: **~ball** *n* Wasserball *m*; **~ buggy** *n* Strandbuggy *m*; **~comber** *n* Strandgutsammler *m*; **~wear** *n* Badesachen *pl*.

beacon ['biːkən] *n (fire, light)* Leuchtfeuer *nt*; *(radio ~)* Funkfeuer *nt*; *(one of a series of lights, radio ~s)* Bake *f*.

bead [biːd] *n (also sweat)* Perle *f*. **(string of) ~s** Perlenschnur *f*; *(necklace)* Perlenkette *f*.

beady ['biːdɪ] *adj* **I've got my ~ eye on you** *(col)* ich beobachte Sie genau!

beak [biːk] *n* Schnabel *m*.

beaker ['biːkəʳ] *n* Becher *m*; *(Chem etc)* Becherglas *nt*.

beam [biːm] **1** *n* **(a)** *(Build)* Balken *m*. **(b) to be broad in the ~** *(ship)* sehr breit sein; *(person)* breit gebaut sein. **(c)** *(of light etc)* Strahl *m*. **on main ~** mit Fernlicht. **(d)** *(radio ~)* Leitstrahl *m*. **(e)** *(smile)* Strahlen *nt*. **2** *vi* strahlen. **to ~ down** *(sun)* niederstrahlen; **her face was ~ing with joy** sie strahlte übers ganze Gesicht; **to ~ at sb** jdn anstrahlen. **3** *vt (Rad, TV)* ausstrahlen.

bean [biːn] *n* Bohne *f*. **to be full of ~s** *(col)* putzmunter sein *(col)*.

bean: **~pole** *n (lit, fig)* Bohnenstange *f*; **~sprout** *n* Sojabohnensprosse *f*.

bear[1] [bɛəʳ] *n* **(a)** Bär *m*; *(fig: person)* Brummbär *m (col)*. **(b)** *(Astron)* **the Great/Little B~** der Große/Kleine Bär.

bear[2] *pret* **bore,** *ptp* **borne 1** *vt* **(a)** *burden, weight, responsibility, fruit* tragen; *gift, message* bei sich tragen. **he was borne along by the crowd** die Menge trug ihn mit (sich). **(b)** *inscription, signature, name, title* tragen; *mark, traces also, likeness, relation* aufweisen. **(c)** *(have in heart or mind) love, hatred, grudge* empfinden. **(d)** *(endure, tolerate)* ertragen; *criticism, noise etc also* vertragen. **could you ~ to stay a little longer?** können Sie es noch ein bißchen länger hier aushalten?; **it doesn't ~ thinking about** man darf gar nicht daran denken. **(e)** *(give birth to)* gebären; *see* **born.**

2 *vi* **(a)** *(move)* **to ~ right/left/north** sich rechts/links/nach Norden halten. **(b)** *(fruit-tree etc)* tragen. **(c) to bring one's mind to ~ on sth** seinen Verstand *or* Geist für etw anstrengen; **to bring pressure to ~ on sb/sth** Druck auf jdn/etw ausüben.

3 *vr* sich halten. **he bore himself with dignity** er hat Würde gezeigt.

♦ **bear down** *vi* **to ~ ~ on sb/sth** *(driver etc)* auf jdn/etw zuhalten.

♦ **bear out** *vt sep* bestätigen.

♦ **bear up** *vi* sich halten. **he bore ~ well under the death of his father** er trug den Tod seines Vaters mit Fassung; **how are you? — ~ing ~!** wie geht's? — man lebt!

♦ **bear with** *vi +prep obj* tolerieren. **if you would ~ ~ me for a couple of minutes** wenn Sie sich vielleicht noch zwei Minuten gedulden wollen.

bearable ['bɛərəbl] *adj* erträglich.

beard [bɪəd] **1** *n* Bart *m*; *(full-face)* Vollbart *m*. **2** *vt* **to ~ the lion in his den** *(fig)* sich in die Höhle des Löwen wagen.

bearded ['bɪədɪd] *adj man, animal* bärtig.

bearer ['bɛərə[r]] *n (carrier)* Träger(in *f*) *m*; *(of news, banknote)* Überbringer *m*; *(of passport)* Inhaber(in *f*) *m*.

bearing ['bɛərɪŋ] *n* **(a)** *(posture)* Haltung *f*; *(behaviour)* Verhalten *nt*. **(b)** *(relevance)* **to have some/no ~ on sth** von Belang/belanglos für etw sein; *(be/not be connected with)* einen gewissen/keinen Bezug zu etw haben. **(c)** *(direction)* **to take a compass ~** den Kompaßkurs feststellen; **to lose one's ~s** die Orientierung verlieren; **to get one's ~s** sich orientieren. **(d)** *(Tech)* Lager *nt*.

beast [bi:st] *n* **(a)** Tier *nt*. **(b)** *(col: person)* Biest, Ekel *nt*. **it's a ~ (of a problem)** das (Problem) hat's in sich *(col)*.

beastly ['bi:stlɪ] *adj (col)* scheußlich *(col)*; *person, conduct also* gemein.

beat [bi:t] *(vb: pret ~, ptp ~en)* **1** *n* **(a)** *(of heart etc) (single ~)* Schlag *m*; *(repeated beating)* Schlagen *nt*. **(b)** *(of policeman, sentry)* Runde *f*, Rundgang *m*; *(district)* Revier *nt*. **to be on one's ~** seine Runde machen. **(c)** *(Mus, Poet)* Takt *m*; *(of metronome, baton)* Taktschlag *m*.

2 *vt* **(a)** *(hit)* schlagen; *person* (ver)prügeln; *carpet* klopfen. **~ it!** *(fig col)* hau ab! *(col)*, verschwinde! **(b)** *(hammer) metal* hämmern. **(c)** *(defeat)* schlagen; *record* brechen. **to ~ sb at chess/tennis** jdn im Schach/Tennis schlagen; **coffee ~s tea any day** Kaffee ist allemal besser als Tee; **that ~s everything** das ist doch wirklich der Gipfel *(col)*; *(is very good)* darüber geht nichts; **that ~s me** *(col)* das ist mir ein Rätsel *(col)*. **(d)** *(be before) budget, crowds* zuvorkommen *(+dat)*. **to ~ sb to it** jdm zuvorkommen. **(e) the bird ~s its wings** der Vogel schlägt mit den Flügeln. **(f)** *(Mus)* **to ~ time** den Takt schlagen. **(g)** *cream, eggs* schlagen.

3 *vi* **(a)** *(heart etc)* schlagen. **to ~ on the door (with one's fists)** (mit den Fäusten) gegen die Tür hämmern; **with ~ing heart** mit pochendem *or* klopfendem Herzen. **(b)** *(wind, waves)* schlagen; *(rain also)* trommeln; *(sun)* brennen.

4 *adj* **(a)** *(col: exhausted)* **to be (dead) ~** total geschafft *or* erledigt sein *(col)*. **(b)** *(col: defeated)* **to be ~(en)** aufgeben müssen *(col)*, sich geschlagen geben müssen; **this problem's got me ~** mit dem Problem komme ich nicht klar *(col)*.

♦ **beat back** *vt sep flames, enemy* zurückschlagen.

♦ **beat down** **1** *vi (rain)* herunterprasseln; *(sun)* herunterbrennen. **2** *vt sep* **(a)** *prices* herunterhandeln; *opposition* kleinkriegen *(col)*. **I managed to ~ him ~** ich konnte den Preis herunterhandeln. **(b)** *(flatten) door* einrennen.

♦ **beat off** *vt sep attack, attacker* abwehren.

♦ **beat out** *vt sep fire* ausschlagen; *dent* aushämmern; *rhythm* schlagen; *(on drum)* trommeln.

♦ **beat up** *vt sep* **(a)** *person* zusammenschlagen. **(b)** *(Cook) eggs, cream* schlagen.

beaten ['bi:tn] **1** *ptp of* **beat. 2** *adj* **(a)** *metal* gehämmert. **(b) to be off the ~ track** abgelegen sein.

beater ['bi:tə[r]] *n (carpet ~)* Klopfer *m*; *(egg ~)* Schneebesen *m*.

beating ['bi:tɪŋ] *n* **(a)** *(series of blows)* Schläge, Prügel *pl*. **to give sb a ~** jdn verprügeln; **to get a ~** verprügelt werden; *(as punishment also)* Prügel bekommen. **(b)** *(of drums, heart, wings)* Schlagen *nt*. **(c)** *(defeat)* Niederlage *f*. **to take a ~** eine Schlappe einstecken *(col)*. **(d) to take some ~** seines-/ihresgleichen suchen.

beat-up ['bi:tʌp] *adj (col)* ramponiert *(col)*.

beautiful ['bju:tɪfʊl] *adj* schön; *weather also, idea, meal* herrlich; *piece of work* hervorragend.

beautifully ['bju:tɪfəlɪ] *adv* schön; *warm, simple* herrlich; *(well) sew, sing* hervorragend.

beautify ['bju:tɪfaɪ] *vt* verschönern.

beauty ['bju:tɪ] *n* **(a)** Schönheit *f*. **~ is only skin-deep** *(prov)* der äußere Schein kann trügen; **~ is in the eye of the beholder** *(Prov)* schön ist, was gefällt; **the ~ of it is that ...** das Schöne daran ist, daß ... **(b)** *(beautiful person)* Schönheit *f*. **(c)** *(good example)* Prachtexemplar *nt*.

beauty *in cpds* Schönheits-; **~ contest** *n* Schönheitswettbewerb *m*; **~ queen** *n* Schönheitskönigin *f*; **~ spot** *n* **(a)** Schönheitsfleck *m*; **(b)** *(place)* schönes *or* hübsches Fleckchen (Erde).

beaver ['bi:və[r]] *n* Biber *m*. **to work like a ~** wie ein Wilder/eine Wilde arbeiten.

becalm [bɪ'kɑ:m] *vt (Naut)* **to be ~ed** in eine Flaute geraten.

became [bɪ'keɪm] *pret of* **become.**

because [bɪ'kɒz] **1** *conj* weil. **it was the more surprising ~ we were not expecting it** es war um so überraschender, als wir es nicht erwartet hatten. **2** *prep* **~ of** wegen *(+gen or (col) dat)*; **I only did it ~ of you** ich habe es nur deinetwegen getan.

beckon ['bekən] *vti* winken. **he ~ed me in/back/over** er winkte mich herein/zurück/herüber.

become [bɪ'kʌm] *pret* **became,** *ptp* **~ 1** *vi* werden. **to ~ old/fat/tired** alt/dick/müde werden; **to ~ accustomed to sb/sth** sich an jdn/etw gewöhnen; **to ~ interested in sb/sth** anfangen, sich für jdn/etw zu interessieren; **to ~ king/a doctor** König/Arzt werden; **what has ~ of him?** was ist aus ihm geworden? **2** *vt (suit)* stehen *(+dat)*; *(befit)* sich schicken für.

becoming [bɪ'kʌmɪŋ] *adj (fitting)* schicklich; *(flattering)* vorteilhaft. **that dress/colour is very ~** das Kleid/die Farbe steht ihr/dir *etc* sehr gut.

bed [bed] **1** *n* **(a)** Bett *nt*. **to go to ~** zu *or* ins Bett gehen; **to go to ~ with sb** mit jdm ins Bett gehen; **to put sb to ~** jdn ins Bett bringen; **he must have got out of ~ on the wrong side** *(col)* er ist wohl mit dem linken Fuß zuerst aufgestanden; **to be in ~** im Bett sein; **his life is not exactly a ~ of roses** er ist nicht gerade auf Rosen gebettet; **can I have a ~ for the night?** kann ich hier/bei euch *etc* übernachten? **(b)** *(sea ~)* Grund, Boden *m*; *(river ~)* Bett *nt*. **(c)** *(oyster ~, coral ~)* Bank *f*. **(d)** *(flower ~)* Beet *nt*. **2** *vt plant* setzen, pflanzen.

♦ **bed down** *vi* sein Lager aufschlagen.

bed and breakfast *n* Übernachtung *f* mit Frühstück. **"~"** „Fremdenzimmer".

bed *in cpds* Bett-; **~-bath** *n* (Kranken)wäsche *f* im Bett; **to give sb a ~-bath** jdn im Bett waschen; **~-bug** *n* Wanze *f*; **~-clothes** *npl* Bettzeug *nt*; **~cover** *n* Bettdecke *f*.

bedding ['bedɪŋ] *n* Bettzeug *nt*; *(for horses)* Streu *f*.

bedevil [bɪ'devl] *vt* erschweren. **~led by misfortune/bad luck** vom Schicksal/Pech verfolgt.

bedfellow ['bed,feləʊ] *n* **to be** *or* **make strange ~s** *(fig)* ein merkwürdiges Gespann sein.

bedlam ['bedləm] *n* Chaos *nt*. **it was sheer ~ in the class** in der Klasse ging es zu wie im Irrenhaus.

bed: ~-linen *n* Bettwäsche *f*; **~-pan** *n* Bettpfanne *f*; **~post** *n* Bettpfosten *m*.

bedraggled [bɪ'drægld] *adj (wet)* trief- *or* tropfnaß; *(dirty)* verdreckt; *(untidy) person, appearance* ungepflegt.

bed-ridden ['bedrɪdn] *adj* bettlägerig.
bedroom ['bedru:m] *n* Schlafzimmer *nt*.
bedroom *in cpds* Schlafzimmer-; ~ **slipper** *n* Hausschuh *m*.
bedside ['bedsaɪd] *n* **to be/sit at sb's** ~ an jds Bett *(dat)* sein/sitzen.
bedside: ~ **lamp** *n* Nachttischlampe *f*; ~ **manner** *n* **he has a good/bad** ~ **manner** er kann gut/nicht gut mit den Kranken umgehen; ~ **rug** *n* Bettvorleger *m*; ~ **table** *n* Nachttisch *m*.
bed: ~**-sit(ter)** *(col)*, ~**-sitting room** *n (Brit)* möbliertes Zimmer; ~**spread** *n* Tagesdecke *f*; ~**time** *n* **it's** ~**time** es ist Schlafenszeit; **his** ~**time is 10 o'clock** er geht um 10 Uhr schlafen; **it's past your** ~**time** du müßtest schon lange im Bett sein; ~**time story** *n* Gutenachtgeschichte *f*; ~**-wetting** *n* Bettnässen *nt*.
bee [bi:] *n* Biene *f*. **he's got a** ~ **in his bonnet about cleanliness** er hat einen Sauberkeitstick *(col)*.
beech [bi:tʃ] *n (tree, wood)* Buche *f*.
beef [bi:f] **1** *n* **(a)** *(meat)* Rindfleisch *nt*. **roast** ~ Roastbeef *nt*. **(b)** *(col) (flesh)* Speck *m (col)*; *(muscles)* Muskeln *pl*. **2** *vi (col: complain)* meckern *(col) (about* über *+acc)*.
beef: ~**burger** *n* Hamburger *m*; ~**eater** *n* **(a)** Beefeater *m*; **(b)** *(US col)* Engländer(in *f*) *m*; ~**steak** *n* Beefsteak *nt*.
beefy ['bi:fɪ] *adj (+er)* fleischig.
bee: ~**hive** *n* **(a)** Bienenstock *m*; *(dome-shaped)* Bienenkorb *m*; **(b)** *(hairstyle)* toupierte Hochfrisur; ~**keeper** *n* Bienenzüchter(in *f*), Imker(in *f*) *m*; ~**-line** *n* **to make a** ~**-line for sb/sth** schnurstracks auf jdn/etw zugehen.
been [bi:n] *ptp of* **be.**
beer [bɪəʳ] *n* Bier *nt*. **two** ~**s, please** zwei Bier, bitte.
beer *in cpds* Bier-; ~**-bottle** *n* Bierflasche *f*; ~ **can** *n* Bierdose *f*; ~ **glass** *n* Bierglas *nt*; ~**mat** *n* Bierdeckel *m*.
beeswax ['bi:zwæks] *n* Bienenwachs *nt*.
beet [bi:t] *n* Rübe *f*.
beetle ['bi:tl] *n* Käfer *m*.
beetle-browed ['bi:tl,braʊd] *adj* mit buschigen Augenbrauen.
beetroot ['bi:t,ru:t] *n (Brit)* rote Bete *or* Rübe.
befall [bɪ'fɔ:l] *pret* **befell** [bɪ'fel], *ptp* **befallen** [bɪ'fɔ:lən] *vt* widerfahren *(+dat) (geh)*.
befitting [bɪ'fɪtɪŋ] *adj* geziemend *(dated)*. ~ **for a lady** für eine Dame schicklich.
before [bɪ'fɔ:ʳ] **1** *prep* **(a)** *(earlier than)* vor *(+dat)*. **the day** ~ **yesterday** vorgestern; ~ **Christ** *(abbr* **BC***)* vor Christi Geburt *(abbr* v. Chr.*)*; ~ **now** früher; ~ **long** bald. **(b)** *(in place, rank, in the presence of)* vor *(+dat)*. ~ **my (very) eyes** vor meinen Augen; **the question** ~ **us** die uns vorliegende Frage; **ladies** ~ **gentlemen** Damen haben den Vortritt; **to appear** ~ **a court/judge** vor Gericht/einem Richter erscheinen. **(c)** *(rather than)* **he would die** ~ **betraying his country** er würde eher sterben als sein Land verraten.
2 *adv* **(a)** *(in time) (~ that)* davor; *(at an earlier time, ~ now)* vorher. **I have read** *etc* **this** ~ ich habe das schon einmal gelesen *etc*; **it has never happened** ~ das ist noch nie passiert; **two days** ~ zwei Tage davor *or* zuvor. **(b)** *(indicating order)* davor. **that chapter and the one** ~ dieses Kapitel und das davor.
3 *conj* **(a)** *(in time)* bevor. ~ **doing sth** bevor man etw tut; **it will be a long time** ~ **he comes back** es wird lange dauern, bis er zurückkommt. **(b)** *(rather than)* **he will die** ~ **he surrenders** eher will er sterben als sich geschlagen geben.
beforehand [bɪ'fɔ:hænd] *adv* im voraus. **you must tell me** ~ Sie müssen mir vorher Bescheid sagen.
befriend [bɪ'frend] *vt* sich annehmen *(+gen)*.
befuddled [bɪ'fʌdld] *adj (confused)* durcheinander *(pred)*.
beg [beg] **1** *vt* **(a)** *money, alms* betteln um. **(b)** *forgiveness, mercy* bitten um. **he** ~**ged to be allowed to ...** er bat darum, ... zu dürfen; **I** ~ **to differ** ich erlaube mir, anderer Meinung zu sein. **(c)** *(entreat) sb* anflehen. **(d) to** ~ **the question** an der eigentlichen Frage vorbeigehen. **2** *vi* **(a)** *(beggar)* betteln; *(dog)* Männchen machen. **(b)** *(for help, time etc)* bitten *(for* um*)*. **(c)** *(entreat)* **I** ~ **of you** ich bitte Sie. **(d) to go** ~**ging** *(col)* noch zu haben sein; *(to be unwanted)* keine Abnehmer finden.
began [bɪ'gæn] *pret of* **begin.**
beggar ['begəʳ] *n* **(a)** Bettler(in *f*) *m*. ~**s can't be choosers** *(prov)* wer arm dran ist, kann nicht wählerisch sein. **(b)** *(col)* Kerl *m (col)*. **poor** ~**!** armer Kerl! *(col)*; **a lucky** ~ ein Glückspilz *m*.
begin [bɪ'gɪn] *pret* **began,** *ptp* **begun 1** *vt* **(a)** beginnen, anfangen; *song also* anstimmen; *bottle* anbrechen; *book* anfangen; *rehearsals, work* anfangen mit; *task* in Angriff nehmen. **to** ~ **to do sth** *or* **doing sth** anfangen *or* beginnen, etw zu tun; **that doesn't even** ~ **to compare with ...** das läßt sich nicht mal annähernd mit ... vergleichen; **I can't** ~ **to thank you for what you've done** ich kann Ihnen gar nicht genug dafür danken, was Sie getan haben. **(b)** *(initiate)* anfangen; *fashion, custom, policy* einführen; *society, firm, movement* gründen; *(cause) war* auslösen.
2 *vi* anfangen, beginnen; *(new play etc)* anlaufen; *(custom)* entstehen; *(river)* entspringen. **to** ~ **by doing sth** etw zuerst (einmal) tun; **he began by saying that ...** er sagte einleitend, daß ...; ~**ning from Monday** ab Montag, von Montag an; **to** ~ **with there were only three** anfänglich waren es nur drei; **to** ~ **with, this is wrong, and ...** erstens einmal ist das falsch, dann ...; **to** ~ **on sth** mit etw anfangen *or* beginnen; **since the world began** seit (An)beginn *or* Anfang der Welt.
beginner [bɪ'gɪnəʳ] *n* Anfänger(in *f*) *m*. ~**'s luck** Anfängerglück *nt*.
beginning [bɪ'gɪnɪŋ] *n* Anfang *m*. *(temporal also)* Beginn *m*; *(of custom, movement)* Entstehen *nt no pl*; *(of river)* Ursprung *m*. **at the** ~ **of sth** am Anfang *or (temporal also)* zu Beginn einer Sache *(gen)*; **the** ~ **of time/the world** der Anbeginn der Welt; **in the** ~ *(Bibl)* am Anfang; **from the** ~ von Anfang an; **from** ~ **to end** von vorn bis hinten; *(temporal)* von Anfang bis Ende; **to begin at the** ~ ganz vorn anfangen; **Nazism had its** ~**s in Germany** der Nazizismus hatte seine Anfänge in Deutschland.
begonia [bɪ'gəʊnɪə] *n* Begonie *f*.
begrudge [bɪ'grʌdʒ] *vt* **(a)** *(be reluctant)* **to** ~ **doing sth** etw widerwillig tun. **(b)** *(envy)* mißgönnen *(sb sth* jdm etw*)*. **no one** ~**s you your good fortune** wir gönnen dir ja dein Glück. **(c)** *(give unwillingly)* nicht gönnen *(sb sth* jdm etw*)*. **I shan't** ~ **you £5** du sollst die £ 5 haben.
beguile [bɪ'gaɪl] *vt (deceive)* betören *(geh)*.
begun [bɪ'gʌn] *ptp of* **begin.**
behalf [bɪ'ha:f] *n* **on** *or (US also)* **in** ~ **of** *(as spokesman)* im Namen von; *(as authorized representative)* im Auftrag von.
behave [bɪ'heɪv] **1** *vi* sich verhalten; *(people also)* sich benehmen. **to** ~ **well towards sb** jdn gut behandeln; ~! benimm dich!; **the car** ~**s well at high speeds** das Auto zeigt bei hoher Geschwindigkeit ein gutes Fahrverhalten. **2** *vr* **to** ~ **oneself** sich benehmen; ~ **yourself!** benimm dich!
behaviour, *(US)* **behavior** [bɪ'heɪvjəʳ] *n* **(a)** *(manner, bearing)* Benehmen *nt*; *(esp of children also)* Betragen *nt*. **to be on one's best** ~ sich von seiner besten Seite zeigen. **(b)** *(towards others, of car)* Verhalten *nt (to(wards)* gegenüber*)*.
behaviourism, *(US)* **behaviorism** [bɪ'heɪvjərɪzəm] *n* Behaviorismus *m*.

behead [bɪ'hed] *vt* enthaupten, köpfen.
beheld [bɪ'held] *prep, ptp of* **behold.**
behest [bɪ'hest] *n (liter)* Geheiß *nt (liter)*. **at his ~** auf sein Geheiß *nt (liter)*.
behind [bɪ'haɪnd] **1** *prep* **(a)** *(stationary)* hinter *(+dat)*; *(with motion)* hinter *(+acc)*. **come out from ~ the door** komm hinter der Tür (her)vor; **he came up ~ me** er trat von hinten an mich heran; **he has the Communists ~ him** er hat die Kommunisten hinter sich *(dat)*; **to be ~ an idea** eine Idee unterstützen; **what is ~ this?** was steckt dahinter? **(b)** *(more backward than)* **to be ~ sb** hinter jdm zurücksein. **(c)** *(in time)* **to be ~ time** *(train etc)* Verspätung haben; *(with work etc)* im Rückstand sein; **to be ~ schedule** im Verzug sein; **to be ~ the times** *(fig)* hinter seiner Zeit zurück(geblieben) sein. **2** *adv* **(a)** *(in or at rear)* hinten; *(~ this, sb etc)* dahinter. **from ~** von hinten; **to look ~** zurückblicken. **(b)** *(late)* **to be ~ with one's studies/payments** mit seinen Studien/Zahlungen im Rückstand sein. **3** *n (col)* Hintern *m (col)*.
behold [bɪ'həʊld] *pret, ptp* **beheld** *vt (liter)* sehen, erblicken *(liter)*. **~!** und siehe (da); *(Rel)* siehe.
beige [beɪʒ] **1** *adj* beige. **2** *n* Beige *nt*.
being ['biːɪŋ] *n* **(a)** *(existence)* Dasein, Leben *nt*. **to come into ~** entstehen; *(club etc also)* ins Leben gerufen werden; **to bring into ~** ins Leben rufen. **(b)** *(that which exists)* Geschöpf *nt*.
belabour, *(US)* **belabor** [bɪ'leɪbə[r]] *vt* einschlagen auf *(+acc)*; *(with insults etc)* überhäufen.
belated [bɪ'leɪtɪd] *adj* verspätet.
belch [beltʃ] **1** *vi (person)* rülpsen, aufstoßen; *(volcano)* Lava ausstoßen; *(smoke, fire)* herausquellen. **2** *vt (also ~* **forth** *or* **out**) *smoke, flames* ausstoßen. **3** *n* Rülpser *m (col)*.
beleaguer [bɪ'liːgə[r]] *vt* belagern; *(fig)* umgeben.
belfry ['belfrɪ] *n* Glockenstube *f*.
Belgian ['beldʒən] **1** *n* Belgier(in *f*) *m*. **2** *adj* belgisch.
Belgium ['beldʒəm] *n* Belgien *nt*.
belie [bɪ'laɪ] *vt* **(a)** *(prove false) words, proverb* Lügen strafen, widerlegen. **(b)** *(give false impression of)* hinwegtäuschen über *(+acc)*.
belief [bɪ'liːf] *n* **(a)** Glaube *m (in* an *+acc)*. **it is beyond ~** es ist nicht zu glauben; **in the ~ that ...** im Glauben, daß ...; **it is my ~ that ...** ich bin der Überzeugung, daß ...; **strong ~s** feste Überzeugungen.
believe [bɪ'liːv] **1** *vt* **(a)** *sth* glauben; *sb* glauben *(+dat)*. **I don't ~ you** das glaube ich (Ihnen) nicht; **don't you ~ it** wer's glaubt, wird selig *(col)*; **I would never have ~d it of him** das hätte ich nie von ihm geglaubt; **he could hardly ~ his eyes/ears** er traute seinen Augen/Ohren nicht. **(b)** *(think)* glauben. **I ~ so/not** ich glaube schon/ nicht. **2** *vi (have a religious faith)* an Gott glauben.
♦ **believe in** *vi +prep obj* glauben an *(+acc)*. **he doesn't ~ ~ medicine/doctors** er hält nicht viel von Medikamenten/Ärzten.
believer [bɪ'liːvə[r]] *n* **(a)** *(Rel)* Gläubige(r) *mf*. **(b) to be a (firm) ~ in sth** (grundsätzlich) für etw sein.
belittle [bɪ'lɪtl] *vt* herabsetzen.
bell [bel] **1** *n* **(a)** Glocke *f*; *(small: on toys etc)* Glöckchen *nt*, Schelle *f*; *(school ~, door~, of cycle)* Klingel *f*; *(Boxing)* Gong *m*. **(b)** *(sound of ~)* Läuten *nt*; *(of door~, telephone etc)* Klingeln *nt*. **was that the ~?** hat es gerade geklingelt *or* geläutet?
bell: ~-bottomed trousers, ~-bottoms *npl* ausgestellte Hosen; **~-boy** *n (US)* Page, Hoteljunge *m*.
belle [bel] *n* Schöne, Schönheit *f*. **the ~ of the ball** die Ballkönigin.
bellhop ['bel,hɒp] *n (US)* = **bell-boy.**
bellicose ['belɪkəʊs] *adj nation, mood* kriegerisch.
belligerent [bɪ'lɪdʒərənt] **1** *adj* **(a)** *nation* kriegerisch; *person, attitude* streitlustig; *speech* aggressiv. **(b)** *(waging war)* kriegführend. **2** *n (nation)* kriegführendes Land; *(person)* Streitende(r) *mf*.
bell-jar ['beldʒɑː[r]] *n* (Glas)glocke *f*.
bellow ['beləʊ] **1** *vi (animal, person)* brüllen; *(singing also)* grölen *(col)*. **2** *vt (also ~* **out**) brüllen; *song also* grölen *(col)*. **3** *n* Brüllen *nt*.
bellows ['beləʊz] *npl* Blasebalg *m*.
bell: ~push *n* Klingel *f*; **~-ringer** *n* Glöckner *m*; **~-shaped** *adj* glockenförmig, kelchförmig; **~tower** *n* Glockenturm *m*.
belly ['belɪ] *n* Bauch *m*.
belly: ~-ache 1 *n (col)* Bauchweh *nt (col)*, Bauchschmerzen *pl*; **2** *vi (col: complain)* murren *(about* über *+acc)*; **~ button** *n (col)* Bauchnabel *m*.
belong [bɪ'lɒŋ] *vi* **(a)** gehören *(to sb* jdm*)*. **who does it ~ to?** wem gehört es?; **the lid ~s to this box** der Deckel gehört zu dieser Schachtel; **to ~ to a club** einem Club angehören. **(b)** *(be in right place)* gehören. **to feel that one doesn't ~** das Gefühl haben, daß man nicht dazugehört; **where does this one ~?** wo gehört das hin?
belongings [bɪ'lɒŋɪŋz] *npl* Besitz *m*, Habe *f (geh)*. **personal ~** persönliches Eigentum, persönlicher Besitz; **all his ~** sein ganzes Hab und Gut.
beloved [bɪ'lʌvɪd] **1** *adj* geliebt; *memory* lieb, teuer. **2** *n* Geliebte(r) *mf*.
below [bɪ'ləʊ] **1** *prep* **(a)** *(under)* unterhalb *(+gen)*; *(with line, level etc also)* unter *(+dat or with motion +acc)*. **the sun disappeared ~ the horizon** die Sonne verschwand hinter dem Horizont; **to be ~ sb** *(in rank)* (rangmäßig) unter jdm stehen. **(b)** *(downstream from)* unterhalb *(+gen)*. **2** *adv* unten. **they live one floor ~** sie wohnen ein Stockwerk tiefer; **the flat ~** die Wohnung darunter; *(below us)* die Wohnung unter uns; **see ~** siehe unten; **15 degrees ~** 15 Grad unter Null, 15 Grad minus.
belt [belt] **1** *n* **(a)** *(on clothes)* Gürtel *m*; *(for holding etc, seat~)* Gurt *m*. **that was below the ~** das war ein Schlag unter die Gürtellinie; **to tighten one's ~** *(fig)* (sich *dat*) den Gürtel *or* Riemen enger schnallen *(col)*. **(b)** *(Tech)* (Treib)riemen *m*; *(conveyor ~)* Band *nt*. **(c)** *(tract of land)* Gürtel *m*. **industrial ~** Industriegürtel *m*. **(d)** *(col: hit)* Schlag *m*. **2** *vt (col: hit)* knallen *(col)*. **she ~ed him one in the eye** sie verpaßte ihm eins aufs Auge *(col)*. **3** *vi (col: rush)* rasen *(col)*. **to ~ out** hinaus-/herausrasen *(col)*; **we were really ~ing along** wir sind wirklich gerast *(col)*.
♦ **belt out** *vt sep (col) tune* schmettern *(col)*.
♦ **belt up 1** *vt sep jacket* den Gürtel *(+gen)* zumachen. **2** *vi* **(a)** *(col)* die Klappe *(col)* halten; *(stop making noise)* mit dem Krach aufhören *(col)*. **(b)** *(hum: put seatbelt on)* sich anschnallen.
bemoan [bɪ'məʊn] *vt* beklagen.
bemused [bɪ'mjuːzd] *adj (puzzled)* verwirrt.
bench [bentʃ] *n* **(a)** *(seat)* Bank *f*. **(b)** *(Jur: office of a judge)* Richteramt *nt*; *(judges generally)* Richter *pl*; *(court)* Gericht *nt*. **to be on the ~** *(permanent office)* Richter sein; *(when in court)* der Richter sein. **(c)** *(work ~)* Werkbank *f*; *(in lab)* Experimentiertisch *m*.
bend [bend] *(vb: pret, ptp* **bent***)* **1** *n (in river, tube etc)* Krümmung, Biegung *f*; *(in road also)* Kurve *f*. **to drive sb round the ~** *(col)* jdn verrückt *or* wahnsinnig machen *(col)*. **2** *vt* **(a)** biegen; *arm, knee also* beugen; *(forwards) back also, head* beugen. **on ~ed knees** auf Knien; *(fig also)* kniefällig. **(b)** *(fig) rules* frei auslegen. **3** *vi* **(a)** sich biegen; *(pipe, rail also)* sich krümmen; *(forwards also) (tree, corn etc)* sich neigen; *(person)* sich beugen. **this metal ~s easily** *(a bad thing)* dieses Metall verbiegt sich leicht; *(a good thing)* dieses Metall läßt sich leicht biegen. **(b)** *(river)* eine Biegung machen; *(road also)* eine Kurve machen. **(c)** *(fig: submit)* sich beugen, sich fügen *(to* dat*)*.

♦ **bend down** *vi (person)* sich bücken.
♦ **bend over 1** *vi (person)* sich bücken. **2** *vt sep* umbiegen.
bends [bendz] *n* **the ~** Taucherkrankheit *f.*
beneath [bɪ'ni:θ] **1** *prep* **(a)** unter *(+dat or with motion +acc); (with line, level etc also)* unterhalb *(+gen); see* **below 1 (a). (b)** *(unworthy of)* **it is ~ him** das ist unter seiner Würde. **2** *adv* unten; *see also* **below 2.**
benediction [,benɪ'dɪkʃən] *n* Segen *m; (act of blessing)* Segnung *f.*
benefactor ['benɪfæktəʳ] *n* Wohltäter *m; (giver of money also)* Gönner *m.*
beneficial [,benɪ'fɪʃəl] *adj* gut *(to* für*); climate also* zuträglich *(geh) (to* dat*); influence also* vorteilhaft; *advice* nützlich *(to* für*).*
beneficiary [,benɪ'fɪʃərɪ] *n* Nutznießer(in *f*) *m; (of will, insurance etc)* Begüngstigte(r) *mf.*
benefit ['benɪfɪt] **1** *n* **(a)** *(advantage)* Vorteil *m; (profit)* Gewinn *m.* **for the ~ of your health** Ihrer Gesundheit zuliebe; **it is for his ~ that this was done** das ist seinetwegen geschehen; **to give sb the ~ of the doubt** im Zweifel zu jds Gunsten entscheiden. **(b)** *(allowance)* Unterstützung *f; (sickness ~)* Krankengeld *nt; (social security ~)* Sozialhilfe *f.* **(c)** *(special performance)* Benefizveranstaltung *f.* **2** *vt* nützen *(+dat); (health-wise)* guttun *(+dat).* **3** *vi* profitieren *(from, by* von*); (from experience also)* Nutzen ziehen *(from* aus*).* **who will ~ from that?** wem wird das nützen?
Benelux ['benɪlʌks] *n* Beneluxländer *pl.*
benevolence [bɪ'nevələns] *n see adj* Wohlwollen *nt;* Gutmütigkeit *f;* Güte *f.*
benevolent [bɪ'nevələnt] *adj* wohlwollend; *smile* gutmütig; *(as character trait)* gütig.
benign [bɪ'naɪn] *adj* **(a)** gütig; *influence* günstig; *climate* mild. **(b)** *(Med)* gutartig.
bent [bent] **1** *pret, ptp of* **bend. 2** *adj* **(a)** *metal etc* gebogen; *(out of shape)* verbogen. **(b)** *(Brit col: dishonest) person* korrupt. **(c)** *(col: homosexual)* andersrum *pred (col).* **(d) to be ~ on sth/doing sth** etw unbedingt wollen/tun wollen. **3** *n (aptitude)* Neigung *f (for* zu*); (type of mind, character)* Schlag *m.*
bequeath [bɪ'kwi:ð] *vt* vermachen; *(fig also)* hinterlassen *(to sb* jdm*).*
bequest [bɪ'kwest] *n (legacy)* Nachlaß *m; (to museum)* Stiftung *f.*
berate [bɪ'reɪt] *vt (liter)* schelten.
bereaved [bɪ'ri:vd] *npl* **the ~** die Hinterbliebenen *pl.*
bereavement [bɪ'ri:vmənt] *n (death in family)* Trauerfall *m.* **to feel a sense of ~ at sth** etw als schmerzlichen Verlust empfinden.
bereft [bɪ'reft] *adj* **to be ~ of sth** einer Sache *(gen)* bar sein *(geh);* **~ of reason** ohne jede Vernunft.
beret ['bereɪ] *n* Baskenmütze *f.*
Berlin [bɜ:'lɪn] *n* Berlin *nt.* **the ~ wall** die Mauer.
Bermuda [bɜ:'mju:də] *n* Bermuda *nt.* **~ shorts** Bermudashorts *pl.*
berry ['berɪ] *n* Beere *f.* **as brown as a ~** ganz braungebrannt.
berserk [bə'sɜ:k] *adj* wild. **to go ~** wild werden; *(audience)* zu toben anfangen; *(go mad)* überschnappen *(col).*
berth [bɜ:θ] **1** *n* **(a)** *(on ship)* Koje *f; (on train)* Bett *nt.* **(b)** *(Naut: place for ship)* Liegeplatz *m.* **to give sb/sth a wide ~** *(fig)* einen (weiten) Bogen um jdn/etw machen. **2** *vi* anlegen.
beseech [bɪ'si:tʃ] *pret, ptp* **~ed** *or (liter)* **besought** *vt person* anflehen, beschwören.
beset [bɪ'set] *pret, ptp* **~** *vt (difficulties, dangers)* (von allen Seiten) bedrängen; *(doubts)* befallen; *(temptations, trials)* heimsuchen. **to be ~ with danger** *(journey etc)* voller Gefahren sein.
besetting [bɪ'setɪŋ] *adj* **his ~ sin** eine ständige Untugend von ihm.
beside [bɪ'saɪd] *prep* **(a)** neben *(+dat or with motion +acc); (at the edge of) road, river* an *(+dat or with motion +acc).* **~ the road** am Straßenrand. **(b)** *(compared with)* neben *(+dat).* **(c) to be ~ oneself** *(with anger)* außer sich sein *(with* vor*).*
besides [bɪ'saɪdz] **1** *adv* außerdem. **have you got any others ~?** haben Sie noch andere *or* noch welche? **2** *prep* außer *(+dat).* **others ~ ourselves** außer uns noch andere; **~ which he was unwell** außerdem fühlte er sich nicht wohl.
besiege [bɪ'si:dʒ] *vt (Mil, fig)* belagern; *(with offers)* überhäufen; *(pester)* bestürmen.
besotted [bɪ'sɒtɪd] *adj* völlig vernarrt *(with* in *+acc).*
besought [bɪ'sɔ:t] *(liter) pret, ptp of* **beseech.**
bespatter [bɪ'spætəʳ] *vt* bespritzen.
bespectacled [bɪ'spektɪkld] *adj* bebrillt.
bespoke [bɪ'spəʊk] **1** *prep, ptp of* **bespeak. 2** *adj garment* Maß-. **a ~ tailor** ein Maßschneider *m.*
best [best] **1** *adj, superl of* **good** beste(r,s) *attr; (most favourable) route, price also* günstigste(r, s) *attr.* **to be ~** am besten/günstigsten sein; **the ~ thing about her** das Beste an ihr; **may the ~ man win!** dem Besten der Sieg!; **the ~ part of the year** fast das ganze Jahr.
2 *adv, superl of* **well (a)** am besten; *like* am liebsten; *enjoy* am meisten. **the ~ known title** der bekannteste Titel; **~ of all** am allerbesten/-liebsten/-meisten; **I helped him as ~ I could** ich half ihm, so gut ich konnte; **do as you think ~** tun Sie, was Sie für richtig halten; **you know ~** Sie müssen es (am besten) wissen. **(b) you had ~ go now** am besten gehen Sie jetzt.
3 *n* **(a) the ~** der/die/das beste; **the ~ of the bunch** *(col)* der/die/das beste; **he can sing with the ~ of them** er kann sich im Singen mit den Besten messen; **to be in one's (Sunday) ~** im Sonntagsstaat sein. **(b) to do one's (level) ~** sein Bestes *or* möglichstes tun; **to make the ~ of it/a bad job** das Beste daraus machen; **the ~ of it is that ...** das beste daran ist, daß ...; **I meant it for the ~** ich habe es doch nur gut gemeint; **to the ~ of my ability** so gut ich kann/konnte; **to the ~ of my knowledge** meines Wissens; **to look one's ~** besonders gut aussehen; **he is at his ~ at about 8 in the evening** so gegen 8 Uhr abends ist seine beste Zeit; **at ~** bestenfalls; **all the ~** alles Gute!
bestial ['bestɪəl] *adj acts, cruelty* bestialisch; *person, appearance* brutal; *(carnal)* tierisch.
best man *n* Trauzeuge *m* (des Bräutigams).
bestow [bɪ'stəʊ] *vt (on or upon sb* jdm*) (grant, give)* schenken; *honour* erweisen; *title, medal* verleihen.
best-seller [,best'seləʳ] *n* Verkaufs- *or* Kassenschlager *m; (book)* Bestseller *m.*
bet [bet] *(vb: pret, ptp ~)* **1** *n* Wette *f (on* auf *+acc); (money etc staked)* Wetteinsatz *m.* **to have a ~ with sb** mit jdm wetten; **it's a safe ~ that ...** *(fig)* höchstwahrscheinlich ... **2** *vt* **(a)** wetten, setzen *(against* gegen, *on* auf *+acc).* **I ~ him £5** ich habe mit ihm (um) £ 5 gewettet. **(b)** *(col)* wetten. **you can ~ your boots** *or* **your bottom dollar that ...** Siekönnen Gift darauf nehmen, daß ... *(col).* **3** *vi* wetten. **to ~ on a horse** auf ein Pferd setzen; **you ~!** *(col)* und ob! *(col).*
betray [bɪ'treɪ] *vt* verraten *(also Pol) (to dat or (Pol)* an *+acc); trust* enttäuschen; *sb's secrets also* preisgeben. **his accent ~ed him as a foreigner** sein Akzent verriet, daß er Ausländer war.
betrayal [bɪ'treɪəl] *n* Verrat *m (of gen); (instance)* Verrat *m (of* an *+dat); (of trust)* Enttäuschung *f; (of friends also)* Untreue *f (of* gegenüber*); (of plans also)* Preisgabe *f.*
betrothal [bɪ'trəʊðəl] *n (liter, hum)* Verlobung *f.*
better 1 *adj, comp of* **good** besser; *route, way also* günstiger. **he's much ~** es geht ihm viel besser; **that's ~!** *(approval)* so ist es besser!; *(relief etc)* endlich!; **the ~ part of an hour** fast eine Stunde;

to go one ~ einen Schritt weiter gehen; *(in offer)* höher gehen.

2 *adv, comp of* **well (a)** besser; *like* lieber; *enjoy* mehr. **they are ~ off than we are** sie sind besser dran als wir; **all the ~, so much the ~** um so besser; **to think ~ of it** es sich *(dat)* noch einmal überlegen. **(b) I had ~ go** ich gehe jetzt wohl besser; **you'd ~ do what he says** tun Sie lieber, was er sagt.

3 *n* **(a) one's ~s** Leute, die über einem stehen; *(socially also)* Höhergestellte. **(b)** *(person, object)* **the ~** der/die/das Bessere. **(c) it's a change for the ~** es ist eine Wendung zum Guten; **it's done now, for ~ or worse** so oder so, es ist geschehen; **to get the ~ of sb** *(person)* jdn unterkriegen *(col)*; *(illness)* jdn erwischen *(col)*; *(problem etc)* jdm schwer zu schaffen machen.

4 *vt (improve on)* verbessern; *(surpass)* übertreffen.

5 *vr* **to ~ oneself** sich verbessern.

betting: ~ man *n* **I'm not a ~ man** ich wette eigentlich nicht; **~ shop** *n* Wettannahme *f*.

between [bɪ'twiːn] **1** *prep* **(a)** zwischen *(+dat)*; *(with movement)* zwischen *(+acc)*. **sit down ~ those two boys** setz dich zwischen diese beiden Jungen; **in ~** zwischen *(+dat/acc)*; **~ now and next week we must ...** bis nächste Woche müssen wir ...; **there's nothing ~ them** *(they're equal)* sie sind gleich gut; *(no feelings, relationship)* zwischen ihnen ist nichts. **(b)** *(amongst)* unter *(+dat/acc)*. **we shared an apple ~ us** wir teilten uns *(dat)* einen Apfel; **~ you and me he is not very clever** unter uns *(dat)* (gesagt), er ist nicht besonders gescheit; **that's just ~ ourselves** das bleibt aber unter uns; **we have a car ~ the two/three of us** wir haben zu zweit/dritt ein Auto. **2** *adv (place)* dazwischen; *(time also)* zwischendurch. **in ~** dazwischen; **the space/time ~** der Zwischenraum/die Zwischenzeit, der Raum/die Zeit dazwischen.

bevelled edge ['bevld'edʒ] Schrägkante *f*.

beverage ['bevərɪdʒ] *n* Getränk *nt*.

bevy ['bevɪ] *n (of girls)* Schar *f*.

bewail [bɪ'weɪl] *vt (deplore)* beklagen; *(lament also)* bejammern; *sb's death also* betrauern.

beware [bɪ'weəʳ] *vti imper and infin only* **to ~ (of) sb/sth** sich vor jdm/etw hüten, sich vor jdm/etw in acht nehmen; **~ of falling** passen Sie auf, daß Sie nicht fallen; **"~ of the dog"** „Vorsicht, bissiger Hund".

bewilder [bɪ'wɪldəʳ] *vt (confuse)* verwirren; *(baffle)* verblüffen.

bewildered [bɪ'wɪldəd] *adj* verwirrt; *(baffled)* verblüfft, perplex *(col)*.

bewildering [bɪ'wɪldərɪŋ] *adj see vt* verwirrend; verblüffend.

bewilderment [bɪ'wɪldəmənt] *n see vt* Verwirrung *f*; Verblüffung *f*. **in ~** verwundert.

bewitch [bɪ'wɪtʃ] *vt* verzaubern; *(fig)* bezaubern.

beyond [bɪ'jɒnd] **1** *prep* **(a)** *(on the other side of)* hinter *(+dat)*, jenseits *(+gen) (geh)*; *(further than)* über *(+acc)* ... hinaus, weiter als. **~ the Alps** jenseits der Alpen. **(b)** *(in time)* **~ 6 o'clock** nach 6 Uhr; **~ the middle of June/the week** über Mitte Juni/der Woche hinaus. **(c) a task ~ her abilities** eine Aufgabe, die über ihre Fähigkeiten geht; **that's almost ~ belief** das ist fast unglaublich *or* nicht zu glauben; **that's ~ me** *(I don't understand)* das geht über meinen Verstand. **2** *adv (on the other side of)* jenseits davon *(geh)*. **the world ~** das Jenseits.

bi- [baɪ] *pref* bi, Bi-.

biannual [baɪ'ænjuəl] *adj* halbjährlich.

bias ['baɪəs] *(vb: pret, ptp* **~(s)ed) 1** *n* **(a)** Voreingenommenheit *f*; *(of course, newspaper etc)* (einseitige) Ausrichtung *f (towards* auf *+acc)*; *(of person)* Vorliebe *f (towards* für*)*. **to have a ~ against sth** *(course, newspaper etc)* gegen etw eingestellt sein; *(person)* ein Vorurteil *nt* gegen etw haben; **to have a left-wing/right-wing ~** nach links/rechts ausgerichtet sein. **(b)** *(Sew)* **on the ~** schräg zum Fadenlauf. **2** *vt report, article etc* (einseitig) färben.

bias(s)ed ['baɪəst] *adj* voreingenommen.

bib [bɪb] *n* Latz *m*; *(for baby)* Lätzchen *nt*.

Bible ['baɪbl] *n* Bibel *f*.

biblical ['bɪblɪkəl] *adj* biblisch.

bibliography [ˌbɪblɪ'ɒgrəfɪ] *n* Bibliographie *f*.

bicarbonate of soda [baɪˌkɑːbənɪtəv'səʊdə] *n (Cook)* Natron *nt*; *(Chem)* doppelt kohlensaures Natrium.

bi-: ~centenary, *(US)* **~centennial** *n* Zweihundertjahrfeier *f (of gen)*.

biceps ['baɪseps] *n* Bizeps *m*.

bicker ['bɪkəʳ] *vi* sich zanken. **they are always ~ing** sie liegen sich dauernd in den Haaren.

bicycle ['baɪsɪkl] *n* Fahrrad *nt*. **to ride a ~** Fahrrad fahren, radfahren; *see* **cycle.**

bid [bɪd] **1** *vti* **(a)** *pret, ptp* **~** *(at auction)* bieten *(for* auf *+acc)*. **(b)** *pret, ptp* **~** *(Cards)* reizen, bieten. **(c)** *pret* **bade,** *ptp* **~den** *(say)* **to ~ sb good-morning** jdm einen guten Morgen wünschen; **to ~ farewell to sb** jdm Lebewohl sagen *(geh)*. **2** *vi pret* **bad,** *ptp* **~den everything ~s fair to be successful** es sieht alles recht erfolgversprechend aus. **3** *n* **(a)** *(at auction)* Gebot *nt (for* auf *+acc)*; *(Comm)* Angebot *nt (for* für*)*. **(b)** *(Cards)* Ansage *f*. **(c)** *(attempt)* Versuch *m*. **to make a ~ for power** nach der Macht greifen; **to make a ~ for freedom** versuchen, die Freiheit zu erlangen.

bidden ['bɪdn] *ptp of* **bid.**

bidder ['bɪdəʳ] *n* Bietende(r) *mf*. **to sell to the highest ~** an den Meistbietenden verkaufen.

bidding ['bɪdɪŋ] *n* **(a)** *(at auction)* Steigern, Bieten *nt*. **(b)** *(Cards)* Bieten, Reizen *nt*.

bide [baɪd] *vt* **to ~ one's time** den rechten Augenblick abwarten.

bidet ['biːdeɪ] *n* Bidet *nt*.

biennial [baɪ'enɪəl] **1** *adj (every two years)* zweijährlich. **2** *n (Bot)* zweijährige Pflanze.

bier [bɪəʳ] *n* Bahre *f*.

biff [bɪf] *n (col)* Stoß, Puff *(col) m*. **a ~ on the nose** eins auf die Nase *(col)*.

bifocal [baɪ'fəʊkəl] **1** *adj* Bifokal-. **2** *n* **~s** *pl* Bifokalbrille *f*.

big [bɪg] **1** *adj (+er)* groß. **a ~ man** ein großer, schwerer Mann; **my ~ brother** mein großer Bruder; **that's really ~ of you** *(iro)* wirklich nobel von dir *(iro)*; **he is too ~ for his boots** *(col)* der ist ja größenwahnsinnig; **to have a ~ head** *(col)* eingebildet sein; **to earn ~ money** das große Geld verdienen *(col)*; **to have ~ ideas** große Pläne haben; **to have a ~ mouth** *(col)* eine große Klappe haben *(col)*; **to do things in a ~ way** alles im großen (Stil) tun; **~ deal!** *(iro col)* na und? *(col)*; *(that's not much etc)* ist ja toll! *(iro col)*. **2** *adv* **to talk ~** große Töne spucken *(col)*; **to think ~** im großen (Maßstab) planen.

bigamist ['bɪgəmɪst] *n* Bigamist *m*.

bigamy ['bɪgəmɪ] *n* Bigamie *f*.

big: ~ business *n (high finance)* Großkapital *nt*; **~ dipper** *n (Brit: at fair)* Achterbahn *f*; **~ game** *n (Hunt)* Großwild *nt*; **~head** *n (col: person)* Angeber *m (col)*; **~-headed** *adj (col)* angeberisch *(col)*; **~ noise** *n (col)* hohes Tier *(col)*.

bigoted ['bɪgətɪd] *adj* engstirnig.

big: ~ shot *n* hohes Tier *(col)*; **~-time** *n (col)* **to make** *or* **hit the ~-time** groß einsteigen *(col)*; **~ toe** *n* große Zehe; **~ top** *n (circus)* Zirkus *m*; *(main tent)* Hauptzelt *nt*; **~ wheel** *n* **(a)** *(US col)* = **~ shot; (b)** *(Brit: at fair)* Riesenrad *nt*; **~wig** *n (col)* hohes Tier *(col)*.

bike [baɪk] *(col)* **1** *n* (Fahr)rad *nt*; *(motor ~)* Motorrad *nt*. **2** *vi* radeln *(col)*.

bikini [bɪ'kiːnɪ] *n* Bikini *m*.

bilateral [baɪ'lætərəl] *adj* bilateral.
bilberry ['bɪlbərɪ] *n* Heidelbeere *f.*
bile [baɪl] *n (Med)* Galle *f.*
bilingual [baɪ'lɪŋgwəl] *adj* zweisprachig.
bilious ['bɪlɪəs] *adj (Med)* Gallen-. ~ **attack** Gallenkolik *f.*
bill[1] [bɪl] **1** *n (of bird, turtle)* Schnabel *m.* **2** *vi* **to ~ and coo** *(birds)* schnäbeln und gurren.
bill[2] **1** *n* **(a)** *(statement of charges)* Rechnung *f.* **could we have the ~ please** zahlen bitte!, wir möchten bitte zahlen. **(b)** *(US: banknote)* Banknote *f,* Schein *m.* **(c)** *(poster)* Plakat *nt*; *(on notice board)* Anschlag *m*; *(public announcement)* Aushang *m*; **"stick no ~s"** „Plakate ankleben verboten". **(d)** *(Theat)* Programm *nt.* **to top the ~** Star *m* des Abends/der Saison sein; *(act)* die Hauptattraktion sein. **(e) ~ of fare** Speisekarte *f.* **(f)** *(Parl)* Gesetzentwurf *m.* **(g)** *(Comm)* **~ of lading** Frachtbrief *m*; **~ of exchange** Wechsel *m*; **~ of sale** Verkaufsurkunde *f*; **to fit** *or* **fill the ~** *(fig)* der/die/das richtige sein, passen.
2 *vt* **(a)** *customers* eine Rechnung ausstellen *(+dat).* **(b)** *play, actor* ankündigen. **he's ~ed at the Apollo** er tritt im Apollo auf.
billboard ['bɪlbɔːd] *n* Reklametafel *f.*
billet ['bɪlɪt] **1** *n (Mil)* Quartier *nt,* Unterkunft *f.* **2** *vt (Mil)* einquartieren *(on sb* bei jdm*).*
billfold ['bɪl,fəʊld] *n (US)* Brieftasche *f.*
billiards ['bɪljədz] *n* Billard *nt.*
billion ['bɪljən] *n* **(a)** *(Brit)* Billion *f.* **(b)** *(US)* Milliarde *f.*
billow ['bɪləʊ] **1** *n (of smoke)* Schwaden *m.* **2** *vi (sail)* sich blähen; *(dress etc)* sich bauschen.
billy(-goat) ['bɪlɪ(gəʊt)] *n* Ziegenbock *m.*
bin [bɪn] *n (esp Brit) (for bread)* Brotkasten *m*; *(rubbish~)* Mülleimer *m*; *(dust~)* Mülltonne *f*; *(litter-~)* Abfallbehälter *m.*
binary ['baɪnərɪ] *adj* binär.
bind [baɪnd] *pret, ptp* **bound 1** *vt* **(a)** *(make fast, tie together)* binden *(to* an *+acc)*; *person* fesseln; *(fig)* verbinden *(to* mit*).* **bound hand and foot** an Händen und Füßen gefesselt. **(b)** *wound, arm etc* verbinden; *bandage* wickeln. **(c)** *(secure edge of)* einfassen. **(d)** *book* binden. **(e)** *(oblige)* **to ~ sb to sth/to do sth** jdn zu etw verpflichten/jdn verpflichten, etw zu tun; *see* **bound**[3]. **2** *n (col: nuisance)* **to be (a bit of) a ~** recht lästig sein.
♦ **bind over** *vt sep (Jur)* **to ~ sb ~ (to keep the peace)** jdn verwarnen; **he was bound ~ for six months** er bekam eine sechsmonatige Bewährungsfrist.
♦ **bind together** *vt sep (lit)* zusammenbinden; *(fig)* verbinden.
♦ **bind up** *vt sep wound* verbinden; *hair* hochbinden. **to be bound ~ in** *(work etc)* verwachsen sein mit; **to be bound ~ with** *(person)* eng verbunden sein mit.
binder ['baɪndə^r] *n* **(a)** *(machine)* Bindemaschine *f.* **(b)** *(for papers)* Hefter *m.*
binding ['baɪndɪŋ] **1** *n (of book)* Einband *m*; *(Sew)* Band *nt; (on skis)* Bindung *f.* **2** *adj agreement* bindend, verbindlich *(on* für*).*
binge [bɪndʒ] *n (col)* Gelage *nt.* **to go on a ~** *(drinking)* auf Sauftour *(col)* gehen; *(eating)* eine Freßtour *(col)* machen.
bingo ['bɪŋgəʊ] *n* Bingo *nt.*
bin liner *n* Mülltüte *f.*
binoculars [bɪ'nɒkjʊləz] *npl* Fernglas *nt.*
bio- [baɪəʊ-]: **~chemist** *n* Biochemiker(in *f*) *m*; **~chemistry** *n* Biochemie *f*; **~degradable** *adj* biologisch abbaubar.
biographer [baɪ'ɒgrəfə^r] *n* Biograph(in *f*) *m.*
biographic(al) [,baɪəʊ'græfɪk(əl)] *adj* biographisch.
biography [baɪ'ɒgrəfɪ] *n* Biographie *f.*
biological [,baɪə'lɒdʒɪkəl] *adj* biologisch.
biologist [baɪ'ɒlədʒɪst] *n* Biologe *m,* Biologin *f.*
biology [baɪ'ɒlədʒɪ] *n* Biologie *f.*
biophysics [,baɪəʊ'fɪzɪks] *n sing* Biophysik *f.*
birch [bɜːtʃ] *n* Birke *f; (for whipping)* Rute *f.*
bird [bɜːd] *n* **(a)** Vogel *m.* **a little ~ told me** *(col)* das hat mir mein kleiner Mann im Ohr erzählt; **the early ~ catches the worm** Morgenstund hat Gold im Mund *(Prov)*; **a ~ in the hand is worth two in the bush** *(Prov)* der Spatz in der Hand ist besser als die Taube auf dem Dach *(Prov)*; **they are ~s of a feather** sie sind vom gleichen Schlag; **~s of a feather flock together** gleich und gleich gesellt sich gern; **to tell sb about the ~s and the bees** jdm erzählen, wo die kleinen Kinder herkommen. **(b)** *(Brit col: girl)* Biene *f (col).* **(c) he's an odd ~** *(col)* er ist ein komischer Kauz.
bird ~-cage *n* Vogelkäfig *m;* **~ sanctuary** *n* Vogelschutzgebiet *nt*; **~seed** *n* Vogelfutter *nt.*
bird's: ~-eye view *n* Vogelperspektive *f*; **~ nest** *n* Vogelnest *nt.*
bird watcher *n* Vogelbeobachter(in *f*) *m.*
Biro ® ['baɪərəʊ] *n (Brit)* Kugelschreiber, Kuli *(col) m.*
birth [bɜːθ] *n* **(a)** Geburt *f.* **to give ~ to** zur Welt bringen; **to give ~** entbinden; *(animal)* jungen. **(b)** *(parentage)* Abstammung, Herkunft *f.* **Scottish by ~** gebürtiger Schotte, gebürtige Schottin; **of good/low** *or* **humble ~** aus guter Familie/von niedriger Geburt. **(c)** *(fig)* Geburt *f*; *(of movement, fashion etc)* Aufkommen *nt*; *(of nation, party, company also)* Entstehen *nt*; *(of new era)* Anbruch *m; (of planet)* Entstehung *f.*
birth: ~ certificate *n* Geburtsurkunde *f*; **~ control** *n* Geburtenkontrolle *f.*
birthday ['bɜːθdeɪ] *n* Geburtstag *m.* **what did you get for your ~?** was hast du zum Geburtstag bekommen?
birthday: ~ cake *n* Geburtstagskuchen *m or* -torte *f*; **~ card** *n* Geburtstagskarte *f*; **~ party** *n* Geburtstagsfeier *f*; *(with dancing etc)* Geburtstagsparty *f*; *(for child)* Kindergeburtstag *m*; **~ present** *n* Geburtstagsgeschenk *nt*; **~ suit** *n (col)* Adams-/Evaskostüm *nt (col).*
birth: ~mark *n* Muttermal *nt*; **~place** *n* Geburtsort *m*; **~rate** *n* Geburtenrate *or* -ziffer *f*; **~right** *n (fig: right)* angeborenes Recht.
biscuit ['bɪskɪt] **1** *n* **(a)** *(Brit)* Keks *m.* **that takes/you take the ~!** *(col)* das übertrifft alles; *(negatively)* das schlägt dem Faß den Boden aus! **(b)** *(US)* Brötchen *nt.* **2** *adj (colour)* beige.
bisect [baɪ'sekt] *vt* in zwei Teile teilen; *(Math)* halbieren.
bishop ['bɪʃəp] *n* Bischof *m; (Chess)* Läufer *m.*
bison ['baɪsn] *n (American)* Bison *m*; *(European)* Wisent *m.*
bit[1] [bɪt] *n* **(a)** *(for horse)* Gebiß(stange *f*) *nt.* **(b)** *(of drill)* Bohrer *m.*
bit[2] **1** *n* **(a)** *(piece)* Stück *nt*; *(smaller)* Stückchen; *(of glass also)* Scherbe *f*; *(part or place in book etc)* Stelle *f.* **a ~** *(not much, small amount)* ein bißchen, etwas; **would you like a ~ of ice cream?** möchten Sie etwas Eis?; **there's a ~ of truth in what he says** daran ist schon etwas Wahres; **a ~ of advice/news** ein Rat *m*/eine Neuigkeit; **we had a ~ of trouble** wir hatten ein wenig Ärger; **it wasn't a ~ of help/use** das war überhaupt keine Hilfe/hat überhaupt nichts genützt; **there's quite a ~ of bread left** es ist noch eine ganze Menge Brot übrig; **in ~s and pieces** in tausend Stücken; **bring all your ~s and pieces** bring deine Siebensachen; **to come** *or* **fall to ~s** kaputtgehen.
(b) *(with time)* **a ~** ein Weilchen *nt.*
(c) *(with cost)* **a ~** eine ganze Menge.
(d) to do one's ~ sein(en) Teil tun.
(e) he's a ~ of a rogue/musician/expert er ist ein ziemlicher Schlingel/er ist gar kein schlechter Musiker/er versteht einiges davon.
(f) ~ by ~ Stück für Stück; *(gradually)* nach und nach; **he's every ~ a soldier** er ist durch und

durch Soldat; **it/he is every ~ as good as ...** es/er ist genauso gut wie ...; **not a ~ of it** keine Spur *(col).*

(g) when it comes to the ~ wenn es drauf ankommt.

(h) *(coin) (Brit)* Stück *nt,* Münze *f.* **2/4/6 ~s** *(US)* 25/50/75 Cent(s).

(i) *(Comp)* Bit *nt.*

2 *adv* **a ~** ein bißchen, etwas; **I'm not a ~ surprised** das wundert mich kein bißchen *(col) or* keineswegs; **he's improved quite a ~** er hat sich ziemlich gebessert.

bit[3] *pret of* **bite.**

bitch [bɪtʃ] **1** *n* **(a)** *(of dog)* Hündin *f.* **terrier ~** weiblicher Terrier. **(b)** *(col: woman)* Miststück *nt (col); (spiteful)* Hexe *f.* **2** *vi (col: complain)* meckern *(col) (about* über *+acc).*

bitchy ['bɪtʃɪ] *adj (+er) (col) woman* gehässig, gemein; *remark also* bissig.

bite [baɪt] *(vb: pret* **bit,** *ptp* **bitten***)* **1** *n* **(a)** Biß *m.* **(b)** *(insect ~)* Stich *m; (flea ~)* Biß *m; (love ~)* (Knutsch)fleck *m (col).* **(c)** *(Fishing)* **I think I've got a ~** ich glaube, es hat einer angebissen. **(d)** *(of food)* Happen *m.* **there's not a ~ to eat** es ist überhaupt nichts zu essen da; **do you fancy a ~ (to eat)**? möchten Sie etwas essen? **2** *vt (person, dog)* beißen; *(insect)* stechen. **to ~ one's nails** an den Nägeln kauen; **to ~ the dust** *(col)* ins Gras beißen *(col);* **once bitten twice shy** *(Prov)* (ein) gebranntes Kind scheut das Feuer *(Prov).* **3** *vi (dog etc)* beißen; *(insects)* stechen; *(fish, fig col)* anbeißen.

♦ **bite into** *vi +prep obj (person)* (hinein)beißen in *(+acc); (teeth)* (tief) eindringen in *(+acc); (acid, saw)* sich hineinfressen in *(+acc); (screw, drill)* sich hineinbohren in *(+acc).*

♦ **bite off** *vt sep* abbeißen. **he won't ~ your head ~** er wird dir schon nicht den Kopf abreißen; **to ~ ~ more than one can chew** *(prov)* sich *(dat)* zuviel zumuten.

♦ **bite through** *vt insep* durchbeißen.

biting ['baɪtɪŋ] *adj* beißend; *cold, wind also* schneidend.

bitten ['bɪtn] *ptp of* **bite.**

bitter ['bɪtə[r]] **1** *adj (+er)* bitter; *weather, wind* eisig; *enemy, struggle, opposition* erbittert. **it was a ~ pill to swallow** es war eine bittere Pille; **he's still ~ about it** er nimmt es mir/ihnen *etc* noch übel; **to the ~ end** bis zum bitteren Ende. **2** *n (Brit: beer)* ≈ Altbier *nt.*

bitterly ['bɪtəlɪ] *adv* bitter; *complain also, weep* bitterlich; *oppose* erbittert; *criticize* scharf; *jealous* sehr; *(showing embitteredness)* verbittert; *criticize* erbittert.

bitterness ['bɪtənɪs] *n see adj* Bitterkeit *f;* eisige Kälte; Erbitterheit *f.*

bitter-sweet ['bɪtə,swi:t] *adj (lit, fig)* bittersüß.

bitty ['bɪtɪ] *adj (+er) (Brit col: scrappy)* zusammengestückelt *(col).*

bitumen ['bɪtjʊmɪn] *n* Bitumen *nt.*

bivouac ['bɪvʊæk] *(vb: pret, ptp* **~ked***)* **1** *n* Biwak *nt.* **2** *vi* biwakieren.

bizarre [bɪ'zɑ:[r]] *adj* bizarr.

blab [blæb] *vi* quatschen *(col); (talk fast, tell secret)* plappern; *(criminal)* singen *(col).*

black [blæk] **1** *adj (+er)* **(a)** schwarz. **~ man/woman** Schwarze(r) *mf;* **a ~ eye** ein blaues Auge; **~ and blue** grün und blau; **~ and white film** Scharzweißfilm *m;* **he's not so ~ as he's painted** *(prov)* er is nicht so schlecht wie sein Ruf. **(b)** *future, prospects, mood* düster, finster. **things are looking ~** es sieht düster aus. **(c)** *(fig: angry) looks* böse. **he looked as ~ as thunder** er machte ein bitterböses Gesicht.

2 *n* **(a)** *(colour)* Schwarz *nt.* **he is dressed in ~** er trägt Schwarz; **to wear ~ for sb** für jdn Trauer tragen; **it's written down in ~ and white** es steht schwarz auf weiß geschrieben; **in the ~** *(Fin)* in den schwarzen Zahlen. **(b)** *(negro)* Schwarze(r) *mf.*

3 *vt* **(a)** schwärzen. **to ~ sb's eye** jdm ein blaues Auge schlagen. **(b)** *(Brit: trade union)* bestreiken; *goods* boykottieren.

♦ **black out 1** *vi* das Bewußtsein verlieren, ohnmächtig werden. **2** *vt sep* **(a)** *building, stage* verdunkeln. **(b)** *(with ink, paint)* schwärzen.

black: ~berry *n* Brombeere *f;* **~bird** *n* Amsel *f;* **~board** *n* Tafel *f;* **to write sth on the ~board** etw an die Tafel schreiben; **~ box** *n (Aviat)* Flugschreiber *m;* **~currant** *n* schwarze Johannisbeere; **B~ Death** *n (Hist)* Schwarzer Tod.

blacken ['blækən] **1** *vt* schwarz machen; *one's face* schwarz anmalen; *(fig) character* verunglimpfen. **to ~ sb's name** jdn schlechtmachen. **2** *vi* schwarz werden.

black: B~ Forest *n* Schwarzwald *m;* **~head** *n* Mitesser *m;* **~ hole** *n (Astron)* schwarzes Loch; **~ humour** *(Brit) or* **humor** *(US) n* schwarzer Humor; **~ ice** *n* Glatteis *nt;* **~jack** *n (Cards)* Siebzehn und Vier; **~leg** *(Brit Ind) n* Streikbrecher(in *f) m;* **~ list** *n* schwarze Liste; **~ magic** *n* Scharze Magie *f;* **~mail 1** *n* Erpressung *f;* **2** *vt* erpressen; **to ~mail sb into doing sth** jdn durch Erpressung dazu zwingen, etw zu tun; **B~ Maria** *n* grüne Minna *(col);* **~ mark** *n* Tadel *m; (in school register)* Eintrag *m;* **~ market 1** *n* Schwarzmarkt *m;* **2** *adj attr* Schwarzmarkt-.

blackness ['blæknɪs] *n* Schwärze *f.*

black: ~out *n* **(a)** *(Med)* Ohnmacht(sanfall *m) f no pl;* **(b)** *(light failure)* Stromausfall *m; (during war)* Verdunkelung *f; (TV)* Ausfall *m;* **(c)** *(news ~out)* (Nachrichten)sperre *f;* **~ pudding** *n* ≈ Blutwurst *f;* **B~ Sea** *n* Schwarzes Meer; **~ sheep** *n (fig)* schwarzes Schaf; **B~shirt** *n* Schwarzhemd *nt;* **~smith** *n* Schmied *m;* **~ spot** *n (also* **accident ~ spot***)* Gefahrenstelle *f;* **"~ tie"** *n (on invitation)* Abendanzug *m.*

bladder ['blædə[r]] *n (Anat, Bot)* Blase *f.*

blade [bleɪd] *n (of knife, tool)* Klinge *f; (of oar, saw, propeller)* Blatt *nt; (of plough)* Schar *f; (of turbine, paddle wheel)* Schaufel *f; (of grass, corn)* Halm *m.*

blame [bleɪm] **1** *vt* **(a)** *(hold responsible)* die Schuld geben *(+dat).* **to ~ sb for sth/sth on sb** jdm die Schuld an etw *(dat)* geben; **you only have yourself to ~** du bist ganz allein (daran) schuld; **I'm to ~ for this** daran bin ich schuld. **(b)** *(reproach)* Vorwürfe machen *(sb for* jdm für *or* wegen*).* **nobody is blaming you** es macht Ihnen ja niemand einen Vorwurf. **(c) he decided to turn down the offer — well, I can't say I ~ him** er entschloß sich, das Angebot abzulehnen — das kann man ihm wahrhaftig nicht verdenken. **2** *n (responsibility)* Schuld *f.* **to put the ~ for sth on sb** jdm die Schuld an etw *(dat)* geben; **to take the ~** die Schuld auf sich *(acc)* nehmen; *(for sb's mistakes also)* den Kopf hinhalten; **the ~ lies with him** er hat *or* ist schuld (daran).

blameless ['bleɪmlɪs] *adj* schuldlos; *life* untadelig.

blanch [blɑ:ntʃ] **1** *vt (Cook) vegetables* blanchieren. **2** *vi (with* vor *+dat) (person)* blaß werden.

bland [blænd] *adj (+er)* **(a)** *person* verbindlich; *face* ausdruckslos-höflich. **(b)** *food* mild, fade *(pej).* **(c)** *(mild, lacking distinction)* nichtssagend.

blandishment ['blændɪʃmənt] *n* Schmeichelei *f.*

blank [blæŋk] **1** *adj (+er)* **(a)** *piece of paper, page, wall* leer. **~ cheque** Blankoscheck *m; (fig)* Freibrief *m;* **there is a ~ space after each question** nach jeder Frage ist eine Lücke (gelassen). **(b)** *(expressionless) face, look* ausdruckslos; *(stupid)* verständnislos; *(puzzled)* verdutzt, verblüfft. **he just looked ~** er guckte mich nur groß an *(col);* **my mind went ~** ich hatte Mattscheibe *(col).* **(c) ~ verse** Blankvers *m.* **2** *n* **(a)** *(in document)* freier Raum, leere Stelle; *(~ document)* Formular *nt; (gap)* Lücke *f.* **(b) my mind was/went a complete ~** ich hatte totale Mattscheibe *(col);* **to**

draw a ~ kein Glück haben. **(c)** *(also ~* **cartridge***)* Platzpatrone *f.*

blanket ['blæŋkɪt] **1** *n (lit, fig)* Decke *f.* **a ~ of snow/fog** eine Schnee-/Nebeldecke. **2** *adj attr statement* pauschal; *insurance etc* umfassend. **3** *vt (snow, smoke)* zudecken.

blare [blɛəʳ] **1** *n (of car horn etc)* lautes Hupen; *(of trumpets etc)* Schmettern *nt.* **2** *vi see n* laut hupen; schmettern. **the music ~d through the hall** die Musik schallte durch den Saal.

♦ **blare out 1** *vi (loud voice, music)* schallen; *(trumpets)* schmettern. **2** *vt sep (trumpets) tune* schmettern; *(radio) music* plärren; *(person) order, warning etc* brüllen.

blasé ['blɑːzeɪ] *adj* blasiert.

blaspheme [blæs'fiːm] *vi* Gott lästern.

blasphemous ['blæsfɪməs] *adj (lit, fig)* blasphemisch; *(lit also)* gotteslästerlich.

blasphemy ['blæsfɪmɪ] *n see adj* Blasphemie *f*; Gotteslästerung *f.*

blast [blɑːst] **1** *n* **(a)** Windstoß *m*; *(of hot air)* Schwall *m.* **(b)** *(sound: of trumpets)* Geschmetter *nt*; *(of foghorn)* Tuten *nt.* **(c)** *(noise, explosion)* Explosion *f*; *(shock wave)* Druckwelle *f.* **to get the full ~ of sb's anger** jds Wut in voller Wucht abbekommen. **(d)** *(in quarrying etc)* Sprengung *f.* **(e) at full ~** *(lit, fig)* auf Hochtouren; **with the radio turned up (at) full ~** mit dem Radio voll aufgedreht. **2** *vt hole* sprengen; *rocket* schießen. **3** *interj (col)* **~ (it)!** verdammt! *(col).*

♦ **blast off** *vi (rocket, astronaut)* abheben, starten.

blasted ['blɑːstɪd] *adj (col)* verdammt *(col).*

blast furnace *n* Hochofen *m.*

blasting ['blɑːstɪŋ] *n (Tech)* Sprengen *nt.* **"danger ~ in progress"** „Achtung! Sprengarbeiten!"

blast-off ['blɑːstɒf] *n* Abschuß *m.*

blatant ['bleɪtənt] *adj (very obvious)* offensichtlich; *injustice also* eklatant; *error also* kraß; *liar* unverfroren; *disregard* offen.

blaze[1] [bleɪz] **1** *n (fire)* Feuer *nt*; *(of building etc also)* Brand *m; (of sun)* Glut *f.* **a ~ of lights/colour** ein Lichtermeer *nt*/Meer *nt* von Farben; **he went out in a ~ of glory** er trat mit Glanz und Gloria ab; **go to ~s** *(col)* scher dich zum Teufel! *(col)*; **what/how the ~s ...?** *(col)* was/wie zum Teufel ...? *(col)*; **like ~s** *(col)* wie verrückt *(col).* **2** *vi* **(a)** *(sun)* brennen; *(fire also)* lodern. **to ~ with anger** vor Zorn glühen. **(b)** *(guns)* feuern.

♦ **blaze away** *vi* **(a)** *(soldiers, guns)* drauflos feuern *(at* auf *+acc).* **(b)** *(fire etc)* lodern.

♦ **blaze up** *vi* auflodern.

blaze[2] *vt* **to ~ a trail** *(fig)* den Weg bahnen.

blazer ['bleɪzəʳ] *n* Blazer *m.*

blazing ['bleɪzɪŋ] *adj building etc* brennend; *fire, torch* lodernd; *sun (hot)* brennend; *(fig) eyes* funkelnd *(with* vor *+dat)*; *red* knall-, leuchtend.

bleach [bliːtʃ] **1** *n* Bleichmittel *nt.* **2** *vt linen, bones, hair* bleichen.

bleachers ['bliːtʃəz] *npl (US)* unüberdachte Zuschauertribüne.

bleak [bliːk] *adj (+er)* **(a)** öde, trostlos. **(b)** *weather, wind* rauh, kalt. **(c)** *(fig) future etc* trostlos.

bleary ['blɪərɪ] *adj (+er) eyes* trübe; *(after sleep)* verschlafen.

bleary-eyed ['blɪərɪ,aɪd] *adj (after sleep)* verschlafen.

bleat [bliːt] *vi (sheep, calf)* blöken; *(goat, fig col)* meckern.

bleed [bliːd] *pret, ptp* **bled** [bled] **1** *vi* bluten. **to ~ to death** verbluten; **my heart ~s for you** *(iro)* ich fang' gleich an zu weinen. **2** *vt* **(a)** *person* zur Ader lassen. **(b)** *(fig col)* schröpfen *(col) (for* um*).* **(c)** *(Aut) brakes* lüften.

bleeding ['bliːdɪŋ] **1** *n* **(a)** *(loss of blood)* Blutung *f.* **(b)** *(taking blood)* Aderlaß *m.* **(c)** *(of brakes)* Lüftung *f.* **2** *adj* **(a)** *wound* blutend; *(fig) heart* gebrochen. **(b)** *(Brit col!)* verdammt *(col).* **just a ~ minute** nu mal sachte *(col).*

bleep [bliːp] **1** *n (Rad, TV)* Piepton *m.* **2** *vi (transmitter)* piepen. **3** *vt (in hospital) doctor* rufen.

bleeper ['bliːpəʳ] *n* Funkrufempfänger *m.*

blemish ['blemɪʃ] **1** *n (lit, fig)* Makel *m.* **2** *vt object* beschädigen; *work* beeinträchtigen; *reputation* beflecken.

blend [blend] **1** *n* Mischung *f.* **2** *vt* **(a)** *teas, colours etc* (ver)mischen. **(b)** *(Cook) (stir)* einrühren; *(in blender) liquids* mixen; *semi-solids* pürieren. **3** *vi* **(a)** *(voices, colours)* verschmelzen. **(b)** *(also ~* **in***: go together, harmonize)* harmonieren *(with* mit*)*, passen *(with* zu*).*

blender ['blendəʳ] *n* Mixer *m*, Mixgerät *nt.*

bless [bles] *vt* segnen. **~ you, you're an angel** *(col)* du bist wirklich ein Engel *(col)*; **~ you!** *(to sneezer)* Gesundheit!; **~ my soul!** *(col)* du meine Güte! *(col)*; **to be ~ed with** gesegnet sein mit.

blessed ['blesɪd] **1** *adj* **(a)** *(Rel)* heilig. **B~ Virgin** Heilige Jungfrau (Maria). **(b)** *(euph col: cursed)* verflixt *(col).* **the whole ~ day** den lieben langen Tag *(col).* **2** *n* **the ~, the Blest** die Seligen *pl.*

blessing ['blesɪŋ] *n (Rel, fig)* Segen *m.* **he can count his ~s** da kann er von Glück sagen; **what a ~ that ...** welch ein Segen *or* Glück, daß ...; **it was a ~ in disguise** es war Glück im Unglück.

blew [bluː] *pret of* **blow**[2].

blight [blaɪt] **1** *n (on plants)* Braunfäule *f.* **these slums are a ~ upon the city** diese Slums sind ein Schandfleck für die Stadt. **2** *vt plants* zerstören; *(fig) hopes* zunichte machen.

blind [blaɪnd] **1** *adj (+er) person, obedience, fury* blind; *corner* unübersichtlich. **a ~ man/woman** ein Blinder/eine Blinde; **~ in one eye** auf einem Auge blind; **he was ~ to her faults** er sah ihre Fehler einfach nicht; **to be ~ to the possibilities** die Möglichkeiten nicht sehen; **to turn a ~ eye to sth** bei etw ein Auge zudrücken; **but he didn't take a ~ bit of notice** *(col)* aber er hat sich nicht die Spur darum gekümmert *(col).*

2 *vt* blenden; *(love, hate etc)* blind machen *(to* für, gegen*).* **he was ~ed in the war** er ist kriegsblind; **to ~ sb with science** jdn mit Fachjargon beeindrucken (wollen).

3 *n* **(a) the ~** die Blinden *pl*; **it's the ~ leading the ~** *(fig)* das hieße, einen Lahmen einen Blinden führen lassen. **(b)** *(window shade) (cloth)* Rollo *nt*; *(slats)* Jalousie *f*; *(outside)* Rolladen *m.*

4 *adv* **(a)** *(Aviat) fly* blind. **(b) ~ drunk** *(col)* sinnlos betrunken.

blind: ~ alley *n (lit, fig)* Sackgasse *f*; **~ date** *n* Rendezvous *nt* mit einem/einer Unbekannten.

blindfold ['blaɪndfəʊld] **1** *vt* die Augen verbinden *(+dat).* **2** *n* Augenbinde *f.* **3** *adj* mit verbundenen Augen. **I could do it ~** *(col)* das mach' ich mit links *(col).*

blindly ['blaɪndlɪ] *adv (lit, fig)* blind(lings).

blind man's buff *n* Blindekuh *no art.*

blindness ['blaɪndnɪs] *n (lit, fig)* Blindheit *f (to* gegenüber*).*

blind spot *n (Med)* blinder Fleck; *(Aut, Aviat)* toter Winkel; *(Rad)* tote Zone.

blink [blɪŋk] **1** *n* Blinzeln *nt.* **to be on the ~** *(col)* kaputt sein *(col).* **2** *vi* blinzeln; *(light)* blinken. **3** *vt* **to ~ one's eyes** mit den Augen zwinkern.

blinkers ['blɪŋkəz] *npl* Scheuklappen *pl.*

blinkered ['blɪŋkəd] *adj (fig)* engstirnig. **they are all so ~** sie laufen alle mit Scheuklappen herum.

bliss [blɪs] *n* Glück *nt.* **this is ~!** das ist eine Wohltat!; **a life of marital ~** ein glückliches Eheleben; **ignorance is ~** *(prov)* was ich *etc* nicht weiß, macht mich *etc* nicht heiß *(prov).*

blissful ['blɪsfʊl] *adj time* herrlich; *respite also* wohltuend; *happiness* höchste(s); *state, look, smile* (glück)selig; *moments* selig.

blissfully ['blɪsfəlɪ] *adv stretch* wohlig; *peaceful* herrlich; *smile* selig. **~ happy** überglücklich; **to be ~ ignorant** herrlich ahnungslos sein.

blister ['blɪstəʳ] **1** *n (on skin, paint)* Blase *f.* **2** *vi* *(skin)* Blasen bekommen; *(paintwork, metal)* Blasen werfen. **3** *vt* Blasen hervorufen auf *(+dat)*.

blithely ['blaɪðlɪ] *adv ignore, carry on* munter. **he ~ ignored the problem** er setzte sich ungeniert über das Problem hinweg.

blitz [blɪts] **1** *n* **(a)** Blitzkrieg *m*; *(aerial)* Luftangriff *m*. **the B~** *deutscher Luftangriff auf britische Städte 1940-41*. **(b)** *(fig col)* Blitzaktion *f*. **2** *vt* heftig bombardieren.

blizzard ['blɪzəd] *n* Schneesturm, Blizzard *m*.

bloated ['bləʊtɪd] *adj* aufgedunsen. **I feel absolutely ~** *(col)* ich bin zum Platzen voll *(col)*.

blob [blɒb] *n (of water, honey, wax)* Tropfen *m*; *(of ink)* Klecks *m*; *(of paint)* Tupfer *m*; *(of ice-cream, mashed potatoes)* Klacks *m*.

bloc [blɒk] *n* **(a)** *(Pol)* Block *m*. **(b) en ~** en bloc.

block [blɒk] **1** *n* **(a)** Block, Klotz *m*. **(b)** *(building, of shares, seats, for notes)* Block *m*. **~ of flats** *(Brit)* Wohnblock *m*; **to take a stroll around the ~** einen Spaziergang um den Block machen; **she lived in the next ~/three ~s from us** *(esp US)* sie wohnte im nächsten Block/drei Blocks *or* Straßen weiter. **(c)** *(obstruction: in pipe, Med)* Verstopfung *f*. **I've a mental ~ about it** dabei habe ich totale Mattscheibe *(col)*. **(d)** *(col: head)* **to knock sb's ~ off** jdm eins überziehen *(col)*. **2** *vt road* blockieren; *traffic also, progress* aufhalten; *pipe* verstopfen; *(Ftbl)* blocken; *ball* stoppen; *credit* sperren. **to ~ sb's way/view** jdm den Weg/die Sicht versperren.

♦ **block off** *vt sep street* absperren; *fireplace* abdecken.

♦ **block out** *vt sep* **(a)** *(obscure) light* nicht durchlassen; *sun also* verdecken. **(b)** *(obliterate) part of picture* wegretuschieren.

♦ **block up** *vt sep* **(a)** *(obstruct) gangway* blockieren; *pipe* verstopfen. **my nose is all ~ed ~** meine Nase ist völlig verstopft. **(b)** *(close, fill in) window* zumauern; *hole* zustopfen.

blockade [blɒ'keɪd] **1** *n (Mil)* Blockade *f*. **2** *vt* blockieren, sperren.

blockage ['blɒkɪdʒ] *n* Verstopfung *f*.

block: ~ and tackle *n* Flaschenzug *m*; **~ booking** *n* Gruppenbuchung *f*; *(Theat)* Gruppenbestellung *f*; **~ capitals** *npl* Blockschrift *f*.

bloke [bləʊk] *n (Brit col)* Kerl *(col)*, Typ *(col) m*.

blond [blɒnd] *adj man, hair* blond.

blonde [blɒnd] **1** *adj woman* blond. **2** *n (woman)* Blondine *f*.

blood [blʌd] *n* Blut *nt*. **to give ~** Blut spenden; **it makes my ~ boil** das macht mich rasend; **she's after his ~** sie will ihm an den Kragen *(col)*; **his ~ ran cold** es lief ihm eiskalt über den Rücken; **it's like trying to get ~ out of a stone** *(prov)* das ist verlorene Liebesmüh; **there is bad ~ between them** sie haben ein gestörtes Verhältnis; **it's in his ~** das liegt ihm im Blut; **~ is thicker than water** *(prov)* Blut ist dicker als Wasser *(prov)*.

blood *in cpds* Blut-; **~ bank** *n* Blutbank *f*; **~bath** *n* Blutbad *nt*; **~ brother** *n* Blutsbruder *m*; **~ clot** *n* Blutgerinnsel *nt*; **~curdling** *adj* grauenerregend; **~ donor** *n* Blutspender(in *f*) *m*; **~ group** *n* Blutgruppe *f*; **~hound** *n* **(a)** *(Zool)* Bluthund *m*; **(b)** *(fig: detective)* Schnüffler *m (col)*.

bloodless ['blʌdlɪs] *adj victory, coup* unblutig; *(pallid)* blutleer, bleich.

blood: ~ money *n* schmutziges Geld; **~ orange** *n* Blutorange *f*; **~-poisoning** *n* Blutvergiftung *f*; **~ pressure** *n* Blutdruck *m*; **to have (high) ~ pressure** hohen Blutdruck haben; **~-red** *adj* blutrot; **~shed** *n* Blutvergießen *nt*; **~shot** *adj* blutunterlaufen; **~ sports** *npl Jagdsport, Hahnenkampf etc*; **~stain** *n* Blutfleck *m*; **~stained** *adj* blutig, blutbefleckt; **~stream** *n* Blut *nt*, Blutkreislauf *m*; **~ test** *n* Blutprobe *f*; **~thirsty** *adj* blutrünstig; **~ transfusion** *n* (Blut)transfusion *f*; **~ vessel** *n* Blutgefäß *nt*.

bloody ['blʌdɪ] **1** *adj (+er)* **(a)** *(lit)* blutig. **(b)** *(Brit col!: damned)* verdammt *(col)*, Scheiß- *(col!)*; *(in positive sense) genius, wonder* echt *(col)*, verdammt *(col)*. **~ hell!** verdammt nochmal! *(col)*; **he is a ~ marvel** er ist verdammt gut *(col)*. **2** *adv (Brit col!)*; verdammt *(col)*; *cold, stupid* sau- *(col)*; *(in positive sense) good, brilliant* echt *(col)*, verdammt *(col)*.

bloody-minded ['blʌdɪ'maɪndɪd] *adj (Brit col)* stur *(col)*.

bloom [blu:m] **1** *n* **(a)** Blüte *f*. **to be in (full) ~** in (voller) Blüte stehen; **in the ~ of youth** in der Blüte der Jugend. **(b)** *(on fruit)* satter Schimmer; *(on peaches)* Flaum *m*. **2** *vi (lit, fig)* blühen.

bloomers ['blu:məz] *npl* Pumphose *f*.

blossom ['blɒsəm] **1** *n* Blüte *f*. **in ~** in Blüte. **2** *vi (lit, fig)* blühen; *(person, trade etc also)* aufblühen. **to ~ into sth** zu etw aufblühen.

♦ **blossom out** *vi (fig)* aufblühen *(into* zu*)*.

blot [blɒt] **1** *n* **(a)** *(of ink)* (Tinten)klecks *m*. **(b)** *(fig: on honour, reputation)* Fleck *m (on* auf *+dat)*. **a ~ on the landscape** ein Schandfleck in der Landschaft. **2** *vt* **(a)** *(make ink spots on)* beklecksen.**to ~ one's copybook** *(fig)* sich danebenbenehmen; *(with sb)* es sich *(dat)* verderben. **(b)** *(dry) ink, page* löschen.

♦ **blot out** *vt sep* **(a)** *(lit) words* verschmieren. **(b)** *(hide from view) landscape* verdecken; *(obliterate) memories* auslöschen.

blotch [blɒtʃ] *n (on skin)* Fleck *m*; *(of ink, colour also)* Klecks *m*.

blotchy ['blɒtʃɪ] *adj (+er) skin* fleckig; *drawing, paint* klecksig.

blotting paper ['blɒtɪŋ,peɪpə^r] *n* Löschpapier *nt*.

blouse [blaʊz] *n* Bluse *f*.

blow[1] [bləʊ] *n (lit, fig)* Schlag *m (for, to* für*)*. **to come to ~s** handgreiflich werden; **at one ~** *(fig)* mit einem Schlag *(col)*.

blow[2] *(vb: pret* **blew,** *ptp* **~n)** **1** *vi* **(a)** *(wind)* wehen, blasen. **(b)** *(person)* blasen, pusten *(col) (on* auf *+acc)*. **(c)** *(move with the wind)* fliegen. **the door blew open/shut** die Tür flog auf/zu. **(d)** *(bugle)* blasen; *(whistle)* pfeifen. **(e)** *(fuse, light bulb)* durchbrennen; *(gasket)* platzen.

2 *vt* **(a)** *(breeze)* wehen; *(strong wind, draught)* blasen; *(gale etc)* treiben; *(person)* blasen, pusten *(col)*. **the wind blew the ship off course** der Wind trieb das Schiff vom Kurs ab; **to ~ sb a kiss** jdm eine Kußhand zuwerfen; **to ~ one's nose** sich *(dat)* die Nase putzen. **(b)** *glass, trumpet* blasen; *bubbles* machen; *(Hunt, Mil) horn* blasen in *(+acc)*. **the referee blew his whistle** der Schiedsrichter pfiff. **(c)** *(burn out, ~ up) safe, bridge etc* sprengen; *valve, gasket* platzen lassen; *transistor* zerstören. **I've ~n a fuse/light bulb** mir ist eine Sicherung/Birne durchgebrannt; **to be ~n to pieces** *(bridge, car)* in die Luft gesprengt werden; *(person)* zerfetzt werden. **(d)** *(col: spend extravagantly) money* verpulvern *(col)*. **(e)** *(col: reveal) secret* verraten. **(f)** *(col: damn)* **~!** Mist! *(col)*; **~ the expense** das ist doch wurscht, was es kostet *(col)*.

♦ **blow away** **1** *vi (hat, paper etc)* wegfliegen. **2** *vt sep* wegblasen; *(breeze also)* wegwehen.

♦ **blow down** **1** *vi (tree etc)* umgeweht werden. **2** *vt sep (lit)* umwehen.

♦ **blow in** **1** *vi* **(a)** *(lit) (be blown down: window etc)* eingedrückt werden; *(be ~n inside: dust etc)* hereingeweht werden; *(wind)* hereinwehen, hereinblasen. **(b)** *(col: arrive unexpectedly)* hereinschneien *(col) (+prep obj, -to* in *+acc)*. **2** *vt sep window, door etc* eindrücken; *dust etc* hereinwehen *(+prep obj, -to* in *+acc)*.

♦ **blow off** **1** *vi* wegfliegen. **2** *vt sep (+prep obj)* blasen von. **3** *vt insep (fig) steam* ablassen *(col)*.

♦ **blow out** **1** *vi (candle etc)* ausgehen. **2** *vt sep candle* ausblasen; *cheeks* aufblasen. **to ~ one's brains ~** sich *(dat)* eine Kugel durch den Kopf

jagen. **3** *vr (wind, storm)* sich legen.
♦ **blow over** *vi (lit, fig: storm, dispute)* sich legen.
♦ **blow up 1** *vi (be exploded)* in die Luft fliegen; *(bomb)* explodieren; *(gale, crisis, row)* ausbrechen; *(fig col: person)* explodieren *(col)*. **2** *vt sep mine, bridge, person* in die Luft jagen; *tyre, balloon* aufblasen; *photo* vergrößern; *(exaggerate) event* aufbauschen *(into* zu*)*.
blow: ~**-by-**~ *adj account* detailliert; ~**-dry 1** *n* **to have a** ~**-dry** sich fönen lassen; **2** *vt* fönen; ~**lamp** *n* Lötlampe *f*.
blown [bləʊn] *ptp of* **blow**[2].
blow: ~**-out** *n* **(a)** *(col: meal)* Schlemmerei *f*; **(b)** *(burst tyre)* **he had a** ~**-out** ihm ist ein Reifen geplatzt; **(c)** *(Elec)* **there's been a** ~**-out** die Sicherung ist durchgebrannt; ~ **pipe** *n (weapon)* Blasrohr *nt*.
blowy ['bləʊɪ] *adj (+er)* windig.
blubber ['blʌbəʳ] **1** *n* Walfischspeck *m*. **2** *vi (col)* flennen *(col)*, heulen *(col)*.
blue [bluː] **1** *adj (+er)* **(a)** blau. ~ **with cold** blau vor Kälte; **until you're** ~ **in the face** *(col)* bis zur Vergasung *(col)*; **once in a** ~ **moon** alle Jubeljahre (einmal). **(b)** *(col: miserable)* melancholisch, trübsinnig. **to feel** ~ niedergeschlagen sein. **(c)** *(col: obscene) joke* schlüpfrig; *film* Porno-, Sex-. **(d)** *(Pol)* konservativ. **2** *n* **(a)** Blau *nt*. **(b)** *(liter: sky)* Himmel *m*. **out of the** ~ *(fig col)* aus heiterem Himmel *(col)*. **(c)** *(Pol)* Konservative(r) *mf*. **(d)** *(col)* **to have (a fit of) the** ~**s** den Moralischen haben *(col)*. **(e)** *(Mus)* **the** ~**s** *pl* der Blues.
blue: ~ **baby** *n* Baby *nt* mit angeborenem Herzfehler; ~**bell** *n* Sternhyazinthe *f*; *(Scot)* Glockenblume *f*; ~**berry** *n* Blau- *or* Heidelbeere *f*; ~ **blood** *n* blaues Blut; ~**bottle** *n* Schmeißfliege *f*; ~ **cheese** *n* Blauschimmelkäse *m*; ~**-collar** *adj* ~**-collar worker/union/jobs** Arbeiter *m*/Arbeitergewerkschaft *f*/Stellen *pl* für Arbeiter; ~**-eyed** *adj* blauäugig; **sb's** ~**-eyed boy** *(fig)* jds Liebling *m*; ~**print** *n* Blaupause *f*; *(fig)* Plan, Entwurf *m*; ~**tit** *n* Blaumeise *f*.
bluff[1] [blʌf] **1** *n (headland)* Kliff *nt*; *(inland)* Felsvorsprung *m*. **2** *adj* rauh aber herzlich *(col)*; *honesty, answer* aufrichtig.
bluff[2] **1** *vti* bluffen. **2** *n* Bluff *m*. **to call sb's** ~ es darauf ankommen lassen; *(make prove)* jdn auf die Probe stellen.
♦ **bluff out** *vt sep* **to** ~ **it** ~ sich rausreden *(col)*.
blunder ['blʌndəʳ] **1** *n* Schnitzer *m (col)*; *(socially)* Fauxpas *m*. **to make a** ~ einen Bock schießen *(col)*; *(socially)* einen Fauxpas begehen. **2** *vi* **(a)** einen Bock schießen *(col)*; *(socially)* sich blamieren. **(b)** *(move clumsily)* tappen *(into* gegen*)*.
blunt [blʌnt] **1** *adj (+er)* **(a)** stumpf. **with a** ~ **instrument** mit einem stumpfen Gegenstand. **(b)** *(outspoken) person* geradeheraus *pred*; *speech* unverblümt; *fact* nackt. **to be** ~ **about sth** sich unverblümt zu etw äußern. **2** *vt knife etc* stumpf machen; *(fig) palate, senses* abstumpfen.
bluntly ['blʌntlɪ] *adv speak* freiheraus.
bluntness ['blʌntnɪs] *n* **(a)** *(of blade)* Stumpfheit *f*. **(b)** *(outspokenness)* Unverblümtheit *f*
blur [blɜːʳ] **1** *n* verschwommener Fleck. **2** *vt* **(a)** *inscription* verwischen; *writing also* verschmieren; *outline, photograph* unscharf machen; *sound* verzerren. **to be/become** ~**red** undeutlich sein/werden; *(image etc also)* verschwommen sein/verschwimmen. **(b)** *(fig) senses, mind* trüben; *meaning* verwischen.
blurb [blɜːb] *n* Material *nt*, Informationen *pl*; *(on book cover)* Klappentext *m*.
blurt (out) [blɜːt('aʊt)] *vt sep* herausplatzen mit *(col)*.
blush [blʌʃ] **1** *vi* rot werden *(with* vor *+dat)*. **2** *n* Erröten *nt no pl*. **with a** ~ errötend.
bluster ['blʌstəʳ] *vi (wind)* toben; *(person)* ein großes Geschrei machen; *(angrily also)* toben.
blustery ['blʌstərɪ] *adj wind, day* stürmisch.
BO [ˌbiː'əʊ] *(col)* = **body odour** Körpergeruch *m*.
boa ['bəʊə] *n* Boa *f*. ~ **constrictor** Boa constrictor *f*.
boar [bɔːʳ] *n (male pig)* Eber *m*; *(wild)* Keiler *m*.
board [bɔːd] **1** *n* **(a)** Brett *nt*; *(black*~*)* Tafel *f*; *(notice*~*)* Schwarzes Brett; *(sign*~*)* Schild *nt*; *(floor*~*)* Diele(nbrett *nt*) *f*. **(b)** *(provision of meals)* Verpflegung *f*. ~ **and lodging** Kost und Logis; **full/half** ~ *(Brit)* Voll-/Halbpension *f*. **(c)** *(group of officials)* Ausschuß *m*; *(with advisory function,* ~ *of trustees)* Beirat *m*; *(permanent official institution: gas*~*, harbour* ~ *etc)* Behörde *f*; *(of company: also* ~ **of directors***)* Vorstand *m*; *(including shareholders, advisers)* Aufsichtsrat *m*. **B**~ **of Trade** *(Brit)* Handelsministerium *nt*. **(d)** *(Naut, Aviat)* **on** ~ an Bord; **to go on** ~ an Bord gehen. **(e)** *(fig phrases)* **across the** ~ *(fig)* allgemein, pauschal; **to go by the** ~ *(dreams, hopes)* zunichte werden; *(principles)* über Bord geworfen werden.
2 *vt ship, plane* besteigen, an Bord *(+gen)* gehen/kommen; *train, bus* einsteigen in *(+acc)*; *(Naut: in attack)* entern.
3 *vi* **(a)** *(live)* in Pension sein *(with* bei*)*. **(b)** *(Sch)* Internatsschüler(in *f*) *m* sein. **(c)** *(Aviat)* die Maschine besteigen. **flight ZA173 now** ~**ing through gate 13** Aufruf für Passagiere des Fluges ZA173, sich zum Flugsteig 13 zu begeben.
♦ **board up** *vt sep* mit Brettern vernageln.
boarder ['bɔːdəʳ] *n* **(a)** Pensionsgast *m*. **(b)** *(Sch)* Internatsschüler(in *f*) *m*.
boarding ['bɔːdɪŋ-]: ~ **card** *n* Bordkarte *f*; ~ **house** *n* Pension *f*; ~ **party** *n (Naut)* Enterkommando *nt*; ~ **school** *n* Internat *nt*.
board: ~ **meeting** *n* Vorstandssitzung *f*; ~**room** *n* Sitzungssaal *m*; ~**walk** *n (US)* Holzsteg *m*; *(on beach)* hölzerne Uferpromenade.
boast [bəʊst] **1** *n* Prahlerei *f*. **it is their** ~ **that ...** sie rühmen sich, daß ... **2** *vi* angeben *(about, of* mit, *to sb* jdm gegenüber*)*. **don't** ~ gib nicht so an. **3** *vt (possess)* sich rühmen *(+gen) (geh)*.
boaster ['bəʊstəʳ] *n* Angeber(in *f*) *m*.
boastful ['bəʊstfʊl] *adj* angeberisch.
boasting ['bəʊstɪŋ] *n* Angeberei *f*.
boat [bəʊt] *n* Boot *nt*; *(sea-going, passenger* ~*)* Schiff *nt*; *(pleasure steamer etc)* Dampfer *m*. **by** ~ mit dem Schiff; **to miss the** ~ *(fig col)* den Anschluß verpassen; **we're all in the same** ~ *(fig col)* wir sitzen alle im gleichen Boot.
boater ['bəʊtəʳ] *n* **(a)** *(hat)* steifer Strohhut. **(b)** *(person boating)* Bootsfahrer(in *f*) *m*.
boat: ~**hook** *n* Bootshaken *m*; ~ **race** *n* Regatta *f*.
boatswain, bosun, bo's'n ['bəʊsn] *n* Bootsmann *m*.
boat train *n* Zug *m* mit Fährenanschluß.
bob[1] [bɒb] *vi* sich auf und ab bewegen; *(rabbit)* hoppeln; *(bird's tail)* wippen; *(boxer)* tänzeln. **to** ~ **(up and down) in** *or* **on the water** auf dem Wasser schaukeln.
♦ **bob up** *vi (lit, fig)* auftauchen.
bob[2] *n, pl* - *(Brit col)* Shilling *m*. **that will cost a few** ~ das wird einiges kosten.
bob[3] *n (haircut)* Bubikopf *m*.
bob[4] *n (sleigh)* Bob *m*.
bobbin ['bɒbɪn] *n* Spule *f*; *(cotton reel)* Rolle *f*.
bobble ['bɒbl] *n* Bommel *f*, Pompon *m*.
bobby ['bɒbɪ] *n (dated Brit col)* Bobby *m*.
bob: ~**cat** *n (US)* Luchs *m*; ~**sleigh 1** *n* Bob *m*; **2** *vi* Bob fahren.
bode [bəʊd] *vi*: **to** ~ **well/ill** ein gutes/schlechtes Zeichen sein.
bodice ['bɒdɪs] *n* **(a)** *(of dress)* Oberteil *nt*. **(b)** *(vest)* Unterhemd *nt*.
bodily ['bɒdɪlɪ] **1** *adj (physical)* körperlich. ~

needs leibliche Bedürfnisse *pl*; ~ **harm** Körperverletzung *f*. **2** *adv (forcibly)* gewaltsam.

body ['bɒdɪ] *n* **(a)** Körper *m*; *(of human also)* Leib *m (geh)*. **to keep ~ and soul together** Leib und Seele zusammenhalten. **(b)** *(corpse)* Leiche *f*. **(c)** *(of plane, ship)* Rumpf *m*; *(of speech, army)* Hauptteil *m*. **the main ~ of his readers/the students** das Gros seiner Leser/der Studenten. **(d)** *(of car)* Karosserie *f*. **(e)** *(group of people)* Gruppe *f*. **the student ~** die Studentenschaft. **(f)** *(organization)* Organ *nt*; *(committee)* Gremium *nt*; *(corporation)* Körperschaft *f*. **(g)** *(of wine)* Körper *m*; *(of hair, paper, cloth)* Festigkeit *f*.

body: ~building *n* Bodybuilding *nt*; **~guard** *n (one person)* Leibwächter *m*; *(group)* Leibwache *f*; **~work** *n (Aut)* Karosserie *f*.

bog [bɒg] *n* **(a)** Sumpf *m*; *(peat ~)* (Torf)moor *nt*. **(b)** *(Brit col: toilet)* Klo *nt (col)*.

♦**bog down** *vt sep* **to be** *or* **get ~ged ~** *(lit)* steckenbleiben; *(fig)* sich festgefahren haben; *(in details)* sich verzettelt haben.

boggle ['bɒgl] *vi (col)* **the mind ~s** *(faced with fact)* da bist du baff *(col) or* platt *(col)*; *(faced with possibility)* das kann man sich *(dat)* kaum ausmalen.

bogus ['bəʊgəs] *adj doctor* falsch; *money, pearls* gefälscht; *company* Schwindel-; *claim* erfunden.

Bohemia [bəʊ'hiːmɪə] *n* Böhmen *nt*

Bohemian [bəʊ'hiːmɪən] **1** *n* **(a)** Böhme *m*, Böhmin *f*. **(b)** *(fig)* **b~** Bohemien *m*. **2** *adj* **(a)** böhmisch. **(b)** *(fig)* **b~** *lifestyle* unkonventionell, unbürgerlich.

boil[1] [bɔɪl] *n (Med)* Furunkel *m*.

boil[2] **1** *vi* **(a)** kochen; *(water also, Phys)* sieden. **the kettle is ~ing** das Wasser kocht. **(b)** *(fig col: be angry)* kochen, schäumen *(with* vor *+dat)*. **2** *vt* kochen. **~ed/hard ~ed egg** weich-/hartgekochtes Ei; **~ed potatoes** Salzkartoffeln *pl*. **3** *n* **to bring to the ~** zum Kochen bringen; **he's gone off the ~** *(fig col)* er hat kein Interesse mehr.

♦**boil down 1** *vt sep* eindicken lassen. **2** *vi* **(a)** *(jam etc)* dickflüssig werden. **(b)** *(fig)* **what it ~s ~ to is that ...** das läuft darauf hinaus, daß ...

♦**boil over** *vi* **(a)** *(lit)* überkochen. **(b)** *(fig) (situation, quarrel)* den Siedepunkt erreichen.

boiler ['bɔɪləʳ] *n* **(a)** *(domestic)* Boiler, Warmwasserbereiter *m*; *(in ship, engine)* (Dampf)kessel *m*. **(b)** *(chicken)* Suppenhuhn *nt*.

boiler: ~maker *n* Kesselschmied *m*; **~suit** *n* Overall, Blaumann *(col) m*.

boiling ['bɔɪlɪŋ]: **~ hot** *adj* kochendheiß; **I'm ~ hot** mir ist schrecklich heiß; **~ point** *n (lit, fig)* Siedepunkt *m*.

boisterous ['bɔɪstərəs] *adj (exuberant) person* ausgelassen; *game etc also* wild.

bold [bəʊld] *adj (+er)* **(a)** *(valiant)* kühn. **(b)** *(impudent)* dreist. **to make so ~ as to ...** sich erlauben, zu ... **(c)** *(striking) colours etc* kräftig; *handwriting, style* kraftvoll. **(d)** *(Typ)* fett. **~ type** Fettdruck *m*.

boldness ['bəʊldnɪs] *n see adj* Kühnheit *(geh) f*; Dreistigkeit *f*; Kräftigkeit *f*.

Bolivia [bə'lɪvɪə] *n* Bolivien *nt*.

bollard ['bɒlɑːd] *n (on quay)* Poller *m*.

Bolshevik ['bɒlʃəvɪk] **1** *n* Bolschewik *m*. **2** *adj* bolschewistisch.

Bolshevism ['bɒlʃəvɪzəm] *n* Bolschewismus *m*.

bolshy ['bɒlʃɪ] *(col) adj (+er) (uncooperative)* stur, störrisch; *(aggressive)* pampig *(col)*.

bolster ['bəʊlstəʳ] **1** *n (on bed)* Nackenrolle *f*. **2** *vt (also ~* **up***) (fig) person* Mut machen *(+dat)*; *status* aufbessern; *currency* stützen.

bolt [bəʊlt] **1** *n* **(a)** *(on door etc)* Riegel *m*. **(b)** *(Tech)* Bolzen *m*. **(c)** *(of lightning)* Blitzstrahl *m*. **it came/was like a ~ from the blue** *(fig)* das war wie ein Blitz aus heiterem Himmel. **(d)** *(of crossbow)* Bolzen *m*. **(e)** *(of rifle)* Kammer *f*. **(f)** *(sudden dash)* Satz *m (col)*. **he made a ~ for the door** er machte einen Satz zur Tür; **to make a ~ for it** abhauen *(col)*. **2** *adv*: **~ upright** kerzengerade. **3** *vi* **(a)** *(horse)* durchgehen; *(person)* Reißaus nehmen *(col)*, abhauen *(col)*. **(b)** *(move quickly)* sausen, rasen. **4** *vt* **(a)** *door, window* verriegeln. **(b)** *(Tech) machine parts* verschrauben *(to* mit*)*. **to ~ together** verschrauben. **(c)** *(also ~* **down***) one's food* hinunterschlingen.

bomb [bɒm] **1** *n* Bombe *f*. **his party went like a ~** *(col)* seine Party war ein Bombenerfolg *(col)*; **the car goes like a ~** *(col)* der Wagen läuft verdammt gut *(col)*. **2** *vt town* bombardieren.

bombard [bɒm'bɑːd] *vt (Mil, fig)* bombardieren *(with* mit*)*; *(Phys)* beschießen.

bombardment [bɒm'bɑːdmənt] *n (Mil)* Bombardierung *f (also fig)*, Bombardement *nt*.

bombastic [bɒm'bæstɪk] *adj* bombastisch.

bomb disposal squad *n* Bombenräumtrupp *m*.

bomber ['bɒməʳ] *n* **(a)** *(aircraft)* Bomber *m*, Bombenflieger *m*. **(b)** *(person) (Aviat)* Bombenschütze *m*; *(terrorist)* Bombenattentäter(in *f*) *m*.

bomber jacket *n* Blouson *m or nt*.

bomb: ~shell *n* **this news was a ~shell** die Nachricht schlug wie eine Bombe ein; **~ site** *n* Trümmergrundstück *nt*.

bona fide ['bəʊnə'faɪdɪ] *adj* bona fide; *traveller, word, antique* echt. **it's a ~ offer** es ist ein Angebot auf Treu und Glauben.

bonanza [bə'nænzə] *n* **(a)** *(US Min)* reiche Erzader. **(b)** *(fig)* Goldgrube *f*. **the oil ~** der Ölboom.

bond [bɒnd] **1** *n* **(a)** *(agreement)* Übereinkommen *nt*. **to enter into a ~ with sb** ein Übereinkommen mit jdm treffen. **(b)** *(fig: link)* Band *nt (geh)*, Bindung *f*. **(c) ~s** *pl (lit, fig: chains)* Bande *pl (geh)*. **(d)** *(Comm, Fin)* Obligation *f*, Pfandbrief *m*. **government ~** Staatsanleihe *f*. **(e)** *(Comm: custody of goods)* Zollverschluß *m*. **goods in ~** Zollgut *nt*. **(f)** *(adhesion between surfaces)* Haftfestigkeit *f*. **2** *vt (Comm) goods* unter Zollverschluß nehmen. **3** *vi (glue)* binden.

bondage ['bɒndɪdʒ] *n* **(a)** *(lit)* Sklaverei *f*; *(in Middle Ages)* Leibeigenschaft *f*. **(b)** *(fig liter)* Versklavung *f*.

bonded warehouse ['bɒndɪd'wɛəhaʊs] Zollager *nt*.

bone [bəʊn] **1** *n* Knochen *m*; *(of fish)* Gräte *f*. **~s** *pl (of the dead)* Gebeine *pl*; **chilled to the ~** völlig durchgefroren; **~ of contention** Zankapfel *m*; **to have a ~ to pick with sb** *(col)* mit jdm ein Hühnchen zu rupfen haben *(col)*; **he made no ~s about saying what he thought** *(col)* er hat kein Blatt vor den Mund genommen; **I can feel it in my ~s** ich spüre es in den Knochen. **2** *vt* die Knochen lösen aus; *fish* entgräten.

bone china *n* feines Porzellan.

bone: ~-dry *adj (col)* knochentrocken; **~-idle** *adj (col)* stinkfaul *(col)*; **~ meal** *n* Knochenmehl *nt*.

bonfire ['bɒnfaɪəʳ] *n* Feuer *nt*; *(as beacon)* Leuchtfeuer *nt*.

bonnet ['bɒnɪt] *n* **(a)** *(woman's)* Haube *f*; *(baby's)* Häubchen *nt*; *(esp Scot: man's)* Mütze *f*. **(b)** *(Brit Aut)* Motor- *or* Kühlerhaube *f*.

bonny ['bɒnɪ] *adj (esp Scot)* schön; *baby* prächtig.

bonus ['bəʊnəs] *n* **(a)** Prämie *f*; *(on output, production also)* Zulage *f*; *(cost-of-living ~)* Zuschlag *m*; *(Christmas ~)* Gratifikation *f*. **(b)** *(Fin: on shares)* Extradividende *f*. **(c)** *(col: sth extra)* Zugabe *f*.

bony ['bəʊnɪ] *adj (+er) (of bone)* knöchern; *(like bone)* knochenartig; *person, knee, hips* knochig; *fish* mit viel Gräten; *meat* mit viel Knochen.

boo [buː] **1** *interj* buh. **he wouldn't say ~ to a goose** *(col)* er ist ein schüchternes Pflänzchen. **2** *vt actor, play, speaker* auspfeifen, ausbuhen. **to be ~ed off the stage** ausgepfiffen *or* ausgebuht werden. **3** *vi* buhen. **4** *n* Buhruf *m*.

boob [buːb] **1** *n* **(a)** *(Brit col: mistake)* Schnitzer *m*.

(b) *(col: woman's breast)* Brust *f.* **2** *vi (Brit col)* einen Schnitzer machen; *(fail)* Mist bauen *(col).*
booby: ~ **prize** *n Trostpreis m für den schlechtesten Teilnehmer;* ~ **trap 1** *n* **(a)** *(als Schabernack versteckt angebrachte)* Falle *f;* **(b)** *(Mil etc)* versteckte Bombe; **2** *vt* **the suitcase was ~-trapped** in dem Koffer war eine Bombe versteckt.
book [bʊk] **1** *n* **(a)** Buch *nt; (exercise ~)* Heft *nt.* **to bring sb to ~** jdn zur Rechenschaft ziehen; **he does everything by the ~** er hält sich bei allem strikt an die Vorschriften; **to be in sb's good/bad ~s** bei jdm gut/schlecht angeschrieben sein *(col);* **to throw the ~ at sb** *(col)* jdn fertigmachen *(col);* **in my ~** für mich; **he knows every trick in the ~** *(col)* er ist mit allen Wassern gewaschen *(col).* **(b)** *(of tickets)* Heft *nt; (thicker)* Block *m; (of matches)* Briefchen *nt.* **(c)** *(Comm, Fin)* **~s** *pl* Büch er *pl;* **to keep the ~s of a firm** die Bücher einer Firma führen. **2** *vt* **(a)** bestellen; *seat, room* buchen; *artiste* engagieren. **(b)** *driver* aufschreiben *(col);* einen Strafzettel verpassen *(+dat) (col); football player* verwarnen. **3** *vi see vt (a)* bestellen; buchen.
♦ **book in 1** *vi (in hotel etc)* sich eintragen. **we ~ed ~ at the Hilton** wir sind im Hilton abgestiegen. **2** *vt sep* **(a)** *(register)* eintragen. **(b)** *(make reservation for)* **to ~ sb ~to a hotel** jdm ein Hotelzimmer reservieren lassen.
♦ **book up 1** *vi* buchen. **2** *vt sep (usu pass)* reservieren lassen. **to be (fully) ~ed ~** (voll) ausgebucht sein.
book: **~case** *n* Bücherregal *nt; (with doors)* Bücherschrank *m;* **~end** *n* Buchstütze *f.*
bookie ['bʊkɪ] *n (col)* Buchmacher *m.*
booking ['bʊkɪŋ] *n (Brit)* Buchung, Reservierung *f; (of artiste)* Engagement *nt.* **to make a ~** buchen.
booking: ~ **clerk** *n* Fahrkartenverkäufer(in *f*) *m;* ~ **office** *n (Brit) (Rail)* Fahrkartenschalter *m; (Theat)* Theaterkasse *f.*
bookish ['bʊkɪʃ] *adj* gelehrt *(pej, hum); language, expression (pej)* trocken.
book: **~-keeper** *n* Buchhalter(in *f*) *m;* **~-keeping** *n* Buchhaltung *or* -führung *f.*
booklet ['bʊklɪt] *n* Broschüre *f.*
book: **~maker** *n* Buchmacher *m;* **~mark** *n* Lesezeichen *nt;* **~seller** *n* Buchändler(in *f*) *m;* **~shelf** *n* Bücherbord *or* -regal *nt;* **~shop** *(Brit),* **~store** *(US) n* Buchhandlung *f;* **~stall** *n* Bücherstand *m;* **~-token** *n* Büchergutschein *m;* **~worm** *n* Bücherwurm *m.*
boom[1] [buːm] *n (across river etc)* Sperre *f; (at factory gate etc)* Schranke *f; (Naut)* Baum *m; (jib of crane)* Ausleger *m; (for microphone)* Galgen *m.*
boom[2] **1** *n (of sea, waves, wind)* Brausen *nt; (of thunder)* Grollen *nt; (of guns)* Donnern *nt; (of organ, voice)* Dröhnen *nt.* **2** *vi* **(a)** *(sea, wind)* brausen; *(thunder)* grollen. **(b)** *(also ~* **out***)* *(organ, person, voice)* dröhnen; *(guns)* donnern. **3** *interj* bum.
♦ **boom out 1** *vi see* **boom**[2] **2 (b). 2** *vt sep (person) order* brüllen.
boom[3] **1** *vi (trade, sales)* einen Aufschwung nehmen. **business is ~ing** das Geschäft blüht *or* floriert. **2** *n (of business, fig)* Boom, Aufschwung *m; (period of economic growth)* Hochkonjunktur *f.*
boomerang ['buːməræŋ] **1** *n (lit, fig)* Bumerang *m.* **2** *vi (fig col: words, actions)* wie ein Bumerang zurückkommen *(on zu).*
boom town *n* Goldgräberstadt *f.*
boon [buːn] *n (blessing, advantage)* Segen *m.*
boor [bʊəʳ] *n* Rüpel, Flegel *m.*
boorish ['bʊərɪʃ] *adj* rüpelhaft, flegelhaft.
boost [buːst] **1** *n* Auftrieb *m no pl; (Elec, Aut)* Verstärkung *f; (for rocket)* Zusatzantrieb *m.* **to give sb/sth a ~** jdm/einer Sache Auftrieb geben. **2** *vt production, economy* ankurbeln; *electric charge, heart etc* verstärken; *confidence, sb's ego* stärken; *morale* heben.
booster ['buːstəʳ] *n* **(a)** *(Elec)* Puffersatz *m; (Rad)* Zusatzverstärker *m; (TV)* Zusatzgleichrichter *m; (Aut) (supercharger)* Kompressor *m; (for heating)* Gebläse *nt; (~ rocket)* Booster *m.* **(b)** *(Med: also ~* **shot***)* Wiederholungsimpfung *f.*
boot [buːt] **1** *n* **(a)** Stiefel *m.* **the ~ is on the other foot** *(fig)* es ist genau umgekehrt; **to give sb the ~** *(fig col)* jdn rausschmeißen *(col).* **(b)** *(Brit: of car)* Kofferraum *m.* **2** *vt* **(a)** *(col: kick)* einen (Fuß)tritt geben *(+dat); ball* kicken. **(b)** *(Comp)* laden.
booth [buːð] *n* **(a)** *(at fair)* (Markt)bude *f.* **(b)** *(telephone ~)* Zelle *f; (polling ~, in language laboratory)* Kabine *f.*
boot: **~lace** *n* Schnürsenkel *m;* **~leg** *adj whisky etc* schwarz gebrannt; **~legger** *n (US)* Bootlegger *m; (producer also)* Schwarzbrenner *m;* ~ **polish** *n* Schuhcreme *f.*
booty ['buːtɪ] *n (lit, fig)* Beute *f.*
booze [buːz] *(col)* **1** *n* Alkohol *m.* **bring some ~** bring was zu trinken mit. **2** *vi* saufen *(col).*
boozer ['buːzəʳ] *n* **(a)** *(pej col: drinker)* Säufer(in *f*) *(pej col) m.* **(b)** *(Brit col: pub)* Kneipe *f (col).*
border ['bɔːdəʳ] **1** *n* **(a)** *(edge, side)* Rand *m.* **(b)** *(boundary, frontier)* Grenze *f.* **north/south of the ~** *(Brit)* in/nach Schottland/England; ~ **dispute** Grenzstreitigkeit *f; (incident)* Grenzzwischenfall *m.* **(c)** *(in garden)* Rabatte *f.* **(d)** *(edging: on dress)* Bordüre *f; (of carpet)* Einfassung *f; (of picture)* Umrahmung *f.* **black ~** *(on notepaper)* schwarzer Rand, Trauerrand *m.* **2** *vt* **(a)** *road* säumen; *garden etc* begrenzen; *(on all sides)* umschließen. **(b)** *(land etc)* grenzen an *(+acc).*
♦ **border on** *vi +prep obj (lit, fig)* grenzen an *(+acc).*
border: **~line 1** *n (lit, fig)* Grenzlinie, Grenze *f;* **to be on the ~line** an der Grenze liegen; **2** *adj* **~line case** Grenzfall *m;* ~ **town** *n* Grenzstadt *f.*
bore[1] [bɔːʳ] **1** *vt hole etc* bohren. **2** *vi* bohren *(for* nach*).* **3** *n (hole)* Bohrloch *nt; (of tube, pipe)* Durchmesser *m; (of shotgun, cannon)* Kaliber *nt.*
bore[2] **1** *n* **(a)** *(person)* Langeweiler *m.* **the club/office ~** der Langweiler vom Dienst. **(b)** *(thing, profession, situation etc)* **to be a ~** langweilig sein. **(c)** *(nuisance)* **don't be a ~** nun hab dich doch nicht so!; **oh what a ~!** das ist aber auch zu dumm! **2** *vt* langweilen. **to ~ sb stiff** *or* **to death** *or* **to tears** jdn zu Tode langweilen; **I'm ~d** ich langweile mich.
bore[3] *pret of* **bear**[1].
boredom ['bɔːdəm] *n* Lang(e)weile *f.*
boring ['bɔːrɪŋ] *adj* langweilig.
born [bɔːn] *adj* **to be ~** geboren werden; *(fig)* entstehen; *(idea)* geboren werden; **I was ~ in 1948** ich bin 1948 geboren; **I wasn't ~ yesterday** *(col)* ich bin nicht von gestern *(col);* **he is Chicago-~** er ist ein gebürtiger Chicagoer; **high-/low-~** von vornehmer/niedriger Geburt; **he is a ~ poet/teacher** er ist der geborene Dichter/Lehrer; **an Englishman ~ and bred** ein echter *or* waschechter *(col)* Engländer.
borne [bɔːn] *ptp of* **bear**[1].
borough ['bʌrə] *n (also* **municipal ~***)* Bezirk *m.*
borrow ['bɒrəʊ] *vt* **(a)** sich *(dat)* leihen *(from* von*); library book* ausleihen; *word* entlehnen; *(fig) idea* übernehmen *(from* von*).* **to ~ money from the bank** einen Kredit bei der Bank aufnehmen.
borrower ['bɒrəʊəʳ] *n (of books)* Entleiher(in *f*) *m; (of capital, loan etc)* Kreditnehmer(in *f*) *m.*
borrowing ['bɒrəʊɪŋ] *n see vt* Leihen *nt;* Ausleihen *nt;* Entlehnung *f;* Übernahme *f.* **~s** *pl (Fin)* Anleihen *pl.*
borstal ['bɔːstl] *n (Brit Jur)* Besserungsanstalt *f.*
bosom ['bʊzəm] **1** *n (lit, fig: of person)* Busen *m.* **in the ~ of his family** im Schoß der Familie. **2** *adj attr friend etc* Busen-.
boss [bɒs] *n* Chef, Boß *(col) m.* **industrial/union ~es** Industrie-/Gewerkschaftsbosse *pl (col);*

OK, you're the ~ okay, du bestimmst.
♦ **boss about** *or* **around** *vt sep (col)* rumkommandieren *(col)*.
bossy ['bɒsɪ] *adj (+er)* herrisch. **don't you get ~ with me!** kommandier mich nicht so rum! *(col)*.
botanical [bə'tænɪkəl] *adj* botanisch, Pflanzen-. **~ gardens** botanischer Garten.
botanist ['bɒtənɪst] *n* Botaniker(in *f*) *m*.
botany ['bɒtənɪ] *n* Botanik, Pflanzenkunde *f*.
botch [bɒtʃ] *(col) vt (also* **~ up***)* verpfuschen *(col)*.
both [bəʊθ] **1** *adj* beide. **~ (the) boys** beide Jungen. **2** *pron* beide; *(two different things)* beides. **~ of them were there, they were ~ there** sie waren (alle) beide da; **come in ~ of you** kommt beide herein. **3** *adv* **~ ... and ...** sowohl ... als auch ...; **~ you and I** wir beide; **John and I ~ came** John und ich sind beide gekommen; **she was ~ laughing and crying** sie lachte und weinte zugleich *or* gleichzeitig; **is it black or white? — ~** ist es schwarz oder weiß? — beides.
bother ['bɒðəʳ] **1** *vt* **(a)** stören; *(pester)* belästigen; *(worry)* Sorgen machen *(+dat)*; *(back, teeth etc)* zu schaffen machen *(+dat)*; *(problem, question)* beschäftigen. **I'm sorry to ~ you but ...** es tut mir leid, daß ich Sie damit belästigen muß, aber ...; **I shouldn't let it ~ you** machen Sie sich mal keine Sorgen; **don't ~ me!** laß mich in Frieden!; **could I ~ you for a light?** dürfte ich Sie vielleicht um Feuer bitten?; **what's ~ing you?** was haben Sie denn? **(b) I can't be ~ed with doing that** ich habe einfach keine Lust dazu; **do you want to stay or go? — I'm not ~ed** willst du blei ben oder gehen? — das ist mir egal.
2 *vti* sich kümmern *(about* um*)*. **don't ~!** nicht nötig!; *(sarcastic)* machen Sie sich *(dat)* keine Mühe!; **she didn't even ~ to ask/check** sie hat nicht einmal gefragt/nachgesehen; **you needn't ~ to come** Sie brauchen wirklich nicht (zu) kommen; **I didn't ~ about lunch** ich habe das Mittagessen ausgelassen.
3 *n* **(a)** *(nuisance)* Plage *f*. **it's such a ~** das ist wirklich lästig; **I've forgotten it, what a ~** ich habe es vergessen, wie ärgerlich. **(b)** *(trouble etc)* Ärger *m*; *(difficulties)* Schwierigkeiten *pl*. **we had a spot** *or* **bit of ~ with the car** wir hatten Ärger mit dem Auto; **it wasn't any ~** *(don't mention it)* gern geschehen; *(not difficult)* das war ganz einfach; **the children were no ~ at all** wir hatten mit den Kindern überhaupt keine Probleme; **to go to a lot of ~ to do sth** sich *(dat)* mit etw viel Mühe geben.
4 *interj* so was Dummes! *(col)*.
bottle ['bɒtl] **1** *n* Flasche *f*. **a ~ of wine** eine Flasche Wein; **to take to the ~** zur Flasche greifen. **2** *vt* in Flaschen abfüllen. **~d in ...** abgefüllt in ...
♦ **bottle up** *vt sep emotion* in sich *(dat)* aufstauen.
bottled ['bɒtld] *adj wine* in Flaschen (abgefüllt); *beer* Flaschen-; *fruit* eingemacht.
bottle: ~ bank *n* Altglasbehälter *m*; **~-feed** *vt* mit der Flasche ernähren; **~ green** *adj* flaschengrün; **~neck** *n (fig)* Engpaß *m*; **~ opener** *n* Flaschenöffner *m*; **~ party** *n* Bottle-Party *f*.
bottom ['bɒtəm] **1** *n* **(a)** *(of receptacle)* Boden *m*; *(of mountain, pillar, spire)* Fuß *m*; *(of well, canyon)* Grund *m*; *(of page, screen, wall)* (unteres) Ende; *(of list, road)* Ende *nt*. **at the ~ (of)** unten *(an/in +dat)*; **to be (at the) ~ of the class** der/die Letzte in der Klasse sein; **~s up!** hoch die Tassen *(col)*; **at ~** *(fig)* im Grunde; **the ~ fell out of his world** *(col)* für ihn brach eine Welt zusammen. **(b)** *(underneath, underside)* Unterseite *f*, untere Seite. **(c)** *(of sea, lake, river)* Grund, Boden *m*. **(d)** *(of person)* Hintern *(col)*, Po *(col) m*; *(of trousers etc)* Hosenboden *m*. **(e)** *(fig: cause)* **to be at the ~ of sth** *(person)* hinter etw *(dat)* stecken; *(thing)* einer Sache *(dat)* zugrunde liegen; **to get to the ~ of sth** einer Sache *(dat)* auf den Grund kommen. **(f)** *(Brit Aut: gear)* **in ~** im ersten Gang.
2 *adj attr (lower)* untere(r, s); *(lowest)* unterste(r, s); *(Fin)* Tiefst-; *pupil* schlechteste(r, s). **~ half** *(of box)* untere Hälfte; *(of list, class)* zweite Hälfte.
bottom: ~ drawer *n (Brit)* **to put sth away in one's ~ drawer** etw für die Aussteuer sparen; **~ gear** *n (Brit Aut)* erster Gang; **~less** *adj (lit)* bodenlos; **a ~less pit** *(fig)* ein Faß ohne Boden; **~most** *adj* allerunterste(r, s).
bough [baʊ] *n* Ast *m*.
bought [bɔːt] *pret, ptp of* **buy.**
boulder ['bəʊldəʳ] *n* Felsblock, Felsbrocken *m*.
bounce [baʊns] **1** *vi* **(a)** *(ball etc)* springen; *(Sport: ball)* aufspringen. **the child ~d up and down on the bed** das Kind hüpfte auf dem Bett herum. **(b)** *(col: cheque)* platzen *(col)*. **2** *vt* aufprallen lassen, prellen *(Sport)*. **he ~d the baby on his knee** er ließ das Kind auf den Knien reiten. **3** *n* **(a)** *(of ball: rebound)* Aufprall *m*. **(b)** *no pl (of ball)* Sprungkraft *f*; *(of rubber)* Elastizität *f*; *(col: of person)* Schwung *m (col)*.
♦ **bounce back** *vi* abprallen, zurückprallen; *(fig col: person)* sich nicht unterkriegen lassen *(col)*.
♦ **bounce off** *vt always separate* **to ~ sth ~ sth** etw von etw abprallen lassen; **to ~ an idea ~ sb** eine Idee an jdm testen *(col)*.
bouncer ['baʊnsəʳ] *n (col)* Rausschmeißer *m (col)*.
bouncing ['baʊnsɪŋ] *adj* **~ baby** strammes Baby.
bouncy ['baʊnsɪ] *adj (+er)* **(a)** *ball* gut springend; *mattress* federnd; *springs* elastisch; *ride* holpernd. **(b)** *(fig col: exuberant)* übermütig.
bound[1] [baʊnd] **1** *n usu pl (lit, fig)* Grenze *f*. **to keep within the ~s of propriety** im Rahmen bleiben; **within the ~s of probability** im Bereich des Wahrscheinlichen; **there are no ~s to his ambition** sein Ehrgeiz kennt keine Grenzen; **out of ~s** gesperrt. **2** *vt usu pass country* begrenzen.
bound[2] **1** *n* Sprung, Satz *m*. **2** *vi* springen; *(rabbit)* hoppeln. **the dog came ~ing up** der Hund kam angesprungen.
bound[3] **1** *pret, ptp of* **bind. 2** *adj* **(a)** *(prisoner, book)* gebunden. **~ hand and foot** an Händen und Füßen gebunden. **(b)** *(sure)* **to be ~ to do sth** etw bestimmt tun; **he's ~ to be late** er kommt garantiert zu spät; **it's ~ to happen** das muß so kommen. **(c)** *(obliged) person* verpflichtet; *(by contract, word, promise)* gebunden. **but I'm ~ to say ...** *(col)* aber ich muß schon sagen ...
bound[4] *adj pred* **to be ~ for London** *(heading for)* auf dem Weg nach London sein; **where are you ~ for?** wohin geht die Reise?, wohin wollen Sie?; **we were northward-/California-~** wir waren nach Norden/Kalifornien unterwegs.
boundary ['baʊndərɪ] *n* Grenze *f*.
boundless ['baʊndlɪs] *adj (lit, fig)* grenzenlos.
bountiful ['baʊntɪfʊl] *adj* großzügig; *sovereign, god* gütig; *harvest, gifts* (über)reich.
bounty ['baʊntɪ] *n* **(a)** *(generosity)* Freigebigkeit *f*; *(of nature)* reiche Fülle *(geh)*. **(b)** *(reward money)* Kopfgeld *nt*. **~ hunter** Kopfgeldjäger *m*.
bouquet ['bʊkeɪ] *n* **(a)** Strauß *m*, Bukett *nt (geh)*. **(b)** *(of wine)* Bukett *nt*, Blume *f*.
bourgeois ['bʊəʒwɑː] **1** *n* Bürger(in *f*) *m*; *(pej)* Spießbürger(in *f*) *m*. **2** *adj* bürgerlich; *(pej)* spießbürgerlich.
bourgeoisie [ˌbʊəʒwɑː'ziː] *n* Bürgertum *nt*, Bourgeoisie *f*.
bout [baʊt] *n* **(a)** *(of flu etc)* Anfall *m*; *(of negotiations)* Runde *f*. **a ~ of fever** ein Fieberanfall *m*; **a drinking ~** eine Zecherei. **(b)** *(Boxing, Wrestling, Fencing)* Kampf *m*.
boutique [buː'tiːk] *n* Boutique *f*.
bow[1] [bəʊ] *n* **(a)** *(for arrows, Mus)* Bogen *m*. **a ~ and arrow** Pfeil und Bogen *pl*. **(b)** *(of ribbon etc)* Schleife *f*.
bow[2] [baʊ] **1** *n (with head, body)* Verbeugung *f*; *(by young boy)* Diener *m*. **2** *vi* **(a)** sich verbeugen *(to sb* vor jdm*)*; *(young boy)* einen Diener machen. **to**

~ **and scrape** katzbuckeln *(pej)*. **(b)** *(bend: branches etc)* sich biegen. **(c)** *(fig: defer, submit)* sich beugen *(before* vor *+dat, under* unter *+dat, to dat)*. **to ~ to the inevitable** sich in das Unvermeidliche fügen. **3** *vt* **to ~ one's head** den Kopf senken; *(in prayer)* sich verneigen.

♦ **bow out** *vi (fig)* sich verabschieden.

bow[3] [baʊ] *n (also:* **~s***)* Bug *m*. **on the port ~** backbord voraus.

bowel ['baʊəl] *n usu pl (Anat) (of person)* Eingeweide *nt usu pl*; *(of animal also)* Innereien *pl*. **a ~ movement** Stuhl(gang) *m*; **the ~s of the earth** das Erdinnere.

bowl[1] [bəʊl] *n* **(a)** Schüssel *f*; *(smaller, shallow also, finger~)* Schale *f*; *(for sugar etc)* Schälchen *nt*; *(for animals, prisoners also)* Napf *m*. **(b)** *(of pipe)* Kopf *m*; *(of lavatory)* Becken *nt*. **(c)** *(Geog)* Becken *nt*. **(d)** *(US: stadium)* Stadion *nt*.

bowl[2] **1** *n (Sport: ball)* Kugel *f*. **2** *vi (Cricket) (mit gestrecktem Arm)* werfen. **3** *vt* **(a)** *(roll) ball* rollen; *hoop also* treiben. **(b)** *(Cricket) ball* werfen; *batsman* ausschlagen.

♦ **bowl over** *vt sep (lit, fig)* umwerfen. **he was ~ed ~ by the news** die Nachricht hat ihn überwältigt *or* umgehauen *(col)*.

bow-legged [ˌbəʊ'legɪd] *adj* O-beinig.

bowler ['bəʊləʳ] *n* **(a)** *(Cricket)* Werfer *m*. **(b)** *(Brit: also* **~ hat***)* Melone *f*.

bowling ['bəʊlɪŋ] *n* **(a)** *(Cricket)* Werfen *nt*. **(b)** *(tenpin ~)* Bowling *nt*; *(skittles)* Kegeln *nt*. **to go ~** bowlen/kegeln gehen.

bowling: ~ alley *n* Kegelbahn *f*; **~ green** *n* Rasenfläche *f* für Bowling.

bowls [bəʊlz] *n sing* Bowling *nt*.

bow: ~ tie *n* Fliege *f*; **~ window** *n* Erkerfenster *nt*.

box[1] [bɒks] **1** *vti (Sport)* boxen. **to ~ sb's ears** jdn ohrfeigen, jdm eine Ohrfeige geben. **2** *n* **a ~ on the ear** eine Ohrfeige.

box[2] *n* **(a)** Kiste *f*; *(cardboard ~)* Karton *m*; *(smaller)* Schachtel *f*; *(snuff~, cigarette ~ etc, biscuit tin)* Dose *f*; *(chocolates etc)* Schachtel *f*; *(jewellery ~)* Schatulle *f*, Kasten *m*; *(collection ~)* (Sammel)büchse *f*; *(in church)* Opferbüchse *f*; *(fixed to wall etc)* Opferstock *m*. **(b)** *(two-dimensional)* (umrandetes) Feld; *(Baseball)* Box *f*; *(in road junction) gelb schraffierter Kreuzungsbereich*. **(c)** *(Theat)* Loge *f*; *(jury ~)* Geschworenenbank *f*; *(witness ~)* Zeugenstand *m*; *(press ~)* Pressekabine *f*. **(d)** *(Tech: housing)* Gehäuse *nt*. **gear ~** Getriebe *nt*. **(e)** *(sentry ~)* Schilderhaus *nt*; *(signal ~)* Häuschen *nt*. **(f)** *(horse ~)* Box *f*. **(g)** **PO B~** Postfach *nt*. **(h)** *(Brit: phone ~)* Zelle *f*. **(i)** *(Brit col: TV)* Glotze *f (col)*.

♦ **box in** *vt sep player* in die Zange nehmen; *parked car* einklemmen; *(fig)* einengen.

boxer ['bɒksəʳ] *n (Sport, dog)* Boxer *m*.

boxing ['bɒksɪŋ] *n* Boxen *nt*.

boxing *in cpds* Box-; **~ Day** *n (Brit)* zweiter Weihnachts(feier)tag; **~ match** *n* Boxkampf *m*; **~ ring** *n* Boxring *m*.

box: ~ number *n (at post office)* Postfach *nt*; **~ office** *n* Kasse, Theater-/Kinokasse *f*; **~room** *n (Brit)* Abstellraum *m*.

boy [bɔɪ] *n* Junge *m*; *(lift~)* Boy *m*. **~s will be ~s** Jungen sind nun mal so; **a school for ~s** eine Jungenschule; **the old ~** *(boss)* der Alte *(col)*; *(father)* mein *etc* alter Herr; **old ~** *(col)* alter Junge *(col)*; **oh ~!** *(col)* Junge, Junge! *(col)*.

boycott ['bɔɪkɒt] **1** *n* Boykott *m*. **2** *vt* boykottieren.

boy: ~friend *n* Freund *m*; **~hood** *n* Kindheit *f*; *(as teenager)* Jugend(zeit) *f*.

boyish ['bɔɪɪʃ] *adj* jungenhaft; *(of woman) figure, appearance* knabenhaft.

Boy Scouts *n sing* Pfadfinder *pl*.

BR = British Rail.

bra [brɑː] *n* = **brassière** BH *m*.

brace[1] [breɪs] *n, pl - (pair: of pheasants etc)* Paar *nt*.

brace[2] **1** *n* **(a)** *(Build)* Strebe *f*. **(b)** *(tool) (wheel ~)* Radschlüssel *m*; *(to hold bit)* Bohrwinde *f*. **~ and bit** Bohrer *m* (mit Einsatz). **(c)** *(on teeth)* Klammer, Spange *f*; *(Med)* Stützapparat *m*. **2** *vt* **(a)** (ab)stützen; *(horizontally)* verstreben; *(in vice etc)* verklammern. **3** *vr* **to ~ oneself for sth** sich auf etw *(acc)* gefaßt machen.

bracelet ['breɪslɪt] *n* Armband *nt*; *(bangle)* Armreif *m*.

braces ['breɪsɪz] *npl (Brit)* Hosenträger *pl*.

bracing ['breɪsɪŋ] *adj* anregend; *climate* Reiz-.

bracken ['brækən] *n* Adlerfarn *m*.

bracket ['brækɪt] **1** *n* **(a)** *(angle ~)* Winkelträger *m*; *(Archit)* Konsole *f*. **(b)** *(Typ)* Klammer *f*. **in ~s** in Klammern. **(c)** *(group)* Gruppe, Klasse *f*. **the lower income ~** die untere Einkommensgruppe. **2** *vt* **(a)** *(put in ~s)* einklammern. **(b)** *(also* **~ together***)* mit einer Klammer versehen; *(fig: group together)* zusammenfassen.

brackish ['brækɪʃ] *adj water* brackig.

brag [bræg] *vti* prahlen, angeben *(about, of* mit*)*.

braggart ['brægət] *n* Prahler, Angeber *m*.

braid [breɪd] **1** *n* **(a)** *(of hair)* Zopf *m*. **(b)** *(trimming)* Borte *f*; *(self-coloured)* Litze *f*. **(c)** *(Mil)* Tressen *pl*. **gold ~** Goldtressen *pl*. **2** *vt (plait) hair, straw etc* flechten.

braille [breɪl] *n* Blinden- *or* Brailleschrift *f*.

brain [breɪn] **1** *n* **(a)** *(Anat, of machine)* Gehirn *nt*. **he's got cars on the ~** *(col)* er hat nur Autos im Kopf. **(b)** **~s** *pl (Anat)* Gehirn *nt*; *(Cook)* Hirn *nt*. **(c)** *(mind)* Verstand *m*. **~s** *pl (intelligence)* Intelligenz *f*, Grips *m (col)*, Köpfchen *nt (col)*. **he didn't have the ~s to warn us** er ist nicht einmal darauf gekommen, uns zu warnen; **he's the ~s of the family** er ist das Genie in der Familie. **2** *vt* **stop it or I'll ~ you!** *(col)* hör auf oder ich knall dir eine! *(col)*.

brain: ~child *n (invention)* Erfindung *f*; **~less** *adj plan, idea* hirnlos, dumm; *person also* unbedarft; **~storm** *n* **(a)** *(Brit)* **to have a ~storm** geistig weggetreten sein *(col)*; **(b)** *(US: ~wave)* Geistesblitz *m*; **~ teaser** *n* Denksportaufgabe *f*; **~ tumour** *(Brit) or* **tumor** *(US) n* Gehirntumor *m*; **~wash** *vt* einer Gehirnwäsche *(dat)* unterziehen; **to ~wash sb into believing that ...** jdm (ständig) einreden, daß ...; **~washing** *n* Gehirnwäsche *f*; **~wave** *n (Brit)* Geistesblitz *m*.

brainy ['breɪnɪ] *adj (+er) (col)* gescheit, helle *pred (col)*.

braise [breɪz] *vt (Cook)* schmoren.

brake [breɪk] **1** *n (Tech)* Bremse *f*. **to put the ~s on** *(lit, fig)* bremsen; **to put the ~s on sth** *(fig)* etw bremsen. **2** *vi* bremsen.

brake *in cpds* Brems-; **~ drum** *n* Bremstrommel *f*; **~light** *n* Bremslicht *nt*; **~ lining** *n* Bremsbelag *m*.

braking ['breɪkɪŋ] *n* Bremsen *nt*. **~ distance** Bremsweg *m*.

bramble ['bræmbl] *n* **(a)** *(thorny shoot)* Dornenzweig *m*. **(b)** *(blackberry)* Brombeere *f*; *(bush)* Brombeerstrauch *m*.

bran [bræn] *n* Kleie *f*.

branch [brɑːntʃ] **1** *n* **(a)** *(Bot)* Zweig *m*; *(growing straight from trunk)* Ast *m*. **(b)** *(of river, pipe, duct)* Arm *m*; *(of road)* Abzweigung *f*; *(of family, race, language)* Zweig *m*; *(of railway)* Abzweig *m*. **(c)** *(Comm)* Filiale *f*; *(of company, bank also)* Geschäftsstelle *f*. **~ manager** Filialleiter *m*/Geschäftsstellenleiter *m*. **2** *vi (divide: river, road etc)* sich gabeln; *(in more than two)* sich verzweigen.

♦ **branch off** *vi (road)* abzweigen; *(driver)* abbiegen.

♦ **branch out** *vi (company)* sein Geschäft erweitern *or* ausdehnen *(into* auf *+acc)*. **to ~ ~ on one's own** sich selbständig machen

branch: ~ line *n (Rail)* Zweiglinie, Nebenlinie *f*; **~ office** *n* Filiale, Geschäftsstelle *f*.

brand [brænd] **1** *n* **(a)** *(make)* Marke *f*. **(b)** *(mark) (on cattle)* Brandzeichen *nt*; *(on criminal, prisoner, fig)* Brandmal *nt*. **2** *vt* **(a)** *(Comm) goods* mit seinem Warenzeichen versehen. **(b)** *cattle, property* mit einem Brandzeichen kennzeichnen. **(c)** *(stigmatize) person* brandmarken.

brandish ['brændɪʃ] *vt* schwingen, fuchteln mit *(col)*.

brand: ~ **name** *n* Markenname *m*; ~**-new** *adj* nagelneu, brandneu *(col)*.

brandy ['brændɪ] *n* Weinbrand *m*.

brash [bræʃ] *adj (+er)* frech, dreist; *(tasteless) colour etc* aufdringlich.

brass [brɑːs] **1** *n* **(a)** Messing *nt*. **(b) the** ~ *(Mus)* die Blechbläser *pl*. **(c)** *(col)* **the top** ~ die hohen Tiere *(col)*. **(d)** *(col: money)* Moos *nt (col)*, Kies *m (col)*. **2** *adj (made of* ~*)* Messing-. ~ **section** Blechbläser *pl*; **to get down to** ~ **tacks** *(col)* zur Sache kommen.

brass band *n* Blaskapelle *f*.

brassière ['bræsɪə^r] *n (dated, form)* Büstenhalter *m*.

brat [bræt] *n (pej col)* Balg *m or nt (col)*, Gör *nt (col)*.

bravado [brə'vɑːdəʊ] *n (showy bravery)* Wagemut *m*; *(hiding fear)* gespielte Tapferkeit.

brave [breɪv] **1** *adj (+er)* mutig, unerschrocken; *(suffering pain) smile* tapfer. **be** ~! nur Mut!; *(more seriously)* sei tapfer! **2** *n (Indian)* Krieger *m*. **3** *vt* die Stirn bieten *(+dat)*; *weather* trotzen *(+dat)*; *death* tapfer ins Auge sehen *(+dat)*.

♦ **brave out** *vt sep* **you have to** ~ **it** ~ das mußt du durchstehen.

bravery ['breɪvərɪ] *n see adj* Mut *m*; Tapferkeit *f*.

bravo [brɑː'vəʊ] *interj* bravo!

brawl [brɔːl] **1** *vi* sich schlagen. **2** *n* Schlägerei *f*.

brawn [brɔːn] *n* **(a)** *(Cook)* Preßkopf *m*, Sülze *f*. **(b)** Muskeln *pl*, Muskelkraft *f*.

brawny ['brɔːnɪ] *adj (+er)* muskulös, kräftig.

bray [breɪ] **1** *n (of ass)* (Esels)schrei *m*. **2** *vi (ass)* schreien; *(col: person)* wiehern.

brazen ['breɪzn] *adj (impudent)* unverschämt, dreist; *lie* schamlos.

♦ **brazen out** *vt sep* **to** ~ **it** ~ durchhalten; *(by lying)* sich durchmogeln *(col)*.

brazier ['breɪzɪə^r] *n* (Kohlen)feuer *nt* (im Freien); *(container)* Kohlenbecken *nt*.

brazil [brə'zɪl] *n (also* ~ **nut***)* Paranuß *f*.

Brazil [brə'zɪl] *n* Brasilien *nt*.

Brazilian [brə'zɪlɪən] **1** *n* Brasilianer(in *f*) *m*. **2** *adj* brasilianisch.

breach [briːtʃ] **1** *n* **(a)** *(of law)* Übertretung *f (of gen)*, Verstoß *m (of* gegen*)*. **a** ~ **of contract** ein Vertragsbruch *m*; ~ **of the peace** *(Jur)* öffentliche Ruhestörung. **(b)** *(in friendship etc)* Bruch *m*. **(c)** *(in wall etc, in security)* Lücke *f*. **to step into the** ~ *(fig)* in die Bresche springen. **2** *vt wall* eine Bresche schlagen *(in +acc)*; *defences, security* durchbrechen.

bread [bred] **1** *n* **(a)** Brot *nt*. **a piece of** ~ **and butter** ein Butterbrot *nt*; **it's my** ~ **and butter** *(fig)* davon lebe ich; **he knows which side his** ~ **is buttered (on)** er weiß, wo was zu holen ist; **to earn one's daily** ~ (sich *dat*) sein Brot verdienen. **(b)** *(col: money)* Moos *nt (col)*, Kohle *f (col)*. **2** *vt* panieren.

bread: ~**bin** *n* Brotkasten *m*; ~**board** *n* Brot(schneide)brett *nt*; ~**crumb** *n* Brotkrume *f or* -krümel *m*; ~**crumbs** *npl (Cook)* Paniermehl *nt*; ~**knife** *n* Brotmesser *nt*; ~**line** *n* **to be on the** ~**line** *(fig)* nur das Allernotwendigste zum Leben haben.

breadth [bretθ] *n* Breite *f*; *(of ideas, of theory)* (Band)breite *f*. **a hundred metres in** ~ hundert Meter breit; **his** ~ **of outlook** *(open-mindedness)* seine Aufgeschlossenheit; *(variety of interests)* seine Vielseitigkeit.

breadwinner ['bredwɪnə^r] *n* Ernährer *m*.

break [breɪk] *(vb: pret* **broke,** *ptp* **broken***)* **1** *n* **(a)** *(in bone, pipe, end of relations etc)* Bruch *m*; *(in wall, line)* Lücke *f*; *(in clouds)* Spalt *m*. ~ **in the circuit** Stromkreisunterbrechung *f*. **(b)** *(pause, rest: Brit Sch)* Pause *f*. **without a** ~ ununterbrochen; **to take** *or* **have a** ~ (eine) Pause machen. **(c)** *(change) (in contest etc)* Wende *f*; *(holiday, change of activity etc)* Abwechslung *f*. **it makes a nice** ~ das ist mal etwas anderes; ~ **in the weather** Wetterumschwung *m*. **(d) at** ~ **of day** bei Tagesanbruch. **(e)** *(col: escape)* Ausbruch *m*. **they made a** ~ **for it** sie versuchten zu entkommen. **(f)** *(col: luck, opportunity)* **to have a good/bad** ~ Glück *or* Schwein *(col) nt*/Pech *nt* haben; **we had a few lucky** ~**s** wir haben ein paarmal Glück *or* Schwein *(col)* gehabt; **give me a** ~! gib mir ein Chance! **(g)** *(Snooker)* Ballfolge, Serie *f*.

2 *vt* **(a)** brechen; *stick, glass* zerbrechen; *window* einschlagen; *egg* aufschlagen; *surface, shell* durchbrechen. **to** ~ **a leg** sich *(dat)* das Bein brechen; **to** ~ **surface** *(submarine)* auftauchen. **(b)** *rule* verletzen; *appointment* nicht einhalten. **(c)** *journey, current, silence etc* unterbrechen; *monotony, routine* auflockern. **(d)** *sound barrier* durchbrechen. **(e) he couldn't** ~ **the habit of smoking** er konnte sich das Rauchen nicht abgewöhnen. **(f)** *code* entziffern; *(Sport) serve* durchbrechen. **to** ~ **sb** *(financially)* jdn ruinieren; *(with grief)* jdn seelisch brechen; **to** ~ **the bank** die Bank sprengen. **(g)** *fall* dämpfen, abfangen. **(h)** *jail, one's bonds* ausbrechen aus. **(i)** *news* mitteilen. **how can I** ~ **it to her?** wie soll ich es ihr bloß beibringen?

3 *vi* **(a)** brechen; *(rope)* zerreißen; *(smash)* kaputtgehen; *(cup, glass etc)* zerbrechen. **(b)** *(stop working etc: toy, watch)* kaputtgehen. **(c)** *(pause)* (eine) Pause machen. **(d)** *(wave)* sich brechen. **(e)** *(day, dawn)* anbrechen; *(suddenly: storm)* losbrechen. **(f)** *(change: weather, luck)* umschlagen. **(g)** *(disperse: clouds)* aufreißen. **(h)** *(stamina)* gebrochen werden; *(under interrogation etc)* zusammenbrechen. **after 6 months her health broke** nach 6 Monaten war ihre Gesundheit ruiniert. **(i)** *(voice: with emotion)* brechen. **his voice is beginning to** ~ *(boy)* er kommt in den Stimmbruch. **(j)** *(story, news, scandal)* bekannt werden. **(k) to** ~ **even** seine (Un)kosten decken. **(l) he's broken with her** er hat mit ihr Schluß gemacht.

♦ **break away 1** *vi* **(a)** *(chair leg, handle etc)* abbrechen *(from* von*)*; *(railway coaches, boats)* sich losreißen *(from* von*)*. **(b)** *(dash away)* weglaufen *(from* von*)*; *(prisoner)* sich losreißen *(from* von*)*; *(Ftbl)* sich freispielen. **(c)** *(cut ties)* sich trennen *(from* von*)*. **2** *vt sep* abbrechen *(from* von*)*.

♦ **break down 1** *vi* **(a)** *(vehicle)* eine Panne haben; *(machine)* ausfallen. **(b)** *(negotiations, plan)* scheitern; *(communications)* zum Erliegen kommen; *(law and order)* zusammenbrechen; *(marriage)* in die Brüche gehen. **(c)** *(argument, resistance, person: start crying)* zusammenbrechen. **(d)** *(be analysed) (expenditure)* sich aufschlüsseln *or* -gliedern; *(theory)* sich aufgliedern (lassen). **2** *vt sep* **(a)** *door* einrennen; *wall* niederreißen; *opposition* brechen; *reserve, shyness* überwinden; *suspicion* zerstreuen. **(b)** *expenditure* aufschlüsseln; *theory, argument* untergliedern; *substance* aufspalten.

♦ **break in 1** *vi* **(a)** *(interrupt)* unterbrechen *(on sb/sth* jdn/etw*)*. **(b)** *(enter illegally)* einbrechen. **2** *vt sep* **(a)** *door* aufbrechen. **(b)** *horse* zureiten; *shoes* einlaufen.

♦ **break into** *vi +prep obj* **(a)** *house* einbrechen in *(+acc)*; *safe, car* aufbrechen. **(b)** *(use part of) savings, £5 note* anbrechen. **(c)** *(begin suddenly)* **to** ~ ~ **song/a trot** zu singen/traben anfangen.

♦ **break off 1** *vi* abbrechen; *(stop also)* aufhören. **we** ~ ~ **at 5 o'clock** wir hören um 5 Uhr auf. **2** *vt* *sep* abbrechen; *engagement* lösen. **she's broken it ~** sie hat sich von ihm getrennt.

♦ **break out** *vi* **(a)** *(epidemic, fire, war)* ausbrechen. **(b) to ~ ~ in a rash/in(to) spots** einen Ausschlag/Pickel bekommen; **he broke ~ in a cold sweat** ihm brach der Angstschweiß aus. **(c)** *(escape)* ausbrechen *(from, of* aus*)*.

♦ **break through** *vi* durchbrechen.

♦ **break up 1** *vi* **(a)** *(road)* aufbrechen; *(ice also)* bersten; *(ship in storm)* zerbersten. **(b)** *(clouds)* sich lichten; *(crowd, group)* auseinanderlaufen; *(meeting, partnership)* sich auflösen; *(marriage, relationship)* in die Brüche gehen; *(friends, partners)* sich trennen. **(c)** *(Brit Sch) (school)* aufhören. **when do you ~ ~?** wann hört bei euch die Schule auf? **2** *vt sep* **(a)** *ground, road* aufbrechen; *ship (in breaker's yard)* abwracken. **(b)** *estate* aufteilen; *room also, paragraph, sentence* unterteilen; *empire* auflösen; *lines, expanse of colour (make more interesting)* auflockern. **(c)** *marriage, home* zerstören; *meeting* auflösen; *crowd (police)* zerstreuen, auseinandertreiben. **~ it ~!** auseinander!

breakable ['breɪkəbl] **1** *adj* zerbrechlich. **2** *n* **~s** *pl* zerbrechliche Ware.

breakage ['breɪkɪdʒ] *n* Bruch *m*. **to pay for ~s** für zerbrochene Ware bezahlen.

breakaway ['breɪkəˌweɪ] **1** *n* **(a)** *(Pol)* Absplitterung *f*; *(of state also)* Loslösung *f*. **(b)** *(Sport)* Aus- *or* Durchbruch *m*. **(c)** *(US Sport: false start)* Fehlstart *m*. **2** *adj* **~ group** Splittergruppe *f*.

breakdown ['breɪkdaʊn] *n* **(a)** *(of machine)* Betriebsschaden *m*; *(of vehicle)* Panne *f*. **(b)** *(of communications, Med)* Zusammenbruch *m*. **(c)** *(of figures, expenditure etc)* Aufschlüsselung *f*; *(of thesis, theory etc)* Auf- *or* Untergliederung *f*. **(d)** *(Chem)* Aufspaltung *f*.

breakdown: ~ service *n (Brit)* Pannendienst *m*; **~ truck** *or* **van** *n (Brit)* Abschleppwagen *m*.

breaker ['breɪkəʳ] *n (wave)* Brecher *m*.

breakfast ['brekfəst] **1** *n* Frühstück *nt*. **to have ~** frühstücken, Frühstück essen; **for ~** zum Frühstück. **2** *vi* frühstücken.

break-in ['breɪkɪn] *n* Einbruch *m*.

breaking ['breɪkɪŋ] *n* **~ and entering** *(Jur)* Einbruch *m*.

breaking point *n* **(a)** *(Tech)* Festigkeitsgrenze *f*. **(b)** *(fig)* **she is at ~** sie ist nervlich am Ende.

break: ~neck *adj*: **at ~neck speed** mit halsbrecherischer Geschwindigkeit; **~-out** *n* Ausbruch *m*; **~through** *n (Mil, fig)* Durchbruch *m*; **~-up** *n* **(a)** *(lit) (of ship)* Zerbersten *nt*; *(of ice)* Bersten *nt*; **(b)** *(fig) (of friendship)* Bruch *m*; *(of marriage)* Zerrüttung *f*; *(of political party)* Zersplitterung *f*; *(of partnership, meeting)* Auflösung *f*; **~water** *n* Wellenbrecher *m*.

breast [brest] *n (lit, fig)* Brust *f*.

breast: ~fed *adj* **to be ~fed** gestillt werden; **~feed** *vti* stillen; **~ stroke** *m* Brustschwimmen *nt*; **to do the ~ stroke** brustschwimmen.

breath [breθ] *n* **(a)** Atem *m*. **to take a deep ~** einmal tief Luft holen; **bad ~** Mundgeruch *m*; **with one's dying ~** mit dem letzten Atemzug; **out of ~** außer Atem, atemlos; **in the same ~** im selben Atemzug; **to take sb's ~ away** jdm den Atem verschlagen; **to say sth under one's ~** etw vor sich *(acc)* hin murmeln; **to go out for a ~ of (fresh) air** an die frische Luft gehen. **(b)** *(slight stirring)* **~ of wind** Lüftchen *nt*, Hauch *m*.

breathalyzer ['breθəlaɪzəʳ] *n (Brit)* Röhrchen *nt (col)*. **to give sb a ~** jdn ins Röhrchen blasen lassen.

breathe [bri:ð] **1** *vi* atmen; *(col: rest)* verschnaufen, Luft holen. **now we can ~ again** jetzt können wir wieder aufatmen; *(have more space)* jetzt haben wir wieder Luft. **2** *vt air* einatmen. **to ~ one's last** seinen letzten Atemzug tun; **he ~d garlic all over me** er verströmte einen starken Knoblauchgeruch; **he ~d new life into the firm** er brachte neues Leben in die Firma; **don't ~ a word** sag kein Sterbenswörtchen!

♦ **breathe in** *vi, vt sep* einatmen.

♦ **breathe out** *vi, vt sep* ausatmen.

breather ['bri:ðəʳ] *n (short rest)* Atempause, Verschnaufpause *f*.

breathing ['bri:ðɪŋ] *n (respiration)* Atmung *f*. **~ space** *(fig)* Atempause, Ruhepause *f*.

breathless ['breθlɪs] *adj* atemlos; *(with exertion also)* außer Atem. **it left me ~** *(lit, fig)* es verschlug mir den Atem.

breathtaking ['breθteɪkɪŋ] *adj* atemberaubend.

bred [bred] *pret, ptp of* **breed.**

breeches ['brɪtʃɪz] *npl* Kniehose *f*; *(riding ~)* Reithose *f*.

breed [bri:d] *(vb: pret, ptp* **bred***)* **1** *n (lit, fig) (species)* Art, Sorte *f*. **2** *vt* **(a)** *animals, flowers* züchten. **(b)** *(fig: give rise to)* erzeugen. **3** *vi (animals)* Junge haben; *(birds)* brüten.

breeder ['bri:dəʳ] *n* **(a)** *(person)* Züchter *m*. **(b)** *(Tech: also* **~ reactor***)* Brutreaktor, Brüter *m*.

breeding ['bri:dɪŋ] *n* **(a)** *(reproduction)* Fortpflanzung und Aufzucht *f* der Jungen. **(b)** *(rearing)* Zucht *f*. **(c)** *(upbringing, good manners: also* **good ~***)* gute Erziehung, Kinderstube *f*.

breeze [bri:z] **1** *n* Brise *f*. **2** *vi* **to ~ in/out** fröhlich angetrabt kommen/vergnügt abziehen *(of* aus*)*.

breezy ['bri:zɪ] *adj (+er)* **(a)** *weather, day* windig; *corner also* luftig. **(b)** *manner* forsch-fröhlich.

brevity ['brevɪtɪ] *n* Kürze *f*.

brew [bru:] **1** *n (beer)* Bräu *nt*; *(of tea)* Tee *m*, Gebräu *nt (iro)*; *(of herbs)* Kräutermischung *f*. **witch's ~** Zaubertrank *m*. **2** *vt beer* brauen; *tea* aufgießen; *(fig) scheme, plot* ausbrüten. **3** *vi (beer)* gären; *(tea)* ziehen; *(make beer)* brauen. **there's something ~ing** da braut sich etwas zusammen.

brewery ['bru:ərɪ] *n* Brauerei *f*.

bribe [braɪb] **1** *n* Bestechung *f*; *(money)* Bestechungsgeld *nt*. **to take a ~** sich bestechen lassen. **2** *vt* bestechen. **to ~ sb to do sth** jdn bestechen, damit er etw tut.

bribery ['braɪbərɪ] *n* Bestechung *f*.

bric-à-brac ['brɪkəbræk] *n* Nippes *m*.

brick [brɪk] *n* **(a)** Ziegel- *or* Backstein *m*. **he came down on me like a ton of ~s** *(col)* er hat mich völlig fertiggemacht *(col)*; **to drop a ~** *(fig col)* ins Fettnäpfchen treten; **to drop sb/sth like a hot ~** *(col)* jdn/etw wie eine heiße Kartoffel fallenlassen. **(b)** *(toy)* (Bau)klotz *m*. **box of (building) ~s** Baukasten *m*.

♦ **brick in** *or* **up** *vt sep door, window* zumauern.

brick: ~layer *n* Maurer *m*; **~ wall** *n (fig col)* **I might as well be talking to a ~ wall** ich könnte genausogut gegen eine Wand reden.

bridal ['braɪdl] *adj* Braut-; *procession, feast* Hochzeits-.

bride [braɪd] *n* Braut *f*. **the ~ and groom** Braut und Bräutigam, das Hochzeitspaar.

bridegroom ['braɪdgru:m] *n* Bräutigam *m*.

bridesmaid ['braɪdzmeɪd] *n* Brautjungfer *f*.

bridge[1] [brɪdʒ] **1** *n* **(a)** *(lit, fig)* Brücke *f*. **(b)** *(Naut)* (Kommando)brücke *f*. **2** *vt river, railway* eine Brücke schlagen *or* bauen über *(+acc)*; *(fig)* überbrücken. **to ~ the gap** *(fig)* die Zeit überbrücken; *(between people)* die Kluft überbrücken.

bridge[2] *n (Cards)* Bridge *nt*.

bridgehead ['brɪdʒˌhed] *n* Brückenkopf *m*.

bridging loan ['brɪdʒɪŋˌləʊn] *n (Brit)* Überbrückungskredit *m*.

bridle ['braɪdl] **1** *n (of horse)* Zaum *m*. **2** *vt horse* aufzäumen; *(fig) emotions* im Zaum halten.

bridlepath ['braɪdlˌpɑ:θ] *n* Reitweg *m*.

brief [bri:f] **1** *adj (+er)* kurz; *(curt also) manner* kurz angebunden. **in ~** kurz (und gut). **2** *n* **(a)**

(Jur) Auftrag *m (an einen Anwalt)*; *(document)* Unterlagen *pl* zu dem/einem Fall; *(instructions)* Instruktionen *pl.* **(b)** *(instructions)* Auftrag *m.* **3** *vt (employ) lawyer* beauftragen; *(give instructions to)* instruieren *(on* über *+acc)*; *(give information)* informieren *(on* über *+acc).*

briefcase ['bri:fkeɪs] *n* (Akten)tasche *f.*

briefing ['bri:fɪŋ] *n (instructions)* Instruktionen *pl,* Anweisungen *pl; (also* ~ **session***)* Einsatzbesprechung *f.*

briefly ['bri:flɪ] *adv* kurz.

briefs [bri:fs] *npl* Slip *m.* **a pair of** ~ ein Slip.

brigade [brɪ'geɪd] *n (Mil)* Brigade *f.*

brigadier (general) [,brɪgə'dɪə('dʒenərəl)] *n* Brigadegeneral *m.*

bright [braɪt] *adj (+er)* **(a)** hell; *colour* leuchtend; *sunshine also, eyes* strahlend; *day, weather* heiter. ~ **red** knallrot; ~ **intervals** *or* **periods** *(Met)* Aufheiterungen *pl*; **the** ~ **lights** *(col)* Großstadtluft *f.* **(b)** *(cheerful) person, smile* fröhlich, heiter. **I wasn't feeling too** ~ es ging mir nicht besonders gut; ~ **and early** in aller Frühe. **(c)** *(intelligent) person* intelligent; *child* aufgeweckt; *idea* glänzend; *(iro)* intelligent. **(d)** *future, prospects* glänzend.

brighten (up) ['braɪtn(ʌp)] **1** *vt (sep)* **(a)** *(make cheerful) spirits, person* aufheitern; *room, atmosphere* aufhellen; *prospects, situation* verbessern. **(b)** *(make bright) colour, hair* aufhellen; *metal* aufpolieren. **2** *vi (weather, sky, face)* sich aufheitern; *(person)* fröhlicher werden; *(eyes)* aufleuchten; *(prospects)* besser werden; *(future)* freundlicher aussehen.

brightly ['braɪtlɪ] *adv shine* hell; *smile* fröhlich.

brightness ['braɪtnɪs] *n see adj* **(a)** Helligkeit *f*; Leuchten *nt*; Strahlen *nt*; Heiterkeit *f.* **(b)** Fröhlichkeit, Heiterkeit *f.* **(c)** Intelligenz *f*; Aufgewecktheit *f.*

brilliance ['brɪljəns] *n* **(a)** *(of light)* heller Glanz, Strahlen *nt.* **(b)** *(of idea, achievement)* Großartigkeit *f*; *(of person)* Brillianz *f.* **a man of such** ~ ein Mann von so hervorragender Intelligenz.

brilliant ['brɪljənt] *adj* **(a)** *sunshine, colour* strahlend. **(b)** *idea etc* großartig *(also iro)*; *scientist, achievement also* glänzend, brilliant. **she is a** ~ **woman** sie ist eine sehr intelligente Frau.

brim [brɪm] **1** *n (of cup)* Rand *m*; *(of hat also)* Krempe *f.* **2** *vi* sprühen *(with* von *or* vor *+dat).* **her eyes were** ~**ming with tears** ihre Augen standen voll Tränen.

♦ **brim over** *vi (lit, fig)* überfließen *(with* vor *+dat).*

brimful ['brɪm'fʊl] *adj (lit)* randvoll; *(fig)* voll *(of, with* von*).* **he is** ~ **of energy** er sprüht vor Energie.

brine [braɪn] *n* **(a)** *(salt water)* Sole *f*; *(for pickling)* Lake *f.* **(b)** *(sea water)* Salzwasser *nt.*

bring [brɪŋ] *pret, ptp* **brought** *vt* **(a)** bringen; *(also:* ~ **with one***)* mitbringen. **did you** ~ **your guitar?** haben Sie Ihre Gitarre mitgebracht?; **to** ~ **tears to sb's eyes** jdm die Tränen in die Augen treiben. **(b) I cannot** ~ **myself to speak to him** ich kann es nicht über mich bringen, mit ihm zu sprechen.

♦ **bring about** *vt sep* **(a)** *(cause)* herbeiführen, verursachen. **(b)** *(Naut)* wenden.

♦ **bring back** *vt sep* **(a)** *(lit) person, object, memories* zurückbringen. **(b)** *custom, hanging* wieder einführen; *government* wiederwählen. **to** ~ **sb** ~ **to life** jdn wieder lebendig machen.

♦ **bring down** *vt sep* **(a)** *(out of air) (shoot down) bird, plane* herunterholen; *(land) plane, kite* herunterbringen. **(b)** *opponent, government* zu Fall bringen; *(by shooting) animal* zur Strecke bringen; *person* niederschießen. **(c)** *(reduce) temperature, prices* senken; *swelling* zurückgehen lassen.

♦ **bring forward** *vt sep* **(a)** *(lit) person, chair* nach vorne bringen. **(b)** *(fig: present) witness* vorführen; *evidence, argument* vorbringen. **(c)** *(advance time of) meeting* vorverlegen. **(d)** *(Comm) figure* übertragen.

♦ **bring in** *vt sep* **(a)** *(lit) person, object* hereinbringen *(prep obj, -to* in *+acc)*; *harvest* einbringen. **(b)** *(fig: introduce) fashion, custom* einführen. **(c)** *(involve, call in) police etc* einschalten *(on* bei*).* **(d)** *(Fin) income, money* (ein)bringen *(-to sb* jdm*)*; *(Comm) business* bringen. **(e)** *(Jur: jury) verdict* fällen.

♦ **bring off** *vt sep* **(a)** *people from wreck* retten, wegbringen *(prep obj* von*).* **(b)** *(succeed with) plan* zustande *or* zuwege bringen. **he brought it** ~**!** er hat es geschafft! *(col).*

♦ **bring on** *vt sep* **(a)** *(cause) illness, quarrel* herbeiführen, verursachen; *attack also* auslösen. **(b)** *(help develop) pupil* weiterbringen. **(c)** *(Theat) person* auftreten lassen; *thing* auf die Bühne bringen; *(Sport) player* einsetzen. **(d) you brought it** ~ **yourself** das hast du dir selbst zuzuschreiben.

♦ **bring out** *vt sep (lit, fig)* herausbringen; *(also* ~ ~ **on strike***) workers* in den Streik treten lassen.

♦ **bring round** *vt sep* **(a)** *(to one's house etc)* vorbeibringen. **(b)** *discussion* bringen *(to* auf *+acc).* **(c)** *unconscious person* wieder zu Bewußtsein bringen. **(d)** *(convert)* herumkriegen *(col).*

♦ **bring to** *vt always separate unconscious person* wieder zu Bewußtsein bringen.

♦ **bring up** *vt sep* **(a)** *(to a higher place)* heraufbringen. **(b)** *(raise, increase) amount* erhöhen *(to* auf *+acc)*; *level, standards* anheben. **to** ~ **sb** ~ **to a certain standard** jdn auf ein gewisses Niveau bringen. **(c)** *(rear) child, animal* groß- *or* aufziehen; *(educate)* erziehen. **a well brought-**~ **child** ein gut erzogenes Kind. **(d)** *(vomit up)* brechen. **(e)** *(mention) fact, problem* erwähnen.

brink [brɪŋk] *n (lit, fig)* Rand *m.* **on the** ~ **of sth/doing sth** *(lit, fig)* am Rande von etw/nahe daran, etw zu tun.

briny ['braɪnɪ] **1** *adj* salzhaltig, salzig. **2** *n (col)* See *f.*

brisk [brɪsk] *adj (+er)* **(a)** *person, way of speaking* forsch; *walk, pace* flott. **(b)** *(fig) trade, betting* lebhaft, rege. **(c)** *wind, weather* frisch.

bristle ['brɪsl] **1** *n (of brush, boar etc)* Borste *f*; *(of beard)* Stoppel *f.* **2** *vi* **(a)** *(animal's hair)* sich sträuben. **(b)** *(fig: person)* zornig werden. **to** ~ **with anger** vor Wut schnauben. **(c)** *(fig)* **to be bristling with police** von Polizisten wimmeln; **bristling with difficulties** mit Schwierigkeiten gespickt.

bristly ['brɪslɪ] *adj (+er) animal, hair* borstig; *chin* Stoppel-, stoppelig.

Britain ['brɪtən] *n* Großbritannien *nt.*

British ['brɪtɪʃ] **1** *adj* britisch. **I'm** ~ ich bin Brite/Britin; **the** ~ **Isles** die Britischen Inseln. **2** *n* **the** ~ *pl* die Briten *pl.*

Britisher ['brɪtɪʃəʳ] *n (US)* Brite *m,* Britin *f.*

Briton ['brɪtən] *n* Brite *m,* Britin *f.*

Brittany ['brɪtənɪ] *n* die Bretagne.

brittle ['brɪtl] *adj* spröde, zerbrechlich. ~ **bones** schwache Knochen.

broach [brəʊtʃ] *vt* **(a)** *barrel* anstechen, anzapfen. **(b)** *subject, topic* anschneiden.

broad [brɔ:d] *adj (+er)* **(a)** *(wide)* breit. **it's as** ~ **as it is long** *(fig)* es ist Jacke wie Hose *(col).* **(b)** *(widely applicable) theory* umfassend; *(general)* allgemein. **(c)** *(not detailed) idea, outline* grob; *sense* weit. **as a very** ~ **rule** als Faustregel. **(d)** *(liberal) mind, attitude* großzügig, tolerant. **(e)** *hint* deutlich. **(f)** *(strongly marked) accent* stark.

broad bean *n* dicke Bohne, Saubohne *f.*

broadcast ['brɔ:dkɑ:st] *(vb: pret, ptp* ~*)* **1** *n (Rad, TV)* Sendung *f*; *(of match etc)* Übertragung *f.* **2** *vt* **(a)** *(Rad, TV)* senden, ausstrahlen; *football* *match, event* übertragen. **(b)** *(fig) news, rumour etc* verbreiten. **3** *vi (Rad, TV: station)* senden.

broadcaster ['brɔːdkɑːstəʳ] *n (Rad, TV) (announcer)* Rundfunk-/Fernsehsprecher(in *f*) *m*; *(personality)* Mitarbeiter(in *f*) *m* beim Rundfunk/Fernsehen.

broadcasting ['brɔːdkɑːstɪŋ] **1** *n (Rad, TV)* Sendung *f*; *(of event)* Übertragung *f*. **2** *attr (Rad)* Rundfunk-; *(TV)* Fernseh-. ~ **station** *(Rad)* Rundfunkstation *f*; *(TV)* Fernsehstation *f*.

broaden (out) ['brɔːdn(aʊt)] **1** *vt (sep) road etc* verbreitern. **to ~ one's mind/one's horizons** *(fig)* seinen Horizont erweitern. **2** *vi* breiter werden, sich verbreitern.

broadly ['brɔːdlɪ] *adv* **(a)** *(in general terms)* allgemein, in großen Zügen. ~ **speaking** ganz allgemein gesprochen. **(b)** *(greatly, widely) differ* beträchtlich. **(c)** *grin, smile, laugh* breit.

broad: ~-minded *adj* großzügig, tolerant; **~sheet** *n* Flugblatt *nt*; **~-shouldered** *adj* breitschult(e)rig; **~side** *(Naut) n* Breitseite *f*; *(fig also)* Attacke *f*; **to fire a ~side** eine Breitseite abfeuern.

brocade [brəʊ'keɪd] *n* Brokat *m*.

broccoli ['brɒkəlɪ] *n* Brokkoli *pl*.

brochure ['brəʊʃjʊəʳ] *n* Broschüre *f*, Prospekt *m*.

brogue [brəʊg] *n (Irish accent)* irischer Akzent.

broil [brɔɪl] *vti (Cook)* grillen.

broke [brəʊk] **1** *pret of* **break. 2** *adj pred (col)* abgebrannt *(col)*, pleite *(col)*.

broken ['brəʊkən] **1** *ptp of* **break. 2** *adj* **(a)** kaputt *(col)*; *twig* geknickt; *bone* gebrochen; *rope also* gerissen; *(smashed) cup, glass etc also* zerbrochen. **(b)** *heart, spirit, man, promise* gebrochen; *health, marriage* zerrüttet. **from a ~ home** aus zerrütteten Familienverhältnissen. **(c)** *road, surface, ground* uneben; *coastline* zerklüftet. **(d)** *(interrupted) journey, line on road* unterbrochen; *line on paper* gestrichelt; *sleep* unruhig. **(e)** *English, German etc* gebrochen.

broken: ~-down *adj machine, car* kaputt *(col)*; **~-hearted** *adj* untröstlich.

broker ['brəʊkəʳ] *n* Makler *m*.

brolly ['brɒlɪ] *n (Brit col)* (Regen)schirm *m*.

bromide ['brəʊmaɪd] *n (Chem)* Bromid *nt*.

bronchial ['brɒŋkɪəl] *adj* bronchial. ~ **tubes** Bronchien *pl*.

bronchitis [brɒŋ'kaɪtɪs] *n* Bronchitis *f*.

bronze [brɒnz] **1** *n* Bronze *f*. **2** *vi (person)* braun werden. **3** *vt face, skin* bräunen. **4** *adj* Bronze-.

Bronze Age *n* Bronzezeit *f*.

bronzed [brɒnzd] *adj* (sonnen)gebräunt.

brooch [brəʊtʃ] *n* Brosche *f*.

brood [bruːd] **1** *n (lit, fig)* Brut *f*. **2** *vi* **(a)** *(bird)* brüten. **(b)** *(fig: person)* grübeln.

♦ **brood over** *or* **(up)on** *vi +prep obj* nachgrübeln über *(+acc)*; *(despondently also)* brüten über *(+dat)*.

broody ['bruːdɪ] *adj* **(a) the hen is ~** die Henne gluckt; **she is feeling ~** *(hum col)* sie will (unbedingt) ein Kind. **(b)** *person* grüblerisch.

brook [brʊk] *n* Bach *m*.

broom [bruːm] *n* Besen *m*. **a new ~ sweeps clean** *(Prov)* neue Besen kehren gut *(Prov)*.

broom: ~ cupboard *n* Besenschrank *m*; **~stick** *n* Besenstiel *m*.

Bros *npl (Comm)* = **Brothers** Gebr.

broth [brɒθ] *n* Fleischbrühe *f*; *(thickened soup)* Suppe *f*.

brothel ['brɒθl] *n* Bordell *nt*, Puff *m (col)*.

brother ['brʌðəʳ] *n* **(a)** Bruder *m*. **my/his ~s and sisters** meine/seine Geschwister; **oh ~!** *(esp US col)* Junge, Junge! *(col)*. **(b)** *(in trade unions)* Kollege *m*.

brother: ~hood *n* **(a)** Brüderlichkeit *f*; **(b)** *(organization)* Bruderschaft *f*; **~hood of man** Gemeinschaft *f* der Menschen; **~-in-law** *n, pl* **~s-in-law** Schwager *m*.

brotherly ['brʌðəlɪ] *adj* brüderlich.

brought [brɔːt] *pret, ptp of* **bring.**

brow [braʊ] *n* **(a)** *(eyebrow)* Braue *f*. **(b)** *(forehead)* Stirn *f*. **(c)** *(of hill)* (Berg)kuppe *f*.

browbeat ['braʊbiːt] *pret* ~, *ptp* **~en** *vt* unter Druck setzen.

brown [braʊn] **1** *adj (+er)* braun. **2** *n* Braun *nt*. **3** *vt (sun) skin, person* bräunen; *(Cook)* (an)bräunen; *meat also* anbraten. **4** *vi* braun werden.

♦ **brown off** *vt* **to be ~ed ~ with sb/sth** *(esp Brit col)* jdn/etw satt haben *(col)*.

brown: ~ ale *n* Malzbier *nt*; **~ bear** *n* Braunbär *m*; **~ bread** *n* Grau- *or* Mischbrot *nt*; *(from wholemeal)* Vollkornbrot *nt*; *(darker)* Schwarzbrot *nt*.

brownie ['braʊnɪ] *n* **(a)** *(fairy)* Heinzelmännchen *nt*. **(b) B~** Pfadfinderin *f*.

brownish ['braʊnɪʃ] *adj* bräunlich.

brown: ~owl *n* **(a)** *(Orn)* Waldkauz *m*; **(b) B~ Owl** *(in Brownies)* die Weise Eule; **~ paper** *n* Packpapier *nt*; **~ rice** *n* ungeschälter Reis.

browse [braʊz] **1** *vi* **to ~ among the books** in den Büchern schmökern; **to ~ (around)** sich umsehen. **2** *n* **to have a ~ (around)** sich umsehen.

bruise [bruːz] **1** *n* blauer Fleck; *(on fruit)* Druckstelle *f*. **2** *vt person* einen blauen Fleck/blaue Flecke(n) schlagen *(+dat)*; *fruit* beschädigen; *(fig) feelings* verletzen. **3** *vi* **he ~s easily** er bekommt leicht blaue Flecken.

brunette [bruː'net] **1** *n* Brünette *f*. **2** *adj* brünett.

brunt [brʌnt] *n* **to bear the ~ of the costs/attack** die Hauptlast der Kosten tragen/die volle Wucht des Angriffs mitbekommen.

brush [brʌʃ] **1** *n* **(a)** Bürste *f*; *(artist's ~, paint ~, shaving ~)* Pinsel *m*; *(with dustpan)* Handbesen *or* -feger *m*. **(b)** *(action)* **to give sth a ~** etw bürsten; *jacket, shoes* etw abbürsten. **(c)** *(light touch)* leichte Berührung. **(d)** *(Mil: skirmish)* Zusammenstoß *m*. **to have a ~ with sb** mit jdm aneinandergeraten. **2** *vt* **(a)** bürsten; *(with hand)* wischen. **to ~ one's teeth/hair** sich *(dat)* die Zähne putzen/das Haar bürsten. **(b)** *(sweep) dirt* fegen, kehren; *(with hand, cloth)* wischen. **(c)** *(touch lightly)* streifen.

♦ **brush against** *vi +prep obj* streifen.

♦ **brush aside** *vt sep obstacle, person* (einfach) zur Seite schieben; *objections* (einfach) abtun.

♦ **brush away** *vt sep* abbürsten; *(with hand, cloth)* wegwischen; *insects* verscheuchen.

♦ **brush off** *vt sep* **(a)** *mud, snow* abbürsten; *insect* verscheuchen. **(b)** *(col: reject) person* abblitzen lassen *(col)*; *suggestion, criticism* zurückweisen.

♦ **brush past** *vi* streifen *(prep obj acc)*.

♦ **brush up** *vt sep* **(a)** *crumbs, dirt* auffegen, aufkehren. **(b)** *(fig: also ~ ~* **on***) subject, one's German etc* auffrischen.

brush: ~-off *n (col)* Abfuhr *f*; **to give sb the ~-off** jdn abblitzen lassen *(col)*, jdm einen Korb geben *(col)*; **~work** *n (Art)* Pinselführung *f*.

brusque [bruːsk] *adj (+er)* brüsk, schroff.

brusqueness ['bruːsknɪs] *n* Schroffheit *f*.

Brussels ['brʌslz] *n* Brüssel *nt*. ~ **sprouts** Rosenkohl *m*.

brutal ['bruːtl] *adj* brutal.

brutality [bruː'tælɪtɪ] *n* Brutalität *f*.

brute [bruːt] **1** *n* **(a)** Tier, Vieh *(pej) nt*. **(b)** *(person)* brutaler Kerl; *(savage)* Bestie *f*. **(c)** *(col: thing)* **it's a ~ of a thing to lift** es ist verdammt schwer, das hochzuheben *(col)*. **2** *adj attr strength* roh; *passion* tierisch. **by ~ force** mit roher Gewalt.

BSc = **Bachelor of Science.**

bubble ['bʌbl] **1** *n* Blase *f*. **to blow ~s** Blasen machen. **2** *vi (liquid)* sprudeln; *(wine)* perlen; *(gas)* Blasen bilden.

♦ **bubble over** *vi (lit)* überschäumen; *(fig)* übersprudeln *(with* vor *+dat)*.

bubble: ~ bath *n* Schaumbad *nt*; **~ gum** *n* Kaugummi *m or nt*.

bubbly ['bʌblɪ] **1** *adj (+er) (lit)* sprudelnd; *(fig col) personality* temperamentvoll, lebendig. **2** *n (col)* Schampus *m (col).*
buck [bʌk] *n* **(a)** *(male of deer)* Bock *m.* **(b)** *(US col: dollar)* Dollar *m.* **(c) to pass the ~** den Schwarzen Peter weitergeben; *(responsibility also)* die Verantwortung abschieben.
♦ **buck up** *(col)* **1** *vi* **(a)** *(hurry up)* sich ranhalten *(col),* rasch *or* fix machen *(col).* **~ ~!** halt dich ran! *(col).* **(b)** *(cheer up)* aufleben. **~ ~!** Kopf hoch! **2** *vt sep* **(a)** *(make cheerful)* aufmuntern. **(b) to ~ one's ideas ~** sich zusammenreißen *(col).*
bucket ['bʌkɪt] **1** *n* Eimer *m*; *(of excavator)* Schaufel *f.* **a ~ of water** ein Eimer Wasser. **2** *vi (col)* **it's ~ing!, the rain is ~ing (down)!** es gießt wie aus Kübeln *(col).*
buckle ['bʌkl] **1** *n* **(a)** *(on belt, shoe)* Schnalle, Spange *f.* **(b)** *(in metal etc)* Beule *f*; *(concave also)* Delle *f.* **2** *vt* **(a)** *belt, shoes* zuschnallen. **(b)** *wheel, girder etc* verbiegen; *(dent)* verbeulen. **3** *vi* **(a)** *(belt, shoe)* mit einer Schnalle *or* Spange geschlossen werden, geschnallt werden. **(b)** *(wheel, metal)* sich verbiegen.
♦ **buckle down** *vi (col)* sich dranmachen *(to* an *+dat) (col).*
buck: ~skin *n* Wildleder *nt;* **~tooth** *m* vorstehender Zahn; **~wheat** *n* Buchweizen *m.*
bud [bʌd] **1** *n* Knospe *f.* **to be in ~** knospen, Knospen treiben. **2** *vi (plant, flower)* knospen, Knospen treiben; *(tree also)* ausschlagen.
Buddha ['bʊdə] *n* Buddha *m.*
Buddhism ['bʊdɪzəm] *n* Buddhismus *m.*
Buddhist ['bʊdɪst] **1** *n* Buddhist(in *f*) *m.* **2** *adj* buddhistisch.
budding ['bʌdɪŋ] *adj* knospend; *(fig) poet etc* angehend.
buddy ['bʌdɪ] *n (US col)* Kumpel *m.*
budge [bʌdʒ] **1** *vi* **(a)** *(move)* sich rühren, sich bewegen. **(b)** *(fig: give way)* nachgeben, weichen. **I will not ~ an inch** ich werde keinen Fingerbreit nachgeben. **2** *vt (move)* (von der Stelle) bewegen. **we can't ~ him** *(fig)* er läßt sich durch nichts erweichen.
budgerigar ['bʌdʒərɪgɑːʳ] *n* Wellensittich *m.*
budget ['bʌdʒɪt] **1** *n* Etat *m,* Budget *nt*; *(Parl also)* Haushalt(splan) *m.* **2** *vi* wirtschaften.
♦ **budget for** *vi +prep obj* (im Etat) einplanen.
budgie ['bʌdʒɪ] *n (col)* = **budgerigar.**
buff [bʌf] **1** *n* **(a)** *(colour)* Gelbbraun *nt.* **(b)** *(col: movie ~ etc)* Fan *m.* **2** *adj* gelbbraun.
buffalo ['bʌfələʊ] *n, pl* **-es,** *collective pl* **-** Büffel *m.*
buffer ['bʌfəʳ] *n (lit, fig)* Puffer *m*; *(Rail: at terminus)* Prellbock *m*; *(Comp)* Pufferspeicher *m.* **old ~** *(col)* alter Heini *(col).*
buffer state *n (Pol)* Pufferstaat *m.*
buffet[1] ['bʌfɪt] **1** *n (blow)* Schlag *m.* **2** *vt* hin und her werfen. **~ed by the wind** vom Wind gerüttelt.
buffet[2] ['bʊfeɪ] *n* Büfett *nt*; *(Brit Rail)* Speisewagen *m*; *(meal)* Stehimbiß *m*; *(cold ~)* kaltes Büfett.
buffet car ['bʊfeɪ-] *n (Brit Rail)* Speisewagen *m.*
buffet ['bʊfeɪ-]: **~ lunch/supper** *n* Stehimbiß *m.*
bug [bʌg] **1** *n* **(a)** Wanze *f*; *(col: any insect)* Käfer *m.* **~s** *pl* Ungeziefer *nt.* **(b)** *(bugging device)* Wanze *f.* **(c)** *(col: germ, virus)* Bazillus *f.* **he picked up a ~ while on holiday** er hat sich *(dat)* im Urlaub eine Krankheit geholt. **(d)** *(col: obsession)* **she's got the travel ~** die Reiselust hat sie gepackt. **(e)** *(col: fault)* Fehler *m.* **2** *vt* **(a)** *room, building* Wanzen *pl* einbauen in *(+acc) (col)*; *conversation, telephone lines* abhören. **(b)** *(col) (worry)* stören; *(annoy)* nerven *(col),* den Nerv töten *(+dat) (col).* **don't let it ~ you** mach dir nichts draus *(col).*
bugbear ['bʌgbɛəʳ] *n* Schreckgespenst *nt.*
bugger ['bʌgəʳ] **1** *n (col!)* Scheißkerl *m (col!),* Arschloch *nt (col!)*; *(when not contemptible)* Kerl *(col),* Typ *(col) m*; *(thing)* Scheißding *nt (col!).* **you lucky ~!** du hast vielleicht ein Schwein! *(col)*; **to play silly ~s** *(col)* Scheiß machen *(col).* **2** *interj (col!)* Mist! *(col).* **~ him** dieser Scheißkerl *(col!).*
♦ **bugger off** *vi (Brit col!)* abhauen *(col).*
♦ **bugger up** *vt sep (Brit col!)* versauen *(col!).*
bugle ['bjuːgl] *n* Signalhorn *nt.*
build [bɪld] *(vb: pret, ptp* **built***)* **1** *n* Körperbau *m.* **2** *vt* **(a)** bauen. **the house is being built** das Haus ist im Bau. **(b)** *(fig) new nation, relationship etc* aufbauen; *a better future* schaffen. **3** *vi* bauen.
♦ **build on 1** *vt sep* anbauen. **2** *vi +prep obj* bauen auf *(+acc).*
♦ **build up 1** *vi* **(a)** entstehen; *(anticyclone, atmosphere also)* sich aufbauen; *(increase)* zunehmen; *(Tech: pressure)* sich erhöhen. **the music ~s ~ to a huge crescendo** die Musik steigert sich zu einem gewaltigen Crescendo. **(b)** *(traffic)* sich verdichten; *(queue, line of cars)* sich bilden. **2** *vt sep* **(a)** aufbauen *(into zu)*; *finances* aufbessern. **to ~ ~ a reputation** sich *(dat)* einen Namen machen. **(b)** *(increase) ego, muscles* aufbauen; *production, pressure* steigern, erhöhen; *forces (mass)* zusammenziehen; *health* kräftigen; *sb's confidence* stärken. **to ~ ~ sb's hopes** jdm Hoffnung(en) machen. **(c)** *(with houses) area, land* (ganz) bebauen. **(d)** *(publicize) person* aufbauen.
builder ['bɪldəʳ] *n (worker)* Bauarbeiter(in *f*) *m*; *(contractor)* Bauunternehmer *m.*
building ['bɪldɪŋ] *n* **(a)** Gebäude *nt*; *(usually big also)* Bau *m.* **(b)** *(act of constructing)* Bau *m,* Bauen *nt.*
building: ~ contractor *n* Bauunternehmer *m*; **~ site** *n* Baustelle *f*; **~ society** *n (Brit)* Bausparkasse *f*; **~ trade** *n* Baugewerbe *nt.*
build-up ['bɪldʌp] *n* **(a)** *(publicity)* Werbung *f.* **they gave the play a good ~** sie haben das Stück ganz groß herausgebracht *(col).* **(b)** *(of pressure)* Steigerung *f*; *(Tech also)* Verdichtung *f.* **~ of troops** Truppenmassierungen *pl.*
built [bɪlt] *pret, ptp of* **build.**
built: ~in *adj* **(a)** *cupboard etc* eingebaut, Einbau-; **(b)** *(instinctive)* instinktmäßig; **~-up area** *n* bebautes Gebiet; *(Mot)* geschlossene Ortschaft.
bulb [bʌlb] *n* **(a)** Zwiebel *f.* **(b)** *(Elec)* (Glüh)birne *f.* **(c)** *(of thermometer etc)* Kolben *m.*
bulbous ['bʌlbəs] *adj nose* Knollen-; *growth etc* knotig, Knoten-.
Bulgaria [bʌl'gɛərɪə] *n* Bulgarien *nt.*
Bulgarian [bʌl'gɛərɪən] **1** *adj* bulgarisch. **2** *n* **(a)** Bulgare *m,* Bulgarin *f.* **(b)** *(language)* Bulgarisch *nt.*
bulge [bʌldʒ] **1** *n (in surface)* Wölbung *f*; *(irregular)* Unebenheit *f,* Buckel *m (col)*; *(in line)* Bogen *m*; *(in tyre)* Wulst *m*; *(in birth rate etc)* Zunahme *f (in gen).* **2** *vi* **(a)** *(also ~ out) (swell)* (an)schwellen; *(metal, sides of box)* sich wölben; *(stick out)* vorstehen. **(b)** *(pocket, sack)* prall gefüllt sein; *(with* mit*).*
bulk [bʌlk] *n* **(a)** *(size)* Größe *f*; *(large shape) (of thing)* massige Form; *(of person, animal)* massige Gestalt. **(b)** *(also* **great ~***)* größter Teil; *(of debt, loan also)* Hauptteil *m*; *(of work, mineral deposits also)* Großteil *m*; *(of people, votes also)* Gros *nt*; *(of property, legacy etc also)* Masse *f.* **(c)** *(Comm)* **in ~** im großen, en gros.
bulky ['bʌlkɪ] *adj (+er) object* sperrig; *book* dick; *sweater* unförmig; *person* massig, wuchtig.
bull [bʊl] *n* **(a)** Stier *m*; *(for breeding)* Bulle *m.* **to take the ~ by the horns** *(fig)* den Stier bei den Hörnern packen; **like a ~ in a china shop** *(col)* wie ein Elefant im Porzellanladen *(col).* **(b)** *(male of elephant, whale etc)* Bulle *m.*
bulldog ['bʊldɒg] *n* Bulldogge *f.*
bulldoze ['bʊldəʊz] *vt* **to ~ sb into doing sth** jdn zwingen, etw zu tun; **she ~d her way through the crowd** sie boxte sich durch die Menge.
bulldozer ['bʊldəʊzəʳ] *n* Planierraupe *f,* Bulldozer *m.*

bullet ['bʊlɪt] *n* Kugel *f.* **~hole** Einschuß(loch *nt*) *m.*
bulletin ['bʊlɪtɪn] *n* Bulletin *nt*, amtliche Bekanntmachung. **health ~** Krankenbericht *m*, Bulletin *nt*; **~ board** *(US)* Schwarzes Brett.
bullet: ~proof *adj* kugelsicher; **~ wound** *n* Schußwunde *or* -verletzung *f.*
bull: ~fight *n* Stierkampf *m*; **~fighter** *n* Stierkämpfer *m*; **~finch** *n* Dompfaff, Gimpel *m*; **~frog** *n* Ochsenfrosch *m.*
bullion ['bʊljən] *n no pl* Gold-/Silberbarren *pl.*
bull-necked ['bʊlnekt] *adj* stiernackig.
bullock ['bʊlək] *n* Ochse *m.*
bull: ~ring *n* Stierkampfarena *f*; **~'s eye** *n (of target)* Scheibenmittelpunkt *m*, Scheibenzentrum *nt*; *(hit)* Schuß *m* ins Schwarze *or* Zentrum; **~shit** *n (col!)* Scheiß *(col) m.*
bully ['bʊlɪ] **1** *n* Tyrann *m*; *(esp Sch)* Rabauke *m.* **you great big ~** du Rüpel. **2** *vt* tyrannisieren, schikanieren; *(using violence)* drangsalieren, traktieren. **to ~ sb into doing sth** jdn so unter Druck setzen, daß er *etc* etw tut.
♦ **bully about** *or* **around** *vt sep* herumkommandieren, tyrannisieren.
bulrush ['bʊlrʌʃ] *n* Rohrkolben *m.*
bulwark ['bʊlwək] *n (lit, fig)* Bollwerk *nt.*
bum[1] [bʌm] *n (esp Brit col)* Hintern *m (col).*
bum[2] *(col) n* **(a)** *(good-for-nothing)* Rumtreiber *m (col)*; *(young)* Gammler *m*; *(down-and-out)* Penner *m (col).* **(b)** *(despicable person)* Saukerl *m (col).*
♦ **bum about** *or* **around** *vi (col)* rumgammeln *(col).*
bumble-bee ['bʌmblbi:] *n* Hummel *f.*
bumf [bʌmf] *n (Brit col)* Papierkram *m (col).*
bump [bʌmp] **1** *n* **(a)** *(blow, noise, jolt)* Bums *m (col)*; *(of sth falling also)* Plumps *m (col).* **to get a ~ on the head** sich *(dat)* den Kopf anschlagen. **(b)** *(on any surface)* Unebenheit *f*; *(on head, knee etc)* Beule *f*; *(on car)* Delle *f.* **2** *vt* stoßen; *car wing etc, one's own car* eine Delle fahren in *(+acc)*; *another car* auffahren auf *(+acc).* **to ~ one's head** sich *(dat)* den Kopf anstoßen *or* anschlagen *(on, against* an *+dat).* **3** *vi (move joltingly)* holpern. **4** *adv* **to go ~** bumsen *(col).*
♦ **bump into** *vi +prep obj* **(a)** stoßen gegen; *(driver, car)* fahren gegen; *another car* fahren auf *(+acc).* **(b)** *(col: meet)* zufällig treffen.
♦ **bump off** *vt sep (col)* abmurksen *(col).*
bumper ['bʌmpə^r] **1** *n (of car)* Stoßstange *f.* **2** *adj* **~ crop** Rekordernte *f.*
bumpkin ['bʌmpkɪn] *n (also* **country ~***)* (Bauern)tölpel *m.*
bumpy ['bʌmpɪ] *adj (+er) surface* holp(e)rig; *flight* unruhig.
bun [bʌn] *n* **(a)** *(bread)* süßes Brötchen; *(iced ~ etc)* süßes Teilchen. **to have a ~ in the oven** *(col)* ein Kind kriegen *(col).* **(b)** *(hair)* Knoten *m.*
bunch [bʌntʃ] *n* **(a)** *(of flowers)* Strauß *m*; *(of radishes)* Bund *nt*; *(of bananas)* Büschel *nt.* **a ~ of grapes** eine (ganze) Weintraube; **~ of keys** Schlüsselbund *m*; **to wear one's hair in ~es** Rattenschwänze haben. **(b)** *(col: of people)* Haufen *m (col).*
♦ **bunch together 1** *vt sep* **~ed ~** dicht zusammen. **2** *vi (people)* einen Haufen bilden.
♦ **bunch up** *vi* **(a)** Haufen bilden. **(b)** *(material)* sich bauschen.
bundle ['bʌndl] **1** *n* Bündel *nt.* **he is a ~ of nerves** er ist ein Nervenbündel; **that child is a ~ of mischief** das Kind hat nichts als Unfug im Kopf. **2** *vt* **(a)** bündeln. **(b)** *(put, send hastily) things* stopfen; *people* verfrachten, schaffen; *(into vehicle)* packen *(col).*
♦ **bundle off** *vt sep* **he was ~d ~ to Australia** er wurde nach Australien verfrachtet.
♦ **bundle up** *vt sep (tie into bundles)* bündeln.
bung [bʌŋ] **1** *n (of cask)* Spund(zapfen) *m.* **2** *vt (Brit col: throw)* schmeißen *(col).*
♦ **bung up** *vt sep (col) pipe* verstopfen. **I'm all ~ed ~** meine Nase ist verstopft.
bungalow ['bʌŋgələʊ] *n* Bungalow *m.*
bungle ['bʌŋgl] *vt* verpfuschen.
bungler ['bʌŋglə^r] *n* Stümper *m.*
bungling ['bʌŋglɪŋ] *adj person* ungeschickt, dusselig *(col)*; *attempt* stümperhaft.
bunk[1] [bʌŋk] *n*: **to do a ~** *(col)* türmen *(col).*
bunk[2] *n (in ship)* Koje *f*; *(in train, dormitory)* Bett *nt.*
bunk-beds [bʌŋk'bedz] *npl* Etagenbett *nt.*
bunker ['bʌŋkə^r] *n (Naut, Golf, Mil)* Bunker *m.*
bunkum ['bʌŋkəm] *n (col)* Quatsch *(col) m.*
bunny ['bʌnɪ] *n (also* **~ rabbit***)* Hase *m*, Häschen *nt.*
bunting ['bʌntɪŋ] *n (flags)* bunte Fähnchen *pl*, Wimpel *pl.*
buoy [bɔɪ] *n* Boje *f.*
♦ **buoy up** *vt sep (lit)* über Wasser halten; *(fig) person* Auftrieb geben *(+dat)*; *hopes* beleben.
buoyancy ['bɔɪənsɪ] *n* **(a)** *(of ship, object)* Schwimmfähigkeit *f.* **(b)** *(fig: cheerfulness)* Schwung, Elan *m.*
buoyant ['bɔɪənt] *adj* **(a)** *ship, object* schwimmend. **(b)** *(fig) person, mood* heiter; *(energetic) step* federnd. **(c)** *market* rege.
burden ['bɜ:dn] **1** *n* **(a)** *(lit)* Last *f.* **beast of ~** Lasttier *nt.* **(b)** *(fig)* Belastung *f (on, to* für*).* **I don't want to be a ~ on you** ich möchte Ihnen nicht zur Last fallen; **the ~ of proof lies with him** er muß den Beweis dafür erbringen; *(Jur)* er trägt die Beweislast. **2** *vt* belasten.
bureau [bjʊə'rəʊ] *n* **(a)** *(Brit: desk)* Sekretär *m.* **(b)** *(US: chest of drawers)* Kommode *f.* **(c)** *(office)* Büro *nt.* **(d)** *(government department)* Amt *nt.*
bureaucracy [bjʊə'rɒkrəsɪ] *n* Bürokratie *f.*
bureaucrat ['bjʊərəʊkræt] *n* Bürokrat *m.*
bureaucratic [,bjʊərəʊ'krætɪk] *adj* bürokratisch.
burger ['bɜ:gə^r] *n (col)* Hamburger *m.*
burglar ['bɜ:glə^r] *n* Einbrecher(in *f*) *m.* **~ alarm** Alarmanlage *f.*
burglarize ['bɜ:gləraɪz] *vt (US)* einbrechen in *(+acc).* **he was ~d** bei ihm wurde eingebrochen.
burglary ['bɜ:glərɪ] *n* Einbruch *m.*
burgle ['bɜ:gl] *vt* einbrechen in *(+acc).* **he was ~d** bei ihm wurde eingebrochen.
burial ['berɪəl] *n* Beerdigung *f*; *(~ ceremony also)* Begräbnis *nt*; *(in cemetery also)* Beisetzung *f (form).*
burlesque [bɜ:'lesk] *n* **(a)** *(parody)* Parodie *f*; *(Theat)* Burleske *f.* **(b)** *(US Theat)* Varieté *nt*; *(show)* Varietévorstellung *f.*
burly ['bɜ:lɪ] *adj (+er)* kräftig, stramm.
Burma ['bɜ:mə] *n* Birma *nt.*
Burmese [bɜ:'mi:z] **1** *adj* birmanisch. **2** *n* Birmane *m*, Birmanin *f*; *(language)* Birmanisch *nt.*
burn *(vb: pret, ptp* **~ed** *or* **~t***)* **1** *n (on skin)* Brandwunde *f*; *(on material)* verbrannte Stelle, Brandfleck *m.* **severe ~s** schwere Verbrennungen *pl.*
2 *vt* **(a)** verbrennen; *village, building* niederbrennen. **to ~ oneself** sich verbrennen; **to be ~t to death** *(at stake)* verbrannt werden; *(in accident)* verbrennen; **to ~ a hole in sth** ein Loch in etw *(acc)* brennen; **to ~ one's boats** *or* **bridges** *(fig)* alle Brücken hinter sich *(dat)* abbrechen; **to ~ the midnight oil** *(fig)* bis tief in die Nacht arbeien. **(b)** *meat, toast etc* verbrennen lassen; *(slightly)* anbrennen lassen. **(c)** *(acid)* ätzen. **(d)** *(use as fuel: ship etc)* befeuert werden mit; *(use up) petrol, electricity* verbrauchen.
3 *vi* **(a)** brennen. **(b)** *(meat, pastry etc)* verbrennen; *(slightly)* anbrennen. **she ~s easily** sie bekommt leicht einen Sonnenbrand. **(c) to be ~ing to do sth** darauf brennen, etw zu tun; **he was ~ing with anger** er kochte wor Wut. **(d)** *(Space: rockets)* zünden.
♦ **burn down 1** *vi* **(a)** *(house etc)* ab- *or* niederbrennen. **(b)** *(fire, candle, wick)* herunterbrennen. **2** *vt sep* ab- *or* niederbrennen.

♦ **burn off** *vt sep paint etc* abbrennen.
♦ **burn out 1** *vi (fire, candle)* ausgehen; *(fuse)* durchbrennen; *(rocket)* den Treibstoff verbraucht haben. **2** *vr* **(a)** *(candle, lamp)* herunterbrennen; *(fire)* ab- *or* ausbrennen. **(b)** *(fig col)* **to ~ oneself** ~ sich völlig verausgaben. **3** *vt sep usu pass* **~t ~ lorries/houses** ausgebrannte Lastwagen/Häuser.
♦ **burn up 1** *vi* **(a)** *(fire etc)* auflodern. **(b)** *(rocket etc)* verglühen. **2** *vt sep rubbish* verbrennen; *fuel, energy* verbrauchen; *excess fat also* abbauen.
burner ['bɜːnə^r] *n (of cooker, lamp)* Brenner *m.*
burning ['bɜːnɪŋ] **1** *adj (lit, fig)* brennend. **2** *n* **I can smell ~** es riecht verbrannt.
burnish ['bɜːnɪʃ] *vt metal* polieren.
burnt [bɜːnt] *adj* verbrannt.
burp [bɜːp] *(col)* **1** *vi* rülpsen *(col); (baby)* aufstoßen. **2** *vt baby* aufstoßen lassen. **3** *n* Rülpser *m (col).*
burrow ['bʌrəʊ] **1** *n (of rabbit etc)* Bau *m.* **2** *vti (rabbits, dogs etc)* graben, buddeln *(col); (person: in papers etc)* wühlen.
bursar ['bɜːsə^r] *n* Schatzmeister *m.*
bursary ['bɜːsərɪ] *n* **(a)** *(grant)* Stipendium *nt.* **(b)** *(office)* Schatzamt *nt.*
burst [bɜːst] *(vb: pret, ptp ~)* **1** *n* **(a)** *(of shell etc)* Explosion *f.* **(b)** *(in pipe etc)* Bruch *m.* **(c)** *(of anger, enthusiasm, activity etc)* Ausbruch, Anfall *m.* **~ of laughter** Lachsalve *f;* **~ of applause** Beifallsturm *m;* **~ of speed** Spurt *m; (of cars etc)* Riesenbeschleunigung *f (col);* **a ~ of automatic gunfire** eine Maschinengewehrsalve.
2 *vi* **(a)** platzen. **to ~ open** *(box, door etc)* aufspringen; *(abscess, wound)* aufplatzen. **(b)** *(be very full)* platzen. **to fill sth to ~ing point** etw bis zum Platzen füllen; **to be ~ing with pride** vor Stolz platzen; **he was ~ing to tell us** *(col)* er brannte darauf, uns das zu sagen; **I'm ~ing** *(col)* ich platze gleich *(col).* **(c) to ~ into tears/flames** in Tränen ausbrechen/in Flammen aufgehen; **he ~ into song** er fing plötzlich an zu singen; **he ~ into the room** er platzte ins Zimmer; **the sun ~ through the clouds** die Sonne brach durch die Wolken; **to ~ out laughing/crying** in Gelächter/Tränen ausbrechen.
3 *vt balloon, bubble* zum Platzen bringen, platzen lassen; *boiler, pipe, dyke* sprengen. **the river has ~ its banks** der Fluß ist über die Ufer getreten; **to ~ one's sides with laughter** vor Lachen platzen.
bury ['berɪ] *vt* **(a)** *person, animal, differences* begraben; *(with ceremony also)* beerdigen; *(hide in earth) treasure, bones* vergraben; *(put in earth) end of post, roots* eingraben. **buried by an avalanche** von einer Lawine verschüttet *or* begraben; **to ~ one's head in the sand** *(fig)* den Kopf in den Sand stecken; **to ~ one's face in one's hands** das Gesicht in den Händen vergraben. **(b)** *(put, plunge) hands, fingers* vergraben *(in* in *+dat); claws, teeth* schlagen *(in* in *+acc); dagger* stoßen *(in* in *+acc).* **(c) to ~ oneself in one's books** sich in seinen Büchern vergraben; **buried in thought** in Gedanken versunken.
bus [bʌs] *n, pl* **-es** *or (US)* **-ses** (Omni)bus *m.* **by ~** mit dem Bus.
bus: ~ conductor *n* Busschaffner *m;* **~ depot** *n* Busdepot *nt;* **~ driver** *n* Busfahrer(in *f*) *m.*
bush [bʊʃ] *n* **(a)** *(shrub)* Busch, Strauch *m; (thicket: also* **~es***)* Gebüsch *nt.* **to beat about the ~** *(fig)* wie die Katze um den heißen Brei herumschleichen. **(b)** *(in Africa, Australia)* Busch *m.*
bushy ['bʊʃɪ] *adj (+er)* buschig.
busily ['bɪzɪlɪ] *adv* eifrig.
business ['bɪznɪs] *n* **(a)** Geschäft *nt; (enterprise also)* Betrieb *m; (line of ~)* Branche *f.* **to be in the plastics/insurance ~** in der Plastikbranche/im Versicherungsgewerbe sein; **to set up in ~** ein Geschäft gründen; **to go out of ~** zumachen; **to do ~ with sb** Geschäfte *pl* mit jdm machen; **~ is ~** Geschäft ist Geschäft; **he is here/away on ~** er ist geschäftlich hier/unterwegs; **to get down to ~** zur Sache kommen; **now we're in ~** *(fig col)* jetzt kann's losgehen *(col);* **to mean ~** *(col)* es ernst meinen. **(b)** *(concern, col: affair)* Sache *f; (task, duty also)* Aufgabe *f.* **that's my ~** das ist meine Sache or Angelegenheit; **that's none of my/your ~** das geht mich/dich nichts an; **to make it one's ~ to do sth** es sich *(dat)* zur Aufgabe machen, etw zu tun; **you've no ~ doing that** du hast kein Recht, das zu tun.
business: ~ address *n* Geschäftsadresse *f;* **~ card** *n* Visitenkarte *f;* **~ expenses** *npl* Spesen *pl;* **~ hours** *npl* Geschäftsstunden *pl,* Geschäftszeit *f.*
businesslike ['bɪznɪslaɪk] *adj (good at doing business)* geschäftstüchtig; *person, manner* geschäftsmäßig; *prose* nüchtern.
business: ~man *n* Geschäftsmann *m;* **~ sense** *n* Geschäftssinn *m;* **~ studies** *npl* Wirtschaftslehre *f;* **~ trip** *n* Geschäftsreise *f;* **~woman** *n* Geschäftsfrau *f.*
busker ['bʌskə^r] *n* Straßenmusikant *m.*
bus: ~man *n:* **a ~man's holiday** *(fig)* Fortsetzung *f* der Arbeit im Urlaub; **~ service** *n* Busverbindung *f; (network)* Busverbindungen *pl;* **~ shelter** *n* Wartehäuschen *nt;* **~ station** *n* Busbahnhof *m;* **~ stop** *n* Bushaltestelle *f.*
bust[1] [bʌst] *n* Büste *f; (Anat also)* Busen *m.* **~ measurement** Brustumfang *m,* Oberweite *f.*
bust[2] *(vb: pret, ptp ~) (col)* **1** *adj* **(a)** *(broken)* kaputt *(col).* **(b)** *(bankrupt)* pleite *(col).* **2** *adv (bankrupt)* **to go ~** pleite gehen *or* machen *(col).* **3** *vt* kaputtmachen *(col); drugs ring* auffliegen lassen *(col).*
bustle ['bʌsl] **1** *n* Betrieb *m (of* in *+dat); (of fair, streets also)* reges Treiben *(of* auf *or* in *+dat).* **2** *vi* **to ~ about** geschäftig hin und her eilen.
bustling ['bʌslɪŋ] *adj person* geschäftig; *place, scene* belebt, voller Leben.
busy ['bɪzɪ] **1** *adj (+er)* **(a)** *(occupied) person* beschäftigt. **a very ~ man** ein vielbeschäftigter Mann; **are you ~?** haben Sie gerade Zeit?; **I was ~ studying when you called** ich war gerade beim Lernen, als Sie kamen; **let's get ~** an die Arbeit! **(b)** *(active) life, time* bewegt; *place, street, town* belebt; *street (with traffic)* stark befahren. **it's been a ~ day/week** heute/diese Woche war viel los. **(c)** *telephone line* besetzt. **2** *vr* **to ~ oneself doing sth** sich damit beschäftigen, etw zu tun; **to ~ oneself with sth** sich mit etw beschäftigen.
busybody ['bɪzɪ'bɒdɪ] *n* **don't be such a ~** misch dich nicht überall ein.
but [bʌt] **1** *conj* **(a)** aber. **(b) not X ~ Y** nicht X sondern Y. **(c) never a week passes ~ she is ill** keine Woche vergeht, ohne daß sie krank ist.
2 *adv* **she's ~ a child** sie ist doch noch ein Kind; **I cannot (help) ~ think that ...** ich kann nicht umhin, zu denken, daß ...; **you can ~ try** du kannst es immerhin versuchen; **she left ~ a few minutes ago** sie ist erst vor ein paar Minuten gegangen.
3 *prep* **no one ~ me could do it** niemand außer mir konnte es tun; **anything ~ that!** (alles,) nur das nicht!; **he/it was nothing ~ trouble** er/das hat nichts als *or* hat nur Schwierigkeiten gemacht; **the last house ~ one/two/three** das vorletzte/vorvorletzte/drittletzte Haus; **the next street ~ one** die übernächste Straße; **~ for you I would be dead** ohne Sie wäre ich tot, wenn Sie nicht gewesen wären, wäre ich tot.
4 *n* **no ~s about it** kein Aber *nt.*
butane ['bjuːteɪn] *n* Butan *nt.*
butch [bʊtʃ] *adj (col)* maskulin.
butcher ['bʊtʃə^r] **1** *n* **(a)** Fleischer, Metzger *m.* **~'s (shop)** *(Brit)* Fleischerei, Metzgerei *f;* **at the**

~'s *(Brit)* beim Fleischer *or* Metzger. **(b)** *(fig: murderer)* Schlächter *m.* **2** *vt animals* schlachten; *people* abschlachten.
butchery ['bʊtʃərɪ] *n (slaughter)* Gemetzel *nt.*
butler ['bʌtlə^r] *n* Butler *m.*
butt[1] [bʌt] *n (for wine)* großes Faß; *(for rainwater)* Tonne *f.*
butt[2] *n (also* ~ **end)** dickes Ende; *(of rifle)* (Gewehr)kolben *m*; *(of cigarette)* Stummel *m.*
butt[3] *n (US col: cigarette)* Kippe *f (col).*
butt[4] *n* **(a)** *(target)* Schießscheibe *f.* **(b)** *usu pl (on shooting range)* Schießstand *m.* **(c)** *(fig: person)* **she's always the ~ of his jokes** sie ist immer (die) Zielscheibe seines Spottes.
butt[5] **1** *n* (Kopf)stoß *m.* **2** *vt* mit dem Kopf stoßen; *(goat also)* mit den Hörnern stoßen.
♦ **butt in** *vi* sich einmischen *(on* in *+acc).*
butter ['bʌtə^r] **1** *n* Butter *f.* **she looks as if ~ wouldn't melt in her mouth** sie sieht aus, als ob sie kein Wässerchen trüben könnte. **2** *vt bread etc* mit Butter bestreichen, buttern.
butter: ~ bean *n* Mondbohne *f*; **~cup** *n* Butterblume *f,* Hahnenfuß *m*; **~dish** *n* Butterdose *f*; **~-fingers** *n sing (col)* Schussel *m (col).*
butterfly ['bʌtəflaɪ] *n* Schmetterling *m.* **I've got/I get butterflies (in my stomach)** mir ist/wird ganz flau im Magen *(col).*
butterfly stroke *n* Schmetterlingsstil *m.*
buttock ['bʌtək] *n* (Hinter)backe, Gesäßhälfte *(form) f.* **~s** *pl* Gesäß *nt,* Hintern *m (col).*
button ['bʌtn] **1** *n* Knopf *m.* **2** *vt garment* zuknöpfen. **3** *vi (garment)* geknöpft werden.
♦ **button up** *vt sep* zuknöpfen.
button: ~hole 1 *n* **(a)** *(in garment)* Knopfloch *nt*; **(b)** *(flower)* Blume *f* im Knopfloch; **2** *vt (fig)* zu fassen bekommen, sich *(dat)* schnappen *(col)*; **~ mushroom** *n* junger Champignon.
buttress ['bʌtrɪs] *n (Archit)* Strebepfeiler *m*; *(fig)* Pfeiler *m.*
buxom ['bʌksəm] *adj* drall.
buy [baɪ] *(vb: pret, ptp* **bought)** **1** *vt* **(a)** kaufen; *(Rail) ticket also* lösen. **(b)** *(fig) victory, fame* sich *(dat)* erkaufen; *time* gewinnen. **the victory was dearly bought** der Sieg war teuer erkauft. **(c) to ~ sth** *(col) (accept)* etw akzeptieren; *(believe)* jdm etw abnehmen *(col) or* abkaufen *(col)*; **I'll ~ that** das ist o.k. *(col)*; *(believe)* ja, das glaube ich. **2** *vi* kaufen. **3** *n (col)* Kauf *m.* **to be a good ~** ein guter Kauf sein; *(clothes also, food)* preiswert sein.
♦ **buy back** *vt sep* zurückkaufen.
♦ **buy in** *vt sep (acquire supply of) goods* einkaufen.
♦ **buy off** *vt sep (col: bribe)* kaufen *(col).*
♦ **buy out** *vt sep shareholders etc* auszahlen; *firm* aufkaufen.
♦ **buy up** *vt sep* aufkaufen.
buyer ['baɪə^r] *n* Käufer *m*; *(agent)* Einkäufer *m.* **~'s market** Käufermarkt *m.*
buzz [bʌz] **1** *vi* summen. **my head is ~ing** mir schwirrt der Kopf; *(from noise)* mir dröhnt der Kopf; **the town is ~ing** in der Stadt ist viel los. **2** *vt* **(a)** *(call) secretary* (mit dem Summer) rufen. **(b)** *(col: telephone)* anrufen. **(c)** *(plane) plane, building* dicht vorbeifliegen an *(+dat).* **3** *n* **(a)** Summen *nt.* **(b)** *(of conversation)* Stimmengewirr *nt.* **(c)** *(col)* **to give sb a ~** jdn anrufen; *secretary etc* jdn (mit dem Summer) rufen.
♦ **buzz off** *vi (Brit col)* abzischen *(col).*
buzzard ['bʌzəd] *n* Bussard *m.*
buzzer ['bʌzə^r] *n* Summer *m.*
buzz word *n* Modewort *nt.*
by [baɪ] **1** *prep* **(a)** *(close to)* bei, an *(+dat)*; *(with movement)* an *(+acc)*; *(next to)* neben *(+dat)*; *(with movement)* neben *(+acc).* **a holiday ~ the sea** Ferien *pl* an der See; **come and sit ~ me** komm, setz dich neben mich.
(b) *(via)* über *(+acc).*
(c) *(past)* **to go/rush** *etc* **~ sb/sth** an jdm/etw vorbeigehen/-eilen *etc.*
(d) *(time: during)* **~ day/night** bei Tag/Nacht.
(e) *(time: not later than)* bis. **can you do it ~ tomorrow?** kannst du es bis morgen machen?; **~ tomorrow I'll be in France** morgen werde ich in Frankreich sein; **~ the time I got there ...** bis ich dorthin kam ...; **~ that time** *or* **~ then it will be too late** bis dahin *or* dann ist es schon zu spät; **~ now** inzwischen.
(f) *(indicating amount)* **~ the metre/kilo/hour** meter-/kilo-/stundenweise; **one ~ one** einer nach dem anderen.
(g) *(indicating agent, cause)* von, durch. **killed ~ a bullet** durch eine *or* von einer Kugel getötet; **a painting ~ Picasso** ein Bild von Picasso; **surrounded ~** umgeben von.
(h) *(indicating method, means, manner)* **~ bus/car** mit dem *or* per Bus/Auto; **~ land and (~) sea** zu Land und zu Wasser; **to pay ~ cheque** mit Scheck bezahlen; **made ~ hand/machine** handgearbeitet/maschinell hergestellt; **~ daylight/moonlight** bei Tag(eslicht)/im Mondschein; **to know sb ~ sight** jdn vom Sehen her kennen; **to be known ~ the name of ...** unter dem Namen ... bekannt sein; **to lead ~ the hand** an der Hand führen; **to grab sb ~ the collar** jdn am Kragen packen; **he had a daughter ~ his first wife** von seiner ersten Frau hatte er eine Tochter; **~ myself/himself** *etc* allein; **~ saving hard he managed to ...** durch eisernes Sparen gelang es ihm, zu ...; **~ saying that I didn't mean ...** ich habe damit nicht gemeint ...
(i) *(according to)* nach. **to judge ~ appearances** allem Anschein nach; **it's all right ~ me** von mir aus gern.
(j) *(measuring difference)* um. **broader ~ a meter** um einen Meter breiter; **it missed me ~ inches** es verfehlte mich um Zentimeter.
(k) *(Math, Measure)* **to divide/multiply ~** dividieren durch/multiplizieren mit; **a room 20 metres ~ 30** ein Zimmer 20 auf *or* mal 30 Meter.
(l) *(points of compass)* **South ~ South West** Südsüdwest.
(m) *(in oaths)* bei. **I swear ~ Almighty God** ich schwöre beim allmächtigen Gott.
(n) ~ the way *or* **by(e)** übrigens.
2 *adv* **(a)** *(past)* **to pass/wander/rush** *etc* **~** vorbei- *or* vorüberkommen/-wandern/-eilen *etc.* **(b)** *(in reserve)* **to put** *or* **lay ~** beiseite legen. **(c)** *(phrases)* **~ and ~** irgendwann; *(with past tense)* nach einiger Zeit; **~ and large** im großen und ganzen.
bye [baɪ] *interj (col)* tschüs. **~ for now!** bis bald!
bye-bye ['baɪ'baɪ] **1** *interj (col)* Wiedersehen *(col).* **2** *n* **to go ~s** *(baby-talk)* in die Heia gehen *(baby-talk).*
by(e)-election [baɪɪ'lekʃən] *n* Nachwahl *f.*
bygone ['baɪgɒn] **1** *adj* längst vergangen. **2** *n* **to let ~s be ~s** die Vergangenheit ruhen lassen.
by: ~law *n (also* **bye-law)** Verordnung *f*; **~pass 1** *n (road)* Umgehungsstraße *f*; *(Tech: pipe etc)* Bypass *m*; **2** *vt town, village* umgehen; *(Tech) fluid, gas* umleiten; *(fig) person* übergehen; *intermediate stage also* überspringen; *difficulties* umgehen; **~pass operation** *n* Bypass-Operation *f*; **~-product** *n (lit, fig)* Nebenprodukt *nt*; **~stander** *n* Zuschauer *m.*
byte [baɪt] *n (Comp)* Byte *nt.*
by: ~way *n* Seitenweg *m*; **~word** *n* **to be/become a ~word for sth** gleichbedeutend mit etw sein/werden.
Byzantium [baɪ'zæntɪəm] *n* Byzanz *nt.*

C

C, c [siː] C, c *nt.* **C sharp/flat** Cis, cis *nt*/Ces, ces *nt.*
c = **(a) cent** c, ct. **(b) circa** ca.
CA = **chartered accountant.**
cab [kæb] *n* **(a)** *(taxi)* Taxi *nt.* **(b)** *(of lorry etc)* Führerhaus *nt.*
cabaret ['kæbəreɪ] *n* Varieté *nt*; *(satire)* Kabarett *nt.*
cabbage ['kæbɪdʒ] *n* **(a)** Kohl *m.* **(b)** *(col: person)* **to become a ~** *(sick person)* dahinvegetieren.
cabby ['kæbɪ] *n (col: of taxi)* Taxifahrer *m.*
cabin ['kæbɪn] *n* **(a)** *(hut)* Hütte *f.* **(b)** *(Naut)* Kabine *f.* **(c)** *(of lorries, buses etc)* Führerhaus *nt.* **(d)** *(Aviat)* Passagierraum *m.*
cabin-: **~boy** *n* Schiffsjunge *m*; *(steward)* Kabinensteward *m*; **~ crew** *n* *(Aviat)* Flugpersonal *nt*; **~ cruiser** *n* Kajütboot *nt.*
cabinet ['kæbɪnɪt] *n* **(a)** Schränkchen *nt*; *(for display)* Vitrine *f*; *(for TV, record-player)* Schrank *m*; *(loudspeaker ~)* Box *f.* **(b)** *(Pol)* Kabinett *nt.*
cabinet: **~maker** *n* (Möbel)schreiner *m*; **~ meeting** *n* Kabinettssitzung *f*; **~ minister** *n* Mitglied *nt* des Kabinetts.
cable ['keɪbl] **1** *n* **(a)** Tau *nt*; *(of wire)* Drahtseil *nt.* **(b)** *(Elec)* Kabel *nt.* **(c)** *(~gram)* Telegramm *nt.* **2** *vt information* telegrafisch durchgeben. **to ~ sb** jdm telegrafieren. **3** *vi* telegrafieren, ein Telegramm schicken.
cable: **~-car** *n* *(hanging)* Drahtseilbahn *f*; *(streetcar)* Straßenbahn *f*; **~ laying** *n* Kabelverlegung *f*; **~ television** *n* Kabelfernsehen *nt.*
caboodle [kə'buːdl] *n*: **the whole ~** *(col)* der ganze Kram *(col).*
cache [kæʃ] **1** *n* geheimes (Waffen-/Proviant)lager *nt.* **2** *vt* verstecken.
cack-handed ['kæk'hændəd] *adj* *(Brit col)* tolpatschig *(col).*
cackle ['kækl] **1** *n (of hens)* Gackern *nt*; *(laughter)* meckerndes Gelächter. **2** *vi* *(hens)* gackern; *(laugh)* meckernd lachen.
cacophony [kæ'kɒfənɪ] *n* Mißklang *m.*
cactus ['kæktəs] *n* Kaktus *m.*
cad [kæd] *n (dated)* Schurke *m (dated).*
cadaver [kə'deɪvə^r] *n* Kadaver *m*; *(of humans)* Leiche *f.*
cadaverous [kə'dævərəs] *adj* *(corpse-like)* Kadaver-, Leichen-; *(gaunt)* ausgemergelt; *(pale)* leichenblaß.
caddie ['kædɪ] *n (Golf~)* Caddie, Golfjunge *m.*
caddy ['kædɪ] *n (tea ~)* Behälter *m*, Dose *f.*
cadence ['keɪdəns] *n* *(Mus)* Kadenz *f*; *(of voice)* Tonfall *m*, Melodie *f*; *(rhythm)* Rhythmus *m*, Melodie *f.*
cadenza [kə'denzə] *n (Mus)* Kadenz *f.*
cadet [kə'det] *n (Mil etc)* Kadett *m.*
cadge [kædʒ] **1** *vt* (er)betteln, schnorren *(col)* *(from sb* bei *or* von jdm*).* **could I ~ a lift?** könnten Sie mich vielleicht mitnehmen? **2** *vi* schnorren *(col).*
cadger ['kædʒə^r] *n* Schnorrer *(col) m.*
Caesar ['siːzə^r] *n* Cäsar *m*; *(emperor)* Kaiser *m.*
Caesarean, Caesarian [siː'zeərɪən] *n, adj* **~ (section)** *(Med)* Kaiserschnitt *m.*
café ['kæfeɪ] *n* Café *nt.*
cafeteria [ˌkæfɪ'tɪərɪə] *n* Cafeteria *f.*
caffein(e) ['kæfiːn] *n* Koffein *nt.*
caftan ['kæftæn] *n* Kaftan *m.*
cage [keɪdʒ] **1** *n* **(a)** Käfig *m*; *(small bird~)* Bauer *nt or m.* **(b)** *(of lift)* Aufzug *m*; *(Min)* Förderkorb *m.* **2** *vt (also ~* **up***)* in einen Käfig sperren.
cagey ['keɪdʒɪ] *adj* *(col)* vorsichtig; *(evasive)* ausweichend. **what are you being so ~ about?** warum tust du so geheimnisvoll?
cagily ['keɪdʒɪlɪ] *adv see* **cagey.**
caginess ['keɪdʒɪnɪs] *n* *(col)* Vorsicht *f*; *(evasiveness)* ausweichende Art.
cagoule [kə'guːl] *n* Windhemd *nt.*
cahoots [kə'huːts] *n (col)*: **to be in ~ with sb** mit jdm unter einer Decke stecken.
Cairo ['kaɪərəʊ] *n* Kairo *nt.*
cajole [kə'dʒəʊl] *vt* gut zureden *(+dat)*, beschwatzen *(col).* **to ~ sb into doing sth** jdn dazu bringen, etw zu tun.
cake [keɪk] **1** *n* **(a)** Kuchen *m*; *(gateau)* Torte *f.* **a piece of ~** *(fig col)* ein Kinderspiel *nt*, ein Klacks *m (col)*; **to sell like hot ~s** weggehen wie warme Semmeln *(col)*; **you can't have your ~ and eat it** *(prov)* man kann nicht beides (gleichzeitig) haben. **(b)** *(of soap)* Stück *nt*; *(of chocolate)* Tafel *f.* **2** *vt* überkrusten. **my shoes are ~d with mud** meine Schuhe sind dreckverkrustet. **3** *vi* eine Kruste bilden.
cake: **~ shop** *n* Konditorei *f*; **~ tin** *n (for baking)* Kuchenform *f*; *(for storage)* Kuchendose *f.*
calamine ['kæləmaɪn] *n* Galmei *m.* **~ lotion** Galmeilotion *f.*
calamity [kə'læmɪtɪ] *n* Katastrophe *f.*
calcify ['kælsɪfaɪ] **1** *vt* Kalk *m* ablagern auf/in *(+dat).* **2** *vi* verkalken.
calcium ['kælsɪəm] *n* Kalzium *nt.*
calculate ['kælkjʊleɪt] **1** *vt* **(a)** *costs* berechnen. **(b)** *(fig: estimate)* kalkulieren, schätzen. **(c) to be ~d to do sth** *(be intended)* auf etw *(acc)* abzielen. **(d)** *(US col: suppose)* schätzen. **2** *vi* *(Math)* rechnen.
♦ **calculate on** *vi +prep obj* rechnen mit. **I had ~d ~ finishing by this week** ich hatte damit gerechnet, noch in dieser Woche fertig zu werden.
calculated ['kælkjʊleɪtɪd] *adj* *(deliberate)* berechnet. **to take a ~ risk** ein kalkuliertes Risiko eingehen.
calculating ['kælkjʊleɪtɪŋ] *adj* berechnend.
calculation [ˌkælkjʊ'leɪʃən] *n* Berechnung *f*; *(critical estimation)* Schätzung *f.* **to do a quick ~** die Sache schnell überschlagen.
calculator ['kælkjʊleɪtə^r] *n* Rechner *m.*
calculus ['kælkjʊləs] *n* *(Math)* Differential- und Integralrechnung *f.*
calendar ['kæləndə^r] *n* **(a)** Kalender *m.* **~ month** Kalendermonat *m.* **(b)** *(schedule)* Terminkalender *m.* **Church ~** Kirchenkalender *m.*
calf[1] [kɑːf] *n, pl* **calves (a)** Kalb *nt.* **a cow in** *or* **with ~** eine trächtige Kuh. **(b)** *(young elephant, seal etc)* Elefanten-/Robbenjunge(s) *etc nt.* **(c)** *(leather)* Kalb(s)leder *nt.*
calf[2] *n, pl* **calves** *(Anat)* Wade *f.*
caliber *n (US)* = **calibre.**
calibrate ['kælɪbreɪt] *vt gun* kalibrieren; *meter, instrument* eichen.
calibration [ˌkælɪ'breɪʃən] *n see vt* Kalibrieren *nt*; Eichen *nt*; *(mark)* Kalibrierung *f*; Eichung *f.*
calibre, *(US)* caliber ['kælɪbə^r] *n (lit)* Kaliber *nt*; *(fig also)* Format *nt.* **a man of his ~** ein Mann

seines Kalibers.
calico ['kælɪkəʊ] *n* Kattun *m.*
California [kælɪ'fɔːnɪə] *n* Kalifornien *nt.*
calipers ['kælɪpəz] *npl (US)* = **callipers.**
call [kɔːl] **1** *n* **(a)** *(shout, cry) (of person, bird etc)* Ruf *m*; *(of bugle)* Signal *nt.* **to give sb a ~** jdn (herbei)rufen; *(wake sb)* jdn wecken; **within ~** in Rufweite *f*; **a ~ for help** *(lit, fig)* ein Hilferuf *m.*
(b) *(telephone ~)* Anruf *m.* **I'll give you a ~** ich rufe Sie an; **to take a ~** ein Gespräch entgegennehmen.
(c) *(fig: summons)* Aufruf *m*; *(of religion)* Berufung *f*; *(fig: lure)* Verlockung *f.* **to be on ~** (Bereitschafts)dienst haben; **the ~ of duty** der Ruf der Pflicht.
(d) *(visit)* Besuch *m.* **to make** *or* **pay a ~ on sb** jdn besuchen; **port of ~** Anlaufhafen *m*; *(fig)* Station *f*; **to pay a ~** *(euph)* mal verschwinden *(col).*
(e) *(demand, claim)* Beanspruchung *f*; *(Comm)* Nachfrage *f (for* nach*).* **to have many ~s on one's purse/time** finanziell/zeitlich sehr in Anspruch genommen sein.
(f) at *or* **on ~** *(Fin)* auf Abruf.
(g) *(need, occasion)* Grund *m*, Veranlassung *f.* **there is no ~ for you to worry** es besteht kein Grund zur Sorge; **there was no ~ for that!** das war wirklich nicht nötig!
(h) *(Cards)* Ansage *f.*
2 *vt* **(a)** *(shout out)* rufen. **(b)** *(name, consider)* nennen. **to be ~ed** heißen; **what's he ~ed?** wie heißt er?; **what's this ~ed in German?** wie heißt das auf deutsch?; **~ it £5** sagen wir £5; **would you ~ German a difficult language?** würden Sie Deutsch als schwierige Sprache bezeichnen? **(c)** *(summon) person, doctor* rufen; *meeting* einberufen; *strike* ausrufen; *(Jur) witness* aufrufen; *(subpoena)* vorladen; *(waken)* wecken. **(d)** *(telephone)* anrufen. **(e)** *(Fin) bond* aufrufen; *loan* abrufen.
3 *vi* **(a)** *(shout: person, animal)* rufen. **to ~ for help** um Hilfe rufen; **to ~ to sb** jdm zurufen. **(b)** *(visit)* vorbeigehen/-kommen. **(c)** *(Telec)* anrufen. **who's ~ing, please?** wer spricht bitte?; **London ~ing!** *(Rad)* hier ist London; **thanks for ~ing** vielen Dank für den Anruf.
♦**call aside** *vt sep person* beiseite rufen.
♦**call at** *vi +prep obj (person)* vorbeigehen bei; *(Rail)* halten in *(+dat)*; *(Naut)* anlaufen.
♦**call away** *vt sep* weg- *or* abrufen. **I was ~ed ~ on business** ich wurde geschäftlich abgerufen.
♦**call back 1** *vti sep* zurückrufen. **2** *vi (come back)* **I'll ~ ~ later** ich komme später noch einmal wieder.
♦**call by** *vi* vorbeikommen.
♦**call for** *vi +prep obj* **(a)** *(send for) person* rufen; *food, drink* kommen lassen; *(ask for)* verlangen (nach). **(b)** *(need) courage, endurance* erfordern. **that ~s ~ a drink/celebration!** darauf müssen wir einen trinken!/das muß gefeiert werden! **(c)** *(collect) person, goods* abholen. **"to be ~ed ~"** *(goods sent by rail)* „bahnlagernd"; *(by post)* „postlagernd"; *(in shop)* „wird abgeholt".
♦**call in 1** *vt sep* **(a)** *doctor* zu Rate ziehen. **(b)** *(withdraw)* aus dem Verkehr ziehen. **2** *vi* vorbeischauen *(at, on* bei*).*
♦**call off** *vt sep* **(a)** *(cancel)* absagen; *deal* rückgängig machen; *engagement* lösen. **(b)** *dog* zurückrufen.
♦**call on** *vi +prep obj* **(a)** *(visit)* besuchen. **(b)** = **call upon.**
♦**call out 1** *vi* rufen. **2** *vt sep* **(a)** *names* aufrufen; *(announce)* ansagen. **(b)** *doctor* rufen; *troops, fire brigade* alarmieren. **(c)** *(order to strike)* zum Streik aufrufen.
♦**call out for** *vi +prep obj food, drink* verlangen; *help* rufen um.
♦**call round** *vi (col)* vorbeikommen.
♦**call up 1** *vt sep* **(a)** *(Mil) reservist* einberufen; *reinforcements* mobilisieren. **(b)** *(Telec)* anrufen. **(c)** *(fig)* (herauf)beschwören; *memories* wachrufen. **2** *vi (Telec)* anrufen.
♦**call upon** *vi +prep obj* **(a)** *(ask)* **to ~ ~ sb to do sth** jdn bitten, etw zu tun. **(b)** *(invoke)* **to ~ ~ sb's generosity** an jds Großzügigkeit *(acc)* appellieren; **to ~ ~ God** Gott anrufen.
callbox ['kɔːl,bɒks] *n (Brit)* Telefonzelle *f.*
caller ['kɔːləʳ] *n* **(a)** *(visitor)* Besuch(er) *m.* **(b)** *(Telec)* Anrufer *m.*
callgirl ['kɔːlgɜːl] *n* Callgirl *nt.*
calligraphy [kə'lɪgrəfɪ] *n* Kalligraphie, Schönschreibkunst *f.*
callipers, *(US)* **calipers** ['kælɪpəz] *npl* **(a)** Tastzirkel *m.* **(b)** *(Med)* Beinschienen *pl.*
callous ['kæləs] *adj (cruel)* gefühllos.
callousness ['kæləsnɪs] *n* Gefühllosigkeit *f.*
callow ['kæləʊ] *adj* unreif.
calm [kɑːm] **1** *adj (+er)* ruhig; *weather* windstill. **keep ~!** bleib ruhig! **2** *n* Ruhe *f*; *(at sea)* Flaute *f*; *(of wind)* Windstille *f.* **the ~ before the storm** *(lit, fig)* die Ruhe vor dem Sturm. **3** *vt* beruhigen.
♦**calm down 1** *vt sep* beruhigen. **2** *vi* sich beruhigen; *(wind)* abflauen.
calmly ['kɑːmlɪ] *adv speak, act* ruhig, gelassen.
calorie ['kælərɪ] *n* Kalorie *f.*
calorific [,kælə'rɪfɪk] *adj* wärmeerzeugend. **~ value** Heizwert *m.*
calumny ['kæləmnɪ] *n* Verunglimpfung *f.*
calve [kɑːv] *vi* kalben.
calves [kɑːvz] *pl of* **calf**[1], **calf**[2].
cam [kæm] *n* Nocken *m.*
camber ['kæmbəʳ] *n* Wölbung *f.*
Cambodia [kæm'bəʊdɪə] *n* Kambodscha *nt.*
came [keɪm] *pret of* **come.**
camel ['kæməl] *n* Kamel *nt.*
camel *in cpds (colour)* kamelhaarfarben.
camellia [kə'miːlɪə] *n* Kamelie *f.*
cameo ['kæmɪəʊ] *n* **(a)** *(jewellery)* Kamee *f.* **(b) ~ part** Mini(atur)rolle *f.*
camera[1] ['kæmərə] *n* Kamera *f*; *(for stills also)* Fotoapparat *m.*
camera[2] *n (Jur)*: **in ~** unter Ausschluß der Öffentlichkeit; *(fig)* hinter verschlossenen Türen.
cameraman ['kæmərə'mæn] *n, pl* **-men** [-mən] Kameramann *m.*
camomile ['kæməʊmaɪl] *m* Kamille *f.* **~ tea** Kamillentee *f.*
camouflage ['kæməflɑːʒ] **1** *n (Mil, fig)* Tarnung *f.* **2** *vt (Mil, fig)* tarnen.
camp[1] [kæmp] **1** *n (lit, fig)* Lager *nt.* **to pitch ~** ein Lager aufschlagen; **to strike** *or* **break ~** das Lager abbrechen. **2** *vi* zelten, campen; *(Mil)* lagern. **to go ~ing** zelten (gehen).
♦**camp out** *vi* zelten.
camp[2] *adj (theatrical, stagey)* übertrieben; *person's appearance* aufgedonnert; *(homosexual)* schwul *(col).*
campaign [kæm'peɪn] **1** *n* **(a)** *(Mil)* Feldzug *m.* **(b)** *(fig)* Kampagne *f.* **2** *vi* **(a)** *(Mil)* einen Feldzug unternehmen. **(b)** *(fig) (for* für, *against* gegen*)* sich einsetzen; *(politician, candidate)* den Wahlkampf führen.
campaigner [kæm'peɪnəʳ] *n* **(a)** *(Mil)* Krieger *m.* **old ~** Kriegsveteran *m*; *(fig)* alter Hase *(col).* **(b)** *(fig)* Befürworter(in *f*) *m (for gen)*; Gegner(in *f*) *m (against gen)*; *(Pol)* Wahlwerber(in *f*) *m.*
camp bed *n (Brit)* Campingliege *f.*
camper ['kæmpəʳ] *n* Camper(in *f*) *m (col)*; *(vehicle)* Campingwagen *m.*
camp: ~fire *n* Lagerfeuer *nt*; **~ follower** *n* Marketender(in *f*) *m*; **~ followers** *(fig)* Gefolge *nt no pl.*
camphor ['kæmfəʳ] *n* Kampfer *m.*
camping ['kæmpɪŋ] *n* Zelten, Camping *nt.*
camping *in cpds* Camping-; **~ site** *n (also* **camp**

site) Campingplatz *m.*

campus ['kæmpəs] *n* Campus *m,* Universitätsgelände *nt.*

camshaft ['kæmʃɑːft] *n* Nockenwelle *f.*

can[1] [kæn] *pret* **could** *modal aux* können; *(may also)* dürfen. ~ **you speak German?** können *or* sprechen Sie Deutsch?; ~ **I come too?** kann ich mitkommen?; ~ **you hear me?** hören Sie mich?; **how ~/could you say such a thing!** wie können/konnten Sie nur so etwas sagen!; **he could be on the next train** er könnte im nächsten Zug sein; **you could have told me** das hättest du mir sagen können; **she was as happy as could be** sie war über alle Maßen glücklich; **he ~'t** *or* **couldn't have done that** er kann das unmöglich getan haben; **as soon as it ~ be arranged** sobald es sich machen läßt.

can[2] **1** *n* **(a)** *(container)* Kanister *m*; *(milk~)* Kanne *f*; *(esp US: garbage ~)* (Müll)eimer *m.* **to carry the ~** *(fig col)* die Sache ausbaden *(col).* **(b)** *(tin)* Dose *f*; *(of food also)* Büchse *f.* **a ~ of beer** eine Dose Bier. **2** *vt foodstuffs* in Dosen füllen.

Canada ['kænədə] *n* Kanada *nt.*

Canadian [kə'neɪdɪən] **1** *adj* kanadisch. **2** *n* Kanadier(in *f*) *m.*

canal [kə'næl] *n* **(a)** Kanal *m.* **(b)** *(Anat)* Gang *m.*

Canaries [kə'nɛərɪz] *npl* Kanarische Inseln *pl.*

canary [kə'nɛərɪ] *n* Kanarienvogel *m.*

canary *in cpds (colour: also* ~ **yellow)** kanariengelb.

cancel ['kænsəl] *vt* **(a)** *(call off)* absagen; *(Comm)* stornieren; *plans* aufgeben; *train, bus* streichen; *invitation, deal* rückgängig machen; *subscription* kündigen. **the last train has been ~led** der letzte Zug fällt aus. **(b)** *cheque* entwerten; *(cross out) name etc* (durch)streichen. **(c)** *(Math)* kürzen.

♦ **cancel out 1** *vt sep (Math)* aufheben; *(fig)* zunichte machen. **to ~ each other ~** *(Math)* sich aufheben; *(fig)* sich die Waage halten. **2** *vi (Math)* sich aufheben.

cancellation [ˌkænsə'leɪʃən] *n see vt* **(a)** Absage *f*; Stornierung *f*; Aufgabe *f*; Streichung *f*; Kündigung *f.* **(b)** Entwertung *f.* **(c)** *(Math)* Kürzung *f.*

cancer ['kænsəʳ] *n (Med)* Krebs *m*; *(fig)* Krebsgeschwür *nt.* **C~** *(Astrol)* Krebs *m*; ~ **research** Krebsforschung *f.*

cancerous ['kænsərəs] *adj* krebsartig.

candelabra [ˌkændɪ'lɑːbrə] *n* Leuchter *m.*

candid ['kændɪd] *adj* offen, ehrlich.

candidacy ['kændɪdəsɪ] *n* Kandidatur *f.*

candidate ['kændɪdeɪt] *n (Pol)* Kandidat(in *f*) *m.*

candle ['kændl] *n* Kerze *f.* **he's burning the ~ at both ends** er arbeitet Tag und Nacht; **he can't hold a ~ to his brother** *(col)* er kann seinem Bruder nicht das Wasser reichen.

candle *in cpds* Kerzen-; **~light** *n* Kerzenlicht *nt*; **~stick** *n* Kerzenhalter *m.*

candour, *(US)* **candor** ['kændəʳ] *n* Offenheit, Ehrlichkeit *f.*

candy ['kændɪ] **1** *n (US) (sweet)* Bonbon *m or nt*; *(sweets)* Süßigkeiten *pl*; *(bar of chocolate)* (Tafel) Schokolade *f*; *(individual chocolate)* Praline *f.* **2** *vt sugar* kristallisieren lassen; *fruit etc* kandieren.

candy: ~floss *n (Brit)* Zuckerwatte *f*; ~ **store** *n (US)* Süßwarenhandlung *f.*

cane [keɪn] **1** *n* **(a)** *(stem of bamboo, sugar etc)* Rohr *nt*; *(of raspberry)* Zweig *m*; *(for supporting plants)* Stock *m.* **a chair made of ~** ein Rohrstuhl *m.* **(b)** *(walking stick)* (Spazier)stock *m*; *(instrument of punishment)* (Rohr)stock *m.* **to get the ~** Stockschläge bekommen. **2** *vt* mit dem Stock schlagen.

canine ['keɪnaɪn] **1** *n* **(a)** *(animal)* Hund *m.* **(b)** *(also ~* **tooth)** Eckzahn *m.* **2** *adj* Hunde-.

canister ['kænɪstəʳ] *n* Behälter *m.*

cannabis ['kænəbis] *n* Cannabis *m.*

canned [kænd] **(a)** *food* Dosen-, in Dosen. ~ **music** *(col)* Musikberieselung *f (col).* **(b)** *(col: drunk)* voll *(col).*

cannibal ['kænɪbəl] **1** *n (person)* Kannibale, Menschenfresser *m.* **2** *adj* kannibalisch.

cannibalism ['kænɪbəlɪzəm] *n* Kannibalismus *m.*

cannibalize ['kænɪbəlaɪz] *vt old car etc* ausschlachten.

cannon ['kænən] *n (Mil)* Kanone *f.*

♦ **cannon into** *vi +prep obj* prallen gegen.

cannon: ~ball *n* Kanonenkugel *f*; ~ **fodder** *n* Kanonenfutter *nt.*

cannot ['kænɒt] = **can not.**

canoe [kə'nuː] **1** *n* Kanu *nt.* **2** *vi* Kanu fahren.

canoeist [kə'nuːɪst] *n* Kanufahrer(in *f*) *m.*

canon[1] ['kænən] *n (all senses)* Kanon *m.*

canon[2] *n (priest)* Kanoniker *m.*

canonize ['kænənaɪz] *vt (Eccl)* heiligsprechen.

can opener *n* Dosen- *or* Büchsenöffner *m.*

canopy ['kænəpɪ] *n (awning)* Markise *f*; *(over entrance)* Vordach *nt*; *(of bed, throne)* Baldachin *m.*

can't [kɑːnt] = **can not.**

cantankerous [kæn'tæŋkərəs] *adj* verdrießlich.

canteen [kæn'tiːn] *n* **(a)** *(restaurant)* Kantine *f.* **(b)** *(Mil) (flask)* Feldflasche *f*; *(mess tin)* Kochgeschirr *nt.* **(c)** *(of cutlery)* Besteckkasten *m.*

canter ['kæntəʳ] **1** *n* Kanter *m.* **2** *vi* langsam galoppieren.

cantilever ['kæntɪliːvəʳ] *n* Ausleger *m*; *(support also)* Freiträger *m.*

cantilever *in cpds* Ausleger-; ~ **bridge** *n* Auslegerbrücke *f.*

canton ['kæntɒn] *n* Kanton *m.*

canvas ['kænvəs] *n* Leinwand *f*; *(for sails)* Segeltuch *nt*; *(set of sails)* Segel *pl*; *(painting)* Gemälde *nt.* **under ~** *(in a tent)* im Zelt; *(Naut)* mit gehißtem Segel.

canvass ['kænvəs] **1** *vt* **(a)** *(Pol) district* Wahlwerbung machen in *(+dat).* **to ~ voters** Wahlwerbung machen. **(b)** *customers, citizens etc* werben; *district* bereisen; *(sound out) opinions* erforschen. **2** *vi* **(a)** *(Pol)* um Stimmen werben *(for sb* für jdn*).* **(b)** *(Comm)* eine Werbekampagne durchführen.

canvasser ['kænvəsəʳ] *n* **(a)** *(Pol)* Wahlhelfer(in *f*) *m.* **(b)** *(Comm)* Vertreter(in *f*) *m.*

canyon ['kænjən] *n* Cañon *m.*

cap [kæp] **1** *n* **(a)** *(hat)* Mütze *f*; *(nurse's ~)* Haube *f*; *(for swimming)* Badekappe *f.* ~ **in hand** *(fig)* kleinlaut; **if the ~ fits(, wear it)** *(prov)* wem der Schuh paßt(, der soll ihn sich anziehen); **he's got his ~ for England, he's an English ~** *(Sport)* er ist/war in der englischen Nationalmannschaft. **(b)** *(lid, cover: of bottle)* Deckel *m*; *(of fountain pen)* (Verschluß)klappe *f*; *(Mil: of shell, fuse)* Kapsel *f*; *(Aut: petrol ~, radiator ~)* Verschluß *m.* **(c)** *(contraceptive)* Pessar *nt.* **(d)** *(of tooth)* (Jacket)krone *f.*

2 *vt* **(a)** *(put ~ on) bottle etc* verschließen. **(b)** *(do or say better)* überbieten. **and then to ~ it all** ... und um dem Ganzen die Krone aufzusetzen, ... **(c) he's been ~ped twice for England** er war zweimal in der englischen Nationalmannschaft.

capability [ˌkeɪpə'bɪlɪtɪ] *n (potential ability)* Fähigkeit *f*; *(no pl: capableness also)* Kompetenz *f.*

capable ['keɪpəbl] *adj* **(a)** *(skilful, competent)* fähig. **(b) to be ~ of doing sth** etw tun können; **it's ~ of speeds of up to ...** es erreicht Geschwindigkeiten bis zu ...; **thank you but I'm quite ~ of doing that myself** danke, ich bin durchaus imstande, das allein zu machen.

capacitor [kə'pæsɪtəʳ] *n* Kondensator *m.*

capacity [kə'pæsɪtɪ] *n* **(a)** *(cubic content etc)* Fassungsvermögen *nt*; *(maximum output)* Kapazität *f*; *(maximum weight)* Höchstlast *f*; *(Aut: engine ~)* Hubraum *m.* **filled to ~** randvoll; *(hall)* bis auf den letzten Platz besetzt; **seating ~ of 400** 400 Sitzplätze; **working at full ~** voll ausgelastet; **to play to a ~ audience** vor ausverkauftem Saal spielen. **(b)** *(ability)* Fähigkeit *f.* **this work is**

beyond his ~ diese Arbeit übersteigt seine Fähigkeiten. **(c)** *(role, position)* Eigenschaft *f*. **in my ~ as a doctor** (in meiner Eigenschaft) als Arzt.

cape[1] [keɪp] *n* Cape *nt*, Umhang *m*.

cape[2] *n (Geog)* Kap *nt*.

caper[1] ['keɪpəʳ] **1** *vi* herumtollen. **2** *n (prank)* Kapriole *f*. **all this ~ with the garage** *(col)* das ganze Theater mit der Werkstatt *(col)*.

caper[2] *n (Bot, Cook)* Kaper *f*.

capillary [kə'pɪlərɪ] **1** *adj* kapillar, Kapillar-. ~ **action** Kapillarwirkung *f*. **2** *n* Kapillare *f*.

capital ['kæpɪtl] **1** *n* **(a)** *(also ~* **city***)* Hauptstadt *f*. **(b)** *(also ~* **letter***)* Großbuchstabe *m*. **please write in ~s** bitte in Blockschrift schreiben! **(c)** *no pl (Fin)* Kapital *nt*. **to make ~ out of sth** *(fig)* aus etw Kapital schlagen. **2** *adj* **(a)** *letter* Groß-. **(b)** *(dated: excellent)* prächtig.

capital *in cpds* Kapital-; ~ **expenditure** *n* Kapitalaufwendungen *pl*; ~ **gains tax** *n* Kapitalertragssteuer *f*; ~ **goods** *npl* Investitionsgüter *pl*; **~-intensive** *adj* kapitalintensiv.

capitalism ['kæpɪtəlɪzəm] *n* Kapitalismus *m*.

capitalist ['kæpɪtəlɪst] **1** *n* Kapitalist(in *f*) *m*. **2** *adj* kapitalistisch.

capitalize ['kæpɪtəˌlaɪz] *vt* **(a)** *(Fin)* kapitalisieren. **(b)** *(Typ) word* groß schreiben.

♦ **capitalize on** *vi +prep obj (fig)* Kapital schlagen aus.

capital: ~ offence *(Brit) or* **offense** *(US) n* Kapitalverbrechen *nt*; ~ **punishment** *n* Todesstrafe *f*.

capitulate [kə'pɪtjʊleɪt] *vi* kapitulieren *(also Mil) (to* vor *+dat)*, aufgeben *(to* gegenüber*)*.

caprice [kə'priːs] *n* Laune(nhaftigkeit), Kaprice *(geh) f*.

capricious [kə'prɪʃəs] *adj* launisch, kapriziös *(geh)*.

Capricorn ['kæprɪkɔːn] *n* Steinbock *m*.

capsize [kæp'saɪz] **1** *vi* kentern. **2** *vt* zum Kentern bringen.

capstan ['kæpstən] *n* Poller *m*.

capsule ['kæpsjuːl] *n* Kapsel *f*.

captain ['kæptɪn] *(abbr* **Capt***)* **1** *n (Mil)* Hauptmann *m*; *(Naut, Aviat, Sport)* Kapitän *m*; *(US: in restaurant)* Oberkellner *m*. ~ **of industry** Industriekapitän *m*. **2** *vt (Sport) team* anführen; *(Naut) ship* befehligen. **he ~ed the team for years** er war jahrelang Kapitän der Mannschaft.

caption ['kæpʃən] *n* Überschrift *f*; *(under cartoon)* Bildunterschrift *f*; *(Film: subtitle)* Untertitel *m*.

captivate ['kæptɪveɪt] *vt* bezaubern.

captivating ['kæptɪveɪtɪŋ] *adj* bezaubernd.

captive ['kæptɪv] **1** *n* Gefangene(r) *mf*. **to take sb ~** jdn gefangennehmen. **2** *adj person* gefangen. **a ~ audience** unfreiwillige Zuhörer/Zuschauer *pl*.

captivity [kæp'tɪvɪtɪ] *n* Gefangenschaft *f*.

captor ['kæptəʳ] *n* **his ~s were British** er wurde von Briten gefangengehalten; **his ~s treated him kindly** er wurde nach seiner Gefangennahme gut behandelt.

capture ['kæptʃəʳ] **1** *vt* **(a)** *town* einnehmen, erobern; *person* gefangennehmen; *animal* (ein)fangen. **(b)** *(fig: painter etc) atmosphere* einfangen; *attention, sb's interest* erregen. **2** *n* Eroberung *f*; *(of soldier, escapee)* Gefangennahme *f*; *(of animal)* Einfangen *nt*.

car [kɑːʳ] *n* **(a)** Auto *nt*, Wagen *m*. **by ~** mit dem Auto. **(b)** *(Rail, tram~)* Wagen *m*. **(c)** *(US: of elevator)* Fahrkorb *m*.

carafe [kə'ræf] *n* Karaffe *f*.

caramel ['kærəməl] *n (substance)* Karamel *m*; *(sweet)* Karamelbonbon *nt or m*.

carat ['kærət] *n* Karat *nt*. **nine ~ gold** neunkarätiges Gold.

caravan ['kærəvæn] *n* **(a)** *(Brit: Aut)* Wohnwagen, Caravan *m*. **(b)** *(gipsy ~)* Zigeunerwagen *m*. **(c)** *(desert ~)* Karawane *f*.

caravanning ['kærəvænɪŋ] *n (Brit)* Urlaub *m* im Wohnwagen.

caravan site *n (Brit)* Campingplatz *m* für Wohnwagen.

caraway ['kærəweɪ] *n* Kümmel *m*.

carbohydrate ['kɑːbəʊ'haɪdreɪt] *n* Kohlehydrat *nt*.

carbolic [kɑː'bɒlɪk] *adj* ~ **acid** Karbolsäure *f*.

carbon ['kɑːbən] *n (Chem)* Kohlenstoff *m*.

carbon: ~ copy *n* Durchschlag *m*; **to be a ~ copy of sth/sb** einer Sache/jdm aufs Haar gleichen *(col)*; ~ **dioxide** *n* Kohlendioxyd *nt*.

carbonize ['kɑːbənaɪz] *vt* karbonisieren.

carbon: ~ monoxide *n* Kohlenmonoxyd *nt*; ~ **paper** *n* Kohlepapier *nt*.

carbuncle ['kɑːˌbʌŋkl] *n (Med)* Karbunkel *m*.

carburettor, *(US)* **carburetor** [ˌkɑːbə'retəʳ] *n* Vergaser *m*.

carcass ['kɑːkəs] *n* **(a)** *(corpse)* Leiche *f*; *(of animal)* Kadaver *m*; *(at butcher's)* Rumpf *m*. **(b)** *(of ship)* Skelett *nt*.

carcinogenic [ˌkaːsɪnə'dʒenɪk] *adj* krebserregend.

card [kɑːd] *n* **(a)** *no pl (~board)* Pappe *f*. **(b)** *(greetings, visiting ~ etc)* Karte *f*. **(c)** *(playing ~)* (Spiel)karte *f*. **to play ~s** Karten spielen. **(d)** *(fig uses)* **to put one's ~s on the table** seine Karten auf den Tisch legen; **to play one's ~s right** taktisch geschickt vorgehen; **it's on the ~s** es ist zu erwarten.

card: ~board *n* Karton *m*, Pappe *f*; **~board box** *n* (Papp)karton *m*; ~ **game** *n* Kartenspiel *nt*.

cardiac ['kɑːdɪæk] *adj* Herz-. ~ **arrest** Herzstillstand *m*.

cardigan ['kɑːdɪgən] *n* Strickjacke *f*.

cardinal ['kɑːdɪnl] *n (Eccl)* Kardinal *m*.

cardinal: ~ **number** *n* Kardinalzahl *f*; ~ **sin** *n* Todsünde *f*.

card index *n* Kartei *f*; *(in library)* Katalog *m*.

cardiology [ˌkɑːdɪ'ɒlədʒɪ] *n* Kardiologie *f*.

care [kɛəʳ] **1** *n* **(a)** *(worry, anxiety)* Sorge *f (of* um*)*. **he hasn't a ~ in the world** er hat keinerlei Sorgen.

(b) *(carefulness, attentiveness)* Sorgfalt *f*. **to drive with due ~ and attention** umsichtig fahren; **"fragile, with ~", "handle with ~"** „Vorsicht, zerbrechlich"; **to take ~** aufpassen, achtgeben; **bye-bye, take ~** tschüs, mach's gut; **to take ~ to do sth** sich bemühen, etw zu tun; **take ~ not to drop it** paß auf, daß du es nicht fallenläßt; **you should take more ~ with** *or* **over the details** Sie sollten sich sorgfältiger mit den Einzelheiten befassen.

(c) *(of teeth, car etc)* Pflege *f*. **to take ~ of sth** auf etw *(acc)* aufpassen; *of one's appearance, hair, car* etw pflegen; *(not treat roughly) car, health* etw schonen.

(d) *(of old people, children)* Fürsorge *f*. **he needs medical ~** er muß ärztlich behandelt werden; **to take ~ of sb** sich um jdn kümmern; *of patients* jdn versorgen; *of one's family* für jdn sorgen; **he can take ~ of himself** *(in a fight)* er kann sich verteidigen.

(e) ~ **of** *(abbr* **c/o***)* bei; **to take a child into ~** ein Kind in Pflege nehmen.

(f) to take ~ of sb/sth *(see to)* sich um jdn/etw kümmern; *of arrangements also* etw erledigen.

(g) *(caringness, concern) (of person)* Anteilnahme *f*; *(of state, council)* soziale Einstellung.

2 *vi (be concerned)* sich kümmern *(about* um*)*. **money is all he ~s about** er interessiert sich nur fürs Geld; **he ~s deeply about her** sie bedeutet ihm sehr viel; **I don't ~** das ist mir egal; **for all I ~** meinetwegen, von mir aus; **who ~s?** na und?

3 *vt* **(a)** *(mind, be concerned)* **I don't ~ what people say** es ist mir egal, was die Leute sagen; **what do I ~?** was geht mich das an?; **I couldn't ~ less** es ist mir doch völlig egal. **(b)** *(like)* **would you ~ to take off your coat?** möchten Sie nicht

(Ihren Mantel) ablegen?
♦**care for** *vi +prep obj* **(a)** *(look after)* sich kümmern um; *invalid also* versorgen; *hands, furniture etc* pflegen. **(b)** *(like)* **I don't ~ ~ your tone of voice** wie reden Sie denn mit mir?; **would you ~ ~ a cup of tea?** hätten *or* möchten Sie gerne eine Tasse Tee?; **I never have much ~d ~ his films** ich habe mir noch nie viel aus seinen Filmen gemacht.
career [kəˈrɪəʳ] **1** *n* Karriere *f*; *(profession)* Beruf *m*; *(working life)* Laufbahn *f*. **~s officer** Berufsberater(in *f*) *m*; **to make a ~ for oneself** Karriere machen. **2** *attr* Karriere-; *soldier, diplomat* Berufs-. **~ woman** Karrierefrau *f*. **3** *vi* rasen. **to ~ along** rasen.
carefree [ˈkɛəfriː] *adj* sorglos; *song* heiter.
careful [ˈkɛəfʊl] *adj* sorgfältig; *(with money etc)* sparsam. **~!** Vorsicht!; **to be ~** aufpassen *(of* auf *+acc)*; **be ~ what you do** nimm dich in acht; **be ~ (that) they don't hear you** gib acht, daß sie dich nicht hören.
carefully [ˈkɛəfəlɪ] *adv see adj.*
careless [ˈkɛəlɪs] *adj (negligent, heedless)* nachlässig; *driver* unvorsichtig; *driving* leichtsinnig; *remark* gedankenlos. **~ mistake** Flüchtigkeitsfehler *m*.
carelessly [ˈkɛəlɪslɪ] *adv see adj.*
carelessness [ˈkɛəlɪsnɪs] *n see adj* Nachlässigkeit *f*; Unvorsicht(igkeit) *f*, Leichtsinn *m*; Gedankenlosigkeit *f*.
caress [kəˈres] **1** *n* Liebkosung *f*, Streicheln *nt no pl*. **2** *vt* streicheln, liebkosen.
care: **~taker** *n* Hausmeister *m*; **~taker government** *n* geschäftsführende Regierung; **~worn** *adj* von Sorgen gezeichnet.
car ferry *n* Autofähre *f*.
cargo [ˈkɑːgəʊ] *n* (Schiffs)ladung *f*. **~ boat** Frachter *m*, Frachtschiff *nt*.
Caribbean [ˌkærɪˈbiːən, *(US)* kæˈrɪbiːən] **1** *adj* karibisch. **~ Sea** Karibisches Meer. **2** *n* Karibik *f*.
caricature [ˈkærɪkətjʊəʳ] **1** *n* Karikatur *f*. **2** *vt* karikieren.
caries [ˈkɛərɪiːz] *n* Karies *f*.
caring [ˈkɛərɪŋ] *adj person* liebevoll; *government, society* sozial eingestellt.
carnage [ˈkɑːnɪdʒ] *n* Gemetzel *nt*.
carnal [ˈkɑːnl] *adj* fleischlich, körperlich.
carnation [kɑːˈneɪʃən] *n* Nelke *f*.
carnival [ˈkɑːnɪvəl] *n* Karneval *m*; *(in S Ger)* Fasching *m*.
carnivore [ˈkɑːnɪvɔːʳ] *n (animal)* Fleischfresser *m*; *(plant)* fleischfressende Pflanze.
carnivorous [kɑːˈnɪvərəs] *adj* fleischfressend.
carol [ˈkærəl] *n* Lied *nt*. **Christmas ~** Weihnachtslied *nt*; **~ singers** *npl* ≈ Sternsinger *pl*.
carouse [kəˈraʊz] *vi (old)* zechen.
carousel [ˌkæruːˈsel] *n* = **car(r)ousel.**
carp[1] [kɑːp] *n (fish)* Karpfen *m*.
carp[2] *vi* etwas auszusetzen haben *(at* an *+dat)*.
car park *n (Brit) (open air)* Parkplatz *m*; *(covered)* Parkhaus *nt*.
carpenter [ˈkɑːpɪntəʳ] *n* Zimmermann *m*; *(for furniture)* Tischler *m*.
carpentry [ˈkɑːpɪntrɪ] *n* Zimmerhandwerk *nt*; *(as hobby)* Tischlern *nt*.
carpet [ˈkɑːpɪt] **1** *n (lit, fig)* Teppich *m*; *(fitted ~)* Teppichboden *m*. **2** *vt floor* (mit Teppichen/Teppichboden) auslegen.
carpet: **~ slippers** *npl* Pantoffeln *pl*; **~ sweeper** *n* Teppichkehrer *m*.
carport [ˈkɑːpɔːt] *n* Einstellplatz *m*.
carriage [ˈkærɪdʒ] *n* **(a)** *(horse-drawn vehicle)* Kutsche *f*; *(esp US: baby ~)* Kinderwagen *m*. **(b)** *(Brit Rail)* Wagen *m*. **(c)** *(Comm: conveyance)* Beförderung *f*. **~ free** frachtfrei; **~ paid** frei Haus. **(d)** *(Typ)* Wagen *m*. **~ return** Rücklauftaste *f*. **(e)** *(of person: bearing)* Haltung *f*.
carriageway [ˈkærɪdʒˈweɪ] *n (Brit)* Fahrbahn *f*.
carrier [ˈkærɪəʳ] *n* **(a)** *(goods haulier)* Spediteur *m*. **(b)** *(of disease)* Überträger *m*. **(c)** *(aircraft ~)* Flugzeugträger *m*; *(troop ~)* Transportflugzeug *nt*/-schiff *nt*. **(d)** *(Chem)* Träger(substanz *f*) *m*. **(e)** *(Brit also ~* **bag***)* Tragetüte *f*.
carrion [ˈkærɪən] *n* Aas *nt*. **~ crow** Rabenkrähe *f*.
carrot [ˈkærət] *n* Karotte, Möhre *f*; *(fig)* Köder *m*.
car(r)ousel [ˌkæruːˈsel] *n* Karussell *nt*.
carry [ˈkærɪ] **1** *vt* **(a)** tragen; *message* (über)bringen.
(b) *(vehicle: convey)* befördern. **the wind carried the sound to him** der Wind trug die Laute zu ihm hin.
(c) *(have on person) documents, money* bei sich haben.
(d) *(fig)* **his voice carries conviction** seine Stimme klingt überzeugend; **the offence carries a penalty of £5** darauf steht eine Geldstrafe von £5; **it carries interest at 8%** es wirft 8% Zinsen ab; **you're ~ing things too far** *(fig)* du treibst es zu weit; **he carries himself well** er hat eine gute Haltung.
(e) *(bridge etc: support)* tragen. **he carries his drink well** er kann viel vertragen.
(f) *(Comm) goods, stock* führen, (auf Lager) haben; *(newspaper) story* bringen.
(g) *(Tech: pipe)* führen; *(wire)* (weiter)leiten.
(h) *(win)* einnehmen, erobern. **to ~ the day** den Sieg davontragen; **the motion was carried unanimously** der Antrag wurde einstimmig angenommen.
2 *vi (voice, sound)* tragen. **the sound of the alphorn carried for miles** der Klang des Alphorns war meilenweit zu hören.
♦**carry away** *vt sep* **(a)** *(lit)* (hin)wegtragen; *(torrent, flood)* (hin)wegspülen. **(b)** *(fig)* **to get carried ~** sich nicht mehr bremsen können; **don't get carried ~!** übertreib's nicht!
♦**carry back** *vt sep (fig) person* zurückversetzen *(to* in *+acc)*.
♦**carry forward** *vt sep (Fin)* vortragen.
♦**carry off** *vt sep* **(a)** *(seize, carry away)* wegtragen. **(b)** *(win) prizes, medals* gewinnen. **(c) to ~ it ~** es hinkriegen *(col)*.
♦**carry on 1** *vi* **(a)** *(continue)* weitermachen; *(life)* weitergehen. **(b)** *(col) (talk)* reden und reden; *(make a scene)* ein Theater machen *(col)*. **to ~ ~ about sth** sich über etw *(acc)* auslassen. **(c)** *(have an affair)* etwas haben *(col) (with sb* mit jdm*)*. **2** *vt sep* **(a)** *(continue) tradition* fortführen. **(b)** *(conduct) conversation, correspondence* führen; *profession, trade* ausüben.
♦**carry out** *vt sep* **(a)** *(lit)* heraustragen. **(b)** *order* ausführen; *plan, experiment* durchführen; *threats* wahrmachen.
♦**carry through** *vt sep (carry out)* zu Ende führen.
carry: **~-all** *n* (Reise)tasche *f*; **~cot** *n (Brit)* Babytragetasche *f*; **~-on** *n (col)* Theater *nt (col)*.
carsick [ˈkɑːsɪk] *adj* **I get ~** mir wird beim Autofahren immer übel.
cart [kɑːt] **1** *n* Wagen, Karren *m*; *(US) (in supermarket)* Einkaufswagen *m*; *(for baggage)* Gepäckwagen *m*. **to put the ~ before the horse** *(prov)* das Pferd am Schwanz aufzäumen *(prov)*. **2** *vt (fig col)* mit sich schleppen.
♦**cart away** *or* **off** *vt sep* abtransportieren.
carte blanche [ˈkɑːtˈblɑ̃ʃ] *n no pl* **to give sb ~ ~** jdm (eine) Blankovollmacht geben.
cartel [kɑːˈtel] *n* Kartell *nt*.
carthorse [ˈkɑːthɔːs] *n* Zugpferd *nt*.
cartilage [ˈkɑːtɪlɪdʒ] *n* Knorpel *m*.
cartography [kɑːˈtɒgrəfɪ] *n* Kartographie *f*.
carton [ˈkɑːtən] *n* Karton *m*; *(of cigarettes)* Stange *f*; *(of milk)* Tüte *f*.
cartoon [kɑːˈtuːn] *n* **(a)** *(in newspaper etc)* Karikatur *f*; *(strip ~)* Comics *pl*. **(b)** *(Film, TV)*

(Zeichen)trickfilm *m.*
cartoonist [ˌkɑːˈtuːnɪst] *n* **(a)** *(in newspaper etc)* Karikaturist(in *f*) *m.* **(b)** *(Film, TV)* Trickzeichner(in *f*) *m.*
cartridge [ˈkɑːtrɪdʒ] *n (for rifle, pen)* Patrone *f*; *(Phot, for tape recorder)* Kassette *f*; *(for record player)* Tonabnehmer *m.*
cartridge paper *n* Zeichenpapier *nt.*
cartwheel [ˈkɑːtˌwiːl] *n (lit)* Wagenrad *nt*; *(Sport)* Rad *nt.* **to turn** *or* **do ~s** radschlagen.
carve [kɑːv] **1** *vt* **(a)** *(Art: cut) wood* schnitzen; *stone etc* (be)hauen. **to ~ sth on a stone** etw in einen Stein einmeißeln. **(b)** *(Cook)* tranchieren. **2** *vi (Cook)* tranchieren.
♦ **carve out** *vt sep* **to ~ ~ a career for oneself** sich *(dat)* eine Karriere aufbauen.
♦ **carve up** *vt sep meat* aufschneiden; *body, (fig) country* zerstückeln.
carving [ˈkɑːvɪŋ] *n (Art) (thing carved)* Skulptur *f*; *(in wood)* Holzschnitt *m.* **~ knive** Tranchiermesser *nt.*
cascade [kæsˈkeɪd] **1** *n* Kaskade *f.* **2** *vi (also* **~ down***)* *(onto* auf *+acc)* (in Kaskaden) herabfallen; *(hair)* wallend herabfallen; *(boxes etc)* herunterpurzeln *(col).*
case[1] [keɪs] *n* **(a)** *(Med, Jur, instance)* Fall *m.* **if that's the ~** wenn das der Fall ist; **as the ~ may be** je nachdem; **it's a clear ~ of lying** das ist eindeutig gelogen; **in ~** falls; **(just) in ~** für alle Fälle; **in ~ of emergency** im Notfall *m*; **in any ~** sowieso; **in this/that ~** in dem Fall; **the ~ for the defence/prosecution** die Verteidigung/Anklage; **in the ~ Higgins v Schwarz** in der Sache Higgins gegen Schwarz; **the ~ for/against the abolition of capital punishment** die Argumente für/gegen die Abschaffung der Todesstrafe; **to put the ~ for sth** etw vertreten; **you've got a good ~** was Sie sagen, ist durchaus gerechtfertigt; **there's a strong ~ for legalizing pot** es spricht viel für die Legalisierung von Marihuana.
(b) *(Gram)* Fall, Kasus *m.* **in the genitive ~** im Genitiv.
(c) *(col: person)* Type *f (col).* **he's a ~** das ist vielleicht 'ne Type *(col)*; **a hard ~** ein schwieriger Fall.
case[2] *n* **(a)** *(suit~)* Koffer *m*; *(crate, packing ~)* Kiste *f*; *(display ~)* Vitrine *f.* **(b)** *(box)* Schachtel *f*; *(for spectacles)* Etui *nt*; *(pillow~)* Bezug *m*; *(for musical instrument)* Kasten *m.*
case: ~ history *n (Med)* Krankengeschichte *f*; *(Sociol, Psych)* Vorgeschichte *f*; **~ study** *n* Fallstudie *f*; **~work** *n (Sociol)* ≈ Sozialarbeit *f.*
cash [kæʃ] **1** *n* **(a)** Bargeld *nt.* **~ in hand** Barbestand *m*; **to pay (in) ~** bar bezahlen; **ready ~** verfügbares Geld. **(b)** *(immediate payment)* Barzahlung *f*; *(not credit)* Sofortzahlung *f.* **~ on delivery** per Nachnahme. **(c)** *(money)* Geld *nt.* **to be short of ~** knapp bei Kasse sein *(col).* **2** *vt cheque* einlösen.
♦ **cash in 1** *vt sep* einlösen. **2** *vi* **to ~ ~ on sth** aus etw Kapital schlagen.
cash: ~-and-carry 1 *adj* Cash-and-carry-; **2** *n (for retailers)* Cash and Carry *m*; *(for public)* Verbrauchermarkt *m*; **~ desk** *n* Kasse *f*; **~ dispenser** *n* Geldautomat *m.*
cashew [kæˈʃuː] *n (tree)* Nierenbaum *m*; *(nut)* Cashewnuß *f.*
cashflow [ˈkæʃfləʊ] *n* Cash-flow *m.* **~ problems** Liquiditätsprobleme.
cashier [kæˈʃɪəʳ] *n* Kassierer(in *f*) *m.*
cashless [ˈkæʃləs] *adj* bargeldlos.
cashmere [kæʃˈmɪəʳ] *n* Kaschmir *m.*
cash: ~ payment *n* Barzahlung *f*; **~ prize** *n* Geldpreis *m*; **~ register** *n* Registrierkasse *f.*
casing [ˈkeɪsɪŋ] *n (Tech)* Gehäuse *nt.*
casino [kəˈsiːnəʊ] *n* (Spiel)kasino *nt.*
cask [kɑːsk] *n* Faß *nt.*
casket [ˈkɑːskɪt] *n* Schatulle *f*; *(US: coffin)* Sarg *m.*
casserole [ˈkæsərəʊl] **1** *n (Cook)* Kasserolle *f.* **2** *vt (Brit)* schmoren.
cassette [kæˈset] *n* Kassette *f.* **~ deck** Kassettendeck *nt*; **~ recorder** Kassettenrecorder *m.*
cassock [ˈkæsək] *n* Soutane *f.*
cast [kɑːst] *(vb: pret, ptp ~)* **1** *n* **(a)** *(of dice, net, line)* Wurf *m.* **(b)** *(mould)* (Guß)form *f*; *(object moulded)* Abdruck *m*; *(in metal)* (Ab)guß *m.* **~ iron** Gußeisen *nt.* **(c)** *(plaster ~)* Gipsverband *m.* **(d)** *(Theat)* Besetzung *f.* **~ (in order of appearance***)* Mitwirkende *pl* (in der Reihenfolge ihres Auftritts). **(e) ~ of mind** Gesinnung *f.* **(f)** *(Med: squint)* schielender Blick. **2** *vt* **(a)** werfen; *anchor, net* auswerfen; *vote* abgeben. **to ~ one's eyes over sth** einen Blick auf etw *(acc)* werfen. **(b)** *(shed)* **to ~ its skin** sich häuten. **(c)** *(Tech, Art)* gießen. **(d)** *(Theat) parts, play* besetzen. **he was ~ for the part of Hamlet** er sollte den Hamlet spielen. **3** *vi* **(a)** *(Fishing)* die Angel auswerfen. **(b)** *(Theat)* die Rollen verteilen.
♦ **cast about** *or* **around for** *vi +prep obj* suchen nach; *for new job etc* sich umsehen nach.
♦ **cast aside** *vt sep cares, inhibitions* ablegen; *old clothes etc* ausrangieren.
♦ **cast away** *vt sep* wegwerfen. **to be ~ ~** *(Naut)* gestrandet sein.
♦ **cast down** *vt sep eyes* niederschlagen. **to be ~ ~** *(fig)* niedergeschlagen sein.
♦ **cast off 1** *vt sep* **(a)** *(get rid of)* abwerfen; *friends* fallenlassen. **(b)** *stitches* abketten. **(c)** *(Naut)* losmachen. **2** *vi* **(a)** *(Naut)* ablegen. **(b)** *(in knitting)* abketteln.
♦ **cast on** *vti sep (Knitting)* anschlagen.
♦ **cast up** *vt sep* **to ~ sth ~ at sb** jdm etw vorhalten.
castanets [ˌkæstəˈnets] *npl* Kastagnetten *pl.*
castaway [ˈkɑːstəweɪ] *n (lit, fig)* Schiffbrüchige(r) *mf.*
caste [kɑːst] *n* Kaste *f.*
caster [ˈkɑːstəʳ] *n* = **castor.**
castigate [ˈkæstɪgeɪt] *vt person (old: physically)* züchtigen; *(verbally)* geißeln.
casting vote [ˈkɑːstɪŋˈvəʊt] *n* ausschlaggebende Stimme.
cast-iron [ˈkɑːstˌaɪən] *adj* **(a)** *(lit)* gußeisern. **(b)** *(fig) will, constitution* eisern; *case, alibi* hieb- und stichfest.
castle [ˈkɑːsl] **1** *n* **(a)** Schloß *nt*; *(fortress)* Burg *f.* **to build ~s in the air** Luftschlösser bauen. **(b)** *(Chess)* Turm *m.* **2** *vi (Chess)* rochieren.
cast: ~-off 1 *adj clothes* abgelegt *attr*; **2** *npl* **~-offs** *(col)* abgelegte Kleider.
castor [ˈkɑːstəʳ] *n* **(a)** *(Brit: for sugar, salt etc)* Streuer *m.* **(b)** *(wheel)* Rolle *f*, Rad *nt.*
castor: ~ oil *n* Rizinus(öl) *nt*; **~ sugar** *n (Brit)* Kristallzucker *m.*
castrate [kæsˈtreɪt] *vt* kastrieren.
casual [ˈkæʒjʊl] **1** *adj* **(a)** *(not planned)* zufällig; *acquaintance, glance* flüchtig. **(b)** *(offhand, careless)* lässig; *attitude* gleichgültig; *remark* beiläufig. **(c)** *(informal)* zwanglos; *clothes* leger. **~ wear** Freizeitkleidung *f.* **(d)** *(irregular) work, labourer* Gelegenheits-. **2** *n (~ worker)* Gelegenheitsarbeiter(in *f*) *m.* **~s** Aushilfen *pl.*
casually [ˈkæʒjʊlɪ] *adv (without planning)* zufällig; *(in an offhand manner)* beiläufig; *(informally)* zwanglos; *dressed* leger.
casualty [ˈkæʒjʊltɪ] *n* **(a)** *(lit, fig)* Opfer *nt*; *(injured also)* Verletzte(r) *mf*; *(dead also)* Tote(r) *mf.* **(b)** *(also* **~ ward***)* Unfallstation *f.*
cat [kæt] *n* Katze *f.* **to let the ~ out of the bag** die Katze aus dem Sack lassen; **they fight like ~ and dog** die vertragen sich wie Hund und Katze; **there isn't room to swing a ~ (in)** *(col)* man kann sich nicht rühren(, so eng ist es); **to be like a ~ on hot bricks** (wie) auf glühenden Kohlen sitzen; **that's put the ~ among the pigeons!** da hast du *etc* aber was (Schönes) angerichtet!; **when the**

~'s away the mice will play *(prov)* wenn die Katze aus dem Haus ist, tanzen die Mäuse.
cataclysm ['kætəklɪzəm] *n* Verheerung *f*; *(fig)* Umwälzung *f*.
catacombs ['kætəku:mz] *npl* Katakomben *pl*.
catalogue ['kætəlɒg] **1** *n* Katalog *m*. **2** *vt* katalogisieren.
catalyst ['kætəlɪst] *n (lit, fig)* Katalysator *m*.
catamaran [,kætəmə'ræn] *n* Katamaran *m*.
catapult ['kætəpʌlt] **1** *n (slingshot)* Schleuder *f*; *(Mil, Aviat)* Katapult *nt or m*. **2** *vt* schleudern; *(Aviat)* katapultieren.
cataract ['kætərækt] *n* **(a)** *(rapids)* Katarakt *m*. **(b)** *(Med)* grauer Star.
catarrh [kə'tɑ:ʳ] *n* Katarrh *m*.
catastrophe [kə'tæstrəfɪ] *n* Katastrophe *f*.
catastrophic [,kætə'strɒfɪk] *adj* katastrophal.
cat: ~ burglar *n* Fassadenkletterer *m*; **~call** *n (Theat)* **~calls** Pfiffe und Buhrufe *pl*.
catch [kætʃ] *(vb: pret, ptp* **caught***)* **1** *n* **(a)** *(of ball etc)* **to make a (good) ~** (gut) fangen. **(b)** *(Fishing, Hunt)* Fang *m*. **(c)** *(trick, snag)* Haken *m*. **there's a ~ in it somewhere** die Sache hat irgendwo einen Haken; **a ~-22 situation** *(col)* eine Zwickmühle; **~ question** Fangfrage *f*. **(d)** *(device for fastening)* Verschluß(vorrichtung *f*) *m*; *(hook)* Haken *m*; *(latch)* Riegel *m*.
2 *vt* **(a)** fangen; *thief* fassen, schnappen *(col)*; *(col: manage to see)* erwischen *(col)*. **to ~ sight/a glimpse of sb/sth** jdn/etw erblicken/flüchtig zu sehen bekommen; **he caught the waiter's eye** er machte den Ober auf sich aufmerksam; **this dress caught my eye** das Kleid ist mir ins Auge gefallen; **to ~ one's breath** *(after exercise etc)* Luft holen, verschnaufen *(col)*.
(b) *(take by surprise)* erwischen, ertappen. **to ~ sb at sth** jdn bei etw erwischen; **you won't ~ me doing that again!** *(col)* das mache ich bestimmt nicht wieder!; **caught in the act** auf frischer Tat ertappt.
(c) *train, bus* erreichen, kriegen *(col)*.
(d) *(get entangled) coat* hängenbleiben mit. **I caught my finger in the car door** ich habe mir den Finger in der Wagentür eingeklemmt.
(e) *(understand, hear)* mitkriegen *(col)*.
(f) to ~ an illness sich *(dat)* eine Krankheit holen *(col)*; **he's always ~ing cold(s)** er erkältet sich leicht.
(g) *(hit)* treffen. **the blow/ball caught him on the arm** der Schlag/Ball traf ihn am Arm; **you'll ~ it!** *(col)* du kannst was erleben!
3 *vi* **(a)** *(with ball)* fangen. **(b)** *(fire)* in Gang kommen; *(wood etc)* Feuer fangen; *(Cook)* anbrennen. **(c)** *(get stuck)* sich verklemmen; *(get entangled)* hängenbleiben. **her dress caught in the door** sie blieb mit ihrem Kleid in der Tür hängen.
♦ **catch on** *vi (col)* **(a)** *(become popular)* (gut) ankommen. **(b)** *(understand)* kapieren *(col)*.
♦ **catch out** *vt sep (fig)* durchschauen; *(with trick question etc)* hereinlegen *(col)*. **I caught you ~ there!** du bist durchschaut; *(with trick question)* jetzt bist du aber reingefallen *(col)*.
♦ **catch up 1** *vi* aufholen. **to ~ ~ on sth** etw nachholen; **to ~ ~ on one's sleep** Schlaf nachholen; **to ~ ~ with sb** *(running, in work etc)* jdn einholen. **2** *vt sep* **(a) to ~ sb ~** *(walking, working etc)* jdn einholen. **(b) to get caught ~ in sth** *(entangled)* sich in etw *(dat)* verfangen; *in traffic* in etw *(acc)* geraten; *in discussion* in etw *(acc)* verwickelt werden.
catching ['kætʃɪŋ] *adj (Med, fig)* ansteckend.
catchment area ['kætʃmənt'ɛərɪə] *n* Einzugsgebiet *nt*.
catch phrase *n* Slogan *m*.
catchy ['kætʃɪ] *adj (+er) tune* eingängig.
catechism ['kætɪkɪzəm] *n (book)* Katechismus *m*.
categorical [,kætɪ'gɒrɪkəl] *adj* kategorisch.
categorize ['kætɪgəraɪz] *vt* kategorisieren.
category ['kætɪgərɪ] *n* Kategorie *f*.
cater ['keɪtəʳ] *vi (provide food)* die Speisen und Getränke liefern.
♦ **cater for** *vi +prep obj* **(a)** *(serve)* mit Speisen und Getränken versorgen; *functions* ausrichten. **(b)** eingestellt sein auf *(+acc)*; *(also* **cater to***) needs, tastes* gerecht werden *(+dat)*. **we ~ ~ all sizes** wir führen alle Größen; **this magazine ~s ~ all ages** diese Zeitschrift hat jeder Altersgruppe etwas zu bieten; **a dictionary which ~s ~ the user** ein benutzerfreundliches Wörterbuch.
catering ['keɪtərɪŋ] *n* Versorgung *f* mit Speisen und Getränken *(for gen)*; *(trade)* Gastronomie *f*. **who's doing the ~?** welche Firma liefert das Essen?; **~ trade** (Hotel- und) Gaststättengewerbe *nt*.
caterpillar ['kætəpɪləʳ] *n (Zool)* Raupe *f*; *(Tech)* Raupe(nkette) *f*; *(vehicle)* Raupenfahrzeug *nt*. **~-track** Raupenkette *f*.
caterwauling ['kætəwɔ:lɪŋ] *n* Gejaule *nt*.
cathedral [kə'θi:drəl] *n* Dom *m*, Kathedrale *f*.
Catherine wheel ['kæθərɪn,wi:l] *n* Feuerrad *nt*.
cathode ['kæθəʊd] *n* Kathode *f*. **~-ray tube** Kathodenstrahlröhre *f*.
catholic ['kæθəlɪk] *adj (varied, all-embracing)* vielseitig. **he's a man of very ~ tastes** er ist (ein) sehr vielseitig interessiert(er Mensch).
Catholic 1 *adj (Eccl)* katholisch. **the ~ Church** die katholische Kirche. **2** *n* Katholik(in *f*) *m*.
Catholicism [kə'θɒlɪsɪzəm] *n* Katholizismus *m*.
cat: ~kin *n (Bot)* Kätzchen *nt*; **~'s eye** *n* Katzenauge *nt*.
cattle ['kætl] *npl* Rind(vieh) *nt*. **~ breeding** Rinderzucht *f*; **~ market** *(lit)* Viehmarkt *m*; *(fig col)* Fleischbeschau *f (col)*.
catty ['kætɪ] *adj (+er)* gehässig, boshaft.
catwalk ['kætwɔ:k] *n* Steg *m*; *(for models)* Laufsteg *m*.
Caucasian [kɔ:'keɪzɪən] **1** *adj* kaukasisch. **2** *n* Kaukasier(in *f*) *m*.
caucus ['kɔ:kəs] *n (committee)* Gremium *nt*; *(US: meeting)* Sitzung *f*.
caught [kɔ:t] *pret, ptp of* **catch.**
cauldron ['kɔ:ldrən] *n* großer Kessel.
cauliflower ['kɒlɪflaʊəʳ] *n* Blumenkohl *m*.
cause [kɔ:z] **1** *n* **(a)** Ursache *f (of* für*)*. **~ and effect** Ursache und Wirkung. **(b)** *(reason)* Grund *m*. **there's no ~ for alarm** es besteht kein Grund zur Aufregung. **(c)** *(purpose, ideal)* Sache *f*. **in the ~ of justice** im Namen der Gerechtigkeit; **it's all in a good ~** es ist für eine gute Sache. **2** *vt* verursachen. **to ~ grief to sb** jdm Kummer machen; **to ~ sb to do sth** jdn veranlassen, etw zu tun.
causeway ['kɔ:zweɪ] *n* Damm *m*.
caustic ['kɔ:stɪk] *adj (Chem, fig)* ätzend; *remark* bissig. **~ soda** Ätznatron *nt*.
cauterize ['kɔ:təraɪz] *vt (Med)* ausbrennen.
caution ['kɔ:ʃən] **1** *n* **(a)** Vorsicht *f*. **"~!"** „Vorsicht!"; **to act with ~** umsichtig *or* vorsichtig vorgehen. **(b)** *(warning)* Warnung *f*; *(official)* Verwarnung *f*. **2** *vt (warn)* **to ~ sb** jdn warnen *(against* vor *+dat)*; *(officially)* jdn verwarnen.
cautious ['kɔ:ʃəs] *adj* vorsichtig *(of* in bezug auf *+acc)*.
cavalier [,kævə'lɪəʳ] **1** *n* Kavalier *m*. **2** *adj person, nature* unbekümmert.
cavalry ['kævəlrɪ] *n* Kavallerie *f*.
cave [keɪv] *n* Höhle *f*.
♦ **cave in** *vi (ground, ceiling)* einstürzen.
cave: ~-in *n* Einsturz *m*; **~man** *n* Höhlenmensch *m*.
cavern ['kævən] *n* Höhle *f*.
cavernous ['kævənəs] *adj pit* tief; *hole* gähnend; *eyes* tiefliegend; *cheeks* eingefallen.
caviar(e) ['kævɪɑ:ʳ] *n* Kaviar *m*.

cavil ['kævɪl] *vi* kritteln. **to ~ at sth** an etw *(dat)* herumkritteln.
cavity ['kævɪtɪ] *n* Hohlraum *m*; *(in tooth)* Loch *nt*. **nasal/chest ~** *(Anat)* Nasen-/Brusthöhle *f*; **~ wall** Hohlwand *f*; **~ wall insulation** Schaumisolierung *f*.
cavort [kə'vɔːt] *vi* tollen, toben.
caw [kɔː] **1** *vi* krächzen. **2** *n* (heiserer) Schrei.
cayenne pepper ['keɪen'pepəʳ] *n* Cayennepfeffer *m*.
CB = **Citizens' Band** CB.
CBI *(Brit)* = **Confederation of British Industry** ≃ BDI.
cc = **cubic centimetre** ccm, cm³.
cease [siːs] **1** *vi* aufhören. **2** *vt* beenden; *fire, production* einstellen. **to ~ to exist** aufhören zu bestehen; **~ fire!** Feuer halt!
ceasefire [ˌsiːs'faɪəʳ] *n* Feuerpause *f*; *(longer)* Waffenruhe *f*.
ceaseless ['siːslɪs] *adj* unaufhörlich; *(relentless) vigilance* unablässig.
cedar ['siːdəʳ] *n (tree)* Zeder *f*.
cede [siːd] *vt territory* abtreten *(to* an *+acc)*. **to ~ a point** in einem Punkt nachgeben.
ceiling ['siːlɪŋ] *n* **(a)** (Zimmer)decke *f*. **(b)** *(Aviat) (cloud ~)* Wolkengrenze *f*; *(aircraft's ~)* maximale Flughöhe. **(c)** *(fig: upper limit)* ober(st)e Grenze. **to put a ~ on sth** etw nach oben begrenzen.
celebrate ['selɪbreɪt] **1** *vt* **(a)** feiern. **(b)** *mass, ritual* zelebrieren. **2** *vi* feiern.
celebrated ['selɪbreɪtɪd] *adj* berühmt *(for* für*)*.
celebration [ˌselɪ'breɪʃən] *n* **(a)** *(party, festival)* Feier *f*. **(b)** *(of mass)* Zelebration *f*.
celebrity [sɪ'lebrɪtɪ] *n* Berühmtheit *f*; *(person also)* berühmte Persönlichkeit.
celeriac [sə'lerɪæk] *n* (Knollen)sellerie *m*.
celery ['selərɪ] *n* Stangensellerie *m*.
celestial [sɪ'lestɪəl] *adj (heavenly)* himmlisch; *(Astron)* Himmels-.
celibacy ['selɪbəsɪ] *n* Zölibat *nt or m*; *(fig)* Enthaltsamkeit *f*.
celibate ['selɪbɪt] *adj (Rel)* ehelos; *(fig)* enthaltsam.
cell [sel] *n* Zelle *f*.
cellar ['seləʳ] *n* Keller *m*.
cellist ['tʃelɪst] *n* Cellist(in *f*) *m*.
cello, 'cello ['tʃeləʊ] *n* Cello *nt*.
cellophane ® ['seləfeɪn] *n* Cellophan ® *nt*.
cellular ['seljʊləʳ] *adj* zellular, Zell-. **~ phone** drahtloses Telefon.
celluloid ['seljʊlɔɪd] *n* Zelluloid *nt*.
cellulose ['seljʊləʊs] **1** *n* Zellulose *f*. **2** *adj* Zellulose-.
Celsius ['selsɪəs] *adj* Celsius.
Celt [kelt, selt] *n* Kelte *m*, Keltin *f*.
Celtic ['keltɪk, 'seltɪk] *adj* keltisch.
cement [sə'ment] **1** *n* **(a)** *(Build)* Zement *m*. **~ mixer** Betonmischmaschine *f*. **(b)** *(glue)* Klebstoff *m*; *(for holes etc, fig)* Kitt *m*. **2** *vt (Build, fig)* zementieren; *(glue)* kleben; *holes* kitten.
cemetery ['semɪtrɪ] *n* Friedhof *m*.
cenotaph ['senətɑːf] *n* Kriegerdenkmal *nt*.
censor ['sensəʳ] **1** *n* Zensor *m*. **2** *vt* zensieren.
censorship ['sensəʃɪp] *n* Zensur *f*.
censure ['senʃəʳ] **1** *vt* tadeln. **2** *n* Tadel *m*. **vote of ~** Tadelsantrag *m*.
census ['sensəs] *n* Volkszählung *f*. **traffic ~** Verkehrszählung *f*.
cent [sent] *n* Cent *m*. **I haven't a ~** *(US)* ich habe keinen Pfennig.
centenarian [ˌsentɪ'nɛərɪən] *n* Hundertjährige(r) *mf*.
centenary [sen'tiːnərɪ] *n (anniversary)* hundertster Jahrestag; *(birthday)* hundertster Geburtstag; *(100 years)* Jahrhundert *nt*.
centennial [sen'tenɪəl] **1** *adj* hundertjährig, hundertjährlich. **2** *n (esp US)* Hundertjahrfeier *f*.
center *n (US)* = **centre.**
centigrade ['sentɪgreɪd] *adj* Celsius-. **one degree ~** ein Grad Celsius.
centimetre, *(US)* **centimeter** ['sentɪˌmiːtəʳ] *n* Zentimeter *m or nt*.
centipede ['sentɪpiːd] *n* Tausendfüßler *m*.
central ['sentrəl] **1** *adj* **(a)** zentral, Zentral-; *(main, chief)* Haupt-. **~ station** Hauptbahnhof *m*; **~ government** Zentralregierung *f*. **(b)** *(fig)* wesentlich; *importance, figure* zentral. **2** *n (US: exchange, operator)* (Telefon)zentrale *f*.
central: C~ America *n* Mittelamerika *nt*; **C~ Europe** *n* Mitteleuropa *nt*; **~ heating** *n* Zentralheizung *f*.
centralize ['sentrəlaɪz] *vt* zentralisieren.
central: ~ nervous system *n* Zentralnervensystem *nt*; **~ reservation** *n (Brit)* Mittelstreifen *m*; *(with grass)* Grünstreifen *m*.
centre, *(US)* **center** ['sentəʳ] **1** *n* **(a)** Zentrum *nt*. **(b)** *(middle)* Mitte *f*; *(of circle)* Mittelpunkt *m*; *(town ~)* Stadtmitte *f*. **~ of gravity** Schwerpunkt *m*; **~ of attraction** Hauptattraktion *f*; **he always wants to be the ~ of attraction** er will immer im Mittelpunkt stehen. **2** *vt* **(a)** *(put in the middle, Typ)* zentrieren; *ball* zur Mitte spielen *or* flanken. **(b)** *(concentrate)* konzentrieren.
♦**centre (up)on** *vi +prep obj (thoughts, talk etc)* sich drehen um.
centre-forward ['sentə'fɔːwəd] *n (Sport)* Mittelstürmer *m*.
centrifugal [ˌsentrɪ'fjʊːgəl] *adj* zentrifugal. **~ force** Zentrifugalkraft, Fliehkraft *f*.
centrifuge ['sentrɪfjuːʒ] *n (Tech)* Zentrifuge *f*.
centurion [sen'tjʊərɪən] *n* Zenturio *m*.
century ['sentjʊrɪ] *n* Jahrhundert *nt*. **in the 20th ~** im 20. Jahrhundert.
ceramic [sɪ'ræmɪk] **1** *adj* keramisch, Keramik-. **2** *n* Keramik *f*.
ceramics [sɪ'ræmɪks] *n* **(a)** *sing (art)* Keramik *f*. **(b)** *pl (articles)* Keramiken *pl*.
cereal ['sɪərɪəl] *n* **(a)** *(crop)* Getreide *nt*. **(b)** *(food)* Getreideprodukt *nt*; *(breakfast ~) Corn-flakes, Haferflocken etc*, Cerealien *pl*.
cerebral ['serɪbrəl] *adj (Physiol)* zerebral; *(intellectual)* geistig. **~ haemorrhage** Gehirnblutung *f*.
ceremonial [ˌserɪ'məʊnɪəl] **1** *adj* zeremoniell. **2** *n* Zeremoniell *nt*.
ceremonious [ˌserɪ'məʊnɪəs] *adj* förmlich.
ceremony ['serɪmənɪ] *n* **(a)** *(event etc)* Zeremonie *f*. **(b)** *(formality)* Förmlichkeit(en *pl*) *f*. **to stand on ~** förmlich sein.
cert [sɜːt] *n (col)* **a (dead) ~** eine todsichere Sache *(col)*.
certain ['sɜːtən] *adj* **(a)** *(positive, convinced)* sicher; *(inevitable, guaranteed)* bestimmt. **is he ~** weiß er das genau?; **I don't know for ~, but ...** ich bin mir nicht ganz sicher, aber ...; **I can't say for ~** ich kann das nicht mit Sicherheit sagen; **he is ~ to come** er wird ganz bestimmt kommen; **to make ~ of sth** *(check)* etw nachprüfen; *(ensure)* für etw sorgen; **be ~ to tell him** vergessen Sie bitte nicht, ihm das zu sagen; **that was ~ to happen** das mußte ja so kommen. **(b)** *(attr: not named or specified)* gewiß; *reason, conditions* bestimmt. **a ~ gentleman** ein gewisser Herr; **to a ~ extent** in gewissem Maße.
certainly ['sɜːtənlɪ] *adv (admittedly)* sicher(lich); *(positively, without doubt)* bestimmt. **~ not!** ganz bestimmt nicht!; **~!** gewiß!
certainty ['sɜːtəntɪ] *n (sure fact)* Gewißheit *f*. **to know for a ~ that ...** mit Sicherheit wissen, daß ...; **the ultimate ~ of death** die Gewißheit des Todes.
certifiable [ˌsɜːtɪ'faɪəbl] *adj* **(a)** *fact, claim* nachweisbar. **(b)** *(Psych)* unzurechnungsfähig; *(col: mad)* nicht ganz bei Trost *(col)*.
certificate [sə'tɪfɪkɪt] *n* Bescheinigung *f*; *(of qualifications, health)* Zeugnis *nt*.

certify ['sɜːtɪfaɪ] *vt* **(a)** bescheinigen; *(Jur)* beglaubigen. **this is to ~ that ...** hiermit wird bescheinigt *or* bestätigt, daß ...; **certified public accountant** *(US)* geprüfter Buchhalter; **by certified mail** *(US)* per Einschreiben. **(b)** *(Psych)* für unzurechnungsfähig erklären.
cervical ['sɜːvɪkəl] *adj* zervikal *(spec)*. **~ cancer** Gebärmutterhalskrebs *m*; **~ smear** Abstrich *m*.
cervix ['sɜːvɪks] *n (of uterus)* Gebärmutterhals *m*.
cessation [se'seɪʃən] *n* Ende *nt*; *(of hostilities)* Einstellung *f*.
cesspit ['sespɪt] *n* = **cesspool (a).**
cesspool ['sespuːl] *n* **(a)** Senkgrube *f*. **(b)** *(fig)* Sumpf *m*.
cf = **confer** vgl.
chafe [tʃeɪf] **1** *vt (rub)* (auf)scheuern. **his shirt ~d his neck** sein (Hemd)kragen scheuerte. **2** *vi* **(a)** *(rub)* sich aufscheuern; *(cause soreness)* scheuern. **her skin ~s easily** ihre Haut wird leicht wund. **(b)** *(fig)* sich ärgern, wütend werden *(at, against* über *+acc)*.
chaff [tʃɑːf] *n* **(a)** *(husks of grain)* Spreu *f*. **(b)** *(straw)* Häcksel *m or nt*.
chaffinch ['tʃæfɪntʃ] *n* Buchfink *m*.
chagrin ['ʃægrɪn] **1** *n* Verdruß *m*. **2** *vt* verdrießen.
chain [tʃeɪn] **1** *n* **(a)** *(lit, fig)* Kette *f*. **~s** *(lit, fig: fetters)* Ketten *pl*. **(b)** *(of mountains)* (Gebirgs)kette *f*. **2** *vt (lit, fig)* anketten. **to ~ sb/sth to sth** jdn/etw an etw *(acc)* ketten.
chain: ~ reaction *n* Kettenreaktion *f*; **~saw** *n* Kettensäge *f*; **~-smoke** *vi* eine nach der anderen rauchen *(col)*; **~-smoker** *n* Kettenraucher(in *f*) *m*; **~ store** *n* Ladenkette *f*; *(individual shop)* Geschäft *m* einer Ladenkette.
chair [tʃɛəʳ] **1** *n* **(a)** *(seat)* Stuhl *m*; *(arm~)* Sessel *m*. **(b)** *(in committees etc)* Vorsitz *m*. **to be in/take the ~** den Vorsitz führen. **(c)** *(professorship)* Lehrstuhl *m (of* für*)*. **(d)** *(electric ~)* (elektrischer) Stuhl. **2** *vt meeting* den Vorsitz führen bei.
chair: ~lift *n* Sessellift *m*; **~man** *n* Vorsitzende(r) *mf*; **~manship** *n* Vorsitz *m*; **~person** *n* Vorsitzende(r) *mf*; **~woman** *n* Vorsitzende *f*.
chalet ['ʃæleɪ] *n* Chalet *nt*.
chalice ['tʃælɪs] *n (poet, Eccl)* Kelch *m*.
chalk [tʃɔːk] **1** *n* Kreide *f*. **not by a long ~** *(Brit col)* bei weitem nicht; **they're as different as ~ and cheese** sie sind so verschieden wie Tag und Nacht. **2** *vt message etc* mit Kreide schreiben.
♦**chalk up** *vt sep* **(a)** *(lit) (mit Kreide)* aufschreiben. **(b)** *(fig) success, victory* verbuchen. **(c)** *(fig: mark up as credit)* anschreiben *(col)*.
challenge ['tʃælɪndʒ] **1** *n* **(a)** *(to duel, match etc)* Herausforderung *f (to* an *+acc)*; *(fig: demands)* Anforderung(en *pl*) *f*. **to issue a ~ to sb** jdn herausfordern; **the ~ of the unknown** der Reiz des Unbekannten. **(b)** *(bid: for leadership etc)* Griff *m (for* nach*)*. **a direct ~ to his authority** eine direkte Infragestellung seiner Autorität. **(c)** *(Mil: of sentry)* Anruf *m*. **(d)** *(Jur: of witness)* Ablehnung *f*. **2** *vt* **(a)** *person* herausfordern; *world record etc* überbieten wollen. **(b)** *(fig: make demands on)* fordern. **(c)** *(fig) remarks, sb's authority* in Frage stellen. **(d)** *(sentry)* anrufen. **(e)** *(Jur) witnesses* ablehnen; *evidence, verdict* anfechten.
challenger ['tʃælɪndʒəʳ] *n (to duel, match etc)* Herausforderer *m*.
challenging ['tʃælɪndʒɪŋ] *adj (provocative)* herausfordernd; *(thought-provoking)* reizvoll; *book* anregend; *(demanding)* anspruchsvoll. **I don't find this work very ~** diese Arbeit fordert mich nicht genügend.
chamber ['tʃeɪmbəʳ] *n* **(a)** *(old: room)* Kammer *f (old)*. **(b) C~ of Commerce** Handelskammer *f*; **the Upper/Lower C~** *(Parl)* die Erste/Zweite Kammer. **(c)** *(Anat)* (Herz)kammer *f*.
chamber: ~maid *n (Brit)* Zimmermädchen *nt*; **~ music** *n* Kammermusik *f*; **~ pot** *n* Nachttopf *m*.
chameleon [kə'miːlɪən] *n (Zool, fig)* Chamäleon *nt*.
chamois ['ʃæmwɑː] *n* **(a)** *also* ['ʃæmɪ] *(leather)* Gamsleder *nt*. **a ~ (leather)** ein Ledertuch *nt*, ein Fensterleder *nt*. **(b)** *(Zool)* Gemse *f*.
champagne [ʃæm'peɪn] *n* Sekt *m*; *(French ~)* Champagner *m*.
champion ['tʃæmpjən] **1** *n* **(a)** *(Sport)* Meister(in *f*) *m*. **~s** *(team)* Meister *m*; **world ~** Weltmeister(in *f*) *m*. **(b)** *(of a cause)* Verfechter *m*. **2** *adj* **(a)** *(prize-winning)* siegreich; *show animal* preisgekrönt. **~ boxer** Boxmeister. **(b)** *(NEngl col)* klasse *inv (col)*. **3** *vt person, action, cause* sich engagieren für.
championship ['tʃæmpjənʃɪp] *n* **(a)** *(Sport)* Meisterschaft *f*. **(b) ~s** *pl (event)* Meisterschaftskämpfe *pl*. **(c)** *(support)* Engagement *nt (of* für*)*.
chance [tʃɑːns] **1** *n* **(a)** *(coincidence)* Zufall *m*; *(luck, fortune)* Glück *nt*. **by ~** zufällig; **would you by any ~ be able to help?** könnten Sie mir vielleicht behilflich sein?
(b) *(possibility)* Chance(n *pl*) *f*; *(probability, likelihood)* Möglichkeit *f*. **the ~s are that ...** wahrscheinlich ...; **he has not much/a good ~ of winning** er hat wenig/gute Aussicht zu gewinnen; **to be in with a ~** ein Chance haben; **he doesn't stand a ~** er hat keine Chance(n); **no ~!** *(col)* (das) ist nicht drin *(col)*, nichts zu machen *(col)*; **the ~ of a lifetime** eine einmalige Chance; **you won't get another ~** das ist eine einmalige Gelegenheit; **now's your ~!** das ist deine Chance!; **give me a ~!** nun mach aber mal langsam! *(col)*; **you never gave me a ~ to explain** du hast mir ja nie Gelegenheit gegeben, das zu erklären.
(c) *(risk)* Risiko *nt*. **to take a ~** ein Risiko eingehen.
2 *attr* zufällig. **~ meeting** zufällige Begegnung.
3 *vt* **I'll ~ it!** *(col)* ich versuch's mal *(col)*; **to ~ one's luck** *(have a try)* sein Glück versuchen; *(risk)* das Glück herausfordern.
♦**chance (up)on** *vi +prep obj person* zufällig treffen; *thing* zufällig stoßen auf *(+acc)*.
chancel ['tʃɑːnsəl] *n* Chor, Altarraum *m*.
chancellor ['tʃɑːnsələʳ] *n (Jur, Pol, Univ)* Kanzler *m*. **C~ (of the Exchequer)** *(Brit)* Schatzkanzler *m*.
chancy ['tʃɑːnsɪ] *adj (col)* riskant.
chandelier [ˌʃændə'lɪəʳ] *n* Kronleuchter *m*.
change [tʃeɪndʒ] **1** *n* **(a)** Veränderung *f*; *(modification)* Änderung *f (to gen)*. **a ~ of air** eine Luftveränderung; **a ~ is as good as a rest** *(prov)* Abwechslung wirkt Wunder; **no ~** unverändert; **a ~ for the better/worse** eine Verbesserung/Verschlechterung; **the ~ of life** die Wechseljahre *pl*; **he needs a ~ of clothes** er müßte sich mal was anderes anziehen. **(b)** *(variety)* Abwechslung *f*. **(just) for a ~** zur Abwechslung (mal); **that makes a ~** das ist mal was anderes; *(iro)* das ist ja was ganz Neues! **(c)** *(of one thing for another)* Wechsel *m*. **a ~ of government** ein Regierungswechsel. **(d)** *no pl (money)* Wechselgeld *nt*; *(small ~)* Kleingeld *nt*. **can you give me ~ for a pound?** können Sie mir ein Pfund wechseln?; **keep the ~** stimmt so!; **you won't get much ~ out of £5** von £5 wird nicht viel übrigbleiben.
2 *vt* **(a)** *(replace)* wechseln; *address, name* ändern. **to ~ train/buses** *etc* umsteigen; **to ~ one's clothes** sich umziehen; **to ~ a wheel/the oil** ein Rad/das Öl wechseln; **to ~ hands** den Besitzer wechseln; **to ~ places with sb** mit jdm den Platz tauschen. **(b)** *(alter)* ändern; *(transform)* verwandeln. **to ~ sb/sth into sth** jdn/etw in etw *(acc)* verwandeln. **(c)** *(exchange: in shop etc)* umtauschen. **(d)** *money* wechseln; *(into other currency also)* (um)tauschen. **(e)** *(Aut)* **to ~ gear** schalten.
3 *vi* **(a)** sich ändern; *(town, person also)* sich

verändern. **you've ~d!** du hast dich aber verändert!; **to ~ into sth/sb** sich in etw *(acc)*/jdn verwandeln. **(b)** *(~ clothes)* sich umziehen. **she ~d into an old skirt** sie zog sich *(dat)* einen alten Rock an. **(c)** *(~ trains etc)* umsteigen. **all ~!** Endstation!, alles aussteigen! **(d)** *(~ gear)* schalten. **(e)** *(from one thing to another) (seasons)* wechseln. **to ~ to a different system** zu einem anderen System übergehen.

♦**change down** *vi (Aut)* in einen niedrigeren Gang schalten.

♦**change over** *vi* **(a)** *(change to sth different)* sich umstellen auf *(+acc)*. **(b)** *(exchange places, activities etc)* wechseln. **do you mind if I ~ ~?** *(TV)* hast du was dagegen, wenn ich umschalte?

♦**change up** *vi (Aut)* in einen höheren Gang schalten.

changeable ['tʃeɪndʒəbl] *adj weather* unbeständig, wechselhaft; *person* wankelmütig.

changing ['tʃeɪndʒɪŋ] **1** *adj* sich verändernd. **2** *n* **the ~ of the Guard** die Wachablösung.

changing-room ['tʃeɪndʒɪŋ'ru:m] *n (Brit) (in store)* Ankleideraum *m*; *(Sport)* Umkleideraum *m*.

channel ['tʃænl] **1** *n* **(a)** *(watercourse)* (Fluß)bett *nt*; *(strait)* Kanal *m*; *(deepest part of river etc)* Fahrrinne *f*. **the (English) C~** der Ärmelkanal; **C~ Islands** Kanalinseln *pl*. **(b)** *(fig, usu pl) (of bureaucracy etc)* Dienstweg *m*; *(of information etc)* Kanal *m*; *(of thought, interest etc)* Bahn *f*. **if you go through the right ~s** wenn Sie sich an die richtigen Stellen wenden. **(c)** *(groove)* Rinne *f*. **(d)** *(TV, Rad)* Kanal *m*, Programm *nt*. **2** *vt* **(a)** *(dig out, furrow) way, course* sich *(dat)* bahnen. **(b)** *(direct) water, river* (hindurch)leiten *(through* durch*)*. **(c)** *(fig) efforts, interest* lenken *(into* auf *+acc)*.

chant [tʃɑ:nt] **1** *n (Eccl, Mus)* Gesang *m*; *(monotonous song)* Sprechgesang *m*; *(of football fans)* Sprechchor *m*. **2** *vt* im (Sprech)chor rufen; *(Eccl)* singen. **3** *vi* Sprechchöre anstimmen; *(Eccl)* singen.

chaos ['keɪɒs] *n* Chaos, Durcheinander *nt*.

chaotic [keɪ'ɒtɪk] *adj* chaotisch.

chap[1] [tʃæp] *n (Med: of skin)* **he's got ~s on his hands** seine Hände sind aufgesprungen.

chap[2] *n (Brit col: man)* Kerl *(col)*, Typ *(col) m*. **old ~** alter Junge *(col)*. **the poor little ~** der arme Kleine.

chapel ['tʃæpəl] *n* Kapelle *f*.

chaperon(e) ['ʃæpərəʊn] **1** *n* **(a)** *(for propriety)* Anstandsdame *f*. **(b)** *(escort)* Begleiter(in *f*) *m*. **2** *vt* **(a)** *(for propriety)* Anstandsdame spielen bei. **(b)** *(escort)* begleiten.

chaplain ['tʃæplɪn] *n* Kaplan *m*.

chapter ['tʃæptə[r]] *n (of book)* Kapitel *nt*. **to give ~ and verse (for sth)** *(fig)* etw genau belegen; **a ~ of accidents** eine Serie von Unfällen.

char[1] [tʃɑ:[r]] *vt (burn black)* verkohlen.

char[2] *(Brit col)* **1** *n (charwoman)* Putzfrau *f*. **2** *vi* putzen.

character ['kærɪktə[r]] *n* **(a)** *(nature)* Charakter *m*; *(of people)* Wesen *nt no pl*. **it is out of ~ for him to behave like that** solches Benehmen ist untypisch für ihn; **to be of good/bad ~** ein guter/schlechter Mensch sein; **a man of ~** ein Mann von Charakter; **he's quite a ~** er ist ein Original. **(b)** *no pl (individuality) (of towns etc)* Charakter *m*; *(of person)* Persönlichkeit *f*. **(c)** *(in novel, Theat)* Figur *f*. **(d)** *(Typ)* Buchstabe *m*.

character actor *n* Charakterdarsteller *m*.

characteristic ['kærɪktə'rɪstɪk] **1** *adj* charakteristisch, typisch *(of* für*)*. **2** *n* (typisches) Merkmal.

characterization [,kærɪktəraɪ'zeɪʃən] *n (in a novel etc)* Personenbeschreibung *f*; *(of one character)* Charakterisierung *f*.

characterize ['kærɪktəraɪz] *vt (be characteristic of)* kennzeichnen, charakterisieren; *(describe)* beschreiben.

charade [ʃə'rɑ:d] *n* Scharade *f*; *(fig)* Farce *f*.

charcoal ['tʃɑ:kəʊl] *n* Holzkohle *f*; *(drawing)* Kohlezeichnung *f*; *(pencil)* Kohle(stift *m*) *f*.

charge [tʃɑ:dʒ] **1** *n* **(a)** *(Jur: accusation)* Anklage *f* *(of* wegen*)*. **to bring a ~ against sb** gegen jdn Anklage erheben; **he was arrested on a ~ of murder** er wurde wegen Mordverdacht festgenommen; **to be on a ~** *(soldier)* eine Disziplinarstrafe verbüßen.

(b) *(attack: of soldiers, bull etc)* Angriff *m*.

(c) *(fee)* Gebühr *f*. **what's the ~?** was kostet das?; **free of ~** kostenlos.

(d) *(explosive ~)* (Spreng)ladung *f*; *(in firearm, Elec, Phys)* Ladung *f*.

(e) *(position of responsibility)* Verantwortung *f* *(of* für*)*. **to be in ~** verantwortlich sein; **who's in ~ here?** wer ist hier der Verantwortliche?; **the children were placed in their aunt's ~** die Kinder wurden ihrer Tante anvertraut; **to take ~ of sth** etw übernehmen; **he took ~ of the situation** er nahm die Sache in die Hand.

2 *vt* **(a)** *(with gen) (Jur)* anklagen; *(fig)* beschuldigen. **(b)** *(attack)* stürmen; *troops* angreifen. **(c)** *(ask in payment)* berechnen. **I won't ~ you for that** dafür berechne ich Ihnen nichts. **(d)** *(record as debt)* in Rechnung stellen. **~ it to the company** stellen Sie das der Firma in Rechnung. **(e)** *firearm* laden; *(Phys, Elec), battery* (auf)laden.

3 *vi* **(a)** *(attack)* stürmen; *(at people)* angreifen *(at sb* jdn*)*. **~!** vorwärts! **(b)** *(col: rush)* rennen. **he ~d into the room/upstairs** er stürmte ins Zimmer/die Treppe hoch.

charge account *n* Kunden(kredit)konto *nt*.

chargé d'affaires ['ʃɑ:ʒeɪdæ'fɛə[r]] *n* Chargé d'affaires *m*.

charger ['tʃɑ:dʒə[r]] *n (battery ~)* Ladegerät *nt*.

chariot ['tʃærɪət] *n* Streitwagen *m*.

charisma [kæ'rɪzmə] *n* Charisma *nt*.

charitable ['tʃærɪtəbl] *adj* gütig; *organization* Wohltätigkeits-; *(financially generous, tolerant)* großzügig; *thought, remark etc* freundlich.

charity ['tʃærɪtɪ] *n* **(a)** *(Christian virtue)* Nächstenliebe *f*; *(tolerance, kindness)* Güte *f*. **~ begins at home** *(Prov)* man sollte zuerst an seine eigene Familie/sein eigenes Land *etc* denken; **to live on ~** von Almosen leben. **(b)** *(charitable society)* Wohltätigkeitsverein *m*; *(charitable purposes)* Wohlfahrt *f*. **a collection for ~** eine Sammlung für wohltätige Zwecke.

charm [tʃɑ:m] **1** *n* **(a)** *(attractiveness)* Charme *m no pl*; *(of village, countryside)* Reiz *m*. **feminine ~s** weibliche Reize *pl*; **to turn on the ~** seinen (ganzen) Charme spielen lassen. **(b)** *(spell)* Bann *m*. **it worked like a ~** das hat hervorragend geklappt. **(c)** *(amulet)* Talisman *m*; *(trinket)* Anhänger *m*. **~ bracelet** Armband *nt* mit Anhängern. **2** *vt* **(a)** *(attract, please)* bezaubern. **(b) to lead a ~ed life** einen Schutzengel haben.

charming ['tʃɑ:mɪŋ] *adj* reizend, charmant. **~!** *(iro)* wie reizend! *(iro)*.

chart [tʃɑ:t] **1** *n* **(a)** Tabelle *f*; *(graph)* Schaubild *nt*; *(map, weather ~)* Karte *f*. **(b) ~s** *pl (top twenty)* Hitliste *f*. **2** *vt (make a map of)* kartographisch erfassen; *(record progress of)* auswerten; *(keep a ~ of)* aufzeichnen; *(plan)* festlegen.

charter ['tʃɑ:tə[r]] **1** *n* **(a)** Charta *f*; *(of a society)* Satzung *f*; *(permission to become established)* Charter *f or m*, Freibrief *m*. **(b)** *(Naut, Aviat: hire)* **on ~** gechartert. **2** *vt plane, bus etc* chartern. **~ed accountant** *(Brit)* Bilanzbuchhalter *m*; **~ flight** *n* Charterflug *m*.

charwoman ['tʃɑ:,wʊmən] *n (Brit)* Putzfrau *f*.

chary ['tʃɛərɪ] *adj (+er) (cautious)* vorsichtig; *(sparing)* zurückhaltend *(of* mit*)*. **he is ~ of giving praise** er spart mit Lob.

chase [tʃeɪs] **1** *n* Verfolgungsjagd *f*; *(Hunt)* Jagd *f*. **to give ~** die Verfolgung aufnehmen. **2** *vt* jagen; *(follow)* verfolgen. **he's been chasing that**

woman for months er ist schon seit Monaten hinter der Frau her. **3** *vi* **to ~ after sb** hinter jdm herrennen *(col)*; *(in vehicle)* hinter jdm herrasen *(col)*; **to ~ around** herumrasen *(col)*.

♦ **chase away** *or* **off 1** *vi* losrasen *(col)*. **2** *vt sep* wegjagen; *(fig) sorrow etc* vertreiben.

♦ **chase up** *vt sep person* rankriegen *(col)*; *information etc* ranschaffen *(col)*.

chasm ['kæzəm] *n (Geol, fig)* Kluft *f*. **a yawning ~** ein gähnender Abgrund.

chassis ['ʃæsɪ] *n* Chassis *nt*; *(Aut)* Fahrgestell *nt*.

chaste [tʃeɪst] *adj (+er)* keusch.

chastening ['tʃeɪsnɪŋ] *adj experience* ernüchternd.

chastise [tʃæs'taɪz] *vt* züchtigen *(geh)*; *(scold)* schelten.

chastity ['tʃæstɪtɪ] *n* Keuschheit *f*.

chat [tʃæt] *n* Unterhaltung *f*. **could we have a ~ about it?** können wir uns mal darüber unterhalten?; **she dropped in for a ~** sie kam zu einem Schwätzchen rein *(col)*.

♦ **chat up** *vt sep (col) person* einreden auf *(+acc)*; *girl, boy* sich heranmachen an *(+acc)*, anmachen *(col)*.

chat show *n (Brit)* Talkshow *f*.

chattels ['tʃætlz] *npl* **all his (goods and) ~** seine gesamte Habe.

chatter ['tʃætə^r] **1** *n (of person)* Geschwätz *nt*; *(of birds)* Gezwitscher *nt*; *(of teeth)* Klappern *nt*. **2** *vi see n* schwatzen; zwitschern; klappern.

chatterbox ['tʃætəbɒks] *n* Quasselstrippe *f (col)*.

chatty ['tʃætɪ] *adj (+er) person* geschwätzig.

chauffeur ['ʃəʊfə^r] *n* Chauffeur *m*.

chauvinism ['ʃəʊvɪnɪzəm] *n* Chauvinismus *m*.

chauvinist ['ʃəʊvɪnɪst] *n (jingoist)* Chauvinist(in *f*) *m*. **(male) ~ pig** Pascha *(col)*, Chauvi *(col) m*.

cheap [tʃiːp] *adj,adv (+er)* billig. **to buy sth on the ~** *(col)* etw für einen Pappenstiel kaufen *(col)*; **it's ~ at the price** es ist spottbillig; **to feel ~** sich *(dat)* schäbig vorkommen.

cheapen ['tʃiːpən] **1** *vt (lit, fig)* herabsetzen. **2** *vi* billiger werden.

cheaply ['tʃiːplɪ] *adv see adj*.

cheapskate ['tʃiːpskeɪt] *n (col)* Knicker *m (col)*.

cheat [tʃiːt] **1** *vt* betrügen. **to ~ sb out of sth** jdn um etw betrügen. **2** *vi* betrügen; *(in exam, game etc)* mogeln *(col)*, schummeln *(Sch sl)*. **3** *n* **(a)** *(person)* Betrüger(in *f*) *m*; *(in exam, game etc)* Mogler(in *f*) *(col)*, Schummler(in *f*) *(Sch sl) m*. **(b)** *(dishonest trick)* Betrug *m*.

check [tʃek] **1** *n* **(a)** *(examination)* Kontrolle *f*. **a random ~** eine Stichprobe; **to keep a ~ on sb/sth** jdn/etw überwachen *or* kontrollieren. **(b)** *(restraint)* Hemmnis *nt*. **to keep one's temper in ~** sich beherrschen; **to act as a ~ on sth** etw unter Kontrolle *(dat)* halten. **(c)** *(pattern)* Karomuster *nt*; *(square)* Karo *nt*. **(d)** *(Chess)* Schach *nt*. **to be in ~** im Schach stehen; **to put sb in ~** jdm Schach bieten. **(e)** *(US) (cheque)* Scheck *m*; *(bill)* Rechnung *f*. **~ please** bitte (be)zahlen! **2** *vt* **(a)** *(examine)* überprüfen; *(in book)* nachschlagen; *tickets* kontrollieren. **(b)** *(act as control on)* kontrollieren; *anger* unterdrücken. **(c)** *(Chess)* Schach bieten *(+dat)*. **(d)** *(US: tick)* abhaken. **3** *vi (make sure)* nachprüfen; *(ask also)* nachfragen *(with* bei*)*; *(have a look)* nachsehen.

♦ **check in 1** *vi (at airport)* einchecken; *(at hotel)* sich anmelden. **2** *vt sep (at airport) luggage* abfertigen lassen; *(at hotel) person* anmelden.

♦ **check out 1** *vi* sich abmelden; *(leave hotel)* abreisen. **2** *vt sep figures, facts* überprüfen.

♦ **check up** *vi* überprüfen.

♦ **check up on** *vi +prep obj* überprüfen; *(keep a check on) sb* kontrollieren.

checkered *adj (US)* = **chequered.**

checkers ['tʃekəz] *n (US)* Damespiel *nt*.

check-in (desk) ['tʃekɪn('desk)] *n* Abfertigung *f*.

checking account ['tʃekɪŋə'kaʊnt] *n (US)* Girokonto *nt*.

check: ~ list *n* Prüf- *or* Checkliste *f*; **~mate** *n* Schachmatt *nt*; **~-out** *n (in supermarket)* Kasse *f*; **~point** *n* Kontrollpunkt *m*; **~room** *n (US) (Theat)* Garderobe *f*; *(Rail)* Gepäckaufbewahrung *f*; **~-up** *n (Med)* Untersuchung *f*; **to have a ~-up** sich untersuchen lassen.

cheddar ['tʃedə^r] *n* Cheddar(käse) *m*.

cheek [tʃiːk] *n* **(a)** Backe, Wange *(geh) f*. **(b)** *(buttock)* Backe *f*. **(c)** *(impudence)* Frechheit *f*. **what (a) ~!** was für eine *or* so eine Frechheit!

cheeky ['tʃiːkɪ] *adj (+er)* frech.

cheep [tʃiːp] **1** *n* Piepser *m*. **2** *vi* piepsen.

cheer [tʃɪə^r] **1** *n* Beifallsruf *m*; *(cheering)* Hurrageschrei *nt*. **three ~s for Mike!** ein dreifaches Hurra für Mike!; **~s!** *(Brit col) (your health)* prost!; *(goodbye)* tschüs! *(col)*; *(thank you)* danke schön! **2** *vt* **(a)** *person* zujubeln. **(b)** *(gladden)* aufmuntern. **3** *vi* jubeln.

♦ **cheer on** *vt sep* anfeuern.

♦ **cheer up 1** *vt sep* aufmuntern; *room, place* freundlicher gestalten. **2** *vi* **he ~ed ~** seine Stimmung hob sich; **~ ~!** laß den Kopf nicht hängen!

cheerful ['tʃɪəfʊl] *adj* vergnügt; *colour etc* heiter; *room* freundlich; *prospect, news* erfreulich; *(iro)* heiter. **you're a ~ one!** *(iro)* du bist vielleicht ein Miesmacher! *(col)*.

cheerio ['tʃɪərɪ'əʊ] *interj (esp Brit col)* Wiedersehen *(col)*; *(to friends)* tschüs *(col)*; *(your health)* prost.

cheerless ['tʃɪəlɪs] *adj person* trübselig; *prospect* trübe; *scenery* grau.

cheery ['tʃɪərɪ] *adj (+er)* fröhlich.

cheese [tʃiːz] *n* Käse *m*.

cheese *in cpds* Käse-; **~board** *n* Käsebrett *nt*; *(course)* Käseplatte *f*; **~burger** *n* Cheeseburger *m*; **~cake** *n (Cook)* Käsekuchen *m*; **~cloth** *n (Tex)* Baumwollkrepp *m*.

cheesed-off [tʃiːzd'ɒf] *adj (Brit col)* angeödet *(col)*.

cheetah ['tʃiːtə] *n* Gepard *m*.

chef [ʃef] *n* Küchenchef *m*; *(as profession)* Koch *m*.

chemical ['kemɪkəl] **1** *adj* chemisch. **2** *n* Chemikalie *f*.

chemist ['kemɪst] *n* **(a)** *(scientist)* Chemiker(in *f*) *m*. **(b)** *(Brit: in shop)* Drogist(in *f*) *m*; *(dispensing)* Apotheker(in *f*) *m*. **~'s shop** Drogerie *f*; Apotheke *f*.

chemistry ['kemɪstrɪ] *n* Chemie *f*.

cheque, *(US)* **check** [tʃek] *n* Scheck *m*. **a ~ for £10** ein Scheck über £10; **to pay by ~** mit (einem) Scheck bezahlen; **~book** Scheckbuch *nt*; **~ card** *(Brit)* Scheckkarte *f*.

chequered, *(US)* **checkered** ['tʃekəd] *adj (lit)* kariert; *(fig) career, history* bewegt.

cherish ['tʃerɪʃ] *vt* **(a)** *person* liebevoll sorgen für. **(b)** *feelings, hope* hegen.

cherry ['tʃerɪ] *n* Kirsche *f*. **~ brandy** Cherry Brandy *m*; **~ red** kirschrot.

cherub ['tʃerəb] *n (fig: baby)* Engelchen *nt*.

chess [tʃes] *n* Schach(spiel) *nt*. **~ board** Schachbrett *nt*; **~man** Schachfigur *f*.

chest[1] [tʃest] *n (for tea, tools etc)* Kiste *f*; *(piece of furniture)* Truhe *f*. **~ of drawers** Kommode *f*.

chest[2] *n (Anat)* Brust *f*. **to get sth off one's ~** *(fig col)* sich *(dat)* etw von der Seele reden; **to have a weak ~** schwach auf der Brust sein *(col)*; **~ specialist** Facharzt *m* für Lungenkrankheiten.

chestnut ['tʃesnʌt] **1** *n* **(a)** *(nut, tree)* Kastanie *f*. **(b)** *(colour)* Kastanienbraun *nt*. **(c)** *(horse)* Fuchs *m*. **(d) old ~** *(joke)* olle Kamelle *(col)*. **2** *adj (colour) hair* kastanienbraun.

chew [tʃuː] *vt* kauen.

♦ **chew over** *vi +prep obj (col) facts, problem* sich *(dat)* durch den Kopf gehen lassen.

♦ **chew up** *vt sep pencil etc* zerkauen; *ground, road surface* zerstören.

chewing gum ['tʃuːɪŋgʌm] *n* Kaugummi *m or nt*.

chewy ['tʃuːwɪ] *adj meat* zäh.
chic [ʃiːk] *adj (+er)* schick, elegant.
chick [tʃɪk] *n (of chicken)* Küken *nt*; *(young bird)* Junge(s) *nt*; *(col: girl)* Mädchen *nt*.
chicken ['tʃɪkɪn] **1** *n* **(a)** Huhn *nt*; *(for roasting, frying)* Hähnchen *nt*. **she's no ~** *(col)* sie ist nicht mehr die Jüngste; **don't count your ~s (before they're hatched)** *(Prov)* man soll den Tag nicht vor dem Abend loben *(Prov)*. **(b)** *(col: coward)* feiges Huhn *(col)*. **2** *adj (col)* feig.
♦ **chicken out** *vi (col)* kneifen *(col)*.
chicken *in cpds* Hühner-; **~feed** *n* **(a)** *(lit)* Hühnerfutter *nt*; **(b)** *(col: insignificant sum)* ein Pappenstiel *(col)*; **~pox** *n* Windpocken *pl*.
chickpea ['tʃɪk,piː] *n* Kichererbse *f*.
chicory ['tʃɪkərɪ] *n* Chicorée *f or m*; *(in coffee)* Zichorie *f*.
chief [tʃiːf] **1** *n, pl* **-s** *(of department or organization)* Leiter *m*; *(of tribe)* Häuptling *m*; *(of gang)* Anführer *m*; *(col: boss)* Chef *m*. **~ of police** Polizeipräsident *m*; **~ of staff** *(Mil)* Stabschef *m*. **2** *adj* **(a)** *(most important)* Haupt-, wichtigste(r, s). **the ~ thing** die Hauptsache. **(b)** *(most senior)* Haupt-. **~ clerk** Bürochef *m*; **~ constable** *(Brit)* Polizeipräsident *m*; **~ justice** *(Brit)* ≈ Oberrichter *m*; *(US)* Oberster Bundesrichter.
chiefly ['tʃiːflɪ] *adv* hauptsächlich, vor allem.
chieftain ['tʃiːftən] *n (of tribe)* Häuptling *m*.
chiffon ['ʃɪfɒn] **1** *n* Chiffon *m*. **2** *adj* Chiffon-.
chilblain ['tʃɪlbleɪn] *n* Frostbeule *f*.
child [tʃaɪld] *n, pl* **children** *(lit, fig)* Kind *nt*. **when I was a ~** in meiner Kindheit.
child: ~ bearing *adj* **of ~-bearing age** im gebärfähigen Alter; **~birth** *n* Geburt *f*; **to die in ~birth** bei der Geburt sterben; **~ care** *n* Kinderpflege *f*; **~hood** *n* Kindheit *f*.
childish ['tʃaɪldɪʃ] *adj (pej)* kindisch.
child: ~ labour *(Brit) or* **labor** *(US) n* Kinderarbeit *f*; **~less** *adj* kinderlos; **~like** *adj* kindlich; **~minder** *n* Tagesmutter *f*.
children ['tʃɪldrən] *pl of* **child.**
child: ~ prodigy *n* Wunderkind *nt*; **~'s play** *n* ein Kinderspiel *nt*; **~ welfare** *n* Jugendfürsorge *f*.
Chile ['tʃɪlɪ] *n* Chile *nt*.
Chilean ['tʃɪlɪən] **1** *adj* chilenisch. **2** *n* Chilene *m*, Chilenin *f*.
chill [tʃɪl] **1** *n* **(a)** Kälte *f*. **there's quite a ~ in the air** es ist ziemlich frisch draußen. **(b)** *(Med)* fieberhafte Erkältung; *(shiver)* Schauder *m*. **to catch a ~** sich verkühlen. **2** *adj (lit, fig)* kühl. **3** *vt* **(a)** *(lit) wine etc* kalt stellen. **I was ~ed to the bone** *etc* die Kälte ging mir bis auf die Knochen. **(b)** *(fig) blood* gefrieren lassen.
chil(l)i ['tʃɪlɪ] *n* Peperoni *pl*; *(spice, meal)* Chili *m*.
chilly ['tʃɪlɪ] *adj (+er) (lit, fig)* kühl. **I feel ~** mir ist kühl.
chime [tʃaɪm] **1** *n* Geläut *nt*; *(of door-bell)* Läuten *nt no pl*. **2** *vt* schlagen. **3** *vi* läuten.
♦ **chime in** *vi (col)* sich einschalten.
chimney ['tʃɪmnɪ] *n* Schornstein *n*.
chimney: ~pot *n* Schornsteinkopf *m*; **~ sweep** *n* Schornsteinfeger *m*.
chimp [tʃɪmp] *(col)*, **chimpanzee** [,tʃɪmpæn'ziː] *n* Schimpanse *m*.
chin [tʃɪn] *n* Kinn *nt*. **keep your ~ up!** Kopf hoch!; **he took it on the ~** *(fig col)* er hat's mit Fassung getragen.
China ['tʃaɪnə] *n* China *nt*. **the People's Republic of ~** die Volksrepublik China.
china ['tʃaɪnə] **1** *n* Porzellan *nt*. **2** *adj* Porzellan-.
china: ~ clay *n* Kaolin *m*; **C~man** *n* Chinese *m*.
Chinese [tʃaɪ'niːz] **1** *n* **(a)** *(person)* Chinese *m*, Chinesin *f*. **(b)** *(language, fig: gibberish)* Chinesisch *nt*. **2** *adj* chinesisch.
chink[1] [tʃɪŋk] *n* **(a)** Ritze *f*; *(in door)* Spalt *m*. **(b)** *(pej, hum: Chinaman)* **C~** Schlitzauge *m (col)*.
chink[2] **1** *n (sound)* Klimpern *nt*. **2** *vt* klimpern mit. **3** *vi* klimpern.
chintz [tʃɪnts] **1** *n* Chintz *m*. **2** *attr* Chintz-.
chip [tʃɪp] **1** *n* **(a)** Splitter *m*; *(of wood)* Span *m*. **he's a ~ off the old block** er ist ganz der Vater; **to have a ~ on one's shoulder** einen Komplex haben *(about* wegen*)*. **(b)** *(Brit: potato ~)* **~s** Pommes frites *pl*; *(US: crisps)* Chips *pl*. **(c)** *(in crockery, furniture etc)* abgeschlagene Stelle *f*. **(d)** *(in poker etc)* Chip *m*. **when the ~s are down** wenn es drauf ankommt. **(e)** *(micro~)* Chip *m*. **2** *vt cup, stone* anschlagen; *varnish, paint* abstoßen. **3** *vi (cup, china etc)* angeschlagen werden; *(paint, varnish)* abspringen.
♦ **chip in** *vi (col)* **(a)** *(interrupt)* sich einschalten. **(b)** *(contribute)* **he ~ped ~ with £3** er steuerte £3 bei.
♦ **chip off 1** *vt sep paint etc* wegschlagen; *piece of china* abschlagen. **2** *vi (paint etc)* absplittern.
chipboard ['tʃɪpbɔːd] *n* Spanholz *nt*.
chipmunk ['tʃɪpmʌŋk] *n* Backenhörnchen *nt*.
chiropodist [kɪ'rɒpədɪst] *n* Fußpfleger(in *f*) *m*.
chiropody [kɪ'rɒpədɪ] *n* Fußpflege *f*.
chirp [tʃɜːp] *vi (birds)* zwitschern; *(crickets)* zirpen.
chirpy ['tʃɜːpɪ] *adj (+er) (col)* munter.
chirrup ['tʃɪrəp] = **chirp.**
chisel ['tʃɪzl] **1** *n* Meißel *m*; *(for wood)* Beitel *m*. **2** *vt* meißeln; *(in wood)* stemmen. **her finely ~led features** ihr fein geschnittenes Gesicht.
chit [tʃɪt] *n (also* **~ of paper***)* Zettel *m*.
chivalrous ['ʃɪvəlrəs] *adj* ritterlich.
chivalry ['ʃɪvəlrɪ] *n* Ritterlichkeit *f*.
chives [tʃaɪvz] *n* Schnittlauch *m*.
chloride ['klɔːraɪd] *n* Chlorid *nt*.
chlorinate ['klɒrɪneɪt] *vt water* chloren.
chlorine ['klɔːriːn] *n* Chlor *nt*.
chloroform ['klɒrəfɔːm] *n* Chloroform *nt*.
chlorophyll ['klɒrəfɪl] *n* Chlorophyll *nt*.
choc-ice ['tʃɒkaɪs] *n* Eis *nt* mit Schokoladenüberzug.
chock [tʃɒk] *n* Bremskeil *m*.
chock-a-block ['tʃɒkəblɒk], **chock-full** ['tʃɒkfʊl] *adj (col)* gerammelt voll *(col)*.
chocolate ['tʃɒklɪt] **1** *n* Schokolade *f*. **a ~** eine Praline; **a box of ~s** eine Schachtel Pralinen. **2** *adj* Schokoladen-; *(also* **~-coloured** *(Brit) or* **~-colored** *US)* schokoladenbraun.
choice [tʃɔɪs] **1** *n* **(a)** Wahl *f*. **to make a ~** eine Wahl treffen; **he had no ~ but to ...** es blieb ihm nichts anders übrig, als zu ...; **take your ~** such dir etwas/eine *etc* aus; **it was your ~** du wolltest es ja so. **(b)** *(variety to choose from)* Auswahl *f (of* an *+dat,* von*)*. **2** *adj goods, fruit, wine* Qualitäts-. **~ fruit** Obst erster Wahl.
choir ['kwaɪə[r]] *n* Chor *m*. **~boy** Sängerknabe *m*.
choke [tʃəʊk] **1** *vt* **(a)** *(stifle)* ersticken; *(throttle)* (er)würgen, erdrosseln. **(b)** *(fig) pipe etc* verstopfen. **2** *vi* ersticken *(on* an *+dat)*. **3** *n (Aut)* Choke *m*.
♦ **choke back** *vt sep tears, reply* unterdrücken.
choker ['tʃəʊkə[r]] *n (collar)* Vatermörder *m*; *(of velvet etc)* enganliegendes Halsband.
cholera ['kɒlərə] *n* Cholera *f*.
cholesterol [kɒ'lestərəl] *n* Cholesterin *nt*.
choose [tʃuːz] *pret* **chose,** *ptp* **chosen 1** *vt* (aus)wählen. **to ~ to do sth** es vorziehen, etw zu tun. **2** *vi* **to ~ (between** *or* **among/from)** wählen (zwischen *+dat*/aus *or* unter *+dat*); **there is nothing to ~ between them** sie sind gleich gut; **I'll do it when I ~** ich mache es, wann es mir paßt *(col)*.
choos(e)y ['tʃuːzɪ] *adj (+er)* wählerisch.
chop[1] [tʃɒp] **1** *n* **(a)** *(blow)* Schlag *m*. **(b)** *(Cook)* Kotelett *nt*. **(c)** *(col)* **to get the ~** *(be axed)* gestrichen werden; *(be fired)* rausgeschmissen werden *(col)*. **2** *vt* hacken; *meat, vegetables etc* kleinschneiden.
♦ **chop down** *vt sep tree* fällen.
♦ **chop off** *vt sep* abhacken.

chop[2] *vi (fig)* **to ~ and change** ständig seine Meinung ändern.
chopper ['tʃɒpəʳ] *n* **(a)** *(axe)* Hackbeil *nt.* **(b)** *(col: helicopter)* Hubschrauber *m.* **(c)** *(bicycle ®)* Fahrrad *nt.*
chopping ['tʃɒpɪŋ]: **~ block** *n* Hackklotz *m*; *(for wood)* Block *m*; **~ board** *n* Hackbrett *nt.*
choppy ['tʃɒpɪ] *adj (+er) sea* kabbelig; *wind* böig.
chopstick ['tʃɒpstɪk] *n* Stäbchen *nt.*
choral ['kɔːrəl] *adj* Chor-. **~ society** Gesangverein *m.*
chord [kɔːd] *n (Mus)* Akkord *m.* **to strike the right/a sympathetic ~** *(fig)* den richtigen Ton treffen/auf Verständnis stoßen.
chore [tʃɔːʳ] *n* lästige Pflicht. **~s** *pl* Hausarbeit *f*; **to do the ~s** den Haushalt machen.
choreographer [ˌkɒrɪ'ɒgrəfəʳ] *n* Choreograph(in *f*) *m.*
choreography [ˌkɒrɪ'ɒgrəfɪ] *n* Choreographie *f.*
chortle ['tʃɔːtl] *vi* glucksen.
chorus ['kɔːrəs] **1** *n* **(a)** *(refrain)* Refrain *m.* **(b)** Chor *m*; *(dancers)* Tanzgruppe *f.* **in ~** im Chor. **2** *vi* im Chor singen/sprechen/rufen.
chorus girl *n* (Revue)tänzerin *f.*
chose [tʃəʊz] *pret of* **choose.**
chosen ['tʃəʊzn] **1** *ptp of* **choose. 2** *adj* **the ~ people** das auserwählte Volk.
chowder ['tʃaʊdəʳ] *n (US)* sämige Fischsuppe.
Christ [kraɪst] *n* Christus *m.*
christen ['krɪsn] *vt* taufen.
christening ['krɪsnɪŋ] *n* Taufe *f.*
Christian ['krɪstɪən] **1** *n* Christ *m.* **2** *adj (lit, fig)* christlich.
Christianity [ˌkrɪstɪ'ænɪtɪ] *n (faith, religion)* Christentum *nt*; *(body of Christians)* Christenheit *f.*
Christian name *n* Vorname *m.*
Christmas ['krɪsməs] *n* Weihnachten *nt.* **happy** *or* **merry ~!** fröhliche Weihnachten!
Christmas: ~ card *n* Weihnachtskarte *f*; **~ carol** *n* Weihnachtslied *nt*; **~ Day** *n* der erste Weihnachtstag; **~ Eve** *n* Heiligabend *m*; **~ present** *n* Weihnachtsgeschenk *nt*; **~ tree** *n* Weihnachtsbaum, Christbaum *m.*
chromatic [krə'mætɪk] *adj (Art, Mus)* chromatisch.
chrome [krəʊm] *n* Chrom *nt.* **~-plated** verchromt.
chromosome ['krəʊməsəʊm] *n* Chromosom *nt.*
chronic ['krɒnɪk] *adj* **(a)** *(Med, fig)* chronisch. **(b)** *(col: terrible)* miserabel *(col).*
chronicle ['krɒnɪkl] **1** *n* Chronik *f.* **2** *vt* aufzeichnen.
chronological [ˌkrɒnə'lɒdʒɪkəl] *adj* chronologisch.
chronology [krə'nɒlədʒɪ] *n* zeitliche Abfolge; *(list of dates)* Zeittafel *f.*
chrysalis ['krɪsəlɪs] *n, pl* **-es** *(Biol)* Puppe *f.*
chrysanthemum [krɪ'sænθəməm] *n* Chrysantheme *f.*
chubby ['tʃʌbɪ] *adj (+er)* pummelig, rundlich.
chuck [tʃʌk] *vt (col)* **(a)** *(throw)* schmeißen *(col).* **(b)** *(also:* **~ away***)* wegschmeißen *(col).* **(c)** *(also:* **~ in***) boyfriend* Schluß machen mit *(col)*; *job* hinschmeißen *(col).*
♦ **chuck out** *vt sep (col)* rausschmeißen *(col)*; *old clothes etc* wegschmeißen.
chuckle ['tʃʌkl] **1** *n* leises Lachen. **2** *vi* in sich *(acc)* hineinlachen.
chuffed [tʃʌft] *adj (Brit col)* vergnügt und zufrieden; *(flattered)* gebauchpinselt *(col) (about* wegen*).*
chug [tʃʌg] **1** *n* Tuckern *nt.* **2** *vi* tuckern.
♦ **chug along** *vi* dahintuckern.
chum [tʃʌm] *n (col)* Kamerad, Kumpel *(col) m.*
chunk [tʃʌŋk] *n* großes Stück; *(of stone)* Brocken *m.*
chunky ['tʃʌŋkɪ] *adj (+er) (col) legs, arms* stämmig; *knitwear* grob gestrickt; *meat* grob geschnitten; *book, format* kompakt; *glasses* solide.
church [tʃɜːtʃ] *n* Kirche *f*; *(service)* die Kirche. **to go to ~** in die Kirche gehen; **the C~ of England** die Anglikanische Kirche; **he has entered the C~** er ist Geistlicher geworden.
church *in cpds* Kirchen-; **~-goer** *n* Kirchgänger(in *f*) *m*; **~ service** *n* Gottesdienst *m*; **~yard** *n* Kirchhof *m.*
churlish ['tʃɜːlɪʃ] *adj* ungehobelt.
churn [tʃɜːn] **1** *n (for butter)* Butterfaß *nt*; *(Brit: milk-~)* Milchkanne *f.* **2** *vt* **to ~ butter** buttern. **3** *vi (water)* wirbeln.
♦ **churn out** *vt sep* am laufenden Band produzieren.
♦ **churn up** *vt sep* aufwühlen.
chute [ʃuːt] *n* **(a)** Rutsche *f*; *(garbage ~)* Müllschlucker *m.* **(b)** *(in playground)* Rutschbahn *f.*
chutney ['tʃʌtnɪ] *n* Chutney *m.*
CIA = Central Intelligence Agency CIA *m.*
cicada [sɪ'kɑːdə] *n* Zikade *f.*
CID = Criminal Investigation Department.
cider ['saɪdəʳ] *n* Apfelwein, Cidre *m.*
cigar [sɪ'gɑːʳ] *n* Zigarre *f.*
cigarette [ˌsɪgə'ret] *n* Zigarette *f.*
cigarette: ~ case *n* Zigarettenetui *nt*; **~ end** *n* Zigarettenstummel *m*; **~ lighter** *n* Feuerzeug *nt.*
cinch [sɪntʃ] *n (col)* **it's a ~** *(easy)* das ist ein Klacks *(col)*; *(esp US: certain)* es ist todsicher *(col).*
cinder ['sɪndəʳ] *n* **~s** *pl* Asche *f.* **burnt to a ~** *(fig)* verkohlt.
Cinderella [ˌsɪndə'relə] *n* Aschenputtel *nt.*
cinder track *n* Aschenbahn *f.*
cine-camera [ˌsɪnɪ'kæmərə] *n (Brit)* (Schmal)filmkamera *f.*
cinema ['sɪnəmə] *n (esp Brit)* Kino *nt.* **at/to the ~** im/ins Kino.
cinnamon ['sɪnəmən] *n* Zimt *m.*
cipher ['saɪfəʳ] *n* **(a)** Ziffer *f*; *(zero)* Null *f.* **(b)** *(code)* Chiffre *f.*
circle ['sɜːkl] **1** *n* **(a)** Kreis *m.* **we're just going around in ~s** *(fig)* wir bewegen uns nur im Kreis; **to come full ~** *(fig)* zum Ausgangspunkt zurückkehren; **the family ~** der engste Familienkreis; **he's moving in different ~s now** er verkehrt jetzt in anderen Kreisen. **(b)** *(Brit: Theat)* Rang *m.* **2** *vt* **(a)** *(surround)* umgeben. **(b)** *(move around)* kreisen um. **(c)** *(draw a ~ round)* einen Kreis machen um. **3** *vi (fly in a ~)* kreisen.
circuit ['sɜːkɪt] *n* **(a)** *(journey around etc)* Rundgang *m*/-fahrt *f*/-reise *f (of* um*).* **three ~s of the racetrack** drei Runden auf der Rennbahn. **(b)** *(Elec)* Stromkreis *m*; *(apparatus)* Schaltung *f.* **(c)** *(Sport: track)* Rennbahn *f.*
circuit: ~ breaker *n* Stromkreisunterbrecher *m*; **~ diagram** *n* Schaltplan *m.*
circuitous [sɜː'kjʊɪtəs] *adj* umständlich.
circular ['sɜːkjʊləʳ] **1** *adj object* rund. **~ saw** Kreissäge *f*; **~ tour** Rundfahrt *f*/-reise *f*; **~ letter** Rundschreiben *nt*, Rundbrief *m.* **2** *n (in firm)* Rundschreiben *nt*; *(advertisement)* Wurfsendung *f.*
circulate ['sɜːkjʊleɪt] **1** *vi (blood, money)* zirkulieren; *(rumour)* kursieren; *(news)* sich verbreiten; *(person: at party)* die Runde machen. **2** *vt memo etc* zirkulieren lassen.
circulation [ˌsɜːkjʊ'leɪʃən] *n* **(a)** *(Med)* Kreislauf *m*; *(of traffic)* Fluß *m*; *(of money)* Umlauf *m*; *(of news, rumour)* Kursieren *nt.* **to have poor ~** Kreislaufstörungen haben; **to put notes into ~** Banknoten in Umlauf bringen; **new words which come into ~** neue Wörter, die in den Sprachgebrauch eingehen; **he's back in ~ now** *(col)* er mischt wieder mit *(col).* **(b)** *(of newspaper etc)* Auflage(nziffer) *f.*
circumcise ['sɜːkəmsaɪz] *vt* beschneiden.
circumcision [ˌsɜːkəm'sɪʒən] *n* Beschneidung *f.*
circumference [sə'kʌmfərəns] *n* Umfang *m.*
circumflex ['sɜːkəmfleks] *n* Zirkumflex *m.*
circumscribe ['sɜːkəmskraɪb] *vt* **(a)** *(Math)* einen

Kreis beschreiben um. **(b)** *(restrict)* eingrenzen.
circumspect ['sɜːkəmspekt] *adj* umsichtig.
circumstance ['sɜːkəmstəns] *n* Umstand *m.* **in** *or* **under the ~s** unter diesen Umständen; **under no ~s** unter gar keinen Umständen; **in certain ~s** unter Umständen.
circumstantial [ˌsɜːkəm'stænʃəl] *adj* **(a)** *report* ausführlich. **(b)** *(Jur)* ~ **evidence** Indizien/-beweis *m.*
circumvent [ˌsɜːkəm'vent] *vt* umgehen.
circus ['sɜːkəs] *n* Zirkus *m*; *(in place names)* Platz *m.*
cirrhosis [sɪ'rəʊsɪs] *n* Zirrhose *f.*
cissy ['sɪsɪ] *n* = **sissy.**
cistern ['sɪstən] *n* Zisterne *f*; *(of WC)* Spülkasten *m.*
citadel ['sɪtədl] *n* Zitadelle *f.*
cite [saɪt] *vt (quote)* zitieren.
citizen ['sɪtɪzn] *n* Bürger(in *f*) *m.*
citizenship ['sɪtɪznʃɪp] *n* Staatsbürgerschaft *f.*
citric ['sɪtrɪk] *adj* Zitrus-. ~ **acid** Zitronensäure *f.*
citrus ['sɪtrəs] ~ **fruits** Zitrusfrüchte *pl.*
city ['sɪtɪ] *n* **(a)** Großstadt *f.* **the ~ of Glasgow** die Stadt Glasgow. **(b)** *(in London)* **the C~** die City, das Banken- und Börsenviertel.
city: ~ **centre** *(Brit) or* **center** *(US) n* Stadtmitte *f*; ~ **hall** *n* Rathaus *nt*; ~ **page** *n (Brit)* Wirtschaftsseite *f*; ~ **slicker** *n (pej col)* feiner Pinkel aus der (Groß)stadt *(pej col).*
civic ['sɪvɪk] *adj rights* bürgerlich, Bürger-; *authorities* Stadt-, städtisch. ~ **centre** *(Brit)* Verwaltungszentrum *nt* einer Stadt.
civil ['sɪvl] *adj* **(a)** *(of society)* bürgerlich; *duties* Bürger-. **(b)** *(polite)* höflich. **(c)** *(Jur)* zivilrechtlich.
civil: ~ **defence** *(Brit) or* **defense** *(US) n* ziviler Bevölkerungsschutz; ~ **disobedience** *n* ziviler Ungehorsam; ~ **engineer** *n* Hoch- und Tiefbauingenieur *m*; ~ **engineering** *n* Hoch- und Tiefbau *m.*
civilian [sɪ'vɪlɪən] **1** *n* Zivilist *m.* **2** *adj* zivil, Zivil-. **in ~ clothes** in Zivil.
civility [sɪ'vɪlɪtɪ] *n* Höflichkeit *f.*
civilization [sɪvɪlaɪ'zeɪʃən] *n* **(a)** Zivilisation *f.* **(b)** *(of Greeks etc)* Kultur *f.*
civilize ['sɪvɪlaɪz] *vt* zivilisieren.
civilized ['sɪvɪlaɪzd] *adj* **(a)** zivilisiert. **(b)** *(cultured) lifestyle etc* kultiviert.
civil: ~ **law** *n* Bürgerliches Recht; ~ **marriage** *n* standesamtliche Trauung; ~ **rights** *npl* (staats)bürgerliche Rechte *pl*; ~ **servant** *n* ≈ Staatsbeamte(r) *mf*; ~ **service** *n* ≈ Staatsdienst *m (ohne Richter und Lehrer)*; *(~ servants collectively)* Beamtenschaft *f*; ~ **war** *n* Bürgerkrieg *m.*
clad [klæd] **1** *(old) pret, ptp of* **clothe. 2** *adj (liter)* gekleidet.
claim [kleɪm] **1** *vt* **(a)** *(demand as one's own or due)* Anspruch erheben auf *(+acc)*; *benefits, sum of money (apply for)* beantragen; *lost property* abholen. **he ~ed diplomatic immunity** er berief sich auf seine diplomatische Immunität. **(b)** *(profess, assert)* behaupten. **the advantages ~ed for this technique** die Vorzüge, die man dieser Methode zuschreibt.

2 *vi* **(a)** *(Insur)* Ansprüche geltend machen; *(for damage done by people)* Schadenersatz verlangen. **(b)** *(for expenses etc)* **to ~ for sth** sich *(dat)* etw zurückzahlen lassen; **you can ~ for your travelling expenses** Sie können sich *(dat)* Ihre Reisekosten (zurück)erstatten lassen.

3 *n* **(a)** Anspruch *m*; *(pay~, Ind)* Forderung *f.* **to lay ~ to the title/property** *etc* Anspruch auf den Titel/das Grundstück *etc* erheben; **to put in a ~ (for sth)** etw beantragen; **he put in an expenses ~ for £100** er reichte Spesen in Höhe von £100 ein; **the ~s were all paid** *(Insur)* der Schaden wurde voll ersetzt. **(b)** *(assertion)* Behauptung *f.* **the book makes no ~ to be original** das Buch erhebt keinen Anspruch auf Originalität.
♦ **claim back** *vt sep* zurückfordern. **to ~ sth ~ (as expenses)** sich *(dat)* etw zurückzahlen *or* -erstatten lassen.
claimant ['kleɪmənt] *n (for social security etc)* Antragsteller(in *f*) *m*; *(for inheritance etc)* Anspruchsteller(in *f*) *m (to* auf *+acc)*; *(Jur)* Kläger(in *f*) *m.*
claim form *n* Antragsformular *nt.*
clairvoyant [klɛə'vɔɪənt] **1** *n* Hellseher(in *f*) *m.* **2** *adj* hellseherisch.
clam [klæm] *n* Venusmuschel *f.*
♦ **clam up** *vi (col)* keinen Piep (mehr) sagen *(col).*
clamber ['klæmbə[r]] *vi* klettern. **to ~ up a hill** einen Berg hinaufklettern.
clammy ['klæmɪ] *adj (+er)* feucht, klamm.
clamour, *(US)* **clamor** ['klæmə[r]] **1** *n* **(a)** *(noise)* Lärm *m.* **(b)** *(demand)* lautstark erhobene Forderung *(for* nach*).* **2** *vi* **to ~ for sth** lautstark etw fordern.
clamp [klæmp] **1** *n* Schraubzwinge *f*; *(Med, Elec)* Klemme *f.* **2** *vt* (ein)spannen.
♦ **clamp down 1** *vt sep (lit)* festmachen. **2** *vi (fig col: on expenses etc)* gewaltig bremsen *(col)*; *(police, government)* rigoros durchgreifen.
♦ **clamp down on** *vi +prep obj (col) person* an die Kandare nehmen; *expenditure, activities* einen Riegel vorschieben *(+dat)*; *crime etc* zum Schlag ausholen gegen.
clan [klæn] *n (lit, fig)* Clan *m.*
clandestine [klæn'destɪn] *adj* geheim.
clang [klæŋ] **1** *n* Klappern *nt*; *(of hammer)* Dröhnen *nt.* **2** *vi* klappern; *(hammer)* dröhnen. **3** *vt* mit etw klappern.
clanger ['klæŋə[r]] *n (Brit col)* Schnitzer *(col) m.* **to drop a ~** ins Fettnäpfchen treten *(col).*
clank [klæŋk] **1** *n* Klirren *nt.* **2** *vt* klirren mit. **3** *vi* klirren.
clap klæp] **1** *n* Klatschen *nt no pl*; *(no pl: applause)* (Beifall)klatschen *nt.* **a ~ of thunder** ein Donnerschlag *m.* **2** *vt* **(a)** *(applaud)* Beifall klatschen *(sb* jdm*).* **(b) to ~ one's hands** in die Hände klatschen. **(c) to ~ sb into prison** jdn ins Gefängnis stecken; **to ~ eyes on sb/sth** *(col)* jdn/etw zu Gesicht bekommen. **3** *vi* (Beifall) klatschen.
clapping ['klæpɪŋ] *n* Klatschen *nt.*
claptrap ['klæptræp] *n (col)* Geschwafel *nt (col).*
claret ['klærət] *n (wine)* roter Bordeauxwein.
clarification [ˌklærɪfɪ'keɪʃən] *n* Klarstellung *f.*
clarify ['klærɪfaɪ] *vt* klären; *text* erklären.
clarinet [ˌklærɪ'net] *n* Klarinette *f.*
clarity ['klærɪtɪ] *n* Klarheit *f.*
clash [klæʃ] **1** *vi* **(a)** *(armies, demonstrators)* zusammenstoßen. **(b)** *(colours)* sich beißen; *(interests)* aufeinanderprallen; *(programmes, films)* sich überschneiden. **(c)** *(cymbals etc: also ~* **together***)* aneinanderschlagen; *(metal)* klirren. **2** *vt cymbals* schlagen. **3** *n* **(a)** *(of armies, demonstrators etc)* Zusammenstoß *m.* **(b)** *(of personalities)* grundsätzliche Verschiedenheit. **it's such a ~ of personalities** sie sind charakterlich grundverschieden. **(c)** *(of swords)* Aufeinanderprallen *nt*; *(between people)* Konflikt *m.* **there's a ~ of dates** die Termine überschneiden sich.
clasp [klɑːsp] **1** *n* **(a)** *(on brooch, purse etc)* (Schnapp)verschluß *m.* **(b)** *(with one's arms)* Umklammerung *f*; *(with hand)* Griff *m.* **2** *vt* **(a)** (er)greifen. **with his hands ~ed** mit gefalteten Händen; **to ~ sb in one's arms** jdn in die Arme schließen. **(b)** *(to fasten with a ~)* befestigen.
class [klɑːs] **1** *n* **(a)** *(group, division)* Klasse *f.* **in a ~ by himself/itself** weitaus der/das Beste. **(b)** *(social rank)* Schicht, Klasse *f.* **(c)** *(Sch, Univ)* Klasse *f.* **to give** *or* **take a Latin ~** Latein unterrichten; **the French ~** *(lesson)* die Französischstunde; *(people)* die Französischklasse; **an evening ~** ein Abendkurs *m.* **(d)** *(col:*

quality, tone) Stil *m.* **to have ~** Stil haben; *(person)* Format haben. **2** *vt* einordnen, klassifizieren.
class: ~ conscious *adj* klassenbewußt, standesbewußt; **~ distinction** *n* Klassenunterschied *m.*
classic ['klæsɪk] **1** *adj (lit, fig)* klassisch. **2** *n* Klassiker *m.*
classical ['klæsɪkəl] *adj* klassisch; *education* humanistisch.
classics ['klæsɪks] *n sing (Univ)* Altphilologie *f.*
classification [ˌklæsɪfɪ'keɪʃən] *n* Klassifizierung *f.*
classified ['klæsɪfaɪd] *adj* in Klassen eingeteilt. **~ ad(vertisement)** Kleinanzeige *f;* **~ information** *(Mil)* Verschlußsache *f; (Pol)* Geheimsache *f.*
classify ['klæsɪfaɪ] *vt* klassifizieren.
class: ~less *adj* klassenlos; **~room** *n* Klassenzimmer *nt;* **~ war(fare)** *n* Klassenkrieg *m.*
classy ['klɑːsɪ] *adj (+er) (col)* nobel *(col).* **~ woman** Klassefrau *f.*
clatter ['klætə^r] **1** *n* Klappern *nt.* **2** *vi* klappern. **the cart ~ed over the cobbles** der Wagen rumpelte über das Pflaster.
clause [klɔːz] *n* **(a)** *(Gram)* Satz *m.* **(b)** *(Jur etc)* Klausel *f.*
claustrophobia [ˌklɔːstrə'fəʊbɪə] *n* Platzangst *f.*
claustrophobic [ˌklɔːstrə'fəʊbɪk] *adj* klaustrophob(isch) *(Psych).* **I get this ~ feeling** ich kriege Platzangst *(col).*
claw [klɔː] **1** *n* Kralle *f; (of lions, birds of prey also)* Klaue *f; (of lobster etc)* Schere *f.* **to get one's ~s into sb** *(col)* jdn in die Krallen bekommen *(col).* **2** *vt* kratzen. **he ~ed back the sheets** er riß die Laken weg. **3** *vi* **to ~ at sth** sich an etw *(acc)* krallen.
clay [kleɪ] *n* Lehm *m.* **potter's ~** Ton *m.*
clay: ~ pigeon shooting *n* Tontaubenschießen *nt;* **~ pipe** *n* Tonpfeife *f.*
clean [kliːn] **1** *adj (+er)* sauber. **to wipe sth ~** etw abreiben; **~ licence** Führerschein *m* ohne Strafeintrag; **to make a ~ start** ganz von vorne anfangen; *(in life)* ein neues Leben anfangen; **to make a ~ breast of sth** sich *(dat)* etw von der Seele reden; **to give sb a ~ bill of health** *(doctor)* jdm gute Gesundheit bescheinigen; *(authorities)* jdn für unbedenklich erklären.

2 *adv* glatt. **I ~ forgot** das habe ich glatt(weg) vergessen *(col);* **he got ~ away** er verschwand spurlos; **I'm ~ out of cigarettes** *(col)* meine Zigaretten sind alle *(col);* **to cut ~ through sth** etw ganz durchschneiden/durchschlagen *etc;* **to come ~** *(col)* auspacken *(col).*

3 *vt* saubermachen; *carpets, clothes, buildings* reinigen; *window, shoes* putzen; *fish, wound* säubern; *chicken* ausnehmen; *car* waschen. **to ~ one's teeth** sich *(dat)* die Zähne putzen.
♦**clean off** *vt sep (wash)* abwaschen; *(wipe)* abwischen.
♦**clean out** *vt sep* **(a)** *(lit)* gründlich saubermachen. **(b)** *(col: leave penniless) person* ausnehmen (wie eine Weihnachtsgans) *(col).*
♦**clean up 1** *vt sep* saubermachen; *old building, old painting* reinigen. **2** *vi (tidy up)* aufräumen; *(wash)* sich waschen; *(col: make money)* absahnen *(col).*
cleaner ['kliːnə^r] *n* **(a)** *(person)* Raumpfleger (in *f*) *m.* **a firm of office ~s** eine Büroreinigungsfirma. **(b)** *(shop)* **~'s** Reinigung *f;* **to take sb to the ~'s** *(col)* jdn übers Ohr hauen *(col).* **(c)** *(substance)* Reinigungsmittel *nt.*
cleaning lady ['kliːnɪŋ'leɪdɪ] *n* Raumpflegerin, Putzfrau *(col) f.*
cleanliness ['klenlɪnɪs] *n* Reinlichkeit *f.*
cleanness ['kliːnnɪs] *n* Sauberkeit *f.*
cleanse [klenz] *vt* reinigen; *(spiritually)* läutern *(of* von*).*
cleanser ['klenzə^r] *n* Reinigungsmittel *nt.*
clean-shaven ['kliːn'ʃeɪvn] *adj* glattrasiert.
cleansing ['klenzɪŋ] *adj agent* Reinigungs-.
clear [klɪə^r] **1** *adj (+er)* **(a)** klar; *complexion, conscience* rein; *photograph* scharf. **on a ~ day** bei klarem Wetter.

(b) *(distinct, obvious)* klar. **it's still not ~ to me why** es ist mir immer noch nicht klar, warum; **to make it ~ to sb that ...** es jdm klarmachen, daß ...; **let's get this ~, I'm the boss** eins wollen wir mal klarstellen: ich bin hier der Chef; **as ~ as day** sonnenklar; **as ~ as mud** *(col)* klar wie Kloßbrühe *(col).*

(c) to be ~ on sth über etw *(acc)* im klaren sein; **I'm not ~ on the implications** ich bin mir nicht sicher, was das bedeutet.

(d) *road, way* frei. **I want to keep the weekend ~** ich möchte mir das Wochenende freihalten; **all ~!** (alles) frei!; **is it all ~ now?** ist alles in Ordnung?; **at last we were ~ of London** endlich hatten wir London hinter uns; **the mortars landed well ~ of us** die Mörser schlugen ein ganzes Stück neben uns ein; **a ~ profit** ein Reingewinn *m;* **three ~ days** drei volle Tage; **a ~ majority** eine Mehrheit; **to have a ~ lead** klar führen.

2 *n* **to be in the ~** nichts zu verbergen haben; **we're not in the ~ yet** *(not out of debt, difficulties)* wir sind noch nicht aus allem heraus; **this puts Harry in the ~** damit ist Harry entlastet.

3 *adv* **to keep ~ of sb/sth** jdm aus dem Wege gehen/etw meiden; **keep ~ of the testing area** Versuchsgebiet nicht betreten!; **stand ~ of the doors!** bitte von den Türen zurücktreten!

4 *vt* **(a)** *(remove obstacles etc from) pipe* reinigen; *blockage* beseitigen; *road, snow* räumen; *one's conscience* erleichtern. **to ~ the table** den Tisch abräumen; **to ~ a space for sth** für etw Platz schaffen; **to ~ the way for sb/sth** den Weg für jdn/etw freimachen; **to ~ the ground for further talks** den Boden für weitere Gespräche bereiten.

(b) *(free from guilt etc, Jur: find innocent) person* freisprechen; *one's/sb's name* reinwaschen.

(c) *(get past or over)* **he ~ed the bar easily** er übersprang die Latte mit Leichtigkeit.

(d) *debt* begleichen; *profit* machen.

(e) *(pass, OK)* abfertigen; *ship* klarieren; *expenses, appointment* bestätigen; *goods* zollamtlich abfertigen. **he's been ~ed by security** er ist von den Sicherheitsbehörden für unbedenklich erklärt worden; **you'll have to ~ that with the boss** das müssen Sie mit dem Chef abklären.

(f) *(Sport)* **to ~ the ball** klären.

5 *vi (weather)* aufklaren; *(mist)* sich lichten.
♦**clear off 1** *vt sep debts* begleichen; *stock* räumen. **2** *vi (col)* verschwinden *(col).*
♦**clear out 1** *vt sep cupboard, room* ausräumen. **2** *vi (col)* verschwinden *(col).*
♦**clear up 1** *vt sep* **(a)** *point, matter* klären; *mystery, crime* aufklären. **(b)** *(tidy)* aufräumen. **2** *vi* **(a)** *(weather)* sich aufklären; *(rain)* aufhören. **(b)** *(tidy up)* aufräumen.
clearance ['klɪərəns] *n* **(a)** *(act of clearing)* Beseitigung *f.* **slum ~** Slumsanierung *f.* **(b)** *(free space)* Spielraum *m; (headroom)* lichte Höhe. **(c)** *(by customs)* Abfertigung *f; (by security)* Unbedenklichkeitserklärung *f; (authorization)* Genehmigung *f.* **~ for take-off** Startfreigabe *f.* **(d)** *(Sport)* Klärung *f.*
clearance sale *n (Comm)* Räumungsverkauf *m.*
clear-cut ['klɪə'kʌt] *adj* klar.
clearing ['klɪərɪŋ] *n (in forest)* Lichtung *f.*
clearing bank *n* Clearingbank *f.*
clearly ['klɪəlɪ] *adv* **(a)** *(distinctly)* klar. **~ visible** gut zu sehen; **to stand out ~ from the rest** sich deutlich von den anderen abheben. **(b)** *(obviously)* eindeutig. **~ we cannot allow ...** wir können keinesfalls zulassen, ...
cleavage ['kliːvɪdʒ] *n* **(a)** *(split)* Spalte *f; (fig)*

Kluft *f.* **(b)** *(of woman's breasts)* Dekolleté *nt.*
cleaver ['kliːvəʳ] *n* Hackbeil *nt.*
clef [klef] *n* (Noten)schlüssel *m.*
cleft [kleft] *adj* gespalten. ~ **palate** Gaumenspalte *f*; **to be in a ~ stick** in der Klemme sitzen *(col).* **2** *n* Spalte *f.*
clemency ['klemənsɪ] *n (of person)* Nachsicht *f (towards sb* jdm gegenüber*)*; *(of weather)* Milde *f.*
clench [klentʃ] *vt fist* ballen; *teeth* zusammenbeißen. **to ~ sth between one's teeth** etw zwischen die Zähne klemmen; **to ~ sth in one's hands** etw mit den Händen umklammern.
clergy ['klɜːdʒɪ] *npl* Klerus *m*, Geistlichkeit *f.*
clergyman ['klɜːdʒɪmən] *n, pl* **-men** [-mən] Geistlicher *m.*
clerical ['klerɪkəl] *adj* **(a)** *(Eccl)* geistlich. **(b)** ~ **staff** Büropersonal *nt*; ~ **error** Versehen *nt.*
clerk [klɑːk, *(US)* klɜːrk] *n* **(a)** (Büro)angestellte(r) *mf.* **(b)** **C~ of the Court** *(Jur)* Protokollführer(in *f*) *m.* **(c)** *(US: in shop)* Verkäufer(in *f*) *m.*
clever ['klevəʳ] *adj* **(a)** *(mentally bright)* klug; *machine also* clever. **to be ~ at French** gut in Französisch sein; **how ~ of you to remember my birthday!** wie aufmerksam von dir, daß du an meinen Geburtstag gedacht hast! **(b)** *(ingenious, skilful)* **to be ~ at sth** Geschick zu etw haben, in etw *(dat)* geschickt sein; **to be ~ with one's hands** geschickte Hände haben. **(c)** *(cunning, smart)* schlau, clever *(col).*
cleverly ['klevəlɪ] *adv* geschickt; *(wittily)* schlau.
cleverness ['klevənɪs] *n see adj* **(a)** Klugheit *f.* **(b)** Geschicktheit *f.* **(c)** Schläue, Cleverness *f.*
cliché ['kliːʃeɪ] *n* Klischee *nt.*
click [klɪk] **1** *n* Klicken *nt*; *(of latch, key in lock)* Schnappen *nt*; *(of tongue)* Schnalzen *nt.* **2** *vi* **(a)** *see n* klicken; schnappen; schnalzen. **(b)** *(col: be understood)* funken *(col).* **suddenly it all ~ed (into place)** plötzlich hatte es gefunkt *(col).* **(c)** *(col: get on well)* **they ~ed right from the moment they first met** zwischen ihnen hatte es vom ersten Augenblick an gefunkt *(col).* **3** *vt heels* zusammenklappen; *fingers* schnippen mit; *tongue* schnalzen mit. **to ~ sth into place** etw einschnappen lassen.
client ['klaɪənt] *n* Kunde *m*, Kundin *f*; *(of lawyer)* Mandant *m*, Mandantin *f.*
clientele [ˌkliːɑ̃ːnˈtel] *n* Kundschaft *f.* **the regular ~** die Stammkundschaft.
cliff [klɪf] *n* Klippe *f*; *(inland also)* Felsen *m.* **the ~s of Dover** die Felsen von Dover.
cliffhanger ['klɪfˌhæŋə] *n* Superthriller *m (col).*
climate ['klaɪmɪt] *n (lit, fig)* Klima *nt.* **the two countries have very different ~s** die beiden Länder haben (ein) sehr unterschiedliches Klima; **to move to a warmer ~** in eine wärmere Gegend ziehen; **the ~ of popular opinion** das öffentliche Klima.
climax ['klaɪmæks] *n (all senses)* Höhepunkt *m.*
climb [klaɪm] **1** *vt* **(a)** *(also ~ up)* klettern auf *(+acc)*; *wall also, hill* steigen auf *(+acc)*; *Everest* besteigen; *ladder, steps* hinaufsteigen; *pole, cliffs* hochklettern. **my car can't ~ that hill** mein Auto schafft den Berg nicht; **to ~ a rope** an einem Seil hochklettern. **(b)** *(also ~ over) wall etc* steigen *or* klettern über *(+acc).* **2** *vi* klettern; *(into train, car etc)* steigen; *(road)* ansteigen; *(aircraft)* (auf)steigen. **3** *n* **(a) the long ~ up Pitt Street** die lange Kletterei die Pittstraße hinauf; **we're going out for a ~** wir machen eine Klettertour; **this face is a difficult ~** diese Steilwand ist schwer zu besteigen. **(b)** *(of aircraft)* Steigflug *m.* **the plane went into a steep ~** das Flugzeug zog steil nach oben.
♦**climb down** *vi* **(a)** *(lit) (person) (from tree, wall)* herunterklettern; *(from horse, mountain)* absteigen. **(b)** *(admit error)* klein beigeben.
climber ['klaɪməʳ] *n* **(a)** *(mountaineer)* Bergsteiger(in *f*) *m.* **(b)** *(socially)* Aufsteiger *m.*
climbing ['klaɪmɪŋ] **1** *adj club* Berg(steiger)-. ~ **frame** Klettergerüst *nt*; ~ **plant** Kletterpflanze *f.* **2** *n* Bergsteigen *nt*; *(rock ~)* Klettern *nt.* **we did a lot of ~** wir sind viel geklettert.
clinch [klɪntʃ] **1** *vt argument* zum Abschluß bringen. **to ~ the deal** den Handel perfekt machen; **that ~es it** damit ist der Fall erledigt. **2** *n (Boxing)* Clinch *m.*
cling [klɪŋ] *pret, prep* **clung** *vi (hold on tightly)* sich festklammern *(to* an *+dat)*; *(to opinion also)* festhalten *(to* an *+dat)*; *(remain close)* sich halten *(to* an *+acc)*; *(clothes, fabric)* eng anliegen; *(smell)* haften *(to* an *+dat).* **the boat clung to the shoreline** das Schiff hielt sich dicht an die Küste.
clinging ['klɪŋɪŋ] *adj garment* enganliegend. **she's the ~ sort** sie ist wie eine Klette *(col).*
clinic ['klɪnɪk] *n* Klinik *f.*
clinical ['klɪnɪkəl] *adj* **(a)** *(Med)* klinisch. **(b)** *(fig)* nüchtern.
clink[1] [klɪŋk] **1** *vt* klirren lassen. **to ~ glasses with sb** mit jdm anstoßen. **2** *vi* klirren; *(jingle)* klimpern. **3** *n no pl* Klirren *nt*; Klimpern *nt.* **the ~ of glasses** das Klingen der Gläser.
clink[2] *n (col: prison)* Knast *m (col).*
clip[1] [klɪp] **1** *n* **(a)** *(for holding things)* Klammer *f.* **(b)** *(jewel)* Klips *m.* **2** *vt* **to ~ on** anklemmen; *papers* anheften.
clip[2] **1** *vt* scheren; *dog* trimmen; *hedge, fingernails* schneiden; *wings* stutzen; *(Brit) ticket* entwerten. **2** *n* **(a)** *see vt* Scheren *nt*; Trimmen *nt*; Schneiden *nt*; Stutzen *nt.* **(b)** *(from film)* Ausschnitt *m.* **(c) to give sb a ~ on the ear** jdm eine Ohrfeige geben.
clip: ~board *n* Klemmbrett *nt*; **~-on** *adj brooch* mit Klips; **~-on earrings** Clips *pl.*
clipped [klɪpt] *adj accent* abgehackt.
clipper ['klɪpəʳ] *n (Naut)* Klipper *m.*
clippers ['klɪpəz] *npl (also* **pair of ~s***)* Schere *f*; *(for fingernails)* Zwicker *m.*
clipping ['klɪpɪŋ] *n (newspaper ~)* Ausschnitt *m.*
clique [kliːk] *n* Clique *f.*
cloak [kləʊk] **1** *n (lit)* Umhang *m*; *(fig) (disguise)* Deckmantel *m*; *(veil: of secrecy etc)* Schleier *m.* **under the ~ of darkness** im Schutz der Dunkelheit. **2** *vt (fig)* hüllen.
cloak: ~-and-dagger *adj* mysteriös; **a ~-and-dagger operation** eine Nacht-und-Nebel-Aktion; **~room** *n* **(a)** *(for coats)* Garderobe *f*; **(b)** *(Brit euph)* Waschraum *m (euph).*
clock [klɒk] **1** *n* **(a)** Uhr *f.* **around the ~** rund um die Uhr; **to work against the ~** gegen die Uhr arbeiten. **(b)** *(col) (speedometer, milometer)* Tacho *m (col)*; *(of taxi)* Uhr *f.* **it's got 100 on the ~** es hat einen Tachostand von 100. **2** *vt (Sport)* **he's ~ed the fastest time this year** er ist die schnellste Zeit dieses Jahres gelaufen/gefahren.
♦**clock in** *or* **on** *vi* (den Arbeitsbeginn) stempeln.
♦**clock off** *or* **out** *vi* (das Arbeitsende) stempeln.
♦**clock up** *vt sep* **(a)** *(athlete, competitor) time* laufen, schwimmen *etc.* **(b)** *speed, distance* zurücklegen. **(c)** *(col) success* verbuchen.
clock *in cpds* Uhr(en)-; ~ **face** *n* Zifferblatt *nt*; **~-radio** *n* Radiouhr *f*; **~wise** *adj, adv* im Uhrzeigersinn; **~work 1** *n (of clock)* Uhrwerk *nt*; *(of toy)* Aufziehmechanismus *m*; **like ~work** wie am Schnürchen; **2** *attr train, car* zum Aufziehen.
clod [klɒd] *n (of earth)* Klumpen *m.*
clog [klɒg] **1** *n (shoe)* Holzschuh *m.* **~s** *(modern)* Clogs *pl.* **2** *vt (also ~ up) pipe, drain etc* verstopfen; *mechanism, wheels* blockieren. **3** *vi (also ~ up) (pipe etc)* verstopfen; *(mechanism etc)* blockiert werden.
cloister ['klɔɪstəʳ] *n* **(a)** *(covered walk)* Kreuzgang *m.* **(b)** *(monastery)* Kloster *nt.*
cloistered ['klɔɪstəd] *adj (fig)* weltabgeschieden.
clone [kləʊn] **1** *n* Klon *m.* **2** *vt* klonen.
close[1] [kləʊs] **1** *adj (+er)* **(a)** *(near)* in der Nähe *(to gen,* von*)*; *(in time)* nahe (bevorstehend); *(fig)*

friend, co-operation, connection etc eng; *relative* nahe; *resemblance* stark; *fight, result* knapp. **is Glasgow ~ to Edinburgh?** liegt Glasgow in der Nähe von Edinburgh?; **in ~ proximity** in unmittelbarer Nähe *(to gen)*; **it's ~r to what we want** das kommt unseren Vorstellungen näher; **you're very ~** *(in guessing etc)* du bist dicht dran; **~ combat** Nahkampf *m*.

(b) *(not spread out) handwriting, print* eng; *ranks* geschlossen.

(c) *examination, study* eingehend; *translation* originalgetreu. **to keep a ~ watch on sb** jdn scharf bewachen; **now pay ~ attention to me** jetzt hör mir gut zu!

(d) *(stuffy)* schwül; *(inside)* stickig.

(e) ~ on nahezu; **~ on sixty/midnight** an die sechzig/kurz vor Mitternacht.

2 *adv (+er)* nahe; *(spatially also)* dicht. **~ by** in der Nähe; **stay ~ to me** bleib dicht bei mir; **~ to the water/ground** nahe *or* dicht am Wasser/Boden; **to be ~ to tears** den Tränen nahe sein.

close[2] [kləʊz] **1** *vt* **(a)** schließen, zumachen; *(col) factory* stillegen. **to ~ one's eyes/ears to sth** sich einer Sache gegenüber blind/taub stellen. **(b)** *(bring to an end) meeting* schließen, beenden; *bank account etc* auflösen. **2** *vi (shut, come together)* sich schließen; *(door, box, lid also)* zugehen; *(shop, factory)* schließen; *(come to an end)* schließen; *(tourist season)* zu Ende gehen. **3** *n* Ende *nt*. **to come to a ~** zu Ende gehen; **to bring sth to a ~** etw beenden.

♦**close down 1** *vi* **(a)** *(business, shop etc)* schließen, zumachen *(col)*; *(factory: permanently)* stillgelegt werden. **(b)** *(Rad, TV)* das Programm beenden. **2** *vt sep shop etc* schließen; *factory (permanently)* stillegen.

♦**close in** *vi (night, darkness)* hereinbrechen; *(days)* kürzer werden; *(enemy etc)* bedrohlich nahekommen. **the police are closing ~ on him** die Polizei zieht das Netz um ihn zu.

♦**close off** *vt sep* (ab)sperren; *(separate off)* abteilen.

♦**close up 1** *vi* **(a)** *(line of people)* zusammenrücken. **(b)** *(lock up)* ab- *or* zuschließen. **2** *vt sep* **(a)** *shop* zumachen; *house* verschließen. **(b)** *(block up) hole* zumachen.

closed-circuit television ['kləʊzd,sɜːkɪt-'telɪ,vɪʒən] *n* interne Fernsehanlage; *(for supervision)* Fernsehüberwachungsanlage *f*.

close-down ['kləʊzdaʊn] *n* **(a)** *(of shop, business etc)* (Geschäfts)schließung *f*; *(of factory)* Stillegung *f*. **(b)** *(Rad, TV)* Sendeschluß *m*.

closed shop ['kləʊzd'ʃɒp] *n* Closed Shop *m*. **we have a ~** wir haben Gewerkschaftszwang.

closely ['kləʊslɪ] *adv* eng, dicht; *work, connect* eng; *related* nah(e); *follow (in time)* dicht; *(attentively) watch, listen etc* genau; *guard* scharf, streng.

closeness ['kləʊsnɪs] *n (nearness, in time)* Nähe *f*; *(fig) (of friendship)* Innigkeit *f*; *(of examination, interrogation)* Genauigkeit *f*; *(of translation)* Texttreue *f*; *(of air, atmosphere)* Schwüle *f*; *(indoors)* stickige Luft.

closet ['klɒzɪt] *(vb: pret, ptp* **~ed** ['klɒzɪtɪd]*)* **1** *n* Wandschrank *m*. **to come out of the ~** *(fig col)* sich als Homosexueller bekennen. **2** *vt* **to be ~ed** hinter verschlossenen Türen sitzen *(with sb* mit jdm*)*.

close-up ['kləʊsʌp] *n* Nahaufnahme *f*. **in ~** in Nahaufnahme; *(of face)* in Großaufnahme.

closing ['kləʊzɪŋ] *adj remarks* abschließend. **~ time** Ladenschluß *m*; *(Brit: in pub)* Polizeistunde *f*; **~ prices** *(St Ex)* Schlußnotierungen *pl*.

closure ['kləʊʒə^r] *n* **(a)** Schließung *f*; *(of road)* Sperrung *f*; *(of factory, mine etc also)* Stillegung *f* **(b)** *(object, stopper)* Verschluß *m*.

clot [klɒt] **1** *n* **(a)** *(of blood)* (Blut)gerinnsel *nt*. **(b)** *(col: person)* Trottel *m*. **2** *vi (blood, milk)* gerinnen.

cloth [klɒθ] *n* Tuch *nt*; *(for cleaning)* Lappen *m*; *(table~)* Tischdecke *f*. **a gentleman of the ~** ein geistlicher Herr.

clothe [kləʊð] *pret, ptp* **clad** *(old) or* **~d** *vt (usu pass: dress)* kleiden.

clothes [kləʊðz] *npl (garments)* Kleider *pl*; *(clothing, outfit also)* Kleidung *f no pl*. **to put on/take off one's ~** sich anziehen/ausziehen.

clothes: ~ hanger *n* Kleiderbügel *m*; **~ horse** *n* Wäscheständer *m*; **~line** *n* Wäscheleine *f*; **~ peg** *(Brit)*, **~ pin** *(US) n* Wäscheklammer *f*; **~ shop** *n* Bekleidungsgeschäft *nt*.

clothing ['kləʊðɪŋ] *n* Kleidung *f*.

cloud [klaʊd] **1** *n* Wolke *f*. **to have one's head in the ~s** in höheren Regionen schweben; **to be on ~ nine** *(col)* im siebten Himmel sein *(col)*; **~ of dust/smoke** Staub-/Rauchwolke *f*; **he's been under a ~ for weeks** *(under suspicion)* seit Wochen haftet ein Verdacht an ihm; *(in disgrace)* er ist seit Wochen in einem schlechten Ruf. **2** *vt* **(a)** *(lit) sky, view* verhängen *(geh)*; *mirror* trüben. **a ~ed sky** ein bewölkter Himmel. **(b)** *(fig) prospect, sb's enjoyment, mind, judgement etc* trüben; *friendship, sb's future* überschatten. **to ~ the issue** *(complicate)* die Dinge unnötig kompliziert machen.

♦**cloud over** *vi (sky)* sich bewölken; *(mirror etc)* sich beschlagen.

cloud: ~burst *n* Wolkenbruch *m*; **~-cuckoo-land** *n* Wolkenkuckucksheim *nt*.

cloudless ['klaʊdlɪs] *adj sky* wolkenlos.

cloudy ['klaʊdɪ] *adj (+er) sky* bewölkt; *liquid* trüb.

clout [klaʊt] **1** *n* **(a)** *(col: blow)* Schlag *m*. **(b)** *influence* Schlagkraft *f*. **2** *vt (col)* hauen *(col)*. **to ~ sb one** jdm eine runterhauen *(col)*.

clove [kləʊv] *n* **(a)** Gewürznelke *f*. **(b) ~ of garlic** Knoblauchzehe *f*.

clover ['kləʊvə^r] *n* Klee *m*. **~ leaf** *(Bot, Mot)* Kleeblatt *nt*.

clown [klaʊn] **1** *n* Clown *m*; *(pej)* Trottel *m*. **to act the ~** den Hanswurst spielen. **2** *vi (also* **~ about** *or* **around***)* herumblödeln *(col)*.

club [klʌb] **1** *n* **(a)** *(weapon)* Knüppel *m*; *(golf~)* Golfschläger *m*. **(b)** *(Cards)* **~s** *pl* Kreuz *nt*; *(Bridge)* Treff *nt*. **nine of ~s** (die) Kreuz-/Treff-Neun. **(c)** *(society)* Klub, Verein *m*. **to be in the ~** *(col)* ein Kind kriegen *(col)*. **2** *vt* einknüppeln auf *(+acc)*.

♦**club together** *vi* zusammenlegen.

clubhouse ['klʌb,haʊs] *n* Klubhaus *nt*.

cluck [klʌk] *vi (hen)* glucken.

clue [kluː] *n* Anhaltspunkt *m*; *(in crosswords)* Frage *f*. **I'll give you a ~** ich gebe dir einen Tip; **I haven't a ~!** (ich hab') keine Ahnung!

clued-up [,kluːd'ʌp] *adj (col)* im Bilde; *(about subject)* vertraut *(about* mit*)*.

clueless ['kluːlɪs] *adj (col)* unbedarft *(col)*.

clump [klʌmp] **1** *n (of trees, flowers etc)* Gruppe *f*; *(of earth)* Klumpen *m*. **2** *vi* **to ~ about** herumtrampeln.

clumsy ['klʌmzɪ] *adj (+er)* **(a)** ungeschickt. **(b)** *(unwieldy)* plump; *tool* unhandlich; *(ungainly)* schwerfällig.

clung [klʌŋ] *pret, ptp of* **cling.**

cluster ['klʌstə^r] *n (of trees, flowers, houses)* Gruppe *f*; *(of grapes)* Traube *f*.

♦**cluster around** *vi +prep obj* sich scharen (um *+acc*).

clutch [klʌtʃ] **1** *n* **(a)** *(Aut)* Kupplung *f*. **to let in/out the ~** ein-/auskuppeln. **(b)** *(fig)* **to fall into sb's ~es** jdm in die Hände fallen. **2** *vt* umklammern.

♦**clutch at** *vi +prep obj (lit)* schnappen nach *(+dat)*; *(fig)* sich klammern an *(+acc)*.

clutter ['klʌtə^r] **1** *n (confusion)* Durcheinander *nt*; *(disorderly articles)* Kram *m (col)*. **2** *vt (also* **~ up***) cupboard* vollstopfen. **to be ~ed up with sth** mit etw vollgestopft sein; *(floor, desk etc)* mit etw übersät sein.

CND = **Campaign for Nuclear Disarma-**

ment.
Co = **(a) company** KG *f.* **(b) county.**
c/o = **care of** bei, c/o.
co- [kəʊ-] *pref* Mit-, mit-.
coach [kəʊtʃ] **1** *n* **(a)** *(horsedrawn)* Kutsche *f*; *(state ~)* (Staats)karosse *f*; *(Rail)* (Eisenbahn)wagen *m*; *(motor ~)* (Reise)bus *m*. **(b)** *(tutor)* Nachhilfelehrer(in *f*) *m*; *(Sport)* Trainer *m*. **2** *vt* **(a)** *(Sport)* trainieren. **(b) to ~ sb for an exam** jdn aufs Examen vorbereiten.
coagulate [kəʊ'ægjʊleɪt] **1** *vi* gerinnen. **2** *vt* gerinnen lassen.
coal [kəʊl] *n* Kohle *f*. **to carry ~s to Newcastle** *(Prov)* Eulen nach Athen tragen *(Prov)*.
coal *in cpds* Kohlen-; **~ black** *adj* kohlrabenschwarz; **~-cellar** *n* Kohlenkeller *m*; **~-face** *n*: **to work at the ~-face** vor Ort arbeiten; **~field** *n* Kohlenrevier *nt*; **~ fire** *n* Kamin *m*.
coalition [ˌkəʊɪ'lɪʃən] *n* Koalition *f*.
coal: ~man *n* Kohlenauslieferer *m*; **~-mine** *n* Grube, Zeche *f*; **~-miner** *n* Bergmann, Kumpel *(col) m*; **~-mining** *n* Kohle(n)bergbau *m*; **~ scuttle** *n* Kohleneimer *m*; **~shed** *n* Kohlenschuppen *m*.
coarse [kɔːs] *adj (+er)* **(a)** *(in texture)* grob. **(b)** *(uncouth)* gewöhnlich; *person, manners* ungehobelt; *joke, language* derb.
coarsen ['kɔːsn] **1** *vt* derb(er) machen; *skin* gerben. **2** *vi (person)* derb(er) werden.
coast [kəʊst] **1** *n* Küste *f*. **at/on the ~** an der Küste; **the ~ is clear** *(fig)* die Luft ist rein. **2** *vi (car, cyclist) (in neutral)* im Leerlauf fahren; *(cruise effortlessly)* dahinrollen.
coastal ['kəʊstəl] *adj* Küsten-.
coaster ['kəʊstə[r]] *n* **(a)** *(Naut)* Küstenmotorschiff *nt*. **(b)** *(drip mat)* Untersetzer *m*.
coast: ~guard *n* Küstenwache *f*; **~line** *n* Küste *f*.
coat [kəʊt] **1** *n* **(a)** Mantel *m*; *(doctor's ~ etc also)* (Arzt)kittel *m*; *(jacket of suit etc)* Jacke *f*. **(b)** *(Her)* **~ of arms** Wappen *nt*. **(c)** *(of animal)* Fell *nt*. **(d)** *(of paint)* Anstrich *m*. **2** *vt (with paint etc)* streichen; *(with chocolate, icing etc)* überziehen. **~ed tongue** belegte Zunge.
coat-hanger ['kəʊtˌhæŋə[r]] *n* Kleiderbügel *m*.
coating ['kəʊtɪŋ] *n* Überzug *m*; *(of paint)* Anstrich *m*.
co-author ['kəʊˌɔːθə[r]] *n* Mitverfasser *m*.
coax [kəʊks] *vt*: **to ~ sb into doing sth** jdn dazu bringen, etw zu tun; **to ~ sth out of sb** jdm etw entlocken.
cobalt ['kəʊbɒlt] *n* Kobalt *nt*.
cobble ['kɒbl] **1** *n (also ~stone)* Kopfstein *m*. **2** *vt* **a ~d street** eine Straße mit Kopfsteinpflaster.
♦**cobble together** *vt sep (col) essay etc* zusammenschustern.
cobbler ['kɒblə[r]] *n* Schuster *m*.
cobra ['kəʊbrə] *n* Kobra *f*.
cobweb ['kɒbweb] *n* Spinn(en)webe *f*.
cocaine [kə'keɪn] *n* Kokain *nt*.
cock [kɒk] **1** *n* **(a)** *(rooster)* Hahn *m*. **(b)** *(male bird)* Männchen *nt*. **(c)** *(tap)* (Wasser)hahn *m*. **fuel ~** Treibstoffhahn *m*. **(d)** *(col!: penis)* Schwanz *m (col!)*. **2** *vt ears* spitzen; *gun* entsichern. **the parrot ~ed its head on one side** der Papagei legte seinen Kopf schief.
cock: ~-a-doodle-doo *interj* Kikeriki; **~-a-hoop** *adj* ganz aus dem Häuschen; **~-and-bull** *adj*: **~-and-bull story** Lügengeschichte *f*.
cockatoo [ˌkɒkə'tuː] *n* Kakadu *m*.
cockchafer ['kɒkˌtʃeɪfə[r]] *n* Maikäfer *m*.
cockerel ['kɒkərəl] *n* junger Hahn.
cock-eyed [ˌkɒk'aɪd] *adj (col)* **(a)** *(crooked)* schief. **(b)** *(absurd)* verrückt.
cockle ['kɒkl] *n (shellfish)* Herzmuschel *f*.
cockney ['kɒknɪ] *n* Cockney *nt*; *(person)* Cockney *m*.
cockpit ['kɒkpɪt] *n (Aviat, Naut, of racing car)* Cockpit *nt*.
cockroach ['kɒkrəʊtʃ] *n* Küchenschabe *f*.
cocksure ['kɒk'ʃʊə[r]] *adj* fest überzeugt.
cocktail ['kɒkteɪl] *n* **(a)** Cocktail *m*. **(b) fruit ~** Obstsalat *m*.
cocktail *in cpds n* Cocktail-; **~ bar** *n* Cocktail-Bar *f*; **~ cabinet** *n* Hausbar *f*.
cock-up ['kɒkʌp] *n (Brit col!)* **to make a ~ of sth** bei etw Scheiße bauen *(col!)*.
cocky ['kɒkɪ] *adj (+er) (col)* großspurig.
cocoa ['kəʊkəʊ] *n* Kakao *m*.
coconut ['kəʊkənʌt] **1** *n* Kokosnuß *f*. **2** *attr* Kokos-. **~ matting** Kokosmatte *f*; **~ palm, ~ tree** Kokospalme *f*.
cocoon [kə'kuːn] **1** *n* Kokon *m*; *(fig: of scarves, blankets etc)* Hülle *f*. **2** *vt* einhüllen.
COD = **cash** *(Brit) or* **collect** *(US)* **on delivery** per Nachnahme.
cod [kɒd] *n* Kabeljau *m*.
coddle ['kɒdl] *vt child* verhätscheln.
code [kəʊd] *n* **(a)** *(cipher)* Kode, Code *m*. **in ~** verschlüsselt; **to put into ~** verschlüsseln; **~-name** Deckname *m*; **~-number** Kennziffer *f*. **(b)** *(rules)* **~ of honour/behaviour** Ehren-/Sittenkodex *m*. **(c) post** *(Brit) or* **zip** *(US)* **~** Postleitzahl *f*.
codeine ['kəʊdiːn] *n* Kodein *nt*.
codger ['kɒdʒə[r]] *n (col)*: **old ~** alter Kauz.
cod-liver-oil ['kɒdlɪvər'ɔɪl] *n* Lebertran *m*.
co-driver ['kəʊdraɪvə[r]] *n* Beifahrer *m*.
co-ed, coed ['kəʊ'ed] *n (col) (Brit: school)* gemischte Schule; *(US: girl student)* Schülerin *f* einer gemischten Schule.
coeducation ['kəʊˌedjʊ'keɪʃən] *n* Koedukation *f*.
coerce [kəʊ'ɜːs] *vt* zwingen. **to ~ sb into doing sth** jdn zwingen, etw zu tun.
coercion [kəʊ'ɜːʃən] *n* Zwang *m*; *(Jur)* Nötigung *f*.
coexist [ˌkəʊɪg'zɪst] *vi* nebeneinander bestehen.
coexistence [ˌkəʊɪg'zɪstəns] *n* Koexistenz *f*.
C of E = **Church of England.**
coffee ['kɒfɪ] *n* Kaffee *m*. **two ~s, please** zwei Kaffee, bitte.
coffee *in cpds* Kaffee-; **~ bar** *n (Brit)* Café *nt*; **~ break** *n* Kaffeepause *f*; **~ pot** *n* Kaffeekanne *f*; **~ table** *n* Couchtisch *m*.
coffin ['kɒfɪn] *n* Sarg *m*.
cog [kɒg] *n* Zahn *m*; *(~wheel)* Zahnrad *nt*. **he's only a ~ in the wheel** *(fig)* er ist nur ein Rädchen im Getriebe.
cogent ['kəʊdʒənt] *adj argument, reason* zwingend; *reasoning* überzeugend.
cogitate ['kɒdʒɪteɪt] *vi* nachsinnen.
cognac ['kɒnjæk] *n* Kognak *m*; *(French)* Cognac *m*.
cognate ['kɒgneɪt] *adj* verwandt.
cohabit [kəʊ'hæbɪt] *vi (esp Jur)* in eheähnlicher Gemeinschaft leben.
coherence [kəʊ'hɪərəns] *n* **(a)** *(lit)* Kohärenz *f*. **(b)** *(of community)* Zusammenhalt *m*; *(of essay, symphony etc)* Geschlossenheit *f*. **his speech lacked ~** seiner Rede *(dat)* fehlte der Zusammenhang.
coherent [kəʊ'hɪərənt] *adj* **(a)** *(comprehensible)* verständlich. **(b)** *(cohesive)* zusammenhängend; *logic, reasoning etc* schlüssig.
cohesive [kəʊ'hiːsɪv] *adj (fig)* geschlossen.
coil [kɔɪl] **1** *n* **(a)** *(of rope, wire etc)* Rolle *f*; *(on loop)* Windung; *f (of smoke)* Kringel *m*. **~ spring** Sprungfeder *f*. **(b)** *(Elec)* Spule *f*. **(c)** *(contraceptive)* Spirale *f*. **2** *vt (also ~ up)* aufwickeln. **to ~ sth around sth** etw um etw wickeln; **the python ~ed itself up** die Pythonschlange rollte sich zusammen. **3** *vi* sich ringeln; *(river)* sich schlängeln.
coin [kɔɪn] **1** *n* Münze *f*. **~-box** *(telephone)* Münzfernsprecher *m*; **~-operated** Münz-; **the other side of the ~** *(fig)* die Kehrseite der Medaille. **2** *vt money, phrase* prägen. **..., to ~ a phrase** ..., um es mal so auszudrücken.
coincide [ˌkəʊɪn'saɪd] *vi (in time, place)* zusammenfallen; *(in area)* sich decken; *(agree)*

übereinstimmen.
coincidence [kəʊ'ınsıdəns] *n* Zufall *m*.
coke [kəʊk] *n* Koks *m*.
Coke ® [kəʊk] *n (col)* Cola *f*, Coke ® *nt*.
colander ['kʌləndəʳ] *n* Durchschlag *m*, Sieb *nt*.
cold [kəʊld] **1** *adj (+er)* kalt *(also fig)*; *reception, personality* kühl. **I am ~** ich friere; **my hands are ~/are getting ~** ich habe/bekomme kalte Hände; **to be ~ to sb** jdn kühl behandeln; **that leaves me ~** das läßt mich kalt; **to be out ~** bewußtlos sein; *(knocked out)* k.o. sein; **in ~ blood** kaltblütig; **to have ~ feet** *(fig col)* kalte Füße gekriegt haben *(col)*; **to give sb the ~ shoulder** *(col)* jdm die kalte Schulter zeigen. **2** *n* **(a)** Kälte *f*. **to feel the ~** kälteempfindlich sein; **to be left out in the ~** *(fig)* ausgeschlossen werden. **(b)** *(Med)* Erkältung *f*; *(runny nose)* Schnupfen *m*. **to have a ~** erkältet sein; **to get** *or* **catch a ~** sich erkälten.
cold: ~-blooded *adj (Zool, fig)* kaltblütig; **~ cream** *n* Cold Cream *f or nt*, Feuchtigkeitscreme *f*; **~-hearted** *adj* kaltherzig.
coldly ['kəʊldlı] *adv (lit, fig)* kalt; *answer, receive* betont kühl.
cold: ~-shoulder *vt (col)* links liegenlassen *(col)*; **~ storage** *n* **to put sth into ~ storage** *(lit) food* etw kühl lagern; *(fig) idea, plan* etw auf Eis legen.
coleslaw ['kəʊlslɔː] *n* Krautsalat *m*.
collaborate [kə'læbəreıt] *vi* **(a)** zusammenarbeiten. **(b)** *(with enemy)* kollaborieren.
collaboration [kə,læbə'reıʃən] *n* **(a)** Zusammenarbeit *f*; *(of one party)* Mitarbeit *f*. **(b)** *(with enemy)* Kollaboration *f*.
collaborator [kə'læbəreıtəʳ] *n* **(a)** Mitarbeiter(in *f*) *m*. **(b)** *(with enemy)* Kollaborateur(in *f*) *m*.
collapse [kə'læps] **1** *vi (lit, fig)* zusammenbrechen; *(building, wall, roof)* einstürzen; *(negotiations)* scheitern. **they all ~d with laughter** sie konnten sich alle vor Lachen nicht mehr halten; **his whole world ~d about him** für ihn brach eine Welt zusammen. **2** *n* Zusammenbruch *m*; *(heart attack)* Kollaps *m*; *(of building etc)* Einsturz *m*; *(of negotiations)* Scheitern *nt*.
collapsible [kə'læpsəbl] *adj bicycle, chair* zusammenklappbar, Klapp-.
collar ['kɒləʳ] **1** *n* Kragen *m*; *(for dogs)* Halsband *nt*; *(Mech: on pipe etc)* Bund *m*. **~bone** Schlüsselbein *nt*. **2** *vt (capture)* fassen.
collate [kɒ'leıt] *vt* vergleichen.
collateral [kɒ'lætərəl] *n (Fin)* (zusätzliche) Sicherheit.
colleague ['kɒliːg] *n* Kollege *m*, Kollegin *f*.
collect ['kɒlekt] **1** *vt* **(a)** *stamps etc, one's thoughts, money, facts* sammeln; *(accumulate)* ansammeln; *(furniture) dust etc* anziehen; *empty glasses, tickets etc* einsammeln; *litter* aufsammeln; *belongings* zusammenpacken; *taxes* einziehen; *rent, fares* kassieren. **(b)** *(pick up, fetch)* abholen *(from* bei*)*. **2** *vi (gather)* sich ansammeln; *(dust)* sich absetzen; *(~ money)* kassieren; *(for charity)* sammeln. **3** *adj (esp US)* **~ call** R-Gespräch *nt*. **4** *adv (esp US)* **to call ~** ein R-Gespräch führen.
collected [kə'lektıd] *adj* **(a) the ~ works of Oscar Wilde** Oscar Wildes gesammelte Werke. **(b)** *(calm)* ruhig, gelassen.
collection [kə'lekʃən] *n* **(a)** *(group of people, objects)* Ansammlung *f*; *(of stamps, coins etc)* Sammlung *f*. **(b)** *(collecting) (of facts, information)* Zusammentragen *nt*; *(of goods)* Abholung *f*; *(from letterbox)* Leerung *f*; *(of stamps, coins)* Sammeln *nt*; *(of money, jumble for charity)* Sammlung *f*; *(in church)* Kollekte *f*; *(of rent, fares)* Kassieren *nt*; *(of taxes)* Einzug *m*. **(c)** *(Fashion)* Kollektion *f*.
collective [kə'lektıv] **1** *adj* kollektiv, Kollektiv-. **~ bargaining** Tarifverhandlungen *pl*. **2** *n* Kollektiv *nt*.
collector [kə'lektəʳ] *n* **(a)** *(of taxes)* Einnehmer(in *f*) *m*; *(of rent, cash)* Kassierer(in *f*) *m*; *(ticket ~)* Fahrkartenkontrolleur *m*. **(b)** *(of stamps, coins etc)* Sammler(in *f*) *m*. **~'s item** Sammler-; *price* Liebhaber-.
college ['kɒlıdʒ] *n* **(a)** *(Univ)* College *nt*. **to go to ~** *(university)* studieren. **(b)** *(of music, technology)* Fachhochschule *f*. **~ of Art** Kunstakademie *f*.
collide [kə'laıd] *vt* zusammenstoßen.
collie ['kɒlı] *n* Collie *m*.
colliery ['kɒlıərı] *n* Grube, Zeche *f*.
collision [kə'lıʒən] *n (lit)* Zusammenstoß *m*; *(fig)* Konflikt *m*, Kollision *f*. **on a ~ course** *(lit, fig)* auf Kollisionskurs.
colloquial [kə'ləʊkwıəl] *adj* umgangssprachlich.
collusion [kə'luːʒən] *n* (geheime) Absprache.
Cologne [kə'ləʊn] *n* Köln *nt*.
cologne [kə'ləʊn] *n* Kölnisch Wasser *nt*.
colon[1] ['kəʊlən] *n (Anat)* Dickdarm *m*.
colon[2] *n (Gram)* Doppelpunkt *m*.
colonel ['kɜːnl] *n* Oberst *m*.
colonial [kə'ləʊnıəl] **1** *adj* Kolonial-, kolonial. **2** *n* Bewohner(in *f*) *m* einer Kolonie/der Kolonien.
colonialism [kə'ləʊnıəlızəm] *n* Kolonialismus *m*.
colonist ['kɒlənıst] *n* Siedler(in *f*) *m*.
colonize ['kɒlənaız] *vt* kolonisieren.
colony ['kɒlənı] *n (also Zool)* Kolonie *f*; *(of ants, bees)* Staat *m*.
color *etc (US)* = **colour** *etc*.
Colorado beetle [,kɒlə'rɑːdəʊ'biːtl] *n* Kartoffelkäfer *m*.
colossal [kə'lɒsl] *adj* riesig; *prices, mistake* gewaltig.
colour, *(US)* **color** ['kʌləʳ] **1** *n* **(a)** *(lit, fig)* Farbe *f*. **what ~ is it?** welche Farbe hat es?; **let's see the ~ of your money first** *(col)* zeig erst mal dein Geld her *(col)*. **(b)** *(complexion)* (Gesichts)farbe *f*. **to get one's ~ back** wieder Farbe bekommen. **(c)** *(racial)* Hautfarbe *f*. **(d)** *(flag)* **~s** Fahne *f*; **to nail one's ~s to the mast** *(fig)* Farbe bekennen; **to show one's true ~s** *(fig)* sein wahres Gesicht zeigen. **2** *vt* **(a)** *(lit)* anmalen. **(b)** *(fig)* beeinflussen; *(bias)* färben. **3** *vi* **(a)** *(leaves)* sich (ver)färben. **(b)** *(person: also* **~ up***)* rot werden.
♦ **colour in** *vt sep* anmalen; *(Art)* kolorieren.
colour *in cpds* Farb-; *(racial)* Rassen-; *(Mil)* Fahnen-; **~-bar** *n* Rassenschranke *f*; **~-blind** *adj* farbenblind.
coloured, *(US)* **colored** ['kʌləd] **1** *adj* **(a)** bunt. **(b)** *(fig: biased)* gefärbt. **(c)** *person, race* farbig. **2** *n* Farbige(r) *mf*.
-coloured, *(US)* **-colored** *adj suf* **straw-/dark-~** strohfarben/dunkel.
colourful, *(US)* **colorful** ['kʌləfʊl] *adj* **(a)** *(lit)* bunt. **(b)** *account etc* anschaulich; *life* bewegt; *personality* schillernd.
colouring, *(US)* **coloring** ['kʌlərıŋ] *n (complexion)* Gesichtsfarbe *f*; *(substance)* Farbstoff *m*; *(coloration)* Farben *pl*. **~ book** Malbuch *nt*.
colourless, *(US)* **colorless** ['kʌləlıs] *adj (lit, fig)* farblos.
colour: ~ photograph *n* Farbfoto *nt*; **~ scheme** *n* Farbzusammenstellung *f*; **~ supplement** *n (Press)* Farbbeilage; **~ television** *n* Farbfernsehen *nt*; *(set)* Farbfernseher *m*.
colt [kəʊlt] *n* Fohlen *nt*.
column ['kɒləm] *n* **(a)** *(Archit, of smoke)* Säule *f*. **(b)** *(division of page)* Spalte; *(article in newspaper)* Kolumne *f*.
columnist ['kɒləmnıst] *n* Kolumnist(in *f*) *m*.
coma ['kəʊmə] *n* Koma *nt*. **to go into a ~** ins Koma fallen; **to be in a ~** im Koma liegen.
comatose ['kəʊmətəʊs] *adj* im Koma.
comb [kəʊm] **1** *n* Kamm *m*. **2** *vt* **(a)** kämmen. **to ~ one's hair** sich *(dat)* die Haare kämmen. **(b)** *(search)* durchkämmen.
combat ['kɒmbæt] **1** *n* Kampf *m*. **2** *vt (lit, fig)* bekämpfen.
combatant ['kɒmbətənt] *n (lit, fig))* Kämpfer *m*.
combination [,kɒmbı'neıʃən] *n* **(a)** Kombination *f*;

(combining: of organizations, people etc) Zusammenschluß *m*; *(of events)* Verkettung *f*. **in ~** zusammen. **(b)** *(for lock)* Kombination *f*. **~ lock** Kombinationsschloß *nt*.

combine [kəm'baɪn] **1** *vt* verbinden, kombinieren. **2** *vi* sich zusammenschließen; *(Chem)* sich verbinden. **3** ['kɒmbaɪn] *n* **(a)** Konzern *m*; *(in socialist countries)* Kombinat *nt*. **(b)** *(also* **~ harvester***)* Mähdrescher *m*.

combined [kəm'baɪnd] *adj* gemeinsam; *talents, efforts* vereint. **~ with** in Kombination mit; *(esp clothes, furniture)* kombiniert mit.

combustible [kəm'bʌstɪbl] *adj* brennbar.

combustion [kəm'bʌstʃən] *n* Verbrennung *f*. **~ chamber** Verbrennungsraum *m*.

come [kʌm] *pret* **came,** *ptp* **~ 1** *vi* **(a)** kommen. **~ and see me soon** besuchen Sie mich bald einmal; **he has ~ a long way** er kommt von weit her; *(fig)* er ist weit gekommen; **the project has ~ a long way** das Projekt ist schon ziemlich weit; **he came running/hurrying into the room** er kam ins Zimmer gerannt/er eilte ins Zimmer; **coming!** ich komme; **~ ~!, ~ now!** *(fig)* komm, komm; **Christmas is coming** bald ist Weihnachten; **they came to a town/castle** sie kamen in eine Stadt/an ein Schloß; **it came into my head that ...** ich habe mir gedacht, daß ...; **May ~s before June** Mai kommt vor Juni; **it came as a shock to me** es war ein Schock für mich; **~ what may** ganz gleich, was geschieht; **you could see it coming** das war ja zu erwarten; **she had it coming to her** *(col)* das mußte ja so kommen; **people were coming and going all day** es war den ganzen Tag ein Kommen und Gehen; **to ~ for sb** *(collect)* jdn abholen; **we'll ~ after you** wir kommen nach; **he came third in the race** er wurde Dritter in dem Rennen; **it all came right in the end** am Ende ergab sich alles; **how ~?** *(col)* wieso?

(b) *(be, become)* werden. **his dreams came true** seine Träume wurden wahr; **no good will ~ of it** das wird nicht gut ausgehen; **nothing came of it** es wurde nichts daraus; **that's what ~s of being careless** das kommt davon, wenn man unvorsichtig ist; **the handle has ~ loose** der Griff hat sich gelockert.

(c) *(Comm: be available)* erhältlich sein. **milk now ~s in plastic bottles** es gibt jetzt Milch in Plastikflaschen.

(d) I have ~ to believe him mittlerweile glaube ich ihm; **I'm sure you will ~ to agree with me** ich bin sicher, daß du mir schließlich zustimmst; **(now I) ~ to think of it** wenn ich es mir recht überlege; **the years/weeks to ~** die kommenden Jahre/Wochen; **the life to ~** das ewige Leben.

(e) *(col uses)* **~ next week** nächste Woche; **I've known him for three years ~ January** im Januar kenne ich ihn drei Jahre; **~ again?** wie bitte?; **she is as vain as they ~** sie ist so eingebildet wie nur was *(col)*.

2 *vt* **don't ~ the innocent with me** *(col)* komm mir bloß nicht auf die unschuldige Tour *(col)*!

♦ **come about** *vi impers (happen)* passieren.

♦ **come across 1** *vi* **(a)** *(cross)* herüberkommen. **(b)** *(be understood)* verstanden werden; *(message, speech)* ankommen. **(c)** *(make an impression)* wirken. **2** *vi +prep obj (find)* finden. **if you ~ ~ my watch** wenn du zufällig meine Uhr siehst.

♦ **come along** *vi* **(a) ~ ~!** (nun) komm doch! **(b)** *(accompany)* mitkommen. **(c)** *(progress)* **to be coming ~** sich machen; **my play isn't coming ~ at all well** mein Stück macht überhaupt keine Fortschritte; **how's the thesis coming ~?** was macht die Doktorarbeit?

♦ **come apart** *vi* auseinandergehen; *(to be able to be taken apart)* zerlegbar sein.

♦ **come around** *vi* **(a)** *(call round)* vorbeikommen. **(b)** *(recur)* **Christmas has ~ ~ again** nun ist wieder Weihnachten. **(c)** *(change one's opinions)* es sich *(dat)* anders überlegen. **eventually he came ~ to our way of thinking** schließlich schloß er sich unserer Auffassung an. **(d)** *(regain consciousness)* wieder zu sich *(dat)* kommen.

♦ **come away** *vi* **(a)** *(leave)* (weg)gehen. **~ ~ from there!** komm da weg! **(b)** *(become detached)* abgehen.

♦ **come back** *vi* **(a)** zurückkommen. **can I ~ ~ to you on that one?** kann ich später darauf zurückkommen? **(b)** *(return to one's memory)* **ah yes, it's all coming ~** ach ja, jetzt fällt mir alles wieder ein; **your German will very quickly ~ ~** du wirst ganz schnell wieder ins Deutsche reinkommen *(col)*.

♦ **come by 1** *vi +prep obj (obtain)* kommen zu; *idea* kommen auf *(+acc)*. **2** *vi (visit)* vorbeikommen.

♦ **come down** *vi* **(a)** *(from ladder, stairs)* herunterkommen. **(b)** *(be demolished: building etc)* abgerissen werden; *(fall down)* herunterfallen. **(c)** *(drop: prices)* sinken; *(seller)* heruntergehen *(to* auf *+acc)*. **(d)** *(be a question of)* ankommen *(to* auf *+acc)*. **it all ~s ~ to something very simple** das ist im Grunde ganz einfach. **(e)** *(lose social rank)* sinken. **you've ~ ~ in the world a bit** du bist aber ganz schön tief gesunken.

♦ **come down on** *vi +prep obj (rebuke)* zusammenstauchen *(col)*.

♦ **come down with** *vi +prep obj illness* bekommen.

♦ **come forward** *vi* **(a)** sich melden. **(b) to ~ ~ with help/money** Hilfe/Geld anbieten.

♦ **come in** *vi* **(a)** hereinkommen. **~ ~!** herein! **(b)** *(arrive)* ankommen; *(train)* einfahren; *(ship)* einlaufen. **(c)** *(be received as income)* **he has £10,000 coming ~ every year** er hat £ 10.000 im Jahr. **(d)** *(have a part to play)* **where do I ~ ~?** welche Rolle spiele ich dabei?; **that will ~ ~ useful** das kann ich/man gut gebrauchen.

♦ **come in for** *vi +prep obj attention, admiration* erregen; *criticism etc* einstecken müssen.

♦ **come into** *vi +prep obj* **(a)** *legacy etc (inherit)* erben. **to ~ ~ one's own** zeigen, was in einem steckt. **(b)** *(be involved)* **I don't see where I ~ ~ all this** ich verstehe nicht, was ich mit der ganzen Sache zu tun habe; **money doesn't ~ ~ it** das hat nichts mit Geld zu tun.

♦ **come off 1** *vi* **(a)** *(off bicycle etc)* herunterfallen. **(b)** *(button, handle, paint etc)* abgehen; *(stains, marks)* weggehen. **(c)** *(take place)* **her wedding didn't ~ ~ after all** aus ihrer Hochzeit ist nun doch nichts geworden. **(d)** *(col: succeed)* klappen *(col)*. **(e)** *(acquit oneself)* abschneiden. **2** *vi +prep obj* **(a)** *bicycle, horse etc* fallen von. **(b)** *(button, paint, stain)* abgehen von. **(c)** *(col)* **~ ~ it!** nun mach mal halblang! *(col)*.

♦ **come on 1** *vi* **(a)** *(follow)* nachkommen. **(b) ~ ~!** komm!; **~ *on!*** komm schon! **(c)** *(continue to advance)* zukommen *(towards* auf *+acc)*. **(d)** *(start) (night)* hereinbrechen; *(storm)* einsetzen. **I feel a cold coming ~** ich spüre die ersten Anzeichen einer Erkältung. **(e)** *(actor)* auftreten. **(f)** *(col)* **to ~ ~ strong** groß auftreten *(col)*. **(g)** = **~ along (c).**

♦ **come out** *vi* **(a)** herauskommen; *(book, magazine also)* erscheinen; *(new product)* auf den Markt kommen; *(film)* (in den Kinos) anlaufen; *(exam results, news also)* bekannt werden. **(b)** *(Ind)* **to ~ ~ (on strike)** in den Streik treten. **(c)** *(Phot: film, photograph)* **let's hope the photos ~ ~** hoffentlich sind die Bilder etwas geworden. **(d)** *(stains, dye etc)* herausgehen. **(e) he came ~ in a rash** er bekam einen Ausschlag; **to ~ ~ against/in favour of sth** sich gegen/für etw aussprechen; **to ~ ~ of sth badly/well** bei etw schlecht/nicht schlecht wegkommen.

♦ **come out with** *vi +prep obj truth, facts* herausrücken mit; *(col) remarks, nonsense* von sich geben.

♦ **come over 1** *vi* herüberkommen. **he came ~ to England** er kam nach England; **he came ~ to our side** er trat auf unsere Seite über; **she came ~ giddy** *(col)* ihr wurde schwindelig; **it came ~ cloudy** es bewölkte sich. **2** *vi +prep obj (feelings)* überkommen. **what's ~ ~ you?** was ist denn in dich gefahren?

♦ **come round** *vi* = **come around.**

♦ **come through 1** *vi* **(a)** *(phone-call, order)* durchkommen. **your papers haven't ~ ~ yet** *(be cleared)* Ihre Papiere sind noch nicht fertig. **(b)** *(survive)* durchkommen. **2** *vi +prep obj (survive) illness, danger* überstehen.

♦ **come to 1** *vi (regain consciousness)* wieder zu sich *(dat)* kommen. **2** *vi +prep obj* **(a) he will never ~ ~ much** aus ihm wird nie etwas werden. **(b)** *(impers)* **if it ~s ~ that we're sunk** wenn es dazu kommt, sind wir verloren; **~ ~ that** *or* **if it ~s ~ that, he's just as good** was das betrifft, ist er genauso gut; **when it ~s ~ mathematics** wenn es um Mathematik geht; **it ~s ~ the same thing** das läuft auf dasselbe hinaus. **(c)** *(price, bill)* **how much does it ~ ~?** wieviel macht das? **(d)** *(touch on) point, subject etc* kommen auf *(+acc)*; *(tackle) problem, job etc* herangehen an *(+acc)*.

♦ **come together** *vi* zusammenkommen. **he and his wife have ~ ~ again** er ist wieder mit seiner Frau zusammen.

♦ **come under** *vi +prep obj* **(a) to ~ ~ sb's influence** unter jds Einfluß geraten; **this shop has ~ ~ new management** dieser Laden hat eine neue Geschäftsführung. **(b)** *category, heading* kommen unter *(+acc)*.

♦ **come up** *vi* **(a)** *(lit)* hochkommen; *(diver, submarine)* nach oben kommen; *(sun, moon)* aufgehen. **you've ~ ~ in the world** du bist ja richtig vornehm geworden!; **he came ~ to me with a smile** er kam lächelnd auf mich zu. **(b)** *(Jur) (case)* verhandelt werden; *(accused)* vor Gericht stehen. **(c)** *(for discussion)* aufkommen; *(name)* erwähnt werden. **(d)** *(number in lottery etc)* gewinnen. **to ~ ~ for sale/auction** zum Verkauf/zur Auktion *etc* kommen. **(e)** *(post, job)* frei werden.

♦ **come up against** *vi +prep obj* stoßen auf *(+acc)*; *opposing team* treffen auf *(+acc)*. **the new teacher keeps coming ~ ~ the headmaster** der neue Lehrer gerät ständig mit dem Direktor aneinander.

♦ **come (up)on** *vi +prep obj (find)* stoßen auf *(+acc)*.

♦ **come up to** *vi +prep obj* **(a)** *(reach up to)* gehen *or* reichen bis zu *or* an *(+acc)*. **(b)** *expectations* entsprechen *(+dat)*. **(c)** *(col: approach)* **it's just coming ~ ~ 10** es ist gleich 10.

♦ **come up with** *vi +prep obj answer* haben; *plan* sich *(dat)* ausdenken; *suggestion* machen; *money (raise)* aufbringen; *(pay)* herausrücken *(col)*.

comeback ['kʌmbæk] *n* **(a)** *(Theat etc, fig)* Comeback *nt*. **(b)** *(col: redress)* Anspruch *m* auf Schadenersatz; *(reaction)* Reaktion *f*. **we have no ~** wir können nichts machen.

comedian [kə'mi:dıən] *n* Komiker *m*.

comedienne [kə,mi:dı'en] *n* Komikerin *f*.

comedown ['kʌmdaʊn] *n (col)* Abstieg *m*. **that's a bit of a ~ for you** du bist ganz schön heruntergekommen *(col)*.

comedy ['kɒmıdı] *n* Komödie *f*.

comer ['kʌmə[r]] *n* **"open to all ~s"** „Teilnahme für jedermann".

comet ['kɒmıt] *n* Komet *m*.

come-uppance [,kʌm'ʌpəns] *n (col)*: **to get one's ~** die Quittung kriegen *(col)*.

comfort ['kʌmfət] **1** *n* **(a)** Komfort *m no pl*. **to live in ~** komfortabel leben; **that car was a little too close for ~** für meine Begriffe ist dieses Auto zu nahe herangefahren. **(b)** *(consolation)* Trost *m*. **to take ~ from the fact that ...** sich damit trösten, daß ...; **your presence is a great ~ to me** es beruhigt mich sehr, daß Sie da sind; **small ~** schwacher Trost. **(c)** *(US)* **~ station** öffentliche Toilette. **2** *vt (console)* trösten.

comfortable ['kʌmfətəbl] *adj* **(a)** *armchair, shoes, life* bequem; *room, hotel etc* komfortabel; *temperature* angenehm. **to make sb/oneself ~** es jdm/sich bequem machen; *(make at home)* es jdm/sich gemütlich machen. **(b)** *(fig) income, pension* ausreichend; *life* angenehm; *majority, lead* sicher. **I don't feel too ~ about it** mir ist nicht ganz wohl bei dem Gedanken.

comfortably ['kʌmfətəblı] *adv* **(a)** *sit, dress etc* bequem; *furnished* komfortabel. **(b)** *(fig) win, lead* sicher; *live* angenehm; *afford* gut und gern; *claim, say* ruhig. **they are ~ off** es geht ihnen gut.

comforter ['kəmfətə[r]] *n (US) (on bed)* Deckbett *nt*; *(scarf)* Wollschal *m*.

comforting ['kʌmfətıŋ] *adj* tröstlich.

comfy ['kʌmfı] *adj (+er) (col)* bequem; *room* gemütlich.

comic ['kɒmık] **1** *adj* komisch. **~ strip** Comic strip *m*. **2** *n* **(a)** *(person)* Komiker(in *f*) *m*. **(b)** *(magazine)* Comic-Heft(chen) *nt*. **(c)** *(US)* **~s** Comics *pl*.

comical ['kɒmıkəl] *adj* komisch.

coming ['kʌmıŋ] **1** *n* Kommen *nt*. **~ and going/~s and goings** Kommen und Gehen *nt*. **2** *adj (lit, fig)* kommend.

comma ['kɒmə] *n* Komma *nt*.

command [kə'ma:nd] **1** *vt* **(a)** befehlen. **(b)** *army, ship* befehligen. **(c)** *resources, vocabulary* verfügen über *(+acc)*. **to ~ sb's admiration/respect** jdm Bewunderung/Respekt abnötigen; **he ~s our admiration** wir bewundern ihn. **(d)** *view* bieten *(of* über *+acc)*. **2** *n* **(a)** *(order)* Befehl *m*. **at/by the ~ of** auf Befehl *+gen;* **on ~** auf Befehl. **(b)** *(Mil: power, authority)* Kommando *nt*. **to be in ~** das Kommando haben *(of* über *+acc)*; **to take ~** das Kommando übernehmen *(of gen)*. **(c)** *(fig: possession, mastery)* Beherrschung *f*. **he has a ~ of three foreign languages** er beherrscht drei Fremdsprachen; **to have sb/sth at one's ~** über jdn/etw verfügen; **I am at your ~** ich stehe zu Ihrer Verfügung.

commandant ['kɒmən'dænt] *n (Mil)* Kommandant *m*.

commandeer [,kɒmən'dıə[r]] *vt (Mil) men* einziehen; *(lit, fig) stores, ship, car* beschlagnahmen.

commander [kə'ma:ndə[r]] *n* Führer *m*; *(Mil, Aviat)* Kommandant *m*; *(Naut)* Fregattenkapitän *m*. **~/~s-in-chief** Oberbefehlshaber *m/pl*.

commanding [kə'ma:ndıŋ] *adj* **(a) ~ officer** *(Mil)* befehlshabender Offizier. **(b)** *personality, voice, tone* gebieterisch. **(c)** *(of place)* beherrschend.

commandment [kə'ma:ndmənt] *n (Bibl)* Gebot *nt*.

command module *n (Space)* Kommandokapsel *f*.

commando [kə'ma:ndəʊ] *n, pl* **-s** *(Mil: soldier)* Angehöriger *m* eines Kommando(trupp)s.

command performance *n (Theat)* königliche Galavorstellung.

commemorate [kə'meməreıt] *vt* gedenken *(+gen)*.

commemoration [kə,memə'reıʃən] *n* Gedenken *nt*. **in ~ of** zum Gedenken an *(+acc)*.

commemorative [kə'memərətıv] *adj* Gedenk-. **~ plaque** Gedenktafel *f*.

commence [kə'mens] *vti (form)* beginnen.

commencement [kə'mensmənt] *n (form)* Beginn *m*.

commend [kə'mend] **1** *vt (praise)* loben; *(recommend)* empfehlen. **2** *vr* **to ~ itself** sich empfehlen *(to dat)*.

commendable [kə'mendəbl] *adj* lobenswert.

commendation [,kɒmen'deıʃən] *n (award)* Auszeichnung *f*.

commensurate [kə'menʃərɪt] *adj* entsprechend *(with dat)*. **to be ~ with sth** einer Sache *(dat)* entsprechen.
comment ['kɒmment] **1** *n (remark)* Bemerkung *f (on, about* über *+acc,* zu*)*; *(official)* Kommentar *m (on* zu*)*. **no ~** kein Kommentar! **2** *vi* sich äußern *(on* über *+acc,* zu*)*. **3** *vt* bemerken.
commentary ['kɒməntərɪ] *n* Kommentar *m (on* zu*)*.
commentate ['kɒmenteɪt] *vi (Rad, TV)* Reporter(in) sein *(on* bei*)*.
commentator ['kɒmenteɪtə^r] *n (Rad, TV)* Reporter(in *f*) *m*. **political ~** politischer Kommentator.
commerce ['kɒmɜːs] *n* Handel *m*.
commercial ['kə'mɜːʃəl] **1** *adj* Handels-; *ethics, training* kaufmännisch; *premises, vehicle* Geschäfts-; *production, radio, project, success, attitude etc* kommerziell. **the ~ world** die Geschäftswelt. **2** *n (Rad, TV)* Werbespot *m*.
commercial: ~ art *n* Werbegraphik *f*; **~ college** *n* Fachschule *f* für kaufmännische Berufe.
commercialism [kə'mɜːʃəlɪzəm] *n* Kommerzialisierung *f*.
commercialize [kə'mɜːʃəlaɪz] *vt* kommerzialisieren.
commercial: ~ television *n* Werbefernsehen *nt*; **~ traveller** *(Brit) or* **traveler** *(US) n* Handelsvertreter(in *f*) *m*.
commiserate [kə'mɪzəreɪt] *vi* mitfühlen *(with* mit*)*.
commiseration [kəˌmɪzə'reɪʃən] *n* (An)teilnahme *f no pl*. **my ~s** herzliches Beileid *(on* zu*)*.
commission [kə'mɪʃən] **1** **(a)** *(for building, painting etc)* Auftrag *m*. **(b)** *(Comm: payment)* Provision *f*. **on ~** auf Provision. **(c)** *(Mil)* Patent *nt*. **(d)** *(special committee)* Kommission *f*. **the (EEC) C~** die EG-Kommission. **(e)** *(use)* **in/out of ~** in/außer Betrieb. **2** *vt* **(a)** *person* beauftragen; *book, painting* in Auftrag geben. **to ~ sb to do sth** jdn damit beauftragen, etw zu tun. **(b)** *(Mil) sb* zum Offizier ernennen. **~ed officer** Offizier *m*. **(c)** *(Naut) ship* in Dienst stellen.
commissionaire [kəˌmɪʃə'nɛə^r] *n* Portier *m*.
commissioner [kə'mɪʃənə^r] *n* **(a)** *(member of commission)* Ausschußmitglied *nt*. **(b)** *(of police)* Polizeipräsident *m*.
commit [kə'mɪt] **1** *vt* **(a)** *crime, suicide* begehen. **(b) to have sb ~ted (to an asylum)** jdn in eine Anstalt einweisen lassen; **to ~ sb for trial** jdn einem Gericht überstellen; **to ~ to writing** zu Papier bringen. **2** *vr* sich festlegen *(to* auf *+acc)*. **to ~ oneself on an issue** sich in einer Frage festlegen; **... without ~ting myself to the whole contract ...** ohne damit an den ganzen Vertrag gebunden zu sein.
commitment [kə'mɪtmənt] *n (obligation)* Verpflichtung *f*; *(dedication)* Engagement *nt*.
committed [kə'mɪtɪd] *adj (dedicated)* engagiert.
committee [kə'mɪtɪ] *n* Ausschuß *m*, Komitee *nt*. **~ meeting** Ausschußsitzung *f*; **~ member** Ausschußmitglied *nt*.
commodity [kə'mɒdɪtɪ] *n* Ware *f*; *(agricultural)* Erzeugnis *nt*. **~ market** Rohstoffmarkt *m*.
common ['kɒmən] **1** *adj (+er)* **(a)** *(shared by many)* gemeinsam. **it is ~ knowledge that ...** es ist allgemein bekannt, daß ... **(b)** *(frequently seen or heard etc)* häufig; *word* geläufig; *experience also* allgemein; *belief, custom, animal, bird* (weit)verbreitet; *(customary, usual)* normal. **(c)** *(ordinary)* gewöhnlich. **the ~ man** der Normalbürger; **the ~ people** die einfachen Leute; **it's only ~ decency** das gehört sich einfach. **(d)** *(vulgar, low-class)* gewöhnlich. **2** *n* **(a)** *(land)* Gemeindewiese *f*. **(b) to have sth in ~** etw miteinander gemein haben.
common denominator *n (Math, fig)* gemeinsamer Nenner.
commoner ['kɒmənə^r] *n* Bürgerliche(r) *mf*.
common-law ['kɒmənlɔː] *adj* **she is his ~-law wife** sie lebt mit ihm in eheähnlicher Gemeinschaft.
commonly ['kɒmənlɪ] *adv* **(a)** *(often)* häufig; *(widely)* weithin. **a ~ held belief** eine weitverbreitete Ansicht. **(b)** *(vulgarly)* ordinär.
common: C~ Market *n* Gemeinsamer Markt; **~-or-garden** *adj* Durchschnitts-, Feld-, Wald- und Wiesen- *(esp pej col)*; *topic, novel etc* ganz gewöhnlich; **~place 1** *adj* alltäglich; *(banal) remark* banal; **2** *n* Gemeinplatz *m*; **~room** *n* Aufenthaltsraum *m*; *(for teachers)* Lehrerzimmer *nt*; *(Univ)* Dozentenzimmer *nt*.
Commons ['kɒmənz] *npl* **the ~** *(Parl)* das Unterhaus.
common: ~ sense *n* gesunder Menschenverstand; **~sense** *adj* vernünftig; **C~wealth** *n* **the (British) C~wealth, the C~wealth of Nations** das Commonwealth.
commotion [kə'məʊʃən] Aufruhr *f*; *(noise)* Lärm *m*. **to cause a ~** Aufsehen erregen.
communal ['kɒmjuːnl] *adj* **(a)** *(of a community)* Gemeinde-. **~ life** Gemeinschaftsleben *nt*. **(b)** *(owned, used in common)* gemeinsam.
commune ['kɒmjuːn] **1** *n* Kommune *f*. **2** [kə'mjuːn] *vi* **to ~ with nature** mit der Natur Zwiesprache halten.
communicable [kə'mjuːnɪkəbl] *adj disease* übertragbar.
communicant [kə'mjuːnɪkənt] *n (Eccl)* Kommunikant(in *f*) *m*.
communicate [kə'mjuːnɪkeɪt] **1** *vt news etc* übermitteln; *ideas, feelings* vermitteln; *illness* übertragen *(to* auf *+acc)*. **2** *vi* **(a)** *(be in communication)* in Verbindung stehen. **(b)** *(convey or exchange thoughts)* sich verständigen. **he can't ~** er hat keine Kommunikationsfähigkeit. **(c)** *(rooms)* verbunden sein. **communicating rooms** Zimmer *pl* mit einer Verbindungstür.
communication [kəˌmjuːnɪ'keɪʃən] *n* **(a)** Kommunikation *f*; *(of ideas, information)* Vermittlung *f*; *(of disease)* Übertragung *f*; *(between people)* Verständigung *f*; *(contact)* Verbindung *f*. **to be in ~ with sb** mit jdm in Verbindung stehen *(about* wegen*)*; **to get into ~ with sb about sth** sich mit jdm wegen etw in Verbindung setzen. **(b)** *(letter, message)* Mitteilung *f*. **(c) ~s** *(roads, railways, telegraph lines etc)* Kommunikationswege *pl*; *(Telec)* Nachrichtenwesen *nt*.
communication: ~ cord *n (Brit Rail)* ≃ Notbremse *f*; **~ network** *n* Kommunikationsnetz *nt*; **~s satellite** *n* Nachrichtensatellit *m*; **~ studies** *npl* Kommunikationswissenschaften *pl*.
communicative [kə'mjuːnɪkətɪv] *adj* gesprächig. **~ skills** Kommunikationsfähigkeit *f*.
communion [kə'mjuːnɪən] *n* **(a)** *(intercourse, exchange of feelings etc)* Zwiesprache *f*. **(b)** *(Eccl: also* **C~***) (Protestant)* Abendmahl *nt*; *(Catholic)* Kommunion *f*. **to receive** *or* **take ~** die Kommunion/das Abendmahl empfangen.
communiqué [kə'mjuːnɪkeɪ] *n* Kommuniqué *nt*, (amtliche) Verlautbarung.
communism ['kɒmjʊnɪzəm] *n* Kommunismus *m*.
communist ['kɒmjʊnɪst] **1** *n* Kommunist(in *f*) *m*. **2** *adj* kommunistisch.
community [kə'mjuːnɪtɪ] *n* **(a)** *(social etc group)* Gemeinde *f*. **(b)** *(the public)* Allgemeinheit *f*.
community: ~ centre *(Brit) or* **center** *(US) n* Gemeindezentrum *nt*; **~ chest** *n (US)* Hilfsfonds *m*; **~ relations** *npl* das Verhältnis zwischen den Bevölkerungsgruppen; **~ spirit** *n* Gemeinschaftsgeist *m*.
commute [kə'mjuːt] **1** *vt* umwandeln. **2** *vi (be commuter)* pendeln.
commuter [kə'mjuːtə^r] *n* Pendler(in *f*) *m*. **~ train** Pendlerzug *m*; **the ~ belt** das Einzugsgebiet.
compact[1] [kəm'pækt] *adj (+er)* kompakt; *soil, snow* fest. **~ disk** Compact-disc *f*.
compact[2] ['kɒmpækt] *n* **(a)** *(powder ~)* Puderdose

f. **(b)** *(US: car)* Kompaktauto *nt.*
compact[3] ['kɒmpækt] *n (form: agreement)* Übereinkunft *f.*
companion [kəm'pænjən] *n* **(a)** Begleiter(in *f*) *m.* **travelling ~** Reisegefährte *m,* Reisegefährtin *f.* **(b)** *(friend)* Freund(in *f*) *m.* **(c)** *(one of pair of objects)* Pendant *nt.* **(d)** *(lady's)* Betreuerin *f.*
companionable [kəm'pænjənəbl] *adj* freundlich.
companionship [kəm'pænjənʃɪp] *n* Gesellschaft *f.*
company ['kʌmpənɪ] **1** *n* Gesellschaft *f*; *(guests)* Besuch *m*; *(Comm also)* Firma *f*; *(Theat)* (Schauspiel)truppe *f.* **ship's ~** *(Naut)* Besatzung *f*; **to keep sb ~** jdm Gesellschaft leisten; **she is not fit ~ for your sister** sie ist nicht der richtige Umgang für deine Schwester; **to get into bad ~** in schlechte Gesellschaft geraten; **we have ~ this evening** wir haben heute abend Besuch. **2** *attr* **~ car** Firmenwagen *m*; **~ secretary** *(Brit)* ≃ Prokurist *m.*
comparable ['kɒmpərəbl] *adj* vergleichbar *(with, to* mit*).*
comparative [kəm'pærətɪv] *adj* **(a)** *religion, philology etc* vergleichend. **the ~ form** *(Gram)* der Komparativ. **(b)** *(relative)* relativ. **to live in ~ luxury** relativ luxuriös leben.
comparatively [kəm'pærətɪvlɪ] *adv (relatively)* verhältnismäßig.
compare [kəm'peəʳ] **1** *vt* vergleichen *(with, to* mit*).* **~d with** verglichen mit; **they cannot be ~d** man kann sie nicht vergleichen; **to ~ notes** Eindrücke/Erfahrungen austauschen. **2** *vi* sich vergleichen lassen *(with* mit*).* **it ~s badly/well** es schneidet vergleichsweise schlecht/gut ab. **3** *n:* **beyond ~** unvergleichlich.
comparison [kəm'pærɪsn] *n* Vergleich *m (to* mit*).* **in ~ with** im Vergleich zu.
compartment [kəm'pɑːtmənt] *n (in fridge, desk etc)* Fach *nt*; *(Rail)* Abteil *nt.*
compass ['kʌmpəs] *n* **(a)** Kompaß *m.* **(b) ~es** *pl* **pair of ~es** Zirkel *m.* **(c)** *(fig: extent)* Rahmen *m*; *(of human mind, experience)* Bereich *m.*
compassion [kəm'pæʃən] *n* Mitgefühl *nt (for* mit*).*
compassionate [kəm'pæʃnɪt] *adj* mitfühlend. **on ~ grounds** aus familiären Gründen; **~ leave** Beurlaubung *f* wegen einer dringenden Familienangelegenheit.
compatibility [kəm,pætɪ'bɪlɪtɪ] *n* Vereinbarkeit *f*; *(Med)* Verträglichkeit *f*; *(Tech)* Kompatibilität *f.*
compatible [kəm'pætɪbl] *adj* vereinbar; *(Med)* verträglich; *people* zueinander passend; *colours, furniture* passend; *(Tech)* kompatibel.
compatriot [kəm'pætrɪət] *n* Landsmann *m,* Landsmännin *f.*
compel [kəm'pel] *vt* zwingen. **I feel ~led to tell you ...** ich sehe mich (dazu) gezwungen, Ihnen mitzuteilen, ...
compelling [kəm'pelɪŋ] *adj reason* zwingend; *performance* bezwingend.
compendium [kəm'pendɪəm] *n* Handbuch *nt.*
compensate ['kɒmpənseɪt] *vt (recompense)* entschädigen.
♦ **compensate for** *vi +prep obj (in money etc)* ersetzen; *(make up for, offset)* wieder wettmachen.
compensation [,kɒmpən'seɪʃən] *n (damages)* Entschädigung *f*; *(fig)* Ausgleich *m.*
compère ['kɒmpeəʳ] *(Brit)* **1** *n* Conférencier *m.* **2** *vt* **to ~ a show** bei einer Show der Conférencier sein.
compete [kəm'piːt] *vi* **(a)** konkurrieren. **to ~ with each other** sich (gegenseitig) Konkurrenz machen; **he can't ~ with her** er kann sich nicht mit ihr messen. **(b)** *(Sport)* teilnehmen.
competence ['kɒmpɪtəns], **competency** ['kɒmpɪtənsɪ] *n* Fähigkeit *f*; *(of doctor etc also)* Kompetenz *f.*
competent ['kɒmpɪtənt] *adj* fähig, befähigt *(in* zu*)*; *(in a particular field)* kompetent.
competition [,kɒmpɪ'tɪʃən] *n* **(a)** *no pl* Konkurrenz *f (for* um*).* **(b)** *(contest)* Wettbewerb *m*; *(in newspapers etc)* Preisausschreiben *nt.* **beauty ~** Schönheitswettbewerb *m.*
competitive [kəm'petɪtɪv] *adj* **(a)** *person, attitude* vom Konkurrenzdenken geprägt; *sport* (Wett)kampf-. **a ~ examination** eine Auswahlprüfung. **(b)** *(Comm) business, prices, salaries* konkurrenzfähig.
competitor [kəm'petɪtəʳ] *n* **(a)** Teilnehmer(in *f*) *m.* **(b)** *(Comm)* **our ~s** unsere Konkurrenten.
compile [kəm'paɪl] *vt* zusammenstellen; *material* zusammentragen; *dictionary* verfassen.
complacency [kəmp'leɪsnsɪ] *n* Selbstgefälligkeit *f.*
complacent [kəm'pleɪsənt] *adj* selbstgefällig.
complain [kəm'pleɪn] *vi* sich beklagen *(about* über *+acc)*; *(to make a formal complaint)* sich beschweren *(about* über *+acc, to* bei*).* **(I) can't ~** *(col)* ich kann nicht klagen *(col).*
complaint [kəm'pleɪnt] *n* **(a)** Klage *f*; *(formal ~)* Beschwerde *f.* **(b)** *(illness)* Beschwerden *pl.* **a very rare ~** eine sehr seltene Krankheit.
complement ['kɒmplɪmənt] **1** *n* **(a)** *(also Gram)* Ergänzung *f (to gen).* **(b)** *(full number)* volle Stärke; *(crew of ship)* Besatzung *f.* **2** ['kɒmplɪment] *vt* ergänzen. **to ~ each other** sich ergänzen.
complementary [,kɒmplɪ'mentərɪ] *adj* **they have ~ interests** ihre Interessen ergänzen sich.
complete [kəm'pliːt] **1** *adj* **(a)** *(entire, whole)* ganz *attr*; *wardrobe, deck of cards* komplett; *(having the required numbers)* vollzählig; *edition* Gesamt-. **~ with** komplett mit; **the ~ works of Shakespeare** die gesammelten Werke Shakespeares; **my happiness was ~** mein Glück war vollkommen. **(b)** *attr (total, absolute)* völlig; *failure, disaster, victory* total; *satisfaction, approval* voll. **a ~ idiot** ein Vollidiot *m*; **we were ~ strangers** wir waren uns völlig fremd. **(c)** *(finished)* fertig. **2** *vt* **(a)** *(make whole) collection, set* vervollständigen. **(b)** *(fig) happiness* vollkommen machen. **and to ~ their misery ...** und zu allem Unglück ... **(c)** *(finish)* abschließen. **(d)** *form, questionnaire* ausfüllen.
completely [kəm'pliːtlɪ] *adv* völlig, vollkommen.
completion [kəm'pliːʃən] *n (finishing)* Fertigstellung *f*; *(of project, course, education)* Abschluß *m.* **on ~ of the contract/sale** bei Vertrags-/Kaufabschluß.
complex ['kɒmpleks] **1** *adj* komplex. **2** *n* **(a)** Komplex *m.* **industrial ~** Industriekomplex. **(b)** *(Psych)* Komplex *m.* **he has a ~ about his big ears** er hat Komplexe wegen seiner großen Ohren.
complexion [kəm'plekʃən] *n* **(a)** Teint *m*; *(skin colour)* Gesichtsfarbe *f.* **(b)** *(fig: aspect)* Aspekt *m.* **to put a new/different/sinister** *etc* **~ on sth** etw in einem neuen/anderen/düsteren *etc* Licht erscheinen lassen.
complexity [kəm'pleksɪtɪ] *n* Komplexität *f.*
compliance [kəm'plaɪəns] *n* Einverständnis *nt*; *(with rules etc)* Einhalten *nt (with gen).* **in ~ with the law/our wishes** *etc* dem Gesetz/unseren Wünschen *etc* gemäß.
complicate ['kɒmplɪkeɪt] *vt* komplizieren.
complicated ['kɒmplɪkeɪtɪd] *adj* kompliziert.
complication [,kɒmplɪ'keɪʃən] *n* Komplikation *f*; *(condition)* Kompliziertheit *f.*
complicity [kəm'plɪsɪtɪ] *n* Mittäterschaft *f (in* bei*).*
compliment ['kɒmplɪmənt] **1** *n* **(a)** Kompliment *nt (on* zu, wegen*).* **to pay sb a ~** jdm ein Kompliment machen. **(b)** *(form)* **~s** *pl* Grüße *pl*; **"the ~s of the season"** „frohes Fest"; **"with the ~s of Mr X/the management"** „mit den besten Empfehlungen von Herrn X/der Geschäftsleitung"; **~s slip** *(Comm)* Empfehlungszettel *m.* **2** ['kɒmplɪment] *vt* ein Kompliment/Komplimente machen *(+dat) (on* wegen, zu*).*
complimentary [,kɒmplɪ'mentərɪ] *adj* **(a)** *(prais-*

ing) schmeichelhaft. ~ **close** *(in letter)* Schlußformel *f.* **(b)** *(gratis) seat, ticket* Frei-.

comply [kəm'plaɪ] *vi (person)* einwilligen; *(object, system etc)* den Bedingungen entsprechen. **to ~ with a request/a wish/instructions** einer Bitte/ einem Wunsch/den Anordnungen entsprechen *(form).*

component [kəm'pəʊnənt] *n* Bestandteil *m*; *(Chem, Phys)* Komponente *f.*

compose [kəm'pəʊz] *vt* **(a)** *music* komponieren; *letter, poem* verfassen. **(b)** *(constitute, make up)* bilden. **to be ~d of** sich zusammensetzen aus. **(c) to ~ oneself** sich sammeln.

composed [kəm'pəʊzd] *adj* gefaßt.

composer [kəm'pəʊzə^r] *n* **(a)** *(Mus)* Komponist(in *f*) *m.* **(b)** *(of letter, poem etc)* Verfasser(in *f*) *m.*

composition [ˌkɒmpə'zɪʃən] *n* **(a)** *(act) (of music)* Komponieren *nt*; *(of letter, poem etc)* Verfassen *nt.* **(b)** *(arrangement, Mus, Art)* Komposition *f.* **(c)** *(Sch: essay)* Aufsatz *m.* **(d)** *(constitution, make-up)* Zusammensetzung *f.* **(e) ~ soles** Kunststoffsohlen *pl.*

compositor [kəm'pɒzɪtə^r] *n (Typ)* (Schrift)setzer(in *f*) *m.*

compost ['kɒmpɒst] *n* Kompost *m.*

composure [kəm'pəʊʒə^r] *n* Fassung *f.*

compote ['kɒmpəʊt] *n* Kompott *nt.*

compound ['kɒmpaʊnd] **1** *n (Chem)* Verbindung *f*; *(Gram)* zusammengesetztes Wort; *(enclosed area)* Lager *nt.* **2** *adj* **~ interest** Zinseszins *m*; **~ fracture** komplizierter Bruch. **3** [kəm'paʊnd] *vt (make worse)* verschlimmern.

comprehend [ˌkɒmprɪ'hend] *vt* verstehen.

comprehensible [ˌkɒmprɪ'hensəbl] *adj* verständlich.

comprehension [ˌkɒmprɪ'henʃən] *n (understanding)* Verständnis *nt*; *(school exercise)* Fragen *pl* zum Textverständnis.

comprehensive [ˌkɒmprɪ'hensɪv] *adj* umfassend, ausführlich; *measures, knowledge* umfassend. **~ school** *(Brit)* Gesamtschule *f*; **~ policy** *(Insur)* Vollkasko(versicherung *f*) *nt.*

compress[1] [kəm'pres] **1** *vt* komprimieren *(into* auf *+acc)*; *materials* zusammenpressen *(into* zu*).* **2** *vi* sich komprimieren lassen.

compress[2] ['kɒmpres] *n (Med)* Kompresse *f.*

compressed air [kəm'prest'ɛə^r] *n* Preßluft *f.*

compression [kəm'preʃən] *n* Kompression *f.*

compressor [kəm'presə^r] *n* Kompressor *m.*

comprise [kəm'praɪz] *vt* umfassen.

compromise ['kɒmprəmaɪz] **1** *n* Kompromiß *m.* **2** *adj attr* Kompromiß-. **~ solution** Kompromißlösung *f.* **3** *vi* Kompromisse schließen *(about* in *+dat).* **not prepared to ~** nicht kompromißbereit. **4** *vt* kompromittieren.

compulsion [kəm'pʌlʃən] *n* Zwang *m*; *(Psych)* innerer Zwang. **under ~** unter Druck; **you are under no ~** niemand zwingt Sie.

compulsive [kəm'pʌlsɪv] *adj* Zwangs-; *behaviour* zwanghaft. **he is a ~ eater** er leidet an einem Eßzwang; **he is a ~ liar** er hat einen krankhaften Trieb zu lügen; **he's a ~ smoker** das Rauchen ist bei ihm zur Sucht geworden; **it makes ~ viewing** das muß man unbedingt sehen.

compulsory [kəm'pʌlsərɪ] *adj* obligatorisch; *measures* Zwangs-; *subject* Pflicht-. **that is ~** das ist Pflicht; **education is ~** es besteht (allgemeine) Schulpflicht; **~ purchase** Enteignung *f.*

compunction [kəm'pʌŋkʃən] *n (liter)* Schuldgefühle *pl.* **with no ~** ohne sich schuldig zu fühlen.

computation ['kɒmpjʊ'teɪʃən] *n* Berechnung *f.*

compute [kəm'pjuːt] *vt* berechnen *(at* auf *+acc).*

computer [kəm'pjuːtə^r] *n* Computer, Rechner *m.*

computerization [kəmˌpjuːtəraɪ'zeɪʃən] *n (of information etc)* Computerisierung *f.* **the ~ of the factory** die Umstellung der Fabrik auf Computer.

computerize [kəm'pjuːtəraɪz] *vt information* computerisieren; *company, accounting methods* auf EDV umstellen.

computer: ~-operated *adj* computergesteuert; **~ program** *n* Programm *nt*; **~ programmer** *n* Programmierer(in *f*) *m*; **~ science** *n* Informatik *f.*

comrade ['kɒmrɪd] *n* Kamerad *m*; *(Pol)* Genosse *m*, Genossin *f.*

con [kɒn] *(col)* **1** *n* Schwindel *m.* **~ man** Schwindler *m.* **2** *vt* hereinlegen *(col).* **he ~ned her out of all her money** er hat sie um ihr ganzes Geld gebracht.

concave ['kɒn'keɪv] *adj* konkav; *mirror* Hohl-.

conceal [kən'siːl] *vt (hide)* verbergen; *(keep secret)* verheimlichen.

concealed [kən'siːld] *adj* verborgen; *lighting* indirekt; *entrance* verdeckt.

concede [kən'siːd] *vt* **(a)** *(yield) privilege* aufgeben; *lands* abtreten *(to* an *+acc)*; *(Sport) corner, penalty* verursachen. **to ~ victory to sb** vor jdm kapitulieren; **to ~ a point to sb** *(in debate)* jdm in einem Punkt recht geben. **(b)** *(admit, grant)* einräumen. **to ~ defeat** sich geschlagen geben.

conceit [kən'siːt] *n (pride)* Einbildung *f.*

conceited [kən'siːtɪd] *adj* eingebildet.

conceivable [kən'siːvəbl] *adj* denkbar. **the worst ~ thing to say** das denkbar Schlechteste, was man sagen kann.

conceivably [kən'siːvəblɪ] *adv* **she may ~ be right** es ist durchaus denkbar, daß sie recht hat.

conceive [kən'siːv] **1** *vt* **(a)** *child* empfangen. **(b)** *(imagine)* sich *(dat)* vorstellen; *idea, plan* haben; *novel* die Idee haben zu. **I can't ~ why** ich verstehe nicht, warum. **2** *vi (woman)* empfangen.

concentrate ['kɒnsəntreɪt] **1** *vt* konzentrieren *(on* auf *+acc).* **2** *vi* **(a)** *(give one's attention)* sich konzentrieren. **(b)** *(people)* sich sammeln. **3** *n (Chem)* Konzentrat *nt.*

concentration [ˌkɒnsən'treɪʃən] *n* Konzentration *f.* **powers of ~** Konzentrationsfähigkeit *f.*

concentration camp *n* Konzentrationslager, KZ *nt.*

concept ['kɒnsept] *n* Begriff *m*; *(conception)* Vorstellung *f.*

conception [kən'sepʃən] *n* **(a)** *(idea)* Vorstellung *f*; *(way sth is conceived)* Auffassung *f.* **the writer's powers of ~** die Vorstellungskraft des Schriftstellers. **he has no ~ of how difficult it is** er macht sich *(dat)* keinen Begriff davon, wie schwer das ist. **(b)** *(of child)* die Empfängnis.

concern [kən'sɜːn] **1** *n* **(a)** *(connection)* **to have no ~ with sth** mit etw nichts zu tun haben. **(b)** *(business, affair)* Angelegenheit(en *pl*) *f*; *(matter of importance to a person)* Anliegen *nt.* **it's no ~ of his** das geht ihn nichts an; **what ~ is it of yours?** was geht Sie das an? **(c)** *(Comm)* Konzern *m.* **(d)** *(anxiety)* Sorge *f.* **a look of ~** ein besorgter Blick; **there's some/no cause for ~** es besteht Grund/ kein Grund zur Sorge; **he showed great ~ for your safety** er zeigte sich sehr um Ihre Sicherheit besorgt.

2 *vt* **(a)** *(be about)* handeln von.

(b) *(be the business of, involve)* angehen, betreffen. **that doesn't ~ you** das betrifft Sie nicht; *(as snub)* das geht Sie nichts an; **to whom it may ~** *(on letter)* an den betreffenden Sachbearbeiter; *(on certificate)* Bestätigung *f*; *(on reference)* Zeugnis *nt*; **as far as I'm ~ed** was mich betrifft; **as far as I'm ~ed you can do what you like** von mir aus kannst du tun und lassen, was du willst; **the persons ~ed** die Betroffenen.

(c) *(interest)* **he is only ~ed with facts** ihn interessieren nur die Fakten; *(is only dealing with)* ihm geht es nur um die Fakten.

(d) *(worry)* **there's no need for you to ~ yourself about that** darum brauchen Sie sich nicht zu kümmern; **to be ~ed about sth** sich *(dat)* um etw Sorgen machen, um etw besorgt sein;

don't ~ yourself machen Sie sich keine Sorgen; **I was very ~ed about** *or* **for your safety** ich war sehr um Ihre Sicherheit besorgt.
concerning [kən'sɜːnɪŋ] *prep* bezüglich *(+gen)*, hinsichtlich *(+gen)*. **~ your request ...** was Ihre Anfrage betrifft ...
concert ['kɒnsət] *n (Mus)* Konzert *nt*. **in ~** *(fig)* gemeinsam.
concerted [kən'sɜːtɪd] *adj efforts* vereint; *action* gemeinsam.
concert: ~goer *n* Konzertbesucher(in *f*) *m*; **~ grand** *n* Konzertflügel *m*; **~ hall** *n* Konzertsaal *m*.
concertina [ˌkɒnsə'tiːnə] *n* Konzertina *f*.
concertmaster ['kɒnsətmæstəʳ] *n (esp US)* Konzertmeister *m*.
concerto [kən'tʃɛːtəʊ] *n* Konzert, Concerto *nt*.
concert: ~ pianist *n* Pianist(in *f*) *m*: **~ pitch** *n* Kammerton *m*; **~ tour** *n* Konzerttournee *f*.
concession [kən'seʃən] *n* Zugeständnis *nt (to* an *+acc)*; *(Comm)* Konzession *f*.
concessionary [kən'seʃənərɪ] *adj (Comm)* Konzessions-.
conciliate [kən'sɪlɪeɪt] *vt* **(a)** *(placate)* besänftigen. **(b)** *(reconcile) opposing views* in Einklang bringen.
conciliatory [kən'sɪlɪətərɪ] *adj* versöhnlich; *(placatory)* beschwichtigend.
concise [kən'saɪs] *adj* präzis(e). **~ dictionary** Handwörterbuch *nt*.
conclude [kən'kluːd] **1** *vt* **(a)** *(end) meeting, letter, speech* schließen. **(b)** *(arrange) treaty, deal* abschließen. **(c)** *(decide)* **to ~ that ...** zu dem Schluß kommen, daß ...; **what do you ~ from this?** was schließen Sie daraus? **2** *vi (meetings, events)* enden; *(letter, speech)* schließen. **the concluding paragraph** der letzte Abschnitt.
conclusion [kən'kluːʒən] *n* **(a)** *(end, settling)* Abschluß *m*; *(of essay, novel etc)* Schluß *m*. **in ~** zum (Ab)schluß. **(b)** *(deduction)* Schluß(folgerung *f*) *m*. **to come to the ~ that ...** zu dem Schluß kommen, daß ...
conclusive [kən'kluːsɪv] *adj (convincing)* überzeugend; *(decisive, final)* endgültig; *(Jur) evidence* einschlägig; *proof* schlüssig.
concoct [kən'kɒkt] *vt* **(a)** *(Cook etc)* zusammenstellen. **(b)** *(fig)* sich *(dat)* zurechtlegen; *new dress, hat* zaubern; *story, alibi* sich *(dat)* ausdenken.
concoction [kən'kɒkʃən] *n (food)* Zusammenstellung *f*; *(drink)* Gebräu *nt*; *(story)* Lügengeschichte *f*; *(fashion)* Spielerei *f*.
concord ['kɒŋkɔːd] *n (harmony)* Eintracht *f*.
concourse ['kɒŋkɔːs] *n (place)* Eingangshalle *f*. **station ~** Bahnhofshalle *f*.
concrete[1] ['kɒŋkriːt] *adj object, example* konkret.
concrete[2] *n (Build)* Beton *m*. **~ mixer** Betonmischmaschine *f*. **2** *adj* Beton-. **3** *vt wall, floor* betonieren.
concur [kən'kɜːʳ] *vi* **(a)** *(agree)* übereinstimmen; *(with a suggestion etc)* beipflichten *(with dat)*. **I ~ with that** ich pflichte dem bei. **(b)** *(happen together)* zusammentreffen.
concurrent [kən'kʌrənt] *adj* gleichzeitig.
concuss [kən'kʌs] *vt (usu pass)* **to be ~ed** eine Gehirnerschütterung haben.
concussion [kən'kʌʃən] *n* Gehirnerschütterung *f*.
condemn [kən'dem] *vt* **(a)** *(censure, Jur, fig)* verurteilen. **to ~ sb to death** jdn zum Tode verurteilen. **(b)** *(declare unfit) building, slums* für abbruchreif erklären; *food* für den Verzehr ungeeignet erklären.
condemnation [ˌkɒndem'neɪʃən] *n* Verurteilung *f*.
condensation [ˌkɒnden'seɪʃən] *n* **(a)** *(of vapour)* Kondensation *f*; *(liquid formed)* Kondensat *nt*. **the windows/walls are covered with ~** die Fenster/Wände sind beschlagen. **(b)** *(short form)* Kurzfassung *f*.
condense [kən'dens] **1** *vt* **(a)** kondensieren. **~d milk** (gesüßte) Kondensmilch *f*. **(b)** *(Phys) gas* kondensieren; *(compress)* verdichten. **(c)** *(shorten)* zusammenfassen. **2** *vi (gas)* kondensieren.
condenser [kən'densəʳ] *n (Elec, Phys)* Kondensator *m*.
condescend [ˌkɒndɪ'send] *vi* sich herablassen.
condescending [ˌkɒndɪ'sendɪŋ] *adj (pej)* herablassend.
condescension [ˌkɒndɪ'senʃən] *n (pej)* Herablassung *f*.
condition [kən'dɪʃən] **1** *n* **(a)** *(determining factor)* Bedingung *f (also Jur, Comm)*; *(prerequisite)* Voraussetzung *f*. **on ~ that ...** unter der Voraussetzung, daß ...; **on no ~** auf keinen Fall; **to make ~s** Bedingungen stellen.
(b) ~s *pl (circumstances)* Verhältnisse *pl*; **working ~s** Arbeitsbedingungen *pl*; **living ~s** Wohnverhältnisse *pl*.
(c) *no pl (state)* Zustand *m*. **he is in good/bad ~** er ist in guter/schlechter Verfassung; **it is in good/bad ~** es ist in gutem/schlechtem Zustand; **you're in no ~ to drive** du bist nicht fahrtüchtig; **to be in/out of ~** eine gute/keine Kondition haben; **to keep in/get into ~** in Form bleiben/kommen.
(d) *(Med)* Beschwerden *pl*. **he has a heart ~** er ist herzkrank.
2 *vt* **(a)** *(esp pass: determine)* bedingen. **to be ~ed by** bedingt sein durch. **(b)** *(Psych etc: train)* konditionieren; *(accustom)* gewöhnen. **~ed reflex** bedingter Reflex.
conditional [kən'dɪʃənl] *adj* **(a)** mit Vorbehalt, bedingt. **to be ~ (up)on sth** von etw abhängen. **(b)** *(Gram)* konditional, Bedingungs-. **the ~ mood/tense** das Konditional.
conditioner [kən'dɪʃənəʳ] *n (for hair)* Haarschnellkur *f*; *(for fabrics)* Weichspüler *m*.
condolence [kən'dəʊləns] *n* Beileid *nt no pl*.
condom ['kɒndəm] *n* Kondom *nt or m*.
condominium [ˌkɒndə'mɪnɪəm] *n (US)* Eigentumswohnung *f*; *(block)* Eigenstumsblock *m*.
condone [kən'dəʊn] *vt (overlook)* hinwegsehen über *(+acc)*; *(tacitly approve)* (stillschweigend) dulden.
conducive [kən'djuːsɪv] *adj* dienlich *(to dat)*.
conduct ['kɒndʌkt] **1** *n* **(a)** *(behaviour)* Verhalten, Benehmen *nt (towards* gegenüber*)*. **(b)** *(management)* Führung *f*. **2** [kən'dʌkt] *vt* **(a)** *(guide)* führen. **~ed tour (of)** *(Brit) (of country)* Gesellschaftsreise *f* (durch); *(of building)* Führung *f* (durch). **(b)** *(direct, manage)* führen; *meeting* leiten; *investigation* durchführen. **(c)** *(Mus)* dirigieren. **(d)** *(Phys, Physiol)* leiten; *lightning* ableiten. **3** [kən'dʌkt] *vr* **to ~ oneself** sich benehmen.
conduction [kən'dʌkʃən] *n (Phys)* Leitung *f*.
conductivity [ˌkɒndʌk'tɪvɪtɪ] *n (Phys)* Leitfähigkeit *f*.
conductor [kən'dʌktəʳ] *n* **(a)** *(Mus)* Dirigent(in *f*) *m*. **(b)** *(bus, tram ~)* Schaffner *m*; *(US Rail: guard)* Zugführer *m*. **(c)** *(Phys)* Leiter *m*; *(lightning ~)* Blitzableiter *m*.
conductress [kən'dʌktrɪs] *n (on bus etc)* Schaffnerin *f*.
conduit ['kɒndɪt] *n* Leitungsrohr *nt*.
cone [kəʊn] *n* **(a)** Kegel *m*. **(b)** *(Bot)* Zapfen *m*. **(c)** *(ice-cream ~)* (Eis)tüte *f*.
cone-shaped ['kəʊn'ʃeɪpt] *adj* kegelförmig.
confab ['kɒnfæb] *n (col)* kleine Besprechung.
confectioner's [kən'fekʃənəz] *n (Brit)* Süßwarenladen *m*.
confectionery [kən'fekʃənərɪ] *n* Süßwaren *pl*; *(chocolates)* Konfekt *nt*.
confederate [kən'fedərɪt] **1** *adj system* konföderiert; *nations* verbündet. **2** *n (Pol: ally)* Verbündete(r) *m*; *(pej: accomplice)* Komplize *m (pej)*.

confederation [kənˌfedə'reɪʃən] *n* **(a)** *(Pol) (alliance)* Bündnis *nt*; *(system of government)* Staatenbund *m*. **the Swiss C~** die Schweizer Eidgenossenschaft. **(b)** *(association)* Bund *m*. **C~ of British Industry** Bund *m* britischer Industrieller.
confer [kən'fɜːʳ] **1** *vt title, degree* verleihen *(on, upon sb* jdm*)*. **2** *vi* sich beraten.
conference ['kɒnfərəns] *n* Konferenz *f*; *(more informal)* Besprechung *f*.
confess [kən'fes] **1** *vt* **(a)** *(acknowledge)* gestehen. **(b)** *(Eccl) sins* bekennen; *(to priest)* beichten; *(priest) penitent* die Beichte abnehmen *(+dat)*. **2** *vi* **(a)** gestehen *(to acc)*. **to ~ to sth** etw gestehen. **(b)** *(Eccl)* beichten.
confession [kən'feʃən] *n* **(a)** Eingeständnis *nt*; *(of guilt, crime etc)* Geständnis *nt*. **I have a ~ to make** ich muß dir etwas gestehen. **(b)** *(Eccl: of sins)* Beichte *f*. **~ of faith** Glaubensbekenntnis *nt*; **to make one's ~** seine Sünden bekennen.
confessional [kən'feʃənl] *n* Beichtstuhl *m*.
confessor [kən'fesəʳ] *n (Eccl)* Beichtvater *m*.
confetti [kən'fetiː] *n no pl* Konfetti *nt*.
confidant [ˌkɒnfɪ'dænt] *n* Vertraute(r) *m*.
confidante [ˌkɒnfɪ'dænt] *n* Vertraute *f*.
confide [kən'faɪd] **1** *vt* anvertrauen *(to sb* jdm*)*. **2** *vi* **to ~ in sb** jdn ins Vertrauen ziehen.
confidence ['kɒnfɪdəns] *n* **(a)** *(trust)* Vertrauen *nt*; *(confident expectation)* Zuversicht *f*. **to have (every/no) ~ in sb/sth** (volles/kein) Vertrauen zu jdm/etw haben; **I have every ~ that ...** ich bin ganz zuversichtlich, daß ...; **to give/ask for a vote of ~** *(Parl)* das Vertrauen aussprechen/die Vertrauensfrage stellen; **motion/vote of no ~** Mißtrauensantrag *m*/-votum *nt*. **(b)** *(self-~)* (Selbst)vertrauen *nt*. **(c)** *(confidential relationship)* Vertrauen *nt*. **in (strict) ~** (streng) vertraulich; **to take sb into one's ~** jdn ins Vertrauen ziehen. **(d)** *(information confided)* vertrauliche Mitteilung.
confidence: ~ trick, ~trickster *n* = **con trick, con-man.**
confident ['kɒnfɪdənt] *adj* **(a)** *(sure)* überzeugt; *look etc* zuversichtlich. **(b)** *(self-assured)* (selbst)sicher.
confidential [ˌkɒnfɪ'denʃəl] *adj information* vertraulich. **~ secretary** Privatsekretär(in *f*) *m*.
confidentially [ˌkɒnfɪ'denʃəlɪ] *adv* im Vertrauen.
confine [kən'faɪn] *vt* **(a)** *(keep in)* (ein)sperren. **~d to bed/the house** ans Bett/ans Haus gefesselt; **to be ~d to barracks** Kasernenarrest haben. **(b)** *(limit)* beschränken *(to* auf *+acc)*. **to ~ oneself to doing sth** sich darauf beschränken, etw zu tun.
confined [kən'faɪnd] *adj space* beschränkt; *atmosphere* beengend.
confinement [kən'faɪnmənt] *n* **(a)** *(imprisonment) (act)* Einsperren *nt*; *(in jail)* Haft *f*. **(b)** *(dated: childbirth)* Niederkunft *(dated) f*.
confines ['kɒnfaɪnz] *npl* Grenzen *pl*.
confirm [kən'fɜːm] *vt* **(a)** *(verify)* bestätigen. **(b)** *(strengthen)* bestärken; *one's resolve* bekräftigen. **(c)** *(Eccl)* konfirmieren; *Roman Catholic* firmen.
confirmation [ˌkɒnfə'meɪʃən] *n* **(a)** Bestätigung *f*. **(b)** *(Eccl)* Konfirmation *f*; *(of Roman Catholics)* Firmung *f*.
confirmed [kən'fɜːmd] *adj* erklärt; *bachelor* eingefleischt.
confiscate ['kɒnfɪskeɪt] *vt* beschlagnahmen.
conflict ['kɒnflɪkt] **1** *n* Konflikt *m*; *(between two accounts etc)* Widerspruch *m*; *(fighting)* Zusammenstoß *m*. **to come into ~ with sb/sth** mit jdm/etw in Konflikt geraten; **~ of interests/opinions** Interessen-/Meinungskonflikt *m*. **2** [kən'flɪkt] *vi* im Widerspruch stehen *(with* zu*)*.
conflicting [kən'flɪktɪŋ] *adj* widersprüchlich.
conform [kən'fɔːm] *vi (things: comply with)* entsprechen *(to dat)*; *(people: socially)* sich anpassen *(to* an *+acc)*; *(things, people: to rules etc)* sich richten *(to* nach*)*.
conformity [kən'fɔːmɪtɪ] *n* **(a)** *(uniformity)* Konformismus *m*. **(b)** *(compliance)* Übereinstimmung *f*; *(socially)* Anpassung *f (with* an *+acc)*. **to be in ~ with sth** einer Sache *(dat)* entsprechen; **in ~ with** entsprechend *(+dat)*.
confound [kən'faʊnd] *vt (amaze)* verblüffen; *(throw into confusion)* verwirren. **~ it!** *(col)* verflixt noch mal! *(col)*.
confounded [kən'faʊndɪd] *adj (col)* verflixt *(col)*; *noise* Heiden- *(col)*.
confront [kən'frʌnt] *vt* **(a)** *(face)* gegenübertreten *(+dat)*; *(problems, decisions)* sich stellen *(+dat)*. **(b)** *(bring face to face with)* konfrontieren. **to ~ sb with sb/sth** jdn mit jdm/etw konfrontieren.
confrontation [ˌkɒnfrən'teɪʃən] *n* Konfrontation *f (also Pol)*; *(with witnesses, evidence etc)* Gegenüberstellung *f*.
confuse [kən'fjuːz] *vt* **(a)** *(bewilder, perplex)* verwirren, durcheinanderbringen. **(b)** *(mix up)* verwechseln.
confused [kən'fjuːzd] *adj (muddled)* konfus; *person also* verwirrt; *(through old age, after anaesthetic etc)* wirr im Kopf; *idea, report, situation* verworren.
confusing [kən'fjuːzɪŋ] *adj* verwirrend.
confusion [kən'fjuːʒən] *n* **(a)** *(disorder)* Durcheinander *nt*; *(jumble)* Wirrwarr *m*. **(b)** *(perplexity)* Verwirrung *f*; *(mental ~: after drugs, blow on head etc)* Verwirrtheit *f*; *(through old age etc)* Wirrheit *f*. **in the ~ of the moment** im Eifer des Gefechts. **(c)** *(mixing up)* Verwechslung *f*.
congeal [kən'dʒiːl] *vi* erstarren; *(glue, mud)* hart werden; *(blood)* gerinnen.
congenial [kən'dʒiːnɪəl] *adj (pleasant)* angenehm.
congenital [kən'dʒenɪtl] *adj deficiency, disease* angeboren. **~ defect** Geburtsfehler *m*; **~ idiot** *(col)* Vollidiot *m (col)*.
congested [kən'dʒestɪd] *adj* überfüllt; *(with traffic)* verstopft.
congestion [kən'dʒestʃən] *n (traffic, pedestrians)* Stau *m*; *(overpopulation)* Übervölkerung *f*; *(Med)* Blutstau *m*.
conglomerate [kən'glɒmərɪt] *n (also Geol, Comm)* Konglomerat *nt*.
conglomeration [kənˌglɒmə'reɪʃən] *n* Ansammlung *f*.
congratulate [kən'grætjʊleɪt] *vt* gratulieren *(+dat) (on* zu*)*.
congratulations [kənˌgrætjʊ'leɪʃənz] **1** *npl* Glückwünsche *pl*. **2** *interj* (ich) gratuliere!; **~ (on your success)!** herzlichen Glückwunsch (zu deinem Erfolg)!
congregate ['kɒŋgrɪgeɪt] *vi* sich sammeln; *(on a particular occasion)* sich versammeln.
congregation [ˌkɒŋgrɪ'geɪʃən] *n* **(a)** Versammlung *f*. **(b)** *(Eccl)* Gemeinde *f*.
congress ['kɒŋgres] *n* **(a)** *(meeting)* Kongreß *m*; *(of political party)* Parteitag *m*. **(b) C~** *(US etc Pol)* der Kongreß.
Congressman ['kɒŋgresmən] *n, pl* **-men** [-mən] Kongreßabgeordnete(r) *m*.
Congresswoman ['kɒŋgresˌwʊmən] *n, pl* **-women** [-ˌwɪmɪn] Kongreßabgeordnete *f*.
conic ['kɒnɪk] *adj* **(a)** *(Math)* konisch. **~ section** Kegelschnitt *m*. **(b)** *(also* **~al***)* kegelförmig.
conifer ['kɒnɪfəʳ] *n* Nadelbaum *m*. **~s** Nadelhölzer *pl*.
coniferous [kə'nɪfərəs] *adj tree, forest* Nadel-.
conjecture [kən'dʒektʃəʳ] **1** *vt* mutmaßen *(geh)*. **2** *vi* Mutmaßungen anstellen. **3** *n* Mutmaßung *f*.
conjugal ['kɒndʒʊgəl] *adj bliss, duties* ehelich.
conjugate ['kɒndʒʊgeɪt] *vt (Gram)* konjugieren.
conjugation [ˌkɒndʒʊ'geɪʃən] *n (Gram)* Konjugation *f*.
conjunction [kən'dʒʌŋkʃən] **(a)** *(Gram)* Konjunk-

tion *f.* **(b)** *(association)* Verbindung *f.* **in ~** zusammen.
conjunctivitis [kən,dʒʌŋktɪ'vaɪtɪs] *n (Med)* Bindehautentzündung *f.*
conjure ['kʌndʒəʳ] *vti* zaubern.
♦ **conjure up** *vt sep ghost, spirits* beschwören; *(fig) memories etc* heraufbeschwören.
conjurer, conjuror ['kʌndʒərəʳ] *n* Zauberkünstler(in *f*) *m.*
conjuring ['kʌndʒərɪŋ] *n* Zaubern *nt;* **~ set** Zauberkasten *m;* **~ trick** Zauberkunststück *nt.*
♦ **conk out** [,kɒŋk'aʊt] *vi (col)* den Geist aufgeben; *(person)* umkippen *(col).*
conker ['kɒŋkəʳ] *n (Brit col)* (Roß)kastanie *f.*
con-man ['kɒnmæn] *n, pl* **-men** [-men] *(col)* Schwindler *m; (pretending to have social status)* Hochstapler *m; (promising marriage)* Heiratsschwindler *m.*
connect [kə'nekt] **1** *vt* **(a)** *(join)* verbinden *(to, with* mit); *(Elec etc: also* **~ up***) appliances, subscribers* anschließen *(to* an *+acc).* **I'll ~ you** *(Telec)* ich verbinde (Sie); **to be ~ed** *(two things)* miteinander verbunden sein. **(b)** *(fig: associate)* in Verbindung bringen. **(c)** *(esp pass: link) ideas, theories etc* verbinden. **to be ~ed with** eine Beziehung haben zu; *(be related to)* verwandt sein mit. **2** *vi (rooms)* eine Verbindung haben *(to, with* zu); *(train, plane)* Anschluß haben *(with* an *+acc).* **his punch didn't ~** sein Schlag hat nicht getroffen.
connection, connexion [kə'nekʃən] *n* **(a)** Verbindung *f (to, with* zum, mit); *(wire)* Leitung *f; (to mains)* Anschluß *m (to* an *+acc); (connecting part)* Verbindung(sstück *nt*) *f.* **parallel/series ~** Parallel-/Reihenschaltung *f.* **(b)** *(fig: link)* Zusammenhang *m.* **the two events are not ~ed** zwischen den beiden Ereignissen besteht kein Zusammenhang; **in this ~** in diesem Zusammenhang; **in ~ with** in Zusammenhang mit. **(c)** *(relationship, business ~)* Beziehung *f (with* zu); *(family ~)* familiäre Beziehung. **to have ~s** Beziehungen haben; **there is some family ~ between them** sie sind weitläufig miteinander verwandt. **(d)** *(Rail etc)* Anschluß *m.*
conning tower ['kɒnɪŋtaʊəʳ] *n* Kommandoturm *m.*
connivance [kə'naɪvəns] *n (tacit consent)* stillschweigendes Einverständnis.
connive [kə'naɪv] *vi* **(a)** *(conspire)* sich verschwören. **(b)** *(deliberately overlook)* **to ~ at sth** etw stillschweigend dulden.
connoisseur [,kɒnə'sɜːʳ] *n* Kenner *m.*
connotation [,kɒnəʊ'teɪʃən] *n* Assoziation *f.*
conquer ['kɒŋkəʳ] *vt* **(a)** *(lit) country, the world* erobern; *enemy, nation* besiegen. **(b)** *(fig) mountain* bezwingen; *people, sb's heart* erobern.
conquering ['kɒŋkərɪŋ] *adj hero* siegreich.
conqueror ['kɒŋkərəʳ] *n (of country, heart)* Eroberer *m; (fig)* Sieger *m (of* über *+acc); (of mountain)* Bezwinger *m (of gen).*
conquest ['kɒŋkwest] *n* Eroberung *f; (of enemy etc, disease)* Sieg *m (of* über *+acc); (col: person)* Eroberung *f; (of mountain)* Bezwingung *f.*
conscience ['kɒnʃəns] *n* Gewissen *nt.* **to have a clear/easy/bad ~** ein reines/gutes/schlechtes Gewissen haben *(about* wegen); **to have sth on one's ~** etw auf dem Gewissen haben; **with an easy ~** mit ruhigem Gewissen; **in (all) ~** allen Ernstes.
conscience-stricken ['kɒnʃəns,strɪkən] *adj* schuldbewußt.
conscientious [,kɒnʃɪ'enʃəs] *adj (diligent)* gewissenhaft; *(conscious of one's duty)* pflichtbewußt. **~ objector** Kriegsdienstverweigerer *m (aus Gewissensgründen).*
conscientiousness [,kɒnʃɪ'enʃəsnɪs] *n* Gewissenhaftigkeit *f; (sense of duty)* Pflichtbewußtsein *nt.*
conscious ['kɒnʃəs] *adj* **(a)** *(Med)* bei Bewußtsein. **(b)** *(aware)* bewußt *(also Psych).* **to be/become ~ of sth** sich *(dat)* einer Sache *(gen)* bewußt sein/werden. **(c)** *(deliberate)* bewußt.
consciousness ['kɒnʃəsnɪs] *n* **(a)** *(Med)* Bewußtsein *nt.* **to lose/regain ~** das Bewußtsein verlieren/wiedererlangen. **(b)** *(awareness)* Wissen *nt (of* um).
conscript [kən'skrɪpt] **1** *vt* einziehen; *army* ausheben. **2** ['kɒnskrɪpt] *n* Wehrpflichtige(r) *m.*
conscription [kən'skrɪpʃən] *n* Wehrpflicht *f; (act of conscripting)* Einberufung *f; (of army)* Aushebung *f.*
consecrate ['kɒnsɪkreɪt] *vt (lit, fig)* weihen.
consecration [,kɒnsɪ'kreɪʃən] *n* Weihe *f; (in mass)* Wandlung *f.*
consecutive [kən'sekjʊtɪv] *adj* aufeinanderfolgend; *numbers* fortlaufend. **on four ~ days** vier Tage hintereinander.
consensus [kən'sensəs] *n* Übereinstimmung *f.* **the ~ is that ...** man ist allgemein der Meinung, daß ...; **that's the ~ of opinion** das ist die allgemeine Meinung.
consent [kən'sent] **1** *vi* zustimmen *(to dat).* **to ~ to do sth** sich bereit erklären, etw zu tun. **2** *n* Zustimmung *(to* zu*) f.* **by mutual ~** in gegenseitigem Einverständnis; **the age of ~** das Ehemündigkeitsalter; **she's below the age of ~** sie ist noch minderjährig.
consequence ['kɒnsɪkwəns] *n* **(a)** *(result, effect)* Folge *f.* **in ~** folglich; **in ~ of** infolge *(+gen);* **in ~ of which** infolgedessen; **to take the ~s** die Konsequenzen tragen. **(b)** *(importance)* Bedeutung *f.* **it's of no ~** das spielt keine Rolle.
consequent ['kɒnsɪkwənt] *adj attr* daraus folgend; *(temporal)* darauffolgend.
consequently ['kɒnsɪkwəntlɪ] *adv* folglich.
conservation [,kɒnsə'veɪʃən] *n (preservation)* Erhaltung *f.* **~ area** *(in the country)* Naturschutzgebiet *nt; (in town)* unter Denkmalschutz stehendes Gebiet.
conservationist [,kɒnsə'veɪʃənɪst] *n* Umweltschützer(in *f*) *m; (as regards old buildings etc)* Denkmalpfleger(in *f*) *m.*
conservative [kən'sɜːvətɪv] *adj (also Pol)* konservativ. **at a ~ estimate** bei vorsichtiger Schätzung.
conservatory [kən'sɜːvətrɪ] *n* **(a)** *(Hort)* Wintergarten *m.* **(b)** *(esp US: Mus etc)* Konservatorium *nt.*
conserve [kən'sɜːv] *vt* erhalten; *one's strength* schonen; *energy* sparen.
consider [kən'sɪdəʳ] *vt* **(a)** *(reflect upon) plan, idea, offer* nachdenken über *(+acc).* **I'll ~ the matter** ich werde mir die Sache durch den Kopf gehen lassen; **have you ~ed the possibility of ...?** haben Sie an die Möglichkeit gedacht, zu...?; **I wouldn't even ~ it!** ich denke nicht daran! **(b)** *(bear in mind)* in Erwägung ziehen; *(take into account)* denken an *(+acc),* berücksichtigen; *person, feelings also* Rücksicht nehmen auf *(+acc).* **~ how much you owe him** bedenken Sie, wieviel Sie ihm schulden; **all things ~ed** alles in allem. **(c)** *(regard as)* betrachten als; *person* halten für. **to ~ oneself lucky** sich glücklich schätzen.
considerable [kən'sɪdərəbl] *adj* beträchtlich.
considerably [kən'sɪdərəblɪ] *adv* beträchtlich.
considerate [kən'sɪdərɪt] *adj* rücksichtsvoll *(to(wards)* gegenüber); *(kind)* aufmerksam.
consideration [kən,sɪdə'reɪʃən] *n* **(a)** *no pl (careful thought)* Überlegung *f.* **I'll give it my ~** ich werde es mir überlegen. **(b)** *no pl (regard, account)* **to take sth into ~** etw berücksichtigen; **to leave sth out of ~** etw außer acht lassen; **he's under ~ for the job** er wird für die Stelle in Erwägung gezogen; **it's under ~** es wird zur Zeit geprüft. **(c)** *no pl (thoughtfulness)* Rücksicht *f (for* auf *+acc).* **to have ~ for sb's feelings** Rücksicht auf

jds Gefühle nehmen; **his lack of ~ (for others)** seine Rücksichtslosigkeit (anderen gegenüber). **(d)** *(sth taken into account)* Faktor *m*. **money is no ~** Geld spielt keine Rolle; **his first ~ is his family** seine Familie spielt für ihn die größte Rolle. **(e)** *(payment)* **for a ~** gegen Entgelt.

considered [kən'sɪdəd] *adj attr opinion* ernsthaft.

considering [kən'sɪdərɪŋ] **1** *prep* **~ my age** für mein Alter, wenn man mein Alter bedenkt. **2** *conj* **~ (that) he's been ill ...** wenn man bedenkt, daß er krank war ...

consign [kən'saɪn] *vt* **(a)** *(Comm: send)* versenden. **(b)** *(entrust)* anvertrauen *(to +dat)*.

consignee [ˌkɒnsaɪ'niː] *n* Empfänger *m*.

consignment [kən'saɪnmənt] *n (Comm) (goods)* Sendung *f*; *(bigger)* Ladung *f*. **~ note** Frachtbrief *m*.

consist [kən'sɪst] *vi* **to ~ of** bestehen aus; **to ~ in sth** in etw *(dat)* bestehen.

consistency [kən'sɪstənsɪ] *n* **(a)** *see adj (a)* Konsequenz *f*; Übereinstimmung *f*; Folgerichtigkeit *f*; Beständigkeit *f*. **his statements lack ~** seine Aussagen widersprechen sich. **(b)** *(of substance)* Konsistenz *f*.

consistent [kən'sɪstənt] *adj* **(a)** konsequent; *statements* übereinstimmend; *argument* folgerichtig; *quality* beständig. **(b)** *(in agreement)* **to be ~ with sth** einer Sache *(dat)* entsprechen.

consistently [kən'sɪstəntlɪ] *adv* **(a)** *argue* konsequent. **(b)** *(uniformly)* durchweg. **(c)** *(in agreement)* entsprechend *(with dat)*.

consolation [ˌkɒnsə'leɪʃən] *n* Trost *m no pl*. **words of ~** tröstende Worte; **~ prize** Trostpreis *m*.

console[1] [kən'səʊl] *vt* trösten.

console[2] ['kɒnsəʊl] *n* **(a)** *(control panel)* (Kontroll)pult *nt*; *(of organ)* Spieltisch *m*. **(b)** *(cabinet)* Schrank *m*. **(c)** *(ornamental bracket)* Konsole *f*.

consolidate [kən'sɒlɪdeɪt] *vt* **(a)** *(confirm)* festigen. **(b)** *(combine)* zusammenlegen; *companies* zusammenschließen; *funds, debts* konsolidieren.

consolidation [kənˌsɒlɪ'deɪʃən] *n see vt* **(a)** Festigung *f*. **(b)** Zusammenlegung *f*; Zusammenschluß *m*; Konsolidierung *f*.

consommé [kɒn'sɒmeɪ] *n* Kraftbrühe *f*.

consonant ['kɒnsənənt] *n (Phon)* Konsonant *m*. **~ shift** Lautverschiebung *f*.

consort ['kɒnsɔːt] **1** *n (form: spouse)* Gemahl(in *f*) *m (form)*. **2** [kən'sɔːt] *vi (form)* verkehren *(with* mit*)*.

consortium [kən'sɔːtɪəm] *n* Konsortium *nt*.

conspicuous [kən'spɪkjʊəs] *adj* auffällig; *road signs* deutlich sichtbar; *lack of sth* offensichtlich; *bravery* bemerkenswert. **to be/make oneself ~** auffallen; **to be/not to be ~ for sth** sich/sich nicht gerade durch etw auszeichnen; **he was ~ by his absence** er glänzte durch Abwesenheit.

conspiracy [kən'spɪrəsɪ] *n* Verschwörung *f*. **a ~ of silence** ein verabredetes Schweigen.

conspirator [kən'spɪrətə^r] *n* Verschwörer *m*.

conspire [kən'spaɪə^r] *vi* sich verschwören *(against* gegen*)*; *(events)* zusammenkommen.

constable ['kʌnstəbl] *n (Brit: police ~)* Polizist(in *f*) *m*.

constabulary [kən'stæbjʊlərɪ] *n (Brit)* Polizei *f no pl*.

constant ['kɒnstənt] **1** *adj* **(a)** *(continuous)* ständig. **(b)** *(unchanging)* gleichbleibend, konstant. **(c)** *(steadfast)* beständig. **2** *n (Math, Phys, fig)* Konstante *f*.

constantly ['kɒnstəntlɪ] *adv* ständig.

constellation [ˌkɒnstə'leɪʃən] *n* Sternbild *nt*.

consternation ['kɒnstə'neɪʃən] *n (dismay)* Bestürzung *f*; *(worry)* Sorge *f*; *(confusion)* Aufruhr *m*. **to my great ~** zu meiner großen Bestürzung; **with a look of ~ on his face** mit bestürzter Miene; **the news filled me with ~** ich war bestürzt, als ich das hörte.

constipated ['kɒnstɪpeɪtɪd] *adj* verstopft. **he is ~** er hat Verstopfung.

constipation [ˌkɒnstɪ'peɪʃən] *n no pl* Verstopfung *f*.

constituency [kən'stɪtjʊənsɪ] *n (Pol)* Wahlkreis *m*.

constituent [kən'stɪtjʊənt] **1** *n* **(a)** *(Pol)* Wähler(in *f*) *m*. **(b)** *(part, element)* Bestandteil *m*. **2** *adj* **(a)** *(Pol) assembly* konstituierend. **(b)** *attr part, element* einzeln.

constitute ['kɒnstɪtjuːt] *vt* **(a)** *(make up)* bilden. **(b)** *(amount to)* darstellen. **(c)** *(set up)* gründen.

constitution [ˌkɒnstɪ'tjuːʃən] *n* **(a)** *(Pol)* Verfassung *f*; *(of club etc)* Satzung *f*. **(b)** *(of person)* Konstitution *f*. **(c)** *(way sth is made)* Aufbau *m*; *(what sth is made of)* Zusammensetzung *f*. **(d)** *(setting up)* Gründung *f*.

constitutional [ˌkɒnstɪ'tjuːʃənl] **1** *adj* **(a)** *(Pol) reform, crisis* Verfassungs-; *monarchy* konstitutionell; *government, action* verfassungsmäßig. **~ law** Verfassungsrecht *nt*; **it's not ~** das ist verfassungswidrig. **(b)** *(Med)* konstitutionell. **2** *n (hum col)* Spaziergang *m*.

constrain [kən'streɪn] *vt* zwingen; *one's temper* zügeln. **to find oneself/feel ~ed to ...** sich gezwungen sehen/fühlen, zu ...

constraint [kən'streɪnt] *n* **(a)** *(compulsion)* Zwang *m*. **(b)** *(restriction)* Beschränkung *f*. **to place ~s on sth** einer Sache *(dat)* Zwänge auferlegen. **(c)** *(in manner etc)* Gezwungenheit *f*; *(embarrassment)* Befangenheit *f*.

constrict [kən'strɪkt] *vt* **(a)** einengen; *muscle* zusammenziehen; *vein* verengen. **(b)** *movements* einschränken *(also fig)*.

constriction [kən'strɪkʃən] *n* **(a)** *(of muscles)* Zusammenziehen *nt*. **(b)** *(of movements etc)* Einschränkung *f*.

construct [kən'strʌkt] *vt* bauen; *geometrical figure* konstruieren; *sentence* bilden; *theory* entwickeln.

construction [kən'strʌkʃən] *n* **(a)** *see vt* Bau *m*; Konstruktion *f*; Entwicklung *f*. **under ~** in *or* im Bau. **(b)** *(way sth is constructed)* Struktur *f*; *(of building)* Bauweise *f*; *(of machine, bridge)* Konstruktion *f*. **(c)** *(sth constructed)* Bau *m*; *(bridge, machine)* Konstruktion *f*. **(d)** *(interpretation)* Deutung *f*. **to put a wrong ~ on sth** etw falsch auffassen. **(e)** *(Gram)* Konstruktion *f*. **sentence ~** Satzbau *m*.

construction industry *n* Bauindustrie *f*.

constructive [kən'strʌktɪv] *adj* konstruktiv.

construe [kən'struː] *vt (interpret)* auffassen.

consul ['kɒnsəl] *n* Konsul *m*.

consular ['kɒnsjʊlə^r] *adj* konsularisch.

consulate ['kɒnsjʊlɪt] *n* Konsulat *nt*.

consult [kən'sʌlt] **1** *vt* sich besprechen mit; *lawyer, doctor etc* konsultieren; *dictionary* nachschlagen in *(+dat)*; *map* nachsehen auf *(+dat)*; *oracle* befragen; *horoscope* nachlesen. **he did it without ~ing anyone** er hat das getan, ohne jemanden zu fragen. **2** *vi (confer)* sich beraten *(with* mit*)*.

consultancy [kən'sʌltənsɪ] *n (act)* Beratung *f*; *(business)* Beratungsbüro *nt*.

consultant [kən'sʌltənt] **1** *n* **(a)** *(Brit Med)* Facharzt *m*, Fachärztin *f*. **~ gynaecologist** Facharzt/-ärztin für Frauenkrankheiten. **(b)** *(other professions)* Berater(in *f*) *m*. **2** *adj attr* beratend.

consultation [ˌkɒnsəl'teɪʃən] *n* Besprechung *f*; *(of doctor, lawyer)* Konsultation *f (of gen)*. **in ~ with** in gemeinsamer Beratung mit.

consulting [kən'sʌltɪŋ] *adj* **~ hours/room** *(Brit)* Sprechstunde *f*/-zimmer *nt*.

consume [kən'sjuːm] *vt* **(a)** *food, drink* zu sich nehmen; *(Econ)* konsumieren. **(b)** *(destroy)* vernichten; *(use up)* verbrauchen. **he was ~d with jealousy** er wurde von Eifersucht verzehrt *(geh)*.

consumer [kən'sjuːmə^r] *n* Verbraucher(in *f*) *m*.

consumer *in cpds* Verbraucher-; **~ durables** *npl* Gebrauchsgüter *pl*; **~ goods** *npl* Konsumgüter *pl*; **~ protection** *n* Verbraucherschutz *m*;

~s' advice centre *(Brit) or* **center** *(US) n* Verbraucherzentrale *f*; **~ society** *n* Konsumgesellschaft *f*.
consummate [kən'sʌmɪt] **1** *adj* vollendet. **with ~ ease** mit spielender Leichtigkeit. **2** ['kɒnsəmeɪt] *vt marriage* vollziehen.
consumption [kən'sʌmpʃən] *n* **(a)** Konsum *m*; *(of non-edible products)* Verbrauch *m*. **this letter is for private ~ only** *(col)* der Brief ist nur für den privaten Gebrauch; **not fit for human ~** zum Verzehr ungeeignet. **(b)** *(Med old)* Schwindsucht *f*.
contact ['kɒntækt] **1** *n* **(a)** Kontakt *m*; *(communication also)* Verbindung *f*. **to be in ~ with sb/sth** *(be touching)* jdn/etw berühren; *(in communication)* mit jdm/etw in Kontakt stehen; **to come into ~ with sb/sth** *(lit, fig)* mit jdm/etw in Berührung kommen; **he has no ~ with his family** er hat keinen Kontakt zu seiner Familie; **to make ~ with sb/sth** *(get in touch with)* sich mit jdm/etw in Verbindung setzen; **I finally made ~ with him at his office** ich habe ihn schließlich im Büro erreicht; **to lose ~ (with sb/sth)** den Kontakt (zu jdm/etw) verlieren; **point of ~** *(Math, fig)* Berührungspunkt *m*.
(b) *(Elec) (act)* Kontakt *m*; *(equipment)* Kontaktstück *nt*. **to make/break ~** den Kontakt herstellen/unterbrechen.
(c) *(person)* Kontaktperson *f (also Med)*; *(in espionage)* Verbindungsmann, V-Mann *m*. **~s** *pl* Kontakte *pl*; **to make ~s** Kontakte herstellen.
2 *vt person, agent* sich in Verbindung setzen mit. **I've been trying to ~ you for hours** ich versuche schon seit Stunden, Sie zu erreichen.
contact: ~ adhesive *n* Kontaktklebstoff *m*; **~-breaker** *n* Unterbrecher *m*; **~ lens** *n* Kontaktlinse *f*.
contagion [kən'teɪdʒən] *n (contact)* Ansteckung *f*; *(disease)* Ansteckungskrankheit *f*; *(epidemic)* Seuche *f (also fig)*; *(fig: spreading influence)* schädlicher Einfluß.
contagious [kən'teɪdʒəs] *adj (Med, fig)* ansteckend.
contain [kən'teɪn] *vt* **(a)** *(hold within itself)* enthalten. **(b)** *(have capacity for)* fassen. **(c)** *emotions, oneself* beherrschen; *disease, inflation* in Grenzen halten; *epidemic, flood* unter Kontrolle bringen.
container [kən'teɪnə^r] **1** *n* **(a)** Behälter *m*. **(b)** *(Comm)* Container *m*. **2** *adj attr* Container-.
containerize [kən'teɪnəraɪz] *vt freight* in Container verpacken; *port* auf Container umstellen.
contaminate [kən'tæmɪneɪt] *vt* verunreinigen; *(poison)* vergiften; *(radioactivity)* verseuchen; *(fig) mind* verderben.
contd = continued Forts., Fortsetzung *f*.
contemplate ['kɒntempleɪt] *vt* **(a)** *(look at)* betrachten. **(b)** *(reflect upon)* nachdenken über (+*acc*); *(consider) a purchase, action* in Erwägung ziehen; *a holiday* denken an (+*acc*).
contemplation [,kɒntem'pleɪʃən] *n* **(a)** *(looking)* Betrachtung *f*. **(b)** *(thinking)* Nachdenken *nt (of* über +*acc)*; *(deep thought)* Betrachtung, Kontemplation *(esp Rel) f*.
contemplative [kən'templətɪv] *adj look* nachdenklich; *life* beschaulich, kontemplativ *(esp Rel)*.
contemporary [kən'tempərərɪ] **1** *adj* **(a)** *(of the same time) events* gleichzeitig; *literature* zeitgenössisch; *(of the same age)* gleich alt. **(b)** *(of the present time) life* heutig; *art* zeitgenössisch, modern. **2** *n* Altersgenosse *m*/-genossin *f*; *(in history)* Zeitgenosse *m*/-genossin *f*.
contempt [kənt'tempt] *n* **(a)** Verachtung *f*; *(disregard also)* Geringschätzung *f (for* von*)*. **to hold in ~** verachten; **beneath ~** unter aller Kritik. **(b)** *(Jur: also* **~ of court***)* Mißachtung *f* des Gerichts.
contemptible [kən'temptəbl] *adj* verachtenswert.
contemptuous [kən'temptjʊəs] *adj manner, look* verächtlich. **to be ~ of sb/sth** jdn/etw verachten.
contend [kən'tend] **1** *vi* **(a)** kämpfen. **to ~ for sth** um etw kämpfen; **then you'll have me to ~ with** dann bekommst du es mit mir zu tun. **(b)** *(cope)* **to ~ with sb/sth** mit jdm/etw fertig werden. **2** *vt* behaupten.
contender [kən'tendə^r] *n* Anwärter(in *f*) *m (for* auf +*acc)*; *(Sport)* Wettkämpfer(in *f*) *m (for* um*)*.
content[1] [kən'tent] **1** *adj* zufrieden *(with* mit*)*. **2** *n* Zufriedenheit *f*; *see* **heart (a)**. **3** *vt person* zufriedenstellen. **to ~ oneself with** sich zufriedengeben mit.
content[2] ['kɒntent] *n* **(a) ~s** *pl* Inhalt *m*; **(table of) ~s** Inhaltsverzeichnis *nt*. **(b)** *no pl (substance)* Gehalt *m*.
contented [kən'tentɪd] *adj* zufrieden.
contention [kən'tenʃən] *n* **(a)** *(dispute)* Streit *m*. **the matter in ~** die strittige Angelegenheit. **(b)** *(assertion)* Behauptung *f*.
contentment [kən'tentmənt] *n* Zufriedenheit *f*.
contest ['kɒntest] **1** *n* Kampf *m (for* um*)*; *(beauty ~ etc)* Wettbewerb *m*. **boxing ~** Boxkampf *m*; **election ~** Wahlkampf *m*. **2** [kən'test] *vt* **(a)** *(fight over)* kämpfen um; *(Pol: candidate) seat* sich bewerben um; *(oppose)* kämpfen gegen. **(b)** *statement* bestreiten; *(Jur) will* anfechten.
contestant [kən'testənt] *n* (Wettbewerbs)teilnehmer(in *f*) *m*; *(Parl, in quiz)* Kandidat(in *f*) *m*; *(Sport)* (Wettkampf)teilnehmer(in *f*) *m*. **the ~s in the election** die Wahlkandidaten.
context ['kɒntekst] *n* Zusammenhang *m*. **out of ~** aus dem Zusammenhang gerissen.
continent ['kɒntɪnənt] *n* Kontinent *m*; *(mainland)* Festland *nt*. **the C~** *(Brit)* Kontinentaleuropa *nt*; **on the C~** auf dem europäischen Festland.
continental [,kɒntɪ'nentl] **1** *adj* **(a)** *(Geog)* kontinental. **(b)** *(Brit: European)* europäisch. **2** *n* (Festlands)europäer(in *f*) *m*.
continental: ~ breakfast *n* kleines Frühstück *(Kaffee und Brötchen)*; **~ quilt** *n (Brit)* Federbett *nt*.
contingency [kən'tɪndʒənsɪ] *n* möglicher Fall. **in this ~** in diesem Fall; **~ fund** Eventualfonds *m*; **a ~ plan** ein Ausweichplan *m*.
contingent [kən'tɪndʒənt] **1** *adj* **~ upon** *(form)* abhängig von; **to be ~ upon** abhängen von. **2** *n* Kontingent *nt*; *(Mil)* Trupp *m*.
continual [kən'tɪnjʊəl] *adj (frequent)* dauernd; *(unceasing)* ununterbrochen.
continuance [kən'tɪnjʊəns] *n* **(a)** *(duration)* Dauer *f*. **(b)** *(continuation)* Fortsetzung *f*.
continuation [kən,tɪnjʊ'eɪʃən] *n* Fortsetzung *f*.
continue [kən'tɪnju:] **1** *vt* fortsetzen. **to ~ to read, to ~ reading** weiterlesen; **to be ~d** Fortsetzung folgt. **2** *vi (go on) (person)* weitermachen; *(crisis, speech)* (an)dauern; *(weather)* anhalten; *(road etc)* sich fortsetzen; *(concert etc)* weitergehen. **he ~s (to be) optimistic** er ist nach wie vor optimistisch.
continuity [,kɒntɪ'nju:ɪtɪ] *n* **(a)** Kontinuität *f*. **the story lacks ~** der Geschichte fehlt der rote Faden. **(b)** *(Film)* **~ girl** Scriptgirl *nt*.
continuous [kən'tɪnjʊəs] *adj* dauernd, ständig; *line* ununterbrochen. **~ performance** *(Film)* durchgehende Vorstellung.
continuously [kən'tɪnjʊəslɪ] *adv see adj* dauernd, ständig; ununterbrochen.
contort [kən'tɔ:t] *vt features* verziehen *(into* zu*)*; *limbs* verrenken. **a face ~ed by pain** ein schmerzverzerrtes Gesicht.
contortion [kən'tɔ:ʃən] *n (esp of acrobat)* Verrenkung *f*; *(of features)* Verzerrung *f*.
contortionist [kən'tɔ:ʃənɪst] *n* Schlangenmensch *m*.
contour ['kɒntʊə^r] *n* Kontur *f*.
contour: ~ line *n (Geog)* Höhenlinie *f*; **~ map** *n* Höhenlinienkarte *f*.

contraband ['kɒntrəbænd] **1** *n no pl (goods)* Schmuggelware *f*; *(form: smuggling)* Schleichhandel *m*. **2** *adj* Schmuggel-.
contraception [ˌkɒntrə'sepʃən] *n* Empfängnisverhütung.
contraceptive [ˌkɒntrə'septɪv] **1** *n* empfängnisverhütendes Mittel. **2** *adj* empfängnisverhütend; *pill* Antibaby-.
contract[1] ['kɒntrækt] **1** *n* **(a)** Vertrag *m*; *(Comm: order)* Auftrag *m*. **to enter into a ~ (with sb)** (mit jdm) einen Vertrag schließen; **to put work out to ~** Arbeiten außer Haus machen lassen. **(b)** *(Bridge)* Kontrakt *m*. **~ bridge** Kontrakt-Bridge *nt*. **2** *adj price, date* vertraglich festgelegt. **3** [kən'trækt] *vt* **(a)** *debts* machen; *illness* erkranken an *(+dat)*. **(b)** *(enter into) marriage, alliance* eingehen. **4** [kən'trækt] *vi (Comm)* **to ~ to do sth** sich vertraglich verpflichten, etw zu tun.
♦ **contract in** *vi* sich anschließen *(-to dat)*; *(into insurance scheme)* beitreten *(-to dat)*.
♦ **contract out 1** *vi (withdraw)* austreten *(of* aus*)*; *(not join)* sich nicht anschließen *(of dat)*; *(of insurance scheme)* nicht beitreten *(of dat)*. **2** *vt sep (Comm) work* vergeben *(to* an *+acc)*.
contract[2] [kən'trækt] **1** *vt* zusammenziehen. **2** *vi (muscle, metal etc)* sich zusammenziehen.
contraction [kən'trækʃən] *n* **(a)** *(shrinking)* Zusammenziehung *f*. **(b)** *(in childbirth)* Wehe *f*.
contractor [kən'træktə[r]] *n* *(individual)* Auftragnehmer *m*; *(building ~)* Bauunternehmer *m*.
contractual [kən'træktʃʊəl] *adj* vertraglich.
contradict [ˌkɒntrə'dɪkt] *vt* widersprechen *(+dat)*.
contradiction [ˌkɒntrə'dɪkʃən] *n* Widerspruch *m (of* zu*)*. **full of ~s** voller Widersprüchlichkeiten.
contradictory [ˌkɒntrə'dɪktərɪ] *adj* widersprüchlich.
contra-flow ['kɒntrə'fləʊ] *n (Mot)* Gegenverkehr *m*.
contralto [kən'træltəʊ] **1** *n (voice)* Alt *m*. **2** *adj voice* Alt-. **the ~ part** die Altstimme.
contraption [kən'træpʃən] *n (col)* Apparat *m (col)*; *(vehicle)* Vehikel *nt (col)*.
contrary[1] ['kɒntrərɪ] **1** *adj (opposite)* entgegengesetzt. **2** *n* Gegenteil *nt*. **on the ~** im Gegenteil; **do you have information to the ~?** liegen Ihnen gegenteilige Informationen vor?; **unless you hear to the ~** sofern Sie nichts Gegenteiliges hören. **3** *adv* **~ to expectations** wider Erwarten; **~ to what he said** im Gegensatz zu dem, was er gesagt hat.
contrary[2] [kən'treərɪ] *adj (awkward)* widerspenstig.
contrast ['kɒntrɑːst] **1** *n* **(a)** Gegensatz *m (with, to* zu*)*; *(visual)* Kontrast *m (with, to* zu*)*. **by** *or* **in ~** im Gegensatz dazu. **(b)** *(Art, Phot, TV)* Kontrast *m*. **2** [kən'trɑːst] *vt* gegenüberstellen *(with dat)*. **3** [kən'trɑːst] *vi* im Gegensatz stehen *(with* zu*)*; *(colours)* sich abheben *(with* von*)*.
contrasting [kən'trɑːstɪŋ] *adj* gegensätzlich.
contravene [ˌkɒntrə'viːn] *vt* verstoßen gegen.
contravention [ˌkɒntrə'venʃən] *n* Verstoß *m (of* gegen*)*. **to act in ~ of sth** einer Sache *(dat)* zuwiderhandeln.
contretemps ['kɒntrəˌtɒŋ] *n no pl* Zwischenfall *m*.
contribute [kən'trɪbjuːt] **1** *vt* beitragen *(to* zu*)*; *money, supplies* beisteuern *(to* zu*)*; *(to charity)* spenden *(to* für*)*. **to ~ one's share** sein(en) Teil (dazu) beitragen. **2** *vi* beitragen *(to* zu*)*; *(to pension fund etc, to newspaper)* einen Beitrag leisten *(to* zu*)*; *(to present)* beisteuern *(to* zu*)*; *(to charity)* spenden *(to* für*)*.
contribution [ˌkɒntrɪ'bjuːʃən] *n* Beitrag *m (to* zu*)*; *(to charity)* Spende *f*. **the beer is my ~** das Bier stelle ich.
contributor [kən'trɪbjʊtə[r]] *n (to magazine)* Mitarbeiter(in *f*) *m (to* an *+dat)*; *(of goods, money)* Spender(in *f*) *m*.
contributory [kən'trɪbjʊtərɪ] *adj* **(a) that's a ~ factor** dieser Faktor spielt eine Rolle; **~ negligence** *(Jur)* Mitverschulden *nt*. **(b)** *pension scheme* beitragspflichtig.
con trick *n (col)* Schwindel *m*.
contrite ['kɒntraɪt] *adj* reuig.
contrition [kən'trɪʃən] *n* Reue *f*. **act of ~** *(Eccl)* Buße *f*.
contrivance [kən'traɪvəns] *n (device)* Vorrichtung *f*; *(mechanical)* Gerät *nt*.
contrive [kən'traɪv] *vt* **(a)** *plan* ersinnen. **to ~ a means of doing sth** einen Weg finden, etw zu tun. **(b)** *(manage, arrange)* bewerkstelligen. **to ~ to do sth** *(also iro)* es fertigbringen, etw zu tun; **he always ~s to get his own way** er versteht (es) immer, seinen Kopf durchzusetzen.
contrived [kən'traɪvd] *adj* gestellt; *style* gekünstelt.
control [kən'trəʊl] **1** *n* **(a)** *no pl (supervision)* Aufsicht *f (of* über *+acc)*; *(of situation, emotion)* Beherrschung *f (of gen)*; *(authority, power)* Gewalt *f (over* über *+acc)*; *(of prices)* Kontrolle *f (of gen)*; *(of traffic)* Regelung *f (of gen) etc*. **to be in ~ of sth** *business, office* etw leiten; *group of children* etw beaufsichtigen; **to have sth under ~** etw in der Hand haben; **to be in ~ of one's emotions** Herr seiner Gefühle sein; **to have no ~ over sb** keinen Einfluß auf jdn haben; **to lose ~ (of sth)** (über etw *acc*) die Gewalt verlieren; **to lose ~ of the situation** nicht mehr Herr der Lage sein; **to be/get out of ~** *(child, class)* außer Rand und Band sein/geraten; *(situation)* außer Kontrolle sein/geraten; **the car went out of ~** das Auto geriet außer Kontrolle; **under state ~** unter staatlicher Aufsicht; **to be under ~** unter Kontrolle sein; **he was beyond parental ~** er war seinen Eltern über den Kopf gewachsen; **circumstances beyond our ~** nicht in unserer Hand liegende Umstände; **his ~ of the ball** seine Ballführung.
(b) *(check)* Kontrolle *f (on gen,* über *+acc)*. **wages/price ~s** Lohn-/Preiskontrolle *f*.
(c) *(~ room)* die Zentrale; *(Aviat)* der Kontrollturm.
(d) *(knob, switch)* Regler *m*; *(of vehicle, machine)* Schalter *m*. **to be at the ~s** *(of spaceship, airliner)* am Kontrollpult sitzen; *(of small plane, car)* die Steuerung haben; **to take over the ~s** die Steuerung übernehmen.
(e) *(Sci: group)* Kontrollgruppe *f*. **~ experiment** Kontrollversuch *m*.
2 *vt* **(a)** *(direct, manage)* kontrollieren; *business* führen; *organization* in der Hand haben; *child, class* fertigwerden mit; *car* lenken; *traffic* regeln; *emotions* beherrschen; *hair* bändigen. **to ~ oneself/one's temper** sich beherrschen; **~ yourself!** nimm dich zusammen! **(b)** *(regulate) temperature, speed* regulieren; *prices etc* kontrollieren; *disease* unter Kontrolle bringen; *population* eindämmen.
control column *n* Steuerknüppel *m*.
controlled [kən'trəʊld] *adj emotion* beherrscht; *conditions* kontrolliert; *prices* gebunden; *temperature* geregelt.
controller [kən'trəʊlə[r]] *n* **(a)** *(Rad)* Intendant *m*; *(Aviat)* (Flug)lotse *m*. **(b)** *(Tech)* Regler *m*.
controlling [kən'trəʊlɪŋ] *adj attr factor* beherrschend; *body* Aufsichts-. **~ interest** Mehrheitsanteil *m*.
control: ~ panel *n* Schalttafel *f*; *(on aircraft, TV)* Bedienungsfeld *nt*; *(on car)* Armaturenbrett *nt*; **~ point** *n* Kontrollpunkt *m*; **~ room** *n* Kontrollraum *m*; *(Mil)* (Operations)zentrale *f*; *(of police)* Zentrale *f*; **~ tower** *n (Aviat)* Kontrollturm *m*.
controversial [ˌkɒntrə'vɜːʃəl] *adj* umstritten.
controversy ['kɒntrəvɜːsɪ, kən'trɒvəsɪ] *n* Kontroversen *pl*. **to give rise to ~** Anlaß zu Kontroversen geben.

contusion [kən'tjuːʒən] *n* Quetschung *f*.
conundrum [kə'nʌndrəm] *n (lit, fig)* Rätsel *nt*.
conurbation [ˌkɒnɜː'beɪʃən] *n* Ballungsgebiet *nt*.
convalesce [ˌkɒnvə'les] *vi* genesen *(from, after* von*)*.
convalescence [ˌkɒnvə'lesəns] *n* Genesung *f*; *(period)* Genesungszeit *f*.
convalescent [ˌkɒnvə'lesənt] **1** *n* Genesende(r) *mf*. **2** *adj* genesend. **to be ~** auf dem Wege der Besserung sein; **~ home** Genesungsheim *nt*.
convection [kən'vekʃən] *n* Konvektion *f*.
convector [kən'vektəʳ] *n (also* **~ heater***)* Heizlüfter *m*.
convene [kən'viːn] **1** *vt meeting* einberufen. **2** *vi* sich versammeln.
convener [kən'viːnəʳ] *n Person, die Versammlungen einberuft*.
convenience [kən'viːnɪəns] *n* **(a)** *no pl (usefulness)* Annehmlichkeit *f*; *(expediency)* Zweckmäßigkeit *f*. **~ foods** Fertiggerichte *pl*. **(b)** *no pl* **these chairs are for the ~ of customers** diese Stühle sind für unsere Kunden gedacht; **at your own ~** wann es Ihnen paßt; **at your earliest ~** *(Comm)* möglichst bald. **(c)** *(convenient thing, amenity)* Annehmlichkeit *f*. **a house with every ~** ein Haus mit allem Komfort. **(d)** *(Brit form: public* **~***)* (öffentliche) Toilette.
convenient [kən'viːnɪənt] *adj (useful)* praktisch; *area, house (for shops etc)* günstig gelegen; *time* günstig. **if it is ~ for you** wenn es Ihnen (so) paßt; **is tomorrow ~ (for you)?** paßt (es) Ihnen morgen?; **the trams are very ~** *(nearby)* die Straßenbahnhaltestellen liegen sehr günstig; *(useful)* die Straßenbahn ist sehr praktisch.
conveniently [kən'viːnɪəntlɪ] *adv* günstigerweise; *situated* günstig; *(usefully) designed* praktisch.
convent ['kɒnvənt] *n* (Frauen)kloster *nt*. **~ school** Klosterschule *f*.
convention [kən'venʃən] *n* **(a)** Sitte *f*; *(social rule)* Konvention *f*. **it's a ~ that ...** es ist so üblich *or* Sitte, daß ... **(b)** *(conference)* Tagung *f*; *(Pol)* Konvent *m*.
conventional [kən'venʃənl] *adj dress* konventionell; *beliefs* herkömmlich; *style* traditionell.
converge [kən'vɜːdʒ] *vi (road, lines)* zusammenlaufen *(at* in *+dat)*; *(fig: views etc)* sich aneinander annähern. **to ~ on sb/sth/New York** von überallher zu jdm/etw/nach New York strömen.
convergence [kən'vɜːdʒəns] *n see vi* Zusammenlaufen *nt*; Annäherung *f*. **point of ~** Schnittpunkt *m*; *(of rays)* Brennpunkt *m*.
conversation [ˌkɒnvə'seɪʃən] *n* Gespräch *nt*; *(Sch)* Konversation *f*. **to make ~** sich unterhalten; **to get into/be in ~ with sb** mit jdm ins Gespräch kommen/im Gespräch sein; **deep in ~** ins Gespräch vertieft; **his ~ is so amusing** er ist ein unterhaltsamer Geprächspartner; **a subject of ~** ein Gesprächsthema *nt*; **~ piece** Gesprächsgegenstand *m*; **that was a ~ stopper** *(col)* das hat uns die Sprache verschlagen *(col)*; **the art of ~** die Kunst des (guten) Gespräch(e)s.
conversational [ˌkɒnvə'seɪʃənl] *adj tone, style* Unterhaltungs-. **~ German** gesprochenes Deutsch.
conversationalist [ˌkɒnvə'seɪʃnəlɪst] *n* guter Gesprächspartner, gute Gesprächspartnerin.
converse[1] [kən'vɜːs] *vi (form)* sich unterhalten.
converse[2] ['kɒnvɜːs] **1** *adj* umgekehrt; *opinions etc* gegenteilig. **2** *n (opposite)* Gegenteil *nt*.
conversely [kɒn'vɜːslɪ] *adv* umgekehrt.
conversion [kən'vɜːʃən] *n* **(a)** Konversion *f (into* in *+acc)*; *(Rugby, US Ftbl)* Verwandlung *f*; *(of measures)* Umrechnung *f (into* in *+acc)*; *(of building)* Umbau *m (into* zu*)*. **~ table** Umrechnungstabelle *f*. **(b)** *(Rel, fig)* Bekehrung *f (to* zu*)*.
convert ['kɒnvɜːt] **1** *n (lit, fig)* Bekehrte(r) *mf*; *(to another denomination)* Konvertit *m*. **2** [kən'vɜːt] *vt* **(a)** konvertieren *(into* in *+acc)*; *(Rugby, US Ftbl)* verwandeln; *measures* umrechnen *(into* in *+acc)*; *attic* ausbauen *(into* zu*)*; *building* umbauen *(into* zu*)*. **(b)** *(Rel, fig)* bekehren *(to* zu*)*; *(to another denomination)* konvertieren. **3** [kən'vɜːt] *vi* sich verwandeln lassen *(into* in *+acc)*.
converter [kən'vɜːtəʳ] *n (Elec)* Konverter *m*; *(for AC/DC)* Stromgleichrichter *m*.
convertible [kən'vɜːtəbl] **1** *adj* verwandelbar; *currency* konvertibel. **~ sofa** Bettcouch *f*. **2** *n (car)* Kabriolett *nt*.
convex [kɒn'veks] *adj lens, mirror* konvex.
convey [kən'veɪ] *vt* **(a)** befördern; *goods* spedieren; *water* leiten. **(b)** *idea* vermitteln; *meaning* klarmachen; *best wishes* übermitteln. **words cannot ~ what I feel** was ich empfinde, läßt sich nicht mit Worten ausdrücken; **the name ~s nothing to me** der Name sagt mir nichts. **(c)** *(Jur) property* übertragen *(to* auf *+acc)*.
conveyance [kən'veɪəns] *n (transport)* Beförderung *f*. **~ of goods** Güterverkehr *m*; **means of ~** Beförderungsmittel *nt*.
conveyancing [kən'veɪənsɪŋ] *n (Jur)* (Eigentums)übertragung *f*.
conveyor [kən'veɪəʳ] *n (of message etc)* Überbringer(in *f*) *m*; *(Tech)* Förderer *m*. **~ belt** Fließband *nt*; *(for transport, supply)* Förderband *nt*.
convict ['kɒnvɪkt] **1** *n* Strafgefangene(r) *mf*. **2** [kən'vɪkt] *vt (Jur) person* verurteilen *(of* wegen*)*. **a ~ed criminal** ein überführter Verbrecher. **3** [kən'vɪkt] *vi* jdn verurteilen.
conviction [kən'vɪkʃən] *n* **(a)** *(Jur)* Verurteilung *f*. **(b)** *(belief, act of convincing)* Überzeugung *f*. **to carry ~** überzeugend klingen; *see* **courage**.
convince [kən'vɪns] *vt* überzeugen.
convincing *adj*, **~ly** *adv* [kən'vɪnsɪŋ, -lɪ] überzeugend.
convivial [kən'vɪvɪəl] *adj* heiter und unbeschwert; *(sociable)* gesellig.
convoluted ['kɒnvəluːtɪd] *adj (involved)* verwickelt; *style* gewunden.
convoy ['kɒnvɔɪ] *n* **(a)** *(escort)* Geleit *nt*. **under ~** mit Geleitschutz; **to be on ~ duty** als Geleitschutz abgeordnet sein. **(b)** *(vehicles under escort, fig)* Konvoi *m*. **in ~** im Konvoi.
convulse [kən'vʌls] *vt land* erschüttern; *muscles* krampfhaft zusammenziehen. **to be ~d with laughter/pain** sich vor Lachen schütteln/vor Schmerzen krümmen.
convulsion [kən'vʌlʃən] *n* **(a)** *(Med)* Schüttelkrampf *m no pl*. **(b)** *(caused by social upheaval etc)* Erschütterung *f*. **(c)** *(col: of laughter)* **to go into/be in ~s** sich biegen vor Lachen.
convulsive [kən'vʌlsɪv] *adj* Krampf-. **~ laughter** Lachkrämpfe *pl*.
coo [kuː] **1** *vi (pigeon, fig)* gurren. **2** *n* Gurren *nt*.
cook [kʊk] **1** *n* Koch *m*, Köchin *f*. **too many ~s spoil the broth** *(Prov)* viele Köche verderben den Brei *(Prov)*. **2** *vt* **(a)** *food, meal* zubereiten; *(in water, milk etc)* kochen; *(fry, roast)* braten; *pie, pancake* backen. **to ~ sb's goose** *(fig)* jdm die Suppe versalzen. **(b)** *(col: falsify) accounts* frisieren *(col)*. **3** *vi (person, food)* kochen; *(fry, roast)* braten; *(pie)* backen. **what's ~ing?** *(fig col)* was ist los?
♦**cook up** *vt sep (fig col) story, excuse* zurechtbasteln *(col)*. **~ed ~ story** Lügenmärchen *nt*.
cookbook ['kʊkbʊk] *n* Kochbuch *nt*.
cooker ['kʊkəʳ] *n (Brit)* **(a)** *(stove)* Herd *m*. **(b)** *(apple)* Kochapfel *m*.
cookery ['kʊkərɪ] *n* Kochen *nt (also Sch)*. **~ book** Kochbuch *nt*.
cookhouse ['kʊkhaʊs] *n (Naut)* Kombüse *f*; *(Mil)* Feldküche *f*.
cookie, cooky ['kʊkɪ] *n* **(a)** *(US: biscuit)* Keks *m*. **(b)** *(col: smart person)* Typ *m*. **he's a pretty sharp ~** er ist ein richtiger Schlauberger.

cooking ['kʊkɪŋ] *n* Kochen *nt*; *(food)* Essen *nt*. **plain** ~ Hausmannskost *f*; **French** ~ die französische Küche.

cooking *in cpds* Koch-; ~ **apple** *n* Kochapfel *m*; ~ **chocolate** *n* Blockschokolade *f*.

cookout ['kʊkaʊt] *n (US)* Kochen *nt* am Lagerfeuer; *(on charcoal brazier)* Grillparty *f*.

cool [ku:l] **1** *adj (+er)* **(a)** *weather, drink* kühl; *person* besonnen; *clothes* luftig. **"keep in a ~ place"** „kühl aufbewahren"; **keep ~!** reg dich nicht auf!; **to be ~ to(wards) sb** sich jdm gegenüber kühl verhalten; **play it ~!** immer mit der Ruhe! **(b)** *(audacious)* unverfroren. **a ~ customer** *(col)* ein lässiger Typ *(col)*; **that was very ~ of him** da hat er sich ein starkes Stück geleistet. **(c)** *(col: of money)* glatt *(col)*. **he earns a ~ ten thousand a year** er verdient glatte zehntausend im Jahr *(col)*. **(d)** *disco, dress etc* stark *(col)*. ~ **jazz** Cool Jazz *m*.

2 *n* **(a)** *(lit, fig)* Kühle *f*. **the ~ of the evening** die Abendkühle. **(b)** *(col)* **keep your ~!** reg dich nicht auf!; **to lose one's ~** durchdrehen *(col)*.

3 *vt* **(a)** kühlen; *(~ down)* abkühlen; *wine* kaltstellen. **(b) ~ it!** *(relax)* reg dich ab; *(don't cause trouble)* mach keinen Ärger! *(col)*.

4 *vi (lit, fig)* abkühlen; *(anger)* sich legen; *(interest)* nachlassen.

♦**cool down 1** *vi* **(a)** *(lit)* abkühlen. **(b)** *(feelings, fig: person)* sich abkühlen; *(critical situation)* sich beruhigen. **to let things ~ ~** die Sache etwas ruhen lassen. **2** *vt sep food, drink* abkühlen; *(let ~ ~)* abkühlen lassen.

♦**cool off** *vi* **(a)** *(liquid, food)* abkühlen; *(person)* sich abkühlen. **(b)** *(fig)* (sich) abkühlen; *(enthusiasm, interest)* nachlassen; *(become less angry)* sich abreagieren; *(become less friendly)* kühler werden *(towards sb* jdm gegenüber*)*.

coolant ['ku:lənt] *n* Kühlmittel *nt*.

cool: ~ **bag** *n* Kühltasche *f*; ~ **box** *n* Kühlbox *f*.

cooler ['ku:ləʳ] *n* **(a)** *(for wine)* Kühler *m*. **(b)** *(col: solitary)* Bau *m (col)*.

cooling ['ku:lɪŋ] *adj drink, shower* kühlend.

cooling-off ['ku:lɪŋ'ɒf] **1** *n (in relationship etc)* Abkühlung *f*. **2** *adj* ~ **period** *Zeitraum für Schlichtungsverhandlungen (bei Arbeitskämpfen)*.

cooling tower *n* Kühlturm *m*.

coolly ['ku:lɪ] *adv* **(a)** *(calmly)* ruhig, gefaßt. **(b)** *(unenthusiastically, in an unfriendly way)* kühl. **(c)** *(audaciously)* unverfroren.

coolness ['ku:lnɪs] *n see adj* **(a)** Kühle *f*; Besonnenheit *f*; Luftigkeit *f*. **(b)** Unverfrorenheit *f*.

coop [ku:p] *n (also* **hen** ~*)* Hühnerstall *m*.

♦**coop up** *vt sep person* einsperren; *several people* zusammenpferchen.

co-op ['kəʊ'ɒp] *n* Genossenschaft *f*; *(shop)* Coop *m*.

cooperate [kəʊ'ɒpəreɪt] *vi* zusammenarbeiten; *(not be awkward)* mitmachen.

cooperation [kəʊ,ɒpə'reɪʃən] *n* Kooperation, Zusammenarbeit *f*; *(help)* Mitarbeit *f*.

cooperative [kəʊ'ɒpərətɪv] **1** *adj* **(a)** *(willing to comply)* kooperativ; *(willing to help)* hilfsbereit. **(b)** ~ **society** Genossenschaft *f*; ~ **farm** Bauernhof *m* auf Genossenschaftsbasis. **2** *n* Genossenschaft *f*; *(also* ~ **farm***)* Bauernhof *m* auf Genossenschaftsbasis.

coopt [kəʊ'ɒpt] *vt* (hinzu)wählen. **he was ~ed onto the committee** er wurde vom Komitee dazugewählt.

coordinate [kəʊ'ɔ:dnɪt] **1** *n (Math etc)* Koordinate *f*. **~s** *(clothes)* Kleidung *f* zum Kombinieren. **2** [kəʊ'ɔ:dɪneɪt] *vt* koordinieren.

coordination [kəʊ,ɔ:dɪ'neɪʃən] *n* Koordination *f*.

coordinator [kəʊ'ɔ:dɪneɪtəʳ] *n* Koordinator *m*.

cop [kɒp] **1** *n* **(a)** *(col: policeman)* Polizist(in *f*), Bulle *(pej col) m*. **(b)** *(Brit col)* **it's not much ~** das ist nichts Besonderes. **2** *vt (col: catch) sb* schnappen *(col)*. **you'll ~ it when your dad gets home** warte nur, bis dein Vater nach Haus kommt!; **hey, ~ a load of this!** he, hör/sieh dir das mal an! *(col)*.

♦**cop out** *vi (col)* aussteigen *(of* aus*)*.

cope [kəʊp] *vi* zurechtkommen; *(with work)* es schaffen. **to ~ with** fertigwerden mit; **she can't ~ with the stairs any more** sie schafft die Treppe nicht mehr.

Copenhagen [,kəʊpn'heɪgən] *n* Kopenhagen *nt*.

copier ['kɒpɪəʳ] *n (copyist)* Kopist(in *f*) *m*; *(machine)* Kopierer *m*, Kopiergerät *nt*.

co-pilot ['kəʊ'paɪlət] *n* Kopilot *m*.

copious ['kəʊpɪəs] *adj supply* reichlich; *information, illustrations* zahlreich.

copper ['kɒpəʳ] *n* **(a)** *(metal)* Kupfer *nt*. **(b)** *(colour)* Kupferrot *nt*. **(c)** *(coin)* Pfennig *m*. **~s** Kleingeld *nt*. **(d)** *(col: policeman)* Polizist(in *f*), Bulle *(pej col) m*.

copper: ~ **beech** *n* Rotbuche *f*; **~-coloured** *(Brit) or* **~-colored** *(US) adj* kupferfarben.

copse [kɒps] *n* Wäldchen *nt*.

copulate ['kɒpjʊleɪt] *vi* kopulieren.

copulation [,kɒpjʊ'leɪʃən] *n* Kopulation *f*.

copy ['kɒpɪ] **1** *n* **(a)** Kopie *f*; *(carbon)* Durchschlag *m*; *(Phot)* Abzug *m*. **to write out a fair ~** etw ins reine schreiben. **(b)** *(of book etc)* Exemplar *nt*. **(c)** *(Press etc) (material)* Stoff *m*; *(text)* Text *m*. **that's always good ~** das zieht immer. **(d)** *(in advertising)* Werbetext *m*. **2** *vi* **(a)** *(imitate)* nachahmen. **(b)** *(Sch etc)* abschreiben. **3** *vt* **(a)** *(make a ~ of) see n* kopieren; einen Durchschlag machen von; abziehen; *(write out again)* abschreiben. **(b)** *(imitate)* nachmachen; *accent etc* nachahmen. **(c)** *(Sch etc) sb else's work* abschreiben.

copy: **~book 1** *n* Schönschreibheft *nt*; **2** *adj attr* mustergültig; **~cat** *n (col)* **she's a terrible ~cat** sie macht immer alles nach.

copyright ['kɒpɪraɪt] **1** *n* Urheberrecht, Copyright *nt*. **2** *adj* urheberrechtlich geschützt.

copy: ~ **typist** *n* Schreibkraft *f*; **~writer** *n* Werbetexter(in *f*) *m*.

coral ['kɒrəl] *n* **(a)** Koralle *f*. **(b)** *(colour)* Korallenrot *nt*.

coral *in cpds* Korallen-; ~ **necklace** *n* Korallenkette *f*; ~ **reef** *n* Korallenriff *nt*.

cord [kɔ:d] *n* **(a)** Schnur *f*; *(for clothes)* Kordel *f*. **(b) ~s** *pl (also* **a pair of ~s***)* Kordhosen *pl*. **(c)** *(Tex)* = **corduroy**.

cordial ['kɔ:dɪəl] **1** *adj* herzlich. **2** *n (soft drink)* Fruchtsaftkonzentrat *nt*; *(alcoholic)* Fruchtlikör *m*.

cordon ['kɔ:dn] *n* Postenkette *f*. **to put a ~ around sth** etw (hermetisch) abriegeln.

♦**cordon off** *vt sep area, building* abriegeln.

corduroy ['kɔ:dərɔɪ] *n* Kordsamt *m*. **~s** Kordhosen *pl*.

core [kɔ:ʳ] **1** *n (lit, fig)* Kern *m*; *(of apple, pear)* Kerngehäuse *nt*; *(of rock)* Innere(s) *nt*. **rotten/English to the ~** *(fig)* durch und durch schlecht/englisch; **to get to the ~ of the matter** *(fig)* zum Kern der Sache kommen. **2** *vt fruit* entkernen; *apple, pear* das Kerngehäuse *(+gen)* ausschneiden.

co-respondent ['kəʊrɪs'pɒndənt] *n (Jur)* Mitbeklagte(r) *mf (im Scheidungsprozeß)*.

coriander [,kɒrɪ'ændəʳ] *n* Koriander *m*.

cork [kɔ:k] **1** *n* **(a)** *no pl (substance)* Kork *m*. **(b)** *(stopper)* Korken *m*. **(c)** *(Fishing: also* ~ **float***)* Schwimmer *m*. **2** *vt (also* ~ **up***) bottle, wine* verkorken. **3** *adj* Kork-.

corked [kɔ:kt] *adj* **the wine is ~** der Wein schmeckt nach Kork.

cork: **~screw** *n* Korkenzieher *m*; **~screw curls** *npl* Korkenzieherlocken *pl*; ~ **tile** *n* Korkfliese *f*; **~-tipped** *adj cigarette* mit Korkfilter; ~ **tree** *n* Korkbaum *m*.

corn[1] [kɔ:n] *n* **(a)** *no pl (Brit: cereal)* Getreide *nt*. **(b)** *(seed of ~)* Korn *nt*. **(c)** *no pl (esp US: sweet ~)* Mais *m*; ~ **on the cob** Maiskolben *m*.

corn[2] *n* Hühnerauge *nt*. ~ **plaster** Hühneraugenpflaster *nt*.
cornea ['kɔːnɪə] *n* Hornhaut *f*.
corned beef ['kɔːnd'biːf] *n* Corned beef *nt*.
corner ['kɔːnəʳ] **1** *n* **(a)** Ecke *f*; *(of sheet)* Zipfel *m*; *(of mouth, eye)* Winkel *m*; *(in road)* Kurve *f*. **at** *or* **on the** ~ an der Ecke; **it's just around the** ~ es ist gleich um die Ecke; **to turn the** ~ *(lit)* um die Ecke biegen; **we've turned the** ~ **now** *(fig)* wir sind jetzt über den Berg; **out of the** ~ **of one's eye** aus dem Augenwinkel (heraus); **to cut** ~**s** *(lit)* Kurven schneiden; *(fig)* das Verfahren abkürzen; **to drive sb into a** ~ *(fig)* jdn in die Enge treiben; **all four** ~**s of the world** die ganze Welt. **(b)** *(out-of-the-way place)* Winkel *m*. **(c)** *(Ftbl)* Eckball *m*, Ecke *f*. **to take a** ~ eine Ecke ausführen.
2 *vt* **(a)** *(lit, fig: trap)* in die Enge treiben. **(b)** *(Comm) the market* monopolisieren.
3 *vi (take a* ~*) (person)* Kurven/die Kurve nehmen. **this car** ~**s well** dieses Auto hat eine gute Kurvenlage.
corner *in cpds* Eck-; ~ **cupboard** *n* Eckschrank *m*; ~ **kick** *n (Ftbl)* Eckstoß *m*; ~ **seat** *n (Rail)* Eckplatz *m*; ~ **shop** *n* Laden *m* an der Ecke; ~**stone** *n (lit, fig)* Eckstein *m*.
cornet ['kɔːnɪt] *n* **(a)** *(Mus)* Kornett *nt*. **(b)** *(ice-cream* ~*)* (Eis)tüte *f*.
corn: ~**field** *n (Brit)* Weizenfeld *nt*; *(US)* Maisfeld *nt*; ~**flakes** *npl* Corn-flakes ® *pl*; ~**flour** *n (Brit)* Stärkemehl *nt*; ~**flower** *n* Kornblume *f*.
cornice ['kɔːnɪs] *n (Archit: of wall, column)* (Ge)sims *nt*; *(fig: of snow)* Wächte *f*.
Cornish ['kɔːnɪʃ] **1** *adj* aus Cornwall. **2** *n (dialect)* Kornisch *nt*.
corn: ~**meal** *n (US)* Maismehl *nt*; ~ **oil** *n* (Mais)keimöl *nt*; ~ **pone** *n (US)* Maisbrot *nt*; ~**starch** *n (US)* Stärkemehl *nt*; ~ **whiskey** *n (US)* Maiswhiskey *m*.
corny ['kɔːnɪ] *adj (+er) (col) joke* blöd *(col)*; *(sentimental)* kitschig. **what a** ~ **old joke!** der Witz hat (so) einen Bart *(col)*.
corollary [kə'rɒlərɪ] *n* (logische) Folge, Korollar *nt (also Math)*.
coronary ['kɒrənərɪ] **1** *adj (Med)* Koronar- *(spec)*. ~ **thrombosis** Herzinfarkt *m*. **2** *n* Herzinfarkt *m*.
coronation [ˌkɒrə'neɪʃən] *n* Krönung *f*.
coroner ['kɒrənəʳ] *n Beamter, der Todesfälle untersucht, die nicht eindeutig eine natürliche Ursache haben.*
coronet ['kɒrənɪt] *n* Krone *f*; *(jewellery)* Krönchen *nt*.
corporal[1] ['kɔːpərəl] *n (abbr* **corp***) (Mil)* Stabsunteroffizier *m*.
corporal[2] *adj* körperlich. ~ **punishment** Prügelstrafe *f*.
corporate ['kɔːpərɪt] *adj* **(a)** *(of a group)* gemeinsam. **(b)** *(of a corporation)* korporativ; *(of a company)* Firmen-. ~ **body** Körperschaft *f*.
corporation [ˌkɔːpə'reɪʃən] *n* **(a)** *(municipal* ~*)* Gemeinde *f*. **(b)** *(Brit Comm: incorporated company)* Handelsgesellschaft *f*; *(US Comm: limited liability company)* Gesellschaft *f* mit beschränkter Haftung. **(c)** *(Brit hum: large belly)* Schmerbauch *m*.
corps [kɔːʳ] *n, pl* - *(Mil)* Korps *nt*. ~ **de ballet** Corps de ballet *nt*.
corpse [kɔːps] *n* Leiche *f*.
corpulence ['kɔːpjʊləns] *n* Korpulenz *f*.
corpulent ['kɔːpjʊlənt] *adj* korpulent.
corpuscle ['kɔːpʌsl] *n* Korpuskel *nt (spec)*. **blood** ~ Blutkörperchen *nt*.
correct [kə'rekt] **1** *adj (right)* richtig; *(proper)* korrekt. **am I** ~ **in thinking ...?** gehe ich recht in der Annahme, daß ...; **you are** ~ Sie haben recht; **it's the** ~ **thing to do** das gehört sich so. **2** *vt* korrigieren; *bad habit* sich/jdm abgewöhnen. ~ **me if I'm wrong** Sie können mich gern berichtigen; **I stand** ~**ed** ich nehme alles zurück.
correction [kə'rekʃən] *n see vt* Korrektur *f*; Abgewöhnung *f*.
correctly [kə'rektlɪ] *adv* richtig; *behave* korrekt.
correlate ['kɒrɪleɪt] **1** *vt two things* zueinander in Beziehung setzen. **to** ~ **sth with sth** etw mit etw in Beziehung setzen. **2** *vi (two things)* sich entsprechen. **to** ~ **with sth** mit etw in Beziehung stehen.
correlation [ˌkɒrɪ'leɪʃən] *n (interdependence)* Wechselbeziehung *f*; *(Math, Statistics)* Korrelation *f*.
correspond [ˌkɒrɪs'pɒnd] *vi* **(a)** *(be equivalent)* entsprechen *(to, with dat)*; *(to one another)* sich entsprechen. **(b)** *(exchange letters)* korrespondieren *(with* mit*)*.
correspondence [ˌkɒrɪs'pɒndəns] *n* **(a)** *(agreement, equivalence)* Übereinstimmung *f (between* zwischen, *with* mit*)*. **(b)** *(letter-writing, letters)* Korrespondenz *f*. **to be in** ~ **with sb** mit jdm in Briefwechsel stehen.
correspondence: ~ **column** *n (Press)* Leserbriefspalte *f*; ~ **course** *n* Fernkurs *m*.
correspondent [ˌkɒrɪs'pɒndənt] *n* **(a)** *(letter-writer)* Briefschreiber(in *f*) *m*. **to be a bad** ~ schreibfaul sein. **(b)** *(Press)* Korrespondent(in *f*) *m*.
corresponding [ˌkɒrɪs'pɒndɪŋ] *adj* entsprechend.
corridor ['kɒrɪdɔːʳ] *n* Korridor *m*; *(in train, bus)* Gang *m*.
corroborate [kə'rɒbəreɪt] *vt* bestätigen.
corroboration [kəˌrɒbə'reɪʃən] *n* Bestätigung *f*.
corrode [kə'rəʊd] **1** *vt metal* zerfressen; *(fig)* zerstören. **2** *vi (metal)* korrodieren.
corrosion [kə'rəʊʒən] *n* Korrosion *f*; *(fig)* Zerstörung *f*.
corrosive [kə'rəʊzɪv] **1** *adj* korrosiv; *(fig)* zerstörend. **2** *n* Korrosion verursachendes Mittel.
corrugated ['kɒrəgeɪtɪd] *adj* gewellt. ~ **cardboard** dicke Wellpappe; ~ **iron** Wellblech *nt*.
corrupt [kə'rʌpt] **1** *adj* verdorben; *(open to bribery)* korrupt. **2** *vt (morally)* verderben; *(ethically)* korrumpieren; *(form: bribe)* bestechen.
corruption [kə'rʌpʃən] *n* **(a)** *(act: of person)* Korruption *f*. **(b)** *(corrupt nature)* Verdorbenheit *f*; *(by bribery)* Bestechlichkeit *f*; *(of morals)* Verfall *m*.
corset ['kɔːsɪt] *n (also* ~**s***)* Korsett *nt*. **surgical** ~ Stützkorsett *nt*.
Corsica ['kɔːsɪkə] *n* Korsika *nt*.
Corsican ['kɔːsɪkən] **1** *adj* korsisch. **2** *n* Korse *m*, Korsin *f*.
cortège [kɔː'teɪʒ] *n (retinue)* Gefolge *nt*; *(procession)* Prozession *f*; *(funeral* ~*)* Leichenzug *m*.
cortisone ['kɔːtɪzəʊn] *n* Kortison *nt*.
cos [kɒs] *n (also* ~ **lettuce***)* römischer Salat.
cosh [kɒʃ] *(Brit col)* **1** *vt* eins über den Schädel ziehen *(+dat) (col)*. **2** *n (instrument)* Totschläger *m*.
cosmetic [kɒz'metɪk] **1** *adj* kosmetisch. **she's had** ~ **surgery** sie hat eine Schönheitsoperation gehabt. **2** *n* Kosmetikum *nt*.
cosmic ['kɒzmɪk] *adj* kosmisch.
cosmonaut ['kɒzmənɔːt] *n* Kosmonaut(in *f*) *m*.
cosmopolitan [ˌkɒzmə'pɒlɪtən] **1** *adj* kosmopolitisch. **2** *n* Kosmopolit *m*.
cosmos ['kɒzmɒs] *n* Kosmos *m*.
cosset ['kɒsɪt] *vt* verwöhnen.
cost [kɒst] *(vb: pret, ptp* ~*)* **1** *vt* **(a)** *(lit, fig)* kosten. **how much does it** ~**?** wieviel kostet es?; **how much will it** ~ **to have it repaired?** wieviel kostet die Reparatur?; **it** ~ **(him) a lot of money** das hat (ihn) viel Geld gekostet; **it** ~ **him a great effort** es kostete ihn viel Mühe; ~ **what it may** koste es, was es wolle; **politeness doesn't** ~ **(you) anything** es kostet (dich) nichts, höflich zu sein. **(b)**

(Comm: put a price on) pret, ptp **~ed** *articles for sale* auszeichnen *(at* zu); *piece of work* veranschlagen *(at* mit).

2 *n* **(a)** Kosten *pl (of* für). **to bear the ~ of sth** die Kosten für etw tragen; **to buy sth at ~** etw zum Selbstkostenpreis kaufen. **(b)** *(fig)* Preis *m.* **at all ~s** um jeden Preis; **whatever the ~** kostet es, was es wolle; **at the ~ of one's health/job/marriage** *etc* auf Kosten seiner Gesundheit/Stelle/Ehe *etc*; **he found out to his ~ that ...** er machte die bittere Erfahrung, daß ... **(c)** *(Jur)* **~s** *pl* Kosten *pl*; **to be ordered to pay ~s** zur Übernahme der Kosten verurteilt werden.

co-star ['kəʊstɑːʳ] **1** *n (Film, Theat)* einer der Hauptdarsteller. **2** *vi* **she was ~ring with Robert Redford** sie spielte neben Robert Redford in einer der Hauptrollen.

cost: ~-conscious *adj* kostenbewußt; **~-effective** *adj* rentabel.

costing ['kɒstɪŋ] *n* Kalkulation *f.*

costly ['kɒstlɪ] *adj* kostspielig.

cost: ~ of living n Lebenshaltungskosten *pl*; **~-of-living index** *n* Lebenshaltungskostenindex *m*; **~ price** *n (Brit)* Selbstkostenpreis *m.*

costume ['kɒstjuːm] *n* Kostüm *nt*; *(bathing ~)* Badeanzug *m.* **national ~** Nationaltracht *f.*

costume: ~ ball *n* Kostümfest *nt*; **~ jewellery** *(Brit) or* **jewelry** *(US) n* Modeschmuck *m.*

cosy, *(US)* **cozy** ['kəʊzɪ] **1** *adj (+er) room, atmosphere* behaglich; *(warm)* mollig warm. **warm and ~** mollig warm. **2** *n (tea ~)* Wärmer *m.*

cot [kɒt] *n (esp Brit: child's bed)* Kinderbett *nt*; *(US: camp bed)* Feldbett *nt.*

cottage ['kɒtɪdʒ] *n* Cottage, Häuschen *nt*; *(US: in institution)* Wohneinheit *f.*

cottage: ~ cheese *n* Hüttenkäse *m*; **~ hospital** *n (Brit) kleines Krankenhaus für leichtere Fälle*; **~ industry** *n* Heimindustrie *f.*

cotter-pin ['kɒtəpɪn] *n* Splint *m.*

cotton ['kɒtn] **1** *n* Baumwolle *f*; *(plant)* Baumwollstrauch *m*; *(sewing thread)* (Baumwoll)garn *nt.* **absorbent ~** *(US)* Watte *f.* **2** *adj* Baumwoll-.

♦ **cotton on** *vi (col)* es kapieren *(col).*

cotton *in cpds* Baumwoll-; **~ batting** *n (US)* Gaze *f*; **~ candy** *n (US)* Zuckerwatte *f*; **~ mill** *n* Baumwollspinnerei *f*; **~-picking** *adj (US col)* verdammt *(col)*; **~ print** *n (fabric)* bedruckter Baumwollstoff; **~tail** *n (US)* Kaninchen *nt*; **~wool** *n (Brit)* Watte *f*; **to wrap sb in ~wool** *(fig)* jdn in Watte packen.

couch [kaʊtʃ] **1** *n* Couch *f.* **2** *vt (put in words)* formulieren.

couchette [kuː'ʃet] *n (Rail)* Liegewagenplatz *m.*

cough [kɒf] **1** *n* Husten *m.* **2** *vti* husten.

♦ **cough up 1** *vt sep (lit)* aushusten. **2** *vt insep (fig col) money* rausrücken *(col).* **3** *vi (fig col)* blechen *(col).*

cough: ~ drop *n* Hustenpastille *f*; **~ mixture** *n* Hustensaft *m*; **~ sweet** *n* Hustenbonbon *nt.*

could [kʊd] *pret of* **can**[1].

couldn't ['kʊdnt] = **could not.**

council ['kaʊnsl] **1** *n* Rat *m.* **city/town ~** Stadtrat *m.* **2** *attr estate (Brit)* ≈ des sozialen Wohnungsbaus. **~ house/housing** ≈ *(Brit)* Sozialwohnung *f*/sozialer Wohnungsbau; **~ chamber** Sitzungssaal *m* des Rats; **~man** *n (US)* = **councillor**; **~ meeting** Ratssitzung *f.*

councillor, *(US)* **councilor** ['kaʊnsələʳ] *n* Ratsmitglied *nt*; *(town ~)* Stadtrat *m*/-rätin *f.*

counsel ['kaʊnsəl] **1** *n* **(a)** *(form: advice)* Rat(schlag) *m.* **(b)** *(Jur)* Rechtsanwalt *m.* **~ for the defence/prosecution** Verteidiger(in *f*) *m*/Vertreter(in *f*) *m* der Anklage, ≈ Staatsanwalt *m*/-anwältin *f.* **2** *vt (form) person* beraten; *course of action* raten zu.

counsellor, *(US)* **counselor** ['kaʊnsələʳ] *n* **(a)** *(adviser)* Berater(in *f*) *m.* **(b)** *(US, Ir: lawyer)* Rechtsanwalt *m*/-anwältin *f.*

count[1] [kaʊnt] **1** *n* **(a)** Zählung *f*; *(of votes)* (Stimmen)auszählung *f.* **she lost ~ when she was interrupted** sie kam mit dem Zählen durcheinander, als sie unterbrochen wurde; **I've lost all ~** ich habe völlig die Übersicht verloren; **he was out for the ~** *(Sport)* er wurde ausgezählt; *(fig)* er war k.o. **(b)** *(Jur: charge)* Anklagepunkt *m.* **on that ~** *(fig)* in dem Punkt; **on all ~s** in jeder Hinsicht.

2 *vt* **(a)** (ab)zählen; *(~ again)* nachzählen; *votes* (aus)zählen. **to ~ the cost** *(lit)* auf die Kosten achten. **(b)** *(consider)* betrachten; *(include)* mitzählen. **to ~ sb among one's friends** jdn zu seinen Freunden zählen; **~ yourself lucky that ...** Sie können von Glück sagen, daß ...; **ten people ~ing the children** zehn Leute, die Kinder mitgerechnet.

3 *vi* **(a)** zählen. **~ing from today** von heute an (gerechnet). **(b)** *(be considered)* betrachtet werden; *(be included)* mitgezählt werden; *(be important)* wichtig sein. **that doesn't ~** das zählt nicht; **to ~ against sb** gegen jdn sprechen.

♦ **count in** *vt sep* mitzählen. **you can ~ me ~!** da bin ich dabei.

♦ **count on** *vi +prep obj (depend on)* rechnen mit. **you can ~ ~ him to help you** du kannst auf seine Hilfe zählen.

♦ **count out** *vt sep* **(a)** *(Sport)* auszählen. **(b)** *money, books etc* abzählen. **(c)** *(col: exclude)* **(you can) ~ me ~ (of that)!** ohne mich!, da mache ich nicht mit!

♦ **count up** *vt sep* zusammenzählen.

♦ **count upon** *vi +prep obj* = **count on.**

count[2] *n* Graf *m.*

countable ['kaʊntəbl] *adj* zählbar *(also Gram).*

countdown ['kaʊntdaʊn] *n* Countdown *m.* **to start the ~** mit dem Countdown beginnen.

countenance ['kaʊntɪnəns] **1** *n (old, form; face)* Antlitz *nt (old).* **to keep one's ~** *(fig)* die Haltung bewahren. **2** *vt behaviour* gutheißen.

counter ['kaʊntəʳ] **1** *n* **(a)** *(in shop)* Ladentisch *m*; *(in cafe)* Theke *f*; *(in bank, post office)* Schalter *m.* **under-the-~ dealings** *(fig)* undurchsichtige Geschäfte. **(b)** *(for games)* Spielmarke *f.* **(c)** *(Tech)* Zähler *m.* **2** *vt (retaliate against)* antworten auf *(+acc).* **3** *vi* kontern *(also Sport).* **4** *adv* **~ to** gegen *(+acc)*; **to run ~ to sb's wishes** jds Wünschen *(dat)* zuwiderlaufen.

counter: ~act *vt (make ineffective)* neutralisieren; *(act in opposition to)* entgegenwirken *(+dat)*; *disease* bekämpfen; **~action** *n see vt* Neutralisierung *f*; Gegenwirkung *f*; Bekämpfung *f*; **~attack 1** *n* Gegenangriff *m*; **2** *vi* einen Gegenangriff starten; **~balance 1** *n* Gegengewicht *nt*; **2** *vt* ausgleichen; **~clockwise** *adj, adv (US)* = **anti-clockwise; ~espionage** *n* Gegenspionage *f.*

counterfeit ['kaʊntəfiːt] **1** *adj* gefälscht; *(fig)* falsch. **~ money** Falschgeld *nt.* **2** *n* Fälschung *f.* **3** *vt* fälschen.

counterfoil ['kaʊntəfɔɪl] *n (Brit)* Kontrollabschnitt *m.*

counterintelligence [,kaʊntərɪn'telɪdʒəns] *n* Gegenspionage *f.*

countermand ['kaʊntəmɑːnd] *vt order* aufheben; *attack, plan* rückgängig machen.

counter: ~measure *n* Gegenmaßnahme *f*; **~offensive** *n (Mil)* Gegenoffensive *f*; **~-offer** *n* Gegenangebot *nt*; **~pane** *n* Tagesdecke *f*; **~part** *n (equivalent)* Gegenüber *nt*; *(complement)* Gegenstück *nt*; **~-productive** *adj* widersinnig; *measures* destruktiv; **that'd be ~-productive** das würde den Zweck verfehlen; **that runs the risk of being ~-productive** es besteht die Gefahr, daß dadurch das Gegenteil bewirkt wird; **~sign** *vt cheque etc* gegenzeichnen; **~sink** *vt hole* senken; *screw* versenken; **~weight** *n* Gegengewicht *nt.*

countess ['kaʊntɪs] *n* Gräfin *f.*

countless ['kaʊntlɪs] *adj* unzählig *attr*, zahllos *attr*.

country ['kʌntrɪ] *n* **(a)** *(state)* Land *nt*. **his own ~** seine Heimat; **to die for one's ~** für sein Land sterben; **to go to the ~** *(Pol)* Wahlen ausschreiben. **(b)** *no pl (as opposed to town)* Land *nt*. **in/to the ~** auf dem/aufs Land; **the surrounding ~** die Umgebung; **there's some lovely ~ up north** die Gegend im Norden ist herrlich.

country *in cpds* Land-; **~-and-western** *n* Country-music *f*; **~ bumpkin** *n (pej)* Bauerntölpel *(col) m*; *(girl)* Bauerntrampel *m (col)*; **~ cousin** *n* Vetter *m*/Cousine *f* vom Lande; **~ dancing** *n* Volkstanz *m*; **~ dweller** *n* Landbewohner(in *f*) *m*; **~ house** *n* Landhaus *nt*; **~man** *n* **(a)** Landsmann *m*; **his fellow ~men** seine Landsleute; **(b)** *(country-dweller)* Landbewohner *m*; **~ people** *npl* Leute *pl* vom Land(e); **~side** *n (scenery)* Landschaft *f*; **it's beautiful ~side** das ist eine herrliche Landschaft; **~ town** *n* Kleinstadt *f*; **~-wide** *adj* landesweit; **~woman** *n* **(a)** Landsmännin *f*; **(b)** *(country dweller)* Landbewohnerin *f*.

county ['kaʊntɪ] *n (Brit)* Grafschaft *f*; *(US)* (Verwaltungs)bezirk *m*.

county: ~ council *n (Brit)* Grafschaftsrat *m*; **~ town** *n (Brit) Hauptstadt f einer Grafschaft.*

coup [kuː] *n* **(a)** *(successful action)* Coup *m*. **(b)** *(~ d'état)* Staatsstreich *m*.

coupé ['kuːpeɪ] *n (car)* Coupé *nt*.

couple ['kʌpl] **1** *n* **(a)** *(pair)* Paar *nt*; *(married ~)* Ehepaar *nt*. **(b)** *(col)* **a ~** *(two)* zwei; *(several)* ein paar; **a ~ of friends** ein paar Freunde; **a ~ of times** ein paarmal. **2** *vt ideas etc* verbinden; *carriages etc* koppeln.

coupling ['kʌplɪŋ] *n* **(a)** *(linking)* Verbindung *f*; *(of carriages etc)* Kopplung *f*. **(b)** *(device)* Kupplung *f*.

coupon ['kuːpɒn] *n* **(a)** *(voucher)* Gutschein *m*. **(b)** *(Ftbl)* Wettschein *m*.

courage ['kʌrɪdʒ] *n* Mut *m*. **I haven't the ~ to refuse** ich habe einfach nicht den Mut, nein zu sagen; **to have the ~ of one's convictions** Zivilcourage haben; **to take one's ~ in both hands** sein Herz in beide Hände nehmen.

courageous [kə'reɪdʒəs] *adj* mutig.

courgette ['kʊəʒet] *n (Brit)* Zucchini *f*.

courier ['kʊrɪə^r] *n (messenger)* Kurier *m*; *(tourist guide)* Reiseleiter(in *f*) *m*.

course[1] [kɔːs] *n* **(a)** *(direction)* Kurs *m*; *(of river, history)* Lauf *m*; *(fig: of illness)* Verlauf *m*. **to set ~ for a place** Kurs auf einen Ort nehmen; **to change ~** den Kurs ändern; **to be on/off ~** auf Kurs sein/vom Kurs abgekommen sein; **to let sth take its ~** einer Sache *(dat)* ihren Lauf lassen; **the ~ of true love ne'er did run smooth** *(prov)* Liebe geht oft seltsame Wege *(prov)*; **which ~ of action did you take?** wie sind Sie vorgegangen?; **the best ~ would be ...** das beste wäre ...; **we have no other ~ (of action) but to ...** es bleibt uns nichts anderes übrig als zu ...

(b) in the ~ of his life/the next few weeks/the meeting *etc* während seines Lebens/der nächsten paar Wochen/der Versammlung *etc*; **in the ~ of time/the conversation** im Laufe der Zeit/Unterhaltung; **in the ordinary ~ of things** unter normalen Umständen; **in the ~ of construction** im Bau.

(c) of ~ *(admittedly)* natürlich; *(obviously)* selbstverständlich; **of ~ I will!** aber natürlich; **of ~ I'm coming** natürlich komme ich.

(d) *(Sch, Univ)* Kurs(us) *m*; *(at work)* Lehrgang *m*; *(Med: of treatment)* Kur *f*. **to go to/on a French ~** einen Französischkurs(us) besuchen; **a ~ of lectures** eine Vorlesungsreihe; **a ~ of treatment** eine Behandlung.

(e) *(Sports) (race ~)* Kurs *m*; *(golf ~)* Platz *m*.

(f) *(Cook)* Gang *m*. **a three-~ meal** ein Essen mit drei Gängen.

course[2] *vi (blood, tears)* strömen.

court [kɔːt] **1** *n* **(a)** *(Jur)* Gericht *nt*; *(room)* Gerichtssaal *m*. **to appear in ~** vor Gericht erscheinen; **his suggestion was ruled out of ~** *(fig)* sein Vorschlag wurde verworfen; **to take sb to ~** jdn vor Gericht bringen. **(b)** *(royal)* Hof *m*. **(c)** *(Sport)* Platz *m*. **2** *vt* **(a)** *(dated) woman* den Hof machen *(+dat)*. **(b)** *(fig) danger* herausfordern. **3** *vi (dated)* **she's ~ing** sie hat einen Freund; **~ing couple** Liebespaar *nt*.

court card *n (Brit)* Bildkarte *f*.

courteous ['kɜːtɪəs] *adj* höflich.

courtesy ['kɜːtɪsɪ] *n* Höflichkeit *f*. **by ~ of ...** freundlicherweise zur Verfügung gestellt von ...; **you might have had the ~ to ...** sie hätten doch so freundlich sein können und ...

courtesy: ~ coach *n* gebührenfreier Bus; **~ light** *n (Aut)* Innenleuchte *f*; **~ visit** *n* Höflichkeitsbesuch *m*.

courthouse ['kɔːthaʊs] *n (Jur)* Gerichtsgebäude *nt*.

courtier ['kɔːtɪə^r] *n* Höfling *m*.

court-martial ['kɔːt'mɑːʃəl] **1** *n (Mil)* Kriegsgericht *nt*. **2** *vt* vor das/ein Kriegsgericht stellen.

courtship ['kɔːtʃɪp] *n (dated)* (Braut)werbung *f (dated) (of* um*)*.

court: ~ shoe *n* Pumps *m*; **~yard** *n* Hof *m*.

cousin ['kʌzn] *n (male)* Vetter, Cousin *m*; *(female)* Cousine *f*.

cove[1] [kəʊv] *n (Geog)* (kleine) Bucht.

cove[2] *n (dated Brit col: fellow)* Kerl *m (col)*.

covenant ['kʌvɪnənt] **1** *n* Schwur *m*; *(Bibl)* Bund *m*; *(Jur)* Verpflichtung *f* zu regelmäßigen Spenden. **2** *vt* **to ~ to do sth** durch ein Abkommen versprechen, etw zu tun.

Coventry ['kɒvəntrɪ] *n*: **to send sb to ~** *(Brit col)* jdn schneiden *(col)*.

cover ['kʌvə^r] **1** *n* **(a)** *(lid)* Deckel *m*; *(of lens)* (Schutz)kappe *f*; *(on chair etc)* Bezug *m*; *(for typewriter etc)* Hülle *f*; *(on lorries, tennis court)* Plane *f*; *(over merchandise)* Decke *f*; *(quilt)* (Bett)decke *f*.

(b) *(of book)* Einband *m*; *(of magazine)* Umschlag *m*. **to read a book from ~ to ~** ein Buch von der ersten bis zur letzten Seite lesen.

(c) *(Comm: envelope)* Umschlag *m*. **under separate ~** mit getrennter Post.

(d) *no pl (shelter, protection)* Schutz *m (from* vor *+dat*, gegen*)*; *(Mil)* Deckung *f (from* vor *+dat*, gegen*)*. **to take ~** *(from rain)* sich unterstellen; *(Mil)* in Deckung gehen *(from* vor *+dat)*; **under the ~ of the trees** im Schutz der Bäume; **under ~ of darkness** im Schutz(e) der Dunkelheit; **to give sb ~** *(Mil)* jdm Deckung geben.

(e) *(Hunt)* Deckung *f*. **to break ~** aus der Deckung hervorbrechen.

(f) *(place at meal)* Gedeck *nt*.

(g) *(Comm, Fin)* Deckung *f*; *(insurance ~)* Versicherung *f*. **to take out ~ against fire** eine Feuerversicherung abschließen; **do you have adequate ~?** sind Sie ausreichend versichert?

2 *vt* **(a)** bedecken; *(cover over)* zudecken; *(with loose cover) chair etc* beziehen. **to ~ oneself in** *or* **with glory** *(iro)* sich mit Ruhm bekleckern *(iro col)*; **~ed in** *or* **with shame** zutiefst beschämt.

(b) *(hide)* verbergen.

(c) *(Mil, Sport, Chess: protect)* decken. **he only said that to ~ himself** er hat das nur gesagt, um sich zu decken; **I'll keep you ~ed** ich gebe dir Deckung.

(d) *(point a gun at etc) door etc* sichern; *sb* in Schach halten; *(be on guard near)* sichern. **to keep sb ~ed** jdn in Schach halten; **I've got you ~ed!** *(with gun etc)* ich hab auf dich angelegt; *(fig: Chess etc)* ich hab' dich.

(e) *(Fin) loan* decken; *(Insur)* versichern. **will £3 ~ the petrol?** reichen £3 für das Benzin?; **we've ~ed most eventualities** wir haben die meisten Eventualitäten abgedeckt.

(**f**) *(Press: report on)* berichten über *(+acc)*.
(**g**) *(travel) miles, distance* zurücklegen; *(deal with) topics* behandeln. **we've ~ed a lot today** wir haben heute viel geschafft.
(**h**) *(salesman etc) territory* zuständig sein für.

♦**cover for** *vi + prep obj* vertreten.
♦**cover over** *vt sep* zudecken.
♦**cover up 1** *vi* **(a)** *(wrap up)* sich einmummen. **(b)** *(conceal a fact)* alles vertuschen. **to ~ ~ for sb** jdn decken. **2** *vt sep* **(a)** *child* zudecken. **(b)** *(hide) truth, facts* vertuschen.
coverage ['kʌvərɪdʒ] *n no pl* **(a)** *(in media)* Berichterstattung *f (of* über *+acc).* **to give full ~ to an event** ausführlich über ein Ereignis berichten. **(b)** *(Insur)* Versicherung *f.*
cover: ~all *n usu pl (US)* Overall *m*; **~ charge** *n* Kosten *pl* für ein Gedeck; **~ girl** *n* Titelmädchen *nt.*
covering ['kʌvərɪŋ] *n* Decke *f*; *(floor ~)* Belag *m.* **a ~ of dust/snow** eine Staub-/Schneedecke.
covering letter *n* Begleitbrief *m.*
cover note *n* vorläufiger Versicherungsschein.
covert ['kʌvət] *adj threat, attack* versteckt; *glance* verstohlen.
cover-up ['kʌvərʌp] *n* Vertuschung *f.*
covet ['kʌvɪt] *vt* begehren.
covetous ['kʌvɪtəs] *adj* begehrlich.
cow[1] [kaʊ] *n* **(a)** Kuh *f.* **~ elephant** Elefantenkuh *f*; **you'll be waiting till the ~s come home** *(fig col)* da kannst du warten, bis du schwarz wirst *(col)*. **(b)** *(pej col: woman) (stupid)* Kuh *f (col)*; *(nasty)* gemeine Ziege *(col)*.
cow[2] *vt person, animal* einschüchtern. **she had a ~ed look about her** sie machte einen eingeschüchterten Eindruck.
coward ['kaʊəd] *n* Feigling *m.*
cowardice ['kaʊədɪs], **cowardliness** ['kaʊədlɪnɪs] *n* Feigheit *f.*
cowardly ['kaʊədlɪ] *adj* feig(e).
cow: ~boy *n* Cowboy *m*; **~catcher** *n (Rail)* Schienenräumer *m.*
cower ['kaʊə^r] *vi* sich ducken; *(squatting)* kauern.
cowhide ['kaʊhaɪd] *n* **(a)** *(untanned)* Kuhhaut *f*; *(no pl: leather)* Rindsleder *nt.* **(b)** *(US: whip)* Lederpeitsche *f.*
cowl [kaʊl] *n* **(a)** *(monk's hood)* Kapuze *f.* **(b)** *(chimney ~)* (Schornstein)kappe *f.*
cowman ['kaʊmən] *n, pl* **-men** [-mən] *(farm labourer)* Stallbursche *m*; *(US: cattle rancher)* Viehzüchter *m.*
cow: ~shed *n* Kuhstall *m*; **~slip** *n (Brit: primrose)* Schlüsselblume *f*; *(US: kingcup)* Sumpfdotterblume *f.*
cox [kɒks] **1** *n* Steuermann *m.* **2** *vt crew* Steuermann sein für. **3** *vi* steuern.
coy [kɔɪ] *adj (+er) (affectedly shy)* verschämt; *(coquettish)* kokett.
cozy *adj (US)* = **cosy.**
crab [kræb] *n* Krabbe *f.*
crab apple *n* Holzapfel *m.*
crack [kræk] **1** *n* **(a)** Riß *m*; *(between floorboards etc)* Ritze *f*; *(wider hole etc)* Spalte *f*; *(in pottery etc)* Sprung *m.* **at the ~ of dawn** in aller Frühe. **(b)** *(sharp noise) (of wood etc breaking)* Knacks *m*; *(of gun, whip)* Knall(en *nt no pl) m*; *(of thunder)* Schlag *m.* **(c)** *(sharp blow)* Schlag *m.* **to give sb/oneself a ~ on the head** jdm eins auf den Kopf geben/sich *(dat)* den Kopf anschlagen. **(d)** *(col) (gibe)* Stichelei *f*; *(joke)* Witz *m.* **(e)** *(col: attempt)* **to have a ~ at sth** etw mal probieren *(col)*.
2 *adj attr* erstklassig; *(Mil)* Elite-. **~ shot** Meisterschütze *m.*
3 *vt nuts, (col) safe, (fig) code* knacken; *problem, case* lösen; *joke* reißen; *whip* knallen mit. **I think I've ~ed it** ich glaub, ich hab's.
4 *vi* **(a)** *(get a ~) (pottery)* springen; *(ice, road)* einen Riß/Risse bekommen; *(lips, skin)* spröde werden; *(bones)* einen Knacks bekommen *(col)*; *(break)* brechen. **(b)** *(twigs, joints)* knacken; *(whip, gun)* knallen. **(c)** *(col)* **to get ~ing** loslegen *(col)*.

♦**crack down** *vi (clamp down)* hart durchgreifen *(on* bei*)*.
♦**crack up 1** *vi* **(a)** *(break into pieces)* zerbrechen. **(b)** *(fig col: person)* zusammenbrechen. **2** *vt sep (col)* **he's not all he's ~ed ~ to be** so toll ist er dann auch wieder nicht.
cracked [krækt] *adj* **(a)** *plate* gesprungen; *rib* angebrochen; *walls* rissig. **(b)** *(col: mad)* übergeschnappt *(col)*.
cracker ['krækə^r] *n* **(a)** *(biscuit)* Kräcker *m.* **(b)** *(fire~)* Knallkörper *m*; *(Christmas ~)* Knallbonbon *nt.*
crackers ['krækəz] *adj pred (Brit col)* übergeschnappt *(col)*.
crackle ['krækl] **1** *vi (dry leaves, paper)* rascheln; *(fire)* knistern; *(twigs, telephone line)* knacken. **2** *n (crackling noise) see vi* Rascheln *nt*; Knistern *nt*; Knacken *nt.*
crackling ['kræklɪŋ] *n no pl* **(a)** = **crackle 2. (b)** *(Cook)* Kruste *f (des Schweinebratens)*.
cradle ['kreɪdl] **1** *n* Wiege *f*; *(of phone)* Gabel *f.* **from the ~ to the grave** von der Wiege bis zur Bahre. **2** *vt (hold closely)* an sich *(acc)* drücken. **he was cradling his injured arm** er hielt sich *(dat)* seinen verletzten Arm; **to ~ sb/sth in one's arms** jdn/etw fest in den Armen halten.
cradle-song ['kreɪdlsɒŋ] *n* Wiegenlied *nt.*
craft [krɑːft] *n* **(a)** *(handicraft)* Kunst *f*; *(trade)* Handwerk *nt*; *(weaving, pottery etc)* Kunstgewerbe *nt.* **(b)** *no pl (skill)* Geschick(lichkeit *f) nt*, Kunstfertigkeit *f.* **(c)** *no pl (cunning)* List *f.* **(d)** *pl - (boat)* Boot *nt.*
craftsman ['krɑːftsmən] *n, pl* **-men** [-mən] Handwerker *m.*
craftsmanship ['krɑːftsmənʃɪp] *n* Handwerkskunst *f*; *(of person)* handwerkliches Können.
crafty ['krɑːftɪ] *adj (+er) (shrewd)* schlau; *(sly)* durchtrieben.
crag [kræg] *n* Fels *m.*
craggy ['krægɪ] *adj (+er) (rocky)* felsig; *(jagged)* zerklüftet; *face* kantig.
cram [kræm] **1** *vt* **(a)** *(fill)* vollstopfen; *(stuff in)* hineinstopfen *(in(to)* in *+acc)*; *people* hineinzwängen *(in(to)* in *+acc)*. **the room was ~med** der Raum war gestopft voll; **he ~med his hat (down) over his eyes** er zog sich *(dat)* den Hut tief ins Gesicht. **(b)** *Latin etc* pauken *(col)*, büffeln *(col)*; *pupil* pauken mit *(col)*. **2** *vi (swot)* pauken *(col)*, büffeln *(col)*.
cramp [kræmp] **1** *n (Med)* Krampf *m.* **2** *vt (also ~* **up***) persons* zusammenpferchen. **to ~ sb's style** jdm im Weg sein.
cramped [kræmpt] *adj* **(a)** *space* beschränkt. **we are very ~ (for space)** wir sind räumlich sehr beschränkt. **(b)** *position* verkrampft.
cranberry ['krænbərɪ] *n* Preiselbeere *f.*
crane [kreɪn] **1** *n* **(a)** Kran *m.* **~ driver** *n* Kranführer *m.* **(b)** *(Orn)* Kranich *m.* **2** *vt*: **to ~ one's neck** den Hals recken. **3** *vi (also ~* **forward***)* den Hals *or* den Kopf recken.
crank[1] [kræŋk] *n (eccentric)* Spinner(in *f) m (col)*; *(US: cross person)* Griesgram *m.*
crank[2] **1** *n (Mech)* Kurbel *f.* **2** *vt (also: ~* **up***)* ankurbeln.
crankshaft ['kræŋkʃɑːft] *n (Aut)* Kurbelwelle *f.*
cranky ['kræŋkɪ] *adj (+er)* **(a)** *(eccentric)* verrückt. **(b)** *(US: bad-tempered)* griesgrämig.
crap [kræp] *n (lit, fig: col!)* Scheiße *f (col!)*. **to go for a ~** aufs Scheißhaus gehen *(col!)*.
crap game *n (US)* Würfelspiel *nt (mit zwei Würfeln)*.
crappy ['kræpɪ] *adj (col!)* beschissen *(col!)*.
crash [kræʃ] **1** *n* **(a)** *(noise)* Krach(en *nt) m no pl*; *(of thunder etc)* Schlag *m.* **(b)** *(accident)* Unfall *m*;

(collision also) Zusammenstoß *m*; *(with several cars)* Karambolage *f*; *(plane ~)* (Flugzeug)unglück *nt*. **to have a ~** (mit dem Auto) verunglücken. **(c)** *(Fin)* Zusammenbruch *m*. **2** *vt car* einen Unfall haben mit; *plane* abstürzen mit. **to ~ one's car/plane into sth** mit dem Auto/Flugzeug gegen etw krachen. **3** *vi* **(a)** *(have an accident)* verunglücken; *(plane)* abstürzen. **to ~ into sth** gegen etw krachen. **(b)** *(move with a ~)* krachen. **to ~ to the ground/through sth** zu Boden/durch etw krachen; **his whole world ~ed about him** eine Welt brach für ihn zusammen. **(c)** *(Fin)* pleite machen *(col)*; *(stock market)* zusammenbrechen.

♦ **crash out** *vi (col: fall asleep)* sich hinhauen *(col)*; *(without meaning to)* wegtreten *(col)*.

crash: ~ barrier *n (Brit)* Leitplanke *f*; **~ course** *n* Intensivkurs *m*; **~ diet** *n* Radikalkur *f*; **~ dive 1** *n* Schnelltauchmanöver *nt*; **2** *vti* schnelltauchen; **~ helmet** *n* Sturzhelm *m*; **~-land** *vi* eine Bruchlandung machen; **~-landing** *n* Bruchlandung *f*.

crass [kræs] *adj (+er) (unsubtle)* kraß.

crate [kreɪt] *n (also col: car, plane)* Kiste *f*; *(of bottles)* Kasten *m*.

crater ['kreɪtəʳ] *n* Krater *m*.

cravat(te) [krə'væt] *n* Halstuch *nt*.

crave [kreɪv] *vt (liter: beg)* erbitten; *attention, drink etc* sich sehnen nach.

craving ['kreɪvɪŋ] *n* Verlangen *nt*. **to have a ~ for sth** Verlangen nach etw haben.

crawfish ['krɔːfɪʃ] *n* Languste *f*.

crawl [krɔːl] **1** *n* **(a)** *(on hands and knees)* Kriechen *nt*; *(slow speed)* Kriechtempo *nt*. **(b)** *(swimming stroke)* Kraulstil *m*. **to do the ~** kraulen. **2** *vi* **(a)** kriechen; *(baby, insects)* krabbeln. **(b)** *(be infested)* wimmeln *(with* von*)*. **the place is ~ing!** hier wimmelt es von Ungeziefer! **(c)** *(col: suck up)* kriechen *(to* vor *+dat)*.

crawler lane ['krɔːləleɪn] *n (Brit Aut)* Kriechspur *f*.

crayfish ['kreɪfɪʃ] *n* **(a)** *(freshwater)* Flußkrebs *m*. **(b)** *(saltwater: also* **crawfish***)* Languste *f*.

crayon ['kreɪən] *n (pencil)* Buntstift *m*; *(wax ~)* Wachs(mal)stift *m*; *(chalk ~)* Pastellstift *m*.

craze [kreɪz] **1** *n (of person)* Fimmel *m (col)*. **it's the latest ~** es ist jetzt in *(col)*. **2** *vt* **(a)** *(make insane)* **to be half ~d with grief** vor Schmerz halb wahnsinnig sein; **he had a ~d look** er sah wie wahnsinnig aus. **(b)** *glazing* rissig machen.

crazy ['kreɪzɪ] *adj (+er)* **(a)** verrückt *(with* vor *+dat)*. **to drive sb ~** jdn verrückt machen; **to go ~** verrückt werden. **(b)** *(col: enthusiastic)* verrückt *(col)*. **to be ~ about sb/sth** ganz verrückt auf jdn/etw sein *(col)*. **(c)** *angle, tilt* unwahrscheinlich.

crazy paving *n* Mosaikpflaster *nt*.

creak [kriːk] **1** *n* Knarren *nt no pl*; *(of hinges, bed)* Quietschen *nt no pl*; *(of knees etc)* Knacken *nt no pl*. **2** *vi* knarren; *(hinges, bed)* quietschen; *(knees etc)* knacken.

cream [kriːm] **1** *n* **(a)** Sahne *f*; *(~ pudding, artificial ~)* Creme *f*. **~ of tomato/chicken soup** Tomaten-/Hühnercremesuppe *f*. **(b)** *(lotion)* Creme *f*. **(c)** *(colour)* Creme(farbe *f*) *nt*. **(d)** *(fig: best)* **the ~** die Besten; *(of society)* die Elite *f*. **2** *adj (colour)* cremefarben. **3** *vt* **(a)** *(put ~ on) face etc* eincremen. **(b)** *butter etc* cremig rühren; *potatoes* pürieren. **~ed potatoes** Kartoffelpüree *nt*. **(c)** *milk* entrahmen.

♦ **cream off** *vt sep (lit)* abschöpfen; *(fig)* absahnen.

cream: ~ cake *n* Sahnetorte *f*; **~ cheese** *n* (Doppelrahm)frischkäse *m*.

creamery ['kriːmərɪ] *n* Molkerei *f*.

creamy ['kriːmɪ] *adj (+er) (tasting of cream)* sahnig; *(smooth)* cremig.

crease [kriːs] **1** *n* Falte *f*. **to put a ~ in a pair of trousers** eine Falte in eine Hose bügeln. **2** *vt (deliberately) clothes* Falten/eine Falte machen in *(+acc)*; *paper* falzen; *(unintentionally)* zerknittern. **3** *vi* knittern. **his face ~d with laughter** er fing an zu lachen.

crease-resistant ['kriːsrɪzɪstənt] *adj* knitterfrei.

create [kriː'eɪt] **1** *vt* **(a)** schaffen; *fashion* kreieren; *the world, man* erschaffen; *fuss* verursachen; *difficulties, impression* machen. **to ~ a sensation** eine Sensation sein; **to ~ a fuss** Theater machen *(col)*. **(b)** *peer* ernennen. **2** *vi (Brit col)* Theater machen *(col)*.

creation [kriː'eɪʃən] *n* **(a)** *no pl see vt* Schaffung *f*; Kreation *f*; Erschaffung *f*; Verursachung *f*; Ernennung *f*. **(b)** *no pl* **the C~** die Schöpfung. **(c)** *(Art)* Werk *nt*; *(Fashion)* Kreation *f*.

creative [krɪː'eɪtɪv] *adj* kreativ.

creativity [ˌkriːeɪ'tɪvɪtɪ] *n* Kreativität *f*.

creator [krɪ'eɪtəʳ] *n* Schöpfer(in *f*) *m*.

creature ['kriːtʃəʳ] *n* Geschöpf *nt*. **she's a poor/funny ~** sie ist ein armes/komisches Geschöpf.

creature comforts *npl* leibliches Wohl.

crèche [kreɪʃ] *n (Brit)* (Kinder)krippe *f*.

credentials [krɪ'denʃəlz] *npl (references)* Referenzen *pl*; *(papers of identity)* (Ausweis)papiere *pl*.

credibility [ˌkredə'bɪlɪtɪ] *n* Glaubwürdigkeit *f*. **there's a ~ gap** es besteht ein Mangel an Glaubwürdigkeit.

credible ['kredɪbl] *adj* glaubwürdig.

credit ['kredɪt] **1** *n* **(a)** *no pl (Fin)* Kredit *m*. **the bank will let me have £5,000 ~** die Bank räumt mir einen Kredit von £ 5.000 ein; **his ~ is good** er ist kreditwürdig; **to give sb ~** jdm Kredit geben; **to be in ~** Geld auf dem Konto haben. **(b)** *no pl (honour)* Ehre *f*; *(recognition)* Anerkennung *f*; *(Sch, Univ: distinction)* Auszeichnung *f*. **he's a ~ to his family** er macht seiner Familie Ehre; **that's to his ~** das muß man ihm hoch anrechnen; **to take the ~ for sth** das Verdienst für etw in Anspruch nehmen; **I gave you ~ for more sense** ich habe Sie für vernünftiger gehalten. **(c)** *(esp US Univ)* Schein *m*. **(d) ~s** *pl (Film etc)* Vor-/Nachspann *m*.

2 *vt* **(a)** *(believe)* glauben. **would you ~ it!** ist das denn die Möglichkeit! **(b)** *(attribute)* zuschreiben *(+dat)*. **I ~ed him with more sense** ich habe ihn für vernünftiger gehalten; **it's ~ed with (having) magic powers** ihm werden Zauberkräfte zugeschrieben. **(c)** *(Fin)* gutschreiben. **to ~ a sum to sb's account** jds Konto *(dat)* einen Betrag gutschreiben.

creditable ['kredɪtəbl] *adj (praiseworthy)* lobenswert.

credit: ~ card *n* Kreditkarte *f*; **~ facilities** *npl* Kreditmöglichkeiten *pl*; **~ note** *n (Brit)* Gutschrift *f*.

creditor ['kredɪtəʳ] *n* Gläubiger *m*.

credit: ~ squeeze *n* Kreditbeschränkung *f*; **~ terms** *npl* Kreditbedingungen *pl*; **~-worthy** *adj* kreditwürdig.

credulity [krɪ'djuːlɪtɪ] *n no pl* Leichtgläubigkeit *f*.

credulous ['kredjʊləs] *adj* leichtgläubig.

creed [kriːd] *n (Eccl)* Glaubensbekenntnis *nt*.

creek [kriːk] *n (esp Brit: inlet)* (kleine) Bucht; *(US: brook)* Bach *m*. **to be up the ~** *(col: be in trouble)* in der Tinte sitzen *(col)*.

creep [kriːp] *(vb: pret, ptp* **crept***)* **1** *vi* **(a)** schleichen; *(crawl)* kriechen. **ivy is a ~ing plant** Efeu ist eine Kletterpflanze; **time's ~ing on** die Zeit verrinnt. **(b) the story made my flesh ~** bei der Geschichte überlief es mich kalt. **2** *n* **(a)** *(col: unpleasant person)* fieser Typ *(col)*. **(b) this old house gives me the ~s** *(col)* in dem alten Haus kriege ich das kalte Grausen *(col)*.

♦ **creep in** *vi (mistakes, new tone etc)* sich einschleichen *(-to* in *+acc)*.

♦ **creep over** *vi +prep obj (pleasant feeling)* überkommen.

♦**creep up** *vi* **(a)** *(person)* sich heranschleichen *(on* an *+acc)*; *(prices)* (in die Höhe) klettern. **(b) to ~ ~ on sb** *(time, exam)* langsam auf jdn zukommen; **old age is ~ing ~ on him** er wird langsam alt.

creeper ['kriːpəʳ] *n* **(a)** *(plant) (along ground)* Kriechpflanze *f*; *(upwards)* Kletterpflanze *f*. **(b) ~s** *pl (US: shoes)* Leisetreter *pl (col)*.

creepy ['kriːpɪ] *adj (+er) (frightening)* unheimlich.

creepy-crawly ['kriːpɪ'krɔːlɪ] *(col) n* Krabbeltier *nt (col)*.

cremate [krɪ'meɪt] *vt* einäschern.

cremation [krɪ'meɪʃən] *n* Einäscherung *f*.

crematorium [ˌkremə'tɔːrɪəm], *(esp US)* **crematory** ['kreməˌtɔːrɪ] *n* Krematorium *nt*.

creosote ['krɪəsəʊt] **1** *n* Kreosot *nt (ein Holzschutzmittel)*. **2** *vt* mit Kreosot streichen.

crêpe [kreɪp]: **~ bandage** *n* elastischer Verband; **~ paper** *n* Kreppapier *nt*; **~ rubber 1** *n* Kreppgummi *m*; **2** *adj* Kreppgummi-; **~-soled** [kreɪp'səʊld] *adj* mit Kreppsohle(n).

crept [krept] *pret, ptp of* **creep.**

crescendo [krɪ'ʃendəʊ] *n (Mus)* Crescendo *nt*; *(fig)* Zunahme *f*.

crescent ['kresnt] **1** *n* Halbmond *m*; *(street)* Straße *f (halbmondförmig verlaufend)*. **2** *adj* **~-shaped** *adj* halbmondförmig; **the ~ moon** die Mondsichel.

cress [kres] *n* (Garten)kresse *f*; *(water~)* Brunnenkresse *f*.

crest [krest] *n* **(a)** *(of bird)* Haube *f*; *(of cock)* Kamm *m*; *(on hat etc)* Federbusch *m*. **(b)** *(Her)* Helmzierde *f*; *(coat of arms)* Wappen *nt*. **(c)** *(of wave, hill, Anat: of horse etc)* Kamm *m*; *(fig: of excitement, popularity)* Höhepunkt *m*; *(Phys: of oscillation)* Scheitel(punkt) *m*. **he's riding on the ~ of a wave** *(fig)* er schwimmt im Augenblick oben.

crestfallen ['krestˌfɔːlən] *adj* niedergeschlagen.

Crete [kriːt] *n* Kreta *nt*.

cretin ['kretɪn] *n (Med)* Kretin *m*; *(col)* Schwachkopf *m (col)*.

crevasse [krɪ'væs] *n* (Gletscher)spalte *f*.

crevice ['krevɪs] *n* Spalte *f*.

crew[1] [kruː] **1** *n* **(a)** Mannschaft *(also Sport) f*; *(including officers: of ship also, of plane, tank)* Besatzung *f*. **50 passengers and 20 ~** 50 Passagiere und 20 Mann Besatzung; **the ground ~** *(Aviat)* das Bodenpersonal. **(b)** *(col: gang)* Bande *f*. **they were a motley ~** sie waren ein bunt zusammengewürfelter Haufen *(col)*. **2** *vt yacht* die Mannschaft sein von. **3** *vi* **to ~ for sb** *(Sailing)* bei jdm den Vorschotmann machen.

crew[2] *(old) pret of* **crow.**

crew-cut ['kruːkʌt] *n* Bürstenschnitt *m*.

crib [krɪb] **1** *n* **(a)** *(manger, nativity scene)* Krippe *f*; *(US: cot)* Kinderbett *nt*. **(b)** *(Sch: cheating aid)* Spickzettel *m (col)*. **2** *vti (esp Sch col)* spicken *(col)*.

crick [krɪk] **1** *n* **a ~ in one's neck** ein steifes Genick. **2** *vt* **to ~ one's neck** sich *(dat)* ein steifes Genick zuziehen.

cricket[1] ['krɪkɪt] *n (insect)* Grille *f*.

cricket[2] *n (Sport)* Kricket *nt*. **that's not ~** *(fig col)* das ist nicht fair.

cricket *in cpds* Kricket-; **~ bat** *n* (Kricket)schlagholz *nt*.

crime [kraɪm] *n* Straftat *f*; *(robbery etc also, fig)* Verbrechen *nt*. **it's a ~ to throw away all that good food** es ist eine Sünde, all das gute Essen wegzuwerfen.

crime: ~ prevention *n* Verbrechensverhütung *f*; **~ rate** *n* Verbrechensrate *f*; **~ wave** *n* Welle *f* von Straftaten.

criminal ['krɪmɪnl] **1** *n* Straftäter(in *f*) *m*; *(guilty of capital crimes also, fig)* Verbrecher(in *f*) *m*. **2** *adj* **(a)** kriminell, verbrecherisch. **C~ Investigation Department** Kriminalpolizei *f*; **~ code** Strafgesetzbuch *nt*; **~ lawyer** Anwalt *m* für Strafsachen; *(specializing in defence)* Strafverteidiger *m*; **to have a ~ record** vorbestraft sein. **(b)** *(fig)* kriminell.

criminology [ˌkrɪmɪ'nɒlədʒɪ] *n* Kriminologie *f*.

crimson ['krɪmzn] **1** *adj* purpurrot; *sky* blutrot. **to turn ~** *(person, face)* knallrot *(col) or* dunkelrot anlaufen. **2** *n* Purpurrot *nt*.

cringe [krɪndʒ] *vi* **(a)** *(shrink back)* zurückschrecken *(at* vor *+dat)*; *(fig)* schaudern. **to ~ before sb** vor jdm zurückschrecken; **he ~d at the thought** er *or* ihn schauderte bei dem Gedanken; **his jokes make me ~** bei seinen Witzen kriege ich zuviel. **(b)** *(fawn)* kriechen *(to* vor *+dat)*. **cringing behaviour** kriecherisches Benehmen.

crinkle ['krɪŋkl] **1** *n* (Knitter)falte *f*. **2** *vt paper, dress etc* (zer)knittern. **3** *vi (paper, foil, dress etc)* knittern; *(face, skin)* (Lach)fältchen bekommen; *(edges of paper)* sich wellen; *(curl: hair)* sich krausen.

crinkly ['krɪŋklɪ] *adj (+er) (col) paper etc* zerknittert; *hair* kraus.

cripple ['krɪpl] **1** *n* Krüppel *m*. **2** *vt person* zum Krüppel machen; *legs etc* verkrüppeln; *ship, plane* aktionsunfähig machen; *(fig) industry* lahmlegen. **the ship was ~d** das Schiff war nicht mehr aktionsfähig; **~d with rheumatism** von Rheuma praktisch gelähmt.

crippling ['krɪplɪŋ] *adj taxes* erdrückend.

crisis ['kraɪsɪs] *n, pl* **crises** ['kraɪsiːz] Krise *f*.

crisp [krɪsp] **1** *adj (+er) apple, lettuce* knackig; *bread, biscuits, bacon* knusprig; *snow* verharscht; *leaves* trocken; *appearance* adrett; *style* knapp; *air* frisch. **2** *n (Brit: potato ~)* Chip *m usu pl*.

crispbread ['krɪspbred] *n* Knäckebrot *nt*.

criss-cross ['krɪskrɒs] **1** *adv* kreuz und quer. **2** *adj pattern* Kreuz-. **3** *vi (lines)* sich kreuzen.

criterion [kraɪ'tɪərɪən] *n, pl* **criteria** [kraɪ'tɪərɪə] Kriterium *nt*.

critic ['krɪtɪk] *n* Kritiker(in *f*) *m*.

critical ['krɪtɪkəl] *adj* kritisch. **to be ~ of sb/sth** *(criticize)* jdn/etw kritisieren; *(have ~ attitude)* jdm/einer Sache kritisch gegenüberstehen; **that's ~** *(crucial)* das ist entscheidend.

critically ['krɪtɪkəlɪ] *adv* **(a)** kritisch. **(b)** *ill* schwer.

criticism ['krɪtɪsɪzəm] *n* Kritik *f*.

criticize ['krɪtɪsaɪz] *vti* kritisieren.

critique [krɪ'tiːk] *n* Kritik *f*.

croak [krəʊk] **1** *n (of frog)* Quaken *nt no pl*; *(of raven, person)* Krächzen *nt no pl*. **2** *vti (frog)* quaken; *(raven, person)* krächzen.

croaky ['krəʊkɪ] *adj (+er) (col) voice* heiser.

crochet ['krəʊʃeɪ] **1** *n* Häkelei *f*. **~ hook** Häkelnadel *f*. **2** *vti* häkeln.

crock[1] [krɒk] *n (jar)* Topf *m*.

crock[2] *n (col) (vehicle)* Kiste *f (col)*; *(person)* Wrack *nt (col)*.

crockery ['krɒkərɪ] *n (Brit)* Geschirr *nt*.

crocodile ['krɒkədaɪl] *n* **(a)** Krokodil *nt*. **~ tears** Krokodilstränen. **(b)** *(Brit Sch)* **to walk in a ~** zwei und zwei hintereinandergehen.

crocus ['krəʊkəs] *n* Krokus *m*.

croft [krɒft] *n (esp Scot)* kleines Pachtgrundstück; *(house)* Kate *f*.

crofter ['krɒftəʳ] *n (esp Scot)* Kleinpächter(in *f*) *m*.

croissant ['krwɑːsɒŋ] *n* Hörnchen *nt*.

crony ['krəʊnɪ] *n* Freund(in *f*) *m*.

crook [krʊk] **1** *n* **(a)** *(dishonest person)* Gauner(in *f*) *m (col)*. **(b)** *(of shepherd)* Hirtenstab *m*; *(of bishop)* Bischofsstab *m*. **(c)** *(bend: in road, river)* Biegung *f*; *(in arm)* Beuge *f*. **2** *vt finger* krümmen; *arm* beugen.

crooked ['krʊkɪd] *adj (lit) (bent)* krumm; *smile* schief; *(fig col: dishonest) method* krumm; *person* unehrlich.

croon [kruːn] *vti (sing softly)* leise singen; *(sentimentally)* schmalzig singen *(pej col)*.
crooner [ˈkruːnəʳ] *n* Schnulzensänger *m (pej col)*.
crop [krɒp] **1** *n* **(a)** *(produce)* Ernte *f*; *(species grown)* (Feld)frucht *f*; *(fig: large number)* Schwung *m*. **a good ~ of potatoes** eine gute Kartoffelernte. **(b)** *(of bird)* Kropf *m*. **(c)** *(of whip)* Stock *m*; *(hunting ~)* Reitpeitsche *f*. **(d)** *(hairstyle)* Kurzhaarschnitt *m*. **2** *vt hair* stutzen.
♦ **crop up** *vi* aufkommen. **something's ~ped ~** es ist etwas dazwischengekommen.
cropper [ˈkrɒpəʳ] *n (col)* **to come a ~** *(lit: fall)* hinfliegen *(col)*; *(fig: fail)* auf die Nase fallen.
crop spraying *n* Schädlingsbekämpfung *f (durch Besprühen)*.
croquet [ˈkrəʊkeɪ] *n* Krocket(spiel) *nt*.
croquette [krəʊˈket] *n* Krokette *f*.
cross[1] [krɒs] **1** *n* **(a)** Kreuz *nt*. **we all have our ~ to bear** wir haben alle unser Kreuz zu tragen. **(b)** *(bias)* **on the ~** schräg. **(c)** *(hybrid)* Kreuzung *f*; *(fig)* Mittelding *nt*.
2 *attr (transverse) street etc* Quer-.
3 *vt* **(a)** *road, river, Channel* überqueren; *(on foot)* überschreiten; *country, desert* durchqueren. **to ~ the road** über die Straße gehen; **to ~ sb's path** *(fig)* jdm über den Weg laufen; **it ~ed my mind that ...** es fiel mir ein, daß ...; **we'll ~ that bridge when we come to it** lassen wir das Problem erst mal auf uns zukommen. **(b)** *(intersect)* kreuzen. **to ~ one's legs** die Beine übereinanderschlagen; **the lines are ~ed** *(Telec)* die Leitungen überschneiden sich; **I'm keeping my fingers ~ed for you** *(col)* ich drücke dir die Daumen *(col)*. **(c) to ~ oneself** sich bekreuzigen; **~ my/your heart** *(col)* Ehrenwort. **(d)** *(mark with a ~)* ankreuzen. **~ed cheque** Verrechnungsscheck *m*. **(e)** *(go against) plans* durchkreuzen. **to ~ sb** jdn verärgern. **(f)** *animal, fruit* kreuzen.
4 *vi* **(a)** *(across road)* hinübergehen; *(across Channel etc)* hinüberfahren. **(b)** *(lines, letters)* sich kreuzen. **our paths have ~ed several times** *(fig)* unsere Wege haben sich öfters gekreuzt.
♦ **cross off** *vt sep* streichen *(prep obj* aus, von*)*.
♦ **cross out** *vt sep* ausstreichen.
cross[2] *adj (+er)* böse. **to be ~ with sb** mit jdm *or* auf jdn böse sein.
cross: ~bar *n (of bicycle)* Stange *f*; *(Sport)* Querlatte *f*; **~breed** *(Zool, Biol)* **1** *n* Kreuzung *f*; **2** *vt* kreuzen; **~-Channel** *attr ferries* Kanal-; **~-check 1** *n* Gegenprobe *f*; **2** *vt facts, figures* überprüfen; **~-country 1** *adj* Querfeldein-; **2** *adv* querfeldein; **3** *n (race)* Querfeldeinrennen *nt*; **~-country skiing** Langlauf *m*; **~-examination** *n* Kreuzverhör *nt (of* über *+acc)*; **~-examine** *vt* ins Kreuzverhör nehmen; **~-eyed** *adj* schielend; **~fire** *n* Kreuzfeuer *nt*; **to be caught in the ~fire** *(lit, fig)* ins Kreuzfeuer geraten.
crossing [ˈkrɒsɪŋ] *n* **(a)** *(act)* Überquerung *f*; *(sea ~)* Überfahrt *f*. **(b)** *(~ place)* Übergang *m*; *(crossroads)* Kreuzung *f*.
cross-legged [ˌkrɒsˈlegɪd] *adj, adv* mit gekreuzten Beinen; *(on ground)* im Schneidersitz.
crossly [ˈkrɒslɪ] *adv* böse, verärgert.
cross: ~patch *n (col)* Brummbär *m (col)*; **~-purposes** *npl* **to be at ~-purposes** aneinander vorbeireden; **~-reference** *n* Querverweis *m (to* auf *+acc)*; **~roads** *n sing or pl (lit)* Kreuzung *f*; *(fig)* Scheideweg *m*; **~ section** *n* Querschnitt *m (of* durch*)*; **~walk** *n (US)* Fußgängerüberweg *m*; **~wind** *n* Seitenwind *m*; **~word (puzzle)** *n* Kreuzworträtsel *nt*.
crotch [krɒtʃ] *n* **(a)** *(in tree etc)* Gabelung *f*. **(b)** *(of trousers)* Schritt *m*; *(Anat)* Unterleib *m*.
crotchet [ˈkrɒtʃɪt] *n (Mus)* Viertelnote *f*.
crouch [kraʊtʃ] *vi* sich zusammenkauern. **to ~ down** sich niederkauern.
croupier [ˈkruːpɪeɪ] *n* Croupier *m*.
crouton [ˈkruːtɒn] *n* Crouton *m*.
crow[1] [krəʊ] *n (Orn)* Krähe *f*. **as the ~ flies** (in der) Luftlinie.
crow[2] **1** *n (of cock, baby)* Krähen *nt*. **2** *vi* **(a)** *pret* **~ed** *or (old)* **crew,** *ptp* **~ed** *(cock)* krähen. **(b)** *pret, ptp* **~ed** *(baby)* krähen; *(boast)* sich brüsten *(about* mit*)*.
crowbar [ˈkrəʊbɑːʳ] *n* Brecheisen *nt*.
crowd [kraʊd] **1** *n* **(a)** Menschenmenge *f*; *(Sport, Theat)* Zuschauermenge *f*. **~s of people** Menschenmassen *pl*; **~ scene** *(Theat)* Massenszene *f*. **(b)** *(set)* Clique *f*. **the university ~** die Leute von der Uni; **they're a nice ~** sie sind alle sehr nett. **(c)** *no pl (the masses)* **the ~** die (breite) Masse; **to go with** *or* **follow the ~** mit der Herde laufen. **2** *vi* (sich) drängen. **to ~ together/in** sich zusammendrängen/(sich) hereindrängen; **to ~ around sb/sth** (sich) um jdn/etw herumscharen. **3** *vt* **to ~ the streets** die Straßen bevölkern.
♦ **crowd out** *vt sep (not let in)* wegdrängen. **the pub was ~ed ~** das Lokal war gerammelt voll *(col)*.
crowded [ˈkraʊdɪd] *adj train etc* überfüllt.
crown [kraʊn] **1** *n* **(a)** Krone *f*. **the C~** die Krone. **(b)** *(of head)* Wirbel *m*; *(of hat)* Kopf *m*; *(of road)* Wölbung *f*; *(of tooth)* Krone *f*. **2** *vt* **(a)** *(lit, fig)* krönen. **he was ~ed king** er ist zum König gekrönt worden; **~ed head** gekröntes Haupt; **to be ~ed with success** von Erfolg gekrönt sein; **to ~ it all it began to snow** *(col)* zur Krönung des Ganzen begann es zu schneien. **(b)** *(in draughts etc)* eine Dame bekommen mit. **(c)** *tooth* eine Krone machen für. **(d)** *(col: hit)* **I'll ~ you!** ich hau dir gleich eine runter! *(col)*.
crown court *n (Brit) Bezirksgericht nt für Strafsachen.*
crowning [ˈkraʊnɪŋ] **1** *n* Krönung *f*. **2** *adj achievement* krönend.
crown: ~ jewels *npl* Kronjuwelen *pl*; **~ prince** *n* Kronprinz *m*; **~ princess** *n* Kronprinzessin *f*; **~ witness** *n (Brit)* Zeuge *m*/Zeugin *f* der Anklage.
crow's: ~ feet *npl* Krähenfüße *pl*; **~ nest** *n (Naut)* Mastkorb *m*; *(on foremast)* Krähennest *nt*.
crucial [ˈkruːʃəl] *adj* **(a)** *(decisive)* entscheidend *(to* für*)*. **(b)** *(col: very important)* sehr wichtig.
crucible [ˈkruːsɪbl] *n* (Schmelz)tiegel *m*.
crucifix [ˈkruːsɪfɪks] *n* Kruzifix *nt*.
crucifixion [ˌkruːsɪˈfɪkʃən] *n* Kreuzigung *f*.
crucify [ˈkruːsɪfaɪ] *vt* **(a)** kreuzigen. **(b)** *(fig) play, author* verreißen; *person* in der Luft zerreißen *(col)*. **(c)** *(mortify) the flesh* abtöten.
crude [kruːd] *adj (+er)* **(a)** *(unprocessed)* Roh-. **(b)** *expression etc* ordinär. **(c)** *implement* primitiv; *manners* ungehobelt, grob.
crudeness [ˈkruːdnɪs], **crudity** [ˈkruːdɪtɪ] *n* **(a)** *(vulgarity)* Derbheit *f*. **(b)** *see adj (c)* Primitivität *f*; Ungehobelte(s) *nt (of gen,* in *+dat)*.
cruel [ˈkrʊəl] *adj* grausam *(to* zu*)*. **that is ~ to animals** das ist Tierquälerei.
cruelty [ˈkrʊəltɪ] *n* Grausamkeit *f (to* gegenüber*)*. **~ to children** Kindesmißhandlung *f*; **~ to animals** Tierquälerei *f*; **physical/mental ~** Grausamkeit *f*/seelische Grausamkeit.
cruet [ˈkruːɪt] *n (set)* Gewürzständer *m*; *(for oil)* Krug *m*.
cruise [kruːz] **1** *vi* eine Kreuzfahrt/Kreuzfahrten machen; *(ship)* kreuzen; *(car)* Dauergeschwindigkeit fahren. **cruising speed** *(Aut)* Reisegeschwindigkeit *f*. **2** *n* Kreuzfahrt *f* **to go for a ~** eine Kreuzfahrt machen.
cruise missile *n* Cruise-Missile *nt*, Marschflugkörper *m*.
cruiser [ˈkruːzəʳ] *n (Naut)* Kreuzer *m*; *(pleasure ~)* Vergnügungsjacht *f*.
crumb [krʌm] **1** *n* **(a)** *(of bread etc)* Krümel *m*; *(inside of loaf)* Krume *f*. **a few ~s of information** ein paar Informationsbrocken; **that's one ~ of comfort** das ist (wenigstens) ein winziger Trost. **(b)** *(col: fool)* Depp *m (col)*. **2** *interj* **~s!** *(col)*

Mensch! *(col)*.
crumble ['krʌmbl] **1** *vt* zerkrümeln. **2** *vi (brick)* bröckeln; *(bread etc)* krümeln; *(also* ~ **away***)* *(earth, building)* zerbröckeln; *(opposition)* sich auflösen. **3** *n (Cook)* Obst *nt* mit Streusel; *(topping)* Streusel *pl*.
crumpet ['krʌmpɪt] *n* **(a)** *(Cook) kleiner dicker Pfannkuchen*. **(b)** *(esp Brit col: women)* Miezen *pl (col)*.
crumple ['krʌmpl] **1** *vt (also* ~ **up***) paper, dress* zerknittern; *(screw up)* zusammenknüllen; *metal* eindrücken. **2** *vi (lit, fig: collapse)* zusammenbrechen.
crumple zone *n* Knautschzone *f*.
crunch [krʌntʃ] **1** *vt apple, biscuit etc* mampfen *(col)*. **2** *vi (gravel, snow etc)* knirschen; *(gears)* krachen. **3** *n (sound)* Krachen *nt*; *(of footsteps, gravel etc)* Knirschen *nt*. **when it comes to the** ~ wenn es darauf ankommt.
crunchy ['krʌntʃɪ] *adj (+er) apple* knackig; *biscuit* knusprig; *snow* verharscht.
crusade [kruː'seɪd] *n (Hist, fig)* Kreuzzug *m*.
crusader [kruː'seɪdəʳ] *n (Hist)* Kreuzritter *m*.
crush [krʌʃ] **1** *n* **(a)** *(crowd)* Gedrängel *nt*. ~ **barrier** Absperrung *f*. **(b)** *(col)* **to have a** ~ **on sb** für jdn schwärmen. **2** *vt* **(a)** *(squeeze)* quetschen; *fruit etc* zerdrücken; *(kill)* zu Tode quetschen; *spices, garlic* (zer)stoßen; *stone* zerkleinern; *scrap metal* zusammenpressen; *(crease)* zerknittern; *(screw up)* zerknüllen. **(b)** *(fig) hopes, sb* vernichten; *people* unterdrücken. **3** *vi (clothes)* knittern.
crushing ['krʌʃɪŋ] *adj defeat, reply* vernichtend.
crust [krʌst] *n (all senses)* Kruste *f*. **the earth's** ~ die Erdkruste.
crustacean [krʌs'teɪʃən] *n* Schalentier *nt*.
crusty ['krʌstɪ] *adj (+er)* knusprig; *(fig: irritable)* barsch.
crutch [krʌtʃ] **(a)** *n (for walking)* Krücke *f*. **(b)** = **crotch (b).**
crux [krʌks] *n (of problem)* Kern *m*. **the** ~ **of the matter** der springende Punkt.
cry [kraɪ] **1** *n* **(a)** Schrei *m*; *(call)* Ruf *m*. **to utter a** ~ einen Schrei ausstoßen; **a** ~ **of pain** ein Schmerzensschrei *m*; **a** ~ **for help** ein Hilferuf *m*. **(b)** *(slogan)* Parole *f*. **(c)** *(weep)* **a** ~ **will do you good** weine ruhig, das wird dir guttun. **2** *vi* **(a)** *(weep)* weinen; *(baby)* schreien. **she was** ~**ing for her mother** sie weinte nach ihrer Mutter. **(b)** *(call)* rufen; *(louder, animal, bird)* schreien. **to** ~ **for help** um Hilfe rufen/schreien. **3** *vt* **(a)** *(shout out)* rufen; *(louder)* schreien. **(b)** *bitter tears etc* weinen. **to** ~ **one's heart out** herzzerreißend weinen; **to** ~ **oneself to sleep** sich in den Schlaf weinen.
♦ **cry off** *vi* einen Rückzieher machen.
♦ **cry out** *vi* **(a)** aufschreien. **to** ~ ~ **to sb** jdm etwas zuschreien. **(b)** *(fig)* **this door is** ~**ing** ~ **for a coat of paint** diese Tür schreit danach, gestrichen zu werden.
crying ['kraɪɪŋ] **1** *adj (fig) injustice* schreiend; *need* dringend. **it is a** ~ **shame** es ist ein Jammer. **2** *n (weeping)* Weinen *nt*.
crypt [krɪpt] *n* Krypta *f*; *(burial* ~*)* Gruft *f*.
cryptic ['krɪptɪk] *adj remark* hintergründig; *riddle* verschlüsselt.
crystal ['krɪstl] **1** *n* **(a)** *(Chem, Rad)* Kristall *m*. **(b)** *(on watch)* (Uhr)glas *nt*. **(c)** *(*~ *glass)* Kristall *nt*. **2** *adj* **(a)** *(crystalline)* kristallin; *(*~*-glass)* Kristall-; *(quartz)* Quarzkristall-. **(b)** *(fig) waters, lake* kristallklar.
crystal: ~ **ball** *n* Glaskugel *f*; ~**-clear** *adj (lit, fig)* glasklar; ~**-gazing** *n* Hellseherei *f*.
crystallization [ˌkrɪstəlaɪ'zeɪʃən] *n* Kristallisierung *f*.
crystallize ['krɪstəlaɪz] **1** *vt (lit)* zum Kristallisieren bringen; *(fig)* feste Form geben *(+dat)*. **2** *vi (lit)* kristallisieren; *(fig)* feste Form annehmen.
crystallized ['krɪstəlaɪzd] *adj fruit* kandiert.
cub [kʌb] *n* **(a)** *(of animal)* Junge(s) *nt*. **(b)** *(also* ~ **scout***)* Wölfling *m*.
Cuba ['kjuːbə] *n* Kuba *nt*.
cubby-hole ['kʌbɪhəʊl] *n* **(a)** *(compartment)* Fach *nt*. **(b)** *(room)* Kabäuschen *nt (col)*.
cube [kjuːb] *n* **(a)** *(shape, object)* Würfel *m*. ~ **sugar** Würfelzucker *m*. **(b)** *(Math)* dritte Potenz. ~ **root** Kubikwurzel *f*.
cubic ['kjuːbɪk] *adj* **(a)** *(of volume)* Kubik-. ~ **capacity** Fassungsvermögen *nt*; *(of engine)* Hubraum *m*. **(b)** *(Math)* kubisch. ~ **equation** Gleichung *f* dritten Grades.
cubicle ['kjuːbɪkəl] *n* Kabine *f*.
cubism ['kjuːbɪzəm] *n* Kubismus *m*.
cuckoo ['kʊkuː] **1** *n* Kuckuck *m*. **2** *adj pred (col)* meschugge *(col)*. ~ **clock** *n* Kuckucksuhr *f*.
cucumber ['kjuːkʌmbəʳ] *n* (Salat)gurke *f*. **as cool as a** ~ seelenruhig.
cud [kʌd] *n* **to chew the** ~ *(lit)* wiederkäuen; *(fig)* vor sich hingrübeln.
cuddle ['kʌdl] **1** *n* Liebkosung *f*. **to give sb a** ~ jdn in den Arm nehmen; **to have a** ~ schmusen. **2** *vt* in den Arm nehmen.
♦ **cuddle down** *vi* sich kuscheln.
♦ **cuddle up** *vi* sich kuscheln *(to, against* an *+acc)*.
cuddly ['kʌdlɪ] *adj (+er) (wanting a cuddle)* anschmiegsam; *(good to cuddle) toy, doll* zum Liebhaben, knuddelig *(col)*.
cudgel ['kʌdʒəl] **1** *n* Knüppel *m*. **to take up the** ~**s for sb/sth** *(fig)* für jdn/etw eine Lanze brechen. **2** *vt* prügeln. **to** ~ **one's brains** *(fig)* sich *(dat)* das (Ge)hirn zermartern.
cue [kjuː] *n* **(a)** *(Theat, fig)* Stichwort *nt*; *(action)* (Einsatz)zeichen *nt*; *(Mus)* Einsatz *m*. **to take one's** ~ **from sb** sich nach jdm richten; **right on** ~ *(Theat)* genau aufs Stichwort; *(fig)* wie gerufen. **(b)** *(Billiards)* Queue *nt*.
♦ **cue in** *vt sep* den Einsatz geben *(+dat)*; *(TV, Film) scene* abfahren lassen; *tape etc* (rechtzeitig) einspielen.
cuff[1] [kʌf] *n* **(a)** Manschette *f*. **off the** ~ *(fig)* aus dem Stegreif; *remark* aus dem Handgelenk. **(b)** *(US: of trousers)* (Hosen)aufschlag *m*.
cuff[2] *vt (strike)* einen Klaps geben *(+dat)*.
cuff-link ['kʌflɪŋk] *n* Manschettenknopf *m*.
cuisine [kwɪ'ziːn] *n* Küche *f*.
cul-de-sac ['kʌldəsæk] *n (esp Brit)* Sackgasse *f*.
culinary ['kʌlɪnərɪ] *adj* kulinarisch; *skill etc* Koch-.
cull [kʌl] **1** *n* **(a)** *(selection)* Auswahl *f*. **(b)** *(killing of surplus)* ~ **of seals** Robbenschlag *m*. **2** *vt* **(a)** *(pick) flowers* pflücken. **(b)** *(collect)* entnehmen *(from dat)*. **(c)** *(kill as surplus)* **to** ~ **seals** Robbenschlag *m* betreiben.
culminate ['kʌlmɪneɪt] *vi* gipfeln *(in* in *+dat)*.
culmination [ˌkʌlmɪ'neɪʃən] *n* Höhepunkt *m*; *(end)* Ende *nt*.
culottes [kjuː'lɒts] *npl* Hosenrock *m*. **a pair of** ~ ein Hosenrock.
culpable ['kʌlpəbl] *adj (form)* schuldig. ~ **homicide** *(Jur)* fahrlässige Tötung; ~ **negligence** grobe Fahrlässigkeit.
culprit ['kʌlprɪt] *n* Schuldige(r) *mf*; *(Jur)* Täter(in *f*) *m*.
cult [kʌlt] *n (Rel, fig)* Kult *m*. **to make a** ~ **of sth** (einen) Kult mit etw treiben.
cultivate ['kʌltɪveɪt] *vt* **(a)** *soil* bebauen; *crop* anbauen. **(b)** *(fig) friendship, links etc* pflegen; *skill, taste* entwickeln.
cultivation [ˌkʌltɪ'veɪʃən] *n see vt* **(a)** Bebauung *f*; Anbau *m*. **(b)** Pflege *f (of* von*)*; Entwicklung *f*.
cultural ['kʌltʃərəl] *adj* Kultur-; *differences, events* kulturell.
culture ['kʌltʃəʳ] *n* **(a)** Kultur *f*. **(b)** *(Agr, Biol, Med)* Kultur *f*; *(of animals)* Zucht *f*.
cultured ['kʌltʃəd] *adj* kultiviert; *(Agr)* Kultur-; *(Biol, Med)* gezüchtet. ~ **pearl** Zuchtperle *f*.
cumbersome ['kʌmbəsəm] *adj clothing* hinder-

lich; *vehicle* schwer zu manövrieren; *suitcases, parcels* sperrig; *procedure* beschwerlich.

cumin [ˈkʌmɪn] *n* Kreuzkümmel *m*.

cumulative [ˈkjuːmjʊlətɪv] *adj* kumulativ. **the ~ debts of ten years** die Schulden, die sich im Lauf von zehn Jahren angehäuft haben/hatten.

cunning [ˈkʌnɪŋ] **1** *n (cleverness)* Schlauheit *f*. **2** *adj* schlau; *person also* gerissen; *expression* verschmitzt; *gadget* raffiniert.

cup [kʌp] **1** *n* **(a)** Tasse *f*; *(goblet)* Pokal *m*; *(mug)* Becher *m*. **a ~ of tea** eine Tasse Tee; **that's just/that's not my ~ of tea** *(fig col)* das ist genau/ist nicht mein Fall *(col)*. **(b)** *(prize, football ~ etc)* Pokal *m*. **(c)** *(of bra)* Körbchen *nt*. **2** *vt hands* hohl machen. **~ped hand** hohle Hand; **he ~ped his chin in his hand** er stützte das Kinn in die Hand; **to ~ one's hands around sth** etw mit der hohlen Hand umfassen.

cupboard [ˈkʌbəd] *n* Schrank *m*. **~ love** fauler Schmus *(col)*.

cup: C~ Final *n* Pokalendspiel *nt*; **~ful** *n, pl* **~sful** *or* **~fuls** Tasse *f*; **~ size** *n (of bra)* Körbchengröße *f*; **~ tie** *n* Pokalspiel *nt*.

curate [ˈkjʊərɪt] *n (Catholic)* Kurat *m*; *(Protestant)* Vikar *m*.

curator [kjʊəˈreɪtəʳ] *n (of museum etc)* Kustos *m*.

curb [kɜːb] **1** *n* **(a)** *(of harness) (bit)* Kandare *f*; *(chain)* Kinnkette *f*. **(b)** *(fig)* Behinderung *f*; *(deliberate)* Beschränkung *f*. **(c)** *(esp US: curbstone)* = **kerb**. **2** *vt horse, (fig)* zügeln; *immigration etc* in Schranken halten.

curd [kɜːd] *n (often pl)* Quark *m*. **~ cheese** Quark *m*.

curdle [ˈkɜːdl] **1** *vt (lit, fig)* gerinnen lassen. **2** *vi* gerinnen. **his blood ~d** das Blut gerann ihm in den Adern.

cure [kjʊəʳ] **1** *vt* **(a)** *(Med) illness, person* heilen. **to be/get ~d (of sth)** (von etw) geheilt sein/werden; **to ~ sb (of sth)** jdn (von etw) heilen. **(b)** *(fig) inflation, ill etc* abhelfen *(+dat)*. **to ~ sb of sth** jdn von etw kurieren. **(c)** *food* haltbar machen; *(salt)* pökeln; *(smoke)* räuchern; *skins, tobacco* trocknen. **2** *n* **a** *(Med) (remedy)* (Heil)mittel *nt (for* gegen); *(treatment)* Heilverfahren *nt (for sb* für jdn, *for sth* gegen etw); *(recovery)* Heilung *f*; *(health ~)* Kur *f*; *(fig: remedy)* Mittel *nt (for* gegen*)*. **to take** *or* **follow a ~** zur *or* in Kur gehen.

cure-all [ˈkjʊərɔːl] *n (lit, fig)* Allheilmittel *nt*.

curfew [ˈkɜːfjuː] *n* Ausgangssperre *f*.

curio [ˈkjʊərɪəʊ] *n* Kuriosität *f*.

curiosity [ˌkjʊərɪˈɒsɪtɪ] *n* **(a)** *no pl (inquisitiveness)* Neugier *f*. **~ killed the cat** *(Prov)* sei nicht so neugierig. **(b)** *(object, person)* Kuriosität *f*.

curious [ˈkjʊərɪəs] *adj* **(a)** *(inquisitive)* neugierig. **I'm ~ to know what he'll do** ich bin mal gespannt, was er macht; **I'd be ~ to know ...** ich wüßte gern, ... **(b)** *(odd)* sonderbar.

curiously [ˈkjʊərɪəslɪ] *adv* **(a)** neugierig. **(b)** *behave, speak etc* eigenartig. **~ enough** merkwürdigerweise.

curl [kɜːl] **1** *n (of hair)* Locke *f*. **a ~ of smoke** ein Rauchkringel *m*. **2** *vt hair* locken; *(with curlers)* in Locken legen; *lips* kräuseln. **3** *vi (hair)* sich locken; *(tightly)* sich kräuseln; *(naturally)* lockig sein. **his lips ~ed** er kräuselte die Lippen.

♦**curl up** *vi (animal)* sich zusammenrollen; *(person)* sich zusammenkuscheln; *(leaf)* sich hochbiegen. **to ~ ~ in an armchair** sich in einen Sessel kuscheln; **to ~ ~ with a good book** es sich *(dat)* mit einem guten Buch gemütlich machen.

curler [ˈkɜːləʳ] *n (hair ~)* Lockenwickler *m*. **to put one's ~s in** sich *(dat)* die Haare eindrehen.

curlew [ˈkɜːljuː] *n* Brachvogel *m*.

curling [ˈkɜːlɪŋ] *n (Sport)* Curling, Eisschießen *nt*.

curling-tongs [ˈkɜːlɪŋˌtɒŋz] *npl* Lockenschere *f*; *(electric)* Lockenstab *m*.

curly [ˈkɜːlɪ] *adj (+er) hair* lockig; *(tighter)* kraus; *tail* Ringel-.

currant [ˈkʌrənt] *n* **(a)** *(dried fruit)* Korinthe *f*. **~ bun** Rosinenbrötchen *nt*. **(b)** *(Bot)* Johannisbeere *f*.

currency [ˈkʌrənsɪ] *n* **(a)** *(Fin)* Währung *f*. **foreign ~** Devisen *pl*. **(b)** *(of ideas etc)* Verbreitung *f*; *(of expression)* Gebräuchlichkeit *f*. **to be in ~** in Umlauf sein.

current [ˈkʌrənt] **1** *adj (present)* gegenwärtig; *edition* letzte(r, s); *opinion* verbreitet. **to be no longer ~** nicht mehr aktuell sein; *(coins)* nicht mehr in Umlauf sein; **~ affairs** aktuelle Fragen *pl*; **in ~ use** allgemein gebräuchlich. **2** *n* **(a)** *(Elec)* Strom *m*; *(of water also)* Strömung *f*; *(of air)* Luftströmung *f*. **(b)** *(fig: of events, opinions etc)* Tendenz *f*. **to go against the ~ of popular opinion** gegen den Strom der öffentlichen Meinung anschwimmen.

current: ~ account *n (Brit)* Girokonto *nt*; **~ assets** *npl* Umlaufvermögen *nt*.

currently [ˈkʌrəntlɪ] *adv* zur Zeit.

curriculum [kəˈrɪkjʊləm] *n, pl* **curricula** Lehrplan *m*. **~ vitae** Lebenslauf *m*.

curry[1] [ˈkʌrɪ] *(Cook) n* Curry *m or nt*. **~-powder** Currypulver *nt*.

curry[2] *vt horse* striegeln. **to ~ favour** *(Brit) or* **favor** *(US)* **(with sb)** sich (bei jdm) einschmeicheln.

curse [kɜːs] **1** *n (lit, fig)* Fluch *m*. **to put sb under a ~** jdn mit einem Fluch belegen; **~s!** *(col)* verflucht! *(col)*; **it's the ~ of my life** das ist der Fluch meines Lebens; **the ~** *(col: menstruation)* die Tage *pl (col)*; **she has the ~** sie hat ihre Tage *(col)*. **2** *vt* **(a)** *(to put a curse on)* verfluchen. **~ you/it!** *(col)* verflucht! *(col)*; **~ these trains!** *(col)* diese verfluchten Züge! *(col)*. **(b)** *(swear at or about)* fluchen über *(+acc)*. **(c)** *(fig: to afflict)* **to be ~d with sb/sth** mit jdm/etw gestraft sein. **3** *vi* fluchen.

cursor [ˈkɜːsəʳ] *n (Comp)* Cursor *m*.

cursory [ˈkɜːsərɪ] *adj glance* flüchtig.

curt [kɜːt] *adj (+er) person* kurz angebunden; *nod, refusal* kurz.

curtail [kɜːˈteɪl] *vt* kürzen.

curtain [ˈkɜːtn] *n* Vorhang *m (also Theat)*. **to draw the ~s** *(open)* den Vorhang/die Vorhänge aufziehen; *(close)* den Vorhang/die Vorhänge zuziehen; **the ~ rises/falls** der Vorhang hebt sich/fällt; **if you get caught it'll be ~s for you** *(col)* wenn sie dich erwischen, bist du weg vom Fenster *(col)*.

♦**curtain off** *vt sep* durch einen Vorhang abtrennen.

curtain: ~-call *n (Theat)* Vorhang *m*; **to get/take a ~-call** einen Vorhang bekommen/vor den Vorhang treten; **~ hook** *n* Gardinengleithaken *m*; **~-raiser** *n (Theat)* kurzes Vorspiel; **~ ring** *n* Gardinenring *m*; **~ rod** *n* Gardinenstange *f*.

curts(e)y [ˈkɜːtsɪ] *n* Knicks *m*; *(to royalty)* Hofknicks *m*. **to drop a ~** einen Knicks machen.

curvaceous [kɜːˈveɪʃəs] *adj figure, woman* kurvenreich.

curvature [ˈkɜːvətʃəʳ] *n* Krümmung *f*; *(misshapen)* Verkrümmung *f*. **~ of the spine** *(normal)* Rückgratkrümmung *f*; *(abnormal)* Rückgratverkrümmung *f*.

curve [kɜːv] **1** *n* Kurve *f*; *(of body, vase etc)* Rundung *f*; *(of river)* Biegung *f*; *(of archway)* Bogen *m*. **there's a ~ in the road** die Straße macht einen Bogen. **2** *vt* biegen; *arch, roof* wölben. **3** *vi* **(a)** *(road)* einen Bogen machen; *(river)* eine Biegung machen. **the road ~s around the city** die Straße macht einen Bogen um die Stadt. **(b)** *(be curved) (arch)* sich wölben; *(hips, breasts)* sich runden; *(metal strip etc)* sich biegen.

curved [kɜːvd] *adj line* gebogen; *arch* gewölbt; *hips* rund.

cushion [ˈkʊʃən] **1** *n* Kissen *nt*; *(pad, fig: buffer)* Polster *nt*; *(Billiards)* Bande *f*. **2** *vt fall, blow* auffangen. **to ~ sb against sth** jdn gegen etw abschirmen.

cushy ['kʊʃɪ] *adj (+er) (col)* bequem. **to be onto a ~ number** eine ruhige Kugel schieben *(col)*.

custard ['kʌstəd] *n (pouring ~)* ≃ Vanillesoße *f*; *(set)* ≃ Vanillepudding *m*.

custard: ~ cream (biscuit) *n* Doppelkeks *m* (mit Vanillecremefüllung); **~ powder** *n* ≃ Vanillepuddingpulver *nt*; **~-tart** *n* ≃ Puddingteilchen *nt*.

custodian [kʌs'təʊdɪən] *n (of park, museum)* Aufseher *m*; *(of treasure)* Hüter *m*.

custody ['kʌstədɪ] *n* **(a)** *(keeping, guardianship)* Obhut *f*; *(Jur: of children)* Vormundschaft *f (of* für, über *+acc)*. **to place sth in sb's ~** etw jdm zur Aufbewahrung anvertrauen; **the money is in safe ~** das Geld ist gut aufgehoben; **the mother was awarded ~ of the children** die Kinder wurden der Mutter zugesprochen. **(b)** *(police)* Haft *f*. **to take sb into ~** jdn verhaften.

custom ['kʌstəm] *n* **(a)** *(convention)* Sitte *f*, Brauch *m*; *(habit)* (An)gewohnheit *f*. **as was his ~** wie er es gewohnt war. **(b)** *no pl (Comm)* Kundschaft *f*. **to get sb's ~** jdn als Kunden gewinnen. **(c) ~s** *pl* Zoll *m*; **(the) C~s** der Zoll; **to go through ~s** durch den Zoll gehen.

customary ['kʌstəmərɪ] *adj (conventional)* üblich; *(habitual)* gewohnt. **it's ~ to wear a tie** man trägt gewöhnlich eine Krawatte.

custom-built ['kʌstəmbɪlt] *adj* spezialgefertigt.

customer ['kʌstəmə^r] *n* **(a)** *(Comm: patron)* Kunde *m*, Kundin *f*. **our ~s** unsere Kundschaft. **(b)** *(col: person)* Kunde *m (col)*.

custom-made ['kʌstəmmeɪd] *adj* maßgefertigt; *clothes* maßgeschneidert; *furniture, car* spezialgefertigt.

customs: ~ clearance *n* Zollabfertigung *f*; **~ declaration** *n* Zollerklärung *f*; **~ duty** *n* Zoll(abgabe *f*) *m*; **~ inspection** *n* Zollkontrolle *f*; **~ officer** *n* Zollbeamte(r) *m*.

cut [kʌt] *(vb: pret, ptp ~)* **1** *n* **(a)** Schnitt *m*. **to make a ~ in sth** in etw *(acc)* einen Einschnitt machen; **the ~ and thrust of politics** das Spannungsfeld der Politik; **the ~ and thrust of the debate** die Hitze der Debatte. **(b)** *(reduction) (in gen) (in prices)* Senkung *f*; *(in financial matters)* Kürzung *f*; *(in production, output)* Einschränkung *f*. **he had to take a ~ in (his) salary** er mußte eine Gehaltskürzung hinnehmen. **(c)** *(of meat)* Stück *nt*. **(d)** *(col: share)* Anteil *m*. **(e)** *(short route)* Abkürzung *f*. **(f)** *(Elec)* Unterbrechung *f (in gen)*. **power ~** Stromausfall *m*. **(g)** *(Cards)* **it's your ~** du hebst ab. **(h) he's a ~ above the rest of them** er ist den anderen um einiges überlegen.

2 *adj usu attr flowers* Schnitt-; *bread* geschnitten; *grass* gemäht; *prices* herabgesetzt.

3 *vt* **(a)** schneiden; *grass* mähen; *cake* anschneiden; *(~ out) fabric, suit* zuschneiden; *(~ off)* abschneiden. **to ~ one's finger** *(with knife etc)* sich *(dat)* in den Finger schneiden; **to ~ one's nails** sich *(dat)* die Nägel schneiden; **to ~ sth in half/three** etw halbieren/dritteln; **to ~ to pieces** zerstückeln; **to get one's hair ~** sich *(dat)* die Haare schneiden lassen; **to ~ sb free/loose** jdn losschneiden.

(b) *(shape) steps* schlagen; *channel, trench* ausheben; *figure (in wood)* schnitzen *(in* aus*)*; *(in stone)* hauen *(in* aus*)*; *diamond* schleifen; *key* anfertigen. **to ~ one's coat according to one's cloth** *(Prov)* sich nach der Decke strecken.

(c) *(fig: break off) electricity* abstellen; *ties, links* abbrechen. **to ~ a long story short** der langen Rede kurzer Sinn.

(d) *person* schneiden. **to ~ sb dead** jdn wie Luft behandeln.

(e) *class* schwänzen *(col)*.

(f) *(intersect)* schneiden.

(g) *(reduce) prices* senken; *expenses, salary* kürzen; *production, output* einschränken.

(h) *part of text or film* streichen.

(i) *(cause pain to)* **it ~ me to the quick** es schnitt mir ins Herz.

(j) to ~ a tooth einen Zahn bekommen.

(k) *(Cards)* **to ~ the cards/the pack** abheben.

(l) aren't you ~ting it a bit fine? ist das nicht ein bißchen knapp?

4 *vi* **(a)** *(knife, scissors)* schneiden. **to ~ both ways** *(fig)* auch umgekehrt zutreffen; *(have disadvantages too)* ein zweischneidiges Schwert sein. **(b)** *(intersect: lines, roads)* sich schneiden. **(c)** *(Cards)* abheben. **(d) to ~ and run** abhauen *(col)*.

♦**cut away** *vt sep* wegschneiden.

♦**cut back 1** *vi* **(a)** *(go back)* zurückgehen/-fahren. **(b)** *(reduce expenditure etc)* sich einschränken. **to ~ ~ on smoking** weniger rauchen. **2** *vt sep* **(a)** *plants, shrubs* zurückschneiden. **(b)** *production* zurückschrauben.

♦**cut down 1** *vt sep* **(a)** *tree* fällen. **(b)** *number, expenses* einschränken. **to ~ sb ~ to size** jdn auf seinen Platz verweisen. **2** *vi (reduce intake, expenditure etc)* sich einschränken. **to ~ ~ on sth** etw einschränken.

♦**cut in** *vi* **(a)** *(interrupt)* sich einschalten. **(b)** *(Aut)* **to ~ ~ in front of sb** jdn schneiden.

♦**cut into** *vi +prep obj savings* ein Loch reißen in *(+acc)*.

♦**cut off** *vt sep* **(a)** *(lit, fig)* abschneiden; *allowance* sperren. **to ~ ~ the enemy's retreat** dem Feind den Rückzug abschneiden; **we're very ~ ~ out here** wir leben hier draußen sehr abgeschieden. **(b)** *(disinherit)* enterben. **to ~ sb ~ without a penny** jdn völlig enterben. **(c)** *(disconnect) telephone etc* abstellen. **operator, I've been ~ ~** wir sind unterbrochen worden.

♦**cut out 1** *vi (engine)* aussetzen. **2** *vt sep* **(a)** *(remove by cutting)* ausschneiden; *malignant growth etc* herausschneiden. **(b)** *dress* zuschneiden. **(c)** *(delete)* (heraus)streichen; *(not bother with)* verzichten auf *(+acc)*; *smoking, swearing etc* aufhören mit. **~ it ~!** *(col)* laß das (sein)! *(col)*. **(d)** *(fig)* **to be ~ ~ for sth** zu etw gemacht sein. **(e) to have one's work ~ ~** alle Hände voll zu tun haben.

♦**cut up 1** *vi* **to ~ ~ rough** Krach schlagen *(col)*. **2** *vt sep* **(a)** *meat* aufschneiden; *wood* spalten. **(b)** *pass (col: upset)* **he was very ~ ~ about it** das hat ihn schwer getroffen.

cut-and-dried [ˌkʌtən'draɪd] *adj* **it's ~** *(fixed beforehand)* das ist eine abgemachte Sache; *(unchangeable)* das ist festgelegt.

cut-back ['kʌtbæk] *n* **(a)** Kürzung *f*. **(b)** *(Film)* Rückblende *f*.

cute [kjuːt] *adj (+er)* **(a)** *(col: sweet)* süß. **(b)** *(esp US col: clever) idea, gadget* dufte *(col)*; *(shrewd) person, move* clever *(col)*.

cut glass *n* geschliffenes Glas.

cuticle ['kjuːtɪkl] *n (of nail)* Nagelhaut *f*. **~ remover** Nagelhautentferner *m*.

cutie ['kjuːtɪ] *n (esp US col: attractive)* dufte Biene *(col)*.

cutlery ['kʌtlərɪ] *n no pl (esp Brit)* Besteck *nt*.

cutlet ['kʌtlɪt] *n (boneless chop)* Schnitzel *nt*; *(of chopped meat)* (paniertes) Hacksteak.

cut: ~-off *n* **(a)** *(Tech: device)* Ausschaltmechanismus *m*; **(b)** *(also* **~-off point***)* Trennlinie *f*; **~-out** *n (of engine)* Aussetzen *nt*; **it has an automatic ~-out** es setzt automatisch aus; **~-price** *adj (Brit)*, **~-rate** *adj (US)* zu herabgesetzten Preisen.

cut-throat ['kʌtθrəʊt] **1** *n (murderous type)* Verbrechertyp *(col) m*. **2** *adj* **(a)** *competition* mörderisch. **(b) ~ razor** (offenes) Rasiermesser.

cutting ['kʌtɪŋ] **1** *n* **(a)** Schneiden *nt*; *(~ off)* Abschneiden *nt*; *(of prices)* Senkung *f*; *(of expenses, salary)* Kürzung *f*; *(of production)* Drosselung *f*; *(of part of text)* Streichung *f*; *(of film)* Schnitt *m*. ~

room *(Film)* Schneideraum *m.* **(b)** *(from newspaper)* Ausschnitt *m.* **(c)** *(Hort)* Ableger *m.* **to take a ~** einen Ableger nehmen. **2** *adj* **(a)** *edge* scharf. **(b)** *(fig) wind, cold* schneidend; *remark, tongue* spitz.

cuttlefish ['kʌtlfɪʃ] *n* Tintenfisch *m.*

cwt = hundredweight.

cyanide ['saɪənaɪd] *n* Zyanid *nt.* **~ poisoning** Blausäurevergiftung *f.*

cybernetics [ˌsaɪbə'netɪks] *n sing* Kybernetik *f.*

cyclamen ['sɪkləmən] *n* Alpenveilchen *nt.*

cycle ['saɪkl] **1** *n* **(a)** Zyklus *m*; *(of events)* Gang *m.* **(b)** *(bicycle)* (Fahr)rad *nt*; *(col: motorbike)* Maschine *f (col).* **~ path** Radweg *m*; **~ race** Radrennen *nt.* **2** *vi* mit dem (Fahr)rad fahren.

cycling ['saɪklɪŋ] *n* Radfahren *nt.* **I enjoy ~** ich fahre gern Rad.

cycling: ~ holiday *n* Urlaub *m* mit dem Fahrrad; **~ tour** *n* Radtour *f.*

cyclist ['saɪklɪst] *n* (Fahr)radfahrer(in *f*) *m.*

cyclone ['saɪkləʊn] *n* Zyklon *m.*

cygnet ['sɪgnɪt] *n* Schwanjunge(s) *nt.*

cylinder ['sɪlɪndəʳ] *n (Math, Aut)* Zylinder *m.* **a four-~ car** ein Vierzylinder *m.*

cylinder: ~ block *n (Aut)* Zylinderblock *m*; **~ head** *n (Aut)* Zylinderkopf *m*; **~ head gasket** *n* Zylinderkopfdichtung *f.*

cylindrical [sɪ'lɪndrɪkəl] *adj* zylindrisch.

cymbal ['sɪmbəl] *n* Beckenteller *m.* **~s** Becken *nt.*

cynic ['sɪnɪk] *n* Zyniker(in *f*) *m.*

cynical ['sɪnɪkəl] *adj* zynisch.

cynicism ['sɪnɪsɪzəm] *n* **(a)** *no pl* Zynismus *m.* **(b)** *(cynical remark)* zynische Bemerkung.

cypress ['saɪprɪs] *n* Zypresse *f.*

Cypriot ['sɪprɪət] **1** *adj* zypriotisch. **2** *n* Zypriot(in *f*) *m.*

Cyprus ['saɪprəs] *n* Zypern *nt.*

cyst [sɪst] *n* Zyste *f.*

cystitis [sɪs'taɪtɪs] *n* Blasenentzündung *f.*

czar [zɑːʳ] *n* Zar *m.*

czarina [zɑː'riːnə] *n* Zarin *f.*

Czech [tʃek] **1** *adj* tschechisch. **2** *n* **(a)** Tscheche *m*, Tschechin *f.* **(b)** *(language)* Tschechisch *nt.*

Czechoslovakia ['tʃekəʊslə'vækɪə] *n* die Tschechoslowakei.

Czechoslovak(ian) ['tʃekəʊslə'væk(ɪən)] **1** *adj* tschechoslowakisch. **2** *n* Tschechoslowake *m*, Tschechoslowakin *f.*

D

D, d [diː] *n* D, d *nt*. **D sharp/flat** Dis, dis *nt*/Des, des *nt*.

dab[1] [dæb] **1** *n* Klecks *m*; *(of powder, cream etc)* Tupfer *m*; *(of liquid, perfume, glue etc)* Tropfen *m*; *(of butter)* Klacks *m*. **a ~ of ointment** ein bißchen Salbe; **to give sth a ~ of paint** etw überstreichen. **2** *vt (with powder etc)* betupfen; *(with towel etc)* tupfen. **to ~ one's eyes** sich *(dat)* die Augen tupfen.

♦ **dab at** *vi +prep obj* betupfen.

♦ **dab on** *vt sep* auftragen *(prep obj* auf *+acc)*.

dab[2] *adj (col)* **to be a ~ hand at sth/doing sth** gut in etw *(dat)* sein/sich darauf verstehen, etw zu tun.

dabble [ˈdæbl] *vi* **to ~ in sth** sich nebenbei mit etw beschäftigen.

dachshund [ˈdækshʊnd] *n* Dackel *m*.

dad [dæd], **daddy** [ˈdædɪ] *n (col)* Vater, Papa *(col)*, Vati *m (col)*.

daddy-long-legs [ˌdædɪˈlɒŋlegz] *n, pl* - *(Brit)* Schnake *f*; *(US)* Weberknecht *m*.

daffodil [ˈdæfədɪl] *n* Osterglocke, Narzisse *f*.

daft [dɑːft] *adj (+er)* doof *(col)*, blöd *(col)*. **he's ~ about her** *(col)* er ist verrückt nach ihr *(col)*.

dagger [ˈdægəʳ] *n* Dolch *m*. **to be at ~s drawn with sb** *(fig)* mit jdm auf Kriegsfuß stehen; **to look ~s at sb** jdn mit Blicken durchbohren.

dago [ˈdeɪgəʊ] *n (pej)* Südländer *m*.

dahlia [ˈdeɪlɪə] *n* Dahlie *f*.

daily [ˈdeɪlɪ] **1** *adj* täglich; *wage, newspaper* Tages-. **~ grind** täglicher Trott; **on a ~ basis** tageweise. **2** *adv* täglich. **3** *n* **(a)** *(newspaper)* Tageszeitung *f*. **(b)** *(also* **~ help***)* Putzfrau *f*.

dainty [ˈdeɪntɪ] *adj (+er)* zierlich; *manners* geziert; *lace, handkerchief* fein; *movement, music* anmutig; *food* appetitlich. **~ morsel** Leckerbissen *m*.

dairy [ˈdɛərɪ] *n* Molkerei *f*; *(on farm)* Milchkammer *f*; *(shop)* Milchgeschäft *nt*.

dairy: ~ butter *n* Markenbutter *f*; **~ cow** *n* Milchkuh *f*; **~ farming** *n* Milchviehhaltung *f*; **~ ice cream** *n* Milchspeiseeis *nt*.

dais [ˈdeɪɪs] *n* Podium *nt*.

daisy [ˈdeɪzɪ] *n* Gänseblümchen *nt*. **as fresh as a ~** taufrisch; **to be pushing up the daisies** *(col)* sich *(dat)* die Radieschen von unten besehen *(col)*; **~ wheel** Typenrad *nt*; *(printer)* Typenraddrucker *m*.

dale [deɪl] *n (N Engl, liter)* Tal *nt*.

dally [ˈdælɪ] *vi (waste time)* (herum)trödeln.

Dalmatian [dælˈmeɪʃən] *n (dog)* Dalmatiner *m*.

dam [dæm] **1** *n (lit, fig)* Damm *m*; *(reservoir)* Stausee *m*. **2** *vt (also* **~ up***) river, lake* stauen.

damage [ˈdæmɪdʒ] **1** *n* **(a)** Schaden *m (to* an *+dat)*. **to do a lot of ~** großen Schaden anrichten; **to do sb/sth a lot of ~** jdm/einer Sache *(dat)* großen Schaden zufügen; **that did a lot of ~ to his reputation** das hat seinem Ruf sehr geschadet. **(b)** *(Jur)* **~s** Schaden(s)ersatz *m*. **(c)** *(col: cost)* **what's the ~?** was kostet der Spaß? *(col)*. **2** *vt* beschädigen; *health, reputation, relations* schaden *(+dat)*, schädigen. **to ~ one's eyesight** sich *(dat)* die Augen verderben; **smoking can ~ your health** Rauchen schadet Ihrer Gesundheit.

damaging [ˈdæmɪdʒɪŋ] *adj* schädlich *(to* für*)*.

dame [deɪm] *n* **(a)** **D~** *britischer Titel*. **(b)** *(Theat)* (komische) Alte. **(c)** *(US col)* Weib *nt (col)*.

damn [dæm] **1** *interj (col)* verdammt *(col)*.

2 *n (col)* **he doesn't care** *or* **give a ~** er schert sich einen Dreck (darum) *(col)*; **I don't give a ~** das ist mir scheißegal *(col!)*.

3 *adj attr (col)* verdammt. **I couldn't see a ~ thing** so ein Mist *(col)*, ich konnte überhaupt nichts sehen.

4 *adv (col)* verdammt. **I should ~ well hope so** das will ich aber auch stark hoffen; **~-all** nicht die Bohne *(col)*; **I've done ~-all today** ich hab heute überhaupt nichts gemacht *(col)*.

5 *vt* **(a)** *(Rel)* verdammen. **(b)** *(judge and condemn)* verurteilen; *book etc also* verreißen. **(c)** *(col)* **~ him/you!** der kann/du kannst mich mal! *(col)*; **~ it!** verdammt (noch mal)! *(col)*; **well, I'll be ~ed!** Donnerwetter! *(col)*; **I'll be ~ed if I'll go there** ich denke nicht daran, da hinzugehen; **I'll be ~ed if I know** weiß der Teufel *(col)*.

damnation [dæmˈneɪʃən] **1** *n (Eccl)* Verdammnis *f*. **2** *interj (col)* verdammt *(col)*.

damned [dæmd] **1** *adj* **(a)** *soul* verdammt. **(b)** *(col)* = **damn 3. 2** *adv* = **damn 4.**

damnedest [ˈdæmdɪst] *n* **to do** *or* **try one's ~** *(col)* sein möglichstes tun.

damning [ˈdæmɪŋ] *adj* vernichtend; *evidence* belastend.

damp [dæmp] **1** *adj (~er)* feucht. **a ~ squib** *(fig)* ein Reinfall *m*. **2** *n* Feuchtigkeit *f*. **3** *vt* **(a)** befeuchten. **(b)** *(fig) enthusiasm etc* dämpfen. **to ~ sb's spirits** jdm einen Dämpfer aufsetzen. **(c)** *sounds, vibrations* dämpfen; *(also* **~ down***) fire* ersticken.

damp course *n* Dämmschicht, Isolierschicht *f*.

dampen [ˈdæmpən] *vt* = **damp 3 (a, b).**

damper [ˈdæmpəʳ] *n* **(a)** *(of chimney)* (Luft)klappe *f*; *(of piano)* Dämpfer *m*. **(b)** **to put a ~ on sth** einer Sache *(dat)* einen Dämpfer aufsetzen.

damson [ˈdæmzən] *n (fruit)* Damaszenerpflaume *f*.

dance [dɑːns] **1** *n* Tanz *m*; *(occasion also)* Tanzabend *m*; *(school etc)* Ball *m*. **she's led him a fine ~** sie hat ihn ganz schön an der Nase herumgeführt. **2** *vti* tanzen. **to ~ for joy** einen Freudentanz aufführen.

dance *in cpds* Tanz-; **~ band** *n* Tanzkapelle *f*; **~ floor** *n* Tanzboden *m*; *(in restaurant)* Tanzfläche *f*; **~ hall** *n* Tanzsaal *m*; **~ music** *n* Tanzmusik *f*.

dancer [ˈdɑːnsəʳ] *n* Tänzer(in *f*) *m*.

dancing [ˈdɑːnsɪŋ] **1** *n* Tanzen *nt*. **2** *attr* Tanz-.

dandelion [ˈdændɪlaɪən] *n* Löwenzahn *m*.

dandruff [ˈdændrəf] *n* Schuppen *pl*.

dandy [ˈdændɪ] **1** *n* Dandy, Geck *m*. **2** *adj (esp US col)* prima *(col)*.

Dane [deɪn] *n* Däne *m*, Dänin *f*.

danger [ˈdeɪndʒəʳ] *n* **(a)** Gefahr *f*. **to put sb/sth in ~** jdn/etw in Gefahr bringen; **to be in ~ of doing sth** Gefahr laufen, etw zu tun; **out of ~** außer Gefahr; **there is no ~ of that** die Gefahr besteht nicht; **to be a ~ to sb/sth** für jdn/etw eine Gefahr bedeuten. **(b)** **"~"** „Achtung, Lebensgefahr!"; **"~, ice"** „Glatteisgefahr".

danger: ~ area *n* Gefahrenzone *f or* -bereich *m*; **~ list** *n*: **on/off the ~ list** in/außer Lebensgefahr; **~ money** *n* Gefahrenzulage *f*.

dangerous [ˈdeɪndʒrəs] *adj* gefährlich.

dangerously [ˈdeɪndʒrəslɪ] *adv* gefährlich. **the**

deadline is getting ~ close der Termin rückt bedenklich nahe; **to be ~ ill** schwerkrank sein.
danger: ~ **signal** *n (lit, fig)* Warnsignal *nt*; ~ **zone** *n* Gefahrenzone *f*.
dangle ['dæŋgl] **1** *vt* baumeln lassen. **to ~ sth before sb** *(fig)* jdm etw in Aussicht stellen. **2** *vi* baumeln.
Danish ['deɪnɪʃ] **1** *adj* dänisch. ~ **blue (cheese)** Edelpilzkäse *m*; ~ **pastry** Plundergebäck *nt*. **2** *n (language)* Dänisch *nt*.
dank [dæŋk] *adj* (unangenehm) feucht.
Danube ['dænju:b] *n* Donau *f*.
dapper ['dæpəʳ] *adj* gepflegt, gediegen.
dappled ['dæpld] *adj* gefleckt; *(with small flecks)* gesprenkelt; *horse* scheckig.
dare [dɛəʳ] **1** *vi (be bold enough)* es wagen; *(have the confidence)* sich trauen. **he wouldn't ~!** er wird sich schwer hüten; **you ~!** untersteh dich!; **how ~ you!** was fällt dir ein! **2** *vt* **(a) to ~ (to) do sth** (es) wagen, etw zu tun, sich trauen, etw zu tun; **he ~ not** *or* **doesn't ~** *or* **~n't do it** das wagt er nicht; **don't (you) ~ say that to me** untersteh dich, das zu mir zu sagen. **(b) I ~ say it gets quite cold here in winter** ich nehme an, daß es hier im Winter ziemlich kalt wird; **I ~ say he'll be there** es kann (gut) sein, daß er dort ist; **he was very sorry — I ~ say** es tat ihm sehr leid — das glaube ich gerne. **(c)** *(challenge)* **I ~ you to jump off** wetten, daß du dich nicht zu springen traust! **3** *n* **to do sth for a ~** etw als Mutprobe tun.
daredevil ['dɛə,devl] **1** *n* Draufgänger *m*. **2** *adj* waghalsig.
daring ['dɛərɪŋ] **1** *adj* kühn; *(in physical matters)* waghalsig; *opinion, dress* gewagt. **2** *n* Kühnheit *f*; *(in physical matters)* Waghalsigkeit *f*.
dark [dɑ:k] **1** *adj (+er) (lit, fig)* dunkel; *thoughts, threats* finster. **it's getting ~** es wird dunkel; **~ blue** dunkelblau; **D~ Ages** finsteres Mittelalter; **to keep sth ~** etw geheimhalten. **2** *n* **(a)** Dunkelheit *f*. **after ~** nach Einbruch der Dunkelheit; **until ~** bis zum Einbruch der Dunkelheit. **(b)** *(fig)* **to be in the ~** keine Ahnung haben *(about* von*)*; **he has kept me in the ~** er hat mich im dunkeln gelassen; **it was a shot in the ~** das war nur auf gut Glück gesagt/geraten *etc*.
darken ['dɑ:kən] **1** *vt* dunkel machen; *sky also* verdunkeln; *(before storm)* verfinstern; **never ~ my door again!** lassen Sie sich hier nicht mehr blicken! **2** *vi see vt* dunkel werden; sich verdunkeln; sich verfinstern.
dark: **~-eyed** ['dɑ:kaɪd] *adj* dunkeläugig; **~ horse** *n (fig)* stilles Wasser; *(unexpected winner)* Außenseiter *m*.
darkly ['dɑ:klɪ] *adj (lit, fig)* dunkel.
darkness ['dɑ:knɪs] *n* Dunkelheit *f*. **the house was in ~** das Haus lag im Dunkeln.
dark: **~room** *n (Phot)* Dunkelkammer *f*; **~-skinned** ['dɑ:kskɪnd] *adj* dunkelhäutig.
darling ['dɑ:lɪŋ] **1** *n* Liebling, Schatz *m*. **be a ~ and** ... sei so lieb und ... **2** *adj wife etc* lieb.
darn[1] [dɑ:n] *(Sew)* **1** *n* gestopfte Stelle. **2** *vt* stopfen.
darn[2] *(col)* **1** *adj, adv, interj* verflixt *(col)*. **2** *vt* **~ him!** zum Kuckuck mit ihm! *(col)*.
darning ['dɑ:nɪŋ] *n* Stopfen *nt*; *(things to be darned)* Stopfsachen *pl*. **I've a lot of ~ to do** ich habe viel zu stopfen; **~ needle** Stopfnadel *f*.
dart [dɑ:t] **1** *n* **(a)** *(movement)* **to make a sudden ~ at sb/sth** einen plötzlichen Satz auf jdn/etw zu machen. **(b)** *(weapon)* Pfeil *m*; *(Sport)* (Wurf)pfeil *m*. **(c)** *(Sew)* Abnäher *m*. **2** *vi* flitzen; *(fish)* schnellen. **to ~ out** *(person)* heraus-/hinausflitzen; *(fish, tongue)* hervorschnellen; **he ~ed behind a bush** er hechtete hinter einen Busch. **3** *vt* **to ~ a glance at sb** jdm einen Blick zuwerfen.
dart board *n* Dartscheibe *f*.
darts [dɑ:ts] *n sing* Darts, Pfeilwurfspiel *nt*.
dash [dæʃ] **1** *n* **(a)** *(sudden rush)* **he made a ~ for the door** er stürzte auf die Tür zu; **she made a ~ for it** sie rannte, so schnell sie konnte. **(b)** *(style, vigour)* Schwung, Elan *m*. **to cut a ~** eine Figur machen. **(c)** *(small amount)* etwas, ein bißchen; *(of wine, vinegar, spirits also)* Schuß *m*; *(of seasoning etc also)* Prise *f*. **(d)** *(Typ)* Gedankenstrich *m*. **(e)** = **dashboard**. **2** *vt* **(a)** *(throw violently)* schleudern. **to ~ sth to pieces** etw in tausend Stücke zerschlagen; **to ~ one's head against sth** mit dem Kopf gegen etw schlagen. **(b)** *sb's hopes* zunichte machen. **3** *vi* **(a) to ~ into a room** in ein Zimmer stürzen; **to ~ away/back/up** fort-/zurück-/hinaufstürzen. **(b)** *(knock, be hurled)* schlagen; *(waves also)* peitschen. **4** *interj* **~ (it)!** *(col)* verflixt! *(col)*.
♦**dash off** **1** *vt sep letter* hinwerfen. **2** *vi* losstürzen.
dashboard ['dæʃbɔ:d] *n* Armaturenbrett *nt*.
dashing ['dæʃɪŋ] *adj* flott, schneidig.
data ['deɪtə] *pl of* **datum** *usu with sing vb* Daten *pl*. **a piece of ~** eine Angabe.
data: **~ bank** *n* Datenbank *f*; **~base** *n* Datenbank *f*; **~ processing** *n* Datenverarbeitung *f*; **~ protection** *n* Datenschutz *m*; **~ transmission** *n* Datenübertragung *f*.
date[1] [deɪt] *n (fruit)* Dattel *f*; *(tree)* Dattelpalme *f*.
date[2] **1** *n* **(a)** Datum *nt*; *(historical ~)* Jahreszahl *f*; *(for appointment)* Termin *m*. **~ of birth** Geburtsdatum *nt*; **what's the ~ today?** der wievielte ist heute?, welches Datum haben wir heute?; **what ~ is he coming on?** an welchem Tag kommt er?; **to ~** bis heute. **(b)** *(appointment)* Verabredung *f*; **who's his ~?** mit wem trifft er sich?; **to make a ~ with sb** sich mit jdm verabreden; **she's out on a ~** sie hat eine Verabredung.
2 *vt* **(a)** mit dem Datum versehen; *letter etc also* datieren. **a coin ~d 1390** eine Münze von 1390. **(b)** *(establish age of) work of art etc* datieren. **that really ~s you** daran merkt man, wie alt Sie sind. **(c)** *(take out) girlfriend etc* ausgehen mit; *(regularly also)* gehen mit *(col)*.
3 *vi* **(a) to ~ back to** zurückdatieren auf *(+acc)*; **to ~ from** zurückgehen auf *(+acc)*. **(b)** *(become old-fashioned)* veralten.
dated ['deɪtɪd] *adj* altmodisch, veraltet.
date: **~ line** *n (Geog)* Datumsgrenze *f*; **~ stamp** *n* Datumsstempel *m*.
dative ['deɪtɪv] *n* Dativ *m*. **in the ~** im Dativ.
daub [dɔ:b] *vt walls, canvas, face* beschmieren; *paint, slogans, make-up* schmieren.
daughter ['dɔ:təʳ] *n* Tochter *f*. **~-in-law** Schwiegertochter *f*.
daunt [dɔ:nt] *vt* entmutigen. **nothing ~ed** unverzagt.
daunting ['dɔ:ntɪŋ] *adj* entmutigend.
dauntless ['dɔ:ntlɪs] *adj* unerschrocken, beherzt.
dawdle ['dɔ:dl] *vi (be too slow)* trödeln; *(stroll)* bummeln.
dawdler ['dɔ:dləʳ] *n* Trödler(in *f*) *m*.
dawn [dɔ:n] **1** *n* (Morgen)dämmerung *f*; *(time of day)* Tagesanbruch *m*; *(fig)* Anbruch *m*. **at ~** bei Tagesanbruch; **it's almost ~** es dämmert schon bald; **from ~ to dusk** von morgens bis abends. **2** *vi* **(a) day was already ~ing** es dämmerte schon; **the day will ~ when ...** *(fig)* der Tag wird kommen, wo ... **(b)** *(fig: new age etc)* dämmern, anbrechen. **(c) it suddenly ~ed on him that ...** es dämmerte ihm, daß ...
dawn chorus *n* Morgenkonzert *nt* der Vögel.
day [deɪ] *n* **(a)** Tag *m*. **it will arrive any ~ now** es muß jeden Tag kommen; **what ~ is it today?** welcher Tag ist heute?; **what ~ of the month is it?** der wievielte ist heute?; **the ~ before yesterday** vorgestern; **the ~ before her birthday** der Tag vor ihrem Geburtstag; **(on) the ~ after/before** am Tag danach/zuvor; **two years ago to the ~** heute/morgen *etc* auf den Tag genau vor

zwei Jahren; **one ~** eines Tages; **one of these ~s** irgendwann (einmal), eines Tages; **~ in, ~ out** tagein, tagaus; **they went to London for the ~** sie machten einen Tagesausflug nach London; **for ~s on end** tagelang; **~ after ~** Tag für Tag; **~ by ~** jeden Tag, täglich; **the other ~** neulich; **at the end of the ~** *(fig)* letzen Endes; **to live from ~ to ~** von einem Tag auf den andern leben; **I remember it to this ~** daran erinnere ich mich noch heute; **for ~s on end** tagelang; **he's fifty if he's a ~** er ist mindestens fünfzig; **to travel during the** *or* **by ~** tagsüber *or* am Tag reisen; **good ~!** guten Tag!; *(good-bye)* auf Wiedersehen; **to be paid by the ~** tageweise bezahlt werden; **let's call it a ~** machen wir Schluß; **to have a nice/lazy ~** einen schönen Tag verbringen/einen Tag faulenzen; **have a nice ~!** schönen Tag noch!; **did you have a nice ~?** na, wie war's?; **to have a good/bad ~** einen guten/schlechten Tag haben; **that'll be the ~** das möcht' ich sehen *or* erleben.

(b) *(period of time: often pl)* **these ~s** heute, heutzutage; **what are you doing these ~s?** was machst du denn so?; **in this ~ and age** heutzutage; **in ~s to come** in künftigen Zeiten; **in his younger ~s** als er noch jünger war; **in Queen Victoria's ~, in the ~s of Queen Victoria** zu Königin Viktorias Zeiten; **the happiest ~s of my life** die glücklichste Zeit meines Lebens; **those were the ~s** das waren noch Zeiten; **in the old ~s** früher; **in the good old ~s** in der guten alten Zeit; **it's early ~s yet** es ist noch zu früh; **he/this machine has seen better ~s** er/diese Maschine hat (auch) schon bessere Tage gesehen; **to end one's ~s in misery** im Elend sterben.

(c) *(with poss adj: lifetime, best time)* **famous in her ~** in ihrer Zeit berühmt; **it has had its ~** das hat seine Glanzzeit überschritten; **his ~ will come** sein Tag wird kommen.

(d) *no pl (contest, battle)* **to win** *or* **carry the ~** siegen. **to lose the ~** (den Kampf) verlieren; **that saved the ~** das war die Rettung.

day: ~ boy *n (Sch)* Externe(r) *m*; **~break** *n* Tagesanbruch *m*; **at ~break** bei Tagesanbruch; **~dream 1** *n* Tagtraum *m*; **2** *vi* mit offenen Augen träumen; **~ girl** *n (Sch)* Externe *f*.

daylight ['deɪlaɪt] *n* Tageslicht *nt*. **at ~** bei Tage; **it is still ~** es ist noch hell; **it was broad ~** es war hellichter Tag; **in broad ~** am hellichten Tage; **I began to see ~** *(fig) (to understand)* mir ging ein Licht auf; *(to see the end appear)* so langsam habe ich Land gesehen *(col)*; **to beat the living ~s out of sb** *(col)* jdn windelweich schlagen *(col)*; **to scare the living ~s out of sb** *(col)* jdm einen fürchterlichen Schreck einjagen *(col)*.

daylight: ~ robbery *n (col)* Halsabschneiderei *f (col)*; **~ saving time** *n* Sommerzeit *f*.

day: ~ nursery *n* Kindertagesstätte *f*; *(in private house)* Kinderzimmer *nt*; **~ release course** *n* Fortbildungskurs *m (für den man 1 Tag pro Woche freigestellt wird)*; **~ return (ticket)** *n (Brit Rail)* Tagesrückfahrkarte *f*; **~ school** *n* Tagesschule *f*; **~ shift** *n* Tagschicht *f*; **to be on ~ shift** Tagschicht arbeiten.

daytime ['deɪtaɪm] **1** *n* Tag *m*. **in the ~** bei Tage, tagsüber. **2** *attr* am Tage.

day: ~-to-day *adj occurrence* alltäglich. **on a ~-to-day basis** tageweise; **~ trip** *n* Tagesausflug *m*; **~ tripper** *n* Tagesausflügler(in *f*) *m*.

daze [deɪz] **1** *n* **in a ~** ganz benommen. **2** *vt* benommen machen.

dazzle ['dæzl] *vt (lig, fig)* blenden.

dazzling ['dæzlɪŋ] *adj (lit)* blendend.

D-day ['di:deɪ] *n (Hist) Tag der Invasion durch die Alliierten (6.6.44)*; *(fig)* der Tag X.

DDT [di:di:'ti:] *n* DDT *nt*.

deacon ['di:kən] *n* Diakon *m*.

dead [ded] **1** *adj* **(a)** *(lit, fig)* tot; *plant also* abgestorben. **to drop (down) ~** tot umfallen; **over my ~ body** *(col)* nur über meine Leiche *(col)*. **(b)** *(not sensitive) limbs* abgestorben, taub. **my fingers are ~** meine Finger sind wie abgestorben; **to be ~ from the neck up** *(col)* nur Stroh im Kopf haben *(col)*, gehirnamputiert sein *(col)*; **to be ~ to the world** vollkommen weggetreten sein *(col)*. **(c)** *(Elec) cable* stromlos; *(Telec)* tot. **to go ~** ausfallen; **the line went ~** die Leitung war plötzlich tot. **(d)** *(burnt out) fire* aus *pred*; *match* abgebrannt. **(e)** *(absolute, exact)* total, vollig. **~ silence** Totenstille *f*; **~ calm** *(Naut)* totale Windstille; **to come to a ~ stop** völlig zum Stillstand kommen; **to hit sth ~ centre** etw genau in der Mitte treffen. **(f)** *(col: exhausted)* völlig kaputt *(col)*.

2 *adv* **(a)** *(exactly)* genau. **~ straight** schnurgerade; **to be ~ on time** auf die Minute pünktlich kommen; **~ on course** voll *or* genau auf Kurs. **(b)** *(col: very)* total *(col)*, völlig. **~ drunk/tired** total betrunken/todmüde; **you're ~ right** Sie haben völlig recht; **~ slow** ganz langsam; **to be ~ certain about sth** bei etw todsicher sein. **(c) to stop ~** abrupt stehenbleiben *or (talking)* innehalten.

3 *n* **(a) the ~** *pl* die Toten *pl*. **(b) at ~ of night** mitten in der Nacht; **in the ~ of winter** mitten im Winter.

dead-beat ['ded'bi:t] *adj (col)* völlig kaputt *(col)*.

deaden ['dedn] *vt sound, noise* dämpfen; *pain* mildern; *force, blow* abschwächen; *nerve* abtöten.

dead: ~end *n* Sackgasse *f*; **a ~-end job** ein Job *m* ohne Aufstiegsmöglichkeiten; **~ heat** *n* totes Rennen; **~line** *n* (letzter) Termin; *(for application etc)* Abgabetermin *m*; **to set a ~line** eine Frist setzen; **to work to a ~line** auf einen Termin hinarbeiten; **~lock** *n* **to reach (a) ~lock** sich festfahren; **to break the ~lock** aus der Sackgasse herauskommen.

deadly ['dedlɪ] **1** *adj (+er)* **(a)** tödlich; *sin, enemy* Tod-; *wit, sarcasm* vernichtend. **he's in ~ earnest** er meint es todernst, es ist sein voller Ernst. **(b)** *(col: boring)* todlangweilig. **2** *adv boring* tod-. **~ pale** totenbleich.

dead: ~pan *adj face* unbewegt; *style, humour* trocken; **D~ Sea** *n* Totes Meer.

deaf [def] *adj (+er)* taub. **as ~ as a (door)post** stocktaub; **to turn a ~ ear to sb/sth** sich jdm/einer Sache *(dat)* gegenüber taub stellen.

deaf: ~-aid *n* Hörgerät *nt*; **~-and-dumb** *adj* taubstumm; *language* Taubstummen-.

deafen ['defn] *vt (lit)* taub machen; *(fig)* betäuben.

deafening ['defnɪŋ] *adj noise* ohrenbetäubend; *row* lautstark. **a ~ silence** ein eisiges Schweigen.

deaf-mute ['def'mju:t] *n* Taubstumme(r) *mf*.

deafness ['defnɪs] *n (lit, fig)* Taubheit *f (to* gegenüber*)*.

deal[1] [di:l] **1** *n* **a good** *or* **great ~** eine Menge, (ziemlich) viel; **not a great ~** nicht (besonders) viel; **there's a great** *or* **good ~ of truth in what he says** es ist schon ziemlich viel Wahres an dem, was er sagt; **and that's saying a good ~** und damit ist schon viel gesagt; **to mean a great ~ to sb** jdm viel bedeuten. **2** *adv* **a good** *or* **great ~** viel; **not a great ~** nicht viel.

deal[2] *(vb: pret, ptp* **dealt***)* **1** *n* **(a)** *(Comm: also* **business ~***)* Geschäft *nt*; *(arrangement)* Abmachung *f*; *(official)* Abkommen *nt*. **to do a ~ with sb** mit jdm ein Geschäft abschließen; **it's a ~** abgemacht!; **I'll make a ~ with you** ich schlage Ihnen ein Geschäft vor; **to give sb a fair ~** jdn anständig behandeln; **a better ~ for the lower paid** bessere Bedingungen für die schlechter bezahlten Arbeiter. **(b)** *(Cards)* **it's your ~** Sie geben. **2** *vti (Cards)* geben, austeilen.

♦ **deal in** *vi +prep obj (Comm)* handeln mit.

♦ **deal out** *vt sep gifts, money* verteilen *(to* an *+acc)*; *cards* geben *(to dat)*. **to ~ ~ justice** Recht sprechen.

♦**deal with** *vi +prep obj* **(a)** *(do business with)* verhandeln mit. **(b)** *(manage, handle)* sich kümmern um; *(with job)* sich befassen mit; *(successfully)* fertigwerden mit; *(Comm) orders* erledigen; *(be responsible for)* zuständig sein für. **to know how to ~ ~ sb** wissen, wie man mit jdm umgeht; **I'll ~ ~ you later!** dich knöpf' ich mir später vor *(col)*. **(c)** *(be concerned with) (book, film etc)* handeln von; *(author)* sich befassen mit.

deal[3] *n (wood)* Kiefern- *or* Tannenholz *nt*.

dealer ['diːləʳ] *n (Comm)* Händler *m*. **a ~ in furs** ein Pelzhändler.

dealing ['diːlɪŋ] *n* **(a)** *(trading)* Handel *m*. **there's some crooked ~ involved here** da ist irgend etwas gemauschelt worden *(col)*. **(b) ~s** *pl (Comm)* Geschäfte *pl*; *(generally)* Umgang *m*; **to have ~s with sb** mit jdm zu tun haben.

dealt [delt] *pret, ptp of* **deal**[2].

dean [diːn] *n (Eccl, Univ)* Dekan *m*.

dear [dɪəʳ] **1** *adj (+er)* **(a) I hold him/it ~** er/es ist mir lieb und teuer; **that is my ~est wish** das ist mein sehnlichster Wunsch; **my ~ chap** mein lieber Freund. **(b)** *(in letter-writing)* **~ Daddy/John** lieber Vati/John!; **~ Sir/Madam** sehr geehrter Herr X/sehr geehrte Frau X; **~ Sirs** sehr geehrte Damen und Herren; **~ Mr Kemp** sehr geehrter Herr Kemp; *(less formal)* lieber Herr Kemp! **(c)** *(expensive)* teuer. **2** *interj* **~ ~!, ~ me!** (du) meine Güte!; **oh ~!** oje! **3** *n* **hello/thank you ~** hallo/vielen Dank; **yes, ~** ja, Liebling; **be a ~** *(col)* sei so lieb *or* gut; **poor ~** der/die Arme. **4** *adv (lit, fig) buy, pay, sell* teuer.

dearly ['dɪəlɪ] *adv* **(a)** *love* von ganzem Herzen. **I should ~ like to live here** ich würde für mein Leben gern hier wohnen. **(b)** *(lit, fig) pay etc* teuer.

dearth [dɜːθ] *n* Mangel *m (of* an *+dat)*. **~ of ideas** Ideenarmut *f*.

death [deθ] *n* Tod *m*; *(of plans, hopes etc)* Ende *nt*. **the number of ~s** die Todesfälle; **to be afraid of ~** sich vor dem Tod fürchten; **a fight to the ~** ein Kampf auf Leben und Tod; **to put sb to ~** jdn hinrichten; **to drink oneself to ~** sich zu Tode trinken; **to be at ~'s door** an der Schwelle des Todes stehen; **it will be the ~ of you** *(col)* das wird dein Tod sein; **he will be the ~ of me** *(col) (he's so funny)* ich lach' mich noch einmal über ihn *(col)*; *(he's annoying)* er bringt mich noch ins Grab; **to catch one's ~ (of cold)** *(col)* sich *(dat)* den Tod holen; **I am sick to ~ of all this** *(col)* das alles hängt mir gründlich zum Halse raus.

death: ~bed *n* Sterbebett *nt*; **~-blow** *n (lit, fig)* Todesstoß *m*; **~ certificate** *n* Totenschein *m*; **~ duties** *npl (Brit)* Erbschaftssteuer *f*.

deathly ['deθlɪ] **1** *adj (+er)* **~ hush** Totenstille *f*; **~ silence** eisiges Schweigen; **~ pallor** Totenblässe *f*. **2** *adv* **~ pale** totenblaß.

death: ~-mask *n* Totenmaske *f*; **~ penalty** *n* Todesstrafe *f*; **~ rate** *n* Sterbeziffer *f*; **~ sentence** *n* Todesurteil *nt*; **~ throes** *npl* Todeskampf *m*; **~-trap** *n* Todesfalle *f*; **~-watch beetle** *n* Klopfkäfer *m*; **~-wish** *n* Wunsch *m* zu sterben.

debar [dɪ'bɑːʳ] *vt* ausschließen *(from* von*)*.

debase [dɪ'beɪs] *vt person* erniedrigen; *qualities* mindern, herabsetzen; *coinage* den Wert mindern von; *language* entstellen.

debatable [dɪ'beɪtəbl] *adj* fraglich.

debate [dɪ'beɪt] **1** *vti* debattieren, diskutieren *(with* mit, *about* über *+acc)*. **he was debating with himself whether to go or not** er überlegte hin und her, ob er gehen sollte; **debating society** Debattierklub *m*. **2** *n* Debatte *f*. **after much ~** nach langer Debatte *or* Diskussion.

debauched [dɪ'bɔːtʃt] *adj* verkommen; *life* ausschweifend.

debauchery [dɪ'bɔːtʃərɪ] *n* Ausschweifung *f*. **a life of ~** ein ausschweifendes Leben.

debenture [dɪ'bentʃəʳ] *n (Fin)* Schuldschein *m*.

debilitate [dɪ'bɪlɪteɪt] *vt* schwächen.

debility [dɪ'bɪlɪtɪ] *n* Schwäche *f*.

debit ['debɪt] **1** *n* Debetposten *m*, Soll *nt*. **~s** Debet, Soll *nt*; **~ balance** Debetsaldo *m*; **~ note** Lastschrift *f*; **on the ~ side there's the weather** *(fig)* als Minuspunkt ist das Wetter zu erwähnen. **2** *vt* **to ~ sb/sb's account with a sum** jdn/jds Konto mit einem Betrag belasten.

debonair [ˌdebə'nɛəʳ] *adj* flott.

debrief [ˌdiː'briːf] *vt* befragen. **to be ~ed** Bericht erstatten.

debris ['debriː] *n* Trümmer *pl*, Schutt *m*.

debt [det] *n* Schuld *f*. **~ of honour** Ehrenschuld *f*; **National D~** Staatsschulden *pl*; **to be in ~** verschuldet sein *(to* gegenüber*)*; **to be £5 in ~** £5 Schulden haben *(to* bei*)*; **to get into ~** Schulden machen; **to be out of ~** schuldenfrei sein; **to repay a ~** *(lit, fig)* eine Schuld begleichen; **I shall always be in your ~** das werde ich Ihnen nie vergessen.

debt collector *n* Inkassobeauftragte(r) *mf*, Schuldeneintreiber *(col) m*.

debtor ['detəʳ] *n* Schuldner(in *f*) *m*.

debunk [ˌdiː'bʌŋk] *vt claim* entlarven; *politician* vom Sockel stoßen.

début ['deɪbjuː] *n (lit, fig)* Debüt *nt*. **to make one's ~** sein Debüt geben.

débutante ['debjuːtɑ̃ːnt] *n* Debütantin *f*.

decade ['dekeɪd] *n* Jahrzehnt *nt*.

decadence ['dekədəns] *n* Dekadenz *f*.

decadent ['dekədənt] *adj* dekadent.

decaffeinated [ˌdiː'kæfɪneɪtɪd] *adj* koffeinfrei.

decal [dɪ'kæl] *n (US)* Aufkleber *m*.

decamp [dɪ'kæmp] *vi (col)* sich aus dem Staube machen.

decant [dɪ'kænt] *vt* umfüllen.

decanter [dɪ'kæntəʳ] *n* Karaffe *f*.

decapitate [dɪ'kæpɪteɪt] *vt* enthaupten, köpfen.

decarbonize [ˌdiː'kɑːbənaɪz] *vt* dekarbonisieren, entkohlen.

decathlete [dɪ'kæθliːt] *n* Zehnkämpfer *m*.

decathlon [dɪ'kæθlən] *n* Zehnkampf *m*.

decay [dɪ'keɪ] **1** *vi* verfallen; *(rot)* verwesen, verfaulen; *(food)* schlecht werden, verderben; *(beauty)* verblühen, vergehen; *(civilization, race)* untergehen; *(one's faculties)* verkümmern. **2** *n see vi* Verfall *m*; Verwesung *f*; Verderben *nt*; *(of civilization)* Untergang *m*; *(of one's faculties)* Verkümmern *nt*. **to fall into ~** in Verfall geraten.

decease [dɪ'siːs] *n (Jur, form)* Ableben *nt (form)*.

deceased [dɪ'siːst] *(Jur, form)* **1** *adj* verstorben. **2** *n*: **the ~** der/die Tote *or* Verstorbene; die Toten *or* Verstorbenen *pl*.

deceit [dɪ'siːt] *n* Betrug *m no pl*, Täuschung *f*.

deceitful [dɪ'siːtfʊl] *adj* falsch, betrügerisch.

deceitfulness [dɪ'siːtfʊlnɪs] *n* Falschheit *f*; *(deceitful acts)* Betrügereien *pl*.

deceive [dɪ'siːv] *vt* täuschen, irreführen; *one's wife, husband* betrügen. **to ~ sb into thinking sth** jdm etw einreden; **are my eyes deceiving me?** täuschen mich meine Augen?; **to ~ oneself** sich *(dat)* selbst etwas vormachen.

decelerate [diː'seləreit] *vi (car, train)* langsamer werden; *(driver)* die Geschwindigkeit herabsetzen.

December [dɪ'sembəʳ] *n* Dezember *m*; *see* **September**.

decency ['diːsənsɪ] *n* Anstand *m*. **it's only common ~ to ...** es gehört sich einfach, zu ...; **have you no sense of ~?** haben Sie denn kein Anstandsgefühl!; **they didn't even have the ~ ...** sie haben es nicht einmal für nötig gehalten, ...

decent ['diːsənt] *adj* anständig. **are you ~?** *(col)* bist du schon angezogen?

decentralization ['diːˌsentrəlaɪ'zeɪʃən] *n* Dezentralisierung *f*.

decentralize [diːˈsentrəlaɪz] *vti* dezentralisieren.

deception [dɪˈsepʃən] *n* Betrug *m no pl* (*of* an +*dat*); *(of public etc)* Täuschung *f*.

deceptive [dɪˈseptɪv] *adj* irreführend; *similarity* täuschend; *simplicity* trügerisch. **to be ~** täuschen, trügen *(geh)*; **appearances can be ~** der Schein trügt.

deceptively [dɪˈseptɪvlɪ] *adv* täuschend.

decibel [ˈdesɪbel] *n* Dezibel *nt*.

decide [dɪˈsaɪd] **1** *vt* **(a)** *(come to a decision)* (sich) entscheiden; *(take it into one's head)* beschließen. **did you ~ anything?** habt ihr irgendwelche Entscheidungen getroffen?; **I have ~d we are making a big mistake** ich bin zu der Ansicht gekommen, daß wir einen großen Fehler machen; **I'll ~ what we do!** ich bestimme, was wir tun! **(b)** *(settle) question, war* entscheiden. **that ~s it** damit ist die Sache entschieden; **that eventually ~d me** das hat schließlich für mich den Ausschlag gegeben. **2** *vi* (sich) entscheiden. **I don't know, *you* ~** ich weiß nicht, entscheiden *or* bestimmen *Sie*!; **to ~ for/against sth** (sich) für/gegen etw entscheiden.

♦ **decide on** *vi +prep obj* sich entscheiden für.

decided [dɪˈsaɪdɪd] *adj* **(a)** *(clear, definite)* entschieden; *difference* deutlich. **(b)** *(determined) manner* entschlossen, bestimmt.

decidedly [dɪˈsaɪdɪdlɪ] *adv (definitely)* entschieden.

deciding [dɪˈsaɪdɪŋ] *adj* entscheidend.

deciduous [dɪˈsɪdjʊəs] *adj* **~ tree** Laubbaum *m*.

decimal [ˈdesɪməl] **1** *adj* Dezimal-. **to three ~ places** auf drei Dezimalstellen; **~ point** Komma *nt*. **2** *n* Dezimalzahl *f*.

decimate [ˈdesɪmeɪt] *vt* dezimieren.

decipher [dɪˈsaɪfəʳ] *vt (lit, fig)* entziffern.

decision [dɪˈsɪʒən] *n* **(a)** Entscheidung *f* (*on* über +*acc*), Entschluß *m*; *(esp of committee etc)* Beschluß *m*. **to make a ~** eine Entscheidung treffen *or* fällen, einen Entschluß/Beschluß fassen; **it's your ~** das mußt du entscheiden; **to come to a ~** zu einer Entscheidung kommen. **(b)** *no pl (of character)* Entschlossenheit *f*.

decision-maker [dɪˈsɪʒən,meikəʳ] *n* Entscheidungsträger *m*.

decisive [dɪˈsaɪsɪv] *adj* **(a)** entscheidend; *factor also* ausschlaggebend. **(b)** *manner, answer* entschlossen; *person* entschlußfreudig.

deck [dek] **1** *n* **(a)** *(Naut)* Deck *nt*. **on ~** auf Deck; **to go up on ~** an Deck gehen; **to go (down) below ~(s)** unter Deck gehen. **(b)** *(of bus)* **top** *or* **upper ~** Oberdeck *nt*. **(c)** *(of cards)* Spiel *nt*. **(d)** *(of record-player)* Laufwerk *nt*; *(part of hi-fi unit)* Plattenspieler *m*. **tape ~** Tape-deck *nt*. **2** *vt (also* **~ out***)* schmücken.

deckchair [ˈdektʃɛəʳ] *n* Liegestuhl *m*.

declaim [dɪˈkleɪm] *vi* deklamieren.

declaration [dekləˈreɪʃən] *n* Erklärung *f*.

declare [dɪˈklɛəʳ] *vt* erklären; *results* bekanntgeben; *goods* angeben. **have you anything to ~?** haben Sie etwas zu verzollen?; **to ~ one's income** sein Einkommen angeben; **to ~ war (on sb)** (jdm) den Krieg erklären; **to ~ sb the winner** jdn zum Sieger erklären; **he ~d that ...** er behauptete, daß ...

declared [dɪˈklɛəd] *adj* erklärt.

declassify [diːˈklæsɪfaɪ] *vt information* freigeben.

declension [dɪˈklenʃən] *n (Gram)* Deklination *f*.

decline [dɪˈklaɪn] **1** *n* **(a)** Rückgang *m*; *(of empire, a party's supremacy)* Untergang, Niedergang *m*. **to be on the ~** *see vi*. **(b)** *(Med)* Verfall *m*. **2** *vt* **(a)** *invitation, honour* ablehnen. **he ~d to come** er hat es abgelehnt, zu kommen. **(b)** *(Gram)* deklinieren. **3** *vi* **(a)** *(prices, value)* sinken; *(popularity, enthusiasm, interest)* abnehmen; *(population, influence, business)* zurückgehen; *(empire)* verfallen; *(fame)* verblassen; *(health)* sich verschlechtern. **in his declining years** gegen Ende seines Lebens. **(b)** *(refuse, say no)* ablehnen. **(c)** *(Gram)* dekliniert werden.

declutch [,diːˈklʌtʃ] *vi* auskuppeln.

decode [,diːˈkəʊd] *vt* entschlüsseln.

decompose [,diːkəmˈpəʊz] *vi (Chem, Phys)* zerlegt werden; *(rot)* sich zersetzen.

decomposition [,diːkɒmpəˈzɪʃən] *n (Chem, Phys)* Zerlegung *f*; *(rotting)* Zersetzung *f*.

decompression [,diːkəmˈpreʃən] *n* Dekompression, Druckverminderung *f*. **~ chamber** *n* Dekompressionskammer *f*.

decontaminate [,diːkənˈtæmɪneɪt] *vt* entgiften; *(from radioactivity)* entseuchen.

decontrol [,diːkənˈtrəʊl] *vt prices* freigeben.

décor [ˈdeɪkɔːʳ] *n (in room)* Ausstattung *f*; *(Theat)* Bühnenbild *nt*.

decorate [ˈdekəreɪt] *vt* **(a)** *cake, hat* verzieren; *street, Christmas tree* schmücken; *room* tapezieren; *(paint)* (an)streichen. **(b)** *soldier* dekorieren, auszeichnen.

decoration [,dekəˈreɪʃən] *n* **(a)** *(act: of room etc)* Tapezieren *nt*; (An)streichen *nt*. **(b)** *(on cake, hat etc)* Verzierung *f*; *(on Christmas tree, in street)* Schmuck *m no pl*. **Christmas ~s** Weihnachtsdekorationen *pl or* -schmuck *m*; **interior ~** Innenausstattung *f*. **(c)** *(Mil)* Auszeichnung *f*.

decorative [ˈdekərətɪv] *adj* dekorativ.

decorator [ˈdekəreɪtəʳ] *n (Brit)* Maler und Tapezierer *m*.

decorous [ˈdekərəs] *adj* schicklich.

decorum [dɪˈkɔːrəm] *n* Anstand *m*.

decoy [ˈdiːkɔɪ] *n (lit, fig)* Köder *m*; *(person)* Lockvogel *m*.

decrease [diːˈkriːs] **1** *vi* abnehmen; *(figures, output, birthrate, production)* zurückgehen; *(strength, enthusiasm, intensity)* nachlassen. **it ~s in value** es verliert an Wert. **2** *vt* verringern, reduzieren. **3** [ˈdiːkriːs] *n see vi* Abnahme *f*; Rückgang *m*; Nachlassen *nt*. **to be on the ~** *see vi*.

decreasingly [diːˈkriːsɪŋlɪ] *adv* immer weniger.

decree [dɪˈkriː] **1** *n (Pol, of king etc)* Erlaß *m*; *(of tribunal, court)* Entscheid *m*, Urteil *nt*. **~ nisi/absolute** vorläufiges/endgültiges Scheidungsurteil. **2** *vt* verordnen, verfügen.

decrepit [dɪˈkrepɪt] *adj* altersschwach; *building also* baufällig.

decry [dɪˈkraɪ] *vt* schlechtmachen.

dedicate [ˈdedɪkeɪt] *vt* **(a)** *church* weihen. **(b)** *book, music* widmen (*to sb* jdm). **to ~ oneself** *or* **one's life to sth** sich *or* sein Leben einer Sache widmen.

dedicated [ˈdedɪkeɪtɪd] *adj attitude* hingebungsvoll; *service* treu; *teacher etc* engagiert. **she's a ~ nurse** sie ist Krankenschwester mit Leib und Seele.

dedication [,dedɪˈkeɪʃən] *n* **(a)** *(quality)* Hingabe *f* (*to* an +*acc*); *(to work)* Engagement *nt*. **(b)** *(of church)* Weihe *f*. **(c)** *(in book)* Widmung *f*.

deduce [dɪˈdjuːs] *vt* folgern, schließen (*from* aus).

deduct [dɪˈdʌkt] *vt* abziehen (*from* von); *(from wages also)* einbehalten. **to ~ sth from the price** etw vom Preis nachlassen.

deductible [dɪˈdʌktəbl] *adj* abziehbar; *(tax ~)* absetzbar.

deduction [dɪˈdʌkʃən] *n* **(a)** *(act of deducting)* Abzug *m*; *(sth deducted) (from price)* Nachlaß *m*; *(from wage)* Abzug *m*. **(b)** *(sth deduced)* (Schluß)folgerung *f*.

deed [diːd] *n* **(a)** Tat *f*. **good ~** gute Tat; **in word and ~** in Wort und Tat. **(b)** *(Jur)* Urkunde *f*. **~ of covenant** Vertragsurkunde *f*.

deem [diːm] *vt* **to ~ sb/sth (to be) sth** jdn/etw für etw erachten *(geh) or* halten.

deep [diːp] **1** *adj (+er)* tief; *(profound) thinker, book, remark* tiefsinnig; *concern, interest* groß; *sorrow* tief (empfunden). **two metres ~ in snow/water** mit zwei Meter Schnee bedeckt/zwei Meter tief unter Wasser; **to go off (at) the ~ end** *(col)* an die

Decke gehen *(col)*; **to plunge in at the ~ end** *(col)* sich kopfüber in die Sache stürzen; **to be thrown in at the ~ end** *(col)* gleich zu Anfang richtig ranmüssen *(col)*; **~ in thought/a book** in Gedanken/in ein Buch vertieft; **he's a ~ one** *(col)* er ist ein stilles Wasser. **2** *adv (+er)* tief. **~ into the night** bis tief in die Nacht hinein; **they stood ten ~** sie standen in zehn Reihen hintereinander. **3** *n (liter)* **the ~** das Meer, die See.

deepen ['diːpən] **1** *vt (lit, fig)* vertiefen. **2** *vi (lit, fig)* tiefer werden; *(concern, interest)* zunehmen; *(mystery)* größer werden.

deep: ~-freeze 1 *n* Tiefkühltruhe *f*; *(upright)* Gefrierschrank *m*; **2** *vt* einfrieren; **~-fry** *vt* fritieren, in schwimmendem Fett ausbacken.

deeply ['diːplɪ] *adv* **(a)** *dig, cut, breathe* tief; *think, consider also* gründlich. **(b)** *grateful, concerned* zutiefst; *offended also, indebted* tief; *love* innig; *interested* höchst; *aware* voll(kommen).

deep: ~-rooted *adj (fig)* tiefverwurzelt; **~-sea** *adj plant, current, animal* Meeres-; **~-sea diver** *n* Tiefseetaucher *m*; **~-sea fishing** *n* Hochseefischerei *f*; **~-seated** *adj* tiefsitzend; **~-set** *adj* tiefliegend; **D~ South** *n* Tiefer Süden.

deer [dɪəʳ] *n, pl* - Hirsch *m*; *(roe ~)* Reh *nt*. **are there any ~ here?** gibt es hier Wild?

deer: ~skin *n* Hirsch-/Rehleder *nt*; **~stalker** *n (hat)* ≈ Sherlock-Holmes-Mütze *f*; **~stalking** *n* Pirschen *nt*, Pirsch *f*.

deface [dɪ'feɪs] *vt* verunstalten.

de facto [deɪ'fæktəʊ] *adj, adv* de facto.

defamation [ˌdefə'meɪʃən] *n* Diffamierung, Verleumdung *f*. **~ of character** Rufmord *m*.

defamatory [dɪ'fæmətərɪ] *adj* diffamierend.

default [dɪ'fɔːlt] **1** *n* **(a)** *(failure to appear) (Jur)* Nichterscheinen *nt* vor Gericht; *(Sport)* Nichtantreten *nt*; *(failure to perform duty)* Versäumnis *f*. **to win by ~** *(Sport)* kampflos gewinnen. **(b) in ~ of** in Ermangelung *(+gen)*. **2** *vi (not appear) (Jur)* nicht erscheinen; *(Sport)* nicht antreten; *(not perform duty, not pay)* säumig sein. **to ~ in one's payments** seinen Zahlungsverpflichtungen nicht nachkommen.

defeat [dɪ'fiːt] **1** *n (defeating)* Sieg *m (of* über *+acc)*; *(of motion, bill)* Ablehnung *f*; *(being defeated)* Niederlage *f*. **to admit ~** sich geschlagen geben. **2** *vt army, team* besiegen, schlagen; *government also* eine Niederlage beibringen *(+dat)*; *motion, bill* ablehnen; **that would be ~ing the purpose** das würde den Zweck verfehlen.

defeatism [dɪ'fiːtɪzəm] *n* Defätismus *m*.

defeatist [dɪ'fiːtɪst] **1** *n* Defätist *m*. **2** *adj* defätistisch.

defecate ['defəkeit] *vi* den Darm entleeren.

defect[1] ['diːfekt] *n* Fehler, Schaden *m*; *(in mechanism also)* Defekt *m*. **physical ~** Mißbildung *f*; *(less serious)* Schönheitsfehler *m*; **a character ~** ein Charakterfehler *m*.

defect[2] [dɪ'fekt] *vi* sich absetzen; *(fig)* abtrünnig werden. **to ~ to the enemy** zum Feind übergehen *or* überlaufen.

defection [dɪ'fekʃən] *n (Pol)* Überlaufen *nt*, *(fig)* Abtrünnigkeit *f*, Abfall *m*.

defective [dɪ'fektɪv] *adj* fehlerhaft; *machine also* defekt; *hearing, sight* mangelhaft, gestört.

defence, *(US)* **defense** [dɪ'fens] *n* Verteidigung *f*; *(Sport also)* Abwehr *f*. **in his ~** zu seiner Verteidigung; **to come to sb's ~** jdn verteidigen; **to put up a stubborn ~** sich hartnäckig verteidigen; **his only ~ was ...** seine einzige Rechtfertigung war ...; **counsel for the ~** Verteidiger(in *f*) *m*; **as a ~ against** als Schutz gegen; **~s** *(Mil)* Verteidigungsanlagen *pl*; **Ministry of D~** Verteidigungsministerium *nt*.

defence: ~less *adj* schutzlos; **~ mechanism** *n* Abwehrmechanismus *m*.

defend [dɪ'fend] *vt* verteidigen *(also Jur) (against* gegen*)*. **to ~ oneself** sich verteidigen.

defendant [dɪ'fendənt] *n* Angeklagte(r) *mf*; *(in civil cases)* Beklagte(r) *mf*.

defender [dɪ'fendəʳ] *n* Verteidiger *m*.

defending [dɪ'fendɪŋ] *adj*: **~ counsel** Verteidiger(in *f*) *m*.

defense *etc* [dɪ'fens] *(US)* = **defence** *etc*.

defensive [dɪ'fensɪv] **1** *adj* defensiv *(also fig)*, Verteidigungs-. **2** *n (Mil)* Abwehraktion *f*. **to be on the ~** *(Mil, fig)* in der Defensive sein.

defer[1] [dɪ'fɜːʳ] *vt (delay)* verschieben; *event also* verlegen. **~red terms** Ratenkauf *m*.

defer[2] *vi* **to ~ to sb/sb's wishes** sich jdm beugen *or* fügen/sich jds Wünschen *(dat)* fügen.

deference ['defərəns] *n* Achtung *f*, Respekt *m*. **out of ~ to** aus Achtung *or* Respekt vor *(+dat)*.

deferential [ˌdefə'renʃəl] *adj* ehrerbietig, respektvoll.

deferment [dɪ'fɜːmənt] *n see* **defer**[1] Verschiebung *f*; Verlegung *f*.

defiance [dɪ'faɪəns] *n* Trotz *m*; *(of danger)* Mißachtung *f*. **in ~ of sb/sb's orders** jdm/jds Anordnungen zum Trotz.

defiant [dɪ'faɪənt] *adj* aufsässig; *esp child also, answer* trotzig; *(challenging) attitude* herausfordernd.

deficiency [dɪ'fɪʃənsɪ] *n* Mangel *m*; *(in character, system)* Schwäche *f*.

deficient [dɪ'fɪʃənt] *adj* unzulänglich. **sb/sth is ~ in sth** jdm/einer Sache fehlt es an etw *(dat)*.

deficit ['defɪsɪt] *n* Defizit *nt*.

defile[1] ['diːfaɪl] *n* Hohlweg *m*.

defile[2] [dɪ'faɪl] *vt (pollute)* verschmutzen; *(desecrate)* schänden, entweihen.

define [dɪ'faɪn] *vt* **(a)** festlegen, bestimmen; *word* definieren. **to ~ one's position** seinen Standpunkt klarmachen. **(b) to be clearly ~d against the sky** sich klar gegen den Himmel abzeichnen.

definite ['defɪnɪt] *adj answer, decision* klar, eindeutig; *date, agreement, plan* fest, definitiv; *improvement, lisp* deutlich; *manner, tone* bestimmt. **is that ~?** ist das sicher?; **the date is not ~ yet** der Termin steht noch nicht fest; **she was very ~ about it** sie war sich *(dat)* sehr sicher; *(insistent)* sie bestand darauf; **can't you be more ~?** können Sie sich etwas genauer festlegen?; **~ article** *(Gram)* bestimmter Artikel.

definitely ['defɪnɪtlɪ] *adv* bestimmt; *decide, arrange* fest, definitiv. **he ~ wanted to come** er wollte bestimmt kommen; **that's ~ an improvement** das ist ganz sicherlich eine Verbesserung.

definition [ˌdefɪ'nɪʃən] *n* **(a)** *(of word, concept)* Definition *f*. **(b)** *(of powers, duties, boundaries)* Festlegung, Bestimmung *f*. **(c)** *(Phot, TV)* Bildschärfe *f*; *(Opt: of lens)* Schärfe *f*.

definitive [dɪ'fɪnɪtɪv] *adj victory, answer* entschieden; *(authoritative) book* maßgeblich *(on* für*)*.

deflate [ˌdiː'fleɪt] *vt tyre* etwas Luft/die Luft ablassen aus. **to ~ the currency** eine Deflation herbeiführen; **he was a bit ~d** es war ein ziemlicher Dämpfer für ihn.

deflation [ˌdiː'fleɪʃən] *n (Fin)* Deflation *f*.

deflationary [ˌdiː'fleɪʃənərɪ] *adj (Fin)* deflationär.

deflect [dɪ'flekt] *vt* ablenken; *(Phys) light* beugen.

deflower [ˌdiː'flaʊəʳ] *vt* entjungfern, deflorieren.

deforestation [diːˌfɒrɪ'steɪʃən] *n* Abholzung *f*.

deform [dɪ'fɔːm] *vt* deformieren, verunstalten.

deformed [dɪ'fɔːmd] *adj limb, body* mißgebildet.

deformity [dɪ'fɔːmɪtɪ] *n* Mißbildung *f*.

defraud [dɪ'frɔːd] *vt* **to ~ sb of sth** jdn um etw betrügen.

defray [dɪ'freɪ] *vt* tragen, übernehmen.

defrock [ˌdiː'frɒk] *vt* aus dem Priesteramt verstoßen.

defrost [ˌdiː'frɒst] *vt* entfrosten; *fridge* abtauen; *food* auftauen.

defroster [ˌdiːˈfrɒstəʳ] *n (US)* Gebläse *nt.*
deft [deft] *adj (+er)* flink, geschickt.
defunct [dɪˈfʌŋkt] *adj institution etc* eingegangen; *law* außer Kraft.
defuse [ˌdiːˈfjuːz] *vt (lit, fig)* entschärfen.
defy [dɪˈfaɪ] *vt* **(a)** *(disobey) person* sich widersetzen *(+dat)*; *orders, law, death, danger* trotzen *(+dat)*. **(b)** *(fig) efforts* widerstehen *(+dat)*. **to ~ definition** sich nicht erklären *or* definieren lassen; **to ~ description** jeder Beschreibung spotten. **(c)** *(challenge)* **I ~ you to do better** machen Sie es doch besser, wenn Sie können.
degeneracy [dɪˈdʒenərəsɪ] *n* Degeneriertheit *f.*
degenerate [dɪˈdʒenərɪt] **1** *adj* degeneriert; *race, morals also* entartet. **2** *n* degenerierter Mensch. **3** [dɪˈdʒenəreɪt] *vi* degenerieren; *(people, morals also)* entarten.
degradation [ˌdegrəˈdeɪʃən] *n* Erniedrigung *f.*
degrade [dɪˈgreɪd] *vt* erniedrigen.
degrading [dɪˈgreɪdɪŋ] *adj* erniedrigend.
degree [dɪˈgriː] *n* **(a)** Grad *m no pl.* **it was 35 ~s in the shade** es waren 35 Grad im Schatten. **(b)** *(extent)* **to some ~, to a (certain) ~** zu einem gewissen Grad, in gewissem Maße; **to a high ~** in hohem Maße; **to such a ~ that ...** so sehr, daß ...; **to what ~ was he involved?** wieweit war er verwickelt?; **by ~s** nach und nach; **first/second ~ murder** *(Jur)* Mord *m*/Totschlag *m.* **(c)** *(Univ)* akademischer Grad. **when did you do your ~?** wann haben Sie das Examen gemacht?; **he has a ~ in English** er hat Anglistik studiert; **she has a ~** sie hat einen Universitätsabschluß.
dehydrate [ˌdiːhaɪˈdreɪt] *vt* Wasser entziehen *(+dat).*
dehydrated [ˌdiːhaɪˈdreɪtɪd] *adj vegetables, milk* Trocken-; *person, skin* ausgetrocknet.
de-ice [ˌdiːˈaɪs] *vt* enteisen.
de-icer [ˌdiːˈaɪsəʳ] *n* Enteiser *m*; *(spray for cars)* Defroster *m.*
deign [deɪn] *vt* **to ~ to do sth** geruhen *or* sich herablassen, etw zu tun.
deity [ˈdiːɪtɪ] *n* Gottheit *f.* **the D~** Gott *m.*
déjà vu [ˈdeɪʒɑːˈvjuː] *n* Déjà-vu-Erlebnis *nt.* **a feeling of ~** das Gefühl, das schon einmal gesehen *or* erlebt zu haben.
dejected [dɪˈdʒektɪd] *adj* niedergeschlagen, deprimiert.
dejection [dɪˈdʒekʃən] *n* Niedergeschlagenheit *f.*
de jure [ˌdiːˈdʒʊərɪ] *adj, adv* de jure.
delay [dɪˈleɪ] **1** *vt* **(a)** *(postpone)* verschieben, aufschieben. **he ~ed writing the letter** er schob den Brief auf. **(b)** *(hold up) person, train* aufhalten. **the flight was ~ed** das Flugzeug hatte Verspätung; *(leaving)* der Abflug verzögerte sich; **we'll be ~ed** wir werden uns verspäten. **2** *vi* **to ~ in doing sth** es aufschieben, etw zu tun; **don't ~!** verlieren Sie keine Zeit! **3** *n (hold-up)* Verzögerung *f*; *(to train, plane)* Verspätung *f*; **there are ~s to all trains** alle Züge haben Verspätung; **without ~** unverzüglich; **without further ~** gleich.
delayed-action [dɪˈleɪdˌækʃən] *adj attr bomb, mine* mit Zeitzünder.
delectable [dɪˈlektəbl] *adj* köstlich; *(fig)* reizend.
delegate [ˈdelɪgeɪt] **1** *vt* delegieren. **to ~ sb to do sth** jdn damit beauftragen, etw zu tun. **2** *vi* delegieren. **3** [ˈdelɪgət] *n* Delegierte(r) *mf.*
delegation [ˌdelɪˈgeɪʃən] *n* Delegation *f (to* an *+acc).*
delete [dɪˈliːt] *vt* streichen *(from* von*).*
deletion [dɪˈliːʃən] *n* Streichung *f.*
deliberate [dɪˈlɪbərɪt] **1** *adj* **(a)** *(intentional)* absichtlich; *action, insult, lie also* bewußt. **(b)** *(cautious, thoughtful)* besonnen; *action* (wohl)überlegt; *(slow) movement, step* bedächtig. **2** [dɪˈlɪbəreɪt] *vi (ponder)* nachdenken *(on* über *+acc)*; *(discuss)* sich beraten *(on* über *+acc,* wegen*).* **3** [dɪˈlɪbəreɪt] *vt (ponder)* bedenken, überlegen; *(discuss)* beraten.
deliberately [dɪˈlɪbərɪtlɪ] *adv* **(a)** absichtlich, bewußt. **(b)** *(purposefully, slowly)* bedächtig.
deliberation [dɪˌlɪbəˈreɪʃən] *n* **(a)** *(consideration)* Überlegung *f.* **(b)** *(discussion)* Beratungen *pl (of, on* in *+dat,* über *+acc).*
delicacy [ˈdelɪkəsɪ] *n see adj* **(a)** Feinheit *f*; Zerbrechlichkeit *f*; Zartheit *f*; Empfindlichkeit *f.* **the ~ of his health** seine schwächliche Konstitution. **(b)** Feinfühligkeit *f*; Empfindlichkeit *f*; Empfindsamkeit *f.* **(c)** Heikle *nt (of* an *+dat).* **(d)** *(food)* Delikatesse *f.*
delicate [ˈdelɪkɪt] *adj* **(a)** *fabric etc* fein, zart; *(fragile)* zerbrechlich; *person* zart; *liver* empfindlich. **to have very ~ health** sehr anfällig sein. **(b)** *(sensitive) person* feinfühlig; *instrument* empfindlich; *playing* empfindsam. **(c)** *operation, situation* heikel, delikat.
delicatessen [delɪkəˈtesn] *n* Feinkostgeschäft *nt.*
delicious [dɪˈlɪʃəs] *adj* köstlich, lecker *(col).*
delight [dɪˈlaɪt] **1** *n* Freude *f.* **to my ~** zu meiner Freude; **he takes great ~ in doing that** es bereitet ihm große Freude, das zu tun; **he's a ~ to watch** es ist eine Freude, ihm zuzusehen. **2** *vt* erfreuen. **3** *vi* sich erfreuen *(in* an *+dat).*
delighted [dɪˈlaɪtɪd] *adj* **to be ~** sich sehr freuen *(at* über *+acc, that* daß*)*; **I'd be ~ to help you** ich würde Ihnen sehr gern helfen.
delightful [dɪˈlaɪtfʊl] *adj* reizend; *weather, party, meal* wunderbar.
delimit [diːˈlɪmɪt] *vt* abstecken, abgrenzen.
delineate [dɪˈlɪnɪeɪt] *vt (draw)* skizzieren; *(describe)* beschreiben.
delinquency [dɪˈlɪŋkwənsɪ] *n* Kriminalität *f.*
delinquent [dɪˈlɪŋkwənt] **1** *adj* **(a)** straffällig. **(b)** *(US) bill* überfällig; *account* rückständig. **2** *n* Delinquent *m.*
delirious [dɪˈlɪrɪəs] *adj (Med)* im Delirium; *(fig)* im Taumel. **~ with joy** im Freudentaumel.
deliriously [dɪˈlɪrɪəslɪ] *adv* **~ happy** überglücklich.
delirium [dɪˈlɪrɪəm] *n (Med)* Delirium *nt.*
deliver [dɪˈlɪvəʳ] **1** *vt* **(a)** *goods* liefern; *note, message* überbringen; *(on regular basis) letters, papers etc* zustellen; **to ~ sth to sb** jdm etw liefern/zustellen; **he ~ed me right to the door** er brachte mich bis zur Tür; **to ~ the goods** *(fig col)* es bringen *(col)*, es schaffen. **(b)** *(liter: rescue)* befreien. **(c)** *(pronounce) speech* halten; *ultimatum* stellen; *verdict* verkünden. **(d)** *baby* zur Welt bringen. **(e)** *(aim) blow* versetzen. **2** *vi* liefern.
deliverance [dɪˈlɪvərəns] *n (liter)* Erlösung *(from* von*) f.*
delivery [dɪˈlɪvərɪ] *n* **(a)** *(of goods)* Lieferung *f*; *(of parcels, letters)* Zustellung *f.* **to take ~ of sth** etw in Empfang nehmen; **to pay on ~** bei Empfang zahlen. **(b)** *(Med)* Entbindung *f.* **(c)** *(of speaker)* Vortragsweise *f.*
delivery: ~ boy *n* Bote *m*; **~ note** *n* Lieferschein *m*; **~ van** *n (Brit)* Lieferwagen *m.*
delphinium [delˈfɪnɪəm] *n* Rittersporn *m.*
delta [ˈdeltə] *n* Delta *nt.* **~ wing** Deltaflügel *m.*
delude [dɪˈluːd] *vt* täuschen, irreführen *(with* mit*).* **to ~ sb into thinking sth** jdm etw weismachen; **to ~ oneself** sich *(dat)* Illusionen machen, sich *(dat)* etwas vormachen.
deluge [ˈdeljuːdʒ] **1** *n* Überschwemmung *f*; *(of rain)* Wolkenbruch *m*; *(fig: of letters etc)* Flut *f.* **2** *vt (lit, fig)* überschwemmen, überfluten.
delusion [dɪˈluːʒən] *n* Illusion *f*, Irrglaube *m no pl.*
de luxe [dɪˈlʌks] *adj* Luxus-.
delve [delv] *vi* sich vertiefen *(into* in *+acc).*
demagogue [ˈdeməgɒg] *n* Demagoge *m*, Demagogin *f.*
demand [dɪˈmɑːnd] **1** *vt* verlangen, fordern *(of, from* von*)*; *(situation, task etc)* erfordern; **he ~ed to see my passport** er verlangte meinen Paß. **2** *n*

(a) Forderung *f (for* nach*)*. **by popular ~** auf allgemeinen Wunsch; **to make ~s on sb** Forderungen an jdn stellen; **I have many ~s on my time** ich habe sehr viele Verpflichtungen. **(b)** *no pl (Comm)* Nachfrage *f*, Bedarf *m (for* nach*)*. **to be in great ~** *(article, person)* sehr gefragt sein.
demanding [dɪ'mɑːndɪŋ] *adj child* anstrengend; *task also, teacher, boss* anspruchsvoll. **physically ~** körperlich anstrengend.
demarcation [ˌdiːmɑː'keɪʃən] *n* Abrenzung, Demarkation *f*. **~-line** Demarkationslinie *f*; **~ dispute** Streit *m* um den Zuständigkeitsbereich.
demeanour, *(US)* **demeanor** [dɪ'miːnəʳ] *n (behaviour)* Benehmen, Auftreten *nt*.
demented [dɪ'mentɪd] *adj* verrückt, wahnsinnig.
demerara (sugar) [ˌdemə'rɛərə('ʃʊgəʳ)] *n* brauner Rohrzucker.
demi ['demɪ-] *pref* Halb-, halb-. **~god** Halbgott *m*.
demilitarize [ˌdiː'mɪlɪtəraɪz] *vt* demilitarisieren.
demise [dɪ'maɪz] *n (form)* Ableben *nt (geh)*; *(fig: of institution, newspaper etc)* Ende *nt*.
demist [ˌdiː'mɪst] *vt windscreen* freimachen.
demister [ˌdiː'mɪstəʳ] *n (Brit)* Gebläse *nt*.
demitasse ['demɪtæs] *n (US) (cup)* Mokkatasse *f*; *(coffee)* Kaffee *m*.
demo ['deməʊ] *n* = **demonstration** Demo(nstration) *f*.
democracy [dɪ'mɒkrəsɪ] *n* Demokratie *f*.
democrat ['deməkræt] *n* Demokrat(in *f*) *m*.
democratic [ˌdemə'krætɪk] *adj* demokratisch.
demography [dɪ'mɒgrəfɪ] *n* Demographie *f*.
demolish [dɪ'mɒlɪʃ] *vt building* ab- *or* einreißen; *(fig) opponent, theory* zunichte machen, vernichten; *(hum) cake etc* vertilgen.
demolition [ˌdemə'lɪʃən] *n* Abbruch *m*.
demon ['diːmən] *n* Dämon *m*; *(col: child)* Teufel *m*. **to be a ~ for work** ein Arbeitstier sein.
demonstrable ['demənstrəbl] *adj* offensichtlich.
demonstrate ['demənstreɪt] **1** *vt* **(a)** zeigen, beweisen. **(b)** *appliance etc* vorführen. **2** *vi (Pol)* demonstrieren.
demonstration [ˌdemən'streɪʃən] *n* **(a)** Beweis *m*; *(of appliance)* Vorführung *f*. **(b)** *(Pol)* Demonstration *f*.
demonstrative [dɪ'mɒnstrətɪv] *adj* demonstrativ. **he's not very ~** er zeigt seine Gefühle nicht.
demonstrator ['demənstreɪtəʳ] *n (Pol)* Demonstrant(in *f*) *m*.
demoralize [dɪ'mɒrəlaɪz] *vt* entmutigen; *troops etc* demoralisieren.
demote [dɪ'məʊt] *vt* degradieren *(to* zu*)*.
demur [dɪ'mɜːʳ] *(form)* **1** *vi* Einwände erheben *(at* gegen*)*. **2** *n* **without ~** widerspruchslos.
demure [dɪ'mjʊəʳ] *adj (+er) (coy)* spröde; *(sedate)* ernst, gesetzt.
den [den] *n* **(a)** *(of lion etc)* Höhle *f*; *(of fox)* Bau *m*. **~ of iniquity** Lasterhöhle *f*; **~ of thieves** Spelunke, Räuberhöhle *(hum) f*. **(b)** *(room)* Bude *f (col)*.
denationalize [ˌdiː'næʃnəlaɪz] *vt* entstaatlichen.
denial [dɪ'naɪəl] *n* **(a)** *(of accusation, guilt)* Leugnen *nt*. **an official ~** ein offizielles Dementi. **(b)** *(of request etc)* Ablehnung *f*; *(official)* abschlägiger Bescheid; *(of rights)* Verweigerung *f*.
denier ['denɪəʳ] *n (of stockings)* Denier *nt*.
denigrate ['denɪgreɪt] *vt* verunglimpfen.
denim ['denɪm] *n* **(a)** Jeansstoff *m*. **~ jacket** Jeansjacke *f*. **(b) ~s** *pl* (Blue) Jeans *pl*.
Denmark ['denmɑːk] *n* Dänemark *nt*.
denomination [dɪˌnɒmɪ'neɪʃən] *n* **(a)** *(Eccl)* Konfession *f*. **(b)** *(of money)* Nennwert *m*.
denominator [dɪ'nɒmɪneɪtəʳ] *n (Math)* Nenner *m*.
denote [dɪ'nəʊt] *vt* bedeuten.
dénouement [dɪ'nuːmɒŋ] *n* Ausgang *m*.
denounce [dɪ'naʊns] *vt* **(a)** *(accuse)* anprangern; *(inform against)* anzeigen, denunzieren *(sb to sb* jdn bei jdm*)*. **(b)** *(condemn) alcohol, habit etc* verurteilen.
dense [dens] *adj (+er)* **(a)** dicht. **(b)** *(col: stupid)* beschränkt.
densely ['denslɪ] *adv* **~ populated** dicht bevölkert.
density ['densɪtɪ] *n* Dichte *f*. **population ~** Bevölkerungsdichte *f*.
dent [dent] **1** *n (in metal)* Beule, Delle *(col) f*. **that made a ~ in his savings** *(col)* das hat ein Loch in seine Ersparnisse gerissen. **2** *vt car* eindellen, verbeulen; *(col) pride* anknacksen *(col)*.
dental ['dentl] *adj* Zahn-; *treatment* zahnärztlich. **~ floss** Zahnseide *f*; **~ surgeon** Zahnarzt *m*/-ärztin *f*.
dentifrice ['dentɪfrɪs] *n* Zahnpasta *f*.
dentist ['dentɪst] *n* Zahnarzt *m*, Zahnärztin *f*.
dentistry ['dentɪstrɪ] *n* Zahnmedizin *f*.
dentures ['dentʃəz] *npl (partial ~)* Zahnprothese *f*; *(full ~)* Gebiß *nt*.
denude [dɪ'njuːd] *vt* entblößen *(of gen)*.
denunciation [dɪˌnʌnsɪ'eɪʃən] *n see* **denounce** Anprangerung *f*; Denunziation *f*; Verurteilung *f*.
deny [dɪ'naɪ] *vt* **(a)** *charge, accusation etc* bestreiten, leugnen; *(officially)* dementieren. **do you ~ having said that?** leugnen *or* bestreiten Sie, das gesagt zu haben?; **I don't ~ it** das streite ich gar nicht ab. **(b)** *(refuse)* **to ~ sb a request/his rights** jdm eine Bitte abschlagen/jdm seine Rechte vorenthalten; **I can't ~ her anything** ich kann ihr nichts abschlagen; **to ~ oneself sth** auf etw *(acc)* verzichten. **(c)** *religion, principles* verleugnen.
deodorant [diː'əʊdərənt] *n* De(s)odorant *m*.
depart [dɪ'pɑːt] *vi* **(a)** *(go away)* weggehen; *(on journey)* abreisen; *(by bus, car etc)* wegfahren; *(train, bus etc)* abfahren. **(b)** *(deviate: from opinion etc)* abweichen, abgehen.
departed [dɪ'pɑːtɪd] *n* **the (dear) ~** der/die (liebe) Verstorbene; die (lieben) Verstorbenen *pl*.
department [dɪ'pɑːtmənt] *n* **(a)** Abteilung *f*; *(in civil service)* Ressort *nt*. **D~ of Employment** *(Brit)* Arbeitsministerium *nt*; **D~ of State** *(US)* Außenministerium *nt*; **that's not my ~** *(fig)* dafür bin ich nicht zuständig. **(b)** *(Univ)* Seminar *nt*.
departmental [ˌdiːpɑːt'mentl] *adj* **(a)** Abteilungs-. **(b)** *(Univ)* Seminar-.
department store *n* Kaufhaus, Warenhaus *nt*.
departure [dɪ'pɑːtʃəʳ] *n* **(a)** *(of person)* Weggang *m*; *(on journey)* Abreise *f (from* aus*)*; *(of vehicle)* Abfahrt *f*; *(of plane)* Abflug *m*. **~ lounge** Abflughalle *f*; **point of ~** *(fig)* Ausgangspunkt *m*. **(b)** *(fig: from custom, truth)* Abweichen *nt (from* von*)*. **a new ~** eine neue Richtung.
depend [dɪ'pend] *vi* **(a)** abhängen *(on sb/sth* von jdm/etw*)*. **it all ~s (on whether ...)** das hängt ganz davon ab(, ob ...); **that ~s** das kommt darauf an; **~ing on his mood/how late we arrive** je nach seiner Laune/je nachdem, wie spät wir ankommen. **(b)** *(rely)* sich verlassen *(on, upon* auf *+acc)*. **you can ~ (up)on it!** darauf können Sie sich verlassen! **(c)** *(person: be dependent on)* **to ~ on** angewiesen sein auf *(+acc)*.
dependable [dɪ'pendəbl] *adj* zuverlässig, verläßlich.
dependant, dependent [dɪ'pendənt] *n* Abhängige(r) *mf*. **do you have ~s?** haben Sie (abhängige) Angehörige?
dependence [dɪ'pendəns] *n* Abhängigkeit *f (on* von*)*.
dependent [dɪ'pendənt] **1** *adj* abhängig *(on, upon* von*)*. **to be ~ on sb's good will** auf jds Wohlwollen *(acc)* angewiesen sein. **2** *n* = **dependant.**
depict [dɪ'pɪkt] *vt* schildern.
depilatory [dɪ'pɪlətərɪ] *n* Enthaarungsmittel *nt*.
deplete [dɪ'pliːt] *vt (exhaust)* erschöpfen; *(reduce)* aufbrauchen.
deplorable [dɪ'plɔːrəbl] *adj* beklagenswert, bedauerlich.
deplore [dɪ'plɔːʳ] *vt (regret)* bedauern, beklagen;

(disapprove of) mißbilligen.
deploy [dɪ'plɔɪ] *vt (Mil, fig)* einsetzen.
deployment [dɪ'plɔɪmənt] *n* Einsatz *m*.
depopulate [ˌdiː'pɒpjʊleɪt] *vt* entvölkern.
depopulation ['diːˌpɒpjʊ'leɪʃən] *n* Entvölkerung *f*.
deport [dɪ'pɔːt] *vt prisoner* deportieren; *alien* abschieben.
deportation [ˌdiːpɔː'teɪʃən] *n see vt* Deportation *f*; Abschiebung *f*.
deportment [dɪ'pɔːtmənt] *n* Haltung *f*; *(behaviour)* Verhalten, Benehmen *nt*.
depose [dɪ'pəʊz] *vt* absetzen.
deposit [dɪ'pɒzɪt] **1** *vt* **(a)** *(put down)* hinlegen; *(upright)* hinstellen. **(b)** *money, valuables* deponieren *(with* bei*)*. **2** *n* **(a)** *(Fin: in bank)* Einlage *f*, Guthaben *nt*. **(b)** *(Comm) (part payment)* Anzahlung *f*; *(returnable security)* Kaution *f*; *(for bottle)* Pfand *nt*. **to lose one's ~** *(Pol)* seine Kaution verlieren. **(c)** *(Chem: in wine, Geol)* Ablagerung *f*; *(of ore, coal, oil)* (Lager)stätte *f*.
deposit account *n (Brit)* Sparkonto *nt*.
depositor [dɪ'pɒzɪtə[r]] *n* Einzahler(in *f*) *m*.
depository [dɪ'pɒzɪtərɪ] *n* Lagerhaus *nt*.
depot ['depəʊ] *n (bus garage etc)* Depot *nt*; *(store also)* Lager(haus) *nt*.
depraved [dɪ'preɪvd] *adj* verkommen.
depravity [dɪ'prævɪtɪ] *n* Verkommenheit *f*.
deprecate ['deprɪkeɪt] *vt (form)* mißbilligen.
depreciate [dɪ'priːʃɪeɪt] *vi* an Wert verlieren; *(currency)* an Kaufkraft verlieren.
depreciation [dɪˌpriːʃɪ'eɪʃən] *n* Wertminderung *f*; *(of currency)* Kaufkraftverlust *m*.
depress [dɪ'pres] *vt* **(a)** *person* deprimieren; *(discourage)* entmutigen. **(b)** *(form) lever* niederdrücken.
depressant [dɪ'presnt] *n* Beruhigungsmittel *nt*.
depressed [dɪ'prest] *adj* **(a)** *person* deprimiert. **don't get ~** sei nicht deprimiert. **(b)** *industry* notleidend. **~ area** strukturschwaches Gebiet.
depressing [dɪ'presɪŋ] *adj* deprimierend.
depression [dɪ'preʃən] *n* **(a)** Depressionen *pl*. **(b)** *(in ground)* Vertiefung, Senke *f*. **(c)** *(Met)* Tief(druckgebiet) *nt*. **(d)** *(Econ)* Flaute *f*; *(St Ex)* Baisse *f*. **the D~** die Weltwirtschaftskrise.
deprivation [ˌdeprɪ'veɪʃən] *n* **(a)** *(depriving)* Entzug *m*; *(Psych)* Deprivation *f*; *(of rights)* Beraubung *f*. **(b)** *(state)* Entbehrung *f*.
deprive [dɪ'praɪv] *vt* **to ~ sb of sth** jdm etw nehmen; **they had been ~d of ...** *(had lacked)* ihnen fehlte ...; **to ~ oneself of sth** auf etw *(acc)* verzichten.
deprived [dɪ'praɪvd] *adj* benachteiligt.
dept = **department** Abt.
depth [depθ] *n (lit, fig)* Tiefe *f*. **the ~s of the ocean** die Tiefen des Ozeans; **at a ~ of 3 metres** in einer Tiefe von 3 Metern, in 3 Meter Tiefe; **to get out of one's ~** *(lit, fig)* den Boden unter den Füßen verlieren; **sorry, I'm out of my ~ there** es tut mir leid, aber da muß ich passen; **with great ~ of feeling** sehr gefühlvoll; **in ~** eingehend, intensiv; **in the ~s of despair** in tiefster Verzweiflung; **in the ~s of winter/the forest** im tiefsten Winter/Wald; **~ charge** Wasserbombe *f*.
deputation [ˌdepjʊ'teɪʃən] *n* Abordnung *f*.
deputize ['depjʊtaɪz] *vi* vertreten *(for sb* jdn*)*.
deputy ['depjʊtɪ] **1** *n* Stellvertreter(in *f*) *m*. **2** *adj attr* stellvertretend.
derail [dɪ'reɪl] *vt* zum Entgleisen bringen, entgleisen lassen. **to be ~ed** entgleisen.
derailment [dɪ'reɪlmənt] *n* Entgleisung *f*.
deranged [dɪ'reɪndʒd] *adj mind* gestört. **to be (mentally) ~** geistesgestört sein.
Derby ['dɜːbɪ] *n (US: also* **~ hat***)* Melone *f*.
derelict ['derɪlɪkt] *adj (abandoned)* verlassen; *(ruined)* verfallen, heruntergekommen.
dereliction [ˌderɪ'lɪkʃən] *n* **~ of duty** Pflichtversäumnis *nt*.
deride [dɪ'raɪd] *vt* verhöhnen.
derision [dɪ'rɪʒən] *n* Hohn, Spott *m*. **object of ~** Zielscheibe *f* des Spotts.
derisive [dɪ'raɪsɪv] *adj* spöttisch, höhnisch.
derisory [dɪ'raɪsərɪ] *adj* **(a)** *amount, offer* lächerlich. **(b)** = **derisive.**
derivation [ˌderɪ'veɪʃən] *n* Ableitung *f*.
derivative [dɪ'rɪvətɪv] **1** *adj* abgeleitet; *literary work etc* nachgeahmt, imitiert. **2** *n* Ableitung *f*.
derive [dɪ'raɪv] **1** *vt ideas, names* her- *or* ableiten *(from* von*)*; *profit* ziehen *(from* aus*)*; *satisfaction, comfort* beziehen *(from* aus*)*. **this word is ~d from the Greek** dieses Wort stammt aus dem Griechischen; **to ~ pleasure from sth** Freude haben an etw *(dat)*. **2** *vi* **to ~ from** sich her- *or* ableiten von; *(power, fortune)* beruhen auf *(+dat)*, *(ideas)* stammen von.
dermatitis [ˌdɜːmə'taɪtɪs] *n* Hautentzündung, Dermatitis *f*.
dermatology [ˌdɜːmə'tɒlədʒɪ] *n* Dermatologie *f*.
derogatory [dɪ'rɒgətərɪ] *adj* abfällig, abschätzig.
derrick ['derɪk] *n* Kran *m*; *(above oilwell)* Bohrturm *m*.
descant ['deskænt] *n (Mus)* Diskant *m*.
descend [dɪ'send] **1** *vi* **(a)** *(go down)* herunter-/hinuntergehen; *(lift, vehicle)* herunter-/hinunterfahren; *(hill)* abfallen. **(b)** *(attack, visit)* **to ~ (up)on sb** jdn überfallen. **(c)** *(lower oneself)* **to ~ to sth** sich zu etw herablassen; **he even ~ed to bribery** er scheute selbst vor Bestechung nicht zurück. **2** *vt* **(a)** *stairs* hinunter-/heruntergehen. **(b) to be ~ed from** abstammen von.
descendant [dɪ'sendənt] *n* **(a)** Nachkomme *m*. **(b)** *(Astron, Astrol)* **in the ~** im Deszendenten.
descent [dɪ'sent] *n* **(a)** Abstieg *m*. **(b)** *(ancestry)* Abstammung, Herkunft *f*. **(c)** *(fig: into crime etc)* Absinken *nt (into* in *+acc)*.
describe [dɪ'skraɪb] *vt* **(a)** beschreiben. **(b)** *(+ as)* bezeichnen. **he ~s himself as a doctor** er bezeichnet sich als Arzt.
description [dɪ'skrɪpʃən] *n* **(a)** Beschreibung *f*. **beyond ~** unbeschreiblich. **(b)** *(+ as)* Bezeichnung *f*. **(c)** *(sort)* **vehicles of every ~** Fahrzeuge aller Art.
descriptive [dɪ'skrɪptɪv] *adj* **(a)** beschreibend; *account, adjective, passage* anschaulich. **(b)** *linguistics, science etc* deskriptiv.
desecrate ['desɪkreɪt] *vt* entweihen, schänden.
desert[1] ['dezət] **1** *n (lit, fig)* Wüste *f*. **2** *adj attr* Wüsten-. **~ island** einsame *or* verlassene Insel.
desert[2] [dɪ'zɜːt] **1** *vt (leave)* verlassen; *cause, party* im Stich lassen. **the place was ~ed** es war niemand da. **2** *vi (Mil)* desertieren. **to ~ to the rebels** zu den Rebellen überlaufen.
deserter [dɪ'zɜːtə[r]] *n (Mil, fig)* Deserteur *m*.
desertion [dɪ'zɜːʃən] *n* **(a)** *(act)* Verlassen *nt*; *(Mil)* Fahnenflucht *f*. **(b)** *(state)* Verlassenheit *f*.
deserts [dɪ'zɜːts] *npl* **to get one's just ~** bekommen, was einem zusteht.
deserve [dɪ'zɜːv] *vt* verdienen. **he ~s to win** er verdient den Sieg; **he ~s to be punished** er verdient es, bestraft zu werden.
deservedly [dɪ'zɜːvɪdlɪ] *adv* verdientermaßen.
deserving [dɪ'zɜːvɪŋ] *adj person, cause* verdienstvoll. **to be ~ of sth** etw verdienen.
desiccated ['desɪkeɪtɪd] *adj* getrocknet; *(fig)* vertrocknet.
design [dɪ'zaɪn] **1** *n* **(a)** Design *nt*, Ausführung *f*; *(of plane, machine)* Konstruktion *f*; *(plan: of building etc)* Entwurf *m*. **a new ~** *(Aut)* ein neues Modell. **(b)** *(pattern)* Muster *nt*. **(c)** *(intention)* Plan *m*, Absicht *f*. **by ~** absichtlich; **to have ~s on sb/sth** es auf jdn/etw abgesehen haben. **2** *vt* **(a)** entwerfen; *machine* konstruieren. **(b)** *(intend)* **to be ~ed for sb/sth** für jdn/etw vorgesehen *or* bestimmt sein.
designate ['dezɪgneɪt] **1** *vt* bezeichnen; *(appoint)* ernennen. **to ~ sb as sth** jdn zu etw ernennen. **2** ['dezɪgnɪt] *adj* **the Prime Minister ~** der desi-

gnierte Premierminister.
designation [ˌdezɪg'neɪʃən] *n see vt* Bezeichnung; Ernennung *f*.
designer [dɪ'zaɪnəʳ] *n* Designer(in *f*) *m*; *(fashion* ~*)* Modeschöpfer(in *f*) *m*; *(of machines etc)* Konstrukteur(in *f*) *m*; *(Theat)* Bühnenbildner(in *f*) *m*.
desirable [dɪ'zaɪərəbl] *adj* wünschenswert, erwünscht; *position, offer, house, area* reizvoll, attraktiv; *woman* begehrenswert.
desire [dɪ'zaɪəʳ] **1** *n (for* nach*)* Wunsch *m*; *(longing)* Sehnsucht *f*; *(sexual)* Verlangen, Begehren *nt*. **I have no ~ to see him** ich habe kein Verlangen, ihn zu sehen; **I have no ~ to cause you any trouble** ich möchte Ihnen keine Unannehmlichkeiten bereiten. **2** *vt* wünschen; *woman* begehren; *peace* wollen. **it leaves much to be ~d** das läßt viel zu wünschen übrig.
desirous [dɪ'zaɪərəs] *adj* **to be ~ of sth** *(form)* nach etw verlangen.
desist [dɪ'zɪst] *vi (form)* Abstand nehmen, absehen *(from doing sth* davon, etw zu tun*)*.
desk [desk] *n* Schreibtisch *m*; *(for pupils, master)* Pult *nt*; *(Brit: in shop, restaurant)* Kasse *f*; *(in hotel)* Empfang *m*. **information ~** Information(sschalter *m*) *f*; **~ job** *n* Bürojob *m*.
desolate ['desəlɪt] **1** *adj* **(a)** *place (devastated)* verwüstet; *(barren)* trostlos; *(fig) outlook* trostlos. **(b)** *(grief-stricken)* tieftraurig, zu Tode betrübt. **2** ['desəleɪt] *vt country* verwüsten.
desolation [ˌdesə'leɪʃən] *n* **(a)** *(by war)* Verwüstung *f*. **(b)** *(of landscape, grief)* Trostlosigkeit *f*.
despair [dɪ'spɛəʳ] **1** *n* Verzweiflung *f (about, at* über *+acc)*. **in ~** aus Verzweiflung. **2** *vi* verzweifeln, alle Hoffnung aufgeben. **to ~ of doing sth** alle Hoffnung aufgeben, etw zu tun.
despairing [dɪs'pɛərɪŋ] *adj* verzweifelt.
despatch [dɪ'spætʃ] *vt, n* = **dispatch.**
desperate ['despərɪt] *adj* verzweifelt; *criminal* zum Äußersten entschlossen; *(urgent) need etc* dringend; *measures* extrem. **to get ~** verzweifeln, in Verzweiflung geraten; **to be ~ for sth** etw dringend brauchen; **I'm/it's not that ~!** so dringend ist es nicht!; **I was ~ to get the job** ich wollte die Stelle unbedingt haben; **things are getting ~** die Lage wird allmählich verzweifelt.
desperately ['despərɪtlɪ] *adv* verzweifelt; *(urgently) need* dringend. **~ in love** verliebt bis über beide Ohren; **~ ill** schwer krank; **do you want ...? — not ~** möchten Sie ...? — nicht unbedingt.
desperation [ˌdespə'reɪʃən] *n* Verzweiflung *f*. **an act of ~** eine Verzweiflungsstat; **in (sheer) ~** aus (reiner) Verzweiflung; **to drive sb to ~** jdn zur Verzweiflung bringen.
despicable [dɪ'spɪkəbl] *adj* abscheulich.
despise [dɪ'spaɪz] *vt* verachten.
despite [dɪ'spaɪt] *prep* trotz *(+gen)*. **~ what she says** trotz allem, was sie sagt.
despondency [dɪ'spɒndənsɪ] *n* Niedergeschlagenheit *f*.
despondent [dɪ'spɒndənt] *adj* niedergeschlagen *(about* wegen*)*.
despot ['despɒt] *n (lit, fig)* Despot *m*.
despotic [des'pɒtɪk] *adj (lit, fig)* despotisch.
despotism ['despətɪzəm] *n* Despotie *f*.
dessert [dɪ'zɜːt] *n* Nachtisch *m*, Dessert *nt*. **~spoon** Dessertlöffel *m*.
destination [ˌdestɪ'neɪʃən] *n* Reiseziel *nt*; *(of goods)* Bestimmungsort *m*.
destined ['destɪnd] *adj* **to be ~d to do sth** dazu bestimmt *or* ausersehen sein, etw zu tun; **we were ~d to meet** das Schicksal wollte es, daß wir uns begegnen; **I was ~d never to see them again** ich sollte sie nie (mehr) wiedersehen; **~ for** *(ship)* unterwegs nach.
destiny ['destɪnɪ] *n* Schicksal *nt*.
destitute ['destɪtjuːt] *adj (poverty-stricken)* mittellos. **to be utterly ~** bettelarm sein.
destroy [dɪ'strɔɪ] *vt* zerstören; *documents, manuscripts etc also* vernichten; *(fire also)* verwüsten; *(kill)* vernichten; *animal* töten; *influence, hopes, chances* zunichte machen; *reputation* ruinieren.
destroyer [dɪ'strɔɪəʳ] *n (Naut)* Zerstörer *m*.
destruction [dɪ'strʌkʃən] *n* Zerstörung *f*; *(of enemy, people, documents)* Vernichtung *f*.
destructive [dɪ'strʌktɪv] *adj wind, fire, war* zerstörerisch; *tendencies, criticism* destruktiv.
desultory ['desəltərɪ] *adj reading* flüchtig; *manner, attempt* halbherzig; *conversation* zwanglos.
detach [dɪ'tætʃ] *vt (separate, unfasten)* lösen *(from* von*)*; *section of form* abtrennen *(from* von*)*; *part of machine, hood* abnehmen *(from* von*)*. **to become ~ed from sth** sich lösen von etw.
detachable [dɪ'tætʃəbl] *adj* abnehmbar.
detached [dɪ'tætʃt] *adj* **(a)** *(unbiased)* objektiv; *(unemotional)* kühl, distanziert. **(b) ~ house** Einfamilienhaus *nt*.
detachment [dɪ'tætʃmənt] *n* **(a)** *(emotionlessness)* Distanz *f*; *(objectivity)* Abstand *m*. **(b)** *(Mil)* Sonderkommando *nt*, Abordnung *f*.
detail ['diːteɪl] **1** *n* **(a)** Detail *nt*; *(particular)* Einzelheit *f*; *(part of painting, photo etc)* Ausschnitt *m*; *(insignificant circumstance)* unwichtige Einzelheit. **in ~** im Detail, in Einzelheiten; **in great ~** in allen Einzelheiten, ausführlich; **there's one little ~ you've forgotten** eine Kleinigkeit haben Sie vergessen; **further ~s** nähere *or* weitere Einzelheiten; **to go into ~s** ins Detail gehen; **his attention to ~** seine Sorgfalt. **(b)** *(Mil)* Sondertrupp *m*. **2** *vt* **(a)** ausführlich *or* detailliert beschreiben. **(b)** *(Mil) troops* abkommandieren.
detailed ['diːteɪld] *adj* ausführlich, detailliert.
detain [dɪ'teɪn] *vt* aufhalten; *(police)* in Haft nehmen.
detainee [dɪteɪ'niː] *n* Häftling *m*.
detect [dɪ'tekt] *vt* entdecken; *(see, make out)* ausfindig machen; *crime* aufdecken; *a tone of sadness, movement* wahrnehmen; *gas* aufspüren.
detection [dɪ'tekʃən] *n* Entdeckung *f*; *(of gases)* Aufspüren *nt*. **to escape ~** nicht entdeckt werden.
detective [dɪ'tektɪv] *n* Kriminalbeamte(r) *mf*; *(private ~)* Detektiv *m*. **~ story** Kriminalgeschichte *f*, Krimi *(col) m*.
detector [dɪ'tektəʳ] *n (Rad, Tech)* Detektor *m*.
détente [deɪ'tɑːnt] *n* Entspannung *f*.
detention [dɪ'tenʃən] *n (captivity)* Haft *f*, Gewahrsam *m*; *(act)* Festnahme *f*; *(Sch)* Nachsitzen *nt*. **he's in ~** *(Sch)* er muß nachsitzen.
deter [dɪ'tɜːʳ] *vt* **to ~ sb from doing sth** jdn davon abhalten, etw zu tun.
detergent [dɪ'tɜːdʒənt] *n (soap powder etc)* Waschmittel *nt*.
deteriorate [dɪ'tɪərɪəreɪt] *vi* sich verschlechtern; *(materials)* verschleißen; *(building)* verfallen.
deterioration [dɪˌtɪərɪə'reɪʃən] *n see vi* Verschlechterung *f*; Verschleiß *m*; Verfall *m*.
determination [dɪˌtɜːmɪ'neɪʃən] *n* **(a)** *(firmness)* Entschlossenheit *f*. **(b)** *(establishing)* Determinierung *f*; *(of character, future also)* Bestimmung *f*; *(of cause, nature, position)* Ermittlung, Bestimmung *f*; *(of frontiers)* Festsetzung *f*.
determine [dɪ'tɜːmɪn] *vt* **(a)** *sb's character, future* bestimmen. **(b)** *(settle, fix) conditions, price* festsetzen. **(c)** *(ascertain)* ermitteln, bestimmen. **(d)** *(resolve) issue* entscheiden.
determined [dɪ'tɜːmɪnd] *adj* entschlossen. **he's ~ to make me lose my temper** *(col)* er legt es darauf an, mich wütend zu machen.
deterrent [dɪ'terənt] **1** *n* Abschreckungsmittel *nt*. **2** *adj attr* Abschreckungs-.
detest [dɪ'test] *vt* verabscheuen, hassen.
detestable [dɪ'testəbl] *adj* widerwärtig, abscheulich.
detestation [ˌdiːtes'teɪʃən] *n* Abscheu *m (of* vor

+*dat*).

detonate ['detəneɪt] *vt* zur Explosion bringen.

detonator ['detəneɪtə^r] *n* Zünd- *or* Sprengkapsel *f*.

detour ['diːˌtʊə^r] *n* Umweg *m*; *(for traffic)* Umleitung *f*.

detract [dɪ'trækt] *vi* **to ~ from sth** etw beeinträchtigen; *pleasure, merit also* etw schmälern.

detriment ['detrɪmənt] *n* Schaden, Nachteil *m*. **to the ~ of** zum Schaden *(+gen)*; **without ~ to** ohne Schaden für.

detrimental [ˌdetrɪ'mentl] *adj (to health, reputation)* schädlich *(to dat)*; *effect also* nachteilig *(to* für*)*; *(to case, cause)* abträglich *(to dat)*.

deuce [djuːs] *n* **(a)** *(Cards)* Zwei *f*. **(b)** *(Tennis)* Einstand *m*. **(c) why the ~ ...?** *(col)* warum zum Teufel ...? *(col)*.

devaluation [ˌdɪvæljʊ'eɪʃən] *n* Abwertung *f*.

devalue [diː'væljuː] *vt* abwerten.

devastate ['devəsteɪt] *vt (lit) town, land* verwüsten; *(fig) opposition* vernichten. **I was ~d** *(col)* das hat mich umgehauen *(col)*.

devastating ['devəsteɪtɪŋ] *adj (lit, fig)* verheerend, vernichtend; *news* niederschmetternd; *wit, humour* umwerfend, überwältigend.

devastatingly ['devəsteɪtɪŋlɪ] *adv beautiful, funny* umwerfend.

devastation [ˌdevə'steɪʃən] *n* Verwüstung *f*.

develop [dɪ'veləp] **1** *vt* **(a)** *(also Phot)* entwickeln. **(b)** *idea, thesis* (weiter)entwickeln; *plot of novel (unfold)* entfalten; *(Mus) theme* durchführen. **(c)** *natural resources, region* erschließen; *old part of town* sanieren; *business (expand)* ausbauen; *(from scratch)* aufziehen. **2** *vi* sich entwickeln. **to ~ into sth** sich zu etw entwickeln; **it later ~ed that ...** später stellte sich heraus, daß ...

developer [dɪ'veləpə^r] *n* **(a)** = **property ~**. **(b)** *(Phot)* Entwickler *m*. **(c) late ~** Spätentwickler *m*.

developing [dɪ'veləpɪŋ] **1** *adj crisis, storm* aufkommend; *industry* neu entstehend; *interest* wachsend. **~ country** Entwicklungsland *nt*. **2** *n (Phot)* Entwickeln *nt*.

development [dɪ'veləpmənt] *n* **(a)** Entwicklung *f*. **to await ~s** die Entwicklung abwarten. **(b)** *(of subject, plot etc)* Ausführung *f*; *(of interests also)* Entfaltung *f*; *(of argument etc)* (Weiter)entwicklung *f*; *(Mus)* Durchführung *f*. **(c)** *(of site, new town)* Erschließung *f*; *(of old part of town)* Sanierung *f*; *(of industry) (from scratch)* Entwicklung *f*; *(expansion)* Ausbau *m*. **we live in a new ~** wir leben in einer neuen Siedlung.

deviant ['diːvɪənt] *adj behaviour* abweichend.

deviate ['diːvɪeɪt] *vi* abweichen *(from* von*)*.

deviation [ˌdiːvɪ'eɪʃən] *n* Abweichung *f*.

device [dɪ'vaɪs] *n* **(a)** *(gadget etc)* Gerät *nt*; *(extra fitment)* Vorrichtung *f*. **nuclear ~** atomarer Sprengkörper. **(b) to leave sb to his own ~s** jdn sich *(dat)* selbst überlassen.

devil ['devl] *n* **(a)** *(lit, fig col)* Teufel *m*. **be a ~!** riskier mal was!; **he's a ~ for changing his mind** er ändert ständig seine Meinung.

(b) *(col: as intensifier)* **I had the ~ of a job getting here** es war verdammt schwierig, hierher zu kommen; **how/what/why/who the ~ ...?** wie/was/warum/wer zum Teufel ...?; **to work like the ~** wie ein Pferd schuften *(col)*; **the ~ of a noise** ein Höllenlärm; **there will be the ~ to pay** das dicke Ende kommt nach.

(c) *(in expressions)* **(to be) between the D~ and the deep blue sea** (sich) in einer Zwickmühle (befinden); **go to the ~!** *(col)* scher dich zum Teufel! *(col)*; **talk of the ~!** wenn man vom Teufel spricht!; **give the ~ his due** das muß der Neid ihm lassen; **to have the ~'s own luck** *(col)* ein Schweineglück *(col) or* unverschämtes Glück haben; **better the ~ you know (than the ~ you don't)** *(prov)* von zwei Übeln wählt man besser das, was man schon kennt; **(the) ~ take the hindmost** den Letzten beißen die Hunde *(Prov)*.

devilish ['devlɪʃ] *adj* **(a)** teuflisch. **(b)** *(col: terrible)* schrecklich.

devil-may-care [ˌdevlmeɪ'kɛə^r] *adj* leichtsinnig.

devilment ['devlmənt] *n* **out of sheer ~** aus lauter Übermut.

devil's advocate *n* Advocatus Diaboli *m*.

devious ['diːvɪəs] *adj* **(a)** *path, argumentation* gewunden. **by a ~ route** auf einem Umweg. **(b)** *(dishonest)* krumm *(col)*, fragwürdig; *person* verschlagen, hinterhältig.

devise [dɪ'vaɪz] *vt* sich *(dat)* ausdenken.

devoid [dɪ'vɔɪd] *adj*: **~ of** bar *(+gen)*, ohne.

devolution [ˌdiːvə'luːʃən] *n (of power)* Übertragung *f (from ... to* von ... auf +*acc)*; *(Pol)* Dezentralisierung *f*.

devote [dɪ'vəʊt] *vt* widmen *(to dat)*; *resources* bestimmen *(to* für*)*.

devoted [dɪ'vəʊtɪd] *adj* ergeben; *followers, service* treu; *admirer* eifrig. **she's ~ to him/her family** sie liebt ihn/ihre Familie über alles.

devotee [ˌdevəʊ'tiː] *n* Anhänger(in *f*) *m*; *(of a writer)* Verehrer(in *f*) *m*; *(of music also, poetry)* Liebhaber(in *f*) *m*.

devotion [dɪ'vəʊʃən] *n (to friend, wife etc)* Ergebenheit *f (to* gegenüber*)*; *(to work)* Hingabe *f (to* an +*acc)*. **~ to duty** Pflichteifer *m*.

devour [dɪ'vaʊə^r] *vt (lit, fig)* verschlingen.

devout [dɪ'vaʊt] *adj (+er) person* fromm; *hope* sehnlich(st).

dew [djuː] *n* Tau *m*. **~drop** *n* Tautropfen *m*.

dewy-eyed ['djuːɪaɪd] *adj (innocent, naive)* naiv; *(trusting)* vertrauensselig. **to go all ~** feuchte Augen bekommen.

dexterity [deks'terɪtɪ] *n* Geschick *nt*.

dext(e)rous ['dekstrəs] *adj (skilful)* geschickt.

DHSS *(Brit)* = **Department of Health and Social Security.**

diabetes [ˌdaɪə'biːtiːz] *n* Diabetes *m*, Zucker *no art (col)*.

diabetic [ˌdaɪə'betɪk] **1** *adj* **(a)** zuckerkrank. **(b)** *beer, chocolate* Diabetiker-. **2** *n* Zuckerkranke(r) *mf*, Diabetiker(in *f*) *m*.

diabolic(al) [ˌdaɪə'bɒlɪk(əl)] *adj* **(a)** diabolisch, teuflisch. **(b)** *(col) weather, heat* saumäßig *(col)*.

diadem ['daɪədem] *n* Diadem *nt*.

diagnose ['daɪəgnəʊz] *vt (Med, fig)* diagnostizieren.

diagnosis [ˌdaɪəg'nəʊsɪs] *n, pl* **diagnoses** [ˌdaɪəg'nəʊsiːz] Diagnose *f*.

diagnostic [ˌdaɪəg'nɒstɪk] *adj* diagnostisch.

diagonal [daɪ'ægənl] **1** *adj* diagonal. **2** *n* Diagonale *f*.

diagonally [daɪ'ægənəlɪ] *adv cut, fold* diagonal. **~ across sth** schräg über etw *(acc)*; **~ opposite sth** einer Sache *(dat)* schräg gegenüber.

diagram ['daɪəgræm] *n* Schaubild *nt*, graphische Darstellung; *(Math)* Diagramm *nt*.

dial ['daɪəl] **1** *n (of clock)* Zifferblatt *nt*; *(of speedometer, pressure gauge)* Skala *f*; *(Telec)* Wählscheibe *f*. **2** *vti (Telec)* wählen. **you can ~ London direct** man kann nach London durchwählen; **to ~ 999** den Notruf wählen.

dialect ['daɪəlekt] *n* Dialekt *m*; *(local, rural also)* Mundart *f*.

dialling ['daɪəlɪŋ]: **~ code** *n* Vorwahl *f*; **~ tone** *n (Brit Telec)* Amtszeichen *nt*.

dialogue ['daɪəlɒg] *n* Dialog *m*.

dialysis [daɪ'æləsɪs] *n* Dialyse *f*.

diameter [daɪ'æmɪtə^r] *n* Durchmesser *m*. **it is one metre in ~** es hat einen Durchmesser von einem Meter.

diametrically [ˌdaɪə'metrɪkəlɪ] *adv* **~ opposed (to)** diametral entgegengesetzt *(+dat)*.

diamond ['daɪəmənd] *n* **(a)** Diamant *m*. **~ wedding** *n* diamantene Hochzeit. **(b) ~s** *(Cards)* Karo *nt*; **the King of ~s** der Karokönig.

diaper ['daɪəpə^r] *n (US)* Windel *f*.

diaphanous [daɪ'æfənəs] *adj* durchscheinend.

diaphragm ['daɪəfræm] *n (Anat, Phys, Med)* Diaphragma *nt*; *(abdominal also)* Zwerchfell *nt*; *(contraceptive also)* Pessar *nt*.
diarrhoea, *(US)* **diarrhea** [ˌdaɪə'riːə] *n* Durchfall *m*. **to have verbal ~** die Laberkrankheit haben *(col)*.
diary ['daɪərɪ] *n (of personal experience)* Tagebuch *nt*; *(for noting dates)* (Termin)kalender *m*.
diatribe ['daɪətraɪb] *n* Schmährede *f*.
dice [daɪs] **1** *n, pl* - Würfel *m*. **2** *vi* **to ~ with death** sein Leben riskieren. **3** *vt (Cook)* in Würfel schneiden.
dicey ['daɪsɪ] *adj (Brit col)* riskant.
dichotomy [dɪ'kɒtəmɪ] *n* Trennung, Dichotomie *f*.
dicky ['dɪkɪ] *adj (col) heart* angeknackst *(col)*.
dickybird ['dɪkɪbɜːd] *n (baby-talk)* Piepmatz *m (baby-talk)*.
dictate [dɪk'teɪt] **1** *vti* diktieren. **2** ['dɪkteɪt] *n usu pl* Diktat *nt*; *(of reason)* Gebote *pl*.
♦ **dictate to** *vi +prep obj person* diktieren *(+dat)*, Vorschriften machen *(+dat)*. **I won't be ~d ~** ich lasse mir keine Vorschriften machen.
dictation [dɪk'teɪʃən] *n (also Sch)* Diktat *nt*.
dictator [dɪk'teɪtə^r] *n (Pol, fig)* Diktator *m*.
dictatorial [ˌdɪktə'tɔːrɪəl] *adj (Pol, fig)* diktatorisch.
dictatorship [dɪk'teɪtəʃɪp] *n (Pol, fig)* Diktatur *f*.
diction ['dɪkʃən] *n (way of speaking)* Diktion *f*.
dictionary ['dɪkʃənrɪ] *n* Wörterbuch *nt*.
did [dɪd] *pret of* **do.**
didactic [dɪ'dæktɪk] *adj* didaktisch.
diddle ['dɪdl] *vt (col)* übers Ohr hauen *(col)*.
didn't ['dɪdənt] = **did not;** *see* **do.**
die[1] [daɪ] **1** *vi* **(a)** sterben *(of sth* an etw *dat)*; *(love)* vergehen; *(memory)* (ent)schwinden; *(custom)* aussterben. **the secret ~d with him** er nahm das Geheimnis mit ins Grab; **old habits ~ hard** der Mensch ist ein Gewohnheitstier; **to ~ of hunger** verhungern; **to be dying** im Sterben liegen; **never say ~!** nur nicht aufgeben!; **to ~ laughing** *(col)* sich totlachen *(col)*. **(b) to be dying to do sth** *(fig)* darauf brennen, etw zu tun; **I'm dying to know what happened** ich will unbedingt wissen, was passiert ist. **2** *vt* **to ~ a hero's/a violent death** den Heldentod/eines gewaltsamen Todes sterben.
♦ **die away** *vi (sound, voice)* leiser werden; *(wind, anger)* sich legen.
♦ **die down** *vi* nachlassen; *(fire)* herunterbrennen; *(storm, wind also)* sich legen.
♦ **die off** *vi* wegsterben.
♦ **die out** *vi* aussterben.
die[2] *n, pl* **dice**: **the ~ is cast** *(fig)* die Würfel sind gefallen.
die-hard ['daɪhɑːd] *adj* zäh; *(pej)* reaktionär; *conservative* Erz-.
diesel ['diːzəl] *n (fuel)* Dieselöl *nt*, Diesel *no art*.
diesel: ~ engine *n* Dieselmotor *m*; **~ oil** *n* Dieselkraftstoff *m*; **~ train** *n* Dieseltriebwagen *m*.
diet ['daɪət] **1** *n* Ernährung *f*; *(special ~)* Diät *f*; *(slimming ~)* Abmagerungs- *or* Schlankheitskur *f*. **to be/go on a ~** eine Schlankheitskur machen. **2** *vi* eine Schlankheitskur machen.
dietician [ˌdaɪə'tɪʃən] *n* Ernährungswissenschaftler(in *f*) *m*; *(in hospital)* Diätassistent(in *f*) *m*.
differ ['dɪfə^r] *vi* **(a)** *(be different)* sich unterscheiden *(from* von*)*. **tastes ~** die Geschmäcker sind verschieden. **(b)** *(disagree)* **to ~ with sb over sth** über etw *(acc)* anderer Meinung sein als jd.
difference ['dɪfrəns] *n* **(a)** Unterschied *m (in, between* zwischen *+dat)*. **that makes a big ~ to me** das ist für mich eine großer Unterschied; **that makes a big ~** das ändert die Sache völlig; **what ~ does it make if ...?** was macht es schon, wenn ...?; **what ~ is that to you?** was macht dir das aus?; **it makes no ~ to me** das ist mir egal; **cooperation makes all the ~** gute Zusammenarbeit ist alles; **a car with a ~** *(col)* das besondere Auto. **(b)** *(between numbers, amounts)* Differenz *f*. **(c)** *(quarrel)* **a ~ of opinion** eine Meinungsverschiedenheit; **to settle one's ~s** die Meinungsverschiedenheiten beilegen.
different ['dɪfrənt] *adj* andere(r, s), anders *pred (from, to* als*)*; *two people, things* verschieden, unterschiedlich. **completely ~** völlig verschieden; *(changed)* völlig verändert; **that's ~!** das ist was anderes!; **in what way are they ~?** worin unterscheiden sie sich?
differential [ˌdɪfə'renʃəl] *n* **(a)** *(difference)* Unterschied *m*. **wage ~** Gehaltsunterschiede *pl*. **(b)** *(Aut)* Differential(getriebe) *nt*.
differentiate [ˌdɪfə'renʃɪeɪt] *vti* unterscheiden. **to ~ between people** einen Unterschied zwischen Menschen machen.
differently ['dɪfrəntlɪ] *adv* anders *(from* als*)*; *(from one another)* verschieden, unterschiedlich.
difficult ['dɪfɪkəlt] *adj* schwierig, schwer; *writer* kompliziert, schwierig; *neighbour, child* schwierig. **I find it ~ to believe that** es fällt mir schwer, das zu glauben; **he's just trying to be ~** er will nur Schwierigkeiten machen; **she is ~ to get on with** es ist schwer, mit ihr auszukommen.
difficulty ['dɪfɪkəltɪ] *n* Schwierigkeit *f*. **with/without ~** mit/ohne Schwierigkeiten *pl*; **a slight ~ in breathing** leichte Atembeschwerden *pl*; **there was some ~ in finding him** es war schwierig, ihn zu finden; **to get into difficulties** in Schwierigkeiten geraten.
diffidence ['dɪfɪdəns] *n* Bescheidenheit *f*.
diffident ['dɪfɪdənt] *adj* bescheiden; *smile* zaghaft.
diffuse [dɪ'fjuːz] **1** *vt* ausstrahlen; *light* streuen; *knowledge, news* verbreiten. **2** [dɪ'fjuːs] *adj (verbose) style, writer* langatmig, weitschweifig.
diffusion [dɪ'fjuːʒən] *n* Ausbreitung *f*; *(of light)* Streuung *f*; *(of knowledge, news)* Verbreitung *f*.
dig [dɪg] *(vb: pret, ptp* **dug***)* **1** *vt* **(a)** *ground* graben. **(b)** *(poke, thrust)* bohren *(sth into sth* etw in etw *acc)*. **(c)** *(col) (enjoy)* stehen auf *(+acc)*; *(understand)* kapieren *(col)*. **2** *vi* graben; *(dog, pig also)* wühlen; *(Tech)* schürfen; *(Archeol)* Ausgrabungen machen. **to ~ for minerals** Erz schürfen; **to ~ in one's pockets for sth** in seinen Taschen nach etw suchen *or* wühlen. **3** *n* **(a) to give sb a ~ in the ribs** jdm einen Rippenstoß geben. **(b)** *(sarcastic remark)* Seitenhieb *m*, Spitze *f*. **to have a ~ at sb/sth** eine Spitze gegen jdn loslassen *(col)*. **(c)** *(Archeol)* (Aus)grabung *f*; *(site)* Ausgrabungsstätte *f*.
♦ **dig in 1** *vi* **(a)** *(also ~ oneself ~)* *(Mil, fig)* sich eingraben. **(b)** *(col: eat)* reinhauen *(col)*. **2** *vt sep compost* untergraben. **to ~ one's heels ~** *(fig)* sich stur stellen.
♦ **dig out** *vt sep (lit, fig)* ausgraben *(of* aus*)*.
♦ **dig up** *vt sep (lit, fig)* ausgraben; *earth* aufwühlen; *lawn, garden* umgraben; *weeds* jäten. **where did you ~ her ~?** *(col)* wo hast du die denn aufgegabelt? *(col)*.
digest [daɪ'dʒest] **1** *vt (lig, fig)* verdauen. **2** ['daɪdʒest] *n (of book, facts)* Zusammenfassung *f*.
digestible [dɪ'dʒestəbl] *adj* verdaulich.
digestion [dɪ'dʒestʃən] *n* Verdauung *f*.
digestive [dɪ'dʒestɪv] *adj* Verdauungs-. **~ (biscuit)** *(Brit) Keks m aus Vollkornschrot*.
digit ['dɪdʒɪt] *n (Math)* Ziffer *f*.
digital ['dɪdʒɪtəl] *adj* Digital-, digital.
dignified ['dɪgnɪfaɪd] *adj person* würdig; *behaviour, manner* würdevoll.
dignitary ['dɪgnɪtərɪ] *n* Würdenträger(in *f*) *m*. **the local dignitaries** die Honoratioren am Ort.
dignity ['dɪgnɪtɪ] *n* Würde *f*. **that would be beneath my ~** das wäre unter meiner Würde.
digress [daɪ'gres] *vi* abschweifen.
digression [daɪ'greʃən] *n* Abschweifung *f*, Exkurs *(geh) m*.

digs [dɪgz] *npl (Brit)* Bude *f (col).* **to be in ~** ein möbliertes Zimmer *or* eine Bude *(col)* haben.
dike [daɪk] *n, vt* = **dyke.**
dilapidated [dɪ'læpɪdeɪtɪd] *adj house* verfallen, baufällig; *clothes* verschlissen, schäbig.
dilapidation [dɪˌlæpɪ'deɪʃən] *n* Baufälligkeit *f,* Verfall *m.*
dilate [daɪ'leɪt] **1** *vt* weiten. **2** *vi (pupils)* sich erweitern.
dilation [daɪ'leɪʃən] *n (of pupils)* Erweiterung *f.*
dilatory ['dɪlətərɪ] *adj* **(a)** *person* langsam; *reply* verspätet. **to be ~** sich *(dat)* Zeit lassen. **(b)** *action, policy* Verzögerungs-, Hinhalte-.
dilemma [daɪ'lemə] *n* Dilemma *nt.* **to be in a ~** sich in einem Dilemma befinden, in der Klemme sitzen *(col).*
dilettante [ˌdɪlɪ'tæntɪ] *m, pl* **dilettanti** [ˌdɪlɪ'tæntɪ] Amateur(in *f*), Dilettant(in *f*) *m.*
diligence ['dɪlɪdʒəns] *n* Eifer *m; (in work also)* Fleiß *m.*
diligent ['dɪlɪdʒənt] *adj person* eifrig; *(in work also)* fleißig; *search, work* sorgfältig, genau.
dilute [daɪ'luːt] *vt orange juice etc* verdünnen; *(fig)* mildern, (ab)schwächen.
dim [dɪm] **1** *adj (+er)* **(a)** *light, eyesight, sound* schwach; *colour* matt; *memory, outline, shape* verschwommen. **the room grew ~** im Zimmer wurde es dunkel. **(b)** *(col: stupid)* schwer von Begriff. **(c)** *(col)* **to take a ~ view of sb/sth** nicht viel von jdm/etw halten. **2** *vt light* abdunkeln. **to ~ one's headlights** *(esp US)* abblenden. **3** *vi (lamps)* schwächer werden; *(memory)* nachlassen.
dime [daɪm] *n (US)* Zehncentstück *nt.*
dimension [daɪ'menʃən] *n* Dimension *f; (measurement)* Abmessung(en *pl*) *f,* Maß *nt.*
-dimensional [-daɪ'menʃənl] *adj suf* -dimensional.
diminish [dɪ'mɪnɪʃ] **1** *vt* verringern, herabsetzen; *value* mindern. **~ed responsibility** *(Jur)* verminderte Zurechnungsfähigkeit; **~ed** *(Mus)* vermindert. **2** *vi* sich verringern; *(authority, strength also)* abnehmen; *(value also)* sich vermindern.
diminutive [dɪ'mɪnjʊtɪv] **1** *adj* winzig, klein. **2** *n (Gram)* Verkleinerungsform *f,* Diminutiv(um) *nt.*
dimly ['dɪmlɪ] *adv shine* schwach; *hear, remember also* undeutlich; *see* verschwommen.
dimple ['dɪmpl] *n (on cheek, chin)* Grübchen *nt.*
din [dɪn] **1** *n* Lärm *m,* Getöse *nt.* **2** *vt* **to ~ sth into sb** jdm etw einbleuen.
dine [daɪn] **1** *vi* speisen, dinieren *(geh) (on* etw*).* **2** *vt* bewirten, beköstigen.
diner ['daɪnəʳ] *n* **(a)** *(person)* Speisende(r) *mf; (in restaurant)* Gast *m.* **(b)** *(US)* Eßlokal *nt.* **(c)** *(Rail)* Speisewagen *m.*
dinghy ['dɪŋgɪ] *n* Ding(h)i *nt; (collapsible)* Schlauchboot *nt.*
dingo ['dɪŋgəʊ] *n* Dingo *m,* australischer Wildhund.
dingy ['dɪndʒɪ] *adj place, furniture* schmuddelig.
dining ['daɪnɪŋ]: **~ car** *n* Speisewagen *m;* **~ room** *n* Eßzimmer *nt; (in hotel)* Speiseraum *m;* **~ table** *n* Eßtisch *m.*
dinner ['dɪnəʳ] *n* (Haupt)mahlzeit *f,* Abendessen *nt; (formal)* (Abend)essen *nt; (lunch)* Mittagessen *nt.* **to be at ~** beim Essen sein.
dinner: ~ jacket *n* Smokingjacke *f;* **~ party** *n* Abendgesellschaft *f* (mit Essen); **to have a small ~ party** ein kleines Essen geben; **~ service** *n* Tafelservice *nt.*
dinosaur ['daɪnəsɔːʳ] *n* Dinosaurier *m.*
dint [dɪnt] *n* **by ~ of** durch.
diocese ['daɪəsɪs] *n* Diözese *f,* Bistum *nt.*
diode ['daɪəʊd] *n* Diode *f.*
dioxide [daɪ'ɒksaɪd] *n* Dioxyd *nt.*
dip [dɪp] **1** *vt* **(a)** *(in(to)* in *+acc) (into liquid)* tauchen; *pen, hand* eintauchen; *bread* (ein)tunken, stippen *(col).* **(b)** *(into bag, basket) hand* stecken. **(c)** *(Brit Aut) headlights* abblenden. **2** *vi (ground)* sich senken; *(temperature, pointer on scale)* fallen. **the sun ~ped behind the mountains** die Sonne verschwand hinter den Bergen. **3** *n* **(a)** *(swim)* **to go for a ~** kurz schwimmen gehen. **(b)** *(for cleaning animals)* Desinfektionslösung *f.* **(c)** *(in ground)* Mulde *f.* **(d)** *(Cook)* Dip *m.*
♦ **dip into** *vi +prep obj* **(a)** *(lit)* **she ~ped ~ her handbag** sie griff in ihre Handtasche. **(b) to ~ ~ one's savings** an seine Ersparnisse gehen. **(c)** *book* einen kurzen Blick werfen in *(+acc).*
diphtheria [dɪf'θɪərɪə] *n* Diphtherie *f.*
diphthong ['dɪfθɒŋ] *n* Diphthong *m.*
diploma [dɪ'pləʊmə] *n* Diplom *nt.*
diplomacy [dɪ'pləʊməsɪ] *n (Pol, fig)* Diplomatie *f.*
diplomat ['dɪpləmæt] *n (Pol, fig)* Diplomat *m.*
diplomatic [ˌdɪplə'mætɪk] *adj (lit, fig)* diplomatisch.
diplomatic: ~ bag *n* Diplomatenpost *f;* **~ corps** *n* diplomatisches Korps; **~ immunity** *n* Immunität *f;* **~ service** *n* diplomatischer Dienst.
dipsomania [ˌdɪpsəʊ'meɪnɪə] *n* Trunksucht *f.*
dipsomaniac [ˌdɪpsəʊ'meɪnɪæk] *n* Trunksüchtige(r) *mf.*
dipstick ['dɪpstɪk] *n* Ölmeßstab *m.*
dire [daɪəʳ] *adj* schrecklich, furchtbar; *poverty* äußerste(r, s). **~ necessity** dringende Notwendigkeit; **to be in ~ need of sth** etw dringend brauchen.
direct [daɪ'rekt] **1** *adj* direkt; *train* durchgehend; *opposite* genau. **~ current** Gleichstrom *m;* **~ hit** Volltreffer *m;* **~ object** direktes Objekt, Akkusativobjekt *nt;* **~ speech** direkte Rede. **2** *vt* **(a)** *(address, aim) remark, letter* richten *(to* an *+acc); efforts* richten *(towards* auf *+acc).* **can you ~ me to the town hall?** können Sie mir sagen, wie ich zum Rathaus komme? **(b)** *person's work, business* leiten, lenken; *traffic* regeln. **(c)** *(order)* anweisen *(sb to do sth* jdn, etw zu tun*),* befehlen *(sb to do sth* jdm, etw zu tun*); (Jur) jury* Rechtsbelehrung erteilen *(+dat).* **(d)** *film, play* Regie führen bei; *radio/TV programme* leiten. **3** *adv* direkt.
direction [dɪ'rekʃən] *n* **(a)** *(lit, fig: way)* Richtung *f.* **in the wrong/right ~** *(lit, fig)* in die falsche/richtige Richtung; **in the ~ of Hamburg** in Richtung Hamburg; **a sense of ~** *(lit)* Orientierungssinn *m; (fig)* ein Ziel *nt* (im Leben). **(b)** *(management: of company etc)* Leitung *f.* **(c)** *(of film, actors)* Regie *f; (of radio/TV programme)* Leitung *f.* **(d) ~s** *pl (instructions)* Anweisungen *pl; (to a place)* Angaben *pl; (for use)* (Gebrauchs)anweisung *f.*
directive [dɪ'rektɪv] *n* Direktive, Weisung *f.*
directly [dɪ'rektlɪ] **1** *adv* direkt, unmittelbar; *(in a short time)* sofort, gleich. **2** *conj* sobald. **he'll come ~ he's ready** er kommt, sobald er fertig ist.
directness [daɪ'rektnɪs] *n* Direktheit *f.*
director [dɪ'rektəʳ] *n* **(a)** *(of company)* Direktor, Leiter *m; (Univ)* Rektor *m.* **(b)** *(Rad, TV)* Direktor *m; (Film, Theat)* Regisseur *m.*
directory [dɪ'rektərɪ] *n* Adreßbuch *nt; (telephone ~)* Telefonbuch *nt; (trade ~)* Branchenverzeichnis *nt.* **~ enquiries** *or (US)* **assistance** *(Telec)* (Fernsprech)auskunft *f.*
dirge [dɜːdʒ] *n* Klagegesang *m.*
dirt [dɜːt] *n (lit, fig)* Schmutz, Dreck *m; (soil)* Erde *f.* **to treat sb like ~** jdn wie (den letzten) Dreck behandeln *(col).*
dirt cheap ['dɜːt'tʃiːp] *adj, adv (col)* spottbillig.
dirty ['dɜːtɪ] **1** *adj (+er)* **(a)** schmutzig; *wound* verschmutzt. **~ weather** Sauwetter *nt (col);* **to give sb a ~ look** *(fig)* jdm einen bösen Blick zuwerfen. **(b)** *(fig: obscene)* schmutzig, unanständig; *story, joke also* zotig. **to have a ~ mind** eine schmutzige Phantasie haben; **~ old man** geiler Bock *(col!);* **they're having a ~ weekend**

(col) sie sind zusammen übers Wochenende weggefahren. **2** *vt* beschmutzen. **3** *n* **to do the ~ on sb** *(Brit col)* jdn reinlegen *(col)*.
disability [ˌdɪsəˈbɪlɪtɪ] *n* Behinderung *f.* **~ pension** *n* Invalidenrente *f.*
disable [dɪsˈeɪbl] *vt tank, gun* unbrauchbar machen; *ship* kampfunfähig machen.
disabled [dɪsˈeɪbld] **1** *adj* **(a)** behindert. **(b)** *tank, gun* unbrauchbar; *ship* nicht seetüchtig. **2** *npl* **the ~** die Behinderten *pl.*
disadvantage [ˌdɪsədˈvɑːntɪdʒ] *n* Nachteil *m.* **to his ~** zu seinem Nachteil. **to be at a ~** sich im Nachteil befinden, benachteiligt sein.
disadvantaged [dɪsədˈvɑːntɪdʒd] *adj* benachteiligt.
disadvantageous *adj* [ˌdɪsædvɑːnˈteɪdʒəs] nachteilig.
disagree [ˌdɪsəˈgriː] *vi* **(a)** *(with person, views, figures)* nicht übereinstimmen; *(with plan, suggestion etc)* nicht einverstanden sein; *(two people)* sich nicht einig sein. **(b)** *(quarrel)* eine Meinungsverschiedenheit haben. **(c)** *(climate, food)* **to ~ with sb** jdm nicht bekommen.
disagreeable [ˌdɪsəˈgriːəbl] *adj* unangenehm; *person* unsympathisch.
disagreement [ˌdɪsəˈgriːmənt] *n* **(a)** *(with opinion, between opinions)* Uneinigkeit *f.* **(b)** *(quarrel)* Meinungsverschiedenheit *f.* **(c)** *(between reports)* Diskrepanz *f.*
disallow [ˌdɪsəˈlaʊ] *vt evidence, goal* nicht anerkennen; *claim also* zurückweisen.
disappear [ˌdɪsəˈpɪəʳ] *vi* verschwinden.
disappearance [ˌdɪsəˈpɪərəns] *n* Verschwinden *nt.*
disappoint [ˌdɪsəˈpɔɪnt] *vt* enttäuschen.
disappointed [ˌdɪsəˈpɔɪntɪd] *adj* enttäuscht.
disappointing [ˌdɪsəˈpɔɪntɪŋ] *adj* enttäuschend.
disappointment [ˌdɪsəˈpɔɪntmənt] *n* Enttäuschung *f.*
disapproval [ˌdɪsəˈpruːvl] *n* Mißbilligung *f.*
disapprove [ˌdɪsəˈpruːv] **1** *vt* mißbilligen. **2** *vi* dagegen sein. **he ~s of children smoking** er mißbilligt es, wenn Kinder rauchen.
disapproving [ˌdɪsəˈpruːvɪŋ] *adj* mißbilligend.
disarm [dɪsˈaːm] **1** *vt (lit, fig)* entwaffnen. **2** *vi (Mil)* abrüsten.
disarmament [dɪsˈɑːməmənt] *n* Abrüstung *f.*
disarray [ˌdɪsəˈreɪ] *n* Unordnung *f.*
disaster [dɪˈzɑːstəʳ] *n* Katastrophe *f; (Aviat, Min, Rail also)* Unglück *nt.* **~ area** Katastrophengebiet *nt.*
disastrous [dɪˈzaːstrəs] *adj* katastrophal.
disband [dɪsˈbænd] **1** *vt* auflösen. **2** *vi (soldiers, club members)* auseinandergehen.
disbelief [ˈdɪsbəˈliːf] *n* **in ~** ungläubig.
disbelieve [ˈdɪsbəˈliːv] *vt* nicht glauben.
disc, *(esp US)* **disk** [dɪsk] *n* **(a)** Scheibe *f; (Anat)* Bandscheibe *f.* **(b)** *(record)* Platte *f.* **(c)** *(Comp)* Diskette *f.*
discard [dɪˈskaːd] *vt unwanted article* ausrangieren; *person* abschieben; *idea, plan* verwerfen.
disc brake *n* Scheibenbremse *f.*
discern [dɪˈsɜːn] *vt* erkennen.
discerning [dɪˈsɜːnɪŋ] *adj clientele, reader* anspruchsvoll, kritisch. **to the ~ eye** für den Kenner.
discernment [dɪˈsɜːnmənt] *n (ability to discern)* feines Gespür. **a man of ~** ein Mann mit Geschmack.
discharge [dɪsˈtʃɑːdʒ] **1** *vt* **(a)** *prisoner, patient, soldier* entlassen; *accused* freisprechen. **(b)** *(emit) (Elec)* entladen; *liquid, gas (pipe etc)* ausstoßen; *(Med)* absondern. **(c)** *(unload) ship, cargo* löschen. **(d)** *(gun)* abfeuern. **(e)** *debt* begleichen; *obligation, duty* nachkommen *(+dat)*; *function* erfüllen. **2** *vi (wound, sore)* eitern. **3** [ˈdistʃɑːdʒ] *n* **(a)** *(dismissal) see vt (a)* Entlassung *f;* Freispruch *m; (of soldier)* Abschied *m.* **(b)** *(Elec)* Entladung *f; (of gas)* Ausströmen *nt; (of liquid, Med: vaginal ~)* Ausfluß *m; (of pus)* Absonderung *f.* **(c)** *(of debt)* Begleichung *f; (of obligation, duty, function)* Erfüllung *f.*
disciple [dɪˈsaɪpl] *n (lit, fig)* Jünger *m.*
disciplinary [ˈdɪsɪplɪnərɪ] *adj* Disziplinar-, disziplinarisch. **to take ~ action against sb** ein Disziplinarverfahren gegen jdn einleiten.
discipline [ˈdɪsɪplɪn] **1** *n* Disziplin *f.* **2** *vt* **(a)** *(train, make obedient)* disziplinieren. **(b)** *(punish)* bestrafen; *(physically)* züchtigen.
disc jockey *n* Diskjockey *m.*
disclaim [dɪsˈkleɪm] *vt* abstreiten.
disclaimer [dɪsˈkleɪməʳ] *n* Dementi *nt.*
disclose [dɪsˈkləʊz] *vt secret* enthüllen; *intentions, news* bekanntgeben.
disclosure [dɪsˈkləʊʒəʳ] *n* **(a)** *see vt* Enthüllung *f;* Bekanntgabe *f.* **(b)** *(fact revealed)* Mitteilung *f.*
disco [ˈdɪskəʊ] *n* Disko *f.*
discoloration [dɪsˌkʌləˈreɪʃən] *n (mark)* Verfärbung *f.*
discomfort [dɪsˈkʌmfət] *n (lit)* Beschwerden *pl; (fig: uneasiness, embarrassment)* Unbehagen *nt.*
disconcert [ˌdɪskənˈsɜːt] *vt* aus der Fassung bringen.
disconnect [ˈdɪskəˈnekt] *vt pipe etc* trennen; *(cut off supply of) gas, electricity* abstellen. **I've been ~ed** *(for non-payment)* man hat mir das Telefon/ den Strom/das Gas *etc* abgestellt. **to ~ an appliance** den Stecker eines Geräts herausziehen.
disconsolate [dɪsˈkɒnsəlɪt] *adj* niedergeschlagen.
discontent [ˈdiskənˈtent] *n* Unzufriedenheit *f.*
discontent(ed) [ˈdiskənˈtent(ɪd)] *adj* unzufrieden *(with, about* mit*)*.
discontinue [ˈdɪskənˈtɪnjuː] *vt* aufgeben; *class, project, conversation* abbrechen; *(Comm) line* auslaufen lassen.
discord [ˈdɪskɔːd] *n* **(a)** Uneinigkeit *f.* **(b)** *(Mus)* Dissonanz *f.*
discordant [dɪsˈkɔːdənt] *meeting, atmosphere* unharmonisch; *(Mus)* dissonant.
discotheque [ˈdɪskəʊtek] *n* Diskothek *f.*
discount [ˈdɪskaʊnt] **1** *n* Rabatt *m; (for cash)* Skonto *nt or m.* **to give a ~ on sth** Rabatt auf etw *(acc)* geben. **2** *vt* **(a)** *(Comm)* nachlassen. **(b)** [dɪsˈkaʊnt] *(dismiss)* abtun; *person's opinion* unberücksichtigt lassen.
discourage [dɪsˈkʌrɪdʒ] *vt* **(a)** *(dishearten)* entmutigen. **(b)** *(dissuade)* **to ~ sb from sth** jdm von etw abraten; *(successfully)* jdn von etw abbringen.
discouragement [dɪsˈkʌrɪdʒmənt] *n* **(a)** *(depression)* Mutlosigkeit *f.* **(b) to be a ~** entmutigend sein.
discouraging [dɪsˈkʌrɪdʒɪŋ] *adj* entmutigend.
discourteous [dɪsˈkɜːtɪəs] *adj* unhöflich.
discourtesy [dɪsˈkɜːtɪsɪ] *n* Unhöflichkeit *f.*
discover [dɪsˈkʌvəʳ] *vt* entdecken; *(notice) mistake, loss also* festellen, bemerken.
discovery [dɪsˈkʌvərɪ] *n* Entdeckung *f.*
discredit [dɪsˈkredɪt] **1** *vt* **(a)** *report, theory* in Mißkredit bringen. **(b)** *(disbelieve)* keinen Glauben schenken *(+dat)*. **2** *n* **(a)** *no pl* **to bring ~ on sb** jdn in Mißkredit bringen. **(b) to be a ~ to sb** eine Schande für jdn sein.
discreet [dɪˈskriːt] *adj* diskret; *(in quiet taste also)* dezent.
discrepancy [dɪˈskrepənsɪ] *n* Diskrepanz *f* *(between* zwischen *+dat)*.
discretion [dɪˈskreʃən] *n* **(a)** Diskretion *f.* **(b) to leave sth to sb's ~** etw jdm anheimstellen; **use your own ~** es steht in Ihrem Ermessen.
discriminate [dɪˈskrɪmɪneɪt] *vi* **(a)** *(distinguish)* unterscheiden *(between* zwischen *+dat)*. **(b) to ~ against/in favour of sb** jdn diskriminieren/ bevorzugen.
discriminating [dɪˈskrɪmɪneɪtɪŋ] *adj person, judgement, mind* kritisch.

discrimination [dɪˌskrɪmɪ'neɪʃən] *n* **(a)** Diskriminierung *f*. **racial ~** Rassendiskriminierung *f*; **sexual ~** Diskriminierung auf Grund des Geschlechts. **(b)** *(discernment)* kritisches Urteilsvermögen.
discus ['dɪskəs] *n* Diskus *m*.
discuss [dɪ'skʌs] *vt* besprechen; *politics, theory* erörten, diskutieren.
discussion [dɪ'skʌʃən] *n* Diskussion *f*; *(meeting)* Besprechung *f*.
disdain [dɪs'deɪn] **1** *vt* verachten. **he ~ed to notice them** er hielt es für unter seiner Würde, ihnen Beachtung zu schenken. **2** *n* Verachtung *f*.
disease [dɪ'ziːz] *n (lit, fig)* Krankheit *f*.
diseased [dɪ'ziːzd] *adj (lit, fig)* krank.
disembark [ˌdɪsɪm'bɑːk] **1** *vt* ausschiffen. **2** *vi* von Bord gehen.
disembarkation [ˌdɪsembɑː'keɪʃən] *n* Landung *f*.
disembodied ['dɪsɪm'bɒdɪd] *adj* körperlos; *voice* geisterhaft.
disenchanted ['dɪsɪn'tʃɑːntɪd] *adj* **to be ~ with sb/sth** von jdm/etw enttäuscht sein; **I've become ~ with it** ich halte nicht mehr viel davon.
disengage [ˌdɪsɪn'geɪdʒ] *vt* **to ~ the clutch** *(Aut)* auskuppeln.
disentangle ['dɪsɪn'tæŋgl] *vt (lit, fig)* entwirren.
disfavour, *(US)* disfavor [dɪs'feɪvəʳ] *n (displeasure)* Ungnade *f*; *(dislike)* Mißfallen *nt*. **to fall into/be in ~** in Ungnade fallen/sein *(with* bei*)*.
disfigure [dɪs'fɪgəʳ] *vt* verunstalten; *person also* entstellen.
disfigurement [dɪs'fɪgəmənt] *n see vt* Verunstaltung *f*; Entstellung *f*.
disgorge [dɪs'gɔːdʒ] *vt* ausspeien.
disgrace [dɪs'greɪs] **1** *n* Schande *f*; *(person)* Schandfleck *m (to gen)*. **to be in/fall into ~** in Ungnade (gefallen) sein/fallen *(with* bei*)*. **2** *vt* Schande machen *(+dat)*; *country, family also* Schande bringen über *(+acc)*. **to ~ oneself** sich blamieren.
disgraceful [dɪs'greɪsfʊl] *adj* erbärmlich (schlecht); *behaviour, performance* skandalös.
disgruntled [dɪs'grʌntld] *adj* verstimmt.
disguise [dɪs'gaɪz] **1** *vt* verkleiden; *voice* verstellen; *interest, feelings* verbergen. **there's no disguising the fact that ...** es läßt sich nicht verhehlen, daß ... **2** *n (lit)* Verkleidung *f*; *(fig)* Deckmantel *m*. **in ~** verkleidet.
disgust [dɪs'gʌst] **1** *n* Ekel *m*; *(at sb's behaviour)* Entrüstung, Empörung *f*. **2** *vt (person, sight)* anekeln, anwidern; *(actions)* empören.
disgusted [dɪs'gʌstɪd] *adj* angeekelt; *(at sb's behaviour)* empört. **I am ~ with you** ich bin empört über dich.
disgusting [dɪs'gʌstɪŋ] *adj* widerlich; *(physically nauseating also)* ekelhaft. **that's ~** das ist eine Schweinerei *(col)*.
dish [dɪʃ] *n* **(a)** Schale *f*; *(for serving also)* Schüssel *f*. **(b) ~es** *pl (crockery)* Geschirr *nt*; **to do the ~es** abwaschen. **(c)** *(food)* Gericht *nt*.
♦ **dish out** *vt sep (col)* austeilen.
♦ **dish up** *vt sep (lit, fig)* auftischen.
disharmony ['dɪs'hɑːmənɪ] *n (lit, fig)* Disharmonie *f*.
dishcloth ['dɪʃklɒθ] *n* Geschirrtuch *nt*; *(for washing)* Spültuch *nt*.
dishearten [dɪs'hɑːtn] *vt* entmutigen. **don't be ~ed** nur Mut.
disheartening [dɪs'hɑːtnɪŋ] *adj* entmutigend.
dished [dɪʃt] *adj (Tech)* konkav (gewölbt); *wheels* gestürzt.
dishevelled, *(US)* disheveled [dɪ'ʃevəld] *adj* ramponiert *(col)*, unordentlich; *hair* zerzaust.
dishonest [dɪs'ɒnɪst] *adj* unehrlich.
dishonesty [dɪs'ɒnɪstɪ] *n* Unehrlichkeit *f*.
dishonour, *(US)* dishonor [dɪs'ɒnəʳ] *n* Schande *f*. **to bring ~ upon sb** Schande über jdn bringen.
dishonourable, *(US)* dishonorable [dɪs'ɒnərəbl] *adj* unehrenhaft.
dish: ~washer *n (person)* Tellerwäscher(in *f*) *m*; *(machine)* Geschirrspülmaschine *f*; **~water** *n* Abwasch- *or* Spülwasser *nt*; **this coffee is like ~water** der Kaffee schmeckt wie Spülwasser.
dishy ['dɪʃɪ] *adj (+er) (Brit col)* dufte *(col)*.
disillusion [ˌdɪsɪ'luːʒən] *vt* desillusionieren.
disillusionment [ˌdɪsɪ'luːʒənmənt] *n* Desillusionierung *f*.
disincentive [ˌdɪsɪn'sentɪv] *n* Entmutigung *f*. **it acts as a ~** es wirkt abschreckend.
disinclination [ˌdɪsɪnklɪ'neɪʃən] *n* Abneigung, Unlust *f*.
disinclined ['dɪsɪn'klaɪnd] *adj* abgeneigt.
disinfect [ˌdɪsɪn'fekt] *vt* desinfizieren.
disinfectant [dɪsɪn'fektənt] *n* Desinfektionsmittel *nt*.
disinherit ['dɪsɪn'herɪt] *vt* enterben.
disintegrate [dɪs'ɪntɪgreɪt] *vi* zerfallen; *(rock, cement)* auseinanderbröckeln; *(car)* sich in seine Bestandteile auflösen; *(group also, institution)* sich auflösen.
disintegration [dɪsˌɪntɪ'greɪʃən] *n see vi* Zerfall *m*; Auseinanderbröckeln *nt*; Auflösung *f*.
disinterested [dɪs'ɪntrɪstɪd] *adj (unbiased)* unvoreingenommen.
disjointed *adj* [dɪs'dʒɔɪntɪd] zusammenhanglos.
disk *n* [dɪsk] *(Comp)* Diskette *f*; *(video etc)* Platte *f*. **~ drive** Diskettenlaufwerk *nt*; **hard ~** Festplatte *f*.
diskette [dɪs'ket] *n* Diskette *f*.
dislike [dɪs'laɪk] **1** *vt* nicht mögen, nicht gern haben. **to ~ doing sth** etw ungern tun. **I don't ~ him** ich habe nichts gegen ihn. **2** *n* Abneigung *f (of* gegen*)*. **to take a ~ to sb/sth** eine Abneigung gegen jdn/etw entwickeln.
dislocate ['dɪsləʊkeɪt] *vt (Med)* verrenken; *(fig) plans* durcheinanderbringen. **to ~ one's shoulder** sich *(dat)* den Arm auskugeln.
dislodge [dɪs'lɒdʒ] *vt obstruction, stone* entfernen; *(accidentally)* verschieben; *enemy* verdrängen.
disloyal [dɪs'lɔɪəl] *adj* treulos; *(esp Pol)* illoyal *(to* gegenüber*)*.
disloyalty [dɪs'lɔɪəltɪ] *n* Treulosigkeit *f*; *(esp Pol)* Illoyalität *f (to* gegenüber*)*.
dismal ['dɪzməl] *adj* trübe, trist; *person* trübsinnig; *failure, result* kläglich.
dismantle [dɪs'mæntl] *vt* auseinandernehmen; *scaffolding* abbauen; *(fig) system* demontieren.
dismay [dɪs'meɪ] **1** *n* Bestürzung *f*. **in ~** bestürzt. **2** *vt* bestürzen.
dismiss [dɪs'mɪs] *vt* **(a)** *(from job)* entlassen. **(b)** *(allow to go)* entlassen; *assembly* auflösen. **(c)** *objection* abtun. **(d)** *(Jur) accused* entlassen; *appeal* abweisen. **to ~ a case** eine Klage abweisen.
dismissal [dɪs'mɪsəl] *n* Entlassung *f*; *(of assembly)* Auflösung *f*; *(of objection)* Zurückweisung *f*; *(of appeal)* Abweisung *f*.
dismount [dɪs'maʊnt] *vi* absteigen.
disobedience [ˌdɪsə'biːdɪəns] *n* Ungehorsam *m (to* gegenüber*)*.
disobedient [ˌdɪsə'biːdɪənt] *adj* ungehorsam.
disobey ['dɪsə'beɪ] *vt* nicht gehorchen *(+dat)*; *rule* übertreten.
disobliging [ˌdɪsə'blaɪdʒɪŋ] *adj* ungefällig.
disorder [dɪs'ɔːdəʳ] *n* **(a)** Durcheinander *nt*; *(in room etc also)* Unordnung *f*. **in ~** durcheinander; in Unordnung. **(b)** *(rioting)* Unruhen *pl*. **(c)** *(Med)* Störung *f*.
disordered [dɪs'ɔːdəd] *adj room, thoughts* unordentlich; *plans* wirr; *existence* ungeordnet.
disorderly [dɪs'ɔːdəlɪ] *adj desk, room* unordentlich; *life* unsolide; *mind* wirr; *(unruly) crowd* aufrührerisch. **~ conduct** *(Jur)* ungebührliches Benehmen.
disorganized [dɪs'ɔːgənaɪzd] *adj* durcheinander *pred*, desorganisiert; *life, person* chaotisch.
disorientated [dɪs'ɔːrɪənteɪtɪd] *adj* desorientiert.
disown [dɪs'əʊn] *vt* verleugnen. **I'll ~ you if you go**

out in that hat wenn du mit dem Hut ausgehst, tue ich so, als ob ich nicht zu dir gehöre.
disparage [dɪ'spærɪdʒ] *vt* herabsetzen.
disparaging [dɪ'spærɪdʒɪŋ] *adj* abschätzig.
disparity [dɪ'spærɪtɪ] *n* Ungleichheit *f*.
dispassionate [dɪs'pæʃənɪt] *adj* objektiv.
dispatch [dɪ'spætʃ] **1** *vt* **(a)** senden, schicken; *person, troops etc also* entsenden. **(b)** *(deal with) job etc* (prompt) erledigen. **(c)** *(kill)* töten. **2** *n* **(a)** *see vt* Senden, Schicken *nt;* Entsendung *f;* prompte Erledigung; Tötung *f.* **date of ~** Absendedatum *nt;* **with ~** prompt. **(b)** *(message)* Depesche *f; (Press)* Bericht *m.* **to be mentioned in ~es** *(Mil)* in den Kriegsberichten erwähnt werden; **~ rider** *(Mil)* Melder *m.*
dispel [dɪ'spel] *vt clouds, fog* auflösen, vertreiben; *doubts, fears* zerstreuen; *sorrows* vertreiben.
dispensable [dɪ'spensəbl] *adj* entbehrlich.
dispensary [dɪ'pensərɪ] *n (in hospital)* (Krankenhaus)apotheke *f.*
dispensation [ˌdɪspen'seɪʃən] *n (handing out)* Verteilung *f.* **~ of justice** Rechtsprechung *f;* **by a special ~** durch besondere Verfügung.
dispense [dɪ'spens] *vt* **(a)** verteilen, austeilen *(to* an *+acc).* **(b)** *medicine* abgeben; *prescription* zubereiten. **dispensing chemist's** *(Brit)* Apotheke *f.*
♦**dispense with** *vi +prep obj* verzichten auf *(+acc).*
dispenser [dɪ'spensəʳ] *n (container)* Spender *m; (slot-machine)* Automat *m.*
dispersal [dɪ'spɜːsəl] *n see vb* Verstreuen *nt;* Verteilung *f;* Verbreitung *f;* Auflösung *f.*
disperse [dɪ'spɜːs] **1** *vt (scatter widely)* verstreuen; *(Bot) seed* verteilen; *(fig) knowledge etc* verbreiten. **2** *vi* sich auflösen.
dispirited [dɪ'spɪrɪtɪd] *adj* entmutigt.
displace [dɪs'pleɪs] *vt (move)* verschieben; *(replace)* ablösen, ersetzen; *water, air* verdrängen. **~d person** Verschleppte(r) *mf.*
displacement [dɪs'pleɪsmənt] *n see vt* Verschiebung *f;* Ablösung *f;* Verdrängung *f.*
display [dɪ'spleɪ] **1** *vt* **(a)** zeigen; *(ostentatiously) new clothes etc also* vorführen; *exam results, notice* aushängen. **(b)** *(Comm) goods* ausstellen. **2** *n* **(a) to make a great ~ of sth** etw groß zur Schau stellen; **a ~ of temper** ein Wutanfall *m.* **(b)** *(of paintings etc)* Ausstellung *f; (dancing ~ etc)* Vorführung *f; (military, air ~)* Schau *f.* **(c)** *(Comm)* Auslage *f.* **the goods on ~** die ausgestellte Ware; **~ case** Vitrine *f.* **(d)** *(visual ~: on calculator etc)* Anzeige *f.*
displease [dɪs'pliːz] *vt* mißfallen *(+dat),* nicht gefallen *(+dat).*
displeasure [dɪs'pleʒəʳ] *n* Mißfallen *nt (at* über *+acc).*
disposable [dɪ'spəʊzəbl] *adj* **(a)** *(to be thrown away)* Wegwerf-; *handkerchief, nappy also* Papier-; *bottle, syringe* Einweg-. **(b)** *(available)* verfügbar.
disposal [dɪ'spəʊzəl] *n* **(a)** *see* **dispose of (a)** Loswerden *nt;* Beseitigung *f;* Erledigung *f.* **(waste) ~ unit** Müllschlucker *m.* **(b) to be at sb's ~** jdm zur Verfügung stehen; **to put sth at sb's ~** jdm etw zur Verfügung stellen.
dispose [dɪ'spəʊz] *vt (form: arrange)* anorden; *troops* aufstellen. **to be well/ill ~d towards sb** jdm wohlwollen/übelwollen.
♦**dispose of** *vi +prep obj* **(a)** *(get rid of)* loswerden; *rubbish* beseitigen; *opponent, difficulties* aus dem Weg räumen; *matter* erledigen. **(b)** *(have at disposal) fortune, time* verfügen über *(+acc).*
disposition [ˌdɪspə'zɪʃən] *n (temperament)* Veranlagung *f.* **her cheerful/friendly ~** ihre fröhliche/freundliche Art.
dispossess ['dɪspə'zes] *vt* enteignen.
disproportionate [ˌdɪsprə'pɔːʃnɪt] *adj* **a ~ amount of money** ein unverhältnismäßig hoher/niedriger Geldbetrag.
disprove [dɪs'pruːv] *vt* widerlegen.
disputable [dɪ'spjuːtəbl] *adj* sehr zweifelhaft.
dispute [dɪ'spjuːt] **1** *vt* **(a)** *statement* bestreiten; *claim to sth, will* anfechten. **(b) the issue was hotly ~d** das Thema wurde heftig diskutiert. **(c)** *(contest) championship* jdm streitig machen. **2** *vi (argue)* streiten. **3** *n also* ['dɪspjuːt] **(a)** *no pl (arguing, controversy)* Disput *m,* Kontroverse *f.* **to be beyond ~** außer Frage stehen; **without ~** zweifellos; **to be open to ~** umstritten sein. **(b)** *(argument)* Streit *m; (debate)* Kontroverse *f.* **industrial ~** Arbeitskampf *m;* **to be in ~** *(on strike)* im Ausstand sein.
disqualification [dɪsˌkwɒlɪfɪ'keɪʃən] *n* **(a)** Ausschluß *m; (Sport also)* Disqualifikation *f.* **~ (from driving)** Führerscheinentzug *m.* **(b)** *(disqualifying factor)* Grund *m* zur Disqualifikation.
disqualify [dɪs'kwɒlɪfaɪ] *vt* ungeeignet machen *(from* für*); (Sport etc)* disqualifizieren. **to ~ sb from driving** jdm den Führerschein entziehen.
disquiet [dɪs'kwaɪət] *n* Unruhe *f.*
disregard ['dɪsrɪ'gɑːd] **1** *vt* ignorieren; *remark, feelings also* nicht beachten *(+acc); danger, advice, authority also* mißachten. **2** *n* Mißachtung *f (for gen); (for money)* Geringschätzung *f (for gen).*
disrepair ['dɪsrɪ'pɛəʳ] *n* Baufälligkeit *f.* **in a state of ~** baufällig; **to fall into ~** verfallen.
disreputable [dɪs'repjʊtəbl] *adj* verrufen, berüchtigt.
disrepute ['dɪsrɪ'pjuːt] *n* schlechter Ruf. **to bring sth into ~** etw in Verruf bringen; **to fall into ~** in Verruf kommen *or* geraten.
disrespect ['dɪsrɪs'pekt] *n* Respektlosigkeit *f (for* gegenüber*).*
disrespectful *adj* [ˌdɪsrɪs'pektfʊl] respektlos *(to* gegenüber*).*
disrupt [dɪs'rʌpt] *vt* stören; *train service, communications* unterbrechen.
disruption [dɪs'rʌpʃən] *n see vt* Störung *f;* Unterbrechung *f.*
disruptive [dɪs'rʌptɪv] *adj* störend.
dissatisfaction ['dɪsˌsætɪs'fækʃən] *n* Unzufriedenheit *f.*
dissatisfied [dɪs'sætɪsfaɪd] *adj* unzufrieden.
dissect [dɪ'sekt] *vt plant* präparieren; *animal also* sezieren.
dissection [dɪ'sekʃən] *n see vt* Präparieren *nt;* Sezieren *nt.*
disseminate [dɪ'semɪneɪt] *vt* verbreiten.
dissension [dɪ'senʃən] *n* Meinungsverschiedenheit, Differenz *f.*
dissent [dɪ'sent] **1** *vi* anderer Meinung sein, differieren *(geh).* **2** *n* Meinungsverschiedenheit *f.* **to voice/express one's ~ (with sth)** erklären, daß man (mit etw) nicht übereinstimmt.
dissenter [dɪ'sentəʳ] *n* Abweichler(in *f*) *m.*
dissertation [ˌdɪsə'teɪʃən] *n* wissenschaftliche Arbeit; *(PhD)* Dissertation *f.*
disservice [dɪs'sɜːvɪs] *n* **to do sb a ~** jdm einen schlechten Dienst erweisen.
dissident ['dɪsɪdənt] **1** *n* Dissident(in *f*), Regimekritiker(in *f*) *m.* **2** *adj* regimekritisch.
dissimilar ['dɪ'sɪmɪləʳ] *adj* verschieden *(to* von*).*
dissimilarity [ˌdɪsɪmɪ'lærɪtɪ] *n* Verschiedenheit *f.*
dissipate ['dɪsɪpeɪt] *vt* **(a)** *doubts, fears* zerstreuen. **(b)** *energy, fortune* verschwenden.
dissipated ['dɪsɪpeɪtɪd] *adj behaviour, society* zügellos; *person also* leichtlebig; *(in appearance)* verlebt; *life* ausschweifend.
dissipation [ˌdɪsɪ'peɪʃən] *n see vt* **(a)** Zerstreuung *f.* **(b)** Verschwendung *f.* **(c)** *(debauchery)* Ausschweifung *f.*
dissociate [dɪ'səʊʃɪeɪt] *vt* trennen. **to ~ oneself from sb/sth** sich von jdm/etw distanzieren.
dissolute ['dɪsəluːt] *adj person* zügellos; *way of life also* ausschweifend; *appearance* verlebt.

dissolution [ˌdɪsəˈluːʃən] *n* Auflösung *f*.
dissolve [dɪˈzɒlv] **1** *vt* auflösen. **2** *vi* sich (auf)lösen; *(fig)* sich in nichts auflösen. **it ~s in water** es ist wasserlöslich.
dissuade [dɪˈsweɪd] *vt* **to ~ sb from doing sth** jdn davon abbringen, etw zu tun.
distance [ˈdɪstəns] *n* Entfernung *f; (gap, interval)* Abstand *m; (distance covered)* Strecke *f*, Weg *m*. **at a ~ of two metres** in zwei Meter(n) Entfernung; **what's the ~ from London to Glasgow?** wie weit ist es von London nach Glasgow?; **in the (far) ~** (ganz) in der Ferne, (ganz) weit weg; **he admired her at a ~** *(fig)* er bewunderte sie aus der Ferne; **it's within walking ~** es ist zu Fuß erreichbar; **it's no ~** es ist überhaupt nicht weit; **seen from a ~ it looks different** von weitem sieht das ganz anders aus; **quite a ~ (away)** ziemlich weit (entfernt); **the fight went the ~** der Kampf ging über alle Runden; **to go the ~** durchhalten; **to keep one's ~** *(lit, fig)* auf Distanz bleiben; **at this ~ in time** nach einem so langen Zeitraum; **to keep sb at a ~** jdn auf Distanz halten.
distance: ~ event *n* Langstreckenlauf *m*; **~ runner** *n* Langstreckenläufer(in *f*) *m*.
distant [ˈdɪstənt] *adj* **(a)** *country* weit entfernt, fern. **we had a ~ view of the church** wir sahen in der Ferne die Kirche. **(b)** *(with time) age* fern, weit zurückliegend; *recollection* entfernt. **that was in the ~ past** das liegt weit zurück; **in the ~ future** in ferner Zukunft. **(c)** *relationship, likeness, cousin* entfernt. **(d)** *(fig: aloof) person, manner* distanziert, reserviert.
distaste [dɪsˈteɪst] *n* Widerwille *m (for* gegen).
distasteful [dɪsˈteɪstfʊl] *adj task* unangenehm; *photo, magazine* geschmacklos. **to be ~ to sb** jdm zuwider *or* unangenehm sein.
distemper[1] [dɪsˈtempəʳ] *n (paint)* Temperfarbe *f*.
distemper[2] *n (Vet)* Staupe *f*.
distend [dɪˈstend] **1** *vt sails, stomach* (auf)blähen. **2** *vi* sich blähen.
distil, *(US)* distill [dɪˈstɪl] *vt (Chem)* destillieren; *whisky etc also* brennen.
distiller [dɪˈstɪləʳ] *n* Destillateur, (Branntwein)brenner *m*.
distillery [dɪˈstɪlərɪ] *n* (Branntwein)brennerei *f*.
distinct [dɪˈstɪŋkt] *adj* **(a)** deutlich, klar; *landmark, shape also* klar erkennbar; *accent, likeness also* ausgeprägt. **I had the ~ feeling that ...** ich hatte das bestimmte Gefühl, daß ... **(b)** *(different)* verschieden; *(separate)* getrennt. **as ~ from** im Unterschied zu.
distinction [dɪˈstɪŋkʃən] *n* **(a)** *(difference)* Unterschied *m; (act of distinguishing)* Unterscheidung *f*. **to make a ~ (between two things)** (zwischen zwei Dingen) einen Unterschied machen. **(b)** *no pl (preeminence)* **to win ~** sich hervortun *or* auszeichnen; **a pianist of ~** ein Pianist von Rang. **(c)** *(Sch, Univ: grade)* **he got a ~ in French** er hat das Französischexamen mit Auszeichnung bestanden.
distinctive [dɪˈstɪŋktɪv] *adj colour, plumage* auffällig; *(unmistakable)* unverkennbar; *characteristic, feature* besondere(s).
distinctly [dɪˈstɪŋktlɪ] *adv* deutlich; *prefer also, rude* ausgesprochen; *better* entschieden.
distinguish [dɪˈstɪŋgwɪʃ] **1** *vt* **(a)** unterscheiden. **(b)** *(make out) landmark, shape* erkennen. **2** *vi* **to ~ between** unterscheiden zwischen *(+dat)*. **3** *vr* **to ~ oneself** sich auszeichnen.
distinguished [dɪˈstɪŋgwɪʃt] *adj* **(a)** *(eminent) pianist, scholar* von hohem Rang; *career* hervorragend. **(b)** *(refined, elegant) person, manner* distinguiert *(geh)*, vornehm.
distinguishing [dɪˈstɪŋgwɪʃɪŋ] *adj* kennzeichnend, charakteristisch. **the ~ feature of his work is ...** was seine Arbeit kennzeichnet, ist ...
distort [dɪˈstɔːt] *vt* verzerren; *truth, words* verdrehen.
distortion [dɪˈstɔːʃən] *n see vt* Verzerrung *f*; Verdrehung *f*.
distract [dɪˈstrækt] *vt* ablenken.
distracted [dɪˈstræktɪd] *adj (worried)* besorgt, beunruhigt; *(distraught)* außer sich *(with* vor *+dat)*.
distraction [dɪˈstrækʃən] *n* **(a)** *(from work etc)* Ablenkung *f*. **(b)** *(entertainment)* Zerstreuung *f*. **(c)** *(anxiety)* Ruhelosigkeit, Unruhe *f*; *(distraughtness)* Verstörtheit *f*. **to drive sb to ~** jdn wahnsinnig machen.
distraught [dɪˈstrɔːt] *adj* verzweifelt.
distress [dɪˈstres] **1** *n* **(a)** *(physical)* Leiden *nt*; *(mental)* Kummer *m*, Sorge *f*. **to be in great ~** sehr leiden. **(b)** *(danger)* **a ship/plane in ~** ein Schiff in Seenot/ein Flugzeug in Not; **~ signal** Notsignal *nt*. **2** *vt* Sorge bereiten *(+dat)*. **please don't ~ yourself** machen Sie sich *(dat)* bitte keine Sorgen!
distressed [dɪˈstrest] *adj (upset)* bekümmert; *(grief-stricken)* verzweifelt *(about* über *+acc)*.
distressing [dɪˈstresɪŋ] *adj (upsetting)* besorgniserregend; *(stronger)* erschütternd.
distribute [dɪˈstrɪbjuːt] *vt* verteilen; *(Comm) goods* vertreiben.
distribution [ˌdɪstrɪˈbjuːʃən] *n see vt* Verteilung *f*; Vertrieb *m*.
distributor [dɪˈstrɪbjʊtəʳ] *n* Verteiler *m (also Aut)*; *(Comm)* Großhändler *m*.
district [ˈdɪstrɪkt] *n* Gegend *f; (of town also)* Viertel *nt; (administrative)* (Verwaltungs)bezirk *m*.
district: ~ attorney *n (US)* Bezirksstaatsanwalt *m*; **~ council** *n (Brit)* Bezirksrat *m*; **~ manager** *n* Bezirksleiter *m*; **~ nurse** *n* Gemeindeschwester *f*.
distrust [dɪsˈtrʌst] **1** *vt* mißtrauen *(+dat)*. **2** *n* Mißtrauen *nt (of* gegenüber*)*.
distrustful [dɪsˈtrʌstfʊl] *adj* mißtrauisch *(of* gegenüber*)*.
disturb [dɪˈstɜːb] **1** *vt* **(a)** stören. **(b)** *(alarm) person* beunruhigen. **(c)** *waters* bewegen; *sediment* aufwirbeln; *papers* durcheinanderbringen. **2** *vi* **"please do not ~"** „bitte nicht stören".
disturbance [dɪˈstɜːbəns] *n* **(a)** *(political)* Unruhe *f; (in pub, street)* (Ruhe)störung *f*. **to cause a ~** eine Ruhestörung verursachen. **(b)** *(in work, routine)* Störung *f*.
disturbed [dɪˈstɜːbd] *adj* **(a)** *(mentally)* geistig gestört; *(socially)* verhaltensgestört. **(b)** *(worried)* beunruhigt *(at, by* über *+acc*, von*)*.
disturbing [dɪˈstɜːbɪŋ] *adj (alarming)* beunruhigend; *(distracting)* störend. **some viewers may find these scenes ~** einige Zuschauer könnten an diesen Szenen Anstoß nehmen.
disuse [ˈdɪsˈjuːs] *n* **to fall into ~** nicht mehr benutzt werden.
disused [ˈdɪsˈjuːzd] *adj building* leerstehend; *mine, railway line* stillgelegt.
ditch [dɪtʃ] **1** *n* Graben *m*. **2** *vt (col: get rid of) person* loswerden; *boyfriend* abservieren *(col)*; *project* fallenlassen.
dither [ˈdɪðəʳ] **1** *n* **to be all of a ~** ganz aufgeregt sein. **2** *vi* zaudern, schwanken.
ditto [ˈdɪtəʊ] *n* **I'd like coffee — ~ (for me)** *(col)* ich möchte Kaffee — ich auch.
ditty [ˈdɪtɪ] *n* Liedchen *nt*.
divan [dɪˈvæn] *n* Diwan *m*. **~ bed** Liege *f*.
dive [daɪv] *(vb: pret* **~d** *or (US)* **dove**, *ptp* **~d)** **1** *n* **(a)** *(by swimmer)* Sprung *m; (by plane)* Sturzflug *m; (Ftbl)* Hechtsprung *m*. **the deepest ~ yet made** die bisher größte Tauchtiefe; **to make a ~ for sth** *(fig col)* sich auf etw *(acc)* stürzen; **the dollar took a ~** *(col)* der Dollar sackte ab *(col)*. **(b)** *(pej col: club etc)* Spelunke *f (col)*. **2** *vi* **(a)** *(person)* springen; *(under water)* tauchen; *(submarine)* untertauchen; *(plane)* einen Sturzflug machen; *(goalkeeper etc)* hechten. **to ~**

for pearls nach Perlen tauchen. **(b)** *(col)* **he ~d into the crowd/under the table** er verschwand blitzschnell in der Menge/unter dem Tisch; **to ~ for cover** blitzschnell in Deckung gehen; **he ~d under the sheets** er machte einen Satz unter die Decke.

dive: ~-bomb *vt* im Sturzflug bombardieren; **~-bomber** *n* Sturzkampfbomber, Stuka *m.*

diver ['daɪvəʳ] *n (also bird)* Taucher *m*; *(off high board)* Turmspringer(in *f*) *m*; *(off springboard)* Kunstspringer(in *f*) *m.*

diverge [daɪ'vɜːdʒ] *vi* abweichen *(from* von*)*; *(two things)* auseinandergehen.

divergence [daɪ'vɜːdʒəns] *n* Abweichung *f.*

divergent [daɪ'vɜːdʒənt] *adj opinions etc* auseinandergehend.

diverse [daɪ'vɜːs] *adj* verschieden(artig).

diversify [daɪ'vɜːsɪfaɪ] **1** *vt* abwechslungsreich(er) gestalten; *business etc* diversifizieren *(Comm)*. **2** *vi (Comm)* diversifizieren.

diversion [daɪ'vɜːʃən] *n* **(a)** *(of stream, esp Brit: of traffic)* Umleitung *f.* **(b)** *(relaxation)* Unterhaltung *f.* **(c)** *(Mil, fig)* Ablenkung *f.* **to create a ~** ablenken.

diversity [daɪ'vɜːsɪtɪ] *n* Vielfalt *f.*

divert [daɪ'vɜːt] *vt* **(a)** *traffic, stream* umleiten; *attention* ablenken; *conversation* in eine andere Richtung lenken; *blow* abwenden. **(b)** *(amuse)* unterhalten.

divide [dɪ'vaɪd] **1** *vt* **(a)** *(separate)* trennen. **(b)** *(split into parts: also ~* **up***)* *money, work* teilen *(into* in *+acc)*; *(in order to distribute)* aufteilen. **(c)** *(Math)* dividieren, teilen *(by* durch*)*. **what is 12 ~d by 3?** wieviel ist 12 (geteilt) durch 3? **2** *vi* **(a)** *(river, road, cells)* sich teilen. **to ~ into groups** sich in Gruppen aufteilen. **(b)** *(Brit Parl)* **the House ~d** das Parlament stimmte durch Hammelsprung ab.

♦ **divide off** *vt sep* (ab)trennen.

♦ **divide out** *vt sep* aufteilen *(among* unter *+acc or dat)*.

divided [dɪ'vaɪdɪd] *adj* geteilt. **~ highway** *(US)* Schnellstraße *f*; **a people ~ against itself** ein gespaltenes Volk.

dividend ['dɪvɪdend] *n (Fin)* Dividende *f.* **to pay ~s** *(fig)* sich bezahlt machen.

dividers [dɪ'vaɪdəz] *npl* Stechzirkel *m.*

dividing [dɪ'vaɪdɪŋ] *adj* **~ wall** Trennwand *f*; **~ line** *(lit, fig)* Trennungslinie *f.*

divine [dɪ'vaɪn] **1** *adj (Rel)* göttlich; *(fig col)* bezaubernd. **2** *vt* **(a)** *the future* weissagen, prophezeien; *sb's intentions* erahnen. **(b)** *water, metal* aufspüren.

diving ['daɪvɪŋ] *n (under water)* Tauchen *nt*; *(into water)* Springen *nt*; *(Sport)* Wasserspringen *nt.*

diving: ~-bell *n* Taucherglocke *f*; **~-board** *n* Sprungbrett *nt*; **~-suit** *n* Taucheranzug *m.*

divinity [dɪ'vɪnɪtɪ] *n* **(a)** *(divine being)* Gottheit *f.* **(b)** *(Sch)* Religion *f.*

divisible [dɪ'vɪzəbl] *adj* teilbar *(by* durch*)*.

division [dɪ'vɪʒən] *n* **(a)** Teilung *f*; *(Math)* Teilen *nt*, Division *f.* **the ~ of labour** die Arbeitsteilung. **(b)** *(Mil)* Division *f.* **(c)** *(in administration)* Abteilung *f.* **(d)** *(in room)* Trennwand *f*; *(fig: between social classes etc)* Schranke *f*; *(dividing line: lit, fig)* Trennungslinie *f.* **(e)** *(fig: discord)* Uneinigkeit *f.* **(f)** *(Brit Parl)* Abstimmung *f* durch Hammelsprung. **(g)** *(Sport)* Liga *f.*

divisive [dɪ'vaɪsɪv] *adj* **to be ~** Uneinigkeit schaffen.

divorce [dɪ'vɔːs] **1** *n* Scheidung *f (from* von*)*; *(fig)* Trennung *f.* **he wants a ~** er will sich scheiden lassen; **to get a ~ (from sb)** sich (von jdm) scheiden lassen. **2** *vt* **(a)** sich scheiden lassen von. **to get ~d** sich scheiden lassen. **(b)** *(fig)* trennen.

divorced [dɪ'vɔːst] *adj* geschieden *(from* von*)*.

divorcee [dɪˌvɔː'siː] *n* geschiedener Mann, geschiedene Frau. **he is a ~** er ist geschieden.

divulge [daɪ'vʌldʒ] *vt* preisgeben *(sth to sb* jdm etw*)*.

DIY = **do-it-yourself.**

dizziness ['dɪzɪnɪs] *n* Schwindel *m.*

dizzy ['dɪzɪ] *adj (+er)* **(a)** *(lit, fig) person* schwind(e)lig; *height* schwindelerregend. **~ spell** Schwindelanfall *m*; **I feel ~** mir ist schwindlig. **(b)** *(col: foolish)* verrückt.

DJ = **dinner jacket; disc jockey.**

do [duː] *(vb: pret* **did**, *ptp* **done***)* **1** *aux* **(a)** **~ you understand?** verstehen Sie?; **I ~ not** *or* **don't understand** ich verstehe nicht; **didn't you know?, did you not know?** haben Sie das nicht gewußt?

(b) *(for emphasis: with stress on do)* **~ come!** kommen Sie doch (bitte)!; **~ shut up!** (nun) sei doch (endlich) ruhig!; **~ I remember him!** und ob ich mich an ihn erinnere!; **but I ~ like it** aber es gefällt mir wirklich; **so you ~ know them!** Sie kennen sie also tatsächlich!; *(and were lying etc)* Sie kennen sie also doch!

(c) *(used to avoid repeating vb)* **you speak better than I ~** Sie sprechen besser als ich; **he likes cheese and so ~ I** er ißt gern Käse und ich auch; **neither ~ I** ich auch nicht.

(d) *(in question tags)* oder. **you know him, don't you?** Sie kennen ihn doch, oder?; **he didn't go, did he?** er ist (doch) nicht gegangen, oder?

(e) *(in answers: replacing vb)* **do you see them often? — yes, I ~/no, I don't** sehen Sie sie oft? — ja/nein; **they speak French — oh, ~ they?** sie sprechen Französisch — ja?, wirklich?; **may I come in? — ~!** darf ich hereinkommen? — ja, bitte; **shall I open the window? — no, don't!** soll ich das Fenster öffnen? — nein, bitte nicht!

2 *vt* **(a)** tun, machen; *puzzle, housework, military service, translation, film* machen. **what are you ~ing on Saturday?** was machen Sie am Sonnabend?; **I've got nothing to ~** ich habe nichts zu tun; **are you ~ing anything this evening?** haben Sie heute abend schon etwas vor?; **what shall we ~ for money?** wo kriegen wir jetzt (das) Geld her?; **we'll have to ~ something about this** wir müssen da etwas unternehmen; **how do you ~ it?** wie macht man das?; *(in amazement)* wie machen Sie das bloß?; **what's to be done?** was ist da zu tun?; **what can you ~?** was kann man da machen?; **sorry, it can't be done** tut mir leid, es läßt sich nicht machen; **what can I ~ for you?** was kann ich für Sie tun?; *(by shop assistant also)* was darf's sein?; **can you ~ it by yourself?** schaffst du das allein?; **what do you want me to ~ (about it)?** und was soll ich da tun *or* machen?; **Brecht doesn't ~ anything for me** Brecht sagt mir nichts; **that's done it** *(col)* da haben wir's, da haben wir die Bescherung; **that does it!** jetzt reicht's mir!; **now what have you done!** was hast du jetzt wieder angestellt?; **we don't ~ lunches** wir haben keinen Mittagstisch.

(b) *(arrange, fix etc)* **to ~ the flowers** die Blumen arrangieren; **to ~ one's hair** sich *(dat)* die Haare machen *(col)*; **who does your hair?** zu welchem Friseur gehen Sie?; **to ~ one's nails** sich *(dat)* die Nägel schneiden *or (varnish)* lackieren; **you ~ the painting and I'll ~ the papering** du streichst und ich tapeziere; **I'll ~ the talking** ich übernehme das Reden.

(c) *(Sch etc: study)* **we've done Milton** wir haben Milton durchgenommen; **I've never done any German** ich habe nie Deutsch gelernt.

(d) *(in pret, ptp only: complete, accomplish)* **the work's done now** die Arbeit ist gemacht *or* getan *or* fertig; **what's done cannot be undone** was geschehen ist, kann man nicht ungeschehen machen; **done!** abgemacht!

(e) *(visit) city, museum* besuchen; *(take in also)* mitnehmen *(col)*.

(f) *(Aut etc)* schaffen, machen *(col)*. **this car does 130** das Auto schafft *or* macht *(col)* 130; **we did London to Edinburgh in 8 hours** wir haben es in 8 Stunden von London bis Edinburgh geschafft.

(g) *(be suitable)* passen *(sb* jdm*)*; *(be sufficient for)* reichen *(sb* jdm*)*. **that will ~ me nicely** *(enough)* das reicht dicke *(col)*; *(just right)* das paßt mir gut.

(h) *(take off, mimic)* nachmachen.

(i) *(col: cheat)* übers Ohr hauen *(col)*.

(j) *(Cook)* machen *(col)*. **to ~ the cooking/food** kochen; **how do you like your steak done?** wie möchten Sie Ihr Steak?; **well done** durch(gebraten).

(k) *(col: in prison) 6 years* (ab)sitzen.

3 *vi* **(a)** *(act)* **~ as I ~** mach es wie ich; **he did well to take advice** er tat gut daran, sich beraten zu lassen. **(b)** *(get on, fare)* **how are you ~ing?** wie geht's (Ihnen)?; **the patient is ~ing very well** dem Patienten geht es recht ordentlich; **he's ~ing well at school** er ist gut in der Schule; **his business is ~ing well** sein Geschäft geht gut. **(c)** *(finish)* **the meat, is it done?** ist das Fleisch fertig *or* durch?; **have you done?** sind Sie endlich fertig? **(d)** *(suit, be convenient)* gehen. **that will never ~!** das geht nicht!; **this room will ~** das Zimmer ist in Ordnung; **will she/it ~?** geht die/das?; **this coat will ~ as a cover** dieser Mantel muß als Decke herhalten; **you'll have to make ~ with £10** Sie werden mit £ 10 auskommen müssen. **(e)** *(be sufficient)* reichen. **will £1 ~?** reicht £ 1?; **yes, that'll ~** ja, das reicht; **that'll ~!** jetzt reicht's aber! **(f)** *(col: char)* putzen *(for* bei*)*.

4 *n (col)* **(a)** Veranstaltung *f*; *(party)* Fete *f (col)*. **(b)** *(in phrases)* **it's a poor ~!** *(col)* das ist ja ein schwaches Bild! *(col)*; **the ~s and don'ts** was man wissen sollte; *(for behaviour)* Verhaltensregeln *pl*; **fair ~s all round** *(col)* gleiches Recht für alle.

♦ **do away with** *vi +prep obj* **(a)** *custom, law* abschaffen; *building* abreißen. **(b)** *(kill)* umbringen.

♦ **do by** *vi +prep obj* **to ~ well/badly ~ sb** jdn gut/schlecht behandlen.

♦ **do for** *vi +prep obj (col: finish off) person* fertigmachen *(col)*; *project* zunichte machen. **to be done ~** *(person)* erledigt *or* fertig *(col)* sein; *(project)* gestorben sein *(col)*.

♦ **do in** *vt sep (col)* **(a)** *(kill)* um die Ecke bringen *(col)*. **(b) to be done ~** *(exhausted)* fertig sein *(col)*.

♦ **do out** *vt sep* **(a)** *room* auskehren. **(b) to ~ sb ~ of a job/£100** jdn um eine Stelle/£ 100 bringen.

♦ **do up 1** *vi (dress etc)* zugemacht werden. **2** *vt sep* **(a)** *(fasten)* zumachen. **(b)** *(parcel together) goods* zusammenpacken. **to ~ sth ~ in a parcel** etw einpacken. **(c)** *house, room* renovieren. **to ~ oneself ~** sich zurechtmachen.

♦ **do with** *vi +prep obj* **(a)** *(with can or could: need)* brauchen. **it could ~ ~ a clean** es müßte mal saubergemacht werden. **(b) what has that got to ~ ~ it?** was hat das damit zu tun?; **that has nothing to ~ ~ you!** das geht Sie gar nichts an!; **it's to ~ ~ this letter you sent** es geht um den Brief, den Sie geschickt haben; **money has a lot to ~ ~ it** Geld spielt eine große Rolle dabei. **(c) what have you done ~ my gloves/your face?** was haben Sie mit meinen Handschuhen/Ihrem Gesicht gemacht? **(d) he doesn't know what to ~ ~ himself** er weiß nicht, was er mit sich anfangen soll. **(e) to be done ~ sb/sth** *(finished)* mit jdm/etw fertig sein.

♦ **do without** *vi +prep obj* auskommen ohne. **I can ~ ~ your advice** Sie können sich Ihre Ratschläge sparen; **I could have done ~ that!** das hätte mir (wirklich) erspart bleiben können; **you'll have to ~ ~** Sie müssen so zurechtkommen.

docile ['dəʊsaɪl] *adj* sanftmütig; *horse* fromm; *(pej) engine* schwach.

dock[1] [dɒk] **1** *n* Dock *nt*; *(for berthing)* Pier, Kai *m*. **~s** *pl* Hafen *m*. **2** *vt* docken; *(Space also)* ankoppeln. **3** *vi (Naut)* anlegen; *(Space)* ankoppeln.

dock[2] *n (Jur)* Anklagebank *f*.

dock[3] *vt* **(a)** *dog's tail* kupieren; *horse's tail* stutzen. **(b)** *wages* kürzen.

docker ['dɒkəʳ] *n (Brit)* Hafenarbeiter, Docker *m*.

docket ['dɒkɪt] *n (on parcel etc)* Warenbegleitschein *m*.

docking ['dɒkɪŋ] *n (Space)* Ankoppelung *f*.

dockyard ['dɒkjɑːd] *n* Werft *f*.

doctor ['dɒktəʳ] **1** *n* **(a)** *(Med)* Arzt *m*, Ärztin *f*. **D~ Smith** Dr. Schmidt; **it's just what the ~ ordered** *(fig col)* das ist genau das richtige. **(b)** *(Univ etc)* Doktor *m*. **Dear Dr Smith** Sehr geehrter Herr Dr./Sehr geehrte Frau Dr. Smith. **2** *vt* **(a)** *(col: castrate)* kastrieren. **(b)** *(tamper with) accounts* frisieren; *text, document* verfälschen. **the wine's been ~ed** dem Wein ist etwas beigemischt worden.

doctorate ['dɒktərɪt] *n* Doktortitel *m*; *see* **PhD.**

doctrinaire [ˌdɒktrɪ'nɛəʳ] *adj* doktrinär.

doctrine ['dɒktrɪn] *n* Doktrin, Lehre *f*.

document ['dɒkjʊmənt] **1** *n* Papier *nt*; *(certificate)* Dokument *nt*, Urkunde *f*. **2** *vt* belegen.

documentary [ˌdɒkjʊ'mentərɪ] *n* Dokumentarfilm *m*.

documentation [ˌdɒkjʊmen'teɪʃən] *n* Dokumentation *f*.

dodderer ['dɒdərəʳ] *n (col)* Tattergreis *(col) m*.

doddery ['dɒdərɪ] *adj* tatterig *(col)*. **the ~ old fool** *(col)* der vertrottelte alte Opa *(col)*.

dodge [dɒdʒ] **1** *n (trick)* Trick, Kniff *m*. **to be up to all the ~s** mit allen Wassern gewaschen sein; **a tax ~** ein Steuertrick. **2** *vt blow, question* ausweichen *(+dat)*; *tax* umgehen; *(shirk) work, military service* sich drücken vor *(+dat)*. **to ~ the issue** dem Problem ausweichen. **3** *vi* **to ~ out of the way** zur Seite springen; *(to escape notice)* blitzschnell verschwinden; **to ~ through the traffic** sich durch den Verkehr schlängeln.

dodgem ['dɒdʒəm] *n (Brit)* (Auto)skooter *m*.

dodgy ['dɒdʒɪ] *adj (+er) (Brit col: tricky) situation* vertrackt *(col)*; *(dubious)* zweifelhaft; *engine* defekt; *translation, spelling* fehlerhaft.

doe [dəʊ] *n (roe deer)* Ricke *f*; *(red deer)* Hirschkuh *f*; *(rabbit)* Weibchen *nt*.

does [dʌz] *3rd pers sing of* **do.**

doesn't ['dʌznt] = **does not.**

doff [dɒf] *vt hat* ziehen, lüften.

dog [dɒg] **1** *n* **(a)** Hund *m*. **(b)** *(fig phrases)* **it's a ~'s life** es ist ein Hundeleben; **to go to the ~s** vor die Hunde gehen *(col)*; **~ in the manger** Spielverderber(in *f*) *m*; **~-in-the-manger attitude** mißgünstige Einstellung; **every ~ has his day** jeder hat einmal Glück; **you can't teach an old ~ new tricks** der Mensch ist ein Gewohnheitstier; **~'s breakfast** *(fig col)* Schlamassel *m (col)*. **(c)** *(male fox, wolf)* Rüde *m*. **(d)** *(col: man)* **lucky ~** Glückspilz *m*; **dirty ~** gemeiner Hund; **sly ~** gerissener Hund *(col)*. **2** *vt* **to ~ sb's footsteps** jdm hart auf den Fersen sein/bleiben; **~ged by misfortune** vom Pech verfolgt.

dog: ~ biscuit *n* Hundekuchen *m*; **~-collar** *n (lit)* Hundehalsband *nt*; *(vicar's) steifer, hoher Kragen*; **~-eared** ['dɒgɪəd] *adj* mit Eselsohren; **~fight** *n (Aviat)* Luftkampf *m*; **~fish** *n* Hundshai *m*; **~ food** *n* Hundefutter *nt*.

dogged ['dɒgɪd] *adj* beharrlich, zäh.

doggerel ['dɒgərəl] *n* Knittelvers *m*.

doggie bag ['dɒgɪˌbæg] *n* Tüte *f für Essensreste, die nach Hause mitgenommen werden.*

doggo ['dɒgəʊ] *adv (col)*: **to lie ~** sich nicht mucksen *(col)*.

dog house *n* **he's in the ~** *(col)* er ist in Ungnade; *(with wife)* bei ihm hängt der Haussegen schief.

dogma ['dɒgmə] *n* Dogma *nt.*
dogmatic [dɒg'mætɪk] *adj* dogmatisch *(about* in *+dat).*
do-gooder ['duː'gʊdəʳ] *n (pej)* Weltverbesserer *m.*
dogsbody ['dɒgzbɒdɪ] *n* **she's/he's the general** ~ sie/er ist Mädchen für alles.
dog: ~ **tag** *n (US Mil col)* Hundemarke *(col) f;* **~-tired** *adj* hundemüde.
doing ['duːɪŋ] *n* **this is your** ~ das ist dein Werk; **that takes some** ~ da gehört (schon) etwas dazu; **~s** *pl* Taten *pl.*
doings ['duːɪŋz] *n sing (Brit col)* Dingsbums *nt (col).*
do-it-yourself ['duːɪtjə'self] **1** *adj shop* Bastler-, Hobby-. **2** *n* Heimwerken, Do-it-yourself *nt.*
doldrums ['dɒldrəmz] *npl* **to be in the** ~ Trübsal blasen; *(business etc)* in einer Flaute stecken.
dole [dəʊl] *n (Brit col)* Arbeitslosenunterstützung *f.* **to go/be on the** ~ stempeln (gehen).
♦ **dole out** *vt sep* austeilen, verteilen.
doleful ['dəʊlfʊl] *adj* traurig.
doll [dɒl] *n* **(a)** Puppe *f.* **~'s house** Puppenhaus *nt.* **(b)** *(esp US col: girl)* Mädchen *nt; (pretty girl)* Puppe *f (col).*
♦ **doll up** *vt sep (col)* **to** ~ **oneself** ~, **to get** ~**ed** ~ sich herausputzen *or* aufdonnern *(col).*
dollar ['dɒləʳ] *n* Dollar *m.*
dollop ['dɒləp] *n (col)* Schlag *m (col).*
dolly-bird ['dɒlɪbɜːd] *n (col)* Puppe *f (col).*
dolphin ['dɒlfɪn] *n* Delphin *m.*
dolt [dəʊlt] *n* Tölpel *m.*
domain [dəʊ'meɪn] *n* **(a)** *(estate)* Gut *nt; (belonging to state, Crown)* Domäne *f.* **(b)** *(fig)* Domäne *f.*
dome [dəʊm] *n (Archit)* Kuppel *f; (of heaven, skull)* Gewölbe *nt.*
domed [dəʊmd] *adj forehead* gewölbt.
domestic [də'mestɪk] *adj* **(a)** *bliss, life* häuslich. **(b)** *policy* Innen-; *news* Inland-, aus dem Inland; *produce* einheimisch; *trade* Binnen-; *flight* Inlands-. **(c)** *animal* Haus-.
domesticate [də'mestɪkeɪt] *vt* zähmen; *(house-train)* stubenrein machen.
domesticated [də'mestɪkeɪtɪd] *adj* zahm; *cat, dog* stubenrein. **she's very** ~ sie ist sehr häuslich.
domestic science *n* Hauswirtschaftslehre *f.*
domicile ['dɒmɪsaɪl] *n (Admin)* Wohnsitz *m.*
dominance ['dɒmɪnəns] *n* Vorherrschaft, Dominanz *f (also Biol) (over* über *+acc).*
dominant ['dɒmɪnənt] **1** *adj* beherrschend, dominierend; *feature also* hervorstechend; *gene, (Mus)* dominant. **2** *n (Mus)* Dominante *f.*
dominate ['dɒmɪneɪt] **1** *vi* dominieren. **2** *vt* beherrschen; *(species, gene)* dominieren.
domination [ˌdɒmɪ'neɪʃən] *n* (Vor)herrschaft *f.*
domineer [ˌdɒmɪ'nɪəʳ] *vi* tyrannisieren *(over sb* jdn*).*
domineering [ˌdɒmɪ'nɪərɪŋ] *adj* herrisch; *mother-in-law, husband etc also* herrschsüchtig.
dominion [də'mɪnɪən] *n* **(a)** *no pl* Herrschaft *f (over* über *+acc).* **(b)** *(territory)* Herrschaftsgebiet *nt; (Brit Pol)* Dominion *nt.*
don[1] [dɒn] *n (Brit Univ)* Universitätsdozent *m.*
don[2] *vt garment* anziehen.
donate [dəʊ'neɪt] *vt* spenden.
donation [dəʊ'neɪʃən] *n* Spende *f; (large scale)* Stiftung *f.*
done [dʌn] **1** *ptp of* **do. 2** *adj* **(a)** *(finished) work* erledigt; *(cooked) vegetables* gar; *meat* durch. **to get sth** ~ *(finished)* etw fertigkriegen. **(b) it's not the** ~ **thing** das tut man nicht.
donkey ['dɒŋkɪ] *n* Esel *m.* **~'s years** *(col)* eine Ewigkeit.
donkey: ~ **jacket** *n dicke (gefütterte) Jacke;* **~work** *n* Routinearbeit, Dreckarbeit *(pej) f.*
donor ['dəʊnəʳ] *n (Med)* Spender(in *f*) *m.*
don't [dəʊnt] = **do not.**
donut ['dəʊnʌt] *n (esp US)* = **doughnut.**
doodle ['duːdl] **1** *vti* kritzeln. **2** *n* Gekritzel *nt.*
doom [duːm] **1** *n (fate)* Schicksal *nt; (ruin)* Verhängnis *nt.* **2** *vt* verurteilen, verdammen. **to be** ~**ed** verloren sein; **the project was** ~**ed from the start** das Vorhaben war von Anfang an zum Scheitern verurteilt.
doomsday ['duːmzdeɪ] *n* der Jüngste Tag. **otherwise we'll be here till** ~ *(col)* sonst sind wir in zwanzig Jahren noch hier.
door [dɔːʳ] *n* **(a)** Tür *f; (entrance: to cinema etc)* Eingang *m.* **was that the** ~**?** hat es geklingelt/geklopft?; **to pay at the** ~ *(Theat etc)* an der Kasse zahlen; **he lives three** ~**s away** er wohnt drei Häuser weiter. **(b)** *(phrases)* **to lay sth at sb's** ~ jdm etw anlasten; **to leave the** ~ **open for further negotiations** die Tür für weitere Verhandlungen offen lassen; **to open the** ~ **to sth** einer Sache *(dat)* Tür und Tor öffnen; **to show sb the** ~ jdm die Tür weisen; **out of** ~**s** im Freien.
door *in cpds* Tür-; **~bell** *n* Türklingel *f;* ~ **knob** *n* Türklinke *f;* **~keeper,** ~**man** *n* Portier *m;* **~mat** *n* Fußmatte *f; (fig)* Fußabtreter *m;* **~nail** *n:* **as dead as a** ~**nail** mausetot; **~post** *n* **deaf as a** ~**post** stocktaub; **~step** *n* (Tür)schwelle *f;* **on my** ~**step** *(fig)* direkt vor meiner Tür; **~-to-~** *adj* **(a)** ~**-to-~ salesman** Vertreter *m;* **(b)** *delivery* ins Haus; **~way** *n (of room)* Tür *f; (of building, shop)* Eingang *m.*
dope [dəʊp] **1** *n* **(a)** *no pl (col: drugs)* Stoff *m (col),* Dope *nt (col); (Sport)* Aufputschmittel *nt.* **(b)** *no pl (col: information)* Information(en *pl*) *f.* **(c)** *(col: stupid person)* Esel *m (col).* **2** *vt* dopen.
dopey, dopy ['dəʊpɪ] *adj (+er) (col) (stupid)* bekloppt *(col); (sleepy, half-drugged)* benebelt *(col).*
dormant ['dɔːmənt] *adj (Zool, Bot)* ruhend; *volcano* untätig; *energy* verborgen. **to lie** ~ *(evil etc)* schlummern.
dormer (window) ['dɔːmə('wɪndəʊ)] *n* Mansardenfenster *nt.*
dormitory ['dɔːmɪtrɪ] *n* Schlafsaal *m; (US: building)* Wohnheim *nt.* ~ **town** *n* Schlafstadt *f.*
dormouse ['dɔːmaʊs] *n, pl* **dormice** ['dɔːmaɪs] Haselmaus *f.*
dorsal ['dɔːsl] *adj* ~ **fin** Rückenflosse *f.*
dosage ['dəʊsɪdʒ] *n* Dose, Dosis *f.*
dose [dəʊs] **1** *n (Med)* Dosis *f.* **a** ~ **of flu** eine Grippe; **he's all right in small** ~**s** er ist nur (für) kurze Zeit zu ertragen. **2** *vt person* Arznei geben *(+dat).* **she's always dosing herself** sie nimmt *or* schluckt ständig Medikamente.
doss [dɒs] *vi (Brit col: also* ~ **down***)* pennen *(col),* sich hinhauen *(col).*
dosshouse ['dɒshaʊs] *n (Brit col)* Bleibe *f (col).*
dossier ['dɒsɪeɪ] *n* Dossier *m or nt.*
dot [dɒt] **1** *n* Punkt *m.* **to arrive on the** ~ auf die Minute pünktlich (an)kommen. **2** *vt* **to** ~ **one's i's and cross one's t's** genau sein; **~ted line** punktierte Linie; **to sign on the** ~**ted line** *(fig)* seine Zustimmung geben; **a field** ~**ted with flowers** ein mit Blumen übersätes Feld; ~**ted about the country** über das ganze Land verstreut.
dotage ['dəʊtɪdʒ] *n* **in one's** ~ senil.
♦ **dote on** ['dəʊtɒn] *vi +prep obj* abgöttisch lieben.
doting ['dəʊtɪŋ] *adj* **her** ~ **parents** ihre Eltern, die sie abgöttisch lieb(t)en.
dot matrix (printer) *n* Matrixdrucker *m.*
dotty ['dɒtɪ] *adj (+er) (Brit col)* kauzig, schrullig.
double ['dʌbl] **1** *adj (twice as much)* doppelt; *(having two similar parts, for two)* Doppel-. **a** ~ **whisky** ein doppelter Whisky; **her salary is** ~ **what it was ten years ago** ihr Gehalt hat sich in den letzten zehn Jahren verdoppelt; ~ **bottom** doppelter Boden; ~ **"p"** Doppel-p; ~ **seven five four/**~ **seven five** *(Telec)* siebenundsiebzig vierundfünfzig/sieben sieben fünf; ~ **room** Doppelzimmer *nt;* **it has a** ~ **meaning** es ist zwei- *or* doppeldeutig; ~ **standards** Doppelmoral *f;* **to lead a** ~ **life** ein Doppelleben führen.

2 *adv* **(a)** *(twice)* doppelt. **I have ~ what you have** ich habe doppelt soviel wie du; **to see ~** doppelt sehen. **(b) to be bent ~ with pain** sich vor Schmerzen krümmen; **fold the paper ~** falte das Papier (einmal).

3 *n* **(a)** *(twice)* das Doppelte, das Zweifache. **(b)** *(person)* Ebenbild *nt*, Doppelgänger(in *f*) *m*; *(Film, Theat: stand-in)* Double *nt*. **(c) at the ~** *(also Mil)* im Laufschritt; *(fig)* auf der Stelle.

4 *vt (increase twofold)* verdoppeln.

5 *vi* **(a)** sich verdoppeln. **(b)** *(Film, Theat)* **to ~ for sb** jds Double sein, jdn doubeln; **he ~s as the butler and the duke** er hat eine Doppelrolle als Butler und Herzog.

♦**double back 1** *vi* kehrtmachen; *(road, river)* sich zurückschlängeln. **2** *vt sep blanket* umschlagen.

♦**double up** *vi* **(a)** *(with pain)* sich krümmen; *(with laughter)* sich biegen. **he ~d ~ when the bullet hit him** er brach zusammen, als die Kugel ihn traf. **(b)** *(share room)* das Zimmer/Büro *etc* teilen; *(share bed)* in einem Bett schlafen.

double: ~ agent *n* Doppelagent *m*; **~ bar** *n (Mus)* Doppelstrich *m*; **~-barrelled,** *(US)* **~-barreled** [ˌdʌblˈbærəld] *adj surname* Doppel-; **~-barrel(l)ed shotgun** *n* doppelläufiges Gewehr, Zwilling *m*; **~ bass** *n* Kontrabaß *m*; **~ bed** *n* Doppelbett *nt*; **~ bend** *n* S-Kurve *f*; **~-breasted** *adj* zweireihig; **~-breasted jacket/suit** Zweireiher *m*; **~-check** *vti* noch einmal (über)prüfen; **~ chin** *n* Doppelkinn *nt*; **~ cream** *n* Schlagsahne *f*; **~-cross** *vt (col)* ein falsches Spiel treiben mit; **~-dealing** *n* Betrügerei(en *pl*) *f*; **~-decker** *n* Doppeldecker *m*; **~-declutch** *vi (Aut)* mit Zwischengas schalten; **~ dutch** *n (Brit)* Kauderwelsch *nt*; **it's ~ dutch to me** das sind böhmische Dörfer für mich; **~-edged** *adj (lit, fig)* zweischneidig; **~ entendre** [ˈduːblɑ̃ːnˈtɑ̃ːndr] *n* Zweideutigkeit *f*; **~ fault** *n (Tennis)* Doppelfehler *m*; **~ glazing** *n* Doppelfenster *pl*; **~-jointed** *adj* sehr gelenkig; **~ park** *vi* in zweiter Reihe parken; **~-quick** *adj (col)* **in ~-quick time** in Null Komma nichts *(col)*.

doubles [ˈdʌblz] *n sing or pl (Sport)* Doppel *nt*.

double: ~ take *n* **he did a ~ take** er mußte zweimal hinsehen; **~talk** *n (ambiguous)* doppeldeutiges Gerede; *(deceitful)* doppelzüngiges Gerede.

doubly [ˈdʌblɪ] *adv* doppelt.

doubt [daʊt] **1** *n* Zweifel *m*. **his honesty is in ~** seine Ehrlichkeit wird angezweifelt; **I am in no ~ as to what he means** ich bin mir völlig im klaren darüber, was er meint; **I have my ~s whether he will come** ich bezweifle, daß er kommt; **there's no ~ about it** daran gibt es keinen Zweifel; **I have no ~s about taking the job** ich habe keine Bedenken, die Stelle anzunehmen; **no ~ he will come tomorrow** höchstwahrscheinlich kommt er morgen; **without (a) ~** ohne Zweifel; **yes, no ~** ja, zweifellos; **it's beyond ~ that ...** es steht außer Zweifel, daß ...; **when in ~** im Zweifelsfall. **2** *vt* bezweifeln; *sb's honesty, truth of statement* anzweifeln, Zweifel haben an *(+dat)*. **I ~ it (very much)** das bezweifle ich (sehr).

doubter [ˈdaʊtəʳ] *n* Skeptiker, Zweifler *m*.

doubtful [ˈdaʊtfʊl] *adj* **(a)** *(uncertain)* unsicher, zweifelhaft; *outcome, result, future* ungewiß. **to be ~ about sb/sth** wegen jdm/etw Bedenken haben; **I'm a bit ~** ich habe so meine Bedenken; **to look ~** *(person)* skeptisch dreinblicken; **the weather looked a bit ~** es sah nach schlechtem Wetter aus. **(b)** *(of questionable character)* zweifelhaft; *person, affair also* zwielichtig.

doubtfully [ˈdaʊtfəlɪ] *adv* skeptisch.

doubtfulness [ˈdaʊtfʊlnɪs] *n see adj* **(a)** Unsicherheit *f*; Ungewißheit *f*. **(b)** Zweifelhaftigkeit *f*; Zwielichtigkeit *f*.

doubtless [ˈdaʊtlɪs] *adj* zweifelsohne.

douche [duːʃ] *n* Spülung *f*.

dough [dəʊ] *n* Teig *m*; *(col: money)* Kohle *f (col)*.

doughnut [ˈdəʊnʌt] *n* Berliner *m*.

dour [ˈdʊəʳ] *adj* mürrisch, verdrießlich; *struggle* hart, hartnäckig.

douse [daʊs] *vt* **(a)** Wasser schütten über *(+acc)*; *plants* reichlich wässern. **(b)** *light* ausmachen.

dove[1] [dʌv] *n (lit, fig)* Taube *f*.

dove[2] [dəʊv] *(US) pret of* **dive.**

dovecot(e) [ˈdʌvkɒt] *n* Taubenschlag *m*.

dovetail [ˈdʌvteɪl] **1** *n* **~ joint** Schwalbenschwanzverbindung *f*. **2** *vt plans* koordinieren. **3** *vi (plans)* übereinstimmen.

dowager [ˈdaʊədʒəʳ] *n* (adelige) Witwe.

dowdy [ˈdaʊdɪ] *adj (+er)* ohne jeden Schick.

down[1] [daʊn] **1** *adv* **(a)** *(towards speaker)* herunter, herab; *(away from speaker)* hinunter, hinab; *(downstairs also)* nach unten. **~!** *(to dog)* Platz!; **to jump ~** hinunter-/herunterspringen; **~ with traitors!** nieder mit den Verrätern!; **on his way ~ from the hilltop** beim Abstieg; **all the way ~ to the bottom** bis ganz nach unten.

(b) *(position)* unten. **~ there** da unten; **~ here** hier unten; **don't kick a man when he's ~** man soll jemanden nicht fertigmachen, wenn es ihm schon schlecht geht; **the sun is ~** die Sonne ist untergegangen; **I'll be ~ in a minute** ich komme sofort runter; **I've been ~ with flu** ich habe mit Grippe im Bett gelegen; **he was (feeling) a bit ~** er fühlte sich ein wenig niedergeschlagen *or* down *(col)*; **they'll be ~ on you** *(police etc)* du bekommst Ärger mit ihnen.

(c) he came ~ from London yesterday er kam gestern aus London; **~ South** im Süden/in den Süden; **~ here in Italy** hier unten in Italien; **he's ~ at his brother's** er ist bei seinem Bruder; **from 1700 ~ to the present** von 1700 bis zur Gegenwart.

(d) *(in volume, degree, activity, status)* **the tyres are ~** die Reifen sind platt; **his temperature has gone ~** sein Fieber ist zurückgegangen; **the price is ~ on last week** der Preis ist gegenüber der letzten Woche gefallen; **I'm £2 ~ on what I expected** ich habe £ 2 weniger, als ich dachte; **they're still three goals ~** sie liegen immer noch mit drei Toren zurück.

(e) *(in writing, planning)* **I've got it ~ in my diary** ich habe es in meinem Kalender notiert; **to be ~ for the next race** für das nächste Rennen gemeldet sein; **it's ~ for next month** es steht für nächsten Monat auf dem Programm.

(f) to pay £2 ~ £ 2 anzahlen; **how much do they want ~?** was verlangen sie als Anzahlung?

2 *prep* **(a)** *(indicating movement to)* **to go/come ~ the hill/street** den Berg/die Straße hinuntergehen/herunterkommen; **she let her hair fall ~ her back** sie ließ ihr Haar über die Schultern fallen; **he ran his finger ~ the list** er ging mit dem Finger die Liste durch. **(b)** *(at a lower part of)* **the other skiers were further ~ the slope** die anderen Skifahrer waren weiter unten; **she lives ~ the street** sie wohnt hier in der Straße. **(c) ~ the ages/centuries** Jahrhunderte (hindurch). **(d)** *(along)* **he was walking/coming ~ the street** er ging/kam die Straße entlang. **(e)** *(Brit col: to, in, at)* **he's gone ~ the pub** er ist in die Kneipe gegangen; **she's ~ the shops** sie ist einkaufen gegangen.

3 *n* **to have a ~ on sb** *(col)* jdn auf dem Kieker haben *(col)*.

4 *vt opponent* niederschlagen; *beer* runterkippen *(col)*. **to ~ tools** die Arbeit niederlegen.

down[2] *n (feathers)* Daunen, Flaumfedern *pl*; *(youth's beard)* Flaum *m*.

down[3] *n usu pl* **on the ~(s)** im Hügelland.

down: ~-and-out 1 *n (tramp)* Penner *m (col)*; **2** *adj* heruntergekommen; **~cast** *adj* niedergeschlagen; **~fall** *n* **(a)** Sturz, Fall *m*; *(of empire also)*

Untergang *m*; *(cause of ruin: drink etc)* Ruin *m*; **(b)** *(of rain)* heftiger Niederschlag, Platzregen *m*; **~grade** *vt hotel, job* herunterstufen; *person also* degradieren; **~-hearted** *adj* niedergeschlagen; **~hill** *adv* **to go ~hill** *(road)* bergab führen *or* gehen; *(fig) (person)* auf dem absteigenden Ast sein; *(work, health)* sich verschlechtern; **~market** *adj product* Massen-; *area, shop etc* weniger vornehm; **~ payment** *n* Anzahlung *f*; **~pour** *n* Wolkenbruch *m*; **~right 1** *adj refusal, lie* glatt; *rudeness, scoundrel, liar* ausgesprochen; **2** *adv rude* ausgesprochen; **~stairs 1** *adv go, come* nach unten; *be* unten; **2** *adj* **the ~stairs rooms** die unteren Zimmer; **our ~stairs neighbours** die Nachbarn unter uns; **~stream** *adv* flußabwärts *(from* von*)*; **~-to-earth** *adj* nüchtern; *advice* praktisch; **~town 1** *adj* **~town district** Zentrum *nt*, Innenstadt *f*; *(US)* Geschäftsviertel *nt*; **2** *adv* **to go ~town** in die Stadt *or* ins Zentrum gehen; **~ train** *n Zug, der von der Stadt aufs Land fährt oder von der Hauptstadt abgeht;* **~-trodden** *adj people* unterdrückt; **~ under** *n (Brit col)* Australien *nt*.

downward ['daʊnwəd] **1** *adj movement, pull* nach unten. **2** *adv (also* **downwards***) go, look* nach unten. **to slope gently ~** sanft abfallen; **from the President ~** beim Präsidenten angefangen.

dowry ['daʊrɪ] *n* Mitgift *f*.

doz = dozen.

doze [dəʊz] **1** *n* Nickerchen *nt*. **2** *vi* (vor sich hin) dösen.

♦ **doze off** *vi* einschlafen, einnicken.

dozen ['dʌzn] *n* Dutzend *nt*. **half a ~** ein halbes Dutzend; **~s** *(fig col)* eine ganze Menge; **~s of times** *(col)* x-mal *(col)*.

dozy ['dəʊzɪ] *adj (+er) (sleepy)* verschlafen.

DPP = Director of Public Prosecutions.

dpt = department Abt.

Dr = doctor Dr.

drab [dræb] *adj (+er)* trist; *colour also* düster.

draft [drɑːft] **1** *n* **(a)** *(rough outline)* Entwurf *m*. **(b)** *(Fin, Comm)* Wechsel *m*. **(c)** *(US Mil: conscription)* Einberufung (zum Wehrdienst). **(d)** *(US)* = **draught. 2** *vt* **(a)** *letter, contract* entwerfen. **(b)** *(US Mil) conscript* einberufen.

drag [dræg] **1** *n* **(a)** *(aerodynamic)* Luftwiderstand *m*. **(b)** *(col: hindrance)* **to be a ~ on sb** für jdn ein Klotz am Bein sein. **(c)** *(col)* **what a ~!** *(boring)* Mann, ist der/die/das langweilig! *(col)*; *(nuisance)* so'n Mist *(col)*; **(d)** *(col: pull on cigarette)* Zug *m (on, at* an *+dat)*. **(e)** *(women's clothing)* **in** *or* **wearing ~** in Frauenkleidung. **2** *vt* **(a)** *person, object* schleppen, schleifen. **to ~ one's feet** *(fig)* alles/die Sache schleifen lassen; **to ~ the truth out of sb** die Wahrheit mühsam aus jdm herausholen. **(b)** *river* absuchen. **3** *vi (time, work)* sich hinziehen; *(play, book, conversation)* sich in die Länge ziehen.

♦ **drag along** *vt sep person* mitschleppen.

♦ **drag away** *vt sep (lit, fig)* wegschleppen. **you'll have to ~ him ~ from the television** den muß man mit Gewalt vom Fernseher wegziehen.

♦ **drag down** *vt sep (lit)* herunterziehen; *(fig)* mit sich ziehen. **to ~ sb ~ to one's level** *(fig)* jdn auf sein eigenes Niveau herunterziehen.

♦ **drag in** *vt sep (fig) subject* aufs Tapet bringen; *remark* anbringen.

♦ **drag on** *vi* sich in die Länge ziehen; *(meeting, lecture also)* sich hinziehen. **it ~ged ~ for 3 hours** es zog sich über 3 Stunden hin.

dragon ['drægən] *n (lit, fig col)* Drache *m*.

dragonfly ['drægən,flaɪ] *n* Libelle *f*.

drain [dreɪn] **1** *n* **(a)** *(pipe)* Rohr *nt*; *(under sink etc)* Abfluß(rohr *nt) m*; *(under the ground)* Kanalisationsrohr *nt*; *(~ cover)* Rost *m*. **~s** *(system)* Kanalisation *f*; **open ~** (Abfluß)rinne *f*; **to throw one's money down the ~** *(fig col)* das Geld zum Fenster hinauswerfen; **this country's going down the ~** *(col)* dieses Land geht vor die Hunde *(col)*. **(b)** *(on resources etc)* Belastung *f (on gen)*. **it has been a great ~ on her strength** das hat sehr an ihren Kräften gezehrt.

2 *vt* **(a)** *land, marshes* entwässern; *vegetables* abgießen; *reservoir* trockenlegen; *boiler, radiator* das Wasser ablassen aus; *engine oil* ablassen. **(b)** *(fig)* **to feel ~ed (of energy)** sich ausgelaugt fühlen; **to ~ a country of resources** ein Land ausbeuten; **to ~ sb dry** jdn ausnehmen *(col)*. **(c)** *glass* austrinken, leeren.

3 *vi (vegetables, dishes)* abtropfen.

♦ **drain away** *vi (liquid)* ablaufen; *(strength)* dahinschwinden.

♦ **drain off** *vt sep* abgießen.

drainage ['dreɪnɪdʒ] *n* **(a)** *(draining)* Dränage *f*; *(of land also)* Entwässerung *f*. **(b)** *(system)* Entwässerungssystem *nt*; *(in house, town)* Kanalisation *f*. **(c)** *(sewage)* Abwasser *nt*.

drain: ~ing board, *(US)* **~ board** *n* Ablauf *m*; **~ pipe** *n* Abflußrohr *nt*.

drake [dreɪk] *n* Erpel, Enterich *m*.

drama ['drɑːmə] *n* Drama *nt*. **the ~ of the situation** die Dramatik der Situation.

drama: ~ critic *n* Theaterkritiker(in *f*) *m*; **~ student** *n* Schauspielschüler(in *f*) *m*.

dramatic [drə'mætɪk] *adj* dramatisch.

dramatist ['dræmətɪst] *n* Dramatiker(in *f*) *m*.

dramatize ['dræmətaɪz] **1** *vt* **(a)** *novel* für die Bühne/das Fernsehen bearbeiten. **(b)** *(make vivid)* dramatisieren. **2** *vi (exaggerate)* übertreiben.

drank [dræŋk] *pret of* **drink.**

drape [dreɪp] **1** *vt* drapieren; *person* hüllen. **2** *n* **~s** *pl (US)* Vorhänge *pl*.

draper ['dreɪpə^r] *n (Brit)* Textilkaufmann *m*.

drapery ['dreɪpərɪ] *n (Brit) (cloth etc)* Stoff *m*; *(business: also* **~ shop***)* Stoffgeschäft *nt*.

drastic ['dræstɪk] *adj* drastisch. **things are getting ~** die Sache wird kritisch.

drat [dræt] *interj (col)* **~ (it)!** verflixt! *(col)*.

draught, *(US)* **draft** [drɑːft] *n* **(a)** (Luft)zug *m*; **there's a terrible ~ in here** hier zieht es fürchterlich; **are you in a ~?** zieht es Ihnen?; **a nice cool ~** etwas frische Luft. **(b)** *(swallow, drink)* Zug *m*. **(c)** *(~ beer)* Faß- *or* Schankbier *nt*. **on ~** vom Faß. **(d)** *(Naut)* Tiefgang *m*. **(e)** *(Brit: game)* **~s** *(+sing vb)* Damespiel *nt*; *(+pl vb: pieces)* Damesteine *pl*.

draughtsman, *(US)* **draftsman** [drɑːftsmən] *n, pl* **-men** [-mən] *(Tech)* Zeichner *m*.

draughtsmanship, *(US)* **draftsmanship** [drɑːftsmənʃɪp] *n* zeichnerisches Können.

draughty, *(US)* **drafty** [drɑːftɪ] *adj (er)* zugig. **it's ~ in here** hier zieht es.

draw[1] [drɔː] *pret* **drew**, *ptp* **drawn 1** *vt (lit, fig)* zeichnen; *line* ziehen. **we must ~ the line somewhere** *(fig)* irgendwo muß Schluß sein. **2** *vi* zeichnen.

draw[2] *(vb: pret* **drew**, *ptp* **drawn***)* **1** *vt* **(a)** *(pull)* ziehen; *bolt* zurückschieben; *bow* spannen; *curtains (open)* aufziehen; *(shut)* zuziehen; *(Med) abscess* schneiden; *cork* herausziehen. **he drew his hat over his eyes** er zog sich *(dat)* den Hut ins Gesicht.

(b) *(obtain from source)* holen; *salary* beziehen. **to ~ a bath** das Badewasser einlassen; **to ~ money from the bank** Geld (vom Konto) abheben; **he's bitten her — has he ~n blood?** er hat sie gebissen — blutet sie?; **to ~ comfort from sth** sich mit etw trösten; **to ~ a smile from sb** jdm ein Lächeln entlocken; **to ~ a (deep) breath** (tief) Luft holen.

(c) *(attract) interest* erregen; *customer, crowd* anlocken. **to feel ~n towards sb** sich zu jdm hingezogen fühlen.

(d) he refuses to be ~n *(will not speak)* aus ihm ist nichts herauszubringen; *(will not be provoked)* er läßt sich auf nichts ein; **I won't be**

~n on that one dazu möchte ich mich nicht äußern.

(e) *conclusion, comparison* ziehen; *distinction* treffen.

(f) *(Sport)* **to ~ a match** unentschieden spielen.

(g) France has been ~n against Scotland Frankreich ist für die Begegnung mit Schottland ausgelost worden.

(h) *(Cook) fowl* ausnehmen.

2 *vi* **(a)** *(move, come)* kommen. **he drew towards the door** er bewegte sich zur Tür; **he drew to one side** er ging/fuhr zur Seite; **he drew over to the kerb** er fuhr an den Straßenrand; **to ~ around the table** sich um den Tisch versammeln; **to ~ to an end** zu Ende gehen; **he drew ahead of** *or* **away from the other runners** er zog den anderen Läufern davon. **(b)** *(allow airflow: of chimney, pipe)* ziehen. **(c)** *(Sport)* unentschieden spielen. **they drew 2-2** sie trennten sich 2:2 unentschieden. **(d)** *(infuse: tea)* ziehen.

3 *n* **(a)** *(lottery)* Ziehung, Ausspielung *f*; *(for sports competitions)* Auslosung *f*. **(b)** *(Sport)* Unentschieden *nt*. **the match ended in a ~** das Spiel endete unentschieden. **(c)** *(attraction: play, film etc)* (Kassen)schlager, Knüller *(col) m*; *(person)* Attraktion *f*. **(d) to be quick on the ~** *(lit)* schnell mit der Pistole sein; *(fig)* schlagfertig sein.

♦ **draw back 1** *vi* zurückweichen. **2** *vt sep* zurückziehen; *curtains also* aufziehen.

♦ **draw in 1** *vi* **(a)** *(train)* einfahren; **to ~ ~ at the kerb** am Bordstein (an)halten. **(b)** *(get shorter: days)* kürzer werden. **2** *vt sep* **(a)** *breath, air* einziehen. **(b)** *(attract, gain) crowds* anziehen. **(c) to ~ ~ one's claws** *(lit, fig)* die Krallen einziehen.

♦ **draw on 1** *vi* **as the night drew ~** mit fortschreitender Nacht; **winter ~s ~** der Winter naht; **time is ~ing ~** es wird spät. **2** *vi +prep obj (use as source: also* **~ upon***)* sich stützen auf *(+acc)*. **3** *vt sep stockings, gloves* anziehen.

♦ **draw out 1** *vi* **(a)** *(train)* ausfahren; *(car)* herausfahren *(of* aus*)*. **(b)** *(days)* länger werden. **2** *vt sep* **(a)** *(take out)* herausziehen. **(b)** *(prolong)* in die Länge ziehen, hinausziehen. **(c) to ~ sb ~ (of his shell)** jdn aus der Reserve locken.

♦ **draw together** *vt sep threads* miteinander verknüpfen.

♦ **draw up 1** *vi (stop: car)* (an)halten. **2** *vt sep* **(a)** *(formulate)* entwerfen; *contract, agreement also, will* aufsetzen; *list* aufstellen. **(b)** *chair* heranziehen; **to ~ oneself ~ (to one's full height)** sich (zu seiner vollen Größe) aufrichten. **(c)** *(set in line) troops* aufstellen.

draw: ~back *n* Nachteil *m*; **~bridge** *n* Zugbrücke *f*.

drawer *n* **(a)** [drɔːʳ] *(in desk etc)* Schublade *f*. **(b)** [ˈdrɔːəʳ] *(person: of pictures)* Zeichner *m*. **(c)** [ˈdrɔːəʳ] *(of cheque etc)* Aussteller *m*.

drawing [ˈdrɔːɪŋ] *n* Zeichnung *f*. **I'm no good at ~** ich kann nicht gut zeichnen.

drawing: ~-board *n* Reißbrett *nt*; **well, it's back to the ~-board** *(fig)* das muß noch einmal ganz neu überdacht werden; **~-pin** *n (Brit)* Reißzwecke *f*; **~ room** *n* Wohnzimmer *nt*; *(in mansion)* Salon *m*.

drawl [drɔːl] **1** *vi* schleppend sprechen. **2** *vt* schleppend aussprechen. **3** *n* schleppende Sprache.

drawn [drɔːn] **1** *ptp of* **draw¹**, **draw²**. **2** *adj* **(a)** *(from tiredness)* abgespannt; *(from worry)* abgehärmt, verhärmt; *(with pain)* schmerzverzerrt. **(b)** *game, match* unentschieden.

dread [dred] **1** *vt* sich fürchten vor *(+dat)*, große Angst haben vor *(+dat)*. **I ~ to think what may happen** ich wage nicht daran zu denken, was passieren könnte. **2** *n* Furcht *f*.

dreadful [ˈdredfʊl] *adj* schrecklich, furchtbar. **I feel ~** *(ill)* ich fühle mich schrecklich *or* scheußlich; *(mortified)* es ist mir schrecklich peinlich.

dreadfully [ˈdredfəlɪ] *adv* schrecklich.

dream [driːm] *(vb: pret, ptp* **dreamt** *or* **~ed***)* **1** *n* Traum *m*. **to have a bad ~** schlecht träumen; **sweet ~s!** träum was Schönes!; **to have a ~ about sb/sth** von jdm/etw träumen; **in a ~** *(fig)* wie im Traum; **the house of his ~s** das Haus seiner Träume, sein Traumhaus; **happy beyond her wildest ~s** glücklicher als in ihren kühnsten Träumen; **to have ~s of becoming rich** davon träumen, reich zu werden; **it worked like a ~** *(col)* es hat hervorragend geklappt; **you're a ~!** du bist ein Schatz; **a ~ of a hat** ein traumhaft schöner Hut.

2 *vi (lit, fig)* träumen *(about, of* von*)*. **I'm sorry, I was ~ing** Verzeihung, ich habe gerade geträumt.

3 *vt (lit, fig)* träumen; *dream* haben. **I wouldn't ~ of it** das würde mir nicht im Traum einfallen; **I never ~t (that) he would come** ich hätte mir nie träumen lassen, daß er kommen würde.

4 *adj attr car, holiday* Traum-.

♦ **dream up** *vt sep (col) idea* sich *(dat)* ausdenken.

dreamer [ˈdriːməʳ] *n* Träumer(in *f*) *m*.

dreamt [dremt] *pret, ptp of* **dream.**

dreamy [driːmɪ] *adj (+er)* verträumt.

dreary [ˈdrɪərɪ] *adj (+er)* eintönig; *weather* trüb; *person, speech* langweilig.

dredge [dredʒ] *vt river, canal* ausbaggern.

♦ **dredge up** *vt sep (lit)* ausbaggern; *(fig) unpleasant facts* ausgraben.

dredger [ˈdredʒəʳ] *n* Bagger *m*.

dregs [dregz] *npl* **(a)** (Boden)satz *m*. **(b)** *(fig)* Abschaum *m*.

drenched [drentʃt] *adj* völlig durchnäßt.

dress [dres] **1** *n* **(a)** *(for woman)* Kleid *nt*. **(b)** *no pl (clothing)* Kleidung *f*. **in eastern ~** orientalisch gekleidet. **2** *vt* **(a)** *(clothe)* anziehen. **to get ~ed** sich anziehen; **to ~ sb in sth** jdm etw anziehen; **~ed in black** schwarz gekleidet. **(b)** *(Naut) ship* beflaggen. **(c)** *(Cook) salad* anmachen; *chicken* bratfertig machen. **(d)** *skins* gerben; *material* appretieren; *timber* hobeln; *stone* schleifen. **(e)** *wound* verbinden. **3** *vi* sich anziehen, sich kleiden. **to ~ in black** sich schwarz kleiden.

♦ **dress up 1** *vi (smartly)* sich feinmachen; *(in fancy dress)* sich verkleiden. **~ed ~ as Father Christmas** als Weihnachtsmann (verkleidet). **2** *vt sep (disguise)* verkleiden.

dressage [ˈdresɑːʒ] *n* Dressur *f*.

dress: ~ circle *n* erster Rang; **~ designer** *n* Modezeichner(in *f*) *m*.

dresser¹ [ˈdresəʳ] *n* **(a)** *(Theat)* Garderobier *m*, Garderobiere *f*. **(b) she's a stylish ~** sie ist immer sehr elegant (gekleidet).

dresser² *n* **(a)** Anrichte *f*. **(b)** *(US: dressing-table)* Frisierkommode *f*.

dressing [ˈdresɪŋ] *n* **(a)** *(Med: bandage, ointment)* Verband *m*. **(b)** *(Cook)* Soße *f*.

dressing: ~ down *n* **to give sb a ~ down** jdn herunterputzen *(col)*; **~-gown** *n* Morgenrock *m*; **~-room** *n (Theat)* (Künstler)garderobe *f*; *(Sport)* Umkleidekabine *f*; **~-table** *n* Frisierkommode *f*.

dress: ~maker *n* (Damen)schneider(in *f*) *m*; **~making** *n* Schneidern *nt*; **~ rehearsal** *n (lit, fig)* Generalprobe *f*; **~ shirt** *n* Frackhemd *nt*; **~ uniform** *n* Galauniform *f*.

dressy [ˈdresɪ] *adj (+er) (col) person* fein angezogen; *clothes* elegant.

drew [druː] *pret of* **draw¹**, **draw²**.

dribble [ˈdrɪbl] **1** *vi* **(a)** *(liquids)* tropfen; *(baby, person)* sabbern; *(animal)* geifern. **(b)** *(Sport)* dribbeln. **(c)** *(people)* **to ~ back/in** nach und nach zurückkommen/hereinkommen. **2** *vt* **(a)** *(Sport)* **to ~ the ball** mit dem Ball dribbeln. **(b)** *(baby etc)* kleckern.

dribs and drabs ['drɪbzən'dræbz] *npl:* **in ~** kleckerweise *(col).*
dried [draɪd] *adj* getrocknet; *fruit also* Dörr-. **~ milk** Trockenmilch *f,* Milchpulver *nt.*
drier *n* = **dryer.**
drift [drɪft] **1** *vi* **(a)** *(Naut)* treiben; *(sand)* wehen. **to ~ off course** abtreiben; **as the smoke ~ed away** als der Rauch abzog. **(b)** *(fig: person)* sich treiben lassen. **to let things ~** die Dinge treiben lassen; **he ~ed into marriage** er ist in die Ehe hineingeschlittert *(col);* **the nation was ~ing towards a crisis** das Land trieb auf eine Krise zu; **young people are ~ing away from the villages** junge Leute wandern aus den Dörfern ab; **to ~ apart** *(people)* sich auseinanderleben. **2** *n* **(a)** *(of air, water)* Strömung *f; (of events)* Lauf *m.* **(b)** *(of sand, snow)* Verwehung *f.* **(c)** *(of ship, aircraft)* (Ab)drift, Abweichung *f.* **(d) continental ~** Kontinentalverschiebung *f.* **(e)** *(of questions)* Richtung, Tendenz *f.* **if I get your ~** wenn ich Sie recht verstehe.
drifter ['drɪftəʳ] *n (person)* Gammler *m.* **he's a bit of a ~** er hält es nirgends lange aus.
driftwood ['driftwʊd] Treibholz *nt.*
drill[1] [drɪl] **1** *n* Bohrer *m.* **2** *vti* bohren *(for* nach*).*
drill[2] **1** *n no pl (esp Mil, fig)* Drill *m; (marching etc)* Exerzieren *nt.* **2** *vt* **(a)** *soldiers* drillen; *(in marching etc)* exerzieren lassen. **(b) to ~ pupils in grammar** mit den Schülern Grammatik pauken; **I ~ed it into him** ich habe es ihm eingebleut *(col).* **3** *vi (Mil)* gedrillt werden; *(marching etc)* exerzieren.
drill[3] *n (Tex)* Drillich *m.*
drilling ['drɪlɪŋ] *n (for oil)* Bohrung *f.* **~ rig** Bohrturm *m; (at sea)* Bohrinsel *f.*
drily ['draɪlɪ] *adv* trocken.
drink [drɪŋk] *(vb: pret* **drank,** *ptp* **drunk***)* **1** *n* **(a)** Getränk *nt.* **food and ~** Essen und Getränke; **may I have a ~?** kann ich etwas zu trinken haben?; **would you like a ~ of water?** möchten Sie etwas Wasser?; **to give sb a ~** jdm etwas zu trinken geben. **(b)** *(alcoholic)* Drink *m.* **let's have a ~** trinken wir was; **I need a ~!** ich brauche was zu trinken!; **he likes a ~** er trinkt gern (einen); **to ask friends in for ~s** Freunde auf ein Glas *or* einen Drink einladen; **he's got a few ~s in him** *(col)* er hat einige Gläser intus *(col).* **(c)** *no pl (alcoholic liquor)* Alkohol *m.* **he has a ~ problem** er trinkt; **his worries/she drove him to ~** vor Kummer fing er an zu trinken/sie trieb ihn in den Alkohol; **to smell of ~** eine Fahne haben.

2 *vt* trinken. **would you like something to ~?** möchten Sie etwas zu trinken (haben)?; **this coffee isn't fit to ~** diesen Kaffee kann man nicht trinken.

3 *vi* trinken. **he doesn't ~** er trinkt nicht; **his father drank** sein Vater war Trinker; **one shouldn't ~ and drive** nach dem Trinken soll man nicht fahren; **~ing and driving** Alkohol am Steuer; **to ~ to sb/sth** auf jdn/etw trinken.
♦ **drink in** *vt sep air* tief einatmen; *(fig) a sight, his words etc* (begierig) in sich *(acc)* aufnehmen.
♦ **drink up** *vti* austrinken.
drinkable ['drɪŋkəbl] *adj* trinkbar.
drinker ['drɪŋkəʳ] *n* Trinker(in *f*) *m.*
drinking ['drɪŋkɪŋ] *n* Trinken *nt.*
drinking: ~ fountain *n* Trinkwasserbrunnen *m;* **~-up time** *n (Brit) die letzten zehn Minuten vor der Polizeistunde;* **~-water** *n* Trinkwasser *nt.*
drip [drɪp] **1** *vi* tropfen. **to be ~ping with sweat/blood** schweißgebadet/blutüberströmt sein. **2** *vt liquid* träufeln, tropfen. **you're ~ping paint over my coat** du tropfst mir Farbe auf den Mantel. **3** *n* **(a)** *(sound)* Tropfen *nt.* **(b)** *(drop)* Tropfen *m.* **(c)** *(Med)* Tropf *(col) m.* **to be on a ~** eine Infusion bekommen, am Tropf hängen *(col).* **(d)** *(col: silly person)* Flasche *f (col).*
drip-dry ['drɪp'draɪ] *adj shirt* bügelfrei.
dripping ['drɪpɪŋ] **1** *n (Cook)* Bratenfett *nt.* **2** *adj* **(a)** *tap* tropfend; *washing* tropfnaß. **(b)** *(col: also* **~ wet***) coat, clothes* klatschnaß *(col).*
drive [draɪv] *(vb: pret* **drove,** *ptp* **driven***)* **1** *n* **(a)** *(Aut: journey)* Fahrt *f.* **to go for a ~** (ein bißchen) spazierenfahren; **to go for a ~ to the coast** ans Meer fahren; **one hour's ~ from London** eine Autostunde von London (entfernt). **(b)** *(into house: also* **~way***)* Einfahrt *f; (longer)* Auffahrt, Zufahrt *f.* **(c)** *(Golf, Tennis)* Treibschlag *m.* **(d)** *(Psych etc)* Trieb *m; (energy)* Schwung, Elan *m.* **sex ~** Sexualtrieb *m.* **(e)** *(Comm, Pol etc)* Aktion *f; (Mil)* Offensive *f.* **sales ~** Verkaufskampagne *f.* **(f)** *(Mech: power transmission)* Antrieb *m; (Comp)* Laufwerk *nt.* **(g)** *(Aut)* Steuerung *f.* **left-hand ~** Linkssteuerung *f.*

2 *vt* **(a)** *animals, dust, clouds etc* treiben. **to ~ a nail into sth** einen Nagel in etw *(acc)* einschlagen; **the gale drove the ship off course** der Sturm trieb das Schiff vom Kurs ab. **(b)** *car, train* fahren. **he ~s a taxi** er fährt Taxi; **I'll ~ you home** ich fahre Sie nach Hause. **(c)** *(provide power for) (belt, shaft)* antreiben; *(electricity, fuel)* betreiben. **(d)** *(cause to become)* treiben. **to ~ sb mad** jdn verrückt machen; **to ~ sb to desperation** jdn zur Verzweiflung treiben; **I was ~n to it** ich wurde dazu getrieben. **(e)** *(force to work hard)* **you're driving him too hard** Sie nehmen ihn zu hart ran; **he ~s himself very hard** er fordert viel von sich.

3 *vi* **(a)** fahren; *(go by car)* mit dem Auto fahren. **he's learning to ~** er lernt Auto fahren. **(b) the rain was driving in our faces** der Regen peitschte uns *(dat)* ins Gesicht.
♦ **drive along 1** *vi (vehicle, person)* dahinfahren. **2** *vt sep (wind, current) person, boat* (voran)treiben.
♦ **drive at** *vi +prep obj* hinauswollen auf *(+acc).* **what are you driving ~?** worauf wollen Sie hinaus?
♦ **drive away 1** *vi (car, person)* wegfahren. **2** *vt sep (lig, fig) person, cares* vertreiben.
♦ **drive back 1** *vti (in vehicle)* zurückfahren. **2** *vt sep enemy* zurücktreiben.
♦ **drive home** *vt sep nail, argument* einhämmern. **how can I ~ it ~ to him that ...?** wie kann ich (es) ihm nur klarmachen, daß ...?
♦ **drive off 1** *vi (person, car)* weg- *or* abfahren. **2** *vt sep person, enemy* vertreiben.
♦ **drive on 1** *vi (person, car)* weiterfahren. **2** *vt sep (encourage)* antreiben; *(to sth bad)* anstiften.
♦ **drive out** *vt sep person* hinaustreiben *or* -jagen; *evil thoughts* austreiben.
♦ **drive up** *vi (car, person)* vorfahren.
drive-in ['draɪv,ɪn] *adj* **~ cinema** Autokino *nt.*
drivel ['drɪvl] *n (pej)* Blödsinn *m.*
driven ['drɪvn] *ptp of* **drive.**
driver ['draɪvəʳ] *n* Fahrer(in *f*) *m; (Brit: of locomotive)* Führer *m.* **to be in the ~'s seat** *(fig)* die Zügel in der Hand haben.
driver's license *n (US)* Führerschein *m.*
drive: ~ shaft *n* Antriebswelle *f; (Aut)* Kardanwelle *f;* **~way** *n* Auffahrt *f; (longer)* Zufahrtsstraße *f.*
driving ['draɪvɪŋ] **1** *n* Fahren *nt.* **his ~ is awful** er fährt kriminell; **dangerous ~** *(Jur)* verkehrsgefährdendes (Fahr)verhalten. **2** *adj* **the ~ force** die treibende Kraft; **~ rain** peitschender Regen.
driving: ~ instructor *n* Fahrlehrer(in *f*) *m;* **~ lesson** *n* Fahrstunde *f;* **~ licence** *n (Brit)* Führerschein *m;* **~ mirror** *n* Rückspiegel *m;* **~ school** *n* Fahrschule *f;* **~ test** *n* Fahrprüfung *f.*
drizzle ['drɪzl] **1** *n* Nieselregen *m.* **2** *vi* nieseln.
droll [draʊl] *adj* drollig, ulkig.
dromedary ['drɒmɪdərɪ] *n* Dromedar *nt.*
drone [drəʊn] **1** *n* **(a)** *(bee, fig)* Drohne *f.* **(b)** *(sound) (of bees)* Summen *nt; (of engine)* Brummen *nt; (way of speaking)* monotone

Stimme. **2** *vi (bee)* summen; *(engine)* brummen; *(speak: also* ~ **away** *or* **on***)* eintönig sprechen; *(in reciting)* leiern. **he ~d on for hours** er redete stundenlang in seinem monotonen Tonfall.

drool [dru:l] *vi* sabbern.

♦**drool over** *vi +prep obj sb* vernarrt sein in *(+acc)*; *sb's remarks* in Ekstase geraten über *(+acc)*; *porno magazine* sich aufgeilen an *(+dat) (col!)*.

droop [dru:p] *vi* **(a)** *(lit) (person)* vornüber gebeugt stehen; *(shoulders)* herabhängen; *(head)* herunterfallen; *(eyelids)* herunterhängen; *(with sleepiness)* zufallen; *(flowers)* die Köpfe hängen lassen; *(one's hand, breasts)* schlaff herunterhängen. **(b)** *(fig: interest, energy)* erlahmen; *(audience etc)* abschlaffen. **don't let your spirits** ~ laß den Mut nicht sinken.

drop [drɒp] **1** *n* **(a)** *(of liquid, also fig)* Tropfen *m*. **a ~ of blood** ein Blutstropfen *m*; **it's a ~ in the ocean** *(fig)* das ist ein Tropfen auf den heißen Stein; **a ~ of wine?** ein Schlückchen Wein?; **he's had a ~ too much** er hat einen über den Durst getrunken. **(b)** *(sweet)* Drops *m*. **(c)** *(fall: in temperature, prices)* Rückgang *m*; *(sudden)* Sturz *m*. **a ~ in prices** ein Preissturz *m*/-rückgang *m*; **a ~ in salary** eine Gehaltseinbuße. **(d)** *(difference in level)* Höhenunterschied *m*; *(fall)* Sturz, Fall *m*; *(parachute jump)* (Ab)sprung *m*. **there's a ~ of ten metres down to the ledge** bis zu dem Felsvorsprung geht es zehn Meter hinunter; **it's a long ~** es geht tief hinunter. **(e)** *(of supplies, arms)* Abwurf *m*.

2 *vt* **(a)** *(allow to fall)* fallen lassen; *bomb, supplies, burden* abwerfen; *parachutist* absetzen; *voice* senken; *(Knitting) stitch* fallen lassen; *(lower) hemline* herunterlassen. **I ~ped my watch** meine Uhr ist (mir) runtergefallen.

(b) *(set down) (from car) person* absetzen; *thing* abliefern; *(from boat) cargo* löschen.

(c) *(utter casually) remark, name* fallenlassen; *clue* geben; *hint* machen. **he let ~ that ...** *(deliberately)* er erwähnte so nebenbei, daß ...

(d) *(send) postcard* schreiben.

(e) *(omit) word, reference* auslassen; *(deliberately also)* weglassen *(from* in *+dat)*; *programme* absetzen. **to ~ sb from a team** jdn aus einer Mannschaft nehmen.

(f) *candidate, minister, friend* fallenlassen; *girlfriend* Schluß machen mit.

(g) *(give up)* aufgeben; *idea, plan also* fallenlassen; *(Jur) case* niederschlagen. **you'll find it hard to ~ the habit** es wird Ihnen schwerfallen, sich *(dat)* das abzugewöhnen; **let's ~ the subject** lassen wir das Thema; **you'd better ~ the idea** schlagen Sie sich *(dat)* das aus dem Kopf; **~ it!** *(col)* hör auf (damit)!; **~ everything!** *(col)* laß alles stehen und liegen!

(h) *(lose) money, game, point* verlieren.

3 *vi* **(a)** *(fall: object)* (herunter)fallen. **don't let it ~** laß es nicht fallen; **to ~ to one's knees** auf die Knie fallen *or* sinken; **I'm ready to ~ (with fatigue)** ich bin zum Umfallen müde; **she ~ped into an armchair** sie ließ sich in einen Sessel fallen; **to ~ (down) dead** tot umfallen. **(b)** *(rate, temperature etc)* sinken; *(wind)* sich legen; *(voice)* sich senken. **(c) you can't just let the matter ~** Sie können die Sache nicht einfach auf sich beruhen lassen; **shall we let it ~?** sollen wir es darauf beruhen lassen?

♦**drop back** *or* **behind** *vi* zurückfallen.

♦**drop by** *vi (col)* vorbeikommen, hereinschauen.

♦**drop down** *vi (fall)* herunterfallen. **we ~ped ~ to the coast for a few days** wir sind für ein paar Tage an die Küste gefahren.

♦**drop in** *vi (col: visit casually)* **to ~ ~ on sb** bei jdm vorbeischauen; **to ~ ~ at the grocer's** beim Lebensmittelgeschäft vorbeigehen.

♦**drop off 1** *vi* **(a)** *(fall off)* abfallen; *(come off)* abgehen. **(b)** *(fall asleep)* einschlafen; *(for brief while)* einnicken. **(c)** *(sales)* zurückgehen; *(speed, interest, popularity)* nachlassen. **2** *vt sep (from car etc) person* absetzen; *parcel* abliefern.

♦**drop out** *vi* **(a)** *(of box etc)* herausfallen *(of* aus*)*. **(b)** *(from competition etc)* ausscheiden *(of* aus*)*; *(of society)* aussteigen. **to ~ ~ of university** sein Studium abbrechen.

droplet ['drɒplɪt] *n* Tröpfchen *nt*.

dropout ['drɒpaʊt] *n* Aussteiger *m (col)*.

droppings ['drɒpɪŋz] *npl* Kot *m*.

drop shot *n (Tennis)* Stoppball *m*.

dross [drɒs] *n no pl (fig)* Tand *m*. **everything else is ~** alles andere ist eitel und nichtig.

drought [draʊt] *n* Dürre *f*.

drove [drəʊv] **1** *pret of* **drive. 2** *n (of animals)* Herde *f*; *(of people)* Schar *f*.

drown [draʊn] **1** *vi* ertrinken. **a ~ing man will clutch at a straw** *(Prov)* dem Verzweifelten ist jedes Mittel recht. **2** *vt* **(a)** *animal, sorrows* ertränken. **to be ~ed** ertrinken. **(b)** *(also* **~ out***) noise, voice* übertönen; *speaker* niederschreien.

drowse [draʊz] *vi* (vor sich *(acc)* hin) dösen.

drowsiness ['draʊzɪnɪs] *n* Schläfrigkeit *f*.

drowsy ['draʊzɪ] *adj (+er)* schläfrig; *(after sleep)* verschlafen; *afternoon* träge.

drudge [drʌdʒ] *n (person)* Arbeitstier *nt (col)*.

drudgery ['drʌdʒərɪ] *n* stumpfsinnige Plackerei. **it's sheer ~** es ist eine einzige Plackerei.

drug [drʌg] **1** *n* Medikament, Arzneimittel *nt*; *(addictive)* Droge *f*. **to be on ~s** drogenabhängig sein; *(Med)* Medikamente nehmen. **2** *vt person* betäuben; *food, drink* ein Betäubungsmittel mischen in *(+acc)*. **to be in a ~ged sleep** in tiefer Betäubung liegen.

drug: ~ addict *n* Drogenabhängige(r) *mf*; **~ addiction** *n* Drogenabhängigkeit, Drogensucht *f*.

druggist ['drʌgɪst] *n (US)* Drogist(in *f*) *m*.

drugstore ['drʌgstɔ:r] *n (US)* Drugstore *m*.

drum [drʌm] **1** *n* **(a)** *(Mus)* Trommel *f*. **the ~s** *(in pop, jazz)* das Schlagzeug. **(b)** *(for oil, petrol)* Tonne *f*; *(cylinder, machine part)* Trommel *f*. **2** *vi (Mus, with fingers, rain)* trommeln. **the noise is still ~ming in my ears** das Geräusch dröhnt mir noch in den Ohren. **3** *vt* **to ~ one's fingers on the table** mit den Fingern auf den Tisch trommeln.

♦**drum into** *vt always separate* **to ~ sth ~ sb** jdm etw eintrichtern *(col)*.

♦**drum up** *vt sep enthusiasm* erwecken; *support* auftreiben. **to ~ ~ business** Aufträge anbahnen.

drummer ['drʌmə[r]] *n* Trommler *m*; *(in band, pop-group)* Schlagzeuger *m*.

drumstick ['drʌmstɪk] *n* **(a)** *(Mus)* Trommelschlegel *or* -stock *m*. **(b)** *(on chicken etc)* Keule *f*.

drunk [drʌŋk] **1** *ptp of* **drink. 2** *adj* betrunken. **to get ~ (on)** betrunken werden (von); *(on purpose)* sich betrinken (mit); **to arrest sb for being ~ and disorderly** *(Jur)* jdn wegen Trunkenheit und ruhestörenden Lärms verhaften; **~ with success** vom Erfolg berauscht. **3** *n* Betrunkene(r) *mf*; *(habitually)* Trinker(in *f*), Säufer(in *f*) *(col) m*.

drunkard ['drʌŋkəd] *n* Säufer(in *f*) *m (col)*.

drunken ['drʌŋkən] *adj* betrunken; *orgy* feuchtfröhlich, Sauf-; *brawl* mit/von Betrunkenen. **~ driving** *(Jur)* Trunkenheit *f* am Steuer.

drunkenness ['drʌŋkənnɪs] *n (state)* Betrunkenheit *f*; *(habit, problem)* Trunksucht *f*.

dry [draɪ] **1** *n* **come into the ~** komm ins Trockene; **to give sth a ~** etw trocknen. **2** *adj (+er)* trocken. **the river ran ~** der Fluß trocknete aus; **to be on ~ land** festen Boden unter den Füßen haben; **as ~ as a bone** *land, clothes* knochentrocken *(col)*; *mouth, ditches* völlig ausgetrocknet; **to feel/to be ~** *(thirsty)* eine trockene Kehle haben *(col)*. **3** *vt* trocknen; *skin* austrocknen; *fruit also* dörren; *dishes, one's hands* abtrocknen. **to ~ one's eyes** sich *(dat)* die Tränen abwischen; **to ~ oneself**

sich abtrocknen. **4** *vi* trocken werden.

♦ **dry off** *vi* trocknen.

♦ **dry out 1** *vi (clothes)* trocknen; *(ground, skin etc)* austrocknen; *(col: alcoholic)* eine Entziehungskur machen. **2** *vt sep clothes* trocknen; *ground, skin* austrocknen.

♦ **dry up 1** *vi* **(a)** *(stream, well)* austrocknen, versiegen; *(moisture)* trocknen; *(inspiration, source of income)* versiegen. **(b)** *(dishes)* abtrocknen. **(c)** *(actor)* steckenbleiben *(col)*. **(d)** *(col: be quiet)* ~ ~! halt den Mund! *(col)*. **2** *vt sep mess* aufwischen; *dishes* abtrocknen.

dry: ~**-clean** *vt* chemisch reinigen; ~**-cleaner** *n* chemische Reinigung; ~ **dock** *n (Naut)* Trockendock *nt*.

dryer, drier ['draɪəʳ] *n (for clothes)* Wäschetrockner *m*; *(spin ~)* Wäscheschleuder *f*; *(for hair)* Fön, Haartrockner *m*; *(hood)* Trockenhaube *f*.

dry: ~ **goods** *npl (Comm)* Kurzwaren *pl*; ~ **ice** *n* Trockeneis *nt*.

drying-up ['draɪɪŋ'ʌp] *n* Abtrocknen *nt*. **to do the** ~ abtrocknen.

dryness ['draɪnɪs] *n* Trockenheit *f*.

dry: ~ **rot** *n* (Haus- *or* Holz)schwamm *m*; ~ **run** *n* Probe *f*; ~ **ski slope** *n* Trockenskipiste *f*.

DTs ['diː'tiːz] **to have the** ~ das Zittern haben.

dual ['djʊəl] *adj (double)* doppelt, Doppel-. ~ **carriageway** *(Brit)* Schnellstraße *f*; ~ **nationality** doppelte Staatsangehörigkeit.

duality [djʊ'ælɪtɪ] *n* Dualität *f*.

dual-purpose ['djʊəl'pɜːpəs] *adj* zweifach verwendbar.

dub dʌb] *vt* **(a)** *(nickname)* taufen. **(b)** *film* synchronisieren.

dubious ['djuːbɪəs] *adj* zweifelhaft; *matter also* dubios; *look* zweifelnd. **I'm very ~ about it** ich habe da (doch) starke Zweifel.

dubiously ['djuːbɪəslɪ] *adv look* zweifelnd; *behave* zweifelhaft, fragwürdig.

duchess ['dʌtʃɪs] *n* Herzogin *f*.

duck [dʌk] **1** *n* **(a)** *(bird)* Ente *f*. **he took to it like a ~ to water** da war er sofort in seinem Element; **it's like water off a ~'s back** das läuft alles an ihm/ihr *etc* ab. **(b)** *(Cricket)* **to be out for a** ~ ohne Punktgewinn aus sein. **2** *vi* **(a)** *(also* ~ **down)** sich ducken. **he ~ed under the water** er tauchte (im Wasser) unter. **(b) he ~ed out of the room** er verschwand aus dem Zimmer. **3** *vt* **(a)** *(push under water)* untertauchen. **(b) to ~ one's head** den Kopf einziehen. **(c)** *(avoid) difficult question etc* ausweichen *(+dat)*.

duckling ['dʌklɪŋ] *n* Entenküken, Entlein *nt*.

duct [dʌkt] *n* **(a)** *(Anat)* Röhre *f*. **tear** ~ Tränenkanal *m*. **(b)** *(for liquid, gas)* Leitung *f*.

dud [dʌd] *(col)* **1** *adj* **(a)** ~ **shell/bomb** Blindgänger *m*. **(b)** *tool* nutzlos; *actor, teacher* mies *(col)*, schlecht; *coin* falsch; *cheque* ungedeckt; *(forged)* gefälscht. ~ **note** Blüte *f (col)*. **2** *n* **(a)** *(shell, bomb)* Blindgänger *m*. **(b)** *(cheque)* ungedeckter *or (forged)* gefälschter Scheck; *(banknote)* Blüte *f (col)*. **(c)** *(person)* Blindgänger *(col)*, Versager *m*.

dudgeon ['dʌdʒən] *n*: **in high** ~ sehr empört.

due [djuː] **1** *adj* **(a)** *(to be paid, owing)* fällig. **the sum which is ~ to him** die Summe, die ihm zusteht; **the amount ~ as compensation** der Betrag, der als Schadenersatz gezahlt werden soll; **to fall** ~ fällig werden *or* sein; **I am ~ six days off/(for) a rise** mir stehen sechs Tage Urlaub zu/mir steht eine Gehaltserhöhung zu.

(b) *(expected, scheduled)* **to be ~ to do sth** etw tun sollen; **the train is ~ at midday** der Zug soll laut Fahrplan um zwölf Uhr ankommen; **I'm ~ in London tomorrow** ich soll morgen in London sein; **he's ~ back tomorrow** er müßte morgen zurück sein; **when is the baby/she ~?** wann soll das Baby kommen/bekommt sie ihr Baby?

(c) *(proper, suitable)* gebührend. **with all ~ respect** bei allem Respekt; **we'll let you know in ~ course** wir werden Sie zu gegebener Zeit benachrichtigen; **he was, in ~ course, to become ...** im Laufe der Zeit wurde er ...; **after ~ consideration** nach reiflicher Überlegung.

(d) ~ **to** aufgrund *(+gen)*, wegen *(+gen or dat)*; **what's it ~ to?** worauf ist dies zurückzuführen?; **it is ~ to you that ...** wir haben es euch zu verdanken, daß ...

2 *adv* ~ **west** direkt nach Westen; ~ **east of the village** genau im Osten des Dorfes.

3 *n* **(a)** ~**s** *pl (fees)* Gebühr *f*, Gebühren *pl*. **(b)** *no pl* **(to) give him his ~, he did try hard** das muß man ihm lassen, er hat sich wirklich angestrengt.

duel ['djʊəl] **1** *n (lit, fig)* Duell *nt*. **2** *vi* sich duellieren.

duet [djuː'et] *n* Duo *nt*; *(for voices)* Duett *nt*.

duffel ['dʌfl]: ~ **bag** *n* Matchbeutel *or* -sack *m*; ~**-coat** *n* Dufflecoat *m*.

dug *pret, ptp of* **dig.**

duke [djuːk] *n* Herzog *m*.

dull [dʌl] **1** *adj (+er)* **(a)** *colour, light* trüb, matt; *weather* trüb; *sound* dumpf. **(b)** *(boring)* langweilig; *person, evening also* lahm; *(lacking spirit) person, mood* lustlos. **as ~ as ditchwater** stinklangweilig *(col)*. **(c)** *(slow-witted) person* schwerfällig. **(d)** *blade* stumpf; *pain* dumpf. **(e)** *market* flau; *trade, business* schleppend. **2** *vt* **(a)** *sense, powers of memory* schwächen; *mind* abstumpfen. **(b)** *pain, grief* betäuben; *pleasure* dämpfen. **(c)** *sound* dämpfen. **(d)** *edge, blade* stumpf machen.

duly ['djuːlɪ] *adv* entsprechend; *(properly)* gebührend, wie es sich gehört; *(according to regulations etc)* vorschriftsmäßig. **and the parcel ~ arrived the next morning** und das Paket kam dann auch am nächsten Morgen.

dumb [dʌm] *adj (+er)* **(a)** stumm. **the** ~ die Stummen *pl*; ~ **animals** die Tiere *pl*; **he was struck** ~ es verschlug ihm die Sprache; ~ **waiter** Speiseaufzug *m*; *(trolley)* Serviertisch *m*, stummer Diener. **(b)** *(esp US col: stupid)* doof *(col)*, dumm.

dumbfound ['dʌmfaʊnd] *vt* verblüffen. **I'm ~ed!** ich bin sprachlos!

dumbness ['dʌmnɪs] *n* **(a)** Stummheit *f*. **(b)** *(esp US col: stupidity)* Doofheit *(col)*, Dummheit *f*.

dummy ['dʌmɪ] **1** *n* **(a)** *(sham object)* Attrappe *f*; *(for clothes)* (Kleider)puppe *f*. **(b)** *(Brit: baby's teat)* Schnuller *m*. **(c)** *(Ftbl etc)* Finte *f*. **2** *adj attr* unecht. **a ~ rifle** eine Gewehrattrappe; ~ **run** Probe *f*.

dump [dʌmp] **1** *n* **(a)** *(pile of rubbish)* Abfallhaufen *m*; *(place)* Müllkippe *f*. **(b)** *(Mil)* Depot *nt*. **(c)** *(pej col: town)* Kaff *nt (col)*; *(house, building)* Loch *nt (pej col)*. **(d)** *(col)* **to be (down) in the ~s** deprimiert sein. **2** *vt* **(a)** *rubbish* abladen; *(col) person, girlfriend* abschieben; *car* abstellen, loswerden. **(b)** *(put down) load* abladen; *bags etc (drop)* fallen lassen; *(leave)* lassen. **(c)** *(Comm) goods* zu Dumpingpreisen verkaufen.

dumpling ['dʌmplɪŋ] *n* **(a)** *(Cook)* Kloß, Knödel *m*. **(b)** *(col: person)* Dickerchen *nt (col)*.

dump truck *n* Kipper *m*.

dumpy ['dʌmpɪ] *adj person* pummelig.

dun [dʌn] *adj* graubraun.

dunce [dʌns] *n (Sch)* langsamer Schüler; *(stupid person)* Dummkopf *m*.

dune [djuːn] *n* Düne *f*.

dung [dʌŋ] **1** *n* Dung *m*. **2** *vt field* düngen.

dungarees [,dʌŋgə'riːz] *npl* Latzhose *f*.

dungeon ['dʌndʒən] *n* Verlies *nt*, Kerker *m*.

dunk [dʌŋk] *vt* (ein)tunken.

dunno ['dʌnəʊ] = **(I) don't know.**

duodenal [,djuːəʊ'diːnl] *adj* ~ **ulcer** Zwölffingerdarmgeschwür *nt*.

dupe [djuːp] **1** *vt* betrügen. **he was ~d into be-**

lieving it er fiel darauf rein. **2** *n* Betrogene(r) *mf.*

duplex ['dju:pleks] *n (esp US: also:* ~ **apartment***)* zweistöckige Wohnung.

duplicate ['dju:plɪkeɪt] **1** *vt document* ein Duplikat *nt* anfertigen von; *(repeat) action* wiederholen; *(wastefully)* doppelt *or* zweimal machen. **2** ['dju:plɪkɪt] *n (of document)* Duplikat *nt*; *(of work of art)* Kopie *f*; *(of key)* Zweitschlüssel *m.* **3** ['dju:plɪkɪt] *adj* doppelt, zweifach.

duplication [ˌdju:plɪ'keɪʃən] *n (of efforts, work)* Wiederholung *f.*

duplicity [dju:'plɪsɪtɪ] *n* Doppelspiel *nt.*

durability [ˌdjʊərə'bɪlɪtɪ] *n (of material)* Haltbarkeit *f*; *(of metal)* Widerstandsfähigkeit *f.*

durable ['djʊərəbl] *adj friendship* dauerhaft; *material* haltbar; *metal* widerstandsfähig.

duration [djʊə'reɪʃən] *n (of play, war etc)* Länge, Dauer *f.* **for the** ~ bis zum Ende.

duress [djʊə'res] *n* **under** ~ unter Zwang.

durex ® ['djʊəreks] *n* Gummi *(col) m.*

during ['djʊərɪŋ] *prep* während *(+gen).*

dusk [dʌsk] *n (twilight)* (Abend)dämmerung *f*; *(gloom)* Finsternis *f.* **at** ~ bei Einbruch der Dunkelheit.

dusky ['dʌskɪ] *adj (+er) maiden* dunkelhäutig.

dust [dʌst] **1** *n no pl* **(a)** Staub *m.* **when the** ~ **had settled** *(fig)* als sich die Wogen wieder etwas geglättet hatten. **(b) to give sth a** ~ etw abstauben. **2** *vt* **(a)** *furniture* abstauben; *room* Staub wischen in *(+dat).* **(b)** *(Cook)* bestäuben.

dust: ~**bin** *n (Brit)* Mülltonne *f*; ~ **bowl** *n* Trockengebiet *nt*; ~**cart** *n (Brit)* Müllauto *nt*; ~**cover** *n (on furniture)* Schonbezug *m.*

duster [dʌstəʳ] *n* Staubtuch *nt*; *(Sch)* (Tafel)schwamm *m.*

dust: ~ **jacket** *n* (Schutz)umschlag *m*; ~**man** *n (Brit)* Müllmann *m (col)*; **the** ~**men come on Fridays** freitags ist Müllabfuhr; ~**pan** *n* Kehrschaufel *f.*

dusty [dʌstɪ] *adj (er) table, path* staubig.

Dutch [dʌtʃ] **1** *adj* holländisch, niederländisch *(esp form).* **I need a little** ~ **courage** *(col)* ich muß mir ein bißchen Mut antrinken; ~ **elm disease** Ulmenkrankheit *f*; **to talk to sb like a** ~ **uncle** *(col)* jdm eine Standpauke halten. **2** *adv* **to go** ~ *(col)* getrennte Kasse machen. **3** *n* **(a) the** ~ die Holländer *or* Niederländer *pl.* **(b)** *(language)* Holländisch, Niederländisch *(esp form) nt.*

Dutchman ['dʌtʃmən] *n, pl* **-men** [-mən] Holländer, Niederländer *(esp form) m.* **he did say that or I'm a** ~ *(col)* ich fresse einen Besen, wenn er das nicht gesagt hat *(col).*

Dutchwoman ['dʌtʃˌwʊmən] *n, pl* **-women** [-ˌwɪmɪn] Holländerin, Niederländerin *(esp form) f.*

dutiable [dju:tɪəbl] *adj* zollpflichtig.

dutiful [dju:tɪfʊl] *adj child* gehorsam; *husband, employee* pflichtbewußt.

duty ['dju:tɪ] *n* **(a)** Pflicht *f.* **to do one's** ~ **by sb** seine Pflicht gegenüber jdm tun *or* erfüllen; **I am (in)** ~ **bound to say that ...** es ist meine Pflicht zu sagen, daß ...; **to make it one's** ~ **to do sth** es sich *(dat)* zur Pflicht machen, etw zu tun. **(b)** *(often pl: responsibility)* Aufgabe, Pflicht *f.* **to take up one's duties** seine Pflichten aufnehmen; **to be on** ~ *(doctor etc)* im Dienst sein; *(Sch etc)* Aufsicht haben; **who's on** ~ **tomorrow?** wer hat morgen Dienst/Aufsicht?; **to be off** ~ nicht im Dienst sein. **(c)** *(Fin: tax)* Zoll *m.*

duty: ~**-free 1** *adj* zollfrei; ~**-free shop** Duty-free-Shop *m*; **2** *n* zollfreie Ware; ~ **officer** *n* Offizier *m* vom Dienst.

duvet ['dju:veɪ] *n (Brit)* Daunendecke *f.*

dwarf [dwɔ:f] **1** *n, pl* **dwarves** [dwɔ:vz] Zwerg *m.* **2** *adj tree, star* Zwerg-. **3** *vt* überragen; *(through achievements, ability etc)* in den Schatten stellen.

dwell [dwel] *pret, ptp* **dwelt** *vi (liter: live)* leben, wohnen.

♦**dwell (up)on** *vi +prep obj* **(a)** verweilen bei; *(stress unnecessarily etc)* herumreiten auf *(+dat).* **(b)** *(Mus) note* halten.

dwelling ['dwelɪŋ] *n (form: also* ~ **place***)* Wohnsitz *m (form)*, Wohnung *f.*

dwelt [dwelt] *pret, ptp of* **dwell.**

dwindle ['dwɪndl] *vi (strength, interest)* schwinden; *(numbers, audiences)* zurückgehen; *(supplies)* zur Neige gehen.

dwindling ['dwɪndlɪŋ] *adj* schwindend; *resources* versiegend.

dye [daɪ] **1** *n* Farbstoff *m.* **hair** ~ Haarfärbemittel *nt*; **the** ~ **will come out in the wash** die Farbe geht beim Waschen heraus. **2** *vt* färben.

dyed-in-the-wool ['daɪdɪnðəˌwʊl] *adj* durch und durch *pred*; *attitude* eingefleischt; *conservative* Erz-.

dying ['daɪɪŋ] *adj person* sterbend; *tradition, race, civilization* aussterbend; *embers* verglühend. **to my** ~ **day** bis an mein Lebensende; ~ **wish** letzter Wunsch; ~ **words** letzte Worte.

dyke, dike [daɪk] *n* **(a)** *(channel)* (Entwässerungs)graben, Kanal *m.* **(b)** *(barrier)* Deich, Damm *m.* **(c)** *(col: lesbian)* Lesbe *f (col).*

dynamic [daɪ'næmɪk] *adj* dynamisch.

dynamism ['daɪnəmɪzəm] *n* Dynamismus *m*; *(of person)* Dynamik *f.*

dynamite ['daɪnəmaɪt] **1** *n (lit)* Dynamit *nt*; *(fig)* Sprengstoff *m.* **she's** ~ sie ist eine Wucht *(col)*; **this story's** ~ diese Geschichte wird wie eine Bombe einschlagen. **2** *vt bridge* sprengen.

dynamo ['daɪnəməʊ] *n* Dynamo *m.*

dynasty ['dɪnəstɪ] *n* Dynastie *f.*

dysentery ['dɪsɪntrɪ] *n* Dysenterie, Ruhr *f.*

dyslexia [dɪs'leksɪə] *n* Legasthenie *f.*

dyslexic [dɪs'leksɪk] **1** *adj* legasthenisch. **2** *n* Legastheniker(in *f*) *m.*

dyspepsia [dɪs'pepsɪə] *n* Verdauungsstörung *f.*

E

E, e [iː] *n* E, e *nt*; *(Mus)* E, e *nt*. **E flat/sharp** Es, es *nt*/Eis, eis *nt*.
E = east O.
each [iːtʃ] **1** *adj* jede(r, s). **~ one of us/ ~ and every one of us** jeder einzelne von uns. **2** *pron* **(a)** jede(r, s). **a little of ~ please** von jedem etwas, bitte; **we ~ had our own ideas about it** jeder von uns hatte seine eigene Vorstellung davon. **(b) ~ other** einander; **they get on ~ other's nerves** sie gehen sich *(dat) or* einander auf die Nerven; **we visit ~ other** wir besuchen uns (gegenseitig); **on top of ~ other/next to ~ other** aufeinander/nebeneinander. **3** *adv* je. **two classes of 20 pupils ~** zwei Klassen mit je 20 Schülern; **the books are £1 ~** die Bücher kosten je £ 1; **carnations at one mark ~** Nelken zu einer Mark das Stück; **it cost them £10 ~** das hat sie pro Person £ 10 gekostet.
eager ['iːgəʳ] *adj* eifrig. **to be ~ to do sth** etw unbedingt tun wollen; **~ to learn** lernbegierig; **to be ~ for sth** auf etw *(acc)* erpicht sein; **~ beaver** *(col)* Arbeitstier *nt (col)*.
eagerly ['iːgəlɪ] *adv* eifrig; *look, wait* gespannt.
eagerness ['iːgənɪs] *n* Eifer *m*.
eagle ['iːgl] *n* Adler *m*.
eagle-eyed ['iːgl'aɪd] *adj* **the ~ detective** der Detektiv mit seinen Adleraugen.
ear[1] [ɪəʳ] *n (Anat, fig)* Ohr *nt*. **to keep one's ~s open** die Ohren offenhalten; **to keep an ~ to the ground** die Ohren aufsperren; **to be all ~s** ganz Ohr sein; **your ~s must have been burning** Ihnen müssen die Ohren geklungen haben; **it goes in one ~ and out the other** das geht zum einen Ohr hinein und zum anderen wieder heraus; **to be up to the ~s in debt** bis über beide Ohren verschuldet sein; **he'll be out on his ~** *(col)* dann fliegt er raus *(col)*; **to have a good ~ for music** musikalisch sein; **to play by ~** *(lit)* nach Gehör spielen; **to play it by ~** *(fig)* improvisieren.
ear[2] *n (of grain)* Ähre *f*.
ear: ~ache *n* Ohrenschmerzen *pl*; **~-drum** *n* Trommelfell *nt*.
earl [ɜːl] *n* Graf *m*.
early ['ɜːlɪ] **1** *adj (+er)* früh; *(sooner than expected)* zu früh; *fruit, vegetable* Früh-. **it was ~ in the morning** es war früh am Morgen; **to be an ~ riser** Frühaufsteher sein; **in the ~ hours** in den frühen Morgenstunden; **in the ~ morning/afternoon** am frühen Morgen/Nachmittag; **in ~ spring/summer** zu Beginn des Frühjahrs/im Frühsommer; **in his ~ youth** in seiner frühen Jugend; **from an ~ age** von frühester Jugend an; **she's in her ~ forties** sie ist Anfang Vierzig; **to take ~ retirement** sich vorzeitig pensionieren lassen; **at the earliest possible moment** so bald wie (irgend) möglich.

2 *adv* früh. **you're ~ today** Sie sind heute ja früh dran; **sorry, am I ~?** bin ich zu früh?; **earlier on this evening** zuvor am Abend; **I saw him earlier on this week** ich habe ihn Anfang der Woche gesehen; **earlier on that year Jim had ...** Jim hatte früher in dem Jahr ...; **the earliest he can come is ...** er kann frühestens ... kommen; **as ~ as 1935** schon 1935; **she left ten minutes ~** sie ist zehn Minuten früher gegangen.
early: ~ bird *n (in morning)* Frühaufsteher(in *f*) *m*; *(arriving etc)* Frühankömmling *m*; **~ closing** *n* **it's ~ closing today** die Geschäfte haben heute nachmittag geschlossen; **~-warning system** *n* Frühwarnsystem *nt*.
ear: ~mark *vt (fig)* vorsehen; **~-muffs** *npl* Ohrenschützer *pl*.
earn [ɜːn] *vt* verdienen; *(Fin) interest* bringen.
earnest ['ɜːnɪst] **1** *adj* ernsthaft; *hope* aufrichtig. **2** *n* **in ~** *(with determination)* ernsthaft; *(without joking)* im Ernst; **this time I'm in ~** diesmal meine ich es ernst; **it is snowing in ~ now** jetzt schneit es richtig.
earnestness ['ɜːnɪstnɪs] *n* Ernsthaftigkeit *f*; *(of voice)* Ernst *m*.
earnings ['ɜːnɪŋz] *npl* Verdienst *m*.
ear: ~-phones *npl* Kopfhörer *pl*; **~-plug** *n* Ohropax ® *nt*; **~-ring** *n* Ohrring *m*; **~shot** *n*: **out of/within ~shot** außer/in Hörweite; **~-splitting** *adj* ohrenbetäubend.
earth [ɜːθ] **1** *n* **(a)** *(also Brit Elec)* Erde *f*. **on ~** auf der Erde; **to the ends of the ~** bis ans Ende der Welt; **where/who** *etc* **on ~?** *(col)* wo/wer *etc* ... bloß?; **nothing on ~ will stop me now** keine Macht der Welt hält mich jetzt noch auf; **you look like nothing on ~** *(col)* du siehst unmöglich aus *(col)*; **it cost the ~** *(col)* das hat eine schöne Stange Geld gekostet *(col)*; **to bring sb down to ~ (with a bump)** *(fig)* jdn (unsanft) wieder auf den Boden der Tatsachen zurückholen. **(b)** *(of fox)* Bau *m*. **to go to ~** im Bau verschwinden; *(criminal)* untertauchen; **to run sb to ~** *(fig)* jdn ausfindig machen. **2** *vt (Elec)* erden.
earthenware ['ɜːθənwɛəʳ] **1** *n (material)* Ton *m*; *(dishes etc)* Tongeschirr *nt*. **2** *adj* aus Ton, Ton-.
earthly ['ɜːθlɪ] **1** *adj* **(a)** irdisch. **(b)** *(col)* **there is no ~ reason to think ...** es besteht nicht der geringste Grund für die Annahme ... **2** *n (col)* **she hasn't an ~** sie hat nicht die geringste Chance.
earth: ~-moving equipment *n* Erdbewegungsmaschinen *pl*; **~quake** *n* Erdbeben *nt*; **~worm** *n* Regenwurm *m*.
earthy ['ɜːθɪ] *adj (+er)* **(a)** *taste, smell* erdig. **(b)** *person, humour* derb.
earwig ['ɪəwɪg] *n* Ohrwurm *m*.
ease [iːz] **1** *n* **(a)** Behagen *nt*. **I am never at ~ in his company** in seiner Gegenwart bin ich immer etwas befangen; **to put** *or* **set sb at his ~** jdm die Befangenheit nehmen; **to put** *or* **set sb's mind at ~** jdn beruhigen; **to feel at ~ with sb** sich bei jdm wohlfühlen; **(stand) at ~!** *(Mil)* rührt euch! **(b) with ~** mit Leichtigkeit; **a life of ~** ein beschauliches Dasein. **2** *vt* **(a)** *pain* lindern; *mind* erleichtern. **(b)** *rope, strap* lockern; *pressure, tension* verringern. **(c) to ~ in the clutch** *(Aut)* die Kupplung langsam kommen lassen; **he ~d the lid off** er löste behutsam den Deckel. **3** *vi* nachlassen; *(situation)* sich entspannen.
♦ **ease off** *or* **up** *vi (slow down, relax)* langsamer werden; *(driver)* verlangsamen; *(situation)* sich entspannen; *(pain, rain)* nachlassen. **the doctor told him to ~ ~** der Arzt riet ihm, etwas kürzer zu treten.
easel ['iːzl] *n* Staffelei *f*.
easily ['iːzɪlɪ] *adv* leicht. **he is ~ the best** er ist mit Abstand der beste; **it's ~ 25 miles** es sind gut und gerne 25 Meilen.

easiness ['i:zɪnɪs] *n* Leichtigkeit *f.*
east [i:st] **1** *n* **(a)** Osten *m.* **in/to the ~** im Osten/ nach Osten; **from the ~** von Osten; **to the ~ of** östlich von. **(b)** *(Geog, Pol)* **the E~** der Osten; **from the E~** aus dem Osten. **2** *adv* nach Osten, ostwärts. **~ of** östlich von. **3** *adj* östlich, Ost-. **~ wind** Ostwind *m;* **E~ Berlin** *n* Ostberlin *nt.*
Easter ['i:stəʳ] **1** *n* Ostern *nt.* **at ~** an *or* zu Ostern. **2** *adj attr week, egg* Oster-. **~ Monday** Ostermontag *m;* **~ Sunday, ~ Day** Ostersonntag *m.*
easterly ['i:stəlɪ] *adj* östlich, Ost-.
eastern ['i:stən] *adj* Ost-, östlich; *attitude* orientalisch. **the ~ bloc** der Ostblock.
east: E~ German *adj* ostdeutsch *(dated),* DDR-; **E~ Germany** *n* die DDR; **~ward(s)** *adv* ostwärts, nach Osten.
easy ['i:zɪ] **1** *adj (+er)* **(a)** leicht. **it's ~ for you to say that** du hast gut reden; **he was an ~ winner** er hat mühelos gewonnen; **he is ~ to get on with** mit ihm kann man gut auskommen; **~ money** leicht verdientes Geld. **(b)** *(free from discomfort etc)* bequem, leicht; *manners, movement* ungezwungen; *style* flüssig. **in ~ stages** in bequemen Etappen; **on ~ terms** *(Comm)* zu günstigen Bedingungen; **I'm ~** *(col)* mir ist alles recht. **2** *adv* **~!, ~ does it!** immer sachte!; **to take things** *or* **it ~** *(healthwise)* sich schonen; **take it ~!** *(don't worry)* nimm's nicht so schwer; *(don't get carried away, don't rush)* immer mit der Ruhe!; **to go ~ on sth** sparsam mit etw umgehen; **to go ~ on sb** nicht zu hart mit jdm sein; **stand ~!** *(Mil)* rührt euch!
easy: ~ chair *n* Sessel *m;* **~ come ~ go** *interj* wie gewonnen, so zerronnen *(Prov);* **~-going** *adj (not anxious)* gelassen; *(lax)* lässig.
eat [i:t] *(vb: pret* **ate,** *ptp* **eaten)** *vti (person)* essen; *(animal)* fressen. **to ~ one's breakfast** frühstücken; **he's ~ing us out of house and home** *(col)* der frißt uns noch die Haare vom Kopf *(col);* **to ~ one's words** alles zurücknehmen; **he won't ~ you** *(col)* er wird dich schon nicht fressen *(col);* **what's ~ing you?** *(col)* was hast du denn?
♦**eat away** *vt sep (sea)* auswaschen; *(acid)* zerfressen.
♦**eat into** *vi +prep obj metal* anfressen; *capital* angreifen.
♦**eat out 1** *vi* essen gehen. **2** *vt sep* **to ~ one's heart ~** Trübsal blasen.
♦**eat up 1** *vt sep* **(a)** aufessen; *(animal)* auffressen. **(b)** *(fig: use up)* verbrauchen. **this car ~s ~ the miles** der Wagen gibt ganz schön was her *(col).* **2** *vi* aufessen.
eatable ['i:təbl] *adj* eßbar, genießbar.
eaten ['i:tn] *ptp of* **eat.**
eater ['i:təʳ] *n* Esser(in *f*) *m.*
eating: ~ apple *n* Eßapfel *m;* **~ place** *n* Eßlokal *nt.*
eau de Cologne ['əʊdəkə'ləʊn] *n* Kölnisch Wasser *nt.*
eaves ['i:vz] *npl* Dachvorsprung *m.*
eavesdrop ['i:vzdrɒp] *vi* (heimlich) lauschen. **to ~ on a conversation** ein Gespräch belauschen.
ebb [eb] **1** *n* Ebbe *f.* **~ and flow** Ebbe und Flut *f; (fig)* Auf und Ab *nt;* **at a low ~** *(fig)* in einem Tief. **2** *vi* **(a)** *(tide)* zurückgehen. **to ~ and flow** *(lit, fig)* kommen und gehen. **(b)** *(fig: also* **~ away)** *(enthusiasm etc)* verebben.
ebony ['ebənɪ] *n* Ebenholz *nt.*
ebullient [ɪ'bʌlɪənt] *adj* überschwenglich; *mood* übersprudelnd.
eccentric [ɪk'sentrɪk] **1** *adj* exzentrisch. **2** *n* Exzentriker(in *f*) *m.*
eccentricity [ˌeksən'trɪsɪtɪ] *n* Exzentrizität *f.*
ecclesiastical [ɪˌkli:zɪ'æstɪkəl] *adj* kirchlich.
echo ['ekəʊ] **1** *n* Echo *nt.* **2** *vt sound* zurückwerfen; *(fig)* wiedergeben. **3** *vi* widerhallen *(with* von*); (room)* hallen. **it ~es in here** hier ist ein Echo.
éclair [eɪ'klɛəʳ] *n* Eclair *nt,* Liebesknochen *m.*
eclipse [ɪ'klɪps] **1** *(Astron)* **~ of the sun/moon** Sonnen-/Mondfinsternis *f.* **2** *vt (Astron)* verfinstern; *(fig)* in den Schatten stellen.
ecological [ˌi:kəʊ'lɒdʒɪkəl] *adj* ökologisch.
ecologist [ɪ'kɒlədʒɪst] *n* Ökologe *m,* Ökologin *f.*
ecology [ɪ'kɒlədʒɪ] *n* Ökologie *f.*
economic ['i:kə'nɒmɪk] *adj* wirtschaftlich, ökonomisch; *development, system also, miracle* Wirtschafts-.
economical [ˌi:kə'nɒmɪkəl] *adj* wirtschaftlich, ökonomisch; *person* sparsam. **to be ~ with sth** mit etw haushalten; **to be ~ (to run)** *(car)* wirtschaftlich sein.
economics [ˌi:kə'nɒmɪks] *n* **(a)** *with sing or pl vb* Volkswirtschaft *f; (management studies)* Betriebswirtschaft *f.* **(b)** *pl (economic aspect)* Wirtschaftlichkeit *f.* **the ~ of the situation** die wirtschaftliche Seite der Situation.
economist [ɪ'kɒnəmɪst] *n see* **economics** Volkswirt(in *f*); Betriebswirt(in *f*) *m.*
economize [ɪ'kɒnəmaɪz] *vi* sparen.
♦**economize on** *vi +prep obj* sparen.
economy [ɪ'kɒnəmɪ] *n* **(a)** *(system)* Wirtschaft *f no pl; (from a monetary aspect)* Konjunktur *f.* **(b)** *(in time, money)* Einsparung *f.* **a false ~** falsche Sparsamkeit. **(c)** *(thrift)* Sparsamkeit *f.* **~ of effort** geringer Kräfteaufwand.
economy: ~ class *n* Touristenklasse *f;* **~ drive** *n* Sparmaßnahmen *pl;* **~ size** *n* Sparpackung *f.*
ecstasy ['ekstəsɪ] *n* Ekstase *f.* **to go into ecstasies over sth** über etw *(acc)* in Verzückung geraten.
ecstatic [eks'tætɪk] *adj* ekstatisch, verzückt.
Ecuador ['ekwədɔ:ʳ] *n* Ecuador, Ekuador *nt.*
ecumenical [ˌi:kjʊ'menɪkəl] *adj* ökumenisch.
eczema ['eksɪmə] *n* (Haut)ausschlag *m.*
eddy ['edɪ] **1** *n* Wirbel *m.* **2** *vi* wirbeln.
edge [edʒ] **1** *n* **(a)** *(of knife)* Schneide *f.* **to take the ~ off sth** *(fig) sensation* etw *(dat)* die Wirkung nehmen; **that took the ~ off my appetite** das nahm mir erst einmal den Hunger; **the noise/ taste sets my teeth on ~** das Geräusch geht mir durch und durch/der Geschmack ist mir widerlich; **to be on ~** nervös sein; **to have the ~ on sb/sth** jdm/etw überlegen sein. **(b)** *(outer limit)* Rand *m; (of cloth, table, of brick)* Kante *f; (of lake, river also)* Ufer *nt.*
2 *vt* **(a)** *(put a border on)* besetzen, einfassen. **(b) to ~ one's way towards sth** *(slowly)* sich allmählich auf etw *(acc)* zubewegen; *(carefully)* sich vorsichtig auf etw *(acc)* zubewegen; **she ~d her way through the crowd** sie schlängelte sich durch die Menge.
3 *vi* sich schieben. **to ~ away from sb/sth** sich allmählich immer weiter von jdm/etw entfernen; **to ~ up to sb** sich an jdn heranmachen; **he ~d past me** er schob sich an mir vorbei.
edgeways ['edʒweɪz] *adv* mit der Schmalseite voran. **I couldn't get a word in ~** ich bin überhaupt nicht zu Wort gekommen.
edging ['edʒɪŋ] *n* Borte, Einfassung *f.*
edgy ['edʒɪ] *adj (+er) person* nervös.
edible ['edɪbl] *adj* eßbar, genießbar.
edict ['i:dɪkt] *n* Erlaß *m.*
edifice ['edɪfɪs] *n* Gebäude *nt.*
edify ['edɪfaɪ] *vt* erbauen.
edifying ['edɪfaɪɪŋ] *adj* erbaulich.
edit ['edɪt] *vt series, newspaper, magazine* herausgeben; *book, text* redigieren; *film, tape* schneiden.
edition [ɪ'dɪʃən] *n* Ausgabe *f; (printing)* Auflage *f.*
editor [edɪtəʳ] *n* Herausgeber(in *f*) *m; (publisher's)* (Verlags)lektor(in *f*) *m; (Film)* Cutter(in *f*) *m.* **political/sports ~** politischer Redakteur/Sportredakteur *m.*
editorial [edɪ'tɔ:rɪəl] **1** *adj* redaktionell, Redaktions-. **~ assistant** Redaktionsassistent(in *f*) *m;* **~ office** Redaktion *f; (Publishing also)* (Verlags)lektorat *nt.* **2** *n* Leitartikel *m.*

educate ['edjʊkeɪt] *vt* erziehen; *the mind* schulen; *one's tastes* (aus)bilden. **he was ~d at Eton** er ist in Eton zur Schule gegangen.
educated ['edjʊkeɪtɪd] *adj* gebildet.
education [ˌedjʊ'keɪʃən] *n* Erziehung *f*; *(studies, training)* Ausbildung *f*; *(knowledge, culture)* Bildung *f*. **College of E~** Pädagogische Hochschule; *(for graduates)* Studienseminar *nt*; **~ is free** die Schulausbildung ist kostenlos.
educational [edjʊ'keɪʃənl] *adj* pädagogisch; *films, games also* Lehr-; *publisher also* Schulbuch-; *experience* lehrreich.
educator ['edjʊkeɪtə^r] *n* Pädagoge, Erzieher *m*.
Edwardian [ed'wɔːdɪən] *adj* aus der Zeit Eduards VII.
EEC = European Economic Community EG *f*.
eel [iːl] *n* Aal *m*.
eerie ['ɪərɪ] *adj (+er)* unheimlich.
efface [ɪ'feɪs] *vt* auslöschen.
effect [ɪ'fekt] **1** *n* **(a)** *(result)* Wirkung *f*, Effekt *m*; *(repercussion)* Auswirkung *f*. **the ~ of this is that ...** das hat zur Folge, daß ...; **to feel the ~s of an accident/of drink** die Folgen eines Unfalls/des Trinkens spüren; **to no ~** ohne Erfolg; **to have an ~ on sb/sth** eine Wirkung auf jdn/etw haben; **to take ~** *(drug)* wirken. **(b)** *(impression)* Wirkung *f*, Effekt *m*. **to create an ~** eine Wirkung *or* einen Effekt erzielen; **it's all done solely for ~** das wird alles bloß des Effekts wegen getan. **(c)** *(meaning)* **an announcement to the ~ that ...** eine Erklärung des Inhalts, daß ...; **... or words to that ~ ...** oder etwas in diesem Sinne. **(d) ~s** *pl (property)* Effekten *pl*. **(e) in ~** effektiv. **(f)** *(of laws)* **to be in ~** gültig *or* in Kraft sein; **to come into ~** in Kraft treten; **to put sth into ~** etw in Kraft setzen.
2 *vt* bewirken, herbeiführen; *(form) sale* tätigen.
effective [ɪ'fektɪv] *adj* **(a)** wirksam, effektiv. **to become ~** *(law)* in Kraft treten; *(drug)* wirken. **(b)** *(creating impression)* wirkungsvoll, effektvoll. **(c)** *(real) contribution* tatsächlich; *profit also* effektiv.
effectiveness [ɪ'fektɪvnɪs] *n see adj* **(a)** Wirksamkeit *f*. **(b)** Wirkung *f*, Effekt *m*.
effectual [ɪ'fektjʊəl] *adj* wirksam.
effeminate [ɪ'femɪnɪt] *adj* weibisch.
effervesce [efə'ves] *vi* sprudeln.
effervescence [efə'vesns] *n (lit)* Sprudeln *nt*; *(fig)* überschäumendes Temperament.
effervescent [ˌefə'vesnt] *adj* sprudelnd; *(fig)* überschäumend.
effete [ɪ'fiːt] *adj* schwach; *person* saft- und kraftlos.
efficacious [efɪ'keɪʃəs] *adj* wirksam.
efficacy ['efɪkəsɪ] *n* Wirksamkeit *f*.
efficiency [ɪ'fɪʃənsɪ] *n (of person)* Tüchtigkeit *f*; *(of machine, factory)* Leistungsfähigkeit *f*; *(of method, organization)* Rationalität, Effizienz *(geh) f*.
efficient [ɪ'fɪʃənt] *adj person* fähig; *worker, secretary etc also* tüchtig; *machine, factory, company* leistungsfähig; *method, organization* rationell. **to be ~ at sth/at doing sth** etw gut verstehen/es gut verstehen, etw zu tun; **the ~ working of a machine** das gute Funktionieren einer Maschine.
efficiently [ɪ'fɪʃəntlɪ] *adj* gut. **they handled the sale ~** sie haben den Verkauf gekonnt abgewickelt.
effigy ['efɪdʒɪ] *n* Bildnis *nt*.
effluent ['eflʊənt] *(sewage)* Abwasser *nt*.
effort ['efət] *n* **(a)** *(attempt)* Bemühung *f*; *(strain, hard work)* Anstrengung, Mühe *f*. **to make an ~ to do sth** sich bemühen *or* anstrengen, etw zu tun; **to make every possible ~ to do sth** sich *(dat)* die größte Mühe geben, etw zu tun; **he made no ~ to be polite** er gab sich *(dat)* keine Mühe, höflich zu sein; **it's an ~** es kostet einige Mühe; **if it's not too much of an ~ for you** *(iro)* wenn es dir nicht zu viel Mühe macht; **come on, make an ~** komm, streng dich ein bißchen an. **(b)** *(col)* **it was a poor ~** das war eine schwache Leistung; **his first ~ at making a film** sein erster Versuch, einen Film zu drehen.
effortless ['efətlɪs] *adj* mühelos, leicht; *style* flüssig.
effrontery [ɪ'frʌntərɪ] *n* Unverschämtheit *f*.
effusive [ɪ'fjuːsɪv] *adj* überschwenglich.
eg = for example z.B.
egalitarian [ɪˌgælɪ'tɛərɪən] *adj* egalitär *(geh)*; *principle also* Gleichheits-.
egg [eg] *n* Ei *nt*. **to put all one's ~s in one basket** *(prov)* alles auf eine Karte setzen.
♦ **egg on** *vt sep* anstacheln.
egg: ~-cup *n* Eierbecher *m*; **~head** *n (pej col)* Intellektuelle(r) *mf*, Eierkopf *m (col)*; **~-plant** *n* Aubergine *f*; **~shell** *n* Eierschale *f*; **~-white** *n* Eiweiß *nt*; **~ yolk** *n* Eidotter *m*, Eigelb *nt*.
ego ['iːgəʊ] *n (Psych)* Ego, Ich *nt*; *(col)* Selbstbewußtsein *nt*; *(conceit)* Einbildung *f*. **this will boost his ~** das wird ihm Auftrieb geben.
egocentric(al) [egəʊ'sentrɪk(əl)] *adj* egozentrisch.
egoism ['egəʊɪzəm] *n* Egoismus *m*, Selbstsucht *f*.
egotism ['egəʊtɪzəm] *n* Egotismus *m*.
egotist ['egəʊtɪst] *n* Egotist *m*.
egotistic(al) [ˌegəʊ'tɪstɪk(əl)] *adj* ichbezogen.
ego-trip ['iːgəʊtrɪp] *n (col)* **he's on one of his ~s** er gibt wieder so an; **it won't last long, it's just some sort of ~** das dauert nicht lange, er will nur sein Selbstgefühl aufpäppeln.
Egypt ['iːdʒɪpt] *n* Ägypten *nt*.
Egyptian [ɪ'dʒɪpʃən] **1** *adj* ägyptisch. **2** *n* **(a)** Ägypter(in *f*) *m*. **(b)** *(language)* Ägyptisch *nt*.
eiderdown ['aɪdədaʊn] *n (quilt)* Daunendecke *f*.
eight [eɪt] **1** *adj* acht. **2** *n* Acht *f*; *see* **six.**
eighteen ['eɪ'tiːn] *adj* achtzehn.
eighteenth ['eɪ'tiːnθ] *adj* achtzehnte(r, s); *see* **sixteenth.**
eighth [eɪtθ] **1** *adj* achte(r, s). **2** *n (fraction)* Achtel *nt*; *(of series)* Achte(r,s); *see* **sixth.**
eightieth ['eɪtɪəθ] *adj* achtzigste(r, s); *see* **sixtieth.**
eighty ['eɪtɪ] *adj* achtzig; *see* **sixty.**
Eire ['ɛərə] *n* Irland *nt*.
either ['aɪðə^r] **1** *adj, pron* **(a)** *(one or other)* eine(r, s) (von beiden). **there are two boxes, take ~** hier sind zwei Schachteln, nimm eine davon. **(b)** *(each, both)* jede(r, s), beide *pl*. **~ day would suit me** beide Tage passen mir; **which bus will you take? — ~ (will do)** welchen Bus wollen Sie nehmen? — das ist egal; **on ~ side of the street** auf beiden Seiten der Straße; **it wasn't in ~ (box)** es war in keiner der beiden (Kisten); **~ way we lose out** wir machen auf jeden Fall einen Verlust.
2 *adv, conj* **(a)** *(after neg statement)* auch nicht. **he can't act ~** schauspielern kann er auch nicht; **I haven't ~** ich auch nicht. **(b) ~ ... or** entweder ... oder; *(after a negative)* weder ... noch; **~ be quiet or go out!** entweder bist du ruhig oder du gehst!; **I have never been to Paris, nor to Rome ~** ich bin bisher weder in Paris noch in Rom gewesen.
ejaculate [ɪ'dʒækjʊleɪt] *vi* aufschreien; *(Physiol)* ejakulieren.
ejaculation [ɪˌdʒækjʊ'leɪʃən] *n (cry)* Ausruf *m*; *(Physiol)* Ejakulation *f*, Samenerguß *m*.
eject [ɪ'dʒekt] **1** *vt heckler, tenant* hinauswerfen; *cartridge* auswerfen. **2** *vi (pilot)* den Schleudersitz betätigen.
ejection [ɪ'dʒekʃən] *n* Hinauswurf *m*; *(of cartridge)* Auswerfen *nt*.
ejector seat [i'dʒektəˌsiːt] *n (Aviat)* Schleudersitz *m*.
♦ **eke out** ['iːkaʊt] *vt sep* strecken. **to ~ ~ a living** sich recht und schlecht durchschlagen.

elaborate [ɪ'læbərɪt] **1** *adj design, hairstyle, pattern, drawing* kunstvoll; *style (of writing) also* ausführlich, detailliert; *plan* ausgeklügelt; *preparations* kompliziert. **an ~ meal** ein großes Menü. **2** [ɪ'læbəreɪt] *vt (work out)* ausarbeiten; *(describe)* ausführen. **3** [ɪ'læbəreɪt] *vi* **could you ~ (on that)?** könnten Sie das etwas näher ausführen?
elapse [ɪ'læps] *vi* vergehen, verstreichen.
elastic [ɪ'læstɪk] **1** *adj (lit, fig)* elastisch. **~ band** *(Brit)* Gummiband *nt.* **2** *n* Gummi(band *nt) m*; *(US: rubber band)* Gummi *m.*
elasticity [ˌiːlæs'tɪsɪtɪ] *n* Elastizität *f.*
elated [ɪ'leɪtɪd] *adj* begeistert.
elation [ɪ'leɪʃən] *n* Begeisterung *f (at* über *+acc).*
elbow ['elbəʊ] **1** *n* Ellbogen *m.* **out at the ~s** an den Ellbogen durchgewetzt. **2** *vt* **he ~ed his way through the crowd** er boxte sich durch die Menge; **to ~ sb aside** jdn beiseite stoßen.
elbow: ~-grease *n (col)* Muskelkraft *f*; **~-room** *n (col: lit, fig)* Ellbogenfreiheit *f (col).*
elder[1] ['eldə^r] **1** *adj attr comp of* **old** *brother* ältere(r, s). **~ statesman** erfahrener Staatsmann. **2** *n* **(a) respect your ~s and betters** du mußt Respekt vor Älteren haben. **(b)** *(of tribe, Church)* Älteste(r) *m.*
elder[2] ['eldə^r] *n (Bot)* Holunder *m.*
elderberry ['eldəˌberɪ] *n* Holunderbeere *f.*
elderly ['eldəlɪ] *adj* ältlich, ältere(r, s) *attr.*
eldest ['eldɪst] *adj attr superl of* **old** älteste(r, s).
elect [ɪ'lekt] **1** *vt* **(a)** wählen. **he was ~ed chairman** er wurde zum Vorsitzenden gewählt. **(b)** *(choose)* **to ~ to do sth** sich dafür entscheiden, etw zu tun. **2** *adj* **the president ~** der designierte Präsident.
election [ɪ'lekʃən] *n* Wahl *f.* **~ campaign** Wahlkampf *m.*
electioneering [ɪˌlekʃə'nɪərɪŋ] *n* Wahlkampf *m*; *(propaganda)* Wahlpropaganda *f.*
elector [ɪ'lektə^r] *n* Wähler(in *f*) *m.*
electoral [ɪ'lektərəl] *adj* Wahl-. **~ college** Wahlmännergremium *nt*; **~ roll** Wählerverzeichnis *nt.*
electorate [ɪ'lektərɪt] *n* Wähler *pl*, Wählerschaft *f.*
electric [ɪ'lektrɪk] *adj* elektrisch. **the atmosphere was ~** es herrschte Hochspannung; **the effect was ~** *(col)* das hatte eine tolle Wirkung.
electrical [ɪ'lektrɪkəl] *adj* Elektro-, elektrisch. **~ engineer** Elektrotechniker *m*; **~ engineering** Elektrotechnik *f.*
electric: ~ blanket *n* Heizdecke *f*; **~ chair** *n* elektrischer Stuhl; **~ cooker** *n* Elektroherd *m*; **~ fire** *n* elektrisches Heizgerät.
electrician [ɪlek'trɪʃən] *n* Elektriker *m.*
electricity [ɪlek'trɪsɪtɪ] *n* Elektrizität *f*; *(electric power for use)* Strom *m.* **to turn off the ~** den Strom abschalten; **~ meter** Stromzähler *m.*
electric: ~ light *n* elektrisches Licht; **~ motor** *n* Elektromotor *m*; **~ shock** *n* elektrischer Schlag; **~ shock treatment** (Elektro)schocktherapie *f.*
electrify [ɪ'lektrɪfaɪ] *vt* **(a)** *(Rail)* elektrifizieren. **(b)** *(charge with electricity)* unter Strom setzen. **(c)** *(fig)* elektrisieren.
electrifying [ɪ'lektrɪfaɪɪŋ] *adj (fig)* elektrisierend.
electrocute [ɪ'lektrəkjuːt] *vt* durch einen (Strom)schlag töten; *(execute)* auf dem elektrischen Stuhl hinrichten.
electrode [ɪ'lektrəʊd] *n* Elektrode *f.*
electrolysis [ɪlek'trɒlɪsɪs] *n* Elektrolyse *f.*
electromagnetic [ɪ'lektrəʊmæg'netɪk] *adj* elektromagnetisch.
electron [ɪ'lektrɒn] *n* Elektron *nt.* **~ microscope** Elektronenmikroskop *nt.*
electronic [ɪlek'trɒnɪk] *adj* elektronisch.
electronics [ɪlek'trɒnɪks] *n* Elektronik *f.*
electroplated [ɪ'lektrəʊpleɪtɪd] *adj* (galvanisch) versilbert/verchromt *etc.*
elegance ['elɪgəns] *n* Eleganz *f.*
elegant ['elɪgənt] *adj* elegant.
elegy ['elɪdʒɪ] *n* Elegie *f.*
element ['elɪmənt] *n (also Elec)* Element *nt*; *(usu pl: of a subject also)* Grundbegriff *m.* **the ~ of chance** das Zufallselement; **to be in one's ~** in seinem Element sein; **to be out of one's ~** *(with people)* sich fehl am Platz fühlen; *(with subject)* sich nicht auskennen.
elementary [ˌelɪ'mentərɪ] *adj* **(a)** *(simple)* einfach, elementar. **(b)** *(basic)* elementar, Grund-. **~ course** Grundkurs *m*; **~ school** Grundschule *f.*
elephant ['elɪfənt] *n* Elefant *m.*
elevate ['elɪveɪt] *vt* **(a)** heben. **(b) elevating reading** erbauliche Lektüre.
elevated ['elɪveɪtɪd] *adj* **(a)** *position* hoch(liegend), höher; *platform* erhöht. **(b)** *(fig) position, style* gehoben; *thoughts* erhaben.
elevation [ˌelɪ'veɪʃən] *n* **(a)** *(lit)* Hebung *f.* **(b)** *(of thought)* Erhabenheit *f*; *(of position, style)* Gehobenheit *f.* **(c)** *(above sea level)* Höhe *f* über dem Meeresspiegel; *(hill)* Anhöhe *f.* **(d)** *(Archit: drawing)* Aufriß *m.* **front ~** Frontansicht *f.*
elevator ['elɪveɪtə^r] *n (US)* Fahrstuhl, Aufzug *m.*
eleven [ɪ'levn] **1** *n* **(a)** *(number)* Elf *f.* **the ~ plus** *(Brit Sch) Aufnahmeprüfung in eine weiterführende Schule.* **(b)** *(Sport)* Elf *f.* **the second ~** die zweite Mannschaft. **2** *adj* elf; *see* **six.**
elevenses [ɪ'levnzɪz] *n sing or pl (Brit)* zweites Frühstück.
eleventh [ɪ'levnθ] *adj* elfte(r, s). **at the ~ hour** *(fig)* in letzter Minute; *see* **sixth.**
elf [elf] *n, pl* **elves** Elf *m*, Elfe *f*; *(mischievous)* Kobold *m.*
elicit [ɪ'lɪsɪt] *vt* entlocken *(from sb* jdm*).*
eligibility [ˌelɪdʒə'bɪlɪtɪ] *n* Berechtigung *f.* **graded in order of ~** nach Eignung geordnet.
eligible ['elɪdʒəbl] *adj* in Frage kommend; *(for competition etc also)* teilnahmeberechtigt; *(for grants etc also)* berechtigt; *(for membership)* aufnahmeberechtigt. **an ~ bachelor** ein begehrter Junggeselle.
eliminate [ɪ'lɪmɪneɪt] *vt* **(a)** ausschließen; *competitor* ausschalten. **our team was ~d in the second round** unsere Mannschaft schied in der zweiten Runde aus. **(b)** *(kill)* ausschalten, eliminieren.
elimination [ɪˌlɪmɪ'neɪʃən] *n see vt* **(a)** Ausschluß *m*; Ausschaltung *f.* **by (a) process of ~** durch negative Auslese. **(b)** Ausschaltung, Eliminierung *f.*
élite [eɪ'liːt] *n* Elite *f.*
élitism [eɪ'liːtɪzəm] *n* Elitedenken *nt.*
élitist [eɪ'liːtɪst] *adj* elitär.
elixir [ɪ'lɪksə^r] *n* Elixier *nt*, Auszug *m.*
Elizabethan [ɪˌlɪzə'biːθən] *adj* elisabethanisch.
elk [elk] *n* Elch *m.*
ellipse [ɪ'lɪps] *n* Ellipse *f.*
elm [elm] *n* Ulme *f.*
elocution [ˌelə'kjuːʃən] *n* Sprechtechnik *f.* **~ classes** Sprecherziehung *f.*
elongate ['iːlɒŋgeɪt] *vt* verlängern.
elope [ɪ'ləʊp] *vi* durchbrennen.
elopement [ɪ'ləʊpmənt] *n* Durchbrennen *nt.*
eloquence ['eləkwəns] *n see adj* Wortgewandtheit *f*; Wohlgesetztheit *f*; Beredtheit *f.*
eloquent ['eləkwənt] *adj* wortgewandt; *speech* wohlgesetzt; *(fig) gesture* beredt, vielsagend.
else [els] *adv* **(a)** *(after pron)* andere(r, s). **anybody ~ would have done it** jeder andere hätte es gemacht; **somebody ~** *(in addition)* sonst jemand; *(somebody different)* jemand anders; **have you anything ~?** haben Sie sonst noch etwas?; **something ~** sonst etwas; etwas anderes; **anywhere ~** sonstwo; **but they haven't got anywhere ~ to go** aber sie können sonst nirgends anders hingehen; **somewhere ~** woanders, anderswo; *(with motion)* woandershin, anderswohin.

(b) *(after pron, neg)* **nobody ~, no one ~** sonst niemand, niemand anders; **nobody ~ understood** niemand anders hat es verstanden; **nothing ~** sonst nichts, nichts anderes; **nothing ~, thank you** danke, nichts weiter; **nowhere ~** sonst nirgends, nirgendwo anders; **there's nothing ~ for it but to go** da gibt es keinen anderen Ausweg, als zu gehen.

(c) *(after interrog)* **where ~?** wo sonst?; **who ~?** wer sonst?; **what ~?** was sonst?; **what ~ could I do?** was konnte ich sonst tun?

(d) *(adv of quantity)* **and much ~** und vieles andere; **there is little ~ to be done** da bleibt nicht viel zu tun übrig.

(e) *(otherwise, if not)* sonst, andernfalls. **do it now (or) ~ you'll be punished** tu es jetzt oder es setzt Strafe; **you better had, or ~ ...!** mach das bloß, sonst ...!

elsewhere [ˌels'weəʳ] *adv* woanders, anderswo; *(to another place)* woandershin, anderswohin. **in Wales and ~** unter anderem in Wales.

elucidate [ɪ'luːsɪdeɪt] *vt text* erklären; *mystery* aufklären.

elude [ɪ'luːd] *vt observation, justice* sich entziehen *(+dat)*; *question* ausweichen *(+dat)*; *police, enemy* entkommen *(+dat)*. **success has ~d him** der Erfolg wollte sich nicht einstellen.

elusive [ɪ'luːsɪv] *adj* schwer faßbar; *concept, meaning also* schwer definierbar; *thoughts, memory* flüchtig; *happiness* unerreichbar; *answer* ausweichend; *fox etc* schwer zu fangen.

elves [elvz] *pl of* **elf.**

emaciated [ɪ'meɪsɪeɪtɪd] *adj* ausgezehrt.

emanate ['eməneɪt] *vi* ausgehen *(from* von*)*; *(light also)* ausstrahlen *(from* von*)*; *(documents, instructions etc)* stammen *(from* aus*)*.

emancipate [ɪ'mænsɪpeɪt] *vt (lit, fig)* emanzipieren.

emancipated [ɪ'mænsɪpeɪtɪd] *adj (lit, fig)* emanzipiert.

emancipation [ɪˌmænsɪ'peɪʃən] *n (lit, fig)* Emanzipation *f.*

embalm [ɪm'bɑːm] *vt corpse* einbalsamieren.

embankment [ɪm'bæŋkmənt] *n* Böschung *f*; *(for railway)* Bahndamm *m*; *(holding back water)* Deich *m*; *(road beside a river)* Uferstraße *f.*

embargo [ɪm'bɑːgəʊ] *n, pl* **-es** Embargo *nt.* **to put an ~ on sth** ein Embargo über etw *(acc)* verhängen.

embark [ɪm'bɑːk] **1** *vt* einschiffen. **2** *vi* **(a)** *(Naut)* sich einschiffen; *(troops)* eingeschifft werden. **(b)** *(fig)* **to ~ up(on) sth** mit etw anfangen.

embarkation [ˌembɑː'keɪʃən] *n* Einschiffung *f.* **~ papers** Bordpapiere *pl.*

embarrass [ɪm'bærəs] *vt* in Verlegenheit bringen; *(generosity etc also)* beschämen. **I feel so ~ed about it** das ist mir so peinlich; **she was ~ed by the question** die Frage war ihr peinlich.

embarrassed [ɪm'bærəst] *adj* verlegen.

embarrassing [ɪm'bærəsɪŋ] *adj* peinlich.

embarrassment [ɪm'bærəsmənt] *n* Verlegenheit *f.* **to cause ~ to sb** jdn in Verlegenheit bringen; **much to my ~ she ...** sie ..., was mir sehr peinlich war; **financial ~** finanzielle Verlegenheit.

embassy ['embəsɪ] *n* Botschaft *f.*

embed [ɪm'bed] *vt* **the screws were so firmly ~ded that ...** die Schrauben steckten so fest, daß ...; **to be ~ded in sth** *(fig)* fest in etw *(dat)* verwurzelt sein.

embellish [ɪm'belɪʃ] *vt (adorn)* schmücken; *(fig) tale, account* ausschmücken; *truth* beschönigen.

embers ['embəz] *npl* Glut *f.*

embezzle [ɪm'bezl] *vt* unterschlagen.

embezzlement [ɪm'bezlmənt] *n* Unterschlagung *f.*

embittered [ɪm'bɪtəd] *adj person* verbittert; *relations* vergiftet.

emblem ['embləm] *n* Emblem *nt.*

embodiment [ɪm'bɒdɪmənt] *n* Verkörperung *f.* **to be the ~ of virtue** die Tugend in Person sein.

embody [ɪm'bɒdɪ] *vt* **(a)** *ideal etc* verkörpern. **(b)** *(include)* enthalten.

emboss [ɪm'bɒs] *vt metal, leather* prägen. **~ed wallpaper** Prägetapete *f*; **an ~ed silver tray** ein Silbertablett mit Relief.

embrace [ɪm'breɪs] **1** *vt* **(a)** *(hug)* umarmen, in die Arme schließen. **(b)** *religion* annehmen; *cause* sich annehmen *(+gen)*. **(c)** *(include)* umfassen, erfassen. **2** *vi* sich umarmen. **3** *n* Umarmung *f.*

embroider [ɪm'brɔɪdəʳ] *vt* **(a)** besticken; *pattern* sticken. **(b)** *(fig) facts, truth* ausschmücken.

embroidery [ɪm'brɔɪdərɪ] *n* **(a)** Stickerei *f.* **(b)** *(fig)* Ausschmückungen *pl.*

embroil [ɪm'brɔɪl] *vt* **to become ~ed in a dispute** in einen Streit verwickelt werden.

embryo ['embrɪəʊ] *n (lit, fig)* Embryo *m*; *(fig)* Keim *m.* **in ~** *(lit, fig)* im Keim.

embryonic [ˌembrɪ'ɒnɪk] *adj* embryonisch; *(fig)* keimhaft.

emend [ɪ'mend] *vt text* verbessern, korrigieren.

emerald ['emərəld] **1** *n (stone)* Smaragd *m*; *(colour)* Smaragdgrün *nt.* **2** *adj* Smaragd-. **the E~ Isle** die Grüne Insel.

emerge [ɪ'mɜːdʒ] *vi* **(a)** auftauchen. **he ~d the winner** er ging als Sieger hervor; **we ~d into the bright daylight** wir kamen heraus in das helle Tageslicht; **one arm ~d from beneath the blanket** ein Arm kam unter der Decke hervor. **(b)** *(come into being: life, new nation)* entstehen. **(c)** *(truth, nature of problem etc)* sich herausstellen. **it now ~s that ...** es stellt sich jetzt heraus, daß ...

emergence [ɪ'mɜːdʒəns] *n* Auftauchen *nt*; *(of new nation etc)* Entstehung *f*; *(of school of thought)* Aufkommen *nt.*

emergency [ɪ'mɜːdʒənsɪ] *n* Notfall *m*; *(state of ~)* Notlage *f.* **in case of ~** im Notfall; **to declare a state of ~** den Notstand ausrufen.

emergency *in cpds* Not-; **~ brake** *n* Notbremse *f*; **~ exit** *n* Notausgang *m*; **~ landing** *n* Notlandung *f*; **~ service** *n* Notdienst *m*; **~ stop** *n (Aut)* Vollbremsung *f*; **~ ward** *n* Unfallstation *f.*

emergent [ɪ'mɜːdʒənt] *adj nations* aufstrebend.

emery ['emərɪ]: **~ board** *n* Papiernagelfeile *f*; **~ paper** *n* Schmirgelpapier *nt.*

emetic [ɪ'metɪk] *n* Brechmittel *nt.*

emigrant ['emɪgrənt] *n* Auswanderer *m*; *(esp for political reasons)* Emigrant(in *f*) *m.*

emigrate ['emɪgreɪt] *vi* auswandern; *(esp for political reasons)* emigrieren.

emigration [ˌemɪ'greɪʃən] *n* Auswanderung *f*; *(esp for political reasons)* Emigration *f.*

émigré ['emɪgreɪ] *n* Emigrant(in *f*) *m.*

eminence ['emɪnəns] *n* **(a)** *(distinction)* hohes Ansehen. **(b)** *(of ground)* Erhebung *f.* **(c)** *(Eccl)* **His/Your E~** Seine/Eure Eminenz.

eminent ['emɪnənt] *adj person* (hoch)angesehen; *suitability, fairness* ausgesprochen, eminent.

eminently ['emɪnəntlɪ] *adv* ausgesprochen.

emissary ['emɪsərɪ] *n* Abgesandte(r) *mf.*

emission [ɪ'mɪʃən] *n* Ausstrahlung *f*; *(of heat also, of sound, smoke)* Abgabe *f*; *(of liquid)* Ausströmen *nt*; *(of lava)* Ausstoßen *nt.*

emit [ɪ'mɪt] *vt light* ausstrahlen; *radiation also* emittieren; *heat also, sound, smoke* abgeben; *lava, cry* ausstoßen.

emotion [ɪ'məʊʃən] *n* **(a)** Gefühl *nt*, Emotion *f.* **(b)** *no pl (state of being moved)* Bewegtheit *f.* **to show no ~** unbewegt bleiben; **in a voice full of ~** mit bewegter Stimme.

emotional [ɪ'məʊʃənl] *adj* **(a)** emotional, emotionell; *story, film, speech also* gefühlsbetont; *moment, writing also* gefühlvoll; *decision also* gefühlsmäßig; *day, experience* erregend; *letter* erregt. **~ state** Zustand *m* der Erregung; **it has an ~ appeal** es appelliert an das Gefühl. **(b)** *person* (leicht) erregbar, emotional. **don't get so ~ about it** reg dich nicht so darüber auf.

emotionalism [ɪ'məʊʃnəlɪzəm] *n* Gefühlsbetontheit *f*. **the article was sheer ~** der Artikel war reine Gefühlsduselei.
emotionally [ɪ'məʊʃnəlɪ] *adv behave, react* gefühlsmäßig, emotional; *(with feeling) speak* gefühlvoll; *(showing one is upset)* erregt. **an ~ deprived child** ein Kind *nt* ohne Nestwärme; **to be ~ disturbed** seelisch gestört sein; **I don't want to get ~ involved (with her)** ich will mich (bei ihr) nicht ernsthaft engagieren.
emotive [ɪ'məʊtɪv] *adj* gefühlsbetont; *word also* emotional gefärbt; *force of a word* emotional.
empathy ['empəθɪ] *n* Einfühlungsvermögen *nt*.
emperor ['empərə[r]] *n* Kaiser *m*.
emphasis ['emfəsɪs] *n* Betonung *f*. **to say sth with ~** etw mit Nachdruck betonen; **to lay ~** *or* **put the ~ on sth** etw betonen; **this year the ~ is on ...** dieses Jahr liegt der Akzent auf ...; **there is too much ~ on ...** ... wird zu sehr betont; **a change of ~** eine Akzentverschiebung.
emphasize ['emfəsaɪz] *vt* betonen.
emphatic [ɪm'fætɪk] *adj tone, manner* nachdrücklich, entschieden; *denial also* energisch.
emphatically [ɪm'fætɪkəlɪ] *adv state* mit Nachdruck, ausdrücklich; *deny, refuse* strikt, energisch. **most ~ not** auf gar keinen Fall.
empire ['empaɪə[r]] *n* Reich *nt*; *(fig: esp Comm)* Imperium *nt*.
empirical [em'pɪrɪkəl] *adj* empirisch.
employ [ɪm'plɔɪ] *vt* **(a)** beschäftigen; *(take on)* anstellen; *private detective* beauftragen. **he's ~ed in a bank** er arbeitet bei einer Bank. **(b)** *(use) method* anwenden; *time* verbringen.
employee [ˌɪmplɔɪ'iː] *n* Angestellte(r) *mf*. **~s and employers** Arbeitnehmer und Arbeitgeber; **the ~s** *(of one firm)* die Belegschaft.
employer [ɪm'plɔɪə[r]] *n* Arbeitgeber(in *f*) *m*.
employment [ɪm'plɔɪmənt] *n* **(a)** *(work)* Stellung, Arbeit *f*. **to take up ~ with sb** eine Stelle bei jdm annehmen; **to seek ~ with sb** sich bei jdm bewerben; **to be in ~** angestellt sein; **place of ~** Arbeitsplatz *m*. **(b)** *(act of employing)* Beschäftigung *f*; *(taking on)* Einstellen *nt*. **(c)** *(use: of method)* Anwendung *f*; *(of word)* Verwendung *f*.
employment: ~ agency *n* Stellenvermittlung *f*; **~ exchange** *n* Arbeitsamt *nt*.
empower [ɪm'paʊə[r]] *vt* **to ~ sb to do sth** jdn ermächtigen, etw zu tun.
empress ['emprɪs] *n* Kaiserin *f*.
empties ['emptɪz] *npl* Leergut *nt*.
emptiness ['emptɪnɪs] *n* Leere *f*.
empty ['emptɪ] **1** *adj (+er)* leer; *(not occupied) house* leerstehend *attr*; *head* hohl. **2** *vt* leeren; *box, room also* ausräumen; *house* räumen; *glass, bottle also (by drinking)* austrinken. **he emptied it into another container** er goß es in ein anderes Gefäß um. **3** *vi (water)* abfließen; *(rivers)* münden *(into* in *+acc)*; *(theatre, streets)* sich leeren.
empty: ~-handed *adj* **to return ~-handed** mit leeren Händen zurückkehren; **~-headed** *adj* strohdumm.
emu ['iːmjuː] *n* Emu *m*.
emulate ['emjʊleɪt] *vt* nacheifern *(+dat)*.
emulsion [ɪ'mʌlʃən] *n* **(a)** Emulsion *f*. **(b)** *(also ~ paint)* Emulsionsfarbe *f*.
enable [ɪ'neɪbl] *vt* **to ~ sb to do sth** es jdm ermöglichen, etw zu tun.
enact [ɪ'nækt] *vt* **(a)** *(Pol) law* erlassen. **(b)** *(perform) play* aufführen. **the drama which was ~ed yesterday** *(fig)* das Drama, das sich gestern abgespielt hat.
enamel [ɪ'næməl] **1** *n* Emaille *f*; *(paint)* Emaillelack *m*; *(of teeth)* Zahnschmelz *m*. **2** *vt* emaillieren.
encampment [ɪn'kæmpmənt] *n* Lager *nt*.
encase [ɪn'keɪs] *vt* verkleiden *(in* mit*)*; *wires* umgeben *(in* mit*)*.
enchant [ɪn'tʃɑːnt] *vt* **(a)** *(delight)* bezaubern, entzücken. **(b)** *(put under spell)* verzaubern.
enchanting *adj* [ɪn'tʃɑːntɪŋ] bezaubernd.
enchantment [ɪn'tʃɑːntmənt] *n* **(a)** *(delight)* Entzücken *nt*. **(b)** *(charm)* Zauber *m*.
enchantress [ɪn'tʃɑːntrɪs] *n* Zauberin *f*.
encircle [ɪn'sɜːkl] *vt* umgeben, umfassen; *(troops)* einkreisen; *building* umstellen.
enc(l) = enclosure(s) Anl.
enclave ['enkleɪv] *n* Enklave *f*.
enclose [ɪn'kləʊz] *vt* **(a)** *(shut in)* einschließen; *(surround)* umgeben; *(with fence etc)* einzäunen. **the garden is completely ~d** der Garten ist völlig abgeschlossen. **(b)** *(in envelope)* beilegen, beifügen. **please find ~d** ... in der Anlage übersenden wir Ihnen ...; **to ~ sth in a letter** einem Brief etw beilegen; **the ~d cheque** der beiliegende Scheck.
enclosure [ɪn'kləʊʒə[r]] *n* **(a)** *(for animals)* Gehege *nt*; *(on racecourse)* Zuschauerbereich. **(b)** *(act)* Einzäunung *f*. **(c)** *(with letter)* Anlage *f*.
encompass [ɪn'kʌmpəs] *vt (include)* umfassen.
encore ['ɒŋkɔː[r]] **1** *interj* da capo, Zugabe. **2** *n* Zugabe *f*. **to give an ~** eine Zugabe spielen/singen.
encounter [ɪn'kaʊntə[r]] **1** *vt* stoßen auf *(+acc)*; *(liter) person* begegnen *(+dat)*, treffen. **2** *n* Begegnung *f*, Treffen *nt*; *(in battle)* Zusammenstoß *m*.
encourage [ɪn'kʌrɪdʒ] *vt person* ermutigen, ermuntern *(to* zu*)*; *(motivate)* anregen; *arts, industry* fördern; *team* anfeuern; *sb's bad habits* unterstützen. **you'll only ~ him to think there's still hope** er wird dann nur noch eher glauben, daß noch Hoffnung besteht; **this ~s me to think that ...** das läßt mich vermuten, daß ...
encouragement [ɪn'kʌrɪdʒmənt] *n* Ermutigung *f*; *(motivation)* Anregung *f*; *(support)* Unterstützung, Förderung *f*. **to give sb ~** jdn ermuntern.
encouraging [ɪn'kʌrɪdʒɪŋ] *adj* ermutigend. **you are not very ~** du machst mir/uns *etc* nicht gerade Mut.
encroach [ɪn'krəʊtʃ] *vi* **to ~ (up)on** *land* vordringen in *(+acc)*; *sphere, rights* eingreifen in *(+acc)*; *time* in Anspruch nehmen.
encrusted [ɪn'krʌstɪd] verkrustet; *(with pearls etc)* besetzt.
encumber [ɪn'kʌmbə[r]] *vt* **to be ~ed with sth** *(person)* mit etw beladen sein; *with debts* mit etw belastet sein; *(room)* mit etw überladen sein.
encumbrance [ɪn'kʌmbrəns] *n (also Jur)* Belastung *f*.
encyclop(a)edia [ɪnˌsaɪkləʊ'piːdɪə] *n* Lexikon *nt*, Enzyklopädie *f*.
end [end] **1** *n* **(a)** Ende *nt*; *(of finger)* Spitze *f*. **at the ~ of the procession** am Schluß der Prozession; **the fourth from the ~** der/die/das vierte von hinten; **from ~ to ~** von einem Ende zum anderen; **to stand on ~** *(box etc)* hochkant stehen; *(hair)* zu Berge stehen; **for hours on ~** stundenlang ununterbrochen; **~ to ~** mit den Enden aneinander; **to change ~s** *(Sport)* die Seiten wechseln; **to make ~s meet** *(fig)* durchkommen *(col)*.
(b) *(remnant) (of rope)* Ende *nt*; *(of candle, cigarette)* Stummel *m*. **just a few odd ~s left** nur noch ein paar Reste.
(c) *(conclusion)* Ende *nt*. **the ~ of the month** das Monatsende; **at/towards the ~ of December** Ende/gegen Ende Dezember; **is there no ~ to this?** hört das denn nie auf?; **we shall never hear the ~ of it** das werden wir noch lange zu hören kriegen; **to be at an ~** zu Ende sein; **to be at the ~ of one's patience** mit seiner Geduld am Ende sein; **to see a film/read a book to the ~** einen Film/ein Buch bis zu Ende sehen/lesen; **that's the ~ of him** er ist erledigt; **that's the ~ of that** das ist damit erledigt; **to come to an ~** zu Ende gehen; **in the ~** schließlich, zum Schluß; **to put**

an ~ to sth einer Sache *(dat)* ein Ende setzen; **to come to a bad ~** ein böses Ende nehmen; **to meet one's ~** den Tod finden.

(d) *(col phrases)* **no ~ of famous people** irrsinnig viele berühmte Leute *(col)*; **it's done him no ~ of harm** es hat ihm irrsinnig geschadet *(col)*; **to think no ~ of sb** große Stücke auf jdn halten; **you're the ~** du bist wirklich das Letzte.

(e) *(purpose)* Ziel *nt*, Zweck *m*. **with this ~ in view** mit diesem Ziel vor Augen; **an ~ in itself** Selbstzweck *no art;* **the ~ justifies the means** *(prov)* der Zweck heiligt die Mittel *(prov)*.

2 *adj attr* letzte(r, s); *house also* End-.

3 *vt* beenden; *speech, broadcast, series also, one's days* beschließen. **the novel to ~ all novels** der größte Roman aller Zeiten.

4 *vi* enden. **we'll have to ~ soon** wir müssen bald Schluß machen; **to be ~ing** zu Ende gehen; **where's it all going to ~?** wo soll das nur enden?

♦ **end up** *vi* enden, landen *(col)*. **to ~ ~ doing sth** schließlich etw tun; **to ~ ~ as a lawyer/an alcoholic** schließlich Rechtsanwalt werden/als Alkoholiker enden.

endanger [ɪn'deɪndʒəʳ] *vt* gefährden.

endear [ɪn'dɪəʳ] *vt* beliebt machen *(to* bei*)*.

endearing [ɪn'dɪərɪŋ] *adj smile, personality* gewinnend; *characteristic also* liebenswert.

endearment [ɪn'dɪəmənt] *n* **term of ~** Kosename *m*.

endeavour, *(US)* **endeavor** [ɪn'devəʳ] **1** *n* Anstrengung, Bemühung *f*. **to make every ~ to do sth** sich nach Kräften bemühen, etw zu tun. **2** *vt* sich bemühen.

endemic [en'demɪk] *adj (lit, fig)* endemisch.

ending ['endɪŋ] *n (of book, events)* Ausgang *m*; *(last part)* Ende *nt*, Schluß *m*; *(of word)* Endung *f*. **happy ~** Happy-End *nt*.

endive ['endaɪv] *n* Endiviensalat *m*.

endless ['endlɪs] *adj* endlos; *possibilities* unendlich. **this job is ~** diese Arbeit nimmt kein Ende.

endorse [ɪn'dɔːs] *vt* **(a)** *cheque* auf der Rückseite unterzeichnen. **(b)** *(Brit) driving licence* eine Strafe vermerken auf *(+dat)*. **(c)** *(approve)* billigen. **I ~ that** dem stimme ich zu.

endorsement [ɪn'dɔːsmənt] *n* **(a)** *(on cheque)* Indossament *nt*. **(b)** *(Brit: on driving licence)* Strafvermerk *m* auf dem Führerschein. **(c)** *(of opinion)* Billigung *f*.

endow [ɪn'daʊ] *vt institution* eine Stiftung machen an *(acc)*; *prize* stiften. **~ed with sth** *(fig: with characteristic)* mit etw ausgestattet.

endowment [ɪndaʊmənt] *n* **(a)** Stiftung *f*. **(b)** *(talent)* Begabung *f*; *(physical)* Merkmal *nt*.

end: ~product *n* Endprodukt *nt*; *(fig)* Produkt *nt*; **~ result** *n* Endergebnis *nt*.

endurable [ɪn'djʊərəbl] *adj* erträglich.

endurance [ɪn'djʊərəns] *n (powers of ~)* Durchhaltevermögen *nt*. **tried beyond ~** über die Maßen gereizt; **~ test** Belastungsprobe *f*.

endure [ɪn'djʊəʳ] **1** *vt* **(a)** *(undergo) pain, insults* (er)leiden. **(b)** *(put up with)* ertragen. **she can't ~ being laughed at** sie kann es nicht vertragen, wenn man über sie lacht. **2** *vi* Bestand haben.

enduring [ɪn'djʊərɪŋ] *adj value, fame* bleibend; *friendship, peace* dauerhaft; *hardship* anhaltend.

enema ['enɪmə] *n* Klistier *nt*.

enemy ['enəmɪ] **1** *n (lit, fig)* Feind *m*. **to make enemies** sich *(dat)* Feinde machen; **he is his own worst ~** er schadet sich *(dat)* selbst am meisten. **2** *adj attr* feindlich; *position, advance, morale* des Feindes. **~ action** Feindeinwirkung *f*.

energetic [,enə'dʒetɪk] *adj* voller Energie, energiegeladen; *(active)* aktiv; *manager, government* tatkräftig; *dancing, music, prose* schwungvoll; *protest, denial* energisch. **she is a very ~ person** sie steckt voller Energie.

energize ['enədʒaɪz] *vt* Antrieb geben *(+dat)*; *(Elec)* unter Strom setzen.

energy ['enədʒɪ] *n* Energie *f*; **~ crisis** *n* Energiekrise *f*; **~-saving** *adj* energiesparend.

enervating ['enɜːveɪtɪŋ] *adj* strapaziös.

enforce [ɪn'fɔːs] *vt* durchführen; *one's claims, rights* geltend machen; *silence, discipline* sorgen für, schaffen; *obedience* sich *(dat)* verschaffen. **the police ~ the law** die Polizei sorgt für die Einhaltung der Gesetze.

engage [ɪn'geɪdʒ] **1** *vt* **(a)** *workers* einstellen; *actor* engagieren; *lawyer* sich *(dat)* nehmen. **(b)** *the attention* in Anspruch nehmen. **to ~ sb in conversation** jdn in ein Gespräch verwickeln. **(c)** *the enemy* angreifen. **(d)** *(Tech) gears* ineinandergreifen lassen. **to ~ a gear** einen Gang einlegen; **to ~ the clutch** (ein)kuppeln. **2** *vi* **(a) to ~ in sth** sich an etw *(dat)* beteiligen; **to ~ in politics** sich politisch betätigen. **(b)** *(gears)* ineinandergreifen; *(clutch)* fassen.

engaged [ɪn'geɪdʒd] *adj* **(a)** verlobt. **to get ~** sich verloben *(to* mit*)*; **the ~ couple** die Verlobten *pl*. **(b)** *(occupied)* beschäftigt. **(c) the parties ~ in this dispute** die streitenden Parteien. **(d)** *(Brit) toilet, phone* besetzt. **~ tone** Besetztzeichen *nt*.

engagement [ɪn'geɪdʒmənt] *n* **(a)** *(appointment)* Verabredung *f*; *(of actor etc)* Engagement *nt*. **public ~s** öffentliche Verpflichtungen *pl*. **(b)** *(to marry)* Verlobung *f*. **~ ring** Verlobungsring *m*. **(c)** *(form: undertaking)* Verpflichtung *f*. **(d)** *(Mil)* Gefecht *nt*.

engaging [ɪn'geɪdʒɪŋ] *adj personality* einnehmend; *smile, look, tone* gewinnend.

engender [ɪn'dʒendəʳ] *vt (fig)* erzeugen.

engine ['endʒɪn] *n* **(a)** Maschine *f*; *(of car, plane etc)* Motor *m*. **(b)** *(Rail)* Lokomotive, Lok *f*.

engine driver *n (Brit)* Lok(omotiv)führer(in *f*) *m*.

engineer [,endʒɪ'nɪəʳ] **1** *n* **(a)** Techniker(in *f*) *m*; *(with university degree etc)* Ingenieur(in *f*) *m*. **the E~s** *(Mil)* die Pioniere *pl*. **(b)** *(Naut: on merchant ships)* Maschinist *m*; *(in Navy)* Schiffsingenieur *m*. **(c)** *(US Rail)* Lokführer(in *f*) *m*. **2** *vt* **(a)** konstruieren. **(b)** *(fig) election, campaign* organisieren; *downfall* einfädeln.

engineering [,endʒɪ'nɪərɪŋ] *n* Technik *f*; *(mechanical ~)* Maschinenbau *m*; *(engineering profession)* Ingenieurwesen *nt*. **the ~ of the Tay Bridge** die Konstruktion der Tay-Brücke.

engine room *n (Naut)* Maschinenraum *m*.

England ['ɪŋglənd] *n* England *nt*.

English ['ɪŋglɪʃ] **1** *adj* englisch. **he is ~** er ist Engländer. **2** *n* **(a) the ~** *pl* die Engländer *pl*. **(b)** Englisch *nt*; *(as university subject)* Anglistik *f*. **can you speak ~?** können Sie Englisch?; **he doesn't speak ~** er spricht kein Englisch; **they were speaking ~** sie sprachen englisch; **in ~** auf englisch; **to translate sth into/from (the) ~** etw ins Englische/aus dem Englischen übersetzen.

English: ~ Channel *n* Ärmelkanal *m*; **~man** *n* Engländer *m*; **~woman** *n* Engländerin *f*.

engrave [ɪn'greɪv] *vt* eingravieren. **it is ~d on my memory** *(fig)* es hat sich mir (unauslöschlich) eingeprägt.

engraving [ɪn'greɪvɪŋ] *n (picture)* Stich *m*.

engrossed [ɪn'grəʊst] *adj* **to be ~ in sth** in etw *(dat)* vertieft sein.

engrossing [ɪn'grəʊsɪŋ] *adj* fesselnd.

engulf [ɪn'gʌlf] *vt* verschlingen.

enhance [ɪn'hɑːns] *vt* verbessern; *chances also, price, value, attraction* erhöhen.

enigma [ɪ'nɪgmə] *n* Rätsel *nt*.

enigmatic [,enɪg'mætɪk] *adj* rätselhaft.

enjoy [ɪn'dʒɔɪ] **1** *vt* **(a)** genießen. **he ~s swimming/reading** er schwimmt/liest gern; **I ~ed the book/film** das Buch/der Film hat mir gefallen; **he ~ed the meal** das Essen hat ihm gut geschmeckt; **I've ~ed talking to you** es war mir eine Freude, mich mit Ihnen zu unterhalten; **I**

didn't ~ it at all es hat mir überhaupt keinen Spaß gemacht. **(b)** *good health* sich erfreuen *(+gen) (geh)*; *rights, advantages* genießen. **2** *vr* **to ~ oneself** sich amüsieren; **~ yourself!** viel Spaß!

enjoyable [ɪn'dʒɔɪəbl] *adj* nett; *film, book also* unterhaltsam; *evening also, meal* angenehm.

enjoyment [ɪn'dʒɔɪmənt] *n* Vergnügen *nt*, Spaß *m* *(of* an *+dat)*. **he got a lot of ~ from this book** das Buch machte ihm großen Spaß.

enlarge [ɪn'lɑːdʒ] **1** *vt* vergrößern; *hole, field of knowledge* erweitern. **2** *vi* **to ~ (up)on sth** sich über etw *(acc)* genauer äußern.

enlargement [ɪn'lɑːdʒmənt] *n* Vergrößerung *f*.

enlighten [ɪn'laɪtn] *vt* aufklären *(on, as to, about* über *+acc)*.

enlightened [ɪn'laɪtnd] *adj* aufgeklärt.

enlightening [ɪn'laɪtnɪŋ] *adj* aufschlußreich.

enlightenment [ɪn'laɪtnmənt] *n* Aufklärung *f*. **the age of E~** das Zeitalter der Aufklärung.

enlist [ɪn'lɪst] **1** *vi (Mil etc)* sich melden *(in* zu*)*. **2** *vt soldiers* einziehen; *supporters, sympathy, support* gewinnen. **~ed man** *(US)* gemeiner Soldat.

enliven [ɪn'laɪvn] *vt* beleben.

enmity ['enmɪtɪ] *n* Feindschaft *f*.

enormity [ɪ'nɔːmɪtɪ] *n no pl (of offence)* ungeheures Ausmaß.

enormous [ɪ'nɔːməs] *adj* gewaltig, enorm; *person* riesig; *patience* enorm. **an ~ number of people** ungeheuer viele Menschen; **an ~ amount of money/time** eine Unmenge Geld/Zeit.

enormously [ɪ'nɔːməslɪ] *adv* enorm, ungeheuer.

enough [ɪ'nʌf] **1** *adj, n* genug, genügend *attr*. **to be ~** genügen, reichen; **is there ~ milk?** ist genug Milch da?; **will that be ~?** reicht das?; **I've had ~, I'm going home** mir reicht's, ich gehe nach Hause; **I've had ~ of your impudence** jetzt habe ich aber genug von deiner Frechheit; **now children, that's ~!** Kinder, jetzt reicht es aber!; **this noise is ~ to drive me mad** dieser Lärm macht mich noch ganz verrückt; **~ is ~** was zuviel ist, ist zuviel. **2** *adv (+adj)* genug; *(+vb also)* genügend. **not big ~** nicht groß genug; **he knows well ~ what I said** er weiß ganz genau, was ich gesagt habe; **she's pleasant ~** sie ist so weit ganz nett; **he sings well ~** er singt ganz ordentlich; **funnily ~** komischerweise; **and sure ~, he didn't come** und er kam auch prompt nicht.

enquire [ɪn'kwaɪəʳ] **1** *vt* **he ~d what/whether/when** *etc* ... er erkundigte sich, was/ob/wann *etc* ... **2** *vi* sich erkundigen *(about* nach*)*.

♦**enquire into** *vi +prep obj* untersuchen.

enquiring [ɪn'kwaɪərɪŋ] *adj* fragend. **he has an ~ mind** er ist eine Forschernatur.

enquiry [ɪn'kwaɪərɪ, *(US)* 'ɪnkwɪrɪ] *n* **(a)** *(question)* Anfrage *f (about* über *+acc)*; *(for tourist information, direction etc)* Erkundigung *f (about* über *+acc,* nach*)*. **to make enquiries** Erkundigungen einziehen; *(police etc)* Nachforschungen anstellen *(about sb* über jdn, *about sth* nach etw*)*. **(b)** *(investigation)* Untersuchung *f*.

enrage [ɪn'reɪdʒ] *vt* wütend machen.

enrich [ɪn'rɪtʃ] *vt* bereichern; *soil, food* anreichern.

enrichment [ɪn'rɪtʃmənt] *n* Bereicherung *f*; *(of soil)* Anreicherung *f*.

enrol, (US) enroll [ɪn'rəʊl] **1** *vt* einschreiben; *members also* aufnehmen; *(Univ)* immatrikulieren. **2** *vi* sich einschreiben; *(in the army)* sich melden *(in* zu*)*; *(for course also, at school)* sich anmelden; *(Univ also)* sich immatrikulieren.

enrolment [ɪn'rəʊlmənt] *n see vt* Einschreibung *f*; Aufnahme *f*; Immatrikulation *f*.

en route [ɒŋ'ruːt] *adv* unterwegs. **~ to Paris** auf dem Weg nach Paris.

ensconce [ɪn'skɒns] *vr* sich häuslich niederlassen *(in* in *+dat)*.

ensemble [ɑ̃ːn'sɑ̃ːmbl] *n* Ensemble *nt*.

ensign ['ensaɪn] *n* **(a)** *(flag)* Nationalflagge *f*. **(b)** *(US Naut)* Fähnrich *m* zur See.

enslave [ɪn'sleɪv] *vt* zum Sklaven machen.

ensnare [ɪn'snɛəʳ] *vt (lit)* fangen; *(fig) (woman)* umgarnen; *(charms)* berücken, bestricken.

ensue [ɪn'sjuː] *vi* folgen *(from* aus*)*.

ensuing [ɪn'sjuːɪŋ] *adj* folgend.

ensure [ɪn'ʃʊəʳ] *vt* sicherstellen; *(secure)* sichern.

entail [ɪn'teɪl] *vt expense, suffering* mit sich bringen; *risk, difficulty also* verbunden sein mit.

entangle [ɪn'tæŋgl] *vt* **to become ~d in sth** sich in etw *(dat)* verfangen; *(fig)* sich in etw *(acc)* verstricken.

entanglement [ɪn'tæŋglmənt] *n* **(a)** *(barbed wire)* Verhau *m*. **(b)** *(fig: in affair etc)* Verwicklung *f*.

enter ['entəʳ] **1** *vt* **(a)** *(towards speaker)* hereinkommen in *(+acc)*; *(away from speaker)* hineingehen in *(+acc)*; *(walk into) building etc also* betreten; *(drive into) car park, motorway* einfahren in *(+acc)*; *(turn into) road etc* einbiegen in *(+acc)*; *(river etc)* münden in *(+acc)*; *(penetrate: bullet etc)* eindringen in *(+acc)*; *(climb into) bus* einsteigen in *(+acc)*; *(cross border of) country* einreisen in *(+acc)*. **the thought never ~ed my mind** so etwas wäre mir nie eingefallen. **(b) to ~ the Army/Navy** zum Heer/zur Marine gehen; **to ~ the Church** Geistlicher werden; **to ~ a university** auf die Universität gehen. **(c)** *(write down, record)* eintragen *(in* in *+acc)*. **(d)** *(enrol) pupil* anmelden; *horse* melden. **(e)** *race, contest* sich beteiligen an *(+dat)*. **(f)** *(submit) appeal, plea* einlegen.

2 *vi* **(a)** *(towards speaker)* hereinkommen; *(away from speaker)* hineingehen; *(walk in)* eintreten. **(b)** *(Theat)* auftreten. **(c)** *(for race, exam etc)* sich melden *(for* zu*)*.

♦**enter into** *vi +prep obj* **(a)** *negotiations* aufnehmen; *contract, alliance* schließen, eingehen; *conversation* anknüpfen. **(b)** *(figure in)* eine Rolle spielen bei. **that doesn't ~ ~ it** das spielt dabei keine Rolle.

♦**enter (up)on** *vi +prep obj (begin)* antreten; *new era* eintreten in *(+acc)*.

enterprise ['entəpraɪz] *n* Unternehmen *nt*; *(initiative)* Initiative *f*; *(adventurousness)* Unternehmungsgeist *m*. **free/private ~** freies/privates Unternehmertum.

enterprising ['entəpraɪzɪŋ] *adj* unternehmungslustig; *idea, venture* kühn.

entertain [ˌentə'teɪn] **1** *vt* **(a)** *(offer hospitality to)* einladen; *(to meal)* bewirten. **to ~ sb to dinner** jdn zum Essen einladen. **(b)** *(amuse)* unterhalten. **(c)** *thought* sich tragen mit; *suspicion, doubt* hegen; *hope* nähren; *proposal, offer, idea* in Erwägung ziehen. **2** *vi (have visitors)* Gäste haben.

entertainer [ˌentə'teɪnəʳ] *n* Entertainer(in *f*) *m*.

entertaining [ˌentə'teɪnɪŋ] **1** *adj* unterhaltsam. **2** *n* **she does a lot of ~** sie hat sehr oft Gäste.

entertainment [ˌentə'teɪnmənt] *n* **(a)** Unterhaltung *f*. **for my own ~** nur so zum Vergnügen. **(b)** *(performance)* Darbietung *f*. **(c)** *(of guests)* Bewirtung *f*. **~ allowance** Aufwandspauschale *f*.

enthral(l) [ɪn'θrɔːl] *vt* begeistern; *(exiting story etc also)* fesseln.

enthralling [ɪn'θrɔːlɪŋ] *adj* spannend.

enthuse [ɪn'θjuːz] *vi* schwärmen *(over* von*)*.

enthusiasm [ɪn'θjuːzɪæzəm] *n* Begeisterung *f*, Enthusiasmus *m (for* für*)*.

enthusiast [ɪn'θjuːzɪæst] *n* Enthusiast *m*. **sports/jazz ~** begeisterter Sport-/Jazzfan *m*.

enthusiastic [ɪnˌθjuːzɪ'æstɪk] *adj* begeistert, enthusiastisch. **to be/get ~ about sth** von etw begeistert sein/sich für etw begeistern.

entice [ɪn'taɪs] *vt* locken; *(lead astray)* verführen, verleiten. **to ~ sb into doing sth** jdn dazu verleiten, etw zu tun; **to ~ sb away** jdn weglocken.

enticement [ɪn'taɪsmənt] *n (lure)* Verlockung *f.*
enticing [ɪn'taɪsɪŋ] *adj* verlockend.
entire [ɪn'taɪəʳ] *adj* ganz; *set, waste of time* vollständig.
entirely [ɪn'taɪəlɪ] *adv* ganz. **I'm not ~ surprised** das kommt für mich nicht ganz überraschend.
entirety [ɪn'taɪərətɪ] *n* **in its ~** in seiner Gesamtheit.
entitle [ɪn'taɪtl] *vt* **(a) it is ~d ...** es hat den Titel ... **(b)** *(give the right)* **to ~ sb to sth/to do sth** jdn zu etw berechtigen/jdn dazu berechtigen, etw zu tun; *(to compensation, legal aid)* jdm den Anspruch auf etw *(acc)* geben; **to be ~d to sth/to do sth** das Recht auf etw *(acc)* haben/das Recht haben, etw zu tun; *to compensation, legal aid, holiday* Anspruch *m* auf etw *(acc)* haben.
entitlement [ɪntaɪtlmənt] *n* Berechtigung *f (to* zu*)*; *(to compensation, holiday etc)* Anspruch *m (to* auf *+acc)*.
entity ['entɪtɪ] *n* Wesen *nt.*
entomology [,entə'mɒlədʒɪ] *n* Insektenkunde *f.*
entourage [,ɒntʊ'rɑːʒ] *n* Gefolge *nt.*
entrails ['entreɪlz] *npl* Eingeweide *pl.*
entrance[1] [ɪn'trɑːns] *vt* in Entzücken versetzen.
entrance[2] ['entrəns] *n* **(a)** *(way in)* Eingang *m*; *(for vehicles)* Einfahrt *f*; *(hall)* Eingangshalle *f.* **(b)** *(entering)* Eintritt *m*; *(Theat)* Auftritt *m.* **to make one's ~** *(Theat)* auftreten; *(fig also)* erscheinen. **(c)** *(admission)* Eintritt *m (to* in *+acc)*; *(to club etc)* Zutritt *m (to* zu*)*.
entrance: ~ fee *n* Eintrittsgeld *nt*; *(for club)* Aufnahmegebühr *f*; **~ visa** *n* Einreisevisum *nt.*
entrancing [ɪn'trɑːnsɪŋ] *adj* bezaubernd.
entrant ['entrənt] *n (in contest)* Teilnehmer(in *f*) *m*; *(in exam)* Prüfling *m.*
entreat [ɪn'triːt] *vt* anflehen *(for* um*)*.
entreaty [ɪn'triːtɪ] *n* dringende Bitte.
entrenched [ɪn'trentʃt] *adj idea, belief etc* (fest) verwurzelt; *position* festgefahren.
entrepreneur [,ɒntrəprə'nɜːʳ] *n* Unternehmer *m.*
entrepreneurial [,ɒntrəprə'nɜːrɪəl] *adj* unternehmerisch.
entrust [ɪn'trʌst] *vt* anvertrauen *(to sb* jdm*)*. **to ~ sb with a task** jdn mit einer Aufgabe betrauen.
entry ['entrɪ] *n* **(a)** *(into* in *+acc)* Eintritt *m*; *(by car etc)* Einfahrt *f*; *(into country)* Einreise *f*; *(Theat)* Auftritt *m.* **"no ~"** *(on door etc)* „Zutritt verboten"; *(on one-way street)* „keine Einfahrt". **(b)** *(way in, doorway)* Eingang *m*; *(for vehicles)* Einfahrt *f.* **(c)** *(in diary, account book etc)* Eintrag *m.* **(d)** *(for race etc)* Meldung *f.*
entry: ~ form *n* Anmeldeformular *nt*; **~ permit** *n* Passierschein *m*; *(into country)* Einreiseerlaubnis *f.*
entwine [ɪn'twaɪn] *vt* ineinanderschlingen.
enumerate [ɪ'njuːməreɪt] *vt* aufzählen.
enunciate [ɪ'nʌnsɪeɪt] *vti* artikulieren.
enunciation [ɪ,nʌnsɪ'eɪʃən] *n* Artikulation *f.*
envelop [ɪn'veləp] *vt* einhüllen.
envelope ['envələʊp] *n* Umschlag *m.*
enviable ['envɪəbl] *adj* beneidenswert.
envious ['envɪəs] *adj* neidisch *(of* auf *+acc)*.
environment [ɪn'vaɪərənmənt] *n* Umwelt *f*; *(of town etc, physical surroundings)* Umgebung *f*; *(social, cultural also)* Milieu *nt.* **Department of the E~** *(Brit)* ≃ Umweltministerium *nt.*
environmental [ɪn,vaɪərən'mentl] *adj* Umwelt-.
environmentalist [ɪn,vaɪərən'mentəlɪst] *n* Umweltschützer(in *f*) *m.*
envisage [ɪn'vɪzɪdʒ] *vt* sich *(dat)* vorstellen; *(expect)* erwarten.
envoy ['envɔɪ] *n* Bote *m*; *(diplomat)* Gesandte(r) *mf.*
envy ['envɪ] **1** *n* Neid *m.* **his house was the ~ of his friends** seine Freunde beneideten ihn um sein Haus. **2** *vt person* beneiden. **to ~ sb sth** jdn um etw beneiden.
enzyme ['enzaɪm] *n* Enzym, Ferment *nt.*
ephemeral [ɪ'femərəl] *adj* flüchtig.
epic ['epɪk] **1** *adj poetry* episch; *film, novel* Monumental-; *performance, match* gewaltig; *journey* lang und abenteuerlich. **2** *n (poem, film)* Epos *nt*; *(match)* gewaltiges Spiel.
epicentre, *(US)* **epicenter** ['epɪsentəʳ] *n* Epizentrum *nt.*
epidemic [epɪ'demɪk] **1** *n* Epidemie *(also fig)*, Seuche *f.* **2** *adj* epidemisch.
epigram ['epɪgræm] *n* Epigramm, Sinngedicht *nt.*
epilepsy ['epɪlepsɪ] *n* Epilepsie *f.*
epileptic [epɪ'leptɪk] **1** *adj* **~ fit** epileptischer Anfall. **2** *n* Epileptiker(in *f*) *m.*
epilogue ['epɪlɒg] *n* Epilog *m*, Nachwort *nt.*
Epiphany [ɪ'pɪfənɪ] *n* das Dreikönigsfest.
episcopal [ɪ'pɪskəpəl] *adj* bischöflich, Bischofs-.
episode ['epɪsəʊd] *n* Episode *f*; *(of story, TV, Rad)* Fortsetzung *f*; *(incident also)* Begebenheit *f.*
epistle [ɪ'pɪsl] *n (Bibl)* Brief *m (to* an *+acc)*.
epitaph ['epɪtɑːf] *n* Epitaph *nt*; *(on grave)* Grabinschrift *f.*
epithet ['epɪθet] *n* Beiname *m.*
epitome [ɪ'pɪtəmɪ] *n* Inbegriff *m (of gen,* an *+dat)*.
epitomize [ɪ'pɪtəmaɪz] *vt* verkörpern.
epoch ['iːpɒk] *n* Zeitalter *nt (also Geol)*, Epoche *f.*
epoch-making ['iːpɒk'meɪkɪŋ] *adj* epochemachend, epochal.
equable ['ekwəbl] *adj* gleichmäßig, ausgeglichen.
equal ['iːkwəl] **1** *adj* **(a)** gleich *(to +dat)*. **they are about ~ in value** sie haben ungefähr den gleichen Wert; **to be on ~ terms** auf der gleichen Stufe stehen *(with* mit*)*; **~ opportunities** Chancengleichheit *f*; **(all) other things being ~** unter sonst gleichen Umständen; **now we're ~** jetzt sind wir quitt. **(b) to be ~ to the situation/task** der Situation/Aufgabe gewachsen sein; **to feel ~ to sth** sich zu etw imstande *or* in der Lage fühlen.

2 *n (in rank)* Gleichgestellte(r) *mf.* **she is his ~** sie ist ihm ebenbürtig; **he has no ~** er hat nicht seinesgleichen; **our ~s** unseresgleichen; **to treat sb as an ~** jdn als ebenbürtig behandeln.

3 *vt (be same as, Math)* gleichen; *(match, measure up to)* gleichkommen *(+dat)*; *record* erreichen. **three times three ~s nine** drei mal drei (ist) gleich neun; **not to be ~led** unvergleichlich.
equality [ɪ'kwɒlɪtɪ] *n* Gleichheit *f.*
equalize ['iːkwəlaɪz] *vti* ausgleichen.
equalizer ['iːkwəlaɪzəʳ] *n (Sport)* Ausgleich *m*; *(Ftbl etc also)* Ausgleichstreffer *m.*
equally ['iːkwəlɪ] *adv* **(a)** *divide, distribute* gleichmäßig. **~ gifted** gleich begabt *pred*, gleichbegabt *attr.* **(b)** *(just as)* genauso. **(c) but then, ~, one must concede ...** aber dann muß man ebenso zugestehen, daß ...
equanimity [,ekwə'nɪmɪtɪ] *n* Gleichmut *m.*
equate [ɪ'kweɪt] *vt (identify)* gleichsetzen; *(treat as the same)* auf die gleiche Stufe stellen.
equation [ɪ'kweɪʒən] *n (Math, fig)* Gleichung *f.*
equator [ɪ'kweɪtəʳ] *n* Äquator *m.*
equestrian [ɪ'kwestrɪən] *adj* Reit-.
equidistant ['iːkwɪ'dɪstənt] *adj* gleich weit entfernt.
equilibrium [,iːkwɪ'lɪbrɪəm] *n* Gleichgewicht *nt.*
equine ['ekwaɪn] *adj* Pferde-.
equinox ['iːkwɪnɒks] *n* Tagundnachtgleiche *f.*
equip [ɪ'kwɪp] *vt* ausrüsten; *kitchen* ausstatten; *laboratory* einrichten. **he's well ~ped for the job** *(fig)* er hat das nötige Rüstzeug für die Stelle.
equipment [ɪ'kwɪpmənt] *n no pl* Ausrüstung *f.* **office ~** Büroeinrichtung *f*; **electrical/kitchen ~** Elektro-/Küchengeräte *pl.*
equitable ['ekwɪtəbl] *adj* fair, gerecht.
equity ['ekwɪtɪ] *n* **(a)** Fairneß *f.* **(b)** *(Brit Fin)* **equities** *pl* Stammaktien *pl.*
equivalence [ɪ'kwɪvələns] *n* Entsprechung *f.*
equivalent [ɪ'kwɪvələnt] **1** *adj* **(a)** *(equal)* gleichwertig. **that's ~ to saying ...** das ist

gleichbedeutend damit, zu sagen ... **(b)** *(corresponding)* entsprechend, äquivalent. **it is ~ to £30** das entspricht £30; **that's ~ to lying** das ist soviel wie gelogen. **2** *n* Äquivalent *nt*; *(counterpart)* Pendant *nt*. **what is the ~ in German marks?** was ist der Gegenwert in DM?; **the German ~ of the English word** die deutsche Entsprechung des englischen Wortes.

equivocal [ɪ'kwɪvəkəl] *adj* zweideutig; *outcome* nicht eindeutig.

equivocate [ɪ'kwɪvəkeɪt] *vi* ausweichen.

equivocation [ɪˌkwɪvə'keɪʃən] *n* Ausflüchte *pl*.

era ['ɪərə] *n* Ära *f*; *(Geol)* Erdzeitalter *nt*.

eradicate [ɪ'rædɪkeɪt] *vt* ausrotten.

erase [ɪ'reɪz] *vt* ausradieren; *(from tape, computer)* löschen; *(from the mind)* streichen *(from* aus*)*.

eraser [ɪ'reɪzə[r]] *n* Radiergummi *nt or m*.

erect [ɪ'rekt] **1** *adj* aufrecht, gerade. **2** *vt* errichten *(to sb* jdm*)*; *flats, factory* bauen; *collapsible furniture, scaffolding* aufstellen; *tent* aufschlagen; *mast* aufrichten.

erection [ɪ'rekʃən] *n* **(a)** *see vt* Errichten *nt*; Bauen *nt*; Aufstellen *nt*; Aufschlagen *nt*; Aufrichten *nt*. **(b)** *(building, structure)* Gebäude *nt*, Bau *m*. **(c)** *(Physiol)* Erektion *f*.

ergonomics [ˌɜːgəʊ'nɒmɪks] *n sing* Ergonomie *f*.

ermine ['ɜːmɪn] *n* Hermelin *nt*; *(fur)* Hermelin *m*.

erode [ɪ'rəʊd] *vt (sea)* auswaschen; *(rust)* zerfressen; *(fig) confidence* untergraben.

erogenous [ɪ'rɒdʒənəs] *adj* erogen.

erosion [ɪ'rəʊʒən] *n (by water)* Erosion *f*; *(fig: of love etc)* Schwinden *nt*.

erotic [ɪ'rɒtɪk] *adj* aufreizend; *book, film* erotisch.

eroticism [ɪ'rɒtɪsɪzəm] *n* Erotik *f*.

err [ɜː[r]] *vi* **(a)** sich irren. **it is better to ~ on the side of caution** man sollte im Zweifelsfall lieber zu vorsichtig sein. **(b)** *(sin)* sündigen.

errand ['erənd] *n (shopping etc)* Besorgung *f*; *(to give a message etc)* Botengang *m*. **to run ~s (for sb)** (für jdn) Besorgungen/Botengänge machen; **~ of mercy** Rettungsaktion *f*; **~ boy** Laufjunge *m*.

erratic [ɪ'rætɪk] *adj* unberechenbar; *results* stark schwankend; *work* ungleichmäßig.

erroneous [ɪ'rəʊnɪəs] *adj* falsch; *belief* irrig.

error ['erə[r]] *n* Fehler *m*. **to be in ~** sich im Irrtum befinden; **in ~** aus Versehen, irrtümlicherweise; **to see the ~ of one's ways** seine Fehler einsehen.

erstwhile ['ɜːstwaɪl] *adj (old, liter)* ehemalig.

erudite ['erʊdaɪt] *adj* gelehrt; *person also* gebildet.

erudition [ˌerʊ'dɪʃən] *n* Gelehrsamkeit *f*.

erupt [ɪ'rʌpt] *vi (volcano, war)* ausbrechen; *skin* aufbrechen; *(fig: person)* explodieren.

eruption [ɪ'rʌpʃən] *n (of volcano, anger, violence)* Ausbruch *m*; *(rash etc)* Hautausschlag *m*.

escalate ['eskəleɪt] **1** *vt war* ausweiten; *costs* sprunghaft erhöhen. **2** *vi* sich ausweiten, eskalieren; *(costs)* sprunghaft ansteigen.

escalation [ˌeskə'leɪʃən] *n* Eskalation *f*.

escalator ['eskəleɪtə[r]] *n* Rolltreppe *f*.

escapade [ˌeskə'peɪd] *n* Eskapade *f*.

escape [ɪ'skeɪp] **1** *vi* **(a)** *(from pursuers)* entkommen *(from dat)*; *(from prison, cage)* ausbrechen *(from* aus*)*; *(water)* auslaufen *(from* aus*)*; *(gas)* ausströmen *(from* aus*)*. **he was shot while trying to ~** er wurde bei einem Fluchtversuch erschossen; **an ~d prisoner/tiger** ein entsprungener Häftling/Tiger; **he ~d from the fire** er ist dem Feuer entkommen; **a room which I can ~ to** ein Zimmer, in das ich mich zurückziehen kann. **(b)** *(get off, be spared)* **to ~ with a warning/a few cuts** mit einer Verwarnung/ein paar Schnittwunden davonkommen; **the others were killed, but he ~d** die anderen kamen um, aber er kam mit dem Leben davon.

2 *vt* **(a)** *pursuers* entkommen *(+dat)*. **(b)** *(avoid) consequences, punishment, disaster* entgehen *(+dat)*. **he narrowly ~d being run over** er wäre um ein Haar überfahren worden; **but you can't ~ the fact that ...** aber du kannst nicht abstreiten, daß ... **(c) his name ~s me** sein Name ist mir entfallen; **nothing ~s him** ihm entgeht nichts; **to ~ sb's notice** jdm entgehen.

3 *n* **(a)** *(from prison etc)* Flucht *f*. **to make an ~** ausbrechen; **there's been an ~** jemand ist ausgebrochen; **to have a miraculous ~** *(from accident, illness)* auf wunderbare Weise davonkommen; **fishing is his ~** Angeln ist seine Zuflucht; **there's no ~** *(fig)* es gibt keinen Ausweg. **(b)** *(of water)* Ausfließen *nt*; *(of gas)* Ausströmen *nt*; *(of steam, gas, in a machine)* Entweichen *nt*.

ecape: ~ bid *n* Fluchtversuch *m*; **~ clause** *n (Jur)* Befreiungsklausel *f*; **~ hatch** *n (Naut)* Notluke *f*; **~ route** *n* Fluchtweg *m*; **~ velocity** *n (Space)* Fluchtgeschwindigkeit *f*.

escapism [ɪ'skeɪpɪzəm] *n* Wirklichkeitsflucht *f*.

escapist [ɪ'skeɪpɪst] *adj* **~ literature** eine Phantasiewelt vorgaukelnde Literatur.

escapologist [ˌeskə'pɒlədʒɪst] *n* Entfesselungskünstler(in *f*) *m*.

escarpment [ɪ'skɑːpmənt] *n* Steilhang *m*; *(as fortification)* Böschung *f*.

escort ['eskɔːt] **1** *n* **(a)** Geleitschutz *m*; *(vehicles, ships etc)* Eskorte *f*. **under ~** unter Bewachung. **(b)** *(male companion)* Begleiter *m*; *(hired female)* Hostess *f*. **2** [ɪ'skɔːt] *vt* begleiten; *(Mil, Naut)* Geleit(schutz) geben *(+dat)*.

escort: ~ agency *n* Hostessenagentur *f*; **~ duty** *n* Geleitdienst *m*; **to be on ~ duty** Geleitschutz geben müssen; **~ vessel** *n (Naut)* Geleitschiff *nt*.

Eskimo ['eskɪməʊ] **1** *adj* Eskimo-. **2** *n* **(a)** Eskimo *m*, Eskimofrau *f*. **(b)** *(language)* Eskimosprache *f*.

esophagus *n (esp US)* = **oesophagus.**

esoteric [ˌesəʊ'terɪk] *adj* esoterisch.

ESP = **extra-sensory perception** außersinnliche Wahrnehmung.

especial [ɪ'speʃəl] *adj* besondere(r, s).

especially [ɪ'speʃəli] *adv* besonders. **you ~ ought to know** gerade du solltest wissen; **I came ~ to see you** ich bin eigens gekommen, um dich zu besuchen.

espionage [ˌespɪə'nɑːʒ] *n* Spionage *f*.

esplanade [ˌesplə'neɪd] *n* (Strand)promenade *f*.

espouse [ɪ'spaʊz] *vt cause* Partei ergreifen für.

espresso [e'spresəʊ] *n* Espresso *m*.

esquire [ɪ'skwaɪə[r]] *n (Brit: on envelope, abbr* **Esq***)* **James Jones, Esq** Herrn James Jones.

essay[1] [e'seɪ] *n (form: attempt)* Versuch *m*.

essay[2] ['eseɪ] *n* Essay *m or nt*; *(esp Sch)* Aufsatz *m*.

essence ['esəns] *n* **(a)** Wesen *nt*. **in ~** im wesentlichen; **speed is of the ~** Geschwindigkeit ist äußerst wichtig. **(b)** *(Chem, Cook)* Essenz *f*. **meat ~** Fleischextrakt *m*.

essential [ɪ'senʃəl] **1** *adj* **(a)** *(necessary, vital)* (unbedingt) erforderlich. **it is ~ that you understand this** du mußt das unbedingt verstehen; **the ~ thing is to ...** wichtig ist vor allem, zu ... **(b)** *(of the essence, basic)* wesentlich; *question* entscheidend. **2** *n* **the ~s** das Wesentliche; *(most important points)* die wichtigen Punkte, die Essentials *pl*. **with only the bare ~s** nur mit dem Allernotwendigsten ausgestattet.

essentially [ɪ'senʃəli] *adv (basically)* im Grunde genommen; *(in essence)* im wesentlichen.

establish [ɪ'stæblɪʃ] **1** *vt* **(a)** *(found, set up)* gründen; *government* bilden; *custom, new procedure* einführen; *relations* aufnehmen; *post* einrichten; *power, authority, reputation* sich *(dat)* verschaffen; *peace* stiften; *order* (wieder)herstellen; *precedent* setzen; *committee* einsetzen. **(b)** *(prove) fact, innocence* beweisen; *claim* unter Beweis stellen. **(c)** *(determine) identity, facts* ermitteln. **(d)** *(gain acceptance for) product, ideas* Anerkennung finden für. **2** *vr (in business)* **to**

~ oneself sich niederlassen.
established [ɪ'stæblɪʃt] *adj* **(a)** *reputation* gefestigt. **well-~ business** gut eingeführte Firma. **(b)** *(accepted) fact* feststehend; *procedure, author* anerkannt; *belief* herrschend; *laws, order* bestehend.
establishment [ɪ'stæblɪʃmənt] *n* **(a)** *see vt (a)* Gründung *f*; Bildung *f*; Einführung *f*; Aufnahme *f*; Einrichtung *f*; *(of power, authority)* Festigung *f*; Stiftung *f*; (Wieder)herstellung *f*; Setzen *nt*; Einsetzen *nt*. **(b)** *(proving)* Beweis *m*. **(c)** *(determining)* Ermittlung *f*. **(d)** *(institution etc)* Institution *f*; *(hospital, school etc also)* Anstalt *f*. **commercial ~** kommerzielles Unternehmen. **(e)** *(Mil, Naut etc: personnel)* Truppenstärke *f*. **(f)** *(Brit)* **the E~** das Establishment.
estate [ɪ'steɪt] *n* **(a)** *(land)* Gut *nt*. **(b)** *(Jur)* Besitz(tümer *pl*) *m*, Eigentum *nt*; *(of deceased)* Nachlaß *m*, Erbmasse *f*. **(c)** *(esp Brit) (housing ~)* Siedlung *f*; *(trading ~)* Industriegelände *nt*.
estate: ~ agent *n (Brit)* Immobilienmakler(in *f*) *m*; **~ car** *n (Brit)* Kombi(wagen) *m*.
esteem [ɪ'stiːm] **1** *vt (form: consider)* betrachten. **2** *n* Wertschätzung *f*. **to hold sb/sth in (high) ~** von jdm/etw eine hohe Meinung haben.
esthete *etc (US)* = **aesthete** *etc*.
estimate ['estɪmɪt] **1** *n* **(a)** Schätzung *f*. **it's just an ~** das ist nur geschätzt; **at a rough ~** grob geschätzt. **(b)** *(Comm: of cost)* (Kosten)voranschlag *m*. **2** ['estɪmeɪt] *vt* schätzen. **his wealth is ~d at ...** sein Vermögen wird auf ... geschätzt.
estimation [ˌestɪ'meɪʃən] *n* **(a) in my ~** meiner Einschätzung nach. **(b)** *(esteem)* Achtung *f*. **he went up/down in my ~** er ist in meiner Achtung gestiegen/gesunken.
estrange [ɪ'streɪndʒ] *vt person* entfremden *(from +dat)*. **to be/become ~d from sb** sich jdm entfremdet haben/entfremden.
estrangement [ɪ'streɪndʒmənt] *n* Entfremdung *f (from* von*)*.
estrogen ['iːstrəʊdʒən] *n (US)* Östrogen *nt*.
estuary ['estjʊərɪ] *n* Mündung *f*.
ETA = estimated time of arrival geschätzte Ankunft.
etch [etʃ] *vti* ätzen; *(in copper)* stechen; *(in other metals)* radieren.
etching ['etʃɪŋ] *n see vb* **(a)** Ätzen *nt*; Stechen *nt*; Radieren *nt*. **(b)** *(picture)* Ätzung *f*; Stich *m*; Radierung *f*.
eternal [ɪ'tɜːnl] *adj (lit, fig)* ewig. **the ~ triangle** *(fig)* das Dreiecksverhältnis.
eternity [ɪ'tɜːnɪtɪ] *n (lit, fig)* Ewigkeit *f*. **from here to ~** bis in alle Ewigkeit.
ether ['iːθəʳ] *n (Chem, poet)* Äther *m*.
ethic ['eθɪk] *n* Ethik *f*, Ethos *nt*.
ethical ['eθɪkəl] *adj* ethisch *attr*. **it is not ~ to ...** es ist unmoralisch, zu ...
ethics ['eθɪks] *n* **(a)** *sing* Ethik *f*. **(b)** *pl (morality)* Moral *f*. **the ~ of abortion** die moralischen Aspekte der Abtreibung.
Ethiopia [ˌiːθɪ'əʊpɪə] *n* Äthiopien *nt*.
Ethiopian [ˌiːθɪ'əʊpɪən] **1** *adj* äthiopisch. **2** *n* Äthiopier(in *f*) *m*.
ethnic ['eθnɪk] *adj* ethnisch, Volks-; *atmosphere, pub* urtümlich, urwüchsig. **~ groups/minority** ethnische Gruppen *pl*/Minderheit *f*.
ethos ['iːθɒs] *n* Gesinnung *f*, Ethos *nt*.
etiquette ['etɪket] *n* Etikette *f*.
etymology [ˌetɪ'mɒlədʒɪ] *n* Etymologie *f*.
eucalyptus [ˌjuːkə'lɪptəs] *n* Eukalyptus *m*.
eulogy ['juːlədʒɪ] *n* Lobensrede *f*.
eunuch ['juːnək] *n* Eunuch *m*.
euphemism ['juːfəmɪzəm] *n* beschönigender Ausdruck, Euphemismus *m*.
euphemistic [ˌjuːfə'mɪstɪk] *adj* euphemistisch.
euphoria [juː'fɔːrɪə] *n* Euphorie *f*.
euphoric [juː'fɒrɪk] *adj* euphorisch.
eureka [jʊə'riːkə] *interj* heureka, ich hab's!
Eurocrat ['jʊərəʊkræt] *n* Eurokrat(in *f*) *m*.
Eurodollar ['jʊərəʊdɒləʳ] *n* Eurodollar *m*.
Europe ['jʊərəp] *n* Europa *nt*.
European [ˌjʊərə'piːən] **1** *adj* europäisch. **~ Economic Community** Europäische Wirtschaftsgemeinschaft. **2** *n* Europäer(in *f*) *m*.
euthanasia [ˌjuːθə'neɪzɪə] *n* Euthanasie *f*.
evacuate [ɪ'vækjʊeɪt] *vt* räumen; *people* evakuieren.
evacuation [ɪˌvækjʊ'eɪʃən] *n see vt* Räumung *f*; Evakuierung *f*.
evacuee [ɪˌvækjʊ'iː] *n* Evakuierte(r) *mf*.
evade [ɪ'veɪd] *vt blow, question, sb's eyes* ausweichen *(+dat)*; *pursuit, pursuers, justice* sich entziehen *(+dat)*.
evaluate [ɪ'væljʊeɪt] *vt house, worth etc* schätzen *(at* auf *+acc)*; *chances, usefulness* einschätzen; *evidence, results* auswerten; *pros and cons* (gegeneinander) abwägen; *achievement* bewerten.
evaluation [ɪˌvæljʊ'eɪʃən] *n see vt* Schätzung *f*; Einschätzung *f*; Auswertung *f*; Abwägung *f*; Bewertung *f*.
evangelic(al) [ˌiːvæn'dʒelɪk(əl)] *adj* evangelisch.
evangelist [ɪ'vændʒəlɪst] *n (Bibl)* Evangelist(in *f*) *m*; *(preacher)* Prediger(in *f*) *m*.
evaporate [ɪ'væpəreɪt] **1** *vi* **(a)** *(liquid)* verdunsten. **(b)** *(fig: disappear)* sich in Luft auflösen. **2** *vt* **~d milk** Kondensmilch *f*.
evaporation [ɪˌvæpə'reɪʃən] *n* Verdampfen *nt*; *(fig)* Schwinden *nt*.
evasion [ɪ'veɪʒən] *n* Ausweichen *nt (of* vor *+dat)*.
evasive [ɪ'veɪzɪv] *adj answer* ausweichend; *meaning, truth* schwer zu fassen. **he was very ~ about it** er wollte (dazu) nicht mit der Sprache herausrücken; **to take ~ action** *(Mil, fig)* ein Ausweichmanöver machen.
eve [iːv] *n* Vorabend *m*. **on the ~ of** am Tage vor *(+dat)*; am Vorabend *(+gen)*.
even ['iːvən] **1** *adj* **(a)** *surface, ground* eben. **to be ~ with sth** mit etw abschließen. **(b)** *(regular) layer etc* gleichmäßig; *progress* stetig; *temper* ausgeglichen. **(c)** *quantities, distances, values* gleich. **the score is ~** es steht unentschieden; **I will get ~ with you for that** das werde ich dir heimzahlen; **that makes us ~** *(in game)* damit steht es unentschieden; *(fig)* damit sind wir quitt. **(d)** *number* gerade.
2 *adv* **(a)** sogar, selbst. **they ~ denied its existence** sie leugneten sogar seine Existenz; **~ better/more beautiful** sogar (noch) besser/schöner. **(b) not ~** nicht einmal; **with not ~ a smile** ohne auch nur zu lächeln. **(c) ~ if/though** selbst wenn; **~ as I spoke ...** noch während ich redete ...; **~ so** (aber) trotzdem.
♦ **even out 1** *vi* **(a)** *(prices)* sich einpendeln. **(b)** *(ground)* eben werden. **2** *vt sep* **(a)** *prices* ausgleichen. **that should ~ things ~ a bit** dadurch müßte ein gewisser Ausgleich erzielt werden. **(b)** *ground, cement* ebnen.
evening ['iːvnɪŋ] *n* Abend *m*. **in the ~** abends, am Abend; **this/tomorrow ~** heute/morgen abend; **one ~** eines Abends; **every Monday ~** jeden Montagabend.
evening *in cpds* Abend-; **~ class** *n* Abendkurs *m*; **~ dress** *n (men's)* Abendanzug *m*; *(women's)* Abendkleid *nt*.
evenly ['iːvənlɪ] *adv* gleichmäßig. **they were ~ matched** sie waren einander ebenbürtig.
evensong ['iːvənsɒŋ] *n* Abendgottesdienst *m*.
event [ɪ'vent] *n* **(a)** *(happening)* Ereignis *nt*. **in the normal course of ~s** normalerweise. **(b)** *(function)* Veranstaltung *f*. **what is your best ~?** *(Sport)* in welcher Disziplin sind Sie am besten? **(c) in the ~ of war/fire** im Falle eines Krieges/Brandes; **in any ~** ohnehin, sowieso; **in the ~** im Endeffekt; **at all ~s** auf jeden Fall.
even-tempered ['ivən'tempəd] *adj* ausgeglichen.
eventful [ɪ'ventfʊl] *adj* ereignisreich.

eventual [ɪ'ventʃʊəl] *adj* **the decline and ~ collapse of ...** der Niedergang und schließliche vollkommene Zerfall des ...; **his ~ arrival ...** als er schließlich kam, ...
eventuality [ɪ,ventʃʊ'ælɪtɪ] *n* möglicher Fall. **be ready for any ~** sei auf alle Eventualitäten gefaßt.
eventually [ɪ'ventʃʊəlɪ] *adv* schließlich, endlich.
ever ['evəʳ] *adv* **(a)** je(mals). **not ~** nie; **nothing ~ happens** es passiert nie etwas; **it hardly ~ snows here** hier schneit es kaum (jemals); **if I ~ catch you doing that again** wenn ich dich noch einmal dabei erwische; **seldom, if ~** selten, wenn überhaupt; **he's a rascal if ~ there was one** er ist ein richtiggehender kleiner Halunke; **as if I ~ would** als ob ich das jemals täte; **don't you ~ say that again!** sag das ja nie mehr!; **have you ~ been to Glasgow?** bist du schon einmal in Glasgow gewesen?; **more beautiful than ~** schöner denn je; **the first ~** der *etc* allererste; **the coldest night ~** die kälteste Nacht aller Zeiten.
(b) ~ since then seit der Zeit, seitdem; **for ~** für immer; **it seemed to go on for ~ (and ~)** es schien ewig zu dauern; **~ increasing powers** ständig wachsende Macht.
(c) *(intensive)* **no government be it ~ so powerful** keine noch so mächtige Regierung; **the best grandmother ~** die beste Großmutter, die es gibt; **did you ~!** *(col)* also so was!; **why ~ not?** warum denn bloß nicht?
(d) *(col)* **~ so/such** unheimlich; **~ so slightly drunk** ein ganz klein wenig betrunken; **I am ~ so sorry** es tut mir schrecklich leid; **thank you ~ so much** ganz herzlichen Dank.
evergreen ['evəgriːn] **1** *adj* immergrün; *(fig) topic* immer aktuell. **2** *n* Nadelbaum *m.*
everlasting [,evə'lɑːstɪŋ] *adj (lit, fig)* ewig.
every ['evrɪ] *adj* jede(r, s). **he is ~ bit as clever as his brother** er ist ganz genauso schlau wie sein Bruder; **I have ~ reason to believe that ...** ich habe allen Grund anzunehmen, daß ...; **I have ~ confidence in him** ich habe uneingeschränktes Vertrauen in ihn; **we wish you ~ success/ happiness** wir wünschen Ihnen alles Gute/viel Glück; **his ~ word** jedes Wort, das er sagte; **~ fifth day, ~ five days** jeden fünften Tag, alle fünf Tage; **~ other day** jeden zweiten Tag, alle zwei Tage; **~ so often, ~ now and then** *or* **again** hin und wieder, ab und zu.
everybody ['evrɪbɒdɪ], **everyone** *pron* jeder(mann), alle *pl.* **~ knows ~ else here** hier kennt jeder jeden.
everyday ['evrɪdeɪ] *adj* alltäglich; *language* Umgangs-.
everyone ['evrɪwʌn] *pron* = **everybody.**
everything ['evrɪθɪŋ] *n* alles. **~ possible** alles Mögliche; **~ you have** alles, was du hast.
everywhere ['evrɪwɛəʳ] *adv* überall; *(with direction)* überallhin. **from ~** überallher, von überall; **~ you look** wo man auch hinsieht.
evict [ɪ'vɪkt] *vt tenants* zur Räumung zwingen *(from gen).*
eviction [ɪ'vɪkʃən] *n* Vertreibung *f (from* aus*).*
evidence ['evɪdəns] **1** *n* **(a)** Beweis(e *pl*) *m*; *(Jur) (object)* Beweisstück *nt*; *(testimony)* Aussage *f.* **there wasn't enough ~** die Beweise reichten nicht aus; **all the ~ was against his claim** alles sprach gegen seine Behauptung; **to give ~ (for/ against sb)** (für/gegen jdn) aussagen; **the ~ for the defence** die Beweisführung für die Verteidigung. **(b) to be in ~** sichtbar sein; **ideas which have been very much in ~ recently** Ideen, die in letzter Zeit deutlich in Erscheinung getreten sind. **2** *vt* zeugen von.
evident *adj*, **~ly** *adv* ['evɪdənt, -lɪ] offensichtlich.
evil ['iːvl] **1** *adj* böse; *person also, reputation, influence* schlecht; *(col) smell* übel. **2** *n* Böse *nt.* **an ~** ein Übel *nt*; **the lesser of two ~s** das kleinere von zwei Übeln; **social ~s** soziale Mißstände.
evil: ~-doer *n* Übeltäter(in *f*) *m*; **~-minded** *adj* bösartig.
evince [ɪ'vɪns] *vt* an den Tag legen.
evocation [,evə'keɪʃən] *n* Heraufbeschwören *nt.*
evocative [ɪ'vɒkətɪv] *adj* evokativ *(geh).* **to be ~ of sth** etw heraufbeschwören.
evoke [ɪ'vəʊk] *vt* heraufbeschwören; *memory also* wachrufen; *admiration* hervorrufen.
evolution [,iːvə'luːʃən] *n* Entwicklung *f*; *(Biol etc)* Evolution *f.*
evolve [ɪ'vɒlv] **1** *vt* entwickeln. **2** *vi* sich entwickeln, sich herausbilden.
ewe [juː] *n* Mutterschaf *nt.*
ex- [eks-] *pref* ehemalig, Ex-. **~-wife** frühere Frau, Exfrau *f.*
exacerbate [ek'sæsəbeɪt] *vt pain, disease* verschlimmern; *situation* verschärfen.
exact [ɪg'zækt] **1** *adj* genau; *figures, analysis etc also* exakt. **it's the ~ opposite** es ist genau umgekehrt. **2** *vt money, ransom* fordern *(from* von*).*
exacting [ɪg'zæktɪŋ] *adj* anspruchsvoll. **to be too/ very ~ with sb** zu viel/sehr viel von jdm verlangen.
exactly [ɪg'zæktlɪ] *adj* genau. **I'm not ~ sure who he is** ich bin mir nicht ganz sicher, wer er ist; **it's not ~ a detective story** es ist eigentlich keine Kriminalgeschichte; **he wasn't ~ pleased** er war nicht gerade erfreut.
exaggerate [ɪg'zædʒəreɪt] *vti* übertreiben; *(intensify) effect* verstärken.
exaggerated [ɪg'zædʒəreɪtɪd] *adj* übertrieben. **to have an ~ opinion of oneself** eine übertrieben hohe Meinung von sich haben.
exaggeration [ɪg,zædʒə'reɪʃən] *n* Übertreibung *f.*
exalted [ɪg'zɔːltɪd] *adj position, style* hoch.
exam [ɪg'zæm] *n* Prüfung *f.*
examination [ɪg,zæmɪ'neɪʃən] *n* **(a)** *(Sch etc)* Prüfung *f*; *(Univ also)* Examen *nt.* **(b)** *(study, inspection)* Prüfung, Untersuchung *f*; *(of machine, passports)* Kontrolle *f*; *(of question)* Untersuchung *f*; *(of accounts)* Prüfung *f.* **the matter is still under ~** die Angelegenheit wird noch geprüft *or* untersucht. **(c)** *(of accused, witness)* Verhör *nt*; *(of case)* Untersuchung *f.*
examine [ɪg'zæmɪn] *vt* **(a)** *(for* auf *+acc)* untersuchen; *document, accounts* prüfen; *machine, passports, luggage* kontrollieren. **(b)** *pupil, candidate* prüfen *(in* in *+dat, on* über *+acc).* **(c)** *accused, witness* verhören.
examiner [ɪg'zæmɪnəʳ] *n (Sch, Univ)* Prüfer *m.*
example [ɪg'zɑːmpl] *n* Beispiel *nt.* **for ~** zum Beispiel; **to set a good/bad ~** ein gutes/schlechtes Beispiel geben; **to make an ~ of sb** an jdm ein Exempel statuieren.
exasperate [ɪg'zɑːspəreɪt] *vt* zur Verzweiflung bringen. **to get ~d** verzweifeln *(with* an *+dat)*; **~d at** *or* **by** verärgert über *(+acc).*
exasperating [ɪg'zɑːspəreɪtɪŋ] *adj* ärgerlich; *delay, difficulty, job* leidig *attr.* **it's so ~!** es ist wirklich zum Verzweifeln!
exasperation [ɪg,zɑːspə'reɪʃən] *n* Verzweiflung *f (with* über *+acc).*
excavate ['ekskəveɪt] **1** *vt ground* ausschachten; *(machine)* ausbaggern; *(Archeol) remains* ausgraben. **2** *vi (Archeol)* Ausgrabungen machen.
excavation [,ekskə'veɪʃən] *n (Archeol)* (Aus)grabung *f*; *(of tunnel etc)* Graben *nt.* **~s** *(site)* Ausgrabungsstätte *f.*
excavator ['ekskəveɪtəʳ] *n (machine)* Bagger *m.*
exceed [ɪk'siːd] *vt (in value, amount, length of time)* übersteigen *(by* um*)*; *(go beyond)* hinausgehen über *(+acc)*; *expectations, desires* übertreffen; *limits, powers, speed limit* überschreiten.
exceedingly [ɪk'siːdɪŋlɪ] *adv* äußerst.
excel [ɪk'sel] **1** *vi* sich auszeichnen, sich hervortun *(in* in *+dat, at* bei*).* **2** *vr* **to ~ oneself** *(oft iro)* sich

selbst übertreffen.

excellence [ˈeksələns] *n* Vorzüglichkeit *f*.

Excellency [ˈeksələnsɪ] *n* **Your ~** Eure Exzellenz.

excellent [ˈeksələnt] *adj* ausgezeichnet.

except [ɪkˈsept] **1** *prep* außer *(+dat)*. **what can they do ~ wait?** was können sie anders tun als warten?; **~ for** abgesehen von, bis auf *(+acc)*; **~ that ...** außer daß ...; **~ for the fact that** abgesehen davon, daß ...; **~ if** außer wenn; **~ when** außer wenn. **2** *conj* **I'd refuse ~ I need the money** ich würde ablehnen, doch ich brauche das Geld. **3** *vt* ausnehmen. **not ~ing X** X nicht ausgenommen.

exception [ɪkˈsepʃən] *n* **(a)** Ausnahme *f*. **to make an ~** eine Ausnahme machen; **with the ~ of** mit Ausnahme von; **as an ~** ausnahmsweise; **the ~ proves the rule** *(prov)* Ausnahmen bestätigen die Regel *(prov)*. **(b) to take ~ to sth** Anstoß *m* an etw *(dat)* nehmen.

exceptional [ɪkˈsepʃənl] *adj* außergewöhnlich. **apart from ~ cases** abgesehen von Ausnahmefällen.

exceptionally [ɪkˈsepʃənəlɪ] *adv (outstandingly)* außergewöhnlich.

excerpt [ˈeksɜːpt] *n* Auszug *m*.

excess [ɪkˈses] *n* **(a)** Übermaß *nt* *(of* an *+dat)*. **to drink to ~** übermäßig trinken; **to carry sth to ~** etw übertreiben. **(b) ~es** *pl* Exzesse *pl*; *(brutalities also)* Ausschreitungen *pl*. **(c)** *(amount left over)* Überschuß *m*. **(d) to be in ~ of** überschreiten.

excess *in cpds weight, production* Über-; **~ baggage** *n* Übergewicht *nt*; **~ fare** *n* Nachlösegebühr *f*; **I had to pay ~ fare** ich mußte nachlösen.

excessive [ɪkˈsesɪv] *adj* übermäßig; *praise also* übertrieben. **I think you're being ~** ich finde, Sie übertreiben.

excessively [ɪkˈsesɪvlɪ] *adv* **(a)** *(to excess) (+vb) eat, drink* übermäßig; *(+adj) optimistic, severe* allzu. **(b)** *(extremely)* äußerst.

exchange [ɪksˈtʃeɪndʒ] **1** *vt books, glances, seats* tauschen; *foreign currency* umtauschen *(for* in *+acc)*; *ideas, experiences etc* austauschen. **to ~ words/letters/blows** einen Wortwechsel haben/einen Briefwechsel führen/sich schlagen; **to ~ one thing for another** eine Sache gegen eine andere austauschen *or (in shop)* umtauschen.

2 *n* **(a)** *(of goods, stamps)* Tausch *m*; *(of prisoners, views)* Austausch *m*; *(of one bought item for another)* Umtausch *m*. **in ~** dafür; **in ~ for money** gegen Geld; **in ~ for lending me your car** dafür, daß Sie mir Ihr Auto geliehen haben. **(b)** *(Fin: place)* Wechselstube *f*. **~ rate** Wechselkurs *m*. **(c) (telephone) ~** Fernamt *nt*; *(in office etc)* (Telefon)zentrale *f*.

3 *adj attr student, teacher* Austausch-.

exchequer [ɪksˈtʃekəʳ] *n* Finanzministerium *nt*; *(esp in GB)* Schatzamt *nt*.

excise [ˈeksaɪz] *n* Verbrauchssteuer *f*.

excitable [ɪkˈsaɪtəbl] *adj* (leicht) erregbar.

excite [ɪkˈsaɪt] *vt* aufregen, aufgeregt machen; *(rouse enthusiasm in)* begeistern; *sentiments, (sexually)* erregen; *imagination* anregen.

excited [ɪkˈsaɪtɪd] *adj* aufgeregt; *(worked up, not calm also, sexually)* erregt; *(enthusiastic)* begeistert. **don't get ~!** *(angry etc)* reg dich nicht auf!; **aren't you ~ about what might happen?** sind Sie nicht gespannt, was passieren wird?

excitement [ɪkˈsaɪtmənt] *n* Aufregung *f*; *(not being calm etc also, sexual)* Erregung *f*. **a mood of ~** eine spannungsgeladene Stimmung; **what's all the ~ about?** wozu die ganze Aufregung?; **his novel has caused great ~** sein Roman hat große Begeisterung ausgelöst.

exciting [ɪkˈsaɪtɪŋ] *adj* aufregend; *story, film, event, adventure also* spannend; *new author* sensationell. **isn't that ~!** ist das nicht prima?; **how ~ for you** prima!, wie aufregend *(also iro)*.

exclaim [ɪkˈskleɪm] *vt* ausrufen.

exclamation [ˌekskləˈmeɪʃən] *n* Ausruf *m* *(also Gram)*. **~ mark** *or* **point** *(US)* Ausrufezeichen *nt*.

exclude [ɪkˈskluːd] *vt* ausschließen. **to ~ sb from the team** jdn aus der Mannschaft ausschließen; **excluding petrol** außer *or* ausgenommen Benzin.

exclusion [ɪkˈskluːʒən] *n* Ausschluß *m* *(from* von*)*. **you can't just think about your job to the ~ of everything else** du kannst nicht ausschließlich an deine Arbeit denken.

exclusive [ɪkˈskluːsɪv] *adj* **(a)** *group, club etc* exklusiv; *right, inverview also* Exklusiv-. **they are mutually ~** sie schließen einander aus. **(b)** *(sole)* ausschließlich, einzig. **(c) from 15th to 20th June ~** vom 15. bis zum 20. Juni ausschließlich; **~ of** ausschließlich *(+gen)*, exklusive *(+gen)*.

exclusively [ɪkˈskluːsɪvlɪ] *adv* ausschließlich.

excommunicate [ˌekskəˈmjuːnɪkeɪt] *vt* exkommunizieren.

excrement [ˈekskrɪmənt] *n* Kot *m*, Exkremente *pl*.

excruciating [ɪkˈskruːʃɪeɪtɪŋ] *adj pain, noise* gräßlich, entsetzlich.

excruciatingly [ɪkˈskruːʃɪeɪtɪŋlɪ] *adv* **it was ~ painful** es hat scheußlich weh getan *(col)*; **~ funny** urkomisch.

excursion [ɪkˈskɜːʃən] *n* Ausflug *m*. **to go on an ~** einen Ausflug machen; **~ ticket** verbilligte Fahrkarte.

excuse [ɪkˈskjuːz] **1** *vt* **(a)** entschuldigen. **he ~d himself for being late** er entschuldigte sich, daß er zu spät kam; **to ~ sb for having done sth** jdm verzeihen, daß er etwas getan hat; **I think I can be ~d for believing him** man kann es mir wohl nicht übelnehmen, daß ich ihm geglaubt habe; **if you will ~ the expression** wenn Sie mir den Ausdruck gestatten; **~ me!** *(to get attention, sorry)* Entschuldigung!, entschuldigen Sie!; *(indignant)* erlauben Sie mal! **(b)** *(from obligation)* **to ~ sb from (doing) sth** jdn von einer Sache befreien, jdm etw erlassen; **you are ~d** ihr könnt gehen; **can I be ~d?** darf ich mal verschwinden *(col)*?

2 [ɪksˈkjuːs] *n* Entschuldigung *f*. **there's no ~ for it** dafür gibt es keine Entschuldigung; **to make ~s for sb** jdn entschuldigen; **he's only making ~s** er sucht nur nach einer Ausrede; **a good ~ for a party** ein guter Grund, eine Party zu feiern.

ex-directory [ˌeksdaɪˈrektərɪ] *adj (Brit)* **to be ~** nicht im Telefonbuch stehen.

execute [ˈeksɪkjuːt] *vt* **(a)** *plan, order* ausführen; *duties* erfüllen. **beautifully ~d** *(concerto)* wunderbar gespielt. **(b)** *criminal* hinrichten. **(c)** *(Jur) will* vollstrecken.

execution [ˌeksɪˈkjuːʃən] *n* **(a)** *see vt (a)* Ausführung *f*; Erfüllung *f*. **in the ~ of his duties** bei der Ausübung seines Amtes. **(b)** *(Mus)* Vortrag *m*; *(musician's skill)* Ausführung *f*. **(c)** *(as punishment)* Hinrichtung *f*. **(d)** *(Jur: of will)* Vollstreckung *f*.

executioner [ˌeksɪˈkjuːʃnəʳ] *n* Henker *m*.

executive [ɪgˈzekjʊtɪv] **1** *adj powers, committee etc* Exekutiv-; *(Comm)* geschäftsführend. **~ position** leitende Stellung *or* Position. **2** *n* **(a)** leitender Angestellter, leitende Angestellte, Manager *m*. **~ (brief)case** Diplomatenköfferchen *nt*. **(b)** *(of government)* Exekutive *f*; *(of association)* Vorstand *m*.

executor [ɪgˈzekjʊtəʳ] *n (of will)* Testamentsvollstrecker *m*.

exemplary [ɪgˈzemplərɪ] *adj* vorbildlich, beispielhaft. **~ punishment** exemplarische Strafe.

exemplify [ɪgˈzemplɪfaɪ] *vt* erläutern.

exempt [ɪgˈzempt] **1** *adj* befreit *(from* von*)*. **2** *vt person* befreien.

exemption [ɪgˈzempʃən] *n* Befreiung *f*.

exercise [ˈeksəsaɪz] **1** *n* **(a)** *no pl (of right)* Wahrnehmung *f*; *(of physical, mental power)*

Ausübung *f.* **(b)** *(bodily or mental, drill, Mus etc)* Übung *f.* **to do one's ~s in the morning** Morgengymnastik machen. **(c)** *no pl (physical)* Bewegung *f.* **physical ~** (körperliche) Bewegung; **you should take more ~** Sie sollten mehr Bewegung haben; **what do you do for ~?** wie halten Sie sich fit? **(d)** *(Mil: usu pl)* Übung *f.* **2** *vt* **(a)** *body, mind* üben, trainieren; *(Mil) troops* exerzieren; *dog* spazierenführen. **(b)** *(use) control, power* ausüben; *a right also* geltend machen; *tact, discretion* üben. **3** *vi* **if you ~ regularly** wenn Sie sich viel bewegen.

exercise book *n* Heft *nt.*

exert [ɪg'zɜːt] **1** *vt pressure* ausüben *(on* auf *+acc); authority* geltend machen *(on* bei*).* **2** *vr* **to ~ oneself** sich anstrengen.

exertion [ɪg'zɜːʃən] *n* **(a)** *(effort)* Anstrengung *f.* **after the day's ~s** nach des Tages Mühen. **(b)** *(of pressure, influence)* Ausübung *f (on* auf *+acc).*

exeunt ['eksɪʌnt] *(in stage directions)* ab.

ex gratia [eks'greɪʃə] *adj payment* Sonder-.

exhale [eks'heɪl] *vti* ausatmen.

exhaust [ɪg'zɔːst] **1** *vt (use up, tire)* erschöpfen. **2** *n (Aut etc)* Auspuff *m*; *(gases)* Auspuffgase *pl.*

exhausted [ɪg'zɔːstɪd] *adj* erschöpft.

exhaust fumes *npl* Abgase *pl.*

exhausting [ɪg'zɔːstɪŋ] *adj* anstrengend.

exhaustion [ɪg'zɔːstʃən] *n* Erschöpfung *f.*

exhaustive [ɪg'zɔːstɪv] *adj* erschöpfend.

exhaust: ~ pipe *n* Auspuffrohr *nt*; **~ system** *n* Auspuff *m.*

exhibit [ɪg'zɪbɪt] **1** *vt* **(a)** ausstellen; *merchandise also* auslegen. **(b)** *skill, ingenuity* zeigen, an den Tag legen. **2** *vi* ausstellen. **3** *n (in an exhibition)* Ausstellungsstück *nt*; *(Jur)* Beweisstück *nt.*

exhibition [ˌeksɪ'bɪʃən] *n* **(a)** Ausstellung *f*; *(of articles for sale)* Auslage *f.* **(b) to make an ~ of oneself** sich danebenbenehmen *(col).*

exhibitionist [ˌeksɪ'bɪʃənɪst] *n* Exhibitionist(in *f*) *m.*

exhibitor [ɪg'zɪbɪtə^r] *n* Aussteller *m.*

exhilarate [ɪg'zɪləreɪt] *vt* in Hochstimmung versetzen; *(sea air etc)* beleben, erfrischen.

exhilarated [ɪg'zɪləreɪtɪd] *adj* erregt. **to feel ~** in Hochstimmung sein.

exhilarating [ɪg'zɪləreɪtɪŋ] *adj sensation, speed* erregend; *music* anregend; *air etc* belebend.

exhilaration [ɪgˌzɪlə'reɪʃən] *n* Hochgefühl *nt.*

exhort [ɪg'zɔːt] *vt* ermahnen.

exhume [eks'hjuːm] *vt* exhumieren.

exile ['eksaɪl] **1** *n (person)* Verbannte(r) *mf*; *(banishment)* Exil *nt*, Verbannung *f.* **in ~** im Exil. **2** *vt* verbannen *(from* aus*).*

exist [ɪg'zɪst] *vi* **(a)** existieren, bestehen. **it doesn't ~** das gibt es nicht; **to continue to ~** fortbestehen; **there ~s a tradition that ...** es gibt den Brauch, daß ...; **she ~s on very little** sie kommt mit sehr wenig aus; **we manage to ~** wir kommen gerade aus. **(b)** *(be found: plants, minerals etc)* vorkommen.

existence [ɪg'zɪstəns] *n* **(a)** Existenz *f*; *(of custom, tradition, institution also)* Bestehen *nt.* **to be in ~** existieren, bestehen; **to come into ~** entstehen; *(person)* auf die Welt kommen; **to go out of ~** zu existieren aufhören; **the only one in ~** der einzige, den es gibt. **(b)** *(life)* Dasein *nt*, Existenz *f.*

existential [ˌegzɪs'tenʃəl] *adj* existentiell.

existentialism [ˌegzɪs'tenʃəlɪzəm] *n* Existentialismus *m.*

existing [ɪg'zɪstɪŋ] *adj law* bestehend; *director* gegenwärtig.

exit ['eksɪt] **1** *n* Ausgang *m*; *(for vehicles)* Ausfahrt *f.* **he made a very dramatic ~** sein Abgang war sehr dramatisch; **~ visa** Ausreisevisum *nt.* **2** *vi (from stage)* abgehen.

exodus ['eksədəs] *n* Auszug *m*; *(Bibl, fig)* Exodus *m.* **general ~** allgemeiner Aufbruch.

exonerate [ɪg'zɒnəreɪt] *vt* entlasten *(from* von*).*

exorbitant [ɪg'zɔːbɪtənt] *adj price* astronomisch; *demands* maßlos, übertrieben. **that's ~!** das ist Wucher!

exorcism ['eksɔːsɪzəm] *n* Exorzismus *m.*

exorcize ['eksɔːsaɪz] *vt* exorzieren; *evil spirit also* austreiben.

exotic [ɪg'zɒtɪk] *adj* exotisch.

expand [ɪk'spænd] **1** *vt* ausdehnen, erweitern; *ideas* entwickeln. **2** *vi (gases, universe)* sich ausdehnen; *(business)* expandieren, sich ausweiten; *(knowledge, influence, market)* wachsen. **could you ~ on that?** könnten Sie das näher ausführen?

expanse [ɪk'spæns] *n* Fläche *f*; *(of sea)* Weite *f no pl.*

expansion [ɪk'spænʃən] *n (of gas, metal, property)* Ausdehnung *f*; *(of business, production, knowledge)* Erweiterung *f*; *(territorial, economic)* Expansion *f*; *(of subject, idea)* Entwicklung *f*; *(of experience, influence)* Vergrößerung *f.*

expansionism [ɪk'spænʃənɪzəm] *n* Expansionspolitik *f.*

expansionist [ɪk'spænʃənɪst] *adj* expansionistisch.

expansive [ɪk'spænsɪv] *adj person* mitteilsam.

expatriate [eks'pætrɪət] **1** *adj* im Ausland lebend. **2** *n* im Ausland Lebende(r) *mf.* **the ~s in Abu Dhabi** die Ausländer in Abu Dhabi.

expect [ɪk'spekt] **1** *vt* **(a)** *(anticipate)* erwarten; *esp sth bad also* rechnen mit. **that was to be ~ed** das war zu erwarten; **I know what to ~** ich weiß, was mich erwartet; **I ~ed as much** das habe ich erwartet; **I was ~ing him to come** ich habe eigentlich erwartet, daß er kommt.

(b) *(suppose)* annehmen. **will they be on time? — yes, I ~ so** kommen sie pünktlich? — ja, ich glaube schon; **I ~ it will rain** es wird wohl regnen; **I ~ he turned it down** ich nehme an, er hat abgelehnt; **well, I ~ he's right** er wird schon recht haben.

(c) *(demand)* **to ~ sth of** *or* **from sb** etw von jdm erwarten; **to ~ sb to do sth** erwarten, daß jd etw tut; **are we ~ed to tip the waiter?** müssen wir dem Kellner Trinkgeld geben?; **what do you ~ me to do about it?** was soll ich da machen?

(d) *(await)* erwarten; *baby also* bekommen. **we'll ~ you when we see you** *(col)* wenn ihr kommt, dann kommt ihr *(col).*

2 *vi* **she's ~ing** sie ist in anderen Umständen.

expectancy [ɪk'spektənsɪ] *n* Erwartung *f.*

expectant [ɪk'spektənt] *adj* erwartungsvoll; *mother* werdend.

expectation [ˌekspek'teɪʃən] *n* **(a)** Erwartung *f.* **in ~ of** in Erwartung *(+gen)*; **contrary to all ~(s)** wider Erwarten; **beyond all ~(s)** über Erwarten; **to come up to sb's ~s** jds Erwartungen entsprechen. **(b)** *(prospect)* Aussicht *f.*

expedience [ɪk'spiːdɪəns], **expediency** [ɪk'spiːdɪənsɪ] *n* **(a)** *(self-interest)* Zweckdenken *nt*, Berechnung *f.* **(b)** *(of measure etc)* Zweckdienlichkeit *f*; *(advisability)* Ratsamkeit *f.*

expedient [ɪk'spiːdɪənt] *adj (politic)* zweckdienlich; *(advisable)* angebracht, ratsam.

expedite ['ekspɪdaɪt] *vt* beschleunigen.

expedition [ˌekspɪ'dɪʃən] *n* Expedition *f*; *(Mil)* Feldzug *m.*

expeditionary [ˌekspɪ'dɪʃənrɪ] *adj* **~ force** Expeditionskorps *nt.*

expel [ɪk'spel] *vt* vertreiben; *(from country)* ausweisen *(from* aus*)*; *(from school)* verweisen *(from* von, *gen)*; *(from party)* ausschließen *(from* aus*).*

expend [ɪk'spend] *vt time, energy* aufwenden *(on* für*)*; *(use up) resources* verbrauchen.

expendable [ɪk'spendəbl] *adj* entbehrlich; *people* überflüssig.

expenditure [ɪk'spendɪtʃə^r] *n (money spent)*

Ausgaben *pl*; *(of time, energy)* Aufwand *m (of* an +*dat)*.

expense [ɪk'spens] *n* **(a)** Kosten *pl*. **at my ~** auf meine Kosten; **at great ~** mit hohen Kosten; **it's a big ~** es ist eine große Ausgabe; **to go to great ~ to repair the house** es sich *(dat)* etwas kosten lassen, das Haus instand zu setzen; **don't go to any ~ of over our visit** stürz dich nicht in Unkosten wegen unseres Besuchs; **at sb's ~/at the ~ of sth** *(fig)* auf jds Kosten *(acc)*/auf Kosten einer Sache *(gen)*. **(b)** *(Comm: usu pl)* Spesen *pl*. **to incur ~s** Unkosten haben; **it's on ~s** das geht auf Spesen; **~ account** Spesenkonto *nt*.

expensive [ɪk'spensɪv] *adj* teuer.

experience [ɪk'spɪərɪəns] **1** *n* **(a)** Erfahrung *f*. **~ shows that ...** die Erfahrung lehrt, daß ...; **from my own personal ~** aus eigener Erfahrung; **he has no ~ of living in the country** er kennt das Landleben nicht; **to have a lot of teaching ~** große Erfahrung als Lehrer haben. **(b)** *(event experienced)* Erlebnis *nt*. **I had a nasty ~** mir ist etwas Unangenehmes passiert; **to go through** *or* **have a painful ~** Schreckliches erleben; **to have an ~** eine Erfahrung machen; **what an ~!** das war vielleicht was!; **it was a new ~ for me** es war völlig neu für mich.

2 *vt* **(a)** erleben; *pain, hunger also* erfahren; *difficult times* durchmachen. **to ~ difficulties** Schwierigkeiten haben. **(b)** *(feel)* empfinden.

experienced [ɪk'spɪərɪənst] *adj* erfahren *(in* in +*dat)*; *eye, ear* geschult.

experiment [ɪk'sperɪmənt] **1** *n* Versuch *m*, Experiment *nt*. **to do an ~** einen Versuch *or* ein Experiment machen. **2** *vi* experimentieren *(on* mit*)*.

experimental [ɪk,sperɪ'mentl] *adj* experimentell; *also method, science* Experimental-; *farm, engine, period* Versuchs-; *theatre, cinema* Experimentier-. **at the ~ stage** im Versuchsstadium.

experimentation [ɪk,sperɪmen'teɪʃən] *n* Experimentieren *nt*.

expert ['ekspɜːt] **1** *n* Fachmann, Experte *m*, Expertin *f*; *(Jur)* Sachverständige(r) *mf*. **2** *adj work* ausgezeichnet, geschickt; *driver etc* erfahren; *approach, advice* fachmännisch; *opinion* eines Fachmanns/Sachverständigen. **~ witness** sachverständiger Zeuge; **the ~ touch** die Meisterhand.

expertise [,ekspə'tiːz] *n* Sachkenntnis *f (in* auf dem Gebiet +*gen)*; *(manual)* Geschick *nt (in* bei*)*.

expire [ɪk'spaɪəʳ] *vi* **(a)** *(passport, time limit)* ablaufen. **(b)** *(liter: die)* seinen Geist aufgeben *(liter)*.

expiry [ɪk'spaɪərɪ] *n* Ablauf *m*. **~ date** Ablauftermin *m*; *(of special offer)* Verfallsdatum *nt*.

explain [ɪk'spleɪn] *vt* erklären *(to sb* jdm*)*; *situation also* erläutern; *mystery* aufklären. **he'd better ~ himself** ich hoffe, er kann das erklären.

♦ **explain away** *vt sep* wegerklären *(col)*.

explanation [,eksplə'neɪʃən] *n see vt* Erklärung *f*; Erläuterung *f*; Aufklärung *f*. **what can you say in ~ of this?** wie erklären Sie das?

explanatory [ɪk'splænətərɪ] *adj* erklärend. **a few ~ remarks** ein paar Worte zur Erklärung.

expletive [ɪk'spliːtɪv] *n* Kraftausdruck *m*.

explicit [ɪk'splɪsɪt] *adj* deutlich, explizit *(geh)*; *text, meaning also* klar; *sex scene* deutlich, unverhüllt.

explicitly [ɪk'splɪsɪtlɪ] *adv* deutlich.

explode [ɪk'spləʊd] **1** *vi (lit, fig)* explodieren. **to ~ with laughter** in schallendes Gelächter ausbrechen. **2** *vt* **(a)** *bomb, mine* sprengen; *dynamite, gas* zur Explosion bringen. **(b)** *(fig) theory, argument* zu Fall bringen.

exploit ['eksplɔɪt] **1** *n (heroic)* Heldentat *f*. **~s** *(adventures)* Abenteuer *pl*. **2** [ɪks'plɔɪt] *vt coal seam, (pej) workers* ausbeuten; *situation, (pej) friend, good nature* ausnutzen; *product* nutzen.

exploitation [,eksplɔɪ'teɪʃən] *n see vt* Ausbeutung *f*; Ausnutzung *f*; Nutzung *f*.

exploration [,eksplɔː'reɪʃən] *n* Erforschung, Erkundung *f*; *(of topic, Med)* Untersuchung *f*. **a voyage of ~** *(lit, fig)* eine Entdeckungsreise.

exploratory [ɪk'splɒrətərɪ] *adj drilling* Probe-. **~ operation** *(Med)* Explorationsoperation *f*; **~ talks** Sondierungsgespräche *pl*.

explore [ɪk'splɔːʳ] **1** *vt (lit, fig)* erforschen; *(Med)* untersuchen. **2** *vi* **to go exploring** auf Entdeckungsreise gehen.

explorer [ɪk'splɔːrəʳ] *n* Forscher(in *f*) *m*.

explosion [ɪk'spləʊʒən] *n (lit, fig)* Explosion *f*; *(fig: of anger)* Wutausbruch *m*.

explosive [ɪk'spləʊzɪv] **1** *adj (lit, fig)* explosiv. **~ device** Sprengkörper *m*. **2** *n* Sprengstoff *m*.

exponent [ɪk'spəʊnənt] *n* Vertreter(in *f*) *m*.

export 1 [ɪk'spɔːt] *vti* exportieren. **2** ['ekspɔːt] *n* Export *m*. **~ drive** Exportkampagne *f*.

exporter [ɪk'spɔːtəʳ] *n* Exporteur *m (of* von*)*; *(country also)* Exportland *nt (of* für*)*.

expose [ɪk'spəʊz] *vt* **(a)** *rocks, remains* freilegen; *electric wire, nerve also* bloßlegen. **to be ~d to view** sichtbar sein. **(b)** *(to danger, sunlight, radiation, criticism)* aussetzen *(to dat)*. **"not to be ~d to heat"** „vor Hitze schützen". **(c)** *(display) one's ignorance* offenbaren; *(indecently) oneself* entblößen. **(d)** *abuse, treachery* aufdecken; *imposter, thief* entlarven. **to ~ sb/sth to the press** jdn/etw der Presse ausliefern. **(e)** *(Phot)* belichten.

exposed [ɪk'spəʊzd] *adj* **(a)** *(to weather) place* ungeschützt. **~ to the wind** dem Wind ausgesetzt. **(b)** *(insecure)* **to feel ~** sich allen Blicken ausgesetzt fühlen. **(c)** *(visible)* sichtbar. **the ~ parts of a motor** die freiliegenden Teile eines Motors.

exposition [ekspə'zɪʃən] *n (of theory)* Darlegung *f*; *(Mus)* Exposition *f*.

expostulate [ɪk'spɒstjʊleɪt] *vi* protestieren.

expostulation [ɪk,spɒstjʊ'leɪʃən] *n* Protest *m*.

exposure [ɪk'spəʊʒəʳ] *n* **(a)** *(to sunlight, air, danger)* Aussetzung *f (to dat)*. **to be suffering from ~** an Unterkühlung leiden; **to die of ~** erfrieren. **(b)** *(displaying)* Entblößung *f*. **indecent ~** Exhibitionismus *m*. **(c)** *(unmasking)* Bloßstellung *f*; *(of thief, murderer)* Entlarvung *f*; *(of abuses, vices, scandals, crime)* Aufdeckung *f*. **(d)** *(Phot)* Belichtung(szeit) *f*. **~ meter** Belichtungsmesser *m*. **(e)** *(Media)* Publicity *f*.

expound [ɪk'spaʊnd] *vt* darlegen, erläutern.

express [ɪk'spres] **1** *vt* ausdrücken. **to ~ oneself** sich ausdrücken. **2** *adj instructions* ausdrücklich; *intention* bestimmt. **3** *adv* **to send sth ~** etw per Expreß schicken. **4** *n (train)* Schnellzug *m*.

expression [ɪk'spreʃən] *n* Ausdruck *m*. **as an ~ of our gratitude** zum Ausdruck unserer Dankbarkeit; **you could tell by his ~ that ...** man konnte an seinem Gesichtsausdruck erkennen, daß ...

expressionism [ɪk'spreʃənɪzəm] *n* Expressionismus *m*.

expressive [ɪk'spresɪv] *adj* ausdrucksvoll.

expressly [ɪk'spreslɪ] *adv deny etc* ausdrücklich.

express: ~ train *n* Schnellzug *m*; **~way** *n* Schnellstraße *f*.

expulsion [ɪk'spʌlʃən] *n (from country)* Ausweisung *f (from* aus*)*; *(from school)* Verweisung *f* (von der Schule); *(from party)* Ausschluß *m (from* aus*)*.

expurgate ['ekspɜːgeɪt] *vt* zensieren. **~d edition** gereinigte Fassung.

exquisite [ɪk'skwɪzɪt] *adj workmanship* ausgezeichnet; *dress, painting* exquisit; *taste* gepflegt; *view* herrlich; *food, wine, sense of humour, satisfaction, pleasure* köstlich.

extant [ek'stænt] *adj* noch vorhanden.

extempore [ɪks'tempərɪ] *adj* **to give an ~ speech**

eine Rede aus dem Stegreif halten.
extemporize [ɪk'stempəraɪz] *vti* aus dem Stegreif sprechen; *(Mus, with makeshift)* improvisieren.
extend [ɪk'stend] **1** *vt* **(a)** *(stretch out) arms* ausstrecken. **(b)** *line, visit, passport, holidays* verlängern. **(c)** *(enlarge) research, powers, limits, knowledge* erweitern; *house* anbauen an *(+acc)*; *frontiers of a country* ausdehnen. **(d)** *(offer) (to sb* jdm*) help* gewähren; *hospitality, friendship* erweisen; *condolences* aussprechen. **to ~ a welcome to sb** jdn willkommen heißen. **2** *vi (wall, garden)* sich erstrecken *(to, as far as* bis*)*; *(over period of time)* sich hinziehen.
extension [ɪk'stenʃən] *n* **(a)** *(of property)* Vergrößerung *f*; *(of business, knowledge also)* Erweiterung *f*; *(of powers, franchise, research, frontiers)* Ausdehnung *f*; *(of road, line, period of time)* Verlängerung *f*; *(of house)* Anbau *m*. **(b)** *(Telec)* (Neben)anschluß *m*. **~ 3714** Apparat 3714; **~ cable** Verlängerungskabel *nt*; **~ ladder** Ausziehleiter *f*.
extensive [ɪk'stensɪv] *adj land, forest* ausgedehnt; *knowledge, press coverage, research, enquiries, operations, alterations* umfangreich; *damage* beträchtlich; *use* häufig; *plans, reforms, influence* weitreichend.
extensively [ɪk'stensɪvlɪ] *adv* weit; *study, investigate, cover* ausführlich; *altered, reformed, damaged* beträchtlich; *used* häufig, viel; *travel* viel.
extent [ɪk'stent] *n (length)* Länge *f*; *(size)* Ausdehnung *f*; *(range, scope)* Umfang *m*; *(of damage, commitments also)* Ausmaß *nt*. **to some ~** bis zu einem gewissen Grade; **to what ~** inwieweit; **to a certain ~** in gewissem Maße; **to a large ~** in hohem Maße; **to such an ~ that ...** dermaßen, daß ...
extenuating [ɪk'stenjʊeɪtɪŋ] *adj* **~ circumstances** mildernde Umstände *pl*.
exterior [ɪk'stɪərɪə^r] **1** *adj surface* äußere(r, s), Außen-. **2** *n (of house etc)* Außenseite *f*; *(of person)* Äußere(s) *nt*. **on the ~** außen.
exterminate [ɪk'stɜːmɪneɪt] *vt* ausrotten.
external [ek'stɜːnl] **1** *adj wall* äußere(r, s), Außen-; *factors, help* extern. **for ~ use only** *(Med)* nur äußerlich (anzuwenden); **~ trade** Außenhandel *m*. **2** *n (fig)* **~s** *pl* Äußerlichkeiten *pl*.
externally [ek'stɜːnəlɪ] *adv* äußerlich.
extinct [ɪk'stɪŋkt] *adj volcano, love* erloschen; *species* ausgestorben.
extinction [ɪk'stɪŋkʃən] *n (of race)* Aussterben *nt*; *(annihilation)* Vernichtung *f*.
extinguish [ɪk'stɪŋgwɪʃ] *vt fire* löschen; *hopes, passion* zerstören.
extinguisher [ɪk'stɪŋgwɪʃə^r] *n* Feuerlöscher *m*.
extol [ɪk'stəʊl] *vt* preisen, rühmen.
extort [ɪk'stɔːt] *vt* erpressen *(from* von*)*.
extortion [ɪk'stɔːʃən] *n* Erpressung *f*. **this is sheer ~!** *(col)* das ist ja Wucher!
extortionate [ɪk'stɔːʃənɪt] *adj prices* Wucher-; *tax, demand* ungeheuer.
extra ['ekstrə] **1** *adj* zusätzlich. **we need an ~ chair** wir brauchen noch einen Stuhl; **to make an ~ effort** sich besonders anstrengen; **~ charge** Zuschlag *m*; **there will be no ~ charge** das wird nicht extra berechnet; **~ time** *(Brit Ftbl)* Verlängerung *f*; **~ pay** eine Zulage; **for ~ safety** zur größeren Sicherheit; **we need an ~ 10 minutes** wir brauchen 10 Minuten mehr; **I have brought an ~ pair of shoes** ich habe ein extra Paar Schuhe mitgebracht. **2** *adv* **(a)** *(especially)* extra, besonders. **(b)** *(in addition)* extra. **3** *n* **(a)** *(perk)* Zusatzleistung *f*; *(for car)* Extra *nt*. **they regard it as an ~** sie betrachten es als Luxus. **(b) ~s** *pl (~ expenses)* zusätzliche Kosten *pl*; *(in restaurant)* Zusätzliches *nt*. **(c)** *(Film, Theat)* Statist(in *f*) *m*. **(d)** *(remainder)* Rest *m*.
extract [ɪk'strækt] **1** *vt* **(a)** herausziehen *(from* aus*)*; *juice, minerals, oil* gewinnen *(from* aus*)*; *tooth* ziehen. **(b)** *(fig) information, confession, money* herausholen *(from* aus*)*. **(c)** *quotation, passage* herausziehen. **2** ['ekstrækt] *n (from book etc)* Auszug *m*. **beef ~** Fleischextrakt *m*.
extraction [ɪk'strækʃən] *n* **(a)** *see vt* Herausziehen *nt*; Gewinnung *f*; Ziehen *nt*; Herausholen *nt*. **he had to have three ~s** ihm mußten drei Zähne gezogen werden. **(b) of Spanish ~** spanischer Abstammung.
extracurricular ['ekstrəkə'rɪkjʊlə^r] *adj* außerhalb des Stundenplans.
extradite ['ekstrədaɪt] *vt* ausliefern.
extradition [,ekstrə'dɪʃən] *n* Auslieferung *f*. **~ treaty** Auslieferungsvertrag *m*.
extramarital ['ekstrə'mærɪtl] *adj* außerehelich.
extramural ['ekstrə'mjʊərəl] *adj courses* Volkshochschul-.
extraneous [ɪk'streɪnɪəs] *adj influence* extern. **~ to** *(unrelated)* irrelevant für.
extraordinary [ɪk'strɔːdnrɪ] *adj* **(a)** *(beyond what is common)* außerordentlich; *(not usual)* ungewöhnlich. **(b)** *(odd, peculiar)* sonderbar, seltsam; *(amazing)* erstaunlich. **(c)** *(special)* **an ~ meeting** eine Sondersitzung.
extrapolate [ek'stræpəleɪt] *vti* extrapolieren *(from* aus*)*.
extrasensory ['ekstrə'sensərɪ] *adj* **~ perception** außersinnliche Wahrnehmung.
extra-special ['ekstrə'speʃəl] *adj* ganz besondere(r, s).
extraterrestrial ['ekstrətɪ'restrɪəl] *adj* außerirdisch.
extravagance [ɪk'strævəgəns] *n* **(a)** Luxus *m no pl*. **her ~** ihre Verschwendungssucht. **(b)** *(wastefulness)* Verschwendung *f*. **(c)** *(of ideas, theories)* Ausgefallenheit *f*; *(of claim, demand)* Übertriebenheit *f*. **(d)** *(extravagant action)* Extravaganz *f*.
extravagant [ɪk'strævəgənt] *adj* **(a)** *taste, habit* teuer, kostspielig; *wedding, lifestyle* aufwendig; *price* überhöht. **she is ~** sie gibt das Geld mit vollen Händen aus; **go on, be ~** gönn dir doch den Luxus. **(b)** *(wasteful)* verschwenderisch. **(c)** *behaviour* extravagant; *ideas, tie also* ausgefallen; *claim, demand* übertrieben.
extreme [ɪk'striːm **1** *adj* äußerste(r, s); *(exaggerated, drastic, Pol)* extrem; *praise, flattery* übertrieben; *exaggeration, demands* maßlos; *penalty* höchste(r, s). **to the ~ right** ganz rechts; **~ old age** ein äußerst hohes Alter; **an ~ case** ein Extremfall *m*. **2** *n* Extrem *nt*. **~s of temperature** extreme Temperaturen *pl*; **in the ~** im höchsten Grade; **to go from one ~ to the other** von einem Extrem ins andere fallen; **to go to ~s** es übertreiben; **to drive sb to ~s** jdn zum Äußersten treiben.
extremely [ɪk'striːmlɪ] *adv* äußerst, höchst. **was it difficult? — ~** war es schwierig? — sehr!
extremist [ɪk'striːmɪst] **1** *adj* extremistisch. **2** *n* Extremist(in *f*) *m*.
extremity [ɪk'stremɪtɪ] *n* **(a)** *(furthest point)* äußerstes Ende. **(b)** *(state of distress)* Not *f*. **(c) to resort to extremities** zu extremen Mitteln greifen. **(d) extremities** *pl (hands and feet)* Extremitäten *pl*.
extricate ['ekstrɪkeɪt] *vt* befreien *(from* aus*)*.
extrovert ['ekstrəʊvɜːt] **1** *adj* extrovertiert. **2** *n* extrovertierter Mensch.
exuberance [ɪg'zuːbərəns] *n (of person)* Überschwenglichkeit *f*; *(of joy, youth, feelings)* Überschwang *m*; *(joy)* überschwengliche Freude *(at* über *+acc)*; *(of prose, style)* Vitalität *f*.
exuberant [ɪg'zuːbərənt] *adj* überschwenglich; *style* übersprudelnd, vital; *music* mitreißend.
exude [ɪg'zjuːd] *vt (liquid)* ausscheiden; *confidence* ausstrahlen; *(pej) charm* triefen vor *(+dat)*.
exult [ɪg'zʌlt] *vi* frohlocken.
exultant [ɪg'zʌltənt] *adj* jubelnd; *shout also* Jubel-.

to be ~ jubeln.

exultation [ˌegzʌlˈteɪʃən] *n* Jubel *m*.

eye [aɪ] **1** *n* Auge *nt*; *(of needle)* Öhr *nt*. **with one's ~s closed/open** mit geschlossenen/offenen Augen; *(fig)* blind/mit offenen Augen; **an ~ for an ~** Auge um Auge; **to be all ~s** große Augen machen; **that's one in the ~ for him** *(col)* da hat er eins aufs Dach gekriegt *(col)*; **to cast** *or* **run one's ~s over sth** etw überfliegen; **to look sb (straight) in the ~** jdm in die Augen sehen; **to set** *or* **clap** *(col)* **~s on sb/sth** jdn/etw zu Gesicht bekommen; **(why don't you) use your ~s!** hast du keine Augen im Kopf?; **with one's own ~s** mit eigenen Augen; **before my very ~s** (direkt) vor meinen Augen; **under the watchful ~ of the guard** unter der Aufsicht des Wächters; **to keep an ~ on sb/sth** *(look after)* auf jdn/etw aufpassen; **to keep one's ~ on the ball/main objective** sich auf den Ball/die Hauptsache konzentrieren; **never to take one's ~s off sb/sth** kein Auge von jdm/etw wenden; **he couldn't take his ~s off her/the cake** er konnte einfach den Blick nicht von ihr/dem Kuchen lassen; **to keep one's ~s open** die Augen offenhalten; **to keep an ~ out for a hotel** nach einem Hotel Ausschau halten; **to keep an ~ on expenditure** auf seine Ausgaben achten; **to open sb's ~s to sb/sth** jdm die Augen über jdn/etw öffnen; **to close one's ~s to sth** die Augen vor etw *(dat)* verschließen; **to see ~ to ~ with sb** mit jdm einer Meinung sein; **to make ~s at sb** jdm schöne Augen machen; **to catch sb's ~** jds Aufmerksamkeit erregen; **that colour caught my ~** die Farbe fiel mir ins Auge; **in the ~s of the law** in den Augen des Gesetzes; **in my ~s** in meinen Augen; **with an ~ to the future** im Hinblick auf die Zukunft; **with an ~ to buying sth** in der Absicht, etw zu kaufen; **I've got my ~ on you** ich beobachte dich genau; **to have one's ~ on sth** *(want)* auf etw *(acc)* ein Auge geworfen haben; **to have an ~ on sb for a job** jdn für eine Stelle im Auge haben; **he has a good ~ for colour** er hat ein Auge für Farbe; **you need an ~ for detail** man muß einen Blick fürs Detail haben; **to be up to the ~s in work** *(col)* in Arbeit ersticken *(col)*.

2 *vt* anstarren. **to ~ sb up and down** jdn von oben bis unten mustern.

♦**eye up** *vt sep girls, boys* mustern, begutachten.

eye *in cpds* Augen-; **~ball** *n* Augapfel *m*; **~brow** *n* Augenbraue *f*; **he never raised an ~brow** *(col)* er hat sich nicht einmal gewundert; **~brow pencil** *n* Augenbrauenstift *m*; **~-catching** *adj* auffallend; *publicity, poster also* auffällig; **~ drops** Augentropfen *pl*.

eyeful [ˈaɪfʊl] *n (col)* **to get an ~** *(get sth in eye)* etw ins Auge bekommen; **get an ~ of this** guck dir das mal an *(col)*.

eye: ~glasses *npl (US)* Brille *f*; **~lash** *n* Augenwimper *f*; **~let** [ˈaɪlɪt] *n* Öse *f*; **~-level** *adj attr grill* in Augenhöhe; **~lid** *n* Augenlid *nt*; **~ liner** *n* Eyeliner *m*; **~-opener** *n* **that was a real ~-opener to me** das hat mir die Augen geöffnet; **~shadow** *n* Lidschatten *m*; **~sight** *n* Sehkraft *f*; **to have good ~sight** gute Augen haben; **to lose one's ~sight** das Augenlicht verlieren *(geh)*, erblinden; **~sore** *n* Schandfleck *m*; **this carpet is a real ~sore** dieser Teppich beleidigt das Auge; **~strain** *n* Überanstrengung *f* der Augen; **~ tooth** *n* Eckzahn *m*; **~wash** *n (fig col)* Gewäsch *nt (col)*; *(deception)* Augenwischerei *f*; **~witness** *n* Augenzeuge *m*.

eyrie [ˈɪərɪ] *n* Horst *m*.

F

F, f [ef] *n* F, f *nt.* ~ **sharp** Fis, fis *nt.*
F = Fahrenheit F.
fable ['feɪbl] *n* Fabel *f*; *(fig: lie)* Märchen *nt.*
fabric ['fæbrɪk] *n* **(a)** *(Tex)* Stoff *m.* **(b)** *(of building)* Bausubstanz *f*; *(of society)* Struktur *f.*
fabricate ['fæbrɪkeɪt] *vt* **(a)** *story* erfinden. **(b)** *(manufacture)* herstellen.
fabrication [ˌfæbrɪ'keɪʃən] *n* **(a)** *(lie etc)* Erfindung *f.* **(b)** *(manufacture)* Herstellung *f.*
fabulous ['fæbjʊləs] *adj* sagenhaft *(also col).*
façade [fə'sɑːd] *n (lit, fig)* Fassade *f.*
face [feɪs] **1** *n* Gesicht *nt*; *(of clock)* Zifferblatt *nt*; *(rock ~)* (Steil)wand *f*; *(coal~)* Streb *m*; *(of playing card)* Bildseite *f*; *(of coin)* Vorderseite *f.* **I don't want to see your ~ here again** ich möchte Sie hier nie wieder sehen; **we were standing ~ to ~** wir standen einander gegenüber; **to bring two people ~ to ~** zwei Leute einander gegenüberstellen; **to come ~ to ~ with sb/death** jdn treffen/dem Tod ins Auge sehen; **he told him so to his ~** er sagte ihm das (offen) ins Gesicht; **he shut the door in my ~** er schlug mir die Tür vor der Nase zu; **he laughed in my ~** er lachte mir ins Gesicht; **to look/be able to look sb in the ~** jdn ansehen/jdm in die Augen sehen können; **in the ~ of great difficulties** trotz größter Schwierigkeiten; **courage in the ~ of the enemy** Tapferkeit vor dem Feind; **to make** *or* **pull a ~** das Gesicht verziehen; **to make** *or* **pull ~s** Grimassen schneiden *(at sb* jdm*)*; **to put a good ~ on it** gute Miene zum bösen Spiel machen; **to put a brave ~ on it** sich *(dat)* nichts anmerken lassen; *(do sth one dislikes)* (wohl oder übel) in den sauren Apfel beißen; **to save/lose ~** das Gesicht wahren/verlieren; **to be ~ up/down** *(person)* mit dem Gesicht nach oben/unten liegen; *(thing)* mit der Vorderseite nach oben/unten liegen; **to work at the (coal)~** vor Ort arbeiten; **the ~ of the town** das Stadtbild; **he vanished off the ~ of the earth** *(col)* er war wie vom Erdboden verschwunden; **on the ~ of it** so, wie es aussieht; **to have the ~ to do sth** *(col)* die Stirn haben, etw zu tun.

2 *vt* **(a)** *(be opposite)* gegenübersein/-stehen/-liegen *etc (+dat)*; *(window, door) north, south* gehen nach; *street, garden etc* liegen zu; *(building, room) north, south* liegen nach. ~ **this way!** bitte sehen Sie hierher!; **he was facing me at dinner** er saß mir beim Essen gegenüber; **the picture facing page 16** die Abbildung gegenüber Seite 16; **to sit facing the engine** in Fahrtrichtung sitzen.

(b) *(fig) possibility, prospect* rechnen müssen mit. **to be ~d with sth** sich einer Sache *(dat)* gegenübersehen; **he is facing a charge of murder** er steht unter Mordanklage.

(c) *situation, danger, criticism* sich stellen *(+dat)*; *person, enemy* gegenübertreten *(+dat).* **to ~ (the) facts** den Tatsachen ins Auge sehen; **let's ~ it** machen wir uns doch nichts vor; **I can't ~ it** ich bringe es einfach nicht über mich; **I couldn't ~ another drink** ich könnte jetzt nichts Alkoholisches mehr verkraften.

(d) *building, wall* verkleiden.

3 *vi (house, room)* liegen *(towards park* dem Park zu, *onto road* zur Straße, *away from road* nicht zur Straße*)*; *(window)* gehen *(onto, towards* auf *+acc,* zu, *away from* nicht auf *+acc).* **in which direction was he facing?** in welche Richtung stand er?
♦**face up to** *vi +prep obj fact, truth* ins Gesicht sehen *(+dat)*; *possibility* sich abfinden mit; *responsibility* auf sich *(acc)* nehmen. **he won't ~ ~ ~ the fact that ...** er will es nicht wahrhaben, daß ...
face *in cpds* Gesichts-; **~cloth** *n (Brit)* Waschlappen *m*; **~ cream** *n* Gesichtscreme *f*; **~less** *adj (fig)* anonym; **~lift** *n (lit)* Gesichts(haut)straffung *f*; *(fig: for car, building etc)* Verschönerung *f*; **to have a ~lift** sich *(dat)* das Gesicht liften lassen; *(fig)* ein neues Aussehen bekommen; **~ pack** *n* Gesichtspackung *f*; **~-saving** *adj* **a ~-saving excuse** eine Entschuldigung, um das Gesicht zu wahren.
facet ['fæsɪt] *n (lit)* Facette *f*; *(fig)* Aspekt *m.*
facetious [fə'siːʃəs] *adj* witzelnd. **to be ~ (about sth)** (über etw *acc*) Witze machen.
face: ~-to-~ *adj* persönlich; *confrontation* direkt; **~ value** *n (Fin)* Nennwert *m*; **to take sth at (its) ~ value** *(fig)* etw für bare Münze nehmen; **to take sb at ~ value** jdm unbesehen glauben.
facial ['feɪʃəl] **1** *adj* Gesichts-. **2** *n (col)* kosmetische Gesichtsbehandlung.
facile ['fæsaɪl] *adj* **(a)** *(glib, superficial)* oberflächlich. **(b)** *(easy) victory* leicht.
facilitate [fə'sɪlɪteɪt] *vt* erleichtern; *(make possible)* ermöglichen.
facility [fə'sɪlɪtɪ] *n* **(a)** Einrichtung *f*; *(possibility)* Möglichkeit *f.* **facilities for the disabled** Einrichtungen für Behinderte; **cooking facilities** Kochgelegenheit *f.* **(b)** *no pl (ease)* Leichtigkeit *f*; *(dexterity)* Gewandtheit *f.*
facing ['feɪsɪŋ] *n (on wall)* Verkleidung *f*; *(Sew)* Besatz *m.*
facsimile [fæk'sɪmɪlɪ] *n* **(a)** Faksimile *nt.* **(b)** *(Telec)* Telebrief *m.*
fact [fækt] *n* Tatsache *f.* **to know for a ~ that** (es) ganz sicher wissen, daß; **the ~ is that ...** die Sache ist die, daß ...; **to stick to the ~s** bei den Tatsachen bleiben; **is that a ~?** tatsächlich?; **the ~ that ...** (die Tatsache,) daß ...; **~ and fiction** Dichtung und Wahrheit; **founded on ~** auf Tatsachen beruhend; **to tell sb the ~s of life** jdn aufklären; **the ~s of the case** der Sachverhalt; **in ~, as a matter of ~** eigentlich; *(to intensify previous statement)* sogar; **I bet you haven't done that! — as a matter of ~ I have!** du hast das bestimmt nicht gemacht! — oh doch!; **do you know Sir Charles? — as a matter of ~ he's my uncle** kennen Sie Sir Charles? — ja, er ist nämlich mein Onkel.
fact-finding ['fæktfaɪndɪŋ] *adj commission* Untersuchungs-; *mission* Erkundungs-.
faction ['fækʃən] *n (group)* Gruppe *f*; *(Pol)* Fraktion *f*; *(splinter group)* Splittergruppe *f.*
factor ['fæktə^r^] *n* Faktor *m.*
factory ['fæktərɪ] *n* Fabrik *f.*
factory: ~ farming *n Aufzucht f von Tieren in automatisierten Farmen;* **~ inspector** *n* Gewerbeaufsichtsbeamte(r) *m*; **~ worker** *n* Fabrikarbeiter(in *f*) *m.*
factual ['fæktjʊəl] *adj* sachlich, Tatsachen-. **~ er-**

ror Sachfehler *m.*

faculty ['fækəltı] *n* **(a)** Fähigkeit *f.* ~ **of reason** Vernunft *f;* ~ **of speech/sight** Sprechvermögen/ Sehvermögen *nt;* **to be in (full) possession of one's faculties** im Vollbesitz seiner Kräfte sein. **(b)** *(Univ)* Fakultät *f.* **the F~** *(staff)* der Lehrkörper.

fad [fæd] *n* Tick *m (col); (fashion)* Masche *f (col).*

fade [feıd] *vi* verblassen; *(flower, beauty)* verblühen. **he ~d from sight** er verschwand; *see* **fade away.**

♦ **fade away** *vi (memory)* verblassen; *(hopes)* zerrinnen; *(interest, strength, inspiration)* nachlassen; *(sound)* verklingen; *(voice)* immer schwächer werden.

♦ **fade in** *vt sep (TV, Film)* allmählich einblenden.

♦ **fade out 1** *vi* **(a)** *(TV, Film)* abblenden. **(b) to ~ ~ of sb's life** aus jds Leben verschwinden. **2** *vt sep (TV, Film)* abblenden.

faeces, *(US)* **feces** ['fi:si:z] *n pl* Kot *m.*

fag [fæg] *(col)* **1** *n* **(a)** *(Brit: cigarette)* Zigarette *f,* Glimmstengel *m (col).* **(b)** *(Brit Sch) junger Internatsschüler, der einem älteren bestimmte Dienste zu leisten hat.* **(c)** *(esp US col: homosexual)* Schwule(r) *m (col).* **2** *vt* **to be ~ged (out)** kaputt *or* geschafft sein *(col).*

fag end *n* **(a)** *(Brit col: cigarette end)* Kippe *f (col).* **(b)** *(col: last part)* letztes Ende.

faggot, *(US)* **fagot** ['fægət] *n* **(a)** Reisigbündel *nt.* **(b)** *(Cook)* Frikadelle *f.* **(c)** *(esp US col: homosexual)* Schwule(r) *m (col).*

Fahrenheit ['færənhaıt] *n* Fahrenheit *nt.*

fail [feıl] **1** *vi* **(a)** keinen Erfolg haben; *(in mission, life etc)* versagen; *(plan, experiment, marriage)* scheitern; *(undertaking, attempt)* fehlschlagen; *(applicant, application)* nicht angenommen werden; *(election candidate, in exam, play)* durchfallen; *(business)* eingehen. **they ~ed (in doing sth)** es gelang ihnen nicht(, etw zu tun); **to ~ in one's duty** seine Pflicht nicht tun; **to ~ by 5 votes** *(person)* um 5 Stimmen geschlagen werden; **if all else ~s** wenn alle Stricke reißen. **(b)** *(health)* sich verschlechtern; *(hearing, eyesight)* nachlassen. **he is ~ing fast** sein Zustand verschlechtert sich zusehends. **(c)** *(generator, battery)* ausfallen; *(brakes, heart)* versagen; *(supply)* ausbleiben. **the crops ~ed** die Ernte fiel aus.

2 *vt* **(a)** *candidate* durchfallen lassen. **to ~ an exam** eine Prüfung nicht bestehen. **(b)** *(let down: person, memory)* im Stich lassen; *(not live up to sb's expectations)* enttäuschen. **words ~ me** mir fehlen die Worte. **(c) to ~ to do sth** etw nicht tun; *(neglect)* (es) versäumen, etw zu tun; **I ~ to see why** es ist mir völlig unklar, warum; *(indignantly)* ich sehe gar nicht ein, warum.

3 *n* **without** ~ ganz bestimmt; *(inevitably)* garantiert.

failing ['feılıŋ] **1** *n* Schwäche *f.* **2** *prep* ~ **an answer** mangels (einer) Antwort *(geh);* ~ **him see if Harry knows** und wenn er es nicht weiß, versuch es bei Harry; ~ **this/that** (oder) sonst, und wenn das nicht möglich ist.

fail-safe ['feılseıf] *adj device* (ab)gesichert.

failure ['feıljə^r] *n* **(a)** Mißerfolg *m; (of plan, experiment, marriage)* Scheitern *nt; (of undertaking, attempt)* Fehlschlag *m; (in exam, Theat: of play also)* Durchfall *m; (of business)* Eingehen *nt.* **it ended in ~** es schlug fehl. **(b)** *(person)* Versager *m,* Niete *f (col) (at* in *+dat).* **(c)** *(omission, neglect)* **because of his ~ to reply** weil er es versäumt hat zu antworten; ~ **to observe a law** Nichtbeachtung *f* eines Gesetzes; **that was a ~ on my part** das war mein Fehler. **(d)** *(of generator, engine)* Ausfall *m; (of brakes, heart)* Versagen *nt; (of supply)* Ausbleiben *nt.* ~ **of crops** Ernteausfall *m.*

faint [feınt] **1** *adj (+er)* **(a)** schwach; *voice (feeble)* matt; *(distant, not loud)* leise. **I haven't the ~est (idea)** ich habe keinen blassen Schimmer *(col).* **(b) I feel a bit ~** mir ist ganz schwach; **she felt ~** ihr wurde schwach; ~ **with hunger** schwach vor Hunger. **2** *n* Ohnmacht *f.* **3** *vi* ohnmächtig werden *(with, from* vor *+dat).*

faint-hearted [ˌfeınt'hɑ:tıd] *adj* zaghaft.

faintly ['feıntlı] *adv* schwach; *hope, sound* leise; *smell, smile, interested* leicht; *similar, resemble* entfernt.

faintness ['feıntnıs] *n (dizziness)* Schwächegefühl *nt.*

fair[1] [fɛə^r] **1** *adj (+er)* **(a)** *(just)* fair *(to/on sb* jdm gegenüber, gegen jdn*).* **that's a ~ comment** das stimmt; **it's only ~ to ask him** man sollte ihn fairerweise fragen; **it's only ~ to expect ...** man kann doch wohl zu Recht erwarten ...; **~ enough!** na gut; **that's ~ enough** das ist nur recht und billig; **~'s ~!** wir wollen doch fair bleiben; **by ~ means or foul** ohne Rücksicht auf Verluste *(col);* **that's a ~ sample of ...** das ist ziemlich typisch für ...

(b) *(reasonable)* ganz ordentlich. **only ~** nur mäßig; **he's a ~ judge of character** er hat eine gute Menschenkenntnis; **to have a ~ idea of sth** eine ungefähre Vorstellung von etw haben; **a ~ chance of success** recht gute Erfolgsaussichten *pl.*

(c) *(reasonably large, fast, strong) sum, number* ansehnlich; *wind* frisch. **a ~ amount** ziemlich viel; **at a ~ speed** ziemlich schnell.

(d) *(fine) weather* heiter. **the ~ sex** das schöne Geschlecht.

(e) *person (light-haired)* blond; *(light-skinned)* hell.

2 *adv* **to play ~** *(Sport)* fair spielen; *(fig)* fair sein; **~ and square** *(honestly)* offen und ehrlich; *(accurately, directly)* direkt; **it ~ took my breath away** *(col)* das hat mir glatt den Atem verschlagen.

fair[2] *n* (Jahr)markt *m; (Brit: fun ~)* Volksfest *nt,* Rummel *m (col); (Comm)* Messe *f.*

fair: ~ **copy** *n* Reinschrift *f;* **to write out a ~ copy of sth** etw ins reine schreiben; ~ **game** *n (lit)* jagdbares Wild; *(fig)* Freiwild *nt;* **~ground** *n see* **fair**[2] Markt(platz) *m;* Rummelplatz *m;* **~-haired** *adj* blond; **~-haired boy** *n (US)* Liebling *m.*

fairly ['fɛəlı] *adv* **(a)** *(justly)* gerecht. **~ and squarely beaten** nach allen Regeln der Kunst geschlagen. **(b)** *(rather)* ziemlich. **it's ~ freezing** *(col)* es ist ganz schön kalt *(col).*

fair-minded ['fɛəmaındıd] *adj* gerecht.

fairness ['fɛənıs] *n* **(a)** Fairneß *f.* **in all ~** fairerweise; **in (all) ~ to him, he didn't have the same chance;** fairerweise muß man sagen, daß er nicht die gleichen Chancen hatte. **(b)** *(of hair)* Blondheit *f; (of skin)* Hellhäutigkeit *f.*

fair: ~ **play** *n (Sport, fig)* faires Verhalten, Fair play *nt;* **~-sized** *adj* recht groß; **~-weather** *adj friends* nur in guten Zeiten.

fairy ['fɛərı] *n* **(a)** Fee *f.* **(b)** *(pej col: homosexual)* Schwule(r) *m (col),* Tunte *f (col).*

fairy: ~ **godmother** *n (lit, fig)* gute Fee; **~land** *n* Märchenland *nt;* ~ **lights** *npl* bunte Lichter *pl;* ~ **queen** *n* Elfenkönigin *f;* ~ **story, ~-tale** *n (lit, fig)* Märchen *nt.*

fait accompli [ˌfetə'kɒmpli:] *n* **to present sb with a ~** jdn vor vollendete Tatsachen stellen.

faith [feıθ] *n* **(a)** *(trust)* Vertrauen *nt (in* zu*); (in human nature, science etc, religious ~)* Glaube *m (in* an *+acc).* **to have ~ in sb** jdm (ver)trauen; **to have ~ in sth** Vertrauen in etw *(acc)* haben; **act of ~** Vertrauensbeweis *m;* **to keep/break ~ with sb** jdm treu bleiben/untreu werden; **to act in good/bad ~** in gutem Glauben/böser Absicht handeln. **(b)** *(religion)* Glaube *m no pl.*

faithful ['feıθfʊl] **1** *adj* **(a)** treu *(to +dat).* **(b)** *account, translation* getreu. **2** *npl* **the ~** *(Rel)* die Gläubigen *pl.*

faithfully ['feıθfəlı] *adv* **(a)** treu; *promise* fest. **(b)**

report etc genau; *translate* wortgetreu.
faithfulness ['feɪθfʊlnɪs] *n (loyalty)* Treue *f (to* zu*)*.
faith: ~ healer *n* Gesundbeter(in *f*) *m*; **~ healing** *n* Gesundbeten *nt*; **~less** *adj* treulos.
fake [feɪk] **1** *n (object)* Fälschung *f*; *(jewellery)* Imitation *f*; *(person: trickster)* Schwindler(in *f*) *m*. **2** *vt* vortäuschen; *picture, document, results etc* fälschen; *bill, burglary, crash* fingieren.
falcon ['fɔːlkən] *n* Falke *m*.
fall [fɔːl] *(vb: pret* **fell,** *ptp* **fallen***)* **1** *n* **(a)** Sturz, Fall *m*; *(of empire etc)* Untergang *m*. **the F~ (of Man)** *(Eccl)* der Sündenfall; **to have a ~** (hin)fallen, stürzen; **it's a long ~ from up here** von hier oben geht es tief hinunter. **(b)** *(of town, fortress etc)* Einnahme *f*; *(of country)* Zusammenbruch *m*; *(of government)* Sturz *m*. **(c) ~ of rain/snow** Regen-/Schneefall *m*; **~ of rock** Steinschlag *m*. **(d)** *(in gen) (lowering)* Sinken *nt*; *(sudden)* Sturz *m*; *(in population, membership)* Abnahme *f*; *(of prices, currency) (gradual)* Sinken *nt*; *(sudden)* Sturz *m*. **(e)** *(of roof, ground)* Gefälle *nt*; *(steeper)* Abfall *m*. **(f)** *(water~: also ~s)* Wasserfall *m*. **the Niagara F~s** die Niagarafälle. **(g)** *(Wrestling)* Schultersieg *m*. **(h)** *(US: autumn)* Herbst *m*. **in the ~** im Herbst.

2 *vi* **(a)** fallen; *(Sport, from a height, badly)* stürzen; *(object: to the ground)* herunter-/hinunterfallen.

(b) *(temperature, price)* fallen; *(population, membership etc)* abnehmen; *(wind)* sich legen; *(land)* abfallen. **his face fell** er machte ein langes Gesicht; **to ~ in sb's estimation** *or* **eyes** in jds Achtung *(dat)* sinken.

(c) *(country)* eingenommen werden; *(government, ruler)* gestürzt werden. **three seats fell to the SDP** drei Sitze gingen an die SDP.

(d) *(night)* hereinbrechen.

(e) *(birthday, Easter etc)* fallen *(on* auf *+acc)*. **that ~s outside the scope ...** das fällt nicht in den Bereich ...; **to ~ into three sections** sich in drei Teile gliedern.

(f) *(phrases)* **her eyes fell on a strange object** ihr Blick fiel auf einen merkwürdigen Gegenstand; **the responsibility ~s on you** Sie tragen die Verantwortung; **it ~s to** *or* **on me to ...** es fällt mir zu, zu ...; **the blame for that ~s on him** ihn trifft die Schuld daran; **to ~ asleep** einschlafen; **to ~ ill** krank werden, erkranken *(geh)*; **to ~ silent** still werden; **it's all ~ing into place now** jetzt wird mir das Ganze klar; **to ~ into a deep sleep** in tiefen Schlaf fallen; **to ~ into bad ways** auf die schiefe Bahn geraten; **to ~ to doing sth** anfangen, etw zu tun.

3 *vt* **to ~ a victim to sb/sth** jdm/einer Sache zum Opfer fallen.
♦**fall about** *vi (laughing)* sich krank lachen *(col)*.
♦**fall apart** *vi* auseinanderfallen; *(fig: marriage etc)* auseinanderbrechen.
♦**fall away** *vi* **(a)** *(ground)* abfallen. **(b)** *(crumble: plaster, river bank)* abbröckeln *(from* von*)*.
♦**fall back** *vi* zurückweichen *(also Mil)*.
♦**fall back on** *vi +prep obj* zurückgreifen auf *(+acc)*.
♦**fall behind** *vi (in race, school etc)* zurückbleiben *(prep obj* hinter *+dat)*; *(with rent, work etc)* in Rückstand geraten.
♦**fall down** *vi (person)* hinfallen; *(statue, vase)* herunterfallen; *(house, scaffolding)* einstürzen. **where he/the plan ~s ~ is ...** *(fig)* woran es ihm/dem Plan fehlt, ist ...; **that was where we fell ~** *(fig)* daran sind wir gescheitert; **he's been ~ing ~ on the job** *(fig)* er hat schlechte Arbeit geleistet.
♦**fall for** *vi +prep obj* **(a)** *(fall in love with)* sich verknallen in *(+acc) (col)*. **I really fell ~ him/it** er/das hatte es mir angetan. **(b)** *(be taken in by)* hereinfallen auf *(+acc)*.
♦**fall in** *vi* **(a)** *(into water etc)* hineinfallen. **(b)** *(collapse)* einstürzen. **(c)** *(Mil)* (in Reih und Glied) antreten; *(one soldier)* ins Glied treten.
♦**fall in with** *vi +prep obj* **(a)** *(meet)* sich anschließen *(+dat)*; *bad company* geraten in *(+acc)*. **(b)** *(agree to)* mitmachen bei; *request* unterstützen.
♦**fall off** *vi* **(a)** *(lit)* herunterfallen *(prep obj* von*)*. **(b)** *(decrease)* zurückgehen; *(supporters)* abfallen; *(support, enthusiasm)* nachlassen.
♦**fall out** *vi* **(a)** *(of bed, boat, window)* herausfallen. **to ~ ~ of sth** aus etw fallen. **(b)** *(quarrel)* sich (zer)streiten. **(c)** *(Mil)* wegtreten. **(d)** *(happen)* **just wait and see how things ~ ~** wart erst mal ab, wie alles wird; **if everything ~s ~ all right** wenn alles wunschgemäß verläuft.
♦**fall over** *vi* **(a)** *(person)* hinfallen; *(collapse)* umfallen. **(b)** *+prep obj (trip over) stone, sb's legs* fallen über *(+acc)*. **to ~ ~ oneself to do sth** sich *(dat)* die größte Mühe geben, etw zu tun.
♦**fall through** *vi (plan)* ins Wasser fallen.
♦**fall to** *vi (col) (start eating)* sich dranmachen *(col)*; *(start fighting, working)* loslegen *(col)*.
fallacious [fə'leɪʃəs] *adj* irrig; *argument* trugschlüssig.
fallacy ['fæləsɪ] *n* Irrtum *m*; *(in logic)* Trugschluß *m*.
fallen ['fɔːlən] **1** *ptp of* **fall. 2** *adj women, angel* gefallen; *leaf* abgefallen. **3** *npl* **the F~** *(Mil)* die Gefallenen *pl*.
fallible ['fæləbl] *adj* fehlbar.
falling star ['fɔːlɪŋ'stɑː[r]] *n* Sternschnuppe *f*.
fall-off ['fɔːlɒf] *n (in gen)* Rückgang *m*; *(in numbers, attendances)* Abfall *m*; *(in support)* Nachlassen *nt*.
Fallopian tube [fə'ləʊpɪən'tjuːb] *n* Eileiter *m*.
fall-out ['fɔːlaʊt] *n* radioaktiver Niederschlag, Fallout *m*. **~ shelter** Atombunker *m*.
fallow ['fæləʊ] *adj land* brach. **to lie ~** brachliegen.
false [fɔːls] *adj* falsch; *lover* treulos; *ceiling, floor* Zwischen-. **under ~ pretences** *(Brit) or* **pretenses** *(US)* unter Vorspiegelung falscher Tatsachen; **a box with a ~ bottom** ein Kiste mit doppeltem Boden.
false alarm *n* blinder Alarm.
falsehood ['fɔːlshʊd] *n (lie)* Unwahrheit *f*.
falsely ['fɔːlslɪ] *adv* falsch; *believe, claim, declare* fälschlicherweise; *accuse* zu Unrecht.
falseness ['fɔːlsnɪs] *n* Falschheit *f*; *(of lover etc)* Untreue *f*.
false: ~ start *n* Fehlstart *m*; **~ teeth** *npl (Brit)* (künstliches) Gebiß.
falsetto [fɔːl'setəʊ] **1** *n (voice)* Fistelstimme *f*. **2** *adv sing* im Falsett.
falsies ['fɔːlsɪz] *npl (col)* Gummibusen *m (col)*.
falsify ['fɔːlsɪfaɪ] *vt records, evidence* fälschen; *report, story* entstellen.
falter ['fɔːltə[r]] *vi (speaking)* stocken; *(steps, horse)* zögern.
fame [feɪm] *n* Ruhm *m*. **to win ~** sich *(dat)* einen Namen machen.
familiar [fə'mɪljə[r]] *adj* **(a)** *surroundings, sight, scene* vertraut; *street, person, feeling, phrase, song* bekannt; *complaint, event* häufig. **his face is ~** das Gesicht ist mir bekannt; **it looks very ~** es kommt mir sehr bekannt vor; **that sounds ~** das habe ich schon mal gehört; **to be on ~ ground with sth** in etw *(dat)* zu Hause sein; **to be ~ with sb/sth** mit jdm/etw vertraut sein; **to make oneself ~ with sth** sich mit etw vertraut machen. **(b)** *(friendly) language, gesture* familiär; *(overfriendly)* plump-vertraulich. **the ~ term of address** die vertraute Anrede; **to be on ~ terms with sb** mit jdm auf vertrautem Fuß stehen; **~ language/expressions** Umgangssprache *f*/umgangssprachliche Ausdrücke *pl*.
familiarity [fə,mɪlɪ'ærɪtɪ] *n* **(a)** *no pl (knowledge)* Vertrautheit *f*. **(b)** *(between people)* vertrautes Verhältnis; *(of language etc)* Familiarität *f*; *(pej)* plumpe Vertraulichkeit. **~ breeds contempt**

(Prov) allzu große Vertrautheit erzeugt Verachtung.
familiarize [fəˈmɪlɪəraɪz] *vt* **to ~ sb/oneself with sth** jdn/sich mit etw vertraut machen.
family [ˈfæmɪlɪ] *n* Familie *f*; *(including cousins, aunts etc)* Verwandtschaft *f*. **to start a ~** eine Familie gründen; **has he any ~?** hat er Familie?; **it runs in the ~** das liegt in der Familie; **he's one of the ~** er gehört zur Familie.
family: ~ allowance *n* Kindergeld *nt*; **~ doctor** *n* Hausarzt *m*/-ärztin *f*; **~ man** *n (home-loving)* häuslich veranlagter Mann; *(with a ~)* Familienvater *m*; **~ planning** *n* Familienplanung *f*; **~ planning clinic** *n* Familienberatungsstelle *f*; **~-size** *adj* in Haushaltsgröße; *car, packets* Familien-; **~ tree** *n* Stammbaum *m*.
famine [ˈfæmɪn] *n* Hungersnot *f*.
famished [ˈfæmɪʃt] *adj (col)* **I'm absolutely ~** ich sterbe vor Hunger *(col)*.
famous [ˈfeɪməs] *adj* berühmt *(for* durch, für*)*.
famously [ˈfeɪməslɪ] *adv (dated col)* famos *(dated)*.
fan[1] [fæn] **1** *n (hand-held)* Fächer *m*; *(mechanical, extractor ~, Aut)* Ventilator *m*. **2** *vt (wind)* umwehen; *(person)* fächeln *(+dat)*. **to ~ sb/oneself** jdm/sich (Luft) zufächeln; **to ~ the flames** *(fig)* Öl ins Feuer gießen.
♦ **fan out** *vi (troops, searchers)* ausschwärmen.
fan[2] *n (supporter)* Fan *m*.
fanatic [fəˈnætɪk] *n* Fanatiker(in *f*) *m*.
fanatic(al) [fəˈnætɪk(əl)] *adj* fanatisch.
fanaticism [fəˈnætɪsɪzəm] *n* Fanatismus *m*.
fan belt *n* Keilriemen *m*.
fancier [ˈfænsɪəʳ] *n* Liebhaber(in *f*) *m*.
fanciful [ˈfænsɪfʊl] *adj story, idea* phantastisch; *explanation* weit hergeholt; *pattern* phantasievoll.
fan club *n* Fanclub *m*.
fancy [ˈfænsɪ] **1** *n* **a passing ~** nur so eine Laune; **he's taken a ~ to her** sie hat es ihm angetan; **to take** *or* **catch sb's ~** jdm gefallen; **to tickle sb's ~** jdn reizen; **just as the ~ takes me/you** ganz nach Lust und Laune.
2 *vt* **(a) ~ that!** so was!; **~ seeing you here!** so was, Sie hier zu sehen!; **~ him winning!** wer hätte gedacht, daß er gewinnt!; **I rather ~ he has gone out** ich glaube, er ist weggegangen.
(b) *(like)* **he fancies the idea/her** die Idee/sie gefällt ihm; **he fancies a house on Crete** *(would like to have)* er hätte gern ein Haus auf Kreta; **he fancies a walk/steak** er hat Lust zu einem Spaziergang/auf ein Steak; **I don't ~ the idea** ich habe keine Lust dazu; **I didn't ~ that job** die Stelle hat mich nicht gereizt; **he fancies his chances** er meint, er hätte Chancen; **I don't ~ my chances of getting that job** ich rechne mir keine großen Chancen aus, die Stelle zu bekommen; **he really fancies himself** er ist stark von sich eingenommen; **he fancies himself as an actor** er hält sich für einen (guten) Schauspieler.
3 *adj (+er) (elaborate) hairdo, footwork* kunstvoll; *(unusual) food, pattern, cigarettes, furnishings* ausgefallen; *baking, cakes, bread* fein; *(col) gadget, car etc* schick *(col)*; *idea* überspannt; *cure* seltsam; *price* gepfeffert *(col)*. **nothing ~** etwas ganz Einfaches.
fancy: ~ dress *n* (Masken)kostüm *nt*; **in ~ dress** verkleidet, kostümiert; **~-dress ball/party** *n* Maskenball *m*/Kostümfest *nt*; **~ goods** *npl* Geschenkartikel *pl*; **~ man** *n (col: lover)* Liebhaber *m*; **~ woman** *n (col)* Freundin *f*.
fanfare [ˈfænfɛəʳ] *n* Fanfare *f*.
fang [fæŋ] *n* Fang *m*; *(of snake)* Giftzahn *m*.
fan: ~ heater *n* Heizlüfter *m*; **~light** *n* Oberlicht *nt*; **~ mail** *n* Verehrerpost *f*.
fantasize [ˈfæntəsaɪz] *vi* phantasieren.
fantastic [fænˈtæstɪk] *adj* phantastisch.
fantasy [ˈfæntəzɪ] *n* Phantasie *f*.
far [fɑːʳ] *see also comp* **further, farther,** *superl* **furthest, farthest 1** *adv* weit. **not ~ (away) from here** nicht weit von hier; **I'll go with you as ~ as the gate** ich komme/gehe bis zum Tor mit; **~ and wide** weit und breit; **from ~ and wide** von nah und fern; **~ above** hoch über *(+dat)*; **~ away** weit weg; **~ away in the distance** weit in der Ferne; **~ into the jungle** weit in den Dschungel hinein; **I won't be ~ away** ich bin ganz in der Nähe; **~ out** weit draußen; **have you come ~?** kommen Sie von weit her?; **as ~ back as I can remember** so weit ich mich erinnern kann; **as ~ back as 1945;** schon (im Jahr) 1945; **~ into the night** bis spät in die Nacht; **~ longer/better** weit länger/besser; **it's ~ beyond what I can afford** das übersteigt meine Mittel bei weitem; **as** *or* **so ~ as I'm concerned** was mich betrifft; **it's all right as ~ as it goes** das ist soweit ganz gut; **in so ~ as** insofern als; **~ and away the best, by ~ the best** bei weitem der/die/das Beste; **~ from satisfactory** alles andere als befriedigend; **~ from liking him I find him quite unpleasant** nicht nur, daß ich ihn nicht leiden kann, ich finde ihn sogar ausgesprochen unsympatisch; **~ from it!** ganz und gar nicht; **~ be it from me to ...** es sei mir fern, zu ...; **so ~** *(up to now)* bis jetzt; *(up to this point)* soweit; **so ~ so good** so weit, so gut; **so ~ and no further** bis hierher und nicht weiter; **to go ~** *(money, supplies etc)* weit reichen; *(person: succeed)* es weit bringen; **I would go so ~ as to say ...** ich würde so weit gehen zu sagen ...; **that's going too ~** das geht zu weit; **to carry a joke too ~** einen Spaß zu weit treiben; **not ~ out** *(in guess)* nicht schlecht; **not ~ off** *(in guess, aim)* fast; **~ gone** *(col: drunk)* schon ziemlich hinüber *(col)*.
2 *adj country* weit entfernt. **the ~ end of the room** das andere Ende des Zimmers; **the ~ window/wall** das Fenster/die Wand am anderen Ende des Zimmers; **the ~ one** das da drüben; **in the ~ distance** in weiter Ferne; **it's a ~ cry from ...** *(fig)* das ist etwas ganz anderes als ...; **it's a ~ cry from what she promised at first** ursprünglich hat sie etwas ganz anderes versprochen.
faraway [ˈfɑːrəweɪ] *adj attr place* abgelegen; *(fig: dreamy)* verträumt.
farce [fɑːs] *n (Theat, fig)* Farce *f*.
farcical [ˈfɑːsɪkəl] *adj (fig: absurd)* absurd.
fare [fɛəʳ] **1** *n* **(a)** *(charge)* Fahrpreis *m*; *(on plane)* Flugpreis *m*; *(on boat)* Preis *m* für die Überfahrt; *(money)* Fahrgeld *nt*. **what is the ~?** was kostet die Fahrt/der Flug/die Überfahrt? **(b)** *(old, form: food)* Kost *f*. **2** *vi* **he ~d well** es ging ihm gut; **how did you ~** wie erging es dir?
Far East *n* **the ~** der Ferne Osten.
fare stage *n* Fahrzone *f*.
farewell [fɛəˈwel] **1** *n* Abschied *m*. **to bid sb ~** jdm auf Wiedersehen sagen. **2** *interj (old)* leb(e) wohl *(dated)*.
farewell *in cpds* Abschieds-.
far: ~-fetched *adj* weithergeholt *attr*, weit hergeholt *pred*; **~-flung** *adj (distant)* abgelegen.
farm [fɑːm] **1** *n* Bauernhof *m*; *(bigger)* Gut(shof *m*) *nt*; *(in US, Australia)* Farm *f*. **2** *attr produce, buildings* Landwirtschafts-; *labourer* Land-. **~ animals** Tiere auf dem Bauernhof. **3** *vt land* bebauen. **4** *vi* Landwirtschaft betreiben.
♦ **farm out** *vt sep work* vergeben *(on, to* an *+acc)*; *children* in Pflege geben *(to dat,* bei*)*.
farmer [ˈfɑːməʳ] *n* Bauer *m*; *(in US, Australia)* Farmer *m*; *(gentleman ~)* Gutsherr *m*; *(tenant ~)* Pächter *m*. **~'s wife** Bäuerin *f*.
farm: ~hand *n* Landarbeiter *m*; *(living on small farm)* Knecht *m*; **~house** *n* Bauernhaus *nt*.
farming [ˈfɑːmɪŋ] *n* Landwirtschaft *f*; *(animals also)* Viehzucht *f*.
farm: ~ land *n* Ackerland *nt*; **~yard** *n* Hof *m*.
Far North *n* **the ~** der Hohe Norden.
far: ~-off *adj* (weit)entfernt; **~-reaching** *adj* weitreichend; **~-sighted** *adj (lit)* weitsichtig;

(fig) person weitblickend; *(taking precautionary measures)* umsichtig; *measures* auf weite Sicht geplant.

fart [fɑːt] *(col)* **1** *n* Furz *m (col!)*. **2** *vi* furzen *(col!)*.

farther [ˈfɑːðəʳ] *comp of* **far 1** *adv see* **further 1 (a). 2** *adj* **at the ~ end** am anderen Ende.

farthest [ˈfɑːðɪst] *adj, adv superl of* **far** *see* **furthest 1, 2.**

farthing [ˈfɑːðɪŋ] *n (old Brit)* Viertelpenny *m*.

fascia [ˈfeɪʃə] *n (Brit Aut)* Armaturentafel *f*.

fascinate [ˈfæsɪneɪt] *vt* faszinieren. **it ~s me how ...** ich finde es erstaunlich, wie ...

fascinating [ˈfæsɪneɪtɪŋ] *adj* faszinierend.

fascination [ˌfæsɪˈneɪʃən] *n* Faszination *f*. **to have a ~ for sb** auf jdn einen besonderen Reiz ausüben; **his ~ with the cinema** die Faszination, die das Kino auf ihn ausübt.

fascism [ˈfæʃɪzəm] *n* Faschismus *m*.

fascist [ˈfæʃɪst] **1** *n* Faschist(in *f*) *m*. **2** *adj* faschistisch.

fashion [ˈfæʃən] **1** *n* **(a)** *no pl (manner)* Art (und Weise) *f*. **in the Indian ~** nach Art der Indianer; **in the usual ~** wie üblich; **well, after a ~** na ja, so einigermaßen; **to do sth after** *or* **in a ~** etw schlecht und recht machen. **(b)** *(in clothing, latest style)* Mode *f*. **in ~** modern; **it's the/all the ~** es ist Mode/große Mode; **to come into/go out of ~** in Mode/aus der Mode kommen; **ladies' ~s** die Damenmode. **(c)** *(custom)* **it was the ~ in those days** das war damals Sitte. **2** *vt* gestalten.

fashionable [ˈfæʃnəbl] *adj clothes, person* modisch; *illness, colour* Mode-; *area, address* vornehm; *pub, artist, author* in Mode. **it's (very) ~** es ist (große) Mode.

fashion *in cpds* Mode-; **~ designer** *n* Modezeichner(in *f*) *m*; **~ model** *n* Mannequin *nt*; *(man)* Dressman *m*; **~ parade** *n* Mode(n)schau *f*; **~ show** *n* Mode(n)schau *f*.

fast[1] [fɑːst] **1** *adj (+er)* **(a)** schnell; *film* hochempfindlich. **he's a ~ worker** *(lit)* er arbeitet schnell; *(fig)* er geht mächtig ran *(col)*; **to pull a ~ one (on sb)** *(col)* jdn übers Ohr hauen *(col)*; **~ lane** Überholspur *f*; **~ train** D-Zug *m*. **(b) to be ~** *(clock, watch)* vorgehen. **(c)** *(fig: immoral)* locker. **~ woman** leichtlebige Frau. **(d)** *(firm)* fest; *friend* gut. **(e)** *colour, dye* farbecht. **2** *adv* **(a)** schnell. **(b)** *(firmly)* fest. **to stick ~** festsitzen; *(with glue)* festkleben; **to hold ~ to sth** an etw *(dat)* festhalten; **to play ~ and loose with sb** mit jdm ein falsches Spiel treiben; **to be ~ asleep** tief schlafen.

fast[2] **1** *vi (not eat)* fasten. **2** *n* Fasten *nt*; *(period of fasting)* Fastenzeit *f*.

fast breeder reactor *n* schneller Brüter.

fasten [ˈfɑːsn] **1** *vt (attach)* befestigen *(to, onto* an *+dat)*; *buttons, dress etc* zumachen; *(lock) door* (ab)schließen. **to ~ two things together** zwei Dinge aneinander befestigen; **to ~ the blame on sb** die Schuld auf jdn schieben. **2** *vi (door etc)* sich schließen lassen. **the dress ~s at the back** das Kleid wird hinten zugemacht; **this piece ~s in here** dieses Teil wird hier befestigt.

♦ **fasten down** *vt sep* festmachen.

♦ **fasten on 1** *vt sep* befestigen *(+prep obj, -to* an *+dat)*. **2** *vi +prep obj (fig)* **the teacher always ~s ~ Smith** der Lehrer hackt immer auf Smith herum *(col)*.

♦ **fasten onto** *vi +prep obj (fig)* **to ~ ~ sb** sich an jdn hängen; **to ~ ~ an idea** eine Idee aufgreifen.

♦ **fasten up** *vt sep dress etc* zumachen.

fastener [ˈfɑːsnəʳ], **fastening** [ˈfɑːsnɪŋ] *n* Verschluß *m*.

fastidious [fæsˈtɪdɪəs] *adj* wählerisch *(about* in bezug auf *+acc)*.

fat [fæt] **1** *n (Anat, Cook)* Fett *nt*. **to live off the ~ of the land** *(fig)* wie die Made im Speck leben *(col)*; **to put on ~** Speck ansetzen; **to run to ~** in die Breite gehen *(col)*. **2** *adj (+er)* **(a)** dick, fett *(pej)*. **to get ~** dick werden. **(b)** *meat* fett. **(c)** *(fig) volume, wallet, cigar* dick; *salary, cheque, profit* üppig, fett *(col)*; *part in play* umfangreich. **(d)** *(iro col)* **a ~ lot of good you are!** Sie sind ja 'ne schöne Hilfe! *(iro col)*; **a ~ lot he knows!** er hat doch überhaupt keine Ahnung!; **a ~ chance he's got** da hat er ja Mordschancen *(iro col)*.

fatal [ˈfeɪtl] *adj (lit)* tödlich *(to* für*)*; *(fig)* verheerend; *day, decision* schicksalsschwer. **that would be ~** das wäre das Ende *(to gen)*; **to deal sb/sth a ~ blow** *(fig)* jdm/einer Sache einen schweren Schlag versetzen; **it's ~ to say that** das ist fatal, so was zu sagen.

fatalism [ˈfeɪtəlɪzəm] *n* Fatalismus *m*.

fatalist [ˈfeɪtəlɪst] *n* Fatalist(in *f*) *m*.

fatalistic [ˌfeɪtəˈlɪstɪk] *adj* fatalistisch.

fatality [fəˈtælɪtɪ] *n* Todesfall *m*; *(in accident, war etc)* (Todes)opfer *nt*.

fatally [ˈfeɪtəlɪ] *adv wounded* tödlich. **to be ~ attracted to sb** jdm hoffnungslos verfallen sein.

fate [feɪt] *n* Schicksal *nt*. **to leave sb to his ~** jdn seinem Schicksal überlassen; **to meet one's ~** *(die)* vom Schicksal ereilt werden.

fated [ˈfeɪtɪd] *adj* unglückselig; *project, plan* zum Scheitern verurteilt. **to be ~** unter einem ungünstigen Stern stehen; **they were ~ never to meet again** es war ihnen bestimmt, sich nie wiederzusehen.

fateful [ˈfeɪtfʊl] *adj (disastrous)* verhängnisvoll; *(momentous)* schicksalsschwer.

fathead [ˈfæthed] *n (col)* Blödian *m (col)*.

father [ˈfɑːðəʳ] **1** *n* **(a)** *(lit, fig)* Vater *m (to sb* jdm*)*. **from ~ to son** vom Vater auf den Sohn; **like ~ like son** der Apfel fällt nicht weit vom Stamm; **F~'s Day** Vatertag *m*. **(b)** *(priest)* Pfarrer *m*. **yes, ~** ja, Herr Pfarrer. **2** *vt child* zeugen.

father: F~ Christmas *n* der Weihnachtsmann; **~-figure** *n* Vaterfigur *f*; **~hood** *n* Vaterschaft *f*; **~-in-law** *n, pl* **~s-in-law** Schwiegervater *m*; **~land** *n* Vaterland *nt*; **~less** *adj* vaterlos.

fatherly [ˈfɑːðəlɪ] *adj* väterlich.

fathom [ˈfæðəm] **1** *n* Faden *m*. **2** *vt (also* **~ out***)* verstehen. **I just can't ~ him (out)** er ist mir ein Rätsel.

fatigue [fəˈtiːg] **1** *n* **(a)** Erschöpfung *f*; *(metal ~)* Ermüdung *f*. **(b)** *(Mil: ~ duty)* **to be on ~** Arbeitsdienst haben. **2** *vt (tire)* ermüden; *(exhaust)* erschöpfen.

fatigue: ~ dress *n* Arbeitsanzug *m*; **~ party** *n* Arbeitskommando *nt*.

fatso [ˈfætsəʊ] *n (col)* Dicke(r) *mf (col)*.

fatten [ˈfætn] *vt (also* **~ up***) animals* mästen; *people* herausfüttern *(col)*.

fattening [ˈfætnɪŋ] *adj* **chocolate is ~** Schokolade macht dick.

fatty [ˈfætɪ] **1** *adj* fett; *(greasy)* fettig; *acid, tissue* Fett-. **~ degeneration** *(Med)* Verfettung *f*. **2** *n (col)* Dickerchen *nt (col)*.

fatuous [ˈfætjʊəs] *adj* blöd.

faucet [ˈfɔːsɪt] *n (US)* Hahn *m*.

fault [fɔːlt] **1** *n* **(a)** Fehler *m*; *(Tech)* Defekt *m*; *(Geol)* Verwerfung *f*; *(Tennis)* Fehler *m*. **generous to a ~** übermäßig großzügig; **to find ~ with sb/sth** etwas an jdm/etw auszusetzen haben; **he/my memory was at ~** er war im Unrecht/mein Gedächtnis hat mich getrogen. **(b)** *no pl* **it's my ~** es ist meine Schuld; **whose ~ is it?** wer ist schuld?; **it's all your own ~** Sie sind selbst schuld. **2** *vt* etwas auszusetzen haben an *(+dat)*. **I can't ~ it** ich habe nichts daran auszusetzen; *(can't disprove it)* ich kann es nicht widerlegen.

fault: ~-finder *n* Krittler(in *f*) *m*; **~-finding** *n* Krittelei *f*.

faultless [ˈfɔːltlɪs] *adj appearance* tadellos; *(without mistakes)* fehlerlos; *English* fehlerfrei.

faulty [ˈfɔːltɪ] *adj (+er)* fehlerhaft; *(Tech)* defekt.

fauna [ˈfɔːnə] *n* Fauna *f*.

faux pas [fəʊˈpɑː] *n* Fauxpas *m*.

favour, *(US)* **favor** ['feɪvəʳ] **1** *n* **(a)** *no pl (goodwill)* Gunst *f.* **to find ~ with sb** bei jdm Anklang finden; **to be in ~ with sb** bei jdm gut angeschrieben sein; *(fashion, pop star, writer etc)* bei jdm beliebt sein; **to be/fall out of ~** in Ungnade (gefallen) sein/fallen; *(fashion, pop star, writer etc)* nicht mehr beliebt sein *(with* bei*)*/nicht mehr ankommen *(with* bei*)*.

(b) to be in ~ of sth für etw sein; **in his ~** zu seinen Gunsten; **all those in ~ raise their hands** alle, die dafür sind, Hand hoch; **I'm in ~ of staying** ich bin dafür zu bleiben.

(c) *(partiality)* Vergünstigung *f.* **to show ~ to sb** jdn bevorzugen.

(d) *(kindness)* Gefallen *m.* **to ask a ~ of sb** jdn um einen Gefallen bitten; **to do sb a ~** jdm einen Gefallen tun; **do me a ~!** *(col)* sei so gut!; **do me the ~ of shutting up!** *(col)* tu mir den Gefallen und halt den Mund!; **as a ~** aus Gefälligkeit; **as a ~ to him** ihm zuliebe.

2 *vt* **(a)** *plan, idea (be in ~ of)* für gut halten; *(prefer)* bevorzugen. **(b)** *(oblige, honour)* beehren *(form).* **(c)** *(US: resemble)* ähneln *(+dat).*

favourable, *(US)* **favorable** ['feɪvərəbl] *adj* günstig *(for, to* für*)*; *(expressing approval)* positiv.

favourably, *(US)* **favorably** ['feɪvərəblɪ] *adv see adj* vorteilhaft; positiv.

favoured, *(US)* **favored** ['feɪvəd] *adj* **the/a ~ few** die wenigen Auserwählten/einige (wenige) Auserwählte.

favourite, *(US)* **favorite** ['feɪvərɪt] **1** *n (person)* Liebling *m*; *(Sport)* Favorit(in *f*) *m.* **this one is my ~** das habe ich am liebsten; **we sang all the old ~s** wir haben all die alten Lieder gesungen. **2** *adj attr* Lieblings-.

favouritism, *(US)* **favoritism** ['feɪvərɪtɪzəm] *n* **giving it to Daphne was just ~ on his part** Daphne hat es nur deshalb bekommen, weil er seine Lieblingskinder bevorzugt behandelt.

fawn[1] [fɔːn] **1** *n* **(a)** Hirschkalb *nt*; *(of roe deer)* Rehkitz *nt.* **(b)** *(colour)* Beige *nt.* **2** *adj* beige.

fawn[2] *vi (dog)* (mit dem Schwanz) wedeln; *(fig: person)* katzbuckeln *(on* vor *+dat).*

fax [fæks] *n (document, machine)* Fax *nt.*

faze [feɪz] *vt (esp US col)* aus der Fassung bringen.

FBI *(US)* = **Federal Bureau of Investigation** FBI *nt.*

fear [fɪəʳ] **1** *n* **(a)** Angst *f (or* vor *+dat).* **in ~ and trembling** mit schlotternden Knien; **to go in ~ of one's life** ständig um sein Leben bangen; **for ~ that ...** aus Angst, daß ...; **she talked quietly for ~ of waking the child** sie sprach leise, um das Kind nicht aufzuwecken; **without ~ or favour** *(Brit) or* **favor** *(US)* ganz gerecht; **to put the ~ of God into sb** *(col)* jdm gewaltig Angst einjagen *(col).* **(b) no ~!** *(col)* nie im Leben! *(col)*; **there's no ~ of that happening again** keine Angst, das passiert so leicht nicht wieder; **there's not much ~ of his coming** wir brauchen kaum Angst zu haben, daß er kommt.

2 *vt* (be)fürchten; *God* Ehrfurcht haben vor *(+dat).* **I ~ the worst** ich befürchte das Schlimmste; **he's a man to be ~ed** er ist ein Mann, vor dem man Angst haben muß.

3 *vi* **to ~ for** fürchten um; **never ~!** keine Angst.

fearful ['fɪəfʊl] *adj* **(a)** *(terrible)* furchtbar. **(b)** *(apprehensive)* ängstlich. **to be ~ for one's/sb's life** um sein/jds Leben fürchten.

fearless ['fɪəlɪs] *adj* furchtlos. **to be ~ of sth** keine Angst vor etw *(dat)* haben.

fearsome ['fɪəsəm] *adj* furchterregend.

feasibility [ˌfiːzə'bɪlɪtɪ] *n* **(a)** *(of plan etc)* Machbarkeit *f.* **~ study** Machbarkeitsstudie *f*; **the ~ of doing sth** die Möglichkeit, etw zu tun. **(b)** *(plausibility: of story etc)* Wahrscheinlichkeit *f.*

feasible ['fiːzəbl] *adj* **(a)** machbar; *plan* realisierbar. **(b)** *(likely) excuse* plausibel.

feast [fiːst] **1** *n* **(a)** Festessen *nt*; *(Hist)* Festgelage *nt.* **a ~ for the eyes** eine Augenweide. **(b)** *(Eccl)* Fest *nt.* **~ day** *n* Feiertag *m.* **2** *vi (lit)* ein Festgelage halten. **to ~ on sth** sich an etw *(dat)* gütlich tun. **3** *vt* **to ~ one's eyes on sth** seine Augen an etw *(dat)* weiden.

feat [fiːt] *n* Leistung *f*; *(heroic, courageous etc)* Heldentat *f*; *(skilful)* Meisterleistung *f.*

feather ['feðəʳ] **1** *n* Feder *f.* **~s** *(plumage)* Gefieder *nt*; **as light as a ~** federleicht; **that's a ~ in his cap** das ist ein Ruhmesblatt *nt* für ihn; **you could have knocked me down with a ~** *(col)* ich war wie vom Donner gerührt; **birds of a ~ flock together** *(Prov)* gleich und gleich gesellt sich gern *(Prov).* **2** *vt* **to ~ one's nest** *(fig)* sein Schäfchen ins trockene bringen.

feather: ~-bed *n* mit Federn gefüllte Matratze; **~brained** *adj* dümmlich; **~ duster** *n* Staubwedel *m*; **~weight** *(Boxing)* **1** *n* Federgewicht *nt*; *(fig)* Leichtgewicht *nt*; **2** *adj* Federgewicht-.

feature ['fiːtʃəʳ] **1** *n* **(a)** *(facial)* (Gesichts)zug *m.* **(b)** *(characteristic)* Merkmal, Kennzeichen *nt.* **a ~ of his style is ...** sein Stil ist durch ... gekennzeichnet; **a ~ of this book is ...** das Buch zeichnet sich durch ... aus. **(c)** *(focal point: of room etc)* Charakteristikum *nt.* **to make a ~ of sth** etw besonders hervorheben. **(d)** *(Press)* (Sonder)beitrag *m*; *(Rad, TV)* (Dokumentar)bericht *m.* **(e)** *(film)* Spielfilm *m.* **2** *vt (Press) story, picture* bringen. **this film ~s ...** in diesem Film spielt ... mit. **3** *vi* vorkommen; *(Film)* (mit)spielen. **it ~s prominently in ...** es spielt in *(+dat)* ... eine bedeutende Rolle.

feature: ~ fireplace *n* offener Kamin; **~-length** *adj film* mit Spielfilmlänge; **~less** *adj* ohne besondere Merkmale; **~ story** *n* Sonderbericht *m*, Feature *nt*; **~ writer** *n* Journalist, der Features schreibt.

February ['februərɪ] *n* Februar *m*; *see* **September.**

feces ['fiːsiːz] *npl (US)* = **faeces.**

feckless ['feklɪs] *adj* nutzlos.

fed [fed] *pret, ptp of* **feed.**

federal ['fedərəl] **1** *adj* Bundes-; *system etc* föderalistisch. **~ state** *(in US)* (Einzel)staat *m*; **the F~ Republic of Germany** die Bundesrepublik Deutschland. **2** *n (US col)* FBI-Mann *m.*

federation [ˌfedə'reɪʃən] *n (act)* Zusammenschluß *m*; *(league)* Föderation *f*, Bund *m.*

fed up ['fed'ʌp] *adj (col)* **I'm ~** ich habe die Nase voll *(col)*; **I'm ~ with him/it** er/es hängt mir zum Hals heraus *(col)*; **I'm ~ waiting for him** ich habe es satt, auf ihn zu warten.

fee [fiː] *n* Gebühr *f*; *(of doctor, lawyer, artist, tutor)* Honorar *nt*; *(of stage performer)* Gage *f.* **(school) ~s** Schulgeld *nt.*

feeble ['fiːbl] *adj (+er)* schwach.

feeble-minded [ˌfiːbl'maɪndɪd] *adj* dümmlich.

feed [fiːd] *(vb: pret, ptp* **fed***)* **1** *n (of animals)* Futter *nt*; *(col: of person)* Essen *nt.* **when is the baby's next ~?** wann wird das Baby wieder gefüttert?; **to have a good ~** *(col)* tüchtig futtern *(col).* **2** *vt* **(a)** *(provide food for)* verpflegen; *family* ernähren. **(b)** *(give food to)* füttern. **to ~ oneself** *(child)* allein essen (können); **to ~ sth to sb/an animal** jdm/einem Tier etw zu essen/fressen geben. **(c)** *machine* versorgen; *furnace* beschicken; *meter* Geld einwerfen in *(+acc)*; *(fig) hope, imagination* nähren. **to ~ sth into a machine** etw in eine Maschine geben; **to ~ sb with information** jdn mit Informationen versorgen; **the data is fed into the computer** die Daten werden in den Computer eingegeben. **(d)** *(Tech: insert)* führen. **3** *vi (animal)* fressen; *(baby)* gefüttert werden.

♦ **feed back** *vt sep information* zurückleiten *(to* an *+acc).*

♦ **feed on 1** *vi +prep obj* sich (er)nähren von. **2** *vt sep +prep obj animal, baby* füttern mit; *person* ernähren mit.

feedback ['fi:dbæk] Reaktion *f*, Feedback *nt*. ~ **of information** Rückinformation *f*; **to provide more ~ about sth** ausführlicher über etw *(acc)* berichten.

feeding ['fi:dɪŋ]: ~ **bottle** *n (Brit)* Flasche *f*; ~ **time** *n (for animal)* Fütterungszeit *f*; *(for baby)* Zeit *f* für die Mahlzeit.

feel [fi:l] *(vb: pret, ptp* **felt***)* **1** *vt* **(a)** *(touch)* fühlen; *(examining)* befühlen. **to ~ one's way** sich vortasten; **to ~ one's way into sth** sich in etw *(acc)* einfühlen. **(b)** *(be aware of)* fühlen, spüren; *pain, emotions, loss* empfinden; *(be affected by) heat, cold, insult* leiden unter *(+dat)*. **I can't ~ anything in my left leg** ich habe kein Gefühl im linken Bein; **I felt it move** ich spürte, wie es sich bewegte; **I could ~ him getting angry** ich merkte, daß er wütend wurde; **I bet she felt that!** das hat bestimmt weh getan. **(c)** *(think)* glauben. **what do you ~ about him/it?** was halten Sie von ihm/davon?; **it was felt that ...** man war der Meinung, daß ...; **he felt it necessary** er hielt es für notwendig; **don't ~ you have to ...** glauben Sie nicht, Sie müßten ...

2 *vi* **(a)** *(physically or mentally)* sich fühlen. **to ~ well/ill** sich wohl/elend fühlen; **to ~ convinced/certain** überzeugt/sicher sein; **to ~ hungry/thirsty/sleepy** hungrig/durstig/müde sein; **I ~ hot/cold** mir ist heiß/kalt; **he doesn't ~ quite himself today** er ist heute nicht ganz auf der Höhe; **I felt sad/strange** mir war traurig/komisch zumute; **I felt as though I'd never been away** mir war, als ob ich nie weggewesen wäre; **I felt as if I was going to be sick** ich dachte, mir würde schlecht werden; **how do you ~ about him?** *(emotionally)* was empfinden Sie für ihn?; **you can imagine how I felt** Sie können sich *(dat)* vorstellen, wie mir zumute war; **what does it ~ like** *or* **how does it ~ to be all alone?** wie fühlt man sich *or* wie ist das so ganz allein?; **it ~s like flying** es ist wie Fliegen.

(b) *(to the touch)* sich anfühlen. **to ~ hard** sich hart anfühlen; **the room/air ~s warm** das Zimmer/die Luft kommt einem warm vor.

(c) *(think, have opinions)* meinen. **how do you ~ about these developments?** was meinen Sie zu dieser Entwicklung?; **that's just how I ~** das meine ich auch.

(d) to ~ like *(have desire for)* Lust haben auf *(+acc)*; *(for food)* Appetit haben auf *(+acc)*; **I ~ like eating something/going for a walk** ich könnte jetzt etwas essen/ich habe Lust spazierenzugehen; **I felt like screaming/giving up** ich hätte am liebsten geschrien/aufgegeben; **if you ~ like it** wenn Sie Lust haben.

3 *n* **let me have a ~ (of it)!** laß (mich) mal fühlen!; **it has a velvety ~** es fühlt sich samten an; **he recognizes things by their ~** er erkennt Dinge daran, wie sie sich anfühlen; **to get/have a ~ for sth** *(fig)* ein Gefühl für etw bekommen/haben.

♦**feel about** *or* **around** *vi* umhertasten; *(in drawer, bag etc)* herumtasten.

♦**feel for** *vi +prep obj* **(a)** *(sympathize with)* Mitgefühl haben mit. **I ~ ~ you** Sie tun mir leid. **(b)** *(search for)* tasten nach.

♦**feel up to** *vi +prep obj* sich gewachsen fühlen *(+dat)*.

feeler ['fi:ləʳ] *n (Zool, fig)* Fühler *m*. **to put out ~s** seine Fühler ausstrecken.

feeling ['fi:lɪŋ] *n* **(a)** Gefühl *nt*. **I've lost all ~ in my right arm** ich habe kein Gefühl mehr im rechten Arm; **I've a funny ~ she won't come** ich hab so das Gefühl, daß sie nicht kommt. **(b)** *(opinion: also* **~s***)* Meinung, Ansicht *f (on zu)*. **there was a general ~ that ...** man war allgemein der Ansicht, daß ...; **bad/good ~** Verstimmung *f*/Wohlwollen *nt*; **there's been a lot of bad ~ about this decision** wegen dieser Entscheidung hat es viel böses Blut gegeben. **(c) ~s** Gefühle *pl*; **you've hurt his ~s** Sie haben ihn verletzt; **no hard ~s!** ich nehme es dir nicht übel; **no hard ~s?** nimm es mir nicht übel.

fee-paying ['fi:,peɪɪŋ] *adj school* Privat-; *pupils* deren Eltern Schulgeld zahlen.

feet [fi:t] *pl of* **foot.**

feign [feɪn] *vt* vortäuschen.

feint [feɪnt] *n (Sport)* Finte *f*.

feline ['fi:laɪn] *adj (lit)* Katzen-; *(fig)* katzenhaft.

fell[1] [fel] *pret of* **fall.**

fell[2] *n (skin)* Fell *nt*.

fell[3] *adj* **with one ~ blow** mit einem einzigen gewaltigen Hieb; **at one ~ swoop** mit einem Schlag.

fell[4] *vt tree* fällen; *person* niederstrecken; *animal* zur Strecke bringen.

fell[5] *n (Brit)* Berg *m*; *(moor)* Moorland *nt*.

fellow ['feləʊ] *n* **(a)** Mann, Typ *(col) m*. **(b)** *(comrade)* Kamerad *m*; *(colleague)* Kollege *m*, Kollegin *f*. **(c)** *(of a society)* Mitglied *nt*; *(Univ)* Fellow *m*.

fellow: ~ **citizen** *n* Mitbürger(in *f*) *m*; ~ **countryman** *n* Landsmann *m*/-männin *f*; ~ **countrymen** *npl* Landsleute *pl*; ~ **feeling** *n* Mitgefühl *nt*; *(togetherness)* Zusammengehörigkeitsgefühl *nt*; ~ **men** *npl* Mitmenschen *pl*; ~ **passenger** *n* Mitreisende(r) *mf*.

fellowship ['feləʊʃɪp] *n* **(a)** *no pl* Kameradschaft *f*; *(company)* Gesellschaft *f*. **(b)** *(society, club etc)* Gesellschaft *f*. **(c)** *(Univ: scholarship)* Forschungsstipendium *nt*; *(job)* Position *f* eines Fellow.

fellow: ~ **student** *n* Kommilitone *m*, Kommilitonin *f*; ~ **sufferer** *n* Leidensgenosse *m*/-genossin *f*; ~ **traveller** *(Brit) or* **traveler** *(US) n* **(a)** *(lit)* Mitreisende(r) *mf*; **(b)** *(Pol)* Sympathisant(in *f*) *m*; ~ **worker** *n* Kollege *m*, Kollegin *f*, Mitarbeiter(in *f*) *m*.

felon ['felən] *n* (Schwer)verbrecher *m*.

felony ['felənɪ] *n* (schweres) Verbrechen.

felt[1] [felt] *pret, ptp of* **feel.**

felt[2] *n* Filz *m*.

felt-tip (pen) ['felttɪp('pen)] *n* Filzstift *m*.

female ['fi:meɪl] **1** *adj* weiblich; *labour, rights* Frauen-. **a ~ doctor/student/slave/dog** eine Ärztin/Studentin/Sklavin/Hündin; ~ **impersonator** Frauenimitator *m*; **a typical ~ attitude** typisch Frau. **2** *n* **(a)** *(animal)* Weibchen *nt*. **(b)** *(col: woman)* Frau *f*; *(pej)* Weib *nt (pej)*.

feminine ['femɪnɪn] **1** *adj (also Gram)* weiblich, feminin. **2** *n (Gram)* Femininum *nt*. **in the ~** in der weiblichen *or* femininen Form.

femininity [,femɪ'nɪnɪtɪ] *n* Weiblichkeit *f*.

feminism ['femɪnɪzəm] *n* Feminismus *m*.

feminist ['femɪnɪst] *n* Feminist(in *f*) *m*.

femur ['fi:məʳ] *n* Oberschenkelknochen *m*.

fen [fen] *n* Moorland, Sumpfland *nt*.

fence [fens] **1** *n* **(a)** Zaun *m*; *(Sport)* Hindernis *nt*. **to sit on the ~** *(fig)* nicht Partei ergreifen; **don't sit on the ~** entscheiden Sie sich. **(b)** *(col: receiver of stolen goods)* Hehler *m*. **2** *vt (also* **~ in***) land* einzäunen, umzäunen. **3** *vi (Sport)* fechten.

♦**fence in** *vt sep* einzäunen, umzäunen. **to ~ sb ~** *(fig)* jds Freiheit beschneiden.

♦**fence off** *vt sep piece of land* abzäunen.

fencer ['fensəʳ] *n* Fechter(in *f*) *m*.

fencing ['fensɪŋ] *n* **(a)** *(Sport)* Fechten *nt*. **(b)** *(fences)* Einzäunung *f*.

fend [fend] *vi* **to ~ for oneself** *(provide)* für sich (selbst) sorgen; **could she ~ for herself in the big city?** könnte sie sich in der großen Stadt allein durchschlagen?

♦**fend off** *vt sep* abwehren.

fender ['fendəʳ] *n* **(a)** *(in front of fire)* Kamingitter *nt*. **(b)** *(US Aut)* Kotflügel *m*; *(of bicycle etc)* Schutzblech *nt*.

fennel ['fenl] *n (Bot)* Fenchel *m*.

ferment ['fɜːment] **1** *n (fig)* Unruhe *f*. **the city/he was in a state of ~** es gärte in der Stadt/in ihm. **2** [fə'ment] *vi (lit, fig)* gären. **3** [fə'ment] *vt (lit)* fermentieren; *(fig)* anwachsen lassen.
fermentation [,fɜːmen'teɪʃən] *n* Gärung *f*.
fern [fɜːn] *n* Farn(kraut *nt*) *m*.
ferocious [fə'rəʊʃəs] *adj appearance, animal* wild; *glance, look* grimmig; *criticism, competition* scharf; *fight, temper, attack* heftig.
ferocity [fə'rɒsɪtɪ] *n see adj* Wildheit *f*; Grimmigkeit *f*; Schärfe *f*; Heftigkeit *f*.
ferret ['ferɪt] **1** *n* Frettchen *nt*. **2** *vi (also ~* **about** *or* **around***)* herumstöbern, herumschnüffeln *(pej)*.
♦ **ferret out** *vt sep* aufstöbern.
ferry ['ferɪ] **1** *n* Fähre *f*. **2** *vt (by boat: also ~* **across** *or* **over***)* übersetzen; *(by plane, car etc)* transportieren. **to ~ sb across a river** jdn über einen Fluß setzen; **to ~ sb/sth back and forth** jdn/etw hin- und herbringen.
ferry: ~boat *n* Fährboot *nt*; **~man** *n* Fährmann *m*.
fertile ['fɜːtaɪl] *adj (lit, fig)* fruchtbar.
fertility [fə'tɪlɪtɪ] **1** *n (lit, fig)* Fruchtbarkeit *f*. **2** *attr cult, symbol* Fruchtbarkeits-. **~ drug** Fruchtbarkeitspille *f*.
fertilization [,fɜːtɪlaɪ'zeɪʃən] *n* Befruchtung *f*.
fertilize ['fɜːtɪlaɪz] *vt* befruchten; *land* düngen.
fertilizer ['fɜːtɪlaɪzə^r] *n* Dünger *m*. **artificial ~** Kunstdünger *m*.
fervent ['fɜːvənt], **fervid** ['fɜːvɪd] *adj* leidenschaftlich; *tone of voice, expression, prayer* inbrünstig.
fervour, *(US)* **fervor** ['fɜːvə^r] *n* Leidenschaft *f*.
fester ['festə^r] *vi (wound)* eitern.
festival ['festɪvəl] *n* **(a)** *(Eccl etc)* Fest *nt*. **(b)** *(cultural)* Festspiele *pl*; *(esp pop ~)* Festival *nt*.
festive ['festɪv] *adj* festlich. **the ~ season** die Festzeit.
festivity [fe'stɪvɪtɪ] *n* **(a)** *(gaiety)* Feststimmung *f*. **(b)** *(celebration)* Feier *f*. **festivities** *pl* Feierlichkeiten *pl*.
festoon [fe'stuːn] *vt* **to ~ sb/sth with sth** jdn mit etw behängen/etw mit etw schmücken.
fetal *adj (esp US)* = **foetal.**
fetch [fetʃ] *vt* **(a)** *(bring)* holen; *(collect) person, thing* abholen. **(b)** *sigh, groan* ausstoßen. **(c)** *(bring in) money* (ein)bringen. **(d)** *(col)* **to ~ sb a blow/one** jdm eine langen *(col)*.
♦ **fetch back** *vt sep* zurückholen.
♦ **fetch in** *vt sep* hereinbringen.
♦ **fetch up 1** *vi (col)* landen *(col)*. **2** *vt sep (Brit: vomit)* brechen.
fetching ['fetʃɪŋ] *adj* bezaubernd, reizend.
fête [feɪt] **1** *n* Fest *nt*. **2** *vt (make much of) sb, sb's success* feiern.
fetid ['fetɪd] *adj* übelriechend.
fetish ['fetɪʃ] *n* Fetisch *m*. **to have a ~ about cleanliness** einen Sauberkeitstick haben *(col)*.
fetishist ['fetɪʃɪst] *n* Fetischist *m*.
fetter ['fetə^r] **1** *vt prisoner* fesseln; *goat* anpflocken; *(fig)* in Fesseln legen. **2** *n* **~s** *pl* (Fuß)fesseln *pl*; *(fig)* Fesseln *pl*.
fettle ['fetl] *n* **to be in fine ~** in bester Form sein.
fetus *n (US)* = **foetus.**
feud [fjuːd] **1** *n (lit, fig)* Fehde *f*. **2** *vi (lit, fig)* sich befehden.
feudal ['fjuːdl] *adj* Feudal-, feudal.
feudalism ['fjuːdəlɪzəm] *n* Feudalismus *m*.
fever ['fiːvə^r] *n (lit, fig)* Fieber *nt no pl*. **to have a ~** eine Fieberkrankheit haben; *(high temperature)* Fieber haben; **in a ~ of excitement** in fieberhafter Erregung; **to reach ~ pitch** am Siedepunkt angelangt sein; **to be working at ~ pitch** auf Hochtouren arbeiten.
feverish ['fiːvərɪʃ] *adj (Med)* fiebernd *attr*; *(fig) activity* fieberhaft. **he's still ~** er hat noch Fieber.
few [fjuː] *adj (+er), pron* **(a)** *(not many)* wenige. **we are very ~** wir sind nur sehr wenige; **~ and far between** dünn gesät; **as ~ books as you** genauso wenig(e) Bücher wie du; **as ~ as six objections** bloß sechs Einwände; **there were 3 too ~** es waren 3 zuwenig da; **he is one of the ~ people who ...** er ist einer der wenigen, die ...; **its days are ~** es hat nur ein kurzes Leben; **the lucky ~** die wenigen Glücklichen; **as ~ as you** genauso wenig wie du; **however ~ there may be** wie wenig auch immer da ist; **I've got too ~ as it is** ich habe sowieso schon zu wenig(e); **there are too ~ of you** ihr seid zu wenige; **the ~ who knew him** die wenigen, die ihn kannten.
(b) a ~ ein paar; **a ~ more days** noch ein paar Tage; **a ~ times** ein paar Male; **he's had a good ~ drinks** er hat ziemlich viel getrunken; **quite a ~ books** ziemlich viele Bücher; **in the next ~ days** in den nächsten paar Tagen; **every ~ days** alle paar Tage.
fewer ['fjuːə^r] *adj, pron comp of* **few** weniger. **no ~ than** nicht weniger als.
fewest ['fjuːɪst] *adj, pron superl of* **few** die wenigsten.
fiancé [fɪ'ɑ̃ːŋseɪ] *n* Verlobte(r) *m*.
fiancée [fɪ'ɑ̃ːŋseɪ] *n* Verlobte *f*.
fiasco [fɪ'æskəʊ] *n* Fiasko *nt*.
fib [fɪb] *(col)* **1** *n* **(that's a) ~!** das ist geflunkert! *(col)*; **don't tell ~s** flunker nicht! *(col)*. **2** *vi* flunkern *(col)*.
fibber ['fɪbə^r] *n (col)* Flunkerer *m (col)*.
fibre, *(US)* **fiber** ['faɪbə^r] *n* Faser *f*. **moral ~** Charakterstärke *f*.
fibreglass, *(US)* **fiberglass** ['faɪbəglɑːs] **1** *n* Fiberglas *nt*. **2** *adj* Fiberglas-.
fibre optics *(Brit)*, **fiber optics** *(US)* *n* Faseroptik *f*.
fibrositis [,faɪbrə'saɪtɪs] *n* Bindegewebsentzündung *f*.
fibrous ['faɪbrəs] *adj* faserig.
fickle ['fɪkl] *adj* unbeständig, launenhaft.
fiction ['fɪkʃən] *n no pl (Liter)* Prosaliteratur *f*; *(category)* Belletristik *f*. **work of ~** Erzählung *f*; *(longer)* Roman *m*; **light ~** (leichte) Unterhaltungsliteratur; **that's pure ~** *(fig)* das ist frei erfunden.
fictional ['fɪkʃənl] *adj* erfunden. **a ~ character** eine Gestalt aus der Literatur.
fictitious [fɪk'tɪʃəs] *adj* **(a)** *(imaginary)* frei erfunden. **(b)** *(false)* falsch.
fiddle ['fɪdl] **1** *n* **(a)** *(Mus col)* Geige *f*. **to play second ~ (to sb)** *(fig)* in jds Schatten *(dat)* stehen; **he refuses to play second ~** *(fig)* er will immer die erste Geige spielen; **as fit as a ~** kerngesund. **(b)** *(Brit col: cheat)* Schiebung *f*; *(with money)* faule Geschäfte *pl (col)*. **it's a ~** das ist Schiebung!; **there are so many ~s going on** es wird so viel getrickst *(col)*; **tax ~** Steuermanipulation *f*. **2** *vi (fidget, play around)* herumspielen. **to ~ with sth** an etw *(dat)* herumspielen *(col)*. **3** *vt (col) accounts, results* frisieren *(col)*; *election* manipulieren. **he ~d it so that ...** er hat es so getrickst, daß ... *(col)*. **4** *interj* ach du liebe Zeit.
fiddler ['fɪdlə^r] *n* **(a)** *(Mus col)* Geiger(in *f*) *m*. **(b)** *(col: cheat)* Schwindler(in *f*) *m*.
fiddlesticks ['fɪdlstɪks] *interj (nonsense)* Unsinn, Quatsch *(col)*; *(bother)* du liebe Zeit.
fiddling ['fɪdlɪŋ] *adj (trivial)* läppisch.
fiddly ['fɪdlɪ] *adj (+er) (col: intricate)* knifflig *(col)*.
fidelity [fɪ'delɪtɪ] *n* **(a)** Treue *f (to* zu*)*. **(b)** *(Rad etc)* Klangtreue *f*.
fidget ['fɪdʒɪt] **1** *vi* zappeln. **to ~ with sth** mit etw herumfummeln; **don't ~** zappel nicht so rum! **2** *n (person)* Zappelphilipp *m (col)*.
fidgety ['fɪdʒɪtɪ] *adj* zappelig; *audience etc* unruhig.
field [fiːld] **1** *n* **(a)** *(lit, fig)* Feld *nt*; *(for root vegetables)* Acker *m*; *(area of grass)* Wiese *f*; *(for cows, horses etc)* Weide *f*. **he's working in the ~s** er arbeitet auf dem Feld *or* Acker; **~ of battle**

Schlachtfeld *nt*; ~ **of vision** Blickfeld *nt*; **magnetic** ~ Magnetfeld *nt*; **to lead the** ~ führend sein. **(b)** *(Sport: ground)* Platz *m*; *(competitors)* Feld *nt*. **there's a very strong** ~ das Feld der Teilnehmer ist sehr stark; **the rest of the** ~ *(runners)* die übrigen Läufer; **to take the** ~ auf den Platz kommen. **(c)** *(of study, work etc)* Gebiet *nt*. **to be first in the** ~ **with sth** *(Comm)* etw als Erster auf den Markt bringen; **studies in the** ~ **of medicine** Studien auf dem Gebiet der Medizin; **this is, of course, a very broad** ~ das ist natürlich ein weites Feld; **what** ~ **are you in?** auf welchem Gebiet arbeiten Sie?; **to test sth in the** ~ etw in der Praxis ausprobieren.

2 *vt (Cricket, Baseball etc) ball* auffangen und zurückwerfen; *(fig) question etc* abblocken, abwehren; *team, side* aufs Feld *or* auf den Platz schicken.

field day *n* **I had a** ~ ich hatte meinen großen Tag.

fielder ['fiːldəʳ] *n (Cricket, Baseball etc)* Fänger *m*.

field: ~ **events** *npl (Athletics)* Sprung- und Wurfdisziplinen *pl*; ~ **glasses** *npl* Feldstecher *m*; ~ **goal** *n (US Ftbl)* Feldtor *nt*; ~ **gun** *n (Mil)* Feldgeschütz *nt*; ~ **hockey** *n (US)* Hockey *nt*; ~ **marshal** *n (Mil)* Feldmarschall *m*; ~**mouse** *n* Feldmaus *f*; ~ **study** *n* Feldforschung *f*; **a** ~ **study** eine Feldstudie; ~**work** *n (of geologist etc)* Arbeit *f* im Gelände; *(of sociologist etc)* Feldarbeit *f*.

fiend [fiːnd] *n* Teufel *m*. **tennis** ~ *(col)* Tennisnarr *m*; **a fresh-air** ~ *(col)* ein Frischluftfanatiker *m*.

fiendish ['fiːndɪʃ] *adj* teuflisch; *(col) pace, heat* höllisch *(col)*; *problem* verteufelt *(col)*.

fierce [fɪəs] *adj (+er) appearance* wild; *glance, look* böse, grimmig; *dog* bissig; *criticism, competition* scharf; *fight, resistance, temper, attack (lit, fig)* heftig; *heat, sun* glühend.

fierceness ['fɪəsnɪs] *n see adj* Wildheit *f*; Grimmigkeit *f*; Bissigkeit *f*; Schärfe *f*; Heftigkeit *f*; Glut *f*.

fiery ['faɪərɪ] *adj (+er) (lit, fig)* feurig; *sunset* rotglühend. **to have a** ~ **temper** ein Hitzkopf *m* sein.

fife [faɪf] *n (Mus)* Querpfeife *f*.

fifteen ['fɪf'tiːn] **1** *adj* fünfzehn. **2** *n* Fünfzehn *f*.

fifteenth ['fɪf'tiːnθ] *adj* fünfzehnte(r, s); *see* **sixteenth.**

fifth [fɪfθ] **1** *adj* fünfte(r, s). **2** *n* Fünfte(r, s); *(part, fraction)* Fünftel *nt*; *(Mus)* Quinte *f*; *see* **sixth.**

fiftieth ['fɪftɪɪθ] *adj* fünfzigste(r, s); *see* **sixtieth.**

fifty ['fɪftɪ] **1** *adj* fünfzig. **2** *n* Fünfzig *f*; *see* **sixty.**

fifty-fifty ['fɪftɪ'fɪftɪ] **1** *adj* halbe-halbe, fifty-fifty. **we have a** ~ **chance of success** unsere Chancen stehen fifty-fifty. **2** *adv* **to go** ~ **(with sb)** (mit jdm) halbe-halbe machen.

fig [fɪg] *n* Feige *f*. **I don't care a** ~ *(col)* ich kümmere mich einen Dreck darum *(col)*.

fight [faɪt] *(vb: pret, ptp* **fought***)* **1** *n (lit, fig)* Kampf *m*; *(fist* ~*, scrap)* Schlägerei *f*; *(argument, row)* Streit *m*. **to have a** ~ **with sb** sich mit jdm schlagen; *(argue)* sich mit jdm streiten; **to put up a good** ~ *(lit, fig)* sich tapfer schlagen; **he won't give in without a** ~ er ergibt sich nicht kampflos; **there was no** ~ **left in him** sein Kampfgeist war erloschen.

2 *vi* kämpfen; *(have punch-up etc)* sich schlagen; *(argue)* sich streiten. **to** ~ **for one's life** um sein Leben kämpfen.

3 *vt person* kämpfen mit; *(have punch-up with)* sich schlagen mit; *fire, disease, cuts, policy* bekämpfen; *decision* ankämpfen gegen. **I'm prepared to** ~ **the government** ich bin bereit, das mit der Regierung durchzukämpfen; **you can't** ~ **the whole company** du kannst es nicht mit der ganzen Firma aufnehmen; **to** ~ **an action at law** einen Prozeß vor Gericht durchfechten; **to** ~ **one's way out of the crowd** sich aus der Menge freikämpfen.

♦**fight back 1** *vi (in fight)* zurückschlagen; *(Mil)* sich verteidigen; *(in argument)* sich wehren; *(after illness)* zu Kräften kommen; *(Sport)* einen Gegenangriff unternehmen; *(pull back)* aufholen. **2** *vt sep tears etc* unterdrücken.

♦**fight down** *vt sep anxiety* unterdrücken.

♦**fight off** *vt sep (Mil, fig) attack, disease* abwehren; *sleep* ankämpfen gegen; *a cold* ankämpfen gegen.

♦**fight on** *vi* weiterkämpfen.

♦**fight out** *vt sep* **to** ~ **it** ~ es untereinander ausfechten.

fighter ['faɪtəʳ] *n* **(a)** Kämpfer *m*; *(Boxing)* Fighter *m*. **he's a** ~ *(fig)* er ist eine Kämpfernatur. **(b)** *(Aviat: plane)* Jagdflugzeug *nt*.

fighter: ~**-aircraft** *n* Kampfflugzeug *nt*; ~**-bomber** *n* Jagdbomber *m*; ~**-interceptor** *n* Abfangjäger *m*; ~**-pilot** *n* Jagdflieger *m*.

fighting ['faɪtɪŋ] *n (Mil)* Kampf *m*; *(punch-ups etc)* Schlägereien *pl*; *(between husband and wife etc)* Streit *m*. ~ **broke out** Kämpfe brachen aus.

fighting: ~ **chance** *n* faire Chancen *pl*; **he's in with** *or* **he has a** ~ **chance** er hat eine Chance, wenn er sich anstrengt; ~ **forces** *npl* Kampftruppen *pl*; ~ **spirit** *n* Kampfgeist *m*; ~ **strength** *n (Mil)* Kampfstärke *f*.

figment ['fɪgmənt] *n* **a** ~ **of the imagination** pure Einbildung.

figurative ['fɪgjʊrətɪv] *adj use, sense* übertragen.

figure ['fɪgəʳ] **1** *n* **(a)** *(number)* Zahl; *(digit also)* Ziffer *f*; *(sum)* Summe *f*. **he's good at** ~**s** er ist ein guter Rechner; **three-**~ **number** dreistellige Zahl; **he earns well into four** ~**s** er hat gut und gern ein vierstelliges Einkommen. **(b)** *(in geometry, dancing, drawing)* Figur *f*. ~ **of eight** Acht *f*. **(c)** *(human form)* Gestalt *f*. **(d)** *(shapeliness)* Figur *f*. **she has a good** ~ sie hat eine gute Figur; **he's a fine** ~ **of a man** er ist ein Bild von einem Mann. **(e)** *(personality)* Persönlichkeit *f*; *(character in novel etc)* Gestalt *f*. **(f)** ~ **of speech** Redensart *f*.

2 *vt (imagine)* sich *(dat)* vorstellen; *(US col: think, reckon)* schätzen *(col)*.

3 *vi* **(a)** *(appear)* erscheinen. **he** ~**d prominently in the talks** er spielte eine bedeutende Rolle bei den Gesprächen. **(b)** *(col: make sense)* hinkommen *(col)*. **that** ~**s** das hätte ich mir denken können.

♦**figure on** *vi +prep obj (esp US)* rechnen mit.

♦**figure out** *vt sep* **(a)** *(understand)* schlau werden aus. **(b)** *(work out)* ausrechnen; *answer, how to do sth* herausbekommen; *solution* finden.

figure: ~**-conscious** *adj* figurbewußt; ~**head** *n (Naut, fig)* Galionsfigur *f*; ~**-skater** *n* Eiskunstläufer(in *f*) *m*; ~**-skating** *n* Eiskunstlaufen *nt*.

Fiji ['fiːdʒiː] *n* Fidschiinseln *pl*.

filament ['fɪləmənt] *n (Elec)* (Glüh)faden *m*.

filch [fɪltʃ] *vt* mausen *(col)*.

file[1] [faɪl] **1** *n (tool)* Feile *f*. **2** *vt* feilen. **to** ~ **one's fingernails** sich *(dat)* die Fingernägel feilen.

file[2] **1** *n* **(a)** *(holder)* Aktenordner *m*; *(for card index)* Karteikasten *m*. **it's in the** ~**s somewhere** das muß irgendwo bei den Akten sein. **(b)** *(documents, information)* Akte *f (on sb* über jdn, *on sth* zu etw*)*. **on** ~ aktenkundig; **to keep a** ~ **on sb/sth** eine Akte über jdn/etw führen. **(c)** *(Comp)* Datei *f*. **data on** ~ auf Abruf gespeicherte Daten. **2** *vt* **(a)** *letters* ablegen. **(b)** *(Jur) petition* einreichen.

♦**file away** *vt sep papers* zu den Akten legen.

file[3] **1** *n (row)* Reihe *f*. **in single** ~ im Gänsemarsch; *(Mil)* in Reihe. **2** *vi* **to** ~ **in** hereinmarschieren; **they** ~**d out of the classroom** sie gingen/kamen nacheinander aus dem Klassenzimmer; **the troops** ~**d past the general** die Truppen marschierten am General vorbei.

file clerk *n (US)* Angestellte(r) *mf* in der Registratur.

filial ['fɪlɪəl] *adj* Kindes-. **with due** ~ **respect** mit

dem Respekt, den eine Tochter/ein Sohn schuldig ist.
filibuster ['fɪlɪbʌstəʳ] *vi (esp US)* Obstruktion betreiben.
filigree ['fɪlɪgriː] *n* Filigran(arbeit *f*) *nt*.
filing: ~ cabinet *n* Aktenschrank *m*; **~ clerk** *n (Brit)* Angestellte(r) *mf* in der Registratur.
filings ['faɪlɪŋz] *npl* Späne *pl*.
Filipino [fɪlɪ'piːnəʊ] *n* Filipino *m*.
fill [fɪl] **1** *vt* füllen; *pipe* stopfen; *teeth* plombieren; *(wind) sails* blähen; *post, position (employer)* besetzen; *(employee)* einnehmen; *need* entsprechen *(+dat)*. **~ed with anger/admiration** voller Zorn/Bewunderung; **the thought ~ed him with horror** der Gedanke erfüllte ihn mit Entsetzen. **2** *vi* sich füllen. **3** *n* **to drink one's ~** seinen Durst löschen; **to eat one's ~** sich satt essen; **I've had my ~ of him/it** *(col)* ich habe von ihm/davon die Nase voll *(col)*.
♦ **fill in 1** *vi* **to ~ ~ for sb** für jdn einspringen. **2** *vt sep* **(a)** *hole* auffüllen; *door, fireplace* zumauern; *(fig) gaps* stopfen. **(b)** *form* ausfüllen; *name, details, missing word* eintragen. **(c) to ~ sb ~ (on sth)** jdn (über etw *acc*) aufklären *or* ins Bild setzen.
♦ **fill out 1** *vi* **(a)** *(sails etc)* sich blähen. **(b)** *(person: become fatter)* fülliger werden; *(cheeks, face)* voller werden. **2** *vt sep form* ausfüllen; *essay, article etc* strecken.
♦ **fill up 1** *vi (Aut)* (auf)tanken; *(hall, barrel etc)* sich füllen. **2** *vt sep tank, cup* vollfüllen; *(driver)* volltanken; *hole* stopfen; *(Brit) form* ausfüllen. **~ her ~!** *(Aut col)* volltanken bitte!
filler ['fɪləʳ] *n (for cracks)* Spachtelmasse *f*.
fillet ['fɪlɪt] **1** *n* Filet *nt*. **~ steak** Filetsteak *nt*. **2** *vt* filetieren.
filling ['fɪlɪŋ] **1** *n* **(a)** *(in tooth)* Füllung, Plombe *f*. **I had to have three ~s** ich mußte mir drei Zähne plombieren lassen. **(b)** *(in pie, tart)* Füllung *f*. **2** *adj food* sättigend.
filling station *n* Tankstelle *f*.
fillip ['fɪlɪp] *n (fig)* Ansporn *m*.
filly ['fɪlɪ] *n* Stutfohlen *nt*; *(dated col)* Mädel *nt (dated)*.
film [fɪlm] **1** *n* **(a)** Film *m*; *(of dust, of ice)* Schicht *f*; *(of mist, on the eye)* Schleier *m*; *(thin membrane)* Häutchen *nt*; *(on teeth)* Belag *m*. **(b)** *(Phot)* Film *m*. **to make a ~** einen Film drehen; **to go to the ~s** ins Kino gehen. **2** *vt play* verfilmen; *scene* filmen; *people* einen Film machen von.
film: ~ camera *n* Filmkamera *f*; **~ clip** *n* Filmausschnitt *m*; **~-maker** *n* Filmemacher(in *f*) *m*; **~ rights** *npl* Filmrechte *pl*; **~ script** *n* Drehbuch *nt*; **~star** *n* Filmstar *m*; **~strip** *n* Filmstreifen *m*; **~ studio** *n* Filmstudio *nt*; **~ version** *n* Verfilmung *f*.
filter ['fɪltəʳ] **1** *n* Filter *m*; *(Brit: for traffic)* Abbiegespur *f*. **2** *vt liquids, air* filtern. **3** *vi (light)* durchscheinen. **to ~ to the left** *(Brit Aut)* sich links einordnen.
♦ **filter back** *vi (refugees, prisoners etc)* allmählich zurückkommen.
♦ **filter in** *vi (people)* allmählich eindringen; *(news)* durchsickern.
♦ **filter out** *vt sep (lit)* herausfiltern.
♦ **filter through** *vi (liquid, sound, news)* durchsickern; *(light)* durchscheinen.
filter: ~ lane *n (Brit)* Abbiegespur *f*; **~ paper** *n* Filterpapier *nt*; **~-tipped** *adj cigarette* Filter-.
filth [fɪlθ] *n (lit)* Schmutz, Dreck *m*; *(fig)* Schweinerei *f*.
filthy ['fɪlθɪ] *adj (+er)* schmutzig, dreckig; *(col) weather* Sau- *(col)*; *day* Mist-; *temper* übel; *(obscene)* unanständig. **don't be ~** du Ferkel!; **a ~ habit** eine widerliche Angewohnheit; **~ rich** *(col)* stinkreich *(col)*.
fin [fɪn] *n (of fish)* Flosse *f*; *(Aviat)* Seitenflosse *f*; *(of bomb, rocket, ship)* Stabilisierungsfläche *f*.
final ['faɪnl] **1** *adj (last)* letzte(r, s); *examination, chord* Schluß-; *(definite) decision, version* endgültig. **~ score** Schlußstand *m*; **~ round/lap** Endrunde *f*; **that's not ~ yet** das steht noch nicht endgültig fest; **you're not going and that's ~** du gehst nicht, und damit Schluß! **2** *n* **(a) ~s** *pl (Univ)* Abschlußprüfung *f*. **(b)** *(Sport)* Finale *nt*; *(in quiz)* Endrunde *f*. **the ~s** das Finale.
finale [fɪ'nɑːlɪ] *n (Mus, fig)* Finale *nt*.
finalist ['faɪnəlɪst] *n (Sport)* Endrundenteilnehmer(in *f*), Finalist(in *f*) *m*.
finality [faɪ'nælɪtɪ] *n (of decision etc)* Endgültigkeit *f*; *(of tone of voice)* Entschiedenheit *f*.
finalize ['faɪnəlaɪz] *vt* fertigmachen; *plans, arrangements* endgültig festlegen; *deal* zum Abschluß bringen; *draft* die endgültige Form geben *(+dat)*. **to ~ a decision** eine endgültige Entscheidung treffen.
finally ['faɪnəlɪ] *adv* schließlich; *(expressing relief etc)* endlich.
finance [faɪ'næns] **1** *n* Finanzen *pl*. **high ~** Hochfinanz *f*; **it's a question of ~** das ist eine Geldfrage. **2** *vt* finanzieren.
financial [faɪ'nænʃəl] *adj* finanziell; *crisis* Finanz-; *news, page* Wirtschafts-. **~ director** Leiter *m* der Finanzabteilung; **the ~ year** das Rechnungsjahr.
financier [faɪ'nænsɪəʳ] *n* Finanzier *m*.
finch [fɪntʃ] *n* Fink *m*.
find [faɪnd] *(vb: pret, ptp* **found***)* **1** *vt* **(a)** finden. **this flower is found all over England** diese Blume findet man in ganz England; **do you know where there is a chemist's to be found?** wissen Sie, wo hier eine Apotheke ist?; **there wasn't one to be found** es war keine(r) zu finden; **we left everything as we found it** wir haben alles so gelassen, wie wir es vorgefunden haben; **he was found dead in bed** er wurde tot im Bett aufgefunden; **where am I going to ~ the money/time?** wo nehme ich nur das Geld/die Zeit her?; **I ~ myself in an impossible situation** ich befinde mich in einer unmöglichen Situation; **he awoke to ~ himself in prison/hospital** er erwachte und fand sich im Gefängnis/Krankenhaus wieder; **I found myself unable/forced to ...** ich sah mich außerstande/gezwungen, zu ...

(b) *(supply)* besorgen *(sb sth* jdm etw*)*. **go and ~ me a needle** hol mir doch mal eine Nadel!

(c) *(discover, ascertain)* feststellen. **we found the car wouldn't start** es stellte sich heraus, daß das Auto nicht ansprang; **if you still ~ you can't do it** wenn Sie feststellen, daß Sie es immer noch nicht können.

(d) *(consider to be)* finden. **I ~ Spain too hot** ich finde Spanien zu heiß; **I don't ~ it easy to tell you this** es fällt mir nicht leicht, Ihnen das zu sagen; **did you ~ her a good worker?** fanden Sie, daß sie gut arbeitet?; **I ~ it impossible to understand him** ich kann ihn einfach nicht verstehen.

(e) £100 per week all found £ 100 pro Woche, (und freie) Kost und Logis.

(f) *(Jur)* **to ~ sb guilty** jdn für schuldig befinden; **how do you ~ the accused?** wie lautet Ihr Urteil?

2 *vi (Jur)* **to ~ for/against the accused** den Angeklagten freisprechen/verurteilen.

3 *n* Fund *m*.
♦ **find out 1** *vt sep* answer, *sb's secret* herausfinden. **don't get found ~** laß dich nicht erwischen; **you've been found ~** du bist ertappt. **2** *vi* es herausfinden. **to ~ ~ about sb/sth** *(learn facts)* etwas über jdn/etw erfahren; **if his wife ~s ~ about it/her** wenn seine Frau dahinterkommt, wenn seine Frau davon/von ihr erfährt.
findings ['faɪndɪŋz] *n pl* Ergebnis(se *pl*) *nt*; *(medical)* Befund *m*.
fine[1] [faɪn] **1** *n (Jur)* Geldstrafe *f*. **2** *vt* zu einer Geldstrafe verurteilen. **he was ~d £10** er mußte £ 10 Strafe bezahlen; **he was ~d for speeding** er

mußte Strafe für zu schnelles Fahren zahlen.

fine[2] *adj (+er)* **(a)** *weather* schön. **one ~ day** eines schönen Tages. **(b)** *(good)* gut; *person* fein; *specimen, chap, woman* prächtig; *pianist, novel, painting, shot* großartig; *holiday, meal, view* herrlich; *(elegant) clothes, manners etc* fein. **a ~ time to ...** *(iro)* genau der richtige Augenblick, zu ...; **a ~ friend you are** *(iro)* du bist mir ja ein schöner Freund!; **that's a ~ thing to say** *(iro)* das ist ja wirklich nett, so was zu sagen!; **this is a ~ state of affairs** *(iro)* das sind ja schöne Zustände!; **that's ~ by me** ich habe nichts dagegen; **(that's) ~** gut, in Ordnung; **I'm/he is ~ now** es geht mir/ihm wieder gut; **how are you? — ~** wie, geht's? — gut. **(c)** *(delicate, thin) workmanship, dust, distinction* fein. **to appeal to sb's ~r feelings** an jds besseres Ich appellieren; **there's a very ~ line between ...** es besteht ein feiner Unterschied zwischen ...

fine art *n* **(a)** *usu pl* schöne Künste *pl.* **(b) he's got it down to a ~** er hat den Bogen heraus *(col).*

finely ['faɪnlɪ] *adv* fein; *worked* schön.

finery ['faɪnərɪ] *n (of dress)* Staat *m.*

finesse [fɪ'nes] *(skill)* Gewandtheit *f; (cunning)* Finesse *f.*

fine-tooth comb ['faɪn'tu:θkəʊm] *n:* **to go through sth with a ~** etw genau unter die Lupe nehmen.

finger ['fɪŋgə[r]] **1** *n* Finger *m.* **she can twist him around her little ~** sie kann ihn um den (kleinen) Finger wickeln; **to have a ~ in every pie** überall die Finger im Spiel haben; **I didn't lay a ~ on her** ich habe sie nicht angerührt; **he wouldn't lift a ~ to help me** er würde keinen Finger rühren, um mir zu helfen; **he didn't lift a ~** er hat keinen Finger krumm gemacht; **I can't put my ~ on it, but ...** ich kann es nicht genau ausmachen, aber ...; **you've put your ~ on it there** da haben Sie den kritischen Punkt berührt; **to get** *or* **pull one's ~ out** *(col) (do properly)* Nägel mit Köpfen machen; *(speed up)* Dampf dahinter machen *(col).* **2** *vt* anfassen; *(toy, meddle with)* herumfingern an *(+dat).*

finger: ~ board *n* Griffbrett *nt;* **~bowl** *n* Fingerschale *f.*

fingering ['fɪŋgərɪŋ] *n (Mus) (in the notation)* Fingersatz *m; (of keys, strings)* (Finger)technik *f.*

finger: ~mark *n* Fingerabdruck *m;* **~nail** *n* Fingernagel *m;* **~ print 1** *n* Fingerabdruck *m;* **2** *vt* **to ~print sb/sth** jdm Fingerabdrücke *pl* abnehmen/von etw Fingerabdrücke *pl* abnehmen; **~tip** *n* Fingerspitze *f;* **to have sth at one's ~tips** *(fig) (know very well)* etw aus dem Effeff kennen *(col); (have at one's disposal)* etw parat haben; **~tip control** *n (of steering wheel etc)* mühelose Steuerung.

finicky ['fɪnɪkɪ] *adj person* schwer zufriedenzustellen, pingelig *(col); work, job* kniff(e)lig *(col); detail* winzig.

finish ['fɪnɪʃ] **1** *n* **(a)** *(end)* Schluß *m,* Ende *nt; (of race)* Finish *nt; (~ing line)* Ziel *nt.* **to be in at the ~** *(fig)* den Schluß miterleben; **to fight to the ~** bis zum letzten Augenblick kämpfen. **(b)** *(of products)* Finish *nt; (of material)* Appretur *f.* **paint with a gloss/matt~** Farbe mit Hochglanzeffekt/mattem Glanz; **this one has a better ~** das ist besser verarbeitet.

2 *vt* **(a)** beenden; *course, work, business also* abschließen. **to ~/have ~ed doing sth** mit etw fertig werden/sein; **to ~ writing/reading sth** etw zu Ende schreiben/lesen; **to have ~ed sth** etw fertig haben; *task, course* mit etw fertig sein; **when do you ~ work?** wann machen Sie Feierabend?; **give me time to ~ my drink** laß mich austrinken; **~ what you're doing** mach das erst fertig; **that last kilometre nearly ~ed me** *(col)* dieser letzte Kilometer hat mich beinahe geschafft *(col).*

(b) *(give ~ to)* den letzten Schliff geben *(+dat); piece of handiwork* verarbeiten; *industrial product* ein schönes Finish geben *(+dat).* **the paintwork isn't very well ~ed** der Lack hat keine besonders schöne Oberfläche.

3 *vi* **(a)** zu Ende sein; *(person: with task etc)* fertig sein; *(come to an end, ~ work)* aufhören; *(piece of music, story etc)* enden. **when does the film ~?** wann ist der Film aus?; **we'll ~ by singing a song** wir wollen mit einem Lied schließen, zum Schluß singen wir ein Lied; **I've ~ed** ich bin fertig. **(b)** *(Sport)* das Ziel erreichen. **to ~ second** als zweiter durchs Ziel gehen.

♦**finish off 1** *vi* aufhören, Schluß machen. **2** *vt sep* **(a)** *piece of work* fertigmachen. **a liqueur to ~ ~ the meal** zum Abschluß des Essens noch einen Likör. **(b)** *food* aufessen; *drink* austrinken. **(c)** *(kill)* den Gnadenstoß geben *(+dat); (by shooting)* den Gnadenschuß geben *(+dat).* **(d)** *(do for) person* den Rest geben *(+dat).*

♦**finish up 1** *vi (end up in a place)* landen *(col).* **he ~ed ~ a nervous wreck** er war zum Schluß ein Nervenbündel; **I'll just ~ ~ by doing it all again** zum Schluß muß ich doch alles noch mal machen. **2** *vt sep* = **finish off 2 (b).**

♦**finish with** *vi +prep obj* **have you ~ed ~ the paper?** haben Sie die Zeitung fertiggelesen?; **I've ~ed ~ him** ich will nichts mehr mit ihm zu tun haben; *(with boyfriend)* ich habe mit ihm Schluß gemacht.

finished ['fɪnɪʃt] *adj* **(a)** *item, product* fertig; *(polished)* poliert; *performance* ausgereift; *appearance* vollendet. **~ goods** Fertigprodukte *pl;* **beautifully ~ dolls** wunderschön gearbeitete Puppen. **(b) to be ~** *(person, task etc)* fertig sein; *(exhausted, done for etc)* erledigt sein; **the wine is ~** es ist kein Wein mehr da; **I'm ~ with politics** mit der Politik ist es für mich vorbei; **it's all ~ (between us)** es ist alles aus (zwischen uns).

finishing ['fɪnɪʃɪŋ]: **~ line** *n* Ziellinie *f;* **~ school** *n* (Mädchen)pensionat *nt.*

finite ['faɪnaɪt] *adj (limited)* begrenzt; *number* endlich.

Finland ['fɪnlənd] *n* Finnland *nt.*

Finn [fɪn] *n* Finne *m,* Finnin *f.*

Finnish ['fɪnɪʃ] **1** *adj* finnisch. **2** *n* Finnisch *nt.*

fiord [fjɔ:d] *n* Fjord *m.*

fir [fɜ:[r]] *n* Tanne *f; (~ wood)* Tanne(nholz *nt*) *f.* **~ cone** Tannenzapfen *m.*

fire [faɪə[r]] **1** *n (lit, fig, Mil)* Feuer *nt; (electric, gas)* Ofen; *(destructive: forest ~, house ~)* Brand *m.* **the house was on ~** das Haus brannte; **to set ~ to sth, to set sth on ~** etw anzünden; *(so as to destroy)* etw in Brand stecken; **to catch ~** Feuer fangen; **you're playing with ~** *(fig)* du spielst mit dem Feuer; **there was a ~ next door** nebenan hat es gebrannt; **to come under ~** *(lit, fig)* unter Beschuß geraten.

2 *vt* **(a)** *gun* abschießen; *shot* abfeuern; *rocket* zünden. **to ~ a gun at sb** auf jdn schießen; **to ~ questions at sb** Fragen auf jdn abfeuern. **(b)** *pottery* brennen. **(c)** *(fig) imagination* beflügeln. **(d)** *(col: dismiss)* feuern *(col).*

3 *vi* **(a)** *(shoot)* schießen *(at* auf *+acc).* **~!** Feuer! **(b)** *(engine)* zünden. **the engine is only firing on three cylinders** der Motor läuft nur auf drei Zylindern.

♦**fire away** *vi (col: begin)* losschießen *(col).*

fire: ~ alarm *n* Feueralarm *m; (apparatus)* Feuermelder *m;* **~arm** *n* Schußwaffe *f;* **~ brigade** *n (Brit)* Feuerwehr *f;* **~cracker** *n* Knallkörper *m;* **~ department** *n (US)* Feuerwehr *f;* **~ drill** *n (for firemen)* Feuerwehrübung *f; (for passengers etc)* Probealarm *m;* **~-eater** *n* Feuerschlucker *m;* **~-engine** *n* Feuerwehrauto *nt;* **~ escape** *n (staircase)* Feuertreppe *f; (ladder)* Feuerleiter *f;* **~ extinguisher** *n* Feuerlöscher *m;* **~guard** *n* (Schutz)gitter *nt (vor dem Kamin);* **~ hazard** *n* **to be a ~ hazard** feuergefährlich sein; **~light** *n*

Schein *m* des Feuers; ~**man** *n* Feuerwehrmann *m*; ~**place** *n* Kamin *m*; ~**power** *n (of guns, aircraft, army)* Feuerkraft *f*; ~**proof** *adj* feuerfest; ~**side** *n* **to sit by the** ~**side** am Kamin sitzen; ~ **station** *n* Feuerwehrzentrale *f*; ~**wood** *n* Brennholz *nt*; ~**works** *npl* Feuerwerkskörper *pl*; *(display)* Feuerwerk *nt*; **there'll be** ~**works if he finds out** *(col)* wenn er das erfährt, dann kracht's.

firing ['faɪrɪŋ] *n* **(a)** *(of pottery)* Brennen *nt*. **(b)** *(Mil)* Feuer *nt*; *(of gun, shot, rocket)* Abfeuern *nt*. **(c)** *(Aut: of engine)* Zündung *f*.

firing: ~ **line** *n (lit, fig)* Schußlinie *f*; ~ **squad** *n* Exekutionskommando *nt*.

firm[1] [fɜːm] *n* Firma *f*.

firm[2] **1** *adj (+er)* fest. **to be** ~ **with sb** jdm gegenüber bestimmt auftreten. **2** *adv* **to stand** ~ **on sth** *(fig)* fest bei etw bleiben.

firmly ['fɜːmlɪ] *adv* fest; *say* bestimmt.

firmness ['fɜːmnɪs] *n* Festigkeit *f*.

first [fɜːst] **1** *adj* erste(r, s). **who's** ~? wer ist der erste?; **I'm** ~, **I've been waiting longer than you** ich bin zuerst an der Reihe, ich warte schon länger als Sie; ~ **things** ~ eins nach dem anderen; **you have to put** ~ **things** ~ du mußt wissen, was dir am wichtigsten ist; **he doesn't know the** ~ **thing about it/cars** davon/von Autos hat er keinen blassen Schimmer *(col)*; **in the** ~ **place** zunächst einmal; **why didn't you say so in the** ~ **place?** warum hast du denn das nicht gleich gesagt?

2 *adv* **(a)** zuerst; *arrive, leave* als erste(r, s); *(in listing)* erstens. ~ **come** ~ **served** *(prov)* wer zuerst kommt, mahlt zuerst *(Prov)*; **ladies** ~ Ladies first!; **you** ~ du zuerst; **he says** ~ **one thing then another** er sagt mal so, mal so; **my health comes** ~ meine Gesundheit ist mir am wichtigsten; **he always puts his job** ~ seine Arbeit kommt bei ihm immer vor allem anderen; ~ **and foremost** zunächst; **I must finish this** ~ ich muß das erst fertigmachen; **think** ~ überlegen Sie es sich. **(b)** *(for the* ~ *time)* zum ersten Mal. **when did you** ~ **meet him?** wann haben Sie ihn das erste Mal getroffen?; **when it** ~ **became known that ...** als zuerst bekannt wurde, daß ... **(c)** *(in preference)* eher, lieber. **I'd die** ~! eher würde ich sterben!

3 *n* **(a) the** ~ der/die/das Erste; **they were the** ~ **to come** sie kamen als erste; **this is the** ~ **I've heard of it** das ist mir ja ganz neu; **at** ~ zuerst; **from the** ~ von Anfang an; **from** ~ **to last** von Anfang bis Ende. **(b)** *(Brit Univ)* **he got a** ~ er bestand (sein Examen) mit „sehr gut". **(c)** *(Aut)* ~ **(gear)** der erste (Gang). **in** ~ im ersten (Gang); *see* **sixth.**

first: ~ **aid** *n* Erste Hilfe; ~ **aid box** *n* Verbandskasten *m*; ~ **aid post** *n* Sanitätswache *f*; ~**-class 1** *adj* erstklassig; ~**-class compartment** Abteil *nt* erster Klasse; ~**-class mail** *bevorzugt beförderte Post*; **he's** ~**-class at tennis** er ist ein erstklassiger Tennisspieler; **that's absolutely** ~**-class** das ist einfach Spitze *(col)*; ~**-class degree** *(Brit)* sehr gutes Examen; **2** *adv travel* erster Klasse; ~ **cousin** *n* Vetter *m* ersten Grades; ~ **edition** *n* Erstausgabe *f*; ~ **form** *n (Brit Sch)* erste Klasse; ~**-generation** *adj citizen, computer* der ersten Generation; ~**-hand** *adj, adv* aus erster Hand; **F**~ **Lady** First Lady *f*.

firstly ['fɜːstlɪ] *adv* erstens, zunächst (einmal).

first: ~ **name** *n* Vorname *m*; ~ **night** *n (Theat)* Premiere *f*; ~ **offender** *n* **he is a** ~ **offender** er ist nicht vorbestraft; ~ **officer** *n (Naut)* Erster Offizier; ~ **performance** *n (Theat)* Premiere *f*; *(first ever)* Uraufführung *f*; ~**-rate** *adj* erstklassig.

firth [fɜːθ] *n (Scot)* Meeresarm *m*.

fir tree *n* Tannenbaum *m*.

fiscal ['fɪskəl] *adj* Finanz-.

fish [fɪʃ] **1** *n, pl* - *or (esp for different types)* **-es** Fisch *m*. ~ **and chips** Fisch und Pommes frites; **to drink like a** ~ *(col)* wie ein Loch saufen *(col)*; **like a** ~ **out of water** wie ein Fisch auf dem Trockenen; **a queer** ~! *(col)* ein komischer Kauz. **2** *vi* fischen; *(with rod)* angeln. **to go** ~**ing** fischen/angeln gehen; **to go salmon** ~**ing** auf Lachsfang gehen. **3** *vt* fischen; *(with rod)* angeln; *river* fischen/angeln in *(+dat)*.

♦ **fish for** *vi +prep obj* fischen/angeln; *(fig) compliments* fischen nach. **they were** ~**ing** ~ **information** sie waren auf Informationen aus.

♦ **fish out** *vt sep* herausfischen *(of or from sth* aus etw*)*.

♦ **fish up** *vt sep (from water)* herausziehen.

fish: ~**bone** *n* (Fisch)gräte *f*; ~**cake** *n* Fischfrikadelle *f*.

fisherman ['fɪʃəmən] *n, pl* **-men** [mən] Fischer *m*; *(amateur)* Angler *m*.

fishery ['fɪʃərɪ] *n (area)* Fischereizone *f*; *(industry)* Fischerei *f*.

fish: ~ **farm** *n* Fischzucht *f*; ~ **finger** *n (Brit)* Fischstäbchen *nt*; ~**hook** *n* Angelhaken *m*.

fishing ['fɪʃɪŋ] *n* Fischen *nt*; *(with rod)* Angeln *nt*; *(as industry)* Fischerei *f*.

fishing: ~ **boat** *n* Fischerboot *nt*; ~ **grounds** *npl* Fischgründe *pl*; ~ **industry** *n* Fischindustrie *f*; ~**-line** *n* Angelschnur *f*; ~**-net** *n* Fischnetz *nt*; ~ **port** *n* Fischereihafen *m*; ~**-rod** *n* Angelrute *f*; ~ **tackle** *n (for sport)* Angelgeräte *pl*; *(for industry)* Fischereigeräte *pl*; ~ **village** *n* Fischerdorf *nt*.

fish: ~ **knife** *n* Fischmesser *nt*; ~**monger** *n (Brit)* Fischhändler(in *f*) *m*; ~ **slice** *n* (Braten)wender *m*; ~ **stick** *n (US)* Fischstäbchen *nt*.

fishy ['fɪʃɪ] *adj (+er)* **(a)** *smell* Fisch-. **(b)** *(col)* verdächtig; *excuse, story* faul *(col)*.

fission ['fɪʃən] *n (Phys)* Spaltung *f*.

fissure ['fɪʃəʳ] *n* Spalt(e *f*) *m*; *(deep)* Kluft *f*.

fist [fɪst] *n* Faust *f*.

fistful ['fɪstfʊl] *n* Handvoll *f*.

fit[1] [fɪt] **1** *adj (+er)* **(a)** *(suitable)* geeignet. ~ **to eat** eßbar; **is this meat still** ~ **to eat?** kann man dieses Fleisch noch essen?; ~ **for habitation** bewohnbar; **to be** ~ **to be seen** sich sehen lassen können; **you're not** ~ **to be spoken to** du verdienst es nicht, daß man sich mit dir unterhält; **I'll do as I think** ~ ich handle, wie ich es für richtig halte; **to see** ~ **do do sth** es für angebracht halten, etw zu tun; **it is only** ~ es ist nur recht und billig; **he did not see** ~ **to apologize** er hat es nicht für nötig gehalten, sich zu entschuldigen; **to be** ~ **to drop (with tiredness)** zum Umfallen müde sein. **(b)** *(in health)* gesund; *sportsman etc* fit, in Form. **she is not yet** ~ **to travel** sie ist noch nicht reisefähig.

2 *n (of clothes)* **it is a very good** ~ es sitzt *or* paßt sehr gut; **it's a bit of a tight** ~ *(suitcase, parking)* es geht gerade (noch); **in order to ensure a smooth** ~ *(of parts)* damit es genau paßt.

3 *vt* **(a)** *(cover, sheet, nut etc)* passen auf *(+acc)*; *(key etc)* passen in *(+acc)*; *(clothes etc)* passen *(+dat)*. **this coat** ~**s you better** dieser Mantel paßt Ihnen besser; **to make a ring** ~ **sb** jdm einen Ring anpassen. **(b)** *(be suitable for) sb's plans, a theory etc* passen in *(+acc)*. **(c) to** ~ **a dress on sb** jdm ein Kleid anprobieren. **(d)** *(put on, attach)* anbringen *(to* an *+dat)*; *tyre* montieren; *(put in)* einbauen *(in* in *+acc)*; *(furnish, provide with)* ausstatten. **to** ~ **a key in the lock** einen Schlüssel ins Schloß stecken. **(e)** *(match) description, facts* entsprechen *(+dat)*; *(person)* passen auf *(+acc)*.

4 *vi (clothes, parts)* passen. **the facts don't** ~ die Fakten sind widersprüchlich; **it all** ~**s** es paßt alles zusammen.

♦ **fit in 1** *vt sep* **(a)** *(find space for)* unterbringen. **(b)** *(find time for) person* einen Termin geben *(+dat)*; *meeting* unterbringen. **(c)** *(make harmonize)* **to** ~ **sth** ~ **with sth** etw mit etw in Einklang bringen. **(d)** *(fit, put in)* einbauen.

2 *vi* **(a)** *(go into place)* hineinpassen. **(b)** *(plans, ideas, word)* passen; *(facts etc)* übereinstimmen; *(match)* dazupassen. **how does this ~ ~?** wie paßt das ins Ganze?; **I see, it all ~s ~ now** jetzt paßt alles zusammen; **does that ~ ~ with your plans?** läßt sich das mit Ihren Plänen vereinbaren?; **he wants everybody to ~ ~ with him** er will, daß sich jedermann nach ihm richtet; **he doesn't ~ ~ here/with the others** er paßt hier nicht her/nicht zu den anderen; **the new director didn't ~ ~** der neue Direktor hat nicht in die Firma gepaßt; **try to ~ ~ (with the others)** versuche, dich den anderen anzupassen.

♦ **fit out** *vt sep (for expedition)* ausrüsten; *person, ship* ausstatten.

fit[2] *n (Med, fig)* Anfall *m*. **~ of coughing/anger** Husten-/Wutanfall *m*; **in a ~ of anger** in einem Anfall von Wut; **in ~s and starts** sporadisch; **to be in ~s of laughter** sich vor Lachen biegen; **he'd have a ~** *(fig col)* er würde (ja) einen Anfall kriegen *(col)*.

fitful ['fɪtfʊl] *adj sleep* unruhig; *enthusiasm* sporadisch.

fitment ['fɪtmənt] *n (furniture)* Einrichtungsgegenstand *m*; *(of machine, car)* Zubehörteil *nt*.

fitness ['fɪtnɪs] *n* **(a)** *(health)* Gesundheit *f*; *(condition)* Fitness, Fitneß *f*. **(b)** *(suitability)* Eignung *f*; *(of remark etc)* Angemessenheit *f*.

fitted ['fɪtɪd] *adj garment* tailliert. **~ carpet** Teppichboden *m*; **~ kitchen/cupboards** Einbauküche *f*/Einbauschränke *pl*.

fitter ['fɪtə^r] *n (Tech)* Monteur *m*; *(for machines)* (Maschinen)schlosser *m*.

fitting ['fɪtɪŋ] **1** *adj (suitable)* passend. **it is not ~ for a lady ...** es schickt sich nicht für eine Dame ... **2** *n* **(a)** *(of suit etc)* Anprobe *f*. **(b)** *(part)* Zubehörteil *nt*. **~s** Ausstattung *f*; *(furniture)* Einrichtung *f*; **bathroom/office ~s** Badezimmer-/Büroeinrichtung *f*; **electrical ~s** Elektroinstallationen.

five [faɪv] **1** *adj* fünf. **2** *n* Fünf *f*; *see* **six**.

five: ~-and-ten *n (US)* billiges Kaufhaus; **~-o'clock shadow** *n nachmittäglicher Anflug von Bartstoppeln.*

fiver ['faɪvə^r] *n (col)* Fünfpfund-/Fünfdollarschein *m*.

fix [fɪks] **1** *vt* **(a)** *(make firm)* befestigen *(sth to sth* etw an/auf etw *+dat)*; *(install) new aerial, new dynamo* anbringen; *(fig) ideas, images* festsetzen; *attention* richten *(on* auf *+acc)*. **to ~ a stake in the ground** einen Pfahl im Boden verankern; **to ~ sth in one's mind** sich *(dat)* etw fest einprägen; **to ~ one's eyes on sb/sth** jdn/etw fixieren. **(b)** *(arrange)* arrangieren; *date, price, limit* festsetzen; *(agree on)* ausmachen; *tickets, taxi etc* besorgen. **(c)** *(straighten out)* regeln. **I'll ~ him** *(col)* dem werd' ich's besorgen *(col)*. **(d)** *(repair)* in Ordnung bringen; *(put in good order, adjust)* machen *(col)*. **(e)** *drink, meal* machen. **to ~ one's hair** sich frisieren. **(f)** *(col) race, fight* manipulieren. **the whole thing was ~ed** das war eine abgekartete Sache *(col)*.

2 *n* **(a)** *(col)* **to be in a ~** in der Klemme sitzen *(col)*; **to get oneself into a ~** sich *(dat)* eine schöne Suppe einbrocken *(col)*. **(b)** *(Naut)* **to take a ~ on sth** etw orten. **(c)** *(col: of drugs)* Fix *m (col)*. **to give oneself a ~** fixen *(col)*. **(d)** *(col)* **the fight was a ~** der Kampf war eine abgekartete Sache *(col)*.

♦ **fix on 1** *vt sep* festmachen *(prep obj* auf *+dat)*; *(fit on)* anbringen. **2** *vi +prep obj (decide on)* sich entscheiden für; *(US col: intend)* vorhaben.

♦ **fix up** *vt sep* **(a)** *shelves* anbringen. **(b)** *(arrange)* arrangieren; *holidays etc* festmachen. **have you got anything ~ed ~ for this evening?** haben Sie (für) heute abend schon etwas vor? **(c) to ~ sb ~ with sth** jdm etw besorgen; **when you get yourself ~ed ~ (with a room)** wenn du ein Zimmer hast.

fixation [fɪk'seɪʃən] *n (Psych)* Fixierung *f*. **a ~ about cleanliness** ein Sauberkeitsfimmel *m (col)*.

fixative ['fɪksətɪv] *n* Fixativ *nt*.

fixed [fɪkst] *adj* **(a)** fest; *idea* fix; *smile* starr. **~ assets** feste Anlagen *pl*; **~ capital** Anlagekapital *nt*; **~ price** Festpreis *m*. **(b)** *(col)* **how are you ~ for money** *etc*? wie steht's (denn) bei dir mit Geld *etc*? *(col)*; **how are you ~ for tonight?** was hast du heute abend vor?

fixedly ['fɪksɪdlɪ] *adv stare, look* starr.

fixings ['fɪksɪŋz] *npl (US Cook)* Beilagen *pl*.

fixture ['fɪkstʃə^r] *n* **(a)** *(of a building etc)* **~s** Ausstattung *f*; **~s and fittings** Anschlüsse und unbewegliches Inventar *(form)*. **(b)** *(Brit Sport)* Spiel *nt*.

fizz [fɪz] *vi (champagne etc)* perlen, sprudeln.

♦ **fizzle out** *vi (firework, enthusiasm)* verpuffen; *(plan)* im Sand verlaufen.

fizzy ['fɪzɪ] *adj (+er)* sprudelnd. **to be ~** sprudeln; **a ~ drink** eine Brause.

fjord [fjɔːd] *n* Fjord *m*.

flab [flæb] *n (col)* Speck *m*.

flabbergasted ['flæbəgɑːstɪd] *adj (col)* platt *(col)*.

flabby ['flæbɪ] *adj (+er)* schlaff; *(fat) stomach* wabbelig.

flag[1] [flæg] *n* Fahne *f*; *(small, on map, chart, for charity)* Fähnchen *nt*; *(national also, Naut)* Flagge *f*. **to keep the ~ flying** die Fahne hochhalten.

♦ **flag down** *vt sep taxi etc* anhalten.

flag[2] *vi (grow weaker etc)* nachlassen; *(person)* ermüden.

flag[3] *n (also* **~stone***)* Steinplatte *f*.

flag: ~ day *n (Brit) Tag m, an dem für einen wohltätigen Zweck gesammelt wird;* **F~ Day** *(US) 14. Juni, Gedenktag der Einführung der amerikanischen Nationalflagge;* **~pole** *n* Fahnenstange *f*.

flagrant ['fleɪgrənt] *adj* eklatant, kraß; *injustice* himmelschreiend; *disregard* unverhohlen.

flag: ~ship *n* Flaggschiff *nt*; **~stone** *n* (Stein)platte *f*; **~ stop** *n (US)* Bedarfshaltestelle *f*.

flail [fleɪl] *vt* **he ~ed his arms about** er schlug (mit den Armen) wild um sich.

flair [flɛə^r] *n (talent)* Talent *nt*; *(stylishness)* Flair *nt*.

flak [flæk] *n* Flakfeuer *nt*. **~ jacket** kugelsichere Weste.

flake [fleɪk] **1** *n (of snow, soap)* Flocke *f*; *(of paint, rust)* Splitter *m*; *(of skin)* Schuppe *f*. **2** *vi (also* **~ off***) (plaster)* abbröckeln; *(paint)* abblättern.

♦ **flake out** *vi (col) (pass out, fall over)* aus den Latschen kippen *(col)*; *(fall asleep)* einpennen *(col)*.

flaky ['fleɪkɪ] *adj (+er)* **~ pastry** Blätterteig *m*.

flamboyance [flæm'bɔɪəns] *n* Extravaganz *f*; *(of colour)* Pracht *f*.

flamboyant [flæm'bɔɪənt] *adj* extravagant; *colours* prächtig.

flame [fleɪm] *n (also fig col: sweetheart)* Flamme *f*. **the house was in ~s** das Haus stand in Flammen.

flamethrower ['fleɪm,θrəʊə^r] *n* Flammenwerfer *m*.

flaming ['fleɪmɪŋ] *adj* **(a)** *(lit)* lodernd; *(fig) passion* glühend; *row* heftig. **he was in a ~ temper** *(col)* er kochte vor Wut *(col)*. **(b)** *(Brit col!: bloody)* verdammt *(col)*.

flamingo [flə'mɪŋgəʊ] *n, pl* **-(e)s** Flamingo *m*.

flammable ['flæməbl] *adj* feuergefährlich.

flan [flæn] *n (Brit)* Kuchen *m*. **fruit ~** Obstkuchen *m*.

Flanders ['flɑːndəz] *n* Flandern *nt*.

flange [flændʒ] *n* Flansch *m*.

flank [flæŋk] **1** *n (of animal, Mil)* Flanke *f*. **2** *vt* flankieren.

flannel ['flænl] **1** *n* **(a)** Flanell *m*. **~s** *pl (trousers)* Flanellhose *f*. **(b)** *(Brit: face-~)* Waschlappen *m*. **(c)** *(Brit col: waffle)* Geschwafel *nt (col)*. **2** *adj trousers etc* Flanell-.

flannelette [ˌflænə'let] *n* Baumwollflanell *m.* ~ **sheet** Biberbettuch *nt.*

flap [flæp] **1** *n* **(a)** *(of pocket, Aviat)* Klappe *f*; *(of table)* ausziehbarer Teil. **a ~ of skin** *(Med)* ein Hautlappen *m.* **(b)** *(sound) (of sails etc)* Flattern *nt*; *(of wings)* Schlagen *nt.* **(c) to give sth a ~** *(shake out)* etw ausschütteln. **(d)** *(col)* **to get in(to) a ~** in Panik geraten; **there's a big ~ on** es herrscht große Panik. **2** *vi* **(a)** *(wings)* schlagen; *(sails, tarpaulin etc)* flattern. **his ears were ~ping** *(col)* er spitzte die Ohren. **(b)** *(col)* in Panik sein. **to start to ~** in Panik geraten; **don't ~** reg dich nicht auf! **3** *vt* **to ~ its wings** mit den Flügeln schlagen.

flare [flɛəʳ] **1** *n* **(a)** Auflodern *nt.* **(b)** *(signal)* Leuchtsignal *nt*; *(from pistol)* Leuchtrakete *f*; *(landing ~)* Leuchtfeuer *nt.* **(c)** *(Fashion)* ausgestellter Schnitt. **(d)** *(solar ~)* Sonneneruption *f.* **2** *vi* **(a)** *(match, torch)* aufleuchten. **(b)** *(nostrils)* sich blähen.

♦ **flare up** *vi* auflodern; *(fig) (person)* aufbrausen; *(fighting, epidemic)* ausbrechen.

flared [flɛəd] *adj trousers, skirt* ausgestellt.

flare: ~ path *n (Aviat)* Leuchtpfad *m*; **~ pistol** *n* Leuchtpistole *f*; **~-up** *n (sudden dispute)* (plötzlicher) Krach; *(fighting)* (plötzlicher) Ausbruch von Kämpfen.

flash [flæʃ] **1** *n* **(a)** Aufblinken *nt no pl*; *(very bright)* Aufblitzen *nt no pl*; *(of metal, jewels etc)* Blinken *nt no pl*; *(Mot)* Lichthupe *f no pl.* **to give sb a ~** *(Mot)* jdn (mit der Lichthupe) anblinken; **~ of lightning** Blitz *m.* **(b)** *(fig: news ~)* Kurzmeldung *f.* **~ of wit/inspiration** Geistesblitz *m*; **in a ~** im Nu; **as quick as a ~** blitzschnell; **a ~ in the pan** *(col)* ein Strohfeuer *nt.* **(c)** *(Phot)* Blitz(licht *nt*) *m.* **to use a ~** Blitzlicht benutzen. **(d)** *(US col: torch)* Taschenlampe *f.*

2 *vi* **(a)** aufblinken; *(very brightly)* aufblitzen; *(repeatedly: indicators etc)* blinken; *(metal, jewels, eyes)* blitzen. **(b)** *(move quickly) (vehicle)* sausen. **to ~ past** *or* **by** vorbeisausen; *(holidays etc)* vorbeifliegen. **the thought ~ed through my mind that ...** es schoß mir durch den Kopf, daß ...

3 *vt* **(a)** *light* aufblitzen lassen; *SOS, message* blinken. **to ~ one's headlights** die Lichthupe betätigen; **to ~ one's headlights at sb, to ~ sb** jdn mit der Lichthupe anblinken; **she ~ed him a look of contempt** sie blitzte ihn verächtlich an. **(b)** *(col: show off: also* **~ around***)* protzen mit; *diamond ring* blitzen lassen. **don't ~ all that money around** wedel nicht so mit dem vielen Geld herum! *(col).*

flash: ~back *n (Film)* Rückblende *f*; **~cube** *n (Phot)* Blitz(licht)würfel *m.*

flasher ['flæʃəʳ] *n (Brit col)* Exhibitionist *m.*

flash: ~ gun *n* Elektronenblitzgerät *nt*; **~ Harry** *n (col)* Lackaffe *m (pej col)*; **~light** *n* **(a)** *(Phot)* Blitzlicht *nt*; **(b)** *(esp US: torch)* Taschenlampe *f.*

flashy ['flæʃɪ] *adj (+er)* auffällig.

flask [flɑːsk] *n* Flakon *m*; *(Chem)* Glaskolben *m*; *(vacuum ~)* Thermosflasche *f.*

flat[1] [flæt] **1** *adj (+er)* **(a)** flach; *tyre, nose, feet* platt; *surface* eben; *battery* leer. **as ~ as a pancake** *(col) (tyre)* total platt; *(countryside)* total flach; *(girl)* flach wie ein Brett; **to fall ~ on one's face** auf die Nase fallen. **(b)** *(fig: dull)* fad(e); *painting, photo* kontrastarm; *colour* matt; *joke* abgedroschen; *business, market* lau; *beer, wine* schal, abgestanden. **she felt a bit ~** sie hatte zu nichts Lust; **to fall ~** *(joke)* nicht ankommen; *(play etc)* durchfallen. **(c)** *refusal, denial* glatt. **and that's ~** und damit basta. **(d)** *(Mus) instrument* zu tief (gestimmt); *voice* zu tief. **A~** As *nt.* **(e)** *(Comm)* Pauschal-. **~ rate of pay** Pauschallohn *m*; **~ rate** Pauschale *f.*

2 *adv (+er)* **(a)** *refuse* rundweg; *tell* klipp und klar. **in ten seconds ~** in sage und schreibe (nur) zehn Sekunden; **~ broke** *(Brit col)* total pleite *(col).* **(b)** *(Mus)* **to sing/play ~** zu tief singen/spielen. **(c) ~ out** *(col: asleep, drunk)* hinüber *(col)*; **to go ~ out** voll aufdrehen *(col)*; *(in car also)* Spitze fahren *(col)*; **to work** *or* **go ~ out** auf Hochtouren arbeiten; **to be lying ~ out** platt am Boden liegen.

3 *n* **(a)** *(of hand)* Fläche *f.* **(b)** *(Mus)* Erniedrigungszeichen, b *nt.* **(c)** *(Aut)* Platte(r) *m (col)*, (Reifen)panne *f.*

flat[2] *n (Brit: apartment)* Wohnung *f.*

flat: ~-chested *adj* flachbrüstig; **~fish** *n* Plattfisch *m*; **~-footed** *adj* plattfüßig; **~let** *n (Brit)* kleine Wohnung.

flatly ['flætlɪ] *adv deny, refuse* rundweg; *say* klipp und klar.

flatmate ['flætmeɪt] *n (Brit)* Mitbewohner(in *f*) *m.*

flatness ['flætnɪs] *n (of land etc)* Flachheit *f.*

flat: ~ race *n* Flachrennen *nt*; **~ season** *n* Flachrennsaison *f.*

flatten ['flætn] **1** *vt path, road, field* ebnen; *(storm etc) crops* zu Boden drücken; *trees* umwerfen; *town* dem Erdboden gleichmachen. **that'll ~ him** *(fig col)* das wird bei ihm die Luft rauslassen *(col).* **2** *vr* **to ~ oneself against sth** sich platt gegen etw drücken.

♦ **flatten out 1** *vi* eben(er) werden. **2** *vt sep path* ebnen; *metal* glatt hämmern; *map, paper, fabric* glätten.

flatter ['flætəʳ] *vt* schmeicheln *(+dat).* **it ~s your figure** das ist sehr vorteilhaft; **you can ~ yourself on being ...** Sie können sich *(dat)* etwas darauf einbilden, daß Sie ...

flatterer ['flætərəʳ] *n* Schmeichler(in *f*) *m.*

flattering ['flætərɪŋ] *adj* schmeichelhaft; *clothes* vorteilhaft.

flattery ['flætərɪ] *n* Schmeicheleien *pl.*

flatulence ['flætjʊləns] *n* Blähung(en *pl*) *f.*

flatware ['flætwɛəʳ] *n (US) (cutlery)* Besteck *nt*; *(plates etc)* Geschirr *nt.*

flaunt [flɔːnt] *vt* zur Schau stellen.

flautist ['flɔːtɪst] *n* Flötist(in *f*) *m.*

flavour, *(US)* **flavor** ['fleɪvəʳ] **1** *n (taste)* Geschmack *m*; *(flavouring)* Aroma *nt*; *(fig: atmosphere)* Atmosphäre *f.* **20 ~s** 20 Geschmackssorten. **2** *vt* Geschmack geben *(+dat).* **pineapple-~ed** mit Ananasgeschmack.

flavouring, *(US)* **flavoring** ['fleɪvərɪŋ] *n (Cook)* Aroma *nt.* **vanilla ~** Vanillearoma *nt.*

flaw [flɔː] *n* Fehler *m*; *(in diamond)* Unreinheit *f.*

flawless ['flɔːlɪs] *adj* fehlerlos; *complexion* makellos; *diamond* lupenrein.

flax [flæks] *n (Bot)* Flachs *m.*

flaxen-haired ['flæksənˌhɛəd] *adj* flachsblond.

flay [fleɪ] *vt (skin) animal* abziehen; *(whip)* auspeitschen; *(fig: criticize)* kein gutes Haar lassen an *(+dat).*

flea [fliː] *n* Floh *m.*

fleck [flek] **1** *n (of red etc)* Tupfen *m*; *(of mud, paint)* Fleck(en) *m.* **a ~ of dust** ein Stäubchen *nt.* **2** *vt* sprenkeln; *(with mud etc)* bespritzen. **blue ~ed with white** blau mit weißen Tupfen.

fled [fled] *pret, ptp of* **flee.**

fledg(e)ling ['fledʒlɪŋ] *n (bird)* Jungvogel *m.*

flee [fliː] *pret, ptp* **fled 1** *vi* fliehen, flüchten *(from* vor *+dat).* **2** *vt town, country* flüchten aus; *danger* entfliehen *(+dat).*

fleece [fliːs] **1** *n* Vlies *nt*; *(fabric) (natural)* Schaffell *nt*; *(artificial)* Webpelz *m.* **2** *vt (fig col: rob)* schröpfen.

fleecy ['fliːsɪ] *adj (+er) blanket, lining* flauschig. **~ clouds** Schäfchenwolken *pl.*

fleet [fliːt] *n* **(a)** *(Naut)* Geschwader *nt*; *(entire naval force)* Flotte *f.* **(b)** *(of buses etc)* (Fuhr)park *m.*

fleeting ['fliːtɪŋ] *adj* flüchtig; *beauty* vergänglich.

Flemish ['flemɪʃ] **1** *adj* flämisch. **2** *n* **(a) the ~** *pl* die Flamen *pl.* **(b)** *(language)* Flämisch *nt.*

flesh [fleʃ] *n* Fleisch *nt*; *(of fruit)* (Frucht)fleisch *nt.*

one's own ~ and blood sein eigen(es) Fleisch und Blut; **it was more than ~ and blood could bear** das war einfach nicht zu ertragen; **in the ~** in Person; **~pots** *pl* Fleischtöpfe *pl*; **~ wound** Fleischwunde *f*.

fleshy ['fleʃɪ] *adj (+er)* fleischig.

flew [flu:] *pret of* **fly**², **fly**³.

flex [fleks] **1** *n (Brit)* Schnur *f*; *(heavy duty)* Kabel *nt*. **2** *vt body, knees* beugen; *muscles (lit, fig)* spielen lassen.

flexibility [,fleksɪ'bɪlɪtɪ] *n see adj* Biegsamkeit *f*; Flexibilität *f*.

flexible ['fleksəbl] *adj wire* biegsam; *(fig)* flexibel. **~ working hours** gleitende Arbeitszeit.

flex(i)time ['fleks(ɪ)taɪm] *n* Gleitzeit *f*.

flick [flɪk] **1** *n (of tail)* kurzer Schlag. **hot water at the ~ of a switch** auf Knopfdruck heißes Wasser; **she gave the room a quick ~ with the duster** sie ging kurz mit dem Staublappen durch das Zimmer. **2** *vt whip* schnalzen mit; *switch* anknipsen; *dust, ash* wegschnipsen; *(with cloth)* wegwedeln. **she ~ed her hair out of her eyes** sie strich sich *(dat)* die Haare aus den Augen. **3** *vi* **the snake's tongue ~ed in and out** die Schlange züngelte.

♦ **flick off** *vt sep* wegschnipsen.

♦ **flick through** *vi +prep obj* (schnell) durchblättern.

flicker ['flɪkəʳ] **1** *vi (flame, candle)* flackern; *(TV)* flimmern; *(needle on dial)* zittern; *(eyelid)* zucken. **2** *n see vi* Flackern *nt*; Flimmern *nt*; Zittern *nt*; Zucken *nt*. **a ~ of hope** ein Hoffnungsschimmer *nt*.

flick knife *n* Klappmesser *nt*.

flight¹ [flaɪt] *n* **(a)** Flug *m*. **in ~** *(birds)* im Flug; *(Aviat)* in der Luft; **~s of fancy** geistige Höhenflüge *pl*. **(b) ~ (of stairs)** Treppe *f*; **he lives six ~s up** er wohnt sechs Treppen hoch.

flight² *n* Flucht *f*. **to put the enemy to ~** den Feind in die Flucht schlagen; **to take (to) ~** die Flucht ergreifen.

flight: ~ deck *n (Naut)* Flugdeck *nt*; *(Aviat)* Cockpit *nt*; **~ engineer** *n* Bordingenieur *m*; **~less** *adj* nicht flugfähig; **~ path** *n* Flugbahn *f*; *(of individual plane)* Flugroute *f*; **incoming/outgoing ~ path** Einflug-/Ausflugschneise *f*; **~ recorder** *n* Flugschreiber *m*.

flighty ['flaɪtɪ] *adj (+er) (fickle)* flatterhaft.

flimsy ['flɪmzɪ] *adj (+er) material* dünn; *clothing* dürftig; *house, aircraft* leicht gebaut; *excuse* fadenscheinig.

flinch [flɪntʃ] *vi* zurückzucken. **without ~ing** ohne mit der Wimper zu zucken; **to ~ from a task** vor einer Aufgabe zurückschrecken.

fling [flɪŋ] *(vb: pret, ptp* **flung)** **1** *n (fig col)* **to have a ~ at sth, to give sth a ~** etw (aus)probieren; **to have a ~ at doing sth** einen Anlauf machen, etw zu tun *(col)*; **to have a** *or* **one's ~** sich austoben. **2** *vt (lit, fig)* schleudern. **to ~ the window open/shut** das Fenster aufstoßen/zuwerfen; **the door was flung open** die Tür flog auf; **to ~ one's arms around sb's neck** jdm die Arme um den Hals werfen; **to ~ on one's coat** sich *(dat)* den Mantel überwerfen; **to ~ oneself into a job** sich auf eine Aufgabe stürzen; **to ~ oneself out of the window/into a chair** sich aus dem Fenster stürzen/sich in einen Sessel werfen.

♦ **fling away** *vt sep* wegwerfen; *(fig) money* verschwenden.

♦ **fling back** *vt sep one's head* zurückwerfen.

♦ **fling down** *vt sep (lit)* herunterwerfen.

♦ **fling out** *vt sep object* wegwerfen; *person* hinauswerfen.

flint [flɪnt] *n* Feuerstein *m*.

flip [flɪp] **1** *vt* schnippen, schnipsen. **to ~ a book open** ein Buch aufschlagen; **to ~ one's lid** *(col)* durchdrehen *(col)*. **2** *vi (col)* durchdrehen *(col)*. **3** *interj (Brit col)* verflixt *(col)*.

♦ **flip off** *vt sep* wegschnipsen; *ash from cigarette* abschnippen.

♦ **flip over 1** *vt sep* umdrehen; *pages of book* wenden. **2** *vi* sich (um)drehen.

♦ **flip through** *vi +prep obj book* durchblättern.

flip pack *n* Klappschachtel *f*.

flippancy ['flɪpənsɪ] *n* Leichtfertigkeit *f*.

flippant ['flɪpənt] *adj* leichtfertig.

flipper ['flɪpəʳ] *n* Flosse *f*.

flipping ['flɪpɪŋ] *adj, adv (Brit col)* verflixt *(col)*.

flip: ~side *n (of record)* B-Seite *f*; **~ top** *n* Klappdeckel *m*.

flirt [flɜ:t] **1** *vi* flirten; *(with idea, death)* spielen. **2** *n* **he/she is just a ~** er/sie will nur flirten.

flirtation [flɜ:'teɪʃən] *n* Flirt *m*.

flit [flɪt] **1** *vi* **(a)** *(bats, butterflies etc)* flattern; *(person, image)* huschen. **to ~ in and out** *(person)* rein- und rausflitzen. **(b)** *(Brit: move house secretly)* sich bei Nacht und Nebel davonmachen. **2** *n (Brit)* **to do a (moonlight) ~** bei Nacht und Nebel umziehen.

float [fləʊt] **1** *n* **(a)** *(on fishing-line, Tech)* Schwimmer *m*; *(on trawl net)* Korken *m*. **(b)** *(vehicle) (in procession)* Festwagen *m*; *(for deliveries)* kleiner Elektrolieferwagen. **(c)** *(ready cash: in till)* Wechselgeld *nt no indef art*; *(loan to start business)* Startkapital *nt*. **2** *vi* **(a)** *(on water)* schwimmen; *(move gently)* treiben; *(in air)* schweben. **(b)** *(Comm: currency)* floaten. **3** *vt* **(a)** *boat* zu Wasser bringen. **(b)** *(Comm, Fin) company* gründen; *shares* auf den Markt bringen; *bond issue* ausgeben; *currency* freigeben, floaten lassen.

♦ **float away** *or* **off** *vi (on water)* abtreiben; *(in air)* davonschweben; *(fig: person)* hinwegschweben.

floating ['fləʊtɪŋ] *adj raft, logs* treibend; *population* wandernd; *kidney* Wander-; *decimal point* Gleit-. **~ voter** Wechselwähler *m*.

flock [flɒk] **1** *n (of sheep, geese, Eccl)* Herde *f*; *(of birds, people)* Schar *f*. **2** *vi* in Scharen kommen. **to ~ in** hinein-/hereinströmen; **to ~ around sb** sich um jdn scharen.

floe [fləʊ] *n* Eisscholle *f*.

flog [flɒg] *vt* **(a)** prügeln; *thief, mutineer* auspeitschen. **you're ~ging a dead horse** *(col)* Sie verschwenden Ihre Zeit; **to ~ sth to death** *(fig)* etw zu Tode reiten. **(b)** *(Brit col: sell)* verkloppen *(col)*.

flogging ['flɒgɪŋ] *n* Tracht *f* Prügel; *(Jur)* Prügelstrafe *f*; *(of thief, mutineer)* Auspeitschen *nt*.

flood [flʌd] **1** *n (of water, fig)* Flut *f*. **~s** Hochwasser *nt*; **the F~** die Sintflut; **the river is in ~** der Fluß führt Hochwasser; **she had a ~ in the kitchen** ihre Küche stand unter Wasser; **she was in ~s of tears** sie war in Tränen gebadet; **bathed in a ~ of light** lichtüberflutet. **2** *vt (lit, fig, Comm)* überschwemmen. **to ~ the carburettor** den Motor absaufen lassen *(col)*; **~ed with light** lichtdurchflutet. **3** *vi* **(a)** *(river)* über die Ufer treten; *(bath etc)* überlaufen. **(b)** *(people)* strömen.

♦ **flood in** *vi (lit, fig)* hinein-/hereinströmen. **the letters just ~ed ~** wir/sie *etc* hatten eine Flut von Briefen.

♦ **flood out** *vt sep house* überfluten. **the villagers were ~ed ~** die Dorfbewohner wurden durch das Hochwasser obdachlos.

floodgate ['flʌdgeɪt] *n* Schleusentor *nt*. **to open the ~s** *(fig)* Tür und Tor öffnen *(to dat)*.

flooding ['flʌdɪŋ] *n* Überschwemmung *f*.

flood: ~light *(vb: pret, ptp* **~lit)** **1** *vt buildings* anstrahlen; *football pitch* mit Flutlicht beleuchten; **2** *n* **under ~lights** unter *or* bei Flutlicht; **~lit 1** *pret, ptp of* **~light; 2** *adj* **~lit football** Fußball bei Flutlicht; **~-tide** *n* Flut *f*.

floor [flɔ:ʳ] **1** *n* **(a)** Boden *m*; *(of room)* (Fuß)boden *m*; *(dance-~)* Tanzboden *m*. **to take the ~** *(dance)* aufs Parkett gehen; *(speak)* das Wort ergreifen; **to have the ~** *(speaker)* das Wort haben; **a question from the ~** ein Frage aus der Zuhörerschaft; *(Parl)* eine Frage aus dem Haus. **(b)** *(storey)* Stock(werk *nt*) *m*. **first** ~ *(Brit)* erster Stock; *(US)* Erdgeschoß *nt*; **on the second** ~ *(Brit)* im zweiten Stock; *(US)* im ersten Stock. **2** *vt* **(a)** *room etc* mit einem (Fuß)boden versehen. **(b)** *(knock down) opponent* zu Boden schlagen. **(c)** *(silence)* die Sprache verschlagen *(+dat)*; *(puzzle)* verblüffen; *(defeat: question, problem etc)* schaffen *(col)*.

floor: ~**board** *n* Diele *f*; ~**cloth** *n* Putzlappen *m*; ~ **polish** *n* Bohnerwachs *nt*; ~ **show** *n* Show *f (im Nachtklub oder Kabarett)*; ~**-walker** *n (Comm)* Ladenaufsicht *f*.

flop [flɒp] **1** *vi* **(a)** *(col: person: into chair etc)* sich hinplumpsen lassen. **(b)** *(col: fail)* durchfallen. **2** *n (col: failure)* Reinfall *m*; *(person)* Niete *f*.

floppy ['flɒpɪ] *adj (+er)* schlaff; *hat, ears* Schlapp-; *clothes* weit. ~ **disk** Floppy-Disk, Diskette *f*.

flora ['flɔːrə] *n* Flora *f*.

floral ['flɔːrəl] *adj arrangement* Blüten-; *fabric, dress* geblümt.

florid ['flɒrɪd] *adj* **(a)** *complexion* kräftig. **(b)** *style, writing* blumig.

florist ['flɒrɪst] *n* Florist(in *f*) *m*.

flotilla [fləʊ'tɪlə] *n* Flotille *f*.

flotsam ['flɒtsəm] *n (lit, fig)* ~ **and jetsam** Strandgut *nt*.

flounce[1] [flaʊns] *vi* **to** ~ **in/out** herein-/herausstolzieren.

flounce[2] *n (frill)* Volant *m*, Rüsche *f*.

flounder[1] ['flaʊndə^r] *n (fish)* Flunder *f*.

flounder[2] *vi* **to** ~ **through the mud/snow** sich durch den Schlamm/Schnee schleppen; **to start to** ~ *(speaker etc)* ins Schwimmen kommen.

flour ['flaʊə^r] *n* Mehl *nt*.

flourish ['flʌrɪʃ] **1** *vi (plants, person)* (prächtig) gedeihen; *(business)* blühen, florieren; *(type of literature, painting)* seine Blütezeit haben. **2** *vt (wave about)* schwenken. **3** *n* **(a)** *(curve, decoration etc)* Schnörkel *m*. **(b)** *(movement)* schwungvolle Bewegung. **(c)** *(Mus) (fanfare)* Fanfare *f*; *(decorative passage)* Verzierung *f*.

flourishing ['flʌrɪʃɪŋ] *adj plant, person* blühend *attr*; *business* florierend *attr*.

flout [flaʊt] *vt* mißachten.

flow [fləʊ] **1** *vi* **(a)** *(lit, fig)* fließen; *(prose)* flüssig sein. **where the river** ~**s into the sea** wo der Fluß ins Meer mündet; **to keep the conversation** ~**ing** das Gespräch in Gang halten; **to keep the traffic** ~**ing** den Verkehr nicht ins Stocken kommen lassen; **to** ~ **in** *(water, people, money)* hinein-/hereinströmen. **(b)** *(tide)* steigen. **2** *n* Fluß *m*. **the** ~ **of traffic/information** der Verkehrs-/Informationsfluß; **the tide is on the** ~ die Flut kommt; **the** ~ **of his style** sein flüssiger Stil; ~**chart** Flußdiagramm *nt*.

flower ['flaʊə^r] **1** *n* Blume *f*; *(blossom, fig)* Blüte *f*. **in** ~ in Blüte; **to be in the** ~ **of youth** in der Blüte seiner Jugend stehen. **2** *vi (lit, fig)* blühen.

flower: ~ **arrangement** *n* Blumengesteck *nt*; ~**bed** *n* Blumenbeet *nt*; ~ **garden** *n* Blumengarten *m*; ~**pot** *n* Blumentopf *m*; ~ **power** *n* Flowerpower *f*; ~ **show** *n* Blumenschau *f*.

flowery ['flaʊərɪ] *adj perfume, (fig) language* blumig; *dress, material* geblümt.

flown [fləʊn] *ptp of* **fly**[2], **fly**[3].

flu, 'flu [fluː] *n* Grippe *f*. **to have (the)** ~ (die *or* eine) Grippe haben.

fluctuate ['flʌktjʊeɪt] *vi* schwanken.

fluctuation [ˌflʌktjʊ'eɪʃən] *n* Schwankung *f*; *(fig: of opinions)* Schwanken *nt no pl*.

flue [fluː] *n* Rauchabzug *m*.

fluency ['fluːənsɪ] *n* Flüssigkeit *f*; *(of speaker)* Gewandtheit *f*. **because of his** ~ **in English ...** da er fließend Englisch spricht/sprach ... .

fluent ['fluːənt] *adj style* flüssig; *speaker, writer* gewandt. **to be** ~ **in Italian, to speak** ~ **Italian** fließend Italienisch sprechen; **his** ~ **Italian** sein gutes Italienisch.

fluently ['fluːəntlɪ] *adv speak a language* fließend; *express oneself* gewandt.

fluff [flʌf] **1** *n no pl (on young animals)* Flaum *m*; *(from material)* Fusseln *pl*; *(dust)* Staubflocken *pl*. **a bit of** ~ eine Staubflocke/Fussel; *(hum col)* eine Mieze *(col)*. **2** *vt* **(a)** *(also* ~ **out***) feathers* aufplustern; *pillows* aufschütteln. **(b)** *(col: make mistake in)* vermasseln *(col)*.

fluffy ['flʌfɪ] *adj (+er) bird* flaumig; *material, toy* kuschelig, weich; *hair* duftig.

fluid ['fluːɪd] **1** *adj substance, style* flüssig; *(fig) situation* ungewiß. **the situation is still** ~ die Dinge sind noch im Fluß. **2** *n* Flüssigkeit *f*.

fluke [fluːk] *n (col)* Dusel *m (col)*. **it was a (pure)** ~ das war (einfach) Dusel *(col)*.

flung [flʌŋ] *pret, ptp of* **fling.**

flunk [flʌŋk] *vt (col)* **to** ~ **German/an exam** in Deutsch/bei einer Prüfung durchsausen *(col)*.

flunk(e)y ['flʌŋkɪ] *n* Lakai *m*.

fluorescent [flʊə'resənt] *adj* Leucht-; *lighting, tube* Neon-.

fluoride ['flʊəraɪd] *n* Fluorid *nt*. ~ **toothpaste** Fluorzahnpasta *f*.

flurry ['flʌrɪ] *n* **(a)** *(of snow)* Gestöber *nt*; *(of wind)* Stoß *m*. **(b)** *(fig)* **all in a** ~ in großer Aufregung; **a** ~ **of activity** eine Hektik.

flush[1] [flʌʃ] **1** *n* **(a)** *(lavatory* ~*)* (Wasser)spülung *f*. **(b)** *(blush)* Röte *f*. **hot** ~**es** *(Med)* fliegende Hitze. **(c)** *(of beauty, youth)* Blüte *f*; *(of excitement)* Welle *f*. **in the (first)** ~ **of victory** im (ersten) Siegestaumel; **in the first** ~ **of youth** in der ersten Jugendblüte. **2** *vi (person, face)* rot werden *(with* vor *+dat)*. **3** *vt* spülen. **to** ~ **the lavatory** spülen; **to** ~ **sth down the lavatory** etw die Toilette hinunterspülen.

♦ **flush away** *vt sep* wegspülen.

♦ **flush out** *vt sep bottle* ausspülen; *dirt* wegspülen; *birds, spies* aufstöbern.

flush[2] *adj pred* **(a)** bündig. ~ **against the wall** direkt an die/der Wand. **(b)** *(col: with money)* **to be** ~ gut bei Kasse sein *(col)*.

flush[3] *n (Cards)* Flöte, Sequenz *f*; *(Poker)* Flush *m*.

flushed [flʌʃt] *adj person* rot *(with* vor*)*.

fluster ['flʌstə^r] **1** *vt* nervös machen; *(confuse)* durcheinanderbringen. **she got** ~**ed** sie wurde nervös; das brachte sie durcheinander. **2** *n* **in a (real)** ~ (ganz) nervös; *(confused)* (völlig) durcheinander.

flute [fluːt] *n* Querflöte *f*.

flutter ['flʌtə^r] **1** *vi (flag, wings, heart)* flattern. **to** ~ **away** davonflattern. **2** *vt (birds) wings* flattern mit. **to** ~ **one's eyelashes at sb** mit den Wimpern klimpern. **3** *n* Flattern *nt (also Med)*. **(all) in** *or* **of a** ~ *(fig)* in heller Aufregung; **to have a** ~ *(Brit col: gamble)* sein Glück (beim Wetten) versuchen.

flux [flʌks] *n* **in a state of** ~ im Fluß.

fly[1] [flaɪ] *n* Fliege *f*. **he wouldn't hurt a** ~ er könnte keiner Fliege etwas zuleide tun; **he's the** ~ **in the ointment** er ist Sand im Getriebe; **there are no flies on him** *(col)* ihn legt man nicht so leicht rein *(col)*.

fly[2] *(vb: pret* **flew,** *ptp* **flown***)* **1** *vi* **(a)** fliegen. **(b)** *(move quickly) (time)* (ver)fliegen; *(people)* sausen *(col)*; *(sparks)* stieben, fliegen. **time flies!** wie die Zeit vergeht!; **to** ~ **past** *(car, person)* vorbeisausen *(col)*; **I must** ~ ich muß jetzt wirklich sausen *(col)*; **the door flew open** die Tür flog auf; **to** ~ **into a rage** einen Wutanfall bekommen; **to (let)** ~ **at sb** *(col)* auf jdn losgehen; **he really let** ~ er legte kräftig los; **to knock sb/sth** ~**ing** jdn/etw umwerfen. **(c)** *(flag)* wehen. **2** *vt aircraft, route* fliegen; *kite* steigen lassen; *Atlantic* überfliegen; *flag* führen.

♦ **fly away** *vi (person, plane, bird)* wegfliegen; *(fig: cares)* schwinden.

♦ **fly in** *vti sep* einfliegen. **she flew** ~ **from New York** sie ist mit dem Flugzeug aus New York angekommen.

♦**fly off** *vi* **(a)** *(plane, person)* abfliegen; *(bird)* wegfliegen. **(b)** *(come off: hat, lid etc)* wegfliegen; *(button)* abspringen.

♦**fly out 1** *vi* ausfliegen. **I'll ~ ~ and come back by ship** ich werde hin fliegen und mit dem Schiff zurückkommen. **2** *vt sep (to an area)* hinfliegen; *(out of an area)* ausfliegen.

fly[3] *pret* **flew,** *ptp* **flown 1** *vi (flee)* fliehen. **to ~ for one's life** um sein Leben laufen/fahren *etc.* **2** *vt* **to ~ the country** aus dem Land flüchten.

fly[4] *n (on trousers: also* **flies***)* (Hosen)schlitz *m.*

fly[5] *adj (col: crafty)* clever, gerissen.

fly-away ['flaɪəweɪ] *adj hair* fliegend.

flying ['flaɪɪŋ] *n* Fliegen *nt.* **he likes ~** er fliegt gerne.

flying: ~ colours *(Brit) or* **colors** *(US) npl* **to come through/pass** *etc* **with ~ colours** glänzend abschneiden; **~ fish** *n* fliegender Fisch; **~ jump** *n* **to take a ~ jump** einen großen Satz machen; **~ saucer** *n* fliegende Untertasse; **~ start** *n (Sport)* **to get off to a ~ start** *(Sport)* hervorragend wegkommen; *(fig)* einen glänzenden Start haben; **~-time** *n* Flugzeit *f*; **~ visit** *n* Blitzbesuch *m.*

fly: ~leaf *n* Vorsatzblatt *nt*; **~over** *n* Überführung *f*; **~paper** *n* Fliegenfänger *m*; **~-past** *n* Luftparade *f*; **~sheet** *n (entrance)* Überdach *nt*; *(outer tent)* Überzelt *nt*; **~-swat(ter)** *n* Fliegenklatsche *f*; **~weight** *n (Boxing)* Fliegengewicht *nt*; **~wheel** *n* Schwungrad *nt.*

FM = **frequency modulation** UKW.

foal [fəʊl] *n* Fohlen, Füllen *nt.*

foam [fəʊm] **1** *n* Schaum *m.* **2** *vi* schäumen. **to ~ at the mouth** *(lit)* Schaum vorm Mund/Maul haben; *(fig: person)* schäumen vor Wut.

foam rubber *n* Schaumgummi *m.*

fob ['efəʊbiː] = **free on board.**

♦**fob off** [fɒb'ɒf] *vt sep* **to ~ sb ~ (with promises)** jdn (mit leeren Versprechungen) abspeisen; **to ~ sb ~ with sth** jdm etw andrehen.

focal ['fəʊkəl] *adj* **~ length** Brennweite *f*; **~ point** *(lit, fig)* Brennpunkt *m.*

fo'c'sle ['fəʊksl] *n* = **forecastle** Vorschiff *nt.*

focus ['fəʊkəs] **1** *n, pl* **foci** ['fəʊkɪ] *(Phys, Math, fig)* Brennpunkt *m*; *(of earthquake, Med)* Herd *m.* **in ~** *camera* (scharf) eingestellt; *photo* scharf; **out of ~** *(lit) camera* unscharf eingestellt; *photo* unscharf; **he was the ~ of attention** er stand im Mittelpunkt. **2** *vt instrument* einstellen *(on* auf *+acc)*; *(fig) one's efforts* konzentrieren *(on* auf *+acc)*; **to ~ one's attention on sth** sich auf etw *(acc)* konzentrieren. **3** *vi* **to ~ on sth** sich auf etw *(acc)* konzentrieren; **his eyes ~ed on the book** sein Blick richtete sich auf das Buch; **I can't ~ properly** ich kann nicht mehr klar sehen.

fodder ['fɒdə^r] *n (lit, fig)* Futter *nt.*

foe [fəʊ] *n (liter)* Feind, Widersacher *(geh) m.*

foetal, *(esp US)* **fetal** ['fiːtl] *adj* fötal.

foetus, *(esp US)* **fetus** ['fiːtəs] *n* Fötus *m.*

fog [fɒg] *n* Nebel *m.*

fogbound ['fɒgbaʊnd] *adj ship, plane* durch Nebel festgehalten; *airport* wegen Nebel(s) geschlossen.

fogey ['fəʊgɪ] *n (col)* **old ~** alter Kauz *(col).*

foggy ['fɒgɪ] *adj (+er)* neb(e)lig. **I haven't the foggiest (idea)** *(col)* ich habe keinen blassen Schimmer *(col).*

fog: ~horn *n (Naut)* Nebelhorn *nt*; **~ light** *n* Nebellampe *f.*

foible ['fɔɪbl] *n* Eigenheit *f.*

foil[1] [fɔɪl] *n (metal)* Folie *f.* **to act as a ~ to sb** *(fig)* jdm als Hintergrund dienen.

foil[2] *n (Fencing)* Florett *nt.*

foil[3] *vt plans* durchkreuzen; *attempts* vereiteln; *person* einen Strich durch die Rechnung machen *(+dat).*

foist [fɔɪst] *vt* **to ~ sth (off) on sb** *goods* jdm etw andrehen; **to ~ oneself on(to) sb** sich jdm aufdrängen.

fold[1] [fəʊld] **1** *n* Falte *f.* **2** *vt paper* (zusammen)falten; *blanket* zusammenlegen. **to ~ sth in two/four** etw falten/zweimal falten; **to ~ one's arms** die Arme verschränken; **he ~ed the book in some paper** er schlug das Buch in Papier ein. **3** *vi* **(a)** *(chair, table)* sich zusammenklappen lassen. **(b)** = **fold up.**

♦**fold away 1** *vi (table, bed)* zusammenklappbar sein. **2** *vt sep table, bed* zusammenklappen; *clothes* zusammenlegen.

♦**fold up 1** *vi (business)* eingehen *(col)*; *(play)* abgesetzt werden. **2** *vt sep paper* zusammenfalten.

fold[2] *n (pen)* Pferch *m.*

foldaway ['fəʊldəweɪ] *adj attr* zusammenklappbar.

folder ['fəʊldə^r] *n* **(a)** *(for papers)* Aktenmappe *f.* **(b)** *(brochure)* Informationsblatt *nt.*

folding ['fəʊldɪŋ] *adj attr* **~ bed** Klappbett *nt*; **~ chair** Klappstuhl *m*; **~ doors** Falttür *f.*

foliage ['fəʊlɪɪdʒ] *n* Blätter *pl*; *(of tree)* Laub *nt.*

folk [fəʊk] *npl* Leute *pl.* **the young/old ~** die Jungen/Alten; **my ~s** *(col)* meine Leute *(col).*

folk: ~-dance *n* Volkstanz *m*; **~lore** *n* Folklore *f*; **~-music** *n* Volksmusik *f*; *(modern)* Folk *m*; **~-singer** *n* Sänger(in *f*) *m* von Volksliedern/Folksongs; **~-song** *n* Volkslied *nt*; *(modern)* Folksong *m.*

follow ['fɒləʊ] **1** *vt (also understand)* folgen *(+dat)*; *(pursue also)* verfolgen; *advice, instructions also* befolgen; *profession* ausüben; *career, serial, speech, news* verfolgen; *athletics etc* sich interessieren für. **he ~ed me about** er folgte mir überall hin; **he ~ed me out** er folgte mir nach draußen; **we're being ~ed** wir werden verfolgt; **to have sb ~ed** jdn verfolgen lassen; **the reaction that ~ed this** die darauf folgende Reaktion; **do you ~ me?** können Sie mir folgen?; **which team do you ~?** für welchen Verein sind Sie?

2 *vi* **(a)** folgen *(on sth* auf etw acc*)*. **as ~s** wie folgt; **what is there to ~?** was gibt es anschließend?; **what ~s** das Folgende. **(b)** *(results, deduction)* folgen *(from* aus*)*. **it doesn't ~ that ...** daraus folgt nicht, daß ...; **that doesn't ~** nicht unbedingt! **(c)** *(understand)* folgen. **I don't ~** das verstehe ich nicht.

♦**follow on** *vi (come after)* später kommen.

♦**follow through 1** *vt sep argument* durchdenken; *idea, plan* (zu Ende) verfolgen. **2** *vi (Sport)* durchschwingen.

♦**follow up** *vt sep* **(a)** *(take further action on) request* nachgehen *(+dat)*; *offer, suggestion* aufgreifen. **(b)** *(investigate further)* sich näher befassen mit; *matter* weiterverfolgen; *rumour* nachgehen *(+dat)*. **(c)** *(reinforce) success, victory* fortsetzen; *advantage* ausnutzen. **you should ~ ~ the letter with a phonecall** zusätzlich zu dem Brief sollten Sie noch anrufen.

follower ['fɒləʊə^r] *n (fan etc)* Anhänger(in *f*) *m.*

following ['fɒləʊɪŋ] **1** *adj* **(a)** folgend. **the ~ day** der (darauf)folgende Tag. **(b) a ~ wind** Rückenwind *m.* **2** *n* **(a)** *(followers)* Anhängerschaft *f.* **(b) he said the ~** er sagte folgendes.

follow-up ['fɒləʊˌʌp] *n* Weiterverfolgen *nt*; *(event, programme etc coming after)* Fortsetzung *f (to gen)*. **what was the ~ to this?** was folgte darauf?

follow-up: ~ advertising *n* Nachfaßwerbung *f*; **~ care** *n (Med)* Nachbehandlung *f*; **~ letter** *n* Nachfaßschreiben *nt.*

folly ['fɒlɪ] *n* Torheit *f.*

fond [fɒnd] *adj (+er)* **(a) to be ~ of sb** jdn gern mögen; **to be ~ of sth** etw mögen; **to be ~ of doing sth** etw gern tun. **(b)** *(loving)* liebevoll; *hope* sehnsüchtig. **(c)** *(vain) illusion* verloren; *hope* kühn.

fondant ['fɒndənt] *n* Fondant *m.*

fondle ['fɒndl] *vt* (zärtlich) spielen mit; *(stroke)* streicheln; *person* schmusen mit.

fondly ['fɒndlɪ] *adv look etc* liebevoll. **he ~ believed that ...** er hoffte vergebens, daß ...

fondness ['fɒndnɪs] *n* Begeisterung *f*; *(for people)* Zuneigung *f (for* zu); *(for food, place)* Vorliebe *f (for* für).

font [fɒnt] *n* **(a)** *(Eccl)* Taufstein *m*. **(b)** *(Typ)* Schrift *f*.

food [fu:d] *n* Essen *nt*; *(for animals)* Futter *nt*; *(nourishment)* Nahrung *f*; *(~stuff)* Nahrungsmittel *nt*; *(groceries)* Lebensmittel *pl*. **canned ~s** Konserven *pl*; **I haven't any ~ in the house** ich habe nichts zu essen im Haus; **to be off one's ~** keinen Appetit haben; **~ for thought** *(fig)* Stoff *m* zum Nachdenken.

food: ~ poisoning *n* Lebensmittelvergiftung *f*; **~ shop** *(Brit) or* **store** *n* Lebensmittelgeschäft *nt*; **~stuff** *n* Nahrungsmittel *nt*.

fool [fu:l] **1** *n* Dummkopf, Narr *(also jester) m*. **don't be a ~!** sei nicht (so) dumm!; **some ~ of a civil servant** irgend so ein blöder Beamter; **I was a ~ not to realize** wie konnte ich nur so dumm sein und das nicht merken; **to play** *or* **act the ~** herumalbern; **to make a ~ of sb** jdn lächerlich machen; **he made a ~ of himself in the discussion** er hat sich in der Diskussion blamiert; **to live in a ~'s paradise** in einem Traumland leben. **2** *vi* herumalbern. **I was only ~ing** das war doch nur Spaß. **3** *vt (trick)* hereinlegen *(col)*; *(disguise, phoney accent etc)* täuschen. **you had me ~ed** ich habe das tatsächlich geglaubt; **they ~ed him into believing that ...** sie haben ihm weisgemacht, daß ...; **you could have ~ed me!** *(iro)* was du nicht sagst!

♦ **fool about** *or* **around** *vi* **(a)** *(waste time)* herumtrödeln. **(b)** *(play the fool)* herumalbern. **(c) to ~ ~ with sth** mit etw Blödsinn machen.

foolhardy ['fu:l,hɑ:dɪ] *adj* tollkühn.

foolish ['fu:lɪʃ] *adj* dumm. **he's afraid of looking ~** er will sich nicht blamieren.

foolishly ['fu:lɪʃlɪ] *adv* **~, I assumed ...** törichterweise habe ich angenommen, ...

foolishness ['fu:lɪʃnɪs] *n* Dummheit *f*.

foolproof ['fu:lpru:f] *adj* narrensicher.

foolscap ['fu:lskæp] *n* ≈ Kanzleipapier *nt*.

foot [fʊt] **1** *n, pl* **feet (a)** *(also bottom, measure)* Fuß *m*. **to be on one's feet** *(lit, fig)* auf den Beinen sein; **to put sb (back) on his feet (again)** *(lit,fig)* jdm (wieder) auf die Beine helfen; **on ~** zu Fuß; **the first time he set ~ in the office** als er das erste Mal das Büro betrat; **to rise/jump to one's feet** aufstehen/aufspringen; **to put one's feet up** *(lit)* die Füße hochlegen; *(fig)* es sich *(dat)* bequem machen. **(b)** *(fig phrases)* **he never puts a ~ wrong** er macht nie einen Fehler; **to catch sb on the wrong ~** jdn überrumpeln; **to put one's ~ down** *(act with decision)* ein Machtwort sprechen; *(forbid, refuse)* es strikt verbieten; *(Aut)* Gas geben; **to put one's ~ in it** ins Fettnäpfchen treten *(col)*; **to put one's best ~ forward** *(hurry)* die Beine unter den Arm nehmen; *(do one's best)* sich anstrengen; **to find one's feet** sich eingewöhnen; **to fall on one's feet** auf die Füße fallen; **to have one ~ in the grave** mit einem Bein im Grabe stehen; **to get/be under sb's feet** jdm in Wege stehen; **to get off on the right/wrong ~** einen guten/schlechten Start haben; **to stand on one's own feet** auf eigenen Füßen stehen.

2 *vt bill* bezahlen.

foot-and-mouth (disease) ['fʊtən'maʊθ(dɪ,zi:z)] *n* Maul- und Klauenseuche *f*.

football ['fʊtbɔ:l] *n (also ball)* Fußball *m*. **~ pools** Fußballtoto *nt*.

footballer ['fʊtbɔ:lə[r]] *n* Fußball(spiel)er *m*.

foot: ~bridge *n* Fußgängerbrücke *f*; **~hills** *npl* (Gebirgs)ausläufer *pl*; **~hold** *n* Halt *m*; *(fig)* sichere (Ausgangs)position.

footing ['fʊtɪŋ] *n* **(a)** *(lit)* Halt *m*. **to lose one's ~** den Halt verlieren; **to miss one's ~** danebentreten. **(b)** *(fig)* Basis *f*; *(relationship)* Beziehung *f*. **on an equal ~ (with each other)** auf gleicher Basis.

footlights ['fʊtlaɪts] *npl (Theat)* Rampenlicht *nt*.

footling ['fu:tlɪŋ] *adj* albern, läppisch.

foot: ~loose *adj* **~loose and fancy-free** frei und ungebunden; **~man** *n* Lakai *m*; **~mark** *n* Fußabdruck *m*; **~note** *n* Fußnote *f*; **~path** *n* Fußweg *m*; *(Brit: pavement)* Bürgersteig *m*; **~print** *n* Fußabdruck *m*; **~prints** *npl* Fußspuren *pl*; **~step** *n* Schritt *m*; **to follow in sb's ~steps** *(fig)* in jds Fußstapfen treten; **~wear** *n* Schuhwerk *nt*; **~work** *n no pl (Boxing)* Beinarbeit *f*.

for [fɔ:[r]] **1** *prep* **(a)** für. **what ~?** wofür?, wozu?; **what is this knife ~?** wozu dient dieses Messer?; **he does it ~ pleasure** er macht es zum Vergnügen; **what did you do that ~?** warum haben Sie das getan?; **a room ~ working in** ein Zimmer zum Arbeiten; **this will do ~ a hammer** das kann man als Hammer nehmen; **the train ~ Stuttgart** der Zug nach Stuttgart; **to leave ~ the USA** nach den USA abreisen; **he swam ~ the shore** er schwamm in Richtung Küste; **to make ~ home** sich auf den Heimweg machen; **to do sth ~ oneself** etw alleine tun; **you're ~ it!** *(col)* jetzt bist du dran! *(col)*; **oh ~ a cup of tea!** jetzt eine Tasse Tee, das wäre schön!

(b) *(indicating suitability)* **it's not ~ you to blame him** Sie haben kein Recht, ihm die Schuld zu geben; **it's not ~ me to say** es steht mir nicht zu, mich dazu zu äußern.

(c) *(representing, instead of)* **I'll see her ~ you if you like** wenn Sie wollen, gehe ich an Ihrer Stelle zu ihr; **to act ~ sb** für jdn handeln; **D ~ Daniel** D wie Daniel.

(d) *(in defence, in favour of)* für. **are you ~ or against it?** sind Sie dafür oder dagegen?; **I'm all ~ it** ich bin ganz dafür.

(e) *(with regard to)* **anxious ~ sb** um jdn besorgt; **~ my part** was mich betrifft; **as ~ him/that** was ihn/das betrifft; **young ~ a president** jung für einen Präsidenten; **it's all right** *or* **all very well ~ you (to talk)** Sie haben gut reden.

(f) *(because of)* **~ this reason** aus diesem Grund; **he did it ~ fear of being left** er tat es aus Angst, zurückgelassen zu werden; **he is famous ~ his big nose** er ist wegen seiner großen Nase berühmt; **to shout ~ joy** vor Freude jauchzen; **to go to prison ~ theft** wegen Diebstahls ins Gefängnis wandern; **to choose sb ~ his ability** jdn wegen seiner Fähigkeiten wählen; **if it were not ~ him** wenn er nicht wäre; **do it ~ me** tu es für mich.

(g) *(in spite of)* trotz *(+gen or (col) +dat)*. **~ all his wealth** trotz all seines Reichtums; **~ all that** trotz allem.

(h) *(in contrast)* **~ one man who would do it there are ten who wouldn't** auf einen, der es tun würde, kommen zehn, die es nicht tun würden.

(i) *(in time)* seit; *(with future tense)* für. **I have not seen her ~ two years** ich habe sie seit zwei Jahren nicht gesehen; **he's been here ~ ten days** er ist seit zehn Tagen hier; **then I did not see her ~ two years** dann habe ich sie zwei Jahre lang nicht gesehen; **he walked ~ two hours** er ist zwei Stunden lang marschiert; **I am going away ~ a few days** ich werde (für) ein paar Tage wegfahren; **he won't be back ~ a week** er wird erst in einer Woche zurück sein; **can you get it done ~ Monday/this time next week?** können Sie es bis Montag/bis in einer Woche fertig haben?; **~ a while/time** (für) eine Weile/einige Zeit.

(j) *(distance)* **the road is lined with trees ~ two miles** die Straße ist auf zwei Meilen mit Bäumen gesäumt; **we walked ~ two miles** wir sind zwei Meilen weit gelaufen.

(k) *(with infin clauses)* ~ **this to be possible** damit dies möglich wird/wurde; **I brought it ~ you to see** ich habe es mitgebracht, damit Sie es sich *(dat)* ansehen können; **the best would be ~ you to go** das beste wäre, wenn Sie weggingen; **their one hope is ~ him to return** ihre einzige Hoffnung ist, daß er zurückkommt.

2 *conj* denn. ~ **it was he who ...** denn es war er, der ...

forage ['fɒrɪdʒ] *vi* nach Futter suchen; *(fig: rummage)* herumwühlen *(for* nach*)*. **~-cap** Schiffchen *nt*.

foray ['fɒreɪ] *n* (Raub)überfall *m*; *(fig)* Exkurs *m (into* in *+acc)*.

forbad(e) [fɔː'bæd] *pret of* **forbid.**

forbearance [fɔː'bɛərəns] *n* Nachsicht *f*.

forbid [fə'bɪd] *pret* **forbad(e),** *ptp* **forbidden** [fə'bɪdn] *vt* verbieten. **to ~ sb to do sth** jdm verbieten, etw zu tun; **smoking ~den** Rauchen verboten; **it is ~den to ...** es ist verboten, zu ...

forbidding [fə'bɪdɪŋ] *adj rocks, cliffs* bedrohlich; *sky* düster; *prospect* grauenhaft; *look, person* streng.

force [fɔːs] **1** *n* **(a)** *no pl (physical strength, power)* Kraft *f*; *(of blow, of impact)* Wucht *f*; *(physical coercion)* Gewalt *f*. **to resort to ~** Gewalt anwenden; **by ~** gewaltsam; **a ~ 5 wind** Windstärke 5; **they came in ~** sie kamen in großer Zahl; **~s of Nature** Naturgewalten *pl*; **there are various ~s at work here** hier sind verschiedene Kräfte am Werk; **to come into/be in ~** *(law etc)* in Kraft treten/sein. **(b)** *no pl (of argument)* Überzeugungskraft *f*; *(of music, phrase)* Eindringlichkeit *f*; *(of character)* Stärke *f*; *(of words, habit)* Macht *f*. **(c)** *(body of men)* **the ~s** *(Mil)* die Streitkräfte *pl*; **work ~** Arbeitskräfte *pl*; **sales ~** Verkaufspersonal *nt*; **the (police) ~** die Polizei; **to join** *or* **combine ~s** sich zusammentun.

2 *vt* **(a)** *(compel)* zwingen. **to ~ sb/oneself to do sth** jdn/sich zwingen, etw zu tun; **he was ~d to resign** er wurde gezwungen zurückzutreten; *(felt obliged to)* er sah sich gezwungen zurückzutreten; **to ~ sth (up)on sb** *present, one's company* jdm etw aufdrängen; *conditions* jdm etw auferlegen; *decision, war* jdm etw aufzwingen; **I don't want to ~ myself on you** ich möchte mich Ihnen nicht aufdrängen.

(b) *(break open) lock* aufbrechen. **to ~ an entry** sich *(dat)* gewaltsam Zutritt verschaffen.

(c) *(push, squeeze)* **to ~ books into a box** Bücher in eine Kiste zwängen; **if it won't go in, don't ~ it** versuche es nicht mit Gewalt, wenn es nicht hineinpaßt; **to ~ one's way through** sich gewaltsam einen Weg bahnen; **to ~ a car off the road** ein Auto von der Fahrbahn drängen.

(d) to ~ a smile gezwungen lächeln; **to ~ a confession out of sb** ein Geständnis von jdm erzwingen.

♦**force back** *vt sep* zurückdrängen; *tear* unterdrücken.

♦**force down** *vt sep food* hinunterquälen; *aeroplane* zur Landung zwingen.

forced [fɔːst] *adj smile, translation* gezwungen. **~ landing** Notlandung *f*; **~ march** Gewaltmarsch *m*.

force-feed ['fɔːsfiːd] *vt* zwangsernähren.

forceful ['fɔːsfʊl] *adj person* energisch; *character* stark; *language, style* eindringlich; *argument* wirkungsvoll.

forceps ['fɔːseps] *npl (also* **pair of ~***)* Zange *f*.

forcible ['fɔːsəbl] *adj* **(a)** *entry* gewaltsam. **(b)** *language, style* eindringlich; *argument, reason* zwingend.

ford [fɔːd] **1** *n* Furt *f*. **2** *vt* durchqueren.

fore [fɔːʳ] **1** *n* **to the ~** im Vordergrund; **to come to the ~** ins Blickfeld geraten. **2** *adv (Naut)* **~ and aft** längsschiffs.

fore: ~arm *n* Unterarm *m*; **~bear** *n* Vorfahr(in *f*), Ahn(e *f*) *m*; **~boding** [fɔː'bəʊdɪŋ] *n (presentiment)* (Vor)ahnung *f*; **~cast 1** *vt* vorhersagen; **2** *n* Vorhersage *f*; **~close** *vi (on loan, mortgage)* ein Darlehen/eine Hypothek kündigen; **to ~close on sth** etw kündigen; **~court** *n* Vorhof *m*; **~father** *n* Ahn, Vorfahr *m*; **~finger** *n* Zeigefinger *m*; **~front** *n* **in the ~ of** im Vorfeld *(+gen)*; **~go** *pret* **~went,** *ptp* **~gone** verzichten auf *(+acc)*; **~going** *adj* vorhergehend; **~gone 1** *ptp of* **~go; 2** *adj*: **it was a ~gone conclusion** es stand von vornherein fest; **~ground** *n* Vordergrund *m*; **in the ~ground** im Vordergrund; **~hand** *n (Sport)* Vorhand *f*; **~head** ['fɔːhed, 'fɒrɪd] *n* Stirn *f*.

foreign ['fɒrən] *adj* ausländisch; *customs, appearance* fremdartig; *policy, trade* Außen-. **is he ~?** ist er Ausländer?; **~ countries** das Ausland; **lying is ~ to him** Lügen ist ihm fremd.

foreign: ~ affairs *npl* Außenpolitik *f*; **~ currency** *n* Devisen *pl*.

foreigner ['fɒrənəʳ] *n* Ausländer(in *f*) *m*.

foreign: ~ exchange *n* Devisen *pl*; **~ exchange market** *n* Devisenmarkt *m*; **~ language** *n* Fremdsprache *f*; **~ legion** *n* Fremdenlegion *f*; **F~ Minister** *n* Außenminister *m*; **F~ Office** *n (Brit)* Außenministerium *nt*; **F~ Secretary** *n (Brit)* Außenminister *m*.

fore: ~ leg *n* Vorderbein *nt*; **~man** [-mən] *n*, *pl* **~men** [-mən] *(in factory)* Vorarbeiter *m*; *(on building site)* Polier *m*; *(Jur: of jury)* Obmann *m*; **~most** *adj (lit)* erste(r, s), vorderste(r, s); *(fig) writer, politician etc* führend; **~name** *n* Vorname *m*.

forensic [fə'rensɪk] *adj* forensisch. **~ science** Kriminaltechnik *f*; **~ medicine** Gerichtsmedizin *f*; **~ expert** Spurensicherungsexperte *m*.

fore: ~play *n* Vorspiel *nt*; **~runner** *n* Vorläufer *m*; **~see** *pret* **~saw,** *ptp* **~seen** *vt* vorhersehen; **~seeable** *adj* voraussehbar; **in the ~seeable future** in absehbarer Zeit; **~shadow** *vt* ahnen lassen, andeuten; **~shorten** *vt* perspektivisch zeichnen/fotografieren; **this has a ~shortening effect** das läßt es kürzer erscheinen; **~sight** *n* Weitblick *m*; **~skin** *n* Vorhaut *f*.

forest ['fɒrɪst] *n* Wald *m*. **~ ranger** *(US)* Förster *m*.

forestall [fɔː'stɔːl] *vt sb, rival* zuvorkommen *(+dat)*; *objection* vorwegnehmen.

forester ['fɒrɪstəʳ] *n* Förster *m*.

forestry ['fɒrɪstrɪ] *n* Forstwirtschaft *f*.

fore: ~taste *n* Vorgeschmack *m*; **~tell** *pret, ptp* **~told** *vt* vorhersagen; **~thought** *n* Vorbedacht *m*.

forever [fər'evəʳ] *adv* **(a)** *(constantly)* ständig, ewig *(col)*. **(b)** *(eternally)* ewig.

fore: ~warn *vt* vorher warnen; **~warned is forearmed** *(Prov)* Gefahr erkannt, Gefahr gebannt *(prov)*; **~went** *pret of* **~go; ~woman** *n*, *pl* **~women** Vorarbeiterin *f*; **~word** *n* Vorwort *nt*.

forfeit ['fɔːfɪt] **1** *vt (esp Jur)* verwirken; *(fig) health, sb's respect* einbüßen. **2** *n (in game)* Pfand *nt*.

forgave [fə'geɪv] *pret of* **forgive.**

forge [fɔːdʒ] **1** *n (workshop)* Schmiede *f*; *(furnace)* Esse *f*. **2** *vt* **(a)** *metal, (fig) friendship* schmieden. **(b)** *signature, banknote* fälschen. **3** *vi* **to ~ ahead** vorwärtskommen; *(in one's career)* seinen Weg machen; *(Sport)* vorstoßen.

forger ['fɔːdʒəʳ] *n* Fälscher(in *f*) *m*.

forgery ['fɔːdʒərɪ] *n (act, thing)* Fälschung *f*.

forget [fə'get] *pret* **forgot,** *ptp* **forgotten 1** *vt* vergessen; *ability, language* verlernen. **never to be forgotten** unvergeßlich; **and don't you ~ it!** und daß du das ja nicht vergißt!; **I ~ his name** sein Name ist mir entfallen; **I ~ what I wanted to say** es ist mir entfallen, was ich sagen wollte; **to ~ past quarrels** vergangene Streitigkeiten ruhen lassen; **~ it!** schon gut!; **you might as well ~ it** *(col)* das kannst du vergessen *(col)*. **2** *vi* es vergessen. **don't ~!** vergiß es nicht!

♦**forget about** *vi +prep obj* vergessen.

forgetful [fə'getfʊl] *adj (absent-minded)* vergeßlich; *(of one's duties etc)* nachlässig *(of* gegenüber*)*.
forget-me-not [fə'getmɪnɒt] *n* Vergißmeinnicht *nt*.
forgive [fə'gɪv] *pret* **forgave,** *ptp* **forgiven** [fə'gɪvn] *vti sth* verzeihen, vergeben *(also Eccl)*. **to ~ sb for sth** jdm etw verzeihen *or* vergeben; **to ~ sb for doing sth** jdm verzeihen *or* vergeben, daß er etw getan hat; **~ me, but ...** Entschuldigung, aber ...
forgiveness [fə'gɪvnɪs] *n, no pl (willingness to forgive)* Versöhnlichkeit *f*. **to ask/beg (sb's) ~** (jdn) um Verzeihung *or* Vergebung *(esp Eccl)* bitten.
forgiving [fə'gɪvɪŋ] *adj* versöhnlich.
forgot [fə'gɒt] *pret of* **forget.**
forgotten [fə'gɒtn] *ptp of* **forget.**
fork [fɔːk] **1** *n (implement)* Gabel *f*; *(in road)* Gabelung *f*. **2** *vi (roads, branches)* sich gabeln. **to ~ right** *(road)* nach rechts abzweigen; *(driver)* nach rechts abbiegen.
♦**fork out** *vti sep (col: pay)* blechen *(col)*.
forked [fɔːkt] *adj branch, road, tail* gegabelt; *lightning* zickzackförmig; *tongue* gespalten.
fork-lift truck [,fɔːklɪft'trʌk] *n* Gabelstapler *m*.
forlorn [fə'lɔːn] *adj (deserted)* verlassen; *person* einsam und verlassen; *attempt* verzweifelt; *hope* schwach.
form [fɔːm] **1** *n* **(a)** Form *f*. **~ of government** Regierungsform *f*; **a human ~** eine menschliche Gestalt; **in the ~ of** in Form von *or +gen; (with reference to people)* in Gestalt von *or +gen;* **to take ~** *(lit, fig)* Form annehmen; **to be in fine/good ~** gut in Form sein, in guter Form sein; **to be on/off ~** in/nicht in Form sein; **he was in great ~ that evening** er war an dem Abend in Hochform; **on past ~** auf dem Papier. **(b)** *no pl (etiquette)* **he did it for ~'s sake** er tat es der Form halber; **it's bad ~** so etwas tut man einfach nicht; **what's the ~?** *(col)* was ist üblich? **(c)** *(questionnaire, document)* Formular *nt*. **application ~** Bewerbungsbogen *m*. **(d)** *(esp Brit: bench)* Bank *f*. **(e)** *(Brit Sch)* Klasse *f*.
2 *vt* **(a)** *object, character* formen *(into* zu*)*. **(b)** *(develop) liking* entwickeln; *friendship* schließen; *opinion* sich *(dat)* bilden; *impression* gewinnen; *plan* entwerfen. **(c)** *(constitute, make up) part, basis, government, circle, queue, (Gram)* bilden; *company* gründen.
3 *vi (take shape)* Gestalt annehmen.
formal ['fɔːməl] *adj* **(a)** formell; *reception, welcome* feierlich; *education, training* offiziell. **~ dance/dress** Gesellschaftstanz *m*/-kleidung *f*. **(b)** *(in form) distinction etc* formal.
formality [fɔː'mælɪtɪ] *n* **(a)** *no pl (of person, dress etc)* Förmlichkeit *f*. **(b)** *(matter of form)* Formalität *f*. **it's a mere ~** es ist (eine) reine Formsache.
formalize ['fɔːməlaɪz] *vt rules, grammar* formalisieren; *agreement, relationship* formell machen.
format ['fɔːmæt] **1** *n (as regards size)* Format *nt*; *(as regards content)* Aufmachung *f*; *(Rad, TV: of programme)* Struktur *f*. **2** *vt (Comp) text* formatieren.
formation [fɔː'meɪʃən] *n* **(a)** *(act of forming, of character)* Formung *f*; *(of government, committee; Gram)* Bildung *f*; *(of company, society)* Gründung *f*. **(b)** *(of aircraft, dances)* Formation *f*.
formative ['fɔːmətɪv] *adj* formend. **it had a ~ influence on him** es hat ihn entscheidend geprägt; **~ years** Entwicklungsjahre *pl*.
former ['fɔːməʳ] **1** *adj* **(a)** früher, ehemalig. **in a ~ life** in einem früheren Leben; **in ~ times/days** früher. **(b)** *(first-mentioned)* erstere(r, s). **2** *n* **the ~** der/die/das erstere.
formerly ['fɔːməlɪ] *adv* früher.
formica ® [fɔː'maɪkə] *n* Resopal ® *nt*.
formidable ['fɔːmɪdəbl] *adj person, rock-face* furchterregend; *opponent* gefährlich; *obstacles, debts, problems, task* gewaltig, enorm; *piece of work* beeindruckend.
formula ['fɔːmjʊlə] *n, pl* **-s** *or* **-e** ['fɔːmjʊliː] Formel *f*; *(for lotion, medicine, soap powder)* Rezeptur *f*. **all his books use the same ~** alle seine Bücher sind nach demselben Rezept geschrieben.
formulate ['fɔːmjʊleɪt] *vt* formulieren.
fornicate ['fɔːnɪkeɪt] *vi* Unzucht treiben.
forsake [fə'seɪk] *pret* **forsook** [fə'sʊk], *ptp* **forsaken** [fə'seɪkn] *vt* verlassen; *bad habits* aufgeben.
fort [fɔːt] *n (Mil)* Fort *nt*. **to hold the ~** *(fig)* die Stellung halten.
forte ['fɔːtɪ] *n (strong point)* Stärke *f*.
forth [fɔːθ] *adv* **to set ~** *(liter)* ausziehen *(liter)*; **from this day ~** *(liter)* von diesem Tag an; **and so ~** und so weiter.
forthcoming [fɔːθ'kʌmɪŋ] *adj* **(a)** *event* bevorstehend; *book* in Kürze erscheinend; *film, play* in Kürze anlaufend. **(b) to be ~** *(money)* kommen; *(help)* erfolgen. **(c)** *(esp Brit: informative)* mitteilsam.
forthright ['fɔːθraɪt] *adj* offen.
forthwith [,fɔːθ'wɪθ] *adv (form)* umgehend.
fortieth ['fɔːtɪɪθ] *adj* vierzigste(r, s); *see* **sixtieth.**
fortification [,fɔːtɪfɪ'keɪʃən] *n (often pl: Mil)* Festungsanlagen *pl*.
fortify ['fɔːtɪfaɪ] *vt (Mil) town* befestigen; *(food, drink)* stärken. **fortified wine** *süßer, starker Wein.*
fortitude ['fɔːtɪtjuːd] *n* (innere) Stärke.
fortnight ['fɔːtnaɪt] *n (Brit)* vierzehn Tage.
fortnightly ['fɔːtnaɪtlɪ] *(Brit)* **1** *adj* vierzehntägig. **2** *adv* alle vierzehn Tage.
fortress ['fɔːtrɪs] *n* Festung *f*.
fortuitous [fɔː'tjuːɪtəs] *adj* zufällig.
fortunate ['fɔːtʃənɪt] *adj* glücklich. **to be ~** *(person)* Glück haben; **it was ~ that ...** es war ein Glück, daß ...
fortunately ['fɔːtʃənɪtlɪ] *adv* zum Glück.
fortune ['fɔtʃuːn] *n* **(a)** *(fate)* Geschick *nt*; *(chance)* Zufall *m*. **he had the good ~ to have rich parents** er hatte das Glück, reiche Eltern zu haben; **by good ~** glücklicherweise. **(b)** *(money)* Vermögen *nt*. **to make a ~** ein Vermögen erwerben; **it costs a ~** es kostet ein Vermögen.
fortune: ~ hunter *n* Mitgiftjäger *m*; **~-teller** *n* Wahrsager(in *f*) *m*.
forty ['fɔːtɪ] **1** *adj* vierzig. **to have ~ winks** *(col)* ein Nickerchen machen *(col)*. **2** *n* Vierzig *f*; *see* **sixty.**
forum ['fɔːrəm *n* Forum *nt*.
forward ['fɔːwəd] **1** *adv (also* **~s***) (ahead)* vorwärts; *(to the front)* nach vorn. **please step ~** bitte vortreten; **backward(s) and ~(s)** hin und her; **from this time ~** *(from then)* seitdem; *(from now)* von jetzt an. **2** *adj* **(a)** *(in place)* vordere(r, s); *(in direction)* Vorwärts-. **this seat is too far ~** dieser Sitz ist zu weit vorn. **(b)** *planning* Voraus-; *(Comm) buying* Termin-. **good ~ thinking!** gut vorausgedacht! **(c)** *(presumptuous, pert)* dreist; *(precocious)* frühreif. **3** *n (Sport)* Stürmer *m*. **4** *vt* **(a)** *(advance) plans* vorantreiben. **(b)** *(dispatch) goods* senden; *(send on) letter* nachsenden; *(to another office etc)* weiterleiten. **please ~** bitte nachsenden.
forwarding ['fɔːwədɪŋ]: **~ address** *n* Nachsendeadresse *f*; **~ agent** *n* Spediteur *m*.
forward-looking ['fɔːwədlʊkɪŋ] *adj person* fortschrittlich, progressiv; *plan* vorausblickend.
forwards ['fɔːwədz] *adv* = **forward 1.**
fossil ['fɒsl] *n* Fossil *nt*. **~ fuels** fossile Brennstoffe *pl*.
fossilized ['fɒsɪlaɪzd] *adj* versteinert; *(fig) customs* verkrustet.
foster ['fɒstəʳ] **1** *vt* **(a)** *child (parents)* in Pflege nehmen; *(authorities:* **~ out***)* in Pflege geben *(with* bei*)*. **(b)** *(encourage, promote)* fördern. **2** *adj*

attr father etc Pflege-.
fought [fɔːt] *pret, ptp of* **fight.**
foul [faʊl] **1** *adj (+er) smell* übel; *water* faulig; *air* schlecht; *food* verdorben; *(horrible) day, weather, mood* ekelhaft; *person, behaviour* gemein, fies *(col)*; *language* unflätig. **a lot of ~ play** *(Sport)* eine Menge Fouls; **the police suspect ~ play** es besteht Verdacht auf einen unnatürlichen Tod; **to fall ~ of sb/the law** mit jdm/dem Gesetz in Konflikt geraten. **2** *n (Sport)* Foul *nt.* **3** *vt* **(a)** *(pollute) air* verpesten; *(dog) pavement* verunreinigen. **(b)** *(entangle) fishing line* verheddern; *(seaweed etc) propeller* sich verheddern in *(+dat)*. **(c)** *also vi (Sport)* foulen.
foul-mouthed ['faʊlmaʊðd] *adj* unflätig.
found[1] [faʊnd] *pret, ptp of* **find.**
found[2] *vt* **(a)** *(set up)* gründen. **(b) to ~ sth on sth** *opinion, belief* etw auf etw *(dat)* gründen; **to be ~ed on sth** auf etw *(dat)* basieren.
foundation [faʊn'deɪʃən] *n* **(a)** *(of business, colony)* Gründung *f.* **(b)** *(institution)* Stiftung *f.* **(c) ~s** *pl (of house etc)* Fundament *nt*; *(of road)* Unterbau *m*; *(fig: basis)* Grundlage *f.* **it has no ~ in fact** es beruht nicht auf Tatsachen.
foundation: ~ cream *n* Grundierungscreme *f*; **~ stone** *n* Grundstein *m.*
founder[1] ['faʊndəʳ] *n (of school etc)* Gründer(in *f*) *m*; *(of charity, museum)* Stifter(in *f*) *m.*
founder[2] *vi (ship)* sinken; *(fig: project)* scheitern.
Founding Fathers ['faʊndɪŋ,fɑːðəz] *npl (US)* Väter *pl.*
foundry ['faʊndrɪ] *n* Gießerei *f.*
fount [faʊnt] *n* **(a)** *(lit liter, fig)* Quelle *f.* **(b)** *(Typ)* Schrift *f.*
fountain ['faʊntɪn] *n* Brunnen *m*; *(with upward jets)* Springbrunnen *m*; *(fig: source)* Quelle *f.*
fountain-pen ['faʊntɪn,pen] *n* Füllfederhalter, Füller *m.*
four [fɔːʳ] **1** *adj* vier. **2** *n* Vier *f.* **on all ~s** auf allen vieren; *see* **six.**
four: ~-door *attr* viertürig; **~-footed** *adj* vierfüßig; **~-letter word** *n* Vulgärausdruck *m*; **~-poster (bed)** *n* Himmelbett *nt*; **~some** *n* Quartett *nt*; *(Sport)* Viererspiel *nt*; **to go out in a ~some** zu viert ausgehen.
fourteen ['fɔː'tiːn] **1** *adj* vierzehn. **2** *n* Vierzehn *f.*
fourteenth ['fɔː'tiːnθ] *adj* vierzehnte(r, s); *see* **sixteenth.**
fourth [fɔːθ] **1** *adj* vierte(r, s). **2** *n (fraction)* Viertel *nt*; *(in series)* Vierte(r, s). **to drive in ~** im vierten Gang fahren; *see* **sixth.**
four-wheel drive ['fɔːwiːl'draɪv] *n* Vierradantrieb *m.*
fowl [faʊl] *n (poultry)* Geflügel *nt*; *(one bird)* Huhn *nt*; Gans *f etc.*
fox [fɒks] **1** *n (lit, fig)* Fuchs *m.* **2** *vt (deceive)* täuschen; *(bewilder)* verblüffen.
fox: ~glove *n (Bot)* Fingerhut *m*; **~-hunting** *n* Fuchsjagd *f*; **~ terrier** *n* Foxterrier *m*; **~trot** *n* Foxtrott *m.*
foyer ['fɔɪeɪ] *n (in theatre)* Foyer *nt*; *(esp US: in apartment house)* Diele *f.*
fracas ['frækɑː] *n* Aufruhr, Tumult *m.*
fraction ['frækʃən] *n (Math)* Bruch *m*; *(fig)* Bruchteil *m.* **a ~ better/shorter** (um) eine Spur besser/kürzer; **for a ~ of a second** einen Augenblick lang; **it missed me by a ~ of an inch** es verfehlte mich um Haaresbreite.
fractional ['frækʃənl] *adj (fig)* geringfügig.
fractious ['frækʃəs] *adj* verdrießlich.
fracture ['fræktʃəʳ] **1** *n* Bruch *m.* **2** *vti* brechen. **he ~d his shoulder** er hat sich *(dat)* die Schulter gebrochen; **~d skull** Schädelbruch *m.*
fragile ['frædʒaɪl] *adj china, glass, relationship* zerbrechlich; *material, plant* zart; *(with age)* brüchig; *(fig) person (in health)* gebrechlich; *health* anfällig; *ego* labil. **he's feeling a bit ~ this morning** *(col)* er fühlt sich heute morgen ein bißchen mitgenommen.
fragment ['frægmənt] **1** *n* **(a)** Bruchstück *nt*; *(of china, glass)* Scherbe *f*; *(of paper, letter)* Schnipsel *m*; *(of programme, opera etc)* Bruchteil *m.* **~s of conversation** Gesprächsfetzen *pl.* **(b)** *(esp Liter, Mus: unfinished work)* Fragment *nt.* **2** [fræg'ment] *vi (rock, glass)* (zer)brechen.
fragmentary ['frægməntərɪ] *adj (lit, fig)* fragmentarisch.
fragrance ['freɪgrəns] *n* Duft *m.*
fragrant ['freɪgrənt] *adj* duftend. **~ smell** Duft *m.*
frail [freɪl] *adj (+er)* zart; *health* anfällig; *(fig) hope* schwach.
frailty ['freɪltɪ] *n see adj* Zartheit *f*; Anfälligkeit *f*; Schwäche *f.*
frame [freɪm] **1** *n (basic structure, of picture, window, door, bicycle)* Rahmen *m*; *(of building, of ship)* Gerippe *nt*; *(of spectacles: also* **~s***)* Gestell *nt*; *(of human, animal)* Gestalt *f*; *(Film, Phot)* (Einzel)bild *nt.* **his massive ~** sein massiver Körper; **~ of mind** *(mental state)* Verfassung *f*; *(mood)* Stimmung *f*; **~ of reference** Bezugssystem *nt.* **2** *vt* **(a)** *picture* rahmen; *(fig) face etc* umrahmen. **(b)** *law, plan* entwerfen; *idea* entwickeln; *(express) answer, excuse* formulieren; *sentence* bilden. **(c) he's been ~ed** *(col)* die Sache wurde ihm angehängt *(col)*.
frame: ~house *n* Holzhaus *nt*; **~-up** *n (col)* Komplott *nt*; **~work** *n (lit)* Grundgerüst *nt*; *(fig) (of novel etc also)* Gerippe *nt*; *(of society, government etc)* grundlegende Struktur; **within the ~work of ...** im Rahmen *(+gen)* ...; **outside the ~work of ...** außerhalb des Rahmens *(+ gen)* ...
franc [fræŋk] *n* Franc *m.*
France [frɑːns] *n* Frankreich *nt.*
franchise ['fræntʃaɪz] *n* **(a)** *(Pol)* Wahlrecht *nt.* **(b)** *(Comm)* Lizenz *f.* **~ system** Franchise-System *nt.*
Franconia [fræŋ'kəʊnɪə] *n* Franken *nt.*
frank[1] [fræŋk] *adj (+er)* offen. **to be (perfectly) ~** ehrlich gesagt.
frank[2] *vt letter* frankieren; *(postmark, cancel) stamp, letter* stempeln.
frankfurter ['fræŋk,fɜːtəʳ] *n* Frankfurter (Würstchen *nt*) *f.*
frankincense ['fræŋkɪnsens] *n* Weihrauch *m.*
frankly ['fræŋklɪ] *adv* offen; *(to tell the truth)* ehrlich gesagt.
frankness ['fræŋknɪs] *n* Offenheit *f.*
frantic ['fræntɪk] *adj effort, cry, scream* verzweifelt; *activity* fiebrig; *desire* übersteigert; *person* außer sich *(with* vor *+dat)*. **to drive sb ~** jdn zur Verzweiflung treiben.
fraternal [frə'tɜːnl] *adj* brüderlich.
fraternity [frə'tɜːnɪtɪ] *n* **(a)** *no pl* Brüderlichkeit *f.* **(b)** *(community)* Vereinigung *f*; *(US Univ)* Verbindung *f.* **the legal/medical ~** die Juristen *pl*/Mediziner *pl.*
fraternize ['frætənaɪz] *vi* freundschaftlichen Umgang haben.
fraud [frɔːd] *n* Betrug *m*; *(person)* Betrüger(in *f*) *m*; *(thing)* (reiner) Schwindel. **~ squad** Betrugsdezernat *nt.*
fraudulent ['frɔːdjʊlənt] *adj* betrügerisch.
fraught [frɔːt] *adj* geladen *(with* mit*)*; *(col: atmosphere)* gespannt. **~ with danger** gefahrvoll.
fray[1] [freɪ] *n* Schlägerei *f*; *(Mil)* Kampf *m.* **ready for the ~** *(lit, fig)* kampfbereit.
fray[2] **1** *vt cloth* ausfransen; *cuff, rope* durchscheuern. **my nerves are ~ed** ich bin mit den Nerven herunter *(col)*; **tempers were ~ed** die Gemüter waren erhitzt. **2** *vi (cloth)* (aus)fransen; *(cuff, trouser turn-up, rope)* sich durchscheuern.
freak [friːk] **1** *n (plant)* Mißbildung *f*; *(person, animal also)* Mißgeburt *f*; *(event)* außergewöhnlicher Zufall; *(snowstorm etc)* Anomalie *f*; *(col: weird person)* Irre(r) *mf.* **~ of nature** Laune *f* der Natur; **movie ~** *(col)* Kinofan *m*; **health ~** *(col)*

Gesundheitsapostel *m (col).* **2** *adj weather, conditions* anormal; *(Statisics) values* extrem; *victory* Überraschungs-.

♦**freak out** *vi (col)* ausflippen *(col)*; *(of society)* aussteigen.

freakish ['fri:kɪʃ] *adj* **(a)** *see* **freak 2. (b)** *(changeable) weather* launisch; *person* ausgeflippt *(col)*; *hairstyle, idea* verrückt *(col).*

freaky ['fri:kɪ] *adj (+er) (col)* irre *(col).*

freckle ['frekl] *n* Sommersprosse *f.*

freckled ['frekld] *adj* sommersprossig.

free [fri:] **1** *adj (+er)* **(a)** frei. **to set sb/an animal ~** jdn/ein Tier freilassen; **he is ~ to go** es steht ihm frei zu gehen; **the fishing is ~ here** diese Stelle hier ist zum Fischen freigegeben; **you're ~ to choose** die Wahl steht Ihnen frei; **you're ~ to refuse** Sie können auch ablehnen; **I'm not ~ to do it** es steht mir nicht frei, es zu tun; **feel ~!** *(col)* bitte, gerne!; **to give sb a ~ hand** jdm freie Hand lassen; **are you ~ tonight?** hast du heute abend Zeit?; **am I ~ to speak here?** kann ich hier unbesorgt reden?; **he left one end of the string ~** er ließ ein Ende des Bindfadens lose; **~ from pain/worry** schmerzfrei/sorgenfrei; **~ from blame/responsibility** frei von Schuld/Verantwortung; **~ of sth** frei von etw.

(b) *(costing nothing)* kostenlos; *(Comm)* gratis. **it's ~** das kostet nichts; **admission ~** Eintritt frei; **to get sth ~** etw umsonst bekommen; **we got in ~** *or* **for ~** *(col)* wir kamen umsonst rein; **~ sample** Gratisprobe *f*; **~ on board** *(Comm)* frei Schiff.

(c) *(lavish)* großzügig; *language, behaviour* lose; *(over-familiar)* plump-vertraulich.

2 *vt prisoner (release)* freilassen; *(help escape)* befreien; *nation* befreien; *(untie) person* losbinden; *pipe* freimachen. **to ~ oneself from sth** sich von etw frei machen.

freebie ['fri:bi:] *n (col)* Werbegeschenk *nt.*

free collective bargaining *n* Tarifautonomie *f.*

freedom ['fri:dəm] *n* Freiheit *f.* **~ of speech** Redefreiheit *f*; **~ of the press** Pressefreiheit *f*; **the ~ of the city** die (Ehren)bürgerrechte *pl*; **to give sb the ~ of one's house** jdm sein Haus zur freien Verfügung stellen.

freedom fighter *n* Freiheitskämpfer(in *f*) *m.*

free: ~ enterprise *n* freies Unternehmertum; **~-for-all** *n* Gerangel *nt (col)*; *(fight)* Schlägerei *f*; **wages ~-for-all** Tarifgerangel *nt*; **~hold** *n* **to own sth ~hold** etw besitzen; **~hold property** *n* (freier) Grundbesitz; **~ house** *n (Brit) Wirtshaus nt, das nicht an eine bestimmte Brauerei gebunden ist*; **~ kick** *n (Sport)* Freistoß *m*; **~lance 1** *n* Freiberufler(in *f*) *m*; *(with particular firm)* freier Mitarbeiter, freie Mitarbeiterin; **2** *adj* frei(schaffend); **3** *adv* freiberuflich; **4** *vi* freiberuflich tätig sein; *(with particular firm)* als freier Mitarbeiter/freie Mitarbeiterin tätig sein; **~load** *vi (esp US col)* schmarotzen *(col) (on* bei*).*

freely ['fri:lɪ] *adv* frei; *give* großzügig. **I ~ admit ...** ich gebe offen zu ...

free: ~mason *n* Freimaurer *m*; **~-range** *adj (Brit) chicken* Farmhof-; *eggs* Land-.

freesia ['fri:zɪə] *n (Bot)* Freesie *f.*

free: ~ speech *n* Redefreiheit *f*; **~style** *n* Kür *f*; *(Swimming)* Freistil *m*; **~-trade** *n* Freihandel *m*; **~way** *n (US)* Autobahn *f*; **~wheel** *vi* im Freilauf fahren.

freeze [fri:z] *(vb: pret* **froze,** *ptp* **frozen***)* **1** *vi* **(a)** *(Met)* frieren; *(water)* gefrieren; *(rivers)* zufrieren; *(pipes)* einfrieren. **I'm/my hands are freezing** mir ist/meine Hände sind eiskalt; **to ~ to death** *(lit)* erfrieren; *(fig)* sich zu Tode frieren. **(b)** *(fig) (blood, smile)* erstarren. **(c)** *(keep still)* **he froze in his tracks** er blieb wie angewurzelt stehen; **~!** keine Bewegung! **2** *vt water* gefrieren; *food, wages* einfrieren; *assets* festlegen; *(stop) film* anhalten. **3** *n (Met)* Frost *m.* **a wages ~** ein Lohnstopp *m.*

♦**freeze over** *vi (lake)* überfrieren; *(windows)* vereisen.

♦**freeze up** *vi* zufrieren; *(lock also, pipes)* einfrieren; *(windows)* vereisen.

freeze-dried ['friz,draɪd] *adj* gefriergetrocknet.

freezer ['fri:zə^r] *n* Gefriertruhe *f*; *(upright)* Gefrierschrank *m*; *(in fridge)* Gefrierfach *nt.*

freezing ['fri:zɪŋ] **1** *adj* eiskalt. **2** *n* **below ~** unter dem Gefrierpunkt.

freight [freɪt] **1** *n* Fracht *f.* **2** *vt (transport)* verfrachten.

freighter ['freɪtə^r] *n (Naut)* Frachter *m*; *(Aviat)* Frachtflugzeug *nt.*

freight: ~ plane *n* Frachtflugzeug *nt*; **~ train** *n* Güterzug *m.*

French [fren*t*ʃ] **1** *adj* französisch. **2** *n* **(a) the ~** *pl* die Franzosen *pl.* **(b)** *(language)* Französisch *nt*; *see* **English.**

French: ~ bean *n* grüne Bohne; **~-Canadian 1** *adj* frankokanadisch; **2** *n* Frankokanadier(in *f*) *m*; **~ dressing** *n* Vinaigrette *f*; **~ fries** *npl* Pommes frites *pl*; **~ horn** *n (Mus)* (Wald)horn *nt*; **~ letter** *n (Brit col)* Pariser *m (col)*; **~man** *n* Franzose *m*; **~ polish** *vt* lackieren; **~ window(s** *pl***)** *n* Verandatür *f*; **~woman** *n* Französin *f.*

frenetic [frə'netɪk] *adj* frenetisch, rasend.

frenzy ['frenzɪ] *n* Raserei *f.* **in a ~** in heller Aufregung.

frequency ['fri:kwənsɪ] *n* Häufigkeit *f*; *(Phys)* Frequenz *f.* **high/low ~** Hoch-/Niederfrequenz *f.*

frequency: ~ band *n* Frequenzband *nt*; **~ modulation** *n (wavelength)* Ultrakurzwelle *f.*

frequent ['fri:kwənt] **1** *adj* häufig. **he's a ~ visitor to our house** er kommt uns oft besuchen. **2** [fri'kwent] *vt* oft besuchen.

frequently ['fri:kwəntlɪ] *adv* oft, häufig.

fresco ['freskəʊ] *n* Fresko(gemälde) *nt.*

fresh [freʃ] **1** *adj (+er)* **(a)** *food, breeze* frisch. **it's still ~ in my memory** es ist mir noch frisch in Erinnerung; **~ water** *(not salt)* Süßwasser *nt*; **in the ~ air** an der frischen Luft. **(b)** *(new) supplies, sheet of paper, ideas, approach, courage* neu. **to make a ~ start** einen neuen Anfang machen. **(c)** *(esp US: cheeky)* frech. **don't get ~ with me!** werd nicht frech! **2** *adv (+er) baked, picked* frisch. **~ from the oven** frisch aus dem Ofen; **~ out of college** frisch von der Schule; **to come ~ to sth** neu zu etw kommen.

freshen ['freʃn] *vi (wind)* auffrischen.

♦**freshen up** *vir* **to ~ ~** *(person)* sich frischmachen.

fresher ['freʃə^r] *n (Brit Univ col)* Erstsemester *nt.*

freshly ['freʃlɪ] *adv* frisch.

freshman ['freʃmən] *n, pl* **-men** [-mən] *(US)* = **fresher.**

freshness ['freʃnɪs] *n see adj* **(a)** Frische *f.* **(b)** Neuheit *f.* **(c)** Frechheit *f.*

freshwater ['freʃwɑ:tə^r] *adj attr* Süßwasser-.

fret[1] [fret] *vi* sich *(dat)* Sorgen machen. **don't ~** beruhige dich; **the child is ~ting for his mother** das Kind jammert nach seiner Mutter.

fret[2] *n (on guitar etc)* Bund *m.*

fretful ['fretfʊl] *adj child* quengelig.

fret: ~saw *n* Laubsäge *f*; **~work** *n (in wood)* Laubsägearbeit *f.*

Freudian ['frɔɪdɪən] *adj (Psych, fig)* Freudsch *attr.* **~ slip** Freudscher Versprecher.

friar ['fraɪə^r] *n* Mönch *m.*

fricassee ['frɪkəseɪ] *n* Frikassee *nt.*

friction ['frɪkʃən] **(a)** Reibung *f.* **~ tape** *(US)* Isolierband *nt.* **(b)** *(fig)* Reibereien *pl.*

Friday ['fraɪdɪ] *n* Freitag *m*; *see* **Tuesday.**

fridge [frɪdʒ] *n (Brit)* Kühlschrank *m.*

fried [fraɪd] *adj* gebraten; *potatoes, chicken* Brat-; *egg* Spiegel-.

friend [frend] *n* Freund(in *f*) *m*; *(less intimate)* Bekannte(r) *mf*. **to make ~s with sb** sich mit jdm anfreunden; **to be ~s with sb** mit jdm befreundet sein; **we're just (good) ~s** wir sind nur gut befreundet; **Society of F~s** Quäker *pl*.

friendliness ['frendlɪnɪs] *n see adj* Freundlichkeit *f*; Freundschaftlichkeit *f*.

friendly ['frendlɪ] **1** *adj (+er) person, smile, welcome* freundlich; *advice, feelings* freundschaftlich. **to be ~ to sb** zu jdm freundlich sein; **to be ~ with sb** mit jdm befreundet sein. **2** *n (Sport)* Freundschaftsspiel *nt*.

friendship ['frendʃɪp] *n* Freundschaft *f*.

Friesian ['fri:ʒən] *adj* friesisch.

frieze [fri:z] *n (picture)* Fries *m*; *(thin band)* Zierstreifen *m*.

frigate ['frɪgɪt] *n (Naut)* Fregatte *f*.

fright [fraɪt] *n* Schreck(en) *m*. **to get a ~** einen Schreck bekommen; **to give sb a ~** jdm einen Schreck(en) einjagen; **to take ~** es mit der Angst zu tun bekommen; **she looks a ~** *(col)* sie sieht verboten aus *(col)*.

frighten ['fraɪtn] *vt* Angst machen *(+dat)*; *(give a sudden fright)* erschrecken. **to be ~ed of sth** vor etw *(dat)* Angst haben; **to be ~ed of doing sth** Angst davor haben, etw zu tun; **I was ~ed out of my wits/to death** ich war zu Tode erschrocken.

♦ **frighten away** *or* **off** *vt sep* abschrecken; *(deliberately)* verscheuchen.

frightening ['fraɪtnɪŋ] *adj* furchterregend.

frightful *adj*, **~ly** *adv* ['fraɪtfʊl, -fəlɪ] furchtbar.

frigid ['frɪdʒɪd] *adj manner, welcome* kühl; *(Physiol, Psych)* frigid(e).

frill [frɪl] *n (on dress, shirt etc)* Rüsche *f*. **with all the ~s** mit allem Drum und Dran *(col)*.

fringe [frɪndʒ] *n (on shawl)* Fransen *pl*; *(Brit: hair)* Pony *m*; *(fig: periphery)* Rand *m*. **on the ~(s) of society** am Rande der Gesellschaft.

fringe: ~ benefits *npl* zusätzliche Leistungen *pl*; **~ group** *n* Randgruppe *f*.

frisk [frɪsk] **1** *vi (leap about)* umhertollen. **2** *vt suspect etc* durchsuchen.

frisky ['frɪskɪ] *adj (+er)* verspielt.

fritter[1] ['frɪtəʳ] *vt (also* **~ away**) *money, time* vergeuden.

fritter[2] *n (Cook)* Schmalzgebackene(s) *nt no pl* mit Füllung.

frivolity [frɪ'vɒlɪtɪ] *n* Frivolität *f*.

frivolous ['frɪvələs] *adj* frivol; *person, life, remark* leichtfertig.

frizz(l)y ['frɪz(l)ɪ] *adj (+er) hair* kraus.

fro [frəʊ] *adv see* **to 4, to-ing and fro-ing.**

frock [frɒk] *n* Kleid *nt*; *(of monk)* Kutte *f*.

frog [frɒg] *n* **(a)** Frosch *m*. **to have a ~ in one's throat** einen Frosch im Hals haben. **(b) F~** *(Brit pej col: French person)* Franzose *m*, Französin *f*.

frog: ~man *n* Froschmann *m*; **~march** *vt (Brit)* (weg)schleifen; *(carry)* zu viert wegtragen; **they ~marched him in** sie schleppten ihn herein *(col)*.

frolic ['frɒlɪk] *vi pret, ptp* **~ked** *(also* **~ about** *or* **around**) umhertoben.

from [frɒm] *prep* **(a)** *(indicating starting place)* von *(+dat)*; *(indicating place of origin)* aus *(+dat)*. **where has he come ~ today?** von wo ist er heute gekommen?; **where is he ~?** woher kommt er?; **he comes ~ York** er kommt aus York; **~ London to Edinburgh** von London nach Edinburgh; **~ house to house** von Haus zu Haus.

(b) *(indicating time) (in past)* seit *(+dat)*; *(in future)* ab *(+dat)*, von *(+dat)* ... an. **~ now on** von jetzt an; **commencing as ~ the 6th May** vom 6. Mai an.

(c) *(indicating distance)* von *(+dat)* (... weg); *(from town etc also)* von *(+dat)* ... entfernt. **the house is 10 km ~ the coast** das Haus ist 10 km von der Küste entfernt; **to go away ~ home** von zu Haus weggehen.

(d) *(indicating origin)* von *(+dat)*; *(out of)* aus *(+dat)*. **tell him ~ me** richten Sie ihm von mir aus; **an invitation ~ the Smiths** eine Einladung von den Smiths; **"~ ..."** *(on envelope, parcel)* „Absender ...“, „Abs. ...“; **where did you get that ~?** wo hast du das her?; **I got it ~ the library/Gloria** ich habe es aus der Bibliothek/von Gloria; **to drink ~ a stream/glass** aus einem Bach/Glas trinken; **a quotation ~ Shakespeare** ein Zitat nach Shakespeare; **translated ~ the English** aus dem Englischen übersetzt; **painted ~ life** nach dem Leben gemalt.

(e) *(indicating lowest amount)* ab *(+dat)*. **~ £2 (upwards)** ab £ 2; **dresses (ranging) ~ £20 to £30** Kleider zwischen £ 20 und £ 30; **there were ~ 10 to 15 people there** es waren zwischen 10 und 15 Leute da.

(f) *(indicating change)* **things went ~ bad to worse** es wurde immer schlimmer; **he went ~ office boy to director** er stieg vom Laufjungen zum Direktor auf; **a price increase ~ 1 mark to 1.50 marks** eine Preiserhöhung von 1 DM auf 1,50 DM.

(g) *(indicating difference)* **he is quite different ~ the others** er ist ganz anders als die andern; **to tell black ~ white** Schwarz und Weiß auseinanderhalten.

(h) *(because of, due to)* **to act ~ conviction** aus Überzeugung handeln; **to die ~ fatigue** an Erschöpfung sterben; **weak ~ hunger** schwach vor Hunger; **~ experience** aus Erfahrung; **~ what I heard** nach dem, was ich gehört habe; **~ what I can see ...** nach dem, was ich sehen kann, ...; **~ the look of things ...** (so) wie die Sache aussieht, ...

(i) *(+prep)* **~ above** *or* **over sth** über etw *(acc)* hinweg; **~ beneath** *or* **underneath sth** unter etw *(dat)* hervor; **~ out of sth** aus etw heraus; **~ among the trees** zwischen den Bäumen hervor; **~ inside/outside the house** von drinnen/draußen.

front [frʌnt] **1** *n* **(a)** Vorderseite *f*; *(forward part)* Vorderteil *nt*. **in ~** vorne; *(in line, race etc also)* an der Spitze; **in ~ of sb/sth** vor jdm/etw; **at the ~ of** *(inside)* vorne in *(+dat)*; *(outside)* vor *(+dat)*; *(at the head of)* an der Spitze *(+gen)*; **to be in ~** vorne sein; *(Sport)* vorn(e) liegen; **in** *or* **at the ~ of the class** vorne im Klassenzimmer. **(b)** *(Mil, Pol, Met)* Front *f*. **they were attacked on all ~s** *(Mil)* sie wurden an allen Fronten angegriffen; *(fig)* sie wurden von allen Seiten angegriffen; **cold ~** *(Met)* Kalt(luft)front *f*; **we must present a united ~** wir müssen eine geschlossene Front bilden. **(c)** *(Brit: at sea)* Strandpromenade *f*. **(d)** *(outward appearance)* Fassade *f*. **to put on a bold ~** eine tapfere Miene zur Schau stellen; **it's just a ~** das ist nur Fassade; **the fruit shop was just a ~** das Obstgeschäft diente nur zur Tarnung.

2 *vi* **the house/windows ~ onto the steet** die Häuser liegen/die Fenster gehen auf die Straße hinaus.

3 *adj* vorderste(r, s); *row, page also* erste(r, s); *tooth, wheel, view* Vorder-. **~ seat** Platz *m* in der ersten Reihe; *(Aut)* Vordersitz *m*.

frontage ['frʌntɪdʒ] *n (of building)* Front *f*.

frontal ['frʌntl] *adj (Mil)* Frontal-. **~ view** Vorderansicht *f*.

front: ~ bench *n (Parl)* vorderste *or* erste Reihe *(wo die führenden Politiker sitzen)*; **~ door** *n* Haustür *f*.

frontier ['frʌntɪəʳ] *n (lit, fig)* Grenze *f*.

frontispiece ['frʌntɪspi:s] *n* Titelseite *f*; *(illustration)* Bildseite *f*.

front: ~ line *n* Front(linie) *f*; **~ man** *n* Mann *m* an der Spitze; *(pej)* Strohmann *m*; **~ page** *n* Titelseite *f*; **~-page** *adj news* auf der ersten Seite; **~-runner** *n (fig)* Spitzenreiter, Favorit *m*.

frost [frɒst] **1** *n* Frost *m*; *(on leaves etc)* Rauhreif *m*. **ten degrees of ~** zehn Grad Kälte. **2** *vt (esp US) cake* glasieren.

frost: ~**bite** *n* Frostbeulen *pl*; *(more serious)* Erfrierungen *pl*; ~**bitten** *adj hands, feet* erfroren.

frosted ['frɒstɪd] *adj* **(a)** ~ **glass** Milchglas *nt; (textured)* geriffeltes Glas. **(b)** *(esp US) cake* mit Zuckerguß überzogen, glasiert.

frosting ['frɒstɪŋ] *n (esp US: icing)* Zuckerguß *m*.

frosty ['frɒstɪ] *adj (+er) (lit, fig)* frostig.

froth [frɒθ] **1** *n (on liquids, Med)* Schaum *m*. **2** *vi* schäumen. **the dog was ~ing at the mouth** der Hund hatte Schaum vor dem Maul.

frown [fraʊn] **1** *n* Stirnrunzeln *nt no pl*. **to give a** ~ die Stirn(e) runzeln; **angry** ~ finsterer Blick; **worried/puzzled** ~ sorgenvoller/verdutzter Gesichtsausdruck. **2** *vi (lit, fig)* die Stirn(e) runzeln *(at* über *+acc)*. **to** ~ **at sb** jdn finster ansehen.

♦ **frown (up)on** *vi +prep obj (fig) suggestion, idea* mißbilligen.

froze [frəʊz] *pret of* **freeze.**

frozen ['frəʊzn] **1** *ptp of* **freeze. 2** *adj river* zugefroren. **I'm absolutely** ~ **stiff** ich bin total steifgefroren; ~ **foods** Tiefkühlkost *f*; ~ **peas** gefrorene Erbsen *pl*.

frugal ['fru:gəl] *adj person* sparsam; *meal* einfach.

fruit [fru:t] *n (as collective)* Obst *nt*; *(Bot)* Frucht *f*. **what is your favourite ~?** welches Obst magst du am liebsten?; **to bear** ~ *(lit, fig)* Früchte tragen; **the ~(s) of my labour** die Früchte *pl* meiner Arbeit.

fruiterer ['fru:tərə^r] *n (esp Brit)* Obsthändler(in *f*) *m*.

fruitful ['fru:tfʊl] *adj (lit, fig)* fruchtbar.

fruition [fru:'ɪʃən] *n* **to come to** ~ sich verwirklichen.

fruitless ['fru:tlɪs] *adj (fig)* fruchtlos.

fruit: ~ **machine** *n (Brit)* Spielautomat *m*; ~ **salad** *n* Obstsalat *m*; ~ **tree** *n* Obstbaum *m*.

fruity ['fru:tɪ] *adj (+er) (like fruit)* fruchtartig; *taste, wine* fruchtig; *voice* rauchig. **to get** ~ *(fig col)* keck werden.

frump [frʌmp] *n (pej)* Vogelscheuche *f (col)*.

frustrate [frʌ'streɪt] *vt hopes* zunichte machen; *plans, plot* durchkreuzen; *person* frustrieren.

frustrated [frʌ'streɪtɪd] *adj person* frustriert.

frustrating [frʌ'streɪtɪŋ] *adj* frustrierend.

frustration [frʌ'streɪʃən] *n* Frustration *f no pl*; *(of hopes, plans, plot)* Zerschlagung *f*.

fry[1] [fraɪ] *npl* **small** ~ *(unimportant people)* kleine Fische *pl (col)*.

fry[2] *vt* (in der Pfanne) braten; *see* **fried.**

frying pan ['fraɪɪŋ,pæn] *n* Bratpfanne *f*. **to jump out of the** ~ **into the fire** *(Prov)* vom Regen in die Traufe kommen *(Prov)*.

ft = **foot** ft; **feet** ft.

fuchsia ['fju:ʃə] *n* Fuchsie *f*.

fuck [fʌk] *(col!!)* **1** *vt* **(a)** *(lit)* ficken *(col!!)*. **(b)** ~ **you!** leck mich am Arsch *(col!!)*. **2** *interj* (verdammte) Scheiße *(col!)*.

♦ **fuck off** *vi (col!!)* ~ ~! verpiß dich! *(col!!)*.

fucking ['fʌkɪŋ] *adj (col!!)* Scheiß- *(col!)*.

fuddled ['fʌdld] *adj (muddled)* verwirrt; *(tipsy)* beschwipst.

fudge [fʌdʒ] *n (Cook)* ≃ Karamel *m*.

fuel [fjʊəl] **1** *n* Brennstoff *m*; *(for vehicle)* Kraftstoff *m*; *(petrol)* Benzin *nt*; *(Aviat, Space)* Treibstoff *m*. **to add** ~ **to the flames** *(fig)* Öl ins Feuer gießen. **2** *vt stove, furnace etc (fill)* mit Brennstoff versorgen; *(drive, propel)* antreiben.

fuel: ~ **cell** *n* Brennstoffzelle *f*; ~ **gauge** *n* Benzinuhr *f*; ~ **injection** *n* (Benzin)einspritzung *f*; **engine with** ~ **injection** Einspritzmotor *m*; ~ **pump** *n* Benzinpumpe *f*; ~ **tank** *n* Tank *m*; *(for oil)* Öltank *m*.

fug [fʌg] *n (esp Brit col)* Mief *m (col)*.

fugitive ['fju:dʒɪtɪv] **1** *n* Flüchtling *m*. **he is a** ~ **from the law** er ist auf der Flucht vor dem Gesetz. **2** *adj* flüchtig.

fugue [fju:g] *n (Mus)* Fuge *f*.

fulfil, *(US)* **fulfill** [fʊl'fɪl] *vt* erfüllen. **to be ~led** *(wish etc)* sich erfüllen; **to feel ~led** Erfüllung finden.

fulfilment, *(US)* **fulfillment** [fʊl'fɪlmənt] *n* Erfüllung *f*.

full [fʊl] **1** *adj (+er)* voll; *description, report* vollständig; *understanding, sympathy* vollste(r, s); *figure, skirt* füllig. ~ **of ...** voller *(+gen)* ...; **he's** ~ **of good ideas** er steckt voll(er) guter Ideen; **a look** ~ **of hate** ein haßerfüllter Blick; **I am** ~ **(up)** *(col)* ich bin voll bis obenhin *(col)*; **we are** ~ **up for July** wir sind für Juli völlig ausgebucht; **for the ~er figure** für vollschlanke Damen; **at** ~ **speed** in voller Fahrt; **to fall** ~ **length** der Länge nach hinfallen; **roses in** ~ **bloom** Rosen in voller Blüte; **I waited two** ~ **hours** ich habe zwei ganze Stunden gewartet; **the** ~ **particulars** die genauen Einzelheiten; ~ **employment** Vollbeschäftigung *f*; ~ **member** vollberechtigtes Mitglied; ~ **name** Vor- und Zuname *m*; **to be** ~ **of oneself** von sich (selbst) eingenommen sein; **she was** ~ **of it** sie hat gar nicht mehr aufgehört, davon zu reden; **the papers were** ~ **of it for weeks** die Zeitungen waren wochenlang voll davon.

2 *adv* **it is a** ~ **five miles from here** es sind volle fünf Meilen von hier; **I know** ~ **well that ...** ich weiß sehr wohl, daß ...; **to hit sb** ~ **in the face** jdn voll ins Gesicht schlagen.

3 *n* **in** ~ vollständig; **to write one's name in** ~ seinen Namen ausschreiben; **to pay in** ~ den vollen Betrag bezahlen; **to the** ~ vollständig.

full: ~**-back** *n (Sport)* Verteidiger *m*; ~**-blooded** [,fʊl'blʌdɪd] *adj (vigorous)* kräftig; ~**-blown** *adj (fig) doctor, theory* richtiggehend; ~**-bodied** *adj wine* vollmundig; ~**-grown** *adj* ausgewachsen; ~**-length** *adj portrait* lebensgroß; *film* abendfüllend; ~ **moon** *n* Vollmond *m*.

fullness ['fʊlnɪs] *n (of detail)* Vollständigkeit *f*; *(of skirt, sound)* Fülle *f*. **in the** ~ **of time** *(eventually)* zu gegebener Zeit; *(at predestined time)* als die Zeit gekommen war.

full: ~**-scale** *adj drawing* in Originalgröße; *operation, search* großangelegt; *revision* umfassend; *attack* General-; ~ **stop** *n* Punkt *m*; ~**-time 1** *adv work* ganztags; **2** *adj employment* Ganztags-.

fully [fʊlɪ] *adv* völlig; *equipped* vollständig; *dressed* fertig. **it's** ~ **two years ago** es ist gut zwei Jahre her; **I** ~ **expected that ...** ich habe fest damit gerechnet, daß ...

fully: ~**-fledged** *adj bird* flügge; *(fig: qualified)* richtiggehend; ~**-qualified** *adj* vollqualifiziert *attr*.

fulsome ['fʊlsəm] *adj praise* übertrieben.

fumble ['fʌmbl] **1** *vi (also* ~ **about***)* umhertasten. **to** ~ **in the dark** im Dunkeln herumtasten; **to** ~ **in one's pockets** in seinen Taschen wühlen; **to** ~ **with sth** an etw *(dat)* herumfummeln. **2** *vt* verpfuschen *(col)*. **to** ~ **the ball** den Ball nicht sicher fangen.

fume [fju:m] **1** *vi (liquids)* dampfen; *(fig col: person)* kochen *(col)*. **2** *npl* ~**s** Dämpfe *pl*; *(of car)* Abgase *pl*.

fumigate ['fju:mɪgeɪt] *vt* ausräuchern.

fun [fʌn] *n* Spaß *m*. **for** *or* **in** ~ *(as a joke)* als Scherz; **it's** ~ es macht Spaß; **it's no** ~ es macht keinen Spaß; **we just did it for** ~ wir haben das nur zum Spaß gemacht; **to spoil the** ~ den Spaß verderben; **he's good** ~ er ist ganz lustig; **have ~!** viel Spaß!; **that should be** ~ **and games** das kann ja (noch) heiter werden *(col)*; **to make** ~ **of** *or* **poke** ~ **at sb/sth** sich über jdn/etw lustig machen.

function ['fʌŋkʃən] **1** *n* **(a)** *(purpose, Math)* Funktion *f*. **in his** ~ **as judge** in seiner Eigenschaft als Richter. **(b)** *(reception)* Empfang *m*; *(official ceremony)* Feier *f*. **2** *vi* funktionieren. **to** ~ **as** fungieren als; *(thing also)* dienen als.

functional ['fʌŋkʃənəl] *adj* funktionell.

fund [fʌnd] **1** *n* **(a)** *(Fin)* Fonds *m*. ~**s** *pl* Mittel *pl*. **(b)** *(of wisdom, humour etc)* Schatz *(of* von*)*,

Vorrat *(of* an *+dat) m.* **2** *vt scheme, project* das Kapital aufbringen für.

fundamental [ˌfʌndəˈmentl] **1** *adj (basic)* grundlegend; *indifference, problem* grundsätzlich. **to be ~ to sth** für etw von grundlegender Bedeutung sein; **our ~ needs/beliefs** unsere Grundbedürfnisse *pl*/Grundüberzeugungen *pl.* **2** *n usu pl* Grundlage *f.*

fundamentally [ˌfʌndəˈmentəlɪ] *adv* grundlegend; *(in essence)* im Grunde.

funeral [ˈfjuːnərəl] *n* Beerdigung *f.* **well that's your ~** *(col)* na ja, das ist dein Problem *(col).*

funeral: ~ director *n* Beerdigungsunternehmer *m;* **~ procession** *n* Leichenzug *m.*

funereal [fjuːˈnɪərɪəl] *adj* trübselig.

funfair [ˈfʌnfɛəʳ] *n (Brit)* Kirmes *f.*

fungus [ˈfʌŋgəs] *n, pl* **fungi** [ˈfʌŋgaɪ] Pilz *m.*

funicular (railway) [fjuːˈnɪkjulə(ˈreɪlweɪ)] *n* Seilbahn *f.*

funk [fʌŋk] *n* **to be in a (blue) ~** *(col)* ganz schön Bammel haben *(col).*

funnel [ˈfʌnl] *n (for pouring)* Trichter *m; (Naut, Rail)* Schornstein *m.*

funnily [ˈfʌnɪlɪ] *adv* **~ enough** komischerweise.

funny [ˈfʌnɪ] *adj (+er)* **(a)** *(comic)* komisch. **are you being ~?** das soll wohl ein Witz sein?; **it's not ~** das ist *or* das finde ich überhaupt nicht komisch. **(b)** *(strange)* seltsam, komisch. **it's a ~ thing, only last week ...** (das ist doch) komisch, erst letzte Woche ...; **~ business** *(col)* faule Sache *(col);* **I felt all ~** *(col)* mir war ganz komisch; **~ bone** *n* Musikantenknochen *m.*

fur [fɜːʳ] **1** *n (on animal)* Fell *nt; (for clothing)* Pelz *m; (in kettle)* Kesselstein *m.* **2** *attr coat, stole* Pelz-.

furious [ˈfjʊərɪəs] *adj person* wütend; *struggle* wild; *speed* rasend. **to be ~ with sb** auf jdn wütend sein.

furlong [ˈfɜːlɒŋ] *n* Achtelmeile *f.*

furnace [ˈfɜːnɪs] *n* Hochofen *m; (Metal)* Schmelzofen *m.*

furnish [ˈfɜːnɪʃ] *vt* **(a)** *house* einrichten. **~ed room** möbliertes Zimmer; **~ing fabrics** Dekorationsstoffe *pl.* **(b)** *information, reason, excuse* liefern. **to ~ sb with sth** jdn mit etw versorgen.

furnishings [ˈfɜːnɪʃɪŋz] *npl* Mobiliar *nt; (with carpets etc)* Einrichtung *f.*

furniture [ˈfɜːnɪtʃəʳ] *n* Möbel *pl.* **a piece of ~** ein Möbelstück *nt;* **he's part of the ~** *(fig col)* er gehört zum Inventar.

furore [fjʊəˈrɔːrɪ], *(US)* **furor** [ˈfjʊrɔːʳ] *n* Protest(e *pl*) *m.* **to cause a ~** einen Skandal verursachen.

furrier [ˈfʌrɪəʳ] *n* Kürschner(in *f*) *m.*

furrow [ˈfʌrəʊ] **1** *n (Agr)* Furche *f; (on brow)* Runzel *f.* **2** *vt brow* runzeln.

furry [ˈfɜːrɪ] *adj (+er) animal* Pelz-; *toy* Plüsch-; *tongue* belegt.

further [ˈfɜːðəʳ] **1** *adv, comp of* **far (a)** *(in place, time, fig)* weiter. **~ on** weiter entfernt; **~ back** *(in place, time)* weiter zurück; *(in time)* früher; **nothing is ~ from my thoughts** nichts liegt mir ferner. **(b)** *(more)* **he didn't question me ~** er hat mich nichts weiter gefragt; **until you hear ~** bis auf weiteres; **and ~ ...** und darüber hinaus ...; **~ to your letter of ...** *(Comm)* in bezug auf Ihren Brief vom ... *(form).* **2** *adj* **(a)** *see* **farther. (b)** *(additional)* weiter. **until ~ notice** bis auf weiteres; **~ particulars** nähere Einzelheiten *pl;* **~ education** Fortbildung; *(at university)* Hochschulausbildung *f.* **3** *vt one's interests, a cause* fördern.

furtherance [ˈfɜːðərəns] *n* Förderung *f.*

furthermore [ˈfɜːðəmɔːʳ] *adv* außerdem.

furthermost [ˈfɜːðəməʊst] *adj* äußerste(r, s).

furthest [ˈfɜːðɪst] **1** *adv* **the ~ north you can go** soweit nach Norden wie möglich. **2** *adj* am weitesten entfernt. **5 km at the ~** höchstens 5 km.

furtive [ˈfɜːtɪv] *adj action* heimlich; *behaviour* heimlichtuerisch; *look* verstohlen.

fury [ˈfjʊərɪ] *n (of person)* Wut *f; (of storm)* Ungestüm *nt.* **she flew into a ~** sie kam in Rage; **like ~** *(col)* wie verrückt *(col).*

fuse, *(US)* **fuze** [fjuːz] **1** *vt* **(a)** *metals* verschmelzen. **(b)** *(Brit Elec)* **to ~ the lights** die Sicherung durchbrennen lassen. **2** *vi* **(a)** *(metals)* sich verbinden; *(fig)* verschmelzen. **(b)** *(Brit Elec)* durchbrennen. **the lights ~d** die Sicherung war durchgebrannt. **3** *n (Elec)* Sicherung *f; (Brit Elec: act of fusing)* Kurzschluß *m; (in bombs)* Zündschnur *f.*

fuse box *n* Sicherungskasten *m.*

fuselage [ˈfjuːzəlɑːʒ] *n* (Flugzeug)rumpf *m.*

fuse wire *n* Schmelzdraht *m.*

fusillade [ˌfjuːzɪˈleɪd] *n* Salve *f.*

fusion [ˈfjuːʒən] *n (of metal, fig)* Verschmelzung *f.*

fuss [fʌs] **1** *n* Theater *nt (col); (bother)* Umstände *pl (col),* Aufheben(s) *nt.* **don't go to a lot of ~** mach dir keine Umstände; **to make a ~, to kick up a ~** Krach schlagen *(col);* **to make a ~ about** *or* **over sth** viel Aufhebens um etw machen; **to make a ~ of sb** *(spoil) VIP, guest* um jdn viel Wirbel machen *(col); children* jdn verwöhnen; **a lot of ~ about nothing** viel Lärm um nichts. **2** *vi* sich (unnötig) aufregen; *(get into a ~)* Umstände *pl* machen. **3** *vt person* nervös machen; *(pester)* keine Ruhe lassen *(+dat).*

♦ **fuss about** *vi* herumfuhrwerken *(col).*

♦ **fuss over** *vi +prep obj* sich *(dat)* große Umstände machen mit.

fussy [ˈfʌsɪ] *adj (+er) (finicky)* kleinlich, pingelig *(col); (elaborate) dress, pattern* verspielt. **what do you want to do? — I'm not ~** was willst du machen? — ist mir egal.

futile [ˈfjuːtaɪl] *adj* sinnlos.

futility [fjuːˈtɪlɪtɪ] *n* Sinnlosigkeit *f.*

future [ˈfjuːtʃəʳ] **1** *n* Zukunft *f.* **in the near ~** bald; **there's no ~ in it** das hat keine Zukunft. **2** *adj* zukünftig. **at some ~ date** zu einem späteren Zeitpunkt; **the ~ tense** *(Gram)* das Futur, die Zukunft.

futuristic [ˌfjuːtʃəˈrɪstɪk] *adj* futuristisch.

fuze *n (US)* = **fuse.**

fuzz [fʌz] *n* **(a)** *(fluff)* Flaum *m.* **(b) the ~** *(col)* die Polypen *pl (col).*

fuzzy [ˈfʌzɪ] *adj (+er)* **(a)** *hair* kraus. **(b)** *(col) picture, sound, memory* verschwommen.

G

G, g [dʒiː] *n* G, g *nt.* ~ **sharp/flat** Gis, gis *nt*/Ges, ges *nt.*

g = **gram(s), gramme(s)** g.

gab [gæb] *(col)* **1** *n* **to have the gift of the** ~ nicht auf den Mund gefallen sein. **2** *vi* quatschen *(col).*

gabardine [ˌgæbəˈdiːn] *n* Gabardine *m.*

gabble [ˈgæbl] **1** *vi (geese)* schnattern. **don't** ~ red' nicht so schnell. **2** *vt* herunterrasseln *(col).*

♦ **gabble away** *vi* drauflosschnattern *(col).*

gable [ˈgeɪbl] *n* Giebel *m.* ~ **end** Giebelwand *f.*

♦ **gad about** [ˈgædəˈbaʊt] *vi (col)* herumziehen. **to** ~ ~ **the country** im Land herumziehen.

gadget [ˈgædʒɪt] *n* Gerät *nt.* **with a lot of** ~**s** mit allen Schikanen *(col).*

gadgetry [ˈgædʒɪtrɪ] *n* Vorrichtungen *pl*; *(superfluous equipment)* technische Spielereien *pl.*

Gaelic [ˈgeɪlɪk] **1** *adj* gälisch. **2** *n (language)* Gälisch *nt.*

gaff [gæf] *n*: **to blow the** ~ *(col)* nicht dichthalten *(col).*

gaffe [gæf] *n* Fauxpas *m*; *(verbal)* taktlose Bemerkung. **to make a** ~ einen Fauxpas begehen.

gaffer [ˈgæfəʳ] *n (col) (boss)* Boß *(col) m*; *(old man)* Opa *m (col).*

gag [gæg] **1** *n* **(a)** Knebel *m.* **(b)** *(col: joke)* Gag *m.* **2** *vt* knebeln *(auch fig).*

gaga [ˈgɑːˈgɑː] *adj (col) old person* verkalkt *(col).*

gage [geɪdʒ] *n, vt (US)* = **gauge.**

gaggle [ˈgægl] *n (of geese)* Herde *f.*

gaiety [ˈgeɪɪtɪ] *n* Fröhlichkeit *f.*

gaily [ˈgeɪlɪ] *adv* fröhlich. ~ **coloured** farbenfroh.

gain [geɪn] **1** *n no pl (advantage)* Vorteil *m*; *(profit)* Gewinn *m*; *(increase)* Zunahme *f (in gen).* **it will be to your** ~ es wird zu Ihrem Vorteil sein; **to do sth for** ~ etw des Geldes wegen tun; **his loss is our** ~ wir profitieren von seinem Verlust; **the SDP made several** ~**s** die SDP gewann einige Sitze.

2 *vt* **(a)** *(obtain, win)* gewinnen; *knowledge, wealth* erwerben; *advantage, respect, entry* sich *(dat)* verschaffen. **what does he hope to** ~ **by it?** was erhofft er sich *(dat)* davon?; **to** ~ **experience** Erfahrung sammeln; **we have nothing to** ~ **by staying** wir haben nichts davon, noch länger dazubleiben. **(b)** *(reach) shore, summit* erreichen. **(c)** *(increase)* **to** ~ **height** (an) Höhe gewinnen; **to** ~ **speed** schneller werden; **she has** ~**ed weight** sie hat zugenommen; **as he** ~**ed confidence** als seine Selbstsicherheit zunahm; **my watch** ~**s five minutes each day** meine Uhr geht fünf Minuten pro Tag vor.

3 *vi* **(a)** *(watch)* vorgehen. **(b)** *(profit: person)* profitieren *(by* von*).* **society/you would** ~ **from that** das wäre für die Gesellschaft/für Sie von Vorteil. **(c) to** ~ **in prestige** an Ansehen gewinnen.

♦ **gain on** *vi +prep obj (close gap)* einholen.

gainful [ˈgeɪnfʊl] *adj occupation etc* einträglich. **to be in** ~ **employment** erwerbstätig sein.

gait [geɪt] *n* Gang *m*; *(of horse)* Gangart *f.*

gal = **gallon(s).**

gala [ˈgɑːlə] *n (festive occasion)* großes Fest; *(Theat, Film, ball)* Galaveranstaltung *f.* ~ **performance** Galavorstellung *f.*

galaxy [ˈgæləksɪ] *n (Astron)* Milchstraße *f.*

gale [geɪl] *n* Sturm *m.* **it was blowing a** ~ ein Sturm wütete; ~ **force 8** Windstärke 8; ~**-force winds** orkanartige Winde.

gall [gɔːl] **1** *n* **(a)** *(Physiol, Bot)* Galle *f.* **(b)** *(col)* **of all the** ~**!** so eine Frechheit! **2** *vt (fig: anger)* maßlos ärgern.

gallant [ˈgælənt] *adj (brave)* tapfer; *(chivalrous, noble)* edel, ritterlich; *(to women)* galant.

gallantry [ˈgæləntrɪ] *n (bravery)* Tapferkeit *f*; *(chivalry)* Edelmut *m*; *(to women)* Galanterie *f.*

gall bladder *n* Gallenblase *f.*

galleon [ˈgælɪən] *n* Galeone *f.*

gallery [ˈgælərɪ] *n (balcony, Art)* Galerie *f*; *(Theat)* oberster Rang. **to play to the** ~ *(fig)* sich in Szene setzen.

galley [ˈgælɪ] *n* **(a)** *(Naut) (ship)* Galeere *f*; *(kitchen)* Kombüse *f.* ~ **slave** Galeerensklave *m.* **(b)** *(Typ) (also* ~ **proof***)* Fahne(nabzug *m*) *f.*

Gallic [ˈgælɪk] *adj* gallisch.

galling [ˈgɔːlɪŋ] *adj* äußerst ärgerlich.

gallivant [ˌgælɪˈvænt] *vi* **to** ~ **about** *(col)* sich herumtreiben.

gallon [ˈgælən] *n* Gallone *f.*

gallop [ˈgæləp] **1** *n* Galopp *m.* **at full** ~ im gestreckten Galopp. **2** *vi* galoppieren. **to** ~ **through a book/one's work** ein Buch im Eiltempo lesen *(col)*/seine Arbeit im Eiltempo erledigen *(col).*

galloping [ˈgæləpɪŋ] *adj (lit, fig)* galoppierend.

gallows [ˈgæləʊz] *n* Galgen *m.*

gallstone [ˈgɔːlstəʊn] *n* Gallenstein *m.*

Gallup poll ® [ˈgæləpˌpəʊl] *n* Meinungsumfrage *f.*

galore [gəˈlɔːʳ] *adv* in Hülle und Fülle.

galvanize [ˈgælvənaɪz] *vt* **(a)** *(Elec)* galvanisieren. **(b)** *(fig)* elektrisieren. **to** ~ **sb into action** jdn plötzlich aktiv werden lassen.

gambit [ˈgæmbɪt] *n* **(a)** *(Chess)* Gambit *nt.* **(b)** *(fig)* (Schach)zug *m.* **his favourite conversational** ~ **is ...** er fängt eine Unterhaltung am liebsten mit ... an.

gamble [ˈgæmbl] **1** *n (fig)* Risiko *nt.* **it's a** ~ es ist riskant; **I'll take a** ~ **on it** ich riskiere es. **2** *vi* **(a)** *(lit)* (um Geld) spielen *(with* mit*)*; *(on horses etc)* wetten. **to** ~ **on the stock exchange** an der Börse spekulieren. **(b)** *(fig)* **she was gambling on him being late** sie hat sich darauf verlassen, daß er sich verspäten würde; **to** ~ **with sth** etw aufs Spiel setzen.

♦ **gamble away** *vt sep* verspielen.

gambler [ˈgæmbləʳ] *n (lit, fig)* Spieler(in *f*) *m.*

gambling [ˈgæmblɪŋ] *n* Spielen *nt* (um Geld); *(on horses etc)* Wetten *nt.* **to disapprove of** ~ gegen das Glückspiel/Wetten sein; ~ **debts** Spielschulden *pl.*

gambol [ˈgæmbəl] *vi* herumspringen.

game[1] [geɪm] *n* **(a)** Spiel *nt*; *(of table tennis)* Satz *m*; *(of billiards, board-games etc, informal tennis match)* Partie *f.* ~**s** *(Sch)* Sport *m*; **to have** *or* **play a** ~ **of football/tennis/chess** *etc* Fußball/Tennis/Schach *etc* spielen; **he plays a good** ~ er spielt gut; **to have a** ~ **with sb, to give sb a** ~ mit jdm spielen; **to be off one's** ~ nicht in Form sein; ~ **of chance** Glücksspiel *nt*; ~ **set and match to X** Satz und Spiel (geht an) X.

(b) *(fig)* Spiel *nt.* **to play the** ~ sich an die Spielregeln halten; **to play** ~**s with sb** mit jdm spielen; **the** ~ **is up** das Spiel ist aus; **to play sb's**

~ jdm in die Hände spielen; **two can play at that ~** wie du mir, so ich dir *(col)*; **to beat sb at his own ~** jdn mit seinen/ihren eigenen Waffen schlagen; **to give the ~ away** alles verderben; **to spoil sb's little ~** jdm die Suppe versalzen *(col)*; **I wonder what his little ~ is?** ich frage mich, was er im Schilde führt.

(c) *(col: business, profession)* Branche *f*. **how long have you been in this ~?** wie lange machen Sie das schon?; **to be/go on the ~** auf den Strich gehen *(col)*.

(d) *(Hunt)* Wild *nt*; *(Cook also)* Wildbret *nt*.

game[2] *adj (brave)* mutig. **to be ~ for sth** (bei) etw mitmachen; **to be ~ for anything** für alles zu haben sein *(col)*.

game: ~ bird *n* Federwild *nt no pl*; **~keeper** *n* Wildhüter *m*.

gamesmanship ['geɪmzmənʃɪp] *n* Spieltaktik *f*.

gammon ['gæmən] *n* Schinken *m*.

gamut ['gæmət] *n (fig)* Skala *f*. **to run the (whole) ~ of emotion(s)** die ganze Skala der Gefühle durchlaufen.

gander ['gændəʳ] *n* Gänserich *m*.

gang [gæŋ] *n* Schar *f*; *(of workers, prisoners)* Kolonne *f*; *(of criminals, youths, terrorists)* Bande *f*; *(of friends etc, clique)* Clique *f (col)*.

♦ **gang up** *vi* sich zusammentun. **to ~ ~ on sb** sich gegen jdn verschwören.

gangling ['gæŋglɪŋ] *adj* schlaksig.

gangplank ['gæŋplæŋk] *n* Laufplanke *f*.

gangrenous ['gæŋgrɪnəs] *adj* brandig.

gangster ['gæŋstəʳ] *n* Gangster *m*.

gangway ['gæŋweɪ] **1** *n* **(a)** *(Naut) (gangplank)* Landungsbrücke *f*; *(ladder)* Fallreep *nt*. **(b)** *(aisle)* Gang *m*. **2** *interj* Platz da.

gantry ['gæntrɪ] *n (for crane)* Portal *nt*; *(on motorway)* Schilderbrücke *f*; *(Rail)* Signalbrücke *f*; *(for rocket)* Abschußrampe *f*.

gaol [dʒeɪl] *n, vt* = **jail**.

gap [gæp] *n (lit, fig)* Lücke *f*; *(chink)* Spalt *m*; *(in surface)* Ritze *f*; *(Tech: spark ~)* Abstand *m*; *(fig) (in conversation, narrative, time)* Pause *f*; *(gulf)* Kluft *f*.

gape [geɪp] *vi* **(a)** *(person)* den Mund aufreißen; *(chasm etc)* gähnen; *(seam, wound)* klaffen. **(b)** *(stare: person)* starren. **to ~ at sb/sth** jdn/etw (mit offenem Mund) anstarren.

gaping ['geɪpɪŋ] *adj* **(a)** klaffend; *chasm* gähnend. **(b)** *(staring)* gaffend; *(astonished)* staunend.

garage ['gærɑːʒ, *(US)* gə'rɑːʒ] *n (for parking)* Garage *f*; *(for petrol)* Tankstelle *f*; *(for repairs etc)* (Reparatur)werkstatt *f*.

garb [gɑːb] *n* Gewand *nt*; *(col)* Kluft *f (col)*.

garbage ['gɑːbɪdʒ] *n (lit: esp US)* Abfall, Müll *m*; *(fig) (useless things)* Schund *m (col)*; *(nonsense)* Quatsch *m (col)*.

garbage: ~ can *n (US)* Mülleimer *m*; *(outside)* Mülltonne *f*; **~ disposal unit** *n* Müllschlucker *m*.

garbled ['gɑːbld] *adj* entstellt. **the message got ~ on its way** die Nachricht kam völlig entstellt an; **the facts got a little ~** die Tatsachen sind etwas durcheinandergeraten.

garden ['gɑːdn] Garten *m*; *(often pl: park)* Gartenanlagen *pl*.

gardener ['gɑːdnəʳ] *n* Gärtner(in *f*) *m*.

gardening ['gɑːdnɪŋ] *n* Gartenarbeit *f*.

garden *in cpds* Garten-; **~ party** *n* Gartenfest *nt*; **~ path** *n*: **to lead sb up the ~ path** *(col)* jdn an der Nase herumführen; **~ shears** *npl* Heckenschere *f*.

gargle ['gɑːgl] **1** *vi* gurgeln. **2** *n (liquid)* Gurgelwasser *nt*. **to have a ~** gurgeln.

gargoyle ['gɑːgɔɪl] *n* Wasserspeier *m*.

garish ['geərɪʃ] *adj lights etc* grell; *colour etc also* knallig *(col)*; *clothes* knallbunt.

garland ['gɑːlənd] *n* Kranz *m*; *(festoon)* Girlande *f*.

garlic ['gɑːlɪk] *n* Knoblauch *m*.

garment ['gɑːmənt] *n* Kleidungsstück *nt*. **~ industry** *(US)* Bekleidungsindustrie *f*.

garnish ['gɑːnɪʃ] *vt* garnieren.

garret ['gærət] *n* Dachboden *m*; *(room)* Dachkammer *f*.

garrison ['gærɪsən] **1** *n* Garnison *f*. **2** *vt troops* in Garnison legen; *town* mit einer Garnison belegen.

garrulous ['gærʊləs] *adj* geschwätzig.

garter ['gɑːtəʳ] *n* Strumpfband *nt*; *(US: suspender)* Strumpfhalter *m*.

gas [gæs] **1** *n* **(a)** Gas *nt*. **(b)** *(US: petrol)* Benzin *nt*. **(c)** *(anaesthetic)* Lachgas *nt*. **to have ~** Lachgas bekommen. **2** *vt* vergasen. **to ~ oneself** sich mit Gas vergiften. **3** *vi (col: talk)* schwafeln *(col)*.

gas *in cpds* Gas-; **~bag** *n (col)* Schwätzer(in *f*) *m (col)*; **~ chamber** *n* Gaskammer *f*; **~ cooker** *n* Gasherd *m*; **~ fire** *n* Gasofen *m*.

gash [gæʃ] **1** *n (wound)* klaffende Wunde; *(in earth, tree)* (klaffende) Spalte; *(in upholstery)* tiefer Schlitz. **2** *vt* aufschlitzen; *furniture, wood* tief einkerben. **he ~ed his knee** er hat sich *(dat)* das Knie aufgeschlagen.

gasket ['gæskɪt] *n (Tech)* Dichtung *f*.

gas: ~ lighter *n* Gasanzünder *m*; **~man** *n* Gasmann *m (col)*; **~ mask** *n* Gasmaske *f*; **~ meter** *n* Gaszähler *m*.

gasoline ['gæsəʊliːn] *n (US)* Benzin *nt*.

gasometer [gæ'sɒmɪtəʳ] *n* Gasometer *m*.

gasp [gɑːsp] **1** *n (for breath)* tiefer Atemzug. **to give a ~ of surprise** vor Überraschung die Luft anhalten; **to be at one's last ~** in den letzten Zügen liegen. **2** *vi (continually)* keuchen; *(once)* tief einatmen; *(with surprise etc)* nach Luft schnappen *(col)*. **to make sb ~** jdm den Atem nehmen; **to ~ for breath** nach Atem ringen.

gas: ~ station *n (US)* Tankstelle *f*; **~ stove** *n* Gasherd *m*; **~ tank** *n (US)* Benzintank *m*.

gastric: ~ flu *n* Darmgrippe *f*; **~ ulcer** *n* Magengeschwür *nt*.

gastritis [gæs'traɪtɪs] *n* Gastritis *f*.

gastroenteritis ['gæstrəʊˌentə'raɪtɪs] Magen-Darm-Entzündung *f*.

gastronomic [ˌgæstrə'nɒmɪk] *adj* gastronomisch.

gasworks ['gæswɜːks] *n sing or pl* Gaswerk *nt*.

gate [geɪt] *n* **(a)** Tor *nt*; *(small, garden ~)* Pforte *f*; *(five-barred ~)* Gatter *nt*; *(in airport)* Flugsteig *m*; *(of level-crossing)* Schranke *f*; *(sports ground entrance)* Einlaß *m*. **(b)** *(Sport) (attendance)* Zuschauerzahl *f*; *(entrance money)* Einnahmen *pl*.

gateau ['gætəʊ] *n* Torte *f*.

gate: ~crash *(col)* **1** *vt* **to ~crash a party** in eine Party hineinplatzen; **2** *vi* einfach so hingehen *(col)*; **~crasher** *n* ungeladener Gast; **~post** *n* Torpfosten *m*; **between you, me and the ~post** *(col)* unter uns gesagt; **~way** *n (lit, fig)* Tor *nt (to* zu*)*; *(archway)* Torbogen *m*.

gather ['gæðəʳ] **1** *vt* **(a)** *(collect, bring together)* sammeln; *people* versammeln; *flowers, fruit* pflücken; *potatoes, corn etc* ernten; *harvest* einbringen; *taxes* einziehen; *(collect up) broken glass, pins etc* aufsammeln; *one's belongings* (zusammen)packen. **to ~ one's strength/thoughts** Kräfte sammeln/seine Gedanken ordnen; **to ~ dust** verstauben.

(b) *(increase)* **to ~ speed** schneller werden; **to ~ strength** stärker werden.

(c) *(infer)* schließen *(from* aus*)*. **I ~ed that** das dachte ich mir; **I ~ from the papers that he has ...** wie ich aus den Zeitungen ersehe, hat er ...; **as far as I can ~** (so) wie ich es sehe; **I ~ she won't be coming** ich nehme an, daß sie nicht kommt; **as you will have/might have ~ed ...** wie Sie bestimmt/vielleicht bemerkt haben ...

(d) she ~ed her mink around her sie hüllte sich in ihren Nerz.

(e) *(Sew)* raffen.

2 *vi* **(a)** *(people)* sich versammeln; *(objects, dust etc)* sich (an)sammeln; *(clouds)* sich zusammenziehen; *(storm)* sich zusammenbrauen.

(**b**) *(increase: darkness etc)* zunehmen *(in an +dat)*.

♦ **gather around** *vi* **come on, children, ~ ~!** kommt alle her, Kinder!; **they ~ed ~ the fire** sie scharten sich um das Feuer.

♦ **gather up** *vt sep* aufsammeln; *one's belongings* zusammenpacken; *hair* hochstecken; *(fig) pieces* auflesen.

gathering ['gæðərɪŋ] *n* Versammlung *f*; *(meeting)* Treffen *nt*.

gauche [gəʊʃ] *adj* ungeschickt.

gaudy ['gɔːdɪ] *adj (+er)* knallig *(col)*.

gauge [geɪdʒ] **1** *n* (**a**) *(instrument)* Meßgerät *nt*; *(to measure diameter, width etc)* (Meß)lehre *f*; *(dial)* Anzeiger *m*. **pressure/wind ~** Druck-/Windmesser *m*; **oil ~** Ölstandsanzeiger *m*. (**b**) *(of wire, sheet metal etc)* Stärke *f*; *(of tube)* Durchmesser *m*; *(Rail)* Spurweite *f*. (**c**) *(fig)* Maßstab *m (of* für). **2** *vt* (**a**) *(measure)* messen. (**b**) *(fig: appraise) character* beurteilen; *reaction* abschätzen.

gaunt [gɔːnt] *adj (+er)* hager; *(from suffering)* abgezehrt.

gauntlet ['gɔːntlɪt] *n* (Stulpen)handschuh *m*; *(of armour)* Panzerhandschuh *m*. **to throw down the ~** *(fig)* den Fehdehandschuh hinwerfen; **to run the ~** *(fig)* Spießruten laufen; **to (have to) run the ~ of sth** einer Sache *(dat)* ausgesetzt sein.

gauze [gɔːz] *n* Gaze *f*; *(Med also)* Mull *m*.

gave [geɪv] *pret of* **give.**

gawky ['gɔːkɪ] *adj (+er) person, movement* schlaksig, staksig *(col)*; *animal* staksig *(col)*.

gawp [gɔːp] *vi (col)* glotzen *(col)*. **to ~ at sb/sth** jdn/etw anglotzen *(col)*.

gay [geɪ] **1** *adj (+er)* (**a**) *(happy)* fröhlich; *colours also* bunt; *company, occasion* lustig; *life* flott. **~ dog** *(col)* lockerer Vogel *(col)*. (**b**) *(homosexual)* schwul *(col)*. **2** *n* Schwule(r) *mf*.

gaze [geɪz] **1** *n* Blick *m*. **2** *vi* starren. **to ~ at sb/sth** jdn/etw anstarren.

gazelle [gə'zel] *n* Gazelle *f*.

gazette [gə'zet] *n* Zeitung *f*; *(government publication)* Amtsblatt *nt*.

gazetteer [ˌgæzɪ'tɪəʳ] *n* alphabetisches Ortsverzeichnis *(mit Ortsbeschreibung)*.

gazump [gə'zʌmp] *vt (Brit) entgegen mündlicher Zusage ein Haus an einen Höherbietenden verkaufen.*

GB = Great Britain GB, Großbritannien *nt*.

GCE *(Brit)* = **General Certificate of Education.**

Gdns = Gardens.

GDR = German Democratic Republic DDR *f*.

gear [gɪəʳ] **1** *n* (**a**) *(Aut etc)* Gang *m*. **~s** *pl (mechanism)* Getriebe *nt*; *(on bicycle)* Gangschaltung *f*; **to put the car into ~** einen Gang einlegen; **to leave the car in ~/out of ~** den Gang eingelegt lassen/das Auto im Leerlauf lassen; **to change ~** schalten; **to change into third ~** in den dritten Gang schalten. (**b**) *(equipment)* Ausrüstung *f*; *(tools)* Gerät *nt*; *(belongings, clothes)* Sachen *pl*. **2** *vt (fig)* **to be ~ed to sth** auf etw *(acc)* ausgerichtet sein; *(have facilities for)* auf etw *(acc)* eingerichtet sein.

gear: ~box *n* Getriebe *nt*; **~lever** *n (Brit)* Schaltknüppel *m*; *(column-mounted)* Schalthebel *m*; **~ shift** *(esp US) n* = **~ lever; ~ wheel** *n* Zahnrad *nt*.

gee [dʒiː] *interj* (**a**) *(esp US col)* Mann! *(col)*. **~ whiz!** Mensch Meier! *(col)*. (**b**) **~ up!** hü!

geese [giːs] *pl of* **goose.**

Geiger counter ['gaɪgəˌkaʊntəʳ] *n* Geigerzähler *m*.

gel [dʒel] **1** *n* Gel *nt*. **2** *vi* gelieren; *(fig: plan, idea)* Gestalt annehmen.

gelatin(e) ['dʒelətiːn] *n* Gelatine *f*.

gelding ['geldɪŋ] *n (horse)* Wallach *m*.

gelignite ['dʒelɪgnaɪt] *n* Plastiksprengstoff *m*.

gem [dʒem] *n* Edelstein *m*; *(cut also)* Juwel *nt*; *(fig) (person)* Juwel *nt*; *(of collection etc)* Prachtstück *nt*. **be a ~ and ...** sei ein Schatz und ...; **it's a real ~** *(fig)* es ist einmalig gut.

Gemini ['dʒemɪniː] *n* Zwillinge *pl*. **he's a ~** er ist Zwilling.

gen [dʒen] *n (Brit col)* Informationen *pl*.

gender ['dʒendəʳ] *n* Geschlecht *nt*.

gene [dʒiːn] *n* Gen *nt*, Erbfaktor *m*.

genealogy [ˌdʒiːnɪ'ælədʒɪ] *n* Stammbaumforschung *f*; *(ancestry)* Stammbaum *m*.

general ['dʒenərəl] **1** *adj* (**a**) allgemein; *view, enquiry also* generell; *agency* General-; *user, reader* Durchschnitts-; *(vague)* unbestimmt. **as a ~ rule** im allgemeinen; **in ~ use** allgemein in Gebrauch; **for ~ use** für den allgemeinen Gebrauch; *(for use by everybody)* für die Allgemeinheit; **~ headquarters** *(Mil)* Generalhauptquartier *nt*; **to explain sth in ~ terms** etw allgemein erklären; **the ~ idea is that ...** wir/sie *etc* hatten uns/sich *(dat)* das so gedacht, daß ...; **that was the ~ idea** so war das (auch) gedacht; **the ~ idea is to wait and see** wir/sie *etc* wollen einfach mal abwarten; **to give sb a ~ idea of sth** jdm eine ungefähre Vorstellung von etw geben; **OK, I've got the ~ idea** OK, ich hab' verstanden, um was es geht.

(**b**) *(after official title)* Ober-. **Consul ~** Generalkonsul *m*.

2 *n* (**a**) **in ~** im allgemeinen. (**b**) *(Mil)* General *m*; *(Caesar, Napoleon etc)* Feldherr *m*.

general: ~ anaesthetic *(Brit)*, **~ anesthetic** *(US) n* Vollnarkose *f*; **~ delivery** *adv (US)* postlagernd; **~ election** *n* Parlamentswahlen *pl*.

generality [ˌdʒenə'rælɪtɪ] *n* **to talk in generalities** ganz allgemein sprechen.

generalization [ˌdʒenərəlaɪ'zeɪʃən] *n* Verallgemeinerung *f*.

generalize ['dʒenərəlaɪz] *vti* verallgemeinern. **to ~ about sth** etw verallgemeinern.

general knowledge *n* Allgemeinbildung *f*.

generally ['dʒenərəlɪ] *adv (usually)* im allgemeinen; *(for the most part also)* im großen und ganzen; *(widely, not in detail)* allgemein. **~ speaking** im großen und ganzen.

general: ~ practitioner *n* praktischer Arzt, praktische Ärztin; **~ public** *n* Öffentlichkeit *f*; **~-purpose** *adj* Mehrzweck-; **~ staff** *n (Mil)* Generalstab *m*; **~ store** *n* Gemischtwarenhandlung *f*; **~ strike** *n* Generalstreik *m*.

generate ['dʒenəreɪt] *vt (lit, fig)* erzeugen. **generating station** Kraftwerk *nt*.

generation [ˌdʒenə'reɪʃən] *n* (**a**) *(lit, fig)* Generation *f*. **~ gap** Generationsunterschied *m*. (**b**) *(act of generating)* Erzeugung *f*.

generator ['dʒenəreɪtəʳ] *n* Generator *m*.

generic [dʒɪ'nerɪk] *adj (Biol)* Gattungs-. **~ name** *or* **term** Oberbegriff *m*.

generosity [ˌdʒenə'rɒsɪtɪ] *n* Großzügigkeit *f*.

generous ['dʒenərəs] *adj* (**a**) großzügig. (**b**) *(large, plentiful)* reichlich; *figure* üppig.

genesis ['dʒenɪsɪs] *n* Entstehung *f*. **(the Book of) G~** die Schöpfungsgeschichte.

genetic [dʒɪ'netɪk] *adj* genetisch. **~ engineering** experimentelle Genetik.

genetics [dʒɪ'netɪks] *n sing* Genetik *f*.

Geneva [dʒɪ'niːvə] *n* Genf *nt*. **Lake ~** der Genfer See; **~ Convention** Genfer Konvention *f*.

genial ['dʒiːnɪəl] *adj (lit, fig)* freundlich; *company* angenehm.

geniality [ˌdʒiːnɪ'ælɪtɪ] *n* Freundlichkeit *f*.

genitals ['dʒenɪtlz] *npl* Geschlechtsorgane *pl*.

genitive ['dʒenɪtɪv] *n (Gram)* Genitiv *m*. **in the ~** im Genitiv.

genius ['dʒiːnɪəs] *n, pl* **-es** *or* **genii** Genie *nt*; *(mental or creative capacity also)* schöpferische Kraft. **a man of ~** ein genialer Mensch; **to have a ~ for sth** eine besondere Gabe für etw haben; **he has a ~ for saying the wrong thing** er hat ein

Talent dafür, immer das Falsche zu sagen.

genocide ['dʒenəʊsaɪd] *n* Völkermord *m*.

genre ['ʒɑ̃:ŋrə] *n* Gattung *f*.

gent [dʒent] *n (col)* = **gentleman. ~s' shoes** *(Comm)* Herrenschuhe *pl*; **"G~s"** *(Brit)* „Herren"; **where is the ~s?** wo ist die Herrentoilette?

genteel [dʒen'ti:l] *adj* vornehm, fein.

gentile ['dʒentaɪl] **1** *n* Nichtjude *m*. **2** *adj* nichtjüdisch.

gentle ['dʒentl] *adj (+er)* sanft; *smack, breeze also, exercise* leicht; *knock, sound* leise; *rebuke also, heat* mild; *person, disposition* sanftmütig; *animal* zahm. **the ~ sex** das zarte Geschlecht; **to be ~ with sb** mit jdm sanft umgehen; **to be ~ with sth** mit etw behutsam umgehen.

gentleman ['dʒentlmən] *n, pl* **-men** [-mən] *(man)* Herr *m*; *(well-mannered, well-born)* Gentleman *m*. **gentlemen's agreement** Gentlemen's Agreement *nt*; **gentlemen!** meine Herren!

gentlemanly ['dʒentlmənlɪ] *adj* zuvorkommend.

gently ['dʒentlɪ] *adv see adj*. **to handle sb/sth ~** mit jdm/etw behutsam umgehen; **~ does it!** sachte, sachte!

gentry ['dʒentrɪ] *npl* (niederer) Adel *m*.

genuine ['dʒenjʊɪn] *adj* echt; *manuscript* Original-; *offer* ernstgemeint; *(sincere)* aufrichtig.

genuinely ['dʒenjʊɪnlɪ] *adv* wirklich; *(sincerely also)* aufrichtig.

genus ['dʒenəs] *n, pl* **genera** *(Biol)* Gattung *f*.

geographer [dʒɪ'ɒgrəfəʳ] *n* Geograph(in *f*) *m*.

geographical [dʒɪə'græfɪkəl] *adj* geographisch.

geography [dʒɪ'ɒgrəfɪ] *n* Geographie *f*; *(Sch also)* Erdkunde *f*.

geological [dʒɪəʊ'lɒdʒɪkəl] *adj* geologisch.

geologist [dʒɪ'ɒlədʒɪst] *n* Geologe *m*, Geologin *f*.

geology [dʒɪ'ɒlədʒɪ] *n* Geologie *f*.

geometric(al) [dʒɪəʊ'metrɪk(əl)] *adj* geometrisch.

geometry [dʒɪ'ɒmɪtrɪ] *n* Geometrie *f*.

geophysics [ˌdʒi:əʊ'fɪzɪks] *n sing* Geophysik *f*.

Georgian ['dʒɔ:dʒɪən] *adj (Brit Hist)* georgianisch.

geranium [dʒɪ'reɪnɪəm] *n* Geranie *f*.

geriatric [ˌdʒerɪ'ætrɪk] **1** *adj* geriatrisch; *nurse, nursing* Alten-; *home* Alters-; *patient* der Geriatrie. **~ medicine** Altersheilkunde *f*. **2** *n* alter Mensch.

geriatrics [ˌdʒerɪ'ætrɪks] *n sing* Geriatrie *f*.

germ [dʒɜ:m] *n (lit, fig)* Keim *m*; *(of particular illness)* Krankheitserreger *m*; *(esp of cold)* Bazillus *m*. **don't spread your ~s around** behalte deine Bazillen für dich.

German ['dʒɜ:mən] **1** *adj* deutsch. **2** *n* **(a)** Deutsche(r) *mf*. **(b)** *(language)* Deutsch *nt*; *see* **English.**

German Democratic Republic *n* Deutsche Demokratische Republik.

Germanic [dʒɜ:'mænɪk] *adj* germanisch.

German: ~ measles *n sing* Röteln *pl*; **~ shepherd** *n* deutscher Schäferhund.

Germany ['dʒɜ:mənɪ] *n* Deutschland *nt*.

germinate ['dʒɜ:mɪneɪt] *vi (lit, fig)* keimen.

germination [ˌdʒɜ:mɪ'neɪʃən] *n* Keimung *f*.

germ warfare *n* bakteriologische Kriegführung.

gerund ['dʒerənd] *n* Gerundium *nt*.

gestation [dʒe'steɪʃən] *n (of animals)* Trächtigkeit *f*; *(of humans)* Schwangerschaft *f*; *(fig)* Reifwerden *nt*.

gesticulate [dʒe'stɪkjʊleɪt] *vi* gestikulieren.

gesture ['dʒestʃəʳ] **1** *n (lit, fig)* Geste *f*. **as a ~ of support** als Zeichen der Unterstützung. **2** *vi* gestikulieren. **to ~ to sb to do sth** jdm bedeuten, etw zu tun.

get [get] *pret* **got,** *ptp* **got** *or (US)* **gotten 1** *vt* **(a)** *(receive)* bekommen, kriegen *(col)*; *wealth, glory* kommen zu; *time, personal characteristics, idea* haben *(from* von*)*. **where did you ~ it (from)?** woher hast du das?; **this country ~s very little rain** in diesem Land regnet es sehr wenig; **where do you ~ that idea (from)?** wie kommst du denn auf die Idee?; **I got quite a surprise/shock** ich war ziemlich überrascht/ich habe einen ziemlichen Schock bekommen *or* gekriegt *(col)*; **I don't ~ much from his lectures** seine Vorlesungen geben mir nicht viel; **he's only in it for what he can ~** er will nur dabei profitieren; **you'll ~ it!** *(col: be in trouble)* du wirst was erleben! *(col)*.

(b) *(obtain by one's own efforts) object* sich *(dat)* besorgen; *visa, money also* sich *(dat)* beschaffen; *(find) staff, partner, job* finden; *(buy)* kaufen; *(buy and keep) large item, car, cat* sich *(dat)* anschaffen. **not to be able to ~ sth** etw nicht bekommen *or* kriegen *(col)*; **to ~ sb/oneself sth, to ~ sth for sb/oneself** jdm/sich etw besorgen; **to need to ~ sth** etw brauchen; **I've still three to ~** ich brauche noch drei; **you'll have to ~ a job/flat** Sie müssen zusehen, daß Sie eine Stelle/Wohnung bekommen *or* finden; **why don't you ~ a flat of your own?** warum schaffen Sie sich *(dat)* nicht eine eigene Wohnung an?; *(rent)* warum nehmen Sie sich *(dat)* nicht eine eigene Wohnung?; **what are you ~ting her for Christmas?** was schenkst du ihr zu Weihnachten?; **I got her a doll for Christmas** ich habe für sie eine Puppe zu Weihnachten besorgt; **we could ~ a taxi** wir könnten (uns *dat*) ein Taxi nehmen; **could you ~ me a taxi?** könnten Sie mir ein Taxi besorgen?; **could you ~ that?** *(telephone)* gehst du ran?; *(door)* gehst du?

(c) *(fetch) person, doctor, object* holen. **to ~ sb from the station** jdn vom Bahnhof abholen; **I got him a drink** ich habe ihm etwas zu trinken geholt; **can I ~ you a drink?** möchten Sie etwas zu trinken?

(d) *(catch)* bekommen, kriegen *(col)*; *cold, illness also* sich *(dat)* holen; *(hit)* treffen, erwischen *(col)*. **to ~ sb by the arm/leg** jdn am Arm/Bein packen; **it** *or* **the pain ~s me here** *(col)* es tut hier weh; **~ him/it!** *(to dog)* faß!; **the bullet got him in the neck** die Kugel traf ihn in den Hals; **(I've) got him/it!** *(col)* ich hab' ihn/ich hab's *(col)*; **got you!** *(col)* hab' dich (erwischt)! *(col)*; **he's out to ~ you** *(col)* er hat's auf dich abgesehen *(col)*; **we'll ~ them yet!** *(col)* die werden wir schon noch kriegen! *(col)*; **I'll ~ you for that!** *(col)* das wirst du mir büßen!; **you've got me there!** *(col)* da bin ich überfragt.

(e) *(Telec) (contact)* erreichen; *number* bekommen; *(put through to, get for sb)* geben. **~ me Mr Johnston please** verbinden Sie mich bitte mit Herrn Johnston.

(f) *(prepare) meal* machen. **I'll ~ you some breakfast** ich mache dir etwas zum Frühstück.

(g) *(send, take)* bringen. **to ~ sb to hospital** jdn ins Krankenhaus bringen; **to ~ sth to sb** jdm etw zukommen lassen; *(take it oneself)* jdm etw bringen; **where does that ~ us?** *(col)* was bringt uns *(dat)* das? *(col)*; **this discussion isn't ~ting us anywhere** diese Diskussion führt zu nichts; **we'll ~ you there somehow** irgendwie kriegen wir dich schon dahin *(col)*; **how am I going to ~ myself home?** wie komme ich nach Hause?

(h) *(manage to move)* kriegen *(col)*. **we'll never ~ this piano upstairs** das Klavier kriegen wir nie nach oben *(col)*.

(i) *(understand)* kapieren *(col)*; *(hear)* mitbekommen, mitkriegen *(col)*. **I don't ~ it/you** *(col)* da komme ich nicht mit *(col)*/ich verstehe nicht, was du meinst; **~ it?** kapiert? *(col)*.

(j) *(col) (annoy)* ärgern, aufregen; *(upset)* an die Nieren gehen *(+dat) (col)*.

(k) to ~ sb to do sth *(have sth done by sb)* etw von jdm machen lassen; *(persuade sb)* jdn dazu bringen, etw zu tun; **I'll ~ him to phone you back** ich sage ihm, er soll Sie zurückrufen; **you'll never ~ him to understand** du wirst es nie schaffen, daß er das versteht.

(l) to ~ sth done *(do)* etw machen; *(cause to be done)* etw machen lassen; **to ~ one's hair cut** sich *(dat)* die Haare schneiden lassen; **I'll ~ the grass cut soon** der Rasen wird bald gemäht; *(by sb else)* ich lasse bald den Rasen mähen; **I'm not going to ~ much done** ich werde nicht viel schaffen; **to ~ things done** etwas fertigkriegen *(col)*; **you'll ~ me thrown out** du bringst es noch so weit, daß ich hinausgeworfen werde.

(m) I can't ~ the car to start/door to open ich kriege das Auto nicht an *(col)*/die Tür nicht auf *(col)*; **once I've got this machine to work** wenn ich die Maschine erst einmal zum Laufen gebracht habe; **to ~ sb talking** jdn zum Sprechen bringen; **to ~ sth clean/shut** etw sauber-/zukriegen *(col)*; **that'll ~ it clean/shut** damit wird es sauber/geht es zu; **to ~ sb drunk** jdn betrunken machen; **to ~ one's arm broken** sich *(dat)* den Arm brechen; **to ~ one's hands dirty** sich *(dat)* die Hände schmutzig machen; **to ~ one's things packed** seine Sachen packen.

(n) to have got sth *(have)* etw haben.

2 *vi* **(a)** *(go, arrive)* kommen; gehen. **to ~ home/here** nach Hause kommen/hier ankommen; **I've got as far as page 16** ich bin auf Seite 16; **~ (lost)!** verschwinde!; **to ~ there** *(succeed)* es schaffen *(col)*; *(understand)* dahinterkommen *(col)*; **now we're ~ting there** *(to the truth)* jetzt kommt's raus! *(col)*; **to ~ somewhere/nowhere** *(in job, career etc)* es zu etwas/nichts bringen; *(with work, in discussion etc)* weiterkommen/nicht weiterkommen; **to ~ somewhere/nowhere (with sb)** (bei jdm) etwas/nichts erreichen.

(b) *(become, be, to form passive)* werden. **to ~ old/tired/paid** *etc* alt/müde/bezahlt *etc* werden; **I'm/the weather is ~ting cold/warm** mir wird es/es wird kalt/warm; **to ~ dressed/shaved/washed** *etc* sich anziehen/rasieren/waschen *etc*; **you could ~ killed** du riskierst dein Leben; **how do people ~ that way?** *(col)* wie wird man nur so? *(col)*.

(c) *(start)* **I got to like him** er ist mir sympathisch geworden; **to ~ to like sth** an etw *(dat)* Gefallen finden; **to ~ to be ...** (mit der Zeit) ... werden; **to ~ working/scrubbing** *etc* anfangen zu arbeiten/schrubben *etc*; **I got talking to him** ich kam mit ihm ins Gespräch; **let's ~ started** fangen wir an!; **we got to talking about that** wir kamen darauf zu sprechen; **I got to thinking ...** ich habe mir überlegt, ...

(d) *(~ chance to)* **to ~ to do sth** die Möglichkeit haben, etw zu tun; **to ~ to see sb** jdn zu sehen bekommen.

(e) *(be obliged to)* **to have got to do sth** etw tun müssen; **I've got to** ich muß.

♦ **get about** *vi (after illness)* auf den Beinen sein; *(socially)* herumkommen; *(news, rumour)* sich verbreiten *(prep obj* in *+dat)*.

♦ **get across 1** *vi* **(a)** *(cross)* hinüber-/herüberkommen; *(+prep obj) road, river* kommen über *(+acc)*. **(b)** *(play, comedian etc)* ankommen *(to* bei*)*; *(teacher etc)* sich verständlich machen *(to dat)*; *(idea, meaning)* klarwerden *(to dat)*. **2** *vt always separate* **(a)** *(transport)* hinüber-/herüberbringen. **to ~ sth ~ sth** etw über etw *(acc)* (hinüber-/herüber)bringen. **(b)** *(communicate)* klarmachen *(to sb* jdm*)*.

♦ **get along** *vi* **(a)** gehen. **I must be ~ting ~** ich muß jetzt gehen; **~ ~ with you!** *(col)* jetzt hör aber auf! *(col)*. **(b)** *(manage)* zurechtkommen. **(c)** *(progress)* vorankommen; *(work, patient, wound etc)* sich machen. **(d)** *(be on good terms)* auskommen *(with* mit*)*. **they ~ ~ quite well** sie kommen ganz gut miteinander aus.

♦ **get around 1** *vi +prep obj problem etc* herumkommen um; *law, regulations* umgehen. **to ~ ~ the conference table** sich an einen Tisch setzen. **2** *vt always separate* **(a)** *(make agree)* herumbringen *or* -kriegen *(col)*. **I'm sure I can ~ her ~ to my way of thinking** ich bin sicher, daß ich sie überzeugen kann. **(b)** *+prep obj* **to ~ people (together) ~ the conference table** Leute an einem Tisch zusammenbringen.

♦ **get around to** *vi +prep obj (col)* **to ~ ~ ~ sth/doing sth** zu etw kommen/dazu kommen, etw zu tun.

♦ **get at** *vi +prep obj* **(a)** *(gain access to, reach)* herankommen an *(+acc)*; *town, house* erreichen; *(take, eat etc) food, money* gehen an *(+acc)*. **put it where the dog/child won't ~ ~ it** stellen Sie es irgendwohin, wo der Hund/das Kind nicht drankommt *(col)*; **let me ~ ~ him!** *(col)* na, wenn ich den erwische! *(col)*; **the mice have been ~ting ~ the cheese again** die Mäuse waren wieder am Käse. **(b)** *(ascertain) truth* herausfinden; *facts* kommen an *(+acc)*. **(c)** *(col: mean)* **what are you ~ting ~?** worauf wollen Sie hinaus? **(d) to ~ ~ sb** *(col) (criticize)* an jdm etwas auszusetzen haben *(col)*; *(nag)* an jdm herumnörgeln *(col)*.

♦ **get away** *vi (leave)* wegkommen; *(prisoner, thief)* entkommen *(from sb* jdm*)*. **there's no ~ting ~ from the fact that ...** man kommt nicht um die Tatsache herum, daß ...; **to ~ ~ from it all** sich von allem frei machen; **~ ~ (with you)!** *(col)* ach, hör auf! *(col)*.

♦ **get away with** *vi +prep obj* **(a)** *(steal)* entkommen mit. **(b)** *(col: escape punishment)* **you'll/he'll** *etc* **never ~ ~ ~ that** das wird nicht gutgehen; **he got ~ ~ it** er ist ungeschoren davongekommen *(col)*; **the things he ~s ~ ~!** was er sich *(dat)* alles erlauben kann!

♦ **get back 1** *vi* zurückkommen; zurückgehen. **I must be ~ting ~ (home)** ich muß nach Hause; **~ ~!** zurück(treten)! **2** *vt sep* **(a)** *possessions* zurückbekommen; *strength* zurückgewinnen. **now that I've got you/it ~** jetzt, wo ich dich/es wiederhabe. **(b)** *(bring back)* zurückbringen.

♦ **get back at** *vi +prep obj (col)* sich rächen an *(+dat)*. **to ~ ~ ~ sb for sth** jdm etw heimzahlen *(col)*.

♦ **get back to** *vi +prep obj (esp Comm)* sich wieder in Verbindung setzen mit. **I'll ~ ~ ~ you on that** ich werde darauf zurückkommen.

♦ **get behind** *vi (with work, payments)* in Rückstand kommen.

♦ **get by** *vi* **(a)** *(move past)* vorbeikommen *(prep obj* an *+dat)*. **(b)** *(manage)* **she ~s ~ on very little money** sie kommt mit sehr wenig Geld aus; **I can just about ~ ~ in German** ich komme mit meinem Deutsch gerade so durch.

♦ **get down 1** *vi* **(a)** *(descend)* hinunter-/heruntersteigen *(prep obj, from* von*)*; *(from horse, bicycle)* absteigen *(from* von*)*. **~ ~!** runter! *(col)*. **(b)** *(leave table)* aufstehen. **2** *vt sep* **(a)** *(take down)* herunternehmen. **(b)** *(reduce) inflation etc* herunterbekommen *(to* auf *+acc)*. **(c)** *(swallow) food* hinunterbringen. **~ this ~ (you)!** *(col)* trink/iß das! **(d)** *(make a note of)* aufschreiben. **(e)** *(col: depress)* fertigmachen *(col)*. **don't let it ~ you ~** laß dich davon nicht unterkriegen *(col)*.

♦ **get down to** *vi +prep obj* sich machen an *(+acc)*; *(find time to do)* kommen zu.

♦ **get in 1** *vi* **(a)** *(enter)* hinein-/hereinkommen *(prep obj, -to* in *+acc)*; *(into car, train etc)* einsteigen *(prep obj, -to* in *+acc)*. **to ~ ~(to) the bath** in die Badewanne steigen; **he can't ~ ~** er kommt nicht herein/hinein. **(b)** *(arrive: train, bus)* ankommen. **(c)** *(be admitted)* angenommen werden; *(be elected)* gewählt werden. **(d)** *(get home)* nach Hause kommen. **2** *vt* **(a)** *sep (bring in)* hinein-/hereinbringen *(prep obj, -to* in *+acc)*; *(fetch)* herein-/hineinholen *(-to* in *+acc)*; *(col) groceries, drink, supplies* sich eindecken mit. **(b)** *sep (submit) forms* einreichen. **(c)** *sep (insert into,* *find room for)* hineinbringen; *(fig) punch, request, words* anbringen. **(d)** *sep (send for) doctor etc* holen. **(e)** *always separate* **to ~ one's eye/hand ~** in Übung kommen.

♦ **get in on** *vi +prep obj (col)* mitmachen bei. **to ~ ~ the act** mitmachen.

♦ **get into 1** *vi +prep obj* **(a)** *rage, debt, company* geraten in *(+acc)*. **what's got ~ him?** *(col)* was ist bloß in ihn gefahren? *(col)*. **(b)** *bad habits* sich *(dat)* angewöhnen. **(c)** *(get involved in) book* sich einlesen bei; *work* sich einarbeiten in *(+acc)*. **(d)** *(put on) clothes* anziehen. **2** *vt +prep obj always separate* **you'll ~ me ~ difficulties** wegen dir komme ich noch in Schwierigkeiten; **to ~ sb ~ bad habits** jdm schlechte Angewohnheiten beibringen.

♦ **get in with** *vi +prep obj bad company* geraten in *(+acc)*; *(ingratiate)* sich gut stellen mit.

♦ **get off 1** *vi* **(a)** *(from bus, train etc)* aussteigen *(prep obj* aus*)*; *(from bicycle, horse)* absteigen *(prep obj* von*)*. **~ ~ the grass!** gehen Sie vom Rasen runter!; **to tell sb where to ~ ~** *(col)* jdm gründlich die Meinung sagen *(col)*; **he knows where he can ~ ~!** *(col)* der kann mich mal! *(col!)*. **(b)** *(leave)* wegkommen. **it's time you got ~ to school** es ist Zeit, daß ihr in die Schule geht; **to ~ ~ to a good/bad start** einen guten/schlechten Anfang machen. **(c)** *(escape, be let off)* davonkommen *(col)*. **to ~ ~ with a fine** mit einer Geldstrafe davonkommen; **I got ~ having to do the work** ich bin um die Arbeit herumgekommen. **(d)** *(fall asleep)* **to ~ ~ (to sleep)** einschlafen. **(e)** *(from work etc)* gehen können. **what time do you ~ ~ work?** wann hören Sie mit der Arbeit auf?

2 *vt* **(a)** *sep (remove)* wegbekommen, wegkriegen *(col) (prep obj* von*)*; *clothes, shoes* ausziehen; *lid, wrapping* abmachen *(prep obj* von*)*; *(manage to ~ ~)* abbekommen *(prep obj* von*)*; *stains* herausmachen *(prep obj* aus*)*; *(manage to ~ ~)* herausbekommen *or* -kriegen *(col) (prep obj* aus*)*. **~ your dirty hands ~ that** nimm deine schmutzigen Hände da weg! **(b)** *always separate (send off) mail, children* losschicken. **to ~ sb/sth ~ to a good start** jdm/einer Sache zu einem guten Start verhelfen; **when she'd got the children ~ to school** als sie die Kinder versorgt und in die Schule geschickt hatte; **to ~ sb ~ (to sleep)** jdn zum Schlafen bringen. **(c)** *sep (lawyer) accused* freibekommen. **(d)** *always separate (from work etc) day, afternoon* freibekommen.

♦ **get off with** *vi +prep obj (col: start a relationship with)* aufreißen *(col)*.

♦ **get on 1** *vi* **(a)** *(climb on)* hinauf-/heraufsteigen *(prep obj* auf *+acc)*; *(on bus, train etc)* einsteigen *(prep obj, -to* in *+acc)*; *(on bicycle, horse etc)* aufsteigen *(prep obj, -to* auf *+acc)*. **to ~ ~ sth** auf etw *(acc)* aufsteigen *etc*.

(b) *(continue: with work etc)* weitermachen. **~ ~ with it!** nun mach schon! *(col)*; **this will do to be ~ting ~ with** das tut's wohl für den Anfang *(col)*.

(c) *(get late, old)* **time is ~ting ~** es wird langsam spät; **he is ~ting ~ (in years)** er wird langsam alt; **he's ~ting ~ for 40** er geht auf die 40 zu; **there were ~ting ~ for 60** es waren fast 60.

(d) = get along (a).

(e) *(progress)* vorankommen; *(work also, patient, pupil)* Fortschritte machen. **to ~ ~ in the world** es zu etwas bringen; **how did you ~ ~ in the exam?** wie ging's (dir) in der Prüfung?; **how are you ~ting ~?** wie geht's?; **to ~ ~ without sb/sth** ohne jdn/etw zurechtkommen.

(f) *(have a good relationship)* sich verstehen, auskommen *(with* mit*)*. **they don't ~ ~ (with each other)** sie kommen nicht miteinander aus.

2 *vt sep (prep obj* auf *+acc) clothes, shoes* anziehen; *hat, kettle* aufsetzen; *lid, cover* drauftun.

♦ **get on to** *vi +prep obj (col)* **(a)** *new subject* übergehen zu. **(b)** *(contact)* sich in Verbindung setzen mit. **I'll ~ ~ ~ him about it** ich werde ihn daraufhin ansprechen.

♦ **get out 1** *vi* **(a)** heraus-/hinauskommen *(of* aus*)*; *(climb out)* hinaus-/heraussteigen *(of* aus*)*; *(of bus, train, car)* aussteigen *(of* aus*)*; *(of business, contract)* aussteigen *(col) (of* aus*)*. **he has to ~ ~ of the country** er muß das Land verlassen; **let's ~ ~ (of here)!** bloß weg hier! *(col)*; **~ ~ (of my room)!** raus (aus meinem Zimmer)! *(col)*; **to ~ ~ of bed** aufstehen; **I don't ~ ~ much these days** ich komme in letzter Zeit nicht viel raus *(col)*. **(b)** *(lit, fig: escape, leak out) (of* aus*)* herauskommen; *(animal, prisoner also)* entkommen; *(news)* an die Öffentlichkeit dringen.

2 *vt sep* **(a)** *(remove) (of* aus*) cork, splinter, stain etc* herausmachen; *people* hinaus-/herausbringen; *(send out)* hinausschicken. **~ him ~ of my house** schaff mir ihn aus dem Haus! **(b)** *(take out) car, wallet* herausholen *(of* aus*)*. **(c)** *(withdraw) money* abheben *(of* von*)*. **(d)** *(borrow from library)* ausleihen *(of* aus*)*. **(e) you only ~ ~ what you put in** Sie bekommen nur das zurück, was Sie hineinstecken.

♦ **get out of 1** *vi +prep obj see also* **get out 1** *duty, obligation* herumkommen um; *difficulty* herauskommen aus. **you can't ~ ~ ~ it now** jetzt kannst du nicht mehr zurück. **2** *vt +prep obj always separate see also* **get out 2 (a-c)** *words, confession, truth* herausbekommen *or* -kriegen *(col)* aus; *profit* machen bei; *benefit, little, nothing* haben von; *pleasure* haben an *(+dat)*. **to ~ the best/most ~ ~ sth** etw voll ausnutzen; **and what I ~ ~ ~ it?** und was habe ich davon?

♦ **get over 1** *vi* **(a)** *(cross)* hinüber-/herübergehen *(prep obj* über *+acc)*; *(climb over)* hinüber-/herübersteigen; *(+prep obj)* steigen über *(+acc)*. **they got ~ to the other side** sie gelangten auf die andere Seite. **(b)** *+prep obj (lit, fig: recover from) disappointment, loss, fact, experience* (hin)wegkommen über *(+acc)*; *shock, illness* sich erholen von. **I can't ~ ~ the fact that ...** ich komme gar nicht darüber hinweg, daß ...; **I can't ~ ~ it** *(col)* da komm ich nicht drüber weg *(col)*. **(c)** *+prep obj (overcome) problem, nervousness* überwinden.

2 *vt* **(a)** *always separate (transport across)* hinüber-/herüberbringen *(prep obj* über *+acc)*; *(fetch)* holen; *(help sb to cross, climb)* hinüber-/herüberhelfen *(sb* jdm*) (prep obj* über *+acc)*. **(b)** *sep information, ideas etc* verständlich machen *(to dat)*; *(impress upon)* klarmachen *(to dat)*. **she ~s her songs ~ well** sie kommt mit ihren Liedern gut an.

♦ **get over with** *vt always separate* hinter sich *(acc)* bringen. **let's ~ it ~ (~)** bringen wir's hinter uns.

♦ **get round (to) = get around (to).**

♦ **get through 1** *vi* **(a)** *(person, thing)* durchkommen *(prep obj* durch*)*; *(news)* durchdringen; *(Telec)* durchkommen *(col) (to sb* zu jdm, *to London* nach London*)*. **to ~ ~ to the second round/final** in die zweite Runde/Endrunde kommen. **(b)** *(communicate, be understood) (person)* durchdringen zu; *(idea etc)* klarwerden *(to dat)*. **(c)** *+prep obj (finish) work* fertigmachen, erledigen; *(manage to ~ ~)* schaffen *(col)*; *book* fertiglesen, auslesen. **when I've got ~ this** wenn ich damit fertig bin. **(d)** *+prep obj (survive) days, time* herumbekommen, herumkriegen *(col)*. **(e)** *+prep obj (consume, use up)* verbrauchen; *clothes, shoes* abnutzen; *food* aufessen; *fortune* durchbringen *(col)*.

2 *vt always separate* **(a)** *person, object, proposal* durchbekommen, durchbringen *(prep obj* durch); *message* durchgeben *(to dat)*; *supplies* durchbringen. **it was his English that got him ~** er hat das nur aufgrund seines Englisch geschafft; **he got the team ~ to the finals** er hat die Mannschaft in die Endrunde gebracht. **(b)** *(make understand)* **to ~ sth ~ (to sb)** jdm etw klarmachen.

♦ **get through with** *vi +prep obj (col: finish)* hinter sich bringen; *job also, formalities, subject* erledigen; *(col) person* fertig werden mit.

♦ **get to** *vi +prep obj* **(a)** *(arrive at)* kommen zu; *hotel, town also* ankommen in *(+dat)*. **where have you got ~ with that book?** wie weit seid ihr mit dem Buch? **(b)** *(col: annoy, upset)* aufregen.

♦ **get together 1** *vi* zusammenkommen; *(estranged couple)* sich versöhnen; *(combine forces)* sich zusammenschließen. **to ~ ~ about sth** zusammenkommen und etw beraten; **why don't we ~ ~ later and have a drink?** warum treffen wir uns nicht später und trinken einen? **2** *vt sep people, parts, collection* zusammenbringen; *documents* zusammensuchen; *thoughts, ideas* sammeln. **to ~ one's things ~** seine Sachen zusammenpacken; **to ~ it ~** *(col)* es bringen *(col)*.

♦ **get up 1** *vi* **(a)** *(stand up, get out of bed)* aufstehen. **(b)** *(climb up)* hinauf-/heraufsteigen *(prep obj* auf *+acc)*. **(c)** *(wind)* aufkommen; *(sea)* stürmisch werden. **2** *vt* **(a)** *always separate (get out of bed)* aus dem Bett holen; *(help stand up)* aufhelfen *(+dat)*. **(b)** *sep steam* aufbauen. **to ~ ~ speed** sich beschleunigen. **(c)** *sep (organize)* organisieren; *play also* auf die Beine stellen *(col)*. **(d)** *always separate (dress up)* zurechtmachen. **to ~ oneself ~ as sb/sth** sich als jd/etw verkleiden; **to ~ sth ~ to look like sth** etw als etw aufmachen.

♦ **get up to** *vi +prep obj* **(a)** *(lit, fig: reach)* erreichen; *standard* herankommen an *(+acc)*; *page* kommen bis. **(b)** *(be involved in)* anstellen *(col)*. **to ~ ~ ~ mischief** etwas anstellen; **what have you been ~ting ~ ~?** was hast du getrieben? *(col)*.

get: ~-at-able [ˌget'ætəbl] *adj (col)* leicht erreichbar; **~away 1** *n* Flucht *f*; **to make one's ~away** sich davonmachen *(col)*; **2** *adj attr* Flucht-; **~-together** *n* Treffen *nt*; **~-up** *n (col)* Aufmachung *f (col)*; **~-up-and-go** *n (col)* Elan *m*.

geyser ['giːzə[r]] *n* **(a)** *(Geol)* Geiser, Geysir *m*. **(b)** *(domestic ~)* Durchlauferhitzer *m*.

Ghana ['gɑːnə] *n* Ghana *nt*.

Ghanaian [gɑː'neɪən] **1** *adj* ghanaisch. **2** *n (person)* Ghanaer(in *f*) *m*.

ghastly ['gɑːstlɪ] *adj* **(a)** *crime etc* entsetzlich; *mistake* schrecklich. **(b)** *(col: awful)* gräßlich *(col)*, scheußlich *(col)*.

gherkin ['gɜːkɪn] *n* Gewürzgurke *f*.

ghetto ['getəʊ] *n* G(h)etto *nt*.

ghettoblaster ['getəʊblaːstə[r]] *n (col)* großes Kofferradio.

ghost [gəʊst] **1** *n (apparition)* Gespenst *nt*; *(of sb)* Geist *m*. **I haven't the ~ of a chance** ich habe nicht die geringste Chance; **to give up the ~** *(col)* den Geist aufgeben *(col)*. **2** *vt* **to ~ sb's speeches** für jdn Reden (als Ghostwriter) schreiben.

ghostly ['gəʊstlɪ] *adj (+er)* gespenstisch.

ghost *in cpds* Geister-; **~ story** *n* Gespenstergeschichte *f*; **~ town** *n* Geisterstadt *f*; **~writer** *n* Ghostwriter *m*.

ghoulish ['guːlɪʃ] *adj* makaber; *laughter, interest* schaurig.

G.I. *n* GI, US-Soldat *m*.

giant ['dʒaɪənt] **1** *n* Riese *m*; *(fig)* Größe *f*; *(company)* Gigant *m*. **2** *adj* riesig, Riesen-. **~ (-size) packet** Riesenpackung *f*; **~ panda** *n* Großer Panda *n*.

gibber ['dʒɪbə[r]] *vi (ape)* schnattern; *(idiot)* brabbeln. **~ing idiot** *(col)* Blödmann *m (col)*.

gibberish ['dzɪbərɪʃ] *n* Kauderwelsch *nt*.

gibbet ['dʒɪbɪt] *n* Galgen *m*.

gibbon ['gɪbən] *n* Gibbon *m*.

gibe [dʒaɪb] **1** *n* Stichelei *f*. **2** *vi* sticheln. **to ~ at sb/sth** höhnische Bemerkungen über jdn/etw machen.

giblets ['dʒɪblɪts] *npl* Geflügelinnereien *pl*.

Gibraltar [dʒɪ'brɔːltə[r]] *n* Gibraltar *nt*.

giddiness ['gɪdɪnɪs] *n* Schwindelgefühl *nt*.

giddy ['gɪdɪ] *adj (+er)* schwind(e)lig; *feeling* Schwindel-. **I feel ~** mir ist schwind(e)lig.

gift [gɪft] *n* **(a)** Geschenk *nt*. **a free ~** ein Geschenk *nt*; **it was a ~** *(col: easy)* das war ja geschenkt *(col)*. **(b)** *(talent)* Begabung *f*. **to have a ~ for sth** ein Talent für etw haben.

gifted ['gɪftɪd] *adj* begabt *(in* für*)*.

gift: ~ horse *n*: **don't look a ~ horse in the mouth** *(prov)* einem geschenkten Gaul schaut man nicht ins Maul *(prov)*; **~ token** *n* Geschenkgutschein *m*; **~-wrap** *vt* in Geschenkpapier einwickeln.

gig [gɪg] *n (col: concert)* Konzert *nt*.

gigantic [dʒaɪ'gæntɪk] *adj* riesig, riesengroß.

giggle ['gɪgl] **1** *n* Gekicher *nt no pl*. **it was a bit of a ~** *(col)* es war ganz lustig; **to get the ~s** anfangen herumzukichern *(col)*; **she's got the ~s** sie kann nicht aufhören zu kichern. **2** *vi* kichern.

gigolo ['ʒɪgələʊ] *n* Gigolo *m*.

gild [gɪld] *vt* vergolden. **to ~ the lily** des Guten zuviel tun.

gill[1] [gɪl] *n (of fish)* Kieme *f*.

gill[2] [dʒɪl] *n (Measure)* Gill *nt*.

gilt [gɪlt] *n (material)* Vergoldung *f*.

gilt-edged [ˌgɪlt'edʒd] *adj (Fin)* mündelsicher; *(fig)* solide.

gimlet ['gɪmlɪt] *n* Vorbohrer *m*.

gimmick ['gɪmɪk] *n* Gag *m (col)*; *(gadget)* Spielerei *f*.

gimmickry ['gɪmɪkrɪ] *n* Effekthascherei *f*; *(advertising, sales)* Gags *pl*; *(gadgetry)* Spielereien *pl*.

gimmicky ['gɪmɪkɪ] *adj* effekthascherisch.

gin [dʒɪn] *n (drink)* Gin *m*. **~ and tonic** Gin Tonic *m*.

ginger ['dʒɪndʒə[r]] **1** *n* Ingwer *m*. **2** *adj biscuit etc* Ingwer-; *hair* kupferrot; *cat* rötlichgelb.

♦ **ginger up** *vt sep (col)* in Schwung bringen *(col)*.

ginger: ~-ale *n* Ginger Ale *nt*; **~ beer** *n (Brit)* Ingwerlimonade *f*; **~bread** *n* Lebkuchen *m mit Ingwergeschmack*.

gingerly ['dʒɪndʒəlɪ] *adv* behutsam; *(because sth is cold, hot etc)* zaghaft.

gingham ['gɪŋəm] *n* Gingan *m*.

gipsy ['dʒɪpsɪ] *n* Zigeuner(in *f*) *m*.

giraffe [dʒɪ'rɑːf] *n* Giraffe *f*.

girder ['gɜːdə[r]] *n* Träger *m*.

girdle ['gɜːdl] *n (corset)* Hüfthalter *m*.

girl [gɜːl] *n* Mädchen *nt*; *(daughter also)* Tochter *f*. **an English ~** eine Engländerin; **factory ~** Fabrikarbeiterin *f*; **shop ~** Verkäuferin *f*; **the ~s** *(colleagues)* die Damen; **the old ~** die Alte *(col)*; *(col: wife, mother)* meine/seine *etc* Alte *(col)*.

girl: ~ Friday *n* Allround-Sekretärin *f*; **~friend** *n* Freundin *f*; **~guide** *n (Brit)* Pfadfinderin *f*.

girlish ['gɜːlɪʃ] *adj* mädchenhaft.

girl scout *n (US)* Pfadfinderin *f*.

giro ['dʒaɪrəʊ] *n (Brit) (bank ~)* Giro(verkehr *m*) *nt*; *(post-office ~)* Postscheckdienst *m*.

girth [gɜːθ] *n* **(a)** *(circumference, of waist)* Umfang *m*. **(b)** *(harness)* (Sattel)gurt *m*.

gismo *n (US col)* = **gizmo**.

gist [dʒɪst] *n no pl* Wesentliche(s) *nt*. **that was the ~ of what he said** das war im wesentlichen, was er gesagt hat.

git [gɪt] *n (Brit col)* Idiot *m*.

give [gɪv] *(vb: pret* **gave**, *ptp* **given***)* **1** *vt* **(a)** geben *(sb sth, sth to sb* jdm etw*)*; *(as present)* schenken *(sb sth, sth to sb* jdm etw*)*; *one's name, particulars* angeben; *(let sb know by phone, letter etc) decision, results* mitteilen; *(produce) results* bringen; *pleasure, joy, pain* bereiten; *trouble* machen; *one's* *love, attention* schenken; *punishment* erteilen. **they gave us roast beef for lunch** sie servierten uns Roastbeef zum (Mittag)essen; **what will you ~ me for it?** was gibst du mir dafür; **what did you ~ for it?** was hast du dafür bezahlt?; **11 o'clock, ~ or take a few minutes** so gegen 11 Uhr; **six foot, ~ or take a few inches** ungefähr sechs Fuß; **to ~ as good as one gets** sich kräftig wehren; **he gave everything he'd got** *(fig)* er holte das Letzte aus sich heraus; **to ~ sb one's cold** *(col)* jdn mit seiner Erkältung anstecken; **I'd ~ a lot/the world/anything to know ...** ich würde viel darum geben, wenn ich wüßte, ...; **what gave you that idea** wie kommst du denn auf die Idee?; **to ~ sb five years** jdm fünf Jahre aufbrummen *(col)*; **~ me Spain (every time)!** *(col)* es geht doch nichts über Spanien; **~ yourself more time/half an hour** lassen Sie sich mehr Zeit/rechnen Sie mit einer halben Stunde; **how long do you ~ that marriage?** wie lange gibst du dieser Ehe? *(col)*; **I'll ~ you that** zugegeben; **he's a good worker, I'll ~ him that** eines muß man ihm lassen, er arbeitet gut; **he wouldn't ~ me his decision/opinion** er wollte mir seine Meinung/Entscheidung nicht sagen.

(b) *(hold, perform) party, dinner, play* geben; *speech* halten; *song* singen; *toast* ausbringen *(to sb* auf jdn*)*. **~ us a song** sing uns was vor; **I ~ you Mary** *(as toast)* auf Mary!; *(as speaker)* ich gebe Mary das Wort.

(c) *(devote)* widmen *(to dat)*. **he has ~n himself entirely to medicine** er hat sich ganz der Medizin verschrieben.

(d) to ~ a cry/groan/laugh/sigh schreien/stöhnen/lachen/seufzen; **to ~ sb a look/smile** jdn ansehen/anlächeln; **to ~ sb a push/kick** jdm einen Stoß/Tritt geben; **to ~ one's hair a brush/wash** sich *(dat)* die Haare bürsten/waschen.

2 *vi* **(a)** *(~ money etc)* spenden. **you have to be prepared to ~ and take** man muß zu Kompromissen bereit sein. **(b)** *(also ~* **way***) (lit, fig: collapse, yield)* nachgeben; *(health, nerve, voice)* versagen; *(break: rope, cable)* reißen. **something's got to ~** *(col)* etwas muß sich einfach ändern. **(c)** *(lit, fig: bend, be flexible)* nachgeben; *(bed)* federn; *(shoe)* sich weiten.

3 *n* Nachgiebigkeit *f*; *(of floor, bed, chair)* Federung *f*.

♦**give away** *vt sep* **(a)** weggeben; *(as present)* verschenken. **at £5 I'm practically giving it ~** ich will £5 dafür, das ist fast geschenkt. **(b)** *bride (als Brautvater etc)* zum Altar führen. **(c)** *(fig: betray)* verraten *(to sb* an jdn*)*. **to ~ the game ~** *(col)* alles verraten.

♦**give back** *vt sep* zurückgeben.

♦**give in 1** *vi (surrender)* sich ergeben *(to sb* jdm*)*; *(in guessing game etc)* aufgeben; *(accede, back down)* nachgeben *(to dat)*. **to ~ ~ to blackmail** auf Erpressung eingehen. **2** *vt sep document, essay* einreichen; *parcel* abgeben.

♦**give off** *vt sep heat, gas* abgeben; *smell* verbreiten; *rays* ausstrahlen.

♦**give on to** *vi +prep obj (window)* hinausgehen auf *(+acc)*; *(door) garden* hinausführen in *(+acc)*.

♦**give out 1** *vi (supplies, strength)* zu Ende gehen *or (in past tense)* sein; *(engine)* versagen. **2** *vt sep* **(a)** *(distribute)* verteilen. **(b)** *(announce)* bekanntgeben. **to ~ oneself ~ as sth** sich als etw ausgeben. **3** *vt insep* = **give off.**

♦**give over 1** *vt sep* **(a)** *(hand over)* übergeben *(to dat)*. **(b)** *(set aside, use for)* **to be ~n ~ to sth** für etw beansprucht werden. **2** *vi (col: stop)* **~ ~!** hör auf!

♦**give up 1** *vi* aufgeben. **I ~ ~** ich gebe auf, ich geb's auf *(col)*. **2** *vt sep* **(a)** aufgeben; *claim also* verzichten auf *(+acc)*. **I'm trying to ~ ~ smoking** ich versuche, das Rauchen aufzugeben; **to ~ sb ~ as dead** jdn für tot halten; **I'd ~n you ~** *(expected visitor etc)* ich hatte nicht mehr damit gerechnet, daß du kommst. **(b)** *land, territory* abgeben *(to dat)*; *seat, place* freimachen *(to* für*)*; *ticket* abgeben *(to* bei*)*. **(c)** *(to authorities)* übergeben *(to dat)*. **to ~ oneself ~** sich stellen; *(after siege)* sich ergeben. **(d)** *(devote)* widmen. **to ~ ~ one's life to music** sein Leben ganz der Musik widmen. **(e)** *(disclose) secret, treasure* enthüllen *(geh)*.

♦**give way** *vi* **(a)** *(lit)* = **give 2 (b). (b)** *(fig: yield)* nachgeben *(to dat)*. **to ~ ~ to intimidation** sich einschüchtern lassen; **don't ~ ~ to despair** überlaß dich nicht der Verzweiflung. **(c)** *(be superseded)* **to ~ ~ to sth** von etw abgelöst werden. **(d)** *(Brit Mot)* **who has to ~ ~ here?** wer hat hier Vorfahrt?; **"~ ~"** „Vorfahrt beachten".

give: ~ and take *n* Entgegenkommen *nt*; *(in personal relationships)* Geben und Nehmen *nt*; **~-away** *n (col)* **the expression on her face was a ~-away** ihr Gesichtsausdruck verriet alles; **that exam question was a ~-away** diese Prüfungsfrage war geschenkt *(col)*; **~-away price** *n (col)* Schleuderpreis *m*.

given ['gɪvn] **1** *ptp of* **give. 2** *adj* **(a)** *(with indef art)* bestimmt; *(with def art)* angegeben. **(b) ~ name** *(esp US)* Vorname *m*. **(c) to be ~ to sth** zu etw neigen; **to be ~ to doing sth** gewohnt sein, etw zu tun. **3** *conj* **~ sth** *(with)* vorausgesetzt, man/er *etc* hat etw; *(in view of)* angesichts einer Sache *(gen)*; **~ that he ...** *(in view of the fact)* angesichts der Tatsache, daß er ...; *(assuming)* vorausgesetzt (daß) er ...; **~ these circumstances/conditions** unter diesen Umständen/Voraussetzungen.

giver ['gɪvəʳ] *n* Spender(in *f*) *m*.

gizmo ['gɪzməʊ] *n (US col)* Ding *nt (col)*.

glacial ['gleɪsɪəl] *adj (cold) look, wind* eisig.

glacier ['glæsɪəʳ] *n* Gletscher *m*.

glad [glæd] *adj (+er)* froh. **to be ~ at** *or* **about sth** sich über etw *(acc)* freuen; **I'm so ~!** das freut mich; **you'll be ~ to hear that ...** es wird Sie freuen, daß ...; **we would be ~ of your help** wir wären froh, wenn Sie helfen könnten; **I'd be ~ to** aber gern!

gladden ['glædn] *vt person, heart* erfreuen.

glade [gleɪd] *n* Lichtung *f*.

gladiator ['glædɪeɪtəʳ] *n* Gladiator *m*.

gladiolus [ˌglædɪ'əʊləs] *n, pl* **gladioli** [ˌglædɪ'əʊlaɪ] Gladiole *f*.

gladly ['glædlɪ] *adv (willingly)* gern.

glamorize ['glæməraɪz] *vt author, war* glorifizieren; *the mundane* idealisiert darstellen.

glamorous ['glæmərəs] *adj* bezaubernd; *film star, life* glamourös; *job* Traum-.

glamour, (US) glamor ['glæməʳ] *n* Glamour *m*; *(of occasion, situation)* Glanz *m*.

glance [glɑːns] **1** *n* Blick *m*. **at a ~** auf einen Blick; **at first ~** auf den ersten Blick; **to take a (quick) ~ at sth** einen kurzen Blick auf etw *(acc)* werfen. **2** *vi* **to ~ at sb/sth** einen kurzen Blick auf jdn/etw *(acc)* werfen; **to ~ at/through the newspaper** einen kurzen Blick in die Zeitung werfen; **he ~d around the room** er sah sich kurz im Zimmer um.

♦**glance off** *vi (bullet etc)* abprallen *(prep obj* von*)*.

glancing ['glɑːnsɪŋ] *adj* **to strike sth a ~ blow** etw streifen.

gland [glænd] *n* Drüse *f*.

glandular ['glændjʊləʳ] *adj* Drüsen-. **~ fever** Drüsenfieber *nt*.

glare [glɛəʳ] **1** *n* **(a)** greller Schein; *(from sun, bulb, lamp also)* grelles Licht. **the ~ of the sun** das grelle Sonnenlicht; **to avoid the ~ of publicity** das grelle Licht der Öffentlichkeit scheuen. **(b)** *(stare)* stechender Blick. **2** *vi* **(a)** *(light, sun)* grell scheinen; *(headlights)* grell leuchten. **(b)** *(stare)* **to ~ at sb/sth** jdn/etw zornig anstarren.

glaring ['glɛərɪŋ] *adj sun, colour* grell; *(fig) omission* eklatant; *mistake* grob; *contrast* kraß;

injustice (himmel)schreiend.
glass [glɑːs] *n* Glas *nt*; *(dated: mirror)* Spiegel *m*; *(barometer)* Barometer *nt*. **a ~ of wine** ein Glas Wein; **~es** *pl (spectacles)* Brille *f*; *(binoculars)* Fernglas *nt*.
glass *in cpds* Glas-; **~-blower** *n* Glasbläser(in *f*) *m*; **~ fibre** *(Brit) or* **fiber** *(US) n* Glasfaser *f*; **~house** *n (Brit Hort)* Gewächshaus *nt*; *(Mil sl)* Bau *m (col)*; **~ware** *n* Glaswaren *pl*; **~ wool** *n* Glaswolle *f*.
glassy ['glɑːsɪ] *adj (+er) surface, sea etc* spiegelglatt; *eye, look* glasig.
glaze [gleɪz] **1** *n (on pottery, tiles, Cook)* Glasur *f*; *(on paper, fabric)* Appretur *f*; *(on painting)* Lasur *f*. **2** *vt* **(a)** *door, window* verglasen. **(b)** *pottery, tiles* glasieren; *fabric, paper* appretieren; *painting* lasieren. **~d tile** Kachel *f*. **(c)** *(Cook)* glasieren. **3** *vi (eyes: also* **~ over**) glasig werden.
glazier ['gleɪzɪə[r]] *n* Glaser *m*.
gleam [gliːm] **1** *n* **(a)** Schimmer *m*; *(of metal, water)* Schimmern *nt*. **(b)** *(fig)* **a ~ of humour/intelligence** ein Anflug *m* von Humor/Intelligenz; **he had a ~ in his eye** seine Augen funkelten. **2** *vi* schimmern; *(hair also)* glänzen; *(eyes)* funkeln.
glean [gliːn] *vt (lit) corn* nachlesen; *(fig) facts, news* ausfindig machen. **to ~ sth from sb/sth** etw von jdm in Erfahrung bringen/etw einer Sache *(dat)* entnehmen.
glee [gliː] *n* Freude *f*; *(malicious)* Schadenfreude *f*. **~ club** *(esp US)* Chor *m*.
gleeful ['gliːfʊl] *adj* fröhlich; *(malicious)* schadenfroh.
glen [glen] *n* Tal *nt*.
glib [glɪb] *adj (pej)* zungenfertig; *reply, remark* leichtfertig; *talker, speech, style* glatt. **don't be so ~** sei nicht so oberflächlich.
glide [glaɪd] *vi* **(a)** gleiten; *(through the air also)* schweben. **(b)** *(plane)* im Gleitflug fliegen; *(glider)* gleiten.
glider ['glaɪdə[r]] *n (Aviat)* Segelflugzeug *nt*.
gliding ['glaɪdɪŋ] *n (Aviat)* Segelfliegen *nt*.
glimmer ['glɪmə[r]] **1** *n (of light, candle etc)* Schimmer *m*; *(of fire)* Glimmen *nt*. **a ~ of hope** ein Hoffnungsschimmer *m*. **2** *vi (light, water)* schimmern; *(fire)* glimmen.
glimpse [glɪmps] **1** *n* Blick *m*. **to catch a ~ of sb/sth** einen flüchtigen Blick von jdm/etw erhaschen. **2** *vt* flüchtig sehen.
glint [glɪnt] **1** *n (of light, metal)* Glitzern *nt no pl*; *(of cat's eyes)* Funkeln *nt no pl*. **he has a wicked/merry ~ in his eyes** seine Augen funkeln böse/lustig. **2** *vi* glitzern; *(eyes)* funkeln.
glisten ['glɪsn] *vi* glitzern.
glitter ['glɪtə[r]] **1** *n* Glitzern *nt*; *(of eyes, diamonds)* Funkeln *nt*; *(fig)* Glanz, Prunk *m*. **2** *vi* glitzern; *(eyes, diamonds)* funkeln. **all that ~s is not gold** *(Prov)* es ist nicht alles Gold, was glänzt *(Prov)*.
gloat [gləʊt] *vi* sich großtun *(over* mit*)*; *(over sb's misfortune)* sich hämisch freuen *(over* über *+acc)*. **to ~ over one's possessions** sich an seinen Reichtümern weiden; **there's no need to ~!** das ist kein Grund zur Schadenfreude!
global ['gləʊbl] *adj* global; *peace, war* Welt-.
globe [gləʊb] *n (sphere)* Kugel *f*; *(map)* Globus *m*. **all over the ~** auf der ganzen Erde *or* Welt; **~-trotter** Globetrotter *m*.
globule ['glɒbjuːl] *n* Kügelchen *nt*; *(of oil, water)* Tröpfchen *nt*.
gloom [gluːm] *n* **(a)** *(darkness)* Düsterkeit *f*. **(b)** *(sadness)* düstere *or* gedrückte Stimmung. **a life of ~** ein trauriges Leben.
gloomy ['gluːmɪ] *adj (+er) room etc* düster; *atmosphere also* gedrückt; *thoughts also, character* trübsinnig; *news also* bedrückend; *outlook on life* pessimistisch. **to take a ~ view of things** schwarzsehen; **to feel ~** bedrückt sein.
glorification [ˌglɔːrɪfɪ'keɪʃən] *n* Verherrlichung *f*.
glorified ['glɔːrɪfaɪd] *adj* **just a ~ snack-bar** nur eine bessere Imbißstube.
glorify ['glɔːrɪfaɪ] *vt* verherrlichen.
glorious ['glɔːrɪəs] *adj weather, sky* herrlich; *deed, victory* ruhmreich.
glory ['glɔːrɪ] **1** *n* **(a)** *(honour, fame)* Ruhm *m*. **covered in ~** ruhmbedeckt. **(b)** *(beauty, magnificence)* Herrlichkeit *f*. **the rose in all its ~** die Rose in ihrer ganzen Pracht; **the glories of Nature** die Schönheiten der Natur; **Rome at the height of its ~** Rom in seiner Blütezeit. **2** *vi* **to ~ in one's strength/ability** sich an seiner Kraft/Fähigkeit weiden; **to ~ in one's/sb's success** sich in seinem/jds Erfolg sonnen; **to ~ in the name of ...** den stolzen Namen ... führen.
gloss[1] [glɒs] *n* Glanz *m*; *(fig: of respectability etc)* Schein *m*.
♦**gloss over** *vt sep (try to conceal)* vertuschen; *(make light of)* beschönigen.
gloss[2] *n (note)* Anmerkung *f*.
glossary ['glɒsərɪ] *n* Glossar *nt*.
gloss (paint) *n* Glanzlack(farbe *f*) *m*.
glossy ['glɒsɪ] *adj (+er)* glänzend; *paper, paint* Glanz-. **~ (magazine)** Illustrierte *f*.
glove [glʌv] *n* Handschuh *m*. **to fit (sb) like a ~** (jdm) wie angegossen passen; **~ box** *or* **compartment** Handschuhfach *nt;* **~ puppet** Handpuppe *f*.
glow [gləʊ] **1** *vi* glühen; *(colour, hands of clock)* leuchten; *(lamp also, candle)* scheinen. **she/her cheeks ~ed with health** sie hatte ein blühendes Aussehen. **2** *n* Glühen *nt*; *(of colour, clock hands)* Leuchten *nt*; *(of lamp, candle)* Schein *m*; *(of fire, sunset, passion)* Glut *f*.
glower ['glaʊə[r]] *vi* ein finsteres Gesicht machen. **to ~ at sb** jdn finster ansehen.
glowing ['gləʊɪŋ] *adj* **(a)** glühend; *candle, colour, eyes* leuchtend; *cheeks, complexion* blühend. **(b)** *(fig) account, description* begeistert; *praise, report* überschwenglich. **to paint sth in ~ colours** *(fig)* etw in den leuchtendsten Farben schildern.
glow-worm ['gləʊˌwɜːm] *n* Glühwürmchen *nt*.
glucose ['gluːkəʊs] *n* Traubenzucker *m*.
glue [gluː] **1** *n* Klebstoff *m*. **2** *vt* kleben. **to ~ sth together** etw zusammenkleben; **to ~ sth down/on** etw fest-/ankleben; **to ~ sth to sth** etw an etw *(acc)* kleben; **to keep one's eyes ~d to sb/sth** jdn/etw nicht aus den Augen lassen; **his eyes were ~d to the screen** seine Augen hingen an der Leinwand; **he's ~d to the TV all evening** er hängt den ganzen Abend vorm Fernseher *(col)*; **he stood there as if ~d to the spot** er stand wie angewurzelt da.
glue-sniffing ['gluːˌsnɪfɪŋ] *n* Schnüffeln *nt (col)*.
glum [glʌm] *adj (+er)* niedergeschlagen, bedrückt. **to feel ~** bedrückt sein.
glut [glʌt] **1** *vt (Comm) market* überschwemmen. **2** *n* Schwemme *f*; *(of manufactured goods also)* Überangebot *nt (of* an *+dat)*. **a ~ of apples** eine Apfelschwemme.
glutinous ['gluːtɪnəs] *adj* klebrig.
glutton ['glʌtn] *n* Vielfraß *m*. **a ~ for work/punishment** ein Arbeitstier *nt (col)*/Masochist *m*.
gluttony ['glʌtənɪ] *n* Völlerei *f*.
glycerin(e) ['glɪsəriːn] *n* Glyzerin *nt*.
gm = gram(s), gramme(s) g.
GMT = Greenwich Mean Time WEZ.
gnarled [nɑːld] *adj tree* knorrig; *hand* knotig.
gnash [næʃ] *vt* **to ~ one's teeth** mit den Zähnen knirschen.
gnat [næt] *n* (Stech)mücke *f*.
gnaw [nɔː] **1** *vi* nagen. **to ~ at sb/sth** an etw *(dat)* nagen; *(fig)* jdn/etw quälen. **2** *vt* nagen an *(+dat)*; *hole* nagen.
gnawing ['nɔːɪŋ] *adj (fig)* quälend.
gnome [nəʊm] *n* Gnom *m*.
GNP = gross national product.
gnu [nuː] *n* Gnu *nt*.
go [gəʊ] *(vb: pret* **went**, *ptp* **gone***)* **1** *vi* **(a)** gehen;

(vehicle, by vehicle) fahren; *(plane)* fliegen; *(road)* führen. **to ~ to France** nach Frankreich fahren; **I have to ~ to the doctor/London** ich muß zum Arzt (gehen)/nach London; **to ~ for a swim** schwimmen gehen; **to ~ fishing/shopping** angeln/einkaufen gehen; **where do we ~ from here?** *(fig)* und was (wird) jetzt?; **you're ~ing too fast for me** *(lit, fig)* du bist mir zu schnell; **just look at him ~!** schau mal, wie schnell er ist! **the favourite is ~ing well** der Favorit liegt gut im Rennen; **to ~ looking for sb/sth** nach jdm/etw suchen; **to ~ for a doctor/newspaper** einen Arzt/eine Zeitung holen (gehen); **there he ~es!** da ist er ja!; **who ~es there?** *(guard)* wer da?; **you ~ first** geh du zuerst!; **you ~ next** du bist der nächste; **there you ~ again!** *(col)* du fängst ja schon wieder an!; **here we ~ again!** *(col)* jetzt geht das schon wieder los! *(col)*; **~ and shut the door** mach mal die Tür zu; **he's gone and lost his new watch** *(col)* er hat seine neue Uhr verloren; **don't ~ telling him** geh jetzt nicht hin und erzähl ihm das *(col)*.

(b) *(depart)* gehen; *(vehicle, by vehicle also)* (ab)fahren; *(plane, by plane also)* (ab)fliegen. **has he gone yet?** ist er schon weg?; **I must ~** *or* **get ~ing now** ich muß jetzt gehen *or* weg; **when I'm gone** *(left)* wenn ich weg bin; *(dead)* wenn ich (einmal) nicht mehr (da) bin; **~!** *(Sport)* los!; **here ~es!** jetzt geht's los! *(col)*.

(c) *(disappear, vanish)* verschwinden; *(pain, spot, mark etc also)* weggehen; *(be used up)* aufgebraucht werden; *(time)* vergehen. **it has gone** *(disappeared)* es ist weg; *(used up, eaten etc)* es ist alle *(col)*; **where has it gone?** wo ist es hin *or* geblieben?; **gone are the days when ...** die Zeiten sind vorbei, wo ...; **I don't know where the money ~es** ich weiß nicht, wo all das Geld bleibt; **all his money ~es on records** sein ganzes Geld geht für Schallplatten drauf *(col)*; **£30 a week ~es in** *or* **on rent** £ 30 die Woche sind für die Miete (weg); **how is the time ~ing?** wie steht's mit der Zeit?; **it's just gone three** es ist gerade drei vorbei; **two days to ~ till ...** noch zwei Tage bis ...; **only two more patients to ~** nur noch zwei Patienten; **he'll have to ~** er wird gehen müssen; **that settee will have to ~** das Sofa muß weg.

(d) *(be sold)* **the hats aren't ~ing very well** die Hüte gehen nicht sehr gut; **to be ~ing cheap** billig sein; **it went for £5** es ging für £ 5 weg; **they are ~ing at 20p each** sie werden zu 20 Pence das Stück verkauft; **~ing, ~ing, gone!** zum ersten, zum zweiten, und zum dritten!

(e) *(prize, 1st place etc)* gehen *(to* an *+acc)*; *(inheritance)* zufallen *(to sb* jdm*)*.

(f) *(extend)* gehen. **the garden ~es down to the river** der Garten geht bis zum Fluß hinunter; **£5 won't ~ far** mit £ 5 kommt man nicht weit.

(g) *(run, function)* gehen; *(car, machine also)* laufen; *(workers)* arbeiten. **to get ~ing** in Schwung kommen; **to get sth ~ing, to make sth ~** etw in Gang bringen; *party* etw in Fahrt bringen; *business* etw auf Vordermann bringen; **to get sb ~ing** jdn in Fahrt bringen; **to get ~ing with sth** etw in Angriff nehmen; **to keep ~ing** *(person)* weitermachen; *(machine, engine, business)* weiterlaufen; *(car)* weiterfahren; **keep ~ing!** weiter!; **this medicine/prospect kept her ~ing** dieses Medikament/diese Aussicht hat sie durchhalten lassen; **here's £50/some work to keep you ~ing** hier hast du erst mal £ 50/etwas Arbeit.

(h) *(happen, turn out) (project, things)* gehen; *(event, evening)* verlaufen. **I've forgotten how the words ~** ich habe den Text vergessen; **how does the story/tune ~?** wie war die Geschichte doch noch mal/wie geht die Melodie?; **the decision went in his favour/against him** die Entscheidung fiel zu seinen Gunsten/Ungunsten aus; **how's it ~ing?, how ~es it?** *(col)* wie geht's (denn so)?; **how did it ~?** wie war's?; **how did the exam/your holiday ~?** wie ging's in der Prüfung/wie war der Urlaub?; **how's the essay ~ing?** was macht der Aufsatz?; **everything is ~ing well** alles läuft gut; **if everything ~es well** wenn alles gutgeht; **we'll see how things ~** *(col)* wir werden sehen, wie es läuft *(col)*; **she has a lot ~ing for her** sie ist gut dran.

(i) *(fail, break, wear out)* kaputtgehen; *(health, strength, eyesight etc)* nachlassen; *(fail: brakes, steering)* versagen. **the jumper has gone at the elbows** der Pullover ist an den Ärmeln durch *(col)*; **his mind is ~ing** er läßt geistig sehr nach; **there ~es another bulb/button!** schon wieder eine Birne kaputt/ein Knopf ab!

(j) *(be permitted, accepted)* gehen *(col)*. **anything ~es!** alles ist erlaubt; **what I say ~es!** was ich sage, wird gemacht!; **that ~es for me too** *(that applies to me)* das gilt auch für mich; *(I agree with that)* das meine ich auch.

(k) *(be available)* **there are no jobs ~ing** es sind keine Stellen zu haben; **is there any tea ~ing?** gibt es Tee?; **I'll have whatever is ~ing** ich nehme, was es gibt; **he's not bad as boys ~** verglichen mit anderen Jungen ist er nicht übel.

(l) *(be, become)* werden. **to ~ deaf/mad/grey** taub/verrückt/grau werden; **I went cold** mir wurde kalt; **to ~ Labour** Labour wählen.

(m) *(fit)* passen; *(belong, be placed)* hingehören; *(in drawer, cupboard etc)* (hin)kommen. **the books ~ in that cupboard** die Bücher kommen in den Schrank dort; **4 into 3 won't ~** 3 durch 4 geht nicht.

(n) *(match)* dazu passen. **to ~ with sth** zu etw passen.

(o) *(contribute)* **the money ~es to help the poor** das Geld soll den Armen helfen; **the money will ~ towards the holiday** das ist Geld für den Urlaub; **the qualities that ~ to make a great man** die Eigenschaften, die einen großen Mann ausmachen.

(p) *(make a sound or movement)* machen. **to ~ bang/ticktock** peng/ticktack machen; **there ~es the bell** es klingelt; **as the bell went** als es klingelte.

(q) *(US)* **food to ~** Essen zum Mitnehmen.

2 *aux vb* **I'm ~ing to do it** ich werde es tun; **I was ~ing to do it** ich wollte es tun; **I had been ~ing to do it** ich hatte es tun wollen; **I wasn't ~ing to do it (anyway)** ich hätte es sowieso nicht gemacht.

3 *vt (col)* **to ~ it** *(~ fast)* ein tolles Tempo draufhaben *(col)*; *(work hard)* sich hineinknien *(col)*; **to ~ it alone** einen Alleingang machen; *(in business)* sich selbständig machen; **I could ~ a beer** ich könnte ein Bier vertragen *(col)*.

4 *n, pl* **-es (a)** *(col: energy)* Schwung *m*. **(b) to be on the ~** auf Trab sein *(col)*; **to keep sb on the ~** jdn auf Trab halten; **he's got two books on the ~** er schreibt zwei Bücher gleichzeitig; **it's all ~** es ist immer was los *(col)*. **(c)** *(attempt)* Versuch *m*. **it's your ~** du bist dran *(col)*; **you've had your ~** du warst schon dran *(col)*; **to have a ~** es probieren; **to have a ~ at sb** *(criticize)* jdn runterputzen *(col)*; *(fight)* es mit jdm aufnehmen; **to have a ~ at doing sth** versuchen, etw zu tun; **at** *or* **in one ~** auf einen Schlag *(col)*; *drink* in einem Zug *(col)*; **can I have a ~?** darf ich mal? **(d)** *(success)* **to make a ~ of sth** in etw *(dat)* Erfolg haben; **(it's) no ~** *(col)* das ist nicht drin *(col)*. **(e) from the word ~** von Anfang an; **all systems (are) ~** (es ist) alles klar.

♦ **go about 1** *vi* herumgehen; *(by vehicle)* herumfahren; *(rumour, flu etc)* umgehen; *(ship)* wenden. **2** *vi +prep obj task, problem* anpacken. **we must ~ ~ it carefully** wir müssen vorsichtig vorgehen; **how does one ~ ~ getting seats?** wie bekommt man Plätze?; to ~ ~ **one's business** seinen Geschäften nachgehen.

♦ **go after** *vi +prep obj* nachgehen *(+dat)*, nachlaufen *(+dat)*; *(in vehicle)* nachfahren *(+dat)*; *criminal* jagen; *job, girl* sich bemühen um; *(Sport) record* einstellen wollen.

♦ **go against** *vi +prep obj* **(a)** *(luck)* sein gegen; *(events)* ungünstig verlaufen für; *(evidence, appearance)* sprechen gegen. **the verdict went ~ her** das Urteil fiel zu ihren Ungunsten aus. **(b)** *(be contrary to)* im Widerspruch stehen zu; *principles, conscience* gehen gegen.

♦ **go ahead** *vi* **(a)** *(in race)* sich an die Spitze setzen. **(b)** *(work, project)* vorangehen. **he just went ~ and did it** er hat es einfach gemacht; **~ ~!** nur zu!; **to ~ ~ with sth** etw durchführen.

♦ **go along** *vi* **(a)** *(walk along)* entlanggehen. **as one ~es ~** *(while walking)* unterwegs; *(bit by bit)* nach und nach; *(at the same time)* nebenbei. **(b)** *(accompany)* mitgehen *(with* mit*)*. **(c)** *(agree)* zustimmen *(with dat)*.

♦ **go around** *vi* **(a)** *(turn, spin)* sich drehen. **(b)** *(make a detour)* **we went ~ by Winchester** wir fuhren bei Winchester herum. **(c)** *(visit)* vorbeigehen *(to* bei*)*. **(d)** *(tour: round museum etc)* herumgehen *(prep obj* in *+dat)*. **(e)** *(be sufficient)* (aus)reichen. **there's enough food to ~ ~** es ist genügend zu essen da. **(f)** = **go about 1.**

♦ **go at** *vi +prep obj (col: attack) person* losgehen auf *(+acc) (col)*; *task* sich machen an *(+acc)*. **he really went ~ it** er hat richtig losgelegt *(col)*.

♦ **go away** *vi* (weg)gehen; *(for a holiday)* wegfahren.

♦ **go back** *vi* zurückgehen; *(to a subject)* zurückkommen *(to* auf *+acc)*; *(revert: to habits, methods etc)* zurückkehren *(to* zu*)*; *(clock: be put back)* zurückgestellt werden. **to ~ ~ to the beginning** wieder von vorn anfangen; **there's no ~ing ~ now** jetzt gibt es kein Zurück mehr; **we ~ ~ a long way** wir kennen uns schon seit langem.

♦ **go back on** *vi +prep obj* zurücknehmen; *decision* rückgängig machen.

♦ **go before** *vi (live before)* in früheren Zeiten leben; *(happen before)* vorangehen.

♦ **go by** *vi (person, opportunity)* vorbeigehen *(prep obj* an *+dat)*; *(vehicle)* vorbeifahren *(prep obj* an *+dat)*; *(time)* vergehen. **as time went ~** mit der Zeit. **2** *vi +prep obj* **(a)** *(base judgement on)* gehen nach; *compass, watch etc* sich richten nach; *(stick to) rules* sich halten an *(+acc)*. **if that's anything to ~ ~** wenn man danach gehen kann; **~ing ~ what he said** nach dem, was er sagte; **that's not much to ~ ~** das will nicht viel heißen. **(b) to ~ ~ the name of X** X heißen.

♦ **go down** *vi* **(a)** hinuntergehen *(prep obj acc)*; *(by vehicle, lift)* hinunterfahren *(prep obj acc)*; *(sun, moon)* untergehen; *(Theat: curtain)* fallen; *(fall: boxer etc)* zu Boden gehen.

(b) *(ship, person: sink)* untergehen; *(be defeated)* geschlagen werden *(to* von*)*.

(c) *(Brit Univ)* die Universität verlassen; *(for vacation)* in die Semesterferien gehen.

(d) *(be accepted, approved)* ankommen *(with* bei*)*. **that won't ~ ~ well with him** das wird er nicht gut finden; **he went ~ big in the States** *(col)* in den Staaten kam er ganz groß heraus *(col)*.

(e) *(floods, temperature etc)* zurückgehen; *(taxes, value)* weniger werden; *(prices)* sinken; *(balloon, tyre)* Luft verlieren; *(deteriorate: neighbourhood)* herunterkommen. **he has gone ~ in my estimation** er ist in meiner Achtung gesunken.

(f) *(be noted)* vermerkt werden. **to ~ ~ to posterity/in history** der Nachwelt überliefert werden/in die Geschichte eingehen.

(g) to ~ ~ with a cold eine Erkältung bekommen.

♦ **go for** *vi +prep obj* **(a)** *(col: attack)* losgehen auf *(+acc) (col)*; *(verbally)* herziehen über *(+acc)*. **(b)** *(col: admire, like)* gut finden. **(c)** *(aim at)* zielen auf *(+acc)*; *(fig)* aussein auf *(+acc) (col)*.

♦ **go in** *vi (enter, fit in)* hineingehen; *(sun)* verschwinden.

♦ **go in for** *vi +prep obj* **(a)** *(enter for)* teilnehmen an *(+dat)*. **(b)** *(be interested in)* stehen auf *(+acc) (col)*; *(as career)* gewählt haben. **to ~ ~ ~ sports/tennis** *(play oneself)* Sport treiben/Tennis spielen; *(be interested in)* sich für Sport/Tennis interessieren; **to ~ ~ ~ growing vegetables** sich auf den Gemüseanbau verlegen.

♦ **go into** *vi +prep obj* **(a)** *house, hospital, politics* gehen in *(+acc)*; *the army, navy etc* gehen zu. **to ~ ~ teaching** Lehrer werden. **(b)** *(crash into) car* (hinein)fahren in *(+acc)*; *wall* fahren gegen. **(c)** *explanation, description etc* geben. **(d)** *trance, coma* fallen in *(+acc)*. **(e)** *(look into)* sich befassen mit; *(treat, explain at length)* abhandeln. **I don't want to ~ ~ that now** darauf möchte ich jetzt nicht (näher) eingehen.

♦ **go off 1** *vi* **(a)** *(leave)* weggehen; *(by vehicle)* wegfahren. **he went ~ to the States** er fuhr in die Staaten; **to ~ ~ with sth** *(steal)* mit etw auf und davon gehen *(col)*. **(b)** *(light)* ausgehen; *(water, electricity, gas)* wegbleiben. **(c)** *(gun, bomb, alarm, alarm clock)* losgehen. **(d)** *(food)* schlecht werden; *(person, work)* nachlassen. **(e)** *(go to sleep)* einschlafen. **(f)** *(take place)* verlaufen. **to ~ ~ well/badly** gut/schlecht gehen. **2** *vi +prep obj (lose liking for)* nicht mehr mögen. **I've gone ~ him/it** ich mache mir nichts mehr aus ihm/daraus.

♦ **go on 1** *vi* **(a)** *(walk on etc)* weitergehen; *(by vehicle)* weiterfahren; *(ahead of others)* vorausgehen.

(b) *(light, power)* angehen.

(c) *(carry on, continue)* weitergehen; *(person)* weitermachen. **to ~ ~ with sth** mit etw weitermachen; **to ~ ~ working** weiterarbeiten; **I want to ~ ~ being a teacher** ich möchte weiterhin Lehrer bleiben; **~ ~, tell me/try!** na, sag schon/na, versuch's doch!; **to have enough to be ~ing ~ with** fürs erste genug haben; **he went ~ to say that ...** dann sagte er, daß ...; **I can't ~ ~** ich kann nicht mehr; **as time ~es ~** im Laufe der Zeit; **don't ~ ~ (about it)** nun hör aber (damit) auf; **you do ~ ~ a bit** du weißt manchmal nicht, wann du aufhören solltest; **to ~ ~ about sb/sth** *(talk a lot)* stundenlang von jdm/etw erzählen; *(complain)* dauernd über jdn/etw schimpfen; **to ~ ~ at sb** an jdm herumnörgeln.

(d) *(happen)* vor sich gehen; *(party, argument etc)* im Gange sein. **this has been ~ing ~ for a long time** das geht schon lange so; **what's ~ing ~ here?** was geht hier vor?

2 *vi +prep obj (be guided by)* gehen nach. **we haven't got much to ~ ~** wir haben nicht viel, worauf wir uns stützen können.

♦ **go on for** *vi +prep obj fifty, one o'clock* zugehen auf *(+acc)*. **there were ~ing ~ ~ twenty people there** es waren fast zwanzig Leute da.

♦ **go out** *vi* **(a)** *(leave)* hinausgehen. to **~ ~ of a room** aus einem Zimmer gehen. **(b)** *(shopping etc)* weggehen; *(socially, to theatre etc, with girl-/boyfriend)* ausgehen. **to ~ ~ for a meal** essen gehen. **(c)** *(fire, light)* ausgehen. **(d)** *(tide)* zurückgehen. **(e) my heart went ~ to him** ich fühlte mit ihm mit. **(f)** *(Sport: be defeated)* ausscheiden. **(g)** *(circular)* (hinaus)gehen; *(Rad, TV: programme)* ausgestrahlt werden.

♦ **go over 1** *vi* **(a)** *(cross)* hinübergehen; *(by vehicle)* hinüberfahren. **(b)** *(change sides etc)* übergehen *(to* zu*)*; *(to another party)* überwechseln *(to* zu*)*. **(c)** *(TV, Rad: to news desk etc)* umschalten. **(d)** *(be received: play, remarks etc)* ankommen. **2** *vi +prep obj* **(a)** *(examine) accounts* durchgehen; *house, luggage* durchsuchen;

(*medically*) *person* untersuchen; (*see over*) *house etc* sich (*dat*) ansehen. **(b)** *lesson, facts* durchgehen. **to ~ ~ sth in one's mind** etw überdenken.

♦ **go past** *vi* (*prep obj* an +*dat*) vorbeigehen; (*vehicle*) vorbeifahren; (*time*) vergehen.

♦ **go round** *vi* = **go around.**

♦ **go through 1** *vi* (*lit, fig*) durchgehen; (*business deal*) abgeschlossen werden. **2** *vi* +*prep obj* **(a)** *hole, door, customs etc* gehen durch. **(b)** *illness, formalities etc* durchmachen. **(c)** (*examine, discuss*) durchgehen. **(d)** (*search*) *pocket, suitcase* durchsuchen. **(e)** (*use up*) aufbrauchen; *money* ausgeben; *shoes* durchlaufen (*col*). **he has gone ~ the seat of his trousers** er hat seine Hose durchgesessen.

♦ **go through with** *vi* +*prep obj plan* durchziehen (*col*). **she couldn't ~ ~ ~ it** sie brachte es nicht fertig.

♦ **go together** *vi* (*harmonize*) zusammenpassen; (*events, conditions*) zusammen auftreten.

♦ **go under 1** *vi* (*sink*) untergehen; (*businessman*) scheitern; (*company*) eingehen (*col*). **2** *vi* +*prep obj* **to ~ ~ the name of X** als X bekannt sein.

♦ **go up** *vi* **(a)** (*price, temperature etc*) steigen. **(b)** (*climb*) hinaufsteigen (*prep obj acc*). **(c)** (*lift*) hochfahren; (*balloon*) aufsteigen; (*Theat: curtain*) hochgehen; (*be built: new flats etc*) gebaut werden. **(d)** (*explode*) in die Luft gehen. **to ~ ~ in flames** in Flammen aufgehen.

♦ **go without 1** *vi* +*prep obj* **to ~ ~ sth** auf etw (*acc*) verzichten. **2** *vi* darauf verzichten.

goad [gəʊd] *vt* (*taunt*) aufreizen. **to ~ sb into sth** jdn zu etw anstacheln.

♦ **goad on** *vt sep* anstacheln.

go-ahead ['gəʊəhed] **1** *adj* fortschrittlich. **2** *n* **to give sb/sth the ~** jdm/für etw freie Fahrt geben.

goal [gəʊl] *n* **(a)** (*Sport*) Tor *nt*. **(b)** (*aim, objective*) Ziel *nt*.

goalie ['gəʊlɪ] *n* (*col*) Tormann *m*.

goal: ~keeper *n* Torwart *m*; **~-kick** *n* Abstoß *m* (vom Tor); **~-post** *n* Torpfosten *m*; **~-scorer** *n* Torschütze *m*.

goat [gəʊt] *n* Ziege *f*. **to get sb's ~** (*col*) jdn auf die Palme bringen (*col*).

gob [gɒb] *n* (*Brit col!: mouth*) Schnauze *f* (*col!*).

♦ **gobble down** *vt sep* hinunterschlingen.

♦ **gobble up** *vt sep* (*lit, fig*) verschlingen.

gobbledygook ['gɒbldɪ,gu:k] *n* (*col*) Kauderwelsch *nt*.

go-between ['gəʊbɪ,twi:n] *n* Vermittler(in *f*) *m*.

goblin ['gɒblɪn] *n* Kobold *m*.

god [gɒd] *n* Gott *m*. **G~ forbid** (*col*) Gott behüte; **G~ (only) knows** (*col*) wer weiß; **(my) G~!** (*col*), **good G~!** (*col*) O Gott! (*col*), großer Gott! (*col*); **for G~'s sake!** (*col*) um Gottes willen! (*col*); **the ~s** (*Brit Theat col*) die Galerie, der Olymp (*col*).

god: ~child *n* Patenkind *nt*; **~daughter** *n* Patentochter *f*.

goddess ['gɒdɪs] *n* Göttin *f*.

god: ~father *n* Pate *m*; **~forsaken** *adj* (*col*) gottverlassen; **~less** *adj* gottlos.

godly ['gɒdlɪ] *adj* (+*er*) fromm, gottesfürchtig.

god: ~mother *n* Patin *f*; **~parent** *n* Pate *m*, Patin *f*; **~send** *n* Geschenk *nt* des Himmels; **~son** *n* Patensohn *m*.

go-getter ['gəʊ'getə^r] *n* (*col*) Tatmensch *m*.

goggle ['gɒgl] *vi* **to ~ at sb/sth** jdn/etw anstarren.

goggle-box ['gɒglbɒks] *n* (*Brit col*) Glotze *f* (*col*).

goggles ['gɒglz] *npl* Schutzbrille *f*.

going ['gəʊɪŋ] **1** *n* **it's slow ~** es geht nur langsam; **that's good ~** das ist ein flottes Tempo; **the ~ is good/hard** (*in racing*) die Bahn ist gut/hart; **the road was heavy/rough ~** man kam auf der Straße nur schwer/mit Mühe voran; **it's heavy ~ talking to him** es ist sehr mühsam, sich mit ihm zu unterhalten; **while the ~ is good** solange es noch geht. **2** *adj attr business* gutgehend; *price* aktuell.

goings-on [,gəʊɪŋ'zɒn] *npl* (*col*) Dinge *pl*. **there have been strange ~** da sind seltsame Dinge passiert.

goitre, (*US*) **goiter** ['gɔɪtə^r] *n* Kropf *m*.

go-kart ['gəʊ,kɑ:t] *n* Go-Kart *m*.

gold [gəʊld] **1** *n* **(a)** Gold *nt*. **(b)** (*colour*) Goldton *m*. **2** *adj* golden; (*made of ~ also*) Gold-.

golden ['gəʊldən] *adj* (*lit, fig*) golden; *opportunity* einmalig. **~ brown** goldbraun; **~ eagle** Steinadler *m*; **~ handshake** (*col*) Abstandssumme *f*; **~ jubilee** goldenes Jubiläum; **~ labrador** Goldener Labrador; **~ rule** goldene Regel; **~ wedding (anniversary)** goldene Hochzeit.

gold: ~finch *n* Stieglitz, Distelfink *m*; **~fish** *n* Goldfisch *m*; **~ medal** *n* Goldmedaille *f*; **~mine** *n* (*lit, fig*) Goldgrube *f*; **~ plate** *n* (*plating*) Vergoldung *f*; (*articles*) vergoldetes Gerät; **~smith** *n* Goldschmied *m*.

golf [gɒlf] *n* Golf *nt*.

golf: ~ball *n* Golfball *m*; (*on typewriter*) Kugelkopf *m*; **~ club** *n* Golfschläger *m*; (*association*) Golfklub *m*; **~ course** *n* Golfplatz *m*.

golfer ['gɒlfə^r] *n* Golfer(in *f*), Golfspieler(in *f*) *m*.

gondola ['gɒndələ] *n* Gondel *f*.

gone [gɒn] *ptp of* **go.**

goner ['gɒnə^r] *n* (*col*) **to be a ~** (*car etc*) kaputt sein (*col*); (*patient*) es nicht mehr lange machen; (*professionally: person, company*) weg vom Fenster sein (*col*).

gong [gɒŋ] *n* Gong *m*.

gonorrhoea [,gɒnə'rɪə] *n* Gonorrhö *f*, Tripper *m*.

goo [gu:] *n* (*col*) Papp *m* (*col*).

good [gʊd] **1** *adj, comp* **better,** *superl* **best (a)** gut. **that's a ~ one!** (*joke*) der ist gut!, das ist ein guter Witz (*also iro*); (*excuse*) wer's glaubt, wird selig! (*col*); **it's no ~ doing it like that** es hat keinen Sinn, das so zu machen; **that's no ~** das ist nichts; **to be ~ at sport/languages** gut im Sport/in Sprachen sein; **to be ~ at sewing/typing** gut nähen/maschineschreiben können; **I'm not very ~ at that** das kann ich nicht besonders gut; **to be ~ for sb** jdm guttun; (*be healthy also*) gesund sein; **to be ~ for toothache/one's health** gut gegen Zahnschmerzen/für die Gesundheit sein; **to drink more than is ~ for one** mehr trinken, als einem guttut; **to be ~ with people** mit Menschen umgehen können; **it's too ~ to be true** es ist zu schön, um wahr zu sein; **to feel ~** sich wohl fühlen; **I don't feel too ~** ich fühle mich nicht wohl; **that's (not) ~ enough** das reicht (nicht); **if he gives his word, that's ~ enough for me** wenn er sein Wort gibt, reicht mir das; **it's just not ~ enough!** so geht das nicht!; . **his attitude/behaviour is just not ~ enough** er hat einfach nicht die richtige Einstellung/sein Benehmen ist nicht akzeptabel; **~ morning/afternoon** guten Morgen/Tag; **that's ~!** gut!, prima!; **(it's) ~ to see you/to be here** (es ist) schön, dich zu sehen/hier zu sein; **~, I think that'll be all** gut, ich glaube das reicht; **very ~, sir** jawohl; **~ for you/him!** gut!, prima!; (*iro also*) das ist ja toll!

(b) (*favourable*) *moment, chance, opportunity* günstig, gut. **a ~ day for a picnic** ein guter Tag für ein Picknick; **it's a ~ thing** *or* **job I was there** (nur) gut, daß ich dort war.

(c) (*enjoyable*) *holiday, evening* schön. **the ~ life** das süße Leben; **to have a ~ time** sich gut amüsieren; **have a ~ time!** viel Spaß *or* Vergnügen!; **did you have a ~ day?** wie ging's (dir) heute?; **have a ~ day!** schönen Tag noch!

(d) (*kind*) gut, lieb. **to be ~ to sb** gut zu jdm sein; **that's very ~ of you** das ist sehr lieb *or* nett von Ihnen; **(it was) ~ of you to come** nett, daß Sie gekommen sind; **would you be ~ enough to tell me ...** wären Sie so nett, mir zu sagen ... (*also iro*); **she was ~ enough to help us** sie war so gut und hat uns geholfen; **with every ~ wish** mit den besten Wünschen.

(e) *(well-behaved, obedient)* artig, brav *(col).* **(as) ~ as gold** mustergültig; **be a ~ girl/boy** sei artig *or* brav *(col);* **be a ~ girl/boy and ...** sei so lieb und ...; **my ~ man** *(dated)* mein guter Mann *(dated);* **~ girl/boy!** das ist lieb!; *(well done)* gut!; **~ old Charles!** der gute alte Charles!

(f) is his credit ~? ist er kreditfähig?; **what** *or* **how much is he ~ for?** *(will he give us)* mit wieviel kann man bei ihm rechnen?; *(does he have)* wieviel hat er?; **he/the car is ~ for another few years** mit ihm kann man noch ein paar Jahre rechnen/das Auto hält *or* tut's *(col)* noch ein paar Jahre.

(g) *(thorough)* gut, gründlich. **to give sth a ~ clean** etw gründlich reinigen; **to have a ~ laugh** ordentlich lachen; **to take a ~ look at sth** sich *(dat)* etw gut ansehen.

(h) *(considerable, not less than) hour, while* gut; *amount, distance, way also* schön. **it's a ~ 8 km** es sind gute 8 km; **a ~ deal of effort/money** beträchtliche Mühe/ziemlich viel Geld; **a ~ many/few people** ziemlich viele/nicht gerade wenig Leute.

(i) as ~ as so gut wie; **as ~ as new/settled** so gut wie neu/abgemacht; **he was as ~ as his word** er hat sein Wort gehalten; **he as ~ as called me a liar** er nannte mich praktisch einen Lügner.

2 *adv* schön. **a ~ strong stick/old age** ein schön(er) starker Stock/ein schön(es) hohes Alter; **~ and strong** *(col)* schön stark *(col).*

3 *n* **(a)** *(what is morally right)* Gute(s) *nt.* **to do ~** Gutes tun; **to be up to no ~** *(col)* nichts Gutes im Schilde führen *(col).*

(b) *(advantage, benefit)* Wohl *nt.* **the common ~** das Gemeinwohl; **for the ~ of the nation** zum Wohl(e) der Nation; **I did it for your own ~** es war nur zu deinem Besten; **for the ~ of one's health** *etc* seiner Gesundheit *etc* zuliebe; **that's all to the ~** auch gut!; **he'll come to no ~** mit ihm wird es noch ein böses Ende nehmen; **what's the ~ of hurrying?** wozu eigentlich die Eile?; **he's no ~ to us** er nützt uns *(dat)* nichts; **it's no ~ complaining to me** es ist sinnlos, sich bei mir zu beklagen; **if that is any ~ to you** wenn es dir hilft; **the applicant was no ~** der Bewerber war nicht gut; **he wasn't any ~ for the job** er eignete sich nicht für die Arbeit; **is this one any ~?** was ist mit dieser/diesem?; **it's no ~, it won't start** es hat keinen Zweck, es springt nicht an; **what ~ will that do you?** was hast du davon?; **that won't do you much/any ~** das hilft dir auch nicht viel/nichts; *(will be unhealthy etc)* das ist nicht gut für dich; **a (fat) lot of ~ that will do!** *(iro col)* als ob das etwas helfen würde! *(iro).*

(c) *(for ever)* **for ~ (and all)** für immer (und ewig).

good: ~bye, *(US)* **~by 1** *n* Abschied *m;* **to say ~bye (to sb)** sich (von jdm) verabschieden; **to say ~bye to sth** einer Sache *(dat)* Lebewohl sagen; **2** *interj* auf Wiedersehen; **~-for-nothing 1** *n* Nichtsnutz *m;* **2** *adj* nichtsnutzig; **G~ Friday** *n* Karfreitag *m;* **~-humoured,** *(US)* **~-humored** *adj* gut gelaunt; *(~-natured)* gutmütig; **~-looking** *adj* gutaussehend; **~-natured** *adj* gutmütig.

goodness ['gʊdnɪs] *n* Güte *f.* **~ knows** *(col)* weiß der Himmel *(col);* **for ~' sake** *(col)* um Himmels willen *(col);* **I wish to ~ I had gone** *(col)* wenn ich doch bloß gegangen wäre!; **(my) ~!, ~ gracious!** *(col)* ach du meine Güte *(col).*

goods [gʊdz] *npl* Güter *pl (also Comm); (merchandise also)* Waren *pl; (possessions also)* Habe *f (geh).* **~ train/yard** *(Brit)* Güterzug *m*/-bahnhof *m;* **one's ~ and chattels** sein Hab und Gut *(also Jur).*

good: ~-sized *adj* ziemlich groß; **~-tempered** *adj person* verträglich; *animal* gutartig; **~will** *n* Wohlwollen *nt; (between nations, Comm)* Goodwill *m;* **a gesture of ~will** ein Zeichen seines/ihres *etc* guten Willens; **to gain sb's ~will** jds Gunst gewinnen; **~will mission/tour** Goodwill-reise *f.*

goody-goody ['gʊdɪ,gʊdɪ] *n (col)* Tugendlamm *nt (col).*

gooey ['gu:ɪ] *adj (+er) (col) (sticky)* klebrig; *toffees, centres of chocolates* weich und klebrig.

goof [gu:f] *vi (col: blunder)* danebenhauen *(col).*

goose [gu:s] *n, pl* **geese** *(lit, fig col)* Gans *f.*

gooseberry ['gʊzbərɪ] *n* Stachelbeere *f.* **to play ~** Anstandswauwau spielen *(col).*

goose: ~flesh *n,* **~pimples** *npl* Gänsehaut *f;* **~-step** *n* Stechschritt *m.*

gore[1] [gɔ:ʳ] *n (liter: blood)* Blut *nt.*

gore[2] *vt* aufspießen.

gorge [gɔ:dʒ] **1** *n (Geog)* Schlucht *f.* **2** *vr* sich vollessen; *(animal)* gierig fressen. **to ~ oneself on sth** etw verschlingen.

gorgeous ['gɔ:dʒəs] *adj* großartig, sagenhaft *(col).*

gorilla [gə'rɪlə] *n* Gorilla *m.*

gormless ['gɔ:mlɪs] *adj (Brit col)* doof *(col).*

gorse [gɔ:s] *n* Stechginster *m.*

gory ['gɔ:rɪ] *adj (+er) battle etc* blutig. **the ~ details** *(fig)* die peinlichen Einzelheiten.

gosh [gɒʃ] *interj* Mensch! *(col),* Mann! *(col).*

go-slow ['gəʊsləʊ] *n (Brit)* Bummelstreik *m.*

gospel ['gɒspəl] *n (Bibl)* Evangelium *nt.* **to take sth as ~** etw für bare Münze nehmen *(col);* **the ~ truth** *(col)* die reine Wahrheit.

gossamer ['gɒsəməʳ] **1** *n* **(a)** Spinnfäden *pl.* **(b)** *(Tex)* hauchdünne Gaze. **2** *adj* hauchdünn.

gossip ['gɒsɪp] **1** *n* **(a)** Klatsch *(col) m; (chat)* Schwatz *m.* **to have a ~ with sb** mit jdm schwatzen. **(b)** *(person)* Klatschbase *f.* **2** *vi* schwatzen *(col); (maliciously)* klatschen.

gossip: ~ column *n* Klatschspalte *f;* **~ columnist** *n* Klatschkolumnist(in *f*) *m.*

got [gɒt] *pret, ptp of* **get.**

Goth [gɒθ] *n* Gote *m.*

Gothic ['gɒθɪk] *adj* gotisch. **~ novel** Schauerroman *m.*

gotten ['gɒtn] *(esp US) ptp of* **get.**

gouge [gaʊdʒ] **1** *n (tool)* Hohlmeißel *m; (groove)* Furche *f.* **2** *vt* bohren. **the river ~d a channel in the mountainside** der Fluß grub sich *(dat)* sein Bett in den Berg.

♦ **gouge out** *vt sep* herausbohren. **to ~ sb's eyes ~** jdm die Augen ausstechen.

goulash ['gu:læʃ] *n* Gulasch *nt.*

gourmand ['gʊəmənd] *n* Schlemmer *m.*

gourmet ['gʊəmeɪ] *n* Feinschmecker, Gourmet *m.*

gout [gaʊt] *n (Med)* Gicht *f.*

govern ['gʌvən] *vt* **(a)** *(rule) country* regieren; *province, colony, school etc* verwalten. **(b)** *(control)* bestimmen; *(legislation)* regeln. **(c)** *(Mech)* regulieren. **(d)** *(Gram) case* regieren.

governess ['gʌvənɪs] *n* Gouvernante *f.*

governing ['gʌvənɪŋ] *adj* **(a)** *(ruling)* regierend. **the ~ party** die Regierungspartei; **~ body** Vorstand *m.* **(b)** *(guiding, controlling)* entscheidend. **~ principle** Leitgedanke *m.*

government ['gʌvənmənt] *n* Regierung *f.*

government *in cpds* Regierungs-, der Regierung.

government: ~ department *n* Ministerium *nt;* **~ grant** *n* (staatliche) Subvention; **~ securities** *npl (Fin)* Staatspapiere *pl.*

governor ['gʌvənəʳ] *n* **(a)** *(of colony, state etc)* Gouverneur *m.* **(b)** *(esp Brit: of bank, prison)* Direktor *m; (of school)* ≃ Mitglied *nt* des Schulbeirats *m.* **the (board of) ~s** der Vorstand; *(of bank also)* das Direktorium; *(of school)* ≃ der Schulbeirat. **(c)** *(Brit col) (boss)* Chef *m (col).* **(d)** *(Mech)* Regler *m.*

govt = government Reg.

gown [gaʊn] *n* **(a)** Kleid *nt; (evening ~)* Abendkleid *nt.* **(b)** *(academic)* Robe *f; (of clergyman, judge)*

Talar *m.*

GP *(Brit)* = **general practitioner.**

grab [græb] **1** *n* **(a)** Griff *m.* **to make a ~ at sth** nach etw greifen. **(b)** *(Mech)* Greifer *m.* **2** *vt (seize)* packen; *(greedily also)* sich *(dat)* schnappen *(col)*; *(take)* wegschnappen *(col)*; *(col: catch) person* schnappen *(col)*; *chance* beim Schopf ergreifen *(col)*. **he ~bed my sleeve** er packte mich am Ärmel; **to ~ sth away from sb** jdm etw wegreißen; **how does that ~ you?** *(col)* was hältst du davon? **3** *vi* **to ~ at** greifen nach, packen *(+acc)*.

grace [greɪs] **1** *n* Anmut *f.* **to do sth with good/bad ~** etw anstandslos/widerwillig tun; **he took it with good/bad ~** er machte gute Miene zum bösen Spiel/er war sehr ungehalten darüber; **he had the ~ to apologize** er war so anständig, sich zu entschuldigen; **he didn't even have the ~ to apologize** er brachte es nicht einmal fertig, sich zu entschuldigen; **social ~s** (gesellschaftliche) Umgangsformen *pl*; **to give sb a few days' ~** jdm ein paar Tage Zeit lassen; *(Comm)* jdm ein paar Tage Aufschub gewähren; **to say ~** das Tischgebet sprechen; **by the ~ of God** durch die Gnade Gottes; **to fall from ~** in Ungnade fallen; **~ note** *(Mus)* Verzierung *f.*

2 *vt* **(a)** *(adorn)* zieren *(geh)*. **(b)** *(honour)* beehren *(with* mit*)* *(geh)*. **to ~ the occasion with one's presence** sich *(dat)* die Ehre geben.

graceful ['greɪsfʊl] *adj* anmutig; *outline, appearance also, behaviour* gefällig.

gracefully ['greɪsfəlɪ] *adv see adj accept, give in etc* gelassen. **he gave in ~** er gab gelassen nach.

gracious ['greɪʃəs] **1** *adj* gnädig *(also iro)*; *buildings etc* stilvoll, elegant. **~ living** feudaler Lebensstil. **2** *interj* **(good) ~!** *(col)* du meine Güte!

grade [greɪd] **1** *n* **(a)** *(standard)* Niveau *nt*; *(of goods)* (Güte)klasse *f.* **high-/low-~ goods** hoch-/minderwertige Ware; **to make the ~** *(fig)* es schaffen *(col)*. **(b)** *(job ~)* Position, Stellung *f*; *(Mil)* Rang, (Dienst)grad *m; (salary ~)* Klasse, Stufe *f.* **(c)** *(Sch) (mark)* Note *f*; *(esp US: class)* Klasse *f.* **(d)** *(US)* = **gradient. 2** *vt* **(a)** klassifizieren; *eggs, goods also* sortieren; *students* einstufen. **(b)** *(Sch: mark)* benoten.

grade: ~ crossing *n (US)* Bahnübergang *m*; **~ school** *n (US)* ≃ Grundschule *f.*

gradient ['greɪdɪənt] *n* Neigung *f*; *(upward also)* Steigung *f*; *(downward also)* Gefälle *nt.* **a ~ of 1 in 10** eine Steigung/ein Gefälle von 10%.

gradual ['grædjʊəl] *adj* allmählich; *slope* sanft.

gradually ['grædjʊəlɪ] *adv* nach und nach, allmählich; *slope* sanft.

graduate[1] ['grædjʊɪt] *n (Univ)* (Hochschul)absolvent(in *f*) *m*; *(US Sch)* Schulabgänger(in *f*) *m.* **high-school ~** ≃ Abiturient(in *f*) *m.*

graduate[2] ['grædjʊeɪt] **1** *vi (Univ)* graduieren; *(US Sch)* die Abschlußprüfung bestehen *(from* an *+dat)*. **2** *vt (mark)* einteilen.

graduation [ˌgrædjʊ'eɪʃən] *n* **(a)** *(Univ, US Sch: ceremony)* (Ab)schlußfeier *f (mit feierlicher Überreichung der Zeugnisse)*. **(b)** *(mark)* (Maß)einteilung *f.*

graffiti [grə'fiːtɪ] *npl* Graffiti *pl.*

graft [grɑːft] **1** *n* **(a)** *(Bot)* (Pfropf)reis *nt*; *(Med)* Transplantat *nt.* **(b)** *(col: corruption)* Schiebung *f.* **(c)** *(col: hard work)* Schufterei *(col) f.* **2** *vt (Bot)* (auf)pfropfen *(on* auf *+acc)*; *(Med)* übertragen *(on* auf *+acc)*, einpflanzen *(in* in *+acc)*; *(fig: incorporate)* einbauen *(onto* in *+acc)*. **3** *vi (col: work hard)* schuften *(col) (at* an *+dat)*.

grain [greɪn] *n* **(a)** *no pl* Getreide, Korn *nt.* **(b)** *(of corn, sand etc)* Korn *nt*; *(fig)* Spur *f*; *(of truth also)* Körnchen *nt.* **(c)** *(of leather)* Narben *m*; *(of cloth)* Strich *m*; *(of wood, marble)* Maserung *f*; *(Phot)* Korn *nt.* **it goes against the ~ (with sb)** *(fig)* es geht jdm gegen den Strich.

grainy ['greɪnɪ] *adj (+er) texture* körnig.

gram(me) [græm] *n* Gramm *nt.*

grammar ['græmə^r^] *n* Grammatik *f.* **that's bad ~** das ist grammat(ikal)isch falsch.

grammar school *n (Brit)* ≃ Gymnasium *nt.*

grammatical [grə'mætɪkəl] *adj* grammat(ikal)isch; *rules, mistakes also* Grammatik-. **this is not ~** das ist grammatisch *or* grammatikalisch falsch.

gramophone ['græməfəʊn] *n (Brit)* Grammophon ® *nt.* **~ record** Schallplatte *f.*

gran [græn] *n (col)* Oma *(col) f.*

granary ['grænərɪ] *n* Getreidespeicher *m.*

grand [grænd] **1** *adj (+er)* großartig; *building, display* prachtvoll; *(lofty) idea* hochfliegend; *(dignified) air, person* würdevoll; *(posh) dinner party, person* vornehm. **to have a ~ time** sich sehr gut amüsieren. **2** *n (col)* ≃ Riese *m (col) (1000 Dollar/Pfund)*. **50 ~** 50 Riesen *(col)*.

grand: ~child *n* Enkel(kind *nt*) *m*; **~(d)ad** *n (col)* Opa *(col)*, Opi *(col) m*; **~daughter** *n* Enkelin *f.*

grandeur ['grændjə^r^] *n (of scenery, music)* Erhabenheit *f*; *(of manner also)* Würde *f*; *(of position, event also)* Glanz *m.*

grand: ~father *n* Großvater *m*; **~father clock** *n* Standuhr *f*; **~ finale** *n* großes Finale.

grandiose ['grændɪəʊz] *adj house, idea, speech* grandios *(also pej)*, großartig; *(pej: pompous) style* schwülstig, bombastisch.

grand jury *n (US Jur)* Großes Geschworenengericht.

grand: ~ma *n (col)* Oma *(col) f*; **~mother** *n* Großmutter *f*; **G~ National** *n* Grand National *nt (bedeutendes Pferderennen in GB)*.

grand: ~ opera *n* große Oper; **~pa** *n (col)* Opa *m (col)*; **~parent** *n* Großvater *m*/-mutter *f*; **~parents** *npl* Großeltern *pl*; **~ piano** *n* Flügel *m*; **G~ Prix** *n* Grand Prix *m*; **~ slam** *n* Großschlemm *m*; **~son** *n* Enkel(sohn) *m*; **~stand** *n* Haupttribüne *f*; **to have a ~stand view of sth** (direkten) Blick auf etw *(acc)* haben.

granite ['grænɪt] *n* Granit *m.*

granny, grannie ['grænɪ] *n* **(a)** *(col)* Oma *(col) f.* **(b)** *(also* **~ knot***)* Altweiberknoten *m.*

grant [grɑːnt] **1** *vt* **(a)** gewähren *(sb* jdm*)*; *privilege also* zugestehen *(sb* jdm*)*; *prayer* erhören; *honour* erweisen *(sb* jdm*)*; *permission* erteilen *(sb* jdm*)*; *(fulfil) wish* erfüllen. **(b)** *(admit, agree)* zugeben, zugestehen. **~ing** *or* **~ed that this is true ...** angenommen, das ist wahr ...; **I ~ you that** da gebe ich dir recht; **to take sb/sth for ~ed** jdn/etw als selbstverständlich hinnehmen; **to take it for ~ed that ...** es als selbstverständlich betrachten, daß ...; **you take too much for ~ed** für dich ist zu vieles (einfach) selbstverständlich. **2** *n (of money)* Subvention *f*; *(for studying etc)* Stipendium *nt.*

granular ['grænjʊlə^r^] *adj* körnig.

granulated sugar ['grænjʊleɪtɪd'ʃʊgə^r^] *n* Zuckerraffinade *f.*

granule ['grænjuːl] *n* Körnchen *nt.*

grape [greɪp] *n* (Wein)traube *f.*

grape: ~fruit *n* Grapefruit *f*; **~vine** *n* Weinstock *m*; *(col)* Nachrichtendienst *m (col)*; **I heard it on the ~vine** es ist mir zu Ohren gekommen.

graph [grɑːf] *n* Diagramm, Schaubild *nt.* **~ paper** Millimeterpapier *nt.*

graphic['græfɪk] *adj* **(a)** graphisch. **~ arts** Grafik, Graphik *f*; **~ designer** Graphiker(in *f*) *m.* **(b)** *(vivid) description* anschaulich.

graphics ['græfɪks] *n* **(a)** *pl (drawings)* graphische Darstellungen *pl.* **(b)** *(Comp)* Grafik *f.*

graphite ['græfaɪt] *n* Graphit *m.*

grapple ['græpl] *vi (lit)* ringen, kämpfen. **to ~ with a problem** sich mit einem Problem auseinandersetzen.

grappling iron ['græplɪŋˌaɪən] *n* Haken *m*; *(Naut)* Enterhaken *m.*

grasp [grɑːsp] **1** *n* **(a)** *(hold)* Griff *m.* **to be within**

sb's ~ (für jdn) in greifbare Nähe gerückt sein. **(b)** *(fig: understanding)* Verständnis *nt*. **to have a good ~ of sth** etw gut beherrschen; **it is beyond/within his ~** das geht über seinen Verstand/das kann er begreifen. **2** *vt* **(a)** *(catch hold of)* ergreifen, greifen nach; *(hold tightly)* festhalten. **(b)** *(fig: understand)* begreifen, erfassen.

grasping ['grɑːspɪŋ] *adj (fig)* habgierig.

grass [grɑːs] *n* **(a)** Gras *nt*; *(lawn)* Rasen *m*; *(pasture)* Weide(land *nt*) *f*. **to let the ~ grow under one's feet** lange zögern; **to put out to ~** auf die Weide führen *or* treiben. **(b)** *(col: marijuana)* Gras *nt (col)*. **(c)** *(Brit col: informer)* Spitzel *m (col)*.

grass: ~hopper *n* Heuschrecke *f*, Grashüpfer *m (col)*; **~land** *n* Grasland *nt*; **~-roots 1** *npl* Volk *nt*; *(of a party)* Basis *f*; **2** *adj attr* an der Basis; **at ~-roots level** an der Basis; **a ~-roots movement** eine Bürgerinitiative; **~ snake** *n* Ringelnatter *f*; **~ widow** *n* Strohwitwe *f*; **~ widower** *n* Strohwitwer *m*.

grassy ['grɑːsɪ] *adj (+er)* mit Gras bewachsen.

grate[1] [greɪt] *n* Gitter *nt*; *(in fire)* (Feuer)rost *m*; *(fireplace)* Kamin *m*.

grate[2] **1** *vt* **(a)** *(Cook)* reiben; *vegetables also* raspeln. **(b)** *(scrape)* streifen; *(make a grating noise with)* kratzen mit; *one's teeth* knirschen mit. **2** *vi (make a noise)* kratzen; *(chalk also, rusty door)* quietschen. **to ~ on sb's nerves** jdm auf die Nerven gehen; **it ~s on the ears** es tut in den Ohren weh.

grateful ['greɪtfʊl] *adj* dankbar *(to sb* jdm*)*.

grater ['greɪtəʳ] *n* Reibe *f*; *(for vegetable also)* Raspel *f*.

gratification [ˌgrætɪfɪ'keɪʃən] *n (pleasure)* Genugtuung *f*; *(of desires)* Befriedigung *f*.

gratify ['grætɪfaɪ] *vt (give pleasure)* erfreuen; *(satisfy)* befriedigen, zufriedenstellen.

gratifying ['grætɪfaɪɪŋ] *adj* (sehr) erfreulich.

grating[1] ['greɪtɪŋ] *n* Gitter *nt*.

grating[2] *adj* kratzend; *sound (squeaking)* quietschend; *(rasping)* knirschend; *voice* schrill.

gratis ['grætɪs] *adj, adv* gratis.

gratitude ['grætɪtjuːd] *n* Dankbarkeit *f (to* gegenüber*)*.

gratuitous [grə'tjuːɪtəs] *adj* überflüssig, unnötig.

gratuity [grə'tjuːɪtɪ] *n* Gratifikation, (Sonder)zuwendung *f*; *(form: tip)* Trinkgeld *nt*.

grave[1] [greɪv] *n (lit, fig)* Grab *nt*. **he's digging his own ~** *(fig)* er schaufelt sich selbst sein Grab; **to turn in one's ~** sich im Grabe herumdrehen.

grave[2] *adj (+er)* ernst; *danger, risk* groß; *error* schwer, gravierend; *news* schlimm.

grave-digger ['greɪvˌdɪgəʳ] *n* Totengräber *m*.

gravel ['grævəl] **1** *n* Kies *m*; *(large chippings)* Schotter *m*. **~ path** Kiesweg *m*.

gravelly ['grævəlɪ] *adj (fig) voice* rauh.

gravely ['greɪvlɪ] *adv* ernst; *mistaken* schwer.

grave: ~stone *n* Grabstein *m*; **~yard** *n* Friedhof *m*.

gravitate ['grævɪteɪt] *vi* **to ~ towards sth** von etw angezogen werden.

gravitation [ˌgrævɪ'teɪʃən] *n (Phys)* Gravitation, Schwerkraft *f*; *(fig)* Tendenz *f (towards* zu*)*.

gravitational [ˌgrævɪ'teɪʃənl] *adj* Gravitations-. **~ field** Gravitations- *or* Schwerefeld *nt*; **~ force** Schwerkraft *f*; **~ pull** Anziehungskraft *f*.

gravity ['grævɪtɪ] *n* **(a)** *(Phys)* Schwere, Schwerkraft *f*. **centre of ~** Schwerpunkt *m*; **force of ~** Schwerkraft *f*; **specific ~** spezifisches Gewicht. **(b)** *(seriousness) see* **grave**[2] Ernst *m*; Größe *f*; Schwere *f*. **such was the ~ of the news that ...** die Nachricht war so schlimm, daß ...

gravy ['greɪvɪ] *n (juice)* Fleischsaft, Bratensaft *m*; *(sauce)* Soße *f*. **~ boat** Sauciere, Soßenschüssel *f*. **to get on the ~ train** *(col)* auch ein Stück vom Kuchen abbekommen *(col)*.

gray [greɪ] *(esp US)* = **grey**.

graze[1] [greɪz] *vi (cattle etc)* grasen, weiden.

graze[2] **1** *vt (touch lightly)* streifen. **to ~ one's knees** sich *(dat)* die Knie aufschürfen. **2** *n* Schürfwunde *f*.

grease [griːs] **1** *n* Fett *nt*; *(lubricant)* Schmierfett *nt*. **2** *vt* fetten; *(Aut, Tech)* schmieren.

grease: ~-gun *n* Fettpresse *f*; **~paint** *n (Theat)* (Fett)schminke *f*; **~proof paper** *n (Brit)* Butterbrotpapier *nt*.

greasy ['griːsɪ] *adj (+er)* **(a)** fettig; *food* fett; *machinery, axle* ölig; *hands, clothes* schmierig; *(slippery) road* rutschig. **(b)** *(fig pej) person* schmierig.

great [greɪt] **1** *adj (+er)* **(a)** groß. **~ big** *(col)* riesig, Mords- *(col)*; **a ~ friend of ours** ein guter Freund von uns; **of no ~ importance** ziemlich unwichtig; **a ~ number of, a ~ many** eine große Anzahl, sehr viele; **he lived to a ~ age** er erreichte ein hohes Alter; **to take a ~ interest in** sich sehr interessieren für; **Frederick the G~** Friedrich der Große; **the ~ thing is ...** das Wichtigste ist ...; **~ minds think alike** *(col)* große Geister denken gleich. **(b)** *(col: excellent)* Klasse *(col)*, Spitze *(col)*. **to be ~ at football/singing** ein großer Fußballspieler/Sänger sein; **he's a ~ one for criticizing others** im Kritisieren anderer ist er (ganz) groß. **2** *n usu pl (~ person)* Größe *f*.

great: ~-aunt *n* Großtante *f*; **G~ Britain** *n* Großbritannien *nt*; **G~ Dane** *n* Deutsche Dogge.

greater ['greɪtəʳ] *adj, comp of* **great** größer. **to pay ~ attention** besser aufpassen; **G~ London** Groß-London *nt*.

greatest ['greɪtɪst] *adj, superl of* **great** größte(r, s). **he's the ~** *(col)* er ist der Größte.

great: ~-grandchild *n* Urenkel *m*; **~-grandparents** *npl* Urgroßeltern *pl*.

greatly ['greɪtlɪ] *adv* außerordentlich, sehr; *improved* bedeutend; *superior* bei weitem.

greatness ['greɪtnɪs] *n* Größe *f*.

great: ~-uncle *n* Großonkel *m*; **the G~ War** *n* der Erste Weltkrieg.

Grecian ['griːʃən] *adj* griechisch.

Greece [griːs] *n* Griechenland *nt*.

greed [griːd] *n* Gier *f (for* nach *+dat)*; *(for material wealth also)* Habsucht, Habgier *f*; *(gluttony)* Gefräßigkeit *f*. **~ for power** Machtgier *f*.

greedy ['griːdɪ] *adj (+er)* gierig *(for* auf *+acc,* nach*)*; *(for material wealth also)* habgierig; *(gluttonous)* gefräßig. **~ for power** machtgierig.

Greek [griːk] **1** *adj* griechisch. **2** *n* **(a)** Grieche *m*, Griechin *f*. **(b)** *(language)* Griechisch *nt*. **it's all ~ to me** *(col)* das sind für mich böhmische Dörfer *(col)*.

green [griːn] **1** *adj (+er) (lit, fig, Pol)* grün; *(gullible)* naiv. **to turn ~** *(lit)* grün werden; *(fig: person)* (ganz) grün im Gesicht werden; *(with envy)* blaß *or* grün vor Neid werden. **2** *n* **(a)** *(colour)* Grün *nt*. **(b)** *(piece of land)* Rasen *m*, Grünfläche *f*; *(Golf)* Grün *nt*; *(village ~)* (Dorf)wiese *f*. **(c) ~s** *pl (Cook)* Grüngemüse *nt*. **(d)** *(Pol)* Grüne(r) *mf*.

green: ~back *n (US col)* Lappen *(col)*, Geldschein *m*; **~ belt** *n* Grüngürtel *m*.

greenery ['griːnərɪ] *n* Grün *nt*; *(foliage)* grünes Laub.

green: ~ fingers *npl* **to have ~ fingers** eine Hand für Pflanzen haben; **~fly** *n* Blattlaus *f*; **~gage** *n* Reneklode *f*; **~grocer** *n (esp Brit)* (Obst- und) Gemüsehändler *m*; **~house** *n* Gewächshaus *nt*.

Greenland ['griːnlənd] *n* Grönland *nt*.

green light *n* **to give sb the ~** jdm grünes Licht geben.

green pepper *n* (grüne) Paprikaschote.

greet [griːt] *vt (welcome)* begrüßen; *(receive, meet)* empfangen; *(say hallo to)* grüßen; *news, decision* aufnehmen. **a terrible sight ~ed his eyes/him** ihm bot sich ein fürchterlicher Anblick.

greeting ['griːtɪŋ] *n* Gruß *m*; *(welcoming)* Be-

grüßung *f*; *(receiving, meeting)* Empfang *m*. ~**s card/telegram** Grußkarte *f*/-telegramm *nt*.
gregarious [grɪ'gɛərɪəs] *adj animal* Herden-; *person* gesellig.
grenade [grɪ'neɪd] *n* Granate *f*.
grew [gruː] *pret of* **grow.**
grey, *(esp US)* **gray** [greɪ] **1** *adj (+er) (lit, fig)* grau. **to go** *or* **turn** ~ grau werden; **little** ~ **cells** *(col)* kleine graue Zellen *pl (col)*; ~ **matter** *(col)* graue Masse *or* Substanz; **a** ~ **area** *(fig)* eine Grauzone. **2** *n (colour)* Grau *nt*. **3** *vi* grau werden. **his** ~**ing hair** sein graumeliertes Haar.
grey: ~**-haired** *adj* grauhaarig; ~**hound** *n* Windhund *m*.
grid [grɪd] *n (grating)* Gitter *nt*; *(on barbecue)* Rost *m*; *(on map)* Gitter, Netz *nt*; *(electricity, gas network)* Verteilernetz *nt*; *(Motor-racing: starting* ~*)* Start(platz) *m*; *(US Ftbl)* Spielfeld *nt*. **the (national)** ~ *(Elec)* das Überland(leitungs)netz.
gridiron ['grɪd,aɪən] *n (Cook)* (Brat)rost *m*.
grief [griːf] *n* Leid *nt*, Kummer *m*; *(because of loss)* große Trauer, Schmerz *m*. **to come to** ~ Schaden erleiden; *(be hurt, damaged)* zu Schaden kommen; *(fail)* scheitern.
grievance ['griːvəns] *n* Beschwerde *f*; *(resentment)* Groll *m*. ~ **procedure** Beschwerdeweg *m*; **to air one's** ~**s** seine Beschwerden vorbringen.
grieve [griːv] **1** *vt* Kummer bereiten *(+dat)*, betrüben. **it** ~**s me to see that ...** es stimmt mich traurig, daß ... **2** *vi* trauern *(at, about* über *+acc)*. **to** ~ **for sb/sth** um jdn/etw trauern.
grievous ['griːvəs] *adj* ~ **bodily harm** *(Jur)* schwere Körperverletzung.
grill [grɪl] **1** *n* **(a)** *(on cooker)* Grill *m*; *(food)* Grillgericht *nt*. **(b)** = **grille. 2** *vt* **(a)** *(Cook)* grillen. **(b)** *(col: interrogate)* in die Zange nehmen *(col)*.
grille [grɪl] *n* Gitter *nt*; *(on window)* Fenstergitter *nt*; *(to speak through)* Sprechgitter *nt*; *(Aut)* Kühlergrill *m*.
grilling ['grɪlɪŋ] *n* strenges Verhör. **to give sb a** ~ jdn in die Zange nehmen *(col)*.
grim [grɪm] *adj (+er) struggle* erbittert, unerbittlich; *(stern) face, smile* grimmig; *(fig) landscape, prospects, weather* trostlos; *news, tale, task* grauenhaft; *winter, times* hart; *determination* eisern; *necessity, truth* bitter. **to look** ~ *(person)* ein grimmiges Gesicht machen; *(things, prospects)* trostlos aussehen; **to hold on (to sth) like** ~ **death** sich verbissen (an etw *dat*) festhalten.
grimace ['grɪməs] **1** *n* Grimasse *f*. **to make a** ~ eine Grimasse schneiden. **2** *vi* Grimassen schneiden.
grime [graɪm] *n* (festsitzender) Schmutz; *(on buildings)* Ruß *m*.
grimy ['graɪmɪ] *adj (+er)* verschmutzt.
grin [grɪn] **1** *n see vi* Lächeln *nt*; Grinsen *nt*. **2** *vi (with pleasure)* lächeln; *(in scorn, cheekily)* grinsen. **to** ~ **and bear it** gute Miene zum bösen Spiel machen; **to** ~ **at sb** jdn anlächeln/angrinsen.
grind [graɪnd] *(vb: pret, ptp* **ground***)* **1** *vt* **(a)** *corn, coffee* mahlen. **to** ~ **one's teeth** mit den Zähnen knirschen. **(b)** *gem, lens, knife* schleifen. **(c) ground down by poverty** von Armut niedergedrückt. **2** *vi (brakes, teeth, gears)* knirschen. **to** ~ **to a halt** *(lit)* quietschend zum Stehen kommen; *(fig)* stocken; *(production etc)* zum Erliegen kommen; *(negotiations)* sich festfahren. **3** *n (col)* **the daily** ~ der tägliche Trott; **it's a bit of a** ~ das ist ganz schön mühsam *(col)*.
grinder ['graɪndəʳ] *n (meat*~*)* Fleischwolf *m*; *(coffee*~*)* Kaffeemühle *f*; *(for sharpening)* Schleifmaschine *f*.
grinding ['graɪndɪŋ] *adj* ~ **poverty** drückende Armut.
grindstone ['graɪndstəʊn] *n*: **to keep one's/sb's nose to the** ~ hart arbeiten/jdn hart arbeiten lassen.
grip [grɪp] **1** *n* **(a)** Griff *m*; *(on rope also, on road)* Halt *m*. **to get a** ~ **on oneself** *(col)* sich zusammenreißen *(col)*; **to have a good** ~ **of a subject** ein Thema im Griff haben; **to release one's** ~ loslassen *(on sth* etw*)*; **to lose one's** ~ *(lit)* den Halt verlieren; *(fig)* nachlassen; **I must be losing my** ~ mit mir geht's bergab; **the country is in the** ~ **of winter** der Winter herrscht im Land; **to get** *or* **come to** ~**s with sth** etw in den Griff bekommen; **to get** *or* **come to** ~**s with sb** jdm auf den Leib rücken *(col)*. **(b)** *(handle)* Griff *m*. **(c)** *(travelling-bag)* Reisetasche *f*.

2 *vt* packen; *hand also, (fig: fear etc also)* ergreifen; *(film, story etc also)* fesseln. **the car/tyre** ~**s the road well** der Wagen liegt gut auf der Straße/der Reifen greift gut.
gripe [graɪp] **1** *vi (col: grumble)* meckern *(col)*. **to** ~ **at sb** jdn anmotzen *(col)*. **2** *n* **(a) the** ~**s** *pl* Darmkrämpfe *pl*. **(b)** *(col: complaint)* Meckerei *f (col)*.
gripping ['grɪpɪŋ] *adj story* spannend, fesselnd.
grisly ['grɪzlɪ] *adj (+er)* grausig, gräßlich.
grist [grɪst] *n* **it's all** ~ **to his mill** das kann er alles verwerten.
gristle ['grɪsl] *n* Knorpel *m*.
grit [grɪt] **1** *n* **(a)** *(dust, in eye)* Staub *m*; *(gravel)* Splitt *m*; *(for roads)* Streusand *m*. **(b)** *(courage)* Mut *m*. **2** *vt* **(a)** *road* streuen. **(b) to** ~ **one's teeth** die Zähne zusammenbeißen.
grizzly ['grɪzlɪ] *n (also* ~ **bear***)* Grisly(bär), Grizzly(bär) *m*.
groan [grəʊn] **1** *n* Stöhnen *nt no pl*; *(of pain also, of planks etc)* Ächzen *nt no pl*. **to let out** *or* **give a** ~ (auf)stöhnen. **2** *vi* stöhnen *(with* vor *+dat)*; *(with pain also, beneath weight)* ächzen *(with* vor *+dat)*.
grocer ['grəʊsəʳ] *n* Lebensmittelhändler, Kaufmann *m*.
grocery ['grəʊsərɪ] *n* **(a)** Lebensmittelgeschäft *nt*. **(b) groceries** *pl (goods)* Lebensmittel *pl*.
grog [grɒg] *n* Grog *m*.
groggy ['grɒgɪ] *adj (+er) (col)* groggy *inv (col)*.
groin [grɔɪn] *n (Anat)* Leiste *f*.
groom [gruːm] **1** *n* **(a)** *(in stables)* Reitknecht *m*. **(b)** *(bride*~*)* Bräutigam *m*. **2** *vt* **(a)** *horse* striegeln. **well** ~**ed** *(person)* gepflegt. **(b) to** ~ **sb for an office** jdn auf *or* für ein Amt vorbereiten.
groove [gruːv] *n* Rille *f*; *(in face)* Furche *f*.
grope [grəʊp] **1** *vi (also* ~ **around** *or* **about***)* (herum)tasten *(for* nach*)*; *(for words)* suchen *(for* nach*)*. **2** *vt (col) girl* befummeln *(col)*. **to** ~ **one's way in/out** sich hinein-/hinaustasten.
gross¹ [grəʊs] *n no pl* Gros *nt*.
gross² **1** *adj (+er)* **(a)** *(fat)* fett, feist. **(b)** *(coarse, vulgar)* derb. **(c)** *(extreme, flagrant)* grob; *impertinence* ungeheuerlich. **(d)** *(total)* brutto; *income, weight* Brutto-. **he earns £250** ~ er verdient £250 brutto; ~ **national product** Bruttosozialprodukt *nt*. **2** *vt* brutto verdienen.
grotesque [grəʊ'tesk] *adj* grotesk.
grotto ['grɒtəʊ] *n, pl* **-(e)s** Grotte *f*.
grotty ['grɒtɪ] *adj (+er) (col)* mies *(col)*.
grouch [graʊtʃ] *(col)* **1** *n* **(a)** *(complaint)* Beschwerde *f*. **she's always got a** ~ sie hat immer was zu meckern *(col)*. **(b)** *(person)* Meckerer *m (col)*. **2** *vi* meckern *(col)*.
grouchy ['graʊtʃɪ] *adj (+er)* griesgrämig.
ground¹ [graʊnd] **1** *n* **(a)** *(soil, terrain, fig)* Boden *m*. **snow on high** ~ Schnee in höheren Lagen; **hilly** ~ hügeliges Gelände; **there is common** ~ **between us** uns verbindet einiges; **to be on dangerous** ~ *(fig)* sich auf gefährlichem Boden bewegen; **to meet sb on his own** ~ zu jdm kommen; **to cut the** ~ **from under sb's feet** jdm den Boden unter den Füßen wegziehen; **to gain/lose** ~ Boden gewinnen/verlieren; *(disease, rumour)* um sich greifen/im Schwinden begriffen sein; **to break new** ~ *(fig)* etwas völlig Neuartiges darstellen; *(person)* Neuland betreten; **to go over the** ~ *(fig)* alles durchgehen; **to cover a lot of** ~ *(lit)* eine weite Strecke zurücklegen; *(fig)* eine Menge Dinge

behandeln; **to hold** *or* **stand one's ~** *(lit)* nicht von der Stelle weichen; *(fig)* seinen Mann stehen, sich nicht unterkriegen lassen; **to shift one's ~** *(fig)* seine Haltung ändern; **above/below ~** über/unter der Erde; *(Min)* über/unter Tage; **to fall to the ~** zu Boden fallen; **to burn sth to the ~** etw niederbrennen; **it suits me down to the ~** das paßt mir ausgezeichnet; **to get off the ~** *(plane etc)* abheben; *(plans, project etc)* ins Rollen kommen; **to get sth off the ~** etw ins Rollen bringen; **to go to ~** *(fox)* im Bau verschwinden; *(person)* untertauchen *(col)*; **to run sb/sth to ~** jdn/etw ausfindig machen; **to run sb/oneself into the ~** *(col)* jdn/sich selbst fertigmachen *(col)*; **to run a car into the ~** ein Auto schrottreif fahren.

(b) *(pitch)* Feld *nt*, Platz *m*; *(parade ~, drill~)* Platz *m*.

(c) ~s *pl (premises, land)* Gelände *nt*; *(gardens)* Anlagen *pl*.

(d) ~s *pl (sediment)* Satz *m*.

(e) *(US Elec)* Erde *f*.

(f) *(reason)* Grund *m*. **to have ~s for sth** Grund zu etw haben; **to be ~(s) for sth** Grund für *or* zu etw sein; **~s for divorce** Scheidungsgrund *m*; **on the ~(s) of** aufgrund *(+gen)*, auf Grund von; **on the ~s that** auf Grund der Tatsache, daß; **on health ~s** aus gesundheitlichen Gründen.

2 *vt* **(a)** *ship* auf Grund setzen. **to be ~ed** aufgelaufen sein. **(b)** *plane (for mechanical reasons)* aus dem Verkehr ziehen; *pilot* sperren. **to be ~ed by bad weather** wegen schlechten Wetters nicht starten können. **(c)** *(US Elec)* erden. **(d)** *(base)* **to be ~ed on sth** sich auf etw *(acc)* gründen.

ground[2] **1** *pret, ptp of* **grind. 2** *adj coffee* gemahlen. **~ beef** *(US)* Hackfleisch *m*; **~ glass** geschliffenes Glas; *(particles)* Glaspulver *nt*; **~ rice** Reismehl *nt*.

ground: ~ control *n (Aviat)* Bodenkontrolle *f*; **~ crew** *n* Bodenpersonal *nt*; **~ floor** *n* Erdgeschoß *nt*; **~ frost** *n* Bodenfrost *m*.

grounding ['graʊndɪŋ] *n (basic knowledge)* Grundwissen *nt*. **to give sb a ~ in English** jdm die Grundlagen *pl* des Englischen beibringen.

ground: ~less *adj* grundlos, unbegründet; **~ level** *n* Boden *m*; **below ~ level** unter dem Boden; **at ~ level** *live* im Erdgeschoß; **~nut** *n* Erdnuß *f*; **~ plan** *n* Grundriß *m*; **~sheet** *n* Zeltboden(plane *f*) *m*.

groundsman ['graʊndzmən] *n, pl* **-men** *(esp Brit)* Platzwart *m*.

ground: ~ staff *n* Bodenpersonal *nt*; **~-to-air missile** *n* Boden-Luft-Rakete *f*; **~work** *n* Vorarbeit *f*.

group [gru:p] **1** *n* Gruppe *f*; *(Comm also)* Konzern *m*; *(theatre ~ also)* Ensemble *nt*. **2** *attr* Gruppen-; *discussion, activities* in der Gruppe. **3** *vt* gruppieren. **to ~ together** *(in one ~)* zusammentun; *(in several ~s)* in Gruppen einteilen; **the books were ~ed according to subject** die Bücher standen nach Sachgruppen geordnet.

group: ~ captain *n (Aviat)* Oberst *m*; **~ therapy** *n* Gruppentherapie *f*.

grouse[1] [graʊs] *n, pl* - Rauhfußhuhn *nt*; *(red ~)* Schottisches Moorhuhn.

grouse[2] *(col)* **1** *n (complaint)* Klage *f*. **to have a good ~** herummeckern *(col)*. **2** *vi* meckern *(col)* *(about* über *+acc)*.

grouting ['graʊtɪŋ] *n* Fugenkitt *m*.

grove [grəʊv] *n* Hain *m*, Wäldchen *nt*.

grovel ['grɒvl] *vi* kriechen *(to sb* vor jdm*)*.

grow [grəʊ] *pret* **grew,** *ptp* **grown 1** *vt* **(a)** *plants* ziehen; *(commercially) potatoes, coffee etc* anbauen; *(cultivate) flowers* züchten. **(b) to ~ one's beard/hair** sich *(dat)* einen Bart/die Haare wachsen lassen. **2** *vi* **(a)** wachsen; *(hair also)* länger werden; *(in numbers)* zunehmen; *(in size also)* sich vergrößern; *(fig: become more mature)* sich weiterentwickeln. **to ~ in stature/wisdom** an Ansehen/Weisheit zunehmen; **to ~ in popularity** immer beliebter werden; **it'll ~ on you** du wirst schon noch Geschmack daran finden. **(b)** *(become)* werden. **to ~ to hate/love sb** jdn hassen/lieben lernen; **to ~ to enjoy sth** langsam Gefallen an etw *(dat)* finden.

♦**grow apart** *vi (fig)* sich auseinanderentwickeln.

♦**grow away** *vi (fig)* **to ~ ~ from sb** sich jdm entfremden.

♦**grow into** *vi +prep obj* **(a)** *clothes, job* hineinwachsen in *(+acc)*. **(b)** *(become)* sich entwickeln zu, werden zu. **to ~ ~ a man/woman** zum Mann/zur Frau heranwachsen.

♦**grow out of** *vi +prep obj* **(a)** *clothes* herauswachsen aus; *habit* ablegen. **(b)** *(arise from)* entstehen aus.

♦**grow up** *vi (spend childhood)* aufwachsen; *(become adult)* erwachsen werden; *(fig) (custom, hatred)* aufkommen; *(city)* entstehen. **what are you going to do when you ~ ~?** was willst du mal werden, wenn du groß bist?; **~ ~!** werde endlich erwachsen!

grower ['grəʊə^r] *n (of fruit, vegetables)* Anbauer *m*; *(of flowers)* Züchter *m*; *(of tobacco, coffee)* Pflanzer *m*.

growing ['grəʊɪŋ] *adj (lit, fig)* wachsend; *child* heranwachsend. **~ pains** *(Med)* Wachstumsschmerzen *pl*; *(fig)* Kinderkrankheiten *pl*.

growl [graʊl] **1** *n* Knurren *nt no pl*; *(of bear)* Brummen *no pl*. **2** *vi* knurren; *(bear)* böse brummen. **to ~ at sb** jdn anknurren/anbrummen.

grown [grəʊn] **1** *ptp of* **grow. 2** *adj* erwachsen. **fully ~** ausgewachsen.

grown-up [,grəʊn'ʌp] **1** *adj* erwachsen; *clothes, shoes* Erwachsenen-. **2** *n* Erwachsene(r) *mf*.

growth [grəʊθ] *n* **(a)** Wachstum *nt*; *(of person also)* Entwicklung *f*; *(increase in quantity, fig: of love, interest etc)* Anwachsen *nt*; *(increase in size also)* Vergrößerung *f*; *(of capital etc)* Zuwachs *m*. **~ industry** Wachstumsindustrie. **(b) with a two days' ~ on his face** mit zwei Tage alten Bartstoppeln. **(c)** *(Med)* Wucherung *f*.

groyne [grɔɪn] *n* Buhne *f*.

grub [grʌb] **1** *n* **(a)** *(larva)* Larve *f*. **(b)** *(col: food)* Fressalien *pl (hum, col)*. **~('s) up!** antreten zum Essenfassen *(col)*. **2** *vi (also* **~ about** *or* **around***)* wühlen *(in* in *+dat)*.

grubby ['grʌbɪ] *adj (+er)* schmuddelig *(col)*; *hands* dreckig *(col)*.

grudge [grʌdʒ] **1** *n* Groll *m (against* gegen*)*. **to bear sb a ~, to have a ~ against sb** jdm böse sein; **I bear him no ~** ich nehme ihm das nicht übel; **to bear ~s** nachtragend sein. **2** *vt* **to ~ sb sth** jdm etw nicht gönnen; **I don't ~ you your success/these pleasures** ich gönne Ihnen Ihren Erfolg/das Vergnügen; **to ~ doing sth** etw mit Widerwillen tun.

grudging ['grʌdʒɪŋ] *adj person, attitude* unwirsch; *contribution, gift* widerwillig gegeben; *admiration, praise, support* widerwillig.

gruel [grʊəl] *n* Schleimsuppe *f*.

gruelling, *(US)* **grueling** ['grʊəlɪŋ] *adj task, day etc* aufreibend; *climb, race* äußerst strapaziös.

gruesome ['gru:səm] *adj* grausig, schaurig.

gruff [grʌf] *adj (+er)* barsch, schroff.

grumble ['grʌmbl] **1** *n (complaint)* Murren *nt no pl*. **2** *vi* murren *(about, over* über *+acc)*; *(thunder, gunfire)* grollen.

grumbler ['grʌmblə^r] *n* Nörgler(in *f*) *m*.

grumpy ['grʌmpɪ] *adj (+er)* brummig, grantig.

grunt [grʌnt] **1** *n* Grunzen *nt no pl*; *(of pain, in exertion)* Ächzen *nt no pl*. **2** *vi* grunzen; *(with pain, exertion)* ächzen. **3** *vt reply* brummen, knurren.

G-string ['dʒi:strɪŋ] *n (clothing)* Minislip *m*.

guarantee [,gærən'ti:] **1** *n* Garantie *f (of* für*)*. **to**

have a 6-month ~ 6 Monate Garantie haben; **while it is under** ~ solange noch Garantie darauf ist; **that's no** ~ **that ...** das heißt noch lange nicht, daß ...; **I give you my** ~ das garantiere ich Ihnen. **2** *vt* garantieren. **to be** ~**d for three months** drei Monate Garantie haben; **I** ~ **to come tomorrow** ich komme garantiert morgen; **that's a** ~**d success** das wird garantiert ein Erfolg.

guarantor [ˌgærənˈtɔːʳ] *n* Garant *m*; *(Jur)* Bürge *m*.

guard [gɑːd] **1** *n* **(a)** *(Mil)* Wache *f*; *(single soldier also)* Wachtposten *m*; *(no pl: squad also)* Wachmannschaft *f*; *(security*~*)* Sicherheitsbeamte(r) *m*, Sicherheitsbeamtin *f*; *(at factory gates, in park etc)* Wächter(in *f*) *m*; *(esp US: prison* ~*)* Gefängniswärter(in *f*) *m*; *(Brit Rail)* Schaffner(in *f*) *m*. **the G**~**s** *(Brit)* das Garderegiment; ~ **of honour** *(Brit)* or **honor** *(US)* Ehrenwache *f*; **to change** ~ Wachablösung machen; **under** ~ unter Bewachung; **to be under** ~ bewacht werden; **to keep sb/sth under** ~ jdn/etw bewachen; **to be on** ~, **to stand** *or* **keep** ~ Wache halten; **to put a** ~ **on sb/sth** jdn/etw bewachen lassen.

(b) *(Boxing, Fencing)* Deckung *f*. **to take** ~ in Verteidigungsstellung gehen; **to drop** *or* **lower one's** ~ *(col)* seine Deckung vernachlässigen; *(fig)* seine Reserve aufgeben; **to catch sb off (his/her)** ~ jdn überrumpeln; **to be on one's** ~ **(against sth)** *(fig)* (vor etw *dat*) auf der Hut sein; **to put sb on his/her** ~ **(against sth)** jdn (vor etw *dat*) warnen.

(c) *(safety device, for protection)* Schutz *m* *(against* gegen); *(on machinery also)* Schutzvorrichtung *f*; *(fire* ~*)* Schutzgitter *nt*.

2 *vt prisoner, place, valuables* bewachen; *treasure also, secret* hüten; *luggage* aufpassen auf *(+acc)*; *(protect) person, place* schützen *(from, against* vor *+dat)*.

♦ **guard against** *vi +prep obj (take care to avoid) suspicion* sich in acht nehmen vor *(+dat)*; *hasty reaction, bad habit* sich hüten vor *(+dat)*; *illness, misunderstandings* vorbeugen *(+dat)*; *accidents* verhüten. **you must** ~ ~ **catching cold** Sie müssen aufpassen, daß Sie sich nicht erkälten; **in order to** ~ ~ **this** um dem vorzubeugen.

guard: ~ **dog** *n* Wachhund *m*; ~ **duty** *n* Wachdienst *m*; **to be on** ~ **duty** Wache haben.

guarded [ˈgɑːdɪd] *adj reply* zurückhaltend.

guardhouse [ˈgɑːdhaʊs] *n (Mil)* Wachstube *f*; *(for prisoners)* Bunker *m*.

guardian [ˈgɑːdɪən] *n* Hüter, Wächter *m*; *(Jur)* Vormund *m*.

guard-rail [ˈgɑːdreɪl] *n* Schutzgeländer *nt*.

guardsman [ˈgɑːdzmən] *n, pl* **-men** [-mən] Wachtposten *m*; *(member of guards regiment)* Gardist *m*; *(US: in National Guard)* Nationalgardist *m*.

guard's van [ˈgɑːdzvæn] *n (Brit Rail)* Schaffnerabteil *nt*, Dienstwagen *m*.

guer(r)illa [gəˈrɪlə] **1** *n* Guerillakämpfer(in *f*) *m*. **2** *attr* Guerilla-.

guess [ges] **1** *n* Vermutung, Annahme *f*; *(estimate)* Schätzung *f*. **to have a** ~ **(at sth)** (etw) raten; *(estimate)* (etw) schätzen; **it was just a** ~ ich habe nur geraten; **it was just a lucky** ~ das war ein Zufallstreffer *m*; **I'll give you three** ~**es** dreimal darfst du raten; **at a rough** ~ grob geschätzt; **my** ~ **is that ...** ich schätze *or* vermute, daß ...; **your** ~ **is as good as mine!** *(col)* da kann ich auch nur raten!; **it's anybody's** ~ *(col)* das wissen die Götter *(col)*.

2 *vi* **(a)** raten. **to keep sb** ~**ing** jdn im ungewissen lassen; **he's only** ~**ing** das ist eine reine Vermutung von ihm; **you'll never** ~! das wirst du nie erraten; **to** ~ **at sth** etw raten. **(b)** *(esp US)* **I** ~ **not** wohl nicht; **he's right, I** ~ er hat wohl recht; **is he coming?** — **I** ~ **so** kommt er? — ich glaube schon.

3 *vt* raten; *(correctly)* erraten; *(estimate) weight* schätzen. **I** ~**ed as much** das habe ich mir schon gedacht; ~ **what!** *(col)* stell dir vor! *(col)*.

guesswork [ˈgeswɜːk] *n* (reine) Vermutung.

guest [gest] *n* Gast *m*. ~ **of honour** *(Brit) or* **honor** *(US)* Ehrengast *m*; **be my** ~ *(col)* nur zu! *(col)*.

guest *in cpds* Gast-; ~**appearance** *n* Gastauftritt *m*; ~**-house** *n* Pension *f*; ~ **list** *n* Gästeliste *f*; ~**-room** *n* Gästezimmer *nt*.

guffaw [gʌˈfɔː] **1** *n* schallendes Lachen *no pl*. **2** *vi* schallend (los)lachen.

guidance [ˈgaɪdəns] *n (direction)* Führung, Leitung *f*; *(counselling)* Beratung *f (on* über *+acc)*; *(from superior, parents, teacher etc)* Anleitung *f*. **for your** ~ zu Ihrer Orientierung; ~ **system** *(on rocket)* Steuerungssystem *nt*.

guide [gaɪd] **1** *n* **(a)** *(person)* Führer(in *f*) *m*; *(fig: indication, pointer)* Anhaltspunkt *m (to* für); *(model)* Leitbild *nt*. **(b)** *(Tech)* Leitvorrichtung *f*. **(c)** *(Brit: girl* ~*)* Pfadfinderin *f*. **(d)** *(instructions)* Anleitung *f*; *(manual)* Handbuch *nt (to gen)*; *(travel* ~*)* (Reise)führer *m*. **2** *vt people, blind man etc* führen; *discussion also* leiten; *missile, sb's behaviour* lenken. **to** ~ **a plane in** ein Flugzeug einweisen; **to be** ~**d by sb/sth** *(person)* sich von jdm/etw leiten lassen.

guide-book [ˈgaɪdbʊk] *n* Reiseführer *m*.

guided missile [ˌgaɪdɪdˈmɪsaɪl] *n* ferngelenktes Geschoß.

guide-dog [ˈgaɪddɒg] *n* Blindenhund *m*.

guided tour [ˌgaɪdɪdˈtʊəʳ] *n* Führung *f (of* durch).

guidelines [ˈgaɪdlaɪnz] *npl n* Richtlinien *pl*.

guiding [ˈgaɪdɪŋ]: ~ **hand** *n* leitende Hand; ~ **principle** *n* Leitmotiv *nt*.

guild [gɪld] *n (Hist)* Zunft, Gilde *f*; *(association)* Verein *m*.

guildhall [ˈgɪldhɔːl] *n (townhall)* Rathaus *nt*.

guile [gaɪl] *n* Tücke, (Arg)list *f*.

guillotine [ˌgɪləˈtiːn] *n* Guillotine *f*; *(for paper)* (Papier)schneidemaschine *f*.

guilt [gɪlt] *n* Schuld *f (for, of* an *+dat)*. **to feel** ~ **about sth** sich wegen etw schuldig fühlen; ~ **complex** Schuldkomplex *m*.

guiltless [ˈgɪltlɪs] *adj* schuldlos *(of* an *+dat)*.

guilty [ˈgɪltɪ] *adj (+er)* schuldig *(of gen)*; *look, voice* schuldbewußt; *conscience, thought* schlecht. **the** ~ **person/party** der/die Schuldige/die schuldige Partei; **verdict of** ~ Schuldspruch *m*; **to find sb** ~**/not** ~ **(of a crime)** jdn (eines Verbrechens) für schuldig/nicht schuldig befinden; **we're all** ~ **of neglecting the problem** uns alle trifft Schuld, daß das Problem vernachlässigt wurde; **I've been** ~ **of that myself** den Fehler habe ich auch schon begangen; **I feel very** ~ **(about ...)** ich habe ein sehr schlechtes Gewissen(, daß ...).

guinea [ˈgɪnɪ] *n (Brit old)* Guinee *f (21 Shillings)*.

guinea-pig [ˈgɪnɪˌpɪg] *n* Meerschweinchen *nt*; *(fig)* Versuchskaninchen *nt*.

guise [gaɪz] *n* **in the** ~ **of a clown/swan** als Clown verkleidet/in Gestalt eines Schwans.

guitar [gɪˈtɑːʳ] *n* Gitarre *f*.

guitarist [gɪˈtɑːrɪst] *n* Gitarrist(in *f*) *m*.

gulch [gʌltʃ] *n (US)* Schlucht *f*.

gulf [gʌlf] *n (bay)* Golf, Meerbusen *m*; *(lit, fig: chasm)* tiefe Kluft. **G**~ **stream** Golfstrom *m*; **the (Persian) G**~ der Persische Golf.

gull [gʌl] *n (sea*~*)* Möwe *f*.

gullet [ˈgʌlɪt] *n* Speiseröhre, Kehle *f*.

gullible [ˈgʌlɪbl] *adj* leichtgläubig.

gully [ˈgʌlɪ] *n (ravine)* Schlucht *f*; *(narrow channel)* Rinne *f*.

gulp [gʌlp] **1** *n* Schluck *m*. **at a/one** ~ auf einen Schluck. **2** *vt (also* ~ **down)** *drink* runterstürzen; *food* runterschlingen; *medicine* hinunterschlucken. **what?, he** ~**ed** was?, preßte er hervor.

gum[1] [gʌm] *n (Anat)* Zahnfleisch *nt no pl*.

gum[2] **1** *n (Bot)* Gummi *nt*; *(glue)* Klebstoff *m*; *(chewing* ~*)* Kaugummi *m*; *(sweet)* Weingummi *m.* **2** *vt (stick together)* kleben; *(spread ~ on)* gummieren.

♦ **gum up** *vt sep* verkleben. **to ~ ~ the works** *(fig col)* die Sache vermasseln *(col).*

gum: ~boil *n* Zahnfleischabszeß *m*; **~boot** *n* Gummistiefel *m.*

gumption ['gʌmpʃən] *n (col)* Grips *m (col).* **to have the ~ to do sth** geistesgegenwärtig genug sein, etw zu tun.

gum: ~-shield *n* Zahnschutz *m*; **~-tree** *n* **to be up a ~-tree** *(Brit col)* aufgeschmissen sein *(col).*

gun [gʌn] **1** *n* **(a)** *(cannon etc)* Kanone *f*, Geschütz *nt*; *(rifle)* Gewehr *nt*; *(pistol etc)* Pistole *f.* **to carry a ~** (mit einer Schußwaffe) bewaffnet sein; **to draw a ~ on sb** jdn mit einer Schußwaffe bedrohen; **big ~** *(fig col)* hohes Tier *(col) (in* in *+dat)*; **to stick to one's ~s** nicht nachgeben; **to jump the ~** *(Sport)* Frühstart machen; *(fig)* voreilig sein *or* handeln. **(b)** *(spray~)* Pistole *f.* **grease ~** Fettpresse *f.* **2** *vi (col)* **to be ~ning for sb** *(fig)* jdn auf dem Kieker haben *(col)*; *for opponent* jdn auf die Abschußliste gesetzt haben.

♦ **gun down** *vt sep* niederschießen.

gun: ~boat *n* Kanonenboot *nt*; **~ carriage** *n* Lafette *f*; **~ crew** *n* Geschützbedienung *f*; **~ dog** *n* Jagdhund *m*; **~-fight** *n* Schießerei *f*; *(Mil)* Feuergefecht *nt*; **~fire** *n* Schießerei *f*, Schüsse *pl*; *(Mil)* Geschützfeuer *nt.*

gunge [gʌndʒ] *n (Brit col)* klebriges Zeug *(col).*

gunman ['gʌnmən] *n, pl* **-men** Bewaffnete(r) *m.* **they saw the ~** sie haben den Schützen gesehen.

gunner ['gʌnə^r] *n (Mil)* Artillerist *m*; *(title)* Kanonier *m*; *(Naut)* Geschützführer *m*; *(in plane)* Bordschütze *m.*

gun: ~point *n* **to hold sb at ~ point** jdn mit einer Pistole/einem Gewehr bedrohen; **to force sb to do sth at ~point** jdn mit Waffengewalt zwingen, etw zu tun; **to surrender at ~ point** sich unter Waffengewalt ergeben; **~ powder** *n* Schießpulver *nt*; **~running** *n* Waffenschmuggel *m*; **~shot** *n* Schuß *m*; *(range)* Schußweite *f*; **~shot wound** Schußwunde *f*; **~smith** *n* Büchsenmacher *m*; **~wale** ['gʌnl] *n* Schandeck *nt.*

gurgle ['gɜːgl] **1** *n (of liquid)* Gluckern *nt no pl.* **2** *vi (liquid)* gluckern; *(person)* glucksen *(with* vor *+dat).*

guru ['gʊruː] *n* Guru *m.*

gush [gʌʃ] **1** *n (of liquid)* Strahl, Schwall *m*; *(of words)* Schwall *m*; *(of emotion)* Ausbruch *m.* **2** *vi* **(a)** *(also* **~out***) (water)* heraussprudeln; *(smoke, blood)* hervorquellen; *(flames)* herausschlagen. **(b)** *(col: talk)* schwärmen *(col) (about, over* von*).*

gushing ['gʌʃɪŋ] *adj (fig)* überschwenglich.

gusset ['gʌsɪt] *n (in garment)* Keil, Zwickel *m.*

gust [gʌst] *n (of wind, day)* Böe *f.*

gusto ['gʌstəʊ] *n* Begeisterung *f.* **to do sth with ~** etw mit Genuß tun.

gusty ['gʌstɪ] *adj (+er) wind, day* böig, stürmisch.

gut [gʌt] **1** *n* **(a)** *(Anat)* Darm *m*; *(stomach, paunch)* Bauch *m*; *(for racket, violin)* Darmsaiten *pl.* **(b)** *usu pl (col: stomach)* Eingeweide *nt usu pl.* **to hate sb's ~s** *(col)* jdn auf den Tod nicht ausstehen können *(col)*; **~ reaction** rein gefühlsmäßige Reaktion. **(c)** *(col: courage)* **~s** *pl* Mut, Mumm *m (col).* **2** *vt* **(a)** *animal* ausnehmen. **(b) it was completely ~ted by the fire** es war völlig ausgebrannt.

gutter ['gʌtə^r] **1** *n (on roof)* Dachrinne *f*; *(in street, fig)* Gosse *f.* **2** *vi (candle, flame)* flackern.

gutter: ~-press *n* Boulevardpresse *f*; **~snipe** *n* Gassenkind *nt.*

guttural ['gʌtərəl] *adj* guttural, kehlig.

guy[1] [gaɪ] *n (col: man)* Typ *(col)*, Kerl *(col) m.* **hey you ~s** he Leute *(col).*

guy[2] *n (also* **~-rope***) (for tent)* Zeltschnur *f.*

guzzle ['gʌzl] *vti (eat)* futtern *(col)*; *(drink)* schlürfen.

gym [dʒɪm] *n (gymnasium)* Turnhalle *f*; *(gymnastics)* Turnen *nt.*

gymkhana [dʒɪm'kɑːnə] *n* Reiterfest *nt.*

gymnasium [dʒɪm'neɪzɪəm] *n* Turnhalle *f.*

gymnast ['dʒɪmnæst] *n* Turner(in *f*) *m.*

gymnastics [dʒɪm'næstɪks] *n* **(a)** *sing (discipline)* Gymnastik *f no pl*; *(with apparatus)* Turnen *nt no pl.* **(b)** *pl (exercises)* Übungen *pl.*

gym: ~ shoe *n (Brit)* Turnschuh *m*; **~slip** *n (Brit)* Schulträgerrock *m.*

gynaecological, *(US)* **gynecological** [ˌgaɪnɪkə'lɒdʒɪkəl] *adj* gynäkologisch. **~ illness** Frauenleiden *nt.*

gynaecologist, *(US)* **gynecologist** [ˌgaɪnɪ'kɒlədʒɪst] *n* Gynäkologe *m*, Gynäkologin *f*, Frauenarzt *m*/-ärztin *f.*

gynaecology, *(US)* **gynecology** [ˌgaɪnɪ'kɒlədʒɪ] *n* Gynäkologie, Frauenheilkunde *f.*

gypsy ['dʒɪpsɪ] *n* Zigeuner(in *f*) *m.*

gyrate [ˌdʒaɪə'reɪt] *vi (rotate)* sich drehen; *(dancer)* sich drehen und winden.

gyrocompass ['dʒaɪərəʊ'kʌmpəs] *n* Kreisel-Magnetkompaß *m.*

gyroscope ['dʒaɪərəˌskəʊp] *n* Gyroskop *nt.*

H

H, h [eɪtʃ] *n* H, h *nt*.
habeas corpus ['heɪbɪəs'kɔːpəs] *n (Jur)* **to issue a writ of** ~ einen Vorführungsbefehl erteilen.
haberdashery [ˌhæbə'dæʃərɪ] *n (Brit)* Kurzwaren *pl*; *(US)* Herrenartikel *pl*.
habit ['hæbɪt] *n* **(a)** Gewohnheit *f*. **to be in the ~ of doing sth** die Angewohnheit haben, etw zu tun; **it became a ~** es wurde zur Gewohnheit; **out of sheer ~** aus reiner Gewohnheit; **I don't make a ~ of asking strangers in** (für) gewöhnlich bitte ich Fremde nicht herein; **don't make a ~ of it** lassen Sie (sich *dat*) das nicht zur Gewohnheit werden; **to get into/to get sb into the ~ of doing sth** sich/jdm angewöhnen, etw zu tun; **to get into bad ~s** schlechte Gewohnheiten annehmen; **to get out of/to get sb out of the ~ of doing sth** sich/jdm abgewöhnen, etw zu tun. **(b)** *(costume)* Gewand *nt*; *(monk's also)* Habit *nt or m*. **(riding) ~** Reitkleid *nt*.
habitable ['hæbɪtəbl] *adj* bewohnbar.
habitat ['hæbɪtæt] *n* Heimat *f*; *(of animals also)* Lebensraum *m*; *(of plants also)* Standort *m*.
habitation [ˌhæbɪ'teɪʃən] *n* **unfit for human ~** für Wohnzwecke nicht geeignet.
habitual [hə'bɪtjʊəl] *adj* gewohnt; *drinker, gambler, liar* gewohnheitsmäßig.
habitually [hə'bɪtjʊəlɪ] *adv* ständig.
habitué [hə'bɪtjʊeɪ] *n* regelmäßiger Besucher, regelmäßige Besucherin.
hack[1] [hæk] **1** *n* **(a)** *(cut)* Kerbe *f*; *(action)* Hieb *m*; *(kick)* Tritt *m*. **(b)** *(cough)* trockener Husten. **2** *vt* hacken. **to hack sb/sth to pieces** jdn zerstückeln/ etw (in Stücke) hacken; **to ~ one's way through (sth)** sich *(dat)* einen Weg (durch etw) schlagen.
♦ **hack down** *vt sep bushes etc* umhauen; *people also* niedermetzeln.
hack[2] *n* **(a)** *(hired horse)* Mietpferd *nt*; *(worn-out horse)* Klepper *m*. **(b)** *(pej: writer)* Schundliterat(in *f*) *m*; *(journalist also)* Schmierfink *m*.
hacker ['hækəʳ] *n (Comp)* Hacker *m*.
hacking [hækɪŋ] *adj* **(a) ~ cough** trockener Husten. **(b) ~ jacket** Sportsakko *m or nt*; *(for riding)* Reitjacke *f*.
hackle ['hækl] *n* **to get sb's ~s up** jdn auf die Palme bringen *(col)*; **to have one's ~s up** auf (hundert)achtzig sein *(col)*.
hackney carriage ['hæknɪˌkærɪdʒ] *n (also form: taxi)* Droschke *f*.
hackneyed ['hæknɪd] *adj* abgedroschen.
hacksaw ['hæksɔː] *n* Metallsäge *f*.
had [hæd] *pret, ptp of* **have**.
haddock ['hædək] *n* Schellfisch *m*.
hadn't ['hædnt] = **had not**.
haematology, *(US)* **hematology** [ˌhiːmə'tɒlədʒɪ] *n* Hämatologie *f*.
haemoglobin, *(US)* **hemoglobin** [ˌhiːməʊ'gləʊbɪn] *n* Hämoglobin *nt*, roter Blutfarbstoff.
haemophilia, *(US)* **hemophilia** [ˌhiːməʊ'fɪlɪə] *n* Bluterkrankheit *f*.
haemorrhage, *(US)* **hemorrhage** ['hemərɪdʒ] **1** *n* Blutung *f*. **2** *vi* bluten.
haemorrhoids, *(US)* **hemorrhoids** ['hemərɔɪdz] *npl* Hämorrhoiden *pl*.
hag [hæg] *n* Hexe *f*.
haggard ['hægəd] *adj* ausgezehrt; *(from tiredness)* abgespannt; *(from worry)* abgehärmt.
haggis ['hægɪs] *n schottisches Gericht aus gehackten Schafsinnereien und Haferschrot.*
haggle ['hægl] *vi (bargain)* feilschen *(about or over* um*)*; *(argue also)* sich streiten *(over* wegen*)*.
Hague [heɪg] *n* **the ~** Den Haag *nt*.
hail[1] [heɪl] **1** *n (lit, fig)* Hagel *m*. **2** *vi* hageln.
♦ **hail down** *vi (stones etc)* niederhageln *(on sb/sth* auf jdn/etw*)*.
hail[2] **1** *vt* **(a) to ~ sb/sth as sth** jdn/etw als etw feiern. **(b)** *(call)* zurufen *(+dat)*; *ship* anrufen; *taxi* rufen. **within ~ing distance** in Rufweite. **2** *vi* **a ship ~ing from London** ein Schiff *nt* mit (dem) Heimathafen London; **he ~s from Ireland** er stammt aus Irland. **3** *interj* **~ Caesar** heil dir Cäsar; **the H~ Mary** das Ave Maria.
hail-fellow-well-met ['heɪlfeləʊˌwel'met] *adj* plumpvertraulich.
hail: ~stone *n* Hagelkorn *nt*; **~storm** *n* Hagel(schlag) *m*.
hair [hɛəʳ] **1** *n* Haar *nt*; *(collective: on head)* Haare *pl*, Haar *nt*. **a fine head of ~** schönes volles Haar; **to do one's ~** sich frisieren, sich *(dat)* die Haare (zurecht)machen *(col)*; **to have one's ~ cut/done** sich *(dat)* die Haare schneiden/frisieren lassen; **her ~ is always perfect** sie ist immer sehr gut frisiert; **to let one's ~ down** *(fig)* aus sich *(dat)* herausgehen; **keep your ~ on!** *(col)* ruhig Blut!; **that film really made my ~ stand on end** bei dem Film lief es mir eiskalt den Rücken herunter; **not a ~ of his head was harmed** ihm wurde kein Haar gekrümmt; **not a ~ out of place** *(fig)* wie aus dem Ei gepellt; **body ~** Körperbehaarung *f*; **the best cure for a hangover is a ~ of the dog (that bit you)** einen Kater kuriert man am besten, wenn man mit dem anfängt, womit man aufgehört hat.
2 *attr mattress, sofa* Roßhaar-.
hair: ~brush *n* Haarbürste *f*; **~ clip** *n* Clip *m*; *(for ponytail etc)* Haarspange *f*; **~ cream** *n* Haarpomade *f*; **~cut** *n* Haarschnitt *m*; *(hairdo)* Frisur *f*; **to have** *or* **get a ~cut** sich *(dat)* die Haare schneiden lassen; **I need a ~cut** ich muß mir die Haare schneiden lassen; **~do** *n (col)* Frisur *f*; **~dresser** *n* Friseur *m*, Friseuse *f*; **~-drier** *n* Haartrockner *m*; *(hand-held also)* Fön ® *m*; *(over head also)* Trockenhaube *f*; **~-grip** *n (Brit)* Haarklemme *f*; **~-line** *n* **(a)** Haaransatz *m*; **(b)** *(thin line)* haarfeine Linie; *(in telescope, on sight)* Faden *m*; **~-line crack** *n* Haarriß *m*; **~net** *n* Haarnetz *nt*; **~ oil** *n* Haaröl *nt*; **~-piece** *n* Haarteil *nt*; *(for men)* Toupet *nt*; **~pin** *n* Haarnadel *f*; **~pin (bend)** *n* Haarnadelkurve *f*; **~-raising** *adj* haarsträubend; **~'s breadth** *n* **by a ~'s breadth** um Haaresbreite; **~-splitting 1** *n* Haarspalterei *f*; **2** *adj* haarspalterisch; **~spray** *n* Haarspray *nt*; **~style** *n* Frisur *f*.
hairy ['hɛərɪ] *adj (+er)* **(a)** stark behaart. **(b)** *(col) situation* brenzlig *(col)*; *film etc* gruselig *(col)*; *driving* kriminell *(col)*.
hake [heɪk] *n* Seehecht *m*.
halcyon ['hælsɪən] *adj*: **~ days** glückliche Tage *pl*.
hale [heɪl] *adj* kräftig. **~ and hearty** gesund und munter.
half [hɑːf] **1** *n, pl* **halves (a)** Hälfte *f*. **to cut in ~** halbieren; **to break/tear sth in ~** etw entzweibrechen/-reißen; **~ of it/them** die Hälfte davon/

von ihnen; ~ **the book/money** die Hälfte des Buches/Geldes; ~ **a cup/an hour** eine halbe Tasse/Stunde; ~ **a second!** (einen) Augenblick mal!; **to go halves** halbe-halbe machen *(col)*; **he is too clever by** ~ *(col)* das ist ein richtiger Schlaumeier; **not** ~ **enough** längst nicht genug; **one and a** ~ eineinhalb, anderthalb; **an hour and a** ~ eineinhalb *or* anderthalb Stunden; **not to do things by halves** keine halben Sachen machen; ~ **and** ~ halb und halb; **that's not the** ~ **of it** *(col)* und das ist noch nicht einmal die Hälfte *(col)*.

(b) *(Sport) (of match)* Halbzeit *f*; *(player)* Läufer(in *f*) *m*.

(c) *(of ticket)* Abschnitt *m* der Fahrkarte; *(travel, admission fee)* halbe Karte *(col)*.

(d) *(beer)* kleines Bier.

2 *adj* halb. **a** ~ **cup** eine halbe Tasse; **he's not** ~ **the man he used to be** er ist längst nicht mehr das, was er einmal war.

3 *adv* **(a)** halb. **I** ~ **thought ...** ich hätte fast gedacht ...; **I was** ~ **afraid that ...** ich habe fast befürchtet, daß ...; **the work is only** ~ **done** die Arbeit ist erst zur Hälfte erledigt; **that's** ~ **right** das ist zur Hälfte richtig. **(b)** *(Brit col)* **he's not** ~ **stupid/rich** er ist unheimlich dumm/reich *(col)*; **not** ~ **bad** gar nicht schlecht; **not** ~! und wie!, und ob! **(c) it's** ~ **past three** *or* ~ **three** es ist halb vier. **(d)** ~ **as big as** halb so groß wie; ~ **as big again** anderthalbmal so groß.

half: ~ **back** *n (Sport)* Läufer(in *f*) *m*; ~**-baked** *adj (fig col) person, plan* blöd; ~**-breed** *n (person)* Mischling *m*; *(animal)* Rassenmischung *f*; *(horse)* Halbblut *nt*; ~ **brother** *n* Halbbruder *m*; ~**-caste** *n* Mischling *m*; ~**-cock** *n*: **to go off at** ~**-cock** *(col)* ein Reinfall *m* sein *(col)*; ~**-crown** *n (in old Brit system)* Zweieinhalbschillingstück *nt*; ~**-cut** *adj (Brit col: drunk)* besoffen *(col!)*; ~**-day** *(holiday) n* halber freier Tag; **we've got a** ~**-day (holiday)** wir haben einen halben Tag frei; ~**-empty** *adj* halbleer *attr*, halb leer *pred;* ~**-fare 1** *n* halber Fahrpreis; **2** *adv* zum halben Preis; ~**-hearted** *adj* halbherzig; *manner* lustlos; ~**-heartedly** *adv agree* mit halbem Herzen; **to do sth** ~**-heartedly** etw ohne rechte Lust tun; ~**-holiday** *n (Brit)* halber Urlaubstag/Feiertag; **we've got a** ~**-holiday tomorrow morning** wir haben morgen vormittag frei; ~**-hour** *n* halbe Stunde; ~**-mast** *n:* **at** ~**-mast** *(also hum)* (auf) halbmast; ~**-moon** *n* Halbmond *m*; ~**-note** *n (US Mus)* halbe Note; ~**penny** ['heɪpnɪ] *n* halber Penny; ~**-pint** *n* **(a)** ≃ Viertelliter *m or nt; (of beer also)* kleines Bier; **(b)** *(col: person)* halbe Portion *(col)*; ~**-price** *n* **at** ~**-price** zum halben Preis; ~**-sister** *n* Halbschwester *f*; ~**-term** *n (Brit)* Ferien *pl* in der Mitte des Trimesters; ~**-timbered** *adj* Fachwerk-; ~**-time** *n* **(a)** *(Sport)* Halbzeit *f*; **(b)** *(Ind)* **to be on** ~**-time** auf Kurzarbeit sein; ~**-truth** *n* Halbwahrheit *f*.

halfway ['hɑːf,weɪ] **1** *adj attr* **when we reached the** ~ **stage on our journey** als wir die Hälfte der Reise hinter uns *(dat)* hatten; **the project is at the** ~ **stage** das Projekt ist zur Hälfte abgeschlossen. **2** *adv* ~**way to** auf halbem Weg nach; **we drove** ~ **to London** wir fuhren die halbe Strecke nach London; ~ **between two points** (in der Mitte *or* genau) zwischen zwei Punkten; ~ **up the hill** auf halber Höhe des Berges; **we went** ~ **up the hill** wir gingen den Berg halb hinauf; ~ **through a book** halb durch ein Buch (durch); **this money will go** ~ **towards paying ...** diese Summe wird die Hälfte der Kosten für ... decken; **to meet sb** ~ *(lit, fig)* jdm (auf halbem Weg) entgegenkommen. **3** *attr* ~ **house** *n (fig)* Zwischending *nt*.

half: ~**-wit** *n (fig)* Schwachkopf *m*; ~**-witted** ['hɑːf,wɪtɪd] *adj* schwachsinnig; ~**-yearly** *adj* halbjährlich.

halibut ['hælɪbət] *n* Heilbutt *m*.

halitosis [,hælɪ'təʊsɪs] *n* Mundgeruch *m*.

hall [hɔːl] *n* **(a)** *(of house)* Flur *m*; *(large)* Diele *f*. **(b)** *(large building)* Halle *f*; *(large room)* Saal *m*; *(village* ~*)* Gemeindehalle *f*; *(school assembly* ~*)* Aula *f*. **(c)** *(mansion)* Herrenhaus *nt*; *(students' also* ~ **of residence***)* Studenten(wohn)heim *nt*.

hallelujah [,hælɪ'luːjə] *interj* halleluja.

hallmark [,hɔːlmɑːk] *n* **(a)** (Feingehalts)stempel *m*. **(b)** *(fig)* Kennzeichen *nt (of gen,* für*)*.

hallo [hə'ləʊ] *interj, n* = **hello.**

Hallowe'en [,hæləʊ'iːn] *n* Tag *m* vor Allerheiligen.

hall: ~ **porter** *n* Portier *m;* ~**-stand** *n* (Flur)garderobe *f*; *(treelike)* Garderobenständer *m*.

hallucinate [hə'luːsɪneɪt] *vi* halluzinieren.

hallucination [hə,luːsɪ'neɪʃən] *n* Halluzination *f*.

hallway ['hɔːlweɪ] *n* Korridor *m*.

halo ['heɪləʊ] *n, pl* **-(e)s** *(of saint)* Heiligenschein *m; (Astron)* Hof *m*.

halt [hɒlt] **1** *n* **(a)** *(stop)* Pause *f*; *(Mil)* Halt *m; (in production)* Stopp *m*. **to come to a** ~ zum Stillstand kommen; **to call a** ~ **to sth** einer Sache *(dat)* ein Ende bereiten; **shall we call a** ~ **now?** wollen wir jetzt Schluß machen?; ~ **sign** Stoppschild *nt*. **(b)** *(small station)* Haltepunkt *m*. **2** *vi* zum Stillstand kommen; *(person)* stehenbleiben; *(Mil)* halten. **to** ~ **briefly** kurz haltmachen. **3** *vt* anhalten; *production, traffic also* zum Stehen bringen. **4** *interj* halt; *(traffic sign)* stop.

halter ['hɒltə[r]] *n (horse's)* Halfter *nt*.

halting ['hɒltɪŋ] *adj walk* unsicher; *speech* stockend; *verse* holp(e)rig.

halve [hɑːv] *vt* **(a)** halbieren. **(b)** *(reduce by one half)* auf die Hälfte reduzieren.

halves [hɑːvz] *pl of* **half.**

ham [hæm] **1** *n* **(a)** *(Cook)* Schinken *m*. **(b)** *(Theat)* Schmierenkomödiant(in *f*) *m*. **(c)** *(Rad col)* Funkamateur *m*. **2** *adj attr acting* übertrieben. **3** *vi (Theat)* chargieren, übertrieben spielen.

♦ **ham up** *vt sep (col)* **to** ~ **it** ~ zu dick auftragen.

hamburger ['hæm,bɜːgə[r]] *n* (flache) Frikadelle *f*; *(with bread)* Hamburger *m*.

ham-fisted [,hæm'fɪstɪd] *adj* ungeschickt.

hamlet ['hæmlɪt] *n* Weiler *m*, kleines Dorf.

hammer ['hæmə[r]] **1** *n* Hammer *m*. **to go at it** ~ **and tongs** *(col)* sich ins Zeug legen *(col)*; *(quarrel)* sich in die Haare kriegen *(col)*; **to come under the** ~ *(auction)* unter den Hammer kommen; **in the** ~ **(throwing)** *(Sport)* im Hammerwurf. **2** *vt* **(a)** *nail, metal* hämmern. **to** ~ **a nail into a wall** einen Nagel in die Wand schlagen; **to** ~ **sth into shape** *metal* etw zurechthämmern; *(fig) plan, agreement* etw ausarbeiten; **to** ~ **sth into sb's head, to** ~ **it home to sb** jdm etw einbleuen *(col)*. **(b)** *(col: defeat badly)* eine Schlappe beibringen +*dat (col)*. **3** *vi* hämmern. **to** ~ **(away) at the door** an die Tür hämmern.

♦ **hammer out** *vt sep (fig) plan, solution* ausarbeiten; *tune* hämmern.

hammering ['hæmərɪŋ] *n* **our team took a** ~ *(col)* unsere Mannschaft mußte eine Schlappe einstecken *(col)*.

hammock ['hæmək] *n* Hängematte *f*.

hamper[1] ['hæmpə[r]] *n* Korb *m; (as present)* Geschenkkorb *m*.

hamper[2] *vt* behindern. **to be** ~**ed** gehandikapt sein.

hamster ['hæmstə[r]] *n* Hamster *m*.

hamstring ['hæmstrɪŋ] *(vb: pret, ptp* **hamstrung** ['hæmstrʌŋ]*)* **1** *n (Anat)* Kniesehne *f*. **2** *vt (fig)* **to be hamstrung** außer Gefecht gesetzt sein; *(project)* lahmliegen.

hand [hænd] **1** *n* **(a)** Hand *f*; *(of clock)* Zeiger *m*. **on** ~**s and knees** auf allen vieren; **to take sb by the** ~ jdn bei der Hand nehmen; ~**s up!** Hände hoch!; *(Sch)* meldet euch!; ~**s off** *(col)* Hände weg!; **keep your** ~**s off it** laß die Finger davon!; **made by** ~ handgearbeitet; **to raise an animal by** ~ ein Tier mit der Flasche aufziehen; **to live**

from ~ to mouth von der Hand in den Mund leben; **with a heavy/firm ~** *(fig)* mit harter/ starker Hand.

(b) *(side, direction, position)* Seite *f.* **on the right ~** auf der rechten Seite, rechts; **on my right ~** rechts von mir; **on all ~s** auf allen Seiten; **on the one ~ ... on the other ~ ...** einerseits ..., andererseits ...

(c) *(agency, possession etc)* **it's the ~ of God** das ist die Hand Gottes; **it's in your own ~s what you do now** Sie haben es selbst in der Hand, was Sie jetzt tun; **to put sth into sb's ~s** jdm etw in die Hand geben; **to leave sb/sth in sb's ~s** jdn in jds Obhut lassen/jdm etw überlassen; **I'm in your ~s** ich verlasse mich ganz auf Sie; **to fall into the ~s of sb** jdm in die Hände fallen; **to be in good ~s** in guten Händen sein; **he has too much time on his ~s** er hat zuviel Zeit zur Verfügung; **I've got enough on my ~s already** ich habe schon genug am Hals *(col)*; **to get sb/sth off one's ~s** jdn/etw loswerden; **to take sb/sth off sb's ~s** jdm jdn/etw abnehmen.

(d) *(applause)* **they gave him a big ~** er bekam großen Applaus.

(e) *(worker)* Arbeitskraft *f*; *(Naut)* Besatzungsmitglied *nt.* **to take on ~s** Leute einstellen; *(Naut)* Leute anheuern; **~s** Belegschaft *f*; **all ~s on deck!** alle Mann an Deck!; **to be an old ~ (at sth)** ein alter Hase (in etw *dat*) sein.

(f) *(Measure: of horse)* ≈ 10 cm.

(g) *(handwriting)* Handschrift *f.*

(h) *(Cards)* Blatt *nt*; *(person)* Mann *m*; *(game)* Runde *f.* **3 ~s** *(people)* 3 Mann.

(i) Christmas is (close) at ~ Weihnachten steht vor der Tür; **at first/second ~** aus erster/ zweiter Hand; **according to the information on ~** laut den vorliegenden Informationen; **to keep sth at ~** etw in Reichweite haben; **it's quite close at ~** es ist ganz in der Nähe; **he had the situation well in ~** er hatte die Situation im Griff; **to take sb in ~** *(discipline)* jdn zur Räson bringen; *(look after)* nach jdm sehen; **stock in ~** *(Comm)* Warenlager *nt*; **he still had £600/a couple of hours in ~** er hatte £ 600 übrig/noch zwei Stunden Zeit; **the matter in ~** die zur Debatte stehende Angelegenheit; **work in ~** Arbeit, die zur Zeit erledigt wird; **a matter/project** *etc* **is in ~** eine Sache/ein Projekt *nt etc* ist in Bearbeitung; **to put sth in ~** zusehen, daß etw erledigt wird; **the children got out of ~** die Kinder waren nicht mehr zu bändigen; **matters got out of ~** die Dinge sind außer Kontrolle geraten; **I don't have the letter to ~** ich habe den Brief gerade nicht zur Hand.

(j) *(phrases)* **to keep one's ~ in** in Übung bleiben; **to eat out of sb's ~** *(lit, fig)* jdm aus der Hand fressen; **to force sb's ~** auf jdn Druck ausüben; **to wait on sb ~ and foot** jdn von vorne und hinten bedienen; **he never does a ~'s turn** er rührt keinen Finger; **to have a ~ in sth** *(in decision)* an etw *(dat)* beteiligt sein; *(in crime)* die Hand bei etw im Spiel haben; **to lend** *or* **give sb a ~** jdm zur Hand gehen; **give me a ~!** hilf mir mal!; **to be ~ in glove with sb** mit jdm unter einer Decke stecken; **to have one's ~s full with sth** mit etw alle Hände voll zu tun haben; **to win ~s down** spielend gewinnen; **he is making money ~ over fist** er scheffelt das Geld nur so; **we're losing money/staff ~ over fist** wir verlieren haufenweise Geld/Personal; **to have the upper ~** die Oberhand behalten; **to gain the upper ~** die Oberhand gewinnen; **to ask for a lady's ~ (in marriage)** um die Hand einer Dame anhalten.

2 *vt (give)* reichen, geben *(sth to sb, sb sth* jdm etw*).* **you've got to ~ it to him** *(fig)* das muß man ihm lassen *(col)*.

♦ **hand back** *vt sep* zurückgeben.

♦ **hand down** *vt sep* **(a)** *(lit)* herunter-/hinunterreichen *or* -geben *(to sb* jdm*).* **(b)** *(fig)* weitergeben; *tradition, story also* überliefern *(to* an *+acc)*; *heirloom etc* vererben *(to dat)*.

♦ **hand in** *vt sep* abgeben; *forms, resignation* einreichen.

♦ **hand on** *vt sep* weitergeben *(to* an *+acc)*.

♦ **hand out** *vt sep* austeilen *(to sb* an jdn*)*; *advice* erteilen *(to sb* jdm*)*.

♦ **hand over 1** *vt sep (pass over)* (herüber-/ hinüber)reichen *(to dat)*; *(give up)* (her)geben *(to dat)*; *(to third party)* (ab)geben *(to dat)*; *criminal, prisoner* übergeben *(to dat)*; *(from one state to another)* ausliefern; *leadership* abtreten *(to* an *+acc)*; *the controls, business* übergeben *(to dat,* an *+acc)*. **2** *vi* **when the Conservatives ~ed ~ to Labour** als die Konservativen die Regierung an Labour abgaben; **when the chairman ~ed ~ to his successor** als der Vorsitzende das Amt an seinen Nachfolger abgab.

♦ **hand round** *vt sep* herumreichen; *(distribute) papers* austeilen.

hand: ~bag *n* Handtasche *f*; **~ baggage** *n* Handgepäck *nt*; **~ball** *n* **(a)** Handball *m*; **(b)** *(Ftbl: foul)* Handspiel *nt*; **~bill** *n* Handzettel *m*; **~book** *n* Handbuch *nt*; *(tourist's)* Reiseführer *m*; **~brake** *n (Brit)* Handbremse *f*; **~cuff** *vt* Handschellen anlegen *(+dat)*; **~cuffs** *npl* Handschellen *pl.*

handful ['hændfʊl] *n* **(a)** Handvoll *f*; *(of hair, fur)* Büschel *nt.* **by the ~, in ~s** büschelweise. **(b)** *(small number)* Handvoll *f.* **(c)** *(fig)* **those children are a ~** die Kinder können einen ganz schön in Trab halten.

hand-grenade ['hændgrɪneɪd] *n* Handgranate *f.*

handicap ['hændɪkæp] **1** *n* Handikap *nt*; *(in horse racing, golf also)* Vorgabe *f*; *(physical, mental also)* Behinderung *f.* **to be under a great ~** stark gehandikapt sein. **2** *vt* ein Handikap *nt* darstellen für. **to be (physically/mentally) ~ped** (körperlich/geistig) behindert sein; **~ped children** behinderte Kinder *pl.*

handicraft ['hændɪkrɑːft] *n* **(a)** *(work)* Kunsthandwerk *nt*; *(needlework etc)* Handarbeit *f*; *(woodwork, modelling etc)* Werken *nt.* **(b)** *(skill)* Geschick *nt,* Handfertigkeit *f.*

handiness ['hændɪnɪs] *n (of shops etc)* günstige Lage.

handiwork ['hændɪwɜːk] *n no pl* **(a)** *(lit)* Arbeit *f*; *(Sch: subject)* Werken *nt*; *(needlework etc)* Handarbeit *f.* **(b)** *(fig)* Werk *nt*; *(pej)* Machwerk *nt.*

handkerchief ['hæŋkətʃɪf] *n* Taschentuch *nt.*

handle ['hændl] **1** *n* Griff *m*; *(of door also)* Klinke *f*; *(of broom, comb)* Stiel *m*; *(of basket, bucket, cup etc)* Henkel *m.* **to fly off the ~** *(col)* an die Decke gehen *(col)*.

2 *vt* **(a)** *(touch, use hands on)* anfassen; *(Ftbl) ball* mit der Hand berühren. **be careful how you ~ that** gehen Sie vorsichtig damit um; **"~ with care"** „Vorsicht Glas/Blumen/lebende Tiere etc".

(b) *(deal with) person, animal, tool, weapon, machine etc* umgehen mit; *legal or financial matters* erledigen; *legal case, order, contract* bearbeiten; *applicant, matter, problem* sich befassen mit; *material for essay etc* bearbeiten; *(tackle) problem, interview etc* anpacken; *(cope with) child, drunk, situation, problem* fertigwerden mit; *vehicle, plane, ship* steuern. **how would you ~ the situation?** wie würden Sie sich in der Situation verhalten?; **you keep quiet, I'll ~ this** sei mal still und laß mich nur machen *(col)*; **who's handling the publicity for this?** wer macht die Öffentlichkeitsarbeit dafür?

3 *vi (ship, plane)* sich steuern lassen; *(car, motorbike)* sich fahren.

4 *vr* **he ~s himself well in a fight** er kann sich in einer Schlägerei behaupten.

handle: **~bar moustache** *n* Schnauzbart *m*; **~bar(s)** *n(pl)* Lenkstange *f*.

handler ['hændlə^{r}] *n (dog-~)* Hundeführer *m*.

handling ['hændlɪŋ] *n* **(a)** *(touching)* Berühren *nt*. **(b)** *(of plant, problem)* Behandlung *f*; *(of person, patient etc also)* Umgang *m (of* mit); *(of tool, weapon, machine)* Handhabung *f*; *(of legal or financial matters)* Erledigung *f*; *(of order, contract, legal case)* Bearbeitung *f*. **his ~ of the situation** die Art, wie er die Situation angepackt hat; **he/it needs careful ~** man muß vorsichtig mit ihm/damit umgehen. **(c)** *(of vehicle)* Fahrverhalten *nt*. **what's its ~ like?** wie fährt es sich?

hand: **~luggage** *n* Handgepäck *nt*; **~-made** *adj* handgearbeitet; **this is ~-made** das ist Handarbeit; **~-me-down** *n (col)* abgelegtes Kleidungsstück; **~out** *n (col: money)* (Geld)zuwendung *f*; *(leaflet)* Flugblatt *nt*; *(publicity ~)* Reklamezettel *m*; **~-picked** *adj (specially selected)* handverlesen; **~rail** *n (of stairs etc)* Geländer *nt*; *(of ship)* Reling *f*; **~shake** *n* Händedruck *m*.

handsome ['hænsəm] *adj* gutaussehend; *furniture, building* schön; *(noble, generous)* großzügig, nobel *(col)*; *profit, inheritance etc* stattlich, beträchtlich. **he is ~/he has a ~ face** er sieht gut aus.

handsomely ['hænsəmlɪ] *adv* **(a)** *(elegantly)* elegant. **(b)** *(generously)* großzügig.

hand: **~-stand** *n* Handstand *m*; **~-to-~** *adj* **~-to-~ fighting** Nahkampf *m*; **~-to-mouth** *adj existence* kümmerlich, armselig; **to lead a ~-to-mouth existence** von der Hand in den Mund leben; **~writing** *n* Handschrift *f*; **~written** *adj* handgeschrieben.

handy ['hændɪ] *adj (+er)* **(a)** *person* geschickt. **to be ~ at doing sth** ein Geschick *nt* für etw haben. **(b)** *pred (close at hand)* in der Nähe *(for +gen)*. **to keep sth ~** etw griffbereit haben. **(c)** *(convenient, useful)* praktisch. **it'll come in ~** das kann ich gut gebrauchen; **he's a very ~ person to have around** man kann ihn gut (ge)brauchen *(col)*; **he's very ~ about the house** er kann im Haus alles selbst erledigen.

handyman ['hændɪmæn] *n, pl* **-men** [-mən] *(do-it-yourself)* Bastler *m*.

hang [hæŋ] *(vb: pret, ptp* **hung)** **1** *vt* **(a)** hängen; *painting* aufhängen; *door, gate* einhängen; *wallpaper* kleben. **to ~ wallpaper** tapezieren; **to ~ sth from sth** etw an etw *(dat)* aufhängen; **the walls were hung with tapestries** die Wände waren mit Gobelins behängt; **to ~ one's head** den Kopf hängen lassen. **(b)** *pret, ptp* **hanged** *criminal* hängen. **to ~ oneself** sich erhängen; **~ him** *(col)* zum Kuckuck mit ihm! *(col)*; **I'm ~ed if I know** *(col)* weiß der Kuckuck *(col)*; **~ it!** *(col)* so ein Mist! *(col)*.

2 *vi* **(a)** hängen *(on* an *(+dat), from* von); *(drapery, clothes, hair)* fallen. **time ~s heavy on my hands** die Zeit wird mir sehr lang. **(b)** *(criminal)* gehängt werden. **(c) it/he can go ~!** *(col)* es/er kann mir gestohlen bleiben *(col)*.

3 *n* **(a)** *(of drapery)* Fall *m*; *(of suit)* Sitz *m*. **(b) you'll soon get the ~ of it** *(col)* du wirst bald den richtigen Dreh (dabei) herauskriegen *(col)*.

♦ **hang about** *or* **around** **1** *vi (col) (wait)* warten; *(loiter)* sich herumtreiben *(col)*. **to keep sb ~ing ~** jdn warten lassen; **~ about, I didn't say that** Moment mal, das habe ich nicht gesagt *(col)*; **he doesn't ~ ~** *(is fast)* er ist einer von der schnellen Truppe. **2** *vi +prep obj* **to ~ ~ a place** sich an einem Ort herumtreiben *(col)*.

♦ **hang back** *vi (lit)* sich zurückhalten; *(hesitate)* zögern.

♦ **hang in** *vi (col)* **just ~ ~ there!** bleib am Ball *(col)*.

♦ **hang on** **1** *vi* **(a)** *(hold)* sich festhalten *(to sth* an etw *dat)*. **(b)** *(hold out)* durchhalten; *(Telec)* am Apparat bleiben; *(col: wait)* warten. **~ ~ (a minute)** wart mal, einen Augenblick (mal). **2** *vi +prep obj* **(a) to ~ ~ sb's arm** an jds Arm *(dat)* hängen; **he ~s ~ her every word** er hängt an ihren Lippen. **(b)** *(depend on)* **it all ~s ~ his decision** alles hängt von seiner Entscheidung ab.

♦ **hang on to** *vi +prep obj (keep)* behalten.

♦ **hang out** **1** *vi* **(a)** *(tongue, shirt tails etc)* heraushängen *(of* aus *+dat)*. **(b)** *(col: live)* sich aufhalten; *(be usually found also)* sich herumtreiben *(col)*. **(c) they hung ~ for more pay** sie hielten an ihrer Lohnforderung fest. **(d)** *(col)* **to let it all ~ ~** die Sau rauslassen *(col)*. **2** *vt sep* hinaushängen.

♦ **hang together** *vi (people)* zusammenhalten; *(argument, report)* zusammenhängend sein; *(alibi etc)* keine Widersprüche aufweisen.

♦ **hang up** **1** *vi (Telec)* auflegen. **he hung ~ on me** er legte einfach auf. **2** *vt sep* aufhängen.

hangar ['hæŋə^{r}] *n* Flugzeughalle *f*.

hangdog ['hæŋdɒg] *adj look* niedergeschlagen; *(ashamed)* zerknirscht.

hanger ['hæŋə^{r}] *n (for clothes)* (Kleider)bügel *m*; *(loop on garment)* Aufhänger *m*.

hanger-on [,hæŋər'ɒn] *n, pl* **-s-on** *(sponger)* Schmarotzer *m*. **he came with all his hangers-on** er kam mit seinem ganzen Gefolge.

hanging ['hæŋɪŋ] **1** *n* **(a)** Todesstrafe *f*; *(of criminal)* Erhängen *nt*; *(event)* Hinrichtung *f* (durch den Strang). **(b)** *(curtains etc)* **~s** *pl* Vorhänge *pl*; *(on wall)* Tapete *f*; *(tapestry)* Wandbehang *m*. **2** *attr* hängend; *bridge* Hänge-.

hang: **~man** *n* Henker *m*; **~-out** *n (col) (place where one lives)* Bude *f (col)*; *(pub, café etc)* Stammlokal *nt*; *(of group)* Treff *m (col)*; **~over** *n* **(a)** Kater *(col) m*; **(b)** *(sth left over)* Überbleibsel *nt*; **~up** *n (col)* Komplex *m (about* wegen); *(obsession)* Fimmel *m (col) (about* mit).

hank [hæŋk] *n (of wool etc)* Strang *m*; *(of hair, fur)* Büschel *nt*.

hanker ['hæŋkə^{r}] *vi* Verlangen haben *(for or after sth* nach etw).

hankering ['hæŋkərɪŋ] *n* Verlangen *nt*. **to have a ~ for sth** Verlangen nach etw haben.

hanky ['hæŋkɪ] *n (col)* Taschentuch *nt*.

hanky-panky ['hæŋkɪ'pæŋkɪ] *n (col)* **(a)** *(dishonest dealings)* Mauscheleien *pl (col)*. **there's some ~ going on** hier ist was faul *(col)*. **(b)** *(love affair)* Techtelmechtel *nt (col)*. **(c)** *(sexy behaviour)* Gefummel *nt (col)*.

Hanover ['hænəʊvə^{r}] *n* Hannover *nt*.

Hanseatic [,hænzɪ'ætɪk] *adj towns* Hanse-. **~ League** Hansebund *m*.

haphazard [,hæp'hæzəd] *adj* willkürlich.

happen ['hæpən] *vi* **(a)** geschehen; *(special or important event also)* sich ereignen; *(esp unexpected, unintentional or unpleasant event also)* passieren; *(process also)* vor sich gehen. **it all ~ed like this ...** das Ganze war so ...; **it's all ~ing here today** *(col)* heute ist hier ganz schön was los *(col)*; **what's ~ing?** was ist los?; **you can't just let things ~** du kannst die Dinge nicht einfach laufen lassen; **don't let it ~ again** daß das nicht noch mal passiert!; **these things ~** so was kommt (schon mal) vor; **what has ~ed to him?** was ist mit ihm passiert?; *(in accident etc)* was ist ihm passiert?; **what's ~ed to your leg?** was ist mit deinem Bein passiert?; **if anything should ~ to me** wenn mir etwas passieren sollte; **it all ~ed so quickly** es ging alles so schnell.

(b) *(chance)* **how does it ~ that ...?** wie kommt es, daß ...?; **it might ~ that ...** es könnte sein, daß ...; **how do you ~ to know?** wie kommt es, daß du das weißt?; **to ~ to do sth** zufälligerweise etw tun; **do you ~ to know whether ...?** wissen Sie zufällig, ob ...?; **I just ~ed to come along when ...** ich kam zufällig (gerade) vorbei, als ...; **as it ~s I'm going there today** zufällig(erweise) gehe ich heute (dort)hin; **he ~s to be the boss** er ist nun einmal der Chef.

♦ **happen (up)on** *vi +prep obj* zufällig stoßen auf *(+acc)*; *person* zufällig treffen.

happening ['hæpnɪŋ] *n* Ereignis *nt*; *(not planned)* Vorfall *m*; *(Theat)* Happening *nt*.

happily ['hæpɪlɪ] *adv* **(a)** glücklich; *(cheerfully also)* fröhlich; *(contentedly also)* zufrieden. **they lived ~ ever after** *(in fairy-tales)* und wenn sie nicht gestorben sind, dann leben sie noch heute. **(b)** *(fortunately)* glücklicherweise. **(c)** *(worded)* treffend.

happiness ['hæpɪnɪs] *n* Glück *nt*; *(disposition)* Fröhlichkeit *f*.

happy ['hæpɪ] *adj (+er)* **(a)** *(about* über *+acc)* glücklich; *(cheerful also)* fröhlich. **a ~ event** ein freudiges Ereignis; **that's all right, ~ to help** schon gut, ich helfe (doch) gern; **yes, I'd be ~ to** ja, sehr gern(e); **to be ~ to do sth** sich freuen, etw tun zu können; **I'm very ~ for you** ich freue mich für dich; **the ~ few** die wenigen Auserwählten. **(b)** *phrase, solution* glücklich. **(c)** *(content)* zufrieden. **we're not ~ with it** wir sind damit nicht zufrieden. **(d) ~ anniversary** herzlichen Glückwunsch zum Hochzeitstag; **~ birthday** alles Gute zum Geburtstag!; **~ Easter** frohe Ostern; **~ New Year** ein gutes neues Jahr.

happy-go-lucky ['hæpɪgəʊ'lʌkɪ] *adj* unbekümmert.

harangue [hə'ræŋ] **1** *n (scolding)* (Straf)predigt *f*; *(encouraging)* Appell *m*. **2** *vt see n* eine (Straf)predigt halten *(+dat)*; einen Appell richten an *(+acc)*.

harass ['hærəs] *vt* belästigen; *(mess around)* schikanieren; *(Mil)* immer wieder überfallen. **don't ~ me** dräng mich doch nicht so!; **they eventually ~ed him into resigning** sie setzten ihm so lange zu, bis er schließlich zurücktrat.

harassed ['hærəst] *adj* mitgenommen; *(worried)* von Sorgen gequält.

harassment ['hærəsmənt] *n (act)* Belästigung *f*; *(messing around)* Schikanierung *f*; *(state)* Bedrängnis *f*; *(Mil)* Kleinkrieg *m*.

harbour, *(US)* **harbor** ['hɑːbəʳ] **1** *n* Hafen *m*. **~ master** *n* Hafenmeister *m*. **2** *vt* **(a)** *criminal etc* Unterschlupf gewähren *(+dat)*. **(b)** *suspicions, grudge* hegen.

hard [hɑːd] **1** *adj (+er)* **(a)** hart; *voice, tone also* schroff. **a ~ man** ein harter Mann; *(ruthless)* ein knallharter Typ *(col)*; **don't be ~ on the boy** sei nicht zu streng zu dem Jungen. **(b)** *(difficult)* schwer, *(complicated also)* schwierig; *(~ to endure)* hart. **~ of hearing** schwerhörig; **I find it ~ to believe that ...** ich kann es kaum glauben, daß ...; **I know it's ~ for you, but ...** ich weiß, es ist hart für Sie, aber ...; **he is ~ to get on with** es ist schwierig, mit ihm auszukommen; **it's ~ going** es ist mühsam; **~ luck!, ~ lines!** (so ein) Pech!

2 *adv (+er)* **(a)** mit aller Kraft; *(violently)* heftig; *run* schnell; *breathe, work* schwer. **to listen ~** genau hinhören; **think ~** denk mal scharf nach; **think ~er** denk mal ein bißchen besser nach; **he has obviously thought ~ about this** er hat es sich *(dat)* offensichtlich gut überlegt; **if you try ~** wenn du dich richtig bemühst; **try ~er** gib dir doch ein bißchen mehr Mühe; **you're not trying ~ enough** du strengst dich nicht genügend an; **you're trying too ~** du bemühst dich zu sehr; **he tried as ~ as he could** er hat sich nach Kräften bemüht; **to look ~ at sb/sth** sich jdn/etw genau ansehen; **to be ~ at it** *(col)* schwer am Werk sein *(col)*.

(b) *(in, with difficulty)* **to be ~ put to it to do sth** es sehr schwer finden, etw zu tun; **to be ~ up** *(col)* knapp bei Kasse sein *(col)*; **he's ~ up for ...** *(col)* es fehlt ihm an ... *(+dat)*; **to be ~ done by** übel dran sein; **he took it pretty ~** es traf ihn ziemlich schwer; **old traditions die ~** alte Traditionen lassen sich nicht so leicht abschaffen.

(c) *rain, snow* stark. **it was freezing ~** es herrschte strenger Frost.

hard: ~ and fast *adj* fest; *rules also* bindend; **~-back 1** *adj book* gebunden; **2** *n* gebundene Ausgabe; **~-bitten** *adj person* abgebrüht; *manager* knallhart *(col)*; **~board** *n* Hartfaserplatte *f*; **~-boiled** *adj* **(a)** *egg* hartgekocht; **(b)** *(fig: shrewd)* ausgekocht *(col)*; *(unsentimental)* abgebrüht *(col)*; **~ cash** *n* Bargeld *nt*; **~ core** *n* **(a)** *(for road)* Schotter *m*; **(b)** *(fig)* harter Kern; *(pornography)* harter Porno *(col)*; **~ court** *n* Hartplatz *m*; **~ disk** *n (Comp)* Festplatte *f*; **~ drinker** *n* starker Trinker; **~ drug** *n* harte Droge; **~-earned** *adj wages* sauer verdient; *victory* hart erkämpft.

harden ['hɑːdn] **1** *vt steel* härten; *body, muscles* kräftigen. **this ~ed his attitude** dadurch hat sich seine Haltung verhärtet; **to ~ oneself to sth** *(physically)* sich gegen etw abhärten; *(emotionally)* gegen etw unempfindlich werden. **2** *vi (substance)* hart werden; *(attitude)* sich verhärten.

hardened ['hɑːdnd] *adj steel* gehärtet; *criminal* Gewohnheits-; *troops* abgehärtet; *sinner* verstockt. **to be ~ to** *or* **against the cold/sb's insensitivity/life** gegen die Kälte abgehärtet sein/an jds Gefühllosigkeit *(acc)* gewöhnt sein/vom Leben hart gemacht sein.

hardening ['hɑːdnɪŋ] *n* **~ of the arteries** Arterienverkalkung *f*.

hard: ~-fought *adj battle* erbittert; *game* hart; **~ hat** *n* Schutzhelm *m*; *(worker)* Bauarbeiter *m*; **~-headed** *adj* nüchtern; **~-hearted** *adj* hartherzig *(towards sb* jdm gegenüber*)*; **~ labour** *(Brit) or* **labor** *(US) n* Zwangsarbeit *f*; **~ line** *n* harte Linie; **to take a ~ line** eine harte Linie verfolgen; **~-liner** *n* Vertreter *m* der harten Linie; **~ liquor** *n* Schnaps *m*.

hardly ['hɑːdlɪ] *adv* kaum. **I need ~ tell you** ich muß Ihnen wohl kaum sagen; **~ ever** fast nie; **he had ~ gone** *or* **~ had he gone when ...** er war kaum gegangen, als ...; **he would ~ have said that** das hat er wohl kaum gesagt; **~!** (wohl) kaum; **~ ideal conditions** wohl kaum ideale Bedingungen.

hardness ['hɑːdnɪs] *n* **(a)** Härte *f*. **(b)** *see adj (b)* Schwere *f*; Schwierigkeit *f*; Härte *f*. **~ of hearing** Schwerhörigkeit *f*.

hard sell *n* aggressive Verkaufstaktik, Hard selling *nt*.

hardship ['hɑːdʃɪp] *n (condition)* Not *f*; *(instance)* Härte *f*; *(deprivation)* Entbehrung *f*. **a temporary ~** eine vorübergehende Notlage; **to suffer great ~s** große Not leiden; **if it's not too much (of a) ~ for you** wenn es dir nicht zuviel Mühe macht.

hard: ~ shoulder *n (Brit)* Seitenstreifen *m*; **~top** *n* Hardtop *nt or m*; **~ware** *n* **(a)** Eisenwaren *pl*; *(household goods)* Haushaltswaren *pl*; **(b)** *(Comp)* Hardware *f*; **(c)** *(Mil)* (Wehr)material *nt*; **~ware store** *n* Eisenwarenhandlung *f*; *(including household goods)* Haushalt- und Eisenwarengeschäft *nt*; **~-wearing** *adj* widerstandsfähig; *cloth, clothes* strapazierfähig; **~-won** *adj* schwer erkämpft; **~-working** *adj person* fleißig; *engine* leistungsfähig.

hardy ['hɑːdɪ] *adj (+er)* **(a)** *(tough)* zäh; *person also* abgehärtet; *plant* (frost)unempfindlich. **~ annual** winterharte einjährige Pflanze. **(b)** *(bold) person* unerschrocken.

hare [hɛəʳ] **1** *n* (Feld)hase *m*. **2** *vi (col)* flitzen*(col)*.

hare: ~-brained *adj* behämmert *(col)*; **~lip** *n* Hasenscharte *f*.

harem [hɑː'riːm] *n* Harem *m*.

haricot ['hærɪkəʊ] *n* **~ bean** *(Brit)* Gartenbohne *f*.

hark [hɑːk] *vi* **~!** *(liter)* horch(t)!; **~ at him!** *(col)* hör sich einer den an! *(col)*.

♦ **hark back** *vi* zurückkommen *(to* auf *+acc)*. **he's** always ~**ing** ~ **to the good old days** er fängt immer wieder von der guten alten Zeit an.

harm [hɑːm] **1** *n (bodily)* Verletzung *f*; *(material, to relations, psychological)* Schaden *m*. **to do ~ to sb** jdm eine Verletzung zufügen/jdm Schaden zufügen; **to do ~ to sth** einer Sache *(dat)* schaden; **you will come to no ~** es wird Ihnen nichts geschehen; **it will do more ~ than good** es wird mehr schaden als nützen; **it won't do you any ~** es wird dir nicht schaden; **I see no ~ in the odd cigarette** ich finde nichts dabei, wenn man ab zu eine Zigarette raucht; **to mean no ~** es nicht böse meinen; **I don't mean him any ~** ich meine es nicht böse mit ihm; **there's no ~ in asking/trying** es kann nicht schaden, zu fragen/es zu versuchen; **where's** *or* **what's the ~ in that?** was kann denn das schaden?; **out of ~'s way** in Sicherheit; **to stay out of ~'s way** der Gefahr *(dat)* aus dem Weg gehen.
2 *vt* schaden *(+dat)*; *person* verletzen.

harmful ['hɑːmfʊl] *adj* schädlich *(to* für*)*; *remarks* verletzend.

harmless ['hɑːmlɪs] *adj* harmlos.

harmonica [hɑː'mɒnɪkə] *n* Harmonika *f*.

harmonious [hɑː'məʊnɪəs] *adj* harmonisch.

harmonium [hɑː'məʊnɪəm] *n* Harmonium *nt*.

harmonize ['hɑːmənaɪz] **1** *vt (Mus)* harmonisieren; *plans, colours* aufeinander abstimmen. **2** *vi (notes, colours, people etc)* harmonieren; *(sing)* mehrstimmig singen.

harmony ['hɑːmənɪ] *n* Harmonie *f*; *(fig: harmonious relations)* Eintracht *f*. **to be in/out of ~ with** *(lit)* harmonieren/nicht harmonieren mit; *(fig also)* in Einklang/nicht in Einklang sein mit; **to sing in ~** mehrstimmig singen.

harness ['hɑːnɪs] **1** *n* Geschirr *nt*; *(of parachute)* Gurtwerk *nt*; *(for baby)* Laufgurt *m*. **to die in ~** *(fig, often hum)* in den Sielen sterben. **2** *vt* **(a)** *horse* anschirren. **to ~ a horse to a carriage** ein Pferd vor einen Wagen spannen. **(b)** *(utilize) river etc* nutzbar machen; *resources* (aus)nutzen.

harp [hɑːp] *n* Harfe *f*.

♦**harp on** *vi (col)* **don't ~ ~ so** reite nicht so darauf herum!; **to ~ ~ about sth** immer wieder mit etw kommen *(col)*.

harpoon [hɑː'puːn] **1** *n* Harpune *f*. **2** *vt* harpunieren.

harpsichord ['hɑːpsɪkɔːd] *n* Cembalo *nt*.

harrow ['hærəʊ] **1** *n* Egge *f*. **2** *vt* eggen.

harrowed ['hærəʊd] *adj look* gequält.

harrowing ['hærəʊɪŋ] *adj* grauenhaft.

harry ['hærɪ] *vt* zusetzen *(+dat)*.

harsh [hɑːʃ] *adj (+er)* rauh. **(a)** *(severe)* hart; *words, tone of voice also* barsch; *(too strict)* streng. **don't be too ~ with him** sei nicht zu streng mit ihm. **(b)** *colour, light, sound* hart; *taste* herb.

harvest ['hɑːvɪst] **1** *n* Ernte *f*; *(of wines, berries also)* Lese *f*. **2** *vt (also fig)* ernten; *vines also* lesen; *(bring in)* einbringen. **3** *vi* ernten.

harvester ['hɑːvɪstə[r]] *n (person)* Erntearbeiter(in *f*) *m*; *(machine)* Mähmaschine *f*; *(combine ~)* Mähdrescher *m*.

harvest: ~ festival *n* Erntedankfest *nt*; **~ time** *n* Erntezeit *f*.

has [hæz] *3rd pers sing pres of* **have.**

has-been ['hæzbiːn] *n (pej)* vergessene Größe.

hash [hæʃ] *n* **(a)** *(Cook)* Haschee *nt*. **(b)** *(col: mess)* **to make a ~ of sth** etw verpfuschen *(col)*. **(c)** *(col: hashish)* Hasch *nt (col)*.

hashish ['hæʃɪʃ] *n* Haschisch *nt*.

hasn't ['hæznt] = **has not.**

hassle ['hæsl] *n (col)* Ärger *m*; *(bother, fuss)* Theater *nt (col)*. **getting there is such a ~** es ist so umständlich, dorthin zu kommen; **we had a bit of ~ with the police** wir hatten ein bißchen Ärger mit der Polizei.

hassock ['hæsək] *n* Kniekissen *nt*.

haste [heɪst] *n* Eile *f*. **to make ~** sich beeilen; **more ~ less speed** *(Prov)* eile mit Weile *(Prov)*.

hasten ['heɪsn] **1** *vi* sich beeilen. **I ~ to add that ...** ich muß allerdings hinzufügen, daß .... **2** *vt* beschleunigen. **the strain of office ~ed his death** die Belastung seines Amtes trug zu seinem vorzeitigen Tod bei; **to ~ sb's departure** jdn zum Aufbruch drängen.

hastily ['heɪstɪlɪ] *adv* **(a)** *(hurriedly)* hastig. **(b)** *(rashly)* vorschnell.

hastiness ['heɪstɪnɪs] *n* **(a)** Eile *f*. **(b)** *(rashness)* Voreiligkeit *f*.

hasty ['heɪstɪ] *adj (+er)* **(a)** *(hurried)* eilig. **they made a ~ exit** sie gingen eilig hinaus. **don't be so ~** nicht so hastig! **(b)** *(rash)* vorschnell.

hat [hæt] *n* **(a)** Hut *m*. **(b)** *(fig phrases)* **I'll eat my ~ if ...** ich fresse einen Besen, wenn ... *(col)*; **I take my ~ off to him** Hut ab vor ihm!; **to talk through one's ~** *(col)* dummes Zeug reden; **to keep sth under one's ~** *(col)* etw für sich behalten; **at the drop of a ~** auf der Stelle; **that's old ~** *(col)* das ist ein alter Hut *(col)*; **to pass around the ~ for sb** für jdn den Hut rumgehen lassen *(col)*.

hatch[1] [hætʃ] *(also ~ out)* **1** *vt* ausbrüten; *(fig) plot also* aushecken. **2** *vi (bird)* ausschlüpfen. **when will the eggs ~?** wann schlüpfen die Jungen aus?

hatch[2] *n (Naut)* Luke *f*. **(service) ~** *(Brit)* Durchreiche *f*. **down the ~!** *(col)* hoch die Tassen! *(col)*.

hatchback ['hætʃbæk] *n* Hecktürmodell *nt*; *(door)* Hecktür *f*.

hatchet ['hætʃɪt] *n* Beil *nt*. **to bury the ~** das Kriegsbeil begraben; **~ man** *n (killer)* gedungener Mörder; *(fig)* Vollstreckungsbeamte(r) *m*.

hatching ['hætʃɪŋ] *n (Art)* Schraffur *f*.

hate [heɪt] **1** *vt* hassen; *(detest also)* verabscheuen; *(dislike also)* nicht leiden können. **to ~ the sound of sth** etw nicht hören können; **to ~ to do sth** *or* **doing sth** es hassen, etw zu tun; *(weaker)* etw äußerst ungern tun; **I ~ seeing her in pain** ich kann es nicht ertragen, sie leiden zu sehen; **I ~ the idea of leaving** der Gedanke, wegzumüssen, ist mir äußerst zuwider; **I ~ to bother you** es ist mir sehr unangenehm, daß ich Sie belästigen muß; **I ~ having to say it but ...** es fällt mir sehr schwer, das sagen zu müssen, aber ...; **I should ~ to keep you waiting** ich möchte Sie auf keinen Fall warten lassen. **2** *n* Haß *m (for, of* auf *+ acc)*. **it's one of his pet ~s** das kann er auf den Tod nicht ausstehen.

hateful ['heɪtfʊl] *adj* abscheulich.

hatpin ['hætpɪn] *n* Hutnadel *f*.

hatred ['heɪtrɪd] *n* Haß *m (for* auf *+acc)*.

hatter ['hætə[r]] *n* Hutmacher(in *f*) *m*; *(seller)* Hutverkäufer(in *f*) *m*.

hat-trick ['hættrɪk] *n* Hattrick *m*.

haughty ['hɔːtɪ] *adj (+er)* hochmütig; *(towards people)* überheblich.

haul [hɔːl] **1** *n* **(a)** *(journey)* Strecke *f*. **it's a long ~** es ist ein weiter Weg; **short/long ~ aircraft** Kurz-/Langstreckenflugzeug *nt*. **(b)** *(Fishing)* (Fisch)fang *m*; *(from robbery)* Beute *f*; *(col: of presents)* Ausbeute *f (col)*. **2** *vt* ziehen; *heavy objects also* schleppen.

♦**haul down** *vt sep flag, sail* einholen.

haulage ['hɔːlɪdʒ] *n* **(a)** Transport *m*. **~ contractor** *(firm)* Spedition(sfirma) *f*; *(person)* Spediteur *m*. **(b)** *(charges)* Transportkosten *pl*.

haulier ['hɔːlɪə[r]] *n* Spediteur *m*; *(company)* Spedition *f*.

haunch [hɔːntʃ] *n (of person)* Hüfte *f*; *(of animal) (hindquarters)* Hinterbacke *f*; *(top of leg)* Keule *f*; *(Cook)* Lendenstück *nt*. **~es** Gesäß *nt*; *(of animal)* Hinterbacken *pl*; **he was sitting on his ~es** er saß in der Hocke; **~ of venison** *(Cook)* Rehkeule *f*.

haunt [hɔːnt] **1** *vt* **(a)** *(ghost) house* spuken in *(+dat)*, umgehen in *(+dat)*. **(b)** *(fig: memory etc)* verfolgen. **the nightmares which ~ed him**

die Alpträume, die ihn heimsuchten. **(c)** *(frequent)* häufig besuchen. **2** *n* **this is one of his favourite ~s** hier hält er sich sehr gerne auf.

haunted ['hɔːntɪd] *adj* **(a)** Spuk-. **a ~ house** ein Haus *nt*, in dem es spukt; **this place is ~** hier spukt es. **(b)** *look* gehetzt; *person* ruhelos.

haunting ['hɔːntɪŋ] *adj doubt* quälend; *tune, visions, poetry* eindringlich. **these ~ final chords** diese Schlußakkorde, die einen nicht loslassen.

have ['hæv] *pret, ptp* **had,** *3rd pers sing pres* **has 1** *vt* **(a)** *(possess)* haben. **she has (got** *esp Brit*) **blue eyes** sie hat blaue Augen; **~ you (got** *esp Brit) or* **do you ~ a suitcase?** hast du einen Koffer?; **I ~n't (got** *esp Brit) or* **I don't ~ a pen** ich habe keinen Kugelschreiber.

(b) to ~ breakfast/lunch/dinner frühstücken/zu Mittag essen/zu Abend essen; **what will you ~? — I'll ~ the steak** was möchten Sie gern(e)? — ich möchte gern das Steak; **he had a cigarette/a drink/a steak** er rauchte eine Zigarette/trank etwas/aß ein Steak; **will you ~ some more?** möchten Sie gern (noch etwas) mehr?; **~ another one** nimm noch eine/einen/eines; trink noch einen; rauch noch eine.

(c) *(receive, obtain, get)* haben. **I ~ it from the tax office that ...** ich habe vom Finanzamt erfahren, daß ...; **to let sb ~ sth** jdm etw geben; **it's nowhere to be had** es ist nirgends zu haben *or* kriegen *(col)*; **she's having a baby** sie bekommt ein Kind.

(d) *(maintain, insist)* **he will ~ it that Paul is guilty** er besteht darauf, daß Paul schuldig ist; **he won't ~ it that Paul is guilty** er will nichts davon hören, daß Paul schuldig ist; **as Professor James would ~ it** *(according to)* laut Professor James; *(as he would put it)* um es mit Professor James zu sagen.

(e) *(neg: refuse to allow)* **I won't ~ this nonsense** dieser Unsinn kommt (mir) nicht in Frage!; **I won't ~ it!** das lasse ich mir nicht bieten!

(f) *(hold)* (gepackt) haben. **the dog had (got) him by the ankle** der Hund hatte ihn am Knöchel gepackt; **I ~ (got) him where I want him** ich habe ihn endlich soweit; **I'll ~ you** *(col)* dich krieg ich (beim Kragen); **you ~ me there** da bin ich überfragt.

(g) *(causative)* **to ~ sth done** etw tun lassen; **to ~ one's hair cut/a suit made** sich *(dat)* die Haare schneiden lassen/einen Anzug machen lassen; **to ~ sb do sth** jdn etw tun lassen; **they had him shot** sie ließen ihn erschießen; **I'd ~ you understand ...** Sie müssen nämlich wissen ...; **what would you ~ me say?** was soll ich dazu sagen?; **they soon had the carpet down** sie waren schnell mit dem Teppichverlegen fertig; **when she had the lid off** als sie den Deckel herunterhatte.

(h) *(experience, suffer)* **he had his car stolen** man hat ihm sein Auto gestohlen; **I've had three windows broken** (bei) mir sind drei Fenster eingeworfen worden; **I had my friends turn against me** ich mußte es erleben, wie *or* daß sich meine Freunde gegen mich wandten.

(i) to ~ a walk spazierengehen; **to ~ a dream** träumen.

(j) *party* geben, machen; *meeting* abhalten. **are you having a reception?** gibt es einen Empfang?

(k) *(phrases)* **let him ~ it!** gib's ihm! *(col)*; **he/that coat has had it** *(col)* der ist weg vom Fenster *(col)*/der Mantel ist im Eimer *(col)*; **if I miss the last bus, I've had it** *(col)* wenn ich den letzten Bus verpasse, bin ich geliefert *(col)*; **to ~ a pleasant evening** einen netten Abend verbringen; **~ a good time!** viel Spaß!; **you've been had!** *(col)* da hat man dich übers Ohr gehauen *(col)*; **thanks for having me** vielen Dank für Ihre Gastfreundschaft.

2 *aux* **(a)** haben; *(esp with vbs of motion)* sein. **to ~ been** gewesen sein; **to ~ seen/heard** gesehen/gehört haben; **to ~ gone/run** gegangen/gelaufen sein; **I ~ /had been** ich bin/war gewesen; **I ~ /had seen** ich habe/hatte gesehen; **had I seen him** hätte ich ihn gesehen; **having seen him** *(since)* da ich ihn gesehen habe/hatte; *(after)* als ich ihn gesehen hatte; **I ~ lived** *or* **~ been living here for 10 years/since January** ich wohne schon 10 Jahre/seit Januar hier; **you *have* grown** du bist aber gewachsen.

(b) *(in tag questions etc)* **you've seen her, ~n't you?** du hast sie gesehen, oder nicht?; **you ~n't seen her, ~ you?** du hast sie nicht gesehen, oder?; **you ~n't seen her — yes, I ~** du hast sie nicht gesehen — doch; **you've made a mistake — no I ~n't** du hast einen Fehler gemacht — nein(, hab' ich nicht *col*); **you've dropped your book — so I ~** du hast dein Buch fallen lassen — tatsächlich!; **I ~ seen a ghost — ~ you?** ich habe ein Gespenst gesehen — tatsächlich?; **I've lost it — you ~n't** *(disbelieving)* ich habe es verloren — das darf doch nicht wahr sein!

3 *modal aux (+infin)* **I ~ to do it, I ~ got to do it** *(Brit)* ich muß es tun; **I don't ~ to do it, I ~n't got to do it** *(Brit)* ich muß es nicht tun, ich brauche es nicht zu tun; **do you ~ to go now?, ~ you got to go now?** *(Brit)* müssen Sie jetzt unbedingt gehen?; **you didn't ~ to tell her** das mußten Sie ihr nicht unbedingt sagen; **it has to be a mistake!** das muß wohl ein Irrtum sein!

♦ **have around** *vt always separate* **(a)** (bei sich*)* zu Besuch haben; *(invite)* einladen. **(b) he's useful to ~ ~** es ist ganz praktisch, ihn zur Hand zu haben.

♦ **have in** *vt always separate* **(a)** *decorators etc* im Haus haben; *doctor* holen. **(b) to ~ it ~ for sb** *(col)* jdn auf dem Kieker haben *(col)*.

♦ **have off** *vt always separate* **to ~ it ~ with sb** *(col)* es mit jdm treiben *(col)*.

♦ **have on 1** *vt sep clothes, radio* anhaben. **2** *vt always separate* **(a)** *(have sth arranged)* vorhaben; *(be busy with)* zu tun haben. **~ you got anything ~ for tonight?** hast du heute abend etwas vor? **(b)** *(col: deceive)* übers Ohr hauen *(col)*; *(tease)* auf den Arm nehmen *(col)*. **(c) to ~ nothing ~ sb** gegen jdn nichts in der Hand haben; **they've got nothing ~ me!** mir kann keiner! *(col)*.

♦ **have out** *vt always separate* **(a) he was having his tonsils ~** ihm wurden die Mandeln herausgenommen. **(b)** *(discuss)* **to ~ it ~ with sb** etw mit jdm ausdiskutieren; **I'll ~ it ~ with him** ich werde mit ihm reden.

♦ **have up** *vt always separate (col: in court)* **to be had ~ for sth** wegen etw vors Gericht kommen.

haven ['heɪvn] *n (fig)* Zufluchtsstätte *f*.

haves [hævz] *npl (col)* **the ~ and the have-nots** die Betuchten und die Habenichtse *(col)*.

havoc ['hævək] *n* verheerender Schaden; *(devastation also)* Verwüstung *f*; *(chaos)* Chaos *nt*. **to wreak ~ in** *or* **with sth, to play ~ with sth** bei etw verheerenden Schaden anrichten.

Hawaii [hə'waiː] *n* Hawaii *nt*.

hawk[1] [hɔːk] *n (Orn)* Habicht *m*; *(sparrow ~)* Sperber *m*; *(falcon)* Falke *m*. **the ~s and the doves** *(fig)* die Falken und die Tauben.

hawk[2] *vt* hausieren (gehen) mit; *(in street)* verkaufen.

hawker ['hɔːkəʳ] *n (pedlar) (door-to-door)* Hausierer(in *f*) *m*; *(in street)* Straßenhändler(in *f*) *m*.

hawk-eyed ['hɔːkaɪd] *adj* scharfsichtig. **to be ~** Adleraugen haben.

hawser ['hɔːzəʳ] *n (Naut)* Trosse *f*.

hawthorn ['hɔːθɔːn] *n* Weiß- *or* Rotdorn *m*.

hay [heɪ] *n* Heu *nt*. **to make ~** Heu machen; **to hit the ~** *(col)* sich in die Falle hauen *(col)*; **to make**

~ **while the sun shines** *(Prov)* das Eisen schmieden, solange es heiß ist *(Prov)*.

hay: ~ **fever** *n* Heuschnupfen *m*; ~**stack** *n* Heuhaufen *m*.

haywire ['heɪwaɪəʳ] *adj pred (col)* **to be (all)** ~ ein Wirrwarr sein *(col)*; **to go** ~ *(plans)* durcheinandergeraten; *(machinery)* verrückt spielen *(col)*.

hazard ['hæzəd] **1** *n* **(a)** *(danger)* Gefahr *f*; *(risk)* Risiko *nt*. **it's a fire** ~ es stellt eine Feuergefahr dar. **(b)** *(chance)* **by** ~ durch Zufall; **game of** ~ Glücksspiel *nt*. **2** *vt life, reputation* riskieren, aufs Spiel setzen. **if I might** ~ **a suggestion** wenn ich mir einen Vorschlag erlauben darf; **to** ~ **a guess** (es) wagen, eine Vermutung anzustellen.

hazardous ['hæzədəs] *adj* gefährlich, risikoreich.

haze [heɪz] *n* Dunst *m*.

hazel ['heɪzl] **1** *n (Bot)* Haselnußstrauch *m*. **2** *adj (colour)* haselnußbraun.

hazelnut ['heɪzlnʌt] *n* Haselnuß *f*.

hazy ['heɪzɪ] *adj (+er)* **(a)** dunstig, diesig; *mountains* im Dunst (liegend). **(b)** *(unclear)* verchwommen. **I'm** ~ **about what happened** ich kann mich nur verschwommen daran erinnern, was geschah.

he [hiː] **1** *pers pron* er. **so** ~**'s the one** der *(col) or* er ist es also!; **Harry Rigg? who's** ~**?** Harry Rigg? wer ist das denn?; ~ **who** *(liter)* derjenige, der. **2** *n* **it's a** ~ *(col: baby)* es ist ein er.

head [hed] **1** *n* **(a)** Kopf *m*. **from** ~ **to foot** von Kopf bis Fuß; ~ **downwards** mit dem Kopf nach unten; **to stand on one's** ~ auf dem Kopf stehen; **you could do it standing on your** ~ *(col)* das kann man ja im Schlaf machen; **to fall** ~ **over heels in love with sb** sich bis über beide Ohren in jdn verlieben; **to keep one's** ~ **above water** *(fig)* sich über Wasser halten; **to talk one's** ~ **off** *(col)* reden wie ein Wasserfall *(col)*; **to shout one's** ~ **off** *(col)* sich *(dat)* die Lunge aus dem Leib schreien *(col)*; **I've got some** ~ **this morning** *(col)* ich habe einen ziemlichen Brummschädel heute morgen *(col)*; **to give sb his** ~ jdn machen lassen; **on your (own)** ~ **be it** auf Ihre eigene Verantwortung; **he gave orders over my** ~ er hat über meinen Kopf (hin)weg Anordnungen gegeben; **to go to one's** ~ einem zu Kopf steigen; **I can't make** ~ **nor tail of it** daraus werde ich nicht schlau.

(b) *(mind, intellect)* Kopf, Verstand *m*. **use your** ~ streng deinen Kopf an; **to get sth into one's** ~ *(understand)* etw begreifen; **he won't get it into his** ~ **that ...** es will ihm nicht in den Kopf, daß ...; **to take it into one's** ~ **to do sth** sich *(dat)* in den Kopf setzen, etw zu tun; **it never entered his** ~ **that ...** es kam ihm nie in den Sinn, daß ...; **what put that idea into his** ~**?** wie kommt er denn darauf?; **to get sth out of one's** ~ sich *(dat)* etw aus dem Kopf schlagen; **he has a good business** ~ er hat einen ausgeprägten Geschäftssinn; **he has a good** ~ **on his shoulders** er ist ein kluger Kopf; **he has an old** ~ **on young shoulders** er ist sehr reif für sein Alter; **two** ~**s are better than one** *(prov)* besser zwei als einer allein; **we put our** ~**s together** wir haben unsere Köpfe zusammengesteckt; **to be above** *or* **over sb's** ~ über jds Horizont *(acc)* gehen; **to keep one's** ~ den Kopf nicht verlieren; **to lose one's** ~ den Kopf verlieren; **he is off his** ~ *(col)* er ist (ja) nicht (ganz) bei Trost *(col)*; **to be soft in the** ~ *(col)* einen (kleinen) Dachschaden haben *(col)*.

(c) twenty ~ **of cattle** zwanzig Stück Vieh; **to pay 10 marks a** ~ 10 Mark pro Kopf bezahlen.

(d) *(of flower, lettuce, nail, page)* Kopf *m*; *(of arrow, spear)* Spitze *f*; *(of bed)* Kopf(ende *nt*) *m*; *(on beer)* Blume *f*; *(of corn)* Ähre *f*; *(of stream)* *(upper area)* Oberlauf *m*; *(source)* Ursprung *m*; *(of tape-recorder)* Tonkopf *m*. ~ **of steam** Dampfdruck *m*; **at the** ~ **of the list/stairs** oben auf der Liste/an der Treppe; **at the** ~ **of the table** am Kopf(ende) des Tisches; **at the** ~ **of the queue/procession** an der Spitze der Schlange/des Zuges; **if things come to a** ~ wenn sich die Sache zuspitzt.

(e) *(of family)* Oberhaupt *nt*; *(of business, organization)* Chef *m*; *(Sch col)* Schulleiter *m*. ~ **of department** *(in business)* Abteilungsleiter *m*; *(Sch, Univ)* Fachbereichsleiter(in *f*) *m*; ~ **of state** Staatsoberhaupt *nt*.

(f) *(~ing, in essay etc)* Rubrik *f*.

(g) *(of coin)* ~**s or tails?** Kopf oder Zahl?; ~**s I win** bei Kopf gewinne ich.

2 *vt* **(a)** *(lead)* anführen; *(be in charge of also)* führen; *list also* an der Spitze stehen von. **(b)** *(direct)* steuern *(towards, for* in Richtung*)*. **(c) in the chapter** ~**ed ...** in dem Kapitel mit der Überschrift ...; ~**ed writing paper** Schreibpapier mit Briefkopf. **(d)** *(Ftbl)* köpfen.

3 *vi* gehen; fahren. **where are you** ~**ing** *or* ~**ed?** wo gehen/fahren Sie hin?

♦**head back** *vi* zurückgehen/-fahren. **to be** ~**ing** ~ auf dem Rückweg sein.

♦**head for** *vi +prep obj place, person* zugehen/zufahren auf *(+acc)*; *town, country* gehen/fahren in Richtung *(+gen)*; *(ship also)* Kurs halten auf *(+acc)*. **where are you** ~**ing** *or* ~**ed** ~**?** wo gehen/fahren Sie hin?; **you're** ~**ing** ~ **trouble** du bist auf dem besten Weg, Ärger zu bekommen.

♦**head off** *vt sep* abfangen; *war, strike* abwenden.

♦**head up** *vt sep delegation* leiten.

head *in cpds (top, senior)* Ober-; ~**ache** *n* Kopfschmerzen *pl*; *(col: problem)* Problem *nt*; **to have a** ~**ache** Kopfschmerzen haben; **this is a bit of a** ~**ache** das macht mir/uns ziemliches Kopfzerbrechen; ~**band** *n* Stirnband *nt*; ~**dress** *n* Kopfschmuck *m*.

header ['hedəʳ] *n* **(a)** *(dive)* Kopfsprung *m*. **(b)** *(Ftbl)* Kopfball *m*.

head: ~**first** *adv (lit, fig)* kopfüber; ~**gear** *n* Kopfbedeckung *f*; ~**-hunter** *n (lit, fig)* Kopfjäger *m*.

heading ['hedɪŋ] *n* Überschrift *f*; *(on letter, document)* Kopf *m*; *(in encyclopedia)* Stichwort *nt*.

head: ~**lamp,** ~**light** *n* Scheinwerfer *m*; ~**land** *n* Landspitze *f*; ~**line** *n (Press)* Schlagzeile *f*; **to hit the** ~**lines** Schlagzeilen machen; **the news** ~**lines** *npl* das Wichtigste in Kürze; ~**long** *adj, adv fall* mit dem Kopf voran; *rush* Hals über Kopf; ~**master** *n* Schulleiter *m*; ~**mistress** *n* Schulleiterin *f*; ~ **office** *n* Zentrale *f*; ~**-on 1** *adj collision* frontal; **2** *adv* frontal; ~**phones** *npl* Kopfhörer *pl*; ~**quarters** *n sing or pl (Mil)* Hauptquartier *nt*; *(Comm)* Zentrale *f*; *(of political party)* Parteizentrale *f*; **police** ~**quarters** Polizeipräsidium *nt*; ~**rest** *n* Kopfstütze *f*; ~**room** *n* lichte Höhe; *(in car)* Kopfraum *m*; ~**scarf** *n* Kopftuch *nt*; ~**set** *n* Kopfhörer *pl*; ~ **start** *n* Vorsprung *m (on sb* jdm gegenüber*)*; ~**stone** *n (on grave)* Grabstein *m*; ~**strong** *adj* dickköpfig; ~ **teacher** *n (Brit)* = ~**master,** ~**mistress;** ~ **waiter** *n* Oberkellner *m*; ~**way** *n* **to make** ~**way** *(lit, fig)* vorankommen; ~**wind** *n* Gegenwind *m*.

heady ['hedɪ] *adj (+er) (lit, fig)* berauschend.

heal [hiːl] **1** *vi (Med, fig)* heilen. **2** *vt (Med)* heilen; *(fig) differences etc* beilegen.

♦**heal up 1** *vi* zuheilen. **2** *vt sep* zuheilen lassen.

health [helθ] *n* Gesundheit *f*. **in good/poor** ~ bei guter/schlechter Gesundheit; **how is his** ~**?** wie geht es ihm gesundheitlich?; **to be good/bad for one's** ~ gesund/ungesund sein; **Ministry of H**~ Gesundheitsministerium *nt*; **to drink (to) sb's** ~ auf jds Wohl *(acc)* trinken; **your** ~**!** zum Wohl!

health: ~ **club** *n* Fitness-Center *nt*; ~ **food** *n* Reformkost *f*; ~ **food shop** *(Brit) or* **store** *(esp US) n* Reformhaus *nt*; *(modern)* Bioladen *m*; ~ **hazard** *n* Gefahr *f* für die Gesundheit; ~ **insurance** *n*

Krankenversicherung *f*; ~ **resort** *n* Kurort *m*; **H~ Service** *n (Brit)* Gesundheitswesen *nt*; **H~ Service doctor** Kassenarzt *m*/-ärztin *f*; ~ **visitor** *n* Sozialarbeiter(in *f*) *m (in der Gesundheitsfürsorge)*.

healthy ['helθı] *adj (+er) (lit, fig)* gesund.

heap [hi:p] **1** *n* **(a)** Haufen *m*; *(col: old car)* Klapperkiste *f (col)*. **he fell in a ~ on the floor** er sackte zu Boden. **(b) ~s of** *(col)* eine Menge *(col)*; **we've got ~s of time** wir haben jede Menge Zeit *(col)*. **2** *vt* häufen. **to ~ praises on sb** jdn mit Lob überschütten; **~ed spoonful** gehäufter Löffel.

♦ **heap up 1** *vt sep* aufhäufen. **2** *vi* sich häufen.

hear [hıə[r]] *pret, ptp* **heard 1** *vt (also learn)* hören. **to make oneself ~d** sich *(dat)* Gehör verschaffen; **you're not going, do you ~ me!** du gehst nicht, hörst du (mich)!; **to ~ him speak you'd think ...** wenn man ihn so reden hört, könnte man meinen, ...; **I've often ~d say** *or* **it said that ...** ich habe oft sagen hören, daß ...; **I ~ (tell) you're going away** ich höre, Sie gehen weg; **I must be ~ing things** ich glaube, ich höre nicht richtig; **to ~ a case** *(Jur)* einen Fall verhandeln.

2 *vi* **(a)** hören. **~, ~!** (sehr) richtig!; *(Parl)* hört!, hört! **(b)** *(get news)* hören. **yes, so I ~** ja, ich habe es gehört; **you'll be ~ing from me!** *(threatening)* Sie werden noch von mir hören!; **to ~ about sth** von etw hören *or* erfahren; **have you ~d about John? he's getting married** haben Sie schon gehört? John heiratet; **never ~d of him/it** nie (von ihm/davon) gehört; **I've ~d of him** ich habe schon von ihm gehört; **he was never ~d of again** man hat nie wieder etwas von ihm gehört; **I've never ~d of such a thing!** das ist ja unerhört!; **I won't ~ of it** *(allow)* ich will davon nichts hören.

♦ **hear out** *vt sep person* ausreden lassen.

heard [hɜ:d] *pret, ptp of* **hear.**

hearing ['hıərıŋ] *n* **(a)** *(sense)* Gehör *nt*. **(b) within/out of ~** in/außer Hörweite. **(c)** *(Pol)* Hearing *nt*, Anhörung *f*; *(Jur)* Verhandlung *f*. **to give sb a ~** jdn anhören; **he didn't get a fair ~** man hörte ihn nicht richtig an; *(Jur)* er bekam keinen fairen Prozeß.

hearing aid *n* Hörgerät *nt*.

hearsay ['hıəseı] *n* Gerüchte *pl*. **to have sth on ~** etw vom Hörensagen wissen.

hearse [hɜ:s] *n* Leichenwagen *m*.

heart [hɑ:t] *n* **(a)** *(lit, fig)* Herz *nt*. **to break sb's ~** jdm das Herz brechen; **to break one's ~ over sth** sich über etw *(acc)* zu Tode grämen; **you're breaking my ~** *(iro)* ich fang' gleich an zu weinen *(iro)*; **after my own ~** ganz nach meinem Herzen; **to have a change of ~** sich anders besinnen; **to learn/know sth by ~** etw auswendig lernen/kennen; **in my ~ of ~s** im Grunde meines Herzens; **with all my ~** von ganzem Herzen; **from the bottom of one's ~** aus tiefstem Herzen; **to take sth to ~** sich *(dat)* etw zu Herzen nehmen; **we have your interests at ~** Ihre Interessen liegen uns am Herzen; **to set one's ~ on sth** sein Herz an etw *(acc)* hängen *(geh)*; **to one's ~'s content** nach Herzenslust; **most men are boys at ~** die meisten Männer sind im Grunde (ihres Herzens) noch richtige Kinder; **his ~ isn't in it** er ist nicht mit dem Herzen dabei; **to lose ~** den Mut verlieren; **to take ~** Mut fassen; **to put new ~ into sb** jdn mit neuem Mut erfüllen; **his ~ is in the right place** *(col)* er hat das Herz auf dem rechten Fleck *(col)*; **to have a ~ of stone** ein Herz aus Stein haben; **to wear one's ~ on one's sleeve** *(prov)* aus seinem Herzem keine Mördergrube machen *(col)*; **my ~ was in my mouth** *(col)* mir schlug das Herz bis zum Hals; **have a ~!** *(col)* gib deinem Herzen einen Stoß! *(col)*; **not to have the ~ to do sth** es nicht übers Herz bringen, etw zu tun; **she has a ~ of gold** sie hat ein goldenes Herz; **my ~ sank** *(apprehension)* mir rutschte das Herz in die Hose *(col)*; *(sadness)* das Herz wurde mir schwer; *(discouraged)* mein Mut sank; **the ~ of the matter** der Kern der Sache; **in the ~ of the forest** mitten im Wald.

(b) *(Cards)* **~s** *pl* Herz *nt*; *(Bridge)* Coeur *nt*; **queen of ~s** Herzdame *f*.

heart: ~ache *n* Kummer *m*; **~ attack** *n* Herzinfarkt *m*; **I nearly had a ~ attack** *(fig col: shock)* ich habe fast einen Herzschlag gekriegt *(col)*; **~beat** *n* Herzschlag *m*; **~break** *n* großer Kummer; **~breaking** *adj* herzzerreißend; **it's a ~breaking job** es bricht einem das Herz; **~broken** *adj* todunglücklich; **~burn** *n* Sodbrennen *nt*.

heartening ['hɑ:tnıŋ] *adj news* ermutigend.

heart: ~ failure *n* Herzversagen *nt*; **~felt** *adj* tief empfunden; *sympathy* herzlichst.

hearth [hɑ:θ] *n* Feuerstelle *f*; *(whole fireplace)* Kamin *m*; *(fig: home)* (häuslicher) Herd. **~rug** Kaminvorleger *m*.

heartily ['hɑ:tılı] *adv* herzlich; *sing* kräftig; *eat* herzhaft. **I ~ agree** ich stimme voll und ganz zu.

heart: ~less *adj* herzlos; *(cruel also)* grausam; **~rending** *adj* herzzerreißend; **~-searching** *n* Gewissenserforschung *f*; **~strings** *npl* **to pull** *or* **tug at the/sb's ~strings** auf die/bei jdm auf die Tränendrüsen drücken *(col)*; **~-throb** *n (col)* Schwarm *m (col)*; **~-to-~** *adj* **to have a ~-to-~ talk with sb** sich mit jdm ganz offen aussprechen; **~ transplant** *n* Herztransplantation *f*; **~-trouble** *n* Herzbeschwerden *pl*; **~-warming** *adj* herzerfreuend.

hearty ['hɑ:tı] *adj (+er)* herzlich; *slap also, meal, appetite* herzhaft, kräftig; *dislike* tief; *person (robust)* kernig; *(cheerful)* laut und herzlich.

heat [hi:t] **1** *n* **(a)** *(lit, fig)* Hitze *f*; *(pleasant, Phys)* Wärme *f*; *(of curry etc)* Schärfe *f*; *(~ing)* Heizung *f*. **in the ~ of the day** wenn es heiß ist; **in the ~ of the moment** in der Hitze des Gefechts; *(when upset)* in der Erregung; **to take the ~ out of the situation** die Situation entschärfen; **to put the ~ on** *(col)* Druck machen *(col)*; **to put the ~ on sb** *(col)* jdn unter Druck setzen; **the ~ is off** *(col)* der Druck ist weg *(col)*; *(danger is past)* die Gefahr ist vorbei. **(b)** *(Sport)* Vorlauf *m*; *(Boxing etc)* Vorkampf *m*. **final ~** Ausscheidungskampf *m*. **(c)** *(Zool)* Brunst *f*; *(of dogs, cats)* Läufigkeit *f*. **on ~** brünstig; läufig. **2** *vt* erhitzen; *room* heizen; *pool, house* beheizen.

♦ **heat up 1** *vi* warm werden; *(get very hot)* sich erhitzen; *(discussion)* hitzig werden. **2** *vt sep* erwärmen; *food* heiß machen.

heated ['hi:tıd] *adj (lit)* geheizt; *pool* beheizt; *(fig) words, discussion* hitzig, erregt. **things got rather ~** die Gemüter erhitzten sich sehr.

heater ['hi:tə[r]] *n* Ofen *m*; *(electrical also)* Heizgerät *nt*; *(in car)* Heizung *f*.

heath [hi:θ] *n* Heide *f*.

heathen ['hi:ðən] **1** *adj* heidnisch, Heiden-; *(fig)* unkultiviert. **2** *n* Heide *m*, Heidin *f*; *(fig)* unkultivierter Mensch.

heather ['heðə[r]] *n* Heidekraut *nt*, Erika *f*.

Heath Robinson [,hi:θ'robınsən] *adj (col) gadget* phantastisch *(col)*.

heating ['hi:tıŋ] *n (in house etc)* Heizung *f*.

heat: ~-resistant *adj* hitzebeständig; **~ shield** *n* Hitzeschild *m*; **~stroke** *n* Hitzschlag *m*; **~ treatment** *n (Med)* Wärmebehandlung *f*; **~wave** *n* Hitzewelle *f*.

heave [hi:v] **1** *vt (lift)* (hoch)hieven *(onto* auf *+acc)*; *(drag)* schleppen; *(throw)* werfen; *sigh, sob* ausstoßen. **to ~ anchor** den Anker lichten. **2** *vi* **(a)** *(pull)* ziehen. **(b)** *(bosom, sea)* sich heben und senken; *(stomach)* sich umdrehen. **(c)** *pret, ptp* **hove** *(Naut)* **to ~ in(to) sight** in Sicht kommen.

♦ **heave to** *(Naut) vi* beidrehen.

heave ho *interj* hau ruck.
heaven ['hevn] *n* **(a)** *(lit, fig col)* Himmel *m*. **in ~** im Himmel; **to go to ~** in den Himmel kommen; **he is in (his seventh) ~** er ist im siebten Himmel; **to move ~ and earth** Himmel und Hölle in Bewegung setzen; **it was ~** es war einfach himmlisch; **the ~s opened** der Himmel öffnete seine Schleusen. **(b)** *(col)* **(good) ~s!** (du) lieber Himmel! *(col)*; **would you like to? — (good) ~s no!** möchten Sie? — um Himmels willen, bloß nicht!; **~ knows what ...** weiß der Himmel, was ... *(col)*; **for ~'s sake!** um Himmels willen!
heavenly ['hevnlɪ] *adj (lit, fig col)* himmlisch. **~ body** Himmelskörper *m*.
heavily ['hevɪlɪ] *adv* schwer; *move, walk* schwerfällig; *rain, smoke, drink, rely, populated, influenced, in debt* stark; *lose, tax* hoch; *sleep* tief. **~ built** kräftig gebaut; **time hung ~ on his hands** die Zeit verging ihm nur langsam; **~ committed** stark engagiert; **to be ~ subscribed** viele Abonnenten haben.
heaviness ['hevɪnɪs] *n* Schwere *f*.
heavy ['hevɪ] **1** *adj (+er)* **(a)** schwer; *features* grob; *rain, cold also, traffic, drinker, smoker* stark; *expenses, taxes* hoch; *line* dick; *sleep* tief; *crop* reich; *(~-handed) manner, style* schwerfällig; *silence* bedrückend; *weather, air* drückend, schwül; *sky* bedeckt; *(tiring) day* anstrengend. **with a ~ heart** schweren Herzens, mit schwerem Herzen; **~ goods vehicle** Lastkraftwagen *m*; **~ industry** Schwerindustrie *f*; **~ artillery** schwere Artillerie; **to be ~ on petrol** viel Benzin brauchen; **the going was ~** wir kamen nur schwer voran; **the conversation was ~ going** die Unterhaltung war mühsam; **this book is very ~ going** das Buch liest sich schwer. **(b)** *(col: strict)* streng *(on* mit*)*. **2** *n (col: thug)* Schlägertyp *m*.
heavy: ~-duty *adj tyres etc* strapazierfähig; *boots* Arbeits-; *machine* Hochleistungs-; **~-handed** *adj* ungeschickt; **~weight** *n (Boxing)* Schwergewicht *nt*; *(fig col)* großes Tier *(col)*.
Hebrew ['hi:bru:] **1** *adj* hebräisch. **2** *n* **(a)** Hebräer(in *f*) *m*. **(b)** *(language)* Hebräisch *nt*.
Hebrides ['hebrɪdi:z] *npl* Hebriden *pl*.
heck [hek] *interj (col)* **oh ~!** zum Kuckuck! *(col)*; **I've a ~ of a lot to do** ich habe irrsinnig viel zu tun *(col)*.
heckle ['hekl] **1** *vt speaker* (durch Zwischenrufe) stören. **2** *vi* Zwischenrufe machen.
heckler ['heklə^r] *n* Zwischenrufer *m*.
heckling ['heklɪŋ] *n* Zwischenrufe *pl*.
hectare ['hektɑ:^r] *n* Hektar *m or nt*.
hectic ['hektɪk] *adj* hektisch.
he'd [hi:d] = **he would; he had.**
hedge [hedʒ] **1** *n* Hecke *f*; *(fig: protection)* Schutz *m*. **2** *vi* Fragen ausweichen, kneifen *(col) (at* bei*)*. **3** *vt investment* absichern. **to ~ one's bets** *(lit, fig)* sich absichern.
hedgehog ['hedʒhɒg] *n* Igel *m*.
hedge: ~hop *vi* tief fliegen; **~row** *n* Hecke *f*.
hedonism ['hi:dənɪzəm] *n* Hedonismus *m*.
hedonist ['hi:dənɪst] *n* Hedonist(in *f*) *m*.
heebie-jeebies ['hi:bɪ'dʒi:bɪz] *npl* **he gives me the ~** *(col)* wenn ich ihn sehe, bekomm' ich eine Gänsehaut *(col)*.
heed [hi:d] **1** *n* **to take ~** achtgeben; **to take ~/no ~ of sb/sth** jdn/etw beachten/nicht beachten. **2** *vt* beachten; *advice* hören auf *(+acc)*.
heedless ['hi:dlɪs] *adj* rücksichtslos. **to be ~ of sth** auf etw *(acc)* nicht achten.
heel [hi:l] **1** *n* **(a)** Ferse *f*; *(of shoe)* Absatz *m*. **to be right on sb's ~s** jdm auf den Fersen folgen; *(fig: chase)* jdm auf den Fersen sein; **to follow hard upon sb's ~s** jdm dicht auf den Fersen sein; **to be down at ~** *(person)* heruntergekommen sein; *(shoes)* abgelaufen sein; **to take to one's ~s** sich aus dem Staub(e) machen; **~!** *(to dog)* (bei) Fuß!; **to turn on one's ~** auf dem Absatz kehrtmachen; **to cool** *or* **kick one's ~s** *(col) (wait)* warten; *(do nothing)* Däumchen drehen; **~ bar** Absatzbar *f*. **(b)** *(pej col: person)* Scheißkerl *m (col!)*. **2** *vt* **to ~ shoes** auf Schuhe neue Absätze machen; **to be well ~ed** *(col)* betucht sein *(col)*.
hefty ['heftɪ] *adj (+er) (col)* kräftig; *book* dick; *object, workload* schwer; *sum of money, amount* ganz schön *(col)*.
heifer ['hefə^r] *n* Färse *f*.
height [haɪt] *n* **(a)** Höhe *f*; *(of person)* Größe *f*. **what ~ are you?** wie groß sind Sie? **(b)** *(high place)* **~s** *pl* Höhen *pl*; **to scale the ~s of Everest** den Mount Everest besteigen; **fear of ~s** Höhenangst *f*; **to be afraid of ~s** nicht schwindelfrei sein. **(c)** *(fig)* Höhe *f*; *(of success, stupidity also)* Gipfel *m*. **at the ~ of his power** auf der Höhe seiner Macht; **at the ~ of the season** in der Hauptsaison; **at the ~ of the storm** als das Gewitter am heftigsten war; **dressed in the ~ of fashion** nach der neuesten Mode gekleidet; **at the ~ of summer** im Hochsommer.
heighten ['haɪtn] *vt (raise)* höher stellen; *(emphasize) colour etc* hervorheben; *(increase) anger, effect etc* verstärken; *intensity* steigern.
heinous ['heɪnəs] *adj* abscheulich.
heir [ɛə^r] *n* Erbe *m (to gen)*. **~ apparent** gesetzlicher Erbe; **~ to the throne** Thronfolger *m*.
heiress ['ɛəres] *n* Erbin *f*.
heirloom ['ɛəlu:m] *n* Erbstück *nt*.
heist [haɪst] *n (esp US col)* Raubüberfall *m*.
held [held] *pret, ptp of* **hold.**
helicopter ['helɪkɒptə^r] *n* Hubschrauber *m*.
heliport ['helɪpɔ:t] *n* Hubschrauberlandeplatz *m*.
helium ['hi:lɪəm] *n* Helium *nt*.
hell [hel] *n* **(a)** Hölle *f*. **to go to ~** *(lit)* in die Hölle kommen.
(b) *(fig uses)* **all ~ was let loose** die Hölle war los; **it's ~ working there** es ist die reinste Hölle, dort zu arbeiten; **life became ~** das Leben wurde zur Hölle; **she made his life ~** sie machte ihm das Leben zur Hölle; **to give sb ~** *(col)* jdm die Hölle heiß machen; *(make life unpleasant)* jdm das Leben zur Hölle machen; **there'll be (all) ~ when he finds out** *(col)* wenn er das erfährt, ist der Teufel los *(col)*; **to play ~ with sth** *(col)* etw total durcheinanderbringen; **for the ~ of it** *(col)* nur zum Spaß *or* aus Jux.
(c) *(col: intensifier)* **a ~ of a noise** ein Höllenlärm *(col)*; **to work like ~** wie wild arbeiten *(col)*; **to run like ~** laufen, was die Beine hergeben; **we had a ~ of a time** *(bad, difficult)* es war grauenhaft; *(good)* wir haben uns prima amüsiert *(col)*; **a ~ of a lot** verdammt viel *(col)*; **that's one** *or* **a ~ of a problem/difference/bruise** das ist ein verdammt schwieriges Problem/ein wahnsinniger Unterschied/Bluterguß *(col)*; **to ~ with him** hol ihn der Teufel *(col)*, der kann mich mal *(col)*; **to ~ with it!, ~!** verdammt noch mal *(col!)*; **go to ~!** scher dich zum Teufel! *(col)*; **what the ~ do you want?** was willst du denn, verdammt noch mal? *(col!)*; **oh, what the ~!** ach, was soll's! *(col)*.
he'll [hi:l] = **he shall, he will.**
hellish ['helɪʃ] *adj (col)* höllisch *(col)*; *exams* verteufelt schwer *(col)*.
hello [hə'ləʊ] *interj* hallo. **say ~ to your parents (from me)** grüß deine Eltern (von mir).
helm [helm] *n* Ruder *nt*. **to be at the ~** *(lit, fig)* am Ruder sein.
helmet ['helmɪt] *n* Helm *m*; *(Fencing)* Maske *f*.
help [help] **1** *n* Hilfe *f*. **with the ~ of** mit Hilfe *(+gen)*; **he is beyond ~** ihm ist nicht mehr zu helfen; **to go/come to sb's ~** jdm zu Hilfe eilen/kommen; **to be of ~ to sb** jdm behilflich sein; *(thing also)* jdm nützen; **you're a great ~!** *(iro)* du bist mir eine schöne Hilfe!; **we are short of ~ in the shop** wir haben nicht genügend (Hilfs)kräfte im Geschäft; **there's no ~ for it** da ist nichts zu

machen.

2 *vti* **(a)** helfen *(+dat)*. **to ~ sb (to) do sth** jdm (dabei) helfen, etw zu tun; **~!** Hilfe!; **can I ~ you?** kann ich (Ihnen) behilflich sein?; **that won't ~ you** das wird Ihnen nichts nützen; **this will ~ the pain** das wird gegen die Schmerzen helfen; **it will ~ the crops to grow** es wird das Wachstum des Getreides fördern.

(b) to ~ sb down jdm hinunter-/herunterhelfen; **to ~ sb off with his coat** jdm aus dem Mantel helfen; **to ~ sb over the street** jdm über die Straße helfen; **to ~ sb through a difficult time** jdm in einer schwierigen Zeit beistehen; **to ~ sb up** *(from floor, chair etc)* jdm aufhelfen *or (up stairs etc)* hinaufhelfen.

(c) she ~ed him to potatoes sie gab ihm Kartoffeln; **to ~ oneself to sth** sich mit etw bedienen; **~ yourself!** bedienen Sie sich doch!

(d) he can't ~ it, he was born with it er kann nichts dafür, das ist angeboren; **he can't ~ it!** *(col: he's stupid)* er ist nun mal so (doof); **don't say more than you can ~** sagen Sie nicht mehr als unbedingt nötig; **not if I can ~ it** nicht, wenn ich es irgendwie vermeiden kann; **I couldn't ~ laughing** ich mußte (einfach) lachen; **I had to do it, I couldn't ~ myself** ich mußte es einfach tun; **one cannot ~ wondering whether ...** man muß sich wirklich fragen, ob ...; **it can't be ~ed** das ist nun mal so.

♦ **help out 1** *vi* aushelfen *(with* bei*)*. **2** *vt sep* helfen *(+dat) (with* mit*)*.

helper ['helpəʳ] *n* Helfer(in *f*) *m*; *(assistant)* Gehilfe *m*, Gehilfin *f*.

helpful ['helpfʊl] *adj person* hilfsbereit; *(useful) gadget, advice* nützlich. **you have been very ~** Sie haben mir sehr geholfen.

helpfully ['helpfəlɪ] *adv* hilfreich.

helping ['helpɪŋ] **1** *n (at table)* Portion *f*. **to take a second ~ of sth** sich *(dat)* noch einmal von etw nehmen. **2** *adj attr* **to lend a ~ hand to sb** jdm behilflich sein.

helpless ['helplɪs] *adj* hilflos. **she was ~ with laughter** sie konnte sich vor Lachen kaum halten.

helter-skelter ['heltə'skeltəʳ] **1** *adv* Hals über Kopf *(col)*. **2** *n (Brit: on fairground)* Rutschbahn *f*.

hem [hem] **1** *n* Saum *m*. **2** *vt* säumen.

♦ **hem in** *vt sep troops* einschließen; *(fig)* einengen.

he-man ['hiːmæn] *n, pl* **-men** [-men] *(col)* sehr männlicher Typ.

hematology *n (US)* = **haematology.**

hemisphere ['hemɪsfɪəʳ] *n* Hemisphäre *f*.

hemlock ['hemlɒk] *n (poison)* Schierling(saft) *m*.

hemp [hemp] *n* Hanf *m*.

hen [hen] *n* Huhn *nt*, Henne *f*; *(female bird)* Weibchen *nt*.

hence [hens] *adv* **(a)** *(for this reason)* also. **~ the name** daher der Name. **(b)** *(from now)* **two years ~** in zwei Jahren.

henceforth [ˌhens'fɔːθ] *adv (from then on)* von da an; *(from now on)* von nun an.

henchman ['hentʃmən] *n, pl* **-men** [-mən] *(pej)* Kumpan *m*.

henna ['henə] **1** *n* Henna *f*. **2** *vt* mit Henna färben.

hen: ~-party *n (col)*=Kaffeeklatsch *m (col)*; *(before wedding) für die Braut arrangierte Damengesellschaft;* **~peck** *vt* **a ~pecked husband** ein Pantoffelheld *m (col)*; **he is ~pecked** er steht unterm Pantoffel *(col)*.

hepatitis [ˌhepə'taɪtɪs] *n* Hepatitis *f*.

her [hɜːʳ] **1** *pers pron* **(a)** *(dir obj, with prep +acc)* sie; *(indir obj, with prep +dat)* ihr. **with her books about ~** mit ihren Büchern um sich. **(b) it's ~** sie ist's; **who, ~?** wer, sie? **2** *poss adj* ihr; *see* **my.**

herald ['herəld] **1** *n (Hist)* Herold *m*; *(fig)* (Vor)bote *m (geh)*. **2** *vt* ankündigen.

heraldic [he'rældɪk] *adj* heraldisch, Wappen-.

heraldry ['herəldrɪ] *n (science)* Wappenkunde *f*.

herb [hɜːb] *n* Kraut *nt*. **~ garden** Kräutergarten *m*.

herbaceous [hɜː'beɪʃəs] *adj* **~ border** Staudenrabatte *f*.

herbal ['hɜːbəl] *adj* Kräuter-.

herd [hɜːd] **1** *n* Herde *f*; *(of deer)* Rudel *nt*. **the common ~** die breite Masse. **2** *vt (drive) cattle, prisoners* treiben; *(tend) cattle* hüten.

♦ **herd together 1** *vi* sich zusammendrängen. **2** *vt sep* zusammentreiben.

herd instinct *n* Herdentrieb *m*.

here [hɪəʳ] *adv* **(a)** hier; *(with motion)* hierher; **~ I am** hier bin ich; **spring is ~** der Frühling ist da; **~ and now** auf der Stelle; **this one ~** der/die/das hier; **I won't be ~ for lunch** ich bin zum Mittagessen nicht da; **~ and there** hier und da; **~, there and everywhere** überall; **around/about ~** hier herum; **up/down to ~** bis hierher; **it's in/over ~** es ist hier (drin)/hier drüben; **put it in/over ~** stellen Sie es hier herein/hierüber; **from ~ on in** *(esp US)* von nun an.

(b) *(phrases)* **~ you are** *(giving sb sth)* hier (bitte); *(on finding sb)* da bist du ja!; *(on finding sth)* da ist es ja; **~ we are, home again** so, da wären wir wieder zu Hause; **~ he comes** da kommt er ja; **look out, ~ he comes** Vorsicht, er kommt!; **~ goes!** *(before attempting sth)* dann mal los; **~, let me do that** komm, laß mich das mal machen; **~'s to you!** *(in toasts)* auf Ihr Wohl!; **it's neither ~ nor there** es spielt keine Rolle.

here: ~abouts ['hɪərəbaʊts] *adv* hier herum; **~after 1** *adv (in books, contracts)* im folgenden. **2** *n* **the ~after** das Jenseits; **~by** *adv (form)* hiermit.

hereditary [hɪ'redɪtərɪ] *adj* erblich, Erb-.

heredity [hɪ'redɪtɪ] *n* Vererbung *f*.

heresy ['herəsɪ] *n* Ketzerei *f*.

heretic ['herətɪk] *n* Ketzer(in *f*) *m*.

heretical [hɪ'retɪkəl] *adj* ketzerisch.

here: ~upon *adv* daraufhin; **~with** *adv (form)* hiermit.

heritage ['herɪtɪdʒ] *n (lit, fig)* Erbe *nt*.

hermaphrodite [hɜː'mæfrədaɪt] *n* Zwitter *m*.

hermetic [hɜː'metɪk] *adj* hermetisch.

hermetically [hɜː'metɪkəlɪ] *adv* **~ sealed** hermetisch verschlossen *or (fig)* abgeriegelt.

hermit ['hɜːmɪt] *n* Einsiedler *m (also fig)*.

hernia ['hɜːnɪə] *n* (Eingeweide)bruch *m*.

hero ['hɪərəʊ] *n, pl* **-es** Held *m*; *(fig: object of hero-worship also)* Idol *nt*.

heroic [hɪ'rəʊɪk] *adj* heldenhaft; *behaviour, action also, words* heroisch; *effort* gewaltig.

heroin ['herəʊɪn] *n* Heroin *nt*. **~ addict** Heroinsüchtige(r) *mf*.

heroine ['herəʊɪn] *n* Heldin *f*.

heroism ['herəʊɪzəm] *n* (Helden)mut *m*.

heron ['herən] *n* Reiher *m*.

hero-worship ['hiːrəʊˌwɜːʃɪp] **1** *n* Verehrung *f*; *(of popstar etc)* Schwärmerei *f*. **2** *vt* verehren; *popstar etc* schwärmen für.

herring ['herɪŋ] *n* Hering *m*.

herringbone pattern ['herɪŋbəʊn'pætən] *n* Fischgrät(en)muster *nt*.

hers [hɜːz] *poss pron* ihre(r, s); *see* **mine**[1].

herself [hɜː'self] *pers pron* **(a)** *(dir and indir obj, with prep)* sich; *see* **myself. (b)** *(emph)* (sie) selbst.

he's [hiːz] = **he is; he has.**

hesitant ['hezɪtənt] *adj answer, smile* zögernd; *person also* unentschlossen. **I was rather ~ about doing it** ich war (mir) ziemlich unschlüssig, ob ich es tun sollte.

hesitate ['hezɪteɪt] *vi* zögern. **he who ~s is lost** *(Prov)* wer lange zögert, hat das Nachsehen; **even he would ~ at murder** selbst er hätte bei einem Mord Bedenken; **he ~s at nothing** er schreckt vor nichts zurück; **I am still hesitating about what to do** ich bin mir immer noch nicht schlüssig, was ich tun soll; **I wouldn't ~ to say so** ich hätte keine Hemmungen, es zu sagen; **don't ~ to ask me** fragen Sie ruhig; **please don't ~ to get in touch** wenden Sie sich bitte an mich/uns.

hesitation [ˌhezɪ'teɪʃən] *n* Zögern *nt*. **without the slightest ~** ohne auch nur einen Augenblick zu zögern.

hessian ['hesɪən] *n* Sackleinen *nt*.

heterogeneous [ˌhetərəʊ'dʒiːnɪəs] *adj* heterogen.

heterosexual [ˌhetərəʊ'seksjʊəl] **1** *adj* heterosexuell. **2** *n* Heterosexuelle(r) *mf*.

het up ['hetˌʌp] *adj (col)* aufgeregt.

hew [hjuː] *pret* **~ed,** *ptp* **hewn** *or* **~ed** *vt* hauen; *(shape)* behauen.

hex [heks] *n* **to put a ~ on sth** etw verhexen.

hexagon ['heksəgən] *n* Sechseck *nt*.

hey [heɪ] *interj* he.

heyday ['heɪdeɪ] *n* Glanzzeit, Blütezeit *f*. **in his ~** in seiner Glanzzeit.

hi [haɪ] *interj* hallo.

hiatus [haɪ'eɪtəs] *n (gap)* Lücke *f*.

hibernate ['haɪbəneɪt] *vi* Winterschlaf halten.

hibernation [ˌhaɪbə'neɪʃən] *n* Winterschlaf *m*.

hiccough, hiccup ['hɪkʌp] *n* Schluckauf *m; (col: in plans etc)* kleines Problem. **to have the ~s** den Schluckauf haben.

hick [hɪk] *n (US col)* Hinterwäldler *m (col)*.

hide[1] [haɪd] *(vb: pret* **hid** [hɪd], *ptp* **hidden** ['hɪdn] *or* **hid***)* **1** *vt (from* vor *+dat)* verstecken; *truth, tears, feelings, face* verbergen; *(from view) moon, rust* verdecken. **2** *vi* sich verstecken *(from sb* vor jdm*)*. **he was hiding in the cupboard** er hielt sich im Schrank versteckt. **3** *n* Versteck *nt*.

♦ **hide away 1** *vi* sich verstecken. **2** *vt sep* verstecken.

♦ **hide out** *vi* sich verstecken.

hide[2] *n (of animal)* Haut *f*; *(of furry animal)* Fell *nt*; *(processed)* Leder *nt*. **I haven't seen ~ nor hair of him for weeks** *(col)* den habe ich in den letzten Wochen nicht mal von weitem gesehen.

hide: ~-and-seek *n* Versteckspiel *nt*; **~away** *n* Versteck *nt*; **~bound** *adj person, views* engstirnig.

hideous ['hɪdɪəs] *adj* grauenhaft, scheußlich.

hideout ['haɪdaʊt] *n* Versteck *nt*.

hiding[1] ['haɪdɪŋ] *n* **to be in ~** sich versteckt halten; **to go into ~** untertauchen; **~ place** Versteck *nt*.

hiding[2] *n (beating)* **to give sb a good ~** jdm eine Tracht Prügel geben.

hierarchy ['haɪərɑːkɪ] *n* Hierarchie *f*.

hieroglyphic ['haɪərə'glɪfɪk] **1** *adj* hieroglyphisch. **2** *n* **~s** *pl* Hieroglyphen(schrift *f*) *pl*.

hi-fi ['haɪˌfaɪ] *n* Hi-Fi *nt*; *(system)* Hi-Fi-Anlage *f*.

higgledy-piggledy ['hɪgldɪ'pɪgldɪ] *adv* wie Kraut und Rüben (durcheinander) *(col)*.

high [haɪ] **1** *adj (+er)* **(a)** hoch *pred*, hohe(r, s) *attr*; *altitude* groß; *wind* stark; *complexion, colour* (hoch)rot. **a building 80 metres ~** ein 80 Meter hohes Gebäude; **on one of the ~er floors** in einem der oberen Stockwerke; **the river is quite ~** der Fluß führt ziemlich viel Wasser; **he left her ~ and dry** er hat sie sitzen lassen; **to be left ~ and dry** auf dem Trockenen sitzen *(col)*; **on the ~est authority** von höchster Stelle; **to act ~ and mighty** erhaben tun; **to be on one's ~ horse** *(fig)* auf dem hohen Roß sitzen; **to pay a ~ price for sth** *(lit, fig)* etw teuer bezahlen; **in ~ spirits** in Hochstimmung; **to have a ~ old time** *(col)* mächtig Spaß haben *(col)*; **it's ~ time you went home** es wird höchste Zeit, daß du nach Hause gehst.

(b) *(col) (on drugs)* high *(col)*.

(c) *meat* angegangen.

2 *adv (+er)* hoch. **~ up** *(position)* hoch oben; *(motion)* hoch hinauf; **one floor ~er** ein Stockwerk höher; **to go as ~ as £200** bis zu £ 200 (hoch)gehen; **feelings ran ~** die Gemüter erhitzten sich; **to search ~ and low** überall suchen.

3 *n* **(a) the orders come from on ~** *(hum col)* der Befehl kommt von oben. **(b) unemployment has reached a new ~** die Arbeitslosenziffern haben einen neuen Höchststand erreicht. **(c)** *(Met)* Hoch *nt*. **(d)** *(US Aut: top gear)* **in ~** im höchsten Gang. **(e)** *(US col: high school)* Penne *f (col)*.

high: ~ altar *n* Hochaltar *m*; **~ball** *n (US)* Highball *m*; **~brow 1** *n* Intellektuelle(r) *mf*; **2** *adj interests* intellektuell; *tastes, music* anspruchsvoll; **~chair** *n* Hochstuhl *m*; **~-class** *adj* hochwertig; **~ commissioner** *n* Hochkommissar *m*; **~ court** *n* oberstes Gericht.

higher ['haɪə[r]] *adj mathematics, life-forms* höher.

high: ~ explosive *n* hochexplosiver Sprengstoff; **~ flier** *n (col)* Senkrechtstarter *m*; **~-flown** *adj style, speech* hochtrabend; **~ frequency** *adj* Hochfrequenz-; **H~ German** *n* Hochdeutsch *nt*; **~-grade** *adj* hochwertig; *ore* gediegen; **~-handed** *adj* eigenmächtig; *character* überheblich; **~-heeled** *adj* hochhackig; **~ heels** *npl* hohe Absätze *pl*; **~ jump** *n (Sport)* Hochsprung *m*; **to be for the ~ jump** *(fig col)* dran sein *(col)*; **H~lands** *npl* schottisches Hochland; *(generally)* Berg- *or* Hochland *nt*; **~-level** *adj talks* auf höchster Ebene; **~ life** *n* Leben *nt* in großem Stil; **~light 1** *n (Art, Phot)* Glanzlicht *nt*; *(in hair)* Strähne *f*; *(fig)* Höhepunkt *m*; **~lights** *(in hair)* Strähnchen *pl*; **2** *vt need, problem* hervorheben.

highly ['haɪlɪ] *adv* hoch-. **to be ~ paid** hoch bezahlt werden; **to think ~ of sb** eine hohe Meinung von jdm haben; **to speak ~ of sb** sich sehr positiv über jdn äußern; **~-strung** nervös.

high: H~ Mass *n* Hochamt *nt*; **~-minded** *adj* hochgeistig; *ideals* hoch.

highness ['haɪnɪs] *n* **Her H~** Ihre Hoheit.

high: ~-pitched *adj sound* hoch; **~-powered** *adj* **(a)** *car* stark, Hochleistungs-; **(b)** *(fig) businessman, politician, academic* Spitzen-; *conversation* sehr anspruchsvoll; **~-pressure** *adj* **(a) ~-pressure area** Hochdruckgebiet *nt*; **(b)** *(fig) salesman* aufdringlich; *sales technique* aggressiv; **~ priest** *n (lit, fig)* Hohepriester *m*; **~-ranking** *adj* von hohem Rang; **~-rise flats** *npl* Hochhaus *nt*; **~ school** *n (US)* Oberschule *f*; **the ~ seas** *npl* die Meere *pl*; **on the ~ seas** auf hoher See; **~ society** *n* High-Society *f*; **~-speed** *adj* Schnell-; *drill* mit hoher Umdrehungszahl; **~-speed film** hoch(licht)empfindlicher Film; **~-spirited** *adj* in Hochstimmung; **~ spot** *n* Höhepunkt *m*; **~ street** *n (Brit)* Hauptstraße *f*; **~ summer** *n* Hochsommer *m*; **~ tea** *n* (frühes) Abendessen; **~-tension** *adj (Elec)* Hochspannungs-; **~ treason** *n* Hochverrat *m*; **~way** *n* Landstraße *f*; **public ~way** öffentliche Straße; **~way code** *n* Straßenverkehrsordnung *f*; **~wayman** *n* Wegelagerer *m*.

hijack ['haɪdʒæk] **1** *vt* entführen; *lorry* überfallen. **2** *n see vt* Entführung *f*; Überfall *m (of* auf *+acc)*.

hijacker ['haɪdʒækə[r]] *n* Entführer *m*.

hike [haɪk] **1** *vi* wandern. **2** *n* Wanderung *f*.

hiker ['haɪkə[r]] *n* Wanderer *m*, Wanderin *f*.

hiking ['haɪkɪŋ] *n* Wandern *nt*.

hilarious [hɪ'lɛərɪəs] *adj* sehr komisch.

hilariously [hɪ'lɛərɪəslɪ] *adv* **~ funny** zum Schreien.

hilarity [hɪ'lærɪtɪ] *n* **his statement caused some ~** seine Behauptung löste Heiterkeit aus.

hill [hɪl] *n* Hügel *m*; *(higher)* Berg *m*; *(incline)* Hang *m*. **built on a ~** am Hang *or* Berg gebaut; **up ~ and down dale** bergauf und bergab; **that joke's as old as the ~s** der Witz hat so einen Bart; **to be over the ~** *(fig col)* die besten Jahre hinter sich *(dat)* haben.

hillbilly ['hɪlbɪlɪ] *(US col) n* Hinterwäldler *m (pej)*.

hillock ['hɪlək] *n* Anhöhe *f*.

hillside ['hɪlsaɪd] *n* Hang *m*.

hilly ['hɪlɪ] *adj (+er)* hüg(e)lig; *(higher)* bergig.

hilt [hɪlt] *n* Heft *nt*. **up to the ~** *(fig)* voll und ganz; *(involved, in debt also)* bis über beide Ohren *(col)*.

him [hɪm] *pers pron* **(a)** *(dir obj, with prep +acc)* ihn; *(indir obj, with prep +dat)* ihm. **with his things around ~** mit seinen Sachen um sich. **(b)** *(emph)* er. **it's ~** er ist's; **who, ~?** wer, er?

Himalayas [ˌhɪmə'leɪəz] *npl* Himalaya *m*.

himself [hɪm'self] *pers pron* **(a)** *(dir and indir obj, with prep)* sich; *see* **myself. (b)** *(emph)* (er) selbst.

hind[1] [haɪnd] *n (Zool)* Hirschkuh *f*.

hind[2] *adj, superl* **hindmost** hintere(r, s). **~ legs** Hinterbeine *pl*; **she could talk the ~ legs off a donkey** *(col)* sie redet wie ein Buch *(col)*.

hinder ['hɪndəʳ] *vt (obstruct)* behindern; *(delay) person* aufhalten. **to ~ sb from doing sth** jdn daran hindern, etw zu tun.

Hindi ['hɪndiː] *n* Hindi *nt*.

hindquarters ['haɪnd,kwɔːtəz] *npl* Hinterteil *nt*; *(of horse)* Hinterhand *f*.

hindrance ['hɪndrəns] *n* Behinderung *f*. **to be a ~** hinderlich sein.

hindsight ['haɪndsaɪt] *n*: **with ~** im nachhinein.

Hindu ['hɪnduː] **1** *adj* hinduistisch, Hindu-. **~ people** Hindu(s) *pl*. **2** *n* Hindu *m*.

Hinduism ['hɪnduːɪzəm] *n* Hinduismus *m*.

hinge [hɪndʒ] **1** *n (of door)* Angel *f*; *(of box etc)* Scharnier *nt*. **2** *vi (fig)* abhängen *(on* von*)*.

hint [hɪnt] **1** *n* **(a)** *(suggestion)* Andeutung *f*, Wink *m*. **to give a/no ~ of sth** etw andeuten/nicht andeuten; **give me a ~** gib mir einen Anhaltspunkt; **to drop a ~** eine Andeutung machen; **OK, I can take a ~** schon recht, ich habe den Wink verstanden. **(b)** *(trace)* Spur *f*. **a ~ of garlic** eine Spur Knoblauch; **not a ~ of tiredness** keine Spur von Müdigkeit; **with the ~ of a smile** mit dem Anflug eines Lächelns. **(c)** *(tip, piece of advice)* Tip *m*. **~s for travellers** Reisetips *pl*. **2** *vt* andeuten *(to* gegenüber*)*. **what are you ~ing (at)?** was wollen Sie damit andeuten?

hip [hɪp] *n* Hüfte *f*.

hip *in cpds* Hüft-; **~ bath** *n* Sitzbad *nt*; **~-flask** *n* Flachmann *(col) m*; **~ joint** *n (Anat)* Hüftgelenk *nt*; **~ pocket** *n* Gesäßtasche *f*.

hippopotamus [ˌhɪpə'pɒtəməs] *n, pl* **-es** *or* **hippopotami** [ˌhɪpə'pɒtəmaɪ] Nilpferd *nt*.

hippy, hippie ['hɪpɪ] *n* Hippie *m*.

hire [haɪəʳ] **1** *n* Mieten *nt*; *(of car also, suit)* Leihen *nt*. **for ~** *(taxi)* frei; **it's on ~** es ist geliehen/gemietet. **2** *vt* mieten; *cars also, suits* leihen; *staff* einstellen. **~d assassin** gedungener Mörder; **~d car** *(Brit)* Mietwagen *m*; **~d hand** Lohnarbeiter *m*.

♦ **hire out** *vt sep* vermieten, verleihen.

hire purchase *n (Brit)* Ratenkauf *m*. **on ~** auf Raten *or* Teilzahlung.

his [hɪz] **1** *poss adj* sein; *see* **my. 2** *poss pron* seine(r, s); *see* **mine**[1].

hiss [hɪs] **1** *vi* zischen; *(cat)* fauchen. **2** *vt actor* auszischen.

historian [hɪs'tɔːrɪən] *n* Historiker(in *f*) *m*.

historic [hɪs'tɒrɪk] *adj* historisch.

historical [hɪs'tɒrɪkəl] *adj* historisch; *studies, investigation also* geschichtlich, Geschichts-.

history ['hɪstərɪ] *n* Geschichte *f*. **to make ~** Geschichte machen; **he has a ~ of violence** er hat eine Vorgeschichte als Gewalttäter; **the family has a ~ of heart disease** in der Familie hat es schon immer Fälle von Herzleiden gegeben.

hit [hɪt] *(vb: pret, ptp ~)* **1** *n* **(a)** *(blow)* Schlag *m*; *(on target, Fencing)* Treffer *m*. **(b)** *(success, also Theat)* Erfolg, Knüller *(col) m*; *(song)* Schlager, Hit *m*. **to be** *or* **make a ~ with sb** bei jdm gut ankommen.

2 *vt* **(a)** *(strike)* schlagen; *(missile, bullet etc)* treffen. **to ~ sb a blow** jdm einen Schlag versetzen; **to ~ one's head against sth** sich *(dat)* den Kopf an etw *(dat)* stoßen; **the car ~ a tree** das Auto fuhr gegen einen Baum; **he was ~ by a stone** er wurde von einem Stein getroffen; **he was ~ in the leg** er wurde ins Bein getroffen; **the commandos ~ the town at dawn** die Kommandos griffen die Stadt im Morgengrauen an; **it ~s you (in the eye)** *(fig)* das springt einem ins Auge; **that ~ home** *(fig)* das saß *(col)*; **then it ~ me** dann wurde es mir plötzlich klar.

(b) *(affect adversely)* treffen. **to be hard ~ by sth** von etw schwer getroffen werden; **this tax will ~ the poor** diese Steuer wird die Armen treffen.

(c) *(achieve, reach) likeness, top* C treffen; *speed, level etc* erreichen. **to ~ the papers** in die Zeitungen kommen; **to ~ town** *(col)* die Stadt erreichen; **we're going to ~ the rush hour** wir geraten direkt in den Stoßverkehr; **the driver ~ a patch of ice** der Fahrer geriet auf eine vereiste Stelle; **to ~ a problem** auf ein Problem stoßen.

(d) *(fig col phrases)* **to ~ the bottle** zur Flasche greifen; **to ~ the ceiling** *or* **roof** an die Decke *or* in die Luft gehen *(col)*; **to ~ the road** sich auf den Weg *or* die Socken *(col)* machen.

3 *vi* **(a)** *(strike)* schlagen. **he ~s hard** er schlägt hart zu. **(b)** *(collide)* zusammenstoßen.

♦ **hit back 1** *vi (lit, fig)* zurückschlagen. **he ~ ~ at his critics** er gab seinen Kritikern Kontra. **2** *vt sep* zurückschlagen.

♦ **hit off** *vt sep* **(a) he ~ him ~ beautifully** er hat ihn ausgezeichnet getroffen. **(b) to ~ it ~ with sb** *(col)* prima mit jdm auskommen *(col)*.

♦ **hit out** *vi (lit)* losschlagen *(at sb* auf jdn*)*; *(fig)* scharf angreifen *(at or against sb* jdn*)*.

♦ **hit (up)on** *vi +prep obj* stoßen auf *(+acc)*.

hit-and-run ['hɪtən'rʌn] *n* **there was a ~ here last night** hier hat heute nacht jemand einen Unfall gebaut und Fahrerflucht begangen.

hitch [hɪtʃ] **1** *n* Schwierigkeit *f*. **without a ~** reibungslos; **but there's one ~** aber die Sache hat einen Haken. **2** *vt* **(a)** *(fasten)* anbinden *(to* an *+dat)*. **(b)** *(col)* **to get ~ed** heiraten. **(c) to ~ a lift** trampen, per Anhalter fahren. **3** *vi (~-hike)* trampen, per Anhalter fahren.

♦ **hitch up** *vt sep* **(a)** *horses* anschirren. **(b)** *trousers* hochziehen.

hitch: ~-hike *vi* per Anhalter fahren, trampen; **~-hiker** *n* Anhalter(in *f*), Tramper(in *f*) *m*; **~-hiking** *n* Trampen *nt*.

hither ['hɪðəʳ] *adv (obs)* hierher. **~ and thither** *(liter)* hierhin und dorthin.

hitherto [ˌhɪðə'tuː] *adv* bisher, bis jetzt.

hit: ~man *n (col)* Killer *m (col)*; **~-or-miss** *adj* auf gut Glück *pred*; *methods, planning* schlampig; **~ parade** *n* Hitparade *f*; **~ record** *n* Schlagerplatte *f*; **~ song** *n* Schlager *m*; **~ tune** *n* Schlagermelodie *f*.

hive [haɪv] *n (bee ~)* Bienenstock *m*. **the office was a ~ of activity** in dem Büro ging es wie in einem Bienenstock zu.

♦ **hive off 1** *vt sep department* ausgliedern. **2** *vi* **(a)** *(branch out)* sich absetzen. **(b)** *(col: slip away)* abschwirren *(col)*.

hoard [hɔːd] **1** *n* Vorrat *m*; *(treasure)* Hort *m*. **a ~ of weapons** ein Waffenlager *nt*. **2** *vt (also* **~ up***) food etc* hamstern; *money* horten.

hoarding *n (Brit) (fence)* Bretterzaun *m*. **(advertisement) ~** Plakatwand *f*.

hoarfrost ['hɔː'frɒst] *n* (Rauh)reif *m*.

hoarse [hɔːs] *adj (+er)* heiser.

hoax [həʊks] **1** *n (joke)* Streich *m*; *(false alarm)* blinder Alarm. **2** *vt* anführen. **he ~ed him into paying money** er hat ihm Geld abgeschwindelt.

hoaxer ['həʊksəʳ] *n (in bomb scares etc) jd, der einen blinden Alarm auslöst.*

hob [hɒb] *n (on modern cooker)* Kochmulde *f*.

hobble ['hɒbl] *vi* humpeln.

hobby ['hɒbɪ] *n* Hobby *nt*.

hobby-horse ['hɒbɪhɔːs] *n (lit, fig)* Steckenpferd *nt*.

hobnailed ['hɒbneɪld] *adj* ~ **boots** genagelte Schuhe *pl.*
hobnob ['hɒbnɒb] *vi* **the people he ~s with** die Leute mit denen er oft zusammen ist.
hobo ['həʊbəʊ] *n (US: tramp)* Penner *m (col).*
hock[1] [hɒk] *n (Brit: wine)* weißer Rheinwein.
hock[2] *n (col)* **in ~** *(pawned)* versetzt.
hockey ['hɒkɪ] *n* Hockey *nt; (US)* Eishockey *nt.* ~ **stick** Hockeyschläger *m.*
hocus-pocus ['həʊkəs'pəʊkəs] *n* Hokuspokus *m.*
hoe [həʊ] *n* Hacke *f.*
hog [hɒg] **1** *n* (Mast)schwein *nt; (US: pig)* Schwein *nt; (pej col: person)* Schwein *nt (col); (greedy)* Vielfraß *m (col).* **2** *vt (col)* in Beschlag nehmen.
Hogmanay [,hɒgmə'neɪ] *n (Scot)* Silvester *nt.*
hoi polloi ['hɔɪpə'lɔɪ] *n (pej)* Pöbel *m.*
hoist [hɔɪst] **1** *vt* hochheben; *(pull up)* hochziehen; *flag, sails* hissen. **to be ~ with one's own petard** *(prov)* in die eigene Falle gehen. **2** *n* Hebevorrichtung *f; (lift)* (Lasten)aufzug *m.*
hoity-toity ['hɔɪtɪ'tɔɪtɪ] *(col) adj* hochnäsig.
hold [həʊld] *(vb: pret, ptp* **held***)* **1** *n* **(a)** Griff *m (also Wrestling); (Mountaineering)* Halt *m; (fig)* Einfluß *m (over* auf *+acc).* **to seize** *or* **grab ~ of sb/sth** *(lit)* jdn/etw fassen *or* packen; **to get (a) ~ of sth** sich an etw *(dat)* festhalten; **to have/catch ~ of sth** *(lit)* etw festhalten/etw fassen *or* packen; **to get ~ of sb** *(fig)* jdn finden; *(on phone etc)* jdn erreichen; **to get** *or* **lay ~ of sth** *(fig)* etw auftreiben *(col);* **where did you get ~ of that idea?** wie kommst du denn auf die Idee?; **to have a ~ over** *or* **on sb** *(fig)* (großen) Einfluß auf jdn ausüben; **to get (a) ~ of oneself** *(fig)* sich in den Griff bekommen; **get (a) ~ of yourself!** reiß dich zusammen! **(b)** *(Naut, Aviat)* Laderaum *m.*

2 *vt* **(a)** *(grasp)* halten. **to ~ hands** sich an der Hand halten; *(lovers, children etc)* Händchen halten; **this car ~s the road well** dieses Auto hat eine gute Straßenlage; **to ~ oneself upright** sich aufrecht halten.

(b) *(contain)* enthalten; *(have capacity of: tank etc)* fassen; *(bus, hall etc)* Platz haben für. **this room ~s twenty people** in diesem Raum haben zwanzig Personen Platz; **the box will ~ all my books** in der Kiste ist Platz für alle meine Bücher; **what does the future ~?** was bringt die Zukunft?

(c) *(believe)* meinen; *(maintain also)* behaupten. **to ~ sth to be true/immoral** *etc* etw für wahr/unmoralisch *etc* halten; **to ~ the belief that ...** glauben, daß ...; **to ~ the view that ...** die Meinung vertreten, daß ...; **she held her grandchild dear** ihr Enkelkind bedeutete ihr sehr viel.

(d) *(keep back) train* aufhalten; *one's breath* anhalten; *suspect, hostages etc* festhalten; *confiscated goods etc* zurückhalten; *(discontinue) fire* einstellen. **to ~ sb (prisoner)** jdn gefangenhalten; **there's no ~ing him** er ist nicht zu bremsen *(col);* **~ it!** *(col)* Moment mal *(col); (taking photograph)* so ist gut; **~ everything!** *(col)* stop!

(e) *(possess, occupy) post, position* innehaben; *passport* haben; *shares* besitzen; *(Sport) record* halten; *(Mil) position* halten.

(f) *(keep, not let go)* **to ~ its value** seinen Wert behalten; **to ~ one's ground** *or* **own** sich behaupten (können); **I'll ~ you to that!** ich werde Sie beim Wort nehmen.

(g) he can't ~ his whisky/liquor er verträgt keinen Whisky/nichts; **she can ~ her drink** sie verträgt was.

(h) *meeting* abhalten.

3 *vi* **(a)** *(rope, nail etc)* halten. **~ still!** halt still!; **~ tight!** festhalten!; **will the good weather ~?** wird sich das gute Wetter wohl halten?; **if his luck ~s** wenn ihm das Glück treu bleibt. **(b)** *(be valid)* gelten.

♦ **hold against** *vt always separate* **to ~ sth ~ sb** jdm etw übelnehmen.
♦ **hold back 1** *vi* sich zurückhalten; *(fail to act)* zögern. **to ~ ~ from doing sth** es unterlassen, etw zu tun. **2** *vt sep* zurückhalten; *floods* (auf)stauen; *tears also* unterdrücken; *emotions* verbergen, unterdrücken; *information* geheimhalten. **to ~ sb ~ from doing sth** jdn daran hindern, etw zu tun; **nothing can ~ him ~ now** jetzt ist er nicht mehr aufzuhalten; **he was ~ing something ~ from me** er verheimlichte mir etwas.
♦ **hold down** *vt sep (keep on ground)* unten halten; *(keep in place)* (fest)halten; *(keep low) prices* niedrig halten. **he can't ~ any job ~ for long** er kann sich in keiner Stellung lange halten.
♦ **hold forth** *vi* sich auslassen *(on* über *+acc).*
♦ **hold in** *vt sep stomach* einziehen.
♦ **hold off 1** *vi (keep away)* sich fernhalten *(from von); (not act)* warten; *(enemy)* nicht angreifen; *(rain, storm)* ausbleiben. **I hope the rain ~s ~** ich hoffe, daß es nicht regnet. **2** *vt sep enemy, attack* abwehren; *visitor etc* hinhalten.
♦ **hold on 1** *vi (maintain grip)* sich festhalten; *(endure, resist)* durchhalten; *(wait)* warten. **~ ~** Moment (mal)!; *(Telec)* einen Moment bitte. **2** *vt sep* **to be held ~ by sth** mit etw befestigt sein.
♦ **hold on to** *vi +prep obj* **(a) to ~ ~ ~ sth** an etw *(dat)* festhalten. **(b)** *hope* nicht aufgeben; *idea* festhalten an *(+dat).* **(c)** *(keep)* behalten. **to ~ ~ ~ the lead** in Führung bleiben.
♦ **hold out 1** *vi* **(a)** *(supplies etc)* reichen. **(b)** *(endure, resist)* durchhalten. **to ~ ~ against sb** sich gegen jdn behaupten; **to ~ ~ for sth** auf etw *(dat)* bestehen. **2** *vt sep* **(a)** ausstrecken. **to ~ ~ sth to sb** jdm etw hinhalten; **~ your hand ~** halt die Hand auf; **she held ~ her arms** sie breitete die Arme aus. **(b)** *(fig) prospects* bieten. **I don't ~ ~ much hope** ich habe nicht mehr viel Hoffnung.
♦ **hold out on** *vi +prep obj (col)* **you've been ~ing ~ ~ me** du verheimlichst mir doch was *(col).*
♦ **hold over** *vt sep question, matter* vertagen; *decision* verschieben *(until* auf *+acc).*
♦ **hold up 1** *vi* **(a)** *(tent, wall etc)* stehen bleiben; *(light fitting, tile etc)* halten. **(b)** *(belief)* standhalten; *(theory)* sich halten lassen. **2** *vt sep* **(a)** hochhalten; *face* nach oben wenden. **~ ~ your hand** hebt die Hand; **to ~ sth ~ to the light** etw gegen das Licht halten. **(b)** *(support)* halten; *(from the side)* stützen; *(from beneath)* tragen. **(c) to ~ sb ~ as sth** jdn als etw hinstellen. **(d)** *(stop)* anhalten; *(delay) people* aufhalten; *talks, delivery* verzögern. **(e)** *(rob)* überfallen.
♦ **hold with** *vi +prep obj (col)* **I don't ~ ~ that** ich bin gegen so was *(col).*
holdall ['həʊldɔːl] *n (Brit)* Reisetasche *f.*
holder ['həʊldə^r] *n (of title, office, record, passport)* Inhaber(in *f*) *m; (object)* Halter *m.*
holding ['həʊldɪŋ] *n (land)* Land *nt; (with buildings)* Gut *nt.* **~s** *pl* (Grund)besitz *m; (Fin)* **~s** *pl* Anteile *pl; (stocks)* Aktienbesitz *m;* **~ company** Dachgesellschaft *f.*
hold-up ['həʊldʌp] *n* **(a)** *(delay)* Verzögerung *f; (Brit: of traffic)* Stockung *f.* **what's the ~?** warum dauert das so lange?; **there's been a ~ in our plans** unsere Pläne haben sich verzögert. **(b)** *(robbery)* bewaffneter Raubüberfall.
hole [həʊl] **1** *n* Loch *nt; (rabbit's, fox's)* Bau *m,* Höhle *f; (pej col)* Loch *nt (col); (town)* Kaff *(col) nt.* **to make a ~ in sb's savings** ein Loch in jds Ersparnisse reißen; **he's talking through a ~ in his head** *(col)* er quatscht lauter Blödsinn *(col).* **2** *vt* ein Loch machen in *(+acc).* **to be ~d** ein Loch bekommen; **the ship was ~d by an iceberg** der Eisberg schlug das Schiff leck.
♦ **hole up** *vi* sich verkriechen.

holiday ['hɒlədɪ] *n* **(a)** *(day off)* freier Tag; *(public ~)* Feiertag *m.* **to take a ~** einen Tag frei nehmen. **(b)** *(esp Brit: period) often pl* Urlaub *m,* Ferien *pl (esp Sch).* **on ~** in den Ferien; auf Urlaub; **to go on ~** Urlaub machen; **where are you going for your ~?** wohin fahren Sie in den Ferien *or* im Urlaub?; **to take a ~** Urlaub nehmen; **I need a ~** ich bin urlaubsreif.

holiday: ~ camp *n* Feriendorf *nt;* **~maker** *n (esp Brit)* Urlauber(in *f*) *m;* **~ resort** *n* Ferienort *m.*

holiness ['həʊlɪnɪs] *n* **His H~** Seine Heiligkeit.

Holland ['hɒlənd] *n* Holland *nt.*

hollow ['hɒləʊ] **1** *adj (+er) (lit, fig)* hohl; *person* innerlich hohl; *life* inhaltslos; *sympathy, praise* unaufrichtig; *promise* leer; *victory* wertlos; *eyes* tiefliegend. **2** *adv sound* hohl. **they beat us ~** *(col)* sie haben uns fertiggemacht *(col).* **3** *n (in ground)* Mulde *f.* **the ~ of one's hand** die hohle Hand.

♦ **hollow out** *vt sep* aushöhlen.

holly ['hɒlɪ] *n* Stechpalme *f.*

hollyhock ['hɒlɪhɒk] *n* Malve *f.*

holocaust ['hɒləkɔːst] *n* Inferno *nt.* **nuclear ~** atomare Katastrophe.

hologram ['hɒləgræm] *n* Hologramm *nt.*

holster ['həʊlstə[r]] *n* (Pistolen)halfter *nt or f.*

holy ['həʊlɪ] *adj (+er)* heilig; *bread, ground* geweiht. **~ water** Weihwasser *nt;* **the H~ Bible** die Bibel; **H~ Ghost** Heiliger Geist; **H~ Week** Karwoche *f;* **~ smoke** *(col)* heiliger Strohsack! *(col).*

homage ['hɒmɪdʒ] *n* Huldigung *f; (for elders)* Ehrerbietung *f.* **to pay ~ to sb** jdm huldigen; **in silent ~** in stummer Ehrerbietung.

home [həʊm] **1** *n* **(a)** *(house)* Heim *nt; (country, area etc)* Heimat *f.* **gadgets for the ~** praktische Haushaltsgeräte; **his ~ is in Brussels** er ist in Brüssel zu Hause; **Bournemouth is his second ~** Bournemouth ist seine zweite Heimat (geworden); **haven't you got a ~ to go to?** hast du kein Zuhause?; **he invited us around to his ~** er hat uns zu sich (nach Hause) eingeladen; **away from ~** von zu Hause weg; **a long way from ~** weit von zu Hause weg; **to live away from ~** nicht zu Hause wohnen; **hasn't this hammer got a ~?** gehört der Hammer nicht irgendwohin?; **to find a ~ for sth** etw irgendwo unterbringen; **it's a ~ from ~** es ist wie zu Hause; **at ~** zu Hause; *(Sport)* auf eigenem Platz; **he doesn't feel at ~ in English** er fühlt sich im Englischen nicht sicher; **to make oneself at ~** es sich *(dat)* bequem machen; **to make sb feel at ~** es jdm gemütlich machen; **~ sweet ~** *(Prov)* trautes Heim, Glück allein *(Prov).*

(b) *(institution)* Heim *nt.*

(c) *(Zool, Bot)* Heimat *f.*

2 *adv* **(a)** *(position)* zu Hause, daheim; *(with verb of motion)* nach Hause, heim. **to go ~** nach Hause gehen/fahren; *(to country)* heimfahren; **on the way ~** auf dem Heimweg *or* Nachhauseweg; **to return ~ from abroad** aus dem Ausland zurückkommen. **(b) to drive a nail ~** einen Nagel einschlagen; **to bring** *or* **get sth ~ to sb** jdm etw klarmachen; **his words went ~** seine Worte hatten ihre Wirkung.

♦ **home in on** *vi +prep obj target* sich ausrichten auf *(+acc); essential point* herausgreifen.

home: ~ address *n* Heimatadresse *or* -anschrift *f; (as opposed to business address)* Privatanschrift *f;* **~-brew** *n* selbstgebrautes Bier; **~ comforts** *npl* häuslicher Komfort; **~-coming** *n* Heimkehr *f;* **H~ Counties** *npl Grafschaften, die an London angrenzen;* **~ economics** *n sing* Hauswirtschaft(slehre) *f;* **~ front** *n* **on the ~ front** *(Mil, Pol)* im eigenen Land; *(in business contexts)* im eigenen Betrieb; *(in personal, family contexts)* zu Hause; **~ game** *n (Sport)* Heimspiel *nt;* **~ ground** *n (Sport)* eigener Platz; **to be on ~ ground** *(fig)* sich auf vertrautem Terrain bewegen; **~-grown** *adj vegetables* selbstgezogen; *(not imported)* einheimisch; **~ help** *n* (Haushalts)hilfe *f;* **~ land** *n* Heimat(land *nt*) *f;* **~less** *adj* heimatlos; *tramp* obdachlos; **~ life** *n* Familienleben *nt.*

homely ['həʊmlɪ] *adj (+er)* **(a)** *(home-loving)* häuslich; *atmosphere* heimelig; *style* anspruchslos; *advice* einfach. **(b)** *(US: plain) person* unscheinbar; *face* reizlos.

home: ~-made *adj* selbstgemacht; **~maker** *n (US) (housewife)* Hausfrau *f; (social worker)* Familienfürsorger(in *f*) *m;* **~ market** *n* Inlandsmarkt *m;* **~ news** *n* Meldungen *pl* aus dem Inland; **H~ Office** *n (Brit)* Innenministerium *nt; (with relation to aliens)* Einwanderungsbehörde *f;* **H~ Secretary** *n (Brit)* Innenminister *m;* **~sick** *adj* **to be ~sick** Heimweh haben *(for* nach*);* **~stead** *n* **(a)** Heimstätte *f;* **(b)** *(US)* Heimstätte *f* für Siedler; **~ straight, ~ stretch** *n (Sport)* Zielgerade *f;* **~ team** *n (Sport)* Gastgeber *pl;* **~ town** *n* Heimatort *m;* **~ truth** *n* **to tell sb some ~ truths** jdm die Augen öffnen.

homeward ['həʊmwəd] *adj journey, flight* Heim-. **we are ~-bound** es geht Richtung Heimat.

homeward(s) ['həʊmwəd(z)] *adv* nach Hause; *(to country also)* in Richtung Heimat.

home: ~ work *n (Sch)* Hausaufgaben *pl;* **to give sb sth for ~work** jdm etw aufgeben; **what have you got for ~work?** was hast du auf?; **he hadn't done his ~work** *(fig col)* er hatte sich mit der Materie nicht vertraut gemacht.

homey ['həʊmɪ] *adj (+er) (US col)* gemütlich.

homicidal [ˌhɒmɪ'saɪdl] *adj* gemeingefährlich.

homicide ['hɒmɪsaɪd] *n* Totschlag *m.* **culpable ~** Mord *m;* **~ (squad)** Mordkommission *f.*

homing ['həʊmɪŋ] *adj* **~ pigeon** Brieftaube *f;* **~ instinct** Heimfindevermögen *nt;* **~ device** Zielsucheinrichtung *f.*

homoeopath, *(US)* **homeopath** ['həʊmɪəʊpæθ] *n* Homöopath(in *f*) *m.*

homoeopathy, *(US)* **homeopathy** [ˌhəʊmɪ'ɒpəθɪ] *n* Homöopathie *f.*

homogeneous [ˌhɒmə'dʒiːnɪəs] *adj* homogen.

homogenize [hə'mɒdʒənaɪz] *vt* homogenisieren.

homosexual [ˌhɒməʊ'seksjʊəl] **1** *adj* homosexuell. **2** *n* Homosexuelle(r) *mf.*

homosexuality [ˌhɒməʊseksjʊ'ælɪtɪ] *n* Homosexualität *f.*

honest ['ɒnɪst] *adj* ehrlich; *business, action also* anständig; *truth* rein. **he made an ~ woman of her** *(col)* er machte sie zu seiner Frau.

honestly ['ɒnɪstlɪ] *adv* ehrlich. **~!** *(in exasperation)* also ehrlich!

honesty ['ɒnɪstɪ] *n* Ehrlichkeit *f.* **in all ~** ganz ehrlich; **~ is the best policy** *(Prov)* ehrlich währt am längsten *(Prov).*

honey ['hʌnɪ] *n* Honig *m; (col)* Schätzchen *nt.*

honeycomb ['hʌnɪkəʊm] **1** *n* (Bienen)wabe *f.* **2** *vt usu pass* durchlöchern.

honeymoon ['hʌnɪmuːn] *n* Flitterwochen *pl; (trip)* Hochzeitsreise *f.* **to be on one's ~** in den Flitterwochen/auf Hochzeitsreise sein.

honeysuckle ['hʌnɪˌsʌkl] *n* Geißblatt *nt.*

honk [hɒŋk] **1** *vi (car)* hupen; *(geese)* schreien. **2** *vt horn* drücken auf *(+acc).*

honky ['hɒŋkɪ] *n (negro pej sl)* Weiße(r) *mf.*

honorary ['ɒnərərɪ] *adj secretary* ehrenamtlich; *member, president* Ehren-. **~ degree** *ehrenhalber verliehener akademischer Grad.*

honour, *(US)* **honor** ['ɒnə[r]] **1** *n* **(a)** Ehre *f.* **he made it a point of ~** er betrachtete es als Ehrensache; **you're on your ~** Sie haben Ihr Ehrenwort gegeben; **to put sb on his ~** jdm vertrauen; **man of ~** Ehrenmann *m;* **to be an ~ to sth** einer Sache *(dat)* Ehre machen; **in ~ of sb/sth** zu Ehren von jdm/etw; *(of dead person, past thing)* in ehrendem Andenken an jdn/etw; **he is ~ bound to do it** es ist Ehrensache für ihn, das zu tun; **to do the ~s** *(col)* die Honneurs machen. **(b)** *(title)* **Your H~**

Hohes Gericht; **His H~** das Gericht. **(c)** *(distinction, award)* **~s** Auszeichnung(en *pl*) *f*; *(Univ: also* **~s degree***) akademischer Grad mit Prüfung im Spezialfach.*

2 *vt* **(a)** *person* ehren. **to ~ sb with a title** jdm einen Titel verleihen; **I should be ~ed if you ...** ich würde mich geehrt fühlen, wenn Sie ...; **he ~ed us with his presence** *(also iro)* er beehrte uns mit seiner Gegenwart. **(b)** *cheque* annehmen; *obligation* nachkommen *(+dat)*; *commitment* stehen zu.

honourable, (US) honorable ['ɒnərəbl] *adj* ehrenhaft; *peace, discharge* ehrenvoll. **to receive ~ mention** lobend erwähnt werden; **the H~ member** *(Parl)* Herr/Frau X.

hood [hʊd] *n* **(a)** Kapuze *f*; *(Aut: roof)* Verdeck *nt*; *(US Aut)* (Motor)haube *f*; *(on cooker)* Abzugshaube *f*. **(b)** *(esp US col)* Gangster *m (col)*.

hoodlum ['hu:dləm] *n* Rowdy *m*; *(member of gang)* Gangster *m (col)*.

hoodwink ['hʊdwɪŋk] *vt (col)* (he)reinlegen *(col)*.

hoof [hu:f] *n*, *pl* **-s** *or* **hooves** Huf *m*.

hook [hʊk] **1** *n* Haken *m (also Boxing)*. **he swallowed the story ~, line and sinker** er hat die Geschichte tatsächlich ganz geschluckt *(col)*; **by ~ or by crook** auf Biegen und Brechen; **to get sb off the ~** *(col)* jdn herausreißen *(col)*; **that lets me off the ~** *(col)* damit bin ich aus dem Schneider *(col)*; **to leave the phone off the ~** nicht auflegen. **2** *vt* **(a) he ~ed the door back** er hakte die Tür fest; **to ~ a trailer to a car** einen Anhänger an ein Auto hängen. **(b)** *fish* an die Angel bekommen; *husband* sich *(dat)* angeln. **(c) to be/get ~ed (on sth)** *(on drugs)* (von etw) abhängig sein/werden; *(on food, place)* auf etw *(acc)* stehen *(col)*; **he's ~ed on the idea** er ist von der Idee besessen.

♦ **hook on 1** *vi* (an)gehakt werden *(to* an *+acc)*; *(with tow-bar)* angekoppelt werden *(to* an *+acc)*. **2** *vt sep* **to ~ sth ~ to sth** *(with tow-bar)* etw an etw *(acc)* (an)koppeln.

♦ **hook up 1** *vi (Rad, TV)* **to ~ ~ with sb** sich jdm anschließen. **2** *vt sep dress etc* zuhaken; *(Rad, TV)* anschließen *(with* an *+acc)*; *trailer* anhängen.

hook and eye *n* Haken und Öse *no art, pl vb.*

hooked nose ['hʊkt' nəʊz] *n* Hakennase *f*.

hooker ['hʊkə^r] *n (esp US col)* Nutte *f (col!)*.

hooligan ['hu:lɪgən] *n* Rowdy *m*.

hooliganism ['hu:lɪgənɪzəm] *n* Rowdytum *nt*.

hoop [hu:p] *n* Reifen *m*; *(on animal)* Ring *m*. **to put sb through the ~s** *(fig col)* jdn durch die Mangel drehen *(col)*.

hoot [hu:t] **1** *n* **(a)** *(of owl)* Ruf *m*. **~s of laughter** johlendes Gelächter; **I don't care two ~s** *(col)* das ist mir völlig schnuppe *(col)*; **to be a ~** *(col) (person, event etc)* zum Schießen sein *(col)*. **(b)** *(Aut)* Hupen *nt no pl*; *(of train, hooter)* Pfeifen *nt no pl*. **2** *vi* **(a)** *(owl)* schreien. **(b)** *(Aut)* hupen; *(train, factory hooter)* pfeifen.

hooter ['hu:tə^r] *n* **(a)** *(Brit Aut)* Hupe *f*; *(at factory)* Sirene *f*. **(b)** *(Brit col: nose)* Zinken *m (col)*.

hoover ® ['hu:və^r] *(Brit)* **1** *n* Staubsauger *m*. **2** *vti* (staub)saugen.

hooves [hu:vz] *pl of* **hoof.**

hop[1] [hɒp] **1** *n* **(a)** (kleiner) Sprung; *(of person, bird also)* Hüpfer *m*; *(of rabbit also)* Satz *m*. **to catch sb on the ~** *(fig col)* jdn überraschen; **to keep sb on the ~** *(fig col)* jdn in Trab halten. **(b)** *(col: dance)* Tanz *m*. **(c)** *(Aviat col)* Sprung *m*. **a short ~** ein Katzensprung *m (col)*. **2** *vi (animal)* hüpfen. **~ in, said the driver** steigen Sie ein, sagte der Fahrer; **~ it!** *(col)* zieh Leine *(col)*.

hop[2] *n (Bot)* Hopfen *m*.

hope [həʊp] **1** *n* Hoffnung *f*. **past** *or* **beyond all ~** hoffnungslos; **the patient is beyond all ~** für den Patienten besteht keine Hoffnung mehr; **to have ~s of doing sth** hoffen, etw zu tun; **well, we live in ~** nun, wir hoffen eben (weiter); **there's no ~ of that** da braucht man sich gar keine Hoffnungen zu machen; **to lose ~ of doing sth** die Hoffnung aufgeben, etw zu tun; **what a ~!** *(col)*, **some ~(s)!** *(col)* schön wär's! *(col)*.

2 *vi* hoffen *(for* auf *+acc)*. **to ~ for the best** das Beste hoffen; **I ~ so/not** hoffentlich/hoffentlich nicht; **to ~ against hope that ...** trotz allem die Hoffnung nicht aufgeben, daß ...

3 *vt* hoffen. **I ~ to see you** hoffentlich sehe ich Sie; **hoping to hear from you** ich hoffe, von Ihnen zu hören.

hopeful ['həʊpfʊl] **1** *adj* hoffnungsvoll; *situation, sign* vielversprechend. **they weren't very ~** sie hatten keine große Hoffnung; **to be ~ that ...** hoffen, daß ...; **you're ~!** du bist vielleicht ein Optimist! *(col)*. **2** *n (col)* **a young ~** *(hopes to succeed)* ein hoffnungsvoller junger Mensch.

hopefully ['həʊpfəlɪ] *adv* **(a)** hoffnungsvoll. **(b) ~ it won't rain** hoffentlich regnet es nicht.

hopeless ['həʊplɪs] *adj situation, outlook* hoffnungslos; *liar, drunkard etc* unverbesserlich; *weather, food* unmöglich *(col)*. **it's ~ even to try** es hat gar keinen Wert, es überhaupt zu versuchen; **you're ~** du bist ein hoffnungsloser Fall; **he's ~ at maths** in Mathematik ist er ein hoffnungsloser Fall.

hopelessly ['həʊplɪslɪ] *adv* hoffnungslos. **we were ~ lost** wir hatten uns ganz und gar verirrt.

hopper ['hɒpə^r] *n (Tech)* Einfülltrichter *m*.

hopping mad ['hɒpɪŋ'mæd] *adj (col)* fuchsteufelswild *(col)*.

hop: ~scotch *n* Himmel-und-Hölle(-Spiel) *nt*; **~, step and jump** *n* Dreisprung *m*.

horde [hɔ:d] *n (of animals, children)* Horde *f*.

horizon [hə'raɪzn] *n (lit, fig)* Horizont *m*. **on the ~** am Horizont.

horizontal [ˌhɒrɪ'zɒntl] *adj* horizontal.

hormone ['hɔ:məʊn] *n* Hormon *nt*.

horn [hɔ:n] *n (of cattle, Mus)* Horn *nt*; *(Aut)* Hupe *f*; *(Naut)* (Signal)horn *nt*; *(of snail, insect)* Fühler *m*. **~s** *pl (of deer)* Geweih *nt*; **to sound the ~** *(Aut)* hupen; *(Naut)* das Horn ertönen lassen; **to draw in one's ~s** *(fig: spend less)* den Gürtel enger schnallen.

hornet ['hɔ:nɪt] *n* Hornisse *f*.

horn-rimmed ['hɔ:n'rɪmd] *adj spectacles* Horn-.

horny ['hɔ:nɪ] *adj (+er) hands etc* schwielig; *(col: randy)* geil *(col)*.

horoscope ['hɒrəskəʊp] *n* Horoskop *nt*.

horrendous [hɒ'rendəs] *adj crime* abscheulich; *prices* horrend.

horrible ['hɒrɪbl] *adj* schrecklich. **don't be ~** sei nicht so gemein *(col)*.

horribly ['hɒrɪblɪ] *adv* schrecklich.

horrid ['hɒrɪd] *adj* entsetzlich, schrecklich.

horrific [hɒ'rɪfɪk] *adj* entsetzlich; *documentary* erschreckend.

horrify ['hɒrɪfaɪ] *vt* entsetzen.

horrifying ['hɒrɪfaɪɪŋ] *adj* schrecklich, entsetzlich.

horror ['hɒrə^r] **1** *n* Entsetzen *nt*; *(strong dislike)* Horror *m (of* vor *+dat)*; *(of war etc)* Greuel *m*. **she shrank back in ~** sie fuhr entsetzt zurück; **to be a real ~** *(col)* furchtbar sein *(col)*; **you little ~!** *(col)* du kleines Ungeheuer! *(col)*. **2** *attr comics, films* Horror-.

horror-stricken ['hɒrəstrɪkn], **horror-struck** ['hɒrəstrʌk] *adj* von Entsetzen gepackt.

hors d'oeuvre [ɔ:'dɜ:v] *n* Vorspeise *f*.

horse [hɔ:s] *n* Pferd *(also Gymnastics)*, Roß *(liter, pej) nt*. **wild ~s would not drag me there** keine zehn Pferde würden mich dahin bringen; **I could eat a ~** ich könnte ein ganzes Pferd essen; **information straight from the ~'s mouth** Informationen aus erster Hand.

horse: ~back: on ~back *adv* zu Pferd; **~-box** *n* Pferdetransporter *m*; **~ chestnut** *n* Roßkastanie *f*; **~hair** *n* Roßhaar *nt*; **~man** *n* Reiter *m*; **~man-**

ship *n* Reitkunst *f*; **~play** *n* Balgerei *f*; **~power** *n* Pferdestärke *f*; **~-racing** *n (races)* Pferderennen *pl*; **~radish** *n* Meerrettich *m*; **~shoe** *n* Hufeisen *nt*; **~-trading** *n (fig)* Kuhhandel *m*; **~whip** *vt* auspeitschen; **~woman** *n* Reiterin *f*.
hors(e)y ['hɔːsɪ] *adj (+er) (col) (fond of horses)* pferdenärrisch; *appearance* pferdeähnlich.
horticultural [ˌhɔːtɪ'kʌltʃərəl] *adj* Garten(bau)-.
horticulture ['hɔːtɪkʌltʃəʳ] *n* Gartenbau *m*.
hose[1] [həʊz] **1** *n (also* **~pipe***)* Schlauch *m*. **2** *vt (also* **~ down***)* abspritzen.
hose[2] *n no pl (Comm: stockings)* Strumpfwaren *pl*.
hosiery ['həʊʒərɪ] *n* Strumpfwaren *pl*.
hospice ['hɒspɪs] *n* Hospiz *nt*.
hospitable [hɒs'pɪtəbl] *adj* gastfreundlich.
hospital ['hɒspɪtl] *n* Krankenhaus *nt*, Klinik *f*. **in** *or (US)* **in the ~** im Krankenhaus; **he's got to go to** *or (US)* **to the ~** er muß ins Krankenhaus (gehen).
hospitality [ˌhɒspɪ'tælɪtɪ] *n* Gastfreundschaft *f*.
hospitalize ['hɒspɪtəlaɪz] *vt* ins Krankenhaus einweisen.
host[1] [həʊst] **1** *n* Gastgeber *m*; *(in own home also)* Hausherr *m*. **2** *vt TV programme, games* Gastgeber sein bei.
host[2] *n* Menge *f*. **for a whole ~ of reasons** aus einer ganzen Reihe von Gründen.
hostage ['hɒstɪdʒ] *n* Geisel *f*.
hostel ['hɒstəl] *n* (Wohn)heim *nt*.
hostess ['həʊstes] *n* Gastgeberin *f*; *(in own home also)* Hausherrin *f*; *(in night-club)* Hosteß *f*; *(air-~)* Stewardeß *f*.
hostile ['hɒstaɪl] *adj* feindlich; *person also* feindlich gesinnt; *reception, looks* feindselig. **to be ~ to sb** sich jdm gegenüber feindselig verhalten; **don't be so ~** seien sie nicht so aggressiv!
hostility [hɒs'tɪlɪtɪ] *n* Feindseligkeit *f*; *(between people)* Feindschaft *f*. **hostilities** *pl (warfare)* Feindseligkeiten *pl*.
hot [hɒt] *adj (+er)* **(a)** heiß; *meal, tap* warm; *curry* scharf. **I am** *or* **feel ~** mir ist (es) heiß. **(b)** *(col: good, competent)* stark *(col)*; *person also* fähig. **he's ~ at German** er ist gut in Deutsch; **he/it isn't (all) that ~** so umwerfend ist er/das auch wieder nicht *(col)*; **I'm not feeling too ~** mir geht's nicht besonders *(col)*. **(c)** *(fig)* **~ favourite** der große Favorit; **~ news** das Neueste vom Neuen; **the pace was so ~** das Tempo war so scharf; **to get into ~ water** in Teufels Küche kommen *(col)*; **to be all ~ and bothered** *(col)* ganz aufgeregt sein *(about* wegen*)*; **to be in ~ pursuit of sb** jdm nacheilen; **it's getting too ~ for him here** hier wird ihm der Boden unter den Füßen zu heiß. **(d)** *(col: stolen)* heiß *(col)*.
♦**hot up** *vi (col) (pace)* schneller werden; *(situation)* zuspitzen; *(party)* in Schwung kommen.
hot: ~ air *n (fig)* leeres Gerede; **~bed** *n (fig)* Nährboden *m (of* für*)*; **~-blooded** *adj* heißblütig.
hotchpotch ['hɒtʃpɒtʃ] *n* Mischmasch *m*.
hot dog *n* Hot dog *m*.
hotel [həʊ'tel] *n* Hotel *nt*.
hotelier [həʊ'telɪəʳ] *n* Hotelier *m*.
hot: ~foot *adv* eilig; **~head** *n* Hitzkopf *m*; **~headed** *adj* hitzköpfig; **~house** *n (lit, fig)* Treibhaus *nt*; **~ line** *n (Pol)* heißer Draht.
hotly ['hɒtlɪ] *adv contested* heiß.
hot: ~plate *n* Kochplatte *f*; *(plate-warmer)* Warmhalteplatte *f*; **~pot** *n (esp Brit)* Fleischeintopf *m* mit Kartoffeleinlage; **~ potato** *n (fig col)* heißes Eisen; **~rod** *n (Aut)* hoch frisiertes Auto; **~ seat** *n* **to be in the ~ seat** auf dem Schleudersitz sein; **~ stuff** *n (col)* **it's/he's ~ stuff** das/er ist große Klasse *(col)*; **~-tempered** *adj* jähzornig; **~-water bottle** *n* Wärmflasche *f*.
hound [haʊnd] **1** *n (Hunt)* (Jagd)hund *m*; *(any dog)* Hund *m*. **the ~s** die Meute. **2** *vt* hetzen.
♦**hound down** *vt sep* Jagd machen auf *(+acc)*; *(criminal also)* zur Strecke bringen.
♦**hound out** *vt sep* vertreiben *(of* aus*)*.
hour ['aʊəʳ] *n* Stunde *f*. **~ by ~** mit jeder Stunde; **on the ~** zur vollen Stunde; **every ~ on the ~** jede volle Stunde; **at an early/a late ~** früh/spät; **at all ~s (of the day and night)** zu jeder (Tages- und Nacht)zeit; **to drive at 80 kilometres an ~** 80 Stundenkilometer fahren; **to be paid by the ~** stundenweise bezahlt werden; **for ~s** stundenlang; **he took ~s to do it** er brauchte stundenlang dazu; **~s** *pl (of banks, shops etc)* Geschäftszeit(en *pl*) *f*; **after ~s** *(in pubs)* nach der Polizeistunde; *(in office etc)* nach Dienstschluß; **the man of the ~** der Mann der Stunde.
hour: ~ glass *n* Sanduhr *f*; **~ hand** *n* kleiner Zeiger.
hourly ['aʊəlɪ] *adj, adv* stündlich.
house [haʊs] **1** *n, pl* **houses** ['haʊzɪz] **(a)** Haus *nt*. **at my ~** bei mir (zu Hause); **to my ~** zu mir (nach Hause); **to set up ~** einen eigenen Hausstand gründen; *(in particular area)* sich niederlassen; **to put one's ~ in order** *(fig)* seine Angelegenheiten in Ordnung bringen; **he's getting on like a ~ on fire** *(col)* er kommt prima voran *(col)*; **they get on like a ~ on fire** *(col)* sie kommen ausgezeichnet miteinander aus; **as safe as ~s** *(Brit)* bombensicher *(col)*; **on the ~** auf Kosten des Hauses; *(on the company)* auf Kosten der Firma; **he brought the ~ down** *(col)* er riß alle von den Sitzen *(col)*; **full ~** *(Cards)* Full House *nt*. **(b)** *(Pol)* **the upper/lower ~** das Ober-/Unterhaus; **H~ of Commons/Lords** *(Brit)* (britisches) Unter-/Oberhaus; **H~ of Representatives** *(US)* Repräsentantenhaus *nt*; **the H~s of Parliament** das Parlament(sgebäude).
2 [haʊz] *vt people, goods* unterbringen.
house *in cpds* Haus-; **~ arrest** *n* Hausarrest *m*; **~boat** *n* Hausboot *nt*; **~bound** *adj* ans Haus gefesselt; **~breaker** *n* Einbrecher *m*; **~coat** *n* Morgenmantel *m*; **~guest** *n* (Haus)gast *m*.
household ['haʊshəʊld] *n* Haushalt *m*. **~ name** *or* **word** Begriff *m*.
householder ['haʊsˌhəʊldəʳ] *n* Haus-/Wohnungsinhaber(in *f*) *m*.
house: ~-hunting *n* Haussuche *f*; **~keeper** *n* Haushälterin *f*; **~keeping** *n* Haushalten *nt*; *(also* **~keeping money***)* Haushaltsgeld *nt*; **~man** *n (Brit)* Assistenzarzt *m*; **~-proud** *adj* **she is ~-proud** sie ist eine penible Hausfrau; **~room** *n* **I wouldn't give it ~room** *(col)* das wollte ich nicht geschenkt haben; **~-to-~** *adj collection* Haus-; **a ~-to-~ search** eine Suche von Haus zu Haus; **~-trained** *adj* stubenrein; **~ warming (party)** *n* Einzugsparty *f*; **~wife** *n* Hausfrau *f*; **~wifely** *adj* hausfraulich; **~work** *n* Hausarbeit *f*.
housing ['haʊzɪŋ] *n* **(a)** *(act)* Unterbringung *f*. **(b)** *(houses)* Wohnungen *pl*; *(temporary)* Unterkunft *f*. **(c)** *(building of houses)* Wohnungsbau *m*. **(d)** *(Tech)* Gehäuse *nt*.
housing *in cpds* Wohnungs-; **~ conditions** *npl* Wohnbedingungen *pl*; **~ estate** *n (Brit)* Wohnsiedlung *f*.
hove [həʊv] *pret, ptp of* **heave** *(Naut)*.
hovel ['hɒvəl] *n* armselige Hütte; *(fig pej)* Bruchbude *f (col)*.
hover ['hɒvəʳ] *vi* schweben; *(stand around)* herumstehen. **a smile ~ed on her lips** ein Lächeln lag auf ihren Lippen; **he ~ed between two alternatives** er schwankte zwischen zwei Möglichkeiten.
♦**hover about** *or* **around** *vi (persons)* herumlungern; *(helicopter etc)* (in der Luft) kreisen.
hover: ~craft *n* Luftkissenboot, Hovercraft *nt*; **~port** *n* Anlegestelle *f* für Hovercrafts.
how [haʊ] *adv* **(a)** wie. **~'s that?, ~ come?** *(col)* wie kommt (denn) das?; **~ is it that ...?** wie kommt es, daß ...?; **~ do you know that?** woher wissen Sie das?; **~ much** wieviel; **I know ~ much he**

loves her ich weiß wie sehr er sie liebt; ~ **many** wie viele; ~ **do you do?** Guten Tag/Abend!, angenehm! *(form)*; ~ **are you?** wie geht es Ihnen?; ~**'s work?** was macht die Arbeit? *(col)*; ~ **are things at school?** wie geht's in der Schule? ~ **about ...** wie wäre es mit ...; ~ **about it?** wie wäre es damit? **(b) and** ~! und ob!; ~ **he's grown!** er ist aber groß geworden; ~ **strange!** seltsam!; ~ **kind of him!** wie nett von ihm! **(c)** *(that)* daß. **she told me** ~ **she had seen him there** sie sagte mir, daß sie ihn dort gesehen hat.

however [haʊ'evəʳ] **1** *conj* jedoch, aber. **2** *adv* ~ **strong he is** wie stark er auch ist; ~ **you do it** wie du es auch machst; **do it** ~ **you like** mach's, wie du willst; ~ **much you cry** und wenn du noch so weinst; ~ **did you manage it?** wie hast du das bloß geschafft?

howl [haʊl] **1** *n* Schrei *m*; *(of animal, wind)* Heulen *nt no pl.* ~**s of protest** Protestgeschrei *nt*. **2** *vi* brüllen; *(animal)* jaulen; *(wind)* heulen. **to** ~ **with laughter** in brüllendes Gelächter ausbrechen.

♦ **howl down** *vt sep* niederbrüllen.

howler ['haʊləʳ] *n (col)* Hammer *m (col)*.

HP, hp = **(a) hire purchase. (b) horse power** ≃ PS.

HQ = **headquarters.**

hub [hʌb] *n* (Rad)nabe *f*; *(fig)* Zentrum *nt*.

hubbub ['hʌbʌb] *n* Tumult *m*.

hubcap ['hʌbkæp] *n* Radkappe *f*.

huddle ['hʌdl] **1** *n (of people)* Gruppe *f*. **in a** ~ dicht zusammengedrängt; **to go into a** ~ *(col)* die Köpfe zusammenstecken. **2** *vi* (sich) kauern.

♦ **huddle together** *vi* sich aneinanderkauern. **to be** ~**d** ~ aneinanderkauern.

♦ **huddle up** *vi* sich zusammenkauern. **to be** ~**d** ~ zusammenkauern.

hue[1] [hju:] *n* Farbe *f*; *(shade, fig)* Schattierung *f*.

hue[2] *n*: ~ **and cry** Zeter und Mordio *nt*.

huff [hʌf] *n* **to be in a** ~ eingeschnappt sein *(col)*; **to go into a** ~ einschnappen *(col)*.

hug [hʌg] **1** *n* Umarmung *f*. **2** *vt* umarmen; *coast etc* sich dicht halten an *(+acc)*.

huge [hju:dʒ] *adj (+er)* riesig.

hulk [hʌlk] *n (col: person)* Klotz *m (col)*.

hulking ['hʌlkɪŋ] *adj*: ~ **great** massig; **a** ~ **great wardrobe** ein Ungetüm *nt* von einem Kleiderschrank.

hull [hʌl] *n (Naut)* Schiffskörper *m*.

hullabaloo [ˌhʌləbə'lu:] *n (col: noise)* Radau *m*.

hullo [hʌ'ləʊ] *interj* = **hello.**

hum [hʌm] **1** *n see vi (a)* Summen *nt*; Surren *nt*; *(of voices)* Gemurmel *nt*. **2** *vi* **(a)** *(insect, person)* summen; *(small machine, camera etc)* surren. **HQ was** ~**ming with activity** im Hauptquartier ging es zu wie in einem Bienenstock; **to** ~ **and haw** *(col)* herumdrucksen *(col) (over, about* um*)*. **(b)** *(col: smell)* stinken *(col)*. **3** *vt tune* summen.

human ['hju:mən] **1** *adj* menschlich. **I'm only** ~ ich bin auch nur ein Mensch; ~ **nature** die menschliche Natur. **2** *n (also* ~ **being***)* Mensch *m*.

humane [hju:'meɪn] *adj* human, menschlich. ~ **killer** Mittel *nt* zum schmerzlosen Töten.

humanism ['hju:mənɪzəm] *n* Humanismus *m*.

humanist ['hju:mənɪst] **1** *n* Humanist *m*. **2** *adj* humanistisch.

humanitarian [hju:ˌmænɪ'tɛərɪən] *adj* humanitär.

humanity [hju:'mænɪtɪ] *n* **(a)** *(mankind)* die Menschheit. **(b)** *(humaneness)* Menschlichkeit *f*. **(c) humanities** *pl* Geisteswissenschaften *pl*; *(Latin and Greek)* Altphilologie *f*.

humanly ['hju:mənlɪ] *adv* menschlich. **to do all that is** ~ **possible** alles menschenmögliche tun.

humble ['hʌmbl] **1** *adj (+er) (unassuming)* bescheiden; *(meek, Rel)* demütig. **in my** ~ **opinion** meiner bescheidenen Meinung nach; **to eat** ~ **pie** klein beigeben. **2** *vt* demütigen.

humbug ['hʌmbʌg] *n* **(a)** *(col)* Humbug *m*. **(b)** *(Brit: sweet)* Pfefferminzbonbon *nt*.

humdinger ['hʌmdɪŋəʳ] *n (col: person, thing)* **to be a** ~ Spitze sein *(col)*.

humdrum ['hʌmdrʌm] *adj* stumpfsinnig.

humid ['hju:mɪd] *adj* feucht.

humidifier [hju:'mɪdɪfaɪəʳ] *n* Luftbefeuchter *m*.

humidity [hju:'mɪdɪtɪ] *n* (Luft)feuchtigkeit *f*.

humiliate [hju:'mɪlɪeɪt] *vt see n* demütigen; beschämen.

humiliation [hju:ˌmɪlɪ'eɪʃən] *n* Demütigung *f*; *(because of one's own actions)* Beschämung *f no pl.*

humility [hju:'mɪlɪtɪ] *n* Demut *f*; *(unassumingness)* Bescheidenheit *f*.

hummingbird ['hʌmɪŋˌbɜ:d] *n* Kolibri *m*.

humorist ['hju:mərɪst] *n* Humorist(in *f*) *m*.

humorous ['hju:mərəs] *adj person* humorvoll; *story etc also, situation* lustig; *idea* witzig.

humour, *(US)* **humor** ['hju:məʳ] **1** *n* **(a)** Humor *m*. **a sense of** ~ (Sinn *m* für) Humor *m*; **a story full of** ~ eine humorvolle Geschichte. **(b)** *(mood)* Stimmung, Laune *f*. **to be in a good** ~ in guter Stimmung sein; **he took it with good** ~ er nahm es gelassen auf. **2** *vt whims* nachgeben *(+dat)*. **to** ~ **sb** jdm seinen Willen lassen.

humourless, *(US)* **humorless** ['hju:məlɪs] *adj* humorlos, ohne jeden Humor.

hump [hʌmp] **1** *n* **(a)** *(Anat)* Buckel *m*; *(of camel)* Höcker *m*. **(b)** *(hillock)* Hügel, Buckel *(esp S Ger) m*. **(c)** *(Brit col)* **he's got the** ~ er ist sauer *(col)*. **2** *vt (col: carry)* schleppen.

humpbacked ['hʌmpˌbækt] *adj person* buck(e)lig; *(Brit) bridge* gewölbt.

hunch [hʌntʃ] **1** *n (feeling)* Gefühl *nt*, Ahnung *f*. **to have a** ~ **that ...** das (leise) Gefühl haben, daß ... **2** *vt (also* ~ **up***) back* krümmen; *shoulders* hochziehen. **he was** ~**ed (up) over his desk** er saß über seinen Schreibtisch gebeugt.

hunchback ['hʌntʃˌbæk] *n (person)* Buck(e)lige(r) *mf*; *(back)* Buckel *m*.

hundred ['hʌndrɪd] **1** *adj* hundert. **a** *or* **one** ~ **years** (ein)hundert Jahre; **two** ~ **years** zweihundert Jahre; **a** *or* **one** ~ **and one** (ein)hundert(und)eins; **not a** ~ **per cent fit** nicht hundertprozentig fit. **2** *n* hundert *num*; *(written figure)* Hundert *f*. ~**s** *(lit, fig)* Hunderte *pl*; **one in a** ~ einer unter hundert; ~**s of times** *(fig)* hundertmal; **they came in their** ~**s** sie kamen zu Hunderten.

hundredth ['hʌndrɪdθ] **1** *adj (in series)* hundertste(r, s). **2** *n (fraction)* Hundertstel *nt*.

hundredweight ['hʌndrɪdweɪt] *n* Zentner *m*; *(Brit)* 50,8 kg; *(US)* 45,4 kg.

hung [hʌŋ] *pret, ptp of* **hang.**

Hungarian [hʌŋ'gɛərɪən] **1** *adj* ungarisch. **2** *n* **(a)** Ungar(in *f*) *m*. **(b)** *(language)* Ungarisch *nt*.

Hungary ['hʌŋgərɪ] *n* Ungarn *nt*.

hunger ['hʌŋgəʳ] *n (lit, fig)* Hunger *m (for* nach*)*. **to go on (a)** ~ **strike** in (den) Hungerstreik treten.

hungrily ['hʌŋgrɪlɪ] *adv (lit, fig)* hungrig.

hungry ['hʌŋgrɪ] *adj (+er) (lit, fig)* hungrig. **to be/get** ~ Hunger haben/bekommen; **to go** ~ hungern; ~ **for power** machthungrig.

hunk [hʌŋk] *n* Stück *nt*. **a gorgeous** ~ **(of a man)** *(col)* ein *Mann*! *(col)*.

hunky-dory ['hʌŋkɪ'dɔ:rɪ] *adj (col)* **that's** ~ das ist prima *(col)*.

hunt [hʌnt] **1** *n* Jagd *f*; *(fig: search)* Suche *f*. **to have a** ~ **for sth** nach etw fahnden *(col)*. **2** *vt* jagen; *criminal also* fahnden nach; *missing article, person* suchen. **3** *vi* **(a)** jagen. **to go** ~**ing** jagen, auf die Jagd gehen. **(b)** *(search)* suchen *(for* nach*)*.

♦ **hunt down** *vt sep* (unerbittlich) Jagd machen auf *(+acc)*; *(capture)* zur Strecke bringen.

♦ **hunt out** *vt sep sth* hervorkramen *(col)*.

♦ **hunt up** *vt sep history, origins* forschen nach.

hunter ['hʌntəʳ] *n* Jäger *m*; *(horse)* Jagdpferd *nt*.

hunting ['hʌntɪŋ] *n* die Jagd. **to go** ~ auf die Jagd gehen.

huntsman ['hʌntsmən] *n, pl* **-men** [-mən] Jagdreiter *m*.

hurdle ['hɜːdl] *(Sport, fig)* Hürde *f.* ~**s** *sing (race)* Hürdenlauf *m.*
hurdler ['hɜːdləʳ] *n (Sport)* Hürdenlätufer(in *f*) *m.*
hurl [hɜːl] *vt* schleudern. **to ~ oneself at sb** sich auf jdn stürzen; **to ~ abuse at sb** jdn wüst beschimpfen *(col).*
hurly-burly ['hɜːlɪ'bɜːlɪ] *n* Rummel *m (col).*
hurrah [hʊ'rɑː], **hurray** [hʊ'reɪ] *interj* hurra.
hurricane ['hʌrɪkən] *n* Orkan *m; (tropical)* Wirbelsturm *m.* ~ **lamp** Sturmlaterne *f.*
hurried ['hʌrɪd] *adj* eilig; *letter, essay* hastig geschrieben; *work* in Eile gemacht.
hurry ['hʌrɪ] **1** *n* Eile *f.* **in my ~ to get it finished ...** vor lauter Eile, damit fertig zu werden ...; **to do sth in a ~** etw hastig tun; **I need it in a ~** ich brauche es dringend; **to be in a ~** es eilig haben; **I won't do that again in a ~!** *(col)* das mache ich so schnell nicht wieder!; **what's the ~?** warum so eilig?; **is there any ~ for it?** eilt das?; **there's no ~** es eilt nicht.
2 *vi* sich beeilen; *(run/go quickly)* laufen. **there's nc need to ~** kein Grund zur Eile; **can't you make her ~?** kannst du sie nicht zur Eile antreiben?; **don't ~!** immer mit der Ruhe!; **I must ~ back** ich muß schnell zu rück.
3 *vt work etc* schneller machen; *(do too quickly)* überstürzen. **troops were hurried to the spot** es wurden schleunigst Truppen dorthin gebracht; **don't ~ me** hetz mich nicht so!; **don't ~ your meal** lassen Sie sich Zeit beim Essen!
♦ **hurry along 1** *vi* sich beeilen. **to ~ ~ the road** die Straße entlanglaufen. **2** *vt sep person* weiterdrängen; *(with work etc)* zur Eile antreiben; *things, work etc* vorantreiben.
♦ **hurry away** *or* **off 1** *vi* schnell weggehen. **2** *vt sep* schnell wegbringen.
♦ **hurry on** *vi* weiterlaufen.
♦ **hurry up 1** *vi* sich beeilen. **~ ~!** beeil dich! **2** *vt sep* zur Eile antreiben; *work* vorantreiben.
hurt [hɜːt] *(vb: pret, ptp ~)* **1** *vt* **(a)** *(lit, fig)* weh tun *(+dat); (injure)* verletzen. **to ~ oneself** sich *(dat)* weh tun; **to ~ one's arm** sich *(dat)* am Arm weh tun; *(injure)* sich *(dat)* den Arm verletzen. **(b)** *(harm)* schaden *(+dat).* **it wouldn't ~ you to say sorry** du solltest dich wirklich entschuldigen; **it won't ~ him to wait** es schadet ihm nicht(s), wenn er etwas warten muß. **2** *vi* **(a)** *(be painful)* weh tun; *(fig also)* verletzend sein. **that ~s!** *(lit, fig)* das tut weh! **(b) but surely a little drink won't ~** aber ein kleines Gläschen kann doch wohl nicht schaden. **3** *adj limb, feelings* verletzt; *tone, look* gekränkt.
hurtful ['hɜːtfʊl] *adj* verletzend.
hurtle ['hɜːtl] *vi* rasen. **he came hurtling around the corner** er kam um die Ecke gerast.
husband ['hʌzbənd] *n* Ehemann *m.* **my/her ~** mein/ihr Mann.
hush [hʌʃ] **1** *n* Stille *f.* **2** *interj* pst!
♦ **hush up** *vt sep scandal* vertuschen.
hushed [hʌʃt] *adj voices* gedämpft; *words* leise.
hush-hush ['hʌʃ'hʌʃ] *adj (col)* streng geheim.
husk [hʌsk] *n* Schale *f; (of rice also)* Hülse *f.*
husky[1] ['hʌskɪ] *adj (+er)* rauh.
husky[2] *n (dog)* Schlittenhund *m.*
hustings ['hʌstɪŋz] *npl (Brit)* **on the ~** im Wahlkampf; *(at election meeting)* bei einer Wahlveranstaltung.
hustle ['hʌsl] **1** *n* **the ~ and bustle** das geschäftige Treiben. **2** *vt* **to ~ sb out of the building** jdn schnell aus einem Gebäude bringen; **to ~ things (along)** die Dinge vorantreiben. **3** *vi* **(a)** *(move busily)* hasten, eilen. **(b)** *(prostitute)* auf den Strich gehen *(col).* **to ~ for business** *(salesman etc)* Aufträgen nachjagen.
hut [hʌt] *n* Hütte *f; (Mil)* Baracke *f.*
hutch [hʌtʃ] *n* Verschlag *m.*
hyacinth ['haɪəsɪnθ] *n* Hyazinthe *f.*
hyaena, hyena [haɪ'iːnə] *n* Hyäne *f.*
hybrid ['haɪbrɪd] *n (Bot, Zool)* Kreuzung *f; (fig)* Mischform *f.*
hydrangea [haɪ'dreɪndʒə] *n* Hortensie *f.*
hydrant ['haɪdrənt] *n* Hydrant *m.*
hydraulic [haɪ'drɒlɪk] *adj* hydraulisch.
hydraulics [haɪ'drɒlɪks] *n sing* Hydraulik *f.*
hydro-: ['haɪdrəʊ-] ~**chloric acid** *n* Salzsäure *f;* ~**electric** *adj* hydroelektrisch; ~**electric power station** *n* Wasserkraftwerk *nt;* ~**foil** *n (boat)* Tragflächenboot *nt.*
hydrogen ['haɪdrɪdʒən] *n* Wasserstoff *m.* ~ **bomb** Wasserstoffbombe *f.*
hydrophobia [ˌhaɪdrə'fəʊbɪə] *n* Wasserscheu *f; (rabies)* Tollwut *f.*
hyena [haɪ'iːnə] *n* = **hyaena.**
hygiene ['haɪdʒiːn] *n* Hygiene *f.* **personal ~** Körperpflege *f.*
hygienic [haɪ'dʒiːnɪk] *adj* hygienisch.
hymn [hɪm] *n* Hymne *f.*
hymnbook ['hɪmbʊk] *n* Gesangbuch *nt.*
hyper- ['haɪpəʳ] *pref* Hyper-, hyper-, Über-, über-.
hyper-: ~**active** *adj* äußerst aktiv; ~**critical** *adj* übertrieben kritisch; ~**market** *n (Brit)* großer Supermarkt; ~**sensitive** *adj* überempfindlich; ~**tension** *n* Hypertonie *f,* erhöhter Blutdruck.
hyphen ['haɪfən] *n* Bindestrich *m; (at end of line)* Trenn(ungs)strich *m.*
hyphenate ['haɪfəneɪt] *vt* mit Bindestrich schreiben; *(insert hyphen)* trennen.
hypnosis [hɪp'nəʊsɪs] *n* Hypnose *f.*
hypnotic [hɪp'nɒtɪk] *adj* hypnotisch; *(hypnotizing, fig)* hypnotisierend.
hypnotism ['hɪpnətɪzəm] *n* Hypnotismus *m.*
hypnotist ['hɪpnətɪst] *n* Hypnotiseur *m,* Hypnotiseuse *f.*
hypnotize ['hɪpnətaɪz] *vt* hypnotisieren.
hypochondria [ˌhaɪpəʊ'kɒndrɪə] *n* Hypochondrie *f.*
hypochondriac [ˌhaɪpəʊ'kɒndrɪæk] *n* Hypochonder *m.*
hypocrisy [hɪ'pɒkrɪsɪ] *n* Heuchelei *f; (pretending innocence)* Scheinheiligkeit *f.*
hypocrite ['hɪpəkrɪt] *n* Heuchler(in *f*) *m.*
hypocritical [ˌhɪpə'krɪtɪkəl] *adj* heuchlerisch.
hypodermic (needle) [ˌhaɪpə'dɜːmɪk (niːdl)] *n* Spritze *f.*
hypotenuse [haɪ'pɒtɪnjuːz] *n* Hypotenuse *f.*
hypothermia [ˌhaɪpəʊ'θɜːmɪə] *n* Unterkühlung *f.*
hypothesis [haɪ'pɒθɪsɪs] *n, pl* **hypotheses** [haɪ'pɒθɪsiːz] Hypothese *f.*
hypothetical [ˌhaɪpəʊ'θetɪkəl] *adj* hypothetisch. **purely ~** reine Hypothese.
hysterectomy [ˌhɪstə'rektəmɪ] *n* Totaloperation *f.*
hysteria [hɪ'stɪərɪə] *n* Hysterie *f.*
hysterical [hɪ'sterɪkəl] *adj* hysterisch; *(col: very funny)* wahnsinnig komisch *(col).*
hysterics [hɪ'sterɪks] *npl* hysterischer Anfall. **to go into ~** *(col: laugh)* sich (halb) totlachen.

I

I, i [ai] *n* I, i *nt.*
I *pers pron* ich. **it is ~** *(form)* ich bin es.
Iberian [aɪ'bɪərɪən] *adj* **~ Peninsula** Iberische Halbinsel.
ice [aɪs] **1** *n* **(a)** Eis *nt*; *(on roads)* (Glatt)eis *nt*. **to be as cold as ~** eiskalt sein; **to keep** *or* **put sth on ~** *(lit)* etw kalt stellen; *(fig)* etw auf Eis legen; **to break the ~** *(fig)* das Eis brechen; **to be skating on thin ~** *(fig)* sich aufs Glatteis begeben; **to cut no ~ with sb** *(col)* auf jdn keinen Eindruck machen. **(b)** *(Brit: ice-cream)* (Speise)eis *nt.* **2** *vt cake* glasieren.
♦ **ice over** *vi* zufrieren; *(windscreen)* vereisen.
♦ **ice up** *vi (aircraft wings etc)* vereisen; *(pipes etc)* einfrieren.
ice *in cpds* Eis-; **~ age** *n* Eiszeit *f*; **~ axe** *(Brit) or* **~ ax** *(US) n* Eispickel *m*; **~berg** *n (lit, fig)* Eisberg *m*; **~bound** *adj port* zugefroren; *ship* vom Eis eingeschlossen; *road* vereist; **~box** *n (Brit: in refrigerator)* Eisfach *nt*; *(US)* Eisschrank *m*; *(insulated box)* Kühltasche *f*; **~breaker** *n* Eisbrecher *m*; **~ bucket** *n* Eiskühler *m*; **~cap** *n* Eiskappe *f*; **~-cold** *adj* eiskalt; **~-cream** *n* Eis *nt*; **~ cube** *n* Eiswürfel *m*; **~ hockey** *n* Eishockey *nt.*
Iceland ['aɪslənd] *n* Island *nt.*
Icelander ['aɪsləndə[r]] *n* Isländer(in *f*) *m.*
Icelandic [aɪs'lændɪk] **1** *adj* isländisch. **2** *n (language)* Isländisch *nt.*
ice: ~lolly *n (Brit)* Eis *nt* am Stiel; **~ pick** *n* Eispickel *m*; **~ rink** *n* Schlittschuhbahn *f*; **~-skate** *vi* Schlittschuh laufen; **~-skating** *n* Schlittschuhlaufen *nt.*
icicle ['aɪsɪkl] *n* Eiszapfen *m.*
icily ['aɪsɪlɪ] *adv (lit, fig)* eisig. **to look ~ at sb** jdm einen eisigen Blick zuwerfen.
icing ['aɪsɪŋ] *n (Cook)* Zuckerguß *m.* **~ sugar** *(Brit)* Puderzucker *m.*
icon ['aɪkɒn] *n* Ikone *f.*
iconoclastic [aɪˌkɒnə'klæstɪk] *adj* bilderstürmerisch.
icy ['aɪsɪ] *adj (+er) (lit, fig)* eisig; *road* vereist.
I'd [aɪd] = **I would; I had.**
id [ɪd] *n (Psych)* Es *nt.*
idea [aɪ'dɪə] *n* Idee *f.* **good ~!** gute Idee!; **that's not a bad ~** das ist keine schlechte Idee; **the very ~!** (nein), so was!; **the very ~ of eating horsemeat revolts me** der bloße Gedanke an Pferdefleisch ekelt mich; **the ~ never entered my head!** auf den Gedanken bin ich überhaupt nicht gekommen; **to hit upon the ~ of doing sth** den plötzlichen Einfall haben, etw zu tun; **that gives me an ~, we could ...** da fällt mir ein, wir könnten ...; **the ~ for the book** die Idee zu dem Buch; **he's somehow got the ~ into his head that ...** er bildet sich *(dat)* irgendwie ein, daß ...; **don't go getting ~s about promotion** machen Sie sich *(dat)* nur keine falschen Hoffnungen auf eine Beförderung; **to put ~s into sb's head** jdm einen Floh ins Ohr setzen; **what's the big ~?** *(col)* was soll das denn?; **that's the ~** genau (das ist's)!; **if that's your ~ of fun** wenn Sie das lustig finden; **he has some very strange ~s** er hat merkwürdige Vorstellungen; **his ~ of a pleasant evening is ...** seine Vorstellung von einem angenehmen Abend ist, ...; **you've no ~ how worried I've been** du kannst dir nicht vorstellen, welche Sorgen ich mir gemacht habe; **(I've) no ~** (ich habe) keine Ahnung; **I have an ~ that ...** ich habe so das Gefühl, daß ...; **could you give me an ~ of how long ...?** könnten Sie mir ungefähr sagen, wie lange ...?
ideal [aɪ'dɪəl] **1** *adj* ideal. **2** *n* Idealvorstellung *f*, Ideal *nt.*
idealism [aɪ'dɪəlɪzəm] *n* Idealismus *m.*
idealist [aɪ'dɪəlɪst] *n* Idealist(in *f*) *m.*
ideally [aɪ'dɪəlɪ] *adv* ideal. **they are ~ suited for each other** sie passen ausgezeichnet zueinander; **~, ...** idealerweise *or* im Idealfall ...
identical [aɪ'dentɪkəl] *adj (exactly alike)* identisch; *(same)* derselbe/dieselbe/dasselbe. **~ twins** eineiige Zwillinge *pl.*
identification [aɪˌdentɪfɪ'keɪʃən] *n* Identifizierung *f*; *(papers)* Ausweispapiere *pl.*
identify [aɪ'dentɪfaɪ] **1** *vt* **(a)** identifizieren; *plant, species etc* bestimmen; *(mark identity of)* kennzeichnen; *(recognize, pick)* erkennen *(by* an *+dat).* **(b)** *(consider as the same)* gleichsetzen *(with* mit*).* **2** *vr* **(a) to ~ oneself** sich ausweisen. **(b) to ~ oneself with sb/sth** sich mit jdm/etw identifizieren. **3** *vi (with film hero etc)* sich identifizieren *(with* mit*).*
identikit [aɪ'dentɪkɪt] *n*: **~ (picture)** Phantombild *nt.*
identity [aɪ'dentɪtɪ] *n* Identität *f.* **to prove one's ~** sich ausweisen.
identity: ~ card *n* (Personal)ausweis *m*; **~ parade** *n* Gegenüberstellung *f* (zur Identifikation des Täters).
ideological [ˌaɪdɪə'lɒdʒɪkəl] *adj* ideologisch.
ideology [ˌaɪdɪ'ɒlədʒɪ] *n* Weltanschauung, Ideologie *f.*
idiom ['ɪdɪəm] *n* idiomatische Wendung.
idiomatic [ˌɪdɪə'mætɪk] *adj* idiomatisch.
idiosyncrasy [ˌɪdɪə'sɪŋkrəsɪ] *n* Eigenheit, Eigenart *f.*
idiosyncratic [ˌɪdɪəsɪŋ'krætɪk] *adj* **he has a very ~ way of ...** er hat eine eigene Art zu ...
idiot ['ɪdɪət] *n* Idiot, Dummkopf *m.* **you (stupid) ~!** du Idiot!; **what an ~ I am/was!** ich Idiot!
idiotic [ˌɪdɪ'ɒtɪk] *adj* idiotisch. **don't be ~!** sei nicht so blöd!
idle ['aɪdl] **1** *adj* **(a)** *(not working) person* untätig. **the ~ rich** die reichen Müßiggänger; **in my ~ moments** in stillen Augenblicken; **~ life** faules Leben; **money lying ~** totes Kapital; **his car was lying ~ most of the time** sein Auto stand meistens unbenutzt herum. **(b)** *(lazy)* faul. **(c)** *(in industry) person* unbeschäftigt; *machine* außer Betrieb. **to be made ~** *(worker)* seine Arbeit einstellen müssen; **the whole factory stood ~** die ganze Fabrik hatte die Arbeit eingestellt; **the machine stood ~** die Maschine stand still. **(d)** *promise, words* leer; *(useless)* nutzlos. **~ curiosity** pure Neugier. **2** *vi (engine)* leerlaufen. **when the engine is idling** wenn der Motor im Leerlauf ist.
♦ **idle away** *vt sep one's time etc* vertrödeln.
idleness ['aɪdlnɪs] *n* **(a)** *(not working)* Untätigkeit *f*; *(pleasurable)* Muße *f.* **(b)** *(laziness)* Faulheit *f.*
idler ['aɪdlə[r]] *n (pej)* Faulenzer(in *f*) *m.*
idly ['aɪdlɪ] *adv* **(a)** *(without working)* untätig; *(pleasurably)* müßig. **to stand ~ by** untätig herumstehen. **(b)** *(lazily)* faul.

idol ['aɪdl] *n (lit)* Götzenbild *nt*; *(fig)* Idol *nt*.

idolize ['aɪdəlaɪz] *vt* vergöttern; *(star)* zum Idol machen.

I'd've ['aɪdəv] = **I would have.**

idyll ['ɪdɪl] *n* Idyll *nt*.

idyllic [ɪ'dɪlɪk] *adj* idyllisch.

i.e. *abbr* d.h.

if [ɪf] **1** *conj* wenn; *(in case also)* falls; *(whether, in indirect clause)* ob. **I would be pleased ~ you could do it** wenn Sie das tun könnten, wäre ich sehr froh; **(even) ~** auch wenn; **(even) ~ they are poor, at least they are happy** sie sind zwar arm, aber wenigstens glücklich; **~ only I had known!** wenn ich das nur gewußt hätte!; **I would like to see him, ~ only for a few hours** ich würde ihn gerne sehen, wenn auch nur für ein paar Stunden; **as ~** als ob; **he acts as ~ he were** *or* **was rich** er tut so, als ob er reich wäre; **~ necessary** falls nötig; **~ so** wenn ja; **~ not** wenn nicht; **~ I were you/him** wenn ich Sie/er wäre. **2** *n* **it's a big ~** das ist die große Frage; **~s and buts** Wenn und Aber *nt*.

igloo ['ɪglu:] *n* Iglu *m or nt*.

ignite [ɪg'naɪt] **1** *vt* entzünden. **2** *vi* sich entzünden.

ignition [ɪg'nɪʃən] *n* Entzünden *nt*; *(Aut)* Zündung *f*. **to switch on the ~** starten.

ignoble [ɪg'nəʊbl] *adj* unehrenhaft.

ignominious [,ɪgnə'mɪnɪəs] *adj* schmachvoll; *behaviour* schändlich.

ignominy ['ɪgnəmɪnɪ] *n* Schmach, Schande *f*.

ignoramus [,ɪgnə'reɪməs] *n* Ignorant *m*.

ignorance ['ɪgnərəns] *n* Unwissenheit *f*; *(of particular subject)* Unkenntnis *f*. **to keep sb in ~ of sth** jdn in Unkenntnis über etw *(acc)* lassen.

ignorant ['ɪgnərənt] *adj* **(a)** unwissend; *(of plan etc)* nicht informiert *(of* über *+acc)*. **to be ~ of geography** sich in Geographie nicht auskennen; **to be ~ of the facts** die Tatsachen nicht kennen. **(b)** *(ill-mannered)* ungehobelt.

ignore [ɪg'nɔ:ʳ] *vt* ignorieren; *(pay no attention to)* nicht beachten; *remark also* übergehen.

ill [ɪl] **1** *adj* **(a)** *pred (sick)* krank. **to fall** *or* **be taken ~** erkranken *(with sth* an etw *dat)*, krank werden; **to feel ~** sich krank fühlen. **(b)** *(bad)* schlecht. **~ feeling** böses Blut; **no ~ feeling?** ist es wieder gut?; **no ~ feeling!** (ist) schon vergessen!; **due to ~ health** aus Gesundheitsgründen; **as ~ luck would have it** wie es der Teufel so will; **~ will** böses Blut; **I don't bear them any ~ will** ich trage ihnen nichts nach; **it's an ~ wind (that blows nobody any good)** *(Prov)* so hat alles seine guten Seiten. **2** *n* **to think ~ of sb** schlecht von jdm denken; **to speak ~ of sb** schlecht über jdn reden. **3** *adv* schlecht. **he can ~ afford to refuse** er kann es sich *(dat)* schlecht leisten abzulehnen.

I'll [aɪl] = **I will; I shall.**

ill: ~-advised *adj* unklug; **you would be ~-advised to trust her** Sie wären schlecht beraten, wenn Sie ihr trauten; **~-at-ease** *adj* unbehaglich; **~-bred** *adj* schlecht erzogen; **~-considered** *adj action, words* unüberlegt; **~-disposed** *adj* **to be ~-disposed to(wards) sb** jdm übel gesinnt sein.

illegal [ɪ'li:gəl] *adj* unerlaubt; *(against a specific law)* gesetzwidrig; *trade, possession etc* illegal; *(Sport)* regelwidrig.

illegality [,ɪli:'gælɪtɪ] *n see adj* Ungesetzlichkeit *f*; Gesetzwidrigkeit *f*; Illegalität *f*.

illegally [ɪ'li:gəlɪ] *adv* **~ imported** illegal eingeführt; **you're ~ parked** Sie stehen im Parkverbot.

illegible [ɪ'ledʒəbl] *adj* unleserlich.

illegitimate [,ɪlɪ'dʒɪtɪmɪt] *adj* **(a)** *child* unehelich. **(b)** *(contrary to law)* unzulässig; *government* unrechtmäßig.

ill: ~-fated *adj* **(a)** *person* vom Unglück verfolgt; **(b)** *(doomed)* unglückselig; **~-founded** *adj* unbegründet; **~-gotten gains** *npl* unrechtmäßiger Gewinn; **~-humoured,** *(US)* **~-humored** *adj* schlecht gelaunt.

illicit [ɪ'lɪsɪt] *adj* illegal; *spirits* schwarz gebrannt.

ill-informed ['ɪlɪn,fɔ:md] *adj person* schlecht informiert; *criticism, speech* wenig sachkundig.

illiterate [ɪ'lɪtərət] **1** *adj* **to be ~** Analphabet sein; *(uncultured) person* ungebildet. **2** *n* Analphabet(in *f*) *m*.

ill: ~-mannered *adj* unhöflich; **~-natured** *adj* bösartig.

illness ['ɪlnɪs] *n* Krankheit *f*.

illogical [ɪ'lɒdʒɪkəl] *adj* unlogisch.

ill: ~-suited *adj (to one another)* nicht zusammenpassend; *(to sth)* ungeeignet *(to* für*)*; **~-timed** *adj* ungelegen; **~-treat** *vt* schlecht behandeln; **~-treatment** *n* schlechte Behandlung.

illuminate [ɪ'lu:mɪneɪt] *vt* **(a)** *room, street* beleuchten; *(spotlight etc)* anstrahlen. **~d sign** Leuchtzeichen *nt*. **(b)** *(fig) question, subject* erläutern.

illuminating [ɪ'lu:mɪneɪtɪŋ] *adj (instructive)* aufschlußreich.

illumination [ɪ,lu:mɪ'neɪʃən] *n* **(a)** *(of street etc)* Beleuchtung *f*. **(b) ~s** *pl* festliche Beleuchtung *f*. **(c)** *(fig)* Erläuterung *f*.

illusion [ɪ'lu:ʒən] *n* Illusion *f*. **to be under an ~** einer Täuschung *(dat)* unterliegen; **to be under the ~ that ...** sich *(dat)* einbilden, daß ...; **to have no ~s** sich *(dat)* keine Illusionen machen.

illusive [ɪ'lu:sɪv], **illusory** [ɪ'lu:sərɪ] *adj* trügerisch.

illustrate ['ɪləstreɪt] *vt* illustrieren; *(fig)* veranschaulichen. **~d (magazine)** Illustrierte *f*.

illustration [,ɪləs'treɪʃən] *n (picture)* Abbildung *f*, Illustration *f*. **by way of ~** als Beispiel.

illustrative ['ɪləstrətɪv] *adj* veranschaulichend.

illustrator ['ɪləstreɪtəʳ] *n* Illustrator *m*.

illustrious [ɪ'lʌstrɪəs] *adj* glanzvoll, gefeiert; *deeds* glorreich.

I'm [aɪm] = **I am.**

image [ɪmɪdʒ] *n* **(a)** *(carved etc)* Standbild *nt*; *(painted)* Bild *nt*; *(likeness)* Ebenbild *nt*. **(b)** *(mental picture)* Vorstellung *f*, Bild *nt*. **(c) (public) ~** Image *nt*.

imagery ['ɪmɪdʒərɪ] *n* Metaphorik *f*.

imaginable [ɪ'mædʒɪnəbl] *adj* denkbar. **the fastest way ~** der denkbar schnellste Weg.

imaginary [ɪ'mædʒɪnərɪ] *adj danger* eingebildet, imaginär; *characters* frei ersonnen, erfunden.

imagination [ɪ,mædʒɪ'neɪʃən] *n (creative)* Phantasie, Vorstellungskraft *f*; *(self-deceptive)* Einbildung *f*. **to have (a vivid) ~** (eine lebhafte) Phantasie haben; **use your ~** lassen Sie Ihre Phantasie spielen; **it's only (your) ~!** das bilden Sie sich *(dat)* nur ein!

imaginative [ɪ'mædʒɪnətɪv] *adj* phantasievoll; *plan, idea also* einfallsreich.

imagine [ɪ'mædʒɪn] *vt* **(a)** *(picture)* sich *(dat)* vorstellen. **I can't ~ what you mean** ich kann mir nicht vorstellen, was Sie meinen; **you can't ~ how ...** Sie können sich nicht vorstellen, wie ...; **you can't ~ it!** Sie machen sich keine Vorstellungen! **(b)** *(be under illusion)* sich *(dat)* eineinbilden. **don't ~ that ...** bilden Sie sich nur nicht ein, daß ...; **you're (just) imagining things** *(col)* Sie bilden sich das alles nur ein. **(c)** *(suppose)* annehmen. **is it time now? — I would ~ so** ist es soweit? — ich denke schon; **I would never have ~d he would have done that** ich hätte nie gedacht, daß er das tun würde.

imbalance [ɪm'bæləns] *n* Unausgeglichenheit *f*.

imbecile ['ɪmbəsi:l] *n* Idiot, Schwachkopf *m*; *(Med)* Schwachsinnige(r) *mf*.

imbibe [ɪm'baɪb] *vt (form, hum)* trinken, bechern *(hum)*.

imbue [ɪm'bju:] *vt (fig)* erfüllen.

IMF = **International Monetary Fund** IWF *m*, Internationaler Währungsfonds.

imitate ['ɪmɪteɪt] *vt* imitieren, nachahmen.
imitation [ˌɪmɪ'teɪʃən] **1** *n* Imitation, Nachahmung *f*. **to do an ~ of sb** jdn imitieren *or* nachahmen. **2** *adj* unecht. **~ leather** Kunstleder *nt*.
imitative ['ɪmɪtətɪv] *adj* imitativ *(geh)*.
imitator ['ɪmɪteɪtə[r]] *n* Nachahmer, Imitator *m*.
immaculate [ɪ'mækjʊlɪt] *adj* tadellos. **the I~ Conception** die Unbefleckte Empfängnis.
immaterial [ˌɪmə'tɪərɪəl] *adj (unimportant)* unwesentlich. **it is quite ~ to me (whether) ...** es ist für mich unwichtig, (ob) ...; **that's (quite) ~** das spielt (überhaupt) keine Rolle.
immature [ˌɪmə'tjʊə[r]] *adj (lit, fig)* unreif.
immaturity [ˌɪmə'tjʊərɪtɪ] *n* Unreife *f*.
immeasurable [ɪ'meʒərəbl] *adj* unermeßlich.
immediacy [ɪ'mi:dɪəsɪ] *n* Unmittelbarkeit *f*; *(urgency)* Dringlichkeit *f*.
immediate [ɪ'mi:dɪət] *adj* **(a)** *(instant)* umgehend. **to take ~ action** sofort handeln. **(b)** *future etc* unmittelbar; *cause, successor also* direkt; *vicinity also* nächste. **the ~ family** die engste Familie.
immediately [ɪ'mi:dɪətlɪ] **1** *adv* sofort; *reply, return, depart also* umgehend. **~ after/before** unmittelbar danach/davor. **2** *conj (Brit)* sobald als ...
immemorial [ˌɪmɪ'mɔ:rɪəl] *adj*: **from time ~** seit undenklichen Zeiten.
immense [ɪ'mens] *adj* enorm, immens.
immensely [ɪ'menslɪ] *adv* unheimlich *(col)*, enorm; *grateful* äußerst.
immensity [ɪ'mensɪtɪ] *n* Unermeßlichkeit *f*.
immerse [ɪ'mɜ:s] *vt* eintauchen *(in* in *+acc)*. **to be ~d in water** unter Wasser sein; **to ~ oneself in sth** *(fig)* sich in etw *(acc)* vertiefen.
immersion [ɪ'mɜ:ʃən] *n* **(a)** Eintauchen *nt*. **~ heater** *(Brit)* Wasserboiler *m*; *(for jug etc)* Tauchsieder *m*. **(b)** *(fig)* Vertieftsein *nt*.
immigrant ['ɪmɪgrənt] **1** *n* Einwanderer *m*, Einwanderin *f*. **2** *attr* **~ workers** ausländische Arbeitnehmer *pl*; *(esp BRD also)* Gastarbeiter *pl*.
immigration [ˌɪmɪ'greɪʃən] *n* Einwanderung, Immigration *f*; *(~ authorities)* Einwanderungsbehörde *f*. **to go through ~** die Einwanderungsformalitäten erledigen.
imminent ['ɪmɪnənt] *adj* **to be ~** nahe bevorstehen.
immobile [ɪ'məʊbaɪl] *adj* unbeweglich; *(not able to move) person* bewegungslos.
immobilize [ɪ'məʊbɪlaɪz] *vt traffic* zum Erliegen bringen; *army* bewegungsunfähig machen; *(Fin) capital* festlegen.
immoderate [ɪ'mɒdərɪt] *adj desire* übermäßig; *demands also* überzogen; *views* übersteigert.
immodest [ɪ'mɒdɪst] *adj* unbescheiden.
immodesty [ɪ'mɒdɪstɪ] *n* Unbescheidenheit *f*.
immoral [ɪ'mɒrəl] *adj action* unmoralisch; *behaviour also* unsittlich; *person also* sittenlos.
immorality [ˌɪmə'rælɪtɪ] *n* Unmoral *f*; *(of person also)* Sittenlosigkeit *f*; *(immoral act)* Unsittlichkeit *f*.
immortal [ɪ'mɔ:tl] *adj* unsterblich.
immortality [ˌɪmɔ:'tælɪtɪ] *n* Unsterblichkeit *f*.
immortalize [ɪ'mɔ:təlaɪz] *vt* unsterblich machen.
immovable [ɪ'mu:vəbl] *adj (lit)* unbeweglich; *(fig) obstacle* unüberwindlich.
immune [ɪ'mju:n] *adj (Med)* immun *(to* gegen*)*; *(fig)* sicher *(from* vor *+dat)*.
immunity [ɪ'mju:nɪtɪ] *n (Med, diplomatic)* Immunität *f*; *(fig)* Sicherheit *f*.
immunization [ˌɪmjʊnaɪ'zeɪʃən] *n* Immunisierung *f*.
immunize ['ɪmjʊnaɪz] *vt* immunisieren.
immutable [ɪ'mju:təbl] *adj* unveränderlich.
imp [ɪmp] *n* Kobold *m*; *(col: child also)* Schlingel *m (col)*.
impact ['ɪmpækt] *n* Aufprall *m (on* auf *+acc)*; *(of two moving objects)* Zusammenprall *m*; *(of falling object) (on house)* Einschlag *m (on* in *+acc)*; *(on ground)* Aufschlag *m (on* auf *+dat)*; *(force)* Wucht *f*; *(fig)* (Aus)wirkung *f (on* auf *+acc)*. **on ~ (with)** beim Aufprall (auf *+acc*)/Zusammenprall (mit) *etc*; **his speech had a great ~ on his audience** seine Rede machte großen Eindruck auf seine Zuhörer.
impair [ɪm'pɛə[r]] *vt* beeinträchtigen.
impale [ɪm'peɪl] *vt* aufspießen *(on* auf *+dat)*.
impart [ɪm'pɑ:t] *vt* **(a)** *information* mitteilen; *knowledge* vermitteln. **(b)** *(bestow)* verleihen *(to dat)*.
impartial [ɪm'pɑ:ʃəl] *adj person, attitude* unvoreingenommen; *decision also* gerecht.
impartiality [ɪmˌpɑ:ʃɪ'ælɪtɪ] *n see adj* Unvoreingenommenheit *f*; Gerechtigkeit *f*.
impassable [ɪm'pɑ:səbl] *adj* unpassierbar.
impasse [ɪm'pɑ:s] *n (fig)* Sackgasse *f*. **to have reached an ~** sich festgefahren haben.
impassioned [ɪm'pæʃnd] *adj* leidenschaftlich.
impassive [ɪm'pæsɪv] *adj* gelassen.
impatience [ɪm'peɪʃəns] *n* Ungeduld *f*; *(intolerance)* Unduldsamkeit *f*.
impatient [ɪm'peɪʃənt] *adj* ungeduldig; *(intolerant)* unduldsam *(of* gegenüber*)*.
impeach [ɪm'pi:tʃ] *vt* **(a)** *(Jur: accuse) public official* (eines Amtsvergehens) anklagen. **(b)** *sb's character, motives* in Frage stellen.
impeccable [ɪm'pekəbl] *adj* tadellos.
impede [ɪm'pi:d] *vt person* hindern; *action, traffic* behindern.
impediment [ɪm'pedɪmənt] *n* Hindernis *nt*; *(Med)* Behinderung *f*. **speech ~** Sprachfehler *m*.
impel [ɪm'pel] *vt* **(a)** *(force)* **to ~ sb to do sth** jdn (dazu) nötigen, etw zu tun. **(b)** *(drive on)* (voran)treiben.
impending [ɪm'pendɪŋ] *adj* bevorstehend; *storm also* heraufziehend; *danger* drohend.
impenetrable [ɪm'penɪtrəbl] *adj* undurchdringlich; *fortress* uneinnehmbar; *mind, mystery* unergründlich; *theory* undurchschaubar.
imperative [ɪm'perətɪv] **1** *adj* **to be ~** unbedingt nötig sein. **2** *n (Gram)* Imperativ *m*. **in the ~** im Imperativ.
imperceptible [ˌɪmpə'septəbl] *adj* nicht wahrnehmbar; *difference also* unmerklich.
imperfect [ɪm'pɜ:fɪkt] **1** *adj* **(a)** *(faulty)* unvollkommen; *(Comm) goods* fehlerhaft. **(b)** *(incomplete)* unvollständig. **2** *n (Gram)* Imperfekt *nt*.
imperfection [ˌɪmpə'fekʃən] *n* **(a)** *no pl see adj* Unvollkommenheit *f*; Unvollständigkeit *f*. **(b)** *(fault, defect)* Mangel *m*.
imperial [ɪm'pɪərɪəl] *adj* **(a)** *(of empire)* Reichs-; *(of emperor)* kaiserlich, Kaiser-. **(b)** *(Brit) weights, measures* englisch.
imperialism [ɪm'pɪərɪəlɪzəm] *n* Imperialismus *m*.
imperious [ɪm'pɪərɪəs] *adj* gebieterisch.
impermeable [ɪm'pɜ:mɪəbl] *adj* undurchlässig.
impersonal [ˌɪm'pɜ:snl] *adj* unpersönlich.
impersonate [ɪm'pɜ:səneɪt] *vt* sich ausgeben als; *(take off)* imitieren, nachahmen.
impersonation [ɪmˌpɜ:sə'neɪʃən] *n see vt* Verkörperung *f*; Imitation, Nachahmung *f*. **he does ~s of politicians** er imitiert Politiker.
impersonator [ɪm'pɜ:səneɪtə[r]] *n (Theat)* Imitator(in *f*) *m*.
impertinence [ɪm'pɜ:tɪnəns] *n* Unverschämtheit *f*.
impertinent [ɪm'pɜ:tɪnənt] *adj* unverschämt *(to* zu, gegenüber*)*.
imperturbable [ˌɪmpə'tɜ:bəbl] *adj* unerschütterlich.
impervious [ɪm'pɜ:vɪəs] *adj (fig)* unzugänglich *(to* für*)*; *(criticism)* unberührt *(to* von*)*.
impetuosity [ɪmˌpetjʊ'ɒsɪtɪ] *n* **(a)** *see adj* Ungestüm *nt*; Impulsivität *f*. **(b)** *(impetuous behaviour)* ungestümes Handeln.
impetuous [ɪm'petjʊəs] *adj act, person* ungestüm; *decision* impulsiv.

impetus ['ɪmpɪtəs] *n (lit, fig)* Impuls *m*; *(force)* Kraft *f*; *(momentum)* Schwung *m*.

♦**impinge on** [ɪm'pɪndʒɒn] *vi +prep obj* sich auswirken auf *(+acc)*, beeinflussen; *(on sb's rights etc also)* einschränken.

impish ['ɪmpɪʃ] *adj* schelmisch.

implacable [ɪm'plækəbl] *adj* unerbittlich.

implant [ɪm'plɑːnt] **1** *vt* **(a)** *(fig)* einimpfen *(in sb* jdm*)*. **(b)** *(Med)* einpflanzen. **2** ['ɪmplɑːnt] *n* Implantat *nt*.

implausible [ɪm'plɔːzəbl] *adj* nicht plausibel; *story, excuse also* unglaubwürdig.

implement ['ɪmplɪmənt] **1** *n* Gerät *nt*; *(tool also)* Werkzeug *nt*. **2** [ɪmplɪ'ment] *vt law* vollziehen; *promise* erfüllen; *plan etc* durchführen.

implicate ['ɪmplɪkeɪt] *vt* **to ~ sb in sth** jdn in etw verwickeln.

implication [ˌɪmplɪ'keɪʃən] *n* Implikation *f*; *(of law, agreement etc also)* Auswirkung *f*. **the possible ~s of his decision** die ganze Tragweite seiner Entscheidung; **by ~** implizit(e).

implicit [ɪm'plɪsɪt] *adj* **(a)** *(implied)* implizit; *threat also* indirekt; *recognition also* stillschweigend. **to be ~ in sth** durch etw impliziert werden; *(in contract etc)* in etw *(dat)* impliziert sein. **(b)** *(unquestioning) confidence* absolut.

implore [ɪm'plɔːʳ] *vt person* anflehen.

imploring [ɪm'plɔːrɪŋ] *adj* flehend; *beg also* inständig.

imply [ɪm'plaɪ] *vt* **(a)** andeuten, implizieren. **are you ~ing ...?** wollen Sie damit vielleicht andeuten, daß ...?; **it implies that he has changed his mind** das deutet darauf hin, daß er es sich *(dat)* anders überlegt hat. **(b)** *(involve)* bedeuten.

impolite [ˌɪmpə'laɪt] *adj* unhöflich.

impoliteness [ˌɪmpə'laɪtnɪs] *n* Unhöflichkeit *f*.

imponderable [ɪm'pɒndərəbl] *adj* unberechenbar.

import ['ɪmpɔːt] **1** *n* **(a)** *(Comm)* Import *m*, Einfuhr *f*. **(b)** *(meaning)* Bedeutung *f*. **2** [ɪm'pɔːt] *vt goods* einführen, importieren.

importance [ɪm'pɔːtəns] *n* Wichtigkeit *f*; *(significance also)* Bedeutung *f*; *(influence also)* Einfluß *m*. **to be of no (great) ~** nicht (besonders) wichtig sein; **to attach the greatest ~ to sth** einer Sache *(dat)* größte Bedeutung beimessen.

important [ɪm'pɔːtənt] *adj* wichtig; *(significant also)* bedeutend; *(influential)* einflußreich. **it's not ~** *(doesn't matter)* das macht nichts; **to try to look ~** sich *(dat)* ein gewichtiges Aussehen geben.

importantly [ɪm'pɔːtəntlɪ] *adj* **(a)** *(usu pej)* wichtigtuerisch *(pej)*. **(b) it is ~ different** das ist entscheidend anders.

import *in cpds* Einfuhr-, Import-; **~ duty** *n* Einfuhrzoll *m*.

importer [ɪm'pɔːtəʳ] *n* Importeur(in *f*) *m (of* von*)*.

import licence *(Brit)* or **license** *(US) n* Einfuhrlizenz *f*.

impose [ɪm'pəʊz] **1** *vt task, conditions* auferlegen *(on sb* jdm*)*; *sanctions, fine* verhängen *(on* gegen*)*; *tax* erheben. **to ~ oneself on sb** sich jdm aufdrängen. **2** *vi* zur Last fallen *(on sb* jdm*)*. **to ~ on sb's kindness** jds Freundlichkeit ausnützen.

imposing [ɪm'pəʊzɪŋ] *adj* beeindruckend; *appearance, building also* stattlich.

imposition [ˌɪmpə'zɪʃən] *n* **(a)** *no pl see vt* Auferlegung *f*; Verhängung *f*. **(b)** *(tax)* Steuer *f* *(on* für, auf *+dat)*. **(c)** *(taking advantage)* Zumutung *f*.

impossibility [ɪmˌpɒsə'bɪlɪtɪ] *n* Unmöglichkeit *f*.

impossible [ɪm'pɒsəbl] **1** *adj* unmöglich. **~!** ausgeschlossen! **2** *n* Unmögliche(s) *nt*. **to ask for the ~** Unmögliches verlangen; **to do the ~** Unmögliches tun.

impostor [ɪm'pɒstəʳ] *n* Hochstapler(in *f*) *m*.

impotence ['ɪmpətəns] *n see adj* Schwäche *f*; Impotenz *f*; Machtlosigkeit *f*.

impotent ['ɪmpətənt] *adj (physically)* schwach; *(sexually)* impotent; *(fig)* machtlos; *rage* ohnmächtig.

impound [ɪm'paʊnd] *vt* **(a)** *(seize) goods* beschlagnahmen. **(b)** *cattle* einsperren; *car* abschleppen (lassen).

impoverished [ɪm'pɒvərɪʃt] *adj* verarmt; *soil* ausgelaugt.

impracticable [ɪm'præktɪkəbl] *adj* impraktikabel; *design, size* unbrauchbar; *road* schwer befahrbar.

impractical [ɪm'præktɪkəl] *adj* unpraktisch; *scheme also* unbrauchbar.

imprecise [ˌɪmprɪ'saɪs] *adj* ungenau, unpräzis(e).

imprecision [ˌɪmprɪ'sɪʒən] *n* Ungenauigkeit *f*.

impregnable [ɪm'pregnəbl] *adj fortress* uneinnehmbar; *(fig) position* unerschütterlich.

impregnate ['ɪmpregneɪt] *vt* **(a)** *(saturate)* tränken. **(b)** *(Biol: fertilize)* befruchten; *humans also* schwängern.

impresario [ˌɪmpre'sɑːrɪəʊ] *n* Theater-/Operndirektor *m*.

impress [ɪm'pres] *vt* **(a)** beeindrucken; *(memorably also)* Eindruck machen auf *(+acc)*; *(arouse admiration in)* imponieren *(+dat)*. **he ~ed me favourably/unfavourably** er hat einen/keinen guten Eindruck auf mich gemacht. **(b) to ~ a pattern onto sth** ein Muster auf etw *(acc)* aufdrücken.

impression [ɪm'preʃən] *n* **(a)** Eindruck *m*. **to make a good ~ on sb** einen guten Eindruck auf jdn machen; **first ~s** der erste Eindruck; **to give sb the ~ that ...** jdm den Eindruck vermitteln, daß ...; **I was under the ~ that ...** ich hatte den Eindruck, daß ... **(b)** *(on wax etc)* Abdruck *m*. **(c)** *(of book etc)* Nachdruck *m*. **first ~** Erstdruck *m*. **(d)** *(take-off)* Nachahmung, Imitation *f*. **to do an ~ of sb** jdn imitieren.

impressionable [ɪm'preʃnəbl] *adj* für Eindrücke empfänglich. **at an ~ age** in einem Alter, in dem man für Eindrücke besonders empfänglich ist.

impressionism [ɪm'preʃənɪzəm] *n* Impressionismus *m*.

impressionist [ɪm'preʃənɪst] *n* Impressionist(in *f*) *m*.

impressive [ɪm'presɪv] *adj* beeindruckend; *performance, personality also* eindrucksvoll.

imprint [ɪm'prɪnt] **1** *vt seal, paper etc* aufprägen *(on* auf *+acc)*; *(on paper)* aufdrucken *(on* auf *+acc)*. **to ~ itself on sb's mind** sich jdm einprägen. **2** ['ɪmprɪnt] *n* **(a)** *(on wax etc)* Abdruck *m*. **(b)** *(Typ)* Impressum *nt*.

imprison [ɪm'prɪzn] *(lit)* inhaftieren; *(fig)* gefangenhalten.

imprisonment [ɪm'prɪznmənt] *n (action)* Inhaftierung *f*; *(state)* Gefangenschaft *f*. **to sentence sb to one month's ~** jdn zu einem Monat Gefängnis verurteilen.

improbability [ɪmˌprɒbə'bɪlɪtɪ] *n* Unwahrscheinlichkeit *f*.

improbable [ɪm'prɒbəbl] *adj* unwahrscheinlich.

impromptu [ɪm'prɒmptjuː] **1** *adj* improvisiert. **2** *adv* improvisiert; *perform* aus dem Stegreif.

improper [ɪm'prɒpəʳ] *adj (unsuitable)* unpassend; *(unseemly)* unschicklich; *(indecent)* unanständig; *use* unsachgemäß; *conduct* unehrenhaft.

impropriety [ˌɪmprə'praɪətɪ] *n* Unschicklichkeit *f*.

improve [ɪm'pruːv] **1** *vt* verbessern; *production* steigern; *knowledge* erweitern; *low salaries* aufbessern. **to ~ one's mind** sich weiterbilden. **2** *vi see vt* besser werden; sich steigern. **the patient is improving** dem Patienten geht es besser.

♦**improve (up)on** *vi +prep obj* übertreffen; *offer* überbieten.

improvement [ɪm'pruːvmənt] *n see vt* Verbesserung *f*; Steigerung *f*; Erweiterung *f*; Aufbesserung *f*; *(in health)* Besserung *f*; *(in studies also)* Fortschritte *pl*. **to carry out ~s to a house**

Ausbesserungsarbeiten an einem Haus vornehmen; **it's an ~ on the old one** es ist eine Verbesserung gegenüber dem/der alten.

improvisation [ˌɪmprəvaɪ'zeɪʃən] *n* Improvisation *f*.

improvise ['ɪmprəvaɪz] *vti* improvisieren.

imprudent [ɪm'pruːdənt] *adj* unklug.

impudence ['ɪmpjʊdəns] *n* Unverschämtheit, Frechheit *f*.

impudent ['ɪmpjʊdənt] *adj* unverschämt.

impulse ['ɪmpʌls] *n* Impuls *m*. **on ~** aus einem Impuls heraus; **~ buying** spontanes Kaufen.

impulsive [ɪm'pʌlsɪv] *adj* impulsiv; *action, remark also* spontan.

impunity [ɪm'pjuːnɪtɪ] *n*: **with ~** ungestraft.

impure [ɪm'pjʊəʳ] *adj water, food* verunreinigt; *thoughts, motives* unsauber.

impurity [ɪm'pjʊərɪtɪ] *n see adj* Unreinheit *f*; Unsauberkeit *f*.

impute [ɪm'pjuːt] *vt* zuschreiben *(to sb/sth* jdm/einer Sache*)*.

in [ɪn] **1** *prep* **(a)** *(position)* in *(+dat)*; *(with motion)* in *(+acc)*. **it was ~ the car** es war im Auto; **he put it ~ the car** er legte es ins Auto; **~ the street** auf der/die Straße; **~ Thompson Street** in der Thompsonstraße; **~ bed/prison** im Bett/Gefängnis; **~ Germany/Iran/Switzerland/the United States** in Deutschland/im Iran/in der Schweiz/in den Vereinigten Staaten.

(b) we find it ~ Dickens wir finden das bei Dickens; **rare ~ a child of that age** selten bei einem Kind in diesem Alter; **we've got a good recruit ~ her** sie ist für uns eine gute neue Mitarbeiterin.

(c) *(time)* in *(+dat)*; *(within)* innerhalb von. **~ 1974** (im Jahre) 1974; **~ the sixties** in den sechziger Jahren; **~ June** im Juni; **~ (the) spring** im Frühling; **~ the morning(s)** morgens, am Morgen; **~ the afternoon** am Nachmittag; **~ the daytime** tagsüber; **~ the evening** am Abend; **three o'clock ~ the afternoon** drei Uhr nachmittags; **~ those days** damals; **~ a week('s time)** in einer Woche; **I haven't seen him ~ years** ich habe ihn seit Jahren nicht mehr gesehen.

(d) *(manner, state, condition)* **~ German** auf Deutsch; **to pay ~ dollars** in Dollar bezahlen; **to walk ~ twos** zu zweit gehen; **~ anger** im Zorn; **~ poverty** in Armut; **dressed ~ white** weiß gekleidet; **the lady ~ green** die Dame in Grün; **to write ~ ink** mit Tinte schreiben; **to die ~ hundreds** zu Hunderten sterben.

(e) *(ratio)* **there are 12 inches ~ a foot** ein Fuß hat 12 Zoll; **one ~ ten** jeder zehnte.

(f) *(in respect of)* **blind ~ the left eye** auf dem linken Auge *or* links blind; **a rise ~ prices** ein Preisanstieg *m*; **ten feet ~ height** zehn Fuß hoch; **five ~ number** fünf an der Zahl.

(g) *(occupation)* **he is ~ the army** er ist beim Militär; **he is ~ banking** er ist im Bankwesen (tätig).

(h) ~ saying this, I ... wenn ich das sage, ... ich; **~ trying to escape** beim Fluchtversuch; **~ that** insofern als.

2 *adv* **(a)** da; *(at home also)* zu Hause. **the train is ~** der Zug ist da *or* angekommen; **the harvest is ~** die Ernte ist eingebracht; **we were asked ~** wir wurden hereingebeten. **(b) miniskirts are ~** Miniröcke sind in *(col)*. **(c)** *(phrases)* **we are ~ for trouble** wir können uns auf was gefaßt machen *(col)*; **we are ~ for rain** uns *(dat)* steht Regen bevor; **he's ~ for it!** der kann sich auf was gefaßt machen *(col)*; **you don't know what you are ~ for** Sie wissen nicht, was Ihnen bevorsteht; **he hasn't got it ~ him** er hat nicht das Zeug dazu; **to have it ~ for sb** *(col)* es auf jdn abgesehen haben *(col)*; **to be ~ on sth** an einer Sache beteiligt sein; *on secret etc* über etw *(acc)* Bescheid wissen.

3 *adj attr* **(a) "~" tray** Ablage *f* für Eingänge. **(b)** *(col)* in *inv (col)*. **an ~ subject** ein Modefach *nt*; **the ~ thing is to ...** es ist in *(col) or* zur Zeit Mode, zu ...

4 *n* **to know the ~s and outs of a matter** bei einer Sache genau Bescheid wissen.

inability [ˌɪnə'bɪlɪtɪ] *n* Unfähigkeit *f*.

inaccessibility ['ɪnækˌsesə'bɪlɪtɪ] *n* Unzugänglichkeit *f*.

inaccessible [ˌɪnæk'sesəbl] *adj* unzugänglich.

inaccuracy [ɪn'ækjʊrəsɪ] *n see adj* Ungenauigkeit *f*; Unrichtigkeit *f*.

inaccurate [ɪn'ækjʊrɪt] *adj* ungenau; *(not correct)* unrichtig.

inaction [ɪn'ækʃən] *n* Untätigkeit *f*.

inactive [ɪn'æktɪv] *adj* untätig; *volcano* erloschen.

inactivity [ˌɪnæk'tɪvɪtɪ] *n* Untätigkeit *f*; *(of mind)* Trägheit *f*; *(Comm)* Flaute *f*.

inadequacy [ɪn'ædɪkwəsɪ] *n see adj* Unzulänglichkeit *f*; Unangemessenheit *f*.

inadequate [ɪn'ædɪkwɪt] *adj* unzulänglich; *supplies, reasons also* unzureichend; *measures* unangemessen. **she makes him feel ~** sie gibt ihm das Gefühl der Unzulänglichkeit.

inadmissible [ˌɪnəd'mɪsəbl] *adj* unzulässig.

inadvertent [ˌɪnəd'vɜːtənt] *adj* unbeabsichtigt, ungewollt.

inadvertently [ˌɪnəd'vɜːtəntlɪ] *adv* versehentlich.

inadvisable [ˌɪnəd'vaɪzəbl] *adj* unratsam.

inane [ɪ'neɪn] *adj* dumm.

inanimate [ɪn'ænɪmɪt] *adj* leblos; *nature* unbelebt.

inanity [ɪ'nænɪtɪ] *n* Dummheit *f*.

inapplicable [ɪn'æplɪkəbl] *adj answer* unzutreffend; *rules* nicht anwendbar *(to sb* auf jdn*)*.

inappropriate [ˌɪnə'prəʊprɪɪt] *adj* unpassend; *action also* unangemessen.

inarticulate [ˌɪnɑː'tɪkjʊlɪt] *adj essay* schlecht *or* unklar ausgedrückt. **she's very ~** sie kann sich nur schlecht ausdrücken.

inattention [ˌɪnə'tenʃən] *n* Unaufmerksamkeit *f*. **~ to detail** Ungenauigkeit *f* im Detail.

inattentive [ˌɪnə'tentɪv] *adj* unaufmerksam.

inaudible [ɪn'ɔːdəbl] *adj* unhörbar.

inaugural [ɪ'nɔːgjʊrəl] *adj lecture* Antritts-.

inaugurate [ɪ'nɔːgjʊreɪt] *vt president, official* (feierlich) in sein/ihr Amt einführen; *building* einweihen; *exhibition* eröffnen; *era* einleiten.

inauspicious [ˌɪnɔːs'pɪʃəs] *adj* unheilverheißend.

in-between [ɪnbɪ'twiːn] *(col) adj* Mittel-, Zwischen-. **it is sort of ~** es ist so ein Mittelding; **~ stage** Zwischenstadium *nt*; **~ times** zwischendurch.

inborn ['ɪn'bɔːn] *adj* angeboren.

inbreeding ['ɪn'briːdɪŋ] *n* Inzucht *f*.

Inc *(US)* = **Incorporated.**

incalculable [ɪn'kælkjʊləbl] *adj amount* unermeßlich; *consequences* unabsehbar.

incantation [ˌɪnkæn'teɪʃən] *n* Zauber(spruch) *m*; *(act)* Beschwörung *f*.

incapable [ɪn'keɪpəbl] *adj person* unfähig; *(physically)* hilflos. **to be ~ of doing sth** unfähig sein, etw zu tun; **~ of working** arbeitsunfähig; **~ of tenderness** zu Zärtlichkeit nicht fähig.

incapacitate [ˌɪnkə'pæsɪteɪt] *vt* unfähig machen. **physically ~d** körperlich behindert.

incapacity [ˌɪnkə'pæsɪtɪ] *n* Unfähigkeit *f (for* für*)*.

incarcerate [ɪn'kɑːsəreɪt] *vt* einkerkern.

incarnate [ɪn'kɑːnɪt] *adj (Rel)* menschgeworden; *(personified)* leibhaftig *attr*, in Person. **the devil ~** der leibhaftige Teufel.

incarnation [ˌɪnkɑː'neɪʃən] *n (Rel)* Menschwerdung *f*; *(fig)* Verkörperung *f*.

incendiary [ɪn'sendɪərɪ] **1** *adj (lit) bomb* Brand-. **~ device** Brandsatz *m*. **2** *n (bomb)* Brandbombe *f*.

incense[1] [ɪn'sens] *vt* wütend machen. **~d** wütend, erbost *(at, by* über *+acc)*.

incense[2] ['ɪnsens] *n (Eccl)* Weihrauch *m*.

incentive [ɪn'sentɪv] *n* Anreiz *m*. **~ scheme** *(Ind)*

Leistungsförderungsprogramm *nt*.

inception [ɪn'sepʃən] *n* Beginn, Anfang *m*. **from its ~** von Anfang an.

incessant [ɪn'sesnt] *adj* unaufhörlich; *noise* ununterbrochen.

incest ['ɪnsest] *n* Inzest *m*.

incestuous [ɪn'sestjʊəs] *adj* blutschänderisch.

inch [ɪntʃ] **1** *n* Zoll, Inch *m*. **a few ~es** ein paar Zentimeter; **~ by ~** Zentimeter um Zentimeter; **he came within an ~ of victory** er hätte um ein Haar gewonnen; **the lorry missed me by ~es** der Lastwagen hat mich um Haaresbreite verfehlt; **he is every ~ a soldier** er ist vom Scheitel bis zur Sohle ein Soldat; **give him an ~ and he'll take a mile** *(prov)* wenn man ihm den kleinen Finger gibt, nimmt er die ganze Hand *(prov)*. **2** *vi* **to ~ forward** sich millimeterweise vorwärtsbewegen; **because prices are ~ing up** weil die Preise allmählich ansteigen; **the Dutch swimmer is ~ing ahead** der holländische Schwimmer schiebt sich langsam an die Spitze.

incidence ['ɪnsɪdəns] *n (of crime)* Häufigkeit *f*. **angle of ~** *(Opt)* Einfallswinkel *m*.

incident ['ɪnsɪdənt] *n (event)* Ereignis *nt*, Vorfall *m*; *(diplomatic etc)* Zwischenfall *m*.

incidental [ˌɪnsɪ'dentl] *adj (secondary etc)* nebensächlich; *remark* beiläufig. **~ music** Begleitmusik *f*; **~ expenses** Nebenkosten *pl*.

incidentally [ˌɪnsɪ'dentəlɪ] *adv (by the way)* übrigens.

incinerate [ɪn'sɪnəreɪt] *vt* verbrennen.

incinerator [ɪn'sɪnəreɪtə[r]] *n* (Müll)verbrennungsanlage *f*; *(garden ~)* Verbrennungsofen *m*.

incipient [ɪn'sɪpɪənt] *adj* beginnend.

incision [ɪn'sɪʒən] *n* Schnitt *m*; *(Med)* Einschnitt *m*.

incisive [ɪn'saɪsɪv] *adj style* prägnant; *criticism* treffend; *mind* scharf; *person* scharfsinnig.

incisor [ɪn'saɪzə[r]] *n* Schneidezahn *m*.

incite [ɪn'saɪt] *vt* aufhetzen *(to* zu *+dat)*.

incitement [ɪn'saɪtmənt] *n* Aufhetzung *f*.

inclement [ɪn'klemənt] *adj weather* unfreundlich.

inclination [ˌɪnklɪ'neɪʃən] *n* **(a)** Neigung *f*. **he follows his (own) ~s** er tut das, wozu er Lust hat; **I have no ~ to see him again** ich habe kein Bedürfnis, ihn wiederzusehen; **he showed no ~ to leave** er schien nicht gehen zu wollen. **(b)** *(of hill, slope etc)* Gefälle *nt*.

incline [ɪn'klaɪn] **1** *vt* **(a)** *head, roof* neigen. **(b)** *(dispose)* veranlassen, bewegen. **this ~s me to think that he must be lying** das läßt mich vermuten, daß er lügt. **2** *vi* **(a)** *(slope)* sich neigen; *(ground also)* abfallen. **(b)** *(tend)* **to ~ to sth** zu etw neigen. **3** ['ɪnklaɪn] *n* Neigung *f*; *(of hill)* Abhang *m*; *(gradient: Rail etc)* Gefälle *nt*.

inclined [ɪn'klaɪnd] *adj* **to be ~ to do sth** *(wish to)* etw tun wollen; *(tend to)* dazu neigen, etw zu tun; **they are ~ to be late** sie kommen gern zu spät; **I am ~ to think that ...** ich neige zu der Ansicht, daß ...; **if you feel ~** wenn Sie Lust haben; **if you're ~ that way** wenn Ihnen so etwas liegt; **I'm ~ to disagree** ich möchte da doch widersprechen; **it's ~ to break** das bricht leicht.

include [ɪn'kluːd] *vt* einschließen; *(on list, in group etc)* aufnehmen. **the tip is not ~d in the bill** Trinkgeld ist in der Rechnung nicht inbegriffen; **the invitation ~s everybody** die Einladung betrifft alle; **the children ~d** einschließlich der Kinder; **does that ~ me?** gilt das auch für mich?

including [ɪn'kluːdɪŋ] *prep* einschließlich *(+gen)*. **~ service** inklusive Bedienung; **not ~ service** Bedienung nicht inbegriffen; **up to and ~ March 4th** bis einschließlich 4. März.

inclusive [ɪn'kluːsɪv] *adj* einschließlich; *price* Pauschal-. **to be ~ of** einschließlich *(+gen)* sein; **from 1st to 6th May ~** vom 1. bis einschließlich 6. Mai.

incognito [ˌɪnkɒg'niːtəʊ] *adv* inkognito.

incoherent [ˌɪnkəʊ'hɪərənt] *adj style, argument* zusammenhanglos; *speech, also* wirr; *drunk etc* schwer verständlich. **he was totally ~** man konnte ihn überhaupt nicht verstehen.

income ['ɪnkʌm] *n* Einkommen *nt*; *(receipts)* Einkünfte *pl*.

income: ~ group *n* Einkommensklasse *f*; **~s policy** *n* Lohnpolitik *f*; **~ tax** *n* Lohnsteuer *f*; **~ tax return** *n* Steuererklärung *f*.

incoming ['ɪnˌkʌmɪŋ] *adj* ankommend; *train also* einfahrend; *mail, orders etc* eingehend. **~ tide** Flut *f*.

incommunicado [ˌɪnkəmjʊnɪ'kɑːdəʊ] *adj pred* abgesondert. **he was held ~** er hatte keinerlei Verbindung zur Außenwelt.

incomparable [ɪn'kɒmpərəbl] *adj* nicht vergleichbar *(with* mit*)*; *beauty, skill* unvergleichlich.

incompatibility ['ɪnkəmˌpætə'bɪlɪtɪ] *n* Unvereinbarkeit *f*.

incompatible [ˌɪnkəm'pætəbl] *adj characters, ideas* unvereinbar; *technical systems also* nicht zueinander passend; *(Comp)* nicht kompatibel; *blood groups* nicht miteinander verträglich. **they are ~** sie passen überhaupt nicht zueinander.

incompetence [ɪn'kɒmpɪtəns] *n* Unfähigkeit *f*; *(for job)* Untauglichkeit *f*.

incompetent [ɪn'kɒmpɪtənt] *adj person* unfähig; *(for sth)* untauglich; *piece of work* unzulänglich.

incomplete [ˌɪnkəm'pliːt] *adj collection, series* unvollkommen, unvollständig; *(not finished also) painting* unfertig.

incomprehensible [ɪnˌkɒmprɪ'hensəbl] *adj* unverständlich; *act also* unbegreiflich.

inconceivable [ˌɪnkən'siːvəbl] *adj* unvorstellbar.

inconclusive [ˌɪnkən'kluːsɪv] *adj result* unbestimmt; *action, investigation* ergebnislos; *(not convincing) argument* nicht überzeugend.

incongruous [ɪn'kɒŋgrʊəs] *adj couple, mixture* nicht zusammenpassend *attr*; *thing to do, behaviour, remark* unpassend; *(out of place)* fehl am Platz.

inconsequential [ɪnˌkɒnsɪ'kwenʃəl] *adj* irrelevant; *(not logical)* unlogisch; *(unimportant)* unwichtig.

inconsiderable [ˌɪnkən'sɪdərəbl] *adj* **a not ~ amount** ein nicht unbedeutender Betrag.

inconsiderate [ˌɪnkən'sɪdərɪt] *adj* rücksichtslos; *(in less critical sense)* unaufmerksam.

inconsistency [ˌɪnkən'sɪstənsɪ] *n see adj* **(a)** Widersprüchlichkeit *f*. **(b)** Unbeständigkeit *f*.

inconsistent [ˌɪnkən'sɪstənt] *adj* **(a)** *(contradictory)* widersprüchlich. **to be ~ with sth** mit etw nicht übereinstimmen. **(b)** *(uneven, irregular) work* unbeständig; *person also* inkonsequent.

inconsolable [ˌɪnkən'səʊləbl] *adj* untröstlich.

inconspicuous [ˌɪnkən'spɪkjʊəs] *adj* unauffällig. **he tried to make himself ~** er versuchte möglichst nicht aufzufallen.

inconstant [ɪn'kɒnstənt] *adj person* unbeständig.

incontestable [ˌɪnkən'testəbl] *adj* unbestreitbar.

incontinent [ɪn'kɒntɪnənt] *adj (Med)* unfähig, Stuhl und/oder Harn zurückzuhalten.

incontrovertible [ɪnˌkɒntrə'vɜːtəbl] *adj* unbestreitbar.

inconvenience [ˌɪnkən'viːnɪəns] **1** *n* Unannehmlichkeit *f (to sb* für jdn*)*. **it was something of an ~ not having a car** es war ziemlich lästig, kein Auto zu haben; **I don't want to cause you any ~** ich möchte Ihnen keine Umstände bereiten. **2** *vt* Umstände bereiten *(+dat)*. **don't ~ yourself** machen Sie keine Umstände.

inconvenient [ˌɪnkən'viːnɪənt] *adj time* ungelegen; *house, design* unpraktisch; *location* ungünstig; *journey* beschwerlich. **3 o'clock is very ~ for me** 3 Uhr kommt mir sehr ungelegen.

incorporate [ɪn'kɔːpəreɪt] *vt* **(a)** *(integrate)* aufnehmen, integrieren *(into* in *+acc)*. **(b)** *(contain)*

(in sich *dat*) enthalten.
incorporated [ɪn'kɔːpəreɪtɪd] *adj (US Comm)* als Aktiengesellschaft eingetragen.
incorrect [ˌɪnkə'rekt] *adj* **(a)** falsch; *wording, calculation also* fehlerhaft. **that is ~** das stimmt nicht. **(b)** *dress, behaviour* inkorrekt.
incorrectly [ˌɪnkə'rektlɪ] *adv see adj; assume* fälschlich(erweise).
incorrigible [ɪn'kɒrɪdʒəbl] *adj* unverbesserlich.
increase [ɪn'kriːs] **1** *vi* zunehmen; *(taxes)* erhöht werden; *(strength, friendship)* wachsen; *(price, demand)* steigen; *(business, town)* sich vergrößern. **to ~ in volume/weight** an Umfang/Gewicht zunehmen; **to ~ in size/number** sich vergrößern/vermehren.
2 *vt* vergrößern; *possessions, riches also* vermehren; *sales also* erweitern; *numbers, taxes, price, speed* erhöhen. **he ~d his efforts** er strengte sich mehr an; **~d standard of living** höherer Lebensstandard; **~d efficiency** Leistungssteigerung *f*.
3 *n* Zunahme, Steigerung *f*; *(in size)* Vergrößerung, Erweiterung *f*; *(in number)* Zuwachs *m*, Zunahme *f*; *(in speed)* Erhöhung, Steigerung *f (in gen)*; *(of business)* Erweiterung *f*; *(in sales)* Aufschwung *m*; *(of effort etc)* Steigerung *f*; *(of demand)* Steigen *nt*; *(of violence)* Anwachsen *nt*. **to get an ~ of £15 per week** eine Lohnerhöhung von £ 15 pro Woche bekommen; **to be on the ~** ständig zunehmen; **rent ~** Mieterhöhung *f*.
increasing [ɪn'kriːsɪŋ] *adj* zunehmend, (an)wachsend. **an ever ~ number of people are changing to ...** mehr und mehr Leute steigen auf *(+acc)* ... um.
increasingly [ɪn'kriːsɪŋlɪ] *adv* zunehmend, immer mehr.
incredible [ɪn'kredəbl] *adj* unglaublich; *(col also)* unwahrscheinlich gut/schlecht *(col)*. **this music is ~** diese Musik ist sagenhaft *(col)*; **you're ~** du bist wirklich unschlagbar.
incredibly [ɪn'kredəblɪ] *adv* unglaublich, unwahrscheinlich.
incredulity [ˌɪnkrɪ'djuːlɪtɪ] *n* Ungläubigkeit, Skepsis *f*.
incredulous [ɪn'kredjʊləs] *adj* ungläubig, skeptisch.
increment ['ɪnkrɪmənt] *n (in salary)* Gehaltserhöhung *f*.
incriminate [ɪn'krɪmɪneɪt] *vt* belasten.
incriminating [ɪn'krɪmɪneɪtɪŋ] *adj* belastend.
incubate ['ɪnkjʊbeɪt] **1** *vt egg* ausbrüten; *bacteria* züchten. **2** *vi (lit)* ausgebrütet werden.
incubation [ˌɪnkjʊ'beɪʃən] *n see vb* Ausbrüten *nt*; Züchten *nt*. **~ period** *(Med)* Inkubationszeit *f*.
incubator ['ɪnkjʊbeɪtəʳ] *n (for babies)* Brutkasten *m*; *(for chickens)* Brutapparat *m*.
inculcate ['ɪnkʌlkeɪt] *vt* einimpfen *(in sb* jdm*)*.
incumbent [ɪn'kʌmbənt] *(form)* **1** *adj* **to be ~ upon sb** jdm obliegen *(form)*. **2** *n* Amtsinhaber *m*.
incur [ɪn'kɜːʳ] *vt anger, injury* sich *(dat)* zuziehen; *loss* erleiden; *debts, expenses* machen.
incurable [ɪn'kjʊərəbl] *adj (Med)* unheilbar; *(fig)* unverbesserlich.
incursion [ɪn'kɜːʃən] *n* Eindringen *nt (into* in *+acc)*.
indebted [ɪn'detɪd] *adj* **to be ~ to sb for sth** jdm für etw (zu Dank) verpflichtet sein.
indecency [ɪn'diːsnsɪ] *n* Unanständigkeit *f*.
indecent [ɪn'diːsnt] *adj* unanständig, anstößig; *(Jur) act* unsittlich.
indecipherable [ˌɪndɪ'saɪfərəbl] *adj* nicht zu entziffern *pred*, nicht zu entziffernd *attr*; *handwriting* unleserlich.
indecision [ˌɪndɪ'sɪʒən] *n* Unentschlossenheit *f*.
indecisive [ˌɪndɪ'saɪsɪv] *adj person, manner* unschlüssig, unentschlossen; *discussion* ergebnislos; *argument, battle* nicht entscheidend *attr*.
indeed [ɪn'diːd] *adv* **(a)** tatsächlich, wirklich. **I feel, ~ I know he is right** ich habe das Gefühl, ja ich weiß (sogar), daß er recht hat; **isn't that wrong? — ~** ist das nicht falsch? — allerdings; **are you coming? — ~ I am!** kommst du? — aber sicher *or* natürlich; **may I open the window? — you may ~** darf ich das Fenster öffnen? — ja bitte!; **very ... ~** wirklich sehr ...; **thank you very much ~** vielen herzlichen Dank. **(b)** *(admittedly)* zwar. **there are ~ mistakes in it, but ...** es sind zwar Fehler darin, aber ... **(c)** *(expressing possibility)* **I may ~ come** es kann gut sein, daß ich komme.
indefatigable [ˌɪndɪ'fætɪgəbl] *adj* unermüdlich.
indefensible [ˌɪndɪ'fensəbl] *adj behaviour etc* unentschuldbar; *town etc* unhaltbar; *cause, theory* unvertretbar.
indefinable [ˌɪndɪ'faɪnəbl] *adj* undefinierbar; *feeling* unbestimmt.
indefinite [ɪn'defɪnɪt] *adj* unbestimmt; *(vague)* unklar, undeutlich.
indefinitely [ɪn'defɪnɪtlɪ] *adv wait etc* unendlich lange, endlos; *postpone* auf unbestimmte Zeit. **we can't go on like this ~** wir können nicht immer so weitermachen.
indelible [ɪn'deləbl] *adj ink* wasserfest; *(fig) impression* unauslöschlich. **~ pencil** Kopierstift *m*.
indelicate [ɪn'delɪkət] *adj person* taktlos; *(crude)* geschmacklos.
indemnify [ɪn'demnɪfaɪ] *vt* **(a)** *(compensate)* entschädigen; *expenses* erstatten. **(b)** *(safeguard)* absichern *(from, against* gegen*)*; *(insure)* versichern *(against, from* gegen*)*.
indemnity [ɪn'demnɪtɪ] *n* **(a)** *(compensation) (for damage, loss etc)* Schadensersatz *m*, Entschädigung *f*; *(after war)* Wiedergutmachung *f*. **(b)** *(insurance)* Versicherung(sschutz *m*) *f*.
indent [ɪn'dent] *vt (Typ) line* einrücken.
indentation [ˌɪnden'teɪʃən] *n (in border)* Einschnitt *m*; *(Typ)* Einrückung *f*; *(in metal)* Delle *f*.
independence [ˌɪndɪ'pendəns] *n see adj* Unabhängigkeit *f (of* von*)*; Selbständigkeit *f*. **I~ Day** *(US)* der Unabhängigkeitstag.
independent [ˌɪndɪ'pendənt] *adj* unabhängig *(of* von*) (also Pol)*; *person (in attitude, spirit also)* selbständig; *development* eigenständig. **a man of ~ means** ein Mann mit Privateinkommen; **~ suspension** *(Aut)* Einzel(rad)aufhängung *f*.
independently [ˌɪndɪ'pendəntlɪ] *adv (on own initiative)* von allein(e).
in-depth ['ɪndepθ] *adj* eingehend, gründlich.
indescribable [ˌɪndɪ'skraɪbəbl] *adj* unbeschreiblich; *(col: terrible)* schrecklich.
indestructible [ˌɪndɪ'strʌktəbl] *adj* unzerstörbar.
indeterminate [ˌɪndɪ'tɜːmɪnɪt] *adj* unbestimmt.
index ['ɪndeks] *n* **(a)** *pl* **-es** *(in book)* Register *nt*; *(of sources)* Quellenverzeichnis *nt*. **(b)** *pl* **indices** *(on scale)* (An)zeiger *m*. **cost-of-living ~** Lebenshaltungskosten-Index *m*.
index: ~ card *n* Karteikarte *f*; **~ finger** *n* Zeigefinger *m*; **~-linked** *adj salaries* der Inflationsrate *(dat)* angeglichen; *pensions* dynamisch.
India ['ɪndɪə] *n* Indien *nt*. **~ ink** Tusche *f*.
Indian ['ɪndɪən] **1** *adj* **(a)** indisch. **(b)** *(American ~)* indianisch, Indianer-. **~ Ocean** Indischer Ozean; **~ summer** Altweibersommer, Spätsommer *m*. **2** *n* **(a)** Inder(in *f*) *m*. **(b)** *(American ~)* Indianer(in *f*) *m*.
India rubber *n* Gummi, Kautschuk *m*.
indicate ['ɪndɪkeɪt] **1** *vt* **(a)** *(point out, mark)* zeigen, bezeichnen; *(register) temperature etc* anzeigen. **(b)** *(show) feelings etc* andeuten, zeigen. **(c)** *(be a sign of, suggest)* schließen lassen auf *(+acc)*, (hin)deuten auf *(+acc)*. **this would definitely ~ that ...** das würde bestimmt darauf hindeuten, daß ...; **what does it ~ to you?** was schließen Sie daraus? **2** *vi (Aut)* blinken. **to ~**

right rechts blinken.

indication [ˌɪndɪ'keɪʃən] *n (sign)* (An)zeichen *nt (also Med) (of* für*)*, Hinweis *m (of* auf *+acc)*. **we had no ~ that ...** es gab kein Anzeichen dafür, daß ...; **if you could give me a rough ~ of ...** wenn Sie mir eine ungefähre Vorstellung davon geben könnten ...

indicative [ɪn'dɪkətɪv] **1** *adj* **(a) to be ~ of sth** auf etw *(acc)* schließen lassen; *of sb's character* für etw bezeichnend sein. **(b)** *(Gram)* indikativisch. **2** *n (Gram)* **in the ~** im Indikativ.

indicator ['ɪndɪkeɪtə^r] *n (gauge)* Anzeiger *m*; *(needle)* Zeiger *m*; *(Aut)* Blinker *m*. **~ board** *(Rail)* (Anzeige)tafel *f*.

indices ['ɪndɪsiːz] *pl of* **index.**

indict [ɪn'daɪt] *vt (charge)* anklagen, unter Anklage stellen; *(US Jur)* Anklage erheben gegen *(for* wegen *+gen)*.

indictable [ɪn'daɪtəbl] *adj offence* strafbar.

indictment [ɪn'daɪtmənt] *n (of person)* Anklage, Anschuldigung *f*. **to be an ~ of sth** *(fig)* ein Armutszeugnis für etw sein.

indifference [ɪn'dɪfrəns] *n see adj* **(a)** Gleichgültigkeit *f (to, towards* gegenüber*)*. **(b)** Mittelmäßigkeit *f*.

indifferent [ɪn'dɪfrənt] *adj* **(a)** gleichgültig, indifferent *(geh) (to, towards* gegenüber*)*. **he is quite ~ to her** sie ist ihm ziemlich gleichgültig. **(b)** *(mediocre)* mittelmäßig, durchschnittlich.

indigenous [ɪn'dɪdʒɪnəs] *adj* einheimisch *(to* in *+dat)*.

indigestible [ˌɪndɪ'dʒestəbl] *adj* unverdaulich.

indigestion [ˌɪndɪ'dʒestʃən] *n* Magenverstimmung *f*.

indignant [ɪn'dɪgnənt] *adj* entrüstet, empört *(at, about, with* über *+acc)*.

indignation [ˌɪndɪg'neɪʃən] *n* Entrüstung, Empörung *f (at, about, with* über *+acc)*.

indignity [ɪn'dɪgnɪtɪ] *n* Demütigung *f*.

indigo ['ɪndɪgəʊ] **1** *n* Indigo *nt or m*. **2** *adj* indigofarben.

indirect [ˌɪndɪ'rekt] *adj* indirekt. **by an ~ route** auf einem Umweg; **to make an ~ reference to sth** auf etw anspielen; **~ object** Dativobjekt *nt*; **~ speech** *or (US)* **discourse** indirekte Rede.

indiscreet [ˌɪndɪ'skriːt] *adj* indiskret; *(tactless)* taktlos.

indiscretion [ˌɪndɪ'skreʃən] *n see adj* Indiskretion *f*; Taktlosigkeit *f*; *(affair)* Affäre *f*.

indiscriminate [ˌɪndɪ'skrɪmɪnɪt] *adj* wahllos; *reader, shopper* unkritisch; *tastes* unausgeprägt.

indispensable [ˌɪndɪ'spensəbl] *adj* unentbehrlich *(to* für*)*. **~ to life** lebensnotwendig.

indisposed [ˌɪndɪ'spəʊzd] *adj (unwell)* unwohl.

indisputable [ˌɪndɪ'spjuːtəbl] *adj* unbestreitbar; *evidence* unanfechtbar.

indistinct [ˌɪndɪ'stɪŋkt] *adj* unklar, undeutlich.

indistinguishable [ˌɪndɪ'stɪŋgwɪʃəbl] *adj* nicht unterscheidbar *(from* von*)*.

individual [ˌɪndɪ'vɪdjʊəl] **1** *adj* **(a)** *(separate)* einzeln. **~ cases** Einzelfälle *pl*; **~ tastes differ** die Geschmäcker sind verschieden. **(b)** *(own)* eigen; *(for one person) portion etc* einzeln, Einzel-. **(c)** *(distinctive)* eigen, individuell. **2** *n* Individuum *nt*, Einzelne(r) *mf*.

individualist [ˌɪndɪ'vɪdjʊəlɪst] *n* Individualist(in *f*) *m*.

individuality ['ɪndɪˌvɪdjʊ'ælɪtɪ] *n* Individualität *f*.

individually [ˌɪndɪ'vɪdjʊəlɪ] *adv* individuell; *(separately)* einzeln.

indivisible [ˌɪndɪ'vɪzəbl] *adj* unteilbar *(also Math)*.

Indo- ['ɪndəʊ-] *pref* Indo-. **~-China** *n* Indochina *nt*.

indoctrinate [ɪn'dɒktrɪneɪt] *vt* indoktrinieren.

indoctrination [ɪnˌdɒktrɪ'neɪʃən] *n* Indoktrination *f*.

indolence ['ɪndələns] *n* Trägheit *f*.

indolent ['ɪndələnt] *adj* träge.

Indonesia [ˌɪndəʊ'niːzɪə] *n* Indonesien *nt*.

Indonesian [ˌɪndəʊ'niːzɪən] **1** *adj* indonesisch. **2** *n* **(a)** Indonesier(in *f*) *m*. **(b)** *(language)* Indonesisch *nt*.

indoor ['ɪndɔː^r] *adj plant* Zimmer-; *clothes* Haus-; *photography* Innen-; *sport* Hallen-; *swimming pool* Hallen-; *(private)* überdacht. **~ games** Spiele *pl* für drinnen; *(Sport)* Hallenspiele *pl*.

indoors [ɪn'dɔːz] *adv* drinnen, innen; *(at home)* zu Hause. **to stay ~** im Haus bleiben, drin bleiben *(col)*; **to go ~** ins Haus gehen.

induce [ɪn'djuːs] *vt* **(a)** *(persuade)* dazu bewegen *or* bringen. **(b)** *reaction* bewirken, hervorrufen; *sleep* herbeiführen; *birth* einleiten. **this drug ~s sleep** dieses Mittel hat eine einschläfernde Wirkung. **(c)** *(Elec) current* induzieren.

inducement [ɪn'djuːsmənt] *n (no pl: persuasion)* Überredung *f*; *(incentive)* Anreiz *m*. **as an added ~** als besonderer Anreiz.

induction [ɪn'dʌkʃən] *n* **(a)** *(of sleep, reaction etc)* Herbeiführen *nt*; *(of birth)* Einleitung *f*. **(b)** *(Philos, Elec)* Induktion *f*. **~ coil** *n (Elec)* Induktionsspule *f*.

indulge [ɪn'dʌldʒ] **1** *vt desires etc* nachgeben *(+dat)*; *person also* nachsichtig sein mit; *(over~) children* verwöhnen. **to ~ oneself in sth** sich *(dat)* etw gönnen. **2** *vi* **to ~ in sth** sich *(dat)* etw gönnen *or* genehmigen *(col)*; *(in vice, drink)* einer Sache *(dat)* frönen. **I don't ~** ich trinke/rauche *etc* nicht.

indulgence [ɪn'dʌldʒəns] *n* **(a)** Nachsicht *f*; *(of appetite etc)* Nachgiebigkeit *f (of* gegenüber*)*; *(over~)* Verwöhnung *f*. **the ~ of his wishes** das Erfüllen seiner Wünsche. **(b)** *(in activity, drink etc)* **~ in drink** übermäßiges Trinken. **(c)** *(thing indulged in)* Luxus *m*; *(food, drink, pleasure)* Genuß *m*.

indulgent [ɪn'dʌldʒənt] *adj (to* gegenüber*)* nachsichtig; *mother etc also* nachgiebig; *(to one's own desires etc)* zu nachgiebig.

industrial [ɪn'dʌstrɪəl] *adj worker, equipment, state* Industrie-; *production also* industriell; *training, accident* Betriebs-. **~ action** Arbeitskampfmaßnahmen *pl*; **to take ~ action** in den Ausstand treten; **~ dispute** Auseinandersetzungen *pl* zwischen Arbeitgebern und Arbeitnehmern; **~ estate** *(Brit)* Industriegebiet *nt*; **~ injury** Arbeitsunfall *m*; **~ relations** Beziehungen *pl* zwischen Arbeitgebern und Gewerkschaften; *(in particular company also)* Betriebsklima *nt*; **I~ Revolution** Industrielle Revolution; **~ tribunal** Arbeitsgericht *nt*; **~ unrest** Arbeitsunruhen *pl*.

industrialist [ɪn'dʌstrɪəlɪst] *n* Industrielle(r) *mf*.

industrialize [ɪn'dʌstrɪəlaɪz] *vti* industrialisieren.

industrious [ɪn'dʌstrɪəs] *adj* fleißig.

industry ['ɪndəstrɪ] *n* **(a)** Industrie *f*. **heavy/light ~** Schwer-/Leichtindustrie *f*. **(b)** *(industriousness)* Fleiß *m*.

inebriated [ɪ'niːbrɪeɪtɪd] *adj* **(a)** *(form)* unter starkem Alkoholeinfluß *(form)*. **(b)** *(fig)* berauscht.

inedible [ɪn'edɪbl] *adj* nicht eßbar; *(unpleasant)* ungenießbar.

ineffective [ˌɪnɪ'fektɪv] *adj* unwirksam, ineffektiv; *person* unfähig, untauglich.

ineffectual [ˌɪnɪ'fektjʊəl] *adj* ineffektiv.

inefficiency [ˌɪnɪ'fɪʃənsɪ] *n see adj* Unfähigkeit *f*; Inkompetenz *f*; Leistungsunfähigkeit *f*.

inefficient [ˌɪnɪ'fɪʃənt] *adj person* unfähig, inkompetent; *machine, company* leistungsunfähig.

inelegant [ɪn'elɪgənt] *adj* unelegant; *clothes also* ohne Schick.

ineligible [ɪn'elɪdʒəbl] *adj (for benefits, grant)* nicht berechtigt *(for* zu *+dat)*; *(for job)* ungeeignet. **~ for a pension** nicht pensionsberechtigt.

inept [ɪ'nept] *adj behaviour* ungeschickt, linkisch; *remark* unpassend; *attempt* plump; *comparison* ungeeignet.

ineptitude [ɪ'neptɪtjuːd] *n see adj* Ungeschicktheit

f; Ungeeignetheit *f*.
inequality [ˌɪnɪˈkwɒlɪtɪ] *n* Ungleichheit *f*.
inequitable [ɪnˈekwɪtəbl] *adj* ungerecht.
inert [ɪˈnɜːt] *adj* unbeweglich; *(Phys) matter* träge; *(Chem) substance* inaktiv. ~ **gas** Edelgas *nt*.
inertia [ɪˈnɜːʃə] *n (lit, fig)* Trägheit *f*. **~-reel seat belt** Automatikgurt *m*.
inescapable [ˌɪnɪsˈkeɪpəbl] *adj* unvermeidlich.
inevitability [ɪnˌevɪtəˈbɪlɪtɪ] *n* Unvermeidlichkeit *f*.
inevitable [ɪnˈevɪtəbl] *adj* unvermeidlich.
inexact [ˌɪnɪgˈzækt] *adj* ungenau.
inexcusable [ˌɪnɪksˈkjuːzəbl] *adj* unverzeihlich.
inexhaustible [ˌɪnɪgˈzɔːstəbl] *adj source* nie versiegend; *wealth, patience* unerschöpflich.
inexorable [ɪnˈeksərəbl] *adj (relentless)* unerbittlich; *(not to be stopped)* unaufhaltsam.
inexpensive [ˌɪnɪkˈspensɪv] *adj* billig, preisgünstig.
inexperience [ˌɪnɪkˈspɪərɪəns] *n* Unerfahrenheit *f*.
inexperienced [ˌɪnɪkˈspɪərɪənst] *adj* unerfahren; *skier etc* ungeübt.
inexplicable [ˌɪnɪkˈsplɪkəbl] *adj* unerklärlich.
inexpressible [ˌɪnɪkˈspresəbl] *adj* unbeschreiblich; *pain, joy also* unsagbar.
inexpressive [ˌɪnɪkˈspresɪv] *adj face* ausdruckslos; *word* nichtssagend; *style* ohne Ausdruckskraft.
inextricable [ˌɪnɪkˈstrɪkəbl] *adj tangle* unentwirrbar; *confusion* unüberschaubar; *difficulties* unlösbar.
infallibility [ɪnˌfæləˈbɪlɪtɪ] *n* Unfehlbarkeit *f*.
infallible [ɪnˈfæləbl] *adj* unfehlbar.
infamous [ˈɪnfəməs] *adj* berüchtigt, verrufen; *deed* niederträchtig.
infamy [ˈɪnfəmɪ] *n see adj* Verrufenheit *f*; Niedertracht *f*.
infancy [ˈɪnfənsɪ] *n* frühe Kindheit; *(fig)* Anfangsstadium *nt*. **data processing is no longer in its ~** die Datenverarbeitung steckt nicht mehr in den Kinderschuhen.
infant [ˈɪnfənt] *n (baby)* Säugling *m*; *(young child)* Kleinkind *nt*. ~ **mortality** Säuglingssterblichkeit *f*; ~ **school** *(Brit) Grundschule f für die ersten beiden Jahrgänge*.
infantile [ˈɪnfəntaɪl] *adj (childish)* kindisch, infantil.
infantry [ˈɪnfəntrɪ] *n (Mil)* Infanterie *f*.
infatuated [ɪnˈfætjʊeɪtɪd] *adj* vernarrt, verknallt *(col) (with* in *+acc)*. **to become ~ with sb** sich in jdn vernarren; ~ **with sth** von etw besessen.
infatuation [ɪnˌfætjʊˈeɪʃən] *n* Vernarrtheit *f (with* in *+acc)*.
infect [ɪnˈfekt] *vt wound* infizieren; *water* verseuchen; *meat* verderben; *(fig: with enthusiasm etc)* anstecken. **his wound became ~ed** seine Wunde entzündete sich.
infection [ɪnˈfekʃən] *n (illness)* Infektion, Entzündung *f*; *(of water)* Verseuchung *f*.
infectious [ɪnˈfekʃəs] *adj (Med, fig)* ansteckend.
infer [ɪnˈfɜːʳ] *vt* **(a)** schließen, folgern *(from* aus*)*. **(b)** *(imply)* andeuten.
inference [ˈɪnfərəns] *n* Schluß(folgerung *f*) *m*.
inferior [ɪnˈfɪərɪəʳ] *adj (in quality)* minderwertig; *quality also* geringer; *person* unterlegen; *court* untergeordnet.
inferiority [ɪnˌfɪərɪˈɒrɪtɪ] *n (in quality)* Minderwertigkeit *f*; *(of person)* Unterlegenheit *f (to* gegenüber*)*. ~ **complex** Minderwertigkeitskomplex *m*.
infernal [ɪnˈfɜːnl] *adj (lit)* Höllen-; *(fig) scheme* teuflisch; *(col) noise* höllisch.
inferno [ɪnˈfɜːnəʊ] *n (hell)* Hölle *f*, Inferno *nt*; *(blazing house etc)* Flammenmeer *nt*. **a blazing ~** ein flammendes Inferno.
infertile [ɪnˈfɜːtaɪl] *adj soil, womb* unfruchtbar; *mind* ideenlos.
infertility [ˌɪnfɜːˈtɪlɪtɪ] *n see adj* Unfruchtbarkeit *f*; Ideenlosigkeit *f*.
infest [ɪnˈfest] *vt (rats)* herfallen über *(+acc)*; *(plague)* befallen. **to be ~ed with disease/rats** verseucht/mit Ratten verseucht sein; **to be ~ed** *(with lice etc)* mit Ungeziefer verseucht sein.
infidelity [ˌɪnfɪˈdelɪtɪ] *n* Untreue *f*.
in-fighting [ˈɪnfaɪtɪŋ] *n (fig)* interner Machtkampf.
infiltrate [ˈɪnfɪltreɪt] **1** *vt troops* infiltrieren; *(Pol) organization also* unterwandern; *spies* einschleusen. **2** *vi (Mil)* eindringen *(into* in *+acc)*; *(spy also)* sich einschleusen *(into* in *+acc)*.
infiltration [ˌɪnfɪlˈtreɪʃən] *n (Mil)* Infiltration *f*; *(Pol also)* Unterwanderung *f*.
infinite [ˈɪnfɪnɪt] *adj (lit)* unendlich; *(fig also) trouble, pleasure* grenzenlos. **an ~ amount of time** unendlich viel Zeit.
infinitely [ˈɪnfɪnɪtlɪ] *adv* unendlich; *(fig also)* grenzenlos; *improved* ungeheuer; *better, worse* unendlich viel.
infinitesimal [ˌɪnfɪnɪˈtesɪməl] *adj* unendlich klein.
infinitive [ɪnˈfɪnɪtɪv] *n* Infinitiv *m*.
infinity [ɪnˈfɪnɪtɪ] *n (lit)* Unendlichkeit *f*; *(fig also)* Grenzenlosigkeit *f*; *(Math)* das Unendliche. **to ~** (bis) ins Unendliche; **"~"** *(Phot)* „unendlich".
infirm [ɪnˈfɜːm] *adj* gebrechlich, schwach.
infirmary [ɪnˈfɜːmərɪ] *n* Krankenhaus *nt*; *(in school etc)* Krankenzimmer *nt*; *(in prison, barracks)* Krankenstation *f*.
inflame [ɪnˈfleɪm] *vt* **(a)** *(Med)* entzünden. **to become ~d** sich entzünden. **(b)** *person* aufbringen; *feelings* entflammen; *anger* erregen.
inflammable [ɪnˈflæməbl] *adj (lit)* feuergefährlich, (leicht) entzündbar; *(fig) situation* brisant.
inflammation [ˌɪnfləˈmeɪʃən] *n (Med)* Entzündung *f*.
inflammatory [ɪnˈflæmətərɪ] *adj speech* aufrührerisch.
inflatable [ɪnˈfleɪtɪbl] *adj* aufblasbar; *dinghy* Schlauch-.
inflate [ɪnˈfleɪt] *vt* **(a)** aufpumpen; *(by mouth)* aufblasen. **(b)** *(Econ) prices* steigern, hochtreiben. **(c)** *(fig)* steigern.
inflated [ɪnˈfleɪtɪd] *adj prices* überhöht, inflationär; *pride* übersteigert; *style* geschwollen. **to have an ~ opinion of oneself** ein übertriebenes Selbstbewußtsein haben.
inflation [ɪnˈfleɪʃən] *n (Econ)* Inflation *f*. **to fight ~** die Inflation bekämpfen; **5% ~** eine Inflationsrate von 5%.
inflationary [ɪnˈfleɪʃənərɪ] *adj* inflationär, inflationistisch *(pej)*. **the ~ spiral** die Inflationsspirale.
inflect [ɪnˈflekt] *vt (Gram)* flektieren, beugen.
inflexibility [ɪnˌfleksɪˈbɪlɪtɪ] *n (lit)* Unbiegsamkeit, Steifheit *f*; *(fig)* Unbeugsamkeit *f*.
inflexible [ɪnˈfleksəbl] *adj person, attitude, opinion* unbeugsam; *substance, object* unbiegsam, steif.
inflict [ɪnˈflɪkt] *vt punishment* verhängen *(on, upon* gegen*)*; *suffering* zufügen *(on or upon sb* jdm*)*; *wound* beibringen *(on or upon sb* jdm*)*. **to ~ oneself on sb** sich jdm aufdrängen.
in-flight [ˈɪnflaɪt] *adj attr* während des Fluges.
influence [ˈɪnflʊəns] **1** *n* Einfluß *m*. **to have an ~ on sb/sth** *(person)* Einfluß auf jdn/etw haben; *(fact, weather etc also)* Auswirkungen *pl* auf jdn/etw haben; **to have a great deal of ~ with sb** großen Einfluß bei jdm haben; **he's been a bad ~ on you** er war ein schlechter Einfluß für Sie; **she is a good ~ on the pupils** sie hat einen guten Einfluß auf die Schüler; **to exert an ~ on sb** Einfluß auf jdn ausüben; **under the ~ of drink** unter Alkoholeinfluß; **under the ~** *(col)* betrunken. **2** *vt* beeinflussen. **to be easily ~d** leicht beeinflußbar sein.
influential [ˌɪnflʊˈenʃəl] *adj* einflußreich.
influenza [ˌɪnflʊˈenzə] *n* Grippe *f*.

influx ['ɪnflʌks] *n (of capital)* Zufuhr *f*; *(of people)* Zustrom *m*; *(of ideas etc)* Zufluß *m*.

inform [ɪn'fɔːm] **1** *vt* benachrichtigen, informieren *(about* über *+acc)*; unterrichten. **to ~ sb of sth** jdn von etw unterrichten, jdn über etw informieren; **I am pleased to ~ you that ...** ich freue mich, Ihnen mitteilen zu können, daß ...; **to ~ the police** die Polizei benachrichtigen; **to keep sb/oneself ~ed** jdn/sich auf dem laufenden halten *(of* über *+acc)*; **why was I not ~ed?** warum wurde mir das nicht mitgeteilt? **2** *vi* **to ~ against** *or* **on sb** jdn anzeigen *or* denunzieren *(pej)*.

informal [ɪn'fɔːməl] *adj (not official) meeting* informell; *visit* inoffiziell; *(without ceremony) meeting, language* ungezwungen; *manner* leger; *restaurant* gemütlich. **"dress ~"** „zwanglose Kleidung".

informality [ˌɪnfɔː'mælɪtɪ] *n see adj* informeller Charakter; inoffizieller Charakter; Ungezwungenheit *f*; legere Art; Gemütlichkeit *f*.

informally [ɪn'fɔːməlɪ] *adv (unofficially)* inoffiziell; *(casually, without ceremony)* zwanglos, ungezwungen.

informant [ɪn'fɔːmənt] *n* Informant *m*.

information [ˌɪnfə'meɪʃən] *n* Auskunft *f*, Informationen *pl*. **a piece of ~** eine Auskunft, eine Information; **for your ~** zu Ihrer Information; *(indignantly)* damit Sie es wissen!; **to give sb ~ about** *or* **on sb/sth** jdm Auskunft *or* Informationen über jdn/etw geben; **to get ~ about** *or* **on sb/sth** sich über jdn/etw informieren; **detailed ~** Einzelheiten *pl*.

information: ~ bureau *n* Auskunft(sbüro *nt*) *f*, Verkehrsbüro *nt*; **~ science** *n* Informatik *f*; **~ technology** Datentechnik *f*.

informative [ɪn'fɔːmətɪv] *adj* aufschlußreich; *book, lecture also* lehrreich. **he's not very ~ about his plans** er ist nicht sehr mitteilsam, was seine Pläne betrifft.

informed [ɪn'fɔːmd] *adj observers* informiert, (gut) unterrichtet; *(educated)* gebildet.

informer [ɪn'fɔːmə^r] *n* Informant, Denunziant *(pej) m*. **police ~** Polizeispitzel *m (pej)*; **to turn ~** seine Mittäter verraten.

infra-red ['ɪnfrə'red] *adj* infrarot.

infrastructure ['ɪnfrə'strʌktʃə^r] *n* Infrastruktur *f*.

infrequent [ɪn'friːkwənt] *adj* selten. **at ~ intervals** in großen Abständen.

infringe [ɪn'frɪndʒ] **1** *vt* verstoßen gegen; *law, copyright also* verletzen. **2** *vi* **to ~ (up)on sb's privacy** in jds Privatsphäre *(acc)* eingreifen.

infringement [ɪn'frɪndʒmənt] *n* **(a) an ~ (of a rule)** ein Regelverstoß *m*; **~ of the law** Gesetzesverletzung *or* -übertretung *f*; **~ of a patent/copyright** Patentverletzung *f*/Verletzung *f* des Urheberrechts. **(b)** *(of privacy)* Eingriff *m (of* in *+acc)*.

infuriate [ɪn'fjʊərɪeɪt] *vt* wütend *or* rasend machen. **to be/get ~d** wütend *or* rasend sein/werden.

infuriating [ɪn'fjʊərɪeɪtɪŋ] *adj* (äußerst) ärgerlich. **an ~ habit** eine Unsitte; **an ~ person** ein Mensch, der einen zur Raserei bringen kann.

infuse [ɪn'fjuːz] **1** *vt* **(a)** *courage etc* einflößen *(into sb* jdm*)*. **they were ~d with new hope** sie waren von neuer Hoffnung erfüllt. **(b)** *(Cook) tea* aufgießen. **2** *vi (tea)* ziehen.

infusion [ɪn'fjuːʒən] *n* **(a)** *(of hope etc)* Einflößen *nt*. **(b)** *(Cook)* Aufguß *m*; *(tea-like)* Tee *m*. **(c)** *(Med)* Infusion *f*.

ingenious [ɪn'dʒiːnɪəs] *adj* genial; *person also* erfinderisch; *device also* raffiniert.

ingenuity [ˌɪndʒɪ'njuːɪtɪ] *n* Genialität *f*; *(of person also)* Einfallsreichtum *m*; *(of device also)* Raffiniertheit *f*.

ingenuous [ɪn'dʒenjʊəs] *adj* **(a)** *(candid)* aufrichtig. **(b)** *(naive)* naiv.

ingot ['ɪŋgət] *n* Barren *m*.

ingrained [ˌɪn'greɪnd] *adj* **(a)** *habit* fest, eingefleischt; *belief* unerschütterlich. **(b)** *dirt* tiefsitzend *(attr)*.

ingratiate [ɪn'greɪʃɪeɪt] *vr* **to ~ oneself with sb** sich bei jdm einschmeicheln.

ingratiating [ɪn'greɪʃɪeɪtɪŋ] *adj person, speech* schmeichlerisch; *smile* schmeichlerisch süßlich.

ingratitude [ɪn'grætɪtjuːd] *n* Undank *m*. **sb's ~** jds Undankbarkeit *f*.

ingredient [ɪn'griːdɪənt] *n* Bestandteil *m*; *(for recipe)* Zutat *f*. **all the ~s of success** alles, was man zum Erfolg braucht.

ingrowing ['ɪngrəʊɪŋ] *adj toenail* eingewachsen.

inhabit [ɪn'hæbɪt] *vt* bewohnen; *(animals)* leben in *(+dat)*.

inhabitable [ɪn'hæbɪtəbl] *adj* bewohnbar.

inhabitant [ɪn'hæbɪtənt] *n* Bewohner(in *f*) *m*; *(of island, town also)* Einwohner(in *f*) *m*.

inhale [ɪn'heɪl] **1** *vt* einatmen; *(Med)* inhalieren. **2** *vi (in smoking)* Lungenzüge machen.

inherent [ɪn'hɪərənt] *adj* innewohnend. **the ~ hardness of diamonds** die den Diamanten eigene Härte; **the ~ risks of the test** die mit dem Test verbundenen Gefahren.

inherently [ɪn'hɪərəntlɪ] *adv* von Natur aus.

inherit [ɪn'herɪt] *vt (lit, fig)* erben.

inheritance [ɪn'herɪtəns] *n* Erbe *nt (also fig)*, Erbschaft *f*.

inhibit [ɪn'hɪbɪt] *vt* hemmen. **to ~ sb from doing sth** jdn daran hindern, etw zu tun.

inhibited [ɪn'hɪbɪtɪd] *adj* gehemmt.

inhibition [ˌɪnhɪ'bɪʃən] *n* Hemmung *f*.

inhospitable [ˌɪnhɒ'spɪtəbl] *adj* ungastlich; *region* unwirtlich.

in-house [ɪn'haʊs] *adj* hausintern.

inhuman [ɪn'hjuːmən] *adj cruelty etc* unmenschlich.

inhumane [ˌɪnhjuː'meɪn] *adj* inhuman; *(to people also)* menschenunwürdig.

inhumanity [ˌɪnhjuː'mænɪtɪ] *n* Unmenschlichkeit *f*. **the ~ of man to man** die Unmenschlichkeit der Menschen untereinander.

inimitable [ɪ'nɪmɪtəbl] *adj* unnachahmlich.

iniquitous [ɪ'nɪkwɪtəs] *adj* ungeheuerlich.

initial [ɪ'nɪʃəl] **1** *adj* anfänglich, Anfangs-. **my ~ reaction** meine anfängliche Reaktion; **in the ~ stages** im Anfangsstadium. **2** *n* Initiale *f*. **3** *vt letter* mit seinen Initialen unterzeichnen; *(Comm)* abzeichnen; *(Pol)* paraphieren.

initially [ɪ'nɪʃəlɪ] *adv* anfangs, am Anfang.

initiate [ɪ'nɪʃɪeɪt] **1** *vt* **(a)** *(set in motion)* den Anstoß geben zu. **(b)** *(into club)* feierlich aufnehmen; *(in tribal society) adolescents* initiieren. **2** *n (in club)* Neuaufgenommene(r) *mf*.

initiation [ɪˌnɪʃɪ'eɪʃən] *n* **(a)** *(of project etc)* Initiierung *f*. **(b)** *(into society)* Aufnahme *f*; *(as tribal member)* Initiation *f*. **~ ceremony** Aufnahmezeremonie *f*.

initiative [ɪ'nɪʃətɪv] *n* Initiative *f*. **to take the ~** die Initiative ergreifen; **on one's own ~** aus eigener Initiative; **use your ~!** hast du keine Initiative?

inject [ɪn'dʒekt] *vt* (ein)spritzen; *(fig) comment* einwerfen; *money* pumpen. **he ~ed new life into the club** er brachte neues Leben in den Verein.

injection [ɪn'dʒekʃən] *n* Injektion, Spritze *f*. **an ~ of capital** eine Finanzspritze.

injudicious [ˌɪndʒʊ'dɪʃəs] *adj* unklug.

injunction [ɪn'dʒʌŋkʃən] *n* Anordnung *f*; *(Jur)* gerichtliche Verfügung.

injure ['ɪndʒə^r] *vt (lit, fig)* verletzen. **to ~ one's leg** sich *(dat)* das Bein verletzen; **he was ~d** er verletzte sich; **is he ~d?** ist er verletzt?; **the ~d** die Verletzten; **the ~d party** *(Jur)* der/die Geschädigte.

injurious [ɪn'dʒʊərɪəs] *adj* schädlich.

injury ['ɪndʒərɪ] *n* Verletzung *f (to gen)*; *(fig also)* Kränkung *f (to gen)*. **to do sb/oneself an ~** jdn/

sich verletzen; **to play ~ time** *(Brit Sport)* nachspielen.

injustice [ɪn'dʒʌstɪs] *n (unfairness, inequality)* Ungerechtigkeit *f*; *(violation of sb's rights)* Unrecht *nt no pl*. **to do sb an ~** jdm Unrecht tun.

ink [ɪŋk] *n* Tinte *f*; *(Art)* Tusche *f*.

inkling ['ɪŋklɪŋ] *n* dunkle Ahnung. **he hadn't an ~** er hatte nicht die leiseste Ahnung; **to give sb an ~** jdm eine Andeutung geben.

inkpad ['ɪnkpæd] *n* Stempelkissen *nt*.

inky ['ɪŋkɪ] *adj (+er) (lit)* tintenbeschmiert; *(fig) darkness* tintenschwarz; *black* tintig.

inlaid [ɪn'leɪd] *adj* eingelegt. **~ table** Tisch *m* mit Einlegearbeit.

inland ['ɪnlænd] **1** *adj waterway, trade* Binnen-; *mail* Inland(s)-. **I~ Revenue** *(Brit)* ≃ Finanzamt *nt*. **2** *adv* landeinwärts.

inlaws ['ɪnlɔːz] *npl (parents-in-law)* Schwiegereltern *pl*; *(others)* angeheiratete Verwandte *pl*.

inlet ['ɪnlet] *n* **(a)** *(of sea)* Meeresarm *m*; *(of river)* Flußarm *m*. **(b)** *(Tech)* Zuleitung *f*; *(of ventilator)* Öffnung *f*. **~ pipe** *n* Zuleitung(srohr *nt*) *f*; **~ valve** *n* Einlaßventil *nt*.

inmate ['ɪnmeɪt] *n* Insasse *m*, Insassin *f*.

inmost ['ɪnməʊst] *adj* innerst.

inn [ɪn] *n* Gasthaus *nt*; *(old: hotel)* Herberge *f (old)*.

innards ['ɪnədz] *npl* Innereien *pl (also fig)*, Eingeweide *pl*.

innate [ɪ'neɪt] *adj* angeboren.

inner ['ɪnəʳ] *adj* innere(r,s); *surface, door, city, ear also* Innen-; *meaning* verborgen; *life* Seelen-. **~ harbour** Innenbecken *nt*; **the needs of the ~ man** die inneren Bedürfnisse.

innermost ['ɪnəməʊst] *adj* innerst. **in the ~ depths of the forest** im tiefsten Wald.

inner tube *n* Schlauch *m*.

innings ['ɪnɪŋz] *n (Cricket)* Innenrunde *f*. **he has had a good ~** *(fig col)* er war lange an der Reihe; *(life)* er hatte ein langes, ausgefülltes Leben.

innkeeper ['ɪnˌkiːpəʳ] *n* (Gast)wirt *m*.

innocence ['ɪnəsəns] *n* **(a)** Unschuld *f*. **in all ~** in aller Unschuld. **(b)** *(ignorance)* Unkenntnis *f*.

innocent ['ɪnəsənt] *adj* **(a)** unschuldig *(of* an *+dat)*; *mistake* unabsichtlich. **to put on an ~ air** eine Unschuldsmiene aufsetzen. **(b) ~ of** *(ignorant)* nicht vertraut mit.

innocuous [ɪ'nɒkjʊəs] *adj* harmlos.

innovate ['ɪnəʊveɪt] *vi* Neuerungen einführen.

innovation [ˌɪnəʊ'veɪʃən] *n* Innovation *f*; *(introduction also)* Neueinführung *f (of gen)*; *(thing introduced also)* Neuerung *f*.

innovative [ɪnə'veɪtɪv] *adj* innovativ *(geh)*, innovatorisch *(geh)*.

innuendo [ˌɪnjʊ'endəʊ] *n, pl* **-es** versteckte Andeutung. **to make ~es about sb** über jdn Andeutungen fallenlassen.

innumerable [ɪ'njuːmərəbl] *adj* unzählig.

inoculate [ɪ'nɒkjʊleɪt] *vt person* impfen *(against* gegen*)*.

inoculation [ɪˌnɒkjʊ'leɪʃən] *n* Impfung *f*.

inoffensive [ˌɪnə'fensɪv] *adj* harmlos.

inopportune [ɪn'ɒpətjuːn] *adj* inopportun; *moment also* ungelegen. **to be ~** ungelegen kommen.

inordinate [ɪ'nɔːdɪnɪt] *adj* unmäßig; *number, sum of money* ungeheuer.

inorganic [ˌɪnɔː'gænɪk] *adj* anorganisch.

in-patient ['ɪnpeɪʃnt] *n* stationär behandelter Patient/behandelte Patientin.

input ['ɪnpʊt] **1** *n (Comp)* Eingabe *f*, Input *m or nt*; *(power ~)* Energiezufuhr *f*; *(of energy, work etc)* Aufwand *m*. **2** *vt (Comp)* eingeben.

inquest ['ɪnkwest] *n (into death)* gerichtliche Untersuchung der Todesursache.

inquire [ɪn'kwaɪəʳ] *etc (esp US)* = **enquire** *etc*.

inquisition [ˌɪnkwɪ'zɪʃən] *n (Hist, fig)* Inquisition *f*.

inquisitive [ɪn'kwɪzɪtɪv] *adj* neugierig; *(for knowledge)* wißbegierig.

inquisitiveness [ɪn'kwɪzɪtɪvnɪs] *n* Neugier *f*.

inroad ['ɪnrəʊd] *n (Mil)* Einfall *m (into* in *+acc)*. **to make ~s into sth** *into time* etw stark in Anspruch nehmen; *into savings* etw stark angreifen; **the Japanese are making ~s into the British market** die Japaner dringen in den britischen Markt ein.

insane [ɪn'seɪn] **1** *adj* geisteskrank; *(fig)* wahnsinnig. **2** *npl* **the ~** die Geisteskranken *pl*.

insanitary [ɪn'sænɪtərɪ] *adj* unhygienisch.

insanity [ɪn'sænɪtɪ] *n* Geisteskrankheit *f*; *(fig)* Wahnsinn *m*.

insatiable [ɪn'seɪʃəbl] *adj* unersättlich.

inscribe [ɪn'skraɪb] *vt (on sth* in etw *acc) words etc (on ring etc)* eingravieren; *(on stone)* einmeißeln.

inscription [ɪn'skrɪpʃən] Inschrift *f*; *(on coin)* Aufschrift *f*; *(in book)* Widmung *f*.

inscrutable [ɪn'skruːtəbl] *adj* unergründlich. **~ face** undurchdringlicher Gesichtsausdruck.

insect ['ɪnsekt] *n* Insekt *nt*. **~ bite** *n* Insektenstich *m*.

insecticide [ɪn'sektɪsaɪd] *n* Insektizid *nt*.

insecure [ˌɪnsɪ'kjʊəʳ] *adj* unsicher.

insecurity [ˌɪnsɪ'kjʊərɪtɪ] *n* Unsicherheit *f*.

insensible [ɪn'sensəbl] *adj* unempfindlich *(to* gegen*)*.

insensitive [ɪn'sensɪtɪv] *adj* **(a)** *(emotionally)* gefühllos. **(b)** *(unappreciative)* unempfänglich *(to* für*)*. **(c)** *(physically)* unempfindlich. **~ to pain/light** schmerz-/lichtunempfindlich.

insensitivity [ɪnˌsensɪ'tɪvɪtɪ] *n* **(a)** *(emotional)* Gefühllosigkeit *f (towards* gegenüber*)*. **(b)** *(unappreciativeness)* Unempfänglichkeit *f (to* für*)*. **(c)** *(physical)* Unempfindlichkeit *f*.

inseparable [ɪn'sepərəbl] *adj* untrennbar; *friends* unzertrennlich.

insert [ɪn'sɜːt] **1** *vt (stick into)* hineinstecken; *(place in)* hineinlegen; *(place between)* einfügen; *thermometer* einführen; *coin* einwerfen. **to ~ a paragraph** einen weiteren Absatz einfügen. **2** ['ɪnsɜːt] *n (in book)* Einlage *f*; *(in magazine)* Beilage *f*.

insertion [ɪn'sɜːʃən] *n see vt* Hineinstecken *nt*; Hineinlegen *nt*; Einfügen *nt*; Einführen *nt*; Einwerfen *nt*.

inset [ɪn'set] *n (also* **~ map***)* Nebenkarte *f*; *(on diagram)* Nebenbild *nt*.

inshore ['ɪn'ʃɔːʳ] *adj* Küsten-. **~ fishing** Küstenfischerei *f*.

inside ['ɪn'saɪd] **1** *n* **(a)** Innere(s) *nt*; *(of pavement)* Innenseite *f*. **on the ~** innen; **to know a company from the ~** interne Kenntnisse über eine Firma haben; **locked from the ~** von innen verschlossen. **(b) the wind blew the umbrella ~ out** der Wind hat den Schirm umgestülpt; **your jumper's ~ out** du hast deinen Pullover verkehrt herum an; **to turn sth ~ out** etw umdrehen; *(fig) flat etc* etw auf den Kopf stellen; **to know sth ~ out** etw in- und auswendig kennen. **(c)** *(col) (~s: stomach)* Eingeweide, Innere(s) *nt*.

2 *adj* Innen-, innere(r, s). **~ information** interne Informationen *pl*; **it looks like an ~ job** *(crime)* es sieht nach dem Werk von Insidern aus *(col)*; **~ lane** *(Sport)* Innenbahn *f*; *(Aut)* Innenspur *f*; **~ pocket** Innentasche *f*; **~ story** *(Press)* Inside-Story *f*; **~ forward** Halbstürmer *m*; **~ left** Halblinke(r) *m*; **~ right** Halbrechte(r) *m*.

3 *adv* innen; *(indoors)* drin(nen); *(direction)* nach innen, hinein/herein. **look ~** sehen Sie hinein; **let's go ~** gehen wir hinein; **there is something ~** es ist etwas (innen) drin; **to be ~** *(col: in prison)* sitzen *(col)*.

4 *prep* **(a)** *(place)* innen in *(+dat)*; *(direction)* in *(+acc)* ... (hinein). **he was waiting ~ the house** er wartete im Haus; **he went ~ the house** er ging ins Haus (hinein). **(b)** *(time)* innerhalb. **he was 5 secs ~ the record** er ist 5 Sekunden unter dem Rekord geblieben.

insider [ɪn'saɪdəʳ] *n* Eingeweihte(r) *m*.

insidious [ɪn'sɪdɪəs] *adj* heimtückisch.

insight ['ɪnsaɪt] *n* **his ~ into my problems** sein Verständnis *nt* für meine Probleme; **to gain an ~ into sth** in etw *(acc)* (einen) Einblick gewinnen.
insignificance [,ɪnsɪg'nɪfɪkəns] *n see adj* Belanglosigkeit *f*; Geringfügigkeit *f*; Unscheinbarkeit *f*.
insignificant [,ɪnsɪg'nɪfɪkənt] *adj* belanglos; *sum, difference also* geringfügig; *person* unscheinbar.
insincere [,ɪnsɪn'sɪəʳ] *adj* unaufrichtig.
insincerity [,ɪnsɪn'serɪtɪ] *n* Unaufrichtigkeit *f*.
insinuate [ɪn'sɪnjʊeɪt] *vt* **(a)** andeuten *(sth to sb* etw jdm gegenüber*)*. **what are you insinuating?** was wollen Sie damit sagen? **(b) to ~ oneself into sb's favour** sich bei jdm einschmeicheln.
insinuation [ɪn,sɪnjʊ'eɪʃən] *n* Anspielung *f (about* auf *+acc)*.
insipid [ɪn'sɪpɪd] *adj* fad; *person, novel also* geistlos.
insist [ɪn'sɪst] *vti* bestehen. **I ~!** ich bestehe darauf!; **if you ~** wenn Sie darauf bestehen; *(if you like)* wenn's unbedingt sein muß; **I must ~ that you stop** ich muß darauf bestehen, daß Sie aufhören; **he ~s that he is innocent** er behauptet beharrlich, unschuldig zu sein; **I ~ on the best** ich bestehe auf bester Qualität; **if you will ~ on smoking, ...** wenn Sie schon unbedingt rauchen müssen, ...
insistence [ɪn'sɪstəns] *n* Bestehen *nt (on* auf *+dat)*. **I did it at his ~** ich tat es, weil er darauf bestand.
insistent [ɪn'sɪstənt] *adj* **(a)** *person* beharrlich; *salesman etc* aufdringlich. **he was most ~ about it** er beharrte darauf. **(b)** *(urgent) demand, tone* nachdrücklich.
insole ['ɪnsəʊl] *n* Einlegesohle *f*.
insolence ['ɪnsələns] *n* Unverschämtheit *f*.
insolent ['ɪnsələnt] *adj* unverschämt.
insoluble [ɪn'sɒljʊbl] *adj* **(a)** *substance* unlöslich. **(b)** *problem* unlösbar.
insolvency [ɪn'sɒlvənsɪ] *n* Zahlungsunfähigkeit *f*.
insolvent [ɪn'sɒlvənt] *adj* zahlungsunfähig.
insomnia [ɪn'sɒmnɪə] *n* Schlaflosigkeit *f*.
insomniac [ɪn'sɒmnɪæk] *n* **to be an ~** an Schlaflosigkeit leiden.
inspect [ɪn'spekt] *vt* **(a)** *(examine)* prüfen. **to ~ sth for sth** etw auf etw *(acc)* (hin) prüfen. **(b)** *(Mil etc: review)* inspizieren.
inspection [ɪn'spekʃən] *n* **(a)** Prüfung *f*; *(of school)* Inspektion *f*. **on ~** bei näherer Betrachtung; **for your ~** zur Prüfung. **(b)** *(Mil)* Inspektion *f*.
inspector [ɪn'spektəʳ] *n (factory ~, Brit: on buses)* Kontrolleur(in *f*) *m*; *(of schools)* Schulrat *m*, Schulrätin *f*; *(of police)* Polizeiinspektor *m*; *(of taxes)* Steuerinspektor *m*.
inspiration [,ɪnspə'reɪʃən] *n* Inspiration *(for* zu *or* für*)*, Eingebung *(for* zu*) f*. **he gets his ~ from ...** er läßt sich von ... inspirieren.
inspire [ɪn'spaɪəʳ] *vt* **(a)** *respect, awe* einflößen *(in sb* jdm*)*. **to ~ sb with confidence** jdm mit Vertrauen erfüllen. **(b)** *(be inspiration to) person* inspirieren.
inspired [ɪn'spaɪəd] *adj* genial. **in an ~ moment** in einem Augenblick der Inspiration; *(iro)* in einem lichten Moment; **it was an ~ guess** das war genial geraten.
inspiring [ɪn'spaɪərɪŋ] *adj speech* inspirierend.
instability [,ɪnstə'bɪlɪtɪ] *n* Instabilität *f*; *(of character also)* Labilität *f*.
install [ɪn'stɔːl] *vt* installieren; *telephone also* anschließen; *person* (in ein Amt) einsetzen.
installation [,ɪnstə'leɪʃən] *n* **(a)** *see vt* Installation *f*; Anschluß *m*; Amtseinsetzung *f*. **(b)** *(machine etc)* Anlage *f*. **(c) military ~** militärische Anlage.
instalment, (US) installment [ɪn'stɔːlmənt] *n* **(a)** *(of serial)* Fortsetzung *f*; *(TV)* (Sende)folge *f*. **(b)** *(Fin)* Rate *f*. **monthly ~** Monatsrate *f*; **to pay in** *or* **by ~s** in Raten bezahlen.
installment plan *n (US)* Ratenzahlung(splan *m*) *f*. **to buy on the ~** auf Raten kaufen.
instance ['ɪnstəns] *n (example)* Beispiel *nt*; *(case)* Fall *m*. **for ~** zum Beispiel; **in the first ~** zunächst (einmal).
instant ['ɪnstənt] **1** *adj* **(a)** unmittelbar; *relief, result also* sofortig *attr*. **(b)** *(Cook)* Instant-. **~ coffee** Pulverkaffee *m*; **~ food** Schnellgerichte *pl*. **2** *n* Augenblick *m*. **this (very) ~** sofort; **at that very ~** genau in dem Augenblick.
instantaneous [,ɪnstən'teɪnɪəs] *adj* unmittelbar.
instantly ['ɪnstəntlɪ] *adv* sofort.
instead [ɪn'sted] **1** *prep* **~ of** statt *(+gen or (col) +dat)*, anstelle von. **~ of going to school** (an)statt zur Schule zu gehen; **his brother came ~ of him** sein Bruder kam an seiner Stelle. **2** *adv* statt dessen. **if he doesn't want to go, I'll go ~** wenn er nicht gehen will, gehe ich statt dessen.
instep ['ɪnstep] *n (Anat)* Spann *m*; *(of shoe)* Blatt *nt*.
instigate ['ɪnstɪgeɪt] *vt* anstiften; *reform etc* initiieren.
instigation [,ɪnstɪ'geɪʃən] *n see vt* Anstiftung *f*; Initiierung *f*. **at sb's ~** auf jds Betreiben.
instil [ɪn'stɪl] *vt* einflößen *(into sb* jdm*)*.
instinct ['ɪnstɪŋkt] *n* Instinkt *m*. **by** *or* **from ~** instinktiv.
instinctive [ɪn'stɪŋktɪv] *adj* instinktiv.
institute ['ɪnstɪtjuːt] **1** *vt* **(a)** *reforms* einführen; *search* einleiten. **(b)** *(Jur) an action* einleiten; *proceedings* anstrengen *(against* gegen*)*. **2** *n* Institut *nt*; *(home)* Anstalt *f*.
institution [,ɪnstɪ'tjuːʃən] *n (organization, custom)* Institution *f*; *(building, home etc)* Anstalt *f*.
institutional [,ɪnstɪ'tjuːʃənl] *adj life etc* Anstalts-.
instruct [ɪn'strʌkt] *vt* **(a)** *(teach) person* unterrichten. **(b)** *(tell, direct) person* anweisen; *(command)* die Anweisung erteilen *(+dat)*; *(appoint) lawyer* beauftragen.
instruction [ɪn'strʌkʃən] *n* **(a)** *(teaching)* Unterricht *m*. **(b)** *(command)* Anweisung, Instruktion *f*; **~s for use** Gebrauchsanweisung *f*; **~ manual** Bedienungsanleitung *f*.
instructive [ɪn'strʌktɪv] *adj* aufschlußreich; *(of educational value)* lehrreich.
instructor [ɪn'strʌktəʳ] *n (also Sport)* Lehrer *m*; *(US)* Dozent *m*; *(Mil)* Ausbilder *m*.
instrument ['ɪnstrʊmənt] *n (Mus, Tech)* Instrument *nt*; *(domestic)* Gerät *nt*; *(person)* Werkzeug *nt*. **to fly an aircraft on ~s** ein Flugzeug nach den (Bord)instrumenten fliegen; **~ panel** *n (Aviat, Aut)* Armaturenbrett *nt*.
instrumental [,ɪnstrʊ'mentl] *adj* **(a) he was ~ in getting her the job** er hat ihr zu dieser Stelle verholfen; **to be ~ in sth** bei etw mitwirken. **(b)** *music* Instrumental-.
instrumentalist [,ɪnstrʊ'mentəlɪst] *n* Instrumentalist(in *f*) *m*.
insubordinate [,ɪnsə'bɔːdənɪt] *adj* aufsässig.
insubordination ['ɪnsə,bɔːdɪ'neɪʃən] *n* Aufsässigkeit *f*; *(Mil)* Gehorsamsverweigerung *f*.
insufferable *adj* [ɪn'sʌfərəbl] unerträglich.
insufficient [,ɪnsə'fɪʃənt] *adj* ungenügend *pred*; *work, insulation also* unzulänglich.
insular ['ɪnsjələʳ] *adj (narrow)* engstirnig.
insularity [,ɪnsjʊ'lærɪtɪ] *n* Engstirnigkeit *f*.
insulate ['ɪnsjʊleɪt] *vt room, (Elec)* isolieren; *(fig: shelter)* abschirmen *(from* gegen*)*.
insulating tape ['ɪnsjʊleɪtɪŋ,teɪp] *n (Brit)* Isolierband *nt*.
insulation [,ɪnsjʊ'leɪʃən] *n* Isolation *f*; *(material also)* Isoliermaterial *nt*; *(fig)* Geschütztheit *f (from* gegen*)*.
insulin ['ɪnsjʊlɪn] *n* Insulin *nt*.
insult [ɪn'sʌlt] **1** *vt* beleidigen; *(by words also)* beschimpfen. **2** ['ɪnsʌlt] *n (to* für *+acc)* Beleidigung *f*; *(with words also)* Beschimpfung *f*. **to add ~ to injury** das Ganze noch schlimmer machen.
insulting [ɪn'sʌltɪŋ] *adj* beleidigend.
insuperable [ɪn'suːpərəbl] *adj* unüberwindlich.
insupportable [,ɪnsə'pɔːtəbl] *adj* unerträglich.
insurance [ɪn'ʃʊərəns] *n* Versicherung *f*. **to take**

out ~ eine Versicherung abschließen.

insurance: ~ **company** *n* Versicherungsgesellschaft *f*; ~ **policy** *n* Versicherungspolice *f*; *(fig)* Sicherheitsvorkehrung *f*; ~ **salesman** Versicherungsvertreter *m*.

insure [ɪn'ʃʊəʳ] *vt house* versichern (lassen). **to** ~ **oneself** *or* **one's life** eine Lebensversicherung abschließen.

insurgent [ɪn'sɜːdʒənt] **1** *adj* aufständisch. **2** *n* Aufständische(r) *mf*.

insurmountable [ˌɪnsə'maʊntəbl] *adj* unüberwindlich.

insurrection [ˌɪnsə'rekʃən] *n* Aufstand *m*.

intact [ɪn'tækt] *adj* unversehrt.

intake ['ɪnteɪk] *n (of water, electric current, Sch)* Aufnahme *f*; *(pipe)* Zuflußrohr *nt*. **air** ~ Luftzufuhr *f*; **food** ~ Nahrungsaufnahme *f*.

intangible [ɪn'tændʒəbl] *adj* **(a)** nicht greifbar. **(b)** *longings* unbestimmbar. **(c)** *(Jur, Comm)* ~ **assets** immaterielle Werte *pl*.

integer ['ɪntɪdʒəʳ] *n* ganze Zahl.

integral ['ɪntɪgrəl] *adj part* wesentlich.

integrate ['ɪntɪgreɪt] *vt* integrieren. **to** ~ **sth into sth** etw in etw *(acc)* integrieren; **to** ~ **sth with sth** etw auf etw *(acc)* abstimmen.

integrated ['ɪntɪgreɪtɪd] *adj plan* einheitlich; *school* ohne Rassentrennung. **a fully** ~ **personality** eine in sich ausgewogene Persönlichkeit; ~ **circuit** integrierter Schaltkreis.

integration [ˌɪntɪ'greɪʃən] *n* Integration *f (into* in *+acc)*. **(racial)** ~ Rassenintegration *f*.

integrity [ɪn'tegrɪtɪ] *n* **(a)** *(honesty)* Integrität *f*. **(b)** *(wholeness)* Einheit *f*.

intellect ['ɪntɪlekt] *n* Intellekt *m*.

intellectual [ɪntɪ'lektjʊəl] **1** *adj* intellektuell; *interests also* geistig. **something a little more** ~ etwas geistig Anspruchsvolleres. **2** *n* Intellektuelle(r) *mf*.

intelligence [ɪn'telɪdʒəns] *n* **(a)** Intelligenz *f*. **(b)** *(news, information)* Informationen *pl*. **(c)** *(Mil etc)* Geheimdienst *m*.

intelligent [ɪn'telɪdʒənt] *adj* intelligent.

intelligentsia [ɪnˌtelɪ'dʒentsɪə] *n* Intelligenz *f*.

intelligible [ɪn'telɪdʒəbl] *adj* verständlich.

intemperate [ɪn'tempərɪt] *adj climate* extrem; *person* unmäßig.

intend [ɪn'tend] *vt* **(a)** *(+n)* beabsichtigen, wollen. **I** ~ **him to go with me** ich habe vor, ihn mitzunehmen; *(insist)* er soll mit mir mitkommen; **I** ~**ed no harm** es war (von mir) nicht böse gemeint; *(with action)* ich hatte nichts Böses beabsichtigt; **I didn't** ~ **it as an insult** das sollte keine Beleidigung sein; **that remark was** ~**ed for you** mit dieser Bemerkung waren Sie gemeint; **this film was never** ~**ed for children** dieser Film war nie für Kinder bestimmt. **(b)** *(+vb)* beabsichtigen, fest vorhaben. **he** ~**s to win** er hat fest vor, zu gewinnen; **what do you** ~ **to do about it?** was beabsichtigen Sie, dagegen zu tun?

intense [ɪn'tens] *adj* intensiv; *disappointment* äußerst groß; *person* ernsthaft.

intensely [ɪn'tenslɪ] *adv angry* äußerst; *study* intensiv.

intensify [ɪn'tensɪfaɪ] **1** *vt* intensivieren; *meaning* verstärken. **2** *vi* zunehmen; *(pain, heat also)* stärker werden.

intensity [ɪn'tensɪtɪ] *n* Intensität *f*; *(of feeling, storm also)* Heftigkeit *f*.

intensive [ɪn'tensɪv] *adj* intensiv, Intensiv-. ~ **care unit** Intensivstation *f*; **they came under** ~ **fire** sie kamen unter heftigen Beschuß.

intent [ɪn'tent] **1** *n* Absicht *f*. **to all** ~**s and purposes** im Grunde; **with** ~ **to** *(Jur)* mit dem Vorsatz zu. **2** *adj look* durchdringend. **to be** ~ **on achieving sth** fest entschlossen sein, etw zu erreichen.

intention [ɪn'tenʃən] *n* Absicht *f*. **I have every** ~ **of doing that** ich habe die feste Absicht, das zu tun; **I have no** *or* **haven't the least** ~ **of staying!** ich habe nicht die geringste Absicht hierzubleiben; **with the best of** ~**s** in der besten Absicht; **with the** ~ **of ...** mit dem Vorsatz zu ...

intentional [ɪn'tenʃənl] *adj* absichtlich, vorsätzlich *(esp Jur)*. **it wasn't** ~ das war keine Absicht.

intentionally [ɪn'tenʃnəlɪ] *adv* absichtlich.

inter- ['ɪntəʳ] *pref* zwischen-, Zwischen-.

interact [ˌɪntər'ækt] *vi* aufeinander einwirken; *(Phys)* wechselwirken; *(Psychol)* interagieren.

interaction [ˌɪntər'ækʃən] *n see vi* gegenseitige Einwirkung, Wechselwirkung *f (also Phys)*; Interaktion *f*.

intercede [ˌɪntə'siːd] *vi* sich einsetzen, sich verwenden *(with* bei, *on behalf of* für*)*.

intercept [ˌɪntə'sept] *vt message, plane* abfangen; *phone call also* abhören. **they** ~**ed the enemy** sie schnitten dem Feind den Weg ab.

interception [ˌɪntə'sepʃən] *n* Abfangen *nt*.

interchange ['ɪntəˌtʃeɪndʒ] **1** *n* **(a)** *(of roads)* Kreuzung *f*; *(of motorways)* (Autobahn)kreuz *nt*. **(b)** *(exchange)* Austausch *m*. **2** [ˌɪntə'tʃeɪndʒ] *vt* **(a)** *(switch round)* (aus)tauschen. **(b)** *ideas etc* austauschen *(with* mit*)*.

interchangeable [ˌɪntə'tʃeɪndʒəbl] *adj* austauschbar. **x is** ~ **with y** x und y sind austauschbar.

interchangeably [ˌɪntə'tʃeɪndʒəblɪ] *adv* austauschbar. **they are used** ~ sie können ausgetauscht werden.

inter-city [ˌɪntə'sɪtɪ] *n* Intercity *m*.

intercom ['ɪntəkɒm] *n* (Gegen)sprechanlage *f*; *(in ship, plane)* Bordverständigungsanlage *f*; *(in schools etc)* Lautsprecheranlage *f*.

intercontinental ['ɪntəˌkɒntɪ'nentl] *adj* interkontinental, Interkontinental-.

intercourse ['ɪntəkɔːs] *n* **(sexual)** ~ (Geschlechts)verkehr *m*. **social** ~ gesellschaftlicher Verkehr.

interdependent [ˌɪntədɪ'pendənt] *adj* wechselseitig voneinander abhängig.

interest ['ɪntrɪst] **1** *n* **(a)** Interesse *nt*. **to take an** ~ **in sb/sth** sich für jdn/etw interessieren; **just for** ~ nur interessehalber; **he has lost** ~ er hat das Interesse verloren; **his** ~**s are ...** er interessiert sich für ...; **of vital** ~ **to the economy** von lebenswichtigem Interesse für die Wirtschaft; **to act in sb's/one's own** ~**(s)** in jds/im eigenen Interesse handeln; **in the public** ~ im öffentlichen Interesse. **(b)** *(Fin)* Zinsen *pl*. **rate of** ~, ~ **rate** Zinssatz *m*; **to bear** ~ **at 4%** 4% Zinsen tragen, mit 4% verzinst sein. **(c)** *(Comm) (share, stake)* Anteil *m*; *(~ group)* Kreise *pl*, Interessentengruppe *f*. **he has a financial** ~ **in the company** er ist finanziell an der Firma beteiligt; **British trading** ~**s** britische Handelsinteressen *pl*.

2 *vt* interessieren *(in* für, an *+dat)*. **to** ~ **sb in doing sth** jdn dafür interessieren, etw zu tun; **can I** ~ **you in a little drink?** kann ich Sie zu etwas Alkoholischem überreden?

interested ['ɪntrɪstɪd] *adj* interessiert *(in* an *+dat)*. **I'm not** ~ ich bin nicht (daran) interessiert; **to be** ~ **in sb/sth** sich für jdn/etw interessieren; **I'm going to the cinema, are you** ~ **(in coming)?** ich gehe ins Kino, haben Sie Lust mitzukommen?; **she was** ~ **to see what he would do** sie war gespannt, was er wohl tun würde; **he is an** ~ **party** er ist daran beteiligt.

interest-free ['ɪntrɪst'friː] *adj loan* zinsfrei.

interesting ['ɪntrɪstɪŋ] *adj* interessant.

interestingly ['ɪntrɪstɪŋlɪ] *adv* ~ **enough, ...** interessanterweise ...

interface ['ɪntəfeɪs] **1** *n (Comp)* Schnittstelle *f*, Interface *nt*; *(fig)* Grenzfläche *f*. **the man/machine** ~ die Interaktion von Mensch und Maschine. **2** [ɪntə'feɪs] *vt* koppeln.

interfere [ˌɪntə'fɪəʳ] *vi (in sb's affairs)* sich einmischen *(in* in *+acc)*. **don't** ~ **with the machine** laß

die Finger von der Maschine; **who's been interfering with my books?** wer war an meinen Büchern?; **to ~ with sth** *(disrupt)* etw stören *(also Rad)*; **to ~ with sb's plans** jds Pläne durchkreuzen.
interference [ˌɪntə'fɪərəns] *n (meddling)* Einmischung *f*; *(disruption, Rad)* Störung *f (with gen)*.
interfering [ˌɪntə'fɪərɪŋ] *adj* **don't be so ~** misch dich nicht immer ein.
interim ['ɪntərɪm] **1** *n* **in the ~** in der Zwischenzeit. **2** *adj* vorläufig; *arrangements also, government* Übergangs-; *report, payment* Zwischen-.
interior [ɪn'tɪərɪə^r] **1** *adj (inside)* Innen-; *(inland, domestic)* Binnen-. **2** *n (of country)* Innere(s) *nt*; *(of house)* Innenausstattung *f*. **deep in the ~** tief im Landesinneren; **Department of the I~** *(US)* Innenministerium *nt*.
interior: ~ decorator *n* Innenausstatter(in *f*) *m*; **~ design** *n* Innenarchitektur *f*; **~ designer** *n* Innenarchitekt(in *f*) *m*.
interjection [ˌɪntə'dʒekʃən] *n (exclamation)* Ausruf *m*; *(remark)* Einwurf *m*.
interlocking [ˌɪntə'lɒkɪŋ] *adj* ineinandergreifend.
interloper ['ɪntələʊpə^r] *n* Eindringling *m*.
interlude ['ɪntəlu:d] *n* Periode *f*; *(Theat)* Pause *f*.
intermarry [ˌɪntə'mærɪ] *vi* Mischehen eingehen.
intermediary [ˌɪntə'mi:dɪərɪ] *n* (Ver)mittler(in *f*) *m*.
intermediate [ˌɪntə'mi:dɪət] *adj* Zwischen-; *French etc* für fortgeschrittene Anfänger.
interminable [ɪn'tɜ:mɪnəbl] *adj* endlos. **after what seemed an ~ journey** nach einer Reise, die nicht enden zu wollen schien.
intermingle [ˌɪntə'mɪŋgl] *vi* sich mischen *(with* unter *+acc)*.
intermission [ˌɪntə'mɪʃən] *n* **(a)** Unterbrechung *f*. **(b)** *(Theat, Film)* Pause *f*.
intermittent [ˌɪntə'mɪtənt] *adj* periodisch auftretend; *(Tech)* intermittierend.
intern[1] [ɪn'tɜ:n] *vt person* internieren.
intern[2] ['ɪntɜ:n] *(US) n* Assistenzarzt *m*, Assistenzärztin *f*.
internal [ɪn'tɜ:nl] *adj (inner)* innere(r, s); *diameter* Innen-; *trade etc* Binnen-; *policy, mail* intern; **~ combustion engine** Verbrennungsmotor *m*; **I~ Revenue Service** *(US)* Finanzamt *nt*; **~ affairs** innere Angelegenheiten *pl*.
internally [ɪn'tɜ:nəlɪ] *adv* innen, im Inneren; *(in body)* innerlich; *(in country)* landesintern; *(in organization)* intern. **"not to be taken ~"** „nicht zur inneren Anwendung".
international [ˌɪntə'næʃnəl] **1** *adj* international. **~ law** Völkerrecht *nt*; **~ money order** Auslandsanweisung *f*. **2** *n (Sport) (match)* Länderspiel *nt*; *(player)* Nationalspieler(in *f*) *m*.
internment [ɪn'tɜ:nmənt] *n* Internierung *f*. **~ camp** Internierungslager *nt*.
interplanetary [ˌɪntə'plænɪtərɪ] *adj* interplanetar.
interplay ['ɪntəpleɪ] *n* Zusammenspiel *nt*.
Interpol ['ɪntəpɒl] *n* Interpol *f*.
interpret [ɪn'tɜ:prɪt] **1** *vt* **(a)** dolmetschen. **(b)** *(explain)* auslegen, interpretieren; *(Theat, Mus)* interpretieren. **how would you ~ what he said?** wie würden Sie seine Worte auffassen? **2** *vi* dolmetschen.
interpretation [ɪnˌtɜ:prɪ'teɪʃən] *n see vt (b)* Auslegung, Interpretation *f*; Interpretation *f*.
interpreter [ɪn'tɜ:prɪtə^r] *n* Dolmetscher(in *f*) *m*; *(Theat, Mus)* Interpret(in *f*) *m*.
interrelated [ˌɪntərɪ'leɪtɪd] *adj* **to be ~** zueinander in Beziehung stehen, zusammenhängen.
interrogate [ɪn'terəgeɪt] *vt (police)* verhören.
interrogation [ɪnˌterə'geɪʃən] *n* Verhör *nt*.
interrogative [ˌɪntə'rɒgətɪv] *adj (Gram)* Frage-, Interrogativ-.
interrogator [ɪn'terəgeɪtə^r] *n* Vernehmungsbeamte(r) *mf*.
interrupt [ˌɪntə'rʌpt] *vti* unterbrechen *(also Elec)*; *work also* stören. **stop ~ing (me)!** fall mir nicht dauernd ins Wort!
interruption [ˌɪntə'rʌpʃən] *n* Unterbrechung *f*; *(of work also)* Störung *f*.
intersect [ˌɪntə'sekt] **1** *vt* durchschneiden; *(Geometry)* schneiden. **2** *vi* sich kreuzen; *(Geometry)* sich schneiden.
intersection [ˌɪntə'sekʃən] *n (crossroads)* Kreuzung *f*; *(Geometry)* Schnittpunkt *m*.
intersperse [ˌɪntə'spɜ:s] *vt* **woods ~d with fields** Wald mit Feldern dazwischen; **a speech ~d with quotations** eine mit Zitaten gespickte Rede.
interval ['ɪntəvəl] *n* **(a)** *(space, time)* Abstand *m*. **at ~s** in Abständen; **sunny ~s** Aufheiterungen *pl*. **(b)** *(Sch, Theat)* Pause *f*. **(c)** *(Mus)* Intervall *nt*.
intervene [ˌɪntə'vi:n] *vi (person)* einschreiten *(in* bei*)*, intervenieren; *(event, fate)* dazwischenkommen. **in the intervening weeks** in den dazwischenliegenden Wochen.
intervention [ˌɪntə'venʃən] *n* Eingreifen *nt*, Intervention *f*.
interview ['ɪntəvju:] **1** *n (for job)* Vorstellungsgespräch *nt*; *(with authorities etc)* Gespräch *nt*; *(TV etc)* Interview *nt*. **2** *vt job applicant* ein/das Vorstellungsgespräch führen mit; *(TV etc)* interviewen. **he is being ~ed on Monday for the job** er hat am Montag sein Vorstellungsgespräch.
interviewer ['ɪntəvju:ə^r] *n (for job)* Leiter(in *f*) *m* des Vorstellungsgesprächs; *(TV etc)* Interviewer(in *f*) *m*.
intestate [ɪn'testɪt] *adj (Jur)* **to die ~** sterben, ohne ein Testament zu hinterlassen.
intestinal [ɪn'testɪnl] *adj* Darm-.
intestine [ɪn'testɪn] *n* Darm *m*. **small/large ~** Dünn-/Dickdarm *m*.
intimacy ['ɪntɪməsɪ] *n* Vertrautheit *f*; *(euph: sexual ~)* Intimität *f*.
intimate[1] ['ɪntɪmɪt] *adj friend* eng, vertraut; *(sexually)* intim; *knowledge* gründlich. **to be on ~ terms with sb** mit jdm auf vertraulichem Fuß stehen; **to be/become ~ with sb** mit jdm vertraut sein/werden.
intimate[2] ['ɪntɪmeɪt] *vt* andeuten. **he ~d to them that they should stop** er gab ihnen zu verstehen, daß sie aufhören sollten.
intimately ['ɪntɪmɪtlɪ] *adv acquainted* bestens; *speak* vertraulich; *connected* eng; *know* genau.
intimation [ˌɪntɪ'meɪʃən] *n* Andeutung *f*.
intimidate [ɪn'tɪmɪdeɪt] *vt* einschüchtern.
intimidation [ɪnˌtɪmɪ'deɪʃən] *n* Einschüchterung *f*.
into ['ɪntʊ] *prep* in *(+acc)*; *crash* gegen. **to translate sth ~ French** etw ins Französische übersetzen; **to divide 3 ~ 9** 9 durch 3 teilen; **far ~ the night** bis tief in die Nacht hinein; **it turned ~ a nice day** es wurde ein schöner Tag; **I'm not really ~ the job yet** *(col)* ich bin noch nicht ganz in der Ar beit drin *(col)*; **he's (heavily) ~ jazz** *(col)* er steht (schwer) auf Jazz *(col)*.
intolerable [ɪn'tɒlərəbl] *adj* unerträglich.
intolerance [ɪn'tɒlərəns] *n* Intoleranz *f (of* gegenüber*)*.
intolerant [ɪn'tɒlərənt] *adj* intolerant *(of* gegenüber*)*.
intonation [ˌɪntəʊ'neɪʃən] *n* Intonation *f*.
intoxicate [ɪn'tɒksɪkeɪt] *vt (lit, fig)* berauschen.
intoxicated [ɪn'tɒksɪkeɪtɪd] *adj* betrunken, berauscht *(also fig)*.
intoxication [ɪnˌtɒksɪ'keɪʃən] *n* Rausch *m (also fig)*.
intractable [ɪn'træktəbl] *adj problem, illness* hartnäckig; *child* widerspenstig.
intransigence [ɪn'trænsɪdʒəns] *n* Unnachgiebigkeit *f*.
intransigent [ɪn'trænsɪdʒənt] *adj* unnachgiebig.
intransitive [ɪn'trænsɪtɪv] *adj verb* intransitiv.
intravenous [ˌɪntrə'vi:nəs] *adj* intravenös.
intrepid [ɪn'trepɪd] *adj* unerschrocken.
intricacy ['ɪntrɪkəsɪ] *n* Kompliziertheit *f*; *(of a law*

etc) Feinheit *f.*
intricate ['ɪntrɪkɪt] *adj* kompliziert; *(involved also)* verwickelt.
intrigue [ɪn'tri:g] **1** *vi* intrigieren. **2** *vt (arouse interest of)* faszinieren; *(arouse curiosity of)* neugierig machen. **I'd be ~d to know why ...** es würde mich schon interessieren, warum ... **3** ['ɪntri:g] *n (plot)* Intrige *f*; *(no pl: plotting)* Intrigen(spiel *nt*) *pl.*
intriguing [ɪn'tri:gɪŋ] *adj* faszinierend, interessant.
intrinsic [ɪn'trɪnsɪk] *adj value* immanent; *(essential)* wesentlich.
introduce [ˌɪntrə'dju:s] *vt* **(a)** *(to person)* vorstellen *(to sb* jdm*)*, bekannt machen *(to* mit*)*; *(to subject)* einführen *(to* in *+acc).* **have you two been ~d?** hat man Sie bekannt gemacht?; **to ~ oneself** sich vorstellen. **(b)** *reform* einführen; *(Parl) bill* einbringen; *programme, (also TV)* ankündigen. **(c)** *(insert)* einführen *(into* in *+acc).*
introduction [ˌɪntrə'dʌkʃən] *n* **(a)** *(to person)* Vorstellung *f.* **(b)** *(in book)* Einleitung *f (to* zu*).* **(c)** *(to subject, of reform etc)* Einführung *f (to* in *+acc)*; *(of bill)* Einbringen *nt*; *(of programme)* Ankündigung *f.* **(d)** *(insertion)* Einführung *f (into* in *+acc).*
introductory [ˌɪntrə'dʌktərɪ] *adj chapter* einleitend; *remarks* einführend; *talk* Einführungs-.
introspection [ˌɪntrəʊ'spekʃən] *n* Selbstbeobachtung *f.*
introspective [ˌɪntrəʊ'spektɪv] *adj person* selbstbeobachtend; *novel* introspektiv.
introvert ['ɪntrəʊvɜ:t] *n* Introvertierte(r) *mf.* **to be an ~** introvertiert sein.
introverted ['ɪntrəʊvɜ:tɪd] *adj* introvertiert.
intrude [ɪn'tru:d] *vi* sich eindrängen. **to ~ in sb's affairs** sich in jds Angelegenheiten *(acc)* einmischen; **am I intruding?** störe ich?; **to ~ on sb's privacy** jds Privatsphäre verletzen.
intruder [ɪn'tru:dəʳ] *n* Eindringling *m.*
intrusion [ɪn'tru:ʒən] *n (disturbance)* Störung *f.* **forgive the ~** entschuldigen Sie, wenn ich hier so eindringe.
intrusive [ɪn'tru:sɪv] *adj person* aufdringlich.
intuition [ˌɪntju:'ɪʃən] *n* Intuition *f*; *(of future events etc)* (Vor)ahnung *f (of* von*).*
intuitive [ɪn'tju:ɪtɪv] *adj* intuitiv; *guess, feeling* instinktiv.
inundate ['ɪnʌndeɪt] *vt (lit, fig)* überschwemmen; *(with work)* überhäufen.
inure [ɪn'jʊəʳ] *vt* gewöhnen *(to* an *+acc)*; *(physically)* abhärten *(to* gegen*).*
invade [ɪn'veɪd] *vt* einmarschieren in *(+acc)*; *(fig)* überfallen; *privacy* eindringen in *(+acc).*
invader [ɪn'veɪdəʳ] *n* Invasor *m.*
invalid[1] ['ɪnvəlɪd] **1** *adj* krank; *(disabled)* körperbehindert. **~ chair** Rollstuhl *m*; **~ car** Invaliden(kraft)fahrzeug *nt.* **2** *n* Kranke(r) *mf*; *(disabled person)* Invalide, Körperbehinderte(r) *mf.*
♦**invalid out** *vt sep* **to be ~ed ~ of the army** wegen Dienstuntauglichkeit aus dem Heer entlassen werden.
invalid[2] [ɪn'vælɪd] *adj* ungültig; *argument* nicht stichhaltig.
invalidate [ɪn'vælɪdeɪt] *vt* ungültig machen; *theory* entkräften.
invaluable [ɪn'væljʊəbl] *adj* unbezahlbar; *service* unschätzbar.
invariable [ɪn'vɛərɪəbl] *adj* unveränderlich.
invariably [ɪn'vɛərɪəblɪ] *adv* ständig.
invasion [ɪn'veɪʒən] *n (lit, fig)* Invasion *f*; *(of privacy etc)* Eingriff *m (of* in *+acc).* **the German ~ of Poland** der Einmarsch der Deutschen in Polen.
invective [ɪn'vektɪv] *n* Beschimpfungen *pl (against gen).*
invent [ɪn'vent] *vt* erfinden.
invention [ɪn'venʃən] *n* Erfindung *f.*
inventive [ɪn'ventɪv] *adj (creative) mind* schöpferisch; *novel, design* einfallsreich; *(resourceful)* erfinderisch.
inventiveness [ɪn'ventɪvnɪs] *n* Einfallsreichtum *m.*
inventor [ɪn'ventəʳ] *n* Erfinder(in *f*) *m.*
inventory ['ɪnvəntrɪ] *n* Inventar *nt*, Bestandsaufnahme *f.* **to take an ~ of sth** den Bestand einer Sache *(gen)* aufnehmen.
inverse ['ɪn'vɜ:s] *adj* umgekehrt. **in ~ order** in umgekehrter Reihenfolge; **to be in ~ proportion to ...** im umgekehrten Verhältnis zu ... stehen.
inversion [ɪn'vɜ:ʃən] *n* Umkehrung *f.*
invert [ɪn'vɜ:t] *vt* umkehren. **~ed commas** *(Brit)* Anführungszeichen *pl.*
invertebrate [ɪn'vɜ:tɪbrɪt] *n* Wirbellose(r) *m.*
invest [ɪn'vest] **1** *vt* **(a)** *(Fin, fig)* investieren *(in* in *+acc or dat)*; *(Fin also)* anlegen *(in* in *+dat).* **(b)** *(form: in office) president etc* einsetzen. **2** *vi* investieren, Geld anlegen *(in* in *+acc or dat, with* bei*).* **to ~ in a new car** sich *(dat)* ein neues Auto anschaffen.
investigate [ɪn'vestɪgeɪt] **1** *vt* untersuchen; *(research also)* erforschen; *business affairs* überprüfen; *complaint* nachgehen *(+dat).* **2** *vi* nachforschen; *(police)* Ermittlungen anstellen.
investigation [ɪnˌvestɪ'geɪʃən] *n* **(a)** *(to determine cause)* Untersuchung *f (into gen)*; *(by police)* Ermittlungen *pl*; *(of applicants, political beliefs etc)* Überprüfung *f.* **on ~** bei näherer Untersuchung; **to be under ~** überprüft werden; **he is under ~** *(by police)* gegen ihn wird ermittelt. **(b)** *(research)* Forschung *f*; *(of bacteria etc)* Erforschung *f (into gen).*
investigative [ɪn'vestɪgətɪv] *adj journalism* Enthüllungs-.
investigator [ɪn'vestɪgeɪtəʳ] *n* Ermittler *m*; *(private ~)* (Privat)detektiv *m.*
investiture [ɪn'vestɪtʃəʳ] *n* Amtseinführung *f.*
investment [ɪn'vestmənt] *n (Fin)* Investition *f.* **to make an ~** investieren *(of sth* etw*)*; **oil is a good ~** Öl ist eine gute (Kapital)anlage.
investor [ɪn'vestəʳ] *n* Kapitalanleger, Investor *m.* **the small ~** der Kleinanleger.
inveterate [ɪn'vetərɪt] *adj hatred* tief verwurzelt; *enemies* unversöhnlich; *criminal, smoker* Gewohnheits-; *gambler* unverbesserlich.
invidious [ɪn'vɪdɪəs] *adj remark* gehässig; *task* unangenehm; *distinctions* ungerecht.
invigilate [ɪn'vɪdʒɪleɪt] *vti (Brit) exam* Aufsicht führen (bei).
invigilator [ɪn'vɪdʒɪleɪtəʳ] *n (Brit)* Aufsicht, Aufsichtsperson *f.*
invigorating [ɪn'vɪgəreɪtɪŋ] *adj climate* gesund; *air, shower* erfrischend; *tonic* kräftigend; *(fig) attitude* (herz)erfrischend.
invincible [ɪn'vɪnsəbl] *adj army etc* unbesiegbar; *courage, determination* unerschütterlich.
invisible [ɪn'vɪzəbl] *adj* unsichtbar. **~ earnings** *(Econ)* unsichtbare Einkünfte *pl*; **~ ink** Geheimtinte *f*; **~ mending** Kunststopfen *nt*; **~ to the naked eye** mit dem bloßen Auge nicht erkennbar.
invitation [ˌɪnvɪ'teɪʃən] *n* Einladung *f.* **by ~ (only)** nur auf Einladung; **at sb's ~** auf jds Aufforderung *(acc)* (hin).
invite [ɪn'vaɪt] **1** *vt person* einladen; *suggestions* bitten um. **to ~ sb to do sth** jdn bitten, etw zu tun; **to ~ sb in** jdn hereinbitten; **that's inviting trouble** das gibt bestimmt Ärger. **2** ['ɪnvaɪt] *n (col)* Einladung *f.*
♦**invite out** *vt sep* einladen. **I ~d her ~** ich habe sie gefragt, ob sie mit mir ausgehen möchte.
inviting [ɪn'vaɪtɪŋ] *adj* einladend; *prospect, meal* verlockend.
invoice ['ɪnvɔɪs] **1** *n* Rechnung *f.* **2** *vt goods* in Rechnung stellen, berechnen. **to ~ sb for sth** jdm für etw eine Rechnung ausstellen.

invoke [ɪn'vəʊk] *vt the law etc* anrufen; *treaty etc* sich berufen auf *(+acc)*.

involuntary [ɪn'vɒləntərɪ] *adj* unbeabsichtigt; *reaction etc* unwillkürlich.

involve [ɪn'vɒlv] *vt* **(a)** *(entangle)* verwickeln *(sb in sth* jdn in etw *acc)*; *(include)* beteiligen *(sb in sth* jdn an etw *dat)*; *(concern)* betreffen. **to get ~d in sth** in etw *(acc)* verwickelt werden; **I didn't want to get ~d** ich wollte damit nichts zu tun haben; **I didn't want to get too ~d** ich wollte mich nicht zu sehr engagieren; **we are all ~d in the battle against inflation** der Kampf gegen die Inflation geht uns alle an; **to be ~d with sb** mit jdm zu tun haben; *(sexually)* mit jdm ein Verhältnis haben; **to get ~d with sb** mit jdm Kontakt bekommen; **he got ~d with a girl** er hat eine Beziehung mit einem Mädchen angefangen.

(b) *(entail)* zur Folge haben; *(mean)* bedeuten. **what does your job ~?** worin besteht Ihre Arbeit?; **to ~ a lot of hard work** mit viel Arbeit verbunden sein; **it would ~ moving to Germany** das würde bedeuten, nach Deutschland zu ziehen.

involved [ɪn'vɒlvd] *adj* kompliziert, umständlich *(pej)*; *story also* verwickelt; *style* komplex.

involvement [ɪn'vɒlvmənt] *n (being concerned with)* Beteiligung *f (in* an *+dat)*; *(in quarrel, crime etc)* Verwicklung *f (in* in *+acc)*; *(commitment)* Engagement *nt*; *(sexually)* Verhältnis *nt*; *(complexity)* Kompliziertheit *f*. **the extent of his ~ with her/with his work** das Maß, in dem er sich bei ihr/bei seiner Arbeit engagiert hat; **we don't know the extent of his ~ in the plot** wir wissen nicht, wie weit er an dem Komplott beteiligt ist/war.

invulnerable [ɪn'vʌlnərəbl] *adj* unverwundbar; *(lit, fig) position* unangreifbar.

inward ['ɪnwəd] *adj (inner)* innere(r, s); *life* innerlich; *thoughts* innerste(r, s).

inwardly ['ɪnwədlɪ] *adv* innerlich.

inward(s) ['ɪnwəd(z)] *adv* nach innen.

iodine ['aɪədiːn] *n* Jod *nt*.

iota [aɪ'əʊtə] *n* Jota *nt*. **not one ~** nicht ein Jota; **not an ~ of truth** kein Körnchen *nt* Wahrheit.

IOU [,aɪəʊ'juː] = **I owe you** Schuldschein *m*.

IQ = **intelligence quotient** IQ, Intelligenzquotient *m*.

IRA = **Irish Republican Army** IRA *f*.

Iran [ɪ'rɑːn] *n* (der) Iran.

Iranian [ɪ'reɪnɪən] **1** *adj* iranisch. **2** *n* **(a)** Iraner(in *f*) *m*. **(b)** *(language)* Iranisch *nt*.

Iraq [ɪ'rɑːk] *n* der Irak.

Iraqi [ɪ'rɑːkɪ] **1** *adj* irakisch. **2** *n* Iraker(in *f*) *m*.

irascible [ɪ'ræsɪbl] *adj* reizbar, jähzornig.

irate [aɪ'reɪt] *adj* zornig; *crowd* wütend.

Ireland ['aɪələnd] *n* Irland *nt*.

iris ['aɪərɪs] *n* **(a)** *(of eye)* Iris *f*. **(b)** *(Bot)* Iris, Schwertlilie *f*.

Irish ['aɪərɪʃ] **1** *adj* **(a)** irisch. **~man** Ire *m*; **~ Sea** Irische See; **~woman** Irin *f*. **(b)** *(hum col: illogical)* unlogisch. **2** *n* **(a)** *pl* **the ~** die Iren *pl*. **(b)** *(language)* Irisch *nt*.

irksome ['ɜːksəm] *adj* lästig.

iron ['aɪən] **1** *n* **(a)** Eisen *nt (also Golf)*. **a will of ~** ein eiserner Wille; **to rule with a rod of ~** mit eiserner Faust herrschen. **(b)** *(electric ~)* Bügeleisen *nt*. **to have more than one ~ in the fire** *(fig)* mehrere Eisen im Feuer haben; **he has too many ~s in the fire** er macht zuviel auf einmal; **to strike while the ~ is hot** *(Prov)* das Eisen schmieden, solange es heiß ist *(Prov)*. **2** *adj (lit, fig)* eisern; *(lit also)* Eisen-. **3** *vt clothes* bügeln.

♦**iron out** *vt sep (lit, fig)* ausbügeln.

iron: I~ Age *n* Eisenzeit *f*; **I~ Curtain** *n* Eiserner Vorhang; **the I~ Curtain countries** die Länder hinter dem Eisernen Vorhang.

ironic(al) [aɪ'rɒnɪk(əl)] *adj* ironisch; *situation* paradox.

ironically [aɪ'rɒnɪkəlɪ] *adv* ironisch. **and then, ~ enough, he turned up** komischerweise tauchte er dann auf.

ironing ['aɪənɪŋ] *n (process)* Bügeln *nt*; *(clothes)* Bügelwäsche *f*. **to do the ~** (die Wäsche) bügeln; **~ board** Bügelbrett *nt*.

iron: ~ lung *n* eiserne Lunge; **~monger** *n (Brit)* Eisen(waren)händler(in *f*) *m*; **~ ore** *n* Eisenerz *nt*. **~works** *n sing or pl* Eisenhütte *f*.

irony ['aɪərənɪ] *n* Ironie *f no pl*. **the ~ of it is that ...** das Ironische daran ist, daß ...

irrational [ɪ'ræʃənl] *adj* irrational; *(not sensible)* unvernünftig.

irreconcilable [ɪ,rekən'saɪləbl] *adj enemy* unversöhnlich; *differences* unvereinbar.

irredeemable [,ɪrɪ'diːməbl] *adj sinner* (rettungslos) verloren; *loss* unwiederbringlich.

irrefutable [,ɪrɪ'fjuːtəbl] *adj* unwiderlegbar.

irregular [ɪ'regjʊlə^r] *adj* **(a)** *(uneven, Gram)* unregelmäßig; *surface* uneben. **to keep ~ hours** keine festen Zeiten haben. **(b)** *behaviour* ungehörig. **this is most ~!** das ist äußerst ungewöhnlich!

irregularity [ɪ,regjʊ'lærɪtɪ] *n see adj* **(a)** Unregelmäßigkeit *f*; Unebenheit *f*. **(b)** Ungehörigkeit *f*. **a slight ~ in the proceedings** ein kleiner Formfehler.

irrelevance [ɪ'reləvəns] *n* Irrelevanz *f no pl*; *(of details also)* Unwesentlichkeit *f*; *(of titles, individuals)* Bedeutungslosigkeit *f*.

irrelevant [ɪ'reləvənt] *adj* irrelevant *(to* für*)*; *information* unwesentlich; *titles etc* bedeutungslos. **it is ~ whether he agrees or not** es ist belanglos, ob er zustimmt; **that's ~** das spielt keine Rolle.

irreparable [ɪ'repərəbl] *adj damage* irreparabel, nicht wiedergutzumachend *attr*.

irreplaceable [,ɪrɪ'pleɪsəbl] *adj* unersetzlich.

irrepressible [,ɪrɪ'presəbl] *adj urge* unbezähmbar; *optimism* unerschütterlich; *person* nicht unterzukriegen; *delight* unbändig.

irreproachable [,ɪrɪ'prəʊtʃəbl] *adj* tadellos.

irresistible [,ɪrɪ'zɪstəbl] *adj* unwiderstehlich.

irresolute [ɪ'rezəluːt] *adj* unentschlossen.

irrespective [,ɪrɪ'spektɪv] *adj*: **~ of** ungeachtet *(+gen)*, unabhängig von; **candidates should be chosen ~ of sex** bei der Auswahl der Kandidaten sollte das Geschlecht keine Rolle spielen; **~ of whether they want to or not** gleichgültig, ob sie wollen oder nicht.

irresponsibility ['ɪrɪ,spɒnsə'bɪlɪtɪ] *n see adj* Unverantwortlichkeit *f*; Verantwortungslosigkeit *f*.

irresponsible [,ɪrɪ'spɒnsəbl] *adj behaviour* unverantwortlich; *person* verantwortungslos.

irretrievable [,ɪrɪ'triːvəbl] *adj* nicht mehr wiederzubekommen; *loss* unersetzlich. **~ breakdown of marriage** (unheilbare) Zerrüttung der Ehe.

irretrievably [,ɪrɪ'triːvəblɪ] *adv* **~ lost** für immer verloren.

irreverent [ɪ'revərənt] *adj behaviour, remark* respektlos; *(towards religion)* ehrfurchtslos.

irreversible [,ɪrɪ'vɜːsəbl] *adj judgment* unwiderruflich.

irrevocable [ɪ'revəkəbl] *adj* unwiderruflich.

irrigate ['ɪrɪgeɪt] *vt land, crop* bewässern.

irrigation [,ɪrɪ'geɪʃən] *n (Agr)* Bewässerung *f*. **~ canal** Bewässerungskanal *m*.

irritable ['ɪrɪtəbl] *adj (as characteristic)* reizbar; *(on occasion)* gereizt.

irritant ['ɪrɪtənt] *n (Med)* Reizerreger *m*.

irritate ['ɪrɪteɪt] *vt (annoy)* ärgern; *(deliberately)* reizen; *(get on nerves)* irritieren.

irritating ['ɪrɪteɪtɪŋ] *adj* ärgerlich; *cough* lästig. **I find his jokes most ~** seine Witze regen mich wirklich auf; **you really are the most ~ person** du kannst einem wirklich auf die Nerven gehen.

irritation [,ɪrɪ'teɪʃən] *n* **(a)** *(state)* Ärger *m*; *(act)*

Ärgern *nt*; *(deliberate)* Reizen *nt*; *(thing that irritates)* Ärgernis *nt*. **(b)** *(Med)* Reizung *f*.

is [ɪz] *3rd person sing pres of* **be.**

Islam ['ɪzlɑːm] *n (religion)* der Islam; *(Moslems collectively)* Mohammedaner *pl*.

Islamic [ɪz'læmɪk] *adj* islamisch.

island ['aɪlənd] *n (lit, fig)* Insel *f*.

islander ['aɪləndəʳ] *n* Inselbewohner(in *f*) *m*.

isle [aɪl] *n (poet)* Eiland *nt (poet)*. **the I~ of Man** die Insel Man.

isn't ['ɪznt] = **is not.**

isolate ['aɪsəʊleɪt] *vt* **(a)** isolieren; *(cut off also)* abschneiden. **to ~ oneself from the world** sich von der Welt zurückziehen. **(b)** *(pinpoint)* herausfinden; *essential factor* herauskristallisieren.

isolated ['aɪsəʊleɪtɪd] *adj* **(a)** *(cut off)* abgeschnitten, isoliert; *(remote)* abgelegen; *existence* zurückgezogen. **(b)** *(single)* einzeln. **~ instances** Einzelfälle *pl*.

isolation [,aɪsəʊ'leɪʃən] **(a)** *(act)* *(separation)* Absonderung, Isolierung *(esp Med) f*; *(pinpointing)* Herausfinden *nt*; *(of essential factor)* Herauskristallisierung *f*. **(b)** *(state)* Isolation *f*; *(remoteness)* Abgeschiedenheit *f*. **to keep a patient in ~** einen Patienten isolieren; **to live in ~** zurückgezogen leben; **to consider sth in ~** etw gesondert betrachten; **it doesn't make much sense in ~** ohne Zusammenhang ist es ziemlich unverständlich.

isolation: ~ hospital *n* Krankenhaus *nt* für ansteckende Krankheiten; **~ ward** *n* Isolierstation *f*.

isotope ['aɪsəʊtəʊp] *n* Isotop *nt*.

Israel ['ɪzreɪl] *n* Israel *nt*.

Israeli [ɪz'reɪlɪ] **1** *adj* israelisch. **2** *n* Israeli *mf*.

issue ['ɪʃuː] **1** *vt passport* ausstellen; *shares, banknotes, rations* ausgeben; *order, warning* erteilen *(to dat)*; *details* bekanntgeben; *(publish) book* herausgeben. **to ~ sth to sb/to ~ sb with sth** etw an jdn ausgeben; **to ~ sb with a visa** jdm ein Visum ausstellen; **a warrant for his arrest was ~d** gegen ihn wurde Haftbefehl erlassen.

2 *vi (liquid, gas)* austreten; *(smoke)* (heraus)quellen; *(sound)* (heraus)dringen; *(people etc)* (heraus)strömen.

3 *n* **(a)** *(question)* Frage *f*; *(matter also)* Angelegenheit *f*; *(problematic)* Problem *nt*. **the ~ is whether ...** die Frage ist, ob ...; **what is at ~?** worum geht es?; **that's not at ~** das steht nicht zur Debatte; **to take ~ with sb over sth** jdm in etw *(dat)* widersprechen; **to make an ~ of sth** etw aufbauschen; **to evade the ~** ausweichen; **to face the ~** den Tatsachen ins Auge sehen.

(b) *(outcome)* Ergebnis *nt*. **that decided the ~** das war ausschlaggebend; **to force the ~** eine Entscheidung erzwingen.

(c) *(of banknotes, shares etc)* Ausgabe *f*; *(of shares also)* Emission *f*. **place of ~** *(of tickets)* Ausgabestelle *f*; *(of passports)* Ausstellungsort *m*; **date of ~** *(of tickets)* Ausstellungsdatum *nt*; *(of stamps)* Ausgabetag *m*. **the ~ of blankets/guns to the troops** die Versorgung der Truppen mit Decken/die Ausrüstung der Truppen mit Gewehren.

(d) *(of book etc)* Herausgabe *f*; *(book etc)* Ausgabe *f*.

(e) *(Jur: offspring)* Nachkommenschaft *f*.

it [ɪt] *pron* **(a)** *(when replacing noun)* *(subject)* er/sie/es; *(dir obj)* ihn/sie/es; *(indir obj)* ihm/ihr/ihm. **of ~** davon; **behind/over** *etc* **~** dahinter/darüber *etc*; **who is ~? — ~'s me** wer ist da? — ich (bin's); **what is ~?** was ist es *or* das?; *(matter)* was ist los?; **that's not ~** *(not the trouble)* das ist es (gar) nicht; **the worst of ~ is that ...** das Schlimmste daran ist, daß ...

(b) *(indef subject)* es. **~'s raining** es regnet; **if ~ hadn't been for her, we would have come** wenn sie nicht gewesen wäre, wären wir gekommen; **why is ~ always me who has to ...?** warum muß (ausgerechnet) immer ich ...?; **I've known ~ happen** ich habe es (schon) erlebt; **~'s Friday tomorrow** morgen ist Freitag; **~ was him who asked her** *er* hat sie gefragt; **~'s his appearance I object to** ich habe nur etwas gegen sein Äußeres; **~ was for his sake that she lied** nur um seinetwillen hat sie gelogen.

(c) *(col phrases)* **that's ~!** *(agreement)* ja, genau!; *(annoyed)* jetzt reicht's mir!; **that's ~ (then)!** *(achievement)* (so,) das wär's!; *(disappointment)* ja, das war's dann wohl.

IT = **information technology.**

Italian [ɪ'tæljən] **1** *adj* italienisch. **2** *n* **(a)** Italiener(in *f*) *m*. **(b)** *(language)* Italienisch *nt*.

italic [ɪ'tælɪk] **1** *adj* kursiv. **2** *n* **~s** *pl* Kursivschrift *f*; **in ~s** kursiv (gedruckt).

Italy ['ɪtəlɪ] *n* Italien *nt*.

itch [ɪtʃ] **1** *n* **(a)** Jucken *nt*, Juckreiz *m*. **I have an ~** mich juckt es. **(b)** *(col: urge)* Lust *f*. **I have an ~ to do sth** es juckt *(col)* mich, etw zu tun. **2** *vi* **(a)** jucken. **my back ~es** mein Rücken juckt (mich). **(b)** *(col)* **he is ~ing to ...** es juckt *(col)* ihn, zu ...; **he's ~ing for a fight** er ist auf Streit aus.

itchy ['ɪtʃɪ] *adj (+er)* *(itching)* juckend. **it's ~** es juckt; **I've got ~ feet** *(col)* ich will hier weg *(col)*; *(want to travel also)* mich packt das Fernweh.

it'd ['ɪtəd] = **it would; it had.**

item ['aɪtəm] *n* **(a)** *(on agenda etc)* Punkt *m*; *(Comm: in account book)* (Rechnungs)posten *m*; *(article)* Gegenstand *m*; *(in catalogue etc)* Artikel *m*; *(Brit: in variety show)* Nummer *f*. **(b)** *(of news)* Bericht *m*; *(short, Rad, TV also)* Meldung *f*. **a short news ~** eine Zeitungsnotiz/eine Kurzmeldung.

itemize ['aɪtəmaɪz] *vt* einzeln aufführen. **~d account** spezifizierte Rechnung.

itinerant [ɪ'tɪnərənt] *adj* umherziehend, Wander-; *worker* Saison-. **~ theatre group** Wandertruppe *f*.

itinerary [aɪ'tɪnərərɪ] *n (route)* (Reise)route *f*.

it'll ['ɪtl] = **it will; it shall.**

its [ɪts] *poss adj* sein(e)/ihr(e)/sein(e).

it's [ɪts] = **it is; it has** *(as aux)*.

itself [ɪt'self] *pron* **(a)** *(reflexive)* sich. **(b)** *(emph)* selbst. **and now we come to the text ~** und jetzt kommen wir zum Text selbst; **the frame ~ is worth £1,000** der Rahmen allein ist £1.000 wert; **the amount in ~** der Betrag an sich. **(c) by ~** *(alone)* allein; *(automatically)* von selbst, selbsttätig.

ITV *(Brit)* = **Independent Television.**

IUD = **intra-uterine device** Pessar *nt*.

I've [aɪv] = **I have.**

ivory ['aɪvərɪ] **1** *n (also colour)* Elfenbein *nt*. **2** *adj* elfenbeinern; *(colour)* elfenbeinfarben.

Ivory Coast *n* Elfenbeinküste *f*.

ivory tower *n (fig)* Elfenbeinturm *m*.

ivy ['aɪvɪ] *n* Efeu *m*.

Ivy League *n (US) Eliteuniversitäten der USA.*

J

J, j [dʒeɪ] *n* J, j *nt.*

jab [dʒæb] **1** *vt (with stick, elbow etc)* stoßen; *(with knife also)* stechen. **he ~bed his elbow into my side** er stieß mir den Ellbogen in die Seite; **a sharp ~bing pain** ein scharfer, stechender Schmerz. **2** *vi* stoßen *(at sb with sth* mit etw nach jdm*)*. **3** *n (with stick, elbow)* Stoß *m*; *(with needle, knife)* Stich *m*; *(col: injection)* Spritze *f*; *(Boxing)* (kurze) Gerade.

jabber ['dʒæbəʳ] **1** *vt* (daher)plappern *(col)*; *poem* herunterrasseln *(col)*. **2** *vi (also ~* **away***)* plappern, quasseln *(col)*. **they were ~ing away in Spanish** sie quasselten *(col)* Spanisch.

jack [dʒæk] *n* **(a)** *(Aut)* Wagenheber *m*. **(b)** *(Cards)* Bube *m*.

♦ **jack in** *vt sep (col) job etc* aufgeben; *girlfriend* Schluß machen mit *(col)*.

♦ **jack up** *vt sep car* aufbocken.

jackal ['dʒækɔːl] *n* Schakal *m*.

jackass ['dʒækæs] *n (col: person)* Esel *m (col)*.

jackdaw ['dʒækdɔː] *n* Dohle *f*.

jacket ['dʒækɪt] *n* **(a)** *(garment)* Jacke *f*; *(man's ~ also)* Jackett *nt*. **(b)** *(of book, US: of record)* Hülle *f*. **(c)** *(esp US: for papers etc)* Umschlag *m*. **(d) ~ potatoes** in der Schale gebackene Kartoffeln *pl*. **(e)** *(Tech: of boiler etc)* Mantel *m*.

jack: ~-in-the-box *n* Kastenteufel *m*; **~knife** *vi* **the lorry ~knifed** der Sattelschlepper hat sich quergestellt; **~-of-all-trades** *n* Alleskönner *m*; **to be (a) ~-of-all-trades (and master of none)** *(prov)* ein Hansdampf *m* in allen Gassen sein; **~pot** *n* Pott *m (col)*; *(in lottery etc)* Hauptgewinn *m*; **to hit the ~pot** *(in lottery)* den Hauptgewinn bekommen; *(fig)* das große Los ziehen; **J~ Robinson** [ˌdʒæk'rɒbɪnsən] *n*: **before you could say J~ Robinson** *(col)* im Nu.

jacuzzi [dʒə'kuːzɪ] *n* Whirlpool *m*.

jade [dʒeɪd] **1** *n (stone)* Jade *m or f*; *(colour)* Jadegrün *nt*. **2** *adj* Jade-; *(colour)* jadegrün.

jaded ['dʒeɪdɪd] *adj (physically)* abgespannt; *(permanently)* verbraucht; *(mentally)* abgestumpft; *appearance* verbraucht.

jagged ['dʒægɪd] *adj* zackig; *wound, tear* ausgefranst; *coastline* zerklüftet.

jaguar ['dʒægjʊəʳ] *n* Jaguar *m*.

jail [dʒeɪl] **1** *n* Gefängnis *nt*. **in ~** im Gefängnis; **to go to ~** ins Gefängnis kommen. **2** *vt* einsperren.

jail: ~bird *n (col)* Knastbruder *m (col)*; **~break** *n* Ausbruch *m (aus dem Gefängnis)*.

jailer ['dʒeɪləʳ] *n* Gefängniswärter(in *f*) *m*.

jalop(p)y [dʒə'lɒpɪ] *n (col)* alte Mühle *(col)*.

jam[1] [dʒæm] *n* Marmelade *f*. **you want ~ on it too, do you?** *(Brit col)* du kriegst wohl nie genug? *(col)*.

jam[2] **1** *n* **(a)** *(crowd)* Gedränge *nt*. **(b)** *(traffic ~)* (Verkehrs)stau *m*. **(c)** *(blockage in machine etc)* Stockung *f*. **(d)** *(col: tight spot)* **to be in a ~** in der Klemme sitzen *(col)*; **to get into a ~ with sth** mit etw Schwierigkeiten haben; **to get sb out of a ~** jdm aus der Klemme helfen *(col)*.

2 *vt* **(a)** *(make stick) window etc* verklemmen; *brakes etc* blockieren; *(wedge)* festklemmen; *(between two things)* einklemmen. **it's ~med** es klemmt; **he ~med his finger in the door** er hat sich *(dat)* den Finger in der Tür eingeklemmt. **(b)** *(cram)* stopfen, quetschen *(into* in *+acc)*. **we were ~med together** wir waren zusammengedrängt. **(c)** *(block) street etc* verstopfen, blockieren; *radio station* stören. **a street ~med with cars** eine verstopfte Straße; **all the lines are ~med** alle Leitungen sind besetzt.

3 *vi* **(a) the crowd ~med into the bus** die Menschenmenge zwängte sich in den Bus. **(b)** *(become stuck) (brake)* sich verklemmen; *(door etc)* klemmen.

♦ **jam in** *vt sep* **(a)** *(wedge in)* einkeilen. **he was ~med ~ by the crowd** er war in der Menge eingekeilt. **(b)** *(press in)* (herein)stopfen in *(+acc)*.

♦ **jam on 1** *vt sep* **to ~ ~ the brakes** eine Vollbremsung machen. **2** *vi (brakes)* klemmen.

Jamaica [dʒə'meɪkə] *n* Jamaika *nt*.

Jamaican [dʒə'meɪkən] *adj* jamaikanisch.

jam: ~ jar *n* Marmeladenglas *nt*; **~-packed** *adj* überfüllt, proppenvoll *(col)*.

jangle ['dʒæŋgl] **1** *vi (money)* klimpern *(col)*; *(bells)* bimmeln *(col)*; *(chains)* rasseln. **2** *vt money* klimpern mit; *keys also, chains* rasseln mit.

janitor ['dʒænɪtəʳ] *n* Hausmeister *m*; *(of flats also)* Hauswart *m*.

January ['dʒænjʊərɪ] *n* Januar *m*; *see* **September.**

Japan [dʒə'pæn] *n* Japan *nt*.

Japanese [ˌdʒæpə'niːz] **1** *adj* japanisch. **2** *n* **(a)** Japaner(in *f*) *m*. **(b)** *(language)* Japanisch *nt*.

jar[1] [dʒɑːʳ] *n (for jam etc)* Glas *nt*; *(without handle)* Topf *m*; *(with handle)* Krug *m*.

jar[2] **1** *n (jolt)* Ruck *m*; *(fig)* Schock *m*. **2** *vi (note)* schauerlich klingen; *(colours)* sich beißen *(col)*; *(ideas)* sich nicht vertragen, nicht harmonieren *(with* mit*)*. **this ~s stylistically** das fällt stilmäßig aus dem Rahmen; **this noise ~s on my nerves** dieser Lärm geht mir auf die Nerven; **her voice ~s on my ears** ihre Stimme geht mir durch und durch. **3** *vt building etc* erschüttern; *back* sich *(dat)* stauchen; *(fig)* einen Schock versetzen *(+dat)*. **he must have ~red the camera** er muß mit dem Fotoapparat gewackelt haben.

jargon ['dʒɑːgən] *n* Jargon *m (pej)*, Fachsprache *f*.

jarring ['dʒɑːrɪŋ] *adj sound* gellend; *accent* störend; *colours* sich beißend *attr (col)*.

jasmin(e) ['dʒæzmɪn] *n* Jasmin *m*.

jaundice ['dʒɔːndɪs] *n* Gelbsucht *f*.

jaundiced ['dʒɔːndɪst] *adj* **(a)** *(lit)* gelbsüchtig. **(b)** *attitude* zynisch. **to take a ~ view of sth** in bezug auf etw *(acc)* zynisch sein.

jaunt [dʒɔːnt] *n* Trip *m*, Spritztour *f*. **to go for a ~** eine Spritztour machen.

jaunty ['dʒɔːntɪ] *adj (+er)* fröhlich; *hat* flott; *attitude* sorglos, unbekümmert. **he wore his hat at a ~ angle** er hatte den Hut keck aufgesetzt.

javelin ['dʒævlɪn] *n* Speer *m*. **(throwing) the ~** Speerwerfen *nt*.

jaw [dʒɔː] *n* **(a)** Kiefer *m*. **with its prey between its ~s** mit der Beute im Maul; **the ~s of death** die Klauen *pl* des Todes. **(b)** *(of vice)* Backe *f*.

jawbone ['dʒɔːbəʊn] *n* Kieferknochen *m*.

jay [dʒeɪ] *n* Eichelhäher *m*.

jaywalker ['dʒeɪˌwɔːkəʳ] *n* unachtsamer Fußgänger, unachtsame Fußgängerin.

jazz [dʒæz] **1** *n (Mus)* Jazz *m*. **... and all that ~** ... und all so'n Zeug *(col)*. **2** *attr band, music* Jazz-.

♦ **jazz up** *vt sep* aufmöbeln *(col)*.

jealous ['dʒeləs] *adj lover etc* eifersüchtig; *(envious: of sb's success etc)* neidisch. **to be ~ of sb** auf jdn eifersüchtig sein/jdn beneiden.
jealousy ['dʒeləsɪ] *n see adj (of* auf *+acc)* Eifersucht *f*; Neid *m*.
jeans [dʒi:nz] *npl* Jeans *pl*.
jeep [dʒi:p] *n* Jeep ® *m*.
jeer [dʒɪəʳ] **1** *n (remark)* höhnische Bemerkung; *(shout)* Buhruf *m*; *(laughter)* Hohngelächter *nt*. **2** *vi see n* höhnische Bemerkungen machen; buhen; höhnisch lachen. **to ~ at sb** jdn (laut) verhöhnen.
jeering ['dʒɪərɪŋ] **1** *adj* höhnisch. **2** *n see* **jeer 1.**
jelly ['dʒelɪ] *n* Gelee *nt*; *(esp Brit: dessert)* Wackelpeter *m (col)*.
jellyfish ['dʒelɪfɪʃ] *n* Qualle *f*.
jeopardize ['dʒepədaɪz] *vt* gefährden.
jeopardy ['dʒepədɪ] *n* Gefahr *f*. **in ~** gefährdet; **to put sb/sth in ~** jdn/etw gefährden.
jerk [dʒɜ:k] **1** *n* **(a)** Ruck *m*; *(jump)* Satz *m*; *(twitch)* Zuckung *f*. **to give sth a ~** einer Sache *(dat)* einen Ruck geben; *rope* an etw *(dat)* ruckartig ziehen; **the train stopped with a ~** der Zug hielt mit einem Ruck an. **(b)** *(col: person)* Trottel *(col) m*. **2** *vt* rucken an *(+dat)*. **the impact ~ed his head forward** beim Aufprall wurde sein Kopf nach vorn geschleudert; **he ~ed the book out of my hand** er riß mir das Buch aus der Hand. **3** *vi (rope)* rucken; *(move jerkily)* ruckeln *(col)*; *(body, muscle)* zucken; *(head)* zurückzucken. **he ~ed away from me** er sprang mit einem Satz von mir weg; **the car ~ed forward** der Wagen machte einen Satz nach vorn; **the car ~ed to a stop** das Auto hielt ruckweise an.
jerky ['dʒɜ:kɪ] *adj (+er)* ruckartig; *speech also, style* abgehackt. **a ~ ride** eine holprige Fahrt.
Jerry ['dʒerɪ] *n (col)* Deutsche(r) *m*.
jerry: ~ built *adj* schlampig gebaut; **~ can** *n* großer (Blech)kanister.
jersey ['dʒɜ:zɪ] *n* Pullover *m*; *(Ftbl etc)* Trikot *nt*.
jest [dʒest] **1** *n (joke)* Scherz, Witz *m*. **in ~** im Spaß. **2** *vi* scherzen. **to ~ about sth** über etw *(acc)* Witze machen.
jester ['dʒestəʳ] *n* **(a)** *(Hist)* Narr *m*. **(b)** *(joker)* Spaßvogel, Witzbold *(col) m*.
Jesuit ['dʒezjʊɪt] *n* Jesuit *m*.
Jesus ['dʒi:zəs] *n* Jesus *m*. **~ Christ** Jesus Christus; **~ Christ!** *(col)* Herrgott (noch mal)! *(col)*.
jet[1] [dʒet] *n* **(a)** Strahl *m*. **a ~ of water** ein Wasserstrahl. **(b)** *(nozzle)* Düse *f*. **(c)** *(also* **~ plane***)* Düsenflugzeug *nt*, Jet *m (col)*.
jet[2] *n (Miner)* Gagat *m*. **~ black** pechschwarz.
jet: ~ engine *n* Düsentriebwerk *nt*; **~lag** *n* Schwierigkeiten *pl* durch den Zeitunterschied; **~lagged** *adj* **to be ~lagged** durch den Zeitunterschied völlig fertig sein; **~ plane** *n* Düsenflugzeug *nt*; **~-propelled** *adj* mit Düsenantrieb, Düsen-; **~ set** *n* Jet-set *m*.
jettison ['dʒetɪsn] *vt (lit, fig)* über Bord werfen; *unwanted articles* wegwerfen.
jetty ['dʒetɪ] *n (breakwater)* Hafendamm *m*; *(landing pier)* Pier *m*, Landungsbrücke *f*.
Jew [dʒu:] *n* Jude *m*, Jüdin *f*.
jewel ['dʒu:əl] *n* **(a)** *(gem)* Edelstein *m*, Juwel *nt (geh)*; *(piece of jewellery)* Schmuckstück *nt*. **(b)** *(of watch)* Stein *m*.
jeweller, *(US)* **jeweler** ['dʒu:ələʳ] *n* Juwelier *m*; *(making jewellery)* Goldschmied *m*.
jewellery, *(US)* **jewelry** ['dʒu:əlrɪ] *n* Schmuck *m no pl*. **a piece of ~** ein Schmuckstück *nt*.
Jewess ['dʒu:ɪs] *n* Jüdin *f*.
Jewish ['dʒu:ɪʃ] *adj* jüdisch; *(pej col: mean)* knickerig *(col)*.
jib [dʒɪb] **1** *n (of crane)* Dreharm *m*; *(Naut)* Klüver *m*. **2** *vi* **to ~ at sth** sich gegen etw sträuben.
jibe [dʒaɪb] *n, vi* = **gibe.**
jiffy ['dʒɪfɪ], **jiff** [dʒɪf] *n (col)* Minütchen *nt (col)*. **I won't be a ~** ich komme sofort; *(back soon)* ich bin sofort wieder da; **in a ~** sofort.
jig [dʒɪg] *n* **(a)** *(dance) lebhafter Volkstanz*. **(b)** *(Tech)* Spannvorrichtung *f*.
jigsaw ['dʒɪgsɔ:] *n (also* **~ puzzle***)* Puzzle(spiel) *nt*.
jilt [dʒɪlt] *vt lover* den Laufpaß geben *(+dat)*. **~ed** verschmäht.
jingle ['dʒɪŋgl] **1** *n* **(a)** *(of keys etc)* Klimpern *nt*; *(of bells)* Bimmeln *nt*. **(b)** *(catchy verse)* Spruch *m*; *(for remembering)* Merkspruch *m*. **advertising ~** Werbespruch *m*. **2** *vi (keys etc)* klimpern; *(bells)* bimmeln. **3** *vt keys* klimpern mit; *bells* bimmeln lassen.
jingoism ['dʒɪŋgəʊɪzəm] *n* Hurrapatriotismus *m*.
jinx [dʒɪŋks] *n* **there's a ~ on it** das ist verhext.
jitters ['dʒɪtəz] *npl (col)* **the ~** das große Zittern *(col)*; **to give sb the ~** jdn ganz rappelig machen *(col)*.
jittery ['dʒɪtərɪ] *adj (col)* nervös, rappelig *(col)*.
jive [dʒaɪv] **1** *n (dance)* Swing *m*. **2** *vi* Swing tanzen.
job [dʒɒb] *n* **(a)** *(piece of work)* Arbeit *f*. **I have a ~ to do** ich habe zu tun; **it's quite a ~ to paint the house** das Haus zu streichen ist eine Heidenarbeit *(col)*; **he's on the ~** *(col: at work)* er ist bei der Arbeit; **he made a good job of it** er hat dabei gute Arbeit geleistet; **we have a lot of ~s on just now** wir haben zur Zeit viele Aufträge; **he knows his ~** er versteht sein Handwerk.

(b) *(employment)* Stelle *f*, Job *m (col)*. **500 ~s lost** 500 Arbeitsplätze verlorengegangen; **to bring new ~s to a region** in einer Gegend neue Arbeitsplätze schaffen.

(c) *(duty)* Aufgabe *f*. **I'm only doing my ~** ich tue nur meine Pflicht.

(d) that's a good ~! so ein Glück; **it's a good ~ I brought my cheque book** nur gut, daß ich mein Scheckbuch mitgenommen habe; **to give sb/sth up as a bad ~** jdn/etw aufgeben; **that should do the ~** das müßte hinhauen *(col)*; **this is just the ~** das ist genau das richtige; **she has a ~ getting up the stairs** es ist gar nicht einfach für sie, die Treppe raufzukommen.

(e) *(col: crime)* Ding *nt (col)*. **remember that bank ~?** erinnerst du dich an das große Ding in der Bank? *(col)*.

(f) *(col: person, thing)* Ding *nt*. **his new car's a lovely little ~** sein neues Auto ist wirklich große Klasse *(col)*.
job: ~ centre *n (Brit)* Arbeitsamt *nt*; **~ creation scheme** *n* Arbeitsbeschaffungsprogramm *nt*; **~ description** *n* Tätigkeitsbeschreibung *f*; **~ hunting** *n* Arbeitssuche *f*; **~less 1** *adj* arbeitslos; **2** *n* **the ~less** *pl* die Arbeitslosen *pl*; **~ lot** *n (Comm)* (Waren)posten *m*; **~ satisfaction** *n* Zufriedenheit *f* am Arbeitsplatz.
jockey ['dʒɒkɪ] **1** *n* Jockey, Rennreiter(in *f*) *m*. **2** *vi* **to ~ for position** *(lit)* sich in eine gute Position zu drängeln versuchen; *(fig)* rangeln.
jockstrap ['dʒɒkstræp] *n* Suspensorium *nt*.
jocular ['dʒɒkjʊləʳ] *adj* lustig, spaßig. **to be in a ~ mood** zu Scherzen aufgelegt sein.
jodhpurs ['dʒɒdpəz] *npl* Reithose(n *pl*) *f*.
jog [dʒɒg] **1** *vt elbow etc* stoßen an *(+acc) or* gegen; *person* anstoßen. **to ~ sb's memory** jds Gedächtnis *(dat)* nachhelfen. **2** *vi* trotten; *(Sport)* Dauerlauf machen, joggen. **3** *n (run)* trabender Lauf, Trott *m*; *(Sport)* Dauerlauf *m*. **to go for a ~** *(Sport)* einen Dauerlauf machen, joggen (gehen).
♦ **jog along** *vi (person, worker, industry)* vor sich *(acc)* hinwursteln *(col)*; *(work)* seinen Gang gehen.
jogging ['dʒɒgɪŋ] *n* Dauerlauf *m*, Joggen *nt*. **he goes ~** er macht Jogging.
join [dʒɔɪn] **1** *vt* **(a)** *(lit, fig: connect)* verbinden *(to* mit*)*; *(attach also)* anfügen *(to* an *+acc)*. **to ~ battle (with the enemy)** den Kampf mit dem Feind aufnehmen; **to ~ hands** *(lit, fig)* sich *(dat)* die Hände reichen.

(b) *(become member of) army* gehen zu; *political party, club* beitreten *(+dat)*, eintreten in *(+acc)*; *university (as student)* anfangen an *(+dat)*; *(as staff) firm* anfangen bei; *group of people* sich anschließen *(+dat)*.

(c) he ~ed us in France er stieß in Frankreich zu uns; **I ~ed him at the station** ich traf mich mit ihm am Bahnhof; **I'll ~ you in five minutes** ich bin in fünf Minuten bei Ihnen; *(follow you)* ich komme in fünf Minuten nach; **may I ~ you?** kann ich mich Ihnen anschließen?; *(sit with you)* darf ich mich zu Ihnen setzen?; **will you ~ us?** machen Sie mit?; *(sit with us)* wollen Sie uns nicht Gesellschaft leisten?; *(come with us)* kommen Sie mit?; **do ~ us for lunch** wollen Sie nicht mit uns essen?; **will you ~ me in a drink?** trinken Sie ein Glas mit mir?

(d) *(river) another river, the sea* münden *or* fließen in *(+acc)*; *(road) another road* münden auf *(+acc)*.

2 *vi* **(a)** *(also ~* **together**) *(two parts) (be attached)* (miteinander) verbunden sein; *(be attachable)* sich (miteinander) verbinden lassen; *(meet, be adjacent)* zusammentreffen; *(estates)* aneinander grenzen; *(rivers)* zusammenfließen; *(roads)* sich treffen. **they all ~ed together to get her a present** sie taten sich alle zusammen, um ihr ein Geschenk zu kaufen. **(b)** *(club member)* beitreten, Mitglied werden.

3 *n* Naht(stelle) *f*; *(in pipe, knitting)* Verbindungsstelle *f*.

♦ **join in** *vi (in activity)* mitmachen *(prep obj* bei*)*; *(in game also)* mitspielen *(prep obj* bei*)*; ~ ~, **everybody!** *(in song etc)* alle (mitmachen)!; **everybody ~ed ~ the chorus** sie sangen alle zusammen den Refrain.

♦ **join up 1** *vi* **(a)** *(Mil)* zum Militär gehen. **(b)** *(meet: road etc)* sich treffen; *(join forces)* sich zusammenschließen, sich zusammentun *(col)*. **2** *vt sep* (miteinander) verbinden.

joiner ['dʒɔɪnə^r] *n* Tischler, Schreiner *m*.

joinery ['dʒɔɪnərɪ] *n (trade)* Tischlerei *f*.

joint [dʒɔɪnt] **1** *n* **(a)** *(Anat)* Gelenk *nt*. **(b)** *(join) (in woodwork)* Fuge *f*; *(in pipe etc)* Verbindung(sstelle) *f*; *(welded etc)* Naht(stelle) *f*. **(c)** *(Cook)* Braten *m*. **a ~ of beef** ein Rinderbraten *m*. **(d)** *(col: place)* Laden *(col) m*. **(e)** *(col: of marijuana)* Joint *m (col)*. **2** *adj attr* gemeinsam; *action, work also* Gemeinschafts-; *owner(ship)* Mit-. **~ account** gemeinsames Konto; **the essay was a ~ effort** der Aufsatz ist in Gemeinschaftsarbeit entstanden; **~ heir** Miterbe *m*, Miterbin *f*; **~ stock company** Aktiengesellschaft *f*; **~ venture** Gemeinschaftsunternehmen, Joint-venture *nt*.

jointly ['dʒɔɪntlɪ] *adv* gemeinsam.

joist [dʒɔɪst] *n* Balken *m*.

joke [dʒəʊk] **1** *n* Witz *m*; *(prank)* Streich *m*; *(laughing stock)* Gespött *nt*. **for a ~** zum Spaß, aus Jux *(col)*; **I don't see the ~** ich möchte wissen, was daran so lustig sein soll; **he treats it as a big ~** für ihn ist das ein Witz; **he can't take a ~** er versteht keinen Spaß; **it's no ~** das ist nicht witzig; **this is getting beyond a ~** das geht (langsam) zu weit; **the ~ was on me** der Spaß ging auf meine Kosten; **to play a ~ on sb** jdm einen Streich spielen; **to make ~s about sth** sich über etw lustig machen. **2** *vi* Witze machen *(about* über *+acc)*; *(pull sb's leg)* Spaß machen. **I'm not joking** ich meine das ernst; **you must be joking!** das ist ja wohl nicht Ihr Ernst!

joker ['dʒəʊkə^r] *n* **(a)** *(person)* Witzbold, Spaßvogel *m*. **(b)** *(Cards)* Joker *m*.

joking ['dʒəʊkɪŋ] **1** *adj tone* scherzhaft, spaßend. **2** *n* Witze *pl*. **~ apart** Spaß beiseite.

jolly ['dʒɒlɪ] **1** *adj (+er) (merry)* fröhlich, vergnügt. **2** *adv (Brit col)* **you are ~ lucky** Sie haben vielleicht Glück *(col)*; **~ good** prima *(col)*; **that's ~ kind of you** das ist furchtbar nett von Ihnen; **you ~ well will go!** und ob du gehst!

jolt [dʒəʊlt] **1** *vi (vehicle)* holpern; *(give one ~)* einen Ruck machen. **to ~ along** rüttelnd entlangfahren; **to ~ to a halt** ruckweise anhalten. **2** *vt (lit) (shake)* durchrütteln; *(once)* einen Ruck geben *(+dat)*; *(fig)* aufrütteln. **it ~ed him into action** das hat ihn aufgerüttelt. **3** *n (jerk)* Ruck *m*. **it gave me a ~** *(fig)* das hat mir einen Schock versetzt.

Jordan ['dʒɔːdn] *n* Jordanien *nt*; *(river)* Jordan *m*.

joss stick ['dʒɒsstɪk] *n* Räucherstäbchen *nt*.

jostle ['dʒɒsl] **1** *vi* drängeln. **he ~d against me** er rempelte mich an. **2** *vt* anrempeln, schubsen. **he was ~d along with the crowd** die Menge schob ihn mit sich.

jot [dʒɒt] *n (of truth)* Funken *m*, Körnchen *nt*.

♦ **jot down** *vt sep* sich *(dat)* notieren.

jotter ['dʒɒtə^r] *n (note pad)* Notizblock *m*; *(notebook)* Notizheft(chen) *nt*.

jottings ['dʒɒtɪŋz] *npl* Notizen *pl*.

journal ['dʒɜːnl] *n (periodical)* Zeitschrift *f*; *(diary)* Tagebuch *nt*.

journalese [ˌdʒɜːnə'liːz] *n* Zeitungsjargon *m*.

journalism ['dʒɜːnəlɪzəm] *n* Journalismus *m*.

journalist ['dʒɜːnəlɪst] *n* Journalist(in *f*) *m*.

journey ['dʒɜːnɪ] **1** *n* Reise *f*; *(by train, car also)* Fahrt *f*. **to go on a ~** eine Reise machen, verreisen; **it is a 50 mile ~** es liegt 50 Meilen entfernt; **a two day ~** eine Zwei-Tage-Reise; **a train ~** eine Zugfahrt; **the ~ home** die Heimfahrt. **2** *vi* reisen.

jovial ['dʒəʊvɪəl] *adj* fröhlich; *welcome* herzlich.

jowl [dʒaʊl] *n (jaw)* (Unter)kiefer *m*; *(often pl: cheek)* Backe *f*.

joy [dʒɔɪ] *n* Freude *f*. **to my great ~** zu meiner großen Freude; **I wish you ~ (of it)!** *(iro)* na dann viel Spaß!; **I didn't get much ~** *(Brit col)* ich hatte nicht viel Erfolg; **did you get any ~?** hat es geklappt? *(col)*.

joyful ['dʒɔɪfʊl] *adj* freudig, froh.

joyous ['dʒɔɪəs] *adj (liter)* freudig, froh.

joy: ~-ride *n* Spritztour *f (in einem gestohlenen Auto)*; **~stick** *n (Aviat)* Steuerknüppel *m*; *(Comp)* Joystick *m*.

JP *(Brit)* = **Justice of the Peace.**

Jr = **junior** jr., jun.

jubilant ['dʒuːbɪlənt] *adj mood* Jubel-; *crowd* jubelnd; *face* strahlend *attr*. **they gave him a ~ welcome** sie empfingen ihn mit Jubel; **he was ~ at the news** er war überglücklich, als er die Nachricht hörte.

jubilation [ˌdʒuːbɪ'leɪʃən] *n* Jubel *m*.

jubilee ['dʒuːbɪliː] *n* Jubiläum *nt*.

judge [dʒʌdʒ] **1** *n (Jur)* Richter(in *f*) *m*; *(of competition)* Preisrichter(in *f*) *m*; *(Sport)* Schiedsrichter(in *f*) *m*; *(fig)* Kenner *m*. **to be a good ~ of character** ein guter Menschenkenner sein; **to be a good ~ of wine** ein Weinkenner sein.

2 *vt* **(a)** *(Jur) person* die Verhandlung führen über *(+acc)*; *case* verhandeln; *(God)* richten. **(b)** *competition* beurteilen, bewerten; *(Sport)* Schiedsrichter sein bei. **(c)** *(fig: pass judgement on)* ein Urteil fällen über *(+acc)*. **you shouldn't ~ people by appearances** Sie sollten Menschen nicht nach ihrem Äußeren beurteilen. **(d)** *(consider, assess)* halten für. **you can ~ for yourself how upset I was** Sie können sich *(dat)* denken, wie bestürzt ich war; **I can't ~ whether he was right or wrong** ich kann nicht beurteilen, ob er recht oder unrecht hatte. **(e)** *(estimate) distance etc* einschätzen. **he ~d the moment well** er hat den richtigen Augenblick abgepaßt.

3 *vi (Jur)* Richter sein; *(God)* richten; *(at competition)* Preisrichter sein; *(Sport)* Schiedsrichter sein; *(fig) (pass judgement)* ein Urteil fällen; *(form an opinion)* (be)urteilen. **as far as one can ~** soweit man (es) beurteilen kann; **judging by** *or*

from sth nach etw zu urteilen; **judging by appearances** dem Aussehen nach; **(you can) ~ for yourself** beurteilen Sie das selbst.
judg(e)ment ['dʒʌdʒmənt] *n (Jur)* (Gerichts)urteil *nt*; *(opinion)* Ansicht *f*, Urteil *nt*; *(value ~)* Werturteil *nt*; *(estimation)* Einschätzung *f*; *(discernment)* Urteilsvermögen *nt*. **to pass ~** *(lit, fig)* ein Urteil fällen, das Urteil sprechen *(on* über *+acc)*; **an error of ~** eine Fehleinschätzung; **in my ~** meiner Meinung nach; **against my better ~** gegen meine Überzeugung; **it's a question of ~** das ist Ansichtssache.
Judg(e)ment Day *n* Tag *m* des Jüngsten Gerichts.
judicial [dʒuː'dɪʃəl] *adj (Jur)* gerichtlich, Justiz-.
judiciary [dʒuː'dɪʃɪərɪ] *n (branch of administration)* Gerichtsbehörden *pl*; *(judges)* Richterstand *m*.
judicious [dʒuː'dɪʃəs] *adj* klug, umsichtig.
judo ['dʒuːdəʊ] *n* Judo *nt*.
jug [dʒʌg] **1** *n* **(a)** *(with lid)* Kanne *f*; *(without lid)* Krug *m*; *(small)* Kännchen *nt*. **(b)** *(col: prison)* Knast *m (col)*. **2** *vt* **~ged hare** ≃ Hasenpfeffer *m*.
juggernaut ['dʒʌgənɔːt] *n (Brit: lorry)* Schwerlaster *m*.
juggle ['dʒʌgl] *vti* jonglieren. **to ~ (with) the figures** die Zahlen so hindrehen, daß sie passen.
juggler ['dʒʌgləʳ] *n* Jongleur *m*.
Jugoslavia [ˌjuːgəʊ'slɑːvɪə] = **Yugoslavia.**
jugular ['dʒʌgjʊləʳ] *n (also* **~ vein***)* Drosselvene *f*.
juice [dʒuːs] *n (lit, fig col)* Saft *m*.
juicy ['dʒuːsɪ] *adj (+er)* saftig; *story* pikant, schlüpfrig; *scandal also* gepfeffert *(col)*.
jujitsu [ˌdʒuː'dʒɪtsuː] *n* Jiu-Jitsu *nt*.
jukebox ['dʒuːkbɒks] *n* Musikbox *f*.
July [dʒuː'laɪ] *n* Juli *m*; *see* **September.**
jumble ['dʒʌmbl] **1** *vt (also* **~ up***) (lit)* durcheinanderwerfen. **~d up** durcheinander; *(fig) facts* durcheinanderbringen. **2** *n* **(a)** Durcheinander *nt*; *(of ideas also)* Wirrwarr *m*. **(b)** *no pl (for ~ sale)* gebrauchte Sachen *pl*. **~ sale** *(Brit)* ≃ Flohmarkt *m*; *(for charity)* Wohltätigkeitsbasar *m*.
jumbo ['dʒʌmbəʊ] *n (~ jet)* Jumbo(-Jet) *m*.
jump [dʒʌmp] **1** *n (lit, fig)* Sprung *m*; *(with parachute)* Absprung *m*; *(on race-course)* Hindernis *nt*; *(of prices)* (sprunghafter) Anstieg. **the movie is full of ~s** der Film ist sprunghaft; **to be one ~ ahead** *(fig)* einen Schritt voraus sein.

2 *vi* **(a)** springen; *(parachutist)* (ab)springen; *(typewriter)* Buchstaben überspringen; *(prices, shares)* sprunghaft ansteigen. **to ~ for joy** einen Freudensprung machen; **to ~ up and down on the spot** auf der Stelle hüpfen; **to ~ to conclusions** vorschnelle Schlüsse ziehen; **go and ~ in the lake!** *(col)* fahr zum Teufel! *(col)*; **~ to it!** mach schon!; **if you keep ~ing from one thing to another** wenn Sie nie bei einer Sache bleiben. **(b)** *(start)* zusammenzucken. **you made me ~** du hast mich (aber) erschreckt.

3 *vt* **(a)** *ditch etc* überspringen, hinüberspringen über *(+acc)*. **(b)** *(skip)* überspringen, auslassen. **to ~ the rails** *(train)* entgleisen. **(c)** *(col)* **to ~ bail** abhauen *(col) (während man auf Kaution freigelassen ist)*; **to ~ the lights** bei Rot über die Kreuzung fahren; **to ~ the queue** *(Brit)* sich vordrängeln; **to ~ ship** *(Naut) (passenger)* das Schiff vorzeitig verlassen; *(sailor)* heimlich abheuern; **they ~ed a train to Acapulco** sie fuhren schwarz nach Acapulco; **to ~ sb** *(attack)* jdn überfallen.
♦ **jump about** *or* **around** *vi* herumspringen.
♦ **jump at** *vi +prep obj person (lit)* anspringen; *(fig)* anfahren; *object* zuspringen auf *(+acc)*; *offer* sofort zugreifen bei; *chance* sofort beim Schopf ergreifen.
♦ **jump down** *vi* hinunter-/herunterspringen *(from* von*)*. **to ~ ~ sb's throat** jdn anfahren.
♦ **jump in** *vi* hineinspringen/hereinspringen. **~ ~!** *(to car)* steig ein!
♦ **jump off** *vi* herunterspringen *(prep obj* von*)*; *(from train, bus)* aussteigen *(prep obj* aus*)*; *(from bicycle, horse)* absteigen *(prep obj* von*)*.
♦ **jump on** *vi (lit) (onto vehicle)* einsteigen *(prep obj, -to* in *+acc)*; *(onto bicycle, horse)* aufsteigen *(prep obj, -to* auf *+acc)*. **he ~ed ~ (to) his bicycle** er schwang sich auf sein Fahrrad.
♦ **jump out** *vi* hinaus-/herausspringen; *(from vehicle)* aussteigen *(of* aus*)*.
♦ **jump up** *vi* hochspringen; *(from sitting or lying position also)* aufspringen; *(onto sth)* hinaufspringen *(onto* auf *+acc)*.
jumped-up ['dʒʌmpt'ʌp] *adj (col)* **this new ~ manager** dieser kleine Emporkömmling von einem Abteilungsleiter.
jumper ['dʒʌmpəʳ] *n* **(a)** *(garment) (Brit)* Pullover *m*; *(US: dress)* Trägerkleid *nt*. **(b)** *(person, animal)* Springer *m*. **(c) ~ cables** *(US Aut)* Starthilfekabel *nt*.
jump: ~ jet *n* Senkrechtstarter *m*; **~ leads** *npl (Brit Aut)* Starthilfekabel *nt*; **~ suit** *n* Overall *m*.
jumpy ['dʒʌmpɪ] *adj (+er) (col) person* nervös; *(easily startled)* schreckhaft.
Jun = **June; junior** jr., jun.
junction ['dʒʌŋkʃən] *n (Rail)* Gleisanschluß *m*; *(Brit: of roads)* Kreuzung *f*. **railway ~** Eisenbahnknotenpunkt *m*.
juncture ['dʒʌŋktʃəʳ] *n*: **at this ~** zu diesem Zeitpunkt.
June [dʒuːn] *n* Juni *m*; *see* **September.**
jungle ['dʒʌŋgl] *n* Dschungel *(also fig)*, Urwald *m*.
junior ['dʒuːnɪəʳ] **1** *adj* **(a)** *(younger)* jünger. **Hiram Schwarz, ~** Hiram Schwarz junior; **~ classes** *(Sch)* Unterstufe *f*; **~ school** *(Brit)* Grundschule *f*; **~ high (school)** *(US)* ≃ Mittelschule *f*. **(b)** *employee* untergeordnet; *officer* rangniedriger. **~ clerk** zweiter Buchhalter; **~ Minister** Staatssekretär(in *f*) *m*. **2** *n* **(a)** Jüngere(r) *mf*. **he is two years my ~** er ist zwei Jahre jünger als ich. **(b)** *(Brit Sch)* Grundschüler(in *f*) *m*; *(US Univ) Student(in f) m im vorletzten Studienjahr.*
juniper ['dʒuːnɪpəʳ] *n* Wacholder *m*. **~ berry** Wacholderbeere *f*.
junk[1] [dʒʌŋk] *n* **(a)** *(discarded objects)* Trödel *m*, Gerümpel *nt*; *(col: trash)* Schund *m*; *(pej: food)* Fraß *m (col)*. **(b)** *(col: drugs)* Stoff *m (col)*.
junk[2] *n (boat)* Dschunke *f*.
junk foods *npl (pej)* Plastikessen *nt (pej col)*; *(sweets)* Süßkram *m (col)*.
junkie ['dʒʌŋkɪ] *n (col)* Fixer(in *f*) *m (col)*.
junk: ~ room *n* Rumpelkammer *f*; **~ shop** *n* Trödelladen *m*.
junta ['dʒʌntə] *n* Junta *f*.
Jupiter ['dʒuːpɪtəʳ] *n* Jupiter *m*.
jurisdiction [ˌdʒʊərɪs'dɪkʃən] *n* Gerichtsbarkeit *f*; *(range of authority)* Zuständigkeit(sbereich *m*) *f*. **matters that do not fall under the ~ of this court** Fälle, für die dieses Gericht nicht zuständig ist; **that's not (in) my ~** dafür bin ich nicht zuständig.
juror ['dʒʊərəʳ] *n* Schöffe *m*, Schöffin *f*; *(for capital crimes)* Geschworene(r) *mf*.
jury ['dʒʊərɪ] *n* **(a) the ~** die Schöffen *pl*; *(for capital crimes)* die Geschworenen *pl*; **to sit on the ~** Schöffe/Geschworener sein. **(b)** *(for competition)* Jury *f*.
jury: ~box *n* Schöffen-/Geschworenenbank *f*; **~ service** *n* **to be called for ~ service** als Schöffe/ Geschworener berufen werden.
just[1] [dʒʌst] *adj* **(a)** *(with time)* gerade, (so)eben. **they have ~ left** sie sind gerade gegangen; **I met him ~ after lunch** ich habe ihn gleich nach dem Mittagessen getroffen; **hurry up, he's ~ going** beeilen Sie sich, er geht gerade; **I'm ~ coming** ich komme ja schon; **I was ~ going to ...** ich

wollte gerade ...; ~ **as I was going** gerade, als ich gehen wollte.

(b) *(barely, almost not)* gerade noch. **he ~ escaped being run over** er wäre um ein Haar überfahren worden; **I arrived ~ in time** ich bin gerade noch rechtzeitig gekommen.

(c) *(exactly)* genau. **it is ~ five o'clock** es ist genau fünf Uhr; **that's ~ like you** das sieht dir ähnlich; **~ as I expected** genau wie ich es erwartet hatte; **that's ~ it!** das ist es ja gerade!; **that's ~ what I was going to say** genau das wollte ich (auch) sagen; **~ what do you mean by that?** was soll das heißen?; **~ at that moment** genau in dem Augenblick; **everything has to be ~ so** es muß alles seine Ordnung haben.

(d) *(only, simply)* nur, bloß. **~ you and me** nur wir beide; **he's ~ a boy** er ist doch noch ein Junge; **~ like that** einfach so; **it's ~ not good enough** es ist einfach nicht gut genug; **I ~ prefer it this way** ich find's einfach besser so; **~ round the corner** gleich um die Ecke; **~ above the trees** direkt über den Bäumen.

(e) *(absolutely)* einfach, wirklich. **it was ~ fantastic** es war einfach prima; **it's ~ terrible** das ist ja schrecklich!

(f) ~ **as** genauso, ebenso; **the blue hat is ~ as nice as the red one** der blaue Hut ist genauso hübsch wie der rote; **it's ~ as well you didn't go out** nur gut, daß Sie nicht weggegangen sind; **it would be ~ as well if you came** es wäre doch besser, wenn Sie kämen; **come ~ as you are** kommen Sie so, wie Sie sind; **~ as you please** wie Sie wollen; **~ as I thought!** ich habe es mir doch gedacht!

(g) ~ **about** in etwa, so etwa; **I am ~ about ready** ich bin so gut wie fertig; **did he make it in time? — ~ about** hat er's (rechtzeitig) geschafft? — so gerade; **I am ~ about fed up with it!** *(col)* so langsam aber sicher hängt es mir zum Hals raus *(col)*.

(h) ~ **now** *(in past)* gerade erst; **not ~ now** im Moment nicht; **you can go, but not ~ now** Sie können gehen, aber nicht gerade jetzt; **~ think** denk bloß; **~ listen** hör mal; **~ a moment** *or* **minute!** Moment mal!; **I can ~ see him as a soldier** ich kann ihn mir gut als Soldat vorstellen; **can I ~ finish this?** kann ich das eben noch fertigmachen?; **don't I ~!** und ob!; **~ watch it** nimm dich bloß in acht; **~ you dare!** wehe!

just[2] *adj (+er) person, decision* gerecht *(to* gegenüber*)*; *anger* berechtigt; *suspicion* begründet. **as (it) is only ~** wie es recht und billig ist.

justice ['dʒʌstɪs] *n* **(a)** *(quality)* Gerechtigkeit *f*; *(system)* Justiz *f*; *(of claims)* Rechtmäßigkeit *f*. **to bring a thief to ~** einen Dieb vor Gericht bringen; **to do him ~** um ihm gegenüber gerecht zu sein; **this photograph doesn't do me ~** auf diesem Foto bin ich nicht gut getroffen; **she never does herself ~** sie kommt nie richtig zur Geltung; **he complained, with ~, that ...** er hat sich zu Recht beklagt, daß ...; **there's no ~, is there?** das ist doch nicht gerecht. **(b)** *(judge)* Richter *m*. **J~ of the Peace** Friedensrichter *m*.

justifiable [ˌdʒʌstɪ'faɪəbl] *adj* zu rechtfertigen *pred*, berechtigt.

justifiably [ˌdʒʌstɪ'faɪəblɪ] *adv* zu Recht.

justification [ˌdʒʌstɪfɪ'keɪʃən] *n* Rechtfertigung *f*.

justify ['dʒʌstɪfaɪ] *vt* **(a)** rechtfertigen *(sth to sb* etw jdm gegenüber*)*. **am I justified in thinking that ...?** gehe ich recht in der Annahme, daß ...?; **he was justified in doing that** es war gerechtfertigt, daß er das tat; **you're not justified in talking to her like that** Sie haben kein Recht, so mit ihr zu reden. **(b)** *(Typ)* justieren.

jut [dʒʌt] *vi (also ~* **out***)* hervorstehen, herausragen.

jute [dʒuːt] *n* Jute *f*.

juvenile ['dʒuːvənaɪl] **1** *n (Admin)* Jugendliche(r) *mf*. **2** *adj (youthful)* jugendlich; *(for young people)* Jugend-, für Jugendliche; *(pej)* kindisch, unreif.

juvenile: ~ court *n* Jugendgericht *nt*; **~ delinquency** *n* Jugendkriminalität *f*; **~ delinquent** *n* jugendlicher Straftäter.

juxtaposition [ˌdʒʌkstəpə'zɪʃən] *n (act)* Nebeneinanderstellung *f*. **in ~** (direkt) nebeneinander.

K

K, k [keɪ] *n* K, k *nt.*
kale [keɪl] *n* Grünkohl *m.*
kaleidoscope [kə'laɪdəskəʊp] *n* Kaleidoskop *nt.*
kangaroo [,kæŋgə'ru:] *n* Känguruh *nt.* **~ court** inoffizielles Gericht.
kaput [kə'pʊt] *adj (col)* kaputt *(col).*
karate [kə'rɑ:tɪ] *n* Karate *nt.*
kebab [kə'bæb] *n* Kebab *m.*
keel [ki:l] *n (Naut)* Kiel *m.* **to be on an even ~ again** *(fig)* wieder im Lot sein; **he put the business back on an even ~** er brachte das Geschäft wieder auf die Beine *(col).*
♦ **keel over** *vi (ship)* kentern; *(fig col)* umkippen.
keen [ki:n] *adj (+er)* **(a)** *edge, wind, competition, wit* scharf; *appetite* kräftig; *interest* stark; *desire, pain* heftig; *sight, hearing* gut; *(esp Brit) prices* günstig. **(b)** *(enthusiastic)* begeistert; *football fan etc also* leidenschaftlich; *applicant, learner* stark interessiert; *(hardworking)* eifrig. **~ to learn** lernbegierig; **to be ~ on sb** von jdm sehr angetan sein, scharf auf jdn sein *(col)*; *on actor, author* von jdm begeistert sein; **to be ~ on sth** etw sehr gern mögen; **to be ~ on doing sth** *(like to do)* etw gern tun; **to be ~ to do sth** *(want to do)* darauf erpicht sein *or* scharf darauf sein *(col)*, etw zu tun; **to be ~ on mountaineering** sehr gern bergsteigen; **I'm not very ~ on him** ich bin von ihm nicht gerade begeistert; **he's not ~ on her coming** er legt keinen besonderen Wert darauf, daß sie kommt.
keenly ['ki:nlɪ] *adv* **(a)** *(sharply)* scharf; *feel* leidenschaftlich, stark. **(b)** *(enthusiastically)* mit Begeisterung.
keenness ['ki:nnɪs] *n* **(a)** *(of mind, wind)* Schärfe *f.* **(b)** *see adj (b)* Begeisterung *f*; Leidenschaftlichkeit *f*; starkes Interesse; Eifer *m.*
keep [ki:p] *(vb: pret, ptp* **kept***)* **1** *vt* **(a)** *(retain)* behalten. **to ~ a place for sb** einen Platz für jdn freihalten; **you can ~ it!** *(col)* das kannst du dir an den Hut stecken! *(col).*
(b) *shop* haben, führen; *bees etc* halten. **to ~ house for sb** jdm den Haushalt führen.
(c) *(support) family etc* unterhalten. **I earn enough to ~ myself** ich verdiene genug für mich (selbst) zum Leben; **to ~ sb in clothing** für jds Kleidung sorgen.
(d) *(maintain in a certain state)* halten. **to ~ one's dress clean** sein Kleid nicht schmutzig machen; **just to ~ her happy** damit sie zufrieden ist; **to ~ sb waiting** jdn warten lassen; **can't you ~ him talking?** können Sie ihn nicht in ein Gespräch verwickeln?; **to ~ sth tidy** etw sauber *or* in Ordnung halten; **the garden was well kept** der Garten war (gut) gepflegt; **to ~ a machine running** eine Maschine laufen lassen; **to ~ the conversation going** das Gespräch in Gang halten.
(e) *(store, look after)* aufbewahren; *(put aside)* aufheben. **where does he ~ his money?** wo bewahrt er sein Geld auf?; **where do you ~ your spoons?** wo sind die Löffel?; **I've been ~ing it for you** ich habe es für Sie aufgehoben.
(f) *promise* halten; *rule* befolgen; *treaty, appointment* einhalten; *obligations* nachkommen *(+dat).*
(g) *accounts, diary etc* führen *(of* über *+acc).*
(h) *(detain)* aufhalten. **I mustn't ~ you** ich will Sie nicht aufhalten; **what kept you?** wo waren Sie denn so lang?; **to ~ sb in prison** jdn in Haft halten.
(i) *(not disclose)* **can you ~ this from your mother?** können Sie das vor Ihrer Mutter geheimhalten?; **~ it to yourself** behalten Sie das für sich.
(j) to ~ late hours lange aufbleiben.
2 *vi* **(a) to ~ (to the) left** sich links halten; **to ~ to the middle of the road** *(Aut)* immer in der Mitte der Straße fahren. **(b) to ~ doing sth** *(not stop)* etw weiter tun; *(repeatedly)* etw immer wieder tun; *(constantly)* etw dauernd tun; **to ~ walking** weitergehen; **he kept lying to her** er hat sie immer wieder belogen; **if you ~ complaining** wenn Sie sich weiter beschweren; **she ~s talking about you all the time** sie redet dauernd von Ihnen; **~ going** machen Sie weiter; **~ at it!** bleib am Ball! **(c)** *(remain)* bleiben. **to ~ quiet** still sein; **to ~ silent** schweigen; **to ~ calm** ruhig bleiben. **(d)** *(food etc)* sich halten. **(e)** *(state of health)* **how are you ~ing?** wie geht es Ihnen denn so?; **to ~ well** gesund bleiben; **to ~ fit** fit bleiben; **he's ~ing better now** es geht ihm wieder besser. **(f)** *(wait)* **that can ~** das kann warten.
3 *n* **(a)** *(livelihood, food)* Unterhalt *m.* **I got £10 a week and my ~** ich bekam £ 10 pro Woche und freie Kost und Logis; **to earn one's ~** *(fig)* sein Geld verdienen; *(machine etc)* sich rentieren. **(b)** *(in castle)* Bergfried *m*; *(as prison)* Burgverlies *nt.* **(c) for ~s** *(col)* für immer; **it's yours for ~s** das darfst du behalten.
♦ **keep away 1** *vi (lit)* wegbleiben; *(not approach)* nicht näher herankommen *(from* an *+acc).* **~ ~!** kommen Sie nicht näher!; **I just can't ~ ~** es zieht mich immer wieder hin; **~ ~ from him** lassen Sie die Finger von ihm. **2** *vt always separate person, children etc* fernhalten *(from* von*).* **to ~ sth ~ from sth** etw nicht an etw *(acc)* kommen lassen.
♦ **keep back 1** *vi* zurückbleiben. **~ ~!** treten Sie zurück! **2** *vt sep* **(a)** *hair, crowds* zurückhalten; *water* stauen; *tears* unterdrücken. **to ~ sb ~ from doing sth** jdn davon abhalten, etwas zu tun. **(b)** *(withhold) taxes* einbehalten; *information etc* verschweigen *(from sb* jdm*)*; *(from parent, husband etc)* verheimlichen *(from sb* jdm*).* **(c)** *(make late)* aufhalten; *pupil* dabehalten. **(d)** *(hold up, slow down)* behindern.
♦ **keep down 1** *vi* unten bleiben. **~ ~!** bleib unten! **2** *vt sep* **(a)** *(hold down)* unten halten. **~ your voices ~** reden Sie leise! **(b)** *revolt, one's anger* unterdrücken; *rabbits, weeds etc* unter Kontrolle halten. **you can't ~ a good man ~** ein tüchtiger Mann läßt sich nicht unterkriegen. **(c)** *prices* niedrig halten; *spending* einschränken. **to ~ one's weight ~** nicht zunehmen. **(d)** *food etc* bei sich behalten. **(e)** *(Sch)* **he was kept ~** er mußte wiederholen.
♦ **keep from 1** *vt +prep obj* **(a) I couldn't ~ him ~ going there** ich konnte ihn nicht davon abhalten, dort hinzugehen; **the bells ~ me ~ sleeping** die Glocken lassen mich nicht schlafen; **his anorak kept him ~ getting wet** sein Anorak schützte ihn

vor dem Regen; **this will ~ the water ~ freezing** das verhindert, daß das Wasser gefriert. **(b)** *(withhold)* **to ~ sth ~ sb** jdm etw verschweigen; *piece of news also* jdm etw vorenthalten. **2** *vi +prep obj* **to ~ ~ doing sth** etw nicht tun; *(avoid doing also)* es vermeiden, etw zu tun; **she couldn't ~ ~ laughing** sie mußte einfach lachen.

♦ **keep in 1** *vt sep feelings* zügeln; *schoolboy* nachsitzen lassen; *stomach* einziehen. **2** *vi* **he's just trying to ~ ~ with her** er versucht nur, sich mit ihr gut zu stellen.

♦ **keep off 1** *vi (person)* wegbleiben. **if the rain ~s ~** wenn es nicht regnet. **2** *vt sep dog, person* fernhalten *(prep obj* von). **"~ ~ the grass"** „Betreten des Rasens verboten"; **~ your hands ~** Hände weg! **3** *vi +prep obj* vermeiden. **~ ~ the whisky** lassen Sie das Whiskytrinken.

♦ **keep on 1** *vi* **(a)** weitermachen. **to ~ ~ doing sth** etw weiter tun; *(repeatedly)* etw immer wieder tun; *(incessantly)* etw dauernd tun; **if you ~ ~ like this** wenn du so weitermachst; **the rain kept ~ all night** es regnete die ganze Nacht durch. **(b)** *(keep going)* weitergehen/-fahren. **~ ~ past the church** fahren/gehen Sie immer weiter an der Kirche vorbei. **(c) to ~ ~ at sb** *(col)* dauernd an jdm herummeckern *(col)*; **to ~ ~ about sth** *(col)* unaufhörlich von etw reden; **don't ~ ~ so!** *(col)* hören Sie doch endlich auf damit! **2** *vt sep* **(a)** *employee* behalten. **(b)** *coat etc* anbehalten; *hat* aufbehalten.

♦ **keep out 1** *vi (of building)* draußen bleiben; *(of property)* etw nicht betreten. **"~ ~"** „Zutritt verboten"; **to ~ ~ of danger** Gefahr meiden; **to ~ ~ of debt** keine Schulden machen; **that child can never ~ ~ of mischief** das Kind stellt dauernd etwas an; **you ~ ~ of this!** halten Sie sich da raus! **2** *vt sep* **(a)** *person* nicht hereinlassen *(of* in *+acc)*; *light, cold, enemy etc* abhalten. **(b) I wanted to ~ him ~ of this** ich wollte nicht, daß er da mit hineingezogen wird; **~ him ~ of my way** halte ihn mir vom Leib.

♦ **keep to 1** *vi +prep obj* **(a) ~ ~ the main road** bleiben Sie auf der Hauptstraße; **to ~ ~ the schedule** sich an den Zeitplan halten. **(b) to ~ (oneself) ~ oneself** nicht sehr gesellig sein; **they ~ ~ themselves** sie bleiben unter sich. **2** *vt +prep obj* **to ~ sb ~ his word** jdn beim Wort nehmen; **to ~ sth ~ a minimum** etw auf ein Minimum beschränken.

♦ **keep together** *vi (stay together)* zusammenbleiben.

♦ **keep up 1** *vi* **(a)** *(tent)* stehen bleiben. **(b)** *(rain)* (an)dauern; *(weather etc)* anhalten; *(morale, determination)* nicht nachlassen. **(c) to ~ ~ (with sb/sth)** *(in race, work)* (mit jdm/etw) Schritt halten; *(in comprehension)* (jdm/einer Sache) folgen können; **to ~ ~ with the Joneses** mit den Nachbarn mithalten; **to ~ ~ with the times** mit der Zeit gehen; **to ~ ~ with the news** sich auf dem laufenden halten.

2 *vt sep* **(a)** *tent* aufrecht halten. **(b)** *(not stop)* nicht aufhören mit; *study etc* weitermachen; *quality, prices, friendship, tradition, payments* aufrechterhalten; *speed* halten. **I try to ~ ~ my French** ich versuche, mit meinem Französisch nicht aus der Übung zu kommen; **~ it ~!** (machen Sie) weiter so!; **he couldn't ~ it ~** er hat schlapp gemacht *(col)*. **(c)** *(maintain) house* unterhalten; *road* instand halten. **(d)** *(prevent from going to bed)* am Schlafengehen hindern. **that child kept me ~ all night** das Kind hat mich die ganze Nacht nicht schlafen lassen.

keeper ['kiːpəʳ] *n (zoo)* Wärter(in *f*) *m*; *(museum)* Aufseher(in *f*) *m*; *(goal~)* Torhüter *m*.

keep-fit ['kiːp'fɪt] *n* Gymnastik *f*.

keeping ['kiːpɪŋ] *n* **(a)** *(care)* **to put sth in sb's ~** jdm etw zur Aufbewahrung übergeben. **(b) in ~ with** in Einklang mit.

keg [keg] *n (barrel)* kleines Faß.

kennel ['kenl] *n* Hundehütte *f*. **to put a dog in ~s** einen Hund in Pflege geben.

Kenya ['kenjə] *n* Kenia *nt*.

Kenyan ['kenjən] **1** *n* Kenianer(in *f*) *m*. **2** *adj* kenianisch.

kept [kept] *pret, ptp of* **keep.**

kerb [kɜːb] *n (Brit)* Randstein *m*.

kernel ['kɜːnl] *n (lit, fig)* Kern *m*.

kerosene ['kerəsiːn] *n* Kerosin *nt; (paraffin)* Paraffin *nt*.

kestrel ['kestrəl] *n* Turmfalke *m*.

ketchup ['ketʃəp] *n* Ketchup *nt or m*.

kettle ['ketl] *n* Kessel *m*. **I'll put the ~ on** ich stelle mal eben (Kaffee-/Tee)wasser auf; **the ~'s boiling** das Wasser kocht; **a pretty ~ of fish** *(col)* eine schöne Bescherung *(col)*; **that's a different ~ of fish** *(col)* das ist doch was ganz anderes.

kettledrum ['ketldrʌm] *n* (Kessel)pauke *f*.

key [kiː] **1** *n* **(a)** *(lit, fig)* Schlüssel *m*. **the ~ to the mystery** der Schlüssel zum Geheimnis. **(b)** *(for maps etc)* Zeichenerklärung *f*. **(c)** *(of piano, typewriter etc)* Taste *f*. **(d)** *(Mus)* Tonart *f*. **to sing off ~** falsch singen; **change of ~** Tonartwechsel *m*; **in the ~ of C** in C-Dur/c-Moll. **2** *adj attr (vital)* Schlüssel-. **~ point** springender Punkt.

♦ **key in** *vt (Comp)* eingeben.

keyboard ['kiːbɔːd] *n* Tastatur *f*.

keyed up ['kiːd'ʌp] *adj* **she was (all) ~ about the interview** sie war wegen des Interviews ganz aufgedreht *(col)*.

key: ~hole *n* Schlüsselloch *nt*; **~note speech** *n (Pol etc)* programmatische Rede; **~ ring** *n* Schlüsselring *m*.

khaki ['kɑːkɪ] **1** *n* K(h)aki *nt*. **2** *adj* k(h)aki(farben).

kibbutz [kɪ'bʊts] *n, pl* **-im** Kibbuz *m*.

kick [kɪk] **1** *n* Tritt, Stoß *m*; *(of gun)* Rückstoß *m*. **to take a ~ at sb/sth** nach jdm/etw treten; **to give the door a ~** gegen die Tür treten; **it's better than a ~ in the pants** *(col)* das ist besser als ein Tritt in den Hintern *(col)*; **she gets a ~ out of it** *(col)* es macht ihr einen Riesenspaß *(col)*; **to do sth for ~s** *(col)* etw aus Jux *(col)* tun; **this drink has plenty of ~ in it** *(col)* dieses Getränk hat es in sich. **2** *vi (person)* treten; *(struggle)* um sich treten; *(animal)* ausschlagen. **3** *vt (person, horse) sb* treten *(+dat)*; *door, ball* treten gegen; *object* einen Tritt versetzen *(+dat)*. **to ~ the bucket** *(col)* ins Gras beißen *(col)*; **I could have ~ed myself** *(col)* ich hätte mir in den Hintern treten können *(col)*; **to ~ the habit** *(col)* es aufgeben.

♦ **kick about** *or* **around 1** *vi (col) (person)* rumhängen *(col) (prep obj* in *+dat)*; *(thing)* rumliegen *(col) (prep obj* in *+dat)*. **2** *vt sep* **to ~ a ball ~** den Ball herumkicken *(col)*; **you shouldn't let them ~ you ~** Sie sollten sich nicht so herumschubsen lassen.

♦ **kick in** *vt sep door* eintreten. **to ~ sb's teeth ~** jdm die Zähne einschlagen.

♦ **kick off** *vi (Ftbl)* anstoßen; *(fig col)* anfangen.

♦ **kick out 1** *vi* **to ~ ~ at sb** nach jdm treten. **2** *vt sep (col)* rauswerfen *(col) (of* aus*)*.

♦ **kick up** *vt sep* **to ~ ~ a fuss** *(col)* Krach schlagen *(col)*.

kick: ~-off *n (Sport)* Anpfiff, Anstoß *m*; *(col: beginning)* Beginn *m*. **~-start(er)** *n* Kickstarter *m*.

kid [kɪd] **1** *n* **(a)** *(young goat)* Kitz *nt*; *(leather)* Glacéleder *nt*. **to handle sb with ~ gloves** *(fig)* jdn mit Samthandschuhen anfassen. **(b)** *(col: child)* Kind *nt*. **it's ~'s stuff** *(for children)* das ist was für kleine Kinder *(col)*; *(easy)* das ist doch ein Kinderspiel; **his ~ brother** sein kleiner Bruder; **OK, ~!** okay, Junge/Mädchen! **2** *vt (col)* **to ~ sb (on)** *(tease)* jdn aufziehen *(col)*; *(deceive)* jdn an der Nase rumführen *(col)*; **don't ~ yourself!** machen Sie sich doch nichts vor! **3** *vi (col)* Jux machen *(col)*. **no ~ding** ehrlich *(col)*.

kidnap ['kɪdnæp] *vt* entführen, kidnappen.

kidnapper ['kɪdnæpəʳ] *n* Entführer(in *f*), Kidnapper(in *f*) *m*.

kidnapping ['kɪdnæpɪŋ] *n* Entführung *f*.

kidney ['kɪdnɪ] *n (Anat, Cook)* Niere *f*.

kidney: ~ bean *n* Gartenbohne *f*; **~ machine** *n* künstliche Niere.

kill [kɪl] **1** *vt* **(a)** töten, umbringen; *(slaughter)* schlachten; *weeds* vernichten. **to be ~ed in battle** im Kampf fallen; **her brother was ~ed in a car accident** ihr Bruder ist bei einem Autounfall ums Leben gekommen; **how many were ~ed?** wieviel Todesopfer gab es?; **she ~ed herself** sie brachte sich um; **don't ~ me** lassen Sie mich leben; **he was ~ed with poison/a knife** er wurde vergiftet/(mit einem Messer) erstochen; **I'll ~ him!** *(also fig)* den bring' ich um *(col)*.

(b) *(fig) feelings, love etc* zerstören; *(spoil) flavour, performance* verderben, überdecken; *hopes* zunichte machen; *sound* schlucken; *(Press etc) paragraph, story* streichen; *(Tech) engine etc* abschalten. **to ~ time** die Zeit totschlagen; **we have two hours to ~** wir haben noch zwei Stunden übrig; **to ~ two birds with one stone** *(Prov)* zwei Fliegen mit einer Klappe schlagen *(Prov)*; **these stairs are ~ing me** *(col)* diese Treppe bringt mich (noch mal) um *(col)*; **she was ~ing herself (laughing)** *(col)* sie hat sich (fast) totgelacht *(col)*; **my feet are ~ing me** *(col)* mir brennen die Füße.

2 *vi* töten. **cigarettes can ~** Zigaretten können tödliche Folgen haben.

3 *n* **to be in at the ~** *(fig)* den Schlußakt miterleben.

♦ **kill off** *vt sep* vernichten; *cows, pigs* abschlachten; *weeds* vertilgen.

killer ['kɪləʳ] *n (person)* Mörder(in *f*) *m*. **this disease is a ~** diese Krankheit ist tödlich.

killer: the ~ instinct *n (lit)* der Tötungsinstinkt; **a successful businessman needs the ~ instinct** ein erfolgreicher Geschäftsmann muß über Leichen gehen können; **~ whale** *n* Schwertwal *m*.

killing ['kɪlɪŋ] **1** *n (of person)* Töten *nt*. **three more ~s in Belfast** drei weitere Todesopfer in Belfast; **to make a ~** *(fig)* einen Riesengewinn machen. **2** *adj blow etc* tödlich; *pace* mörderisch.

killingly ['kɪlɪŋlɪ] *adv*: **~ funny** zum Totlachen.

killjoy ['kɪldʒɔɪ] *n* Spielverderber *m*.

kiln [kɪln] *n* (Brenn)ofen *m*; *(for bricks)* Trockenofen *m*.

kilo ['kiːləʊ] *n* Kilo *nt*.

kilobyte ['kɪləʊbaɪt] *n* Kilobyte *nt*.

kilogramme, *(US)* **kilogram** ['kɪləʊgræm] *n* Kilogramm *nt*.

kilometre, *(US)* **kilometer** ['kɪləʊˌmiːtəʳ, kɪ'lɒmiːtəʳ] *n* Kilometer *m*.

kilowatt ['kɪləʊwɒt] *n* Kilowatt *nt*.

kilt [kɪlt] *n* Kilt, Schottenrock *m*.

kin [kɪn] *n* Verwandte *pl*, Verwandschaft *f*.

kind[1] [kaɪnd] **1** *n* **(a)** Art *f*; *(of coffee etc)* Sorte *f*. **several ~s of flour** mehrere Mehlsorten; **this ~ of book** diese Art Buch; **what ~ of ...?** was für ein(e) ...?; **the only one of its ~** das einzige seiner Art; **he is not the ~ of man to refuse** er ist nicht der Typ, der nein sagt; **he's not that ~ of person** so ist er nicht; **a strange ~ of feeling** so ein seltsames Gefühl; **they're two of a ~** *(people)* sie sind vom gleichen Schlag; **I know your ~** deinen Typ kenne ich; **this ~ of thing** so etwas; **... of all ~s** alle möglichen ...; **something of the ~** so etwas ähnliches; **nothing of the ~** nichts dergleichen; **you'll do nothing of the ~** du wirst das schön bleiben lassen!; **it's not my ~ of holiday** solche Ferien sind nicht mein Fall *(col)*; **she's my ~ of woman** sie ist mein Typ.

(b) payment in ~ Bezahlung in Naturalien; **I shall pay you in ~** *(fig)* ich werde es Ihnen in gleicher Münze zurückzahlen.

2 *adv (col)* **I was ~ of disappointed** *(a little)* ich war irgendwie enttäuscht; *(very)* ich war ziemlich enttäuscht.

kind[2] *adj (+er)* nett, freundlich *(to* zu*)*. **would you be ~ enough to open the door** wären Sie so nett *or* lieb, die Tür zu öffnen.

kindergarten ['kɪndəˌgɑːtn] *n* Kindergarten *m*.

kind-hearted ['kaɪnd'hɑːtɪd] *adj* gütig.

kindle ['kɪndl] *vt fire* anzünden; *passions* entfachen.

kindly ['kaɪndlɪ] **1** *adv speak, act* freundlich, nett; *treat* liebenswürdig. **they ~ put me up for a night** sie nahmen mich freundlicherweise für eine Nacht auf; **will you ~ do it now** tun Sie das sofort, wenn ich bitten darf!; **~ shut the door** machen Sie doch bitte die Tür zu!; **I don't take ~ to his smoking** sein Rauchen ist mir gar nicht angenehm; **he won't take at all ~ to that** das wird ihm gar nicht gefallen. **2** *adj (+er) person* lieb, nett; *advice* freundlich; *voice* sanft, gütig.

kindness ['kaɪndnɪs] *n no pl* Freundlichkeit, Liebenswürdigkeit *f (towards* gegenüber*)*; *(goodness)* Güte *f (towards* gegenüber*)*; *(act of ~)* Gefälligkeit, Aufmerksamkeit *f*. **out of the ~ of one's heart** aus reiner Nächstenliebe; **to do sb a ~** jdm eine Gefälligkeit erweisen.

kindred ['kɪndrɪd] **1** *n no pl (relatives)* Verwandtschaft *f*. **2** *adj (related)* verwandt. **~ spirit** Gleichgesinnte(r) *mf*.

kinetic [kɪ'netɪk] *adj* kinetisch.

king [kɪŋ] *n* König *m (also Chess, Cards)*; *(Draughts)* Dame *f*.

kingdom ['kɪŋdəm] *n* Königreich *nt*. **you can go on doing that till ~ come** *(col)* Sie können (so) bis in alle Ewigkeit weitermachen.

kingfisher ['kɪŋfɪʃəʳ] *n* Eisvogel *m*.

king: ~pin *n (fig: person)* Stütze *f*; **~-size(d)** *adj (col)* in Großformat; *cigarettes* King-size; *bed* extra groß.

kink [kɪŋk] *n* **(a)** *(in rope etc)* Schlaufe *f*; *(in hair)* Welle *f*. **(b)** *(mental peculiarity)* Tick *m (col)*; *(sexual)* abartige Veranlagung.

kinky ['kɪŋkɪ] *adj (+er)* **(a)** *hair* wellig. **(b)** *(col) person, ideas* verdreht *(col)*; *fashion* verrückt *(col)*; *(sexually)* abartig.

kinship ['kɪnʃɪp] *n* Verwandtschaft *f*.

kinsman ['kɪnzmən] *n, pl* **-men** [-mən] Verwandte(r) *m*.

kinswoman ['kɪnzwʊmən] *n, pl* **-women** [-wɪmɪn] Verwandte *f*.

kiosk ['kiːɒsk] *n* Kiosk *m*; *(Brit Telec)* (Telefon)zelle *f*.

kip [kɪp] *(Brit col)* **1** *n (sleep)* Schläfchen *nt*. **I've got to get some ~** ich muß mal 'ne Runde pennen *(col)*. **2** *vi* pennen *(col)*.

kipper ['kɪpəʳ] *n* Räucherhering *m*.

kiss [kɪs] **1** *n* Kuß *m*. **~ of life** Mund-zu-Mund-Beatmung *f*; **~ of death** *(fig)* Todesstoß *m*. **2** *vt* küssen; *(fig: touch gently)* sanft berühren. **to ~ sb's cheek** jdn auf die Wange küssen; **they ~ed each other** sie küßten sich; **to ~ sb goodbye** jdm einen Abschiedskuß geben. **3** *vi* küssen; *(~ each other)* sich küssen.

kit [kɪt] *n* **(a)** *(equipment)* Ausrüstung *f*; *(Brit Sport)* Sportzeug *nt*, Sportsachen *pl*; *(belongings, luggage etc)* Sachen *pl*. **(b)** *(for self-assembly)* Bastelsatz *m*; **model aircraft ~** Modellflugzeugbaukasten; **in ~ form** zum Selberbauen.

♦ **kit out** *vt sep* ausrüsten *(esp Mil)*, ausstatten.

kitbag ['kɪtbæg] *n* Seesack *m*.

kitchen ['kɪtʃɪn] **1** *n* Küche *f*. **2** *attr* Küchen-. **~ unit** Küchenschrank *m*.

kitchenette [ˌkɪtʃɪ'net] *n (separate room)* kleine Küche; *(part of one room)* Kochnische *f*.

kitchen sink *n* Spüle *f*. **I've packed everything**

but the ~ *(col)* ich habe den ganzen Hausrat eingepackt; ~ **drama** Alltagsdrama *nt.*
kite [kaɪt] *n (Orn)* Milan *m*; *(toy)* Drachen *m.*
kith [kɪθ] *n*: ~ **and kin** Blutsverwandte *pl.*
kitten ['kɪtn] *n* Kätzchen *nt.* **to have** ~**s** *(fig col)* Junge kriegen *(col).*
kitty ['kɪtɪ] *n* **(a)** *(money)* (gemeinsame) Kasse; *(Cards etc also)* Spielkasse *f.* **(b)** *(col: cat)* Mieze *f.*
kleptomaniac [ˌkleptəʊ'meɪnɪæk] *n* Kleptomane *m*, Kleptomanin *f.*
knack [næk] *n* Trick, Kniff *m.* **there's a (special)** ~ **to opening it** da ist ein Trick dabei, wie man das aufbekommt; **to get the** ~ **of doing sth** (es) herausbekommen, wie man etw macht; **you'll soon get the** ~ **of it** Sie werden den Dreh bald raushaben; **I've lost the** ~ ich bekomme das nicht mehr hin; **she's got a** ~ **of saying the wrong thing** sie hat ein Talent dafür, immer das Falsche zu sagen.
knackered ['nækəd] *adj (Brit col)* kaputt *(col).*
knapsack ['næpsæk] *n* Proviantbeutel *m.*
knead [ni:d] *vt dough* kneten.
knee [ni:] **1** *n* Knie *nt.* **to be on one's** ~**s** *(lit, fig)* auf den Knien liegen; **on bended** ~**(s)** *(liter, hum)* kniefällig; **to go down on one's** ~**s (to sb)** *(lit, fig)* sich (vor jdm) auf die Knie werfen; **to bring sb to his** ~**s** *(lit, fig)* jdn in die Knie zwingen. **2** *vt* mit dem Knie stoßen.
knee: ~ **cap** *n* Kniescheibe *f*; ~**-deep** *adj* knietief; ~**-high** *adj* in Kniehöhe.
kneel [ni:l] *pret, ptp* **knelt** *or* ~**ed** *vi (before* vor *+dat)* knien; *(also* ~ **down***)* (sich) hinknien.
knee-length ['ni:leŋθ] *adj skirt* knielang; *boots* kniehoch.
knee pad *n* Knieschützer *m.*
knelt [nelt] *pret, ptp of* **kneel.**
knew [nju:] *pret of* **know.**
knickers ['nɪkəz] *npl* Schlüpfer *m.* **don't get your** ~ **in a twist!** *(col!)* dreh nicht gleich durch! *(col).*
knick-knack ['nɪknæk] *n* nette Kleinigkeit *nt.* ~**s** Krimskrams *m.*
knife [naɪf] **1** *n, pl* **knives** Messer *nt.* ~**, fork and spoon** Besteck *nt*; **he's got his** ~ **into me** *(col)* der hat es auf mich abgesehen *(col)*; **to be balanced on a** ~ **edge** *(fig)* auf Messers Schneide stehen. **2** *vt* einstechen auf *(+acc)*; *(fatally)* erstechen.
knight [naɪt] **1** *n (title, Hist)* Ritter *m*; *(Chess)* Springer *m.* **2** *vt* adeln.
knighthood ['naɪthʊd] *n* **to receive a** ~ in den Adelsstand erhoben werden.
knit [nɪt] *pret, ptp* ~**ted** *or* ~ **1** *vt* **(a)** stricken. **(b) to** ~ **one's brow** die Stirn runzeln. **2** *vi* **(a)** stricken. **(b)** *(bones: also* ~ **together***)* verwachsen.
knitted ['nɪtɪd] *adj* gestrickt; *cardigan etc* Strick-.
knitting ['nɪtɪŋ] *n* Stricken *nt*; *(material being knitted)* Strickzeug *nt.* **she was doing her** ~ sie strickte.
knitting: ~ **machine** *n* Strickmaschine *f*; ~ **needle** *n* Stricknadel *f.*
knitwear ['nɪtwɛəʳ] *n* Strickwaren *pl.*
knives [naɪvz] *pl of* **knife.**
knob [nɒb] *n (on walking stick)* Knauf *m*; *(on door also)* Griff *m*; *(on instrument etc)* Knopf *m*; *(of butter)* Stück *nt.*
knobbly ['nɒblɪ] *adj (+er) wood* knorrig. ~ **knees** Knubbelknie *pl (col).*
knock [nɒk] **1** *n* **(a)** *(blow)* Stoß *m*; *(esp with hand, tool etc)* Schlag *m.* **I got a** ~ **on the head** ich habe einen Schlag auf den Kopf bekommen; **he gave himself a nasty** ~ er hat sich böse angeschlagen. **(b)** *(noise)* Klopfen *nt no pl.* **there was a** ~ **at the door** es hat geklopft. **(c)** *(fig: setback)* (Tief)schlag *m.* ~**s** *(col: criticism)* Kritik *f*; **to (have to) take a lot of** ~**s** viele Tiefschläge einstecken (müssen); *(be criticized)* unter starken Beschuß kommen; **to take a** ~ *(pride etc)* erschüttert werden.
2 *vt* **(a)** *(strike)* stoßen; *(with hand, tool etc)* schlagen; *(jolt)* stoßen gegen; *(collide with: car, driver)* rammen. **to** ~ **one's head** *etc* sich *(dat)* den Kopf *etc* anschlagen; **to** ~ **sb on the head** jdn an *or* auf den Kopf schlagen; **to** ~ **sb to the ground** jdn zu Boden werfen; **to** ~ **sb unconscious** jdn bewußtlos werden lassen; *(person)* jdn bewußtlos schlagen; **to** ~ **holes in an argument** ein Argument zerpflücken; **she** ~**ed the gun out of his hand** sie schlug ihm die Waffe aus der Hand; **she** ~**ed the glass to the ground** sie stieß gegen das Glas, und es fiel zu Boden; **to** ~ **some sense into sb** jdn zur Vernunft bringen. **(b)** *(col: criticize)* (he)runtermachen *(col).*
3 *vi* **(a)** klopfen. **to** ~ **at the door/window** anklopfen/gegen das Fenster klopfen. **(b)** *(collide)* stoßen *(into, against* gegen*).* **(c) his knees were** ~**ing** ihm zitterten die Knie.
♦**knock about** *or* **around 1** *vi (col) (prep obj* in *+dat) (person)* herumziehen; *(object)* herumliegen. **2** *vt sep (ill-treat)* verprügeln; *(damage)* ramponieren *(col).* **to** ~ **a ball** ~ ein paar Bälle schlagen.
♦**knock back** *vt sep (col)* **(a) he** ~**ed** ~ **his whisky** er kippte sich *(dat)* den Whisky hinter die Binde *(col).* **(b)** *(cost)* **this watch** ~**ed me** ~ **£20** ich habe für die Uhr £ 20 hingelegt *(col).*
♦**knock down** *vt sep person, thing* umwerfen; *opponent* niederschlagen; *(car, driver)* anfahren; *(fatally)* überfahren; *building* abreißen; *door* einschlagen.
♦**knock in** *vt sep nail* einschlagen.
♦**knock off 1** *vi (col)* aufhören, Schluß machen *(col).* **let's** ~ ~ **now** Schluß für heute *(col).* **2** *vt sep* **(a)** *(lit) vase, person etc* hinunterstoßen. **the branch** ~**ed the rider** ~ **his horse** der Ast riß den Reiter vom Pferd. **(b) he** ~**ed £5** ~ **the price** *(col)* er hat £ 5 vom Preis nachgelassen. **(c)** *(col: do quickly) essay* hinhauen *(col).* **(d)** *(Brit col: steal)* klauen *(col).* **(e)** *(col: stop)* aufhören mit. **to** ~ ~ **work** Feierabend machen; ~ **it** ~! nun hör schon auf!
♦**knock out** *vt sep* **(a)** *tooth* ausschlagen; *nail* herausschlagen *(of* aus*)*; *pipe* ausklopfen; *contents* herausklopfen *(of* aus*).* **(b)** *(stun)* bewußtlos werden lassen; *(by hitting)* bewußtlos schlagen, k.o. schlagen *(also Boxing).* **(c)** *(from contest)* besiegen *(of* in *+dat).* **to be** ~**ed** ~ ausscheiden *(of* aus*).* **(d)** *(col: exhaust)* schaffen *(col).*
♦**knock over** *vt sep* umwerfen, umstoßen; *(car)* anfahren; *(fatally)* überfahren.
♦**knock together** *vt sep* **(a)** *(make hurriedly)* auf die Beine stellen *(col).* **(b)** *(lit)* aneinanderstoßen. **I'd like to** ~ **their heads** ~ man sollte die beiden zur Räson bringen.
♦**knock up** *vt sep* **(a)** *(Brit: wake)* (auf)wecken. **(b)** *meal* auf die Beine stellen *(col).* **(c)** *(col: make pregnant)* ein Kind anhängen *(+dat) (col).*
knockdown ['nɒkdaʊn] *adj* ~ **price** Schleuderpreis *m*; *(at auction)* Mindestpreis *m.*
knocker ['nɒkəʳ] *n (door* ~*)* (Tür)klopfer *m.*
knocking ['nɒkɪŋ] *n* Klopfen *nt.*
knock: ~**-kneed** [nɒk'ni:d] *adj* **to be** ~**-kneed** X-Beine haben; ~**out 1** *n (Boxing)* Knockout, K.o. *m*; *(col: person, thing)* Wucht *f (col)*; **2** *attr* ~**out competition** Ausscheidungskampf *m*; ~**-up** *n (Brit Sport)* **to have a** ~**-up** ein paar Bälle schlagen.
knot [nɒt] **1** *n (lit, fig, Naut)* Knoten *m*; *(in muscle)* Verspannung *f*; *(in wood)* Ast *m*, Verwachsung *f.* **to tie/untie a** ~ einen Knoten machen/aufmachen; **to tie oneself (up) in** ~**s** *(fig)* sich immer mehr verwickeln. **2** *vt* einen Knoten machen in *(+acc)*; *(*~ *together)* verknoten. **get** ~**ted!** *(col)* du kannst mich mal! *(col).*
knotty ['nɒtɪ] *adj (+er) problem* verwickelt, verzwickt *(col).*
know [nəʊ] *(vb: pret* **knew**, *ptp* **known***)* **1** *vti* **(a)**

(have knowledge about) wissen; *answer, facts etc also* kennen; *French etc* können. **to ~ how to do sth** *(in theory)* wissen, wie man etw macht; *(in practice)* etw tun können; **she ~s all the answers** sie kennt sich aus; *(pej)* sie weiß immer alles besser; **to let sb ~ sth** *(not keep back)* jdn etw wissen lassen; *(tell, inform)* jdm Bescheid geben; **as far as I ~** soviel ich weiß; **not that I ~** nicht daß ich wüßte; **who ~s?** wer weiß?; **there's no ~ing what he'll do** man weiß nie, was er noch tut; **I'd have you ~ that ...** ich möchte doch sehr betonen, daß ...; **to ~ what one is talking about** wissen, wovon man redet; **before you ~ where you are** ehe man sich's versieht; **he just didn't want to ~** er wollte einfach nicht hören; **I ~!** ich weiß!; *(having a good idea)* ich weiß was!; **I wouldn't ~** *(col)* weiß ich (doch) nicht *(col)*; **I knew it** ich wußte es doch!; **how should I ~** wie soll ich das wissen?; **well, what do you ~!** *(col)* sieh mal einer an!; **you never ~** man kann nie wissen; **you ~, we could ...** weißt du/wissen Sie, wir könnten ...; **he didn't come, you ~** er ist nämlich nicht gekommen; **I ~ better than that** ich bin ja nicht ganz dumm; **I ~ better than to say something like that** ich werde mich hüten, so etwas zu sagen; **he should have ~n better than to do that** es war dumm von ihm, das zu tun; **they don't ~ any better** sie kennen's nicht anders; **OK, you ~ best** okay, Sie müssen's wissen.

(b) *(be acquainted with) people, places, book* kennen. **do you ~ him to speak to?** kennen Sie ihn näher?; **if I ~ John, he'll already be there** wie ich John kenne, ist er schon da; **to get to ~ sb/a place** jdn/einen Ort kennenlernen; **to get to ~ sth** *methods etc* etw lernen; *habits, shortcuts etc* etw herausfinden.

(c) *(recognize)* erkennen. **to ~ sb by his voice** *etc* jdn an der Stimme *etc* erkennen; **he ~s a bargain when he sees one** er weiß, was ein guter Kauf ist; **you wouldn't ~ him from his brother** Sie könnten ihn nicht von seinem Bruder unterscheiden; **to ~ the difference between right and wrong** Gut und Böse unterscheiden können; **he wouldn't ~ the difference** das merkt er nicht.

(d) *(experience)* erleben. **I've never ~n it to rain so heavily** so einen starken Regen habe ich noch nie erlebt; **I've never ~n him to smile** ich habe es noch nie erlebt, daß er lächelt; **have you ever ~n such a thing to happen before?** haben Sie je schon so etwas erlebt?

(e) *(in passive)* **to be ~n (to sb)** (jdm) bekannt sein; **it is (well) ~n that ...** es ist (allgemein) bekannt, daß ...; **he is ~n to have been here** man weiß, daß er hier war; **he is ~n as Mr X** man kennt ihn als Herrn X; **to make sb/sth ~n** jdn/etw bekanntmachen; **to make oneself ~n** sich melden *(to sb* bei jdm*)*; **to become ~n** bekannt werden; *(famous)* berühmt werden.

2 *n (col)* **to be in the ~** Bescheid wissen *(col)*.

♦ **know about** *vi +prep obj maths, politics* sich auskennen in *(+dat)*; *Africa* Bescheid wissen über *(+acc)*; *women, cars* sich auskennen mit; *(be aware of)* wissen von. **I didn't ~ ~ that** das wußte ich nicht; **I only knew ~ it yesterday** ich habe erst gestern davon gehört; **did you ~ ~ Maggie?** weißt du über Maggie Bescheid?; **I don't ~ ~ that** *(don't agree)* da bin ich aber nicht so sicher.

♦ **know of** *vi +prep obj café, method* kennen; *(have heard of) sb* gehört haben von. **not that I ~ ~** nicht, daß ich wüßte.

know: ~-all *n* Alleswisser *m*; **~-how** *n* Sachkenntnis *f*, Know-how *nt*.

knowing ['nəʊɪŋ] *adj look* wissend.

knowingly ['nəʊɪŋlɪ] *adv* **(a)** *(consciously)* bewußt, absichtlich. **(b)** *look* wissend.

know-it-all ['nəʊɪtɔːl] *n (US)* = **know-all.**

knowledge ['nɒlɪdʒ] *n* **(a)** Wissen *nt*, Kenntnis *f*. **to have no ~ of** keine Kenntnis haben von; **to (the best of) my ~** meines Wissens; **not to my ~** nicht, daß ich wüßte; **without his ~** ohne sein Wissen; **it has come to my ~ that ...** es ist mir zu Ohren gekommen, daß ... **(b)** *(learning)* Kenntnisse *pl*, Wissen *nt*. **my ~ of English** meine Englischkenntnisse *pl*.

knowledgeable ['nɒlɪdʒəbl] *adj person* bewandert *(about* in *+dat)*; *report* fundiert.

known [nəʊn] **1** *ptp of* **know. 2** *adj* bekannt; *expert also* anerkannt.

knuckle ['nʌkl] *n* (Finger)knöchel *m*; *(of meat)* Haxe *f*.

♦ **knuckle down** *vi (col)* sich dahinterklemmen *(col)*.

♦ **knuckle under** *vi (col)* spuren *(col)*.

knuckleduster ['nʌklˌdʌstəʳ] *n* Schlagring *m*.

KO *n* K.o.(-Schlag) *m*.

koala [kəʊ'ɑːlə] *n (also* **~ bear***)* Koala(bär) *m*.

Koran [kɒ'rɑːn] *n* Koran *m*.

Korea [kə'rɪə] *n* Korea *nt*.

kosher ['kəʊʃəʳ] *adj* koscher.

Kraut [kraʊt] *n (esp pej)* Deutsche(r) *mf*.

Kremlin ['kremlɪn] *n*: **the ~** der Kreml.

kudos ['kjuːdɒs] *n* Ansehen *nt*, Ehre *f*.

L

L, l [el] *n* L, l *nt.*
L *(Brit Mot)* = **Learner** L.
l = **(a) litre(s)** l. **(b) left** l.
lab [læb] = **laboratory.**
label ['leɪbl] **1** *n (lit, fig)* Etikett *nt; (showing contents etc)* Aufschrift *f; (on cage)* Schild *nt; (tied)* Anhänger *m; (adhesive)* Aufkleber *m; (on parcel)* Paketadresse *f.* **on the Pye ~** bei Pye erschienen. **2** *vt* **(a)** etikettieren, mit einem Anhänger/Aufkleber versehen; *(write on)* beschriften. **the bottle was ~led "poison"** die Flasche trug die Aufschrift „Gift". **(b)** *(fig) ideas* bezeichnen; *(pej)* abstempeln.
laboratory [lə'bɒrətərɪ, *(US)* 'læbrəˌtɔːrɪ] *n* Labor *nt.* **~ assistant** Laborant(in *f*) *m.*
laborious [lə'bɔːrɪəs] *adj task* mühsam; *style* schwerfällig.
labour, *(US)* labor ['leɪbəʳ] **1** *n* **(a)** *(work in general)* Arbeit *f; (toil)* Mühe; *(task)* Aufgabe *f.* **it was a ~ of love** ich/er *etc* tat es aus Liebe zur Sache. **(b)** *(persons)* Arbeitskräfte *pl.* **to withdraw one's ~** die Arbeit verweigern; **organized ~** die organisierte Arbeiterschaft. **(c)** *(Brit Pol)* **L~** die Labour Party; **this district is L~** dies ist ein Labourbezirk. **(d)** *(Med)* Wehen *pl.* **to be in ~** in den Wehen liegen, die Wehen haben; **to go into ~** die Wehen bekommen. **2** *vt subject* auswalzen, breittreten *(col).* **I won't ~ the point** ich will nicht darauf herumreiten. **3** *vi (in fields etc)* arbeiten; *(work hard)* sich abmühen *(at, with* mit*).* **to ~ under a delusion** sich einer Täuschung *(dat)* hingeben; **to ~ up a hill** sich einen Hügel hinaufquälen.
labour: ~ camp *n* Arbeitslager *nt;* **L~ Day** *n* der Tag der Arbeit.
labourer, *(US)* laborer ['leɪbərəʳ] *n* (Hilfs)arbeiter *m; (farm ~)* Landarbeiter *m.*
labour: L~ Exchange *n (dated Brit)* Arbeitsamt *nt;* **~ force** *n* Arbeiterschaft *f;* **~-market** *n* Arbeitsmarkt *m;* **~ movement** *n* Arbeiterbewegung *f;* **~ pains** *npl* Wehen *pl;* **~ relations** *npl* die Beziehungen *pl* zwischen Unternehmern und Arbeitern *or* Gewerkschaften; **~-saving** *adj* arbeitssparend.
labyrinth ['læbɪrɪnθ] *n (lit, fig)* Labyrinth *nt.*
lace [leɪs] **1** *n* **(a)** *(fabric)* Spitze *f; (as trimming)* Spitzenbesatz *m.* **(b)** *(of shoe)* Schnürsenkel *m.* **~-up (shoe)** Schnürschuh *m.* **2** *vt* **(a)** schnüren. **(b) to ~ a drink** einen Schuß Alkohol in ein Getränk geben; **~d with brandy** mit einem Schuß Weinbrand.
♦**lace up 1** *vt sep* (zu)schnüren. **2** *vi* geschnürt werden.
lacerate ['læsəreɪt] *vt* verletzen; *(by glass etc)* zerschneiden; *painting* aufschlitzen. **her knee was badly ~d** sie hatte tiefe Wunden am Knie.
laceration [ˌlæsə'reɪʃən] *n* Fleischwunde *f.*
lack [læk] **1** *n* Mangel *m.* **through ~ of sth** aus Mangel an etw *(dat);* **they failed through ~ of support** sie scheiterten, weil es ihnen an Unterstützung mangelte; **~ of water** Wassermangel *m;* **there is no ~ of money in that family** in dieser Familie fehlt es nicht an Geld. **2** *vt* **they ~ the necessary talent** es fehlt ihnen am richtigen Talent; **we ~ time** uns fehlt die nötige Zeit. **3** *vi* **to be ~ing** fehlen; **to be found ~ing** zu wünschen übrig lassen; **he is ~ing in confidence** ihm fehlt es an Selbstvertrauen; **he ~ed for nothing** es fehlte ihm an nichts.
lackadaisical [ˌlækə'deɪzɪkəl] *adj (lacking energy)* schlapp; *(idle)* saumselig.
lackey ['lækɪ] *n (lit, fig)* Lakai *m.*
lacklustre ['lækˌlʌstəʳ] *adj surface* glanzlos; *style* farblos.
laconic [lə'kɒnɪk] *adj* lakonisch; *prose, style* knapp.
lacquer ['lækəʳ] **1** *n* Lack *m; (Brit: hair~)* Haarspray *nt.* **2** *vt* lackieren; *(Brit) hair* sprayen.
lacrosse [lə'krɒs] *n* Lacrosse *nt.*
lad [læd] *n* Junge *m; (in stable etc)* Bursche *m.* **young ~** junger Mann; **listen, ~** hör mir mal zu, mein Junge!; **all together, ~s, push!** alle Mann anschieben!; **he's a bit of a ~** *(col)* er ist ein ziemlicher Draufgänger; **he likes a night out with the ~s** *(col)* er geht abends gern mal mit seinen Kumpels weg *(col).*
ladder ['lædəʳ] **1** *n* **(a)** *(lit, fig)* Leiter *f.* **the climb up the social ~** der gesellschaftliche Aufstieg; **it's a first step up the ~** das ist ein Anfang. **(b)** *(Brit: in stocking)* Laufmasche *f.* **~proof** maschenfest. **2** *vt (Brit) stocking* zerreißen. **3** *vi (Brit: stocking)* Laufmaschen bekommen.
laden ['leɪdn] *adj (lit, fig)* beladen *(with* mit*).*
la-di-da ['lɑːdɪ'dɑː] *adj (col)* affektiert.
ladle ['leɪdl] **1** *n* (Schöpf)kelle *f,* Schöpflöffel *m.* **2** *vt* schöpfen.
lady ['leɪdɪ] *n* **(a)** Dame *f.* **"Ladies"** *(lavatory)* „Damen"; **where is the ladies** *or* **the ladies' room?** wo ist die Damentoilette?; **ladies and gentlemen!** sehr geehrte Damen und Herren!; **the old ~** *(col) (mother)* die alte Dame *(col); (wife)* meine/seine Alte *(col);* **his young ~** seine Freundin; **ladies' man** Charmeur *m.* **(b)** *(noble)* Adlige *f.* **L~** *(title)* Lady *f;* **Our L~** die Jungfrau Maria.
lady: ~bird, *(US)* ~bug *n* Marienkäfer *m;* **~ doctor** *n* Ärztin *f;* **~ friend** *n* Dame *f;* **~-in-waiting** *n* Ehrendame *f;* **~-killer** *n (col)* Herzensbrecher *m;* **~like** *adj* damenhaft; **~ship** *n:* **Your L~ship** Ihre Ladyschaft.
lag[1] [læg] **1** *n (time-~)* Zeitdifferenz *f; (delay)* Verzögerung *f.* **2** *vi (time)* langsam vergehen, dahinkriechen; *(also* **~ behind***)* zurückbleiben; **we ~ behind in space exploration** in der Raumforschung liegen wir (weit) zurück.
lag[2] *vt pipe* isolieren.
lager ['lɑːgəʳ] *n* helles Bier.
lagging ['lægɪŋ] *n* Isolierschicht *f; (material)* Isoliermaterial *nt.*
lagoon [lə'guːn] *n* Lagune *f.*
laid [leɪd] *pret, ptp of* **lay**[3].
laid-back ['leɪd'bæk] *adj (col)* gelassen, cool *(col).*
lain [leɪn] *ptp of* **lie**[2].
lair [lɛəʳ] *n* Lager *nt; (cave)* Höhle *f; (den)* Bau *m.*
laity ['leɪɪtɪ] *n (Eccl)* Laienstand *m.*
lake [leɪk] *n* See *m.*
lamb [læm] **1** *n* Lamm *nt; (meat)* Lamm(fleisch) *nt.* **2** *vi* lammen. **the ~ing season** die Lammungzeit.
lamb chop *n* Lammkotelett *nt.*
lambswool ['læmzwʊl] *n* Lammwolle *f.*
lame [leɪm] **1** *adj (+er)* **(a)** lahm; *(as result of stroke etc)* gelähmt. **the horse went ~** das Pferd fing an zu lahmen. **(b)** *(fig) excuse* faul; *argument* schwach. **~ duck** Niete *f (col).* **2** *vt* lähmen; *horse*

lahm machen.

lament [lə'ment] **1** *n* **(a)** Klage(n *pl*), Wehklage *f*. **(b)** *(Mus)* Klagelied *nt*. **2** *vt* beklagen; *misfortune etc* bejammern. **to ~ sb** um jdn trauern. **3** *vi* (weh)klagen. **to ~ for sb** um jdn trauern; **to ~ over sth** über etw *(acc)* jammern.

lamentable ['læməntəbl] *adj* beklagenswert; *work* erbärmlich.

laminated ['læmɪneɪtɪd] *adj* geschichtet; *windscreen* Verbundglas-; *book cover* laminiert. **~ glass** Verbundglas *nt;* **~ wood** Sperrholz *nt;* **~ plastic** Resopal ® *nt*.

lamp [læmp] *n* Lampe *f; (in street)* Laterne *f; (on ship)* Licht *nt*; *(torch)* Taschenlampe *f*.

lamp: ~light *n* Lampenlicht *nt*; *(in street)* Licht *nt* der Laterne(n); **by ~light** bei Lampenlicht.

lampoon [læm'puːn] **1** *n* Schmähschrift *f*. **2** *vt* verspotten.

lamp: ~post *n* Laternenpfahl *m;* **~shade** *n* Lampenschirm *m;* **~-standard** *n* = **~post.**

lance [lɑːns] **1** *n* Lanze *f*. **~-corporal** Obergefreite(r) *m*. **2** *vt (Med)* aufschneiden.

lancet ['lɑːnsɪt] *n (Med)* Lanzette *f*.

land [lænd] **1** *n* **(a)** *(not sea)* Land *nt*. **by ~** auf dem Landweg; **to see how the ~ lies** *(fig)* die Lage sondieren. **(b)** *(nation, region, fig)* Land *nt*. **to be in the ~ of the living** unter den Lebenden sein. **(c)** *(as property)* Grund und Boden *m*. **(d)** *(Agr)* Land *nt; (soil)* Boden *m*. **to work on the ~** das Land bebauen; **to live off the ~** *(grow own food)* sich von Selbstangebautem ernähren.

2 *vt* **(a)** *passengers* absetzen; *plane, troops* landen; *goods* abladen; *boat, fish on hook* an Land ziehen; *fish at port* anlanden. **(b)** *(col: obtain)* kriegen *(col)*; *contract* sich *(dat)* verschaffen; *prize* sich *(dat)* holen *(col)*. **(c)** *(col)* **he ~ed him a punch on the jaw** er versetzte ihm einen Kinnhaken; **it'll ~ you in jail** das wird dich noch ins Gefängnis bringen; **I've ~ed myself in a real mess** ich bin (ganz schön) in die Klemme geraten *(col)*; **I got ~ed with the job** man hat mir die Arbeit aufgehalst *(col)*; **I got ~ed with him for two hours** ich hatte ihn zwei Stunden lang auf dem Hals.

3 *vi* landen; *(from ship)* an Land gehen. **we're coming in to ~** wir setzen zur Landung an; **to ~ on one's feet** *(lit)* auf den Füßen landen; *(fig)* auf die Füße fallen; **he ~ed awkwardly** er ist ungeschickt aufgekommen.

♦ **land up** *vi (col)* landen *(col)*.

landed ['lændɪd] *adj* **the ~ class** die Großgrundbesitzer *pl;* **~ gentry** Landadel *m*.

landing ['lændɪŋ] *n* **(a)** *(of person, troops, plane)* Landung *f*. **(b)** *(on stairs) (inside house)* Gang *m; (outside flat door)* Treppenabsatz *m*.

landing: ~-card *n* Einreisekarte *f;* **~-craft** *n* Landungsboot *nt;* **~-stage** *n (Brit Naut)* Landesteg *m;* **~-strip** *n* Landebahn *f*.

land: ~lady *n* Vermieterin *f; (in pub)* Wirtin *f;* **~locked** *adj* von Land eingeschlossen; **a ~locked country** ein Binnenstaat *m;* **~lord** *n (of land)* Grundbesitzer *m; (of flat etc)* Vermieter *m; (of pub)* Wirt *m;* **~mark** *n* Wahrzeichen *nt; (fig)* Meilenstein *m;* **~-owner** *n* Grundbesitzer *m;* **~scape** ['lændskeɪp] **1** *n* Landschaft *f;* **2** *vt big area* landschaftlich gestalten; *garden* anlegen; **~scape gardening** *n* Landschafts-/Gartengestaltung *f;* **~slide** *n (lit, fig)* Erdrutsch *m;* **a ~slide victory** ein überwältigender Sieg.

lane [leɪn] *n (in country)* (Feld)weg *m; (in town)* Gasse *f;* Weg *m; (Sport)* Bahn *f; (motorway)* Spur *f*. **"get in ~"** „bitte einordnen".

language ['læŋgwɪdʒ] *n* Sprache *f*. **bad ~** unanständige Ausdrücke *pl;* **strong ~** Kraftausdrücke *pl; (forceful)* harte Worte *pl;* **mind your ~!** so was sagt man nicht! *(col)*; **to talk the same ~ (as sb)** die gleiche Sprache (wie jd) sprechen.

language: ~ course *n* Sprachkurs(us) *m;* **~ lab(oratory)** *n* Sprachlabor *nt;* **~ teacher** *n* Sprachlehrer(in *f*) *m*.

languid ['læŋgwɪd] *adj* träge; *gesture* müde; *appearance, manner* gelangweilt.

languish ['læŋgwɪʃ] *vi* schmachten; *(pine)* sich sehnen *(for* nach).

languor ['læŋgəʳ] *n* Trägheit *f; (weakness)* Mattigkeit *f*.

languorous ['læŋgərəs] *adj* träge; *feeling* wohlig; *tone, voice* schläfrig.

lank [læŋk] *adj person* hager; *hair* strähnig.

lanky ['læŋkɪ] **1** *adj (+er)* schlaksig. **2** *n (col)* Lange(r) *mf (col)*.

lantern ['læntən] *n* Laterne *f*.

lap[1] [læp] *n* Schoß *m*. **it's in the ~ of the gods** es liegt im Schoß der Götter; **to live in the ~ of luxury** ein Luxusleben führen.

lap[2] *(Sport) n (round)* Runde *f*. **we're on the last ~ now** *(fig)* wir haben es bald geschafft.

lap[3] **1** *vt (lick)* lecken. **2** *vi (water)* klatschen *(against* gegen).

♦ **lap up** *vt sep liquid* auflecken; *praise* genießen; *nonsense* schlucken. **she ~ped it ~** *(fig)* das ging ihr runter wie Honig *(col)*.

lapel [lə'pel] *n* Revers *nt or m*.

Lapland ['læplænd] *n* Lappland *nt*.

lapse [læps] **1** *n* **(a)** *(error)* Fehler *m; (moral)* Fehltritt *m; (decline)* Absinken *nt no pl*. **he had a ~ of memory** es ist ihm entfallen; **~ in standards** Niveauabfall *m*. **(b)** *(expiry)* Ablauf *m; (of claim)* Erlöschen *nt*; *(of time)* Zeitraum *m*. **there was a ~ in the conversation** es gab eine Gesprächspause. **2** *vi* **(a)** *(morally)* einen Fehltritt begehen; *(decline)* abgleiten. **to ~ into one's old ways** wieder in seine alten Gewohnheiten verfallen; **he ~d into silence** er verfiel in Schweigen; **his work is lapsing** seine Arbeit läßt nach. **(b)** *(expire)* ablaufen; *(claims)* erlöschen; *(correspondence)* einschlafen.

lapsed [læpst] *adj Catholic* abtrünnig.

larceny ['lɑːsənɪ] *n (Jur)* Diebstahl *m*.

larch [lɑːtʃ] *n* Lärche *f*.

lard [lɑːd] *n* Schweineschmalz *nt*.

larder ['lɑːdəʳ] *n (room)* Speisekammer *f; (cupboard)* Speiseschrank *m*.

large [lɑːdʒ] **1** *adj (+er)* **(a)** *(big)* groß; *person* korpulent. **~ as life** in voller Lebensgröße. **(b)** *(extensive) interests* weitreichend. **2** *adv* groß. **guilt was written ~ all over his face** die Schuld stand ihm deutlich im Gesicht geschrieben. **3** *n* **at ~** *(in general)* im großen und ganzen; **people at ~** die Allgemeinheit; **to be at ~** *(free)* frei herumlaufen; **strewn at ~** kreuz und quer verstreut.

largely ['lɑːdʒlɪ] *adv (mainly)* zum größten Teil.

large: ~-scale *adj* groß angelegt; **~-scale changes** Veränderungen *pl* in großem Umfang; **a ~-scale producer** ein Großhersteller *m;* **~-scale rioting** Massenunruhen *pl;* **a ~-scale map** eine (Land)karte in großem Maßstab.

lark[1] [lɑːk] *n (Orn)* Lerche *f*. **to get up with the ~** mit den Hühnern aufstehen.

lark[2] *n (col) (joke)* Jux *(col)*, Spaß *m*. **to do sth for a ~** etw (nur) aus Jux machen; **this whole agency ~** die ganze Geschichte mit der Agentur *(col)*.

♦ **lark about** *or* **around** *vi (col)* herumalbern. **to ~ ~ with sth** mit etw herumspielen.

larva ['lɑːvə] *n, pl* **-e** ['lɑːvɪ] Larve *f*.

laryngitis [,lærɪn'dʒaɪtɪs] *n* Kehlkopfentzündung *f*.

larynx ['lærɪŋks] *n* Kehlkopf *m*.

lascivious [lə'sɪvɪəs] *adj person, behaviour* lüstern.

laser ['leɪzəʳ] *n* Laser *m*. **~ beam** Laserstrahl *m*.

lash[1] [læʃ] *n (eye~)* Wimper *f*.

lash[2] **1** *n (whip)* Peitsche *f; (thong)* Schnur *f; (stroke, as punishment)* (Peitschen)schlag *m; (~ing) (of tail)* Schlagen *nt; (of waves, rain also)* Peitschen *nt*. **2** *vt* **(a)** *(beat)* peitschen; *(as punishment)* auspeitschen; *(rain)* peitschen gegen; *(tail)* schlagen mit. **the wind ~ed the sea into a fury** wütend peitschte der Wind die See. **(b)** *(tie)* festbinden *(to* an *+dat)*. **to ~ sth together** etw zusammenbinden.

♦ **lash down 1** *vt sep (tie down)* festbinden. **2** *vi (rain etc)* niederprasseln.

♦ **lash out** *vi* **(a)** *(physically)* (wild) um sich schlagen. **to ~ ~ at sb** auf jdn losgehen. **(b)** *(in words)* vom Leder ziehen *(col)*. **to ~ ~ against** *or* **at sb/sth** gegen jdn/etw wettern. **(c)** *(col: with money)* sich in Unkosten stürzen. **to ~ ~ on sth** sich *(dat)* etw was kosten lassen *(col)*.

lashing ['læʃıŋ] *n* **(a)** *(beating)* Prügel *pl; (punishment)* Auspeitschung *f*. **(b) ~s** *pl (col)* eine Unmenge *(col)*; **~s of money** massenhaft Geld *(col)*.

lass [læs] *n* (junges) Mädchen.

lasso [læ'su:] **1** *n, pl* **-(e)s** Lasso *m or nt*. **2** *vt* mit dem Lasso einfangen.

last[1] [lɑ:st] **1** *adj* letzte(r, s). **he was ~ to arrive** er kam als letzter an; **the ~ person** der letzte; **the ~ but one, the second ~ (one)** der/die/das vorletzte; **~ Monday** letzten Montag; **~ year** letztes Jahr; **during the ~ 20 years** in den letzten 20 Jahren; **to have the ~ laugh** zum Schluß das Lachen haben; **~ but not least** nicht zuletzt; **that's the ~ thing I worry about** das ist das letzte, worüber ich mir Sorgen machen würde; **that was the ~ thing I expected** damit hatte ich am wenigsten gerechnet; **he's the ~ person I want to see** er ist der letzte, den ich sehen möchte.

2 *n* der/die/das letzte. **he was the ~ to leave** er ging als letzter; **each one is better than the ~** eins ist besser als das andere; **this is the ~ of the cake** das ist der Rest des Kuchens; **that was the ~ we heard of him** seitdem haben wir nichts mehr von ihm gehört; **we shall never hear the ~ of it** das werden wir noch lange zu hören kriegen; **at ~** endlich; **to the ~** bis zum Schluß.

3 *adv* **I ~ heard from him a month ago** vor einem Monat habe ich das letztemal von ihm gehört; **he spoke ~** er sprach als letzter.

last[2] **1** *vt* **it will ~ me a lifetime** das hält ein Leben lang; **these cigarettes will ~ me a week** diese Zigaretten reichen mir eine Woche. **2** *vi (continue)* dauern; *(remain intact: flowers, food, marriage)* halten; *(rain)* anhalten. **it's too good to ~** das ist zu schön, um wahr zu sein; **the previous boss ~ed only a week** der letzte Chef blieb nur eine Woche.

last-ditch ['lɑ:st,dıtʃ] *adj attr* in letzter Minute.

lasting ['lɑ:stıŋ] *adj relationship* dauerhaft; *shame etc* anhaltend.

lastly ['lɑ:stlı] *adv* schließlich, zum Schluß.

last-minute [,lɑ:st'mınıt] *adj* in letzter Minute. **it was a ~ decision** er/sie *etc* hat sich in letzter Minute dazu entschlossen.

latch [lætʃ] *n* Riegel *m*. **to leave the door on the ~** die Tür nur einklinken.

♦ **latch on** *vi (col)* **(a)** *(get hold)* sich festhalten *(to sth* an etw *dat)*. **he ~ed ~ to the idea of coming with us** er hat es sich *(dat)* in den Kopf gesetzt, mitzukommen. **(b)** *(attach oneself)* sich anschließen *(to dat)*. **she ~ed ~ to me at the party** sie hängte sich auf der Party an mich *(col)*. **(c)** *(understand)* kapieren *(col)*.

latchkey ['lætʃ,ki:] *n* Haus-/Wohnungsschlüssel *m*. **~ child** Schlüsselkind *nt*.

late [leıt] **1** *adj (+er)* **(a)** spät. **to be ~ (for sth)** (zu etw) zu spät kommen; **the train was ~** der Zug hatte Verspätung; **I was ~ in getting up this morning** ich bin heute morgen zu spät aufgestanden; **he is ~ with his rent** er hat seine Miete noch nicht bezahlt; **I don't want to make you ~** ich möchte Sie nicht aufhalten; **due to the ~ arrival of ...** wegen der verspäteten Ankunft ... *(+gen)*. **(b)** *hour* spät; *opening hours* lang; *bus* Spät-. **it's ~** es ist spät; **it's getting ~** es ist schon spät; **at this ~ hour** zu so später Stunde; **he keeps very ~ hours** er geht sehr spät ins Bett; **it happened in the ~ eighties** es geschah Ende der achtziger Jahre; **in the ~ morning** am späten Vormittag; **he came in ~ June** er kam Ende Juni. **(c)** *attr (deceased)* verstorben. **the ~ John F. Kennedy** John F. Kennedy. **(d)** *(former)* **the ~ Prime Minister** der frühere *or* vorige Premierminister.

2 *adv* spät. **to come ~** zu spät kommen; **the train arrived eight minutes ~** der Zug hatte acht Minuten Verspätung; **better ~ than never** besser spät als gar nicht; **to stay up ~** lange aufbleiben; **to work ~ at the office** länger im Büro arbeiten; **~ at night** spät abends; **~ in the afternoon** am späten Nachmittag; **~ in the year** (gegen) Ende des Jahres; **of ~** in letzter Zeit.

latecomer ['leıtkʌmə[r]] *n* Nachzügler(in *f*) *m*.

lately ['leıtlı] *adv* in letzter Zeit. **till ~** bis vor kurzem.

lateness ['leıtnıs] *n (at work etc)* Zuspätkommen *nt; (of train, payments)* Verspätung *f; (of meal)* späte Zeit; *(of harvest, seasons)* spätes Eintreten. **the ~ of the hour** die vorgerückte Stunde.

latent ['leıtənt] *adj* latent; *ability, strength also* verborgen; *energy* ungenutzt.

later ['leitə[r]] **1** *adj* später. **at a ~ date** zu einem späteren Termin; **a ~ edition** eine neuere Auflage; **in his ~ years** in seinem späteren Leben. **2** *adv* später. **~ that night** später in der Nacht; **a moment ~** einen Augenblick später; **see you ~!** bis später!; **not ~ than 1995** spätestens 1995; **~ on** nachher.

lateral ['lætərəl] *adj* seitlich.

latest ['leıtıst] **1** *adj* **(a)** späteste(r, s). **what is the ~ date you can come?** wann kannst du spätestens kommen? **(b)** *(most recent) fashion, version* neu(e)ste(r, s). **the ~ news** das Neu(e)ste. **2** *adv* am spätesten. **3** *n* **(a) what's the ~ (about John)?** was gibt's Neues (über John)?; **wait till you hear the ~!** warte, bis du das Neueste gehört hast! **(b) at the (very) ~** spätestens.

latex ['leıteks] *n* Latex *(spec)*, Milchsaft *m*.

lath [læθ] *n* Latte *f*. **~s** *pl (structure)* Lattenwerk *nt*.

lathe [leıð] *n* Drehbank *f*. **~ operator** Dreher *m*.

lather ['lɑ:ðə[r]] **1** *n* (Seifen)schaum *m; (sweat)* Schweiß *m*. **the horse was in a ~** das Pferd war schweißnaß; **to get into a ~ (about sth)** *(col)* sich (über etw *acc*) aufregen. **2** *vt* einschäumen. **3** *vi* schäumen.

Latin ['lætın] **1** *adj (Roman) civilization* römisch; *poets also* lateinisch; *temperament* südländisch. **~ language** lateinische Sprache. **2** *n (language)* Latein(isch) *nt*.

Latin America *n* Lateinamerika *nt*.

Latin-American ['lætınə'merıkən] **1** *adj* lateinamerikanisch. **2** *n* Lateinamerikaner(in *f*) *m*.

latitude ['lætıtju:d] *n* Breite *f; (fig)* Freiheit *f*.

latrine [lə'tri:n] *n* Latrine *f*.

latter ['lætə[r]] **1** *adj* **(a)** *(second of two)* letztere(r, s). **(b)** *(at the end)* **the ~ part of the book is better** gegen Ende wird das Buch besser; **the ~ part of the week** die zweite Hälfte der Woche; **in his ~ years** in den späteren Jahren seines Lebens. **2** *n* **the ~** der/die/das letztere; die letzteren.

latterly ['lætəlı] *adv* in letzter Zeit.

lattice ['lætıs] *n* Gitter *nt*. **~-work** Gitterwerk *nt*.

laudable ['lɔ:dəbl] *adj* lobenswert.

laugh [lɑ:f] **1** *n* Lachen *nt*. **she gave a loud ~** sie lachte laut auf; **to have a good ~ about sth** sich köstlich über etw *(acc)* amüsieren; **it'll give us a ~** *(col)* das wird lustig; **the ~ was on me** der Witz ging auf meine Kosten; **to have the last ~ (over** *or* **on sb)** es jdm zeigen *(col)*; **what a ~** (das ist ja) zum Totlachen *(col)*!; **just for a ~** nur (so) aus Spaß; **it'll be a good ~** es wird bestimmt lustig;

he's a ~ er ist zum Schreien *(col).*

2 *vi* lachen *(about, at, over* über *+acc).* **to ~ at sb** sich über jdn lustig machen; **to ~ up one's sleeve** sich *(dat)* ins Fäustchen lachen; **it's all very well for you to ~** du hast gut lachen; **you'll be ~ing on the other side of your face soon** dir wird das Lachen bald vergehen; **to ~ in sb's face** jdm ins Gesicht lachen; **he who ~s last ~s longest** *(Prov)* wer zuletzt lacht, lacht am besten *(Prov)*; **don't make me ~!** *(iro col)* daß ich nicht lache! *(col)*; **you've got your own house, you're ~ing** *(col)* du hast ein eigenes Haus, du hast es gut.

3 *vt* **to ~ oneself silly** sich tot- *or* kaputtlachen *(col)*; **he was ~ed out of court** er wurde ausgelacht.

♦ **laugh off** *vt* **(a)** *always separate* **to ~ one's head ~** sich totlachen *(col).* **(b)** *sep (dismiss)* mit einem Lachen abtun.

laughable ['lɑːfəbl] *adj* lächerlich.

laughing ['lɑːfɪŋ] **1** *adj* lachend. **it's no ~ matter** das ist nicht zum Lachen **2** *n* Lachen *nt.*

laughing stock *n* Witzfigur *f.* **his ideas made him a ~** mit seinen Ideen machte er sich lächerlich.

laughter ['lɑːftəʳ] *n* Gelächter *nt.* **~ broke out among the audience** das Publikum brach in Gelächter aus.

launch [lɔːntʃ] **1** *n* **(a)** *(vessel)* Barkasse *f.* **(b)** *(~ing) (of ship)* Stapellauf *m; (of lifeboat)* Aussetzen *nt; (of rocket)* Abschuß *m.* **(c)** *(~ing) (of company)* Gründung *f; (of new product)* Einführung *f.* **2** *vt* **(a)** *new vessel* vom Stapel lassen; *lifeboat* aussetzen; *rocket* abschießen. **Lady X ~ed the new boat** der Stapellauf fand in Anwesenheit von Lady X statt. **(b)** *company* gründen; *new product* auf den Markt bringen. **to ~ an offensive against the enemy** zum Angriff gegen den Feind übergehen.

♦ **launch into** *vi +prep obj (attack)* angreifen. **the author ~es straight ~ his main theme** der Autor kommt gleich zum Hauptthema.

♦ **launch out** *vi (diversify)* sich verlegen *(in* auf *+acc).* **the company ~ed ~ in several new directions** die Firma stieg in einige neue Branchen ein.

launching ['lɔːntʃɪŋ] *n* = **launch 1 (b).**

launching pad *n* Abschußrampe *f; (fig)* Sprungbrett *nt.*

launder ['lɔːndəʳ] *vti* waschen und bügeln.

launderette [ˌlɔːndə'ret] *n (Brit)* Waschsalon *m.*

laundromat ['lɔːndrəʊmæt] *n (US)* Waschsalon *m.*

laundry ['lɔːndrɪ] *n (place)* Wäscherei *f; (clothes) (dirty)* schmutzige Wäsche; *(washed)* Wäsche *f.* **to do the ~** (Wäsche) waschen.

laurel ['lɒrəl] *n* Lorbeer *m.* **to rest on one's ~s** sich auf seinen Lorbeeren ausruhen.

lava ['lɑːvə] *n* Lava *f.*

lavatory ['lævətrɪ] *n* Toilette *f.* **~ seat** Toilettensitz *m.*

lavender ['lævɪndəʳ] *n (flower)* Lavendel *m.*

lavish ['lævɪʃ] **1** *adj gifts* großzügig; *praise, affection* überschwenglich; *banquet, party* üppig; *(pej)* verschwenderisch. **to be ~ with sth** mit etw verschwenderisch umgehen; **to be ~ with one's money** das Geld mit vollen Händen ausgeben. **2** *vt* **to ~ sth on sb** jdn mit etw überhäufen.

lavishly ['lævɪʃlɪ] *adv give* großzügig; *praise* überschwenglich; *put paint on* reichlich; *entertain* üppig. **they entertain ~** sie geben feudale Feste; **~ furnished** aufwendig eingerichtet.

law [lɔː] *n* Gesetz *nt; (system)* Recht *nt; (as study)* Jura *no art.* **~ of nature** Naturgesetz *nt;* **it's the ~** das ist Gesetz; **his word is ~** sein Wort ist Gesetz; **is there a ~ against it?** ist das verboten?; **he is a ~ unto himself** er macht, was er will; **he is above the ~** er steht über dem Gesetz; **to keep within the ~** sich im Rahmen des Gesetzes bewegen; **in ~** vor dem Gesetz; **by ~** gesetzlich; **to go to ~** vor Gericht gehen; **to take the ~ into one's own hands** das Recht selbst in die Hand nehmen; **~ and order** Recht und Ordnung; **I'll have the ~ on you** *(col)* ich rufe die Polizei.

law: ~-abiding *adj* gesetzestreu; **~breaker** *n* Rechtsbrecher *m;* **~ court** *n* Gericht *nt.*

lawful ['lɔːfʊl] *adj* rechtmäßig.

lawless ['lɔːlɪs] *adj act* gesetzwidrig; *person* gesetzlos; *country* ohne Gesetzgebung.

lawlessness ['lɔːlɪsnɪs] *n* Gesetzwidrigkeit *f.*

lawn [lɔːn] *n (grass)* Rasen *m no pl.*

lawn: ~mower *n* Rasenmäher *m;* **~ tennis** *n* Rasentennis *nt.*

law: ~school *n (US)* juristische Fakultät; **~ student** *n* Jurastudent(in *f*) *m;* **~suit** *n* Prozeß *m,* Klage *f;* **he brought a ~suit for damages** er strengte eine Schadenersatzklage an.

lawyer ['lɔːjəʳ] *n* (Rechts)anwalt *m,* (Rechts)anwältin *f.*

lax [læks] *adj (+er)* lax; *discipline* lasch; *morals* locker. **to be ~ about sth** etw vernachlässigen; **he's ~ about washing** er nimmt's mit dem Waschen nicht so genau.

laxative ['læksətɪv] *n* Abführmittel *nt.*

laxity ['læksɪtɪ], **laxness** ['læksnɪs] *n* Laxheit *f; (carelessness)* Nachlässigkeit *f.*

lay[1] [leɪ] *adj* Laien-.

lay[2] *pret of* **lie.**

lay[3] *(vb: pret, ptp* **laid***)* **1** *vt* **(a)** *(place, put)* legen *(sth on sth* etw auf etw *acc).* **to ~ (one's) hands on** *(get hold of)* erwischen; *(find)* finden; **I never laid a hand on him** ich habe ihn überhaupt nicht angefaßt.

(b) *bricks, foundations, track, mines, eggs* legen; *cable* verlegen; *carpet* (ver)legen; *(prepare) fire* herrichten; *(Brit) table* decken; *plans* schmieden. **to ~ breakfast** den Frühstückstisch decken.

(c) *(non-material things) burden* auferlegen *(on sb* jdm*).* **to ~ the blame for sth on sb** jdm die Schuld an etw *(dat)* geben; **to ~ oneself open to criticism** sich der Kritik aussetzen; **the police laid a charge of murder against him** die Polizei erstattete gegen ihn Anzeige wegen Mordes; **he laid his case before them** er trug ihnen seinen Fall vor; **to ~ a bet on sth** auf etw *(acc)* wetten.

(d) *ghost* anstreiben; *fear* zerstreuen.

(e) *(col: sexually)* aufs Kreuz legen *(col).*

2 *vi (hen)* legen.

♦ **lay aside** *vt sep work etc* zur Seite legen; *(save)* beiseite legen; *plans etc* auf Eis legen.

♦ **lay down** *vt sep* **(a)** *book, pen etc* hinlegen *(on* auf *+acc).* **(b)** *(give up) burden* ablegen; *office* niederlegen. **to ~ ~ one's arms** die Waffen niederlegen; **to ~ ~ one's life** sein Leben opfern. **(c)** *policy* festsetzen; *rules* festlegen. **to ~ ~ the law** *(col)* Vorschriften machen *(to sb* jdm*).*

♦ **lay in** *vt sep food etc* einlagern; *supplies also* anlegen.

♦ **lay into** *vi +prep obj (col)* **to ~ ~ sb** auf jdn losgehen; *(verbally)* jdn fertigmachen *(col).*

♦ **lay off 1** *vi (col: stop)* aufhören *(prep obj* mit*).* **~ ~ it!** hör auf damit!; **~ ~ my little brother, will you!** laß bloß meinen kleinen Bruder in Ruhe! **2** *vt sep workers* entlassen; *(temporarily)* Feierschichten machen lassen. **to be laid ~** entlassen werden; Feierschichten einlegen müssen.

♦ **lay on** *vt sep* **(a)** *(apply) paint* auftragen. **(b)** *hospitality* bieten *(for sb* jdm*); entertainment* sorgen für; *excursion* veranstalten; *extra buses* einsetzen; *water, electricity* anschließen.

♦ **lay out** *vt sep* **(a)** *clothes* zurechtlegen; *corpse* aufbahren. **(b)** *(design, arrange)* anlegen; *room* aufteilen; *rooms in house* anordnen; *page* umbrechen; *(in magazines)* das Layout *(+gen)* machen. **(c)** *money* ausgeben. **(d)** *(knock out)* **to ~ sb ~** jdn erledigen *(col).*

♦ **lay up** *vt sep* **(a)** *(store)* lagern; *supply* anlegen;

(amass) anhäufen. **he's ~ing ~ trouble for himself in the future** er wird später noch (viel) Ärger bekommen. **(b)** *(immobilize) ship* auflegen; *car* stillegen. **to be laid ~ (in bed)** im Bett liegen.

lay: ~about *n* Nichtstuer *m;* **~by** *n (Brit) (in town)* Parkbucht *f; (in country)* Parkplatz *m; (big)* Rastplatz *m.*

layer ['leɪəʳ] *n* Schicht *(also Geol),* Lage *f.*

lay: ~man *n* Laie *m;* **to the ~man** für den Laien; **~-off** *n* **further ~-offs were unavoidable** weitere Arbeiter mußten entlassen werden *or (temporarily)* mußten Feierschichten einlegen; **~out** *n* Anordnung *f; (Typ)* Layout *nt;* **we have changed the ~out of this office** wir haben dieses Büro anders aufgeteilt.

laze [leɪz] *vi (also:* **~ about, ~ around***)* faulenzen.

laziness ['leɪzɪnɪs] *n* Faulheit *f; (languor)* Trägheit *f.*

lazy ['leɪzɪ] *adj (+er)* faul; *(slow-moving)* langsam; *(lacking activity)* träge. **we had a ~ holiday** wir haben im Urlaub nur gefaulenzt.

lazybones ['leɪzɪˌbəunz] *n sing (col)* Faulpelz *m.*

lb *n (weight)* ≈ Pfd.

lead[1] [led] *n (metal)* Blei *nt; (in pencil)* Graphit *nt.*

lead[2] [liːd] *(vb: pret, ptp* **led***)* **1** *n* **(a)** *(front position)* Spitzenposition *f; (Sport)* Führung *f; (distance, time ahead)* Vorsprung *m.* **to have two minutes' ~ over sb** zwei Minuten Vorsprung vor jdm haben; **to be in the ~** in Führung liegen; **he took the ~ from the German runner** er ging vor dem deutschen Läufer in Führung; **it's my** *(Cards)* **~** ich fange an. **(b)** *(example)* Beispiel *nt.* **to follow sb's ~** jds Beispiel folgen. **(c)** *(clue)* Anhaltspunkt *m; (in guessing etc)* Tip *m.* **the police have a ~** die Polizei hat eine Spur. **(d)** *(Theat) (part)* Hauptrolle *f; (person)* Hauptdarsteller(in *f*) *m.* **to sing the ~** die tragende Partie singen. **(e)** *(leash)* Leine *f.* **on a ~** an der Leine. **(f)** *(Elec)* Leitung *f,* Kabel *nt.*

2 *vt* **(a)** *(conduct) person, animal* führen. **that road will ~ you to the station** auf dieser Straße kommen Sie zum Bahnhof; **to ~ the way** *(lit, fig)* vorangehen; *(fig: be superior)* führend sein.

(b) *(be the leader of, direct)* (an)führen; *expedition, team* leiten; *movement, revolution* anführen; *orchestra (conductor)* leiten; *(first violin)* führen. **to ~ a government** an der Spitze einer Regierung stehen; **to ~ a party** den Parteivorsitz führen.

(c) *(be first in)* anführen. **they led us by 30 seconds** sie lagen 30 Sekunden vor uns *(dat);* **Britain led the world in textiles** Großbritannien war auf dem Gebiet der Textilproduktion führend in der Welt.

(d) *card* ausspielen.

(e) *life* führen. **to ~ a life of luxury** in Luxus leben, ein Luxusleben führen.

(f) *(influence)* **to ~ sb to do sth** jdn dazu bringen, etw zu tun; **what led him to change his mind?** wie kam er dazu, seine Meinung zu ändern?; **he is easily led** er läßt sich leicht beeinflussen; **this led me to the conclusion that ...** daraus schloß ich, daß ...

3 *vi* **(a)** *(go in front)* vorangehen; *(in race)* in Führung liegen. **to ~ by 10 metres** 10 Meter Vorsprung haben. **(b)** *(be a leader)* führen. **(c)** *(Cards)* ausspielen *(with sth* etw*).* **(d)** *(street etc)* führen. **it ~s into that room** es führt zu diesem Raum. **(e)** *(result in, cause)* führen *(to* zu*).* **remarks like that could ~ to trouble** solche Bemerkungen können unangenehme Folgen haben; **what will all these strikes ~ to?** wo sollen all diese Streiks hinführen?

♦ **lead away** *vt sep* wegführen; *prisoner* abführen.

♦ **lead off 1** *vt sep* abführen. **a policeman led the drunk man ~ the pitch** ein Polizist führte den Betrunkenen vom Platz. **2** *vi* **several streets led ~ the square** mehrere Straßen gingen vom Platz ab.

♦ **lead on 1** *vi usu imper* **~ ~, sergeant!** führen Sie an, Feldwebel! **2** *vt sep (deceive)* hinters Licht führen; *(tease)* aufziehen. **he led us ~ to believe that we would get the money** er hat uns vorgemacht, wir würden das Geld bekommen; **she's just ~ing him ~** sie führt ihn nur an der Nase herum.

♦ **lead up** *vi* **the events that led ~ to the war** die Ereignisse, die dem Krieg vorausgingen; **what are you ~ing ~ to?** worauf willst du hinaus?; **what's all this ~ing ~ to?** was soll das Ganze?

leaded ['ledɪd] *adj window* Bleiglas-.

leader ['liːdəʳ] *n* **(a)** Führer *m; (of union, party also)* Vorsitzende(r) *mf; (military also)* Befehlshaber *m; (of gang, rebels)* Anführer *m; (of expedition, project)* Leiter(in *f*) *m; (Sport) (in league)* Tabellenführer *m; (in race)* der/die/das Erste; *(Mus) (Brit: of orchestra)* Konzertmeister *m; (of choir)* Leiter *m; (of pop group)* Leader *m.* **to be the ~** *(in race, competition)* in Führung liegen; **the ~s** *(in race, competition)* die Spitzengruppe; **~ of the opposition** Oppositionsführer(in *f*) *m;* **the product is a ~ in its field** dieses Produkt ist auf diesem Gebiet führend. **(b)** *(Brit Press)* Leitartikel *m.* **~ writer** Leitartikler *m.*

leadership ['liːdəʃɪp] *n* **(a)** Führung *f.* **under the ~ of** unter (der) Führung von. **(b)** *(quality)* Führungsqualitäten *pl.*

lead-free ['led'friː] *adj* bleifrei.

leading ['liːdɪŋ] *adj* **(a)** *(first)* vorderste(r, s); *runner also* führend. **(b)** *(most important) person, company* führend; *sportsman, product* Spitzen-; *issue; (Theat) part* Haupt-.

leading: ~ lady *n* Hauptdarstellerin *f;* **~ light** *n (person)* Leuchte *f;* **~ man** *n* Hauptdarsteller *m;* **~ question** *n* Suggestivfrage *f.*

lead [led-]: **~ pencil** *n* Bleistift *m;* **~-poisoning** *n* Bleivergiftung *f.*

lead story ['liːd-] *n* Hauptartikel *m.*

leaf [liːf] **1** *n, pl* **leaves (a)** Blatt *nt.* **to be in ~** grün sein. **(b)** *(of paper)* Blatt *nt.* **to take a ~ out of sb's book** sich *(dat)* von jdm eine Scheibe abschneiden; **to turn over a new ~** einen neuen Anfang machen. **(c)** *(of table)* Ausziehplatte *f.* **2** *vi* **to ~ through a book** ein Buch durchblättern.

leaflet ['liːflɪt] *n* Prospekt *m; (with instructions)* Merkblatt *nt; (handout)* Flugblatt *nt; (brochure)* Broschüre *f.*

leafy ['liːfɪ] *adj tree* belaubt; *lane* grün.

league [liːg] *n* **(a)** *(treaty)* Bündnis *nt,* Bund *m; (organization)* Verband *m.* **L~ of Nations** Völkerbund *m;* **to be in ~ with sb** mit jdm gemeinsame Sache machen. **(b)** *(Sport)* Liga *f.* **he's not in the same ~** *(fig)* er hat nicht das gleiche Format.

leak [liːk] **1** *n (lit, fig)* undichte Stelle; *(Naut)* Leck *nt; (escape of liquid)* Leck *nt.* **to have a ~** undicht sein; **a gas ~** eine undichte Stelle in der Gasleitung; **there's been a ~ to the press** man hat der Presse etwas zugespielt. **2** *vt* durchlassen; *(fig) information* zuspielen *(to sb* jdm*).* **3** *vi* **(a)** *(ship, receptacle)* lecken; *(roof, shoes)* nicht dicht sein; *(pen)* auslaufen. **(b)** *(gas)* ausströmen; *(liquid)* auslaufen. **water is ~ing (in) through the roof** Wasser sickert durch das Dach.

leakage ['liːkɪdʒ] *n (act)* Auslaufen *nt.* **the ground was polluted by a ~ of chemicals** der Boden war durch auslaufende Chemikalien verunreinigt.

leaky ['liːkɪ] *adj (+er)* undicht; *boat also* leck.

lean[1] [liːn] *adj (+er)* **(a)** *(thin)* dünn; *face, person* schmal; *(through lack of food)* hager; *meat* mager. **(b)** *(poor) year, harvest* mager.

lean[2] *(vb: pret, ptp* **~ed** *or* **leant***)* **1** *vt (put in sloping position)* lehnen *(against* gegen, an *+acc); (rest)* aufstützen *(on* auf *+dat or acc).* **to ~ one's head on sb's shoulder** seinen Kopf an jds Schulter *(acc)* lehnen; **to ~ one's elbow on sth** sich mit dem Ellbogen auf etw *(acc)* stützen. **2** *vi* **(a)** *(be off vertical)* sich neigen *(to* nach*)*; *(trees)* sich biegen. **he ~t across the counter** er beugte sich über den Ladentisch. **(b)** *(rest)* sich lehnen *(against* gegen *+acc)*. **he ~t on the edge of the table** er stützte sich auf die Tischkante. **(c)** *(tend in opinion etc)* **to ~ towards the left/socialism** nach links/zum Sozialismus tendieren.

♦ **lean back** *vi* sich zurücklehnen.

♦ **lean forward** *vi* sich vorbeugen.

♦ **lean on** *vi (depend)* **to ~ ~ sb** sich auf jdn verlassen; *(col: put pressure on)* jdn bearbeiten *(col) or* beknien *(col)*.

♦ **lean out** *vi* sich hinauslehnen *(of* aus*)*.

♦ **lean over** *vi (be off vertical)* sich (vor)neigen; *(bend)* sich vorbeugen *(sth* über *+acc)*.

leaning ['li:nɪŋ] **1** *adj* schräg, schief. **2** *n* Hang *m.*

leant [lent] *pret, ptp of* **lean.**

lean-to ['li:ntu:] *n* Anbau *m; (shelter)* Wetterschutz *m.*

leap [li:p] *(vb: pret, ptp* **~ed** *or* **leapt***)* **1** *n* Sprung *m.* **in one ~** mit einem Satz; **a great ~ forward** *(fig)* ein großer Sprung nach vorn; **a ~ in the dark** *(fig)* ein Sprung ins Ungewisse; **by ~s and bounds** *(fig)* sprunghaft. **2** *vt* springen über *(+acc)*. **3** *vi* springen. **to ~ to one's feet** aufspringen; **my heart leapt** mein Herz machte einen Sprung.

♦ **leap at** *vi +prep obj offer, opportunity* sich stürzen auf *(+acc)*.

♦ **leap up** *vi (person)* aufspringen; *(flames)* hochschlagen; *(prices)* sprunghaft ansteigen.

leapfrog ['li:pfrɒg] **1** *n* Bockspringen *nt.* **2** *vi* **he ~ged over him** er machte einen Bocksprung über ihn.

leap year *n* Schaltjahr *nt.*

leapt [lept] *pret, ptp of* **leap.**

learn [lɜ:n] *pret, ptp* **~ed** *or* **learnt 1** *vt* lernen; *language also* erlernen; *(be informed)* erfahren. **I ~t (how) to swim** ich habe schwimmen gelernt; **we ~t (how) to write business letters** wir lernten Geschäftsbriefe schreiben. **2** *vi* lernen; *(find out)* erfahren *(about, of* von*)*. **I can't, but I'm hoping to ~** ich kann es nicht, aber ich hoffe, es zu lernen; **he'll never ~!** er lernt es nie!; **to ~ from experience** durch Erfahrung lernen.

learned ['lɜ:nɪd] *adj* gelehrt; *society also, profession* akademisch. **a ~ man** ein Gelehrter *m.*

learner ['lɜ:nəʳ] *n* Anfänger(in *f*) *m; (Brit: ~ driver)* Fahrschüler(in *f*) *m.* **slow ~s** lernschwache Schüler.

learning ['lɜ:nɪŋ] *n (act)* Lernen *nt; (erudition)* Gelehrsamkeit *f.* **a man of ~** ein Gelehrter *m.*

learnt [lɜ:nt] *pret, ptp of* **learn.**

lease [li:s] **1** *n (of land, business premises etc)* Pacht *f; (contract)* Pachtvertrag *m; (of house, office)* Miete *f; (contract)* Mietvertrag *m.* **to take a ~ on a house** ein Haus mieten; **to let sth out on ~** etw verpachten/vermieten; **to give sb a new ~ of life** jdm (neuen) Aufschwung geben. **2** *vt (take) (from* von*)* pachten; mieten; *(give: also* **~ out***) (to* an *+acc)* verpachten; vermieten.

lease: ~hold 1 *n (property)* Pachtbesitz *m*; **2** *adj* gepachtet; *property* Pacht-; **~holder** *n* Pächter *m.*

leash [li:ʃ] *n* Leine *f.* **on a ~** an der Leine.

least [li:st] **1** *adj* geringste(r, s). **2** *adv* am wenigsten; **~ possible expenditure** möglichst geringe Kosten; **the ~ expensive car** das billigste Auto; **he's the ~ aggressive of men** er ist nicht im mindesten aggressiv; **not the ~ bit drunk** kein bißchen betrunken. **3** *n* **the ~** der/die/das Geringste; **it's the ~ one can do** es ist das wenigste, was man tun kann; **at ~ it's not raining** wenigstens regnet es nicht; **there were eight at ~** es waren mindestens acht da; **we need three at the very ~** allermindestens brauchen wir drei; **not in the ~ (upset)** nicht im geringsten (verärgert); **to say the ~** um es milde zu sagen; **the ~ said, the better** *(Prov)* je weniger man darüber spricht, desto besser.

leather ['leðəʳ] **1** *n* Leder *nt.* **2** *adj* Leder-, ledern.

leave [li:v] *(vb: pret, ptp* **left***)* **1** *n* **(a)** *(permission)* Erlaubnis *f.* **to ask sb's ~ to do sth** jdn um Erlaubnis bitten, etw zu tun. **(b)** *(permission to be absent, Mil)* Urlaub *m.* **to be on ~** auf Urlaub sein; **to be on ~ of absence** beurlaubt sein. **(c) to take one's ~** sich verabschieden *(of sb* von jdm*)*; **to take ~ of one's senses** den Verstand verlieren.

2 *vt* **(a)** *(depart from, quit) place, person* verlassen. **the train left the station** der Zug fuhr aus dem Bahnhof; **when he left Rome** als er von Rom wegging/wegfuhr *etc;* **to ~ home** von zu Hause weggehen; **to ~ one's job** seine Stelle aufgeben; **to ~ the road** *(crash)* von der Straße abkommen; **I'll ~ you at the station** *(in car)* ich setze dich am Bahnhof ab.

(b) *(allow or cause to remain)* lassen; *mark, message, scar* hinterlassen; *meal* stehenlassen. **who left the window open?** wer hat das Fenster offengelassen?; **this ~s me free for the afternoon** dadurch habe ich den Nachmittag frei; **~ me alone!** laß mich (in Ruhe)!; **to ~ well alone** die Finger davonlassen *(col)*; **to ~ sb to himself** jdn allein lassen; **to ~ go of** loslassen; **let's ~ it at that** lassen wir es dabei (bewenden); **I was left with the bill** ich saß mit der Rechnung da.

(c) *(forget)* liegenlassen, stehenlassen.

(d) to be left *(remain, be over)* übrigbleiben; **all I have left** alles, was ich noch habe; **3 from 10 ~s 7** 10 minus 3 (ist) gleich 7; **nothing was left for me but to sell it** mir blieb nichts anderes übrig, als es zu verkaufen.

(e) *(entrust)* überlassen *(up to sb* jdm*)*. **~ it to me** laß mich nur machen!; **I ~ it to you** das überlasse ich Ihnen; **to ~ sth to chance** etw dem Zufall überlassen.

(f) *(after death) money, person* hinterlassen.

3 *vi* (weg)gehen, abfahren; *(plane)* abfliegen. **we ~ for Sweden tomorrow** wir fahren morgen nach Schweden.

♦ **leave behind** *vt sep car, children* dalassen; *(outstrip)* hinter sich *(dat)* lassen; *(forget)* liegenlassen, stehenlassen. **we've left all that ~ us** das alles liegt hinter uns.

♦ **leave in** *vt sep scene in play etc* darinlassen.

♦ **leave off 1** *vt sep clothes* nicht anziehen; *lid* nicht darauftun; *lights* auslassen. **you left her name ~ the list** Sie haben ihren Namen nicht in die Liste aufgenommen. **2** *vi +prep obj (col)* aufhören. **we left ~ work after lunch** wir haben nach dem Mittagessen Feierabend gemacht; **~ ~ (doing that)!** hör auf (damit)!

♦ **leave on** *vt sep clothes, lights* anlassen.

♦ **leave out** *vt sep* **(a)** *(not bring in)* draußen lassen. **(b)** *(omit)* auslassen; *(exclude) people* ausschließen *(of* von*)*. **you ~ my wife ~ of this** lassen Sie meine Frau aus dem Spiel! **(c)** *(leave available)* dalassen; *(not put away)* liegen lassen. **I'll ~ the books ~ on my desk** ich lasse die Bücher auf meinem Schreibtisch.

♦ **leave over** *vt sep (leave surplus)* übriglassen. **to be left ~** übrig(geblieben) sein.

leaves [li:vz] *pl of* **leaf.**

Lebanon ['lebənən] *n* **the ~** der Libanon.

lecherous ['letʃərəs] *adj* lüstern; *man also* geil.

lecture ['lektʃəʳ] **1** *n* **(a)** Vortrag *m; (Univ)* Vorlesung *f.* **to give a ~** einen Vortrag/eine Vorlesung halten *(to* für, *on sth* über etw *acc)*. **(b)** *(scolding)* **to give sb a ~** jdm eine Strafpredigt halten *(about* wegen*)*. **2** *vt* **(a) to ~ sb on sth** jdm einen Vortrag/eine Vorlesung über etw *(acc)* halten; **he ~s us in physics** wir hören bei ihm (Vorlesungen in) Physik. **(b)** *(scold)* abkanzeln.

3 *vi* einen Vortrag halten; *(Univ)* eine Vorlesung halten; *(give ~ course)* Vorlesungen halten *(on* über *+acc).* **he ~s in English** er ist Dozent für Anglistik.

lecture: ~ hall *n (Univ)* Hörsaal *nt;* **~ notes** *npl (professor's)* Manuskript *nt; (student's)* Aufzeichnungen *pl.*

lecturer ['lektʃərəʳ] *n (Univ)* Dozent(in *f*) *m; (speaker)* Referent(in *f*) *m.*

led [led] *pret, ptp of* **lead**².

ledge [ledʒ] *n* Leiste, Kante *f; (of window) (inside)* Fensterbrett *nt; (outside)* Sims *nt or m; (shelf)* Ablage *f; (mountain ~)* (Fels)vorsprung *m.*

ledger ['ledʒəʳ] *n* Hauptbuch *nt.*

lee [liː] **1** *adj* Lee-. **2** *n* **(a)** *(Naut)* Lee *f.* **(b)** *(shelter)* Windschatten *m.*

leech [liːtʃ] *n* Blutegel *m; (fig)* Blutsauger *m.*

leek [liːk] *n* Porree, Lauch *m.*

leer [lɪəʳ] **1** *n (knowing, sexual)* anzügliches Grinsen; *(evil)* heimtückischer Blick. **2** *vi* anzüglich grinsen; einen heimtückischen Blick haben. **he ~ed at her** er warf ihr lüsterne Blicke zu.

leeward ['liːwəd] **1** *adj* Lee-. **2** *n* Lee(seite) *f.* **to ~** leewärts.

leeway ['liːweɪ] *n* **(a)** *(Naut)* Leeweg *m.* **(b)** *(fig) (flexibility)* Spielraum *m.* **to make up ~** den Zeitverlust aufholen.

left¹ [left] *pret, ptp of* **leave.**

left² **1** *adj (also Pol)* linke(r, s). **2** *adv* links *(of* von*).* **turn ~** *(Aut)* links abbiegen; **keep ~** links halten. **3** *n* **(a)** Linke(r, s). **on the ~** links *(of* von*);* **on my ~** links von mir. **(b)** *(Pol)* Linke *f.* **to be on the ~** links stehen.

left: ~-hand *adj* **~-hand drive** Linkssteuerung *f;* **~-hand side** linke Seite; **on his ~-hand side** zu seiner Linken; **~-handed** *adj* linkshändig; *tool* für Linkshänder.

leftie ['leftɪ] *n (pej)* Rote(r) *mf (pej col).*

leftist ['leftɪst] **1** *adj* linke(r, s), linksgerichtet. **2** *n* Linke(r) *mf.*

left: ~-luggage (office) *n (Brit)* Gepäckaufbewahrung *f;* **~-luggage locker** *n* Gepäckschließfach *nt;* **~-overs** *n* (Über)reste *pl;* **~-wing 1** *adj (Pol)* linke(r, s); **2** *n* **~ wing** linker Flügel *(also Sport).*

leg [leg] **1** *n* Bein *nt; (of bed also)* Fuß *m; (Cook)* Keule, Hachse *f.* **to pull sb's ~** jdn auf den Arm nehmen; **to be on one's last ~s** in den letzten Zügen liegen *(col); (person)* auf dem letzten Loch pfeifen *(col);* **he hasn't a ~ to stand on** *(fig) (no excuse)* er kann sich nicht herausreden; *(no proof)* das kann er nicht belegen. **2** *vt:* **to ~ it** *(col)* laufen.

legacy ['legəsɪ] *n (lit, fig)* Vermächtnis *nt; (fig also)* Erbe *nt; (fig pej)* Hinterlassenschaft *f.*

legal ['liːgl] *adj* **(a)** *(lawful)* legal; *claim* Rechts-; *(according to the law) tender, limit* gesetzlich; *(allowed by law) speed* zulässig; *will, purchase* rechtsgültig. **to become ~** rechtskräftig werden; **the ~ age for marriage** das gesetzliche Heiratsalter; **to have ~ status** rechtsfähig sein; *(document)* Rechtskraft haben. **(b)** *(relating to the law) matters* juristisch, Rechts-; *advice, mind* juristisch; *fees, decision* Gerichts-; *act, adviser* Rechts-; *inquiry* gerichtlich. **to take ~ action against sb** gegen jdn Klage erheben; **~ aid** Rechtshilfe *f;* **to take ~ advice** juristischen Rat einholen; **the ~ profession** die Juristenschaft.

legality [liː'gælɪtɪ] *n* Legalität *f; (of claim)* Rechtmäßigkeit *f; (of will, marriage, purchase)* Rechtsgültigkeit *f.*

legalize ['liːgəlaɪz] *vt* legalisieren.

legally ['liːgəlɪ] *adv (lawfully) transacted* legal; *married* rechtmäßig; *guaranteed* gesetzlich; *indefensible* rechtlich. **~ binding** rechtsverbindlich; **~ valid** rechtsgültig.

legation [lɪ'geɪʃən] *n (diplomats)* Gesandtschaft *f; (building)* Gesandtschaftsgebäude *nt.*

legend ['ledʒənd] *n* **(a)** Legende *f; (fictitious)* Sage *f.* **(b)** *(inscription, caption)* Legende *f.*

legendary ['ledʒəndərɪ] *adj* **(a)** legendär. **(b)** *(famous)* berühmt.

-legged [-'legd, -'legɪd] *adj suf* -beinig. **bare-~** ohne Strümpfe.

leggy ['legɪ] *adj (+er)* langbeinig; *(gawky)* staksig.

legible ['ledʒɪbl] *adj* lesbar; *writing also* leserlich.

legion ['liːdʒən] *n* Legion *f.*

legislate ['ledʒɪsleɪt] *vi* Gesetze/ein Gesetz erlassen. **to ~ for sth** *(fig)* etw berücksichtigen.

legislation [ˌledʒɪs'leɪʃən] *n (making laws)* Gesetzgebung; *(laws)* Gesetze *pl.*

legislative ['ledʒɪslətɪv] *adj* gesetzgebend. **~ reforms** Gesetzesreformen *pl.*

legislator ['ledʒɪsleɪtəʳ] *n* Gesetzgeber *m.*

legislature ['ledʒɪsleɪtʃəʳ] *n* Legislative *f.*

legitimate [lɪ'dʒɪtɪmət] *adj (lawful)* rechtmäßig, legitim; *(born in wedlock)* ehelich; *(reasonable)* berechtigt; *excuse* begründet.

legitimize [lɪ'dʒɪtɪmaɪz] *vt* legitimieren; *children* für ehelich erklären.

leg-room ['legˌruːm] *n* Platz *m* für die Beine.

leisure ['leʒəʳ] *n* Freizeit *f.* **to lead a life of ~** sich dem (süßen) Nichtstun ergeben; **do it at your ~** *(in own time)* tun Sie es, wenn Sie Zeit dazu haben; *(at own speed)* lassen Sie sich *(dat)* Zeit damit.

leisure: ~ activities *npl* Freizeitbeschäftigungen *pl;* **~ hours** Freizeit *f.*

leisurely ['leʒəlɪ] *adj* geruhsam. **at a ~ pace** gemächlich.

leisure: ~ time *n* Freizeit *f;* **~ wear** *n* Freizeitbekleidung *f.*

lemon ['lemən] *n* **(a)** Zitrone *f; (colour)* Zitronengelb *nt.* **(b)** *(col: fool)* Dussel *m (col).*

lemonade [ˌlemə'neɪd] *n* Limonade *f.*

lemon: ~ curd *n zähflüssiger Brotaufstrich mit Zitronengeschmack;* **~ tea** *n* Zitronentee *m.*

lend [lend] *pret, ptp* **lent 1** *vt (loan)* leihen *(to sb* jdm*); (banks) money* verleihen *(to* an *+acc).* **to ~ a hand** helfen; **it ~s it a certain credibility** das verleiht ihm eine gewisse Glaubwürdigkeit. **2** *vr* **to ~ oneself to sth** *(be suitable)* sich für etw eignen.

length [leŋθ] *n* **(a)** Länge *f; (section) (of cloth, pipe)* Stück *nt; (of pool, wallpaper)* Bahn *f.* **to be 4 metres in ~** 4 Meter lang sein; **what ~ is it?** wie lang ist es?; **of some ~** ziemlich lang; **along the whole ~ of the river** den ganzen Fluß entlang; **over all the ~ and breadth of England** in ganz England; *(travelling)* kreuz und quer durch ganz England; **at full ~** in voller Länge; **to win by half a ~** mit einer halben Länge siegen. **(b)** *(of time)* Dauer *f; (great ~)* lange Dauer. **of some ~** ziemlich lange; **at ~** *(finally)* schließlich; *(for a long time)* lange, ausführlich. **(c) to go to great ~s** sich *(dat)* sehr viel Mühe geben; **to go to the ~ of ...** so weit gehen, daß ...

lengthen ['leŋθən] **1** *vt* verlängern; *clothes* länger machen. **2** *vi* länger werden.

lengthways ['leŋθweɪz], **lengthwise** ['leŋθwaɪz] *adv* der Länge nach.

lengthy ['leŋθɪ] *adj (+er)* lange; *(dragging on)* langwierig; *speech also* langatmig *(pej).*

lenience ['liːnɪəns], **leniency** ['liːnɪənsɪ] *n see adj* Nachsicht *f;* Milde *f.*

lenient ['liːnɪənt] *adj* nachsichtig *(towards* gegenüber*); judge* milde.

lens [lenz] *n (Opt)* Linse *f; (in spectacles)* Glas *nt; (camera part)* Objektiv *nt.*

lent [lent] *pret, ptp of* **lend.**

Lent [lent] *n* Fastenzeit *f.*

lentil ['lentl] *n* Linse *f.*

Leo ['liːəʊ] *n (Astrol)* Löwe *m.*

leopard ['lepəd] *n* Leopard *m.*

leotard ['liːətɑːd] *n* Trikot *nt; (gymnastics)* Gymnastikanzug *m.*

leper ['lepəʳ] *n* Leprakranke(r) *mf.*
leprosy ['leprəsɪ] *n* Lepra *f.*
lesbian ['lezbɪən] **1** *adj* lesbisch. **2** *n* Lesbierin *f.*
lesion ['li:ʒən] *n* Verletzung *f.*
less [les] **1** *adj, adv, n* weniger. **the minister, no ~** kein Geringerer als der Minister; **~ and ~** immer weniger; **she saw him ~ and ~ (often)** sie sah ihn immer seltener; **it's nothing ~ than disgraceful** es ist wirklich eine Schande; **~ quickly** nicht so schnell; **even ~** noch weniger; **none the ~** trotzdem; **the ~ said the better** je weniger man darüber spricht, desto besser; **can't you let me have it for ~?** können Sie es mir nicht etwas billiger geben? **2** *prep* weniger; *(Comm)* abzüglich. **6 ~ 4 is 2** 6 weniger 4 ist 2.
lessee [le'si:] *n* Pächter *m; (of house, flat)* Mieter *m.*
lessen ['lesn] **1** *vt (make less)* verringern; *cost* senken; *effect* abschwächen; *(make less important etc)* herabsetzen. **2** *vi* nachlassen; *(value of money)* abnehmen.
lessening ['lesnɪŋ] *n* Nachlassen *nt (in sth +gen).*
lesser ['lesəʳ] *adj* geringer; *(in names)* klein. **to a ~ extent** in geringerem Maße.
lesson ['lesn] *n (Sch etc)* Stunde *f; (unit of study)* Lektion *f; (fig)* Lehre *f.* **~s** Unterricht *m;* **a French ~** eine Französischstunde; **to give a ~** eine Stunde geben; **to be a ~ to sb** jdm eine Lehre sein; **to teach sb a ~** jdm eine Lektion erteilen.
lessor [le'sɔ:ʳ] *n (form)* Verpächter *m; (of flat etc)* Vermieter *m.*
lest [lest] *conj (form) (for fear that)* aus Furcht, daß; *(in order that ... not)* damit ... nicht; *(in case)* für den Fall, daß. **~ we forget** damit wir nicht vergessen; **I was frightened ~ he should fall** ich hatte Angst, daß er fallen könnte.
let [let] *pret, ptp* ~ *vt* **(a)** *(permit)* lassen. **to ~ sb do sth** jdn etw tun lassen; **~ me help you** kann ich Ihnen behilflich sein?; **~ me know what you think** sagen Sie mir, was Sie davon halten; **to ~ sb be** jdn (in Ruhe) lassen; **to ~ sb/sth go, to ~ go of sb/sth** jdn/etw loslassen; **to ~ oneself go** *(neglect oneself)* sich gehenlassen; *(relax)* aus sich herausgehen; **we'll ~ it pass** *or* **go this once** *(disregard)* wir wollen es einmal durchgehen lassen; **to ~ sb/sth alone** jdn/etw in Ruhe lassen; **we'd better ~ well alone** wir lassen besser die Finger davon; **~ alone ...** *(much less)* geschweige denn ...; **to ~ sb through** jdn durchlassen.
(b) ~'s go! gehen wir!; **~ him try (it)!** das soll er nur versuchen!; **~ me think** *or* **see, where did I put it?** warte mal, wo habe ich das nur hingetan? **~ X be 60** X sei 60.
(c) *(esp Brit: hire out)* vermieten. **"to ~"** „zu vermieten".
♦ **let down** *vt sep* **(a)** *(lower) rope, person* hinunter-/herunterlassen; *seat* herunterklappen; *hair, window* herunterlassen; *(lengthen) dress* länger machen. **(b) to ~ sb** *(fail to help)* jdn im Stich lassen *(over* mit*)*; **to feel ~ ~** enttäuscht sein; **to ~ the school/oneself ~** die Schule/sich blamieren.
♦ **let in 1** *vt sep* **(a)** *water* durchlassen. **(b)** *(admit) air, visitor* hereinlassen. **just ~ yourself ~** geh einfach hinein; **I was just ~ting myself ~** ich schloß gerade die Tür auf. **(c)** *(involve in)* **to ~ oneself ~ for sth** sich auf etw *(acc)* einlassen; **to ~ oneself/sb ~ for trouble** sich/jdm Ärger einhandeln. **(d)** *(allow to know)* **she ~ me ~ on the secret** sie hat es mir verraten. **2** *vi (shoes, tent)* undicht sein.
♦ **let off 1** *vt sep* **(a)** *arrow* abschießen; *gun* abfeuern; *firework, bomb* hochgehen lassen; *(emit) vapour* von sich geben; *gases* absondern. **(b)** *(forgive)* **to ~ sb ~** jdm etw durchgehen lassen; **to ~ sb ~ with a warning** jdn mit einer Verwarnung davonkommen lassen; **to be ~ ~ lightly** glimpflich davonkommen. **(c)** *(allow to go)* gehen lassen. **2** *vi (col: fart)* einen fahren lassen *(col).*
♦ **let on** *vi* **(a)** *also vt* **don't ~ ~ you know** *(col)* laß dir bloß nicht anmerken, daß du das weißt. **(b)** *(pretend)* **to ~ ~ that ...** vorgeben, daß ...
♦ **let out** *vt sep* **(a)** *(allow to go out)* hinaus-/herauslassen; *(from car)* absetzen; *(divulge) news* bekanntgeben; *secret* verraten, ausplaudern *(col)*; *fire* ausgehen lassen. **I'll ~ myself ~** ich finde alleine hinaus; **to ~ ~ a laugh/groan** auflachen/(auf)stöhnen. **(b)** *(make larger) dress* auslassen. **(c)** *(free from responsibility)* **that ~s me ~ (of it)** da komme ich (schon mal) nicht in Frage. **(d)** *(Brit: rent)* vermieten.
♦ **let up** *vi (cease)* aufhören; *(ease up)* nachlassen. **he never ~s ~ about money** er redet unaufhörlich von Geld.
let-down ['letdaʊn] *n (col: disappointment)* Enttäuschung *f.*
lethal ['li:θəl] *adj* tödlich.
lethargic [lɪ'θɑ:dʒɪk] *adj person* träge, lethargisch; *(uninterested)* teilnahmslos.
let's [lets] = **let us.**
letter ['letəʳ] **1** *n* **(a)** *(of alphabet)* Buchstabe *m.* **the ~ of the law** der Buchstabe des Gesetzes; **to the ~** sehr genau; *(as given)* ganz nach Vorschrift. **(b)** *(written message)* Brief *m; (Comm etc)* Schreiben *nt (to* an *+acc).* **by ~** schriftlich; **~ of credit** Akkreditiv *nt.* **(c)** *(Liter)* **~s** Literatur *f;* **man of ~s** Belletrist *m; (writer)* Literat *m.*
letter: ~ bomb *n* Briefbombe *f;* **~ box** *n* Briefkasten *m.*
letterhead ['letəhed] *n* Briefkopf *m; (writing paper)* Geschäftspapier *nt.*
lettering ['letərɪŋ] *n* Beschriftung f.
letterpress ['letəpres] *n* Hochdruck *m.*
lettuce ['letɪs] *n* Kopfsalat *m.*
let-up ['letʌp] *n (col)* Pause *f; (easing up)* Nachlassen *nt.* **if there is a ~ in the rain** wenn der Regen nachläßt.
leukaemia, leukemia [lu:'ki:mɪə] *n* Leukämie *f.*
level ['levl] **1** *adj* **(a)** *(flat) surface* eben; *spoonful* gestrichen; *(at the same height)* auf gleicher Höhe *(with* mit*)*; *(fig)* gleich gut. **the two runners are dead ~** die beiden Läufer sind genau auf gleicher Höhe. **(b)** *(steady) tone of voice* ruhig; *(well-balanced)* ausgeglichen; *judgement* abgewogen; *head* kühl. **(c) I'll do my ~ best** ich werde mein möglichstes tun.
2 *adv* **~ with** in Höhe *(+gen)*; **the pipe runs ~ with the ground** *(parallel)* das Rohr verläuft parallel zum Boden; **they're running absolutely ~** sie laufen auf genau gleicher Höhe; **to draw ~ with sb** mit jdm gleichziehen.
3 *n* **(a)** *(instrument)* Wasserwaage *f.*
(b) *(altitude)* Höhe *f; (standard)* Niveau *nt.* **on a ~ (with)** auf gleicher Höhe (mit); **at eye ~** in Augenhöhe; **to be on a ~ with** auf gleichem Niveau sein wie; **a high ~ of hydrogen** ein hoher Wasserstoffanteil; **the ~ of alcohol in the blood** der Alkoholgehalt im Blut; **a high ~ of intelligence** ein hoher Intelligenzgrad; **the very high ~ of production** das hohe Produktionsniveau; **a high ~ of civilization** eine hohe Kulturstufe; **the talks were held at a very high ~** die Gespräche fanden auf hoher Ebene statt; **at ministerial ~** auf Ministerebene; **a high-~ meeting** ein Spitzentreffen; **on the moral ~** moralisch gesehen; **on a purely personal ~** auf rein persönlicher Ebene.
(c) *(col: straightforward, honest)* **it's on the ~** *(business)* es ist reell; **to be on the ~ (with sb)** (jdm gegenüber) ehrlich sein.
4 *vt* **(a)** *ground etc* einebnen; *building* abreißen; *town* dem Erdboden gleichmachen. **(b)** *blow* versetzen *(at sb* jdm*)*; *weapon* richten *(at* auf *+acc)*; *accusation* erheben *(at* gegen*)*; *remark* richten *(at* gegen*).*

5 *vi* **to ~ with sb** *(col)* jdm keinen Quatsch erzählen *(col)*.

♦ **level out 1** *vi (also* **~ off***) (ground)* eben werden; *(fig)* sich ausgleichen. **2** *vt sep site* planieren, einebnen; *(fig) differences* ausgleichen.

level: ~ crossing *n (Brit)* (beschrankter) Bahnübergang; **~-headed** *adj person* ausgeglichen; *reply, decision* ausgewogen, überlegt.

lever ['li:və[r], *(US)* 'levə[r]] **1** *n* Hebel *m; (crowbar)* Brechstange *f; (fig)* Druckmittel *nt*. **2** *vt* (hoch)stemmen. **he ~ed the box open** er stemmte die Kiste auf.

leverage ['li:vərɪdʒ] *n* Hebelkraft *f; (fig)* Einfluß *m*. **to use sth as ~** *(fig)* etw als Druckmittel benutzen.

levity ['levɪtɪ] *n* Leichtfertigkeit *f*.

levy ['levɪ] **1** *n (act)* (Steuer)einziehung *f; (tax)* Abgaben *pl*. **2** *vt tax* einziehen; *fine* auferlegen *(on sb* jdm*)*; *army* ausheben.

lewd [lu:d] *adj (+er)* unanständig; *(lustful)* lüstern; *remark* anzüglich; *imagination* schmutzig.

liability [ˌlaɪə'bɪlɪtɪ] *n* **(a)** *(burden)* Belastung *f; (proneness)* Anfälligkeit *f (to* für*)*; *(responsibility)* Haftung *f*. **~ for tax** Steuerpflicht *f*; **we accept no ~ for ...** wir übernehmen keine Haftung für ... **(b)** *(Fin)* **liabilities** Verbindlichkeiten *pl*.

liable ['laɪəbl] *adj* **(a)** *(subject to)* **to be ~** unterliegen *(for sth* einer Sache *dat)*; **to be ~ for tax** *(things)* besteuert werden; *(person)* steuerpflichtig sein. **(b)** *(to illness)* anfällig *(to* für *+acc)*. **(c)** *(responsible)* **to be ~** haften *(for* für *+acc)*. **(d)** *(likely to)* **we are ~ to get wet here** wir können hier leicht naß werden; **is he ~ to come?** ist es wahrscheinlich, daß er kommt?; **he's ~ to tell the police** es wäre ihm zuzutrauen, daß er es der Polizei meldet; **the computer is still ~ to make mistakes** der Computer kann durchaus noch Fehler machen.

liaise [li:'eɪz] *vi* als Verbindungsmann auftreten.

liaison [li:'eɪzɒn] *n (coordination)* Zusammenarbeit *f; (person)* Verbindungsmann *m*.

liaison officer *n* Verbindungsmann *m*.

liar ['laɪə[r]] *n* Lügner(in *f*) *m*.

libel ['laɪbəl] **1** *n* (schriftlich geäußerte) Verleumdung *(on gen)*. **2** *vt* verleumden.

libellous, *(US)* **libelous** ['laɪbələs] *adj* verleumderisch.

liberal ['lɪbərəl] **1** *adj* **(a)** *(generous) offer* großzügig; *helping of food* reichlich. **(b)** *(broad-minded, also Pol)* liberal. **2** *n (Pol:* **L~***)* Liberale(r) *mf*.

liberalism ['lɪbərəlɪzəm] *n* Liberalität *f; (Pol:* **L~***)* der Liberalismus.

liberality [ˌlɪbə'rælɪtɪ] *n (generosity)* Großzügigkeit *f*.

liberalize ['lɪbərəlaɪz] *vt* liberalisieren.

liberally ['lɪbərəlɪ] *adv* liberal; *(generously)* großzügig. **apply the paint ~** die Farbe reichlich auftragen.

liberal-minded [ˌlɪbərəl'maɪndɪd] *adj person* liberal (eingestellt); *views* liberal.

liberate ['lɪbəreɪt] *vt (free) prisoner* befreien; *gas etc* freisetzen.

liberation [ˌlɪbə'reɪʃən] *n* Befreiung *f; (of gases)* Freisetzung *f*.

liberator ['lɪbəreɪtə[r]] *n* Befreier *m*.

liberty ['lɪbətɪ] *n* **(a)** Freiheit *f*. **basic liberties** Grundrechte *pl*; **to be at ~** *(criminal etc)* frei herumlaufen; **to be at ~ to do sth** *(be permitted)* etw tun dürfen; **I am not at ~ to comment** es ist mir nicht gestattet, darüber zu sprechen. **(b) I have taken the ~ of giving your name** ich habe mir erlaubt, Ihren Namen anzugeben; **to take liberties with sb** sich jdm gegenüber Freiheiten herausnehmen; **what a ~!** *(col)* so eine Frechheit!

libido [lɪ'bi:dəʊ] *n* Libido *f*.

Libra ['li:brə] *n (Astrol)* Waage *f*.

librarian [laɪ'brɛərɪən] *n* Bibliothekar(in *f*) *m*.

library ['laɪbrərɪ] *n* Bibliothek, Bücherei *f*.

library: ~ book *n* Leihbuch *nt;* **~ ticket** *n* Leserausweis *m*.

libretto [lɪ'bretəʊ] *n* Libretto *nt*.

Libya ['lɪbɪə] *n* Libyen *nt*.

Libyan ['lɪbɪən] **1** *adj* libysch. **2** *n* Libyer(in *f*) *m*.

lice [laɪs] *pl of* **louse.**

licence, *(US)* **license** ['laɪsəns] *n* **(a)** *(permit)* Genehmigung *f; (Comm)* Lizenz *f; (driving ~)* Führerschein *m; (gun ~)* Waffenschein *m; (marriage ~)* Eheerlaubnis *f; (to sell alcohol)* Schankerlaubnis *f*. **you have to have a (television) ~** man muß Fernsehgebühren bezahlen; **to manufacture sth under ~** etw in Lizenz herstellen. **(b)** *(freedom)* Freiheit *f; (excessive freedom)* Zügellosigkeit *f*.

licence: ~ number *n (Aut)* (Kraftfahrzeug)kennzeichen *nt;* **~ plate** *n (Aut)* Nummernschild *nt*.

license ['laɪsəns] **1** *n (US)* = **licence. 2** *vt* eine Lizenz/Konzession vergeben an *(+acc)*. **a car must be ~d every year** die Kfz-Steuer muß jedes Jahr bezahlt werden.

licensed ['laɪsənst] *adj* **~ premises** Lokal *nt* mit Schankerlaubnis.

licensee [ˌlaɪsən'si:] *n (of bar)* Inhaber(in *f*) *m* einer Schankerlaubnis. **postage paid by ~** Gebühr bezahlt Empfänger.

licensing ['laɪsənsɪŋ] *adj* **~ hours** Ausschankzeiten *pl*.

licentious [laɪ'senʃəs] *adj life* ausschweifend; *behaviour* unzüchtig; *person, look* lüstern.

lick [lɪk] **1** *n* **(a)** *(with tongue)* Lecken *nt*. **to give sth a ~** an etw *(dat)* lecken. **(b)** *(col: small quantity)* **it's time we gave the kitchen a ~ of paint** die Küche könnte auch mal wieder etwas Farbe vertragen *(col)*. **(c)** *(col: pace)* **at full ~** mit Volldampf *(col)*. **2** *vt* **(a)** *(with tongue)* lecken; *(flames)* züngeln an *(+dat)*. **he ~ed the stamp** er leckte an der Briefmarke; **to ~ one's lips** sich *(dat)* die Lippen lecken; *(fig)* sich *(dat)* die Finger lecken; **to ~ one's wounds** *(fig)* seine Wunden lecken; **to ~ sb's boots** *(fig)* vor jdm kriechen. **(b)** *(col: defeat)* in die Pfanne hauen *(col)*. **I think we've got it ~ed** ich glaube, wir haben die Sache jetzt im Griff.

licorice *n* = **liquorice.**

lid [lɪd] *n* **(a)** Deckel *m*. **that puts the ~ on it** *(col)* das schlägt dem Faß den Boden aus; **the press took the ~ off the whole plan** die Presse hat den Plan aufgedeckt. **(b)** *(eye~)* Lid *nt*.

lido ['li:dəʊ] *n* Freibad *nt*.

lie[1] [laɪ] **1** *n* Lüge *f*. **to tell a ~** lügen; **to give the ~ to a report** die Unwahrheit eines Berichtes nachweisen; **~ detector** Lügendetektor *m*. **2** *vi* lügen. **to ~ to sb** jdn anlügen. **3** *vt* **to ~ one's way out of sth** sich aus etw herauslügen.

lie[2] *(vb: pret* **lay,** *ptp* **lain***) vi* liegen; *(~ down)* sich legen. **he lay where he had fallen** er blieb liegen, wo er hingefallen war; **~ on your back** leg dich auf den Rücken; **obstacles ~ in the way of our success** unser Weg zum Erfolg ist mit Hindernissen verstellt; **the snow didn't ~** der Schnee blieb nicht liegen; **the runner who is lying third** der Läufer, der auf dem dritten Platz liegt; **it ~s with you to solve the problem** es liegt bei dir, das Problem zu lösen; **that responsibility ~s with your department** dafür ist Ihre Abteilung verantwortlich; **to ~ asleep** schlafen; **to ~ helpless** hilflos daliegen; **to ~ dying** im Sterben liegen; **to ~ resting** ruhen; **the snow lay deep** es lag tiefer Schnee; **the book lay unopened** das Buch lag ungeöffnet da; **to ~ low** untertauchen; **how do things ~?** wie steht die Sache?

♦ **lie about** *or* **around** *vi* herumliegen.

♦ **lie back** *vi* **(a)** *(recline)* sich zurücklehnen. **(b)** *(fig: take no action)* sich ausruhen.

♦ **lie down** *vi* sich hinlegen *(on* auf *+acc)*. **~ ~** *(to*

a dog) leg dich!; **he won't take that lying ~!** das läßt er sich nicht gefallen!
♦ **lie in** *vi (stay in bed)* im Bett bleiben.
♦ **lie up** *vi (hide)* untertauchen. **the robbers are lying ~** die Räuber sind untergetaucht.
lie-down ['laɪdaʊn] *n (col)* Nickerchen *(col) nt.* **to have a ~** ein Nickerchen machen *(col).*
lie-in ['laɪɪn] *n (col)* **to have a ~** (sich) ausschlafen.
lieu [luː] *n* **in ~ of X** anstelle von X.
lieutenant [lef'tenənt, *(US)* luː'tenənt] *n (US)* Leutnant *m; (Brit)* Oberleutnant *m.*
lieutenant: ~-colonel *n* Oberstleutnant *m;* **~-general** *n* Generalleutnant *m.*
life [laɪf] *n, pl* **lives (a)** Leben *nt.* **bird ~** die Vogelwelt; **drawn from ~** lebensnah; **the battle resulted in great loss of ~** bei der Schlacht kamen viele ums Leben; **this is a matter of ~ and death** hier geht es um Leben und Tod; **a ~ and death struggle** ein Kampf auf Leben und Tod; **to come to ~** *(fig)* lebendig werden; **after half an hour the discussion came to ~** nach einer halben Stunde kam Leben in die Diskussion; **to put new ~ into sb** jdm wieder Auftrieb geben; **they swam for dear ~** sie schwammen um ihr Leben; **at my time of ~** in meinem Alter; **he's got a job for ~** er hat eine Stelle auf Lebenszeit; **to take one's ~ in one's hands** mit dem Leben spielen; **the murderer was imprisoned for ~** der Mörder wurde zu lebenslänglicher Freiheitsstrafe verurteilt; **he's doing ~** *(col)* er ist ein Lebenslänglicher *(col)*; **to see ~** *(fig)* die Welt sehen; **there isn't much ~ here in the evenings** hier ist abends nicht viel los; **those children are full of ~!** diese Kinder sind sehr lebhaft!; **he is the ~ and soul of the party** er bringt Leben in die Party.

(b) *(individual life)* **how many lives were lost?** wie viele (Menschen) sind ums Leben gekommen?; **to take sb's ~** jdn umbringen; **to take one's own ~** sich *(dat)* das Leben nehmen; **to save sb's ~** *(lit)* jdm das Leben retten; *(fig)* jdn retten; **early/later in ~** in frühen/späten Jahren; **his ~ won't be worth living!** er wird nichts mehr zu lachen haben!; **all his ~** sein ganzes Leben lang; **I've never been to London in my ~** ich war in meinem ganzen Leben noch nicht in London; **run for your lives!** rennt um euer Leben!; **I can't for the ~ of me ...** *(col)* ich kann beim besten Willen nicht ...; **not on your life!** *(col)* ich bin doch nicht verrückt! *(col).*

(c) *(useful or active life of sth)* Lebensdauer *f.* **during the ~ of the present Parliament** während der Legislaturperiode des gegenwärtigen Parlaments; **there's not much ~ left in the battery** die Batterie macht's nicht mehr lange *(col).*
life: ~ assurance *n (Brit)* Lebensversicherung *f;* **~belt** *n* Rettungsgürtel *m;* **~blood** *n (fig)* Lebensnerv *m;* **~boat** *n* Rettungsboot *nt;* **~buoy** *n* Rettungsring *m;* **~ cycle** *n* Lebenszyklus *m;* **~ expectancy** *n* Lebenserwartung *f;* **~guard** *n (on beach)* Rettungsschwimmer *m;* **~ imprisonment** *n* lebenslängliche Freiheitsstrafe; **~ insurance** *n* Lebensversicherung *f;* **~ jacket** *n* Schwimmweste *f.*
lifeless ['laɪflɪs] *adj* leblos; *planet* ohne Leben; *(fig: dull)* lahm *(col),* langweilig; *hair* schlaff.
life: ~like *adj* lebensecht; *imitation also* naturgetreu; **~line** *n* Rettungsleine *f; (of diver)* Signalleine *f; (fig)* Rettungsanker *m;* **~long** *adj* lebenslang; **they are ~long friends** sie sind schon ihr Leben lang Freunde; **~ raft** *n* Rettungsfloß *nt;* **~saver** *n* **it was a real ~saver!** das hat mich gerettet; **~-size(d)** *adj* in Lebensgröße; **~ support system** *n* Lebenserhaltungssystem *nt;* **~time** *n* **(a)** Lebenszeit *f; (of battery, machine, animal)* Lebensdauer *f;* **once in a ~time** einmal im Leben; **during** *or* **in my ~time** während meines Lebens; **the chance of a ~time** eine einmalige Chance; **the work of a ~time** ein Lebenswerk *nt;* **(b)** *(fig)* Ewigkeit *f.*
lift [lɪft] **1** *n* **(a) give me a ~ with this trunk** hilf mir, den Koffer hochzuheben. **(b)** *(fig: emotional uplift)* **to give sb a ~** jdn aufmuntern. **(c)** *(in car etc)* Mitfahrgelegenheit *f.* **to give sb a ~** *(take along)* jdn mitnehmen; *(as special journey)* jdn fahren; **to get a ~ from sb** von jdm mitgenommen/gefahren werden; **thanks for the ~** danke fürs Mitnehmen. **(d)** *(Brit: elevator)* Aufzug *m.* **(e)** *(Aviat)* Auftrieb *m.* **2** *vt* **(a)** *(also* **~ up)** hochheben; *window* hochschieben; *feet, head* heben; *eyes* aufschlagen; *hat* ziehen. **it's too heavy to ~** es ist zu schwer zum Hochheben. **(b)** *(fig: also* **~ up)** heben; *voice* erheben. **(c)** *(remove) restrictions etc* aufheben. **(d)** *(col: steal)* klauen *(col).* **3** *vi* **(a)** *(mist)* sich lichten. **(b) = ~ up 2.**
♦ **lift down** *vt sep* herunterheben.
♦ **lift off** *vti sep* abheben.
♦ **lift up 1** *vt sep* **= lift 2 (a, b). to ~ ~ one's head** *(fig)* den Kopf hochhalten. **2** *vi* hochgeklappt werden.
lift: ~ attendant *n (Brit)* Fahrstuhlführer *m;* **~-off** *(Space)* Start *m;* **we have ~-off** der Start ist erfolgt; **~shaft** *n* Aufzugsschacht *m.*
ligament ['lɪgəmənt] *n (Anat)* Band *nt.* **he's torn a ~ in his shoulder** er hat einen Bänderriß in der Schulter.
light[1] [laɪt] *(vb: pret, ptp* **lit** *or* **~ ed) 1** *n* **(a)** Licht *nt.* **at first ~** bei Tagesanbruch; **to shed** *or* **throw ~ on sth** *(fig)* Licht in etw *(acc)* bringen; **to cast fresh ~ on sth** neues Licht auf etw *(acc)* werfen; **to stand in sb's ~** *(lit)* jdm im Licht stehen; **in the cold ~ of day** *(fig)* bei Licht besehen; **this story shows him in a bad ~** diese Geschichte wirft ein schlechtes Licht auf ihn; **it revealed him in a different ~** es ließ ihn in einem anderen Licht erscheinen; **to see sth in a new ~** etw mit anderen Augen betrachten; **in the ~ of** angesichts *(+gen)*; **to bring to ~** ans Tageslicht bringen; **to come to ~** ans Tageslicht kommen; **finally I saw the ~** *(col)* endlich ging mir ein Licht auf *(col)*; *(morally)* endlich wurden mir die Augen geöffnet; **according to his ~s** nach bestem Wissen und Gewissen.

(b) *(single ~)* Licht *nt; (lamp)* Lampe *f; (fluorescent ~)* Neonröhre *f.* **to switch the ~ on/off** das Licht anschalten/ausschalten; **(traffic) ~s** Ampel *f;* **the ~s** *(of a car)* die Beleuchtung.

(c) *(flame)* **have you a ~?** haben Sie Feuer?; **to set ~ to sth** etw anzünden.

2 *adj (+er)* hell. **a ~ green dress** ein hellgrünes Kleid; **it is ~ now** es ist jetzt hell *or* Tag.

3 *vt* **(a)** *(illuminate)* beleuchten; *lamp, light* anmachen. **to ~ the way for sb** jdm leuchten; *(fig)* jdm den Weg weisen. **(b)** *(set fire to)* anzünden; *fire also* anmachen.

4 *vi (begin to burn)* brennen.
♦ **light up 1** *vi* **(a)** *(be lit)* aufleuchten. **(b)** *(face)* sich erhellen; *(eyes)* aufleuchten. **2** *vt sep* **(a)** *(illuminate)* beleuchten; *(from inside also)* erhellen. **George Square was all lit ~** der Georgsplatz war hell erleuchtet. **(b)** *cigarette etc* anzünden.
light[2] **1** *adj (+er)* leicht; *taxes* niedrig; *punishment* milde. **to be a ~ eater** kein großer Esser sein; **~ comedy** Lustspiel *nt;* **~ opera** Operette *f;* **~ reading** Unterhaltungslektüre *f;* **as ~ as a feather** federleicht; **to be ~ on one's feet** sich leichtfüßig bewegen; **to make ~ of one's difficulties** seine Schwierigkeiten auf die leichte Schulter nehmen; **to make ~ work of** spielend fertigwerden mit. **2** *adv* **to travel ~** mit leichtem Gepäck reisen.
light: ~ bulb *n* Glühbirne *f;* **~-coloured** *(Brit) or* **~-colored** *(US) adj* hell.

lighten[1] ['laɪtn] **1** *vt* erhellen; *colour, hair* aufhellen; *gloom* aufheitern. **2** *vi* sich aufhellen.
lighten[2] **1** *vt load, (fig) heart* leichter machen. **to ~ sb's burden** jds Lage erleichtern. **2** *vi (load)* leichter werden. **her heart ~ed** ihr wurde leichter ums Herz.
lighter ['laɪtəʳ] *n (cigarette ~)* Feuerzeug *nt.*
light: ~-fingered [ˌlaɪt'fɪŋgəd] *adj* langfingerig; **~ fitting** *n (~bulb holder)* Fassung *f;* **~-haired** *adj* hellhaarig; **~-headed** *adj* benebelt *(col); (dizzy also)* benommen; *(frivolous)* leichtfertig; **~-hearted** *adj* unbeschwert; *chat* zwanglos; *reply* scherzhaft; *book* vergnüglich; **~house** *n* Leuchtturm *m.*
lighting ['laɪtɪŋ] *n* Beleuchtung *f.*
lighting-up time [ˌlaɪtɪŋ'ʌptaɪm] *n (Brit) Zeitpunkt m, zu dem Straßen- und Fahrzeugbeleuchtung eingeschaltet werden muß.* **when is ~?** wann wird die Beleuchtung angemacht?
lightly ['laɪtlɪ] *adv* **(a)** *touch, rain, wounded* leicht; *tread* leise. **to sleep ~** einen leichten Schlaf haben; **to get off ~** glimpflich davonkommen. **(b)** *(casually) say* leichthin. **he spoke ~ of his illness** er nahm seine Krankheit auf die leichte Schulter; **to treat sth too ~** etw nicht ernst genug nehmen; **a responsibility not to be ~ undertaken** eine Verantwortung, die man nicht unüberlegt auf sich nehmen sollte.
light meter *n* Belichtungsmesser *m.*
lightness[1] ['laɪtnɪs] *n* Helligkeit *f.*
lightness[2] *n* **(a)** geringes Gewicht; *(of task, step)* Leichtigkeit *f; (of punishment)* Milde *f; (of soil, cake)* Lockerheit *f.* **(b)** *(lack of seriousness)* Leichtfertigkeit *f.*
lightning ['laɪtnɪŋ] **1** *n* Blitz *m.* **as quick as ~, like (greased) ~** wie der Blitz, wie ein geölter Blitz; **~ conductor** *or (US)* **rod** Blitzableiter *m.* **2** *attr* blitzschnell, Blitz-. **~ attack** Blitzangriff *m;* **~ strike** spontaner Streik.
light: ~weight 1 *adj* leicht; *(boxer)* Leichtgewichts-; *(fig)* schwach; **2** *n* Leichtgewicht *nt (also fig); (boxer)* Leichtgewichtler *m;* **~-year** *n* Lichtjahr *nt.*
like[1] [laɪk] **1** *adj* **(a)** *(similar)* ähnlich. **(b)** *(same)* **of ~ origin** gleicher Herkunft.
2 *prep (similar to)* ähnlich *(+dat); (in comparisons)* wie. **to be ~ sb** jdm ähnlich sein; **they are very ~ each other** sie sind sich sehr ähnlich; **who(m) is he ~?** wem sieht er ähnlich?; **what's he ~?** wie ist er?; **what's your new coat ~?** wie sieht dein neuer Mantel aus?; **she was ~ a sister to me** sie war wie eine Schwester zu mir; **that's just ~ him!** das sieht ihm ähnlich!; **it's not ~ him** es ist nicht seine Art; **I never saw anything ~ it** so (et)was habe ich noch nie gesehen; **that's more ~ it!** so ist es schon besser!; **there's nothing ~ a nice cup of tea!** es geht nichts über eine gute Tasse Tee!; **the Americans are ~ that** so sind die Amerikaner; **do it ~ this** mach es so; **people ~ that** solche Leute; **it will cost something ~ £10** es wird so ungefähr £ 10 kosten; **that sounds ~ a good idea** das hört sich gut an; **~ mad** *(col),* **~ anything** *(col)* wie verrückt *(col);* **he thinks ~ us** er denkt wie wir.
3 *adv (col)* **it's nothing ~ it** das ist nicht zu vergleichen; **as ~ as not** höchstwahrscheinlich.
4 *conj (strictly incorrect)* **~ I said** wie gesagt.
5 *n (equal etc)* **did you ever see the ~?** *(col)* hast du so was schon gesehen?; **and the ~, and such ~** und dergleichen; **I've met the ~s of you before** solche wie dich kenne ich schon.
like[2] **1** *n usu pl* **she tried to find out his ~s and dislikes** sie wollte herausbekommen, was er mochte und was nicht.
2 *vt* **(a)** *person* mögen. **how do you ~ him?** wie gefällt er dir?; **I don't ~ him** ich mag ihn nicht; **he is well ~d here** er ist hier sehr beliebt.
(b) I ~ black shoes mir gefallen schwarze Schuhe; **I ~ it** das gefällt mir; **I ~ chocolate** ich mag Schokolade; **I ~ football** ich mag Fußball; *(playing)* ich spiele gerne Fußball; **I ~ this translation** ich finde diese Übersetzung gut; **how would you ~ a walk?** was hältst du von einem Spaziergang?; **well, I ~ that!** *(col)* das ist ein starkes Stück! *(col).*
(c) *(wish, wish for)* **I should ~ more time** ich würde mir gerne noch etwas Zeit lassen; **they should have ~d to come** sie wären gern gekommen; **I should ~ to know why** ich wüßte (gerne), warum; **I should ~ you to do it** ich möchte, daß du es tust; **I didn't ~ to disturb him** ich wollte ihn nicht stören; **what would you ~?** was hätten *or* möchten Sie gern?; **would you ~ a drink?** möchten Sie etwas trinken?; **how do you ~ your coffee?** wie trinken Sie Ihren Kaffee?
3 *vi* **as you ~** wie Sie wollen; **if you ~** wenn Sie wollen.
lik(e)able ['laɪkəbl] *adj* sympathisch.
likelihood ['laɪklɪhʊd] *n* Wahrscheinlichkeit *f.* **in all ~** aller Wahrscheinlichkeit nach; **there is no ~ of that** das ist nicht wahrscheinlich; **there is little ~ that ...** es ist kaum anzunehmen, daß ...
likely ['laɪklɪ] **1** *adj (+er)* **(a)** *(probable)* wahrscheinlich. **he is not ~ to come** es ist unwahrscheinlich, daß er kommt; **is it ~ that I would do that?** trauen Sie mir das zu?; **an incident ~ to cause trouble** ein Zwischenfall, der möglicherweise Ärger nach sich zieht; **a ~ explanation** eine wahrscheinliche Erklärung; *(iro)* wer's glaubt, wird selig! *(col);* **a ~ story!** *(iro)* das glaubst du doch (wohl) selber nicht! *(col).* **(b)** *(col: suitable)* **a ~ spot for a picnic** ein geeignetes Fleckchen für ein Picknick; **he is a ~ person for the job** er kommt für die Stelle in Frage. **2** *adv* **not ~!** *(col)* wohl kaum *(col);* **as ~ as not** höchstwahrscheinlich; **very ~ they've lost it** höchstwahrscheinlich haben sie es verloren.
like-minded ['laɪk'maɪndɪd] *adj* gleichgesinnt.
liken ['laɪkən] *vt* vergleichen *(to* mit*).*
likeness ['laɪknɪs] *n (resemblance)* Ähnlichkeit *f; (portrait)* Bild(nis) *nt.* **in the ~ of** in der Gestalt *(+gen).*
likewise ['laɪkwaɪz] *adv* ebenso. **he did ~** er machte es ebenso; **have a nice weekend — ~** schönes Wochenende! — danke gleichfalls!
liking ['laɪkɪŋ] *n* **(a)** *(for particular person)* Zuneigung *f; (for types)* Vorliebe *f.* **to have a ~ for sb** Zuneigung für jdn empfinden; **she took a ~ to him** er war ihr sympathisch. **(b)** *(for thing)* Vorliebe *f.* **to take a ~ to sth** eine Vorliebe für etw bekommen; **to be to sb's ~** nach jds Geschmack *m* sein.
lilac ['laɪlək] **1** *n* **(a)** *(plant)* Flieder *m.* **(b)** *(colour)* Lila *nt.* **2** *adj* fliederfarben, lila.
lilt [lɪlt] *n (of song)* munterer Rhythmus; *(of voice)* singender Tonfall.
lily ['lɪlɪ] *n* Lilie *f; (water ~)* Seerose *f.* **~ of the valley** Maiglöckchen *nt.*
limb [lɪm] *n (Anat)* Glied *nt.* **~s** *pl* Gliedmaßen *pl;* **life and ~** Leib und Leben; **to be out on a ~** *(fig)* (ganz) allein (da)stehen.
♦ **limber up** [ˌlɪmbər'ʌp] *vi* Lockerungsübungen machen; *(fig)* sich vorbereiten.
limbo ['lɪmbəʊ] *n (Rel)* Vorhölle *f; (fig)* Übergangs- *or* Zwischenstadium *nt.* **our plans are in ~** unsere Pläne sind in der Schwebe.
lime[1] [laɪm] *n (Geol)* Kalk *m.*
lime[2] *n (Bot: linden, also* **~ tree***)* Linde(nbaum *m*) *f.*
lime[3] *n (Bot: citrus fruit)* Limone *f; (tree)* Limonenbaum *m.*
limelight ['laɪmlaɪt] *n* Rampenlicht *nt.* **to be in the ~** im Rampenlicht stehen.
limerick ['lɪmərɪk] *n* Limerick *m.*
limestone ['laɪmstəʊn] *n* Kalkstein *m.*
limey ['laɪmɪ] *n (US col)* Engländer *m.*
limit ['lɪmɪt] **1** *n* **(a)** Grenze *f; (limitation)* Be-

schränkung *f; (speed ~)* Geschwindigkeitsbegrenzung *f; (Comm)* Limit *nt.* **to put a ~ on sth, to set a ~ to** *or* **on sth** etw beschränken; **there's a ~!** alles hat seine Grenzen!; **there is a ~ to what one person can do** ein Mensch kann nur so viel tun und nicht mehr; **there is no ~ to his stupidity** seine Dummheit kennt keine Grenzen; **there's a ~ to the amount of money we can spend** unseren Ausgaben sind Grenzen gesetzt; **it is true within ~s** es ist bis zu einem gewissen Grade richtig; **without ~s** unbegrenzt; **to know no ~s** keine Grenzen kennen; **over the ~** zuviel; *(in time)* zu lange; **he was driving over the ~** er hat die Geschwindigkeitsbegrenzung überschritten; *(after drinking)* er hat sich mit zuviel Promille ans Steuer gesetzt.

(b) *(col)* **that's the ~!** das ist die Höhe! *(col)*; **that child is the ~!** dieses Kind ist eine Zumutung! *(col)*.

2 *vt* beschränken; *freedom, spending* einschränken; *imagination* hemmen. **to ~ sth to sth** etw auf etw *(acc)* beschränken; **are you ~ed for time?** ist Ihre Zeit begrenzt?

limitation [ˌlɪmɪˈteɪʃən] *n* Beschränkung *f; (of freedom, spending)* Einschränkung *f; (disadvantage)* Handikap *nt.* **to have/know one's ~s** seine Grenzen haben/kennen.

limited [ˈlɪmɪtɪd] *adj* begrenzt. **in a ~ sense** in gewissem Maße; **~ company** *(Brit)* Gesellschaft *f* mit beschränkter Haftung.

limitless [ˈlɪmɪtlɪs] *adj* grenzenlos.

limousine [ˈlɪməziːn] *n* Limousine *f.*

limp[1] [lɪmp] **1** *n* Hinken *nt.* **to walk with a ~** hinken, humpeln. **2** *vi* hinken. **the ship ~ed into port** das Schiff kam mit Müh und Not in den Hafen.

limp[2] *adj (+er)* schlapp, schlaff; *flowers* welk; *material, cloth* weich. **let your body go ~** alle Muskeln entspannen.

limpet [ˈlɪmpɪt] *n* Napfschnecke *f.* **to stick to sb like a ~** *(col)* wie eine Klette an jdm hängen.

limpid [ˈlɪmpɪd] *adj* klar; *liquid also* durchsichtig.

linchpin [ˈlɪntʃpɪn] *n* Achs(en)nagel *m; (fig)* Stütze *f.* **accurate timing is the ~ of the entire operation** das ganze Unternehmen steht und fällt mit genauer Zeiteinteilung.

linden [ˈlɪndən] *n (also ~ tree)* Linde(nbaum *m) f.*

line[1] [laɪn] **1** *n* **(a)** *(rope etc, fishing ~)* Leine *f; (on tennis court etc, on paper)* Linie *f; (on face)* Falte *f.* **the ~ between right and wrong** die Grenze zwischen Recht und Unrecht; **the ship's graceful ~s** die schnittigen Linien des Schiffes.

(b) *(row)* Reihe *f; (of people, cars also)* Schlange *f; (of hills)* Kette *f; (US: queue)* Schlange *f.* **in (a) ~** in einer Reihe; **in a straight ~** geradlinig; **John is next in ~ for promotion** John ist als nächster mit der Beförderung an der Reihe; **he was descended from a long ~ of farmers** er stammte aus einem alten Bauerngeschlecht; **who is fourth in ~ to the throne?** wer steht an vierter Stelle der Thronfolge?; **to be out of ~ with sb/sth** *(fig)* mit jdm/etw nicht übereinstimmen; **to bring sth into ~ with sth** *(fig)* etw mit etw in Einklang bringen; **he refused to fall into ~ with the new proposals** er weigerte sich, mit den neuen Vorschlägen konform zu gehen; **to step out of ~** *(fig)* aus der Reihe tanzen; **to stand in ~** *(US)* Schlange stehen.

(c) *(air~, shipping ~)* Linie *f.*

(d) *(Rail)* Strecke *f.* **~s** *pl* Gleise *pl;* **to reach the end of the ~** *(fig)* am Ende sein.

(e) *(Telec: cable)* Leitung *f.* **the firm has 52 ~s** die Firma hat 52 Anschlüsse; **this is a very bad ~** die Verbindung ist sehr schlecht; **the ~ went dead** die Leitung war auf einmal tot; **to be on the ~ to sb** mit jdm telefonieren; **hold the ~** bleiben Sie am Apparat!; **can I have an outside ~?** geben Sie mir bitte ein Amt.

(f) *(Comp)* **on ~** on line.

(g) *(written)* Zeile *f.* **~s** *(Sch)* Strafarbeit *f;* **~s** *(Theat)* Text *m;* **to drop sb a ~** jdm ein paar Zeilen schreiben; **to read between the ~s** zwischen den Zeilen lesen.

(h) *(direction, course)* **~ of argument** Argumentation *f;* **~ of attack** *(Mil)* Angriffslinie *f; (fig)* Taktik *f;* **enemy ~s** *(Mil)* feindliche Stellungen *pl;* **to be on the right ~s** *(fig)* auf dem richtigen Weg sein, richtig liegen *(col)*; **we must take a firm** *or* **strong ~ with these people** wir müssen diesen Leuten gegenüber sehr bestimmt auftreten; **to lay it on the ~** *(col)* die Karten auf den Tisch legen *(col)*; **to lay it on the ~ to sb** jdm reinen Wein einschenken *(col)*; **the ~ of least resistance** der Weg des geringsten Widerstandes; **he took the ~ that ...** er vertrat den Standpunkt, daß ...; **to be along the ~s of** ungefähr so etwas wie ... sein; **I was thinking along the same ~s** ich hatte etwas ähnliches gedacht; **it's all in the ~ of duty** das gehört zu meinen/seinen *etc* Pflichten.

(i) *(fig: business)* Branche *f; (model)* Modell *nt.* **what ~ is he in?, what's his ~?** was ist er von Beruf?; **that's not in my ~** das liegt mir nicht; **we have a new ~ in spring hats** wir haben eine neue Kollektion Frühjahrshüte.

2 *vt* **(a)** *(cross with ~s)* linieren. **worry had ~d his face** sein Gesicht war von Sorgen gezeichnet. **(b)** *streets* säumen. **a road ~d with trees** eine von Bäumen gesäumte Straße; **the streets were ~d with cheering crowds** eine jubelnde Menge säumte die Straßen.

♦ **line up 1** *vi (stand in line)* sich aufstellen; *(queue)* sich anstellen. **2** *vt sep* **(a)** *troops, prisoners* antreten lassen; *boxes, books etc* in einer Reihe aufstellen. **(b)** *(prepare, arrange) entertainment* sorgen für; *speakers* verpflichten; *support* mobilisieren. **have you anything special ~d ~ for today?** haben Sie für heute etwas Bestimmtes auf dem Programm?; **have you anyone ~d ~ for the job?** haben Sie schon jemanden für die Stelle geplant?

line[2] *vt clothes* füttern; *box* auskleiden. **to ~ one's own pockets** *(fig)* in die eigene Tasche arbeiten.

linear [ˈlɪnɪəʳ] *adj motion* linear; *measure* Längen-.

lined [laɪnd] *adj face etc (of old people)* faltig; *(through worry, etc)* gezeichnet; *paper* liniert.

line drawing *n* Zeichnung *f.*

linen [ˈlɪnɪn] **1** *n* Leinen *nt; (table ~)* Tischwäsche *f; (sheets, garments etc)* Wäsche *f.* **~ cupboard** Wäscheschrank *m.* **2** *adj* Leinen-.

line printer *n* Zeilendrucker *m.*

liner [ˈlaɪnəʳ] *n (ship)* Passagierschiff *nt.*

linesman [ˈlaɪnzmən], *(US also)* **lineman** [ˈlaɪnmən] *n, pl* **-men** [-mən] *(Sport)* Linienrichter *m; (Rail)* Streckenwärter *m.*

line-up [ˈlaɪnʌp] *n (Sport)* Aufstellung *f; (cast)* Besetzung *f; (US: queue)* Schlange *f.*

linger [ˈlɪŋgəʳ] *vi (also ~ on)* (zurück)bleiben; *(delay)* sich aufhalten; *(in dying)* zwischen Leben und Tod schweben; *(custom)* sich halten; *(doubts)* zurückbleiben; *(feeling, pain)* anhalten; *(memory)* bleiben; *(chords)* nachklingen. **the guests ~ed in the hall** die Gäste standen noch im Flur herum; **to ~ on a subject** bei einem Thema verweilen; **to ~ over a meal** sich bei einer Mahlzeit lange aufhalten.

lingerie [ˈlænʒəriː] *n* (Damen)unterwäsche *f.*

lingering [ˈlɪŋgərɪŋ] *adj* lang; *death* langsam; *illness* langwierig; *doubt* zurückbleibend; *look* sehnsüchtig; *kiss* innig.

lingo [ˈlɪŋgəʊ] *n (col)* Sprache *f.*

linguist [ˈlɪŋgwɪst] *n (speaker of languages)* Sprachkundige(r) *mf; (specialist in linguistics)* Linguist(in *f*) *m.* **I'm no ~** ich bin nicht sprachbegabt.

linguistic [lɪŋˈgwɪstɪk] *adj* **(a)** sprachlich; *competence* Sprach-. **(b)** *(of linguistics)* sprachwissenschaftlich.

linguistics [lɪŋ'gwɪstɪks] *n sing* Linguistik *f.*
lining ['laɪnɪŋ] *n (of clothes etc)* Futter *nt; (of brake)* (Brems)belag *m.*
link [lɪŋk] **1** *n (of chain, fig)* Glied *nt; (person)* Verbindungsmann *m.* **he broke all his ~s with his family** er brach alle Beziehungen zu seiner Familie ab; **cultural ~s** kulturelle Beziehungen *pl.* **2** *vt* verbinden; *spaceships also* aneinanderkoppeln. **to ~ arms** sich unterhaken *(with* bei*)*; **do you think these two murders are ~ed?** glauben Sie, daß zwischen den beiden Morden eine Verbindung besteht?. **3** *vi* **to ~ (together)** *(parts of story)* sich zusammenfügen lassen; *(railway lines)* zusammenlaufen.
♦ **link up** *vi* zusammenkommen; *(people)* sich zusammentun; *(facts)* übereinstimmen; *(companies)* sich zusammenschließen; *(spaceships)* ein Kopplungsmanöver durchführen.
links [lɪŋks] *npl (golf course)* Golfplatz *m.*
link-up ['lɪŋkʌp] *n (Telec, general)* Verbindung *f; (of spaceships)* Kopplung(smanöver *nt) f.*
lino ['laɪnəʊ] *n (Brit)* Linoleum *nt.*
linoleum [lɪ'nəʊlɪəm] *n* Linoleum *nt.*
linseed ['lɪnsiːd] *n* Leinsamen *m.* **~ oil** Leinöl *nt.*
lint [lɪnt] *n* Mull *m.*
lintel ['lɪntl] *n (Archit)* Sturz *m.*
lion ['laɪən] *n* Löwe *m.* **the ~'s share** der Löwenanteil.
lioness ['laɪənɪs] *n* Löwin *f.*
lip [lɪp] *n* **(a)** *(Anat)* Lippe *f; (of jug)* Schnabel *m; (of cup)* Rand *m.* **to keep a stiff upper ~** die Haltung bewahren. **(b)** *(col: cheek)* Frechheit(en *pl) f.* **to give sb a lot of ~** jdm gegenüber eine (freche) Lippe riskieren *(col).*
lip: ~read *vti* von den Lippen ablesen; **~ service** *n* **to pay ~ service to an idea** ein Lippenbekenntnis zu einer Idee ablegen; **~stick** *n* Lippenstift *m.*
liquefy ['lɪkwɪfaɪ] **1** *vt* verflüssigen. **2** *vi* sich verflüssigen.
liqueur [lɪ'kjʊəʳ] *n* Likör *m.*
liquid ['lɪkwɪd] **1** *adj* flüssig *(also Comm).* **2** *n* Flüssigkeit *f.*
liquidate ['lɪkwɪdeɪt] *vt* **(a)** *(Comm)* liquidieren; *assets also* flüssig machen; *company also* auflösen. **(b)** *enemy etc* liquidieren.
liquidation [ˌlɪkwɪ'deɪʃən] *n see vt* **(a)** Liquidation *f; (of company also)* Auflösung *f.* **to go into ~** in Liquidation gehen. **(b)** Liquidierung *f.*
liquid crystal *n* Flüssigkristall *nt.*
liquidity [lɪ'kwɪdɪtɪ] *n* Liquidität *f.*
liquidize ['lɪkwɪdaɪz] *vt* (im Mixer) pürieren.
liquidizer ['lɪkwɪdaɪzəʳ] *n* Mixgerät *nt.*
liquor ['lɪkəʳ] *n (whisky, brandy etc)* Spirituosen *pl; (alcohol)* Alkohol *m.*
liquorice, licorice ['lɪkərɪs] *n* Lakritze *f.*
lisp [lɪsp] **1** *n* Lispeln *nt.* **to speak with a ~** lispeln. **2** *vti* lispeln.
lissom ['lɪsəm] *adj* geschmeidig; *person also* gelenkig.
list¹ [lɪst] **1** *n* Liste *f; (shopping ~)* Einkaufszettel *m.* **it's not on the ~** es steht nicht auf der Liste; **it's on my ~ for tomorrow** es steht für morgen auf dem Programm. **2** *vt* notieren; *item* in die Liste aufnehmen. **it is not ~ed** es ist nicht aufgeführt; **~ed building** Gebäude *nt* unter Denkmalschutz.
list² *(Naut)* **1** *n* Schlagseite *f.* **2** *vi* Schlagseite haben.
listen ['lɪsn] *vi* **(a)** hören *(to sth* etw *acc).* **to ~ to the radio** Radio hören; **to ~ for sth** auf etw *(acc)* horchen; **to ~ for sb** hören, ob jd kommt; **OK, I'm ~ing** ich höre zu. **(b)** *(heed)* zuhören. **~ to me!** hör mir zu!; **~, I know what we'll do** hör mal, ich weiß, was wir machen; **don't ~ to him** hör nicht auf ihn; **he wouldn't ~** er wollte nicht hören.
♦ **listen in** *vi* (im Radio) hören *(to sth* etw *acc); (listen secretly)* mithören *(on sth* etw *acc).*
listener ['lɪsnəʳ] *n* Zuhörer(in *f) m; (Rad)* Hörer(in *f) m.* **to be a good ~** gut zuhören können.
listless ['lɪstlɪs] *adj* lustlos; *patient* teilnahmslos.
list price *n* Listenpreis *m.*
lists [lɪsts] *npl (Hist)* Schranken *pl.* **to enter the ~** *(fig)* zum Kampf antreten.
lit [lɪt] *pret, ptp of* **light¹**.
litany ['lɪtənɪ] *n* Litanei *f.*
liter *n (US)* = **litre.**
literacy ['lɪtərəsɪ] *n* Fähigkeit *f,* lesen und schreiben zu können **~ campaign** Alphabetisierungskampagne *f.*
literal ['lɪtərəl] *adj translation* wörtlich; *meaning also* eigentlich. **it was a ~ disaster** es war im wahrsten Sinne des Wortes eine Katastrophe.
literally ['lɪtərəlɪ] *adv (word for word, exactly)* (wort)wörtlich; *(really)* buchstäblich, wirklich. **to take sth ~** etw wörtlich nehmen; **he was ~ a giant** er war im wahrsten Sinne des Wortes ein Riese.
literary ['lɪtərərɪ] *adj* literarisch. **a ~ man** ein Literaturkenner *m; (author)* ein Literat *m.*
literate ['lɪtərɪt] *adj* **to be ~** lesen und schreiben können; *(well-educated)* gebildet sein.
literature ['lɪtərɪtʃəʳ] *n* Literatur *f; (col: brochures etc)* Informationsmaterial *nt.*
lithe [laɪð] *adj (+er)* geschmeidig.
lithograph ['lɪθəʊgrɑːf] *n* Lithographie *f,* Steindruck *m.*
litigation [ˌlɪtɪ'geɪʃən] *n* Prozeß, Rechtsstreit *m.*
litmus ['lɪtməs] *n* **~ paper** Lackmuspapier *nt.*
litre, *(US)* **liter** ['liːtəʳ] *n* Liter *m or nt.*
litter ['lɪtəʳ] **1** *n* **(a)** Abfälle *pl; (papers, wrappings)* Papier *nt.* **(b)** *(Zool)* Wurf *m; (bedding for animals)* Streu *f,* Stroh *nt; (cat ~)* Katzenstreu *f.* **2** *vt* **to be ~ed with sth** *(lit, fig)* mit etw übersät sein.
litter: ~ bin *n* Abfalleimer *m;* **~ bug** *(col),* **~ lout** *(col) n* Schmutzfink *(col) m.*
little ['lɪtl] **1** *adj* klein. **a ~ house** ein Häuschen *nt;* **the ~ ones** die Kleinen *pl;* **a nice ~ profit** ein hübscher Gewinn; **a ~ while ago** vor kurzem; **it's only a ~ while till I ...** es ist nicht mehr lange, bis ich ...; **in a ~ while** bald.

2 *adv, n* **(a)** wenig. **of ~ importance** von geringer Bedeutung; **~ better than** kaum besser als; **~ more than a month ago** vor kaum einem Monat; **~ short of** fast schon, beinahe; **~ did I think that ...** ich hätte kaum gedacht, daß ...; **I walk as ~ as possible** ich laufe so wenig wie möglich; **every ~ helps** wir sind froh um jede Kleinigkeit; **I see very ~ of her nowadays** ich sehe sie in letzter Zeit sehr selten; **there was ~ we could do** wir konnten nicht viel tun; **she did what ~ she could** sie tat das Wenige, das sie tun konnte; **~ by ~** nach und nach; **to make ~ of sth** etw herunterspielen; **I could make ~ of this book** ich konnte mit diesem Buch nicht viel anfangen.

(b) a ~ ein wenig, ein bißchen; **a ~ better** ein bißchen besser; **with a ~ effort** mit etwas Anstrengung; **a ~ after five** kurz nach fünf; **we walked on for a ~** wir liefen noch ein bißchen weiter; **after a ~** nach einer Weile.
liturgy ['lɪtədʒɪ] *n* Liturgie *f.*
live¹ [lɪv] **1** *vt life* führen. **to ~ life to the full** sein Leben auskosten.

2 *vi* **(a)** leben. **will he ~, doctor?** wird er (über)leben, Herr Doktor?; **don't worry, you'll ~, it's only a broken ankle** reg dich nicht auf, du stirbst schon nicht, du hast nur einen gebrochenen Knöchel; **long ~ Queen Anne!** lang lebe Königin Anne!; **we ~ and learn** man lernt nie aus; **to ~ and let ~** leben und leben lassen; **to ~ like a king** wie Gott in Frankreich leben; **to ~ to a ripe old age** ein hohes Alter erreichen; **his name will ~ for ever** sein Ruhm wird nie vergehen; **his poetry will ~ for ever** seine Dichtung ist unvergänglich; **he ~d through two wars** er hat zwei Kriege miterlebt; **to ~ beyond one's income** über seine Verhältnisse leben; **you'll ~**

to regret it das wirst du noch bereuen!; **you'll just have to ~ with it** du mußt eben damit leben; **the other athletes couldn't ~ with him** die anderen Läufer konnten mit ihm nicht mithalten.

(b) *(reside)* wohnen; *(in town etc)* leben. **he ~s at 19 Marktstraße** er wohnt in der Marktstraße Nr.19; **he ~s with his parents** er wohnt bei seinen Eltern.

♦**live down** *vt sep humiliation* hinwegkommen über *(+acc)*, verwinden; *(actively) scandal* Gras wachsen lassen über *(+acc)*. **he'll never ~ it ~** das wird man ihm nie vergessen.

♦**live in** *vi* im Wohnheim wohnen.

♦**live off** *vi +prep obj* **to ~ ~ one's interest** von seinen Zinsen leben; **to ~ ~ one's relations** auf Kosten seiner Verwandten leben.

♦**live on 1** *vi (continue to live)* weiterleben. **2** *vi +prep obj* leben von. **to ~ ~ eggs** sich von Eiern ernähren; **he doesn't earn enough to ~ ~** er verdient nicht genug, um davon zu leben.

♦**live out 1** *vi* außerhalb (des Wohnheims) wohnen. **2** *vt sep life* verbringen; *winter* überleben. **to ~ ~ one's days** seinen Lebensabend verbringen.

♦**live together** *vi (cohabit)* zusammenleben; *(share a flat etc)* zusammenwohnen.

♦**live up** *vt always separate:* **to ~ it ~** *(col)* sich ausleben; *(extravagantly)* in Saus und Braus leben *(col)*.

♦**live up to** *vi +prep obj* **the holidays ~d ~ ~ our expectations** der Urlaub hielt, was wir uns *(dat)* versprochen hatte; **to ~ ~ ~ one's reputation** seinem Ruf gerecht werden; **it didn't ~ ~ ~ our hopes** es entsprach nicht dem, was wir uns *(dat)* erhofft hatten; **he's got a lot to ~ ~ ~** in ihn werden große Erwartungen gesetzt.

live[2] [laɪv] **1** *adj* **(a)** *(alive)* lebend; *issue* aktuell. **a real ~ duke** ein waschechter Herzog. **(b)** *(having power or energy) coal* glühend; *match* ungebraucht; *cartridge, shell* scharf; *(Elec)* geladen. **"danger, ~ wires!"** „Vorsicht Hochspannung!"; **she's a real ~ wire** *(fig)* sie ist ein richtiges Energiebündel. **(c)** *(Rad, TV)* live. **a ~ programme** eine Livesendung. **2** *adv (Rad, TV)* live.

livelihood ['laɪvlɪhʊd] *n* Lebensunterhalt *m*. **to earn a ~** sich *(dat)* seinen Lebensunterhalt verdienen.

liveliness ['laɪvlɪnɪs] *n see adj* Lebhaftigkeit *f*; Lebendigkeit *f*; Dynamik *f*; Aufgewecktheit *f*.

lively ['laɪvlɪ] *adj (+er)* lebhaft; *scene, account* lebendig; *campaign* dynamisch; *pace* flott; *mind* aufgeweckt. **things are getting ~** es geht hoch her *(col)*.

♦**liven up** ['laɪvən'ʌp] **1** *vt sep* beleben, Leben bringen in *(+acc) (col)*. **2** *vi* in Schwung kommen; *(person)* aufleben.

liver ['lɪvə[r]] *n (Anat, Cook)* Leber *f*.

liverish ['lɪvərɪʃ] *adj (bad-tempered)* mürrisch. **to be ~** etwas mit der Leber haben; **I felt a bit ~ after the party** mir ging es nach der Party ziemlich mies *(col)*.

livery ['lɪvərɪ] *n* Livree *f*; *(fig liter)* Kleid *nt*.

lives [laɪvz] *pl of* **life.**

livestock ['laɪvstɒk] *n* Vieh *nt*.

livid ['lɪvɪd] *adj* **(a)** *(col)* fuchsteufelswild *(col)*. **he got ~ with us** er hatte eine Stinkwut auf uns *(col)*. **(b)** *(colour)* bleifarben.

living ['lɪvɪŋ] **1** *adj* lebend; *example, faith* lebendig. **a ~ creature** ein Lebewesen *nt*; **(with)in ~ memory** seit Menschengedenken; **he is ~ proof of ...** er ist der lebende Beweis für ... **2** *n* **(a) the ~** *pl* die Lebenden *pl*. **(b)** *(livelihood)* Lebensunterhalt *m*. **to earn** *or* **make a ~** sich *(dat)* seinen Lebensunterhalt verdienen; **he sells brushes for a ~** er verkauft Bürsten, um sich *(dat)* seinen Lebensunterhalt zu verdienen; **what do you do for a ~?** was machen Sie beruflich?; **to work for one's ~** sich selbst unterhalten.

living: ~ conditions *npl* Wohnverhältnisse *pl*; **~ room** *n* Wohnzimmer *nt*; **~ wage** *n* ausreichender Lohn.

lizard ['lɪzəd] *n* Eidechse *f*.

lo [ləʊ] *interj* **~ and behold!** und siehe da.

load [ləʊd] **1** *n* **(a)** *(sth carried, burden)* Last *f*; *(cargo)* Ladung *f*; *(on axle etc, fig)* Belastung *f*; *(Elec)* Spannung *f*. **an arm-~ of shopping** ein Armvoll Einkäufe; **a train-~ of passengers** ein Zug voll Reisender; **(work) ~** (Arbeits)pensum *nt*; **that's a ~ off my mind!** da fällt mir ein Stein vom Herzen!

(b) *(col usages)* **~s of, a ~ of** jede Menge *(col)*; **it's a ~ of old rubbish** das ist alles Quatsch! *(col)*; *(book)* das ist alles Mist! *(col)*; **get a ~ of this!** *(listen)* hör dir das mal an!; *(look)* guck dir das mal an! *(col)*.

2 *vt* **(a)** *goods, software* laden; *lorry etc, (burden: also* **~ down***)* beladen. **the ship was ~ed with bananas** das Schiff hatte Bananen geladen. **(b)** *gun* laden; *dice* präparieren. **to ~ a camera** einen Film (in einen Fotoapparat) einlegen. **(c)** *(fig)* überhäufen. **to ~ sb with honours** jdn mit Ehrungen überschütten; **we're ~ed (down) with debts** wir stecken bis zum Hals in Schulden; **the dice had been ~ed against him** *(fig)* es war Schiebung *(col) or* ein abgekartetes Spiel.

3 *vi* laden. **~ing bay** Ladeplatz *m*.

♦**load up 1** *vi* aufladen. **2** *vt sep lorry* beladen; *goods* aufladen.

loaded ['ləʊdɪd] *adj* beladen; *dice* präpariert; *camera* mit eingelegtem Film; *gun* geladen. **a ~ question** eine Fangfrage; **he's ~** *(col: rich)* er ist steinreich *(col)*.

loaf [ləʊf] *n, pl* **loaves** Brot *nt*; *(unsliced)* (Brot)laib *m*. **a ~ of bread** ein Brot; **half a ~ is better than none** *(Prov)* (wenig ist) besser als gar nichts; **use your ~!** *(col)* streng deinen Grips an! *(col)*.

♦**loaf about** *or* **around** *vi (col)* faulenzen.

loam [ləʊm] *n* Lehmerde *f*.

loan [ləʊn] **1** *n (thing lent)* Leihgabe *f*; *(from bank etc)* Kredit *m*, Darlehen *nt*; *(public ~)* Anleihe *f*. **I asked for the ~ of the bicycle** ich bat darum, das Fahrrad ausleihen zu dürfen; **he gave me the ~ of his bicycle** er hat mir sein Fahrrad geliehen; **it's on ~** es ist geliehen; *(out on ~)* es ist verliehen. **2** *vt* leihen *(to sb* jdm*)*.

loath [ləʊθ] *adj* **to be ~ to do sth** etw ungern tun.

loathe [ləʊð] *vt thing, person* verabscheuen; *jazz etc* nicht ausstehen können. **I ~ doing it** *(in general)* ich hasse es, das zu tun; *(on particular occasion)* es ist mir zuwider, das zu tun.

loathing ['ləʊðɪŋ] *n* Abscheu *m*.

loathsome ['ləʊðsəm] *adj thing, person* abscheulich, widerlich; *task* verhaßt.

loaves [ləʊvz] *pl of* **loaf.**

lob [lɒb] **1** *n (Tennis)* Lob *m*. **2** *vt ball* lobben. **to ~ sth over to sb** jdm etw zuwerfen.

lobby ['lɒbɪ] **1** *n (entrance hall)* Eingangshalle *f*; *(place in Parliament)* Lobby *f*; *(Pol)* Interessenverband *m*. **2** *vt* **to ~ one's MP** auf seinen Abgeordneten Einfluß nehmen. **3** *vi* **they are ~ing for this reform** die Lobbyisten versuchen, diese Reform durchzubringen.

lobbyist ['lɒbɪɪst] *n* Lobbyist *m*.

lobe [ləʊb] *n (of ear)* Ohrläppchen *nt*.

lobster ['lɒbstə[r]] *n* Hummer *m*. **~ pot** Hummerkorb *m*.

local ['ləʊkəl] **1** *adj* Orts-; *(in this area)* hiesig; *(in that area)* dortig; *radio station* Regional-; *newspaper* Lokal-; *train* Nahverkehrs-; *politician* Kommunal-; *anaesthetic* örtlich. **he's a ~ man** er ist von hier *(col)*; **~ authorities** städtische Behörden *pl*; *(council)* Stadt-/Gemeinde-/Kreisverwaltung *f*; **~ call** Ortsgespräch *nt*; **~ government** Gemeinde-/Kreisverwaltung *f*; **~ branch** Zweigstelle *f*. **2** *n* **(a)** *(Brit: pub)* **the**

~ das Stammlokal; *(in village)* die Dorfkneipe *(col)*. **(b)** *(born in)* Einheimische(r) *mf; (living in)* Einwohner(in *f*) *m*.

locality [ləʊ'kælɪtɪ] *n* Gegend *f*. **in the ~ of the crime** am Ort des Verbrechens.

localize ['ləʊkəlaɪz] *vt* **(a)** *(detect)* lokalisieren **(b)** **~d** *(restricted)* örtlich begrenzt.

locally ['ləʊkəlɪ] *adv* am Ort. **houses are dear ~** Häuser sind hier teuer; **the shops are situated ~** die Geschäfte befinden sich in günstiger Lage; **do you live ~?** wohnen Sie am Ort?

locate [ləʊ'keɪt] *vt* **(a)** *(position)* legen. **to be ~d at** *or* **in** sich befinden in *(+dat)*; **the hotel is centrally ~d** das Hotel liegt zentral. **(b)** *(find)* ausfindig machen; *submarine* orten.

location [ləʊ'keɪʃən] *n* **(a)** *(position, site)* Lage *f; (of ship)* Position *f*. **this would be an ideal ~ for the road/airport** das wäre ein ideales Gelände für die Straße/den Flughafen. **(b)** *(finding)* Auffinden *nt; (of tumour)* Lokalisierung *f; (of star, ship)* Ortung *f*. **(c)** *(Film)* Drehort *m*. **part of the film was done on ~ in Mexico** Außenaufnahmen für den Film wurden in Mexiko gedreht.

loch [lɒx] n *(Scot)* See *m; (sea ~)* Meeresarm *m*.

lock[1] [lɒk] *n (of hair)* Locke *f*.

lock[2] **1** *n* **(a)** *(on door, box, gun)* Schloß *nt*. **to put sb/sth under ~ and key** jdn hinter Schloß und Riegel bringen/etw wegschließen; **he offered me the house ~, stock and barrel** er bot mir das Haus mit allem Drum und Dran an *(col)*; **they rejected the idea ~, stock and barrel** sie lehnten die Idee in Bausch und Bogen ab. **(b)** *(canal ~)* Schleuse *f*. **(c)** *(Aut)* Wendekreis *m*. **the steering wheel was on full ~** das Lenkrad war voll eingeschlagen.

2 *vt door etc* abschließen; *steering wheel* sperren, arretieren; *wheel* blockieren. **the armies were ~ed in combat** die Armeen waren in Kämpfe verwickelt; **they were ~ed in each other's arms** sie hielten sich fest umschlungen; **this bar ~s the wheel in position** diese Stange hält das Rad fest.

3 *vi* schließen; *(wheel)* blockieren. **a suitcase that ~s** ein verschließbarer Koffer.

♦ **lock away** *vt sep* wegschließen; *(in safe)* einschließen; *person* einsperren.

♦ **lock in** *vt sep* einschließen. **to be ~ed ~** eingesperrt sein.

♦ **lock out** *vt sep* aussperren.

♦ **lock up 1** *vt sep* **(a)** *thing, house* abschließen; *person* einsperren. **to ~ sth ~ in sth** etw in etw *(dat)* einschließen; **he ought to be ~ed ~!** den müßte man einsperren! **(b)** *(Comm) capital* fest anlegen. **2** *vi* abschließen.

locker ['lɒkəʳ] *n* Schließfach *nt*. **~ room** Umkleideraum *m*.

locket ['lɒkɪt] *n* Medaillon *nt*.

lock: ~ gate *n* Schleusentor *nt;* **~jaw** *n* Wundstarrkrampf *m;* **~out** *n* Aussperrung *f;* **~smith** *n* Schlosser *m;* **~-up** *n* **(a)** *(shop)* kleiner Laden; *(garage)* Garage *f;* **(b)** *(prison)* Gefängnis *nt*.

locomotion [,ləʊkə'məʊʃən] *n* Fortbewegung *f*.

locomotive [,ləʊkə'məʊtɪv] Lokomotive *f*.

locust ['ləʊkəst] *n* Heuschrecke *f*.

lodge [lɒdʒ] **1** *n (in grounds)* Pförtnerhaus *nt; (skiing ~ etc)* Hütte *f; (porter's ~)* Pförtnerloge *f*. **2** *vt person* unterbringen; *complaint* einlegen *(with* bei*); charge* einreichen; *(insert) spear* stoßen; *jewellery, money* deponieren, hinterlegen. **to be ~d** (fest)stecken. **3** *vi* **(a)** *(live)* (zur *or* in Untermiete) wohnen *(with sb, at sb's* bei jdm*); (at boarding house)* wohnen *(in* in *+dat)*. **(b)** *(object, bullet)* steckenbleiben.

lodger ['lɒdʒəʳ] *n* Untermieter(in *f*) *m*. **she takes ~s** sie vermietet (Zimmer).

lodging ['lɒdʒɪŋ] *n* Unterkunft *f*. **~s** *pl* ein möbliertes Zimmer; möblierte Zimmer *pl;* **we took ~s with Mrs B** wir mieteten uns bei Frau B ein; **~ house** Pension *f*.

loft [lɒft] *n* Dachboden, Speicher *m; (hay~)* Heuboden *m*. **in the ~** auf dem Dachboden.

lofty ['lɒftɪ] *adj (+er)* **(a)** *(high)* hoch. **(b)** *ideals* hoch; *ambitions* hochfliegend; *sentiments* erhaben; *prose* gehoben. **(c)** *(haughty)* hochmütig.

log[1] [lɒg] *n* Baumstamm *m; (short)* Holzblock *m; (for a fire)* Scheit *nt*. **to sleep like a ~** wie ein Stein schlafen; **~ cabin** Blockhütte *f;* **~ fire** Holzfeuer *nt*.

log[2] **1** *n (record)* Aufzeichnungen *pl*. **to make** *or* **keep a ~ of sth** über etw *(acc)* Buch führen; *see* **~book. 2** *vt* **(a)** Buch führen über *(+acc); (Naut)* (ins Logbuch) eintragen. **(b)** *(travel)* zurücklegen.

log[3] = **logarithm** log. **~ tables** Logarithmentafel *f*.

logarithm ['lɒgərɪθəm] *n* Logarithmus *m*.

log book *n (Naut)* Logbuch *nt; (Aviat)* Bordbuch *nt; (of lorries)* Fahrtenbuch *nt; (Aut: registration book)* Kraftfahrzeugbrief *m; (in hospitals etc)* Dienstbuch *nt*.

loggerheads ['lɒgəhedz] *npl:* **to be at ~ (with sb)** Streit (mit jdm) haben; **they were constantly at ~ with the authorities** sie standen mit den Behörden dauernd auf Kriegsfuß.

logic ['lɒdʒɪk] *n* Logik *f*.

logical ['lɒdʒɪkəl] *adj* logisch.

logically ['lɒdʒɪkəlɪ] *adv think, argue* logisch. **~, he may be right** logisch gesehen könnte er recht haben.

logistics [lɒ'dʒɪstɪks] *n sing* Logistik *f*.

logo ['lɒgəʊ] *n* Firmenzeichen *nt*.

loin [lɔɪn] *n* Lende *f*. **~ cloth** Lendenschurz *m*.

loiter ['lɔɪtəʳ] *vi (waste time)* trödeln; *(hang around suspiciously)* herumlungern. **to ~ with intent** sich verdächtig machen.

loll [lɒl] *vi* lümmeln. **to ~ against sth** sich (lässig) gegen *or* an etw *(acc)* lehnen.

♦ **loll about** *or* **around** *vi* herumlümmeln.

lollipop ['lɒlɪpɒp] *n* Lutscher *m; (iced ~)* Eis *nt* am Stiel. **~ man/woman** *(Brit col)* ≃ Schülerlotse *m*.

lolly ['lɒlɪ] *n* **(a)** *(Brit col: lollipop)* Lutscher *m*. **an ice ~** ein Eis *nt* am Stiel. **(b)** *(col: money)* Mäuse *(col) pl*.

London ['lʌndən] **1** *n* London *nt*. **2** *adj* Londoner.

Londoner ['lʌndənəʳ] *n* Londoner(in *f*) *m*.

lone [ləʊn] *adj* einzeln, einsam; *(only)* einzig. **~ wolf** *(fig)* Einzelgänger *m*.

loneliness ['ləʊnlɪnɪs] *n* Einsamkeit *f*.

lonely ['ləʊnlɪ] *adj (+er)* einsam.

loner ['ləʊnəʳ] *n* Einzelgänger(in *f*) *m*.

lonesome ['ləʊnsəm] *adj (esp US)* einsam.

long[1] [lɒŋ] **1** *adj (+er)* **(a)** *(in size)* lang; *glass* hoch; *journey* weit. **it is 6 metres ~** es ist 6 Meter lang; **to pull a ~ face** ein langes Gesicht machen; **it's a ~ way to Hamburg** nach Hamburg ist es weit; **to have a ~ memory** ein gutes Gedächtnis haben; **to be ~ in the tooth** *(col)* nicht mehr der/die Jüngste sein. **(b)** *(in time)* lang; *job* langwierig. **it's a ~ time since I saw her** ich habe sie schon seit längerer Zeit nicht mehr gesehen; **will you need it for a ~ time?** brauchen Sie es lange?; **he's been here (for) a ~ time** er ist schon lange hier; **~ time no see** *(col)* sieht man dich auch mal wieder? *(col)*; **to take a ~ look at sth** etw lange betrachten; **how ~ is the film?** wie lange dauert der Film?; **to take the ~ view** etw auf lange Sicht betrachten; **a ~ drink** *(mixed)* ein Longdrink *m*.

2 *adv* lang(e). **to be ~ in doing sth** lange zu etw brauchen; **don't be ~!** beeil dich!; **I shan't be ~** *(in finishing)* ich bin gleich fertig; *(in returning)* ich bin gleich wieder da; **all night ~** die ganze Nacht; **something he had ~ wished to happen** etwas, was er sich *(dat)* schon lange gewünscht hatte; **~ ago** vor langer Zeit; **not ~ ago** vor kurzem; **~ before** lange vorher; **not ~ before**

that kurz davor; **as ~ as** so lange wie; **we waited as ~ as we could** wir haben gewartet, solange wir konnten; **as ~ as, so ~ as** *(provided that)* solange; **how much ~er can you stay?** wie lange können Sie noch bleiben?; **no ~er** *(not any more)* nicht mehr; **I'll wait no ~er** ich warte nicht länger; **so ~!** *(col)* tschüs *(col)*.

3 *n* **the ~ and the short of it is that ...** der langen Rede kurzer Sinn, ...; **before ~** bald; **are you going for ~?** werden Sie länger weg sein?; **it won't take ~** das dauert nicht lange.

long[2] *vi* sich sehnen *(for* nach*)*; *(less passionately)* kaum erwarten können *(for sth* etw *acc)*. **I am ~ing to go abroad** ich brenne darauf, ins Ausland zu gehen; **I'm ~ing to see that film** ich will den Film unbedingt sehen.

long: ~-distance 1 *adj lorry, call* Fern-; *flight, race* Langstrecken-; **2** *adv* **to call ~ distance** ein Ferngespräch führen; **~-drawn-out** *adj speech* langatmig; *meeting* in die Länge gezogen; **~-haired** *adj person* langhaarig; *dog etc* Langhaar-; **~hand** *n* **in ~hand** handschriftlich.

longing ['lɒŋɪŋ] **1** *adj look* sehnsüchtig; *eyes* sehnsuchtsvoll. **2** *n* Sehnsucht *f (for* nach*)*. **to have a ~ to do sth** sich danach sehnen, etw zu tun.

longingly ['lɒŋɪŋlɪ] *adv* sehnsüchtig.

longitude ['lɒŋgɪtjuːd] *n* Länge *f*.

long: ~-legged *adj* langbeinig; **~-lost** *adj person* verloren geglaubt; *ideals etc* verlorengegangen; **~-playing** *adj* Langspiel-; **~-range** *adj gun* weittragend; *missile, aircraft* Langstrecken-; *forecast* langfristig; **~ shot** *n* **to take a ~ shot** einen gewagten Versuch unternehmen; **not by a ~ shot** bei weitem nicht; **~-sighted** *adj (lit, fig)* weitsichtig; **~-standing** *adj* alt; *friendship also* langjährig; *interest, invitation* schon lange bestehend; **~-suffering** *adj* schwer geprüft; **~-term 1** *adj* langfristig; **2** *n* **in the ~ term** langfristig gesehen; **~ vacation** *n (Univ)* (Sommer)semesterferien *pl; (Sch)* große Ferien *pl*; **~-winded** *adj* umständlich; *story* langatmig.

loo [luː] *n (Brit col)* Klo *nt (col)*. **to go to the ~** aufs Klo gehen *(col)*; **in the ~** auf dem Klo *(col)*.

look [lʊk] **1** *n* **(a)** *(glance)* Blick *m*. **she gave me a dirty ~** sie warf mir einen vernichtenden Blick zu; **she gave me a ~ of disbelief** sie sah mich ungläubig an; **to have** *or* **take a ~ at sth** sich *(dat)* etw ansehen; **can I have a ~?** darf ich mal sehen; **have a ~ at this!** sieh dir das mal an!; **let's have a ~** laß mal sehen!; **to take a good ~ at sth** sich *(dat)* etw genau ansehen; **to have a ~ for sth** sich nach etw umsehen; **to have a ~ around** sich umsehen; **shall we have a ~ around the town?** sollen wir uns *(dat)* die Stadt ansehen?

(b) *(air, appearances)* Aussehen *nt*. **there was a ~ of despair in his eyes** ein verzweifelter Blick war in seinen Augen; **I don't like the ~ of him/this wound** er/die Wunde gefällt mir gar nicht; **by the ~ of him** so, wie er aussieht.

(c) ~s *pl* Aussehen *nt;* **good ~s** gutes Aussehen; **you can't go by ~s alone** man kann nicht nur nach dem Äußeren gehen.

2 *vt* **he is ~ing his age** man sieht ihm sein Alter an; **he's not ~ing himself these days** er sieht in letzter Zeit ganz verändert aus; **to ~ one's best** sehr vorteilhaft aussehen; **~ what you've done!** sieh dir mal an, was du da angestellt hast!; **~ where you're going!** paß auf, wo du hintrittst!

3 *vi* **(a)** *(see, glance)* gucken *(col)*, schauen *(dial)*; *(with prep etc also)* sehen; *(search)* suchen, nachsehen. **to ~ carefully** genau hinsehen *etc;* **~ here!** hör (mal) zu!; **~, I know you're tired, but ...** ich weiß ja, daß du müde bist, aber ...; **just ~!** guck mal! *(col)*; **to ~ over one's shoulder** über die Schulter sehen; **to ~ over sb's shoulder** jdm über die Schulter sehen; **~ before you leap** *(Prov)* erst wägen, dann wagen *(Prov)*.

(b) *(seem)* aussehen. **it ~s all right to me** es scheint mir in Ordnung zu sein; **it ~s suspicious to me** es kommt mir verdächtig vor; **the car ~s about 10 years old** das Auto sieht so aus, als ob es 10 Jahre alt wäre; **it ~s well on you** es steht dir gut; **to ~ like** aussehen wie; **the picture doesn't ~ like him** das Bild sieht ihm nicht ähnlich; **it ~s like rain** es sieht nach Regen aus; **it ~s as if we'll be late** es sieht (so) aus, als würden wir zu spät kommen.

(c) *(face)* gehen nach. **this window ~s north** dieses Fenster geht nach Norden.

♦ **look after** *vi +prep obj* **(a)** *(take care of)* sich kümmern um. **to ~ ~ oneself** *(cook etc)* für sich selbst sorgen; *(be capable, strong etc)* auf sich *(acc)* aufpassen. **(b)** *bags, children* aufpassen auf *(+acc)*.

♦ **look around** *vi* **(a)** sich umsehen. **(b)** *(in shop etc)* sich umsehen. **let's ~ ~ the garden** sehen wir uns den Garten an.

♦ **look at** *vi +prep obj (also examine)* ansehen, angucken *(col)*; *(view)* betrachten, sehen; *(consider) possibilities* sich *(dat)* überlegen; *offer* in Betracht ziehen. **he ~ed ~ his watch** er sah auf die Uhr; **he/it isn't much to ~ ~** *(not attractive)* er/es sieht nicht besonders (gut) aus; *(nothing special)* er/es sieht nach nichts aus.

♦ **look away** *vi* wegsehen.

♦ **look back** *vi* sich umsehen; *(fig)* zurückblicken *(on sth, to sth* auf etw *acc)*. **he's never ~ed ~** *(col)* es ist ständig mit ihm bergauf gegangen.

♦ **look down** *vi* hinunter-/heruntersehen *or* -gucken *(col)*. **we ~ed ~ the hole** wir sahen ins Loch hinunter.

♦ **look down on** *vi +prep obj (lit, fig)* herabsehen auf *(+acc)*.

♦ **look for** *vi +prep obj (seek)* suchen. **he's ~ing ~ trouble** er wird sich *(dat)* Ärger einhandeln; *(actively)* er sucht Streit.

♦ **look forward to** *vi +prep obj* sich freuen auf *(+acc)*. **I'm so ~ing ~ ~ seeing you again** ich freue mich so darauf, dich wiederzusehen; **I ~ ~ ~ hearing from you** ich hoffe, bald von Ihnen zu hören.

♦ **look in** *vi* **(a)** hinein-/hereinsehen *or* -gucken *(col)*. **(b)** *(visit)* vorbeikommen *(on sb* bei jdm*)*.

♦ **look into** *vi +prep obj* untersuchen; *complaint etc* prüfen.

♦ **look on** *vi* **(a)** *(watch)* zusehen, zugucken *(col)*. **(b) to ~ ~to** *(window)* (hinaus)gehen auf *(+acc)*; *(building)* liegen an *(+dat)*. **(c)** *+prep obj (also* **look upon***)* betrachten, ansehen.

♦ **look out 1** *vi* **(a)** hinaus-/heraussehen *or* -gucken *(col)*. **to ~ ~ (of) the window** zum Fenster hinaussehen, aus dem Fenster sehen; **to ~ ~ for sb/troublemakers** nach jdm Ausschau halten/auf Unruhestifter achten. **(b)** *(take care)* aufpassen. **~ ~!** paß auf! **2** *vt sep* heraussuchen.

♦ **look over** *vt sep papers, notes etc* durchsehen; *house* sich *(dat)* ansehen.

♦ **look round** *vi* = **look around.**

♦ **look through 1** *vi* durchsehen *or* -gucken *(col) (prep obj* durch*)*. **he ~ed ~ the window** er sah zum Fenster hinein/herein; **to ~ straight ~ sb** durch jdn hindurchgucken. **2** *vt sep (examine)* durchsehen.

♦ **look to** *vi +prep obj* **(a)** *(look after)* sich kümmern um. **(b)** *(rely on)* sich verlassen auf *(+acc)*. **they ~ed ~ him to solve the problem** sie verließen sich darauf, daß er das Problem lösen würde.

♦ **look up 1** *vi* **(a)** aufsehen, aufblicken. **(b)** *(improve)* besser werden; *(shares, prices)* steigen. **things are ~ing ~** es geht bergauf. **2** *vt sep* **(a) to ~ sb ~ and down** jdn von oben bis unten ansehen. **(b)** *(visit)* **to ~ sb ~** bei jdm vorbeischauen. **(c)** *(seek) word* nachschlagen.

looker-on ['lʊkə'(r)ɒn] Schaulustige(r) *mf (pej)*.

look-in ['lʊkɪn] *n:* **he didn't get a ~** *(col)* er hatte keine Chance.

looking glass ['lʊkɪŋglaːs] *n* Spiegel *m.*

look-out ['lʊk,aʊt] *n* **(a)** *(Mil) (tower etc)* Ausguck *m; (person)* Wachtposten *m.* **to keep a ~ for** Ausschau halten nach. **~post** Beobachtungsposten *m.* **(b)** *(prospect)* Aussichten *pl.* **it's a grim ~ for us** es sieht schlecht aus für uns. **(c)** *(col: worry)* **that's his ~!** das ist sein Problem!

loom[1] [luːm] *n* Webstuhl *m.*

loom[2] *vi (also ~* **ahead** *or* **up**) *(lit, fig)* sich abzeichnen; *(storm)* heraufziehen; *(disaster)* sich zusammenbrauen; *(danger)* drohen; *(difficulties)* sich auftürmen; *(exams)* bedrohlich näherrücken. **the ship ~ed (up) out of the mist** das Schiff tauchte aus dem Nebel (auf); **to ~ large** eine große Rolle spielen.

loony ['luːnɪ] *(col)* **1** *adj (+er)* bekloppt *(col).* **2** *n* Verrückte(r) *(col) mf.* **~ bin** Klapsmühle *f (col).*

loop [luːp] **1** *n* **(a)** *(curved shape)* Schlaufe *f; (of wire)* Schlinge *f; (of river)* Schleife *f.* **(b)** *(Aviat)* Looping *m.* **to ~ the ~** einen Looping machen. **2** *vt rope etc* schlingen *(around* um*).*

loophole ['luːp,həʊl] *n (fig)* Hintertürchen *nt.* **a ~ in the law** eine Lücke im Gesetz.

loose [luːs] **1** *adj (+er)* **(a)** *board, button* lose; *dress, collar* weit; *tooth, bandage, knot, screw, soil, weave* locker; *limbs* beweglich. **~ change** Kleingeld *nt;* **a ~ connection** *(Elec)* ein Wackelkontakt *m;* **to come** *or* **work ~** *(screw, handle etc)* sich lockern; *(button)* abgehen.

(b) *(free)* **to break** *or* **get ~** *(person, animal)* sich losreißen *(from* von*)*; *(break out)* ausbrechen; **to run ~** frei herumlaufen; *(of children)* unbeaufsichtigt herumlaufen; **to be at a ~ end** *(fig)* nichts mit sich anzufangen wissen; **to turn** *or* **set ~** frei herumlaufen lassen; *prisoner* freilassen; **to tie up the ~ ends** *(fig)* ein paar offene Probleme lösen.

(c) *(not exact, vague) translation* frei; *account* ungenau; *connection* lose; *thinking* unlogisch.

(d) *(too free, immoral) conduct* lose; *morals* locker; *person* unmoralisch.

2 *n (col)* **to be on the ~** *(prisoners, dangerous animals)* frei herumlaufen.

3 *vt* **(a)** *(free)* befreien. **(b)** *(untie)* losmachen. **(c)** *(slacken)* lockern.

loose: ~ covers *npl* Überzüge *pl;* **~-fitting** *adj* weit; **~-leaf book** *n* Ringbuch *nt;* **~-limbed** *adj (lithe)* gelenkig.

loosely ['luːslɪ] *adv* lose, locker; *behave* unmoralisch. **~ speaking** grob gesagt; **I was using the word rather ~** ich habe das Wort ziemlich frei gebraucht.

loosen ['luːsn] **1** *vt* **(a)** *(free)* befreien; *tongue* lösen. **(b)** *(untie)* lösen. **(c)** *(slacken)* lockern; *collar* aufmachen. **2** *vi* sich lockern.

♦ **loosen up 1** *vt sep muscles* lockern. **2** *vi (muscles)* locker werden; *(athlete)* sich (auf)lockern; *(relax)* auftauen.

loot [luːt] **1** *n* Beute *f; (col: money)* Zaster *m (col).* **2** *vti* plündern.

looter ['luːtəʳ] *n* Plünderer *m.*

lop [lɒp] *vt (also ~* **off**) abhacken.

lope [ləʊp] *vi* in großen Sätzen springen; *(hare)* hoppeln.

lopsided ['lɒp'saɪdɪd] *adj* schief; *(fig)* einseitig.

loquacious [lə'kweɪʃəs] *adj* redselig.

lord [lɔːd] **1** *n* **(a)** *(master, ruler)* Herr *m.* **~ and master** Herr und Meister *m.* **(b)** *(Brit)* Lord *m.* **the (House of) L~s** das Oberhaus; **my ~** *(to noble) (in English contexts)* Mylord; *(to judge)* Euer Ehren; **L~ Chancellor** Lordkanzler *m;* **L~ Mayor** ≃ Oberbürgermeister *m.* **(c)** *(Rel)* **L~** Herr *m;* **the L~'s prayer** das Vaterunser; **(good) L~!** *(col)* ach, du lieber Himmel! *(col);* **L~ knows** *(col)* wer weiß; **L~ knows I've tried often enough** ich hab's weiß Gott oft genug versucht. **2** *vt* **to ~ it** das Zepter schwingen; **to ~ it over sb** jdn herumkommandieren.

lordship ['lɔːdʃɪp] *n (Brit: title)* Lordschaft *f.* **your ~** Eure Lordschaft; *(to judge)* Euer Ehren.

lore [lɔːʳ] *n* Überlieferungen *pl.* **plant ~** Pflanzenkunde *f.*

lorry ['lɒrɪ] *n (Brit)* Last(kraft)wagen, Lkw, Laster *(col) m.* **~ driver** Last(kraft)wagenfahrer(in *f*) *m.*

lose [luːz] *pret, ptp* **lost 1** *vt* **(a)** verlieren; *pursuer* abschütteln; *one's French* verlernen; *prize* nicht bekommen. **the shares have lost 15% in a month** die Aktien sind in einem Monat um 15% gefallen; **you will ~ nothing by helping them** es kann dir nicht schaden, wenn du ihnen hilfst; **that mistake lost him the game** dieser Fehler kostete ihn den Sieg; **to ~ no time in doing sth** etw sofort tun; **my watch lost three hours in a week** meine Uhr ist innerhalb einer Woche drei Stunden nachgegangen.

(b) *(not catch) train, opportunity* verpassen; *words* nicht mitbekommen. **you've lost me now with all this abstract argument** bei dieser abstrakten Argumentation komme ich nicht mehr mit.

(c) to be lost *(things)* verschwunden sein; *(people)* sich verlaufen haben; *(driver)* sich verfahren haben; *(fig)* verloren sein; *(words)* untergehen; **I can't follow the reasoning, I'm lost** ich kann der Argumentation nicht folgen, ich verstehe nichts mehr; **to get lost** sich verlaufen; *(driver)* sich verfahren; **get lost!** *(col)* verschwinde! *(col);* **to give sb/sth up for lost** jdn verloren geben/etw abschreiben; **I'm lost without my watch** ohne meine Uhr bin ich verloren *or* aufgeschmissen *(col);* **classical music is lost on him** er hat keinen Sinn für klassische Musik; **the remark was lost on her** die Bemerkung kam bei ihr nicht an.

2 *vi* verlieren; *(watch)* nachgehen. **you can't ~** du kannst nichts verlieren

♦ **lose out** *vi (col)* den kürzeren ziehen *(on* bei*) (col).*

loser ['luːzəʳ] *n* Verlierer(in *f*) *m.* **he's a born ~** er ist der geborene Verlierer; **to be a bad ~** ein schlechter Verlierer sein.

losing ['luːzɪŋ] *adj team* Verlierer-. **a ~ battle** ein aussichtsloser Kampf.

loss [lɒs] *n* **(a)** Verlust *m.* **there was a heavy ~ of life** viele kamen ums Leben; **the army suffered heavy ~es** die Armee erlitt schwere Verluste; **his business is running at a ~** er arbeitet mit Verlust; **to sell sth at a ~** etw mit Verlust verkaufen; **it's your ~** es ist deine Sache; **a dead ~** *(col)* ein böser Reinfall *(col); (person)* ein hoffnungsloser Fall *(col).* **(b) to be at a ~** nicht mehr weiterwissen; **to be at a ~ to explain sth** etw nicht erklären können; **to be at a ~ for words** nicht wissen, was man sagen soll.

lost [lɒst] **1** *pret, ptp of* **lose. 2** *adj* verloren; *cause* aussichtslos; *child* verschwunden; *opportunity* verpaßt. **~-and-found (department)** *(US),* **~ property office** *(Brit)* Fundbüro *nt.*

lot[1] [lɒt] *n* **(a)** *(for deciding)* Los *nt.* **to cast** *or* **draw ~s for sth** etw verlosen. **(b)** *(destiny)* Los *nt.* **it falls to my ~ to tell him** mir fällt die Aufgabe zu, es ihm zu sagen; **to throw in one's ~ with sb** sich mit jdm zusammentun. **(c)** *(plot)* Parzelle *f.* **parking ~** *(US)* Parkplatz *m.* **(d)** *(number of articles)* Posten *m; (at auction)* Los *nt.* **where shall I put this ~?** wo soll ich das hier hintun?; **divide the books up into three ~s** teile die Bücher in drei Stapel auf; **he's just given me another ~** er hat mir gerade einen neuen Stoß *or* noch eine Ladung gegeben *(col).* **(e)** *(col: group)* Haufen *m.* **that ~ in the next office** die Typen vom Büro nebenan *(col).* **(f) the ~** alle; alles; **that's the ~** das ist alles; **the whole ~ of them** sie alle; **he's**

eaten the ~ er hat alles aufgegessen.

lot[2] **1** *n* **a ~, ~s** viel; **a ~ of money** viel Geld; **a ~ of books, ~s of books** viele Bücher; **such a ~** so viel; **quite a ~ of books** ziemlich viele Bücher; **he made ~s and ~s of mistakes** er hat eine Unmenge Fehler gemacht; **we see a ~ of John these days** wir sehen John in letzter Zeit sehr oft; **I'd give a ~ to know ...** ich würde viel darum geben, wenn ich wüßte ...; **thanks a ~!** *(also iro)* vielen Dank! **2** *adv* **a ~, ~s** viel; **things have changed a ~** es hat sich vieles geändert; **I feel ~s** *or* **a ~ better** es geht mir sehr viel besser.

lotion ['ləʊʃən] *n* Lotion *f.*

lottery ['lɒtərɪ] *n* Lotterie *f.*

loud [laʊd] **1** *adj (+er)* **(a)** laut. **~ and clear** laut und deutlich. **(b)** *behaviour* aufdringlich; *colour* schreiend; *(in bad taste)* auffällig. **2** *adv* laut. **to say sth out ~** etw laut sagen.

loudhailer [ˌlaʊd'heɪlə[r]] *n* Megaphon *nt; (not hand-held)* Lautsprecher *m.*

loudly ['laʊdlɪ] *adv see adj.* **he was ~ dressed in blue** er war in ein grelles Blau gekleidet.

loud-mouthed ['laʊd,maʊðd] *adj (col)* großmäulig *(col).*

loudspeaker [ˌlaʊd'spiːkə[r]] n Lautsprecher *m; (of hi-fi also)* Box *f.*

lounge [laʊndʒ] **1** *n (in house)* Wohnzimmer *nt; (in hotel)* Gesellschaftsraum *m; (~ bar)* Salon *m; (at airport)* Warteraum *m.* **2** *vi* faulenzen. **to ~ about** herumliegen/-sitzen/-stehen.

lour, lower ['laʊə[r]] *vi (person)* ein finsteres Gesicht machen; *(clouds)* sich türmen. **to ~ at sb** jdn finster *or* drohend ansehen.

louse [laʊs] *n, pl* **lice** *(Zool)* Laus *f.*

lousy ['laʊzɪ] *adj (col: very bad)* saumäßig *(col),* beschissen *(col!); trick etc* fies *(col).* **I'm ~ at arithmetic** in Mathe bin ich miserabel *(col);* **a ~ $3** lausige 3 Dollar *(col).*

lout [laʊt] *n* Rüpel, Flegel *m.*

lovable ['lʌvəbl] *adj* liebenswert.

love [lʌv] **1** *n* **(a)** *(affection)* Liebe *f.* **~ of learning** Freude *f* am Lernen; **~ of books** Liebe *f* zu Büchern; **he studies history for the ~ of it** er studiert Geschichte aus Liebe zur Sache; **to be in ~ (with sb)** (in jdn) verliebt sein; **to fall in ~ (with sb)** sich (in jdn) verlieben; **there is no ~ lost between them** sie können sich nicht ausstehen; **to make ~** *(sexually)* miteinander schlafen; **to make ~ to sb** *(sexually)* mit jdm schlafen. **(b)** *(greetings)* **all my ~** mit herzlichen Grüßen; **give him my ~** grüß ihn von mir; **he sends his ~** er läßt grüßen; **yes, (my) ~** ja, Liebling. **(c)** *(Tennis)* null. **fifteen ~** fünfzehn null.

2 *vt* lieben; *(like) thing* gern mögen. **I ~ tennis** ich mag Tennis sehr gern; *(to play)* ich spiele sehr gern Tennis; **I'd ~ to come** ich würde sehr gerne kommen.

love: ~ affair *n* Verhältnis *nt;* **~ game** *n (Tennis)* Zu-Null-Spiel *nt;* **~-hate relationship** *n* Haßliebe *f;* **~ letter** *n* Liebesbrief *m;* **~ life** *n* Liebesleben *nt.*

lovely ['lʌvlɪ] *adj (+er) (beautiful)* schön; *object also* hübsch; *baby* niedlich; *(delightful)* herrlich; *(likeable)* nett. **we had a ~ time** es war sehr schön; **it's ~ and warm in this room** es ist schön warm in diesem Zimmer; **it's been ~ to see you** es war schön, dich zu sehen.

love-making ['lʌv,meɪkɪŋ] *n (sexual)* Liebe *f.*

lover ['lʌvə[r]] *n* **(a)** Geliebte(r) *mf.* **the ~s** das Liebespaar; **to be a good ~** gut in der Liebe sein. **(b) a ~ of good food** ein Freund *m* von gutem Essen; **music ~** Musikliebhaber *m.*

love: ~sick *adj* **to be ~sick** Liebeskummer *m* haben; **~ story** *n* Liebesgeschichte *f.*

loving ['lʌvɪŋ] *adj* liebend; *look, disposition* liebevoll.

lovingly ['lʌvɪŋlɪ] *adv* liebevoll.

low[1] [ləʊ] **1** *adj (+er)* niedrig; *form of life* nieder; *bow, note, punch* tief; *density, intelligence* gering; *food supplies* knapp; *quality* minderwertig; *light* gedämpft; *rank, position also* untergeordnet; *tastes, manners* gewöhnlich, ordinär *(pej); company* schlecht; *joke, song* geschmacklos; *trick* gemein; *resistance* gering; *morale* schlecht. **to speak in a ~ voice** leise sprechen; **the lamp was ~** die Lampe brannte schwach; **to feel ~** sich nicht wohl *or* gut fühlen; *(emotionally)* niedergeschlagen sein.

2 *adv aim* nach unten; *speak, sing* leise; *fly, bow* tief. **I would never sink so ~ as to ...** so tief würde ich nie sinken, daß ich ...; **share prices went so ~ that ...** die Aktienkurse fielen so sehr, daß ...; **to run** *or* **get ~** knapp werden; **we are getting ~ on petrol** uns *(dat)* geht das Benzin aus.

3 *n* **(a)** *(Met)* Tief *nt; (fig also)* Tiefpunkt *m.* **to reach a new ~** einen neuen Tiefstand erreichen. **(b)** *(Aut: ~ gear)* niedriger Gang.

low[2] **1** *n (of cow)* Muh *nt.* **2** *vi* muhen.

low: ~brow *adj* (geistig) anspruchslos; **~-cost** *adj* preiswert; **the L~ Countries** *npl* die Niederlande *pl;* **~-cut** *adj dress* tief ausgeschnitten; **~-down** *(col)* **1** *n* Informationen *pl;* **he gave me the ~-down on it** er hat mich darüber aufgeklärt; **2** *adj (esp US)* gemein, fies *(col).*

lower[1] ['ləʊə[r]] **1** *adj see* **low**[1] niedriger; tiefer *etc; jaw, arm* Unter-; *limbs, storeys* untere(r, s). **the ~ school** die Unter- und Mittelstufe; **hemlines are ~ this year** die Röcke sind dieses Jahr länger; **the ~ classes** die untere(n) Schicht(en).

2 *adv* tiefer; leiser. **~ down the mountain** weiter unten am Berg; **~ down the scale/the list** weiter unten auf der Skala/Liste.

3 *vt load* herunter-/hinunterlassen; *eyes, gun* senken; *sail, flag* einholen; *bicycle saddle* niedriger machen; *pressure* verringern; *voice, price* senken; *morale, resistance* schwächen; *standard* herabsetzen. **~ your voice** sprich leiser!; **his behaviour ~ed him in my opinion** sein Benehmen ließ ihn in meiner Achtung sinken; **to ~ the tone of the conversation** das Gesprächsniveau senken; **to ~ oneself to do sth** sich herablassen, etw zu tun.

lower[2] ['laʊə[r]] *vi* = **lour.**

lower case ['ləʊəkeɪs] *n* Kleinbuchstaben *pl.*

low: ~-flying *adj* tieffliegend; **~-grade** *adj* minderwertig; **~ key** *adj approach* gelassen; *handling* besonnen; *production* einfach gehalten; *reception* reserviert; **~land** *n* Flachland *nt.*

lowly ['ləʊlɪ] *adj (+er)* bescheiden.

low-lying [ˌləʊ'laɪɪŋ] *adj* tiefgelegen.

low: ~-pitched *adj* tief; **~-rise** *attr* niedrig (gebaut); **~-spirited** *adj* niedergeschlagen; **~ tide, ~ water** *n* Niedrigwasser *nt.*

loyal ['lɔɪəl] *adj (+er)* treu. **he was very ~ to his friends** er hielt (treu) zu seinen Freunden.

loyalist ['lɔɪəlɪst] **1** *n* Loyalist *m.* **2** *adj* loyal; *troops* regierungstreu.

loyally ['lɔɪəlɪ] *adv* treu.

loyalty ['lɔɪəltɪ] *n* Treue *f; (esp Pol also)* Loyalität *f.* **conflicting loyalties** nicht zu vereinbarende Treuepflichten; **his changing political loyalties** seine wechselnden politischen Bekenntnisse.

lozenge ['lɒzɪndʒ] *n* **(a)** *(Med)* Pastille *f.* **(b)** *(shape)* Raute *f.*

LP = long player, long playing record LP *f.*

L-plate ['elpleɪt] *n Schild nt mit der Aufschrift „L" (für Fahrschüler).*

Ltd = Limited GmbH.

lubricant ['luːbrɪkənt] *n* Schmiermittel *nt.*

lubricate ['luːbrɪkeɪt] *vt (lit, fig)* schmieren, ölen. **well-~d** *(hum)* gut abgefüllt *(col).*

lubrication [ˌluːbrɪ'keɪʃən] *n* Schmieren, Ölen *nt.*

lucid ['luːsɪd] *adj (+er) (clear)* klar; *explanation* anschaulich. **~ intervals** lichte Augenblicke.

luck [lʌk] *n* Glück *nt.* **bad ~** Unglück, Pech *nt;* **bad**

~! so ein Pech!; **good ~** Glück *nt;* **good ~!** viel Glück!; **good ~ to them!** *(iro),* **and the best of (British) ~!** *(iro)* na dann viel Glück!; **no such ~!** schön wär's! *(col);* **just my ~!** Pech (gehabt), wie immer!; **it's the ~ of the draw** man muß es eben nehmen, wie's kommt; **with any ~** mit etwas Glück; **worse ~** leider; **better ~ next time!** vielleicht klappt es beim nächsten Mal!; **to be in ~** Glück haben; **to be out of ~** kein Glück haben; **he was a bit down on his ~** er hatte eine Pechsträhne; **to bring sb bad ~** jdm Unglück bringen; **as ~ would have it** wie es der Zufall wollte; **for ~** als Glücksbringer; **to try one's ~** sein Glück versuchen.

luckily ['lʌkɪlɪ] *adv* glücklicherweise. **~ for me** zu meinem Glück.

lucky [lʌkɪ] *adj (+er) (having, bringing luck) person, number* Glücks-; *coincidence* glücklich. **~ charm** Glücksbringer *m;* **~ dip** ≈ Glückstopf *m;* **it must be my ~ day** ich habe wohl heute meinen Glückstag; **you ~ thing!, ~ you!** du Glückliche(r); **to be ~** Glück haben; **I was ~ enough to meet him** ich hatte das Glück, ihn kennenzulernen; **you are ~ to be alive** du kannst von Glück sagen, daß du noch lebst; **you were ~ to catch him** du hast Glück gehabt, daß du ihn erwischt hast; **you'll be ~ to make it in time** wenn du das noch schaffst, hast du (aber) Glück; **I want another £500 — you'll be ~!** ich will nochmal £ 500 haben — viel Glück!; **it was ~ I stopped him in time** zum Glück habe ich ihn rechtzeitig aufgehalten; **that was a ~ escape** da habe ich/hast du *etc* nochmal Glück gehabt.

lucrative ['lu:krətɪv] *adj* einträglich, lukrativ.

ludicrous ['lu:dɪkrəs] *adj* grotesk; *sight, words also* lächerlich.

lug [lʌg] *vt* schleppen.

luggage ['lʌgɪdʒ] *n* Gepäck *nt.*

luggage: ~ rack *n (Rail etc)* Gepäckablage *f; (Aut)* Gepäckträger *m;* **~ trolley** *(Brit),* **~ cart** *(US) n* Kofferkuli *m;* **~ van** *n (Brit Rail)* Gepäckwagen *m.*

lugubrious [lu:'gu:brɪəs] *adj person, song* schwermütig; *expression* kummervoll.

lukewarm ['lu:kwɔ:m] *adj (lit, fig)* lauwarm; *support also* mäßig; *friendship* oberflächlich.

lull [lʌl] **1** *n* Pause *f; (Comm)* Flaute *f.* **a ~ in the wind** eine Windstille; **a ~ in the conversation** eine Gesprächspause. **2** *vt baby* beruhigen; *(fig)* einlullen. **to ~ a baby to sleep** ein Baby in den Schlaf wiegen; **he was ~ed into a sense of false security** er wiegte sich in trügerischer Sicherheit.

lullaby ['lʌləbaɪ] *n* Schlaflied *nt.*

lumbago [lʌm'beɪgəʊ] *n* Hexenschuß *m.*

lumber[1] ['lʌmbə[r]] **1** *n* **(a)** *(timber)* (Bau)holz *nt.* **(b)** *(junk)* Gerümpel *nt.* **2** *vt (Brit col)* **to ~ sb with sth** jdm etw aufhalsen *(col);* **he got ~ed with the job** man hat ihm die Arbeit aufgehalst *(col);* **I got ~ed with her for the evening** ich hatte sie den ganzen Abend auf dem Hals *(col).*

lumber[2] *vi (cart)* rumpeln; *(elephant, person)* trampeln.

lumber: ~jack *n* Holzfäller *m;* **~ room** *n* Rumpelkammer *f;* **~yard** *n (US)* Holzlager *nt.*

luminous ['lu:mɪnəs] *adj* leuchtend; *paint, dial* Leucht-.

lump [lʌmp] **1** *n* Klumpen *m; (of sugar)* Stück *nt; (swelling)* Beule *f.* **with a ~ in one's throat** *(fig)* mit einem Kloß im Hals. **2** *vt (col)* **if he doesn't like it he can ~ it** wenn's ihm nicht paßt, hat er eben Pech gehabt *(col).*

♦**lump together** *vt sep* **(a)** *(put together)* zusammentun; *books* zusammenstellen; *expenses, money* zusammenlegen. **(b)** *(judge together) persons, topics* über einen Kamm scheren. **he ~ed all the soldiers ~ as traitors** er urteilte all die Soldaten pauschal als Verräter ab.

lump: ~ sugar *n* Würfelzucker *m;* **~ sum** *n* Pauschalsumme *f;* **to pay sth in a ~ sum** etw pauschal bezahlen.

lumpy ['lʌmpɪ] *adj (+er)* klumpig.

lunacy ['lu:nəsɪ] *n* Wahnsinn *m.* **it's sheer ~!** das ist reiner Wahnsinn!

lunar ['lu:nə[r]] *adj* Mond-. **~ module** Mondfähre *f.*

lunatic ['lu:nətɪk] **1** *adj* verrückt, wahnsinnig. **~ fringe** radikale Randgruppe. **2** *n* Wahnsinnige(r), Irre(r) *mf.* **~ asylum** Irrenanstalt *f.*

lunch [lʌntʃ] *n* Mittagessen *nt.* **to have ~** (zu) Mittag essen; **he's at ~** er ist beim Mittagessen.

lunch break *n* Mittagspause *f.*

luncheon ['lʌntʃən] *n (form)* Mittagessen *nt.*

lunch: ~ hour *n* Mittagspause *f;* **~time** *n* Mittagspause *f.*

lung [lʌŋ] *n* Lunge *f.* **~ cancer** Lungenkrebs *m.*

lunge [lʌndʒ] **1** *n* Satz *m* nach vorn; *(esp Fencing)* Ausfall *m.* **he made a ~ at his opponent** er stürzte sich auf seinen Gegner. **2** *vi* (sich) stürzen. **to ~ at sb** sich auf jdn stürzen.

lurch[1] [lɜ:tʃ] *n:* **to leave sb in the ~** *(col)* jdn im Stich lassen, jdn hängenlassen *(col).*

lurch[2] **1** *n* Ruck *m; (of boat)* Schlingern *nt.* **to give a ~** einen Ruck machen; *(boat)* schlingern. **2** *vi* **(a)** *see* **to give a ~. (b)** *(move with ~es)* sich ruckartig bewegen; *(boat)* schlingern; *(person)* taumeln. **the train ~ed to a standstill** der Zug kam mit einem Ruck zum Stehen; **to ~ about** hin und her schlingern/hin und her taumeln.

lure [lʊə[r]] **1** *n (bait)* Köder *m; (person, for hawk)* Lockvogel *m; (general)* Lockmittel *nt; (fig: of city, sea etc)* Verlockungen *pl.* **2** *vt* anlocken. **to ~ sb/an animal into a trap** jdn/ein Tier in eine Falle locken; **to ~ sb/an animal out** jdn/ein Tier herauslocken.

lurid ['lʊərɪd] *adj (+er) colour, sky* grell; *dress* grellfarben, in grellen Farben; *posters also* schreiend; *language* reißerisch; *account* sensationslüstern; *detail* grausig; *(sordid)* widerlich.

lurk [lɜ:k] *vi* lauern. **a doubt still ~ed in his mind** ein Zweifel plagte ihn noch.

luscious ['lʌʃəs] *adj* köstlich; *fruit also* saftig; *girl* zum Anbeißen *(col).*

lush [lʌʃ] *adj grass* saftig, satt; *vegetation* üppig.

lust [lʌst] **1** *n (inner sensation)* Wollust *f; (wanting to acquire)* Begierde *f (for* nach*); (greed)* Gier *f (for* nach*).* **~ for power** Machtgier *f.* **2** *vi* **to ~ after, to ~ for** *(sexually)* begehren *(+acc); (greedily)* gieren nach.

lustre, *(US)* luster ['lʌstə[r]] *n* Schimmer *m; (in eyes)* Glanz *m.*

lustrous ['lʌstrəs] *adj* schimmernd, glänzend.

lusty ['lʌstɪ] *adj (+er) person* gesund und munter; *man also, life* urwüchsig; *appetite* herzhaft; *cheer, cry* kräftig; *push, kick etc* kraftvoll.

lute [lu:t] *n* Laute *f.*

Luxembourg ['lʌksəmbɜ:g] *n* Luxemburg *nt.*

luxuriant [lʌg'zjʊərɪənt] *adj* üppig.

luxurious [lʌg'zjʊərɪəs] *adj* luxuriös, Luxus-; *carpet, hotel also* feudal; *food* üppig.

luxury ['lʌkʃərɪ] **1** *n* Luxus *m; (of car, house etc)* luxuriöse Ausstattung. **to live a life of ~** ein Luxusleben führen; **little luxuries** Luxus *m.* **2** *adj (cruise, tax)* Luxus-.

lying ['laɪɪŋ] **1** *adj* verlogen. **2** *n* Lügen *nt.* **that would be ~** das wäre gelogen.

lynch [lɪntʃ] *vt* lynchen.

lynching ['lɪntʃɪŋ] *n* Lynchen *nt.*

lynx [lɪŋks] *n* Luchs *m.*

lyre ['laɪə[r]] *n* Leier *f.*

lyric ['lɪrɪk] **1** *adj* lyrisch. **2** *n (poem)* lyrisches Gedicht; *(often pl: words of pop song)* Text *m.*

lyrical ['lɪrɪkəl] *adj* lyrisch; *(fig)* schwärmerisch. **to get *or* wax ~ about sth** über etw *(acc)* ins Schwärmen geraten.

M

M, m [em] *n* M, m *nt.*

m = million(s) Mio; **metre(s)** m; **mile(s).**

MA = Master of Arts.

ma [mɑː] *n (col)* Mama *(col)*, Mutti *(col) f.*

mac [mæk] *n (Brit col)* Regenmantel *m.*

macabre [mə'kɑːbrə] *adj* makaber.

macaroni [ˌmækə'rəʊnɪ] *n* Makkaroni *pl.* **~ cheese** Käsenudeln *pl.*

macaroon [ˌmækə'ruːn] *n* Makrone *f.*

mace[1] [meɪs] *n (weapon)* Streitkolben *m; (mayor's)* Amtsstab *m.*

mace[2] *n (spice)* Muskatblüte *f.*

machete [mə'tʃeɪtɪ] *n* Machete *f.*

Machiavellian [ˌmækɪə'velɪən] *adj* machiavellistisch.

machination [ˌmækɪ'neɪʃən] *n usu pl* Machenschaften *pl.*

machine [mə'ʃiːn] **1** *n* Maschine *f,* Apparat *m; (vending ~)* Automat *m.* **2** *vt (Tech)* maschinell herstellen; *(treat with machine)* maschinell bearbeiten; *(Sew)* mit der Maschine nähen.

machine: ~ gun *n* Maschinengewehr *nt;* **~ operator** *n* Maschinenarbeiter *m; (skilled)* Maschinist *m.*

machinery [mə'ʃiːnərɪ] *n (lit, fig)* Maschinerie *f; (mechanism)* Mechanismus *m.* **the ~ of government** der Regierungsapparat.

machine: ~ shop *n* Maschinensaal *m;* **~ tool** *n* Werkzeugmaschine *f;* **~ washable** *adj* waschmaschinenfest.

machinist [mə'ʃiːnɪst] *n (Tech) (operator)* Maschinist *m; (Sew)* Näherin *f.*

mackerel ['mækrəl] *n* Makrele *f.*

mackintosh ['mækɪntɒʃ] *n* Regenmantel *m.*

macro- ['mækrəʊ-] *pref* makro-, Makro-.

mad [mæd] **1** *adj (+er)* **(a)** wahnsinnig; *dog* tollwütig; *idea* verrückt. **to go ~** wahnsinnig werden; **to drive sb ~** jdn wahnsinnig *or* verrückt machen; **he's as ~ as a hatter** *or* **a March hare** *(prov)* er ist total verrückt; **you must be ~!** du bist ja wahnsinnig!; **they made a ~ rush for the door** sie stürzten zur Tür; **you ~ fool!** du bist ja wahnsinnig! **(b)** *(col: angry)* sauer *(col).* **to be ~ at sb** auf jdn sauer *(col)* sein; **to be ~ about** *or* **at sth** über etw *(acc)* wütend *or* sauer *(col)* sein. **(c)** *(col: very keen)* **to be ~ about** *or* **on sth** auf etw *(acc)* verrückt sein. **2** *adv (col)* **to be ~ keen on sb/sth** ganz scharf auf jdn/etw sein *(col)*; **to be ~ keen to do sth** ganz versessen darauf sein, etw zu tun; **like ~** wie verrückt.

madam ['mædəm] *n* **(a) yes, ~** sehr wohl, gnädige Frau *(old, form)*; **can I help you, ~?** kann ich Ihnen behilflich sein?; **Dear Sir or M~** Sehr geehrte Damen und Herren. **(b)** *(col: girl)* kleine Madam. **(c)** *(of brothel)* Bordellwirtin *f.*

madden ['mædn] *vt (make angry)* ärgern.

maddening ['mædnɪŋ] *adj* zum Verrücktwerden; *delay also* lästig; *habit* aufreizend. **isn't it ~?** ist das nicht ärgerlich?

made [meɪd] *pret, ptp of* **make.**

Madeira [mə'dɪərə] *n (wine)* Madeira *m.* **~ cake** Sandkuchen *m.*

made-to-measure ['meɪdtə'meʒə^r] *adj* maßgeschneidert. **~ suit** Maßanzug *m.*

madly ['mædlɪ] *adv* wie verrückt; *(col: extremely)* wahnsinnig. **to be ~ in love (with sb)** total (in jdn) verschossen sein *(col)* ; **I'm not ~ keen** ich bin nicht wahnsinnig scharf darauf *(col).*

madman ['mædmən] *n, pl* **-men** [-mən] Verrückter *m.*

madness ['mædnɪs] *n* Wahnsinn *m.* **it's sheer ~!** das ist heller *or* reiner Wahnsinn!

magazine [ˌmægə'ziːn] *n* **(a)** Zeitschrift *f,* Magazin *nt.* **(b)** *(in gun)* Magazin *nt.*

maggot ['mægət] *n* Made *f.*

magic ['mædʒɪk] **1** *n* Magie, Zauberei *f; (mysterious charm)* Zauber *m.* **as if by ~** wie durch Zauberei; **it worked like ~** *(col)* es lief wie am Schnürchen *(col).* **2** *adj* Zauber-; *powers* magisch; *moment* zauberhaft. **the ~ word** *(having special effect)* das Stichwort; *(making sth possible)* das Zauberwort.

magical ['mædʒɪkəl] *adj* magisch.

magician [mə'dʒɪʃən] *n* Zauberer *m; (conjuror)* Zauberkünstler *m.* **I'm not a ~!** ich kann doch nicht hexen!

magistrate ['mædʒɪstreɪt] *n* Friedensrichter *m.* **~s' court** Schiedsgericht *nt.*

magnanimous [mæg'nænɪməs] *adj* großmütig.

magnate ['mægneɪt] *n* Magnat *m.*

magnesia [mæg'niːʃə] *n* Magnesia *f.*

magnesium [mæg'niːzɪəm] *n* Magnesium *nt.*

magnet ['mægnɪt] *n (lit, fig)* Magnet *m.*

magnetic [mæg'netɪk] *adj (lit)* magnetisch; *charms* unwiderstehlich.

magnetism ['mægnɪtɪzəm] *n* Magnetismus *m; (fig: of person)* Anziehungskraft *f.*

magnetize ['mægnɪtaɪz] *vt* magnetisieren.

magnification [ˌmægnɪfɪ'keɪʃən] *n* Vergrößerung *f.*

magnificence [mæg'nɪfɪsəns] *n (excellence)* Größe *f; (splendid appearance)* Pracht *f,* Glanz *m.*

magnificent [mæg'nɪfɪsənt] *adj (wonderful, excellent)* großartig; *food, meal* ausgezeichnet; *(of splendid appearance)* prachtvoll.

magnify ['mægnɪfaɪ] *vt* vergrößern; *(exaggerate)* aufbauschen. **~ing glass** Lupe *f.*

magnitude ['mægnɪtjuːd] *n* Ausmaß *nt; (importance)* Bedeutung *f; (Astron)* Größenklasse *f.* **operations of this ~** Vorhaben dieser Größenordnung.

magpie ['mægpaɪ] *n* Elster *f.*

mahogany [mə'hɒgənɪ] **1** *n* Mahagoni *nt; (tree)* Mahagonibaum *m.* **2** *adj* Mahagoni-.

maid [meɪd] *n (servant)* (Dienst)mädchen *nt; (in hotel)* Zimmermädchen *nt; (lady's ~)* Zofe *f; (old, poet: young girl)* Maid *f (poet).*

maiden ['meɪdn] **1** *n (old, poet)* Mädchen *nt.* **2** *adj flight, voyage etc* Jungfern-.

maiden: ~ aunt *n* unverheiratete, ältere Tante; **~ name** *n* Mädchenname *m;* **~ speech** *n* Jungfernrede *f.*

maid: ~ of honour *(Brit) or* **honor** *(US) n* Brautjungfer *f;* **~servant** *n* Hausangestellte *f.*

mail [meɪl] **1** *n* Post *f.* **to send sth by ~** etw mit der Post schicken; **is there any ~ for me?** ist Post für mich da? **2** *vt* aufgeben; *(put in letterbox)* einwerfen; *(send by ~)* mit der Post schicken. **~ing list** Anschriftenliste *f.*

mail: ~box *n (US, also electronic)* Briefkasten *m;* **~man** *n (US)* Briefträger, Postbote *m;* **~-order catalogue** *n* Versandhauskatalog *m;* **~-order firm** *n* Versandhaus *nt;* **~shot** *n* Mailshot *m;*

~ train *n* Postzug *m;* **~ van** *n (on roads)* Postauto *nt; (Brit Rail)* Postwagen *m.*

maim [meɪm] *vt (mutilate)* verstümmeln; *(cripple)* zum Krüppel machen.

main [meɪn] **1** *adj attr* Haupt-. **the ~ thing is to ...** die Hauptsache ist, daß ...; **the ~ thing is you're still alive** Hauptsache, du lebst noch. **2** *n* **(a)** *(pipe)* Hauptleitung *f.* **the ~s** *(of town)* das öffentliche Versorgungsnetz; *(electricity also)* das Stromnetz; **~s operated** für Netzbetrieb; **the electricity was switched off at the ~s** der Hauptschalter für den Strom wurde abgeschaltet. **(b) in the ~** im großen und ganzen.

main: ~ course *n* Hauptgericht *nt;* **~frame** *n (Comp)* Großrechner *m;* **~land** *n* Festland *nt;* **on the ~land of Europe** auf dem europäischen Festland; **~line train** *n* Schnellzug *m.*

mainly ['meɪnlɪ] *adv* hauptsächlich; *(generally)* überwiegend. **the meetings are held ~ on Tuesdays** die Besprechungen finden meistens dienstags statt.

main: ~ road *n* Hauptstraße *f;* **~spring** *n (Mech)* Triebfeder *f; (fig)* treibende Kraft; **~stay** *n (fig)* Stütze *f;* **~stream** *n* Hauptrichtung *f;* **to be in the ~stream of sth** der Hauptrichtung *(+gen)* angehören.

maintain [meɪn'teɪn] *vt* **(a)** *(keep up)* aufrechterhalten; *law and order etc* wahren; *quality also, speed, attitude* beibehalten; *life* erhalten. **(b)** *(support) family* unterhalten. **(c)** *(in good condition) machine* warten; *roads, building* instand halten; *car* pflegen. **(d)** *(claim)* behaupten.

maintenance ['meɪntɪnəns] *n see vt* **(a)** Aufrechterhaltung *f;* Wahrung *f;* Beibehaltung *f;* Erhaltung *f.* **(b)** *(of family)* Unterhalt *m; (social security)* Unterstützung *f.* **he has to pay ~** er ist unterhaltspflichtig. **(c)** Wartung *f;* Instandhaltung *f;* Pflege *f.*

maintenance costs *npl* Unterhaltskosten *pl.*

maisonette [ˌmeɪzə'net] *n (small flat)* Appartement *nt; (small house)* Häuschen *nt.*

maize [meɪz] *n (Brit)* Mais *m.*

majestic [mə'dʒestɪk] *adj* majestätisch; *proportions* stattlich; *music* getragen.

majesty ['mædʒɪstɪ] *n* Majestät *f.* **Her M~** Ihre Majestät; **Your M~** Eure Majestät.

major ['meɪdʒə^r] **1** *adj* Haupt-; *(of greater importance)* bedeutend(er); *(of greater extent)* größer. **a ~ road** eine Hauptverkehrsstraße; **of ~ importance** von großer Bedeutung. **2** *n* **(a)** *(Mil)* Major *m.* **(b)** *(Jur)* **to become a ~** mündig werden. **(c)** *(US) (subject)* Hauptfach *nt.* **3** *vi (US)* **to ~ in sth** etw als Hauptfach studieren.

majority [mə'dʒɒrɪtɪ] *n* **(a)** Mehrheit *f.* **the ~ of cases** die Mehrzahl der Fälle; **to be in a ~** in der Mehrzahl sein; **to have a ~ of 10** eine Mehrheit von 10 Stimmen haben; **by a small ~** mit knapper Mehrheit. **(b)** *(Jur)* Mündigkeit *f.* **to attain one's ~** mündig werden.

majority: ~ decision *n* Mehrheitsbeschluß *m;* **~ holding** *n (Fin)* Mehrheitsbeteiligung *f;* **~ rule** *n* Mehrheitsregierung *f.*

make [meɪk] *(vb: pret, ptp* **made)** **1** *vt* **(a)** machen; *bread* backen; *cars* herstellen; *dress* nähen; *coffee* kochen; *the world* erschaffen; *speech* halten; *choice, arrangements, decision* treffen. **she made it into a suit** sie machte einen Anzug daraus; **it's made of gold** es ist aus Gold; **made in Germany** in Deutschland hergestellt; **to show what one is made of** zeigen, was in einem steckt; **they're made for each other** sie sind wie geschaffen füreinander; **this car wasn't made to carry 8 people** dieses Auto ist nicht dazu gedacht, 8 Leute zu transportieren.

(b) *(cause to be)* machen; *(appoint)* machen zu; *(cause to do or happen)* lassen; *(compel)* zwingen. **to ~ sb happy** *etc* jdn glücklich *etc* machen; **he was made a judge** man ernannte ihn zum Richter; **it ~s the room look smaller** es läßt den Raum kleiner wirken; **we decided to ~ a day of it** wir beschlossen den ganzen Tag dafür zu nehmen; **let's ~ it Monday** sagen wir Montag; **it all ~s me think that ...** das alles läßt mich denken, daß ...; **to ~ sb laugh** jdn zum Lachen bringen; **what ~s you say that?** warum sagst du das?; **to ~ sb do sth** jdn dazu bringen, etw zu tun; *(force)* jdn zwingen, etw zu tun; **to ~ sth do, to ~ do with sth** mit etw zufrieden sein; **you can't ~ things happen** man kann das nicht erzwingen; **how can I ~ you understand?** wie kann ich es Ihnen verständlich machen?; **that made the cloth shrink** dadurch ging der Stoff ein; **what ~s the engine go?** wie wird der Motor angetrieben?; **what ~s you think you can do it?** weshalb glauben Sie denn, daß Sie es schaffen können?; **the chemical ~s the plant grow faster** die Chemikalie bewirkt, daß die Pflanze schneller wächst; **what made you come to this town?** was hat Sie in diese Stadt geführt?; **to ~ oneself heard/understood** sich *(dat)* Gehör verschaffen/sich verständlich machen.

(c) *(earn) money* verdienen; *profit, loss, fortune* machen *(on* bei*)*; *name, reputation* sich *(dat)* verschaffen.

(d) *(reach, achieve, also Sport)* schaffen *(col)*, erreichen; *connection* schaffen; *summit etc* es schaffen zu *(col)*. **we made good time** wir kamen schnell voran; **he just made it** er hat es gerade noch geschafft; **sorry I couldn't ~ your party last night** tut mir leid, ich habe es gestern abend einfach nicht zu deiner Party geschafft; **his first record didn't ~ the charts** seine erste Platte schaffte es nicht bis in die Hitparade; **we've made it!** wir haben es geschafft!; **we'll never ~ the airport in time** wir schaffen es garantiert nicht mehr rechtzeitig zum Flughafen; **the story made the front page** die Geschichte kam auf die Titelseite.

(e) *(cause to succeed) stars etc* berühmt machen. **this film made her** dieser Film war für sie der Durchbruch; **you'll be made for life** Sie werden ausgesorgt haben; **he's got it made** *(col)* er hat ausgesorgt; **he's a made man** er ist ein gemachter Mann; **that ~s my day!** das freut mich unheimlich!; *(iro)* das hat mir gerade noch gefehlt!; **he can ~ or break you** er hat dich ganz in der Hand.

(f) *(equal)* sein, ergeben; *(constitute also)* machen. **2 plus 2 ~s 4** 2 und 2 ist 4; **how much does that ~ altogether?** was macht das insgesamt?; **he made a good father** er gab einen guten Vater ab; **he'll never ~ a soldier** aus ihm wird nie ein Soldat.

(g) *(estimate) distance, total* schätzen auf. **what time do you ~ it?** wie spät hast du es?; **I ~ it 3.15** auf meiner Uhr ist es 3^{15}; **I ~ it 3 miles** ich schätze 3 Meilen; **how many do you ~ it?** wie viele sind es nach deiner Rechnung?

2 *vi* **(a)** *(go)* **to ~ towards a place** auf einen Ort zuhalten; *(ship)* Kurs auf einen Ort nehmen; **to ~ after sb** jdm nachsetzen. **(b) to ~ as if to do sth** Anstalten machen, etw zu tun; *(as deception)* so tun, als wolle man etw tun.

3 *n* **(a)** *(brand)* Marke *f.* **what ~ of car do you run?** welche (Auto)marke fahren Sie? **(b)** *(pej col)* **on the ~** *(for profit)* profitgierig *(col)*, auf Profit aus; *(ambitious)* karrieresüchtig *(col)*; *(sexually)* sexhungrig *(col)*.

♦ **make away** *vi* = **make off.**

♦ **make away with** *vi +prep obj (kill)* **to ~ ~ ~ sb/oneself** jdn/sich umbringen.

♦ **make for** *vi +prep obj* **(a)** *(head for)* zuhalten auf *(+acc)*; *(vehicle)* losfahren auf *(+acc)*; *(ship)* Kurs halten auf *(+acc)*. **where are you making ~?** wo willst du hin? **(b)** *(promote)* führen zu; *happy marriage etc* den Grund legen für. **the**

trade figures ~ ~ optimism die Handelsziffern geben Anlaß zum Optimismus.
♦ **make of** *vi +prep obj* halten von. **I didn't ~ much ~ it** ich konnte nicht viel dabei finden.
make off *vi* sich davonmachen *(with sth* mit etw*)*.
make out 1 *vt sep* **(a)** *(write out) cheque* ausstellen *(to* auf *+acc)*; *list, bill* aufstellen; *(fill out) form* ausfüllen. **to ~ ~ a case for sth** für etw argumentieren. **(b)** *(see, discern)* ausmachen; *(decipher)* entziffern; *(understand)* verstehen; *person, actions* schlau werden aus. **how do you ~ that ~?** wie kommst du darauf? **(c)** *(imply)* **to ~ ~ that ...** es so hinstellen, als ob ...; **he made ~ that he was hurt** er tat, als sei er verletzt; **to ~ sb ~ to be a genius** jdn als Genie hinstellen. **2** *vi (col) (get on)* zurechtkommen; *(with people)* auskommen; *(succeed)* es schaffen.
♦ **make over** *vt sep (assign)* überschreiben *(to sb dat)*; *(bequeath)* vermachen *(to sb dat)*.
♦ **make up 1** *vt sep* **(a)** *(prepare) food, medicine, bed* zurechtmachen; *parcel also* zusammenpacken; *list, accounts, team* zusammenstellen. **to ~ material ~ into sth** Material zu etw verarbeiten. **(b)** *(constitute)* bilden. **to be made ~ of** bestehen aus. **(c)** *quarrel* beilegen. **to ~ it ~ (with sb)** sich (mit jdm) wieder vertragen. **(d)** *face* schminken. **(e) to ~ ~ one's mind (to do sth)** sich entschließen(, etw zu tun); **to ~ ~ one's mind about sb/sth** sich *(dat)* eine Meinung über jdn/etw bilden. **(f)** *(invent)* erfinden. **you're making that ~!** jetzt schwindelst du aber! *(col)*. **(g)** *(compensate for) loss* ausgleichen; *time* einholen, aufholen; *sleep* nachholen. **to ~ it ~ to sb (for sth)** *(compensate)* jdn (für etw) entschädigen; *(emotionally etc)* jdm etw wiedergutmachen.
2 *vi* **(a)** *(after quarrelling)* sich wieder vertragen. **(b)** *(apply cosmetics)* sich schminken. **(c)** *(catch up)* aufholen. **to ~ ~ on sb** jdn einholen.
♦ **make up for** *vi +prep obj* ausgleichen. **to ~ ~ ~ lost time** verlorene Zeit aufholen; **to ~ ~ ~ the loss of sb/lack of sth** jdn/etw ersetzen.
♦ **make up to** *vi +prep obj (col)* sich heranmachen an *(+acc)*.
make-believe ['meɪkbɪˌliːv] **1** *adj attr* Phantasie-; *world also* Schein-. **2** *n* Phantasie *f*. **a world of ~** eine Phantasiewelt; **it's only ~** das ist doch nur eine Geschichte. **3** *vt* sich *(dat)* vorstellen.
maker ['meɪkəʳ] *n (manufacturer)* Hersteller *m*. **our M~** unser Schöpfer *m*.
make: ~shift *adj* improvisiert; *repairs* behelfsmäßig; **~-up** *n* **(a)** Make-up *nt; (Theat also)* Maske *f*; **(b)** *(composition) (of team, party etc)* Zusammenstellung *f; (character)* Veranlagung *f*; **loyalty is part of his ~-up** er ist loyal veranlagt; **~-up bag** *n* Schminktäschchen *nt*.
making ['meɪkɪŋ] *n* **(a)** *(production)* Herstellung *f; (of food)* Zubereitung *f*. **in the ~** im Entstehen; **here you can see history in the ~** hier wird Geschichte gemacht; **it was the ~ of him** *(made him successful)* das hat ihn zu dem gemacht, was er (heute) ist. **(b) he has the ~s of an actor** *etc* er hat das Zeug zu einem Schauspieler *etc;* **the situation has all the ~s of a strike** die Situation bietet alle Voraussetzungen für einen Streik.
maladjusted [ˌmælə'dʒʌstɪd] *adj (Psych, Sociol)* verhaltensgestört.
maladroit [ˌmælə'drɔɪt] *adj* ungeschickt.
malaise [mæ'leɪz] *n* Unwohlsein *nt; (fig)* Unbehagen *nt*.
malaria [mə'lɛərɪə] *n* Malaria *f*.
male [meɪl] **1** *adj* männlich. **~ nurse** Krankenpfleger *m;* **~ crocodile** Krokodilmännchen *nt;* **~ chauvinist pig** *(col pej)* Chauvi *m (col)*. **2** *n (animal)* Männchen *nt; (col: man)* Mann *m*.
malevolent [mə'levələnt] *adj* boshaft; *action* böswillig.
malformed [mæl'fɔːmd] *adj* mißgebildet.
malfunction [ˌmæl'fʌŋkʃən] **1** *n (of liver etc)* Funktionsstörung *f; (of machine)* Defekt *m*. **2** *vi (liver etc)* nicht richtig arbeiten; *(machine etc)* defekt sein; *(system)* nicht richtig funktionieren.
malice ['mælɪs] *n* Bosheit *f; (of action)* Böswilligkeit *f*. **I bear him no ~** ich bin ihm nicht böse; **with ~ aforethought** *(Jur)* in böswilliger Absicht.
malicious [mə'lɪʃəs] *adj person, words* boshaft; *slander* böswillig; *(Jur) damage* mutwillig.
malign [mə'laɪn] **1** *adj (liter) intent* böse; *influence* unheilvoll. **2** *vt* verleumden; *(run down)* schlecht machen. **to ~ sb's character** jdm Übles nachsagen.
malignant [mə'lɪgnənt] *adj* bösartig. **a ~ growth** *(Med, fig)* ein bösartiges Geschwür.
malingerer [mə'lɪŋgərəʳ] *n* Simulant *m*.
malleable [mæ'lɪəbl] *adj* formbar *(also fig)*, weich.
mallet ['mælɪt] *n* Holzhammer *m; (croquet)* (Krocket)hammer *m; (polo)* (Polo)schläger *m*.
malnutrition [ˌmælnjʊ'trɪʃən] *n* Unterernährung *f*.
malpractice [ˌmæl'præktɪs] *n* Berufsvergehen, Amtsvergehen *nt*.
malt [mɔːlt] *n* Malz *nt*. **~ loaf** ≈ Rosinenbrot *nt;* **~ whisky** Malt Whisky *m*.
Malta ['mɔːltə] *n* Malta *nt*.
maltreat [ˌmæl'triːt] *vt* schlecht behandeln; *(using violence)* mißhandeln.
mam(m)a [mə'mɑː] *n (col)* Mama *(col)*.
mammal ['mæməl] *n* Säugetier *nt*.
mammoth ['mæməθ] **1** *n* Mammut *nt*. **2** *adj* Mammut-; *cost, enterprise* kolossal.
man [mæn] **1** *n, pl* **men** Mann *m; (human race: also* **M~***)* der Mensch; die Menschen; *(Chess)* Figur *f; (in draughts)* Stein *m*. **to make a ~ out of sb** einen Mann aus jdm machen; **that's just like a ~** das ist typisch Mann; **they are ~ and wife** sie sind Mann und Frau; **the ~ in the street** der Mann auf der Straße; **~ of property** vermögender Mann; **he's a ~ about town** er kennt sich aus; **a ~ of the world** ein Mann von Welt; **no ~** keiner, niemand; **any ~** jeder; **men say that ...** die Leute sagen, daß ...; **that ~ Jones** dieser Jones!; **as one ~** geschlossen, wie ein Mann; **they are communists to a ~** sie sind allesamt Kommunisten; **he's not the ~ for the job** er ist nicht der Richtige für diese Aufgabe; **he's not a ~ to ...** er ist nicht der Typ, der ...; **he's a family ~** *(home-loving)* er ist sehr häuslich; **it's got to be a local ~** es muß jemand aus dieser Gegend sein; **I'm not a drinking ~** ich bin kein großer Trinker; **you can't do that, ~** *(col)* Mensch *or* Mann, das kannst du doch nicht machen! *(col)*.
2 *vt ship* bemannen; *fortress* besetzen; *pump, gun* bedienen. **the ship is ~ned by a crew of 30** das Schiff hat 30 Mann Besatzung; **there's someone ~ning the telephone all day** es ist den ganzen Tag über jemand da, der das Telefon bedient.
manacle ['mænəkl] *n usu pl* Handfesseln *pl*.
manage ['mænɪdʒ] **1** *vt* **(a)** *company, organization* leiten; *affairs* regeln; *football team, pop group* managen. **the election was ~d** *(pej)* die Wahl war manipuliert.
(b) *(handle, control) person, animal, car* zurechtkommen mit. **I can ~ him** mit dem werde ich schon fertig.
(c) *task, another portion* bewältigen, schaffen *(col)*. **£5 is the most I can ~** ich kann mir höchstens £5 leisten; **I'll ~ it** das werde ich schon schaffen; **can you ~ the cases?** kannst du die Koffer (allein) tragen?; **she can't ~ the stairs** sie kommt die Treppe nicht hinauf/hinunter; **can you ~ 8 o'clock?** 8 Uhr, ginge das?; **I couldn't ~ another thing** ich könnte keinen Bissen mehr runterbringen; **to ~ to do sth** es schaffen, etw zu tun; **he ~d not to get his feet wet** es ist ihm gelungen, keine nassen Füße zu bekommen; **how**

did you ~ to miss that? wie konnte Ihnen das nur entgehen?; **could you possibly ~ to close the door?** *(iro)* wäre es vielleicht möglich, die Tür zuzumachen?

2 *vi* zurechtkommen, es schaffen *(col)*. **can you ~?** geht es?; **how do you ~?** wie machen Sie das bloß?; **to ~ without sth/sb** ohne etw/jdn auskommen; **how do you ~ on only £20 a week?** wie kommen Sie mit nur £ 20 pro Woche aus?

manageable ['mænɪdʒəbl] *adj child, horse* fügsam; *amount, job* zu bewältigen; *hair* leicht frisierbar; *number* überschaubar; *car* leicht zu handhaben. **pieces of a more ~ size** Stücke, die leichter zu handhaben sind.

management ['mænɪdʒmənt] *n* **(a)** *(act: of company)* Leitung, Führung *f*. **~ studies** Betriebswirtschaft *f*; **~ and workers** Arbeitgeber und Arbeitnehmer *pl*. **(b)** *(persons)* Unternehmensleitung *f*; *(of single unit or smaller factory)* Betriebsleitung *f*; *(non-commercial)* Leitung *f*; **"under new ~"** „neuer Inhaber"; *(shop)* „neu eröffnet".

manager ['mænɪdʒəʳ] *n (Comm etc)* Geschäftsführer *m*; *(of smaller firm or factory)* Betriebsleiter *m*; *(of bank, chain store)* Filialleiter *m*; *(of department)* Abteilungsleiter *m*; *(of pop group etc)* Manager *m*; *(of team)* Trainer *m*. **sales/publicity ~** Verkaufsleiter/Werbeleiter *m*.

manageress [ˌmænɪdʒə'res] *n* Geschäftsführerin *f*; *(of department)* Abteilungsleiterin *f*; *(of chain store)* Filialleiterin *f*.

managerial [ˌmænə'dʒɪərɪəl] *adj* geschäftlich; *(executive)* Management-; *post* leitend. **he has no ~ skills** er ist für leitende Funktionen ungeeignet.

managing director ['mænɪdʒɪŋdɪ'rektəʳ] *n* leitender Direktor.

mandarin ['mændərɪn] *n* **(a)** *(Chinese official)* Mandarin *m*. **(b)** *(language)* **M~** Hochchinesisch *nt*. **(c)** *(fruit)* Mandarine *f*.

mandate ['mændeɪt] *n* Auftrag *m*; *(Pol also)* Mandat *nt*; *(territory)* Mandatsgebiet *nt*. **to give sb a ~ to do sth** jdm den Auftrag geben, etw zu tun.

mandatory ['mændətərɪ] *adj* obligatorisch; *(Pol)* mandatorisch. **union membership is ~** Mitgliedschaft in der Gewerkschaft ist Pflicht.

mandolin(e) ['mændəlɪn] *n* Mandoline *f*.

mane [meɪn] *n (lit, fig)* Mähne *f*.

maneuver *n, vti (US)* = **manoeuvre.**

manful ['mænfʊl] *adj* mannhaft, mutig.

manganese [ˌmæŋgə'niːz] *n* Mangan *nt*.

mangle[1] ['mæŋgl] *n* Mangel *f*.

mangle[2] *vt (also* **~ up***)* (übel) zurichten.

mango ['mæŋgəʊ] *n (fruit)* Mango *f*.

man: ~handle *vt* **(a)** grob behandeln; **he was ~handled into the van** er wurde recht unsanft in den Wagen verfrachtet; **(b)** *piano etc* hieven; **~hole** *n* Kanalschacht *m*.

manhood ['mænhʊd] *n (state)* Mannesalter *nt*.

man: ~-hour *n* Arbeitsstunde *f*; **~hunt** *n* Fahndung *f*; *(for criminal also)* Verbrecherjagd *f*.

mania ['meɪnɪə] *n (madness)* Manie *f*; *(col: enthusiasm)* Manie *f*, Tick *(col) m*. **he has a ~ for punctuality** er hat einen Pünktlichkeitsfimmel *(col)*.

maniac ['meɪnɪæk] **1** *adj* wahnsinnig. **2** *n* **(a)** Wahnsinnige(r), Irre(r) *mf*. **(b)** *(fig)* **these sports ~s** diese Sportfanatiker *pl*.

manic-depressive ['mænɪkdɪ'presɪv] **1** *adj* manisch-depressiv. **2** *n* Manisch-Depressive(r) *mf*.

manicure ['mænɪˌkjʊəʳ] **1** *n* Maniküre *f*. **~ set** Nagelnecessaire *nt*. **2** *vt* maniküren.

manifest ['mænɪfest] **1** *adj* offenkundig; *(definite also)* eindeutig. **he made it ~ that ...** er machte deutlich, daß ... **2** *vr* **to ~ itself** sich zeigen.

manifestation [ˌmænɪfe'steɪʃən] *n (act of showing)* Ausdruck *m*, Bekundung *f*; *(sign)* Anzeichen *nt*.

manifestly ['mænɪfestlɪ] *adv* offensichtlich. **it's so ~ obvious** es ist so völlig offensichtlich.

manifesto [ˌmænɪ'festəʊ] *n, pl* **-(e)s** Manifest *nt*.

manifold ['mænɪfəʊld] **1** *adj* vielfältig. **~ uses** vielseitige Anwendung. **2** *n (Aut: exhaust ~)* Auspuffrohr *nt*.

manipulate [mə'nɪpjʊleɪt] *vt* **(a)** *machine etc* bedienen; *bones* einrenken; *(after fracture)* zurechtrücken. **(b)** *public opinion, prices* manipulieren; *accounts also* frisieren *(col)*.

manipulation [məˌnɪpjʊ'leɪʃən] *n* Manipulation *f*.

mankind [mæn'kaɪnd] *n* die Menschheit.

manliness ['mænlɪnɪs] *n* Männlichkeit *f*.

manly ['mænlɪ] *adj (+er)* männlich.

man-made ['mæn'meɪd] *adj* künstlich, Kunst-. **~ fibres** Kunstfasern *pl*.

manna ['mænə] *n* Manna *nt*.

manned [mænd] *adj satellite etc* bemannt.

mannequin ['mænɪkɪn] *n (fashion)* Mannequin *nt*; *(Art)* Modell *nt*; *(dummy)* Schaufensterpuppe *f*.

manner ['mænəʳ] *n* **(a)** *(mode)* Art (und Weise) *f*. **in this ~** auf diese Art und Weise; **in such a ~ that ...** so ..., daß ...; **in a ~ of speaking** sozusagen; **as to the ~ born** als sei er/sie dafür geschaffen. **(b)** *(behaviour etc)* Art *f*. **he has a very kind ~** er hat ein sehr freundliches Wesen; **I don't like his ~** ich mag seine Art nicht. **(c) ~s** *pl (good, bad etc)* Manieren *pl*; **that's bad ~s** das gehört sich nicht; **it's bad ~s to ...** es gehört sich nicht, zu ...; **he has no ~s** er hat keine Manieren; **to teach sb some ~s** jdm Manieren beibringen. **(d)** *(class, type)* Art *f*. **we saw all ~ of interesting things** wir sahen allerlei Interessantes.

mannerism ['mænərɪzəm] *n (in behaviour)* Eigenheit *f*; *(of style)* Manieriertheit *f*. **his ~s** seine Manierismen.

mannerly ['mænəlɪ] *adj* wohlerzogen.

manoeuvrable, (US) maneuverable [mə'nuːvrəbl] *adj* wendig. **easily ~** leicht zu manövrieren.

manoeuvre, (US) maneuver [mə'nuːvəʳ] **1** *n (Mil)* Feldzug *m*; *(clever plan)* Manöver *nt*, Schachzug *m*. **~s** Manöver *nt or pl*; **the troops were out on ~s** die Truppen befanden sich im Manöver. **2** *vt* manövrieren. **to ~ a gun into position** ein Geschütz in Stellung bringen. **3** *vi* manövrieren; *(Mil)* (ein) Manöver durchführen. **to ~ for position** *(lit, fig)* sich in eine günstige Position manövrieren; **room to ~** Manövrierfähigkeit *f*.

manor ['mænəʳ] *n* Gut(shof *m*) *nt*. **lord of the ~** Gutsherr *m*; **~ house** Herrenhaus *nt*.

manpower ['mænˌpaʊəʳ] *n* Arbeitskräfte *pl*; *(Mil)* Stärke *f*.

mansion ['mænʃən] *n* Villa *f*; *(of ancient family)* Herrenhaus *nt*.

manslaughter ['mænˌslɔːtəʳ] *n* Totschlag *m*.

mantelpiece ['mæntlpiːs] *n* Kaminsims *nt or m*.

mantle ['mæntl] *n* **(a)** Umhang *m*; *(fig)* Deckmantel *m*. **a ~ of snow** eine Schneedecke. **(b)** *(gas ~)* Glühstrumpf *m*.

man-to-man [ˌmæntə'mæn] *adj, adv* von Mann zu Mann.

manual ['mænjʊəl] **1** *adj* manuell; *labour* körperlich. **~ worker** (manueller) Arbeiter *m*; **~ gear change** Schaltgetriebe *nt*, Schaltung *f* von Hand. **2** *n (book)* Handbuch *nt*.

manufacture [ˌmænjʊ'fæktʃəʳ] **1** *n (act)* Herstellung *f*; *(pl: products)* Erzeugnisse *pl*. **2** *vt* herstellen. **~d goods** Fertigware *f*.

manufacturer [ˌmænjʊ'fæktʃərəʳ] *n* Herstelier *m*.

manufacturing [ˌmænjʊ'fæktʃərɪŋ] **1** *adj techniques* Herstellungs-; *industry* verarbeitend. **2** *n* Herstellung *f*.

manure [mə'njʊəʳ] **1** *n* Dung *m*; *(esp artificial)* Dünger *m*. **2** *vt field* düngen.

manuscript ['mænjʊskrɪpt] *n* Manuskript *nt*; *(ancient also)* Handschrift *f*.

many ['menɪ] *adj, n* viele. **~ people** viele (Menschen *or* Leute); **there were as ~ as 20** es waren sogar 20 da; **as ~ again** noch einmal so viele; **there's one too ~** einer ist zuviel; **he's had one too ~** er hat einen zuviel getrunken; **they were too ~ for us** sie waren zu viele für uns; **he made one mistake too ~** er hat einen Fehler zuviel gemacht; **~ a good soldier** so mancher gute Soldat; **~ a time** so manches Mal; **a good/great ~ houses** sehr viele Häuser.

many: ~-coloured *(Brit)*, **~-colored** *(US) adj* vielfarbig; **~-sided** *adj* vielseitig.

map [mæp] **1** *n* (Land)karte *f; (of streets, town)* Stadtplan *m; (showing specific item)* Karte *f.* **this will put Cheam on the ~** *(fig)* das wird Cheam zu einem Namen verhelfen; **it's right off the ~** *(fig)* das liegt (ja) am Ende der Welt; **entire cities were wiped off the ~** ganze Städte wurden ausradiert. **2** *vt (measure)* vermessen; *(make a map of)* eine Karte anfertigen von.

♦ **map out** *vt sep* **(a)** *(lit) see* **map 2. (b)** *(fig: plan)* entwerfen. **our holiday schedule was all ~ped ~ in advance** der Zeitplan für unsere Ferien war schon im voraus genau festgelegt.

maple ['meɪpl] *n (wood, tree)* Ahorn *m.*

mar [mɑːʳ] *vt* verderben; *happiness* trüben; *beauty* mindern.

marathon ['mærəθən] **1** *n (lit)* Marathon(lauf) *m; (fig)* Marathon *nt.* **2** *adj* Marathon-.

marauding [mə'rɔːdɪŋ] *adj* plündernd.

marble ['mɑːbl] **1** *n* Marmor *m; (glass ball)* Murmel *f,* Klicker *m (col).* **2** *adj* Marmor-.

March [mɑːtʃ] *n* März *m; see* **September.**

march [mɑːtʃ] **1** *n* **(a)** *(Mil, Mus)* Marsch *m; (demonstration)* Demonstration *f; (fig: long walk)* Weg *m.* **we had been five days on the ~** wir waren fünf Tage lang marschiert; **it's two days' ~** es ist ein Zwei-Tage-Marsch. **(b)** *(of time, history, events)* Lauf *m.* **(c) to steal a ~ on sb** jdm zuvorkommen. **2** *vt soldiers* marschieren lassen; *distance* marschieren. **to ~ sb off** jdn abführen. **3** *vi* marschieren. **forward ~!** vorwärts(, marsch)!; **quick ~!** im Laufschritt, marsch!; **time ~es on** die Zeit bleibt nicht stehen; **to ~ past sb** an jdm vorbeimarschieren; **she ~ed straight up to him** sie marschierte schnurstracks auf ihn zu.

marching orders ['mɑːtʃɪŋ'ɔːdəz] *npl (Mil)* Marschbefehl *m; (col)* Entlassung *f.* **she gave him his ~** sie hat ihm den Laufpaß gegeben.

marchioness ['mɑːʃənɪs] *n* Marquise *f.*

march past *n* Aufmarsch *m.*

mare [mɛəʳ] *n (horse)* Stute *f; (donkey)* Eselin *f.*

margarine ['mɑːdʒə'riːn], **marge** [mɑːdʒ] *(col) n* Margarine *f.*

margin ['mɑːdʒɪn] *n* **(a)** *(on page)* Rand *m.* **(b)** *(extra amount)* Spielraum *m.* **to allow for a ~ of error** etwaige Fehler mit einkalkulieren; **by a narrow ~** knapp; **(profit) ~** Gewinnspanne *f.*

marginal ['mɑːdʒɪnl] *adj* **(a)** *note* Rand-. **(b)** *improvement, difference* geringfügig; *constituency* mit schwankendem Wählerverhalten.

marginally ['mɑːdʒɪnəlɪ] *adv* geringfügig.

marigold ['mærɪgəʊld] *n* Ringelblume *f.*

marijuana [ˌmæri'hwɑːnə] *n* Marihuana *nt.*

marina [mə'riːnə] *n* Jachthafen *m.*

marinade [ˌmærɪ'neɪd] *n* Marinade *f.*

marinate ['mærɪneɪt] *vt* marinieren.

marine [mə'riːn] **1** *adj* Meeres-, See-. **~ insurance** Seeversicherung *f;* **~ life** Meeresfauna und -flora *f.* **2** *n* **(a)** *(fleet)* Marine *f.* **merchant ~** Handelsmarine *f.* **(b) the ~s** die Marinetruppen *pl;* **tell that to the ~s!** *(col)* das kannst du deiner Großmutter erzählen! *(col).*

mariner ['mærɪnəʳ] *n* Seefahrer, Seemann *m.*

marionette [ˌmærɪə'net] *n* Marionette *f.*

marital ['mærɪtl] *adj* ehelich. **~ status** Familienstand *m.*

marjoram ['mɑːdʒərəm] *n* Majoran *m.*

mark[1] [mɑːk] *n (Fin)* Mark *f.*

mark[2] **1** *n* **(a)** *(stain, spot etc)* Fleck *m; (scratch)* Kratzer *m; (on person)* Mal *nt; (on plane, football pitch etc)* Markierung *f.* **to make a ~ on sth** einen Fleck auf etw *(acc)* machen/etw beschädigen; **dirty ~s** Schmutzflecken *pl;* **with not a ~ on it** in makellosem Zustand; **he didn't have a ~ on him** er wies keine Verletzungen auf; **the ~s of violence** die Spuren der Gewalt.

(b) *(in exam)* Note *f.* **high** *or* **good ~s** gute Noten *pl;* **the ~s are out of 100** insgesamt kann/konnte man 100 Punkte erreichen; **there are no ~s for guessing** *(fig)* das ist ja wohl nicht schwer zu erraten; **he gets full ~s for punctuality** *(fig)* in Pünktlichkeit verdient er eine Eins.

(c) *(sign, indication)* Zeichen *nt.* **it bears the ~s of genius** das trägt geniale Züge; **it's the ~ of a gentleman** daran erkennt man den Gentleman.

(d) *(level)* **expenses have reached the £100 ~** die Ausgaben haben die 100-Pfund-Grenze erreicht.

(e) Cooper M~ II Cooper II.

(f) *(phrases)* **to be quick off the ~** *(Sport)* einen guten Start haben; *(fig)* blitzschnell reagieren; **to be up to the ~** den Anforderungen entsprechen; **to leave one's ~ (on sth)** einer Sache *(dat)* seinen Stempel aufdrücken; **to make one's ~** sich *(dat)* einen Namen machen; **on your ~s!** auf die Plätze!; **to be wide of the ~** *(shooting)* danebenschießen; *(fig: in guessing)* danebentippen; **to hit the ~** *(lit, fig)* ins Schwarze treffen.

2 *vt* **(a)** *(adversely)* beschädigen; *(stain)* schmutzig machen; *(scratch)* zerkratzen.

(b) *(for recognition, identity)* markieren; *(label)* beschriften; *(price)* auszeichnen. **the bottle was ~ed "poison"** die Flasche trug die Aufschrift „Gift"; **the teacher ~ed him absent** der Lehrer trug ihn als fehlend ein; **it's not ~ed on the map** es ist nicht auf der Karte eingezeichnet.

(c) *(characterize)* kennzeichnen. **the new bill ~s a change of policy** das neue Gesetz deutet auf einen politischen Kurswechsel hin.

(d) *exam, paper* korrigieren (und benoten). **to ~ sth wrong** etw anstreichen.

(e) *(heed)* hören auf *(+acc).* **~ my words** eins kann ich Ihnen sagen; *(threatening, warning)* lassen Sie sich das gesagt sein!

(f) *(Sport) player, opponent* decken.

(g) to ~ time *(Mil, fig)* auf der Stelle treten.

3 *vi (get dirty)* schmutzig werden; *(get scratched)* Kratzer bekommen. **she ~s easily** sie bekommt leicht blaue Flecken.

♦ **mark down** *vt sep (note down)* (sich *dat*) notieren; *prices* herabsetzen.

♦ **mark off** *vt sep* kennzeichnen; *boundary* markieren; *danger area etc* absperren.

♦ **mark out** *vt sep* **(a)** *tennis court etc* abstecken. **(b)** *(note)* bestimmen *(for* für*).* **he's been ~ed ~ for promotion** er ist zur Beförderung vorgesehen.

♦ **mark up** *vt sep (write up)* notieren *(on* auf *+dat); price* heraufsetzen.

marked [mɑːkt] *adj* **(a)** *contrast, accent* deutlich; *improvement* spürbar. **(b) he's a ~ man** er steht auf der schwarzen Liste.

markedly ['mɑːkɪdlɪ] *adv* merklich. **it is ~ better** es ist wesentlich besser.

marker ['mɑːkəʳ] *n* **(a)** Marke *f; (to turn at)* Wendemarke *f; (on road)* Schild *nt; (in book)* Lesezeichen *nt.* **(b)** *(for exams)* Korrektor(in *f*) *m.*

market ['mɑːkɪt] **1** *n* Markt *m.* **at the ~** auf dem Markt; **to go to ~** auf den Markt gehen; **to be in the ~ for sth** an etw *(dat)* interessiert sein; **to be on the ~** auf dem Markt sein; **to come on(to) the ~** auf den Markt kommen; **to put on the ~** auf den Markt bringen; *house* zum Verkauf anbieten; **to create a ~** Nachfrage

erzeugen; **to play the ~** (an der Börse) spekulieren. **2** *vt* vertreiben. **to ~ a (new) product** ein (neues) Produkt auf den Markt bringen.
market garden *n (Brit)* Gemüseanbaubetrieb *m.*
marketing ['mɑːkɪtɪŋ] *n* Marketing *nt.*
market: ~place *n* Marktplatz *m; (world of trade)* Markt *m;* **~ price** *n* Marktpreis *m;* **~ research** *n* Marktforschung *f;* **~ town** *n* Marktstädtchen *nt.*
marking ['mɑːkɪŋ] *n* **(a)** Markierung *f; (on animal)* Zeichnung *f.* **~ink** Wäschetinte *f.* **(b)** *(of exams) (correcting)* Korrektur *f; (grading)* Benotung *f.*
marksman ['mɑːksmən] *n, pl* **-men** [-mən] Schütze *m; (police etc)* Scharfschütze *m.*
mark-up ['mɑːkʌp] *n (amount added)* Preiserhöhung *f.* **~ price** Verkaufspreis *m.*
marmalade ['mɑːməleɪd] *n* Marmelade *f* aus Zitrusfrüchten. **(orange) ~** Orangenmarmelade *f.*
maroon[1] [mə'ruːn] *adj* kastanienbraun.
maroon[2] *vt* **~ed** von der Außenwelt abgeschnitten; **~ed by floods** vom Hochwasser eingeschlossen.
marquee [mɑː'kiː] *n* Festzelt *nt.*
marquess ['mɑːkwɪs] *n* Marquis *m.*
marriage ['mærɪdʒ] *n (state)* die Ehe; *(wedding)* Hochzeit, Heirat *f; (~ ceremony)* Trauung *f.* **relations by ~** angeheiratete Verwandte.
marriageable ['mærɪdʒəbl] *adj* heiratsfähig. **of ~ age** im heiratsfähigen Alter.
marriage: ~ guidance Eheberatung *f;* **~ vow** *n* Ehegelübde *nt.*
married ['mærɪd] *adj* verheiratet; *life, state* Ehe-. **~ couple** Ehepaar *nt;* **she is a ~ woman** sie ist verheiratet.
marrow ['mærəʊ] *n* **(a)** *(Anat)* (Knochen)mark *nt.* **to be frozen to the ~** völlig durchfroren sein. **(b)** *(Bot)* Gartenkürbis *m.*
marry ['mærɪ] **1** *vt* heiraten; *(priest)* trauen. **2** *vi (also* **get married***)* heiraten. **to ~ into a rich family** in eine reiche Familie einheiraten.
♦ **marry off** *vt sep* verheiraten.
Mars [mɑːz] *n* Mars *m.*
marsh [mɑːʃ] *n* Sumpf *m.*
marshal ['mɑːʃəl] **1** *n (Mil etc)* Marschall *m; (at demo etc)* Ordner *m; (US)* Bezirkspolizeichef *m.* **2** *vt arguments* ordnen; *soldiers* antreten lassen.
marshalling yard ['mɑːʃəlɪŋ'jɑːd] *n* Rangierbahnhof *m.*
marsh: ~land *n* Marschland *nt;* **~mallow** *n (sweet)* Marshmallow *nt; (Bot)* Eibisch *m.*
marshy ['mɑːʃɪ] *adj (+er)* sumpfig.
marsupial [mɑː'suːpɪəl] *n* Beuteltier *nt.*
martial ['mɑːʃəl] *adj music* kriegerisch, Kampf-; *bearing* soldatisch. **the ~ arts** die Kampfkunst; **~ law** Kriegsrecht *nt.*
martin ['mɑːtɪn] *n* Schwalbe *f.*
martyr ['mɑːtə^{r}] **1** *n* Märtyrer(in *f*) *m.* **to be a ~ to arthritis** entsetzlich unter Arthritis zu leiden haben. **2** *vt* martern.
martyrdom ['mɑːtədəm] *n (suffering)* Martyrium *nt; (death)* Märtyrertod *m.*
marvel ['mɑːvəl] **1** *n* Wunder *nt.* **it's a ~ to me how he does it** *(col)* es ist mir einfach schleierhaft, wie er das macht; **you're a ~!** *(col)* du bist ein Engel!; *(clever)* du bist ein Genie! **2** *vi* staunen *(at* über *+acc).* **to ~ at a sight** einen Anblick bestaunen.
marvellous, *(US)* **marvelous** ['mɑːvələs] *adj* wunderbar, fabelhaft. **isn't it ~?** ist das nicht herrlich?; *(iro)* gut, nicht! *(iro).*
Marxism ['mɑːksɪzəm] *n* der Marxismus.
Marxist ['mɑːksɪst] **1** *adj* marxistisch. **2** *n* Marxist(in *f*) *m.*
marzipan [ˌmɑːzɪ'pæn] *n* Marzipan *nt or m.*
mascara [mæ'skɑːrə] *n* Wimperntusche *f.*
mascot ['mæskət] *n* Maskottchen *nt.*
masculine ['mæskjʊlɪn] **1** *adj* männlich; *woman* maskulin. **2** *n (Gram)* Maskulinum *nt.*
mash [mæʃ] **1** *n* Brei *m; (for animals)* Futterbrei *m.* **2** *vt* zerstampfen. **~ed potatoes** Kartoffelbrei *m or* -püree *nt.*
mask [mɑːsk] **1** *n (lit, fig)* Maske *f.* **2** *vt* maskieren; *(clouds etc)* verdecken; *feelings* verbergen.
masochism ['mæsəʊkɪzəm] *n* Masochismus *m.*
masochist ['mæsəʊkɪst] *n* Masochist(in *f*) *m.*
masochistic [ˌmæsəʊ'kɪstɪk] *adj* masochistisch.
mason ['meɪsn] *n* **(a)** *(builder)* Steinmetz *m.* **(b)** *(free~)* Freimaurer *m.*
masonic [mə'sɒnɪk] *adj* Freimaurer-. **~ lodge** Freimaurerloge *f.*
masonry ['meɪsnrɪ] *n* **(a)** *(stonework)* Mauerwerk *nt.* **(b)** *(free~)* Freimaurertum *nt.*
masquerade [ˌmæskə'reɪd] **1** *n* Maskerade *f.* **2** *vi* **to ~ as ...** sich ausgeben als ...
mass[1] [mæs] *n (Eccl)* Messe *f.* **to go to ~** zur Messe gehen; **to say ~** die Messe lesen.
mass[2] **1** *n (general, Phys)* Masse *f; (of people)* Menge *f.* **a ~ of red hair** ein Wust roter Haare; **he's a ~ of bruises** er ist voller blauer Flecken; **the ~es** die Masse(n *pl*); **the great ~ of the population** die breite Masse der Bevölkerung; **~es (of)** massenhaft, eine Masse *(col).* **2** *vt troops* zusammenziehen. **3** *vi (Mil)* sich massieren; *(clouds)* sich (zusammen)ballen. **they're ~ing for an attack** sie sammeln sich zum Angriff.
massacre ['mæsəkə^{r}] **1** *n* Massaker *nt.* **2** *vt* massakrieren.
massage ['mæsɑːʒ] **1** *n* Massage *f.* **2** *vt* massieren.
masseur [mæ'sɜː^{r}] *n* Masseur *m.*
masseuse [mæ'sɜːz] *n* Masseuse *f.*
massive ['mæsɪv] *adj* riesig, enorm; *wall, heart attack, support* massiv; *task* gewaltig.
mass: ~ media *npl* Massenmedien *pl;* **~ meeting** *n* Massenveranstaltung *f;* **~-produce** *vt* in Massenproduktion herstellen; **~-produced** *adj* **~-produced items** Massenartikel *pl;* **~ production** *n* Massenproduktion *f.*
mast [mɑːst] *n (Naut)* Mast *m; (Rad etc)* Sendeturm *m.* **10 years before the ~** 10 Jahre auf See.
master ['mɑːstə^{r}] **1** *n* **(a)** *(of the house, dog, servants)* Herr *m.* **to be ~ in one's own house** *(also fig)* Herr im Hause sein; **to be one's own ~** sein eigener Herr sein; **to be ~ of sth** etw beherrschen; **to be ~ of the situation** Herr der Lage sein; **~ of ceremonies** *(at function)* Zeremonienmeister *m; (on stage)* Conférencier *m; (TV)* Showmaster *m.* **(b)** *(Naut)* Kapitän *m.* **(c)** *(musician, painter etc)* Meister *m.* **(d)** *(teacher)* Lehrer *m.* **(e)** *(boy's title)* Master *m.* **(f)** *(Univ)* **M~ of Arts/Science** *n* Magister *m* der philosophischen/naturwissenschaftlichen Fakultät. **2** *vt* meistern; *one's emotions* unter Kontrolle bringen; *technique* beherrschen.
master *in cpds* **~ builder** *n* Baumeister *m;* **~ copy** *n* Original *nt.*
masterful ['mɑːstəfʊl] *adj* meisterhaft; *(dominating) personality* gebieterisch.
master key *n* Haupt- *or* Generalschlüssel *m.*
masterly ['mɑːstəlɪ] *adj* meisterhaft.
master: ~mind 1 *n* (führender) Kopf; **2** *vt* **who ~minded the robbery?** wer steckt hinter dem Raubüberfall?; **~piece** *n* Meisterwerk *nt;* **~ switch** *n* Hauptschalter *m.*
mastery ['mɑːstərɪ] *n (of instrument, language etc)* Beherrschung *f; (skill)* Können *nt; (over competitors etc)* Oberhand *f.*
mastiff ['mæstɪf] *n* Dogge *f.*
masturbate ['mæstəbeɪt] *vi* masturbieren, onanieren.
masturbation [ˌmæstə'beɪʃən] *n* Masturbation, Onanie *f.*
mat[1] [mæt] *n* Matte *f; (door~)* Fußabstreifer *m; (on table)* Untersetzer *m.* **place ~** Set *nt.*
mat[2] *adj* = **matt.**
match[1] [mætʃ] *n* Streichholz *nt.*
match[2] **1** *n* **(a)** *(sb/sth similar, suitable etc)* **to be** *or*

make a good ~ gut zusammenpassen. **(b)** *(equal)* **to be a/no ~ for sb** *(be able to compete with)* sich mit jdm messen/nicht messen können; *(be able to handle)* jdm gewachsen/nicht gewachsen sein; **to meet one's ~** seinen Meister finden. **(c)** *(marriage)* Heirat *f.* **she made a good ~** sie hat eine gute Partie gemacht. **(d)** *(Sport) (general)* Wettkampf *m; (team game)* Spiel *nt; (Tennis)* Match *nt; (Boxing)* Kampf *m.*

2 *vt* **(a)** *(pair off)* **they're well ~ed as man and wife** die beiden passen gut zusammen; **the teams are well ~ed** die Mannschaften sind gleichwertig; **~ each diagram with its counterpart** ordnen Sie die Schaubilder einander *(dat)* zu; **to be ~ed against sb** gegen jdn antreten. **(b)** *(equal)* gleichkommen *(+dat) (in* an *+dat).* **I can't ~ him in chess** im Schach kann ich es mit ihm nicht aufnehmen; **the results did not ~ our hopes** die Ergebnisse entsprachen nicht unseren Hoffnungen. **(c)** *(clothes, colours)* passen zu.

3 *vi* zusammenpassen. **with a skirt to ~, with a ~ing skirt** mit (dazu) passendem Rock.

matchbox ['mætʃbɒks] *n* Streichholzschachtel *f.*

match: ~maker *n* Ehestifter(in *f*), Kuppler(in *f*) *(pej) m;* **~ point** *n (Tennis)* Matchball *m;* **~stick** *n* Streichholz *nt.*

mate[1] [meɪt] *(Chess)* **1** *n* Matt *nt.* **2** *vt* matt setzen.

mate[2] **1** *n* **(a)** *(fellow worker)* Kumpel *m; (helper)* Gehilfe *m.* **(b)** *(Naut)* Maat *m.* **(c)** *(of animal) (male)* Männchen *nt; (female)* Weibchen *nt.* **his ~** das Weibchen. **(d)** *(col: friend)* Kamerad(in *f*) *m.* **listen ~!** hör mal, Freundchen! *(col);* **got a light ~?** hast du Feuer, Kumpel? *(col).* **2** *vt animals* paaren; *female* decken lassen. **3** *vi (Zool)* sich paaren.

material [mə'tɪərɪəl] **1** *adj* **(a)** materiell. **~ damage** Sachschaden *m.* **(b)** *(esp Jur: important) difference* wesentlich. **2** *n* **(a)** Material *nt; (for report etc)* Stoff *m.* **~s** Material *nt;* **he's good editorial ~** er hat das Zeug zum Redakteur. **(b)** *(cloth)* Stoff *m.*

materialism [mə'tɪərɪəlɪzəm] *n* der Materialismus.

materialize [mə'tɪərɪəlaɪz] *vi (idea, plan)* sich verwirklichen; *(promises, hopes etc)* wahr werden.

materially [mə'tɪərɪəlɪ] *adv* wesentlich.

maternal [mə'tɜːnl] *adj* mütterlich. **~ grandfather** Großvater mütterlicherseits.

maternity [mə'tɜːnɪtɪ] *n* Mutterschaft *f.*

maternity: ~ benefit *n* Mutterschaftsgeld *nt;* **~ dress** *n* Umstandskleid *nt;* **~ home, ~ hospital** *n* Entbindungsheim *nt;* **~ leave** *n* Schwangerschaftsurlaub *m;* **~ ward** *n* Entbindungsstation *f.*

math [mæθ] *n (US col)* Mathe *f (col).*

mathematical [,mæθə'mætɪkəl] *adj* mathematisch.

mathematician [,mæθəmə'tɪʃən] *n* Mathematiker(in *f*) *m.*

mathematics [,mæθə'mætɪks] *n sing* Mathematik *f.*

maths [mæθs] *n sing (Brit col)* Mathe *f (col).*

matinée ['mætɪneɪ] *n* Matinee *f; (in the afternoon also)* Nachmittagsvorstellung *f.*

mating ['meɪtɪŋ] *n* Paarung *f.*

mating: ~ call *n* Lockruf *m;* **~ season** *n* Paarungszeit *f.*

matriarch ['meɪtrɪɑːk] *n* Matriarchin *f.*

matrices ['meɪtrɪsiːz] *pl of* **matrix.**

matriculate [mə'trɪkjʊleɪt] *vi* sich immatrikulieren.

matrimonial [,mætrɪ'məʊnɪəl] *adj vows* Ehe-.

matrimony ['mætrɪmənɪ] *n (form)* Ehe *f.*

matrix ['meɪtrɪks] *n, pl* **matrices** *or* **-es (a)** *(mould)* Matrize *f.* **(b)** *(Geol, Math)* Matrix *f.*

matron ['meɪtrən] *n (in hospital)* Oberschwester *f; (in school)* Schwester *f.*

matronly ['meɪtrənlɪ] *adj* matronenhaft.

matt [mæt] *adj* mattiert. **~ paint** Mattlack *m.*

matted ['mætɪd] *adj* verfilzt.

matter ['mætə^r] **1** *n* **(a)** *(Phys etc: substance)* die Materie. **advertising ~** Werbung *f;* **printed ~** Drucksache(n *pl*) *f;* **colouring ~** Farbstoff(e *pl*) *m;* **reading ~** Lektüre *f.*

(b) *(Med: pus)* Eiter *m.*

(c) *(content)* Inhalt *m.*

(d) *(question, affair)* Sache, Angelegenheit *f; (topic)* Thema *nt.* **in this ~** in diesem Zusammenhang; **in the ~ of ...** was ... *(+acc)* anbelangt; **in the ~ of clothes** *etc* in puncto Kleidung *etc;* **there's the ~ of my expenses** da wären noch meine Auslagen; **that's quite another ~** das ist etwas (ganz) anderes; **it will be no easy ~ (to) ...** es wird nicht einfach sein, zu ...; **it's a serious ~** das ist eine ernste Angelegenheit; **the ~ in hand** die vorliegende Angelegenheit; **the ~ is closed** der Fall ist erledigt; **for that ~** eigentlich; **business ~s** geschäftliche Dinge *pl,* Geschäftliche(s) *nt;* **money ~s** Geldfragen *pl;* **as ~s stand** wie die Dinge liegen; **to make ~s worse** zu allem Unglück (noch).

(e) a ~ of eine Sache von; **it's a ~ of time** das ist eine Frage der Zeit; **it's a ~ of opinion** das ist Ansichtssache; **it will be a ~ of a few weeks** es wird ein paar Wochen dauern; **in a ~ of minutes** innerhalb von Minuten; **it's a ~ of great concern to us** die Sache ist für uns von großer Bedeutung; **it's a ~ of increasing the money supply** es geht darum, die Geldzufuhr zu erhöhen; **as a ~ of course** selbstverständlich; **no ~!** macht nichts; **I've decided to leave, no ~ what** ich gehe, egal was passiert; **no ~ how/what/when** *etc* ... egal, wie/was/wann *etc* ...; **no ~ how hot it was** selbst bei der größten Hitze; **something is the ~ with sb/sth** etwas ist mit jdm/etw los; *(ill)* etw fehlt jdm; **what's the ~ with you?** was ist denn mit dir los?; **what's the ~ with smoking?** was ist denn dabei, wenn man raucht?; **something's the ~ with the lights** mit dem Licht ist irgend etwas nicht in Ordnung.

2 *vi* **it doesn't ~** (es *or* das) macht nichts; **what does it ~?** was macht das schon?; **I forgot it, does it ~?** ich hab's vergessen, ist das schlimm?; **does it ~ to you if I go?** macht es dir etwas aus, wenn ich gehe?; **it doesn't ~ to me what you do** es ist mir (ganz) egal, was du machst.

matter-of-fact ['mætərəv'fækt] *adj* sachlich.

mattress ['mætrɪs] *n* Matratze *f.*

mature [mə'tjʊə^r] **1** *adj (+er) person, cheese* reif; *child* vernünftig; *wine* ausgereift. **2** *vi (person)* reifer werden; *(wine, cheese)* reifen.

maturity [mə'tjʊərɪtɪ] *n* Reife *f.* **to reach ~** *(person)* erwachsen werden; *(legally)* volljährig werden.

maudlin ['mɔːdlɪn] *adj story* rührselig; *person* gefühlsselig.

maul [mɔːl] *vt* übel zurichten.

mausoleum [,mɔːsə'lɪəm] *n* Mausoleum *nt.*

mauve [məʊv] *adj* malvenfarben.

maverick ['mævərɪk] *n (dissenter)* Abtrünnige(r) *m; (independent person)* Alleingänger *m.*

mawkish ['mɔːkɪʃ] *adj* rührselig, kitschig.

max = maximum max.

maxim ['mæksɪm] *n* Maxime *f.*

maximize ['mæksɪmaɪz] *vt* maximieren.

maximum ['mæksɪməm] **1** *adj attr* Höchst-; *size, costs* maximal. **the ~ salary is ...** das höchste Gehalt ist ...; *(top grade)* das Endgehalt ist... **2** *n, pl* **-s** *or* **maxima** ['mæksɪmə] Maximum *nt.* **up to a ~ of £8** bis zu maximal £8; **temperatures reached a ~ of 34°** die Höchsttemperatur betrug 34°.

May [meɪ] *n* Mai *m.*

may [meɪ] *vi pret* **might** *(see also* **might**[1]*)* **(a)** *(possibility: also* **might***)* können. **it ~ rain** vielleicht regnet es; **it ~ be that ...** vielleicht ..., es könnte sein, daß ...; **he ~ not be hungry** vielleicht hat er keinen Hunger; **I ~ have said so** es kann *or* könnte sein, daß ich das gesagt habe; **you ~ be right** *(doubting)* Sie haben vielleicht recht; *(tentatively agreeing)* da könnten Sie recht haben; **yes, I ~** ja, das ist möglich; **you ~ well ask** das ist eine gute Frage!

(b) *(permission)* dürfen. **~ I go now?** darf ich jetzt gehen?; **yes, you ~** ja, Sie dürfen.

(c) I hope he ~ succeed ich hoffe, daß es ihm gelingt; **I hoped he might succeed** ich hatte gehofft, es würde ihm gelingen; **you ~** *or* **might as well go now** du kannst jetzt ruhig gehen; **if they don't have it we ~** *or* **might as well go to another firm** wenn sie es nicht haben, gehen wir am besten zu einer anderen Firma.

(d) *(in wishes)* **~ you be successful!** (ich wünsche Ihnen) viel Erfolg!; **~ you be very happy together** ich wünsche euch, daß ihr sehr glücklich miteinander werdet.

maybe ['meɪbiː] *adv* vielleicht.

May: ~ Day *n* der 1. Mai; **~day** *n (distress call)* Maydaysignal *nt*, SOS-Ruf *m*.

mayonnaise [ˌmeɪə'neɪz] *n* Mayonnaise *f*.

mayor [mɛəʳ] *n* Bürgermeister(in *f*) m.

mayoress ['mɛəres] *n* Frau *f* des Bürgermeisters; *(lady mayor)* Bürgermeisterin *f*.

maypole ['meɪpəʊl] *n* Maibaum *m*.

maze [meɪz] *n* Irrgarten *m*; *(fig)* Gewirr *nt*.

MC = Master of Ceremonies.

MD = Doctor of Medicine Dr. med.

me [miː] *pron* **(a)** *(dir obj, with prep +acc)* mich; *(indir obj, with prep +dat)* mir. **he's older than ~** er ist älter als ich. **(b)** *(emph)* ich. **who, ~?** wer, ich?; **it's ~** ich bin's.

meadow ['medəʊ] *n* Wiese *f*.

meagre, *(US)* **meager** ['miːgəʳ] *adj* spärlich; *amount* kläglich; *meal* dürftig.

meal[1] [miːl] *n (flour etc)* Schrot(mehl *nt*) *m*.

meal[2] *n* Mahlzeit *f*; *(food)* Essen *nt*. **come around for a ~** komm zum Essen (zu uns); **to go for a ~** essen gehen; **to have a (good) ~** (gut) essen; **hot ~s** warme Mahlzeiten *pl*; **he really made a ~ of it** *(col)* er war nicht mehr zu bremsen *(col)*.

meal: ~-ticket *n (US: lit)* Essensmarke *f*; **she's just his ~-ticket** er ist nur des Geldes wegen mit ihr befreundet; **~time** *n* Essenszeit *f*.

mealy-mouthed ['miːlɪ'maʊðd] *adj* unaufrichtig; *politician* schönfärberisch.

mean[1] [miːn] *adj (+er)* **(a)** *(miserly)* geizig. **he's ~ with his money** er ist geizig mit seinem Geld. **(b)** *(unkind, spiteful)* gemein. **you ~ thing!** du gemeines Stück!, du Miststück! *(col)*; **a ~ trick** eine Gemeinheit. **(c)** *(vicious)* bösartig; *look* gehässig; *criminal* niederträchtig. **(d) he is no ~ player** er ist ein beachtlicher Spieler; **that's no ~ feat** diese Aufgabe ist nicht zu unterschätzen.

mean[2] **1** *n* Durchschnitt *m*. **the golden** *or* **happy ~** der goldene Mittelweg. **2** *adj* mittlere(r, s).

mean[3] *pret, ptp* **meant** *vt* **(a)** bedeuten; *(person: have in mind)* meinen. **what do you ~ by that?** was willst du damit sagen?; **I ~ it!** ich meine das ernst!; **I ~ what I say** es ist mir ernst damit; **the name ~s nothing to me** der Name sagt mir nichts; **it ~s starting all over again** das bedeutet, daß wir/sie wieder ganz von vorne anfangen müssen; **this will ~ great changes** dies wird bedeutende Veränderungen zur Folge haben; **he ~s a lot to me** er bedeutet mir viel.

(b) *(intend)* beabsichtigen. **to ~ to do sth** etw tun wollen; *(do on purpose)* etw absichtlich tun; **to be ~t for sb/sth** für jdn/etw bestimmt sein; **to ~ sb to do sth** wollen, daß jd etw tut; **sth is ~t to be sth** etw soll etw sein; **I ~t it as a joke** das sollte ein Witz sein; **you are ~t to be on time** du solltest pünktlich sein; **he wasn't ~t to be a leader** er war nicht zum Führer bestimmt; **I ~ to be obeyed** ich verlange, daß man mir gehorcht; **this pad is ~t for drawing** dieser Block ist zum Zeichnen gedacht; **you weren't ~t to see it** du solltest das nicht zu sehen bekommen; **he ~s well/no harm** er meint es gut/nicht böse.

meander [mɪ'ændəʳ] *vi (river)* sich (dahin)schlängeln; *(go off subject)* (vom Thema) abschweifen; *(walking)* schlendern.

meaning ['miːnɪŋ] *n* Bedeutung *f*; *(sense: of words, poem etc also)* Sinn *m*. **a look full of ~** ein bedeutsamer Blick; **do you get my ~?** haben Sie mich (richtig) verstanden?; **you don't know the ~ of hunger** du weißt ja gar nicht, was Hunger bedeutet; **what's the ~ of this?** was soll denn das (heißen)?

meaningful ['miːnɪŋfʊl] *adj* sinnvoll; *film* bedeutungsvoll.

meaningless ['miːnɪŋlɪs] *adj sentence* ohne Bedeutung; *life* sinnlos.

meanness ['miːnnɪs] *n see adj* **(a)** Geiz *m*. **(b)** Gemeinheit *f*. **(c)** Bösartigkeit *f*; Gehässigkeit *f*; Niedertracht *f*.

means [miːnz] *n* **(a)** *sing (method)* Möglichkeit *f*; *(instrument)* Mittel *nt*. **a ~ of transport** ein Beförderungsmittel *nt*; **a ~ to an end** ein Mittel *nt* zum Zweck; **there is no ~ of doing it** es ist unmöglich, das zu tun; **we've no ~ of knowing** wir können nicht wissen; **by ~ of sth** durch etw; **by ~ of doing sth** dadurch, daß man etw tut. **(b)** *sing* **by all ~!** (aber) selbstverständlich *or* natürlich!; **by no ~** keineswegs; *(under no circumstances)* auf keinen Fall. **(c)** *pl (wherewithal)* Mittel *pl*; *(financial ~ also)* Gelder *pl*. **a man of ~** ein vermögender Mann; **private ~** private Mittel; **to live beyond/within one's ~** über seine Verhältnisse leben/seinen Verhältnissen entsprechend leben; **~ test** Einkommensveranlagung *f*.

meant [ment] *pret, ptp of* **mean**[3].

meantime ['miːntaɪm] **1** *adv* inzwischen. **2** *n* **in the ~** in der Zwischenzeit, inzwischen.

meanwhile ['miːnwaɪl] *adv* inzwischen.

measles ['miːzlz] *n sing* Masern *pl*.

measly ['miːzlɪ] *adj (+er) (col)* mick(e)rig *(col)*.

measure ['meʒəʳ] **1** *n* **(a)** *(unit of measurement)* Maß(einheit *f*) *nt*; *(amount ~d)* Menge *f*; *(fig: yardstick)* Maßstab *m (of* für*)*. **her joy was beyond ~** ihre Freude kannte keine Grenzen; **to give sb full/short ~** *(barman)* richtig/zuwenig ausschenken; **in full ~** in höchstem Maße; **for good ~** sicherheitshalber; **it gave us some ~ of the difficulty** es gab uns einen Begriff von der Schwierigkeit; **in some ~** in gewisser Hinsicht; **some ~ of** ein gewisses Maß an; **to a** *or* **in large ~** in hohem Maße. **(b)** *(step)* Maßnahme *f*. **to take ~s to do sth** Maßnahmen ergreifen, um etw zu tun.

2 *vt* messen; *length* abmessen; *room* ausmessen; *(take sb's measurements)* Maß nehmen bei. **to ~ one's length** *(fig: fall)* der Länge nach hinfallen.

3 *vi* messen. **what does it ~?** wieviel mißt es?

♦ **measure off** *vt sep* abmessen.

♦ **measure out** *vt sep* abmessen; *weights* abwiegen.

♦ **measure up** *vi (be good enough, compare well)* **he didn't ~ ~** er hat enttäuscht; **to ~ ~ to sth** an etw *(acc)* herankommen.

measured ['meʒəd] *adj tread* gemessen; *tone, way of talking* bedächtig; *words* wohlüberlegt.

measurement ['meʒəmənt] *n* **(a)** *(act)* Messung *f*. **(b)** *(measure)* Maß *nt*; *(figure)* Meßwert m; *(fig)* Maßstab *m*. **to take sb's ~s** bei jdm Maß nehmen.

meat [miːt] *n* Fleisch *nt*. **cold ~s** Aufschnitt *m*. **one man's ~ is another man's poison** *(Prov)* des einen Freud, des andern Leid *(Prov)*.

meat *in cpds* Fleisch-; **~ball** *n* Fleischkloß *m*.

meaty ['miːtɪ] *adj (+er)* **(a)** *taste* Fleisch-. **(b)** *(fig) book* aussagestark.

mechanic [mɪ'kænɪk] *n* Mechaniker *m*.

mechanical [mɪ'kænɪkəl] *adj (lit, fig)* mechanisch. ~ **engineer/engineering** Maschinenbauingenieur *m*/Maschinenbau *m*.

mechanics [mɪ'kænɪks] *n* **(a)** *sing (subject) (engineering)* Maschinenbau *m; (Phys)* Mechanik *f*. **(b)** *pl (technical aspects)* Mechanik *f; (of writing etc)* Technik *f; (of procedure)* Mechanismus *m*.

mechanism ['mekənɪzəm] *n* Mechanismus *m*.

mechanize ['mekənaɪz] *vt* mechanisieren.

medal ['medl] *n* Medaille *f; (decoration)* Orden *m*.

medallist, medalist ['medəlɪst] *n* **gold** ~ Goldmedaillengewinner(in *f*) *m*.

meddle ['medl] *vi (interfere)* sich einmischen *(in* in +*acc); (tamper)* sich zu schaffen machen *(with* an +*dat)*. **he's not a man to** ~ **with** mit ihm ist nicht gut Kirschen essen *(col)*.

meddler ['medləʳ] *n* **he's a terrible** ~ er muß sich immer in alles einmischen.

meddlesome ['medlsəm] *adj*, **meddling** ['medlɪŋ] *adj attr* **she's a** ~ **old busybody** sie mischt sich dauernd in alles ein.

media ['miːdɪə] *n, pl of* **medium** Medien *pl*. **he works in the** ~ er ist im Mediensektor tätig; **all the** ~ **were there** Presse, Funk und Fernsehen waren dort.

mediaeval *adj* = **medieval.**

median strip ['miːdɪən'strɪp] *n (US)* Mittelstreifen *m*.

mediate ['miːdɪeɪt] **1** *vi* vermitteln. **2** *vt settlement* aushandeln.

mediation [,miːdɪ'eɪʃən] *n* Vermittlung *f*.

mediator ['miːdɪeɪtəʳ] *n* Vermittler *m*.

medical ['medɪkəl] **1** *adj* medizinisch; *treatment* ärztlich; *board, inspector* Gesundheits-; *student* Medizin-. ~ **school** ≈ medizinische Fakultät; ~ **card** *(Brit)* Krankenversicherungsschein *m*. **2** *n* (ärztliche) Untersuchung.

Medicare ['medɪ,kɛəʳ] *n (US) staatliche Krankenversicherung und Gesundheitsfürsorge.*

medicated ['medɪkeɪtɪd] *adj* medizinisch.

medication [,medɪ'keɪʃən] *n (act)* (medizinische) Behandlung; *(drugs etc)* Medikamente *pl*.

medicinal [me'dɪsɪnl] *adj* Heil-, heilend.

medicine ['medsɪn, 'medɪsɪn] *n* **(a)** Arznei *f; (particular preparation)* Medikament *nt*. **to give sb a taste of his own** ~ *(fig)* es jdm mit gleicher Münze heimzahlen. **(b)** *(science)* Medizin *f*.

medicine: ~ **chest** *n* Hausapotheke *f;* ~**-man** *n* Medizinmann *m*.

medieval [,medɪ'iːvəl] *adj* mittelalterlich.

mediocre [,miːdɪ'əʊkəʳ] *adj* mittelmäßig.

mediocrity [,miːdɪ'ɒkrɪtɪ] *n* Mittelmäßigkeit *f*.

meditate ['medɪteɪt] *vi* nachdenken *(upon, on* über +*acc); (Rel, Philos)* meditieren.

meditation [,medɪ'teɪʃən] *n* Nachdenken *nt; (Rel, Philos)* Meditation *f*.

Mediterranean [,medɪtə'reɪnɪən] **1** *n* Mittelmeer *nt*. **2** *adj* Mittelmeer-; *person* südländisch.

medium ['miːdɪəm] **1** *adj quality, size etc* mittlere(r, s); *steak* halbdurch; *brown, sized etc* mittel-. **of** ~ **height** mittelgroß. **2** *n, pl* **media** *or* **-s** **(a)** *(means)* Mittel *nt*. **through the** ~ **of the press** durch die Presse; **advertising** ~ Werbeträger *m*. **(b)** *(midpoint)* Mitte *f*. **happy** ~ goldener Mittelweg. **(c)** *(spiritualist)* Medium *nt*.

medium *in cpds* mittel-; ~**-sized** *adj* mittelgroß; ~ **wave** *n* Mittelwelle *f*.

medley ['medlɪ] *n* Gemisch *nt; (Mus)* Medley *nt*.

meek [miːk] *adj (+er)* sanft(mütig); *(pej)* duckmäuserisch; *(uncomplaining)* duldsam.

meet [miːt] *(vb: pret, ptp* **met***)* **1** *vt* **(a)** *(encounter) person* treffen; *(by arrangement)* sich treffen mit; *difficulty* stoßen auf *(+acc)*; **he met his death in 1800** im Jahre 1800 fand er den Tod; **to arrange to** ~ **sb** sich mit jdm verabreden; **his eyes met mine** unsere Blicke trafen sich; **there's more to it than** ~**s the eye** da steckt mehr dahinter, als man auf den ersten Blick meint.

(b) *(get to know)* kennenlernen. **come and** ~ **my brother** komm, ich mache dich mit meinem Bruder bekannt; **pleased to** ~ **you!** angenehm! *(form)*, guten Tag/Abend.

(c) *(await arrival, collect)* abholen *(at* an +*dat*, von*)*. **the car will** ~ **the train** der Wagen steht am Bahnhof bereit.

(d) *expectations, target, deadline* erfüllen; *requirement* gerecht werden *(+dat)*; *expenses, needs* decken; *charge, criticism* begegnen *(+dat)*.

2 *vi* **(a)** *(encounter) (people)* sich begegnen; *(by arrangement)* sich treffen; *(society, committee etc)* tagen. **haven't we met before somewhere?** sind wir uns nicht schon mal begegnet?; **until we** ~ **again!** bis zum nächsten Mal! **(b)** *(join etc)* sich treffen; *(converge)* sich vereinigen; *(rivers)* ineinanderfließen; *(intersect)* sich schneiden; *(fig: come together)* sich treffen. **our eyes met** unsere Blicke trafen sich.

3 *n (Hunt)* Jagd *f; (US Sport)* Sportfest *nt*.

♦ **meet up** *vi* sich treffen.

♦ **meet with** *vi +prep obj* **(a)** *hostility, problems* stoßen auf *(+acc)*; *success, accident* haben; *disaster* erleiden; *approval, untimely death* finden. **(b)** *person* treffen; *(have a meeting)* (zu einer Unterredung) zusammenkommen mit.

meeting ['miːtɪŋ] *n* **(a)** Begegnung *f*; *(arranged)* Treffen *nt; (business* ~*)* Besprechung *f*. **the minister had a** ~ **with the ambassador** der Minister traf zu Gesprächen mit dem Botschafter zusammen. **(b)** *(of committee)* Sitzung *f; (of members, citizens)* Versammlung *f*. **at the last** ~ bei der letzten Sitzung; **Mr Jones is in a** ~ Herr Jones ist (gerade) in einer Sitzung. **(c)** *(Sport)* Veranstaltung *f; (between teams, opponents)* Begegnung *f*.

meeting place *n* Treffpunkt *m*.

megalomaniac [,megələʊ'meɪnɪæk] *n* Größenwahnsinnige(r) *mf*.

megaphone ['megəfəʊn] *n* Megaphon *nt*.

melancholy ['melənkəlɪ] **1** *adj* melancholisch; *duty, sight etc* traurig. **2** *n* Melancholie *f*.

mellow ['meləʊ] **1** *adj (+er) fruit, wine* ausgereift; *colour, light* warm; *sound, voice* weich; *person* gesetzt; *(fig: slightly drunk)* angeheitert. **2** *vi (wine, fruit)* reif werden, *(colours, sounds)* weicher werden; *(person)* gesetzter werden.

melodious [mɪ'ləʊdɪəs] *adj* melodisch.

melodrama ['meləʊ,drɑːmə] *n* Melodrama *nt*.

melodramatic [,meləʊdrə'mætɪk] *adj* melodramatisch.

melody ['melədɪ] *n* Melodie *f*.

melon ['melən] *n* Melone *f*.

melt [melt] **1** *vt* schmelzen; *butter* zerlassen; *(fig) heart etc* erweichen. **her tears** ~**ed my anger** beim Anblick ihrer Tränen verflog mein Zorn. **2** *vi* schmelzen; *(butter also)* zergehen; *(fig: anger)* verfliegen. **it just** ~**s in the mouth** es zergeht einem nur so auf der Zunge; **he** ~**ed into the crowd** er verschwand in der Menge.

♦ **melt away** *vi (lit)* (weg)schmelzen; *(fig)* sich auflösen; *(person)* dahinschmelzen; *(anger)* verfliegen; *(suspicion, money)* zerrinnen.

♦ **melt down** *vt sep* einschmelzen.

meltdown ['meltdaʊn] *n* Kernschmelze *f*.

melting ['meltɪŋ-]: ~ **point** *n* Schmelzpunkt *m;* ~ **pot** *n (lit, fig)* Schmelztiegel *m;* **to be in the** ~ **pot** in der Schwebe sein.

member ['membəʳ] *n* Mitglied *nt; (of tribe, species)* Angehörige(r) *mf; (Parl)* Abgeordnete(r) *mf*. **"**~**s only"** „nur für Mitglieder"; ~ **of the family** Familienmitglied *nt*; **a** ~ **of the audience** ein Zuschauer/Zuhörer *m*; **the** ~ **countries** die Mitgliedsstaaten *pl;* ~ **of parliament** Parlamentsmitglied *nt*.

membership ['membəʃɪp] *n* Mitgliedschaft *f (of* in +*dat); (number of members)* Mitgliederzahl *f*. ~ **card** Mitgliedskarte *f*.

membrane ['membreɪn] *n* Membran(e) *f*.

memento [mə'mentəʊ] *n, pl* **-(e)s** Andenken *nt (of* an *+acc)*.

memo ['meməʊ] *n* **(a)** = **memorandum.** **(b)** ~ **pad** Notizblock *m*.

memoir ['memwɑːʳ] *n* **(a)** Kurzbiographie *f*. **(b)** ~**s** *pl* Memoiren *pl*.

memorable ['memərəbl] *adj* unvergeßlich; *(important)* denkwürdig.

memorandum [,memə'rændəm] *n, pl* **memoranda** [,memə'rændə] *(in business)* Mitteilung *f; (personal reminder)* Notiz *f*.

memorial [mɪ'mɔːrɪəl] **1** *adj plaque, service* Gedenk-. **2** *n* Denkmal *nt (to* für*)*.

memorize ['meməraɪz] *vt* sich *(dat)* einprägen.

memory ['memərɪ] *n* **(a)** Gedächtnis *nt; (faculty)* Erinnerungsvermögen *nt*. **from** ~ aus dem Kopf; **I have a bad** ~ **for faces** ich habe ein schlechtes Personengedächtnis; **if my** ~ **serves me right** wenn ich mich recht entsinne. **(b)** *(that remembered)* Erinnerung *f (of* an *+acc)*. **I have no** ~ **of it** ich kann mich nicht daran erinnern. **(c)** *(Comp)* Speicher *m*. ~ **bank** Datenspeicher *m*. **(d) in** ~ **of** zur Erinnerung *or* zum Gedenken *(form)* an *(+acc)*.

men [men] *pl of* **man.**

menace ['menɪs] **1** *n* **(a)** Bedrohung *f (to gen); (imminent danger)* drohende Gefahr. **(b)** *(col: nuisance)* (Land)plage *f*. **2** *vt* bedrohen.

menacing ['menɪsɪŋ] *adj* drohend.

mend [mend] **1** *n* **to be on the** ~ auf dem Wege der Besserung sein. **2** *vt (repair)* reparieren; *roof, fence also* ausbessern; *hole, clothes* flicken. **my shoes need** ~**ing** ich muß meine Schuhe reparieren lassen; **to** ~ **one's ways** sich bessern. **3** *vi (bone)* (ver)heilen.

menfolk ['menfəʊk] *npl* Männer *pl*.

menial ['miːnɪəl] *adj* niedrig.

meningitis [,menɪn'dʒaɪtɪs] *n* Hirnhautentzündung *f*.

menopause ['menəʊpɔːz] *n* Wechseljahre *pl*.

menstruate ['menstrʊeɪt] *vi* die Menstruation haben.

menstruation [,menstrʊ'eɪʃən] *n* die Menstruation *or* Periode.

mental ['mentl] *adj* **(a)** geistig; *cruelty* seelisch. **to make a** ~ **note of sth** sich *(dat)* etw merken; ~ **blackout** Bewußtseinsstörung *f*; ~ **arithmetic** Kopfrechnen *nt*; ~ **health** Geisteszustand *m*; ~ **home** (Nerven)heilanstalt *f*; ~ **hospital** psychiatrische Klinik *f*; ~ **illness** Geisteskrankheit *f*. **(b)** *(col: mad)* übergeschnappt *(col)*.

mentality [men'tælɪtɪ] *n* Mentalität *f*. **they have an aggressive** ~ sie haben eine aggressive Art.

mentally ['mentəlɪ] *adv* **(a)** geistig. ~ **handicapped/deficient** geistig behindert/geistesschwach; **he is** ~ **ill** er ist geisteskrank. **(b)** *(in one's head)* im Kopf.

menthol ['menθɒl] *n* Menthol *nt*.

mention ['menʃən] **1** *n* Erwähnung *f*. **to get** *or* **receive a** ~ erwähnt werden; **to give sth a** ~ etw erwähnen; **there is a/no** ~ **of it** es wird erwähnt/nicht erwähnt; **it's hardly worth a** ~ es ist kaum erwähnenswert. **2** *vt* erwähnen *(to sb* jdm gegenüber*)*. **not to** ~ ... geschweige denn ...; **too numerous to** ~ zu zahlreich, um sie einzeln erwähnen zu können; **don't** ~ **it!** (bitte,) gern geschehen!; ~**ing no names,** ohne irgendwelche Namen nennen zu wollen; ~ **me to your parents!** viele Grüße an Ihre Eltern!

menu ['menjuː] *n* **(a)** Speisekarte *f*. **what's on the** ~**?** was gibt es heute (zu essen)? **(b)** *(Comp)* Menü *nt*. ~**-driven** menügesteuert.

mercenary ['mɜːsɪnərɪ] **1** *adj* **(a)** *person* geldgierig. **(b)** *(Mil) troops* Söldner-. **2** *n* Söldner *m*.

merchandise ['mɜːtʃəndaɪz] *n* Ware *f*.

merchant ['mɜːtʃənt] *n* Kaufmann *m*. **diamond** ~ Diamantenhändler *m*.

merchant *in cpds* Handels-; ~ **bank** *n (Brit)* Handelsbank *f*; ~ **navy** *n* Handelsmarine *f*; ~ **seaman** *n* Matrose *m* in der Handelsmarine.

merciful ['mɜːsɪfʊl] *adj* gnädig. **his death was a** ~ **release** sein Tod war für ihn eine Erlösung.

mercifully ['mɜːsɪfəlɪ] *adv act* barmherzig; *treat sb* gnädig; *(fortunately)* glücklicherweise.

merciless ['mɜːsɪlɪs] *adj* erbarmungslos; *destruction* schonungslos.

Mercury ['mɜːkjʊrɪ] *n* Merkur *m*.

mercury ['mɜːkjʊrɪ] *n* Quecksilber *nt*.

mercy ['mɜːsɪ] *n no pl (feeling of compassion)* Erbarmen *nt; (in judgment)* Gnade *f; (God's* ~*)* Barmherzigkeit *f*. **to have** ~ **on sb** mit jdm Erbarmen haben; **to show sb** ~**/no** ~ Erbarmen/kein Erbarmen mit jdm haben; **to be at the** ~ **of sb/sth** jdm/einer Sache *(dat)* ausgeliefert sein; **it's a** ~ **nobody was hurt** *(col)* man kann von Glück sagen, daß niemand verletzt wurde.

mercy killing *n* Töten *nt* aus Mitleid.

mere [mɪəʳ] *adj* bloß; *formality also* rein. **he's a** ~ **clerk** er ist bloß ein kleiner Angestellter; **but she's a** ~ **child** aber sie ist doch noch ein Kind!

merely ['mɪəlɪ] *adv* lediglich, bloß.

merge [mɜːdʒ] **1** *vi* **(a)** zusammenkommen; *(colours)* ineinander übergehen; *(roads)* zusammenlaufen. **to** ~ **with sth** mit etw verschmelzen; *(colour)* in etw *(acc)* übergehen; **to** ~ **into sth** in etw *(acc)* übergehen. **(b)** *(Comm)* fusionieren. **2** *vt (Comm)* fusionieren.

merger ['mɜːdʒəʳ] *n (Comm)* Fusion *f*.

meringue [mə'ræŋ] *n* Meringe *f*, Baiser *nt*.

merit ['merɪt] **1** *n (achievement)* Leistung *f*, Verdienst *nt; (advantage)* Vorzug *m*. **to look** *or* **inquire into the** ~**s of sth** etw auf seine Vorteile untersuchen; **to treat a case on its** ~**s** einen Fall gesondert behandeln. **2** *vt* verdienen.

meritocracy [,merɪ'tɒkrəsɪ] *n* Leistungsgesellschaft *f*.

mermaid ['mɜːmeɪd] *n* Nixe, Meerjungfrau *f*.

merriment ['merɪmənt] *n* Heiterkeit *f; (laughter)* Gelächter *nt*.

merry ['merɪ] *adj (+er)* **(a)** *(cheerful)* fröhlich, vergnügt. **M**~ **Christmas!** Fröhliche *or* Frohe Weihnachten! **(b)** *(col: tipsy)* beschwipst *(col)*.

merry: ~**-go-round** *n* Karussel *nt*; ~**making** *n* Feiern *nt*.

mesh [meʃ] *n (hole)* Masche *f; (size of hole)* Maschenweite *f; (wire* ~*)* Maschendraht *m*. **out of/in** ~ *(Mech)* nicht im/im Eingriff.

mesmerize ['mezməraɪz] *vt* hypnotisieren; *(fig)* fesseln. **the audience sat** ~**d** die Zuschauer saßen wie gebannt.

mess[1] [mes] *n* Durcheinander *nt; (untidy also)* Unordnung *f; (dirty)* Schweinerei *f*. **to be (in) a** ~ unordentlich sein; *(disorganized)* ein einziges Durcheinander sein; *(fig: one's life, marriage etc)* vekorkst sein *(col)*; **to look a** ~ *(person)* unmöglich aussehen; *(untidy also, room)* unordentlich aussehen; **to make a** ~ *(untidy)* Unordnung machen; *(dirty)* eine Schweinerei machen; **to make a** ~ **of sth** *(untidy)* etw durcheinanderbringen; *(dirty)* etw verdrecken; *(bungle, botch)* etw verpfuschen; **the cat made a** ~ **on the carpet** die Katze hat auf den Teppich gemacht.

♦ **mess about** *or* **around** *(col)* **1** *vt sep person* an der Nase herumführen *(col)*; *(boss etc)* herumschikanieren; *(by delaying)* hinhalten. **2** *vi (play the fool)* herumalbern *or* -blödeln *(col)*; *(do nothing in particular)* herumgammeln *(col)*; *(fiddle)* herumfummeln *(col) (with* an *+dat)*; *(as hobby etc)* herumbasteln *(with* an *+dat) (col)*.

♦ **mess up** *vt sep* durcheinanderbringen; *(make untidy also)* in Unordnung bringen; *(make dirty)* verdrecken; *(botch, bungle)* verpfuschen, verhunzen *(col)*; *marriage* kaputtmachen *(col)*, ruinieren; *life, person* verkorksen *(col)*.

mess[2] *(Mil) n* Kasino *nt; (on ships)* Messe *f*.

message ['mesɪdʒ] *n* Mitteilung, Nachricht, Botschaft *(form) f.* **to take a ~ to sb** jdm eine Nachricht überbringen; **can I take a ~ (for him)?** *(on telephone)* kann ich (ihm) etwas ausrichten?; **to give sb a ~** *(verbal)* jdm etwas ausrichten; *(written)* jdm eine Nachricht geben; **would you give John a ~ (for me)?** könnten Sie John etwas (von mir) ausrichten?; **to leave a ~ for sb** *(written)* jdm eine Nachricht hinterlassen; *(verbal)* jdm etwas ausrichten lassen; **to get the ~** *(fig col)* kapieren *(col).*
messenger ['mesɪndʒəʳ] *n* Bote *(form)*, Überbringer(in *f*) *m*; *(Mil)* Kurier *m.* **~ boy** Laufbursche *m.*
Messiah [mɪ'saɪə] *n* Messias *m.*
Messrs ['mesəz] *pl of* **Mr** *(on letters etc)* **to ~** ... an die Herren ...
messy ['mesɪ] *adj (+er) (dirty)* dreckig; *(untidy)* unordentlich; *(confused)* durcheinander *pred; (fig: unpleasant)* unschön.
met [met] *pret, ptp of* **meet.**
metal ['metl] *n* Metall *nt; (Brit: on road)* Asphalt *m.*
metallic [mɪ'tælɪk] *adj* metallisch.
metallurgy [me'tælədʒɪ] *n* Metallurgie *f.*
metal *in cpds* Metall-; **~ plating** *n* Metallschicht *f;* **~work** *n* Metall *nt;* **we did ~work at school** wir haben in der Schule Metallarbeiten gemacht.
metamorphosis [ˌmetə'mɔːfəsɪs] *n, pl* **metamorphoses** [ˌmetə'mɔːfəsiːz] Metamorphose *f; (fig)* Verwandlung *f.*
metaphor ['metəfəʳ] *n* Metapher *f.*
metaphorical [ˌmetə'fɒrɪkəl] *adj* metaphorisch.
metaphysical [ˌmetə'fɪzɪkəl] *adj* metaphysisch.
metaphysics [ˌmetə'fɪzɪks] *n sing* Metaphysik *f.*
♦ **mete out** ['miːt'aʊt] *vt sep* zuteil werden lassen *(to sb* jdm*); praise* austeilen; *rewards* verteilen. **to ~ ~ a punishment to sb** jdn bestrafen.
meteor ['miːtɪəʳ] *n* Meteor *m.*
meteoric [ˌmiːtɪ'ɒrɪk] *adj* meteorisch; *(fig)* kometenhaft.
meteorite ['miːtɪəraɪt] *n* Meteorit *m.*
meteorological [ˌmiːtɪərə'lɒdʒɪkəl] *adj* Wetter-, meteorologisch.
meteorologist [ˌmiːtɪə'rɒlədʒɪst] *n* Meteorologe *m,* Meteorologin *f.*
meteorology [ˌmiːtɪə'rɒlədʒɪ] *n* Meteorologie *f.*
meter[1] ['miːtəʳ] *n* Zähler *m; (parking ~)* Parkuhr *f.*
meter[2] *n (US)* = **metre.**
methane ['miːθeɪn] *n* Methan *nt.*
method ['meθəd] *n* Methode *f; (process)* Verfahren *nt.* **~ of payment** Zahlungsweise *f.*
methodology [ˌmeθə'dɒlədʒɪ] *n* Methodik *f.*
meths [meθs] *n sing* Spiritus *m.*
methylated spirits ['meθɪleɪtɪd'spɪrɪts] *n sing* (Brenn)spiritus *m.*
meticulous [mɪ'tɪkjʊləs] *adj* (peinlich) genau. **to be ~ about sth** es mit etw sehr genau nehmen.
metre, *(US)* **meter** ['miːtəʳ] *n* **(a)** *(Measure)* Meter *m or nt.* **(b)** *(Poet)* Metrum *nt.*
metric ['metrɪk] *adj* metrisch. **to go ~** auf das metrische Maßsystem umstellen.
metrication [ˌmetrɪ'keɪʃən] *n* Umstellung *f* auf das metrische Maßsystem.
metropolis [mɪ'trɒpəlɪs] *n* Metropole, Weltstadt *f; (capital)* Hauptstadt *f.*
metropolitan [ˌmetrə'pɒlɪtən] *adj* weltstädtisch; der Hauptstadt.
mettle ['metl] *n (spirit)* Stehvermögen *nt; (of horse)* Zähigkeit *f; (temperament)* Feuer *nt.* **to show one's ~** zeigen, was in einem steckt; **to be on one's ~** auf dem Posten sein.
mew [mjuː] **1** *n* Miau(en) *nt.* **2** *vi* miauen.
Mexican ['meksɪkən] **1** *adj* mexikanisch. **2** *n* Mexikaner(in *f*) *m.*
Mexico ['meksɪkəʊ] *n* Mexiko *nt.*
mezzo-soprano [ˌmetsəʊsə'prɑːnəʊ] *n* Mezzosopran *m.*
miaow [miː'aʊ] **1** *n* Miau(en) *nt.* **2** *vi* miauen.
mica ['maɪkə] *n* Muskovit *m.*
mice [maɪs] *pl of* **mouse.**
mickey ['mɪkɪ] *n (col)*: **to take the ~ (out of sb)** jdn auf den Arm *or* auf die Schippe nehmen *(col).*
micro- ['maɪkrəʊ-] *pref* mikro-, Mikro-.
microbe ['maɪkrəʊb] *n* Mikrobe *f.*
micro: **~biology** *n* Mikrobiologie *f;* **~chip** *n* Mikrochip *m;* **~-computer** *n* Mikrocomputer; **~cosm** *n* Mikrokosmos *m;* **~film** *n* Mikrofilm *m;* **~organism** *n* Mikroorganismus *m;* **~phone** *n* Mikrofon *nt;* **~processor** *n* Mikroprozessor *m;* **~scope** *n* Mikroskop *nt;* **~scopic** [ˌmaɪkrə'skɒpɪk] *adj details, print* mikroskopisch; **~scopic creature** mikroskopisch kleines Lebewesen; **~wave** *n* Mikrowelle *f;* **~wave oven** Mikrowellenherd *m.*
mid [mɪd] *adj* mittel-, Mittel-. **in ~ January** Mitte Januar; **in the ~ 1950s** Mitte der fünfziger Jahre; **he's in his mid 30s** er ist Mitte dreißig; **temperatures in the ~ eighties** Temperaturen um 85° Fahrenheit; **in ~ morning** am Vormittag; **in ~ ocean** mitten auf dem Meer; **in ~ air** in der Luft.
midday ['mɪd'deɪ] **1** *n* Mittag *m.* **at ~** mittags, um die Mittagszeit. **2** *adj attr* mittäglich. **~ meal** Mittagessen *nt.*
middle ['mɪdl] **1** *n* Mitte *f; (central section: of book, film etc)* mittlerer Teil; *(inside of fruit etc)* Innere(s) *nt; (waist)* Taille *f.* **in the ~ of the table** mitten auf dem Tisch; *(in exact centre)* in der Mitte des Tisches; **in the ~ of the night** mitten in der Nacht; **in the ~ of the day** gegen Mittag; **in the ~ of nowhere** am Ende der Welt; **in** *or* **about the ~ of May** Mitte Mai; **we were in the ~ of lunch** wir waren mitten beim Essen; **to be in the ~ of doing sth** mitten dabei sein, etw zu tun; **I'm in the ~ of reading it** ich bin mittendrin. **2** *adj* mittlere(r, s); *part, point, finger* Mittel-.
middle *in cpds* Mittel-, mittel-; **~ age** *n* mittleres Lebensalter; **~-aged** *adj* mittleren Alters; **M~ Ages** *npl* Mittelalter *nt;* **~-class** *adj* bürgerlich, spießig *(pej)*; *(Sociol)* mittelständisch; **~ class(es)** *n* Mittelstand *m or* -schicht *f;* **M~ East** *n* Naher Osten; **~man** *n* Mittelsmann *m; (Comm)* Zwischenhändler *m;* **~-of-the-road** *adj* gemäßigt; *policy, politician* der gemäßigten Mitte.
midge [mɪdʒ] *n* Mücke *f.*
midget ['mɪdʒɪt] *n* Liliputaner *m.*
mid: **the M~lands** *npl* die Midlands; **~night** *n* Mitternacht *f;* **at ~night** um Mitternacht.
midriff ['mɪdrɪf] *n* Taille *f.*
midst [mɪdst] *n* **in the ~ of** mitten in.
mid: **~stream** *n* **in ~stream** *(lit)* in der Mitte des Flusses; *(fig)* auf halber Strecke, **~summer 1** *n* Hochsommer *m;* **M~summer's Day** Sommersonnenwende *f;* **2** *adj days, nights* Hochsommer-; **~-term** *adj* **~-term elections** *(Pol)* Zwischenwahlen *pl;* **~way** *adv* auf halbem Weg; **~way through sth** mitten in etw *(dat)*; **~week** *adv* mitten in der Woche.
midwife ['mɪdwaɪf] *n, pl* **-wives** Hebamme *f.*
midwinter [ˌmɪd'wɪntəʳ] *n* Mitte *f* des Winters.
might[1] [maɪt] *pret of* **may. as you ~ expect** wie zu erwarten war; **you ~ try Smith's** Sie könnten es ja mal bei Smith versuchen; **he ~ at least have apologized** er hätte sich wenigstens entschuldigen können.
might[2] *n* Macht *f.* **with all one's ~** mit aller Kraft.
mighty ['maɪtɪ] **1** *adj (+er)* gewaltig; *(wielding power)* mächtig; *warrior* stark. **2** *adv (col)* mächtig *(col).*
migraine ['miːgreɪn] *n* Migräne *f.*
migrant ['maɪgrənt] **1** *adj* Wander-. **~ bird** Zugvogel *m;* **~ worker** Gastarbeiter *m.* **2** *n* Zugvogel *m;* Gastarbeiter *m.*
migrate [maɪ'greɪt] *vi (animals, workers)* (ab)wandern; *(birds)* nach Süden ziehen.
migration [maɪ'greɪʃən] *n* Wanderung *f; (of birds*

also) (Vogel)zug *m; (seasonal)* Zug *m.*
mike [maɪk] *n (col)* Mikrofon, Mikro *(col) nt.*
mild [maɪld] **1** *adj (+er)* mild; *breeze, criticism* leicht; *character* sanft; *(slight)* leicht. **2** *n (Brit: beer)* leichtes dunkles Bier.
mildew ['mɪldjuː] *n* Schimmel *m; (on plants)* Mehltau *m.*
mildly ['maɪldlɪ] *adv* leicht; *say* sanft; *rebuke* milde. **to put it ~** gelinde gesagt.
mile [maɪl] *n* Meile *f.* **how many ~s per gallon does your car do?** wieviel verbraucht Ihr Auto?; **a fifty-~ journey** eine Fahrt von fünfzig Meilen; **~s (and ~s)** *(col)* meilenweit; **they live ~s away** sie wohnen meilenweit weg; **it sticks out a ~** das sieht ja ein Blinder (mit Krückstock) *(col)*; **he's ~s better at tennis than she is** er spielt hundertmal besser Tennis als sie *(col).*
mileage ['maɪlɪdʒ] *n* Meilen *pl; (on odometer)* Meilenstand *m.* **what ~ does your car do?** wieviel (Benzin) verbraucht Ihr Auto?; **we got a lot of ~ out of it** *(fig col)* das war uns *(dat)* sehr dienlich.
mileometer [maɪ'lɒmɪtəʳ] *n (Brit)* Tacho(meter) *m.*
milestone ['maɪlstəʊn] *n (lit, fig)* Meilenstein *m.*
milieu ['miːljɜː] *n* Milieu *nt.*
militant ['mɪlɪtənt] **1** *adj* militant. **2** *n* militantes Mitglied/militanter Gewerkschaftler *etc.*
militarism ['mɪlɪtərɪzəm] *n* Militarismus *m.*
militaristic [,mɪlɪtə'rɪstɪk] *adj* militaristisch.
military ['mɪlɪtərɪ] **1** *adj* militärisch; *government, band* Militär-. **~ service** Wehrdienst *m.* **2** *n*: **the ~** das Militär.
militate ['mɪlɪteɪt] *vi* **to ~ against sth** gegen etw sprechen.
militia [mɪ'lɪʃə] *n* Miliz, Bürgerwehr *f.*
milk [mɪlk] *n* Milch *f.* **~ of magnesia** Magnesiamilch *f;* **it's no use crying over spilt ~** *(prov)* was passiert ist, ist passiert.
milk *in cpds* Milch-; **~ chocolate** *n* Vollmilchschokolade *f;* **~ churn** *n* Milchkanne *f;* **~ float** *n* Milchwagen *m.*
milking ['mɪlkɪŋ] *n* Melken *nt.* **~ machine** Melkmaschine *f.*
milk: ~man *n* Milchmann *m;* **~ shake** *n* Milchshake *m;* **~ tooth** *n* Milchzahn *m.*
milky ['mɪlkɪ] *adj (+er)* milchig. **~ coffee** Milchkaffee *m.*
Milky Way [,mɪlkɪ'weɪ] *n* Milchstraße *f.*
mill [mɪl] **1** *n* Mühle *f; (paper, steel ~ etc)* Fabrik *f; (cotton~) (for thread)* Spinnerei *f; (for cloth)* Weberei *f.* **he really went through the ~** *(col)* er hat wirklich viel durchmachen müssen. **2** *vt flour, coffee etc* mahlen; *metal, paper* walzen.
♦ **mill about** *or* **around** *vi* umherlaufen.
millennium [mɪ'lenɪəm] *n, pl* **-s** *or* **millennia** [mɪ'lenɪə] *(1,000 years)* Jahrtausend *nt; (state of perfection)* Tausendjähriges Reich *nt.*
miller ['mɪləʳ] *n* Müller *m.*
millet ['mɪlɪt] *n* Hirse *f.*
milli: ~gram(me) *n* Milligramm *nt;* **~litre,** *(US)* **~liter** *n* Milliliter *m or nt.*
milliner ['mɪlɪnəʳ] *n* Hutmacher(in *f*) *m.*
million ['mɪljən] *n* Million *f.* **4 ~ people** 4 Millionen Menschen; **the starving ~s** die Millionen, die Hunger leiden; **she's one in a ~** *(col)* so jemanden wie sie findet man sobald nicht wieder; **to feel like a ~ dollars** *(col)* sich pudelwohl fühlen.
millionaire [,mɪljə'nɛəʳ] *n* Millionär *m.*
millionairess [,mɪljə'nɛəres] *n* Millionärin *f.*
millipede ['mɪlɪpiːd] *n* Tausendfüßler *m.*
mill: ~pond *n* Mühlteich *m;* **~stone** *n* Mühlstein *m;* **it's a ~stone around his neck** das ist für ihn ein Klotz am Bein.
mime [maɪm] **1** *n (acting)* Pantomime *f; (actor)* Pantomime *m; (ancient play, actor)* Mimus *m.* **2** *vt* pantomimisch darstellen.
mimic ['mɪmɪk] **1** *n* Imitator *m.* **2** *vt* nachahmen; *(ridicule)* nachäffen.
mimicry ['mɪmɪkrɪ] *n* Nachahmung *f.*
min = minute(s) min; **minimum** min.
mince [mɪns] **1** *n (Brit)* Hackfleisch, Gehackte(s) *nt.* **2** *vt meat* durch den Fleischwolf drehen. **he doesn't ~ his words** er nimmt kein Blatt vor den Mund. **3** *vi (walk)* tänzeln, trippeln; *(speak)* sich geziert ausdrücken.
mincemeat ['mɪnsmiːt] *n süße Gebäckfüllung aus Dörrobst und Sirup.* **to make ~meat of sb** *(col) (physically)* Hackfleisch aus jdm machen *(col)*; *(verbally)* jdn zur Schnecke machen *(col).*
mincer ['mɪnsəʳ] *n* Fleischwolf *m.*
mind [maɪnd] **1** *n* **(a)** *(intellect)* Geist *(also Philos, person)*, Verstand *m; (type of ~ also)* Kopf *m; (thoughts)* Gedanken *pl; (memory)* Gedächtnis *nt.* **it's a question of ~ over matter** es ist eine Willensfrage; **it's all in the ~** das ist alles Einbildung; **one of the finest ~s of our times** einer der großen Geister unserer Zeit; **to be clear in one's ~ about sth** sich *(dat)* über etw im klaren sein; **he had something on his ~** ihn beschäftigte etwas; **if you put your ~ to it** wenn du dich anstrengst; **she couldn't get him out of her ~** er ging ihr nicht aus dem Kopf; **to take sb's ~ off sth** jdn auf andere Gedanken bringen; **the idea never entered my ~** daran hatte ich überhaupt nicht gedacht; **to bear** *or* **keep sth in ~** etw nicht vergessen; *facts also, application* etw im Auge behalten; **to bear** *or* **keep sb in ~** an jdn denken; **it went right out of my ~** daran habe ich überhaupt nicht mehr gedacht; **to bring** *or* **call sth to ~** etw in Erinnerung rufen.

(b) *(inclination)* Lust *f; (intention)* Absicht *f.* **to have sb/sth in ~** an jdn/etw denken; **to have it in ~ to do sth** beabsichtigen, etw zu tun; **I've half a ~/a good ~ to ...** ich hätte Lust/gute Lust, zu ...; **nothing was further from my ~** nichts lag mir ferner; **his ~ is set on that** er hat sich *(dat)* das in den Kopf gesetzt.

(c) *(opinion)* Meinung, Ansicht *f.* **to change one's ~** es sich *(dat)* anders überlegen; **to be in two ~s about sth** sich *(dat)* über etw *(acc)* nicht im klaren sein; **to be of one** *or* **the same ~** gleicher Meinung sein; **to my ~ he's wrong** meiner Ansicht nach irrt er sich; **to have a ~ of one's own** *(person: not conform)* seinen eigenen Kopf haben; *(hum: machine etc)* seine Mucken haben *(col).*

(d) *(sanity)* Verstand *m.* **to go out of** *or* **lose one's ~** den Verstand verlieren; **to be out of one's ~** nicht bei Verstand sein; *(with worry etc)* vor Sorgen ganz krank sein.

2 *vt* **(a)** *(look after)* aufpassen auf *(+acc)*; *sb's chair, seat* freihalten. **I'm ~ing the shop** *(fig)* ich sehe nach dem Rechten.

(b) *(be careful of)* aufpassen (auf *+acc*); *(pay attention to)* achten auf *(+acc)*; *(act in accordance with)* beachten. **~ the step!** Vorsicht Stufe!; **~ your own business** kümmern Sie sich um Ihre eigenen Angelegenheiten.

(c) *(care, worry about)* sich kümmern um; *(object to)* etwas haben gegen. **she doesn't ~ it** es macht ihr nichts aus; *(is not bothered)* es stört sie nicht; *(is indifferent to)* es ist ihr egal; **would you ~ opening the door?** wären Sie so freundlich, die Tür aufzumachen?; **do you ~ my smoking?** macht es Ihnen etwas aus, wenn ich rauche?; **never ~ the expense** (es ist) egal, was es kostet; **never ~ him** kümmere dich nicht um ihn!; **I wouldn't ~ a cup of tea** ich hätte nichts gegen eine Tasse Tee.

3 *vi* **(a)** *(be careful)* aufpassen. **~ you get that done** sieh zu, daß du das fertigbekommst!

(b) ~ you allerdings; **~ you, he did try** er hat es immerhin versucht.

(c) *(care, worry)* sich kümmern; *(object)* etwas dagegen haben. **do you ~?** macht es Ihnen etwas aus?; **do you ~!** *(iro)* ich möchte doch sehr bitten!; **may I? — I don't ~** darf ich? — meinetwegen; **which one do you want? — I don't ~** welches willst du? — das ist mir egal.

(d) never ~ macht nichts!; *(in exasperation)* ist ja auch egal!; **never ~, you'll find another** mach dir nichts draus, du findest bestimmt einen anderen; **never ~ about that now!** laß das doch jetzt!

♦ **mind out** *vi* aufpassen *(for* auf *+acc).*

mind: ~-blowing *adj (col)* irre *(col)*; **~-boggling** *adj (col)* irrsinnig *(col).*

-minded *adj suf* **an industrially-~ nation** ein auf Industrie ausgerichtetes Land.

mindful ['maɪndfʊl] *adj* **to be ~ of sth** etw berücksichtigen.

mind: ~less *adj (stupid)* ohne Verstand; *(senseless) destruction, crime* sinnlos; *occupation* geistlos; **~ reader** *n* Gedankenleser(in *f*) *m.*

mine[1] [maɪn] *poss pron* meine(r, s). **this car is ~** dieses Auto gehört mir; **is this ~?** gehört das mir?; **his friends and ~** seine und meine Freunde; **a friend of ~** ein Freund von mir; **a favourite expression of ~** einer meiner Lieblingsausdrücke.

mine[2] **1** *n* **(a)** *(Min)* Bergwerk *nt; (copper ~ etc also)* Mine *f; (coal~ also)* Zeche *f.* **to work down the ~s** unter Tage arbeiten. **(b)** *(Mil, Naut etc)* Mine *f.* **to lay ~s** Minen legen. **(c)** *(fig)* **the book is a ~ of information** das Buch ist eine wahre Fundgrube; **he is a ~ of information** er ist ein wandelndes Lexikon *(col).* **2** *vt* **(a)** *coal, metal* fördern, abbauen. **(b)** *(Mil, Naut)* verminen; *ship* eine Mine befestigen an *(+dat)*; *(blow up)* (mit einer Mine) sprengen. **3** *vi* Bergbau betreiben. **to ~ for sth** nach etw graben.

mine: ~-detector *n* Minensuchgerät *nt;* **~field** *n* Minenfeld *nt.*

miner ['maɪnə^r] *n* Bergarbeiter, Bergmann *m.*

mineral ['mɪnərəl] **1** *n* Mineral *nt.* **2** *adj deposit, resources* Mineral-. **~ water** Mineralwasser *nt.*

mine sweeper *n* Minensuchboot *nt.*

mingle ['mɪŋgl] *vi* sich vermischen; *(people, groups)* sich untereinander vermischen. **to ~ with the crowd** sich unters Volk mischen.

mini- ['mɪnɪ-] *pref* Mini-.

miniature ['mɪnɪtʃə^r] **1** *n* Miniaturausgabe *f; (Art)* Miniatur *f.* **2** *adj attr* Miniatur-.

minibus ['mɪnɪ,bʌs] *n* Kleinbus *m.*

minimal ['mɪnɪml] *adj* minimal.

minimize ['mɪnɪmaɪz] *vt expenditure etc* auf ein Minimum reduzieren.

minimum ['mɪnɪməm] **1** *n* Minimum *nt.* **with a ~ of inconvenience** mit einem Minimum an Unannehmlichkeiten; **to reduce sth to a ~** etw auf ein Mindestmaß reduzieren. **2** *adj attr* Mindest-. **~ temperature** Tiefsttemperatur *f;* **~ wage** Mindestlohn *m.*

mining ['maɪnɪŋ] *n* **(a)** *(Min)* Bergbau *m.* **(b)** *(Mil) (of area)* Verminen *nt; (of ship)* Sprengung *f* (mit einer Mine).

mining: ~ engineer *n* Bergbauingenieur *m;* **~ industry** *n* Bergbau *m.*

miniskirt ['mɪnɪ,skɜːt] *n* Minirock *m.*

minister ['mɪnɪstə^r] *n* **(a)** *(Pol)* Minister *m.* **(b)** *(Eccl)* Pastor *m,* protestantischer Geistlicher.

ministerial [,mɪnɪ'stɪərɪəl] *adj (Pol)* ministeriell, Minister-.

ministry ['mɪnɪstrɪ] *n* **(a)** *(Pol)* Ministerium *nt.* **~ of agriculture** Landwirtschaftsministerium. **(b)** *(Eccl)* geistliches Amt. **to join** *or* **go into the ~** Geistlicher werden.

mink [mɪŋk] *n* Nerz *m.* **~ coat** Nerzmantel *m.*

minor ['maɪnə^r] **1** *adj* **(a)** *(of lesser extent)* kleiner; *(of lesser importance)* unbedeutend; *offence, operation* leicht; *importance* geringer; *position, road* Neben-. **a ~ role** eine Nebenrolle. **(b)** *(Mus)* Moll-. **G ~** g-Moll *nt.* **2** *n* **(a)** *(Jur)* Minderjährige(r) *mf.* **(b)** *(US Univ)* Nebenfach *nt.*

minority [maɪ'nɒrɪtɪ] **1** *n* Minderheit *f.* **to be in a ~** in der Minderheit sein. **2** *adj attr* Minderheits-. **~ group** Minderheit *f.*

minstrel ['mɪnstrəl] *n* Spielmann *m.*

mint[1] [mɪnt] **1** *n* Münzanstalt, Münze *f.* **to be worth a ~** steinreich sein. **2** *adj stamp* ungestempelt. **in ~ condition** in tadellosem Zustand. **3** *vt coin* prägen.

mint[2] *n (Bot)* Minze *f; (sweet)* Pfefferminz *nt.* **~ sauce** Minzsoße *f.*

minuet [,mɪnjʊ'et] *n* Menuett *nt.*

minus ['maɪnəs] **1** *prep* **(a)** minus, weniger. **£100 ~ taxes** £ 100 abzüglich (der) Steuern. **(b)** *(without, deprived of)* ohne. **2** *adj quantity, value* negativ; *sign* Minus-; *temperatures* unter Null. **~ three degrees** drei Grad minus.

minute[1] ['mɪnɪt] *n* **(a)** *(of time, degree)* Minute *f.* **in a ~** sofort; **this (very) ~!** auf der Stelle!; **I shan't be a ~, it won't take a ~** es dauert nicht lang; **any ~** jeden Augenblick; **tell me the ~ he comes** sag mir sofort Bescheid, wenn er kommt; **have you got a ~?** hast du mal einen Augenblick Zeit?; **at the last ~** in letzter Minute. **(b)** *(official note)* Notiz *f.* **~s** Protokoll *nt;* **to take the ~s** das Protokoll führen.

minute[2] [maɪ'njuːt] *adj (small)* winzig; *(detailed, exact)* minuziös; *detail* kleinste(r, s).

minute hand *n* Minutenzeiger *m.*

minutely [maɪ'njuːtlɪ] *adv (by a small amount)* ganz geringfügig; *(in detail)* genauestens.

miracle ['mɪrəkəl] *n* Wunder *nt.* **to work** *or* **perform ~s** *(lit)* Wunder vollbringen; **I can't work ~s** ich kann doch nicht hexen!; **it's a ~ he ....** es ist ein Wunder, daß er ....

miraculous [mɪ'rækjʊləs] *adj* wunderbar; *powers* Wunder-.

mirage ['mɪrɑːʒ] *n* Fata Morgana *f; (fig)* Trugbild *nt.*

mirror ['mɪrə^r] **1** *n* Spiegel *m.* **~ image** *(lit, fig)* Spiegelbild *nt.* **2** *vt* widerspiegeln.

mirth [mɜːθ] *n* Frohsinn *m; (laughter)* Heiterkeit *f.*

misadventure [,mɪsəd'ventʃə^r] *n* Mißgeschick *nt.* **death by ~** Tod *m* durch Unfall.

misanthropist [mɪ'zænθrəpɪst] *n* Misanthrop, Menschenfeind *m.*

misapprehension ['mɪs,æprɪ'henʃən] *n* Mißverständnis *nt.* **I think you are under a ~** ich glaube, bei Ihnen liegt (da) ein Mißverständnis vor; **he was under the ~ that ...** er hatte irrtümlicherweise angenommen, daß ...

misappropriate ['mɪsə'prəʊprɪeɪt] *vt* entwenden; *money* veruntreuen.

misappropriation ['mɪsə,prəʊprɪ'eɪʃən] *n see vt* Entwendung *f;* Veruntreuung *f.*

misbehave ['mɪsbɪ'heɪv] *vi* sich schlecht benehmen; *(child also)* ungezogen sein.

misbehaviour, *(US)* **misbehavior** [,mɪsbɪ'heɪvjə^r] *n* schlechtes Benehmen.

miscalculate ['mɪs'kælkjʊleɪt] **1** *vt* falsch berechnen; *(misjudge)* falsch einschätzen. **2** *vi* sich verrechnen; *(estimate wrongly)* sich verkalkulieren.

miscalculation ['mɪs,kælkjʊ'leɪʃən] *n* Rechenfehler *m; (wrong estimation)* Fehlkalkulation *f; (misjudgement)* Fehleinschätzung *f.*

miscarriage ['mɪsː,kærɪdʒ] *n* **(a)** *(Med)* Fehlgeburt *f.* **(b) ~ of justice** Justizirrtum *m.*

miscarry [,mɪs'kærɪ] *vi* **(a)** *(Med)* eine Fehlgeburt haben. **(b)** *(fail: plans)* fehlschlagen.

miscellaneous [,mɪsɪ'leɪnɪəs] *adj* verschieden; *poems* verschiedenerlei; *collection, crowd* bunt. **"~"** „Verschiedenes".

miscellany [mɪ'selənɪ] *n (collection)* (bunte) Sammlung; *(variety)* Vielfalt *f.*

mischance [,mɪs'tʃɑːns] *n* **by some ~** durch einen unglücklichen Zufall.

mischief [,mɪstʃɪf] *n (roguery)* Verschmitztheit *f;*

(naughty behaviour) Unfug *m.* **he's always getting into ~** er stellt dauernd etwas an; **to keep out of ~** keine Dummheiten machen; **to make ~** Unfrieden stiften; **to do sb a ~** jdm etwas (an)tun.

mischievous ['mɪstʃɪvəs] *adj expression, smile* verschmitzt; *rumour* bösartig; *person* boshaft.

misconception ['mɪskən'sepʃən] *n* fälschliche Annahme; *(no pl: misunderstanding)* Verkennung *f.* **to be under a ~ about sth** sich *(dat)* falsche Vorstellungen von etw machen.

misconduct [ˌmɪs'kɒndʌkt] *n (improper behaviour)* schlechtes Benehmen; *(professional)* Berufsvergehen *nt; (sexual)* Fehltritt *m.*

misconstrue ['mɪskən'struː] *vt* mißverstehen.

misdemeanour, *(US)* **misdemeanor** [ˌmɪsdɪ'miːnəʳ] *n* schlechtes Benehmen; *(Jur)* Vergehen *nt.*

miser ['maɪzəʳ] *n* Geizhals, Geizkragen *m.*

miserable ['mɪzərəbl] *adj* **(a)** *(unhappy)* unglücklich. **I feel ~ today** ich fühle mich heute elend *or* miserabel. **(b)** *headache, weather* fürchterlich; *existence, spectacle* erbärmlich, elend. **(c)** *(contemptible)* miserabel, jämmerlich; *person* gemein, erbärmlich; *failure* kläglich. **a ~ £3** miese £ 3 *(col).*

miserably ['mɪzərəblɪ] *adv* **(a)** *(unhappily)* unglücklich. **(b)** *(wretchedly) live, die* jämmerlich; *poor* erbärmlich. **(c)** *(contemptibly) pay* miserabel; *fail* kläglich; *treat, behave* gemein.

miserly ['maɪzəlɪ] *adj* geizig.

misery ['mɪzərɪ] *n (sadness)* Kummer *m,* Trauer *f; (suffering)* Qualen *pl; (wretchedness)* Elend *nt.* **to put an animal out of its ~** ein Tier von seinen Qualen erlösen; **to put sb out of his ~** *(fig)* jdn nicht länger auf die Folter spannen.

misfire ['mɪs'faɪəʳ] *vi (engine, rocket)* fehlzünden; *(plan)* fehlschlagen; *(trick)* danebengehen.

misfit ['mɪsfɪt] *n (person)* Außenseiter(in *f*) *m.*

misfortune ['mɪsfɔːtʃuːn] *n (ill fortune, affliction)* (schweres) Schicksal *or* Los *nt; (bad luck)* Pech *nt no pl; (unlucky incident)* Mißgeschick *nt.* **I had the ~ to ...** ich hatte das Pech, zu ....

misgiving [mɪs'gɪvɪŋ] *n* Bedenken *pl.* **I had (certain) ~s about lending him the money** mir war bei dem Gedanken, ihm das Geld zu leihen, nicht ganz wohl.

misguided [mɪs'gaɪdɪd] *adj* töricht; *decision also, opinions* irrig; *(misplaced) kindness, enthusiasm* unangebracht.

mishandle [mɪs'hændl] *vt case* falsch handhaben.

mishap ['mɪshæp] *n* Mißgeschick *nt.* **he's had a slight ~** ihm ist ein kleines Mißgeschick passiert; **without ~** ohne Zwischenfälle.

mishear ['mɪs'hɪəʳ] *pret, ptp* **misheard** ['mɪs'hɜːd] **1** *vt* falsch hören. **2** *vi* sich verhören.

mishmash ['mɪʃmæʃ] *n* Mischmasch *m.*

misinform ['mɪsɪn'fɔːm] *vt* falsch informieren. **you've been ~ed** man hat Sie falsch informiert.

misinterpret ['mɪsɪn'tɜːprɪt] *vt* falsch auslegen; *novel* fehlinterpretieren. **he ~ed her silence as agreement** er deutete ihr Schweigen fälschlich als Zustimmung.

misjudge ['mɪs'dʒʌdʒ] *vt* falsch einschätzen, sich verschätzen in *(+dat); person also* falsch beurteilen.

mislay [ˌmɪs'leɪ] *pret, ptp* **mislaid** [ˌmɪs'leɪd] *vt* verlegen.

mislead [ˌmɪs'liːd] *pret, ptp* **misled** *vt (give wrong idea)* irreführen. **your description misled me into thinking that ...** aufgrund Ihrer Beschreibung nahm ich (irrtümlich) an, daß...

misleading [ˌmɪs'liːdɪŋ] *adj* irreführend. **the ~ simplicity of his style** die täuschende Einfachheit seines Stils.

misled [ˌmɪs'led] *pret, ptp of* **mislead.**

mismanage ['mɪs'mænɪdʒ] *vt company, finances* schlecht verwalten; *affair* schlecht handhaben.

misnomer ['mɪs'nəʊməʳ] *n* unzutreffende Bezeichnung.

misogynist [mɪ'sɒdʒɪnɪst] *n* Frauenfeind *m.*

misplace ['mɪs'pleɪs] *vt* **(a)** *file etc* falsch einordnen; *(mislay)* verlegen. **(b) to be ~d** *(confidence etc)* unangebracht sein.

misprint ['mɪsprɪnt] *n* Druckfehler *m.*

mispronounce ['mɪsprə'naʊns] *vt* falsch aussprechen.

misquote ['mɪs'kwəʊt] *vt* falsch zitieren.

misread ['mɪs'riːd] *pret, ptp* **misread** ['mɪs'red] *vt* falsch lesen; *(misinterpret)* falsch verstehen.

misrepresent ['mɪsˌreprɪ'zent] *vt* falsch darstellen; *ideas* verfälschen.

miss[1] [mɪs] **1** *n (shot)* Fehltreffer *m.* **it was a near ~** das war sehr knapp; *(shot)* das war knapp daneben; **to give sth a ~** *(col)* sich *(dat)* etw schenken.

2 *vt* **(a)** *(fail to hit, catch, find etc)* verpassen; *(not hit, find) target, ball, vocation, place* verfehlen; *(not hear etc)* nicht mitbekommen. **to ~ breakfast** nicht frühstücken; *(be too late for)* das Frühstück verpassen; **you haven't ~ed much!** da hast du nicht viel verpaßt!; **they ~ed each other in the crowd** sie verfehlten sich in der Menge; **to ~ the boat** *or* **bus** *(fig)* den Anschluß verpassen; **I wouldn't have ~ed it for anything** das hätte ich mir nicht entgehen lassen wollen. **(b)** *(avoid) obstacle* (noch) ausweichen können *(+dat); (escape)* entgehen *(+dat); (leave out)* auslassen; *(overlook)* übersehen. **my heart ~ed a beat** mir stockte das Herz. **(c)** *(notice or regret absence of)* vermissen. **I ~ my old car** mein altes Auto fehlt mir.

3 *vi* nicht treffen; *(shooting also)* danebenschießen; *(not catch)* nicht fangen; *(ball also)* danebengehen.

♦ **miss out 1** *vt sep* auslassen, weglassen. **2** *vi (col)* zu kurz kommen. **to ~ ~ on sth** etw verpassen; *(get less)* bei etw zu kurz kommen.

miss[2] *n* Fräulein *nt.* **M~ Germany 1980** (die) Miß Germany von 1980.

missal ['mɪsəl] *n* Meßbuch *nt.*

missile ['mɪsaɪl] *n* **(a)** *(stone etc)* (Wurf)geschoß *nt.* **(b)** *(rocket)* Rakete *f.* **~ base** *or* **site** Raketenbasis *f;* **~ launcher** Startrampe *f; (vehicle)* Raketenwerfer *m.*

missing ['mɪsɪŋ] *adj (not able to be found) person, boat* vermißt; *object* verschwunden; *(not there)* fehlend. **to be ~/to have gone ~** fehlen; *(mountaineer, boat etc)* vermißt werden; **the coat has two buttons ~** an dem Mantel fehlen zwei Knöpfe; **~ person** Vermißte(r) *mf;* **~ link** fehlendes Glied; *(Biol)* Zwischenform *f.*

mission ['mɪʃən] *n (task)* Auftrag *m; (calling)* Berufung *f; (Mil)* Befehl *m; (operation)* Einsatz *m; (journey)* Mission *f.* **he's on a secret ~** er ist in geheimer Mission unterwegs; **Kissinger's ~ to the Middle East** Kissingers Nahostmission.

missionary ['mɪʃənrɪ] *n* Missionar(in *f*) *m.*

misspell ['mɪs'spel] *pret, ptp* **~ed** *or* **misspelt** *vt* falsch schreiben.

misspent [ˌmɪs'spent] *adj* vergeudet.

mist [mɪst] *n* Nebel *m; (haze)* Dunst *m; (on glass etc)* Beschlag *m.* **through a ~ of tears** durch einen Tränenschleier; **it is lost in the ~s of time** das liegt im Dunkel der Vergangenheit.

♦ **mist over** *vi (become cloudy)* sich trüben; *(glass, mirror: also* **mist up***)* (sich) beschlagen.

mistake [mɪ'steɪk] **1** *n* Fehler *m.* **to make a ~** *(in calculating etc)* einen Fehler machen; *(be mistaken)* sich irren; **to make the ~ of asking too much** den Fehler machen, zuviel zu verlangen; **by ~** aus Versehen, versehentlich; **there must be some ~** da muß ein Irrtum vorliegen; **there's no ~ about it, ...** (es besteht) kein Zweifel, ...; **make no ~, I mean what I say** damit wir uns nicht falsch verstehen: mir ist es Ernst; **it's**

freezing and no ~! *(col)* (ich kann dir sagen,) das ist vielleicht eine Kälte! *(col)*.

2 *vt pret* **mistook,** *ptp* **mistaken** *remarks etc* falsch verstehen; *house, time* sich irren *or* vertun *(col)* in *(+dat)*. **to ~ sb's meaning** jdn falsch verstehen; **there's no mistaking the urgency of the situation** die Dringlichkeit der Situation steht außer Frage; **to ~ A for B** A mit B verwechseln; **to be ~n** sich irren; **if I am not (very much) ~n ...** wenn ich mich nicht (sehr) irre ...

mistaken [mɪ'steɪkən] *adj (wrong) idea* falsch; *(misplaced) loyalty, kindness* unangebracht. **a case of ~ identity** eine Verwechslung.

mistletoe ['mɪsltəʊ] *n* Mistel *f; (sprig)* Mistelzweig *m*.

mistook [mɪ'stʊk] *pret of* **mistake.**

mistranslation ['mɪstrænz'leɪʃən] *n* falsche Übersetzung.

mistreat [mɪs'triːt] *vt* schlecht behandeln; *(violently)* mißhandeln.

mistress ['mɪstrɪs] *n* **(a)** *(of house, dog)* Herrin *f*. **(b)** *(lover)* Geliebte. **(c)** *(Brit: teacher)* Lehrerin *f*.

mistrust ['mɪs'trʌst] **1** *n* Mißtrauen *nt (of* gegenüber*)*. **2** *vt* mißtrauen *(+dat)*.

mistrustful [,mɪs'trʌstfʊl] *adj* mißtrauisch *(of sb/sth* jdm/einer Sache gegenüber*)*.

misty ['mɪstɪ] *adj (+er) day* neblig; *(hazy)* dunstig; *glasses (misted up)* beschlagen.

misunderstand ['mɪsʌndə'stænd] *pret, ptp* **misunderstood** *vt* falsch verstehen, mißverstehen.

misunderstanding ['mɪsʌndə'stændɪŋ] *n* Mißverständnis *nt; (disagreement)* Meinungsverschiedenheit *f*.

misunderstood ['mɪsʌndə'stʊd] **1** *ptp of* **misunderstand. 2** *adj* unverstanden; *artist* verkannt.

misuse ['mɪs'juːs] **1** *n* Mißbrauch *m*. **2** ['mɪs'juːz] *vt* mißbrauchen.

mite [maɪt] *n* **(a)** *(small amount)* bißchen *nt*. **(b)** *(child)* **poor little ~!** armes Wurm! *(col)*.

mitigate ['mɪtɪgeɪt] *vt punishment* mildern. **mitigating circumstances** mildernde Umstände *pl*.

mitigation [,mɪtɪ'geɪʃən] *n* Milderung *f*.

mitre, *(US)* **miter** ['maɪtə^r] *n* **(a)** *(Eccl)* Mitra *f*. **(b)** *(Tech: also* **~-joint***)* Gehrung *f*.

mitt [mɪt] *n* **(a) = mitten. (b)** *(baseball glove)* Baseballhandschuh *m*.

mitten ['mɪtn] *n* Fausthandschuh *m; (with bare fingers)* Handschuh *m* mit halben Fingern.

mix [mɪks] **1** *n* Mischung *f*. **a good social ~** ein bunt gemischtes Publikum; **cake ~** Backmischung *f*. **2** *vt* (ver)mischen; *drinks* mixen; *(Cook) ingredients* verrühren. **you shouldn't ~ business with pleasure** Dienst ist Dienst und Schnaps ist Schnaps *(prov)*. **3** *vi* **(a)** sich mischen lassen; *(chemical substances, races)* sich vermischen. **(b)** *(go together)* zusammenpassen. **(c)** *(people) (get on)* miteinander auskommen; *(associate)* miteinander verkehren. **to ~ with sb** mit jdm auskommen; mit jdm verkehren; **to ~ well** kontaktfreudig sein.

♦ **mix in** *vt sep egg, water* unterrühren.

♦ **mix up** *vt sep* **(a)** vermischen; *ingredients* verrühren; *medicine* mischen. **(b)** *(get in a muddle)* durcheinanderbringen; *(confuse with sb/sth else)* verwechseln. **(c)** *(involve)* **to ~ sb ~ in sth** jdn in etw *(acc)* hineinziehen; **to be ~ed ~ in sth** in etw *(acc)* verwickelt sein.

mixed [mɪkst] *adj* gemischt; *(both good and bad)* unterschiedlich. **I have ~ feelings about it** ich betrachte die Sache mit gemischten Gefühlen.

mixed: ~ blessing *n* **it's a ~ blessing** das ist ein zweischneidiges Schwert; **~ doubles** *npl (Sport)* gemischtes Doppel; **~ grill** *n* Grillteller *m;* **~ metaphor** *n* gemischte Metapher *f;* **~-up** *adj* durcheinander *pred; (muddled) person also, ideas* konfus; **she's just a crazy ~-up kid** sie ist einfach total verdreht.

mixer ['mɪksə^r] *n* **(a)** *(food ~)* Mixgerät *nt; (cement ~)* Mischmaschine *f*. **(b)** *(sociable person)* **to be a good ~** kontaktfreudig sein.

mixture ['mɪkstʃə^r] *n* Mischung *f; (Cook)* Gemisch *nt; (cake ~, dough)* Teig *m*.

mix-up ['mɪksʌp] *n* Durcheinander *nt*. **there must have been a ~** da muß irgend etwas schiefgelaufen sein *(col)*.

moan [məʊn] **1** *n (groan)* Stöhnen *nt; (grumble)* Gejammer *nt no pl (col)*. **2** *vi (groan)* stöhnen; *(grumble)* jammern, schimpfen *(about* über *+acc)*.

moat [məʊt] *n* Wassergraben *m; (of castle also)* Burggraben *m*.

mob [mɒb] **1** *n (crowd)* Horde *f; (riotous, violent)* Mob *m no pl*. **the ~** *(pej: the masses)* die Masse(n *pl)*. **2** *vt* herfallen über *(+acc)*.

mobile ['məʊbaɪl] *adj person* beweglich; *(having means of transport)* beweglich, motorisiert; *(Sociol)* mobil; *X-ray unit etc* fahrbar. **~ home** Wohnwagen *m;* **~ library** Fahrbücherei *f*.

mobility [məʊ'bɪlɪtɪ] *n (of person)* Beweglichkeit *f; (of work force, Sociol)* Mobilität *f*.

moccasin ['mɒkəsɪn] *n* Mokassin *m*.

mock [mɒk] **1** *adj attr emotions* gespielt; *battle* Schein-; *examination* Probe-; *Tudor* Pseudo-. **2** *vt (ridicule)* sich lustig machen über *(+acc); (mimic)* nachäffen; *(defy)* trotzen *(+dat)*. **3** *vi* **to ~ at sb/sth** sich über jdn/etw lustig machen.

mockery ['mɒkərɪ] *n (derision)* Spott *m; (object of ridicule)* Gespött *nt*. **they made a ~ of him** sie machten ihn zum Gespött; **to make a ~ of sth** etw lächerlich machen; **it was a ~ of a trial** der Prozeß war eine einzige Farce.

mocking ['mɒkɪŋ] *adj* spöttisch.

mockingbird ['mɒkɪŋ,bɜːd] *n* Spottdrossel *f*.

mock: ~ turtle soup *n* Mockturtlesuppe *f;* **~-up** *n* Modell *nt* in Originalgröße.

mod cons ['mɒd'kɒnz] = **modern conveniences** Komfort *m*.

mode [məʊd] *n* **(a)** *(way)* Art (und Weise) *f; (form)* Form *f*. **~ of transport** Transportmittel *nt*. **(b)** *(Fashion)* Mode *f*.

model ['mɒdl] **1** *n* Modell *nt; (perfect example)* Muster *nt (of* an *+dat); (fashion ~)* Mannequin *nt; (male ~)* Dressman *m*. **to make sth on the ~ of sth** etw *(acc)* einer Sache *(dat)* nachbilden; **to hold sb up as a ~** jdn als Vorbild hinstellen. **2** *adj railway* Modell-; *home* Muster-; *(perfect)* vorbildlich, Muster-. **3** *vt* **(a) X is ~led on Y** Y dient als Vorlage *or* Muster für X; **the system was ~led on the American one** das System war nach amerikanischem Muster aufgebaut; **to ~ oneself on sb** sich *(dat)* jdn zum Vorbild nehmen. **(b)** *(make a ~)* modellieren, formen. **(c)** *dress etc* vorführen. **4** *vi* **(a)** *(make ~s)* modellieren. **(b)** *(Art, Phot)* als Modell arbeiten; *(fashion)* als Mannequin/Dressman arbeiten. **to ~ for sb** jdm Modell stehen/jds Kreationen vorführen.

modem ['məʊdem] *n* Modem m.

moderate ['mɒdərɪt] **1** *adj* gemäßigt *(also Pol); appetite, speed* mäßig; *price* vernünftig; *eater* maßvoll; *number, income, success* bescheiden; *punishment, winter* mild. **a ~ amount** einigermaßen viel; **~-sized** mittelgroß. **2** *n (Pol)* Gemäßigte(r) *mf*. **3** ['mɒdəreɪt] *vt* mäßigen. **to have a moderating influence on sb** mäßigend auf jdn wirken. **4** ['mɒdəreɪt] *vi* nachlassen.

moderately ['mɒdərɪtlɪ] *adv* einigermaßen. **a ~ expensive suit** ein nicht allzu teurer Anzug; **the house was ~ large** das Haus war mäßig groß.

moderation ['mɒdə'reɪʃən] *n* Mäßigung *f*. **in ~** mit Maß(en).

modern ['mɒdən] *adj* modern *(also Art, Liter); times, world also* heutig; *history* neuere. **~ languages** neuere Sprachen *pl;* **M~ Greek** *etc*

Neugriechisch *etc nt*.

modernity [mɒ'dɜːnɪtɪ] *n* Modernität *f*.

modernization [ˌmɒdənaɪ'zeɪʃən] *n* Modernisierung *f*.

modernize ['mɒdənaɪz] *vt* modernisieren.

modest ['mɒdɪst] *adj* bescheiden; *requirements* gering; *price* mäßig. **to be ~ about one's successes** nicht mit seinen Erfolgen prahlen.

modesty ['mɒdɪstɪ] *n* Bescheidenheit *f*. **in all ~** bei aller Bescheidenheit.

modicum ['mɒdɪkəm] *n* ein wenig *or* bißchen. **a ~ of truth** ein Körnchen Wahrheit.

modification [ˌmɒdɪfɪ'keɪʃən] *n* (Ver)änderung *f*; *(of design)* Abänderung *f*; *(of contract, wording)* Modifizierung *f*. **to make ~s to sth** (Ver)änderungen an etw *(dat)* vornehmen; etw abändern; etw modifizieren.

modify ['mɒdɪfaɪ] *vt* **(a)** *(change)* (ver)ändern; *design* abändern; *contract, wording* modifizieren. **(b)** *(moderate)* mäßigen. **(c)** *(Gram)* näher bestimmen.

modular ['mɒdjʊlə[r]] *adj* **the ~ design of the furniture** die aus Bauelementen bestehenden Möbel.

modulation [ˌmɒdjʊ'leɪʃən] *n (Mus, Rad)* Modulation *f*.

module ['mɒdjuːl] *n* (Bau)element *nt*; *(Space)* Raumkapsel *f*.

mohair ['məʊhɛə[r]] *n* Mohair *m*.

Mohammedan [məʊ'hæmɪdən] **1** *adj* mohammedanisch. **2** *n* Mohammedaner(in *f*) *m*.

moist [mɔɪst] *adj (+er)* feucht *(from, with* vor *+dat)*.

moisten ['mɔɪsn] *vt* anfeuchten. **to ~ sth with sth** etw mit etw befeuchten.

moisture ['mɔɪstʃə[r]] *n* Feuchtigkeit *f*.

moisturizer ['mɔɪstʃəraɪzə[r]], **moisturizing cream** ['mɔɪstʃəraɪzɪŋ'kriːm] *n* Feuchtigkeitscreme *f*.

molar (tooth) ['məʊlə[r](ˌtuːθ)] *n* Backenzahn *m*.

molasses [məʊ'læsɪz] *n* Melasse *f*.

mold *etc (US)* = **mould** *etc*.

mole[1] [məʊl] *n (Anat)* Leberfleck *m*.

mole[2] *n (Zool)* Maulwurf *m*; *(col: secret agent)* Agent *m*.

molecule ['mɒlɪkjuːl] *n* Molekül *nt*.

molest [məʊ'lest] *vt* belästigen.

mollusc ['mɒləsk] *n* Weichtier *nt*.

mollycoddle ['mɒlɪˌkɒdl] *vt* verhätscheln.

molten ['məʊltən] *adj* geschmolzen; *glass, lava* flüssig.

moment ['məʊmənt] *n* **(a)** Augenblick, Moment *m*. **at any ~** jeden Augenblick; **at the ~** im Augenblick, momentan; **not at the ~** im Augenblick *or* zur Zeit nicht; **at the last ~** im letzten Augenblick; **at this (particular) ~ in time** momentan; **for the ~** im Augenblick; **for a ~** (für) einen Moment; **not for a** *or* **one ~ ...** nie(mals)...; **I didn't hesitate for a ~** ich habe keinen Augenblick gezögert; **in a ~** gleich; **half a ~/one ~!** einen Moment!; **just a ~!, wait a ~!** Moment mal!; **I shan't be a ~** ich bin gleich wieder da; *(nearly ready)* ich bin gleich soweit; **I have just this ~ heard of it** ich habe es eben *or* gerade erst erfahren; **not a ~ too soon** keine Minute zu früh; **the ~ it happened** (in dem Augenblick,) als es passierte; **tell me the ~ he comes** sagen Sie mir sofort Bescheid, wenn er kommt; **the man of the ~** der Mann des Tages.

(b) *(Phys)* Moment *nt*.

(c) *(importance)* Bedeutung *f*.

momentarily ['məʊməntərɪlɪ] *adv* **(a)** *(für)* einen Augenblick. **(b)** *(US) (very soon)* jeden Augenblick; *(from moment to moment)* zusehends.

momentary ['məʊməntərɪ] *adj* kurz. **there was a ~ silence** einen Augenblick lang herrschte Stille.

momentous [məʊ'mentəs] *adj (memorable, important)* bedeutsam; *(of great consequence)* von großer Tragweite.

momentum [məʊ'mentəm] *n (of moving object)* Schwung *m*; *(at moment of impact)* Wucht *f*; *(Phys)* Impuls *m*; *(fig)* Schwung *m*. **to gather** *or* **gain ~** *(lit)* sich beschleunigen, in Fahrt kommen *(col)*; *(fig: idea, movement, plan)* in Gang kommen.

monarch ['mɒnək] *n* Monarch(in *f*) *m*.

monarchist ['mɒnəkɪst] **1** *adj* monarchistisch. **2** *n* Monarchist(in *f*) *m*.

monarchy ['mɒnəkɪ] *n* Monarchie *f*.

monastery ['mɒnəstərɪ] *n* (Mönchs)kloster *nt*.

monastic [mə'næstɪk] *adj* mönchisch, klösterlich; *life* Ordens-.

Monday ['mʌndɪ] *n* Montag *m*; *see* **Tuesday**.

monetarism ['mʌnɪtərɪzəm] *n* Monetarismus *m*.

monetarist ['mʌnɪtərɪst] **1** *adj* monetaristisch. **2** *n* Monetarist(in *f*) *m*.

monetary ['mʌnɪtərɪ] *adj* **(a)** währungspolitisch; *policy, system* Währungs-; *reserves* Geld-. **(b)** *(pecuniary)* Geld-; *considerations* geldlich.

money ['mʌnɪ] *n* Geld *nt*. **to make ~** *(person)* (viel) Geld verdienen; *(business)* etwas einbringen; **to lose ~** *(person)* Geld verlieren; *(business)* Verluste machen; **there's ~ in it** das ist sehr lukrativ; **that's the one for my ~!** ich tippe auf ihn/sie *etc*; **it's ~ for jam** *(col) or* **old rope** *(col)* da wird einem das Geld ja nachgeworfen *(col)*; **to be in the ~** *(col)* Geld wie Heu haben; **to earn good ~** gut verdienen; **to get one's ~'s worth** etwas für sein Geld bekommen; **do you think I'm made of ~?** *(col)* ich bin doch kein Krösus!; **that's throwing good ~ after bad** das ist rausgeschmissenes Geld *(col)*; **~ talks** *(col)* mit Geld geht alles; **~ isn't everything** *(prov)* Geld allein macht nicht glücklich *(prov)*.

moneybox ['mʌnɪˌbɒks] *n* Sparbüchse *f*.

moneyed ['mʌnɪd] *adj* begütert.

money: ~grubbing *adj* geldgierig; **~lender** *n* Geld(ver)leiher *m*; **~maker** *n (idea)* einträgliche Sache; *(product)* Verkaufserfolg *m*; **~making** *adj idea, plan* einträglich; **~ market** *n* Geldmarkt *m*; **~ order** *n* Zahlungsanweisung *f*; **~spinner** *n (col)* Verkaufsschlager *m (col)*.

mongol ['mɒŋgəl] *(Med)* **he's a ~** er ist mongoloid.

mongoose ['mɒŋguːs] *n, pl* **-s** Mungo *m*.

mongrel ['mʌŋgrəl] *n (also* **~ dog***)* Promenadenmischung *f*; *(pej)* Köter *m*.

monitor ['mɒnɪtə[r]] **1** *n* **(a)** *(Sch) Schüler(in f) m mit besonderen Pflichten.* **book ~** Bücherwart *m*. **(b)** *(TV, Tech: screen)* Monitor *m*; *(control, observer)* Überwacher *m*; *(Rad)* Mitarbeiter(in *f*) *m* am Monitor-Dienst. **2** *vt foreign station* abhören; *product, progress* überwachen.

monk [mʌŋk] *n* Mönch *m*.

monkey ['mʌŋkɪ] *n* Affe *m*; *(fig: child)* Schlingel *m*.

monkey: ~ business *n (col)* **no ~ business!** mach(t) mir keine Sachen! *(col)*; **there's some ~ business going on here** da ist doch irgend etwas faul *(col)*; **~-nut** *n* Erdnuß *f*; **~-tricks** *npl* Unfug *m*; **~-wrench** *n* verstellbarer Schraubenschlüssel, Engländer *m*.

mono- ['mɒnəʊ] *pref* Mono-, mono-.

monochrome ['mɒnəkrəʊm] *adj* monochrom; *television* Schwarzweiß-.

monocle ['mɒnəkəl] *n* Monokel *nt*.

monogram ['mɒnəgræm] *n* Monogramm *nt*.

monolith ['mɒnəʊlɪθ] *n* Monolith *m*.

monologue ['mɒnəlɒg] *n* Monolog *m*.

monoplane ['mɒnəʊpleɪn] *n* Eindecker *m*.

monopolize [mə'nɒpəlaɪz] *vt (lit) market* beherrschen; *(fig) place, sb's time etc* in Beschlag nehmen; *conversation* an sich *(acc)* reißen.

monopoly [mə'nɒpəlɪ] *n (lit)* Monopol *nt*. **to have a ~ on sth** *(fig)* etw für sich gepachtet haben *(col)*.

mono: ~rail *n* Einschienenbahn *f*; **~syllabic** *adj (lit, fig)* einsilbig; **~syllable** *n* einsilbiges Wort; **to speak/answer in ~syllables** einsilbig sein/einsilbige Antworten geben.

monotone ['mɒnətəʊn] *n* monotoner Klang; *(voice)* monotone Stimme.
monotonous [mə'nɒtənəs] *adj (lit, fig)* eintönig, monoton.
monotony [mə'nɒtənɪ] *n (lit, fig)* Eintönigkeit, Monotonie *f.*
monoxide [mɒ'nɒksaɪd] *n* Monoxyd *nt.*
monsoon [mɒn'suːn] *n* Monsun *m.*
monster ['mɒnstəʳ] **1** *n (big animal, thing)* Ungetüm, Monstrum *nt; (animal, person also)* Ungeheuer *nt; (cruel person)* Unmensch *m.* **2** *attr (enormous)* Riesen-.
monstrosity [mɒn'strɒsɪtɪ] *n (quality)* Ungeheuerlichkeit *f; (thing)* Monstrum *nt.*
monstrous ['mɒnstrəs] *adj (huge)* ungeheuer (groß); *(shocking, horrible)* abscheulich; *suggestion* ungeheuerlich.
month [mʌnθ] *n* Monat *m.* **in the ~ of October** im Oktober; **six ~s** ein halbes Jahr, sechs Monate; **paid by the ~** monatlich bezahlt.
monthly ['mʌnθlɪ] **1** *adj* monatlich; *magazine, ticket* Monats-. **2** *adv* monatlich. **twice ~** zweimal im Monat. **3** *n* Monats(zeit)schrift *f.*
monument ['mɒnjʊmənt] *n* Denkmal *nt; (big also)* Monument *nt; (small, on grave etc)* Gedenkstein *m; (fig)* Zeugnis *nt (to gen).*
monumental [,mɒnjʊ'mentl] *adj (very great)* enorm, monumental *(geh); proportions, achievement* gewaltig; *ignorance* ungeheuer.
moo [muː] **1** *n* Muhen *nt.* **2** *vi* muhen.
mooch [muːtʃ] *(col)* **1** *vi* **to ~ about** *or* **around** herumgammeln *(col).* **2** *vt (US)* abstauben *(col).*
mood[1] [muːd] *n* Stimmung *f; (of person also)* Laune *f; (bad ~)* schlechte Laune. **he was in a good/bad/foul ~** er war gut/schlecht/fürchterlich gelaunt; **to be in a festive ~** feierlich gestimmt sein; **to be in a generous ~** in Geberlaune sein; **to be in the ~ for sth/to do sth** zu etw aufgelegt sein/dazu aufgelegt sein, etw zu tun; **I'm not in the ~ for work** ich habe keine Lust zum Arbeiten; **I'm not in the ~** ich bin nicht in der richtigen Stimmung; **he's in a ~** er hat schlechte Laune.
mood[2] *n (Gram)* Modus *m.*
moody ['muːdɪ] *adj (+er)* launisch; *(bad-tempered)* schlechtgelaunt *attr,* schlecht gelaunt *pred; look, answer* übellaunig.
moon [muːn] *n* Mond *m.* **you're asking for the ~!** du verlangst Unmögliches!; **to be over the ~** *(col)* überglücklich sein.
moon *in cpds* Mond-; **~beam** *n* Mondstrahl *m;* **~light 1** *n* Mondschein *m;* **2** *vi (col)* ≃ schwarzarbeiten; **~lit** *adj object* mondbeschienen; *night, lawn* mondhell; **~shine** *n (~light)* Mondschein *m;* **~shot** *n* Mondflug *m.*
moor[1] [mʊəʳ] *n* (Heide)moor *nt.*
moor[2] **1** *vt* festmachen, vertäuen; *(at permanent moorings)* muren. **2** *vi* festmachen, anlegen.
mooring ['mʊərɪŋ] *n (place)* Anlegeplatz *m.* **~s** *(ropes)* Verankerung *f.*
moose [muːs] *n* Elch *m.*
moot [muːt] **1** *adj:* **a ~ point** *or* **question** eine fragliche Sache. **2** *vt* **it has been ~ed whether ...** es wurde zur Debatte gestellt, ob ...
mop [mɒp] **1** *n (floor ~)* Mop *m; (dish ~)* Spülbürste *f; (col: hair)* Mähne *f.* **2** *vt floor* wischen. **to ~ one's face** sich *(dat)* den Schweiß vom Gesicht wischen.
♦ **mop up** *vt sep* **(a)** aufwischen. **(b)** *(Mil)* säubern *(col).*
mope [məʊp] *vi* Trübsal blasen *(col).*
♦ **mope about** *or* **around** *vi* mit einer Jammermiene herumlaufen.
moped ['məʊped] *n* Moped *nt; (very small)* Mofa *nt.*
moral ['mɒrəl] **1** *adj* moralisch; *principles, philosophy* Moral-; *(virtuous)* moralisch einwandfrei; *(sexually)* tugendhaft. **~ standards** Moral *f;* **~ courage** Charakter *m.* **2** *n* **(a)** *(lesson)* Moral *f.* **(b) ~s** *pl (principles)* Moralvorstellungen *pl.*
morale [mɒ'rɑːl] *n* Moral *f.* **to boost sb's ~** jdm (moralischen) Auftrieb geben.
morality [mə'rælɪtɪ] *n* Moralität *f; (moral system)* Moral, Ethik *f.*
moralize ['mɒrəlaɪz] *vi* moralisieren. **to ~ about sth** sich über etw *(acc)* moralisch entrüsten.
morally ['mɒrəlɪ] *adv* **(a)** *(ethically)* moralisch. **(b)** *(virtuously)* moralisch einwandfrei; *(in sexual matters)* tugendhaft.
morass [mə'ræs] *n* Morast, Sumpf *(also fig) m.*
moratorium [,mɒrə'tɔːrɪəm] *n* Moratorium *nt.* **a ~ on nuclear armament** ein Atomwaffenstopp *m.*
morbid ['mɔːbɪd] *adj* **(a)** *idea etc* krankhaft; *interest* unnatürlich; *imagination, humour etc* makaber; *(gloomy) outlook, thoughts, novel, film* düster; *person* trübsinnig; *(pessimistic)* schwarzseherisch. **(b)** *(Med)* morbid; *growth* krankhaft.
more [mɔːʳ] **1** *n, pron* **(a)** *(greater amount)* mehr; *(additional amount, things)* noch mehr. **~ and ~** immer mehr; **a lot ~** viel mehr; *(in addition)* noch viel mehr; **a few ~** noch ein paar; **a little ~** etwas mehr; *(in addition)* noch etwas mehr; **no ~** nichts mehr; *(countable)* keine mehr; **some ~** noch etwas; *(countable)* noch welche; **any ~?** noch mehr?; **there isn't/aren't any ~** mehr gibt es nicht; *(here, left over)* es ist nichts mehr da/es sind keine mehr da; **is/are there any ~?** gibt es noch mehr?; *(left over)* ist noch etwas da/sind noch welche da?; **even ~** noch mehr; **what ~ do you want?** was willst du denn noch?; **there's ~ to it** da steckt (noch) mehr dahinter; **and what's ~, he ...** und obendrein hat er ... (noch) ...

(b) (all) the ~ um so mehr; **the ~ you give him, the ~ he wants** je mehr du ihm gibst, desto mehr verlangt er; **the ~ the merrier** je mehr desto besser.

2 *adj* mehr; *(in addition)* noch mehr. **two ~ bottles** noch zwei Flaschen; **one ~ day** noch ein Tag; **~ and ~ money** immer mehr Geld; **a lot/a little ~ money** viel/etwas mehr Geld; *(in addition)* noch viel/noch etwas mehr Geld; **a few ~ weeks** noch ein paar Wochen; **no ~ money** kein Geld mehr; **no ~ singing!** Schluß mit der Singerei; **do you want some ~ tea** möchten Sie noch etwas Tee?; **is there any ~ wine in the bottle?** ist noch (etwas) Wein in der Flasche?; **the ~ fool you for giving him the money** daß du auch so dumm bist, ihm das Geld zu geben.

3 *adv* **(a)** mehr. **~ and ~** immer mehr; **it will grow a bit ~** es wird noch etwas wachsen; **£5/2 hours ~ than I thought** £5 mehr/2 Stunden länger, als ich dachte; **he is ~ than satisfied** er ist mehr als zufrieden; **it will ~ than meet the demand** das wird die Nachfrage mehr als genügend befriedigen; **no ~ a duchess than I am** genausowenig eine Herzogin wie ich (eine bin); **once ~** noch einmal, nochmal *(col);* **never ~** nie mehr *or* wieder; **no ~, not any ~** nicht mehr; **if he comes here any ~ ...** wenn er noch weiter hierher kommt ...; **~ or less** mehr oder weniger. **(b)** *(to form comp of adj, adv)* -er *(than* als). **~ beautiful/beautifully** schöner; **~ and ~ beautiful** immer schöner; **no ~ stupid than I am** (auch) nicht dümmer als ich.
moreover [mɔː'rəʊvəʳ] *adv* zudem, außerdem.
morgue [mɔːg] *n* Leichenschauhaus *nt.*
moribund ['mɒrɪbʌnd] *adj customs, way of life* zum Aussterben verurteilt.
morning ['mɔːnɪŋ] **1** *n* Morgen *m; (later part also)* Vormittag *m.* **in the ~** am Morgen; am Vormittag; *(tomorrow)* morgen früh; **early in the ~** früh(morgens); *(tomorrow)* morgen früh; **(at) 7 in the ~** (um) 7 Uhr morgens; *(tomorrow)* morgen (früh) um 7; **this/yesterday/tomorrow ~** heute morgen/gestern morgen/morgen früh; heute/

gestern/morgen vormittag; **on the ~ of November 28th** am Morgen des 28. November. **2** *attr* Morgen-; *train, service etc* Vormittags-; *(early ~) train, news* Früh-.
morning: ~ dress *n no pl* Cut *m;* **~ sickness** *n* (Schwangerschafts)übelkeit *f.*
Morocco [məˈrɒkəʊ] *n* Marokko *nt.*
moron [ˈmɔːrɒn] *n (Med)* Geistesschwache(r) *mf; (col)* Dummkopf *(col) m.*
morose [məˈrəʊs] *adj* verdrießlich, mißmutig.
morphine [ˈmɔːfiːn] *n* Morphium *nt.*
morse [mɔːs] *n (also* **M~ code***)* Morseschrift *f.*
morsel [ˈmɔːsl] *n (food)* Bissen *m; (fig)* bißchen *nt.*
mortal [ˈmɔːtl] **1** *adj* sterblich; *injury, combat* tödlich. **2** *n* Sterbliche(r) *mf.*
mortality [mɔːˈtælɪtɪ] *n* **(a)** Sterblichkeit *f.* **(b)** *(number of deaths)* Todesfälle *pl; (rate)* Sterblichkeit(sziffer) *f.*
mortally [ˈmɔːtəlɪ] *adv (fatally)* tödlich; *(fig: extremely) shocked* zu Tode; *offended* tödlich.
mortar[1] [ˈmɔːtə^r] *n* **(a)** *(bowl)* Mörser *m.* **(b)** *(cannon)* Minenwerfer *m.*
mortar[2] *n (cement)* Mörtel *m.*
mortarboard [ˈmɔːtəˌbɔːd] *n (Univ)* Doktorhut *m.*
mortgage [ˈmɔːgɪdʒ] **1** *n* Hypothek *f (on* auf *+acc/dat).* **2** *vt house, land* mit einer Hypothek belasten.
mortice *n, vt* = **mortise.**
mortician [ˌmɔːˈtɪʃən] *n (US)* Bestattungsunternehmer *m.*
mortification [ˌmɔːtɪfɪˈkeɪʃən] *n* **(a)** Beschämung *f; (humiliation)* Demütigung *f.* **(b)** *(Rel)* Kasteiung *f.*
mortify [ˈmɔːtɪfaɪ] *vt usu pass* **(a)** beschämen. **he was mortified** er empfand das als beschämend. **(b)** *(Rel)* kasteien.
mortise, mortice [ˈmɔːtɪs] *n* Zapfenloch *nt.* **~ lock** Einsteckschloß *nt.*
mortuary [ˈmɔːtjʊərɪ] *n* Leichenhalle *f.*
mosaic [məʊˈzeɪɪk] **1** *n* Mosaik *nt.* **2** *attr* Mosaik-.
Moscow [ˈmɒskəʊ] *n* Moskau *nt.*
Moslem [ˈmɒzlem] **1** *adj* moslemisch. **2** *n* Moslem *m.*
mosque [mɒsk] *n* Moschee *f.*
mosquito [mɒˈskiːtəʊ] *n, pl* **-es** Stechmücke *f; (in tropics)* Moskito *m.* **~ net** Moskitonetz *nt.*
moss [mɒs] *n* Moos *nt.*
mossy [ˈmɒsɪ] *adj (+er) (moss-covered)* bemoost; *lawn* vermoost; *(mosslike)* moosartig.
most [məʊst] **1** *adj superl* **(a)** meiste(r, s); *(greatest) satisfaction, pleasure etc* größte(r, s). **who has (the) ~ money?** wer hat am meisten *or* das meiste Geld?; **for the ~ part** größtenteils; *(by and large)* im großen und ganzen. **(b)** *(the majority of)* die meisten. **~ men/people** die meisten (Menschen/Leute).

2 *n, pron* **~ of it/them** das meiste/die meisten; **~ of the money/his friends** das meiste Geld/die meisten seiner Freunde; **~ of the day** fast den ganzen Tag über; **~ of the time** die meiste Zeit; *(usually)* meist(ens); **do the ~ you can** machen Sie soviel (wie) Sie können; **at (the) ~** höchstens; **to make the ~ of sth** *(make good use of)* etw voll ausnützen; *(enjoy)* etw in vollen Zügen genießen.

3 *adv* **(a)** *superl (+vbs)* am meisten; *(+adj)* -ste(r, s); *(+adv)* am -sten. **the ~ beautiful** der/die/das schönste; **which one did it ~ easily?** wem ist es am leichtesten gefallen?; **what ~ displeased him** ... am meisten mißfiel ihm ...; **~ of all** am allermeisten; **~ of all because ...** vor allem, weil ... **(b)** *(very)* äußerst, überaus. **~ likely** höchstwahrscheinlich.
mostly [ˈməʊstlɪ] *adv (principally)* hauptsächlich; *(most of the time)* meistens; *(by and large)* zum größten Teil.
MOT *(Brit)* **(a)** = **Ministry of Transport. (b) ~ (test)** der TÜV. **it failed its ~** es ist nicht durch den TÜV gekommen.
motel [məʊˈtel] *n* Motel *nt.*
motet [məʊˈtet] *n* Motette *f.*
moth [mɒθ] *n* Nachtfalter *m; (wool-eating)* Motte *f.*
moth: ~ball *n* Mottenkugel *f;* **to put in ~balls** *(lit, fig)* einmotten; *ship* stillegen; **~-eaten** *adj (fig)* ausgedient, vermottet *(col).*
mother [ˈmʌðə^r] **1** *n* Mutter *f.* **M~'s Day** Muttertag *m;* **to be (like) a ~ to sb** wie eine Mutter zu jdm sein. **2** *vt (care for) young* großziehen; *(cosset)* bemuttern.
mother: ~ country *n (native country)* Vaterland *nt; (head of empire)* Mutterland *nt;* **~hood** *n* Mutterschaft *f;* **~-in-law** *n, pl* **~s-in-law** Schwiegermutter *f.*
motherly [ˈmʌðəlɪ] *adj* mütterlich.
mother: ~-of-pearl *n* Perlmutt *nt;* **~ ship** *n* Mutterschiff *nt;* **~-to-be** *n, pl* **~s-to-be** werdende Mutter; **~ tongue** *n* Muttersprache *f.*
motif [məʊˈtiːf] *n (Art, Mus)* Motiv *nt.*
motion [ˈməʊʃən] **1** *n* **(a)** Bewegung *f.* **to be in ~** sich bewegen; *(machine etc)* laufen; *(train etc)* fahren; **to set** *or* **put sth in ~** etw in Gang bringen *or* setzen; **to go through the ~s (of doing sth)** etw der Form halber tun. **(b)** *(proposal)* Antrag *m.* **to propose** *or* **make** *(US)* **a ~** einen Antrag stellen. **2** *vti* **to ~ (to) sb to do sth** jdm ein Zeichen geben, daß er etw tun solle.
motion: ~less *adj* bewegungslos, reg(ungs)los; **~ picture** *n* Film *m.*
motivate [ˈməʊtɪveɪt] *vt* motivieren.
motivation [ˌməʊtɪˈveɪʃən] *n* Motivation *f.*
motive [ˈməʊtɪv] **1** *n* Motiv *nt.* **the profit ~** Gewinnstreben *nt.* **I did it from the best of ~s** ich hatte die besten Absichten. **2** *adj force* Antriebs-.
motley [ˈmɒtlɪ] *adj* kunterbunt; *(varied also)* bunt(gemischt).
motor [ˈməʊtə^r] **1** *n* **(a)** Motor *m.* **(b)** *(col: car)* Auto *nt.* **2** *vi* (mit dem Auto) fahren.
motor: ~bike *n* Motorrad *nt;* **~boat** *n* Motorboot *nt;* **~car** *n (form)* Kraftfahrzeug *(form) nt;* **~-cycle** *n* Motorrad *nt;* **~-cyclist** *n* Motorradfahrer(in *f*) *m.*
motoring [ˈməʊtərɪŋ] **1** *adj attr accident, offence* Verkehrs-; *correspondent* Auto-. **the ~ public** die Autofahrer *pl.* **2** *n* Autofahren *nt.*
motorist [ˈməʊtərɪst] *n* Autofahrer(in *f*) *m.*
motorize [ˈməʊtəraɪz] *vt* motorisieren.
motor: ~ mechanic *n* Kfz-Mechaniker *m;* **~ racing** *n* Rennsport *m;* **~ scooter** *n* Motorroller *m;* **~ show** *n (Brit)* Automobilausstellung *f;* **~way** *n (Brit)* Autobahn *f;* **~way madness** Geschwindigkeitsrausch *m.*
mottled [ˈmɒtld] *adj* gesprenkelt; *complexion* fleckig.
motto [ˈmɒtəʊ] *n, pl* **-es** Motto *nt; (personal also)* Devise *f.*
mould[1], *(US)* **mold** [məʊld] **1** *n (hollow form)* (Guß)form *f; (shape, Cook)* Form *f.* **to be cast in the same ~** *(people)* vom gleichen Schlag sein. **2** *vt* formen *(into* zu*); (cast)* gießen.
mould[2], *(US)* **mold** *n (fungus)* Schimmel *m.*
moulder, *(US)* **molder** [ˈməʊldə^r] *vi (lit)* vermodern; *(food)* verderben; *(building)* zerfallen.
moulding, *(US)* **molding** [ˈməʊldɪŋ] *n (cast)* Abdruck *m; (ceiling ~)* Deckenfries *m.*
mouldy, *(US)* **moldy** [ˈməʊldɪ] *adj (+er)* verschimmelt; *(musty)* mod(e)rig. **to go ~** verschimmeln.
moult, *(US)* **molt** [məʊlt] *vi (bird)* sich mausern; *(mammals)* sich haaren.
mound [maʊnd] *n* **(a)** *(hill, burial ~)* Hügel *m; (earthwork)* Wall *m; (Baseball)* Wurfmal *nt.* **(b)** *(pile)* Haufen *m; (of books)* Stapel *m.*
mount[1] [maʊnt] *n (poet: mountain, hill)* Berg *m.* **M~ Everest** Mount Everest *m.*
mount[2] **1** *n* **(a)** *(horse etc)* Reittier *nt.* **(b)** *(support, base) (of machine)* Sockel *m; (of colour slide)* Rah-

men *m; (of jewel)* Fassung *f; (of photo, picture)* Passepartout *nt; (stamp ~)* Falz *m.* **2** *vt* **(a)** *(climb onto)* besteigen. **(b)** *(place in/on ~)* montieren; *picture* mit einem Passepartout versehen; *(on backing)* aufziehen; *colour slide* rahmen; *specimen* präparieren; *jewel* (ein)fassen; *stamp* aufkleben. **(c)** *(organize) play* inszenieren; *attack* organisieren. **(d) to ~ guard** Wache stehen *(on* vor *+dat).* **3** *vi* **(a)** *(get on)* aufsteigen; *(on horse also)* aufsitzen. **(b)** *(increase: also ~* **up***)* sich häufen.

mountain ['maʊntɪn] *n (lit, fig)* Berg *m.* **in the ~s** im Gebirge; **to make a ~ out of a molehill** aus einer Mücke einen Elefanten machen *(col)*; **~ chain** Gebirgskette *f.*

mountaineer [,maʊntɪ'nɪə^r] *n* Bergsteiger(in *f*) *m.*

mountaineering [,maʊntɪ'nɪərɪŋ] *n* Bergsteigen *nt.*

mountainous ['maʊntɪnəs] *adj* gebirgig.

mountain: ~ range *n* Gebirgszug *m;* **~side** *n* (Berg)hang *m.*

mounted ['maʊntɪd] *adj (on horseback)* beritten.

mourn [mɔːn] **1** *vt person* trauern um; *sb's death* beklagen, betrauern; *(fig)* nachtrauern *(+dat).* **2** *vi* trauern. **to ~ for** *or* **over sb/sth** um jdn trauern/einer Sache *(dat)* nachtrauern.

mourner ['mɔːnə^r] *n* Trauernde(r) *mf; (non-relative at funeral)* Trauergast *m.*

mournful ['mɔːnfʊl] *adj person, occasion* trauervoll; *character, voice, look* weinerlich; *sigh, appearance* kläglich; *sound, cry* klagend.

mourning ['mɔːnɪŋ] *n (act)* Trauer *f,* Trauern *nt (of* um*).* **to be in ~ for sb** um jdn trauern; *(wear ~)* Trauer tragen.

mouse [maʊs] *n, pl* **mice** *(also Comp)* Maus *f.*

mousetrap ['maʊstræp] *n* Mausefalle *f.*

mousse [muːs] *n* Creme(speise) *f.*

moustache, *(US)* **mustache** [mə'stɑːʃ] *n* Schnurrbart *m.*

mousy, mousey ['maʊsɪ] *adj (+er) (timid)* schüchtern; *hair* mausgrau.

mouth [maʊθ] **1** *n (of person)* Mund *m; (of animal)* Maul *nt; (of bottle, cave etc)* Öffnung *f; (of river)* Mündung *f; (of harbour)* Einfahrt *f.* **to keep one's (big) ~ shut** *(col)* die Klappe halten *(col)*; **shut your ~!** *(col!)* halt's Maul! *(col!).* **2** [maʊð] *vt (say affectedly)* (über)deutlich artikulieren; *(soundlessly)* mit Lippensprache sagen.

mouthful ['maʊθfʊl] *n (of drink)* Schluck *m; (of food)* Bissen *m; (fig) (difficult word)* Zungenbrecher *m; (long word)* Bandwurm *m.*

mouth *in cpds* Mund-; **~-organ** *n* Mundharmonika *f;* **~piece** *n* Mundstück *nt; (of telephone)* Sprechmuschel *f; (fig: medium)* Sprachrohr *nt;* **~-to-~ resuscitation** *n* Mund-zu-Mund-Beatmung *f;* **~wash** *n* Mundwasser *nt;* **~-watering** *adj* lecker; **it's really ~-watering** da läuft einem das Wasser im Mund zusammen.

movable ['muːvəbl] *adj* beweglich; *(transportable)* transportierbar.

move [muːv] **1** *n* **(a)** *(in game)* Zug *m; (fig) (step, action)* Schritt *m; (measure taken)* Maßnahme *f.* **it's my** *etc* **~** *(lit, fig)* ich *etc* bin am Zug!; **to make a/the first ~** *(fig)* Schritte unternehmen/den ersten Schritt tun; **that was a bad/good ~** *(fig)* das war taktisch falsch/das war ein guter Schachzug.

(b) *(movement)* Bewegung *f.* **to be on the ~** *(fig: things, developments)* im Fluß sein; *(person: in different places)* unterwegs sein; **to get a ~ on (with sth)** *(col: hurry up)* sich (mit etw) beeilen; **get a ~ on!** nun mach schon! *(col)*; **to make a ~ to do sth** *(fig)* Anstalten machen, etw zu tun; **it's time we made a ~** es wird Zeit, daß wir uns auf den Weg machen.

(c) *(of house etc)* Umzug *m; (to different job)* Stellenwechsel *m; (to different department)* Wechsel *m.*

2 *vt* **(a)** bewegen; *wheel etc* (an)treiben; *(shift about)* umstellen, umräumen; *(transport)* befördern; *hand* wegziehen; *chess piece etc* ziehen mit; *(out of the way)* wegräumen. **to be unable to ~ sth** *(lift)* etw nicht von der Stelle bringen; *screw* etw nicht losbekommen; **I can't ~ this handle** der Griff läßt sich nicht bewegen.

(b) *(change location of) offices, troops* verlegen; *patient* bewegen; *(transport)* transportieren; *employee (to new department)* versetzen. **to ~ house** *(Brit)* umziehen.

(c) *(fig: sway)* **to ~ sb from an opinion** *etc* jdn von einer Meinung *etc* abbringen; **to ~ sb to do sth** jdn veranlassen, etw zu tun; **I shall not be ~d** ich bleibe dabei.

(d) *(cause emotion in)* bewegen; *(upset)* erschüttern, ergreifen. **to ~ sb to tears** jdn zu Tränen rühren.

(e) *(form: propose)* beantragen. **she ~d an amendment to the motion** sie stellte einen Abänderungsantrag.

3 *vi* **(a)** sich bewegen; *(vehicle)* fahren; *(traffic)* vorankommen. **nobody ~d** niemand rührte sich; **the vehicle began to ~** das Fahrzeug setzte sich in Bewegung; **don't ~!** stillhalten!; **to keep moving** nicht stehenbleiben; **to keep sb/sth moving** jdn/etw in Gang halten; **things are moving at last** endlich kommen die Dinge in Gang; **to ~ with the times** mit der Zeit gehen; **they must ~ first** sie müssen den ersten Schritt tun; **he has ~d to another department** er hat die Abteilung gewechselt; **it's time we were moving** es wird Zeit, daß wir gehen; **that's moving!** *(col: fast)* das ist aber ein ganz schönes Tempo! *(col).*

(b) *(~ house)* umziehen.

(c) *(in games) (make a ~)* ziehen; *(have one's turn)* am Zug sein.

♦ **move about 1** *vt sep furniture etc* umstellen; *parts of body* (hin und her) bewegen; *employee* versetzen. **2** *vi* sich (hin und her) bewegen; *(fidget)* herumzappeln; *(travel)* unterwegs sein.

♦ **move along 1** *vt sep* weiterrücken; *bystanders etc* zum Weitergehen veranlassen. **2** *vi (along seat etc)* aufrücken; *(along bus etc)* weitergehen; *(cars)* weiterfahren.

♦ **move away 1** *vt sep* wegräumen; *person* wegschicken. **to ~ sb ~ from sth** jdn von etw entfernen. **2** *vi (move aside)* aus dem Weg gehen; *(leave) (people)* weggehen; *(vehicle)* losfahren; *(move house)* wegziehen *(from* aus, von*).*

♦ **move back 1** *vt sep (to former place)* zurückstellen; *people* zurückbringen; *(to the rear) things* zurückschieben; *car* zurückfahren; *people* zurückdrängen; *troops* zurückziehen. **2** *vi* **(a)** *(to former place)* zurückkommen; *(into one's house)* wieder einziehen *(into* in *+acc).* **(b)** *(to the rear)* zurückweichen; *(troops)* sich zurückziehen; *(car)* zurückfahren. **~ ~, please!** bitte zurücktreten!

♦ **move down 1** *vt sep (downwards)* (weiter) nach unten stellen; *(along)* (weiter) nach hinten stellen. **2** *vi (downwards)* nach unten rücken; *(along)* weiterrücken; *(in bus etc)* nach hinten aufrücken.

♦ **move forward 1** *vt sep person* vorgehen lassen; *table etc* vorrücken; *chess piece* vorziehen; *car* vorfahren; *troops* vorrücken lassen; *event, date* vorverlegen. **2** *vi (person)* vorrücken; *(crowd)* sich vorwärts bewegen; *(car)* vorwärtsfahren; *(troops)* vorrücken.

♦ **move in 1** *vt sep troops* einsetzen *(-to* in *+dat); (take inside)* herein-/hineinstellen *(-to* in *+acc).* **2** *vi* **(a)** *(into house)* einziehen *(-to* in *+acc).* **(b)** *(come closer)* näher herankommen *(on* an *+acc); (police, troops)* anrücken; *(workers)* anfangen. **to ~ ~ on sb** gegen jdn vorrücken.

♦ **move off 1** *vt sep people* wegschicken. **2** *vi* **(a)** *(go away)* weggehen. **(b)** *(start moving)* sich in Bewegung setzen; *(train, car also)* abfahren.

♦**move on 1** *vt sep hands of clock* vorstellen. **the policeman ~d them ~** der Polizist forderte sie auf, weiterzugehen/weiterzufahren. **2** *vi (people)* weitergehen; *(vehicles)* weiterfahren. **it's about time I was moving ~** *(fig)* es wird Zeit, daß ich (mal) etwas anderes mache; **let's ~ ~ to the next point** gehen wir zum nächsten Punkt über.

♦**move out 1** *vt sep car* herausfahren *(of* aus*)*; *troops* abziehen. **~ the table ~ of the corner** rücken Sie den Tisch von der Ecke weg! **2** *vi (leave accommodation)* ausziehen; *(withdraw: troops)* abziehen.

♦**move over 1** *vt sep* herüber-/hinüberschieben. **2** *vi* zur Seite rücken. **~ ~!** rück mal ein Stück! *(col)*.

♦**move up 1** *vt sep* (weiter) nach oben stellen; *(promote)* befördern; *(Sch)* versetzen; *(Sport)* aufsteigen lassen. **2** *vi (fig)* aufsteigen; *(shares, rates etc)* steigen; *(be promoted)* befördert werden; *(Sch)* versetzt werden; *(move along)* aufrücken. **to ~ ~ the social scale** die gesellschaftliche Leiter hinaufklettern.

movement ['muːvmənt] *n* **(a)** Bewegung *f; (fig: trend)* Trend *m (towards* zu*)*; *(of events)* Entwicklung *f*. **a slight upward ~** eine leichte Aufwärtsbewegung; **the police were investigating his ~s** die Polizei stellte Ermittlungen über ihn an. **(b)** *(political etc ~)* Bewegung *f*. **(c)** *(Mus)* Satz *m*.

movie ['muːvɪ] *n (esp US)* Film *m*. **(the) ~s** der Film; **to go to the ~s** ins Kino gehen.

movie *in cpds* Film-; **~ camera** *n* Filmkamera *f*; **~goer** *n* Kinogänger(in *f*) *m*.

moving ['muːvɪŋ] *adj* **(a)** beweglich. **~ staircase** Rolltreppe *f*. **(b)** *(fig: instigating) force* treibend. **(c)** *(causing emotion)* ergreifend; *tribute* rührend.

mow [məʊ] *pret* **~ed**, *ptp* **mown** *or* **~ed** *vti* mähen.

MP = **Member of Parliament.**

mpg = **miles per gallon.**

mph = **miles per hour.**

Mr ['mɪstə^r] = **Mister** Herr *m*.

Mrs ['mɪsɪz] *n* Frau *f*.

Ms [mɪz] Frau *f*.

MSc = **Master of Science.**

much [mʌtʃ] **1** *adj, n* **(a)** viel *inv*. **how ~** wieviel *inv*; **that ~** so viel; **~ of this is true** vieles daran ist wahr; **we don't see ~ of each other** wir sehen uns nicht oft; **he/it isn't up to ~** *(col)* er/es ist nicht gerade berühmt *(col)*; **she's not ~ of a cook** sie ist keine große Köchin; **that wasn't ~ of a party** die Party war nicht gerade besonders; **that's a bit ~!** das ist ja ein starkes Stück! *(col)*; **they are ~ of a muchness** sie nehmen sich nicht viel.

(b) too ~ zuviel *inv*; *(ridiculous)* das Letzte *(col)*; **to be too ~ for sb** *(in quantity)* zuviel für jdn sein; *(too expensive)* jdm zuviel sein; **that insult was too ~ for me** die Beleidigung ging mir zu weit.

(c) (just) as ~ genausoviel *inv*; **not as ~** nicht soviel; **three times as ~** dreimal soviel; **as ~ as you want/can** *etc* soviel du willst/kannst *etc*; **as ~ again** noch einmal soviel; **I feared/thought** *etc* **as ~** (genau) das habe ich befürchtet/mir gedacht *etc*; **it's as ~ as I can do to stand up** es fällt mir schwer genug aufzustehen.

(d) so ~ soviel *inv*; *(emph so, with following that)* so viel; **it's not so ~ a problem of modernization as ...** es ist nicht so sehr ein Problem der Modernisierung, als ...

(e) to make ~ of sb/sth viel Wind um jdn/etw machen; **I couldn't make ~ of that chapter** mit dem Kapitel konnte ich nicht viel anfangen *(col)*.

2 *adv* **(a)** *(with adj, adv)* viel; *(with vb)* sehr; *(with vb of physical action) drive, sleep, talk etc* viel; *come, visit etc* oft, viel *(col)*. **so ~/too ~** soviel/zuviel; so sehr/zu sehr; **I like it very/so ~** es gefällt mir sehr gut/so sehr; **I don't like him/it too ~** ich kann ihn/es nicht besonders leiden; **thank you very ~** vielen Dank; **however ~ he tries** wie sehr er sich auch bemüht; **~ to my astonishment** zu meinem großen Erstaunen; **~ as I should like to** so gern ich möchte; **~ as I like him** sosehr ich ihn mag.

(b) *(by far)* weitaus, bei weitem. **~ the biggest** weitaus der/die/das größte; **I would ~ rather stay** ich würde viel lieber bleiben.

(c) *(almost)* beinahe. **they are ~ the same** sie sind fast gleich.

muck [mʌk] *n* **(a)** *(dirt)* Dreck *m; (manure)* Dung *m*. **(b)** *(rubbish)* Mist *m; (food etc)* Zeug *nt (col)*.

♦**muck about** *or* **around** *(col)* **1** *vt sep* **to ~ sb ~** jdn verarschen *(col)*; *(by not committing oneself)* jdn hinhalten. **2** *vi (lark about)* herumblödeln *(col)*; *(do nothing in particular)* herumgammeln *(col)*; *(tinker with)* herumfummeln *(with* an *+dat)*.

♦**muck in** *vi (col)* mit anpacken *(col)*.

♦**muck up** *vt sep (col)* **(a)** *(dirty)* dreckig machen *(col)*. **(b)** *(spoil)* vermasseln *(col)*.

muck-raking ['mʌk,reɪkɪŋ] *n (fig col)* Sensationsmache(rei) *f (col)*.

mucky ['mʌkɪ] *adj (+er)* dreckig *(col)*, schmutzig.

mucus ['mjuːkəs] *n* Schleim *m*.

mud [mʌd] *n* Schlamm *m*. **his name is ~** *(col)* er ist unten durch *(col)*; **to throw ~ at sb/sth** *(fig col)* jdn mit Schmutz bewerfen/etw in den Schmutz ziehen.

mud bath *n* Schlammbad *nt; (Med)* Moorbad *nt*.

muddle ['mʌdl] **1** *n* Durcheinander *nt*. **to get in(to) a ~** *(things)* durcheinandergeraten; *(person)* konfus werden; **to be in a ~** völlig durcheinander sein; **to make a ~ of sth** etw völlig durcheinanderbringen. **2** *vt (also* **~ up***)* durcheinanderbringen; *(make confused) person also* verwirren.

♦**muddle along** *or* **on** *vi* vor sich *(acc)* hinwursteln *(col)*.

♦**muddle through** *vi* sich durchschlagen.

muddled ['mʌdld] *adj* konfus; *person also* durcheinander *pred; ideas also* verworren.

muddle-headed ['mʌdl,hedɪd] *adj person* zerstreut; *ideas* verworren.

muddy ['mʌdɪ] *adj (+er) floor, shoes etc* schlammbeschmiert; *ground, liquid* schlammig.

mud: ~guard *n (on cycles)* Schutzblech *nt; (on cars)* Kotflügel *m*; **~ pack** *n* Schlammpackung *f*; **~-slinging** *n* Schlechtmacherei *f*.

muff[1] [mʌf] *n* Muff *m*.

muff[2] *(col) vt* vermasseln *(col)*; *exam also* verhauen *(col)*; *lines, text* verpatzen *(col)*.

muffle ['mʌfl] *vt* **(a)** *(wrap warmly: also* **~ up***) person* einmummen. **(b)** *(deaden) shot etc* dämpfen; *noise* abdämpfen; *shouts* ersticken.

muffled ['mʌfld] *adj sound etc* gedämpft; *shouts* erstickt.

muffler ['mʌflə^r] *n* **(a)** *(scarf)* (dicker) Schal. **(b)** *(US Aut)* Auspuff(topf) *m*.

mufti ['mʌftɪ] *n (col)* **in ~** in Zivil.

mug [mʌg] **1** *n* **(a)** *(cup)* Becher *m; (for beer)* Krug *m*. **(b)** *(col: fool)* Trottel *m*. **that's a ~'s game** das ist doch schwachsinnig. **(c)** *(col: face)* Visage *f (col!)*. **~ shot** Verbrecherfoto *nt (col)*. **2** *vt (attack and rob)* überfallen.

♦**mug up** *vt sep (also* **~ ~ on***)* pauken *(col)*.

mugger ['mʌgə^r] *n* Straßenräuber *m*.

mugging ['mʌgɪŋ] *n* Straßenraub *m no pl*. **a lot of ~s** viele Überfälle auf offener Straße.

muggy ['mʌgɪ] *adj (+er)* schwül; *heat* drückend.

mulatto [mjuː'lætəʊ] *n, pl* **-es** Mulatte *m*, Mulattin *f*.

mulberry ['mʌlbərɪ] *n (fruit)* Maulbeere *f; (tree)* Maulbeerbaum *m*.

mule [mjuːl] *n* Maultier *nt*. **(as) stubborn as a ~** (so) störrisch wie ein Maulesel.

mull [mʌl] *vt* **~ed wine** Glühwein *m*.

♦**mull over** *vt sep* sich *(dat)* durch den Kopf gehen lassen.
multi- ['mʌltɪ] *pref* mehr-, Mehr-; *(with Latin stem in German)* Multi-, multi-; **~-coloured,** *(US)* **~-colored** *adj* mehrfarbig; *lights, decorations* bunt; *bird* buntgefiedert.
multifarious [ˌmʌltɪ'fɛərɪəs] *adj* vielfältig.
multi: ~lateral *adj (Pol)* multilateral; **~level parking garage** *n (US)* Parkhaus *nt;* **~lingual** *adj* mehrsprachig; **~millionaire** *n* Multimillionär(in *f*) *m;* **~national 1** *n* multinationaler Konzern; **2** *adj* multinational.
multiple ['mʌltɪpl] **1** *adj* **(a)** *(with sing n: of several parts)* mehrfach. **~ choice** Multiple Choice *no art;* **~ crash** Massenkarambolage *f.* **(b)** *(with pl n: many)* mehrere. **2** *n* **(a)** *(Math)* Vielfache(s) *nt.* **(b)** *(Brit: also* **~ store***)* Ladenkette *f.*
multiple sclerosis *n* multiple Sklerose.
multiplication [ˌmʌltɪplɪ'keɪʃən] *n* **(a)** *(Math)* Multiplikation *f.* **~ table** Multiplikationstabelle *f.* **(b)** *(fig)* Vervielfachung *f.*
multiplicity [ˌmʌltɪ'plɪsɪtɪ] *n* Vielzahl *f.* **for a ~ of reasons** aus vielerlei Gründen.
multiply ['mʌltɪplaɪ] **1** *vt (Math)* multiplizieren, malnehmen. **4 multiplied by 6 is 24** 4 mal 6 ist 24. **2** *vi* **(a)** *(Math)* multiplizieren. **(b)** *(fig)* sich vervielfachen. **(c)** *(breed)* sich vermehren.
multi: ~-purpose *adj* Mehrzweck-; **~racial** *adj* gemischtrassig; **~-stor(e)y** *adj* mehrstöckig; **~-stor(e)y car-park** *(Brit)* Parkhaus *nt.*
multitude ['mʌltɪtjuːd] *n* Menge *f.*
mum[1] [mʌm] *n, adj (col)* **~'s the word!** nichts verraten! *(col);* **to keep ~** den Mund halten *(about* über *+acc) (col).*
mum[2] *n (Brit col: mother)* Mutter *f; (as address)* Mutti *f (col).*
mumble ['mʌmbl] **1** *vt* murmeln. **2** *vi* vor sich *(acc)* hin murmeln; *(speak indistinctly)* nuscheln.
mummify ['mʌmɪfaɪ] *vt* mumifizieren.
mummy[1] ['mʌmɪ] *n (corpse)* Mumie *f.*
mummy[2] *n (Brit col: mother)* Mami *f (col).*
mumps [mʌmps] *n sing* Mumps *m or f (col) no art.*
munch [mʌntʃ] *vti* mampfen *(col).*
mundane [ˌmʌn'deɪn] *adj (worldly)* weltlich; *(pej: humdrum)* banal.
municipal [mjuː'nɪsɪpəl] *adj* städtisch; *council, elections etc* Stadt-, Gemeinde-.
municipality [mjuːˌnɪsɪ'pælɪtɪ] *n* Gemeinde *f.*
Munich ['mjuːnɪk] *n* München *nt.*
munificence [mjuː'nɪfɪsns] *n (form)* Großzügigkeit *f.*
munition [mjuː'nɪʃən] *n usu pl* Kriegsmaterial *nt no pl.*
mural ['mjʊərəl] **1** *n* Wandgemälde *nt.* **2** *adj* Wand-.
murder ['mɜːdəʳ] **1** *n* **(a)** Mord *m.* **to commit ~** einen Mord begehen. **(b)** *(fig col)* **it was ~** es war mörderisch; **to cry blue ~** ein Mordstheater machen *(col);* **to get away with ~** sich *(dat)* alles erlauben können. **2** *vt* ermorden, umbringen; *(slaughter)* morden; *(col) opponents* haushoch schlagen; *(col: ruin) music etc* verhunzen *(col).*
murderer ['mɜdərəʳ] *n* Mörder *m.*
murderous ['mɜːdərəs] *adj deed* Mord-; *(fig)* mörderisch.
murky ['mɜːkɪ] *adj (+er)* trübe; *fog* dicht; *photo, outline etc* unscharf; *past* dunkel.
murmur ['mɜːməʳ] **1** *n* Murmeln *nt; (of discontent)* Murren *nt; (of water, traffic)* Rauschen *nt.* **there was a ~ of approval/disagreement** ein beifälliges/abfälliges Murmeln erhob sich; **not a ~** kein Laut; **without a ~** ohne zu murren. **2** *vt* murmeln; *(with discontent)* murren. **3** *vi* murmeln; *(with discontent)* murren *(about* über *+acc); (fig)* rauschen.
muscle ['mʌsl] *n* Muskel *m; (fig: power)* Macht *f.* **to have financial/industrial ~** finanzkräftig/wirtschaftlich einflußreich sein; **he never moved a ~** er rührte sich nicht.
♦**muscle in** *vi (col)* **to ~ ~ (on sth)** (bei etw) mitmischen.
muscular ['mʌskjʊləʳ] *adj* Muskel-; *strong* muskulös.
muse [mjuːz] **1** *vi* nachgrübeln *(about, on* über *+acc).* **2** *vt* grüblerisch sagen.
museum [mjuː'zɪəm] *n* Museum *nt.* **~ piece** *(lit, hum)* Museumsstück *nt.*
mush [mʌʃ] *n* Brei *m.*
mushroom ['mʌʃrʊm] **1** *n* (eßbarer) Pilz; *(button* **~***)* Champignon *m.* **~ cloud** Atompilz *m.* **2** *vi (grow rapidly)* wie die Pilze aus dem Boden schießen. **his fame ~ed** er wurde schlagartig berühmt; **the smoke ~ed** der Rauch breitete sich pilzförmig in der Luft aus.
mushy ['mʌʃɪ] *adj (+er)* matschig; *liquid, consistency* breiig; *(col) film etc* schmalzig *(col).* **~ peas** Erbsenmus *nt.*
music ['mjuːzɪk] *n* Musik *f; (written score)* Noten *pl.* **to set sth to ~** etw vertonen; **to face the ~** *(fig)* dafür geradestehen.
musical ['mjuːzɪkəl] **1** *adj* musikalisch; *instrument, evening* Musik-; *(tuneful)* melodisch. **~ box** Spieluhr *or* -dose *f;* **~ chairs** *sing* Reise *f* nach Jerusalem. **2** *n* Musical *nt.*
music *in cpds* Musik-; **~ centre** *(Brit) or* **center** *(US) n* Kompaktanlage *f;* **~ hall** *n* Varieté *nt.*
musician [mjuː'zɪʃən] *n* Musiker(in *f*) *m.*
musicologist [ˌmjuːzɪ'kɒlədʒɪst] *n* Musikwissenschaftler(in *f*) *m.*
music-: ~ stand *n* Notenständer *m;* **~-stool** *n* Klavierhocker *m.*
musk [mʌsk] *n (secretion, smell)* Moschus *m.*
musket ['mʌskɪt] *n* Muskete *f.*
musk: ~rat *n* Bisamratte *f;* **~-rose** *n* Moschusrose *f.*
musky ['mʌskɪ] *adj (+er) smell* Moschus-.
Muslim ['mʊzlɪm] *adj, n* = **Moslem.**
musquash ['mʌskwɒʃ] *n* Bisamratte *f.*
muss [mʌs] *vt (US col: also* **~ up***)* durcheinanderbringen *(col).*
mussel ['mʌsl] *n* (Mies)muschel *f.*
must [mʌst] **1** *vb aux present tense only* **(a)** müssen. **if you ~** wenn's sein muß. **(b)** *(in neg sentences)* dürfen. **I ~n't forget that** ich darf das nicht vergessen. **(c)** *(probability)* **he ~ be there by now** er ist wohl inzwischen da; *(more certain)* er ist inzwischen bestimmt da; **I ~ have lost it** ich habe es wohl verloren; **you ~ have heard of him** Sie haben bestimmt schon von ihm gehört; **he ~ be older than that** er muß älter sein; **there ~ be a reason for it** es muß doch eine Erklärung dafür geben! **2** *n (col)* Muß *nt.* **an umbrella is a ~** man braucht unbedingt einen Schirm; **this programme is a ~ for everyone** dieses Programm muß man einfach gesehen haben.
mustache *n (US)* = **moustache.**
mustard ['mʌstəd] *n* Senf *m; (colour)* Senfgelb *nt.*
muster ['mʌstəʳ] **1** *n (esp Mil: assembly)* Appell *m.* **to pass ~** *(fig)* den Anforderungen genügen. **2** *vt* **(a)** *(summon)* zusammenrufen; *(esp Mil)* antreten lassen. **(b)** *(manage to raise: also* **~ up***)* zusammenbekommen; *strength, courage* aufbringen; *all one's strength, courage* zusammennehmen. **3** *vi* sich versammeln; *(esp Mil)* (zum Appell) antreten.
mustiness ['mʌstɪnɪs] *n* Muffigkeit *f.*
mustn't ['mʌsnt] = **must not.**
musty ['mʌstɪ] *adj (+er) air* muffig; *books* moderig.
mutate [mjuː'teɪt] *vi (Biol)* mutieren *(to* zu*).*
mutation [mjuː'teɪʃən] *n (Biol)* Mutation *f.*
mute [mjuːt] **1** *adj* stumm *(also Ling); amazement, rage* sprachlos. **2** *n (dumb person)* Stumme(r) *mf.*
muted ['mjuːtɪd] *adj* gedämpft; *(fig) criticism etc* leicht.
mutilate ['mjuːtɪleɪt] *vt person, animal, story* verstümmeln; *painting etc* verschandeln *(col).*
mutilation [ˌmjuːtɪ'leɪʃən] *n see vt* Verstüm-

melung *f*; Verschandelung *f (col).*
mutineer [ˌmjuːtɪ'nɪəʳ] *n* Meuterer *m.*
mutinous ['mjuːtɪnəs] *adj (Naut)* meuterisch; *(fig)* rebellisch.
mutiny ['mjuːtɪnɪ] *(Naut, fig)* **1** *n* Meuterei *f.* **2** *vi* meutern.
mutter ['mʌtəʳ] **1** *n* Gemurmel *nt; (of discontent)* Murren *nt.* **2** *vt* murmeln, brummeln. **3** *vi* murmeln; *(with discontent)* murren.
mutton ['mʌtn] *n* Hammel(fleisch *nt*) *m.* **leg of ~** Hammelkeule *f;* **she's ~ dressed as lamb** *(col)* sie macht auf jung *(col).*
mutual ['mjuːtjʊəl] *adj respect etc* gegenseitig; *satisfaction* beiderseitig; *friends, dislikes etc* gemeinsam. **it would be for our ~ benefit** es wäre für uns beide von Vorteil; **the feeling is ~** das beruht (ganz) auf Gegenseitigkeit.
mutually ['mjuːtjʊəlɪ] *adv* beide; *distrust* gegenseitig; *satisfactory, beneficial* für beide Seiten; *agreed* von beiden Seiten.
muzzle ['mʌzl] **1** *n* **(a)** *(snout, mouth)* Maul *nt.* **(b)** *(for dog etc)* Maulkorb *m.* **(c)** *(of gun)* Mündung *f; (barrel)* Lauf *m.* **2** *vt animal* einen Maulkorb anlegen *(+dat)*; *(fig) critics, the press* mundtot machen.
muzzy ['mʌzɪ] *adj (+er) (dizzy, dazed)* benommen; *(blurred) view, memory etc* veschwommen.
my [maɪ] *poss adj* mein. **I've hurt ~ leg** ich habe mir das Bein verletzt; **~ father and mother** mein Vater und meine Mutter; **in ~ country** bei uns.
myna(h) bird ['maɪnəˌbɜːd] *n* Hirtenstar *m.*
myopia [maɪ'əʊpɪə] *n* Kurzsichtigkeit *f.*
myopic [maɪ'ɒpɪk] *adj* kurzsichtig.
myself [maɪ'self] *pers pron* **(a)** *(dir obj, with prep +acc)* mich; *(indir obj, with prep +dat)* mir. **I said to ~** ich sagte mir; **I wanted to see (it) for ~** ich wollte es selbst sehen. **(b)** *(emph)* (ich) selbst. **my wife and ~** meine Frau und ich; **I did it ~** ich habe es selbst gemacht; **(all) by ~** (ganz) allein(e); **I'll go there ~** ich gehe selbst hin. **(c)** *(one's normal self)* **I'm not (feeling) ~ today** ich bin heute nicht ganz auf der Höhe.
mysterious [mɪ'stɪərɪəs] *adj* geheimnisvoll; *(puzzling)* mysteriös.
mysteriously [mɪ'stɪərɪəslɪ] *adv vanish, change* auf mysteriöse Weise; *missing* unerklärlicherweise; *(secretively)* geheimnisvoll.
mystery ['mɪstərɪ] *n (puzzle)* Rätsel *nt; (secret)* Geheimnis *nt.* **it's a ~ to me** das ist mir ein Rätsel.
mystic ['mɪstɪk] **1** *adj* mystisch. **2** *n* Mystiker(in *f*) *m.*
mystical ['mɪstɪkəl] *adj* mystisch.
mysticism ['mɪstɪsɪzəm] *n* Mystizismus *m; (of poetry etc)* Mystik *f.*
mystify ['mɪstɪfaɪ] *vt* vor ein Rätsel stellen. **I was mystified by the whole business** die ganze Sache war mir ein Rätsel.
mystifying ['mɪstɪfaɪɪŋ]*adj* rätselhaft.
mystique [mɪ'stiːk] *n* geheimnisvolle Exotik.
myth [mɪθ] *n* Mythos *m; (fig)* Märchen *nt.*
mythical ['mɪθɪkəl] *adj* mythisch; *(fig)* erfunden. **~ figure/character** Sagengestalt *f.*
mythological [ˌmɪθə'lɒdʒɪkəl] *adj* mythologisch.
mythology [mɪ'θɒlədʒɪ] *n* Mythologie *f.*
myxomatosis [ˌmɪksəʊmə'təʊsɪs] *n* Myxomatose *f.*

N

N, n [en] *n* N, n *nt.*
N = north N.
nab [næb] *vt (col)* **(a)** *(catch, speak to)* erwischen; *(police also)* schnappen *(col).* **(b)** *(take for oneself)* sich *(dat)* grapschen *(col),* klauen *(col).*
nadir ['neɪdɪəʳ] *n* **(a)** *(Astron)* Fußpunkt *m.* **(b)** *(fig)* Tiefstpunkt *m.*
nag¹ [næg] **1** *vt* herumnörgeln an *(+dat).* **she ~ged me into buying it** sie ließ mir keine Ruhe, bis ich es gekauft hatte. **2** *vi (find fault)* herumnörgeln, meckern *(col); (be insistent)* keine Ruhe geben. **to ~ at sb** an jdm herumnörgeln, jdm keine Ruhe lassen. **3** *n (fault-finder)* Nörgler(in *f*) *m.*
nag² *n (old horse)* Klepper *m; (col: horse)* Gaul *m.*
nagging ['nægɪŋ] **1** *adj wife* meckernd *(col),* nörglerisch; *(pestering)* ewig drängend; *pain* dumpf; *worry, doubt* quälend. **2** *n (fault-finding)* Meckern *nt (col),* Nörgelei *f; (pestering)* ewiges Drängen.
nail [neɪl] **1** *n (Anat, Tech)* Nagel *m.* **as hard as ~s** knallhart *(col); (physically)* zäh wie Leder; **to pay on the ~** *(fig col)* auf der Stelle bezahlen; **to hit the ~ on the head** *(fig)* den Nagel auf den Kopf treffen; **to be a ~ in sb's coffin** *(fig)* ein Nagel zu jds Sarg sein. **2** *vt* **(a)** nageln. **to ~ sth to the wall** etw an die Wand nageln. **(b)** *(fig col)* **to be ~ed to the spot** *or* **ground** wie auf der Stelle festgenagelt sein; **to ~ sb** sich *(dat)* jdn schnappen *(col); (charge also)* jdn drankriegen *(col).*
♦ **nail down** *vt sep* **(a)** *(lit) box* zunageln; *carpet, lid* festnageln **(b)** *person* festnageln *(to* auf *+acc).*
nail *in cpds* Nagel-; **~-biting** *adj (col) terror* atemberaubend; *suspense also* atemlos; **~-brush** *n* Nagelbürste *f;* **~-file** *n* Nagelfeile *f;* **~ polish** *n* Nagellack *m;* **~ polish remover** *n* Nagellackentferner *m;* **~ scissors** *npl* Nagelschere *f;* **~ varnish** *n (Brit)* Nagellack *m.*
naïve [naɪ'iːv] *adj (+er)* naiv.
naïveté, naïvety [naɪ'iːvɪtɪ] *n* Naivität *f.*
naked ['neɪkɪd] *adj person* nackt; *branch, countryside* kahl; *flame, light* ungeschützt; *truth, facts* nackt. **to/with the ~ eye** für das bloße/mit dem bloßen Auge.
name [neɪm] **1** *n* **(a)** Name *m.* **what's your ~?** wie heißen Sie?, wie ist Ihr Name? *(form);* **my ~ is ...** ich heiße ..., mein Name ist ... *(form);* **a man by the ~ of Gunn** ein Mann namens Gunn; **I know him only by ~** ich kenne ihn nur dem Namen nach; **to refer to sb/sth by ~** jdn/etw namentlich *or* mit Namen nennen; **in ~ alone** *or* **only** nur dem Namen nach; **I won't mention any ~s** ich möchte keine Namen nennen; **he writes under the ~ of X** er schreibt unter dem Namen X; **fill in your ~(s) and address(es)** Namen und Adresse eintragen; **in the ~ of** im Namen *(+gen);* **in the ~ of God** um Gottes willen; **all the big ~s were there** alle großen Namen waren da; **I'll put your ~ down** *(on list, in register etc)* ich trage dich ein; *(for school, excursion etc)* ich melde dich an *(for* zu); **to call sb ~s** jdn beschimpfen; **that's the ~ of the game** *(col)* darum geht es.
(b) *(reputation)* Name, Ruf *m.* **to have a good/bad ~** einen guten/schlechten Ruf haben; **to get a bad ~** in Verruf kommen; **to give sb a bad ~** jdn in Verruf bringen; **to make a ~ for oneself as** sich *(dat)* einen Namen machen als; **to have a ~ for sth** für etw bekannt sein.
2 *vt* **(a)** *(call by a ~, give a ~ to, specify)* nennen *(as* als*); new star etc* benennen; *ship* taufen. **a person ~d Smith** jemand namens Smith; **to ~ a child after** *or (US)* **for sb** ein Kind nach jdm nennen; **~ your price** nennen Sie Ihren Preis; **to ~ the day** den Hochzeitstag festsetzen; **you ~ it, he's done it** es gibt nichts, was er noch nicht gemacht hat.
(b) *(appoint, nominate)* ernennen *(as* als, *for* für*).*
name: ~-drop *vi (col)* berühmte Bekannte in die Unterhaltung einfließen lassen; **she's always ~-dropping** sie muß dauernd erwähnen, wen sie alles kennt; **~less** *adj (unknown) person* unbekannt; *(undesignated)* namenlos; *(undefined) sensation, emotion* unbeschreiblich; *(shocking) vice, crime* unaussprechlich; **a certain person who shall remain ~less** jemand, der nicht genannt werden soll.
namely ['neɪmlɪ] *adv* nämlich.
name: ~-plate *n* Namensschild *nt; (on business premises)* Firmenschild *nt;* **~sake** *n* Namensvetter(in *f*) *m.*
nanny ['nænɪ] *n* **(a)** Kindermädchen *nt.* **(b)** *(col: also* **nanna***)* Oma, Omi *f (col).*
nanny goat *n* Geiß, Ziege *f.*
nap¹ [næp] *n* Nickerchen *nt.* **to have** *or* **take a ~** ein Nickerchen machen.
nap² *n (Tex)* Flor *m.*
napalm ['neɪpɑːm] *n* Napalm *nt.*
nape [neɪp] *n:* **~ of the neck** Nacken *m,* Genick *nt.*
napkin ['næpkɪn] *n* **(a)** *(table~)* Serviette *f.* **~ ring** Serviettenring *m.* **(b)** *(for baby)* Windel *f; (US: sanitary ~)* (Damen)binde *f.*
Naples ['neɪplz] Neapel *nt.*
nappy ['næpɪ] *n (Brit)* Windel *f.*
narcissus [nɑː'sɪsəs] *n, pl* **narcissi** *(Bot)* Narzisse *f.*
narcotic [nɑː'kɒtɪk] *n* Rauschgift *nt.*
nark [nɑːk] *vt (Brit col)* **to get/feel ~ed** wütend werden/sich ärgern.
narrate [nə'reɪt] *vt* erzählen; *events etc* schildern.
narration [nə'reɪʃən] *n* Erzählung *f; (of events etc)* Schilderung *f.*
narrative ['nærətɪv] **1** *n* Erzählung *f.* **three pages of ~** drei Seiten erzählender Text. **2** *adj* erzählend; *ability etc* erzählerisch.
narrator [nə'reɪtəʳ] *n* Erzähler(in *f*) *m.*
narrow ['nærəʊ] **1** *adj (+er)* **(a)** eng; *road, valley also* schmal. **(b)** *(fig) person, attitudes* engstirnig; *sense* eng; *existence* beschränkt; *majority, victory* knapp; *scrutiny* peinlich genau. **to have a ~ mind** engstirnig sein; **to have a ~ escape** mit knapper Not davonkommen. **2** *vt road etc* enger machen. **3** *vi* enger werden, sich verengen.
♦ **narrow down** *(to* auf *+acc)* **1** *vi* sich beschränken; *(be concentrated)* sich konzentrieren. **2** *vt sep (limit)* beschränken; *(concentrate)* konzentrieren. **that ~s it ~ a bit** dadurch wird die Auswahl kleiner.
narrowly ['nærəʊlɪ] *adv* **(a)** *beat* knapp; *escape* mit knapper Not. **he ~ escaped being knocked down** er wäre um ein Haar überfahren worden; **you ~ missed (seeing) him** du hast ihn gerade verpaßt. **(b)** *interpret* eng; *examine* peinlich genau.
narrow: ~ minded *adj* engstirnig; **~-mindedness**

n Engstirnigkeit *f.*
nasal ['neɪzəl] *adj sound* nasal, Nasal-; *voice* näselnd.
nastily ['nɑːstɪlɪ] *adv (unpleasantly)* scheußlich; *speak, say* gehässig; *behave also* gemein.
nastiness ['nɑːstɪnɪs] *n no pl* Scheußlichkeit *f; (of person)* Gemeinheit *f; (behaviour)* gemeines Benehmen *(to* gegenüber*).*
nasturtium [nəs'tɜːʃəm] *n* (Kapuziner)kresse *f.*
nasty ['nɑːstɪ] *adj (+er)* scheußlich, widerlich; *cough, wound* schlimm; *(offensive)* anstößig; *(dirty)* schmutzig; *(dangerous) disease, corner, fog* böse, gefährlich; *person, behaviour* gemein, fies *(col)*; *trick* übel; *(spiteful) remark* gehässig. **she had a ~ fall** sie ist böse hingefallen; **he had a ~ time of it** es ging ihm ganz übel; **to turn ~** unangenehm werden; **he has a ~ temper** mit ihm ist nicht gut Kirschen essen; **he's a ~ piece of work** *(col)* er ist ein übler Typ *(col).*
nation ['neɪʃən] *n* Volk *nt; (people of one country)* Nation *f.*
national ['næʃənəl] **1** *adj* national; *interest, debt, income* Staats-, öffentlich; *strike, scandal* landesweit; *security* Staats-; *team, character* National-; *language* Landes-; *custom, monument* Volks-. **the ~ papers** die überregionale Presse. **2** *n* **(a)** *(person)* Staatsbürger(in *f*) *m.* **foreign ~** Ausländer(in *f*) *m.* **(b)** *(col: newspaper)* überregionale Zeitung.
national: ~ anthem *n* Nationalhymne *f;* **~ costume, ~ dress** *n* Nationaltracht *f;* **N~ Health** *adj attr (Brit)* ≈ Kassen-; **N~ Health (Service)** *n (Brit)* Staatlicher Gesundheitsdienst *m;* **I got it on the N~ Health** ≈ das hat die Krankenkasse bezahlt; **~ insurance** *n (Brit)* Sozialversicherung *f.*
nationalism ['næʃnəlɪzəm] *n* Nationalismus *m.*
nationalist ['næʃnəlɪst] **1** *adj* nationalistisch. **2** *n* Nationalist(in *f*) *m.*
nationality [ˌnæʃə'nælɪtɪ] *n* Staatsangehörigkeit, Nationalität *f.* **what ~ is he?** welche Staatsangehörigkeit hat er?
nationalization [ˌnæʃnəlaɪ'zeɪʃən] *n* Verstaatlichung *f.*
nationalize ['næʃnəlaɪz] *vt* verstaatlichen.
nationally ['næʃnəlɪ] *adv (as a nation)* als Nation; *(nation-wide)* landesweit.
national: ~ park *n* Nationalpark *m;* **~ service** *n (Brit)* Wehrdienst *m;* **N~ Socialism** *n* der Nationalsozialismus.
nation-wide ['neɪʃənˌwaɪd] *adj, adv* landesweit.
native ['neɪtɪv] **1** *adj* **(a)** *town* Heimat-; *language* Mutter-; *product, costume, customs, plants* einheimisch; *(associated with natives) quarters, labour* Eingeborenen-. **a ~ German** ein gebürtiger Deutscher, eine gebürtige Deutsche; **~ speaker** Muttersprachler(in *f*) *m.* **(b)** *(inborn) wit, quality* angeboren. **2** *n* **(a)** *(person)* Einheimische(r) *mf; (in colonial contexts)* Eingeborene(r) *mf; (original inhabitant)* Ureinwohner(in *f*) *m.* **a ~ of Germany** ein gebürtiger Deutscher, eine gebürtige Deutsche. **(b) to be a ~ of ...** *(plant, animal)* in ... beheimatet sein.
native: ~ country *n* Heimatland *nt;* **~ land** *n* Vaterland *nt.*
nativity [nə'tɪvɪtɪ] *n* **the N~** Christi Geburt *no art;* **~ play** Krippenspiel *nt.*
NATO ['neɪtəʊ] = **North Atlantic Treaty Organization** NATO *f.*
natter ['nætəʳ] *(Brit col)* **1** *vi* schwatzen *(col)*; *(chatter also)* quasseln *(col).* **2** *n* **to have a ~** einen Schwatz halten *(col).*
natural ['nætʃrəl] **1** *adj* **(a)** natürlich; *rights* naturgegeben, Natur-; *laws, phenomena, silk* Natur-. **it is ~ for him to think ...** es ist nur natürlich, daß er denkt ...; **~ resources** Naturschätze *pl;* **the ~ world** die Natur; **in its ~ state** im Naturzustand; **to die a ~ death** *or* **of ~ causes** eines natürlichen Todes sterben; **death from ~ causes** *(Jur)* Tod durch natürliche Ursachen. **(b)** *(inborn) gift, ability* angeboren. **to have a ~ talent for sth** eine natürliche Begabung für etw haben. **2** *n* **(a)** *(Mus) (sign)* Auflösungszeichen *nt; (note)* Note *f* ohne Vorzeichen; **B ~/D ~** H, h/D, d. **(b)** *(col: person)* Naturtalent *nt.*
natural: ~ gas *n* Erdgas *nt;* **~ history** *n* Naturkunde *f.*
naturalist ['nætʃrəlɪst] *n* Naturforscher(in *f*) *m.*
naturalization [ˌnætʃrəlaɪ'zeɪʃən] *n* Einbürgerung *f.*
naturalize ['nætʃrəlaɪz] *vt person* einbürgern; *animal, plants* heimisch machen. **to become ~d** eingebürgert werden.
naturally ['nætʃrəlɪ] *adv* **(a) he is ~ lazy** er ist von Natur aus faul. **(b)** *(not taught)* natürlich, instinktiv. **it comes ~ to him** das fällt ihm leicht. **(c)** *(unaffectedly)* natürlich, ungekünstelt. **(d)** *(of course)* natürlich.
nature ['neɪtʃəʳ] *n* **(a)** Natur *f.* **N~** die Natur; **laws of ~** Naturgesetze *pl;* **to paint from ~** nach der Natur malen. **(b)** *(of person)* Wesen(sart *f*) *nt,* Natur *f.* **to have a jealous/happy ~** eine eifersüchtige/fröhliche Natur haben; **it is not in my ~ to say things like that** es entspricht nicht meiner Art, so etwas zu sagen; **cruel by ~** von Natur aus grausam. **(c)** *(type, sort)* Art *f.* **things of this ~** derartiges; **something in the ~ of an apology** so etwas wie eine Entschuldigung; **... or something of that ~** ... oder etwas in der Art.
nature: ~ conservancy *n* Naturschutz *m;* **~-lover** *n* Naturfreund *m;* **~ reserve** *n* Naturschutzgebiet *nt;* **~ study** *n* Naturkunde *f;* **~ trail** *n* Naturlehrpfad *m.*
naturism ['neɪtʃərɪzəm] *n* Freikörperkultur *f,* FKK *no art.*
naturist ['neɪtʃərɪst] *n* Anhänger(in *f*) *m* der Freikörperkultur.
naughtily ['nɔːtɪlɪ] *adv* frech; *(esp of child) remark, behave* ungezogen.
naughtiness ['nɔːtɪnɪs] *n see adj (a)* Frechheit *f;* Unartigkeit, Ungezogenheit *f.*
naughty ['nɔːtɪ] *adj (+er)* **(a)** frech; *child* unartig, ungezogen; *dog* ungehorsam. **you ~ boy!** du böser Junge!; **it was ~ of him to break it** das war aber gar nicht lieb von ihm, daß er das kaputtgemacht hat. **(b)** *joke, word, story* unanständig.
nausea ['nɔːsɪə] *n (Med)* Übelkeit *f; (fig)* Ekel *m.*
nauseate ['nɔːsɪeɪt] *vt* **to ~ sb** *(fig)* jdn anwidern.
nauseating ['nɔːsɪeɪtɪŋ] *adj sight, violence, food* ekelerregend; *film, book* gräßlich; *person* widerlich.
nauseous ['nɔːsɪəs] *adj* **(a)** *(Med)* **that made me (feel) ~** dabei wurde mir übel. **(b)** *(fig)* widerlich.
nautical ['nɔːtɪkəl] *adj* nautisch; *superiority* zur See; *tradition, appearance* seemännisch. **~ mile** Seemeile *f.*
naval ['neɪvəl] *adj* Marine-; *base, parade* Flotten-; *battle, forces* See-.
naval: ~ officer *n* Marineoffizier *m;* **~ power** *n* Seemacht *f.*
nave [neɪv] *n (of church)* Haupt- *or* Mittelschiff *nt.*
navel ['neɪvəl] *n (Anat)* Nabel *m.*
navigable ['nævɪgəbl] *adj waterway* schiffbar.
navigate ['nævɪgeɪt] **1** *vi (in plane, ship)* navigieren; *(in car)* den Fahrer dirigieren. **2** *vt* **(a)** *aircraft, ship* navigieren. **(b)** *(journey through)* durchfahren.
navigation [ˌnævɪ'geɪʃən] **(a)** Navigation *f.* **~ light** Positionslicht *nt.* **(b)** *(shipping)* Schiffsverkehr *m.*
navigator ['nævɪgeɪtəʳ] *n (Naut)* Navigationsoffizier *m; (Aviat)* Navigator *m; (Mot)* Beifahrer *m.*
navvy ['nævɪ] *n (Brit)* Bauarbeiter *m.*
navy ['neɪvɪ] **1** *n* **(a)** (Kriegs)marine *f.* **(b)** *(also ~*

blue) Marineblau *nt*. **2** *adj* **(a)** *attr* Marine-. **(b)** *(also* ~ **blue)** marineblau.

Nazi ['nɑːtsɪ] **1** *n* Nazi *m; (fig pej)* Faschist *m*. **2** *adj* Nazi-.

NB = **nota bene** NB.

NCO = **non-commissioned officer.**

near [nɪəʳ] *(+er)* **1** *adv* **(a)** nahe. **to be** ~ *(person, object)* in der Nähe sein; *(event etc)* bevorstehen; *(danger, end, help etc)* nahe sein; **to be very** ~ ganz in der Nähe sein; *(in time)* unmittelbar bevorstehen; *(danger etc)* ganz nahe sein; **to be ~er/~est** näher/am nächsten sein; *(event etc)* zeitlich näher liegen/zeitlich am nächsten liegen; **to be ~ at hand** zur Hand sein; *(shops)* in der Nähe sein; *(help)* ganz nahe sein; *(event)* unmittelbar bevorstehen; **he lives quite** ~ er wohnt ganz in der Nähe; **that was the ~est I ever got to seeing him** da hätte ich ihn fast gesehen.

(b) *(exactly, accurately)* genau. **as ~ as I can judge** soweit ich es beurteilen kann; **(that's) ~ enough** so geht's ungefähr.

(c) it's nowhere ~ enough/right das ist bei weitem nicht genug/das ist weit gefehlt; **nowhere ~ as much** bei weitem nicht soviel; **he is nowhere ~ as clever as you** er ist bei weitem nicht so klug wie du.

2 *prep (also adv:* ~ **to) (a)** *(close to) (position)* nahe an *(+dat)*, nahe *(+dat)*; *(with motion)* nahe an *(+acc)*; *(in the vicinity of)* in der Nähe von *or* *+gen*. **the hotel is very ~ (to) the station** das Hotel liegt ganz in der Nähe des Bahnhofs; **to come** *or* **get ~ (to) sth** nahe an etw herankommen; **to stand ~ (to) the table** neben dem *or* nahe am Tisch stehen; **she stood too ~ (to) the stove** sie stand zu nahe am Herd; **when we got ~ (to) the house** als wir an das Haus herankamen; **~ here/there** hier/dort in der Nähe; **take the chair ~est (to) you** nehmen Sie den Stuhl direkt neben Ihnen.

(b) *(close in time)* gegen. **come back ~er (to) 3 o'clock** kommen Sie gegen 3 Uhr wieder; **~ (to) the end of the play** gegen Ende des Stücks; **I'm ~ (to) the end of the book/my stay** ich habe das Buch fast zu Ende gelesen/mein Aufenthalt ist fast zu Ende.

(c) *(on the point of)* **to be ~ (to) doing sth** nahe daran sein, etw zu tun; **to be ~ (to) tears/despair** *etc* den Tränen/der Verzweiflung *etc* nahe sein; **the project is ~ (to) completion** das Projekt steht vor seinem Abschluß.

(d) *(similar to)* ähnlich *(+dat)*. **German is ~er (to) Dutch than English is** Deutsch ist dem Holländischen ähnlicher als Englisch; **nobody comes anywhere ~ him at swimming** im Schwimmen kann es niemand mit ihm aufnehmen *(col)*.

3 *adj* **(a)** *(close in space)* nahe. **it looks very** ~ es sieht so aus, als ob es ganz nah wäre; **our ~est neighbours are 5 miles away** unsere nächsten Nachbarn sind 5 Meilen entfernt. **(b)** *relation, friend* nah. **(c)** *escape* knapp; *resemblance* groß. **a ~ disaster** beinahe ein Unglück *nt*; **that was a ~ thing** das war knapp; **a ~ contest** ein Wettkampf *m* mit knappem Ausgang; **to be in a state of ~ collapse** einem Zusammenbruch nahe sein; **£50 or ~est offer** Verhandlungsbasis £50; **this is the ~est equivalent** das kommt dem am nächsten.

4 *vt place* sich nähern *(+dat)*. **to be ~ing sth** *(fig)* auf etw *(acc)* zugehen; **to ~ completion** kurz vor dem Abschluß stehen.

nearby [nɪə'baɪ] **1** *adv* in der Nähe. **2** *adj* nahe gelegen.

nearly ['nɪəlɪ] *adv* beinahe, fast. **I ~ laughed** ich hätte fast gelacht; **she was ~ in tears** sie war den Tränen nahe; **not** ~ bei weitem nicht, nicht annähernd.

nearness ['nɪənɪs] *n* Nähe *f*.

near: ~side 1 *adj* auf der Beifahrerseite, linke(r, s)/rechte(r, s); **2** *n* Beifahrerseite *f;* **~-sighted** *adj* kurzsichtig.

neat [niːt] *adj (+er)* **(a)** *(tidy) person, house, hairstyle* ordentlich; *worker, work, handwriting also* sauber; *appearance also* gepflegt. **to make a ~ job of sth** etwas tadellos machen. **(b)** *(pleasing)* nett; *clothes also* adrett; *person, figure also* hübsch. **(c)** *(skilful) gadget* gelungen; *style* gewandt; *solution* elegant; *trick* schlau. **that's very** ~ das ist sehr schlau. **(d)** *(undiluted) spirits* pur. **(e)** *(US col: excellent)* klasse *inv (col)*.

neatly ['niːtlɪ] *adv see adj (a-c)* **(a)** ordentlich; sauber. **(b)** nett; adrett; hübsch. **(c)** gelungen; gewandt; elegant; schlau. ~ **put** treffend ausgedrückt.

neatness ['niːtnɪs] *n see adj (a-c)* **(a)** Ordentlichkeit *f;* Sauberkeit *f*. **(b)** Nettheit *f*, nettes Aussehen; Adrettheit *f*; hübsches Aussehen. **(c)** Gelungenheit *f*; Gewandtheit *f*; Eleganz *f;* Schlauheit *f*.

nebulous ['nebjʊləs] *adj (fig)* unklar, nebulös.

necessarily ['nesɪsərɪlɪ] *adv* notwendigerweise, unbedingt. **not** ~ nicht unbedingt.

necessary ['nesɪsərɪ] **1** *adj* **(a)** notwendig, nötig *(to, for* für*)*. **it is ~ to ...** man muß ...; **is it ~ for me to come too?** muß ich auch kommen?; **it's not ~ for you to come** Sie brauchen nicht zu kommen; **it is ~ for him to be there** es ist nötig *or* notwendig, daß er da ist, er muß (unbedingt) da sein; **all the ~ qualifications** alle erforderlichen Qualifikationen; **~ condition** Voraussetzung *f;* **to make it ~ for sb to do sth** es erforderlich machen, daß jd etw tut; **if** ~ wenn nötig, nötigenfalls; **to make the ~ arrangements** die erforderlichen Anordnungen treffen; **to do what is** ~ alles Nötige tun; **to do no more than is** ~ nicht mehr tun, als unbedingt nötig ist. **(b)** *(unavoidable) conclusion, result* unausweichlich. **a ~ evil** ein notwendiges Übel.

2 *n* **(a)** *(col: what is needed)* **the** ~ das Notwendige; **will you do the ~?** wirst du das Nötige erledigen? **(b)** *(col: money)* **the** ~ das nötige Kleingeld.

necessitate [nɪ'sesɪteɪt] *vt* notwendig machen, erfordern *(form)*.

necessity [nɪ'sesɪtɪ] *n* **(a)** *no pl* Notwendigkeit *f*. **from** *or* **out of** ~ aus Not; **of** ~ notgedrungen; **it is a case of absolute** ~ es ist unbedingt notwendig; **in case of** ~ im Notfall. **(b)** *(necessary thing)* Notwendigkeit *f*. **the bare necessities (of life)** das Notwendigste (zum Leben).

neck [nek] **1** *n* Hals *m; (of dress etc)* Ausschnitt *m*. **to break one's** ~ sich *(dat)* das Genick brechen; **to risk one's** ~ Kopf und Kragen riskieren; **to save one's** ~ seinen Hals aus der Schlinge ziehen; **a stiff** ~ ein steifer Hals *or* Nacken; **to be up to one's ~ in work** bis über den Hals in der Arbeit stecken; **he's in it up to his** ~ *(col)* er steckt bis über den Hals drin; **to stick one's ~ out** seinen Kopf riskieren; **in this ~ of the woods** *(col)* in diesen Breiten; **it has a high** ~ *(dress etc)* es ist hochgeschlossen. **2** *vi (col)* knutschen *(col)*.

neck and neck *(lit, fig)* **1** *adj attr* Kopf-an-Kopf-. **2** *adv* Kopf an Kopf.

necklace ['neklɪs] *n* (Hals)kette *f*.

neck: ~line *n* Ausschnitt *m;* **~tie** *n (esp US)* Krawatte *f*, Schlips *m*.

nectar ['nektəʳ] *n (lit, fig)* Nektar *m*.

nectarine ['nektərɪn] *n (fruit)* Nektarine *f*.

née [neɪ] *adj* **Mrs Smith, ~ Jones** Frau Smith, geborene Jones.

need [niːd] **1** *n* **(a)** *no pl (necessity)* Notwendigkeit *f* *(for gen)*. **if ~ be** nötigenfalls; **in case of** ~ notfalls, im Notfall; **(there is) no ~ for sth** etw ist nicht nötig; **there is no ~ for sb to do sth** jd braucht etw nicht zu tun; **there's no ~ to get angry** du brauchst nicht gleich wütend zu werden; **to be (badly) in ~ of sth** *(person)* etw (dringend) brauchen; **to be in ~ of repair** reparaturbedürftig sein; **to have no ~ of sth** etw nicht brauchen; **to have no ~ to do sth** etw nicht zu tun brauchen.

(b) *no pl (misfortune, poverty)* Not *f*. **in time(s) of ~** in Zeiten der Not; **those in ~** die Notleidenden *pl*.

(c) *(requirement)* Bedürfnis *nt*. **the body's ~ for oxygen** das Sauerstoffbedürfnis des Körpers; **my ~s are few** ich stelle nur geringe Ansprüche.

2 *vt* **(a)** brauchen. **to ~ no introduction** keine spezielle Einführung brauchen; **much ~ed** dringend notwendig; **just what I ~ed** genau das richtige; **that's all I ~ed** *(iro)* das hat mir gerade noch gefehlt; **it ~s a coat of paint** es muß gestrichen werden; **a visa is ~ed to enter the USA** man braucht für die Einreise in die USA ein Visum; **it ~ed an accident to make him drive carefully** er mußte erst einen Unfall haben, bevor er vernünftig fuhr.

(b) sth ~s doing *or* **to be done** etw muß gemacht werden; **the book ~s careful reading** man muß das Buch genau lesen; **to ~ to do sth** *(have to)* etw tun müssen; **not to ~ to do sth** etw nicht zu tun brauchen; **he doesn't ~ to be told** man braucht es ihm nicht zu sagen; **she ~s to have everything explained to her** man muß ihr alles erklären.

3 *aux* **(a)** *(positive)* müssen. **~ he go?** muß er gehen?; **~ I say more?** mehr brauche ich ja wohl nicht zu sagen; **I ~ hardly say that ...** ich brauche wohl kaum zu erwähnen, daß ...; **you only ~ed (to) ask** du hättest nur (zu) fragen brauchen; **one ~ only look** ein Blick genügt.

(b) *(negative)* brauchen. **you ~n't wait** du brauchst nicht (zu) warten; **we ~n't have come** wir hätten gar nicht kommen brauchen; **I/you ~n't have bothered** das war nicht nötig.

(c) *(logical necessity)* **that ~n't be the case** das muß nicht unbedingt der Fall sein; **it ~ not follow that ...** daraus folgt nicht unbedingt, daß ...

needle ['ni:dl] **1** *n* Nadel *f*. **it's like looking for a ~ in a haystack** es ist, als ob man eine Stecknadel im Heuhaufen suchte; **to give sb the ~** *(col)* jdn reizen. **2** *vt (col: goad)* ärgern, piesacken *(col)*. **what's needling him?** was ist ihm über die Leber gelaufen? *(col)*.

needless ['ni:dlɪs] *adj* unnötig. **~ to say** natürlich; **~ to say, he didn't come** er kam natürlich nicht.

needlessly ['ni:dlɪslɪ] *adv* unnötig(erweise).

needlework ['ni:dlwɜ:k] *n* Handarbeit *f*.

needy ['ni:dɪ] **1** *adj (+er)* ärmlich, bedürftig. **2** *n* **the ~** die Bedürftigen *pl*.

negation [nɪ'geɪʃən] *n* Verneinung *f*.

negative ['negətɪv] **1** *adj* negativ; *answer* verneinend; *(Gram) form* verneint. **2** *n* **(a)** *(also Gram)* Verneinung *f*. **to answer in the ~** eine verneinende Antwort geben; *(refuse)* einen abschlägigen Bescheid geben; **his answer was a curt ~** er antwortete mit einem knappen Nein; **put this sentence into the ~** verneinen Sie diesen Satz. **(b)** *(Gram: word)* Negation *f; (Math)* negative Zahl. **(c)** *(Phot)* Negativ *nt*. **(d)** *(Elec)* negativer Pol.

neglect [nɪ'glekt] **1** *vt* vernachlässigen; *opportunity* versäumen; *advice* nicht befolgen. **to ~ to do sth** es versäumen, etw zu tun. **2** Vernachlässigung *f*; *(negligence)* Nachlässigkeit *f*. **~ of one's duties** Pflichtversäumnis *nt*; **to be in a state of ~** verwahrlost sein, völlig vernachlässigt sein; **the fire started through (his) ~** das Feuer ist durch seine Nachlässigkeit entstanden.

neglected [nɪ'glektɪd] *adj* vernachlässigt. **to feel ~** sich vernachlässigt fühlen.

neglectful [nɪ'glektfʊl] *adj* nachlässig; *father, government etc* pflichtvergessen. **to be ~ of sb/sth** jdn/etw vernachlässigen.

négligé(e) ['neglɪʒeɪ] *n* Negligé *nt*.

negligence ['neglɪdʒəns] *n (carelessness)* Nachlässigkeit *f*; *(causing danger, Jur)* Fahrlässigkeit *f*.

negligent ['neglɪdʒənt] *adj* **(a)** nachlässig; *(causing danger, damage)* fahrlässig. **both drivers were ~** beide Fahrer haben sich fahrlässig verhalten. **(b)** *(off-hand)* lässig.

negligible ['neglɪdʒəbl] *adj* unwesentlich; *quantity also* geringfügig.

negotiable [nɪ'gəʊʃɪəbl] *adj* **(a)** *(Comm) (can be sold)* verkäuflich; *(can be transferred)* übertragbar. **these terms are ~** über diese Bedingungen kann verhandelt werden. **(b)** *road* befahrbar; *river, mountain pass* passierbar; *obstacle, difficulty* überwindbar.

negotiate [nɪ'gəʊʃɪeɪt] **1** *vt* **(a)** verhandeln über *(+acc)*; *(bring about)* aushandeln. **(b)** *bend, (horse) fence* nehmen; *river, mountain* passieren; *obstacle* überwinden. **2** *vi* verhandeln *(for* über *+acc)*.

negotiation [nɪ,gəʊʃɪ'eɪʃən] *n* **(a)** *siehe vt (a)* Verhandlung *f*; Aushandlung *f*. **the matter is still under ~** über diese Sache wird noch verhandelt. **(b)** *usu pl (talks)* Verhandlung *f*. **to enter into ~s with sb** Verhandlungen mit jdm aufnehmen. **(c)** *(of river, mountain)* Passage *f*, Passieren *nt*; *(of obstacle)* Überwindung *f*.

negotiator [nɪ'gəʊʃɪeɪtə[r]] *n* Unterhändler(in *f*) *m*.

Negress ['ni:gres] *n* Negerin *f*.

Negro ['ni:grəʊ] **1** *adj* Neger-. **2** *n* Neger *m*.

neigh [neɪ] **1** *vi* wiehern. **2** *n* Wiehern *nt*.

neighbour, *(US)* **neighbor** ['neɪbə[r]] *n* Nachbar(in *f*) *m*; *(at table)* Tischnachbar(in *f*) *m*; *(Bibl etc)* Nächste(r) *mf*.

neighbourhood, *(US)* **neighborhood** ['neɪbəhʊd] *n (district)* Gegend *f*; *(people)* Nachbarschaft *f*. **in the ~ of sth** in der Nähe von etw.

neighbouring, *(US)* **neighboring** ['neɪbərɪŋ] *adj house(s), village* benachbart, Nachbar-; *fields, community* Nachbar-.

neighbourly, *(US)* **neighborly** ['neɪbəlɪ] *adj action, relations* gutnachbarlich. **they are ~ people** sie sind gute Nachbarn.

neither ['naɪðə[r]] **1** *adv* **~ ... nor** weder ... noch; **he ~ knows nor cares** er weiß es nicht und will es auch nicht wissen. **2** *conj* auch nicht. **if you don't go, ~ shall I** wenn du nicht gehst, gehe ich auch nicht; **I'm not going — ~ am I** ich gehe nicht — ich auch nicht; **he didn't do it (and) ~ did his sister** weder er noch seine Schwester haben es getan. **3** *adj* keine(r, s) (der beiden). **~ one of them** keiner von beiden. **4** *pron* keiner(r, s). **~ of them** keiner von beiden; **which one will you take? — ~** welches nehmen Sie? — keines (von beiden).

neo- ['ni:əʊ-] *pref* neo-, Neo-; **~classical** klassizistisch; **~fascist 1** *adj* neofaschistisch; **2** *n* Neofaschist(in *f*) *m*.

neolithic [,ni:əʊ'lɪθɪk] *adj* jungsteinzeitlich, neolithisch.

neologism [nɪ'ɒlədʒɪzəm] *n (Ling)* (Wort)neubildung *f*, Neologismus *m*.

neon ['ni:ɒn] *n (Chem)* Neon *nt*. **~ sign** *(name)* Neon- *or* Leuchtschild *nt*; *(advertisement)* Leuchtreklame *f no pl*.

nephew ['nevju:, 'nefju:] *n* Neffe *m*.

nepotism ['nepətizəm] *n* Vetternwirtschaft *f*.

nerve [nɜ:v] **1** *n* **(a)** *(Anat)* Nerv *m*. **to suffer from ~s** nervös sein; **to have an attack of ~s** in Panik geraten, durchdrehen *(col)*; **his ~s are bad** er hat schlechte Nerven; **to get on sb's ~s** *(col)* jdm auf die Nerven gehen; **to have ~s of steel** Nerven wie Drahtseile haben. **(b)** *no pl (courage)* Mut *m*. **to lose/keep one's ~** die Nerven verlieren/nicht verlieren; **to have the ~ to do sth** sich trauen, etw zu tun; **a test of ~** eine Nervenprobe. **(c)** *no pl (col: impudence)* Frechheit, Unverschämtheit *f.* **to have the ~ to do sth** die Frechheit besitzen, etw zu tun; **he's got a ~!** der hat Nerven! *(col).*

2 *vtr* **to ~ oneself for sth/to do sth** sich seelisch und moralisch auf etw *(acc)* vorbereiten/darauf vorbereiten, etw zu tun.

nerve-racking ['nɜːvrækɪŋ] *adj* nervenaufreibend.

nervous ['nɜvəs] *adj* **(a)** *(Anat) exhaustion, reflex* nervös. **~ tension** Nervenanspannung *f.* **(b)** *(apprehensive)* nervös; *(overexcited, tense also)* aufgeregt. **to feel ~** nervös sein; **I am ~ about the exam/him** mir ist bange vor dem Examen/um ihn; **I am rather ~ about diving** ich habe einen zeimlichen Bammel vor dem Tauchen *(col).*

nervous *in cpds* Nerven-; **~ breakdown** *n* Nervenzusammenbruch *m;* **~ energy** *n* Vitalität *f.*

nervously ['nɜːvəslɪ] *adv* nervös; *(excitedly also)* aufgeregt.

nervous wreck *n (col)* **to be/look/feel a ~** mit den Nerven völlig am Ende sein.

nervy ['nɜːvɪ] *adj (+er)* **(a)** *(Brit: tense)* nervös. **(b)** *(US col: cheeky)* frech.

nest [nest] **1** *n* Nest *nt.* **to leave the ~** *(lit, fig)* das Nest verlassen; **a ~ of tables** ein Satz *m* Tische. **2** *vi* nisten.

nesting-box ['nestɪŋbɒks] *n* Nistkasten *m.*

nestle ['nesl] *vi* **to ~ down in bed** sich ins Bett kuscheln; **to ~ up to sb** sich an jdn kuscheln; **the village nestling in the hills** das Dorf, das zwischen den Bergen eingebettet liegt.

nestling ['neslɪŋ] *n* Nestling *m.*

net[1] [net] **1** *n* *(lit, fig)* Netz *nt.* **to be caught in the ~** *(fig)* in die Falle gehen. **2** *vt* *fish, butterfly* mit dem Netz fangen; *(fig) criminal* fangen.

net[2] **1** *adj* **(a)** *price, income, weight* netto, Netto-. **~ profit** Reingewinn *m;* **it costs £15 ~** es kostet £ 15 netto. **(b)** *(fig) result* End-, letztendlich. **2** *vt* netto einnehmen; *(in wages, salary)* netto verdienen; *(deal etc)* einbringen.

net: ~ball *n (Brit)* Korbball *m;* **~ curtain** *n* Tüllgardine *f*, Store *m.*

Netherlands ['neðələndz] *npl* **the ~** die Niederlande *pl.*

netting ['netɪŋ] *n* Netz *nt; (wire ~)* Maschendraht *m.*

nettle ['netl] **1** *n (Bot)* Nessel *f.* **2** *vt (fig col) person* wurmen *(col)*, fuchsen *(col).*

network ['netwɜːk] *n* **(a)** *(lit, fig)* Netz *nt.* **(b)** *(Rad, TV)* Sendenetz *nt; (Elec)* Netzwerk *nt.*

neuralgia [njʊə'rældʒə] *n* Neuralgie *f*, Nervenschmerzen *pl.*

neurosis [njʊə'rəʊsɪs] *n, pl* **neuroses** [njʊə'rəʊsiːz] Neurose *f.*

neurotic [njʊə'rɒtɪk] **1** *adj* neurotisch. **to be ~ about sth** *(col)* in bezug auf etw *(acc)* neurotisch sein. **2** *n* Neurotiker(in *f*) *m.*

neuter ['njuːtə[r]] **1** *adj* **(a)** *(Gram)* sächlich. **(b)** *animal, person* geschlechtslos; *(castrated)* kastriert; *plant* ungeschlechtlich. **2** *n* **(a)** *(Gram)* Neutrum *nt.* **(b)** *(animal)* geschlechtloses Wesen; *(castrated)* kastriertes Tier. **3** *vt cat, dog* kastrieren; *female* sterilisieren.

neutral ['njuːtrəl] **1** *adj* neutral. **2** *n (Aut)* Leerlauf *m.* **to be in ~** im Leerlauf sein.

neutrality [njuː'trælɪtɪ] *n* Neutralität *f.*

neutralize ['njuːtrəlaɪz] *vt* neutralisieren; *(fig)* ausgleichen.

neutron ['njuːtrɒn] *n* Neutron *nt.*

neutron bomb *n* Neutronenbombe *f.*

never ['nevə[r]] *adv* **(a)** nie. **I have ~ seen him** ich habe ihn (noch) nie gesehen; **~ again** nie wieder; **I'll ~ try that again** das werde ich nicht noch einmal versuchen; **~ before** noch nie; **I have ~ seen him before** ich habe ihn noch nie gesehen; **~ before have men climbed this peak** nie zuvor haben Menschen diesen Gipfel erklommen; **~ even** nicht einmal; **~ ever** gar nie; **I have ~ ever been so insulted** ich bin noch nie so beleidigt worden.

(b) *(emph: not)* **that will ~ do!** das geht ganz und gar nicht!; **he ~ so much as smiled** er hat nicht einmal gelächelt; **he said ~ a word** er hat kein einziges Wort gesagt; **you've ~ left it behind!** *(col)* du hast es doch wohl nicht etwa liegenlassen! *(col)*; **would you do it again? — ~!** würdest du das noch einmal machen? — bestimmt nicht; **Spurs were beaten — ~!** *(col)* Spurs sind geschlagen worden — das ist doch nicht möglich!; **well I ~ (did)!** *(col)* nein, so was!

never: ~-ending *adj* endlos; **~-never** *n (Brit col)*: **on the ~-never** auf Pump *(col).*

nevertheless [ˌnevəðə'les] *adv* trotzdem, dennoch.

new [njuː] *adj (+er)* neu. **~ moon** Neumond *m;* **there's a ~ moon tonight** heute nacht ist Neumond; **that's nothing ~** das ist nichts Neues; **that's something ~!** das ist wirklich ganz was Neues!; **what's ~?** *(col)* was gibt's Neues? *(col)*; **dressed in ~ clothes** neu eingekleidet; **to make sth (look) like ~** etw wie neu machen; **as ~** wie neu; **this system is ~ to me** dieses System ist mir neu; **he is a ~ man** *(fig)* er ist ein neuer Mensch; **that's a ~ one on me** *(col)* das ist mir ja ganz neu; **a ~ kind of engine** ein neuartiger Motor; **I'm quite ~ to this job** ich bin neu in dieser Stelle; **I am ~ to this place** ich bin erst seit kurzem hier.

new: ~-born *adj* neugeboren; **~comer** *n* Neuankömmling *m; (in job, subject etc)* Neuling *m (to* in *+dat).*

new-fangled ['njuːˌfæŋgld] *adj* neumodisch.

new-laid ['njuːleɪd] *adj* frisch.

newly ['njuːlɪ] *adv* frisch. **~-made** ganz neu; *bread, cake etc* frisch gebacken.

newlyweds ['njuːlɪwedz] *npl (col)* Frischvermählte *pl.*

newness ['njuːnɪs] *n* Neuheit *f.*

news [njuːz] *n no pl* **(a)** *(report, information)* Nachricht *f; (recent development)* Neuigkeit(en *pl*) *f.* **a piece of ~** eine Neuigkeit; **I have ~/no ~ of him** ich weiß Neues/nichts Neues von ihm; **there is no ~** es gibt nichts Neues; **have you heard the ~?** haben Sie schon das Neueste gehört?; **is there any ~?** gibt es etwas Neues?; **I have ~ for you** *(iro)* ich habe eine Überraschung für dich; **bad/good ~** schlechte/gute Nachricht(en); **that is good ~** das sind ja gute Nachrichten; **who will break the ~ to him?** wer wird es ihm beibringen?; **that is ~ to me!** das ist (mir) ganz neu!

(b) *(Press, Film, Rad, TV)* Nachrichten *pl.* **it was on the ~** das kam in den Nachrichten; **to be in the ~** von sich reden machen.

news: ~ agent *n (Brit)* Zeitungshändler *m;* **~cast** *n* Nachrichtensendung *f;* **~caster** *n* Nachrichtensprecher(in *f*) *m;* **~ dealer** *n (US)* Zeitungshändler *m;* **~ editor** *n* Nachrichtenredakteur *m;* **~flash** *n* Kurzmeldung *f;* **~letter** *n* Mitteilungsblatt *nt.*

newspaper ['njuːzˌpeɪpə[r]] *n* Zeitung *f.* **daily/weekly ~** Tageszeitung/Wochenzeitung.

newspaper: ~ article *n* Zeitungsartikel *m;* **~ man** *n* Zeitungsverkäufer *m; (journalist)* Journalist *m;* **~ report** *n* Zeitungsbericht *m.*

news: ~print *n* Zeitungspapier *nt;* **~reader** *n* Nachrichtensprecher(in *f*) *m;* **~reel** *n* Wochenschau *f;* **~room** *n (of newspaper)* Nachrichtenredaktion *f; (TV, Rad)* Nachrichtenstudio *nt;* **~stand** *n* Zeitungsstand *m;* **~worthy** *adj* sensationell; **to be ~ worthy** Neuigkeitswert haben.

newsy ['njuːzɪ] *adj (+er) (col)* voller Neuigkeiten.

newt [njuːt] *n* Wassermolch *m.*

new: N~ Testament 1 *n* **the N~ Testament** das Neue Testament; **2** *adj attr* des Neuen Testaments; **N~ World** *n* Neue Welt.

New Year *n* neues Jahr; *(~'s Day)* Neujahr *nt.* **to see in the ~** das neue Jahr begrüßen; **Happy ~!** (ein) gutes neues Jahr!; **~'s Day,** *(US also)* **~'s** Neujahr *nt;* **~'s Eve** Silvester *nt;* **~ resolution** (guter) Vorsatz für das neue Jahr.

New: ~ Zealand 1 *n* Neuseeland *nt;* **2** *adj attr* neuseeländisch; **~ Zealander** *n* Neuseeländer(in *f*) *m.*

next [nekst] **1** *adj* nächste(r, s). **come back ~ week/Tuesday** kommen Sie nächste Woche/nächsten Dienstag wieder; **he came back the ~ day/week** er kam am nächsten Tag/in der nächsten Woche wieder; **(the) ~ time I see him** wenn ich ihn das nächste Mal sehe; **the ~ time I saw him** als ich ihn das nächste Mal sah; **(the) ~ moment he was gone** im nächsten Moment war er weg; **from one moment to the ~** von einem Augenblick auf den anderen; **this time ~ week** nächste Woche um diese Zeit; **the year/week after ~** übernächstes Jahr/übernächste Woche; **the ~ day but one** der übernächste Tag; **who's ~?** wer ist der nächste?; **you're ~** Sie sind dran *(col) or* an der Reihe; **~ please!** der nächste bitte!; **the ~ but one** der/die/das übernächste; **the ~ best** der/die/das nächstbeste.

2 *adv* **(a)** *(the ~ time)* das nächste Mal; *(afterwards)* danach. **what shall we do ~?** was sollen wir als nächstes machen?; **whatever ~?** *(in surprise)* Sachen gibt's! *(col)*; *(despairingly)* wo soll das nur hinführen? **(b) ~ to sb/sth** neben jdm/etw; *(with motion)* neben jdn/etw; **the ~ to last row** die vorletzte Reihe; **he was ~ to last** er war der vorletzte; **the ~ to bottom shelf** das vorletzte Brett; **~ to the skin** (direkt) auf der Haut; **~ to nothing** so gut wie nichts; **~ to impossible** nahezu unmöglich.

next-door ['neks'dɔːʳ] **1** *adv* nebenan. **they live ~ to us** sie wohnen (direkt) neben uns; **the boy ~** der Junge von nebenan. **2** *adj* **the ~ neighbour/house** der Nachbar/die Nachbarin von nebenan/das Nebenhaus; **we are ~ neighbours** wir wohnen Tür an Tür.

NHS *(Brit)* = **National Health Service.**

nib [nɪb] *n* Feder *f.*

nibble ['nɪbl] **1** *vti* **to ~ (at) sth** an etw *(dat)* knabbern. **2** *vi (fig)* sich interessiert zeigen.

nice [naɪs] *adj (+er)* **(a)** nett; *voice also* sympathisch; *(~-looking) girl, dress, looks etc also* hübsch; *taste, smell, meal* gut; *warmth, weather, feeling, car* schön; *(skilful) workmanship, work* gut, schön. **be ~ to him** sei nett zu ihm; **that's not ~!** das ist aber nicht nett; **to have a ~ time** sich gut amüsieren; **I had a ~ rest** ich habe mich gut *or* schön ausgeruht; **how ~ of you to ...** wie nett von Ihnen, zu ...

(b) *(intensifier)* schön. **a ~ long holiday** schön lange Ferien; **~ and warm/near** schön warm/nahe; **~ and easy** ganz leicht.

(c) *(respectable)* nett; *district* fein; *words* schön; *manners* gut.

(d) *(iro)* schön, sauber. **here's a ~ state of affairs!** das sind ja schöne Zustände!; **you're in a ~ mess** du sitzt schön im Schlamassel *(col).*

(e) *(subtle) distinction* fein, genau. **that was a ~ point** das war eine gute Bemerkung; **one or two ~ points** ein paar gute Gedanken.

nice-looking ['naɪs'lʊkɪŋ] *adj* gutaussehend; *girl also* hübsch. **to be ~** gut aussehen.

nicely ['naɪslɪ] *adv (pleasantly)* nett; *(well) go, speak, behave, placed* gut. **to go ~** wie geschmiert laufen *(col)*; **that will do ~** das reicht vollauf; **how's it going? — ~, thank you** wie geht es so? — danke, ganz gut; **he's getting on ~** ihm geht's ganz gut.

nicety ['naɪsɪtɪ] *n* **(a)** *(subtlety)* Feinheit *f; (of judgement also)* Schärfe *f; (precision)* (peinliche) Genauigkeit. **(b) niceties** *pl* Feinheiten *pl.*

niche [niːʃ] *n (Archit)* Nische *f; (fig)* Plätzchen *nt.*

nick[1] [nɪk] **1** *n* **(a)** Kerbe *f.* **I got a little ~ on my chin** ich habe mich leicht am Kinn geschnitten. **(b) in the ~ of time** gerade noch (rechtzeitig). **(c)** *(Brit col: condition)* **in good/bad ~** gut/nicht gut in Schuß *(col).* **2** *vt* **(a)** *stick* einkerben. **to ~ oneself** *(col)* sich schneiden. **(b)** *(bullet) person, wall* streifen.

nick[2] *(Brit)* **1** *vt (col)* **(a)** *(arrest)* einsperren *(col)*; *(catch)* schnappen *(col).* **he got ~ed** den haben sie sich *(dat)* geschnappt *(col).* **(b)** *(steal)* klauen *(col).* **2** *n (prison)* Knast *m (col)*; *(police station)* Wache *f.*

nickel ['nɪkl] *n* **(a)** *(metal)* Nickel *nt.* **(b)** *(US)* Fünfcentstück *nt.*

nickname ['nɪkneɪm] **1** *n* Spitzname *m.* **2** *vt person* taufen.

nicotine ['nɪkətiːn] *n* Nikotin *nt.*

niece [niːs] *n* Nichte *f.*

nifty ['nɪftɪ] *adj (+er) (col)* flott *(col)*; *gadget, tool* schlau *(col).*

Nigeria [naɪ'dʒɪərɪə] *n* Nigeria *nt.*

niggardly ['nɪgədlɪ] *adj person* knaus(e)rig; *amount, portion also* kümmerlich.

nigger ['nɪgəʳ] *n (pej)* Nigger *m (pej col).*

niggle ['nɪgl] **1** *vi (complain)* herumkritisieren *(about* an *+dat).* **2** *vt (worry)* plagen, zu schaffen machen *(+dat).*

niggling ['nɪglɪŋ] *adj person* überkritisch; *doubt, pain* quälend; *detail* pingelig *(col).*

night [naɪt] *n* Nacht *f; (evening)* Abend *m.* **I saw him last ~** ich habe ihn gestern abend gesehen; **I'll see him tomorrow ~** ich treffe ihn morgen abend; **on Friday ~** Freitag abend/nacht; **on the ~ of (Saturday) the 11th** am (Samstag, dem) 11. nachts; **11/6 o'clock at ~** 11 Uhr nachts/6 Uhr abends; **to travel/see Paris by ~** nachts reisen/Paris bei Nacht sehen; **far into the ~** bis spät in die Nacht; **in/during the ~** in/während der Nacht; **the ~ before last they were ...** vorgestern abend/vorletzte Nacht waren sie ...; **to spend the ~ at a hotel** in einem Hotel übernachten; **I need a good ~'s sleep** ich muß mal wieder ordentlich schlafen; **~ after ~** jede Nacht; **all ~ (long)** die ganze Nacht; **to have a ~ out** (abends) ausgehen; **to have a late/an early ~** spät/früh ins Bett kommen, spät/früh schlafen gehen; **to work ~s** nachts arbeiten; **~ is falling** die Nacht bricht herein; **the last three ~s of Hamlet** die letzten drei Abende von „Hamlet".

night *in cpds* Nacht-; **~-bird** *n* Nachtvogel *m; (fig)* Nachteule *f (col)*, Nachtschwärmer *m (col)*; **~cap** *n* **(a)** *(garment)* Schlafmütze *f;* **(b)** *(drink)* Schlaftrunk *m;* **~-club** *n* Nachtklub *m;* **~dress** *n (Brit)* Nachthemd *nt;* **~fall** *n* Einbruch *m* der Dunkelheit; **~gown** *n* Nachthemd *nt.*

nightie ['naɪtɪ] *n (Brit: col)* Nachthemd *nt.*

nightingale ['naɪtɪŋgeɪl] *n* Nachtigall *f.*

nightly ['naɪtlɪ] **1** *adj (every night)* (all)nächtlich, Nacht-; *(every evening)* (all)abendlich, Abend-. **2** *adv* jede Nacht/jeden Abend. **twice ~** zweimal pro Abend.

night: ~mare *n (lit, fig)* Alptraum *m;* **~owl** *n (col)* Nachteule *f (col)*; **~safe** *n* Nachtsafe *m;* **~school** *n* Abendschule *f;* **~-shift** *n* Nachtschicht *f;* **to be on ~-shift** Nachtschicht haben *or* arbeiten; **~-spot** *n* Nachtlokal *nt;* **~stick** *n (US)* Schlagstock *m;* **~-time** *n* Nacht *f;* **at ~-time** nachts; **~-watchman** *n* Nachtwächter *m.*

nihilism ['naɪɪlɪzəm] *n* Nihilismus *m.*

nil [nɪl] *n* null *(also Sport)*; *(nothing)* nichts. **the score was one-~** es stand eins zu null.

nimble ['nɪmbl] *adj (+er) fingers* flink; *(agile)* gelenkig, beweglich; *(skilful)* geschickt; *mind* beweglich.

nimbly ['nɪmblɪ] *adv work* flink; *dance* leicht(füßig).

nine [naɪn] **1** *adj* neun. **~ times out of ten** so gut wie immer. **2** *n* Neun *f.* **dressed up to the ~s** in Schale *(col)*; *see* **six.**

nineteen ['naɪn'tiːn] *adj* neunzehn. **she talks ~ to the dozen** sie redet wie ein Wasserfall *(col)*.

nineteenth ['naɪn'tiːnθ] *adj* neunzehnte(r, s); *see* **sixteenth.**

ninety ['naɪntɪ] **1** *adj* neunzig. **2** *n* Neunzig *f*; *see* **sixty.**

ninth [naɪnθ] **1** *adj* neunte(r, s). **2** *n (as fraction)* Neuntel *nt*; *(of series)* Neunte(r, s); *see* **sixth.**

nip[1] [nɪp] **1** *n (pinch)* Kniff *m; (bite from animal etc)* Biß *m*. **there's a ~ in the air today** es ist heute ganz schön frisch. **2** *vt* **(a)** *(bite)* zwicken; *(pinch also)* kneifen; *bud, shoot* abknipsen. **to ~ sth in the bud** *(fig)* etw im Keim ersticken. **(b)** *(cold, frost etc) plants* angreifen. **the cold air ~ped our faces** die Kälte schnitt uns ins Gesicht. **3** *vi (Brit col)* sausen *(col)*, flitzen *(col)*. **to ~ up(stairs)/down(stairs)** hoch-/runtersausen *(col)*; **I'll just ~ down to the shops** ich gehe mal kurz einkaufen *(col)*; **I'll just ~ out for a moment** ich gehe nur mal kurz raus.

nip[2] *n (col: drink)* Schlückchen *nt*.

nipple ['nɪpl] *n (Anat)* Brustwarze *f; (on baby's bottle)* Sauger *m*.

nippy ['nɪpɪ] *adj (+er)* **(a)** *(Brit col)* flink, flott; *car* spritzig. **(b)** *weather* frisch.

nit [nɪt] *n* **(a)** *(Zool)* Nisse *f*. **(b)** *(Brit col)* Dummkopf, Blödmann *(col) m*.

nit-picking ['nɪtpɪkɪŋ] *adj (col)* pingelig *(col)*.

nitrogen ['naɪtrədʒən] *n* Stickstoff *m*.

nitroglycerin(e) ['naɪtrəʊ'glɪsəriːn] *n* Nitroglyzerin *nt*.

nitty-gritty ['nɪtɪ'grɪtɪ] *n (col)* **to get down to the ~** zur Sache kommen.

nitwit ['nɪtwɪt] *n (col)* Dummkopf *m*.

No, no = number Nr.

no [nəʊ] **1** *adv* **(a)** *(negative)* nein. **oh ~!** o nein!; **to answer ~** *(to question)* mit Nein antworten; *(to request)* nein sagen; **she can't say ~** sie kann nicht nein sagen. **(b)** *(with comp)* nicht. **I can bear it ~ longer** ich kann es nicht länger ertragen; **I have ~ more money** ich habe kein Geld mehr; **~ fewer than 100** bestimmt 100; **~ later than Monday** spätestens Montag.

2 *adj* kein. **~ one person could do it** keiner könnte das allein tun; **~ two men are alike** zwei Menschen sind immer verschieden; **~ other man** kein anderer; **it's of ~ interest/importance** das ist belanglos/unwichtig; **it's ~ use** *or* **good** das hat keinen Zweck; **~ parking/smoking** Parken/Rauchen verboten; **there's ~ telling what he'll do next** man kann nie wissen, was er als nächstes tun wird; **there's ~ denying it** es läßt sich nicht leugnen; **she's ~ beauty** sie ist nicht gerade eine Schönheit; **I'm ~ expert, but ...** ich bin zwar kein Fachmann, aber ...; **in ~ time** im Nu; **it's ~ small matter** das ist keine Kleinigkeit; **theirs is ~ easy task** sie haben keine leichte Aufgabe; **there is ~ such thing** so etwas gibt es nicht; **it was/we did ~ such thing!** das stimmt überhaupt nicht!

3 *n, pl* **-es** Nein *nt; (~ vote)* Neinstimme *f*. **I won't take ~ for an answer** ich bestehe darauf.

nobble ['nɒbl] *vt (Brit col)* **(a)** *horse* lahmlegen *(col)*. **(b)** *(catch)* sich *(dat)* schnappen *(col)*. **(c)** *(obtain dishonestly) votes etc* sich *(dat)* kaufen; *money* einsacken *(col)*.

Nobel prize ['nəʊbel'praɪz] *n* Nobelpreis *m*.

nobility [nəʊ'bɪlɪtɪ] *n no pl* (Hoch)adel *m*. **she is one of the ~** sie ist eine Adlige.

noble ['nəʊbl] **1** *adj (+er)* **(a)** *person, rank* adlig. **to be of ~ birth** adlig sein. **(b)** *(fine) person, deed etc* edel, nobel; *appearance* vornehm. **(c)** *(col: selfless)* edel, edelmütig. **2** *n* Adlige(r) *mf*.

nobleman ['nəʊblmən] *n, pl* **-men** [-mən] Adlige(r) *m*.

noblewoman ['nəʊblwʊmən] *n, pl* **-women** [-wɪmɪn] Adlige *f*.

nobly ['nəʊblɪ] *adv (aristocratically)* vornehm; *(finely)* edel; *(bravely)* wacker; *(col: selflessly)* nobel, edel(mütig).

nobody ['nəʊbədɪ] **1** *pron* niemand, keiner. **~ knows better than I** niemand *or* keiner weiß besser als ich; **there was ~ else** da war sonst niemand; **~ else could have done it** es kann niemand anders gewesen sein. **2** *n* Niemand *m no pl* **he's a ~** er ist ein Niemand.

nocturnal [nɒk'tɜːnl] *adj* nächtlich; *animal, bird* Nacht-.

nocturne ['nɒktɜːn] *n (Mus)* Nokturne *f*.

nod [nɒd] **1** *n* Nicken *nt*. **to give sb a ~** jdm zunicken; **to answer with a ~** (zustimmend) nicken. **2** *vi* nicken. **to ~ to sb** jdm zunicken; **to ~ in agreement** zustimmend nicken. **3** *vt* **to ~ one's head** mit dem Kopf nicken.

♦ **nod off** *vi* einnicken *(col)*.

node [nəʊd] *n (all senses)* Knoten *m*.

no-go area ['nəʊ'gəʊ,ɛərɪə] *n* Sperrgebiet *nt*.

noise [nɔɪz] *n* Geräusch *nt; (loud, irritating sound)* Lärm, Krach *m; (Elec: interference)* Rauschen *nt*. **what was that ~?** was war das für ein Geräusch?; **the ~ of the traffic/bells** der Straßenlärm/der Lärm der Glocken; **it made a lot of ~** es hat viel Krach gemacht; **don't make a ~!** sei leise!; **stop that ~** hör mit dem Lärm auf; **she made ~s about leaving early** sie wollte unbedingt früh gehen; **a big ~** *(fig col)* ein großes Tier *(col)*.

noiseless ['nɔɪzlɪs] *adj* geräuschlos; *step also* lautlos.

noisily ['nɔɪzɪlɪ] *adv see adj.*

noisy ['nɔɪzɪ] *adj (+er)* laut; *protest, debate* lautstark. **don't be so ~** sei nicht so laut, mach nicht so viel Lärm.

nomad ['nəʊmæd] *n* Nomade *m*, Nomadin *f*.

nomadic [nəʊ'mædɪk] *adj* nomadisch; *tribe* Nomaden-.

no-man's-land ['nəʊmænzlænd] *n (lit, fig)* Niemandsland *nt*.

nom de plume ['nɒmdə'pluːm] *n* Pseudonym *nt*.

nomenclature [nəʊ'menklətʃə[r]] *n* Nomenklatur *f*.

nominal ['nɒmɪnl] *adj* nominell.

nominate ['nɒmɪneɪt] *vt (appoint)* ernennen; *(propose)* nominieren, (als Kandidat) aufstellen. **he was ~d chairman** er wurde zum Vorsitzenden ernannt.

nomination [,nɒmɪ'neɪʃən] *n (appointment)* Ernennung *f; (proposal)* Nominierung *f*.

nominative [,nɒmɪnətɪv] *(Gram)* **1** *n* Nominativ, Werfall *m*. **2** *adj* **(the) ~ case** der Nominativ.

nominee [,nɒmɪ'niː] *n* Kandidat(in *f*) *m*.

non: ~-aggression *n* Nichtangriff *m*; **~-aggression pact** *n* Nichtangriffspakt *m*; **~ alcoholic** *adj* alkoholfrei; **~-aligned** *adj* bündnisfrei; **~-believer** *n* Nichtgläubige(r) *mf*.

nonchalance ['nɒnʃələns] *n* Lässigkeit, Nonchalance *f*.

nonchalant ['nɒnʃələnt] *adj* lässig, nonchalant.

non: ~-combatant 1 *n* Nichtkämpfer *m*; **2** *adj* nicht am Kampf beteiligt; **~-commisssioned officer** *n* Unteroffizier *m*; **~-committal** *adj* zurückhaltend; *answer also* unverbindlich; **to be ~-committal about whether ...** sich nicht festlegen, ob ...; **~conformist 1** *n* Nonkonformist(in *f*) *m*; **2** *adj* nonkonformistisch; **~-co-operation** *n* unkooperative Haltung.

nondescript ['nɒndɪskrɪpt] *adj taste, colour* unbestimmbar; *person, appearance* unauffällig, unscheinbar *(pej)*.

none [nʌn] **1** *pron* keine(r, s); keine; *(on form)* keine. **~ of them is coming** von ihnen kommt keiner; **~ of the boys/them** keiner der Jungen/von ihnen; **~ of this** nichts davon; **~ of this is any good** das ist alles nicht gut; **do you have any bread/apples? — ~ (at all)** haben Sie Brot/Äpfel?— nein, gar keines/keine; **there is ~**

left es ist nichts übrig; **their guest was ~ other than ...** ihr Gast war kein anderer als ...; **(we'll have) ~ of that!** jetzt reicht's aber!; **he would have ~ of it** er wollte davon nichts wissen.

2 *adv* **to be ~ the wiser** auch nicht schlauer sein; **it's ~ too warm** es ist nicht zu warm; **he's ~ the worse for the experience** die Erfahrung hat ihm nichts geschadet; **and ~ too soon either** und auch keineswegs zu früh.

nonentity [nɒ'nentɪtɪ] *n* unbedeutende Figur.

non-essential [nɒnɪ'senʃəl] **1** *adj* unnötig; *workers* nicht unbedingt nötig; *services* nicht lebenswichtig. **2** *n* **~s** *pl* nicht (lebens)notwendige Dinge *pl.*

nonetheless [ˌnʌnðə'les] *adv* nichtsdestoweniger, trotzdem.

non: ~-event *n (col)* Reinfall *m (col)*, Pleite *f (col)*; **~-existence** *n* Nichtvorhandensein *nt;* **~-existent** *adj* nicht vorhanden; **his accent is practically ~-existent** er hat praktisch keinen Akzent; **~-fattening** *adj* nicht dickmachend *attr;* **~-fiction** *n* Sachbücher *pl;* **~-flammable** *adj* nichtentzündbar *attr,* nicht entzündbar; **~-intervention** *n (Pol etc)* Nichteinmischung *f (in* in *+acc)*; **~-iron** *adj* bügelfrei; **~-member** *n* Nichtmitglied *nt;* **open to ~-members** Gäste willkommen; **~-payment** *n* Nichtzahlung *f.*

nonplus ['nɒn'plʌs] *vt* verblüffen.

non: ~-productive *adj meeting, discussion etc* unergiebig; **~-productive industries** Dienstleistungssektor *m;* **~-productive worker** Angestellte(r) *mf* im Dienstleistungssektor; **~-profit** *(US)*, **~-profit-making** *adj* keinen Gewinn anstrebend *attr; charity etc also* gemeinnützig; **~-resident 1** *adj* nicht ansässig; *(in hotel)* nicht im Hause wohnend; **2** *n* Nicht(orts)ansässige(r) *mf; (in hotel)* nicht im Haus wohnender Gast; **open to ~-residents** auch für Nichthotelgäste.

nonsense ['nɒnsəns] *n no pl (also as interjection)* Unsinn, Quatsch *(col) m*; *(verbal also)* dummes Zeug; *(silly behaviour)* Dummheiten *pl.* **a piece of ~** ein Unsinn *or* Quatsch *(col) m;* **that's a lot of ~!** das ist (ja) alles dummes Zeug!; **I've had enough of this ~** jetzt reicht's mir aber; **to make (a) ~ of sth** etw unsinnig *or* sinnlos machen; **no more of your ~!** Schluß mit dem Unsinn!; **he will stand no ~ from anybody** er läßt nicht mit sich spaßen.

nonsensical [nɒn'sensɪkəl] *adj* unsinnig.

non: ~-shrink *adj* nicht einlaufend; **~-skid** *adj* rutschsicher; **~-slip** *adj* rutschfest; **~-smoker** *n* **(a)** *(person)* Nichtraucher(in *f*) *m;* **(b)** *(Rail)* Nichtraucher(abteil *nt*) *m;* **~-smoking** *adj area* Nichtraucher-; **~-starter** *n (fig: person, idea)* Blindgänger *m;* **~-stick** *adj pan, surface* kunststoffbeschichtet, Teflon- ®; **~-stop 1** *adj train* durchgehend; *journey* ohne Unterbrechung; *flight, performances* Nonstop-; **2** *adv talk* ununterbrochen; *fly* nonstop; *travel* ohne Unterbrechung; **~-violent** *adj* gewaltlos; **~-white 1** *n* Farbige(r) *mf;* **2** *adj* farbig; *area* für Farbige.

noodle ['nu:dl] *n (Cook)* Nudel *f.*

nook [nʊk] *n* Winkel *m.* **in every ~ and cranny** in jedem Winkel.

noon [nu:n] *n* Mittag *m.* **at ~** um 12 Uhr mittags.

no-one ['nəʊwʌn] *pron* = **nobody 1.**

noose [nu:s] *n* Schlinge *f.* **to put one's head in the ~** *(fig)* den Kopf in die Schlinge stecken.

nor [nɔ:ʳ] *conj* **(a)** noch. **neither ... ~** weder ... noch. **(b)** *(and not)* und ... auch nicht. **I don't like him — ~ do I** ich mag ihn nicht — ich auch nicht.

norm ['nɔ:m] *n* Norm *f.*

normal ['nɔ:məl] **1** *adj person, situation* normal; *practice, routine also, (customary)* üblich. **it's a perfectly ~ thing** das ist völlig normal; **he is not his ~ self today** er ist heute so anders. **2** *n no pl (of temperature)* Normalwert. **temperatures below ~** Temperaturen unter dem Durchschnitt; **her temperature is above/below ~** sie hat erhöhte Temperatur/sie hat Untertemperatur; **when things are back to ~** wenn sich alles wieder normalisiert hat.

normality [nɔ:'mælɪtɪ] *n* Normalität *f.* **to return to ~** sich wieder normalisieren.

normalize ['nɔ:məlaɪz] *vt* normalisieren; *relations* wiederherstellen.

normally ['nɔ:məlɪ] *adv (usually)* normalerweise, gewöhnlich; *(in normal way)* normal.

north [nɔ:θ] **1** *n* Norden *m.* **in/from the ~** im/aus dem Norden; **to live in the ~** im Norden leben; **to the ~ of** nördlich von, im Norden von; **to veer/go to the ~** in nördliche Richtung *or* nach Norden drehen/gehen; **to face (the) ~** nach Norden liegen; **the N~ (of Scotland/England) Nordschottland/Nordengland** *nt.* **2** *adj attr* Nord-. **3** *adv (towards N~)* nach Norden. **~ of** nördlich *or* im Norden von.

north *in cpds* Nord-; **N~ America** *n* Nordamerika *nt;* **N~ American 1** *adj* nordamerikanisch; **2** *n* Nordamerikaner(in *f*) *m.*

north: ~bound *adj carriageway* nach Norden (führend); *traffic* in Richtung Norden; **~-east 1** *adj* Nordost-, nordöstlich; **2** *adv* nach Nordosten; **~-east of** nordöstlich von; **~-easterly** *adj* nordöstlich; **~-eastern** *adj* nordöstlich.

northerly ['nɔ:ðəlɪ] *adj wind, direction, latitude* nördlich.

northern ['nɔ:ðən] *adj hemisphere, counties* nördlich; *Germany, Italy etc* Nord-. **N~ Ireland** Nordirland *nt;* **with a ~ outlook** mit Blick nach Norden.

northerner ['nɔ:ðənəʳ] *n* **(a)** Bewohner(in *f*) *m* des Nordens; Nordengländer(in *f*) *m*/-deutsche(r) *mf etc.* **he is a ~** er kommt aus dem Norden des Landes. **(b)** *(US)* Nordstaatler(in *f*) *m.*

northernmost ['nɔ:ðənməʊst] *adj* nördlichste(r, s).

north: N~ Pole *n* Nordpol *m;* **N~ Sea 1** *n* Nordsee *f;* **2** *adj* Nordsee-; **N~ Sea gas/oil** Nordseegas *nt*/-öl *nt;* **~ward, ~wardly** *adj* nördlich; **~-west 1** *adj* Nordwest-, nordwestlich; **2** *adv* nach Nordwest(en); **~-west of** nordwestlich von; **~-westerly 1** *adj* nordwestlich; **2** *n* Nordwestwind *m;* **~-western** *adj* nordwestlich.

Norway ['nɔ:weɪ] *n* Norwegen *nt.*

Norwegian [nɔ:'wi:dʒən] **1** *adj* norwegisch. **2** *n* **(a)** Norweger(in *f*) *m.* **(b)** *(language)* Norwegisch *nt.*

nose [nəʊz] **1** *n* **(a)** Nase *f; (fig also)* Riecher *m (col).* **to speak through one's ~** durch die Nase sprechen; **my ~ is bleeding** ich habe Nasenbluten; **follow your ~** immer der Nase nach; **to do sth under sb's very ~** etw vor jds Augen tun; **it was right under his ~ all the time** er hatte es die ganze Zeit direkt vor der Nase; **to lead sb by the ~** jdn an der Nase herumführen; **to poke** *or* **stick one's ~ into sth** *(fig)* seine Nase in etw *(acc)* stecken; **you keep your ~ out of this** *(col)* halt du dich da raus! *(col)*; **to look down one's ~ at sb/sth** auf jdn/etw herabblicken; **to pay through the ~** *(col)* sich dumm und dämlich zahlen *(col)*; **to have a ~ for sth** *(fig)* eine Nase *or* einen Riecher *(col)* für etw haben.

(b) *(of plane)* Nase *f; (of car)* Schnauze *f; (of boat also)* Bug *m.* **~ to tail** *(cars)* Stoßstange an Stoßstange.

2 *vti* **the ship ~d (its way) through the fog** das Schiff tastete sich durch den Nebel; **to ~ into sb's affairs** *(fig)* seine Nase in jds Angelegenheiten *(acc)* stecken *(col).*

♦**nose about** *or* **around** *vi* herumschnüffeln *(col)*; *(person also)* herumspionieren *(col).*

♦**nose out 1** *vt sep* aufspüren; *secret, scandal* ausspionieren *(col)*, ausschnüffeln *(col).* **2** *vi (car)* sich vorschieben.

nose: ~bag *n* Futtersack *m;* **~bleed** *n*

Nasenbluten *nt;* **to have a ~bleed** Nasenbluten haben; **~dive 1** *n (Aviat)* Sturzflug *m;* **to go into a ~dive** zum Sturzflug ansetzen; **the company's affairs took a ~dive** mit der Firma ging es rapide bergab; **2** *vi (plane)* im Sturzflug herabgehen.

nosey *adj* = **nosy.**

nosh [nɒʃ] *n (Brit col) (food)* Futter *nt (col); (meal)* Schmaus *m.*

nosh-up ['nɒʃʌp] *n (Brit col)* Schmaus *m,* Freßgelage *nt (col).*

nostalgia [nɒ'stældʒɪə] *n* Nostalgie *f (for* nach*).*

nostalgic [nɒ'stældʒɪk] *adj* nostalgisch, wehmütig.

nostril ['nɒstrəl] *n* Nasenloch *nt; (of horse etc)* Nüster *f.*

nosy ['nəʊzɪ] *adj (+er) (col)* neugierig.

not [nɒt] *adv* **(a)** nicht. **he told me ~ to come** er sagte, ich solle nicht kommen; **do ~** *or* **don't come** kommen Sie nicht; **~ a sound/word** *etc* nicht *ein* Ton/Wort *etc;* **~ a bit** kein bißchen; **~ a sign of ...** keine Spur von ...; **~ one of them** kein einziger, nicht einer; **~ a thing** überhaupt nichts; **~ any more** nicht mehr; **~ yet** noch nicht.

(b) *(in rhetorical questions)* **it's hot, isn't it?** es ist heiß, nicht wahr *or* nicht?; **isn't it hot?** ist das vielleicht heiß!; **you are coming, aren't you** *or* **are you ~?** Sie kommen doch, oder?; **you are ~ angry — or are you?** Sie sind doch nicht etwa böse?

(c) is he coming? — I hope/I believe ~ kommt er? — ich hoffe/glaube nicht; **it would appear ~** anscheinend nicht; **he's decided not to do it — I should think/hope ~** er hat sich entschlossen, es nicht zu tun — das möchte ich auch meinen/hoffen; **are you cold? — ~ at all** ist dir kalt? — überhaupt nicht; **thank you very much — ~ at all** vielen Dank — keine Ursache; **~ in the least** überhaupt *or* gar nicht; **~ that I know of** nicht, daß ich wüßte.

notable ['nəʊtəbl] *adj person* bedeutend; *success, event also* bemerkenswert, denkwürdig; *difference, improvement* beträchtlich, beachtlich.

notably ['nəʊtəblɪ] *adv* **(a)** *(strikingly)* auffallend; *improved, different* beträchtlich. **(b)** *(in particular)* hauptsächlich, vor allem.

notary (public) ['nəʊtərɪ('pʌblɪk)] *n* Notar(in *f*) *m.*

notation [nəʊ'teɪʃən] *n (system)* Zeichensystem *nt; (symbols)* Zeichen *pl; (Mus)* Notenschrift *f.*

notch [nɒtʃ] **1** *n* Kerbe *f; (of handbrake etc)* Raste *f; (in belt)* Loch *nt; (on damaged blade etc)* Scharte *f.* **2** *vt* einkerben, einschneiden.

♦**notch up** *vt sep points* erzielen, einheimsen *(col); record* verzeichnen; *success* verzeichnen können.

note [nəʊt] **1** *n* **(a)** Notiz *f; (foot~)* Anmerkung, Fußnote *f; (informal letter)* Briefchen *nt,* paar Zeilen *pl.* **~s** *(summary)* Aufzeichnungen *pl; (plan, draft)* Konzept *nt;* **lecture ~s** *(professor's)* Manuskript *nt; (student's)* Aufzeichnungen *pl;* **to speak without ~s** ohne Vorlage sprechen; **to take ~s** Notizen machen; *(in lecture also, in interrogation)* mitschreiben; **to take** *or* **make a ~ of sth** sich *(dat)* etw notieren.

(b) *no pl (notice)* **to take ~ of sth** von etw Notiz nehmen; *(heed)* einer Sache *(dat)* Beachtung schenken; **worthy of ~** beachtenswert, erwähnenswert.

(c) *no pl (importance)* **a man of ~** ein bedeutender Mann; **nothing of ~** nichts Erwähnenswertes.

(d) *(Mus) (sign)* Note *f; (sound, on piano etc)* Ton *m.* **to play the right/wrong ~** richtig/falsch spielen; **to strike the right ~** *(fig)* den richtigen Ton treffen.

(e) *(quality, tone)* Ton, Klang *m.* **a ~ of nostalgia** eine nostalgische Note; **there was a ~ of warning in his voice** seine Stimme hatte einen warnenden Unterton.

(f) *(Brit Fin)* Note *f,* Schein *m.* **a £5 ~, a five-pound ~** ein Fünfpfundschein *m.*

2 *vt* bemerken; *(take note of)* zur Kenntnis nehmen; *(pay attention to)* beachten.

notebook ['nəʊtbʊk] *n* Notizbuch *or* -heft *nt.*

noted ['nəʊtɪd] *adj* bekannt *(for* für, wegen*).*

note: ~pad *n* Notizblock *m;* **~paper** *n* Briefpapier *nt.*

noteworthy ['nəʊtwɜːðɪ] *adj* beachtenswert, erwähnenswert.

nothing ['nʌθɪŋ] **1** *n, pron, adv* nichts. **to eat ~** nichts essen; **~ could be easier** nichts wäre einfacher; **it was reduced to ~** es war nichts übrig; **she is** *or* **means ~ to him** sie bedeutet ihm nichts; **that came to ~** da ist nichts draus geworden; **I can make ~ of it** das sagt mir nichts; **he thinks ~ of doing that** er findet nichts dabei(, das zu tun); **think ~ of it** keine Ursache!; **to say ~ of ...** ganz zu schweigen von ...; **~ doing!** *(col)* da ist nichts drin! *(col);* **for ~** *(free, in vain)* umsonst; **there's ~ (else) for it but to leave** da bleibt einem nichts (anderes) übrig als zu gehen; **there's ~ in the rumour** das Gerücht ist aus der Luft gegriffen, an dem Gerücht ist nichts (Wahres); **there's ~ to it** *(col)* das ist kinderleicht *(col);* **~ but** nur; **he does ~ but eat** er ißt nur *or* ständig; **~ else** sonst nichts; **~ more** sonst nichts; **I'd like ~ more than that** ich möchte nichts lieber als das; **~ much** nicht viel; **~ if not polite** überaus höflich; **~ new** nichts Neues; **it was ~ like as big** es war lange nicht so groß.

2 *n* **(a)** *(Math)* Null *f.* **(b)** *(thing, person of no value)* Nichts *nt.* **it was a mere ~** das war doch nicht der Rede wert; **to whisper sweet ~s to sb** jdm Zärtlichkeiten ins Ohr flüstern.

nothingness ['nʌθɪŋnɪs] *n* Nichts *nt.*

notice ['nəʊtɪs] **1** *n* **(a)** *(warning, communication)* Bescheid *m,* Benachrichtigung *f; (written notification)* Mitteilung *f; (of forthcoming event, film etc)* Ankündigung *f.* **to give sb ~ of sth** jdm etw mitteilen; **without ~** ohne Ankündigung; *(of arrival also)* unangemeldet; **he didn't give us much ~, he gave us rather short ~** er hat uns nicht viel Zeit gelassen *or* gegeben; **at short ~** kurzfristig; **at a moment's ~** jederzeit, sofort; **at three days' ~** innerhalb von drei Tagen; **until further ~** bis auf weiteres.

(b) *(public announcement)* Bekanntmachung *f; (on ~-board etc)* Anschlag *m; (poster also)* Plakat *nt; (sign)* Schild *nt; (in newspaper)* Mitteilung *f; (short)* Notiz *f; (of wedding, vacancy etc)* Anzeige *f.* **the ~ says ...** da steht ...

(c) *(to end employment etc)* Kündigung *f.* **~ to quit** Kündigung *f;* **to give sb ~** jdm kündigen; **to give in one's ~** kündigen; **I am under ~ (to quit), I got my ~** mir ist gekündigt worden; **a month's ~** eine einmonatige Kündigungsfrist.

(d) *(review)* Kritik, Rezension *f.*

(e) *(attention)* **to take ~ of sth** von etw Notiz nehmen; *(heed)* etw beachten, einer Sache *(dat)* Beachtung schenken; **to take no ~ of sb/sth** von jdm/etw keine Notiz nehmen; **take no ~!** kümmern Sie sich nicht darum!; **that has escaped his ~** das hat er nicht bemerkt; **to bring sth to sb's ~** jdn auf etw *(acc)* aufmerksam machen; *(in letter)* jdn von etw in Kenntnis setzen; **it came to his ~ that ...** er hat erfahren, daß ...

2 *vt* bemerken; *(perceive also)* wahrnehmen; *(recognize, acknowledge)* zur Kenntnis nehmen; *difference* feststellen; *(realize also)* merken. **without my noticing it** ohne daß ich etwas gemerkt *or* bemerkt habe; **he pretended not to ~** er tat so, als ob er es nicht bemerken würde; **did he wave? — I never ~d** hat er gewunken? — ich habe es nicht bemerkt.

noticeable ['nəʊtɪsəbl] *adj* erkennbar, wahrnehmbar; *(visible)* sichtbar; *(obvious, considerable)* deutlich; *(relief, pleasure etc)* sichtlich, merklich. **the stain is very ~** der Fleck fällt ziemlich auf; **it is hardly ~** man merkt es kaum.

notice-board ['nəʊtɪsbɔːd] *n (Brit)* Anschlagbrett *nt; (in school etc also)* Schwarzes Brett.

notification [,nəʊtɪfɪ'keɪʃən] *n* Benachrichtigung, Mitteilung *f; (of loss, damage etc)* Meldung *f.* **to send written ~ of sth to sb** jdm etw schriftlich mitteilen.

notify ['nəʊtɪfaɪ] *vt person, candidate* benachrichtigen, unterrichten *(form); change of address, loss etc* melden. **to ~ sb of sth** jdn von etw benachrichtigen; *authorities etc* jdm etw melden.

notion ['nəʊʃən] *n* **(a)** *(idea, thought)* Idee *f; (conception also)* Vorstellung *f; (vague knowledge also)* Ahnung *f; (opinion)* Meinung *f.* **I have no ~** *or* **not the slightest ~ of what he means** ich habe keine Ahnung *or* nicht die leiseste Ahnung, was er meint; **I have no ~ of time** ich habe überhaupt kein Zeitgefühl; **where did you get the ~ that I ...?** wie kommst du denn auf die Idee, daß ich ...?; **I have a ~ that ...** ich habe den Verdacht, daß ...; **to get/have a ~ to do sth** Lust bekommen/haben, etw zu tun. **(b)** *(esp US col)* **~s** *pl* Kurzwaren *pl.*

notoriety [,nəʊtə'raɪətɪ] *n* traurige Berühmtheit.

notorious [nəʊ'tɔːrɪəs] *adj person, fact* berüchtigt; *place also* verrufen; *(well-known) criminal, liar* notorisch. **to be ~ for sth** für etw berüchtigt sein.

notoriously [nəʊ'tɔːrɪəslɪ] *adv* notorisch. **to be ~ violent** für seine Gewalttätigkeit berüchtigt sein.

notwithstanding [,nɒtwɪθ'stændɪŋ] *(form)* **1** *prep* ungeachtet *(+gen) (form).* **2** *adv* nichtsdestotrotz *(form).* **3** *conj* **~ that ...** obgleich ...

nougat ['nuːgɑː] *n* Nougat *m.*

nought [nɔːt] *n* Null *f.* **~s and crosses** *Kinderspiel nt mit Nullen und Kreuzen.*

noun [naʊn] *n* Substantiv(um), Hauptwort *nt.*

nourish ['nʌrɪʃ] *vt* nähren; *person* ernähren.

nourishing ['nʌrɪʃɪŋ] *adj* nahrhaft.

nourishment ['nʌrɪʃmənt] *n* Nahrung *f.*

nouveau riche [,nuːvəʊ'riːʃ] **1** *n, pl* **-x -s** [,nuːvəʊ'riːʃ] Neureiche(r) *mf.* **2** *adj* typisch neureich.

novel[1] ['nɒvəl] *n* Roman *m.*

novel[2] *adj* neu(artig).

novelist ['nɒvəlɪst] *n* Romanschriftsteller(in *f*) *m.*

novelty ['nɒvəltɪ] *n* **(a)** *(newness)* Neuheit *f.* **(b)** *(innovation)* Neuheit *f,* Novum *nt.* **it was quite a ~** das war etwas ganz Neues. **(c)** *(Comm: trinket)* Krimskrams *m.*

November [nəʊ'vembə^r] *n* November *m; see* **September.**

novice ['nɒvɪs] *n (Eccl)* Novize *m,* Novizin *f; (fig)* Neuling, Anfänger(in *f*) *m (at* bei, in *+dat).*

now [naʊ] **1** *adv* **(a)** jetzt, nun; *(immediately)* sofort, gleich; *(at this very moment)* gerade, (so)eben; *(nowadays)* heute, heutzutage. **she ~ realized why ...** da erkannte sie, warum ...; **just ~** gerade; **~ is the time to do it** jetzt ist der richtige Moment dafür; **I'll do it right ~** ich mache es jetzt gleich *or* sofort; **it's ~ or never** jetzt oder nie; **by ~** inzwischen; **for ~** (jetzt) erst einmal, vorläufig; **even ~** selbst jetzt noch; **from ~ on(wards)** von nun an; **in three days from ~** (heute) in drei Tagen; **up to ~, till ~, until ~** bis jetzt; **that's all for ~** das wär's für heute. **(b) ~ ... ~** bald ... bald; **(every) ~ and then, ~ and again** ab und zu, gelegentlich.

2 *conj* **~ (that) you've seen him** jetzt, wo Sie ihn gesehen haben.

3 *interj* also. **~, ~!** na, na!; **well ~** also; **~ then** also (jetzt); **stop that ~!** Schluß jetzt!; **~, why didn't I think of that?** warum habe ich bloß nicht daran gedacht?

nowadays ['naʊədeɪz] *adv* heute, heutzutage.

nowhere ['nəʊwɛə^r] *adv* nirgends; *(with verbs of motion)* nirgendwohin. **~ special** irgendwo; *(with motion)* irgendwohin; **to appear from ~** ganz plötzlich auftauchen; **we're getting ~ (fast)** wir kommen nicht weiter; **rudeness will get you ~** Grobheit bringt dir gar nichts ein.

noxious ['nɒkʃəs] *adj* schädlich; *habit* übel.

nozzle ['nɒzl] *n* Düse *f.*

nth [enθ] *adj* **the ~ degree** die n-te Potenz; **for the ~ time** zum x-ten Mal *(col).*

nuance ['njuːɑ̃ːns] *n* Nuance *f.*

nubile ['njuːbaɪl] *adj (attractive) girl* gut entwickelt.

nuclear ['njuːklɪə^r] *adj* Kern-, Atom- *(esp Mil); fission, reaction, research* Kern-; *fuel* nuklear, atomar; *attack, testing* Kernwaffen-, Atomwaffen-; *submarine, missile* atomgetrieben, Atom-.

nuclear: ~ deterrent *n* nukleares Abschreckungsmittel; **~ family** *n* Kleinfamilie *f;* **~ physics** *n* Kernphysik *f;* **~ power** *n* Atomkraft, Kernenergie *f;* **~-powered** *adj* atomgetrieben; **~ power station** *n* Kern- *or* Atomkraftwerk *nt;* **~ reactor** *n* Kern- *or* Atomreaktor *m;* **~ war** *n* Atomkrieg *m.*

nucleus ['njuːklɪəs] *n, pl* **nuclei** *(Phys, fig)* Kern *m; (Biol: of cell also)* Nukleus *m.*

nude [njuːd] **1** *adj* nackt; *(Art)* Akt-. **~ figure/portrait** Akt *m.* **2** *n (person)* Nackte(r) *mf; (Art) (painting etc)* Akt *m; (model)* Aktmodell *nt.* **in the ~** nackt.

nudge [nʌdʒ] **1** *vt* stupsen. **2** *n* **to give sb a ~** jdm einen Stups geben.

nudist ['njuːdɪst] *n* Anhänger(in *f*) *m* der Freikörperkultur, FKK-Anhänger(in *f*) *m.* **~ colony** FKK-Kolonie *f.*

nudity ['njuːdɪtɪ] *n* Nacktheit *f.*

nugget ['nʌgɪt] *n (of gold etc)* Klumpen *m.*

nuisance ['njuːsns] *n* **(a)** *(person)* Plage *f; (esp pestering)* Nervensäge *f; (esp child)* Quälgeist *m.* **to make a ~ of oneself** lästig werden. **(b)** *(thing, event)* **to be a ~** lästig sein; *(annoying)* ärgerlich sein; **what a ~, having to do it again** wie ärgerlich, das noch einmal machen zu müssen.

nuke [njuːk] *vt (col)* atomar vernichten.

null [nʌl] *adj:* **~ and void** *(Jur)* (null und) nichtig, ungültig.

nullify ['nʌlɪfaɪ] *vt* annullieren, für (null und) nichtig erklären.

numb [nʌm] **1** *adj (+er)* taub, gefühllos; *(emotionally)* benommen, wie betäubt. **hands ~ with cold** Hände, die vor Kälte taub *or* gefühllos sind; **~ with grief** starr *or* wie betäubt vor Schmerz. **2** *vt (cold)* taub *or* gefühllos machen; *(injection, fig)* betäuben.

number ['nʌmbə^r] **1** *n* **(a)** *(Math)* Zahl *f; (numeral)* Ziffer *f; (amount)* Anzahl *f.* **a ~ of applicants** eine Anzahl von Bewerbern; **large ~s of people/books** eine große Anzahl von Leuten/eine ganze Menge Bücher; **on a ~ of occasions** des öfteren; **in a small ~ of cases** in wenigen Fällen; **ten in ~** zehn an der Zahl; **in small/large ~s** in kleinen/großen Mengen; **any ~ of cards** *etc (many)* sehr viele Karten *etc.*

(b) *(of house, phone)* Nummer *f; (of page)* Seitenzahl *f; (of car)* (Auto)nummer *f.* **N~ Ten (Downing Street)** Nummer Zehn (Downing Street); **to take a car's ~** die Nummer eines Autos aufschreiben; **I dialled a wrong ~** ich habe mich verwählt; **it was a wrong ~** ich/er *etc* war falsch verbunden; **the ~ one pop star** *(col)* der Popstar Nummer Eins *(col);* **to look after ~ one** *(col)* (vor allem) an sich *(acc)* selbst denken; **his ~'s up** *(col)* er ist dran *(col).*

(c) *(song, act etc)* Nummer *f; (issue of magazine etc also)* Ausgabe *f,* Heft *nt; (dress)* Kreation *f.*

2 *vt* **(a)** *(give a number to)* numerieren; *(count)* zählen. **to be ~ed** *(limited)* begrenzt sein; **his days are ~ed** seine Tage sind gezählt. **(b)** *(include)* zählen *(among* zu*)*. **we ~ them among our friends** wir zählen sie zu unseren Freunden. **(c)** *(amount to)* zählen. **the group ~ed 50** es waren 50 (Leute in der Gruppe).

number: ~less *adj* zahllos, unzählig; **~-plate** *n (Brit)* Nummernschild *nt.*

numbness ['nʌmnɪs] *n (of limbs etc)* Taubheit *f; (fig: of mind, senses)* Benommenheit *f.*

numeracy ['njuːmərəsɪ] *n* Rechnen *nt.* **his ~** seine rechnerischen Fähigkeiten.

numeral ['njuːmərəl] *n* Ziffer *f.*

numerate ['njuːmərɪt] *adj* rechenkundig.

numerical [njuː'merɪkəl] *adj symbols, equation* numerisch, Zahlen-; *value* Zahlen-; *superiority* zahlenmäßig. **in ~ order** nach Zahlen geordnet.

numerous ['njuːmərəs] *adj* zahlreich; *family* kinderreich.

nun [nʌn] *n* Nonne *f.*

nuptial ['nʌpʃəl] *(liter, hum)* **1** *adj bliss, vow* Ehe-; *feast* Hochzeits-. **2** *n* **~s** *pl* Hochzeit *f.*

nurse [nɜːs] **1** *n* Schwester *f; (as professional title)* Krankenschwester *f; (nanny)* Kindermädchen *nt.* **male ~** Krankenpfleger *m.* **2** *vt* **(a)** pflegen; *(fig) plan* hegen; *(treat carefully)* schonen. **to ~ sb back to health** jdn gesundpflegen; **he stood there nursing his bruised arm** er stand da und hielt seinen verletzten Arm. **(b)** *(suckle) child* stillen; *(cradle)* (in den Armen) wiegen.

nursemaid ['nɜːsmeɪd] *n (nanny, hum: servant)* Kindermädchen *nt.*

nursery ['nɜːsərɪ] *n* **(a)** *(room)* Kinderzimmer *nt; (in hospital)* Säuglingssaal *m.* **(b)** *(institution)* Kindergarten *m; (all-day)* Kindertagesstätte *f.* **(c)** *(Agr, Hort) (for plants)* Gärtnerei *f; (for trees)* Baumschule *f.*

nursery: ~ rhyme *n* Kinderreim *m;* **~ school** *n* Kindergarten *m;* **~ slope** *n (Brit)* Idiotenhügel *(hum)*, Anfängerhügel *m.*

nursing ['nɜːsɪŋ] **1** *n* **(a)** *(care of invalids)* Pflege *f.* **(b)** *(profession)* Krankenpflege *f.* **she's going in for ~** sie will in der Krankenpflege arbeiten. **2** *adj attr staff* Pflege-; *abilities* pflegerisch. **the ~ profession** die pflegerischen Berufe.

nursing: ~ auxiliary *n (Brit)* Schwesternhelferin *f;* **~ bottle** *n (US)* Flasche *f;* **~ home** *n* Privatklinik *f; (Brit: maternity hospital)* Entbindungsklinik *f; (convalescent home)* Pflegeheim *nt;* **~ mother** *n* stillende Mutter; **~ officer** *n* Oberschwester *f.*

nut [nʌt] *n* **(a)** *(Bot)* Nuß *f; (of coal)* kleines Stück. **a packet of ~s and raisins** eine Tüte Studentenfutter. **(b)** *(col: head)* Nuß *(col)*, Birne *(col) f.* **use your ~!** streng deinen Grips an! *(col)*; **to do one's ~** *(Brit col)* durchdrehen *(col)*. **(c)** *(col: person)* Spinner(in *f*) *m (col)*. **he's a tough ~** *(col)* er ist ein harter Brocken *(col)*. **(d)** *(Mech)* (Schrauben)mutter *f.*

nut: ~-case *n (col)* Spinner(in *f*) *m (col)*; **~cracker(s** *pl*) *n* Nußknacker *m;* **~-house** *n (col) (lit, fig)* Irrenhaus *nt (col)*; **~meg** *n* Muskat(nuß *f*) *m.*

nutrient ['njuːtrɪənt] **1** *adj substance* nahrhaft; *properties* Nähr-. **2** *n* Nährstoff *m.*

nutrition [njuː'trɪʃən] *n (diet, science)* Ernährung *f.*

nutritious [njuː'trɪʃəs] *adj* nahrhaft.

nuts [nʌts] *adj pred (col)* **to be ~** spinnen *(col)*; **to go ~** durchdrehen *(col)*; **to be ~ about sb/sth** *(keen on)* ganz wild auf jdn/etw sein *(col)*.

nutshell ['nʌt,ʃel] *n* Nußschale *f.* **in a ~** *(fig)* kurz gesagt.

nutty ['nʌtɪ] *adj (+er)* **(a)** *flavour* Nuß-. **(b)** *(col: crazy)* bekloppt *(col)*.

nuzzle ['nʌzl] *vi* **to ~ (up) against sb, to ~ up to sb** sich an jdn schmiegen *or* drücken.

nylon ['naɪlɒn] **1** *n* **(a)** *(Tex)* Nylon *nt.* **(b) ~s** *pl* Nylonstrümpfe *pl.* **2** *adj* Nylon-.

nymph [nɪmf] *n (Myth)* Nymphe *f.*

nymphomaniac [,nɪmfəʊ'meɪnɪæk] *n* Nymphomanin *f.*

O

O, o [əʊ] *n* **(a)** O, o *nt.* **(b)** [*(Brit)* əʊ, *(US)* 'zɪərəʊ] *(Telec)* Null *f.*
oaf [əʊf] *n, pl* **-s** *or* **oaves** Flegel, Lümmel *m.*
oafish ['əʊfɪʃ] *adj* flegelhaft, lümmelhaft.
oak [əʊk] *n* Eiche *f*; *(wood also)* Eichenholz *nt.*
oak *in cpds* Eichen-; ~ **apple** *n* Gallapfel *m.*
OAP *(Brit)* = **old-age pensioner.**
oar [ɔːʳ] *n* Ruder *nt,* Riemen *(Rowing) m.* **to stick one's ~ in** *(col)* sich einmischen.
oarsman ['ɔːzmən] *n* Ruderer *m.*
oasis [əʊ'eɪsɪs] *n, pl* **oases** [əʊ'eɪsiːz] *(lit, fig)* Oase *f.*
oat [əʊt] *n usu pl* Hafer *m.* **~s** *pl (Cook)* Haferflocken *pl*; **to sow one's wild ~s** *(fig)* sich *(dat)* die Hörner abstoßen.
oath [əʊθ] *n* **(a)** Schwur *m*; *(Jur)* Eid *m.* **to take** *or* **swear an ~** schwören; *(Jur)* einen Eid ablegen *or* leisten; **to be under ~** *(Jur)* unter Eid stehen; **to put sb on ~** *(Jur)* jdn vereidigen; **to take the ~** *(Jur)* vereidigt werden. **(b)** *(curse, profanity)* Fluch *m.*
oatmeal ['əʊtmiːl] *n no pl* Haferschrot *m.*
obdurate ['ɒbdjʊrɪt] *adj (stubborn)* hartnäckig; *sinner* verstockt; *(hardhearted)* unerbittlich.
obedience [ə'biːdɪəns] *n no pl* Gehorsam *m.* **in ~ to the law** dem Gesetz entsprechend.
obedient [ə'biːdɪənt] *adj* gehorsam; *child, dog also* folgsam. **to be ~** gehorchen *(to dat).*
obelisk ['ɒbɪlɪsk] *n (Archit)* Obelisk *m.*
obese [əʊ'biːs] *adj* fettleibig *(form, Med).*
obesity [əʊ'biːsɪtɪ] *n* Fettleibigkeit *f (form, Med).*
obey [ə'beɪ] **1** *vt* gehorchen *(+dat)*; *law, rules, order* befolgen; *(machine)* reagieren auf *(+acc).* **2** *vi* gehorchen; *(child, dog also)* folgen.
obituary [ə'bɪtjʊərɪ] *n* Nachruf *m.* **~ notice** Todesanzeige *f*; **~ column** Sterberegister *nt.*
object[1] ['ɒbdʒɪkt] *n* **(a)** *(thing)* Gegenstand *m*; *(abstract etc)* Objekt, Ding *nt.* **he was an ~ of scorn** er war die Zielscheibe der Verachtung. **(b)** *(aim)* Ziel *nt,* Absicht *f.* **with this ~ in mind** mit diesem Ziel vor Augen; **with the sole ~ (of doing)** mit dem einzigen Ziel (, zu ...); **what's the ~ (of staying here)?** wozu (bleiben wir hier)?; **that defeats the ~** das verfehlt seinen Sinn *or* Zweck. **(c) money/distance (is) no ~** Geld/Entfernung spielt keine Rolle. **(d)** *(Gram)* Objekt *nt.*
object[2] [əb'dʒekt] **1** *vi* dagegen sein; *(protest)* protestieren; *(be against: in discussion etc)* Einwände haben *(to* gegen*)*; *(raise objection)* Einwände erheben; *(disapprove)* sich stören *(to* an *+dat).* **to ~ to sth** *(disapprove)* etw mißbilligen; **if you don't ~** wenn Sie nichts dagegen haben; **do you ~ to my smoking?** stört es (Sie), wenn ich rauche?; **I ~ to your tone/to people smoking in my living room** ich verbitte mir diesen Ton/ich verbitte mir, daß in meinem Wohnzimmer geraucht wird. **2** *vt* einwenden.
objection [əb'dʒekʃən] *n (reason against)* Einwand *m (to* gegen*)*; *(dislike)* Abneigung *f*; *(disapproval)* Einspruch, Widerspruch *m.* **to make** *or* **raise an ~** einen Einwand erheben; **I have no ~ to his going away** ich habe nichts dagegen (einzuwenden), daß er weggeht; **are there any ~s?** irgendwelche Einwände?; **I see no ~ to it** ich sehe nichts, was dagegen spricht; **I have no ~ to him** *(as a person)* ich habe nichts gegen ihn.
objectionable [əb'dʒekʃənəbl] *adj* störend; *conduct, remark, language* anstößig; *smell* übel. **he's a most ~ person** er ist unausstehlich.
objective [əb'dʒektɪv] **1** *adj* objektiv. **2** *n (aim)* Ziel *nt*; *(esp Comm)* Zielvorstellung *f*; *(Mil)* Angriffsziel *nt.*
objectively [əb'dʒektɪvlɪ] *adv* objektiv.
objectivity [ˌɒbdʒek'tɪvɪtɪ] *n* Objektivität *f.*
object lesson *n (fig)* Paradebeispiel *nt (in, on* für, *gen).*
objector [əb'dʒektəʳ] *n* Gegner(in *f*) *m (to gen).*
obligation [ˌɒblɪ'geɪʃən] *n* Verpflichtung, Pflicht *f.* **to be under an ~ to do sth** die Pflicht haben, etw zu tun; **without ~** *(Comm)* unverbindlich.
obligatory [ɒ'blɪgətərɪ] *adj* obligatorisch. **biology is ~** Biologie ist Pflicht; **to make it ~ for sb to do sth** vorschreiben, daß jd etw tut.
oblige [ə'blaɪdʒ] *vt* **(a)** *(compel)* zwingen; *(because of duty)* verpflichten *(sb to do sth* jdn, etw zu tun*).* **to feel ~d to do sth** sich verpflichtet fühlen, etw zu tun; **I was ~d to go** ich sah mich gezwungen zu gehen; **you are not ~d to do it** Sie sind nicht dazu verpflichtet. **(b)** *(do a favour to)* einen Gefallen tun *(+dat).* **could you ~ me with a light?** wären Sie so gut, mir Feuer zu geben?; **anything to ~ a friend** was tut man nicht alles für einen Freund!; **much ~d!** herzlichen Dank!; **I am much ~d to you for this** ich bin Ihnen dafür sehr verbunden.
obliging [ə'blaɪdʒɪŋ] *adj* entgegenkommend, gefällig; *personality* zuvorkommend.
oblique [ə'bliːk] **1** *adj line, look* schief, schräg; *angle* schief; *style, reply, hint, reference* indirekt. **2** *n* Schrägstrich *m.*
obliquely [ə'bliːklɪ] *adv* schräg; *(fig)* indirekt.
obliterate [ə'blɪtəreɪt] *vt (erase)* auslöschen; *city also* vernichten; *(hide) sun, view* verdecken.
oblivion [ə'blɪvɪən] *n* Vergessenheit *f.* **to sink** *or* **fall into ~** in Vergessenheit geraten.
oblivious [ə'blɪvɪəs] *adj* **to be ~ of sth** sich *(dat)* einer Sache *(gen)* nicht bewußt sein; **he was quite ~ of his surroundings** er nahm seine Umgebung gar nicht wahr.
oblong ['ɒblɒŋ] **1** *adj* rechteckig. **2** *n* Rechteck *nt.*
obnoxious [ɒb'nɒkʃəs] *adj* widerlich, widerwärtig; *person also, behaviour* unausstehlich. **an ~ person** ein Ekel *nt (col).*
oboe ['əʊbəʊ] *n* Oboe *f.*
obscene [əb'siːn] *adj* obszön; *(non-sexually, repulsive)* ekelerregend, widerlich.
obscenity [əb'senɪtɪ] *n* Obszönität *f.* **the ~ of these crimes** diese ekelerregenden Verbrechen.
obscure [əb'skjʊəʳ] **1** *adj (+er)* **(a)** *style* unklar; *argument* verworren; *book* schwer verständlich. **(b)** *(indistinct) feeling, memory* dunkel. **for some ~ reason** aus einem unerfindlichen Grund. **(c)** *(little known) poet, village* unbekannt; *beginnings (humble)* unbedeutend; *life* wenig beachtenswert. **2** *vt* **(a)** *(hide) sun, view* verdecken. **(b)** *(confuse) issue, argument* unklar machen.
obscurity [əb'skjʊərɪtɪ] *n (of night, origins)* Dunkel *nt*; *(of style, argument)* Unklarheit *f.* **to live in ~** zurückgezogen leben; **to sink into ~** in Vergessenheit geraten.
obsequious [əb'siːkwɪəs] *adj* unterwürfig *(to(wards)* gegen, gegenüber*).*
observance [əb'zɜːvəns] *n* **(a)** *(of law)* Befolgung,

Beachtung *f.* **(b)** *(Eccl)* Einhaltung *f.*
observant [əb'zɜːvənt] *adj* aufmerksam, wachsam. **that's very ~ of you** das hast du aber gut bemerkt.
observation [ˌɒbzə'veɪʃən] *n* **(a)** Beobachtung *f; (act also)* Beobachten *nt.* **to keep sb/sth under ~** *(by police)* jdn/etw überwachen; **powers of ~** Beobachtungsgabe *f;* **he's in hospital for ~** er ist zur Beobachtung im Krankenhaus; **~ post** Beobachtungsposten *m.* **(b)** *(remark)* Bemerkung *f.*
observatory [əb'zɜːvətrɪ] *n* Sternwarte *f; (Met)* Wetterwarte *f.*
observe [əb'zɜːv] *vt* **(a)** *(watch, notice)* beobachten; *difference also* wahrnehmen; *(by police)* überwachen. **(b)** *(obey)* achten auf *(+acc)*; *rule, custom, ceasefire* einhalten.
observer [əb'zɜːvəʳ] *n (watcher)* Zuschauer(in *f*) *m*; *(Mil, Pol)* Beobachter(in *f*) *m.*
obsess [əb'ses] *vt* **to be ~ed by** *or* **with sb/sth** von jdm/etw besessen sein.
obsession [əb'seʃən] *n* *(fixed idea)* fixe Idee, Manie *f; (fear etc)* Zwangsvorstellung *f; (state)* Besessenheit *f (with* von*).* **it's an ~ with him** *(hobby etc)* er ist davon besessen; **this ~ with order** dieser Ordnungswahn *m;* **because of his ~ with her** weil er ihr gänzlich verfallen ist/war.
obsessive [əb'sesɪv] *adj* zwanghaft. **to become ~** *(activity)* zum Zwang *or* zur Manie werden; **he is an ~ reader** er liest wie besessen.
obsolescence [ˌɒbsə'lesns] *n* Veralten *nt.*
obsolescent [ˌɒbsə'lesnt] *adj* veraltend. **to be ~** anfangen zu veralten.
obsolete ['ɒbsəliːt] *adj* veraltet, überholt. **to become ~** veralten.
obstacle ['ɒbstəkl] *n (lit, fig)* Hindernis *nt.* **to be an ~ to sb/sth** jdm/einer Sache im Weg(e) stehen; **to put an ~ in sb's way** jdm ein Hindernis in den Weg stellen; **all the ~s to peace** *etc* alles, was den Frieden *etc* behindert.
obstetrician [ˌɒbstə'trɪʃən] *n* Geburtshelfer(in *f*) *m.*
obstetrics [ɒb'stetrɪks] *n sing* Geburtshilfe *f.*
obstinacy ['ɒbstɪnəsɪ] *n* Hartnäckigkeit *f,* Starrsinn *m (pej).*
obstinate ['ɒbstɪnɪt] *adj* hartnäckig, starrsinnig; *nail etc* widerspenstig. **to remain ~** stur bleiben.
obstreperous [əb'strepərəs] *adj* aufmüpfig *(col)*; *child* aufsässig.
obstruct [əb'strʌkt] *vt* **(a)** *(block)* blockieren; *road also, view* versperren; *(Med) artery, pipe also* verstopfen. **you're ~ing my view** Sie versperren mir die Sicht. **(b)** *(hinder)* (be)hindern; *traffic, progress also* aufhalten; *(Sport)* behindern.
obstruction [əb'strʌkʃən] *n see vt* **(a)** Blockierung *f; (of view)* Versperren *nt;* Verstopfung *f.* **(b)** Behinderung *f.* **to cause an ~** *(to traffic)* den Verkehr behindern. **(c)** *(obstacle)* Hindernis, Hemmnis *(esp fig) nt.* **there is an ~ in the pipe** das Rohr ist verstopft.
obstructive [əb'strʌktɪv] *adj* obstruktiv *(esp Pol)*, behindernd. **to be ~** *(person)* Schwierigkeiten machen, sich querstellen *(col).*
obtain [əb'teɪn] *vt* erhalten; *result, votes also* erzielen; *information, goods also* beziehen. **to ~ sth by hard work** etw durch harte Arbeit erreichen; **to ~ sth for sb** jdm etw beschaffen.
obtainable [əb'teɪnəbl] *adj* erhältlich.
obtrusive [əb'truːsɪv] *adj person* aufdringlich; *smell also* penetrant; *building, furniture* zu auffällig.
obtuse [əb'tjuːs] *adj* **(a)** *(Geometry)* stumpf. **(b)** *person* begriffsstutzig, beschränkt.
obviate ['ɒbvɪeɪt] *vt* vermeiden; *need* vorbeugen *(+dat).*
obvious ['ɒbvɪəs] *adj* offensichtlich; *difference, fact also* eindeutig; *statement* naheliegend; *reason* (leicht) ersichtlich; *reluctance, surprise* sichtlich; *(not subtle)* plump. **an ~ truth** eine offenkundige Tatsache; **that's the ~ solution** das ist die naheliegendste Lösung; **he was the ~ choice** es lag nahe, ihn zu wählen; **it's quite ~ he doesn't understand** es ist doch klar, daß er es nicht versteht; **there's no need to make it so ~** man braucht das (doch) nicht so deutlich zu zeigen; **I would have thought that was perfectly ~** das liegt doch auf der Hand; **to state the ~** sagen/schreiben, was sich von selbst versteht.
obviously ['ɒbvɪəslɪ] *adv* offensichtlich, offenbar; *(noticeably)* (offen)sichtlich. **he's ~ French** er ist eindeutig ein Franzose; **he's not ~ French** man merkt ihm nicht an, daß er Franzose ist; **~!** selbstverständlich!
occasion [ə'keɪʒən] **1** *n* **(a)** *(point in time)* Gelegenheit *f.* **on that ~** damals, bei jener Gelegenheit; **on ~** gelegentlich; **to rise to the ~** sich der Lage gewachsen zeigen. **(b)** *(special time)* Ereignis *nt.* **it's an ~** es ist ein besonderes Ereignis. **(c)** *(opportunity)* Gelegenheit *f.* **(d)** *(reason)* Grund *m.* **if you have ~ to ...** sollten Sie Veranlassung haben, zu ... **2** *vt (form)* Anlaß geben zu.
occasional [ə'keɪʒənl] *adj* **(a) he likes an ~ cigar** er raucht gelegentlich eine Zigarre. **(b) ~ table** kleiner Wohnzimmertisch.
occasionally [ə'keɪʒənəlɪ] *adv* gelegentlich, hin und wieder. **very ~** sehr selten.
occult [ɒ'kʌlt] **1** *adj* okkult. **2** *n* Okkulte(s) *nt.*
occupant ['ɒkjʊpənt] *n (of house)* Bewohner(in *f*) *m; (of post)* Inhaber(in *f*) *m; (of car)* Insasse *m.*
occupation [ˌɒkjʊ'peɪʃən] *n* **(a)** *(employment)* Beruf *m,* Tätigkeit *f.* **he is a joiner by ~** er ist Tischler von Beruf. **(b)** *(pastime)* Beschäftigung *f.* **(c)** *(Mil)* Okkupation *f; (act also)* Besetzung *f (of* von*)*; *(state also)* Besatzung *f (of* in *+dat).* **army of ~** Besatzungsheer *nt.* **(d)** *(of house etc)* **ready for ~** bezugsfertig.
occupational [ˌɒkjʊ'peɪʃənl] *adj* Berufs-, beruflich. **~ hazard** *or* **risk** Berufsrisiko *nt;* **~ therapy** Beschäftigungstherapie *f.*
occupier ['ɒkjʊpaɪəʳ] *n (of house)* Bewohner(in *f*) *m; (of post)* Inhaber(in *f*) *m.*
occupy ['ɒkjʊpaɪ] *vt* **(a)** *house* bewohnen; *room* belegen. **is this seat occupied?** ist dieser Platz besetzt? **(b)** *(Mil etc)* besetzen. **(c)** *post, position* innehaben, bekleiden *(geh).* **(d)** *(take up)* beanspruchen; *space also* einnehmen; *time also* in Anspruch nehmen. **to ~ one's time** seine Zeit verbringen. **(e)** *(busy)* beschäftigen. **to be occupied (with)** beschäftigt sein (mit); **to ~ oneself** sich beschäftigen; **to keep sb occupied** jdn beschäftigen; **he kept his mind occupied** er beschäftigte sich geistig.
occur [ə'kɜːʳ] *vi* **(a)** *(event)* geschehen, vorkommen; *(difficulty)* sich ergeben; *(change)* stattfinden. **that doesn't ~ very often** das kommt nicht oft vor. **(b)** *(be found: disease)* vorkommen. **(c) it ~s to me that ...** ich habe den Eindruck, daß ...; **the idea just ~red to me** es ist mir gerade eingefallen; **it never ~red to me** darauf bin ich noch nie gekommen.
occurrence [ə'kʌrəns] *n (event)* Ereignis *nt,* Begebenheit *f; (presence, taking place)* Auftreten *nt; (of minerals)* Vorkommen *nt.* **an everyday ~** ein alltägliches Ereignis.
ocean ['əʊʃən] *n* Ozean *m,* Meer *nt.*
ocean: ~ bed *n* Meeresboden *or* -grund *m;* **~-going** *adj* hochseetauglich.
oceanic [ˌəʊʃɪ'ænɪk] *adj* Meeres-.
oceanography [ˌəʊʃə'nɒgrəfɪ] *n* Meereskunde *f.*
ochre, *(US)* **ocher** ['əʊkəʳ] *n* Ocker *m or nt.*
o'clock [ə'klɒk] *adv* **at 5 ~** um 5 Uhr; **it is 5 ~** es ist 5 Uhr.
octagon ['ɒktəgən] *n* Achteck, Oktagon *nt.*
octagonal [ɒk'tægənl] *adj* achteckig.
octane ['ɒkteɪn] *n* Oktan *nt.* **high-~ petrol** Benzin *nt* mit hoher Oktanzahl.

octave ['ɒktɪv] *n (Mus)* Oktave *f.*

October [ɒk'təʊbəʳ] *n* Oktober *m*; *see* **September.**

octogenarian [,ɒktəʊdʒɪ'nɛərɪən] **1** *n* Achtzigjährige(r) *mf.* **2** *adj* achtzigjährig.

octopus ['ɒktəpəs] *n* Tintenfisch *m*, Krake *f.*

oculist ['ɒkjʊlɪst] *n* Augenspezialist(in *f*) *m.*

odd [ɒd] *adj (+er)* **(a)** *(peculiar)* merkwürdig, sonderbar; *person, thing, idea also* eigenartig. **how ~ that we should meet him** (wie) eigenartig *etc*, daß wir ihn trafen; **the ~ thing about it is that ...** das Merkwürdige *etc* daran ist, daß ...; **he's got some ~ ways** er hat eine verschrobene Art. **(b)** *number* ungerade. **(c)** *(one of a pair or a set) shoe, glove* einzeln. **he is (the) ~ man** *or* **one out** er ist das fünfte Rad am Wagen; **underline the word which is the ~ man** *or* **one out** unterstreichen Sie das nicht dazugehörige Wort. **(d) 600 ~ marks** so um die 600 Mark; **at ~ moments** ab und zu; **~ job** (gelegentlich) anfallende Arbeit; **~ job man** Mädchen *nt* für alles.

oddity ['ɒdɪtɪ] *n* **(a)** *(of person)* Eigenartigkeit *f*; *(of thing)* Ausgefallenheit *f.* **(b)** *(odd person)* komischer Kauz; *(thing)* Kuriosität *f.*

oddly ['ɒdlɪ] *adv speak, behave* eigenartig, sonderbar. **they are ~ similar** sie sind sich merkwürdig ähnlich; **~ enough she was at home** seltsamerweise war sie zu Hause.

oddment ['ɒdmənt] *n usu pl* Restposten *m*; *(of cloth)* Rest *m*; *(single piece)* Einzelstück *nt.*

oddness ['ɒdnɪs] *n* Merkwürdigkeit, Seltsamkeit *f.*

odds [ɒdz] *npl* **(a)** *(Betting)* Gewinnquote *f*; *(of bookmaker also)* Kurse *pl.* **the ~ are 6 to 1** die Chancen stehen 6:1; **long/short ~** geringe/hohe Gewinnchancen. **(b)** *(chances for or against)* Chance(n *pl*) *f.* **the ~ were against us** alles sprach gegen uns; **the ~ were in our favour** alles sprach für uns; **against all the ~ he won** wider Erwarten gewann er; **what are the ~ on/against ...?** wie stehen die Chancen, daß .../daß ... nicht?; **to struggle against impossible ~** so gut wie keine Aussicht auf Erfolg haben; **the ~ are that he will come** es sieht ganz so aus, als ob er kommen würde. **(c)** *(col)* **to pay over the ~** einiges mehr bezahlen. **(d)** *(difference)* **what's the ~?** was macht das schon (aus)?; **it makes no ~** es spielt keine Rolle. **(e)** *(variance)* **to be at ~ with sb over sth** mit jdm in etw *(dat)* nicht übereinstimmen.

odds and ends *npl* Krimskrams *m (col).* **bring all your ~** bringen Sie Ihre Siebensachen *(col).*

odds-on ['ɒdzɒn] *adj* **he's ~ favourite for the post** er hat die größten Aussichten, die Stelle zu bekommen.

ode [əʊd] *n* Ode *f (to, on* an *+acc).*

odious ['əʊdɪəs] *adj person* abstoßend, ekelhaft; *action* abscheulich.

odometer [əʊ'dɒmɪtəʳ] *n (US)* Tacho(meter) *m.*

odour, *(US)* **odor** ['əʊdəʳ] *n (lit, fig)* Geruch *m*; *(sweet smell)* Duft *m*; *(bad smell)* Gestank *m.* **to be in bad ~ with sb** schlecht bei jdm angeschrieben sein *(col).*

odourless, *(US)* **odorless** ['əʊdəlɪs] *adj* geruchlos.

Odyssey ['ɒdɪsɪ] *n (Myth, fig)* Odyssee *f.*

Oedipus ['iːdɪpəs] *n* Ödipus *m.* **~ complex** Ödipuskomplex *m.*

oesophagus, *(US)* **esophagus** [iː'sɒfəgəs] *n* Speiseröhre *f.*

of [ɒv,əv] *prep* **(a)** von *(+dat)*, *use of gen.* **the wife ~ the doctor** die Frau des Arztes; **a friend ~ ours** ein Freund von uns; **a painting ~ the Queen** ein Gemälde von der Königin; **a painting ~ the Queen's** *(belonging to her)* ein Gemälde der Königin; **~ it** davon; **the first ~ May** der erste Mai; **it is very kind ~ you** es ist sehr freundlich von Ihnen; **south ~ Paris** südlich von Paris; **within a month ~ his death** einen Monat nach seinem Tod.

(b) *(cause)* **he died ~ poison/cancer** er starb an Gift/Krebs; **it tastes ~ garlic** es schmeckt nach Knoblauch.

(c) *(material)* aus. **dress made ~ wool** Wollkleid *nt*, Kleid *nt* aus Wolle.

(d) *(quality, identity etc)* **man ~ courage** mutiger Mensch; **girl ~ ten** zehnjähriges Mädchen; **the city ~ Paris** die Stadt Paris.

(e) he is a leader ~ men er hat die Fähigkeit, Menschen zu führen; **writer ~ legal articles** Verfasser von juristischen Artikeln; **love ~ money** Liebe zum Geld; **how many ~ them do you want?** wie viele möchten Sie (davon)?; **there were six ~ us** wir waren zu sechst; **he is not one ~ us** er gehört nicht zu uns; **today ~ all days** ausgerechnet heute; **you ~ all people ought to know** gerade Sie sollten das wissen; **what do you think ~ him?** was halten Sie von ihm?; **what ~ it?** ja und?

(f) *(in temporal phrases)* **he's become very quiet ~ late** er ist seit neuestem so ruhig; **they go out ~ an evening** *(col)* sie gehen abends (schon mal) aus.

off [ɒf] **1** *adv* **(a)** *(distance)* **the house is 5km ~** das Haus ist 5 km entfernt; **it's a long way ~** das ist weit weg; *(time)* das liegt in weiter Ferne; **the exams aren't very far ~** es ist nicht mehr lang bis zu den Prüfungen.

(b) *(departure)* **to be/go ~** gehen; **he's ~ to school** er ist zur Schule gegangen; **(be) ~ with you!** fort mit dir!; **I must be ~** ich muß gehen; **where are you ~ to?** wohin gehen Sie denn?, wohin geht's denn *(col)*?; **~ we go!** los!, na denn man los! *(col)*; **he's ~ playing tennis every evening** er geht jeden Abend Tennis spielen.

(c) *(removal)* **he had his coat ~** er hatte den Mantel aus; **~ with those wet clothes!** raus aus den nassen Kleidern!; **the handle is ~** der Griff ist ab *(col) or* ist abgegangen; **there are two buttons ~** es fehlen zwei Knöpfe.

(d) *(discount)* **3% ~** *(Comm)* 3% Nachlaß; **to give sb £5 ~** jdm £ 5 Ermäßigung geben.

(e) *(not at work)* **to have time ~ to do sth** Zeit freibekommen haben, um etw zu tun; **I've got a day ~** ich habe einen Tag frei(bekommen); **she's nearly always ~ on Tuesdays** dienstags hat sie fast immer frei.

(f) *(in phrases)* **~ and on, on and ~** ab und zu; **right** *or* **straight ~** gleich; **3 days straight ~** 3 Tage hintereinander.

2 *adj* **(a)** *attr (substandard)* schlecht. **I'm having an ~ day today** ich bin heute nicht in Form.

(b) *pred (Brit: not fresh)* verdorben, schlecht.

(c) *pred (cancelled) party, talks* abgesagt; *(not available: in restaurant)* aus. **the agreement is ~** die Abmachung gilt nicht (mehr); **their engagement is ~** ihre Verlobung ist gelöst; **the play is ~** das Stück wurde abgesagt.

(d) *TV, light, machine* aus(geschaltet); *tap* zu(gedreht). **the gas/electricity was ~** das Gas/der Strom war abgeschaltet; **the handbrake was ~** die Handbremse war gelöst.

(e) they are badly/well ~ sie sind nicht gut/(ganz) gut gestellt; **how are we ~ for time?** wie sieht es mit der Zeit aus?; **that's a bit ~!** das ist ein dicker Hund! *(col).*

3 *prep* **(a)** *(indicating motion, removal etc)* von *(+dat).* **he jumped ~ the roof** er sprang vom Dach; **they dined ~ a chicken** sie verspeisten ein Hühnchen; **he got £2 ~ the shirt** er bekam das Hemd £ 2 billiger; **the coat has two buttons ~ it** am Mantel fehlen zwei Knöpfe.

(b) a street ~ Piccadilly eine Nebenstraße von Piccadilly; **he lives just ~ the square** er wohnt gleich am Platz; **2 miles ~ the motorway** 2 Meilen von der Autobahn entfernt; **anchored ~**

the coast vor der Küste liegend.

(c) ~ **the map** nicht auf der Karte; **I'm** ~ **beer at the moment** Bier kann mich zur Zeit nicht reizen; **I'm right** ~ **sausages** ich kann keine Wurst mehr sehen.

offal ['ɒfəl] *n no pl* Innereien *pl*.

off: ~**beat** *adj (unusual)* ausgefallen, ungewöhnlich; ~**-centre,** *(US)* ~**-center** *adj (lit)* nicht in der Mitte; ~**-chance** *n* **I just did it on the** ~**-chance** ich habe es auf gut Glück getan; **he bought it on the** ~**-chance that it would come in useful** er kaufte es, weil es vielleicht irgendwann mal nützlich sein könnte; ~**-colour,** *(US)* ~**-color** *adj* **to be** ~**-colour** sich unwohl fühlen.

offence, *(US)* **offense** [ə'fens] *n* **(a)** *(Jur: crime)* Straftat *f*, Delikt *nt*; *(minor also)* Vergehen *nt*. **to commit an** ~ sich strafbar machen; **it is an** ~ **to** ... ... ist bei Strafe verboten; **an** ~ **against** ... ein Verstoß *m* gegen ... **(b)** *no pl (to sb's feelings)* Kränkung *f*. **to cause** *or* **give** ~ **to sb** jdn kränken; **to take** ~ **at sth** wegen etw gekränkt sein; **I meant no** ~ ich habe es nicht böse gemeint

offend [ə'fend] **1** *vt* **(a)** *(hurt feelings of)* kränken; *(be disagreeable to)* Anstoß erregen bei. **don't be** ~**ed** nehmen Sie mir *etc* das nicht übel. **(b)** *ear, eye* beleidigen; *sense of justice* verletzen. **2** *vi* **(a)** *(give offence)* beleidigend sein. **(b)** *(do wrong)* Unrecht tun.

offender [ə'fendə[r]] *n (law-breaker)* Täter(in *f*) *m*; *(against traffic laws)* Verkehrssünder(in *f*) *m*. **young** ~ jugendlicher Straffälliger.

offensive [ə'fensɪv] **1** *adj* **(a)** *weapon (Jur)* Angriffs-; *(Mil also)* Offensiv-. **(b)** *(unpleasant) smell, sight* übel, abstoßend; *language, film* anstößig; *(insulting) remark, behaviour* beleidigend. **to find sb/sth** ~ jdn/etw abstoßend finden; *behaviour, language* Anstoß an etw *(dat)* nehmen; **he was** ~ **to her** er beleidigte sie. **2** *n (Mil, Sport)* Angriff *m*, Offensive *f*. **to take the** ~ in die Offensive gehen; **on the** ~ in der Offensive.

offensively [ə'fensɪvlɪ] *adv (unpleasantly)* übel, widerlich; *(in moral sense)* anstößig; *(abusively)* beleidigend.

offer ['ɒfə[r]] **1** *n* Angebot *nt*. **to make an** ~ **of sth to sb** jdm etw anbieten; **an** ~ **I couldn't refuse** ein Angebot, zu dem ich nicht nein sagen konnte; **on** ~ *(Comm)* im Angebot. **2** *vt* **(a)** anbieten; *reward, prize* aussetzen; *plan, suggestion* unterbreiten; *excuse* vorbringen. **to** ~ **to do sth** anbieten, etw zu tun; **he** ~**ed to help** er bot seine Hilfe an; **to** ~ **one's services** sich anbieten. **(b)** *resistance* bieten.

offering ['ɒfərɪŋ] *n* Gabe *f*; *(Rel) (collection)* Opfergabe *f*; *(sacrifice)* Opfer *nt*.

offertory ['ɒfətərɪ] *n (Eccl) (part of service)* Opferung *f*; *(collection)* Kollekte *f*.

offhand [,ɒf'hænd] **1** *adj remark* lässig. **2** *adv* so ohne weiteres, aus dem Stand *(col)*. **I couldn't tell you** ~ das könnte ich Ihnen auf Anhieb nicht sagen.

offhandedly [,ɒf'hændɪdlɪ] *adv* lässig, leichthin.

office ['ɒfɪs] *n* **(a)** Büro *nt*; *(of lawyer)* Kanzlei *f*; *(part of organization)* Abteilung *f*; *(branch also)* Geschäftsstelle *f*. **at the** ~ im Büro. **(b)** *(public position)* Amt *nt*. **to take** ~ sein Amt antreten; *(political party)* die Regierung übernehmen; **to be in** *or* **hold** ~ im Amt sein; *(party)* an der Regierung sein; **to be out of** ~ nicht mehr an der Regierung sein; *(person)* nicht im Amt sein. **(c)** *usu pl* **through his good** ~**s** durch seine guten Dienste; **through the** ~**s of** ... durch Vermittlung von ... **(d)** *(Eccl)* Gottesdienst *m*.

office: ~ **automation** *n* Büroautomatisierung *f*; ~ **bearer** *n* Amtsträger(in *f*) *m*; ~ **block** *n* Bürogebäude *nt*; ~ **hours** *npl* Dienstzeit *f*; *(on sign)* Geschäftszeiten *pl*; ~ **job** *n* Stelle *f* im Büro.

officer ['ɒfɪsə[r]] *n* **(a)** *(Mil, Naut, Aviat)* Offizier *m*. ~**s' mess** Offizierskasino *nt*. **(b)** *(official)* Beamte(r) *m*, Beamtin *f*; *(police* ~*)* Polizist *m*. **no,** ~ nein(, Herr Wachtmeister).

office worker *n* Büroangestellte(r) *mf*.

official [ə'fɪʃəl] **1** *adj* offiziell; *report, duties, meeting also* amtlich; *robes, visit* Amts-; *ceremony, style* formell. **is that** ~? ist das amtlich?; *(publicly announced)* ist das offiziell? **2** *n* Beamte(r) *m*, Beamtin *f*; *(of club)* Funktionär(in *f*) *m*.

officialdom [ə'fɪʃəldəm] *n (pej)* Beamtentum *nt*.

officialese [ə,fɪʃə'li:z] *n* Amtssprache *f*.

officially [ə'fɪʃəlɪ] *adv* offiziell.

officiate [ə'fɪʃɪeɪt] *vt* amtieren, fungieren *(at* bei*)*. **to** ~ **at a marriage** eine Trauung vornehmen.

officious [ə'fɪʃəs] *adj* übereifrig.

offing ['ɒfɪŋ] *n*: **in the** ~ in Sicht.

off: ~**-key** *adj (Mus)* falsch; ~**-licence** *n (Brit)* Wein- und Spirituosenhandlung *f*; ~**-load** *vt goods* ausladen, entladen; *passengers* aussteigen lassen; ~**-peak** *adj* ~**-peak charges** verbilligter Tarif; *(Elec)* ≈ Nachttarif *m*; ~**-peak ticket** verbilligte Fahrkarte/Flugkarte außerhalb der Stoßzeit; ~**-putting** *adj (Brit) smell, behaviour* abstoßend; *thought, story* wenig ermutigend; *(daunting)* entmutigend; ~**-season** *n* Nebensaison *f*.

offset ['ɒfset] *(vb: pret, ptp* ~*)* **1** *vt (financially, statistically etc)* ausgleichen; *(make up for)* aufwiegen. **2** *n (Typ)* Offsetdruck *m*.

off: ~**shoot** *n* **(a)** *(of plant)* Ausläufer *m*; **(b)** *(fig: of organization)* Nebenzweig *m*; ~**shore** *adj fisheries* Küsten-; *island* küstennah; *rig, installations etc* im Meer; ~**side 1** *adj* **(a)** *(Sport)* im Abseits; **(b)** *(Aut)* auf der Fahrerseite; **2** *n (Aut)* Fahrerseite *f*; **3** *adv (Sport)* abseits, im Abseits; ~**-spring** *n* Sprößling *m*; *(of animal)* Junge(s) *nt*; ~**stage** *adv* hinter den Kulissen; ~**-the-cuff** *adj remark, speech* aus dem Stegreif; ~**-the-peg** *adj (Brit) suit* von der Stange; ~**-white** *adj* gebrochen weiß.

often ['ɒfən] *adv* oft, häufig. **not as** ~ **as twice a week** weniger als zweimal in der Woche; **more** ~ **than not, as** ~ **as not** meistens; **every so** ~ von Zeit zu Zeit; **how** ~? wie oft?

ogle ['əʊgl] *vt* kein Auge lassen von, begaffen *(pej)*; *(flirtatiously)* schöne Augen machen *(+dat)*.

ogre ['əʊgə[r]] *n* Menschenfresser *m*; *(fig)* Unmensch *m*.

oh [əʊ] *interj* ach; *(surprised, disappointed)* oh; *(questioning)* tatsächlich.

OHMS = **On His/Her Majesty's Service.**

oil [ɔɪl] **1** *n* **(a)** Öl *nt*. **to pour** ~ **on troubled waters** die Wogen glätten. **(b)** *(petroleum)* (Erd)öl *nt*. **to strike** ~ *(lit)* auf Öl stoßen; *(get rich)* das große Los ziehen. **2** *vt* ölen, schmieren.

oil *in cpds* Öl-; ~**can** *n* Ölkanne *f*; ~**field** *n* Ölfeld *nt*; ~**-fired** *adj* Öl-; ~ **lamp** *n* Öllampe *f*; ~ **painting** *n* Ölgemälde *nt*; ~**-producing** *adj* ölproduzierend; ~**-rich** *adj* ölreich; ~ **rig** *n* (Öl)bohrinsel *f*; ~**skin** *n (cloth)* Öltuch *nt*; ~**skins** *npl (clothing)* Ölzeug *nt*; ~ **tanker** *n* (Öl)tanker *m*; *(lorry)* Tankwagen *m*; ~ **well** *n* Ölquelle *f*.

oily ['ɔɪlɪ] *adj (+er)* ölig; *food* fettig; *clothes, fingers* voller Öl; *(fig)* aalglatt.

ointment ['ɔɪntmənt] *n* Salbe *f*.

OK, okay ['əʊ'keɪ] *(col)* **1** *interj* okay *(col)*; *(agreed also)* in Ordnung. ~, ~! ist ja gut! *(col)*. **2** *adj* in Ordnung, okay *(col)*. **that's** ~ **with** *or* **by me** *(that's convenient)* das ist mir recht, mir ist's recht; **is it** ~ **with you if** ...? macht es (dir) was aus, wenn ...?; **how's your mother?** — **she's** ~ wie geht's deiner Mutter? — gut *or (not too well)* so einigermaßen; **to be** ~ **(for time/money** *etc***)** (noch) genug (Zeit/Geld *etc*) haben; **is that** ~? geht das?, ist das okay? *(col)*; **he's** ~ er ist in Ordnung *(col)*. **3** *adv (well)* gut; *(not too badly)* einigermaßen. **can you mend/manage it** ~? kannst du das reparieren/kommst du damit klar? **4** *vt plan, suggestion* gutheißen, billigen. **5** *n*

Zustimmung *f*, Okay *nt (col)*.

old [əʊld] **1** *adj (+er)* **(a)** alt. ~ **people** *or* **folk(s)** alte Leute *pl*; ~ **Mr Smith** der alte (Herr) Smith; **he is 40 years** ~ er ist 40 (Jahre alt); **two-year-**~ Zweijährige(r) *mf*; **the** ~ **part of Ulm** die Ulmer Altstadt; **the** ~ **(part of) town** die Altstadt; **my** ~ **school** meine alte *or* ehemalige Schule. **(b)** *(col: as intensifier)* **she dresses any** ~ **how** die ist vielleicht immer angezogen *(col)*; ~ **Mike** der Mike *(col)*; **the same** ~ **excuse** die gleiche alte Entschuldigung. **2** *n* **the** ~ die alten Leute; **in days of** ~ in früheren Zeiten; **I know him of** ~ ich kenne ihn von früher.

old: ~ **age** *n* das Alter; **in one's** ~ **age** auf seine alten Tage *(also hum)*; ~**-age pension** *n* Rente *f*; ~**-age pensioner** *n (Brit)* Rentner(in *f*) *m*; ~ **boy** *n (Brit Sch)* ehemaliger Schüler; **the** ~ **boy network** Beziehungen *pl* (von der Schule her).

olden ['əʊldən] *adj (liter)* **in** ~ **times** *or* **days** früher, vordem *(liter)*.

old: O~ **English 1** *n* Altenglisch *nt*; **2** *adj* altenglisch; ~**-established** *adj family, firm* alteingesessen; *custom* seit langem bestehend, alt.

old: ~**-fashioned** ['əʊld'fæʃnd] *adj* altmodisch; ~ **girl** *n (Brit Sch)* ehemalige Schülerin; ~ **maid** *n* alte Jungfer; ~ **master** *n* alter Meister; ~ **people's home** *n* Altersheim *nt*; ~ **school** *n (fig)* alte Schule; **O**~ **Testament** *n* Altes Testament; ~**-timer** *n* Veteran *m*; ~ **wives' tale** *n* Ammenmärchen *nt*; **O**~ **World** *n* alte Welt.

O Level ['əʊlevl] *n (Brit)* Abschluß *m* der Sekundarstufe 1, ≈ mittlere Reife. **to do one's** ~**s** ≈ die mittlere Reife machen; **3** ~**s** die mittlere Reife in 3 Fächern.

oligarchy ['ɒlɪgɑːkɪ] *n* Oligarchie *f*.

olive ['ɒlɪv] **1** *n* **(a)** Olive *f*; *(also* ~ **tree***)* Olivenbaum *m*. **(b)** *(colour)* Olive *nt*. **2** *adj* olivgrün.

olive: ~ **branch** *n (lit, fig)* Ölzweig *m*; **to hold out the** ~ **branch to sb** *(fig)* jdm seinen Willen zum Frieden bekunden; ~ **oil** *n* Olivenöl *nt*.

Olympic [əʊ'lɪmpɪk] **1** *adj* olympisch. ~ **champion** Olympiasieger(in *f*) *m*. **2** *n* **the** ~**s** *pl* die Olympiade, die olympischen Spiele.

ombudsman ['ɒmbʊdzmən] *n, pl* **-men** [-mən] Ombudsmann *m*.

omelette, *(US)* **omelet** ['ɒmlɪt] *n* Omelett(e) *nt*.

omen ['əʊmen] *n* Omen, Zeichen *nt*.

ominous ['ɒmɪnəs] *adj* bedrohlich; *sign also* verhängnisvoll. **that sounds** ~ das verspricht nichts Gutes.

ominously ['ɒmɪnəslɪ] *adv* bedrohlich; *say* in einem unheilverkündenden Ton.

omission [əʊ'mɪʃən] *n* Auslassen *nt*; *(word etc left out)* Auslassung *f*; *(failure to do sth)* Unterlassung *f*.

omit [əʊ'mɪt] *vt* **(a)** *(leave out)* auslassen. **(b)** *(fail)* es unterlassen *(to do sth* etw zu tun*)*.

omnibus ['ɒmnɪbəs] *n* **(a)** *(form: bus)* Omnibus *m*. **(b)** ~ **edition** *(book)* Sammelband *m*.

omnipotent [ɒm'nɪpətənt] *adj* allmächtig.

omniscient [ɒm'nɪsɪənt] *adj* allwissend.

on [ɒn] **1** *prep* **(a)** *(indicating place, position)* auf *(+dat)*; *(with vb of motion)* auf *(+acc)*; *(on vertical surface, part of body)* an *(+dat/acc)*. **the book is** ~ **the table** das Buch ist auf dem Tisch; **he put the book** ~ **the table** er legte das Buch auf den Tisch; **it was** ~ **the blackboard** es stand an der Tafel; **he hung it** ~ **the wall/nail** er hängte es an die Wand/den Nagel; **he hit his head** ~ **the table/** ~ **the ground** er hat sich *(dat)* den Kopf am Tisch/auf dem *or* am Boden angeschlagen; **I have no money** ~ **me** ich habe kein Geld bei mir; **we had something to eat** ~ **the train** wir haben im Zug etwas gegessen; **a house** ~ **the main road** ein Haus an der Hauptstraße.

(b) *(means)* **we went** ~ **the train** wir fuhren mit dem Zug; ~ **foot/horseback** zu Fuß/Pferd; **he lives** ~ **his income** er lebt von seinem Einkommen.

(c) *(about, concerning)* über *(+acc)*. **a book** ~ **German grammar** ein Buch über deutsche Grammatik; **his views** ~ **that** seine Meinung darüber.

(d) *(time)* ~ **Sunday** (am) Sonntag; ~ **Sundays** sonntags; ~ **December the first** am ersten Dezember; ~ **the minute** auf die Minute genau; ~ **my arrival** bei meiner Ankunft; ~ **examination** bei der Untersuchung; ~ **request** auf Wunsch; ~ **hearing this he left** als er das hörte, ging er; ~ **(receiving) my letter** nach Erhalt meines Briefes.

(e) he is ~ **the committee/the board** er gehört dem Ausschuß/Vorstand an; **I am working** ~ **a new project** ich arbeite gerade an einem neuen Projekt; **we were** ~ **page 72** wir waren auf Seite 72; **this round is** ~ **me** diese Runde geht auf meine Kosten; **prices are up** ~ **last year('s)** im Vergleich zum letzten Jahr sind sie Preise gestiegen; **he played (it)** ~ **the violin/trumpet** er spielte (es) auf der Geige/Trompete; **I'm** ~ **£8,000 a year** ich bekomme £ 8,000 im Jahr; **to be** ~ **a course** *(Sch, Univ)* an einem Kurs teilnehmen; **to be** ~ **drugs/pills** Drogen/Pillen nehmen.

2 *adv see also vb +on* **(a) he put his hat** ~ er setzte seinen Hut auf; **he put his coat** ~ er zog seinen Mantel an; **she had nothing** ~ sie hatte nichts an; **what did he have** ~**?** was hatte er an?

(b) *(continuation)* **move** ~**!** gehen Sie weiter!; **from that day** ~ von diesem Tag an; **it was well** ~ **in the night** es war spät in der Nacht; **to keep** ~ **talking** in einem fort reden; **go** ~ **with your work** machen Sie Ihre Arbeit weiter; **life still goes** ~ das Leben geht weiter; **they talked** ~ **and** ~ sie redeten und redeten; **to read** ~ weiterlesen.

(c) *(in phrases)* **he's always (going)** ~ **at me to get my hair cut** er liegt mir dauernd in den Ohren, daß ich mir die Haare schneiden lassen soll; **she's always** ~ **about her experiences in Italy** sie kommt dauernd mit ihren Italienerfahrungen; **what's he** ~ **about?** wovon redet er nun schon wieder?

3 *adj* **(a)** *lights, TV, radio* an; *brake* angezogen; *electricity, gas* an(gestellt). **the** ~ **switch** der Einschalter; **to leave the engine** ~ den Motor laufen lassen.

(b) to be ~ *(being performed: film etc)* gezeigt werden; **what's** ~ **tonight?** was läuft heute abend?; **I have nothing** ~ **tonight** ich habe heute abend nichts vor; **what's** ~ **in London?** was ist los in London?

(c) *(valid)* **to be** ~ *(bet, agreement)* gelten; **you're** ~**!** abgemacht!; **it's just not** ~ *(not acceptable)* das ist einfach nicht drin *(col)*.

once [wʌns] **1** *adv* **(a)** *(on one occasion)* einmal. ~ **a week** einmal in der Woche; ~ **again** *or* **more** noch einmal; ~ **again we find that ...** wir stellen erneut fest, daß ...; ~ **or twice** *(fig)* nur ein paarmal; ~ **and for all** ein für allemal; **(every)** ~ **in a while** ab und zu mal; **you can come this** ~ dieses eine Mal können Sie kommen; **for** ~ ausnahmsweise einmal. **(b)** *(in past)* einmal. **he was** ~ **famous** er war früher einmal berühmt; ~ **upon a time there was ...** es war einmal ... **(c) at** ~ *(immediately)* sofort, auf der Stelle; *(at the same time)* auf einmal, gleichzeitig; **all at** ~ auf einmal; **they came all at** ~ sie kamen alle gleichzeitig. **2** *conj* wenn; *(with past tense)* als. ~ **you understand, it's easy** wenn Sie es einmal verstehen, ist es einfach.

once-over ['wʌnsəʊvə[r]] *n (col)* **to give sb/sth the** ~ *(appraisal)* jdn/etw mal kurz überprüfen; *(clean)* mal kurz über etw *(acc)* gehen *(col)*.

oncoming ['ɒnkʌmɪŋ] *adj car, traffic* entgegenkommend. **the** ~ **traffic** der Gegenverkehr.

one [wʌn] **1** *adj* **(a)** *(number)* ein/eine/ein. ~ **man in**

a thousand einer von tausend; the baby is ~ (year old) das Kind ist ein Jahr (alt); it is ~ (o'clock) es ist eins, es ist ein Uhr; there is only ~ way of doing it es gibt nur eine Möglichkeit, es zu tun.

(b) *(indefinite)* ~ morning/day he realized ... eines Morgens/Tages bemerkte er ...; you'll regret it ~ day Sie werden das eines Tages bereuen; ~ morning next week nächste Woche einmal morgens.

(c) *(sole, only)* he is the ~ man to tell you er ist der einzige, der es Ihnen sagen kann; no ~ man could do it niemand konnte es allein tun; the ~ and only Brigitte Bardot die unvergleichliche Brigitte Bardot.

(d) *(same)* they all came in the ~ car sie kamen alle in dem einen Auto; they are ~ and the same person das ist ein und dieselbe Person; it is ~ and the same thing das ist ein und dasselbe; it's all ~ das ist einerlei.

2 *pron* (a) eine(r, s). the ~ who ... der(jenige), der .../die(jenige), die .../das(jenige), das ...; do you have ~? haben Sie einen/eine/ein(e)s?; the red/big *etc* ~ der/die/das rote/große *etc*; a bigger ~ ein größerer/eine größere/ein größeres; not ~ of them nicht eine(r, s) von ihnen; every ~ jede(r, s); this ~ diese(r, s); that ~ der/die/das; which ~? welche(r, s)?; I'm not ~ to go out often ich bin nicht der Typ, der oft ausgeht; he's never ~ to say no er sagt nie nein; he's a great ~ for discipline der ist ganz groß, wenn's um Disziplin geht; she is a teacher, and he/her sister wants to be ~ too sie ist Lehrerin, und er möchte auch gern Lehrer werden/ihre Schwester möchte auch gern eine werden; I, for ~, think otherwise ich, zum Beispiel, denke anders; ~ by ~ einzeln; he is ~ of the family er gehört zur Familie; he is ~ of us er ist einer von uns.

(b) *(impers) (nom)* man; *(acc)* einen; *(dat)* einem. ~ must learn to keep quiet man muß lernen, still zu sein; to hurt ~'s foot sich *(dat)* den Fuß verletzen.

3 *n (written figure)* Eins *f*. in ~s and twos in kleinen Gruppen; it was bedroom and sitting-room (all) in ~ es war Schlaf- und Wohnzimmer in einem; to be at ~ with oneself mit sich selbst im Einklang sein; to be ~ up on sb *(col) (know more)* jdm eins voraussein; *(have more)* jdm etwas voraushaben.

one another = **each other**.

one: ~-armed *adj* einarmig; ~-eyed *adj* einäugig; ~-legged *adj* einbeinig; ~-man *adj* Einmann-; ~-man band Einmannkapelle *f*; *(fig col)* Einmannbetrieb *m*; ~-off *adj (Brit col)* einmalig; ~-piece *adj* einteilig.

onerous ['ɒnərəs] *adj responsibility* schwer(wiegend); *task, duty* schwer.

oneself [wʌn'self] *pron* (a) *(dir and indir, with prep)* sich; *(~ personally)* sich selbst *or* selber. (b) *(emph)* (sich) selbst; *see* myself.

one: ~-shot *adj, n (US)* einmalig; ~-sided *adj* einseitig; *judgement, account also* parteiisch; ~-time *adj* ehemalig; ~-to-one *adj correlation* eins-zu-eins; ~-track *adj* he's got a ~-track mind der hat immer nur das eine im Sinn; ~-upmanship [,wʌn'ʌpmənʃɪp] *n* that's just a form of ~-upmanship damit will er *etc* den anderen nur um eine Nasenlänge voraus sein; ~-way *adj traffic, street* Einbahn-; ~-way ticket *(US Rail)* einfache Fahrkarte.

ongoing ['ɒngəʊɪŋ] *adj (in progress)* laufend; *(long-term) development, relationship* andauernd.

onion ['ʌnjən] *n* Zwiebel *f*.

online [ɒn'laɪn] 1 *adj attr* On-line-. 2 *adv* on-line. the computer is operating ~ der Computer arbeitet im On-line-Betrieb.

onlooker ['ɒnlʊkəʳ] *n* Zuschauer(in *f*) *m*.

only ['əʊnlɪ] 1 *adj attr* einzige(r, s). he's an ~ child er ist ein Einzelkind *nt*; he was the ~ one to leave *or* who left er ist als einziger gegangen; that's the ~ thing for it/the ~ thing to do das ist die einzige Möglichkeit; my ~ wish/regret das einzige, was ich mir wünsche/was ich bedaure.

2 *adv* nur. it's ~ five o'clock es ist erst fünf Uhr; I ~ wanted to be with you ich wollte nur mit dir zusammen sein; ~ too true *etc* nur (all)zu wahr *etc*; I'd be ~ too pleased to help ich würde nur zu gerne helfen; if ~ that hadn't happened wenn das bloß nicht passiert wäre; we ~ just caught the train wir haben den Zug gerade noch gekriegt; he has ~ just arrived er ist gerade erst angekommen; I've ~ just got enough ich habe gerade genug; not ~ ... but also ... nicht nur ..., sondern auch ...

3 *conj* bloß, nur. I would do it myself, ~ I haven't time ich würde es selbst machen, ich habe nur keine Zeit.

onomatopoeia [,ɒnəʊmætəʊ'piːə] *n* Lautmalerei *f*.

onrush ['ɒnrʌʃ] *n (of people)* Ansturm *m*; *(of water)* Schwall *m*.

onset ['ɒnset] *n* Beginn *m*; *(of cold weather also)* Einbruch *m*; *(of illness)* Ausbruch *m*.

onslaught ['ɒnslɔːt] *n (Mil)* (heftiger) Angriff *(on* auf *+acc)*. to make an ~ on sb/sth *(fig) (verbally)* jdn/etw angreifen; *(on work)* einer Sache *(dat)* zu Leibe rücken.

onto ['ɒntʊ] *prep* (a) *(upon, on top of)* auf *(+acc)*; *(on sth vertical)* an *(+acc)*. (b) *(in verbal expressions)* to get/come ~ a subject auf ein Thema zu sprechen kommen; to be/get ~ *or* on to sb *(find sb out)* jdm auf die Schliche gekommen sein/kommen *(col)*; I'll get ~ him about it ich werde ihn darauf ansprechen.

onus ['əʊnəs] *n no pl* Pflicht *f*; *(burden)* Last *f*. to shift the ~ for sth onto sb jdm die Verantwortung für etw zuschieben; the ~ to do it is on him es liegt an ihm, das zu tun.

onward ['ɒnwəd] *adv (also ~s)* voran, vorwärts; *march* weiter. from today/this time ~ von heute/der Zeit an.

onyx ['ɒnɪks] 1 *n* Onyx *m*. 2 *adj* Onyx-.

ooze [uːz] 1 *n (mud)* Schlamm *m*. 2 *vi* triefen; *(wound)* nässen; *(resin, mud, glue)* (heraus)quellen. 3 *vt* (a) (aus)schwitzen. (b) *(fig) kindness, charm* triefen von *(pej)*, verströmen.

opal ['əʊpəl] *n (stone)* Opal *m*.

opaque [əʊ'peɪk] *adj* (a) opak; *glass also, liquid* trüb. (b) *(fig) prose* undurchsichtig, unklar.

OPEC ['əʊpek] = **Organization of Petroleum Exporting Countries** OPEC *f*.

open ['əʊpən] 1 *adj* offen; *door, bottle, eye, flower also* auf *pred*, geöffnet; *lines of communication, road* frei; *(public) meeting, trial* öffentlich. to keep/hold the door ~ die Tür offen- *or* auflassen/offen- *or* aufhalten; I can't keep my eyes ~ ich kann die Augen nicht offenhalten; the baker's shop is ~ der Bäckerladen hat geöffnet *or* hat auf *(col)*; to lay oneself ~ to criticism/attack sich der Kritik/Angriffen aussetzen; in the ~ air im Freien; ~ to traffic/shipping für den Verkehr/die Schiffahrt freigegeben; to be ~ to sb *(admission)* jdm freistehen; *(place)* für jdn geöffnet sein; he was ~ with us er war ganz offen mit uns; two possibilities were ~ to him zwei Möglichkeiten standen ihm offen; ~ day Tag *m* der offenen Tür; ~ to the public der Öffentlichkeit zugänglich; to be ~ to advice/suggestions Ratschlägen/Vorschlägen gegenüber offen sein; I'm ~ to offers ich lasse gern mit mir reden; they left the matter ~ sie ließen die Angelegenheit offen; to keep an ~ mind alles offen lassen; to have an ~ mind on sth einer Sache *(dat)* aufgeschlossen gegenüberstehen.

2 *n* in the ~ *(outside)* im Freien; *(on ~ ground)* auf freiem Feld; to bring sth out into the ~ mit

etw nicht länger hinterm Berg halten; **to come out into the ~** *(fig) (person)* Farbe bekennen; *(affair)* herauskommen.

3 *vt* **(a)** *door, mouth, bottle, letter etc* öffnen, aufmachen *(col)*; *book also, newspaper* aufschlagen; *(officially) exhibition* eröffnen; *building* einweihen; *road* dem Verkehr übergeben. **to ~ one's heart to sb** sich jdm eröffnen *(geh)*; **~ your mind to new possibilities** öffnen Sie sich *(dat)* den Blick für neue Möglichkeiten; **to ~ fire** *(Mil)* das Feuer eröffnen *(on* auf *+acc)*. **(b)** *shop, trial, school, account* eröffnen.

4 *vi* **(a)** aufgehen; *(door, flower, wound also)* sich öffnen. **(b)** *(shop, museum)* öffnen, aufmachen. **(c)** *(door)* führen *(into* in *+acc)*. **(d)** *(start)* beginnen *(with* mit*)*; *(Cards, Chess)* eröffnen. **the play ~s next week** das Stück wird ab nächster Woche gegeben.

♦ **open out 1** *vi (river, street)* sich verbreitern *(into* zu*)*; *(valley also, view)* sich weiten, sich öffnen; *(flower)* sich öffnen, aufgehen. **2** *vt sep (unfold) map etc* auseinanderfalten.

♦ **open up 1** *vi (flower)* sich öffnen, aufgehen; *(fig) (prospects, field, new horizons)* sich erschließen; *(person: become expansive)* gesprächiger werden. **2** *vt sep* **(a)** *territory, prospects* erschließen; *new horizons, field of research etc also* auftun; *(unblock) disused tunnel etc* freimachen. **(b)** *(unlock) house, shop, car etc* aufschließen. **(c)** *(start) business* eröffnen; *shop also* aufmachen.

open: ~-air *adj* im Freien; **~-air swimming pool** *n* Freibad *nt*; **~-and-shut** *adj* **it's an ~-and-shut case** es ist ein glasklarer Fall; **~-cast** *adj coalmine* über Tage; **~-cast mining** Tagebau *m*.

opener ['əupnəʳ] *n* Öffner *m*.

open: ~-handed *adj* freigebig; **~ house** *n* **to keep ~ house** ein offenes Haus führen.

opening ['əupnɪŋ] **1** *n* **(a)** Öffnung *f*; *(in traffic)* Lücke *f*; *(forest clearing)* Lichtung *f*. **(b)** *(beginning)* Anfang *m*; *(of debate, speech, trial also, Chess, Cards)* Eröffnung *f*. **(c)** *(official ~) (of exhibition, stores)* Eröffnung *f*. **O~ of Parliament** Parlamentseröffnung *f*. **(d)** *(opportunity)* Möglichkeit, Chance *f*; *(job vacancy)* (freie) Stelle. **2** *attr (initial, first)* erste(r, s); *speech also* Eröffnungs-; *remarks* einführend.

opening: ~ ceremony *n* Eröffnungsfeierlichkeiten *pl*; **~ time** *n* Öffnungszeit *f*; **what are the bank's ~ times?** wann hat die Bank geöffnet?

openly ['əupənlɪ] *adv* offen; *(publicly)* öffentlich.

open: ~-minded *adj* aufgeschlossen; **~-mindedness** *n* Aufgeschlossenheit *f*; **~-mouthed** [,əupn'mauðd] *adj (in surprise or stupidity)* mit offenem Mund; **~-necked** *adj shirt* mit offenem Kragen.

openness ['əupnnɪs] *n (frankness)* Offenheit *f*.

open-plan ['əupən,plæn] *adj office* Großraum-; *flat etc* offen angelegt.

opera ['ɒpərə] *n* Oper *f*. **to go to the ~** in die Oper gehen.

opera *in cpds* Opern-; **~ glasses** *npl* Opernglas *nt*; **~ house** *n* Opernhaus *nt*; **~ singer** *n* Opernsänger(in *f*) *m*.

operate ['ɒpəreɪt] **1** *vi* operieren *(also Mil, Med)*; *(machine)* funktionieren; *(be in operation)* in Betrieb sein; *(buses, planes)* verkehren; *(theory, plan, law)* sich auswirken; *(organization, system)* arbeiten. **I don't like the way he ~s** ich mag seine Methoden nicht; **to be ~d on** *(Med)* operiert werden. **2** *vt* **(a)** *machine* bedienen; *(set in operation)* in Betrieb setzen; *brakes etc also* betätigen. **(b)** *business* führen.

operatic [,ɒpə'rætɪk] *adj singer, music* Opern-.

operating ['ɒpəreɪtɪŋ] *adj attr* **(a)** *(Tech, Comm) pressure, cost* Betriebs-. **(b)** *(Med)* Operations-. **~ theatre** *(Brit) or* **room** Operationssaal, OP *m*.

operation [,ɒpə'reɪʃən] *n* **(a)** *(of machine, system)* Funktionieren *nt*; *(act of operating)* Bedienung *f*; *(of small mechanism)* Betätigung *f*. **to be in ~** *(machine)* in Betrieb sein; *(law)* in Kraft sein; *(plan)* durchgeführt werden; **to be out of ~** außer Betrieb sein; **to come into ~** *(law)* in Kraft treten; *(plan)* zur Anwendung gelangen; **to bring** *or* **put a law into ~** ein Gesetz in Kraft setzen. **(b)** *(Med)* Operation *f (on* an *+dat)*. **to have an ~** operiert werden; **to have an ~ for a hernia** wegen eines Bruchs operiert werden. **(c)** *(enterprise)* Unternehmen *nt*; *(task, stage in undertaking)* Arbeitsgang *m*. **(business) ~s** Geschäfte *pl*; **to cease ~s** den Geschäftverkehr einstellen.

operational [,ɒpə'reɪʃənl] *adj (ready for use) machine, vehicle* betriebsbereit; *army unit, aeroplane etc* einsatzfähig; *(in use or action) machine, vehicle etc* in Betrieb; *army unit etc* im Einsatz.

operative ['ɒpərətɪv] **1** *adj* **(a)** *measure, laws* wirksam. **"if" being the ~ word** wobei ich „wenn" betone. **(b)** *(Med) treatment* operativ. **2** *n (of machinery)* Maschinenarbeiter(in *f*) *m*.

operator ['ɒpəreɪtəʳ] *n (Telec)* ≈ Vermittlung *f*; *(person)* Dame *f*/Herr *m* von der Vermittlung; *(of machinery)* (Maschinen)arbeiter(in *f*) *m*; *(of computer etc)* Operator(in *f*) *m*. **to be a smooth ~** *(col)* raffiniert vorgehen.

ophthalmic [ɒf'θælmɪk] *adj* Augen-.

opinion [ə'pɪnjən] *n* Meinung, Ansicht *f (about, on* zu*)*; *(political, religious)* Anschauung *f*; *(professional advice)* Gutachten *nt*; *(esp Med)* Befund *m*. **in my ~** meiner Meinung nach; **to be of the ~ that ...** der Ansicht sein, daß ...; **to ask sb's ~** jdn nach seiner Meinung fragen; **it is a matter of ~** das ist Ansichtssache; **to have a high/poor ~ of sb/sth** eine hohe/schlechte Meinung von jdm/etw haben; **to form an ~ of sb/sth** sich *(dat)* eine Meinung über jdn/etw bilden; **~ poll** Meinungsumfrage *f*; **to seek** *or* **get a second ~** *(esp Med)* ein zweites Gutachten einholen.

opinionated [ə'pɪnjəneɪtɪd] *adj* rechthaberisch.

opium ['əupɪəm] *n (lit, fig)* Opium *nt*.

opponent [ə'pəunənt] *n* Gegner(in *f*) *m*.

opportune ['ɒpətju:n] *adj time* günstig; *remark* an passender Stelle; *action, event* rechtzeitig.

opportunism [,ɒpə'tju:nɪzəm] *n* Opportunismus *m*.

opportunist [,ɒpə'tju:nɪst] *n* Opportunist *m*.

opportunity [,ɒpə'tju:nɪtɪ] *n* Gelegenheit *f*; *(chance to better oneself)* Chance, Möglichkeit *f*. **at the first** *or* **earliest ~** bei der erstbesten Gelegenheit; **to take the ~ to do sth** *or* **of doing sth** die Gelegenheit nutzen, etw zu tun; **as soon as I get the ~** sobald sich die Gelegenheit ergibt; **opportunities for promotion** Aufstiegsmöglichkeiten *or* -chancen *pl*.

oppose [ə'pəuz] *vt* ablehnen; *(fight against)* sich entgegenstellen *(+dat)*; *leadership, orders* sich widersetzen *(+dat)*; *government* sich stellen gegen. **he ~s our coming** er ist absolut dagegen, daß wir kommen.

opposed [ə'pəuzd] *adj pred* **to be ~ to sb/sth** gegen jdn/etw sein; **I am ~ to your going** ich bin dagegen, daß Sie gehen; **as ~ to** im Gegensatz zu.

opposing [ə'pəuzɪŋ] *adj team* gegnerisch; *army* feindlich; *characters* gegensätzlich.

opposite ['ɒpəzɪt] **1** *adj* **(a)** *(facing)* gegenüberliegend *attr*, gegenüber *pred*. **to be ~** gegenüber liegen/stehen/sitzen *etc*; **on the ~ page** auf der Seite gegenüber, auf der gegenüberliegenden Seite. **(b)** *(other) side, end, opinion* entgegengesetzt *(to, from dat,* zu*)*. **the ~ sex** das andere Geschlecht; **~ number** Pendant *nt*; **they've got quite ~ characters** sie sind ganz gegensätzliche Charaktere. **2** *n* Gegenteil *nt*; *(contrasting: black/white etc)* Gegensatz *m*. **quite the ~!** ganz im Gegenteil! **3** *adv* gegenüber, auf der gegenüberliegenden Seite. **they sat ~** sie saßen uns/ihnen/sich *etc* gegenüber. **4** *prep* gegenüber *(+dat)*. ~ **one another** sich gegenüber; **they live ~ us** sie wohnen uns gegenüber.

opposition [ˌɒpəˈzɪʃən] *n* **(a)** *(resistance)* Widerstand *m*; *(people resisting)* Opposition *f*. **to act in ~ to sth** einer Sache *(dat)* zuwiderhandeln. **(b)** *(esp Brit Parl)* **O~** Opposition(spartei) *f*; **to be in ~** in der Opposition sein.

oppress [əˈpres] *vt* **(a)** *(tyrannize)* unterdrücken. **(b)** *(weigh down)* bedrücken.

oppression [əˈpreʃən] *n (tyranny)* Unterdrückung *f*.

oppressive [əˈpresɪv] *adj* **(a)** *regime, laws* repressiv; *taxes* (er)drückend. **(b)** *(fig) heat* drückend; *thought* bedrückend.

oppressor [əˈpresəʳ] *n* Unterdrücker *m*.

opt [ɒpt] *vi* **to ~ for sth/to do sth** sich für etw entscheiden/sich entscheiden, etw zu tun.

♦ **opt out** *vi* sich anders entscheiden; *(of awkward situation)* abspringen *(of* bei*)*; *(of responsibility, invitation)* ablehnen *(of acc)*; *(give up membership)* austreten *(of* aus*)*; *(of insurance scheme)* kündigen *(of acc)*.

optic [ˈɒptɪk] *adj nerve, centre* Seh-.

optical [ˈɒptɪkəl] *adj* optisch. ~ **illusion** optische Täuschung.

optician [ɒpˈtɪʃən] *n* Optiker(in *f*) *m*.

optics [ˈɒptɪks] *n sing* Optik *f*.

optimism [ˈɒptɪmɪzəm] *n* Optimismus *m*.

optimist [ˈɒptɪmɪst] *n* Optimist(in *f*) *m*.

optimistic [ˌɒptɪˈmɪstɪk] *adj* optimistisch *(about sth* in bezug auf *+acc)*.

optimum [ˈɒptɪməm] *adj* optimal.

option [ˈɒpʃən] *n* **(a)** *(choice)* Wahl *f no pl*; *(possible course of action also)* Möglichkeit *f*. **I have no ~** mir bleibt keine andere Wahl; **he had no ~ but to come** ihm blieb nichts anderes übrig, als zu kommen; **to leave one's ~s open** sich *(dat)* alle Möglichkeiten offenlassen. **(b)** *(Comm)* Option *f (on* auf *+acc)*; *(on house, goods etc also)* Vorkaufsrecht *nt (on* an *+dat)*; *(on shares)* Bezugsrecht *nt (on* für*)*. **with an ~ to buy** mit einer Kaufoption. **(c)** *(Univ, Sch)* Wahlfach *nt*.

optional [ˈɒpʃənl] *adj (not compulsory)* freiwillig; *(Sch, Univ) subject* Wahl-. ~ **extras** Extras *pl*.

opulence [ˈɒpjʊləns] *n no pl see adj* Reichtum *m*; Prunk *m*; Feudalität *f*; Üppigkeit *f*.

opulent [ˈɒpjʊlənt] *adj* reich; *clothes* prunkvoll; *chairs, carpets* feudal; *lifestyle* üppig.

opus [ˈəʊpəs] *n, pl* **opera** [ˈɒpərə] *n (Mus)* Opus *nt*.

or *conj* oder; *(with neg)* noch. **he could not read ~ write** er konnte weder lesen noch schreiben; **you'd better go ~ (else) you'll be late** gehen Sie jetzt besser, sonst kommen Sie zu spät; **you'd better do it ~ else!** tu das lieber, sonst ...!; **in a day ~ two** in ein bis zwei Tagen; **the Congo, ~ rather, Zaire** der Kongo, beziehungsweise Zaire.

oracle [ˈɒrəkl] *n* Orakel *nt*; *(person)* Seher(in *f*) *m*; *(fig)* Alleswisser *m*.

oral [ˈɔːrəl] **1** *adj* **(a)** *(Med)* oral. ~ **vaccination** Schluckimpfung *f*. **(b)** *(verbal)* mündlich. **to improve one's ~ skills in a language** ein Sprache besser sprechen lernen. **2** *n* Mündliche(s) *nt*.

orally [ˈɔːrəlɪ] *adv* **(a)** oral. **not to be taken ~** nicht einnehmen. **(b)** *(verbally)* mündlich.

orange [ˈɒrɪndʒ] **1** *n* *(fruit)* Orange, Apfelsine *f*; *(tree)* Orangenbaum *m*. **2** *adj (in colour)* orange *inv*, orange(n)farben.

orangeade [ˈɒrɪndʒˈeɪd] *n* Orangenlimonade *f*.

orange: ~**juice** *n* Orangensaft *m*; ~ **peel** *n* Orangenschale *f*.

orang-utan [ɔːˌræŋuːˈtæn] *n* Orang-Utan *m*.

oration [ɒˈreɪʃən] *n* Ansprache *f*. **funeral ~** Grabrede *f*.

orator [ˈɒrətəʳ] *n* Redner(in *f*) *m*.

oratorio [ˌɒrəˈtɔːrɪəʊ] *n (Mus)* Oratorium *nt*.

oratory [ˈɒrətərɪ] *n (art)* Redekunst *f*.

orbit [ˈɔːbɪt] **1** *n* **(a)** *(Astron, Space)* Umlaufbahn *f*. **to be in ~** in der Umlaufbahn sein; **to put a satellite into ~** einen Satelliten in die Umlaufbahn schießen; **to go into ~** in die Umlaufbahn eintreten. **(b)** *(fig: sphere of influence)* Einflußsphäre *f*. **2** *vt* umkreisen. **3** *vi* kreisen.

orchard [ˈɔːtʃəd] *n* Obstgarten *m*; *(commercial)* Obstplantage *f*. **apple ~** Obstgarten *m* mit Apfelbäumen.

orchestra [ˈɔːkɪstrə] *n* Orchester *nt*.

orchestral [ɔːˈkestrəl] *adj* Orchester-, orchestral.

orchestra pit *n* Orchestergraben *m*.

orchestration [ˌɔːkɪsˈtreɪʃən] *n* Orchesterbearbeitung *f*.

orchid [ˈɔːkɪd] *n* Orchidee *f*.

ordain [ɔːˈdeɪn] *vt* **(a)** *sb* ordinieren. **(b)** *(destine: God, fate)* wollen, bestimmen. **it was ~ed** das Schicksal hat es so gefügt.

ordeal [ɔːˈdiːl] *n* Tortur *f*; *(stronger, long-lasting)* Martyrium *nt*; *(torment, emotional ~)* Qual *f*.

order [ˈɔːdəʳ] **1** *n* **(a)** *(sequence)* (Reihen)folge *f*. **word ~** Wortstellung *f*; **in ~ of preference** *etc* in der bevorzugten Reihenfolge; **to put sth in (the right) ~** etw ordnen; **to be in the wrong ~** *or* **out of ~** durcheinander sein; *(one item)* nicht am richtigen Platz sein.

(b) *(system, discipline)* Ordnung *f*; *(in school also)* Disziplin *f*. **there's no ~ in his work** seiner Arbeit fehlt die Systematik; **it is in the ~ of things** es liegt in der Natur der Dinge; **his passport was in ~** sein Paß war in Ordnung; **to keep ~** die Ordnung wahren; **to keep the children in ~** die Kinder unter Kontrolle halten.

(c) *(working condition)* Zustand *m*. **to be in good/bad ~** in gutem/schlechtem Zustand sein; *(work well/badly)* in Ordnung/nicht in Ordnung sein; **to be out of/in ~** *(car, radio, telephone)* nicht funktionieren/funktionieren; *(machine, lift)* außer/in Betrieb sein.

(d) *(command)* Befehl *m*. **by ~ of the minister** auf Anordnung des Ministers; **to be under ~s to do sth** Instruktionen haben, etw zu tun.

(e) *(in restaurant etc, for supplies)* Bestellung *f*; *(for goods, services)* Auftrag *m*. **made to ~** auf Bestellung (gemacht); **to place an ~ with sb** eine Bestellung bei jdm aufgeben *or* machen; jdm einen Auftrag geben; **pay to the ~ of** zahlbar an *(+acc)*.

(f) in ~ to do sth um etw zu tun; **in ~ that** damit.

(g) *(correct procedure at meeting, Parl etc)* **a point of ~** eine Verfahrensfrage; **to be out of ~** *(fig)* aus dem Rahmen fallen; **to call the meeting to ~** die Versammlung zur Ordnung rufen; **a drink would seem to be in ~** ein Drink wäre angebracht; **is it in ~ for me to go to Paris?** ist es in Ordnung, wenn ich nach Paris fahre?; **to be the ~ of the day** auf dem Programm stehen *(also fig)*; *(Mil)* der Tagesbefehl sein.

(h) *(Biol)* Ordnung *f*; *(fig: class, degree)* Art *f*. **intelligence of a high ~** hochgradige Intelligenz; **something in the ~ of ten per cent** in der Größenordnung von zehn Prozent.

(i) *(Eccl) (of monks etc)* Orden *m*. **to take (holy) ~s** die Weihen empfangen.

2 *vt* **(a)** *(command, decree) sth* befehlen, anordnen; *(prescribe: doctor)* verordnen *(for sb* jdm*)*. **to ~ sb to do sth** jdm befehlen, etw zu tun; *(esp Mil)* jdn dazu beordern, etw zu tun; **the referee ~ed him off the pitch** der Schiedsrichter verwies ihn des Feldes. **(b)** *(direct, arrange) one's affairs, life* ordnen. **(c)** *(Comm etc) goods, dinner, taxi* bestellen; *(to be manufactured)* in Auftrag geben.

3 *vi* bestellen.

♦ **order about** *or* **around** *vt sep* herumkommandieren.

order: ~ **book** *n (Comm)* Auftragsbuch *nt*; **to have a full ~ book** voll im Geschäft sein; ~ **form** *n* Bestellformular *nt*, Bestellschein *m*.

orderly ['ɔːdəlɪ] **1** *adj* **(a)** *(tidy, methodical)* ordentlich. **(b)** *(disciplined)* ruhig, friedlich. **2** *n* **(medical)** ~ Pfleger(in *f*) *m*; *(Mil)* Sanitäter *m*.

ordinal ['ɔːdɪnl] *(Math)* **1** *adj* Ordnungs-, Ordinal-. **2** *n* Ordnungs- *or* Ordinalzahl *f*.

ordinance ['ɔːdɪnəns] *n (of government)* Verordnung *f*; *(Jur)* Anordnung *f*.

ordinarily ['ɔːdnrɪlɪ] *adv* gewöhnlich; *(+adj)* normal.

ordinary ['ɔːdnrɪ] **1** *adj* **(a)** gewöhnlich, normal. **in the ~ way I would ...** normalerweise *or* gewöhnlich würde ich ...; **my ~ doctor** der Arzt, zu dem ich normalerweise gehe. **(b)** *(average)* durchschnittlich. **2** *n* **out of the ~** außergewöhnlich, außerordentlich.

ordination [ˌɔːdɪ'neɪʃən] *n* Ordination *f*.

ordnance ['ɔːdnəns] *n (Mil) (artillery)* Geschütze *pl*; *(supply)* Material *nt*. **O~ Survey map** *n (Brit)* Meßtischblatt *nt*.

ore [ɔːʳ] *n* Erz *nt*.

organ ['ɔːgən] *n* **(a)** *(Anat)* Organ *nt*. **(b)** *(Mus)* Orgel *f*. **(c)** *(mouthpiece of opinion)* Sprachrohr *nt*; *(newspaper)* Organ *nt*.

organ-grinder ['ɔːgən'graɪndəʳ] *n* Drehorgelspieler *m*.

organic [ɔː'gænɪk] *adj (lit, fig)* organisch; *vegetables, farming* biodynamisch.

organism ['ɔːgənɪzəm] *n* Organismus *m*.

organist ['ɔːgənɪst] *n* Organist(in *f*) *m*.

organization [ˌɔːgənaɪ'zeɪʃən] *n* **(a)** *(act)* Organisation *f (also Pol)*; *(of time)* Einteilung *f*. **(b)** *(arrangement) see vt (a)* Ordnung *f*; Einteilung *f*; Aufbau *m*; Planung *f*. **(c)** *(institution)* Organisation *f*; *(Comm)* Unternehmen *nt*.

organize ['ɔːgənaɪz] *vt* **(a)** *(systematize)* ordnen; *time, work* einteilen; *essay* aufbauen; *one's/sb's life* planen. **to get (oneself) ~d** *(get ready)* alles vorbereiten; *(sort things out)* seine Sachen in Ordnung bringen. **(b)** *(arrange) party, meeting etc* organisieren; *food for party etc* sorgen für. **to ~ things so that ...** es so einrichten, daß ...

organized ['ɔːgənaɪzd] *adj* organisiert; *life* geregelt. **he isn't very ~** bei ihm geht alles drunter und drüber *(col)*.

organizer ['ɔːgənaɪzəʳ] *n* Organisator(in *f*) *m*; *(of event also)* Veranstalter(in *f*) *m*.

orgasm ['ɔːgæzəm] *n* Orgasmus *m*.

orgy ['ɔːdʒɪ] *n (lit, fig)* Orgie *f*. **drunken ~** Sauforgie *f*.

orient ['ɔːrɪənt] *n (also* **O~***)* Orient *m*; *(poet also)* Morgenland *nt*.

oriental [ˌɔːrɪ'entl] **1** *adj* orientalisch. **2** *n (person)* **O~** Orientale *m*, Orientalin *f*.

orientate ['ɔːrɪənteɪt] *vt* ausrichten *(towards* auf *+acc)*. **money-~d** materiell ausgerichtet.

orientation [ˌɔːrɪən'teɪʃən] *n* Orientierung *f*; *(fig also)* Ausrichtung *f*.

orienteering [ˌɔːrɪən'tɪərɪŋ] *n* Orientierungslauf *m*.

orifice ['ɒrɪfɪs] *n* Öffnung *f*.

origin ['ɒrɪdʒɪn] *n* Ursprung *m*; *(of person, family)* Herkunft *f*. **to have its ~ in sth** auf etw *(acc)* zurückgehen; **country of ~** Herkunftsland *nt*; **of humble ~s** aus bescheidenen Verhältnissen.

original [ə'rɪdʒɪnl] **1** *adj* **(a)** *(first, earliest)* ursprünglich. **~ inhabitants of a country** Ureinwohner *pl* eines Landes; **~ text/version** Originaltext *m*/Originalfassung *f*. **(b)** *(not imitative) painting* original; *idea* originell. **~ research** eigene Forschung. **2** *n* Original *nt*; *(of model)* Vorlage *f*. **he reads Kant in the ~** er liest Kant im Original.

originality [əˌrɪdʒɪ'nælɪtɪ] *n* Originalität *f*.

originally [əˌrɪdʒənəlɪ] *adv* **(a)** ursprünglich. **(b)** *(in an original way)* originell.

originate [ə'rɪdʒɪneɪt] **1** *vt* hervorbringen; *policy, company* ins Leben rufen; *product* erfinden. **2** *vi* **(a)** entstehen. **to ~ from** *or* **with sb** von jdm stammen. **(b)** *(US: bus, train etc)* ausgehen *(in* von*)*.

originator [ə'rɪdʒɪneɪtəʳ] *n (of plan, idea)* Urheber(in *f*) *m*; *(of product)* Erfinder(in *f*) *m*.

ornament ['ɔːnəmənt] **1** *n (object)* Ziergegenstand *m*. **2** *vt* verzieren; *room* ausschmücken.

ornamental [ˌɔːnə'mentl] *adj* dekorativ; *garden, plant etc* Zier-.

ornamentation [ˌɔːnəmen'teɪʃən] *n (ornamental detail)* Verzierungen *pl*; *(ornaments)* Schmuck *m*.

ornate [ɔː'neɪt] *adj* kunstvoll; *(of larger objects)* prunkvoll; *language* überladen *(pej)*, reich.

ornithologist [ˌɔːnɪ'θɒlədʒɪst] *n* Ornithologe *m*, Ornithologin *f*.

ornithology [ˌɔːnɪ'θɒlədʒɪ] *n* Ornithologie, Vogelkunde *f*.

orphan ['ɔːfən] **1** *n* Waise *f*. **2** *vt* **to be ~ed** zur Waise werden.

orphanage ['ɔːfənɪdʒ] *n* Waisenhaus *nt*.

orthodox ['ɔːθədɒks] *adj (Rel, fig)* orthodox.

orthodoxy ['ɔːθədɒksɪ] *n* **(a)** Orthodoxie *f*. **(b)** *(fig)* Konventionalität *f*.

orthography [ɔː'θɒgrəfɪ] *n* Rechtschreibung, Orthographie *f*.

orthopaedic, *(US)* **orthopedic** [ˌɔːθəʊ'piːdɪk] *adj* orthopädisch.

orthopaedics, *(US)* **orthopedics** [ˌɔːθəʊ'piːdɪks] *n sing* Orthopädie *f*.

orthopaedist, *(US)* **orthopedist** [ˌɔːθəʊ'piːdɪst] *n* Orthopäde *m*, Orthopädin *f*.

oscillate ['ɒsɪleɪt] *vi (lit, fig)* schwanken.

oscillation [ˌɒsɪ'leɪʃən] *n* Schwanken *nt*; *(individual movement etc)* Schwankung *f*.

osprey ['ɒspreɪ] *n* Fischadler *m*.

ossify ['ɒsɪfaɪ] *vi (lit)* verknöchern; *(fig)* erstarren; *(mind)* unbeweglich werden.

ostensible [ɒ'stensəbl] *adj* vorgeblich; *(alleged)* angeblich.

ostentation [ˌɒsten'teɪʃən] *n (display of wealth etc)* Pomp *m*, Protzerei *f (pej)*; *(of skills etc)* Angeberei *f*.

ostentatious [ˌɒsten'teɪʃəs] *adj* **(a)** *(pretentious)* protzig *(col)*. **(b)** *(conspicuous)* auffällig.

osteopath ['ɒstɪəpæθ] *n* Osteopath(in *f*) *m*.

ostracism ['ɒstrəsɪzəm] *n* Ächtung *f*.

ostracize ['ɒstrəsaɪz] *vt* ächten.

ostrich ['ɒstrɪtʃ] *n* Strauß *m*.

other ['ʌðəʳ] **1** *adj* **(a)** andere(r, s). **~ people** andere (Leute); **some ~ people will come later** später kommen noch ein paar; **do you have any ~ questions?** haben Sie sonst noch Fragen?; **the ~ day** neulich; **some ~ time** *(in future)* ein andermal; *(in past)* ein anderes Mal; **~ people's property** fremdes Eigentum. **(b) every ~** *(alternate)* jede(r, s) zweite. **(c) ~ than** *(except)* außer *(+dat)*; *(different to)* anders als. **(d) some time or ~** irgendwann (einmal); **some writer or ~** irgendein Schriftsteller *m*.

2 *pron* andere(r, s). **he doesn't like hurting ~s** er mag niemanden verletzen; **there are 6 ~s** da sind noch 6 (andere); **are there any ~s there?** sind noch andere da?; **there were no ~s there** es waren sonst keine da; **something/someone or ~** irgend etwas/jemand; **one or ~ of them will come** einer (von ihnen) wird kommen.

3 *adv* **he could do no ~ (than come)** er konnte nicht anders (als kommen); **somehow or ~** irgendwie; **somewhere or ~** irgendwo; **he was none ~ than the Minister** es war niemand anders als der Minister.

otherwise ['ʌðəwaɪz] **1** *adv* **(a)** *(in a different way)* anders. **I am ~ engaged** *(form)* ich bin anderweitig beschäftigt; **except where ~ stated** *(form)* sofern nicht anders angegeben; **Richard I, ~ (known as) the Lionheart** Richard I., auch bekannt als Löwenherz; **you seem to think ~** Sie scheinen anderer Meinung zu sein. **(b)** *(in other respects)* sonst, im übrigen. **2** *conj (or else)* sonst, andernfalls.

other-worldly [ˌʌðəˈwɜːldlɪ] *adj attitude* weltfern; *smile, expression* entrückt.

otter [ˈɒtəʳ] *n* Otter *m.*

ouch [aʊtʃ] *interj* autsch.

ought [ɔːt] *aux* **(a)** *(moral obligation)* **I ~ to do it** ich sollte *or* müßte es tun; **he ~ to have come** er hätte kommen sollen *or* müssen; **he thought you ~ to know** er meinte, Sie sollten das wissen. **(b)** *(desirability)* **you ~ to see that film** den Film sollten Sie sehen; **she ~ to have been a teacher** sie hätte Lehrerin werden sollen. **(c)** *(probability)* **he ~ to win the race** er müßte das Rennen gewinnen; **that ~ to do** das dürfte wohl *or* müßte reichen; **... and I ~ to know!** ... und ich muß es doch wissen!

ounce [aʊns] *n* Unze *f.* **there's not an ~ of truth in it** daran ist kein Fünkchen Wahrheit.

our [ˈaʊəʳ] *poss adj* unser; *see* **my.**

ours [ˈaʊəz] *poss pron* unsere(r, s); *see* **mine**[1].

ourselves [ˌaʊəˈselvz] *pers pron (dir, indir obj +prep)* uns; *(emph)* selbst; *see* **myself.**

oust [aʊst] *vt object* herausbekommen; *government* absetzen; *politician, colleague etc* absägen *(col)*; *rivals* ausschalten; *(take place of)* verdrängen.

out [aʊt] *see also* **~ of 1** *adv* **(a)** *(not in container, car etc)* außen; *(not in building, room)* draußen; *(indicating motion) (seen from inside)* hinaus, raus *(col)*; *(seen from ~side)* heraus, raus *(col)*. **to be ~** weg sein; *(when visitors come)* nicht da sein; **they are ~ shopping** sie sind zum Einkaufen (gegangen); **he's ~ in his car** er ist mit dem Auto unterwegs; **it's cold ~ here/there** es ist kalt hier/da draußen; **he likes to be ~ and about** er ist gern unterwegs; **we had a day ~ in London** wir haben einen Tag in London verbracht; **the journey ~** die Hinreise; *(seen from destination)* die Herfahrt; **the workers are ~** *(on strike)* die Arbeiter streiken; **the tide is ~** es ist Ebbe.

(b) *(indicating distance)* **to go ~ to China** nach China fahren; **~ in the Far East** im Fernen Osten; **the boat was ten miles ~** das Schiff war zehn Meilen weit draußen; **five days ~ from Liverpool** *(Naut) (leaving)* fünf Tage nach dem Auslaufen von Liverpool; *(approaching)* fünf Tage vor Liverpool; **~ at sea** draußen auf dem Meer.

(c) to be ~ *(sun)* draußen sein; *(stars, moon)* dasein; *(flowers)* blühen.

(d) *(light, fire, ball, player)* aus; *(not in fashion)* aus der Mode; *(~ of the question)* ausgeschlossen, nicht drin *(col)*; **to be ~** *(unconscious)* bewußtlos *or* weg *(col)* sein.

(e) the best car ~ das beste Auto, das es zur Zeit gibt; **to be ~** *(be published)* herausgekommen sein; **their secret was ~** ihr Geheimnis war bekannt geworden; **the results are ~** die Ergebnisse sind (he)raus; **~ with it!** heraus damit!; **before the day was ~** noch am selben Tag; **his calculations were ~** er hatte sich in seinen Berechnungen geirrt; **you're not far ~** Sie haben es fast (getroffen); **you're way ~!** weit gefehlt! *(geh)*, da hast du dich völlig vertan *(col)*; **we were £5/20% ~** wir hatten uns um £ 5/20% verrechnet *or* vertan *(col)*; **speak ~ loud** sprechen Sie laut/lauter; **to be ~ for a good time** sich amüsieren wollen; **he's ~ for all he can get** er will haben, was er nur bekommen kann; **he's ~ to get her** er ist hinter ihr her; **he's just ~ to make money** er ist nur auf Geld aus; **~ and away** weitaus, mit Abstand.

2 *n* **(a)** *see* **in. (b)** *(esp US fig col: way ~)* Hintertür *f.*

out-and-out [ˈaʊtənˈaʊt] *adj liar, fool* ausgemacht; *defeat* total.

outback [ˈaʊtbæk] *(in Australia) n*: **the ~** das Hinterland.

out: ~bid *pret, ptp* **~bid** *vt* überbieten; **~board** *adj motor* Außenbord-.

outbreak [ˈaʊtbreɪk] *n (of war, hostility, disease)* Ausbruch *m.* **a recent ~ of fire caused ...** ein Brand verursachte kürzlich ...; **at the ~ of war** bei Kriegsausbruch.

outbuilding [ˈaʊtbɪldɪŋ] *n* Nebengebäude *nt.*

outburst [ˈaʊtbɜːst] *n (of joy, anger)* Ausbruch *m.*

outcast [ˈaʊtkɑːst] *n* Ausgestoßene(r) *mf.* **social ~** Außenseiter *m* der Gesellschaft.

outclass [ˌaʊtˈklɑːs] *vt* in den Schatten stellen.

outcome [ˈaʊtkʌm] *n* Ergebnis *nt.* **what was the ~?** was ist dabei herausgekommen?

outcrop [ˈaʊtkrɒp] *n* **an ~ (of rock)** eine Felsnase.

outcry [ˈaʊtkraɪ] *n* Aufschrei *m (against* über *+acc)*; *(public protest)* Protestwelle *f (against* gegen*)*. **there was a general ~ about the increase in taxes** eine Welle des Protests erhob sich wegen der Steuererhöhung.

out: ~dated *adj idea, theory* überholt; *machine, word, custom* veraltet; **~distance** *vt* hinter sich *(dat)* lassen, abhängen *(col)*.

outdo [ˌaʊtˈduː] *pret* **outdid** [ˌaʊtˈdɪd], *ptp* **outdone** [ˌaʊtˈdʌn] *vt* übertreffen, überbieten *(sb in sth* jdn an etw *dat)*.

outdoor [ˈaʊtdɔːʳ] *adj* **~ shoes** Straßenschuhe *pl*; **~ clothes** wärmere Kleidung; **~ type** sportlicher Typ; **the ~ life** das Leben im Freien; **~ swimming pool** Freibad *nt.*

outdoors [ˈaʊtˈdɔːz] **1** *adv* draußen, im Freien. **to go ~** nach draußen gehen. **2** *n* **the great ~** *(hum)* die freie Natur.

outer [ˈaʊtəʳ] *adj attr* äußere(r, s); *door etc also* Außen-. **~ space** der Weltraum.

outfit [ˈaʊtfɪt] *n* **(a)** *(clothes)* Kleidung *f*; *(Fashion)* Ensemble *nt*; *(uniform)* Uniform *f*; *(of scout)* Kluft *f.* **(b)** *(equipment)* Ausrüstung *f.* **(c)** *(col: organization)* Verein *(col) m.* **(d)** *(Mil)* Einheit, Truppe *f.*

outfitter [ˈaʊtfɪtəʳ] *n (of ships)* Ausrüster *m.* **gentlemen's ~'s** *(esp Brit)* Herrenausstatter *m*; **sports ~'s** *(esp Brit)* Sportartikelgeschäft *nt.*

outgoing [ˈaʊtˈgəʊɪŋ] **1** *adj* **(a)** *tenant* ausziehend; *office-holder* scheidend; *train, boat* hinausfahrend; *plane* hinausgehend. **(b)** *personality* kontaktfreudig. **2** *npl* **~s** *(Brit)* Ausgaben *pl.*

outgrow [ˌaʊtˈgrəʊ] *pret* **outgrew** [ˌaʊtˈgruː], *ptp* **outgrown** [ˌaʊtˈgrəʊn] *vt clothes* herauswachsen aus; *habit* entwachsen *(+dat)*.

outing [ˈaʊtɪŋ] *n* Ausflug *m.* **to go on an ~** einen Ausflug machen.

outlandish [ˌaʊtˈlændɪʃ] *adj* absonderlich; *behaviour also* befremdend; *wallpaper etc* ausgefallen.

outlast [ˌaʊtˈlɑːst] *vt (live longer)* überleben; *(endure longer)* länger durchhalten als; *(thing)* länger halten als; *(idea etc)* überdauern.

outlaw [ˈaʊtlɔː] **1** *n* Geächtete(r) *mf*; *(in western etc)* Bandit *m.* **2** *vt organization* ächten; *newspaper etc* verbieten.

outlay [ˈaʊtleɪ] *n* (Kosten)aufwand *m*; *(recurring, continuous)* Kosten *pl.* **the initial ~** die anfänglichen Aufwendungen; **capital ~** Kapitalaufwand *m.*

outlet [ˈaʊtlet] **1** *n* **(a)** *(for water)* Abfluß *m*; *(for steam)* Abzug *m*; *(US Elec)* Steckdose *f.* **(b)** *(Comm)* Absatzmarkt *m*; *(merchant)* Abnehmer *m*; *(shop)* Verkaufsstelle *f.* **(c)** *(fig) (for talents)* Betätigungsmöglichkeit *f*; *(for emotion)* Ventil *nt.* **2** *attr pipe* Abfluß-; *(for steam)* Abzugs-; *valve* Auslaß-.

outline [ˈaʊtlaɪn] **1** *n* **(a)** *(of objects)* Umriß *m*; *(silhouette)* Silhouette *f*; *(of face)* Züge *pl.* **(b)** *(fig: summary)* Abriß *m.* **in (broad) ~** in groben Zügen; **just give (me) the broad ~s** skizzieren Sie es mir grob. **2** *vt* **(a) the mountain was ~d against the sky** der Berg zeichnete sich gegen den Himmel ab. **(b)** *(give summary of)* umreißen, skizzieren.

outlive [ˌaʊt'lɪv] *vt person* überleben. **to have ~d one's usefulness** ausgedient haben; *(method, system)* sich überlebt haben.

outlook ['aʊtlʊk] *n* **(a)** *(view)* Aussicht *f (over* über +*acc, on to* auf +*acc)*. **(b)** *(prospects, Met)* Aussichten *pl*. **(c)** *(mental attitude)* Einstellung *f*. **his ~ (up)on life** seine Einstellung zum Leben.

out: ~lying *adj (distant)* entlegen, abgelegen; *(outside the town boundary)* umliegend; *district (of town)* Außen-; **~manoeuvre,** *(US)* **~maneuver** *vt (Mil, fig)* ausmanövrieren; *(in rivalry)* ausstechen; **~moded** *adj* unzeitgemäß; *ideas, technology etc also* überholt.

outnumber [ˌaʊt'nʌmbəʳ] *vt* in der Überzahl sein gegenüber. **we were ~ed five to one** sie waren fünfmal so viele wie wir.

out of *prep* **(a)** *(outside, away from) (position)* nicht in *(+dat)*, außerhalb *(+gen)*; *(motion)* aus *(+dat)*. **to go/be ~ the country** außer Landes gehen/sein; **he walked ~ the room** er ging aus dem Zimmer (hinaus); **he went ~ the door** er ging zur Tür hinaus; **to look ~ the window** aus dem Fenster sehen; **I saw him ~ the window** ich sah ihn durchs Fenster; **~ danger/sight** außer Gefahr/Sicht; **he feels ~ it** *(col)* er kommt sich *(dat)* ausgeschlossen vor; **you're well ~ it** so ist es auch besser für dich.

(b) *(cause, motive)* aus *(+dat)*. **~ curiosity** aus Neugier.

(c) *(indicating origins or source)* aus *(+dat)*. **to drink ~ a glass** aus einem Glas trinken; **made ~ silver** aus Silber (gemacht); **to copy sth ~ a book** etw aus einem Buch kopieren.

(d) *(from among)* von *(+dat)*. **in seven cases ~ ten** in sieben von zehn Fällen; **one ~ every four smokers** einer von vier Rauchern.

(e) *(without)* **~ breath** außer Atem; **we are ~ money/bread** wir haben kein Geld/Brot mehr.

out: ~-of-date *adj, pred* **~ of date** *methods, ideas* überholt; *clothes, records* altmodisch; *customs* veraltet; **~-of-the-way** *adj, pred* **~ of the way** *spot* abgelegen; *theory* ungewöhnlich; **~patient** *n* ambulanter Patient, ambulante Patientin; **~patient's (department)** Ambulanz *f*; **~post** *n (Mil, fig)* Vorposten *m*.

output [aʊtpʊt] *n (of machine, factory, person)* Produktion *f*; *(Elec)* Leistung *f*; *(capacity of amplifier)* Ausgangsleistung *f*; *(Comp)* Ausgabe *f*, Output *m or nt*.

outrage ['aʊtreɪdʒ] **1** *n (wicked, violent deed)* Schandtat *f*; *(cruel also)* Greueltat *f*; *(by police, demonstrators etc)* Ausschreitung *f*; *(indecency, injustice)* Skandal *m*. **bomb ~** verbrecherischer Bombenanschlag; **an ~ against humanity** ein Verbrechen *nt* gegen die Menschlichkeit; **it's a public ~** es ist ein öffentlicher Skandal; **an ~ against good taste** eine unerhörte Geschmacklosigkeit. **2** [aʊt'reɪdʒ] *vt sense of decency* beleidigen; *person* empören, entrüsten.

outrageous [aʊt'reɪdʒəs] *adj (cruel, violent)* grauenhaft; *(unjust)* unerhört; *conduct, nonsense* haarsträubend; *language* entsetzlich; *charge etc* ungeheuerlich; *clothes, make-up* unmöglich; *(indecent)* geschmacklos.

outrageously [aʊt'reɪdʒəslɪ] *adv* fürchterlich; *exaggerate also* maßlos.

out: ~ran *pret of* **~run**; **~ride** *pret* **~rode,** *ptp* **~ridden** *vt* besser reiten als; *(on bike)* besser fahren als; *(outdistance)* davonreiten *(+dat)*/davonfahren *(+dat)*; **~rider** *n (on motorcycle)* Kradbegleiter *m*.

outright [aʊt'raɪt] **1** *adv (at once) kill* auf der Stelle; *(openly)* geradeheraus. **2** ['aʊtraɪt] *adj nonsense, disaster* total. **that's ~ arrogance/deception** das ist die reine Arroganz/das ist glatter Betrug; **an ~ error** ganz einfach ein Fehler.

out: ~rode *pret of* **~ride; ~run** *pret* **~ran,** *ptp* **~run** *vt* schneller laufen als; *(outdistance)* davonlaufen *(+dat)*; **~set** *n* Anfang *m*; **at the ~set** am Anfang; **from the ~set** von Anfang an; **~shine** *pret, ptp* **~shone** *vt (fig)* in den Schatten stellen.

outside ['aʊt'saɪd] **1** *n (of house, car, object)* Außenseite *f*. **to open the door from the ~** die Tür von außen öffnen; **to overtake on the ~** außen überholen; **he sees it from the ~** *(fig)* er sieht es als Außenstehender; **at the (very) ~** im äußersten Falle.

2 *adj* **(a)** *(external)* Außen-, äußere(r, s). **an ~ broadcast** eine nicht im Studio produzierte Sendung; **the ~ lane** die äußere Spur; **~ seat** *(in a row)* Platz *m* am Gang. **(b)** *price* äußerste(r, s). **at an ~ estimate** maximal. **(c)** *(very unlikely)* **an ~ chance** eine kleine Chance; **my horse only has an ~ chance** mein Pferd hat nur Außenseiterchancen.

3 *adv (on the outer side)* außen; *(of house, vehicle)* draußen. **to be/go ~** draußen sein/nach draußen gehen.

4 *prep (also* **~ of***)* **(a)** außerhalb *(+gen)*. **to be/go ~ sth** außerhalb einer Sache sein/aus etw gehen; **he is waiting ~ the door** er wartet vor der Tür; **it is ~ our agreement** es geht über unsere Vereinbarung hinaus. **(b)** *(apart from)* außer *(+dat)*.

outsider [ˌaʊt'saɪdəʳ] *n* Außenseiter(in *f*) *m*.

out: ~size *adj* übergroß; **~size clothes** Kleidung *f* in Übergröße; **~skirts** *npl (of town)* Außenbezirke *pl*.

outspoken [ˌaʊt'spəʊkən] *adj person, criticism, book* freimütig; *remark* direkt. **he is ~** er nimmt kein Blatt vor den Mund.

outspread ['aʊtspred] *adj* ausgebreitet.

outstanding [ˌaʊt'stændɪŋ] *adj* **(a)** *(exceptional)* hervorragend; *talent, beauty* außerordentlich; *event* bemerkenswert; *detail* auffallend; *feature* hervorstechend. **(b)** *(Comm, Fin) business, work* unerledigt; *bill, interest* ausstehend.

outstandingly [ˌaʊt'stændɪŋlɪ] *adv* hervorragend.

out: ~stay *vt* **I don't want to ~stay my welcome** ich will eure Gastfreundschaft nicht zu lange in Anspruch nehmen; **~stretched** *adj body* ausgestreckt; **~strip** *vt* **(a)** überholen; **(b)** *(fig)* übertreffen *(in* an +*dat)*.

outward ['aʊtwəd] **1** *adj* **(a)** *appearance, form* äußere(r, s). **it was purely ~ show** es war alles nur Theater *or* Mache *(col)*. **(b)** *movement* nach außen gehend; *freight* ausgehend; *journey, voyage* Hin-. **2** *adv* nach außen. **the door opens ~** die Tür geht nach außen auf.

outwardly ['aʊtwədlɪ] *adv* nach außen hin.

outwards ['aʊtwədz] *adv* nach außen.

out: ~weigh *vt disadvantages* mehr Gewicht haben als; **~wit** *vt* überlisten; *(in card games etc)* austricksen *(col)*; **~worn** *adj idea* abgenutzt.

oval ['əʊvəl] **1** *adj* oval. **~-shaped** oval. **2** *n* Oval *nt*.

ovary ['əʊvərɪ] *n (Anat)* Eierstock *m*; *(Bot)* Fruchtknoten *m*.

ovation [əʊ'veɪʃən] *n* Ovation *f*, stürmischer Beifall. **to get an ~** stürmischen Beifall ernten.

oven ['ʌvn] *n (Cook)* (Back)ofen *m*; *(cooker)* Herd *m*; *(Tech: for drying)* (Trocken)ofen *m*. **it's like an ~ in here** hier ist ja der reinste Backofen.

oven: ~-glove *n (Brit)* Topfhandschuh *m*; **~proof** *adj dish* feuerfest; **~-ready** *adj* bratfertig; **~ware** *n* feuerfeste Formen *pl*.

over ['əʊvəʳ] **1** *prep* **(a)** *(above, across)* über *(+dat)*; *(direction)* über *(+acc)*. **he spread the blanket ~ the bed** er breitete die Decke über das Bett; **he spilled coffee ~ it** er goß Kaffee darüber; **you've got ink all ~ your hands** Ihre Hände sind ganz voller Tinte; **to hit sb ~ the head** jdm auf den Kopf schlagen; **bent ~ one's books** über die Bücher gebeugt; **to look ~ the wall** über die Mauer schauen; **the noise came from ~ the wall** der Lärm kam von der anderen Seite der Mauer; **it's**

~ **the page** es ist auf der nächsten Seite; **it's just ~ the road from us** das ist von uns (aus) nur über die Straße; **the bridge ~ the river** die Brücke über den Fluß; **they came from all ~ England** sie kamen aus ganz England.

(b) *(more than, longer than)* über *(+acc)*. ~ **and above that** darüber hinaus; **an increase of 15% ~ last year** ein Zuwachs von 15% im Vergleich zum letzten Jahr; **that was well ~ a year ago** das ist gut ein Jahr her.

(c) *(during)* während *(+gen)*, in *(+dat)*. ~ **the weekend** übers Wochenende; ~ **the summer/ Christmas** den Sommer über/über Weihnachten; ~ **the years I've come to realize ...** im Laufe der Jahre ist mir klargeworden ...; **the visits were spread ~ several months** die Besuche verteilten sich über mehrere Monate.

(d) they talked ~ a cup of coffee sie unterhielten sich bei einer Tasse Kaffee; **they'll be a long time ~ it** sie werden dazu lange brauchen; **I've got an advantage ~ him** ich habe ihm gegenüber einen Vorteil; **he told me ~ the phone** er hat es mir am Telefon gesagt; **I heard it ~ the radio** ich habe es im Radio gehört; **it's not worth arguing ~** es lohnt (sich) nicht, darüber zu streiten.

2 *adv* **(a)** *(across) (away from speaker)* hinüber; *(towards speaker)* herüber; *(on the other side)* drüben. **they swam ~ to us** sie schwammen zu uns herüber; **he took the fruit ~ to his mother** er brachte das Obst zu seiner Mutter hinüber; **he swam ~ to the other side** er schwamm auf die andere Seite (hinüber); **come ~ tonight** kommen Sie heute abend vorbei; **he is ~ here/there** er ist hier/dort drüben; ~ **to you!** Sie sind daran; **and now ~ to our reporter in Belfast** und nun schalten wir zu unserem Reporter in Belfast um; ~ **in America** drüben in Amerika.

(b) famous the world ~ in der ganzen Welt berühmt; **I've been looking for it all ~** ich habe überall danach gesucht; **I am aching all ~** mir tut alles weh; **he was shaking all ~** er zitterte am ganzen Leib; **that's him/Fred all ~** das ist typisch für ihn/Fred, typisch Fred.

(c) to turn an object ~ einen Gegenstand herumdrehen; **he hit her and ~ she went** er schlug sie, und sie fiel um.

(d) *(ended: film, operation etc)* zu Ende. **the rain is ~** der Regen hat aufgehört; **the danger was ~** die Gefahr war vorüber; **when all this is ~** wenn das alles vorbei ist; **it's all ~ between us** es ist aus zwischen uns.

(e) *(repetition)* **to start (all) ~ again** noch einmal (ganz) von vorn anfangen; ~ **and ~ (again)** immer (und immer) wieder; **he did it five times ~** er hat es fünfmal wiederholt.

(f) *(excessively)* übermäßig, allzu.

(g) *(remaining)* übrig. **there was no meat (left) ~** es war kein Fleisch mehr übrig.

(h) *(more)* **children of 8 and ~** Kinder über 8; **all results of 5.3 and ~** alle Ergebnisse von 5,3 und darüber.

(i) *(Telec)* over. ~ **and out** Ende der Durchsage; *(Aviat)* over and out.

over- *pref* über-.

over: ~abundant *adj* überreichlich; **~act** *vi* übertreiben; **~active** *adj* zu aktiv.

overall[1] [,əʊvər'ɔːl] **1** *adj* **(a)** *width, total* gesamt, Gesamt-. ~ **dimensions** *(Aut)* Außenmaße *pl*; ~ **majority** absolute Mehrheit. **(b)** *(general)* allgemein. **the ~ effect of this was to ...** dies hatte das Endergebnis, daß ... **2** *adv* **(a)** insgesamt. **(b)** *(in general)* im großen und ganzen.

overall[2] ['əʊvərɔːl] *n (Brit)* Kittel *m*.

overalls ['əʊvərɔːlz] *npl* Overall *m*.

over: ~anxious *adj* übertrieben besorgt; *(on particular occasion)* übermäßig aufgeregt; **I'm not exactly ~anxious to go** ich bin nicht gerade scharf darauf zu gehen; **~ate** *pret of* **~eat**; **~awe** *vt (intimidate)* einschüchtern; *(impress)* überwältigen; **~balance 1** *vi* aus dem Gleichgewicht kommen; **2** *vt* umwerfen; *boat* kippen.

overbearing [,əʊvə'bɛərɪŋ] *adj* herrisch.

overboard ['əʊvəbɔːd] *adv* **(a)** *(Naut)* **to fall ~** über Bord gehen; **man ~!** Mann über Bord! **(b)** *(fig: col)* **to go ~** übers Ziel hinausschießen, zu weit gehen; **don't go ~ about it** übertreiben Sie es nicht.

over: ~burden *vt (lit)* überladen; *(fig)* überlasten; **~came** *pret of* **~come**; **~cast** *adj* bedeckt; *sky also* bewölkt; **it's getting rather ~cast** es zieht sich zu; **~cautious** *adj* übervorsichtig.

overcharge [,əʊvə'tʃɑːdʒ] *vt person* zuviel berechnen *(+dat) (for* für*)*.

overcoat ['əʊvəkəʊt] *n* Mantel *m*.

overcome [,əʊvə'kʌm] *pret* **overcame** [,əʊvə'keɪm], *ptp* ~ *vt enemy* überwältigen; *bad habit* sich *(dat)* abgewöhnen; *shyness etc* überwinden; *temptation* widerstehen *(+dat)*; *difficulty, anger* überwinden; *disappointment* hinwegkommen über *(+acc)*. **he was ~ by the fumes** die giftigen Gase machten ihn bewußtlos; **he was quite ~ by grief/emotion** Schmerz/Rührung übermannte ihn; **I'm quite ~** ich bin ganz ergriffen.

over: ~confident *adj* übertrieben selbstsicher; *(too optimistic)* zu optimistisch; **~crowded** *adj* überfüllt; *(overpopulated)* überbevölkert; **~crowding** *n* Überfüllung *f*; *(of town)* Überbevölkerung *f*.

overdo [,əʊvə'duː] *pret* **overdid** [,əʊvə'dɪd], *ptp* **overdone** [,əʊvə'dʌn] *vt (exaggerate)* übertreiben. **you are ~ing it** *or* **things** Sie übertreiben; *(tiring yourself)* Sie übernehmen sich.

over: ~done *adj* **(a)** *(exaggerated)* übertrieben; **(b)** *(Cook)* verkocht; *bacon etc* verbraten; **~dose** *n* Überdosis *f*; **~draft** *n* Konto-Überziehung *f*; **to have an ~draft of £10** sein Konto um £ 10 überzogen haben; **~draw** *pret* **~drew**, *ptp* **~drawn** *vt one's account* überziehen; **~drive** *n (Aut)* Schnellgang(getriebe *nt*) *m*; **~due** *adj* überfällig; **long ~due** schon seit langem fällig; **~eat** *pret* **~ate**, *ptp* **~eaten** *vi* zuviel essen; **~emphasize** *vt* überbetonen; **~enthusiastic** *adj* übertrieben begeistert; **~estimate** *vt price* zu hoch einschätzen; *importance* überbewerten; *chances, danger* überschätzen; **~excited** *adj person* zu aufgeregt; *children* aufgedreht; **~exertion** *n* Überanstrengung *f*; **~expose** *vt (Phot)* überbelichten; **~feed** *pret, ptp* **~fed** *vt* überfüttern.

overflow ['əʊvəfləʊ] **1** *n (outlet)* Überlauf *m*; *(excess: of people, population)* Überschuß *m (of* an *+dat)*. **2** [,əʊvə'fləʊ] *vt area* überschwemmen. **the river has ~ed its banks** der Fluß ist über die Ufer getreten. **3** [,əʊvə'fləʊ] *vi (liquid, river etc)* überlaufen. **full to ~ing** *(bowl, cup)* zum Überlaufen voll; *(room)* überfüllt; **the crowd at the meeting ~ed into the street** die Leute bei der Versammlung standen bis auf die Straße.

over: ~fly *pret* **~flew**, *ptp* **~flown** *vt* **(a)** *(fly over) town* überfliegen; **(b)** *(fly beyond) runway, airport* hinausfliegen über *(+acc)*. **~generous** *adj* zu großzügig; **~grown** *adj* **(a)** überwachsen *(with* von*)*; **(b)** *child* aufgeschossen; **an ~grown schoolboy** ein großes Kind; **~hang** *(vb: pret, ptp* **~hung***)* **1** *vt* hängen über *(+acc)*; *(rocks, balcony)* hinausragen über *(+acc)*, vorstehen über *(+acc)*; **2** *n* Überhang *m*; **~hanging** *adj* überhängend; **~haul 1** *n* Überholung *f*; **2** *vt engine* überholen; *plans* überprüfen.

overhead [,əʊvə'hed] **1** *adv* oben; *(in the sky)* am Himmel. **a plane flew ~** ein Flugzeug flog über uns *etc (acc)* (hinweg). **2** ['əʊvəhed] *adj* ~ **cables** Freileitungen. **3** ['əʊvəhed] *n (US)* = **overheads.**

overheads ['əʊvəhedz] *npl (Brit Comm)* allgemeine Unkosten *pl*.

overhear [ˌəʊvəˈhɪəʳ] *pret, ptp* **overheard** [ˌəʊvəˈhɜːd] *vt* zufällig mit anhören. **he was ~d to say that ...** jemand hat ihn sagen hören, daß ...

over: ~heat *vi (engine)* heißlaufen; **~hung** *pret, ptp of* **~hang.**

overindulge [ˈəʊvərɪnˈdʌldʒ] *vi* zuviel genießen.

overindulgence [ˈəʊvərɪnˈdʌldʒəns] *n (eating)* Völlerei *f.* **~ in wine** übermäßiger Weingenuß.

overjoyed [ˌəʊvəˈdʒɔɪd] *adj* überglücklich *(at, by* über *+acc).* **he wasn't exactly ~** er war nicht gerade erfreut.

over: ~kill *n (Mil)* Overkill *m*; *(fig)* Rundumschlag *m*; **~land** *adv travel etc* über Land.

overlap [ˈəʊvəlæp] **1** *n* Überschneidung *f*; *(of concepts)* teilweise Deckung. **3 inches' ~** 3 Zoll Überappung; **there's quite a lot of ~ between their work** ihre Arbeitsbereiche überschneiden sich in vielen Punkten. **2** [ˌəʊvəˈlæp] *vi* **(a)** *(tiles, boards)* einander überdecken. **(b)** *(dates, responsibilities)* sich überschneiden; *(ideas, work)* sich teilweise decken.

over: ~lay *(vb: pret, ptp* **~laid***)* [ˌəʊvəˈleɪ] *vt* überziehen; **~leaf** *adv* **the illustration ~leaf** die umseitige Abbildung; **~load** *vt* überladen; *lorry, (Elec, Mech)* überlasten.

overlook [ˌəʊvəˈlʊk] *vt* **(a)** *(have view onto)* überblicken. **a room ~ing the park** ein Zimmer mit Blick auf den Park; **the garden is not ~ed** niemand kann in den Garten hineinsehen. **(b)** *(fail to notice)* übersehen. **(c)** *(ignore) mistake* hinwegsehen über *(+acc)*, durchgehen lassen.

overly [ˈəʊvəlɪ] *adv* übermäßig.

over: ~manning *n* zu große Belegschaft(en *pl*); **~much** *adv* übermäßig viel.

overnight [ˈəʊvəˈnaɪt] **1** *adv* **(a)** über Nacht. **to stay ~ (with sb)** bei jdm übernachten. **(b)** *(fig)* von heute auf morgen. **the place had changed ~** der Ort hatte sich über Nacht verändert. **2** *adj* **(a)** *journey* Nacht-. **~ stay** Übernachtung *f*; **~ bag** Reisetasche *f.* **(b)** *(fig: sudden)* ganz plötzlich. **the play was an ~ success** das Stück wurde über Nacht ein Erfolg.

over: ~paid *pret, ptp of* **~pay**; **~particular** *adj* zu genau, pingelig *(col)*; **~pass** *n* Überführung *f*; **~pay** *pret, ptp* **~paid** *vt* überbezahlen; **to ~pay sb by £50** jdm £ 50 zuviel bezahlen; **~populated** *adj* überbevölkert.

overpower [ˌəʊvəˈpaʊəʳ] *vt (emotion, heat)* überwältigen.

overpowering [ˌəʊvəˈpaʊərɪŋ] *adj* überwältigend; *smell* penetrant; *heat* glühend. **he's a bit ~ at times** seine Art kann einem manchmal zuviel werden.

over: ~price *vt* **these goods are ~ priced** diese Waren sind zu teuer; **at £50 it's ~ priced** £ 50 ist zuviel dafür; **~print** *vt stamp, text* überdrucken; *(Phot)* überkopieren; **~produce** *vi* überproduzieren; **~production** *n* Überproduktion *f*; **~protective** *adj parent* überängstlich; **~rate** *vt* überschätzen; *book, system etc* überbewerten; **~reach** *vr* sich übernehmen; **~react** *vi* übertrieben reagieren *(to* auf *+acc).*

override [ˌəʊvəˈraɪd] *pret* **overrode** [ˌəʊvəˈrəʊd], *ptp* **overridden** [ˌəʊvəˈrɪdn] *vt decision, ruling* aufheben, außer Kraft setzen; *objection* ablehnen; *mechanism* abschalten.

overriding [ˌəʊvəˈraɪdɪŋ] *adj principle* vorrangig, wichtigste(r, s). **of ~ importance** von allergrößter Wichtigkeit.

overripe [ˌəʊvəˈraɪp] *adj* überreif.

overrule [ˌəʊvəˈruːl] *vt* ablehnen; *claim* nicht anerkennen; *verdict, decision* aufheben. **he was ~d by the majority** er wurde überstimmt.

overrun [ˌəʊvəˈrʌn] *pret* **overran** [ˌəʊvəˈræn], *ptp* **~ 1** *vt* **(a)** *(weeds)* überwuchern. **~ with tourists** von Touristen überlaufen. **(b)** *(troops etc: invade)* einfallen in *(+dat).* **2** *vi (in time)* überziehen. **his speech overran by ten minutes** seine Rede dauerte zehn Minuten zu lang.

overseas [ˈəʊvəˈsiːz] **1** *adj market, state* ausländisch; *(far away)* Übersee-. **our ~ office** unsere Zweigstelle im Ausland/in Übersee; **~ aid** Entwicklungshilfe *f*; **an ~ visitor** ein Besucher aus dem Ausland/aus Übersee. **2** *adv* **to be ~** im Ausland/in Übersee sein; **to go ~** ins Ausland/nach Übersee gehen.

over: ~see *pret* **~saw,** *ptp* **~seen** *vt* beaufsichtigen; **~seer** *n* Aufseher(in *f*) *m*; *(foreman)* Vorarbeiter(in *f*) *m*; **~sensitive** *adj* überempfindlich; **~shadow** *vt (lit, fig)* überschatten.

overshoot [ˌəʊvəˈʃuːt] *pret, ptp* **overshot** [ˌəʊvəˈʃɒt] *vt runway* hinausschießen über *(+acc).* **to ~ the mark** *(lit, fig)* übers Ziel hinausschießen.

oversight [ˈəʊvəsaɪt] *n* Versehen *nt.* **by** *or* **through an ~** aus Versehen.

over: ~simplification *n* (zu) grobe Vereinfachung; **~simplify** *vt* grob vereinfachen; **~sleep** *pret, ptp* **~slept** *vi* verschlafen; **~spend** *pret, ptp* **~spent** *vi* zuviel ausgeben; **~spill** *n (Brit)* Bevölkerungsüberschuß *m*; **~spill town** Trabantenstadt *f*; **~staffed** *adj* überbesetzt; **~state** *vt facts, case* übertreiben; **~statement** *n* Übertreibung *f*; **~step** *vt* **to ~step the mark** zu weit gehen; **~subscribe** *vt (Fin)* überzeichnen.

overt [əʊˈvɜːt] *adj* offen; *hostility* unverhohlen.

overtake [ˌəʊvəˈteɪk] *pret* **overtook** [ˌəʊvəˈtʊk], *ptp* **overtaken** [ˌəʊvəˈteɪkən] **1** *vt* einholen; *(pass) runner etc, (Brit) car* überholen. **events have ~n us** wir waren auf die Entwicklung der Dinge nicht gefaßt. **2** *vi (Brit)* überholen.

overtaking [ˌəʊvəˈteɪkɪŋ] *n (Brit)* Überholen *nt.* **"No ~"** „Überholverbot".

over: ~tax *vt* **(a)** *(fig) person, heart* überlasten; *patience* überfordern; **to ~tax one's strength** sich übernehmen; **(b)** *(lit)* übermäßig besteuern; **~throw** *(vb: pret* **~threw,** *ptp* **~thrown***)* **1** [ˈəʊvəˌθrəʊ] *n* Sieg *m (of* über *+acc)*; *(being ~thrown)* Niederlage *f*; *(of dictator etc)* Sturz *m*; *(of country)* Eroberung *f*; **2** [ˌəʊvəˈθrəʊ] *vt (defeat) enemy* besiegen; *dictator* stürzen; *country* erobern.

overtime [ˈəʊvətaɪm] **1** *n* **(a)** Überstunden *pl.* **I am on ~** ich mache Überstunden; **he did four hours' ~** er hat vier (Stunden) Überstunden gemacht. **(b)** *(US Sport)* Verlängerung *f.* **2** *adv* **to work ~** Überstunden machen; **my imagination was working ~** meine Phantasie lief auf Hochtouren *(col).*

overtired [ˌəʊvəˈtaɪəd] *adj* übermüdet.

overtone [ˈəʊvətəʊn] *n (fig)* Unterton *m.*

overture [ˈəʊvətjʊəʳ] *n (Mus)* Ouvertüre *f.* **to make ~s to sb** Annäherungsversuche bei jdm machen.

overturn [ˌəʊvəˈtɜːn] **1** *vt* **(a)** umkippen, umwerfen. **(b)** *regime* stürzen. **2** *vi (chair)* umkippen; *(boat also)* kentern.

over: ~use [ˌəʊvəˈjuːz] *vt* zu häufig gebrauchen; **~value** *vt goods* zu hoch schätzen; **~view** *n* Überblick *m (of* über *+acc).*

overweight [ˈəʊvəˈweɪt] *adj thing* zu schwer; *person* übergewichtig. **this box is 5 kilos ~** diese Schachtel hat 5 Kilo Übergewicht; **you're ~** Sie haben Übergewicht.

overwhelm [ˌəʊvəˈwelm] *vt* **(a)** *(overpower: strong feelings)* überwältigen. **he was ~ed when they gave him the present** er war zutiefst gerührt, als sie ihm das Geschenk gaben. **(b)** *enemy* überwältigen; *country* besiegen. **(c)** *(fig) (with favours, praise)* überschütten; *(with questions)* bestürmen; *(with work)* überhäufen.

overwhelming [ˌəʊvəˈwelmɪŋ] *adj* überwältigend; *desire* unwiderstehlich.

overwhelmingly [ˌəʊvəˈwelmɪŋlɪ] *adv see adj.* **they voted ~ for it** sie haben mit überwältigender Mehrheit dafür gestimmt.

overwork [ˌəʊvəˈwɜːk] **1** *n* Überarbeitung *f*. **2** *vt horse etc* schinden; *person* überanstrengen; *idea, theme* überstrapazieren. **we're ~ed** wir sind überarbeitet. **3** *vi* sich überarbeiten.
overwrought [ˌəʊvəˈrɔːt] *adj person* überreizt.
overzealous [ˌəʊvəˈzeləs] *adj* übereifrig.
ovulation [ˌɒvjʊˈleɪʃən] *n* Eisprung *m*.
owe [əʊ] *vt money* schulden, schuldig sein *(sb sth, sth to sb* jdm etw*)*. **I ~ him a meal** ich bin ihm noch ein Essen schuldig; **how much do I ~ you?** *(in shop etc)* was bin ich schuldig?; **I ~ my life to him** ich verdanke ihm mein Leben; **to what do I ~ the honour of your visit?** *(iro)* was verschafft mir die Ehre Ihres Besuches?
owing [ˈəʊɪŋ] **1** *adj* unbezahlt. **how much is still ~?** wieviel steht noch aus? **2** *prep* **~ to** wegen *(+gen or (col) +dat)*, infolge *(+gen)*; **~ to the circumstances** umständehalber; **~ to his being foreign** weil er Ausländer ist/war.
owl [aʊl] *n* Eule *f*.
own[1] [əʊn] *vt* **(a)** *(possess)* besitzen. **who ~s that?** wem gehört das?; **he looks as if he ~s the place** er sieht so aus, als wäre er hier zu Hause. **(b)** *(admit)* zugeben; *(recognize)* anerkennen.
♦**own up** *vi* es zugeben. **to ~ ~ to sth** etw zugeben; **he ~ed ~ to stealing the money** er gab zu, das Geld gestohlen zu haben.
own[2] **1** *adj attr* eigen. **his ~ car** sein eigenes Auto; **one's ~ car** ein eigenes Auto; **he's his ~ man** er geht seinen eigenen Weg; **he does (all) his ~ cooking** er kocht für sich selbst. **2** *pron* **(a) that's my ~** das ist mein eigenes; **those are my ~** die gehören mir; **my ~ is bigger** meine(r, s) ist größer; **my time is my ~** ich kann mit meiner Zeit machen, was ich will; **a house of one's ~** ein eigenes Haus; **I have money of my ~** ich habe selbst Geld; **it has a beauty all its ~** *or* **of its ~** es hat eine ganz eigene Schönheit. **(b)** *(in phrases)* **can I have it for my (very) ~?** darf ich das ganz für mich allein behalten?; **to get one's ~ back (on sb)** es jdm heimzahlen; **(all) on one's ~** (ganz) allein; **on its ~** von selbst, von allein.
owner [ˈəʊnəʳ] *n* Besitzer(in *f*), Eigentümer(in *f*) *m*; *(of shop, factory, firm etc)* Inhaber(in *f*) *m*. **who's the ~ of this umbrella?** wem gehört dieser Schirm?; **at the ~'s risk** auf eigene Gefahr.
owner-occupier [ˌəʊnərˈɒkjʊpaɪəʳ] *n jd, der ein Haus/eine Wohnung besitzt und darin wohnt.*
ownership [ˈəʊnəʃɪp] *n* Besitz *m*. **under new ~** unter neuer Leitung.
ox [ɒks] *n, pl* **-en** Ochse *m*. **as strong as an ~** bärenstark.
oxidation [ˌɒksɪˈdeɪʃən] *n (Chem)* Oxydation *f*.
oxide [ˈɒksaɪd] *n (Chem)* Oxyd *nt*.
oxidize [ˈɒksɪdaɪz] *vti* oxydieren.
oxtail [ˈɒksteɪl] *n*: **~ soup** Ochsenschwanzsuppe *f*.
oxyacetylene [ˈɒksɪəˈsetɪliːn] *adj* Azetylensauerstoff-. **~ burner** Schweißbrenner *m*.
oxygen [ˈɒksɪdʒən] *n* Sauerstoff *m*.
oxygen: ~ mask *n* Sauerstoffmaske *f*; **~ tank** *n* Sauerstoffbehälter *m*; **~ tent** *n* Sauerstoffzelt *nt*.
oyster [ˈɔɪstəʳ] *n* Auster *f*. **the world's his ~** die Welt steht ihm offen.
oz = **ounce(s)**.
ozone [ˈəʊzəʊn] *n* Ozon *nt*. **~ layer** Ozonschicht *f*.

P

P, p [piː] *n* P, p *nt.* **to mind one's P's and Q's** *(col)* sich anständig benehmen.

p = **(a) page** S. **(b) penny, pence.**

PA = **(a) personal assistant. (b) public address (system).**

p.a. = **per annum.**

pace [peɪs] **1** *n* **(a)** *(step)* Schritt *m.* **twelve ~s off** zwölf Schritt(e) entfernt; **to put sb/a new car through his/its ~s** *(fig)* jdn/ein neues Auto auf Herz und Nieren prüfen. **(b)** *(speed)* Tempo *nt.* **at a good** *or* **smart ~** recht schnell; **at a slow ~** langsam; **how long will he keep this ~ up?** wie lange wird er das Tempo durchhalten?; **the present ~ of development** die momentane Entwicklungsrate; **to keep ~** Schritt halten; *(in discussing)* mitkommen; **I can't keep ~ with events** ich komme mit den Ereignissen nicht mehr mit; **to make** *or* **set the ~** das Tempo angeben; **I can't stand the ~ any more** *(col)* ich kann nicht mehr mithalten. **2** *vt (measure) floor, room* mit Schritten ausmessen. **3** *vi* **to ~ up and down** auf und ab gehen.

pace: ~maker *n (Med, Sport, fig)* Schrittmacher *m*; **~-setter** *n (Sport)* Schrittmacher *m.*

Pacific [pəˈsɪfɪk] *n* **the ~ (Ocean)** der Pazifische Ozean, der Pazifik.

pacifier [ˈpæsɪfaɪəʳ] *n (US: dummy)* Schnuller *m.*

pacifism [ˈpæsɪfɪzəm] *n* Pazifismus *m.*

pacifist [ˈpæsɪfɪst] *n* Pazifist(in *f*) *m.*

pacify [ˈpæsɪfaɪ] *vt baby* beruhigen; *angry person* besänftigen. **just to ~ the unions** nur damit die Gewerkschaften stillhalten.

pack [pæk] **1** *n* **(a)** *(bundle)* Bündel *nt*; *(on animal)* Last *f*; *(rucksack)* Rucksack *m*; *(Mil)* Gepäck *nt no pl.* **(b)** *(packet) (washing powder etc)* Paket *nt*; *(US: of cigarettes)* Schachtel *f.* **in ~s of six** im Sechserpack. **(c)** *(Hunt)* Meute *f.* **(d)** *(of wolves)* Rudel *nt.* **(e)** *(pej: group)* Horde, Meute *f.* **he told us a ~ of lies** er tischte uns einen Sack voll Lügen auf. **(f)** *(of cards)* (Karten)spiel *nt.* **(g)** *(Rugby)* Stürmer *pl.*

2 *vt* **(a)** *container etc* vollpacken; *meat in tin etc* abpacken. **~ed in dozens** im Dutzend abgepackt. **(b)** *case* packen; *things in case* einpacken. **(c)** *(wrap, put into parcel)* einpacken. **~ed in polythene** in Cellophan verpackt. **(d)** *(crowd)* packen; *articles also* stopfen. **the box was ~ed full of explosives** die Kiste war voll mit Sprengstoff; **the crowds that ~ed the stadium** die Menschenmassen, die sich im Stadium drängten; **to be ~ed** *(full)* gerammelt voll sein *(col)*; **all this information is ~ed into one chapter** all diese Informationen sind in einem Kapitel konzentriert. **(e)** *(make firm) soil etc* festdrücken. **(f)** *(US col: carry) gun* tragen, dabei haben. **(g)** *(col)* **to ~ a (heavy) punch** kräftig zuschlagen.

3 *vi* **(a)** *(items)* passen; *(person)* packen. **it ~s (in) nicely** es läßt sich gut verpacken; **I'm still ~ing** ich bin noch beim Packen. **(b)** *(crowd)* **the crowds ~ed into the stadium** die Menge drängte sich in das Stadion; **we can't all ~ into one Mini** wir können uns nicht alle in einen Mini zwängen. **(c)** *(col)* **to send sb ~ing** jdn kurz abfertigen.

♦ **pack in 1** *vt sep* **(a)** *clothes etc* einpacken. **(b)** *people* hineinpferchen in *(+acc).* **we can't ~ any more ~ here** *(people)* hier geht keiner mehr rein; *(things)* hier geht nichts mehr rein. **(c)** *(play, actor etc)* in Scharen anziehen. **(d)** *(Brit col: give up) job* hinschmeißen *(col)*; *girlfriend* sausenlassen *(col)*; *work, activity* Feierabend machen mit *(col).* **~ it ~!** hör auf!, laß es gut sein! **2** *vi* **(a)** *(crowd in)* sich hineindrängen. **(b)** *(Brit col: engine etc)* seinen Geist aufgeben *(hum).*

♦ **pack off** *vt sep* **she ~ed them ~ to bed/school** sie schickte sie ins Bett/in die Schule.

♦ **pack up 1** *vt sep clothes etc* zusammenpacken. **2** *vi* **(a)** *(prepare luggage)* packen. **(b)** *(col: stop working) (engine)* seinen Geist aufgeben *(hum)*; *(person)* Feierabend machen *(col).* **(c) the tent ~s ~ easily** das Zelt läßt sich gut verpacken.

package [ˈpækɪdʒ] **1** *n* **(a)** *(parcel, esp US: packet)* Paket *nt*; *(of cardboard)* Schachtel *f.* **(b)** *(esp Comm: group, set)* Paket, Bündel *nt.* **2** *vt* **(a)** verpacken. **(b)** *(to enhance sales)* präsentieren.

package: ~ deal *n* Pauschalangebot *nt*; **~ holiday** *n* Pauschalreise *f.*

packaging [ˈpækɪdʒɪŋ] *n see vt* **(a)** Verpackung *f.* **(b)** Präsentation *f.*

packed lunch [ˈpæktˈlʌntʃ] *n* Lunchpaket *nt.*

packet [ˈpækɪt] *n* **(a)** Paket *nt*; *(of cigarettes)* Päckchen *nt*, Schachtel *f*; *(of potato crisps)* Tüte *f*; *(small box)* Schachtel *f.* **(b)** *(Brit col: lot of money)* **that must have cost a ~** das muß ein Heidengeld gekostet haben *(col).*

pack: ~horse *n* Packpferd *nt*; *(fig)* Packesel *m*; **~ice** *n* Packeis *nt.*

packing [ˈpækɪŋ] *n* **(a)** *(act) (in suitcases)* Packen *nt*; *(in factories etc)* Verpackung *f.* **to do one's ~** packen. **(b)** *(material)* Verpackung *f.*

packing case *n* Kiste *f.*

pact [pækt] *n* Pakt *m.* **to make a ~ with sb** mit jdm einen Pakt schließen.

pad [pæd] **1** *n* **(a)** *(stuffing) (for comfort etc)* Polster *nt*; *(for protection)* Schützer *m.* **(b)** *(of paper)* Block *m.* **(c)** *(for inking)* Stempelkissen *nt.* **(d)** *(of animal's foot)* Ballen *m.* **(e)** *(launching ~)* (Abschuß)rampe *f.* **(f)** *(col: room, home)* Bude *f (col).* **2** *vt shoulders etc* polstern.

♦ **pad about** *vi* umhertapsen.

♦ **pad out** *vt sep* **(a)** *shoulders* polstern. **(b)** *essay etc* auffüllen; *speech* ausdehnen.

padded [ˈpædɪd] *adj shoulders* wattiert; *dashboard* gepolstert.

padding [ˈpædɪŋ] *n* **(a)** *(material)* Polsterung *f.* **(b)** *(fig: in essay etc)* Füllwerk *nt.*

paddle [ˈpædl] **1** *n* **(a)** *(oar)* Paddel *nt*; *(blade of wheel)* Schaufel *f*; *(wheel)* Schaufelrad *nt.* **(b) to go for a ~** durchs Wasser waten. **2** *vti* **(a)** paddeln. **(b)** *(walk in shallow water)* waten.

paddle: ~ boat *n* Raddampfer *m*; *(small, on pond)* Paddelboot *nt*; **~ steamer** *n* Raddampfer *m.*

paddling pool [ˈpædlɪŋˌpuːl] *n (Brit)* Planschbecken *nt.*

paddock [ˈpædək] *n (field)* Koppel *f*; *(of racecourse)* Sattelplatz *m.*

paddy [ˈpædɪ] *n (also* **~ field***)* Reisfeld *nt.*

padlock [ˈpædlɒk] **1** *n* Vorhängeschloß *nt.* **2** *vt* (mit einem Vorhängeschloß) verschließen.

paediatric, *(US)* **pediatric** [ˌpiːdɪˈætrɪk] *adj* Kinder-.

pagan ['peɪgən] **1** *adj* heidnisch. **2** *n* Heide *m*, Heidin *f*.

page[1] [peɪdʒ] **1** *n (also* **~-boy)** Page *m*. **2** *vt* **to ~ sb** jdn ausrufen lassen.

page[2] *n* Seite *f*. **on ~ 14** auf Seite 14; **write on both sides of the ~** beschreiben Sie beide Seiten.

pageant ['pædʒənt] *n (show)* Historienspiel *nt*.

pageantry ['pædʒəntrɪ] *n* Prunk *m*, Gepränge *nt*.

page: ~-boy *n* **(a)** Page *m*; **(b)** *(hairstyle)* Pagenkopf *m*; **~ number** *n* Seitenzahl *f*.

pagoda [pə'gəʊdə] *n* Pagode *f*.

paid [peɪd] **1** *pret, ptp of* **pay. 2** *adj official, work* bezahlt. **to put ~ to sth** etw zunichte machen; **that's put ~ to him** das war's dann wohl für ihn *(col)*.

paid-up ['peɪd'ʌp] *adj share* eingezahlt. **a ~ membership of 500** 500 zahlende Mitglieder; **fully ~ member** Mitglied *m* ohne Beitragsrückstände.

pail [peɪl] *n* Eimer *m*.

pain [peɪn] **1** *n* **(a)** *(physical)* Schmerz *m*; *(mental)* Qualen *pl*. **this will help the ~** das ist gut gegen die Schmerzen; **to be in ~** Schmerzen haben; **he screamed in ~** er schrie vor Schmerzen; **I have a ~ in my leg** mein Bein tut mir weh. **(b) to be at (great) ~s to do sth** sich *(dat)* (große) Mühe geben, etw zu tun; **to take ~s over sth/to do sth** sich *(dat)* Mühe mit etw geben/sich *(dat)* Mühe geben, etw zu tun. **(c)** *(penalty)* **on ~ of death** bei Todesstrafe. **(d)** *(col: also* **~ in the neck** *col)* **to be a (real) ~** einem auf den Wecker gehen *(col)*. **2** *vt (mentally)* schmerzen. **it ~s me to see their ignorance** ihre Unwissenheit tut schon weh.

pained [peɪnd] *adj expression* schmerzerfüllt.

painful ['peɪnfʊl] *adj* **(a)** *(physically)* schmerzhaft. **is it ~?** tut es weh? **(b)** *experience, memory* unangenehm. **it is my ~ duty to tell you that ...** ich habe die traurige Pflicht, Ihnen mitteilen zu müssen, daß ... **(c)** *(col: terrible)* peinlich; *(boring) party etc* zum Sterben langweilig.

painfully ['peɪnfəlɪ] *adv* **(a)** *(physically)* schmerzhaft. **(b)** *(col: very)* schrecklich. **it was ~ obvious** es war nicht zu übersehen.

painkiller ['peɪn,kɪlə[r]] *n* Schmerzmittel *nt*.

painless ['peɪnlɪs] *adj* schmerzlos. **don't worry, it's quite ~** *(col)* keine Angst, es ist ganz einfach.

painstaking ['peɪnz,teɪkɪŋ] *adj person, work* sorgfältig; *accuracy* peinlich.

paint [peɪnt] **1** *n* **(a)** Farbe *f*; *(on car, furniture also)* Lack *m*; *(make-up)* Schminke *f*. **(b) ~s** *pl* Farben *pl*. **2** *vt* **(a)** *wall etc* streichen; *car* lackieren. **to ~ the town red** *(col)* die Stadt unsicher machen *(col)*. **(b)** *picture, person* malen. **he ~ed a very convincing picture** *(fig)* er zeichnete ein sehr überzeugendes Bild. **3** *vi* malen; *(decorate)* (an)streichen.

paint: ~box *n* Farbkasten *m*; **~brush** *n* Pinsel *m*.

painter ['peɪntə[r]] *n* Maler(in *f*) *m*.

painting ['peɪntɪŋ] *n* **(a)** *(picture)* Bild, Gemälde *nt*. **(b)** *no pl (Art)* Malerei *f*. **(c)** *no pl (of flat etc)* Anstreichen *nt*.

paint: ~ pot *n* Farbtopf *m*; **~ roller** *n* Rolle *f*; **~work** *n (on car etc)* Lack *m*; *(on wall, furniture)* Anstrich *m*.

pair [pɛə[r]] **1** *n (of shoes, people)* Paar *nt*; *(of animals, cards)* Pärchen *nt*. **a ~ of trousers/scissors** eine Hose/Schere; **in ~s** paarweise; *arrive, go out* zu zweit; *seated* in Zweiergruppen. **2** *vt* in Paaren *or* paarweise anordnen.

♦ **pair off 1** *vt sep* in Zweiergruppen einteilen. **to ~ sb ~ with sb** *(find boyfriend etc for)* jdn mit jdm zusammenbringen. **2** *vi* Paare bilden. **to ~ ~ with sb** mit jdm gehen.

pajamas [pə'dʒɑːməz] *npl (US)* = **pyjamas.**

Pakistani [,pɑːkɪs'tɑːnɪ] **1** *adj* pakistanisch. **2** *n* Pakistani *mf*, Pakistaner(in *f*) *m*.

pal [pæl] *n (col)* Kumpel *m (col)*.

palace ['pælɪs] *n (lit, fig)* Palast *m*.

palatable ['pælətəbl] *adj (iro)* genießbar; *food also* schmackhaft *(to* für*)*; *(fig)* attraktiv.

palate ['pælɪt] *n (lit)* Gaumen *m*.

palatial [pə'leɪʃəl] *adj (spacious)* palastartig; *(luxurious)* luxuriös, feudal *(hum col)*.

palaver [pə'lɑːvə[r]] *n (col: fuss)* Theater *nt (col)*.

pale[1] [peɪl] **1** *adj (+er)* blaß; *face (unhealthy)* bleich. **~ green** *etc* blaß- *or* zartgrün *etc*; **to go** *or* **turn ~** bleich werden. **2** *vi (person)* erbleichen, blaß werden. **to ~ into insignificance** zur Bedeutungslosigkeit herabsinken.

pale[2] *n (stake)* Pfahl *m*. **those remarks were quite beyond the ~** diese Bemerkungen haben eindeutig die Grenzen überschritten.

paleness ['peɪlnɪs] *n* Blässe *f*.

Palestine ['pælɪstaɪn] *n* Palästina *nt*.

Palestinian [,pælə'stɪnɪən] **1** *adj* palästinensisch. **2** *n* Palästinenser(in *f*) *m*.

palette ['pælɪt] *n* Palette *f*.

pall[1] [pɔːl] *n (over coffin)* Sargtuch *nt*. **a ~ of smoke** eine Dunstglocke; *(rising)* eine Rauchwolke.

pall[2] *vi* an Reiz verlieren.

pall-bearer ['pɔːl,bɛərə[r]] *n* Sargträger *m*.

pallet ['pælɪt] *n (for storage)* Palette *f*.

palliative ['pælɪətɪv] *n* Linderungsmittel *nt*.

pallid ['pælɪd] *adj* blaß, fahl.

pallor ['pælə[r]] *n* Blässe, Fahlheit *f*.

pally ['pælɪ] *adj (+er) (col)* **to be ~ with sb** mit jdm gut Freund sein; **to get ~ with sb** sich mit jdm anfreunden.

palm[1] [pɑːm] *n (Bot)* Palme *f*; *(Eccl)* Palmzweig *m*.

palm[2] *n (Anat)* Handfläche *f*. **to grease sb's ~** jdn schmieren *(col)*; **to read sb's ~** jdm aus der Hand lesen.

♦ **palm off** *vt sep (col) rubbish, goods* andrehen *(on(to)sb* jdm*) (col)*.

palmist ['pɑːmɪst] *n* Handliniendeuter(in *f*) *m*.

palm: P~ Sunday *n* Palmsonntag *m*; **~tree** *n* Palme *f*.

palpable ['pælpəbl] *adj* greifbar; *(clear) lie, error* offensichtlich.

palpably ['pælpəblɪ] *adv (clearly)* eindeutig.

palpitate ['pælpɪteɪt] *vi (heart)* heftig klopfen; *(tremble)* zittern.

palpitation [,pælpɪ'teɪʃən] *n (of heart)* Herzklopfen *nt*; *(trembling)* Zittern *nt*. **to have ~s** Herzklopfen haben.

paltry ['pɔːltrɪ] *adj* armselig, schäbig.

pampas ['pæmpəs] *npl* Pampas *pl*.

pamper ['pæmpə[r]] *vt* verwöhnen; *child also, dog* verhätscheln.

pamphlet ['pæmflɪt] *n (informative)* Broschüre *f*; *(literary)* Druckschrift *f*; *(political)* Flugblatt *nt*.

pan[1] [pæn] **1** *n* **(a)** *(Cook)* Pfanne *f*; *(sauce ~)* Topf *m*. **(b)** *(of scales)* Waagschale *f*; *(of lavatory)* Becken *nt*. **2** *vt* **(a)** *gold* waschen. **(b)** *(US) fish* braten. **(c)** *(US col: slate) new play etc* verreißen. **3** *vi* **to ~ for gold** Gold waschen.

♦ **pan out** *vi (col)* sich entwickeln. **to ~ ~ well** klappen *(col)*.

pan[2] *vi (camera)* schwenken. **a ~ning shot** ein Schwenk *m*.

pan- *pref* pan-, Pan-. **P~-African** panafrikanisch.

panacea [,pænə'sɪə] *n* Allheilmittel *nt*.

panache [pə'næʃ] *n* Schwung, Elan *m*. **she dresses with ~** sie kleidet sich sehr extravagant.

Panama [,pænə'mɑː] *n* Panama *nt*. **~ Canal** Panamakanal *m*.

panama (hat) *n* Panamahut *m*.

pancake ['pænkeɪk] *n* Pfannkuchen *m*. **P~ Day** Fastnachtsdienstag *m*.

pancreas ['pæŋkrɪəs] *n* Bauchspeicheldrüse *f*.

panda ['pændə] *n* Panda *m*.

panda car *n (Brit)* (Funk)streifenwagen *m*.

pandemonium [,pændɪ'məʊnɪəm] *n* Chaos *nt*.

pander ['pændə[r]] *vi* nachgeben *(to dat)*. **to ~ to sb's desires** jds Bedürfnisse befriedigen wollen; **to ~ to sb's ego** jdm um den Bart gehen.

pane [peɪn] *n* Glasscheibe *f*.

panel ['pænl] **1** *n* **(a)** *(wood)* Platte, Tafel *f*; *(in ceiling, door)* Feld *nt*; *(Art)* Tafel *f*; *(of bodywork of a car)* Karosserieteil *nt*; *(of instruments, switches)* Schalttafel *f*. **instrument ~** Armaturenbrett *nt*; *(on machine)* Kontrolltafel *f*. **(b)** *(of interviewers etc)* Gremium *nt*; *(in discussion)* Diskussionsrunde *f*. **a ~ of experts** ein Sachverständigengremium *nt*. **2** *vt wall* täfeln.

panel: ~ beater *n* Autoschlosser *m*; **~ discussion** *n* Podiumsdiskussion *f*; **~ game** *n* Ratespiel *nt*.

panelling, *(US)* **paneling** ['pænəlɪŋ] *n* Täfelung *f*, Paneel *nt*; *(to conceal radiator etc)* Verschalung *f*.

panellist, *(US)* **panelist** ['pænəlɪst] *n* Diskussionsteilnehmer(in *f*) *m*.

pang [pæŋ] *n* **~ of conscience** Gewissensbisse *pl*; **~s of hunger** quälender Hunger.

panic ['pænɪk] **1** *n* Panik *f*. **to flee in ~** panikartig die Flucht ergreifen; **a ~ reaction** eine Kurzschlußreaktion; **at ~ stations** in Alarmbereitschaft. **2** *vi* in Panik geraten. **don't ~!** nur keine Panik! **3** *vt* Panik auslösen bei.

panicky ['pænɪkɪ] *adj person* überängstlich; *act, measure etc* Kurzschluß-.

panic-stricken ['pænɪk,strɪkən] *adj* von panischem Schrecken ergriffen; *look* panisch.

pannier ['pænɪəʳ] *n* Korb *m*; *(on motor-cycle etc)* Satteltasche *f*.

panorama [,pænə'rɑːmə] *n* Panorama *nt (of gen)*; *(survey)* Übersicht *f (of* über *+acc)*.

panoramic [,pænə'ræmɪk] *adj view* Panorama-. **~ shot** *(Phot)* Panoramaaufnahme *f*; **a ~ view of the hills** ein Blick *m* auf das Bergpanorama.

pansy ['pænzɪ] *n* **(a)** *(Bot)* Stiefmütterchen *nt*. **(b)** *(pej: homosexual)* Schwule(r) *m (col)*.

pant [pænt] *vi* keuchen; *(dog)* hecheln. **to be ~ing for a drink** nach etwas zu trinken lechzen.

pantechnicon [pæn'teknɪkən] *n (Brit)* Möbelwagen *m*.

panther ['pænθəʳ] *n* Panther *m*.

panties ['pæntɪz] *npl* Höschen *nt*; *(for women also)* Slip *m*. **a pair of ~** ein Höschen *nt*/ein Slip *m*.

pantomime ['pæntəmaɪm] *n (in GB: Theat)* Weihnachtsmärchen *nt*; *(mime)* Pantomime *f*.

pantry ['pæntrɪ] *n* Speisekammer *f*.

pants [pænts] *npl (trousers)* Hose *f*; *(Brit: under~)* Unterhose *f*. **a pair of ~** eine Hose/Unterhose; **to wear the ~** *(US fig)* die Hosen anhaben *(col)*.

pantyhose ['pæntɪhəʊz] *n (US)* Strumpfhose *f*.

papacy ['peɪpəsɪ] *n* Papsttum *nt*.

papal ['peɪpəl] *adj* päpstlich.

paper ['peɪpəʳ] **1** *n* **(a)** Papier *nt*. **a piece of ~** ein Stück *nt* Papier; **a sheet of ~** ein Blatt *nt* Papier; **to put sth down on ~** etw schriftlich festhalten; **it looks good on ~ but ...** auf dem Papier sieht es gut aus, aber ...; **it's not worth the ~ it's written on** es ist schade um das Papier, auf dem es steht. **(b)** *(newspaper)* Zeitung *f*. **to write to the ~s about sth** Leserbriefe/einen Leserbrief schreiben; **it was in the ~s** es stand in der Zeitung. **(c) ~s** *pl (identity ~s, writings)* Papiere *pl*. **private ~s** private Unterlagen *pl*. **(d)** *(set of questions in exam)* Testbogen *m*; *(exam) (Univ)* Klausur *f*; *(Sch)* Arbeit *f*; *(academic)* Referat *nt*. **to read a ~** ein Referat halten. **(e)** *(wall~)* Tapete *f*. **2** *vt wall, room* tapezieren.

paper *in cpds* Papier-; **~back** *n* Taschenbuch *nt*; **~ bag** *n* Tüte *f*; **~boy** *n* Zeitungsjunge *m*; **~-clip** *n* Büroklammer *f*; **~ knife** *n* Brieföffner *m*; **~ mill** *n* Papierfabrik *f*; **~ money** *n* Papiergeld *nt*; **~-thin** *adj walls* hauchdünn; **~weight** *n* Briefbeschwerer *m*; **~work** *n* Schreibarbeit *f*.

papier mâché ['pæpɪeɪ'mæʃeɪ] *n* Papiermaché *nt*.

papist ['peɪpɪst] *n (pej)* Papist(in *f*) *m*.

paprika ['pæprɪkə] *n* Paprika *m*.

par [pɑːʳ] *n* **to be on a ~ with sb/sth** sich mit jdm/etw messen können; **below ~** *(fig)* unter Niveau; **that's ~ for the course** *(fig)* das ist normal; **I'm not feeling quite up to ~ today** ich bin heute nicht ganz auf dem Posten *(col)*.

parable ['pærəbl] *n* Parabel *f*, Gleichnis *nt*.

parachute ['pærəʃuːt] **1** *n* Fallschirm *m*. **by ~** mit dem Fallschirm; **~ jump** Absprung *m* (mit dem Fallschirm). **2** *vt troops* mit dem Fallschirm absetzen; *supplies* abwerfen. **3** *vi (also* **~ down***)* (mit dem Fallschirm) abspringen. **to ~ to safety** sich mit dem Fallschirm retten.

parachutist ['pærəʃuːtɪst] *n* Fallschirmspringer(in *f*) *m*.

parade [pə'reɪd] **1** *n (procession)* Umzug *m*; *(Mil, circus, display)* Parade *f*; *(political)* Demonstration *f*; *(fashion ~)* Modenschau *f*; *(of wealth etc)* Zurschaustellung *f*; *(Mil: review)* Truppeninspektion *f*. **to be on ~** *(Mil)* eine Parade abhalten. **2** *vt* **(a)** *troops* vorbeimarschieren lassen; *military might* demonstrieren; *placards* vor sich her tragen. **(b)** *(show off)* zur Schau stellen. **3** *vi* ziehen *(through* durch*)*; *(Mil)* vorbeimarschieren; *(political party)* eine Demonstration veranstalten.

parade ground *n* Exerzierplatz *m*.

paradigm ['pærədaɪm] *n* Musterbeispiel *nt*.

paradise ['pærədaɪs] *n (lit, fig)* Paradies *nt*.

paradox ['pærədɒks] *n* Paradox *nt*. **life is full of ~es** das Leben steckt voller Widersprüche.

paradoxical [,pærə'dɒksɪkəl] *adj* paradox; *person* widersprüchlich.

paradoxically [,pærə'dɒksɪkəlɪ] *adv* paradoxerweise; *worded* paradox.

paraffin ['pærəfɪn] *n (Brit: oil)* Paraffin(öl) *nt*; *(US: wax)* Paraffin *nt*.

paraffin: ~ lamp *n* Paraffinlampe *f*; **~ stove** *n (Brit)* Paraffinofen *m*.

paragon ['pærəgən] *n* Muster *nt*. **a ~ of virtue** ein Muster *nt* an Tugendhaftigkeit.

paragraph ['pærəgrɑːf] *n* Absatz *m*.

parakeet ['pærəkiːt] *n* Sittich *m*.

parallel ['pærəlel] **1** *adj* **(a)** *lines, streets* parallel. **the road is ~ to the river** die Straße verläuft parallel zum Fluß; **~ bars** Barren *m*. **(b)** *(fig) case, career, development* vergleichbar. **a ~ case** ein Parallelfall *m*; **the two systems developed along ~ lines** die Entwicklung der beiden Systeme verlief parallel. **2** *adv* **to run ~** *(roads, careers)* parallel verlaufen. **3** *n* **(a)** *(Geometry)* Parallele *f*; *(Geog)* Breitenkreis *m*. **the 49th ~** der 49. Breitengrad. **(b)** *(Elec)* **connected in ~** parallel geschaltet. **(c)** *(fig)* Parallele *f*. **without ~** beispiellos; **to draw a ~ between X and Y** eine Parallele zwischen X und Y ziehen. **4** *vt (fig)* gleichen *(+dat)*.

parallelogram [,pærə'leləʊgræm] *n* Parallelogramm *nt*.

paralysis [pə'ræləsɪs] *n, pl* **paralyses** [pə'ræləsiːz] Lähmung *f*; *(of industry etc)* Lahmlegung *f*.

paralytic [,pærə'lɪtɪk] *adj* **(a)** paralytisch, Lähmungs-. **(b)** *(Brit col: drunk)* total blau *(col)*.

paralyze ['pærəlaɪz] *vt* **(a)** lähmen. **to be ~d (with fright)** vor Schreck wie gelähmt sein. **(b)** *industry* lahmlegen.

parameter [pə'ræmɪtəʳ] *n* **(a)** *(Math)* Parameter *m*. **(b) ~s** *pl (framework, limits)* Rahmen *m*.

paramilitary [,pærə'mɪlɪtərɪ] *adj* paramilitärisch.

paramount ['pærəmaʊnt] *adj* Haupt-. **of ~ importance** von größter Wichtigkeit.

paranoia [,pærə'nɔɪə] *n* Paranoia *f*; *(col)* Verfolgungswahn *m*.

paranoid ['pærənɔɪd] *adj* paranoid. **or am I just being ~ about it?** oder bilde ich mir das nur ein?

paranormal [,pærə'nɔːməl] *adj* paranormal.

parapet ['pærəpɪt] *n* Brüstung *f*.

paraphernalia ['pærəfə'neɪlɪə] *npl* Drum und Dran *nt*.

paraphrase ['pærəfreɪz] **1** *n* Umschreibung *f*. **2** *vt* umschreiben.

paraplegia [,pærə'pliːdʒə] *n* doppelseitige

Lähmung.

paraplegic [ˌpærəˈpliːdʒɪk] **1** *adj* doppelseitig gelähmt. **2** *n* Paraplegiker(in *f*) *m (spec)*.

parasite [ˈpærəsaɪt] *n (lit, fig)* Parasit *m*.

parasitic(al) [ˌpærəˈsɪtɪk(əl)] *adj animal, plant* Schmarotzer-, parasitär *(also fig)*.

parasol [ˈpærəsɒl] *n* Sonnenschirm *m*.

paratrooper [ˈpærətruːpəʳ] *n* Fallschirmjäger *m*.

paratroops [ˈpærətruːps] *npl* Fallschirmjäger *pl*.

parcel [ˈpɑːsl] *n* **(a)** Paket *nt*. **to do sth up in a ~** etw als Paket packen; **~ post** Paketpost *f*. **(b) a ~ of land** ein Stück *nt* Land.

♦ **parcel up** *vt sep* als Paket verpacken.

parched [pɑːtʃt] *adj* ausgetrocknet. **to be ~ (with thirst)** (vor Durst) verschmachten.

parchment [ˈpɑːtʃmənt] *n* Pergament *nt*.

pardon [ˈpɑːdn] **1** *n* **(a)** *(Jur)* Begnadigung *f*. **general ~** Amnestie *f*. **(b) I beg your ~, but could you ...?** verzeihen Sie bitte, könnten Sie ...?; **I beg your ~!** erlauben Sie mal!; **I beg your ~?** *(Brit)* bitte?, wie bitte?; **I beg your ~** *(apology)* Verzeihung. **2** *vt* **(a)** *(Jur)* begnadigen. **(b)** *(forgive)* verzeihen *(sb* jdm, *sth* etw*)*. **to ~ sb sth** jdm etw verzeihen; **~ me?** *(US)* bitte?, wie bitte?

pare [pɛəʳ] *vt nails* schneiden; *fruit, stick* schälen.

♦ **pare down** *vt sep costs etc* einschränken.

parent [ˈpɛərənt] **1** *n* Elternteil *m*. **~s** Eltern *pl*. **2** *attr* **~ company** Muttergesellschaft *f*.

parentage [ˈpɛərəntɪdʒ] *n* Herkunft *f*.

parental [pəˈrentl] *adj care etc* elterlich *attr*.

parenthesis [pəˈrenθɪsɪs] *n, pl* **parentheses** [pəˈrenθɪsiːz] Klammer *f*.

parenthetic(al) [ˌpærənˈθetɪk(əl)] *adj* beiläufig.

parenthood [ˈpɛərənthʊd] *n* Elternschaft *f*.

Paris [ˈpærɪs] *n* Paris *nt*.

parish [ˈpærɪʃ] *n* Gemeinde *f*; *(district)* Pfarrbezirk *m*, Pfarrei *f*.

parish: ~ church *n* Pfarrkirche *f*; **~ council** *n* Gemeinderat *m*.

parishioner [pəˈrɪʃənəʳ] *n* Gemeindemitglied *nt*.

parish priest *n* Pfarrer *m*.

Parisian [pəˈrɪzɪən] **1** *adj* Pariser *inv*. **2** *n* Pariser(in *f*) *m*.

parity [ˈpærɪtɪ] *n (equality)* Gleichstellung *f*; *(of opportunities)* Gleichheit *f*; *(Fin, Sci)* Parität *f*. **the ~ of the dollar** die Dollarparität.

park [pɑːk] **1** *n* Park *m*. **2** *vt* **(a)** *car* parken; *bike* abstellen. **a ~ed car** ein parkendes Auto. **(b)** *(col: put) luggage etc* abstellen. **he ~ed himself right in front of the fire** er pflanzte sich direkt vor den Kamin *(col)*. **3** *vi* parken. **there was nowhere to ~** es gab nirgendwo einen Parkplatz.

parka [ˈpɑːkə] *n* Parka *m*.

parking [ˈpɒːkɪŋ] *n* Parken *nt*.

parking: ~ lights *npl* Standlicht *nt*; **~ lot** *n (US)* Parkplatz *m*; **~ meter** *n* Parkuhr *f*; **~ place** *n* Parkplatz *m*; **~ ticket** *n* Strafzettel *m*.

park: ~keeper *n* Parkwächter *m*; **~way** *n (US)* Allee *f*.

parky [ˈpɑːkɪ] *adj (+er) (Brit col)* kühl, frisch.

parlance [ˈpɑːləns] *n* **in common ~** im allgemeinen Sprachgebrauch; **in technical ~** in der Fachsprache.

parliament [ˈpɑːləmənt] *n* Parlament *nt*. **to get into ~** ins Parlament kommen.

parliamentarian [ˌpɑːləmenˈtɛərɪən] *n* Parlamentarier *m*.

parliamentary [ˌpɑːləˈmentərɪ] *adj* parlamentarisch.

parlour, *(US)* parlor [ˈpɑːləʳ] *n (in house, beauty ~ etc)* Salon *m*. **ice-cream ~** Eisdiele *f*.

Parmesan [ˈpɑːmɪzæn] *n* Parmesan *m*.

parochial [pəˈrəʊkɪəl] *adj* **(a)** *(Eccl)* Pfarr-, Gemeinde-. **(b)** *(fig) attitude, person* engstirnig; *mind, ideas* beschränkt.

parody [ˈpærədɪ] **1** *n* Parodie *f (of* auf *+acc)*. **2** *vt* parodieren.

parole [pəˈrəʊl] **1** *n (Jur)* Bewährung *f*; *(temporary release)* Strafunterbrechung *f*. **let sb out on ~** jdn auf Bewährung entlassen; *(temporarily)* jdm Strafunterbrechung gewähren; **to be on ~** unter Bewährung stehen; *(temporarily)* auf Kurzurlaub sein. **2** *vt prisoner* auf Bewährung entlassen; *(temporarily)* Strafunterbrechung gewähren *(+dat)*.

paroxysm [ˈpærəksɪzəm] *n* Anfall *m*. **~s of laughter** ein Lachkrampf *m*.

parquet [ˈpɑːkeɪ] *n* Parkett *nt*.

parrot [ˈpærət] *n* Papagei *m*. **to repeat sth ~-fashion** etw wie ein Papagei nachplappern.

parry [ˈpærɪ] *vti (Fencing, fig)* parieren; *(Boxing)* abwehren.

parsimonious [ˌpɑːsɪˈməʊnɪəs] *adj* geizig.

parsley [ˈpɑːslɪ] *n* Petersilie *f*.

parsnip [ˈpɑːsnɪp] *n* Pastinake *f*.

parson [ˈpɑːsn] *n* Pfarrer, Pastor *m*.

parsonage [ˈpɑːsənɪdʒ] *n* Pfarrhaus *nt*.

part [pɑːt] **1** *n* **(a)** Teil *m*. **it is ~ and parcel of the job** das gehört zu der Arbeit dazu; **in ~** teilweise, zum Teil; **it is in large ~ true** das ist zum großen Teil wahr; **for the main** *or* **most ~** in erster Linie; *(generally speaking)* im großen und ganzen; **in the latter ~ of the year** gegen Ende des Jahres; **5 ~s of sand to 1 of cement** 5 Teile Sand auf ein(en) Teil Zement.

(b) *(component, Mech)* Teil *nt*. **spare ~** Ersatzteil *nt*; *(Gram)* **~ of speech** Wortart *f*; **principal ~s of a verb** Stammformen *pl*; *(of series)* Folge *f*; *(of serial)* Fortsetzung *f*; **end of ~ one** *(TV)* Ende des ersten Teils.

(c) *(share, role)* (An)teil *m*, Rolle *f*; *(Theat)* Rolle *f*; *(Mus)* Stimme *f*. **to play one's ~** *(fig)* seinen Beitrag leisten; **to take ~ in sth** an etw *(dat)* teilnehmen; **he looks the ~** *(fig)* so sieht er auch aus; **to play no ~ in sth** *(person)* nicht an etw *(dat)* beteiligt sein; *(factor etc)* bei etw keine Rolle spielen.

(d) ~s *pl (region)* Gegend *f*; **he's not from these ~s** er ist nicht aus dieser Gegend.

(e) *(side)* Seite *f*. **to take sb's ~** sich auf jds Seite *(acc)* stellen; **for my ~** was mich betrifft; **on my ~** *etc* meinerseits *etc*; **on the ~ of** von seiten *(+gen)*, seitens *(+gen)*; **to take sth in good/bad ~** etw nicht übelnehmen/etw übelnehmen; **a man of ~s** ein Universalgenie *nt*; **a man of many ~s** ein vielseitiger Mensch.

(f) *(US: in hair)* Scheitel *m*.

2 *adv* teils, teilweise. **it is ~ iron and ~ copper** es ist teils aus Eisen und teils aus Kupfer; **it was ~ eaten** es war halb aufgegessen.

3 *vt* **(a)** *(divide)* teilen; *hair* scheiteln; *curtain* zur Seite schieben. **(b)** *(separate)* trennen. **to ~ sb from sb/sth** jdn von jdm/etw trennen; **to ~ company with sb/sth** sich von jdm/etw trennen; *(in opinion)* mit jdm nicht gleicher Meinung sein.

4 *vi* **(a)** *(divide)* sich teilen; *(curtains)* sich öffnen. **(b)** *(separate) (person)* sich trennen; *(things)* sich lösen, abgehen. **to ~ with sth** sich von etw trennen.

partake [pɑːˈteɪk] *pret* **partook,** *ptp* **partaken** [pɑːˈteɪkn] *vi (form)* **(a) to ~ of** *food, drink* zu sich *(dat)* nehmen. **(b) to ~ in (an activity)** an etw *(dat)* teilnehmen.

part exchange *n (Brit)* **to offer/take sth in ~** etw in Zahlung geben/nehmen.

partial [ˈpɑːʃəl] *adj* **(a)** *(not complete)* Teil-, teilweise; *paralysis, eclipse* teilweise, partiell. **(b)** *(biased)* voreingenommen. **(c) to be ~ to sth** eine Schwäche für etw haben.

partiality [ˌpɑːʃɪˈælɪtɪ] *n* **(a)** *(bias)* Voreingenommenheit *f*. **(b)** *(liking)* Vorliebe *f (for* für*)*.

partially [ˈpɑːʃəlɪ] *adv (partly)* zum Teil, teilweise.

participant [pɑːˈtɪsɪpənt] *n* Teilnehmer(in *f*) *m (in gen,* an *+dat)*.

participate [pɑːˈtɪsɪpeɪt] *vi (take part)* sich beteiligen, teilnehmen *(in* an *+dat).*

participation [pɑːˌtɪsɪˈpeɪʃən] *n* Beteiligung *f; (in competition etc)* Teilnahme *f; (worker ~)* Mitbestimmung *f.*

participle [ˈpɑːtɪsɪpl] *n* Partizip *nt.*

particle [ˈpɑːtɪkl] *n* **(a)** *(of sand etc, Phys)* Teilchen *nt.* **(b)** *(Gram)* Partikel *f.*

particular [pəˈtɪkjʊləʳ] **1** *adj* **(a)** *(as against others)* **this ~ house is very nice** dies (eine) Haus ist sehr hübsch; **in this ~ instance** in diesem besonderen Fall; **is there any one ~ colour you prefer?** bevorzugen Sie eine bestimmte Farbe? **(b)** *(special)* besondere(r, s). **in ~** besonders, vor allem; **nothing in ~** nichts Besonderes *or* Bestimmtes; **is there anything in ~ you'd like?** haben Sie einen besonderen Wunsch?; **he's a ~ friend of mine** er ist ein guter Freund von mir; **for no ~ reason** aus keinem besonderen Grund. **(c)** *(fussy, fastidious)* eigen; *(choosy)* wählerisch. **he is very ~ about cleanliness** er nimmt es mit der Sauberkeit sehr genau; **you can't be too ~** man kann gar nicht wählerisch genug sein; **I'm not too ~ (about it)** es kommt mir nicht so darauf an.

2 *n* **~s** *pl* Einzelheiten *pl; (about person)* Personalien *pl;* **for further ~s apply to the personnel manager** weitere Auskünfte erteilt der Personalchef; **to give ~s** Angaben machen.

particularly [pəˈtɪkjʊləlɪ] *adv* besonders, vor allem; *specify, request* ausdrücklich. **he was not ~ pleased** er war nicht besonders erfreut.

parting [ˈpɑːtɪŋ] **1** *n* **(a)** Abschied *m.* **is this the ~ of the ways then?** das ist also das Ende (unserer Beziehung)? **(b)** *(Brit: in hair)* Scheitel *m.* **2** *adj* Abschieds-, abschließend. **"he knows about it already", was her ~ shot** „er weiß es schon", schleuderte sie ihm nach; **his ~ words** seine Abschiedsworte *pl.*

partisan [ˌpɑːtɪˈzæn] **1** *adj* **(a)** parteiisch *(esp pej),* parteilich. **~ spirit** Parteigeist *m.* **(b)** *(Mil)* Partisanen-. **2** *n (Mil)* Partisan(in *f*) *m.*

partition [pɑːˈtɪʃən] **1** *n* **(a)** Teilung *f.* **(b)** *(wall)* Trennwand *f.* **(c)** *(section)* Abteilung *f.* **2** *vt country* spalten; *room* aufteilen.

♦ **partition off** *vt sep* abteilen, abtrennen.

partly [ˈpɑːtlɪ] *adv* zum Teil, teilweise.

partner [ˈpɑːtnəʳ] **1** *n* Partner(in *f*) *m; (in limited company also)* Gesellschafter(in *f*) *m; (in crime)* Komplize *m,* Komplizin *f.* **~s in crime** Komplizen. **2** *vt* **to ~ sb** jds Partner sein; **to be ~ed by sb** jdn zum Partner haben.

partnership [ˈpɑːtnəʃɪp] *n* **(a)** Partnerschaft *f; (in sport, dancing etc)* Paar *nt.* **in ~ with sb** in Zusammenarbeit mit jdm. **(b)** *(Comm)* Personengesellschaft *f.* **to enter into a ~** in eine Gesellschaft eintreten.

partook [pɑːˈtʊk] *pret of* **partake.**

part: ~ owner *n* Mitbesitzer(in *f*) *m;* **~ payment** *n* Teilzahlung *f.*

partridge [ˈpɑːtrɪdʒ] *n* Rebhuhn *nt.*

part-time [ˈpɑːtˈtaɪm] **1** *adj* Teilzeit-. **I'm just ~** ich arbeite nur Teilzeit. **2** *adv work* stundenweise; *teach* als Teilzeitlehrer(in).

party [ˈpɑːtɪ] *n* **(a)** *(Pol)* Partei *f.* **(b)** *(group)* Gruppe, Gesellschaft *f; (Mil)* Kommando *nt,* Trupp *m.* **a ~ of tourists** eine Reisegesellschaft. **(c)** *(celebration)* Fest *nt,* Party, Fete *(col) f; (more formal)* Gesellschaft *f.* **to have** *or* **give a ~** eine Party geben *or* machen; **at the ~** auf dem Fest *or* der Party; bei der Gesellschaft. **(d)** *(Jur, fig)* Partei *f.* **a/the third ~** ein Dritter *m*/der Dritte; **the parties to a dispute** die streitenden Parteien; **to be a ~ to sth** an etw *(dat)* beteiligt sein.

party line *n* **(a)** *(Pol)* Parteilinie *f.* **(b)** *(Telec)* Gemeinschaftsanschluß *m.*

pass [pɑːs] **1** *n* **(a)** *(permit)* Ausweis *m; (Mil etc)* Passierschein *m.* **(b)** *(Brit Univ)* **to get a ~ in German** seine Deutschprüfung bestehen; *(lowest level)* seine Deutschprüfung mit „ausreichend" bestehen. **(c)** *(Geog, Sport)* Paß *m; (Ftbl: for shot at goal)* Vorlage *f.* **(d) things have come to a pretty ~ when ...** so weit ist es schon gekommen, daß ...; **things had come to such a ~ that ...** die Lage hatte sich so zugespitzt, daß ... **(e) to make a ~ at sb** bei jdm Annäherungsversuche machen.

2 *vt* **(a)** *(move past)* vorbeigehen an *(+dat);* vorbeifahren an *(+dat); (overtake) athlete, car* überholen. **(b)** *(cross) frontier etc* überschreiten, passieren. **not a word ~ed her lips** kein Wort kam über ihre Lippen. **(c)** *(reach, hand)* reichen. **they ~ed the photograph around** sie reichten das Foto herum; **~ (me) the salt, please** reich mir doch bitte das Salz!; *(Sport)* **to ~ the ball to sb** jdm den Ball zuspielen. **(d) it ~es my comprehension that ...** es geht über meinen Verstand, daß ... **(e)** *(Univ etc) exam* bestehen; *candidate* bestehen lassen. **(f)** *(approve) motion* annehmen; *plan* gutheißen; *(Parl)* verabschieden. **(g)** *(spend) time* verbringen. **he did it just to ~ the time** er tat das nur, um sich *(dat)* die Zeit zu vertreiben. **(h)** *remark* von sich geben; *opinion* abgeben; *(Jur) sentence* verhängen; *judgement* fällen.

3 *vi* **(a)** *(move past)* vorbeigehen; vorbeifahren. **we ~ed in the corridor** wir gingen im Korridor aneinander vorbei.

(b) *(overtake)* überholen.

(c) *(move, go)* **~ along the car please!** bitte weiter durchgehen!; **words ~ed between them** es gab einige Meinungsverschiedenheiten; **to ~ out of sight** außer Sichtweite geraten; **when we ~ed over the frontier** als wir die Grenze passierten; **shall we ~ to the second subject on the agenda?** wollen wir zum zweiten Punkt der Tagesordnung übergehen?; **he ~ed under the archway** er ging/fuhr durch das Tor.

(d) *(time) (also* **~ by***)* vergehen.

(e) *(disappear, end: anger, era etc)* vorübergehen; *(storm) (go over)* vorüberziehen; *(abate)* sich legen; *(rain)* vorbeigehen. **it'll ~** das geht vorüber!

(f) *(be acceptable)* gehen. **to let sth ~** etw durchgehen lassen; **let it ~!** vergessen wir's!; **it'll ~** das geht.

(g) *(be considered, be accepted)* angesehen werden *(for or as sth* als etw*).* **she could easily ~ for 25** sie könnte leicht für 25 durchgehen.

(h) *(in exam)* bestehen.

(i) *(Cards, in quiz etc)* passen. **(I) ~!** passe!

♦ **pass away** *vi* **(a)** *(end)* zu Ende gehen. **(b)** *(euph: die)* entschlafen, hinscheiden.

♦ **pass by 1** *vi (go past)* vorbeigehen; *(car etc)* vorbeifahren; *(time, months etc)* vergehen. **I can't let that ~ ~** ich kann das nicht durchgehen lassen. **2** *vi +prep obj* **we ~ed ~ a line of hotels** wir kamen an einer Reihe Hotels vorbei. **3** *vt sep (ignore) problems* übergehen. **life has ~ed her ~** das Leben ist an ihr vorübergegangen.

♦ **pass down** *vt sep traditions, characteristics* weitergeben *(to* an *+acc).*

♦ **pass off 1** *vi* **(a)** *(take place)* ablaufen. **(b)** *(end)* vorübergehen. **(c)** *(be taken as)* durchgehen *(as* als*).* **2** *vt sep* **to ~ oneself/sb ~ as sth** sich/jdn als *or* für etw ausgeben.

♦ **pass on 1** *vi* **(a)** *(euph: die)* entschlafen. **(b)** *(proceed)* übergehen *(to* zu*).* **2** *vt sep news, information* weitergeben; *disease* übertragen.

♦ **pass out** *vi* **(a)** *(become unconscious)* in Ohnmacht fallen, umkippen *(col).* **(b)** *(new officer)* ernannt werden.

♦ **pass over** *vt sep* übergehen. **he's been ~ed ~ again** er ist schon wieder übergangen worden.

♦ **pass through** *vi* **I'm only ~ing ~** ich bin nur auf der Durchreise; **you have to ~ ~ Berlin** du mußt über Berlin fahren.

passable ['pɑːsəbl] *adj* **(a)** passierbar; *road etc also* befahrbar. **(b)** *(tolerable)* passabel.

passage ['pæsɪdʒ] *n* **(a)** *(transition)* Übergang *m.* **with the ~ of time** mit der Zeit. **(b)** *(through country)* Durchreise *f.* **(c)** *(voyage, fare)* Überfahrt *f.* **(d)** *(Parl: process)* parlamentarische Behandlung; *(final)* Verabschiedung *f.* **(e)** *(corridor)* Gang *m.* **(f)** *(in book)* Passage *f*; *(Mus also)* Stück *nt.* **a ~ from the Bible** eine Bibelstelle.

passageway ['pæsɪdʒweɪ] *n* Durchgang *m.*

pass: ~ book *n* Sparbuch *nt*; **~ degree** *n niedrigster Grad an britischen Universitäten,* „Bestanden".

passenger ['pæsɪndʒəʳ] *n (on bus, in taxi)* Fahrgast *m*; *(on train)* Reisende(r) *mf*; *(on ship, plane)* Passagier *m*; *(in car)* Mitfahrer(in *f*) *m*; *(on motorcycle)* Beifahrer(in *f*) *m.* **he's just a ~ in the team** *(fig pej)* er wird von den anderen mit durchgeschleppt.

passer-by ['pɑːsə'baɪ] *n, pl* **passers-by** Passant(in *f*) *m.*

passing ['pɑːsɪŋ] **1** *n* Vorübergehen *nt.* **with the ~ of time** im Lauf(e) der Zeit; **I would like to mention in ~ that ...** ich möchte beiläufig erwähnen, daß ... **2** *adj car* vorbeifahrend; *clouds* vorüberziehend; *years* vergehend; *glance etc, thought* flüchtig; *comments, reference* beiläufig; *fancy* vorübergehend.

passion ['pæʃən] *n* Leidenschaft *f*; *(Rel, Mus)* Passion *f.* **to have a ~ for sth** eine Passion *or* Leidenschaft für etw haben; **music is a ~ with him** die Musik ist bei ihm eine Leidenschaft.

passionate ['pæʃənɪt] *adj* leidenschaftlich.

passion: ~ flower *n* Passionsblume *f*; **~ fruit** *n* Passionsfrucht *f.*

passive ['pæsɪv] **1** *adj* passiv; *acceptance* widerspruchslos. **2** *n (Gram)* Passiv *nt.* **in the ~** im Passiv.

pass key *n* Hauptschlüssel *m.*

Passover ['pɑːsəʊvəʳ] *n* Passah *nt.*

passport ['pɑːspɔːt] *n* (Reise)paß *m*; *(fig)* Schlüssel *m (to* für, zu*).*

password ['pɑːswɜːd] *n* Kennwort *nt*, Parole *f.*

past [pɑːst] **1** *adj* **(a)** frühe(r, s) *attr*, vergangene(r, s) *attr.* **for some time ~** seit einiger Zeit; **in times ~** in früheren Zeiten. **(b)** *(Gram)* **~ tense** Vergangenheit *f*; **~ participle** Partizip Perfekt *nt.*

2 *n (also Gram)* Vergangenheit *f.* **in the ~** in der Vergangenheit *(also Gram)*, früher; **to be a thing of the ~** der Vergangenheit *(dat)* angehören.

3 *prep* **(a)** *(motion)* an *(+dat)* ... vorbei *or* vorüber; *(position: beyond)* hinter *(+dat).* **just ~ the library** kurz hinter der Bücherei; **to run ~ sb** an jdm vorbeilaufen. **(b)** *(time)* nach *(+dat).* **ten (minutes) ~ three** zehn (Minuten) nach drei; **half ~ four** halb fünf; **a quarter ~ nine** Viertel nach neun. **(c)** *(beyond)* **~ forty** über vierzig; **~ belief** unglaublich; **we're ~ caring** es kümmert uns nicht mehr; **to be ~ sth** für etw zu alt sein; **I wouldn't put it ~ him** *(col)* ich würde es ihm schon zutrauen.

4 *adv* vorbei, vorüber. **to walk/run ~** vorbeigehen/vorbeirennen.

pasta ['pæstə] *n* Nudeln *pl.*

paste [peɪst] **1** *n* **(a)** *(for sticking)* Kleister *m.* **(b)** *(spread)* Brotaufstrich *m.* **(c)** *(jewellery)* Straß *m.* **(d) mix to a smooth/firm ~** *(Cook)* zu einem glatten/festen Teig anrühren. **2** *vt (apply ~ to) wallpaper etc* einkleistern; *(affix)* kleben *(to* an *+acc; in* in *+acc).*

pasteboard ['peɪstbɔːd] *n* Karton *m*, Pappe *f.*

pastel ['pæstl] **1** *n (crayon)* Pastellstift *m*; *(drawing)* Pastellzeichnung *f*, Pastell *nt*; *(colour)* Pastellton *m.* **2** *adj attr* Pastell-.

pasteurize ['pæstəraɪz] *vt* pasteurisieren.

pastille ['pæstɪl] *n* Pastille *f.*

pastime ['pɑːstaɪm] *n* Zeitvertreib *m.*

past master *n* **to be a ~ at doing sth** ein Experte darin sein, etw zu tun.

pastor ['pɑːstəʳ] *n* Pfarrer *m.*

pastoral ['pɑːstərəl] *adj* pastoral; *duties also* seelsorgerisch. **~ care** Seelsorge *f.*

pastry ['peɪstrɪ] *n* Teig *m*; *(cake etc)* Stück, Teilchen *(dial) nt.* **pastries** *pl* Gebäck *nt.*

pasture ['pɑːstʃəʳ] *n* **(a)** *(field)* Weide *f.* **to put out to ~** auf die Weide treiben; **to move on to ~s new** *(fig)* sich *(dat)* etwas Neues suchen. **(b)** *no pl (also* **~ land***)* Weideland *nt.*

pasty[1] ['peɪstɪ] *adj consistency* zähflüssig; *material* klebrig; *colour* bläßlich; *look also* kränklich.

pasty[2] ['pæstɪ] *n (esp Brit)* Pastete *f.*

pat[1] [pæt] *n (of butter)* Portion *f.*

pat[2] **1** *adv* **to know** *or* **have sth off ~** etw wie aus dem Effeff können *(col).* **2** *adj answer, explanation* glatt.

pat[3] **1** *n* Klaps *m.* **he gave him a ~ on the shoulder** er tippte ihm auf die Schulter; **to give the dog a ~** den Hund tätscheln; **to give sb/oneself a ~ on the back** *(fig)* jdm/sich selbst auf die Schulter klopfen. **2** *vt (touch lightly)* tätscheln; *(hit gently) ball* leicht schlagen; *sand* festklopfen; *face* abtupfen.

patch [pætʃ] **1** *n* **(a)** *(for mending)* Flicken *m*; *(eye ~)* Augenklappe *f.* **(b) it's/he's not a ~ on ...** *(col)* das/er ist gar nichts gegen ... **(c)** *(small area, stain)* Fleck *m*; *(piece of land)* Stück *nt*; *(subdivision of garden)* Beet *nt*; *(part, section)* Stelle *f*; *(of time)* Phase *f.* **a ~ of blue sky** ein Stückchen *nt* blauer Himmel; **~es of colour** Farbtupfer *pl*; **the cabbage ~** das Kohlbeet; **he's going through a bad ~ at the moment** ihm geht's im Augenblick nicht sonderlich gut. **2** *vt* flicken.

♦ **patch up** *vt sep* zusammenflicken; *quarrel* beilegen. **to ~ things ~ temporarily** die Dinge notdürftig zusammenflicken; *(in relationship)* die Beziehung wieder ins Lot bringen; **they managed to ~ ~ their relationship** sie haben sich schließlich wieder ausgesöhnt.

patchwork ['pætʃwɜːk] *n* **~ quilt** Flickendecke *f*; **a ~ of fields** ein buntes Mosaik von Feldern.

patchy ['pætʃɪ] *adj (+er) work* ungleichmäßig; *knowledge, memory* lückenhaft. **~ fog** stellenweise auftretender Nebel.

pâté ['pæteɪ] *n* Pastete *f.*

patent[1] ['peɪtənt] *adj (obvious)* offensichtlich.

patent[2] **1** *n* Patent *nt.* **~ applied for** *or* **pending** Patent angemeldet; **to take out a ~ (on sth)** ein Patent (auf etw *acc*) erhalten. **2** *vt* patentieren lassen. **3** *adj (~ed) invention* patentiert.

patent leather *n* Lackleder *nt.*

patently ['peɪtəntlɪ] *adv* offensichtlich. **that's ~ obvious** das liegt doch auf der Hand.

patent medicine *n* patentrechtlich geschütztes Arzneimittel.

paternal [pə'tɜːnl] *adv* väterlich. **my ~ grandmother** meine Großmutter väterlicherseits.

paternalist(ic) [pə'tɜːnəlɪst, pə,tɜːnə'lɪstɪk] *adj* patriarchalisch.

paternity [pə'tɜːnɪtɪ] *n* Vaterschaft *f.* **~ suit** Vaterschaftsprozeß *m.*

path [pɑːθ] *n (lit, fig)* Weg *m*; *(smaller)* Pfad *m*; *(in field)* Feldweg *m*; *(trajectory)* Bahn *f.* **the ~ of virtue** der Pfad der Tugend.

pathetic [pə'θetɪk] *adj* **(a)** *(piteous)* mitleiderregend. **it was ~ to see** es war ein Bild des Jammers. **(b)** *(bad)* erbärmlich. **it's ~** es ist zum Heulen *(col).*

pathetically [pə'θetɪkəlɪ] *adv* **(a)** *(piteously)* mitleiderregend. **~ thin/weak** erschreckend dünn/schwach. **(b)** *slow, stupid, inefficient* erbärmlich. **a ~ inadequate answer** eine äußerst dürftige Antwort.

pathological [,pæθə'lɒdʒɪkəl] *adj (lit, fig)* krank-

haft; *studies etc* pathologisch.
pathologist [pəˈθɒlədʒɪst] *n* Pathologe *m*, Pathologin *f*.
pathology [pəˈθɒlədʒɪ] *n (science)* Pathologie *f*.
pathos [ˈpeɪθɒs] *n* Pathos *nt*.
pathway [ˈpɑːθweɪ] *n* Weg *m*; *(smaller)* Pfad *m*.
patience [ˈpeɪʃəns] *n* **(a)** Geduld *f*. **to have ~/no ~ (with sb/sth)** Geduld/keine Geduld (mit jdm/etw) haben; **to lose (one's) ~ (with sb/sth)** (mit jdm/etw) die Geduld verlieren. **(b)** *(Brit Cards)* Patience *f*. **to play ~** eine Patience legen.
patient [ˈpeɪʃənt] **1** *adj* geduldig. **to be ~ with sb** Geduld mit jdm haben. **2** *n* Patient(in *f*) *m*.
patio [ˈpætɪəʊ] *n* Veranda, Terrasse *f*.
patriarch [ˈpeɪtrɪɑːk] *n* Patriarch *m*.
patriot [ˈpeɪtrɪət] *n* Patriot(in *f*) *m*.
patriotic [ˌpætrɪˈɒtɪk] *adj* patriotisch.
patriotism [ˈpætrɪətɪzəm] *n* Patriotismus *m*.
patrol [pəˈtrəʊl] **1** *n (police)* Streife *f*; *(aircraft, ship)* Patrouille *f*. **on ~** *(Mil)* auf Patrouille; *(police)* auf Streife; *(guard dogs, squad car)* im Einsatz. **2** *vt (Mil)* patrouillieren; *(policeman)* seine Runden machen in *(+dat)*; *(police car)* Streife fahren in *(+dat)*. **3** *vi* patrouillieren; *(policemen)* eine Streife/Streifen machen. **to ~ up and down** auf und ab gehen.
patrol: ~ car *n* Streifenwagen *m*; **~man** *n* Wächter *m*; *(US: policeman)* Polizist *m*; **~ wagon** *n (US)* grüne Minna *(col)*, Gefangenenwagen *m*.
patron [ˈpeɪtrən] *n (of shop)* Kunde *m*, Kundin *f*; *(of restaurant, hotel)* Gast *m*; *(of society)* Schirmherr(in *f*) *m*; *(of artist)* Förderer, Gönner(in *f*) *m*; *(~ saint)* Schutzpatron(in *f*) *m*.
patronage [ˈpætrənɪdʒ] *n* **under the ~ of** unter der Schirmherrschaft des/der.
patronize [ˈpætrənaɪz] *vt* **(a)** *pub, cinema etc* besuchen. **the shop is well ~d** das Geschäft hat viel Kundschaft. **(b)** *(treat condescendingly)* herablassend behandeln.
patronizing [ˈpætrənaɪzɪŋ] *adj* gönnerhaft, herablassend. **to be ~ to** *or* **towards sb** jdn von oben herab behandeln.
patter [ˈpætə[r]] **1** *n* **(a)** *(of feet)* Getrippel *nt*; *(of rain)* Plätschern *nt*. **(b)** *(of salesman, comedian, conjurer, disc jockey)* Sprüche *pl (col)*. **sales ~** Vertretersprüche *pl*. **2** *vi (person, feet)* trippeln; *(rain: also* **~ down***)* plätschern.
pattern [ˈpætən] **1** *n* **(a)** Muster *nt*. **to make a ~** ein Muster bilden. **(b)** *(Sew)* Schnittmuster *nt*; *(Knitting)* Strickanleitung *f*. **(c)** *(fig: model)* Vorbild *nt*. **on the Albanian ~** nach albanischem Muster; **to set a** *or* **the ~ for sth** ein Vorbild für etw sein. **(d)** *(fig: in events, behaviour etc)* Muster *nt*; *(recurrent)* Regelmäßigkeit *f*. **the ~ of events** der Ablauf der Ereignisse; **to follow the usual ~** nach dem üblichen Schema verlaufen; **behaviour ~s** Verhaltensmuster *pl*. **2** *vt (model)* machen *(on* nach*)*. **to be ~ed on sth** einer Sache *(dat)* nachgebildet sein; *(music, style etc)* einer Sache *(dat)* nachempfunden sein.
pattern book *n* Musterbuch *nt*.
patterned [ˈpætənd] *adj* gemustert.
paunch [pɔːntʃ] *n* Bauch, Wanst *m*.
pauper [ˈpɔːpə[r]] *n* Arme(r) *mf*.
pause [pɔːz] **1** *n* Pause *f*. **there was a ~ while ...** es entstand eine Pause, während ...; **to have a ~** (eine) Pause machen; **without (a) ~** ununterbrochen; **a ~ for thought** eine Denkpause. **2** *vi* stehenbleiben; *(speaker)* innehalten. **he ~d for breath** er machte eine Pause, um Luft zu holen; **let's ~ here** machen wir hier Pause; **it made him ~** das machte ihn nachdenklich.
pave [peɪv] *vt* pflastern. **to ~ the way for sb/sth** *(fig)* jdm/einer Sache den Weg ebnen.
pavement [ˈpeɪvmənt] *n* **(a)** *(Brit)* Bürgersteig *m*, Trottoir *nt*. **(b)** *(US) (paved road)* Straße *f*; *(surfacing)* Straßendecke *f*.
pavilion [pəˈvɪlɪən] *n* Pavillon *m*; *(Sport) (changing ~)* Umkleideräume *pl*; *(clubhouse)* Klubhaus *nt*.
paving [ˈpeɪvɪŋ] *n* Belag *m*; *(US: of road)* Decke *f*; *(action)* Pflastern *nt*. **~ stone** Platte *f*.
paw [pɔː] **1** *n (of animal, col: hand)* Pfote *f*; *(of lion, bear)* Pranke, Tatze *f*. **2** *vt* **(a)** tätscheln; *(lion etc)* mit der Tatze berühren. **to ~ the ground** *(lit)* scharren; *(fig: be impatient)* ungeduldig werden. **(b)** *(pej col: handle)* betatschen *(col)*.
pawn[1] [pɔːn] *n (Chess)* Bauer *m*; *(fig)* Schachfigur *f*.
pawn[2] **1** *n (security)* Pfand *nt*. **to put sth in ~** etw verpfänden. **2** *vt* verpfänden.
pawn: ~broker *n* Pfandleiher *m*; **~shop** *n* Pfandhaus *nt*.
pay [peɪ] *(vb: pret, ptp* **paid***)* **1** *n* Lohn *m*; *(of salaried employee, civil servant)* Gehalt *nt*; *(Mil)* Sold *m*. **to be in sb's ~** für jdn arbeiten.
2 *vt* **(a)** zahlen; *person, bill, debt* bezahlen. **to ~ sb £10** jdm £ 10 zahlen; **how much is there to ~?** was bin ich schuldig?; **to be** *or* **get paid** *(in regular job)* seinen Lohn/sein Gehalt bekommen; **savings accounts that ~ 5%** Sparkonten, die 5% Zinsen bringen. **(b)** *(lit, fig: be profitable to)* sich lohnen für. **in future it would ~ you to ask** in Zukunft solltest du besser vorher fragen. **(c) to ~ (sb) a visit** *or* **call** jdn besuchen; *(more formal)* jdm einen Besuch abstatten.
3 *vi* **(a)** zahlen. **they ~ well for this sort of work** diese Arbeit wird gut bezahlt; **no, no, I'm ~ing** nein, nein, ich (be)zahle; **to ~ for sth** etw bezahlen; **it's already paid for** es ist schon bezahlt. **(b)** *(be profitable)* sich lohnen. **it's a business that ~s** es ist ein rentables Geschäft; **crime doesn't ~** *(prov)* Verbrechen lohnt sich nicht. **(c)** *(fig: to suffer)* **to ~ for sth (with sth***)* für etw (mit etw) bezahlen; **you'll ~ for that!** dafür wirst du (mir) büßen.
♦**pay back** *vt sep money* zurückzahlen; *compliment, visit* erwidern; *insult, trick* sich revanchieren für. **to ~ sb ~** es jdm heimzahlen.
♦**pay in** *vt sep* einzahlen. **to ~ money ~to an account** Geld auf ein Konto einzahlen.
♦**pay off** *vt sep workmen* auszahlen; *debt* abbezahlen; *HP* ab(be)zahlen; *mortgage* ablösen; *creditor* befriedigen.
♦**pay out** *vt sep* **(a)** *money (spend)* ausgeben; *(count out)* auszahlen. **(b)** *rope* ablaufen lassen.
♦**pay up 1** *vt sep what one owes* zurückzahlen; *subscription* bezahlen. **his account/he is paid ~** er hat alles bezahlt. **2** *vi* zahlen. **come on, ~ ~!** los, bezahl endlich!
payable [ˈpeɪəbl] *adj* zahlbar; *(due)* fällig. **to make a cheque ~ to sb** einen Scheck auf jdn ausstellen.
pay: ~-claim *n* Lohn-/Gehaltsforderung *f*; **~-day** *n* Zahltag *m*.
PAYE *(Brit)* = **pay-as-you-earn** *Steuersystem nt, bei dem die Lohnsteuer direkt einbehalten wird.*
payee [peɪˈiː] *n* Zahlungsempfänger *m*.
pay: ~ freeze *n* Lohnstopp *m*; **~ increase** *n* Lohn-/Gehaltserhöhung *f*.
paying [ˈpeɪɪŋ] *adj* **(a)** *(profitable)* rentabel. **(b) ~ guest** zahlender Gast.
payment [ˈpeɪmənt] *n* Zahlung *f*; *(paying)* Bezahlung *f*; *(of debt, mortgage)* Abtragung, Rückzahlung *f*. **three monthly ~s** drei Monatsraten; **as** *or* **in ~ for his services** als Bezahlung für seine Dienste; **on ~ of** bei Bezahlung von; **to make a ~** eine Zahlung leisten.
payoff [ˈpeɪɒf] *n (col: bribe)* Bestechungsgeld *nt*; *(outcome)* Quittung *f*; *(of joke)* Pointe *f*.
pay: ~ packet *n* Lohntüte *f*; **~ phone** *n* Münzfernsprecher *m*; **~ rise** *n* Lohn-/Gehaltserhöhung *f*; **~slip** *n* Lohn-/Gehaltsstreifen *m*; **~ station** *n (US)* öffentlicher Fernsprecher; **~ talks** *npl* Lohnverhandlungen *pl*; *(for profession, area of industry)* Tarifverhandlungen *pl*.
pc = **(a) post card. (b) per cent.**
PE = **physical education.**

pea [piː] *n* Erbse *f.*

peace [piːs] *n* Frieden *m*; *(tranquillity)* Ruhe *f.* **to be at ~ with sb/sth** mit jdm/etw in Frieden leben; **he is at ~** *(euph: dead)* er ruht in Frieden; **to make (one's) ~ (with sb)** sich (mit jdm) versöhnen; **to make ~ between ...** Frieden stiften zwischen *(+dat)* ...; **to keep the ~** *(Jur) (demonstrator, citizen)* die öffentliche Ordnung wahren; *(policeman)* die öffentliche Ordnung aufrechterhalten; *(fig)* Frieden bewahren; **~ of mind** innere Ruhe; **~ and quiet** Ruhe und Frieden; **to give sb some ~** jdn in Ruhe *or* Frieden lassen; **to give sb no ~** jdm keine Ruhe lassen.

peaceable ['piːsəbl] *adj* friedlich.

peace conference *n* Friedenskonferenz *f.*

peaceful ['piːsfʊl] *adj* friedlich; *nation, person etc* friedfertig; *holiday, sleep etc* ruhig; *death* sanft.

peacefully ['piːsfəlɪ] *adv* friedlich. **to die ~ (in one's sleep)** sanft sterben.

peace: ~-keeping 1 *n* Friedenssicherung *f*; **2** *adj* Friedens-; **~-keeping force** Friedenstruppe *f*; **~-loving** *adj* friedliebend; **~maker** *n* Friedensstifter(in *f*) *m*; **~-offering** *n (lit, fig)* Friedensangebot *nt*; **~ talks** *npl* Friedensverhandlungen *pl*; **~time** *n* Friedenszeiten *pl.*

peach [piːtʃ] **1** *n* **(a)** *(fruit)* Pfirsich *m*; *(tree)* Pfirsichbaum *m.* **(b)** *(col)* **she's a ~** sie ist klasse *(col)*. **2** *adj* pfirsichfarben.

peacock ['piːkɒk] *n* Pfau *m.*

peak [piːk] **1** *n* **(a)** *(of mountain)* Gipfel *m*; *(of roof)* First *m.* **(b)** *(of cap)* Schirm *m.* **(c)** *(maximum)* Höhepunkt *m*; *(on graph)* Scheitelpunkt *m.* **he is at the ~ of fitness** er ist in Höchstform; **when demand is at its ~** wenn die Nachfrage am stärksten ist. **2** *adj attr value* Spitzen-; *production* Höchst-. **3** *vi* den Höchststand erreichen.

peak: ~ hours *npl (of traffic)* Hauptverkehrszeit *f*; *(Telec, Elec)* Hauptbelastungszeit *f*; **~ season** *n* Hochsaison *f.*

peaky ['piːkɪ] *adj (+er) (Brit col) complexion* blaß. **to look ~** angeschlagen aussehen *(col)*.

peal [piːl] **1** *n* **~ of bells** *(sound)* Glockenläuten *nt*; **~s of laughter** schallendes Gelächter; **~ of thunder** Donnerrollen *nt.* **2** *vi (bell)* läuten.

peanut ['piːnʌt] *n* Erdnuß *f.* **~s** *(col) (not much money)* Kleingeld *nt (to sb* für jdn*)*; *(not significant)* Kleinkram *m;* **the pay is ~s** die Bezahlung ist miserabel *or* lächerlich *(col)*; **~ butter** Erdnußbutter *f.*

pear [pɛəʳ] *n* Birne *f*; *(tree)* Birnbaum *m.*

pearl [pɜːl] *n (lit, fig)* Perle *f*; *(mother-of-~, colour)* Perlmutt *nt.* **~ of wisdom** weiser Spruch.

pearl: ~ barley *n* Perlgraupen *pl*; **~ fishing** *n* Perlenfischerei *f*; **~ grey** *adj* silbergrau; **~ oyster** *n* Perlenauster *f.*

pearly ['pɜːlɪ] *adj (+er) (in colour)* perlmuttfarben. **~ white** perlweiß; **P~ Gates** Himmelstür *f.*

pear-shaped ['pɛəʃeɪpt] *adj* birnenförmig.

peasant ['pezənt] **1** *n (lit)* (armer) Bauer; *(pej col) (ignoramus)* Banause *m*; *(pleb)* Prolet *m.* **2** *adj attr* bäuerlich. **~ farmer** (armer) Bauer.

pea: ~shooter *n* Pusterohr *nt*; **~ soup** *n* Erbsensuppe *f.*

peat [piːt] *n* Torf *m.* **~bog** Torfmoor *nt.*

pebble ['pebl] *n* Kieselstein *m.* **he/she is not the only ~ on the beach** *(col)* es gibt noch andere.

pebbly ['peblɪ] *adj* steinig.

peck [pek] **1** *n* **(a)** *(col: kiss)* Küßchen *nt.* **(b) the hen gave him a ~** die Henne hackte nach ihm. **2** *vt (bird)* picken. **3** *vi* picken *(at* nach*)*. **he just ~ed at his food** er stocherte nur in seinem Essen herum.

pecking order ['pekɪŋ,ɔːdəʳ] *n (lit, fig)* Hackordnung *f.*

peckish ['pekɪʃ] *adj (Brit col: hungry)* **I'm (feeling) a bit ~** ich könnte was zwischen die Zähne gebrauchen *(col)*.

peculiar [pɪ'kjuːlɪəʳ] *adj* **(a)** *(strange)* seltsam, eigenartig. **(b)** *(exclusive, special)* eigentümlich *(to* für *+acc)*. **an animal ~ to Africa** ein Tier, das nur in Afrika vorkommt.

peculiarity [pɪ,kjuːlɪ'ærɪtɪ] *n* **(a)** *(strangeness)* Eigenartigkeit *f.* **(b)** *(unusual feature)* Besonderheit *f.*

pecuniary [pɪ'kjuːnɪərɪ] *adj (form) penalties, affairs* Geld-; *gain, problem* finanziell.

pedagogic(al) [,pedə'gɒdʒɪk(əl)] *adj (form)* pädagogisch.

pedal ['pedl] **1** *n* Pedal *nt*; *(on bin etc)* Trethebel *m.* **2** *vi (on bicycle)* treten. **to ~ off** (mit dem Rad) wegfahren.

pedant ['pedənt] *n* Pedant(in *f*) *m.*

pedantic [pɪ'dæntɪk] *adj* pedantisch.

pedantry ['pedəntrɪ] *n* Pedanterie *f.*

peddle ['pedl] *vt* hausieren mit *(pej)*. **to ~ drugs** mit Drogen handeln.

peddler ['pedləʳ] *n (esp US)* = **pedlar.**

pederast ['pedəræst] *n* Päderast *m.*

pedestal ['pedɪstl] *n* Sockel *m.* **to put sb on a ~** *(fig)* jdn in den Himmel heben.

pedestrian [pɪ'destrɪən] **1** *n* Fußgaǵnger(in *f*) *m.* **2** *adj* **(a)** *attr* Fußgänger-. **~ crossing** *(Brit)* Fußgängerüberweg *m*; **~ precinct** *(Brit)* Fußgängerzone *f.* **(b)** *(prosaic)* schwunglos.

pediatric [,piːdɪ'ætrɪk] *(esp US)* = **paediatric.**

pedicure ['pedɪkjʊəʳ] *n* Pediküre *f.*

pedigree ['pedɪgriː] **1** *n (lit, fig)* Stammbaum *m*; *(document)* Ahnentafel *f.* **2** *attr* reinrassig.

pedlar ['pedləʳ] *n* Hausierer(in *f*) *m*; *(of drugs)* Drogenhändler(in *f*) *m.*

pee [piː] *(col)* **1** *n (urine)* Urin *m*, Pipi *(baby-talk) nt.* **to need/have a ~** pinkeln müssen/pinkeln *(col)*. **2** *vi* pinkeln *(col)*.

peek [piːk **1** *n* kurzer Blick; *(furtive)* verstohlener Blick. **to take** *or* **have a ~** kurz/verstohlen gucken *(at* nach*)*. **2** *vi* gucken *(at* nach*)*.

peel [piːl] **1** *n* Schale *f.* **2** *vt* schälen. **3** *vi (wallpaper)* sich lösen; *(paint)* abblättern; *(skin, person)* sich schälen *or* pellen *(col)*.

♦ **peel away 1** *vt sep wallpaper, paint* abziehen *(from* von*)*; *wrapper* abstreifen *(from* von*)*. **2** *vi (lit, fig)* sich lösen *(from* von*)*.

♦ **peel back** *vt sep cover, wrapping* abziehen.

♦ **peel off 1** *vt sep (+prep obj* von*) tape, wallpaper* abziehen; *wrapper, glove etc* abstreifen. **2** *vi* sich lösen.

peeler ['piːləʳ] *n (potato ~)* Schälmesser *nt.*

peelings ['piːlɪŋz] *npl* Schalen *pl.*

peep[1] [piːp] **1** *n (sound) (of bird etc)* Piep *m*; *(of horn, whistle, col: of person)* Ton *m.* **we haven't heard a ~ out of him** *(col)* wir haben keinen Pieps von ihm gehört *(col)*. **2** *vi (bird etc)* piepen; *(horn, car)* tuten; *(whistle)* pfeifen.

peep[2] **1** *n (look)* kurzer Blick; *(furtive)* verstohlener Blick. **to take** *or* **have a ~ (at sth)** kurz/verstohlen (nach etw) gucken. **2** *vi* gucken *(at* nach*)*. **to ~ from behind sth** hinter etw *(dat)* hervorschauen; **to ~ over sth** über etw *(acc)* gucken.

peephole ['piːphəʊl] *n* Guckloch *nt*; *(in door also)* Spion *m.*

peeping Tom ['piːpɪŋ'tɒm] *n* Spanner *(col)*, Voyeur *m.*

peer[1] [pɪəʳ] *n* **(a) ~ (of the realm)** Peer *m.* **(b)** *(equal)* Gleichrangige(r) *mf.* **he was well-liked by his ~s** er war bei seinesgleichen beliebt.

peer[2] *vi* starren; *(inquiringly)* schielen. **to ~ (hard) at sb/sth** jdn/etw anstarren.

peerage ['pɪərɪdʒ] *n* Adelsstand *m*, Peers *pl.* **to give sb a ~** jdm einen Adelstitel verleihen; **to raise sb to the ~** jdn in den Adelsstand erheben.

peer group *n (age group)* Altersgruppe *f*; *(ability group)* Leistungsklasse *f.*

peerless ['pɪəlɪs] *adj* einzigartig.

peeved [piːvd] *adj (col)* eingeschnappt *(col)*, verärgert.

peevish ['pi:vɪʃ] *adj (irritable)* reizbar.
peewit ['pi:wɪt] *n* Kiebitz *m*.
peg [peg] **1** *n (stake)* Pflock *m*; *(for wood joints, in games)* Stift *m*; *(Brit: clothes ~)* (Wäsche)klammer *f*. **off the ~** von der Stange; **to take sb down a ~ or two** *(col)* jdm einen Dämpfer geben; **a ~ on which to hang one's prejudices** *etc* ein guter Aufhänger für seine Vorurteile *etc*. **2** *vt* **(a)** *(fasten)* anpflocken; *clothes* anklammern; *(tent)* festpflocken. **(b)** *prices, wages* festsetzen.
♦ **peg away** *vi (col)* nicht locker lassen *(at* mit*)*.
♦ **peg out 1** *vt sep washing* aufhängen; *(mark out) area* abstecken. **2** *vi (col: die)* abkratzen *(col!)*.
pejorative [pɪ'dʒɒrɪtɪv] *adj* abwertend.
pekinese [,pi:kɪ'ni:z] *n, pl - (dog)* Pekinese *m*.
pelican ['pelɪkən] *n* Pelikan *m*. **~ crossing** Ampelüberweg *m*.
pellet ['pelɪt] *n* Kügelchen *nt*; *(for gun)* Schrotkugel *f*.
pell-mell ['pel'mel] *adv* wie Kraut und Rüben *(col)*.
pelmet ['pelmɪt] *n* Blende *f*.
pelt [pelt] **1** *vt (throw)* schleudern *(at* nach*)*. **to ~ sb/sth (with sth)** jdn/etw (mit etw) bewerfen. **2** *vi (col)* **(a)** *(go fast)* pesen *(col)*. **(b) it ~ed (with rain)** es hat nur so geschüttet *(col)*. **3** *n (col)* **at full ~** volle Pulle *(col)*.
pelvis ['pelvɪs] *n* Becken *nt*.
pen[1] [pen] **1** *n (dip ~)* Feder *f*; *(fountain ~)* Füller *m*; *(ball-point ~)* Kugelschreiber, Kuli *(col) m*. **to put ~ to paper** zur Feder greifen. **2** *vt* niederschreiben.
pen[2] *n* **(a)** *(for cattle etc)* Pferch *m*; *(play ~)* Laufstall *m*. **(b)** *(US col: prison)* Knast *(col) m*.
penal ['pi:nl] *adj law, colony etc* Straf-. **~ code** Strafgesetzbuch *nt*; **~ system** Strafrecht *nt*.
penalize ['pi:nəlaɪz] *vt* bestrafen; *(fig)* benachteiligen.
penalty ['penəltɪ] *n* **(a)** *(punishment)* Strafe *f*; *(fig: disadvantage)* Nachteil *m*. **on ~ of death/£5/imprisonment** bei Todestrafe/bei einer Geldstrafe von £ 5/bei Gefängnisstrafe; **to pay the ~** dafür büßen. **(b)** *(Sport)* Strafstoß *m*; *(Soccer also)* Elfmeter *m*.
penalty: ~ area *n* Strafraum *m*; **~ clause** *n* Strafklausel *f*; **~ kick** *n* Strafstoß *m*; *(soccer also)* Elfmeter *m*.
penance ['penəns] *n (Rel)* Buße *f*; *(fig)* Strafe *f*. **to do ~** Buße tun; *(fig)* büßen.
pence [pens] *n pl of* **penny**.
penchant ['pɑ̃:ŋʃɑ̃:ŋ] *n* Schwäche *f (for* für*)*.
pencil ['pensl] **1** *n* Bleistift *m*; *(eyebrow ~)* Augenbrauenstift *m*. **2** *vt (also ~ in)* mit Bleistift schreiben/zeichnen. **3** *attr drawing* Bleistift-.
pencil: ~ case *n* Federmäppchen *nt*; **~ sharpener** *n* (Bleistift)spitzer *m*.
pendant ['pendənt] *n* Anhänger *m*.
pending ['pendɪŋ] **1** *adj* anstehend; *lawsuit* anhängig. **to be ~** *(decision etc)* noch anstehen; *(trial)* noch anhängig sein. **2** *prep* **~ his arrival/return** bis zu seiner Ankunft/Rückkehr.
pendulum ['pendjʊləm] *n* Pendel *nt*. **the ~ has swung back in the opposite direction** *(fig)* das Pendel ist in die entgegengesetzte Richtung ausgeschlagen.
penetrate ['penɪtreɪt] **1** *vt* eindringen in *(+acc)*; *walls etc* durchdringen; *(Mil) enemy lines* durchbrechen; *(Med) vein* durchstechen. **2** *vi* eindringen; *(go right through)* durchdringen. **the idea just didn't ~** *(fig)* das ist mir/ihm *etc* nicht klargeworden.
penetrating ['penɪtreɪtɪŋ] *adj* durchdringend; *mind* scharf; *insight* scharfsinnig; *light* grell; *pain* stechend.
penetration [,penɪ'treɪʃən] *n see vt* Eindringen *nt (into* in *+acc)*; Durchdringen *nt (of gen)*; Durchbrechung *f*; Durchstechen *nt*.
penfriend ['penfrend] *n (Brit)* Brieffreund(in *f*) *m*.
penguin ['peŋgwɪn] *n* Pinguin *m*.
penicillin [,penɪ'sɪlɪn] *n* Penizillin *nt*.
peninsula [pɪ'nɪnsjʊlə] *n* Halbinsel *f*.
penis ['pi:nɪs] *n* Penis *m*.
penitence ['penɪtəns] *n (also Eccl)* Reue *f*.
penitent ['penɪtənt] **1** *adj* reuig *(also Eccl)*, zerknirscht. **2** *n (Eccl)* Büßer(in *f*) *m*.
penitentiary [,penɪ'tenʃərɪ] *n (esp US: prison)* Strafanstalt *f*.
pen: ~knife *n* Taschenmesser *nt*; **~ name** *n* Pseudonym *nt*.
penniless ['penɪlɪs] *adj* mittellos.
penny ['penɪ] *n, pl (coins)* **pennies** *or (sum)* **pence** Penny *m*; *(US)* Centstück *nt*. **in for a ~, in for a pound** *(prov)* wennschon, dennschon *(col)*; *(morally)* wer A sagt, muß auch B sagen *(prov)*; **I'm not a ~ the wiser** ich bin genauso klug wie zuvor; **take care of the pennies and the pounds will take care of themselves** *(Prov)* spare im kleinen, dann hast du im großen; **a ~ for your thoughts** ich möchte deine Gedanken lesen können; **he keeps turning up like a bad ~** *(col)* der taucht immer wieder auf *(col)*; **the ~ dropped** *(col)* der Groschen ist gefallen *(col)*.
pen pal *n (US)* Brieffreund(in *f*) *m*.
pen-pusher ['pen,pʊʃə^r] *n (col)* Schreiberling *m*.
pension ['penʃən] *n (money)* Rente *f*.
♦ **pension off** *vt sep (col)* vorzeitig pensionieren.
pensioner ['penʃənə^r] *n* Rentner(in *f*) *m*.
pension: ~ fund *n* Rentenfonds *m*; **~ scheme** *n* Rentenversicherung *f*.
pensive ['pensɪv] *adj* nachdenklich; *(sadly serious)* schwermütig.
pentagon ['pentəgən] *n* Fünfeck *nt*. **the P~** das Pentagon.
pentathlon [pen'tæθlən] *n* Fünfkampf *m*.
Pentecost ['pentɪkɒst] *n (Jewish)* Erntefest *nt*; *(Christian)* Pfingsten *nt*.
penthouse ['penthaus] *n (apartment)* Penthouse *nt*.
pent-up ['pent'ʌp] *adj person (with frustration, anger)* geladen *pred*; *(nervous, excited)* innerlich angespannt; *emotions, excitement* aufgestaut.
penultimate [pe'nʌltɪmɪt] *adj* vorletzte(r, s).
penury ['penjʊrɪ] *n* Armut, Not *f*.
peony ['pi:ənɪ] *n* Pfingstrose *f*.
people ['pi:pl] *npl* **(a)** Menschen *pl*; *(not in formal context)* Leute *pl*. **French ~** die Franzosen; **Edinburgh ~** (die) Leute aus/in Edinburgh; **all ~ with red hair** alle Rothaarigen; **why me of all ~?** warum ausgerechnet ich/mich?; **what do you ~ think?** was haltet ihr denn davon?; **poor/blind/disabled ~** Arme/Blinde/Behinderte; **country ~** Menschen *pl* vom Land; **some ~!** Leute gibt's! **(b)** *(inhabitants)* Bevölkerung *f*. **the ~ of Rome** die Bevölkerung von Rom. **(c)** *(one, they)* man; *(~ in general)* die Leute. **~ say that ...** man sagt, daß ... **(d)** *(nation, masses)* Volk *nt*. **the common ~** das einfache Volk; **a man of the ~** ein Mann *m* des Volkes; **the P~'s Republic of ...** die Volksrepublik ...
pep [pep] *n (col)* Schwung, Pep *(col) m*.
♦ **pep up** *vt sep (col)* Schwung bringen in *(+acc)*; *food* pikanter machen; *person* munter machen.
pepper ['pepə^r] **1** *n* Pfeffer *m*; *(green, red ~)* Paprika *m*. **2** *vt* pfeffern. **to ~ a work with quotations** eine Arbeit mit Zitaten spicken.
pepper: ~corn *n* Pfefferkorn *nt*; **~mint** *n* Pfefferminz *nt*; *(Bot)* Pfefferminze *f*; **~ pot** *n* Pfefferstreuer *m*.
peppery ['pepərɪ] *adj* gepfeffert; *(fig) old man etc* hitzköpfig.
pep pill *n* Aufputschpille *f*.
pep talk *n (col)* aufmunternde Worte *pl*.
per [pɜ:^r] *prep* pro. **£20 ~ annum** £ 20 pro Jahr; **60km ~ hour** 60 km pro Stunde *or* in der Stunde; **$2 ~ dozen** das Dutzend für $ 2; **£5 ~ copy** £ 5 pro *or* je Exemplar; **as ~** gemäß *(+dat)*.
perceive [pə'si:v] *vt* wahrnehmen; *(understand,*

recognize) erkennen.

per cent, *(US)* **percent** [pə'sent] *n* Prozent *nt*. **20 ~** 20 Prozent; **a 10 ~ discount** 10 Prozent Rabatt.

percentage [pə'sentɪdʒ] **1** *n* Prozentsatz *m*; *(commission, payment)* Anteil *m*; *(proportion)* Teil *m*. **a small ~ of the population** ein geringer Teil der Bevölkerung; **what ~?** wieviel Prozent?; **to get a ~ on all sales** prozentual am Umsatz beteiligt sein. **2** *attr* prozentual. **on a ~ basis** prozentual; **~ sign** Prozentzeichen *nt*.

perceptible [pə'septəbl] *adj* wahrnehmbar; *improvement, trend etc* spürbar.

perceptibly [pə'septəblɪ] *adv* spürbar; *(to the eye)* sichtbar.

perception [pə'sepʃən] *n* **(a)** *no pl* Wahrnehmung *f*. **(b)** *(mental image, conception)* Auffassung *f (of* von*)*. **one's ~ of the situation** die eigene Einschätzung der Lage. **(c)** *(no pl: perceptiveness)* Einsicht *f*; *(perceptive remark, observation)* Beobachtung *f*. **(d)** *no pl (of difficulties, meaning etc)* Erkennen *nt*.

perceptive [pə'septɪv] *adj (sensitive) person* einfühlsam; *(penetrating) analysis, speech* scharfsinnig; *book* aufschlußreich. **very ~ of you!** *(iro)* du merkst auch alles.

perch[1] [pɜːtʃ] *n (fish)* Barsch *m*.

perch[2] **1** *n (of bird)* Stange *f*; *(in tree)* Ast *m*; *(iro: for person etc)* Hochsitz *m*. **2** *vt* **to ~ sth on sth** etw auf etw *(acc)* setzen *or (upright)* stellen; **to be ~ed on sth** auf etw *(dat)* sitzen. **3** *vi (bird, fig: person)* hocken; *(alight)* sich niederlassen.

percolate ['pɜːkəleɪt] **1** *vt* filtrieren; *coffee* (in einer Kaffeemaschine) zubereiten. **2** *vi (lit, fig)* durchsickern.

percolator ['pɜːkəleɪtə^r] *n* Kaffeemaschine *f*.

percussion [pə'kʌʃən] *n (Mus)* Schlagzeug *nt*. **~ instrument** Schlaginstrument *nt*.

peregrine (falcon) ['perɪgrɪn('fɔːlkən)] *n* Wanderfalke *m*.

peremptory [pə'remptərɪ] *adj command* kategorisch; *voice* gebieterisch; *person* herrisch.

perennial [pə'renɪəl] **1** *adj plant* mehrjährig; *(perpetual)* ewig; *(recurring)* immer wiederkehrend. **2** *n (Bot)* mehrjährige Pflanze.

perfect ['pɜːfɪkt] **1** *adj* **(a)** perfekt; *balance, symmetry also* vollkommen; *work of art also* vollendet; *weather, day also* ideal; *(Comm: not damaged)* einwandfrei. **it was the ~ moment** es war genau der richtige Augenblick. **(b)** *(absolute, utter)* völlig. **he's a ~ stranger to me** er ist mir völlig fremd; **it's a ~ disgrace** es ist wirklich eine Schande. **(c)** *(Gram)* **~ tense** Perfekt *nt*. **2** *n (Gram)* Perfekt *nt*. **in the ~** im Perfekt. **3** [pə'fekt] *vt* vervollkommnen.

perfection [pə'fekʃən] *n* Vollkommenheit, Perfektion *f*. **to do sth to ~** etw perfekt tun.

perfectionist [pə'fekʃənɪst] *n* Perfektionist *m*.

perfectly ['pɜːfɪktlɪ] *adv* **(a)** perfekt. **I understand you ~** ich weiß genau, was Sie meinen. **(b)** *(absolutely)* absolut, vollkommen. **we're ~ happy about it** wir sind damit völlig zufrieden; **a ~ lovely day** ein wirklich herrlicher Tag; **you know ~ well that ...** du weißt ganz genau, daß ...

perforate ['pɜːfəreɪt] *vt (also Med)* perforieren; *(pierce once)* durchstechen, lochen.

perforation [,pɜːfə'reɪʃən] *n (act)* Perforieren *nt*; *(row of holes, Med)* Perforation *f*.

perform [pə'fɔːm] **1** *vt play, concerto* aufführen; *solo* vortragen; *part* spielen; *trick* vorführen; *miracle* vollbringen; *task* verrichten; *duty, function* erfüllen; *operation* durchführen; *ceremony* vollziehen. **2** *vi* **(a)** *(orchestra etc)* auftreten. **to ~ on the violin** Geige spielen. **(b) to ~ well/badly** *(car, football team etc)* eine gute/schlechte Leistung zeigen; *(examination candidate etc)* gut/schlecht abschneiden; **the 2 litre version ~s better** die Zweiliterversion leistet mehr; **how did he ~?** *(actor, musician)* wie war er?; **how did the car ~?** wie ist der Wagen gelaufen?

performance [pə'fɔːməns] *n* **(a)** *(of play, opera etc)* Aufführung *f*; *(cinema)* Vorstellung *f*; *(by actor)* Leistung *f*; *(of a part)* Darstellung *f*. **he gave an excellent ~** er hat ausgezeichnet gespielt/gesungen *etc*; **we are going to hear a ~ of Beethoven's 5th** wir werden Beethovens Fünfte hören. **(b)** *(carrying out) see vt* Aufführung *f*; Vortrag *m*; *(of part)* Darstellung *f*; Vorführung *f*; Vollbringung *f*; Verrichtung, Erfüllung *f*; Durchführung *f*; Vollzug *m*. **in the ~ of his duties** in Ausübung seiner Pflicht. **(c)** *(effectiveness) (of machine, sportsman etc)* Leistung *f*; *(of examination candidate etc)* Abschneiden *nt*. **he put up a good ~** er hat sich gut geschlagen *(col)*. **(d)** *(col)* **what a ~!** was für ein Umstand!

performer [pə'fɔːmə^r] *n (Theat, Mus)* Künstler(in *f) m*.

perfume ['pɜːfjuːm] **1** *n (substance)* Parfüm *nt*; *(smell)* Duft *m*. **2** [pə'fjuːm] *vt* parfümieren.

perfumery [pɜː'fjuːmərɪ] *n (perfume factory)* Parfümerie *f*; *(perfumes)* Parfüm *nt*.

perfunctory [pə'fʌŋktərɪ] *adj* flüchtig.

perhaps [pə'hæps, præps] *adv* vielleicht. **~ so** das mag sein.

peril ['perɪl] *n* Gefahr *f*.

perilous ['perɪləs] *adj* gefährlich.

perilously ['perɪləslɪ] *adv* gefährlich. **she came ~ close to falling** sie wäre um ein Haar heruntergefallen.

perimeter [pə'rɪmɪtə^r] *n (Math)* Umfang *m*; *(of grounds)* Grenze *f*. **~ fence** Umzäunung *f*.

period ['pɪərɪəd] *n* **(a)** *(length of time)* Zeit *f*; *(age)* Zeitalter *nt*, Epoche *f*; *(Geol, Met)* Periode *f*. **for a ~ of eight weeks** für einen Zeitraum von acht Wochen; **at that ~ (of my life)** zu diesem Zeitpunkt (in meinem Leben); **a writer of the ~** ein zeitgenössischer Schriftsteller. **(b)** *(Sch)* Stunde *f*. **(c)** *(esp US: full stop)* Punkt *m*. **you're not going, ~** du gehst nicht, und damit hat sich's; **he just doesn't understand, ~** er versteht einfach überhaupt nichts. **(d)** *(menstruation)* Periode *f*, Tage *pl (col)*.

period: ~ costume *n* zeitgenössische Kostüme *pl*; **~ furniture** *n* antike Möbel *pl*.

periodic [,pɪərɪ'ɒdɪk] *adj* periodisch. **~ table** *(Chem)* Periodensystem *nt*.

periodical [,pɪərɪ'ɒdɪkəl] **1** *adj* = **periodic. 2** *n* Zeitschrift *f*.

periodically [,pɪərɪ'ɒdɪkəlɪ] *adv* von Zeit zu Zeit.

period: ~ pains *npl* Menstruationsschmerzen *pl*; **~ piece** *n* antikes Stück; *(painting, music etc)* Zeitdokument *nt*.

peripatetic [,perɪpə'tetɪk] *adj* umherreisend; *existence* rastlos; *teacher* an mehreren Schulen unterrichtend *attr*.

peripheral [pə'rɪfərəl] *adj* Rand-; *(fig also)* nebensächlich.

periphery [pə'rɪfərɪ] *n* Peripherie *f*.

periscope ['perɪskəʊp] *n* Periskop *nt*.

perish ['perɪʃ] *vi* **(a)** *(die)* umkommen, sterben; *(cities, civilization)* untergehen. **(b)** *(rubber, leather etc)* verschleißen; *(food)* verderben. **(c)** *(col)* **~ the thought!** Gott bewahre!

perishable ['perɪʃəbl] **1** *adj food* verderblich. **2** *npl* **~s** leicht verderbliche Ware(n).

perishing ['perɪʃɪŋ] *adj (col: very cold)* eisig kalt. **I'm ~** ich geh' fast ein vor Kälte *(col)*.

perjure ['pɜːdʒə^r] *vr* **to ~ oneself** einen Meineid leisten.

perjury ['pɜːdʒərɪ] *n* Meineid *m*. **to commit ~** einen Meineid leisten.

perk [pɜːk] *n (esp Brit: benefit)* Vergüngstigung *f*.

♦ **perk up 1** *vt sep* **(a) he ~ed ~ his ears** *(dog, person)* er spitzte die Ohren. **(b) to ~ sb ~** *(make lively)* jdn munter machen; *(make cheerful)* jdn aufheitern. **2** *vi (liven up: person, party)* munter werden; *(cheer up)* aufleben.

perky ['pɜːkɪ] *adj (+er) (cheerful, bright)* munter; *(cheeky, pert)* keß.

perm [pɜːm] **1** *n* Dauerwelle *f*. **2** *vt* **she had her hair ~ed** sie hat sich *(dat)* eine Dauerwelle machen lassen.

permanence ['pɜːmənəns], **permanency** ['pɜːmənənsɪ] *n* Dauerhaftigkeit *f*.

permanent ['pɜːmənənt] **1** *adj* ständig, permanent; *arrangement, position* fest; *job, relationship* dauerhaft; *agreement* unbefristet. **a ~ employee** ein Festangestellter *m*; **I'm not ~ here** ich bin hier nicht fest angestellt; **~ address** ständiger Wohnsitz. **2** *n (US)* = **perm 1.**

permanently ['pɜːmənəntlɪ] *adv* permanent, ständig; *fixed* fest. **are you living ~ in Frankfurt?** ist Frankfurt Ihr ständiger Wohnsitz?

permeable ['pɜːmɪəbl] *adj* durchlässig.

permeate ['pɜːmɪeɪt] **1** *vt (lit, fig)* durchdringen. **2** *vi* dringen *(into* in *+acc, through* durch*)*.

permissible [pə'mɪsɪbl] *adj* erlaubt *(for sb* jdm*)*.

permission [pə'mɪʃən] *n* Erlaubnis *f*. **with your ~** mit Ihrer Erlaubnis; **to give sb ~ (to do sth)** jdm erlauben(, etw zu tun); **to ask sb's ~** jdn um Erlaubnis bitten.

permissive [pə'mɪsɪv] *adj* nachgiebig, permissiv *(geh)*; *(sexually)* freizügig. **the ~ society** die permissive Gesellschaft.

permit [pə'mɪt] **1** *vt sth* erlauben, gestatten. **to ~ sb to do sth** jdm erlauben, etw zu tun; **is it/am I ~ted to smoke?** darf man/ich rauchen? **2** *vi* **(a) if you (will) ~** wenn Sie gestatten; **weather ~ting** wenn es das Wetter zuläßt. **(b)** *(form)* **to ~ of sth** etw zulassen. **3** ['pɜːmɪt] *n* Genehmigung *f*. **~ holder** Inhaber(in *f*) *m* eines Berechtigungsscheins.

permutation [,pɜːmjʊ'teɪʃən] *n* Permutation *f*.

pernicious [pɜː'nɪʃəs] *adj* schädlich.

pernickety [pə'nɪkɪtɪ] *adj (col)* pingelig *(col)*.

perpendicular [,pɜːpən'dɪkjʊlə^r] **1** *adj* senkrecht *(to* zu*)*. **2** *n* Senkrechte *f*.

perpetrate ['pɜːpɪtreɪt] *vt* begehen; *crime also* verüben.

perpetrator ['pɜːpɪtreɪtə^r] *n* Täter *m*. **the ~ of this crime** derjenige, der dieses Verbrechen begangen hat.

perpetual [pə'petjʊəl] *adj* ständig, immerwährend; *joy* stet; *ice, snow* ewig. **~ motion** Perpetuum mobile *nt*.

perpetuate [pə'petjʊeɪt] *vt* aufrechterhalten; *memory* bewahren.

perpetuity [,pɜːpɪ'tjuːɪtɪ] *n* **in ~** auf ewig.

perplex [pə'pleks] *vt* verblüffen.

perplexed [pə'plekst] *adj* verblüfft, perplex.

perplexing [pə'pleksɪŋ] *adj* verblüffend.

perplexity [pə'pleksɪtɪ] *n* Verblüffung *f*.

persecute ['pɜːsɪkjuːt] *vt* verfolgen.

persecution [,pɜːsɪ'kjuːʃən] *n* Verfolgung *f (of* von*)*. **~ complex** Verfolgungswahn *m*.

perseverance [,pɜːsɪ'vɪərəns] *n* Ausdauer *(with* mit*)*, Beharrlichkeit *(with* bei*) f*.

persevere [,pɜːsɪ'vɪə^r] *vi* durchhalten *(with* bei*)*, nicht aufgeben *(with* bei*)*. **to ~ in one's studies** mit seinem Studium weitermachen.

persevering [,pɜːsɪ'vɪərɪŋ] *adj* beharrlich.

Persia ['pɜːʃə] *n* Persien *nt*.

Persian ['pɜːʃən] **1** *adj* persisch. **~ carpet** Perser(teppich) *m*; **~ cat** Perserkatze *f*. **2** *n* **(a)** Perser(in *f*) *m*. **(b)** *(language)* Persisch *nt*.

persist [pə'sɪst] *vi (persevere)* nicht lockerlassen *(with* mit*)*; *(in belief, demand etc)* beharren *(in* auf *+dat)*; *(fog, pain)* anhalten. **if you ~ in misbehaving** wenn du dich weiterhin so schlecht benimmst.

persistence [pə'sɪstəns] *n* Hartnäckigkeit *f*; *(perseverance)* Ausdauer *f*; *(of pain)* Anhalten *nt*.

persistent [pə'sɪstənt] *adj questions* beharrlich; *person* hartnäckig; *efforts* ausdauernd; *offender, drinking* gewohnheitsmäßig; *nagging, lateness, threats* ständig; *rain, illness* anhaltend.

person ['pɜːsn] *n* **(a)** *pl* **people** *or (form)* **-s** *(human being)* Mensch *m*; *(in official contexts)* Person *f*. **I know no such ~** so jemanden kenne ich nicht; **a certain ~** ein gewisser Jemand; **~ to ~ call** Gespräch *nt* mit Voranmeldung; **per ~** pro Person. **(b)** *pl* **-s** *(Gram)* **first ~ singular/plural** erste Person Singular/Plural. **(c)** *pl* **-s** *(body, physical presence)* Körper *m*; *(appearance)* Äußere(s) *nt*. **in ~** persönlich; **in the ~ of** in Gestalt *(+gen)*; **on** *or* **about one's ~** bei sich.

personable ['pɜːsnəbl] *adj* von angenehmer Erscheinung.

personage ['pɜːsənɪdʒ] *n* Persönlichkeit *f*.

personal ['pɜːsənl] *adj* persönlich. **it's nothing ~ but ...** nicht, daß ich etwas gegen Sie persönlich hätte, aber ...; **don't be ~** nun werden Sie mal nicht persönlich; **"~"** *(on letter)* „privat"; **~ column** Familienanzeigen *pl*; **~ property** Privateigentum *nt*; **~ call** Gespräch *nt* mit Voranmeldung; *(private call)* Privatgespräch *nt*; **~ computer** Personal Computer *m*; **~ matter** private Angelegenheit; **~ pronoun** Personalpronomen *nt*.

personality [,pɜːsə'nælɪtɪ] *n (character, person)* Persönlichkeit *f*. **~ cult** Personenkult *m*.

personally ['pɜːsənəlɪ] *adv* persönlich. **~, I think that ...** ich persönlich bin der Meinung, daß ...

personification [pɜː,sɒnɪfɪ'keɪʃən] *n* Verkörperung *f*.

personify [pɜː'sɒnɪfaɪ] *vt* verkörpern. **he is greed personified** er ist der Geiz in Person.

personnel [,pɜːsə'nel] **1** *n sing or pl* **(a)** Personal *nt*; *(on plane, ship)* Besatzung *f*; *(Mil)* Leute *pl*. **(b)** *(~ department)* die Personalabteilung. **2** *attr* Personal-. **~ manager/officer** Personalchef *m*/-leiter *m*.

perspective [pə'spektɪv] *n (lit, fig)* Perspektive *f*. **try to get things in ~** versuchen Sie, das nüchtern und sachlich zu sehen.

Perspex ® ['pɜːspeks] *n (Brit)* Plexiglas ® *nt*.

perspicacious [,pɜːspɪ'keɪʃəs] *adj person, remark etc* scharfsinnig; *decision* weitsichtig.

perspiration [,pɜːspə'reɪʃən] *n (perspiring)* Schwitzen *nt*, Transpiration *f (geh)*; *(sweat)* Schweiß *m*.

perspire [pə'spaɪə^r] *vi* schwitzen.

persuade [pə'sweɪd] *vt* überreden; *(convince)* überzeugen. **to ~ sb to do sth** jdn überreden, etw zu tun; **to ~ sb into doing sth** jdn dazu überreden, etw zu tun; **to ~ sb of sth** jdn von etw überzeugen; **to ~ sb that ...** jdn davon überzeugen, daß ...; **he doesn't take much persuading** ihn braucht man nicht lange zu überreden.

persuasion [pə'sweɪʒən] *n* **(a)** *(persuading)* Überredung *f*. **she tried every possible means of ~** sie setzte ihre ganze Überredungskunst ein. **(b)** *(belief)* Überzeugung *f*; *(sect, denomination)* Glaube(nsrichtung *f*) *m*.

persuasive [pə'sweɪsɪv] *adj salesman, arguments etc* überzeugend.

persuasively [pə'sweɪsɪvlɪ] *adv* überzeugend.

pert [pɜːt] *adj (+er)* keß; *(impudent)* keck.

pertain [pɜː'teɪn] *vi* **to ~ to sth** etw betreffen; *(belong to)* zu etw gehören; **all documents ~ing to the case** alle den Fall betreffenden Dokumente.

pertinence ['pɜːtɪnəns] *n* Relevanz *f (to* für*)*; *(of information)* Sachdienlichkeit *f*.

pertinent ['pɜːtɪnənt] *adj* relevant *(to* für*)*; *information* sachdienlich.

perturb [pə'tɜːb] *vt* beunruhigen.

perturbing [pə'tɜːbɪŋ] *adj* beunruhigend.

Peru [pə'ruː] *n* Peru *nt*.

perusal [pə'ruːzəl] *n* Lektüre *f*.

peruse [pə'ruːz] *vt* (durch)lesen.

Peruvian [pə'ruːvɪən] **1** *adj* peruanisch. **2** *n* Peruaner(in *f*) *m*.

pervade [pɜː'veɪd] *vt* erfüllen.

pervasive [pɜːˈveɪsɪv] *adj smell etc* durchdringend; *influence, ideas* um sich greifend.
perverse [pəˈvɜːs] *adj (contrary) idea* abwegig; *(perverted)* pervers.
perversion [pəˈvɜːʃən] *n (esp sexual, Psych)* Perversion *f*; *(no pl: act of perverting)* Pervertierung *f*; *(distortion: of truth etc)* Verzerrung *f*.
perversity [pəˈvɜːsɪtɪ] *n see adj* Abwegigkeit *f*; Perversität *f*.
pervert [pəˈvɜːt] **1** *vt (deprave) person, mind* verderben, pervertieren; *(distort) truth etc* verzerren. **to ~ the course of justice** *(Jur)* die Rechtsfindung behindern; *(by official)* das Recht beugen. **2** [ˈpɜːvɜːt] *n* Perverse(r) *mf*.
pessimism [ˈpesɪmɪzəm] *n* Pessimismus *m*.
pessimist [ˈpesɪmɪst] *n* Pessimist(in *f*) *m*.
pessimistic [ˌpesɪˈmɪstɪk] *adj* pessimistisch. **I'm rather ~ about it** da bin ich ziemlich pessimistisch.
pest [pest] *n* **(a)** *(Zool)* Schädling *m*. **~ control** Schädlingsbekämpfung *f*. **(b)** *(fig) (person)* Nervensäge *f*; *(thing)* Plage *f*.
pester [ˈpestəʳ] *vt* belästigen; *(keep on at: with requests etc)* plagen.
pesticide [ˈpestɪsaɪd] *n* Schädlingsbekämpfungsmittel, Pestizid *(spec) nt*.
pestilent [ˈpestɪlənt], **pestilential** [ˌpestɪˈlenʃəl] *adj (fig: pernicious)* schädlich; *(col: loathsome)* ekelhaft.
pestle [ˈpestl] *n* Stößel *m*.
pet [pet] **1** *adj attr (favourite) pupil, idea etc* Lieblings-. **he has a ~ monkey** er hält einen Affen als Haustier; **a ~ name** ein Kosename *m*. **2** *n* **(a)** *(animal)* Haustier *nt*. **(b)** *(favourite)* Liebling *m*. **teacher's ~** Lehrers Liebling *m*; **yes, (my) ~** ja, (mein) Schatz. **3** *vt animal* streicheln; *child also* liebkosen. **4** *vi (sexually)* Petting machen.
petal [ˈpetl] *n* Blütenblatt *nt*.
♦ **peter out** [ˌpiːtəˈraʊt] *vi* langsam zu Ende gehen; *(mineral vein)* versiegen; *(river)* versickern; *(song, noise)* verhallen; *(interest)* sich legen.
petit bourgeois [ˈpetɪˈbʊəʒwɑː] **1** *n* Kleinbürger(in *f*) *m*. **2** *adj* kleinbürgerlich.
petite [pəˈtiːt] *adj woman, girl* zierlich.
petition [pəˈtɪʃən] **1** *n* **(a)** *(list of signatures)* Unterschriftenliste *f*. **to get up a ~ against sth** Unterschriften gegen etw sammeln. **(b)** *(request)* Gesuch *nt*, Petition *f*. **~ for divorce** Scheidungsantrag *m*. **2** *vt person, authorities (request, entreat)* ersuchen *(for* um*)*; *(hand ~ to)* eine Unterschriftenliste vorlegen *(+dat)*. **3** *vi* **to ~ for divorce** die Scheidung einreichen.
petrify [ˈpetrɪfaɪ] *vt* **(a)** *(lit)* versteinern. **(b) to be petrified with fear** starr vor Angst sein.
petrochemical [ˈpetrəʊˈkemɪkəl] *adj* petrochemisch.
petrol [ˈpetrəl] *n (Brit)* Benzin *nt*.
petrol: ~ bomb *n* Benzinbombe *f*; **~ can** *n (Brit)* Benzinkanister *m*.
petroleum [pɪˈtrəʊlɪəm] *n* Petroleum *nt*. **~ jelly** Vaseline *f*.
petrol: ~ gauge *n (Brit)* Benzinuhr *f*; **~ pump** *n (Brit)* (in engine) Benzinpumpe *f*; *(at garage)* Zapfsäule *f*; **~ station** *n (Brit)* Tankstelle *f*; **~ tank** *n (Brit)* Benzintank *m*; **~ tanker** *n (Brit)* Tankwagen *m*.
petticoat [ˈpetɪkəʊt] *n* Unterrock *m*; *(stiffened)* Petticoat *m*.
petting [ˈpetɪŋ] *n* Petting *nt*.
petty [ˈpetɪ] *adj (+er)* **(a)** *(trivial)* unbedeutend, belanglos; *excuse* billig; *crime* geringfügig, Bagatell-. **(b)** *(small-minded)* kleinlich; *(spiteful) remark* spitz. **(c)** *(minor) chieftain etc* untergeordnet; *(pej) official also* unbedeutend.
petty: ~ cash *n* Portokasse *f*; **~ larceny** *n* leichter Diebstahl; **~ thief** *n* Dieb(in *f*) *m*; **~ officer** *n* Unteroffizier *m*.
petulance [ˈpetjʊləns] *n* verdrießliche Art; *(of child)* bockige Art *(col)*.
petulant [ˈpetjʊlənt] *adj* verdrießlich; *child* bockig *(col)*.
pew [pjuː] *n (Eccl)* (Kirchen)bank *f*. **have** *or* **take a ~!** *(hum)* laß dich nieder! *(hum)*.
pewter [ˈpjuːtəʳ] *n (alloy)* Zinn *nt*.
phallic [ˈfælɪk] *adj* phallisch; *symbol* Phallus-.
phantom [ˈfæntəm] **1** *n* Phantom *nt*; *(ghost: esp of particular person)* Geist *m*. **2** *adj attr* Geister-; *(mysterious)* Phantom-.
pharmaceutic(al) [ˌfɑːməˈsjuːtɪk(əl)] *adj* pharmazeutisch.
pharmacist [ˈfɑːməsɪst] *n* Apotheker(in *f*) *m*; *(in research)* Pharmazeut(in *f*) *m*.
pharmacology [ˌfɑːməˈkɒlədʒɪ] *n* Pharmakologie *f*.
pharmacy [ˈfɑːməsɪ] *n* **(a)** *(science)* Pharmazie *f*. **(b)** *(shop)* Apotheke *f*.
phase [feɪz] **1** *n* Phase *f*; *(of project, history also)* Abschnitt *m*; *(of illness)* Stadium *nt*. **out of/in ~** *(Tech, Elec)* phasenverschoben/phasengleich; *(fig)* unkoordiniert/koordiniert; **he's just going through a ~** das ist nur so eine Phase bei ihm. **2** *vt (introduce gradually)* schrittweise durchführen; *(coordinate, fit to one another) starting times, etc* aufeinander abstimmen; *machines etc* gleichschalten. **a ~d withdrawal of troops** ein schrittweiser Truppenabzug.
♦ **phase in** *vt sep* allmählich einführen.
♦ **phase out** *vt sep* auslaufen lassen.
PhD *n* Doktor *m*. **~ thesis** Doktorarbeit *f*.
pheasant [ˈfeznt] *n* Fasan *m*.
phenomenal [fɪˈnɒmɪnl] *adj* phänomenal, sagenhaft *(col)*; *boredom, heat* unglaublich.
phenomenon [fɪˈnɒmɪnən] *n*, *pl* **phenomena** Phänomen *nt*.
phew [fjuː] *interj* Mensch, puh.
philanderer [fɪˈlændərəʳ] *n* Schwerenöter *m*.
philanthropic [ˌfɪlənˈθrɒpɪk] *adj* menschenfreundlich; *person also, organization* philanthropisch *(geh)*.
philanthropist [fɪˈlænθrəpɪst] *n* Menschenfreund, Philanthrop *(geh) m*.
philanthropy [fɪˈlænθrəpɪ] *n* Menschenfreundlichkeit *f*.
philately [fɪˈlætəlɪ] *n* Philatelie, Briefmarkenkunde *f*.
philharmonic [ˌfɪlɑːˈmɒnɪk] **1** *adj* philharmonisch. **2** *n* **P ~** Philharmonie *f*.
Philipines [ˈfɪlɪpiːnz] *npl* Philippinen *pl*.
Philips screw ® *n* [ˈfɪlɪpskruː] Kreuzschlitzschraube *f*.
philology [fɪˈlɒlədʒɪ] *n* Philologie *f*.
philosopher [fɪˈlɒsəfəʳ] *n* Philosoph(in *f*) *m*.
philosophic(al) [ˌfɪləˈsɒfɪk(əl)] *adj* philosophisch; *(fig)* gelassen.
philosophize [fɪˈlɒsləfaɪz] *vi* philosophieren *(about, on* über *+acc)*.
philosophy [fɪˈlɒsəfɪ] *n* Philosophie *f*. **~ of life** Lebensphilosophie *f*.
phlegm [flem] *n (mucus)* Schleim *m*; *(fig) (coolness)* Gemütsruhe *f*; *(stolidness)* Trägheit *f*.
phlegmatic [flegˈmætɪk] *adj (cool)* seelenruhig *f*; *(stolid)* träge, phlegmatisch.
phobia [ˈfəʊbɪə] *n* Phobie *f*. **she has a ~ about it** sie hat krankhafte Angst davor.
phoenix, *(US)* **phenix** [ˈfiːnɪks] *n (Myth)* Phönix *m*.
phone [fəʊn] **1** *n* Telefon *nt*. **to pick up/put down the ~** (den Hörer) abnehmen/auflegen. **2** *vt person* anrufen. **3** *vi* anrufen, telefonieren.
♦ **phone in 1** *vi* anrufen. **2** *vt sep* telefonisch übermitteln.
phone: ~ book *n* Telefonbuch *nt*; **~ box** *n* Telefonzelle *f*; **~ call** *n* Anruf *m*; **in our ~ call** in unserem Telefongespräch; **~card** *n* Telefonkarte *f*; **~-in** [ˈfəʊnɪn] *n Rundfunk-/Fernsehprogramm nt, an dem man sich per Telefon beteiligen kann,* Phone-in *nt*.

phonetic [fəʊ'netɪk] *adj* phonetisch.
phonetics [fəʊ'netɪks] *n sing (subject)* Phonetik *f.*
phon(e)y ['fəʊnɪ] *(col)* **1** *adj* unecht; *excuse, deal* faul *(col); name* falsch; *passport, money* gefälscht; *story* erfunden. **2** *n (bogus policeman etc)* Schwindler(in *f*) *m; (doctor)* Scharlatan *m; (pretentious person)* Angeber(in *f*) *m.*
phonograph ['fəʊnəgrɑːf] *n (old)* Phonograph *m; (US)* Plattenspieler *m.*
phonology [fəʊ'nɒlədʒɪ] *n* Phonologie *f.*
phony *adj, n* = **phon(e)y.**
phosphate ['fɒsfeɪt] *n (Chem)* Phosphat *nt; (Agr: fertilizer)* Phosphatdünger *m.*
phosphorescent [ˌfɒsfə'resnt] *adj* phosphoreszierend.
phosphorous ['fɒsfərəs] *adj* phosphorsauer.
photo ['fəʊtəʊ] *n* Foto *nt,* Aufnahme *f.*
photo: ~copier *n* (Foto)kopiergerät *nt;* **~copy 1** *n* Fotokopie *f;* **2** *vt* fotokopieren; **~electric cell** *n* Photozelle *f;* **~ finish** *n* Fotofinish *nt;* **P~fit (picture)** *n* Phantombild *nt.*
photogenic [ˌfəʊtəʊ'dʒenɪk] *adj* fotogen.
photograph ['fəʊtəgræf] **1** *n* Fotografie, Aufnahme *f.* **to take a ~ (of sb/sth)** (jdn/etw) fotografieren, ein Bild (von jdm/etw) machen; **~ album** Fotoalbum *nt.* **2** *vt* fotografieren.
photographer [fə'tɒgrəfə[r]] *n* Fotograf(in *f*) *m.*
photographic [ˌfəʊtə'græfɪk] *adj* fotografisch; *equipment, club* Foto-.
photography [fə'tɒgrəfɪ] *n* Fotografie *f; (in film, book etc)* Fotografien, Bilder *pl.*
photo: ~sensitive *adj* lichtempfindlich; **~stat** ® *n, vt* = **~copy; ~synthesis** *n* Photosynthese *f.*
phrase [freɪz] **1** *n (Gram)* Satzteil *m; (Mus)* Phrase *f; (expression)* Ausdruck *m; (set expression)* Redewendung *f.* **2** *vt* formulieren.
phrasebook ['freɪzbʊk] *n* Sprachführer *m.*
phraseology [ˌfreɪzɪ'ɒlədʒɪ] *n* Ausdrucksweise *f.*
physical ['fɪzɪkəl] *adj* **(a)** *(of the body)* körperlich; *(not psychological also)* physisch; *check-up* ärztlich. **(b)** *(material)* physisch; *world* faßbar. **(c)** *(of physics) laws* physikalisch. **it's a ~ impossibility** es ist ein Ding der Unmöglichkeit *(col).*
physical: ~ education *n (abbr* **PE***)* Sport *m,* Leibesübungen *pl (form);* **~ jerks** *npl (col)* Gymnastik *f.*
physically ['fɪzɪkəlɪ] *adv* körperlich, physisch; *(Sci)* physikalisch. **~ impossible** praktisch unmöglich; **they removed him ~** sie haben ihn mit Gewalt entfernt.
physician [fɪ'zɪʃən] *n* Arzt *m,* Ärztin *f.*
physicist ['fɪzɪsɪst] *n* Physiker(in *f*) *m.*
physics ['fɪzɪks] *n sing (subject)* Physik *f.*
physiological [ˌfɪzɪə'lɒdʒɪkəl] *adj* physiologisch.
physiology [ˌfɪzɪ'ɒlədʒɪ] *n* Physiologie *f.*
physiotherapist [ˌfɪzɪə'θerəpɪst] *n* Physiotherapeut(in *f*) *m.*
physiotherapy [ˌfɪzɪə'θerəpɪ] *n* Physiotherapie *f.*
physique [fɪ'ziːk] *n* Körperbau *m,* Statur *f.*
pianist ['pɪənɪst] *n* Klavierspieler(in *f*) *m; (concert ~)* Pianist(in *f*) *m.*
piano ['pjænəʊ] *n (upright)* Klavier *nt; (grand)* Flügel *m.*
piano: ~ accordion *n* Pianoakkordeon *nt;* **~ lesson** *n* Klavierstunde *f;* **~ stool** *n* Klavierhocker *m.*
piccolo ['pɪkələʊ] *n* Pikkoloflöte *f.*
pick [pɪk] **1** *n* **(a)** *(~axe)* Spitzhacke *f,* Pickel *m; (Mountaineering)* Eispickel *m; (tooth~)* Zahnstocher *m.* **(b)** *(choice)* **to have first ~** die erste Wahl haben; **take your ~!** such dir etwas/einen *etc* aus! **(c)** *(best)* Beste(s) *nt.*
2 *vt* **(a)** *(choose)* (aus)wählen. **to ~ a team** eine Mannschaft aufstellen; **to ~ sides** wählen; **to ~ a winner** *(lit)* den Sieger erraten; *(fig)* das Große Los ziehen; **to ~ one's time** den richtigen Zeitpunkt wählen; **you do ~ 'em** *(iro)* du gerätst auch immer an den Falschen. **(b)** *(pull at) jumper, blanket etc* zupfen an *(+dat); spot, scab* kratzen an *(+dat); hole* bohren. **to ~ one's nose** in der Nase bohren; **to ~ one's teeth** in den Zähnen herumstochern; **to ~ a lock** ein Schloß knacken; **to ~ holes in sth** *(fig)* etw bemäkeln; *in argument* etw in einigen Punkten widerlegen; **to ~ a fight** *or* **quarrel (with sb)** (mit jdm) einen Streit vom Zaun brechen; **to ~ sb's pocket** jdm die Geldbörse/Brieftasche stehlen; **to ~ sb's brains** sich von jdm inspirieren lassen. **(c)** *(pluck) flowers, fruit* pflücken.
3 *vi* **to ~ and choose** wählerisch sein; **to ~ at one's food** im Essen herumstochern.
♦ **pick off** *vt sep* **(a)** *(remove) fluff etc* wegzupfen; *nail polish* abschälen. **(b)** *(shoot)* abschießen.
♦ **pick on** *vi +prep obj (choose)* aussuchen; *(victimize)* herumhacken auf *(+dat).* **why ~ ~ me?** *(col)* warum gerade ich?; **~ ~ somebody your own size!** *(col)* leg dich doch mit einem Gleichstarken an! *(col).*
♦ **pick out** *vt sep* **(a)** *(choose)* aussuchen. **(b)** *(distinguish) person, face* entdecken. **(c)** *(Mus)* **to ~ ~ a tune** eine Melodie improvisieren.
♦ **pick up 1** *vt sep* **(a)** *(take up)* aufheben; *reference, trail* aufnehmen; *(lift momentarily)* hochheben. **to ~ ~ a child in one's arms** ein Kind auf den Arm nehmen; **to ~ oneself ~** aufstehen; **as soon as he ~s ~ a book** sobald er ein Buch in die Hand nimmt; **to ~ ~ the phone** den Hörer abnehmen; **to ~ ~ the bill** *(fig)* die Rechnung bezahlen; **to ~ ~ the pieces** *(lit, fig)* die Scherben aufsammeln.
(b) *(get)* holen; *(buy)* bekommen; *(acquire) habit* sich *(dat)* angewöhnen; *news, gossip* aufschnappen; *illness* sich *(dat)* holen *or* zuziehen; *(col) girl* aufgabeln *(col),* sich *(dat)* anlachen *(col).* **to ~ ~ speed** schneller werden.
(c) *(learn) skill etc* sich *(dat)* aneignen; *language also* lernen; *accent, word* aufschnappen; *information* herausbekommen. **you'll soon ~ it ~** du wirst das schnell lernen.
(d) *(collect) person, goods* abholen; *(bus etc) passengers* aufnehmen; *(in car)* mitnehmen; *(rescue: helicopter, lifeboat)* bergen; *(arrest, catch) criminal* schnappen *(col).*
(e) *(Rad) station* hereinbekommen; *message* empfangen; *(on radar)* ausmachen.
(f) *(correct, put right)* korrigieren.
2 *vi* **(a)** *(improve)* besser werden; *(appetite also)* zunehmen; *(currency)* sich erholen; *(business)* florieren; *(after slump)* sich erholen. **(b)** *(continue)* **to ~ ~ where one left off** da weitermachen, wo man aufgehört hat.
pickaback ['pɪkəbæk] *n* **to give sb a ~** jdn huckepack nehmen.
pickaxe, *(US)* **pickax** [pɪkæks] *n* Spitzhacke, Pickel *m.*
picket ['pɪkɪt] **1** *n* **(a)** *(of strikers)* Streikposten *m.* **(b)** *(Mil)* Feldposten, Vorposten *m.* **2** *vt factory* Streikposten aufstellen vor *(+dat).* **3** *vi* Streikposten aufstellen. **he is ~ing at the front entrance** er ist Streikposten am Vordereingang.
picket: ~ duty *n* Streikpostendienst *m;* **to be on ~ duty** Streikposten sein; **~ line** *n* Streikpostenkette *f;* **to cross a ~ line** eine Streikpostenkette durchbrechen.
pickings ['pɪkɪŋz] *npl* Ausbeute *f; (stolen goods)* Beute *f.* **the ~ are good** es fällt einiges dabei ab.
pickle ['pɪkl] **1** *n* **(a)** *(food)* Pickles *pl.* **(b)** *(solution) (brine)* Salzlake *f; (vinegar)* Essigsoße *f.* **(c)** *(col: predicament)* Klemme *f (col).* **he was in a ~** er saß in der Tinte *(col).* **2** *vt* einlegen.
pick: ~-me-up *n (col)* Muntermacher *m.* **~pocket** *n* Taschendieb(in *f*) *m.*
pick-up ['pɪkʌp] *n* **(a)** Tonabnehmer *m.* **~ arm** Tonarm *m.* **(b)** *(also* **~ truck***)* Kleintransporter *m.*
picnic ['pɪknɪk] **1** *n* Picknick *nt.* **to have a ~** picknicken; **it was no ~** *(fig col)* es war kein

Honiglecken. **2** *vi* picknicken, ein Picknick machen.

picnic basket *or* **hamper** *n* Picknickkorb *m.*

pictorial [pɪk'tɔːrɪəl] *adj calendar* bebildert; *magazine also* illustriert; *description* bildhaft.

picture ['pɪktʃəʳ] **1** *n* **(a)** Bild *nt*; *(mental image also)* Vorstellung *f*; *(painting also)* Gemälde *nt*; *(drawing also)* Zeichnung *f.* **these figures give the general ~** diese Zahlen geben ein allgemeines Bild; **to be in the ~** im Bilde sein; **to put sb in the ~** jdn ins Bild setzen; **I get the ~** ich hab's begriffen *or* kapiert *(col)*; **she looked a ~** sie war bildschön; **the garden is a ~** der Garten ist eine Pracht; **she looked** *or* **was the ~ of happiness** sie sah wie das Glück in Person aus. **(b)** *(Film)* Film *m.* **the ~s** *(Brit)* das Kino; **to go to the ~s** *(Brit)* ins Kino gehen. **2** *vt (imagine)* sich *(dat)* vorstellen.

picture: ~ book *n* Bildband *m*; *(for children)* Bilderbuch *nt*; **~ frame** *n* Bilderrahmen *m*; **~ gallery** *n* Gemäldegalerie *f*; **~ postcard** *n* Ansichtskarte *f.*

picturesque [,pɪktʃə'resk] *adj* malerisch; *(fig) description* anschaulich.

pie [paɪ] *n* Pastete *f*; *(sweet)* Obstkuchen *m*; *(individual)* Tortelett *nt.* **that's all ~ in the sky** *(col)* das sind nur verrückte Ideen; **as easy as ~** *(col)* kinderleicht.

piece [piːs] *n* **(a)** Stück *nt*; *(part, member of a set)* Teil *nt*; *(component part)* Einzelteil *nt*; *(fragment of glass etc also)* Scherbe *f*; *(in draughts etc)* Stein *m*; *(chess)* Figur *f*; *(Press: article)* Artikel *m*; *(col!: woman)* Weib *nt.* **a 50p ~** ein 50-Pence-Stück; **a ~ of cake/land/paper** ein Stück *nt* Kuchen/Land/Papier; **a ~ of furniture/luggage/clothing** ein Möbel-/Gepäck-/Kleidungsstück *nt*; **a ten-~ coffee set** ein zehnteiliges Kaffeeservice; **a ~ of news/information** eine Nachricht/eine Information; **a ~ of work** eine Arbeit; **~ by ~** Stück für Stück; **to take sth to ~s** etw in seine Einzelteile zerlegen; **to come to ~s** sich zerlegen lassen; *(break)* auseinanderfallen; **to fall to ~s** auseinanderfallen; *(glass)* zerbrechen; **to smash sth to ~s** etw kaputtschlagen; **he tore the letter (in)to ~s** er zerriß den Brief (in Stücke).

(b) *(phrases)* **to go to ~s** *(crack up)* durchdrehen *(col)*; **all in one ~** *(intact)* heil, unversehrt; **to give sb a ~ of one's mind** jdm gehörig die Meinung sagen; **to say one's ~** seine Meinung sagen.

♦ **piece together** *vt sep (lit)* zusammenstückeln; *(fig)* sich *(dat)* zusammenreimen; *evidence* zusammenfügen.

piece: ~meal 1 *adv* stückweise; *(haphazardly)* kunterbunt durcheinander; **2** *adj* stückweise; *(haphazard)* wenig systematisch; **~work** *n* Akkordarbeit *f*; **to be on ~work** im Akkord arbeiten.

pier [pɪəʳ] *n* Pier *m or f*; *(landing-place also)* Anlegestelle *f.*

pierce [pɪəs] *vt* durchstechen; *(knife, spear, bullet)* durchbohren; *(fig: sound, coldness etc)* durchdringen. **to ~ a hole in sth** etw durchstechen; **to have one's ears ~d** sich *(dat)* die Ohrläppchen durchstechen lassen.

piercing ['pɪəsɪŋ] *adj* durchdringend; *eyes also* stechend; *cold also, sarcasm* beißend; *wit* scharf.

piety ['paɪətɪ] *n* Pietät, Frömmigkeit *f.*

pig [pɪg] *n (lit, fig col)* Schwein *nt*; *(greedy)* Vielfraß *m (col).* **to buy a ~ in a poke** *(prov)* die Katze im Sack kaufen; **to make a ~ of oneself** sich *(dat)* den Bauch vollschlagen *(col).*

pigeon ['pɪdʒən] *n* **(a)** Taube *f.* **(b)** *(col)* **that's not my ~** das ist nicht mein Bier *(col).*

pigeon: ~hole 1 *n (in desk etc)* Fach *nt*; **2** *vt (lit)* (in Fächer) einordnen; *(fig: categorize)* einordnen, aufteilen; **~-toed** *adj, adv* mit einwärts gerichteten Fußspitzen.

piggyback ['pɪgɪbæk] *n* = **pickaback.**

piggy bank ['pɪgɪbæŋk] *n* Sparschwein *nt.*

pigheaded ['pɪg'hedɪd] *adj* stur.

piglet ['pɪglɪt] *n* Ferkel *nt.*

pigment ['pɪgmənt] *n* Pigment *nt.*

pigmentation [,pɪgmən'teɪʃən] *n* Pigmentierung *f.*

pigmy *n* = **pygmy.**

pig: ~skin *n* Schweinsleder *nt*; **~sty** *n* Schweinestall *m*; *(fig also)* Saustall *m (col)*; **~tail** *n* Zopf *m.*

pike [paɪk] *n (fish)* Hecht *m.*

pilchard ['pɪltʃəd] *n* Sardine *f.*

pile[1] [paɪl] **1** *n* **(a)** *(heap)* Stapel *m.* **to put things in a ~** etw (auf)stapeln; **her things lay** *or* **were in a ~** ihre Sachen lagen auf einem Haufen. **(b)** *(col: large amount)* Haufen *m*, Menge *f.* **~s of food** jede Menge Essen *(col)*; **a ~ of things to do** massenhaft zu tun *(col).* **(c)** *(col: fortune)* Vermögen *nt.* **to make a ~** einen Haufen Geld verdienen. **2** *vt* stapeln. **a table ~d high with books** ein Tisch mit Stapeln von Büchern.

♦ **pile in** *vi (col) (-to* in *+acc)* hereindrängen; *(get in)* einsteigen. **~ ~!** immer herein!

♦ **pile up 1** *vi* **(a)** *(lit, fig)* sich anhäufen; *(traffic)* sich stauen; *(evidence)* sich verdichten. **(b)** *(crash)* aufeinander auffahren. **2** *vt sep* (auf)stapeln; *money* horten; *(fig) debts* anhäufen; *evidence* sammeln.

pile[2] *n* Pfahl *m.*

pile[3] *n (of carpet, cloth)* Flor *m.*

piles [paɪlz] *npl* Hämorrhoiden *pl.*

pile-up ['paɪlʌp] *n (car crash)* (Massen)karambolage *f.*

pilfer ['pɪlfəʳ] *vti* stehlen, klauen *(col).* **there's a lot of ~ing in the office** im Büro wird viel geklaut *(col).*

pilgrim ['pɪlgrɪm] *n* Pilger(in *f*) *m.*

pilgrimage ['pɪlgrɪmɪdʒ] *n* Wallfahrt *f.* **to go on** *or* **make a ~** pilgern, eine Wallfahrt machen.

pill [pɪl] *n* Tablette *f.* **the ~** die Pille; **to be/go on the ~** die Pille nehmen.

pillage ['pɪlɪdʒ] **1** *n (act)* Plünderung *f*; *(booty)* Beute *f.* **2** *vti* plündern.

pillar ['pɪləʳ] *n* Säule *f.* **a ~ of society** eine Stütze der Gesellschaft; **from ~ to post** von Pontius zu Pilatus.

pillar-box ['pɪləbɒks] *n (Brit)* Briefkasten *m.* **~ red** knallrot.

pillion ['pɪljən] **1** *n (on motor-bike)* Beifahrersitz *m.* **~ passenger** Beifahrer(in *f*) *m.* **2** *adv* **to ride ~** auf dem Beifahrersitz mitfahren.

pillow ['pɪləʊ] *n* (Kopf)kissen *nt.*

pillow case *or* **slip** *n* (Kopf)kissenbezug *m.*

pilot ['paɪlət] **1** *n (Aviat)* Pilot(in *f*) *m*; *(Naut)* Lotse *m.* **2** *vt plane* fliegen; *ship* lotsen; *(fig)* führen, leiten.

pilot: ~ boat *n* Lotsenboot *nt*; **~ light** *n* Zündflamme *f*; **~ scheme** *n* Versuchsprojekt *nt.*

pimento [pɪ'mentəʊ] *n* Paprikaschote *f.*

pimp [pɪmp] *n* Zuhälter *m.*

pimple ['pɪmpl] *n* Pickel *m.*

pimply ['pɪmplɪ] *adj (+er)* pickelig.

pin [pɪn] **1** *n (Sew)* Stecknadel *f*; *(tie ~, hair ~)* Nadel *f*; *(Mech)* Bolzen, Stift *m*; *(in grenade)* Sicherungsstift *m*; *(Elec: of plug)* Pol *m.* **a two-~ plug** ein zweipoliger Stecker; **~s and needles** *sing or pl* ein Kribbeln *nt*; **as neat as a new ~** blitzsauber; **for two ~s I'd pack up and go** *(col)* es fehlt nicht mehr viel, dann gehe ich; **you could have heard a ~ drop** man hätte eine Stecknadel fallen hören können. **2** *vt* **(a)** *dress* stecken. **to ~ sth to sth** etw an etw *(acc)* heften. **(b)** *(fig)* **to ~ sb to the ground/against a wall** jdn an den Boden/an eine Wand pressen; **to ~ one's hopes on sb/sth** seine Hoffnungen auf jdn/etw setzen; **to ~ back one's ears** die Ohren spitzen *(col).* **(c)** *(col: accuse of)* **to ~ sth on sb** jdm etw anhängen.

♦ **pin down** *vt sep* **(a)** *(with pins)* an- *or* festheften; *(hold, weight down)* niederhalten; *(person)* zu

Boden drücken. **(b)** *(fig)* **to ~ sb ~** jdn festnageln *(col) or* festlegen; **he wouldn't be ~ned ~ to any particular date** er ließ sich nicht auf ein bestimmtes Datum festlegen; **I've seen him somewhere before but I can't ~ him ~** ich habe ihn schon mal irgendwo gesehen, kann ihn aber nicht einordnen; **we can't ~ ~ the source of the rumours** wir können die Quelle der Gerüchte nicht lokalisieren; **there's something odd here, but I can't ~ it ~** irgend etwas ist hier merkwürdig, aber ich kann nicht genau sagen was.

♦ **pin up** *vt sep notice* anheften; *hair* hochstecken; *dress etc* stecken.

pinafore ['pɪnəfɔːʳ] *n (for children)* Kinderkittel *m*; *(apron)* Schürze *f*. **~ dress** *(Brit)* Trägerkleid *nt*.

pinball ['pɪnbɔːl] *n* Flipper *m*. **~ machine** Flipper *m*.

pincers ['pɪnsəz] *npl* **(a)** Kneifzange *f*. **a pair of ~** eine Kneifzange. **(b)** *(Zool)* Schere, Zange *f*.

pinch [pɪntʃ] **1** *n* **(a)** *(with fingers)* Kneifen *nt no pl*. **to give sb a ~ on the arm** jdn in den Arm kneifen. **(b)** *(Cook)* Prise *f*. **(c)** *(pressure)* **I'm rather feeling the ~ at the moment** ich bin im Augenblick ziemlich knapp bei Kasse *(col)*; **to feel the ~** die schlechte Lage zu spüren bekommen; **if it comes to the ~** wenn es zum Schlimmsten kommt; **at a ~** zur Not. **2** *vt* **(a)** *(with fingers)* kneifen; *(with tool) wire etc* zusammendrücken. **(b)** *(col: steal)* klauen *(col)*. **don't let anyone ~ my seat** paß auf, daß mir niemand den Platz wegnimmt. **3** *vi (shoe, also fig)* drücken. **to ~ and scrape** sich einschränken.

pinched ['pɪntʃt] *adj* **(a)** verhärmt; *(from cold)* verfroren; *(from fatigue)* erschöpft. **~ with cold/hunger** verfroren/verhungert. **(b)** *(col: short)* **to be ~ for money/time/space** knapp bei Kasse sein *(col)*/keine Zeit haben/ein wenig beengt sein.

pincushion ['pɪnˌkʊʃn] *n* Nadelkissen *nt*.

pine[1] [paɪn] *n* Kiefer *f*.

pine[2] *vi* **to ~ for sb/sth** sich nach jdm/etw sehnen.

♦ **pine away** *vi* sich vor Kummer verzehren.

pineapple ['paɪnˌæpl] *n* Ananas *f*.

pine: ~ cone *n* Kiefernzapfen *m*; **~ needle** *n* Kiefernnadel *f*; **~ tree** *n* Kiefer *f*.

ping [pɪŋ] **1** *n (of bell)* Klingeln *nt*; *(of bullet)* Peng *nt*. **2** *vi (bell)* klingeln; *(bullet)* peng machen.

ping-pong ['pɪŋpɒŋ] *n* Pingpong *nt*.

pinion ['pɪnjən] *n (Mech)* Ritzel, Treibrad *nt*.

pink[1] [pɪŋk] **1** *n* **(a)** *(colour)* Rosa *nt*. **(b)** *(plant)* Gartennelke *f*. **(c) to be in the ~** vor Gesundheit strotzen. **2** *adj (colour)* rosa *inv*, rosafarben; *cheeks, face* rosig. **to turn ~** erröten.

pink[2] *vt (Sew)* mit der Zickzackschere schneiden.

pinkie ['pɪŋkɪ] *n (Scot col, US col)* kleiner Finger.

pinnacle ['pɪnəkl] *n (Archit)* Fiale *f*; *(of rock)* Gipfel *m*, Spitze *f*; *(fig)* Gipfel, Höhepunkt *m*.

pin: ~point *vt (locate)* genau an- *or* aufzeigen; *(define, identify)* genau feststellen *or* -legen; **~-prick** *n* Nadelstich *m*; **~stripe** *n (~stripe suit)* Nadelstreifenanzug *m*.

pint [paɪnt] *n (Measure)* Pint *nt*. **to have a ~** *(esp Brit)* ein Bier *nt* trinken.

pinta ['paɪntə] *n (Brit col)* ≈ halber Liter Milch.

pin-up ['pɪnʌp] *n (picture)* Pin-up-Foto *nt*; *(girl)* Pin-up-Girl *nt*; *(man)* Idol *nt*.

pioneer [ˌpaɪə'nɪəʳ] **1** *n (also Mil)* Pionier *m*; *(fig also)* Wegbereiter *m*. **2** *vt way* bahnen; *(fig)* Pionierarbeit *f* leisten für.

pious ['paɪəs] *adj* fromm; *(pej also)* frömmlerisch. **a ~ hope** ein frommer Wunsch.

pip[1] [pɪp] *n* **(a)** *(Bot)* Kern *m*. **(b)** *(on dice)* Auge *nt*; *(Brit Mil col)* Stern *m*; *(radar)* Pip *m*, Echozeichen *nt*. **(c)** *(Rad, Telec)* **the ~s** das Zeitzeichen; *(in public telephone)* das Tut-tut-tut. **to give sb the ~** *(Brit col)* jdn aufregen *(col)*.

pip[2] *vt (Brit col)* knapp besiegen *or* schlagen. **to ~ sb at the post** *(in race)* jdn um Haaresbreite schlagen; *(fig)* jdm um Haaresbreite zuvorkommen.

pipe [paɪp] **1** *n* **(a)** *(for water, gas etc)* Rohr *nt*, Leitung *f*; *(fuel ~)* Leitung *f*. **(b)** *(Mus)* Flöte *f*; *(fife, of organ)* Pfeife *f*. **~s** *(bag~s)* Dudelsack *m*. **(c)** *(for smoking)* Pfeife *f*. **to smoke a ~** Pfeife rauchen; **put that in your ~ and smoke it!** *(col)* steck dir das hinter den Spiegel *(col)*. **2** *vt* **(a)** *water, oil etc* in Rohren leiten; *music, broadcast* ausstrahlen. **~d music** *(pej)* Musikberieselung *f (col)*. **(b)** *(Mus) tune* flöten, pfeifen; *(sing in high voice)* krähen; *(speak in high voice)* piepsen; *(Naut)* pfeifen. **to ~ sb aboard** jdn mit Pfeifensignal an Bord empfangen. **(c)** *(Cook)* spritzen; *cake* mit Spritzguß verzieren. **3** *vi (Mus)* (die) Flöte spielen; *(young bird, anxiously)* piep(s)en.

♦ **pipe down** *vi (col)* die Luft anhalten *(col)*.

♦ **pipe up** *vi (col: person)* den Mund aufmachen, sich melden.

pipe: ~ cleaner *n* Pfeifenreiniger *m*; **~ dream** *n* Hirngespinst *nt*; **that's just a ~ dream** das ist ja wohl nur ein frommer Wunsch; **~line** *n* (Rohr)leitung *f*; *(for oil, gas also)* Pipeline *f*; **to be in the ~line** *(fig)* in Vorbereitung sein.

piper ['paɪpəʳ] *n (bagpipes)* Dudelsackpfeifer *m*.

piping ['paɪpɪŋ] **1** *n* **(a)** *(pipework)* Rohrleitungssystem *nt*; *(pipe)* Rohrleitung *f*. **(b)** *(Sew)* Paspelierung *f*. **2** *adv*: **~ hot** kochendheiß.

pippin ['pɪpɪn] *n* Cox Orange *m*.

piquancy ['piːkənsɪ] *n* Würze *f*; *(fig)* Pikanterie *f*.

piquant ['piːkənt] *adj (lit, fig)* pikant.

pique [piːk] **1** *n* Groll *m*. **he resigned in a fit of ~** er kündigte, weil er vergrämt war. **2** *vt (offend)* kränken, verletzen. **~d** pikiert.

piracy ['paɪərəsɪ] *n* Piraterie *f*; *(of book etc)* Raubdruck *m*; *(of record)* Raubpressung *f*.

pirate ['paɪərɪt] **1** *n* Seeräuber, Pirat *m*. **~ radio** Piratensender *m*. **2** *vt book* einen Raubdruck herstellen von; *invention, idea* stehlen. **a ~d record** eine Raubpressung.

pirouette [ˌpɪrʊ'et] **1** *n* Pirouette *f*. **2** *vi* Pirouetten drehen.

Pisces ['paɪsiːz] *npl (Astrol)* Fische *pl*. **I'm (a) ~** ich bin (ein) Fisch.

piss [pɪs] *(col!)* **1** *n* Pisse *f (col!)*. **2** *vti* pissen *(col!)*.

♦ **piss off** *vi (esp Brit col!)* abhauen *(col)*. **to be ~ed ~ with sb/sth** von jdm/etw die Schnauze voll haben *(col!)*.

pissed [pɪst] *adj (col!) (Brit: drunk)* voll *(col)*, besoffen *(col)*; *(US: angry)* stocksauer *(col)*.

pistol ['pɪstl] *n* Pistole *f*. **~ shot** Pistolenschuß *m*; **to hold a ~ to sb's head** *(fig)* jdm die Pistole auf die Brust setzen.

piston ['pɪstən] *n* Kolben *m*. **~ engine** Kolbenmotor *m*; **~ rod** Kolbenstange *f*.

pit[1] [pɪt] **1** *n* **(a)** Grube *f*; *(motor-racing)* Box *f*; *(Sport: for jump)* Sprunggrube *f*; *(coalmine also)* Zeche *f*; *(trap)* Fallgrube *f*; *(of stomach)* Magengrube *f*. **in the ~ of one's stomach** in der Magengegend; **he works down the ~(s)** er arbeitet unter Tage. **(b)** *(Theat) (usu pl Brit: for audience)* Parkett *nt*; *(orchestra ~)* Orchesterraum *m*.

2 *vt* **(a) to be ~ted with small craters** mit kleinen Kratern übersät sein; **the car was ~ted with rustholes** der Wagen war mit Rostlöchern übersät. **(b) to ~ one's strength/wits against sb/sth** seine Kraft/seinen Verstand an jdm/etw messen; **in the next round A is ~ted against B** in der nächsten Runde stehen sich A und B gegenüber.

pit[2] **1** *n (in fruit)* Stein *m*. **2** *vt* entsteinen.

pitapat ['pɪtə'pæt] *adv (of heart)* poch poch; *(of feet)* tapp tapp. **to go ~** *(heart)* pochen, klopfen.

pitch[1] [pɪtʃ] *n* Pech *nt*. **as black as ~** pechschwarz.

pitch[2] **1** *n* **(a)** *(esp Brit Sport)* Platz *m*, Feld *nt*. **(b)** *(angle, slope: of roof)* Neigung *f*; *(of propeller)* Steigung *f*. **(c)** *(of note)* Tonhöhe *f*; *(of instrument)* Tonlage *f*; *(of voice)* Stimmlage *f*. **to have perfect ~** das absolute Gehör haben. **(d)** *(fig: degree)* **we**

can't keep on working at this ~ much longer wir können dieses Arbeitstempo nicht mehr lange durchhalten; **matters had reached such a ~ that** ... die Sache hatte sich derart zugespitzt, daß ...

2 *vt* **(a)** *(throw) hay* gabeln; *ball* werfen. **he was ~ed from** *or* **off his horse** er wurde vom Pferd geworfen. **(b)** *(Mus) song* anstimmen; *note (give)* angeben; *instrument* stimmen. **(c)** *(fig)* **to ~ one's aspirations too high** seine Erwartungen *or* Hoffnungen zu hoch stecken; **that's ~ing it rather strong** *or* **a bit high** das ist ein bißchen übertrieben. **(d)** *(put up) camp* aufschlagen; *stand* aufstellen.

3 *vi* **(a)** *(fall)* fallen, stürzen. **to ~ forward** vornüberfallen. **(b)** *(Naut)* stampfen; *(Aviat)* absacken. **to ~ and toss** *(ship)* von den Wellen hin und her geworfen werden; *(person)* sich wälzen.

♦ **pitch in 1** *vt sep* hineinwerfen. **2** *vi (col)* einspringen. **so we all ~ed ~ together** also packten wir alle mit an.

♦ **pitch into** *vi +prep obj (attack)* herfallen über *(+acc)*; *food also, work* sich hermachen über *(+acc)*.

pitch black *or* **dark** *adj* pechschwarz.

pitched [pɪtʃt] *adj* **(a)** *roof* Sattel-. **(b)** *battle* offen.

pitcher[1] ['pɪtʃəʳ] *n* Krug *m*.

pitcher[2] *n (Baseball)* Werfer *m*.

pitchfork ['pɪtʃfɔːk] **1** *n* Heugabel *f*; *(for manure)* Mistgabel *f*. **2** *vt* gabeln; *(fig)* hineinwerfen.

piteous ['pɪtɪəs] *adj* mitleiderregend; *sounds* kläglich.

pitfall ['pɪtfɔːl] *n (fig)* Falle *f*. **"P~s of English"** „Hauptschwierigkeiten der englischen Sprache".

pith [pɪθ] *n (Bot)* Mark *nt*; *(of orange etc)* weiße Haut; *(fig: core)* Kern *m*.

pithead ['pɪthed] *n* Übertageanlagen *pl*. **at the ~** über Tage; **~ ballot** Abstimmung *f* der Bergarbeiter.

pithy ['pɪθɪ] *adj (+er) (fig)* markig. **~ remarks** Kraftsprüche *pl*.

pitiable ['pɪtɪəbl] *adj* bemitleidenswert.

pitiful ['pɪtɪfʊl] *adj* **(a)** *sight, story* mitleiderregend; *person* bedauernswert; *cry also* jämmerlich. **(b)** *(poor, wretched)* erbärmlich, jämmerlich.

pitifully ['pɪtɪfəlɪ] *adv see adj*. **it was ~ obvious that ...** es war schon qualvoll offensichtlich, daß ...

pitiless ['pɪtɪlɪs] *adj* mitleidlos; *person also, heat* unbarmherzig; *cruelty also* erbarmungslos.

pittance ['pɪtəns] *n* Hungerlohn *m*.

pitter-patter ['pɪtə'pætəʳ] **1** *n (of rain)* Klatschen *nt*; *(of feet)* Getrappel *nt*. **2** *adv run* tapp tapp. **her heart went ~** ihr Herz klopfte.

pity ['pɪtɪ] **1** *n* **(a)** Mitleid, Erbarmen *nt*. **for ~'s sake!** Erbarmen!; *(less seriously)* um Himmels willen!; **to have** *or* **take ~ on sb, to feel ~ for sb** mit jdm Mitleid haben. **(b) (what a) ~!** (wie) schade!; **more's the ~!** leider; **it is a ~ that ...** es ist schade, daß ... **2** *vt* bedauern.

pitying ['pɪtɪɪŋ] *adj* mitleidig; *(with contempt)* verächtlich.

pivot ['pɪvət] *(vb: pret, ptp* **~ed***)* **1** *n* Drehzapfen *m*; *(fig)* Dreh- und Angelpunkt *m*. **2** *vt* drehbar lagern. **3** *vi* sich drehen.

pixie, pixy ['pɪksɪ] *n* Kobold *m*.

placard ['plækɑːd] *n* Plakat *nt*.

placate [plə'keɪt] *vt* beschwichtigen.

place [pleɪs] **1** *n* **(a)** *(in general)* Platz *m*, Stelle *f*. **this is just the ~ for a picnic** das ist genau der richtige Platz für ein Picknick; **this is the ~ where he was ...** an dieser Stelle wurde er ...; **from ~ to ~** von einem Ort zum anderen; **in another ~** woanders; **some/any ~** irgendwo; **this is no ~ for children** das ist hier für Kinder nicht geeignet; **all over the ~** überall; **water is coming through in several ~s** an mehreren Stellen kommt Wasser durch; **do the spoons have a special ~?** haben die Löffel einen bestimmten Platz?; **make sure the screw is properly in ~** achten Sie darauf, daß die Schraube richtig sitzt; **to be out of ~** nicht an der richtigen Stelle sein; *(fig) (remark)* unangebracht sein; *(person)* fehl am Platze sein; **to feel out of ~** sich fehl am Platz fühlen; **not a hair out of ~** tipptopp frisiert *(col)*; **your ~ is by his side** dein Platz ist an seiner Seite; **everything was in ~** alles war an seiner Stelle; **in the right/wrong ~** an der richtigen/falschen Stelle; **to keep/lose one's ~** *(in book etc)* die richtige Stelle markieren/verlieren; **it was the last ~ I expected to find him** da hätte ich ihn am wenigsten vermutet; **this isn't the ~ to discuss politics** dies ist nicht der Ort, um über Politik zu sprechen; **to go ~s** *(travel)* herumreisen; **he's going ~s** *(fig col)* er bringt's zu was *(col)*.

(b) *(specific ~)* Stätte *f*, Ort *m*. **~ of birth/residence** Geburtsort *m*/Wohnort *m*; **~ of business** *or* **work** Arbeitsstelle *f*.

(c) *(district etc)* Gegend *f*; *(country)* Land *nt*; *(building)* Gebäude *nt*; *(town)* Ort *m*; *(home)* Haus *nt*; Wohnung *f*. **there's nothing to do in this ~** hier kann man nichts unternehmen; **at Jimmy's ~** bei Jimmy; **come round to my ~ some time** besuch mich mal, komm doch mal vorbei; **let's go back to my ~** laß uns zu mir gehen; **where's your ~?** wo wohnst du?

(d) *(seat, in team, school etc)* Platz *m*; *(university ~)* Studienplatz *m*; *(job)* Stelle *f*. **to take one's ~ (at table)** Platz nehmen; **~s for 500 workers** 500 Arbeitsplätze; **to lose one's ~** *(in a queue)* sich wieder hinten anstellen müssen.

(e) *(social position etc)* Rang *m*, Stellung *f*. **people in high ~s** Leute in hohen Positionen; **to know one's ~** wissen, was sich (für jdn) gehört; **it's not my ~ to comment** es steht mir nicht zu, einen Kommentar abzugeben; **to keep** *or* **put sb in his ~** jdn in seine Schranken weisen.

(f) *(in exam, Sport etc)* Platz *m*; *(Math)* Stelle *f*. **to three decimal ~s** auf drei Stellen nach dem Komma; **in the first/second ~** erstens/zweitens; **to win first ~** erste(r, s) sein.

(g) in ~ of statt *(+gen)*; **if I were in your ~** (wenn ich) an Ihrer Stelle (wäre); **to take ~** stattfinden; **to take the ~ of sb/sth** den Platz von jdm/etw einnehmen.

2 *vt* **(a)** *(put)* setzen, stellen; *(lay down)* legen; *person at table etc* setzen; *guards* aufstellen; *(Ftbl, Tennis)* plazieren; *troops* in Stellung bringen; *announcement (in paper)* inserieren *(in* in *+dat)*; *advertisement* setzen *(in* in *+acc)*. **I shall ~ the matter in the hands of a lawyer** ich werde die Angelegenheit einem Rechtsanwalt übergeben; **to ~ too much emphasis on sth** auf etw *(acc)* zuviel Nachdruck legen; **that should be ~d first** das sollte an erster Stelle stehen; **to ~ trust** *etc* **in sb/sth** Vertrauen in jdn/etw setzen.

(b) to be ~d *(shop, town, house etc)* liegen; **we are well ~d for the shops** was Einkaufsmöglichkeiten angeht, wohnen wir günstig; **how are you ~d for time/money?** wie sieht es mit deiner Zeit/deinem Geld aus?; **Liverpool are well ~d in the league** Liverpool liegt gut in der Tabelle; **we are better ~d now than we were last month** wir stehen jetzt besser da als vor einem Monat.

(c) *order* erteilen *(with sb* jdm*)*; *contract* abschließen *(with sb* mit jdm*)*; *money* deponieren; *(Comm) goods* absetzen.

(d) *(in race, competition etc)* **the German runner was ~d third** der deutsche Läufer belegte den dritten Platz.

(e) *(remember, identify)* einordnen. **I can't quite ~ him/his accent** ich kann ihn/seinen Akzent nicht einordnen.

place: ~ **card** *n* Tischkarte *f*; ~ **mat** *n* Set *nt*; ~**-name** *n* Ortsname *m*.

placenta [plə'sentə] *n* Plazenta *f*.

placid ['plæsɪd] *adj* ruhig; *disposition* friedfertig.

plagiarism ['pleɪdʒjərɪzəm] *n* Plagiat *nt*.

plagiarize ['pleɪdʒjəraɪz] *vt book, idea* plagiieren.

plague [pleɪg] **1** *n (Med)* Seuche *f*; *(Bibl, fig)* Plage *f*. **the ~** die Pest; **to avoid sb/sth like the ~** *(col)* jdn/etw wie die Pest meiden *(col)*. **2** *vt* plagen. **to ~ sb with questions** jdn ständig mit Fragen belästigen; **to be ~d by doubts** von Zweifeln geplagt werden.

plaice [pleɪs] *n no pl* Scholle *f*.

plaid [plæd] *n* Plaid *nt*. ~ **skirt** karierter Rock.

plain [pleɪn] **1** *adj (+er)* **(a)** klar; *(obvious also)* offensichtlich; *tracks, differences* deutlich. ~ **to see** offensichtlich; **it's as ~ as the nose on your face** *(col)* das sieht doch ein Blinder (mit Krückstock) *(col)*; **to make sth ~ to sb** jdm etw klarmachen; **I'd like to make it quite ~ that ...** ich möchte gern klarstellen, daß ...

(b) *(frank, straightforward) question, answer* klar; *truth* schlicht. ~ **dealing** Redlichkeit *f*; **in ~ language** *or* **English** unmißverständlich, auf gut Deutsch; **it was ~ sailing** es ging glatt (über die Bühne) *(col)*.

(c) *(simple, with nothing added)* einfach; *living also* schlicht, bescheiden; *cooking also* (gut)bürgerlich; *chocolate* bitter; *paper* unliniert; *colour* einheitlich; *(not patterned) material etc* uni *pred*, einfarbig. **under ~ cover** in neutralem Umschlag.

(d) *(sheer)* rein; *greed also* nackt; *nonsense etc also* völlig, blank *(col)*.

(e) *(not beautiful)* nicht gerade ansprechend; *face also* alltäglich.

2 *adv* **(a)** *(col: simply, completely)* (ganz) einfach. **(b) I can't put it ~er than that** deutlicher kann ich es nicht sagen.

3 *n* **(a)** *(Geog)* Ebene *f*. **(b)** *(Knitting)* rechte Masche.

plain clothes *npl* **in ~** in Zivil.

plainly ['pleɪnlɪ] *adv* **(a)** *(clearly)* eindeutig; *explain, visible* klar, deutlich. **(b)** *(frankly)* offen. **(c)** *(simply, unsophisticatedly)* einfach.

plainness ['pleɪnnɪs] *n* **(a)** *(frankness)* Offenheit *f*. **(b)** *(simplicity)* Einfachheit *f*. **(c)** *(lack of beauty)* Unansehnlichkeit *f*.

plain: ~ **speaking** *n* Offenheit *f*; **some ~ speaking** ein paar offene Worte; ~**-spoken** *adj* offen, direkt; *criticism also* unverhohlen; **to be ~-spoken** sagen, was man denkt.

plaintiff ['pleɪntɪf] *n* Kläger(in *f*) *m*.

plaintive ['pleɪntɪv] *adj* klagend; *voice etc also* wehleidig *(pej)*.

plait [plæt] **1** *n* Zopf *m*. **she wears her hair in ~s** sie trägt Zöpfe. **2** *vt* flechten.

plan [plæn] **1** *n* **(a)** *(scheme)* Plan *m*; *(Pol, Econ also)* Programm *nt*. ~ **of action** *(Mil, fig)* Aktionsprogramm *nt*; ~ **of campaign** *(Mil)* Strategie *f*; **the ~ is to meet at six** es ist geplant, sich um sechs zu treffen; **the best ~ is to tell him first** am besten sagt man es ihm zuerst; **to have great ~s for sb** große Pläne mit jdm haben; **have you any ~s for tonight?** hast du (für) heute abend (schon) etwas vor?; **according to ~** planmäßig, wie vorgesehen. **(b)** *(diagram)* Plan *m*; *(for essay, speech)* Konzept *nt*; *(town ~)* Stadtplan *m*.

2 *vt* planen; *programme etc* erstellen, ausarbeiten; *(intend)* vorhaben. **we weren't ~ning to** wir hatten es nicht vor; **this development was not ~ned** diese Entwicklung war nicht eingeplant; **~ned obsolescence** geplanter Verschleiß.

3 *vi* planen. **to ~ for sth** sich einstellen auf *(+acc)*; **to ~ months ahead** (auf) Monate vorausplanen; **I'm not ~ning on staying** ich habe nicht vor zu bleiben.

plane[1] [pleɪn] *n (also* ~ **tree)** Platane *f*.

plane[2] **1** *adj* eben *(also Math)*. **2** *n* **(a)** *(Math, fig)* Ebene *f*; *(intellectual also)* Niveau *nt*; *(social ~)* Schicht *f*. **(b)** *(tool)* Hobel *m*. **(c)** *(aeroplane)* Flugzeug *nt*. **to go by ~** fliegen. **3** *vt* hobeln. **to ~ sth down** etw glatt hobeln.

planet ['plænɪt] *n* Planet *m*.

planetarium [ˌplænɪ'tɛərɪəm] *n* Planetarium *nt*.

plank [plæŋk] *n* Brett *nt*.

plankton ['plæŋktən] *n* Plankton *nt*.

planner ['plænəʳ] *n* Planer(in *f*) *m*.

planning *in cpds* Planungs-; ~ **permission** Baugenehmigung *f*.

plant [plɑːnt] **1** *n* **(a)** *(Bot)* Pflanze *f*. **rare/tropical ~s** seltene/tropische Gewächse *pl*. **(b)** *(no pl: equipment)* Anlagen *pl*; *(equipment and buildings)* Produktionsanlage *f*; *(factory)* Werk *nt*. **2** *attr* Pflanzen-. ~ **life** Pflanzenwelt *f*. **3** *vt* **(a)** *plants, trees* (an)pflanzen; *field* bepflanzen. **to ~ a field with wheat** auf einem Feld Weizen anbauen. **(b)** *(place in position)* setzen; *bomb* legen; *kiss* drücken; *(in the ground) stick* stecken; *flag* pflanzen. **to ~ sth in sb's mind** jdm etw in den Kopf setzen; **he ~ed himself right in the doorway** er pflanzte sich genau in den Eingang *(col)*. **(c)** *(col)* schmuggeln; *informer, spy etc* (ein)schleusen. **to ~ sth on sb** jdm etw unterjubeln *(col)*.

plantation [plæn'teɪʃən] *n* Plantage *f*; *(of trees)* Anpflanzung *f*.

planter ['plɑːntəʳ] *n (person)* Pflanzer(in *f*) *m*; *(machine)* Pflanzmaschine *f*.

plaque [plæk] *n* **(a)** *(on building etc)* Tafel *f*. **(b)** *(Med: on teeth)* (Zahn)belag *m*.

plasma ['plæzmə] *n* Plasma *nt*.

plaster ['plɑːstəʳ] **1** *n* **(a)** *(Build)* (Ver)putz *m*. **(b)** *(Art, Med: also* ~ **of Paris)** Gips *m*; *(Med:* ~ *cast)* Gipsverband *m*. **to have one's leg in ~** das Bein in Gips haben. **(c)** *(Brit: sticking ~)* Pflaster *nt*. **2** *vt* **(a)** *(Build) wall* verputzen. **(b)** *(col: cover)* vollkleistern. **to ~ a wall with posters** eine Wand mit Plakaten bepflastern *(col)*; **~ed with mud** schlammbedeckt.

plaster: ~**board** *n* Gipskarton(platten *pl*) *m*; ~ **cast** *n (model, statue)* Gipsform *f*; *(of footprint etc)* Gipsabdruck *m*; *(Med)* Gipsverband *m*.

plastered ['plɑːstəd] *adj pred (col: drunk)* voll *(col)*. **to get ~** sich vollaufen lassen *(col)*.

plasterer ['plɑːstərəʳ] *n* Gipser, Stukkateur *m*.

plastic ['plæstɪk] **1** *n* Plastik *nt or f*. **~s** Kunststoffe *pl*. **2** *adj (lit, fig)* Plastik-; *food also* synthetisch. **the ~ arts** die gestaltenden Künste.

plastic: ~ **bag** *n* Plastiktüte *f*; ~ **bullet** *n* Plastikgeschoß *nt*; ~ **explosive** *n* Plastiksprengstoff *m*.

plasticine ® ['plæstɪsiːn] *n* Plastilin *nt*.

plastic: ~ **money** *n* Plastikgeld *nt*; ~ **surgery** *n* plastische Chirurgie; *(esp facial also)* Schönheitsoperation *f*; **he had to have ~ surgery** er mußte sich einer Gesichtsoperation unterziehen.

plate [pleɪt] **1** *n* **(a)** *(also ~ful)* Teller *m*. **cold ~** kalte Platte; **to have sth handed to one on a ~** *(fig col)* etw auf einem Tablett serviert bekommen *(col)*; **to have a lot on one's ~** *(fig col)* viel am Hals haben *(col)*. **(b)** *(gold, silver)* Tafelsilber *nt*; Tafelgold *nt*; *(~d metal)* vergoldetes/versilbertes Metall. **(c)** *(Tech, Phot, Typ)* Platte *f*; *(name~, number~)* Schild *nt*. **(d)** *(illustration)* Tafel *f*. **(e)** *(dental ~)* (Gaumen)platte *f*. **2** *vt (with armour-plating)* panzern. **to ~ (with gold/silver/nickel)** vergolden/-silbern/-nickeln.

plateau ['plætəʊ] *n, pl* **-s** *or* **-x** *(Geog)* Plateau *nt*, Hochebene *f*. **prices have reached a ~** die Preise haben sich eingependelt.

plate glass *n* Tafelglas *nt*.

plate rack *n (Brit)* Geschirrständer *m*.

platform ['plætfɔːm] *n* **(a)** Plattform *f*; *(stage)* Podium *nt*, Bühne *f*. **(b)** *(Rail)* Bahnsteig *m*. **from**

~ 7 von Gleis 7. **(c)** *(Pol)* Plattform *f.*

platform: ~ **shoe** *n* Plateauschuh *m;* ~ **ticket** *n* Bahnsteigkarte *f.*

plating ['pleɪtɪŋ] *n (act)* Vergolden *nt;* Versilbern *nt; (material)* Auflage *f; (armour-~)* Panzerung *f.*

platinum ['plætɪnəm] *n* Platin *nt.* **a ~ blonde** eine Platinblonde.

platitude ['plætɪtjuːd] *n* Platitüde, Plattheit *f.*

platonic [plə'tɒnɪk] *adj love, friendship* platonisch.

platoon [plə'tuːn] *n (Mil)* Zug *m.*

platter ['plætə[r]] *n* Teller *m; (wooden ~ also)* Brett *nt; (serving dish)* Platte *f.*

plausible ['plɔːzəbl] *adj* plausibel; *argument also* einleuchtend; *story, excuse also* glaubwürdig.

play [pleɪ] **1** *n* **(a)** Spiel *nt.* **to be at ~** beim Spielen sein; **to do/say sth in ~** etw aus Spaß tun/sagen; **~ on words** Wortspiel *nt;* **children at ~** spielende Kinder; **to abandon ~** das Spiel abbrechen; **there was some exciting ~ towards the end** gegen Ende gab es einige spannende (Spiel)szenen; **to be in/out of ~** *(ball)* im Spiel/im Aus sein. **(b)** *(Tech, Mech)* Spiel *nt.* **1 mm (of) ~** 1 mm Spiel. **(c)** *(Theat)* (Theater)stück *nt; (Rad)* Hörspiel *nt; (TV)* Fernsehspiel *nt.* **(d)** *(fig phrases)* **to come into ~** ins Spiel kommen; **to give full ~ to one's imagination** seiner Phantasie *(dat)* freien Lauf lassen; **to bring** *or* **call sth into ~** etw einsetzen; **to make great ~ of sth** viel Aufhebens von etw machen.

2 *vt game, card, role, instrument, tune* spielen; *(direct) light, hose* richten. **to ~ sb (at a game)** gegen jdn (ein Spiel) spielen; **to ~ ball** *(fig)* mitmachen; **to ~ a joke on sb** jdm einen Streich spielen; **to ~ a mean trick on sb** jdn auf gemeine Art hereinlegen; **to ~ the piano** Klavier spielen.

3 *vi* spielen; *(fountain)* laufen. **to go out to ~** rausgehen und spielen; **to ~ with the idea of doing sth** mit dem Gedanken spielen, etw zu tun; **we don't have much time/money to ~ with** wir haben zeitlich/finanziell nicht viel Spielraum; **he wouldn't ~** *(fig col)* er wollte nicht mitspielen *(col);* **he was ~ing at being angry** seine Wut war gespielt; **he's just ~ing at it** er tut nur so; **what are you ~ing at?** *(col)* was soll (denn) das? *(col);* **to ~ for money** um Geld spielen; **to ~ for time** *(fig)* Zeit gewinnen wollen; **to ~ into sb's hands** *(fig)* jdm in die Hände spielen; **to ~ to sb** jdm vorspielen; **the firemen's hoses ~ed on the flames** die Schläuche der Feuerwehrmänner waren auf die Flammen gerichtet; **the searchlights ~ed over the roofs** die Suchscheinwerfer strichen über die Dächer; **it's playing at the Old Vic next week** *(Theat)* es läuft nächste Woche im Old Vic.

♦ **play about** *or* **around** *vi* spielen. **to ~ ~ with sth/an idea** mit etw/einer Idee spielen.

♦ **play along 1** *vi* mitspielen. **he ~ed ~ with the system** er arrangierte sich mit dem System. **2** *vt sep* ein falsches Spiel spielen mit; *(in order to gain time)* hinhalten.

♦ **play back** *vt sep tape recording* abspielen. **the conversation was ~ed ~ to us** man spielte uns *(dat)* das Gespräch vor.

♦ **play down** *vt sep* herunterspielen.

♦ **play off** *vt sep* **to ~ X ~ against Y** X gegen Y ausspielen; **he was ~ing them ~ against each other** er spielte sie gegeneinander aus.

♦ **play on 1** *vi* weiterspielen. **2** *vi +prep obj sb's fears, good nature* geschickt ausnutzen. **the author is ~ing ~ words** der Autor spielt mit Worten.

♦ **play out** *vt sep* **(a)** *(Theat) scene* darstellen. **(b) to be ~ed ~** *(mine)* ausgebeutet sein; *(joke etc)* abgedroschen sein. **(c)** *(Mus: accompany)* mit Musik hinausgeleiten.

♦ **play through** *vi +prep obj* durchspielen.

♦ **play up 1** *vi* **(a)** *(Brit col: cause trouble: car, child)* verrückt spielen *(col).* **(b)** *(col: flatter)* **to ~ ~ to sb** jdn umschmeicheln. **2** *vt sep (col)* **(a)** *(cause trouble to)* **to ~ sb ~** jdm Schwierigkeiten machen. **(b)** *(exaggerate)* hochspielen.

play: ~**-act** *vi* Theater spielen; ~**-acting** *n (fig)* Theater(spiel) *nt;* ~**back** *n (switch, recording)* Wiedergabe *f;* ~**boy** *n* Playboy *m.*

player ['pleɪə[r]] *n (Sport, Mus)* Spieler(in *f*) *m; (Theat)* Schauspieler(in *f*) *m.*

playful ['pleɪfʊl] *adj* neckisch; *child, animal* verspielt, munter.

play: ~**ground** *n* Spielplatz *m; (Sch)* (Schul)hof *m;* ~**group** *n* Spielgruppe *f;* ~**house** *n* **(a)** *(US: doll's house)* Puppenstube *f;* **(b)** *(Theat)* Schauspielhaus *nt.*

playing ['pleɪɪŋ]: ~ **card** *n* Spielkarte *f;* ~ **field** *n* Sportplatz *m.*

play: ~**mate** *n* Spielkamerad(in *f*) *m;* ~**-off** *n* Entscheidungsspiel *nt; (extra time)* Verlängerung *f;* ~**pen** *n* Laufstall *m;* ~**room** *n* Spielzimmer *nt;* ~ **school** *n* Kindergarten *m;* ~**thing** *n (lit, fig)* Spielzeug *nt;* ~**time** *n* Zeit *f* zum Spielen; *(Sch)* große Pause.

playwright ['pleɪraɪt] *n* Dramatiker(in *f*) *m; (contemporary also)* Stückeschreiber(in *f*) *m.*

plea [pliː] *n* **(a)** Bitte *f; (general appeal)* Appell *m.* **to make a ~ for sth** zu etw aufrufen; **to make a ~ for leniency** um Milde bitten. **(b)** *(Jur)* Plädoyer *nt.* **to enter a ~ of guilty/not guilty** ein Geständnis ablegen/seine Unschuld erklären.

plead [pliːd] *pret, ptp* ~**ed** *or (Scot, US)* **pled 1** *vt* **(a)** *(argue)* vertreten. **to ~ sb's case, to ~ the case for sb** *(Jur)* jdn vertreten; **to ~ the case for sth** *(fig)* sich für etw einsetzen; **to ~ sb's cause** *(fig)* für jds Sache eintreten. **(b)** *(as excuse) ignorance* sich berufen auf *(+acc).* **2** *vi* **(a)** *(beg)* bitten, nachsuchen *(for* um*).* **to ~ with sb to do sth** jdn bitten *or* ersuchen *(geh),* etw zu tun. **(b)** *(Jur) (counsel)* das Plädoyer halten. **to ~ guilty/not guilty** sich schuldig/nicht schuldig bekennen; **to ~ for sth** *(fig)* für etw plädieren.

pleading ['pliːdɪŋ] **1** *n* Bitten *nt; (Jur)* Plädoyer *nt.* **2** *adj look, voice* flehend.

pleasant ['pleznt] *adj* angenehm; *news* erfreulich; *person also, face* nett; *smile* freundlich.

pleasantry ['plezntrɪ] *n (joking remark)* Scherz *m; (polite remark)* Nettigkeit *f.*

please [pliːz] **1** *interj* bitte. **(yes,) ~** *(acceptance)* (ja,) bitte; *(enthusiastic)* oh ja, gerne; **pass the salt, ~** würden Sie mir bitte das Salz reichen?; **may I? — ~ do!** darf ich? — bitte sehr!

2 *vi* **(a) if you ~** *(form: in request)* wenn ich darum bitten darf; **and then, if you ~, he tried ...** und dann, stell dir vor, versuchte er ...; **(just) as you ~** ganz wie Sie wollen; **to do as one ~s** machen *or* tun, was einem gefällt. **(b)** *(cause satisfaction)* gefallen. **anxious** *or* **eager to ~** darum bemüht, alles richtig zu machen.

3 *vt (give pleasure to)* eine Freude machen *(+dat); (satisfy)* zufriedenstellen; *(do as sb wants)* gefällig sein *(+dat).* **it ~s me to see him so happy** es freut mich, daß er so glücklich ist; **you can't ~ everybody** man kann es nicht allen recht machen; **there's no pleasing him** er ist nie zufrieden; **to be hard to ~** schwer zufriedenzustellen sein; **I was only too ~d to help** es war mir wirklich eine Freude zu helfen.

4 *vr* **to ~ oneself** tun, was einem gefällt; **~ yourself, then!** wie Sie wollen!; **you can ~ yourself where you sit** es ist Ihnen überlassen, wo Sie sitzen.

pleased [pliːzd] *adj (happy)* erfreut; *(satisfied)* zufrieden. **to be ~ (about sth)** sich (über etw *acc*) freuen; **I'm ~ to hear that ...** es freut mich zu hören, daß ...; **~ to meet you** angenehm *(form),* freut mich; **to be ~ with sb/sth** mit jdm/etw zufrieden sein.

pleasing ['pliːzɪŋ] *adj* angenehm.

pleasurable ['plezərəbl] *adj* angenehm.

pleasure ['pleʒəʳ] *n* **(a)** Freude *f.* **it's a ~, (my) ~** gern (geschehen)!; **with ~** gern, mit Vergnügen *(form)*; **it gives me great ~ to be here** *(form)* es ist mir eine große Freude, hier zu sein; **it would give me great ~ to ...** es wäre mir ein Vergnügen, zu ...; **to have the ~ of doing sth** das Vergnügen haben, etw zu tun; **Mrs X requests the ~ of Mr Y's company** *(form)* Frau X gibt sich die Ehre, Herrn Y einzuladen *(form)*. **(b)** *(source of ~)* Vergnügen *nt.* **he's a ~ to teach** es ist ein Vergnügen, ihn zu unterrichten; **the ~s of country life** die Freuden des Landlebens; **all the ~s of London** alle Vergnügungen Londons. **(c)** *(iro, form: will)* Wunsch *m.* **at one's ~** nach Belieben; **to await sb's ~** abwarten, was jd zu tun geruht.

pleasure *in cpds* Vergnügungs-; **~ boat** *n (steamer)* Vergnügungsdampfer *m*; **~-loving** *adj* lebenslustig, leichtlebig *(pej)*.

pleat [pliːt] **1** *n* Falte *f.* **2** *vt* fälteln.

pleb [pleb] *n (pej col)* Plebejer(in *f*) *(pej)*, Prolet(in *f*) *(pej col) m.*

pled [pled] *(US, Scot) pret, ptp of* **plead.**

pledge [pledʒ] **1** *n (in pawnshop, of love)* Pfand *nt*; *(promise)* Versprechen *nt.* **as a ~ of** als Zeichen *(+gen)*; **under (the) ~ of secrecy** unter dem Siegel der Verschwiegenheit; **election ~s** Wahlversprechen *pl*; **to sign** *or* **take the ~** *(hum col)* dem Alkohol abschwören *(usu hum)*. **2** *vt* **(a)** *(give as security, pawn)* verpfänden. **(b)** *(promise)* versprechen, zusichern. **to ~ one's word** sein Wort geben; **to ~ support for sb/sth** jdm/einer Sache seine Unterstützung zusichern; **I am ~d to secrecy** ich bin zum Schweigen verpflichtet.

plenary ['pliːnərɪ] *adj* **~ session** Plenarsitzung *f*; **~ powers** unbeschränkte Vollmachten *pl.*

plenipotentiary [ˌplenɪpə'tenʃərɪ] *n* (General)bevollmächtigte(r) *mf.*

plentiful ['plentɪfʊl] *adj* reichlich; *commodities, gold etc* reichlich vorhanden; *hair* voll. **to be in ~ supply** im Überfluß vorhanden sein.

plenty ['plentɪ] *n* **(a)** eine Menge. **land of ~** Land des Überflusses; **times of ~** Zeiten des Überflusses; **in ~** im Überfluß; **three kilos will be ~** drei Kilo sind reichlich; **take ~** nimm dir reichlich; **there are still ~ left** es sind immer noch eine ganze Menge da. **(b) ~ of** viel, eine Menge; **~ of time/milk/eggs** viel *or* eine Menge Zeit/Milch/viele *or* eine Menge Eier; **a country with ~ of natural resources** ein Land mit umfangreichen Bodenschätzen; **we arrived in ~ of time to get a good seat** wir kamen so rechtzeitig, daß wir einen guten Platz bekamen.

pleurisy ['plʊərɪsɪ] *n* Brustfellentzündung *f.*

pliable ['plaɪəbl] *adj* biegsam; *leather* geschmeidig; *mind, person* formbar.

pliers ['plaɪəz] *npl (also* **pair of ~***)* Zange *f.*

plight [plaɪt] *n* Not *f*, Elend *nt*; *(of economy etc)* Verfall *m.*

plimsoll ['plɪmsəl] *n (Brit)* Turnschuh *m.*

plinth [plɪnθ] *n* Sockel *m.*

plod [plɒd] *vi* **to ~ up a hill** einen Hügel hinaufstapfen; **to ~ along** *or* **on** weiterstapfen; **to ~ away at sth** sich mit etw herumquälen.

plodder ['plɒdəʳ] *n* zähe(r) Arbeiter(in *f*) *m.*

plonk[1] [plɒŋk] **1** *n* Bums *m.* **it fell with a ~ to the floor** es fiel mit einem Bums auf den Boden. **2** *adv fall, land* bums. **3** *vt (col: also* **~ down***) (drop, put down)* hinschmeißen *(col)*; *(bang down)* hinknallen *(col)*. **to ~ oneself (down)** sich hinpflanzen *(col)*.

plonk[2] *n (Brit col: wine)* (billiger) Wein, Gesöff *nt (hum, pej)*.

plop [plɒp] **1** *n* Plumps *m*; *(in water)* Platsch *m.* **2** *vi (make a plopping sound)* platschen.

plot [plɒt] **1** *n* **(a)** *(Agr)* Stück *nt* Land; *(bed: in garden)* Beet *nt*; *(building ~)* Grundstück *nt*; *(allotment)* Schrebergarten *m.* **a ~ of land** ein Stück *nt* Land. **(b)** *(conspiracy)* Komplott *nt.* **(c)** *(Liter, Theat)* Handlung *f.* **2** *vt* **(a)** *(plan)* planen, aushecken *(col)*. **they ~ted to kill him** sie planten gemeinsam, ihn zu töten. **(b)** *position, course* feststellen; *(draw on map)* einzeichnen; *(Math, Med) curve* aufzeichnen. **3** *vi* sich verschwören.

plough, *(US)* **plow** [plaʊ] **1** *n* Pflug *m.* **the P~** *(Astron)* der Wagen. **2** *vt* pflügen.

♦ **plough back** *vt sep (Agr)* unterpflügen; *(Comm) profits* wieder hineinstecken *(into* in *+acc)*.

♦ **plough up** *vt sep field* umpflügen.

plough, *(US)* **plow: ~land** *n* Ackerland *nt*; **~man** *n* Pflüger *m*; **~man's lunch** ≈ Käsebrot *nt.*

ploy [plɔɪ] *n (stratagem)* Trick *m.*

pluck [plʌk] **1** *n (courage)* Mut *m.* **2** *vt fruit, flower* pflücken; *chicken* rupfen; *guitar, eyebrows* zupfen. **to ~ (at) sb's sleeve** jdn am Ärmel zupfen; **to ~ up courage** all seinen Mut zusammennehmen.

plucky ['plʌkɪ] *adj (+er) person, smile* tapfer; *action, person* mutig.

plug [plʌg] **1** *n* **(a)** *(in sink)* Stöpsel *m*; *(for stopping a leak, in barrel)* Propfen *m.* **(b)** *(Elec)* Stecker *m*; *(Aut: spark ~)* (Zünd)kerze *f.* **(c)** *(col: piece of publicity)* Schleichwerbung *f no pl.* **to give sb/sth a ~** für jdn/etw Schleichwerbung machen. **2** *vt* **(a)** *(stop) gap, leak* zustopfen. **(b)** *(insert)* stecken. **(c)** *(col: publicize)* Schleichwerbung machen für *(col)*. **(d)** *(col: push, put forward) idea* hausieren gehen mit.

♦ **plug away** *vi (col)* ackern *(col)*. **to ~ ~ at sth** sich mit etw abrackern *(col)*; **he kept ~ging ~** er hat nicht lockergelassen.

♦ **plug in 1** *vt sep TV, heater etc* einstöpseln, anschließen. **to be ~ged ~** angeschlossen sein. **2** *vi* sich anschließen lassen. **where does the TV ~ ~?** wo wird der Fernseher angeschlossen?

plughole ['plʌghəʊl] *n* Abfluß(loch *nt*) *m.*

plum [plʌm] **1** *n* **(a)** *(fruit, tree)* Pflaume *f*; *(Victoria ~, dark blue)* Zwetsch(g)e *f.* **(b)** *(colour)* Pflaumenblau *nt.* **(c)** *(fig col)* **a real ~ (of a job)** ein Bombenjob *(col)*. **2** *adj attr (col) job, position* Bomben- *(col)*, Mords- *(col)*.

plumage ['pluːmɪdʒ] *n* Gefieder *nt.*

plumb [plʌm] **1** *n (~-line)* Lot *nt.* **out of ~** nicht im Lot. **2** *adv (col) (completely)* total *(col)*; *(exactly)* genau. **~ crazy** vollkommen *or* total *(col)* verrückt; **~ in the middle** (haar)genau in der Mitte. **3** *vt* **(a)** *ocean, depth* (aus)loten. **(b)** *(fig) mystery etc* ergründen. **to ~ the depths of despair** die tiefste Verzweiflung erleben.

plumb bob *n* Lot, Senkblei *nt.*

plumber ['plʌməʳ] *n* Installateur, Klempner *m.*

plumbing ['plʌmɪŋ] *n* **(a)** *(work)* Installieren *nt.* **(b)** *(fittings)* Rohre, Leitungen *pl.*

plumbline ['plʌmlaɪn] *n* Lot.

plume [pluːm] *n* Feder *f*; *(on helmet)* Federbusch *m.* **~ of smoke** Rauchwolke *f.*

plummet ['plʌmɪt] *vi (bird, plane etc)* hinunter-/herunterstürzen; *(sales)* stark zurückgehen; *(currency)* fallen, absacken *(to* auf *+acc)*.

plump [plʌmp] *adj (+er)* rundlich, pummelig *(col)*; *legs etc* stämmig; *face* rundlich, voll.

♦ **plump for** *vi +prep obj* sich entscheiden für.

♦ **plump up** *vt sep pillow* aufschütteln; *chicken* mästen.

plunder ['plʌndəʳ] **1** *n* **(a)** *(act) (of place)* Plünderung *f*; *(of things)* Raub *m.* **(b)** *(loot)* Beute *f.* **2** *vt place* plündern *(also hum)*.

plunge [plʌndʒ] **1** *vt* **(a)** *(thrust)* stecken; *(into water etc)* tauchen. **he ~d his knife into his victim's back** er jagte seinem Opfer das Messer in den Rücken. **(b)** *(fig)* **to ~ the country into debt** das Land in Schulden stürzen; **the room was/we were ~d into darkness** das Zimmer war in Dunkelheit getaucht/tiefe Dunkelheit umfing uns.

2 *vi* **(a)** *(dive)* tauchen; *(goalkeeper)* hechten.

(b) *(rush, esp downward)* stürzen. **to ~ to one's death** zu Tode stürzen. **(c)** *(share prices, currency etc)* stark fallen. **(d)** *(fig: into debate, studies etc)* sich stürzen *(into* in *+acc)*.

3 *vr (into studies, job etc)* sich stürzen *(into in +acc)*.

4 *n (lit, fig)* Sturz *m*; *(dive)* (Kopf)sprung *m*. **to take the ~** *(fig col)* den Sprung wagen.

plunger ['plʌndʒəʳ] *n* **(a)** *(piston)* Tauchkolben *m*. **(b)** *(for clearing drain)* Sauger *m*.

plunging ['plʌndʒɪŋ] *adj neckline, back* tief ausgeschnitten.

pluperfect ['pluː'pɜːfɪkt] *n* Plusquamperfekt *nt*.

plural ['plʊərəl] **1** *adj (Gram)* Mehrzahl-, Plural-. **2** *n* Mehrzahl *f*, Plural *m*. **in the ~** im Plural, in der Mehrzahl.

plus [plʌs] **1** *prep* plus *(+dat)*; *(together with)* und (außerdem). **2** *adj* **~ sign** Pluszeichen *nt*; **a ~ factor** ein Pluspunkt *m*; **on the ~ side** auf der Habenseite; **50 hours ~ a week** mehr als 50 Stunden pro Woche. **3** *n (sign)* Pluszeichen *nt*; *(positive factor)* Pluspunkt *m*; *(extra)* Plus *nt*.

plush [plʌʃ] **1** *n* Plüsch *m*. **2** *adj (+er) (col: luxurious)* feudal *(col)*; *hotel also* Nobel-; *furnishing also* elegant, vornehm.

Pluto ['pluːtəʊ] *n (Astron)* Pluto *m*.

plutocrat ['pluːtəʊkræt] *n* Plutokrat(in *f*) *m*.

plutonium [pluː'təʊnɪəm] *n* Plutonium *nt*.

ply[1] [plaɪ] *n* **three-~** *wood* dreischichtig; *wool* dreifädig; *tissues* dreilagig.

ply[2] **1** *vt* **(a)** *tool, brush etc* gebrauchen; *oars* einsetzen. **(b)** *trade* ausüben, betreiben. **(c)** *(ships) sea, river* befahren. **(d) to ~ sb with questions** jdn mit Fragen überhäufen; **to ~ sb with drink(s)** jdn immer wieder zum Trinken auffordern. **2** *vi (ship)* **to ~ between** verkehren zwischen; **to ~ for hire** seine Dienste anbieten.

plywood ['plaɪwʊd] *n* Sperrholz *nt*.

PM = **Prime Minister.**

pm = **post meridiem** p.m.

pneumatic [njuː'mætɪk] *adj* Luft-. **~ drill** Preßluftbohrer *m*.

pneumonia [njuː'məʊnɪə] *n* Lungenentzündung *f*.

PO = **post office; postal order.**

poach[1] [pəʊtʃ] *vt egg* pochieren; *fish* (blau) dünsten. **~ed eggs** verlorene Eier.

poach[2] *vti* wildern *(for* auf *+acc)*; *ideas etc* klauen *(col)*. **to ~ (on sb's territory)** jdm ins Gehege kommen.

poacher ['pəʊtʃəʳ] *n* Wilderer *m*.

poaching ['pəʊtʃɪŋ] *n* Wildern *nt*, Wilderei *f*.

pocket ['pɒkɪt] **1** *n* **(a)** *(in garment)* Tasche *f*. **to have sb/sth in one's ~** *(fig)* jdn/etw in der Tasche haben *(col)*. **(b)** *(receptacle: in suitcase, file etc)* Fach *nt*; *(Billiards)* Loch *nt*. **to be a drain on one's ~** jds Geldbeutel strapazieren *(col)*; **to be in ~** auf sein Geld kommen *(col)*; **I was £100 in ~ after the sale** nach dem Verkauf war ich um £ 100 reicher; **they live in each others ~s** sie hängen ständig zusammen *(col)*; **to put one's hand in one's ~** tief in die Tasche greifen; **~ of resistance** Widerstandsnest *nt*. **2** *adj comb, edition* Taschen-. **3** *vt* **(a)** *(put in one's pocket)* einstecken. **to ~ one's pride** seinen Stolz überwinden. **(b)** *(gain)* kassieren; *(misappropriate)* einstecken *(col)*.

pocket: ~-book *n* **(a)** *(notebook)* Notizbuch *nt*; **(b)** *(wallet)* Brieftasche *f*; **(c)** *(US: handbag)* Handtasche *f*; **~ calculator** *n* Taschenrechner *m*; **~ handkerchief** *n* Taschentuch *nt*; **~-knife** *n* Taschenmesser *nt*; **~-money** *n* Taschengeld *nt*; **~-size(d)** *adj book* im Taschenformat; *camera* Miniatur-.

pockmarked ['pɒkmɑːkt] *adj face* pockennarbig; *surface* narbig.

pod [pɒd] *n (Bot)* Hülse *f*; *(of peas also)* Schote *f*.

podgy ['pɒdʒɪ] *adj (+er)* rundlich, pummelig; *face* schwammig.

podiatrist [pɒ'diːətrɪst] *n (US)* Fußspezialist(in *f*) *m*.

podium ['pəʊdɪəm] *n* Podest *nt*.

poem ['pəʊɪm] *n* Gedicht *nt*.

poet ['pəʊɪt] *n* Dichter(in *f*) *m*.

poetic [pəʊ'etɪk *adj* poetisch; *talent also* dichterisch; *place* malerisch. **~ justice** poetische Gerechtigkeit; **~ licence** *(Brit) or* **license** *(US)* dichterische Freiheit.

poetry ['pəʊɪtrɪ] *n* Dichtung *f*. **to write ~** Gedichte schreiben; **~ reading** Dichterlesung *f*.

poignancy ['pɔɪnjənsɪ] *n see adj* Ergreifende(s) *nt*; Wehmut *f*; Schmerzlichkeit *f*; Schärfe *f*. **he writes with great ~** er schreibt sehr ergreifend.

poignant ['pɔɪnjənt] *adj* ergreifend; *memories, look* wehmütig; *distress, regret* schmerzlich; *wit* scharf.

point [pɔɪnt] **1** *n* **(a)** Punkt *m*; *(place also)* Stelle *f*; *(sharp end)* Spitze *f*; *(on thermometer)* Grad *m*. **(nought) ~ seven (0.7)** null Komma sieben (0,7); **from all ~s (of the compass)** aus allen (Himmels)richtungen; **up to a ~** bis zu einem gewissen Grad *or* Punkt; **at the ~ of a gun** mit vorgehaltener Pistole; **not to put too fine a ~ on it** *(fig)* um ganz offen zu sein; **the train stops at Slough and all ~s east** der Zug hält in Slough und allen Orten östlich davon; **~ of departure** *(lit, fig)* Ausgangspunkt *m*; **~ of view** Gesichtspunkt *m*; **from my ~ of view** aus meiner Sicht; **from the ~ of view of productivity** von der Produktivität her gesehen; **at this ~** *(spatially)* an dieser Stelle; *(in time) (then)* in diesem Augenblick; *(now)* jetzt; **from that ~ on they were friends** von da an waren sie Freunde; **at no ~** nie; **at no ~ in the book** an keiner Stelle des Buches; **to be (up)on the ~ of doing sth** im Begriff sein, etw zu tun; **to reach the ~ of no return** *(fig)* den Punkt erreichen, von dem an es kein Zurück gibt; **they provoked him to the ~ where he lost his temper** sie reizten ihn so lange, bis er die Geduld verlor; **severe to the ~ of cruelty** streng bis an die Grenze der Grausamkeit; **when it comes to the ~** wenn es darauf ankommt; **to win on ~s** nach Punkten gewinnen; **the ~ at issue** der strittige Punkt; **a 12-~ plan** ein Zwölfpunkte-Plan *m*; **a ~ of interest** ein interessanter Punkt; **to come to the ~** zur Sache kommen; **to keep to the ~** beim Thema bleiben; **beside the ~** irrelevant; **his remarks are very much to the ~** seine Bemerkungen sind sehr sachbezogen; **my ~ was ...** was ich sagen wollte, war ...; **to make a ~** ein Argument *nt* anbringen; **he made the ~ that ...** er betonte, daß ...; **you have a ~ there** darin mögen Sie recht haben, da ist etwas dran *(col)*; **I take your ~, ~ taken** ich habe schon begriffen; **to gain** *or* **carry one's ~** sich durchsetzen; **to get** *or* **see the ~** verstehen, worum es geht; **to miss the ~** nicht verstehen, worum es geht; **he missed the ~ of what I was saying** er hat nicht begriffen, worauf ich hinauswollte; **that's not the ~** darum geht es nicht; **that's the whole ~** das ist es ja gerade; **a case in ~** ein einschlägiger Fall; **the case in ~** der zur Debatte stehende Punkt; **to make a ~ of sth** auf etw *(acc)* Wert legen; **he made a special ~ of being early** er legte besonderen Wert darauf, früh dazusein; **a ~ of principle** eine grundsätzliche Frage; **a ~ of order** eine Frage der Geschäftsordnung; **good/bad ~s** *(characteristics)* gute/schlechte Seiten *pl*; **he has his ~s** er hat auch seine guten Seiten.

(b) *(purpose)* Zweck, Sinn *m*. **there's no ~ in staying** es hat keinen Zweck *or* Sinn zu bleiben; **I don't see the ~ of carrying on** ich sehe keinen Sinn darin, weiterzumachen; **what's the ~?** was soll's?; **the ~ is that ...** die Sache ist die, daß ...; **the ~ of the story** die Pointe (der Geschichte).

(c) ~s *pl (Brit Rail)* Weichen *pl*.

(d) *(Aut: usu pl)* Unterbrecherkontakte *pl.* **(e)** *(Brit Elec)* Steckdose *f.*

2 *vt* **(a)** *(aim, direct) gun, telescope etc* richten *(at* auf *+acc).* **he ~ed his stick in the direction of the house** er zeigte mit dem Stock auf das Haus. **(b)** *(mark, show)* zeigen. **to ~ the way** *(lit, fig)* den Weg weisen. **(c)** *(Build) wall, brickwork* verfugen.

3 *vi* **(a)** *(with finger etc)* zeigen, deuten *(at, to* auf *+acc).* **he ~ed in the direction of the house/towards the house** er zeigte in die Richtung des Hauses/zum Haus; **the compass needle ~s (to the) north** die Kompaßnadel zeigt nach Norden. **(b)** *(indicate, point out)* hinweisen; *(facts, events also)* hindeuten *(to* auf *+acc).* **everything ~s that way** alles weist in diese Richtung. **(c)** *(face, be situated: building, valley etc)* liegen; *(be aimed: gun, vehicle etc)* gerichtet sein. **in which direction is it ~ing?** in welche Richtung zeigt es?

♦ **point out** *vt sep* zeigen auf *(+acc).* **could you ~ him ~ to me?** kannst du mir zeigen, wer er ist?; **to ~ sth ~ (to sb)** (jdn) auf etw *(acc)* hinweisen; **she ~ed ~ that ...** sie wies darauf hin, daß ...

♦ **point up** *vt sep (emphasize)* betonen.

point-blank ['pɔɪnt'blæŋk] **1** *adj* direkt; *refusal* glatt. **at ~ range** aus kürzester Entfernung. **2** *adv fire* aus kürzester Entfernung; *refuse* rundheraus.

pointed ['pɔɪntɪd] *adj* **(a)** *(sharp) stick, roof, nose* spitz; *window, arch* spitzbogig. **(b)** *(obvious in intention) remark, comment* scharf, spitz; *reference* unverblümt; *gesture, departure* ostentativ.

pointer ['pɔɪntəʳ] *n* **(a)** *(indicator)* Zeiger *m*; *(stick)* Zeigestock *m.* **(b)** *(dog)* Pointer, Vorstehhund *m.* **(c)** *(fig)* Hinweis *m*; *(indication also)* Anzeichen *nt.* **a ~ to a possible solution** ein Hinweis auf eine mögliche Lösung.

pointless ['pɔɪntlɪs] *adj* sinnlos.

point duty *n* Verkehrsdienst *m.*

poise [pɔɪz] **1** *n* **(a)** *(carriage of head, body)* Haltung *f*; *(grace)* Grazie *f.* **(b)** *(composure)* Gelassenheit *f*; *(self-possession)* Selbstsicherheit *f.* **2** *vt (balance, hold balanced)* balancieren. **we sat ~d on the edge of our chairs** wir balancierten auf den Stuhlkanten; **the enemy are ~d to attack** der Feind steht bereit zum Angriff.

poison ['pɔɪzn] **1** *n (lit, fig)* Gift *nt.* **to hate sb like ~** jdn wie die Pest hassen *(col).* **2** *vt (lit, fig)* vergiften; *air, rivers* verpesten; *marriage* zerrütten. **it won't ~ you** *(col)* das wird dich nicht umbringen *(col)*; **to ~ sb's mind against sb/sth** jdn gegen jdn/etw aufstacheln.

poison gas *n* Giftgas *nt.*

poisoning ['pɔɪznɪŋ] *n (lit, fig)* Vergiftung *f.*

poison ivy *n* Giftefeu *m.*

poisonous ['pɔɪznəs] *adj* **(a)** giftig; *snake, plants etc also* Gift-. **(b)** *(fig) literature, doctrine* zersetzend; *remark etc* giftig; *propaganda also* Hetz-. **she has a ~ tongue** sie hat eine giftige Zunge.

poke [pəʊk] **1** *n (jab)* Stoß, Schubs *(col) m.* **2** *vt* **(a)** *(jab with stick)* stoßen; *(with finger)* stupsen. **to ~ the fire** das Feuer schüren; **he accidentally ~d me in the eye** er hat mir aus Versehen ins Auge gestoßen. **(b)** *(US col: punch)* hauen *(col).* **(c)** *(thrust)* **to ~ one's head/a stick into sth** seinen Kopf/einen Stock in etw *(acc)* stecken; **he ~d his head around the door** er steckte seinen Kopf durch die Tür. **(d)** *(make by poking) hole* bohren. **3** *vi* **his elbows were poking through his sleeves** an seinen Ärmeln kamen schon die Ellenbogen durch; **to ~ at sth** *(testing)* etw prüfen; *(searching)* in etw *(dat)* stochern; **well, if you will go poking into things that don't concern you ...** na ja, wenn du deine Nase ständig in Dinge steckst, die dich nichts angehen ...

♦ **poke about** *or* **around** *vi* **(a)** *(prod)* herumstochern. **(b)** *(col: nose about)* schnüffeln *(col).*

♦ **poke out 1** *vi* vorstehen. **2** *vt sep* **to ~ sb's eye ~** jdm das Auge ausstechen.

poker[1] ['pəʊkəʳ] *n (for fire)* Schürhaken *m.*

poker[2] *n (Cards)* Poker *nt.*

poker-faced ['pəʊkə,feɪst] *adj* mit einem Pokergesicht; *(bored)* mit unbewegter Miene.

poky ['pəʊkɪ] *adj (+er) (pej) room, house* winzig. **it's so ~ in here** es ist so eng hier.

Poland ['pəʊlənd] *n* Polen *nt.*

polar ['pəʊləʳ] *adj* **(a)** Polar-, polar. **~ bear** Polar- *or* Eisbär *m.* **(b) they are ~ opposites** sie sind absolute Gegensätze.

polarity [pəʊ'lærɪtɪ] *n (Phys, fig)* Polarität *f.*

polarization [,pəʊləraɪzeɪʃən] *n (Phys)* Polarisation *f*; *(fig)* Polarisierung *f.*

polarize ['pəʊləraɪz] **1** *vt* polarisieren. **2** *vi* sich polarisieren.

Pole [pəʊl] *n* Pole *m*, Polin *f.*

pole[1] [pəʊl] *n* Stange *f*; *(flag~, telegraph ~ also)* Mast *m*; *(for vaulting)* Stab *m.*

pole[2] *n (Geog, Astron, Elec)* Pol *m.* **they are ~s apart** sie *(acc)* trennen Welten.

polecat ['pəʊlkæt] *n* Iltis *m*; *(US)* Skunk *m*, Stinktier *nt.*

polemic [pɒ'lemɪk] **1** *adj* polemisch. **2** *n* Polemik *f.*

pole: ~star *n* Polarstern *m*; **~ vault 1** *n* Stabhochsprung *m*; **2** *vi* stabhochspringen.

police [pə'liːs] **1** *n (+sing vb: institution, +pl vb: policemen)* Polizei *f.* **hundreds of ~** Hunderte von Polizisten; **extra ~ were called in** es wurden zusätzliche Polizeikräfte angefordert. **2** *vt road, frontier* kontrollieren.

police: ~ car *n* Polizeiwagen *m*; **~ constable** *n (Brit)* Polizist *m*; **~ dog** *n* Polizeihund *m*; **~ escort** *n* Polizeieskorte *f*; **~ force** *n* Polizei *f*; **~man** *n* Polizist *m*; **~ officer** *n* Polizeibeamter *m*; **~ record** *n* **to have a ~ record** vorbestraft sein; **~ station** *n* (Polizei)wache *f*; **~woman** *n* Polizistin *f.*

policy[1] ['pɒlɪsɪ] *n* Politik *f no pl*; *(of business also)* Geschäftspolitik *f no pl (on* bei*)*, Praktiken *pl (pej) (on* in bezug auf *+acc)*; *(of government, newspaper also)* Linie *f*; *(of political party also)* Programm *nt*; *(principle)* Grundsatz *m.* **our ~ on immigration/recruitment** unsere Einwanderungs-/Einstellungspolitik; **foreign ~** Außenpolitik; **my ~ is to wait and see** meine Devise heißt abwarten; **it was good/bad ~** das war (taktisch) klug/unklug.

policy[2] *n (also* **insurance ~***)* (Versicherungs)police *f.* **~ holder** Versicherungsnehmer *m.*

polio ['pəʊlɪəʊ] *n* Polio, Kinderlähmung *f.*

Polish ['pəʊlɪʃ] **1** *adj* polnisch. **2** *n (language)* Polnisch *nt.*

polish ['pɒlɪʃ] **1** *n* **(a)** *(shoe ~)* Creme *f*; *(floor ~)* Bohnerwachs *nt*; *(furniture ~)* Politur *f*; *(metal ~)* Poliermittel *nt*; *(nail ~)* Lack *m.* **to give sth a ~** etw polieren; *shoes, silver also* etw putzen; *floor* etw bohnern. **(b)** *(shine)* Glanz *m*; *(of furniture)* Politur *f.* **high ~** starker Glanz; **to put a ~ on sth** Glanz auf etw *(acc)* bringen. **(c)** *(fig: refinement)* Schliff *m*; *(of performance)* Brillanz *f.* **he lacks ~** ihm fehlt der Schliff/die Brillanz. **2** *vt* **(a)** polieren; *silver, shoes also* putzen; *floor* bohnern. **(b)** *(fig) performance* den letzten Schliff geben *(+dat)*; *manner, style also* verfeinern.

♦ **polish off** *vt sep (col) food* verputzen *(col)*; *drink* wegputzen *(col)*; *work* erledigen.

♦ **polish up** *vt sep* **(a)** *floor, silver etc* auf Hochglanz bringen. **(b)** *(fig: improve) style, one's French etc* aufpolieren *(col)*; *work* überarbeiten.

polished ['pɒlɪʃt] *adj* **(a)** *surface, furniture* poliert; *floor* gebohnert; *stone, glass* geschliffen. **(b)** *style etc* verfeinert; *performance, performer* brillant. **(c)** *manners* geschliffen.

polite [pə'laɪt] *adj (+er)* höflich. **it wouldn't be ~** es wäre unhöflich; **be ~ about her cooking** mach ein paar höfliche Bemerkungen über ihre Kochkunst; **I was just being ~** ich wollte nur höflich

sein; **we sat around making ~ conversation** wir saßen zusammen und machten Konversation.
politeness [pə'laɪtnɪs] *n* Höflichkeit *f*.
politic ['pɒlɪtɪk] *adj* (taktisch) klug.
political [pə'lɪtɪkəl] *adj* politisch. **~ asylum** politisches Asyl; **~ prisoner** politischer Gefangener.
politician [ˌpɒlɪ'tɪʃən] *n* Politiker(in *f*) *m*.
politics ['pɒlɪtɪks] *n* **(a)** *(+pl vb)* Politik *f*. **what are his ~?** welche politischen Ansichten hat er? **(b)** *(+ sing or pl vb)* Politik *f*. **to go into ~** in die Politik gehen; **to talk ~** über Politik reden.
polka ['pɒlkə] *n* Polka *f*.
polka dot 1 *n* Tupfen *m*. **2** *adj* gepunktet.
poll [pəʊl] **1** *n* **(a)** *(Pol: voting)* Abstimmung *f*; *(election)* Wahl *f*. **to take a ~** eine Abstimmung durchführen. **(b)** *(total of votes cast)* Wahlbeteiligung *f*; *(for candidate)* Stimmenanteil *m*. **there was an 84% ~** die Wahlbeteiligung betrug 84%; **they got 34% of the ~** sie bekamen 34% der Stimmen. **(c) ~s** *(voting place)* Wahllokale *pl*; *(election)* Wahl *f*; **to go to the ~s** zur Wahl gehen; **a defeat at the ~s** eine Wahlniederlage. **(d)** *(opinion ~)* Umfrage *f*. **2** *vt votes* erhalten; *(in opinion ~)* befragen. **40% of those ~ed supported the Government** 40% der Befragten waren für die Regierung.
pollen ['pɒlən] *n* Blütenstaub, Pollen *m*. **~ count** Pollenzahl *f*.
pollinate ['pɒlɪneɪt] *vt* bestäuben.
pollination [ˌpɒlɪ'neɪʃən] *n* Bestäubung *f*.
polling ['pəʊlɪŋ] *n* Stimmabgabe, Wahl *f*. **~ has been heavy** die Wahlbeteiligung war hoch.
polling: ~ booth *n* Wahlkabine *f*; **~ day** *n* Wahltag *m*; **~ station** *n* Wahllokal *nt*.
pollute [pə'luːt] *vt* verschmutzen, verunreinigen; *(fig) mind* verderben.
pollution [pə'luːʃən] *n* **(a)** Umweltverschmutzung *f*. **(b)** *(of rivers etc)* Verschmutzung, Verunreinigung *f*; *(fig)* Verpestung *f*.
polo ['pəʊləʊ] *n* Polo *nt*.
polo neck *n* Rollkragen *m*; *(sweater)* Rollkragenpullover *m*.
poltergeist ['pɒltəgaɪst] *n* Poltergeist *m*.
poly *(Brit)* = **polytechnic.**
polyester [ˌpɒlɪ'estə^r] *n* Polyester *m*.
polygamy [pɒ'lɪgəmɪ] *n* Polygamie, Vielehe *f*.
polyglot ['pɒlɪglɒt] **1** *adj* vielsprachig. **2** *n (person)* Polyglotte(r) *mf*.
polygon ['pɒlɪgən] *n* Polygon, Vieleck *nt*.
polymer ['pɒlɪmə^r] *n* Polymer *nt*.
polyp ['pɒlɪp] *n* Polyp *m*.
polystyrene [ˌpɒlɪ'staɪriːn] *n* Polystyrol *nt*; *(extended also)* Styropor ® *nt*.
polytechnic [ˌpɒlɪ'teknɪk] *n (Brit)* ≃ Polytechnikum *nt*; *(degree-awarding)* Technische Hochschule, TH *f*.
polythene ['pɒlɪθiːn] *n (Brit)* Polyäthylen *nt*; *(in everyday language)* Plastik *nt*. **~ bag** Plastiktüte *f*.
polyunsaturated [ˌpɒlɪʌn'sætʃəreɪtɪd] *adj* mehrfach ungesättigt.
pomegranate ['pɒməˌgrænɪt] *n* Granatapfel *m*.
pommel ['pʌml] *n (on sword)* Knauf *m*; *(on saddle)* Knopf *m*.
pommy ['pɒmɪ] *n (Austral col)* Engländer(in *f*) *m*.
pomp [pɒmp] *n* Pomp, Prunk *m*. **~ and circumstance** Pomp und Prunk.
pompom ['pɒmpɒm] *n (on hat etc)* Troddel, Bommel *(dial) f*.
pomposity [pɒm'pɒsɪtɪ] *n see adj* Aufgeblasenheit, Wichtigtuerei *f*; Bombast *m*.
pompous ['pɒmpəs] *adj person* aufgeblasen, wichtigtuerisch; *language, remark* bombastisch.
pond [pɒnd] *n* Teich *m*.
ponder ['pɒndə^r] **1** *vt* nachdenken über *(+acc)*. **2** *vi* nachdenken *(on, over* über *+acc)*.
ponderous ['pɒndərəs] *adj style etc* schwerfällig.
pong [pɒŋ] *(Brit col)* **1** *n* Gestank, Mief *(col) m*. **there's a bit of a ~ in here** hier stinkt's. **2** *vi* stinken.
pontiff ['pɒntɪf] *n* Pontifex *m*; *(pope also)* Papst *m*.
pontificate [pɒn'tɪfɪkɪt] **1** *n* Pontifikat *nt*. **2** [pɒn'tɪfɪkeɪt] *vi (fig)* dozieren.
pontoon[1] [pɒn'tuːn] *n* Ponton *m*. **~ bridge** Pontonbrücke *f*.
pontoon[2] *n (Brit Cards)* Siebzehnundvier *nt*.
pony ['pəʊnɪ] *n* Pony *nt*.
pony: ~ tail *n* Pferdeschwanz *m*; **~ trekking** *n* Ponyreiten *nt*.
poodle ['puːdl] *n* Pudel *m*.
poof [pʊf] *n (Brit col)* Schwule(r) *m (col)*.
pooh [puː] *interj (bad smell)* puh; *(disdain)* bah.
pooh-pooh ['puː'puː] *vt* verächtlich abtun.
pool[1] [puːl] *n* **(a)** Teich *m*; *(underground)* See *m*; *(of rain)* Pfütze *f*; *(of spilt liquid)* Lache *f*; *(in river)* Loch *nt*. **a ~ of blood** eine Blutlache. **(b)** *(swimming ~)* (Schwimm)becken *nt*; *(in private garden, hotel also)* Swimming Pool *m*; *(swimming baths)* Schwimmbad *nt*.
pool[2] **1** *n* **(a)** *(common fund)* (gemeinsame) Kasse *f*. **each player put £10 in the ~** jeder Spieler gab £10 in die Kasse. **(b)** *(supply, source)* **typing ~** Schreibzentrale *f*; **~ of labour** Arbeitskraftreserve *f*; **there is a great ~ of untapped resources** es gibt große, noch ungenutzte Reserven. **(c) the ~s** *pl (football ~)* Toto *m or nt*; **to do the ~s** Toto spielen; **to win the ~s** im Toto gewinnen. **(d)** *(form of snooker)* Poolbillard *nt*. **(e)** *(Comm)* Interessengemeinschaft *f*; *(US: monopoly, trust)* Pool *m*, Kartell *nt*. **2** *vt resources, savings* zusammenlegen; *efforts* vereinen *(geh)*.
poor [pʊə^r] **1** *adj (+er)* **(a)** arm. **a country ~ in natural resources** ein an Bodenschätzen armes Land; **~ relation** *(fig)* Sorgenkind *nt*; **you ~ (old) chap** *(col)* du armer Kerl *(col)*; **~ you!** du Ärmste(r)! **(b)** *(not good)* schlecht; *performance also, leadership* schwach. **a ~ chance of success** schlechte Erfolgsaussichten *pl*; **he is a ~ traveller** er verträgt Reisen nicht gut; **it's a ~ thing for Britain if ...** es steht schlecht um Großbritannien, wenn ...; **it's very ~ of them not to have replied** es ist sehr unhöflich, daß sie uns *etc (dat)* nicht geantwortet haben; **she was ~ at languages** sie war schlecht *or* schwach in Sprachen. **2** *npl* **the ~** die Armen *pl*.
poor box *n* Almosenbüchse *f*.
poorly ['pʊəlɪ] **1** *adv* **(a)** arm; *dressed, furnished* ärmlich. **~ off** schlecht gestellt, arm dran *(col)*. **(b)** *(badly)* schlecht. **~ lit/~ paid** schlecht beleuchtet/bezahlt; **to do ~ (at sth)** (in etw *dat*) schwach *or* schlecht abschneiden. **2** *adj pred (ill)* krank, elend. **to be ~** sich schlecht fühlen.
pop[1] [pɒp] *n (esp US col) (father)* Papa *m (col)*; *(elderly man)* Opa *m (hum col)*.
pop[2] *n (~ music)* Popmusik *f*, Pop *m*.
pop[3] **1** *n* **(a)** *(sound)* Knall *m*. **(b)** *(fizzy drink)* Brause, Limo *(col) f*. **2** *adv* **to go ~** *(cork)* knallen; *(balloon)* platzen. **3** *vt* **(a)** *balloon, corn* zum Platzen bringen. **(b)** *(col: put)* stecken. **to ~ a letter into the postbox** einen Brief einwerfen; **he ~ped his head around the door** er streckte den Kopf durch die Tür; **to ~ the question** einen (Heirats)antrag machen. **4** *vi* **(a)** *(col: go ~) (cork)* knallen; *(balloon)* platzen; *(buttons, popcorn)* aufplatzen; *(ears)* knacken. **his eyes were ~ping out of his head** ihm fielen fast die Augen aus dem Kopf *(col)*. **(b)** *(col: go quickly or suddenly)* **to ~ along/down to the baker's** schnell zum Bäcker gehen; **I'll just ~ upstairs** ich laufe mal eben nach oben.
♦**pop in** *(col) vi* schnell hereinkommen/hereingehen; *(visit)* auf einen Sprung vorbeikommen *(col)*.
♦**pop off** *vi (col)* **(a)** *(die)* den Löffel abgeben *(col)*. **(b)** *(go off)* verschwinden *(col) (to* nach*)*.
♦**pop out** *(col) vi (go out)* (schnell) rausgehen

(*col*)/rauskommen (*col*); (*spring, rabbit*) herausspringen (*of* aus). **he has just ~ped ~ to the shops** er ist schnell einkaufen gegangen.
♦**pop up** (*col*) *vi* (*appear suddenly*) auftauchen; (*head, toast*) hochschießen (*col*).
pop: ~ art *n* Pop-art *f*; **~corn** *n* Popcorn *nt*.
Pope [pəup] *n* Papst *m*.
pop: ~ group *n* Popgruppe *f*; **~ gun** *n* Spielzeugpistole *f*.
poplar ['pɒpləʳ] *n* Pappel *f*.
poplin ['pɒplɪn] *n* Popeline *f*.
pop music *n* Popmusik *f*.
popper ['pɒpəʳ] *n* (*Brit col: press-stud*) Druckknopf *m*.
poppet ['pɒpɪt] *n* (*col*) Schatz *m*.
poppy ['pɒpɪ] *n* Mohn *m*.
poppy: P~ Day *n* (*Brit*) ≃ Volkstrauertag *m* (*BRD*); **~-seed** *n* Mohn *m*.
popsicle ® ['pɒpsɪkl] *n* (*US*) Eis *nt* am Stiel.
pop: ~ singer *n* Popsänger(in *f*) *m*; **~ song** *m* Popsong *m*; (*hit*) Schlager *m*; **~ star** *n* Popstar *m*.
populace ['pɒpjʊlɪs] *n* Bevölkerung *f*; (*masses*) breite Öffentlichkeit *f*.
popular ['pɒpjʊləʳ] *adj* **(a)** beliebt (*with* **bei**); *decision, measure* populär. **he was a very ~ choice** seine Wahl fand großen Anklang. **(b)** (*for the general public*) populär; *music* leicht; *prices* erschwinglich; *science* Populär-; *edition* Volks-; *lectures, journal* populärwissenschaftlich. **(c)** (*widespread*) *belief, fallacy* weitverbreitet; (*of or for the people*) *government, approval, support* des Volkes. **by ~ request** auf allgemeinen Wunsch.
popularity [ˌpɒpjʊ'lærɪtɪ] *n* Beliebtheit *f*; (*with the public also*) Popularität *f* (*with* bei).
popularize ['pɒpjʊləraɪz] *vt* populär machen; *science* popularisieren.
popularly ['pɒpjʊləlɪ] *adv* allgemein. **he is ~ believed to be a rich man** nach allgemeiner Ansicht ist er ein reicher Mann.
populate ['pɒpjʊleɪt] *vt* (*inhabit*) bevölkern; (*colonize*) besiedeln. **this area is ~d mainly by immigrants** in diesem Gebiet leben hauptsächlich Einwanderer; **densely ~d cities** dichtbevölkerte Städte *pl*.
population [ˌpɒpjʊ'leɪʃən] *n* (*of region, country*) Bevölkerung *f*; (*of town*) Einwohner *pl*; (*number of inhabitants*) Bevölkerungszahl *f*. **the ~ explosion** die Bevölkerungsexplosion.
populous ['pɒpjʊləs] *adj* dicht besiedelt.
porage *n* = **porridge**.
porcelain ['pɔːsəlɪn] **1** *n* Porzellan *nt*. **2** *adj* Porzellan-.
porch [pɔːtʃ] *n* (*of house*) Vorbau *m*; (*US*) Veranda *f*; (*of church*) Portal *nt*.
porcupine ['pɔːkjʊpaɪn] *n* Stachelschwein *nt*.
pore [pɔːʳ] *n* Pore *f*.
♦**pore over** *vi* +*prep obj* (*scrutinize*) genau studieren; (*meditate*) nachgrübeln über (+*acc*). **to ~ ~ one's books** über seinen Büchern hocken.
pork [pɔːk] *n* Schweinefleisch *nt*.
pork: ~ chop *n* Schweinekotelett *nt*; **~pie** *n* Schweinefleischpastete *f*.
porn [pɔːn], (*esp US*) **porno** ['pɔːnəʊ] *n* (*col*) Porno *m* (*col*). **hard/soft ~** harter/weicher Porno.
pornographic [ˌpɔːnə'græfɪk] *adj* pornographisch.
pornography [pɔː'nɒgrəfɪ] *n* Pornographie *f*.
porous ['pɔːrəs] *adj* *rock, substance* porös.
porpoise ['pɔːpəs] *n* Tümmler *m*.
porridge ['pɒrɪdʒ] *n* Haferbrei *m*. **~ oats** Haferflocken *pl*.
port[1] [pɔːt] *n* Hafen *m*; (*town also*) Hafenstadt *f*. **to come/put into ~** in den Hafen einlaufen; **~ authority** Hafenbehörde *f*; **any ~ in a storm** (*prov*) in der Not frißt der Teufel Fliegen (*Prov*).
port[2] **1** *n* (*Naut, Aviat: left side*) Backbord *m*. **2** *adj* *side* Backbord-.
port[3] *n* (*also* **~ wine**) Portwein *m*.
portable ['pɔːtəbl] *adj* tragbar; *radio, typewriter also* Koffer-. **easily ~** leicht zu tragen; **a ~ television** ein Portable *m or nt*, ein tragbarer Fernseher.
porter ['pɔːtəʳ] *n* (*of office etc*) Pförtner *m*; (*hospital ~*) Assistent *m*; (*at hotel*) Portier *m*; (*Rail, at airport*) Gepäckträger *m*.
portfolio [pɔːt'fəʊlɪəʊ] *n* (Akten)mappe *f*; (*Fin*) Portefeuille *nt*; (*of artist, designer*) Kollektion *f*. (*Pol*) **minister without ~** Minister ohne Geschäftsbereich.
porthole ['pɔːthəʊl] *n* Bullauge *nt*.
portion ['pɔːʃən] *n* (*piece, part*) Teil *m*; (*of ticket*) Abschnitt *m*; (*of food*) Portion *f*.
portly ['pɔːtlɪ] *adj* (+*er*) beleibt, korpulent.
portrait ['pɔːtrɪt] *n* Porträt *nt*. **to have one's ~ painted** sich malen lassen.
portrait painter *n* Porträtmaler(in *f*) *m*.
portray [pɔː'treɪ] *vt* darstellen; (*paint also*) malen.
Portugal ['pɔːtjʊgəl] *n* Portugal *nt*.
Portuguese [ˌpɔːtjʊ'giːz] **1** *adj* portugiesisch. **~ man-of-war** Staatsqualle *f*. **2** *n* **(a)** Portugiese *m*, Portugiesin *f*. **(b)** (*language*) Portugiesisch *nt*.
pose [pəʊz] **1** *n* (*position, attitude*) Haltung *f*; (*of model, pej also*) Pose *f*. **to strike a ~** sich in Positur werfen. **2** *vt* *question, problem* vortragen. **3** *vi* (*model*) posieren; (*sitting also*) Modell sitzen; (*standing also*) Modell stehen.
poser ['pəʊzəʳ] *n* **(a)** (*col: person*) Angeber *m*. **(b)** (*problem*) harte Nuß (*col*).
posh [pɒʃ] (*col*) **1** *adj* (+*er*) piekfein (*col*), vornehm; *neighbourhood, hotel also* nobel. **2** *adv* (+*er*): **to talk ~** mit vornehmem Akzent sprechen.
position [pə'zɪʃən] **1** *n* **(a)** (*location*) (*of person*) Platz *m*; (*of object also*) Stelle *f*; (*of microphone, statue, wardrobe etc*) Standort *m*; (*of spotlight, table*) Anordnung *f*; (*of town, house etc*) Lage *f*; (*of plane, ship, Sport*) Position *f*; (*Mil*) Stellung *f*. **to be in/out of ~** an der richtigen/falschen Stelle sein; **what ~ do you play?** auf *or* in welcher Position spielst du?; **to finish in third ~** Dritter werden.
(b) (*posture*) Haltung *f*; (*in love-making*) Stellung *f*. **in a reclining ~** zurückgelehnt.
(c) (*social standing*) Stellung, Position *f*; (*job*) Stelle *f*. **a man of ~** eine hochgestellte Persönlichkeit; **he has a high ~ in the Ministry** er bekleidet eine hohe Stellung im Ministerium; **a ~ of trust** eine Vertrauensstellung.
(d) (*fig: situation, circumstance*) Lage *f*. **to be in a ~ to do sth** in der Lage sein, etw zu tun; **what is the ~ regarding ...?** wie sieht es mit ... aus?
(e) (*fig: point of view, attitude*) Standpunkt *m*, Haltung *f*. **to take up a ~ on sth** eine Haltung bei einer Sache einnehmen.
2 *vt* *ladder, guards* aufstellen; *soldiers, policemen* postieren. **he ~ed himself where he could see her** er plazierte sich so, daß er sie sehen konnte.
positive ['pɒzɪtɪv] *adj* **(a)** (*Math, Phot, Elec*) positiv; *pole* Plus-. **(b)** (*affirmative, constructive*) positiv; *criticism, suggestion* konstruktiv. **(c)** *person, tone of voice* bestimmt; *instructions* streng; *evidence, answer* eindeutig; *rule* fest. **that is ~ proof** das ist der sichere Beweis; **to be ~ that ...** sicher sein, daß ...; **this is a ~ miracle/disgrace** das ist wirklich ein Wunder/eine Schande.
positively ['pɒzɪtɪvlɪ] *adv* **(a)** positiv. **(b)** (*decisively*) bestimmt; (*definitely*) *prove* eindeutig. **(c)** (*really, absolutely*) wirklich, echt (*col*).
posse ['pɒsɪ] *n* (*US: sheriff's ~*) Aufgebot *nt*; (*fig*) Gruppe, Schar *f*.
possess [pə'zes] *vt* besitzen. **to be ~ed by an idea** von einer Idee besessen sein; **to fight like one ~ed** wie ein Besessener kämpfen; **whatever ~ed you to do that?** was ist bloß in Sie gefahren, so etwas zu tun?
possession [pə'zeʃən] *n* **(a)** (*ownership*) Besitz *m*;

(Sport: of ball) Ballbesitz *m*. **to have sth in one's ~** etw in seinem Besitz haben; **to have/take ~ of sth** etw in Besitz haben/nehmen; **to come into ~ of sth** in den Besitz von etw gelangen; **to get/ have ~ of the ball** in Ballbesitz gelangen/sein; **to be in ~ of sth** im Besitz von etw sein. **(b)** *(thing possessed)* Besitz *m no pl*; *(territory)* Besitzung *f*.

possessive [pə'zesɪv] *adj* **(a) to be ~ about sth** seine Besitzansprüche auf etw *(acc)* betonen; **to be ~ towards sb** an jdn Besitzansprüche stellen. **(b)** *(Gram)* **~ pronoun/adjective** Possessivpronomen *nt*.

possessor [pə'zesəʳ] *n* Besitzer(in *f*) *m*. **to be the proud ~ of sth** der stolze Besitzer von etw sein.

possibility [ˌpɒsə'bɪlɪtɪ] *n* Möglichkeit *f*. **there's not much ~ of success/of his** *or* **him being successful** die Aussichten auf Erfolg/darauf, daß er Erfolg hat, sind nicht sehr groß; **within the bounds of ~** im Bereich des Möglichen; **the ~ of doing sth** die Möglichkeit, etw zu tun; **it's a distinct ~ that ...** es besteht eindeutig die Möglichkeit, daß ...; **he is a ~ for the job** er kommt für die Stelle in Betracht; **there is some** *or* **a ~ that ...** es besteht die Möglichkeit, daß ...; **a job with real possibilities** eine Stelle mit echten Möglichkeiten.

possible ['pɒsəbl] **1** *adj* möglich. **to make sth ~** etw möglich machen; **as soon/often as ~** so bald/ oft wie möglich; **the best/worst ~ ...** der/die/das bestmögliche/schlechtestmögliche ...; **if (at all) ~** falls (irgend) möglich; **it's just ~ that I'll see you before then** eventuell sehe ich dich vorher noch; **it will be ~ for you to return the same day** Sie haben die Möglichkeit, am selben Tag zurückzukommen. **2** *n* **a long list of ~s for the job** eine lange Liste möglicher Kandidaten für die Stelle.

possibly ['pɒsəblɪ] *adv* **(a) that can't ~ be true** das kann unmöglich wahr sein; **how could he ~ have known that?** wie konnte er das nur wissen?; **he did all he ~ could** er tat, was er nur konnte; **if I ~ can** wenn ich irgend kann. **(b)** *(perhaps)* vielleicht, möglicherweise.

post[1] [pəʊst] **1** *n (pole, door ~ etc)* Pfosten *m*; *(lamp~)* Pfahl *m*; *(telegraph ~)* Mast *m*. **starting/ winning** *or* **finishing ~** Start-/Zielpfosten *m*; **he was left at the ~** sie ließen ihn stehen. **2** *vt* **(a)** *(display: also* **~ up)** anschlagen. **(b)** *(announce) concert etc* durch Anschlag bekanntmachen. **to ~ (as) missing** als vermißt melden.

post[2] 1 *n* **(a)** *(job)* Stelle *f*, Posten *m*. **to look for/ take up a ~** eine Stelle suchen/antreten. **(b)** *(Mil)* Posten *m*. **at one's ~** auf seinem Posten; **a frontier ~** ein Grenzposten *m*; **last ~** *(bugle call)* Zapfenstreich *m*. **2** *vt* **(a)** *(position)* postieren. **(b)** *(send, assign)* versetzen.

post[3] 1 *n (esp Brit: mail)* Post *f*. **by ~** mit der Post; **it's in the ~** es ist unterwegs; **to put sth in the ~** etw aufgeben; **to catch/miss the ~** *(letter)* noch/ nicht mehr mit der Post mitkommen; *(person)* rechtzeitig zur Leerung kommen/die Leerung verpassen; **has the ~ been?** war die Post schon da? **2** *vt* **(a)** *(put in the ~)* aufgeben; *(in letter-box)* einwerfen, einstecken; *(send by ~ also)* mit der Post schicken. **I ~ed it to you on Monday** ich habe es am Montag an Sie abgeschickt. **(b)** *(inform)* **to keep sb ~ed** jdn auf dem laufenden halten.

post- [pəʊst-] *pref* nach-.

postage ['pəʊstɪdʒ] *n* Porto *nt*. **~ and packing** *(abbr* **p & p)** Porto und Verpackung.

postage stamp *n* Briefmarke *f*.

postal order *n (Brit) Geldgutschein, der bei der Post gekauft und eingelöst wird.*

post: ~-bag *n (Brit)* Postsack *m*; **~box** *n (Brit)* Briefkasten *m*; **~card** *n* Postkarte *f*; **(picture) ~card** *n* Ansichtskarte *f*; **~ code** *n (Brit)* Postleitzahl *f*; **~date** *vt cheque* vordatieren.

poster ['pəʊstəʳ] *n (advertising)* Plakat *nt*; *(for decoration also)* Poster *nt*.

poste restante ['pəʊst'restɑ̃ːnt] *(Brit)* **1** *n* Aufbewahrungsstelle *f* für postlagernde Sendungen. **2** *adv* postlagernd.

posterior [pɒ'stɪərɪəʳ] *n (hum)* Allerwerteste(r) *m (hum)*.

posterity [pɒ'sterɪtɪ] *n* die Nachwelt.

post: ~-free *adj, adv* portofrei; **~graduate** *n jd, der seine Studien nach dem ersten akademischen Grad weiterführt;* **~haste** *adv* schnellstens.

posthumous ['pɒstjʊməs] *adj* post(h)um.

post: ~man *n* Briefträger *m*; **~mark 1** *n* Poststempel *m*; **2** *vt* (ab)stempeln; **the letter is ~marked "Birmingham"** der Brief ist in Birmingham abgestempelt; **~master** *n* Postmeister *m*; **~master general** *n* ≈ Postminister *m*; **~mistress** *n* Postmeisterin *f*; **~-mortem** [ˌpəʊst'mɔːtəm] *n* Obduktion, Leichenöffnung *f*; *(fig)* nachträgliche Erörterung; **to hold** *or* **have a ~-mortem on sth** etw hinterher erörtern; **~-natal** *adj* nach der Geburt, postnatal *(spec)*; **~ office** *n* Postamt *nt*; **the P~ Office** *(institution)* die Post; **~ office box** *(abbr* **PO Box)** Postfach *nt*; **~-paid** *adj* portofrei; *envelope* frankiert.

postpone [pəʊst'pəʊn] *vt* aufschieben; *(for specified period)* verschieben. **it has been ~d till Tuesday** es ist auf Dienstag verschoben worden.

postponement [pəʊst'pəʊnmənt] *n (act)* Verschiebung *f*; *(result)* Aufschub *m*.

postscript ['pəʊsˌskrɪpt] *n (abbr* **PS:** *to letter)* Postskriptum *nt*; *(to book, article etc)* Nachwort *nt*; *(fig: to affair)* Nachspiel *nt*.

postulate ['pɒstjʊlɪt] **1** *n* Postulat *nt*. **2** ['pɒstjʊleɪt] *vt* postulieren; *theory* aufstellen.

posture ['pɒstʃəʳ] **1** *n (lit, fig)* Haltung *f*; *(pej)* Pose *f*. **2** *vi* sich in Positur werfen.

postwar ['pəʊst'wɔːʳ] *adj* Nachkriegs-. **~ London** das London der Nachkriegszeit.

posy ['pəʊzɪ] *n* Sträußchen *nt*.

pot [pɒt] **1** *n* **(a)** Topf *m*; *(tea~, coffee-~)* Kanne *f*. **~s and pans** Kochgeschirr *nt*; **to go to ~** *(col: person, business)* auf den Hund kommen *(col)*; **to have ~s of money** *(col)* jede Menge Geld haben *(col)*. **(b)** *(col: marijuana)* Gras *nt (col)*. **2** *vt meat* einmachen; *jam* einfüllen; *plant* eintopfen; *(shoot) game* schießen; *(Billiards) ball* einlochen.

potash ['pɒtæʃ] *n* Kali *nt*.

potassium [pə'tæsɪəm] *n* Kalium *nt*.

potato [pə'teɪtəʊ] *n, pl* **-es** Kartoffel *f*. **~ chip** *(US) or* **crisp** *(Brit) n* Kartoffelchip *m*.

potbellied ['pɒt'belɪd] *adj person* spitzbäuchig; *(through hunger)* blähbäuchig.

potency ['pəʊtənsɪ] *n see adj* Stärke *f*; Durchschlagskraft *f*; Potenz *f*; Macht *f*.

potent ['pəʊtənt] *adj drink, motive etc* stark; *argument etc* durchschlagend; *man* potent; *ruler* mächtig.

potentate ['pəʊtənteɪt] *n* Potentat *m*.

potential [pəʊ'tenʃəl] **1** *adj* potentiell. **2** *n* Potential *nt*. **the ~ for growth** das Wachstumspotential; **to have ~** ausbaufähig sein *(col)*; **he shows quite a bit of ~** es steckt einiges in ihm.

potentially [pəʊ'tenʃəlɪ] *adv* potentiell.

pot: ~hole *n* **(a)** *(in road)* Schlagloch *nt*; **(b)** *(Geol)* Höhle *f*; **~holer** *n* Höhlenforscher(in *f*) *m*; **~holing** *n* Höhlenforschung *f*.

potion ['pəʊʃən] *n* Trank *m*.

pot: ~luck *n*: **to take ~luck** nehmen, was es gerade gibt; **we took ~luck and went to the nearest pub** wir gingen aufs Geratewohl in die nächste Kneipe; **~pourri** [ˌpəʊpʊ'riː] *n* **(a)** *(lit)* Duftsträußchen *nt*; **(b)** *(fig: mixture, medley)* bunte Mischung; *(of music)* Potpourri *nt*; **~ roast** *n* Schmorbraten *m*; **~shot** *n* **to take a ~shot at sth** aufs Geratewohl auf etw *(acc)* schießen.

potted ['pɒtɪd] *adj* **(a)** *meat* eingemacht; *fish* eingelegt; *plant* Topf-. **(b)** *(shortened) history* gekürzt.

potter[1] [pɒtəʳ] *n* Töpfer(in *f*) *m*. **~'s wheel** Töpferscheibe *f*.

potter[2] *vi (do little jobs)* herumwerkeln; *(wander aimlessly)* herumschlendern. **she ~s away in the kitchen for hours** sie hantiert stundenlang in der Küche herum; **to ~ around the house** im Haus herumwerkeln.

pottery ['pɒtərɪ] *n (workshop, craft)* Töpferei *f*; *(pots)* Töpferwaren *pl*; *(glazed)* Keramik *f*; *(archaeological remains)* Tonscherbe *f*.

potty[1] ['pɒtɪ] *n (esp Brit)* Töpfchen *nt*. **~-trained** sauber.

potty[2] *adj (+er) (Brit col: mad)* verrückt.

pouch [paʊtʃ] *n* Beutel *m*; *(under eyes)* (Tränen)sack *m*; *(of hamster)* Tasche *f*; *(Mil)* (Patronen)tasche *f*.

pouf(fe) [pu:f] *n* **(a)** *(seat)* Puff *m*. **(b)** *(Brit col)* = **poof.**

poulterer ['pəʊltərəʳ] *n (Brit)* Geflügelhändler(in *f*) *m*.

poultice ['pəʊltɪs] *n* Umschlag, Wickel *m*; *(for boil)* Zugpflaster *nt*.

poultry ['pəʊltrɪ] *n* Geflügel *nt*. **~ farm** Geflügelfarm *f*; **~ farmer** Geflügelzüchter *m*.

pounce [paʊns] **1** *n* Sprung, Satz *m*; *(swoop by bird)* Angriff *m*. **2** *vi (cat, lion etc)* einen Satz machen; *(bird)* niederstoßen; *(fig)* zuschlagen. **to ~ on sb/sth** *(lit, fig)* sich auf jdn/etw stürzen; *(bird)* auf etw *(acc)* niederstoßen; *(police)* sich *(dat)* jdn greifen/in etw *(dat)* eine Razzia machen.

pound[1] [paʊnd] *n* **(a)** *(weight)* ≈ Pfund *nt*. **two ~s of apples** zwei Pfund Äpfel; **by the ~** pfundweise. **(b)** *(money)* Pfund *nt*. **one ~ sterling** ein Pfund Sterling; **five ~s** fünf Pfund; **a five-~ note** ein Fünfpfundschein *m*.

pound[2] **1** *vt (hammer, strike)* hämmern; *earth* feststampfen; *meat* klopfen; *dough* kneten; *corn etc* (zer)stampfen; *piano* hämmern auf *(+dat)*; *table* hämmern auf *(+acc)*; *door, wall* hämmern gegen; *(waves) ship* schlagen gegen; *(guns, bombs)* ununterbrochen beschießen; *(artillery)* unter Beschuß haben. **to ~ sth to pieces** etw kleinstampfen; *(sea) ship* etw zertrümmern; **to ~ sth to a pulp** etw zu Brei stampfen. **2** *vi* **(a)** *(beat)* hämmern; *(heart)* (wild) pochen; *(waves, sea)* schlagen *(on, against* gegen*)*; *(hooves)* stampfen. **he ~ed on the door/on the table** er hämmerte gegen die Tür/auf den Tisch. **(b)** *(run heavily)* stampfen; *(walk heavily, stamp)* stapfen.

pound[3] *n (for stray dogs)* städtischer Hundezwinger; *(for cars)* Abstellplatz *m (für amtlich abgeschleppte Fahrzeuge)*.

pounding ['paʊndɪŋ] *n* Hämmern *nt*; *(of heart)* Pochen *nt*; *(of music, drums)* Dröhnen *nt*; *(of waves, sea)* Schlagen *nt*; *(of hooves, feet etc)* Stampfen *nt*; *(of guns, bombs)* Bombardement *nt*. **to take a ~** *(ship in storm)* stark mitgenommen werden; *(town in war)* schwer bombardiert werden; *(theory)* scharf angegriffen werden.

pour [pɔ:ʳ] **1** *vt liquid* gießen; *sugar, rice etc* schütten; *drink* einschenken. **can I ~ you another drink?** kann ich Ihnen nachschenken?; **to ~ money into a project** Geld in ein Projekt pumpen *(col)*. **2** *vi* **(a)** *(lit, fig)* strömen; *(smoke also)* hervorquellen. **the sweat was ~ing off him** der Schweiß floß in Strömen an ihm herunter; **cars ~ed along the road** Autokolonnen rollten die Straße entlang. **(b) it's ~ing (with rain)** es gießt (in Strömen), es schüttet *(col)*.

♦ **pour away** *vt sep* weggießen.

♦ **pour in** *vi* hinein-/hereinströmen; *(donations, protests)* in Strömen eintreffen.

♦ **pour out 1** *vi* hinaus-/herausströmen *(of* aus*)*; *(smoke also)* hervorquellen *(of* aus*)*; *(words)* heraussprudeln *(of* aus*)*. **2** *vt sep liquid* ausgießen; *sugar etc* ausschütten; *drink* einschenken; *(fig) troubles* sich *(dat)* von der Seele reden. **to ~ ~ one's heart to sb** jdm sein Herz ausschütten.

pouring ['pɔ:rɪŋ] *adj* **~ rain** strömender Regen; **a ~ wet day** ein völlig verregneter Tag.

pout [paʊt] **1** *n (facial expression)* Schmollmund *m*. **2** *vi (with lips)* einen Schmollmund machen; *(sulk)* schmollen.

poverty ['pɒvətɪ] *n* Armut *f*. **~-stricken** notleidend; *conditions* kümmerlich; **to be ~-stricken** Armut leiden; *(hum col)* am Hungertuch nagen *(hum)*.

powder ['paʊdəʳ] **1** *n* Pulver *nt*; *(face, talcum ~ etc)* Puder *m*; *(dust)* Staub *m*. **2** *vt* **(a)** *milk* pulverisieren. **~ed milk** Milchpulver *nt*. **(b)** *face etc* pudern. **to ~ one's nose** *(lit)* sich *(dat)* die Nase pudern; *(euph)* kurz verschwinden *(euph)*.

powder: ~ compact *n* Puderdose *f*; **~ puff** *n* Puderquaste *f*; **~ room** *n* Damentoilette *f*.

powdery ['paʊdərɪ] *adj (like powder)* pulvrig; *(crumbly)* bröckelig; *bones* morsch; *(covered with powder)* gepudert.

power ['paʊəʳ] **1** *n* **(a)** *no pl (physical strength)* Kraft *f*; *(force: of blow, explosion etc)* Stärke, Wucht *f*; *(fig: of argument etc)* Überzeugungskraft *f*. **the ~ of love/tradition** die Macht der Liebe/Tradition.

(b) her ~s of persuasion ihre Überredungskünste *pl*; **his ~s of hearing** sein Hörvermögen *nt*; **mental ~s** geistige Kräfte *pl*.

(c) *(capacity, authority)* Macht *f*; *(Jur, parental)* Gewalt *f*; *(usu pl: authority)* Befugnis *f*. **he did all in his ~ to help them** er tat (alles), was in seiner Macht stand, um ihnen zu helfen; **to be in sb's ~** in jds Gewalt *(dat)* sein; **that is beyond** *or* **outside my ~(s)** das überschreitet meine Befugnisse; **~ of attorney** *(Jur)* (Handlungs)vollmacht *f*; **the party now in ~** die Partei, die im Augenblick an der Macht ist; **to come to ~** an die Macht kommen; **he has been given full ~(s) to make all decisions** man hat ihm volle Entscheidungsgewalt übertragen.

(d) *(person or institution having authority)* Autorität *f*. **to be the ~ behind the throne** die graue Eminenz sein; **the ~s that be** *(col)* die da oben *(col)*; **the ~s of darkness** die Mächte der Finsternis.

(e) *(nation)* Macht *f*. **a naval ~** eine Seemacht.

(f) *(nuclear ~ etc)* Energie *f*; *(of water, steam also)* Kraft *f*; *(of engine, transmitter)* Leistung *f*; *(of lens, drug)* Stärke *f*. **they cut off the ~** *(electricity)* sie haben den Strom abgestellt.

(g) *(Math)* Potenz *f*. **to the ~ (of) 2** hoch 2.

(h) *(col: a lot of)* **that did me a ~ of good** das hat mir unheimlich gut getan *(col)*.

2 *vt (engine)* antreiben; *(fuel)* betreiben.

power: ~boat *n* Rennboot *nt*; **~ cut** *n (Brit)* Stromsperre *f*; *(accidental)* Stromsausfall *m*; **~-driven** *adj tool* Motor-; **~ failure** *n* = **~ cut.**

powerful ['paʊəfʊl] *adj government etc* mächtig; *boxer, engine, drug, emotions* stark; *punch, detergent* kraftvoll; *build* kräftig; *(fig) actor, music, film* mitreißend; *argument* durchschlagend.

powerfully ['paʊəfəlɪ] *adv* kraftvoll. **~ built** kräftig gebaut.

powerhouse ['paʊəhaʊs] *n (fig)* treibende Kraft *(behind* hinter *+dat, of gen)*.

power: ~less *adj committee, person* machtlos; **to be ~less to resist** nicht die Kraft haben, zu widerstehen; **the government is ~less to deal with inflation** die Regierung steht der Inflation machtlos gegenüber; **~ point** *n (Brit Elec)* Steckdose *f*; **~ station** *n* Kraftwerk *nt*; **~ steering** *n (Aut)* Servolenkung *f*.

pp = **(a) pages** S. **(b) on behalf of.**

PR = **proportional representation; public relations.**

practicable ['præktɪkəbl] *adj* durchführbar, praktikabel; *road* befahrbar.

practical ['præktɪkəl] *adj* praktisch; *person* praktisch (veranlagt). **to have a ~ mind** praktisch denken.

practicality [ˌpræktɪ'kælɪtɪ] *n (of person)* praktische Veranlagung; *(of scheme)* Durchführbarkeit *f*; *(practical detail)* praktische Einzelheit.

practical: ~ joke *n* Streich *m*; **~ joker** *n* Witzbold *m (col)*.

practically ['præktɪkəlɪ] *adv (all senses)* praktisch.

practice ['præktɪs] **1** *n* **(a)** *(habit, custom) (of individual)* Gewohnheit *f*; *(of group, in country)* Brauch *m*; *(in business)* Verfahrensweise *f*. **as is my (usual) ~** wie es meine Gewohnheit ist; **that's common ~** das ist allgemein üblich. **(b)** *(exercise, training)* Übung *f*; *(rehearsal, trial run)* Probe *f*; *(Sport)* Training *nt*. **~ makes perfect** *(Prov)* Übung macht den Meister *(Prov)*; **to be out of/in ~** aus der/in Übung sein; **that was just a ~ run** das war nur mal zur Probe. **(c)** *(as opposed to theory)* Praxis *f*. **in ~** in der Praxis; **that won't work in ~** das läßt sich praktisch nicht durchführen; **to put one's ideas into ~** seine Ideen in die Praxis umsetzen. **(d)** *(of doctor etc)* Praxis *f*. **to set up in ~** eine Praxis eröffnen.
2 *vti (US)* = **practise.**

practise, *(US)* **practice** ['præktɪs] **1** *vt* **(a)** *thrift, patience etc* üben; *self-denial* praktizieren. **to ~ what one preaches** *(prov)* seine Lehren in die Tat umsetzen. **(b)** *(in order to acquire skill)* üben; *song, chorus* proben. **to ~ the violin** Geige üben; **to ~ doing sth** etw üben; **I'm practising my German on him** ich probiere mein Deutsch an ihm aus. **(c)** *(follow, exercise) profession, religion* ausüben, praktizieren. **to ~ law/medicine** als Anwalt/Arzt praktizieren. **2** *vi* **(a)** *(in order to acquire skill)* üben. **(b)** *(lawyer, doctor etc)* praktizieren.

practised, *(US)* **practiced** ['præktɪst] *adj* geübt. **with a ~ eye** mit geübtem Auge.

practising, *(US)* **practicing** ['præktɪsɪŋ] *adj doctor, Christian, homosexual* praktizierend; *socialist* aktiv.

practitioner [præk'tɪʃənəʳ] *n (of method)* Benutzer *m*; *(medical ~)* praktischer Arzt, praktische Ärztin; *(dental ~)* Zahnarzt *m*/-ärztin *f*; *(legal ~)* Rechtsanwalt *m*/-anwältin *f*.

pragmatic [præg'mætɪk] *adj* pragmatisch.

prairie ['prɛərɪ] *n* Grassteppe *f*; *(in North America)* Prärie *f*.

praise [preɪz] **1** *vt* loben; *(to others, worshipfully also)* rühmen *(geh)*. **to ~ sb for having done sth** jdn dafür loben, etw getan zu haben. **2** *n* Lob *nt no pl*. **a hymn of ~** eine Lobeshymne; **he spoke in ~ of their efforts** er sprach lobend von ihren Bemühungen; **I have nothing but ~ for him** ich kann ihn nur loben; **~ be to God!** gelobt sei der Herr!

praiseworthy ['preɪzˌwɜːðɪ] *adj* lobenswert.

pram [præm] *n (Brit)* Kinderwagen *m*.

prance [prɑːns] *vi (horse)* tänzeln; *(person) (jump around)* herumhüpfen; *(walk gaily, mince)* tänzeln. **to ~ in/out** *(person)* herein-/hinausspazieren.

prank [præŋk] *n* Streich *m*. **to play a ~ on sb** jdm einen Streich spielen.

prattle ['prætl] **1** *n* Geplapper *nt*. **2** *vi* plappern.

prawn [prɔːn] *n* Garnele *f*. **~ cocktail** Krabbencocktail *m*.

pray [preɪ] *vi (say prayers)* beten. **let us ~** lasset uns beten; **to ~ for sb/sth** für jdn/um etw beten.

prayer [prɛəʳ] *n* Gebet *nt*; *(service, ~ meeting)* Andacht *f*. **to say one's ~s** beten.

prayer: ~ book *n* Gebetbuch *nt*; **~ mat** *n* Gebetsteppich *m*.

pre- [priː-] *pref* vor-; *(esp with Latinate words in German)* prä-. **at ~1980 prices** zu Preisen von vor 1980.

preach [priːtʃ] **1** *vt* predigen; *(fig) advantages etc* propagieren. **to ~ a sermon** *(lit, fig)* eine Predigt halten. **2** *vi (lit, fig)* predigen. **to ~ to/at sb** jdm eine Predigt halten; **to ~ to the converted** *(prov)* offene Türen einrennen.

preacher ['priːtʃəʳ] *n* Prediger *m*; *(fig: moraliser)* Moralprediger(in *f*) *m*.

preamble [priː'æmbl] *n* Einleitung *f*; *(of book)* Vorwort *nt*; *(Jur)* Präambel *f*.

prearrange ['priːə'reɪndʒ] *vt* vorher vereinbaren.

precarious [prɪ'kɛərɪəs] *adj* unsicher; *situation also, relationship* prekär; *theory* anfechtbar.

precariously [prɪ'kɛərɪəslɪ] *adv* **to be ~ balanced** *(lit, fig)* auf der Kippe stehen; **he lived rather ~** er lebte in ziemlich ungesicherten finanziellen Verhältnissen.

precaution [prɪ'kɔːʃən] *n* Vorsichtsmaßnahme *f*. **to take ~s against sth** Vorsichtsmaßnahmen gegen etw treffen; **to take the ~ of doing sth** vorsichtshalber etw tun; **to take ~s** *(use contraceptives)* ein Verhütungsmittel *nt* gebrauchen.

precautionary [prɪ'kɔːʃənərɪ] *adj* Vorsichts-, vorbeugend.

precede [prɪ'siːd] *vt (in order, time)* vorangehen *(+dat)*; *(in importance)* gehen vor *(+dat)*; *(in rank)* stehen über *(+dat)*.

precedence ['presɪdəns] *n (of person)* vorrangige Stellung *(over* gegenüber*)*; *(of problem etc)* Vorrang *m (over* vor *+dat)*. **to take ~ over sb/sth** vor jdm/etw Vorrang haben.

precedent ['presɪdənt] *n* Präzedenzfall *m*. **without ~** noch nie dagewesen; **to set a ~** einen Präzedenzfall schaffen.

preceding [prɪ'siːdɪŋ] *adj* vorhergehend.

precept ['priːsept] *n* Grundsatz *m*, Prinzip *nt*.

precinct ['priːsɪŋkt] *n (pedestrian ~)* Fußgängerzone *f*; *(shopping ~)* Geschäftsviertel *nt*; *(US: police ~)* Revier *nt*. **~s** *pl (grounds, premises)* Gelände; *(environs)* Umgebung *f*.

precious ['preʃəs] **1** *adj (costly)* wertvoll, kostbar; *(treasured)* wertvoll; *(iro)* heißgeliebt. **~ stone/metal** Edelstein *m*/Edelmetall *nt*. **2** *adv (col)* **~ little/few** herzlich wenig/wenige *(col)*.

precipice ['presɪpɪs] *n (lit, fig)* Abgrund *m*.

precipitate [prə'sɪpɪtɪt] **1** *adj (overhasty)* übereilt, überstürzt. **2** [prɪ'sɪpɪteɪt] *vt* **(a)** *(hurl)* schleudern; *(downwards)* hinunterschleudern; *(fig)* stürzen. **(b)** *(hasten)* beschleunigen. **(c)** *(Chem)* (aus)fällen; *(Met)* niederschlagen.

precipitous [prɪ'sɪpɪtəs] *adj* steil; *(hasty)* überstürzt.

précis ['preɪsiː] *n* Zusammenfassung *f*; *(Sch)* Inhaltsangabe *f*.

precise [prɪ'saɪs] *adj* genau; *answer, description etc, worker also* präzis. **at that ~ moment** genau in dem Augenblick; **this was the ~ amount I needed** das war genau der Betrag, den ich brauchte; **please be more ~** drücken Sie sich bitte etwas genauer aus; **or, to be more ~ ...** oder, um es genauer zu sagen, ...

precisely [prɪ'saɪslɪ] *adv* genau; *answer, describe, work also* präzis. **at ~ 7 o'clock, at 7 o'clock ~** genau um 7 Uhr; **what ~ do you mean?** was meinen Sie eigentlich genau?

precision [prɪ'sɪʒən] *n* Genauigkeit *f*; *(of work, movement also)* Präzision *f*.

precision instrument *n* Präzisionsinstrument *nt*.

preclude [prɪ'kluːd] *vt possibility* ausschließen. **to ~ sb from doing sth** jdn daran hindern, etw zu tun.

precocious [prɪ'kəʊʃəs] *adj teenager, behaviour* frühreif; *statement, way of speaking* altklug.

precociousness [prɪ'kəʊʃəsnɪs], **precocity** [prɪ'kɒsɪtɪ] *n see adj* Frühreife *f*; Altklugheit *f*.

preconceived [ˌpriːkən'siːvd] *adj opinion, idea* vorgefaßt.

preconception [ˌpriːkən'sepʃən] *n* vorgefaßte Meinung.

precondition [ˌpriːkənˈdɪʃən] *n* (Vor)bedingung *f*.
precursor [priːˈkɜːsəʳ] *n* Vorläufer *m*; *(in office)* (Amts)vorgänger(in *f*) *m*.
predate [ˌpriːˈdeɪt] *vt (precede)* zeitlich vorangehen *(+dat)*; *cheque, letter* zurückdatieren.
predator [ˈpredətəʳ] *n (animal)* Raubtier *nt*; *(person)* Plünderer *m*.
predecessor [ˈpriːdɪsesəʳ] *n (person)* Vorgänger(in *f*) *m*; *(thing)* Vorläufer *m*. **our ~s** *(ancestors)* unsere Vorfahren *pl*.
predestination [priːˌdestɪˈneɪʃən] *n* Vorherbestimmung *f*.
predestine [priːˈdestɪn] *vt* vorherbestimmen; *person* prädestinieren.
predetermine [ˌpriːdɪˈtɜːmɪn] *vt events, sb's future etc* vorherbestimmen; *price, date etc* im voraus festlegen.
predicament [prɪˈdɪkəmənt] *n* Zwangslage *f*, Dilemma *nt*. **to be in a ~** in einer Zwangslage sein.
predicate [ˈpredɪkɪt] *n (Gram)* Prädikat *nt*.
predict [prɪˈdɪkt] *vt* vorhersagen.
predictable [prɪˈdɪktəbl] *adj* vorhersagbar. **you are so ~** man weiß doch genau, wie Sie reagieren.
predictably [prɪˈdɪktəblɪ] *adv* **~, he was late** wie vorauszusehen, kam er zu spät.
prediction [prɪˈdɪkʃən] *n* Voraussage *f*.
predilection [ˌpriːdɪˈlekʃən] *n* Vorliebe *f (for* für*)*.
predispose [ˌpriːdɪˈspəʊz] *vt* geneigt machen. **to ~ sb in favour of sb/sth** jdn für jdn/etw einnehmen; **I'm not ~d to help him** ich bin nicht geneigt, ihm zu helfen.
predominance [prɪˈdɒmɪnəns] *n (control)* Vorherrschaft *f*; *(prevalence)* Überwiegen *nt*.
predominant [prɪˈdɒmɪnənt] *adj (most prevalent) idea, theory* vorherrschend; *(dominating) person, animal* beherrschend.
predominantly [prɪˈdɒmɪnəntlɪ] *adv* überwiegend.
predominate [prɪˈdɒmɪneɪt] *vi* **(a)** vorherrschen. **(b)** *(in influence etc)* überwiegen. **Good will always ~ over Evil** das Gute wird immer über das Böse siegen.
pre-eminent [priːˈemɪnənt] *adj* herausragend.
pre-eminently [priːˈemɪnəntlɪ] *adv* hauptsächlich, vor allem; *(excellently)* hervorragend.
preen [priːn] **1** *vt feathers* putzen. **2** *vr* **to ~ oneself** *(bird)* sich putzen; *(person: dress up)* sich herausputzen, sich aufputzen.
prefab [ˈpriːfæb] *n* Fertighaus *nt*.
prefabricated [ˌpriːˈfæbrɪkeɪtɪd] *adj* vorgefertigt, Fertig-; *building* Fertig-.
preface [ˈprefɪs] *n* **1** Vorwort *nt*. **2** *vt remarks* einleiten.
prefect [ˈpriːfekt] *n* Präfekt *m*; *(Brit Sch)* Aufsichtsschüler(in *f*) *m*. **form ~** *(Sch)* ≃ Klassensprecher(in *f*) *m*.
prefer [prɪˈfɜːʳ] *vt* **(a)** *(like better)* vorziehen *(to dat)*, lieber mögen *(to* als*)*; *drink, food, music also* lieber trinken/essen/hören *(to* als*)*; *applicant, solution* vorziehen, bevorzugen; *(be more fond of) person* lieber haben *(to* als*)*. **he ~s coffee to tea** er trinkt lieber Kaffee als Tee; **I'd ~ something less ornate** ich hätte lieber etwas Schlichteres; **I ~ to resign rather than ...** eher kündige ich, als daß ...; **I ~ walking/flying** ich gehe lieber zu Fuß/fliege lieber; **I ~ not to say** ich sage es lieber nicht; **I would ~ you to do it today** mir wäre es lieber, wenn Sie es heute täten. **(b)** *(Jur)* **to ~ a charge/charges (against sb)** Klage (gegen jdn) erheben.
preferable [ˈprefərəbl] *adj* **X is ~ to Y** X ist Y *(dat)* vorzuziehen; **it would be ~ to do it that way** es wäre besser, es so zu machen.
preferably [ˈprefərəblɪ] *adv* am liebsten. **tea or coffee? — coffee, ~** Tee oder Kaffee? — lieber Kaffee; **but ~ not Tuesday** aber, wenn möglich, nicht Dienstag.
preference [ˈprefərəns] *n (greater liking)* Vorliebe *f*; *(greater favour)* Vorzug *m*. **for ~** lieber; **to have a ~ for sth** eine Vorliebe für etw haben, etw bevorzugen; **I drink coffee in ~ to tea** ich trinke lieber Kaffee als Tee; **what is your ~?** was wäre Ihnen am liebsten?; **I have no ~** mir ist das eigentlich gleich; **to show ~ to sb** jdn bevorzugen; **to give ~ to sb/sth** jdm/etw den Vorzug geben *(over* gegenüber*)*; **~ shares** *or* **stock** *(Brit Fin)* Vorzugsaktien *pl*.
preferential [prefəˈrenʃəl] *adj treatment* Vorzugs-; *terms* Sonder-. **to give sb ~ treatment** jdn bevorzugt behandeln.
prefix [ˈpriːfɪks] *n (Gram)* Vorsilbe *f*, Präfix *nt*.
pregnancy [ˈpregnənsɪ] *n* Schwangerschaft *f*; *(of animal)* Trächtigkeit *f*. **~ test** Schwangerschaftstest *m*.
pregnant [ˈpregnənt] *adj* **(a)** *woman* schwanger; *animal* trächtig, tragend. **3 months ~** im dritten Monat (schwanger). **(b)** *(fig) remark, silence, pause* bedeutungsschwer. **~ with meaning** bedeutungsgeladen.
prehistoric [ˌpriːhɪˈstɒrɪk] *adj* prähistorisch, vorgeschichtlich.
prehistory [ˌpriːˈhɪstərɪ] *n* Vorgeschichte *f*.
prejudge [priːˈdʒʌdʒ] *vt case, issue* im vorhinein beurteilen; *person* im voraus verurteilen.
prejudice [ˈpredʒʊdɪs] **1** *n* **(a)** *(biased opinion)* Vorurteil *nt*. **his ~ against ...** seine Voreingenommenheit gegen ...; **that's pure ~** das ist reine Voreingenommenheit; **racial ~** Rassenvorurteile *pl*. **(b)** *(esp Jur: detriment, injury)* Schaden *m*. **to the ~ of sb/sth** *(form)* zu jds Schaden/unter Beeinträchtigung *+gen*; **without ~** *(Jur)* ohne Verbindlichkeit. **2** *vt* **(a)** *(bias)* beeinflussen. **(b)** *(injure) case etc* gefährden; *chances also* beeinträchtigen.
prejudiced [ˈpredʒʊdɪst] *adj person* voreingenommen *(against* gegen*)*; *opinion* vorgefaßt; *judge* befangen.
prejudicial [ˌpredʒʊˈdɪʃəl] *adj* abträglich *(to sth* einer Sache *dat)*. **to be ~ to sb's chances** jds Chancen gefährden.
prelate [ˈprelɪt] *n* Prälat *m*.
prelim [ˈpriːˌlɪm] *n (exam)* Vorprüfung *f*.
preliminary [prɪˈlɪmɪnərɪ] **1** *adj talks, enquiry etc* Vor-; *remarks also, chapter* einleitend; *measures* vorbereitend. **2** *n* Einleitung *f (to* zu*)*; *(preparatory measure)* vorbereitende Maßnahme; *(Sport)* Vorspiel *nt*.
prelude [ˈpreljuːd] *n* Vorspiel *nt*; *(fig)* Auftakt *m (to* zu *+dat)*.
premarital [priːˈmærɪtl] *adj* vorehelich.
premature [ˈprematʃʊəʳ] *adj birth, arrival* vorzeitig; *decision, action* verfrüht. **you were a little ~** da waren Sie ein wenig voreilig; **the baby was three weeks ~** das Baby wurde drei Wochen zu früh geboren; **~ baby** Frühgeburt *f*.
premeditate [priːˈmedɪteɪt] *vt* vorsätzlich planen.
premeditated [priːˈmedɪteɪtɪd] *adj* vorsätzlich.
premenstrual [priːmenstruəl] *adj* prämenstruell, vor der Menstruation auftretend.
premier [ˈpremɪəʳ] *n* Premier(minister) *m*.
première [ˈpremɪeəʳ] *n* Premiere *f*; *(first ever also)* Uraufführung *f*.
premise [ˈpremɪs] *n* **(a)** *(esp Logic)* Prämisse *(spec)*, Voraussetzung *f*. **(b) ~s** *pl (of school, factory)* Gelände *nt*; *(building)* Gebäude *nt*; *(shop)* Räumlichkeiten *pl*. **business ~s** Geschäftsräume *pl*.
premium [ˈpriːmɪəm] *n (bonus)* Bonus *m*, Prämie *f*; *(surcharge)* Zuschlag *m*; *(Insur)* Prämie *f*; *(St Ex)* Aufgeld, Agio *nt*. **~ bond** *(Brit)* Lotterieaktie *f*; **to sell sth at a ~** etw über seinem Wert verkaufen; **to be at a ~** *(St Ex)* über Pari stehen; *(fig)* hoch im Kurs stehen; **to put a ~ on sth** *(fig)* etw

hoch einschätzen.
premonition [ˌpriːmə'nɪʃən] *n (presentiment)* (böse) Vorahnung; *(forewarning)* Vorwarnung *f.*
preoccupation [priːˌɒkjʊ'peɪʃən] *n* **her ~ with her appearance** ihre ständige Sorge um ihr Äußeres; **that was his main ~** das war sein Hauptanliegen.
preoccupied [priː'ɒkjʊpaɪd] *adj* gedankenverloren. **to be ~ with sth** nur an etw *(acc)* denken.
preoccupy [priː'ɒkjʊpaɪ] *vt* (stark) beschäftigen.
prep [prep] *(col) n* = **preparation (b).**
prepacked [ˌpriː'pækt] *adj* abgepackt.
prepaid [ˌpriː'peɪd] *adj postage, goods* vorausbezahlt; *envelope* freigemacht.
preparation [ˌprepə'reɪʃən] *n* **(a)** Vorbereitung *f; (of meal, medicine etc)* Zubereitung *f.* **in ~ for sth** als Vorbereitung für etw; **to be in ~** in Vorbereitung sein; **~s for war/a journey** Kriegs-/Reisevorbereitungen *pl*; **to make ~s** Vorbereitungen treffen. **(b)** *(Brit Sch) (homework)* Hausaufgaben *pl.*
preparatory [prɪ'pærətərɪ] *adj* **(a)** *step, measure* vorbereitend. **~ to the conference** um die Konferenz vorzubereiten. **(b) ~ school** *(Brit) private Vorbereitungsschule für die Public School; (US) private Vorbereitungsschule für die Hochschule.*
prepare [prɪ'pɛəʳ] **1** *vt* vorbereiten *(sb for sth* jdn auf etw *(acc), sth for sth* etw für etw *acc)*; *meal, medicine* zubereiten; *guest-room* fertigmachen; *(Sci)* präparieren; *data* aufbereiten. **~ yourself for a shock!** mach dich auf einen Schock gefaßt! **2** *vi* **to ~ for sth** Vorbereitungen für etw treffen; **to ~ for an exam/for war** sich auf eine Prüfung vorbereiten/Kriegsvorbereitungen treffen; **to ~ to do sth** Anstalten machen, etw zu tun.
prepared [prɪ'pɛəd] *adj* **(a)** vorbereitet *(for* auf *+acc)*. **(b)** *(willing)* **to be ~ to do sth** bereit sein, etw zu tun.
preponderance [prɪ'pɒndərəns] *n* Übergewicht *nt.*
preponderant [pri'pɒndərənt] *adj* überwiegend.
preposition [ˌprepə'zɪʃən] *n* Präposition *f.*
prepossessing [ˌpriːpə'zesɪŋ] *adj* anziehend.
preposterous [pri'pɒstərəs] *adj* grotesk, absurd.
prep school *n (Brit) see* **preparatory (b).**
prerecord [ˌpriːrɪ'kɔːd] *vt* vorher aufzeichnen. **~ed cassette** bespielte Kassette.
prerequisite [ˌpriː'rekwɪzɪt] *n* Voraussetzung *f.*
prerogative [prɪ'rɒgətɪv] *n* Vorrecht *nt.*
Presbyterian [ˌprezbɪ'tɪərɪən] **1** *adj* presbyterianisch. **2** *n* Presbyterianer(in *f*) *m.*
preschool ['priː'skuːl] *adj attr* vorschulisch. **a child of ~ age** ein Kind *nt* im Vorschulalter.
prescribe [prɪ'skraɪb] *vt* **(a)** *(order, lay down)* vorschreiben. **~d reading** Pflichtlektüre *f.* **(b)** *(Med, fig)* verschreiben *(sth for sb* jdm etw*)*.
prescription [prɪ'skrɪpʃən] *n (Med)* Rezept *nt*; *(act of prescribing)* Verschreiben *nt.* **to make up** *or* **fill** *(US)* **a ~** eine Medizin zubereiten; **~ charge** Rezeptgebühr *f*; **only available on ~** rezeptpflichtig.
presence ['prezns] *n* Gegenwart, Anwesenheit *f.* **in sb's ~, in the ~ of sb** in jds Gegenwart *(dat)*; **to make one's ~ felt** sich bemerkbar machen; **a military ~** Militärpräsenz *f.*
presence of mind *n* Geistesgegenwart *f.*
present[1] ['preznt] **1** *adj* **(a)** *(in attendance)* anwesend; *(existing)* vorhanden. **to be ~** anwesend sein, da/hier sein; **to be ~ at sth** bei etw anwesend sein; **~ company excepted** Anwesende ausgenommen; **all those ~** alle Anwesenden; **carbon is ~ in organic matter** Kohlenstoff ist in organischen Stoffen vorhanden. **(b)** *(at the ~ time) moment, state of affairs etc* gegenwärtig, derzeitig; *problems, husband etc also* jetzig; *season etc* laufend. **at the ~ moment** zum jetzigen Zeitpunkt; **in the ~ circumstances** unter den gegenwärtigen Umständen; **in the ~ case** im vorliegenden Fall. **(c)** *(Gram)* **in the ~ tense** in der Gegewart, im Präsens; **~ participle** Partizip *nt* Präsens. **2** *n* Gegenwart *f*; *(Gram also)* Präsens *nt.* **at ~** zur Zeit, im Moment; **up to the ~** bislang, bis jetzt.
present[2] **1** *n (gift)* Geschenk *nt.* **to make sb a ~ of sth** jdm etw schenken *(also fig)*; **I was given it as a ~** das habe ich geschenkt bekommen.
2 [prɪ'zent] *vt* **(a)** *medal, prize etc* überreichen; *(as gift)* schenken; *(put forward)* vorlegen; *cheque (for payment)* präsentieren; *proof* erbringen *(of sth* für etw; *proposal* unterbreiten. **to ~ sb with sth, to ~ sth to sb** jdm etw überreichen; *(as a gift)* jdm etw schenken; **~ arms!** *(Mil)* präsentiert das Gewehr! **(b)** *(offer, provide) target, opportunity* bieten. **his action ~ed us with a problem** seine Tat stellte uns vor ein Problem. **(c)** *(Rad, TV)* präsentieren; *(Theat also)* aufführen; *(commentator)* moderieren. **~ing Sabine Citron as ...** *(Film)* und erstmals Sabine Citron als ... **(d)** *(introduce)* vorstellen. **to ~ Mr X to Miss Y** Herrn X Fräulein Y *(dat)* vorstellen.
3 [prɪ'zent] *vr (opportunity, problem etc)* sich ergeben.
presentable [prɪ'zentəbl] *adj* **to be ~** sich sehen lassen können; **to make oneself ~** sich zurechtmachen.
presentation [ˌprezən'teɪʃən] *n* **(a)** *(of gift etc)* Überreichung *f*; *(of prize, medal also, ceremony)* Verleihung *f*; *(gift)* Geschenk *nt.* **to make sb a ~** jdm ein Geschenk überreichen. **(b)** *(act of presenting) (of report, voucher etc)* Vorlage *f*; *(of petition)* Überreichung *f*; *(Jur: of case, evidence)* Darlegung *f.* **on ~ of a certificate** gegen Vorlage einer Bescheinigung. **(c)** *(Theat)* Inszenierung *f*; *(TV also, Rad)* Produktion *f.* **(d)** *(style of ~)* Präsentation *f.*
present-day ['preznt'deɪ] *adj attr* heutig.
presenter [prɪ'zentəʳ] *n (TV, Rad)* Moderator(in *f*) *m.*
presentiment [prɪ'zentɪmənt] *n* (Vor)ahnung *f.* **to have a ~ that ...** das Gefühl haben, daß ...
presently ['prezntlɪ] *adv* **(a)** *(soon)* bald. **(b)** *(at present)* zur Zeit, gegenwärtig.
preservation [ˌprezə'veɪʃən] *n see vt* **(a)** Erhaltung *f*; Wahrung *f*; Aufrechterhaltung *f.* **(b)** Konservierung *f (also of leather, wood)*; Präservierung *f.* **(c)** Einmachen *nt*; Einlegen *nt.* **(d)** Bewahrung *f.*
preservative [prɪ'zɜːvətɪv] *n (Cook)* Konservierungsmittel *nt.*
preserve [prɪ'zɜːv] **1** *vt* **(a)** *(keep intact, maintain) customs, building, position* erhalten; *peace also, dignity, appearances* wahren; *memory* aufrechterhalten. **(b)** *(keep from decay)* konservieren; *specimens etc* präservieren; *leather, wood* schützen. **well ~d** gut erhalten. **(c)** *(Cook)* einmachen; *(pickle)* einlegen. **(d)** *(keep from harm, save)* bewahren. **to ~ sb from sth** jdn vor etw *(dat)* bewahren. **2** *n* **(a)** *(Cook)* **~s** *pl* Eingemachtes *nt.* **(b)** *(special domain)* Ressort *nt.* **game ~** *(Hunt)* Jagdrevier *nt.*
pre-shrunk [priː'ʃrʌŋk] *adj* vorgewaschen.
preside [prɪ'zaɪd] *vi (at meeting etc)* den Vorsitz haben *(at* bei*)*. **to ~ over an organization** *etc* eine Organisation *etc* leiten.
presidency ['prezɪdənsɪ] *n* Präsidentschaft *f*; *(esp US: of company)* Aufsichtsratsvorsitz *m*; *(US Univ)* Rektorat *nt.*
president ['prezɪdənt] *n* Präsident(in *f*) *m*; *(esp US: of company)* Aufsichtsratsvorsitzende(r) *mf*; *(US Univ)* Rektor(in *f*) *m.*
presidential [ˌprezɪ'denʃəl] *adj (Pol)* Präsidenten-; *election also* Präsidentschafts-. **his ~ duties** seine Pflichten als Präsident.
press [pres] **1** *n* **(a)** *(squeeze, push)* Druck *m.* **to give sth a ~** etw drücken; *dress etc* etw bügeln.

(b) *(trouser ~, flower ~)* Presse *f.* **(c)** *(Typ)* (Drucker)presse *f*; *(publishing firm)* Verlag *m*; *(newspapers)* Presse *f.* **to go to ~** in Druck gehen; **to be in the ~** im Druck sein; **the daily ~** die Tagespresse; **the weekly ~** die Wochenzeitungen *pl*; **to get a good/bad ~** eine gute/schlechte Presse bekommen.

2 *vt* **(a)** *(push, squeeze)* drücken *(to* an *+acc)*; *button, doorbell also, brake pedal* drücken auf *(+acc)*; *clutch, piano pedal* treten; *grapes* (aus)pressen; *flowers* pressen. **(b)** *(iron) clothes* bügeln. **(c)** *(urge, persuade)* drängen; *(harass)* bedrängen; *(insist on) claim, argument* bestehen auf *(+dat)*. **to ~ sb hard** jdm (hart) zusetzen; **to ~ the point** darauf beharren *or* herumreiten *(col)*; **to ~ one's views on sb** jdm seine Ansichten aufdrängen; **to ~ sb for an answer** auf jds Antwort drängen; **to be ~ed (for money/time)** in Geldnot/Zeitnot sein; **to ~ sb/sth into service** jdn/etw einspannen. **(d)** *machine part, record etc* pressen. **~ed steel** Preßstahl *m.*

3 *vi* **(a)** *(lit, fig: bear down, exert pressure)* drücken; *(urge, agitate)* drängen; *(be insistent also)* drängeln *(col)*. **to ~ for sth** auf etw *(acc)* drängen; **time ~es** die Zeit drängt. **(b)** *(move, push)* sich drängen. **to ~ ahead (with sth)** *(fig)* (mit etw) weitermachen; *(with plans)* etw weiterführen.

♦**press on** *vi* weitermachen; *(with journey)* weiterfahren.

press: ~ agency *n* Presseagentur *f*; **~ conference** *n* Pressekonferenz *f*; **~ gallery** *n (esp Jur, Parl)* Pressetribüne *f*; **~-gang** *vt (col)* **to ~-gang sb into (doing) sth** jdn drängen, etw zu tun.

pressing ['presɪŋ] *adj (urgent)* dringend; *(insistent) requests* nachdrücklich.

press: ~ photographer *n* Pressefotograf(in *f*) *m*; **~ stud** *n (Brit)* Druckknopf *m*; **~-up** *n* Liegestütz *m.*

pressure ['preʃəʳ] **1** *n* **(a)** Druck *m (also Phys, Met)*. **at high/full ~** *(lit, fig)* unter Hochdruck. **(b)** *(compulsion, influence)* Druck, Zwang *m.* **parental ~** Druck von seiten der Eltern; **social ~s** gesellschaftliche Zwänge *pl*; **to do sth under ~** etw unter Druck tun; **to be under ~ to do sth** unter Druck stehen, etw zu tun; **to put ~ on sb** jdn unter Druck setzen; **to put the ~ on** *(col)* Dampf machen *(col)*; **~ of work prevents me** Arbeitsüberlastung hindert mich daran; **he's under a lot of ~** er ist großen Belastungen ausgesetzt. **2** *vt* = **pressurize (b).**

pressure: ~cooker *n* Druckkochtopf, Schnellkochtopf *m*; **~ group** *n* Pressure-group *f.*

pressurize ['preʃəraɪz] *vt* **(a)** *cabin, spacesuit* auf Normaldruck halten. **(b)** unter Druck setzen. **to ~ sb into doing sth** jdn so unter Druck setzen, daß er etw tut.

prestige [pre'stiːʒ] *n* Prestige *nt.*

prestigious [pre'stɪdʒəs] *adj* Prestige-. **to be (very) ~** (einen hohen) Prestigewert haben.

presumably [prɪ'zjuːməblɪ] *adv* vermutlich. **~ he is very rich, is he?** ich nehme an, er ist sehr reich, oder?

presume [prɪ'zjuːm] **1** *vt* **(a)** *(suppose)* annehmen, vermuten. **(b)** *(venture)* **to ~ to do sth** sich *(dat)* erlauben, etw zu tun. **2** *vi* **(a)** *(suppose)* annehmen, vermuten. **(b)** *(take liberties)* **I didn't want to ~** ich wollte nicht aufdringlich sein; **to ~ on** *or* **upon sth** etw überbeanspruchen.

presumption [prɪ'zʌmpʃən] *n* **(a)** *(assumption)* Annahme, Vermutung *f.* **(b)** *(boldness, arrogance)* Dreistigkeit *f.*

presumptuous [prɪ'zʌmptjuəs] *adj* unverschämt.

presuppose [ˌpriːsə'pəʊz] *vt* voraussetzen.

pretence, *(US)* **pretense** [prɪ'tens] *n* **(a)** *(story)* erfundene Geschichte; *(insincerity)* Verstellung *f*; *(affectation)* Unnatürlichkeit *f*; *(pretext)* Vorwand *m.* **he didn't really shoot me, it was just ~** er hat nicht auf mich geschossen, er hat nur so getan; **to make a ~ of being sth** so tun, als sei man etw; **it's all a ~** das ist alles nur gespielt *or* Mache *(col)*; **his ~ of innocence/friendship** seine gespielte Unschuld/Freundschaft; **let's stop all this ~** hören wir auf, uns *(dat)* etwas vorzumachen; **on** *or* **under the ~ of doing sth** unter dem Vorwand, etw zu tun. **(b) to make no ~ to sth** keinen Anspruch auf etw *(acc)* erheben.

pretend [prɪ'tend] **1** *vt* **(a)** *(make believe)* so tun, als ob; *(feign also)* vortäuschen, vorgeben. **to ~ to be interested** so tun, als ob man interessiert wäre; **to ~ to be sick** eine Krankheit vortäuschen; **to ~ to be asleep** sich schlafend stellen. **(b)** *(claim)* **I don't ~ to ...** ich behaupte nicht, daß ich ... **2** *vi* so tun, als ob; *(keep up facade)* sich verstellen. **he is only ~ing** er tut nur so (als ob).

pretense *n (US)* = **pretence.**

pretension [prɪ'tenʃən] *n* **(a)** *(claim)* Anspruch *m*; *(social, cultural)* Ambition *f.* **he makes no ~(s) to originality** er beansprucht keineswegs, originell zu sein. **(b)** *(ostentation)* Prahlerei *f*; *(affectation)* Anmaßung *f.*

pretentious [prɪ'tenʃəs] *adj* anmaßend; *speech, book* hochtrabend; *(ostentatious)* angeberisch, protzig *(col)*; *restaurant, décor* pompös.

preterite ['pretərɪt] *n* Imperfekt *nt.*

pretext ['priːtekst] *n* Vorwand *m.* **on** *or* **under the ~ of doing sth** unter dem Vorwand, etw zu tun.

pretty ['prɪtɪ] **1** *adj (+er)* **(a)** hübsch, nett. **to make oneself ~** sich hübsch machen; **I'm/she's not just a ~ face!** *(col)* ich bin gar nicht so dumm (wie ich aussehe) *(col)*/sie hat auch Köpfchen; **it wasn't ~/a ~ sight** das war alles andere als schön/das war kein schöner Anblick. **(b)** *(col)* hübsch, schön *(col)*; *price, sum also* stolz. **it'll cost a ~ penny** das wird eine schöne Stange Geld kosten *(col)*. **2** *adv (rather)* ziemlich; *good also* ganz; *(very also)* ganz schön *(col)*. **~ nearly** *or* **well finished** so gut wie fertig *(col)*.

pretzel ['pretsl] *n* Brezel *f.*

prevail [prɪ'veɪl] *vi* **(a)** *(gain mastery)* sich durchsetzen *(over, against* gegenüber*)*. **(b)** *(conditions, wind etc)* vorherrschen; *(be widespread: customs)* weit verbreitet sein. **(c)** *(persuade)* **to ~ (up)on sb to do sth** jdn dazu bewegen, etw zu tun.

prevailing [prɪ'veɪlɪŋ] *adj conditions* derzeitig; *fashion* aktuell; *opinion* herrschend; *wind* vorherrschend.

prevalence ['prevələns] *n (widespread occurrence)* Vorherrschen *nt*; *(of crime, disease)* Häufigkeit *f.*

prevalent ['prevələnt] *adj (widespread)* weit verbreitet; *conditions* herrschend; *fashions, style* beliebt.

prevaricate [prɪ'værɪkeɪt] *vi* Ausflüchte machen.

prevarication [priˌværɪ'keɪʃən] *n* Ausflucht *f*; *(prevaricating)* Ausflüchte *pl.*

prevent [prɪ'vent] *vt sth* verhindern, verhüten; *(through preventive measures)* vorbeugen *(+dat)*. **to ~ sb (from) doing sth** jdn daran hindern, etw zu tun; **to ~ sth (from) happening** verhindern, daß etw geschieht.

prevention [prɪ'venʃən] *n* Verhütung *f*; *(through preventive measures)* Vorbeugung *f (of* gegen*)*.

preventive [prɪ'ventɪv] *adj* vorbeugend, Präventiv-. **~ medicine** Präventivmedizin *f.*

preview ['priːvjuː] *n* **(a)** *(of play, film)* Vorpremiere *f*; *(of exhibition)* Vorbesichtigung *f.* **(b)** *(Film, trailer, TV)* Vorschau *f (of* auf *+acc)*.

previous ['priːvɪəs] *adj* **(a)** vorherig; *page, day* vorhergehend; *year* vorangegangen; *(with indef art)* früher. **the ~ page/day** die Seite/der Tag davor; **in ~ years** in früheren Jahren; **on a ~ occasion** bei einer früheren Gelegenheit; **I have a ~ engagement** ich habe schon einen Termin; **to have a ~ conviction** vorbestraft sein; **~ owner** Vorbesitzer(in *f*) *m.* **(b) ~ to** vor *(+dat)*; **~**

to going out ... bevor ich/er *etc* ausging, ...
previously ['priːvɪəslɪ] *adv* vorher, früher.
pre-war [priː'wɔːʳ] *adj* Vorkriegs-.
prey [preɪ] **1** *n (lit, fig)* Beute *f*. **bird of ~** Raubvogel *m*; **to fall ~ to sb/sth** *(fig)* ein Opfer von jdm/etw werden. **2** *vi* **to ~ (up)on** *(animals)* Beute machen auf *(+acc)*; *(pirates, thieves)* (aus)plündern; *(doubts)* nagen an *(+dat)*; *(anxiety)* quälen.
price [praɪs] **1** *n (lit, fig)* Preis *m*. **the ~ of cars** die Autopreise *pl*; **to go up/down in ~** teurer/billiger werden; **what is the ~ of that?** was kostet das?; **at a ~ of ...** zum Preis(e) von ...; **at a ~** zum entsprechenden Preis; **at a reduced ~** verbilligt, zu herabgesetztem Preis *(form)*; **the ~ of fame** der Preis für den Ruhm; **at any ~** um jeden Preis; **not at any ~** um keinen Preis; **at the ~ of losing his health** um den Preis seiner Gesundheit; **it's too high a ~ to pay** das ist ein zu hoher Preis; **to put a ~ on sth** einen Preis für etw nennen; **to be beyond/without ~** nicht mit Geld zu bezahlen sein; **to put a ~ on sb's head** eine Belohnung auf jds Kopf *(acc)* aussetzen.

2 *vt (fix ~ of)* den Preis festsetzen von; *(label)* auszeichnen *(at* mit*)*. **it was ~d at £5** es kostete £5; **reasonably ~d** angemessen im Preis; **~d too high/low** zu teuer/billig; **to ~ oneself out of the market** sich selbst durch zu hohe Preise konkurrenzunfähig machen.
price: ~cut *n* Preissenkung *f*; **~ fixing** *n* Preisfestlegung *f*; **~ freeze** *n* Preisstopp *m*.
priceless ['praɪslɪs] *adj* unschätzbar, von unschätzbarem Wert; *(col: amusing) joke, film* köstlich; *person* unbezahlbar.
price: ~ limit *n* Preisgrenze *f*; **~ list** *n* Preisliste *f*; **~ range** *n* Preisklasse *f*; **~ rise** *n* Preiserhöhung *f*; **~ tag** *n* Preisschild *nt*.
pricey ['praɪsɪ] *adj (Brit col)* kostspielig.
prick [prɪk] **1** *n* **(a)** *(puncture, pricking sensation)* Stich *m*. **~s of conscience** Gewissensbisse *pl*. **(b)** *(col!: penis)* Schwanz *m (col!)*. **2** *vt (puncture) oneself, sb* stechen; *balloon* durchstechen; **to ~ one's finger (with/on sth)** sich *(dat)* (mit etw) in den Finger stechen/sich *(dat)* (an etw *dat*) den Finger stechen. **3** *vi (thorn, injection etc)* stechen; *(eyes)* brennen.
♦ **prick up** *vt sep* **to ~ ~ its/one's ears** *(lit, fig)* die Ohren spitzen.
prickle ['prɪkl] *n* **(a)** *(sharp point)* Stachel *m*; *(on plants also)* Dorn *m*. **(b)** *(sensation)* Stechen *nt*; *(from wool etc)* Kratzen *nt*; *(tingle)* Prickeln *nt*.
prickly ['prɪklɪ] *adj (+er)* **(a)** *plant, animal* stach(e)lig; *material* kratzig; *sensation* stechend; *(tingling)* prickelnd. **(b)** *(fig) person* bissig.
prickly: ~ heat *n* Hitzepocken *pl*; **~ pear** *n (plant)* Feigenkaktus *m*; *(fruit)* Kaktusfeige *f*.
pride [praɪd] **1** *n* **(a)** Stolz *m*; *(arrogance)* Hochmut *m*. **to take (a) ~ in sth/in one's appearance** auf etw *(acc)* stolz sein/Wert auf sein Äußeres legen; **her ~ and joy** ihr ganzer Stolz; **the ~ of the army** der Stolz der Armee; **to have** *or* **take ~ of place** den Ehrenplatz einnehmen. **(b)** *(of lions)* Rudel *nt*. **2** *vr* **to ~ oneself on sth** sich einer Sache *(gen)* rühmen können; **I ~ myself on being something of an expert in this field** ich darf wohl behaupten, mich auf diesem Gebiet auszukennen.
priest [priːst] *n* Priester, Geistliche(r) *m*.
priestess ['priːstɪs] *n* Priesterin *f*.
priesthood ['priːsthʊd] *n* Priestertum *nt*; *(priests collectively)* Priesterschaft *f*. **to enter the ~** Priester werden.
priestly ['priːstlɪ] *adj* priesterlich; *robes, office also* Priester-.
prig [prɪg] *n (goody-goody)* Tugendlamm *nt (col)*; *(snob)* Schnösel *m (col)*.
prim [prɪm] *adj (+er) (also* **~ and proper***)* etepetete *inv (col)*; *(demure) person, dress* sittsam, züchtig; *(prudish)* prüde.
prima facie ['praɪmə'feɪʃɪ] **1** *adv* allem Anschein nach. **2** *adj* **a ~ case of ...** auf den ersten Blick ein Fall von ...; **the police have a ~ case** die Polizei hat genügend Beweise.
primarily ['praɪmərɪlɪ] *adv* in erster Linie.
primary ['praɪmərɪ] **1** *adj (chief, main)* Haupt-, wesentlich. **of ~ importance** von größter Bedeutung. **2** *n (US: election)* Vorwahl *f*.
primary: ~ colour *(Brit) or* **color** *(US) n* Grundfarbe *f*; **~ education** *n* Grundschul(aus)bildung *f*; **~ school** *n* Grundschule *f*; **~ teacher** *n* Grundschullehrer(in *f*) *m*.
primate ['praɪmeɪt] *n* **(a)** *(Zool)* Primat *m*. **(b)** ['praɪmɪt] *(Eccl)* Primas *m*.
prime [praɪm] **1** *adj* **(a)** *(major, chief)* Haupt-, wesentlich. **of ~ importance** von größter Bedeutung. **(b)** *(excellent)* erstklassig. **in ~ condition** *(meat, fruit etc)* von hervorragender Qualität; *(athlete, car etc)* in erstklassiger Verfassung. **(c)** *(Math)* Prim-.

2 *n* **in the ~ of life** in der Blüte seiner Jahre; **he is in/past his ~** er ist in den besten Jahren/er ist über seine besten Jahre hinaus; *(singer, artist)* er ist an seinem Höhepunkt angelangt/er hat seine beste Zeit hinter sich.

3 *vt* **(a)** *bomb* scharf machen; *pump* vorpumpen; *surface for painting* grundieren. **(b)** *(with advice, information)* instruieren. **to be well ~d for the interview/game** für das Interview/Spiel gut gerüstet sein.
prime: ~ minister *n* Premierminister(in *f*) *m*; **~ number** *n* Primzahl *f*.
primer ['praɪməʳ] *n* **(a)** *(paint, coat)* Grundierung *f*. **(b)** *(book)* Fibel *f*. **(c)** *(explosive)* Zünder *m*.
primeval [praɪ'miːvəl] *adj* urzeitlich; *forest* Ur-.
primitive ['prɪmɪtɪv] *adj* primitiv.
primrose ['prɪmrəʊz] **1** *n (Bot)* Primel *f*; *(colour)* Blaßgelb *nt*. **2** *adj* blaßgelb.
primula ['prɪmjʊlə] *n* Primel *f*.
primus (stove) ® ['praɪməs(ˌstəʊv)] *n* Primuskocher *m*.
prince [prɪns] *n (king's son)* Prinz *m*; *(ruler)* Fürst *m*. **P~ Charming** *(fig)* Märchenprinz *m*; **~ consort/regent** Prinzgemahl *m*/-regent *m*.
princely ['prɪnslɪ] *adj (lit, fig)* fürstlich.
princess [prɪn'ses] *n* Prinzessin *f*; *(wife of ruler)* Fürstin *f*.
principal ['prɪnsɪpəl] **1** *adj* Haupt-, hauptsächlich. **the ~ cities of China** die wichtigsten Städte Chinas; **my ~ concern** mein Hauptanliegen *nt*; **~ horn** erster Hornist, erste Hornistin. **2** *n* **(a)** *(of school, college)* Rektor *m*; *(in play)* Hauptperson *f*. **(b)** *(Fin, of investment)* Kapital(summe *f*) *nt*.
principality [ˌprɪnsɪ'pælɪtɪ] *n* Fürstentum *nt*.
principally ['prɪnsɪpəlɪ] *adv* vornehmlich, in erster Linie.
principle ['prɪnsɪpl] *n (moral precept)* Prinzip *nt*, Grundsatz *m*. **in/on ~** im/aus Prinzip, prinzipiell; **a man of ~(s)** ein Mensch mit Prinzipien; **it's against my ~s** es geht gegen meine Prinzipien; **it's a matter of ~, it's the ~ of the thing** es geht dabei ums Prinzip.
print [prɪnt] **1** *n* **(a)** *(typeface)* Schrift *f*; *(~ed matter)* Gedruckte(s) *nt*. **out of/in ~** vergriffen/gedruckt; **to see sth in cold ~** etw schwarz auf weiß sehen; **he'll never get into ~** er wird nie etwas veröffentlichen; **in big/small ~** groß/klein gedruckt. **(b)** *(picture)* Druck *m*; *(Phot)* Abzug *m*, Kopie *f*; *(fabric)* bedruckter Stoff; *(cotton ~)* Kattun *m*. **(c)** *(impression: of foot etc)* Abdruck *m*. **2** *vt* **(a)** *book, design* drucken; *fabric* bedrucken. **(b)** *(publish) story* veröffentlichen. **(c)** *(write)* in Druckschrift schreiben.
♦ **print out** *vt sep (Comp)* ausdrucken.
printed ['prɪntɪd] *adj* Druck-, gedruckt; *(written in capitals)* in Großbuchstaben; *fabric* bedruckt. **~ matter/papers** Drucksache *f*; **~ circuit** ge-

druckte Schaltung; ~ **circuit board** Leiterplatte *f.*
printer ['prɪntəʳ] *n* Drucker *m.* **~'s error** Druckfehler *m;* **~'s ink** Druckerschwärze *f.*
printing ['prɪntɪŋ] *n* **(a)** *(process)* Drucken *nt.* **(b)** *(unjoined writing)* Druckschrift *f; (characters, print)* Schrift *f.* **(c)** *(quantity printed)* Auflage *f.*
printing: ~ **press** *n* Druckerpresse *f;* ~ **works** *n sing or pl* Druckerei *f.*
printout ['prɪntaʊt] *n (Comp)* Ausdruck *m.*
prior[1] ['praɪəʳ] *adj* **(a)** *knowledge, warning, agreement* vorherig; *(earlier)* früher. ~ **claim** Vorrecht *nt (to* auf*);* **a ~ engagement** eine vorher getroffene Verabredung. **(b)** ~ **to sth** vor etw *(dat);* ~ **to going out ...** bevor ich/er *etc* ausging, ...
prior[2] *n (Eccl)* Prior *m.*
priority [praɪ'ɒrɪtɪ] *n* Vorrang *m,* Priorität *f; (thing having precedence)* vorrangige Angelegenheit. **a top ~** eine Sache von äußerster Dringlichkeit; **to have ~** Vorrang *or* Priorität haben; **to give ~ to sth** etw vorrangig behandeln, einer Sache *(dat)* Priorität geben; **order of ~** nach Dringlichkeit; **we must get our priorities right** wir müssen unsere Prioritäten richtig setzen.
prise, *(US)* **prize** [praɪz] *vt* **to ~ sth open** etw aufbrechen; **to ~ the lid up/off** den Deckel auf-/abbekommen.
prism ['prɪzəm] *n* Prisma *nt.*
prison ['prɪzn] **1** *(lit, fig)* Gefängnis *nt.* **to be in ~** im Gefängnis sein; **to go to ~ for 5 years** für 5 Jahre ins Gefängnis gehen; **to send sb to ~** jdn ins Gefängnis schicken. **2** *attr* Gefängnis-; *system, facilities* Strafvollzugs-. ~ **camp** Gefangenenlager *nt;* ~ **life** das Leben im Gefängnis.
prisoner ['prɪznəʳ] *n* Gefangene(r) *mf; (convicted also)* Häftling *m.* **to hold** *or* **keep sb ~** jdn gefangenhalten; **to take sb ~** jdn gefangennehmen; ~ **of war** Kriegsgefangene(r) *m;* ~ **of war camp** (Kriegs)gefangenenlager *nt.*
pristine ['prɪstaɪn] *adj beauty* unberührt; *condition* tadellos, makellos.
privacy ['prɪvəsɪ, 'praɪvəsɪ] *n* Privatleben *nt.* **there is no ~** man kann kein Privatleben führen; **in the ~ of one's home** im eigenen Heim; **in the strictest ~** *(meeting etc)* unter äußerster Geheimhaltung.
private ['praɪvɪt] **1** *adj* **(a)** privat; *letter, reasons* persönlich; *matter* Privat-, vertraulich; *place* abgelegen; *funeral* im engsten Kreis; *hearing etc* nichtöffentlich *attr.* ~ **property** Privateigentum *nt;* **they wanted to be ~** sie wollten für sich sein; **to keep sth ~** etw für sich behalten; **his ~ life** sein Privatleben *nt;* **with ~ bathroom** mit eigenem Bad. **(b)** ~ **car** Privatwagen *m;* ~ **citizen** Privatperson *f:* ~ **enterprise** Privatunternehmen *nt; (free enterprise)* freies Unternehmertum; ~ **eye** *(col)* Privatdetektiv *m;* ~ **parts** *(genitals)* Geschlechtsteile *pl;* ~ **practice** Privatpraxis *f;* ~ **school** Privatschule *f;* ~ **sector** privater Sektor. **2** *n* **(a)** *(Mil)* Gefreite(r) *mf.* **(b) in ~** privat; **we must talk in ~** wir müssen das unter uns besprechen.
privately ['praɪvɪtlɪ] *adv* **(a)** *(not publicly)* privat. **(b)** *(secretly, personally)* persönlich; *(in confidence)* vertraulich. **but ~ he was very upset** doch innerlich war er sehr aufgebracht.
privation [praɪ'veɪʃən] *n* **(a)** *(state)* Armut, Not *f.* **(b)** *(hardship)* Entbehrung *f.*
privatization [ˌpraɪvətaɪ'zeɪʃən] *n* Privatisierung *f.*
privatize ['praɪvətaɪz] *vt* privatisieren.
privet ['prɪvɪt] *n* Liguster *m.*
privilege ['prɪvɪlɪdʒ] **1** *n* Privileg, Sonderrecht *nt; (honour)* Ehre *f; (Parl)* Immunität *f.* **2** *vt* privilegieren, bevorrechtigen. **I was ~d to talk to him** ich hatte die Ehre, mich mit ihm zu unterhalten.
privileged ['prɪvɪlɪdʒd] *adj person, classes* privilegiert. **for a ~ few** für eine kleine Gruppe von Privilegierten.
privy ['prɪvɪ] *adj* **(a) to be ~ to sth** in etw *(acc)* eingeweiht sein. **(b) P~ Council, P~ Councillor** Geheimer Rat.
prize[1] [praɪz] **1** *n* Preis *m; (in lottery also)* Gewinn *m.* **to win first ~** den ersten Preis gewinnen. **2** *adj* **(a)** *(awarded a ~) entry, essay* preisgekrönt. ~ **idiot** *(col)* Vollidiot *m (col).* **(b)** *(awarded as a ~) trophy* Sieges-. **(c)** *(offering a ~) competition* Preis-. ~ **draw** Lotterie *f.* **3** *vt* (hoch)schätzen. **~d possession** wertvollster Besitz.
prize[2] *vt (US)* = **prise.**
prize: **~-fight** *n* Berufsboxkampf *m;* **~-giving** *n (Sch)* Preisverteilung *f;* ~ **money** *n* Geldpreis *m; (in competition)* Gewinn *m;* **~winner** *n* (Preis)gewinner(in *f*) *m;* **~winning** *adj entry, novel* preisgekrönt; *ticket* Gewinn-.
pro[1] [prəʊ] *n (col: professional)* Profi *m.*
pro[2] **1** *prep (in favour of)* für. **2** *n* **the ~s and the cons** das Für und Wider, das Pro und Kontra.
pro- *pref (in favour of)* pro-. **~-Soviet** prosowjetisch.
probability [ˌprɒbə'bɪlɪtɪ] *n* Wahrscheinlichkeit *f.* **in all ~** höchstwahrscheinlich.
probable ['prɒbəbl] *adj* wahrscheinlich.
probably ['prɒbəblɪ] *adv* wahrscheinlich. **more ~ than not** höchstwahrscheinlich.
probate ['prəʊbɪt] *n (examination)* gerichtliche Testamentsbestätigung; *(will)* beglaubigte Testamentsabschrift.
probation [prə'beɪʃən] *n* **(a)** *(Jur)* Bewährung *f.* **to put sb on ~ (for a year)** jdm (ein Jahr) Bewährung geben; **to be on ~** Bewährung haben; **to be released on ~** auf Bewährung freigelassen werden; ~ **officer** Bewährungshelfer(in *f*) *m.* **(b)** *(of employee)* Probe *f; (~ period)* Probezeit *f.*
probe [prəʊb] **1** *n* **(a)** *(device)* Sonde *f.* **(b)** *(investigation)* Untersuchung *f (into gen).* **2** *vt* untersuchen; *space, sb's past, private life* erforschen; *mystery* ergründen. **3** *vi* suchen, forschen *(for* nach*); (Med)* untersuchen *(for* auf *+acc).* **to ~ into sb's private life** in jds Privatleben *(dat)* herumschnüffeln *(col).*
probing ['prəʊbɪŋ] **1** *n* Untersuchung *f.* **2** *adj question, study* prüfend.
problem ['prɒbləm] *n* Problem *nt; (Math: as school exercise)* Aufgabe *f.* **what's the ~?** wo fehlt's?; **he's got a drinking ~** er trinkt (zuviel); **I had no ~ in getting the money** ich habe das Geld ohne Schwierigkeiten bekommen; **no ~!** *(col)* kein Problem!; ~ **area** Problembereich *m.*
problematic(al) [ˌprɒblə'mætɪk(əl)] *adj* problematisch.
problem: ~ **child** *n* Problemkind *nt;* ~ **page** *n* Problemseite *f.*
procedure [prə'siːdʒəʳ] *n* Verfahren *nt.* **business ~** geschäftliche Verfahrensweise.
proceed [prə'siːd] **1** *vi* **(a)** *(form: go)* gehen; fahren. **(b)** *(form: go on) (person)* weitergehen; *(vehicle, by vehicle)* weiterfahren. **we then ~ed to London** wir fuhren dann nach London weiter. **(c)** *(set about sth)* vorgehen; *(carry on, continue)* fortfahren. **can we now ~ to the next item on the agenda?** können wir jetzt zum nächsten Punkt der Tagesordnung übergehen?; **they ~ed with their plan** sie führten ihren Plan weiter; *(start)* sie gingen nach ihrem Plan vor; **negotiations are ~ing well** die Verhandlungen kommen gut voran; **to ~ on the assumption that ...** von der Voraussetzung ausgehen, daß ... **(d)** *(originate)* **to ~ from** kommen von; *(fig)* herrühren von. **(e)** *(Jur)* **to ~ against sb** gegen jdn gerichtlich vorgehen.

2 *vt* **now, he ~ed** nun, fuhr er fort; **to ~ to do sth** (dann) etw tun.

proceeding [prə'si:dɪŋ] *n* **(a)** *(course of action)* Vorgehen *nt.* **(b)** ~**s** *pl (function)* Veranstaltung *f.* **(c)** ~**s** *pl (esp Jur)* Verfahren *nt;* **to take/start** ~**s against sb** gegen jdn gerichtlich vorgehen; **to take legal** ~**s** einen Prozeß anstrengen. **(d)** ~**s** *pl (written minutes etc)* Protokoll *nt; (published report)* Tätigkeitsbericht *m.*

proceeds ['prəʊsi:dz] *npl (yield)* Ertrag *m; (from sale etc)* Erlös *m; (takings)* Einnahmen *pl.*

process[1] ['prəʊses] **1** *n* **(a)** Prozeß *m.* **in the** ~ **of time** im Laufe der Zeit; **in the** ~ dabei; **in the** ~ **of learning** beim Lernen; **to be in the** ~ **of doing sth** dabei sein, etw zu tun; **in** ~ **of construction** im Bau. **(b)** *(method, technique)* Verfahren *nt.* **2** *vt (treat) raw materials, data* verarbeiten; *food* konservieren; *milk* sterilisieren; *application, loan* bearbeiten; *film* entwickeln. ~**ed cheese,** *(US)* ~ **cheese** Schmelzkäse *m.*

process[2] [prə'ses] *vi (Brit: go in procession)* ziehen, schreiten.

processing ['prəʊsesɪŋ] *n see vt* Verarbeitung *f;* Konservierung *f;* Sterilisierung *f;* Bearbeitung *f;* Entwicklung *f.*

procession [prə'seʃən] *n (organized)* Umzug *m; (solemn)* Prozession *f; (line of people, cars etc)* Reihe, Schlange *f.* **funeral** ~ Trauerzug *m.*

processor ['prəʊsesəʳ] *n (Comp)* Prozessor *m.*

proclaim [prə'kleɪm] *vt* **(a)** erklären; *revolution* ausrufen. **to** ~ **sb king** jdn zum König ausrufen. **(b)** *(reveal)* verraten.

proclamation [,prɒklə'meɪʃən] *n* Erklärung *f; (of laws, measures)* Verkündung *f; (of state of emergency)* Ausrufung *f.*

proclivity [prə'klɪvɪtɪ] *n* Neigung *f (for* zu*).*

procrastinate [prəʊ'kræstɪneɪt] *vi* zögern, zaudern.

procreation [,prəʊkrɪ'eɪʃən] *n* Zeugung *f.*

procure [prə'kjʊəʳ] *vt* **(a)** *(obtain)* beschaffen, sich *(dat)* verschaffen; *(bring about)* bewirken. **to** ~ **sth for sb/oneself** jdm/sich etw beschaffen. **(b)** *(for prostitution)* beschaffen *(for sb* jdm*).*

prod [prɒd] **1** *n* Stoß, Knuff *(col) m.* **to give sb a** ~ jdn anstoßen; *(fig)* jdm einen Stoß geben. **2** *vt* **(a)** stoßen, knuffen *(col).* **he** ~**ded the donkey (on) with his stick** er trieb den Esel mit seinem Stock vorwärts. **(b)** *(fig)* anspornen *(to do sth, into sth* zu etw*).* **to** ~ **sb into action** jdm einen Stoß geben. **3** *vi* **to** ~ **at sth** an etw *(acc)* stoßen.

prodigal ['prɒdɪgəl] *adj* verschwenderisch. **the** ~ **son** *(Bibl, fig)* der verlorene Sohn.

prodigious [prə'dɪdʒəs] *adj (vast)* ungeheuer; *(marvellous)* erstaunlich, wunderbar.

prodigy ['prɒdɪdʒɪ] *n* Wunder *nt.* **child** ~ Wunderkind *nt.*

produce ['prɒdju:s] **1** *n no pl (Agr)* Produkt(e *pl*), Erzeugnis(se *pl*) *nt.* ~ **of Italy** italienisches Erzeugnis. **2** [prə'dju:s] *vt* **(a)** *(manufacture)* produzieren; *cars, steel, paper etc also* herstellen; *energy* erzeugen; *crop, return on capital* abwerfen; *coal also* fördern; *(create) book, article* schreiben; *painting* anfertigen; *ideas also, delinquents etc* hervorbringen. **(b)** *(bring forward, show) gift, wallet etc* hervorholen *(from, out of* aus*); pistol* ziehen *(from, out of* aus*); evidence* liefern; *witness* beibringen; *ticket, documents* vorzeigen. **I can't** ~ **it out of thin air** ich kann es doch nicht aus dem Ärmel schütteln *(col).* **(c)** *play* inszenieren; *film* produzieren. **(d)** *(cause) bitterness, impression* hervorrufen; *interest also, spark* erzeugen.

producer [prə'dju:səʳ] *n* Hersteller *m; (Agr)* Produzent, Erzeuger *m; (Theat)* Regisseur *m; (Film, TV)* Produzent *m.*

product ['prɒdʌkt] *n* Produkt, Erzeugnis *nt; (fig: result, Math, Chem)* Produkt *nt.* **food** ~**s** Nahrungsmittel *pl.*

production [prə'dʌkʃən] *n* **(a)** *see vt (a)* Produktion *f;* Herstellung *f;* Erzeugung *f;* Förderung *f;* Schreiben *nt;* Hervorbringung *f.* **to go into** ~ *(factory)* die Produktion aufnehmen; *(model)* in Produktion gehen; **to take sth out of** ~ etw aus der Produktion nehmen. **(b)** *(output)* Produktion *f.* **(c)** *see vt (b)* Hervorholen *nt;* Lieferung *f;* Vorzeigen *nt.* **on** ~ **of this ticket** gegen Vorlage dieser Eintrittskarte. **(d)** *(of play)* Inszenierung *f; (of film)* Produktion *f.*

production line *n* Fließband *nt.*

productive [prə'dʌktɪv] *adj* produktiv; *land* fruchtbar; *mind* schöpferisch; *business* rentabel.

productivity [,prɒdʌk'tɪvɪtɪ] *n see adj* Produktivität *f;* Fruchtbarkeit *f;* schöpferische Kraft.

productivity: ~ **agreement** *n* Produktivitätsvereinbarung *f;* ~ **bonus** *n* Leistungszulage *f.*

profane [prə'feɪn] **1** *adj* **(a)** *(secular)* weltlich, profan. **(b)** *(irreverent, sacrilegious)* (gottes)lästerlich. **2** *vt* entweihen.

profanity [prə'fænɪtɪ] *n* Gotteslästerlichkeit *f; (act, utterance)* (Gottes)lästerung *f.*

profess [prə'fes] *vt* **(a)** *faith, belief etc* sich bekennen zu. **(b)** *(claim to have) interest, enthusiasm* bekunden; *belief* kundtun; *ignorance* zugeben. **she** ~**es to be 25** sie behauptet, 25 zu sein.

professed [prə'fest] *adj* erklärt; *(pej: purported)* angeblich. **to be a** ~ **Christian** sich zum christlichen Glauben bekennen.

profession [prə'feʃən] *n* **(a)** *(occupation)* Beruf *m.* **the medical/teaching** ~ der Arzt-/Lehrerberuf; *(members of the* ~*)* die Ärzte-/Lehrerschaft; **by** ~ von Beruf; **the** ~**s** die gehobenen Berufe. **(b)** *(declaration)* Bekenntnis *f; (Eccl)* Gelübde *nt.* ~ **of faith** Glaubensbekenntnis *nt.*

professional [prə'feʃənl] **1** *adj* **(a)** Berufs-, beruflich; *army, soldier, tennis player* Berufs-; *opinion* fachmännisch, fachlich. **the** ~ **classes** die gehobenen Berufe; **to take** ~ **advice** fachmännischen Rat einholen; **to turn** *or* **go** ~ Profi werden. **(b)** *(skilled, competent) piece of work etc* fachmännisch, fachgerecht; *company, approach* professionell. **it's not up to** ~ **standards** es entspricht nicht fachlichen Normen; **it wouldn't be** ~ **of me to ...** es wäre nicht korrekt von mir, wenn ich ... **2** *n* Profi *m.*

professionalism [prə'feʃnəlɪzəm] *n* Professionalismus *m; (of job, piece of work)* Perfektion *f.*

professionally [prə'feʃnəlɪ] *adv* beruflich; *(in accomplished manner)* fachmännisch; *work* professionell. **he plays** ~ er ist Berufsspieler *or* Profi; **he is** ~ **recognized as the best ...** er ist in Fachkreisen als der beste ... bekannt.

professor [prə'fesəʳ] *n* Professor(in *f*) *m; (US also: teacher)* Dozent(in *f*) *m.*

proffer ['prɒfəʳ] *vt gift, drink* anbieten; *apologies, thanks etc* aussprechen; *remark* machen.

proficiency [prə'fɪʃənsɪ] *n* **level** *or* **standard of** ~ Leistungsstand *m;* **her** ~ **at teaching** ihre Tüchtigkeit als Lehrerin; ~ **test** Leistungstest *m.*

proficient [prə'fɪʃənt] *adj* tüchtig, fähig. **he is just about** ~ **in German** seine Deutschkenntnisse reichen gerade aus.

profile ['prəʊfaɪl] *n* Profil *nt; (picture, photograph)* Profilbild *nt; (biographical* ~*)* Porträt *nt.* **in** ~ *(person, head)* im Profil; **to keep a low** ~ sich zurückhalten.

profit ['prɒfɪt] **1** *n* Gewinn, Profit *(also pej) m.* ~ **and loss account** Gewinn-und-Verlust-Rechnung *f;* **to make a** ~ **(out of** *or* **on sth)** (mit etw) einen Gewinn machen, (an etw *dat*) verdienen; **to sell sth at a** ~ etw mit Gewinn verkaufen. **2** *vi (gain)* profitieren *(by, from* von*),* Nutzen ziehen *(by, from* aus*).*

profitability [,prɒfɪtə'bɪlɪtɪ] *n* Rentabilität *f.*

profitable ['prɒfɪtəbl] *adj (Comm)* gewinnbringend, rentabel; *(fig: beneficial)* nützlich.

profiteering [,prɒfɪ'tɪərɪŋ] *n* Wucher(ei *f*) *m.*

profit: ~**-making** *adj organization* rentabel;

(~-*orientated)* auf Gewinn gerichtet; ~ **margin** *n* Gewinnspanne *f*; ~**-sharing** *n* Gewinnbeteiligung *f*.

profligate ['prɒflɪgɪt] *adj (dissolute)* lasterhaft; *(extravagant)* verschwenderisch.

pro forma invoice [,prəʊ'fɔːmə'ɪnvɔɪs] *n* Pro-Forma-Rechnung *f*.

profound [prə'faʊnd] *adj* tief; *thought, thinker* tiefgründig; *book* gehaltvoll; *knowledge* profund *(geh)*; *indifference* völlig; *interest* stark; *changes* tiefgreifend *attr*.

profoundly [prə'faʊndlɪ] *adv* zutiefst. ~ **significant** äußerst bedeutsam; ~ **indifferent** vollkommen gleichgültig; **..., he said** ~ ..., sagte er tiefsinnig.

profundity [prə'fʌndɪtɪ] *n* **(a)** *no pl* Tiefe *f*; *(of thought, thinker, book etc)* Tiefgründigkeit *f*; *(of knowledge)* Gründlichkeit *f*. **(b)** *(profound remark)* Tiefsinnigkeit *f*.

profuse [prə'fjuːs] *adj vegetation* üppig; *thanks, praise* überschwenglich; *apologies* überreichlich.

profusely [prə'fjuːslɪ] *adv grow* üppig; *bleed, sweat* stark; *thank, praise* überschwenglich. **he apologized** ~ er entschuldigte sich vielmals.

profusion [prə'fjuːʒən] *n* Überfülle *f*. **trees in** ~ Bäume in Hülle und Fülle.

prognosis [prɒg'nəʊsɪs] *n, pl* **prognoses** [prɒg'nəʊsiːz] Prognose, Voraussage *f*.

program ['prəʊgræm] **1** *n* **(a)** *(Comp)* Programm *nt*. **(b)** *(US)* = **programme 1. 2** *vt* **(a)** *computer* programmieren. **(b)** *(US)* = **programme 2.**

programme, *(US)* **program** ['prəʊgræm] **1** *n* Programm *nt*; *(Rad, TV also)* Sendung *f*. **we've got a very heavy** ~ **of meetings** wir haben sehr viele Besprechungen auf unserem Programm; **what's the** ~ **for tomorrow?** was steht für morgen auf dem Programm? **2** *vt* programmieren.

programmer ['prəʊgræmə^r] *n* Programmierer(in *f*) *m*.

programming ['prəʊgræmɪŋ] *n* Programmieren *nt*. ~ **language** Programmiersprache *f*.

progress ['prəʊgres] **1** *n* **(a)** *no pl (movement forwards)* Vorwärtskommen *nt*; *(Mil)* Vorrücken *nt*. **they made good** ~ **across the open country** sie kamen im offenen Gelände gut vorwärts. **(b)** *no pl (advance)* Fortschritt *m*. **the** ~ **of events** der Gang der Ereignisse; **to make (good/slow)** ~ (gute/langsame) Fortschritte machen; ~ **report** Fortschrittsbericht *m*; **in** ~ im Gange; **the work still in** ~ die noch zu erledigende Arbeit.

2 [prə'gres] *vi* **(a)** *(move, go forward)* sich vorwärts bewegen. **(b)** *(in time)* **as the work** ~**es** mit dem Fortschreiten der Arbeit; **as the game** ~**ed** im Laufe des Spiels. **(c)** *(improve, make progress)* Fortschritte machen. **how far have you** ~**ed since our last meeting?** wie weit sind Sie seit unserer letzten Sitzung vorangekommen?; **investigations are** ~**ing well** die Untersuchungen machen gute Fortschritte.

progression [prə'greʃən] *n* Folge *f*; *(Math)* Reihe *f*; *(Mus)* Sequenz *f*; *(development)* Entwicklung *f*. **sales have shown a continuous upwards** ~ im Absatz wurde eine stete Aufwärtsentwicklung verzeichnet.

progressive [prə'gresɪv] *adj* **(a)** *(increasing)* zunehmend; *disease etc* fortschreitend; *paralysis, taxation* progressiv. **(b)** *(favouring progress)* progressiv, fortschrittlich.

progressively [prə'gresɪvlɪ] *adv* zunehmend.

prohibit [prə'hɪbɪt] *vt* **(a)** verbieten, untersagen. **to** ~ **sb from doing sth** jdm etw verbieten *or* untersagen. **"smoking** ~**ed"** „Rauchen verboten". **(b)** *(prevent)* verhindern. **to** ~ **sb from doing sth** jdn daran hindern, etw zu tun.

prohibition [,prəʊɪ'bɪʃən] *n* Verbot *nt*. **(the) P**~ *(Hist)* die Prohibition; **the** ~ **of smoking** das Rauchverbot.

prohibitive [prə'hɪbɪtɪv] *adj price, cost* unerschwinglich.

project[1] ['prɒdʒekt] *n* Projekt *nt*; *(scheme)* Vorhaben *nt*; *(Sch, Univ)* Referat *nt*.

project[2] [prə'dʒekt] **1** *vt* **(a)** *film, map, figures* projizieren. **to** ~ **oneself/one's personality** sich selbst/seine eigene Person zur Geltung bringen; **to** ~ **one's voice** seine Stimme zum Tragen bringen. **(b)** *(plan)* voraussagen; *costs* überschlagen. **2** *vi* **(a)** *(plan)* planen. **(b)** *(jut out)* hervorragen *(from* aus*)*. **the upper storey** ~**s over the road** das obere Stockwerk ragt über die Straße.

projectile [prə'dʒektaɪl] *n (also Mil)* Geschoß *nt*.

projection [prə'dʒekʃən] *n* **(a)** *(of films, map)* Projektion *f*. ~ **room** Vorführraum *m*. **(b)** *(overhang etc)* Vorsprung *m*. **(c)** *(prediction)* Prognose *f*; *(of cost)* Überschlagung *f*.

projector [prə'dʒektə^r] *n (Film)* Projektor *m*.

proletarian [,prəʊlə'teərɪən] **1** *adj* proletarisch. **2** *n* Proletarier(in *f*) *m*.

proletariat [,prəʊlə'teərɪət] *n* Proletariat *nt*.

proliferate [prə'lɪfəreɪt] *vi (number)* sich stark erhöhen; *(ideas)* um sich greifen; *(animals)* sich stark vermehren; *(weeds, cells)* wuchern.

proliferation [prə,lɪfə'reɪʃən] *n (in numbers)* starke Erhöhung; *(of animals)* zahlreiche Vermehrung; *(of nuclear weapons)* Weitergabe *f*; *(of ideas)* Ausbreitung *f*; *(of weeds)* Wuchern *nt*.

prolific [prə'lɪfɪk] *adj* fruchtbar; *writer* produktiv.

prologue ['prəʊlɒg] *n* Prolog *m*; *(of book)* Vorwort *nt*; *(fig)* Vorspiel *nt*.

prolong [prə'lɒŋ] *vt* verlängern; *(pej) process, pain* hinauszögern.

prolongation [,prəʊlɒŋ'geɪʃən] *n see vt* Verlängerung *f*; Hinauszögern *nt*.

promenade [,prɒmɪ'nɑːd] **1** *n (esp Brit: esplanade)* (Strand)promenade *f*; *(US: ball)* Studenten-/Schülerball *m*. ~ **concert** Konzert *nt (in gelockertem Rahmen)*; ~ **deck** Promenadendeck *nt*. **2** *vi (stroll)* promenieren.

prominence ['prɒmɪnəns] *n* **(a) the** ~ **of his features** seine ausgeprägten Gesichtszüge. **(b)** *(of ideas, beliefs)* Beliebtheit *f*; *(of writer, politician etc)* Bekanntheit *f*. **to come into** ~ in den Vordergrund rücken; *(person)* in Erscheinung treten; **to bring sb/sth into** ~ *(attract attention to)* jdn/etw herausstellen; *(make famous)* jdn/etw berühmt machen. **(c)** *(prominent part)* Vorsprung *m*.

prominent ['prɒmɪnənt] *adj* **(a)** *cheek-bones, teeth* vorstehend *attr*; *crag* vorspringend *attr*. **to be** ~ vorstehen; vorspringen. **(b)** *(conspicuous) markings* auffällig; *feature, characteristic* hervorstechend. **the castle occupies a** ~ **position** das Schloß hat eine exponierte Lage. **(c)** *(leading) role* führend; *(significant)* wichtig. **(d)** *(well-known) personality, publisher* prominent.

prominently ['prɒmɪnəntlɪ] *adv display, place* deutlich sichtbar. **he figured** ~ er spielte eine bedeutende Rolle.

promiscuity [,prɒmɪ'skjuːɪtɪ] *n* Promiskuität *f*.

promiscuous [prə'mɪskjʊəs] *adj (sexually)* **to be** ~ häufig den Partner wechseln; ~ **behaviour** häufiger Partnerwechsel.

promise ['prɒmɪs] **1** *n* **(a)** Versprechen *nt*. **their** ~ **of help** ihr Versprechen zu helfen; **to make sb a** ~ jdm ein Versprechen geben; **to hold** *or* **keep sb to his** ~ jdn an sein Versprechen binden. **(b)** *(hope, prospect)* Hoffnung, Aussicht *f*. **a young man of** ~ ein vielversprechender junger Mann; **to show** ~ zu den besten Hoffnungen berechtigen. **2** *vt* versprechen; *(forecast)* hindeuten auf *(+acc)*. **to** ~ **(sb) to do sth** (jdm) versprechen, etw zu tun; **to** ~ **sb sth, to** ~ **sth to sb** jdm etw versprechen; **to** ~ **sb the earth** jdm das Blaue

vom Himmel herunter versprechen; **it ~s to be a hard day** es sieht nach einem harten Tag aus. **3** *vi* versprechen. **(do you) ~?** versprichst du es?; **I'll try, but I'm not promising** ich werde es versuchen, aber ich kann nichts versprechen.
promising ['prɒmɪsɪŋ] *adj* vielversprechend.
promissory note ['prɒmɪsərɪ'nəʊt] *n* Schuldschein *m*.
promontory ['prɒməntrɪ] *n* Kap *nt*.
promote [prə'məʊt] *vt* **(a)** *(in rank)* befördern *(to* zu +*dat)*. **our team was ~d** *(Ftbl)* unsere Mannschaft ist aufgestiegen. **(b)** *(foster)* fördern; *(organize) conference etc* veranstalten; *(advertise)* werben für; *(put on the market)* auf den Markt bringen.
promoter [prə'məʊtə^r] *n (Sport, of beauty contest etc)* Promoter, Veranstalter *m*; *(of company)* Mitbegründer *m*.
promotion [prə'məʊʃən] *n* **(a)** *(in rank)* Beförderung *f*. **to get** *or* **win ~** befördert werden; *(football team)* aufsteigen. **(b)** *(fostering)* Förderung *f*; *(organization: of conference etc)* Veranstaltung *f*; *(advertising)* Werbung, Promotion *f (of* für); *(advertising campaign)* Werbekampagne *f*; *(marketing)* Einführung *f* auf dem Markt.
promotional [prə'məʊʃənəl] *adj literature etc* Werbe-.
prompt [prɒmpt] **1** *adj* (+*er*) prompt; *action* unverzüglich. **he is always very ~** *(on time)* er ist immer sehr pünktlich. **2** *adv* **at 6 o'clock ~** Punkt 6 Uhr. **3** *vt* **(a)** *(motivate)* veranlassen *(to* zu). **to ~ sb to do sth** jdn (dazu) veranlassen, etw zu tun; **what ~ed you to do it?** was hat Sie dazu veranlaßt? **(b)** *conclusion* nahelegen. **(c)** *(help with speech)* vorsagen *(sb* jdm); *(Theat)* soufflieren *(sb* jdm). **he didn't need any ~ing** *(fig)* das brauchte man ihm nicht zweimal zu sagen.
prompter ['prɒmptə^r] *n* Souffleur *m*, Souffleuse *f*.
promptly ['prɒmptlɪ] *adv* prompt. **they left ~ at 6** sie gingen Punkt 6 Uhr; **of course he ~ forgot it all** er hat natürlich prompt alles vergessen.
prone [prəʊn] *adj* **(a)** *(lying)* **to be** *or* **lie ~** auf dem Bauch liegen. **(b)** *(liable)* **to be ~ to sth/to do sth** zu etw neigen/dazu neigen, etw zu tun.
prong [prɒŋ] *n* **(a)** *(of fork)* Zinke *f*. **(b)** *(fig) (of argument)* Punkt *m*; *(of attack)* (Angriffs)spitze *f*.
-pronged [-prɒŋd] *adj suf (of fork)* -zinkig. **a three-~ attack** ein Angriff mit drei Spitzen.
pronoun ['prəʊnaʊn] *n* Fürwort, Pronomen *nt*.
pronounce [prə'naʊns] **1** *vt* **(a)** *word etc* aussprechen. **(b)** *(declare)* erklären für. **the doctors ~d him unfit for work** die Ärzte erklärten ihn für arbeitsunfähig; **to ~ sentence** das Urteil verkünden. **2** *vi* **to ~ in favour of/against sth** sich für/gegen etw aussprechen; **to ~ on sth** zu etw Stellung nehmen.
pronounced [prə'naʊnst] *adj (marked)* ausgesprochen; *improvement* deutlich; *views* entschieden. **he has a ~ limp** er hinkt sehr stark.
pronouncement [prə'naʊnsmənt] *n* Erklärung *f*; *(Jur: of sentence)* Verkündung *f*. **to make a ~** eine Erklärung abgeben.
pronto ['prɒntəʊ] *adv (col)* fix *(col)*. **do it ~** aber dalli! *(col)*.
pronunciation [prə,nʌnsɪ'eɪʃən] *n* Aussprache *f*.
proof [pru:f] **1** *n* **(a)** Beweis *m (of* für). **as** *or* **in ~ of** als *or* zum Beweis für; **that is ~ that ...** das ist der Beweis dafür, daß ...; **to give** *or* **show ~ of sth** etw nachweisen; **can you give us any ~ of that?** können Sie (uns) dafür Beweise liefern? **(b)** *(test, trial)* Probe *f*. **to put sth to the ~** etw auf die Probe stellen; *(Tech)* etw erproben. **(c)** *(Typ)* (Korrektur)fahne *f*; *(Phot)* Probeabzug *m*. **(d)** *(of alcohol)* Alkoholgehalt *m*. **70 ~** ≈ 40 Vol.-%. **2** *adj* **to be ~ against fire** feuersicher sein; **~ against inflation** inflationssicher.
proof: ~-reader *n* Korrektor(in *f*) *m*; **~-reading** *n* Korrekturlesen *nt*.
prop [prɒp] **1** *n (lit)* Stütze *f*; *(fig also)* Halt *m*. **2** *vt* **to ~ the door open** die Tür offenhalten; **to ~ sth against sth** etw gegen etw lehnen.
♦ **prop up** *vt sep* **(a)** *(rest, lean)* **to ~ oneself/sth ~ against sth** sich/etw gegen etw lehnen. **(b)** *(lit, fig: support)* stützen; *tunnel, wall* abstützen; *organization* unterstützen. **to ~ oneself ~ on sth** sich auf etw *(acc)* stützen.
propaganda [,prɒpə'gændə] *n* Propaganda *f*.
propagate ['prɒpəgeɪt] **1** *vt* fortpflanzen; *(disseminate)* verbreiten; *views also* propagieren. **2** *vi* sich fortpflanzen; *(views)* sich verbreiten.
propagation [,prɒpə'geɪʃən] *n* Fortpflanzung *f*; *(dissemination)* Verbreitung *f*; *(of views)* Propagierung *f*.
propel [prə'pel] *vt* antreiben; *(fuel)* betreiben.
propeller [prə'pelə^r] *n* Propeller *m*.
propelling pencil [prə,pelɪŋ'pensl] *n (Brit)* Drehbleistift *m*.
propensity [prə'pensɪtɪ] *n* Neigung *f (to* zu). **to have a ~ to do sth** dazu neigen, etw zu tun.
proper ['prɒpə^r] **1** *adj* **(a)** *(fitting, suitable)* richtig; *(seemly)* anständig; *(prim and ~)* korrekt. **the ~ time** die richtige Zeit; **in the ~ way** richtig; **as you think ~** wie Sie es für richtig halten; **to do the ~ thing** das tun, was sich gehört; **the ~ thing to do would be to apologize** eigentlich müßte er *etc* sich entschuldigen; **we thought it only ~** wir dachten, es gehört sich einfach. **(b)** *(actual)* eigentlich. **in the ~ sense of the word** in der eigentlichen Bedeutung des Wortes; **he's not a ~ electrician** er ist kein richtiger Elektriker; **not in Berlin ~** nicht in Berlin selbst. **(c)** *(col: real) fool etc* richtig; *(thorough) beating* gehörig, tüchtig *(col)*. **we are in a ~ mess** wir sitzen ganz schön in der Patsche *(col)*.
2 *adv* **(a)** *(dial) cruel, poorly* richtig *(col)*. **(b)** *(incorrect usage) talk* richtig.
properly ['prɒpəlɪ] *adv* **(a)** *(correctly)* richtig. **~ speaking** genaugenommen; **not ~ dressed for walking** nicht richtig angezogen zum Wandern. **(b)** *(in seemly fashion)* anständig. **(c)** *(justifiably)* zu Recht. **(d)** *(col: really, thoroughly)* ganz schön *(col)*.
proper noun *n* Eigenname *m*.
property ['prɒpətɪ] *n* **(a)** *(thing owned)* Eigentum *nt*. **that's my ~** das gehört mir; **a man of ~** ein begüterter Mann. **(b)** *(building)* Haus *nt*; Wohnung *f*; *(office)* Gebäude *nt*; *(land)* Besitztum *nt*; *(estate)* Besitz *m*. **(c)** *(characteristic)* Eigenschaft *f*. **it has healing properties** es besitzt heilende Kräfte. **(d)** *(Theat)* Requisit *nt*.
property: ~ developer *n* Häusermakler *m*; **~ man, ~ manager** *n (Theat)* Requisiteur *m*; **~ owner** *n* Haus- und Grundbesitzer *m*.
prophecy ['prɒfɪsɪ] *n* Prophezeiung *f*.
prophesy ['prɒfɪsaɪ] *vt* prophezeien.
prophet ['prɒfɪt] *n* Prophet *m*.
prophetess ['prɒfɪtɪs] *n* Prophetin *f*.
prophetic [prə'fetɪk] *adj* prophetisch.
propitious [prə'pɪʃəs] *adj* günstig *(to, for* für).
proportion [prə'pɔ:ʃən] **1** *n* **(a)** *(in number)* Verhältnis *nt (of x to y* zwischen x und y). **~s** *(size)* Ausmaß *nt*; *(of building)* Ausmaße *pl*. **to be in/out of ~ to** *or* **with sth** im Verhältnis/in keinem Verhältnis zu etw stehen; *(in size, Art)* in den Proportionen zu etw passen/nicht zu etw passen; **to get sth in ~** *(fig)* etw objektiv betrachten; **he has let it all get out of ~** *(fig)* er hat den Blick für die Proportionen verloren; **it's out of all ~!** das geht über jedes Maß hinaus!; **he has no sense of ~** *(fig)* ihm fehlt der Sinn für das richtige Maß. **(b)** *(part, amount)* Teil *m*. **what ~ of the industry is in private hands?** wie groß ist der Anteil der Industrie, der sich in privater Hand befindet?
2 *vt* **a well ~ed woman/building** eine wohlproportionierte Frau/ein wohlausgewogenes Gebäude.

proportional [prə'pɔːʃənl] *adj* proportional *(to* zu*)*. **~ representation** Verhältniswahlrecht *nt*.

proportionally [prə'pɔːʃnəlɪ] *adv* proportional; *more, less* entsprechend.

proportionate [prə'pɔːʃnɪt] *adj* proportional. **to be/not to be ~ to sth** im Verhältnis/in keinem Verhältnis zu etw stehen.

proposal [prə'pəʊzl] *n* Vorschlag *m (on, about* zu*)*; *(of marriage)* (Heirats)antrag *m*. **to make sb a ~** jdm einen Vorschlag machen.

propose [prə'pəʊz] **1** *vt* **(a)** vorschlagen; *motion* stellen, einbringen. **I ~ that we leave now** ich schlage vor, daß wir jetzt gehen. **(b)** *(have in mind)* beabsichtigen. **but I don't ~ to** ich habe aber nicht die Absicht; **how do you ~ to pay for it?** wie wollen Sie das bezahlen? **2** *vi (~ marriage)* einen (Heirats)antrag machen *(to sb* jdm*)*.

proposer [prə'pəʊzə^r^] *n (in debate)* Antragsteller(in *f*) *m*.

proposition [ˌprɒpə'zɪʃən] **1** *n* **(a)** *(statement)* Aussage *f*. **(b)** *(proposal)* Vorschlag *m*; *(argument)* These *f*. **(c)** *(prospect)* Aussicht *f*. **(d) he/that is a tough ~** er/das ist ein harter Brocken. **2** *vt* **to ~ sb** *(sexually)* jdm einen unanständigen Antrag machen.

propound [prə'paʊnd] *vt* darlegen.

proprietary [prə'praɪətərɪ] *adj rights* Besitz-; *medicine, brand* Marken-.

proprietor [prə'praɪətə^r^] *n (of pub, patent)* Inhaber(in *f*) *m*; *(of house, newspaper)* Besitzer(in *f*) *m*.

propriety [prə'praɪətɪ] *n (correctness)* Korrektheit *f*; *(decency)* Anstand *m*. **breach of ~** Verstoß *m* gegen die guten Sitten.

props [prɒps] *npl (Theat)* Requisiten *pl*.

propulsion [prə'pʌlʃən] *n* Antrieb *m*.

prosaic [prəʊ'zeɪɪk] *adj* prosaisch; *(down-to-earth)* nüchtern; *life, joke* alltäglich.

proscribe [prəʊ'skraɪb] *vt (forbid)* verbieten; *(exile)* verbannen.

prose [prəʊz] *n* Prosa *f*; *(writing, style)* Stil *m*; *(Sch: translation)* Übersetzung *f* in die Fremdsprache.

prosecute ['prɒsɪkjuːt] *vt* **(a)** *person* strafrechtlich verfolgen *(for* wegen*)*. **(b)** *(form: carry on) campaign etc* durchführen; *claim* weiterverfolgen.

prosecution [ˌprɒsɪ'kjuːʃən] *n (Jur) (act of prosecuting)* strafrechtliche Verfolgung; *(in court: case, side)* Anklage *f (for* wegen*)*. **(the) counsel for the ~** der Anklagevertreter.

prosecutor ['prɒsɪkjuːtə^r^] *n* Ankläger(in *f*) *m*.

prospect ['prɒspekt] **1** *n* **(a)** *(outlook)* Aussicht *f (of* auf *+acc)*. **what a ~!** *(iro)* das sind ja schöne Aussichten!; **he has no ~s** er hat keine Zukunft; **a job with no ~s** eine Stelle ohne Zukunft; **to hold out the ~ of sth** etw in Aussicht stellen; **to have sth in ~** etw in Aussicht haben. **(b)** *(person, thing)* **Manchester is a good ~ for the cup** Manchester ist ein aussichtsreicher Kandidat für den Pokal. **2** [prə'spekt] *vi (Min)* nach Bodenschätzen suchen. **to ~ for gold** nach Gold suchen.

prospective [prə'spektɪv] *adj attr (likely to happen)* voraussichtlich; *(future) son-in-law* zukünftig; *buyer* interessiert. **~ candidate** Kandidat *m*.

prospector [prə'spektə^r^] *n* Gold-/Erz-/Ölsucher *m*.

prospectus [prə'spektəs] *n* Verzeichnis *nt*; *(for holidays etc)* Prospekt *m*.

prosper ['prɒspə^r^] *vi (country, crime)* blühen; *(financially also)* florieren.

prosperity [prɒs'perɪtɪ] *n* Wohlstand *m*; *(of business)* Prosperität *f*.

prosperous ['prɒspərəs] *adj* wohlhabend; *business* gutgehend; *economy* florierend, blühend.

prostate (gland) ['prɒsteɪt(ˌglænd)] *n* Prostata *f*.

prostitute ['prɒstɪtjuːt] **1** *n* Prostituierte *f*. **male ~** männliche Prostituierte *(form)*, Strichjunge *m (col)*. **2** *vt one's talents* verkaufen. **to ~ oneself** sich prostituieren.

prostitution [ˌprɒstɪ'tjuːʃən] *n (lit, fig)* Prostitution *f*; *(of talents, ideals)* Verkaufen *nt*.

prostrate ['prɒstreɪt] **1** *adj* ausgestreckt. **2** [prɒ'streɪt] *vt usu pass (lit)* zu Boden werfen; *(fig) (with fatigue)* mitnehmen; *(with shock)* niederschmettern. **to be ~d by** *or* **with grief** vor Gram gebrochen sein. **3** [prɒ'streɪt] *vr* sich niederwerfen *(before* vor *+dat)*.

protagonist [prəʊ'tægənɪst] *n* Protagonist(in *f*) *m*.

protect [prə'tekt] *vt (against* gegen, *from* vor *+dat)* schützen; *(person)* beschützen.

protection [prə'tekʃən] *n* **(a)** Schutz *m (against* gegen, *from* vor *+dat)*; *(of rights)* Wahrung *f*. **to be under sb's ~** unter jds Schutz *(dat)* stehen. **(b)** *(also* **~ money***)* Schutzgeld *nt*. **~ racket** organisiertes Erpresserunwesen.

protective [prə'tektɪv] *adj* Schutz-; *attitude* beschützend. **~ clothing** Schutzkleidung *f*; **~ custody** Schutzhaft *f*; **she is very ~ towards her children** sie ist sehr fürsorglich ihren Kindern gegenüber.

protector [prə'tektə^r^] *n (defender)* Beschützer *m*.

protégé, protégée ['prɒtəʒeɪ] *n* Schützling *m*.

protein ['prəʊtiːn] *n* Eiweiß, Protein *nt*. **a high-~ diet** eine eiweißreiche Kost.

protest ['prəʊtest] **1** *n* Protest *m*; *(demonstration)* Protestkundgebung *f*. **under ~** unter Protest; **in ~ against** aus Protest gegen; **to make a/one's ~** Widerspruch erheben; **~ march** Protestmarsch *m*. **2** [prəʊ'test] *vi (against, about* gegen*)* protestieren; *(demonstrate)* demonstrieren. **3** [prəʊ'test] *vt ' innocence* beteuern. **it's mine, he ~ed** das gehört mir, protestierte er.

Protestant ['prɒtɪstənt] **1** *adj* protestantisch; *(esp in Germany)* evangelisch. **2** *n* Protestant(in *f*) *m*.

protestation [ˌprɒte'steɪʃən] *n* **(a)** *(of loyalty etc)* Beteuerung *f*. **(b)** *(protest)* Protest *m*.

protester [prə'testə^r^] *n* Protestierende(r) *mf*; *(in demonstration)* Demonstrant(in *f*) *m*.

protocol ['prəʊtəkɒl] *n* Protokoll *nt*.

proton ['prəʊtɒn] *n* Proton *nt*.

prototype ['prəʊtəʊtaɪp] *n* Prototyp *m*.

protracted [prə'træktɪd] *adj illness, discussion* langwierig; *dispute* längere(r, s).

protractor [prə'træktə^r^] *n (Math)* Winkelmesser *m*.

protrude [prə'truːd] **1** *vi (out of, from* aus*)* vorstehen; *(eyes)* vortreten; *(ears)* abstehen. **2** *vt* strecken.

protruding [prə'truːdɪŋ] *adj* vorstehend; *eyes* vortretend; *ears* abstehend.

protuberant [prə'tjuːbərənt] *adj* vorstehend; *eyes* vortretend.

proud [praʊd] **1** *adj* stolz *(of* auf *+acc)*. **to be ~ that ...** stolz (darauf) sein, daß ...; **I hope you're ~ of yourself** *(iro)* ich hoffe, du bist stolz auf dich; **that's nothing to be ~ of** das ist nichts, worauf man stolz sein kann. **2** *adv* **to do sb/oneself ~** jdn/sich verwöhnen.

proudly ['praʊdlɪ] *adv* stolz.

prove [pruːv] *pret* **~d**, *ptp* **~d** *or* **proven 1** *vt* **(a)** *(verify)* beweisen. **to ~ sb innocent** *or* **sb's innocence** jds Unschuld beweisen; **he was ~d right in the end** er hat schließlich doch recht behalten. **(b)** *(test) rifle etc* erproben; *one's worth, courage* beweisen. **(c)** *also vi (turn out)* **to ~ (to be) useful** *etc* sich als nützlich *etc* erweisen; **if it ~s otherwise** wenn sich das Gegenteil herausstellt. **2** *vr* **(a)** *(show one's value, courage etc)* sich bewähren. **(b) to ~ oneself innocent** *etc* sich als unschuldig *etc* erweisen.

proverb ['prɒvɜːb] *n* Sprichwort *nt*.

proverbial [prə'vɜːbɪəl] *adj (lit, fig)* sprichwörtlich.

provide [prə'vaɪd] **1** *vt* **(a)** *(make available)* zur Verfügung stellen; *money* bereitstellen; *(see to, bring along) food, records etc* sorgen für; *(produce) ideas, specialist knowledge, electricity* liefern;

shade spenden; *privacy, topic of conversation* sorgen für. **to ~ sth for sb** jdm etw zur Verfügung stellen; *(supply)* jdm etw besorgen; **to ~ sb with sth** *(with food etc)* jdn mit etw versorgen; *(equip)* jdn mit etw ausstatten; *(with excuse, idea)* jdm etw liefern; *(with opportunity, information)* jdm etw verschaffen *or* geben; **this job ~d him with enough money** die Stelle verschaffte ihm genug Geld. **(b)** *(stipulate: clause, agreement)* vorsehen. **2** *vi* **the Lord will ~** *(prov)* der Herr wird's schon geben.

♦ **provide for** *vi +prep obj* **(a)** *family etc* versorgen. **his family was well ~d ~** seine Familie war gut versorgt. **(b) as ~d ~ in the 1970 contract** wie in dem Vertrag von 1970 vorgesehen; **we ~d ~ all emergencies** wir haben für alle Notfälle vorgesorgt.

provided (that) [prə'vaɪdɪd('ðæt)] *conj* vorausgesetzt(, daß).

providence ['prɒvɪdəns] *n (fate)* die Vorsehung.

providential [,prɒvɪ'denʃəl] *adj* glücklich. **to be ~** (ein) Glück sein.

providing (that) [prə'vaɪdɪŋ('ðæt)] *conj* vorausgesetzt(, daß).

province ['prɒvɪns] *n* **(a)** Provinz *f*. **(b) the ~s** *pl* die Provinz. **(c)** *(fig: area of knowledge, activity etc)* Gebiet *nt*, Bereich *m*. **it's not within my ~** das fällt nicht in meinen Bereich; **that is outside my ~** das ist nicht mein Gebiet. **(d)** *(area of authority)* Kompetenzbereich *m*. **that's not my ~** dafür bin ich nicht zuständig.

provincial [prə'vɪnʃəl] **1** *adj* Provinz-; *custom, accent* ländlich; *(pej)* provinziell. **2** *n* Provinzbewohner(in *f*) *m*; *(pej)* Provinzler(in *f*) *m*.

provision [prə'vɪʒən] *n* **(a)** *(act of supplying)* Beschaffung *f*; *(of food, water etc)* Versorgung *f* *(of* mit, *to sb* jds*)*. **(b)** *(supply)* Vorrat *m (of* an *+dat)*. **(c) ~s** *(food)* Lebensmittel *pl*; *(for journey)* Proviant *m*. **(d)** *(allowance)* Berücksichtigung *f*; *(arrangement)* Vorkehrung *f*; *(stipulation)* Bestimmung *f*. **with the ~ that ...** mit der Bedingung, daß...; **there's no ~ for later additions** spätere Erweiterungen sind nicht vorgesehen; **to make ~ for the future** für die Zukunft Vorsorge treffen; **to make ~ for sth** etw vorsehen; *for error etc* etw einkalkulieren; **to make ~ against sth** gegen etw Vorkehrungen treffen.

provisional [prə'vɪʒənl] **1** *adj* provisorisch; *measures also, offer, decision* vorläufig. **~ driving licence** *(Brit)* vorläufige Fahrerlaubnis für Fahrschüler. **2** *n (Ir Pol)* **the P~s** *die Provisorische Irisch-Republikanische Armee.*

provisionally [prə'vɪʒnəlɪ] *adv* vorläufig.

proviso [prə'vaɪzəʊ] *n (condition)* Bedingung *f*; *(clause)* Vorbehaltsklausel *f*.

provocation [,prɒvə'keɪʃən] *n* Provokation *f*.

provocative [prə'vɒkətɪv] *adj* provokatorisch; *remark, behaviour also* herausfordernd.

provoke [prə'vəʊk] *vt sb* provozieren, herausfordern; *animal* reizen; *anger, criticism, smile* hervorrufen; *discussion, revolt* auslösen. **to ~ sb into doing sth** *or* **to do sth** jdn dazu bringen, daß er etw tut; *(taunt)* jdn dazu treiben, daß er etw tut.

provoking [prə'vəʊkɪŋ] *adj* provozierend; *(annoying)* ärgerlich.

provost ['prɒvəst] *n (Scot)* Bürgermeister *m*; *(Univ)* ≃ Dekan *m*.

prow [praʊ] *n* Bug *m*.

prowess ['praʊɪs] *n (skill)* Fähigkeiten *pl*, Können *nt*; *(courage)* Tapferkeit *f*.

prowl [praʊl] *vi (also* **~ about** *or* **around***)* herumstreichen; *(boss, headmaster)* herumschleichen.

prowler ['praʊlə^r] *n* Herumtreiber(in *f*) *m*; *(peeping Tom)* Spanner *m (col)*.

proximity [prɒk'sɪmɪtɪ] *n* Nähe *f*. **in close ~ to** in unmittelbarer Nähe *(+gen)*.

proxy ['prɒksɪ] *n (power)* (Handlungs)vollmacht *f*; *(person)* Stellvertreter(in *f*) *m*. **by ~** durch einen Stellvertreter.

prude [pruːd] *n* **to be a ~** prüde sein.

prudence ['pruːdəns] *n see adj* Umsicht *f*; Klugheit *f*; Überlegtheit *f*.

prudent ['pruːdənt] *adj person* umsichtig; *measure, decision* klug; *answer* wohlüberlegt.

prudish ['pruːdɪʃ] *adj* prüde.

prune[1] [pruːn] *n* Backpflaume *f*.

prune[2] *vt (also* **~ down***)* stutzen; *(fig) expenditure, essay* kürzen; *workforce* reduzieren.

pry[1] [praɪ] *vi* neugierig sein; *(in drawers etc)* (herum)schnüffeln *(in* in *+dat)*. **I don't mean to ~, but ...** es geht mich ja nichts an, aber ...; **to ~ into sb's affairs** seine Nase in jds Angelegenheiten *(acc)* stecken.

pry[2] *vt (US)* = **prise.**

PS = **postscript** PS.

psalm [sɑːm] *n* Psalm *m*.

pseud [sjuːd] *(col) n* Angeber(in *f*) *m*.

pseudo ['sjuːdəʊ] *adj (col: pretended)* unecht; *intellectual etc* Möchtegern- *(col)*, Pseudo-.

pseudo- *pref* Pseudo-, pseudo.

pseudonym ['sjuːdənɪm] *n* Pseudonym *nt*.

psyche ['saɪkɪ] *n* Psyche *f*.

♦ **psyche up** [,saɪk'ʌp] *vt sep (col)* **to ~ oneself ~** sich in Stimmung bringen.

psychedelic [,saɪkɪ'delɪk] *adj* psychedelisch.

psychiatric [,saɪkɪ'ætrɪk] *adj* psychiatrisch; *illness* psychisch.

psychiatrist [saɪ'kaɪətrɪst] *n* Psychiater(in *f*) *m*.

psychiatry [saɪ'kaɪətrɪ] *n* Psychiatrie *f*.

psychic ['saɪkɪk] *adj* übersinnlich; *powers* übernatürlich. **~ research** Parapsychologie *f*; **she is ~** sie besitzt übernatürliche Kräfte; **you must be ~!** du kannst wohl hellsehen!

psycho ['saɪkəʊ] *n (US col)* Verrückte(r) *mf*.

psychoanalyse, *(US)* **psychoanalyze** [,saɪkəʊ'ænəlaɪz] *vt* psychoanalytisch behandeln.

psychoanalysis [,saɪkəʊə'nælɪsɪs] *n* Psychoanalyse *f*.

psychoanalyst [,saɪkəʊ'ænəlɪst] *n* Psychoanalytiker(in *f*) *m*.

psychological [,saɪkə'lɒdʒɪkəl] *adj (mental)* psychisch; *(concerning psychology)* psychologisch. **~ warfare** psychologische Kriegführung; **he's not really ill, it's all ~** er ist nicht wirklich krank, das ist alles psychisch bedingt.

psychologist [saɪ'kɒlədʒɪst] *n* Psychologe *m*, Psychologin *f*.

psychology [saɪ'kɒlədʒɪ] *n (science)* Psychologie *f*; *(make-up)* Psyche *f*.

psychopath ['saɪkəʊpæθ] *n* Psychopath(in *f*) *m*.

psychosis [saɪ'kəʊsɪs] *n, pl* **psychoses** [saɪ'kəʊsiːz] Psychose *f*.

psychosomatic [,saɪkəʊsəʊ'mætɪk] *adj* psychosomatisch. **~ medicine** Psychosomatik *f*.

psychotherapy [,saɪkəʊ'θerəpɪ] *n* Psychotherapie *f*.

psychotic [saɪ'kɒtɪk] **1** *adj* psychotisch. **~ illness** Psychose *f*. **2** *n* Psychotiker(in *f*) *m*.

pto = **please turn over** bitte wenden, b. w.

pub [pʌb] *n (Brit)* Kneipe *(col)*, Wirtschaft *f*; *(in the country also)* Gasthaus *nt*.

pub-crawl ['pʌbkrɔːl] *n (Brit col)* **to go on a ~** einen Kneipenbummel machen *(col)*.

puberty ['pjuːbətɪ] *n* die Pubertät.

pubic ['pjuːbɪk] *adj* Scham-.

public ['pʌblɪk] **1** *adj* öffentlich; *health, library also* Volks-; *spending, debts* der öffentlichen Hand, Staats-. **to be ~ knowledge** allgemein bekannt sein; **in the ~ interest** im öffentlichen Interesse; **it's rather ~ here** es ist nicht gerade privat hier; **he is a ~ figure** er ist eine Persönlichkeit des öffentlichen Lebens; **in the ~ eye** im Blickpunkt der Öffentlichkeit; **to make sth ~** etw bekanntgeben; *(officially)* etw öffentlich bekanntmachen; **to create ~ awareness** öffentliches Interesse wecken; **to go ~** *(Comm)* in eine Aktiengesellschaft umgewandelt werden. **2** *n sing or pl* Öffentlichkeit *f*. **in ~** in der Öffentlichkeit; *speak also* öffentlich; **the theatre-going ~** die theaterinteressierte Öffentlichkeit.

public address system *n* Lautsprecheranlage *f*.

publican ['pʌblɪkən] *n (Brit)* Gastwirt(in *f*) *m*.

publication [ˌpʌblɪ'keɪʃən] *n* Veröffentlichung *f*.

public: ~ company *n* Aktiengesellschaft *f*; **~ convenience** *n (Brit)* öffentliche Toilette; **~ holiday** *n* gesetzlicher Feiertag; **~ house** *n (Brit)* Gaststätte *f*.

publicity [pʌb'lɪsɪtɪ] *n* Publicity *f*; *(Comm: advertising, advertisements)* Werbung *f*. **~ campaign** Publicitykampagne *f*; *(Comm)* Werbekampagne *f*.

publicize ['pʌblɪsaɪz] *vt* **(a)** *(make public)* bekanntmachen. **I don't ~ the fact** ich will das nicht an die große Glocke hängen *(col)*. **(b)** *(get publicity for) film, author* Publicity machen für; *new product* Werbung machen für.

public: ~ opinion *n* die öffentliche Meinung; **~ opinion poll** *n* Meinungsumfrage *f*; **~ ownership** *n* **under ~ ownership** in öffentlichem Besitz; **~ purse** *n* Staatskasse *f*; **~ relations** *npl* Public Relations *pl*, Öffentlichkeitsarbeit *f*; **~ relations officer** *n* Pressesprecher(in *f*) *m*; **~ school** *n (Brit)* Privatschule, Public School *f*; *(US)* staatliche Schule; **~ sector** *n* öffentlicher Sektor; **~ service** *n (Civil Service)* öffentlicher Dienst; *(facility: water, transport etc)* öffentlicher Dienstleistungsbetrieb; *(work)* Dienst *m* an der Allgemeinheit; **~ speaking** *n* **I don't like ~ speaking** ich halte nicht gern Reden; **~-spirited** *adj act* von Gemeinsinn zeugend; **~ transport** *n* öffentliche Verkehrsmittel *pl*.

publish ['pʌblɪʃ] *vt* **(a)** *(issue)* veröffentlichen; *book, magazine etc also* herausbringen. **~ed by Collins** bei Collins erschienen; **"~ed monthly"** „erscheint monatlich"; **who's that book ~ed by?** in welchem Verlag ist das Buch erschienen? **(b)** *(make public) news, banns* bekanntgeben; *decree* herausgeben; *will* eröffnen.

publisher ['pʌblɪʃə^r] *n (person)* Verleger(in *f*) *m*; *(firm: also* **~s***)* Verlag *m*.

publishing ['pʌblɪʃɪŋ] *n (trade)* das Verlagswesen. **~ company** Verlagshaus *nt*.

puce [pjuːs] *adj* braunrot; *(with rage, shame)* rot.

pucker ['pʌkə^r] *vt (also* **~ up***) one's lips, mouth* verziehen; *(for kissing)* spitzen; *one's brow* runzeln; *material* Falten machen in *(+acc)*.

pudding ['pʊdɪŋ] *n (dessert)* Nachspeise *f*. **what's for ~?** was gibt es als Nachtisch?

pudding basin *n* Puddingform *f*.

puddle ['pʌdl] *n* Pfütze *f*.

puerile ['pjʊəraɪl] *adj* infantil.

puff [pʌf] **1** *n* **(a)** *(on cigarette etc)* Zug *m (at, of* an *+dat)*. **a ~ of wind** ein Windstoß *m*; **a ~ of smoke** eine Rauchwolke; **to be out of ~** *(col)* außer Puste sein *(col)*. **(b)** *(powder* **~***)* Quaste *f*. **(c)** *(Cook)* **cream ~** Windbeutel *m*; **~ pastry,** *(US)* **~ paste** Blätterteig *m*. **2** *vt* *smoke* ausstoßen; *(person)* blasen; *cigarette* paffen *(col)*. **3** *vi* *(person, train)* schnaufen; *(chimney, smoke)* qualmen. **the train ~ed into the station** der Zug fuhr schnaufend in den Bahnhof ein; **to ~ at a cigar** an einer Zigarre paffen.

puffin ['pʌfɪn] *n* Papageientaucher *m*.

puffy ['pʌfɪ] *adj (+er) (swollen)* geschwollen; *(from crying)* verquollen.

pug [pʌg] *n (also* **~ dog***)* Mops *m*.

pugnacious [pʌg'neɪʃəs] *adj* kampfeslustig; *(verbally)* streitsüchtig.

pug-nosed ['pʌgneʊzd] *adj* knollennasig.

puke [pjuːk] *vti (col!)* kotzen *(col)*.

pull [pʊl] **1** *n* **(a)** *(tug)* Ziehen *nt*; *(short)* Ruck *m*; *(lit, fig: attraction)* Anziehungskraft *f*; *(of current)* Sog *m*. **he gave her/the rope a ~** er zog sie/am Seil; **I felt a ~ at my sleeve** ich spürte, wie mich jemand am Ärmel zog. **(b)** *(at pipe, beer)* Zug *m*. **he took a ~ at his pipe/glass** er zog an seiner Pfeife/nahm einen Schluck aus seinem Glas. **(c)** **bell ~** Klingelzug *m*. **(d)** *(col: influence)* Beziehungen *pl*. **I've got no ~ with them** ich habe keinen Draht zu ihnen *(col)*.

2 *vt* **(a)** *(draw, drag)* ziehen. **to ~ a door shut** eine Tür zuziehen. **(b)** *(tug) rope, bell* ziehen an *(+dat)*; *boat* rudern. **he ~ed her hair** er zog sie an den Haaren; **to ~ sth to pieces** *(lit)* etw in Stücke reißen; *(fig: criticize)* etw verreißen; **~ the other one** *(col)* das glaubst du doch wohl selber nicht!; **she was the one ~ing the strings** sie war es, die alle Fäden in der Hand hielt; **to ~ one's punches** *(fig)* sich zurückhalten. **(c)** *(extract, draw out) tooth, gun, knife* ziehen; *weeds, lettuce, cork* herausziehen; *beer* zapfen. **to ~ a gun on sb** jdn mit der Pistole bedrohen. **(d)** *(strain) muscle* sich *(dat)* zerren; *(tear) thread* ziehen. **(e)** *(attract) crowd* anziehen. **(f)** *(col)* **what are you trying to ~?** was heckst du wieder aus? *(col)*.

3 *vi* **(a)** ziehen *(on, at* an *+dat)*. **to ~ to the left** *(car)* nach links ziehen; **to ~ on** *or* **at one's cigarette** an seiner Zigarette ziehen. **(b)** *(move: train, car etc)* fahren. **the car ~ed into the driveway** der Wagen fuhr in die Einfahrt; **he ~ed across to the left-hand lane** er wechselte auf die linke Spur über; **to ~ ahead (of sb)** *(car, runner)* (an jdm) vorbeiziehen; *(fig: rival etc)* jdn hinter sich *(dat)* lassen.

♦ **pull apart** *vt sep* **(a)** *(separate)* auseinanderziehen; *sheets of paper also, fighting people* trennen; *radio etc* auseinandernehmen. **(b)** *(fig col) (search thoroughly)* auseinandernehmen *(col)*; *(criticise also)* verreißen.

♦ **pull away 1** *vt sep* wegziehen. **she ~ed it ~ from him** sie zog es von ihm weg; *(from his hands)* sie zog es ihm aus den Händen. **2** *vi (move off)* wegfahren; *(ship)* ablegen.

♦ **pull back 1** *vt sep* zurückziehen. **2** *vi (lit)* sich zurückziehen; *(catch up)* aufholen. **to ~ ~ (from doing sth)** *(fig)* einen Rückzieher machen (und etw nicht tun) *(col)*.

♦ **pull down** *vt sep* **(a)** herunterziehen. **(b)** *(demolish) buildings* abreißen.

♦ **pull in 1** *vt sep* **(a)** *claws etc* einziehen; *(into swimming-pool etc)* hineinziehen. **(b)** *(rein in) horse* zügeln. **(c)** *(attract) crowds* anziehen. **(d)** *(col: take into custody)* einkassieren *(col)*. **2** *vi (into station etc)* einfahren, einlaufen *(into* in *+acc)*; *(into driveway)* hineinfahren *(into* in *+acc)*; *(stop, park)* anhalten. **he ~ed ~ to the side of the road** er fuhr an den Straßenrand.

♦ **pull off** *vt sep* **(a)** *wrapping paper* abziehen; *cover also* abnehmen; *(violently)* abreißen; *clothes, shoes* ausziehen. **(b)** *(col: succeed in)* schaffen *(col)*; *deal also* zuwege bringen *(col)*; *burglary* drehen *(col)*.

♦ **pull on** *vt sep coat etc* sich *(dat)* überziehen; *hat* aufsetzen.

♦ **pull out 1** *vt sep* **(a)** *(extract) (of* aus*)* herausziehen; *tooth* ziehen; *page* heraustrennen. **(b)** *(withdraw)* zurückziehen; *troops* abziehen. **2** *vi* **(a)** *(withdraw)* aussteigen *(of* aus*) (col)*; *(troops)* abziehen. **(b)** *(leave: train etc)* herausfahren *(of* aus*)*. **(c)** *(driver)* herausfahren.

♦ **pull over 1** *vt sep* **(a)** hinüber-/herüberziehen *(prep obj* über *+acc)*. **(b)** *(topple)* umreißen. **2** *vi (car, driver)* zur Seite fahren.

♦ **pull through** *vi (fig: recover)* durchkommen.

♦ **pull together 1** *vi (lit)* gemeinsam ziehen; *(fig: cooperate)* am gleichen Strang ziehen. **2** *vr* sich zusammenreißen. **~ yourself ~** reiß dich zusammen.

♦ **pull up 1** *vt sep* **(a)** *(raise by pulling)* hochziehen; *(up slope also)* nach oben ziehen. **(b)** *(uproot)* herausreißen. **(c)** *(stop)* anhalten. **(d)** *(reprimand) (for behaviour)* zurechtweisen; *(for grammar etc)* korrigieren. **2** *vi (stop)* anhalten.

pulley ['pʊlɪ] *n* Rolle *f*; *(block)* Flaschenzug *m*.

pull: ~-out *n (withdrawal)* Abzug *m*; *(supplement)* heraustrennbarer Teil; **~over** *n* Pullover *m*.

pulp [pʌlp] **1** *n* Brei *m*; *(of fruit)* Fruchtfleisch *nt*. **to beat sb to a ~** *(col)* jdn zu Brei schlagen *(col)*. **2** *vt fruit* zerdrücken; *paper, book* einstampfen; *wood* zu Brei verarbeiten.

pulpit ['pʊlpɪt] *n* Kanzel *f*.

pulsate [pʌl'seɪt] *vi (lit, fig)* pulsieren; *(head, heart)* klopfen; *(voice, building)* beben; *(music)* rhythmisch klingen.

pulse[1] [pʌls] **1** *n (Anat)* Puls *m*; *(Phys)* Impuls *m*; *(fig: of music)* Rhythmus *m*. **to feel** *or* **take sb's ~** jdm den Puls fühlen. **2** *vi* pulsieren; *(machines)* stampfen.

pulse[2] *n (Bot, Cook)* Hülsenfrucht *f*.

puma ['pju:mə] *n* Puma *m*.

pumice (stone) ['pʌmɪs(ˌstəʊn)] *n* Bimsstein *m*.

pummel ['pʌml] *vt* eintrommeln auf *(+acc)*.

pump [pʌmp] **1** *n* Pumpe *f*. **2** *vt* pumpen; *brake pedal* mehrmals treten. **to ~ sth dry** etw leerpumpen; **to ~ sb dry** *(fig)* jdn aussaugen; **to ~ bullets into sb** jdn mit Blei vollpumpen *(col)*; **to ~ money into sth** Geld in etw *(acc)* hineinpumpen; **to ~ information out of sb** Informationen aus jdm herausholen.

♦ **pump in** *vt sep (lit, fig)* hineinpumpen.

♦ **pump out** *vt sep liquid, air* herauspumpen; *boat, cellar* leerpumpen; *stomach* auspumpen.

♦ **pump up** *vt sep tyre etc* aufpumpen.

pumpkin ['pʌmpkɪn] *n* Kürbis *m*.

pun [pʌn] *n* Wortspiel *nt*.

Punch [pʌntʃ] *n* Kasper *m*, Kasperle *nt*. **~-and-Judy show** Kasper(le)theater *nt*; **to be (as) pleased as ~** *(col)* sich wie ein Schneekönig freuen *(col)*.

punch[1] [pʌntʃ] **1** *n* **(a)** *(blow)* Schlag *m*. **(b)** *no pl (fig: vigour)* Schwung *m*. **2** *vti* boxen.

punch[2] **1** *n (for ~ing holes)* Locher *m*; *(for tickets)* Lochzange *f*; *(for stamping metal etc)* Prägestempel *m*. **2** *vt ticket etc* lochen; *metal, holes* stanzen; *(stamp) metal, pattern* prägen.

♦ **punch in** *vt sep (Comp) data* tasten, tippen *(col)*.

punch[3] *n (drink)* Bowle *f*; *(hot)* Punsch *m*.

punch: ~ ball *n* Punchingball *m*; **~ bowl** *n* Bowle *f*; **~ card** *n* Lochkarte *f*; **~-drunk** *adj (fig)* durcheinander *pred*; **~-line** *n* Pointe *f*; **~ tape** *n* Lochstreifen *m*; **~-up** *n (Brit col)* Schlägerei *f*.

punctilious [pʌŋk'tɪlɪəs] *adj (regarding etiquette)* korrekt; *(fastidious)* peinlich genau.

punctual ['pʌŋktjʊəl] *adj* pünktlich. **to be ~** pünktlich kommen.

punctuality [ˌpʌŋktjʊ'ælɪtɪ] *n* Pünktlichkeit *f*.

punctuate ['pʌŋktjʊeɪt] *vt* **(a)** *(Gram)* mit Satzzeichen versehen. **(b)** *(intersperse)* unterbrechen. **he ~d his talk with jokes** er spickte seine Rede mit Witzen.

punctuation [ˌpʌŋktjʊ'eɪʃən] *n* Zeichensetzung, Interpunktion *f*. **~ mark** Satzzeichen *nt*.

puncture ['pʌŋktʃə^r] **1** *n (in tyre, balloon etc)* Loch *nt*; *(in skin)* (Ein)stich *m*; *(flat tyre)* Reifenpanne *f*. **2** *vt* stechen in *(+acc)*; *membrane* durchstechen; *tyre, balloon* Löcher/ein Loch machen in *(+acc)*.

pundit ['pʌndɪt] *n (fig)* Experte *m*, Expertin *f*.

pungency ['pʌndʒənsɪ] *n (lit, fig)* Schärfe *f*.

pungent ['pʌndʒənt] *adj (lit, fig)* scharf; *smell also* stechend.

punish ['pʌnɪʃ] *vt* **(a)** *person, offence* bestrafen. **(b)** *(fig col: drive hard, treat roughly)* strapazieren; *horses, oneself* schinden; *opponent* zusetzen *(+dat)*.

punishable ['pʌnɪʃəbl] *adj* strafbar. **it is a ~ offence** es ist strafbar.

punishing ['pʌnɪʃɪŋ] **1** *adj blow* hart. **2** *n* **to take a ~** *(col) (car, furniture etc)* strapaziert werden; *(team, boxer etc)* vorgeführt werden *(col)*.

punishment ['pʌnɪʃmənt] *n* **(a)** *(penalty)* Strafe *f*; *(punishing)* Bestrafung *f*. **(b)** *(fig col)* **to take a lot of ~** *(car, furniture etc)* stark strapaziert werden; *(Sport)* vorgeführt werden *(col)*.

punk [pʌŋk] *n* **(a)** *(person: also* **~ rocker***)* Punker *m*; *(music: also* **~ rock***)* Punk(-Rock) *m*; *(culture)* Punk *m*. **(b)** *(US col: hoodlum)* Ganove *m (col)*.

punt [pʌnt] **1** *n (boat)* Stechkahn *m*. **2** *vti* staken. **to go ~ing** Stechkahn fahren.

punter ['pʌntə^r] *n* **(a)** *(better)* Wetter *m*; *(gambler)* Spieler(in *f*) *m*. **(b)** *(col)* Typ *m (col)*. **the average ~** Otto Normalverbraucher.

puny ['pju:nɪ] *adj (+er) (weak) person* schwächlich; *effort* kläglich.

pup [pʌp] *n* Junge(s) *nt*.

pupil[1] ['pju:pl] *n (Sch, fig)* Schüler(in *f*) *m*.

pupil[2] *n (Anat)* Pupille *f*.

puppet ['pʌpɪt] *n* Puppe *f*; *(glove ~)* Handpuppe *f*; *(string ~, fig)* Marionette *f*.

puppet: ~government *n* Marionettenregierung *f*; **~-show** *n* Puppenspiel *nt*; **~ state** *n* Marionettenstaat *m*.

puppy ['pʌpɪ] *n* junger Hund. **~ fat** *n* Babyspeck *m*; **~ love** *n* Schwärmerei *f*.

purchase ['pɜ:tʃɪs] **1** *n* **(a)** Kauf *m*; *(of furniture, flat, car also)* Anschaffung *f*. **to make a ~** einen Kauf tätigen; eine Anschaffung machen. **(b)** *(grip)* Halt *m*. **he couldn't get a ~ on the wet rope** er konnte an dem nassen Seil keinen Halt finden. **2** *vt (buy)* kaufen, erwerben *(form)*. **purchasing power** Kaufkraft *f*; **~ price** Kaufpreis *m*.

purchaser ['pɜ:tʃɪsə^r] *n* Käufer(in *f*) *m*.

pure [pjʊə^r] *adj (+er)* rein; *motive* ehrlich, lauter *(geh)*. **she stared at him in ~ disbelief** sie starrte ihn ganz ungläubig an; **malice ~ and simple** reine Bosheit; **a ~ wool dress** ein Kleid aus reiner Wolle.

purée ['pjʊəreɪ] *n* Püree *nt*, Brei *m*. **tomato ~** Tomatenmark *nt*.

purely ['pjʊəlɪ] *adv* rein.

purgative ['pɜ:gətɪv] *n* Abführmittel *nt*.

purgatory ['pɜ:gətərɪ] *n (Rel)* das Fegefeuer; *(fig: state)* die Hölle.

purge [pɜ:dʒ] **1** *n* **(a)** *(Med)* (starkes) Abführmittel. **(b)** *(Pol etc)* Säuberung(saktion) *f*. **2** *vt* reinigen; *body* entschlacken; *guilt, sin* büßen; *(Pol etc) party* säubern *(of* von*)*; *traitor* eliminieren *(from* aus*)*.

purification [ˌpjʊərɪfɪ'keɪʃən] *n* Reinigung *f*.

purify ['pjʊərɪfaɪ] *vt* reinigen.

purist ['pjʊərɪst] *n* Purist(in *f*) *m*.

puritan ['pjʊərɪtən] *(Rel:* **P~***)* **1** *adj* puritanisch. **2** *n* Puritaner(in *f*) *m*.

puritanical [ˌpjʊərɪ'tænɪkəl] *adj* puritanisch.

purity ['pjʊərɪtɪ] *n* Reinheit *f*; *(of motives)* Lauterkeit *(geh)*, Ehrlichkeit *f*.

purl [pɜ:l] *n* linke Masche. **~ two** zwei links.

purple ['pɜ:pl] **1** *adj* violett, lila; *face* hochrot; *(pej) passage* hochtrabend. **to go ~ (in the face)** hochrot werden. **2** *n (colour)* Violett, Lila *nt*.

purport ['pɜ:pət] **1** *n* Tenor *m*. **2** [pɜ:'pɔ:t] *vt* **to ~ to be/do sth** *(person)* vorgeben, etw zu sein/tun; *(thing)* etw sein/tun sollen.

purpose ['pɜ:pəs] *n* **(a)** *(intention)* Absicht *f*; *(goal)* Zweck *m*. **on ~** mit Absicht, absichtlich; **he did it for** *or* **with the ~ of improving his image** er tat es in der Absicht, sein Image zu verbessern; **to have a ~ in life** ein Lebensziel haben; **to answer** *or* **serve sb's ~(s)** jds Zweck(en) dienen; **for our ~s** für unsere Zwecke; **for the ~s of this meeting** zum Zweck dieser Konferenz; **for all practical ~s** in der Praxis; **to the ~** relevant; **to good ~** zu einem guten Zweck; **to no ~** umsonst. **(b)** *no pl* **strength of ~** Entschlußkraft *f*; **sense of ~** Zielbewußtsein *nt*.

purpose-built ['pɜːpəs'bɪlt] *adj* Spezial-; *building also* speziell gebaut.
purposeful ['pɜːpəsfʊl] *adj* entschlossen.
purposely ['pɜːpəslɪ] *adv* bewußt, absichtlich.
purr [pɜːʳ] **1** *vi (cat, fig: person)* schnurren; *(engine)* surren. **2** *n* Schnurren *nt no pl*; Surren *nt no pl.*
purse [pɜːs] **1** *n* **(a)** *(for money)* Portemonnaie *nt*, Geldbörse *f (form).* **to hold the ~ strings** *(fig)* über die Finanzen bestimmen. **(b)** *(US: handbag)* Handtasche *f.* **(c)** *(Sport: prize)* Preisgeld *nt.* **2** *vt* **to ~ one's lips** einen Schmollmund machen.
purser ['pɜːsəʳ] *n* Zahlmeister *m.*
pursue [pə'sjuː] *vt* **(a)** verfolgen; *pleasure, success* nachjagen *(+dat)*, aussein auf *(+acc)*; *happiness* streben nach. **(b)** *(carry on) course of action etc* verfolgen; *inquiry* durchführen; *profession, studies* nachgehen *(+dat)*; *subject* weiterführen.
pursuer [pə'sjuːəʳ] *n* Verfolger(in *f*) *m.*
pursuit [pə'sjuːt] *n* **(a)** *(of person)* Verfolgung *(of gen)*, Jagd *(of* auf *+acc) f*; *(of knowledge, happiness)* Streben *nt (of* nach*)*; *(of pleasure)* Jagd *f (of* nach*).* **in hot ~ of sb** hart auf jds Fersen *(acc)*; **to go in ~ of sb/sth** sich auf die Jagd nach jdm/etw machen; **in (the) ~ of his goal** in Verfolgung seines Ziels. **(b)** *(occupation)* Beschäftigung *f*; *(hobby, pastime)* Zeitvertreib *m.* **his literary ~s** seine Beschäftigung mit der Literatur.
purveyor [pɜː'veɪəʳ] *n (form) (seller)* Händler *m*; *(supplier)* Lieferant *m.*
pus [pʌs] *n* Eiter *m.*
push [pʊʃ] **1** *n* **(a)** Schubs *m (col)*; *(short)* Stoß *m.* **to give sb/sth a ~** jdn/etw schieben; jdm/etw einen Stoß versetzen; **to give a car a ~** einen Wagen anschieben; **to give sb the ~** *(Brit col) employee* jdn rausschmeißen *(col)*; *boyfriend* jdm den Laufpaß geben *(col).* **(b)** *(effort)* Anstrengung *f*; *(sales ~)* Aktion *f*; *(Mil: offensive)* Offensive *f.* **(c)** *(drive, aggression)* Durchsetzungsvermögen *nt.* **(d)** *(col)* **at a ~** notfalls, im Notfall; **if/when it comes to the ~** wenn es darauf ankommt.

2 *vt* **(a)** schieben; *(quickly, violently)* stoßen, schubsen *(col)*; *(press) button* drücken. **to ~ a door open/shut** eine Tür auf-/zudrücken; **he ~ed the book into my hand** er drückte mir das Buch in die Hand.

(b) *(fig) claims, interests* durchzusetzen versuchen; *candidate* die Werbetrommel rühren für; *product* propagieren, pushen *(Comm sl)*; *drugs* schieben, pushen *(Drugs sl).* **to ~ home one's advantage** seinen Vorteil ausnützen; **don't ~ your luck** treib's nicht zu weit!; **he must be ~ing 70** *(col)* er muß auf die 70 zugehen.

(c) *(fig: put pressure on)* drängen, drängeln *(col)*; *pupil, employee* antreiben. **to ~ sb to do sth** jdn dazu drängen, etw zu tun; **they ~ed him to the limits** sie trieben ihn bis an seine Grenzen; **that's ~ing it a bit** *(col)* das ist ein bißchen übertrieben; **to be ~ed for time/money** *(col)* unter Zeitdruck stehen/knapp bei Kasse sein *(col)*; **I'm a bit ~ed just now** *(col)* ich habe momentan wenig Zeit.

3 *vi (shove)* schieben; *(quickly, violently)* stoßen; *(in a crowd, apply pressure)* drängen, drängeln *(col)*; *(fig: be ambitious, assert oneself)* kämpfen. "~" *(on door)* „drücken"; *(on bell)* „klingeln".
♦ **push around** *vt sep* **(a)** herumstoßen. **(b)** *(fig col: bully)* herumschubsen.
♦ **push aside** *vt sep* zur Seite *or* beiseite schieben; *(fig) problems etc* einfach abtun.
♦ **push away** *vt sep* wegschieben; *(quickly)* wegstoßen.
♦ **push back** *vt sep people* zurückdrängen; *(with one push)* zurückstoßen; *curtains, hair* zurückschieben.
♦ **push down** *vt sep* nach unten drücken; *(knock over)* umstoßen; *fence* niederreißen.
♦ **push down on** *vi +prep obj* drücken auf *(+acc).*
♦ **push forward 1** *vi (Mil)* vorwärts drängen. **2** *vt sep (lit)* nach vorn schieben; *(fig) claim* geltend machen; *ideas* hervorheben; *sb, oneself* in den Vordergrund schieben.
♦ **push in 1** *vt sep* **(a)** hineinschieben; *(quickly, violently)* hineinstoßen. **to ~ one's way ~** sich hineindrängen. **(b)** *(break) window, sides of box* eindrücken. **2** *vi (lit: in queue etc)* sich hineindrängen *or* -drängeln *(col).*
♦ **push off 1** *vt sep* hinunterschieben; *(quickly, violently)* hinunterstoßen; *lid, cap* wegdrücken. **to ~ sb/sth ~ sth** jdn/etw von etw schieben/stoßen. **2** *vi* **(a)** *(in boat)* abstoßen. **(b)** *(col: leave)* abhauen *(col).*
♦ **push on 1** *vi (with journey)* weiterfahren; *(walking)* weitergehen; *(with job)* weitermachen. **2** *vt sep top, lid* festdrücken.
♦ **push out** *vt sep* hinausschieben; *(quickly, violently)* hinausstoßen. **to ~ sb/sth ~ of sth** jdn/etw aus etw schieben/stoßen.
♦ **push over** *vt sep* **(a)** *(pass over)* hinüber-/herüberschieben; *(quickly, violently)* hinüber-/herüberstoßen. **to ~ sb/sth ~ sth** jdn/etw über etw *(acc)* schieben/stoßen. **(b)** *(knock over)* umwerfen.
♦ **push through 1** *vt sep* **(a)** *(shove through)* durchschieben; *(quickly, violently)* durchstoßen. **to ~ sb/sth ~ sth** jdn/etw durch etw schieben/stoßen; **to ~ one's way ~ the crowd** sich durch die Menge drängen. **(b)** *(get done quickly) bill, decision* durchpeitschen *(col)*; *business* durchziehen *(col).* **2** *vi (through crowd)* sich durchschieben; *(more violently)* sich durchdrängen; *(new shoots)* sich herausschieben.
♦ **push up** *vt sep* **(a)** *(lit)* hinaufschieben; *(quickly, violently)* hinaufstoßen; *window* hochschieben/-stoßen. **(b)** *(fig: raise, increase)* hochtreiben.
push: ~-bike *n (Brit)* Fahrrad *nt* **~-button** *n* Drucktaste *f*, Knopf *m*; **~-button telephone** Tastentelefon *nt*; **~-button warfare** Krieg *m* auf Knopfdruck; **~chair** *n (Brit)* Sportwagen *m.*
pusher ['pʊʃəʳ] *n (col)* **(a)** *(of drugs)* Pusher(in *f*) *m (col).* **(b)** *(ambitious person)* **he's a ~** er setzt sich durch.
push-over ['pʊʃəʊvəʳ] *n (col) (job etc)* Kinderspiel *nt*; *(person)* leichtes Opfer.
pushy ['pʊʃɪ] *adj (+er) (col)* penetrant *(pej).*
pussy ['pʊsɪ] *n (cat)* Mieze *(col) f.*
pussy: ~-cat *n (baby-talk)* Miezekatze *f (baby-talk)*; **~ willow** *n* Salweide *f.*
put [pʊt] *pret, ptp* **~ 1** *vt* **(a)** *(place)* tun; *(~ down, position)* stellen, setzen; *(lay down)* legen; *(push in)* stecken. **~ the lid on the box** mach den Deckel auf die Schachtel; **to ~ sth in a drawer** etw in eine Schublade tun *or* legen; **he ~ his hand in his pocket** er steckte die Hand in die Tasche; **he ~ some more coal on the fire** er legte Kohle nach; **to ~ sugar in one's coffee** Zucker in den Kaffee tun; **to ~ the ball in the net** *(Ftbl)* den Ball ins Netz setzen; **he ~ his toe in the water** er steckte seinen Zeh ins Wasser; **he ~ his hand on my shoulder** er legte seine Hand auf meine Schulter.

(b) *(thrust)* stecken. **he ~ his head around the door** er steckte den Kopf zur Tür herein; **to ~ one's fist through a window** mit der Faust ein Fenster einschlagen.

(c) to stay ~ liegen-/stehen-/hängen- *etc* bleiben; *(hair)* halten; *(person) (not move)* hier-/dableiben; *(not stand up)* sitzenbleiben.

(d) to ~ a child in a home ein Kind in ein Heim stecken; **to ~ money into sth** (sein) Geld in etw *(acc)* stecken; **he ~ £10/money on Red Rum** er setzte £ 10/setzte auf Red Rum; **to ~ a lot of time into sth** viel Zeit in etw *(acc)* stecken; **to ~ a lot of effort into one's work** viel Mühe in seine Arbeit stecken.

(e) *(cause to be, do etc)* **to ~ sb in a good/bad**

mood jdn fröhlich/mißmutig stimmen; **they ~ her to work on the new project** ihr wurde die Arbeit an dem neuen Projekt zugewiesen; **to be ~ to a lot of inconvenience over sth** mit etw viele Unannehmlichkeiten haben.

(f) *comma, line* machen; *(~ forward) proposal* vorbringen. **to ~ one's signature to a document** seine Unterschrift unter ein Schriftstück setzen; **to ~ a matter before a committee** eine Angelegenheit vor einen Ausschuß bringen; **to ~ the arguments for and against sth** das Für und Wider von etw *(dat)* aufzählen; **to ~ sth on the agenda** etw auf die Tagesordnung setzen; **you might ~ it to him that ...** du könntest ihm nahelegen, daß ...; **to ~ a question/suggestion to sb** jdm eine Frage stellen/einen Vorschlag unterbreiten; **I ~ it to you that ...** ich möchte Ihnen vorhalten, daß ...

(g) *(express)* ausdrücken, sagen. **that's one way of ~ting it** so kann man's auch sagen; **to ~ it bluntly** hart *or* grob ausgedrückt; **how shall I ~ it?** wie soll ich (es) sagen?; **to ~ sth into German** etw ins Deutsche übersetzen.

(h) *(rate)* schätzen *(at* auf *+acc)*. **he ~s money before his family's happiness** er stellt Geld über das Glück seiner Familie; **to ~ a value of £10 on sth** den Wert einer Sache *(gen)* auf £ 10 schätzen.

2 *vi (Naut)* **to ~ to sea** in See stechen.

♦ **put about** *vt sep news, rumour* verbreiten, in Umlauf bringen. **he ~ it ~ that ...** er verbreitete (das Gerücht), daß ...

♦ **put across** *vt sep* **(a)** *(communicate) ideas* verständlich machen *(to sb* jdm*)*, klar zum Ausdruck bringen; *knowledge* vermitteln *(to sb* jdm*)*; *(promote)* an den Mann bringen *(col)*. **to ~ oneself ~** den richtigen Eindruck von sich geben. **(b)** *(col)* = **put over.**

♦ **put aside** *vt sep* **(a)** *book etc* beiseite legen. **(b)** *(save for later use)* zurücklegen. **(c)** *(fig: forget)* ablegen, über Bord werfen *(col)*; *anger* begraben; *thought* aufgeben; *differences* vergessen.

♦ **put away** *vt sep* **(a)** *(in usual place)* einräumen; *(tidy away)* wegräumen. **to ~ the car ~** das Auto in die Garage stellen. **(b)** *(col: consume)* schaffen *(col)*; *food also* verputzen *(col)*. **(c)** *(in prison etc)* einsperren.

♦ **put back** *vt sep* **(a)** *(replace) see* **put 1 (a)** zurücktun/-stellen *or* -setzen/-legen/-stecken. **(b)** *(postpone)* verschieben; *(set back)* zurückwerfen; *(readjust) watch etc* zurückstellen.

♦ **put by** *vt sep* zurücklegen, auf die hohe Kante legen.

♦ **put down 1** *vt sep* **(a)** *(set down) object see* **put 1 (a)** wegtun/-setzen *or* -stellen/weglegen; *surface* verlegen. **I simply couldn't ~ that book ~** ich konnte das Buch einfach nicht aus der Hand legen.

(b) *(lower) umbrella* zumachen; *aerial* einschieben; *car roof* zurückklappen; *lid* zuklappen.

(c) *rebellion* niederschlagen; *rebels* niederwerfen; *crime* besiegen; *(humiliate)* demütigen.

(d) *(pay)* anzahlen; *deposit* machen.

(e) *pets* einschläfern; *injured horse etc* den Gnadenschuß geben *(+dat)*.

(f) *(write down)* aufschreiben; *(on form)* angeben. **~ me ~ for £50** für mich können Sie £ 50 eintragen.

(g) *(attribute)* zurückführen *(to* auf *+acc)*, zuschreiben *(to dat)*.

2 *vi (Aviat)* landen.

♦ **put forward** *vt sep* **(a)** *idea, suggestion* vorbringen; *(nominate)* vorschlagen. **(b)** *(advance) meeting* vorverlegen *(to* auf *+acc)*; *watch* vorstellen.

♦ **put in 1** *vt sep* **(a)** *(place in) see* **put 1 (a)** hineintun/-setzen *or* -stellen/-legen/-stecken; *(pack)* einpacken.

(b) *(insert in book, speech etc)* einfügen; *(add)* hinzufügen.

(c) *(enter) application* einreichen; *claim also* stellen. **to ~ ~ a plea of not guilty** *(Jur)* auf „nicht schuldig" plädieren; **to ~ one's name ~ for sth** sich um etw bewerben; *for evening classes, exam* sich für etw anmelden; **to ~ sb ~ for an exam/an award** jdn für *or* zu einer Prüfung/für eine Ehrung vorschlagen.

(d) *(install) central heating, car radio* einbauen.

(e) *(Pol: elect)* an die Regierung bringen.

(f) *(devote, expend) time* verbringen *(with* mit*)*, verwenden *(with* auf*)*. **could you ~ ~ an extra hour?** könnten Sie eine zusätzliche Stunde Arbeit einschieben?; **he ~ ~ a lot of hard work on the project** er hat eine Menge harter Arbeit in das Projekt gesteckt.

2 *vi* **(a) to ~ ~ for sth** *for job* sich um etw bewerben; *for leave, rise* etw beantragen. **(b)** *(Naut: enter port)* **to ~ ~ to Bremen/harbour** in Bremen/in den Hafen einlaufen.

♦ **put off** *vt sep* **(a)** *(set down) passengers* aussteigen lassen *(prep obj* aus*)*; *(forcibly)* hinauswerfen *(prep obj* aus*)*. **(b)** *(postpone, delay)* verschieben; *visitors* (wieder) ausladen; *decision* aufschieben; *sth unpleasant* hinauszögern. **to ~ sth ~ till later** etw auf später verschieben. **(c)** *(prevent from coming) boyfriend, creditor* hinhalten. **to ~ sb ~ doing sth** jdn davon abbringen, etw zu tun. **(d)** *(repel)* die Lust verderben *(+dat)*. **to ~ sb ~ sth** jdm etw verleiden. **(e)** *(distract)* ablenken *(prep obj* von*)*; *(disturb)* stören.

♦ **put on** *vt sep* **(a)** *coat, shoes etc* anziehen; *hat (sich dat)* aufsetzen; *make-up* auftragen; *accent, manners* annehmen; *facade, front* aufsetzen. **to ~ ~ one's make-up** sich schminken; **to ~ ~ an air of innocence** eine unschuldige Miene aufsetzen; **his sorrow is all ~ ~** sein Kummer ist bloß Schau *(col)*.

(b) *(increase, add)* **to ~ ~ weight/a few pounds** zunehmen/ein paar Pfund zunehmen; **to ~ ~ speed** schneller fahren, beschleunigen; **10p was ~ ~ the price of petrol** der Benzinpreis wurde um 10 Pence erhöht.

(c) *play* aufführen; *exhibition* veranstalten; *film* vorführen; *train, bus* einsetzen; *(fig) act, show* abziehen *(col)*.

(d) *(on telephone)* **to ~ sb ~ to sb** jdn mit jdm verbinden; **would you ~ him ~?** könnten Sie ihn mir geben?

(e) *(switch on) light, TV* anmachen, einschalten. **to ~ the kettle/dinner ~** das Wasser/das Essen aufsetzen.

(f) *watch etc* vorstellen.

(g) to ~ sb ~ to sth *(inform about)* jdm etw vermitteln; **to ~ sb ~ to a plumber/garage** *etc* jdm einen Installateur/eine Reparaturwerkstatt *etc* empfehlen; **what ~ you ~ to it?** was hat dich darauf gebracht?; **to ~ the police ~ to sb** die Polizei auf jds Spur bringen.

(h) *(col: tease, trick)* auf den Arm nehmen *(col)*.

♦ **put out 1** *vt sep* **(a)** *rubbish etc* hinausbringen; *cat* vor die Tür setzen. **to ~ the washing ~ (to dry)** die Wäsche (zum Trocknen) raushängen; **to be ~ ~** *(asked to leave)* vor die Tür gesetzt werden; **to ~ sb ~ of business** jdn aus dem Markt drängen; **she could not ~ him ~ of her thoughts** er ging ihr nicht aus dem Sinn.

(b) *(stretch out) hand, foot* ausstrecken; *tongue, head* herausstrecken. **to ~ one's head ~ of the window** den Kopf zum Fenster hinausstrecken.

(c) *dishes, cutlery* auflegen; *chessmen etc* aufstellen.

(d) *(circulate) pamphlet* herausbringen; *propaganda* machen; *rumour* verbreiten; *regulations* erlassen; *statement* abgeben;

message, appeal durchgeben; *description* bekanntgeben; *TV programme* bringen, senden.

(e) *(extinguish)* löschen.

(f) *(vex)* **to be ~ ~ (by sth)** (über etw *acc*) verärgert sein.

(g) *(inconvenience)* **to ~ oneself ~ (for sb)** sich *(dat)* (wegen jdm) Umstände machen.

(h) *(dislocate) knee, shoulder* ausrenken; *(more severely)* auskugeln; *back* verrenken.

2 *vi (Naut: set sail)* auslaufen. **to ~ ~ to sea** in See stechen; **to ~ ~ from Bremen** von Bremen auslaufen.

♦ **put over** *vt sep* **to ~ one ~ on sb** *(col)* jdn anführen.

♦ **put through** *vt sep* **(a)** *reform, proposal* durchbringen; *(+prep obj)* bringen durch; *claim* weiterleiten. **(b)** *person* verbinden *(to* mit*)*; *call* durchstellen *(to* zu*)*. **to ~ a call ~ to Beirut** ein Gespräch nach Beirut vermitteln *or (caller)* anmelden.

♦ **put together** *vt sep* **(a)** *(in same room etc)* zusammentun; *(seat together)* zusammensetzen. **he's better than all the others ~ ~** er ist besser als alle anderen zusammen. **(b)** *(assemble)* zusammensetzen; *furniture, machine also* zusammenbauen; *essay etc, (Jur) case* zusammenstellen; *collection, evidence* zusammentragen.

♦ **put up 1** *vt sep* **(a)** *(raise) hand* hochheben; *car window* zumachen; *sash window* hochschieben; *umbrella* aufklappen; *hair* hochstecken; *collar* hochschlagen. **(b)** *flag, sail* aufziehen. **(c)** *picture etc* aufhängen; *notice* anschlagen. **(d)** *building, fence* errichten; *ladder, scaffolding* aufstellen; *tent* aufschlagen; *(fig) facade* vortäuschen. **(e)** *missile, flare* hochschießen. **(f)** *(increase) sales, prices* erhöhen. **(g) = put forward (a). (h)** *(offer)* **to ~ sth ~ for sale** etw zum Verkauf anbieten; **to ~ ~ resistance (to sb)** (jdm) Widerstand leisten. **(i)** *(give accommodation to)* unterbringen. **(j)** *(provide) capital* bereitstellen; *reward* aussetzen. **(k) to ~ sb ~ to sth** jdn zu etw anstiften.

2 *vi* **(a)** *(stay)* wohnen; *(for one night)* übernachten. **(b) to ~ ~ for election** sich zur Wahl stellen.

♦ **put upon** *vi +prep obj (impose on)* ausnutzen.

♦ **put up with** *vi +prep obj* sich abfinden mit. **I won't ~ ~ ~ that** das lasse ich mir nicht gefallen.

putrefy ['pju:trɪfaɪ] *vi* verwesen.

putrid ['pju:trɪd] *adj* verfault; *smell* faul.

putt [pʌt] **1** *n (Golf)* Schlag *m (mit dem man einlocht)*. **2** *vti* putten, einlochen.

putting ['pʌtɪŋ] Putten *nt*. **~ green** kleiner Rasenplatz zum Putten.

putty ['pʌtɪ] *n* Kitt *m*. **he was ~ in her hands** er war Wachs in ihren Händen.

put-up ['pʊtʌp] *adj (col)* **a ~ job** ein abgekartetes Spiel.

puzzle ['pʌzl] **1** *n* **(a)** *(wordgame etc)* Rätsel *nt*; *(toy)* Geduldsspiel *nt*; *(jigsaw)* Puzzle(spiel) *nt*. **(b)** *(mystery)* Rätsel *nt*. **2** *vi* **to ~ over sth** sich *(dat)* über etw *(acc)* den Kopf zerbrechen. **3** *vt* verblüffen. **I'm ~d about it** ich bin mir darüber im unklaren; **the police are ~d** die Polizei steht vor einem Rätsel.

♦ **puzzle out** *vt sep* austüfteln.

puzzled ['pʌzld] *adj look* verdutzt, verblüfft.

puzzlement ['pʌzlmənt] *n* Verblüffung *f*.

puzzling ['pʌzlɪŋ] *adj* rätselhaft; *story, mechanism* verwirrend.

PVC = polyvinyl chloride PVC *nt*.

pygmy ['pɪgmɪ] *n* **(a) P~** Pygmäe *m*. **(b)** *(small person, fig)* Zwerg *m*.

pyjamas, *(US)* **pajamas** [pə'dʒɑ:məz] *npl* Schlafanzug, Pyjama *m*.

pylon ['paɪlən] *n* Mast *m*.

pyramid ['pɪrəmɪd] *n* Pyramide *f*.

pyre ['paɪə[r]] *n* Scheiterhaufen *m (zum Verbrennen von Leichen)*.

Pyrenees [pɪrə'ni:z] *npl* Pyrenäen *pl*.

Pyrex ® ['paɪreks] *n* Jenaer Glas ® *nt*.

pyromaniac [,paɪərəʊ'meɪnɪæk] *n* Pyromane *m*, Pyromanin *f*.

pyrotechnics [,paɪrəʊ'teknɪks] *n (sing)* Pyrotechnik *f*; *(pl: display)* Feuerwerk *nt*.

python ['paɪθən] *n* Python(schlange *f*) *m*.

Q

Q, q [kjuː] *n* Q, q *nt.*
quack[1] [kwæk] **1** *n* Schnattern, Quaken *nt no pl.* **2** *vi (duck)* schnattern, quaken, quak machen *(col).*
quack[2] *n* Quacksalber, Kurpfuscher *m*; *(hum: doctor)* Doktor, Medizinmann *(hum) m.*
quad [kwɒd] *n* = **(a) quadrangle** Hof *m.* **(b) quadruplet** Vierling *m.*
quadrangle ['kwɒdræŋgl] *n* **(a)** *(Math)* Viereck *nt.* **(b)** *(Archit)* (viereckiger) (Innen)hof.
quadratic [kwɒ'drætɪk] *adj (Math)* quadratisch.
quadrilateral [ˌkwɒdrɪ'lætərəl] **1** *adj (Math)* vierseitig. **2** *n* Viereck *nt.*
quadruped ['kwɒdrʊped] *n* Vierfüß(l)er *m.*
quadruple ['kwɒdrʊpl] **1** *adj* vierfach. **2** *vt* vervierfachen. **3** *vi* sich vervierfachen.
quadruplet [kwɒ'druːplɪt] *n (child)* Vierling *m.*
quagmire ['kwægmaɪə^{r}] *n* Sumpf, Morast *m*; *(fig) (of vice etc)* Morast *m*; *(difficult situation)* Schlamassel *m (col).*
quail[1] ['kweɪl] *vi* (vor Angst) zittern *or* beben *(before* vor *+dat).*
quail[2] *n (Orn)* Wachtel *f.*
quaint [kweɪnt] *adj (+er) (picturesque)* malerisch; *(charmingly old-fashioned)* urig; *(pleasantly odd) idea* kurios; *old lady, way of speaking* drollig.
quake [kweɪk] **1** *vi* beben *(with* vor *+dat).* **2** *n (col: earth~)* (Erd)beben *nt.*
Quaker ['kweɪkə^{r}] *n* Quäker(in *f*) *m.*
qualification [ˌkwɒlɪfɪ'keɪʃən] *n* **(a)** *(on paper)* Qualifikation *f*; *(document)* Zeugnis *nt*; *(requisite quality)* Voraussetzung *f*; *(act of qualifying)* Abschluß *m* von jds Ausbildung. **what are your ~s?** welche Qualifikationen haben Sie?; **the only ~ needed is a knowledge of French** die einzige Voraussetzung sind Französischkenntnisse. **(b)** *(limitation)* Einschränkung *f*; *(modification)* Modifikation *f.* **to accept a plan with/without ~(s)** einen Plan unter Vorbehalt/vorbehaltlos billigen.
qualified ['kwɒlɪfaɪd] *adj* **(a)** *(having training)* ausgebildet; *engineer* graduiert; *(with university degree) engineer* Diplom-. **highly ~** hochqualifiziert; **to be ~ to do sth** qualifiziert sein, etw zu tun; **he was not ~ for the job** ihm fehlte die Qualifikation für die Stelle. **(b)** *(limited) praise, approval* nicht uneingeschränkt. **a ~ success** kein voller Erfolg; **~ acceptance** *(Comm)* bedingte Annahme; **in a ~ sense** mit Einschränkungen.
qualify ['kwɒlɪfaɪ] **1** *vt* **(a)** *(make competent)* qualifizieren; *(make legally entitled)* berechtigen. **to ~ sb to do sth** *(entitle)* jdn berechtigen, etw zu tun; **he is not qualified to make these decisions** er ist nicht kompetent, diese Entscheidungen zu treffen. **(b)** *(limit) statement, criticism* einschränken; *(change slightly) opinion, remark* modifizieren. **(c)** *(Gram)* näher bestimmen. **2** *vi (also Sport)* sich qualifizieren *(for* für); *(fulfil required conditions)* in Frage kommen *(for* für). **to ~ as a doctor/teacher** sein medizinisches Staatsexamen machen/die Lehrbefähigung erhalten; **he hardly qualifies as a poet** er kann kaum als Dichter angesehen werden.
qualifying ['kwɒlɪfaɪɪŋ] *adj adjective* erläuternd; *round, heat* Qualifikations-. **~ examination** Auswahlprüfung *f.*
qualitative ['kwɒlɪtətɪv] *adj* qualitativ.
quality ['kwɒlɪtɪ] **1** *n* Qualität *f*; *(of justice, education etc)* (hoher) Stand; *(characteristic)* Eigenschaft *f*; *(nature)* Art *f.* **of good/poor ~** von guter/schlechter Qualität; **~ matters more than quantity** Qualität geht vor Quantität; **they vary in ~** sie sind qualitativ unterschiedlich. **2** *attr goods etc* Qualitäts-; *(col: good)* erstklassig *(col)*; *newspaper* angesehen.
qualm [kwɑːm] *n* Bedenken *nt*; *(scruple)* Skrupel *m.* **without a ~** ohne jeden Skrupel; **~s of conscience** Gewissensbisse *pl*; **I had some ~s about his future** ich hatte mancherlei Bedenken wegen seiner Zukunft.
quandary ['kwɒndərɪ] *n* Verlegenheit *f*, Dilemma *nt.* **he was in a ~ about what to do** er wußte nicht, was er tun sollte.
quango ['kwæŋgəʊ] *n* Regierungsausschuß *m.*
quantitative ['kwɒntɪtətɪv] *adj* quantitativ.
quantity ['kwɒntɪtɪ] *n* Quantität *f*; *(amount)* Menge *f*; *(proportion)* Anteil *m (of* an *+dat)*; *(Math, Phys, fig)* Größe *f.* **in ~, in large quantities** in großen Mengen; **in equal quantities** zu gleichen Teilen; **quantities of books** Unmengen von Büchern.
quantity surveyor *n* Baukostenkalkulator *m.*
quantum ['kwɒntəm] *n, pl* **quanta** *(Phys)* Quant *nt.* **~ physics** *n sing* Quantenphysik *f*; **~ theory** *n* Quantentheorie *f.*
quarantine ['kwɒrəntiːn] *n* Quarantäne *f.* **to be in ~** in Quarantäne sein.
quarrel ['kwɒrəl] **1** *n* Streit *m*; *(dispute)* Auseinandersetzung *f.* **they have had a ~** sie haben Streit gehabt; **let's not have a ~ about it** wir wollen uns nicht darüber streiten; **to start** *or* **pick a ~** einen Streit anfangen *(with* mit); **I have no ~ with him** ich habe nichts gegen ihn. **2** *vi* **(a)** *(have a dispute)* sich streiten *(with* mit, *about, over* über *+acc)*; *(more trivially also)* sich zanken. **(b)** *(find fault)* etwas auszusetzen haben *(with* an *+dat).* **you can't ~ with that** daran kann man doch nichts aussetzen.
quarrelling, *(US)* **quarreling** ['kwɒrəlɪŋ] *n* Streiterei *f.*
quarrelsome ['kwɒrəlsəm] *adj* streitsüchtig; *woman also* zänkisch.
quarry[1] ['kwɒrɪ] **1** *n* **(a)** Steinbruch *m.* **sandstone ~** Sandsteinbruch *m.* **(b)** *(fig)* Fundgrube *f.* **2** *vt* brechen, hauen.
quarry[2] *n* **(a)** *(Hunt)* Beute *f.* **(b)** *(fig) (thing)* Ziel *nt*; *(person)* Opfer *nt.*
quart [kwɔːt] *n (Measure)* Quart *nt.*
quarter ['kwɔːtə^{r}] **1** *n* **(a)** Viertel *nt.* **to divide sth into ~s** etw in vier Teile teilen; **the bottle was a ~/three-~s full** die Flasche war viertel/dreiviertel voll; **a ~ (of a pound) of sausages** ein Viertel(pfund) Wurst; **a mile and a ~** eineinviertel Meilen; **a ~ of a mile** eine Viertelmeile; **for a ~ of the price** zu einem Viertel des Preises; **a ~ of an hour** eine Viertelstunde; **a ~ to seven** *(Brit)*, **a ~ of seven** *(US)* Viertel vor sieben; **a ~ past six** *(Brit)*, **a ~ after six** *(esp US)* Viertel nach sechs; **an hour and a ~** eineinviertel Stunden.
(b) *(district, area)* Viertel *nt.* **they came from all ~s of the earth** sie kamen aus allen Teilen der Welt; **in these ~s** in dieser Gegend; **he won't get**

help from that ~ von dieser Seite wird er keine Hilfe bekommen; **at close ~s** in der Nähe; *(from nearby)* aus der Nähe.

(c) *(direction)* (Himmels)richtung *f.* **they came from all ~s** sie kamen aus allen Himmelsrichtungen.

(d) **~s** *pl (lodgings)* Quartier *nt (also Mil)*, Unterkunft *f*; **to be confined to ~s** *(Mil)* Stubenarrest haben.

(e) to give sb no ~ jdn nicht schonen.

2 *adj pound, mile* Viertel-.

3 *vt* **(a)** vierteln. **(b)** *(lodge)* einquartieren *(also Mil) (on* bei*)*.

quarter: ~deck *n (Naut)* Achterdeck *nt*; **~-final** *n* Viertelfinale *nt.*

quarterly ['kwɔːtəlɪ] **1** *adj* vierteljährlich. **2** *n* Vierteljahresschrift *f.* **3** *adv* vierteljährlich.

quartermaster ['kwɔːtəˌmɑːstəʳ] *n (Mil)* Quartiermeister *m*; *(Navy)* Steuermannsmaat *m.*

quartet [kwɔː'tet] *n (Mus)* Quartett *nt.*

quarto ['kwɔːtəʊ] **1** *n (Typ)* Quart(format) *nt.* **2** *attr paper, volume* in Quart.

quartz ['kwɔːts] *n* Quarz *m.* **~ clock** Quarzuhr *f.*

quash [kwɒʃ] *vt* **(a)** *(Jur) verdict* aufheben, annullieren. **(b)** *rebellion* unterdrücken; *suggestion, objection* ablehnen.

quasi- ['kwɑːzɪ] *pref* quasi-, quasi.

quaver ['kweɪvəʳ] **1** *n* **(a)** *(esp Brit Mus)* Achtel(note *f*) *nt.* **(b)** *(in voice)* Beben *nt.* **2** *vi (voice)* beben; *(Mus)* tremolieren.

quay [kiː] *n* Kai *m.* **alongside the ~** am Kai.

quayside ['kiːsaɪd] *n* Kai *m.*

queasy ['kwiːzɪ] *adj (+er)* **I feel ~** mir ist übel.

queen [kwiːn] *n* **(a)** *(also fig)* Königin *f.* **~ bee** Bienenkönigin *f*; **~ mother** Königinmutter *f*; **~'s English** englische Hochsprache. **(b)** *(Cards, Chess)* Dame *f.* **~ of spades** Pik Dame. **(c)** *(col: homosexual)* Schwule(r) *m (col).*

queer [kwɪəʳ] **1** *adj (+er)* **(a)** *(strange)* komisch. **(b)** *(col) (unwell)* unwohl; *(peculiar) feeling* komisch. **I feel ~** mir ist nicht gut/mir ist ganz komisch *(col).* **(c)** *(col: homosexual)* schwul *(col).* **2** *n (col: homosexual)* Schwule(r) *mf (col).* **3** *vt* **to ~ sb's pitch** *(col)* jdm einen Strich durch die Rechnung machen.

quell [kwel] *vt fear* bezwingen; *passion* zügeln; *riot* niederschlagen; *anxieties* überwinden.

quench [kwentʃ] *vt fire* löschen; *thirst also* stillen; *enthusiasm* dämpfen.

querulous ['kwerʊləs] *adj* nörglerisch. **a ~ person** ein Querulant *m.*

query ['kwɪərɪ] **1** *n (question)* Frage *f.* **to raise a ~** eine Frage aufwerfen. **2** *vt* **(a)** *(express doubt about)* bezweifeln; *statement, motives* in Frage stellen; *bill, item* reklamieren. **(b)** *(check)* **to ~ sth with sb** etw mit jdm abklären.

quest [kwest] *n (search)* Suche *f (for* nach*)*; *(for knowledge, happiness etc)* Streben *nt (for* nach*)*.

question ['kwestʃən] **1** *n* Frage *f (to* an *+acc)*; *(Parl also)* Anfrage *f (to* an *+acc)*; *(no pl: doubt also)* Zweifel *m.* **to ask sb a ~** jdm eine Frage stellen; **beyond (all)** *or* **without ~** ohne Frage, ohne (jeden) Zweifel; **without ~ he is ...** er ist zweifellos *or* ohne Zweifel ...; **his honesty is beyond ~** seine Ehrlichkeit steht außer Frage; **your sincerity is not in ~** niemand zweifelt an Ihrer Aufrichtigkeit; **to call sth into ~** etw in Frage stellen; **that's another ~ altogether** das ist etwas völlig anderes; **that's not the ~** darum geht es nicht; **it's not just a ~ of money** es ist nicht nur eine Frage des Geldes; **there's no ~ of that happening** es kann keine Rede davon sein, daß das passiert; **there's no ~ of a strike** von einem Streik kann keine Rede sein; **that's out of the ~** das kommt nicht in Frage; **the matter in ~** die in Frage stehende Angelegenheit.

2 *vt* **(a)** *(ask ~s of)* fragen *(about* nach*)*; *(police etc)* vernehmen, befragen *(about* zu*)*; *(examiner)* prüfen *(on* über *+acc)*. **they were ~ed by the immigration authorities** ihnen wurden von der Einwanderungsbehörde viele Fragen gestellt. **(b)** *(express doubt about)* bezweifeln; *(dispute, challenge)* in Frage stellen. **I ~ whether it's worth it** ich bezweifle, daß es der Mühe wert ist.

questionable ['kwestʃənəbl] *adj (suspect)* fragwürdig; *(open to doubt) statement, figures* fraglich; *value, advantage also* zweifelhaft.

questioner ['kwestʃənəʳ] *n* Fragesteller(in *f*) *m.*

questioning ['kwestʃənɪŋ] **1** *adj look* fragend. **2** *n* Verhör *nt*; *(by police also)* Vernehmung *f.*

question mark *n (lit, fig)* Fragezeichen *nt.*

questionnaire [ˌkwestʃə'nɛəʳ] *n* Fragebogen *m.*

queue [kjuː] **1** *n (Brit: of people, cars)* Schlange *f.* **to form a ~** eine Schlange bilden; **to stand in a ~** Schlange stehen; **to join the ~** sich (hinten) anstellen; **a ~ of cars** eine Autoschlange. **2** *vi (Brit: also* **~ up***)* Schlange stehen; *(form a ~)* eine Schlange bilden; *(people)* sich anstellen. **they were queuing for bread** sie standen um Brot an.

quibble ['kwɪbl] **1** *vi (be petty-minded)* kleinlich sein *(over, about* wegen*)*; *(argue with sb)* sich herumstreiten *(over, about* wegen*)*. **to ~ over details** auf Einzelheiten herumreiten. **2** *n* **I've got a few ~s about the design** ich habe ein paar Kleinigkeiten am Design auszusetzen.

quick [kwɪk] **1** *adj (+er)* **(a)** schnell; *answer also* prompt. **be ~!** mach schnell!; *(on telephone etc)* faß dich kurz!; **and be ~ about it** aber ein bißchen dalli *(col)*; **you were ~** das ging ja schnell; **he was too ~ for me** *(in speech)* das ging mir zu schnell; *(in escaping)* er war zu schnell für mich; **~ march!** *(Mil)* im Eilschritt, marsch!; **it's ~er by train** mit dem Zug geht es schneller; **he is ~ to criticize other people** er ist mit seiner Kritik schnell bei der Hand; **what's the ~est way to the station?** wie komme ich am schnellsten zum Bahnhof?

(b) *(short) kiss* flüchtig; *speech* kurz; *rest* klein, kurz. **let me have a ~ look** laß mich mal schnell sehen; **could I have a ~ word?** könnte ich Sie mal kurz sprechen?; **I'll just write him a ~ note** ich schreibe ihm schnell mal; **a ~ one** eine(r, s) auf die Schnelle *(col)*; *(question)* eine kurze Frage.

(c) *(lively, ~ to understand) mind* wach; *person* schnell von Begriff *(col)*; *child* aufgeweckt; *temper* hitzig; *eye, ear* scharf. **he is ~ at figures** er kann schnell rechnen.

2 *n (Anat)* empfindliches Fleisch *(besonders unter den Fingernägeln)*. **to be cut to the ~** *(fig)* tief getroffen sein.

3 *adv (+er)* schnell.

quicken ['kwɪkən] **1** *vt (also* **~ up***)* beschleunigen. **2** *vi (also* **~ up***)* schneller werden, sich beschleunigen. **the pace ~ed** das Tempo nahm zu.

quickie ['kwɪkɪ] *n (col)* eine(r, s) auf die Schnelle *(col)*; *(question)* kurze Frage.

quicklime ['kwɪklaɪm] *n* ungelöschter Kalk.

quickly ['kwɪklɪ] *adv* schnell.

quickness ['kwɪknɪs] *n* **(a)** *(speed)* Schnelligkeit *f.* **(b)** *(intelligence)* schnelle Auffassungsgabe.

quick: ~sand *n* Treibsand *m*; **~silver** *n* Quecksilber *nt*; **~step** *n* Quickstep *m*; **~-tempered** *adj* hitzig, leicht erregbar; **~-witted** *adj* geistesgegenwärtig; *answer* schlagfertig.

quid [kwɪd] *n, pl* - *(col)* Pfund *nt.* **20 ~** 20 Eier *(col).*

quiet ['kwaɪət] **1** *adj (+er)* **(a)** *(silent)* still; *neighbours, person also, engine* ruhig; *music, car, voice* leise. **he's very ~** er ist sehr still; **(be) ~!** Ruhe!; **to keep ~** *(not speak)* still sein; *(not make noise)* leise sein; **keep ~!** sei/seid still!; **can't you keep your dog ~!** können Sie nicht zusehen, daß Ihr Hund still ist?; **to keep ~ about sth** über etw *(acc)* nichts sagen.

(b) *(peaceful)* ruhig; *smile* leise. **things are**

very ~ at the moment im Augenblick ist nicht viel los; **to lead a ~ life** ein ruhiges Leben führen; **everything was ~ on the Syrian border** an der syrischen Grenze herrschte Ruhe; **to have a ~ drink** sein Bier *etc* in aller Ruhe trinken.

(c) *(gentle) character* sanft; *child* ruhig; *horse* gutwillig; *irony* leise.

(d) *(simple) style, elegance* schlicht; *wedding, dinner* im kleinen Rahmen.

(e) *(not overt) hatred, envy* still; *resentment* heimlich. **I'll have a ~ word with him** ich werde mal ein Wörtchen (im Vertrauen) mit ihm reden; **he kept the matter ~** er behielt die Sache für sich.

2 *n* Ruhe *f*. **the sudden ~ after the bombing** die plötzliche Stille nach dem Bombenangriff; **on the ~** heimlich; **he left on the ~** er ist still und heimlich weggegangen.

3 *vt* = **quieten.**

quieten ['kwaɪətn] *vt sb* zum Schweigen bringen; *noisy class, dog* zur Ruhe bringen; *crying baby* beruhigen; *engine* ruhiger machen; *(calm) person, conscience* beruhigen.

♦**quieten down 1** *vi (become silent)* leiser werden; *(become calm)* sich beruhigen; *(after wild youth)* ruhiger werden. **2** *vt sep* beruhigen.

quietly ['kwaɪətlɪ] *adv (making little noise)* leise; *(peacefully, making little fuss)* ruhig; *(secretly)* still und heimlich. **he's very ~ spoken** er spricht sehr leise; **to be ~ confident** insgeheim sehr sicher sein; **I was sitting here ~ sipping my wine** ich saß da und trank in aller Ruhe meinen Wein; **he slipped off ~** er machte sich in aller Stille davon.

quietness ['kwaɪətnɪs] *n* **(a)** Stille *f*; *(of engine, car)* Geräuscharmut *f*; *(of footsteps etc)* Lautlosigkeit *f*; *(of person)* stille Art. **the ~ of her voice** ihre leise Stimme. **(b)** *(peacefulness)* Ruhe *f*.

quill [kwɪl] *n (feather, pen)* Feder *f*; *(feather stem)* Federkiel *m*; *(of porcupine)* Stachel *m*.

quilt [kwɪlt] **1** *n (continental ~)* Steppdecke *f*; *(unstitched)* Federbett *nt*. **2** *vt* absteppen; *(with padding)* wattieren.

quin [kwɪn] *n (Brit)* = **quintuplet** Fünfling *m*.

quince [kwɪns] *n (fruit, tree)* Quitte *f*. **~ jelly** Quittengelee *nt*.

quinine [kwɪ'ni:n] *n* Chinin *nt*.

quintessence [kwɪn'tesns] *n (fig)* Quintessenz *f*; *(embodiment)* Inbegriff *m*.

quintet [kwɪn'tet] *n (Mus)* Quintett *nt*.

quintuplet [kwɪn'tju:plɪt] *n* Fünfling *m*.

quip [kwɪp] **1** *n* witzige Bemerkung. **2** *vti* witzeln.

quirk [kw3:k] *n* Marotte *f*; *(of nature, fate)* Laune *f*. **by a strange ~ of fate** durch eine Laune des Schicksals.

quirky ['kw3:kɪ] *adj (+er)* schrullig.

quit [kwɪt] *(vb: pret, ptp* **~ted** *or* **~)** **1** *vt* **(a)** *(leave) town, army* verlassen; *(give up) job* aufgeben. **(b)** *(col: stop)* aufhören mit. **to ~ doing sth** aufhören, etw zu tun. **2** *vi* **(a)** *(leave one's job)* kündigen. **(b)** *(go away)* weg- *or* fortgehen. **notice to ~** Kündigung *f*; **they gave me notice to ~** sie haben mir gekündigt. **(c)** *(give up)* aufgeben. **3** *adj* **~ of** frei von, ledig *(+gen) (geh)*; **we are ~ of him** wir sind ihn los.

quite [kwaɪt] *adv* **(a)** *(entirely)* ganz; *(emph)* völlig. **~ unnecessary/wrong** völlig unnötig/falsch; **I am ~ happy where I am** ich fühle mich hier ganz wohl; **I was ~ happy until you came along** bevor du kamst, war ich völlig zufrieden; **it's ~ impossible to do that** das ist völlig unmöglich; **are you ~ finished!** bist du jetzt fertig?; **he's ~ grown up now** er ist jetzt schon richtig erwachsen; **I ~ agree with you** ich stimme völlig mit Ihnen überein; **he ~ understands that he must go** er sieht durchaus ein, daß er gehen muß; **he has ~ recovered** er ist völlig wiederhergestellt; **that's ~ another matter** das ist doch etwas ganz anderes; **that's ~ enough for me** das reicht wirklich; **not ~** nicht ganz; **you weren't ~ early/tall enough** Sie waren ein bißchen zu spät dran/zu klein; **I don't ~ see what he means** ich verstehe nicht ganz, was er meint; **sorry! — that's ~ all right** entschuldige! — das macht nichts; **thank you — that's ~ all right** danke — bitte schön; **~ (so)!** genau!; **~ the thing** *(col)* ganz große Mode.

(b) *(to some degree)* ziemlich. **~ likely** sehr wahrscheinlich; **he's had ~ a lot to drink** er hat ganz schön viel getrunken *(col)*; **~ a few people** ziemlich viele Leute; **he is ~ a good singer** er ist ein ziemlich guter Sänger; **I ~ like this painting** dieses Bild gefällt mir ganz gut.

(c) *(really, truly)* wirklich. **she's ~ a girl/cook** *etc* sie ist ein tolles Mädchen/eine tolle Köchin *etc*; **it's ~ delightful** es ist einfach wunderbar; **it was ~ a shock** es war ein ziemlicher Schock; **that's ~ some bill** *(col)* das ist vielleicht eine Rechnung *(col)*; **it was ~ an experience** das war schon ein Erlebnis; **he's ~ a hero now** jetzt ist er ein richtiger Held.

quits [kwɪts] *adj* quitt. **to be ~ with sb** mit jdm quitt sein; **shall we call it ~?** lassen wir's?

quiver[1] ['kwɪvə^r] **1** *vi* zittern *(with* vor *+dat)*; *(eyelids etc)* zucken. **2** *n* Zittern *nt*; Zucken *nt*.

quiver[2] *n (for arrows)* Köcher *m*.

quixotic [kwɪk'sɒtɪk] *adj* versponnen; *ideals* schwärmerisch. **a ~ gesture** eine Donquichotterie.

quiz [kwɪz] **1** *n* **(a)** Quiz *nt*. **(b)** *(US Sch col)* Prüfung *f*. **2** *vt* **(a)** *(question closely)* ausfragen *(about* über *+acc)*. **(b)** *(US Sch col)* prüfen.

quiz: ~master *n* Quizmaster *m*; **~ show** *n* Quiz *nt*.

quizzical ['kwɪzɪkəl] *adj* **(a)** *air, look* fragend; *smile* zweifelnd. **(b)** *(odd)* eigenartig.

quoit [kwɔɪt] *n* Wurfring *m*.

quorum ['kwɔ:rəm] *n* Quorum *nt*.

quota ['kwəʊtə] *n* **(a)** *(of work)* Pensum *nt*. **(b)** *(of* an *+dat) (permitted amount)* Quantum *nt*; *(share allotted)* Anteil *m*; *(of goods)* Kontingent *nt*. **the ~ of immigrants allowed into the country** die zugelassene Einwanderungsquote.

quotation [kwəʊ'teɪʃən] *n* **(a)** *(passage cited)* Zitat *nt*; *(act)* Zitieren *nt*. **a ~ from Shakespeare** ein Shakespeare-Zitat. **(b)** *(St Ex)* Notierung *f*. **(c)** *(Comm)* Preis *m*; Preise *pl*; *(estimate)* Kostenvoranschlag *m*.

quotation marks *npl* Anführungszeichen *pl*. **open/close ~** Anführungszeichen unten/oben.

quote [kwəʊt] **1** *vt* **(a)** *author, text* zitieren. **you can ~ me (on that)** Sie können das ruhig wörtlich wiedergeben; **he was ~d as saying that ...** er soll gesagt haben, daß ...; **~... un~** Zitat Anfang ... Zitat Ende; **don't ~ me on this** *(I'm not sure)* ich kann mich nicht dafür verbürgen; *(don't repeat)* das sollte unter uns bleiben; **he said, and I ~ ...** er sagte, und zwar wörtlich, ... **(b)** *(cite)* anführen. **to ~ sb/sth as an example** jdn/etw als Beispiel anführen. **(c)** *(Comm) price* nennen; *reference number* angeben. **how much did they ~ you for that?** wieviel haben sie dafür verlangt? **(d)** *(St Ex)* notieren. **the shares are ~d at £2** die Aktien werden mit £2 notiert.

2 *vi* zitieren. **to ~ from an author** einen Schriftsteller zitieren.

3 *n* **(a)** *(from author, politician)* Zitat *nt*. **(b) ~s** *pl (col)* Anführungszeichen *pl*; **in ~s** in Anführungszeichen. **(c)** *(Comm)* Preis *m*; Preise *pl*; *(estimate)* Kostenvoranschlag *m*.

quotient ['kwəʊʃənt] *n (Math)* Quotient *m*.

R

R, r [ɑːʳ] *n* R, r *nt.* **the three Rs** Lesen, Schreiben und Rechnen *(with sing or pl vb).*
rabbi ['ræbaɪ] *n* Rabbiner *m*; *(as title)* Rabbi *m.*
rabbit ['ræbɪt] *n* Kaninchen *nt.*
rabbit *in cpds* Kaninchen-; ~ **burrow** *or* **hole** *n* Kaninchenbau *m*; ~ **hutch** *n* Kaninchenstall *m*; ~ **warren** *n (fig: maze)* Labyrinth *nt.*
♦ **rabbit on** *vi (Brit col)* schwafeln *(col).* **what's he ~ting ~ about?** was schwafelt er da? *(col).*
rabble ['ræbl] *n (disorderly crowd)* lärmender Haufen *(col)*; *(pej: lower classes)* Pöbel *m.*
rabid ['ræbɪd] *adj* **(a)** *(Vet)* tollwütig. **(b)** *(fanatical)* fanatisch; *hatred also* wild.
rabies ['reɪbiːz] *n* Tollwut *f.*
RAC = **Royal Automobile Club.**
raccoon *n* = **racoon.**
race[1] [reɪs] **1** *n* Rennen *nt*; *(on foot also)* (Wett)lauf *m*; *(swimming)* Wettschwimmen *nt.* **100 metres ~** 100-Meter-Lauf *m*; **to run a ~ with** *or* **against sb** mit jdm um die Wette laufen; **to go to the ~s** zum Pferderennen gehen; **a ~ against time** *(fig)* ein Wettlauf *m* gegen die Zeit.
2 *vt (compete with)* um die Wette laufen/fahren/schwimmen *etc* mit; *(Sport)* laufen/fahren/schwimmen *etc* gegen. **I'll ~ you to school** ich mache mit dir ein Wettrennen bis zur Schule.
3 *vi* **(a)** *(compete)* laufen/fahren/schwimmen *etc.* **to ~ with** *or* **against sb** mit jdm um die Wette laufen *etc.* **(b)** *(rush)* rasen, jagen; *(on foot also)* rennen; *(with work)* hetzen. **to ~ after sb/sth** hinter jdm/etw herjagen; **to ~ ahead with sth** etw vorantreiben; **the project is racing ahead** die Arbeit am Projekt geht mit Riesenschritten voran. **(c)** *(engine)* durchdrehen; *(pulse)* jagen, fliegen.
race[2] *n (ethnic group, species)* Rasse *f.* **of mixed ~** gemischtrassig.
race: ~course *n* Rennbahn *f*; **~horse** *n* Rennpferd *nt*; ~ **relations** *n* **(a)** *pl* Beziehungen *pl* zwischen den Rassen; **(b)** *sing (subject)* Rassenintegration *f*; **~track** *n* Rennbahn *f.*
racial ['reɪʃəl] *adj* rassisch, Rassen-. ~ **discrimination** Rassendiskriminierung *f*; ~ **equality** Rassengleichheit *f.*
racialism ['reɪʃəlɪzəm] *n* Rassismus *m.*
racialist ['reɪʃəlɪst] **1** *n* Rassist(in *f*) *m.* **2** *adj* rassistisch.
racial: ~ **minority** *n* rassische Minderheit; ~ **prejudice** *n* Rassenvorurteil *nt.*
racing ['reɪsɪŋ] *n (horse-~)* Pferderennsport *m*; *(motor ~)* Motorrennen *nt.*
racing *in cpds* Renn-.
racism ['reɪsɪzəm] *n* = **racialism.**
racist ['reɪsɪst] *n, adj* = **racialist.**
rack[1] [ræk] **1** *n* **(a)** *(for hats, toast, pipes etc)* Ständer *m*; *(for bottles, plates also)* Gestell *nt*; *(shelves)* Regal *nt*; *(luggage ~)* Gepäcknetz *nt*; *(on car, bicycle)* Gepäckträger *m*; *(Tech)* Zahnstange *f.* **(b)** *(Hist)* Folter(bank) *f.* **2** *vt* **(a)** *(pain)* quälen. **~ed with pain/remorse** von Schmerz/Gewissensbissen geplagt. **(b) to ~ one's brains** sich *(dat)* den Kopf zerbrechen.
rack[2] *n*: **to go to ~ and ruin** *(country, economy)* herunterkommen, vor die Hunde gehen *(col)*; *(building)* verfallen.
rack-and-pinion steering ['rækən'pɪnjən,stiːrɪŋ] *n (Aut)* Zahnstangenlenkung *f.*
racket[1] ['rækɪt] *n (Sport)* Schläger *m.*
racket[2] *n* **(a)** *(uproar)* Krach, Lärm *m.* **to make a ~** Krach machen. **(b)** *(col) (dishonest business)* Schwindelgeschäft *nt (col)*; *(making excessive profit)* Wucher *m.* **the drugs ~** das Drogengeschäft.
racketeer [,rækɪ'tɪəʳ] *n* Gauner *m (col)*; *(making excessive profit)* Halsabschneider *m (col).*
raconteur [,rækɒn'tɜːʳ] *n* Erzähler(in *f*) *m* von Anekdoten.
racoon, raccoon [rə'kuːn] *n* Waschbär *m.*
racquet ['rækɪt] *n* = **racket**[1].
racy ['reɪsɪ] *adj (+er) speech, style* schwungvoll, feurig; *(risqué)* gewagt.
radar ['reɪdɑːʳ] *n* Radar *nt or m.*
radar *in cpds* Radar-; ~ **scanner** *n* Rundsuchradargerät *nt*; ~ **trap** *n* Radarfalle *f.*
radial ['reɪdɪəl] *adj (Tech)* radial. **~(-ply) tyre** *(Brit) or* **tire** *(US)* Gürtelreifen *m.*
radiance ['reɪdɪəns] *n* Leuchten *nt.*
radiant ['reɪdɪənt] *adj (lit, fig)* strahlend *(with* vor *+dat).* **to be ~ with health/joy** vor Gesundheit strotzen/vor Freude strahlen.
radiate ['reɪdɪeɪt] **1** *vi* **(a)** Strahlen aussenden; *(emit heat)* Wärme ausstrahlen; *(heat)* ausgestrahlt werden. **(b)** *(lines, roads)* strahlenförmig ausgehen *(from* von*).* **2** *vt (lit, fig)* ausstrahlen.
radiation [,reɪdɪ'eɪʃən] *n (of heat etc)* (Aus)strahlung *f*; *(rays)* radioaktive Strahlung. ~ **sickness** Strahlenkrankheit *f.*
radiator ['reɪdɪeɪtəʳ] *n (heating)* Heizkörper, Radiator *m*; *(Aut)* Kühler *m.* ~ **grill** Kühlergrill *m.*
radical ['rædɪkəl] **1** *adj (basic)* fundamental; *(extreme) reform* radikal, grundlegend; *rethinking* total; *(Pol)* radikal. **2** *n (Pol)* Radikale(r) *mf.*
radically ['rædɪkəlɪ] *adv see adj.* **there's something ~ wrong with this** hier stimmt etwas ganz und gar nicht.
radio ['reɪdɪəʊ] **1** *n* **(a)** Rundfunk *m*; *(also ~* **set***)* Radio(apparat *m*) *nt.* **to listen to the ~** Radio hören; **to hear sth on the ~** etw im Radio hören. **(b)** *no pl (telegraphy)* Funk *m.* **over the** *or* **by ~** über *or* per Funk. **2** *vt person* über Funk verständigen; *message* funken, durchgeben. **3** *vi* **to ~ for help** per Funk einen Hilferuf durchgeben.
radio: ~active *adj* radioaktiv; **~activity** *n* Radioaktivität *f*; ~ **announcer** *n* Rundfunksprecher(in *f*) *m*; ~ **beacon** *n (Aviat, Naut)* Funkfeuer *nt*; **~-controlled** *adj* ferngesteuert; ~ **engineer** *n* Rundfunktechniker(in *f*) *m.*
radiogram ['reɪdɪəʊgræm] *n (apparatus)* Musiktruhe *f.*
radiography [,reɪdɪ'ɒgrəfɪ] *n* Röntgenographie *f.*
radiology [,reɪdɪ'ɒlədʒɪ] *n* Radiologie *f*; *(X-ray also)* Röntgenologie *f.*
radio: ~ **pager** *n* Funkrufempfänger *m*; ~ **station** *n* Rundfunkstation *f*; **~telephone** *n* Funksprechgerät *nt*; **~therapy** *n* Röntgentherapie *f.*
radish ['rædɪʃ] *n* Rettich *m*; *(small red)* Radieschen *nt.*
radium ['reɪdɪəm] *n* Radium *nt.*
radius ['reɪdɪəs] *n, pl* **radii** ['reɪdɪaɪ] *(Math)* Radius *m.* **within a 6 km ~ (of Hamburg)** in einem Umkreis von 6 km (von Hamburg).

RAF = **Royal Air Force** königliche (britische) Luftwaffe.
raffia ['ræfɪə] *n (for handicraft)* Bast *m*.
raffle ['ræfl] **1** *n* Tombola, Verlosung *f*. ~ **ticket** Los *nt*. **2** *vt (also* ~ **off***)* verlosen.
raft [rɑːft] *n* Floß *nt*.
rafter ['rɑːftə^r] *n* (Dach)sparren *m*.
rag[1] [ræg] *n* **(a)** Lumpen, Fetzen *m*; *(for cleaning)* Lappen *m*. ~**s** Lumpen *pl*; *(col: clothes)* Klamotten *pl (col)*; **in** ~**s** zerlumpt; **to go from** ~**s to riches** vom Tellerwäscher zum Millionär werden. **(b)** *(pej col: newspaper)* Käseblatt *nt*.
rag[2] **1** *n (Brit col: joke)* Jux *m (col)*. ~ **week** *(Univ) Woche, in der Studenten durch Aufführungen Geld für Wohltätigkeitszwecke sammeln.* **2** *vt (tease)* aufziehen, foppen.
rag: ~**-and-bone man** *n* Lumpensammler *m*; ~**bag** *n (fig)* Sammelsurium *nt (col)*; ~ **doll** *n* Flickenpuppe *f*.
rage [reɪdʒ] **1** *n* Wut *f*, Zorn *m*. **to be in a** ~ wütend sein; **to fly into a** ~ einen Wutanfall bekommen; **to be (all) the** ~ *(col)* der letzte Schrei sein *(col)*. **2** *vi* toben.
ragged ['rægɪd] *adj person, clothes* zerlumpt; *beard* zottig; *coastline, rocks* zerklüftet; *edge, cuff* ausgefranst.
raging ['reɪdʒɪŋ] *adj person* wütend; *fever* heftig; *thirst* brennend; *sea, wind* tobend. **he was** ~ er tobte.
rag trade *n (col)* Kleiderbranche *f*.
raid [reɪd] **1** *n* Überfall *m*; *(Mil also)* Angriff *m*; *(air* ~*)* Luftangriff *m*; *(police* ~*)* Razzia *f*; *(by thieves)* Einbruch *m*. **2** *vt* **(a)** überfallen; *(police)* eine Razzia durchführen in *(+dat)*; *(thieves)* einbrechen in *(+acc)*. **(b)** *(fig hum)* plündern.
raider ['reɪdə^r] *n (bandit)* Gangster *m*; *(thief)* Einbrecher *m*; *(in bank)* Bankräuber *m*.
rail [reɪl] *n* **(a)** *(on bridge, stairs etc)* Geländer *nt*; *(Naut)* Reling *f*; *(curtain* ~*)* Schiene *f*; *(towel-*~*)* Handtuchhalter *m*. ~**s** *(fence)* Umzäunung *f*. **(b)** *(for train, tram)* Schiene *f*, Gleis *nt*. **to go off the** ~**s** *(lit)* entgleisen; *(fig: morally)* auf die schiefe Bahn geraten. **(c)** *(*~ *travel,* ~*way)* die (Eisen)bahn. **to travel by** ~ mit der Bahn fahren.
railing ['reɪlɪŋ] *n (rail)* Geländer *nt*; *(Naut)* Reling *f*; *(fence* ~*s)* Zaun *m*.
railroad ['reɪlrəʊd] **1** *n (US)* (Eisen)bahn *f*. **2** *vt* **to** ~ **a bill** eine Gesetzesvorlage durchpeitschen; **to** ~ **sb into doing sth** jdn dazu hetzen, etw zu tun.
rail strike *n* Bahnstreik *m*.
railway ['reɪlweɪ] *n (Brit)* (Eisen)bahn *f*; *(track)* Gleis *nt*.
railway: ~ **carriage** *n (Brit)* Eisenbahnwagen *m*; ~ **crossing** *n (Brit)* Bahnübergang *m*; ~ **engine** *n (Brit)* Lokomotive *f*; ~ **line** *n (Brit)* (Eisen)bahnlinie *f*; *(track)* Gleis *nt*; ~**man** *n (Brit)* Eisenbahner *m*; ~ **station** *n (Brit)* Bahnhof *m*.
rain [reɪn] **1** *n* Regen *m*. **in the** ~ im Regen; **come** ~ **or shine** *(fig)* was auch geschieht; **the** ~**s** die Regenzeit. **2** *vti impers (lit, fig)* regnen. **it is** ~**ing** es regnet; **it never** ~**s but it pours** *(prov)* ein Unglück kommt selten allein *(prov)*; **it's** ~**ing cats and dogs** *(col)* es gießt wie aus Kübeln.
♦**rain down** *vi (blows etc)* niederprasseln *(upon* auf *+acc)*.
rainbow ['reɪnbəʊ] *n* Regenbogen *m*.
rain: ~**-check** *n (US)* **to take a** ~**-check** *(col)* die Sache auf ein andermal verschieben; ~**coat** *n* Regenmantel *m*; ~**drop** *n* Regentropfen *m*; ~**fall** *n* Niederschlag *m*; ~**water** *n* Regenwasser *nt*.
rainy ['reɪnɪ] *adj (+er)* regnerisch, Regen-; *area* regenreich. ~ **season** Regenzeit *f*; **to keep sth for a** ~ **day** *(fig)* etw für schlechte Zeiten aufheben.
raise [reɪz] **1** *vt* **(a)** *(lift) object, arm* heben; *blinds, eyebrow, (Theat) curtain* hochziehen; *(Naut) anchor* lichten; *sunken ship* heben. **to** ~ **one's hat to sb** den Hut vor jdm ziehen; **to** ~ **sb from the dead** jdn von den Toten erwecken; **to** ~ **one's voice** lauter sprechen; *(get angry)* laut werden; **to** ~ **the roof** *(fig: with anger)* fürchterlich toben.
(b) *(increase) (to* auf *+acc) salary, temperature* erhöhen; *price also, standard* anheben. **to** ~ **the tone** das Niveau heben; **to** ~ **to the power 2** *(Math)* in die 2. Potenz erheben.
(c) *(promote)* (er)heben *(to* in *+acc)*.
(d) *(build, erect)* errichten.
(e) *(create, evoke) problem, question* aufwerfen; *objection* erheben; *suspicion, hope* (er)wecken; *spirits* (herauf)beschwören. **to** ~ **sb's/one's hopes** jdm/sich Hoffnung machen; **to** ~ **a laugh/smile** *(in others)* Gelächter/ein Lächeln hervorrufen; *(oneself)* lachen/lächeln; **to** ~ **a protest** protestieren; **to** ~ **hell** *(col)* einen Höllenspektakel machen *(col)*.
(f) *(grow, breed) children, animals* aufziehen; *crops* anbauen. **to** ~ **a family** Kinder großziehen.
(g) *army* aufstellen; *taxes* erheben; *funds, money* aufbringen; *loan* aufnehmen.
(h) *(end) siege, embargo* aufheben.
2 *n (in salary)* Gehaltserhöhung *f*; *(in wages)* Lohnerhöhung *f*.
raisin ['reɪzən] *n* Rosine *f*.
rake[1] [reɪk] **1** *n* Harke *f*. **2** *vt* **(a)** *garden, leaves* harken. **(b)** *(machine gun, searchlight)* bestreichen.
♦**rake in** *vt sep (col) money* kassieren *(col)*. **he's raking it in** er scheffelt das Geld nur so.
♦**rake up** *vt sep memories, grievance* aufwärmen. **to** ~ ~ **the past** in der Vergangenheit wühlen.
rake[2] *n (person)* Lebemann *m*.
rakish ['reɪkɪʃ] *adj person* flott, verwegen.
rally ['rælɪ] **1** *n* **(a)** Versammlung *f*; *(with speaker)* Kundgebung *f*; *(Aut)* Rallye *f*. **(b)** *(Tennis)* Ballwechsel *m*. **2** *vt troops, supporters* (ver)sammeln. **to** ~ **one's strength** all seine Kräfte sammeln. **3** **(a)** *vi (St Ex)* sich erholen. **(b)** *(troops, people)* sich versammeln. ~**ing point** Sammelplatz *m*; **to** ~ **to the support of sb** *(fig)* jdm in Scharen zu Hilfe eilen.
♦**rally around** *vi +prep obj leader* sich scharen um; *person in distress* sich annehmen *(+gen)*.
ram [ræm] **1** *n* **(a)** *(animal)* Widder, Schafbock *m*. **(b)** *(Tech)* Ramme *f*, Rammbock *m*; *(hydraulic)* Stoßheber *m*. **2** *vt* **(a)** *(push) stick, post, umbrella* stoßen; *(with great force)* rammen; *(pack)* zwängen; *(Tech) pile* rammen. **to** ~ **sth down sb's throat** *(col)* jdm etw eintrichtern *(col)*. **(b)** *(crash into) ship, car* rammen. **the car** ~**med a lamppost** das Auto prallte gegen einen Laternenpfahl.
ramble ['ræmbl] **1** *n* Streifzug *m*; *(hike)* Wanderung *f*. **to go for** *or* **on a** ~ einen Streifzug/eine Wanderung machen. **2** *vi* **(a)** *(wander about)* Steifzüge/einen Streifzug machen; *(go on hike)* wandern. **(b)** *(in speech)* faseln *(col)*; *(pej: also* ~ **on***)* schwafeln *(col)*.
rambler ['ræmblə^r] *n* Wanderer *m*, Wanderin *f*.
rambling ['ræmblɪŋ] *adj speech* weitschweifig; *person* schwafelnd *(col)*; *building* weitläufig. ~ **rose** Kletterrose *f*.
ramification [ˌræmɪfɪ'keɪʃən] *n* Verzweigung *f*; *(smaller, of arteries)* Verästelung *f*. **the race question and its many** ~**s** die Rassenfrage und die damit verbundenen Probleme.
ramify ['ræmɪfaɪ] *vi (lit, fig)* sich verzweigen.
ramp [ræmp] *n* Rampe *f*; *(hydraulic* ~*)* Hebebühne *f*; *(Aviat: also* **boarding** ~*)* Gangway *f*.
rampage [ræm'peɪdʒ] **1** *n* **to be/go on the** ~ randalieren. **2** *vi (also* ~ **about***)* herumtoben.
rampant ['ræmpənt] *adj plants, growth* üppig; *evil etc* wild wuchernd *attr*. **the** ~ **growth of** das Wuchern *(+gen)*; **to be** ~ (wild) wuchern.
rampart ['ræmpɑːt] *n* Wall *m*.
ramshackle ['ræmˌʃækl] *adj building* baufällig.
ran [ræn] *pret of* **run**.

ranch [rɑːntʃ] *n* Ranch, Viehfarm *f.*
rancid ['rænsɪd] *adj* ranzig.
rancour, *(US)* **rancor** ['ræŋkə^r] *(of tone)* Verbitterung *f; (of attack)* Boshaftigkeit *f.*
random ['rændəm] **1** *n* **at ~** *speak, walk, drive* aufs Geratewohl; *shoot, drop bombs* ziellos; *take* wahllos; **a few examples taken at ~** ein paar willkürlich gewählte Beispiele; **I (just) chose one at ~** ich wählte einfach irgendeine (beliebige). **2** *adj selection* willkürlich, Zufalls-. **a ~ bullet** eine verirrte Kugel; **a ~ shot** ein Schuß *m* ins Blaue; **he was killed by a ~ shot** er wurde von einer verirrten Kugel getötet; **to make a ~ guess** auf gut Glück raten; **~ sample** Stichprobe *f.*
randy ['rændɪ] *adj (+er) (Brit)* scharf *(col)*, geil.
rang [ræŋ] *pret of* **ring**[2].
range [reɪndʒ] **1** *n* **(a)** *(scope, distance covered)* Aktionsradius *m; (of missile, gun, telescope also)* Reichweite *f; (of vehicle also)* Fahrbereich *m; (of plane also)* Flugbereich *m.* **at a ~ of** auf eine Entfernung von; **at short/long ~** auf kurze/große Entfernung; **to be out of ~** außer Reichweite sein; **within (firing) ~** in Schußweite; **~ of vision** Gesichtsfeld *nt.* **(b)** *(spread, selection)* Reihe *f; (of goods also)* Sortiment *nt; (of colours also)* Skala *f; (of sizes, models)* Auswahl *f (of* an *+dat).* **a wide ~** eine große Auswahl; **in this price ~** in dieser Preisklasse; **out of/within my price ~** außerhalb/innerhalb meiner (finanziellen) Möglichkeiten. **(c)** *(also* **shooting ~***) (Mil)* Schießplatz *m; (rifle ~)* Schießstand *m.* **(d)** *(row)* Reihe *f; (mountain ~)* Kette *f.* **(e)** *(US: grazing land)* Weideland *nt.*
2 *vt (place in a row)* aufstellen; *objects also* anordnen.
3 *vi* **(a)** *(extend) (from ... to)* gehen (von ... bis); *(temperature, value)* liegen (zwischen ... und). **his interests ~ from skiing to chess** seine Interessen reichen vom Skifahren bis zum Schachspielen; **the conversation ~d over a number of subjects** die Unterhaltung kreiste um eine ganze Menge von Themen. **(b)** *(roam)* streifen. **to ~ over the area** im Gebiet umherstreifen.
range-finder ['reɪndʒ'faɪndə^r] *n* Entfernungsmesser *m.*
ranger ['reɪndʒə^r] *n* **(a)** *(of forest etc)* Förster *m.* **(b)** *(US: mounted patrolman)* Ranger *m; (commando)* Überfallkommando *nt.*
rank[1] [ræŋk] **1** *n* **(a)** *(Mil: grade)* Rang *m.* **(b)** *(class, status)* Stand *m*, Schicht *f.* **people of all ~s** Leute *pl* aller Stände. **(c)** *(row)* Reihe *f; (Brit: taxi ~)* Taxistand *m.* **(d)** *(Mil: formation)* Glied *nt.* **to break ~(s)** aus dem Glied treten; **the ~s** *(Brit)* die Mannschaften und die Unteroffiziere; **the ~ and file of the party/union** die Basis der Partei/Gewerkschaft; **the ~ and file workers** die einfachen Arbeiter; **to rise from the ~s** aus dem Mannschaftsstand zum Offizier aufsteigen; *(fig)* sich hocharbeiten. **2** *vt (class, consider)* **to ~ sb among the best/great** *etc* jdn zu den Besten/Großen *etc* zählen. **3** *vi* **to ~ among** zählen zu; **to ~ above sb** bedeutender als jd sein; *(officer)* rangmäßig über jdm liegen; **to ~ 6th** den 6. Rang belegen; **he ~s as a great composer** er gilt als großer Komponist.
rank[2] *adj (+er)* **(a)** *plants* üppig; *grass* verwildert. **to grow ~** wuchern. **(b)** *smell* übel; *fat* ranzig. **(c)** *attr injustice* schreiend; *nonsense* rein; *traitor, liar* übel; *stupidity* ausgesprochen.
rankle ['ræŋkl] *vi* **to ~ with sb** jdn wurmen *(col).*
ransack ['rænsæk] *vt (search)* durchwühlen; *(pillage) house* plündern; *region* herfallen über *(+acc).*
ransom ['rænsəm] **1** *n* Lösegeld *nt.* **to hold sb to ~** *(lit)* jdn als Geisel halten; *(fig)* jdn erpressen. **2** *vt (buy free)* Lösegeld bezahlen für; *(set free)* gegen Lösegeld freilassen.
rant [rænt] *vi (angrily)* eine Schimpfkanonade loslassen; *(talk nonsense)* irres Zeug reden *(col).* **to ~ (and rave)** *(be angry)* herumschimpfen; **to ~ at sb** mit jdm schimpfen.
rap [ræp] **1** *n (noise, blow)* Klopfen *nt no pl.* **there was a ~ at the door** es hat geklopft; **to take the ~** *(col)* die Schuld zugeschoben kriegen *(col).* **2** *vt table* klopfen auf *(+acc); window* klopfen an *(+acc).* **to ~ sb's knuckles** *(lit, fig)* jdm auf die Finger klopfen. **3** *vi* klopfen. **to ~ at the door** kurz (an die Tür) klopfen.
rapacious [rə'peɪʃəs] *adj* habgierig.
rape[1] [reɪp] **1** *n* Vergewaltigung *f.* **2** *vt* vergewaltigen.
rape[2] *n (plant)* Raps *m.*
rapid ['ræpɪd] **1** *adj* schnell; *change also* rapide; *descent, decline, rise* steil. **2** *n* **~s** *pl* Stromschnellen *pl.*
rapidity [rə'pɪdɪtɪ] *n see adj* Schnelligkeit *f;* Rapidheit *f;* Steilheit *f.*
rapier ['reɪpɪə^r] *n* Rapier *nt.*
rapist ['reɪpɪst] *n* Vergewaltiger *m.*
rapport [ræ'pɔː^r] *n* **the ~ I have with my father** das enge Verhältnis zwischen mir und meinem Vater; **in ~ with** in Harmonie mit.
rapt [ræpt] *adj* **(a)** *interest* gespannt. **~ in contemplation** in Betrachtungen versunken. **(b)** *look, smile* verzückt.
rapture ['ræptʃə^r] *n (delight)* Entzücken *nt; (ecstasy)* Verzückung *f.* **to be in ~s** entzückt sein *(over* über *+acc, about* von*);* **to go into ~s** ins Schwärmen geraten.
rapturous ['ræptʃərəs] *adj applause, reception* stürmisch; *exclamation* entzückt; *look* verzückt.
rare [rɛə^r] *adj (+er)* **(a)** selten. **it's ~ for her to come** sie kommt nur selten. **(b)** *atmosphere* dünn. **(c)** *meat* roh; *steak also* blutig, englisch.
rarebit ['rɛəbɪt] *n* = **Welsh ~.**
rarefied ['rɛərɪfaɪd] *adj atmosphere, air* dünn; *(fig)* exklusiv.
rarely ['rɛəlɪ] *adv* selten.
rarity ['rɛərɪtɪ] *n* Seltenheit *f; (rare occurrence also)* Rarität *f.*
rascal ['rɑːskəl] *n* Gauner *m; (child)* Schlingel *m.*
rash[1] [ræʃ] *n (Med)* Ausschlag *m.* **to break out in a ~** einen Ausschlag bekommen.
rash[2] *adj (+er) person* unbesonnen; *act also* überstürzt; *words, decision* voreilig.
rasher ['ræʃə^r] *n* **~ of bacon** Speckstreifen *m.*
rasp [rɑːsp] **1** *n (tool)* Raspel *f; (noise)* Kratzen *nt no pl.* **2** *vt* **(a)** *(Tech)* raspeln. **(b) ... he rasped** ..., krächzte er.
raspberry ['rɑːzbərɪ] **1** *n* Himbeere *f.* **to blow a ~** *(col)* verächtlich schnauben. **2** *adj jam* Himbeer-.
rasping ['rɑːspɪŋ] **1** *adj sound* kratzend; *voice* krächzend; *cough, breath* keuchend. **2** *n (sound)* Kratzen *nt; (of voice)* Krächzen *nt.*
rat [ræt] *n* Ratte *f; (pej col: person)* elender Verräter *(col).* **to smell a ~** den Braten riechen *(col).*
ratchet ['rætʃɪt] *n* Ratsche *f.* **~ wheel** Sperrad *nt.*
rate [reɪt] **1** *n* **(a)** *(ratio, proportion, frequency)* Rate *f; (speed)* Tempo *nt.* **at a ~ of 14 feet per minute** (in einem Tempo von) 14 Fuß pro Minute; **~ of flow** *(of water etc)* Fluß *m;* **pulse ~** Puls *m;* **at a great** *(col)* **~, at a ~ of knots** *(col)* in irrsinnigem Tempo *(col);* **if you continue at this ~** *(lit, fig)* wenn du in diesem Tempo weitermachst; **at any ~** auf jeden Fall. **(b)** *(Comm, Fin)* Satz *m; (St Ex)* Kurs *m.* **~ of exchange** Wechselkurs *m;* **what's the ~ of pay?** wie hoch ist die Bezahlung?; **~ of interest** Zinssatz *m;* **postage ~s** Postgebühren *pl;* **there is a reduced ~ for children** Kinderermäßigung wird gewährt. **(c) ~s** *pl (Brit: municipal tax)* Gemeindesteuern *pl.*
2 *vt* **(a)** *(estimate value or worth of)* (ein)schätzen. **to ~ sb/sth among ...** jdn/etw zu ... zählen; **how do you ~ these results?** was halten Sie von diesen Ergebnissen?; **to ~ sb/sth as sth**

jdn/etw für etw halten; **he is generally ~d as ...** er gilt allgemein als ...; **to ~ sb/sth highly** jdn/etw hoch einschätzen. **(b)** *(Brit)* **a house ~d at £500 per annum** ein Haus, dessen steuerbarer Wert £ 500 pro Jahr ist.

3 *vi* **to ~ as/among ...** gelten als .../zählen zu ...

rateable ['reɪtəbl] *adj (Brit)* **~ value** steuerbarer Wert.

ratepayer ['reɪtˌpeɪəʳ] *n (Brit)* Steuerzahler *m (von Gemeindesteuern)*.

rather ['rɑːðəʳ] *adv* **(a)** *(for preference)* lieber. **~ than wait, he went away** er ging lieber, als daß er wartete; **I would ~ have the blue dress** ich hätte lieber das blaue Kleid; **I would ~ be happy than rich** ich wäre lieber glücklich als reich; **I would ~ you came yourself** mir wäre es lieber, Sie kämen selbst; **I'd ~ not** lieber nicht; **he expects me to phone ~ than (to) write** er erwartet eher, daß ich anrufe, als daß ich schreibe.

(b) *(more accurately)* vielmehr. **he is, or ~ was, a soldier** er ist, beziehungsweise *or* vielmehr war, Soldat; **a car, or ~ an old banger** ein Auto, genauer gesagt eine alte Kiste.

(c) *(to a considerable degree)* ziemlich; *(somewhat)* etwas. **he felt ~ better** er fühlte sich bedeutend wohler; **it's ~ more difficult than you think** es ist um einiges schwieriger, als du denkst; **she's ~ an idiot/a killjoy** sie ist reichlich doof *(col)*/ein richtiger Spielverderber; **I ~ think he's wrong** ich glaube fast, er hat Unrecht; **~!** *(col)* und ob! *(col)*, klar! *(col)*.

ratify ['rætɪfaɪ] *vt* ratifizieren.

rating ['reɪtɪŋ] *n* **(a)** *(assessment)* (Ein)schätzung *f*. **(b)** *(class) (Sport: of yacht, car)* Klasse *f*; *(Fin: also* **credit ~***)* Kreditfähigkeit *f*. **(c)** *(Naut) (rank)* Rang *m*; *(sailor)* Matrose *m*.

ratio ['reɪʃɪəʊ] *n* Verhältnis *nt*. **the ~ of men to women** das Verhältnis von Männern zu Frauen; **in the** *or* **a ~ of 100 to 1** *(written* **100:1***)* im Verhältnis 100 zu 1.

ration ['ræʃən] **1** *n* Ration *f*; *(fig)* Quantum *nt*. **~s** *(food)* Rationen *pl*; **to put sb on short ~s** jdn auf halbe Ration setzen. **2** *vt goods, food* rationieren. **he was ~ed to 1 kg** ihm wurde nur 1 kg erlaubt.

rational ['ræʃənl] *adj (having reason)* vernunftbegabt, rational; *(reasonable)* vernünftig; *person, action also* rational; *(Med: lucid, sane) person* bei klarem Verstand.

rationale [ræʃə'nɑːl] *n* Gründe *pl*.

rationalization [ˌræʃnəlaɪ'zeɪʃən] *n* Rationalisierung *f*.

rationalize ['ræʃnəlaɪz] *vt* rationalisieren; *problem* vernünftig betrachten.

rationing ['ræʃənɪŋ] *n* Rationierung *f*.

rat: ~ poison *n* Rattengift *nt*; **~-race** *n* ständiger Konkurrenzkampf.

rattle ['rætl] **1** *vi* klappern; *(chains)* rasseln; *(bottles)* klirren; *(gunfire)* knattern. **there's something rattling** da klappert etwas. **2** *vt* **(a)** *dice, keys* schütteln; *chains* rasseln mit; *windows* rütteln an *(+dat)*. **(b)** *(col: alarm) person* durcheinanderbringen. **don't get ~d!** reg dich nicht auf! **3** *n* **(a)** *(sound) see vi* Klappern *nt no pl*; Rasseln *nt no pl*; Klirren *nt no pl*; Knattern *nt no pl*. **(b)** *(child's)* Rassel *f*; *(sports fan's)* Schnarre *f*.

♦**rattle off** *vt sep speech, list* herunterrasseln.

♦**rattle on** *vi (col)* (unentwegt) quasseln *(col) (about* über *+acc)*.

rattlesnake ['rætlsneɪk] *n* Klapperschlange *f*.

ratty ['rætɪ] *adj (+er) (col: irritable)* gereizt. **don't get ~** sei nicht so gereizt.

raucous ['rɔːkəs] *adj* rauh, heiser.

ravage ['rævɪdʒ] **1** *n* **~s** *(of war)* Verheerung *f (of* durch*)*; **the ~s of time** die Spuren *pl* der Zeit. **2** *vt (ruin)* verwüsten; *(plunder)* plündern.

rave [reɪv] **1** *vi* phantasieren; *(speak furiously)* toben; *(col: speak, write enthusiastically)* schwärmen *(about, over* von*)*. **2** *attr* **~ review** *(col)* begeisterte Kritik.

raven ['reɪvən] *n* Rabe *m*.

ravenous ['rævənəs] *adj animal* ausgehungert; *person also* heißhungrig; *appetite* gewaltig. **I'm ~** ich habe einen Bärenhunger *(col)*.

ravine [rə'viːn] *n* Schlucht *f*.

raving ['reɪvɪŋ] **1** *adj (frenzied)* wahnsinnig, verrückt; *(delirious)* im Delirium. **a ~ lunatic** *(col)* ein kompletter Idiot *(col)*. **2** *adv* **~ mad** *(col)* total verrückt *(col)*. **3** *n* **~(s)** Phantasien *pl*.

ravishing ['rævɪʃɪŋ] *adj* atemberaubend.

raw [rɔː] **1** *adj (+er)* **(a)** *(uncooked)* roh; *(unprocessed) ore, sugar also* Roh-; *spirit* rein; *cloth* ungewalkt; *leather* ungegerbt; *(fig) statistics* nackt. **~ material** Rohstoff *m*. **(b)** *(inexperienced) troops* neu, unerfahren. **~ recruit** *(fig)* blutiger Anfänger *(col)*. **(c)** *(sore) wound* offen; *skin* wund. **(d)** *wind, air* rauh. **(e)** *(esp US: coarse)* derb. **2** *n* **(a) to touch sb on the ~** *(Brit)* bei jdm einen wunden Punkt berühren. **(b) nature in the ~** die rauhe Seite der Natur.

ray[1] [reɪ] *n* Strahl *m*. **a ~ of hope** ein Hoffnungsschimmer *m*.

ray[2] *n (fish)* Rochen *m*.

rayon ['reɪɒn] **1** *n* Reyon *nt*. **2** *adj* Reyon-.

raze [reɪz] *vt* **to ~ to the ground** dem Erdboden gleichmachen.

razor ['reɪzəʳ] *n* Rasierapparat *m*; *(cutthroat)* Rasiermesser *nt*. **electric ~** Elektrorasierer *m*; **to be on a ~'s edge** auf Messers Schneide stehen.

razor: ~ blade *n* Rasierklinge *f*; **~-sharp** *adj knife* scharf (wie ein Rasiermesser); *(fig) person* sehr scharfsinnig; *mind, wit* messerscharf.

RC = **Roman Catholic** rk, r.-k.

Rd = **Road** Str.

RE = **Religious Education.**

re [riː] *prep (Comm)* betreffs *(+gen)*. **~ your letter of the 16th** Betr(eff): Ihr Brief vom 16.

re- [riː-] *pref* wieder-.

reach [riːtʃ] **1** *n* **(a) within/out of sb's ~** in/außer jds Reichweite *(dat)*; **keep out of ~ of children** von Kindern fernhalten; **within easy ~ of the sea** in unmittelbarer Nähe des Meeres; **I keep it within easy ~** ich habe es in greifbarer Nähe. **(b)** *(of river)* Strecke *f*.

2 *vt* **(a)** *(arrive at)* erreichen; *town* ankommen in *(+dat)*; *agreement* erzielen; *conclusion* kommen zu. **when the news ~ed my ears** als mir die Nachricht zu Ohren kam; **to ~ page 50** bis Seite 50 kommen; **you can ~ me at my hotel** Sie erreichen mich in meinem Hotel. **(b)** *(stretch to get or touch)* **to be able to ~ sth** an etw *(acc)* (heran)reichen können; **can you ~ it?** kommen Sie dran? **(c)** *(come up to, go down to)* reichen bis zu. **he ~es her shoulder** er geht ihr bis zur Schulter.

3 *vi* **(a)** *(to, as far as* bis*)* reichen; *(territory etc also)* sich erstrecken. **(b)** *(stretch out hand or arm)* greifen. **to ~ for sth** nach etw greifen *or* langen *(col)*.

♦**reach out 1** *vt sep* **he ~ed ~ his hand to take the book** er streckte die Hand aus, um das Buch zu nehmen. **2** *vi* die Hand/Hände ausstrecken. **to ~ ~ for sth** nach etw greifen *or* langen *(col)*.

react [riː'ækt] *vi* reagieren *(to* auf *+acc)*. **to ~ against** negativ reagieren auf *(+acc)*.

reaction [riː'ækʃən] *n* Reaktion *f (to* auf *+acc, against* gegen*)*; *(Mil)* Gegenschlag *m*. **what was his ~ to your suggestion?** wie hat er auf Ihren Vorschlag reagiert?

reactionary [riː'ækʃənrɪ] *adj* reaktionär.

reactor [riː'æktəʳ] *n (Phys)* Reaktor *m*.

read[1] [riːd] *(vb: pret, ptp* **read** [red]*)* **1** *vt* **(a)** lesen; *(to sb)* vorlesen *(to dat)*. **do you ~ music?** können Sie Noten lesen?; **to take sth as read** *(fig) (as self-evident)* etw als selbstverständlich voraussetzen; *(as agreed)* etw für abgemacht halten. **(b)** *(interpret) thoughts, feelings* lesen;

dream deuten; *words* verstehen. **to ~ sb's thoughts/mind** jds Gedanken lesen; **to ~ sb's hand** jdm aus der Hand lesen; **these words can be read in several ways** diese Wörter können unterschiedlich verstanden werden; **to ~ something into a text** etwas in einen Text (hinein)lesen. **(c)** *(Univ: study)* studieren. **(d)** *thermometer etc* sehen auf *(+acc)*. **to ~ a meter** einen Zähler(stand) ablesen.

2 *vi* lesen; *(to sb)* vorlesen *(to dat)*; *(have wording)* lauten. **to ~ aloud** laut lesen; **to ~ to oneself** für sich lesen; **he likes being read to** er läßt sich *(dat)* gern vorlesen; **this book ~s well** das Buch liest sich gut; **the letter ~s as follows** der Brief besagt folgendes *or* hat folgenden Wortlaut *(form)*.

3 *n* **she enjoys a good ~** sie liest gern; **this book is quite a good ~** das Buch liest sich gut.

♦**read off** *vt sep* ablesen; *(without pause)* herunterlesen.

♦**read on** *vi* weiterlesen.

♦**read out** *vt sep* vorlesen.

♦**read over** *or* **through** *vt sep* durchlesen.

♦**read up 1** *vt sep* nachlesen über *(+acc)*. **2** *vi* nachlesen *(on* über *+acc)*.

read² [red] **1** *pret, ptp of* **read¹**. **2** *adj* **he is well/badly ~** er ist sehr/wenig belesen.

readable ['ri:dəbl] *adj (legible)* lesbar; *(worth reading)* lesenswert.

readdress [ˌri:ə'dres] *vt* umadressieren.

reader ['ri:dəʳ] *n* **(a)** Leser(in *f*) *m*. **(b)** *(Brit Univ)* ≃ Dozent(in *f*) *m*. **(c)** *(schoolbook)* Lesebuch *nt*; *(to teach reading)* Fibel *f*; *(foreign language text)* Text *m*; *(anthology)* Sammelband *m*.

readership ['ri:dəʃɪp] *n* Leserschaft *f*. **a wide ~** eine große Leserschaft.

readily ['redɪlɪ] *adv* bereitwillig; *(easily)* leicht.

readiness ['redɪnɪs] *n* Bereitschaft *f*. **to be (kept) in ~ (for sth)** (für etw) bereitgehalten werden; **his ~ to help** seine Hilfsbereitschaft.

reading ['ri:dɪŋ] *n* **(a)** *(action)* Lesen *nt*; *(by author)* Lesung *f*. **(b)** *(~ matter)* Lektüre *f*. **this book makes very interesting ~** dieses Buch ist sehr interessant zu lesen. **(c)** *(interpretation)* Interpretation *f*. **my ~ of this sentence** mein Verständnis des Satzes. **(d)** *(from meter)* Thermometer-/Zählerstand *etc m*; *(from instruments)* Anzeige *f*. **to take a ~** den Thermometerstand *etc* ablesen; die Anzeige ablesen.

reading: ~ matter *n* Lesestoff *m*; **~ room** *n* Lesesaal *m*.

readjust [ˌri:ə'dʒʌst] **1** *vt instrument, mechanism* neu einstellen; *(correct)* nachstellen. **2** *vi* sich wieder anpassen *(to* an *+acc)*.

ready ['redɪ] **1** *adj* **(a)** fertig; *(prepared also)* bereit. **~ for use** gebrauchsfertig; **~ to serve** tischfertig; **~ for battle** kampfbereit; **~ for anything** zu allem bereit; **are you ~ to go?** sind Sie soweit?; **I'm ~ for him!** er soll nur kommen!; **everything is ~ for his visit** alles ist für seinen Besuch bereit; **to be ~ with an excuse** eine Entschuldigung bereit haben; **to get (oneself) ~** sich fertigmachen; **to get ~ to do sth** sich bereitmachen, etw zu tun; **to get ~ to go out** sich zum Ausgehen fertigmachen. **(b) ~ to do sth** *(willing)* bereit, etw zu tun; *(quick)* schnell dabei, etw zu tun; **I'm ~ to believe it** ich möchte das fast glauben; **he was ~ to cry** er war den Tränen nahe. **(c)** *(available)* **~ money** jederzeit verfügbares Geld; **~ cash** Bargeld *nt*.

2 *n* **at the ~** *(Mil)* mit dem Gewehr im Anschlag; *(fig)* marsch-/fahrbereit *etc*; **with his pen at the ~** mit gezücktem Federhalter.

ready *in cpds* fertig-; **~-made** *adj curtains* fertig; *clothes* Konfektions-; *solution* Patent-; **~ reckoner** *n* Rechentabelle *f*; **~-to-wear** *adj* Konfektions-, von der Stange *(col)*.

real ['rɪəl] **1** *adj* **(a)** wirklich; *(genuine) gold, flowers, joy* echt; *(as opposed to substitute)* richtig; *(true, actual) owner, reason, purpose also* eigentlich; *(not imaginary) creature, world also, (Econ)* real. **~ coffee** Bohnenkaffee *m*; **in ~ life** im wirklichen Leben; **in ~ terms** effektiv; **it's the ~ thing** *or* **McCoy, this whisky!** dieser Whisky ist das einzig Wahre. **(b) ~ estate** Immobilien *pl*. **2** *adv (esp US col)* echt *(col)*, wirklich. **3** *n* **for ~** wirklich, echt *(col)*; **is that invitation for ~?** ist die Einladung ernst gemeint?

realism ['rɪəlɪzəm] *n* Realismus *m*.

realist ['rɪəlɪst] *n* Realist *m*.

realistic [rɪə'lɪstɪk] *adj* realistisch.

reality [ri:'ælɪtɪ] *n* **(a)** Wirklichkeit, Realität *f*. **to become ~** sich verwirklichen; **(the) ~ is somewhat different** die Wirklichkeit sieht etwas anders aus; **in ~** *(in fact)* in Wirklichkeit; *(actually)* eigentlich. **(b)** *(trueness to life)* Naturtreue *f*.

realization [ˌrɪəlaɪ'zeɪʃən] *n* **(a)** *(of assets)* Realisation *f*; *(of hope, plan)* Realisierung, Verwirklichung *f*. **(b)** *(awareness)* Erkenntnis *f*.

realize ['rɪəlaɪz] *vt* **(a)** *(become aware of)* erkennen, sich *(dat)* bewußt werden *(+gen)*; *(be aware of)* sich *(dat)* klar sein über *(+acc)*; *(appreciate)* begreifen; *(notice)* bemerken; *(discover)* feststellen. **does he ~ the problems?** sind ihm die Probleme bewußt?; **I ~d what he meant** ich habe begriffen, was er meinte; **I ~d how he had done it** ich erkannte, wie er es gemacht hatte; **I'd ~d it was raining** ich hatte gemerkt, daß es regnete; **I ~d I didn't have any money on me** ich stellte fest, daß ich kein Geld dabei hatte; **you couldn't be expected to ~ that** das konnten Sie nicht wissen. **(b)** *hope, plan* verwirklichen. **(c)** *(Fin) assets* realisieren; *price* erzielen; *interest* abwerfen; *(goods)* einbringen.

really ['rɪəlɪ] **1** *adv* **(a)** *(in reality)* wirklich, tatsächlich. **I don't ~ think so** das glaube ich eigentlich nicht. **(b)** *(intensifier)* wirklich, echt *(col)*. **you ~ must visit Paris** Sie müssen wirklich Paris besuchen. **2** *interj* wirklich, ehrlich.

realm [relm] *n (liter: kingdom)* Königreich *nt*; *(fig)* Reich *nt*. **within the ~s of possibility** im Bereich des Möglichen.

realtor ['rɪəltɔ:ʳ] *n (US)* Grundstücksmakler *m*.

ream [ri:m] *n (of paper)* Ries *nt*. **he always writes ~s** *(col)* er schreibt immer ganze Bände *(col)*.

reap [ri:p] *vt* **(a)** *corn (cut)* schneiden, mähen; *(harvest)* ernten. **(b)** *(fig) profit* ernten; *reward* bekommen.

reappear [ˌri:ə'pɪəʳ] *vi* wiederauftauchen.

reappearance [ˌri:ə'pɪərəns] *n* Wiederauftauchen *nt*.

reappraisal [ˌri:ə'preɪzəl] *n* Neubeurteilung *f*.

rear¹ [rɪəʳ] **1** *n (back part)* hinterer Teil; *(col: buttocks)* Hintern *m (col)*. **to be situated at the ~ of the plane** *(inside)* hinten im Flugzeug sein; *(outside)* am hinteren Ende des Flugzeugs sein; **at the ~ of the building** *(outside)* hinter dem Haus; *(inside)* hinten im Haus; **from the ~** von hinten; **to bring up the ~** *(Mil)* die Nachhut bilden; *(fig)* das Schlußlicht bilden. **2** *adj* Hinter-, hintere(r, s); *(Aut) engine, window* Heck-. **~ door** *(of car)* hintere Tür; **~ wheel/lights** *(Aut)* Hinterrad *nt*/Rücklichter *pl*.

rear² **1** *vt* **(a)** *animals, family* großziehen, aufziehen. **(b) to ~ its head** *(animal)* den Kopf zurückwerfen; **racialism ~ed its ugly head** der Rassismus kam zum Durchbruch. **2** *vi (also ~ up) (horse)* sich aufbäumen.

rearm [ˌri:'ɑ:m] **1** *vt country* wiederbewaffnen; *forces* neu ausrüsten. **2** *vi* wieder aufrüsten; sich neu ausrüsten.

rearmament [ˌri:'ɑ:məmənt] *n see vb* Wiederaufrüstung *f*; Neuausrüstung *f*.

rearrange [ˌri:ə'reɪndʒ] *vt furniture, system* umstellen; *plans also, order, ideas* ändern; *meeting* verlegen.

rearrangement [ˌriːəˈreɪndʒmənt] *n see vt* Umstellung *f*; Änderung *f*; Verlegung *f*.

rear-view mirror [ˈrɪəˌvjuːˈmɪrəʳ] *n* Rückspiegel *m*.

reason [ˈriːzn] **1** *n* **(a)** *(cause, justification)* Grund *m* *(for* für*)*. **to give sb ~ for complaint** jdm Anlaß *or* Grund zu Klagen geben; **you have no ~ to interfere** Sie haben keinen Grund, sich einzumischen; **I want to know the ~ why** ich möchte wissen, weshalb; **and that's the ~ why ...** und deshalb ...; **I have (good) ~ to believe that ...** ich habe (guten) Grund zu glauben, daß ...; **there is every ~ to believe ...** es spricht alles dafür ...; **for that very ~ (that)** eben deswegen(, weil); **with (good) ~** mit gutem Grund; **for no particular ~** ohne bestimmten Grund; **all the more ~ for doing it** um so mehr Grund, das zu tun; **by ~ of** wegen *(+gen)*.

(b) *no pl (faculty)* Verstand *m*; *(common sense)* Vernunft *f*. **to lose one's ~** den Verstand verlieren; **he won't listen to ~** er läßt sich *(dat)* nichts sagen; **that stands to ~** das ist logisch; **you can have anything within ~** Sie können alles haben, solange es sich in Grenzen hält.

2 *vi* **(a)** *(think logically)* vernünftig *or* logisch denken. **(b)** *(argue)* **to ~ (with sb)** vernünftig mit jdm reden.

3 *vt* **(a) to ~ why/what ...** sich *(dat)* klarmachen, warum/was ... **(b)** *(also* **~ out***)* *(deduce)* folgern; *(verbally)* argumentieren.

reasonable [ˈriːznəbl] *adj* **(a)** vernünftig; *chance* reell; *claim, doubt* berechtigt; *amount* angemessen; *(acceptable) excuse, offer* akzeptabel. **beyond (all) ~ doubt** ohne (jeden) Zweifel. **(b)** *(quite good)* ordentlich, ganz gut.

reasonably [ˈriːznəblɪ] *adv* **(a)** *behave, act, think* vernünftig. **one could ~ think that ...** man könnte durchaus annehmen, daß ...; **~ priced** preiswert. **(b)** *(quite)* ziemlich, ganz.

reasoned [ˈriːznd] *adj* durchdacht.

reasoning [ˈriːznɪŋ] *n* Argumentation *f*. **~ is not his strong point** logisches Denken ist nicht gerade seine starke Seite.

reassurance [ˌriːəˈʃʊərəns] *n* **(a)** *(feeling of security)* Beruhigung *f*. **safe in the ~ that ...** in der sicheren Gewißheit, daß ...; **to give sb ~** jdn beruhigen. **(b)** *(renewed confirmation)* Bestätigung *f*. **despite his ~(s)** trotz seiner Versicherungen.

reassure [ˌriːəˈʃʊəʳ] *vt* **(a)** *(relieve sb's mind)* beruhigen; *(give feelings of security to)* das Gefühl der Sicherheit geben *(+dat)*. **(b)** *(verbally)* versichern *(+dat)*. **to ~ sb of sth** jdm etw versichern.

reassuring [ˌriːəˈʃʊərɪŋ] *adj* beruhigend.

rebate [ˈriːbeɪt] *n (money back)* Rückvergütung *f*.

rebel [ˈrebl] **1** *n* Rebell(in *f*) *m*. **2** *adj attr* rebellisch. **3** [rɪˈbel] *vi* rebellieren.

rebellion [rɪˈbeljən] *n* Rebellion *f*, Aufstand *m*.

rebellious [rɪˈbeljəs] *adj* rebellisch.

rebirth [ˌriːˈbɜːθ] *n* Wiedergeburt *f*.

rebound [rɪˈbaʊnd] **1** *vi* zurückprallen *(against, off* von*)*. **your violent methods will ~ on you** Ihre rauhen Methoden werden auf Sie zurückfallen. **2** [ˈriːbaʊnd] *n (of ball, bullet)* Rückprall *m*. **to be on the ~** *(fig)* sich über eine Enttäuschung hinwegtrösten; **she married him on the ~** sie heiratete ihn, um sich über einen anderen hinwegzutrösten.

rebuff [rɪˈbʌf] **1** *n* Abfuhr *f*. **to meet with a ~** abgewiesen werden, eine Abfuhr bekommen; *(from opposite sex)* einen Korb bekommen *(col)*. **2** *vt* abweisen; einen Korb geben *(+dat) (col)*.

rebuild [ˌriːˈbɪld] *vt house* wieder aufbauen; *(fig) country, relationship* wiederaufbauen.

rebuke [rɪˈbjuːk] **1** *n* Zurechtweisung *f*. **2** *vt* zurechtweisen *(for* wegen*)*, tadeln *(for* für*)*.

rebut [rɪˈbʌt] *vt contention* widerlegen.

rebuttal [rɪˈbʌtl] *n* Widerlegung *f*.

recalcitrant [rɪˈkælsɪtrənt] *adj* aufsässig.

recall [rɪˈkɔːl] **1** *vt* **(a)** *(summon back, evoke)* zurückrufen; *ambassador* abberufen; *library book, (Fin) capital* zurückfordern. **(b)** *(remember)* sich erinnern an *(+acc)*. **I cannot ~ meeting him** ich kann mich nicht daran erinnern, daß ich ihn kennengelernt habe. **2** *n see vt (a)* Rückruf *m*; Abberufung *f*; Rückforderung *f*. **beyond ~** für immer vorbei.

recant [rɪˈkænt] **1** *vt religious belief* widerrufen; *statement also* zurücknehmen. **2** *vi* widerrufen.

recap [ˈriːkæp] *(col)* **1** *n* kurze Zusammenfassung. **2** *vti* rekapitulieren, kurz zusammenfassen.

recapitulate [ˌriːkəˈpɪtjʊleɪt] *vti* rekapitulieren, kurz zusammenfassen.

recapture [ˌriːˈkæptʃəʳ] *vt animal* wieder einfangen; *prisoner* wiederergreifen; *territory* wiedererobern; *(fig) atmosphere* wieder wachwerden lassen.

recede [rɪˈsiːd] *vi (tide, price)* zurückgehen; *(fig)* sich entfernen; *(hope)* schwinden. **to ~ into the distance** in der Ferne verschwinden.

receding [rɪˈsiːdɪŋ] *adj chin, forehead* fliehend; *hairline* zurückweichend.

receipt [rɪˈsiːt] *n* **(a)** *no pl* Empfang *m*; *(Comm also)* Erhalt, Eingang *m*. **to acknowledge ~ of sth** den Empfang *etc* einer Sache *(gen)* bestätigen; **I am in ~ of** *(on letter)* ich bin im Besitz *(+gen)*. **(b)** *(paper)* Quittung *f*. **(c)** *(Comm, Fin: money taken)* **~s** Einnahmen *pl*.

receive [rɪˈsiːv] *vt* **(a)** *(get)* bekommen, erhalten; *punch* (ab)bekommen; *refusal, setback* erfahren; *impression* gewinnen; *recognition* finden; *(Jur) stolen goods* Hehlerei (be)treiben mit. **"~d with thanks"** *(Comm)* „dankend erhalten“. **(b)** *(welcome) person* empfangen; *(into group)* aufnehmen *(in* in *+acc)*; *offer, news* aufnehmen. **the play has been well ~d** das Stück wurde gut aufgenommen.

receiver [rɪˈsiːvəʳ] *n* **(a)** *(of letter, goods)* Empfänger(in *f*) *m*; *(Jur: of stolen goods)* Hehler(in *f*) *m*. **(b)** *(Fin, Jur)* **(official) ~** Konkursverwalter *m*. **(c)** *(Telec)* Hörer *m*. **(d)** *(Rad)* Empfänger *m*.

recent [ˈriːsənt] *adj* kürzlich *(usu adv)*; *event, development, news* neueste(r, s); *edition, addition* neu; *publication* Neu-. **the ~ improvement** die vor kurzem eingetretene Verbesserung; **most ~** neueste(r, s); **his ~ arrival** seine Ankunft vor kurzem; **in ~ years** in den letzten Jahren; **~ developments** jüngste Entwicklungen.

recently [ˈriːsəntlɪ] *adv (a short while ago)* vor kurzem, kürzlich; *(during the last few days or weeks)* in letzter Zeit. **~ he has been doing it differently** seit kurzem macht er das anders; **as ~ as** erst; **quite ~** erst kürzlich; **until (quite) ~** (noch) bis vor kurzem.

receptacle [rɪˈseptəkl] *n* Behälter *m*.

reception [rɪˈsepʃən] *n (welcome, ceremony, in hotel, Rad, TV)* Empfang *m*; *(into group, of play etc)* Aufnahme *f*. **to give sb a warm ~** jdm einen herzlichen Empfang bereiten, jdn herzlich empfangen; **~ centre** *(Brit) or* **center** *(US)* Durchgangslager *nt*; **~ desk** Empfang *m*, Rezeption *f*.

receptionist [rɪˈsepʃənɪst] *n (in hotel)* Empfangschef *m*, Empfangsdame *f*; *(with firm)* Herr *m*/Dame *f* am Empfang; *(at airport)* Bodenhostess *f*; *(at doctor's etc)* Sprechstundenhilfe *f*.

receptive [rɪˈseptɪv] *adj person, mind* aufnahmefähig; *audience* empfänglich. **~ to** empfänglich für.

recess [rɪˈses] *n* **(a)** *(of Parliament)* (Sitzungs)pause *f*; *(of lawcourts)* Ferien *pl*; *(US Sch)* Pause *f*. **(b)** *(alcove)* Nische *f*.

recession [rɪˈseʃən] *n* **(a)** *no pl* Rückgang *m*. **(b)** *(Econ)* Rezession *f*.

recharge [ˌriːˈtʃɑːdʒ] *vt battery* aufladen; *gun*

nachladen.

recherché [rə'ʃɛəʃeɪ] *adj* gewählt; *book, subject* ausgefallen.

recipe ['resɪpɪ] *n* Rezept *nt.* **~ for success** Erfolgsrezept *nt*; **an easy ~ for ...** *(fig)* ein Patentrezept für ...; **that's a ~ for disaster** das führt mit Sicherheit in die Katastrophe.

recipient [rɪ'sɪpɪənt] *n* Empfänger(in *f*) *m.*

reciprocal [rɪ'sɪprəkəl] *adj (mutual)* gegenseitig; *favour* Gegen-; *(Gram, Math)* reziprok.

reciprocate [rɪ'sɪprəkeɪt] **1** *vt smiles, wishes, help* erwidern. **2** *vi* sich revanchieren. **but she didn't ~** *(emotionally)* aber sie erwiderte seine/ihre Gefühle nicht.

recital [rɪ'saɪtl] *n (of music, poetry)* Vortrag *m*; *(piano ~ etc)* Konzert *nt*; *(account)* Schilderung *f.*

recitation [ˌresɪ'teɪʃən] *n* Vortrag *m.*

recite [rɪ'saɪt] **1** *vt* **(a)** *poetry* vortragen. **(b)** *facts* hersagen; *details* aufzählen. **2** *vi* vortragen, rezitieren.

reckless ['reklɪs] *adj* leichtsinnig; *driver, driving* rücksichtslos; *speed* gefährlich; *attempt* gewagt.

reckon ['rekən] *vt* **(a)** *(calculate)* berechnen. **he ~ed the cost to be £40.51** er berechnete die Kosten auf £ 40,51. **(b)** *(judge)* rechnen, zählen *(among* zu). **she is ~ed a beautiful woman** sie gilt als schöne Frau. **(c)** *(think, suppose)* glauben; *(estimate)* schätzen. **what do you ~?** was meinen Sie?; **I ~ we can start** ich glaube, wir können anfangen; **I ~ he must be about forty** ich schätze, er müßte so um die Vierzig sein.

♦**reckon on** *vi +prep obj* zählen auf *(+acc).* **you can ~ ~ 30** Sie können mit 30 rechnen; **I wasn't ~ing ~ having to do that** ich habe nicht damit gerechnet, daß ich das tun muß.

♦**reckon up** *vt sep* zusammenrechnen.

♦**reckon with** *vi +prep obj* rechnen mit. **he's a person to be ~ed ~** er ist jemand, mit dem man rechnen muß.

reckoning ['rekənɪŋ] *n (calculation)* (Be)rechnung *f.* **to be out in one's ~** sich ziemlich verrechnet haben; **the day of ~** der Tag der Abrechnung.

reclaim [rɪ'kleɪm] **1** *vt* **(a)** *land* gewinnen; *(by irrigation etc)* kultivieren. **(b)** *baggage etc* abholen. **2** *n* **past ~** für immer verloren.

reclamation [ˌreklə'meɪʃən] *n see vt (a)* Gewinnung *f*; Kultivierung *f.*

recline [rɪ'klaɪn] **1** *vt arm* legen *(on* auf *+acc)*; *head also* zurücklehnen *(on* an *+acc)*; *seat* zurückstellen. **2** *vi (person)* liegen; *(seat)* sich verstellen lassen. **reclining chair** Ruhesessel *m*; *(in car, on boat)* Liegesitz *m.*

recluse [rɪ'klu:s] *n* Einsiedler(in *f*) *m.*

recognition [ˌrekəg'nɪʃən] *n* **(a)** *(acknowledgement, Pol)* Anerkennung *f.* **in ~ of** in Anerkennung *(+gen)*; **by your own ~** wie Sie selbst zugeben; **to gain ~** Anerkennung finden. **(b)** *(identification)* Erkennen *nt.* **he has changed beyond all** *or* **out of all ~** er ist nicht wiederzuerkennen.

recognizable ['rekəgnaɪzəbl] *adj* erkennbar. **you're scarcely ~ with that beard** Sie sind mit dem Bart kaum zu erkennen.

recognize ['rekəgnaɪz] *vt* **(a)** *(know again)* wiedererkennen; *(identify)* erkennen *(by* an *+dat).* **(b)** *(acknowledge, Pol)* anerkennen *(as, to be* als). **(c)** *(be aware)* erkennen; *(be prepared to admit)* zugeben, eingestehen.

recognized ['rekəgnaɪzd] *adj* anerkannt.

recoil [rɪ'kɔɪl] *vi* **(a)** *(person) (from* vor *+dat)* zurückweichen; *(in fear)* zurückschrecken; *(in disgust)* zurückschaudern. **he ~ed from doing it** ihm graute davor, das zu tun. **(b)** *(gun)* zurückstoßen; *(spring)* zurückschnellen.

recollect [ˌrekə'lekt] *vt* sich erinnern an *(+acc).* **as far as I can ~** soweit ich mich erinnern kann.

recollection [ˌrekə'lekʃən] *n (memory)* Erinnerung *f (of* an *+acc).* **I have no ~ of it** ich kann mich dessen nicht entsinnen.

recommend [ˌrekə'mend] *vt* empfehlen *(as* als). **what do you ~ for a cough?** was empfehlen Sie gegen Husten?; **to ~ sth to sb** jdm etw empfehlen; **it is not to be ~ed** es ist nicht zu empfehlen; **~ed price** empfohlener Richtpreis; **she has much to ~ her** es spricht sehr viel für sie.

recommendation [ˌrekəmen'deɪʃən] *n* Empfehlung *f.* **on the ~ of** auf Empfehlung von; **to make a ~** jemanden/etwas empfehlen.

recompense ['rekəmpens] **1** *n* **(a)** *(reward)* Belohnung *f.* **in ~ for** als Belohnung für. **(b)** *(Jur, fig)* Entschädigung *f.* **2** *vt* **(a)** *(reward)* belohnen. **(b)** *(Jur, fig: repay) person* entschädigen.

reconcile ['rekənsaɪl] *vt* **(a)** *people* aussöhnen; *differences* beilegen; *dispute* schlichten. **they became ~d** sie versöhnten sich; **to ~ oneself to sth, to become ~d to sth** sich mit etw abfinden. **(b)** *(make compatible) facts, ideas* miteinander in Einklang bringen, miteinander vereinbaren. **to ~ sth with sth** etw mit etw in Einklang bringen.

reconciliation [ˌrekənsɪlɪ'eɪʃən] *n (of persons)* Aussöhnung *f*; *(of opinons, principles)* Versöhnung *f*; *(of differences)* Beilegung *f.*

recondition [ˌri:kən'dɪʃən] *vt* generalüberholen. **a ~ed engine** ein Austauschmotor *m.*

reconnaissance [rɪ'kɒnɪsəns] *n (Aviat, Mil)* Aufklärung *f.* **~ plane** Aufklärungsflugzeug *nt*; **to be on ~** bei einem Aufklärungseinsatz sein.

reconnoitre, *(US)* **reconnoiter** [ˌrekə'nɔɪtə^r] **1** *vt (Aviat, Mil) region* auskundschaften, aufklären. **2** *vi* das Gelände erkunden.

reconsider [ˌri:kən'sɪdə^r] **1** *vt* noch einmal überdenken; *(change)* revidieren; *(Jur) case* wiederaufnehmen. **2** *vi* **there's still time to ~** es ist noch nicht zu spät, es sich *(dat)* anders zu überlegen.

reconstruct [ˌri:kən'strʌkt] *vt* rekonstruieren; *building* wiederaufbauen.

reconstruction [ˌri:kən'strʌkʃən] *n see vt* Rekonstruktion *f*; Wiederaufbau *m.*

record [rɪ'kɔ:d] **1** *vt* **(a)** *(diarist etc)* aufzeichnen; *(documents, diary etc)* dokumentieren; *(in register)* eintragen; *(keep minutes of)* protokollieren; *one's thoughts, feelings etc* niederschreiben; *protest* zum Ausdruck bringen. **(b)** *(on tape etc)* aufnehmen. **a ~ed programme** eine Aufzeichnung.

2 ['rekɔ:d] *n* **(a)** *(account)* Aufzeichnung *f*; *(of attendance)* Liste *f*; *(of meeting)* Protokoll *nt*; *(official document)* Unterlage *f*; *(lit, fig: of the past)* Dokument *nt.* **to keep a ~ of sth** über etw *(acc)* Buch führen; *(official, registrar)* etw registrieren; **it is on ~ that ...** es gibt Belege dafür, daß ...; *(in files)* es ist aktenkundig, daß ...; **there is no similar example on ~** es ist kein ähnliches Beispiel bekannt; **he's on ~ as saying ...**es ist belegt, daß er gesagt hat, ...; **to put sth on ~** etw schriftlich festhalten; **there is no ~ of his having said it** es ist nirgends belegt, daß er es gesagt hat; **to set the ~ straight** für klare Verhältnisse sorgen; **for the ~** der Ordnung halber; **(strictly) off the ~ he did come** ganz im Vertrauen: er ist doch gekommen.

(b) *(history)* Vorgeschichte *f*; *(achievements)* Leistungen *pl*; *(police ~)* Vorstrafen *pl.* **to have an excellent ~** ausgezeichnete Leistungen vorweisen können; **he's got a ~** er ist vorbestraft; **he has a good ~ of service** er ist ein verdienter Mitarbeiter; **he has a bad attendance ~** er fehlt oft; **his past ~** seine bisherigen Leistungen; **to have a good ~ at school** ein guter Schüler sein; **to have a good safety ~** in bezug auf Sicherheit einen guten Ruf haben.

(c) *(Mus)* (Schall)platte *f*; *(~ing)* Aufnahme *f.*

(d) *(Sport, fig)* Rekord *m.* **to beat** *or* **break the ~** den Rekord brechen; **to hold the ~** den Rekord halten; **long-jump ~** Rekord im Weitsprung; **a ~ time** eine Rekordzeit.

record-breaking ['rekɔːd,breɪkɪŋ] *adj (Sport, fig)* Rekord-.

recorded delivery [rɪ'kɔːdɪd dɪ'lɪvrɪ] *n (Brit)* eingeschriebene Sendung. **by ~** per Einschreiben.

recorder [rɪ'kɔːdə^r] *n* **(a)** *(apparatus)* Registriergerät *nt.* **cassette/tape ~** Kassettenrecorder *m*/ Tonbandgerät *nt.* **(b)** *(Mus)* Blockflöte *f.*

record holder *n (Sport)* Rekordinhaber(in *f*) *m.*

recording [rɪ'kɔːdɪŋ] *n (of sound)* Aufnahme *f*; *(programme)* Aufzeichnung *f.* **~ engineer** Aufnahmetechniker *m*; **~ studio** Aufnahmestudio *nt.*

record ['rekɔːd]: **~ library** *n* Plattenverleih *m*; *(collection)* Plattensammlung *f*; **~-player** *n* Plattenspieler *m*; **~ token** *n* Plattengutschein *m.*

recount [rɪ'kaʊnt] *vt (relate)* erzählen, wiedergeben.

re-count [,riː'kaʊnt] **1** *vt* nachzählen. **2** ['riː,kaʊnt] *n (of votes)* Nachzählung *f.*

recoup [rɪ'kuːp] *vt money, amount* wieder hereinbekommen; *losses* wiedergutmachen, wettmachen.

recourse [rɪ'kɔːs] *n* Zuflucht *f.* **to have ~ to sb/sth** sich an jdn wenden/Zuflucht zu etw nehmen; **without ~** *(Fin)* ohne Regreß.

recover [rɪ'kʌvə^r] **1** *vt* wiederfinden; *goods, property* zurückbekommen; *health* wiedererlangen; *wreck* bergen; *(Ind etc) materials* gewinnen; *debt* eintreiben; *(Jur) damages* Ersatz erhalten für; *losses* wiedergutmachen; *expenses* decken. **to ~ one's breath/strength** wieder zu Atem/Kräften kommen; **to ~ consciousness** das Bewußtsein wiedererlangen; **to ~ one's sight** wieder sehen können; **to be quite ~ed** sich ganz erholt haben. **2** *vi (after accident etc, from illness, Fin)* sich erholen; *(regain consciousness)* wieder zu sich kommen.

re-cover [,riː'kʌvə^r] *vt chairs etc* neu beziehen; *book* neu einbinden.

recovery [rɪ'kʌvərɪ] *n* **(a)** *see vt* Wiederfinden *nt*; Zurückbekommen *nt*; Wiedererlangung *f*; Bergung *f*; Gewinnung *f*; Eintreibung *f*; Ersatz *m (of* für*)*; Wiedergutmachung *f*; Deckung *f.* **(b)** *see vi* Erholung *f.* **he is making a good ~** er erholt sich gut; **past ~** nicht mehr zu retten.

recreation [,rekrɪ'eɪʃən] *n* **(a)** *(leisure)* Erholung *f*; *(pastime)* Hobby *nt.* **for ~ I go fishing** zur Erholung gehe ich angeln; **~ period** Freistunde *f*; **~ ground** Freizeitgelände *nt.* **(b)** *(Sch)* Pause *f.*

recreational [,rekrɪ'eɪʃənəl] *adj* Freizeit-.

recriminations [rɪ,krɪmɪ'neɪʃənz] *npl* gegenseitige Beschuldigungen *pl.*

recruit [rɪ'kruːt] **1** *n (Mil)* Rekrut *m (to gen)*; *(to party, club)* neues Mitglied *(to* in *+dat)*; *(to staff)* Neue(r) *mf (to* in *+dat).* **2** *vt soldier* rekrutieren; *member* werben; *staff* einstellen. **he ~ed me to help** er hat mich dazu herangezogen.

recruitment [rɪ'kruːtmənt] *n (of soldiers)* Rekrutierung *f*; *(of members)* Werbung *f*; *(of staff)* Einstellung *f.*

rectangle ['rek,tæŋgl] *n* Rechteck *nt.*

rectangular [rek'tæŋgjʊlə^r] *adj* rechteckig.

rectify ['rektɪfaɪ] *vt* korrigieren.

rector ['rektə^r] *n* **(a)** *(Rel)* Pfarrer *m (der Anglikanischen Kirche).* **(b)** *(Scot) (Sch)* Direktor(in *f*) *m*; *(Univ)* Rektor(in *f*) *m.*

rectory ['rektərɪ] *n (house)* Pfarrhaus *nt.*

rectum ['rektəm] *n, pl* **-s** *or* **recta** Mastdarm *m.*

recuperate [rɪ'kuːpəreɪt] **1** *vi* sich erholen. **2** *vt losses* wettmachen.

recuperation [rɪ,kuːpə'reɪʃən] *n see vb* Erholung *f*; Wiedergutmachung *f.*

recur [rɪ'kɜː^r] *vi* wiederkehren; *(error also, event)* sich wiederholen; *(opportunity)* sich noch einmal bieten; *(idea, theme also)* wieder auftauchen.

recurrence [rɪ'kʌrəns] *n see vi* Wiederkehr *f*; Wiederholung *f*; Wiederauftauchen *nt.*

recurrent [rɪ'kʌrənt] *adj idea, illness* (ständig) wiederkehrend *attr*; *error, problem also* häufig (vorkommend).

recurring [rɪ'kɜːrɪŋ] *adj attr* **(a)** = **recurrent. (b)** *(Math)* **four point nine three ~** vier Komma neun Periode drei.

recycle [,riː'saɪkl] *vt waste* wiederaufbereiten.

recycling [,riːsaɪklɪŋ] *n* Wiederaufbereitung *f*, Recycling *nt.*

red [red] **1** *adj (+er) (also Pol)* rot. **~ meat** Rind-/ Lammfleisch *nt*; **~ as a beetroot** rot wie eine Tomate; **she turned ~ with embarrassment** sie wurde rot vor Verlegenheit; **it's like a ~ rag to a bull** das ist ein rotes Tuch für ihn/sie *etc.* **2** *n* Rot *nt*; *(Pol: person)* Rote(r) *mf.* **to underline sth in ~** etw rot unterstreichen; **to be (£100) in the ~** (mit £ 100) in den roten Zahlen sein; **to see ~** rot sehen.

red *in cpds* Rot-, rot; **~ beet** *n (US)* rote Rübe; **~-blooded** *adj* heißblütig; **~breast** *n* Rotkehlchen *nt*; **~-brick university** *n (Brit) um die Jahrhundertwende erbaute britische Universität*; **~ carpet** *n (lit, fig)* roter Teppich; **a ~-carpet reception** ein Empfang *m* mit rotem Teppich; *(fig also)* ein großer Bahnhof; **R~ Cross** *n* Rotes Kreuz; **~ deer** *n* Rothirsch *m*; *pl* Rotwild *nt.*

redden ['redn] **1** *vt* röten; *sky, foliage* rot färben. **2** *vi (face)* sich röten; *(person)* rot werden; *(sky, foliage)* sich rot färben.

reddish ['redɪʃ] *adj* rötlich.

redeem [rɪ'diːm] *vt trading stamps, coupons etc* einlösen *(for* gegen*)*; *(Fin) debt, mortgage* abzahlen; *shares* verkaufen; *(US) banknote* wechseln *(for* in *+acc)*; *one's honour* retten; *(Rel) sinner* erlösen; *(compensate for) failing* wettmachen. **to ~ oneself** sich reinwaschen.

Redeemer [rɪ'diːmə^r] *n (Rel)* Erlöser *m.*

redeeming [rɪ'diːmɪŋ] *adj quality* ausgleichend. **~ feature** aussöhnendes Moment; **the only ~ feature of this novel is ...** das einzige, was einen mit diesem Roman aussöhnt, ist ...

redemption [rɪ'dempʃən] *n see vt* Einlösung *f*; Abzahlung *f*; Verkauf *m*; Wechsel *m*; Rettung *f*; *(Rel)* Erlösung *f.* **beyond** *or* **past ~** *(fig)* nicht mehr zu retten.

redevelop [,riːdɪ'veləp] *vt building, area* sanieren.

red: **~-faced** *adj* mit rotem Kopf; **~-haired** *adj* rothaarig; **~-handed** *adv*: **to catch sb ~-handed** jdn auf frischer Tat ertappen; **~head** *n* Rothaarige(r) *mf*; **~ herring** *n (fig)* Ablenkungsmanöver *nt*; *(in thrillers, research)* falsche Spur; **~-hot** *adj (lit)* rotglühend; *(very hot)* glühend heiß; *(fig col) (enthusiastic)* Feuer und Flamme *pred (col)*; *news* brandaktuell; **R~ Indian** *n* Indianer(in *f*) *m.*

redirect [,riːdaɪ'rekt] *vt letter* umadressieren; *(forward)* nachsenden; *traffic* umleiten.

redistribute [,riːdɪ'strɪbjuːt] *vt* umverteilen.

red: **~-letter day** *n* besonderer Tag; **~ light** *n (lit) (warning light)* rotes Licht; *(traffic light)* Rotlicht *nt*; **to go through the ~ light** *(Mot)* bei Rot über die Ampel fahren; **the ~-light district** die Strichgegend.

redness ['rednɪs] *n* Röte *f.*

redouble [,riː'dʌbl] *vt efforts, zeal etc* verdoppeln.

redoubtable [rɪ'daʊtəbl] *adj (formidable) task* horrend; *person* respektgebietend *attr.*

redress [rɪ'dres] **1** *vt errors etc* wiedergutmachen; *situation* bereinigen; *grievance* beseitigen; *balance* wiederherstellen. **2** *n* **to seek ~ for** Wiedergutmachung verlangen für; **there is no ~** das steht unumstößlich fest; **to have no ~ in law** keinen Rechtsanspruch haben.

red: **R~ Sea** *n* Rotes Meer; **~skin** *n* Rothaut *f*; **~ tape** *n (fig)* Papierkrieg *m (col)*; *(with authorities also)* Behördenkram *m (col).*

reduce [rɪ'djuːs] *vt pressure, swelling* verringern, reduzieren; *standards, goods, prices* herabsetzen;

taxes, temperature senken; *(shorten)* verkürzen; *expenses, wages* kürzen; *width, staff, photo* verkleinern; *scale of operations* einschränken; *output* drosseln. **to ~ one's weight** abnehmen; **to ~ speed** *(Mot)* langsamer fahren; **to ~ sth to a powder/to its parts** etw pulverisieren/in seine Einzelteile zerlegen; **it has been ~d to nothing** es ist zu nichts zusammengeschmolzen; **to ~ sb to silence/despair/tears** jdn zum Schweigen/zur Verzweiflung/zum Weinen bringen; **to ~ sb to begging** jdn zum Betteln zwingen; **are we ~d to this!** so weit ist es also gekommen!

reduced [rɪ'djuːst] *adj price, fare* ermäßigt; *goods* herabgesetzt; *scale, version* kleiner.

reduction [rɪ'dʌkʃən] *n* **(a)** *no pl (in sth gen)* Reduzierung, Verringerung *f*; *(in authority)* Schwächung *f*; *(in prices also, of goods, items)* Herabsetzung *f*; *(in expenses, wages)* Kürzung *f*; *(in size)* Verkleinerung *f*; *(shortening)* Verkürzung *f*; *(in output also)* Drosselung *f*. **to make a ~ on an article** einen Artikel heruntersetzen; **~ of taxes** Steuersenkung *f*. **(b)** *(amount reduced) (in sth gen)* Abnahme *f*, Rückgang *m*; *(in size)* Verkleinerung *f*; *(in length)* Verkürzung *f*; *(in taxes)* Nachlaß *m*; *(in prices)* Ermäßigung *f*; *(Jur: of sentence)* Kürzung *f*; *(of swelling)* Rückgang *m*.

redundancy [rɪ'dʌndənsɪ] *n* Überflüssigkeit *f*; *(Brit Ind)* Arbeitslosigkeit *f*. **redundancies** Entlassungen *pl*; **~ payment** Abfindung *f*.

redundant [rɪ'dʌndənt] *adj* überflüssig; *(Brit Ind: out of work)* arbeitslos. **to be made ~** *(Brit Ind)* den Arbeitsplatz verlieren.

redwood ['rɛdwʊd] *n* Redwood *nt*.

reed [riːd] *n (Bot)* Schilf(rohr), Ried *nt*; *(of wind instrument)* Rohrblatt *nt*.

reef[1] [riːf] *n (in sea)* Riff *nt*.

reef[2] *(Naut) n* Reff *nt*. **~ knot** Kreuzknoten *m*.

reek [riːk] **1** *n* Gestank *m*. **2** *vi* stinken *(of* nach*)*.

reel [riːl] **1** *n* **(a)** Spule *f*; *(of thread etc also)* Rolle *f*; *(Fishing)* (Angel)rolle *f*. **(b)** *(dance)* Reel *m*. **2** *vi (person)* taumeln; *(drunk also)* torkeln. **the blow sent him ~ing** er taumelte unter dem Schlag; **my head is ~ing** mir dreht sich der Kopf.

♦ **reel in** *vt sep (Fishing)* einrollen; *fish* einholen.

♦ **reel off** *vt sep list* herunterrasseln *(col)*.

re-elect [ˌriːɪ'lekt] *vt* wiederwählen.

re-enact [ˌriːɪ'nækt] *vt* **(a)** *(Jur)* wieder in Kraft setzen. **(b)** *(repeat) scene, crime* nachspielen.

re-entry [ˌriː'entrɪ] *n (also Space)* Wiedereintritt *m*.

re-examine [ˌriːɪg'zæmɪn] *vt* erneut prüfen.

ref[1] [ref] *n (Sport col)* = **referee** Schiedsrichter *m*, Schiri *m (Sport col)*.

ref[2] = **reference (number).**

refectory [rɪ'fektərɪ] *n (in college)* Mensa *f*.

refer [rɪ'fɜːʳ] **1** *vt (pass) matter, problem* weiterleiten *(to* an *+acc)*; *decision* übergeben *(to sb* jdm*)*. **I ~red him to the manager** ich verwies ihn an den Geschäftsführer; **to ~ sb to the article on ...** jdn auf den Artikel über *(+acc)* ... verweisen. **2** *vi* **(a) to ~ to** *(allude to)* sprechen von; *(mention also)* erwähnen; *(words)* sich beziehen auf *(+acc)*; **I am not ~ring to you** ich meine nicht Sie; **~ring to your letter** *(Comm)* mit Bezug auf Ihren Brief. **(b)** *(apply)* **to ~ to** *(orders, rules)* gelten für; *(criticism, remark)* sich beziehen auf *(+acc)*. **(c)** *(consult)* **to ~ to** *to notes, book* nachschauen in *(+dat)*; *to person* sich wenden an *(+acc)*.

referee [ˌrefə'riː] **1** *n* **(a)** *(Ftbl, fig)* Schiedsrichter *m*; *(Boxing)* Ringrichter *m*; *(Judo, Wrestling)* Kampfrichter *m*. **(b)** *(Brit: person giving a reference)* Referenz *f*. **2** *vt (Sport, fig)* Schiedsrichter sein bei; *(Ftbl also)* pfeifen *(col)*.

reference ['refrəns] *n* **(a)** *(act of mentioning)* Erwähnung *f (to sb/sth* jds/einer Sache*)*; *(allusion) (direct)* Bemerkung *f (to* über *+acc)*; *(indirect)* Anspielung *f (to* auf *+acc)*; *(in book etc)* Verweis *m*. **to make (a) ~ to sth** etw erwähnen; **in or with ~ to** was ... anbetrifft; *(Comm)* bezüglich *(+gen)*. **(b)** *(connection)* **to have ~ to** in Beziehung stehen zu; **this has no/little ~ to** das steht in keiner/kaum in Beziehung zu. **(c)** *(testimonial: also* **~s***)* Referenz(en *pl*) *f*. **to give sb a good ~** jdm ein gutes Zeugnis ausstellen.

reference: ~ book *n* Nachschlagewerk *nt*; **~ library** *n* Präsenzbibliothek *f*; **~ number** *n* Nummer *f*; *(file number)* Aktenzeichen *nt*; *(of machine)* Seriennummer *f*.

referendum [ˌrefə'rendəm] *n, pl* **referenda** [ˌrefə'rendə] Volksentscheid *m*, Referendum *nt*. **to hold a ~** einen Volksentscheid durchführen.

refill [ˌriː'fɪl] **1** *vt* nachfüllen. **2** ['riːfɪl] *n (for fountain pen, lighter)* Nachfüllpatrone *f*; *(for ballpoint)* Ersatzmine *f*. **would you like a ~?** *(col: drink)* darf ich nachschenken?

refine [rɪ'faɪn] *vt oil, sugar* raffinieren; *techniques* verfeinern.

♦ **refine upon** *vi +prep obj detail* näher ausführen; *method* verfeinern.

refined [rɪ'faɪnd] *adj* **(a)** *metal, oil* raffiniert, rein. **~ sugar** Raffinade *f*. **(b)** *taste* fein; *person, style* vornehm.

refinement [rɪ'faɪnmənt] *n no pl (of oil, sugar)* Raffination, Reinigung *f*; *(no pl: of person, language, style)* Vornehmheit, Feinheit *f*; *(improvement: in technique, machine etc)* Verfeinerung, Verbesserung *f (in sth gen)*.

refinery [rɪ'faɪnərɪ] *n (oil, sugar ~)* Raffinerie *f*.

refit [ˌriː'fɪt] **1** *vt ship* neu ausrüsten; *factory* neu ausstatten. **2** ['riːfɪt] *n (Naut)* Neuausrüstung *f*.

reflate [ˌriː'fleɪt] *vt (Econ)* ankurbeln.

reflation [riː'fleɪʃən] *n (Econ)* Ankurbelung *f* der Konjunktur.

reflect [rɪ'flekt] **1** *vt* **(a)** *light etc* reflektieren; *(surface, mirror also)* spiegeln; *(fig) views, reality etc* widerspiegeln. **the moon was ~ed in the lake** der Mond spiegelte sich im See; **I saw him ~ed in the mirror** ich sah ihn im Spiegel; **the difficulties ~ed in his report** die Schwierigkeiten, die sich in seinem Bericht spiegeln. **(b)** *(think)* **do you ever ~ that ...?** denken Sie je darüber nach, daß ...? **2** *vi (meditate)* nachdenken, reflektieren *(geh) (on, about* über *+acc)*.

reflection [rɪ'flekʃən] *n* **(a)** *no pl (reflecting)* Reflexion *f*; *(by mirror)* Spiegelung *f*; *(fig)* Widerspiegelung *f*. **(b)** *(image)* Spiegelbild *nt*; *(fig)* Widerspiegelung *f*. **to see one's ~ in a mirror** sich im Spiegel sehen; **a pale ~ of ...** ein matter Abglanz *(+gen)*. **(c)** *no pl (consideration)* Überlegung *f*; *(contemplation)* Reflexion, Betrachtung *f*. **on ~** wenn ich *etc* mir das recht überlege; **this is no ~ on your motives** damit soll gar nichts über Ihre Motive gesagt sein.

reflective [rɪ'flektɪv] *adj person* nachdenklich.

reflectively [rɪ'flektɪvlɪ] *adv say, speak* überlegt.

reflector [rɪ'flektəʳ] *n (on car)* Rückstrahler *m*; *(telescope)* Reflektor *m*.

reflex ['riːfleks] **1** *adj* Reflex-. **~ action** Reflex *m*; **~ camera** *(Phot)* Spiegelreflexkamera *f*. **2** *n (Physiol, Psych, fig)* Reflex *m*.

reflexive [rɪ'fleksɪv] *(Gram) adj* reflexiv.

refloat [ˌriː'fləʊt] *vt ship, business* wieder flottmachen.

reform [rɪ'fɔːm] **1** *n* Reform *f (in sth gen)*; *(of person)* Besserung *f*. **2** *vt institutions, society* reformieren; *person* bessern. **3** *vi (person)* sich bessern.

reformation [ˌrefə'meɪʃən] *n (of person)* Besserung *f*. **the R~** die Reformation.

reformed [rɪ'fɔːmd] *adj church, spelling* reformiert; *person* gewandelt. **he's a ~ character** er hat sich gebessert.

reformer [rɪ'fɔːməʳ] *n (Pol)* Reformer *m*; *(Rel)* Reformator *m*.

refraction [rɪ'frækʃən] *n* Brechung *f.* **angle of ~** Brechungswinkel *m.*
refractory [rɪ'fræktərɪ] *adj* **(a)** *person* störrisch. **(b)** *(Chem, Miner)* hitzebeständig.
refrain[1] [rɪ'freɪn] *vi* **please ~!** bitte unterlassen Sie das!; **he ~ed from comment** er enthielt sich eines Kommentars; **I couldn't ~ from laughing** ich konnte mir das Lachen nicht verkneifen; **please ~ from smoking** bitte nicht rauchen!
refrain[2] *n (Mus, Poet, fig)* Refrain *m.*
refresh [rɪ'freʃ] *vt (drink, rest)* erfrischen; *(meal)* stärken. **to ~ oneself** *(with drink)* eine Erfrischung zu sich *(dat)* nehmen; *(with a bath)* sich erfrischen; *(with rest)* sich ausruhen; **to ~ one's memory** sein Gedächtnis auffrischen.
refreshing [rɪ'freʃɪŋ] *adj (lit, fig)* erfrischend.
refreshment [rɪ'freʃmənt] *n* **(a)** *(of mind, body)* Erfrischung *f.* **(b)** *(food, drink)* **(light) ~s** (kleine) Erfrischungen *pl*; **~ bar** *or* **stall** Büfett *nt.*
refrigerate [rɪ'frɪdʒəreɪt] *vt (chill)* kühlen; *(freeze)* tiefkühlen.
refrigeration [rɪˌfrɪdʒə'reɪʃən] *n see vt* Kühlung *f*; Tiefkühlung *f.*
refrigerator [rɪ'frɪdʒəreɪtə^r] *n* Kühlschrank *m.*
refuel [ˌriː'fjʊəl] *vti* auftanken.
refuge ['refjuːdʒ] *n* **(a)** *(lit, fig)* Zuflucht *f (from* vor *+dat).* **place of ~** Zufluchtsort *m*; **to seek ~** Zuflucht suchen; **to take ~** sich flüchten *(in* in *+acc).* **(b)** *(for climbers etc)* Unterstand *m.*
refugee [ˌrefjʊdʒiː] *n* Flüchtling *m.* **~ camp** Flüchtlingslager *nt.*
refund [rɪ'fʌnd] **1** *vt money, postage* zurückerstatten; *expenses* erstatten. **2** ['riːfʌnd] *n see vt* Rückerstattung *f*; Erstattung *f.* **they wouldn't give me a ~** man wollte mir das Geld nicht zurückgeben.
refurbish [ˌriː'fɜːbɪʃ] *vt* aufpolieren; *dress, furniture also* verschönern; *house* renovieren.
refusal [rɪ'fjuːzəl] *n* Ablehnung *f*; *(to offer also)* Zurückweisung *f*; *(of permission, visa)* Verweigerung *f*; *(to do sth)* Weigerung *f.* **to meet with** *or* **get a ~** eine Absage erhalten; **to have (the) first ~ of sth** etw als erster angeboten bekommen.
refuse[1] [rɪ'fjuːz] **1** *vt invitation, candidate, proposal* ablehnen; *(stronger)* zurückweisen; *offer also* ausschlagen; *permit, permission* verweigern. **to ~ to do sth** sich weigern, etw zu tun; **he was ~d a visa** ihm wurde das Visum verweigert; **to be ~d sth** etw nicht bekommen; **his request was ~d** seine Bitte wurde abgelehnt; **the car ~s to start** das Auto will einfach nicht anspringen. **2** *vi* ablehnen; *(to do sth)* sich weigern; *(horse)* verweigern.
refuse[2] ['refjuːs] *n* Müll *m*; *(food waste)* Abfall *m.*
refuse ['refjuːs] *in cpds* Müll-; **~ bin** *n* Mülleimer *m*; **~ disposal** *n* Müllbeseitigung *f*; **~ disposal unit** *n* Müllschlucker *m*; **~ dump** *n* Müllabladeplatz *m*; **~ lorry** *n* Müllwagen *m.*
refute [rɪ'fjuːt] *vt* widerlegen.
regain [rɪ'geɪn] *vt* wiedererlangen; *lost time* aufholen; *territory* zurückbekommen. **to ~ possession of sth** wieder in den Besitz einer Sache *(gen)* gelangen.
regal ['riːgəl] *adj* königlich; *(fig)* hoheitsvoll.
regale [rɪ'geɪl] *vt (with food, drink)* verwöhnen; *(with stories)* ergötzen *(geh).*
regalia [rɪ'geɪlɪə] *npl* Insignien *pl.* **she was in full ~** *(hum)* sie war in großer Aufmachung *(hum).*
regard [rɪ'gɑːd] **1** *vt* **(a)** *(consider)* betrachten. **to ~ sb/sth as sth** jdn/etw für etw halten; **to ~ sb/sth with favour** jdn/etw wohlwollend betrachten; **to ~ sth with horror** mit Schrecken an etw *(acc)* denken; **to be ~ed as ...** als ... gelten, als ... angesehen werden; **to ~ sb/sth highly** jdn/etw sehr schätzen; **he is highly ~ed** er ist hoch angesehen. **(b)** *(concern)* **as ~s your application** was Ihren Antrag betrifft. **(c)** *(heed)* berücksichtigen. **without ~ing his wishes** ohne Rücksicht auf seine Wünsche.
2 *n* **(a)** *(attention, concern)* Rücksicht *f (for* auf *+acc).* **to show no ~ for sb/sth** keine Rücksichtnahme für jdn/etw zeigen; **with no ~ for his safety** ohne Rücksicht auf seine Sicherheit. **(b) in this ~** diesbezüglich *(form)*, in diesem Zusammenhang; **with** *or* **in ~ to** in bezug auf *(+acc).* **(c)** *(respect)* Achtung *f.* **to hold sb in high ~** jdn sehr schätzen. **(d) ~s** *pl (in message)* Gruß *m.* **to send sb one's ~s** jdn grüßen lassen; **give him my ~s** grüßen Sie ihn von mir; **(kindest) ~s, with kind ~s** mit freundlichen Grüßen.
regarding [rɪ'gɑːdɪŋ] *prep* in bezug auf *(+acc)*, bezüglich *(+gen).*
regardless [rɪ'gɑːdlɪs] **1** *adj* **~ of** ohne Rücksicht auf *(+acc)*, ungeachtet *(+gen)*; **to do sth ~ of the consequences** etw ohne Rücksicht auf die Folgen tun; **~ of what it costs** egal, was es kostet; **~ of the fact that ...** ungeachtet der Tatsache, daß ... **2** *adv* trotzdem. **he did it ~** er hat es trotzdem getan.
regatta [rɪ'gætə] *n* Regatta *f.*
regenerate [rɪ'dʒenəreɪt] *vt (renew, re-create)* erneuern; *tissue also* neu bilden.
regeneration [rɪˌdʒenə'reɪʃən] *n see vt* Erneuerung *f*; Neubildung *f.*
reggae ['regeɪ] *n* Reggae *m.*
regime [reɪ'ʒiːm] *n (Pol)* Regime *nt*; *(fig: management, social system etc)* System *nt.*
regiment ['redʒɪmənt] **1** *n (Mil)* Regiment *nt.* **2** *vt (fig)* reglementieren.
regimental [ˌredʒɪ'mentl] *adj (Mil)* Regiments-.
regimentation [ˌredʒɪmen'teɪʃən] *n (fig)* Reglementierung *f.*
region ['riːdʒən] *n (of country)* Region *f*; *(of body also)* Gegend *f*; *(of atmosphere, fig)* Bereich *m.* **in the ~ of 5 kg** um die 5 kg.
regional ['riːdʒənl] *adj* regional. **~ development** Gebietserschließung *f.*
register ['redʒɪstə^r] **1** *n (book)* Register *nt*; *(at school)* Namensliste *f*; *(in hotel)* Gästebuch *nt*; *(of members etc)* Mitgliedsbuch *nt.* **to take the ~** die Namen aufrufen; **electoral ~** Wählerverzeichnis *nt*; **~ of births, deaths and marriages** Personenstandsbuch *nt.*
2 *vt* **(a)** *(authorities: record formally)* registrieren; *(in book, files)* eintragen; *fact, figure also* erfassen. **he is ~ed as disabled** er ist anerkannter Schwerbeschädigter. **(b)** *(individual: have recorded) birth, (Comm) company, trademark, vehicle etc* anmelden. **to ~ a protest** Protest anmelden. **(c)** *(indicate) speed* anzeigen; *(expression) happiness* zum Ausdruck bringen. **he ~ed surprise** er zeigte sich überrascht. **(d)** *letter* einschreiben lassen.
3 *vi* **(a)** *(on electoral list etc)* sich eintragen; *(in hotel)* sich anmelden; *(student)* sich einschreiben. **to ~ with a doctor** sich bei einem Arzt auf die Patientenliste setzen lassen. **(b)** *(col: be understood)* **it hasn't ~ed (with him)** er hat es noch nicht registriert.
registered ['redʒɪstəd] *adj* **(a)** *student* eingeschrieben; *voter, company* eingetragen; *vehicle* amtlich zugelassen. **~ nurse** *(US)* staatlich geprüfte Krankenschwester; *(male)* staatlich geprüfter Pfleger; **~ trademark** eingetragenes Warenzeichen. **(b)** *letter* eingeschrieben. **by ~ post** per Einschreiben.
registrar [ˌredʒɪ'strɑː^r] *n (Admin)* Standesbeamte(r) *m*; *(Univ)* Kanzler *m*; *(Med)* Krankenhausarzt *m*/-ärztin *f.*
registration [ˌredʒɪ'streɪʃən] *n see vt* **(a)** Registrierung *f*; Eintragung *f*; Erfassung *f.* **(b)** Anmeldung *f.* **~ number** *(Brit Aut)* polizeiliches Kennzeichen.
registry ['redʒɪstrɪ] *n* Sekretariat *nt*; *(in church)*

Sakristei *f*; *(Brit: also* ~ **office***)* Standesamt *nt*. **to get married in a ~ office** standesamtlich heiraten.
regress [rɪ'gres] *vi (deteriorate)* sich rückläufig entwicklen.
regression [rɪ'greʃən] *n* Rückentwicklung *f*.
regret [rɪ'gret] **1** *vt* bedauern; *lost opportunity* nachtrauern *(+dat)*. **I ~ that we will not be coming** ich bedaure, daß wir nicht kommen können; **I ~ to say that ...** ich muß Ihnen leider mitteilen, daß ... **2** *n* Bedauern *nt no pl*. **much to my ~** sehr zu meinem Bedauern; **I have no ~s** ich bereue nichts.
regretfully [rɪ'gretfəlɪ] *adv (sadly)* mit Bedauern; *(reluctantly)* widerstrebend.
regrettable [rɪ'gretəbl] *adj* bedauerlich.
regrettably [rɪ'gretəblɪ] *adv* bedauerlicherweise.
regroup [ˌriː'gruːp] **1** *vt* um- *or* neugruppieren. **2** *vi* sich umgruppieren, sich neu gruppieren.
regular ['regjʊlə^r] **1** *adj* **(a)** regelmäßig; *features also* ebenmäßig; *surface* gleichmäßig; *employment* fest; *way of life* geregelt. **to keep ~ hours** feste Zeiten haben; **she is as ~ as clockwork** bei ihr geht alles auf die Minute genau. **(b)** *(habitual) size, price, time* normal; *staff, customer, pub* Stamm-; *listener* regelmäßig. **our ~ cleaning woman** unsere normale Reinemachefrau; **my ~ dentist** mein Hauszahnarzt *m*. **(c)** *(permissible, accepted) action, procedure* richtig. **it is quite ~ to apply in person** es ist ganz in Ordnung, sich persönlich zu bewerben. **(d)** *(Mil) soldier, army* Berufs-. **(e)** *(col) disaster, clown etc* regelrecht. **2** *n (Mil)* Berufssoldat *m*; *(customer etc)* Stammkunde *m*, Stammkundin *f*; *(in pub, hotel)* Stammgast *m*.
regularity [ˌregjʊ'lærɪtɪ] *n* **(a)** *see adj (a)* Regelmäßigkeit *f*; Ebenmäßigkeit *f*; Gleichmäßigkeit *f*; *(of procedure etc)* Festheit *f*; Geregeltheit *f*. **(b)** *(of action, procedure)* Richtigkeit *f*.
regularize ['regjʊləraɪz] *vt breathing, service* regulieren; *situation, relationship* normalisieren.
regularly ['regjʊləlɪ] *adv* regelmäßig; *breathe, beat also* gleichmäßig.
regulate ['regjʊleɪt] *vt* regulieren; *life-style* regeln; *clock* richtig stellen.
regulation [ˌregjʊ'leɪʃən] **1** *n* **(a)** *(of machine)* Regulierung *f*. **(b)** *(rule)* Vorschrift *f*. **2** *attr boots, dress* vorgeschrieben.
regulator ['regjʊleɪtə^r] *n (instrument)* Regler *m*.
rehabilitate [ˌriːə'bɪlɪteɪt] *vt refugee, ex-criminal, ex-soldier* (in die Gesellschaft) eingliedern; *the disabled also* rehabilitieren.
rehabilitation ['riːəˌbɪlɪ'teɪʃən] *n see vt* Eingliederung *f* in die Gesellschaft; Rehabilitation *f*. **~ centre** *(Admin)* Rehabilitationszentrum *nt*.
rehash [ˌriː'hæʃ] **1** *vt literary material etc* aufbereiten. **2** ['riːhæʃ] *n* Aufguß *m*.
rehearsal [rɪ'hɜːsəl] *n (Theat, Mus)* Probe *f*.
rehearse [rɪ'hɜːs] *vti (Theat, Mus)* proben. **to ~ what one is going to say** einüben, was man sagen will.
rehouse [ˌriː'haʊz] *vt* unterbringen.
reign [reɪn] **1** *n (lit, fig)* Herrschaft *f*. **in the ~ of** während der Herrschaft *(+gen)*. **2** *vi (lit, fig)* herrschen *(over* über *+acc)*. **silence ~s** es herrscht Ruhe; **~ing champion** amtierender Meister.
reimburse [ˌriːɪm'bɜːs] *vt person* entschädigen; *loss, expenses, costs* ersetzen.
rein [reɪn] *n (lit, fig)* Zügel *m*. **~s** *(for child)* Laufgurt *m*; **to hold the ~s** *(lit, fig)* die Zügel in der Hand haben; **to keep a tight ~ on sb/sth** *(lit, fig)* bei jdm/etw die Zügel kurz halten; **to allow sb/sth free ~** *(fig)* jdm/einer Sache freien Lauf lassen.
♦ **rein in** *vt sep (lit, fig)* zügeln.
reincarnation [ˌriːɪnkɑː'neɪʃən] *n* die Wiedergeburt.
reindeer ['reɪndɪə^r] *n, pl* - Ren(tier) *nt*.
reinforce [ˌriːɪn'fɔːs] *vt (lit, fig, Psych)* verstärken; *sb's demands* stärken, stützen; *evidence, opinion* bestätigen. **~d concrete** Stahlbeton *m*.
reinforcement [ˌriːɪn'fɔːsmənt] *n* **(a)** *no pl (act) see vt* Verstärkung *f*; Stärkung, Stützung *f*; Bestätigung *f*. **(b)** *(thing)* Verstärkung *f*. **~s** *(Mil, fig)* Verstärkung *f*.
reinstate [ˌriːɪn'steɪt] *vt person* wieder einstellen *(in* in *+acc)*; *law and order* wiederherstellen *(in* in *+dat)*.
reissue [ˌriː'ɪʃjuː] **1** *vt book* neu auflegen; *stamps, recording, coins* neu herausgeben. **2** *n see vt* Neuauflage *f*; Neuausgabe *f*.
reiterate [riː'ɪtəreɪt] *vt* wiederholen.
reject [rɪ'dʒekt] **1** *vt* **(a)** *damaged goods etc (customer)* zurückweisen; *(maker)* aussortieren. **(b)** *(turn down) application, request etc* ablehnen; *suitor, advances* zurückweisen; *offer also* ausschlagen; *possibility* verwerfen; *candidate (through vote)* durchfallen lassen. **(c)** *(Med) transplant* abstoßen; *(stomach) food* verweigern. **2** ['riːdʒekt] *n (Comm)* Ausschuß *m no pl*. **~ goods** Ausschußware *f*.
rejection [rɪ'dʒekʃən] *n see vt* **(a)** Zurückweisung *f*; Aussortierung *f*. **(b)** Ablehnung *f*; Zurückweisung *f*; Verwerfen *nt*. **(c)** *(Med)* Abstoßung *f*; Verweigerung *f*.
rejoice [rɪ'dʒɔɪs] *vi* sich freuen; *(jubilate)* jubeln; *(Rel)* jauchzen.
rejoicing [rɪ'dʒɔɪsɪŋ] *n* Jubel *m*. **~s** Jubel *m*.
rejoin[1] [ˌriː'dʒɔɪn] *vt person, regiment* sich wieder anschließen *(+dat)*. **to ~ ship** *(Naut)* wieder aufs Schiff kommen; **then we ~ed the motorway** danach fuhren wir wieder auf die Autobahn.
rejoin[2] [rɪ'dʒɔɪn] *vt (reply)* erwidern.
rejoinder [rɪ'dʒɔɪndə^r] *n* Erwiderung *f*.
rejuvenate [rɪ'dʒuːvɪneɪt] *vt* verjüngen; *(fig)* erfrischen.
rekindle [ˌriː'kɪndl] *vt (lit, fig) fire, passions* wieder anzünden; *hope* wiedererwecken.
relapse [rɪ'læps] **1** *n (Med, into vice, crime)* Rückfall *m*; *(in economy)* Rückschlag *m*. **2** *vi (Med)* einen Rückfall haben. **to ~ (into crime)** rückfällig werden.
relate [rɪ'leɪt] **1** *vt* **(a)** *(recount) story* erzählen; *details* aufzählen. **(b)** *(associate)* in Verbindung bringen *(to, with* mit*)*. **2** *vi* **(a)** zusammenhängen *(to* mit*)*. **(b)** *(form relationship)* eine Beziehung finden *(to* zu*)*.
related [rɪ'leɪtɪd] *adj* **(a)** *(in family)* verwandt *(to* mit*)*. **(b)** *(connected)* zusammenhängend; *theories, languages etc* verwandt. **to be ~d to sth** mit etw zusammenhängen/verwandt sein.
relating [rɪ'leɪtɪŋ] *adj* **~ to** in Zusammenhang mit.
relation [rɪ'leɪʃən] *n* **(a)** *(relative)* Verwandte(r) *mf*. **he's a/no ~ (of mine)** er ist/ist nicht mit mir verwandt; **what ~ is she to you?** wie ist sie mit Ihnen verwandt? **(b)** *(relationship)* Beziehung *f*. **to bear a ~ to** in Beziehung stehen zu; **in ~ to** *(as regards)* in bezug auf *(+acc)*; *(compared with)* im Verhältnis zu. **(c) ~s** *pl (dealings, ties, sexual ~s)* Beziehungen *pl*.
relationship [rɪ'leɪʃənʃɪp] *n (in family)* Verwandtschaft *f (to* mit*)*; *(connection: between events etc)* Beziehung *f*; *(relations)* Verhältnis *nt*, Beziehungen *pl*; *(in business)* Verbindung *f*. **to have a (sexual) ~ with** ein Verhältnis haben mit; **to have a good ~ with sb** ein gutes Verhältnis zu jdm haben.
relative ['relətɪv] **1** *adj* **(a)** relativ; *(respective)* respektiv. **to live in ~ luxury** verhältnismäßig *or* relativ luxuriös leben; **the ~ merits of A and B** die respektiven Verdienste von A und B. **(b)** *(relevant)* **~ to** sich beziehend auf *(+acc)*. **(c)** *(Gram)* Relativ-. **2** *n (person)* = **relation (a).**
relatively ['relətɪvlɪ] *adv* relativ, verhältnismäßig. **~ speaking** relativ gesehen.

relativity [ˌreləˈtɪvɪtɪ] *n (Phys, Philos)* Relativität *f.* **the theory of ~** die Relativitätstheorie.

relax [rɪˈlæks] **1** *vt* lockern; *muscles also, person* entspannen; *attention, effort* nachlassen in *(+dat).* **2** *vi* (sich) entspannen; *(rest)* (sich) ausruhen; *(calm down)* sich beruhigen.

relaxation [ˌriːlækˈseɪʃən] *n* **(a)** *see vt* Lockerung *f;* Entspannung *f;* Nachlassen *nt.* **(b)** *(rest)* Entspannung *f; (recreation also)* Erholung *f.*

relaxed [rɪˈlækst] *adj* locker; *person, smile, voice* ruhig; *atmosphere* gelockert. **to feel ~** *(physically)* entspannt sein; *(mentally)* sich wohl fühlen.

relaxing [rɪˈlæksɪŋ] *adj* entspannend; *climate* erholsam.

relay [ˈriːleɪ] **1** *n* **(a)** *(of workers)* Ablösung *f; (of horses)* frisches Gespann. **to work in ~s** sich ablösen. **(b)** *(Sport: also* **~ race***)* Staffel(lauf *m*) *f.* **(c)** *(Rad, TV)* Relais *nt.* **2** *vt* **(a)** *(Rad, TV)* (weiter)übertragen. **(b)** *message* ausrichten *(to sb* jdm*).*

release [rɪˈliːs] **1** *vt* **(a)** *animal, person* freilassen; *(from prison also)* entlassen; *(rescue)* befreien; *(from obligation)* entbinden, befreien. **(b)** *(let go of)* loslassen; *handbrake* losmachen; *(Phot) shutter* auslösen; *grip, clasp* lösen; *confiscated articles* freigeben. **to ~ the clutch** die Kupplung kommen lassen. **(c)** *news, statement* veröffentlichen. **(d)** *(emit) gas, energy* freisetzen; *smell* ausströmen; *pressure, steam* ablassen. **2** *n* **(a)** *see vt (a)* Freilassung *f;* Entlassung *f;* Befreiung *f;* Entbindung *f.* **(b)** *(mechanism)* Auslöser *m.* **(c)** *(of statement etc)* Veröffentlichung *f; (statement)* Verlautbarung *f.* **(d)** *(of gas, energy)* Freisetzung *f.* **(e)** *(film)* Film *m; (record)* Platte *f.* **this film is now on general ~** dieser Film ist nun überall zu sehen; **a new ~** *(record)* eine Neuerscheinung; *(film)* ein neu herausgekommener Film.

relegate [ˈrelɪgeɪt] *vt (lit, fig: downgrade)* degradieren; *(Sport) team* absteigen lassen *(to* in *+acc).* **to be ~d** *(Sport)* absteigen.

relegation [ˌrelɪˈgeɪʃən] *n see vt* Degradierung *f;* Abstieg *m.*

relent [rɪˈlent] *vi (person)* nachgeben; *(pace, pain)* nachlassen; *(weather)* sich bessern.

relentless [rɪˈlentlɪs] *adj* erbarmungslos; *person also* unerbittlich; *pain, cold* nicht nachlassend.

relevance [ˈreləvəns] *n* Relevanz *f.*

relevant [ˈreləvənt] *adj* relevant *(to* für*); authority, person* zuständig.

reliability [rɪˌlaɪəˈbɪlɪtɪ] *n see adj* Zuverlässigkeit *f;* Seriosität *f.*

reliable [rɪˈlaɪəbl] *adv* zuverlässig; *firm* seriös.

reliably [rɪˈlaɪəblɪ] *adv* zuverlässig. **I am ~ informed that …** ich weiß aus zuverlässiger Quelle, daß …

reliance [rɪˈlaɪəns] *n* Vertrauen *nt (on* auf *+acc).*

reliant [rɪˈlaɪənt] *adj* angewiesen *(on, upon* auf *+acc).*

relic [ˈrelɪk] *n* Überbleibsel, Relikt *nt; (Rel)* Reliquie *f.*

relief [rɪˈliːf] **1** *n* **(a)** *(from anxiety, pain)* Erleichterung *f.* **to bring sb ~** *(drug)* jdm Erleichterung verschaffen; **that's a ~!** mir fällt ein Stein vom Herzen; **it was a ~ to find it** ich/er *etc* war erleichtert, als ich/er *etc* es fand. **(b)** *(assistance)* Hilfe *f.* **to provide ~ for the poor** für die Armen sorgen. **(c)** *(esp Mil: act of relieving, replacement forces)* Entsatz *m; (substitute)* Ablösung *f.* **(d)** *(Art, Geog)* Relief *nt; (Typ also)* Hochdruck *m.* **throw sth into ~** *(fig)* etw hervorheben. **2** *attr* **(a)** *fund, organization* Hilfs-. **~ supplies** Hilfsgüter *pl.* **(b)** *driver* Ablöse-; *troops* Entsatz-; *(Brit) bus, road* Entlastungs-. **(c)** *map* Relief-; *printing also* Hoch-.

relieve [rɪˈliːv] *vt* **(a)** *person* erleichtern. **he was ~d to learn that** er war erleichtert, als er das hörte; **to ~ sb's mind** jdn beruhigen; **to ~ sb of sth** *of burden, pain* jdn von etw befreien; *of duty, command* jdn einer Sache *(gen)* entheben *(geh); of suitcase* jdm etw abnehmen. **(b)** *(mitigate) anxiety* mildern, schwächen; *pain* lindern; *(completely)* stillen; *tension* abbauen; *poverty* erleichtern; *(Med) congestion* abhelfen *(+dat); (completely)* beheben. **to ~ oneself** *(euph)* sich erleichtern; **it'll ~ the monotony** das dient der Abwechslung. **(c)** *(take over from, also Mil)* ablösen. **(d)** *(Mil) town* entsetzen.

religion [rɪˈlɪdʒən] *n* Religion *f; (creed)* Glaube(n) *m.* **the Christian ~** der christliche Glaube.

religious [rɪˈlɪdʒəs] *adj* **(a)** religiös; *person also* gläubig; *order* geistlich; *freedom also, wars* Glaubens-. **~ instruction** *(Sch)* Religionsunterricht *m.* **(b)** *(fig: conscientious)* gewissenhaft.

relinquish [rɪˈlɪŋkwɪʃ] *vt hope, plan* aufgeben; *right, possessions also* verzichten auf *(+acc).* **to ~ one's hold on sb/sth** *(lit, fig)* jdn/etw loslassen.

relish [ˈrelɪʃ] **1** *n* **(a)** *(enjoyment)* Gefallen *m (for* an *+dat).* **to do sth with (great) ~** etw mit (großem) Genuß tun. **(b)** *(Cook)* Soße *f.* **2** *vt* genießen; *food, wine also* sich *(dat)* schmecken lassen. **I don't ~ doing that** *(enjoy)* das ist gar nicht nach meinem Geschmack; *(look forward to)* darauf freue ich mich überhaupt nicht.

reluctance [rɪˈlʌktəns] *n* Widerwillen *m.* **to do sth with ~** etw widerwillig *or* ungern tun.

reluctant [rɪˈlʌktənt] *adj* widerwillig. **he is ~ to do it** es widerstrebt ihm, es zu tun; **he seems ~ to admit it** er scheint es nicht zugeben zu wollen.

rely [rɪˈlaɪ] *vi* **to ~ (up)on sb/sth** sich auf jdn/etw verlassen; *(be dependent on)* auf jdn/etw angewiesen sein; **she relied on the trains being on time** sie verließ sich darauf, daß die Züge pünktlich waren; **she is not to be relied upon** man kann sich nicht auf sie verlassen.

remain [rɪˈmeɪn] *vi* bleiben; *(be left over)* übrigbleiben. **much ~s to be done** es bleibt noch viel zu tun; **all that ~s is for me to wish you every success** ich möchte Ihnen nur noch viel Erfolg wünschen; **that ~s to be seen** das bleibt abzuwarten; **the fact ~s that …** das ändert nichts an der Tatsache, daß …; **to ~ silent** weiterhin schweigen; **to ~ behind** zurückbleiben; **"I ~, yours faithfully John Smith"** „mit besten Grüßen verbleibe ich Ihr John Smith".

remainder [rɪˈmeɪndə[r]] *n* Rest *m (also Math).* **~s** *pl (Comm)* Restbestände *pl.*

remaining [rɪˈmeɪnɪŋ] *adj* übrig, restlich. **I have only two ~** ich habe nur noch zwei (übrig).

remains [rɪˈmeɪnz] *npl (of meal)* Reste *pl; (of building)* Überreste *pl; (archaeological ~)* Ruinen *pl.* **human ~** menschliche Überreste *pl.*

remake [ˈriːmeɪk] *n (Film)* Neuverfilmung *f,* Remake *nt (spec).*

remand [rɪˈmɑːnd] **1** *vt (Jur)* **to ~ sb (in custody/on bail)** jdn weiterhin in Untersuchungshaft behalten/unter Kaution halten. **2** *n* **to be on ~** in Untersuchungshaft sein; *(on bail)* auf Kaution freigelassen sein; **~ home** *(Brit)* Untersuchungsgefängnis *nt* für Jugendliche.

remark [rɪˈmɑːk] **1** *n* Bemerkung *f.* **to pass ~s** Bemerkungen machen; **worthy of ~** bemerkenswert. **2** *vt (say)* bemerken. **3** *vi* **to ~ (up)on sth** über etw *(acc)* eine Bemerkung machen.

remarkable [rɪˈmɑːkəbl] *adj (notable)* bemerkenswert; *intelligence, talent also* beachtlich; *(extraordinary)* außergewöhnlich. **to be ~ for sth** sich durch etw auszeichnen.

remarkably [rɪˈmɑːkəblɪ] *adv* außergewöhnlich.

remarry [ˌriːˈmærɪ] *vi* wieder heiraten.

remedial [rɪˈmiːdɪəl] *adj attr action, measures* Hilfs-; *(Med)* Heil-; **~ teaching** Förderunterricht *m*; ~ **class** Förderklasse *f* (für Lernschwache).

remedy ['remədı] **1** *n (Med, fig)* Mittel *nt (for* gegen); *(medication)* Heilmittel *nt (for* gegen*)*. **the situation is beyond** ~ die Lage ist hoffnungslos. **2** *vt (Med)* heilen; *(fig) fault* beheben; *situation* bessern.

remember [rı'membəʳ] **1** *vt* **(a)** *(recall)* sich erinnern an *(+acc)*; *(bear in mind)* denken an *(+acc)*; *(learn) facts* sich *(dat)* merken. **I ~ that he was very tall** ich erinnere mich, daß er sehr groß war; **I ~ her as a beautiful girl** ich habe sie als schönes Mädchen in Erinnerung; **we must ~ that he's only a child** wir sollten bedenken, daß er noch ein Kind ist; **to ~ to do sth** daran denken, etw zu tun; **I can't ~ the word at the moment** das Wort fällt mir im Moment nicht ein; **here's something to ~ me by** da hast du etwas, das dich (immer) an mich erinnern wird; **I can never ~ phone numbers** ich kann mir Telefonnummern einfach nicht merken; **to ~ sb in one's will** jdn in seinem Testament bedenken. **(b)** *(commemorate)* gedenken *(+gen)*. **(c)** *(give good wishes to)* **~ me to your mother** grüßen Sie Ihre Mutter von mir; **he asks to be ~ed to you** er läßt Sie grüßen. **2** *vi* sich erinnern. **if I ~ right(ly)** *or* **aright** wenn ich mich recht erinnere *or* entsinne.

remembrance [rı'membrəns] *n* Erinnerung *f (of* an *+acc)*. **R~Day** *(Brit)* ≈ Volkstrauertag *m*; **in ~ of** zur Erinnerung an *(+acc)*.

remind [rı'maınd] *vt* erinnern *(of* an *+acc)*. **to ~ sb to do sth** jdn daran erinnern, etw zu tun; **that ~s me!** da(bei) fällt mir was ein.

reminder [rı'maındəʳ] *n (note etc)* Gedächtnisstütze *f*. **(letter of) ~** *(Comm)* Mahnung *f*; **to give sb a ~ to do sth** jdn daran erinnern, etw zu tun.

reminisce [,remı'nıs] *vi* sich in Erinnerungen ergehen *(about* über *+acc)*.

reminiscence [,remı'nısəns] *n* Erinnerung *f (of* an *+acc)*.

reminiscent [,remı'nısənt] *adj* **to be ~ of sth** an etw *(acc)* erinnern.

remiss [rı'mıs] *adj* nachlässig.

remission [rı'mıʃən] *n (Jur)* (Straf)erlaß *m*; *(Rel)* Nachlaß *m*. **he got 3 years' ~** ihm wurden 3 Jahre erlassen.

remit [rı'mıt] *vt* **(a)** *(cancel, pardon) debt, sentence, sins* erlassen. **(b)** *(send) money* überweisen. **(c)** *(Jur: transfer) case* verweisen *(to* an *+acc)*.

remittance [rı'mıtəns] *n* Überweisung *f (to* an *+acc)*.

remnant ['remnənt] *n* Rest *m*; *(fig: of splendour, custom)* Überrest *m*.

remonstrance [rı'mɒnstrəns] *n* Protest *m (with* bei, *against* gegen*)*.

remonstrate ['remənstreıt] *vi* protestieren *(against* gegen*)*. **to ~ with sb (about sth)** jdm Vorhaltungen (wegen etw) machen.

remorse [rı'mɔːs] *n* Reue *f (at, over* über *+acc)*. **without ~** *(merciless)* erbarmungslos.

remorseful [rı'mɔːsfʊl] *adj* reumütig, reuig.

remorseless [rı'mɔːslıs] *adj* reuelos; *(fig: merciless)* unbarmherzig.

remote [rı'məʊt] *adj (+er)* **(a)** entfernt; *(isolated)* abgelegen; *(in time)* fern; *(person)* unnahbar. **(b)** *(slight) possibility, resemblance* entfernt; *chance* gering.

remote: ~ control *n* Fernlenkung *f*; *(Rad, TV)* Fernbedienung *f*; **~-controlled** *adj* ferngesteuert; *(Rad, TV)* mit Fernbedienung.

remotely [rı'məʊtlı] *adv situated, related* entfernt. **it's just ~ possible** es ist gerade eben noch möglich; **they're not even ~ similar** sie sind sich nicht im entferntesten ähnlich.

removable [rı'muːvəbl] *adj cover, attachment* abnehmbar; *lining* abknöpfbar.

removal [rı'muːvəl] *n see vt* **(a)** Entfernung *f*; Abnahme *f*; Herausnehmen *nt*; Ausbau *m*. **(b)** Beseitigung *f*; Zerstreuung *f*. **(c)** Entfernung *f*. **(d)** *(move from house)* Umzug *m*.

removal van *n (Brit)* Möbelwagen *m*.

remove [rı'muːv] **1** *vt* **(a)** *(take off/away, Med)* entfernen *(from* aus*)*; *cover, attachments also, bandage, tie* abnehmen; *(take out)* herausnehmen *(from* aus*)*; *(Tech)* ausbauen *(from* aus*)*. **to ~ sth from sb** jdm etw wegnehmen; **to ~ a child from school** ein Kind von der Schule nehmen. **(b)** *(eradicate) threat, obstacle, problem* beseitigen; *doubt, suspicion* zerstreuen. **(c)** *(form: dismiss) official* entfernen. **(d) to be far ~d from ...** weit entfernt sein von ...; **a cousin twice ~d** ein Vetter zweiten Grades. **2** *vi (form: move house)* **to ~ to London** nach London (um)ziehen.

remover [rı'muːvəʳ] *n* **(a)** *(for nail varnish, stains etc)* Entferner *m*. **(b)** *(removal man)* Möbelpacker *m*.

remuneration [rı,mjuːnə'reıʃən] *n* Vergütung *f*; *(reward)* Belohnung *f*.

renaissance [rı'neısɑːns] *n* **the R ~** *(Hist)* die Renaissance.

rename [,riː'neım] *vt* umbenennen. **Petrograd was ~d Leningrad** Petrograd wurde in Leningrad umbenannt.

render ['rendəʳ] *vt* **(a)** *(form: give) service* leisten; *judgement* abgeben; *homage* erweisen. **(b)** *(interpret, translate)* wiedergeben; *(in writing)* übertragen; *music, poem also* vortragen. **(c)** *(form: make)* machen. **to ~ a bomb harmless** eine Bombe entschärfen.

rendering ['rendərıŋ] *n* Wiedergabe *f*; *(in writing)* Übertragung *f*; *(of piece of music, poem)* Vortrag *m*.

rendez-vous ['rɒndıvuː] **1** *n (place)* Treffpunkt *m*; *(agreement to meet)* Rendezvous *nt*. **2** *vi* sich treffen *(with* mit*)*; *(spaceships)* ein Rendezvousmanöver durchführen.

rendition [ren'dıʃən] *n (form)* = **rendering.**

renegade ['renıgeıd] **1** *n* Abtrünnige(r) *mf*. **2** *adj* abtrünnig.

renew [rı'njuː] *vt* erneuern; *contract, passport etc (authority)* verlängern; *(holder)* verlängern lassen; *discussions, attempts* wiederaufnehmen; *one's strength* wiederherstellen; *supplies* auffrischen. **to ~ a library book** ein Buch verlängern lassen; **to ~ one's acquaintance with sb** seine Bekanntschaft mit jdm auffrischen.

renewal [rı'njuːəl] *n see vt* Erneuerung *f*; Verlängerung *f*; Wiederaufnahme *f*; Wiederherstellung *f*; Auffrischung *f*.

renounce [rı'naʊns] *vt right, one's liberty* aufgeben; *religion, devil, opinions, cause* abschwören *(+dat)*; *(Rel) world* entsagen *(+dat)*.

renovate ['renəʊveıt] *vt building* renovieren; *painting, furniture* restaurieren.

renovation [,renəʊ'veıʃən] *n see vt* Renovierung *f*; Restaurierung *f*.

renown [rı'naʊn] *n* guter Ruf, Ansehen *nt*.

renowned [rı'naʊnd] *adj* berühmt *(for* für*)*.

rent [rent] **1** *n (for house, room)* Miete *f*; *(for farm, factory)* Pacht *f*. **for ~** zu vermieten/verpachten/verleihen. **2** *vt* **(a)** *(also vi) house, room* mieten; *farm, factory* pachten; *TV, car etc* leihen. **(b)** *(also* **~ out***)* vermieten; verpachten; verleihen.

rental ['rentl] *n (amount paid) (for house)* Miete *f*; *(for TV, car, boat etc also)* Leihgebühr *f*; *(for land)* Pacht *f*; *(income from rents)* Miet-/Pacht-/Leihgebühreinnahmen *pl*. **~ car** *(US)* Mietauto *nt*; **~ library** *(US)* Leihbücherei *f*.

renunciation [rı,nʌnsı'eıʃən] *n see* **renounce** Aufgabe *f*; Abschwören *nt*; Entsagung *f*.

reopen [,riː'əʊpən] **1** *vt* wieder öffnen; *shop, theatre, hostilities* wiedereröffnen; *debate, negotiations, (Jur) case* wiederaufnehmen. **2** *vi* wieder aufgehen; *(shop, theatre etc)* wieder aufmachen; *(negotiations)* wiederbeginnen.

reorganization [riː,ɔːgənaɪ'zeɪʃən] *n see vt* Umorganisation *f*; Umordnung *f*; Neueinteilung *f*; Neuaufbau *m*.
reorganize [,riː'ɔːgənaɪz] *vt* umorganisieren; *furniture, books* umordnen; *work* neu einteilen; *essay* neu aufbauen.
rep [rep] = **(a)** *(Theat)* **repertory** Repertoire-Theater *nt*. **(b)** *(Comm)* **representative** Vertreter(in *f*) *m*.
repaid [,riː'peɪd] *pret, ptp of* **repay.**
repair [rɪ'pɛəʳ] **1** *vt (lit, fig)* reparieren; *tyre also, clothes* flicken; *roof, wall also, road* ausbessern; *(fig) wrong, damage* wiedergutmachen. **2** *n see vt* Reparatur *f*; Flicken *nt*; Ausbesserung *f*. **to be under ~** *(car, machine)* in Reparatur sein; **to put sth in for ~** etw zur Reparatur bringen; **damaged beyond ~** nicht mehr zu reparieren; **closed for ~s** wegen Reparaturarbeiten geschlossen; **to be in good ~** in gutem Zustand sein; **state of ~** Zustand *m*.
repairable [rɪ'pɛərəbl] *adj* reparabel.
reparable ['repərəbl] *adj damage* reparabel, wiedergutzumachen; *loss* ersetzbar.
reparation [,repə'reɪʃən] *n (for damage)* Entschädigung *f*; *(usu pl: after war)* Reparationen *pl*; *(for wrong)* Wiedergutmachung *f*. **to make ~ for sth** etw wiedergutmachen.
repartee [,repɑː'tiː] *n* Schlagabtausch *m*; *(retort)* schlagfertige Antwort.
repatriate [,riː'pætrɪeɪt] *vt* in das Heimatland zurücksenden, repatriieren.
repatriation ['riː,pætrɪ'eɪʃən] *n* Repatriierung *f*.
repay [,riː'peɪ] *pret, ptp* **repaid** *vt money* zurückzahlen; *expenses* erstatten; *debt* abzahlen; *kindness* vergelten; *visit* erwidern. **how can I ever ~ you?** wie kann ich das jemals wiedergutmachen?
repayable [,riː'peɪəbl] *adj* rückzahlbar.
repayment [,riː'peɪmənt] *n (of money)* Rückzahlung *f*; *(of effort, kindness)* Lohn *m*.
repeal [rɪ'piːl] *vt law* aufheben.
repeat [rɪ'piːt] **1** *vt* wiederholen; *(tell to sb else)* weitersagen *(to sb* jdm*)*. **to ~ oneself** sich wiederholen; **don't ~ it to anyone** sag es nicht weiter; **to ~ an order** *(Comm)* nachbestellen; **this offer will never be ~ed!** dies ist ein einmaliges Angebot! **2** *n (Rad, TV)* Wiederholung *f*.
repeat: ~ order *n (Comm)* Nachbestellung *f*; **~ performance** *n (Theat)* Wiederholungsvorstellung *f*.
repel [rɪ'pel] *vt enemy* zurückschlagen; *sb's advance* abwehren; *water* abstoßen; *(disgust)* abstoßen.
repellent [rɪ'pelənt] *adj* **(a) ~ to water** wasserabstoßend. **(b)** *(disgusting)* abstoßend.
repent [rɪ'pent] *vi* Reue empfinden *(of* über *+acc)*.
repentance [rɪ'pentəns] *n* Reue *f*.
repentant [rɪ'pentənt] *adj look* reuevoll. **he was very ~** es reute ihn sehr.
repercussion [,riːpə'kʌʃən] *n (consequence)* Auswirkung *f (on* auf *+acc)*. **~s** *pl (of misbehaviour etc)* Nachspiel *nt*; **that is bound to have ~s** das wird Kreise ziehen.
repertoire ['repətwɑːʳ] *n* Repertoire *nt*.
repertory ['repətərɪ] *n (also* **~ theatre***)* Repertoire-Theater *nt*. **~ company** Repertoire-Ensemble *nt*.
repetition [,repɪ'tɪʃən] *n* Wiederholung *f*.
repetitious [,repɪ'tɪʃəs] *adj* sich wiederholend.
repetitive [rɪ'petɪtɪv] *adj* sich dauernd wiederholend; *work also* monoton. **to be ~** sich dauernd wiederholen.
replace [rɪ'pleɪs] *vt* **(a)** zurückstellen; *(put flat)* zurücklegen. **to ~ the receiver** *(Telec)* (den Hörer) auflegen. **(b)** *(substitute, renew)* ersetzen; *(employee: temporarily)* vertreten.
replacement [rɪ'pleɪsmənt] *n* **(a)** *see vt (a)* Zurückstellen *nt*; Zurücklegen *nt*. **(b)** *(substituting)* Ersatz *m*; *(by deputy)* Vertretung *f*. **~ part** Ersatzteil *nt*.
replay ['riːpleɪ] *(Sport)* **1** *n (recording)* Wiederholung *f*; *(match)* Wiederholungsspiel *nt*. **2** [,riː'pleɪ] *vt match, game* wiederholen.
replenish [rɪ'plenɪʃ] *vt* ergänzen; *glass* auffüllen.
replete [rɪ'pliːt] *adj (form: supplied)* reichlich versehen *(with* mit*)*.
replica ['replɪkə] *n* Kopie *f*; *(of ship, building etc)* Nachbildung *f*.
reply [rɪ'plaɪ] **1** *n (letter)* Antwort *f*; *(spoken also)* Erwiderung *f*. **in ~** (als Antwort) darauf; **in ~ to your letter** in Beantwortung Ihres Briefes *(form)*. **2** *vti* antworten; *(spoken also)* erwidern.
report [rɪ'pɔːt] **1** *n* **(a)** *(account, statement)* Bericht *m (on* über *+acc)*; *(Press, Rad, TV also)* Reportage *f (on* über *+acc)*. **to give a ~ on sth** Bericht über etw *(acc)* erstatten/eine Reportage über etw *(acc)* machen; **(school) ~** Zeugnis *nt*; **there is a ~ that ...** *(rumour)* es wird gesagt, daß ... **(b)** *(of gun)* Knall *m*.
2 *vt* **(a)** *results, findings* berichten über *(+acc)*; *(announce also)* melden *(to sb* jdm*)*. **he ~ed to me that ...** er meldete mir, daß ...; **the papers ~ed the crime as solved** laut Presseberichten ist das Verbrechen aufgeklärt; **he is ~ed as having said ...** er soll gesagt haben ...; **~ed speech** *(Gram)* indirekte Rede. **(b)** *(to sb* jdm*)* *(notify authorities of) accident, crime* melden; *(to police also)* anzeigen; *one's position* angeben. **to ~ sb for sth** jdn wegen etw melden.
3 *vi* **(a)** *(announce oneself)* sich melden. **to ~ for duty** sich zum Dienst melden; **to ~ sick** sich krank melden. **(b)** *(give a ~)* berichten, Bericht erstatten *(on* über *+acc)*. **(c)** *(be subordinate to)* **to ~ to sb** jdm unterstellt sein.
♦ **report back** *vi* **(a)** *(announce one's return)* sich zurückmelden. **(b)** *(give report)* Bericht erstatten *(to sb* jdm*)*.
reporter [rɪ'pɔːtəʳ] *n (Press, Rad, TV)* Reporter(in *f*); *(on the spot)* Korrespondent(in *f*) *m*.
repose [rɪ'pəuz] **1** *n (liter) (rest, peace)* Ruhe *f*; *(composure)* Gelassenheit *f*. **2** *vi (form, liter: rest, be buried)* ruhen.
reprehensible [,reprɪ'hensɪbl] *adj* tadelnswert.
represent [,reprɪ'zent] *vt* darstellen; *(symbolize also)* symbolisieren; *(act or speak for, Parl, Jur)* vertreten.
representation [,reprɪzen'teɪʃən] *n* **(a)** *no pl see vt* Darstellung *f*; Symbolisierung *f*; Vertretung *f*. **(b)** *(drawing, description, Theat)* Darstellung *f*. **(c) ~s** *pl (esp Pol: remonstrations)* Vorhaltungen *pl*; **the ambassador made ~s to the government** der Botschafter wurde bei der Regierung vorstellig.
representative [,reprɪ'zentətɪv] **1** *adj (of* für*)* repräsentativ; *attitude also* typisch; *(symbolic)* symbolisch. **2** *n (Comm)* Vertreter(in *f*) *m*; *(Jur)* Bevollmächtigte(r) *mf*; *(US Pol)* Abgeordnete(r) *mf* des Repräsentantenhauses.
repress [rɪ'pres] *vt revolt, population, laugh* unterdrücken; *emotions, desires also* zurückdrängen; *(Psych)* verdrängen.
repressed [rɪ'prest] *adj* unterdrückt; *(Psych)* verdrängt.
repression [rɪ'preʃən] *n* Unterdrückung *f*; *(Psych)* Verdrängung *f*.
repressive [rɪ'presɪv] *adj* repressiv.
reprieve [rɪ'priːv] **1** *n (Jur)* Begnadigung *f*; *(postponement)* Strafaufschub *m*; *(fig)* Gnadenfrist *f*. **2** *vt* **he was ~d** *(Jur)* er wurde begnadigt; *(sentence postponed)* seine Strafe wurde aufgeschoben; **the building/firm has been ~d for a while** das Gebäude/die Firma ist vorerst noch einmal verschont geblieben.
reprimand ['reprɪmɑːnd] **1** *n* Tadel *m*; *(official also)* Verweis *m*. **2** *vt* tadeln.
reprint [,riː'prɪnt] **1** *vt* neu auflegen, nachdrucken.

2 ['riːprɪnt] *n* Neuauflage *f*, Nachdruck *m*.
reprisal [rɪ'praɪzəl] *n (for* gegen*)* Vergeltungsmaßnahme *f*, Repressalie *f*. **to take ~s** zu Repressalien greifen; **as a ~ for** als Vergeltung für.
reproach [rɪ'prəʊtʃ] **1** *n (rebuke)* Vorwurf *m*. **above** *or* **beyond ~** über jeden Vorwurf erhaben. **2** *vt* Vorwürfe machen *(+dat)*. **to ~ sb for his mistake** jdm einen Fehler vorwerfen; **to ~ sb for having done sth** jdm Vorwürfe dafür machen, daß er etw getan hat.
reproachful [rɪ'prəʊtʃfʊl] *adj* vorwurfsvoll.
reprobate ['reprəʊbeɪt] *n* verkommenes Subjekt.
reprocessing plant [rɪ'prəʊsesɪŋplɑːnt] *n* Wiederaufbereitungsanlage *f*.
reproduce [ˌriːprə'djuːs] **1** *vt* wiedergeben; *(Art, mechanically also)* reproduzieren. **2** *vi (Biol)* sich vermehren.
reproduction [ˌriːprə'dʌkʃən] *n* **(a)** *(procreation)* Fortpflanzung *f*. **(b)** *(copy)* Reproduktion *f*; *(photo)* Kopie *f*; *(sound~)* Wiedergabe *f*. **~ furniture** (moderne) Stilmöbel *pl*.
reproof[1] ['riː'pruːf] *vt garment* frisch imprägnieren.
reproof[2] [rɪ'pruːf] *n* Tadel *m*, Rüge *f*.
reprove [rɪ'pruːv] *vt person, action* tadeln.
reptile ['reptaɪl] *n* Reptil *nt*.
republic [rɪ'pʌblɪk] *n* Republik *f*.
republican [rɪ'pʌblɪkən] **1** *adj* republikanisch. **2** *n* Republikaner(in *f*) *m*.
repudiate [rɪ'pjuːdɪeɪt] *vt person* verstoßen; *authorship, debt, obligation* nicht anerkennen; *accusation* zurückweisen.
repugnance [rɪ'pʌgnəns] *n* Widerwille *m (towards, for* gegen*)*.
repugnant [rɪ'pʌgnənt] *adj* widerlich, abstoßend.
repulse [rɪ'pʌls] *vt (Mil) enemy* abwehren.
repulsion [rɪ'pʌlʃən] *n (distaste)* Widerwille *m (for* gegen*)*.
repulsive [rɪ'pʌlsɪv] *adj (loathsome)* abstoßend.
reputable ['repjʊtəbl] *adj* ehrenhaft; *occupation* ordentlich, anständig; *dealer, firm* seriös.
reputation [ˌrepjʊ'teɪʃən] *n* Ruf *m*; *(bad ~)* schlechter Ruf. **what sort of ~ does she have?** wie ist ihr Ruf?; **to have a ~ for honesty** als ehrlich gelten.
repute [rɪ'pjuːt] **1** *n* Ruf *m*, Ansehen *nt*. **to be of good ~** einen guten Ruf genießen; **to be held in high ~** in hohem Ansehen stehen. **2** *vt (pass only)* **he is ~d to be ...** man sagt, daß er ... ist.
reputedly [rɪ'pjuːtɪdlɪ] *adj* wie man annimmt. **he is ~ the best player** er gilt als der beste Spieler.
request [rɪ'kwest] **1** *n* Bitte *f*, Ersuchen *nt (geh)*. **at sb's ~** auf jds Bitte *etc*; **by ~** auf Wunsch; **to make a ~ for sth** um etw bitten. **2** *vt* bitten um; *(Rad) record* sich *(dat)* wünschen. **to ~ sth of sb** jdn um etw bitten *or* ersuchen *(geh)*; **to ~ sb to do sth** jdn darum bitten, etw zu tun; **"you are ~ed not to smoke"** „bitte nicht rauchen".
request stop *n (Brit)* Bedarfshaltestelle *f*.
requiem ['rekwɪem] *n* Requiem *nt*.
require [rɪ'kwaɪəʳ] *vt* **(a)** *(need)* brauchen, benötigen; *action* erfordern; *(desire)* wünschen. **I have all I ~** ich habe alles, was ich brauche; **what qualifications are ~d?** welche Qualifikationen werden verlangt?; **to be ~d to do sth** etw machen müssen; **if ~d** falls erforderlich; **as and when ~d** nach Bedarf. **(b)** *(order)* **to ~ sb to do sth** von jdm verlangen, daß er/sie etw tut; **to ~ sth of sb** etw von jdm verlangen.
required [rɪ'kwaɪəd] *adj* erforderlich; *date* vorgeschrieben; *(desired)* gewünscht. **the ~ amount** die benötigte Menge.
requirement [rɪ'kwaɪəmənt] *n (need)* Bedarf *m no pl*; *(desire)* Wunsch *m*; *(condition, thing required)* Erfordernis *nt*. **to meet sb's ~s** jds Ansprüchen gerecht werden; **to fit the ~s** den Erfordernissen entsprechen.
requisite ['rekwɪzɪt] **1** *n* Erfordernis *nt*. **toilet ~s** Toilettenartikel *pl*. **2** *adj* erforderlich.
requisition [ˌrekwɪ'zɪʃən] **1** *n* Anforderung *f*; *(Mil)* Requisition *f*. **to make a ~ for sth** etw anfordern. **2** *vt* anfordern; *(Mil) supplies* requirieren.
rescind [rɪ'sɪnd] *vt* rückgängig machen; *law* aufheben.
rescue ['reskjuː] **1** *n (saving)* Rettung *f*; *(freeing)* Befreiung *f*. **to go/come to sb's ~** jdm zu Hilfe kommen. **2** *vt (save)* retten; *(free)* befreien. **you ~d me from a difficult situation** du hast mich aus einer schwierigen Lage gerettet; **the ~d** die Geretteten.
rescuer ['reskjʊəʳ] *n see vt* Retter(in *f*) *m*; Befreier(in *f*) *m*.
research [rɪ'sɜːtʃ] **1** *n* Forschung *f (into, on* über *+acc)*. **a piece of ~** eine Forschungsarbeit; **to do ~** forschen, Forschung betreiben. **2** *vi* forschen. **3** *vt* erforschen, untersuchen. **a well-~ed book** ein Buch *nt*, das auf solider Forschungsarbeit beruht.
research assistant *n* wissenschaftliche Hilfskraft.
researcher [rɪ'sɜːtʃəʳ] *n* Forscher(in *f*) *m*.
research: ~ student *n (Univ) Student, der Forschungen für einen höheren akademischen Grad betreibt,* ≈ Doktorand(in *f*) *m*; **~ worker** *n* Forscher *m*.
resemblance [rɪ'zembləns] *n* Ähnlichkeit *f*. **to bear a strong/no ~ to sb/sth** starke/keine Ähnlichkeit mit jdm/etw haben.
resemble [rɪ'zembl] *vt* gleichen *(+dat)*, ähnlich sein *(+dat)*.
resent [rɪ'zent] *vt remarks, behaviour* sich ärgern über *(+acc)*; *person* eine Abneigung haben gegen. **he ~ed the fact that ...** er ärgerte sich darüber, daß ...; **to ~ sb's success** jdm seinen Erfolg mißgönnen; **I ~ that** das gefällt mir nicht.
resentful [rɪ'zentfʊl] *adj* verärgert *(of* über *+acc)*; *(jealous)* neidisch *(of* auf *+acc)*. **he felt ~ about her promotion** er nahm es ihr übel, daß sie befördert worden war.
resentment [rɪ'zentmənt] *(of* über *+acc)* Verärgerung *f*; *(jealousy)* Neid *m*.
reservation [ˌrezə'veɪʃən] *n* **(a)** *(qualification of opinion)* Vorbehalt *m*. **without ~** ohne Vorbehalt. **with ~s** unter Vorbehalt(en); **to have ~s about sb/sth** Bedenken in bezug auf jdn/etw haben. **(b)** *(booking)* Reservierung *f*. **to make a ~ at the hotel** ein Zimmer im Hotel reservieren lassen; **to have a ~ (for a room)** ein Zimmer reserviert haben. **(c)** *(area of land)* Reservat *nt*. **(central) ~** *(Brit: on motorway)* Mittelstreifen *m*.
reserve [rɪ'zɜːv] **1** *vt* **(a)** *(keep)* aufsparen, aufheben. **to ~ one's strength** seine Kräfte sparen; **to ~ judgement** mit einem Urteil zurückhalten; **to ~ the right to do sth** sich *(dat)* (das Recht) vorbehalten, etw zu tun. **(b)** *(book in advance)* reservieren lassen. **2** *n* **(a)** *(store) (of* an *+dat)* Reserve *f*, Vorrat *m*; *(Fin)* Reserve *f*. **cash ~** Barreserve *f*; **world ~s of copper** die Weltreserven *pl* an Kupfer; **to have/keep in ~** in Reserve haben/halten. **(b) without ~** ohne Vorbehalt. **(c)** *(piece of land)* Reservat *nt*. **(d)** *(coolness, reticence)* Reserve *f*. **he treated me with some ~** er behandelte mich etwas reserviert. **(e)** *(Mil: force)* Reserve *f*. **the ~s** die Reserveeinheiten; *(Sport)* Reservespieler(in *f*) *m*.
reserved [rɪ'zɜːvd] *adj* **(a)** *(reticent)* zurückhaltend *(about* in bezug auf *+acc)*. **(b)** *room, seat* reserviert. **(c) all rights ~** alle Rechte vorbehalten.
reserve team *n* Reserve(mannschaft) *f*.
reservoir ['rezəvwɑːʳ] *n (lit) (for water)* Reservoir *nt*; *(fig: of knowledge etc)* Fundgrube *f (of* an *+dat)*.
reshuffle [ˌriː'ʃʌfl] *n* **Cabinet ~** *(Pol)* Kabinettsumbildung *f*.
reside [rɪ'zaɪd] *vi* **(a)** *(form: live)* seinen Wohnsitz

haben; *(monarch etc)* residieren. **(b)** *(fig)* **the power ~s in the President** die Macht ruht beim Präsidenten.

residence ['rezıdəns] *n* **(a)** *(house)* Wohnhaus *nt*; *(hostel: for students, nurses)* Wohnheim *nt*; *(of monarch, ambassador etc)* Residenz *f*. **(b)** *no pl* **country/place of ~** Aufenthaltsland *nt*/Wohnort *m*; **after 5 years' ~ in Britain** nach 5 Jahren Aufenthalt in Großbritannien; **to take up ~ in the capital** sich in der Hauptstadt niederlassen; **to be in ~** *(monarch, governor etc)* anwesend sein; **~ permit** Aufenthaltsgenehmigung *f*.

resident ['rezıdənt] **1** *n* Bewohner(in *f*) *m*; *(in town also)* Einwohner(in *f*) *m*; *(of institution also)* Insasse *m*, Insassin *f*; *(in hotel)* Gast *m*. **2** *adj (in country, town)* wohnhaft; *tutor* Haus-; *physician* Anstalts-. **they are ~ in Germany** sie haben ihren Wohnsitz in Deutschland.

residential [ˌrezı'denʃəl] *adj area* Wohn-; *job* im Haus; *college* mit einem Wohnheim verbunden; *course* mit Wohnung im Heim.

residual [rı'zıdjʊəl] *adj* restlich, Rest-.

resign [rı'zaın] **1** *vt* **(a)** *(give up) office, post* zurücktreten von; *claim, rights* verzichten auf *(+acc)*. **to ~ power** abtreten. **(b) to ~ oneself to sth/to doing sth** sich mit etw abfinden/sich damit abfinden, etw zu tun. **2** *vi (from public appointment* zurücktreten; *(employee)* kündigen. **to ~ from office** sein Amt niederlegen.

resignation [ˌrezıg'neıʃən] *n* **(a)** *see vi* Rücktritt *m*; Kündigung *f*. **to hand in** *or* **tender** *(form)* **one's ~** seinen Rücktritt/seine Kündigung einreichen/sein Amt niederlegen. **(b)** *(mental state)* Resignation *f (to* gegenüber *+dat)*.

resigned [rı'zaınd] *adj smile* resigniert. **to become ~ to sth** sich mit etw abfinden; **to be ~ to one's fate** sich in sein Schicksal ergeben haben.

resilience [rı'zılıəns] *n see adj* Federn *nt*; Unverwüstlichkeit *f*.

resilient [rı'zılıənt] *adj* **(a)** *material* federnd *attr*. **to be ~** federn. **(b)** *(fig) person, nature* unverwüstlich.

resin ['rezın] *n* Harz *nt*.

resist [rı'zıst] **1** *vt* **(a)** sich widersetzen *(+dat)*; *arrest, advances, attack, proposal, change also* sich wehren gegen. **(b)** *temptation, sb* widerstehen *(+dat)*. **I couldn't ~ (eating) another cake** ich konnte der Versuchung nicht widerstehen, noch ein Stück Kuchen zu essen. **(c)** *(wall, door)* standhalten *(+dat)*. **2** *vi see vt* **(a)** sich widersetzen; sich wehren. **(b)** widerstehen.

resistance [rı'zıstəns] *n (to* gegen*)* Widerstand *m (also Elec, Phys, Mil)*; *(Med)* Widerstandsfähigkeit *f*. **~ to water/heat** Wasser-/Hitzebeständigkeit *f*; **to meet with ~** auf Widerstand stoßen; **to offer no ~ (to sb/sth)** *(to attacker, advances etc)* (jdm/gegen etw) keinen Widerstand leisten.

resistant [rı'zıstənt] *adj material* strapazierfähig; *(Med)* immun *(to* gegen*)*. **water-~** wasserbeständig.

resolute ['rezəluːt] *adj* energisch; *answer* entschieden, bestimmt.

resolution [ˌrezə'luːʃən] *n* **(a)** *(decision)* Beschluß *m*; *(Pol, Admin etc also)* Resolution *f*; *(governing one's behaviour)* Vorsatz *m*. **good ~s** gute Vorsätze *pl*. **(b)** *no pl (resoluteness)* Entschlossenheit *f*. **(c)** *no pl (of problem)* Lösung *f*.

resolve [rı'zɒlv] **1** *vt* **(a)** *problem* lösen; *doubt* zerstreuen. **(b)** *(decide)* **to ~ that ...** beschließen, daß ...; **to ~ to do sth** beschließen, etw zu tun. **2** *n* **(a)** *(decision)* Beschluß *m*. **to make a ~ to do sth** den Beschluß fassen, etw zu tun. **(b)** *(resoluteness)* Entschlossenheit *f*.

resonance ['rezənəns] *n* Resonanz *f*; *(of voice)* voller Klang.

resonant ['rezənənt] *adj sound* voll; *voice* klangvoll; *room* mit Resonanz.

resort [rı'zɔːt] **1** *n* **(a)** *(recourse)* Ausweg *m*; *(thing, action resorted to also)* Rettung *f*. **without ~ to violence** ohne Gewaltanwendung; **as a last ~** als letztes; **in the last ~** im schlimmsten Fall. **(b)** *(place)* Urlaubsort *m*. **seaside ~** Seebad *nt*; **winter sports ~** Wintersportort *m*. **2** *vi* **to ~ to sth/sb** zu etw greifen/sich an jdn wenden; **to ~ to violence/theft** gewalttätig/zum Dieb werden; **to ~ to lying/swearing** sich aufs Lügen/Fluchen verlegen.

resound [rı'zaʊnd] *vi* (wider)halten *(with* von*)*.

resounding [rı'zaʊndıŋ] *adj noise, shout* widerhallend; *(fig) victory* gewaltig; *success* durchschlagend; *defeat* haushoch. **the response was a ~ "no"** die Antwort war ein überwältigendes „Nein".

resource [rı'sɔːs] *n* **(a) ~s** *pl (wealth, supplies, money etc)* Mittel, Ressourcen *pl*; **financial/mineral/natural ~s** Geldmittel *pl*/Bodenschätze *pl*/Naturschätze *pl*; **left to his own ~s** sich *(dat)* selbst überlassen. **(b)** *(expedient)* Ausweg *m*, Mittel *nt*. **as a last ~** als letzter Ausweg.

resourceful [rı'sɔːsfʊl] *adv person* einfallsreich, findig; *scheme* genial.

respect [rı'spekt] **1** *n* **(a)** *(esteem)* Respekt *m*, Achtung *f (for* vor *+dat)*. **to have/show ~ for** Respekt haben/zeigen vor *(+dat)*; **I have the highest ~ for his ability** ich halte ihn für außerordentlich fähig; **to hold sb in great ~** jdn sehr achten. **(b)** *(consideration)* Rücksicht *f (for* auf *+acc)*. **to treat with ~** *person* rücksichtsvoll behandeln; *dangerous person etc* sich in acht nehmen vor *(+dat)*; **out of ~ for** aus Rücksicht auf *(+acc)*; **with (due) ~, I still think that ...** bei allem Respekt meine ich dennoch, daß ... **(c)** *(reference)* **with ~ to ...** was ... anbetrifft, in bezug auf ... *(+acc)*. **(d)** *(aspect)* Hinsicht, Beziehung *f*. **in many ~s** in vieler Hinsicht. **(e) ~s** *pl (regards)* Empfehlungen *(geh)*, Grüße *pl*; **to pay one's last ~s to sb** jdm die letzte Ehre erweisen.

2 *vt* respektieren; *person, customs, privacy also* achten; *ability* anerkennen. **a ~ed company** eine angesehene Firma.

respectability [rıˌspektə'bılıtı] *n see adj (a)* Ehrbarkeit *f*; Ehrenhaftigkeit *f*; Anständigkeit *f*; Korrektheit *f*.

respectable [rı'spektəbl] *adj* **(a)** *person* ehrbar; *motives also* ehrenhaft; *district* anständig; *clothes, behaviour* korrekt. **in ~ society** in guter Gesellschaft. **(b)** *(large) income* ansehnlich. **(c)** *(fairly good) advantage* beträchtlich; *score* beachtlich.

respectably [rı'spektəblı] *adv dress, behave* anständig.

respectful [rı'spektfʊl] *adj* respektvoll *(towards* gegenüber*)*.

respecting [rı'spektıŋ] *prep* bezüglich *(+gen)*.

respective [rı'spektıv] *adj* jeweilig.

respectively [rı'spektıvlı] *adv* **they cost £50 and £60 ~** sie kosten £ 50 beziehungsweise £ 60.

respiration [ˌrespı'reıʃən] *n (Bot, Med)* Atmung *f*.

respiratory [rı'spaıərətərı] *adj* Atem-; *organs, problem* Atmungs-.

respite ['respaıt] *n (easing off)* Nachlassen *nt*. **without ~** ohne Unterbrechung; **to give sb no ~** jdm keine Ruhe lassen.

resplendent [rı'splendənt] *adj* glänzend, strahlend; *clothes* prächtig.

respond [rı'spɒnd] *vi* **(a)** *(reply)* antworten. **to ~ to a question** eine Frage beantworten. **(b)** *(show reaction)* reagieren *(to* auf *+acc)*. **to ~ to an appeal** einen Appell beantworten; **to ~ to a call** einem Ruf folgen; **the patient did not ~ to the treatment** der Patient sprach auf die Behandlung nicht an.

response [rı'spɒns] *n (reply)* Antwort, Erwiderung *f*; *(reaction)* Reaktion *f*; *(Eccl)* Antwort *f*. **in ~ (to)** in Erwiderung *(+gen)* *(geh)*.

responsibility [rɪˌspɒnsəˈbɪlɪtɪ] *n* **(a)** *no pl* Verantwortung *f*. **to take (full) ~ (for sth)** die (volle) Verantwortung (für etw) übernehmen; **that's his ~** dafür ist er verantwortlich. **(b)** *(duty, burden)* Verpflichtung *f (to* für*)*.

responsible [rɪˈspɒnsəbl] *adj* **(a)** verantwortlich; *(to blame also)* schuld *(for* an *+dat)*. **what's ~ for the hold-up?** woran liegt die Verzögerung?; **she is not ~ for her actions** *(esp Jur)* sie ist für ihre Handlungen nicht voll verantwortlich; **to hold sb ~ for sth** jdn für etw verantwortlich machen; **to be directly ~ to sb** jdm unmittelbar unterstellt sein. **(b)** *(trustworthy)* verantwortungsbewußt; *(involving responsibility) job* verantwortungsvoll.

responsive [rɪˈspɒnsɪv] *adj person, audience* interessiert; *steering* leicht ansprechend. **to be ~ to sth** auf etw *(acc)* reagieren *or* ansprechen; **he wasn't very ~** *(to my complaint)* er ging kaum darauf ein.

rest[1] [rest] **1** *n* **(a)** *(relaxation)* Ruhe *f*; *(pause)* Pause *f*; *(on holiday etc)* Erholung *f*. **a day of ~** ein Ruhetag *m*; **to need ~** Ruhe brauchen; **I need a ~** ich muß mich ausruhen; *(vacation)* ich brauche Urlaub; **to have a ~** *(relax)* (sich) ausruhen; *(pause)* (eine) Pause machen. **(b) to be at ~** *(peaceful)* ruhig sein; *(immobile)* sich in Ruhelage/-stellung befinden; *(euph: dead)* ruhen; **to put** *or* **set sb's mind at ~** jdn beruhigen; **to come to ~** *(ball, car etc)* zum Stillstand kommen; *(bird, insect)* sich niederlassen; *(gaze, eyes)* hängenbleiben *(upon* an *+dat)*. **(c)** *(Mus)* Pause *f*.

2 *vi* **(a)** sich ausruhen; *(pause)* Pause machen; *(euph: be buried)* ruhen. **he will not ~ until he discovers the truth** er wird nicht (eher) ruhen, bis er die Wahrheit gefunden hat; **to let a matter ~** eine Sache auf sich beruhen lassen; **may he ~ in peace** er ruhe in Frieden.

(b) *(decision, responsibility etc)* liegen *(with* bei*)*. **the matter must not ~ there** man kann die Sache so nicht belassen; **~ assured that ...** Sie können versichert sein, daß ...

(c) *(lean: person, head, ladder)* lehnen *(on* an *+dat, against* gegen*)*; *(roof etc, eyes, gaze)* ruhen *(on* auf *+dat)*; *(fig: be based) (argument, case)* sich stützen *(on* auf *+acc)*; *(reputation)* beruhen *(on* auf *+dat)*.

3 *vt one's eyes* ausruhen; *voice* schonen; *horses* ausruhen lassen; *ladder* lehnen *(against* gegen, *on* an *+acc)*; *elbow, (fig) theory, suspicions* stützen *(on* auf *+acc)*. **God ~ his soul** Gott hab ihn selig!

rest[2] *n (remainder)* **the ~** der Rest, das übrige/die übrigen; **the ~ of the money/meal** das übrige Geld/Essen; **the ~ of us/them** die übrigen, die anderen; **all the ~ of the money** das ganze übrige Geld; **all the ~ of the books** alle übrigen Bücher; **and all the ~ of it** *(col)* und so weiter und so fort; **for the ~** im übrigen.

restaurant [ˈrestərɔ̃ːŋ] *n* Restaurant *nt*. **~ car** *(Brit Rail)* Speisewagen *m*.

rest: ~ cure *n* Erholung *f*; *(in bed)* Liegekur *f*; **~ day** *n* Ruhetag *m*.

restful [ˈrestfʊl] *adj occupation, pastime etc* erholsam; *colour* ruhig; *place* friedlich.

rest-home [ˈrest,həʊm] *n* Pflegeheim *nt*.

restitution [ˌrestɪˈtjuːʃən] *n* **(a)** *(giving back)* Rückgabe *f*; *(of money also)* Rückerstattung *f*. **(b)** *(reparation)* Entschädigung *f*.

restive [ˈrestɪv] *adj* unruhig; *(restless) person, manner* rastlos.

restless [ˈrestlɪs] *adj person, sea* unruhig; *(not wanting to stay in one place)* rastlos.

restoration [ˌrestəˈreɪʃən] *n* **(a)** *(return)* Rückgabe *f (to* an *+acc)*; *(of property also)* Rückerstattung *f (to* an *+acc)*; *(of confidence, order etc)* Wiederherstellung *f*; *(to office)* Wiedereinsetzung *f (to* in *+acc)*. **(b) the R~** *(Hist)* die Restauration.

restore [rɪˈstɔːʳ] *vt* **(a)** *(give back)* zurückgeben; *confidence, order* wiederherstellen. **to ~ sb to health** jds Gesundheit wiederherstellen; **~d to health** wiederhergestellt; **to ~ sth to its former condition** etw wiederherstellen. **(b)** *(to former post)* wiedereinsetzen *(to* in *+acc)*. **to ~ to power** wieder an die Macht bringen. **(c)** *(repair)* restaurieren.

restorer [rɪˈstɔːrəʳ] *n (Art)* Restaurator(in *f*) *m*.

restrain [rɪˈstreɪn] *vt person* zurückhalten; *prisoner* mit Gewalt festhalten; *animal, children* bändigen. **to ~ sb from doing sth** jdn davon abhalten, etw zu tun; **to ~ oneself** sich beherrschen.

restrained [rɪˈstreɪnd] *adj emotions* unterdrückt; *manner, words* beherrscht; *tone* verhalten; *criticism* maßvoll.

restraint [rɪˈstreɪnt] *n* **(a)** *(restriction)* Einschränkung, Beschränkung *f*. **without ~** unbeschränkt; *develop* ungehemmt; **wage ~** Zurückhaltung *f* bei Lohnforderungen. **(b)** *(moderation)* Beherrschung *f*. **to show a lack of ~** wenig Beherrschung zeigen.

restrict [rɪˈstrɪkt] *vt* beschränken *(to* auf *+acc)*; *time, number also* begrenzen *(to* auf *+acc)*.

restricted [rɪˈstrɪktɪd] *adj view* beschränkt, begrenzt; *(Admin, Mil) information* geheim; *locality* nur bestimmten Gruppen zugänglich. **~ area** *(Brit Mot)* Strecke *f* mit Geschwindigkeitsbeschränkung; *(Mil etc)* Sperrgebiet *nt*.

restriction [rɪˈstrɪkʃən] *n see vt (on gen)* Beschränkung *f*; Begrenzung *f*. **without ~s** uneingeschränkt; **price ~** Preisbeschränkung *f*.

restrictive [rɪˈstrɪktɪv] *adv* restriktiv, einschränkend *attr*.

result [rɪˈzʌlt] **1** *n* **(a)** Folge *f*. **as a ~ he failed** folglich fiel er durch; **as a ~ of which he ...** was zur Folge hatte, daß er ...; **to be the ~ of** resultieren aus. **(b)** *(outcome)* Ergebnis, Resultat *nt*. **~s** *(of test, experiment)* Werte *pl*; **to get ~s** *(person)* Resultate erzielen; **as a ~ of my inquiry** auf meine Anfrage (hin); **what was the ~?** *(Sport)* wie ist es ausgegangen?; **without ~** ergebnislos. **2** *vi* sich ergeben, resultieren *(from* aus*)*.

♦ **result in** *vi +prep obj* führen zu. **this ~ed ~ his being late** das führte dazu, daß er zu spät kam.

resultant [rɪˈzʌltənt] *adj* resultierend.

resume [rɪˈzjuːm] **1** *vt* **(a)** *(restart) activity* wiederaufnehmen; *journey* fortsetzen. **to ~ work** die Arbeit wiederaufnehmen. **(b)** *command, possession* wieder übernehmen. **to ~ one's seat** seinen Platz wieder einnehmen. **2** *vi (classes, work etc)* wieder beginnen.

résumé [ˈreɪzjuːmeɪ] *n* Zusammenfassung *f*; *(US: curriculum vitae)* Lebenslauf *m*.

resumption [rɪˈzʌmpʃən] *n (of activity)* Wiederaufnahme *f*; *(of command, possession)* erneute Übernahme; *(of journey)* Fortsetzung *f*; *(of classes)* Wiederbeginn *m*.

resurrection [ˌrezəˈrekʃən] *n (revival)* Wiederbelebung *f*; *(Rel)* Auferstehung *f*.

resuscitate [rɪˈsʌsɪteɪt] *vt (Med)* wiederbeleben; *(fig)* beleben.

retail [ˈriːteɪl] **1** *n* Einzelhandel *m*. **2** *vt* im Einzelhandel verkaufen. **3** *vi (goods)* **to ~ at ...** im Einzelhandel ... kosten. **4** *adv* im Einzelhandel.

retailer [ˈriːteɪləʳ] *n* Einzelhändler *m*.

retail: ~ outlet *n* Einzelhandelsverkaufsstelle *f*; **~ price** *n* Einzelhandelspreis *m*.

retain [rɪˈteɪn] *vt* **(a)** *(keep)* behalten; *money, possession, person* zurück(be)halten; *custom* bewahren; *(dam) water* stauen. **to ~ control (of sth)** etw weiterhin in der Gewalt haben. **(b)** *(remember)* sich *(dat)* merken; *(computer) information* speichern.

retainer [rɪˈteɪnəʳ] *n (fee)* Honorar *nt; (advance)* Vorschuß *m*.

retaliate [rɪˈtælɪeɪt] *vi* Vergeltung üben; *(for bad treatment, insults etc)* sich revanchieren *(against*

sb an jdm); *(in battle)* zurückschlagen; *(Sport, in fight, in argument)* kontern.
retaliation [rɪˌtælɪˈeɪʃən] *n* Vergeltung *f*; *(in fight also)* Vergeltungsschlag *m*; *(in argument, diplomacy etc)* Konterschlag *m*. **in ~** zur Vergeltung; **that's my ~ for what you did** das ist meine Revanche für das, was du getan hast.
retarded [rɪˈtɑːdɪd] *adj (Med)* zurückgeblieben.
retch [retʃ] *vi* würgen.
retentive [rɪˈtentɪv] *adj memory* aufnahmefähig.
reticence [ˈretɪsəns] *n* Zurückhaltung *f*.
reticent [ˈretɪsənt] *adj* zurückhaltend.
retina [ˈretɪnə] *n, pl* **-e** [ˈretɪniː] *or* **-s** Netzhaut *f*.
retinue [ˈretɪnjuː] *n* Gefolge *nt*.
retire [rɪˈtaɪəʳ] **1** *vi* **(a)** *(give up work)* aufhören zu arbeiten; *(civil servant)* sich pensionieren lassen; *(self-employed)* sich zur Ruhe setzen; *(soldier)* aus der Armee ausscheiden; *(singer, player etc)* (zu singen/spielen etc*)* aufhören. **(b)** *(withdraw, Mil)* sich zurückziehen; *(Sport)* aufgeben; *(Ftbl etc)* vom Feld gehen. **to ~ into oneself** sich in sich *(acc)* selbst zurückziehen. **2** *vt* aus Altersgründen entlassen; *civil servant, military officer* pensionieren, in den Ruhestand versetzen.
retired [rɪˈtaɪəd] *adj* **(a)** pensioniert, im Ruhestand; *soldier* aus der Armee ausgeschieden. **(b)** *(secluded) life* zurückgezogen.
retiree [ˌrɪtaɪˈriː] *n (US)* Rentner(in *f*) *m*.
retirement [rɪˈtaɪəmənt] *n (stopping work)* Ausscheiden *nt* aus dem Arbeitsleben *(form)*; *(of civil servant, military officer)* Pensionierung *f*; *(state)* Ruhestand *m*. **~ at 65** Altersgrenze bei 65; **to announce one's ~** sein Ausscheiden (aus seinem Beruf/seiner Stellung *etc*) ankündigen; **how will you spend your ~?** was tun Sie, wenn Sie pensioniert *or* im Ruhestand sind?
retirement age *n* Altersgrenze *f*.
retiring [rɪˈtaɪərɪŋ] *adj* **(a)** *(shy)* zurückhaltend. **(b) ~ age = retirement age.**
retort [rɪˈtɔːt] **1** *n* **(a)** *(answer)* scharfe Erwiderung *or* Antwort. **(b)** *(Chem)* Retorte *f*. **2** *vti* scharf erwidern.
retrace [rɪˈtreɪs] *vt past, development* zurückverfolgen. **to ~ one's steps** denselben Weg zurückgehen.
retract [rɪˈtrækt] **1** *vt (withdraw) offer* zurückziehen; *statement* zurücknehmen; *claws, undercarriage* einziehen. **2** *vi* einen Rückzieher machen; *(claws)* eingezogen werden.
retread [ˈriːˌtred] *n (tyre)* laufflächenerneuerter Reifen.
retreat [rɪˈtriːt] **1** *n* **(a)** *(Mil)* Rückzug *m*. **to beat a ~** *(Mil)* den Rückzug antreten; *(fig)* das Feld räumen. **(b)** *(place)* Zuflucht(sort *m*) *f*. **he has gone to his country ~** er hat sich aufs Land zurückgezogen. **2** *vi (Mil)* den Rückzug antreten; *(in fear)* zurückweichen; *(flood, glacier)* zurückgehen.
retrench [rɪˈtrentʃ] **1** *vt expenditure* einschränken; *personnel* einsparen. **2** *vi* sich einschränken.
retrial [riːˈtraɪəl] *n (Jur)* Wiederaufnahmeverfahren *nt*.
retribution [ˌretrɪˈbjuːʃən] *n* Vergeltung *f*. **in ~** als Vergeltung.
retrieval [rɪˈtriːvəl] *n see vt* Zurück-/Hervor-/Heraus-/Herunterholen *nt*; Rettung *f*; Bergung *f*; Rückgewinnung *f*; Abfragen *nt*; Wiedererlangen *nt*; Wiedergutmachen *nt*.
retrieve [rɪˈtriːv] *vt* **(a)** *(recover)* zurück-/hervor-/heraus-/herunterholen; *(rescue)* retten; *(from wreckage etc)* bergen; *material from waste* zurückgewinnen; *(Comp) information* abfragen; *honour, position* wiedererlangen; *loss* wiedergutmachen. **(b)** *(dog)* apportieren.
retriever [rɪˈtriːvəʳ] *n (dog)* Retriever *m*.
retroactive [ˌretrəʊˈæktɪv] *adj* rückwirkend.
retrograde [ˈretrəʊgreɪd] *adj* rückläufig; *policy* rückschrittlich. **~ step** Rückschritt *m*.
retrorocket [ˈretrəʊˈrɒkɪt] *n* Bremsrakete *f*.
retrospect [ˈretrəʊspekt] *n* **in ~** im Rückblick; **everything looks different in ~** im nachhinein sieht alles anders aus.
retrospective [ˌretrəʊˈspektɪv] *adj thought* rückblickend; *(Admin, Jur) pay rise* rückwirkend.
return [rɪˈtɜːn] **1** *vi (come back: person, vehicle)* zurück- *or* wiederkommen; *(go back) (person)* zurückgehen; *(vehicle)* zurückfahren; *(symptoms, doubts, fears)* wieder auftreten. **to ~ to a subject** auf ein Thema zurückkommen; **to ~ home** nach Hause kommen/gehen, heimkehren *(geh)*.

2 *vt* **(a)** *(give back)* zurückgeben *(to sb* jdm*)*; *(bring or take back)* zurückbringen *(to sb* jdm*)*; *(put back)* zurücksetzen/-stellen/-legen; *(send back) (to* an *+acc) letter etc* zurückschicken; *(refuse) cheque* zurückweisen; *ball* zurückschlagen/-werfen; *salute, visit, compliment* erwidern. **to ~ goods to the shop** Waren in das Geschäft zurückbringen; **to ~ fire** *(Mil)* das Feuer erwidern. **(b)** *(reply)* erwidern. **(c)** *(declare) details of income* angeben. **to ~ a verdict of guilty/not guilty (on sb)** *(Jur)* (jdn) schuldig sprechen/freisprechen. **(d)** *(Fin) income* einbringen; *profit, interest* abwerfen. **(e)** *(Brit Parl) candidate* wählen.

3 *n* **(a)** *(of person, vehicle, seasons)* Rückkehr *f*; *(of illness)* Wiederauftreten *nt*. **on my ~** bei meiner Rückkehr; **by ~ (of post)** postwendend; **many happy ~s (of the day)!** herzlichen Glückwunsch zum Geburtstag!

(b) *(giving/bringing/taking/sending back) see vt (a)* Rückgabe *f*; Zurückbringen *nt*; Zurücksetzen/-stellen/-legen *nt*; Zurückschicken *nt*; Zurückweisen *nt*; Zurückschlagen *nt*/-werfen *nt*; Erwiderung *f*.

(c) *(profit)* Einkommen *nt (on* aus*)*; *(from land, mine etc)* Ertrag *m*. **~s** *(profits)* Gewinn *m*; *(receipts)* Einkünfte *pl*; **~ on capital** *(Fin)* Kapitalertrag *m*.

(d) *(fig: recompense)* **in ~** dafür; **in ~ for** für; **to do sb a kindness in ~** sich bei jdm für einen Gefallen revanchieren.

(e) *(act of declaring: of verdict, election results)* Verkündung *f*. **the (election) ~s** das Wahlergebnis; **tax ~** Steuererklärung *f*.

(f) = ~ ticket.
returnable [rɪˈtɜːnəbl] *adj bottle* Mehrweg-; *(with deposit)* Pfand-.
return fare *n* Preis *m* für eine Rückfahrkarte *or (Aviat)* einen Rückflugschein.
returning officer [rɪˈtɜːnɪŋˈɒfɪsəʳ] *n (Brit Parl)* Wahlleiter *m*.
return: ~ journey *n* Rückreise *f*; *(both ways)* Hin- und Rückreise *f*; **~ match** *n* Rückspiel *nt*; **~ ticket** *n (Brit)* Rückfahrkarte *f*; *(Aviat)* Rückflugschein *m*.
reunion [rɪˈjuːnjən] *n* **(a)** *(coming together)* Wiedervereinigung *f*. **(b)** *(gathering)* Zusammenkunft *f*. **a family ~** ein Familientreffen *nt*.
reunite [ˌriːjuːˈnaɪt] **1** *vt* wiedervereinigen. **they were ~d at last** sie waren endlich wieder vereint. **2** *vi (countries, parties)* sich wiedervereinigen; *(people)* wieder zusammenkommen.
Rev [rev] = **Reverend.**
rev [rev] **1** *n* = **revolution** *(Aut)* Umdrehung *f*. **~ counter** Drehzahlmesser *m*. **2** *vti* **to ~ (up)** *(driver)* den Motor auf Touren bringen; *(noisily)* den Motor aufheulen lassen; *(engine)* aufheulen.
revalue [ˌriːˈvæljuː] *vt (Fin)* aufwerten
revamp [ˌriːˈvæmp] *vt (col) book, play* aufpolieren *(col)*; *house, room* aufmöbeln.
reveal [rɪˈviːl] *vt (make visible)* zum Vorschein bringen; *(show)* zeigen; *(make known) truth, facts* enthüllen; *one's identity* zu erkennen geben; *ignorance, knowledge* erkennen lassen. **I cannot ~ to you what he said** ich kann Ihnen nicht verraten, was er gesagt hat.

revealing [rɪ'viːlɪŋ] *adj* aufschlußreich; *dress, neckline* offenherzig *(hum)*.
reveille [rɪ'vælɪ] *n (Mil)* Wecksignal *nt*.
revel ['revl] *vi (make merry)* feiern. **to ~ in doing sth** seine wahre Freude daran haben, etw zu tun.
revelation [ˌrevə'leɪʃən] *n* Enthüllung *f*; *(Rel)* Offenbarung *f*. **it was a ~ to me** das hat mir die Augen geöffnet.
revelry ['revlrɪ] *n usu pl* Festlichkeit *f*.
revenge [rɪ'vendʒ] **1** *n* Rache *f*; *(Sport)* Revanche *f*. **to take ~ on sb (for sth)** sich an jdm (für etw) rächen; **to get one's ~** sich rächen. **2** *vt insult, murder, sb* rächen. **to ~ oneself on sb (for sth)** sich (für etw) an jdm rächen.
revenue ['revənjuː] *n (of state)* Staatseinkünfte *pl*; *(tax ~)* Steueraufkommen *nt*; *(of individual)* Einkünfte *pl*; *(department)* Finanzbehörde *f*.
reverberate [rɪ'vɜːbəreɪt] *vi (sound)* widerhallen.
reverberation [rɪˌvɜːbə'reɪʃən] *n (of sound)* Widerhall *m*.
revere [rɪ'vɪəʳ] *vt* verehren.
reverence ['revərəns] **1** *n* Ehrfurcht *f*. **2** *vt* verehren.
Reverend ['revərənd] *adj* **the ~ Robert Martin** ≃ Pfarrer Robert Martin.
reverent ['revərənt] *adj* ehrfürchtig.
reverie ['revərɪ] *n (liter)* Träumereien *pl*. **he fell into a ~** er kam ins Träumen.
reversal [rɪ'vɜːsəl] *n* Umkehrung *f*; *(of verdict also)* Umstoßung *f*.
reverse [rɪ'vɜːs] **1** *adj (opposite)* umgekehrt; *direction* entgegengesetzt; *(Opt) image* seitenverkehrt. **in ~ order** in umgekehrter Reihenfolge; **~ gear** *(Aut)* Rückwärtsgang *m*.
2 *n* **(a)** *(opposite)* Gegenteil *nt*. **quite the ~!** ganz im Gegenteil! **(b)** *(back)* Rückseite *f*; *(of cloth also)* linke Seite. **(c)** *(setback, loss)* Rückschlag *m*; *(defeat)* Niederlage *f*. **(d)** *(Aut)* Rückwärtsgang *m*. **in ~** im Rückwärtsgang.
3 *vt* **(a)** *(turn about) order, situation* umkehren; *objects, sentences also* umstellen; *garment* wenden; *result also* umdrehen. **to ~ the charges** *(Brit Telec)* ein R-Gespräch führen; **~d charge call** R-Gespräch *nt*. **(b) to ~ one's car into the garage/into a tree** rückwärts in die Garage/gegen einen Baum fahren. **(c)** *trend, policy* umkehren; *verdict also* umstoßen.
4 *vi (car)* rückwärts fahren. **reversing lights** Rückfahrscheinwerfer *pl*.
reversible [rɪ'vɜːsəbl] *adj decision* umstoßbar; *(Phys, Chem)* umkehrbar; *garment* Wende-. **~ cloth** Doubleface *m or nt*.
revert [rɪ'vɜːt] *vi (to former state)* zurückkehren *(to* zu*)*; *(to bad state)* zurückfallen *(to* in *+acc)*; *(to topic)* zurückkommen *(to* auf *+acc)*; *(Jur: property)* zurückfallen *(to* an *+acc)*.
review [rɪ'vjuː] **1** *n* **(a)** *(looking back)* Rückblick *m (of* auf *+acc)*; *(report)* Überblick *m (of* über *+acc)*. **I shall keep your case under ~** ich werde Ihren Fall im Auge behalten. **(b)** *(re-examination)* nochmalige Prüfung. **the agreement comes up for ~ next year** das Abkommen wird nächstes Jahr nochmals geprüft. **(c)** *(Mil: inspection)* Inspektion *f*. **(d)** *(of book, play etc)* Kritik, Rezension *f*. **(e)** *(magazine)* Zeitschrift *f*. **2** *vt* **(a)** *(look back at) one's life etc* zurückblicken auf *(+acc)*. **(b)** *(re-examine) case* erneut (über)prüfen. **(c)** *(Mil) troops* inspizieren. **(d)** *book, play, film* besprechen, rezensieren.
revile [rɪ'vaɪl] *vt* schmähen, verunglimpfen.
revise [rɪ'vaɪz] **1** *vt opinion, estimate* überholen, revidieren; *text* revidieren, überarbeiten. **~d edition** überarbeitete Ausgabe. **2** *vi (Brit)* (den Stoff) wiederholen.
revision [rɪ'vɪʒən] *n* **(a)** *(of opinion, estimate)* Revidieren *nt*. **(b)** *(of proofs)* Revision, Überarbeitung *f*. **(c)** *(Brit: for exam)* Wiederholung *f* (des Stoffs). **(d)** *(revised version)* überarbeitete Ausgabe.
revival [rɪ'vaɪvəl] *n (from faint)* Wiederbelebung *f*. **there has been a ~ of interest in ...** das Interesse an ... ist wieder wach geworden; **an economic ~** ein wirtschaftlicher Wiederaufschwung.
revive [rɪ'vaɪv] **1** *vt person (from fainting, fatigue)* (wieder *or* neu) beleben; *(from near death)* wiederbeleben; *custom, hatred* wiederaufleben lassen; *friendship, word, old play* wiederaufnehmen. **2** *vi (person) (from fainting)* wieder zu sich kommen; *(from fatigue)* wieder aufleben, wieder munter werden; *(hope, feelings)* wiederaufleben; *(business, trade)* wiederaufblühen.
revoke [rɪ'vəʊk] *vt law* aufheben; *order, promise* zurückziehen; *decision* rückgängig machen; *licence* entziehen.
revolt [rɪ'vəʊlt] **1** *n* Revolte *f*, Aufstand *m*. **to be in ~ (against)** rebellieren (gegen). **2** *vi (rebel)* rebellieren *(against* gegen*)*. **3** *vt* abstoßen, anekeln *(col)*. **I was ~ed by it** es hat mich angeekelt.
revolting [rɪ'vəʊltɪŋ] *adj (repulsive)* abstoßend; *meal, story* ekelhaft; *(col: unpleasant) weather, colour* scheußlich; *person* widerlich.
revolution [ˌrevə'luːʃən] *n* **(a)** *(Pol, fig)* Revolution *f*. **(b)** *(turn)* Umdrehung *f*. **4,000 ~s per minute** eine Drehzahl von 4.000 pro Minute.
revolutionary [ˌrevə'luːʃnərɪ] **1** *adj (lit, fig)* revolutionär. **2** *n* Revolutionär *m*.
revolutionize [ˌrevə'luːʃənaiz] *vt* revolutionieren.
revolve [rɪ'vɒlv] **1** *vt* drehen. **2** *vi* sich drehen. **to ~ on an axis/around the sun** sich um eine Achse/um die Sonne drehen; **he thinks everything ~s around him** *(fig)* er glaubt, alles drehe sich nur um ihn.
revolver [rɪ'vɒlvəʳ] *n* Revolver *m*.
revolving [rɪ'vɒlvɪŋ] *in cpds* Dreh-.
revue [rɪ'vjuː] *n (Theat)* Revue *f*; *(satirical)* Kabarett *nt*.
revulsion [rɪ'vʌlʃən] *n (disgust)* Abscheu, Ekel *m (at* vor *+dat)*.
reward [rɪ'wɔːd] **1** *n* Belohnung *f*. **one of the ~s of this job** einer der Vorzüge dieser Arbeit; **~ offered for the return of ...** Finderlohn für ... **2** *vt* belohnen.
rewarding [rɪ'wɔːdɪŋ] *adj (financially)* lohnend, einträglich; *(morally)* lohnend; *work* dankbar.
rewind [ˌriː'waɪnd] *pret, ptp* **rewound** *vt thread* wieder aufwickeln; *film, tape* zurückspulen. **~ button** Rückspultaste *f*.
rewire [ˌriː'waɪəʳ] *vt* neu verkabeln.
rhapsody ['ræpsədɪ] *n (Mus)* Rhapsodie *f*; *(fig)* Schwärmerei *f*.
rhesus ['riːsəs] *n* **~ monkey** Rhesusaffe *m*; **~ factor** Rhesusfaktor *m*.
rhetoric ['retərɪk] *n* Rhetorik *f*; *(pej)* Phrasendrescherei *f (pej)*.
rhetorical [rɪ'tɒrɪkəl] *adj* rhetorisch; *(pej)* phrasenhaft. **~ question** rhetorische Frage.
rheumatic [ruː'mætɪk] *adj pains* rheumatisch; *joint* rheumakrank.
rheumatism ['ruːmətɪzəm] *n* Rheuma(tismus *m*) *nt*.
rheumatoid ['ruːmətɔɪd] *adj* **~ arthritis** Gelenkrheumatismus *m*.
Rhine [raɪn] *n* Rhein *m*.
rhino ['raɪnəʊ] *n* = **rhinoceros.**
rhinoceros [raɪ'nɒsərəs] *n* Nashorn, Rhinozeros *nt*.
rhododendron [ˌrəʊdə'dendrən] *n* Rhododendron *m or nt*.
rhubarb ['ruːbɑːb] *n* Rhabarber *m*.
rhyme [raɪm] **1** *n* Reim *m*; *(poem)* Gedicht *nt*. **without ~ or reason** ohne Sinn und Verstand; **in ~** in Versen. **2** *vi* sich reimen.
rhythm ['rɪðm] *n* Rhythmus *m*.
rhythmic(al) ['rɪðmɪk(əl)] *adj* rhythmisch.
rib [rɪb] **1** *n* **(a)** *(Anat, Cook, of leaf)* Rippe *f*. **(b)**

(Knitting) Rippen *pl.* **2** *vt (tease)* necken, foppen.
ribald ['rɪbəld, 'raɪbəld] *adj* deftig; *behaviour* derb; *company* liederlich.
ribbon ['rɪbən] *n (for hair, dress)* Band *nt*; *(for typewriter)* Farbband *nt*; *(on medal)* Ordensband *nt*; *(fig: narrow strip)* Streifen *m*.
rice [raɪs] *n* Reis *m*.
rice *in cpds* Reis-; ~ **paper** *n* Reispapier *nt*; ~ **pudding** *n* Milchreis *m*.
rich [rɪtʃ] **1** *adj (+er)* reich; *decoration, clothes* prächtig; *food* schwer; *soil* fett; *land* fruchtbar; *colour* satt; *sound, voice* voll; *wine* schwer. ~ **in vitamins** vitaminreich; ~ **in minerals** reich an Bodenschätzen; ~ **in examples** mit vielen Beispielen; **that's** ~! *(iro)* das ist ja großartig! **2** *n* **(a) the** ~ *pl* die Reichen *pl*. **(b)** ~**es** Reichtümer *pl*.
richly ['rɪtʃlɪ] *adv dress, decorate* prächtig. **he was** ~ **rewarded** *(lit)* er wurde reich belohnt; *(fig)* er wurde reichlich belohnt.
richness ['rɪtʃnɪs] *n see adj* Reichtum *m*; Pracht *f*; Schwere *f*; Fruchtbarkeit *f*; Sattheit *f*; Fülle *f*; Schwere *f*.
rickets ['rɪkɪts] *n sing* Rachitis *f*.
rickety ['rɪkɪtɪ] *adj furniture etc* wackelig.
rickshaw ['rɪkʃɔː] *n* Rikscha *f*.
ricochet ['rɪkəʃeɪ] **1** *n* Abprall *m*. **2** *vi* abprallen *(off* von*)*.
rid [rɪd] *pret, ptp* ~ *or* ~**ded** *vt* **to** ~ **oneself of sb/sth** jdn/etw loswerden; *of pests also* sich von etw befreien; *of ideas, prejudice etc* sich von etw lösen; **to get** ~ **of sb/sth** jdn/etw loswerden; **get** ~ **of it** sieh zu, daß du das loswirst; *(throw it away)* schmeiß es weg *(col)*.
riddance ['rɪdəns] *n* **good** ~! *(col)* ein Glück, daß wir das/den *etc* los sind.
ridden ['rɪdn] *ptp of* **ride**.
riddle[1] ['rɪdl] *vt* **to** ~ **sb/sth with bullets** jdn/etw mit Kugeln durchlöchern; ~**d with holes** völlig durchlöchert.
riddle[2] *n* Rätsel *nt*. **to speak in** ~**s** in Rätseln sprechen.
ride [raɪd] *(vb: pret* **rode**, *ptp* **ridden***)* **1** *n (in vehicle, on bicycle)* Fahrt *f*; *(on horse)* Ritt *m*; *(for pleasure)* Ausritt *m*. **to go for a** ~ eine Fahrt machen; reiten gehen; **to go for a** ~ **in the car** eine Fahrt (mit dem Auto) machen; **to take sb for a** ~ *(in car etc)* mit jdm eine Fahrt machen; *(col)* jdn anschmieren *(col)*; **he gave me a** ~ **into town in his car** er nahm mich im Auto in die Stadt mit; **thanks for the** ~ danke fürs Mitnehmen.

2 *vi* **(a)** *(on a horse etc)* reiten *(on* auf *+dat)*; *(go in vehicle, by cycle etc)* fahren. **to go riding** reiten gehen; **to** ~ **on a bus/in a car/in a train** in einem Bus/Wagen/Zug fahren. **(b) he's riding high** *(fig)* er schwimmt ganz oben; **to** ~ **at anchor** *(ship)* vor Anker liegen; **to let things** ~ den Dingen ihren Lauf lassen.

3 *vt horse* reiten. **to** ~ **a bike** Fahrrad fahren; **they had ridden 10 km** sie waren 10 km geritten/gefahren; **we rode the bus into town** *(esp US)* wir fuhren mit dem Bus in die Stadt.

♦**ride out** *vt sep* überstehen. **to** ~ ~ **the storm** *(lit, fig)* den Sturm überstehen.
♦**ride up** *vi* **(a)** *(horseman)* heranreiten; *(motorcyclist etc)* heranfahren. **(b)** *(skirt etc)* hochrutschen.
rider ['raɪdə[r]] *n* **(a)** *(on horse)* Reiter(in *f*) *m*; *(on bicycle, motorcycle)* Fahrer(in *f*) *m*. **(b)** *(addition)* Zusatz *m*; *(to document)* Zusatzklausel *f*.
ridge [rɪdʒ] *n (of hills, mountains)* Rücken, Kamm *m*; *(pointed, steep)* Grat *m*; *(of roof)* First *m*; *(of nose)* Rücken *m*; *(raised edge)* Rand *m*. **a** ~ **of hills** eine Hügelkette; **a** ~ **of high pressure** *(Met)* ein Hochdruckkeil *m*.
ridge pole *n (of tent)* Firststange *f*.
ridicule ['rɪdɪkjuːl] *n* Spott *m*. **to hold sb/sth up to** ~ sich über jdn/etw lustig machen.
ridiculous [rɪ'dɪkjʊləs] *adj* lächerlich. **don't be** ~ red keinen Unsinn.
ridiculously [rɪ'dɪkjʊləslɪ] *adv* lächerlich; *expensive* wahnsinnig *(col)*.
riding ['raɪdɪŋ] *n* Reiten *nt*. **I enjoy** ~ ich reite gern.
rife [raɪf] *adj disease, corruption* weitverbreitet. **to be** ~ grassieren; *(rumour)* umgehen.
riffraff ['rɪfræf] *n* Pöbel *m*, Gesindel *nt*.
rifle[1] ['raɪfl] *vt (also* ~ **through***) sb's pockets, drawer, house* durchwühlen.
rifle[2] *n (gun)* Gewehr *nt*; *(for hunting)* Büchse *f*.
rifle range *n* Schießstand *m*.
rift [rɪft] *n* **(a)** Spalt *m*. **(b)** *(fig: in friendship)* Riß *m*; *(Pol also)* Spalt *m*.
rig [rɪg] **1** *n (oil* ~*)* (Öl)förderturm *m*; *(offshore)* Ölbohrinsel *f*. **2** *vt (fig) election, market etc* manipulieren.
♦**rig out** *vt sep (col: clothe)* ausstaffieren *(col)*.
♦**rig up** *vt sep ship* auftakeln; *equipment* aufbauen; *(fig) (make)* improvisieren; *(arrange)* arrangieren.
rigging ['rɪgɪŋ] *n (Naut)* Tauwerk *nt*.
right [raɪt] **1** *adj* **(a)** *(just, fair)* richtig. **he thought it** ~ **to warn me** er hielt es für richtig, mich zu warnen; **it's only** ~ **(and proper)** es ist nur recht und billig.

(b) *(true, correct) answer, time* richtig. **to be** ~ *(person)* recht haben; *(answer, solution)* richtig sein; *(clock)* richtig gehen; **you're quite** ~ Sie haben ganz recht; **let's get it** ~ **this time** diesmal muß es klappen; **you were** ~ **to refuse** Sie hatten recht, als Sie ablehnten; **on the** ~ **track** *(fig)* auf dem rechten Weg; **to put** ~ *error* korrigieren; *clock* richtig stellen; *situation* wieder in Ordnung bringen; **to put sb** ~ jdn berichtigen.

(c) *(proper) clothes, document* richtig. **what's the** ~ **thing to do in this case?** was tut man da am besten?; **to come at the** ~ **time** zur rechten Zeit kommen; **to do sth the** ~ **way** etw richtig machen; **the** ~**word** das rechte *or* richtige Wort; **the** ~ **man for the job** der richtige Mann für die Stelle; **to know the** ~ **people** die richtigen Leute kennen.

(d) *(well)* **the medicine soon put him** ~ die Medizin hat ihn schnell wieder auf die Beine gebracht; **I don't feel quite** ~ **today** ich fühle mich heute nicht ganz wohl; **to be as** ~ **as rain** *(Brit)* kerngesund sein; **to be in one's** ~ **mind** klar bei Verstand sein.

(e) *(phrases)* ~! ~**-oh!** *(Brit col)*, ~ **you are!** *(Brit col)* gut, okay *(col)*; **that's** ~! *(correct, true)* das stimmt!; ~ **enough!** (das) stimmt!; **it's a** ~ **mess in there** *(col)* das ist vielleicht ein Durcheinander hier *(col)*; **he's a** ~ **fool!** *(col)* er ist wirklich doof *(col)*; **you're a** ~ **one** *(col)* du bist mir der Richtige *(col)*.

(f) *(opposite of left)* rechte(r, s). ~ **hand** rechte Hand; **I'd give my** ~ **hand to know the answer** ich würde was drum geben, wenn ich die Antwort wüßte *(col)*.

2 *adv* **(a)** *(straight, directly)* direkt; *(exactly also)* genau. ~ **in front of you** direkt vor Ihnen; ~ **away** *(immediately)* sofort; ~ **off** *(at the first attempt)* auf Anhieb *(col)*; ~ **now** *(at this very moment)* in diesem Augenblick; *(immediately)* sofort; ~ **here** genau hier; ~ **in the middle** genau in der/die Mitte; ~ **at the beginning** gleich am Anfang.

(b) *(completely, all the way)* ganz. **rotten** ~ **through** durch und durch verfault *or (fig)* verdorben; ~ **the way around the city** um die ganze Stadt.

(c) *(correctly)* richtig. **to answer** ~ richtig antworten; **if I remember** ~ wenn ich mich recht erinnere; **if everything goes** ~ wenn alles klappt *(col)*.

(d) *(Pol)* **the R~ Honourable John Smith MP** der Abgeordnete John Smith.

(e) *(opposite of left)* rechts. **turn ~** biegen Sie rechts ab; **~ of centre** *(Pol)* rechts von der Mitte; **~, left and centre** *(everywhere)* überall.

3 *n* **(a)** *no pl (moral, legal)* Recht *nt*. **he doesn't know ~ from wrong** er kann Recht und Unrecht nicht auseinanderhalten; **to be in the ~** im Recht sein.

(b) *(entitlement)* Recht *nt*; *(to sth also)* Anrecht *nt*. **(to have) a** *or* **the ~ to do sth** ein *or* das Recht haben, etw zu tun; **what ~ have you to say that?** mit welchem Recht sagen Sie das?; **he is within his ~s** das ist sein gutes Recht; **by ~s** von Rechts wegen; **in one's own ~** selber, selbst.

(c) to put *or* **set sth to ~s** etw (wieder) in Ordnung bringen.

(d) *(not left)* rechte Seite; *(punch)* Rechte *f*. **to drive on the ~** rechts fahren; **to keep to the ~** sich rechts halten; **on my ~** rechts (von mir); **the R~** *(Pol)* die Rechte.

4 *vt* **(a)** *(return to upright position)* aufrichten. **(b)** *(make amends for) wrong* wiedergutmachen. **the problem should ~ itself** *(fig)* das Problem müßte sich von selbst lösen.

right: ~ angle *n* rechter Winkel; **at ~ angles (to)** rechtwinklig (zu); **~-angled** ['raɪt,æŋgld] *adj* rechtwinklig.

righteous ['raɪtʃəs] *adj* rechtschaffen; *(pej)* selbstgerecht *(pej)*; *indignation* gerecht.

rightful ['raɪtfʊl] *adj heir, owner* rechtmäßig; *punishment* gerecht.

right: ~-hand drive *adj* rechtsgesteuert; **~-handed** *adj person* rechtshändig; **~-hand man** *n* rechte Hand; **~-hand side** *n* rechte Seite.

rightly ['raɪtlɪ] *adv* **(a)** *(correctly)* **he said, ~, that ...** er sagte sehr richtig, daß ...; **I don't ~ know** ich weiß nicht genau. **(b)** *(justifiably)* mit *or* zu Recht. **~ or wrongly** ob das nun richtig ist/war oder nicht; **and ~ so** und zwar mit Recht.

right: ~-minded *adj* vernünftig; **~ of way** *n (across property)* Durchgangsrecht *nt*; *(Mot: priority)* Vorfahrt *f*; **he has the ~ of way** *(Mot)* er hat Vorfahrt; **~ wing** *n (Sport, Pol)* rechter Flügel; **~-winger** *n (Sport)* Rechtsaußen *m*; *(Pol)* Rechte(r) *mf*.

rigid ['rɪdʒɪd] *adj (lit) material, frame* starr, steif; *(fig) person* streng, stur *(pej)*; *discipline, principles* streng, strikt; *(inflexible)* unbeugsam; *specifications* genau festgelegt, strikt; *system* starr, unbeugsam.

rigmarole ['rigmərəʊl] *n* Gelaber *nt*; *(process)* Gedöns *nt (col)*. **to go through the whole ~ again** nochmal mit demselben Gelaber/Gedöns anfangen.

rigor mortis ['rɪgə'mɔːtɪs] *n* die Leichenstarre.

rigorous ['rɪgərəs] *adj character, discipline* streng, strikt; *measures* rigoros; *(accurate)* peinlich genau; *analysis, tests* gründlich; *climate* streng.

rigour, *(US)* **rigor** ['rɪgəʳ] *n* **(a)** *no pl (strictness)* Strenge, Striktheit *f*. **(b) ~s** *pl (of climate, famine etc)* Unbilden *pl*.

rim [rɪm] *n (of cup, bowl)* Rand *m*; *(of hat also)* Krempe *f*; *(of spectacles also)* Fassung *f*; *(of wheel)* Felge *f*.

rimless ['rɪmlɪs] *adj spectacles* randlos.

rind [raɪnd] *n (of cheese)* Rinde *f*; *(of bacon)* Schwarte *f*; *(of fruit)* Schale *f*.

ring[1] [rɪŋ] **1** *n* **(a)** Ring *m*; *(in tree trunk)* Jahresring *m*. **to stand in a ~** im Kreis stehen; **to run ~s around sb** *(col)* jdn in die Tasche stecken *(col)*. **(b)** *(group) (Pol)* Gruppe *f*; *(of dealers, spies)* Ring *m*. **(c)** *(enclosure) (at circus)* Manege *f*; *(Sport, at exhibition)* Ring *m*. **2** *vt (surround)* umringen; *(put ~ on or round) item on list etc* einkreisen; *bird* beringen.

ring[2] *(vb: pret* **rang,** *ptp* **rung) 1** *n* **(a)** *(sound)* Klang *m*; *(~ing: of bell, alarm)* Läuten *nt*; *(of electric bell, alarm clock, phone)* Klingeln *nt*; *(metallic sound: of swords etc)* Klirren *nt*. **there was a ~ at the door** es hat geklingelt. **(b)** *(esp Brit Telec)* Anruf *m*. **to give sb a ~** jdn anrufen. **(c)** *(fig)* Klang *m*. **his voice had an angry ~ (in** *or* **to it)** seine Stimme klang etwas böse; **that has the ~ of truth (about it)** das klingt sehr wahrscheinlich.

2 *vi* **(a)** *see n (a)* klingen; läuten; klingen; klirren; *(hammers)* schallen. **the (door)bell rang** es hat geklingelt; **to ~ for sb** (nach) jdm läuten; **please ~ for attention** bitte klingeln. **(b)** *(esp Brit Telec)* anrufen. **(c)** *(sound, resound) (words, voice)* tönen; *(music, singing also)* erklingen *(geh)*. **to ~ false/true** falsch/wahr klingen; **my ears are ~ing** mir klingen die Ohren.

3 *vt* **(a)** *bell* läuten. **~ the doorbell** (an der Tür) klingeln; **his name ~s a bell** *(fig col)* sein Name kommt mir bekannt vor; **to ~ the changes (on sth)** *(fig)* etw in allen Variationen durchspielen. **(b)** *(esp Brit: also* **~ up***)* anrufen.

♦ **ring back** *vti sep (esp Brit)* zurückrufen.

♦ **ring off** *vi (esp Brit Telec)* auflegen.

♦ **ring out** *vi* ertönen; *(bell also)* laut erklingen; *(shot also)* krachen; *(sound above others)* herausklingen.

♦ **ring up** *vt sep (esp Brit Telec)* anrufen.

ring binder *n* Ringbuch *nt*.

ring-finger ['rɪŋ'fɪŋgəʳ] *n* Ringfinger *m*.

ringing ['rɪŋɪŋ] **1** *adj voice, tone* schallend. **~ tone** *(Brit Telec)* Rufzeichen *nt*. **2** *n (of bell)* Läuten *nt*; *(of electric bell also, of phone)* Klingeln *nt*; *(in ears)* Klingen *nt*.

ringleader ['rɪŋ,liːdəʳ] *n* Anführer(in *f*) *m*.

ringlet ['rɪŋlɪt] *n* Ringellocke *f*.

ring: ~master *n* Zirkusdirektor *m*; **~ road** *n (Brit)* Umgehung(sstraße) *f*.

rink [rɪŋk] *n* Eisbahn *f*; *(roller-skating ~)* Rollschuhbahn *f*.

rinse [rɪns] **1** *n* Spülung *f*; *(colorant)* Tönung *f*. **2** *vt* **(a)** *clothes, hair* spülen; *plates* abspülen; *cup, mouth, basin* ausspülen. **to ~ one's hands** sich *(dat)* die Hände abspülen. **(b)** *(colour with a ~) hair* tönen.

♦ **rinse out** *vt sep* ausspülen, auswaschen. **to ~ ~ one's mouth** sich *(dat)* den Mund ausspülen.

riot ['raɪət] **1** *n (Pol)* Aufstand, Aufruhr *m no pl*; *(by mob etc)* Krawall *m*; *(fig: wild occasion)* Orgie *f*. **to run ~** *(people)* randalieren; *(vegetation)* wuchern; **his imagination runs ~** seine Phantasie geht mit ihm durch; **to read sb the ~ act** *(fig)* jdm die Leviten lesen; **the ~ police** die Bereitschaftspolizei. **2** *vi* randalieren; *(revolt)* einen Aufruhr machen.

rioter ['raɪətəʳ] *n* Randalierer *m*; *(Pol)* Aufrührer *m*.

riotous ['raɪətəs] *adj* **(a)** *person, crowd* randalierend; *living, behaviour, child* wild. **(b)** *(col)* wild *(col)*; *(hilarious)* urkomisch *(col)*.

riotously ['raɪətəslɪ] *adv behave* wild. **it was ~ funny** *(col)* es war zum Schreien *(col)*.

rip [rɪp] **1** *n* Riß *m*; *(made by knife etc)* Schlitz *m*. **2** *vt material* einen Riß machen in *(+acc)*; *(stronger)* zerreißen; *(vandalize) pictures etc* zerschlitzen. **you've ~ped your jacket** du hast dir die Jacke zerrissen; **to ~ open** aufreißen; *(with knife)* aufschlitzen. **3** *vi* **(a)** *(cloth)* reißen. **(b)** *(col)* **he let ~ at me** er ist auf mich losgegangen *(col)*.

♦ **rip off** *vt sep* **(a)** *(lit)* abreißen *(prep obj* von*)*; *clothing* herunterreißen. **(b)** *(col) person* ausnehmen *(col)*.

♦ **rip up** *vt sep* zerreißen; *road* aufreißen.

rip-cord ['rɪp,kɔːd] *n* Reißleine *f*.

ripe [raɪp] *adj (+er) fruit, cheese* reif. **to live to a ~ old age** ein hohes Alter erreichen; **to be ~ for sth** *(fig)* für etw reif sein.

ripen ['raɪpən] **1** *vt (lit, fig)* reifen lassen. **2** *vi* reifen.

rip-off ['rɪpɒf] *n (col)* Wucher *m*; *(cheat)* Schwindel *m*. **it's a ~** das ist Wucher/Schwindel.

riposte [rɪ'pɒst] *n (retort)* scharfe Antwort.

ripple ['rɪpl] **1** *n* kleine Welle; *(noise)* Plätschern *nt*; *(of waves)* Klatschen *nt*. **2** *vi (undulate: water)* sich kräuseln; *(murmur: water)* plätschern; *(waves)* klatschen. **3** *vt water* kräuseln.

rip-roaring ['rɪp'rɔːrɪŋ] *adj (col)* sagenhaft *(col)*.

rise [raɪz] *(vb: pret* **rose,** *ptp* **risen)** **1** *n* **(a)** *(increase) (in gen)* Anstieg *m*, Steigen *nt no pl*; *(in number)* Zunahme *f*; *(in prices, wages, bank rate also)* Steigerung *f*; *(St Ex)* Aufschwung *m*. **a (pay) ~** *(Brit)* eine Gehaltserhöhung; **a ~ in the population** ein Bevölkerungszuwachs *m*; **to take a ~ out of sb** *(col)* jdn auf den Arm nehmen *(col)*.
(b) *(of theatre curtain)* Heben *nt*; *(of sun)* Aufgehen *nt*; *(to fame, power etc)* Aufstieg *m (to* zu*)*.
(c) *(small hill)* Erhebung *f*; *(slope)* Steigung *f*.
(d) *(origin) (of river)* Ursprung *m*. **to give ~ to sth** etw verursachen; *to questions* etw aufwerfen; *to complaints* Anlaß zu etw geben.
2 *vi* **(a)** *(get up) (from sitting, lying)* aufstehen, sich erheben *(geh)*; *(from the dead)* auferstehen. **to ~ from the table** vom Tisch aufstehen.
(b) *(go up)* steigen; *(smoke also)* aufsteigen; *(prices, temperature etc also)* ansteigen *(to* auf *+acc)*; *(theatre curtain)* sich heben; *(sun, bread)* aufgehen; *(voice) (in volume)* sich erheben; *(in pitch)* höher werden; *(fig) (hopes)* steigen; *(anger)* wachsen. **to ~ to the surface** an die Oberfläche kommen; **he won't ~ to any of your taunts** er läßt sich von dir nicht reizen; **to ~ in price** im Preis steigen; **her spirits rose** ihre Stimmung hob sich.
(c) *(ground)* ansteigen; *(mountains)* sich erheben. **the mountain ~s to 3,000 metres** der Berg erhebt sich auf 3.000 m.
(d) *(fig: in society, rank)* **to ~ from nothing** sich aus dem Nichts hocharbeiten; **he rose to be President** er stieg zum Präsidenten auf.
(e) *(adjourn) (assembly)* auseinandergehen; *(meeting)* beendet sein. **the House rose at 2 a.m.** *(Parl)* das Haus beendete die Sitzung um 2 Uhr morgens.
(f) *(originate: river)* entspringen.
(g) *(also* **~ up)** *(revolt: people)* sich empören, sich erheben. **to ~ (up) in protest/anger (at sth)** *(people)* sich protestierend (gegen etw) erheben/ sich (gegen etw) empören. **to ~ (up) in revolt (against sb/sth)** (gegen jdn/etw) rebellieren.

risen ['rɪzn] *ptp of* **rise.**

riser ['raɪzə^{r}] *n (person)* **to be an early/late ~** Frühaufsteher(in *f*)/Langschläfer(in *f*) *m* sein.

rising ['raɪzɪŋ] **1** *n* **(a)** *(rebellion)* Aufstand *m*. **(b)** *(of sun)* Aufgehen *nt*; *(of barometer, prices)* (An)steigen *nt*; *(from dead)* Auferstehung *f*. **2** *adj* **(a)** *sun* aufgehend; *tide, barometer, prices, hopes* steigend; *anger, fury* wachsend. **~ damp** Bodenfeuchtigkeit *f*. **(b)** *(fig)* **a ~ politician** ein kommender Politiker; **the ~ generation** die kommende Generation.

risk [rɪsk] **1** *n* Risiko *nt*. **to take** *or* **run ~s/a ~** Risiken/ein Risiko eingehen; **to take** *or* **run the ~ of doing sth** das Risiko eingehen, etw zu tun; **there is no ~ of his coming** *or* **that he will come** es besteht keine Gefahr, daß er kommt; **at one's own ~** auf eigene Gefahr; **at the ~ of seeming stupid** auf die Gefahr hin, dumm zu erscheinen; **to put sb/sth at ~** jdn gefährden/etw riskieren; **fire ~** Feuerrisiko. **2** *vt* riskieren, aufs Spiel setzen; *life also* wagen; *defeat, accident* riskieren. **she won't ~ coming today** sie wird es heute nicht riskieren, zu kommen; **I'll ~ it** das riskiere ich, ich lasse es darauf ankommen.

risky ['rɪskɪ] *adj (+er) enterprise, deed* riskant. **it's a ~ business** das ist riskant.

risqué ['riːskeɪ] *adj* pikant, gewagt.

rissole ['rɪsəʊl] *n* ≃ Frikadelle *f*.

rite [raɪt] *n* Ritus *m*. **burial ~s** Bestattungsriten *pl*.

ritual ['rɪtjʊəl] **1** *adj* rituell; *laws, objects, killing* Ritual-. **2** *n* Ritual *nt*.

rival ['raɪvəl] **1** *n* Rivale *m*, Rivalin *f (for* um, *to* für*)*; *(Comm)* Konkurrent(in *f*) *m*. **2** *adj (to* für*) claims, attraction* konkurrierend; *firm* Konkurrenz-. **3** *vt (in love, for affections)* rivalisieren mit; *(Comm)* konkurrieren mit. **I can't ~ that** da kann ich nicht mithalten.

rivalry ['raɪvəlrɪ] *n* Rivalität *f*; *(Comm)* Konkurrenzkampf *m*.

river ['rɪvə^{r}] *n* Fluß *m*; *(major)* Strom *m*. **down/up ~** flußabwärts/-aufwärts; **the ~ Rhine** *(Brit)*, **the Rhine ~** *(US)* der Rhein.

river *in cpds* Fluß-; **~bed** *n* Flußbett *nt*; **~side** *n* Flußufer *nt*; **by the ~side** am Fluß.

rivet ['rɪvɪt] **1** *n* Niete *f*. **2** *vt (lit)* nieten; *two things* vernieten; *(fig) audience, attention* fesseln. **his eyes were ~ed to the screen** sein Blick war auf den Bildschirm geheftet; **~ed (to the spot) with fear** vor Angst wie festgenagelt.

rivet(t)ing ['rɪvɪtɪŋ] *adj (fig)* fesselnd.

RN = **Royal Navy.**

road [rəʊd] *n* **(a)** Straße *f*. **"~ up"** „Straßenbauarbeiten"; **by ~** *(send sth)* per Spedition; *(travel)* mit dem Bus/Auto *etc*; **she lives across the ~ (from us)** sie wohnt gegenüber (von uns); **my car is off the ~ just now** mein Auto ist momentan in der Werkstatt; **this vehicle shouldn't be on the ~** das Fahrzeug ist nicht verkehrstüchtig; **to be on the ~** *(travelling)* unterwegs sein; *(theatre company)* auf Tournee sein; *(car)* fahren; **is this the ~ to London?** geht es hier nach London?; **the London ~** die Straße nach London; **to have one for the ~** *(col)* zum Abschluß noch einen trinken.
(b) *(fig)* Weg *m*. **you're on the right ~** Sie sind auf dem richtigen Weg; **on the ~ to success** auf dem Weg zum Erfolg; **somewhere along the ~ he changed his mind** irgendwann hat er seine Meinung geändert; **(get) out of the ~!** *(dial col)* geh weg!; **any ~** *(dial col)* = **anyhow.**

road *in cpds* Straßen-; **~block** *n* Straßensperre *f*; **~ haulage** *n* Spedition *f*; **~hog** *n (col)* Verkehrsrowdy *m (col)*; **~holding** *n* Straßenlage *f*; *(of tyres)* Griffigkeit *f*; **~roller** *n* Straßenwalze *f*; **~ safety** *n* Verkehrssicherheit *f*; **~ sense** *n* Verkehrssinn *m*; **~side 1** *n* Straßenrand *m*; **by the ~side** am Straßenrand; **2** *adj stall* an der Straße; **~sign** *n* Verkehrszeichen *nt*; **~sweeper** *n* Straßenkehrer(in *f*) *m*; **~ transport** *n* Straßengüterverkehr *m*; **~-user** *n* Verkehrsteilnehmer *m*; **~way** *n* Fahrbahn *f*; **~works** *npl* Straßenbauarbeiten *pl*; **~worthy** *adj* verkehrstüchtig.

roam [rəʊm] **1** *vt streets, countryside* wandern *or* ziehen durch. **2** *vi* (herum)wandern.

roar [rɔː^{r}] **1** *vi (person, crowd, lion)* brüllen *(with* vor *+dat)*; *(fire)* prasseln; *(wind, engine)* heulen; *(sea)* tosen; *(thunder)* toben. **to ~ at sb** jdn anbrüllen; **the trucks ~ed past** die Lastwagen donnerten vorbei; **they ~ed with laughter** sie brüllten vor Lachen. **2** *n* **(a)** *no pl see vi* Gebrüll *nt*; Prasseln *nt*; Heulen *nt*; Tosen *nt*; Toben *nt*. **~s of laughter** brüllendes Gelächter.

roaring ['rɔːrɪŋ] *adj see vi* brüllend; prasselnd; heulend; tosend; tobend. **the ~ Twenties** die wilden zwanziger Jahre; **a ~ success** ein Bombenerfolg *m (col)*; **to do a ~ trade (in sth)** ein Riesengeschäft *nt* (mit etw) machen.

roast [rəʊst] **1** *n* Braten *m*. **pork ~** Schweinebraten *m*. **2** *adj pork, veal* gebraten; *chicken* Brat-, gebraten; *potatoes* in Fett im Backofen gebraten. **~ beef** Roastbeef *nt*. **3** *vt meat* braten; *coffee beans* rösten. **to be ~ed alive** *(fig)* sich totschwitzen *(col)*. **4** *vi (meat)* braten; *(col: person)* irrsinnig schwitzen *(col)*; *(in sun)* in der Sonne braten.

rob [rɒb] *vt person* bestehlen; *(more seriously)* berauben; *shop, bank* ausrauben. **to ~ sb of sth** *(lit fig)* jdm etw rauben; *(lit also)* jdm etw stehlen;

I've been ~bed! ich bin bestohlen worden!; *(had to pay too much)* ich bin geneppt worden *(col).*

robber ['rɒbəʳ] *n* Räuber *m.*

robbery ['rɒbərɪ] *n* Raub *m no pl; (burglary)* Einbruch *m (of* in *+acc).* **~ with violence** *(Jur)* Raubüberfall *m.*

robe [rəʊb] *n (of office)* Robe *f; (esp US: for house wear)* Morgenrock, Bademantel *m.*

robin ['rɒbɪn] *n* Rotkehlchen *nt.*

robot ['rəʊbɒt] *n* Roboter *m; (fig also)* Automat *m.*

robust [rəʊ'bʌst] *adj* robust; *build also* kräftig; *structure* stabil.

rock[1] [rɒk] **1** *vt* **(a)** *(swing)* schaukeln; *(gently: lull)* wiegen. **(b)** *(shake) town* erschüttern; *ship* hin und her werfen; *(fig col) person* erschüttern. **to ~ the boat** *(fig)* für Unruhe sorgen. **2** *vi* schaukeln; *(building, tree)* schwanken; *(ship)* hin und her geworfen werden; *(ground)* beben. **3** *n (Mus)* Rock *m; (dance)* Rock 'n' Roll *m.*

rock[2] *n* **(a)** *(substance)* Stein *m; (~ face)* Fels(en) *m; (Geol)* Gestein *nt.* **(b)** *(large mass)* Fels(en) *m; (boulder also)* Felsbrocken *m; (smaller)* (großer) Stein. **as solid as a ~** *(structure)* massiv wie ein Fels; *(marriage)* sehr beständig *or* stabil; **on the ~s** *(col) (with ice)* mit Eis; *(ruined: marriage etc)* kaputt *(col).*

rock: ~-bottom *n* der Tiefpunkt; **to touch/reach ~-bottom** den Tiefpunkt erreichen; **~-climber** *n* (Felsen)kletterer(in *f*) *m;* **~ climbing** *n* Klettern *nt* (im Fels).

rocker ['rɒkəʳ] *n* **to be/go off one's ~** *(col)* übergeschnappt sein *(col)*/überschnappen *(col).*

rockery ['rɒkərɪ] *n* Steingarten *m.*

rocket ['rɒkɪt] **1** *n* **(a)** Rakete *f.* **(b)** *(Brit col: reprimand)* **to give sb a ~** jdm eine Zigarre verpassen *(col).* **2** *vi (prices)* hochschießen. **to ~ to fame** über Nacht berühmt werden.

rocket *in cpds* Raketen-; **~ launcher** *n* Raketenabschußgerät *nt.*

rock face *n* Felswand *f.*

rocking ['rɒkɪŋ]: **~ chair** *n* Schaukelstuhl *m;* **~ horse** *n* Schaukelpferd *nt.*

rock: ~ plant *n* Steinpflanze *f;* **~ salt** *n* Steinsalz *nt.*

rocky *adj (+er) hill* felsig; *road* steinig. **the R~ Mountains** die Rocky Mountains *pl.*

rococo [rəʊ'kəʊkəʊ] **1** *n* Rokoko *nt.* **2** *adj* Rokoko-.

rod [rɒd] *n* Stab *m,* Stange *f; (in machinery)* Stange *f; (for punishment, fishing)* Rute *f.*

rode [rəʊd] *pret of* **ride.**

rodent ['rəʊdənt] *n* Nagetier *nt.*

rodeo ['rəʊdɪəʊ] *n* Rodeo *nt.*

roe[1] [rəʊ] *n, pl* **-(s)** *(species: also* **~ deer***)* Reh *nt.* **~ buck** Rehbock *m.*

roe[2] *n, pl* **-** *(of fish)* Rogen *m.* **hard ~** Rogen *m;* **soft ~** Milch *f.*

rogue [rəʊg] *n* Schurke *m; (scamp)* Schlingel *m.* **~s' gallery** *(Police col)* Verbrecheralbum *nt;* **~ elephant** Einzelgängerelefant *m.*

roguish ['rəʊgɪʃ] *adj* spitzbübisch.

role [rəʊl] *n (Theat, fig)* Rolle *f.* **~-playing** Rollenspiel *nt;* **~ reversal** Rollentausch *m.*

roll [rəʊl] **1** *n* **(a)** *(of paper, wire etc)* Rolle *f; (of fabric)* Ballen *m; (of banknotes)* Bündel *nt; (of butter, flesh, fat)* Röllchen *nt.* **a ~ of paper** eine Rolle Papier. **(b)** *(Cook) (also* **bread ~***)* Brötchen *nt.* **ham/cheese ~** Schinken-/Käsebrötchen *nt.* **(c)** *(movement, of sea)* Rollen *nt; (of ship also)* Schlingern *nt; (of person's gait)* Wiegen *nt.* **(d)** *(sound) (of thunder)* Rollen *nt; (of drums)* Wirbel *m.* **(e)** *(list, register)* Liste *f,* Register *nt.* **we have 60 pupils on our ~(s)** bei uns sind 60 Schüler angemeldet; **to call the ~** die Namensliste verlesen, die Namen aufrufen; **~ of honour** *(Brit) or* **honor** *(US)* Ehrenliste *f; (plaque)* Ehrentafel *f.*

2 *vi* **(a)** rollen; *(ship)* schlingern; *(presses)* laufen; *(Aviat)* eine Rolle machen. **the stones ~ed down the hill** die Steine rollten den Berg hinunter; **tears were ~ing down her cheeks** Tränen rollten ihr über die Wangen; **heads will ~!** *(fig)* da werden Köpfe rollen!; **he's ~ing in money** *or* **in it** *(col)* er schwimmt im Geld *(col).* **(b)** *(thunder)* grollen; *(drum)* wirbeln.

3 *vt* rollen; *cigarette* drehen; *pastry* ausrollen; *metal, lawn* walzen. **to ~ one's eyes** die Augen rollen; **to ~ one's r's** das R rollen; **the hedgehog ~ed itself into a ball** der Igel rollte sich zu einer Kugel zusammen.

♦ **roll about** *vi (balls)* herumrollen *or* -kugeln *(col); (ship)* schlingern; *(person, dog)* sich wälzen; *(col: with laughter)* sich kugeln (vor Lachen) *(col).*

♦ **roll away 1** *vi (ball, vehicle)* wegrollen; *(clouds)* abziehen. **2** *vt sep trolley* wegrollen.

♦ **roll back** *vt sep* zurückrollen.

♦ **roll by** *vi (vehicle, procession)* vorbeirollen; *(clouds)* vorbeiziehen; *(time, years)* dahinziehen.

♦ **roll in** *vi* herein-/hineinrollen; *(letters, money)* hereinströmen; *(col: person)* eintrudeln *(col).*

♦ **roll on** *vi* weiterrollen; *(time)* verfliegen. **~ ~ the holidays!** wenn doch nur schon Ferien wären!

♦ **roll out** *vt sep barrel* hinaus-/herausrollen; *pastry, dough* ausrollen; *metal* auswalzen.

♦ **roll over 1** *vi (vehicle)* umkippen; *(person)* sich umdrehen. **the dog ~ed ~ onto his back** der Hund rollte auf den Rücken. **2** *vt sep person, animal, object* umdrehen.

♦ **roll up 1** *vi* **(a)** *(animal)* sich zusammenrollen *(into* zu*).* **(b)** *(col: arrive)* auftauchen. **2** *vt sep* auf- *or* zusammenrollen; *sleeves* hochkrempeln.

roller ['rəʊləʳ] *n* **(a)** Rolle *f; (pastry ~)* Teigrolle *f; (for lawn, road)* Walze *f; (paint ~)* Rolle *f.* **(b)** *(hair ~)* (Locken)wickler *m.* **with her ~s in** mit Lockenwicklern (im Haar). **(c)** *(wave)* Brecher *m.*

roller: ~ blind *n* Rollo *nt;* **~ coaster** *n* Achterbahn *f;* **~ skate** *n* Rollschuh *m;* **~-skating** *m* Rollschuhlaufen *nt.*

rolling ['rəʊlɪŋ] *adj sea* wogend; *waves* rollend; *countryside* wellig. **a ~ stone gathers no moss** *(Prov)* ≃ wer rastet, der rostet *(Prov).*

rolling: ~ mill *n (factory)* Walzwerk *nt; (machine)* Walze *f;* **~ pin** *n* Teigrolle *f;* **~ stock** *n (Rail)* rollendes Material.

Roman ['rəʊmən] **1** *n (Hist)* Römer(in *f*) *m.* **2** *adj* römisch. **~ numeral** römische Ziffer.

Roman Catholic 1 *adj* (römisch-)katholisch. **2** *n* Katholik(in *f*) *m,* (Römisch-)Katholische(r) *mf.*

romance [rəʊ'mæns] **1** *n* **(a)** *(book)* Roman *m; (love-story)* Liebesroman *m.* **(b)** *(Mus, love affair)* Romanze *f.* **(c)** *no pl (romanticism)* Romantik *f.* **2** *adj* **R~** *language etc* romanisch.

Romanesque [ˌrəʊmə'nesk] *adj* romanisch.

Romania [ruː'meɪnɪə] *n* Rumänien *nt.*

romantic [rəʊ'mæntɪk] **1** *adj (Art etc: also* **R~***)* romantisch; *person also* romantisch veranlagt. **~ novel** Liebesroman *m.* **2** *n (Art etc: also* **R~***)* Romantiker(in *f*) *m.*

romanticism [rəʊ'mæntɪsɪzəm] *n (Art, Liter, Mus: also* **R~***)* Romantik *f.*

romanticize [rəʊ'mæntɪsaɪz] *vt* romantisieren.

Romany ['rəʊmənɪ] **1** *n* **(a)** Zigeuner(in *f*) *m,* Roma *mf.* **(b)** *(language)* die Zigeunersprache, Romani *nt.* **2** *adj* Zigeuner-.

Rome [rəʊm] *n* Rom *nt.* **when in ~ do as the Romans do** *(prov)* ≃ andere Länder, andere Sitten *(Prov).*

romp [rɒmp] **1** *n* Tollerei *f.* **to have a ~** herumtollen *or* -toben. **2** *vi (children, puppies)* herumtollen *or* -toben. **to ~ home** *(fig: win)* spielend gewinnen; **to ~ through sth** *(fig) exam* mit etw spielend fertig werden.

roof [ruːf] **1** *n* Dach *nt; (of car also)* Verdeck *nt; (of cave)* Gewölbe *nt.* **the ~ of the mouth** der Gaumen; **without a ~ over one's head** ohne Dach über dem Kopf; **a room in the ~** ein Zimmer unter dem Dach; **to go through the ~** *(col) (person)* an die Decke gehen *(col)*; *(prices etc)* in die Höhe schießen. **2** *vt house* mit einem Dach decken. **red-~ed** mit rotem Dach.

roof: ~-rack *n* Dachgepäckträger *m*; **~-top** *n* Dach *nt*; **to shout sth from the ~-tops** *(fig)* etw überall herumposaunen *(col)*.

rook [rʊk] **1** *n (bird)* Saatkrähe *f*; *(Chess)* Turm *m*. **2** *vt (swindle)* übers Ohr hauen *(col)*, betrügen.

room [ruːm] **1** *n* **(a)** Zimmer *nt*, Raum *m*; *(public hall, ball~ etc)* Saal *m*; *(office)* Büro *nt*. **the whole ~ laughed** der ganze Saal lachte; **they used to live in ~s** sie haben früher in möblierten Zimmern gewohnt. **(b)** *no pl (space)* Platz *m*; *(fig)* Spielraum *m*. **is there (enough) ~?** ist da genügend Platz?; **there is no ~ (for you)** es ist nicht genug Platz (für dich); **to make ~ for sb/sth** für jdn/etw Platz machen; **there is no ~ for doubt** es kann keinen Zweifel geben; **there is ~ for improvement in your work** Ihre Arbeit könnte um einiges besser sein. **2** *vi* zur Untermiete wohnen. **~ing house** *(esp US)* Mietshaus *nt (mit möblierten Wohnungen)*.

room: ~mate *n* Zimmergenosse *m*, Zimmergenossin *f*; **~ service** *n* Zimmerservice *m*; **~ temperature** *n* Zimmertemperatur *f*; **wine at ~ temperature** Wein mit Zimmertemperatur.

roomy ['ruːmɪ] *adj (+er)* geräumig; *garment* weit.

roost [ruːst] **1** *n (pole)* Stange *f*; *(henhouse)* Hühnerstall *m*. **to come home to ~** *(fig)* auf den Urheber zurückfallen. **2** *vi (bird)* sich niederlassen.

rooster ['ruːstəʳ] *n* Hahn *m*.

root [ruːt] **1** *n* Wurzel *f*. **~s** *(fig: of person)* Wurzeln; **by the ~s** mit der Wurzel; **to take ~** *(lit, fig)* Wurzeln schlagen; **the ~ of the matter** der Kern der Sache; **to get to the ~(s) of the problem** dem Problem auf den Grund gehen. **2** *vt plant* Wurzeln schlagen lassen bei. **deeply ~ed** *(fig)* tief verwurzelt; **to be** *or* **stand ~ed to the spot** *(fig)* wie angewurzelt dastehen. **3** *vi (plants etc)* Wurzeln schlagen.

♦ **root out** *vt sep* **(a)** *(lit) plant* herausreißen; *(dig up)* ausgraben. **(b)** *(fig) evil* mit der Wurzel ausreißen; *(find)* aufspüren, ausgraben *(col)*.

rope [rəʊp] **1** *n* Seil *nt*; *(Naut)* Tau *nt*; *(of bell)* Glockenstrang *m*. **to give sb more ~** *(fig)* jdm mehr Freiheit lassen; **to know the ~s** *(col)* sich auskennen; **to show sb the ~s** *(col)* jdn in alles einweihen. **2** *vt box, case* verschnüren.

♦ **rope in** *vt sep (fig)* rankriegen *(col)*. **how did you get ~d ~ to that?** wie bist du denn da reingeraten? *(col)*.

♦ **rope off** *vt sep area* mit einem Seil abgrenzen.

♦ **rope up** *vi (climber)* sich anseilen.

rope *in cpds* Seil-; **~ ladder** *n* Strickleiter *f*.

ropy ['rəʊpɪ] *adj (+er) (col) (bad)* miserabel *(col)*; *(worn)* mitgenommen.

rosary ['rəʊzərɪ] *n (Rel)* Rosenkranz *m*.

rose[1] [rəʊz] *pret of* **rise.**

rose[2] **1** *n* **(a)** Rose *f*. **~-bush/-tree** Rosenbusch *m*/-bäumchen *nt*; **my life isn't all ~s** *(col)* ich bin auch nicht auf Rosen gebettet. **(b)** *(nozzle)* Brause *f*. **(c)** *(colour)* Rosarot *nt*. **2** *adj* rosarot.

rose *in cpds* Rosen-; **~-coloured,** *(US)* **~-colored** *adj* rosarot; **to see life through ~-coloured spectacles** das Leben durch die rosarote Brille sehen; **~hip** *n* Hagebutte *f*.

rosemary ['rəʊzmərɪ] *n* Rosmarin *m*.

rosette [rəʊ'zet] *n* Rosette *f*.

roster ['rɒstəʳ] *n* Dienstplan *m*.

rostrum ['rɒstrəm] *n, pl* **rostra** ['rɒstrə] Rednerpult *nt*; *(for conductor)* Dirigentenpult *nt*.

rosy ['rəʊzɪ] *adj (+er) (pink)* rosarot; *cheeks, future* rosig. **to paint a ~ picture of sth** etw in den rosigsten Farben ausmalen.

rot [rɒt] **1** *n* **(a)** Fäulnis *f no pl*; *(in wood also)* Moder *m no pl*. **we must stop the ~** *(fig)* wir müssen energisch durchgreifen; **then the ~ set in** *(fig)* dann setzte der Verfall ein. **(b)** *(col: rubbish)* Blödsinn *m (col)*. **2** *vi (wood, material, rope)* verrotten, faulen; *(teeth, plant)* verfaulen; *(fig)* verrotten.

rota ['rəʊtə] *n* Dienstplan *m*.

rotary ['rəʊtərɪ] **1** *adj motion* rotierend, Dreh-. **2** *n (US)* Kreisverkehr *m*.

rotate [rəʊ'teɪt] **1** *vt* **(a)** *(around axis)* drehen, rotieren lassen. **(b)** *crops* im Wechsel anbauen; *work* turnusmäßig erledigen. **2** *vi* **(a)** sich drehen; *(Math)* rotieren. **(b)** *(crops)* im Wechsel angebaut werden; *(people: take turns)* sich abwechseln.

rotation [rəʊ'teɪʃən] *n* **(a)** *no pl* Drehung, Rotation *f*; *(of crops)* Wechsel *m*; *(taking turns)* turnusmäßiger Wechsel. **in ~** abwechselnd im Turnus. **(b)** *(turn)* (Um)drehung *f*.

rote [rəʊt] *n*: **by ~** *learn* auswendig; *recite* mechanisch.

rotor ['rəʊtəʳ] *n (Aviat, Elec, Aut)* Rotor *m*.

rotten ['rɒtn] *adj* **(a)** faul; *wood also* morsch; *fruit also* verdorben; *(fig: corrupt)* korrupt, verdorben. **(b)** *(col) (bad)* scheußlich *(col)*; *weather, book, film, piece of work also* mies *(col)*; *(mean)* gemein; *(unwell)* elend, mies *(col)*. **what ~ luck!** so ein Pech!; **it's a ~ business** das ist eine üble Sache.

rotund [rəʊ'tʌnd] *adj person* rund(lich).

rouble, *(US)* **ruble** ['ruːbl] *n* Rubel *m*.

rouge [ruːʒ] *n* Rouge *nt*.

rough [rʌf] **1** *adj (+er)* **(a)** *(uneven) ground* uneben; *surface, skin, hands* rauh.

(b) *(coarse, unrefined) person* ungehobelt; *manners also, speech* grob, roh; *taste* sauer.

(c) *(harsh, unpleasant) person* grob, roh; *treatment, words* grob, hart; *life* wüst; *sport, work, sound* hart; *neighbourhood, manners, voice, weather* rauh; *sea crossing* stürmisch. **to be ~ with sb** grob mit jdm umgehen; **to feel ~** sich mies fühlen; **he had a ~ time (of it)** *(fig col)* es ging ihm ziemlich dreckig *(col)*; **to make things ~ for sb** *(col)* jdm Schwierigkeiten machen; **it's ~ on him** *(Brit col)* das ist hart für ihn.

(d) *(approximate) plan, calculation, estimate* grob, ungefähr; *justice* grob. **~ copy** Konzept *nt*; **~ sketch** Faustskizze *f*; **~ paper** Konzeptpapier *nt*.

2 *adv live* wüst; *play* wild. **to sleep ~** im Freien übernachten.

3 *n* **(a)** unwegsames Gelände; *(Golf)* Rauh *nt*. **(b)** *(unpleasant aspect)* **to take the ~ with the smooth** das Leben nehmen, wie es kommt.

4 *vt* **to ~ it** *(col)* primitiv leben.

♦ **rough out** *vt sep plan, drawing* grob entwerfen.

roughage ['rʌfɪdʒ] *n* Ballaststoffe *pl*.

rough: ~-and-ready *adj method, equipment* provisorisch; *work* zusammengehauen *(col)*; *person* rauh(beinig); **~-and-tumble** *n (play)* Balgerei *f*; *(fighting)* Keilerei *f*; **~ diamond** *n* **he's a ~ diamond** er ist rauh aber herzlich.

roughen ['rʌfn] *vt ground* uneben machen; *skin, cloth* rauh machen; *surface* aufrauhen.

roughly ['rʌflɪ] *adv* **(a)** grob; *play* rauh; *answer, order also* hart. **(b)** *(approximately)* ungefähr. **~ (speaking)** grob gesagt.

roughness ['rʌfnɪs] *n see adj* **(a)** Unebenheit *f*; Rauheit *f*. **(b)** Ungehobeltheit *f*; Grobheit, Roheit *f*; saurer Geschmack. **(c)** Grobheit, Roheit *f*; Härte *f*; Rauheit *f*.

rough: ~ note book *n (Sch)* Schmierheft *nt*; **~shod** *adv*: **to ride ~shod over sb** rücksichtslos über jdn hinweggehen.

roulette [ruː'let] *n* Roulett(e) *nt*.

round [raʊnd] **1** *adj (+er)* rund. **~ number** runde Zahl; **in ~ figures, that will cost 20 million** es kostet rund *or* runde 20 Millionen.

2 *adv (esp Brit)* **the long way ~** der Umweg, der längere Weg; **~ and ~** rundherum; **I asked**

him ~ for a drink ich lud ihn auf ein Glas Wein/Bier *etc* bei mir ein; **I'll be ~ at 8 o'clock** ich werde um 8 Uhr da sein; **for the second time ~** zum zweitenmal; **all (the) year ~** das ganze Jahr über; **all ~** *(lit)* ringsherum; *(fig: for everyone)* für alle; **drinks all ~!** eine Runde!

3 *prep (esp Brit)* **(a)** *(of place etc)* um (... herum). **~ the table** um den Tisch (herum); **all ~ the house** *(inside)* im ganzen Haus; *(outside)* um das ganze Haus herum; **to go ~ a corner** um eine Ecke gehen/fahren *etc;* **to look ~ a house** sich *(dat)* ein Haus ansehen; **to show sb ~ a town** jdn in einer Stadt herumführen. **(b)** *(approximately)* **~ (about)** 7 **o'clock** ungefähr um 7 Uhr; **~ (about) £800** um die £ 800.

4 *n* **(a)** *(slice: of bread, meat)* Scheibe *f.* **a ~ of toast** eine Scheibe Toast. **(b)** *(delivery ~, Sport, of election, talks)* Runde *f.* **~(s)** *(of policeman, doctor)* Runde *f;* **to do one's ~(s)** seine Runde machen; *(doctor also)* Hausbesuche machen; **he does a paper ~** er trägt Zeitungen aus; **the daily ~** *(fig)* die tägliche Arbeit, der tägliche Trott *(pej);* **to go the ~s** *(story etc)* reihum gehen; **a ~ (of drinks)** eine Runde; **a new ~ of negotiations** eine neue Verhandlungsrunde; **~ of ammunition** Ladung *f;* **a ~ of applause** ein Applaus *m.*

5 *vt* **(a)** *(make ~)* runden. **(b)** *(go ~) bend* gehen/fahren um; *obstacle* herumgehen/-fahren *etc* um.

♦**round off** *vt sep* **(a)** *edges etc* abrunden. **(b)** *list, series* voll machen; *speech, meal* abrunden; *debate, meeting* abschließen.

♦**round on** *vi +prep obj (verbally)* anfahren; *(in actions)* losgehen auf *(+acc).*

♦**round up** *vt sep* **(a)** *people* zusammentrommeln *(col); cattle* zusammentreiben; *criminals* hochnehmen *(col).* **(b)** *price, number* aufrunden.

roundabout ['raʊndəbaʊt] **1** *adj* **~ route** Umweg *m;* **we came a ~ way** wir haben einen Umweg gemacht; **I found out in a ~ way** ich habe es auf Umwegen herausgefunden. **2** *n (Brit) (merry-go-round)* Karussell *nt; (Mot)* Kreisverkehr *m.*

roundly ['raʊndlɪ] *adv (bluntly)* ohne Umschweife.

round: ~-necked ['raʊnd'nekt] *adj* mit rundem Ausschnitt; **~-shouldered** ['raʊnd'ʃəʊldəd] *adj* mit runden Schultern; **~-the-clock** *adj* rund um die Uhr *not attr;* **~ trip** *n* Rundreise *f;* **~-trip ticket** *n (US)* Rückfahrkarte *f; (Aviat)* Hin- und Rückflug-Ticket *nt;* **~-up** *n (of cattle)* Zusammentreiben *nt; (of criminals)* Hochnehmen *nt (col);* **a ~-up of today's news** eine Zusammenfassung der Nachrichten vom Tage.

rouse [raʊz] *vt* **(a)** *(from sleep)* wecken. **(b)** *(stimulate) person* bewegen; *feeling* wachrufen; *hatred, suspicions* erregen. **to ~ sb (to anger)** jdn reizen; **to ~ sb to action** jdn zum Handeln bewegen; **to ~ the masses** die Massen aufrütteln.

rousing ['raʊzɪŋ] *adj speech* zündend, mitreißend; *applause* stürmisch; *music* schwungvoll.

rout[1] [raʊt] **1** *n (defeating)* Sieg *m (of* über *+acc); (being defeated)* Niederlage *f.* **2** *vt (defeat)* in die Flucht schlagen.

rout[2] *vi (pig: also* **~ about***)* herumwühlen.

♦**rout out** *vt sep (find)* aufstöbern; *(force out)* (heraus)jagen *(of* aus*).*

route [ru:t], *(US)* [raʊt] **1** *n* Strecke, Route *f; (bus service)* Linie *f.* **shipping/air ~s** Schiffahrtsstraßen *or* -wege/Flugwege; **we live on a bus ~** wir wohnen an einer Buslinie; **the ~ to the coast** der Weg zur Küste. **2** *vt train, coach, bus* legen. **my luggage was ~d through Amsterdam** mein Gepäck wurde über Amsterdam geschickt.

routine [ru:'ti:n] **1** *n* **(a)** Routine *f.* **(b)** *(Dancing)* Figur *f; (Gymnastics)* Übung *f.* **2** *adj* Routine-, routinemäßig. **~ duties** tägliche Pflichten *pl;* **to be ~ procedure** Routine(sache) sein.

roving ['rəʊvɪŋ] *adj* **he has a ~ eye** er riskiert gern ein Auge; **~ ambassador** Botschafter *m* für mehrere Vertretungen.

row[1] [rəʊ] *n* Reihe *f.* **4 failures in a ~** 4 Mißerfolge hinter- *or* nacheinander; **arrange them in ~s** stell sie in Reihen auf.

row[2] [rəʊ] **1** *vti (in boat)* rudern. **to ~ sb across** jdn hinüber-/herüberrudern. **~ing boat** *(Brit)* Ruderboot *nt.* **2** *n* **to go for a ~** rudern gehen.

row[3] [raʊ] **1** *n* **(a)** *(noise)* Lärm, Krach *(col) m.* **to make a** *or* **kick up** *(col)* **a ~** Krach schlagen *(col).* **(b)** *(quarrel)* Streit, Krach *(col) m.* **to have a ~ with sb** mit jdm Streit *or* Krach *(col)* haben. **2** *vi (quarrel)* (sich) streiten.

rowan ['raʊən] *n (tree)* Eberesche, Vogelbeere *f.*

rowboat ['rəʊ,bəʊt] *n (US)* Ruderboot *nt.*

rowdy ['raʊdɪ] **1** *adj (+er) (noisy)* laut; *football fans* randalierend. **2** *n* Krawallmacher *m.* **football rowdies** Fußballrowdys *pl.*

rower ['rəʊə^r] *n* Ruderer *m.*

rowing[1] ['rəʊɪŋ] *n* Rudern *nt.*

rowing[2] ['raʊɪŋ] *n (quarrelling)* Streiterei *f.*

royal ['rɔɪəl] *adj* königlich; *family, palace also* Königs-; *(fig also)* fürstlich.

royal: R~ Air Force *n (Brit)* Königliche Luftwaffe; **~ blue 1** *adj* königsblau; **2** *n* Königsblau *nt.*

royalist ['rɔɪəlɪst] **1** *adj* royalistisch. **2** *n* Royalist(in *f*) *m.*

Royal Navy *(Brit)* **1** *n* Königliche Marine. **2** *attr* der Königlichen Marine.

royalty ['rɔɪəltɪ] *n* **(a)** *(rank)* das Königtum; *(collectively)* das Königshaus. **(b) royalties** *pl (from book, records)* Tantiemen *pl (on* auf *+acc).*

rpm = revolutions per minute U/min.

RSPCA = Royal Society for the Prevention of Cruelty to Animals ≈ Tierschutzverein *m.*

RSVP = répondez s'il vous plaît u.A.w.g.

Rt Hon = Right Honourable.

rub [rʌb] **1** *n* **(a) to give sth a ~** etw reiben; *furniture, shoes, silver* etw polieren. **(b)** *(fig)* **there's the ~!** *(old, hum)* da liegt der Hase im Pfeffer. **2** *vt* reiben; *(with towel also)* frottieren; *(polish)* polieren. **to ~ one's hands (together)** sich *(dat)* die Hände reiben; **to ~ sth dry** etw trockenreiben; **to ~ shoulders with all sorts of people** *(fig)* mit allen möglichen Leuten in Berührung kommen. **3** *vi (thing) (against* an *+dat)* reiben; *(shoes, collar)* scheuern. **you must have ~bed against some wet paint** da mußt du an feuchte Farbe gekommen sein.

♦**rub down** *vt sep horse (dry)* abreiben; *(clean)* striegeln; *person* abrubbeln *(col); wall, paint (clean)* abwaschen; *(sandpaper)* abschmirgeln.

♦**rub in** *vt sep* **(a)** *lotion* einreiben *(to* in *+acc).* **(b)** *(fig)* herumreiten auf *(+dat).* **don't ~ it ~** mußt du auch noch Salz in die Wunde streuen?

♦**rub off 1** *vt sep dirt etc* abreiben; *tape* löschen; *(from blackboard)* aus- *or* wegwischen. **2** *vi (lit, fig)* abgehen. **to ~ ~ on sb** *(fig)* auf jdn abfärben.

♦**rub out 1** *vt sep stain etc* herausreiben; *(with eraser)* ausradieren. **2** *vi* herausgehen; *(with eraser)* sich ausradieren lassen.

♦**rub up** *vt sep* **(a)** *table* blank reiben, (auf)polieren. **(b) to ~ sb ~ the wrong way** jdn anfreizen.

rubber[1] ['rʌbə^r] **1** *n (material)* Gummi *m; (Brit: eraser)* (Radier)gummi *m.* **2** *adj* Gummi-.

rubber[2] *n (Cards)* Rubber, Robber *m.*

rubber: ~ band *n* Gummiband *nt;* **~ stamp** *n* Stempel *m;* **~-stamp** *vt (lit)* stempeln; *(fig col)* genehmigen.

rubbery ['rʌbərɪ] *adj material* gummiartig; *meat* zäh, wie Gummi *pred.*

rubbish ['rʌbɪʃ] *n* Abfall *m,* Abfälle *pl; (household ~, in factory also)* Müll *m; (on building site)* Schutt *m; (trashy goods, record etc)* Mist *m (col); (nonsense)* Quatsch *(col),* Blödsinn *m.* **don't talk ~!** red keinen Quatsch! *(col);* **~!** (so ein) Quatsch!

rubbish *in cpds (esp Brit)* Müll-; ~ **bin** *n* Mülleimer *m*; ~ **cart** *n* Müllwagen *m*; ~ **chute** *n* Müllschlucker *m*; ~ **collection** *n* Müllabfuhr *f*; ~ **dump** *n* Müllkippe *f*; *(in garden: also* ~ **heap***)* Abfallhaufen *m*; ~ **tip** *n* Müllkippe *f*.

rubbishy ['rʌbɪʃɪ] *adj (col) goods* wertlos.

rubble ['rʌbl] *n* Trümmer *pl*; *(smaller pieces)* Schutt *m*.

ruby ['ru:bɪ] **1** *n (stone)* Rubin *m*; *(colour: also* ~ **red***)* Rubinrot *nt*. **2** *adj (~-coloured)* rubinrot; *(made of rubies)* Rubin-. ~ **wedding** vierzigster Hochzeitstag.

rucksack ['rʌksæk] *n (esp Brit)* Rucksack *m*.

ruction ['rʌkʃən] *n (col: usu pl)* Krach *m no pl*. **that'll cause ~s** das gibt Krach.

rudder ['rʌdə^r] *n (Naut, Aviat)* Ruder *nt*.

ruddy ['rʌdɪ] *adj (+er)* **(a)** *complexion* gesund, rot; *glow* rötlich. **(b)** *(Brit col!)* verdammt *(col)*.

rude [ru:d] *adj (+er)* **(a)** *(bad-mannered)* unhöflich; *(stronger)* unverschämt; *(uncouth)* grob. **it's ~ to stare** es gehört sich nicht, Leute anzustarren; **don't be so ~!** so was sagt man/tut man nicht! **(b)** *(obscene)* unanständig. **(c)** *(harsh) shock* hart; *reminder* unsanft.

rudeness ['ru:dnɪs] *n see adj* **(a)** Unhöflichkeit *f*; Unverschämtheit *f*; Grobheit *f*. **(b)** Unanständigkeit *f*. **(c)** Härte *f*.

rudiment ['ru:dɪmənt] *n* **~s** *pl* Anfangsgründe *pl*.

rudimentary [ˌru:dɪ'mentərɪ] *adj knowledge* elementar; *system* rudimentär. **a ~ sort of building** ein primitives Gebäude.

rueful ['ru:fʊl] *adj look* reuevoll; *situation* beklagenswert.

ruff [rʌf] *n (on dress etc, of bird)* Halskrause *f*.

ruffian ['rʌfɪən] *n* Rüpel *m*; *(violent)* Schläger *m*.

ruffle ['rʌfl] *vt* **(a)** *hair, feathers* zerzausen; *surface, water* kräuseln. **(b)** *(fig) (upset, disturb)* aus der Ruhe bringen; *(annoy also)* verärgern. **to get ~d** aus der Ruhe kommen.

rug [rʌg] *n* **(a)** Teppich *m*; *(rectangular also)* Läufer *m*; *(valuable also)* Brücke *f*; *(bedside)* (Bett)vorleger *m*. **fireside ~** Kaminvorleger *m*. **(b)** *(blanket)* (Woll)decke *f*.

rugby ['rʌgbɪ] *n* Rugby *nt*.

rugged ['rʌgɪd] *adj* rauh; *mountains* zerklüftet; *ground* felsig; *features* markig; *determination* wild.

rugger ['rʌgə^r] *n (Brit col)* = **rugby.**

ruin ['ru:ɪn] **1** *n* **(a)** *no pl* Untergang *m*; *(of event)* Ende *nt*; *(financial, social)* Ruin *m*. **the palace was going to ~** der Palast verfiel (zur Ruine); **you'll be the ~ of me** du bist mein Ruin. **(b)** *(ruined building)* Ruine *f*. **~s** *(of building)* Ruinen *pl*; *(of reputation, beauty)* Reste *pl*; *(of hopes, career)* Trümmer *pl*; **to be** *or* **lie in ~s** *(lit)* eine Ruine sein; *(fig)* zerstört sein; *(life: financially, socially)* ruiniert sein. **2** *vt (destroy) building, hopes* zerstören; *reputation, health also* ruinieren; *(financially, socially)* ruinieren, zugrunde richten; *(spoil) clothes, event, child* verderben.

ruinous ['ru:ɪnəs] *adj (financially)* ruinös; *price* extrem.

rule [ru:l] **1** *n* **(a)** Regel *f*; *(Admin also)* Bestimmung *f*. **the ~s of the game** *(lit, fig)* die Spielregeln; **to play by the ~s** *(lit, fig)* die Spielregeln einhalten; **running is against the ~s** Rennen ist nicht erlaubt; **by ~ of thumb** über den Daumen gepeilt; **~ book** Regelheft *nt*; **I make it a ~ to get up early** ich habe es mir zur Regel gemacht, früh aufzustehen; **as a ~** in der Regel. **(b)** *(authority, reign)* Herrschaft *f*; *(period also)* Regierungszeit *f*. **the ~ of law** die Rechtsstaatlichkeit. **(c)** *(for measuring)* Metermaß *nt*, Maßstab *m*.

2 *vt* **(a)** beherrschen; *(individual also)* herrschen über; *(fig) emotion also* zügeln; **to ~ the roost** *(fig)* Herr im Haus sein *(col)*. **(b)** *(Jur, Sport, Admin: give decision)* entscheiden. **his question was ~d out of order** seine Frage wurde als unzulässig abgewiesen. **(c)** *(draw lines on) paper* linieren; *(draw) line* ziehen.

3 *vi* **(a)** *(lit, fig: reign)* herrschen *(over* über *+acc)*, regieren *(over acc)*. **(b)** *(Jur)* entscheiden *(against* gegen, *in favour of* für, *on* über *+acc)*.

♦ **rule out** *vt sep (fig: exclude)* ausschließen.

ruler ['ru:lə^r] *n* **(a)** *(for measuring)* Lineal *nt*. **(b)** *(sovereign)* Herrscher *m*.

ruling ['ru:lɪŋ] **1** *adj principle* leitend, Leit-. **the ~ class** die herrschende Klasse. **2** *n (Admin, Jur)* Entscheid *m*. **to give a ~** einen Entscheid fällen.

rum [rʌm] *n* Rum *m*.

Rumania [ru:'meɪnɪə] *n* Rumänien *nt*.

rumble ['rʌmbl] **1** *n see vi* Grollen *nt*; Donnern *nt*; Knacken *nt*; Knurren *nt*; Rumpeln *nt (all no pl)*. **2** *vi (thunder)* grollen; *(cannon)* donnern; *(pipes)* knacken; *(stomach)* knurren; *(train, truck)* rumpeln. **to ~ past** vorbeirumpeln. **3** *vt (col: see through) trick, person* durchschauen.

rumbustious [rʌm'bʌstʃəs] *adj* derb.

ruminate ['ru:mɪneɪt] *vi (lit)* wiederkäuen; *(fig)* grübeln *(over, about, on* über *+acc)*.

rummage ['rʌmɪdʒ] *vi (also* ~ **about,** ~ **around***)* herumstöbern *(among, in* in *+dat, for* nach*)*.

rumour, *(US)* **rumor** ['ru:mə^r] **1** *n* Gerücht *nt*. **~ has it that ...** es geht das Gerücht, daß ... **2** *vt* **it is ~ed that ...** es geht das Gerücht, daß ...; *(through gossip)* man munkelt, daß ...; **he is ~ed to be rich** er soll angeblich reich sein.

rump [rʌmp] *n (of animal)* Hinterbacken *pl*; *(col: of person)* Hinterteil *nt*. **~ (steak)** Rumpsteak *nt*.

rumpus ['rʌmpəs] *n (col)* Krach *m*. **to kick up a ~** *(make noise)* einen Heidenlärm machen *(col)*; *(complain)* Krach schlagen *(col)*; **~ room** *(US)* Spielzimmer *nt*.

run [rʌn] *(vb: pret* **ran,** *ptp ~)* **1** *n* **(a)** *(act of running, Cricket, Baseball)* Lauf *m*. **to go for a 2-km ~** einen 2 km-Lauf machen; **he came in at a ~** er kam hereingelaufen; **he took the fence at a ~** er nahm die Hürde im Lauf; **to break into a ~** zu rennen anfangen; **to make a ~ for it** weglaufen; **on the ~** *(from the police etc)* auf der Flucht; **he has had a good ~ for his money** *(col)* er hat was für sein Geld bekommen; *(on death)* er hat sein Leben gelebt.

(b) *(in vehicle)* Fahrt *f*; *(outing also)* Ausflug *m*. **to go for a ~ in the car** eine Fahrt/einen Ausflug im Auto machen; **on the outward/inward ~** auf der Hinfahrt/Rückfahrt; *(in plane)* auf dem Hinflug/Rückflug; **the ferries on the Dover-Calais ~** die Fähren der Linie Dover-Calais.

(c) to have the ~ of a place einen Ort zur freien Verfügung haben; **to give sb the ~ of one's house** jdm sein Haus überlassen.

(d) in the short/long ~ fürs nächste/auf die Dauer; *plan etc* auf kurz/lange Sicht.

(e) *(series)* Folge, Reihe *f*; *(Cards)* Sequenz *f*; *(Theat)* Spielzeit *f*; *(of film)* Laufzeit *f*. **the play had a long ~** das Stück lief sehr lange; **a ~ of bad luck** eine Pechsträhne; **a ~ of misfortunes** eine Serie von Mißgeschicken.

(f) *(great demand)* **~ on** Ansturm *m* auf *(+acc)*; *(St Ex, Fin also)* Run *m* auf *(+acc)*.

(g) *(track for skiing etc)* Bahn *f*. **ski ~** Abfahrt(sstrecke) *f*.

(h) *(animal enclosure)* Gehege *nt*; *(chicken)* Hühnerhof *m*.

(i) *(in tights)* Laufmasche *f*.

2 *vi* **(a)** laufen, rennen; *(in race)* laufen. **to ~ past/off** vorbei-/davonlaufen *or* -rennen; **she came ~ning out** sie kam herausgelaufen *or* -gerannt; **to ~ down a slope** einen Abhang hinunterlaufen *or* -rennen; **to ~ for the bus** zum Bus laufen *or* rennen; **she ran to meet him** sie lief ihm entgegen; **she ran to help him** sie kam ihm schnell zu Hilfe; **to ~ for one's life** um sein Leben rennen; **to ~ for President** *or* **for the**

Presidency für die Präsidentschaft kandidieren; **a rumour ran through the school** ein Gerücht ging in der Schule um; **a shiver ran down her spine** ein Schauer lief ihr über den Rücken; **don't come ~ning to me if ...** du brauchst nicht bei mir anzukommen, wenn ...

(b) *(become)* **to ~ dry** *(river)* austrocknen; *(pen)* leer werden; *(resources)* ausgehen; **he ran short of ideas** ihm gingen die Ideen aus; **supplies are ~ning low** die Vorräte werden knapp.

(c) *(flow) (river, electric current)* fließen; *(eyes)* tränen; *(nose, tap)* laufen; *(paint)* zerfließen, ineinanderfließen; *(dye: in washing)* färben; *(ink)* fließen. **where the river ~s into the sea** wo der Fluß ins Meer mündet; **the street ~s into the square** die Straße mündet auf den Platz; **inflation is ~ning at 20%** die Inflationsrate beträgt 20%; **your bath is ~ning** Ihr Badewasser läuft ein; **the floor was ~ning with water** der Fußboden schwamm vor Wasser; **his blood ran cold** das Blut gefror ihm in den Adern.

(d) *(play, contract, Jur: sentence)* laufen; *(Fin: interest rate)* gelten. **the contract has 10 months to ~** der Vertrag läuft noch 10 Monate; **the expenditure ~s into thousands of pounds** die Ausgaben gehen in die Tausende (von Pfund); **I can't ~ to a new car** ich kann mir kein neues Auto leisten.

(e) *(bus, train etc)* fahren. **this train ~s between London and Manchester** dieser Zug verkehrt zwischen London und Manchester; **the buses ~ once an hour** die Busse fahren stündlich.

(f) *(function)* laufen; *(factory)* arbeiten. **when the central heating is ~ning** wenn die Zentralheizung angeschaltet ist; **the car is ~ning smoothly** der Wagen läuft ohne Schwierigkeiten; **if everything ~s smoothly** wenn alles glatt geht; **you mustn't leave the engine ~ning** Sie dürfen den Motor nicht laufen lassen; **this model ~s on diesel** dieses Auto fährt mit Diesel; **the radio ~s off the mains/off batteries** das Radio läuft auf Netz/Batterie; **all trains are ~ning late** alle Züge haben Verspätung; **the project is ~ning late** das Projekt hat sich verzögert.

(g) *(road)* gehen, führen; *(mountains)* sich erstrecken; *(river)* fließen; *line* sich ziehen. **the main road ~s north and south** die Hauptstraße führt von Norden nach Süden; **the river ~s for 300 km** der Fluß ist 300 km lang; **this theme ~s through his work** dieses Thema zieht sich durch sein ganzes Werk.

(h) to ~ in the family in der Familie liegen.

(i) *(stocking)* eine Laufmasche bekommen.

(j) *(roll, slide) (drawer, curtains)* laufen, gleiten; *(vehicle)* rollen.

3 *vt* **(a)** *distance* laufen, rennen; *race* laufen. **he ~s 3 km every day** er läuft jeden Tag 3 km; **to ~ errands** Botengänge machen; **to ~ its course** *(event, disease)* seinen Lauf nehmen; **to ~ a temperature** Fieber haben; **to ~ sb off his feet** *(col)* jdn ständig in Trab halten *(col)*; **to ~ sb into debt** jdn in Schulden stürzen.

(b) I'll ~ you a bath ich lasse Ihnen ein Bad einlaufen; **he ~s his words together** bei ihm fließen alle Wörter ineinander über.

(c) *(transport) person, thing* fahren, bringen; *(drive) vehicle* fahren. **he ran her home** er brachte sie nach Hause; **this company ~s a bus service** diese Firma unterhält einen Busdienst; **they ~ trains to London every hour** es besteht stündlicher Zugverkehr nach London.

(d) *(operate) machine* betreiben *(on* mit*)*; *(person)* bedienen. **to ~ a radio off the mains** ein Radio auf Netz laufen lassen; **I can't afford to ~ a car** ich kann es mir nicht leisten, ein Auto zu unterhalten; **he ~s a Rolls** er fährt einen Rolls Royce; **this car is cheap to ~** dieses Auto ist billig im Unterhalt; **to ~ a program** *(Comp)* ein Programm durchlaufen.

(e) *(manage, be in charge of)* leiten; *shop* führen; *(organize) course of study, competition* durchführen. **a well-~ hotel** ein gutgeführtes Hotel; **I want to ~ my own life** ich möchte mein eigenes Leben leben; **she's the one who really ~s everything** sie ist diejenige, die den Laden schmeißt *(col)*.

(f) *(move, put)* **to ~ one's finger down a list** mit dem Finger eine Liste durchgehen; **to ~ a comb through one's hair** sich *(dat)* mit einem Kamm durch die Haare fahren; **to ~ one's eye over a page** eine Seite überfliegen.

(g) *(take, lead etc) rope, road* führen; *line, ditch* ziehen; *pipe, wires* (ver)legen; *(above ground)* führen.

♦ **run about** *or* **around** *vi (lit, fig)* herumlaufen *or* -rennen.

♦ **run across 1** *vi* **(a)** *(lit)* hinüber-/herüberlaufen. **(b)** *(go to see)* kurz rüberlaufen *(to* zu*)*. **2** *vi +prep obj (meet) person* zufällig treffen; *(find) object, reference* stoßen auf *(+acc)*.

♦ **run along** *vi* laufen, rennen; *(go away)* gehen. **~ ~!** nun geht mal schön!

♦ **run away** *vi* **(a)** *(person, animal)* weglaufen; *(horse)* durchgehen. **to ~ ~ from home** von zu Hause weglaufen. **(b)** *(water)* auslaufen.

♦ **run away with** *vi +prep obj (steal) money, object* durchbrennen mit *(col)*; *(Sport etc: win easily) race, prize* spielend gewinnen. **don't ~ ~ ~ the idea that ...** *(fig)* kommen Sie nur nicht auf den Gedanken, daß ...; **he lets his imagination ~ ~ ~ him** seine Phantasie geht leicht mit ihm durch.

♦ **run down 1** *vi* **(a)** *(lit: person)* hinunter-/herunterlaufen. **(b)** *(watch, clock)* ablaufen; *(battery)* leer werden. **to let stocks ~ ~** das Lager leer werden lassen; *(deliberately)* die Vorräte abbauen. **2** *vt sep* **(a)** *(knock down)* umfahren; *(run over)* überfahren. **(b)** *factory, shop* (allmählich) auflösen; *department, stocks, staff* abbauen; *battery* zu stark belasten. **(c)** *(disparage)* schlechtmachen *(col)*.

♦ **run in** *vt sep* **(a)** *(Brit) car* einfahren. **(b)** *(col: arrest)* schnappen *(col)*.

♦ **run into** *vi +prep obj (meet)* zufällig treffen; *(collide with)* rennen/fahren gegen. **to ~ ~ trouble/problems** Ärger bekommen/auf Probleme stoßen; **to ~ ~ danger/debt** in Gefahr/Schulden geraten.

♦ **run off 1** *vi* = **run away (a). 2** *vt sep* **(a)** *water* ablassen. **(b)** *(reproduce) copy* abziehen.

♦ **run on** *vi* **(a)** *(lit)* weiterlaufen. **you ~ ~, I'll catch up** geh schon mal voraus, ich komme nach. **(b) it ran ~ for four hours** das zog sich über vier Stunden hin.

♦ **run out** *vi* **(a)** *(person)* hinaus-/herauslaufen; *(rope, chain)* ablaufen; *(liquid)* herauslaufen; *(through leak)* auslaufen. **(b)** *(come to an end) contract, period of time)* ablaufen; *(money, supplies)* zu Ende gehen. **my patience is ~ning ~** mir geht langsam die Geduld aus.

♦ **run out of** *vi +prep obj* **he ran ~ ~ money/patience/time** ihm ging das Geld/die Geduld aus/er hatte keine Zeit mehr.

♦ **run over 1** *vi* **(a)** *(to neighbour etc)* kurz hinübergehen *or* rübergehen *(col)*. **(b)** *(overflow: liquid, container)* überlaufen. **(c)** *(Rad, TV etc)* überziehen. **2** *vi +prep obj story, part in play, details* durchgehen; *text, notes* durchsehen. **3** *vt sep (in vehicle)* überfahren.

♦ **run through** *vi +prep obj* **(a)** *(use up) money* durchbringen. **(b)** *(rehearse) play* durchspielen; *ceremony also, part* durchgehen. **(c)** = **run over 2.**

♦ **run up 1** *vi (lit) (upstairs etc)* hinauf-/herauflaufen; *(towards sb/sth)* hin-/herlaufen *(to* zu*)*. **to ~ ~ against difficulties** auf Schwierigkeiten stoßen. **2** *vt sep* machen. **to ~ ~ a debt** Schulden machen.

run: ~away 1 *n* Ausreißer(in *f*) *m*; **2** *adj slave* entlaufen; *person, horse* ausgerissen; *car etc* der/die/das sich selbständig gemacht hat; *inflation* unkontrollierbar; **he had a ~away victory** er hatte einen sehr leichten Sieg; **~-down 1** *n (col: summary)* Zusammenfassung *f*; **to give sb a ~-down on sth** jdm einen Bericht über etw *(acc)* geben; **2** *adj (dilapidated)* heruntergekommen; *(tired)* abgespannt; *battery* leer; **to be (feeling) ~-down** abgespannt sein.

rung[1] [rʌŋ] *ptp of* **ring**[2].

rung[2] *n (of ladder)* Sprosse *f*; *(of chair)* Querstab *m*.

runner ['rʌnəʳ] *n* **(a)** *(athlete)* Läufer(in *f*) *m*. **(b)** *(on sledge)* Kufe *f*; *(for curtain)* Röllchen *nt*; *(for drawer, machine part)* Laufschiene *f*. **(c)** *(Bot)* **~ bean** *(Brit)* Stangenbohne *f*.

runner-up ['rʌnər'ʌp] *n* Zweite(r) *mf*. **the runners-up** die weiteren Plätze; *(in competition)* die weiteren Gewinner.

running ['rʌnɪŋ] **1** *n* **(a)** Laufen, Rennen *nt*. **to make the ~** *(lit, fig)* das Rennen machen; **to be in the ~ (for sth)** im Rennen (für etw) liegen. **(b)** *(functioning: of machine)* Laufen *nt*. **(c)** *(management) see* **run 3 (e)** Leitung *f*; Führung *f*; Durchführung *f*. **2** *adj* **(a) ~ jump** Sprung *m* mit Anlauf; **go and take a ~ jump** *(col)* du kannst mich gern haben *(col)*; **~ commentary** *(Rad, TV)* fortlaufender Kommentar. **(b) 4 days ~** 4 Tage hintereinander. **(c)** *(flowing)* fließend; *tap, nose* laufend; *eyes* tränend.

running: ~ battle *n (Mil)* Gefecht *nt*; *(fig)* Kleinkrieg *m*; **~ costs** *npl* Betriebskosten *pl*; *(of car)* Unterhaltskosten *pl*.

runny ['rʌnɪ] *adj (+er)* flüssig; *honey* dünnflüssig; *nose* laufend; *eyes* wässerig.

run: ~-of-the-mill *adj* durchschnittlich; *theme, novel* Feld-Wald-Wiesen *(col)*; **~-up** *n (Sport)* Anlauf *m*; **in the final ~-up to ...** in der letzten Phase vor *(+dat)* ...

runway ['rʌnweɪ] *n (Aviat)* Start- und Landebahn *f*, Runway *f or m*.

rupture ['rʌptʃəʳ] **1** *n (lit, fig)* Bruch *m*; *(Pol: of relations)* Abbruch *m*. **2** *vt* brechen. **to ~ oneself** *(col)* sich *(dat)* einen Bruch heben *(col)*.

rural ['rʊərəl] *adj* ländlich; *life also* Land-.

ruse [ru:z] *n* List *f*.

rush[1] [rʌʃ] **1** *n* **(a)** *(of crowd)* Gedränge *nt*; *(of air)* Stoß *m*; *(Mil: attack)* Sturm *m*. **they made a ~ for the door** sie drängten zur Tür; **to make a ~ at** losstürzen auf *(+acc)*; **there's been a ~ on these goods** diese Waren sind rasend weggegangen; **we have a ~ on in the office just now** bei uns im Büro herrscht zur Zeit Hochbetrieb; **the Christmas ~** der Weihnachtsbetrieb; **we've had a ~ of orders** wir hatten eine Flut von Aufträgen; **water streamed out in a ~** das Wasser schoß in einem Schwall heraus. **(b)** *(hurry)* Eile *f*; *(stronger)* Hetze *f*. **to be in a ~** in Eile sein; **I did it in a ~** ich habe es sehr hastig gemacht; **what's the ~?** wozu die Eile/Hetzerei?; **is there any ~ for this?** eilt das?; **it all happened in such a ~** das ging alles so plötzlich.

2 *vi (hurry)* eilen; *(stronger)* hetzen; *(run)* stürzen; *(wind)* brausen; *(water)* schießen. **they ~ed to help her** sie eilten ihr zu Hilfe; **I'm ~ing to finish it** ich beeile mich, es fertigzumachen; **don't ~, take your time** überstürzen Sie nichts, lassen Sie sich Zeit; **to ~ through** *book* hastig lesen; *meal* hastig essen; *museum, town* hetzen durch; *work* hastig erledigen; **to ~ past** *(person)* vorbeistürzen; *(vehicle)* vorbeischießen; **to ~ in/out** *etc* hinein-/hinausstürzen; **the ambulance ~ed to the scene** der Krankenwagen raste zur Unfallstelle.

3 *vt* **(a) to ~ sb to hospital** jdn schnellstens ins Krankenhaus bringen; **they ~ed more troops to the front** sie schickten eilends mehr Truppen an die Front; **they ~ed the bill through Parlament** sie peitschten die Gesetzesvorlage durch das Parlament.

(b) *(force to hurry)* hetzen, drängen. **don't ~ me!** hetz mich nicht; **he won't be ~ed** er läßt sich nicht drängen; **to be ~ed off one's feet** dauernd auf Trab sein; **to ~ sb off his feet** jdn dauernd auf Trab halten; **to ~ sb into doing sth** jdn dazu treiben, etw überstürzt zu tun.

(c) *(charge at)* stürmen; *fence* zustürmen auf *(+acc)*. **the mob ~ed the line of policemen** der Mob stürmte auf die Polizeikette zu.

(d) *(do hurriedly) job, task* hastig machen; *(do badly)* schludern bei *(col)*. **you can't ~ this sort of work** für solche Arbeit muß man sich *(dat)* Zeit lassen.

♦**rush about** *or* **around** *vi* herumhetzen.

♦**rush out 1** *vi* hinaus-/herauseilen; *(very fast)* hinaus-/herausstürzen. **he ~ed ~ and bought one** er kaufte sofort eines. **2** *vt sep troops, supplies* eilends hintransportieren.

♦**rush through** *vt sep order* durchjagen; *goods, supplies* eilends durchschleusen.

♦**rush up** *vi (lit)* hinauf-/heraufeilen; *(very fast)* hinauf-/heraufstürzen.

rush[2] *n (Bot)* Binse *f*.

rush: ~-hour(s *pl***)** *n* Hauptverkehrszeit(en *pl*), Rush-hour *f*; **~-hour traffic** Stoßverkehr *m*; **~ job** *n* eiliger Auftrag; *(pej: bad work)* Schluderarbeit *f (col)*; **~ matting** *n* Binsenmatte *f*.

rusk [rʌsk] *n* Zwieback *m*.

russet ['rʌsɪt] *adj* rostfarben.

Russia ['rʌʃə] *n* Rußland *nt*.

Russian ['rʌʃən] **1** *adj* russisch. **2** *n* **(a)** Russe *m*, Russin *f*. **(b)** *(language)* Russisch *nt*.

rust [rʌst] **1** *n* Rost *m*. **~-proof** rostfrei. **2** *adj (also* **~-coloured***)* rostfarben. **3** *vi* rosten.

rustic ['rʌstɪk] **1** *n* Bauer *m*. **2** *adj* bäuerlich; *furniture, style* rustikal; *manners* bäurisch *(pej)*.

rustle ['rʌsl] **1** *n* Rascheln *nt*; *(of foliage)* Rauschen *nt*. **2** *vi (leaves, silk, papers)* rascheln; *(foliage, skirts)* rauschen. **3** *vt* **(a)** *paper, leaves on ground etc* rascheln mit; *(wind) leaves on tree* rauschen in *(+dat)*. **(b)** *(US: steal) cattle* klauen *(col)*.

♦**rustle up** *vt sep (col) meal* improvisieren *(col)*.

rustler ['rʌsləʳ] *n (US: cattle-thief)* Viehdieb *m*.

rusty ['rʌstɪ] *adj (+er) (lit)* rostig; *(fig) French, maths* eingerostet; *talent* verkümmert. **I'm a bit ~** ich bin etwas aus der Übung.

rut[1] [rʌt] *n (in track, path)* Spur, Furche *f*; *(fig: routine)* Trott *m (col)*. **to be in a ~** *(fig)* im Trott sein *(col)*; **to get into a ~** *(person)* in einen Trott geraten *(col)*.

rut[2] *n (Zool)* Brunst *f*.

ruthless ['ru:θlɪs] *adj person* rücksichtslos; *treatment, irony* schonungslos. **you'll have to be ~** man muß hart sein.

rye [raɪ] *n (grain)* Roggen *m*; *(US col)* Rye(whisky) *m*; *(bread)* Roggenbrot *nt*. **~ bread** Roggenbrot *nt*.

S

S, s [es] *n* S, s *nt.*
S = (a) south S. **(b) Saint** St.
Sabbath ['sæbəθ] *n* Sabbat *m.*
sabbatical [sə'bætɪkəl] *n (Univ)* Forschungsurlaub *m.* **to be on ~** Forschungsurlaub haben.
sable ['seɪbl] *n* Zobel *m*; *(fur)* Zobelpelz *m.*
sabotage ['sæbətɑːʒ] **1** *n* Sabotage *f.* **2** *vt (lit, fig)* sabotieren.
saboteur [ˌsæbə'tɜːʳ] *n* Saboteur *m.*
sabre, (US) saber ['seɪbəʳ] *n* Säbel *m.*
saccharin ['sækərɪn] *n* Saccharin *nt.*
sachet ['sæʃeɪ] *n* Beutel *m*; *(of powder)* Päckchen *nt*; *(of shampoo, cream)* Briefchen *nt.*
sack[1] [sæk] **1** *n* **(a)** Sack *m.* **two ~s of coal** zwei Sack Kohlen. **(b)** *(col: dismissal)* Entlassung *f*, Rausschmiß *m (col).* **to get the ~** rausfliegen *(col)*; **to give sb the ~** jdn rausschmeißen *(col).* **(c)** *(col: bed)* **to hit the ~** sich in die Falle hauen *(col).* **2** *vt (col: dismiss)* rausschmeißen *(col)*, entlassen.
sack[2] **1** *n (pillage)* Plünderung *f.* **2** *vt* plündern.
sacking ['sækɪŋ] *n* **(a)** *(material)* Sackleinen *nt.* **(b)** *(col: dismissal)* Entlassung *f.*
sacrament ['sækrəmənt] *n* Sakrament *nt.*
sacred ['seɪkrɪd] *adj* heilig; *music* geistlich; *building* sakral. **is nothing ~?** *(col)* ist denn nichts mehr heilig?; **~ cow** *(lit, fig)* heilige Kuh.
sacrifice ['sækrɪfaɪs] **1** *n (lit, fig)* Opfer *nt.* **to make ~s** Opfer bringen. **2** *vt* opfern *(sth to sb* jdm etw*).*
sacrificial [ˌsækrɪ'fɪʃəl] *adj* Opfer-.
sacrilege ['sækrɪlɪdʒ] *n* Sakrileg *nt*; *(fig also)* Frevel *m.* **that's ~** das ist ein Sakrileg.
sacrilegious [ˌsækrɪ'lɪdʒəs] *adj (lit)* gotteslästerlich; *(fig)* frevelhaft.
sacristy ['sækrɪstɪ] *n* Sakristei *f.*
sacrosanct ['sækrəʊˌsæŋkt] *adj (lit, fig)* sakrosankt.
sad [sæd] *adj (+er)* traurig; *loss* schmerzlich; *colour* trist; *result also, mistake, lack* bedauerlich. **to feel ~** traurig sein; **a ~ state of affairs** eine traurige Sache.
sadden ['sædn] *vt* betrüben.
saddle ['sædl] **1** *n (also of hill)* Sattel *m*; *(of meat)* Rücken *m.* **to be in the ~** *(lit)* im Sattel sein; *(fig)* im Sattel sitzen. **2** *vt* **(a)** *horse* satteln. **(b)** *(col)* **to ~ sb with sb/sth** jdm jdn/etw aufhalsen *(col).*
saddlebag ['sædlbæg] *n* Satteltasche *f.*
sadism ['seɪdɪzəm] *n* Sadismus *m.*
sadist ['seɪdɪst] *n* Sadist(in *f*) *m.*
sadistic [sə'dɪstɪk] *adj* sadistisch.
sadly ['sædlɪ] *adv* **(a)** traurig; *(unfortunately)* traurigerweise. **(b)** *(regrettably)* bedauerlich. **he is ~ lacking in any sense of humour** ihm fehlt absolut jeglicher Humor.
sadness ['sædnɪs] *n* Traurigkeit *f.* **our ~ at his death** unsere Trauer über seinen Tod.
sae = stamped addressed envelope.
safari [sə'fɑːrɪ] *n* Safari *f.* **to be/go on ~** auf Safari sein/gehen; **~ park** Safaripark *m.*
safe[1] [seɪf] *n (for valuables)* Safe *m or nt*, Tresor *m.*
safe[2] **1** *adj (+er)* sicher; *method also, player* zuverlässig; *(cautious) policy* vorsichtig; *estimate* realistisch; *(not dangerous)* ungefährlich; *(out of danger)* in Sicherheit; *(not injured)* unverletzt. **to be ~ from sb/sth** vor jdm/etw sicher sein; **to keep sth ~** etw sicher aufbewahren; **all the passengers are ~** alle Passagiere sind in Sicherheit *or (not injured)* unverletzt; **~ journey!** gute Fahrt/Reise!; **~ journey home!** komm gut nach Hause!; **thank God you're ~** Gott sei Dank ist dir nichts passiert; **~ and sound** gesund und wohlbehalten; **the patient is ~ now** der Patient ist jetzt außer Gefahr; **the secret is ~ with me** bei mir ist das Geheimnis gut aufgehoben; **this car is not ~ to drive** das Auto ist nicht verkehrssicher; **she is not ~ on the roads** sie ist eine Gefahr im Straßenverkehr; **it's a ~ assumption that ...** man kann mit ziemlicher Sicherheit annehmen, daß ...; **it's a ~ guess** es ist so gut wie sicher; **I think it's ~ to say ...** ich glaube, man kann wohl sagen ...; **better ~ than sorry** Vorsicht ist besser als Nachsicht *(Prov)*; **just to be on the ~ side** um ganz sicher zu sein.
2 *adv* **to play (it) ~** *(col)* auf Nummer Sicher gehen *(col).*
safe: ~-breaker *n* Safeknacker *m (col)*; **~-conduct** *n* freies Geleit; **~-deposit** *n* Tresorraum *m*; **~-deposit box** *n* Banksafe *m or nt*; **~guard 1** *n* Schutz *m*; **as a ~guard against** zum Schutz gegen; **2** *vt* schützen *(against* vor *+dat)*; *interests* wahrnehmen; **3** *vi* **to ~guard against sth** sich gegen etw absichern; **~-keeping** *n* sichere Verwahrung; **to give sb sth for ~-keeping** jdm etw zur (sicheren) Aufbewahrung geben.
safely ['seɪflɪ] *adv (unharmed) arrive* wohlbehalten; *(without problems also)* sicher, gut; *(without risk)* gefahrlos; *drive* vorsichtig; *(solidly, firmly)* sicher, fest; *(not dangerously)* ungefährlich. **I think I can ~ say ...** ich glaube, ich kann wohl sagen ...; **I got ~ through the first interview** ich bin gut *or* heil durch das erste Interview gekommen; **to put sth away ~** etw an einem sicheren Ort verwahren.
safety ['seɪftɪ] *n* Sicherheit *f.* **in a place of ~** an einem sicheren Ort; **for ~'s sake** aus Sicherheitsgründen; **with complete ~** vollkommen sicher; **~ first!** Sicherheit geht vor!; **to play for ~** *(fig)* sichergehen; **(there's) ~ in numbers** zu mehreren ist man sicherer; **when we reached the ~ of the opposite bank** als wir sicher das andere Ufer erreicht hatten; **to leap to ~** sich in Sicherheit bringen.
safety: ~ belt *n* Sicherheitsgurt *m*; **~ catch** *n (on gun)* (Abzugs)sicherung *f*; **~ curtain** *n (Theat)* eiserner Vorhang; **~ factor** *n* Sicherheitsfaktor *m*; **~ margin** *n* Sicherheitsspielraum *m*; **~ match** *n* Sicherheitsholz *nt*; **~ measure** *n* Sicherheitsmaßnahme *f*; **~ net** *n* Sprungnetz *nt*; **~ pin** *n* Sicherheitsnadel *f*; **~ valve** *n* Sicherheitsventil *nt*; *(fig)* Ventil *nt.*
saffron ['sæfrən] **1** *n* Safran *m.* **2** *adj* Safran-; *(in colour)* safrangelb.
sag [sæg] *vi* absacken; *(in the middle)* durchhängen; *(shoulders)* herabhängen; *(production, rate)* zurückgehen; *(price, spirit)* sinken; *(conversation)* abflauen.
saga ['sɑːgə] *n* Saga *f*; *(novel also)* Generationsroman *m*; *(fig)* Geschichte *f.*
sagacious [sə'geɪʃəs] *adj* weise, klug.
sage[1] [seɪdʒ] *n* Weise(r) *m.*
sage[2] *n (Bot)* Salbei *m.*
Sagittarius [ˌsædʒɪ'tɛərɪəs] *n* Schütze *m.*
sago ['seɪgəʊ] *n* Sago *m.*

Sahara [sə'hɑːrə] *n* Sahara *f.*

said [sed] **1** *pret, ptp of* **say. 2** *adj (form)* besagt.

sail [seɪl] **1** *n* Segel *nt; (of windmill)* Flügel *m; (trip)* Fahrt *f.* **under ~** mit aufgezogenen Segeln; **in** *or* **under full ~** mit vollen Segeln; **to set ~ (for ...)** los- *or* abfahren (nach ...); *(with sailing boat)* absegeln (nach ...); **it's (a) 3 days' ~ from here** von hier aus fährt *or (in yacht)* segelt man 3 Tage; **to go for a ~** segeln gehen.

2 *vt ship* segeln mit; *liner etc* steuern. **they ~ed the ship to Cadiz** sie segelten nach Cadiz; **to ~ the seas** die Meere befahren.

3 *vi* **(a)** *(Naut)* fahren; *(with yacht)* segeln. **are you flying or ~ing?** fliegen Sie, oder fahren Sie mit dem Schiff?; **I went ~ing for a week** ich ging eine Woche segeln; **to ~ around the world** um die Welt segeln. **(b)** *(leave) (for* nach) abfahren; *(yacht, in yacht)* absegeln. **passengers ~ing for New York** Passagiere nach New York. **(c)** *(fig: glider, swan etc)* gleiten; *(moon, clouds)* ziehen; *(ball, object)* fliegen. **she ~ed past/out of the room** sie rauschte vorbei *(col)*/aus dem Zimmer *(col)*; **she ~ed through all her exams** sie schaffte alle Prüfungen spielend; **the holidays just ~ed by** *(col)* die Ferien vergingen wie im Flug.

sailboat ['seɪlbəʊt] *n (US)* Segelboot *nt.*

sailing ['seɪlɪŋ] *n* **(a)** Segeln *nt; (as sport also)* Segelsport *m.* **(b) when is the next ~ for Arran?** wann fährt das nächste Schiff nach Arran?

sailing: ~ boat *n (Brit)* Segelboot *nt;* **~ ship** *n* Segelschiff *nt.*

sailor ['seɪləʳ] *n* **(a)** Seemann *m; (in navy)* Matrose *m; (sportsman)* Segler(in *f*) *m.* **(b) to be a bad ~** *(get seasick)* nicht seefest sein.

saint [seɪnt] *n (also fig)* Heilige(r) *mf; (before name abbr to* **St** [snt]) Sankt. **St John** der heilige Johannes, St. Johannes; **St. Mark's (Church)** die Markuskirche.

saintly ['seɪntlɪ] *adj (+er)* fromm; *(fig pej) person* frömmlerisch; *smile* lammfromm.

sake [seɪk] *n* **for the ~ of ...** um *(+gen)* ... willen; **for your own ~** dir selbst zuliebe; **for your family's ~** um Ihrer Familie willen; **for heaven's ~!** *(col)* um Gottes willen!; **for heaven's** *or* **Christ's ~ shut up** *(col)* nun halt doch endlich die Klappe *(col)*; **for old times' ~** in Erinnerung an alte Zeiten; **for the ~ of those who ...** für diejenigen, die ...; **and all for the ~ of a few pounds** und alles wegen ein paar Pfund.

salad ['sæləd] *n* Salat *m.*

salad: ~ bowl *n* Salatschüssel *f;* **~ cream** *n (Brit)* ≈ Mayonnaise *f;* **~ dressing** *n* Salatsoße *f.*

salami [sə'lɑːmɪ] *n* Salami *f.*

salaried ['sælərɪd] *adj* **~ post** Angestelltenposten *m;* **~ staff** Gehaltsempfänger *pl.*

salary ['sælərɪ] *n* Gehalt *nt.* **~ increase** Gehaltserhöhung *f.*

sale [seɪl] *n* **(a)** *(selling)* Verkauf *m; (instance)* Geschäft *nt; (of insurance, bulk order)* Abschluß *m.* **~s** *pl (turnover)* der Absatz; **for ~** zu verkaufen; **to put sth up for ~** etw zum Verkauf anbieten; **not for ~** nicht verkäuflich; **to be on ~** verkauft werden; **on ~ at all bookshops** in allen Buchhandlungen erhältlich; **on a ~ or return basis** auf Verkaufsbasis mit Rückgaberecht. **(b)** *(at reduced prices)* Ausverkauf *m; (at end of season)* Schlußverkauf *m; (clearance ~)* Räumungsverkauf *m.* **to go to the ~s** zum Ausverkauf *etc* gehen; **they've got a ~ on** da ist Ausverkauf *etc*; **to buy in the ~s** im Ausverkauf *etc* kaufen.

saleable, *(US)* **salable** ['seɪləbl] *adj (marketable)* absatzfähig; *(in ~ condition)* verkäuflich.

sale: ~ price *n* Ausverkaufspreis *m;* **~room** *n* Auktionsraum *m.*

sales: ~ clerk *n (US)* Verkäufer(in *f*) *m;* **~ department** *n* Verkaufsabteilung *f;* **~ figures** *npl* Verkaufs- *or* Absatzziffern *pl;* **~ force** *n* Vertreterstab *m;* **~man** *n* Verkäufer *m; (representative)* Vertreter *m;* **~ manager** *n* Verkaufsleiter, Sales-manager *m.*

salesmanship ['seɪlzmənʃɪp] *n* Verkaufstechnik *f.*

sales: ~ talk *n* Verkaufsgespräch *nt;* **~woman** *n* Verkäuferin *f.*

salient ['seɪlɪənt] *adj (lit)* hervorstehend; *(fig)* hervorstechend. **the ~ points of his argument** die Hauptpunkte *pl* seiner Argumentation.

saline ['seɪlaɪn] *adj* salzig.

saliva [sə'laɪvə] *n* Speichel *m.*

salivate ['sælɪveɪt] *vi* Speichel produzieren; *(animal)* geifern; *(old people, baby)* sabbern.

sallow ['sæləʊ] *adj* bleich; *colour* fahl.

salmon ['sæmən] **1** *n, pl* **-** Lachs *m.* **2** *adj (in colour)* lachs(farben).

salon ['sælɒn] *n (all senses)* Salon *m.*

saloon [sə'luːn] *n* Saal *m; (Naut)* Salon *m; (US: bar)* Wirtschaft *f; (in Westerns)* Saloon *m.*

saloon: ~ bar *n (Brit) vornehmerer Teil eines Lokals;* **~ car** *n (Brit)* Limousine *f.*

salt [sɔːlt] **1** *n (Cook, Chem)* Salz *nt.* **~ of the earth** *(fig)* Salz der Erde; **to take sth with a pinch of ~** *(fig)* etw nicht ganz so wörtlich nehmen; **to rub ~ into the wound** *(fig)* Salz in die Wunde streuen. **2** *adj meat, water etc* Salz-; *butter* gesalzen; *taste* salzig. **it's very ~** es ist sehr salzig.

salt: ~ cellar *n* Salzfäßchen *nt; (shaker)* Salzstreuer *m;* **~ shaker** *n* Salzstreuer *m;* **~ water** *n* Salzwasser *nt;* **~-water** *adj fish* Meeres-; *lake* Salz-.

salty ['sɔːltɪ] *adj (+er)* salzig.

salubrious [sə'luːbrɪəs] *adj* **(a)** *(form) air, climate* gesund. **(b)** *(col) district, friends* ersprießlich.

salutary ['sæljʊtərɪ] *adj* **(a)** *(healthy)* gesund. **(b)** *(beneficial) advice* nützlich; *experience* lehrreich; *effect* günstig.

salute [sə'luːt] **1** *n* Gruß *m; (of guns)* Salut *m.* **to take the ~** die Parade abnehmen. **2** *vt (Mil)* grüßen; *person also* salutieren vor *(+dat)*; *courage* bewundern.

salvage ['sælvɪdʒ] **1** *n (act)* Bergung *f; (objects)* Bergungsgut *nt.* **2** *vt (from wreck, building)* bergen *(from* aus); *(fig)* retten *(from* von). **to ~ sth from the fire** etw aus den Flammen retten; **~ what you can** *(lit, fig)* rettet, was ihr retten könnt.

salvage: ~ operation *n* Bergungsaktion *f; (fig)* Rettungsaktion *f;* **~ vessel** *n* Bergungsschiff *nt.*

salvation [sæl'veɪʃən] *n* Rettung *f.*

Salvation Army 1 *n* Heilsarmee *f.* **2** *attr hostel, band, meeting* der Heilsarmee.

Samaritan [sə'mærɪtən] *n* Samariter *m.* **good ~** *(lit, fig)* barmherziger Samariter.

same [seɪm] **1** *adj* **the ~** der/die/das gleiche; *(one and the ~, identical)* derselbe/dieselbe/dasselbe; **they were both wearing the ~ dress** sie hatten beide das gleiche Kleid an; **they both live in the ~ house** sie wohnen beide in demselben Haus; **they are all the ~** sie sind alle gleich; **she just wasn't the ~ person** sie war ein anderer Mensch; **it's the ~ thing** das ist das gleiche; **see you tomorrow, ~ time ~ place** bis morgen, gleicher Ort, gleiche Zeit; **we sat at the ~ table as usual** wir saßen an unserem üblichen Tisch; **he is the ~ age as his wife** er ist (genau) so alt wie seine Frau; **it happened the ~ day** es ist am gleichen *or* selben Tag passiert; **in the ~ way** (genau) gleich; *(by the ~ token)* ebenso.

2 *pron* **(a) the ~** der/die/das gleiche; derselbe/dieselbe/dasselbe; **and I would do the ~ again** und ich würde es wieder tun; **he left and I did the ~** er ist gegangen, und ich auch; **they are one and the ~** das ist doch dasselbe; *(people)* das ist doch ein und derselbe/dieselbe; **she's much the ~** sie hat sich kaum geändert; *(in health)* es geht ihr kaum besser; **it's always the ~** es ist immer das gleiche.

(b) the ~ gleich; **to pay/treat everybody the ~** alle gleich bezahlen/behandeln; **things go on just the ~ (as always)** es ändert sich nichts; **it's**

not the ~ as before es ist nicht wie früher; if it's all the ~ to you wenn es Ihnen egal ist; it's all the ~ to me (what you do) es ist mir egal(, was du tust); it amounts to the ~ das kommt *or* läuft aufs gleiche hinaus; all *or* just the ~ *(nevertheless)* trotzdem; ~ here ich/wir auch; ~ to you (danke) gleichfalls.

sameness ['seɪmnɪs] *n* Eintönigkeit *f*.

sample ['sɑːmpl] **1** *n (example)* Beispiel *nt (of* für*)*; *(for tasting, fig: of talent, behaviour)* Kostprobe *f*; *(Comm) (of cloth etc)* Muster *nt*; *(of commodities, blood etc)* Probe *f*; *(Statistics)* Stichprobe *f*, Sample *nt*. **a representative ~ of the population** eine repräsentative Auswahl aus der Bevölkerung. **2** *vt wine, food* probieren, kosten; *pleasures* kosten.

sanatorium [ˌsænə'tɔːrɪəm] *n, pl (Brit)* Sanatorium *nt*; *(in cpds)* -heilanstalt *f*.

sanctify ['sæŋktɪfaɪ] *vt (to make holy)* heiligen; *(fig)* sanktionieren; *(consecrate)* weihen.

sanctimonious [ˌsæŋktɪ'məʊnɪəs] *adj* frömmlerisch. **don't be so ~** tu doch nicht so fromm.

sanction ['sæŋkʃən] **1** *n* **(a)** *(permission, approval)* Zustimmung *f*. **(b)** *(enforcing measure)* Sanktion *f*. **to impose (economic) ~s on a country** (wirtschaftliche) Sanktionen gegen ein Land verhängen. **2** *vt* sanktionieren.

sanctity ['sæŋktɪtɪ] *n* Heiligkeit *f*; *(of rights)* Unantastbarkeit *f*.

sanctuary ['sæŋktjʊərɪ] *n* **(a)** *(holy place)* Heiligtum *nt*; *(altar ~)* Altarraum *m*. **(b)** *(refuge)* Zuflucht *f*. **to seek ~ with** Zuflucht suchen bei. **(c)** *(for animals)* Schutzgebiet *nt*.

sand [sænd] **1** *n* Sand *m no pl*. **~s** *(of desert)* Sand *m*; *(beach)* Sandstrand *m*. **2** *vt (smooth)* schmirgeln; *(sprinkle with ~)* streuen.

sandal ['sændl] *n* Sandale *f*.

sand: ~bag *n* Sandsack *m*; **~bank** *n* Sandbank *f*; **~blast** *vt* sandstrahlen; **~boy** *n*: **as happy as a ~boy** quietschvergnügt; **~castle** *n* Sandburg *f*; **~ dune** *n* Sanddüne *f*; **~paper 1** *n* Sand- *or* Schmirgelpapier *nt*; **2** *vt* schmirgeln; **~pit** *n* Sandkasten *m*; **~shoe** *n* Stoffschuh *m*; *(for beach)* Strandschuh *m*; **~stone 1** *n* Sandstein *m*; **2** *adj* Sandstein-, aus Sandstein; **~storm** *n* Sandsturm *m*.

sandwich ['sænwɪdʒ] **1** *n* belegtes Brot, Sandwich *nt*. **open ~** belegtes Brot. **2** *vt (also ~ in)* hineinzwängen; *car* einkeilen. **to be ~ed between two things/people** zwischen zwei Dingen/Menschen eingekeilt sein.

sandwich: ~board *n* Reklametafel *f*; **~ course** *n Ausbildungsgang m, bei dem sich Theorie und Praxis abwechseln.*

sandy ['sændɪ] *adj (+er)* sandig; *beach, soil* Sand-, sandig *pred*; *(in colour)* rötlich; *hair* rotblond.

sane [seɪn] *adj (+er) person* normal; *(Med, Psych etc)* geistig gesund; *(Jur)* zurechnungsfähig; *society etc* gesund; *(sensible) advice, person* vernünftig.

sang [sæŋ] *pret of* **sing.**

sangfroid ['sɑ̃ːŋ'frwɑː] *n* Seelenruhe *f*.

sanguine ['sæŋgwɪn] *adj (optimistic)* optimistisch.

sanitarium [ˌsænɪ'tɛərɪəm] *n (US)* = **sanatorium.**

sanitary ['sænɪtərɪ] *adj* hygienisch; *arrangements, installations* sanitär *attr*; *regulations, expert* Gesundheits-; *questions, principles* der Hygiene.

sanitary napkin *(US) or* **towel** *n* Damenbinde *f*.

sanitation [ˌsænɪ'teɪʃən] *n* Hygiene *f*; *(toilets etc)* sanitäre Anlagen *pl*; *(sewage disposal)* Kanalisation *f*.

sanity ['sænɪtɪ] *n* **(a)** *(mental balance)* geistige Gesundheit; *(of individual also)* gesunder Verstand; *(Jur)* Zurechnungsfähigkeit *f*. **to lose one's ~** den Verstand verlieren; **to doubt sb's ~** an jds Verstand *(dat)* zweifeln. **(b)** *(sensibleness)* Vernünftigkeit *f*. **to return to ~** Vernunft annehmen.

sank [sæŋk] *pret of* **sink**[1].

Santa (Claus) ['sæntə('klɔːz)] *n* der Weihnachtsmann.

sap[1] [sæp] *n (Bot)* Saft *m*; *(fig)* Lebenskraft *f*.

sap[2] *vt (weaken, Mil)* untergraben; *confidence also* schwächen. **to ~ sb's strength** jdn entkräften, jds Kräfte angreifen.

sapling ['sæplɪŋ] *n* junger Baum.

sapper ['sæpə[r]] *n (Mil)* Pionier *m*.

sapphire ['sæfaɪə[r]] **1** *n* Saphir *m*; *(colour)* Saphirblau *nt*. **2** *adj ring* Saphir-.

sarcasm ['sɑːkæzəm] *n* Sarkasmus *m*.

sarcastic [sɑː'kæstɪk] *adj* sarkastisch. **are you being ~?** das soll wohl ein Witz sein *(col)*.

sardine [sɑː'diːn] *n* Sardine *f*. **packed in like ~s** wie die Sardinen.

Sardinia [sɑː'dɪnɪə] *n* Sardinien *nt*.

sardonic [sɑː'dɒnɪk] *adj* süffisant.

sash[1] [sæʃ] *n* Schärpe *f*.

sash[2] *n (in window)* Gewichtsschnur *f*.

sash: ~-cord *n* Gewichtsschnur *f*; **~-window** *n* Schiebefenster *nt*.

sat [sæt] *pret, ptp of* **sit.**

Satan ['seɪtən] *n* Satan *m*.

satanic [sə'tænɪk] *adj* satanisch.

satchel ['sætʃəl] *n* Schultasche *f*.

satellite ['sætəlaɪt] *n* Satellit *m*.

satellite: ~ state *n* Satellitenstaat *m*; **~ town** *n* Trabantenstadt *f*.

satiate ['seɪʃɪeɪt] *vt appetite, desires etc* stillen *(geh)*; *person, animal* sättigen; *(to excess)* übersättigen.

satin ['sætɪn] **1** *n* Satin *m*. **2** *adj* Satin-; *skin* samtig.

satire ['sætaɪə[r]] *n* Satire *f (on* auf *+acc)*.

satirical [sə'tɪrɪkəl] *adj literature, film etc* satirisch; *(mocking, joking)* ironisch.

satirist ['sætərɪst] *n* Satiriker(in *f*) *m*.

satisfaction [ˌsætɪs'fækʃən] *n* **(a)** *(act: of person, needs, curiosity etc)* Befriedigung *f*; *(of ambition)* Verwirklichung *f*; *(of conditions, contract)* Erfüllung *f*. **(b)** *(state)* Zufriedenheit *f (at* mit*)*. **the ~ of having solved a difficult problem** das befriedigende Gefühl, ein schwieriges Problem gelöst zu haben; **to feel a sense of ~ at sth** Genugtuung über etw *(acc)* empfinden; **has it been done to your ~?** ist es zu Ihrer Zufriedenheit erledigt worden? *(form)*; **to get ~ out of sth** Befriedigung in etw *(dat)* finden; *(find pleasure)* Freude an etw *(dat)* haben; **he proved to my ~ that ...** er hat überzeugend bewiesen, daß ...

satisfactory [ˌsætɪs'fæktərɪ] *adj* befriedigend; *account, completion of contract* zufriedenstellend; *(only just good enough)* ausreichend; *reason* triftig; *excuse* angemessen; *(in exams)* ausreichend; befriedigend.

satisfy ['sætɪsfaɪ] **1** *vt* **(a)** *(make contented)* befriedigen; *employer, customers etc* zufriedenstellen; *(meal) person* sättigen. **not satisfied with that he ...** damit noch immer nicht zufrieden, ... er ...; **he's never satisfied** *(always wants more)* er ist mit nichts zufrieden. **(b)** *needs, demand, sb (sexually)* befriedigen; *hunger* stillen; *conditions* erfüllen; *requirements* genügen *(+dat)*; *ambitions* verwirklichen. **(c)** *(convince)* überzeugen. **they were not satisfied with the answers** sie waren mit den Antworten nicht zufrieden.

2 *vr* **to ~ oneself about sth** sich von etw überzeugen; **to ~ oneself that ...** sich davon überzeugen, daß ...

satisfying ['sætɪsfaɪɪŋ] *adj* befriedigend; *food, meal* sättigend. **a cool ~ lager** ein kühles, durststillendes Bier.

saturate ['sætʃəreɪt] *vt* (durch)tränken; *(rain)* durchnässen; *(Chem, fig) solution, market* sättigen. **I'm ~d** *(col)* ich bin klatschnaß *(col)*.

saturation [ˌsætʃə'reɪʃən] *n* Sättigung *f*. **to have reached ~ point** *(fig)* seinen Sättigungsgrad erreicht haben.

Saturday ['sætədɪ] *n* Samstag, Sonnabend *m*; *see* **Tuesday.**

Saturn ['sætən] *n (Astron)* Saturn *m.*
sauce [sɔːs] *n* **(a)** Soße, Sauce *f.* **white ~** Mehlsoße *f;* **what's ~ for the goose is ~ for the gander** *(Prov)* was dem einen recht ist, ist dem anderen billig *(prov).* **(b)** *no pl (col: cheek)* Frechheit *f.* **none of your ~!** werd bloß nicht frech! *(col).*
saucepan ['sɔːspən] *n* Kochtopf *m.*
saucer ['sɔːsəʳ] *n* Untertasse *f.*
saucy ['sɔːsɪ] *adj (+er)* frech.
Saudi Arabia ['saudɪə'reɪbɪə] *n* Saudi-Arabien *nt.*
sauna ['sɔːnə] *n* Sauna *f.* **to have a ~** in die Sauna gehen.
saunter ['sɔːntəʳ] *vi* schlendern. **he ~ed up to me** er schlenderte auf mich zu.
sausage ['sɒsɪdʒ] *n* Wurst *f.*
sausage: ~ dog *n (Brit hum)* Dackel *m;* **~meat** *n* Wurstbrät *nt;* **~ roll** *n* ≈ Bratwurst *f* im Schlafrock.
sauté ['səʊteɪ] **1** *adj* **~ potatoes** Brat- *or* Röstkartoffeln *pl.* **2** *vt potatoes* rösten; *(sear)* (kurz) anbraten.
savage ['sævɪdʒ] **1** *adj* wild; *fighter, punch, revenge* brutal; *custom* grausam; *animal* gefährlich; *competition* scharf; *(drastic) cuts, measures, changes* drastisch; *criticism* schonungslos, brutal *(col).* **to make a ~ attack on sb** brutal über jdn herfallen; *(fig)* jdn scharf angreifen. **2** *n* Wilde(r) *mf.* **3** *vt (animal)* anfallen; *(fatally)* zerfleischen.
savanna(h) [sə'vænə] *n* Savanne *f.*
save[1] [seɪv] **1** *n (Ftbl etc)* Ballabwehr *f.*
2 *vt* **(a)** *(rescue, Rel)* retten. **to ~ sb from sth** jdn vor etw *(dat)* retten; **to ~ sb from disaster/ruin** jdn vor einer Katastrophe/dem Ruin bewahren; **he ~d me from falling/making that mistake** er hat mich davor bewahrt, hinzufallen/den Fehler zu machen; **to ~ sth from sth** etw aus etw retten; **to ~ the day (for sb)** jds Rettung sein; **God ~ the Queen** Gott schütze die Königin.
(b) *(put by)* aufheben, aufsparen; *money* sparen; *(collect) stamps etc* sammeln. **~ some of the cake for me** laß mir etwas Kuchen übrig; **~ me a seat** halte mir einen Platz frei; **~ it!** *(col)* spar dir das! *(col).*
(c) *(avoid using up) time, money* sparen; *(spare) eyes, battery* schonen; *(~ up) strength, fuel etc* aufsparen. **that will ~ you £2 a week** dadurch sparen Sie £ 2 die Woche.
(d) *(prevent) bother, trouble* ersparen. **it'll ~ a lot of hard work if we ...** es erspart uns *(dat)* sehr viel Mühe, wenn wir ...
(e) *goal* verhindern; *penalty* halten.
(f) *(Comp) job* speichern, saven *(col).*
3 *vi* **(a)** *(with money)* sparen. **to ~ for sth** für *or* auf etw *(acc)* sparen. **(b) to ~ on sth** etw sparen.
♦ **save up 1** *vi* sparen *(for* für, auf *+acc).* **2** *vt sep (not spend)* sparen; *(not use)* aufheben, aufbewahren. **he's saving himself ~ for the big match** er schont sich für das große Spiel.
save[2] **1** *prep* außer *+dat.* **2** *conj* **(a)** *(old, liter)* es sei denn *(geh).* **(b) ~ that** nur daß.
saveloy ['sævəlɔɪ] *n* Zervelatwurst *f.*
saving ['seɪvɪŋ] *n* **(a)** *no pl (act: rescue, Rel)* Rettung *f; (of money)* Sparen *nt.* **(b)** *(of cost etc) (act)* Einsparung *f; (amount saved)* Ersparnis *f.* **(c) ~s** *pl* Ersparnisse *pl; (in account)* Spareinlagen *pl;* **post-office ~s** Postsparguthaben *nt.*
savings *in cpds* Spar-; **~ and loan association** *n (US)* Bausparkasse *f;* **~ bank** *n* Sparkasse *f.*
saviour, *(US also)* **savior** ['seɪvjəʳ] *n* Retter(in *f*) *m; (Rel also)* Erlöser *m.*
savour, *(US)* **savor** ['seɪvəʳ] **1** *n* Geschmack *m; (slight trace)* Spur *f; (enjoyable quality)* Reiz *m.* **2** *vt* **(a)** *(form)* kosten *(geh); aroma (of food)* riechen. **(b)** *(fig liter)* genießen, auskosten.
savoury, *(US)* **savory** ['seɪvərɪ] **1** *adj* **(a)** *(appetizing)* lecker; *meal also* schmackhaft. **(b)** *(not sweet)* pikant. **~ omelette** gefülltes Omelett; **~ biscuits** Salzgebäck *nt.* **(c)** *(fig)* angenehm; *sight also* einladend. **2** *n* Häppchen *nt.*
saw[1] [sɔː] *pret of* **see**[1].
saw[2] *(vb: pret* **~ed,** *ptp* **~ed** *or* **sawn) 1** *n* Säge *f.* **2** *vt* sägen. **to ~ sth through** etw durchsägen; **to ~ sth in two** etw entzweisägen.
♦ **saw off** *vt sep* absägen. **a ~n-~ shotgun** ein Gewehr *nt* mit abgesägtem Lauf.
saw: ~dust *n* Sägemehl *nt;* **~mill** *n* Sägewerk *nt.*
sawn [sɔːn] *ptp of* **saw**[2].
Saxon ['sæksn] **1** *n* Sachse *m,* Sächsin *f; (Hist)* (Angel)sachse *m*/-sächsin *f.* **2** *adj* sächsisch; *(Hist)* (angel)sächsisch.
saxophone ['sæksəfəʊn] *n* Saxophon *nt.*
say [seɪ] *(vb: pret, ptp* **said) 1** *n* Mitspracherecht *nt (in* bei*).* **let him have his ~** laß ihn mal reden *or* seine Meinung äußern; **you've had your ~** Sie haben Ihre Meinung äußern können; **to have no/a ~ in sth** bei etw nichts/etwas zu sagen haben, bei etw kein/ein Mitspracherecht haben.
2 *vti* **(a)** sagen; *poem* aufsagen; *prayer, text* sprechen; *(pronounce)* aussprechen; *(dial, gauge)* anzeigen. **~ after me ...** sprechen Sie mir nach ...; **what have you got to ~ for yourself?** was hast du zu deiner Verteidigung zu sagen?; **that's not for him to ~** es steht ihm nicht zu, sich darüber zu äußern; *(to decide)* das kann er nicht entscheiden; **he said to wait here** er hat gesagt, ich soll/wir sollen *etc* hier warten; **do it this way — if you ~ so** machen Sie es so — wenn Sie meinen; **why didn't you ~ so?** warum hast du das nicht gleich gesagt?; **you'd better do it — who ~s?** tun Sie das lieber — wer sagt das?; **what does it mean? — I wouldn't like to ~** was bedeutet das? — das kann ich auch nicht sagen; **so ~ing, he sat down** und mit diesen Worten setzte er sich; **it ~s in the papers that ...** in den Zeitungen steht, daß ...; **what does the paper/this book ~?** was steht in der Zeitung/diesem Buch?; **the rules ~ that ...** in den Regeln heißt es, daß ...; **what does the weather forecast ~?** wie ist der Wetterbericht?; **what does your watch ~?** wie spät ist es auf deiner Uhr?; **that ~s a lot about his character** das läßt tief auf seinen Charakter schließen; **and that's ~ing a lot** und das will schon etwas heißen; **that doesn't ~ much for him** das spricht nicht für ihn.
(b) what would you ~ to a whisky? wie wär's mit einem Whisky?; **I wouldn't ~ no to a cup of tea** ich hätte nichts gegen eine Tasse Tee; **he never ~s no to a drink** er sagt nie nein zu einem Drink; **what did he ~ to your plan?** was hat er zu Ihrem Plan gesagt?; **I'll offer £500, what do you ~ to that?** ich biete £ 500, was meinen Sie dazu?; **what do you ~?** was meinen Sie?; **I ~!** *(to attract attention)* hallo!; **I should ~ (so)!** das möchte ich doch meinen!; **you don't ~!** *(also iro)* nein wirklich?, was du nicht sagst!; **well said!** (ganz) richtig!; **you('ve) said it!** Sie sagen es!; **you can ~ that again!** das kann man wohl sagen!; **~ no more!** ich weiß Bescheid!; **(it's) easier said than done** das ist leichter gesagt als getan; **when all is said and done** letzten Endes; **he is said to be very rich** er soll sehr reich sein; **it goes without ~ing that ...** es versteht sich von selbst, daß ...; **that is to ~** das heißt; *(correcting also)* beziehungsweise; **to ~ nothing of the costs** *etc* von den Kosten *etc* ganz zu schweigen; **that's not to ~ that ...** das soll nicht heißen, daß ...; **they ~ ..., it is said ...** es heißt ...
saying ['seɪɪŋ] *n* Redensart *f; (proverb)* Sprichwort *nt.* **as the ~ goes** wie es so schön heißt.
say-so ['seɪsəʊ] *n (col) (assertion)* Wort *nt; (authority)* Plazet *nt.* **on whose ~?** mit welchem Recht?
scab [skæb] *n* **(a)** *(on cut)* Schorf, Grind *m.* **(b)** *(col: strikebreaker)* Streikbrecher(in *f*) *m.*
scaffolding ['skæfəldɪŋ] *n* Gerüst *nt.* **to put up ~** ein Gerüst aufbauen.
scald [skɔːld] **1** *n* Verbrühung *f.* **2** *vt* **(a)** *oneself,*

skin etc verbrühen. **(b)** *instruments, vegetables* abbrühen; *milk* abkochen.
scalding ['skɔːldɪŋ] *adj* siedend.
scale[1] [skeɪl] *n (of fish)* Schuppe *f*; *(of rust)* Flocke *f*; *(kettle ~)* Kesselstein *m no pl*.
scale[2] *n* **(a)** Skala *f*; *(on ruler)* (Maß)einteilung *f*; *(fig)* Leiter *f*; *(social ~)* Stufenleiter *f*. ~ **of charges** Gebührenordnung *f*, Tarife *pl*. **(b)** *(instrument)* Meßgerät *nt*. **(c)** *(Mus)* Tonleiter *f*. **the ~ of G** die G(-Dur)-Tonleiter. **(d)** *(of map etc)* Maßstab *m*. **on a ~ of 5 km to the cm** in einem Maßstab von 5 km zu 1 cm; **to draw sth to ~** etw im Maßstab *or* maßstabgerecht zeichnen. **(e)** *(fig: size, extent)* Umfang *m*, Ausmaß *nt*. **to entertain on a large/small ~** Feste im größeren/kleineren Rahmen geben; **inflation on an unprecedented ~** Inflation von bisher nie gekanntem Ausmaß; **it's similar but on a smaller ~** es ist ähnlich, nur kleiner; **on a national ~** auf nationaler Ebene.
♦ **scale down** *vt sep (lit)* verkleinern; *(fig)* verringern.
scale[3] *vt mountain, wall* erklettern.
scale: ~ drawing *n* maßstabgetreue Zeichnung; **~ model** *n* maßstabgetreues Modell.
scales [skeɪlz] *npl* **(pair of) ~s** Waage *f*; **to tip the ~s in favour of sb/sth** für jdn/etw den Ausschlag geben.
scallop ['skɒləp] *n (Zool)* Kammuschel *f*.
scalp [skælp] **1** *n* Kopfhaut *f*; *(as Indian trophy)* Skalp *m*. **2** *vt* skalpieren; *(hum: by barber)* kahlscheren *(hum)*.
scalpel ['skælpəl] *n* Skalpell *nt*.
scamp [skæmp] *n* Frechdachs *m (col)*.
scamper ['skæmpəʳ] *vi (person, child, puppy)* trappeln; *(squirrel, rabbit)* hoppeln; *(mice)* huschen.
scan [skæn] **1** *vt* **(a)** *(search with sweeping movement)* schwenken über *(+acc)*; *(person)* seine Augen wandern lassen über *(+acc)*; *newspaper, book* überfliegen; *(examine closely) horizon* absuchen; *(by radar)* absuchen, abtasten. **(b)** *(TV)* abtasten. **(c)** *verse* in Versfüße zerlegen. **2** *vi (verse)* sich reimen *(col)*. **3** *n (Med)* Scan *m*; *(in pregnancy)* Ultraschall-Untersuchung *f*.
scandal ['skændl] *n* **(a)** Skandal *m*. **to create a ~** einen Skandal verursachen; *(amongst neighbours etc)* allgemeines Aufsehen erregen; **it is a ~ that ...** es ist skandalös, daß ... **(b)** *no pl (gossip)* Skandalgeschichten *pl*; *(piece of gossip)* Skandalgeschichte *f*. **the latest ~** der neueste Klatsch *(col)*.
scandalize ['skændəlaɪz] *vt* schockieren. **she was ~d** sie war empört *(by* über *+acc)*.
scandalous ['skændələs] *adj* skandalös. **a ~ report/tale** eine Skandalgeschichte.
Scandinavia [ˌskændɪ'neɪvɪə] *n* Skandinavien *nt*.
Scandinavian [ˌskændɪ'neɪvɪən] **1** *adj* skandinavisch. **2** *n* Skandinavier(in *f*) *m*.
scanner ['skænəʳ] *n (Rad)* Richtantenne *f*.
scant [skænt] *adj (+er)* wenig *inv*; *attention, respect also, chance* gering; *success* mager; *amount* spärlich.
scantily ['skæntɪlɪ] *adv* spärlich.
scanty ['skæntɪ] *adj (+er) amount* spärlich; *vegetation, meal also* kärglich; *clothing* knapp.
scapegoat ['skeɪpgəʊt] *n* Sündenbock *m*. **to make a ~ of sb** jdn zum Sündenbock machen.
scar [skɑːʳ] **1** *n (on skin, tree)* Narbe *f*; *(scratch)* Kratzer *m*; *(burn)* Brandfleck *m*; *(fig) (emotional)* Wunde *f*; *(on good name)* Makel *m*. **2** *vt skin, tree* Narben/eine Narbe hinterlassen auf *(+dat)*; *furniture* zerkratzen; Brandflecken hinterlassen auf *(+dat)*; *(fig) person* zeichnen. **he was ~red for life** *(lit)* er behielt bleibende Narben zurück; *(fig)* er war fürs Leben gezeichnet; **her ~red face** ihr narbiges Gesicht. **3** *vi* Narben/eine Narbe hinterlassen.
scarce [skɛəs] *adj (+er) (in short supply)* knapp; *(rare)* selten. **to make oneself ~** *(col)* verschwinden *(col)*.
scarcely ['skɛəslɪ] *adv* kaum. **~ anybody** kaum jemand; **~ anything** fast nichts; **~ ever** fast nie; **you can ~ expect him to believe that** Sie erwarten doch wohl kaum, daß er das glaubt.
scarceness ['skɛəsnɪs], **scarcity** ['skɛəsɪtɪ] *n (shortage)* Knappheit *f*; *(rarity)* Seltenheit *f*. **a ~ of qualified people** ein Mangel *m* an qualifizierten Kräften; **in times of ~** in schlechten Zeiten.
scare [skɛəʳ] **1** *n (fright, shock)* Schreck(en) *m*; *(general alarm)* Hysterie *f (about* wegen*)*. **to give sb a ~** jdm einen Schrecken einjagen; **to cause a ~** eine Panik auslösen. **2** *vt* einen Schrecken einjagen *(+dat)*; *(worry also)* Angst machen *(+dat)*; *(frighten physically) person, animal* erschrecken; *birds* aufschrecken. **to be ~d** Angst haben *(of* vor *+dat)*; **to be easily ~d** sehr schreckhaft sein; *(easily worried)* sich *(dat)* leicht Angst machen lassen; *(timid: deer etc)* sehr scheu sein; **to be ~d stiff** *or* **to death** *or* **out of one's wits** *(all col)* Todesängste ausstehen; **he's ~d of telling her the truth** er traut sich nicht, ihr die Wahrheit zu sagen.
♦ **scare away** *vt sep* verscheuchen; *people* verjagen.
scare: ~crow *n (lit, fig)* Vogelscheuche *f*; **~monger** *n* Panikmacher *m*.
scarf [skɑːf] *n, pl* **scarves** Schal *m*; *(neck ~)* Halstuch *nt*; *(head~)* Kopftuch *nt*; *(round the shoulders)* Schultertuch *nt*.
scarlet ['skɑːlɪt] **1** *n* Scharlach(rot) *nt*. **~ fever** Scharlach *m*. **2** *adj* (scharlach)rot. **to turn ~** hochrot werden, rot anlaufen *(col)*.
scarves [skɑːvz] *pl of* **scarf**.
scary ['skɛərɪ] *adj (+er) (col)* unheimlich; *film also* grus(e)lig *(col)*. **it was pretty ~** da konnte man schon Angst kriegen *(col)*.
scathing ['skeɪðɪŋ] *adj* bissig; *attack* scharf; *look, criticism* vernichtend. **to be ~** bissige Bemerkungen *pl* machen *(about* über *+acc)*.
scatter ['skætəʳ] **1** *vt* **(a)** verstreuen; *seeds, gravel, (Phys) light* streuen *(on, onto* auf *+acc)*. **the books were ~ed (about) all over the room** die Bücher lagen im ganzen Zimmer verstreut; **his friends were ~ed all over the country** seine Freunde waren über das ganze Land verstreut. **(b)** *(disperse)* auseinandertreiben; *army etc also* zersprengen. **2** *vi* sich zerstreuen *(to* in *+acc)*; *(in a hurry, in fear)* auseinanderlaufen.
scatter: ~brain *n (col)* Schussel *m (col)*; **~brained** ['skætəˌbreɪnd] *adj (col)* schusselig *(col)*.
scattered ['skætəd] *adj population* weit verstreut; *villages* verstreut; *clouds, showers* vereinzelt.
scatty ['skætɪ] *adj (+er) (col)* **(a)** *(scatterbrained)* schusselig *(col)*. **(b)** *(mad)* verrückt.
scavenge ['skævɪndʒ] **1** *vt (lit, fig)* ergattern. **2** *vi (lit)* Nahrung suchen. **jackals live by scavenging** Schakale leben von Aas.
scavenger ['skævɪndʒəʳ] *n (animal)* Aasfresser *m*; *(fig: person)* Dreckwühler *m*.
scenario [sɪ'nɑːrɪəʊ] *n* Szenar(ium) *nt*; *(fig)* Szenario *nt*.
scene [siːn] *n* **(a)** *(place, setting)* Schauplatz *m*; *(of play, novel)* Ort *m* der Handlung. **the ~ of the crime** der Tatort, der Schauplatz des Verbrechens; **the ~ of the battle was a small hill** die Schlacht fand auf einem kleinen Hügel statt; **to set the ~** den Rahmen geben; **the ~ is set in Padua** das Stück/der Roman *etc* spielt in Padua; **to appear on the ~** auftauchen, auf der Bildfläche erscheinen; **the police were first on the ~** die Polizei war als erste zur Stelle. **(b)** *(Theat)* Szene *f*. **Act II, ~ i** Akt II, 1. Szene. **behind the ~s** *(lit, fig)* hinter den Kulissen. **(c)** *(sight)* Anblick *m*; *(landscape)* Landschaft *f*. **(d)** *(fuss, argument)* Szene *f*. **to make a ~** eine Szene machen. **(e)** *(col)* **the drug** *etc* **~** die

Drogenszene *etc (col)*; **that's not my ~** da steh' ich nicht drauf *(col)*.

scenery ['siːnərɪ] *n (landscape)* Landschaft *f*; *(Theat)* Kulissen *pl*.

scenic ['siːnɪk] *adj route etc* landschaftlich; *(picturesque)* malerisch. **~ railway** *(roller coaster)* Achterbahn *f*.

scent [sent] **1** *n (smell)* Duft, Geruch *m*; *(perfume)* Parfüm *nt*; *(of animal)* Fährte *f*. **to be on the ~** *(lit, fig)* auf der Spur sein *(of sb/sth* jdm/einer Sache); **to lose the ~** *(lit, fig)* die Spur verlieren; **to put** *or* **throw sb off the ~** *(lit, fig)* jdn von der Spur abbringen. **2** *vt* **(a)** *(smell, suspect)* wittern. **(b)** *(perfume)* parfümieren. **roses ~ed the air** der Duft von Rosen erfüllte die Luft.

sceptic, *(US)* **skeptic** ['skeptɪk] *n* Skeptiker(in *f*) *m*.

sceptical, *(US)* **skeptical** ['skeptɪkəl] *adj* skeptisch. **he was ~ about it** er war skeptisch.

scepticism, *(US)* **skepticism** ['skeptɪsɪzəm] *n* Skepsis *f (about* gegenüber).

sceptre, *(US)* **scepter** ['septəʳ] *n* Szepter *nt*.

schedule ['ʃedjuːl *(esp Brit)*, 'skedʒʊəl] **1** *n (of events)* Programm *nt*; *(of work)* Zeitplan *m*; *(US: timetable)* Fahr-/Flugplan *m*; *(list)* Verzeichnis *nt*. **what's on the ~ for today?** was steht für heute auf dem Programm?; **according to ~** planmäßig; *(work also)* nach Plan; **the train is behind ~** der Zug hat Verspätung; **the bus was on ~** der Bus war pünktlich; **ahead of ~** dem Zeitplan voraus; **behind ~** im Rückstand; **we are working to a very tight ~** wir arbeiten nach einem sehr knappen Zeitplan. **2** *vt* planen; *(put on programme, timetable)* ansetzen; *(US: list)* aufführen. **the work is ~d for completion in 3 months** die Arbeit soll (laut Zeitplan) in 3 Monaten fertig sein; **this stop was not ~d** dieser Aufenthalt war nicht eingeplant.

scheduled ['ʃedjuːld *(esp Brit)*, 'skedʒʊəld] *adj* vorgesehen, geplant; *departure etc* planmäßig. **~ flight** *(not charter)* Linienflug *m*; *(on timetable)* planmäßiger Flug.

schematic [skɪ'mætɪk] *adj* schematisch.

scheme [skiːm] **1** *n* **(a)** *(plan)* Plan *m*, Programm *nt*; *(project)* Projekt *nt*; *(housing ~)* Siedlung *f*; *(idea)* Idee *f*. **savings ~** Sparprogramm *nt*; **pension ~** Rentenschema *nt*; **the ~ for the new ring road** das neue Umgehungsstraßenprojekt; **a ~ of work** ein Arbeitsprogramm *nt*. **(b)** *(plot)* (raffinierter) Plan; *(political also)* Komplott *nt*; *(at court, in firm etc)* Intrige *f*. **2** *vi* Pläne schmieden; *(at court, in firm etc)* intrigieren.

scheming ['skiːmɪŋ] **1** *n* Tricks *pl (col)*; *(of politicians etc)* Machenschaften *pl*; *(in firm etc)* Intrigen *pl*. **2** *adj methods, businessman* raffiniert; *politician* gewieft *(col)*.

schism ['sɪzəm] *n (Eccl)* Schisma *nt*; *(general)* Spaltung *f*.

schizophrenia [,skɪtsəʊ'friːnɪə] *n* Schizophrenie *f*.

schizophrenic ['skɪtsəʊ'frenɪk] **1** *adj person, reaction* schizophren. **2** *n* Schizophrene(r) *mf*.

schnap(p)s [ʃnæps] *n* Schnaps *m*.

scholar ['skɒləʳ] *n (learned person)* Gelehrte(r) *mf*; *(student)* Student(in *f*) *m*; Schüler(in *f*) *m*. **the foremost ~s of our time** die führenden Wissenschaftler unserer Zeit; **a famous Shakespeare ~** ein bekannter Shakespearekenner.

scholarly ['skɒləlɪ] *adj thesis etc* wissenschaftlich; *(learned)* gelehrt; *interests* hochgeistig.

scholarship ['skɒləʃɪp] *n (learning)* Gelehrsamkeit *f*; *(money award)* Stipendium *nt*.

scholastic [skə'læstɪk] *adj (relative to school)* schulisch, Schul-; *(Univ)* Studien-.

school[1] [skuːl] **1** *n* **(a)** Schule *f*; *(US: college, university)* College *nt*; Universität *f*. **at ~** in der Schule/im College/an der Universität; **to go to ~** in die Schule/ins College/zur Universität gehen; **there's no ~ tomorrow** morgen ist schulfrei *or* keine Schule. **(b)** *(Univ: department)* Fachbereich *m*; *(of medicine, law)* Fakultät *f*. **(c)** *(group of artists etc)* Schule *f*. **he's a diplomat of the old ~** er ist ein Diplomat der alten Schule. **2** *vt* lehren; *animal* dressieren. **to ~ sb in a technique** jdn in einer Technik unterrichten.

school[2] *n (of fish)* Schwarm *m*.

school *in cpds* Schul-; **~ age** *n* schulpflichtiges Alter, Schulalter *nt*; **~ boy** *n* Schüler *m*; **~children** *npl* Schulkinder, Schüler *pl*; **~days** *npl* Schulzeit *f*; **~ fees** *npl* Schulgeld *nt*; **~girl** *n* Schülerin *f*.

schooling ['skuːlɪŋ] *n (education)* Ausbildung *f*. **compulsory ~** die Schulpflicht.

school: ~-leaver *n* Schulabgänger(in *f*) *m*; **~-leaving age** *n* Schulabgangsalter *nt*; **~master** *n* Lehrer *m*; **~mistress** *n (Brit)* Lehrerin *f*; **~room** *n* Klassenzimmer *nt*; **~teacher** *n* Lehrer(in *f*) *m*; **~ year** *n* Schuljahr *nt*.

schooner ['skuːnəʳ] *n* **(a)** *(boat)* Schoner *m*. **(b)** *(sherry glass)* großes Sherryglas; *(US, Austral: beer ~)* hohes Bierglas.

sciatica [saɪ'ætɪkə] *n* Ischias *m or nt*.

science ['saɪəns] *n* **(a)** Wissenschaft *f*; *(natural ~)* Naturwissenschaft *f*. **to study ~** Naturwissenschaften studieren; **a man of ~** ein Wissenschaftler *m*. **(b)** *(systematic knowledge or skill)* Technik *f*.

science fiction *n* Science-fiction *f*. **~ novel** Zukunftsroman, Science-fiction-Roman *m*.

scientific [,saɪən'tɪfɪk] *adj* wissenschaftlich; *(of natural sciences)* naturwissenschaftlich.

scientist ['saɪəntɪst] *n* Wissenschaftler(in *f*) *m*; *(natural ~)* Naturwissenschaftler(in *f*) *m*.

Scillies ['sɪlɪz], **Scilly Isles** ['sɪlɪ,aɪlz] *npl* Scilly-Inseln *pl*.

scintillating ['sɪntɪleɪtɪŋ] *adj* funkelnd *attr*; *(fig) (witty, lively) wit, humour* sprühend *attr*.

scissors ['sɪzəz] *n pl* Schere *f*. **a pair of ~** eine Schere.

sclerosis [sklɪ'rəʊsɪs] *n* Sklerose *f*.

scoff[1] [skɒf] *vi* spotten. **to ~ at sb/sth** jdn/etw verachten; *(verbally)* sich verächtlich über jdn/etw äußern.

scoff[2] *vt (col)* futtern *(col)*. **she ~ed the lot** sie hat alles verputzt *(col)*.

scold [skəʊld] *vt* ausschimpfen *(for* wegen). **she ~ed him for coming home late** sie schimpfte ihn aus, weil er so spät heimkam.

scolding ['skəʊldɪŋ] *n* Schelte *f no pl*; *(act)* Schimpferei *f*. **to give sb a ~** jdn ausschimpfen.

scollop *n* = **scallop.**

scone [skɒn] *n* ≃ Milchbrötchen *nt*; *(with sultanas)* Rosinenbrötchen *nt*.

scoop [skuːp] **1** *n* **(a)** *(instrument)* Schaufel *f*; *(for ice cream, potatoes etc)* Portionierer *m*. **(b)** *(col: lucky gain)* Fang *m (col)*. **(c)** *(Press)* Knüller *m (col)*. **2** *vt* **(a)** schaufeln; *liquid* schöpfen. **(b) The Times ~ed the other papers** die Times ist den anderen Zeitungen zuvorgekommen.

♦ **scoop out** *vt sep* **(a)** *(take out)* herausschaufeln; *liquid* herausschöpfen. **(b)** *(hollow out) marrow etc* aushöhlen; *hole* graben.

♦ **scoop up** *vt sep* aufschaufeln; *liquid* aufschöpfen. **she ~ed the cards/money ~** sie raffte die Karten/das Geld an sich *(acc)*.

scoot [skuːt] *vi (col) (scram)* abzischen *(col)*; *(walk quickly)* rennen.

scooter ['skuːtəʳ] *n* (Tret)roller *m*; *(motor ~)* Motorroller *m*.

scope [skəʊp] *n* **(a)** *(of topic, investigation, knowledge)* Umfang *m*; *(of law, measures)* Reichweite *f*; *(of sb's duties, tribunal)* Kompetenzbereich *m*. **sth is within the ~ of sth** etw hält sich im Rahmen einer Sache *(gen)*; **sth is beyond the ~ of sth** etw geht über etw *(acc)* hinaus; **that is beyond my ~** das übersteigt mein Fassungsvermögen. **(b)** *(opportunity)* Möglichkeit(en *pl*) *f*;

(to develop one's talents) Entfaltungsmöglichkeit *f*; *(to use one's talents)* Spielraum *m*. **there is ~ for improvement** es könnte noch verbessert werden; **to give sb ~ to do sth** jdm den nötigen Spielraum geben, etw zu tun.

scorch [skɔːtʃ] **1** *n (also* **~ mark***)* Brandfleck *m*. **2** *vt* versengen. **the sun ~ed our faces** die Sonne brannte auf unsere Gesichter.

scorcher [ˈskɔːtʃəʳ] *n (col)* **last summer was a real ~** im letzten Sommer war es wirklich heiß.

scorching [ˈskɔːtʃɪŋ] *adj (very hot) sun, iron* glühend heiß; *day, weather* brütend heiß; *(col: very fast) speed* rasend.

score [skɔːʳ] **1** *n* **(a)** *(number of points)* (Punkte)stand *m*; *(of game, Sport)* Spielstand *m*; *(final ~)* Spielergebnis *nt*. **the ~ was Celtic 2, Rangers 1** es stand 2:1 *or* zwei zu eins für Celtic (gegen Rangers); *(final ~)* Celtic schlug Rangers (mit) 2:1; **to keep (the) ~** (mit)zählen; *(officially)* Punkte zählen; *(on scoreboard)* Punkte anschreiben; **what's the ~?** wie steht es?; *(fig also)* wie sieht es aus? *(on* mit*) (col)*; **to make a ~ with sb** *(fig: impress)* jdn stark beeindrucken.

(b) *(reckoning, grudge)* **to pay off old ~s** alte Schulden begleichen; **to have a ~ to settle with sb** mit jdm eine alte Rechnung zu begleichen haben.

(c) *(Mus) (printed music)* Noten *pl*; *(of classical music also)* Partitur *f*; *(of film, musical)* Musik *f*.

(d) *(line, cut)* Kerbe *f*; *(on body)* Kratzer *m*; *(weal)* Striemen *m*.

(e) *(20)* **a ~** zwanzig; **~s of ...** *(many)* Hunderte von ..., jede Menge ... *(col)*; **by the ~** massenweise *(col)*.

(f) *(reason, ground)* Grund *m*. **on that ~** *(connection)* in diesem Zusammenhang.

2 *vt* **(a)** erzielen; *points also* bekommen; *goals also* schießen; *runs also* schaffen. **he ~d an advantage over his opponent** er war gegenüber seinem Gegner im Vorteil; **each correct answer ~s five points** jede richtige Antwort zählt fünf Punkte; **to ~ a point off sb** *(fig)* jdn ausstechen; **to ~ a hit with sb** jdn stark beeindrucken. **(b)** *(groove)* einkerben, Kerben/eine Kerbe machen in *(+acc)*; *(mark)* Kratzer/einen Kratzer machen in *(+acc)*.

3 *vi* **(a)** einen Punkt erzielen; *(Ftbl etc)* ein Tor schießen. **to ~ well/badly** gut/schlecht abschneiden; **that's where he ~s** *(fig)* das ist sein großes Plus. **(b)** *(keep ~)* (mit)zählen. **(c) to ~ with sb** *(col: have sex)* mit jdm bumsen *(col)*.

♦ **score off 1** *vt sep (delete)* ausstreichen. **2** *vi +prep obj* **to ~ ~ sb** jdn als dumm hinstellen.

score: ~board *n* Anzeigetafel *f*; **~keeper** *n (official) (Sport)* Anschreiber *m*; *(in quiz etc)* Punktezähler *m*.

scorer [ˈskɔːrəʳ] *n* **(a)** *(Ftbl etc: player)* Torschütze *m*. **Chelsea were the highest ~s** Chelsea schoß die meisten Tore; **the leading ~ in the quiz** der, der die meisten Punkte im Quiz erzielt. **(b)** = **scorekeeper.**

scorn [ˈskɔːn] **1** *n (disdain)* Verachtung *f*; *(verbal also)* Hohn *m*. **to pour ~ on sth** etw verächtlich abtun. **2** *vt (treat scornfully)* verachten; *(condescendingly)* verächtlich behandeln; *(turn down) gift, advice* verschmähen; *idea* mit Verachtung von sich weisen.

scornful [ˈskɔːnfʊl] *adj* verächtlich; *laughter also, person* spöttisch, höhnisch. **to be ~ of sb/sth** jdn/etw verachten; *(verbally)* jdn/etw verhöhnen.

Scorpio [ˈskɔːpɪəʊ] *n (Astrol)* Skorpion *m*.

scorpion [ˈskɔːpɪən] *n* Skorpion *m*.

Scot [skɒt] *n* Schotte *m*, Schottin *f*.

Scotch [skɒtʃ] **1** *adj* schottisch. **~ egg** *hartgekochtes Ei in Wurstbrät, paniert und ausgebacken;* **~ tape** ® Tesafilm ® *m*. **2** *n* **(a)** *(~ whisky)* Scotch *m*. **(b) the ~** *pl* die Schotten *pl*.

scotch [skɒtʃ] *vt rumour* aus der Welt schaffen; *idea, plan* unterbinden.

scot-free [ˈskɒtˈfriː] *adv*: **to get off ~** ungeschoren davonkommen.

Scotland [ˈskɒtlənd] *n* Schottland *nt*.

Scots [skɒts] *adj* schottisch.

Scots: ~man *n* Schotte *m*; **~woman** *n* Schottin *f*.

Scottish [ˈskɒtɪʃ] **1** *adj* schottisch. **2** *n* **(a)** *(dialect)* Schottisch *nt*. **(b) the ~** *pl* die Schotten *pl*.

scoundrel [ˈskaʊndrəl] *n (dated)* Schurke *m*; *(col)* Bengel *m*.

scour[1] [ˈskaʊəʳ] *vt pans* scheuern.

scour[2] *vt area* absuchen *(for* nach*)*.

scourer [ˈskaʊərəʳ] *n* Topfkratzer *m*.

scourge [skɜːdʒ] **1** *n (lit, fig)* Geißel *f*. **2** *vt* **(a)** geißeln. **(b)** *(fig: punish)* (be)strafen.

scout [skaʊt] **1** *n* **(a)** *(Mil)* Späher *m*. **(b)** Pfadfinder *m*; *(US: girl ~)* Pfadfinderin *f*. **2** *vi* erkunden. **to ~ for sth** nach etw Ausschau halten.

scout: ~ master *n* Gruppenführer *m*; **~ troop** *n* Pfadfindergruppe *f*.

scowl [skaʊl] **1** *n* finsterer Blick, böses Gesicht. **to give sb a ~** jdn böse ansehen. **2** *vi* ein finsteres Gesicht machen. **to ~ at sb** jdn böse ansehen.

scrabble [ˈskræbl] *vi (also* **~ about***)* (herum)tasten; *(among movable objects)* (herum)wühlen.

scraggy [ˈskrægɪ] *adj (+er)* dürr; *meat* sehnig.

scram [skræm] *vi (col)* abhauen *(col)*. **~!** ab!, verschwinde/verschwindet!

scramble [ˈskræmbl] **1** *vt* **(a)** *pieces, letters* (ver)mischen. **(b)** *eggs* verrühren. **~d eggs** Rührei(er *pl*) *nt*. **(c)** *(Telec) message* verschlüsseln.

2 *vi* **(a)** *(climb)* klettern. **he ~d to his feet** er rappelte sich auf *(col)*; **to ~ through the hedge** durch die Hecke krabbeln *(col)*; **to ~ up sth** auf etw *(acc)* hinaufklettern. **(b)** *(struggle)* **to ~ for sth/to get sth** sich um etw raufen/sich raufen, um etw zu bekommen; *for ball etc* um etw kämpfen/darum kämpfen, etw zu bekommen; *for bargains, job, good site* sich um etw drängeln/sich drängeln, um etw zu bekommen.

3 *n* **(a)** *(rush)* Gedrängel *nt (for* nach*)*. **(b)** *(motorcycle ~)* Querfeldeinrennen *nt*.

scrap[1] [skræp] **1** *n* **(a)** *(small piece)* Stückchen *nt*; *(fig)* bißchen *no pl*; *(of papers also, of conversation, news)* Fetzen *m*; *(of truth)* Fünkchen *nt*, Spur *f*. **there isn't a ~ of food in the house** es ist überhaupt nichts zu essen im Haus; **not a ~!** nicht die Spur!; **not a ~ of evidence** nicht der geringste Beweis. **(b)** *(usu pl: leftover)* Rest *m*. **(c)** *(waste material)* Altmaterial *nt*; *(metal)* Schrott *m*; *(paper)* Altpapier *nt*. **are these notes ~?** können die Notizen weggeworfen werden?; **to sell a ship for ~** ein Schiff zum Verschrotten verkaufen. **2** *vt car, ship etc* verschrotten; *furniture, clothes* ausrangieren; *idea, plan etc* fallenlassen; *piece of work* wegwerfen.

scrap[2] *(col)* **1** *n* Balgerei *f*; *(verbal)* Streiterei *f*. **2** *vi* sich balgen; *(verbally)* sich streiten.

scrap: ~book *n* Sammelalbum *nt*; **~ dealer** *n* Altwarenhändler *m*.

scrape [skreɪp] **1** *n* **(a)** *(act)* **to give sth a ~** *see vt (a)*. **(b)** *(mark, graze)* Schramme *f*. **(c)** *(sound)* Kratzen *nt*. **(d)** *(difficulty)* Schwulitäten *pl (col)*. **to get sb out of a ~** jdm aus der Klemme helfen *(col)*. **2** *vt* **(a)** *(make clean or smooth) potatoes etc* schaben; *plate, wall* abkratzen; *saucepan* auskratzen. **that's really scraping the barrel** *(fig)* das ist wirklich das Letzte vom Letzten. **(b)** *gatepost etc* streifen; *paintwork* ankratzen; *knee* aufschürfen. **(c)** *(grate against)* kratzen an *(+dat)*. **(d)** *(make by scraping) hole* scharren. **to ~ a living** gerade so sein Auskommen haben. **3** *vi* **he ~d at the paint for hours** er kratzte stundenlang an der Farbe herum.

♦ **scrape along** *or* **by** *vi* sich schlecht und recht durchschlagen *(col) (on* mit*)*.

♦ **scrape off** *vt sep* abkratzen *(prep obj* von*)*.
♦ **scrape through 1** *vi (lit) (object)* gerade so durchgehen; *(person)* sich durchzwängen; *(in exam)* gerade noch durchkommen *(col)*. **2** *vi +prep obj narrow gap* sich durchzwängen durch; *exam* gerade noch durchkommen durch *(col)*.
♦ **scrape together** *vt sep leaves* zusammenharken; *money* zusammenkratzen; *people* zusammenbringen; *support* organisieren.
scraper ['skreɪpə^r] *n (tool)* Spachtel *m*; *(at door)* Kratzeisen *nt*.
scrap heap *n* Schrotthaufen *m*. **to be thrown on the ~** *(thing)* zum Schrott geworfen werden; *(person)* zum alten Eisen geworfen werden; *(idea)* über Bord geworfen werden.
scrap metal *n* Schrott *m*, Altmetall *nt*.
scrappy ['skræpɪ] *adj (+er)* zusammengestoppelt *(col)*; *knowledge* lückenhaft.
scrap yard *n* Schrottplatz *m*.
scratch [skrætʃ] **1** *n* **(a)** *(mark)* Kratzer *m*. **(b)** *(act)* **the dog enjoys a ~** der Hund kratzt sich gern. **(c) to start from ~** (ganz) von vorn(e) anfangen; **to start sth from ~** etw ganz von vorne anfangen; *business* etw aus dem Nichts aufbauen; **to learn a language/a new trade from ~** eine Sprache von Grund auf erlernen/einen neuen Beruf von der Pike auf erlernen; **to come up to ~** *(col)* den Anforderungen entsprechen.
2 *adj attr meal* improvisiert; *crew, team* zusammengewürfelt.
3 *vt* kratzen; *hole* scharren; *(leave ~es on)* zerkratzen. **to ~ a living** sich *(dat)* einen kümmerlichen Lebensunterhalt verdienen; **to ~ one's head** *(lit, fig)* sich *(dat)* den Kopf kratzen; **if you ~ my back, I'll ~ yours** *(fig)* eine Hand wäscht die andere; **to ~ the surface of sth** *(fig)* etw oberflächlich berühren.
4 *vi* **(a)** *(make ~ing movement/noise)* kratzen; *(in soil etc)* scharren; *(~ oneself)* sich kratzen. **(b)** *(become ~ed)* **the new paint ~es easily** die neue Farbe bekommt leicht Kratzer.
♦ **scratch out** *vt sep* auskratzen; *(cross out)* ausstreichen.
scratchy ['skrætʃɪ] *adj (+er) sound, pen* kratzend *attr*; *record* zerkratzt; *feel, sweater* kratzig.
scrawl [skrɔːl] **1** *n* Gekrakel *nt (col)*; *(handwriting)* Klaue *f (col)*; *(col: message)* gekritzelte Nachricht. **2** *vt* hinkritzeln.
scrawny ['skrɔːnɪ] *adj (+er)* dürr.
scream [skriːm] **1** *n* **(a)** Schrei *m*; *(of tyres)* Kreischen *nt*; *(of engines, siren)* Heulen *nt*. **there were ~s of laughter from the audience** das Publikum kreischte vor Lachen; **to give a ~** einen Schrei ausstoßen. **(b)** *(fig col)* **to be a ~** zum Schreien sein *(col)*. **2** *vt* schreien; *command* brüllen; *(fig: headlines)* ausschreien. **to ~ sth at sb** jdm etw zuschreien; **you idiot, she ~ed at me** du Idiot, schrie sie mich an. **3** *vi* schreien; *(tyres)* kreischen; *(wind, engine, siren)* heulen. **to ~ at sb** jdn anschreien; **to ~ with laughter** vor Lachen kreischen.
scree [skriː] *n* Geröll *nt*.
screech [skriːtʃ] **1** *n* Kreischen *nt no pl*; *(of tyres also, of brakes)* Quietschen *nt no pl*; *(of owl)* Schrei *m*. **the car stopped with a ~ of brakes** das Auto hielt mit quietschenden Bremsen. **2** *vi* kreischen; *(brakes, tyres also)* quietschen.
screen [skriːn] **1** *n* **(a)** *(protective)* Schirm *m*; *(for privacy etc)* Wandschirm *m*; *(as partition)* Trennwand *f*; *(against insects)* Fliegenfenster *nt*; *(fig) (for protection)* Schutz *m*; *(of trees)* Wand *f*; *(of mist, secrecy)* Schleier *m*. **(b)** *(Film)* Leinwand *f*; *(TV, radar ~, Comp)* (Bild)schirm *m*. **the big/small ~** die Leinwand/die Mattscheibe. **2** *vt* **(a)** *(hide)* verdecken; *(protect)* abschirmen *(from* gegen*)*. **he ~ed his eyes from the sun** er schützte die Augen vor der Sonne. **(b)** *TV programme* senden; *film* vorführen. **(c)** *(sift)* sieben. **(d)** *(investigate) applicants, security risks* überprüfen.
screening ['skriːnɪŋ] *n* **(a)** *(of applicants, security risks)* Überprüfung *f*. **(b)** *(of film)* Vorführung *f*; *(TV)* Sendung *f*.
screenplay ['skriːnpleɪ] *n* Drehbuch *nt*.
screw [skruː] **1** *n* **(a)** *(Mech, Naut, Aviat)* Schraube *f*. **he's got a ~ loose** *(col)* bei dem ist eine Schraube locker *(col)*; **to put the ~s on sb** *(col)* jdm die Daumenschrauben anlegen. **(b)** *(Brit col: prison officer)* Schließer *(col)*. **2** *vt* **(a)** schrauben *(to* an *+acc, onto* auf *+acc)*. **(b)** *(col: put pressure on)* **to ~ sb for sth** etw aus jdm herausquetschen *(col)*. **(c)** *(col!: have sex with)* bumsen *(col)*, vögeln *(col!)*.
♦ **screw together** *vt sep* zusammenschrauben.
♦ **screw up** *vt sep* **(a)** *paper, material* zerknüllen; *eyes* zusammenkneifen; *face* verziehen. **to ~ ~ one's courage** seinen ganzen Mut zusammennehmen. **(b)** *(col) (spoil)* vermasseln *(col)*; *(make uptight) sb* neurotisch machen. **to be ~ed ~ about sth** sich wegen etw ganz verrückt machen.
screw: ~ball *(esp US col) n* Spinner(in *f*) *m (col)*; **~driver** *n* Schraubenzieher *m*.
screwy ['skruːɪ] *adj (+er) (col)* verrückt, bekloppt *(col)*; *person, humour* komisch.
scribble ['skrɪbl] **1** *n* Gekritzel *nt no pl*; *(note)* schnell hingekritzelte Nachricht. **2** *vt* hinkritzeln. **to ~ sth on sth** etw auf etw *(acc)* kritzeln; **to ~ sth down** etw hinkritzeln. **3** *vi* kritzeln. **he ~s away all day at his novel** er schreibt den ganzen Tag an seinem Roman herum.
scribe [skraɪb] *n* Schreiber *m*; *(Bibl)* Schriftgelehrte(r) *m*.
scrimmage ['skrɪmɪdʒ] *n (US Ftbl)* Gedränge *nt*; *(col: struggle also)* Rangelei *f (col)*; *(Rugby)* offenes Gedränge.
scrimp [skrɪmp] *vi* sparen, knausern. **to ~ and save** geizen und sparen.
script [skrɪpt] *n* **(a)** *(style of writing)* Schrift *f*; *(handwriting)* Handschrift *f*. **(b)** *(of play, documentary)* Text *m*; *(for film)* Drehbuch *nt*.
scripture ['skrɪptʃə^r] *n* **(a) S~, the S~s** die (Heilige) Schrift. **(b)** *(Sch)* Religion *f*.
scriptwriter ['skrɪpt,raɪtə^r] *n (Film)* Drehbuchautor(in *f*) *m*.
scroll [skrəʊl] *n* Schriftrolle *f*; *(decorative)* Schnörkel *m*.
scrotum ['skrəʊtəm] *n (Anat)* Hodensack *m*.
scrounge [skraʊndʒ] *(col)* **1** *vi (sponge)* schnorren *(col) (off, from* bei*)*. **he ~d off his parents for years** er lag seinen Eltern jahrelang auf der Tasche *(col)*. **2** *vt* schnorren *(col)*, abstauben *(col) (from, off* bei*)*. **3** *n (col)* **to be on the ~** am Schnorren sein *(col)*.
scrounger ['skraʊndʒə^r] *n (col)* Schnorrer *m (col)*.
scrub[1] [skrʌb] *nt (Bot)* Gebüsch, Gestrüpp *nt*.
scrub[2] **1** *n* Schrubben *nt no pl*. **to give sth a ~/a good ~** etw schrubben/gründlich abschrubben. **2** *vt* schrubben; *vegetables* putzen; *(col: cancel)* abblasen *(col)*; *idea* abschreiben *(col)*. **to ~ oneself down** sich abschrubben.
scrubbing brush ['skrʌbɪŋ,brʌʃ] *n* Scheuerbürste *f*; *(for hands)* Handbürste *f*.
scruff[1] [skrʌf] *n* **by the ~ of the neck** am Genick.
scruff[2] *n (col: scruffy person) (man)* schlampig aussehender Typ; *(woman)* Schlampe *f (col)*.
scruffy ['skrʌfɪ] *adj (+er) (col)* vergammelt *(col)*; *house also* verlottert *(col)*, verwahrlost.
scrum [skrʌm] *n (Rugby)* Gedränge *nt*.
scrumptious ['skrʌmpʃəs] *adj (col) meal etc* lecker.
scruple ['skruːpl] *n* Skrupel *m usu pl*. **~s** *(doubts)* (moralische) Bedenken *pl*. **to have no ~s** keine Skrupel haben.
scrupulous ['skruːpjʊləs] *adj (person)* gewissenhaft; *honesty, fairness* unbedingt; *cleanliness* peinlich; *account* (peinlich) genau.

scrupulously ['skru:pjʊləslɪ] *adv (honestly, conscientiously)* gewissenhaft; *(meticulously) exact, clean* peinlich; *fair, careful* äußerst.
scrutinize ['skru:tɪnaɪz] *vt (examine)* (genau) untersuchen; *(check)* genau prüfen; *votes* prüfen; *(stare at)* mustern. **to ~ sth for sth** etw auf etw *(acc)* prüfen.
scrutiny ['skru:tɪnɪ] *n* **(a)** *(examination)* Untersuchung *f*; *(checking)* (Über)prüfung *f*; *(of person)* Musterung *f*; *(stare)* musternder Blick. **it does not stand up to ~** es hält keiner genauen Prüfung stand. **(b)** *(Pol)* Wahlprüfung *f*.
scuba ['sku:bə] *n* (Schwimm)tauchgerät *nt*. **~ diver** (Sport)taucher(in *f*) *m*; **~ diving** Sporttauchen *nt*.
scuff [skʌf] **1** *vt* abwetzen. **2** *n (~ mark)* abgewetzte Stelle.
scuffle ['skʌfl] **1** *n (skirmish)* Rauferei *f (col)*. **2** *vi (have skirmish)* sich raufen. **to ~ with the police** ein Handgemenge *nt* mit der Polizei haben.
scullery ['skʌlərɪ] *n* Spülküche *f*.
sculpt [skʌlpt] **1** *vt* = **sculpture 2. 2** *vi* bildhauern *(col)*.
sculptor ['skʌlptə^r] *n* Bildhauer(in *f*) *m*.
sculptress ['skʌlptrɪs] *n* Bildhauerin *f*.
sculpture ['skʌlptʃə^r] **1** *n (art)* Bildhauerkunst *f*; *(work)* Bildhauerei *f*; *(object)* Skulptur, Plastik *f*. **2** *vt* formen; *(in stone)* hauen, meißeln; *(in clay etc)* modellieren. **he ~d the tombstone out of marble** er haute den Grabstein in Marmor.
scum [skʌm] *n* **(a)** *(on liquid)* Schaum *m*; *(residue)* Rand *m*. **(b)** *(pej col) (collective)* Abschaum *m*; *(one individual)* Dreckskerl *m (col)*. **the ~ of the earth** der Abschaum der Menschheit.
scupper ['skʌpə^r] *vt (Naut)* versenken; *(Brit col: ruin)* zerschlagen. **if he finds out, we'll be ~ed** wenn er das erfährt, sind wir erledigt *(col)*.
scurrilous ['skʌrɪləs] *adj (abusive)* verleumderisch; *(indecent)* unflätig.
scurry ['skʌrɪ] *vi (person)* hasten; *(with small steps)* trippeln; *(animals)* huschen. **to ~ along** entlanghasten/entlangtrippeln/entlanghuschen.
scurvy ['skɜ:vɪ] *n* Skorbut *m*.
scuttle[1] ['skʌtl] *n* Kohleneimer *m*.
scuttle[2] *vi (person)* trippeln; *(animals)* hoppeln; *(spiders, crabs etc)* krabbeln. **she ~d off in a hurry** sie flitzte davon.
scuttle[3] *(Naut)* **1** *n* Luke *f*. **2** *vt* versenken.
scythe [saɪð] **1** *n* Sense *f*. **2** *vt* (mit der Sense) mähen.
SDP = Social Democratic Party.
sea [si:] *n* **(a)** Meer *nt*, See *f*. **by ~** auf dem Seeweg; **to travel by ~** mit dem Schiff fahren; **a town by the ~** eine Stadt am Meer *or* an der See; **(out) at ~** auf See; **as I looked out to ~** als ich aufs Meer hinausblickte; **to be all at ~** *(fig)* nicht durchblicken *(col) (with* bei*)*; **to go to ~** zur See gehen; **to put to ~** in See stechen; **heavy/strong ~s** schwere/rauhe See; **a ~ of faces** ein Meer von Gesichtern; **a ~ of flame** ein Flammenmeer.
sea: ~ air *n* Seeluft *f*; **~ anemone** *n* Seeanemone *f*; **~bed** *n* Meeresboden *m*; **~ bird** *n* Seevogel *m*; **~board** *n (US)* Küste *f*; **~ breeze** *n* Seewind *m*; **~faring** *adj nation, people* seefahrend; *boat* hochseetüchtig; **~food** *n* Meeresfrüchte *pl*; **~ front** *n* Strandpromenade *f*; **~going** *adj boat etc* hochseetüchtig; *nation, family* Seefahrer-; **~gull** *n* Möwe *f*; **~horse** *n* Seepferdchen *nt*.
seal[1] [si:l] *n (Zool)* Seehund *m*; *(~skin)* Seal *m*.
seal[2] **1** *n* **(a)** *(impression in wax etc)* Siegel *nt*; *(against unauthorized opening)* Versiegelung *f*; *(die)* Stempel *m*; *(decorative label)* Aufkleber *m*. **under the ~ of secrecy** unter dem Siegel der Verschwiegenheit; **~ of quality** Gütesiegel *nt*; **to put one's ~ of approval on sth** einer Sache *(dat)* seine offizielle Zustimmung geben. **(b)** *(airtight closure)* Verschluß *m*; *(washer)* Dichtung *f*. **2** *vt* versiegeln; *envelope, parcel also* zukleben; *(make air- or watertight) joint etc* abdichten; *(fig: finalize)* besiegeln. **~ed envelope** verschlossener Briefumschlag; **my lips are ~ed** meine Lippen sind versiegelt; **this ~ed his fate** dadurch war sein Schicksal besiegelt.
♦ **seal off** *vt sep* absperren, abriegeln.
♦ **seal up** *vt sep* versiegeln; *parcel, letter* zukleben; *crack, windows* abdichten.
sea: ~ legs *npl*: **to find one's ~ legs** standfest werden; **~ level** *n* Meeresspiegel *m*; **above/below ~ level** über/unter dem Meeresspiegel.
sealing wax ['si:lɪŋ,wæks] *n* Siegelwachs *nt*.
sea lion *n* Seelöwe *m*.
seam [si:m] *n* **(a)** Naht *f*. **to come apart at the ~s** *(lit, fig)* aus den Nähten gehen; **to be bursting at the ~s** *(lit, fig)* aus allen Nähten platzen *(col)*. **(b)** *(Geol)* Flöz *nt*.
seaman ['si:mən] *n, pl* **-men** [-mən] Seemann *m*.
seamanship ['si:mənʃɪp] *n* Seemannschaft *f*.
seamstress ['semstrɪs] *n* Näherin *f*.
seamy ['si:mɪ] *adj (+er)* düster. **the ~ side of life** die Schattenseite des Lebens.
séance ['seɪɑ̃:ns] *n* spiritistische Sitzung, Séance *f*.
sea: ~ plane *n* Wasserflugzeug *nt*; **~ port** *n* Seehafen *m*; **~ power** *n* Seemacht *f*.
search [sɜ:tʃ] **1** *n (hunt: for lost object, person etc)* Suche *f (for* nach*)*; *(examination: of luggage etc)* Durchsuchung *f (of gen)*. **to go in ~ of sb/sth** auf die Suche nach jdm/etw gehen; **a ~ through the drawers revealed nothing** er *etc* durchsuchte die Schubladen ohne Erfolg. **2** *vt (for* nach*)* durchsuchen; *archives etc* suchen in *(+dat)*, durchforschen; *conscience* erforschen; *memory etc* durchforschen. **to ~ a place for sb/sth** einen Ort nach jdm/etw absuchen; **~ me!** *(col)* was weiß ich? *(col)*. **3** *vi* suchen *(for* nach*)*.
♦ **search through** *vi +prep obj* durchsuchen; *papers, books* durchsehen.
searching ['sɜ:tʃɪŋ] *adj look* forschend; *question* durchdringend.
search: ~light *n* Suchscheinwerfer *m*; **~ party** *n* Suchmannschaft *f*; **~ warrant** *n* Durchsuchungsbefehl *m*.
searing ['sɪərɪŋ] *adj heat* glühend; *pain also* scharf.
sea: ~scape *n* Seestück *nt*; **~ shell** *n* Muschel *f*; **~shore** *n* Strand *m*; **on the ~shore** am Strand; **~sick** *adj* seekrank; **~sickness** *n* Seekrankheit *f*; **~side 1** *n* **at the ~side** am Meer; **to go to the ~side** ans Meer fahren; **2** *attr resort, town* See-.
season ['si:zn] **1** *n* **(a)** *(of the year)* Jahreszeit *f*. **rainy/monsoon ~** Regen-/Monsunzeit *f*. **(b)** *(sporting ~ etc)* Saison *f*. **holiday ~** Urlaubszeit *f*; **close ~** *(Hunt)* Schonzeit *f*; **nesting/hunting ~** Brut-/Jagdzeit *f*; **the football ~** die Fußballsaison; **strawberries are in ~/out of ~ now** für Erdbeeren ist jetzt die richtige/nicht die richtige Zeit; **"S~'s greetings"** „fröhliche Weihnachten und ein glückliches neues Jahr". **2** *vt* **(a)** *food* würzen; *(fig: temper)* durchsetzen. **(b)** *wood* ablagern; *(fig: inure) troops* stählen.
seasonable ['si:zənəbl] *adj dress, weather etc* der Jahreszeit entsprechend *attr*. **to be ~** der Jahreszeit entsprechen.
seasonal ['si:zənl] *adj employment etc* Saison-.
seasoned ['si:znd] *adj* **(a)** *food* gewürzt. **(b)** *timber* abgelagert. **(c)** *(fig: experienced)* erfahren.
seasoning ['si:znɪŋ] *n (Cook)* Gewürz *nt*.
season ticket *n (Rail)* Zeitkarte *f*; *(Theat)* Abonnement *nt*.
seat [si:t] **1** *n* **(a)** *(place to sit)* (Sitz)platz *m*; *(piece of furniture)* Sitz *m*; *(usu pl: ~ing)* Sitzgelegenheit *f*. **driving ~** Fahrersitz *m*; **we'll have to borrow some ~s** wir werden uns wohl ein paar Stühle borgen müssen; **we haven't enough ~s** wir haben nicht genügend Sitzgelegenheiten; **to lose one's ~** seinen Platz verlieren; **will you keep my ~ for me?** würden Sie mir meinen Platz freihalten?; **I've booked two ~s** ich habe zwei Plätze

reservieren lassen. **(b)** *(of chair etc)* Sitz *m*, Sitzfläche *f*; *(of trousers)* Hosenboden *m*. **(c)** *(on committee, of government, in parliament)* Sitz *m*; *(of fire, trouble)* Herd *m*. **to win a ~** ein Mandat gewinnen; **his ~ is in Devon** sein Wahlkreis *m* ist in Devon; **~ of emotions** Sitz der Gefühle; **~ of learning** Lehrstätte *f*.

2 *vt* **(a)** *person etc* setzen. **to ~ oneself** sich setzen; **to be ~ed** sitzen; **please be ~ed** bitte, setzen Sie sich; **to remain ~ed** sitzen bleiben. **(b)** *(have sitting room for)* **the car/table ~s 4** im Auto/am Tisch ist Platz für 4 Personen; **the theatre ~s 900** das Theater hat 900 Sitzplätze.

seat belt *n* Sicherheitsgurt *m*. **to fasten one's ~** sich anschnallen.

seating ['si:tɪŋ] *n* Sitzplätze *pl*. **~ arrangements** Sitzordnung *f*.

sea: **~ urchin** *n* Seeigel *m*; **~ wall** *n* Deich *m*; **~ water** *n* Meerwasser *nt*; **~weed** *n* (See)tang *m*, Seegras *nt*; **~worthy** *adj* seetüchtig.

sec [sek] = **second(s)** Sek.

secateurs [ˌsekə'tɜ:z] *npl (Brit)* Gartenschere *f*.

secession [sɪ'seʃən] *n* Abspaltung *f*; *(US Hist)* Sezession *f*.

secluded [sɪ'klu:dɪd] *adj spot, house* abgelegen; *life* zurückgezogen.

seclusion [sɪ'klu:ʒən] *n (of house, spot)* Abgelegenheit *f*.

second[1] ['sekənd] **1** *adj* zweite(r, s). **a ~ Goethe** ein zweiter Goethe; **every ~ house** jedes zweite Haus; **to be ~** Zweite(r, s) sein; **to be ~ to none** unübertroffen sein; **in ~ place** *(Sport etc)* an zweiter Stelle; **in the ~ place** *(secondly)* zweitens; **to be ~ in command** *(Mil)* stellvertretender Kommandeur sein; *(fig)* der zweite Mann sein; **will you have a ~ cup?** möchten Sie noch eine Tasse? **2** *adv (+adj)* zweit-; *(+vb)* an zweiter Stelle. **the ~ largest house** das zweitgrößte Haus; **to come/lie ~** *(in race, competition)* Zweite(r) werden. **3** *vt motion, proposal* unterstützen. **I'll ~ that!** *(at meeting)* ich unterstütze das; *(in general)* (genau) meine Meinung.

second[2] *n* **(a)** *(of time, Math, Sci)* Sekunde *f*; *(col: short time)* Augenblick *m*. **just a ~!** (einen) Augenblick!; **it won't take a ~** es dauert nicht lange; **I'll only be a ~ (or two)** ich komme gleich; *(back soon)* ich bin gleich wieder da; **at that very ~** genau in dem Augenblick. **(b) the ~** *(in order)* der/die/das zweite; *(in race, class etc)* der/die/das Zweite; **to come a poor/good ~** einen schlechten/guten zweiten Platz belegen; **Elizabeth the S~** Elisabeth die Zweite. **(c)** *(Brit Univ: degree) mittlere Noten bei Abschlußprüfungen.* **(d) ~s** *pl (col: ~ helping)* Nachschlag *m (col)*; **can I have ~s?** kann ich noch etwas nachbekommen? **(e)** *(Comm)* **~s** Waren zweiter Wahl. **(f)** *(Boxing, duelling)* Sekundant *m*.

secondary ['sekəndərɪ] *adj* **(a)** sekundär, Sekundär- *(also Sci)*; *road, effect* Neben-; *industry* verarbeitend; *reason* weniger bedeutend. **of ~ importance** von untergeordneter Bedeutung. **(b)** *(higher) education, school* höher. **~ modern (school)** *(Brit)* ≃ Realschule *f*.

second: **~-best** **1** *n* Zweitbeste(r, s); **(the) ~-best isn't good enough for him** das Beste ist gerade gut genug für ihn; **2** *adj* zweitbeste(r, s); **3** *adv* **to come off ~-best** es nicht so gut haben; *(come off badly)* den kürzeren ziehen; **~ class** *n (Rail etc, mail)* zweite Klasse; **~-class** *adj* **(a)** *also adv travel, mail, citizen* zweiter Klasse *(after noun)*; **(b)** = **~-rate**; **~ cousin** *n* Cousin *m*/Cousine *f* zweiten Grades.

seconder ['sekəndə[r]] *n* Befürworter(in *f*) *m*.

second: **~ hand** *n (of watch)* Sekundenzeiger *m*; **~-hand** **1** *adj* gebraucht; *car also* Gebraucht-; *dealer* Gebrauchtwaren-; *(for cars)* Gebrauchtwagen-; *bookshop* Antiquariats-; *clothes* getragen, Secondhand- *(esp Comm)*; *(fig) information, knowledge* aus zweiter Hand; **2** *adv* gebraucht, aus zweiter Hand; **I only heard it ~-hand** ich habe es nur aus zweiter Hand.

secondly ['sekəndlɪ] *adv* zweitens; *(secondarily)* an zweiter Stelle, in zweiter Linie.

secondment [sɪ'kɒndmənt] *n* Abordnung *f*. **to be on ~** abgeordnet sein.

second: **~ nature** *n* zweite Natur; **to become ~ nature (to sb)** (jdm) in Fleisch und Blut übergehen; **~-rate** *adj (pej)* zweitklassig; **~ thoughts** *npl* **to have ~ thoughts about sth** sich *(dat)* etw anders überlegen; **on ~ thoughts I decided not to** dann habe ich mich doch dagegen entschieden.

secrecy ['si:krəsɪ] *n (of person)* Verschwiegenheit *f*; *(secretiveness)* Heimlichtuerei *f*; *(of event, talks)* Heimlichkeit *f*. **in ~** im geheimen.

secret ['si:krɪt] **1** *adj* geheim; *negotiations, code also* Geheim-. **the ~ ingredient** die geheimnisvolle Zutat; *(fig: of success etc)* die Zauberformel; **to keep sth ~ (from sb)** etw (vor jdm) geheimhalten; **it's all highly ~** es ist alles streng geheim. **2** *n* Geheimnis *nt*. **in ~** im geheimen; **I told you that in ~** *or* **as a ~** ich habe Ihnen das im Vertrauen erzählt; **they always met in ~** sie trafen sich immer heimlich; *(society etc)* sie hatten immer geheime Versammlungen; **there's no ~ about it** das ist kein Geheimnis; **to keep a ~** ein Geheimnis bewahren; **can you keep a ~?** kannst du schweigen?; **to make no ~ of sth** kein Geheimnis aus etw machen.

secret agent *n* Geheimagent(in *f*) *m*.

secretarial [ˌsekrə'tɛərɪəl] *adj* Sekretärinnen-; *job* Sekretariats-; *qualifications* als Sekretärin.

secretariat [ˌsekrə'tɛərɪət] *n* Sekretariat *nt*.

secretary ['sekrətrɪ] *n* Sekretär(in *f*) *m*; *(of society)* Geschäftsführer(in *f*) *m*; *(keeping minutes etc)* Schriftführer(in *f*) *m*; *(esp US Pol: minister)* Minister(in *f*) *m*.

secretary: **~ bird** *n* Sekretär *m*; **S~ General** *n*, *pl* **Secretaries General** *or* **S~ Generals** Generalsekretär *m*; **S~ of State** *n (Brit)* Minister(in *f*) *m*; *(US)* Außenminister(in *f*) *m*.

secrete [sɪ'kri:t] *vt* **(a)** *(hide)* verbergen. **(b)** *(Med)* absondern.

secretion [sɪ'kri:ʃən] *n* **(a)** *(hiding)* Verbergen *nt*. **(b)** *(Med) (act)* Absonderung *f*; *(substance)* Sekret *nt*.

secretive ['si:krətɪv] *adj person (by nature)* verschlossen; *(in action)* geheimnistuerisch; *smile, behaviour* geheimnisvoll. **to be ~ about sth** mit etw geheimnisvoll tun.

secretly ['si:krətlɪ] *adv (in secrecy)* im geheimen; *meet* heimlich; *(privately)* insgeheim. **he was ~ concerned** insgeheim war er beunruhigt.

secret: **~ police** *n* Geheimpolizei *f*; **~ service** *n* Geheimdienst *m*.

sect [sekt] *n* Sekte *f*.

sectarian [sek'tɛərɪən] *adj policy, views* religiös beeinflußt; *school also* konfessionell; *war, differences* Konfessions-; *groups* sektiererisch. **it was a ~ bombing** der Bombenanschlag hing mit den Konfessionsstreitigkeiten zusammen.

section ['sekʃən] *n* **(a)** *(part)* Teil *m*; *(of book, motorway)* Abschnitt *m*; *(of document, law)* Absatz *m*; *(of railway)* Streckenabschnitt *m*. **the string ~ of the orchestra** die Streicher *pl* des Orchesters; **the sports ~** *(Press)* der Sportteil; **the black ~ of the community** die Gruppe der Schwarzen in der Gesellschaft. **(b)** *(department, Mil)* Abteilung *f*. **(c)** *(diagram)* Schnitt *m*. **vertical/longitudinal ~** Quer-/Längsschnitt *m*.

sectional ['sekʃənl] *adj* **(a)** *(in sections) furniture, pipe* zerlegbar, zusammensetzbar. **~ drawing** Darstellung *f* im Schnitt. **(b)** *rivalries* zwischen den Gruppen; *interests* partikularistisch.

sector ['sektə[r]] *n* Sektor *m*.

secular ['sekjʊlə[r]] *adj* weltlich; *music, art* profan.

secure [sɪ'kjʊəʳ] **1** *adj (+er)* sicher; *(emotionally)* geborgen; *existence, income* gesichert; *(firm) grip, knot* fest. ~ **in the knowledge that ...** ruhig in dem Bewußtsein, daß ...; **to be ~ against sth** vor etw *(dat)* sicher sein; **to feel ~** sich sicher fühlen; *(emotionally)* sich geborgen fühlen; **is the window/lid ~?** ist das Fenster fest zu/ist der Deckel fest drauf? **2** *vt* **(a)** festmachen; *(tie up also)* befestigen; *window, door* fest zumachen; *(with bolt etc)* sichern; *tile* befestigen; *(make safe)* sichern *(from, against* gegen), schützen *(from, against vor +dat)*. **(b)** *(obtain)* sich *(dat)* sichern; *votes, order* erhalten; *profits* erzielen; *share, interest in business* erwerben; *(buy)* erstehen; *employee* verpflichten. **(c)** *(guarantee)* sichern; *loan* (ab)sichern.

securely [sɪ'kjʊəlɪ] *adv (firmly)* fest; *(safely)* sicher.

security [sɪ'kjʊərɪtɪ] *n* **(a)** Sicherheit *f*; *(emotional)* Geborgenheit *f*; *(~ measures)* Sicherheitsvorkehrungen *pl*. **for ~** zur Sicherheit; **airports have tightened their ~** die Flughäfen haben ihre Sicherheitsvorkehrungen verschärft. **(b)** *(~ department)* Sicherheitsdienst *m*. **(c)** *(Fin) (guarantee)* Sicherheit *f*; *(guarantor)* Bürge *m*. **to lend money on ~** Geld gegen Sicherheit leihen. **(d)** *(Fin)* **securities** *pl* (Wert)papiere *pl*.

security *in cpds* Sicherheits-; *(Fin)* Wertpapier-; **~ check** *n* Sicherheitskontrolle *f*; **~ guard** *n* Sicherheitsbeamte(r) *m*; **~ risk** *n* Sicherheitsrisiko *nt*.

sedan [sɪ'dæn] *n (US)* Limousine *f*.

sedate [sɪ'deɪt] **1** *adj (+er)* gesetzt; *colour* ruhig; *life* geruhsam; *speed* gemächlich. **2** *vt* Beruhigungsmittel geben *(+dat)*. **he was heavily ~d** er stand stark unter dem Einfluß von Beruhigungsmitteln.

sedation [sɪ'deɪʃən] *n* Beruhigungsmittel *pl*. **to put sb under ~** jdm Beruhigungsmittel geben.

sedative ['sedətɪv] **1** *n* Beruhigungsmittel *nt*. **2** *adj* beruhigend.

sedentary ['sedntərɪ] *adj job* sitzend *attr*; *worker* Sitz-. **to lead a ~ life** sehr viel sitzen.

sediment ['sedɪmənt] *n* (Boden)satz *m*; *(in river)* Ablagerung *f*; *(in solution)* Sediment *nt*.

seditious [sə'dɪʃəs] *adj* aufrührerisch.

seduce [sɪ'djuːs] *vt* verführen. **to ~ sb into doing sth** jdn zu etw verleiten.

seduction [sɪ'dʌkʃən] *n* Verführung *f*.

seductive [sɪ'dʌktɪv] *adj* verführerisch; *offer* verlockend.

see[1] [siː] *pret* **saw**, *ptp* **seen 1** *vt* **(a)** sehen; *(in book etc also)* lesen; *(check also)* nachsehen, gucken *(col)*; *film* sich *(dat)* ansehen. **worth ~ing** sehenswert; **to ~ sb do sth** sehen, wie jd etw macht; **I've never ~n him swim** ich habe ihn nie schwimmen sehen; **he was ~n to enter the building** man hat ihn gesehen, wie er das Gebäude betrat; **I saw it happen** ich habe gesehen, wie es passiert ist; **I don't like to ~ people mistreated** ich kann es nicht sehen, wenn Menschen schlecht behandelt werden; **I'll go and ~ who it is** ich sehe mal nach (, wer das ist); **~ page 8** siehe Seite 8; **there was nothing to be ~n** es war nichts zu sehen; **I don't know what she ~s in him** ich weiß nicht, was sie an ihm findet; **we don't ~ much of them nowadays** wir sehen sie zur Zeit nur selten; **I shall be ~ing them for dinner** ich treffe sie beim Abendessen; **~ you (soon)!** bis bald!; **be ~ing you!, ~ you later!** bis später!; **~ you on Sunday!** bis Sonntag!; **you must be ~ing things** du siehst wohl Gespenster!; **that remains to be ~n** das wird sich zeigen; **now let me ~ how we can solve this** lassen Sie mich mal überlegen, wie wir das lösen können; **let me ~ if I can't find a better way** mal sehen, ob ich nicht etwas Besseres finden kann; **as I ~ it** so, wie ich das sehe; **try to ~ it my way** versuchen Sie doch einmal, es aus meiner Sicht zu sehen; **I don't ~ it that way** ich sehe das anders.

(b) *(visit)* besuchen; *(on business)* aufsuchen. **to go and ~ sb** jdn besuchen (gehen); **to ~ the doctor** zum Arzt gehen; **he is the man to ~ about this** Sie sollten sich damit an ihn wenden.

(c) *(meet with)* sehen; *(talk to)* sprechen; *(receive visit of)* empfangen. **the boss will ~ you now** der Chef läßt jetzt bitten; **I'll have to ~ my wife about that** das muß ich mit meiner Frau besprechen; **have you ~n Personnel yet?** waren Sie schon bei der Personalabteilung?

(d) *(accompany)* begleiten, bringen. **to ~ sb to the door** jdn zur Tür bringen.

(e) *(visualize)* sich *(dat)* vorstellen. **I can't ~ that working** ich kann mir kaum vorstellen, daß das klappt; **I can't ~ myself in that job** ich glaube nicht, daß das eine Stelle für mich wäre.

(f) *(understand)* verstehen; *(understand the reason for)* einsehen; *(realize)* erkennen. **I don't ~ the need for the change** ich sehe nicht ein, warum das geändert werden muß; **I can ~ that it might be a good thing** ich sehe ja ein, daß das eine gute Idee wäre; **I can ~ I'm going to be busy** ich sehe schon, ich werde viel zu tun haben; **I fail to** *or* **don't ~ how anyone could ...** ich begreife einfach nicht, wie jemand nur ... kann; **I don't ~ how it works** es ist mir nicht klar, wie das funktioniert; **I ~ from this report that ...** ich ersehe aus diesem Bericht, daß ...; **(do you) ~ what I mean?** verstehst du(, was ich meine)?; *(didn't I tell you!)* siehst du's jetzt!; **I ~ what you mean** ich verstehe, was du meinst; *(you're quite right)* ja, du hast recht; **to make sb ~ sth** jdm etw klarmachen.

(g) *(ensure)* **~ that it is done by tomorrow** sieh zu, daß es bis morgen fertig ist.

2 *vi* **(a)** sehen. **let me ~, let's ~** laß mich mal sehen; **who was it? — I couldn't/didn't ~** wer war das? — ich konnte es nicht sehen; **can you ~ to read?** ist es Ihnen hell genug zum Lesen?; **as far as the eye can ~** so weit das Auge reicht; **~ for yourself!** sieh doch selbst!

(b) *(check, find out)* nachsehen, gucken *(col)*. **is he there? — I'll ~** ist er da? — ich sehe mal nach; **let me ~** lassen Sie mich mal nachsehen.

(c) *(understand)* verstehen. **as far as I can ~ ...** soweit ich sehen kann ...; **it's all over, ~?** es ist vorbei, verstehst du?; **as I ~ from your report** wie ich aus Ihrem Bericht ersehe; **(you) ~, it's like this** es ist nämlich so; **I ~!** aha!; *(after explanation)* ach so!

(d) *(consider)* **we'll ~** (wir werden *or* wollen) mal sehen; **I don't know, I'll have to ~** ich weiß nicht, ich muß mal sehen; **let me ~, let's ~** lassen Sie mich mal überlegen.

♦ **see about** *vi +prep obj* **(a)** *(attend to)* sich kümmern um. **he came to ~ ~ the TV** er kam, um sich *(dat)* den Fernseher anzusehen; **he came to ~ ~ the rent** er ist wegen der Miete gekommen. **(b)** *(consider)* **I'll ~ ~ it** ich will mal sehen; **we'll ~ ~ that!** *(iro)* das wollen wir mal sehen.

♦ **see in 1** *vi* herein-/hineinsehen. **2** *vt sep New Year* begrüßen.

♦ **see off** *vt sep* **(a)** *(bid farewell to)* verabschieden. **are you coming to ~ me ~?** kommt ihr mit mir (zum Flughafen *etc*)? **(b)** *(chase off)* Beine machen *(+dat) (col)*.

♦ **see out 1** *vi (look out)* heraus-/hinaussehen. **I can't ~ ~ of the window** ich kann nicht zum Fenster hinaussehen. **2** *vt sep* **(a)** *(show out)* hinausbegleiten *(of* aus). **I'll ~ myself ~** ich finde (schon) alleine hinaus. **(b)** *(last to the end of) (coat, car) winter etc* überdauern; *(invalid) year etc* überleben.

♦ **see over** *vi +prep obj house etc* sich *(dat)* ansehen.

♦ **see through 1** *vi* **(a)** *(lit)* (hin)durchsehen *(prep* *obj* durch). **(b)** +*prep obj (fig: not be deceived by)* durchschauen. **I can ~ right ~ you** ich habe dich durchschaut. **2** *vt always separate* **(a)** *(help through difficult time)* beistehen (+*dat*). **I hope £10 will ~ you ~** die £ 10 reichen dir hoffentlich. **(b)** *job* zu Ende bringen; *(Parl) bill* durchbringen.

♦ **see to** *vi* +*prep obj* sich kümmern um. **these shoes need/that cough needs ~ing ~** mit den Schuhen muß etwas gemacht werden/um den Husten muß man sich kümmern; **please ~ ~ it that ...** bitte sorgen Sie dafür, daß ...

see[2] *n* Bistum *nt*. **Holy S~** Heiliger Stuhl.

seed [si:d] **1** *n (Bot) (one single)* Same(n) *m*; *(of grain, poppy etc)* Korn *nt*; *(within fruit)* (Samen)kern *m*; *(collective)* Samen *m*; *(for birds)* Körner *pl*; *(grain)* Saat *f*; *(fig: of unrest, idea etc)* Keim *m (of* zu). **to go to ~** *(vegetables)* schießen; *(flowers)* einen Samenstand bilden; *(fig: person)* herunterkommen. **2** *vt* **(a)** *(sow with ~)* besäen. **(b)** *(extract ~s from)* entkernen. **(c)** *(Sport)* setzen, plazieren. **~ed number one** als Nummer eins gesetzt. **3** *vi (vegetables)* schießen; *(flowers)* Samen entwickeln.

seed: **~bed** *n* Saatbeet *nt*; **~ corn** *n* Saatkorn *nt*; **~less** *adj* kernlos.

seedling ['si:dlɪŋ] *n* Sämling *m*.

seed potato *n* Saatkartoffel *f*.

seedy ['si:dɪ] *adj* (+*er*) *(disreputable) person* zwielichtig; *area, place* übel; *clothes* abgerissen.

seeing ['si:ɪŋ] *conj* **~ (that)** da.

seek [si:k] *pret, ptp* **sought** *vt* suchen; *fame, wealth* streben nach. **to ~ sb's advice** jdn um Rat fragen.

♦ **seek for** *vi* +*prep obj* suchen nach; *reforms, changes* anstreben.

♦ **seek out** *vt sep* ausfindig machen; *opinion* herausfinden.

seem [si:m] *vi* scheinen. **he ~s (to be) honest** er scheint ehrlich zu sein; **he ~s younger than he is** er wirkt jünger, als er ist; **that makes it ~ longer** dadurch wirkt es länger; **things aren't always what they ~** vieles ist anders, als es aussieht; **what ~s to be the trouble?** worum geht es denn?; *(doctor)* was kann ich für Sie tun?; **he has left, it ~s** er ist anscheinend weggegangen; **so it ~s** es sieht (ganz) so aus; **it would ~ that he is coming after all** es sieht so aus, als ob er doch noch kommt; **how does it ~ to you?** was meinen *Sie*?; **it just doesn't ~ right somehow** das ist doch irgendwie nicht richtig; **it only ~s like it** das kommt einem nur so vor; **it all ~s so unreal to me** es kommt mir alles so unwirklich vor; **I ~ to have heard his name before** es kommt mir so vor, als hätte ich seinen Namen schon einmal gehört.

seeming ['si:mɪŋ] *adj attr* scheinbar.

seemingly ['si:mɪŋlɪ] *adv* anscheinend.

seemly ['si:mlɪ] *adj* (+*er*) schicklich. **it isn't ~ (for sb to do sth)** es schickt sich nicht (für jdn, etw zu tun).

seen [si:n] *ptp of* **see**[1].

seep [si:p] *vi* sickern. **to ~ through/into sth** durch etw durchsickern/in etw *(acc)* hineinsickern.

seesaw ['si:sɔ:] **1** *n* Wippe *f*. **2** *vi* wippen; *(fig) (emotional states)* auf und ab gehen; *(prices, public opinion)* schwanken.

seethe [si:ð] *vi (boil)* sieden; *(fig) (be crowded)* wimmeln *(with* von); *(be angry)* kochen *(col)*. **to ~ with anger** vor Wut kochen.

see-through ['si:θru:] *adj* durchsichtig.

segment ['segmənt] *n* Teil *m*; *(of worm)* Glied, Segment *nt*; *(of orange)* Stück *nt*; *(of circle)* Abschnitt *m*, Segment *nt*.

segregate ['segrɪgeɪt] *vt individuals* absondern; *group of population* nach Rassen/Konfessionen *etc* trennen. **to be ~d from sb/sth** von jdm/etw abgesondert sein; **~d** *(racially) school, church* nur für Weiße/Schwarze; *schools* mit Rassentrennung; *society* nach Rassen getrennt.

segregation [ˌsegrɪ'geɪʃən] *n* Trennung *f*. **racial/sexual ~** Rassentrennung *f*/Geschlechtertrennung *f*.

seize [si:z] *vt* **(a)** *(grasp)* packen, ergreifen; *(as hostage)* nehmen; *(confiscate)* beschlagnahmen; *passport* einziehen; *ship (authorities)* beschlagnahmen; *(capture) town* einnehmen; *train, building* besetzen; *criminal* fassen. **to ~ sb's arm** jdn am Arm packen. **(b)** *(fig) (panic, fear)* packen; *power* an sich *(acc)* reißen; *(leap upon) idea* aufgreifen; *opportunity* ergreifen.

♦ **seize on** *or* **upon** *vi* +*prep obj* **(a)** *(clutch at) idea, offer* sich stürzen auf (+*acc*). **(b)** *(pick out for criticism)* herausgreifen.

♦ **seize up** *vi (engine, brakes)* sich verklemmen.

seizure ['si:ʒə^r] *n* **(a)** Beschlagnahmung *f*; *(of passport)* Einzug *m*; *(capture)* Einnahme *f*; *(of train, building)* Besetzung *f*. **(b)** *(Med)* Anfall *m*; *(apoplexy)* Schlaganfall *m*.

seldom ['seldəm] *adv* selten. **~ have I ...** ich habe selten ...

select [sɪ'lekt] **1** *vti* auswählen; *(in buying also)* aussuchen. **2** *adj* exklusiv; *(carefully chosen)* auserlesen. **~ committee** Sonderausschuß *m*.

selection [sɪ'lekʃən] *n* **(a)** *(choosing)* (Aus)wahl *f*; *(Biol)* Auslese *f*. **(b)** *(person, thing selected)* Wahl *f*; *(likely winner)* Tip *m*. **to make one's ~** seine Wahl treffen; **~ committee** Auswahlkomitee *nt*. **(c)** *(range, assortment)* Auswahl *f (of* an +*dat)*.

selective [sɪ'lektɪv] *adj* wählerisch; *reader* kritisch, anspruchsvoll; *school* Elite-. **~ service** *(US)* Wehrdienst *m*.

selectively [sɪ'lektɪvlɪ] *adv* wählerisch; *read, operate* selektiv. **to buy ~** beim Einkaufen kritisch sein.

selector [sɪ'lektə^r] *n* **(a)** *(Tech)* Wählschalter *m*; *(knob)* Schaltknopf *m*. **(b)** *(Sport) jd, der die Mannschaftsaufstellung vornimmt.*

self [self] *n, pl* **selves** Ich, Selbst *(esp Psych) no pl nt*; *(side of character)* Seite *f*. **one's other/better ~** sein anderes/besseres Ich; **he's quite his old ~ again** er ist wieder ganz der alte *(col)*.

self: **~-addressed** *adj envelope* adressiert; **~-adhesive** *adj* selbstklebend; **~-adjusting** *adj* selbstregulierend *attr*; *brakes* selbst-nachstellend *attr*; **~-assertive** *adj* selbstbewußt; *(pej)* von sich selbst eingenommen; **~-assured** *adj* selbstsicher; **~-catering** *adj (Brit)* für Selbstversorger; **~-centred,** *(US)* **~-centered** *adj* egozentrisch, ichbezogen; **~-confessed** *adj* erklärt *attr*; **~-confidence** *n* Selbstvertrauen *nt*; **~-confident** *adj* selbstbewußt; **~-conscious** *adj* befangen, gehemmt; *piece of writing, style etc* bewußt; **~-contained** *adj flat* separat; **~-control** *n* Selbstbeherrschung *f*; **~-critical** *adj* selbstkritisch; **~-criticism** *n* Selbstkritik *f*; **~-defeating** *adj* unsinnig; *argument* sich selbst widerlegend *attr*; **~-defence,** *(US)* **~-defense** *n* Selbstverteidigung *f*; *(Jur)* Notwehr *f*; **to act in ~-defence** in Notwehr handeln; **~-discipline** *n* Selbstdisziplin *f*; **~-effacing** *adj* zurückhaltend; **~-employed** *adj* selbständig; *artist* freischaffend; *journalist* freiberuflich; **~-esteem** *n (~-respect)* Selbstachtung *f*; **~-evident** *adj* offensichtlich; *(not needing proof)* selbstverständlich; **~-explanatory** *adj* unmittelbar verständlich; **this word is ~-explanatory** das Wort erklärt sich selbst; **~-expression** *n* Selbstdarstellung *f*; **~-governing** *adj* selbstverwaltet; **to become ~-governing** eine eigene Regierung bekommen; **~-help** *n* Selbsthilfe *f*; **~-importance** *n* Aufgeblasenheit *f*; **~-important** *adj* aufgeblasen; **~-imposed** *adj* selbstauferlegt *attr*; **~-indulgent** *adj* genießerisch; *(in eating, drinking also)* maßlos; **~-inflicted** *adj wounds* sich *(dat)* selbst zugefügt *attr*; *task, punishment* sich *(dat)* freiwillig auferlegt; **~-interest** *n (selfishness)* Eigennutz *m*; *(personal*

advantage) eigenes Interesse.
selfish ['selfɪʃ] *adj (not sharing)* geizig; *(self-centred)* egoistisch.
selfishness ['selfɪʃnɪs] *n see adj* Geiz *m*; Egoismus *m*.
selfless ['selflɪs] *adj* selbstlos.
self: ~**-made** *adj* ~**-made man** Selfmademan *m*; ~**-opinionated** *adj* rechthaberisch; *nonsense, drivel* selbstherrlich; ~**-pity** *n* Selbstmitleid *nt*; ~**-portrait** *n* Selbstporträt *nt*; ~**-possessed** *adj* selbstbeherrscht; ~**-preservation** *n* Selbsterhaltung *f*; ~**-raising,** *(US)* ~**-rising** *adj flour* selbsttreibend, *mit bereits beigemischtem Backpulver;* ~**-reliance** *n* Selbständigkeit *f*; ~**-reliant** *adj* selbständig; ~**-respect** *n* Selbstachtung *f*; **have you no** ~**-respect?** schämen Sie sich gar nicht?; ~**-respecting** *adj* anständig; **no** ~**-respecting person would ...** niemand, der etwas auf sich hält, würde ...; ~**-righteous** *adj* selbstgerecht; ~**-righteousness** *n* Selbstgerechtigkeit *f*; ~**-sacrifice** *n* Selbstaufopferung *f*; ~**same** *adj* **the** ~**same** genau der-/die-/dasselbe; **on the** ~**same day** noch am selben Tag; ~**-satisfied** *adj (smug)* selbstgefällig; ~**-service 1** *n* Selbstbedienung *f*; **2** *adj* Selbstbedienungs-; ~**-styled** *adj* selbsternannt; ~**-sufficiency** *n (of person)* Selbständigkeit *f*; *(emotional)* Selbstgenügsamkeit *f*; *(of country)* Autarkie *f*; ~**-sufficient** *adj person* selbständig; *(emotionally)* selbstgenügsam; *country* autark; **they are** ~**-sufficient in oil** sie können ihren Ölbedarf selbst decken; ~**-supporting** *adj person* finanziell unabhängig; *structure* freitragend; *chimney* freistehend; **the newspaper is** ~**-supporting** die Zeitung trägt sich selbst; ~**-taught** *adj skills* selbsterlernt; **he is** ~**-taught** er hat sich *(dat)* das selbst beigebracht; *(intellectually)* er hat sich durch Selbstunterricht gebildet.
sell [sel] *(vb: pret, ptp* **sold***)* **1** *vt* **(a)** verkaufen *(sb sth, sth to sb* jdm etw, etw an jdn*)*; *insurance policy* abschließen *(to* mit*)*; *(business) goods also* absetzen. **I was sold this in Valencia** man hat mir das in Valencia verkauft; **the book sold 3,000 copies** von dem Buch wurden 3.000 Exemplare verkauft; **to be sold on sb/sth** *(col)* von jdm/etw begeistert sein. **(b)** *(stock)* führen, haben *(col)*; *(deal in)* vertreiben. **to** ~ **oneself** *(put oneself across)* sich profilieren *(to* bei*)*, sich verkaufen *(to* an *+acc)*. **(c)** *(fig: betray)* verraten. **to** ~ **sb down the river** *(col)* jdn verschaukeln *(col)*.
2 *vi (person)* verkaufen *(to sb* an jdn*)*; *(article)* sich verkaufen (lassen). **his book is** ~**ing well/won't** ~ sein Buch verkauft sich gut/läßt sich nicht verkaufen; **the house sold for £30,000** das Haus wurde für £ 30.000 verkauft.
♦ **sell off** *vt sep* verkaufen; *(get rid of quickly, cheaply)* abstoßen.
♦ **sell out 1** *vt sep* ausverkaufen. **sorry, sold** ~ wir sind leider ausverkauft; **we're sold** ~ **of ice-cream** das Eis ist ausverkauft. **2** *vi* **(a)** *(sell entire stock)* alles verkaufen. **(b)** *(in business)* sein Geschäft/seine Firma/seinen Anteil *etc* verkaufen. **(c)** *(col: betray)* **he sold** ~ **to the enemy** er hat sich an den Feind verkauft.
♦ **sell up 1** *vt sep* zu Geld machen *(col)*; *(Brit Fin)* zwangsverkaufen. **2** *vi* seinen Besitz/seine Firma *etc* verkaufen.
seller ['seləʳ] *n* **(a)** Verkäufer(in *f*) *m*. **it's a** ~**'s market in housing just now** zur Zeit bestimmen die Verkäufer die Hauspreise. **(b)** *(thing sold)* **big** ~ Verkaufsschlager *m*; **bad** ~ schlecht gehender Artikel; *(in shop also)* Ladenhüter *m*; **this book is a good/slow** ~ das Buch verkauft sich gut/schlecht.
selling ['selɪŋ] *adj* Verkaufs-. ~ **price** Verkaufspreis *m*.
sellotape ® ['seləʊteɪp] *(Brit)* **1** *n* Tesafilm ® *m*. **2** *vt* mit Tesafilm ® festkleben.
sell-out ['selaʊt] *n* **(a)** *(col: betrayal)* fauler Handel *(to* mit*)*; *(of one's ideals etc)* Ausverkauf *m (to* an *+acc)*. **(b)** *(Theat, Sport)* ausverkauftes Haus. **to be a** ~ ausverkauft sein.
selvage, selvedge ['selvɪdʒ] *n* Webkante *f*.
selves [selvz] *pl of* **self.**
semantic [sɪ'mæntɪk] *adj* semantisch.
semaphore ['seməfɔːʳ] *n* Signalsprache *f*.
semblance ['sembləns] *n* Anflug *m (of* von*)*; *(of order)* Anschein *m*.
semen ['siːmən] *n* Sperma *nt*.
semester [sɪ'mestəʳ] *n* Semester *nt*.
semi ['semɪ] *n (Brit col)* = **semidetached.**
semi: ~**breve** *n (esp Brit)* ganze Note; ~**circle** *n* Halbkreis *m*; ~**circular** *adj* halbkreisförmig; ~**colon** *n* Semikolon *nt*; ~**conductor** *n* Halbleiter *m*; ~**conscious** *adj* halb bewußtlos; ~**detached** *n* Doppelhaus(hälfte *f*) *nt*; ~**final** *n* Halbfinalspiel *nt*; ~**finalist** *n* Teilnehmer(in *f*) *m* am Halbfinale; ~**finals** *npl* Halbfinale *nt*.
seminal ['semɪnl] *adj* **to be present in a** ~ **state** im Keim vorhanden sein.
seminar ['seminɑːʳ] *n* Seminar *nt*.
seminary ['semɪnərɪ] *n* Priesterseminar *nt*.
semi: ~**precious** *adj* ~**precious stone** Halbedelstein *m*; ~**quaver** *n (esp Brit)* Sechzehntel(note *f*) *nt*; ~**skilled** *adj worker* angelernt; *job* Anlern-; ~**skilled labour** *(workforce)* Angelernte *pl*; *(work)* Arbeit *f* für Angelernte.
semolina [ˌsemə'liːnə] *n* Grieß *m*.
senate ['senɪt] *n* Senat *m*.
senator ['senɪtəʳ] *n* Senator *m*; *(as address)* Herr Senator.
send [send] *pret, ptp* **sent** *vt* **(a)** schicken; *letter, messenger also* senden; *(~ off) letter* abschicken; *(Rad) radio wave* ausstrahlen; *signal* senden; *(through wires)* übermitteln. **to** ~ **sb to prison/to his death** jdn ins Gefängnis/in den Tod schicken; **to** ~ **sb to university** jdn studieren lassen; **to** ~ **sb for sth** jdn nach etw schicken; **she** ~**s her love/congratulations/apologies** *etc* sie läßt grüßen/Ihnen ihre Glückwünsche ausrichten/sich entschuldigen *etc*; ~ **him my love/best wishes** grüßen Sie ihn von mir.
(b) *(propel, make go) ball* schießen; *(hurl)* schleudern; *(conveyor belt)* befördern. **the blow sent him sprawling** der Schlag schleuderte ihn zu Boden; **the fire sent everyone running out of the building** das Feuer ließ alle das Gebäude fluchtartig verlassen; **his speech sent a wave of excitement through the audience** seine Rede ließ eine Woge der Aufregung durch die Zuschauer gehen; **this sent him into fits of laughter** das ließ ihn in einen Lachkrampf ausbrechen.
♦ **send away 1** *vt sep* wegschicken; *letter etc also* abschicken. **I had to** ~ **him** ~ **without an explanation** ich mußte ihn ohne Erklärung weggehen lassen. **2** *vi* schreiben. **to** ~ ~ **for sth** etw anfordern.
♦ **send back** *vt sep* zurückschicken; *food in restaurant* zurückgehen lassen.
♦ **send down** *vt sep* **(a)** *temperature, prices* fallen lassen; *(gradually)* senken. **(b)** *(Brit Univ: expel)* relegieren. **(c)** *prisoner* verurteilen *(for* zu*)*.
♦ **send for** *vi +prep obj* **(a)** kommen lassen; *doctor, police, priest also* rufen; *help* herbeirufen; *(person in authority) pupil, minister* zu sich bestellen. **(b)** *copy, catalogue* anfordern.
♦ **send in** *vt sep* einsenden; *person* herein-/hineinschicken; *troops* einsetzen.
♦ **send off 1** *vt sep* **(a)** *letter* abschicken. **(b)** *children to school* wegschicken. **(c)** = **send away 1. (d)** *(Sport)* vom Platz weisen *(for* wegen*)*. **2** *vi* = **send away 2.**
♦ **send on** *vt sep* **(a)** *(Brit: forward) letter* nachschicken; *(pass on) memo* weiterleiten. **(b)** *(in advance) troops, luggage* vorausschicken. **(c)** *substitute* einsetzen; *actor* auf die Bühne schicken.

♦**send out** *vt sep* **(a)** *(of house, room)* hinaus-/herausschicken *(of* aus). **he sent me ~ to buy a paper** er hat mich losgeschickt, um eine Zeitung zu kaufen. **(b)** *(emit) rays, radio signals* aussenden; *light, heat, smoke* abgeben. **(c)** *leaflets, invitations, application forms* verschicken.

sender ['sendəʳ] *n* Absender(in *f*) *m*. **return to ~** zurück an Absender.

send: **~-off** *n* Verabschiedung *f*; **to give sb a good ~-off** jdn ganz groß verabschieden *(col)*; **~-up** *n (Brit col)* Verulkung *f (col)*; **to do a ~-up of sb/sth** jdn/etw verulken *(col)*.

senile ['siːnaɪl] *adj person* senil; *(physically)* altersschwach.

senior ['siːnɪəʳ] **1** *adj (in age)* älter; *(in rank)* vorgesetzt, übergeordnet; *(with longer service)* dienstälter; *rank, civil servant* höher; *officer* ranghöher; *position, editor, executive etc* leitend; *doctor, nurse etc* Ober-. **he is ~ to me** *(in age)* er ist älter als ich; *(in rank)* er ist mir übergeordnet; *(in length of service)* er arbeitet schon länger hier als ich; **the ~ management** die Geschäftsleitung; **~ partner** Seniorpartner *m*; **~ consultant** Chefarzt *m*/-ärztin *f*; **~ citizen** älterer Mitbürger; **~ school, ~ high school** *(US)* Oberstufe *f*; **can I speak to somebody more ~?** könnte ich bitte jemanden sprechen, der verantwortlich ist?; **J. B. Schwartz, S~** J. B. Schwartz senior.

2 *n (Sch)* Oberstufenschüler(in *f*) *m*; *(US Univ)* Student(in *f*) *m* im 4./letzten Studienjahr. **he is my ~** *(in age)* er ist älter als ich; *(in rank)* er ist mir übergeordnet; *(in length of service)* er arbeitet schon länger hier als ich; **he is two years my ~** er ist zwei Jahre älter als ich.

seniority [ˌsiːnɪ'ɒrɪtɪ] *n (in age)* (höheres) Alter; *(in rank)* (höhere) Position; *(Mil)* (höherer) Rang; *(in civil service etc)* (höherer) Dienstgrad; *(in service)* (längere) Betriebszugehörigkeit; *(in civil service etc)* (höheres) Dienstalter.

sensation [sen'seɪʃən] *n* **(a)** *(feeling)* Gefühl *nt*; *(of heat etc)* Empfindung *f*. **a/the ~ of falling** das Gefühl zu fallen; **a ~ of fear** ein Angstgefühl *nt*. **(b)** *(great success)* Sensation *f*. **to cause a ~** (großes) Aufsehen erregen.

sensational [sen'seɪʃənl] *adj* **(a)** sensationell; *news item* Sensations-; *style, film* reißerisch. **(b)** *(col: very good etc)* sagenhaft *(col)*.

sense [sens] **1** *n* **(a)** *(bodily)* Sinn *m*. **~ of hearing** Gehör(sinn *m*) *nt*; **~ of sight** Sehvermögen *nt*; **~ of smell** Geruchssinn *m*; **~ of taste** Geschmackssinn *m*; **~ of touch** Tastsinn *m*; **~s** *pl (right mind)* Verstand *m*; **to be out of one's ~s** nicht ganz bei Trost sein *(col)*, von Sinnen sein *(geh)*; **to bring sb to his ~s** jdn zur Besinnung bringen; **to come to one's ~s** zur Besinnung kommen, Vernunft annehmen.

(b) *(feeling)* Gefühl *nt*. **~ of duty** Pflichtgefühl *nt*; **a ~ of pleasure** *etc* ein Gefühl der Freude *etc*; **~ of justice** Gerechtigkeitssinn *m*; **these buildings create a ~ of space** diese Gebäude vermitteln den Eindruck von Weite.

(c) *(good ~)* **(common) ~** gesunder Menschenverstand; **he had the (good) ~ to ...** er war so vernünftig und ...; **she didn't even have the ~ to take a key** sie war auch noch zu dumm dazu, einen Schlüssel mitzunehmen; **you should have had more ~ than to ...** du hättest vernünftiger sein sollen und nicht ...; **there is no ~ in that** das hat keinen Sinn; **what's the ~ of doing this?** welchen Sinn hat es denn, das zu tun?; **to talk ~** vernünftig sein; **to make sb see ~** jdn zur Vernunft bringen.

(d) to make ~ *(sentence etc)* (einen) Sinn ergeben; *(be sensible, rational etc)* sinnvoll *or* vernünftig sein; **it doesn't make ~ to spend all that money** es ist doch Unsinn, soviel Geld auszugeben; **it makes good ~** das scheint sehr vernünftig; **it makes good financial ~ to ...** aus finanzieller Sicht gesehen ist es sehr vernünftig, zu ...; **it all makes ~ now** jetzt wird einem alles klar; **to make ~ of sth** etw verstehen, aus etw schlau werden *(col)*.

(e) *(meaning)* Sinn *m no pl*. **in the full ~ of the word** im wahrsten Sinn des Wortes; **it has three distinct ~s** es hat drei verschiedene Bedeutungen; **in every ~ of the word** in der vollen Bedeutung des Wortes; **in a ~** in gewisser Hinsicht; **in every ~** in jeder Hinsicht; **in what ~?** inwiefern?

2 *vt* fühlen, spüren. **I could ~ someone there in the dark** ich fühlte *or* spürte, daß da jemand in der Dunkelheit war.

senseless ['senslɪs] *adj* **(a)** *(unconscious)* besinnungslos, bewußtlos. **to knock sb ~** jdn bewußtlos schlagen. **(b)** *(stupid)* unvernünftig, unsinnig; *(futile) waste, discussion* sinnlos.

sensibility [ˌsensɪ'bɪlɪtɪ] *n (to beauty etc)* Empfindsamkeit *f*; *(artistic ~ also)* Sensibilität *f*; *(emotional ~, susceptibility to insult)* Empfindlichkeit *f*. **sensibilities** Zartgefühl *nt*.

sensible ['sensəbl] *adj* **(a)** vernünftig. **be ~ about it** seien Sie vernünftig. **(b)** *(appreciable)* spürbar.

sensitive ['sensɪtɪv] *adj* **(a)** *(emotionally) person* sensibel, empfindsam; *(easily hurt)* empfindlich; *(understanding)* einfühlsam; *novel, remark* einfühlend. **to be ~ about sth** in bezug auf etw *(acc)* empfindlich sein. **(b)** *instruments, plants* empfindlich; *(Phot) film* lichtempfindlich; *(fig) topic, issue* heikel. **~ to light** lichtempfindlich.

sensitize ['sensɪtaɪz] *vt (Phot)* sensibilisieren.

sensual ['sensjʊəl] *adj* sinnlich.

sensuality [ˌsensjʊ'ælɪtɪ] *n* Sinnlichkeit.

sensuous ['sensjʊəs] *adj* sinnlich.

sent [sent] *pret, ptp of* **send.**

sentence ['sentəns] **1** *n* **(a)** *(Gram)* Satz *m*. **~ structure** Satzbau *m*. **(b)** *(Jur)* Strafe *f*. **to be under ~ of death** zum Tode verurteilt sein; **the judge gave him a 6-month ~** der Richter verurteilte ihn zu 6 Monaten Haft; **to pass ~ (on sb)** (über jdn) das Urteil verkünden; *(fig)* jdn verurteilen. **2** *vt (Jur)* verurteilen *(to* zu).

sentiment ['sentɪmənt] *n* **(a)** *(feeling, emotion)* Gefühl *nt*. **(b)** *(sentimentality)* Sentimentalität *f*. **(c)** *(opinion)* Ansicht *f*. **my ~s exactly!** genau meine Meinung!

sentimental [ˌsentɪ'mentl] *adj* sentimental; *person, mood also* gefühlvoll; *value* Gefühls-. **for ~ reasons** aus Sentimentalität.

sentimentality [ˌsentɪmen'tælɪtɪ] *n* Sentimentalität *f*.

sentry ['sentrɪ] *n* Wachtposten *m*. **to be on ~ duty** auf Wache sein; **~ box** Wachhäuschen *nt*.

separable ['sepərəbl] *adj* trennbar.

separate ['seprət] **1** *adj* **(a)** gesondert *(from* von*)*; *section, piece also* extra *attr inv*; *organization, unit also, existence* eigen *attr*; *provisions, regulations also* besondere(r, s) *attr*; *beds, accounts* getrennt; *entrance, flat* separat. **that is a ~ issue** das ist eine Frage für sich; **on two ~ occasions** bei zwei verschiedenen Gelegenheiten; **on a ~ occasion** bei einer anderen Gelegenheit; **they live ~ lives** sie gehen getrennte Wege; **to keep two things ~** zwei Dinge auseinanderhalten. **(b)** *(individual)* einzeln. **all the ~ questions** alle einzelnen Fragen; **everybody has a ~ task** jeder hat seine eigene Aufgabe.

2 *n* **~s** *pl* Röcke, Blusen, Hosen *etc*.

3 ['sepəreɪt] *vt* trennen; *(divide up)* aufteilen *(into* in +*acc)*. **he is ~d from his wife** er lebt von seiner Frau getrennt.

4 ['sepəreɪt] *vi* sich trennen.

separately ['seprətlɪ] *adv* getrennt, separat; *live* getrennt; *(singly)* einzeln.

separation [ˌsepə'reɪʃən] *n* Trennung *f*; *(of rocket etc)* Abtrennung *(from* von*)*.

separatist ['sepərətɪst] **1** *adj* separatistisch. **2** *n* Separatist(in *f*) *m*.

sepia ['si:pjə] *n* Sepia *f*.

September [sep'tembə^r] **1** *n* September *m*. **the first of ~** der erste September; **on ~ 19th** *(written)*, **on 19th ~** *(written)*, **on the 19th of ~** *(spoken)* am 19. September, am neunzehnten September; **~ 3rd, 1979, 3rd ~ 1979** *(on letter)* 3. September 1979; **in ~** im September; **at the beginning/end of ~** Anfang/Ende September; **there are 30 days in ~** der September hat 30 Tage. **2** *adj attr* September-; *mists etc also* septemberlich.

septic ['septɪk] *adj* vereitert, septisch. **the wound turned ~** die Wunde eiterte; **~ tank** Klärbehälter *m*.

sepulchre, *(US)* **sepulcher** ['sepəlkə^r] *n* Grabstätte *f*.

sequel ['si:kwəl] *n* Folge *f (to* von*)*; *(of book, film)* Fortsetzung *f (to* von*)*. **it had a tragic ~** es hatte ein tragisches Nachspiel.

sequence ['si:kwəns] *n* **(a)** *(order)* Folge, Reihenfolge *f*. **in ~** der Reihe nach; **to do sth in ~** etw in der richtigen Reihenfolge tun. **(b)** *(things following)* Reihe, Folge *f*; *(Mus, Cards)* Sequenz *f*; *(Math)* Reihe *f*.

sequin ['si:kwɪn] *n* Paillette *f*.

serenade [,serə'neɪd] **1** *n* Serenade *f*. **2** *vt* ein Ständchen *nt* bringen *(+dat)*.

serene [sə'ri:n] *adj* gelassen; *sea* ruhig; *sky* heiter.

serenity [sɪ'renɪtɪ] *n* Gelassenheit *f*.

serge [sɜ:dʒ] *n* Serge *f*.

sergeant ['sɑ:dʒənt] *n (Mil)* Feldwebel *m*; *(police)* Polizeimeister *m*. **~ major** Oberfeldwebel *m*.

serial ['sɪərɪəl] *n (novel)* Fortsetzungsroman *m*; *(Rad)* Sendereihe *f*; *(TV)* Serie *f*. **~ number** fortlaufende Nummer; *(on manufactured goods)* Fabrikationsnummer *f*.

serialize ['sɪərɪəlaɪz] *vt* in Fortsetzungen bringen; *(put into serial form)* in Fortsetzungen umarbeiten.

series ['sɪərɪz] *n, pl* **-** Serie *f*; *(Rad)* Sendereihe *f*; *(of books, lectures, films)* Reihe *f*. **a ~ of articles** eine Artikelserie; **in ~** der Reihe nach.

serious ['sɪərɪəs] *adj* **(a)** ernst; *person, manner (not frivolous)* ernsthaft; *newspaper, interest* seriös; *offer, suggestion* ernstgemeint *attr*, ernst gemeint *pred*, seriös; *doubts also* ernsthaft. **to be ~ about doing sth** etw im Ernst tun wollen; **I'm ~ (about it)** das ist mein Ernst; **he is ~ about her** er meint es ernst mit ihr; **you can't be ~!** das kann nicht dein Ernst sein! **(b)** *(critical)* ernst; *accident, mistake, damage, loss* schwer; *situation also* bedenklich. **it's ~** das ist schlimm; **it's getting ~** es wird ernst; **inflation is getting ~** die Inflation nimmt ernste Ausmaße an.

seriously ['sɪərɪəslɪ] *adv* **(a)** ernst; *talk, interested* ernsthaft; *(not jokingly)* im Ernst. **to take sb/sth ~** jdn/etw ernst nehmen; **do you ~ want to do that?** wollen Sie das wirklich *or* im Ernst tun?; **~ though ...** aber mal ganz im Ernst ...; **do you mean that ~?** meinen Sie das ernst?, ist das Ihr Ernst? **(b)** *wounded* schwer; *ill also* ernstlich; *deteriorate* bedenklich.

seriousness ['sɪərɪəsnɪs] *n see adj* **(a)** Ernst *m*; Ernsthaftigkeit *f*; Seriosität *f*. **in all ~** ganz im Ernst. **(b)** Ernst *m*; Schwere *f*; Bedenklichkeit *f*.

sermon ['sɜ:mən] *n (Eccl)* Predigt *f*; *(moralizing)* Moralpredigt *f*; *(scolding)* Strafpredigt *f*.

serpent ['sɜ:pənt] *n* Schlange *f (also fig)*.

serrated [se'reɪtɪd] *adj* gezackt. **~ knife** Sägemesser *nt*.

serum ['sɪərəm] *n* Serum *nt*.

servant ['sɜ:vənt] *n (lit, fig)* Diener(in *f*) *m*; *(also* **~ girl***)* Dienstmädchen *nt*; *(domestic)* Dienstbote *m*.

serve [sɜ:v] **1** *vt* **(a)** dienen *(+dat)*; *(be of use)* nützen *(+dat)*. **he ~d his country well** er hat sich um sein Land verdient gemacht; **if my memory ~s me correctly** wenn ich mich recht erinnere; **to ~ its/sb's purpose** seinen Zweck erfüllen/jds Zwecken *(dat)* dienen; **it ~s no useful purpose** es hat keinen praktischen Wert; **to ~ sb as sth** jdm als etw dienen; **it has ~d us well** es hat uns gute Dienste geleistet.

(b) *years in army etc* ableisten; *term of office* durchlaufen; *apprenticeship* durchmachen; *sentence* verbüßen, absitzen *(col)*.

(c) *(in shop)* bedienen; *(bus, gas etc)* versorgen. **I'm being ~d, thank you** danke, ich werde schon bedient.

(d) *(esp in restaurant) food, drink* servieren; *guests* bedienen; *(waiter)* bedienen; *(pour drink for)* einschenken *(+dat)*; *wine etc* einschenken. **dinner is ~d** *(butler)* das Essen ist aufgetragen; *(hostess)* darf ich zu Tisch bitten?; **"~s three"** *(on packet etc)* „(ergibt) drei Portionen".

(e) *(Tennis etc) ball* aufschlagen.

(f) *(Jur)* zustellen *(on sb* jdm*)*. **to ~ a summons on sb, to ~ sb with a summons** jdn vor Gericht laden; **the landlord ~d notice on his tenants** der Vermieter kündigte den Mietern.

(g) (it) ~s you right! *(col)* das geschieht dir (ganz) recht!; **it ~s him right for being so greedy** *(col)* das geschieht ihm ganz recht, was muß er auch so gierig sein!

2 *vi* **(a)** dienen. **to ~ on the jury** Geschworene(r) *mf* sein; **to ~ on a committee** einem Ausschuß angehören; **to ~ as chairman** das Amt des Vorsitzenden innehaben. **(b)** *(Mil)* dienen. **(c)** *(waiter, butler etc)* servieren *(at table* bei Tisch*)*. **(d) to ~ as, to ~ for** dienen als; **it ~s to show/explain ...** das zeigt/erklärt ... **(e)** *(Tennis etc)* aufschlagen.

3 *n (Tennis etc)* Aufschlag *m*. **whose ~ is it?** wer hat Aufschlag?

♦ **serve up** *vt sep food* servieren; *rations* verteilen.

server ['sɜ:və^r] *n* **(a)** *(fork etc)* Servierlöffel *m*/ Vorlegegabel *f*; *(pie ~)* Tortenheber *m*. **salad ~s** Salatbesteck *nt*. **(b)** *(Tennis)* Aufschläger(in *f*) *m*.

service ['sɜ:vɪs] **1** *n* **(a)** Dienst *m*. **his faithful ~** seine treuen Dienste; **his ~s to industry/the country** seine Verdienste in der Industrie/um das Land; **he has ten years' ~ behind him** er hat zehn Jahre Dienstzeit hinter sich *(dat)*; **to do sb a ~** jdm einen Dienst erweisen; **to do good ~** gute Dienste leisten; **to be of ~ to sb** jdm nützen; **to be at sb's ~** jdm zur Verfügung stehen; **can I be of ~ to you?** kann ich Ihnen behilflich sein?; **out of ~** außer Betrieb; **to need the ~s of a lawyer** einen Anwalt brauchen.

(b) *(Mil)* Militärdienst *m*.

(c) *(to customers)* Service *m*; *(in shop, restaurant etc)* Bedienung *f*.

(d) *(bus, train, plane etc)* Bus-/Zug-/ Flugverbindung *f*. **there's no ~ to Oban on Sundays** sonntags besteht kein Zug-/Busverkehr nach Oban.

(e) *(Eccl)* Gottesdienst *m*.

(f) *(of machines)* Wartung *f*; *(Aut: major ~)* Inspektion *f*. **my car is in for a ~** mein Auto wird gewartet; mein Auto ist bei der Inspektion.

(g) *(tea or coffee set)* Service *nt*.

(h) *(Tennis)* Aufschlag *m*.

(i) ~s *pl (commercial)* Dienstleistungen *pl*; *(gas etc)* Versorgungsnetz *nt*.

2 *vt car, machine* warten. **to send a car to be ~d** ein Auto warten lassen; *(major ~)* ein Auto zur Inspektion geben.

serviceable ['sɜ:vɪsəbl] *adj (practical)* zweckmäßig; *(usable)* brauchbar.

service: ~ area *n* Raststätte *f*; **~ charge** *n (Brit)* Bedienung(sgeld *nt*) *f*; *(of bank)* Bearbeitungsgebühr *f*; **~ industry** *n* Dienstleistungsbranche *f*; **~man** *n* Militärangehörige(r) *m*; **~ station** *n* Tankstelle *f* (mit Reparaturwerkstatt).

serviette [,sɜ:vɪ'et] *n* Serviette *f*.

servile ['sɜːvaɪl] *adj* unterwürfig; *obedience* sklavisch.

session ['seʃən] *n* **(a)** *(meeting)* Sitzung *f*; *(Jur, Parl: period)* Sitzungsperiode *f*; *(Parl: term of office)* Legislaturperiode *f*. **to be in ~** eine Sitzung abhalten; *(Jur, Pol)* tagen; **a ~ of talks/negotiations** Gespräche *pl*/Verhandlungen *pl*; **recording ~** Aufnahme *f*; **we're in for a long ~** das wird lange dauern; **I had a long ~ with him** *(talk)* ich habe lange mit ihm gesprochen. **(b)** *(academic year)* *(Univ)* Studienjahr *nt*; *(Sch)* Schuljahr *nt*; *(term)* Semester/Trimester *nt*; *(division of course)* Stunde, Sitzung *(esp Univ) f*.

set [set] *(vb: pret, ptp ~)* **1** *n* **(a)** Satz *m*; *(of two)* Paar *nt*; *(of cutlery, furniture etc)* Garnitur *f*; *(tea-~ etc)* Service *nt*; *(of tablemats etc)* Set *nt*; *(chess or draughts ~ etc)* Spiel *nt*; *(painting ~)* Malkasten *m*; *(Meccano®, chemistry ~)* Baukasten *m*; *(gift or presentation ~)* Kassette *f*. **~ of rooms** Zimmerflucht *f*; **a ~ of tools** Werkzeug *nt*; **a ~ of teeth** ein Gebiß *nt*.

(b) *(group of people)* Kreis *m*; *(pej)* Bande *f*; *(Brit Sch: stream)* Kurs *m*. **the literary ~** die Literaten *pl*; **the golfing ~** die Golffreunde *pl*.

(c) *(Tennis)* Satz *m*; *(Table-tennis)* Spiel *nt*. **~ point** Satzpunkt *m*.

(d) *(Telec, Rad, TV)* Gerät *nt*, Apparat *m*.

(e) *(hair~)* Frisur, Form *f*. **to have a (shampoo and) ~** sich *(dat)* die Haare (waschen und) legen lassen.

(f) *(Theat)* Bühnenbild *nt*; *(Film)* Szenenaufbau *m*. **to be on the ~** bei den Dreharbeiten sein.

(g) *(Math)* Menge *f*.

2 *adj* **(a)** *pred (ready)* fertig, bereit. **all ~?** alles klar?; **to be all ~ to do sth** sich darauf eingerichtet haben, etw zu tun. **(b)** *(rigid)* starr; *expression* feststehend; *forms also, habit, custom* fest; *(prescribed)* festgesetzt; *essay topic* vorgegeben; *(prearranged) time, place* bestimmt, ausgemacht *(col)*. **~ book(s)** Pflichtlektüre *f*; **~ lunch/meal** Tagesgericht *nt*; **~ menu** Tageskarte *f*; **~ piece** Standardstück *nt*; **to be ~ in one's ways** in seinen Gewohnheiten festgefahren sein. **(c)** *(resolved)* entschlossen. **to be (dead) ~ on sth/doing sth** etw unbedingt haben/tun wollen; **to be (dead) ~ against sth/doing sth** (total) gegen etw sein/etw (absolut) nicht tun wollen.

3 *vt* **(a)** *(put, place)* stellen; *(on its side, flat)* legen; *(deliberately, carefully)* setzen.

(b) *(regulate, adjust)* einstellen *(at* auf *+acc)*; *clock* stellen *(by* nach, *to* auf *+acc)*; *(fix) trap, snare* aufstellen; *(fig)* stellen *(for sb* jdm*)*. **to ~ the alarm for a certain time** den Wecker auf eine bestimmte Zeit stellen.

(c) *(prescribe, impose) target, limit etc* festlegen; *task, question* stellen *(sb* jdm*)*; *homework* aufgeben; *exam* zusammenstellen; *(arrange) time, date* festsetzen, ausmachen *(col)*; *(establish) record* aufstellen; *fashion* bestimmen. **to ~ the date (of the wedding)** die Hochzeit festsetzen; **to ~ a value on sth** einen Wert für etw festsetzen; **to ~ a high value on sth** einer Sache *(dat)* großen Wert beimessen; **to ~ sb a problem** *(lit)* jdm ein Problem aufgeben; *(fig)* jdn vor ein Problem stellen.

(d) *(mount) gem* fassen *(in* in *+dat)*; *piece of jewellery* besetzen *(with* mit*)*; *windowpane* einsetzen *(in* in *+acc)*; *(embed firmly)* einlegen *(in* in *+dat)*; *(in ground)* einlassen *(in* in *+acc)*.

(e) *(Liter)* **the book** *etc* **is ~ in Rome** das Buch *etc* spielt in Rom; **he ~ the book in Rome** er wählte Rom als Schauplatz für sein Buch.

(f) *(Med) bone* einrichten; *dislocated joint* einrenken.

(g) *(lay with cutlery) table* decken. **to ~ places for 14** für 14 decken.

(h) *hair* legen, eindrehen.

(i) to ~ the police/dogs on sb die Polizei/Hunde auf jdn hetzen.

(j) *(Mus)* **to ~ sth to music** etw vertonen.

(k) *(Typ)* setzen.

(l) to ~ sth going/in motion etw in Gang/Bewegung bringen; **to ~ sb doing sth** jdn dazu veranlassen, etw zu tun; **to ~ sb laughing** jdn zum Lachen bringen; **that ~ me thinking** das gab mir zu denken; **that ~ me thinking that ...** das ließ mich denken, daß ...; **to ~ people talking** Anlaß zu Gerede geben; **to ~ sb/oneself to do sth** jdn etw tun lassen/sich daranmachen, etw zu tun.

4 *vi* **(a)** *(sun etc)* untergehen. **(b)** *(jelly, cement)* fest werden; *(jam also)* gelieren; *(bone)* zusammenwachsen.

♦ **set about** *vi +prep obj* **(a)** *(begin)* anfangen; *(tackle)* anfassen, anpacken *(col)*. **to ~ ~ doing sth** *(begin)* sich daranmachen, etw zu tun; **how do I ~ ~ getting a loan?** wie fasse *or* packe *(col)* ich es an, um ein Darlehen zu bekommen? **(b)** *(attack)* herfallen über *(+acc)*.

♦ **set against** *vt sep +prep obj* **(a)** *(influence against)* einnehmen gegen; *(cause trouble between)* Zwietracht säen zwischen *(+dat)*. **(b)** *(balance against) evidence etc* gegenüberstellen *(+dat)*.

♦ **set aside** *vt sep* **(a)** *work, money* beiseite legen; *time* einplanen; *plans* aufschieben; *differences* beiseite schieben; *dislike* vergessen; *mistrust, bitterness* sich freimachen von; *formality* verzichten auf *(+acc)*; *rules, protest* übergehen. **(b)** *(Jur)* aufheben; *will* für ungültig erklären.

♦ **set back** *vt sep* **(a)** *(place at a distance)* zurücksetzen. **the house is ~ ~ from the road** das Haus liegt etwas von der Straße ab. **(b)** *(retard)* verzögern, behindern. **the programme has been ~ ~ (by) 2 years** das Programm ist um 2 Jahre zurückgeworfen. **(c)** *(col: cost)* kosten. **the dinner ~ me ~ £15** das Essen hat mich 15 Pfund gekostet *or* ärmer gemacht *(col)*.

♦ **set down** *vt sep* **(a)** *(put down) suitcase* absetzen; *passenger also* aussteigen lassen. **(b)** *(in writing)* (schriftlich) niederlegen.

♦ **set in** *vi (start) (frost etc)* einsetzen; *(panic)* ausbrechen; *(night)* anbrechen; *(Med: gangrene, complications)* sich einstellen. **the rain has ~ ~** es hat sich eingeregnet.

♦ **set off 1** *vt sep* **(a)** *bomb* losgehen lassen; *alarm, mechanism* auslösen. **(b)** *(offset)* **to ~ sth ~ against sth** etw einer Sache *(dat)* gegenüberstellen. **(c)** *(enhance)* hervorheben. **to ~ sth ~ from sth** etw von etw abheben. **2** *vi (depart)* aufbrechen; *(car, in car etc)* losfahren. **to ~ ~ on a journey** eine Reise antreten; **to ~ ~ for Spain** nach Spanien abfahren *or* losfahren.

♦ **set out 1** *vt sep (display)* ausbreiten; *(arrange) chess pieces* aufstellen; *essay* anlegen. **2** *vi* **(a)** *(depart)* = **set off 2. (b)** *(intend)* beabsichtigen. **I didn't ~ ~ to do that** ich hatte nicht vor, das zu tun.

♦ **set to 1** *vi (start working etc)* loslegen *(col)*. **they ~ ~ and repaired it** sie machten sich an die Arbeit und reparierten es. **2** *vi +prep obj* **to ~ ~ work** sich an die Arbeit machen.

♦ **set up 1** *vi (establish oneself)* **to ~ ~ as a doctor** sich als Arzt niederlassen; **to ~ ~ in business** sein eigenes Geschäft aufmachen; **to ~ ~ for oneself** sich selbständig machen. **2** *vt sep* **(a)** *(place in position) statue, post* aufstellen; *(assemble) tent, stall, apparatus* aufbauen; *(fig: arrange) meeting* vereinbaren; *robbery* planen. **to ~ sth ~ for sb** etw für jdn vorbereiten. **(b)** *(establish)* gründen; *school, office* einrichten; *inquiry* anordnen. **to ~ sb ~ in business** jdm zu einem Geschäft verhelfen; **to ~ sb ~ as sth** (es) jdm ermöglichen, etw zu werden; **to be ~ ~ for life** für sein ganzes Leben ausgesorgt haben. **(c)** *(col: frame)* **to ~ sb ~** jdm etw anhängen; **I've** been ~ ~ das will mir einer anhängen *(col)*.

♦ **set upon** *vi +prep obj* überfallen; *(animal)* anfallen.

set: ~**-back** *n* Rückschlag *m*; ~ **square** *n* Zeichendreieck *nt*; ~ **theory** *n* Mengenlehre *f*.

settee [se'tiː] *n* Couch *f*, Sofa *nt*.

setter ['setəʳ] *n (dog)* Setter *m*.

setting ['setɪŋ] *n* **(a)** *(of sun, moon)* Untergang *m*. **(b)** *(background, atmosphere)* Rahmen *m*; *(surroundings)* Umgebung *f*; *(of novel etc)* Schauplatz *m*. **a film with a medieval** ~ ein Film, der im Mittelalter spielt. **(c)** *(of jewel)* Fassung *f*. **(d)** *(at table)* Gedeck *nt*. **(e)** *(position on dial etc)* Einstellung *f*. **(f)** *(musical arrangement)* Vertonung *f*. **(g)** *(hair)* Legen *nt*. ~ **lotion** (Haar)festiger *m*.

settle ['setl] **1** *vt* **(a)** *(decide)* entscheiden; *(sort out)* regeln; *problem* klären; *dispute, differences* beilegen; *doubts* ausräumen; *date, place* festlegen, ausmachen *(col)*; *venue* festlegen; *deal* abschließen; *price, terms* aushandeln. **when my future is** ~**d** wenn sich meine Zukunft entschieden hat; **to** ~ **one's affairs** seine Angelegenheiten in Ordnung bringen; **to** ~ **an estate** *(Jur)* die Verteilung des Nachlasses regeln; **to** ~ **a case out of court** einen Fall außergerichtlich klären; **that's** ~**d then** das ist also klar; **that** ~**s it** damit wäre der Fall (ja wohl) erledigt; *(angry)* jetzt reicht's.

(b) *(pay) bill* begleichen; *account* ausgleichen.

(c) *(place carefully)* legen; *(in upright position)* stellen; *(make comfortable) child, invalid* versorgen; *(calm) nerves, stomach* beruhigen. **to** ~ **oneself comfortably in an armchair** es sich *(dat)* in einem Sessel bequem machen.

(d) *(colonize) land* besiedeln.

(e) *(form)* **to** ~ **money/property on sb** jdm Geld/Besitz überschreiben; *(in will)* jdm Geld/ Besitz vermachen.

2 *vi* **(a)** *(in country, town, profession)* sich niederlassen; *(as settler)* sich ansiedeln; *(in house)* sich einrichten; *(feel at home in house, town)* sich einleben *(into an +dat)*; *(in job, surroundings)* sich eingewöhnen *(into in +dat)*; *(permanently in area)* seßhaft werden. **to** ~ **into a habit** sich *(dat)* etw angewöhnen.

(b) *(become less variable: weather)* beständig werden. **if the weather would only** ~ wenn das Wetter nicht mehr so unbeständig wäre.

(c) *(become calm) (child, matters, stomach)* sich beruhigen; *(panic, excitement)* sich legen; *(become less excitable)* ruhiger werden. **he couldn't** ~ **to anything** er konnte sich auf nichts konzentrieren.

(d) *(come to rest, sit down) (person, bird)* sich niederlassen *or* setzen; *(dust)* sich setzen *or* legen; *(sink slowly) (building)* sich senken; *(ground, sediment)* sich setzen.

(e) *(Jur)* **to** ~ **(out of court)** sich vergleichen.

(f) *(pay)* bezahlen. **can I** ~ **with you later?** kann ich später mit Ihnen abrechnen?

♦ **settle down** *vi* **(a)** = **settle 2 (a)**. **it's time he** ~**d** ~ es wird Zeit, daß er zur Ruhe kommt; *(got married)* es wird Zeit, daß er heiratet; **to** ~ ~ **at school/job** sich an einer Schule/in einer Stellung eingewöhnen. **(b)** = **settle 2 (c)**. **(c) to** ~ ~ **to work** sich an die Arbeit machen *or* setzen; **to** ~ ~ **for the night** sich schlafen legen.

♦ **settle for** *vi +prep obj* sich zufriedengeben mit. **she won't** ~ ~ **anything less** mit weniger gibt sie sich nicht zufrieden.

♦ **settle in** *vi (in house, town)* sich einleben; *(in job, school)* sich eingewöhnen.

♦ **settle on** *vi +prep obj* sich entscheiden für; *(agree on)* sich einigen auf *(+acc)*.

♦ **settle up 1** *vi* (be)zahlen. **to** ~ ~ **with sb** *(lit, fig)* mit jdm abrechnen. **2** *vt sep bill* bezahlen.

settled ['setld] *adj way of life* geregelt; *(Brit) weather* beständig. **to be** ~ in geregelten Verhältnissen leben; *(established)* etabliert sein; *(in place)* seßhaft sein; *(have permanent job etc)* festen Fuß gefaßt haben; *(in a house)* sich häuslich niedergelassen haben; *(be less restless)* ruhiger sein.

settlement ['setlmənt] *n* **(a)** *(act) (deciding)* Entscheidung *f*; *(sorting out)* Regelung *f*; *(of problem etc)* Klärung *f*; *(of dispute etc)* Beilegung *f*; *(of estate)* Regelung *f*; *(of bill, claim)* Bezahlung *f*; *(of account)* Ausgleich *m*. **a** ~ **out of court** *(Jur)* ein außergerichtlicher Vergleich; **to reach a** ~ sich einigen, einen Vergleich treffen; **in** ~ **of our account** zum Ausgleich unseres Kontos. **(b)** *(colony, village)* Siedlung, Niederlassung *f*; *(colonization)* Besiedlung *f*. **(c)** *(contract, agreement etc)* Übereinkunft *f*.

settler ['setləʳ] *n* Siedler(in *f*) *m*.

set: ~**-to** *n (col)* Krach *m (col)*; **to have a** ~**-to with sb** sich mit jdm in die Wolle kriegen *(col)*; ~**-up** *n* **(a)** *(col: situation)* Zustände *pl*; **I don't like the whole** ~**-up** mir gefällt das ganze Drum und Dran nicht *(col)*; **(b)** *(col: rigged contest)* abgekartete Sache.

seven ['sevn] *adj* sieben; *see* **six**.

seventeen ['sevn'tiːn] *adj* siebzehn.

seventeenth ['sevn'tiːnθ] *adj* siebzehnte(r, s); *see* **sixteenth**.

seventh ['sevnθ] **1** *adj* siebte(r, s). **2** *n (fraction)* Siebtel *nt*; *(in series)* Siebte(r, s); *(Mus)* Septime *f*; *(chord)* Septimenakkord *m*; *see* **sixth**.

seventy ['sevntɪ] *adj* siebzig; *see* **sixty**.

sever ['sevəʳ] *vt (cut through)* durchtrennen; *(violently)* durchschlagen; *(cut off)* abtrennen; *(violently)* abschlagen; *(fig: break off) ties* lösen; *relations* abbrechen; *communications* unterbrechen.

several ['sevrəl] **1** *adj (some)* einige, mehrere;- *(various)* verschiedene. **I've seen him** ~ **times/**~ **times already** ich habe ihn einige Male gesehen/ schon mehrere Male gesehen; **I'll need** ~ **more** ich brauche noch einige. **2** *pron* einige. ~ **of the houses** einige (der) Häuser; ~ **of us** einige von uns.

severance pay ['sevərəns,peɪ] *n* eine Abfindung.

severe [sɪ'vɪəʳ] *adj (+er) person, appearance* streng; *punishment, competition, test* hart; *criticism, reprimand* scharf; *crime, warning* ernst; *illness, injury, blow, frost, loss* schwer, schlimm; *pain, storm* stark, heftig; *weather* rauh. **to be** ~ **with sb** streng mit jdm sein.

severely [sɪ'vɪəlɪ] *adv see adj*. **to be** ~ **critical of sth** sich äußerst kritisch über etw *(acc)* äußern.

severity [sɪ'verɪtɪ] *n see adj* Strenge *f*; Härte *f*; Schärfe *f*; Ernst *m*; Schwere *f*; Stärke, Heftigkeit *f*; Rauheit *f*. **the** ~ **of the cold/drought/frost/loss** die schwere Kälte/Dürre/der starke Frost/der schwere Verlust.

sew [səʊ] *pret* ~**ed**, *ptp* ~**n** *vti* nähen. **to** ~ **sth on/together** etw annähen/zusammennähen.

♦ **sew up** *vt sep* **(a)** nähen *(also Med)*; *opening* zunähen. **(b)** *(fig)* unter Dach und Fach bringen. **it's all** ~**n** ~ es ist unter Dach und Fach.

sewage ['sjuːɪdʒ] *n* Abwasser *nt*. ~ **farm/works** Kläranlage *f*.

sewer ['sjʊəʳ] *n (pipe)* Abwasserleitung *f*; *(main* ~*)* Abwasserkanal *m*; *(fig: smelly place)* Kloake *f*.

sewing ['səʊɪŋ] *n (activity)* Nähen *nt*; *(piece of work)* Näharbeit *f*. ~ **machine** Nähmaschine *f*.

sewn [səʊn] *ptp of* **sew**.

sex [seks] **1** *n* **(a)** *(Biol)* Geschlecht *nt*. **what** ~ **is the baby?** welches Geschlecht hat das Baby? **(b)** *(sexuality)* Sexualität *f*, Sex *m*; *(sexual intercourse)* Sex *(col)*, Geschlechtsverkehr *(form) m*. **to have** ~ (Geschlechts)verkehr haben. **2** *adj attr* Geschlechts-; *hygiene, crime* Sexual-; *film, scandal* Sex-.

sex: ~ **appeal** *n* Sex-Appeal *m*; ~ **discrimination** *n* Diskriminierung *f* auf Grund des Geschlechts; ~ **education** *n* Sexualerziehung *f*.

sexism ['seksɪzm] *n* Sexismus *m.*
sexist ['seksɪst] **1** *n* Sexist(in *f*) *m.* **2** *adj* sexistisch.
sex: ~ **life** *n* Geschlechtsleben *nt*; ~ **maniac** *n* *(criminal)* Triebtäter *m*; *(hum col) (man)* Lustmolch *m (hum)*; *(woman)* Nymphomanin *f*; ~ **shop** *n* Sexshop *m.*
sextet(te) [seks'tet] *n* Sextett *nt.*
sexton ['sekstən] *n* Küster *m.*
sexual ['seksjʊəl] *adj* sexuell; *intercourse, maturity* Geschlechts-; *crime* Sexual-, Trieb-.
sexuality [ˌseksjʊ'ælɪtɪ] *n* Sexualität *f.*
sexy ['seksɪ] *adj (+er) (col)* sexy *pred*; *smile, pose also* aufreizend; *joke, film* erotisch.
shabbiness ['ʃæbɪnɪs] *n (lit, fig)* Schäbigkeit *f.*
shabby ['ʃæbɪ] *adj (+er) (lit, fig)* schäbig.
shack [ʃæk] **1** *n* Hütte *f.* **2** *vi (col)* **to ~ up with sb** mit jdm zusammenziehen.
shackle ['ʃækl] *n usu pl* Kette, Fessel *(also fig) f.*
shade [ʃeɪd] **1** *n* **(a)** Schatten *m.* **30° in the ~** 30 Grad im Schatten; **to give ~** Schatten spenden; **to put sb/sth in the ~** *(fig)* jdn/etw in den Schatten stellen. **(b)** *(lamp~)* (Lampen)schirm *m*; *(esp US: blind)* Jalousie *f*; *(roller blind)* Rollo *nt*; *(outside house)* Markise *f.* **~s** *(esp US: sunglasses)* Sonnenbrille *f.* **(c)** *(of colour)* (Farb)ton *m*; *(fig) (of opinion)* Schattierung *f*; *(of meaning)* Nuance *f.* **a brighter ~ of red** ein leuchtenderer Rotton. **(d)** *(small quantity)* **it's a ~ long/too long** es ist etwas *or* eine Spur zu lang. **2** *vt (protect from light)* abschirmen; *lamp, window* abdunkeln. **that part is ~d by a tree** der Teil liegt im Schatten eines Baumes.
shadow ['ʃædəʊ] **1** *n (lit, fig)* Schatten *m*; *(fig: threat)* (Be)drohung *f.* **in the ~** im Schatten; **in the ~s** im Dunkel; **sb lives under the ~ of sth** etw lastet wie ein Schatten auf jdm; **to be just a ~ of one's former self** nur noch ein Schatten seiner selbst sein; **without a ~ of a doubt** ohne den geringsten Zweifel. **2** *attr (Brit Pol)* Schatten-. **the ~ Foreign Secretary** der Außenminister im Schattenkabinett. **3** *vt (follow)* beschatten *(col).*
shadow: **~-boxing** *n (lit, fig)* Schattenboxen *nt*; ~ **cabinet** *n (Brit)* Schattenkabinett *nt.*
shadowy ['ʃædəʊɪ] *adj* schattig; *(blurred)* verschwommen. **to lead a ~ existence** ein undurchsichtiges Dasein führen.
shady ['ʃeɪdɪ] *adj (+er)* **(a)** *place* schattig; *tree* schattenspendend. **(b)** *(col: of dubious honesty)* zwielichtig.
shaft [ʃɑːft] *n* Schaft *m*; *(of tool, golf club etc)* Stiel *m*; *(of light)* Strahl *m*; *(Mech)* Welle *f.*
shaggy ['ʃægɪ] *adj (+er) (long-haired)* zottig; *(unkempt)* zottelig.
shake [ʃeɪk] *(vb: pret* **shook,** *ptp* **shaken***)* **1** *n (act of shaking)* Schütteln *nt.* **to give a rug a ~** einen Läufer ausschütteln; **give the paint a ~** die Farbe (gut) durchschütteln; **to give sb/oneself a good ~** jdn/sich kräftig schütteln; **with a ~ of her head** mit einem Kopfschütteln; **to be no great ~s** *(col)* nicht umwerfend sein *(at* in *+dat).*
2 *vt* **(a)** schütteln; *building* erschüttern; *cocktail* durchschütteln. **"~ well before using"** „vor Gebrauch gut schütteln"; **to be ~n to pieces** total durchgeschüttelt werden; **to ~ one's fist at sb** jdm mit der Faust drohen; **to ~ one's head** den Kopf schütteln; **to ~ oneself/itself free** sich losmachen; **to ~ hands with sb** jdm die Hand schütteln. **(b)** *(weaken) faith etc* erschüttern; *evidence, reputation, resolve* ins Wanken bringen. **(c)** *(shock, amaze)* erschüttern. **that shook him!** da war er platt *(col)*; **it was a nasty accident, he's still rather badly ~n** ein schlimmer Unfall, der Schreck sitzt ihm noch in den Knochen.
3 *vi* wackeln; *(hand)* zittern; *(earth, voice)* beben. **the whole boat shook as the waves hit** das ganz Boot wurde vom Aufprall der Wellen erschüttert; **to ~ like a leaf** zittern wie Espenlaub; **to ~ with fear** vor Angst zittern; **he was shaking all over** er zitterte am ganzen Körper.
♦ **shake off** *vt sep dust, pursuer* abschütteln; *headache* loswerden.
♦ **shake out** *vt sep* **(a)** herausschütteln; *rug* ausschütteln. **(b)** *(fig: out of complacency etc)* aufrütteln *(of* aus*).*
♦ **shake up** *vt sep* **(a)** *bottle, liquid* schütteln; *pillow* aufschütteln. **(b)** *(upset)* erschüttern. **she's still a bit ~n ~** sie ist immer noch ziemlich mitgenommen. **(c)** *management, recruits* auf Zack bringen *(col)*; *ideas* revidieren.
shaken ['ʃeɪkən] *ptp of* **shake.**
shake-up ['ʃeɪkʌp] *n (col) (reorganization)* Umbesetzung *f.* **to give a department a good ~** eine Abteilung auf Zack bringen *(col).*
shakily ['ʃeɪkɪlɪ] *adv* wacklig; *talk* mit zitteriger Stimme; *walk* mit wackligen Schritten.
shaky ['ʃeɪkɪ] *adj (+er) chair, position* wacklig; *evidence* fragwürdig; *voice, hands, writing* zittrig; *knowledge* unsicher. **his Spanish is rather ~** sein Spanisch ist ziemlich holprig; **to feel ~** sich ganz schwach fühlen.
shale [ʃeɪl] *n* Schiefer *m.*
shall [ʃæl] *pret* **should** *modal aux* **(a)** *(future)* **we ~** *or* **we'll go to France this year** wir werden dieses Jahr nach Frankreich fahren, wir fahren dieses Jahr nach Frankreich; **no, I ~ not** *or* **I shan't/yes, I ~** nein, das werde ich nicht tun *or* das tue ich nicht/jawohl, das werde ich tun *or* das tue ich! **(b)** *(determination, obligation)* **you ~ pay for this!** dafür wirst du büßen!; **but I say you *shall* do it!** aber ich sage dir, du wirst das machen!; **the directors ~ not be disturbed** *(form)* die Direktoren dürfen nicht gestört werden; **I want to go too — and so you ~** ich will auch mitkommen — aber gewiß doch. **(c)** *(in questions, suggestions)* **what ~ we do?** was sollen wir machen?; **let's go in, ~ we?** komm, gehen wir hinein!; **I'll buy 3, ~ I?** soll ich 3 kaufen?, ich kaufe 3, oder?
shallot [ʃə'lɒt] *n* Schalotte *f.*
shallow ['ʃæləʊ] **1** *adj* flach; *water also* seicht; *(fig) talk, person* oberflächlich. **in the ~ end of the pool** am flachen Ende des Beckens. **2** *n* **~s** *pl* Untiefe *f.*
shalt [ʃælt] *(obs) 2nd pers sing of* **shall.**
sham [ʃæm] **1** *n* **(a)** *(pretence)* Heuchelei *f.* **their marriage had become a ~** ihre Ehe war zur Farce geworden. **(b)** *(person)* Scharlatan. **2** *adj diamonds etc* unecht, imitiert; *sympathy etc* vorgetäuscht, gespielt. ~ **battle** Scheingefecht *nt.* **3** *vt* vortäuschen; *sympathy* heucheln. **4** *vi* so tun; *(esp with illness)* simulieren; *(with feelings)* heucheln. **he's just ~ming** er tut nur so.
shambles ['ʃæmblz] *n sing* heilloses Durcheinander. **the room was a ~** im Zimmer herrschte ein heilloses Durcheinander; **the economy is in a ~** die Wirtschaft befindet sich in einem Chaos.
shame [ʃeɪm] **1** *n* **(a)** *(feeling of ~)* Scham *f*; *(cause of ~)* Schande *f.* **to feel ~ at sth** sich für etw schämen; **he hung his head in ~** er senkte beschämt den Kopf; *(fig)* er schämte sich; **to bring ~ upon sb/oneself** jdm/sich Schande machen; **to put sb/sth to ~** *(fig)* jdn/etw in den Schatten stellen; **~ on you!** du solltest dich/ihr solltet euch schämen! **(b)** *(pity)* **it's a ~ you couldn't come** schade, daß du nicht kommen konntest; **what a ~!** (das ist aber) schade!; **what a ~ he ...** schade, daß er ... **2** *vt* Schande machen *(+dat)*; *(fig: by excelling)* in den Schatten stellen. **he ~d us by working so hard** er hat uns alle durch sein hartes Arbeiten beschämt.
shamefaced ['ʃeɪm'feɪst] *adj* betreten.
shameful ['ʃeɪmfʊl] *adj* schändlich. **how ~!** was für eine Schande!; **what ~ behaviour!** dieses Benehmen ist eine Schande.
shameless ['ʃeɪmlɪs] *adj* schamlos. **he was quite ~ about it** er schämte sich überhaupt nicht.

shammy (leather) ['ʃæmɪ('leðə^r)] *n* Fenster-/Autoleder *nt*.
shampoo [ʃæm'puː] **1** *n (liquid)* Shampoo, Schampon *nt*; *(act of washing)* Reinigung *f*; *(of hair)* Waschen *nt*. **to have a ~** sich *(dat)* die Haare waschen lassen. **2** *vt person* die Haare waschen *(+dat)*; *hair* waschen; *carpet* reinigen.
shamrock ['ʃæmrɒk] *n* Klee *m*; *(leaf)* Kleeblatt *nt*.
shandy ['ʃændɪ] *n* Bier *nt* mit Limonade, Radler *m (S Ger)*, Alsterwasser *nt (N Ger)*.
shandygaff ['ʃændɪ,gæf] *n (US)* = **shandy.**
shank [ʃæŋk] *n* **(to go) on S~s' pony** auf Schusters Rappen (reiten).
shan't [ʃɑːnt] = **shall not.**
shanty[1] ['ʃæntɪ] *n (hut)* Baracke, Hütte *f*. **~ town** Slum(vor)stadt *f*.
shanty[2] *n (Mus)* Seemannslied, Shanty *nt*.
shape [ʃeɪp] **1** *n* **(a)** Form *f*. **what ~ is it?** welche Form hat es?; **it's rectangular** *etc* **in ~** es ist rechteckig *etc*; **she's the right ~ for a model** sie hat die richtige Figur für ein Mannequin; **to hammer metal into ~** Metall zurechthämmern; **to knock sth out of ~** etw zerbeulen; **to take ~** *(lit, fig)* Gestalt annehmen; **of all ~s and sizes** jeder Art, in allen Variationen; **I don't accept gifts in any ~ or form** ich nehme überhaupt keine Geschenke an; **we do not know the ~ of things to come** wir wissen nicht, wie sich die Zukunft gestalten wird.
(b) *(unidentified figure)* Gestalt *f*; *(object)* Form *f*.
(c) *(fig: order, condition)* **in good/bad~** *(sportsman)* in Form/nicht in Form; *(mentally, healthwise)* in guter/schlechter Verfassung; *(things, business)* in gutem/schlechtem Zustand; **to get into ~** *(sportsman etc)* in Form kommen; **to get a house into ~** ein Haus in Ordnung bringen; **to get one's affairs into ~** seine Angelegenheiten ordnen; **to knock sb/sth into ~** jdn/etw auf Vordermann bringen.
2 *vt (lit) stone etc* bearbeiten; *clay etc* formen *(into* zu*)*; *(fig) character, ideas* formen, prägen; *one's life* gestalten; *course of history* bestimmen.
3 *vi (also* **~ up***)* sich entwickeln. **to ~ up well** sich gut entwickeln.
shaped [ʃeɪpt] *adj* geformt. **an oddly ~ hat** ein Hut mit einer komischen Form.
-shaped [-ʃeɪpt] *adj suf* -förmig.
shapeless ['ʃeɪplɪs] *adj* formlos; *(ugly)* unförmig.
shapely ['ʃeɪplɪ] *adj (+er) figure, woman* wohlproportioniert; *legs, bust* wohlgeformt.
share [ʃɛə^r] **1** *n* **(a)** *(portion)* Anteil *m (in or of* an *+dat)*. **I want my fair ~** ich will meinen (An)teil; **he didn't get his fair ~** er ist zu kurz gekommen; **I've had more than my fair ~ of bad luck** ich habe mehr (als mein Teil an) Pech gehabt; **I'll give you a ~ in the profit** ich beteilige Sie am Gewinn; **in equal ~s** zu gleichen Teilen; **to take one's ~ of the proceeds/blame** sich *(dat)* seinen Anteil am Gewinn nehmen/sich mitschuldig erklären; **to pay one's ~** seinen (An)teil bezahlen; **to do one's ~** sein(en) Teil beitragen; **to have a ~ in sth** an etw *(dat)* beteiligt sein; **I had no ~ in that** damit hatte ich nichts zu tun. **(b)** *(Fin)* (Geschäfts)anteil *m*; *(in a public limited company)* Aktie *f*.
2 *vt (divide)* teilen; *(have in common also)* gemeinsam haben; *responsibility* gemeinsam tragen. **we ~ the same name/birthday** wir haben den gleichen Namen/am gleichen Tag Geburtstag; **they ~ a room** sie haben ein gemeinsames Zimmer; **I do not ~ that view** diese Ansicht teile ich nicht.
3 *vi* **(a)** teilen. **children have to learn to ~** Kinder müssen lernen, mit anderen zu teilen; **to ~ and ~ alike** (brüderlich) mit (den) anderen teilen. **(b) to ~ in sth** sich an etw *(dat)* beteiligen; *(in profit)* an etw *(dat)* beteiligt werden; *(in enthusiasm)* etw teilen; *(in success, sorrow)* an etw *(dat)* Anteil nehmen.
share: ~holder *n* Aktionär(in *f*) *m*; **~ index** *n* Aktienindex *m*; **~-out** *n* Verteilung *f*; *(St Ex)* (Dividenden)ausschüttung *f*.
shark [ʃɑːk] *n* **(a)** Hai(fisch) *m*. **(b)** *(col: swindler)* Schlitzohr *nt (col)*. **loan ~** Kredithai *m (col)*.
sharp [ʃɑːp] **1** *adj (+er)* **(a)** scharf; *needle, angle* spitz; *air, wind* schneidend; *apple* sauer; *wine* herb; *nose* empfindlich; *(intelligent) person* schlau, auf Draht *(col)*; *child* aufgeweckt; *remark* scharfsinnig. **that was pretty ~ of you** das war ganz schön schlau *or* clever *(col)* von dir; **to keep a ~ watch for mistakes** scharf auf Fehler aufpassen. **(b)** *(sudden, intense) whistle, cry* durchdringend, schrill; *drop in prices* steil; *frost* scharf; *shower, desire, pain* heftig. **after a short, ~ struggle** nach kurzem, heftigem Kampf. **(c)** *(pej: cunning) person* gerissen, raffiniert, clever *(col)*; *trick etc* raffiniert. **(d)** *(harsh, fierce) tongue, retort, tone of voice* scharf; *person* schroff. **he has a ~ temper** er ist jähzornig. **(e)** *(Mus) note (too high)* zu hoch; *(raised a semitone)* (um einen Halbton) erhöht.
2 *adv (+er)* **(a)** *(Mus)* zu hoch. **(b) at 5 o'clock ~** Punkt 5 Uhr; **to turn ~ right** scharf nach rechts abbiegen.
3 *n (Mus)* Kreuz *nt*. **you played F natural instead of a ~** du hast f statt fis gespielt.
sharpen ['ʃɑːpən] *vt* **(a)** *knife* schleifen; *razor* wetzen; *pencil* spitzen; *(fig) appetite* anregen; *wits* schärfen. **(b)** *(Mus) (by a semitone)* (um einen Halbton) erhöhen; *(raise pitch)* höher singen/spielen/stimmen.
sharpener ['ʃɑːpnə^r] *n* Schleifgerät *nt*; *(in rod shape)* Wetzstahl *m*; *(pencil ~)* (Bleistift)spitzer *m*.
sharp: ~-eyed *adj* scharfsichtig; **to be ~-eyed** scharfe Augen haben; **~-featured** *adj* mit scharfen (Gesichts)zügen; **~shooter** *n* Scharfschütze *m*; **~-sighted** *adj* = **~-eyed; ~-tempered** *adj* jähzornig; **~-tongued** *adj* scharfzüngig; **~-witted** *adj* scharfsinnig.
shatter ['ʃætə^r] **1** *vt* **(a)** *(lit)* zertrümmern; *hopes, dreams* zunichte machen; *nerves* zerrütten. **the blast ~ed all the windows** durch die Explosion zersplitterten alle Fensterscheiben; **his hopes were ~ed** seine Hoffnungen hatten sich zerschlagen. **(b)** *(fig col: exhaust)* fertigmachen *(col)*; *(mentally)* mitnehmen. **2** *vi* zerbrechen, zerspringen; *(windscreen)* (zer)splittern.
shattered ['ʃætəd] *adj (col) (exhausted)* fertig *(col)*; *(amazed)* platt *(col)*; *(emotionally exhausted)* mitgenommen.
shattering ['ʃætərɪŋ] *adj* **(a)** *blow, explosion* gewaltig; *defeat* vernichtend. **(b)** *(fig col: exhausting)* anstrengend; *(psychologically)* niederschmetternd.
shatterproof ['ʃætəpruːf] *adj* splitterfrei.
shave [ʃeɪv] *(vb: pret* **~d,** *ptp* **~d** *or* **shaven***)* **1** *n* Rasur *f*. **to have a ~** sich rasieren; *(at a barber's)* sich rasieren lassen; **to have a close ~** *(fig)* mit knapper Not davonkommen; **that was a close ~** das war knapp. **2** *vt face, legs* rasieren; *wood* hobeln. **3** *vi (person)* sich rasieren; *(razor)* rasieren.
♦ **shave off** *vt sep beard* sich *(dat)* abrasieren; *sb's beard* abrasieren; *wood* abhobeln.
shaven ['ʃeɪvn] *adj head* (kahl)geschoren.
shaver ['ʃeɪvə^r] *n (razor)* Rasierapparat *m*.
shaving ['ʃeɪvɪŋ] *n* **~s** *pl* Späne *pl*.
shaving *in cpds* Rasier-; **~ brush** *n* Rasierpinsel *m*; **~ cream** *n* Rasiercreme *f*; **~ point** *n (Brit)* Steckdose *f* für Rasierapparate.
shawl [ʃɔːl] *n* (Umhänge)tuch *nt*; *(covering head)* (Kopf)tuch *nt*.
she [ʃiː] **1** *pron* sie; *(of boats, cars)* es. **~ who ...** *(liter)* diejenige, die ... **2** *n* Sie *f*.

she- *pref* weiblich. **~-bear** weiblicher Bär, Bärin *f*.
sheaf [ʃiːf] *n, pl* **sheaves** *(of wheat, corn)* Garbe *f*; *(of arrows etc, papers, notes)* Bündel *nt*.
shear [ʃɪəʳ] *pret* **~ed,** *ptp* **shorn** *vt sheep* scheren; *wool* (ab)scheren.
shears [ʃɪəz] *npl* (große) Schere; *(for hedges)* Heckenschere *f*; *(for metal)* Metallschere *f*.
sheath [ʃiːθ] *n (for sword etc)* Scheide *f*; *(Bot)* (Blatt)scheide *f*; *(on cable)* Mantel *m*; *(Brit: contraceptive)* Kondom *m or nt*.
sheath knife *n* Fahrtenmesser *nt*.
sheaves [ʃiːvz] *pl of* **sheaf.**
shed[1] [ʃed] *pret, ptp* ~ *vt* **(a)** *leaves, hair etc* verlieren; *horns* abwerfen; *clothes* ausziehen. **to ~ its skin** sich häuten; **you should ~ a few pounds** Sie sollten ein paar Pfund abnehmen *or* loswerden. **(b)** *tears, blood* vergießen. **I won't ~ any tears over him** ich weine ihm keine Träne nach. **(c)** *burden, leader* loswerden; *cares* ablegen; *friend* fallenlassen. **(d)** *light, perfume* verbreiten. **to ~ light on sth** *(fig)* etw erhellen.
shed[2] *n* Schuppen *m*; *(industrial)* Halle *f*; *(cattle ~)* Stall *m*.
she'd [ʃiːd] = **she would; she had.**
sheen [ʃiːn] *n* Glanz *m*.
sheep [ʃiːp] *n, pl* - *(lit, fig)* Schaf *nt*. **to separate the ~ from the goats** *(fig)* die Schafe von den Böcken trennen.
sheep: ~-dip *n* Desinfektionsbad *nt* für Schafe; **~dog** *nt* Hütehund *m*.
sheepish [ˈʃiːpɪʃ] *adj look* verlegen. **I felt a bit ~ about it** das war mir ein bißchen peinlich.
sheepskin [ˈʃiːpskɪn] *n* **(a)** Schaffell *nt*. **(b)** *(US col: diploma)* Pergament *nt*.
sheer [ʃɪəʳ] *adj (+er)* **(a)** *(absolute)* rein; *nonsense also* bar, glatt. **by ~ chance** rein zufällig; **by ~ hard work** durch nichts als harte Arbeit. **(b)** *(steep) cliff, drop* steil, jäh *(geh)*. **there is a ~ drop of 200 metres** es fällt 200 Meter steil ab. **(c)** *(of cloth etc)* (hauch)dünn.
sheet [ʃiːt] *n* **(a)** *(for bed)* (Bett)laken, Bettuch *nt*; *(for covering furniture)* Tuch *nt*. **the furniture was covered with (dust)~s** die Möbel waren verhängt. **(b)** *(of paper, col: a newspaper)* Blatt *nt*; *(big, as of wrapping paper, stamps etc, Typ)* Bogen *m*. **~ of music** Notenblatt *nt*. **(c)** *(of plywood)* Platte *f*; *(of glass also)* Scheibe *f*; *(of metal also)* Blech *nt*; *(baking ~)* (Back)blech *nt*; *(of water, ice etc)* Fläche *f*. **a ~ of ice covered the lake** eine Eisschicht bedeckte den See; **a ~ of flame** eine riesige Flamme.
sheet: ~ feed *n (for printer)* Einzelblattzuführung *f*; **~ lightning** *n* Wetterleuchten *nt*; **~ metal** *n* Walzblech *nt*; **~ music** *n* Notenblätter *pl*.
sheik(h) [ʃeɪk] *n* Scheich *m*.
shelf [ʃelf] *n, pl* **shelves (a)** Brett, Bord *nt*; *(for books)* Bücherbrett *nt*. **shelves** *(unit of furniture)* Regal *nt*; **she was left on the ~** *(col: girl)* sie ist sitzengeblieben. **(b)** *(ledge of rock etc)* Gesims *nt*, (Fels-)vorsprung *m*.
shelf: ~ life *n* Lagerfähigkeit *f*; **~ mark** *n* Standortzeichen *nt*.
shell [ʃel] **1** *n* **(a)** *(of egg, nut, mollusc)* Schale *f*; *(on beach)* Muschel *f*; *(of snail)* (Schnecken)haus *nt*; *(of tortoise, insect)* Panzer *m*; *(pastry ~)* Form *f*. **to come out of one's ~** *(fig)* aus sich *(dat)* herausgehen; **to withdraw into one's ~** *(fig)* sich in sein Schneckenhaus verkriechen. **(b)** *(frame) (of building)* Mauerwerk *nt*; *(unfinished)* Rohbau *m*; *(ruin)* Gemäuer *nt*; *(of car) (unfinished)* Karosserie *f*; *(gutted)* Wrack *nt*; *(of ship)* Gerippe *nt*; *(gutted)* Wrack *nt*. **(c)** *(Mil)* Granate *f*; *(esp US: cartridge)* Patrone *f*. **2** *vt* **(a)** *peas etc* enthülsen; *eggs, nuts* schälen. **(b)** *(Mil)* (mit Granaten) beschießen.
♦ **shell out** *(col)* **1** *vt sep* blechen *(col)*. **2** *vi* **to ~ ~ for sth** für etw blechen *(col)*.
she'll [ʃiːl] = **she will; she shall.**
shellfish [ˈʃɛlfɪʃ] *n* Schaltier(e *pl) nt*; *(Cook)* Meeresfrüchte *pl*.
shelling [ˈʃelɪŋ] *n* Granatfeuer *nt (of* auf *+acc)*.
shell: ~proof *adj* bombensicher; **~ shock** *n* Kriegsneurose *f*.
shelter [ˈʃeltəʳ] **1** *n (protection)* Schutz *m*; *(place)* Unterstand *m*; *(air-raid ~)* (Luftschutz)keller *m*; *(bus ~)* Wartehäuschen *nt*; *(for the night)* Unterkunft *f*. **a night ~ for homeless people** ein Obdachlosenasyl *nt*; **in the ~ of one's home** in der Geborgenheit des Hauses; **under the ~ of the rock** im Schutze des Felsens; **to take ~** sich in Sicherheit bringen; *(from rain, hail etc)* sich unterstellen; **to give sb ~** jdn beherbergen. **2** *vt* schützen *(from* vor *+dat)*; *criminal* verstecken. **to ~ sb from blame** jdn gegen Vorwürfe in Schutz nehmen; **to ~ sb from harm** jdn vor Schaden bewahren. **3** *vi* **there was nowhere to ~** man konnte nirgends Schutz finden; *(from rain etc)* man konnte sich nirgends unterstellen; **a good place to ~** eine Stelle, wo man gut geschützt ist.
sheltered [ˈʃeltəd] *adj place* geschützt; *life* behütet. **~ from the wind** windgeschützt.
shelve [ʃelv] **1** *vi (slope)* abfallen. **2** *vt problem* aufschieben; *plan* ad acta legen.
shelves [ʃelvz] *pl of* **shelf.**
shelving [ˈʃelvɪŋ] *n* Regale *pl*.
shepherd [ˈʃepəd] **1** *n* Schäfer *m*. **~'s pie** *Auflauf m aus Hackfleisch und Kartoffelbrei*. **2** *vt* führen.
sherbet [ˈʃɜːbət] *n (powder)* Brausepulver *nt*; *(drink)* Brause *f*; *(US: water ~ ice)* Fruchteis *nt*.
sheriff [ˈʃerɪf] *n* Sheriff *m*; *(Scot)* Friedensrichter *m*.
sherry [ˈʃerɪ] *n* Sherry *m*.
she's [ʃiːz] = **she is; she has.**
Shetland Islands [ˈʃetlənd'aɪləndz] *npl* Shetlandinseln *pl*.
Shetland pony [ˈʃetlənd'pəʊnɪ] *n* Shetlandpony *nt*.
shield [ʃiːld] **1** *n (Mil, Her)* Schild *m*; *(sporting trophy also)* Trophäe *f*; *(on machine)* Schutzschirm *m*; *(eye~, radiation ~)* Schirm *m*; *(fig)* Schutz *m*. **riot ~** Schutzschild *m*. **2** *vt* schützen *(sb from sth* jdn vor etw *dat)*.
shift [ʃɪft] **1** *n* **(a)** *(change)* Änderung *f*; *(in policy, opinion also)* Wandel *m*; *(from one place to another)* Verlegung *f*. **a ~ in direction** eine Richtungsänderung; **a ~ in public opinion** ein Meinungsumschwung *m* in der Bevölkerung; **a ~ of emphasis** eine Gewichtsverlagerung. **(b)** *(Aut: gear~)* Schaltung *f*; *(on typewriter: also ~* **key***)* Umschalttaste *f*. **(c)** *(period at work, group of workers)* Schicht *f*. **to work in ~s** in Schichten arbeiten; **to do ~ work** Schicht arbeiten. **(d)** *(stratagem)* List *f*; *(expedient)* Ausweg *m*. **to make ~ with sth** sich mit etw behelfen.

2 *vt* **(a)** *(move)* (von der Stelle) bewegen; *nail, cork* rauskriegen; *lid* abkriegen; *furniture also* verrücken; *head, arm* wegnehmen; *(from one place to another)* verschieben; *offices etc* verlegen; *rubble* wegräumen. **to ~ scenery** Kulissen schieben; **to ~ one's ground** seinen Standpunkt ändern; **to ~ sb from an opinion** jdn von einer Meinung abbringen; **to ~ the blame onto somebody else** die Verantwortung auf jemand anders schieben. **(b)** *(col: get rid of)* loswerden. **(c)** *(US Aut)* **to ~ gears** schalten.

3 *vi* **(a)** *(move)* sich bewegen; *(cargo, scene)* sich verlagern; *(scene)* wechseln; *(wind)* umspringen; *(from one's opinion)* abgehen. **he ~ed out of the way** er ging aus dem Weg; **~ over, you're taking up too much room** rück mal rüber, du nimmst zuviel Platz weg!; **he ~ed onto his back** er drehte sich auf den Rücken; **~ing sands** *(Geol)* Flugsand *m*. **(b)** *(Aut)* schalten. **(c)** *(col: move quickly)* rasen.
shiftless [ˈʃɪftlɪs] *adj* träge, energielos.

shifty ['ʃɪftɪ] *adj (+er) (not honest)* unehrlich; *(not reliable)* unzuverlässig; *glance* verstohlen; *reply* ausweichend.

shilling ['ʃɪlɪŋ] *n (Brit old)* Shilling *m.*

shilly-shally ['ʃɪlɪˌʃælɪ] *vi (col)* unschlüssig sein.

shimmer ['ʃɪməʳ] **1** *n* Schimmer *m.* **2** *vi* schimmern.

shin [ʃɪn] **1** *n* Schienbein *nt; (of meat)* Hachse *f.* **2** *vi* **to ~ up/down** (geschickt) hinauf-/hinunterklettern.

shinbone ['ʃɪnbəʊn] *n* Schienbein *nt.*

shindy ['ʃɪndɪ] *n (col)* Radau *m (col); (noise also, dispute)* Krach *m (col).*

shine [ʃaɪn] *(vb: pret, ptp* **shone***)* **1** *n* Glanz *m.* **to give one's shoes a ~** seine Schuhe polieren; **to take the ~ off sth** *(lit, fig)* einer Sache *(dat)* den Glanz nehmen; **she's taken a real ~ to my brother** *(col)* mein Bruder hat es ihr wirklich angetan. **2** *vt* **(a)** *pret, ptp usu* **~d** *(polish: also* **~ up***)* blank putzen; *shoes also* polieren. **(b) to ~ a light on sth** etw beleuchten; **~ the torch this way!** leuchte einmal hierher!; **don't ~ it in my eyes!** blende mich nicht! **3** *vi* **(a)** leuchten; *(stars, eyes also, paint)* glänzen; *(sun, lamp)* scheinen; *(glass)* blitzblank sein. **her face shone with happiness** ihr Gesicht strahlte vor Glück. **(b)** *(fig: excel)* glänzen. **to ~ at/in sth** bei/in etw *(dat)* glänzen.

shingle[1] ['ʃɪŋgl] *n (US col: signboard)* Schild *nt.*

shingle[2] *n no pl (pebbles)* Kieselsteine *pl.*

shingles ['ʃɪŋglz] *n sing (Med)* Gürtelrose *f.*

shining ['ʃaɪnɪŋ] *adj (lit, fig)* leuchtend; *light* strahlend; *eyes also, paint* glänzend; *car* blitzblank.

shiny ['ʃaɪnɪ] *adj (+er)* glänzend.

ship [ʃɪp] **1** *n* **(a)** Schiff *nt.* **on board ~** an Bord; **~'s company** (Schiffs)besatzung *f;* **~'s papers** Schiffspapiere *pl.* **(b)** *(US col: plane)* Maschine *f; (space~)* Raumschiff *nt.* **2** *vt* **(a)** *(take on board) goods* an Bord bringen, laden; *crew, passengers* an Bord nehmen. **to ~ oars** die Riemen einlegen; **to ~ water** leck sein. **(b)** *(transport)* versenden; *grain etc* verfrachten; *(by sea also)* verschiffen.

♦**ship out** *vt sep* versenden; *coal, grain etc* verfrachten. **to ~ supplies ~ to sb** jdn (per Schiff) mit Vorräten versorgen.

ship: ~builder *n* Schiffbauer *m;* **~building** *n* Schiffbau *m;* **~load** *n* Schiffsladung *f;* **~mate** *n* Schiffskamerad *m.*

shipment ['ʃɪpmənt] *n* Sendung *f; (act)* Transport *m; (transporting by sea)* Verschiffung *f.*

shipowner ['ʃɪpəʊnəʳ] *n* Schiffseigner *m; (of many ships)* Reeder *m.*

shipper ['ʃɪpəʳ] *n (company)* Speditionsfirma *f; (sender)* Absender *m.*

shipping ['ʃɪpɪŋ] **1** *n no pl* **(a)** Schiffahrt *f; (ships)* Schiffe *pl.* **(b)** *(transportation)* Verschiffung *f; (by rail etc)* Versand *m.* **2** *adj attr* **~ agent** Spediteur *m;* **~ company, ~ line** Schiffahrtslinie, Reederei *f;* **~ lane** Schiffahrtsstraße *f.*

ship: ~shape *adj, adv* tipptopp *(col);* **~wreck 1** *n (lit, fig)* Schiffbruch *m; (fig also)* Scheitern *nt;* **2** *vt* **to be ~wrecked** *(lit)* schiffbrüchig sein; *(fig)* Schiffbruch erleiden, scheitern; **~yard** *n* (Schiffs)werft *f.*

shire ['ʃaɪəʳ] *n (Brit old)* Grafschaft *f.* **~ horse** Zugpferd *nt.*

shirk [ʃɜːk] **1** *vt* sich drücken vor *(+dat)*, ausweichen *(+dat).* **2** *vi* sich drücken.

shirker ['ʃɜːkəʳ] *n* Drückeberger(in *f*) *m.*

shirt [ʃɜːt] *n (men's)* (Ober)hemd *nt; (Ftbl)* Hemd, Trikot *nt; (woman's: also US* **~waist***)* Hemdbluse *f.* **keep your ~ on** *(col)* reg dich nicht auf!

shirt-sleeves ['ʃɜːtsliːvz] *npl* Hemdsärmel *pl.* **in his/their ~** in Hemdsärmeln.

shirty ['ʃɜːtɪ] *adj (+er) (esp Brit col)* sauer *(col),* verärgert; *(as characteristic)* griesgrämig *(col).*

shit [ʃɪt] *(vb: pret, ptp* **~** *or (hum)* **shat***) (col!)* **1** *n* **(a)** Scheiße *f (col!); (nonsense also)* Scheiß *m (col!).* **(b)** *(person)* Arschloch *nt (col!).* **(c) ~s** *pl (state of fear)* **to have/get the ~s** Schiß haben/kriegen *(col).* **2** *vi* scheißen *(col!).* **3** *interj* Scheiße *(col!).*

shiver ['ʃɪvəʳ] **1** *n* **(a)** *(of cold)* Schauer *m; (of horror also)* Schauder *m.* **the sight sent ~s down my back** bei dem Anblick lief es mir kalt den Rücken hinunter; **it gives me the ~s** ich kriege davon eine Gänsehaut. **2** *vi* zittern *(with* vor *+dat); (with fear also)* schaudern.

shivery ['ʃɪvərɪ] *adj* **to feel ~** frösteln.

shoal [ʃəʊl] *n (of fish)* Schwarm *m.*

shock [ʃɒk] **1** *n* **(a)** *(of explosion, impact)* Wucht *f; (of earthquake)* (Erd)stoß *m.* **(b)** *(Elec)* Schlag *m; (Med)* (Elektro)shock *m.* **to get a ~** einen Schlag bekommen. **(c)** *(emotional disturbance)* Schock, Schlag *m; (state)* Schock(zustand) *m.* **to be suffering from ~** einen Schock (erlitten) haben; **to be in (a state of) ~** unter Schock stehen; **the ~ killed him** den Schock hat er nicht überlebt; **to give sb a ~** jdn erschrecken; **it gave me a nasty ~** es hat mir einen bösen Schreck(en) eingejagt; **to get the ~ of one's life** den Schock seines Lebens kriegen; **he is in for a ~!** *(col)* der wird sich wundern! *(col).*

2 *vt (affect emotionally)* erschüttern; *(make indignant)* schockieren, schocken *(col).* **to be ~ed by sth** über etw *(acc)* bestürzt sein; *(morally)* über etw *(acc)* schockiert sein; **she is easily ~ed** sie ist leicht schockiert; **I was ~ed at the news** ich war bestürzt über die Nachricht.

3 *vi (film, writer etc)* schockieren, schocken *(col).*

shock absorber ['ʃɒkəbˌzɔːbəʳ] *n* Stoßdämpfer *m.*

shocking ['ʃɒkɪŋ] *adj* **(a)** *news* erschütternd, schockierend. **(b)** *(very bad)* entsetzlich, furchtbar. **isn't it ~!** es ist doch furchtbar!

shock: ~proof *adj* stoßfest; **~ therapy** *n* Schocktherapie *f;* **~ wave** *n (lit)* Druckwelle *f; (fig)* Erschütterung *f.*

shod [ʃɒd] *pret, ptp of* **shoe.**

shoddy ['ʃɒdɪ] *adj (+er)* schäbig; *work* schludrig; *goods also* minderwertig.

shoe [ʃuː] *(vb: pret, ptp* **shod***)* **1** *n* **(a)** Schuh *m.* **I wouldn't like to be in his ~s** ich möchte nicht in seiner Haut stecken; **to put oneself in sb's ~s** sich in jds Lage *(acc)* versetzen. **(b)** *(horse~)* (Huf)eisen *nt.* **(c)** *(brake ~)* Bremsschuh *m.* **2** *vt horse* beschlagen.

shoe: ~brush *n* Schuhbürste *f;* **~horn** *n* Schuhanzieher, Schuhlöffel *m;* **~lace** *n* Schnürsenkel *m;* **~maker** *n* Schuhmacher, Schuster *m;* **~ polish** *n* Schuhcreme *f;* **~shop** *n* Schuhgeschäft *nt;* **~string** *n* **(a)** *(US: ~lace)* Schnürsenkel *m;* **(b)** *(fig)* **to live on a ~string** von der Hand in den Mund leben; **~string budget** *n* Minibudget *nt (col);* **~tree** *n* (Schuh)spanner *m.*

shone [ʃɒn] *pret, ptp of* **shine.**

shoo [ʃuː] **1** *interj* sch; *(to dog etc)* pfui; *(to child)* husch. **2** *vt* **to ~ sb away** jdn verscheuchen.

shook [ʃʊk] *pret of* **shake.**

shoot [ʃuːt] *(vb: pret, ptp* **shot***)* **1** *n* **(a)** *(Bot)* Trieb *m; (from seed etc also)* Keim *m; (of bushes, trees)* Schößling *m; (young branch)* Reis *nt.* **(b)** *(hunting expedition)* Jagd *f; (~ing party)* Jagdgesellschaft *f; (competition)* (Wett)schießen *nt.*

2 *vt* **(a)** *(Mil etc)* schießen; *bullet, gun* abfeuern. **(b)** *person, animal (hit)* anschießen; *(wound seriously)* niederschießen; *(kill)* erschießen. **to ~ sb dead** jdn erschießen; **he shot himself** er hat sich erschossen; **he accidentally shot himself in the foot** er schoß sich *(dat)* versehentlich in den Fuß; **he was shot in the leg** er wurde ins Bein getroffen; **you'll get shot for doing that!** *(fig col)* das kann dich Kopf und Kragen kosten! *(col).* **(c)** *(throw, propel)* schleudern; *(Sport)* schießen. **to ~ a question at sb** eine Frage auf jdn abfeuern; **to ~ a glance at sb** jdm einen (schnellen) Blick zuwerfen. **(d)** *(Phot) film, scene* drehen; *snapshot* schießen; *subject* aufnehmen.

3 *vi* **(a)** schießen; *(as hunter)* jagen. **to ~ to kill** gezielt schießen; *(police)* einen gezielten Todesschuß/gezielte Todesschüsse abgeben; **don't ~!** nicht schießen!; **stop or I'll ~!** stehenbleiben oder ich schieße!; **to ~ at sb/sth** auf jdn/etw schießen; **to ~ at goal** aufs Tor schießen. **(b) to ~ into the lead** an die Spitze vorpreschen; **he shot down the stairs** er schoß *or* jagte die Treppe hinunter; **to ~ by** *or* **past** vorbeischießen *or* -jagen; **the pain shot up his leg** der Schmerz durchzuckte sein Bein.

♦ **shoot down** *vt sep plane* abschießen; *person* erschießen; *(fig col) person* fertigmachen *(col)*; *suggestion* abschmettern *(col)*; *argument* in der Luft zerreißen.

♦ **shoot off** *vi* davonschießen *(col)*.

♦ **shoot out 1** *vi (emerge swiftly)* herausschießen *(of* aus*)*. **2** *vt sep* **(a)** *(put out swiftly) hand etc* blitzschnell ausstrecken; *tongue etc* hervorschnellen (lassen). **(b) to ~ it ~** sich *(dat)* ein (Feuer)gefecht liefern.

♦ **shoot up** *vi (hand, prices)* in die Höhe schnellen; *(grow rapidly) (children, plant)* in die Höhe schießen; *(new towns, buildings etc)* aus dem Boden schießen.

shooting ['ʃuːtɪŋ] *n* **(a)** *(shots)* Schießen *nt*; *(by artillery)* Feuer *nt*. **was there any ~?** gab es Schießereien?; **there was a ~ last night** gestern nacht ist jemand erschossen worden. **(b)** *(Sport: Ftbl etc, with guns)* Schießen *nt*; *(Hunt)* Jagen *nt*, Jagd *f*. **(c)** *(Film)* Drehen *nt*.

shooting: ~ brake *n (Aut old)* Kombiwagen *m*; **~ gallery** *n* Schießstand *m*; **~ match** *n*: **the whole ~ match** *(col)* der ganze Laden *(col)*; **~ party** *n* Jagdgesellschaft *f*; **~ star** *m* Sternschnuppe *f*; **~ stick** *n* Jagdstuhl *m*.

shop [ʃɒp] **1** *n* **(a)** Geschäft *nt*, Laden *m*; *(esp Brit: large store)* Kaufhaus *nt*. **I have to go to the ~s** ich muß einkaufen gehen; **to set up ~** ein Geschäft eröffnen; **all over the ~** *(col)* in der ganzen Gegend herum *(col)*; **to talk ~** über die Arbeit reden; *(professional people also)* fachsimpeln. **(b)** *(work~)* Werkstatt *f*; *(workers)* Arbeiterschaft *f*. **2** *vi* einkaufen, Einkäufe machen. **to go ~ping** einkaufen gehen. **3** *vt (Brit col: betray)* **to ~ sb (to sb)** jdn (bei jdm) verpfeifen *(col)*.

♦ **shop around** *vi (lit, fig)* sich umsehen *(for* nach*)*.

shop: ~ assistant *n (Brit)* Verkäufer(in *f*) *m*; **~ floor** *n* **(a)** *(place)* Produktionsstätte *f*; *(for heavier work)* Werkstatt *f*; **he started off working on the ~ floor** er hat (ganz unten) in der Fabrik *or* Produktion angefangen; **on the ~ floor** in der Werkstatt *etc*; unter den Arbeitern; **(b)** *(Brit: workers)* Arbeiter *pl*, Leute *pl* in der Produktion; **~keeper** *n* Ladenbesitzer(in *f*), Geschäftsinhaber(in *f*) *m*; **~lifter** *n* Ladendieb(in *f*) *m*; **~lifting** *n* Ladendiebstahl *m*.

shopper ['ʃɒpəʳ] *n* Käufer(in *f*) *m*.

shopping ['ʃɒpɪŋ] *n (act)* Einkaufen *nt*; *(goods bought)* Einkäufe *pl*. **to do one's ~** einkaufen, Einkäufe machen.

shopping: ~ bag *n* Einkaufstasche *f*; **~ basket** *n* Einkaufskorb *m*; **~ centre,** *(US)* **~ center** *n* Einkaufszentrum *nt*; **~ list** *n* Einkaufszettel *m*.

shop: ~-soiled *adj (Brit) clothes, furniture* angeschmutzt; *goods, material* leicht beschädigt; **~ steward** *n* (gewerkschaftlicher) Vertrauensmann *(im Betrieb)*; **~ window** *n (lit, fig)* Schaufenster *nt*; **~-worn** *adj (US)* = **~-soiled.**

shore[1] [ʃɔːʳ] *n (sea ~, lake ~)* Ufer *nt*; *(beach)* Strand *m*; *(coast)* Küste *f*. **these ~s** *(fig)* dieses Land; **on the ~s of the lake** am Seeufer; **on ~** an Land.

shore[2] *vt (also* **~ up***)* (ab)stützen; *(fig)* stützen.

shore: ~ leave *n (Naut)* Landurlaub *m*; **~line** *n* Uferlinie *f*.

shorn [ʃɔːn] *ptp of* **shear.**

short [ʃɔːt] **1** *adj (+er)* **(a)** kurz; *steps also, person* klein. **a ~ way off** nicht weit entfernt; **to be ~ in the leg** *(person)* kurze Beine haben; *(trousers)* zu kurz sein; **a ~ time ago** vor kurzer Zeit, vor kurzem; **in a ~ while** in Kürze; **time is getting/is ~** die Zeit wird/ist knapp; **to take the ~ view of sth** etw auf kurze Sicht betrachten; **in ~ order** *(US col)* sofort; **~ and sweet** schön kurz; **the ~ answer is that he refused** kurz gesagt, er lehnte ab; **in ~** kurz gesagt; **Pat is ~ for Patricia** Pat ist die Kurzform von Patricia.

(b) *(curt) reply* knapp; *(rude)* barsch, schroff; *manner, person* schroff, kurz angebunden *(col)*. **to have a ~ temper** unbeherrscht sein; **to be ~ with sb** jdn schroff behandeln, jdm gegenüber kurz angebunden sein *(col)*.

(c) *(insufficient)* zuwenig *inv*; *rations* knapp. **to be in ~ supply** knapp sein; *(Comm)* beschränkt lieferbar sein; **to be ~** *(in ~ supply)* knapp sein; *(shot, throw)* nicht weit genug sein; **we are (five/ £3) ~** wir haben (fünf/£ 3) zuwenig, uns *(dat)* fehlen fünf/£ 3; **we are ~ of books** wir haben zuwenig Bücher; **to be ~ of time** wenig Zeit haben; **I'm a bit ~ (of cash)** *(col)* ich bin etwas knapp bei Kasse *(col)*; **we are £2,000 ~ of our target** wir liegen £ 2.000 unter unserem Ziel; **not far ~ of £100** nicht viel weniger als £ 100, knapp unter £ 100; **to be ~ on experience** wenig Erfahrung haben.

2 *adv* **(a) to fall ~** *(arrow, missile etc)* zu kurz landen. **that's where the book falls ~** daran fehlt es dem Buch; **to fall ~ of sth** etw nicht erreichen; *of expectations* etw nicht erfüllen; **it falls far ~ of what we require** das bleibt weit hinter unseren Bedürfnissen zurück; **to go ~ (of money/food** *etc***)** zuwenig (Geld/zu essen *etc*) haben; **we are running ~ (of petrol/time)** wir haben nicht mehr viel (Benzin/Zeit); **I'm running ~ of ideas** mir gehen die Ideen aus; **my patience is running ~** meine Geduld ist bald zu Ende; **to sell sb ~** *(in shop)* jdm zuwenig geben; *(betray, cheat)* jdn betrügen.

(b) *(abruptly, suddenly)* plötzlich, abrupt. **to stop ~** *(while driving)* plötzlich stehenbleiben; *(while talking)* plötzlich *or* unvermittelt innehalten; **I'd stop ~ of** *or* **at murder** vor Mord würde ich haltmachen.

(c) ~ of *(except)* außer *(+dat)*; **it is nothing ~ of robbery** das ist glatter Diebstahl; **nothing ~ of a revolution can ...** nur eine Revolution kann ...; **it's little ~ of madness** das grenzt an Wahnsinn; **I don't see what you can do ~ of asking him yourself** ich sehe keine andere Möglichkeit, als daß Sie ihn selbst fragen; **~ of telling him a lie ...** außer ihn zu belügen ...

3 *n (~ circuit)* Kurzschluß, Kurze(r) *(col) m*; *(col: ~ drink)* Kurze(r) *m (col)*.

4 *vt (Elec)* kurzschließen.

5 *vi (Elec)* einen Kurzschluß haben.

shortage ['ʃɔːtɪdʒ] *n (of goods, objects)* Knappheit *f no pl (of* an *+dat)*; *(of people)* Mangel *m no pl (of* an *+dat)*. **the housing ~** die Wohnungsknappheit; **a ~ of staff** Personalmangel *m*.

short: ~bread *n* Mürb(e)teiggebäck *nt*; **~cake** *n (Brit: ~bread)* Mürb(e)teiggebäck *nt*; *(US: sponge)* Biskuittörtchen *nt*; **~-change** *vt* **to ~-change sb** jdm zuwenig herausgeben; **~-circuit 1** *n* Kurzschluß *m*; **2** *vt* kurzschließen; **3** *vi* einen Kurzschluß haben; **~coming** *n (esp pl)* Mangel *m*; *(of person)* Fehler *m*; **~crust** *n (also* **~crust pastry***)* Mürbeteig *m*; **~ cut** *n* Abkürzung *f*; *(easy solution)* Patentlösung *f*.

shorten ['ʃɔːtn] **1** *vt* verkürzen; *dress, rope* kürzer machen; *book, syllabus etc* kürzen. **2** *vi (days)* kürzer werden.

short: ~hand *n* Kurzschrift, Stenographie *f*; **in ~hand** in Kurzschrift; **to write ~hand** stenographieren; **to take sth down in ~hand** etw stenographieren; **~hand typist** *n (Brit)* Stenotypist(in *f*) *m*; **~ list** *n (esp Brit)* Auswahlliste *f*; **to be on the ~ list** in der engeren Wahl sein; **~-list** *vt (esp Brit)* **to ~-list sb** jdn in die engere Wahl ziehen; **~-lived** *adj (lit, fig)* kurzlebig; *protests, attempts* nicht lange andauernd; **to be ~-lived** *(success, happiness)* von kurzer Dauer sein.

shortly ['ʃɔːtlɪ] *adv* **(a)** *(soon)* bald, in Kürze; *after, before* kurz. **(b)** *(curtly)* barsch.

shorts [ʃɔːts] *npl* **(a)** Shorts *pl*, kurze Hose(n *pl*). **(b)** *(esp US: underpants)* Unterhose *f*.

short: ~-sighted *adj (lit, fig)* kurzsichtig; **~-sleeved** *adj* kurzärmelig; **~-staffed** *adj* **to be ~-staffed** zuwenig Personal haben; **~ story** *n* Kurzgeschichte, Short story *f*; **~-tempered** *adj (in general)* unbeherrscht; *(in a bad temper)* gereizt; **to be ~-tempered with sb** mit jdm ungeduldig sein; **~ term** *n* **in the ~ term** auf kurze Sicht; **~-term** *adj* kurzfristig; **~ time** *n* Kurzarbeit *f*; **to be on ~ time** kurzarbeiten, Kurzarbeit haben; **~wave 1** *n (also* **~wave radio***)* Kurzwelle *f*; **2** *adj transmission* auf Kurzwelle.

shot[1] [ʃɒt] **1** *pret, ptp of* **shoot.**

2 *n* **(a)** *(from gun, bow etc)* Schuß *m*. **to fire** *or* **take a ~ at sb/sth** einen Schuß auf jdn/etw abfeuern *or* abgeben; **to call the ~s** *(fig col)* das Sagen haben *(col)*; **he's a good/bad ~** er ist ein guter/schlechter Schütze. **(b)** *(attempt)* Versuch *m*. **at the first ~** *(col)* auf Anhieb *(col)*; **to take a ~ (at it)** *(try)* es (mal) versuchen; *(guess)* (auf gut Glück) raten. **(c)** *(col: quickly)* **like a ~** *run away* wie der Blitz *(col)*; *do sth* sofort; *agree* sofort, ohne zu überlegen. **(d)** *(injection)* Spritze *f*; *(immunization)* Impfung *f*. **to give a company a ~ in the arm** *(fig)* einer Firma eine Finanzspritze geben. **(e)** *(Sport) (Ftbl, Hockey etc)* Schuß *m*; *(throw)* Wurf *m*; *(Tennis, Golf)* Schlag *m*. **to take a ~ at goal** aufs Tor schießen. **(f)** *(~-putting)* **the ~** *(discipline)* Kugelstoßen *nt*; *(weight)* die Kugel; **to put the ~** kugelstoßen. **(g)** *(Phot)* Aufnahme *f*.

shot[2] *adj (col: rid)* **to be/get ~ of sb/sth** jdn/etw los sein/loswerden.

shot: ~gun *n* Schrotflinte *f*; **~gun wedding** *n* Mußheirat *f*; **~-putter** *n* Kugelstoßer(in *f*) *m*.

should [ʃʊd] *pret of* **shall** *modal aux vb* **(a)** *(expressing duty, advisability, command)* **you ~ do that** du solltest das tun; **you ~n't do that** Sie sollten das nicht tun; **I ~ have done it** ich hätte es tun sollen *or* müssen; **I ~n't have done it** ich hätte es nicht tun sollen *or* dürfen; **he ~ know that it's wrong to lie** er sollte *or* müßte wissen, daß man nicht lügen darf; **you really ~ see that film** den Film sollten *or* müssen Sie wirklich sehen; **~ I go too? — yes you ~** sollte ich auch gehen? — ja, das sollten Sie schon; **was it a good film? — I ~ think it was** war der Film gut? — und ob; **he's coming to apologize — I ~ think so** er will sich entschuldigen — das möchte ich auch hoffen; **... and I ~ know ...** und ich müßte es ja wissen; **how ~ I know?** woher soll ich das wissen?

(b) *(expressing probability)* **he ~ be there by now** er müßte eigentlich schon da sein; **why ~ he suspect me?** warum sollte er mich verdächtigen?; **this book ~ help you** dieses Buch wird Ihnen bestimmt helfen.

(c) *(in tentative statements)* **I ~n't like to say** ich möchte mich nicht festlegen; **I ~ hardly have called him an idiot** ich hätte ihn wohl kaum einen Idioten genannt; **I ~ think there were about 40** ich würde schätzen, daß etwa 40 dort waren; **I ~ like to disagree** da möchte ich widersprechen; **I ~ like to know** ich wüßte gern; **I ~ like to apply for the job** ich würde mich gern um die Stelle bewerben; **thanks, I ~ like to** danke, gern.

(d) *(subjunc, conditional)* **I ~ go if ...** ich würde gehen, wenn ...; **we ~ have come if ...** wir wären gekommen, wenn ...; **I don't know why he ~ behave so strangely** ich weiß nicht, warum er sich so eigenartig benimmt; **if he ~ come, ~ he come** falls er kommen sollte, sollte er kommen; **I ~n't be surprised if he comes** *or* **were to come** ich wäre keineswegs überrascht, wenn er kommen würde; **I ~n't (do it) if I were you** ich würde das an Ihrer Stelle nicht tun; **I ~n't worry about it** ich würde mir darüber keine Gedanken machen; **it is necessary that he ~ be told** es ist nötig, daß man es ihm sagt.

shoulder ['ʃəʊldəʳ] **1** *n (also of meat)* Schulter *f*. **to shrug one's ~s** mit den Schultern *or* Achseln zucken; **to have broad ~s** *(lit)* breite Schultern haben; *(fig)* einen breiten Rücken haben; **to cry on sb's ~** sich an jds Brust *(dat)* ausweinen; **~ to ~** Schulter an Schulter; **he's head and ~s above the rest** er ist einen ganzen Kopf größer als die anderen; **to put one's ~ to the wheel** *(fig)* sich ins Zeug legen. **2** *vt* **(a)** schultern, auf die Schulter nehmen; *(fig) responsibilities* auf sich *(acc)* nehmen; *expense* tragen. **(b)** *(push)* (mit der Schulter) stoßen. **to ~ sb aside** *(lit)* jdn zur Seite stoßen.

shoulder: ~ bag *n* Umhängetasche *f*; **~ blade** *n* Schulterblatt *nt*; **~-length** *adj hair* schulterlang; **~ strap** *n (Mil)* Schulterklappe *f*; *(of dress)* Träger *m*; *(of bag etc)* (Schulter)riemen *m*.

shouldn't ['ʃʊdnt] = **should not.**

shout [ʃaʊt] **1** *n* Ruf, Schrei *m*. **a ~ of protest/pain** ein Protestruf *m*/Schmerzensschrei *m*; **a ~ of excitement** ein aufgeregter Schrei; **~s of applause/laughter** Beifallsrufe *pl*/brüllendes Gelächter; **to give a ~** einen Schrei ausstoßen; **to give sb a ~** jdn rufen; **give me a ~ when you're ready** *(col)* sag mir Bescheid, wenn du fertig bist. **2** *vt* schreien; *(call)* rufen; *order* brüllen. **to ~ abuse at sb** jdn (laut) beschimpfen; **to ~ a warning to sb** jdm eine Warnung zurufen. **3** *vi (call out)* rufen; *(very loudly)* schreien; *(angrily, commanding)* brüllen. **to ~ for sb/sth** nach jdm/etw rufen *or* schreien; **to ~ at sb** jdn anschreien *or* anbrüllen; **to ~ for help** um Hilfe rufen. **4** *vr* **to ~ oneself hoarse** sich heiser schreien.

♦ **shout down** *vt sep person* niederbrüllen; *play* ausbuhen.

♦ **shout out 1** *vi* einen Schrei ausstoßen; *(in pain, rage, protest)* aufschreien. **2** *vt sep* ausrufen; *order* brüllen.

shouting ['ʃaʊtɪŋ] *n (act)* Schreien *nt*; *(sound)* Geschrei *nt*. **it's all over bar the ~** *(col)* es ist so gut wie gelaufen *(col)*.

shove [ʃʌv] **1** *n* Schubs *(col)*, Stoß *m*. **to give sb a ~** jdn schubsen *(col) or* stoßen; **to give sth a ~** etw rücken; *door* gegen etw stoßen; *car* etw anschieben. **2** *vt* **(a)** *(push)* schieben; *(with one short push)* stoßen, schubsen *(col)*; *(jostle)* drängen. **to ~ one's way forward** sich nach vorn durchdrängen. **(b)** *(col: put)* **to ~ sth on(to) sth** etw auf etw *(acc)* werfen *(col)*; **to ~ sth in(to) sth/between sth** etw in etw *(acc)*/zwischen etw *(acc)* stecken; **he ~d a book into my hand** er drückte mir ein Buch in die Hand. **3** *vi* stoßen; *(to move sth)* schieben; *(jostle)* drängeln. **to ~ past sb** sich an jdm vorbeidrängen.

♦ **shove off** *vi (col)* abschieben *(col)*.

♦ **shove over** *(col)* **1** *vt sep* rüberwerfen *(col)*. **2** *vi (also* **shove up***)* rutschen.

shovel ['ʃʌvl] **1** *n* Schaufel *f*; *(with long handle also)* Schippe *f*. **2** *vt* schaufeln; *coal, snow also* schippen. **to ~ food into one's mouth** *(col)* Essen in sich *(acc)* hineinschaufeln *(col)*.

show [ʃəʊ] *(vb: pret* **~ed,** *ptp* **~n***)* **1** *n* **(a)** *(display)* **a fine ~ of roses** eine Rosenpracht; **~ of force** Machtdemonstration *f*; **to have a ~ of hands** eine Abstimmung per Handzeichen vornehmen.

(b) *(outward appearance)* Schau *f*. **to do sth for**

~ etw tun, um Eindruck zu machen; **to make a great ~ of being impressed/overworked** sich *(dat)* ganz den Anschein geben, beeindruckt/überarbeitet zu sein; **without any ~ of emotion** ohne irgendwelche Gefühle zu zeigen; **it was all ~** es war alles nur Schau *(col)*.

(c) *(exhibition)* Ausstellung *f*. **flower/dog ~** Blumen-/Hundeschau *f*; **to be on ~** ausgestellt sein.

(d) *(Theat)* Aufführung *f*; *(TV, variety ~)* Show *f*; *(Rad)* Sendung *f*; *(Film)* Vorstellung *f*. **to go to a ~** ins Theater gehen; **the ~ must go on** *(fig)* es muß trotz allem weitergehen.

(e) *(col: organization)* Laden *m (col)*. **he runs the ~** er schmeißt hier den Laden *(col)*; **to give the (whole) ~ away** alles verraten.

(f) good ~! *(col)* bravo!; **it's a poor ~ when ...** *(col)* es ist ein schwaches Bild, wenn ...; **to put up a good ~** eine gute Leistung zeigen.

2 *vt* **(a)** zeigen; *(at exhibition also)* ausstellen; *passport* vorzeigen; *profit* verzeichnen; *kindness, favour* erweisen; *courage also, loyalty, taste* beweisen; *proof* erbringen. **to ~ sth to sb** jdm etw zeigen; **~ me how to do it** zeigen Sie mir, wie man das macht; **to ~ one's face** sich zeigen; **he had nothing to ~ for it** er hatte am Ende nichts vorzuweisen; **I'll ~ him!** *(col)* dem werd' ich's zeigen!; **it ~s that ...** es zeigt, daß ...; **as ~n in the illustration** wie in der Illustration dargestellt; **the roads are ~n in red** die Straßen sind rot (eingezeichnet); **it just goes to ~ that ...** das zeigt doch nur, daß ...; **it was ~ing signs of rain** es sah nach Regen aus; **to ~ signs of wear** Abnutzungserscheinungen aufweisen; **she's beginning to ~ her age** man sieht ihr allmählich das Alter an; **the carpet ~s the dirt** auf dem Teppich sieht man den Schmutz; **to ~ sb the way** jdm den Weg zeigen; **to ~ sb in/out** jdn hereinbringen/hinausbegleiten; **to ~ sb to his seat** jdn an seinen Platz bringen; **to ~ sb to the door** jdn zur Tür bringen; *(eject)* jdm die Tür weisen; **they were ~n over** *or* **around the factory** sie wurden in der Fabrik herumgeführt.

(b) *(prove)* beweisen. **this ~s him to be a thief** das beweist, daß er ein Dieb ist.

3 *vi* **(a)** *(be visible)* zu sehen sein, sichtbar sein; *(petticoat etc)* vorsehen, rausgucken *(col)*; *(film)* gezeigt werden, laufen; *(exhibit: artist)* ausstellen. **it doesn't ~** man sieht es nicht; **the dirt doesn't ~** man sieht den Schmutz nicht; **his anger ~ed in his eyes** man konnte ihm seinen Ärger von den Augen ablesen; **to ~ through** durchkommen. **(b)** *(prove)* **it just goes to ~!** da sieht man's mal wieder!

♦ **show off 1** *vi* angeben *(to, in front of* vor *+dat)*. **2** *vt sep knowledge, medal* angeben mit; *new car, son* vorführen *(to sb* jdm*)*.

♦ **show up 1** *vi* **(a)** *(be seen)* zu sehen *or* zu erkennen sein; *(stand out)* hervorstechen. **the tower ~ed ~ clearly against the sky** der Turm zeichnete sich deutlich gegen den Himmel ab; **to ~ ~ well/badly** *(fig)* ein gute/schlechte Figur machen. **(b)** *(col: turn up)* auftauchen, sich blicken lassen *(col)*. **2** *vt sep* **(a)** *(highlight)* (deutlich) erkennen lassen. **(b)** *(reveal)* zum Vorschein bringen; *sb's character, intentions* deutlich zeigen; *impostor* entlarven; *fraud* aufdecken; *(humiliate)* bloßstellen; *(shame)* blamieren.

show: ~ business *n* Showbusiness, Showgeschäft *nt*; **~case** *n* Schaukasten *m*, Vitrine *f*; *(fig)* Schaufenster *nt*; **~down** *n (col)* Kraftprobe, Machtprobe *f*; **to have a ~down with sb** sich mit jdm auseinandersetzen.

shower ['ʃaʊəʳ] **1** *n* **(a)** *(of rain etc)* Schauer *m*; *(of arrows, blows etc)* Hagel *m*; *(of questions)* Schwall *m*. **(b)** *(~ bath)* Dusche *f*. **to take** *or* **have a ~** duschen. **(c)** *(US col: party) Party, auf der jeder ein Geschenk für den Ehrengast mitbringt; (for bride-to-be)* ≈ Polterabend *m*. **2** *vt* **to ~ sb with sth** *with curses, blows* etw auf jdn niederprasseln lassen; *with honours, presents, abuse* jdn mit etw überschütten. **3** *vi (wash)* duschen.

shower: ~ cap *n* Duschhaube *f*; **~proof** *adj* regenfest.

showery ['ʃaʊərɪ] *adj* regnerisch.

show: ~girl *n* Revuegirl *nt*; **~ground** *n* Ausstellungsgelände *nt*; *(for circus)* Zirkusgelände *nt*.

showing ['ʃəʊɪŋ] *n* **(a)** *(exhibition)* Ausstellung *f*. **(b)** *(performance)* Aufführung *f*; *(of film)* Vorstellung *f*; *(of programme)* Ausstrahlung *f*. **(c)** *(standard of performance)* **to make a good/poor ~** eine gute/schwache Leistung zeigen.

show-jumping ['ʃəʊ,dʒʌmpɪŋ] *n* Springreiten *nt*.

showman ['ʃəʊmən] *n, pl* **-men** [-mən] Showman *m*; *(fig)* Schauspieler *m*.

shown [ʃəʊn] *ptp of* **show**.

show: ~-off *n (col)* Angeber(in *f*) *m*; **~piece** *n* Schaustück *nt*; *(fine example)* Paradestück *nt*; **~place** *n (tourist attraction)* Sehenswürdigkeit *f*; **~room** *n* Ausstellungsraum *m*.

showy ['ʃəʊɪ] *adj (+er)* protzig; *person, colour* auffallend; *manner* theatralisch; *production, decor* bombastisch.

shrank [ʃræŋk] *pret of* **shrink**.

shrapnel ['ʃræpnl] *n* Schrapnell *nt*.

shred [ʃred] **1** *n (scrap)* Fetzen *m*; *(of vegetable, meat)* Stückchen *nt*; *(fig)* Spur; *f*; *(of truth)* Fünkchen *nt*. **not a ~ of evidence** keinerlei Beweis; **to be in ~s** zerfetzt sein; **to tear sth to ~s** etw in Stücke reißen; *(fig)* etw verreißen; *argument* etw total zerpflücken; **to tear sb to ~s** keinen guten Faden an jdm lassen. **2** *vt* **(a)** *food, paper* schnitzeln; *carrot* raspeln; *cabbage* hobeln; *(in shredder) paper* in den Papierwolf geben. **(b)** *(tear)* in kleine Stücke reißen; *(with claws)* zerfetzen.

shredder ['ʃredəʳ] *n (grater)* Reibe *f*; *(in electric mixer)* Gemüseschneider *m*; *(for waste paper)* Reißwolf *m*.

shrew [ʃruː] *n* Spitzmaus *f*; *(fig)* Xanthippe *f*.

shrewd [ʃruːd] *adj (+er) person* gewitzt, clever *(col)*; *businessman also, plan* clever *(col)*, raffiniert; *investment, argument* taktisch geschickt; *assessment, mind* scharf. **that was a ~ guess** das war gut geraten; **I have a ~ idea that ...** ich habe so das Gefühl, daß ...

shrewdness ['ʃruːdnɪs] *n see adj* Gewitztheit *f*; Cleverness *(col)*, Raffiniertheit *f*; Geschicktheit *f*; Schärfe *f*; *(of guess)* Treffsicherheit *f*.

shriek [ʃriːk] **1** *n* (schriller) Schrei; *(of whistle)* schriller Ton. **a ~ of pain/horror** ein Schmerzens-/Schreckensschrei *m*; **~s of laughter** kreischendes Lachen; **to give a ~** einen schrillen Schrei ausstoßen. **2** *vi* aufschreien. **to ~ at sb** jdn ankreischen; **to ~ with laughter** vor Lachen quietschen.

shrift [ʃrɪft] *n* **to give sb/sth short ~** jdn/etw kurz abfertigen.

shrill [ʃrɪl] *adj (+er)* schrill.

shrimp [ʃrɪmp] *n* Garnele, Krevette *f*.

shrine [ʃraɪn] *n* Schrein *m*; *(tomb)* Grabstätte *f*; *(chapel)* Grabkapelle *f*; *(altar)* Grabaltar *m*.

shrink [ʃrɪŋk] *(vb: pret* **shrank**, *ptp* **shrunk)** **1** *vt* einlaufen lassen. **2** *vi* **(a)** schrumpfen; *(clothes etc)* einlaufen; *(wood)* schwinden; *(fig) (popularity)* abnehmen, schwinden; *(trade)* zurückgehen. **~-proof** nicht einlaufend. **(b)** *(fig: recoil)* **to ~ from doing/saying sth** davor zurückschrecken, etw zu tun/sich davor scheuen, etw zu sagen; **to ~ from the truth** vor der Wahrheit die Augen verschließen; **to ~ back** zurückweichen; **to ~ away from sb** vor jdm zurückweichen.

shrinkage ['ʃrɪŋkɪdʒ] *n (of material, clothes)* Einlaufen *nt*; *(fig: of economic growth etc)* Rückgang *m*; *(Comm)* Einbußen *pl*.

shrink-wrap ['ʃrɪŋk'ræp] *vt* einschweißen.

shrivel ['ʃrɪvl] *(also* **~ up)** **1** *vt plants (frost, dry-*

ness) welk werden lassen; *(heat)* austrocknen; *skin, fruit* runzlig werden lassen; *nylon* zusammenschrumpfen lassen. **2** *vi* schrumpfen; *(balloon, nylon)* zusammenschrumpfen; *(plants)* welk werden; *(through heat)* austrocknen; *(fruit, skin)* runzlig werden.

shroud [ʃraʊd] **1** *n* **(a)** Leichentuch *nt*. **(b)** *(fig)* Schleier *m*. **a ~ of mist** ein Nebelschleier *m*. **2** *vt* *(fig)* hüllen. **the whole thing is ~ed in mystery** die ganze Angelegenheit ist von einem Geheimnis umgeben.

Shrove Tuesday [ˌʃrəʊv'tjuːzdeɪ] *n* Faschingsdienstag *(S Ger)*, Fastnachtsdienstag *m*.

shrub [ʃrʌb] *n* Busch, Strauch *m*.

shrubbery ['ʃrʌbərɪ] *n (shrub bed)* Strauchrabatte *f*; *(shrubs)* Büsche, Sträucher *pl*.

shrug [ʃrʌg] **1** *n* Achselzucken *nt no pl*. **to give a ~** die *or* mit den Achseln zucken. **2** *vt shoulders* zucken (mit).

♦ **shrug off** *vt sep* mit einem Achselzucken abtun.

shrunk [ʃrʌŋk] *ptp of* **shrink.**

shrunken ['ʃrʌŋkən] *adj* (ein)geschrumpft. *old person* geschrumpft. **~ head** Schrumpfkopf *m*.

shudder ['ʃʌdə^r] **1** *n* Schauer, Schauder *m*. **to give a ~** *(person)* sich schütteln, erschaudern *(geh)*; *(ground)* beben. **2** *vi (person)* schaudern, schauern; *(house, ground)* beben, zittern; *(car, train)* rütteln. **the train ~ed to a halt** der Zug kam rüttelnd zum Stehen; **I ~ to think** mir graut, wenn ich nur daran denke.

shuffle ['ʃʌfl] **1** *n* **(a) to walk with a ~** schlurfen. **(b)** *(Cards)* **to give the cards a ~** die Karten mischen. **2** *vt* **(a) he ~d his feet as he walked** er schlurfte beim Gehen. **(b)** *cards* mischen. **he ~d the papers on his desk together** er raffte die Papiere auf seinem Schreibtisch zusammen. **3** *vi (walk)* schlurfen.

shun [ʃʌn] *vt* meiden; *publicity, light* scheuen.

shunt [ʃʌnt] *vt* **(a)** *(Rail)* rangieren. **they ~ed the train off the main line** sie schoben den Zug auf ein Nebengleis. **(b)** *(col) person* schieben.

shush [ʃʊʃ] **1** *interj* pst, sch. **2** *vt* zum Schweigen auffordern.

shut [ʃʌt] *(vb: pret, ptp ~)* **1** *vt* **(a)** zumachen; *door, book, shop also* schließen. **they ~ the office at 6.00** das Büro wird um 18^{00} geschlossen; **~ your eyes** mach die Augen zu; **~ your mouth** *(col!) or* **face** *(col!)* halt's Maul! *(col!)*. **(b) to ~ sb/sth in(to) sth** jdn/etw in etw *(dat)* einschließen; **she was ~ in the cellar** sie wurde im Keller eingesperrt; **to ~ one's fingers in the door** sich *(dat)* die Finger in der Tür einklemmen.

2 *vi (door, window, box)* schließen, zugehen; *(shop, factory)* schließen, geschlossen werden. **it ~s very easily** es läßt sich ganz leicht schließen *or* zumachen *(col)*; **when do the shops ~?** wann schließen die Geschäfte?, wann machen die Geschäfte zu? *(col)*.

3 *adj* geschlossen, zu *pred (col)*. **sorry sir, we're ~** wir haben leider geschlossen; **the door swung ~** die Tür schlug zu; **to find the door ~** vor verschlossener Tür stehen.

♦ **shut away** *vt sep (put away)* wegschließen; *(in sth)* einschließen *(in in +dat)*; *(keep locked away) books, papers etc* aufbewahren; *(safely)* verwahren; *persons* verborgen halten.

♦ **shut down 1** *vt sep shop, factory* zumachen *(col)*, schließen. **Heathrow is completely ~ ~** Heathrow hat seinen gesamten Flugverkehr eingestellt. **2** *vi (shop, factory etc)* zumachen *(col)*, schließen. **the television service ~s ~ at midnight** um Mitternacht ist Sendeschluß im Fernsehen.

♦ **shut in** *vt sep* einschließen *(also fig)*, einsperren *(col) (prep obj, to* in *+dat)*.

♦ **shut off** *vt sep* **(a)** *water, electricity* abstellen; *light, engine* ab- *or* ausschalten; *street* (ab)sperren. **the kettle ~s itself ~** der Wasserkessel schaltet von selbst ab. **(b)** *(isolate)* (ab)trennen. **I feel ~ ~ from civilization** ich komme mir von der Zivilisation abgeschnitten vor.

♦ **shut out** *vt sep* **(a)** *person, oneself* aussperren *(of* aus*)*; *view* versperren; *light* nicht hereinlassen *(of* in *+acc)*. **don't ~ the sun ~** laß doch die Sonne herein! **(b)** *(fig) foreign competition* ausschalten; *memory, foreign broadcasts* unterdrücken. **I can't ~ her ~ of my life** sie spielt immer noch eine Rolle in meinem Leben.

♦ **shut up 1** *vt sep* **(a)** *house* verschließen. **to ~ ~ shop** *(lit)* das Geschäft schließen; *(fig)* Feierabend machen *(col)*. **(b)** *(imprison)* einsperren. **(c)** *(col: silence)* zum Schweigen bringen. **that'll soon ~ him ~** das wird ihm schon den Mund stopfen *(col)*. **2** *vi (col)* den Mund halten *(col)*. **~ ~!** halt die Klappe! *(col)*, halt's Maul! *(col!)*.

shut: ~down *n* Stillegung *f*; *(TV, Rad)* Sendeschluß *m*; **~-eye** *n (col)* Schlaf *m*; **~-in** *adj* **(a)** *(US)* ans Haus/ans Bett gefesselt; **(b) a ~-in feeling** ein Gefühl des Eingeschlossenseins.

shutter ['ʃʌtə^r] **1** *n* (Fenster)laden *m*; *(Phot)* Verschluß *m*. **to put up the ~s** *(fig)* den Laden dichtmachen *(col)*; **~ release** *(Phot)* Auslöser *m*. **2** *vt* **~ed windows** geschlossene (Fenster)läden.

shuttle ['ʃʌtl] **1** *n* **(a)** *(of loom etc)* Schiffchen *nt*. **(b)** *(plane, train etc)* Pendelflugzeug *nt*/-zug *m etc*; *(space ~)* Raumtransporter *m*. **2** *vt passengers, goods* hin- und hertransportieren. **to ~ sb about** jdn herumschieben.

shuttle: ~cock *n* Federball *m*; **~ service** *n* Pendelverkehr *m*.

shy [ʃaɪ] **1** *adj (+er)* **(a)** schüchtern; *animal* scheu. **don't be ~** nur keine Hemmungen! *(col)*; **to be ~ of/with sb** Hemmungen vor/gegenüber jdm haben; **to be ~ of doing sth** Hemmungen haben, etw zu tun; **to feel ~** schüchtern sein. **(b)** *(esp US col: short)* **we're $3 ~** wir haben 3 Dollar zuwenig. **2** *vi (horse)* scheuen *(at* vor *+dat)*.

♦ **shy away** *vi (horse)* zurückscheuen; *(person)* zurückweichen. **to ~ ~ from sb/sth** vor jdm zurückweichen/vor etw *(dat)* zurückschrecken.

shyly ['ʃaɪlɪ] *adv see adj*.

shyness ['ʃaɪnɪs] *n* Schüchternheit *f*; *(esp of animals)* Scheu *f*.

shyster ['ʃaɪstə^r] *n (US col)* Gauner *m*; *(lawyer)* Rechtsverdreher *m (col)*.

Siamese [ˌsaɪə'miːz] *adj* siamesisch. **~ cat** Siamkatze *f*, siamesische Katze; **~ twins** siamesische Zwillinge *pl*.

Siberia [saɪ'bɪərɪə] *n* Sibirien *nt*.

Sicily ['sɪsɪlɪ] *n* Sizilien *nt*.

sick [sɪk] *adj (+er)* **(a)** *(ill)* krank *(also fig)*. **the ~** die Kranken *pl*; **to be (off) ~** (wegen Krankheit) fehlen; **to fall** *or* **take ~** krank werden; **to go ~** krank werden; **to make sb ~** *(fig col)* jdn (ganz) krank machen *(col)*; **it makes you ~ the way he's always right** *(col)* es ist zum Auswachsen, daß er immer recht hat *(col)*; **to be ~ at sth** *(fig) (disgusted)* von etw angewidert sein; *(upset)* wegen etw geknickt sein. **(b)** *(Brit: vomiting or about to vomit)* **to be ~** brechen, sich übergeben; *(esp cat, baby)* spucken; **I felt ~** mir war schlecht *or* übel; **that food makes me ~** von dem Essen wird mir übel *or* schlecht. **(c)** *(col: fed up)* **to be ~ of doing sth** es satt haben, etw zu tun; **I'm ~ and tired of it** ich habe davon die Nase voll *(col)*, ich habe es gründlich satt. **(d)** *(col) joke etc* geschmacklos; *person* abartig, pervers.

sick: ~ bay *n* Krankenrevier *nt*; **~-bed** *n* Krankenlager *nt*.

sicken ['sɪkn] **1** *vt (turn sb's stomach)* anekeln, anwidern; *(upset greatly)* erschüttern, krank machen *(col)*; *(disgust)* anwidern. **2** *vi* **he's definitely ~ing for something** er wird bestimmt krank; **to ~ of sth** *(tire)* einer Sache *(gen)* müde sein *(geh)*, etw satt haben.

sickening ['sɪknɪŋ] *adj (lit)* ekelerregend; *smell*,

sight also widerlich, ekelhaft; *(upsetting)* entsetzlich, erschütternd; *(disgusting, annoying)* ekelhaft; *treatment* abscheulich; *delays* unerträglich.

sickle ['sɪkl] *n* Sichel *f*.

sick: ~ leave *n* **to be on ~ leave** krank geschrieben sein; **~ list** *n* **to be on/off the ~ list** auf der/nicht mehr auf der Krankenliste stehen; *(with injury)* auf der/nicht mehr auf der Verletztenliste stehen.

sickly ['sɪklɪ] *adj (+er) person* kränklich; *complexion, light* blaß; *smell, taste, colour* widerlich, ekelhaft; *smile* matt; *grin* schwach; *climate* ungesund.

sickness ['sɪknɪs] *n (Med)* Krankheit *f (also fig)*; *(nausea)* Übelkeit *f*; *(Brit: vomiting)* Erbrechen *nt*; *(of joke etc)* Geschmacklosigkeit *f*. **~ benefit** Krankengeld *nt*.

sick: ~-pay *n* Krankengeld *nt*; **~-room** *n* Krankenzimmer *nt*.

side [saɪd] **1** *n* **(a)** Seite *f*; *(of cave, trench, mining shaft, boat, caravan)* Wand *f*; *(of cliff, mountain)* Hang *m*. **this ~ up!** *(on parcel etc)* oben!; **right/wrong ~** *(of cloth)* rechte/linke Seite.

(b) *(edge)* Rand *m*. **at the ~ of the road** am Straßenrand; **at the ~ of his plate** auf dem Tellerrand.

(c) *(not back or front)* Seite *f*. **by/at the ~ of sth** seitlich von etw; **to drive on the left ~ of the road** auf der linken Straßenseite fahren; **the path goes down the ~ of the house** der Weg führt seitlich am Haus entlang; **it's this/the other ~ of London** *(out of town)* es ist auf dieser/auf der anderen Seite Londons; *(in town)* es ist in diesem Teil/am anderen Ende von London; **from all ~s** von allen Seiten; **from ~ to ~** von einer Seite zur anderen; **he moved to one ~** er trat zur Seite; **to put sth on one ~** etw beiseite legen; *(shopkeeper)* etw zurücklegen; **to take sb on one ~** jdn beiseite nehmen; **just this ~ of the boundary** (noch) diesseits der Grenze; **on the other ~ of the boundary** jenseits der Grenze; **with one's head on one ~** mit zur Seite geneigtem Kopf; **by sb's ~** neben jdm; **~ by ~** nebeneinander, Seite an Seite; **to stand/sit ~ by ~ with sb** direkt neben jdm stehen/sitzen; **I'll be by your ~** *(fig)* ich werde Ihnen zur Seite stehen; **to be on the safe ~** sichergehen; **we'll take an extra £50 just to be on the safe ~** wir nehmen vorsichtshalber 50 Pfund mehr mit; **to stay on the right ~ of sb** es (sich *dat*) mit jdm nicht verderben; **on the right ~ of the law** auf dem Boden des Gesetzes; **on the right/wrong ~ of 40** diesseits/jenseits der 40, unter/über 40; **on his mother's ~** mütterlicherseits; **to make a bit (of money) on the ~** *(col)* sich *(dat)* etwas nebenbei verdienen; **a problem with many ~s to it** ein vielschichtigtes Problem; **there are always two ~s to every story** alles hat seine zwei Seiten; **let's hear your ~ of the story** erzählen Sie mal Ihre Version (der Geschichte); **to look on the bright ~** *(be optimistic)* zuversichtlich sein; *(look on the positive ~)* etw von der positiven Seite betrachten.

(d) (a bit) on the large/formal *etc* **~** etwas groß/förmlich *etc*; *(for somebody)* etwas zu groß/förmlich *etc*.

(e) *(opposing team) (Sport, in quiz)* Mannschaft *f*; *(fig)* Seite *f*. **there are two ~s in the dispute** in dem Streit stehen sich zwei Parteien gegenüber; **to change ~s** sich auf die andere Seite schlagen; *(Sport)* die Seiten wechseln; **to take ~s** parteiisch sein; **to take ~s with sb** für jdn Partei ergreifen; **he's on our ~** er steht auf unserer Seite; **whose ~ are you on?** *(supporting team)* für wen sind Sie?; *(in argument)* zu wem halten Sie eigentlich?

2 *adj attr (on one ~) entrance, road* Seiten-; *(not main) entrance, room, road, job* Neben-.

3 *vi* **to ~ with/against sb** jds Partei *(acc)*/Partei gegen jdn ergreifen.

side: ~board *n* Anrichte *f*, Sideboard *nt*; **~boards, ~burns** *npl* Koteletten *pl*; *(longer)* Backenbart *m*; **~car** *n* Beiwagen *m*; *(esp Sport)* Seitenwagen *m*; **~ effect** *n* Nebenwirkung *f*; **~kick** *n (esp US col)* Kumpel *m (col)*; *(assistant)* Handlanger *m (pej)*; **~light** *n (Aut)* Parklicht *nt*; *(incorporated in headlight)* Standlicht *nt*; **~line** *n (job etc)* Nebenerwerb *m*; **to do sth as a ~line** etw nebenbei tun; **~lines** *npl* Seitenlinien *pl*; **to be** *or* **stand on the ~lines** *(fig)* unbeteiligter Zuschauer sein; **~long** *adj, adv glance* Seiten-; *(surreptitious)* verstohlen; **to give sb a ~long glance, to glance ~long at sb** jdn kurz aus den Augenwinkeln anblicken; **~-saddle** *adv* **to ride ~-saddle** im Damensitz reiten; **~ salad** *n* Salat *m* (als Beilage); **~ show** *n* Nebenvorstellung *f*; *(exhibition)* Sonderausstellung *f*; **~-splitting** *adj* urkomisch, zum Totlachen *(col)*; **~-step 1** *vt tackle, punch* (seitwärts) ausweichen *(+dat)*; *person, question* ausweichen *(+dat)*; **2** *vi (lit, fig)* ausweichen; **~ street** *n* Seitenstraße *f*; **~track 1** *n (esp US)* = **siding; 2** *vt* ablenken; **I got ~tracked onto something else** ich wurde durch irgend etwas abgelenkt; *(from topic)* ich wurde irgendwie vom Thema abgebracht; **~walk** *n (US)* Bürgersteig, Gehsteig *m*; **~ways 1** *adj movement* zur Seite; *glance* von der Seite; **to give sb/sth a ~ways glance** jdn/etw von der Seite ansehen; **2** *adv move* zur Seite, seitwärts; *look at sb* von der Seite.

siding ['saɪdɪŋ] *n (Rail)* Rangiergleis *nt*.

sidle ['saɪdl] *vi* (sich) schleichen. **to ~ away** (sich) wegschleichen; **to ~ up to sb** sich an jdn heranschleichen.

siege [siːdʒ] *n (of town)* Belagerung *f*; *(by police)* Umstellung *f*. **to lay ~ to a town/a house** eine Stadt/ein Haus belagern/umstellen.

siesta [sɪ'estə] *n* Siesta *f*. **to have a ~** Siesta halten.

sieve [sɪv] **1** *n* Sieb *nt*. **to have a memory like a ~** *(col)* ein Gedächtnis wie ein Sieb haben *(col)*. **2** *vt* = **sift 1 (a).**

sift [sɪft] **1** *vt* **(a)** sieben; *coal* schütteln. **(b)** *(fig) (search)* sichten, durchgehen; *(separate)* trennen. **2** *vi (fig)* **to ~ through the evidence** das Beweismaterial durchgehen.

sigh [saɪ] **1** *n (of person)* Seufzer *m*; *(of wind)* Säuseln *nt no pl*. **to heave a ~ of relief** einen Seufzer der Erleichterung ausstoßen. **2** *vti* seufzen; *(wind)* säuseln. **to ~ with relief** erleichtert aufatmen.

sighing ['saɪɪŋ] *n see vti* Seufzen *nt*; Säuseln *nt*.

sight [saɪt] **1** *n* **(a)** *(faculty)* Sehvermögen *nt*. **to have long/short ~** weit-/kurzsichtig sein; **to lose/regain one's ~** sein Augenlicht verlieren/wiedergewinnen; **he has very good ~** er sieht sehr gut.

(b) to hate sb at first ~ jdn vom ersten Augenblick an nicht leiden können; **at first ~ it seemed easy** auf den ersten Blick erschien es einfach; **to shoot on ~** sofort schießen; **he played the music at ~** er hat vom Blatt gespielt; **love at first ~** Liebe auf den ersten Blick; **at the ~ of the police they ran away** als sie die Polizei sahen, rannten sie weg; **to know sb by ~** jdn vom Sehen kennen; **to catch ~ of sb/sth** jdn/etw sehen; **to lose ~ of sb/sth** *(lit, fig)* jdn/etw aus den Augen verlieren; **don't lose ~ of the fact that ...** Sie dürfen nicht außer acht lassen, daß ...; **payable at ~** *(Comm)* zahlbar bei Sicht; **30 days' ~** *(Comm)* 30 Tage nach Sicht.

(c) *(sth seen)* Anblick *m*. **the ~ of blood makes me sick** wenn ich Blut sehe, wird mir übel; **the most beautiful ~ I've ever seen** das Schönste, was ich je gesehen habe; **I can't bear the ~ of him** ich kann ihn (einfach) nicht ausstehen; **what a horrible ~!** das sieht ja furchtbar aus!; **to be** *or* **look a ~** *(funny)* zum Schreien aussehen *(col)*; *(horrible)* fürchterlich aussehen.

(d) *(range of vision)* Sicht *f*. **to be in** *or* **within ~** in Sicht *or* in Sichtweite sein; **our goal is in ~** unser Ziel ist in greifbarer Nähe; **we came in ~ of the coast** die Küste kam in Sicht; **to keep sb in ~** jdn im Auge behalten; **to keep out of ~** sich verborgen halten; **to keep sb/sth out of ~** jdn/etw versteckt halten; **keep out of my ~!** laß dich bloß bei mir nicht mehr blicken!; **to be out of ~** nicht mehr zu sehen sein; **don't let the children out of your ~** laß die Kinder nicht aus den Augen!; **out of ~, out of mind** *(Prov)* aus den Augen, aus dem Sinn *(Prov)*.

(e) *usu pl (of city etc)* Sehenswürdigkeit *f*. **to see the ~s of a town** eine Stadt besichtigen.

(f) *(on gun etc)* Visier *nt*. **to set one's ~s too high** *(fig)* seine Ziele zu hoch stecken; **to set one's ~s on sth** *(fig)* ein Auge auf etw *(acc)* werfen.

(g) *(col)* **not by a long ~** bei weitem nicht; **we're not finished yet, not by a long ~** wir sind noch lange nicht fertig; **he's a damn ~ cleverer than you think** er ist ein ganzes Ende gescheiter als du meinst *(col)*.

2 *vt (see)* sichten *(also Mil)*; *person* ausmachen.

sighted ['saɪtɪd] *adj* sehend.

sighting ['saɪtɪŋ] *n* Sichten *nt*. **another ~ of the monster was reported** das Ungeheuer soll erneut gesichtet worden sein.

sight: ~-read *vti* vom Blatt spielen/lesen/singen; **~seeing** *n* Besichtigungen *pl*; **to go ~seeing** auf Besichtigungstour gehen; **~seer** *n* Tourist(in *f*) *m*.

sign [saɪn] **1** *n* **(a)** *(with hand etc)* Zeichen *nt*. **he nodded as a ~ of recognition** er nickte zum Zeichen, daß er mich/ihn *etc* erkannt hatte; **to give sb a ~, to make a ~ to sb** jdm ein Zeichen geben.

(b) *(indication, Med)* Anzeichen *nt (of* für *or gen)*; *(evidence)* Zeichen *nt (of* von *or gen)*; *(trace)* Spur *f*. **a sure/good ~** ein sicheres/gutes Zeichen; **it's a ~ of the true expert** daran erkennt man den wahren Experten; **at the first ~ of disagreement** beim ersten Anzeichen von Uneinigkeit; **there is no ~ of their agreeing** nichts deutet darauf hin, daß sie zustimmen werden; **to show ~s of sth** Anzeichen von etw erkennen lassen; **our guest showed no ~s of leaving** unser Gast machte keine Anstalten zu gehen; **the rain showed no ~s of stopping** nichts deutete darauf hin, daß der Regen aufhören würde; **there was no ~ of life in the village** es gab kein Anzeichen von Leben im Dorf; **there was no ~ of him anywhere** von ihm war keine Spur zu sehen.

(c) *(road~, shop~)* Schild *nt*.

(d) *(written symbol, Astron)* Zeichen *nt*.

2 *vt* **(a) to ~ one's name** unterschreiben; **to ~ one's name in a book** sich in ein Buch eintragen; **he ~s himself J.G. Jones** er unterschreibt mit J.G. Jones. **(b)** *letter etc* unterschreiben, unterzeichnen *(form)*; *picture, book* signieren. **to ~ the register** sich eintragen.

3 *vi* **(a)** *(signal)* **to ~ to sb to do sth** jdm Zeichen/ein Zeichen geben, etw zu tun. **(b)** *(with signature)* unterschreiben.

♦ **sign away** *vt sep* verzichten auf *(+acc)*. **she felt she was ~ing ~ her life** sie hatte das Gefühl, ihr ganzes Leben zu überschreiben.

♦ **sign for** *vi +prep obj* den Empfang *(+gen)* bestätigen.

♦ **sign in 1** *vt sep person* eintragen. **to ~ sb ~ at a club** jdn als Gast in einen Klub mitnehmen. **2** *vi* sich eintragen.

♦ **sign off** *vi (in letter)* Schluß machen.

♦ **sign on 1** *vt sep* = **sign up 1. 2** *vi* **(a)** = **sign up 2. (b)** *(for unemployment benefit etc) (apply)* beantragen *(for acc)*; *(register regularly)* sich melden.

♦ **sign out** *vi* sich austragen. **to ~ ~ of a hotel** (aus einem Hotel) abreisen.

♦ **sign over** *vt sep* überschreiben *(to sb* jdm*)*.

♦ **sign up 1** *vt sep (employ, enlist) actors* verpflichten; *workers, employees* anstellen; *sailors* anheuern. **2** *vi* sich verpflichten; *(employees, players also)* unterschreiben; *(sailors)* anheuern; *(for evening class etc)* sich einschreiben.

signal ['sɪgnl] **1** *n* **(a)** *(sign)* Zeichen *nt*; *(as part of code)* Signal *nt*; *(message)* Nachricht *f*. **engaged** *(Brit) or* **busy ~** *(Telec)* Besetztzeichen *nt*; **to give the ~ for sth** das Zeichen/Signal zu etw geben; **the ~ is very weak** *(TV, Rad)* der Empfang ist sehr schlecht. **(b)** *(apparatus, Rail)* Signal *nt*. **the ~ is at red** das Signal steht auf Rot. **2** *vt* **(a)** *(indicate)* anzeigen; *arrival, (fig) future event etc* ankündigen. **to ~ sb to do sth** jdm ein/das Zeichen geben, etw zu tun. **(b)** *message* signalisieren. **3** *vi* Zeichen/ein Zeichen geben. **he ~led for his bill** er winkte zum Zeichen, daß er zahlen wollte; **the driver didn't ~** der Fahrer hat kein Zeichen gegeben.

signal: ~box *n* Stellwerk *nt*; **~man** *n (Rail)* Stellwerkswärter *m*; *(Mil)* Fernmelder, Funker *m*.

signatory ['sɪgnətərɪ] *n* Unterzeichnete(r) *mf (form)*.

signature ['signətʃə[r]] *n* **(a)** Unterschrift *f*; *(of artist)* Signatur *f*. **(b)** *(Mus)* Vorzeichnung *f*. **~ tune** *(Brit)* Erkennungsmelodie *f*.

signboard ['saɪnbɔːd] *n* Schild *nt*.

signet ring ['sɪgnɪt,rɪŋ] *n* Siegelring *m*.

significance [sɪg'nɪfɪkəns] *n* Bedeutung *f*; *(of action also)* Tragweite *f*. **of no ~** belanglos, bedeutungslos.

significant [sɪg'nɪfɪkənt] *adj (considerable, having consequence)* bedeutend; *(important)* wichtig; *(meaningful)* bedeutungsvoll; *look* vielsagend, bedeutsam. **it is ~ that ...** es ist bezeichnend, daß ...; **to be ~ to** *or* **for sth** eine bedeutende *or* wichtige Rolle in etw *(dat)* spielen.

significantly [sɪg'nɪfɪkəntlɪ] *adv (considerably)* bedeutend; *(meaningfully)* bedeutungsvoll; *look* vielsagend, bedeutsam. **it is not ~ different** da besteht kein wesentlicher Unterschied; **~ enough, ...** bezeichnenderweise ...

signify ['sɪgnɪfaɪ] *vt* **(a)** *(mean)* bedeuten. **(b)** *(indicate)* andeuten, erkennen lassen; *(person also)* zu erkennen geben.

sign: ~ language Zeichensprache *f*; **~post 1** *n* Wegweiser *m*; **2** *vt way* beschildern; *diversion* ausschildern.

silage ['saɪlɪdʒ] *n* Silage *f*, Silofutter *nt*.

silence ['saɪləns] **1** *n* Stille *f*; *(quietness also)* Ruhe *f*; *(absence of talk also, of letters etc)* Schweigen *nt*; *(on a particular subject)* (Still)schweigen *nt*. **~!** Ruhe!; **in ~** still; *(not talking also)* schweigend; **there was ~** alles war still; **radio ~** *(Mil)* Funkstille *f*. **2** *vt (lit, fig)* zum Schweigen bringen.

silencer ['saɪlənsə[r]] *n (on gun, Brit: on car)* Schalldämpfer *m*; *(whole fitting on car)* Auspufftopf *m*.

silent ['saɪlənt] *adj* still; *(not talking also)* schweigsam; *engine etc* ruhig; *agreement etc* (still)schweigend *attr*. **~ movie/letter** Stummfilm *m*/stummer Buchstabe; **~ partner** *(US)* stiller Teilhaber; **the ~ majority** die schweigende Mehrheit; **to be ~ (about sth)** (über etw *acc*) schweigen; **to keep** *or* **remain ~** still sein *or* bleiben; *(about sth)* sich nicht äußern.

silently ['saɪləntlɪ] *adv* lautlos; *(without talking)* schweigend; *(with little noise)* leise.

silhouette [,sɪluː'et] **1** *n* Silhouette *f*; *(picture)* Scherenschnitt *m*. **2** *vt* **to be ~d against sth** sich (als Silhouette) gegen etw abzeichnen.

silicon ['sɪlɪkən] *n* Silizium *nt*. **~ chip** Siliziumchip *m*.

silicone ['sɪlɪkəʊn] *n* Silikon *nt*.

silicosis [,sɪlɪ'kəʊsɪs] *n* Staublunge, Silikose *f*.

silk [sɪlk] **1** *n* **(a)** Seide *f*; *(~ dress)* Seidenkleid *nt*. **(b)** *(Brit Jur: barrister)* Kronanwalt *m*. **2** *adj* Seiden-, seiden. **the dress is ~** das Kleid ist aus Seide.

silk: ~ **screen** *n* Seidensieb *nt*; *(also* **~-screen printing***)* Seidensiebdruck *m*; **~worm** *n* Seidenraupe *f*.

silky [ˈsɪlkɪ] *adj (+er)* seidig; *voice* samtig.

sill [sɪl] *n* Sims *m or nt*; *(window~)* (Fenster)sims *m or nt*; *(esp of wood)* Fensterbrett *nt*; *(on car)* Türleiste *f*.

silly [ˈsɪlɪ] *adj (+er)* dumm, doof *(col)*. **don't be** ~ *(do ~ things)* mach keinen Quatsch *(col)*; *(say ~ things)* red keinen Unsinn; *(ask ~ questions)* frag nicht so dumm; **that was a ~ thing to do** das war dumm (von dir); **to make sb look** ~ jdn lächerlich machen.

silo [ˈsaɪləʊ] *n* Silo *nt*; *(for missile)* unterirdische Startrampe.

silt [sɪlt] **1** *n* Schwemmsand *m*; *(river mud)* Schlick *m*. **2** *vi (also* ~ **up***)* verschlammen.

silver [ˈsɪlvəʳ] **1** *n* **(a)** *(metal, tableware)* Silber *nt*. **(b)** *(coins)* Silbergeld *nt*. **2** *adj* Silber-, silbern.

silver: ~ **birch** *n* Weißbirke *f*; ~ **paper** *n (Brit)* Silberpapier *nt*; ~ **plate** *n (plating)* Silberauflage *f*; *(articles)* versilberte Sachen *pl*; ~ **screen** *n* Leinwand *f*; **~smith** *n* Silberschmied *m*; **~ware** *n* Silber *nt*; ~ **wedding** *n* silberne Hochzeit, Silberhochzeit *f*.

silvery [ˈsɪlvərɪ] *adj* silbern; *voice* silberhell.

similar [ˈsɪmɪləʳ] *adj* ähnlich; *amount, size* ungefähr gleich. **she and her sister are very** ~ ihre Schwester und sie sind sich sehr ähnlich; ~ **in size** ungefähr gleich groß.

similarity [ˌsɪmɪˈlærɪtɪ] *n* Ähnlichkeit *f (to* mit*)*.

similarly [ˈsɪmɪləlɪ] *adv* ähnlich; *(equally)* genauso. **~, you could maintain ...** genausogut könnten Sie behaupten ...

simile [ˈsɪmɪlɪ] *n* Gleichnis *nt*.

simmer [ˈsɪməʳ] **1** *vt* auf kleiner Flamme kochen lassen. **2** *vi* auf kleiner Flamme kochen; *(fig) (with rage)* kochen *(col)*; *(with excitement)* fiebern.

♦ **simmer down** *vi* sich beruhigen, sich abregen *(col)*.

simper [ˈsɪmpəʳ] **1** *n* **..., she said with a ~ ...**, sagte sie affektiert. **2** *vi (smile)* geziert lächeln; *(talk)* säuseln.

simple [ˈsɪmpl] *adj (+er)* **(a)** einfach; *decor, dress also* schlicht. **the ~ fact is ...** es ist einfach so, daß ...; **it's as ~ as ABC** das ist kinderleicht. **(b)** *(foolish, mentally deficient)* einfältig.

simple-minded [ˌsɪmplˈmaɪndɪd] *adj* einfältig.

simpleton [ˈsɪmpltən] *n* Einfaltspinsel *m*.

simplicity [sɪmˈplɪsɪtɪ] *n* Einfachheit *f*; *(lack of sophistication, of decor etc also)* Schlichtheit *f*. **it's ~ itself** das ist die einfachste Sache der Welt.

simplification [ˌsɪmplɪfɪˈkeɪʃən] *n* Vereinfachung *f*.

simplify [ˈsɪmplɪfaɪ] *vt* vereinfachen.

simplistic [sɪmˈplɪstɪk] *adj* simpel.

simply [ˈsɪmplɪ] *adv* einfach; *(merely)* nur, bloß.

simulate [ˈsɪmjʊleɪt] *vt emotions* vortäuschen; *enthusiasm also* spielen; *illness also, conditions, environment* simulieren. **~d leather/sheepskin** Lederimitation *f*/falsches Schaffell.

simulation [ˌsɪmjʊˈleɪʃən] *n* Vortäuschung *f*; *(reproduction)* Simulation *f*.

simulator [ˈsɪmjʊleɪtəʳ] *n* Simulator *m*.

simultaneous [ˌsɪməlˈteɪnɪəs] *adj* gleichzeitig. ~ **equations** *(Math)* Simultangleichungen *pl*; ~ **interpreting** Simultandolmetschen *nt*.

simultaneously [ˌsɪməlˈteɪnɪəslɪ] *adv* gleichzeitig, simultan *(geh)*.

sin [sɪn] **1** *n (Rel, fig)* Sünde *f*. **to live in ~** *(col)* in wilder Ehe leben; *(Rel)* in Sünde leben; **to cover a multitude of ~s** *(hum)* viele Schandtaten verdecken. **2** *vi* sündigen *(against* gegen, an *+dat)*, sich versündigen *(against* an *+dat)*; *(against principles etc)* verstoßen *(against* gegen*)*.

since [sɪns] **1** *adv (in the meantime)* inzwischen; *(up to now)* seitdem. **ever ~** seither; **long ~** schon lange; **he died long ~** er ist schon lange tot; **not long ~** erst vor kurzem. **2** *prep* seit. **ever ~ 1900** (schon) seit 1900; **he had been living there ~ 1900** er lebte da schon seit 1900; **I've been coming here ~ 1972** ich komme schon seit 1972 hierher; **it's a long time ~ then** das ist schon lange her. **3** *conj* **(a)** *(time)* seit(dem). **ever ~ I've known him** seit(dem) ich ihn kenne. **(b)** *(because)* da.

sincere [sɪnˈsɪəʳ] *adj* aufrichtig; *person also* offen; *intention also* ernst, ehrlich.

sincerely [sɪnˈsɪəlɪ] *adv see adj* aufrichtig; offen; ernsthaft. **yours ~** mit freundlichen Grüßen, hochachtungsvoll *(form)*.

sincerity [sɪnˈserɪtɪ] *n see adj* Aufrichtigkeit *f*; Offenheit *f*; Ernsthaftigkeit *f*. **in all ~** in aller Offenheit.

sine [saɪn] *n (Math)* Sinus *m*.

sinecure [ˈsɪnɪkjʊəʳ] *n* Sinekure *f (geh)*.

sinew [ˈsɪnjuː] *n* Sehne *f*.

sinewy [ˈsɪnjʊɪ] *adj* sehnig; *(fig) plant, tree* knorrig.

sinful [ˈsɪnfʊl] *adj* sündig; *person, act, thought also* sündhaft *(geh)*.

sing [sɪŋ] *pret* **sang**, *ptp* **sung 1** *vt* singen. **to ~ the praises of sb/sth** ein Loblied auf jdn/etw singen. **2** *vi* singen; *(ears)* dröhnen; *(kettle)* summen.

♦ **sing out** *vi (col: shout)* schreien *(col)*.

Singapore [ˌsɪŋgəˈpɔːʳ] *n* Singapur *nt*.

singe [sɪndʒ] *vt* sengen; *clothes* versengen; *(slightly)* ansengen.

singer [ˈsɪŋəʳ] *n* Sänger(in *f*) *m*.

singing [ˈsɪŋɪŋ] *n* Singen *nt*; *(of person, bird also)* Gesang *m*; *(in the ears)* Dröhnen *nt*; *(of kettle)* Summen *nt*. **he teaches ~** er gibt Gesangstunden; **do you like my ~?** gefällt dir mein Gesang?

single [ˈsɪŋgl] **1** *adj* **(a)** *(one only)* einzige(r, s). **not a ~ one spoke up** nicht ein einziger äußerte sich dazu; **every ~ day was precious** jeder (einzelne) Tag war kostbar; **not a ~ thing** überhaupt nichts. **(b)** *(not double etc)* einzeln; *bed, room* Einzel-; *carburettor, (Brit) ticket* einfach. **(c)** *(not married)* unverheiratet, ledig; *parent* alleinstehend, alleinerziehend. **~ people** Unverheiratete *pl*; **I'm a ~ man/girl** ich bin ledig. **2** *n (Brit: ticket)* Einzelfahrkarte *f*; *(room)* Einzelzimmer *nt*; *(record)* Single *f*. **a ~/two ~s to Bonn** einmal/zweimal einfach nach Bonn.

♦ **single out** *vt sep (choose)* auswählen; *victim, prey* sich *(dat)* herausgreifen; *(distinguish, set apart)* herausheben *(from* über *+acc)*. **to ~ sb ~ for special attention** jdm besondere Aufmerksamkeit zuteil werden lassen.

single: **~-breasted** *adj jacket* einreihig; **~-cell(ed)** *adj (Biol)* einzellig; **~-decker** *n* einstöckiger Omnibus; ~ **file** *n* **in ~ file** im Gänsemarsch; **~-handed 1** *adj* (ganz) allein *(after noun)*; *achievement* ohne (fremde) Hilfe vollbracht; *struggle* einsam; **2** *adv (also* **~-handedly***)* ohne Hilfe, im Alleingang; **~-lens-reflex (camera)** *n* Spiegelreflexkamera *f*; **~-line** *adj* eingleisig; *railway also, traffic* einspurig; **~-minded** *adj* zielstrebig; *devotion* unbeirrbar.

singleness [ˈsɪŋglnɪs] *n* **~ of purpose** Zielstrebigkeit *f*.

single-parent [ˌsɪŋglˈpeərənt] *adj family* mit nur einem Elternteil.

singles [ˈsɪŋglz] *n sing or pl (Sport)* Einzel *nt*. **the ~ finals** das Finale im Einzel; **men's ~** Herreneinzel *nt*.

single-seater [ˌsɪŋglˈsiːtəʳ] *n* Einsitzer *m*.

singlet [ˈsɪŋglɪt] *n (Brit) (Sport)* ärmelloses Trikot; *(underclothing)* (ärmeloses) Unterhemd, Trikothemd *nt*.

single-track [ˈsɪŋglˌtræk] *adj* einspurig; *(Rail also)* eingleisig.

singly [ˈsɪŋglɪ] *adv* einzeln; *(solely)* allein.

singsong [ˈsɪŋsɒŋ] *n* **we often have a ~ at the pub** in der Kneipe singen wir oft zusammen.

singular ['sɪŋgjʊləʳ] **1** *adj* **(a)** *(Gram)* im Singular. **(b)** *(odd)* sonderbar, eigenartig. **(c)** *(outstanding)* einzigartig, einmalig. **2** *n* Singular *m*. **in the ~** im Singular.

singularity [ˌsɪŋgjʊ'lærɪtɪ] *n* *(oddity)* Sonderbarkeit, Eigenartigkeit *f*.

singularly ['sɪŋgjʊləlɪ] *adv* außerordentlich.

sinister ['sɪnɪstəʳ] *adj* unheimlich; *person, scheme also* finster; *music, look also* düster; *fate* böse.

sink[1] [sɪŋk] *pret* **sank**, *ptp* **sunk 1** *vt* **(a)** *ship* versenken. **(b)** *(fig: ruin) theory* zerstören; *hopes also* zunichte machen. **now we're sunk!** *(col)* jetzt sind wir geliefert *(col)*. **(c)** *shaft* senken; *hole* ausheben. **to ~ a post in the ground** einen Pfosten in den Boden einlassen. **(d)** *teeth, claws* schlagen. **(e)** *differences* begraben. **(f) to ~ money in sth** Geld in etw *(acc)* stecken. **(g) to be sunk in thought** in Gedanken versunken sein.

2 *vi* sinken; *(ship also)* untergehen; *(sun also)* versinken; *(voice, building, land etc)* sich senken; *(shares, prices)* fallen. **to ~ to the bottom** auf den Grund sinken; **he was left to ~ or swim** *(fig)* er war ganz auf sich allein angewiesen; **to ~ into a chair** in einen Sessel (nieder)sinken; **the sun sank beneath the horizon** die Sonne versank am Horizont; **to ~ to one's knees** auf die Knie sinken; **to ~ into a deep sleep** in tiefen Schlaf versinken; **my heart sank at the sight of the work** beim Anblick der Arbeit verließ mich der Mut; **with ~ing heart** mutlos; **she has sunk in my estimation** sie ist in meiner Achtung gesunken.

♦ **sink in** *vi* **(a)** *(into mud etc)* einsinken *(prep obj, -to* in *+acc)*. **(b)** *(col: be understood)* kapiert werden *(col)*. **it's only just sunk ~ that it really did happen** ich kapiere/er kapiert *etc* erst jetzt, daß das tatsächlich passiert ist *(col)*.

sink[2] *n* Ausguß *m*; *(in kitchen also)* Spülbecken *nt*. **~ unit** Spüle *f*.

sinking ['sɪŋkɪŋ] **1** *n* *(of ship)* Untergang *m*; *(deliberately)* Versenkung *f*; *(of shaft)* Senken *nt*; *(of well)* Bohren *nt*. **2** *adj* **~ feeling** flaues Gefühl (im Magen) *(col)*.

sinner ['sɪnəʳ] *n* Sünder(in *f*) *m*.

sinuous ['sɪnjʊəs] *adj (lit, fig)* gewunden; *motion of snake* schlängelnd *attr*; *dancing etc* geschmeidig.

sinus ['saɪnəs] *n (in head)* (Nasen)nebenhöhle *f*.

sip [sɪp] **1** *n* Schluck *m*; *(very small)* Schlückchen *nt*. **2** *vt* in kleinen Schlucken trinken; *(suspicious, daintily)* nippen an *(+dat)*; *(savour)* schlürfen.

siphon ['saɪfən] **1** *n* Heber *m*; *(soda~)* Siphon *m*. **2** *vt* absaugen; *(into tank)* umfüllen.

♦ **siphon off** *vt sep* **(a)** *(lit)* absaugen; *petrol* abzapfen; *(into container)* umfüllen, abfüllen. **(b)** *(fig) staff* abziehen; *profits* abschöpfen.

sir [sɜːʳ] *n* **(a)** *(in direct address)* mein Herr *(form)*, Herr X. **Dear S~ (or Madam),** ... sehr geehrte (Damen und) Herren! **(b)** *(knight etc)* **S~** Sir *m*. **(c)** *(Sch: teacher)* **please ~!** Herr X!; **I'll tell ~** ich sag's ihm.

siren ['saɪərən] *n (also Myth)* Sirene *f*.

sirloin ['sɜːlɔɪn] *n* Filet *nt*.

sissy ['sɪsɪ] *n* Waschlappen *m (col)*, Memme *f*.

sister ['sɪstəʳ] *n* **(a)** Schwester *f*; *(in trade union)* Kollegin *f*. **(b)** *(nun)* (Ordens)schwester *f*; *(before name)* Schwester *f*. **(c)** *(Brit: senior nurse)* Oberschwester *f*.

sister *in cpds* Schwester-; **~-in-law**, *pl* **~s-in-law** Schwägerin *f*.

sisterly ['sɪstəlɪ] *adj* schwesterlich.

sit [sɪt] *(vb: pret, ptp* **sat***)* **1** *vi* **(a)** *(be ~ting)* sitzen *(in/on* in/auf *+dat)*; *(~ down)* sich setzen *(in/on* in/auf *+acc)*. **a place to ~** ein Sitzplatz *m*; **~ by/with me** setz dich zu mir/neben mich; **to ~ for a painter** für einen Maler Modell sitzen; **to ~ for an exam** eine Prüfung ablegen *(form) or* machen; **to be ~ting pretty** *(fig col)* gut dastehen *(col)*. **(b)** *(assembly)* tagen; *(have a seat)* einen Sitz haben. **to ~ on a committee** in einem Ausschuß sitzen. **(c)** *(bird: hatch)* sitzen, brüten. **(d)** *(fig: clothes)* sitzen *(on sb* bei jdm*)*.

2 *vt* **(a)** setzen *(in* in *+acc, on* auf *+acc)*; *(place) object also* stellen. **to ~ a child on one's knees** sich *(dat)* ein Kind auf die Knie setzen; **the table/car ~s 5 people** an dem Tisch/in dem Auto haben 5 Leute Platz. **(b)** *examination* ablegen *(form)*, machen.

♦ **sit about** *or* **around** *vi* herumsitzen.

♦ **sit back** *vi (lit, fig)* sich zurücklehnen; *(fig: do nothing)* die Hände in den Schoß legen.

♦ **sit down** *vi* sich (hin)setzen. **to ~ ~ in a chair** sich auf einen Stuhl setzen.

♦ **sit in** *vi* **(a)** *(demonstrators)* ein Sit-in veranstalten. **(b)** *(attend as visitor)* dabeisein, dabeisitzen *(on sth* bei etw*)*.

♦ **sit on** *vi +prep obj (not deal with) document etc* sitzen auf *(+dat)*; *(col: suppress) idea, product* unterdrücken; *person* einen Dämpfer aufsetzen *(+dat) (col)*.

♦ **sit out 1** *vi* draußen sitzen. **2** *vt sep* **(a)** *(stay to end) play* bis zum Ende (sitzen)bleiben bei, bis zum Ende durchhalten *(pej)*; *storm* auf das Ende *(+gen)* warten. **(b)** *dance* auslassen. **to ~ ~ a round** eine Runde aussetzen.

♦ **sit through** *vi +prep obj* durchhalten, aushalten *(pej)*.

♦ **sit up 1** *vi* **(a)** aufrecht sitzen; *(action)* sich aufrichten. **~ ~!** setz dich gerade hin!; **to make sb ~ ~ (and take notice)** *(fig col)* jdn aufhorchen lassen. **(b)** *(not go to bed)* aufbleiben. **she sat ~ with the sick child** sie wachte bei dem kranken Kind. **2** *vt sep* aufrichten; *doll also, baby* hinsetzen.

sitcom ['sɪtkɒm] *n (col)* Situationskomödie *f*.

sit-down ['sɪtdaʊn] *adj attr* **to have a ~ strike** einen Sitzstreik machen; **a ~ meal** eine richtige Mahlzeit.

site [saɪt] **1** *n* **(a)** Stelle *f*, Platz *m*. **(b)** *(Archeol)* Stätte *f*. **(c)** *(building ~)* Baustelle *f*. **missile ~** Raketenbasis *f*. **(d)** *(camping ~)* Campingplatz *m*. **2** *vt* legen, anlegen. **to be ~d** liegen, (gelegen) sein.

sit-in ['sɪtɪn] *n* Sit-in *nt*. **to hold** *or* **stage a ~** ein Sit-in veranstalten.

sitting ['sɪtɪŋ] *n (of committee, for portrait)* Sitzung *f*. **they have two ~s for lunch** sie servieren das Mittagessen in zwei Schüben.

sitting: ~ duck *n (fig)* leichte Beute; **~ room** *n (lounge)* Wohnzimmer *nt*; *(in guest house etc)* Aufenthaltsraum *m*; **~ tenant** *n* (derzeitiger) Mieter.

situate ['sɪtjʊeɪt] *vt* legen.

situated ['sɪtjʊeɪtɪd] *adj* gelegen; *person (financially)* gestellt, situiert *(geh)*. **it is ~ in the High Street** es liegt an der Hauptstraße; **a pleasantly ~ house** ein schön gelegenes Haus; **how are you ~ (for money)?** wie ist Ihre finanzielle Lage?

situation [ˌsɪtjʊ'eɪʃən] *n* **(a)** *(state of affairs)* Lage, Situation *f*; *(financial, marital etc)* Lage *f*, Verhältnisse *pl*; *(in play, novel)* Situation *f*. **to save the ~** die Situation retten; **~ comedy** Situationskomödie *f*. **(b)** *(of house etc)* Lage *f*. **(c)** *(job)* Stelle *f*. **"~s vacant/wanted"** „Stellenangebote/Stellengesuche“.

six [sɪks] **1** *adj* sechs. **she is ~ (years old)** sie ist sechs (Jahre alt); **at (the age of) ~** im Alter von sechs Jahren; **it's ~ (o'clock)** es ist sechs (Uhr); **there are ~ of us** wir sind sechs; **~ and a half/quarter** sechseinhalb/sechseinviertel; **to be ~ feet under** *(hum)* sich *(dat)* die Radieschen von unten besehen *(hum)*; **it's ~ of one and half a dozen of the other** *(col)* das ist Jacke wie Hose *(col)*. **2** *n* Sechs *f*. **to divide sth into ~** etw in sechs Teile teilen; **the are sold in ~es** sie werden in Sechserpackungen verkauft; **to be at ~es and sevens** *(things)* wie Kraut und Rüben durchein-

anderliegen *(col)*; *(person)* völlig durcheinander sein; **to knock sb for ~** *(col)* jdn umhauen.
six: ~fold 1 *adj* sechsfach; **2** *adv* um das Sechsfache; **~ footer** *n* **to be a ~ footer** über 1,80 *(gesprochen:* einsachtzig*)* sein; **~ hundred 1** *adj* sechshundert; **2** *n* Sechshundert *f*; **~ million** *adj, n* sechs Millionen; **~-shooter** *n (col)* sechsschüssiger Revolver.
sixteen ['sɪks'tiːn] **1** *adj* sechzehn. **2** *n* Sechzehn *f*.
sixteenth ['siks'tiːnθ] **1** *adj* sechzehnte(r, s). **a ~ part** ein Sechzehntel *nt*. **2** *n* **(a)** *(fraction)* Sechzehntel *nt*; *(in series)* Sechzehnte(r, s). **(b)** *(date)* **the ~** der Sechzehnte.
sixth [sɪksθ] **1** *adj* sechste(r, s). **a ~ part** ein Sechstel *nt*; **he was** *or* **came ~** er wurde Sechster; **he was ~ from the left** er war der Sechste von links. **2** *n* **(a)** *(fraction)* Sechstel *nt*; *(in series)* Sechste(r, s). **(b)** *(date)* **the ~** der Sechste; **on the ~** am Sechsten; **the ~ of September** der sechste September.
sixth: ~ form *n (Brit)* Abschlußklasse, ≃ Prima *f*; **~-former** *n (Brit)* Schüler(in *f*) *m* der Abschlußklasse, ≃ Primaner(in *f*) *m*.
six thousand 1 *adj* sechstausend. **2** *n* Sechstausend *f*.
sixth sense *n* sechster Sinn.
sixtieth ['sɪkstɪɪθ] **1** *adj* sechzigste(r, s). **2** *n (fraction)* Sechzigstel *nt*; *(in series)* Sechzigste(r, s).
sixty ['sikstɪ] **1** *adj* sechzig. **2** *n* Sechzig *f*. **the sixties** die sechziger Jahre; **to be in one's sixties** in den Sechzigern sein; **to be in one's late/early sixties** Ende/Anfang sechzig sein; **~-four thousand dollar question** *n (hum)* Zehntausendmarkfrage *f (hum)*.
sixty-one ['sɪkstɪ'wʌn] *adj* einundsechzig.
six-year-old ['sɪksjɪə,əʊld] **1** *adj* sechsjährig *attr*, sechs Jahre alt *pred*. **2** *n* Sechsjährige(r) *mf*.
size [saɪz] **1** *n* Größe *f*; *(of problem, operation also)* Ausmaß *nt*. **collar/hip/waist ~** Kragen-/Hüft-/Taillenweite *f*; **it's the ~ of a brick** es ist so groß wie ein Ziegelstein; **he's about your ~** er ist ungefähr so groß wie du; **what ~ is it?** wie groß ist es?; *(clothes, shoes, gloves etc)* welche Größe ist es?; **it's quite a ~** es ist ziemlich groß; **it's two ~s too big** es ist zwei Nummern zu groß; **to cut sth to ~** etw auf die richtige Größe zurechtschneiden; **that's about the ~ of it** *(col)* ja, so ungefähr kann man es sagen. **2** *vt* größenmäßig ordnen.
♦ **size up** *vt sep* abschätzen.
sizeable ['saɪzəbl] *adj* ziemlich groß, größer; *car, estate, jewel also* ansehnlich.
sizzle ['sɪzl] *vi* brutzeln.
skate[1] [skeɪt] *n (fish)* Rochen *m*.
skate[2] **1** *n (shoe)* Schlittschuh *m*; *(blade)* Kufe *f*. **put** *or* **get your ~s on** *(fig col)* mach/macht mal ein bißchen dalli! *(col)*. **2** *vi* eislaufen, Schlittschuh laufen; *(figure-~)* eislaufen; *(roller-~)* Rollschuh laufen. **it went skating across the room** *(fig)* es rutschte durch das Zimmer.
♦ **skate around** *or* **over** *vi +prep obj difficulty, problem* einfach übergehen.
skateboard ['skeɪtbɔːd] *n* Skateboard, Rollbrett *nt*.
skater ['skeɪtə[r]] *n (ice-~)* Schlittschuhläufer(in *f*) *m*; *(figure-~)* Eiskunstläufer(in *f*) *m*; *(roller-~)* Rollschuhläufer(in *f*) *m*.
skating ['skeɪtɪŋ] *n (ice-~)* Eislauf *m*; *(figure-~)* Eiskunstlauf *m*; *(roller-~)* Rollschuhlauf *m*. **~ rink** Eisbahn/Rollschuhbahn *f*.
skein [skeɪn] *n (of wool etc)* Strang *m*.
skeleton ['skelɪtn] **1** *n (lit, fig)* Skelett *nt*; *(esp of ship)* Gerippe *nt*. **a ~ in one's cupboard** *(of public figure)* ein Leiche im Keller. **2** *adj staff, service etc* Not-. **~ key** Dietrich, Nachschlüssel *m*.
skeptic *etc (US)* = **sceptic** *etc*.
sketch [sketʃ] **1** *n (Art, Liter)* Skizze *f*; *(Theat)* Sketch *m*; *(design also)* Entwurf *m*. **2** *vt (lit, fig)* skizzieren.
♦ **sketch in** *vt sep details (verbally)* umreißen.
sketch-book ['sketʃbʊk] *n* Skizzenbuch *nt*.
sketchy ['sketʃɪ] *adj (+er) (inadequate)* flüchtig, oberflächlich; *(incomplete)* bruchstückhaft.
skewer ['skjʊə[r]] **1** *n* Spieß *m*. **2** *vt* aufspießen.
skew-whiff [,skjuː'wɪf] *adj (Brit col)* (wind)schief.
ski [skiː] **1** *n* Ski, Schi *m*. **2** *vi* Ski laufen *or* fahren. **they ~ed down the slope/over the hill** sie fuhren (auf ihren Skiern) den Hang hinunter/sie liefen (mit ihren Skiern) über den Hügel.
skid [skɪd] **1** *n (Aut etc)* Schleudern *nt*. **to go into a ~** ins Schleudern kommen; **to correct a ~** das Fahrzeug wieder in seine Gewalt bekommen. **2** *vi (car, objects)* schleudern; *(person)* ausrutschen. **to ~ across the floor** über den Boden rutschen; **the car ~ded into a tree** der Wagen schleuderte gegen einen Baum.
skid: ~mark *n* Reifenspur *f*; *(from braking)* Bremsspur *f*; **~ row** *n (esp US col)* Pennergegend *f (col)*; **to be on ~ row** heruntergekommen sein.
skier ['skiːə[r]] *n* Skifahrer(in *f*) *m*.
skiff [skɪf] *n* Skiff *nt*; *(Sport)* Einer *m*.
skiing ['skiːɪŋ] *n* Skilaufen, Skifahren *nt*. **to go ~** Ski laufen gehen; **~ instructor** Skilehrer(in *f*) *m*.
ski *in cpds* Ski-; **~-jump** *n (action)* Skisprung *m*; *(place)* Sprungschanze *f*; **~-jumping** *n* Skispringen *nt*.
skilful, *(US)* **skillful** ['skɪlfʊl] *adj* geschickt; *player etc also* gewandt; *painting etc* kunstvoll.
ski-lift ['skiːlɪft] *n* Skilift *m*.
skill [skɪl] *n* **(a)** *no pl (skilfulness)* Geschick *nt*, Geschicklichkeit *f*; *(of sculptor etc)* Kunst(fertigkeit) *f*. **his ~ at billiards/in persuading people** sein Geschick beim Billiard/seine Fähigkeit, andere zu überreden. **(b)** *(acquired technique)* Fertigkeit *f*; *(ability)* Fähigkeit *f*.
skilled [skɪld] *adj (skilful)* geschickt, gewandt *(at* in *+dat)*; *(trained)* ausgebildet, Fach-; *(requiring skill)* fachmännisch.
skillet ['skɪlɪt] *n* Bratpfanne *f*.
skillful *(US)* = **skilful.**
skim [skɪm] **1** *vt* **(a)** *(remove floating matter)* abschöpfen; *milk* entrahmen. **~med** *or (US)* **~ milk** Magermilch *f*. **(b)** *(pass low over)* streifen über *(+acc)*; *(fig: touch on)* berühren. **the book merely ~s the surface of the problem** das Buch berührt das Problem nur an der Oberfläche. **(c)** *(read quickly)* überfliegen. **2** *vi (across, over* über *+acc) (move quickly)* fliegen; *(aircraft also)* rasch gleiten; *(stones)* springen.
skimp [skɪmp] **1** *vt food, material* sparen an *(+dat)*; *work* nachlässig erledigen; *details* zu kurz kommen lassen. **2** *vi* sparen *(on* an *+dat)*.
skimpy ['skɪmpɪ] *adj (+er)* dürftig; *meal, existence also* kärglich; *clothes* knapp. **to be ~ with sth** mit etw sparsam sein.
skin [skɪn] **1** *n* **(a)** Haut *f*. **to be soaked to the ~** bis auf die Haut naß sein; **he's nothing but ~ and bone(s) nowadays** er ist nur noch Haut und Knochen; **that's no ~ off my nose** *(col)* das juckt mich nicht *(col)*; **to save one's own ~** die eigene Haut retten; **to jump out of one's ~** *(col)* erschreckt hochfahren; **to get under sb's ~** *(col) (irritate)* jdm auf die Nerven gehen *(col)*; *(fascinate) (music)* jdm unter die Haut gehen; *(person)* jdn faszinieren; **I've got you under my ~** du hast mir's angetan; **to have a thick ~** *(fig)* ein dickes Fell haben *(col)*; **by the ~ of one's teeth** *(col)* mit knapper Not. **(b)** *(hide)* Haut *f*; *(fur)* Fell *nt*. **(c)** *(of fruit etc)* Schale *f*; *(on sausage, milk)* Haut *f*.

2 *vt animal* häuten; *fruit* schälen; *grapes, tomatoes* enthäuten. **to ~ sb alive** *(col)* jdm den Kopf abreißen *(hum col)*; **to keep one's eyes ~ned (for sth)** die Augen (nach etw) offenhalten.
skin: ~-diver *n* Sporttaucher(in *f*) *m*; **~-diving** *n* Sporttauchen *nt*; **~flint** *n (col)* Geiz-

kragen *m (col)*.
skinful ['skɪnfʊl] *n (col)* **to have had a ~** einen über den Durst getrunken haben.
skin: ~ graft *n* Hauttransplantation *f*; **~head** *n (Brit col)* Skinhead *m*.
skinny ['skɪnɪ] *adj (+er) (col) person, legs* dünn.
skint [skɪnt] *adj (Brit col)* **to be ~** pleite *or* blank sein *(col)*.
skin-tight ['skɪn,taɪt] *adj* hauteng.
skip[1] [skɪp] **1** *n* (kleiner) Sprung *m*; *(in dancing)* Hüpfschritt *m*. **2** *vi* **(a)** hüpfen; *(jump, gambol)* springen; *(with rope)* seilspringen. **(b)** *(move from subject to subject)* springen. **3** *vt* **(a)** *(omit, miss) school etc* schwänzen *(col)*; *chapter etc* auslassen, überspringen. **to ~ lunch** das Mittagessen ausfallen lassen; **let's ~ it** lassen wir das. **(b)** *(US)* **to ~ rope** seilspringen.
skip[2] *n (Build)* Container *m*; *(Min)* Förderkorb *m*.
ski: ~ pants *npl* Skihose(n *pl*) *f*; **~ pole** *n* Skistock *m*.
skipper ['skɪpəʳ] *n* Kapitän *m*.
skipping ['skɪpɪŋ] *n* Seilspringen *nt*. **~ rope** Sprungseil *nt*.
skirmish ['skɜːmɪʃ] *n (Mil)* Gefecht *nt*; *(scrap, fig)* Zusammenstoß *m*.
skirt [skɜːt] **1** *n* Rock *m*; *(of jacket, coat)* Schoß *m*. **2** *vt (also ~* **(a)round***)* umgehen.
skirting (board) ['skɜːtɪŋ(,bɔːd)] *n (Brit)* Fußleiste *f*.
ski: ~-run *n* Skipiste *f*; **~ stick** *n* Skistock *m*.
skit [skɪt] *n* (satirischer) Sketch *(on* über *+acc)*.
skittish ['skɪtɪʃ] *adj (playful)* übermütig; *(flirtatious) woman* neckisch, kokett.
skittle ['skɪtl] *n (Brit)* Kegel *m*. **to play ~s** kegeln.
skive [skaɪv] *(Brit col) vi* blaumachen *(col)*; *(from school etc)* schwänzen *(col)*.
♦ **skive off** *vi (Brit col)* sich drücken *(col) (prep obj* vor *+dat)*.
skulk [skʌlk] *vi (move)* schleichen; *(lurk)* sich herumdrücken.
skull [skʌl] *n* Schädel *m*. **~ and crossbones** Totenkopf *m*.
skunk [skʌŋk] *n* Skunk *m*, Stinktier *nt*.
sky [skaɪ] *n* Himmel *m*. **under the open ~** unter freiem Himmel; **in the ~** am Himmel; **the ~'s the limit!** nach oben sind keine Grenzen gesetzt; **to praise sb to the skies** jdn über den grünen Klee loben *(col)*.
sky: ~ blue *n* Himmelblau *nt*; **~-blue** *adj* himmelblau, **~-high 1** *adj prices* schwindelnd hoch; **2** *adv* zum Himmel; **to blow a bridge ~-high** *(col)* eine Brücke in die Luft sprengen; **to blow a theory ~-high** *(col)* eine Theorie zum Einsturz bringen; **~lark 1** *n* Feldlerche *f*; **2** *vi (col) (frolic)* tollen; *(fool around)* blödeln *(col)*; **~light** *n* Oberlicht *nt*; *(in roof also)* Dachfenster *nt*; **~line** *n (horizon)* Horizont *m*; *(of hills etc)* Silhouette *f*; **~scraper** *n* Wolkenkratzer *m*.
slab [slæb] *n (of wood etc)* Tafel *f*; *(of stone etc)* Platte *f*; *(in mortuary)* Tisch *m*; *(of cake)* großes Stück; *(of chocolate)* Tafel *f*.
slack [slæk] **1** *adj (+er)* **(a)** *(not tight)* locker. **(b)** *(lazy)* bequem, träge; *(negligent)* nachlässig, schlampig *(col)*. **to be ~ about one's work** in bezug auf seine Arbeit nachlässig sein. **(c)** *(Comm) market* flau; *season also* ruhig. **business is ~** das Geschäft geht schlecht. **2** *n* **(a)** *(of rope etc)* **to take up the ~ (on a rope/sail)** ein Seil/Segel straffen *or* spannen; **there is too much ~** das Seil/Segel hängt zu sehr durch; **to take up the ~ in the economy** die brachliegenden Kräfte (der Wirtschaft) nutzen. **(b)** *(coal)* Grus *m*. **3** *vi* bummeln.
slacken ['slækn] **1** *vt* **(a)** *(loosen)* lockern. **(b)** *(reduce)* vermindern, verringern. **2** *vi* **(a)** *(become loose)* sich lockern. **(b)** *(also ~* **off***)* *(speed)* sich verringern; *(rate of development)* sich verlangsamen; *(wind, demand, market)* abflauen.
slackness ['slæknɪs] *n (of rope)* Schlaffheit *f*; *(of business, market etc)* Flaute *f*; *(laziness)* Bummelei *f*; *(negligence)* Nachlässigkeit *f*.
slacks [slæks] *npl* Hose *f*.
slag [slæg] **1** *n* Schlacke *f*. **~ heap** Schlackenhalde *f*. **2** *vt (col: run down)* (he)runtermachen *(col)*.
slain [sleɪn] *ptp of* **slay**.
slake [sleɪk] *vt thirst* stillen.
slam [slæm] **1** *n* **(a)** *(of door etc)* Zuschlagen *nt no pl*. **with a ~** mit voller Wucht. **(b)** *(Cards)* Schlemm *m*. **2** *vt* **(a)** *(close violently)* zuknallen. **to ~ sth shut** etw zuknallen; **to ~ the door in sb's face** jdm die Tür vor der Nase zumachen; **he ~med his fist on the table** er knallte mit der Faust auf den Tisch *(col)*; **to ~ the brakes on** *(col)* auf die Bremse latschen *(col)*. **(b)** *(col: criticize harshly)* verreißen; *person* herunterputzen *(col)*. **3** *vi (door)* zuschlagen.
slander ['slɑːndəʳ] **1** *n* Verleumdung *f*. **2** *vt* verleumden.
slanderous ['slɑːndərəs] *adj* verleumderisch.
slang [slæŋ] **1** *n* Slang *m*; *(army ~, schoolboy ~ etc)* Jargon *m*. **2** *adj* Slang-. **3** *vt (esp Brit col)* **to ~ sb/sth** jdn beschimpfen/über etw *(acc)* schimpfen; **they were having a ~ing match** sie beschimpften sich um die Wette.
slangy ['slæŋɪ] *adj (+er)* salopp.
slant [slɑːnt] **1** *n* **(a)** Schräge *f*. **to be on the ~** sich neigen, schräg sein. **(b)** *(fig) (bias, leaning)* Tendenz, Neigung *f*; *(point of view)* Anstrich *m*. **a right-wing ~** ein Rechtsdrall *m*. **2** *vt (lit)* verschieben; *report* färben. **the book is ~ed towards women** das Buch ist auf Frauen ausgerichtet. **3** *vi* sich neigen.
slanting ['slɑːntɪŋ] *adj* schräg.
slap [slæp] **1** *n* Schlag, Klaps *m*. **to give sb a ~** jdm einen Klaps geben; **a ~ in the face** *(lit, fig)* ein Schlag ins Gesicht; *(lit also)* eine Ohrfeige; **to give sb a ~ on the back** jdm (anerkennend) auf den Rücken klopfen; *(fig)* jdn loben. **2** *adv (col)* direkt. **3** *vt* **(a)** schlagen. **to ~ sb's face** jdn ohrfeigen, jdm eine runterhauen *(col)*. **(b)** *(put noisily)* knallen *(on(to)* auf *+acc)*. **he just ~ped the paint on** er klatschte die Farbe einfach drauf *(col)*.
slap: ~-bang *adv (col) crash* mit Karacho *(col)*; **it was ~-bang in the middle** es war genau in der Mitte; **~dash** *adj* flüchtig, schludrig *(pej)*; **~-happy** *adj* unbekümmert; **~stick** *n* Klamauk *m (col)*; **~stick comedy** Slapstick *m*; **~-up** *adj (col) meal* mit allem Drum und Dran *(col)*.
slash [slæʃ] **1** *n (action)* Streich *m*; *(wound)* Schnitt *m*. **2** *vt* **(a)** *(cut)* zerfetzen; *face also* aufschlitzen; *undergrowth* abhauen; *(with sword)* hauen auf *(+acc)*. **(b)** *(col) price* radikal herabsetzen.
slat [slæt] *n* Leiste *f*; *(in grid etc)* Stab *m*.
slate [sleɪt] **1** *n* **(a)** *(rock)* Schiefer *m*; *(roof ~)* Schieferplatte *f*. **put it on the ~** *(col)* schreiben Sie es an; **to wipe the ~ clean** *(fig)* reinen Tisch machen. **(b)** *(US Pol)* (Kandidaten)liste *f*. **2** *adj* Schiefer-. **3** *vt* **(a)** *roof* (mit Schiefer) decken. **(b)** *(col: criticize harshly)* verreißen; *person* zusammenstauchen *(col)*.
slate: ~-blue *adj* blaugrau; **~-coloured,** *(US)* **~-colored** *adj* schieferfarben; **~-grey,** *(US)* **~-gray** *adj* schiefergrau.
slaughter ['slɔːtəʳ] **1** *(of animals)* Schlachten *nt no pl*; *(of persons)* Gemetzel. **the ~ on the roads** das Massensterben auf den Straßen. **2** *vt* schlachten; *persons (lit)* abschlachten; *(fig)* fertigmachen *(col)*.
slaughterhouse ['slɔːtəhaʊs] *n* Schlachthof *m*.
Slav [slɑːv] **1** *adj* slawisch. **2** *n* Slawe *m*, Slawin *f*.
slave [sleɪv] **1** *n* Sklave *m*, Sklavin *f*. **to be a ~ to sb/sth** jds Sklave sein/Sklave von etw sein. **2** *vi* sich abplagen, schuften *(col)*. **to ~ (away) at sth** sich mit etw herumschlagen.
slave: ~ driver *n (lit, fig)* Sklaventreiber *m*;

~ **labour** *(Brit) or* **labor** *(US) n (work)* Sklavenarbeit *f;* **he uses ~ labour** sein Leute müssen wie die Sklaven arbeiten.
slavery ['sleɪvərɪ] *n* Sklaverei *f; (condition)* Sklavenleben *nt; (fig: addiction)* sklavische Abhängigkeit *(to* von*)*.
slave trade *n* Sklavenhandel *m.*
slavish *adj,* **~ly** *adv* ['sleɪvɪʃ, -lɪ] sklavisch.
slay [sleɪ] *pret* **slew,** *ptp* **slain** *vt* erschlagen; *(with gun etc)* ermorden.
sleazy ['sliːzɪ] *adj (+er) (col)* schäbig.
sledge [sledʒ] *n* Schlitten *m.*
sledge(hammer) ['sledʒ(ˌhæməʳ)] *n* Vorschlaghammer *m.*
sleek [sliːk] **1** *adj (+er) hair, fur, animal* geschmeidig; *(of general appearance)* gepflegt; *car also* schnittig, elegant. **2** *vt* **to ~ one's hair down** sich *(dat)* die Haare glätten.
sleep [sliːp] *(vb: pret, ptp* **slept***)* **1** *n* Schlaf *m.* **to go to ~** *(person, limb)* einschlafen; **to have a ~** (etwas) schlafen; **to have a good night's ~** sich richtig ausschlafen; **to put sb to ~** jdn zum Schlafen bringen; *(drug)* jdn einschläfern; **to put an animal to ~** *(euph)* ein Tier einschläfern; **that film sent me to ~** bei dem Film bin ich eingeschlafen. **2** *vt* **the house ~s 10** in dem Haus können 10 Leute schlafen *or* übernachten. **3** *vi* schlafen. **to ~ late** lange schlafen.
♦ **sleep around** *vi (col)* mit jedem schlafen *(col).*
♦ **sleep in** *vi* ausschlafen; *(col: oversleep)* verschlafen.
♦ **sleep off** *vt sep hangover etc* ausschlafen. **to ~ it ~** seinen Rausch ausschlafen.
♦ **sleep on** *vi +prep obj problem, decision* überschlafen. **why don't you ~ ~ it** schlafen Sie noch einmal darüber.
♦ **sleep with** *vi +prep obj (have sex)* schlafen mit.
sleeper ['sliːpəʳ] *n* **(a) to be a heavy/light ~** einen festen/leichten Schlaf haben. **(b)** *(Brit Rail: on track)* Schwelle *f.* **(c)** *(Brit Rail) (train)* Schlafwagenzug *m; (coach)* Schlafwagen *m; (berth)* Platz *m* im Schlafwagen.
sleeping ['sliːpɪŋ] *adj* schlafend. **S~ Beauty** Dornröschen *nt;* **let ~ dogs lie** *(Prov)* schlafende Hunde soll man nicht wecken *(Prov).*
sleeping: ~ bag *n* Schlafsack *m;* **~ car** *n* Schlafwagen *m;* **~ partner** *n (Brit)* stiller Teilhaber; **~ pill** *n* Schlaftablette *f;* **~ quarters** *npl* Schlafräume *pl.*
sleepless ['sliːplɪs] *adj* schlaflos.
sleep: ~walk *vi* schlafwandeln; **~walker** *n* Schlafwandler(in *f*) *m.*
sleepy ['sliːpɪ] *adj (+er)* **(a)** *(drowsy) person, voice etc* müde, schläfrig; *(not yet awake)* verschlafen. **(b)** *(inactive) person* lahm *(col); place, atmosphere* verschlafen; *climate* schläfrig machend; *afternoons* schläfrig.
sleet [sliːt] **1** *n* Schneeregen *m.* **2** *vi* **it was ~ing** es gab Schneeregen.
sleeve [sliːv] *n* **(a)** *(on garment)* Ärmel *m.* **to roll up one's ~s** *(lit, fig)* die Ärmel aufkrempeln *(col);* **to have sth up one's ~** *(fig col)* etw in petto haben *or* auf Lager haben. **(b)** *(for record)* Hülle *f.*
sleeveless ['sliːvlɪs] *adj* ärmellos.
sleigh [sleɪ] *n* (Pferde)schlitten *m.*
sleight [slaɪt] *n:* **by ~ of hand** durch Taschenspielertricks.
slender ['slendəʳ] *adj* schlank; *hand, waist also* schmal; *resources* knapp, mager; *hope* schwach, gering.
slept [slept] *pret, ptp of* **sleep.**
sleuth [sluːθ] *n (col)* Spürhund *m (col).*
slew [sluː] *pret of* **slay.**
slice [slaɪs] **1** *n* **(a)** Scheibe *f; (of bread also)* Schnitte *f; (fig: of population, profit)* Teil *m.* **a ~ of life** ein Ausschnitt aus dem Leben. **(b)** *(esp Brit: food server)* Wender *m.* **cake ~** Tortenheber *m.* **2** *vt* **(a)** *bread, meat etc* (in Scheiben) schneiden. **to ~ sth in two** etw durchschneiden. **(b)** *ball* anschneiden. **3** *vi* **to ~ through sth** etw durchschneiden.
♦ **slice off** *vt sep* abschneiden.
♦ **slice up** *vt sep* (ganz) in Scheiben schneiden; *(divide)* aufteilen.
slicer ['slaɪsəʳ] *n (cheese-~ etc)* Hobel *m; (machine) (bread-~)* Brotschneider *m; (bacon-~)* ≃ Wurstschneidemaschine *f.*
slick [slɪk] **1** *adj (+er) (col)* **(a)** *(usu pej: clever, smart)* clever *(col); answer, solution, performance, style* glatt. **(b)** *hair* geschniegelt. **(c)** *(US: slippery)* glatt, schlüpfrig. **2** *n* **(a)** *(oil~)* Ölteppich *m.* **(b)** *(US col: glossy magazine)* Hochglanzmagazin *nt.*
slide [slaɪd] *(vb: pret, ptp* **slid** [slɪd]*)* **1** *n* **(a)** *(chute, in playground etc)* Rutschbahn *f.* **(b)** *(fig: fall, drop)* Abfall *m.* **the ~ in share prices** der Preisrutsch bei den Aktien. **(c)** *(esp Brit: for hair)* Spange *f.* **(d)** *(Phot)* Dia *nt; (microscope ~)* Objektträger *m.* **a lecture with ~s** ein Diavortrag *m.* **2** *vt (push)* schieben; *(slip)* gleiten lassen. **3** *vi* **(a)** rutschen; *(deliberately also)* schlittern. **to ~ down the banisters** das Treppengeländer hinunterrutschen. **(b)** *(move smoothly: machine part etc)* sich schieben lassen. **it slid into place** es rutschte an die richtige Stelle. **(c)** *(person: move quietly etc)* schleichen. **(d)** *(fig)* **the days slid by** *or* **past** die Tage schwanden dahin *(geh);* **to let things ~** die Dinge laufen lassen.
slide: ~ film *n* Diafilm *m;* **~ projector** *n* Diaprojektor *m;* **~ rule** *n* Rechenschieber *m;* **~ show** *n* Diavortrag *m.*
sliding ['slaɪdɪŋ] *adj part* gleitend; *door, roof, seat* Schiebe-.
slight [slaɪt] **1** *adj (+er)* **(a)** *person, build* zierlich. **(b)** *(small, trivial)* leicht; *improvement also, change, possibility* geringfügig; *importance, intelligence* gering; *error also* klein; *acquaintance* flüchtig. **he showed some ~ optimism** er zeigte gewisse Ansätze von Optimismus; **he takes offence at the ~est thing** er ist wegen jeder kleinsten Kleinigkeit gleich beleidigt; **I haven't the ~est (idea)** ich habe nicht die geringste Ahnung; **not in the ~est** nicht im geringsten. **2** *n (affront)* Affront *m (on* gegen*).* **a ~ on one's/sb's character** eine persönliche Kränkung. **3** *vt (offend)* kränken; *(ignore)* ignorieren.
slighting ['slaɪtɪŋ] *adj (offensive)* kränkend; *remark* abfällig.
slightly ['slaɪtlɪ] *adv* **(a) ~ built** *person* zierlich. **(b)** *(to a slight extent)* etwas, ein kleines bißchen; *know* flüchtig; *smell* leicht, etwas.
slim [slɪm] **1** *adj (+er)* **(a)** schlank; *waist etc* schmal. **(b)** *resources, profits* mager; *hope also* schwach; *chances* gering; *evidence* dürftig. **2** *vi* eine Schlankheitskur machen.
slime [slaɪm] *n* Schleim *m.*
slimming ['slɪmɪŋ] *adj* schlankmachend *attr.* **crispbread is ~** Knäckebrot macht schlank; **~ foods** kalorienarme Nahrungsmittel *pl.*
slimy ['slaɪmɪ] *adj (+er) (lit, fig)* schleimig; *wall* glitschig; *hands* schmierig.
sling [slɪŋ] *(vb: pret, ptp* **slung***)* **1** *n* Schlinge *f; (for rifle)* (Trag)riemen *m.* **to have one's arm in a ~** den Arm in der Schlinge tragen. **2** *vt (throw)* schleudern; *(col)* schmeißen *(col).* **he slung his coat over his arm** er warf sich *(dat)* den Mantel über den Arm.
♦ **sling out** *vt sep (col)* rausschmeißen *(col).*
slink [slɪŋk] *pret, ptp* **slunk** *vi* schleichen. **to ~ away** *or* **off** sich davonschleichen.
slinky ['slɪŋkɪ] *adj (+er) (col)* aufreizend.
slip [slɪp] **1** *n* **(a)** *(slide)* **he had a nasty ~** er ist ausgerutscht und bös gefallen. **(b)** *(mistake)* Ausrutscher, Patzer *m.* **to make a (bad) ~** sich (übel) vertun *(col);* **a ~ of the pen/tongue** ein

Schreibfehler *m*/Versprecher *m*; **it was just a ~ of the pen** das war nur ein Flüchtigkeitsfehler. **(c) to give sb the ~** jdm entwischen. **(d)** *(pillow~)* Kissenbezug *m*. **(e)** *(undergarment)* Unterrock *m*. **(f)** *(of paper)* Zettel *m*. **~s of paper** Zettel *pl*. **(g) a (mere) ~ of a girl** *(slightly built)* ein zierliches Persönchen.

2 *vt* **(a)** schieben; *(slide)* gleiten lassen; *(Aut) clutch* schleifen lassen. **to ~ sth across to sb** jdm etw zuschieben; *(unobtrusively)* jdm etw zuschmuggeln; **she ~ped the dress over her head** sie streifte sich *(dat)* das Kleid über den Kopf; **to ~ a disc** *(Med)* sich *(dat)* einen Bandscheibenschaden zuziehen; **to ~ sb a fiver** jdm einen Fünfer zustecken. **(b)** *(escape from)* sich losreißen. **the dog ~ped its chain** der Hund hat sich (von der Kette) losgerissen; **the boat had ~ped its moorings** das Boot hatte sich losgerissen; **it ~ped my mind** ich habe es vergessen; **it ~ped my notice** es ist mir entgangen.

3 *vi* **(a)** *(person)* (aus)rutschen; *(feet, tyres)* (weg)rutschen; *(become loose: knot, nut)* sich lösen; *(Aut: clutch)* schleifen. **the knife ~ped** das Messer rutschte ab; **it ~ped from her hand** es rutschte ihr aus der Hand; **the secret ~ped out before he realized** ehe er sich's versah, war ihm das Geheimnis herausgerutscht. **(b)** *(move quickly)* schlüpfen; *(move smoothly)* rutschen. **I'll ~ around to the shop** ich spring' schnell zum Laden. **(c) to let (it) ~ that ...** fallenlassen, daß...; **the police let the thief ~ through their fingers** die Polizei ließ sich *(dat)* den Dieb durch die Finger schlüpfen. **(d)** *(decline: standards, morals etc)* fallen. **you're ~ping!** *(col)* du läßt nach *(col)*.

♦ **slip away** *vi* sich wegschleichen; *(time)* verstreichen; *(chances)* (allmählich) schwinden; *(opportunity)* dahinschwinden.

♦ **slip by** *vi (person)* sich vorbeischleichen *(prep obj* an *+dat)*; *(years)* verfliegen, nur so dahinschwinden.

♦ **slip off 1** *vi (person)* sich wegschleichen. **2** *vt sep clothes* ausziehen, abstreifen.

♦ **slip on** *vt sep* schlüpfen in *(+acc)*; *dress also* überstreifen; *ring* aufziehen; *lid* drauftun *(prep obj* auf *+acc)*.

♦ **slip out** *vi* **(a)** *(leave unobtrusively)* kurz weggehen. **(b)** *(be revealed)* herauskommen.

♦ **slip up** *vi (col: err)* sich vertun *(col) (over, in* bei*)*.

slip: ~ case *n* Schuber *m*; **~cover** *n (esp US)* Schonbezug *m*; **~knot** *n* Schlaufenknoten *m*; **~-ons** *npl (shoes)* Slipper *pl*.

slipper ['slɪpəʳ] *n* Pantoffel, Hausschuh *m*.

slippery ['slɪpərɪ] *adj* **(a)** schlüpfrig; *rope, road* glatt, rutschig; *fish* glitschig. **(b)** *(pej col) person* glatt, windig *(col)*. **a ~ customer** ein aalglatter Typ *(col)*; **he's on the ~ slope** *(col)* er ist auf der schiefen Bahn.

slip-road ['slɪprəʊd] *n (Brit)* Zufahrtsstraße *f*; *(for entering motorway)* (Autobahn)auffahrt *f*; *(for leaving motorway)* (Autobahn)ausfahrt *f*.

slipshod ['slɪpʃɒd] *adj* schludrig.

slip: ~stream *m (Aviat)* Sog *m*; *(Aut)* Windschatten *m*; **~way** *n (Naut)* Gleitbahn *f*; **to come off the ~way** vom Stapel laufen.

slit [slɪt] *(vb: pret, ptp ~)* **1** *n* Schlitz *m*. **2** *vt* (auf)schlitzen. **to ~ a sack open** einen Sack aufschlitzen; **to ~ sb's throat** jdm die Kehle aufschlitzen.

slither ['slɪðəʳ] *vi* rutschen. **to ~ about on the ice** auf dem Eis herumschlittern.

sliver ['slɪvəʳ] *n (of wood etc)* Splitter *m*; *(thin slice)* Scheibchen *nt*.

slob [slɒb] *n (col)* Drecksau *f (col!)*.

slobber ['slɒbəʳ] *vi* sabbern, sabbeln *(also fig)*; *(dog)* geifern.

slog [slɒg] *(col)* **1** *n (effort)* Schinderei *f (col)*. **it's a hard ~ to the top** man muß ganz schön schuften, um nach oben zu kommen. **2** *vt ball* dreschen *(col)*; *opponent* hart treffen. **3** *vi* **to ~ away at sth** *(work)* an etw *(dat)* schuften *(col)*; **we ~ged on for another 5 miles** wir kämpften uns noch 5 Meilen weiter.

slogan ['sləʊgən] *n* Slogan *m*; *(motto)* Motto *nt*; *(political also)* Parole *f*.

slogger ['slɒgəʳ] *n (col: worker)* Arbeitstier *nt*.

slop [slɒp] **1** *vi (spill)* (über)schwappen. **to ~ over (into sth)** überschwappen (in etw *acc*). **2** *vt (spill)* verschütten; *(pour out)* schütten.

slope [sləʊp] **1** *n* **(a)** *(angle)* Neigung *f*; *(downwards also)* Gefälle *nt*; *(of roof also)* Schräge *f*. **(b)** *(sloping ground)* (Ab)hang *m*. **on a ~** am Hang; **halfway up the ~** auf halber Höhe; **the (ski) ~s** die Piste. **2** *vi* geneigt sein; *(road, floor)* sich neigen. **the ground ~s down to the stream** das Land senkt sich zum Fluß hin ab.

♦ **slope off** *vi (col: person)* abziehen *(col)*.

sloping ['sləʊpɪŋ] *adj road (upwards)* ansteigend; *(downwards)* abfallend; *roof, floor* schräg; *garden etc* am Hang; *(not aligned)* schief.

sloppy ['slɒpɪ] *adj (+er)* **(a)** *(col: careless)* schlampig *(col)*; *work also* schlud(e)rig *(col)*. **(b)** *(col: sentimental)* rührselig; *novel also* schmalzig.

slops [slɒps] *npl (dirty water)* Schmutzwasser *nt*; *(food waste)* Abfallbrühe *f*; *(in teapot)* Satz *m*.

slosh [slɒʃ] *(col)* **1** *vt* **(a) to ~ some water over sth** Wasser über etw *(acc)* schütten. **(b)** *(Brit: hit)* hauen. **2** *vi* **to ~ about in the water** im Wasser herumplanschen.

sloshed [slɒʃt] *adj pred (esp Brit col)* blau *(col)*. **to get ~** sich besaufen *(col)*.

slot [slɒt] *n (opening)* Schlitz *m*; *(groove)* Rille *f*; *(col: place)* Plätzchen *nt (col)*; *(TV col)* (gewohnte) Sendezeit. **~ machine** Münzautomat *m*; *(for gambling)* Spielautomat *m*; **~ meter** Münzzähler *m*.

♦ **slot in 1** *vt sep* hineinstecken. **to ~ sth ~ to sth** etw in etw *(acc)* stecken. **2** *vi* sich einfügen lassen. **suddenly everything ~ted ~to place** plötzlich paßte alles zusammen.

sloth [sləʊθ] *n* **(a)** *(laziness)* Faulheit *f*. **(b)** *(Zool)* Faultier *nt*.

slothful ['sləʊθfʊl] *adj* faul; *person, life also* träge.

slouch [slaʊtʃ] *vi (stand, sit)* herumhängen *(col)*; *(move)* latschen. **to ~ off** davonzockeln *(col)*; **he was ~ed over his desk** er hing über seinem Schreibtisch; **he sat ~ed on a chair** er hing auf einem Stuhl.

slovenly ['slʌvnlɪ] *adj* schlampig *(col)*.

slow [sləʊ] **1** *adj (+er)* langsam; *trade* flau. **it's ~ work** das braucht seine Zeit; **he is a ~ worker/learner/reader** er arbeitet/lernt/liest langsam; **to get off to a ~ start** *(race)* schlecht vom Start kommen; *(project)* nur langsam in Gang kommen; **to be ~/not to be ~ to do sth** sich *(dat)* mit etw Zeit lassen/etw prompt erledigen; **he is ~ to make up his mind/~ to anger** er braucht lange, um sich zu entscheiden/er wird nicht so leicht wütend; **they were ~ to act** sie ließen sich *(dat)* Zeit; **to be (20 minutes) ~** *(clock)* (20 Minuten) nachgehen; **bake in a ~ oven** bei schwacher Hitze backen. **2** *adv (+er)* langsam. **to go ~** *(driver)* langsam fahren; *(workers)* einen Bummelstreik machen. **3** *vi* **to ~ (to a stop/standstill)** langsam zum Halten/zum Stillstand kommen.

♦ **slow down** *or* **up 1** *vi* sich verlangsamen; *(drive/walk)* langsamer fahren/gehen; *(worker)* langsamer arbeiten. **2** *vt sep* verlangsamen; *engine* drosseln; *machine* herunterschalten; *programme, project* verzögern.

slow: ~coach *n (Brit col)* Langweiler *m*; *(mentally)* Transuse *f (col)*; **~down** *n (US: go-slow)* Bummelstreik *m*; **~ lane** *n* (äußerste) rechte/linke Spur.

slowly ['sləʊlɪ] *adv* langsam.

slow motion *n* Zeitlupe *f*. **in ~** in Zeitlupe.

slowness ['sləʊnɪs] *n* Langsamkeit *f*. **their ~ to act** ihr Zaudern; **~ of mind** Begriffsstutzigkeit *f*.

slow: ~**-witted** *adj* begriffsstutzig; ~**worm** *n* Blindschleiche *f*.

sludge [slʌdʒ] *n* Schlamm *m*.

slug[1] [slʌg] *n* Nacktschnecke *f*. ~**s and snails** Schnecken *pl* (mit und ohne Gehäuse).

slug[2] **1** *n (bullet)* Kugel *f*; *(blow)* Schlag *m*. **a** ~ **of whisky** ein Schluck *m* Whisky. **2** *vt (col: hit)* eine knallen *(+dat) (col)*.

sluggish ['slʌgɪʃ] *adj (indolent, Med)* träge; *engine, car* lahm, langsam; *business* flau; *market* lustlos.

sluice [slu:s] **1** *n* Schleuse *f*. **2** *vt* **to** ~ **sth (down)** etw abspritzen.

sluice gate *n* Schleusentor *nt*.

slum [slʌm] **1** *n (usu pl: area)* Slum *m*, Elendsviertel *nt*; *(house)* Elendsquartier *nt*. ~ **clearance** ≃ (Stadt)sanierung *f*.

slumber ['slʌmbəʳ] *(liter)* **1** *n* Schlummer *(geh)*, Schlaf *m*. ~**s** Träume *pl*. **2** *vi* schlummern *(geh)*.

slump [slʌmp] **1** *n (in gen) (in numbers, popularity etc)* (plötzliche) Abnahme; *(in production, sales)* Rückgang *m*; *(state)* Tiefstand *m*; *(Fin)* Sturz *m*, Baisse *f (spec)*. ~ **in prices** Preissturz *m (of* bei); **the 1929 S**~ die Weltwirtschaftskrise von 1929. **2** *vi* **(a)** *(Fin, Comm) (prices)* stürzen, fallen; *(sales, production)* plötzlich zurückgehen; *(fig: morale etc)* sinken. **(b)** *(sink)* fallen, sinken. **to** ~ **into a chair** sich in einen Sessel fallen lassen; **he was** ~**ed over the wheel** er war über dem Steuer zusammengesackt.

slung [slʌŋ] *pret, ptp of* **sling.**

slunk [slʌŋk] *pret, ptp of* **slink.**

slur [slɜ:ʳ] **1** *n* **(a)** Makel *m*; *(insult)* Beleidigung *f*. **to cast a** ~ **on sb/sth** jdn/etw in schlechtem Licht erscheinen lassen; *(person)* jdn/etw verunglimpfen. **(b)** *(Mus)* Bindung *f*. **(c) to speak with a** ~ unartikuliert sprechen. **2** *vt (pronounce indistinctly)* (halb) verschlucken.

slurp [slɜ:p] *vti* schlürfen.

slurred [slɜ:d] *adj* undeutlich; *(Mus)* gebunden.

slush [slʌʃ] *n (watery snow)* (Schnee)matsch *m*; *(mud)* Morast *m*; *(col: sentimental nonsense)* Kitsch *m*. ~ **fund** Schmiergeldfonds *m*.

slushy ['slʌʃɪ] *adj (+er) snow, mud, path* matschig; *(col: sentimental)* kitschig.

slut [slʌt] *n* (liederliche) Schlampe.

sly [slaɪ] **1** *adj (+er)* schlau, gerissen; *look, wink* verschmitzt. **2** *n* **on the** ~ heimlich, still und leise *(hum)*, ganz heimlich.

smack[1] [smæk] *vi* **to** ~ **of** *(taste)* leicht schmecken nach; *(fig)* riechen nach.

smack[2] **1** *n* (klatschender) Schlag *m*; *(slap also)* fester Klaps; *(sound)* Klatschen *nt*. **to give a child/the ball a** ~ einem Kind eine knallen *(col)*/auf den Ball dreschen *(col)*; **you'll get a** ~ du kriegst gleich eine *(col)*; **a** ~ **in the eye** *(fig)* ein Schlag ins Gesicht. **2** *vt (slap)* knallen *(col)*. **to** ~ **a child's bottom** einen Kind den Hintern versohlen *(col)*; **he** ~**ed his lips** er leckte sich *(dat)* die Lippen. **3** *adv (col)* direkt. **she ran** ~ **into the door** sie rannte rums! gegen die Tür *(col)*.

small [smɔ:l] **1** *adj (+er)* **(a)** klein; *supply also, importance* gering; *waist* schmal; *letter also* Klein-; *sum also* bescheiden. **the** ~**est possible number of books** so wenig Bücher wie möglich; **to have a** ~ **appetite/be a** ~ **eater** wenig Appetit haben/kein großer Esser sein; **no** ~ **success** ein beachtlicher Erfolg; **to feel/look** ~ *(fig)* sich (ganz) klein (und häßlich) vorkommen/schlecht dastehen; **a few** ~ **matters** ein paar Kleinigkeiten; **to help in a** ~ **way** bescheidene Hilfe leisten; **to start in a** ~ **way** klein anfangen. **(b)** *(fig: mean, petty) person* kleinlich. **2** *n* **(a) the** ~ **of the back** das Kreuz. **(b)** ~**s** *pl (Brit col)* Unterwäsche *f*. **3** *adv* **to chop sth up** ~ etw kleinhacken.

small: ~ **ad** *n (Brit)* Kleinanzeige *f*; ~ **arms** *npl* Handfeuerwaffen *pl*; ~ **change** *n* Kleingeld *nt*; ~**holder** *n* Kleinbauer *m*; ~**holding** *n* kleiner Landbesitz; ~ **hours** *npl* früher Morgen; **in the** ~ **hours** in den frühen Morgenstunden.

smallish ['smɔ:lɪʃ] *adj* (eher) kleiner. **he is** ~ er ist eher klein.

small-minded [ˌsmɔ:l'maɪndɪd] *adj* engstirnig.

smallness ['smɔ:lnɪs] *n* Kleinheit *f*; *(of waist)* Schmalheit *f*; *(of sum, present)* Bescheidenheit *f*; *(pettiness)* Kleinlichkeit *f*.

small: ~**pox** *n* Pocken *pl*; ~ **print** *n* das Kleingedruckte; ~**-scale** *adj map, model* in verkleinertem Maßstab; *project* kleinangelegt; ~ **screen** *n (TV)* **on the** ~ **screen** auf dem Bildschirm; ~**talk** *n* oberflächliche Konversation; ~**-time** *adj (col)* armselig; *crook* klein; *politician* Schmalspur-; *actor* drittrangig; ~**-town** *adj* Kleinstadt-, kleinstädtisch; *mentality also* kleinbürgerlich.

smarmy ['smɑ:mɪ] *adj (+er) (Brit col)* kriecherisch *(pej)*; *voice* einschmeichelnd.

smart [smɑ:t] **1** *adj (+er)* **(a)** schick; *person, clothes, car also* flott; *society* fein. **a** ~**-looking girl/garden** ein flott aussehendes Mädchen/ein gepflegter Garten; **the** ~ **set** die Schickeria *(col)*. **(b)** *(bright, clever)* clever *(col)*, schlau; *thief, trick also* raffiniert; *(pej) person, answer* neunmalklug *(pej col)*. **to get** ~ *(col)* sich am Riemen reißen *(col)*; *(get cheeky)* frech kommen *(with dat)*. **(c)** *(quick)* (blitz)schnell; *pace* flott *(col)*. **and look** ~ **(about it)!** und zwar ein bißchen fix *or* plötzlich! *(col)*. **2** *vi* brennen. **it will make your cut** ~ es wird (dir) in der Wunde brennen; **to** ~ **from sth** *(from blow etc)* von etw brennen; *(fig)* unter etw *(dat)* leiden.

smart-aleck ['smɑ:tˌælɪk] *(col)* **1** *n* Schlauberger *m (col)*. **2** *adj remarks* besserwisserisch.

smarten ['smɑ:tn] *(also* ~ **up)** **1** *vt house, room* herausputzen; *appearance* aufmöbeln *(col)*. **to** ~ **oneself up** *(dress up)* sich in Schale werfen *(col)*; *(generally improve appearance)* mehr Wert auf sein Äußeres legen; **you'd better** ~ **up your ideas** *(col)* du solltest dich am Riemen reißen *(col)*. **2** *vi* = ~ **oneself up.**

smartness ['smɑ:tnɪs] *n* **(a)** Schick *m*. **(b)** *(cleverness)* Cleverness *(col)*, Schlauheit *f*; *(of thief, trick)* Raffiniertheit *f*.

smash [smæʃ] **1** *vt* **(a)** zerschlagen; *window also* einschlagen. **I** ~**ed my glasses** die Brille ist mir kaputtgegangen. **(b)** *(defeat or destroy)* zerschlagen; *rebellion also* niederschlagen; *opponent* zerschmettern; *record* haushoch schlagen. **(c)** *(strike, also Tennis)* schmettern.

2 *vi* **(a)** *(break)* zerbrechen. **it** ~**ed into a thousand pieces** es (zer)sprang in tausend Stücke. **(b)** *(crash)* prallen. **the car** ~**ed into the wall** das Auto krachte gegen die Mauer; **the plane** ~**ed into the houses** das Flugzeug raste in eine Häusergruppe.

3 *n* **(a)** *(noise) nt*; *(of waves)* Klatschen *nt*. **there was a** ~ es hat gekracht. **(b)** *(collision)* Unfall *m*. **(c)** *(blow)* Schlag *m*; *(Tennis)* Schmetterball *m*.

4 *adv (col)* mit Karacho *(col)*.

♦ **smash down** *vt sep door* einschlagen.

♦ **smash in** *vt sep* einschlagen. **the firemen had to** ~ **their way** ~ die Feuerwehrleute mußten gewaltsam eindringen; **to** ~ **sb's face** ~ *(col)* jdm die Schnauze einschlagen *(col!)*.

♦ **smash up** *vt sep* zertrümmern; *car* kaputtfahren.

smash-and-grab (raid) [ˌsmæʃən'græb(reɪd)] *n* Schaufenstereinbruch *m*.

smashed [smæʃt] *adj (col)* stockbesoffen *(col)*.

smasher ['smæʃəʳ] *n (esp Brit col)* toller Typ *(col)*; *(woman)* Klassefrau *f (col)*.

smash hit *n (col)* Superhit *m (col)*.

smashing ['smæʃɪŋ] *adj (esp Brit col)* klasse *inv*, Klasse *pred*, dufte *(all col)*.

smattering ['smætərɪŋ] *n* **a** ~ **of French** ein paar Brocken Französisch.

smear [smɪəʳ] **1** *n* verschmierter Fleck; *(fig)* Beschmutzung *f*; *(defamation)* Verleumdung *f*; *(Med)* Abstrich *m*. **this left a ~ on his name** das hinterließ einen Fleck auf seinem Namen; **~ campaign** Verleumdungskampagne *f*; **~ test** *(Med)* Abstrich *m*. **2** *vt* **(a)** *cream, ointment* schmieren; *(spread)* verschmieren; *(mark, make dirty)* beschmieren; *face* einschmieren. **(b)** *(fig) person* verunglimpfen; *sb's reputation* beschmutzen. **3** *vi (glass)* verschmieren; *(print)* verschmiert *or* verwischt werden; *(biro)* schmieren; *(paint, ink)* verlaufen.

smell [smel] *(vb: pret, ptp* **~ed** *or* **smelt***)* **1** *n (sense of ~, odour)* Geruch *m*; *(unpleasant also)* Gestank *m*; *(fragrant also)* Duft *m*. **it has a nice ~** es riecht gut *or* angenehm; **there's a ~ of gas** hier riecht es nach Gas. **2** *vt* **(a)** riechen. **can you ~ burning?** riechst du, daß etwas brennt *or (Cook)* anbrennt? **(b)** *(fig) danger, treason* wittern. **to ~ trouble** Ärger kommen sehen. **3** *vi* riechen; *(unpleasantly also)* stinken; *(fragrantly also)* duften. **that ~s!** *(lit, fig)* das stinkt!; **to ~ of sth** *(lit, fig)* nach etw riechen; **his breath ~s** er riecht aus dem Mund.

♦ **smell out** *vt sep* **(a)** *rabbit, traitor etc* aufspüren; *plot* aufdecken. **(b) these onions are ~ing the house ~!** die Zwiebeln verpesten das ganze Haus!

smelling salts ['smelɪŋˌsɒlts] *npl* Riechsalz *nt*.

smelly ['smelɪ] *adj (+er)* übelriechend, stinkend. **it's ~ in here** hier drin stinkt es.

smelt[1] [smelt] *pret, ptp of* **smell.**

smelt[2] *vt ore* schmelzen; *(refine)* verhütten.

smile [smaɪl] **1** *n* Lächeln *nt*. **to be all ~s** übers ganze Gesicht strahlen; **to give sb a ~** jdm zulächeln; **take that ~ off your face!** hör auf, so zu grinsen!; **that soon wiped the ~ off his face** dabei verging ihm bald das Lachen. **2** *vi* lächeln. **come on, ~** lach mal!; **to ~ at sb** jdn anlächeln; *(cheerfully)* jdn anlachen; **to ~ at sth** über etw *(acc)* lächeln; **to ~ with joy/happiness** *etc* vor Freude/Glück *etc* strahlen; **fortune ~d on him** *(liter)* ihm lachte das Glück.

smiling ['smaɪlɪŋ] *adj* lächelnd.

smirk [smɜːk] **1** *n* Grinsen *nt*. **2** *vi* grinsen.

smite [smaɪt] *pret* **smote,** *ptp* **smitten** *vt (old, liter)* schlagen.

smith [smɪθ] *n* Schmied *m*.

smithereens [ˌsmɪðə'riːnz] *npl* **to smash sth to ~** etw in tausend Stücke schlagen.

smithy ['smɪðɪ] *n* Schmiede *f*.

smitten ['smɪtn] **1** *ptp of* **smite. 2** *adj* **to be ~ with the plague/remorse** von der Pest heimgesucht/von Reue geplagt werden; **he's really ~ with her** *(col)* er ist wirklich vernarrt in sie *(col)*.

smock [smɒk] *n* Kittel *m*.

smog [smɒg] *n* Smog *m*.

smoke [sməʊk] **1** *n* **(a)** Rauch *m*. **there's no ~ without fire** *(prov)* kein Rauch ohne Flamme *(prov)*; **to go up in ~** in Rauch (und Flammen) aufgehen. **(b)** *(cigarette etc)* was zu rauchen *(col)*. **have you got a ~?** hast du was zu rauchen? *(col)*; *(act)* **to have a ~** eine rauchen. **2** *vt* **(a)** *cigarette* rauchen. **(b)** *fish etc* räuchern. **3** *vi* rauchen; *(oil-lamp etc)* qualmen. **to ~ like a chimney** wie ein Schlot rauchen.

smoke-bomb ['sməʊkbɒm] *n* Rauchbombe *f*.

smoked [sməʊkt] *adj bacon, fish* geräuchert, Räucher-. **~ glass** Rauchglas *nt*.

smokeless ['sməʊklɪs] *adj zone* rauchfrei; *fuel* rauchlos.

smoker ['sməʊkəʳ] *n* **(a)** *(person)* Raucher(in *f*) *m*. **to be a heavy ~** stark rauchen, starker Raucher sein. **(b)** *(Rail)* Raucher(abteil *nt*) *m*.

smoke: ~-ring *n* (Rauch)ring *m*; **~screen** *n* Rauchvorhang *m*; *(fig)* Deckmantel, Vorwand *m*; **~ signal** *n* Rauchzeichen *nt*.

smoking ['sməʊkɪŋ] **1** *adj* rauchend. **2** *n* Rauchen *nt*. **"no ~"** „Rauchen verboten".

smoking: ~ compartment, *(US)* **~ car** *n* Raucherabteil *nt*; **~ jacket** *n* Hausjacke *f*.

smoky ['sməʊkɪ] *adj (+er) chimney, fire* rauchend; *room, atmosphere* verraucht; *flavour* rauchig.

smolder *vi (US)* = **smoulder.**

smooch [smuːtʃ] *(col) vi* knutschen *(col)*.

smooth [smuːð] **1** *adj (+er)* **(a)** *(in texture, surface etc)* glatt; *sea also* ruhig; *outline* sanft; *skin also, hair* weich. **as ~ as glass** spiegelglatt; **worn ~** *steps* glattgetreten; *knife* abgeschliffen; *tyre* abgefahren. **(b)** *(in consistency) paste* sämig; *sauce* glatt. **(c)** *motion, flight, crossing* ruhig; *gearchange* weich; *landing* glatt; *breathing* gleichmäßig; *(trouble-free) transition, functioning* reibungslos, glatt. **the bill had a ~ passage through Parliament** der Gesetzentwurf kam glatt durchs Parlament. **(d)** *(polite, often pej) manners, salesman* glatt; *person also* aalglatt *(pej)*; *(unruffled)* kühl, cool *(col)*. **to be a ~ talker** ein Schönredner sein; **a ~ operator** ein Schlawiner *m (col)*.

2 *vt surface, dress, hair* glätten; *wood* glatthobeln; *(fig) feelings* beruhigen. **to ~ the way for sb** jdm den Weg ebnen.

♦ **smooth out** *vt sep (make smooth) crease, surface* glätten; *(fig) difficulty* aus dem Weg räumen.

♦ **smooth over** *vt sep quarrel* in Ordnung bringen. **to ~ things ~** die Sache geradebiegen *(col)*.

smoothly ['smuːðlɪ] *adv land* weich; *change gear* leicht; *drive* ruhig; *fit* genau; *make transition* unmerklich; *talk* schön; *handle situation* kühl; *behave* aalglatt *(pej)*. **to go ~** *(without problems)* glatt über die Bühne gehen.

smoothness ['smuːðnɪs] *n see adj* **(a)** Glätte *f*; Ruhe *f*; Sanftheit *f*; Weichheit *f*. **(b)** Sämigkeit *f*; Glätte *f*. **(c)** Ruhe *f*; Weichheit *f*; Glätte *f*; Gleichmäßigkeit *f*; Reibungslosigkeit *f*; *(of fit)* Genauigkeit *f*.

smote [sməʊt] *pret of* **smite.**

smother ['smʌðəʳ] *vt* **(a)** *(stifle) person, fire* ersticken; *(fig) criticism also, yawn, sob etc* unterdrücken. **to ~ sb with affection** jdn mit seiner Liebe erdrücken. **(b)** *(cover)* bedecken. **fruit ~ed in cream** Früchte, die in Sahne schwimmen.

smoulder, *(US)* **smolder** ['sməʊldəʳ] *vi (lit, fig)* glimmen, schwelen. **~ing hatred** schwelender Haß.

smudge [smʌdʒ] **1** *n* Fleck *m*; *(of ink)* Klecks *m*. **2** *vt* verwischen. **3** *vi* verschmieren.

smug [smʌg] *adj (+er)* selbstgefällig; *remark also* süffisant.

smuggle ['smʌgl] *vti (lit, fig)* schmuggeln. **to ~ sb/sth in** jdn/etw einschmuggeln; **to ~ sb/sth out** jdn/etw herausschmuggeln.

smuggler ['smʌgləʳ] *n* Schmuggler(in *f*) *m*.

smuggling ['smʌglɪŋ] *n* Schmuggel *m*.

smut [smʌt] *n* **(a)** *(piece of dirt)* Rußflocke *f*. **(b)** *(fig)* Schmutz *m*.

smutty ['smʌtɪ] *adj (+er) (lit, fig)* schmutzig.

snack [snæk] *n* Kleinigkeit *f*, Imbiß *m*. **to have a ~** eine Kleinigkeit essen; **~ bar** Imbißstube *f*.

snafu [snæ'fuː] *n (US col)* Schlamassel *m (col)*.

snag [snæg] *n* Haken *m*, Schwierigkeit *f*. **there's a ~** die Sache hat einen Haken; **what's the ~?** was ist das Problem?; **to run into** *or* **hit a ~** in Schwierigkeiten *(acc)* kommen.

snail [sneɪl] *n* Schnecke *f*. **at a ~'s pace** im Schneckentempo.

snake [sneɪk] *n* Schlange *f*. **a ~ in the grass** *(fig) (woman)* eine listige Schlange; *(man)* ein heimtückischer Kerl.

snake: ~bite *n* Schlangenbiß *m*; **~ charmer** *n* Schlangenbeschwörer *m*; **~skin 1** *n* Schlangenhaut *f*; *(leather)* Schlangenleder *nt*; **2** *adj* Schlangenleder-, aus Schlangenleder.

snap [snæp] **1** *n* **(a)** *(sound)* Schnappen *nt*; *(with fingers)* Schnippen *nt*; *(of sth breaking)* Knacken *nt*. **(b)** *(Phot)* Schnappschuß *m*. **(c)** *(Cards)* ≃ Schnippschnapp *nt*. **2** *adj attr* plötzlich, spontan.

~ **decision** plötzlicher Entschluß. 3 *vt* **(a)** *fingers* schnipsen mit. **to ~ a book shut** ein Buch zuklappen; **to ~ sth into place** etw einschnappen lassen. **(b)** *(break)* zerbrechen. **(c)** *(also ~ out)* **to ~ an order** bellend etwas befehlen; **she ~ped a few words at the children** sie pfiff die Kinder an. **(d)** *(Phot)* knipsen. **4** *vi* **(a)** *(click)* (zu)schnappen; *(crack, break)* zerbrechen. **to ~ shut** zuschnappen; **my patience finally ~ped** dann ist mir aber der Geduldsfaden gerissen. **(b)** *(speak sharply)* bellen *(col)*. **to ~ at sb** jdn anschnauzen *(col)*. **(c)** *(of dog etc, fig)* schnappen *(at* nach*)*.

♦ **snap off** *vt sep (break off)* abbrechen; *(bite off)* abbeißen. **to ~ sb's head ~** *(fig col)* jdm ins Gesicht springen *(col)*.

♦ **snap out 1** *vt sep order* brüllen. **2** *vi* **~ ~ of it!** reiß dich zusammen!; *(cheer up)* Kopf hoch!

♦ **snap up** *vt sep (lit, fig)* wegschnappen.

snapdragon ['snæp,drægən] *n (Bot)* Löwenmaul *nt*.

snappish ['snæpɪʃ] *adj (lit, fig)* bissig.

snappy ['snæpɪ] *adj (+er)* **(a)** *(col)* flott *(col)*. **and make it ~!** und zwar ein bißchen flott! *(col)*. **(b)** *(lit, fig) dog, person* bissig. **(c)** *(col) translation* kurz und treffend; *phrase* zündend.

snapshot ['snæpʃɒt] *n* Schnappschuß *m*.

snare [snɛəʳ] **1** *n (lit, fig: trap)* Falle *f*; *(fig also)* Fallstrick *m*. **2** *vt (lit, fig)* (ein)fangen.

snarl [snɑːl] **1** *n* Knurren *nt no pl*. **2** *vi* knurren. **to ~ at sb** jdn anknurren.

♦ **snarl up** *vt sep (col)* **I got ~ed ~ in a traffic jam** ich bin im Verkehr steckengeblieben.

snarl-up ['snɑːlʌp] *n (col) (in traffic)* Verkehrschaos *nt*; *(in system)* Kuddelmuddel *nt (col)*.

snatch [snætʃ] **1** *n* **(a)** *(act)* Griff *m*. **to make a ~ at sth** nach etw greifen; *(animal)* zuschnappen. **(b)** *(Brit col) (robbery)* Raub *m*; *(kidnapping)* Entführung *f*. **(c)** *(snippet)* Stück *nt*; *(of conversation)* Fetzen *m*. **2** *vt* **(a)** *(grab)* greifen. **to ~ sth from sb** jdm etw entreißen; **to ~ hold of sth** nach etw greifen; **to ~ sth out of sb's hand** jdm etw aus der Hand reißen. **(b)** *some sleep etc* ergattern. **to ~ a quick meal** schnell etwas essen. **(c)** *(Brit col) (steal) money* klauen *(col)*; *handbag* aus der Hand reißen; *(kidnap)* entführen. **3** *vi* greifen *(at* nach*)*. **don't ~!** nicht grapschen! *(col)*.

♦ **snatch away** *vt sep* wegreißen *(sth from sb* jdm etw*)*.

♦ **snatch up** *vt sep* schnappen. **he ~ed ~ his camera** er schnappte sich *(dat)* seine Kamera; **the mother ~ed her child ~** die Mutter riß ihr Kind an sich *(acc)*.

sneak [sniːk] **1** *n* Schleicher *m*; *(Sch col)* Petze(r) *mf (Sch col)*. **~ thief** Langfinger *m (col)*. **2** *vt* **he ~ed a cake off the counter** er klaute einen Kuchen vom Tresen *(col)*; **to ~ sth into a room** etw in ein Zimmer schmuggeln; **to ~ a look at sb/sth** auf jdn/etw schielen *(col)*. **3** *vi* **(a) to ~ away** *or* **off** sich wegschleichen; **to ~ in** sich einschleichen; **to ~ past sb** (sich) an jdm vorbeischleichen. **(b)** *(Sch col: tell tales)* petzen *(col)*. **to ~ on sb** jdn verpetzen *(col)*.

sneakers ['sniːkəz] *npl (US)* Freizeitschuhe *pl*.

sneaking ['sniːkɪŋ] *adj attr* geheim *attr*. **I have a ~ feeling that ...** ich habe das unbestimmte Gefühl, daß ...

sneaky ['sniːkɪ] *adj (+er) (col)* raffiniert, schlau.

sneer [snɪəʳ] **1** *n (expression)* spöttisches Lächeln; *(remark)* spöttische Bemerkung. **2** *vi* spotten; *(look sneering)* spöttisch grinsen. **to ~ at sb** jdn verhöhnen; *(facially also)* jdn auslachen.

sneeze [sniːz] **1** *n* Nieser *m (col)*. **2** *vi* niesen. **not to be ~d at** nicht zu verachten.

snide [snaɪd] *adj (col)* abfällig.

sniff [snɪf] **1** *n* Schniefen *nt no pl (col)*; *(disdainful)* Naserümpfen *nt no pl*; *(of dog)* Schnüffeln *nt no pl*. **we never got a ~ of the vodka** *(col)* wir durften noch nicht einmal an dem Wodka riechen; **have a ~ at this** riech mal hieran! **2** *vt (test by smelling)* riechen, schnuppern an *(+dat) (col)*; *smelling salts* einziehen; *glue* einatmen, schnüffeln *(col)*; *(fig: detect)* wittern, riechen. **3** *vi (person)* schniefen *(col)*; *(dog)* schnuppern. **to ~ at sth** *(lit)* an etw *(dat)* schnuppern; *(fig)* die Nase über etw *(acc)* rümpfen; **not to be ~ed at** nicht zu verachten.

♦ **sniff out** *vt sep (lit, fig)* aufspüren; *crime, plot* aufdecken.

sniffle ['snɪfl] *n, vi* = **snuffle.**

snigger ['snɪgəʳ] **1** *n* Kichern, Gekicher *nt*. **2** *vi* kichern *(at, about* wegen*)*.

snip [snɪp] **1** *n* **(a)** *(cut, cutting action)* Schnitt *m*. **(b)** *(of cloth)* Stück *nt*; *(of paper)* Schnipsel *m (col)*; *(from newspaper)* Ausschnitt *m*. **(c)** *(esp Brit col: bargain)* Geschäft *nt*, günstiger Kauf. **it's a ~ at only £2** für nur £ 2 ist es unheimlich günstig. **(d)** *(US col: insignificant person)* Würstchen *nt (pej col)*. **2** *vt* schnippeln *(col)*. **to ~ sth off** etw abschnippeln *(col)*.

snipe [snaɪp] **1** *n, pl* - *(Orn)* Schnepfe *f*. **2** *vi* **to ~ at sb** *(lit, fig)* aus dem Hinterhalt auf jdn schießen.

sniper ['snaɪpəʳ] *n* Heckenschütze *m*. **~-fire** Heckenschützenfeuer *nt*.

snippet ['snɪpɪt] *n* Stückchen *nt*; *(of paper also)* Schnipsel *m or nt*; *(of information)* (Bruch)stück *nt*. **~s of a conversation** Gesprächsfetzen *pl*.

snivel ['snɪvl] *vi* heulen, flennen *(col)*.

snivelling, *(US)* **sniveling** ['snɪvlɪŋ] *adj* heulend.

snob [snɒb] *n* Snob *m*. **~ value** Snobappeal *m*.

snobbery ['snɒbərɪ] *n* Snobismus *m*.

snobbish ['snɒbɪʃ] *adj* snobistisch, versnobt *(col)*.

snog [snɒg] *vi (Brit col)* rumknutschen *(col)*.

snooker ['snuːkəʳ] **1** *n* Snooker *nt*. **2** *vt* **to be ~ed** *(fig col)* festsitzen *(col)*.

snoop [snuːp] **1** *n* **(a)** = **snooper.** **(b)** *(act)* **I'll have a ~ around** ich gucke mich mal (ein bißchen) um. **2** *vi* schnüffeln. **to ~ around** herumschnüffeln.

snooper ['snuːpəʳ] *n* Schnüffler(in *f*) *m*.

snooty ['snuːtɪ] *adj (+er) (col)* hochnäsig.

snooze [snuːz] **1** *n* Schläfchen, Nickerchen *nt*. **to have a ~** ein Schläfchen machen. **2** *vi* ein Nickerchen machen.

snore [snɔːʳ] **1** *n* Schnarchen *nt no pl*. **2** *vi* schnarchen.

snorkel ['snɔːkl] **1** *n* Schnorchel *m*. **2** *vi* **to go ~ling** *(Brit) or* **~ing** *(US)* schnorcheln gehen.

snort [snɔːt] **1** *n* Schnauben *nt no pl*; *(of boar)* Grunzen *nt no pl*. **he gave a ~ of contempt** er schnaubte verächtlich. **2** *vti* schnauben; *(boar)* grunzen.

snot [snɒt] *n (col)* Rotz *m (col)*.

snotty ['snɒtɪ] *adj (+er) (col)* **(a)** Rotz- *(col)*; *child* rotznäsig *(col)*. **(b)** *(fig: snooty)* rotzig *(col)*.

snout [snaʊt] *n (of animal)* Schnauze *f*; *(col: of person)* Rüssel *(col)*.

snow [snəʊ] **1** *n* **(a)** *(also col: cocaine or heroin)* Schnee *m*; *(~fall)* Schneefall *m*. **the heavy ~s last winter** die heftigen Schneefälle im letzten Winter; **as white as ~** schneeweiß. **(b)** *(TV)* Geflimmer *nt*, Schnee *m*. **2** *vi* schneien.

♦ **snow in** *vt sep (usu pass)* **to be** *or* **get ~ed ~** einschneien.

♦ **snow under** *vt sep (col: usu pass)* **to be ~ed ~** *(with work)* reichlich eingedeckt sein; *(with requests)* überhäuft werden.

snow: **~ball 1** *n* Schneeball *m*; *(drink)* Snowball *m*; **2** *vi* eskalieren; **~ blindness** *n* Schneeblindheit *f*; **~bound** *adj* eingeschneit; **~-capped** *adj* schneebedeckt; **~-covered** *adj* verschneit; **~drift** *n* Schneewehe *f*; **~drop** *n (Bot)* Schneeglöckchen *nt*; **~fall** *n* Schneefall *m*; **~flake** *n* Schneeflocke *f*; **~man** *n* Schneemann *m*; **~plough,** *(US)* **~plow** *n (also Ski)* Schneepflug *m*; **~shoe** *n* Schneeschuh *m*; **~storm** *n* Schneesturm *m*; **~-white** *adj* schneeweiß.

snowy ['snəʊɪ] *adj (+er)* **(a)** *weather, region* schneereich; *hills* verschneit. **it was very ~ yesterday**

gestern hat es viel geschneit. **(b)** *(white as snow)* schneeweiß.

snub [snʌb] **1** *n* Brüskierung *f*. **to give sb a ~** jdn brüskieren, jdn vor den Kopf stoßen; *subordinate, pupil etc (verbally)* jdm über den Mund fahren. **2** *vt* **(a)** *person* brüskieren, vor den Kopf stoßen; *subordinate, pupil (verbally)* über den Mund fahren *(+dat)*; *proposal* kurz abtun. **(b)** *(ignore, not greet)* schneiden.

snub: ~nose *n* Stupsnase *f*; **~-nosed** *adj* stupsnasig.

snuff [snʌf] **1** *n* Schnupftabak *m*. **to take ~** schnupfen. **2** *vt candle (extinguish: also ~ out)* auslöschen. **to ~ it** *(Brit col!: die)* abkratzen *(col!)*.

snuffle ['snʌfl] **1** *n* Schniefen *nt no pl*. **to have the ~s** *(col)* einen leichten Schnupfen haben. **2** *vi* schnüffeln; *(with cold, from crying)* schniefen.

snug [snʌg] *adj (+er) (cosy)* behaglich, gemütlich; *bed, garment, room etc* mollig warm; *(sheltered) spot* geschützt; *(close-fitting)* gutsitzend *attr; (tight)* eng. **to be ~ in bed** es im Bett mollig warm haben; **it is a good ~ fit** es paßt gut.

snuggle ['snʌgl] *vi* sich kuscheln. **to ~ down in bed** sich ins Bett kuscheln; **to ~ up (to sb)** sich (an jdn) ankuscheln.

so [səʊ] **1** *adv* **(a)** so. **~ much tea/ ~ many flies** so viel Tee/so viele Fliegen; **he was ~ stupid (that)** er war so dumm(, daß); **I am not ~ stupid as to believe that** so dumm bin ich nicht, daß ich das glaube(n würde); **would you be ~ kind as to open the door?** wären Sie bitte so freundlich, die Tür zu öffnen?; **~ great a writer as Shakespeare** ein so großer Dichter wie Shakespeare; **he's not been ~ well recently** in letzter Zeit geht es ihm nicht so sonderlich; **how are things? — not ~ bad!** wie geht's? — nicht schlecht!

(b) *(emphatic) glad, sorry etc* so; *pleased, relieved, hope, wish* sehr; *love* so sehr; *hate* so sehr, derart. **I'm ~ very tired** ich bin ja so müde; **it would be ~ much better** *etc* es wäre soviel besser *etc*; **~ much the better/worse (for sb)** um so besser/schlechter (für jdn); **that's ~ kind of you** das ist wirklich sehr nett von Ihnen.

(c) *(replacing longer sentence)* das, es. **I hope ~** hoffentlich; *(emphatic)* das hoffe ich doch sehr; **I think ~** ich glaube schon; **I never said ~** das habe ich nie gesagt; **I told you ~** ich habe es dir doch gesagt; **why should I do it? — because I say ~** warum muß ich das tun? — weil ich es sage, darum; **I didn't say ~** das habe ich nicht gesagt; **~ I believe** ja, ich glaube schon; **~ I see** ja, das sehe ich; **please, do ~** bitte(, tun Sie es ruhig); **it may be ~** es kann schon sein; **~ be it** nun gut; **if ~** wenn ja; **or ~ they say** oder so heißt es jedenfalls; **that is ~** das stimmt; **if that's ~** wenn das stimmt; **he's coming by plane — is that ~?** er kommt mit dem Flugzeug — tatsächlich?; **I didn't say that — you did ~** *(esp US col)* das habe ich nicht gesagt — hast du wohl.

(d) *(thus, in this way)* so. **perhaps it was better ~** vielleicht war es auch besser so; **~ it was that ...** so kam es, daß ...; **and ~ it was** und so war es auch; **by ~ doing he has ...** dadurch hat er ..., indem er das tat, hat er ...; **... and ~ saying he walked out** ... und damit ging er hinaus; **the article is ~ written as to ...** der Artikel ist so geschrieben, daß er ...

(e) *(unspecified amount)* **how high is it? — oh, about ~ high** wie hoch ist das? — oh, ungefähr so; **~ much per head** soviel pro Kopf; **they looked like ~ many gypsies** sie sahen aus wie Zigeuner; **a week or ~** so eine Woche; **50 or ~** etwa 50.

(f) *(likewise)* auch. **~ am/would/do/could** *etc* **I** ich auch; **he's wrong and ~ are you** ihr irrt euch beide.

(g) he walked past and didn't ~ much as look at me er ging vorbei, ohne mich auch nur anzusehen; **~ much for that!** *(col)* das wär's ja wohl gewesen! *(col)*; **~ much for him** *(col)* das war ja wohl nichts mit ihm! *(col)*; **~ much for his help** *(col)* schöne Hilfe! *(col)*.

2 *conj* **(a)** *(expressing purpose)* damit. **~ (that) you don't have to do it again** damit Sie es nicht noch einmal machen müssen; **we hurried ~ as not to be late** wir haben uns beeilt, um nicht zu spät zu kommen.

(b) *(expressing result, therefore)* also. **it rained (and) ~ we couldn't go out** es regnete und deshalb konnten wir nicht weggehen; **he was standing in the doorway ~ (that) no-one could get past** er stand in der Tür, so daß niemand vorbeikonnte; **I told him to leave and ~ he did** ich habe ihm gesagt, er solle gehen, und das hat er auch getan; **the roads are busy ~ be careful** es ist viel Verkehr, also sei vorsichtig; **~ you see ...** wie du siehst, ...

(c) *(in questions, exclamations)* also. **~ that's his wife/the reason!** das ist also seine Frau/der Grund!; **~ you *did* do it!** du hast es also doch gemacht!; **~ (what)?** *(col)* (na) und?; **I'm not going, ~ there!** *(col)* ich geh' nicht, fertig, aus!

soak [səʊk] **1** *vt (wet)* durchnässen. **to be/get ~ed** völlig durchnäßt sein/werden; **to be ~ed to the skin, to be ~ed through** bis auf die Haut durchnäßt sein. **2** *vi* **(a)** *(steep)* **leave it to ~** weichen Sie es ein; *(in dye)* lassen Sie die Farbe einziehen; **to ~ in a bath** sich in der Badewanne aalen *(col)*. **(b)** *(penetrate)* **rain has ~ed through the ceiling** der Regen ist durch die Decke gesickert; **the coffee was ~ing into the carpet** der Kaffee saugte sich in den Teppich.

♦ **soak in** *vi (stain, dye etc)* einziehen.

♦ **soak up** *vt sep liquid* aufsaugen; *sunshine* genießen; *sound* schlucken; *(fig) information* aufsaugen, in sich *(acc)* aufnehmen.

soaking ['səʊkɪŋ] **1** *adj* klitschnaß *(col)*, patschnaß *(col)*. **2** *adv* **~ wet** triefend naß, klitschnaß *(col)*; **a ~ wet day** ein völlig verregneter Tag. **3** *n* **to get a ~** patschnaß werden *(col)*.

so-and-so ['səʊənsəʊ] *n (col)* **(a)** *(unspecified)* **~ up at the shop** Herr/Frau Soundso im Laden. **(b)** *(pej)* **he's an old ~** das ist ein gemeiner Kerl.

soap [səʊp] **1** *n* Seife *f*. **2** *vt* einseifen, abseifen.

soap: ~box *n (lit: packing case)* Seifenkiste *f*; *(fig: platform)* Apfelsinenkiste *f*; **~flakes** *npl* Seifenflocken *pl*; **~ opera** *n (TV, Rad)* Fernseh-/Hörspielserie, Seifenoper *(col) f*; **~ powder** *n* Seifenpulver *nt*; **~suds** *npl (foam)* Seifenschaum *m*.

soapy ['səʊpɪ] *adj (+er)* seifig.

soar [sɔːʳ] *vi* **(a)** *(rise: also ~ up)* aufsteigen; *(bird also)* sich in die Lüfte schwingen. **to ~ (up) into the sky** zum Himmel steigen. **(b)** *(fig) (building)* hochragen; *(price)* hochschnellen; *(popularity, hopes)* einen Aufschwung nehmen.

soaring ['sɔːrɪŋ] *adj bird, plane* in die Luft steigend; *tower* hoch aufragend; *imagination* hochfliegend; *popularity* schnell zunehmend; *prices* in die Höhe schnellend; *inflation* unaufhaltsam; *hopes* wachsend.

sob [sɒb] **1** *n* Schluchzer *m*, Schluchzen *nt no pl*. **to give a ~** (auf)schluchzen; **..., he said with a ~** ..., sagte er schluchzend. **2** *vi* schluchzen *(with* vor *+dat)*. **3** *vt* **to ~ one's heart out** sich *(dat)* die Seele aus dem Leib weinen.

sober ['səʊbəʳ] *adj* **(a)** *(not drunk)* nüchtern. **to be as ~ as a judge** stocknüchtern sein *(col)*. **(b)** *(sedate, serious) life, mood, occasion* ernst; *(sensible, moderate) opinion, judgement* vernünftig; *assessment, facts* nüchtern. **(c)** *(not bright or showy)* schlicht; *colour* gedeckt.

♦ **sober up 1** *vt sep (lit)* nüchtern machen; *(fig)* zur Vernunft bringen. **2** *vi (lit)* nüchtern werden; *(fig)* zur Vernunft kommen; *(after laughing etc)* sich beruhigen.

soberly ['səʊbəlɪ] *adv* nüchtern; *behave* vernünf-

tig; *dress, furnish* schlicht.
sobriety [sə'braɪɪtɪ] *n* **(a)** *(not being drunk)* Nüchternheit *f.* **(b)** *(seriousness, sedateness)* Solidität *f; (of dress)* Schlichtheit *f; (of colour)* Gedecktheit *f.*
soc = **society** Ges.
so-called ['səʊ'kɔːld] *adj* sogenannt; *(supposed)* angeblich.
soccer ['sɒkə^r] *n* Fußball *m.* ~ **player** Fußballer, Fußballspieler(in *f*) *m.*
sociable ['səʊʃəbl] *adj* *(gregarious)* gesellig; *(friendly)* freundlich. ... **just to be** ~ ..., man möchte sich ja nicht ausschließen; **I'm not feeling very** ~ **today** mir ist heute nicht nach Geselligkeit (zumute).
social ['səʊʃəl **1** *adj* **(a)** *(relating to community, Admin, Pol)* sozial; *history, reform, legislation, policy* Sozial-; *system, realism* Gesellschafts-; *structure, conditions, evils also* gesellschaftlich. **the** ~ **services** die Sozialeinrichtungen *pl.*
(b) *engagements, life, superior* gesellschaftlich; *behaviour* in Gesellschaft; *advancement, status also* sozial. ~ **climber** Emporkömmling *m (pej)*, sozialer Aufsteiger; **there isn't much** ~ **life around here** hier in der Gegend läuft nicht viel; **a job which leaves no time for one's** ~ **life** ein Beruf, bei dem man keine Zeit für Freizeitaktivitäten hat.
(c) *(gregarious) evening, person* gesellig; *(living in groups) animals* gesellig lebend.
2 *n* geselliger Abend.
social: ~ **democratic** *adj* sozialdemokratisch; ~ **insurance** *n (US)* Sozialversicherung *f.*
socialism ['səʊʃəlɪzəm] *n* Sozialismus *m.*
socialist ['səʊʃəlɪst] **1** *adj* sozialistisch. **2** *n* Sozialist(in *f*) *m.*
socialite ['səʊʃəlaɪt] *n (col)* Angehörige(r) *mf* der Schickeria *(col)*; *(man also)* Salonlöwe *m (col).*
socialize ['səʊʃəlaɪz] **1** *vt* sozialisieren; *means of production* vergesellschaften. **2** *vi* **to** ~ **with sb** *(meet socially)* mit jdm gesellschaftlich verkehren; *(chat to)* sich mit jdm unterhalten; **she** ~**s a lot** sie hat ein reges gesellschaftliches Leben.
socially ['səʊʃəlɪ] *adv* gesellschaftlich; *deprived etc* sozial; *meet* privat.
social: ~ **science** *n* Sozialwissenschaft *f;* ~ **security** *n* Sozialhilfe *f; (scheme)* Sozialversicherung *f;* **to be on** ~ **security** Sozialhilfeempfänger sein; ~ **work** *n* Sozialarbeit *f;* ~ **worker** *n* Sozialarbeiter(in *f*) *m.*
society [sə'saɪətɪ] *n* **(a)** Gesellschaft *f.* **modern industrial** ~ die moderne Industriegesellschaft. **(b)** *(club, organization)* Verein *m; (learned, Comm)* Gesellschaft *f.*
society *in cpds* Gesellschafts-; ~ **column** *n* Gesellschaftsspalte *f.*
socio- [ˌsəʊsɪəʊ-] *pref* sozio-. ~**economic** sozioökonomisch.
sociological [ˌsəʊsɪə'lɒdʒɪkəl] *adj* soziologisch.
sociologist [ˌsəʊsɪ'ɒlədʒɪst] *n* Soziologe *m*, Soziologin *f.*
sociology [ˌsəʊsɪ'ɒlədʒɪ] *n* Soziologie *f.*
sock[1] [sɒk] *n* Socke *f*, Socken *m (col); (knee-length)* Kniestrumpf *m.* **to pull one's** ~**s up** *(col)* sich am Riemen reißen *(col).*
sock[2] **1** *n (col)* Schlag *m* (mit der Faust). **to give sb a** ~ **in the eye** jdm eine aufs Auge verpassen *(col).* **2** *vt (col: hit)* hauen *(col).* ~ **him one!** knall ihm eine! *(col).*
socket ['sɒkɪt] *n* **(a)** *(of eye)* Augenhöhle *f; (of joint)* Gelenkpfanne *f; (of tooth)* Zahnhöhle *f.* **(b)** *(Brit Elec)* Steckdose *f; (for lightbulb)* Fassung *f; (Mech)* Sockel *m*, Fassung *f.*
sod[1] [sɒd] *n (turf)* Grassode *f.*
sod[2] *n (Brit col!)* Sau *f (col!).* **the poor** ~**s** die armen Schweine *(col).*
soda ['səʊdə] *n* **(a)** *(Chem)* Soda *nt; (sodium oxide)* Natriumoxyd *nt.* **(b)** *(drink)* Soda(wasser) *nt.*
soda: ~**-fountain** *n (US: café)* Erfrischungshalle *f;* ~ **siphon** *n* Siphon *m;* ~**-water** *n* Sodawasser *nt.*
sodden ['sɒdn] *adj* durchnäßt.
sodium ['səʊdɪəm] *n* Natrium *nt.* ~ **chloride** Natriumchlorid, Kochsalz *nt.*
sodomy ['sɒdəmɪ] *n* Analverkehr *m.*
sofa ['səʊfə] *n* Sofa *nt*, Couch *f.*
soft [sɒft] *adj (+er)* **(a)** weich; *meat* zart; *(pej: flabby) muscle* schlaff. ~ **currency** weiche Währung. **(b)** *(smooth) skin* zart; *surface* glatt; *material* weich. **(c)** *(gentle, not harsh)* sanft; *(subdued) music* gedämpft; *(not loud)* leise; *rain, breeze, tap, steps* leicht. **(d)** *character, government* schwach; *treatment, teacher* nachsichtig; *punishment* mild(e). **to be** ~ **on sb** jdm gegenüber nachgiebig sein. **(e)** *(easy) job, life* bequem. **that's a** ~ **option** das ist der Weg des geringsten Widerstandes. **(f)** *drink* alkoholfrei; *drug, pornography* weich. **(g)** *(col: foolish)* doof *(col).* **you must be** ~! du spinnst wohl! *(col).* **(h)** *(col: feeling affection)* **to be** ~ **on sb** für jdn schwärmen; **to have a** ~ **spot for sb** eine Schwäche für jdn haben.
soft-boiled ['sɒftˌbɔɪld] *adj egg* weich(gekocht).
soften ['sɒfn] **1** *vt* weich machen; *light, sound, colour* dämpfen; *effect, sb's anger, reaction, impression* mildern; *outline* weicher machen; *resistance* schwächen; *person* verweichlichen. **to** ~ **the blow** *(fig)* den Schock mildern. **2** *vi (material, person, heart)* weich werden; *(voice, look)* sanft werden; *(anger, resistance)* nachlassen.
softener ['sɒfnə^r] *n (for water)* Enthärtungsmittel *nt; (fabric* ~*)* Weichspülmittel *nt.*
soft-hearted [ˌsɒft'hɑːtɪd] *adj* weichherzig.
softie ['sɒftɪ] *n (col)* Softy *m (col); (weakling)* Weichling *m.*
softly ['sɒftlɪ] *adv (gently, tenderly)* sanft; *(not loud)* leise; *rain, blow* leicht.
softness ['sɒftnɪs] *n see adj* **(a)** Weichheit *f;* Zartheit *f;* Schlaffheit *f.* **(b)** Zartheit *f;* Glätte *f;* Weichheit *f.* **(c)** Sanftheit *f;* Gedämpftheit *f;* leiser Klang; Leichtheit *f.* **(d)** Schwäche *f;* Nachsichtigkeit *f;* Milde *f.* **(e)** Bequemlichkeit *f.*
soft: ~**-pedal** *vi* zurückstecken; ~ **sell** *n* weiche Verkaufstaktik, Soft selling *nt;* ~**-soap** *(fig)* **1** *n* Schmeichelei *f;* **2** *vt* einseifen *(col);* ~**-spoken** *adj person* leise sprechend *attr;* **to be** ~**-spoken** leise sprechen; ~ **touch** *n* **to be a** ~ **touch** nachgiebig sein; ~ **toy** *n* Stofftier *nt;* ~ **verge** *n* **"**~ **verges"** „Seitenstreifen nicht befahrbar"; ~**ware** *n* Software *f.*
softy *n (col)* = **softie.**
soggy ['sɒgɪ] *adj (+er)* durchnäßt, triefnaß; *soil* durchweicht; *food* matschig *(col).*
soil[1] [sɔɪl] *n (earth, ground)* Erde *f*, Erdreich *nt*, Boden *m.* **cover it with** ~ bedecken Sie es mit Erde; **native/foreign** ~ heimatlicher/fremder Boden; **the** ~ *(fig: farmland)* die Scholle.
soil[2] **1** *vt (lit, fig)* beschmutzen; *honour* beflecken; *oneself* besudeln; *minds* verderben. **2** *vi* schmutzig werden.
soiled [sɔɪld] *adj* schmutzig, verschmutzt.
solar ['səʊlə^r] *adj* Sonnen-. ~ **cell** Solarzelle *f;* ~ **eclipse** Sonnenfinsternis *f;* ~ **energy** Sonnenenergie *f;* ~ **panel** Sonnenkollektor *m;* ~ **plexus** Magengrube *f;* ~ **system** Sonnensystem *nt.*
solarium [səʊ'lɛərɪəm] *n, pl* **solaria** [səʊ'lɛərɪə] Solarium *nt.*
sold [səʊld] *pret, ptp of* **sell.**
solder ['səʊldə^r] **1** *n* Lötmittel *nt.* **2** *vt* löten; *(*~ *together)* verlöten.
soldering-iron ['səʊldərɪŋ'aɪən] *n* Lötkolben *m.*
soldier ['səʊldʒə^r] **1** *n* Soldat *m.* **old** ~ altgedienter Soldat; *(fig)* alter Kämpe. **2** *vi* Soldat sein.
♦ **soldier on** *vi* unermüdlich weitermachen.
sole[1] [səʊl] **1** *n* Sohle *f.* **2** *vt* besohlen.
sole[2] *n (fish)* Seezunge *f.*
sole[3] *adj* einzig; *heir also, agency* Allein-; *rights* alleinig.

solely ['səʊllɪ] *adv* (einzig und) allein, nur. **she is ~ responsible** sie allein trägt die Verantwortung.

solemn ['sɒləm] *adj* feierlich; *person, plea, warning* ernst; *architecture* erhaben; *promise, oath* heilig; *(drab) colour* trist.

solemnity [sə'lemnɪtɪ] *n see adj* Feierlichkeit *f*; Ernst *m*; Erhabenheit *f*; heiliger Ernst; Tristheit *f*.

solemnize ['sɒləmnaɪz] *vt* **to ~ a marriage** eine Trauung feierlich vollziehen.

solemnly ['sɒləmlɪ] *adv* feierlich; *walk* gemessenen Schrittes; *look, warn, plead* ernst; *promise* hoch und heilig; *swear* bei allem, was einem heilig ist.

solenoid ['səʊlənɔɪd] *n* Magnetspule *f*.

solicit [sə'lɪsɪt] **1** *vt support etc* bitten um; *person* inständig bitten; *votes* werben; *(prostitute)* ansprechen. **2** *vi (prostitute)* Kunden anwerben.

solicitor [sə'lɪsɪtə^r] *n (Jur) (Brit)* Rechtsanwalt *m*/-anwältin *f (der/die nicht vor Gericht plädiert)*; *(US)* Justizbeamte(r) *m*/-beamtin *f*.

solicitous [sə'lɪsɪtəs] *adj (form) (concerned)* besorgt *(about* um*)*; *(eager)* dienstbeflissen. **to be ~ to do sth** eifrig darauf bedacht sein, etw zu tun.

solid ['sɒlɪd] **1** *adj* **(a)** *(firm, not liquid) fuel, food, substance* fest. **~ body** Festkörper *m*; **to be frozen ~** hartgefroren sein.

(b) *(pure, not hollow, not broken) block, gold, rock* massiv; *matter* fest; *crowd etc* dicht; *row* ununterbrochen; *line of people etc* geschlossen; *week* ganz. **the square was packed ~ with cars** die Autos standen dicht an dicht auf dem Platz; **for two ~ days** *or* **for two days ~** zwei Tage ununterbrochen.

(c) *(stable, secure) bridge, house, car, relationship* stabil; *piece of work, character, education* solide; *foundations also, (lit, fig) ground* fest; *business* solide, reell. **a good ~ meal** eine kräftige Mahlzeit.

(d) *reason, argument* handfest, stichhaltig; *grounds* fundiert.

(e) *(unanimous) vote* einstimmig; *support* geschlossen. **Newtown is ~ for Labour** Newtown wählt fast ausschließlich Labour.

2 *n* **(a)** fester Stoff. **~s and liquids** feste und flüssige Stoffe *pl*; *(Sci)* Festkörper und Flüssigkeiten *pl*. **(b)** *(usu pl: food)* feste Nahrung *no pl*.

solidarity [ˌsɒlɪ'dærɪtɪ] *n* Solidarität *f*.

solidify [sə'lɪdɪfaɪ] **1** *vi* fest werden; *(lava etc)* erstarren; *(fig: support)* sich festigen. **2** *vt see vi* fest werden lassen; erstarren lassen; festigen.

solidly ['sɒlɪdlɪ] *adv* **(a)** *(firmly) secured* fest. **~ built** *house* solide gebaut; *person* kräftig gebaut. **(b)** *(uninterruptedly) work* ununterbrochen. **(c)** *vote* einstimmig; *support* geschlossen. **to be ~ behind sb** geschlossen hinter jdm stehen.

solid-state ['sɒlɪd'steɪt] *adj* Festkörper-; *(Elec)* Halbleiter-.

soliloquy [sə'lɪləkwɪ] *n* Monolog *m (also Theat)*.

solitaire [ˌsɒlɪ'tɛə^r] *n (game, gem)* Solitär *m*.

solitary ['sɒlɪtərɪ] *adj* **(a)** *(alone, secluded) life, person* einsam; *place also* abgeschieden. **a few ~ houses** ein paar vereinzelte Häuser; **in ~ confinement** in Einzelhaft. **(b)** *(sole) case, example* einzig. **not a ~ one** kein einziger.

solitude ['sɒlɪtjuːd] *n* Einsamkeit *f*; *(of place also)* Abgeschiedenheit *f*.

solo ['səʊləʊ] **1** *n* Solo *nt*. **2** *adj flight* Allein-; *violinist* Solo-. **3** *adv* allein; *(Mus)* solo. **to fly ~** einen Alleinflug machen.

soloist ['səʊləʊɪst] *n* Solist(in *f*) *m*.

solstice ['sɒlstɪs] *n* Sonnenwende *f*.

soluble ['sɒljʊbl] *adj* **(a)** löslich. **~ in water** wasserlöslich. **(b)** *problem* lösbar.

solution [sə'luːʃən] *n* **(a)** Lösung *f (to gen)*; *(of crime)* Aufklärung *f*. **(b)** *(Chem)* Lösung *f*.

solve [sɒlv] *vt problem, equation* lösen; *mystery* enträtseln; *crime* aufklären.

solvency ['sɒlvənsɪ] *n (Fin)* Zahlungsfähigkeit, Solvenz *f*.

solvent ['sɒlvənt] **1** *adj* **(a)** *(Chem)* lösend; *agent* Lösungs-. **(b)** *(Fin)* zahlungsfähig, solvent. **2** *n (Chem)* Lösungsmittel *nt*. **~ abuse** Lösungsmittelmißbrauch *m*, Schnüffeln *nt (col)*.

sombre, *(US)* **somber** ['sɒmbə^r] *adj (dark)* dunkel; *(gloomy)* düster.

some [sʌm] **1** *adj* **(a)** *(with plural nouns)* einige; *(a few, emphatic)* ein paar; *(any: in "if" clauses, questions) usu not translated.* **if you have ~ questions** wenn Sie Fragen haben; **did you bring ~ records?** hast du Schallplatten mitgebracht?; **~ records of mine** einige meiner Platten; **would you like ~ more biscuits?** möchen Sie noch (ein paar) Kekse?; **~ few people** einige wenige Leute.

(b) *(with singular nouns)* etwas, *usu not translated*; *(a little, emph)* etwas, ein bißchen. **there's ~ ink on your shirt** Sie haben Tinte auf dem Hemd; **would you like ~ cheese?** möchten Sie (etwas) Käse?; **~ more tea?** möchten Sie noch Tee?; **leave ~ cake for me** laß mir ein Stück Kuchen übrig.

(c) *(certain, in contrast)* manche(r, s). **~ people say ...** manche Leute sagen ...; **in ~ ways** in gewisser Weise; **to ~ extent** in gewissem Maße.

(d) *(vague, indeterminate)* irgendein. **~ book/man or other** irgendein Buch/Mann; **~ woman rang up** da hat eine Frau angerufen; **in ~ way or another** irgendwie; **or ~ such** oder so etwas ähnliches; **or ~ such name** oder so ein ähnlicher Name; **~ time before midnight** irgendwann vor Mitternacht; **~ time or other** irgendwann einmal; **~ other time** ein andermal; **~ day** eines Tages; **~ day next week** irgendwann nächste Woche.

(e) *(intensifier)* ziemlich; *(in exclamations)* vielleicht ein *(col)*. **(that was) ~ party!** das war vielleicht eine Party! *(col)*; **this might take ~ time** das könnte einige Zeit dauern; **quite ~ time** ziemlich lange; **to speak at ~ length** ziemlich lange sprechen; **it's ~ distance from the house** es ist ziemlich weit vom Haus entfernt.

(f) *(iro)* vielleicht ein *(col)*. **~ experts!** das sind vielleicht Experten! *(col)*; **~ help you are/this is** du bist/das ist mir vielleicht eine Hilfe *(col)*; **~ people!** Leute gibt's!

2 *pron* **(a)** *(~ people)* einige; *(certain people)* manche; *(in "if" clauses, questions)* welche. **~ ..., others ...** manche ..., andere ...; **~ of my friends** einige meiner Freunde; **there are still ~ who will never understand** es gibt immer noch Leute, die das nicht begreifen werden; **do you have ~?** haben Sie welche?

(b) *(referring to plural nouns) (a few)* einige; *(certain ones)* manche; *(in "if" clauses, questions)* welche. **~ of these books** einige dieser Bücher; **they're lovely, try ~** die schmecken gut, probieren Sie mal; **if I've still got ~** wenn ich noch welche habe.

(c) *(referring to singular nouns) (a little)* etwas; *(a certain amount, in contrast)* manches; *(in "if" clauses, questions)* welche(r, s). **I drank ~ of the milk** ich habe (etwas) von der Milch getrunken; **have ~!** nehmen Sie sich *(dat)*, bedienen Sie sich; **it's good cake, would you like ~?** das ist ein guter Kuchen, möchten Sie welchen?; **would you like ~ tea? — no, I've got ~** möchten Sie Tee? — nein, ich habe noch; **~ of it had been eaten** einiges (davon) war gegessen worden; **this is ~ of the finest scenery in Scotland** dies ist eine der schönsten Landschaften Schottlands.

3 *adv* **(a)** ungefähr, etwa, zirka. **~ 20 people** ungefähr 20 Leute; **~ few difficulties** einige Schwierigkeiten. **(b)** *(US col) (a little)* etwas, ein bißchen; *(a lot)* viel. **he's traveling ~** er fährt schnell; **that's going** ~ das ist ganz schön schnell *(col)*.

somebody ['sʌmbədɪ] **1** *pron* jemand; *(dir obj)* jemand(en); *(indir obj)* jemandem. ~ **else** jemand anders; ~ **or other** irgend jemand; ~ **knocked at the door** es klopfte jemand an die Tür; **we need** ~ **German** wir brauchen einen Deutschen; **everybody needs** ~ **to talk to** jeder braucht einen, mit dem er sprechen kann. **2** *n* **to be** ~ wer *(col) or* jemand sein.

somehow ['sʌmhaʊ] *adv* irgendwie. **it must be done** ~ **or other** es muß irgendwie gemacht werden.

someone ['sʌmwʌn] *pron* = **somebody 1.**

someplace ['sʌmpleɪs] *adv (US col) be* irgendwo; *go* irgendwohin.

somersault ['sʌməsɔːlt] **1** *n* Purzelbaum *m*; *(Sport, fig)* Salto *m*. **to do a** ~ einen Purzelbaum schlagen/einen Salto machen; *(car)* sich überschlagen. **2** *vi (person)* einen Purzelbaum schlagen; *(Sport)* einen Salto machen; *(car)* sich überschlagen.

something ['sʌmθɪŋ] **1** *pron* etwas. ~ **serious** *etc* etwas Ernstes; ~ **or other** irgend etwas, irgendwas; ~ **of the kind** so (et)was Ähnliches; **she has a certain** ~ sie hat ein gewisses Etwas; **there's** ~ **in what you say** an dem, was du sagst, ist (schon) was dran; **well, that's** ~ das ist immerhin etwas; **she's called Rachel** ~ sie heißt Rachel Soundso; **it was** ~ **else** *or* **quite** ~ das war schon toll *(col)*; **or** ~ *(col)* oder so (was); **are you drunk or** ~? *(col)* bist du betrunken oder was? *(col)*.

2 *adv* **(a)** ~ **over 200** etwas über 200; ~ **like 200** ungefähr 200; **you look** ~ **like him** du siehst ihm irgendwie ähnlich; **this is** ~ **like the one I wanted** so (et)was Ähnliches wollte ich haben. **(b) it's** ~ **of a problem** das ist schon ein Problem; **I feel** ~ **of a stranger here** ich fühle mich hier irgendwie fremd; **he's** ~ **of a musician** er ist ein recht guter Musiker; ~ **of a surprise/drunkard** eine ziemliche Überraschung/ein ziemlicher Säufer. **(c)** *(dial)* **the weather was** ~ **shocking** das Wetter war einfach schrecklich.

sometime ['sʌmtaɪm] **1** *adv* irgendwann. **write to me** ~ **soon** schreib mir (doch) bald (ein)mal; ~ **next year** irgendwann nächstes Jahr. **2** *adj attr (form)* früher, einstig.

sometimes ['sʌmtaɪmz] *adv* manchmal.

somewhat ['sʌmwɒt] *adv* ein wenig. ~ **of a surprise** eine ziemliche Überraschung.

somewhere ['sʌmwɛəʳ] *adv* **(a)** *be* irgendwo; *go* irgendwohin. **I left it** ~ **or other** ich habe es irgendwo liegen-/stehenlassen; **I know** ~ **where ...** ich weiß, wo ... **(b)** *(fig)* ~ **about £50,** ~ **in the region of £50** um (die) £ 50 herum; **she is** ~ **in her fifties** sie muß in den Fünfzigern sein; ~ **between midnight and one o'clock** irgendwann zwischen Mitternacht und ein Uhr.

somnambulist [sɒm'næmbjʊlɪst] *n* Schlafwandler(in *f*) *m*.

somnolent ['sɒmnələnt] *adj* **(a)** *(sleepy)* schläfrig. **(b)** *(causing sleep)* einschläfernd.

son [sʌn] *n (lit, fig)* Sohn *m*; *(as address)* mein Junge.

sonar ['səʊnɑːʳ] *n* Sonar(gerät), Echolot *nt*.

sonata [sə'nɑːtə] *n* Sonate *f*.

song [sɒŋ] *n* Lied *nt*; *(folk~ also, blues-~)* Song *m*; *(singing)* Gesang *m*. **to burst into** ~ ein Lied anstimmen; **to make a** ~ **and dance about sth** *(col)* eine Haupt- und Staatsaktion aus etw machen *(col)*; **to buy sth for a** ~ *(col)* etw für ein Butterbrot kaufen.

song: ~**bird** *n* Singvogel *m*; ~**book** *n* Liederbuch *nt*.

songwriter ['sɒŋ,raɪtəʳ] *n* Texter(in *f*) und Komponist(in *f*) *m*; *(of modern ballads)* Liedermacher(in *f*) *m*.

sonic ['sɒnɪk] *adj* Schall-. ~ **boom** Überschallknall *m*.

son-in-law ['sʌnɪnlɔː] *n, pl* **sons-in-law** Schwiegersohn *m*.

sonnet ['sɒnɪt] *n* Sonett *nt*.

sonny ['sʌnɪ] *n (col)* (mein) Junge *m*.

sonority [sə'nɒrɪtɪ] *n* Klangfülle *f*.

sonorous ['sɒnərəs] *adj* volltönend, sonor *(geh)*; *language, poem* klangvoll.

soon [suːn] *adv* **(a)** *(in a short time from now)* bald; *(early)* früh; *(quickly)* schnell. **it will** ~ **be Christmas** bald ist Weihnachten; ~ **after his death** kurz nach seinem Tode; ~ **afterwards** kurz *or* bald danach; **how** ~ **can you be ready?** wann kannst du fertig sein?; **how** ~ **is the next performance?** wann fängt die nächste Vorstellung an?; **we got there too** ~ wir kamen zu früh an; **he** ~ **changed his mind** er blieb nicht lange bei seiner Meinung; **all too** ~ viel zu schnell; **we were none too** ~ wir kamen gerade rechtzeitig; **as** ~ **as** sobald; **as** ~ **as possible** so schnell wie möglich. **(b) I would as** ~ **not go** *(prefer not to)* ich würde lieber nicht gehen; **I would as** ~ **you didn't tell him** es wäre mir lieber, wenn du es ihm nicht erzählen würdest.

sooner ['suːnəʳ] *adv* **(a)** *(time)* früher. ~ **or later** früher oder später; **the** ~ **the better** je eher *or* früher, desto besser; **no** ~ **had we arrived than ...** wir waren kaum angekommen, da ...; **no** ~ **said than done** gesagt, getan. **(b)** *(preference)* lieber. **I would** ~ **not do it** ich würde es lieber nicht tun.

soot [sʊt] *n* Ruß *m*. **black as** ~ rußschwarz.

soothe [suːð] *vt* beruhigen; *pain* lindern, mildern.

soothing ['suːðɪŋ] *adj* beruhigend; *(pain-relieving)* schmerzlindernd; *massage* wohltuend.

sooty ['sʊtɪ] *adj (+er)* rußig; *deposit* Ruß-.

sop [sɒp] *n* **(a)** *(food)* eingetunktes Brotstück. **(b)** *(to pacify)* **as a** ~ zur Beschwichtigung.

sophisticated [sə'fɪstɪkeɪtɪd] *adj* **(a)** *(worldly, cultivated)* kultiviert; *person, restaurant also* gepflegt, elegant; *dress* raffiniert, schick. **(b)** *(complex, advanced)* hochentwickelt; *method also* durchdacht; *device also* ausgeklügelt. **(c)** *(subtle, refined)* subtil; *prose, style also, discussion* anspruchsvoll; *plan* ausgeklügelt, raffiniert; *system* differenziert.

sophistication [sə,fɪstɪ'keɪʃən] *n see adj* **(a)** Kultiviertheit *f*; Gepflegtheit, Eleganz *f*; Raffiniertheit *f*, Schick *m*. **(b)** hoher Entwicklungsstand; Durchdachtheit *f*; Ausgeklügeltheit *f*. **(c)** Subtilität *f*; hohe Ansprüche *pl*; Ausgeklügeltheit, Raffiniertheit *f*; Differenziertheit *f*.

sophomore ['sɒfəmɔːʳ] *n (US) Student(in f) m im 2. Jahr.*

soporific [,sɒpə'rɪfɪk] *adj* einschläfernd.

sopping ['sɒpɪŋ] *adj (also* ~ **wet**) durchnäßt; *person* klitschnaß *(col)*.

soppy ['sɒpɪ] *adj (col) (sentimental) book, song* schmalzig *(col)*; *person* sentimental; *look* schmachtend; *(effeminate)* weibisch; *(silly)* doof *(col)*.

soprano [sə'prɑːnəʊ] **1** *n (also part)* Sopran *m*; *(person also)* Sopranist(in *f*) *m*. **2** *adj* Sopran-. **3** *adv* im Sopran.

sorbet ['sɔːbeɪ] *n* Fruchteis *nt*.

sorcerer ['sɔːsərəʳ] *n* Hexenmeister, Hexer *m*.

sorcery ['sɔːsərɪ] *n* Hexerei *f*.

sordid ['sɔːdɪd] *adj* eklig; *place also* verkommen; *motive* niedrig; *conditions, life, story* erbärmlich; *crime* gemein.

sore [sɔːʳ] **1** *adj (+er)* **(a)** *(hurting)* weh; *(inflamed)* wund, entzündet. **to have a** ~ **throat** Halsschmerzen haben; **my eyes are** ~ mir tun die Augen weh. **(b)** *(fig)* **a** ~ **point** ein wunder Punkt. **(c)** *(col: angry, upset)* verärgert, sauer *(col) (about sth* über etw *(acc), at sb* über jdn). **now don't get** ~ **at me** werd doch nicht gleich sauer! *(col)*. **2** *n* wunde Stelle. **to open old** ~**s** *(fig)* alte Wunden aufreißen.

sorely ['sɔːlɪ] *adv tempted* sehr, arg *(S Ger, Aus, Sw)*; *needed* dringend; *missed* schmerzlich; *(liter) afflicted, offended* zutiefst; *wounded* schwer.

sorrel ['sɒrəl] *n* **(a)** *(Bot)* Sauerampfer *m*; *(wood-~)* Sauerklee *m*. **(b)** *(horse)* Fuchs *m*.

sorrow ['sɒrəʊ] *n (no pl: sadness)* Traurigkeit *f*; *(no pl: grief)* Kummer *m*; *(care)* Sorge, Kümmernis *f*; *(affliction)* Leiden *nt*. **this was a great ~ to me** das hat mir großen Kummer bereitet; **her ~ at his death** ihre Trauer über seinen Tod; **to drown one's ~s** seine Sorgen ertränken.

sorrowful ['sɒrəʊfʊl] *adj* traurig.

sorry ['sɒrɪ] *adj (+er)* **(a)** *pred (sad)* traurig. **this work is no good, I'm ~ to say** diese Arbeit taugt nichts, das muß ich leider sagen; **to feel ~ for sb/oneself** jdn/sich selbst bemitleiden; **I feel ~ for the child** das Kind tut mir leid; **you'll be ~ for this!** das wird dir noch leid tun! **(b)** *(in apologizing)* **~!** Entschuldigung!, Verzeihung!; **I'm ~** es tut mir leid; **can you lend me £5? — ~** kannst du mir £5 leihen? — bedaure, leider nicht; **~?** *(pardon)* wie bitte?; **to say ~ (to sb for sth)** sich (bei jdm für etw) entschuldigen; **I'm ~ about that vase/your dog** es tut mir leid wegen der Vase/um Ihren Hund. **(c)** *(pitiful) condition, plight* traurig; *excuse* faul.

sort [sɔːt] **1** *n* **(a)** *(kind)* Art *f*; *(species, type, model also)* Sorte *f*. **a ~ of ...** eine Art ..., so ein(e) ...; **this ~ of house** diese Art Haus; **what ~ of** was für ein; **he's not the ~ of man to do that** er ist nicht der Mensch, der das täte; **this ~ of thing** so etwas; **all ~s of things** alles mögliche; **people of all ~s** alle möglichen Leute; **he's a painter of a ~** *or* **of ~s** er ist Maler, sozusagen; **something of the ~** (irgend) so (et)was; **nothing of the ~!** von wegen!; **you'll do nothing of the ~!** das wirst du schön bleiben lassen! **(b)** *(person)* **he's a good ~** er ist ein prima Kerl; **he's not my ~** er ist nicht mein Typ; **I don't trust his ~** solchen Leuten traue ich nicht; **I know your ~** euch Brüder kenn' ich! *(col)*; **it takes all ~s (to make a world)** es gibt solche und solche. **(c) to be out of ~s** nicht ganz auf der Höhe sein.

2 *adv* **~ of** *(col)* irgendwie; **it's ~ of heavy** es ist irgendwie schwer *(col)*; **is this how he did it? — well, ~ of** hat er das so gemacht? — ja, so ungefähr.

3 *vt (also Comp)* sortieren.

♦ **sort out** *vt sep* **(a)** *(arrange)* sortieren; *(select)* aussortieren. **to ~ sth ~ from sth** etw von etw trennen. **(b)** *(straighten out) muddle* in Ordnung bringen; *problem* lösen; *situation* klären. **the problem will ~ itself ~** das Problem wird sich von selbst lösen; **to ~ oneself ~** zur Ruhe kommen. **(c)** *(col)* **to ~ sb ~** sich *(dat)* jdn vorknöpfen *(col)*.

sortie ['sɔːtɪ] *n (Mil)* Ausfall *m*; *(Aviat)* (Einzel)einsatz *m*.

sorting office ['sɔːtɪŋ'ɒfɪs] *n* Sortierstelle *f*.

SOS *n* SOS *nt*.

so-so ['səʊ'səʊ] *adj pred, adv (col)* so la la.

soufflé ['suːfleɪ] *n* Soufflé *nt*.

sought [sɔːt] *pret, ptp of* **seek.**

sought-after ['sɔːtɑːftəʳ] *adj* begehrt. **much ~** vielbegehrt; *rare object* gesucht.

soul [səʊl] *n* **(a)** Seele *f*. **All S~s' Day** Allerheiligen *nt*; **God rest his ~!** Gott hab ihn selig! **(b)** *(inner being)* Innerste(s), Wesen *nt*; *(finer feelings)* Herz, Gefühl *nt*. **he loved her with all his ~** er liebte sie von ganzem Herzen. **(c)** *(person)* Seele *f*. **poor ~!** *(col)* Ärmste(r)!; **not a ~** keine Menschenseele; **the ship was lost with all ~s** das Schiff ging mit allen Passagieren unter; **he's the ~ of discretion** er ist die Diskretion in Person. **(d)** *(music)* Soul *m*.

soul-destroying ['səʊldɪˌstrɔɪɪŋ] *adj* geisttötend; *factory work etc* nervtötend.

soulful ['səʊlfʊl] *adj look* seelenvoll; *person* gefühlvoll.

soul: ~mate *n* **they are ~mates** sie sind verwandte Seelen; **~-searching** *n* Gewissensprüfung *f*.

sound[1] [saʊnd] **1** *adj (+er)* **(a)** *(in good condition) person, animal* gesund; *condition, building, appliance* einwandfrei. **to be as ~ as a bell** kerngesund sein; **to be of ~ mind** *(esp Jur)* bei klarem Verstand sein, im Vollbesitz seiner geistigen Kräfte sein *(Jur)*. **(b)** *(valid, dependable)* solide; *argument, analysis also* vernünftig, fundiert; *economy also* stabil; *person* verläßlich; *idea, move, advice* vernünftig. **to be ~ on sth** *(have good knowledge)* gründliche Kenntnisse in etw *(dat)* haben. **(c)** *(thorough)* gründlich; *beating* gehörig; *defeat* vernichtend. **(d)** *(Jur) decision* rechtmäßig. **(e)** *(deep) sleep* tief, fest. **2** *adv (+er)* **to be ~ asleep** fest schlafen.

sound[2] **1** *n* *(noise)* Geräusch *nt*; *(Ling)* Laut *m*; *(Phys)* Schall *m*; *(Mus, of instruments)* Klang *m*; *(TV, Rad)* Ton *m*. **don't make a ~** still!; **the speed of ~** (die) Schallgeschwindigkeit; **within ~ of** in Hörweite *(+gen)*; **to the ~(s) of the national anthem** zu den Klängen der Nationalhymne; **not a ~ was to be heard** man hörte keinen Ton; **~s/the ~ of laughter** Gelächter *nt*; **we heard the ~ of voices on the terrace** wir hörten Stimmen auf der Terrasse; **I don't like the ~ of it** das klingt gar nicht gut.

2 *vt* **(a) ~ your horn** hupen!; **to ~ the alarm** Alarm schlagen; *(mechanism)* die Alarmanlage auslösen; **to ~ the retreat** zum Rückzug blasen; **to ~ the "r" in "cover"** das „r" in „cover" aussprechen; **his speech ~ed a note of warning** in seiner Rede klang eine Warnung an. **(b)** *(test by tapping, Med)* abklopfen.

3 *vi* **(a)** *(emit ~)* erklingen, ertönen. **feet ~ed in the corridor** im Flur waren Schritte zu hören. **(b)** *(give impression)* klingen, sich anhören. **it ~s hollow** es klingt hohl; **the children ~ happy** es hört sich so an, als ob die Kinder ganz vergnügt sind; **he ~s French (to me)** er hört sich (für mich) wie ein Franzose an; **that ~s very odd** das hört sich sehr seltsam an; **he ~s like a nice man** er scheint ein netter Mensch zu sein; **it ~s like a sensible idea** das klingt ganz vernünftig.

♦ **sound off** *vi (col)* sich auslassen *(about* über *+acc)*.

sound[3] *vt (Naut)* loten, ausloten. **to ~ sb (out) on sth** bei jdm in bezug auf etw *(acc)* vorfühlen.

sound[4] *n (Geog)* Meerenge *f*, Sund *m*.

sound: ~ archives *npl* Tonarchiv *nt*; **~ barrier** *n* Schallmauer *f*; **~ effects** *npl* Toneffekte *pl*; **~ engineer** *n* Toningenieur(in *f*) *m*.

sounding ['saʊndɪŋ] *n (Naut)* Loten *nt*, Peilung *f*. **to take ~s** *(lit)* Lotungen vornehmen; *(fig)* sondieren.

soundless ['saʊndlɪs] *adj* lautlos.

soundly ['saʊndlɪ] *adv built, made* solide; *argue, invest also* vernünftig; *thrash* tüchtig, gehörig. **our team was ~ beaten** unsere Mannschaft wurde eindeutig geschlagen; **to sleep ~** tief und fest schlafen.

sound: ~-proof 1 *adj* schalldicht; **2** *vt* schalldicht machen; **~-track** *n* Ton *m*; Filmmusik *f*, Soundtrack *m*; **~-wave** *n* Schallwelle *f*.

soup [suːp] *n* Suppe *f*. **to be in the ~** *(col)* in der Tinte sitzen *(col)*.

♦ **soup up** *vt sep (col) car* frisieren *(col)*.

soupçon ['suːpsɔ̃ːŋ] *n (of spice etc)* Spur *f*; *(of irony etc)* Anflug *m*.

soup: ~-kitchen *n* Volksküche *f*; *(for disaster area etc)* Feldküche *f*; **~-plate** *n* Suppenteller *m*; **~ spoon** *n* Suppenlöffel *m*.

sour ['saʊəʳ] *adj (+er)* **(a)** *fruit* sauer; *wine* säuerlich. **(b)** *(bad) milk* sauer; *smell* säuerlich. **to go ~** *(lit)* sauer werden; *(fig) (relationship, marriage)* sich radikal verschlechtern; *(plan, investment)* sich als Fehlschlag erweisen. **(c)** *(fig) person* verdrießlich, griesgrämig; *remark* bissig. **he's feeling ~ about being demoted** er ist über seine Absetzung verbittert; **it's just ~ grapes** die Trauben hängen zu hoch.

source [sɔːs] *n (of river, light, information)* Quelle *f*; *(of troubles, problems etc)* Ursache *f*. **a ~ of vitamin C** ein Vitamin-C-Spender *m*; **I have it from a good ~ that ...** ich habe es aus sicherer Quelle, daß ...; **at ~** *(Tax)* unmittelbar, direkt; **from reliable ~s** aus zuverlässiger Quelle.

souse [saʊs] *vt* übergießen. **he ~d himself with water** er übergoß sich mit Wasser.

south [saʊθ] **1** *n* Süden *m*. **in the ~ of** im Süden *+gen*; **to the ~ of** im Süden *or* südlich von; **from the ~** aus dem Süden; *(wind)* aus Süden; **to veer to the ~** nach Süden drehen; **the S~ of France** Südfrankreich *nt*. **2** *adj* südlich, Süd-; *(in names)* Süd-. **3** *adv* im Süden; *(towards the ~)* nach Süden. **to be further ~** weiter südlich sein; **~ of** südlich von, im Süden von.

south *in cpds* Süd-; **S~ Africa** *n* Südafrika *nt*; **S~ African 1** *adj* südafrikanisch; **2** *n* Südafrikaner(in *f*) *m*; **S~ America** *n* Südamerika *nt*; **S~ American 1** *adj* südamerikanisch; **2** *n* Südamerikaner(in *f*) *m*; **~bound** *adj* (in) Richtung Süden; **~-east 1** *n* Südosten, *m*; **2** *adj* südöstlich; *(in names)* Südost-; **3** *adv* nach Südosten; **~-east of** südöstlich von; **~-easterly** *adj direction* südöstlich; **~-easterly wind** Südostwind *m*; **~-eastern** *adj* südöstlich, im Südosten.

southerly ['sʌðəlɪ] *adj* südlich; *wind* aus südlicher Richtung.

southern ['sʌðən] *adj* südlich; *(in names)* Süd-; *(Mediterranean)* südländisch. **S~ Africa** das südliche Afrika; **S~ Europe** Südeuropa *nt*; **S~ Ireland** (Süd)irland *nt*; **S~ States** Südstaaten *pl*.

southerner ['sʌðənəʳ] *n* Bewohner(in *f*) *m* des Südens; Südengländer(in *f*) *m*/-deutsche(r) *mf etc*; *(from the Mediterranean)* Südländer(in *f*) *m*; *(US)* Südstaatler(in *f*) *m*.

southernmost ['sʌðənməʊst] *adj* südlichste(r, s).

south: S~ Pole *n* Südpol *m*; **~ward(s) 1** *adj* südlich; **2** *adv* nach Süden, südwärts; **~-west 1** *n* Südwesten *m*; **2** *adj* Südwest-, südwestlich; *wind* aus südwestlicher Richtung; **3** *adv* nach Südwest(en); **~-west of** südwestlich von; **~-westerly** *adj* südwestlich; *wind* Südwest-; **~-western** *adj* südwestlich.

souvenir [ˌsuːvə'nɪəʳ] *n* Andenken, Souvenir *nt (of* an *+acc)*.

sou'wester [saʊ'westəʳ] *n (hat)* Südwester *m*.

sovereign ['sɒvrɪn] **1** *n (monarch)* Souverän *m*, Herrscher(in *f*) *m*; *(Brit old: coin)* 20-Shilling-Münze *f*. **2** *adj (supreme)* höchste(r, s), oberste(r, s); *state, power* souverän; *contempt* tiefste(r, s), äußerste(r, s).

sovereignty ['sɒvrəntɪ] *n* Oberhoheit *f*; *(right of self-determination)* Souveränität *f*.

soviet ['səʊvɪət] **1** *n* Sowjet *m*. **the S~s** *(people)* die Sowjets. **2** *adj attr* sowjetisch, Sowjet-. **the S~ Union** *n* die Sowjetunion.

sow[1] [səʊ] *pret* **~ed**, *ptp* **~n** *or* **~ed** *vt* **(a)** *corn, plants* säen; *seed* aussäen; *(Mil) mine* legen. **(b)** *(fig)* **to ~ (the seeds of) hatred/discord/rebellion** Haß/Zwietracht säen/Aufruhr stiften.

sow[2] [saʊ] *n* Sau *f*.

sown [səʊn] *ptp of* **sow**[1].

soya ['sɔɪə], *(US)* **soy** [sɔɪ] *n* Soja *f*. **~ bean** Sojabohne *f*; **~ sauce** Sojasoße *f*.

sozzled ['sɒzld] *adj (Brit col)* **to be ~** einen sitzen haben *(col)*; **to get ~** beschwipst werden *(col)*.

spa [spɑː] *n (town)* Kurort *m*; *(spring)* (Mineral)quelle *f*.

space [speɪs] **1** *n* **(a)** Raum *m (also Phys)*; *(outer ~ also)* der Weltraum, das Weltall. **to stare into ~** ins Leere starren. **(b)** *no pl (room)* Platz, Raum *m*. **to take up a lot of ~** viel Platz einnehmen; **to clear/leave some ~ for sb/sth** für jdn/etw Platz schaffen/lassen; **to buy ~** *(Press)* Platz für Anzeigen kaufen; **parking ~** Platz *m* zum Parken. **(c)** *(gap, empty area)* Platz *m no art*; *(between objects, words, lines)* Zwischenraum *m*; *(parking ~)* Lücke *f*. **please answer in the ~ provided** bitte an der dafür vorgesehenen Stelle beantworten. **(d)** *(of time)* Zeitraum *m*. **in a short ~ of time** in kurzer Zeit; **in the ~ of one hour** innerhalb einer Stunde.

2 *vt (also* **~ out***)* in Abständen verteilen; *visits* verteilen; *words* Abstand lassen zwischen *(+dat)*.

space *in cpds* (Welt)raum-; **~ age** *n* Weltraumzeitalter *nt*; **~-age** *adj attr* des Weltraumzeitalters; **~-bar** *n (Typ)* Leertaste *f*; **~craft** *n* Raumfahrzeug *nt*; *(unmanned)* Raumkörper *m*; **~ heater** *n (esp US)* Heizgerät *nt*; **~man** *n* (Welt)raumfahrer *m*; **~ rocket** *n* Weltraumrakete *f*; **~-saving** *adj equipment, gadget* platzsparend; **~ship** *n* Raumschiff *nt*; **~ shuttle** *n* Raumfähre *f*; **~ station** *n* (Welt)raumstation *f*; **~ suit** *n* Raumanzug *m*; **~ travel** *n* die Raumfahrt; **~ walk** *n* Weltraumspaziergang *m*.

spacing ['speɪsɪŋ] *n* Abstände *pl*; *(between two objects)* Abstand *m*; *(also* **~ out***)* Verteilung *f*; *(of payments)* Verteilung *f* über längere Zeit. **double ~** *(Typ)* zweizeiliger Abstand.

spacious ['speɪʃəs] *adj* geräumig; *park* weitläufig.

spade [speɪd] *n* **(a)** *(tool)* Spaten *m*; *(children's ~)* Schaufel *f*. **to call a ~ a ~** *(prov)* das Kind beim Namen nennen *(prov)*. **(b)** *(Cards)* Pik *nt*. **the Queen/two of S~s** die Pik-Dame/Pik-Zwei.

spadework ['speɪdwɜːk] *n (fig)* Vorarbeit *f*.

spaghetti [spə'getɪ] *n* Spaghetti *pl*.

Spain [speɪn] *n* Spanien *nt*.

span[1] [spæn] **1** *n* **(a)** *(of hand)* Spanne *f*; *(wing~, of bridge etc)* Spannweite *f*. **a single-~ bridge** eine eingespannte Bogenbrücke. **(b)** *(time ~)* Zeitspanne *f*; *(of memory)* Gedächtnisspanne *f*; *(of attention)* Konzentrationsspanne *f*; *(range)* Umfang *m*. **2** *vt (rope, rainbow)* sich spannen über *(+acc)*; *(plank)* führen über *(+acc)*; *(Mus) octave etc* greifen; *(encircle)* umfassen; *(in time)* sich erstrecken über *(+acc)*.

span[2] *(old) pret of* **spin.**

Spaniard ['spænjəd] *n* Spanier(in *f*) *m*.

spaniel ['spænjəl] *n* Spaniel *m*.

Spanish ['spænɪʃ] **1** *adj* spanisch. **the ~** die Spanier *pl*. **2** *n (language)* Spanisch *nt*.

Spanish onion *n* Gemüsezwiebel *f*.

spank [spæŋk] **1** *n* Klaps *m*. **to give sb a ~** jdm einen Klaps geben; *(spanking)* jdm den Hintern versohlen. **2** *vt* versohlen.

spanner ['spænəʳ] *n (Brit)* Schraubenschlüssel *m*. **to throw a ~ in the works** *(fig)* jdm Knüppel zwischen die Beine werfen *(col)*; **that's a real ~ in the works** das ist wirklich ein Hemmschuh.

spar[1] [spɑːʳ] *n (Naut)* Rundholz *nt*.

spar[2] *vi (Boxing)* ein Sparring *nt* machen; *(fig)* sich kabbeln *(col) (about* um*)*. **~ring partner** *(lit, fig)* Sparringpartner *m*.

spare [speəʳ] **1** *adj* **(a)** den/die/das man nicht braucht, übrig *pred*; *(surplus)* überzählig, übrig *pred*; *bed, room* Gäste-; *(replacement) part etc* Ersatz-. **have you any ~ string?** kannst du mir (einen) Bindfaden geben?; **I can give you a racket, I have a ~ one** ich kann dir einen Schläger geben, ich habe noch einen; **take some ~ clothes** nehmen Sie Kleider zum Wechseln mit; **it's all the ~ cash I have** mehr Bargeld habe ich nicht übrig; **should you have any ~ time** sollten Sie noch Zeit haben; **we have two ~ seats** wir haben zwei Plätze übrig. **(b) to go ~** *(col)* durchdrehen *(col)*.

2 *n* Ersatzteil *nt*.

3 *vt* **(a)** *usu neg (grudge)* **we must ~ no effort in trying to finish this job** wir dürfen keine Mühe scheuen, um diese Arbeit zu erledigen; **no ex-**

pense was ~d es wurden keine Kosten gescheut.

(b) to ~ sb sth *(give)* jdm etw überlassen *or* geben; *money* jdm etw geben; **can you ~ the time to do it?** haben Sie Zeit, das zu machen?; **I can ~ you five minutes** ich habe fünf Minuten Zeit für Sie (übrig); **to have sth to ~** etw übrig haben; **there are three to ~** es sind drei übrig; **to have a few minutes to ~** ein paar Minuten Zeit haben; **I got to the airport with two minutes to ~** ich war zwei Minuten vor Abflug am Flughafen.

(c) *(do without) person, object* entbehren, verzichten auf *(+acc)*. **I can't ~ it** ich kann es nicht entbehren, ich kann darauf nicht verzichten; **can you ~ this for a moment?** kannst du mir das kurz geben?; **to ~ a thought for sb/sth** an jdn/etw denken.

(d) *(show mercy to)* verschonen; *(refrain from upsetting) sb, sb's feelings* schonen.

(e) *(save)* **to ~ sb/oneself sth** jdm/sich etw ersparen; **~ me the details** verschone mich mit den Einzelheiten; **to ~ him embarrassment** um ihn nicht in Verlegenheit zu bringen.

spare: ~ part *n* Ersatzteil *nt*; **~ room** *n* Gästezimmer *nt*; **~ time 1** *n (leisure time)* Freizeit *f*; **2** *adj attr* Freizeit-; **~ tyre** *(Brit) or* **tire** *(US) n* Ersatzreifen *m*; *(fig col)* Rettungsring *m (col)*; **~ wheel** *n* Ersatzrad *nt*.

sparing ['spɛərɪŋ] *adj* sparsam. **to be ~ of (one's) praise** mit Lob geizen.

sparingly ['spɛərɪŋlɪ] *adv* sparsam; *spend, drink, eat* in Maßen. **to use sth ~** mit etw sparsam umgehen.

spark [spɑːk] **1** *n (from fire, Elec)* Funke *m*; *(fig: glimmer)* Fünkchen *nt*, Funke(n) *m*. **not a ~ of life** kein Fünkchen Leben; **when the ~s start to fly** *(fig)* wenn die Funken anfangen zu fliegen; **a bright ~** *(iro)* ein Intelligenzbolzen *m (iro)*. **2** *vt (also* **~ off***)* entzünden; *explosion* verursachen; *(fig)* auslösen; *interest, enthusiasm* wecken. **3** *vi* Funken sprühen; *(Elec)* zünden.

spark(ing) plug ['spɑːk(ɪŋ)'plʌg] *n* Zündkerze *f*.

sparkle ['spɑːkl] **1** *n* Funkeln *nt*. **he lacks ~** ihm fehlt der (rechte) Schwung. **2** *vi* funkeln *(with* vor *+dat)*; *(fig: person)* vor Leben(sfreude) sprühen; *(with intelligence, wit etc)* brillieren.

sparkling ['spɑːklɪŋ] *adj lights* glänzend, funkelnd; *eyes* funkelnd; *wit* sprühend; *(lively) person* vor Leben sprühend; *(witty) person, speech* vor Geist sprühend; *(bubbling) lemonade etc* perlend; **~ wine** *(as type)* Schaumwein *m*; *(slightly ~)* Perlwein *m*.

sparrow ['spærəʊ] *n* Sperling, Spatz *m*.

sparse [spɑːs] *adj (+er)* spärlich; *covering, population* dünn; *(infrequent) references also* rar.

sparsely ['spɑːslɪ] *adv* spärlich; *wooded also, populated* dünn.

spartan ['spɑːtən] *adj (fig)* spartanisch.

spasm ['spæzəm] *n (Med)* Krampf *m*; *(of asthma, coughing, fig)* Anfall *m*. **to work in ~s** sporadisch arbeiten.

spasmodic [spæz'mɒdɪk] *adj (Med)* krampfartig; *(fig: occasional)* sporadisch; *growth* schubweise.

spastic ['spæstɪk] **1** *adj* spastisch. **2** *n* Spastiker(in *f*) *m*.

spat *pret, ptp of* **spit**[1].

spate [speɪt] *n (of river)* Hochwasser *nt*; *(fig) (of letters, orders etc)* Flut *f*; *(of burglaries, accidents)* Serie *f*; *(of words, abuse)* Schwall *m*. **the river is in (full) ~** der Fluß führt Hochwasser.

spatial ['speɪʃəl] *adj* räumlich.

spatter ['spætəʳ] *vt* bespritzen. **to ~ water over sb, to ~ sb with water** jdn naß spritzen.

spatula ['spætjʊlə] *n* Spachtel *m*; *(Med)* Spatel *m*.

spawn [spɔːn] **1** *n (of fish, frogs)* Laich *m*. **2** *vi* laichen. **3** *vt (fig)* erzeugen.

speak [spiːk] *pret* **spoke,** *ptp* **spoken 1** *vt* **(a)** *(utter)* sagen; *one's thoughts* äußern; *one's lines* aufsagen. **to ~ one's mind** seine Meinung sagen; **nobody spoke a word** niemand sagte ein Wort. **(b)** *language* sprechen. **English spoken here** hier spricht man Englisch.

2 *vi* **(a)** *(talk, be on ~ing terms)* sprechen, reden *(about* über *+acc,* von; *on* zu*)*; *(converse)* reden, sich unterhalten *(with* mit*)*; *(give opinion)* sich äußern *(on, to* zu*)*. **to ~ to** *or* **with sb** mit jdm sprechen; **did you ~?** haben Sie etwas gesagt?; **to ~ in a whisper** flüstern; **I'm not ~ing to you** mit dir rede ich nicht mehr; **I'll ~ to him about it** *(euph: tell off)* ich werde ein Wörtchen mit ihm reden; **I don't know him to ~ to** ich kenne ihn nicht näher; **~ing of dictionaries ...** da wir gerade von Wörterbüchern sprechen ...; **not to ~ of ...** ganz zu schweigen von ...; **it's nothing to ~ of** es ist nicht weiter erwähnenswert; **no money** *etc* **to ~ of** so gut wie kein Geld *etc*; **to ~ well of sb/sth** Gutes über jdn/etw sagen; **so to ~** sozusagen; **strictly ~ing** genau genommen; **legally ~ing** rechtlich gesehen; **generally ~ing** im allgemeinen; **~ing personally ...** was mich betrifft ...

(b) to ~ in public in der Öffentlichkeit reden; **to ~ in the debate** in der Debatte das Wort ergreifen; **to ask sb to ~** jdm das Wort erteilen.

(c) *(Telec)* **~ing!** am Apparat!; **Jones ~ing!** (hier) Jones!; **who is ~ing?** wer ist da, bitte?; *(on extension phone, in office)* wer ist am Apparat?

♦ **speak against** *vi +prep obj (in debate)* sich aussprechen gegen; *(criticize)* kritisieren.

♦ **speak for** *vi +prep obj* **(a)** *(in debate)* unterstützen. **(b) to ~ ~ sb** *(on behalf of)* in jds Namen *(dat)* sprechen; *(in favour of)* ein gutes Wort für jdn einlegen; **~ing ~ myself ...** was mich angeht ...; **let her ~ ~ herself** laß sie selbst reden; **~ ~ yourself!** *(I don't agree)* das meinst auch nur du!; *(don't include me)* du vielleicht!; **to ~ well/badly ~ sth** ein Beweis *m*/nicht gerade ein Beweis für etw sein; **to ~ ~ itself** *(be obvious)* für sich sprechen; **that's already spoken ~** das ist schon vergeben.

♦ **speak out** *vi (audibly)* deutlich sprechen; *(give opinion)* seine Meinung deutlich vertreten. **to ~ ~ against sth** sich gegen etw aussprechen.

♦ **speak up** *vi* **(a)** *(raise one's voice)* lauter sprechen; *(talk loudly)* laut (und verständlich) sprechen. **(b)** *(fig)* seine Meinung sagen *or* äußern. **don't be afraid to ~ ~** sagen Sie ruhig Ihre Meinung; **to ~ ~ for sb/sth** für jdn/etw eintreten.

speaker ['spiːkəʳ] *n* **(a)** *(of language)* Sprecher *m*. **all ~s of German** alle Deutschsprechenden. **(b)** Sprecher(in *f*) *m*; *(in discussion also, in lecture)* Redner(in *f*) *m*. **the last** *or* **previous ~** der Vorredner; **our ~ today is ...** der heutige Referent ist ... **(c)** *(loud~, in record-player)* Lautsprecher *m*; *(on hi-fi etc)* Box *f*. **(d)** *(Parl)* **S~** Sprecher *m*.

speaking ['spiːkɪŋ] *n (act of ~)* Sprechen *nt*; *(speeches)* Reden *pl*.

-speaking *adj suf* -sprechend; *(with native language also)* -sprachig.

speaking: ~ clock *n (Brit)* Zeitansage *f*; **~ terms** *npl* **to be on ~ terms with sb** mit jdm reden.

spear [spɪəʳ] *n* Speer *m*.

spearhead ['spɪəˌhed] **1** *n (of spear)* Speerspitze *f*; *(Mil)* Angriffsspitze *f*; *(fig: person, thing)* Bahnbrecher *m (of* für*)*. **2** *vt (lit, fig)* anführen.

spec [spek] *n (col)* **on ~** auf gut Glück.

special ['speʃəl] **1** *adj* **(a)** besondere(r, s); *(specific, exceptional) purpose, use, friend, favour, occasion also* speziell. **I have no ~ person in mind** ich habe eigentlich an niemanden Bestimmtes gedacht; **take ~ care of it** passen Sie besonders gut darauf auf; **nothing ~** nichts Besonderes; **he expects ~ treatment** er will besonders behandelt werden; **what's so ~ about her?** was ist denn an ihr so besonders?; **what's so ~ about that?** na und? *(col)*, das ist doch nichts Besonderes! **(b)** *(out of the ordinary) permission, edition, powers* Sonder-; *subject, dictionary* Spezial-. ~ **feature** *(Press)* Sonderartikel *m*. **2** *n (constable)* Hilfspolizist(in *f*) *m*; *(train)* Sonderzug *m*; *(Cook)* Tagesgericht *nt*; *(edition)* Sonderausgabe *f*.

special: ~ **agent** *n (spy)* Agent(in *f*) *m*; **S~ Branch** *n (Brit)* Sicherheitspolizei *f*; ~ **case** *n (also Jur)* Sonderfall *m*; ~ **correspondent** *n (Press)* Sonderberichterstatter(in *f*) *m*; ~ **delivery** *n* Eilzustellung *f*; **by ~ delivery** durch Eilboten; ~ **effects** *npl* Tricks *pl*.

specialist ['speʃəlɪst] **1** *n* Fachmann *m (in* für*)*; *(Med)* Spezialist(in *f*) *m*, Facharzt *m*/-ärztin *f (in* für*)*. **2** *adj attr knowledge, dictionary* Fach-.

speciality [ˌspeʃɪ'ælɪtɪ], *(US)* **specialty** ['speʃəltɪ] *n* Spezialität; *(subject also)* Spezialgebiet *nt*. **to make a ~ of sth** sich auf etw *(acc)* spezialisieren.

specialize ['speʃəlaɪz] *vi* sich spezialisieren *(in* auf *+acc)*. **we ~ in ...** wir haben uns auf ... spezialisiert.

specialized ['speʃəlaɪzd] *adj* spezialisiert. **a ~ knowledge of biology** Fachkenntnisse *pl* in Biologie.

specially ['speʃəlɪ] *adv* besonders; *(specifically)* speziell, extra. **a ~ difficult task** eine besonders schwierige Aufgabe; **I had it ~ made** ich habe es extra machen lassen.

special: ~ **offer** *n* Sonderangebot *nt*; ~ **school** *n* Sonderschule *f*; *(for physically handicapped)* Behindertenschule *f*.

specialty ['speʃəltɪ] *n (US)* = **speciality.**

species ['spiːʃiːz] *n, pl* - Art *f*; *(Biol also)* Spezies *f*.

specific [spə'sɪfɪk] **1** *adj* **(a)** *(definite)* speziell; *(precise) statement, instructions* genau; *example* ganz bestimmt. **9.3, to be ~** 9,3, um genau zu sein; **can you be a bit more ~?** können Sie sich etwas genauer äußern? **(b)** *(Sci)* spezifisch. ~ **gravity** spezifisches Gewicht. **2** *n* **~s** *pl* nähere Einzelheiten *pl*.

specifically [spə'sɪfɪkəlɪ] *adv warn, order, state* ausdrücklich; *(specially) designed, request* speziell; *(precisely)* genau.

specification [ˌspesɪfɪ'keɪʃən] *n (detail)* Angabe *f*; *(stipulation)* Bedingung *f*; *(of requirements)* genaue Angabe; *(for patent)* (genaue) Beschreibung; *(design) (for car, machine)* (detaillierter) Entwurf; *(for building)* Bauplan *m*. **~s** *pl* genaue Angaben *pl*; *(of car, machine)* technische Daten *pl*; *(of new building)* Baubeschreibung *f*.

specify ['spesɪfaɪ] **1** *vt* angeben; *(list)* (einzeln) aufführen; *(stipulate)* vorschreiben; *(blueprint, contract etc)* vorsehen. **2** *vi* genaue Angaben machen. **unless otherwise specified** wenn nicht anders angegeben.

specimen ['spesɪmɪn] **1** *n* Exemplar *nt*; *(of urine, blood etc)* Probe *f*; *(sample)* Muster *nt*. **a beautiful** *or* **fine ~** ein Prachtexemplar *nt*; **you're a pretty poor ~** *(col)* du hast ja nicht viel zu bieten *(col)*. **2** *adj attr page* Probe-. **a ~ copy** ein Probeexemplar *nt*; **a ~ signature** eine Unterschriftenprobe.

specious ['spiːʃəs] *adj argument* vordergründig bestechend, Schein-; *claim* fadenscheinig.

speck [spek] *n* Fleck *(m*; *(of blood, paint also)* Spritzer *m*; *(of dust)* Körnchen *nt*; *(of soot)* Flocke *f*; *(of gold, colour etc)* Sprenkel *m*. **a ~ on the horizon** ein Punkt *m* am Horizont.

speckle ['spekl] *vt* sprenkeln. **to be ~d with sth** mit etw gesprenkelt sein.

specs [speks] *npl (col)* Brille *f*.

spectacle ['spektəkl] *n* **(a)** *(show)* Schauspiel *nt*. **a sad ~** ein trauriger Anblick; **to make a ~ of oneself** unangenehm auffallen. **(b) ~s** *pl (also* **pair of ~s***)* Brille *f*.

spectacle case *n* Brillenetui *nt*.

spectacular [spek'tækjʊləʳ] **1** *adj* sensationell; *improvement, success also* spektakulär. **2** *n (Theat)* Show *f*.

spectator [spek'teɪtəʳ] *n* Zuschauer(in *f*) *m*. ~ **sport** Publikumssport *m*.

spectre, *(US)* **specter** ['spektəʳ] *n* Gespenst *nt*; *(fig)* (Schreck)gespenst *nt*.

spectrum ['spektrəm] *n, pl* **spectra** Spektrum *nt*; *(fig: range also)* Skala *f*.

speculate ['spekjʊleɪt] *vi* **(a)** Überlegungen anstellen, spekulieren *(about, on* über *+acc)*. **(b)** *(Fin)* spekulieren *(in* mit, *on* an *+dat)*.

speculation [ˌspekjʊ'leɪʃən] *n* Spekulation *f (on* über *+acc)*; *(guesswork also)* Vermutung *f*. **it is the subject of much ~** darüber sind viele Vermutungen angestellt worden.

speculative ['spekjʊlətɪv] *adj* **(a)** spekulativ; *ideas* rein theoretisch. **(b)** *(Fin)* Spekulations-.

speculator ['spekjʊleɪtəʳ] *n* Spekulant(in *f*) *m*.

sped [sped] *pret, ptp of* **speed.**

speech [spiːtʃ] *n no pl* Sprache *f*; *(act of speaking)* Sprechen *nt*; *(manner of speaking)* Sprechweise *f*; *(oration, Theat)* Rede *f (on, about* über *+acc)*; *(address)* Ansprache *f*. **to lose/recover the power of ~** die Sprache verlieren/zurückgewinnen; **freedom of ~** Redefreiheit *f*; **to give** *or* **make a ~** eine Rede *etc* halten; **direct/indirect** *or* **reported ~** *(Brit Gram)* direkte/indirekte Rede.

speech: ~ **day** *n (Brit)* Schulfeier *f*; ~ **defect,** ~ **impediment** *n* Sprachfehler *m*.

speechless ['spiːtʃlɪs] *adj (at a loss for words)* sprachlos *(with* vor *+dat)*; *anger* stumm. **his remark left me ~** seine Bemerkung verschlug mir die Sprache.

speech: ~ **therapist** *n* Logopäde *m*, Logopädin *f*; ~ **therapy** *n* Sprachtherapie *f*; *(treatment)* logopädische Behandlung.

speed [spiːd] *(vb: pret, ptp* **sped** *or* **~ed***)* **1** *n* **(a)** Geschwindigkeit *f*; *(fast ~ also)* Schnelligkeit *f*; *(of moving object or person also)* Tempo *nt*. **at ~** äußerst schnell; **at a high/low ~** mit hoher/niedriger Geschwindigkeit; **at full** *or* **top ~** mit Höchstgeschwindigkeit; **at a ~ of 50 mph** mit einem Tempo von 50 Meilen pro Stunde; **at the ~ of light** mit Lichtgeschwindigkeit; **to pick up** *or* **gather ~** schneller werden; *(fig: development)* sich beschleunigen; **to lose ~** (an) Geschwindigkeit verlieren; **what ~ were you doing?** wie schnell sind Sie gefahren? **(b)** *(Aut, Tech: gear)* Gang *m*. **a three-~ gear** ein Dreiganggetriebe *nt*. **(c)** *(Phot) (film ~)* Lichtempfindlichkeit *f*; *(shutter ~)* Belichtungszeit *f*.

2 *vt* **to ~ sb on his way** *(person)* jdn verabschieden; *(iro)* jdn hinauskomplimentieren; *(good wishes etc)* jdn auf seinem Weg begleiten.

3 *vi* **(a)** *pret, ptp* **sped** *(move quickly)* jagen; *(arrow)* sausen. **the years sped by** die Jahre vergingen wie im Fluge. **(b)** *pret, ptp* **~ed** *(Aut: exceed ~ limit)* zu schnell fahren.

♦ **speed up** *pret, ptp* **~ed ~ 1** *vi (car, driver etc)* beschleunigen; *(person)* Tempo zulegen; *(work, production etc)* schneller werden. **2** *vt sep* beschleunigen; *person* antreiben; *research also* vorantreiben.

speedboat ['spiːdbəʊt] *n* Rennboot *nt*.

speeding ['spiːdɪŋ] *n* Geschwindigkeitsüberschreitung *f*.

speed limit *n* Geschwindigkeitsbegrenzung *f*. **a 30 mph ~** eine Geschwindigkeitsbegrenzung von 50 km/h.

speedometer [spɪ'dɒmɪtəʳ] *n* Tachometer *m*.

speed: ~ **trap** *n* Radarfalle *f (col)*; **~way** *n* **(a)** *(Sport)* Speedwayrennen *nt*; *(track)* Speedwayrennbahn *f*; **(b)** *(US) (race-track)* Rennstrecke *f*; *(expressway)* Schnellstraße *f*.

speedy ['spiːdɪ] *adj (+er)* schnell; *answer, service also* prompt; *remedy* schnell wirkend.

spell[1] [spel] *n (lit, fig)* Zauber *m*; *(incantation)* Zauberspruch *m*. **to be under a ~** *(lit)* verzaubert *or* verhext sein; *(fig)* wie verzaubert sein; **to cast a ~ over sb** *(lit, fig)* jdn verzaubern; **to be under**

sb's ~ *(fig)* in jds Bann *(dat)* stehen; **to break the ~** *(lit, fig)* den Bann brechen.

spell[2] *n (period)* Weile *f*. **for a ~** eine Weile, eine Zeitlang; **cold/hot ~** Kälte-/Hitzewelle *f*; **a short ~ of sunny weather** eine kurze Schönwetterperiode.

spell[3] *pret, ptp* **~ed** *or* **spelt 1** *vi (in writing)* richtig schreiben; *(aloud)* buchstabieren. **she can't ~** sie kann keine Rechtschreibung. **2** *vt* **(a)** schreiben; *(aloud)* buchstabieren. **how do you ~ "onyx"?** wie schreibt man „Onyx"?; **how do you ~ your name?** wie schreibt sich Ihr Name?, wie schreiben Sie sich? **(b)** *(denote)* bedeuten. **this ~s disaster (for us)** das bedeutet Unglück (für uns).

♦ **spell out** *vt sep (spell aloud)* buchstabieren; *(read slowly)* entziffern; *(explain)* verdeutlichen. **do I have to ~ it ~ for you?** *(col)* muß ich noch deutlicher werden?

spellbound ['spelbaʊnd] *adj, adv (fig)* wie verzaubert, gebannt. **to hold sb ~** jdn fesseln; *(person also)* jdn in seinen Bann schlagen.

spelling ['spelɪŋ] *n* Rechtschreibung; *(of a word)* Schreibweise *f*. **~ mistake** *n* (Recht)schreibfehler *m*.

spelt [spelt] *pret, ptp of* **spell**[3].

spend [spend] *pret, ptp* **spent** *vt* **(a)** *money* ausgeben *(on* für*)*; *energy, strength* verbrauchen; *time* brauchen. **time well spent** sinnvoll genutzte Zeit. **(b)** *(pass) time, evening etc* verbringen. **he ~s his time reading** er verbringt seine Zeit mit Lesen; **to ~ money/time on sth** *(devote to)* Geld/Zeit für etw aufbringen.

spending ['spendɪŋ] *n no pl* Ausgaben *pl*. **government ~ cuts** Kürzungen im Etat; **~ money** Taschengeld *nt*; **~ power** Kaufkraft *f*.

spendthrift ['spendθrɪft] **1** *adv* verschwenderisch. **2** *n* Verschwender(in *f*) *m*.

spent [spent] **1** *pret, ptp of* **spend. 2** *adj ammunition, cartridge, match* verbraucht; *person* erschöpft. **to be a ~ force** nichts mehr zu sagen haben; *(movement)* sich totgelaufen haben.

sperm [spɜːm] *n* Samenfaden *m*, Spermium *nt*; *(fluid)* Sperma *nt*. **~ whale** *n* Pottwal *m*.

sphere [sfɪəʳ] *n* **(a)** Kugel *f*; *(heavenly ~)* Gestirn *nt* *(geh)*. **(b)** *(fig)* Sphäre *f*; *(of person, experience)* Bereich *m*; *(of knowledge etc)* Gebiet, Feld *nt*; *(social etc circle)* Kreis *m*. **in the ~ of politics** in der Welt der Politik; **his ~ of influence** sein Einflußbereich; **~ of activity** *(job, specialism)* Wirkungskreis *m*; **that's outside my ~** *(not my responsibility)* das ist nicht mein Gebiet.

spherical ['sferɪkəl] *adj (in shape)* kugelförmig.

sphinx [sfɪŋks] *n* Sphinx *f*.

spice [spaɪs] **1** *n* **(a)** Gewürz *nt*. **~ rack** Gewürzbord *nt*; **mixed ~ (s)** Gewürzmischung *f*. **(b)** *(fig)* Würze *f*. **variety is the ~ of life** *(prov)* öfter mal was Neues *(col)*. **2** *vt (lit, fig)* würzen. **a highly ~d account** *(fig)* ein reichlich ausgeschmückter Bericht.

spick-and-span ['spɪkən'spæn] *adj house etc* blitzsauber, tipptopp in Ordnung *pred; person* wie aus dem Ei gepellt *(col)*.

spicy ['spaɪsɪ] *adj (+er)* würzig; *sauce, food also* stark gewürzt; *(fig) story etc* pikant.

spider ['spaɪdəʳ] *n* Spinne *f*. **~'s web** Spinnwebe *f*, Spinnennetz *nt*.

spiel [ʃpiːl] *n (col)* Blabla *nt (col)*; *(tall story, excuse)* Geschichte *f (col)*.

spike [spaɪk] **1** *n (on railing, helmet etc)* Spitze *f*; *(nail)* Nagel *m*; *(on plant)* Stachel *m*; *(on shoe etc)* Spike *m*; *(for receipts etc)* Dorn *m*. **2** *vt* **(a)** aufspießen. **(b)** *(fig: frustrate) rumours* den Boden entziehen *(+dat)*. **to ~ sb's guns** jdm einen Strich durch die Rechnung machen *(col)*. **(c)** *(US: lace) drink* einen Schuß zusetzen *(+dat)*. **~d with rum** mit einem Schuß Rum.

spikes [spaɪks] *npl (Sport)* Spikes *pl*.

spiky ['spaɪkɪ] *adj (+er) railings* mit Metallspitzen; *bush, grass, animal* stach(e)lig; *branch* dornig; *flower* mit spitzen Blütenblättern; *leaf* spitz; *writing* steil.

spill [spɪl] *pret, ptp* **~ed** *or* **spilt 1** *vt* verschütten; *blood* vergießen. **to ~ the beans (to sb)** *(col)* (jdm gegenüber) nicht dichthalten *(col)*; **the lorry ~ed its load onto the road** die Ladung fiel vom Lastwagen herunter auf die Straße. **2** *vi* verschüttet werden; *(large quantity)* sich ergießen; *(fig: people)* strömen. **the blood ~ed onto the floor** das Blut floß auf den Boden.

♦ **spill out 1** *vi (of* aus*) (liquid)* herausschwappen; *(grain)* herausrieseln; *(money, jewels)* herausfallen; *(fig: people)* (heraus)strömen. **2** *vt sep* ausschütten; *(by accident)* verschütten.

♦ **spill over** *vi (liquid)* überlaufen; *(grain etc, assembly)* überquellen; *(fig: population)* sich ausbreiten *(into* auf *+acc)*.

spilt [spɪlt] *pret, ptp of* **spill.**

spin [spɪn] *(vb: pret, ptp* **spun***)* **1** *n* **(a)** *(revolution)* Drehung *f*; *(washing machine programme)* Schleudern *nt no pl*. **to give sth a ~** etw (schnell) drehen; **to give sth a long/short ~** *(in washing machine)* etw lange/kurz schleudern; **to be in a (flat) ~** *(fig col)* am Rotieren sein *(col) (about* wegen*)*. **(b)** *(on ball)* Drall *m*; *(Billiards)* Effet *m*. **(c)** *(Aviat)* Trudeln *nt no pl*. **to go into a ~** zu trudeln anfangen. **(d)** *(trip)* Spritztour *f*. **to go for a ~** eine Spritztour machen.

2 *vt* **(a)** spinnen. **(b)** *(turn) wheel* drehen; *(fast)* herumwirbeln; *(in washing machine)* schleudern; *(toss) coin* werfen; *(Sport) ball* einen Drall/Effet geben *(+dat)*; *(with racquet)* (an)schneiden.

3 *vi* **(a)** spinnen. **(b)** *(revolve)* sich drehen; *(fast)* (herum)wirbeln; *(plane etc)* trudeln; *(in washing machine)* schleudern. **the car spun out of control** der Wagen geriet stark ins Schleudern; **my head is ~ning** mir dreht sich alles.

♦ **spin out** *vt sep (col) money, food* strecken *(col)*; *holiday, meeting* in die Länge ziehen; *story* ausspinnen.

spinach ['spɪnɪtʃ] *n* Spinat *m*.

spinal ['spaɪnl] *adj vertebrae* Rücken-; *injury, muscle* Rückgrat-; **~ column** Wirbelsäule *f*.

spindle ['spɪndl] *n (for spinning, Mech)* Spindel *f*.

spindly ['spɪndlɪ] *adj (+er) legs, arms, plant* spindeldürr; *chairs* zierlich.

spin: ~-drier, ~-dryer *n (Brit)* (Wäsche)schleuder *f*; **~-dry** *vti* schleudern.

spine [spaɪn] *n* **(a)** *(Anat)* Rückgrat *nt*; *(of book)* (Buch)rücken *m*. **(b)** *(spike)* Stachel *m*; *(of plant also)* Dorn *m*.

spine: ~-chiller *n (col)* Gruselgeschichte *f*; Gruselfilm *m*; **~-chilling** *adj (col)* gruselig; *noise* unheimlich.

spineless ['spaɪnlɪs] *adj (fig) person* ohne Rückgrat; *compromise, refusal* feige.

spinner ['spɪnəʳ] *n* **(a)** *(of cloth)* Spinner(in *f*) *m*. **(b)** *(col)* = **spin-drier.**

spinney ['spɪnɪ] *n (esp Brit)* Dickicht *nt*.

spinning *in cpds* Spinn-; **~ top** *n* Kreisel *m*; **~ wheel** *n* Spinnrad *nt*.

spin-off ['spɪnɒf] *n (side-product)* Nebenprodukt *nt*.

spinster ['spɪnstəʳ] *n* Unverheiratete *f*; *(pej)* alte Jungfer *(pej)*. **to be a ~** unverheiratet *or* eine alte Jungfer *(pej)* sein.

spiral ['spaɪrəl] **1** *adj* spiralförmig; *shell also* gewunden; *spring* Spiral-; *movement* in Spiralen. **~ staircase** Wendeltreppe *f*. **2** *n (lit, fig)* Spirale *f*. **inflationary ~** Inflationsspirale *f*. **3** *vi (also* **~ up***)* sich hochwinden; *(smoke also)* spiralförmig aufsteigen; *(prices)* (nach oben) klettern.

spire [spaɪəʳ] *n (of church)* Turmspitze *f*.

spirit ['spɪrɪt] *n (soul, ghost)* Geist *m*. **I'll be with you in ~** im Geiste werde ich bei euch sein.

(b) *no pl (courage)* Mut *m*; *(vitality)* Elan *m*. **a man of ~** *(courageous)* ein mutiger Mensch; **to break sb's ~** jds Mut brechen; **to sing with ~** mit Inbrunst singen.

(c) *(attitude: of country, group of people etc)* Geist *m*; *(mood)* Stimmung *f*. **team/community ~** Mannschaftsgeist *m*/Gemeinschaftssinn *m*; **Christmas ~** *(mood)* weihnachtliche Stimmung; **party ~** Partystimmung *f*; **fighting ~** Kampfgeist *m*; **a ~ of optimism** eine optimistische Stimmung; **the ~ of the age** der Zeitgeist; **he has the right ~** er hat die richtige Einstellung; **to enter into the ~ of sth** bei etw mitmachen; **that's the ~!** *(col)* so ist's recht! *(col)*; **the ~ of the law** der Geist des Gesetzes; **to take sth in the right ~** etw richtig auffassen.

(d) ~s *pl (state of mind)* Stimmung *f*. **to be in good/bad ~s** guter/schlechter Laune sein; **to keep up one's ~s** den Mut nicht verlieren; **to raise sb's ~s** jdn aufmuntern.

(e) ~s *pl (alcohol)* Spirituosen *pl*.

spirited ['spɪrɪtɪd] *adj* temperamentvoll; *performance* lebendig; *(courageous) person, attempt* mutig.

spirit: ~ lamp *n* Petroleumlampe *f*; **~ level** *n* Wasserwaage *f*.

spiritual ['spɪrɪtjʊəl] **1** *adj* geistig; *(Eccl)* geistlich. **2** *n (Mus)* Spiritual *nt*.

spiritualism ['spɪrɪtjʊəlɪzəm] *n* Spiritismus *m*.

spiritualist ['spɪrɪtjʊəlɪst] *n* Spiritist(in *f*) *m*.

spit[1] [spɪt] *(vb: pret, ptp* **spat***)* **1** *n (saliva)* Spucke *f*. **2** *vt* spucken. **3** *vi* spucken; *(fat)* spritzen; *(fire)* zischen; *(person: verbally, cat)* fauchen. **it is ~ting (with rain)** es tröpfelt.

♦ **spit out** *vt sep* ausspucken; *words* ausstoßen. **~ it ~!** *(fig col)* heraus mit der Sprache!

spit[2] *n* **(a)** *(Cook)* (Brat)spieß *m*. **on the ~** am Spieß. **(b)** *(of land)* Landzunge *f*.

spite [spaɪt] **1** *n* **(a)** *(ill will)* Gehässigkeit *f*. **to do sth out of** *or* **from ~** etw aus reiner Boshaftigkeit tun. **(b) in ~ of** *(despite)* trotz *(+gen)*; **we went in ~ of him** wir gingen dennoch; **he did it in ~ of himself** er konnte nicht anders; **in ~ of the fact that he ...** obwohl er ... **2** *vt* ärgern. **she just does it to ~ me** sie tut es nur, um mich zu ärgern.

spiteful ['spaɪtfʊl] *adj* boshaft, gemein.

spitting image ['spɪtɪŋ'ɪmɪdʒ] *n (col)* Ebenbild *nt*. **to be the ~ of sb** jdm wie aus dem Gesicht geschnitten sein.

spittle ['spɪtl] *n* Speichel *m*, Spucke *f*.

splash [splæʃ] **1** *n* **(a)** *(spray)* Spritzen *nt no pl*; *(noise)* Platschen *nt no pl*. **to make a ~** *(fig)* Furore machen; *(news)* wie eine Bombe einschlagen; *(book)* einschlagen. **(b)** *(small amount)* Spritzer *m*; *(in drink etc also)* Schuß *m*; *(of colour, light)* Tupfen *m*. **~es of paint** Farbspritzer *pl*. **2** *vt water etc* spritzen; *(pour)* gießen; *person, object* bespritzen. **to ~ water over sb** jdn mit Wasser bespritzen; **the story was ~ed all over the papers** die Geschichte wurde in allen Zeitungen groß rausgebracht *(col)*. **3** *vi (liquid)* spritzen; *(rain, waves)* klatschen; *(tears)* tropfen; *(when diving, walking etc)* platschen; *(when playing)* planschen.

♦ **splash down** *vi (Space)* wassern.

♦ **splash out** *vi (col)* tüchtig in die Tasche greifen *(col)*; *(giving presents etc)* sich nicht lumpen lassen *(col)*. **to ~ ~ on sth** sich *(dat)* etw spendieren *(col)*.

splashdown ['splæʃdaʊn] *n (Space)* Wasserung *f*.

splatter ['splætəʳ] *vt* bespritzen; *(with ink, paint etc)* beklecksen.

splay [spleɪ] *(also* **~ out***)* *vt (spread out) legs, fingers, toes* spreizen; *feet* nach außen stellen.

spleen [spliːn] *n (Anat)* Milz *f*; *(fig)* Zorn *m*. **to vent one's ~** seinem Ärger Luft machen.

splendid ['splendɪd] *adj* **(a)** *(magnificent)* herrlich; *occasion, scale* großartig. **(b)** *(excellent)* hervorragend; *rider etc, idea* glänzend.

splendour, *(US)* **splendor** ['splendəʳ] *n* Pracht *f no pl*; *(of music, achievement)* Großartigkeit *f*.

splice [splaɪs] *vt ropes* spleißen *(spec)*; *tapes, film* (zusammen)kleben; *pieces of wood etc* verfugen.

splint [splɪnt] *n* Schiene *f*. **to put a ~ on sth** etw schienen; **to be in ~s** geschient sein.

splinter ['splɪntəʳ] **1** *n* Splitter *m*. **2** *vt* (zer)splittern; *(with axe) wood* zerhacken. **3** *vi* (zer)splittern.

splinter group *n* Splittergruppe *f*.

split [splɪt] *(vb: pret, ptp ~)* **1** *n* **(a)** Riß *m (in* in *+dat)*; *(in rock, wood also)* Spalt *m (in* in *+dat)*. **(b)** *(fig: division)* Bruch *m (in* in *+dat)*; *(Pol, Eccl)* Spaltung *f (in gen)*. **there is a ~ in the party over ...** die Partei ist in der Frage *(+gen)* ... gespalten. **(c)** *(distinction: in meaning)* Aufteilung *f*. **(d)** *pl* **the ~s** Spagat *m*; **to do the ~s** einen Spagat machen. **(e)** *(col: sweet) (also* **banana ~***)* Bananen-Split *m*. **jam/cream ~** *mit Marmelade/Sahne gefülltes Gebäckstück*.

2 *adj* gespalten *(on, over* in *+dat)*.

3 *vt* **(a)** *(cleave)* (zer)teilen; *wood also, atom* spalten; *fabric* zerreißen; *seam* aufplatzen lassen. **to ~ hairs** *(col)* Haarspalterei treiben *(col)*; **to ~ one's sides (laughing)** *(col)* vor Lachen fast platzen *(col)*; **to ~ sth open** etw aufbrechen; **his head was ~ open when he fell** er hatte sich *(dat)* beim Fallen den Kopf aufgeschlagen. **(b)** *(divide)* spalten; *(share) work, costs etc* (sich *dat*) teilen. **to ~ sth into three parts** etw in drei Teile aufteilen; **to ~ the vote** die Stimmen spalten; **a party ~ three ways** eine in drei Lager gespaltene Partei; **they ~ the profit three ways** sie haben den Gewinn in drei Teile geteilt; **to ~ the difference** *(fig: in argument etc)* sich auf halbem Wege einigen; *(lit: with money etc)* sich *(dat)* die Differenz teilen.

4 *vi* **(a)** *(wood)* (entzwei)brechen; *(trousers, seam etc)* platzen; *(fabric)* zerreißen. **to ~ open** aufplatzen; **my head is ~ting** *(fig)* mir platzt der Kopf. **(b)** *(col: tell tales)* **to ~ on sb** jdn verpfeifen *(col)*.

♦ **split off 1** *vt sep* abtrennen *(prep obj* von*)*; *(break)* abbrechen *(prep obj* von*)*. **2** *vi* abbrechen; *(fig)* sich trennen *(from* von*)*.

♦ **split up 1** *vt sep money, work* (auf)teilen; *party, organization* spalten; *meeting* ein Ende machen *(+dat)*; *two people* trennen; *crowd* zerstreuen. **2** *vi* zerbrechen; *(divide)* sich teilen; *(meeting, crowd)* sich spalten; *(partners)* sich trennen.

split: ~ infinitive *n (Gram)* getrennter Infinitiv; **~-level** *adj (Archit)* mit versetzten Geschossen; **~ peas** *npl* getrocknete (halbe) Erbsen *pl*; **~ personality** *n* gespaltene Persönlichkeit; **~ second 1** *n* **in a ~ second** in Sekundenschnelle; **2** *adj* **~-second timing** Abstimmung *f* auf die Sekunde; *(of actor)* Gefühl *nt* für den richtigen Moment.

splitting ['splɪtɪŋ] **1** *n* Zerteilung *f*; *(of wood)* Spalten *nt*. **the ~ of the atom** die Kernspaltung. **2** *adj headache* rasend.

splodge [splɒdʒ], **splotch** [splɒtʃ] *n* Klecks *m*; *(of cream etc)* Klacks *m*.

splutter ['splʌtəʳ] *vi (person) (spit)* prusten; *(stutter)* stottern; *(engine)* stottern; *(fire, fat)* zischen.

spoil [spɔɪl] *(vb: pret, ptp* **~ed** *or* **spoilt***)* **1** *n usu pl* Beute *f no pl*; *(fig: profits also)* Gewinn *m*. **the ~s of war** die Kriegsbeute. **2** *vt* **(a)** *(ruin, detract from)* verderben; *view also, town, looks etc* verschandeln; *peace of mind* zerstören; *life* ruinieren; *ballot papers* ungültig machen. **to ~ one's appetite** sich *(dat)* den Appetit verderben; **it ~ed our evening** das hat uns *(dat)* den Abend verdorben. **(b)** *person* verwöhnen; *children also* verziehen. **to be ~t for choice** die Qual der Wahl haben. **3** *vi (food)* verderben. **to be ~ing for a**

fight Streit suchen.
spoilsport ['spɔɪlspɔːt] *n (col)* Spielverderber *m (col).*
spoilt [spɔɪlt] **1** *pret, ptp of* **spoil. 2** *adj child* verwöhnt.
spoke[1] [spəʊk] *n* Speiche *f.* **to put a ~ in sb's wheel** *(col)* jdm Knüppel zwischen die Beine werfen *(col).*
spoke[2] *pret of* **speak.**
spoken ['spəʊkən] **1** *ptp of* **speak. 2** *adj language* gesprochen.
spokesman ['spəʊksmən] *n, pl* **-men** [-mən] Sprecher *m.*
spokesperson ['spəʊkspɜːsn] *n* Sprecher(in *f*) *m.*
spokeswoman ['spəʊkswʊmən] *n, pl* **-women** [-wɪmɪn] Sprecherin *f.*
sponge [spʌndʒ] **1** *n* **(a)** Schwamm *m.* **(b)** *(Cook) (also ~* **cake***)* Rührkuchen *m*; *(fatless)* Biskuitkuchen *m.* **2** *vt* **(a)** *(clean)* abwischen; *(wound)* abtupfen. **(b)** *(col: scrounge)* schnorren *(col) (from* bei*).*
♦ **sponge down** *vt sep person* (schnell) waschen; *walls also* abwaschen; *horse* abreiben.
sponge: ~ bag *n (Brit)* Kulturbeutel *m*; **~ cake** *n* Rührkuchen *m*; *(fatless)* Biskuitkuchen *m.*
sponger ['spʌndʒəʳ] *n (col)* Schnorrer *m (col).*
spongy ['spʌndʒɪ] *adj (+er)* weich; *(light) pudding* locker; *skin etc* schwammig.
sponsor ['spɒnsəʳ] **1** *n* Förderer *m*, Förderin *f*; *(for membership)* Bürge *m*, Bürgin *f*; *(for event)* Schirmherr(in *f*) *m*; *(Rad, TV, Sport etc)* Sponsor(in *f*) *m*; *(for fund raising)* Spender(in *f*) *m.* **2** *vt* unterstützen; *(financially also)* fördern; *event also* die Schirmherrschaft *(+gen)* übernehmen; *future member* bürgen für; *membership, bill* befürworten; *(Rad, TV, Sport etc)* sponsern. **he ~ed him at 5p a mile** er verpflichtete sich, ihm 5 Pence pro Meile zu geben.
sponsored ['spɒnsəd] *adj (for charity etc) walk etc: zur Geldbeschaffung abgehalten, wobei die Leistung vom Spender honoriert wird.*
sponsorship ['spɒnsəʃɪp] *n see vt* Unterstützung *f*; Förderung *f*; Schirmherrschaft *f*; Bürgschaft *f*; Befürwortung *f*; *(Rad, TV, Sport etc)* Finanzierung *f.*
spontaneity [ˌspɒntə'neɪətɪ] *n see adj* Spontaneität *f*; Ungezwungenheit *f.*
spontaneous [spɒn'teɪnɪəs] *adj* spontan; *style* ungezwungen. **~ combustion** Selbstentzündung *f.*
spoof [spuːf] *(col) n* **(a)** *(parody)* Parodie *f (of* auf *+acc).* **(b)** *(hoax)* Scherz *m (col).*
spook [spuːk] *n (col)* Gespenst *nt.*
spooky ['spuːkɪ] *adj (+er) (col) castle etc* gruselig *(col).*
spool [spuːl] *n (Phot, on sewing machine)* Spule *f*; *(on fishing line, for thread)* Rolle *f.*
spoon [spuːn] **1** *n* Löffel *m.* **to be born with a silver ~ in one's mouth** *(prov)* mit einem silbernen Löffel im Mund geboren sein *(col).* **2** *vt* löffeln.
spoonerism ['spuːnərɪzəm] *n* lustiger Versprecher.
spoon-feed ['spuːnfiːd] *pret, ptp* **spoon-fed** ['spuːnfed] *vt baby, invalid* füttern; *(fig) (do thinking for)* gängeln; *(supply with)* füttern *(col).*
spoonful ['spuːnfʊl] *n* Löffel *m.* **a ~ of soup** ein Löffel Suppe.
sporadic [spə'rædɪk] *adj* sporadisch.
spore [spɔːʳ] *n* Spore *f.*
sport [spɔːt] **1** *n* **(a)** Sport *m no pl*; *(type of ~)* Sportart *f.* **to be good at ~(s)** sportlich sein; **outdoor/indoor ~s** Sport *m* im Freien/Hallensport *m.* **(b)** *(amusement)* Spaß *m.* **to do sth for/in ~** etw zum Spaß tun. **(c)** *(col: person)* feiner Kerl *(col)*; *(Austral)* Junge *m.* **to be a (good) ~** alles mitmachen; **be a ~!** sei kein Spielverderber! **2** *vt tie, dress* anhaben; *(show off) ring etc* protzen mit. **3** *adj attr (US)* = **sports.**
sporting ['spɔːtɪŋ] *adj* **(a)** *person, interests* sportlich; *gun* Jagd-. **~ events** Wettkämpfe *pl.* **(b)** *(sportsmanlike)* sportlich; *spirit also* Sports-; *(fig) offer, solution* fair; *(decent)* anständig. **to give sb a ~ chance** jdm eine faire Chance geben.
sports, *(US also)* **sport** *in cpds* Sport-; **~ car** *n* Sportwagen *m*; **~ field, ~ ground** *n* Sportplatz *m*; **~ jacket** *n* Sportjackett *nt*; **~man** [-mən] *n (player)* Sportler *m*; **~woman** *n* Sportlerin *f.*
sporty ['spɔːtɪ] *adj (+er) (col)* **(a)** *person, clothes* sportlich. **(b)** *(jaunty)* flott.
spot [spɒt] **1** *n* **(a)** *(dot)* Tupfen, Punkt *m*; *(on dice)* Punkt *m*; *(stain, on fruit)* Fleck *m*; *(fig: on reputation)* Makel *m (on* an *+dat).* **a dress with ~s** ein getupftes *or* gepunktetes Kleid; **~s of blood/grease** Blutflecken *pl*/Fettflecken *pl*; **~s of ink** Tintenkleckse *pl*; **to knock ~s off sb/sth** *(fig col)* jdn/etw in den Schatten stellen; **to have ~s before one's eyes** Sternchen sehen.
(b) *(Med etc)* Fleck *m*; *(pimple)* Pickel *m.* **to break** *or* **come out in ~s** Flecken/Pickel bekommen.
(c) *(place)* Stelle *f*; *(point)* Punkt *m.* **this is the ~ where Karl was murdered** an dieser Stelle ist Karl ermordet worden; **a pleasant ~** ein schönes Fleckchen *(col)*; **on the ~** *(at the scene)* an Ort und Stelle; *(at once)* auf der Stelle; **on-the-~ investigation** Untersuchung *f* an Ort und Stelle; *(immediate)* sofortige Untersuchung; **an on-the-~ report** ein Bericht *m* vom Ort des Geschehens; **weak ~** schwache Stelle.
(d) *(Brit col: small quantity)* **a ~ of** ein bißchen; **we had a ~ of rain/a few ~s of rain** wir hatten ein paar Tropfen Regen; **there was a ~ of trouble/bother** es gab etwas Ärger; **would you like to do a ~ of driving?** möchten Sie ein bißchen fahren?
(e) *(difficulty)* Klemme *f.* **to be in a (tight) ~, to be on the ~** in der Klemme sitzen *(col)*; **to put sb on the ~** jdn in Verlegenheit bringen.
(f) *(in show)* Nummer *f*; *(Rad, TV)* Sendezeit *f*; *(for advertisement)* Werbespot *m.*
(g) *(col: ~light)* Scheinwerfer, Spot *m.*
2 *vt* **(a)** *(notice, see)* entdecken, sehen; *(pick out)* erkennen; *(find) mistake, bargain* finden. **(b)** *(stain)* bespritzen. **blue material ~ted with white** blauer Stoff mit weißen Tupfen.
3 *vi* **it's ~ting (with rain)** es tröpfelt.
spot check *n* Stichprobe *f.*
spotless ['spɒtlɪs] *adj* tadellos sauber, picobello *inv (col)*; *(fig) reputation* makellos.
spotlessly ['spɒtlɪslɪ] *adv:* **~ clean** blitzsauber.
spot: ~light *n (lamp)* Scheinwerfer *m*; **to be in the ~light** *(fig)* im Rampenlicht der Öffentlichkeit stehen; **to turn the ~light on sb/sth** *(fig)* die Aufmerksamkeit auf jdn/etw lenken; **~-on** *adj (Brit col) answer, analysis* exakt, genau, richtig.
spotted ['spɒtɪd] *adj* gefleckt; *(with dots)* getüpfelt; *material* getupft; *(marked, stained)* fleckig.
spotty ['spɒtɪ] *adj (+er)* fleckig; *(pimply)* pick(e)lig, voller Pickel.
spouse [spaʊs] *n (form)* Gatte *m (form)*, Gattin *f (form).*
spout [spaʊt] **1** *n* **(a)** Ausguß *m*; *(on watering can)* Rohr *nt.* **up the ~** *(col: plans etc)* im Eimer *(col).* **(b)** *(jet of water etc)* Fontäne *f.* **2** *vt* **(a)** *water etc* (heraus)spritzen; *(whale also)* ausstoßen; *(volcano)* speien. **(b)** *(col: declaim) poetry, speeches* loslassen *(col) (at sb* auf jdn*)*; *words* hervorsprudeln; *figures* herunterrasseln *(col)*; *nonsense* von sich geben.
sprain [spreɪn] **1** *n* Verstauchung *f.* **2** *vt* verstauchen. **to ~ one's ankle** sich *(dat)* den Fuß verstauchen.
sprang [spræŋ] *pret of* **spring.**
sprawl [sprɔːl] **1** *n (of town etc)* Ausbreitung *f.* **urban ~** wild wuchernde Ausbreitung des Stadtgebietes. **2** *vi (person) (fall)* der Länge nach hinfallen; *(lounge)* sich hinflegeln; *(plant,*

town) (wild) wuchern. **to send sb ~ing** jdn zu Boden werfen.

sprawling [ˈsprɔːlɪŋ] *adj city, suburbs* wildwuchernd; *figure* hingeflegelt.

spray[1] [spreɪ] *n (bouquet)* Strauß *m*; *(buttonhole)* Ansteckblume *f.*

spray[2] **1** *n* **(a)** Sprühregen *m*; *(of sea)* Gischt *m*. **the ~ from the lorries makes it difficult to see** die Lastwagen spritzen so, daß man kaum etwas sehen kann. **(b)** *(implement)* Sprühdose *f*; *(insecticide ~, for irrigation)* Spritze *f*; *(scent~)* Zerstäuber *m*. **(c)** *(hair-~ etc)* Spray *m or nt*. **(d) to give sth a ~** etw besprühen; *(with paint, insecticide)* etw spritzen; *(with hair-~ etc)* etw sprayen. **2** *vt plants, insects etc* besprühen; *(with paint, insecticide)* spritzen; *hair* sprayen; *room* aussprühen; *water, paint, foam* sprühen; *perfume* (ver)sprühen. **to ~ sth with water/bullets** etw mit Wasser besprühen/mit Kugeln übersäen. **3** *vi* sprühen; *(water, mud)* spritzen.

sprayer [ˈspreɪəʳ] *n* = **spray**[2] **1 (b).**

spread [spred] *(vb: pret, ptp ~)* **1** *n* **(a)** *(of wings)* Spannweite *f*; *(range) (of marks)* Verteilung *f*; *(of prices)* Spanne *f*; *(of ideas, interests)* Spektrum *nt*. **middle-age ~** Altersspeck *m (col)*.

(b) *(growth)* Ausbreitung *f*; *(spatial)* Ausdehnung *f*. **the ~ of nuclear weapons** die zunehmende Verbreitung von Atomwaffen.

(c) *(col: of food etc)* Festessen *nt*; *(for bread)* (Brot)aufstrich *m*. **cheese ~** Streichkäse *m*.

(d) *(Press, Typ: two pages)* Doppelseite *f*. **a double-page ~** ein zweiseitiger Bericht; *(advertisement)* eine zweiseitige Anzeige.

2 *vt* **(a)** *(open or lay out: also ~* **out***)* ausbreiten; *fan* öffnen; *hands, legs* spreizen. **the peacock ~ its tail** der Pfau schlug ein Rad; **the view which was ~ before us** die Sicht, die sich uns bot.

(b) *bread, surface* bestreichen; *butter, paint etc* streichen. **~ the paint evenly** verteilen Sie die Farbe gleichmäßig; **to ~ a blanket on sth** eine Decke über etw *(acc)* breiten; **the table was ~ with food** der Tisch war reichlich gedeckt.

(c) *(distribute: also ~* **out***) forces, objects, payments* verteilen; *sand, fertilizer also, muck* streuen. **our resources are ~ very thinly** unsere Mittel sind maximal beansprucht.

(d) *news, panic, rumour* verbreiten.

3 *vi* **(a)** *(extend) (spatially)* sich erstrecken *(over, across* über *+acc)*; *(with movement) (weeds, fire, smile, industry)* sich ausbreiten *(over, across* über *+acc)*; *(towns)* sich ausdehnen; *(knowledge, fear etc, smell, disease, trouble, fire)* sich verbreiten. **to ~ to sth** etw erreichen; *(disease etc)* auf etw *(acc)* übergreifen. **(b)** *(butter etc)* sich streichen lassen.

♦ **spread out 1** *vt sep* = **spread 2 (a, c). 2** *vi* **(a)** *(countryside etc)* sich ausdehnen. **(b)** *(troops, runners)* sich verteilen.

spread-eagle [ˈspred,iːgl] *vt* **to be ~d** alle viere von sich *(dat)* strecken *(col)*.

spreadsheet [ˈspredʃiːt] *n* Arbeitsblatt *nt*.

spree [spriː] *n* **spending** *or* **shopping ~** Großeinkauf *m*; **to be/go on a ~** *(drinking)* eine Zechtour machen; *(spending)* groß einkaufen gehen.

sprig [sprɪg] *n* Zweig *m*. **~ of flowers** Blütenzweig.

sprightly [ˈspraɪtlɪ] *adj (+er) person, tune* munter; *old person* rüstig; *walk* schwungvoll.

spring [sprɪŋ] *(vb: pret* **sprang** *or (US)* **sprung,** *ptp* **sprung***)* **1** *n* **(a)** *(lit, fig liter: source)* Quelle *f*.

(b) *(season)* Frühling. **~ is in the air** der Frühling liegt in der Luft.

(c) *(leap)* Sprung *m*. **in one ~** mit einem Satz.

(d) *(Mech)* Feder *f*. **~s** *(Aut)* Federung *f*.

(e) *no pl (bounciness) (of chair)* Federung *f*; *(of wood etc)* Elastizität *f*. **to walk with a ~ in one's step** mit federnden Schritten gehen.

2 *vt (cause to operate)* auslösen; *mine also* explodieren lassen; *lock, mousetrap etc* zuschnappen lassen. **to ~ a leak** *(pipe)* (plötzlich) undicht werden; *(ship)* (plötzlich) ein Leck bekommen; **to ~ sth on sb** *(fig) idea, decision* jdn mit etw konfrontieren; **to ~ a surprise on sb** jdn völlig überraschen.

3 *vi* **(a)** *(leap)* springen; *(be activated)* ausgelöst werden; *(mousetrap)* zuschnappen. **to ~ at sb** jdn anspringen; **to ~ out at sb** auf jdn losspringen; **to ~ open** aufspringen; **to ~ to one's feet** aufspringen; **to ~ into action** aktiv werden; *(police, fire brigade etc)* in Aktion treten; **to ~ into view** plötzlich in Sicht kommen; **to ~ to mind** einem einfallen; **to ~ to sb's aid/defence** jdm zu Hilfe eilen; **he sprang to fame** er wurde plötzlich berühmt; **to ~ (in)to life** (plötzlich) lebendig werden.

(b) *(issue: also ~* **forth***) (liter) (water, blood)* (hervor)quellen *(from* aus*)*; *(fire, sparks)* sprühen *(from* aus*)*.

(c) *(fig) (idea)* entstehen *(from* aus*)*; *(interest, irritability etc)* herrühren *(from* von*)*. **where did you ~ from?** *(col)* wo kommst du denn her?; **to ~ into existence** (plötzlich *or* rasch) entstehen.

♦ **spring up** *vi (plant)* hervorsprießen; *(weeds, buildings)* aus dem Boden schießen; *(person)* aufspringen; *(fig) (friendship, firm)* (plötzlich) entstehen; *(problem, rumour)* auftauchen.

spring: ~binder *n* Klemmhefter *m*; **~board** *n (lit, fig)* Sprungbrett *nt*; **~-cleaning** *n* Frühjahrsputz *m*; **~ onion** *n* Frühlingszwiebel *f*; **~ tide** *n* **(a)** Springflut *f*; **(b)** *(poet: ~time)* Lenz *m (poet)*; **~time** *n* Frühling *m*.

springy [ˈsprɪŋɪ] *adj (+er) step* federnd; *plank, turf, grass also* nachgiebig, elastisch; *rubber, wood, plastic etc, hair* elastisch; *bed* weich gefedert.

sprinkle [ˈsprɪŋkl] *vt water* sprenkeln; *lawn, plant,* besprengen; *salt, dust, sugar etc* streuen; *cake* bestreuen.

sprinkler [ˈsprɪŋkləʳ] *n (Hort, Agr)* Berieselungsapparat *m*; *(in garden also)* (Rasen)sprenger *m*; *(for fire-fighting)* Sprinkler *m*; *(on watering can etc)* Sprenger *m*; *(sugar ~)* Streuer *m*.

sprinkling [ˈsprɪŋklɪŋ] *n (of rain, dew etc)* ein paar Tropfen; *(of sugar etc)* Prise *f*; *(fig: of humour etc)* Anflug *m*. **there was a ~ of young people** es waren ein paar vereinzelte junge Leute da.

sprint [sprɪnt] **1** *n* Lauf *m*; *(race)* Sprint *m*; *(burst of speed)* Spurt *m*. **the 100-m ~** der 100-m-Lauf. **2** *vi (in race)* sprinten; *(dash)* rennen; *(for train etc also)* spurten *(for* zu*)*.

sprinter [ˈsprɪntəʳ] *n* Sprinter(in *f*) *m*.

sprout [spraʊt] **1** *n* **(a)** *(of plant)* Trieb *m*; *(of tree also)* Schößling, Sproß *m*; *(from seed)* Keim *m*. **(b)** *(Brussels ~)* (Rosenkohl)röschen *nt*. **~s** *pl* Rosenkohl *m*. **2** *vt leaves, buds etc* treiben; *horns etc* entwickeln; *seeds etc* keimen lassen; *(col) beard* sich *(dat)* wachsen lassen. **3** *vi* **(a)** *(grow)* sprießen; *(seed, wheat etc)* keimen; *(potatoes, trees etc)* Triebe bekommen. **(b)** *(lit, fig: also ~* **up***) (plants, weeds)* sprießen; *(new sects, new buildings)* wie Pilze aus dem Boden schießen.

spruce[1] [spruːs] *n (also ~* **fir***)* Fichte *f*.

spruce[2] *adj (+er)* gepflegt; *women, child* adrett.

♦ **spruce up** *vt sep child* herausputzen; *house, garden* auf Vordermann bringen *(col)*. **to ~ oneself ~** *(get dressed up)* sich in Schale werfen; *(woman)* sich zurechtmachen.

sprung [sprʌŋ] **1** *ptp of* **spring. 2** *adj* gefedert.

spry [spraɪ] *adj* rüstig.

spud [spʌd] *n (col: potato)* Kartoffel *f*.

spun [spʌn] *pret, ptp of* **spin.**

spunk [spʌŋk] *n (col)* Courage *f*.

spur [spɜːʳ] **1** *n* Sporn *m*; *(fig)* Ansporn *m (to* für*)*; *(Geog)* Vorsprung *m*. **to win** *or* **gain one's ~s** *(fig)* sich *(dat)* die Sporen verdienen; **on the ~ of the moment** ganz spontan. **2** *vt (also ~* **on***) horse* die Sporen geben *(+dat)*; *(fig)* anspornen. **~red (on) by greed** von Habgier getrieben.

spurious ['spjʊərɪəs] *adj claim* unberechtigt; *document, account* falsch; *emotion* nicht echt.
spurn [spɜːn] *vt* verschmähen.
spurt [spɜːt] **1** *n* **(a)** *(flow)* Strahl *m*. **~s of flame** Stichflammen. **(b)** *(of speed)* Spurt *m*. **to put a ~ on** *(lit, fig)* einen Spurt vorlegen; **there was a ~ of activity** es brach plötzliche Aktivität aus. **2** *vi* *(gush: also* **~ out***)* (heraus)spritzen *(from* aus*)*.
spy [spaɪ] **1** *n* Spion(in *f*) *m*; *(police ~)* Spitzel *m*. **2** *vt* sehen. **3** *vi* spionieren. **to ~ on sb** jdn bespitzeln; *on neighbours* jdm nachspionieren.
♦ **spy out** *vt sep* **to ~ ~ the land** *(Mil)* die Gegend auskundschaften; *(fig)* die Lage peilen.
spying ['spaɪɪŋ] *n* Spionage *f*.
spy story *n* Spionagegeschichte *f*.
Sq = Square.
sq = square. ~ m qm, m².
squabble ['skwɒbl] **1** *n* Zank, Streit *m*. **2** *vi* (sich) zanken, (sich) streiten *(about, over* um*)*.
squad [skwɒd] *n (Mil, police unit etc)* Kommando *nt*; *(police department)* Dezernat *nt*; *(of workmen)* Trupp *m*; *(Sport, fig)* Mannschaft *f*.
squad car *n* Streifenwagen *m*.
squadron ['skwɒdrən] *n (of cavalry)* Schwadron *f*; *(Aviat)* Staffel *f*; *(Naut)* Geschwader *nt*.
squalid ['skwɒlɪd] *adj room, house* schmutzig und verwahrlost; *existence, conditions* elend; *deed, idea etc* niederträchtig; *dispute, gossip* entwürdigend; *affair* schmutzig.
squall [skwɔːl] **1** *n (storm)* Bö(e) *f*; *(fig)* Gewitter *nt*. **2** *vi* schreien.
squalor ['skwɒlə^r] *n* Schmutz *m*; *(moral ~)* Verkommenheit *f*.
squander ['skwɒndə^r] *vt* verschwenden *(on* an *+acc)*; *opportunity* vertun.
square [skwɛə^r] **1** *n* **(a)** Quadrat *nt*; *(piece of material, paper etc also)* Viereck *nt*; *(on chessboard etc)* Feld *nt*; *(on paper, in crossword)* Kästchen *nt*; *(on material etc)* Karo *nt*. **cut it in ~s** schneiden Sie es quadratisch zu; **we're back to ~ one** jetzt sind wir wieder da, wo wir angefangen haben. **(b)** *(in town, Mil)* Platz *m*; *(US: of houses)* Block *m*. **(c)** *(Math)* Quadrat(zahl *f*) *nt*. **the ~ of 3 is 9** 3 hoch 2 ist 9. **(d)** *(col: old-fashioned person)* Spießer *m* *(col)*. **to be a ~** von (vor)gestern sein.
2 *adj (+er)* **(a)** *(in shape)* quadratisch; *picture, lawn etc also, nib* viereckig; *file* Vierkant-; *block of wood etc* vierkantig. **to be a ~ peg in a round hole** am falschen Platz sein. **(b)** *(forming right angle)* *angle* recht *attr*; *corner* rechtwinklig; *bracket, shoulder* eckig; *build* vierschrötig. **(c)** *(Math)* Quadrat-. **3 ~ kilometers** 3 Quadratkilometer; **3 metres ~** 3 Meter im Quadrat. **(d)** *attr (complete)* *meal* ordentlich. **(e)** *(fair) deal* gerecht, fair; *game, person* ehrlich. **to give sb a ~ deal** jdn fair behandeln; **I'll be ~ with you** ich will ehrlich mit dir sein. **(f)** *(fig: even)* **to be ~** *(accounts etc)* in Ordnung sein; **to get ~ with sb** mit jdm abrechnen. **(g)** *(col: old-fashioned)* überholt; *person, ideas* spießig *(col)*. **he's ~** er ist von (vor)gestern.
3 *adv (+er)* **(a)** *(at right angles)* rechtwinklig. **~ with sth** senkrecht zu etw. **(b)** *(directly)* direkt, genau.
4 *vt* **(a)** *(make ~)* quadratisch machen; **to ~ one's shoulders** die Schultern straffen; **to try to ~ the circle** die Quadratur des Kreises versuchen. **(b)** *(Math) number* quadrieren. **3 ~d is 9** 3 hoch 2 ist 9. **(c)** *(adjust) debts* begleichen; *creditors* abrechnen mit; *(reconcile)* in Einklang bringen. **to ~ one's accounts** abrechnen *(with* mit*)*; **to ~ sth with one's conscience** etw mit seinem Gewissen vereinbaren; **I'll ~ it with the porter** *(col)* ich mache das mit dem Portier ab *(col)*.
5 *vi* übereinstimmen *(with* mit*)*.
♦ **square off** *vt sep (make square) corner* rechtwinklig machen.
♦ **square up** *vi* **(a)** Kampfstellung annehmen. **to ~ ~ to sb** sich vor jdm aufpflanzen *(col)*; *(boxer)* vor jdm in Kampfstellung gehen; *(fig)* jdm die Stirn bieten. **(b)** *(lit, fig: settle)* abrechnen.
squarely ['skwɛəlɪ] *adj* **(a)** *(directly)* direkt, genau; *(fig: firmly)* fest. **we must face this ~** wir müssen dieser Sache *(dat)* (fest) ins Auge sehen. **(b)** *(honestly)* ehrlich; *(fairly)* gerecht, fair.
squash[1] [skwɒʃ] **1** *n* **(a)** *(Brit) (fruit concentrate)* Fruchtsaftkonzentrat *nt*; *(drink)* Fruchtsaftgetränk *nt*. **a glass of orange ~** ein Glas Orangensaft. **(b)** *(crowd)* Gedränge *nt*. **it's a bit of a ~** es ist ziemlich eng. **2** *vt* **(a)** *(also* **~ up***)* zerdrücken; *box etc* zusammendrücken. **(b)** *(fig col) (silence) person* über den Mund fahren *(+dat)*; *(quash) protest, argument* vom Tisch fegen *(col)*. **(c)** *(squeeze)* quetschen. **to ~ sb/sth in** jdn einquetschen/etw hineinquetschen; **to be ~ed together** eng zusammengequetscht sein. **3** *vi* **(a)** *(get ~ed)* zerdrückt werden. **(b)** *(squeeze)* sich quetschen. **to ~ in** sich hinein-/ hereinquetschen; **could you ~ up?** könnt ihr etwas zusammenrücken?
squash[2] *n (Sport)* Squash *nt*.
squat [skwɒt] **1** *adj (+er) chair* niedrig; *figure, person* gedrungen. **2** *vi* **(a)** *(person) (animal)* hocken; *(also* **~ down***)* sich (hin)hocken. **(b)** *(on land)* sich (illegal) ansiedeln. **to ~ (in a house)** ein Haus besetzt haben.
squatter ['skwɒtə^r] *n (on land)* illegaler Siedler; *(in house)* Hausbesetzer(in *f*) *m*.
squaw [skwɔː] *n* Squaw *f*.
squawk [skwɔːk] **1** *n* heiserer Schrei; *(of hens)* Gackern *nt*. **2** *vi (bird, person)* kreischen.
squeak [skwiːk] **1** *n (of hinge etc, shoe, pen)* Quietschen *nt no pl*; *(of person, small animal)* Quieken *nt no pl*; *(of bird)* Piepsen *nt no pl*; *(fig col: sound)* Pieps *m (col)*. **the door opened with a ~** die Tür ging quietschend auf. **2** *vi (door, hinge, shoes etc)* quietschen; *(person, small animal)* quieken; *(mouse, bird)* piepsen.
squeaky ['skwiːkɪ] *adj (+er)* quietschend; *voice* piepsig.
squeal ['skwiːl] **1** *n* Schrei *m*; *(of person, tyre, brakes)* Kreischen *nt no pl*; *(of protest)* (Auf)schrei *m*; *(of pig)* Quieken *nt no pl*. **a ~ of pain** ein Schmerzensschrei *m*; **~s/a ~ of laughter** schrilles Gelächter. **2** *vi* **(a)** schreien; *(brakes, tyres)* quietschen; *(pig, puppy)* quieksen; *(fig col)* jammern. **to ~ with pain/pleasure** vor Schmerz kreischen/vor Vergnügen quietschen. **(b)** *(col: confess, inform) (criminal)* singen *(col) (to* bei*)*; *(schoolboy etc)* petzen *(col) (to* bei*)*.
squeamish ['skwiːmɪʃ] *adj person (easily nauseated or shocked)* empfindlich. **I felt a bit ~** *(sick)* mir war leicht übel.
squeeze [skwiːz] **1** *n* **(a)** *(act of squeezing)* Drücken *nt no pl*; *(hug)* Umarmung *f*; *(of hand)* Händedruck *m*; *(in bus etc)* Gedränge *nt*. **to give sth a ~** etw drücken, etw pressen; *lemon, sponge* etw ausdrücken; **to give sb/sb's hand a ~** jdn an sich *(acc)* drücken/jdm die Hand drücken; **it was a tight ~** es war fürchterlich eng; **put a ~ of toothpaste on the brush** drücken Sie etwas Zahnpasta auf die Bürste; **to put the ~ on sb** *(col)* jdm die Daumenschrauben anlegen *(col)*. **(b)** *(credit ~)* Kreditbeschränkung *f*.
2 *vt* drücken; *sponge, tube* ausdrücken; *orange* auspressen; *(squash) person, hand* einquetschen. **to ~ clothes into a case** Kleider in einen Koffer zwängen; **to ~ out water/juice** Wasser/Saft herauspressen *(from* aus*)*; **he ~d the trigger** er drückte ab; **to ~ money/information** *etc* **out of sb** Geld/Informationen *etc* aus jdm herausquetschen.
3 *vi* **to ~ in/out** sich hinein-/hinausdrängen; **to ~ past sb** sich an jdm vorbeidrücken; **to ~ through a crowd** sich durch eine Menge zwängen; **you'll have to ~ up a bit** Sie müssen ein

bißchen zusammenrücken.

squelch [skweltʃ] *vi* platschen; *(shoes, mud)* quatschen.

squid [skwɪd] *n* Tintenfisch *m.*

squint [skwɪnt] **1** *n (Med)* Schielen *nt no pl.* **to have a ~** leicht schielen; **to take a ~ at sb/sth** einen Blick auf jdn/etw werfen; *(obliquely)* nach jdm/etw schielen. **2** *vi* schielen; *(in strong light etc)* blinzeln. **to ~ at sb/sth** nach jdm/etw schielen; *(quickly)* einen kurzen Blick auf jdn/etw werfen.

squire ['skwaɪəʳ] *n (esp Brit: landowner)* Gutsherr *m.*

squirm [skwɜːm] *vi* sich winden; *(in distaste)* schaudern; *(with embarrassment)* sich (drehen und) winden. **spiders make me ~** vor Spinnen graust es mir.

squirrel ['skwɪrəl] *n* Eichhörnchen *nt.*

squirt [skwɜːt] **1** *n* **(a)** Spritzer *m.* **(b)** *(pej col: person)* Pimpf *m (col).* **2** *vt liquid* spritzen; *object, person* bespritzen. **to ~ water at sb** jdn mit Wasser bespritzen. **3** *vi* spritzen.

Sr = **senior** sen.

St. = **(a) Street** Str. **(b) Saint** hl., St.

stab [stæb] **1** *n* **(a)** *(with knife etc, wound, of pain)* Stich *m.* **~ wound** Stichwunde *f*; **to feel a ~ of pain** einen stechenden Schmerz empfinden; **a ~ in the back** *(fig)* ein Dolchstoß *m.* **(b)** *(col: try)* Versuch *m.* **to have a ~ at sth** etw probieren. **2** *vt person* einen Stich versetzen *(+dat)*; *(several times)* einstechen auf *(+acc)*; *(wound seriously)* niederstechen. **to ~ sb (to death)** jdn erstechen; **to ~ sb with a knife** jdn mit einem Messerstich/mit Messerstichen verletzen; **he was ~bed through the arm/heart** er hatte eine Stichwunde am Arm/der Stich traf ihn ins Herz; **to ~ sb in the back** *(lit)* jdm in den Rücken stechen; *(fig)* jdm in den Rücken fallen. **3** *vi* **to ~ at sb/sth** *(with knife etc)* nach jdm/etw stechen; *(with finger)* auf jdn/etw zeigen.

stabbing ['stæbɪŋ] **1** *n* Messerstecherei *f.* **2** *adj pain* stechend.

stability [stə'bɪlɪtɪ] *n* Stabilität *f*; *(of relationship also, of job)* Beständigkeit *f.* **(mental) ~** (seelische) Ausgeglichenheit.

stabilize ['steɪbəlaɪz] **1** *vt (Fin, Naut, Aviat)* stabilisieren. **2** *vi* sich stabilisieren.

stabilizer ['steɪbəlaɪzəʳ] *n (Naut)* Stabilisator *m*; *(Aviat)* Stabilisierungsfläche *f.*

stable[1] ['steɪbl] *adj (+er)* stabil; *relationship also, job* beständig; *character* gefestigt. **mentally ~** ausgeglichen.

stable[2] *n (building)* Stall *m*; *(group of racehorses)* (Renn)stall *m.* **riding ~s** Reitstall *m.*

stack [stæk] **1** *n* **(a)** *(pile)* Haufen *m*; *(neatly piled)* Stoß, Stapel *m.* **to join the ~** *(Aviat)* kreisen. **(b)** *(col: lots)* Haufen *m (col).* **~s** jede Menge *(col)*; **we have ~s of time** wir haben jede Menge Zeit. **2** *vt* **(a)** stapeln. **to ~ up** aufstapeln. **(b)** *(US Cards)* präparieren. **the odds are ~ed against us** *(fig)* wir haben keine großen Chancen. **3** *vi* sich stapeln lassen.

stadium ['steɪdɪəm] *n* Stadion *nt.*

staff [stɑːf] **1** *n* **(a)** Personal *nt*; *(Sch, Univ)* Kollegium *nt*, Lehrkörper *m (form)*; *(of department, on project)* Mitarbeiterstab *m.* **a large ~** viel Personal/ein großes Kollegium/ein großer Mitarbeiterstab; **a member of ~** ein Mitarbeiter *m*; *(Sch)* ein Kollege *m*; **we have 30 typists on the ~** bei uns sind 30 Schreibkräfte angestellt; **to be on the ~** zum Personal/Kollegium/Mitarbeiterstab gehören. **(b)** *(stick, symbol of authority)* Stab *m.* **(c)** *pl* **staves** *(Mus)* Notenlinien *pl.* **2** *vt department* Mitarbeiter finden für; *hospital, shop* mit Personal besetzen; *school* mit Lehrpersonal besetzen. **to be well ~ed** gut besetzt sein; **the kitchens are ~ed by foreigners** das Küchenpersonal besteht aus Ausländern.

staff: ~ meeting *n* Lehrerkonferenz *f*; **~ nurse** *n* ausgebildete Krankenschwester; **~ officer** *n* Stabsoffizier *m*; **~room** *n* Lehrerzimmer *nt.*

stag [stæg] *n (deer)* Hirsch *m.*

stage [steɪdʒ] **1** *n* **(a)** *(Theat, fig)* Bühne *f*; *(platform in hall)* Podium *nt.* **the ~** *(profession)* das Theater; **to be on/go on ~** *(as career)* beim Theater sein/zum Theater gehen; **to go on ~** *(actor)* die Bühne betreten; **the ~ was set** *(fig)* alles war vorbereitet. **(b)** *(period)* Stadium *nt*; *(of disease, process also, of development)* Phase *f.* **at this ~ in the negotiations** an diesem Punkt der Verhandlungen; **at this ~ in the game** *(fig)* zu diesem Zeitpunkt; **in the early/final ~(s)** im Anfangs-/Endstadium; **to go through a difficult ~** eine schwierige Phase durchmachen. **(c)** *(part of journey, race etc)* Abschnitt *m*, Etappe *f*; *(fare~)* Fahrzone *f.* **in** *or* **by (easy) ~s** *(lit, fig)* etappenweise. **(d)** *(section of rocket)* Stufe *f.*

2 *vt play* aufführen; *(fig) accident, scene etc* inszenieren; *welcome* arrangieren; *demonstration, strike etc* veranstalten. **to ~ a recovery/comeback** sich erholen/ein Comeback machen.

stage: ~coach *n* Postkutsche *f*; **~ door** *n* Bühneneingang *m*; **~ fright** *n* Lampenfieber *nt*; **~manage** *vt (lit)* Inspizient sein bei; *(fig) demonstration, argument* inszenieren; **~ manager** *n* Inspizient *m*; **~ name** *n* Künstlername *m*; **~-struck** *adj* theaterbesessen.

stagger ['stægəʳ] **1** *vi* taumeln; *(because of illness, weakness)* wanken; *(drunkenly)* torkeln. **2** *vt* **(a)** *(fig: amaze)* den Atem verschlagen *(+dat)*, umhauen *(col).* **(b)** *hours, holidays* staffeln; *seats etc* versetzt anordnen.

staggered ['stægəd] *adj* **(a)** *(amazed)* verblüfft. **(b)** *working hours etc* gestaffelt.

staggering ['stægərɪŋ] *adj (amazing)* umwerfend *(col).*

stagnant ['stægnənt] *adj (still) air, water* stehend *attr*; *(foul, stale) water* abgestanden; *air* verbraucht; *trade* stagnierend; *mind* träge.

stagnate [stæg'neɪt] *vi (not circulate, business)* stagnieren; *(become foul) (water)* stagnieren; *(air)* verbraucht werden; *(person)* verdummen; *(mind)* einrosten.

stagnation [stæg'neɪʃən] *n (of water)* Stagnieren *nt*; *(of air)* Stau *m*; *(of trade also)* Stagnation *f*; *(of person)* Verdummung *f*; *(of mind)* Verlangsamung *f.*

stag: ~ night *n* Saufabend *m (col) des Bräutigams mit seinen Kumpeln*; **~ party** *n* **(a)** Herrenabend *m*; **(b)** = **~ night.**

staid [steɪd] *adj (+er)* seriös; *person* ernst; *colour* gedeckt.

stain [steɪn] **1** *n* **(a)** *(lit)* Fleck *m*; *(fig also)* Makel *m.* **a blood ~** ein Blutfleck *m*, **~ remover** Fleckenentferner *m.* **(b)** *(colorant)* (Ein)färbemittel *nt*; *(wood~)* Beize *f.* **2** *vt* beflecken; *(colour)* einfärben; *(with wood~)* beizen. **3** *vi* **(a)** *(leave a ~)* Flecken hinterlassen. **(b)** *(become ~ed)* Flecken bekommen.

stained [steɪnd] *adj dress, floor* fleckig; *glass* bemalt; *reputation* befleckt. **~-glass window** Buntglasfenster *nt*; **~ with blood** blutbefleckt.

stainless ['steɪnlɪs] *adj (rust-resistant)* rostfrei. **~ steel** Edelstahl; **"~ steel"** „rostfrei"; **~ steel cutlery** rostfreies Besteck.

stair [stɛəʳ] *n* **(a)** *(step)* Stufe *f.* **(b)** *usu pl (~way)* Treppe *f.* **at the top of the ~s** oben an der Treppe.

stair: ~ carpet *n* Treppenläufer *m*; **~case** *n* Treppe *f*; **~way** *n* Treppe *f*; **~well** *n* Treppenhaus *nt.*

stake [steɪk] **1** *n* **(a)** *(post)* Pfahl *m*; *(for plant)* Stange *f*; *(for animal)* Pflock *m.* **(b)** *(place of execution)* Scheiterhaufen *m.* **to be burnt at the ~** auf dem Scheiterhaufen verbrannt werden. **(c)** *(bet)* Einsatz *m*; *(financial interest)* Anteil *m.* **to be at ~** auf dem Spiel stehen; **he has a lot at ~** er hat viel zu verlieren; **to have a ~ in sth** *in business* einen Anteil an etw *(dat)* haben; **that's precisely**

the issue at ~ genau darum geht es. **2** *vt* **(a)** *animal* anpflocken. **(b)** *(also ~* **up**) *plant* hochbinden; *fence* abstützen. **(c)** *(bet, risk)* setzen *(on* auf *+acc)*; *(US: back financially)* finanziell unterstützen. **to ~ one's life/reputation on sth** seine Hand für etw ins Feuer legen/sein Wort für etw verpfänden; **to ~ a/one's claim to sth** sich *(dat)* ein Anrecht auf etw *(acc)* sichern.

♦ **stake off** *or* **out** *vt sep land* abstecken.

stalactite ['stæləktaɪt] *n* Stalaktit *m.*

stalagmite ['stæləgmaɪt] *n* Stalagmit *m.*

stale [steɪl] *adj (+er)* **(a)** *(old, musty)* alt; *cake also* trocken; *(in taste, smell also)* muffig; *water, beer* schal; *air* verbraucht. **(b)** *(fig) news* veraltet; *joke* abgedroschen; *athlete, pianist* verbraucht.

stalemate ['steɪlmeɪt] *n (Chess, fig)* Patt *nt.* **to reach ~** *(lit)* ein Patt erreichen; *(fig)* in eine Sackgasse geraten.

stalk[1] [stɔːk] **1** *vt game* sich anpirschen an *(+acc)*; *person* sich anschleichen an *(+acc)*; *(animal)* sich heranschleichen an *(+acc)*. **2** *vi (walk haughtily)* stolzieren.

stalk[2] *n (of plant, leaf)* Stiel *m*; *(cabbage ~)* Strunk *m.* **his eyes popped out on ~s** *(col)* er bekam Stielaugen *(col).*

stall [stɔːl] **1** *n* **(a)** *(in stable)* Box *f.* **(b)** *(at market etc)* Stand *m.* **(c)** **~s** *pl (Brit Theat, Film)* Parkett *nt*; **in the ~s** im Parkett. **2** *vt (Aut)* abwürgen; *(Aviat)* überziehen. **3** *vi* **(a)** *(engine)* absterben; *(Aviat)* überziehen. **(b)** *(delay)* Zeit schinden *(col).* **to ~ on a decision** ein Entscheidung hinauszögern; **to ~ for time** versuchen, Zeit zu gewinnen; **stop ~ing** hören Sie auf auszuweichen.

stallion ['stæljən] *n* Hengst *m.*

stalwart ['stɔːlwət] **1** *adj* **(a)** *(in spirit)* treu; *belief* unerschütterlich. **(b)** *(in build)* robust. **2** *n (supporter)* (getreuer) Anhänger.

stamen ['steɪmen] *n* Staubgefäß *nt.*

stamina ['stæmɪnə] *n* Stehvermögen *nt.*

stammer ['stæmə[r]] **1** *n* Stottern *nt.* **to speak with a ~** stottern. **2** *vt* stammeln. **3** *vi* stottern.

stamp [stæmp] **1** *n* **(a)** *(postage ~)* (Brief)marke *f*; *(insurance ~ etc)* Marke *f*; *(trading ~)* (Rabatt)marke *f*; *(airmail ~, sticker)* Aufkleber *m.* **(b)** *(rubber ~ etc)* Stempel *m.* **(c)** *(fig)* **to bear the ~ of authenticity** die Züge der Echtheit tragen. **2** *vt* **(a)** **to ~ one's foot** (mit dem Fuß) aufstampfen; **to ~ the ground** (mit dem Fuß/den Füßen) auf den Boden stampfen. **(b)** *(put postage ~ on)* freimachen. **a ~ed addressed envelope** ein frankierter Rückumschlag. **(c)** *document etc (with rubber ~)* stempeln; *(with embossing machine)* prägen; *name, pattern* aufstempeln; aufprägen *(on* auf *+acc)*; *(fig)* ausweisen *(as* als*).* **the new leader has ~ed his personality on the party** der neue Vorsitzende hat der Partei seine Persönlichkeit aufgeprägt. **3** *vi (walk)* sta(m)pfen; *(disapprovingly, in dancing)* (auf)stampfen; *(horse)* aufstampfen. **you ~ed on my foot!** Sie haben mir auf den Fuß getreten!

♦ **stamp out 1** *vt sep* **(a)** *fire* austreten; *(fig: eradicate) epidemic, crime* ausrotten; *opposition* unterdrücken; *trouble* niederschlagen; *rebels* unschädlich machen. **(b)** *(cut out) pattern* ausstanzen. **2** *vi* heraussta(m)pfen.

stamp: ~ album *n* Briefmarkenalbum *nt*; **~ collection** *n* Briefmarkensammlung *f.*

stampede [stæm'piːd] **1** *n (of cattle)* wilde Flucht; *(of people)* Massenansturm *m (on* auf *+acc)*; *(to escape)* wilde Flucht. **2** *vt horses, crowd* in (wilde *or* helle) Panik versetzen. **to ~ sb into doing sth** *(fig)* jdn dazu drängen, etw zu tun. **3** *vi* durchgehen; *(crowd)* losstürmen *(for* auf *+acc).*

stamp machine *n* Briefmarkenautomat *m.*

stance [stæns] *n (posture, Sport)* Haltung *f*; *(mental attitude also)* Einstellung *f.*

stand [stænd] *(vb: pret, ptp* **stood**) **1** *n* **(a)** **to take a ~ (on a matter)** (zu einer Angelegenheit) eine Einstellung vertreten; **to take a firm ~** einen festen Standpunkt vertreten *(on* zu*).* **(b)** *(Mil) (resistance)* Widerstand *m*; *(battle)* Gefecht *nt.* **to make a ~** *(lit, fig)* Widerstand leisten. **(c)** *(taxi ~)* Stand *m.* **(d)** *(furniture, music ~)* Ständer *m.* **(e)** *(market stall etc)* Stand *m.* **(f)** *(band~)* Podium *nt.* **(g)** *(Sport)* Tribüne *f*; *(US Jur)* Zeugenstand *m.* **(we sat) in the ~** (wir saßen) auf der Tribüne.

2 *vt* **(a)** *(place)* stellen. **(b)** *(withstand) pressure, close examination etc (object)* standhalten *(+dat)*; *(person)* gewachsen sein *(+dat)*; *test* bestehen; *climate* vertragen; *heat, noise* aushalten; *loss, cost* verkraften. **(c)** *(col: put up with) person, noise etc* aushalten. **I can't ~ him/it** *(don't like)* ich kann ihn/es nicht ausstehen; **I can't ~ being kept waiting** ich kann es nicht leiden, wenn man mich warten läßt; **I can't ~ it any longer** ich halte das nicht mehr (länger) aus. **(d)** **to ~ sb a drink** *(col)* jdm einen Drink spendieren.

3 *vi* **(a)** *(be situated, be upright)* stehen; *(get up)* aufstehen. **don't just ~ there!** stehen Sie nicht nur (dumm) rum! *(col)*; **to ~ still** stillstehen; **we stood talking** wir standen da und unterhielten uns; **to be left ~ing** *(house etc)* stehenbleiben; *(fig)* nicht vom Start wegkommen.

(b) **he ~s over 6 feet** er ist über 1,80 m groß; **the tree ~s 20 m high** der Baum ist 20 m hoch.

(c) **to ~ as a candidate** kandidieren.

(d) *(continue to be valid) (offer, argument, contract)* gelten; *(decision, record, account)* stehen. **the theory ~s or falls by this** damit steht und fällt die Theorie.

(e) *(fig: be in a position)* **we ~ to lose/gain a lot** wir laufen Gefahr, eine Menge zu verlieren/wir können sehr viel gewinnen.

(f) *(fig: be placed)* **how do we ~?** wie stehen wir?; **I'd like to know where I ~ (with him)** ich möchte wissen, woran ich (bei ihm) bin; **to ~ accused of sth** einer Sache *(gen)* angeklagt sein; **as things ~** nach Lage der Dinge.

(g) *(fig: be, continue to be)* **to ~ firm** *or* **fast** festbleiben; **to ~ ready** sich bereithalten; **to ~ together** zusammenhalten; **to ~ (as) security for sb** für jdn bürgen; **nothing now ~s between us** es steht nichts mehr zwischen uns.

♦ **stand about** *or* **around** *vi* herumstehen.

♦ **stand aside** *vi (lit)* zur Seite treten; *(fig: withdraw)* zurücktreten.

♦ **stand back** *vi (move back)* zurücktreten; *(be situated at a distance)* abliegen; *(fig: distance oneself)* Abstand nehmen. **to ~ ~ and do nothing** tatenlos zusehen.

♦ **stand by 1** *vi* **(a)** *(remain uninvolved)* (unbeteiligt) danebenstehen. **(b)** *(be on alert)* sich bereithalten. **2** *vi +prep obj* **to ~ ~ a promise/sb** ein Versprechen/zu jdm halten.

♦ **stand down** *vi (retire, withdraw)* zurücktreten; *(before appointment)* verzichten; *(Jur)* den Zeugenstand verlassen.

♦ **stand for** *vi +prep obj* **(a)** *(be candidate for)* kandidieren für. **to ~ ~ election** sich zur Wahl stellen. **(b)** *(represent)* stehen für. **(c)** *(put up with)* hinnehmen.

♦ **stand in** *vi* einspringen.

♦ **stand out** *vi* **(a)** *(project)* hervorstehen; *(land, balcony)* herausragen. **(b)** *(contrast, be noticeable)* auffallen. **to ~ ~ against sth** sich von etw abheben *(oppose)* gegen etw Widerstand leisten; **to ~ ~ for sth** auf etw *(acc)* bestehen.

♦ **stand up 1** *vi* **(a)** *(get up)* aufstehen; *(be standing)* stehen. **(b)** *(argument)* überzeugen; *(Jur)* bestehen. **(c)** **to ~ ~ for sb/sth** für jdn/etw eintreten; **to ~ ~ to sth** *to test, pressure (object)* einer Sache *(dat)* standhalten; *(person)* einer Sache *(dat)* gewachsen sein; *to hard wear* etw *(acc)* aushalten; **to ~ ~ to sb** sich jdm gegenüber behaupten. **2** *vt sep* **(a)** *(put upright)* hinstellen.

(b) *(col) boyfriend etc* versetzen.

standard ['stændəd] **1** *n* **(a)** *(average, established norm)* Norm *f*; *(criterion)* Maßstab *m*. **to set a good ~** Maßstäbe setzen; **to be above/below ~** über/unter der Norm sein; **to be up to ~** den Anforderungen genügen. **(b)** *usu pl (moral ~s)* (sittliche) Maßstäbe *pl*. **he sets himself very high ~s** er stellt hohe Anforderungen an sich *(acc)* selbst. **(c)** *(degree, level)* Niveau *nt*. **~ of living** Lebensstandard *m*; **first-year university ~** Wissensstand *m* des ersten Studienjahrs; **of high/low ~** von hohem/niedrigem Niveau. **(d)** *(measurement)* (Maß)einheit *f*; *(monetary ~)* (Währungs)standard *m*. **(e)** *(flag)* Flagge *f*; *(on car)* Stander *m*. **~-bearer** Fahnenträger *m*.

2 *adj (usual, customary)* üblich; *model, price, practice, reply, reference work* Standard-; *size* Normal-; *(established) weight, size* Norm-. **~ English** korrektes Englisch; **~ German** Hochdeutsch *nt*.

standardize ['stændədaɪz] *vt education, style* vereinheitlichen; *format, sizes etc* normen.

stand-by ['stændbaɪ] **1** *n* **(a)** *(person)* Ersatz, Ersatzmann *m*; *(Sport also)* Auswechselspieler(in *f*) *m*; *(thing)* Reserve *f*; *(Aviat) (plane)* Entlastungsflugzeug *nt*; *(ticket)* Standby-Ticket *nt*. **(b)** *(state of readiness)* **on ~** in Bereitschaft; *(ready for action)* in Einsatzbereitschaft; **to be on 24-hour ~** 24 Stunden Bereitschaftsdienst haben. **2** *adj attr troops, player, generator* Reserve-; *(Aviat) plane* Entlastungs-; *ticket* Standby-.

stand-in ['stændɪn] *n (Film, Theat)* Ersatz *m*.

standing ['stændɪŋ] **1** *n* **(a)** *(social)* Rang *m*, (gesellschaftliche) Stellung; *(professional)* Position *f*; *(financial)* (finanzielle) Verhältnisse *pl*; *(repute)* Ruf *m*. **of high ~** von hohem Rang; *(repute)* von hohem Ansehen; **a man of some ~** ein angesehener Mann; **what is his ~ locally?** was hält man in der Gegend von ihm? **(b)** *(duration)* Dauer *f*. **a treaty of only six months' ~** ein Vertrag, der erst seit sechs Monaten besteht; **of long ~** alt, langjährig.

2 *adj attr* **(a)** *(established, permanent)* ständig; *rule, custom* bestehend; *army also* stehend. **it's a ~ joke** das ist schon zu einem Witz geworden; **to pay sth by ~ order** etw per Dauerauftrag bezahlen. **(b)** *(from a standstill)* aus dem Stand; *(not sitting) ticket* Stehplatz-; *(erect) corn* auf dem Halm (stehend); *stone* (aufrecht) stehend. **~ room only** nur Stehplätze; **to give sb a ~ ovation** jdm im Stehen Beifall klatschen.

stand: ~-offish [,stænd'ɒfɪʃ] *adj (col)* hochnäsig; **~point** *n* Standpunkt *m*; **from the ~point of the teacher** von Standpunkt des Lehrers gesehen; **~still** *n* Stillstand *m*; **to be at a ~still** *(plane, train)* stehen; *(machines, traffic, factory)* stillstehen; *(trade)* ruhen; **to bring production to a ~still** die Produktion zum Erliegen bringen; **to come to a ~still** *(person, vehicle)* anhalten; *(traffic, machines)* zum Stillstand kommen; *(industry etc)* zum Erliegen kommen; **~-up** *adj attr buffet, collar* Steh-; *meal* im Stehen.

stank [stæŋk] *pret of* **stink.**

stanza ['stænzə] *n* Strophe *f*.

staple[1] ['steɪpl] **1** *n* Heftklammer *f*; *(for wires, cables etc)* Krampe *f*. **2** *vt* heften; *wire* mit Krampen befestigen. **to ~ sth together** etw zusammenheften.

staple[2] *adj diet, food* Grund-, Haupt-

stapler ['steɪpləʳ] *n* Heftmaschine *f*.

star [stɑːʳ] **1** *n* **(a)** Stern *m*; *(asterisk also, Sch)* Sternchen *nt*. **the S~s and Stripes** das Sternenbanner; **you can thank your lucky ~s that ...** Sie können von Glück sagen, daß ...; **it's all in the ~s** es steht (alles) in den Sternen; **to see ~s** Sterne sehen; **a four-~ hotel** ein Vier-Sterne-Hotel *nt*. **(b)** *(person)* Star *m*. **2** *adj attr attraction* Haupt-; *performer, pupil* Star-. **3** *vt (Film etc)* **to ~ sb** jdn in der Hauptrolle zeigen; **~ring ...** in der Hauptrollen/den Hauptrollen ... **4** *vi (Film etc)* die Hauptrolle spielen.

starboard ['stɑːbəd] **1** *n* Steuerbord *nt*. **2** *adj* Steuerbord-.

starch [stɑːtʃ] **1** *n* Stärke *f*. **~-reduced** stärkearm. **2** *vt* stärken.

starchy ['stɑːtʃɪ] *adj (+er)* stärkehaltig; *(fig)* steif.

stardom ['stɑːdəm] *n* Ruhm *m*. **where he hoped to find ~** wo er hoffte, ein Star zu werden.

stare [stɛəʳ] **1** *n* (starrer) Blick. **to give sb a ~** jdn anstarren. **2** *vt* **the answer was staring us in the face** die Antwort lag klar auf der Hand. **3** *vi (vacantly etc)* (vor sich hin) starren; *(cow, madman)* stieren; *(in surprise)* große Augen machen; *(eyes)* weit aufgerissen sein. **he ~d in disbelief** er starrte ungläubig; **to ~ at sb/sth** jdn/etw anstarren.

star: ~fish *n* Seestern *m*; **~gazer** *n (hum col)* Sterngucker *m (hum col)*.

stark [stɑːk] **1** *adj (+er) realism, contrast* kraß; *reality, poverty also, truth, terror* nackt; *landscape, cliffs, branches* kahl; *colour* kräftig; *(glaring)* grell. **2** *adv* **~ raving mad** *(col)* total verrückt *(col)*; **~ naked** *(also* **starkers** *col)* splitternackt.

starlet ['stɑːlɪt] *n* (Film)sternchen nt.

starlight ['stɑːlaɪt] *n* Sternenlicht *nt*.

starling ['stɑːlɪŋ] *n* Star *m*.

starlit ['stɑːlɪt] *adj sky, night* stern(en)klar.

starry ['stɑːrɪ] *adj (+er) night* stern(en)klar.

starry-eyed [,stɑːrɪ'aɪd] *adj idealist* blauäugig. **to go all ~** glänzende Augen kriegen.

star: S~-spangled Banner *n* Sternenbanner *nt*; **~-studded** *adj* **(a)** *(liter) night* stern(en)klar; **(b)** *(fig)* **~-studded cast** Starbesetzung *f*.

start[1] [stɑːt] **1** *n (fright etc)* **to give a ~** zusammenfahren; *(start up)* aufschrecken; *(horse)* scheuen; **to give sb a ~** jdn erschrecken; **to wake with a ~** aus dem Schlaf hochschrecken. **2** *vi* zusammenfahren; *(start up)* aufschrecken. **to ~ from one's chair/out of one's sleep** aus dem Stuhl hochfahren/aus dem Schlaf hochschrecken.

start[2] **1** *n* **(a)** *(beginning)* Beginn, Anfang *m*; *(departure)* Aufbruch *m*; *(of race)* Start *m*; *(of rumour, trouble, journey)* Ausgangspunkt *m*. **at the ~** am Anfang, zu Beginn; *(Sport)* am Start; **for a ~** *(to begin with)* fürs erste; *(firstly)* zunächst einmal; **from the ~** von Anfang an; **from ~ to finish** von Anfang bis Ende; **to make a ~ (on sth)** (mit etw) anfangen; **to make an early ~** frühzeitig aufbrechen; **to make a fresh ~ (in life)** (noch einmal) von vorn anfangen. **(b)** *(advantage, Sport)* Vorsprung *m (over* vor *+dat)*.

2 *vt* **(a)** *(begin)* anfangen mit; *argument, career, new life, negotiations* beginnen, anfangen; *new job, journey* antreten. **to ~ work** anfangen zu arbeiten; **he ~ed life as a miner** er hat als Bergmann angefangen; **you ~ed it!** du hast angefangen!; **don't ~ that again!** fang nicht schon wieder (damit) an! **(b)** *(cause to begin) runners, race* starten; *train* abfahren lassen; *rumour* in Umlauf setzen; *conversation* anfangen, anknüpfen; *fight* anfangen; *blaze, collapse, chain reaction* auslösen; *fire* anzünden; *(arsonist)* legen; *(found) enterprise* gründen. **to ~ sb thinking/on a subject** jdn nachdenklich machen/jdn auf ein Thema bringen; **to ~ sb on a career** jdm zu einer Karriere verhelfen. **(c)** *car, machine* starten; *engine also* anlassen; *clock* in Gang setzen.

3 *vi (begin)* anfangen, beginnen; *(car, engine)* anspringen; *(plane)* starten; *(move off)* anfahren; *(bus, train)* abfahren; *(rumour)* in Umlauf kommen; *(violins etc)* einsetzen. **~ing from Tuesday** ab Dienstag; to **~ for home** sich auf den Heimweg machen; **to ~ (off) with** *(firstly)* erstens; *(at the beginning)* zunächst; **to ~ after sb** jdn verfolgen; **to get ~ed** anfangen; *(on trip)* aufbrechen; **to ~ on a task/the food** sich an eine Aufgabe/

ans Essen machen; to ~ **talking** zu sprechen anfangen; **he ~ed by saying ...** er sagte zunächst ...; **don't you ~!** fang du nicht auch noch an!

♦ **start off 1** *vi (begin)* anfangen; *(begin moving: person)* losgehen; *(on journey)* aufbrechen; *(run)* loslaufen; *(drive)* losfahren; *(esp Sport)* starten; *(begin talking etc)* anfangen *(on* mit*)*. **2** *vt sep sth* anfangen. **to ~ sb ~ (talking)** jdm das Stichwort geben; **a few stamps to ~ you ~** ein paar Briefmarken für den Anfang.

♦ **start out** *vi (begin)* (zunächst) beginnen *or* anfangen; *(begin a journey)* aufbrechen *(for* nach*)*. **we ~ed ~ on a long journey** wir machten uns auf eine lange Reise.

♦ **start over** *vi (US)* noch (ein)mal von vorn anfangen.

♦ **start up 1** *vi (begin: music etc)* anfangen; *(machine)* angehen *(col)*, in Gang kommen; *(motor)* anspringen; *(siren)* losheulen. **2** *vt sep* **(a)** *(cause to function)* in Gang bringen; *engine also* anlassen. **(b)** *(begin)* eröffnen; *business also, conversation* anfangen.

starter ['stɑːtəʳ] *n* **(a)** *(Sport)* Starter(in *f*) *m*. **(b)** *(Aut etc: self-~)* Anlasser *m*. **(c)** *(child)* **to be a late** *or* **slow ~** Spätentwickler *m* sein. **(d)** *(col: first course)* Vorspeise *f*. **(e) for ~s** *(col)* für den Anfang *(col)*.

starting ['stɑːtɪŋ] *in cpds (Sport) line, post* Start-; **~ gun** *n* Startpistole *f*; **~ handle** *n* Anlasserkurbel *f*; **~ point** *n (lit, fig)* Ausgangspunkt *m*; **~ post** *n* Startpflock *m*.

startle ['stɑːtl] *vt* erschrecken. **I was ~d to see how old he looked** ich stellte entsetzt fest, wie alt er aussah.

startling ['stɑːtlɪŋ] *adj news* überraschend; *(bad)* alarmierend, bestürzend; *resemblance* erstaunlich; *originality, discovery* aufregend.

starvation [stɑː'veɪʃən] *n (act)* Hungern *nt*; *(of besieged people)* Aushungern *nt*; *(condition)* Hunger *m*. **to die of ~** verhungern; **to go on a ~ diet** *(hum)* eine Hungerkur machen.

starve [stɑːv] **1** *vt* **(a)** *(deprive of food)* hungern lassen; *(also ~* **out***)* aushungern; *(kill: also ~* **to death***)* verhungern lassen; **to ~ oneself** hungern. **(b)** *(fig)* **to ~ sb of sth** jdm etw vorenthalten *or* verweigern; **to be ~d of capital** an akutem Kapitalmangel leiden; **to be ~d of affection** zuwenig Zuneigung erfahren. **2** *vi* hungern; *(die: also ~* **to death***)* verhungern. **I'm simply starving!** *(col)* ich sterbe vor Hunger! *(col)*; **to ~ for sth** *(fig)* nach etw hungern.

starving ['stɑːvɪŋ] *adj (lit)* hungernd *attr*; *(fig)* hungrig.

stash [stæʃ] *vt (also ~* **away***)* *(col) loot* verschwinden lassen *(col)*; *money* beiseite schaffen.

state [steɪt] **1** *n* **(a)** *(condition)* Zustand *m*. **~ of health/mind** Gesundheits-/Geisteszustand *m*; **the ~ of the nation** die Lage der Nation; **the present ~ of the economy** die gegenwärtige Wirtschaftslage; **where animals live in their natural ~** wo Tiere im Naturzustand leben; **in a good/bad ~** in gutem/schlechtem Zustand; **he's in no (fit) ~ to do that** er ist nicht in dem (richtigen) Zustand dafür; **look at the ~ of your hands!** guck dir bloß mal deine Hände an!; **the room was in a terrible ~** im Zimmer herrschte ein fürchterliches Durcheinander.

(b) *(col: anxiety)* **to get into a ~ (about sth)** *(col)* wegen etw durchdrehen *(col)*.

(c) *(pomp)* Aufwand, Pomp *m*. **to be received in great ~** mit großem Staat empfangen werden; **to travel in ~** pompös reisen; **to lie in ~** (feierlich) aufgebahrt sein.

(d) *(Pol)* Staat *m*; *(federal ~)* (Bundes)staat *m*; *(in BRD, Austria)* (Bundes)land *nt*. **the S~s** die (Vereinigten) Staaten; **the S~ of Florida** der Staat Florida; **affairs of ~** Staatsangelegenheiten *pl*.

2 *vt* darlegen, vortragen; *name, price* nennen; *purpose* angeben. **to ~ that ...** feststellen, daß ...; **to ~ one's case** seine Sache vortragen; **to ~ the case for the prosecution** *(Jur)* die Anklage vortragen; **unless otherwise ~d** wenn nicht anders angegeben; **as ~d in my letter I ...** wie in meinem Brief erwähnt, ... ich ...

state *in cpds* Staats-; *control also, industry* staatlich; *(US etc)* bundesstaatlich.

stated ['steɪtɪd] *adj* **(a)** *(declared) sum, date* genannt; *limits* bestimmt. **(b)** *(fixed, regular) times, amount* fest(gesetzt).

state: S~ Department *n (US)* Außenministerium *nt*; **~ education** *n* staatliche Erziehung; *(system)* staatliches Erziehungswesen; **~house** *n (US)* Parlamentsgebäude, Kapitol *nt*; **~less** *adj* staatenlos; **~less person** Staatenlose(r) *mf*.

stately ['steɪtlɪ] *adj (+er) person, bearing* würdevoll; *pace* gemessen. **~ home** herrschaftliches Anwesen, Schloß *nt*.

statement ['steɪtmənt] *n* **(a)** *(of thesis etc)* Darstellung *f*; *(of problem also)* Darlegung *f*. **(b)** *(that said)* Feststellung *f*; *(claim)* Behauptung *f*; *(official ~)* Erklärung *f*; *(in court, to police)* Aussage *f*; *(written)* Protokoll *nt*. **to make a ~ to the press** eine Presseerklärung abgeben. **(c)** *(Fin) (tradesman's)* Rechnung *f*; *(bank ~)* Kontoauszug *m*.

state: ~-of-the-art *adj* neueste(r, s); **~-owned** *adj* staatseigen; **~room** *n (in palace)* Empfangssaal *m*; *(on ship)* Kabine *f*; **~ school** *n* öffentliche Schule; **~ secret** *n* Staatsgeheimnis *nt*; **S~'s evidence** *n (US)* Aussage *f* eines Kronzeugen; **to turn S~'s evidence** als Kronzeuge auftreten.

statesman ['steɪtsmən] *n, pl* **-men** [-mən] Staatsmann *m*.

statesmanship ['steɪtsmənʃɪp] *n* Staatskunst *f*.

static ['stætɪk] **1** *adj* **(a)** *(Phys)* statisch. **(b)** *(not moving or changing)* konstant; *(stationary)* feststehend *attr*; *condition, society* statisch. **2** *n (Phys)* Reibungselektrizität *f*; *(Rad)* atmosphärische Störungen *pl*.

station ['steɪʃən] **1** *n* **(a)** *(railway ~, bus ~)* Bahnhof *m*; *(stop)* Station *f*. **(b)** *(police ~, fire ~)* Wache *f*; *(space ~)* (Raum)station *f*; *(US: gas ~)* Tankstelle *f*. **(c)** *(Mil: post)* Stellung *f*, Posten *m*. **(d)** *(Rad, TV)* Sender *m*. **(e)** *(rank)* Stand *m*. **~ in life** Stellung *f* (im Leben), Rang *m*; **he has got ideas above his ~** er hat Ideen, die jemandem aus seinem Stand gar nicht zukommen. **2** *vt (Mil) troops* stationieren; *sentry* aufstellen.

stationary ['steɪʃənərɪ] *adj (not moving) car* haltend *attr*; *(not movable)* fest(stehend *attr*). **to be ~** *(vehicles)* stehen; *(traffic, fig)* stillstehen; **to remain ~** sich nicht bewegen; *(traffic)* stillstehen.

stationer ['steɪʃənəʳ] *n* Schreibwarenhändler *m*. **~'s (shop)** *(Brit)* Schreibwarenhandlung *f*.

stationery ['steɪʃənərɪ] *n (notepaper)* Briefpapier *nt*; *(writing materials)* Schreibwaren *pl*.

station: ~ house *n (US: police)* (Polizei)wache *f*; **~-master** *n* Bahnhofsvorsteher *m*; **~ wagon** *n (US)* Kombi(wagen) *m*.

statistical [stə'tɪstɪkəl] *adj* statistisch.

statistician [ˌstætɪ'stɪʃən] *n* Statistiker(in *f*) *m*.

statistics [stə'tɪstɪks] *n* **(a)** *sing* Statistik *f*. **(b)** *pl (data)* Statistiken *pl*.

statue ['stætjuː] *n* Statue *f*.

statuesque [ˌstætjʊ'esk] *adj figure* wohlgeformt; *beauty* klassisch.

statuette [ˌstætjʊ'et] *n* Statuette *f*.

stature ['stætʃəʳ] *n* **(a)** Wuchs *m*; *(esp of man)* Statur *f*. **(b)** *(fig)* Format *nt*.

status ['steɪtəs] *n* Stellung *f*; *(legal ~, social ~ also)* Status *m*. **equal ~** Gleichstellung *f*; **marital ~** Familienstand *m*.

status quo ['steɪtəs'kwəʊ] *n* Status quo *m*.

status symbol *n* Statussymbol *nt*.

statute ['stætjuːt] *n* Gesetz *n*; *(of organization)* Satzung *f*, Statut *nt*. **~ book** Gesetzbuch *nt*; **to put sth**

in the ~ **book** etw zum Gesetz machen.

statutory ['stætjʊtərɪ] *adj* gesetzlich; *(in organization)* satzungsgemäß; *right also* verbrieft; *punishment* (vom Gesetz) vorgesehen.

staunch[1] [stɔːntʃ] *adj (+er) Catholic, loyalist* überzeugt; *member, supporter* getreu; *support* standhaft.

staunch[2] *vt flow* stauen; *bleeding* stillen.

stave [steɪv] *n (Mus: staff)* Notenlinien *pl.*

♦ **stave in** *pret, ptp* **stove in** *vt sep* eindrücken; *head* einschlagen.

♦ **stave off** *pret, ptp* **~d off** *vt sep attack* zurückschlagen; *crisis, cold* abwehren; *hunger* lindern.

staves [steɪvz] *pl of* **staff 1 (c).**

stay [steɪ] **1** *n* **(a)** Aufenthalt *m.* **a short ~ in hospital** ein kurzer Krankenhausaufenthalt. **(b)** *(Jur)* Aussetzung *f.* **~ of execution** Vollstreckungsaufschub *m.*

2 *vt* **(a)** *(Jur) order, sentence* aussetzen. **(b) to ~ the course** *(lit, fig)* durchhalten.

3 *vi* **(a)** *(remain)* bleiben. **to ~ for** *or* **to supper** zum Abendessen bleiben; **to have come to ~** nicht nur eine Modeerscheinung sein; **unemployment has come to ~** die Arbeitslosigkeit ist zum Dauerzustand geworden; **if it ~s fine** wenn es schön bleibt; **~ with it!** nicht aufgeben! **(b)** *(reside)* wohnen; *(at youth hostel etc)* übernachten. **to ~ at a hotel** im Hotel wohnen; **I ~ed in Italy for a few weeks** ich habe mich ein paar Wochen in Italien aufgehalten; **he is ~ing at Chequers for the weekend** er verbringt das Wochenende in Chequers; **to ~ with friends** bei Freunden wohnen; **my brother came to ~** mein Bruder ist zu Besuch gekommen.

♦ **stay away** *vi (from* von*)* wegbleiben; *(from person)* sich fernhalten.

♦ **stay behind** *vi* zurückbleiben; *(Sch: as punishment)* nachsitzen.

♦ **stay in** *vi (at home)* zu Hause bleiben; *(in position etc)* drinbleiben; *(Sch)* nachsitzen.

♦ **stay on** *vi (lid etc)* draufbleiben; *(light)* anbleiben; *(people)* (noch) bleiben. **to ~ ~ at school/as manager** (in der Schule) weitermachen/(weiterhin) Geschäftsführer bleiben.

♦ **stay out** *vi* draußen bleiben; *(on strike)* weiterstreiken; *(not come home)* wegbleiben. **to ~ ~ of sth** sich aus etw heraushalten; **he never managed to ~ ~ of trouble** er war dauernd in Schwierigkeiten.

♦ **stay up** *vi* **(a)** *(person)* aufbleiben. **don't ~ ~ for me!** bleib nicht meinetwegen auf! **(b)** *(tent, fence, pole)* stehen bleiben; *(picture, decorations)* hängen bleiben.

stay-at-home ['steɪət,həʊm] *n* Stubenhocker *m.*

stayer ['steɪəʳ] *n* **to be a ~** Stehvermögen *nt* haben.

staying power ['steɪɪŋ,paʊəʳ] *n* Durchhaltevermögen *nt*, Ausdauer *f.*

STD *(Brit Telec)* = **subscriber trunk dialling. ~ code** Vorwahl(nummer) *f.*

stead [sted] *n* **in his ~** an seiner Stelle; **to stand sb in good ~** jdm zugute kommen.

steadfast ['stedfɑːst] *adj* fest; *person, refusal also* standhaft; *belief* unerschütterlich.

steadily ['stedɪlɪ] *adv* **(a)** *(firmly)* ruhig; *balanced* fest; *gaze* unverwandt. **(b)** *(constantly)* ständig; *rain* ununterbrochen. **(c)** *(reliably)* zuverlässig.

steady ['stedɪ] **1** *adj (+er)* **(a)** *(firm, not wobbling) hand, nerves, eye* ruhig; *gaze* unverwandt. **with a ~ hand** mit ruhiger Hand; **to hold sth ~** etw ruhig halten; *ladder* etw festhalten; **the chair is not very ~** der Stuhl ist wacklig. **(b)** *(constant) wind, progress, demand etc* ständig, stet *(geh)*; *drizzle* ununterbrochen; *temperature* beständig. **at a ~ pace/70** in gleichmäßigem Tempo/ständig mit 70. **(c)** *(reliable, regular) worker* zuverlässig. **(d)** *job, boyfriend* fest. **2** *adv* **~!** *(carefully, gently)* vorsichtig!; *(Naut)* Kurs halten!; **~ (on)!** sachte! *(col)*; **to go ~ (with sb)** *(col)* mit jdm (fest) zusammen sein. **3** *vt plane, boat* wieder ins Gleichgewicht bringen; *(stabilize) nerves, person* beruhigen; *(in character)* ausgleichen. **to ~ oneself** festen Halt finden; **she had a ~ing influence on him** durch sie wurde er ausgeglichener.

steak [steɪk] *n* Steak *nt*; *(of fish)* Filet *nt.* **~ and kidney pie** Fleischpastete *f* mit Nieren.

steal [stiːl] *(vb: pret* **stole**, *ptp* **stolen***)* **1** *vt object, idea, heart* stehlen. **to ~ sth from sb** jdm etw stehlen; **to ~ the show/sb's thunder** die Schau stehlen/jdm den Wind aus den Segeln nehmen; **the baby stole all the attention** das Kind zog die ganze Aufmerksamkeit auf sich. **2** *vi* **(a)** *(thieve)* stehlen. **(b)** *(move quietly)* sich stehlen, (sich) schleichen. **to ~ away** sich davonstehlen; **to ~ up on sb** sich an jdn heranschleichen. **3** *n* *(US col: bargain)* Geschenk *nt (col)*. **it's a ~!** das ist (ja) geschenkt! *(col)*.

stealth [stelθ] *n* List *f.* **by ~** durch List.

stealthy ['stelθɪ] *adj (+er)* verstohlen; *footsteps* verhalten.

steam [stiːm] **1** *n* Dampf *m.* **the windows were covered with ~** die Fensterscheiben waren beschlagen; **full ~ ahead!** *(Naut)* volle Kraft voraus!; **to get up ~** *(fig)* in Schwung kommen; **to let off ~** *(lit, fig)* Dampf ablassen; **to run out of ~** *(fig)* Schwung verlieren; **under one's own ~** *(fig)* allein, ohne Hilfe. **2** *vt* dämpfen; *food* dünsten. **to ~ open an envelope** einen Briefumschlag über Dampf öffnen; **~ed pudding** Kochpudding *m.* **3** *vi* **(a)** *(give off ~)* dampfen. **(b)** *(move)* dampfen. **the ship ~ed into the harbour** das Schiff kam in den Hafen gefahren.

♦ **steam up 1** *vt sep window* beschlagen lassen. **to be/get ~ed ~** *(fig col)* hochgehen *(col) (about* wegen*)*. **2** *vi (window)* beschlagen.

steam: ~boat *n* Dampfschiff *nt*, Dampfer *m*; **~ engine** *n (Rail)* Dampflok *f.*

steamer ['stiːməʳ] *n (ship)* Dampfer *m*; *(Cook)* Dampfkochtopf *m.*

steam: ~ iron *n* Dampfbügeleisen *nt*; **~roller** *n* Dampfwalze *f*; **~ship** *n* Dampfschiff *nt.*

steamy ['stiːmɪ] *adj (+er)* dunstig; *room, atmosphere* voll Dampf; *window* beschlagen.

steed [stiːd] *n (liter)* Roß *nt.*

steel [stiːl] **1** *n* Stahl *m.* **2** *adj attr* Stahl-. **3** *vt* **to ~ oneself** sich wappnen *(for* gegen*)*; *(physically)* sich stählen *(for* für*)*; **to ~ oneself to do sth** allen Mut zusammennehmen, um etw zu tun.

steel *in cpds* Stahl-, stahl-; **~ mill** *n* Stahlwalzwerk *nt*; **~works** *n sing or pl* Stahlwerk *nt.*

steely ['stiːlɪ] *adj (+er) grip* stahlhart; *gaze* hart; *determination* eisern; *blue* Stahl-.

steep[1] [stiːp] *adj (+er)* **(a)** steil. **it's a ~ climb** es geht steil hinauf; **there's been a ~ drop in the value of the pound** das Pfund ist stark gefallen. **(b)** *(fig col) demand* unverschämt; *price also, bill* gesalzen *(col)*. **it seems a bit ~ that ...** es ist ein starkes Stück, daß ...

steep[2] *vt* **(a)** *(in liquid)* eintauchen; *(in marinade, dye)* ziehen lassen; *dried food* einweichen. **(b)** *(fig)* **to be ~ed in sth** von etw durchdrungen sein; **~ed in history** geschichtsträchtig.

steeple ['stiːpl] *n* Kirchturm *m.*

steeple: ~chase *n (for horses)* Hindernisrennen *nt*; *(for runners)* Hindernislauf *m*; **~jack** *n* Turmarbeiter *m.*

steer[1] [stɪəʳ] **1** *vt (lit, fig)* lenken; *ship* steuern; *person also* lotsen. **2** *vi (in car)* lenken; *(in ship)* steuern. **to ~ due north** Kurs nach Norden halten; **to ~ for** *or* **towards sth** auf etw *(acc)* zuhalten; *(Naut)* etw ansteuern; *(fig)* auf etw *(acc)* zusteuern.

steer[2] *n* junger Ochse.

steering ['stɪərɪŋ] *n (in car etc)* Lenkung *f*; *(Naut)* Steuerung *f.*

steering: ~ column *n* Lenksäule *f*; **~ committee** *n* vorbereitender Ausschuß; **~ wheel** *n* Steuer(rad) *nt*; *(of car also)* Lenkrad *nt*.

stem [stem] **1** *n (of plant, glass)* Stiel *m*; *(of shrub, word)* Stamm *m*; *(of grain)* Halm *m*; *(of pipe)* Hals *m*. **2** *vt (check, stop)* aufhalten; *flood, tide* eindämmen; *bleeding* zum Stillstand bringen. **3** *vi* **to ~ from sth** *(result from)* von etw herrühren; *(have as origin)* auf etw *(acc)* zurückgehen.

stench [stentʃ] *n* Gestank *m*.

stencil ['stensl] *n* Schablone *f*; *(Printing: for duplicating)* Matrize *f*.

stenographer [ste'nɒgrəfəʳ] *n* Stenograph(in *f*) *m*.

stenography [ste'nɒgrəfɪ] *n* Stenographie *f*.

step [step] **1** *n* **(a)** *(pace, in dancing)* Schritt *m*. **to take a ~** einen Schritt machen; **~ by ~** *(lit, fig)* Schritt für Schritt; **to be in/out of ~** *(fig)* im/nicht im Gleichklang sein *(with* mit*)*.

(b) *(move)* Schritt *m*; *(measure also)* Maßnahme *f*. **it's a great ~ forward** es ist ein großer Schritt nach vorn; **that would be a ~ back/in the right direction for him** das wäre für ihn ein Rückschritt/ein Schritt in die richtige Richtung; **to take ~s to do sth** Maßnahmen ergreifen, (um) etw zu tun.

(c) *(in process, experiment, scale, hierarchy)* Stufe *f*. **~s** *(outdoors)* Treppe *f*; **mind the ~** Vorsicht Stufe.

(d) ~s *pl (~-ladder: also* **pair of ~s***)* Stufenleiter *f*.

2 *vt* **~ two paces to the left** treten Sie zwei Schritte nach links.

3 *vi* gehen. **to ~ into/out of sth** *house, room, puddle* in etw *(acc)*/aus etw treten; *train, dress* in etw *(acc)*/aus etw steigen; **to ~ on(to) sth** *plane, train* in etw *(acc)* steigen; *platform, ladder* auf etw *(acc)* steigen; **to ~ on sth** *object, toy* auf etw *(acc)* treten; **to ~ over sb/sth** über jdn/etw steigen; **~ this way, please** hier entlang, bitte!; **to ~ inside** herein-/hineintreten; **to ~ outside** heraus-/hinaustreten; **~ on it!** mach mal ein bißchen schneller! *(col)*; *(in car)* gib Gas!

♦ **step aside** *vi (lit)* zur Seite treten; *(fig)* Platz machen.

♦ **step back** *vi (lit)* zurücktreten. **to ~ ~ from sth** *(fig)* von etw Abstand gewinnen.

♦ **step down** *vi (fig)* **to ~ ~ in favour of sb** jdm Platz machen.

♦ **step forward** *vi* vortreten; *(fig)* sich melden.

♦ **step in** *vi (lit)* eintreten *(-to, +prep obj* in *+acc)*; *(fig)* einschreiten.

♦ **step off** *vi +prep obj (off bus, plane, boat)* aussteigen *(prep obj* aus*)*. **to ~ ~ the pavement** vom Bürgersteig treten.

♦ **step up** *vt sep* steigern; *efforts also, campaign* verstärken; *volume* erhöhen.

step- *pref brother, mother etc* Stief-.

step-ladder ['step,lædəʳ] *n* Stufenleiter *f*.

steppe [step] *n* Steppe *f*.

stepping stone ['stepɪŋ,stəʊn] *n* (Tritt)stein *m*; *(fig)* Sprungbrett *nt (to* für*)*.

stereo ['sterɪəʊ] **1** *n* Stereo *nt*; *(record-player)* Stereoanlage *f*. **in ~** in Stereo. **2** *adj* Stereo-.

stereophonic [,sterɪəʊ'fɒnɪk] *adj* stereophon.

stereotype ['sterɪə,taɪp] *n (fig)* Klischee(vorstellung *f*) *nt*; *(~ character)* stereotype Figur.

sterile ['steraɪl] *adj* **(a)** *(lit, fig)* unfruchtbar. **(b)** *(germ-free)* steril, keimfrei; *(fig) décor etc* steril.

sterilization [,sterɪlaɪ'zeɪʃən] *n* Sterilisation *f*.

sterilize ['sterɪlaɪz] *vt person, instruments* sterilisieren.

sterling ['stɜːlɪŋ] **1** *adj* **(a)** *(Fin)* Sterling-. **in pounds ~** in Pfund Sterling. **(b)** *(fig)* gediegen; *character* lauter. **(c) ~ silver** Sterlingsilber *nt*. **2** *n no art (money)* das Pfund Sterling. **in ~** in Pfund Sterling. **3** *adj attr* aus (Sterling)silber.

stern[1] [stɜːn] *n (Naut)* Heck *nt*.

stern[2] *adj (+er) (strict)* streng; *words also, character, warning* ernst. **made of ~er stuff** aus härterem Holz geschnitzt.

steroid ['stɪərɔɪd] *n* Steroid *nt*.

stethoscope ['steθəskəʊp] *n* Stethoskop *nt*.

stevedore ['stiːvɪdɔːʳ] *n* Stauer *m*.

stew [stjuː] **1** *n* **(a)** Eintopf(gericht *nt*) *m*. **(b)** *(col)* **to be in a ~ (about sth)** (über etw *(acc) or* wegen etw) ganz aufgeregt sein. **2** *vt meat* schmoren; *fruit* dünsten. **~ed apples** Apfelkompott *nt*. **3** *vi (meat)* schmoren; *(fruit)* dünsten; *(col: tea)* bitter werden. **to let sb ~ (in his/her own juice)** jdn (im eigenen Saft) schmoren lassen.

steward ['stjuːəd] *n* Steward *m*; *(on estate etc)* Verwalter *m*; *(at dance, meeting)* Ordner *m*.

stewardess ['stjuːədes] *n* Stewardess *f*.

stick[1] [stɪk] *n* **(a)** Stock *m*; *(twig)* Zweig *m*; *(hockey ~)* Schläger *m*; *(drum~)* Schlegel *m*. **to give sb/sth (a lot of) ~** *(col: criticize)* jdn/etw heruntermachen *(col)*; **just a few ~s of furniture** nur ein paar Möbelstücke; **to get hold of the wrong end of the ~** *(fig col)* etw falsch verstehen; **in the ~s** *(esp US: backwoods)* in der hintersten Provinz. **(b)** *(of sealing wax, celery, rhubarb, dynamite)* Stange *f*; *(of chalk, shaving soap)* Stück *nt*.

stick[2] *pret, ptp* **stuck 1** *vt* **(a)** *(with glue etc)* kleben. **to ~ an envelope down** einen Briefumschlag zukleben. **(b)** *(pin)* stecken. **he stuck a badge on his lapel** er steckte sich *(dat)* ein Abzeichen ans Revers. **(c)** *(jab) knife, sword etc* stoßen. **(d)** *(col: place, put)* tun *(col)*; *(in sth also)* stecken *(col)*. **~ it on the shelf** tu's aufs Regal; **he stuck his head around the corner** er steckte seinen Kopf um die Ecke; **you know where you can ~ that** *(col!)* du kannst mich mal! *(col!)*. **(e)** *(esp Brit col: tolerate)* aushalten; *pace, pressure of work* durchhalten. **I can't ~ him/that** ich kann ihn/das nicht ausstehen *(col)*.

2 *vi* **(a)** *(glue, object)* kleben *(to* an *+dat)*. **the name seems to have stuck** der Name scheint ihm/ihr *etc* geblieben zu sein. **(b)** *(become caught, wedged etc)* steckenbleiben; *(drawer, window)* klemmen. **(c)** *(sth pointed)* stecken *(in* in *+dat)*. **it stuck in my foot** das ist mir im Fuß steckengeblieben. **(d)** *(project)* **his toes are ~ing through his socks** seine Zehen kommen durch die Socken. **(e)** *(stay)* bleiben; *(slander)* haftenbleiben. **to ~ in sb's mind** jdm im Gedächtnis bleiben; **to make sth ~ (in one's mind)** sich *(dat)* etw einprägen.

♦ **stick around** *vi (col)* hier/da bleiben.

♦ **stick at** *vi +prep obj* **(a)** *(persist)* bleiben an *(+dat) (col)*. **to ~ ~ it** dranbleiben *(col)*. **(b) he will ~ ~ nothing** er macht vor nichts halt.

♦ **stick by** *vi +prep obj sb* halten zu; *promise* stehen zu.

♦ **stick on 1** *vt sep label, cover* aufkleben *(prep obj* auf *+acc)*. **2** *vi (label etc)* kleben, haften *(prep obj* an *+dat)*.

♦ **stick out 1** *vi* vorstehen *(of* aus*)*; *(ears, hair)* abstehen; *(fig: be noticeable)* auffallen. **2** *vt sep* **(a)** *tongue etc* hinaus-/herausstrecken. **(b) to ~ it ~** durchhalten.

♦ **stick out for** *vi +prep obj* sich stark machen für.

♦ **stick to** *vi +prep obj* bleiben bei; *(remain faithful to) principles etc* treu bleiben *(+dat)*.

♦ **stick together** *vi* zusammenkleben; *(fig: partners etc)* zusammenhalten.

♦ **stick up 1** *vt sep* **(a)** *(with tape etc)* zukleben. **(b)** *(col: raise)* **~ 'em ~!** Hände hoch! **(c)** *(col) notice etc* aufhängen, anbringen. **2** *vi (nail etc)* vorstehen; *(hair)* abstehen; *(collar)* hochstehen.

♦ **stick up for** *vi +prep obj sb, one's principles* eintreten für. **to ~ ~ ~ oneself** sich behaupten.

sticker ['stɪkəʳ] *n* **(a)** *(label)* Aufkleber *m*. **(b)** *(col: determined person)* **he's a ~** er ist zäh.

sticking plaster ['stɪkɪŋ,plɑːstəʳ] *n (Brit)* Heftpflaster *nt*.

stick-in-the-mud ['stɪkɪnðə,mʌd] *(col) n* Muffel *m (col)*.

stickleback ['stɪklbæk] *n* Stichling *m*.

stickler ['stɪkləʳ] *n* **to be a ~ for sth** es mit etw peinlich genau nehmen.

stick: **~-on** *adj label* (Auf)klebe-; **~-up** *n (col)* Überfall *m*.

sticky ['stɪkɪ] *adj (+er)* **(a)** klebrig; *label* Klebe-; *paint* feucht; *atmosphere* schwül; *air* stickig; *(sweaty) hands* feucht. **~ tape** Klebeband *nt*. **(b)** *(fig col) problem, person* schwierig; *moment* heikel. **to come to a ~ end** ein böses Ende nehmen; **to be on a ~ wicket** in einer schwierigen Lage sein.

stiff [stɪf] *adj (+er)* **(a)** steif; *brush* hart; *dough, paste* fest. **(b)** *resistance, drink* stark; *competition* hart; *breeze* steif; *climb, test* schwierig; *examination, punishment* schwer; *price, demand* hoch. **that's a bit ~** das ist ganz schön happig *(col)*.

stiffen ['stɪfn] *(also ~ up)* **1** *vt* steif machen; *shirt etc* stärken; *(disease) limb* steif werden lassen; *resistance etc* verstärken. **2** *vi* steif werden; *(fig: resistance)* sich verhärten; *(breeze)* auffrischen.

stiffly ['stɪflɪ] *adv* steif.

stiffness ['stɪfnɪs] *n see adj* **(a)** Steifheit *f*; Härte *f*; Festigkeit *f*. **(b)** Stärke *f*; Härte *f*; Schwierigkeit *f*; Schwere *f*; Höhe *f*.

stifle ['staɪfl] **1** *vt (suffocate)* ersticken; *(fig) cough also, opposition* unterdrücken. **2** *vi* ersticken.

stifling ['staɪflɪŋ] *adj fumes* erstickend; *heat* drückend. **it's ~ in here** es ist ja zum Ersticken hier drin *(col)*.

stigma ['stɪgmə] *n* Brandmal, Stigma *nt*.

stigmatize ['stɪgmətaɪz] *vt* brandmarken.

stile [staɪl] *n* (Zaun)übertritt *m*.

stiletto [stɪ'letəʊ] *n* **(a)** *(knife)* Stilett *nt*. **(b)** *(also ~ heel)* Pfennigabsatz *m*.

still[1] [stɪl] **1** *adj, adv (+er)* **(a)** *(motionless)* bewegungslos; *person also* reglos; *sea, waters* ruhig. **to keep ~** stillhalten; **to hold sth ~** etw ruhig halten; **to be ~** *(vehicle, needle etc)* stillstehen; **to lie ~** reglos daliegen; **to stand ~** still stehen; **my heart stood ~** mir stockte das Herz; **~ waters run deep** *(Prov)* stille Wasser sind tief *(Prov)*. **(b)** *(quiet, calm)* still. **be ~!** sei still! **2** *adj wine* nicht moussierend; *drink* ohne Kohlensäure. **a ~ photograph** ein Standfoto *nt*. **3** *n* **(a)** **in the ~ of the night** in der Stille der Nacht. **(b)** *(Film)* Standfoto *nt*.

still[2] **1** *adv* **(a)** *(temporal)* noch; *(for emphasis, in exasperation, used on its own)* immer noch; *(in negative sentences)* noch immer, immer noch; *(now as in the past)* nach wie vor. **there will ~ be objections** es wird nach wie vor Einwände geben. **(b)** *(nevertheless, all the same)* trotzdem. **~, it was worth it** es hat sich trotzdem gelohnt; **~, he is my brother** er ist trotz allem mein Bruder; **rich but ~ not happy** reich und doch nicht glücklich; **~, at least we didn't lose anything** na ja, wir haben wenigstens nichts dabei verloren; **~, what can you expect?** was kann man auch anderes erwarten? **(c)** *(with comp)* noch. **~ better** noch besser; **better ~, do it this way** oder noch besser, mach es so. **2** *conj* (und) dennoch.

still[3] *n (for alcohol)* Destillierapparat *m*.

still: **~birth** *n* Totgeburt *f*; **~born** *adj (lit, fig)* totgeboren *attr;* **the child was ~born** das Kind kam tot zur Welt; **~ life** *n, pl* **~ lifes** Stilleben *nt*.

stillness ['stɪlnɪs] *n* **(a)** *(motionlessness)* Unbewegtheit *f*; *(of person)* Reglosigkeit *f*. **(b)** *(quietness)* Stille, Ruhe *f*.

stilt [stɪlt] *n* Stelze *f*; *(Archit)* Pfahl *m*.

stilted ['stɪltɪd] *adj* gestelzt, gespreizt.

stimulant ['stɪmjʊlənt] *n* Anregungsmittel *nt*; *(fig)* Ansporn *m*.

stimulate ['stɪmjʊleɪt] *vt* **(a)** *(excite) circulation, mind* anregen; *(cold shower, coffee)* beleben; *(Med also)* stimulieren; *nerve* reizen; *(sexually)* erregen; *(fig) person* anspornen; *(intellectually)* stimulieren; *sb's interest* erregen. **to ~ sb to do sth** jdn anspornen, etw zu tun. **(b)** *(increase) economy, sales etc* ankurbeln; *(incite) response* hervorrufen; *criticism* anregen zu.

stimulating ['stɪmjʊleɪtɪŋ] *adj* anregend; *walk* belebend; *prospect* ermunternd; *experience (physically)* erfrischend; *(mentally)* stimulierend.

stimulation [ˌstɪmjʊ'leɪʃən] *n* **(a)** *(act) (physical, mental)* Anregung *f*; *(from shower, walk etc)* belebende Wirkung; *(state)* Angeregtheit *f*; *(sexual)* Erregung *f*; *(fig: incentive)* Anreiz *m*; *(intellectual)* Stimulation *f*. **(b)** *(of economy, sales etc)* Ankurbelung *f (to gen)*.

stimulus ['stɪmjʊləs] *n, pl* **stimuli** ['stɪmjʊlaɪ] Anreiz *m*; *(inspiration)* Anregung *f*; *(Physiol)* Reiz *m*. **it gave trade new ~** das hat dem Handel neuen Aufschwung gegeben.

sting [stɪŋ] *(vb: pret, ptp* **stung***)* **1** *n* **(a)** *(organ: of insect)* Stachel *m*. **(b)** *(wound) (of insect)* Stich *m*; *(of nettle, jellyfish)* Quaddel *f*. **(c)** *(pain) (from needle etc)* Stechen *nt*; *(of antiseptic, ointment, from nettle etc)* Brennen *nt*; *(of whip)* brennender Schmerz. **(d)** *(fig) (of remark, irony)* Stachel *m*; *(of attack, criticism etc)* Schärfe *f*. **to take the ~ out of sth** etw entschärfen; *(out of remark, criticism also)* einer Sache *(dat)* den Stachel nehmen.

2 *vt* **(a)** *(insect)* stechen; *(jellyfish)* verbrennen. **(b)** *(comments etc)* treffen; *(remorse, conscience)* quälen. **(c)** *(col)* **they really stung you for that** sie haben dich dabei ganz schön ausgenommen; **can I ~ you for a fiver?** kann ich dich um einen Fünfer erleichtern?

3 *vi (insect)* stechen; *(nettle, jellyfish etc)* brennen; *(burn: eyes, cut, ointment etc)* brennen; *(comments etc)* schmerzen. **smoke makes your eyes ~** Rauch brennt in den Augen.

stinging nettle ['stɪŋɪŋ'netl] *n* Brennessel *f*.

stingy ['stɪndʒɪ] *adj (+er) (col) person* geizig, knickerig *(col)*; *sum, portion, donation* schäbig. **to be ~ with sth** mit etw knausern.

stink [stɪŋk] *(vb: pret* **stank,** *ptp* **stunk***)* **1** *n* Gestank *m*. **to kick up a ~** *(col)* Stunk machen *(col)*. **2** *vi* **(a)** stinken *(of* nach*)*. **it ~s in here** hier (drin) stinkt's. **(b)** *(fig col) (be bad)* sauschlecht sein *(col)*; *(be suspicious)* stinken *(col)*.

♦ **stink out** *vt sep (col) room* verstänkern *(col)*.

stink bomb *n* Stinkbombe *f*.

stinker ['stɪŋkəʳ] *n (col) (problem)* harte Nuß *(col)*; *(person)* Ekel *nt*.

stinking ['stɪŋkɪŋ] **1** *adj (col)* beschissen *(col!)*. **keep your ~ money!** du kannst dein Scheißgeld behalten! *(col!)* **2** *adv (col)* **~ rich** stinkreich *(col)*.

stint [stɪnt] **1** *n* **to do one's ~** *(work)* seine Arbeit tun; *(share)* sein(en) Teil beitragen; **would you like to do a ~ at the wheel?** möchtest du auch mal das Steuer übernehmen? **2** *vt* knausern mit. **to ~ sb of sth** *of praise, reward* jdm etw vorenthalten; **to ~ oneself (of sth)** sich (mit etw) einschränken.

stipulate ['stɪpjʊleɪt] *vt* **(a)** *(make a condition)* zur Auflage machen. **(b)** *delivery date, amount, price* festsetzen; *size* vorschreiben; *conditions* stellen.

stipulation [ˌstɪpjʊ'leɪʃən] *n* **(a)** *(condition)* Auflage *f*. **(b)** *see vt (b)* Festsetzung *f*; Vorschreiben *nt*; Stellen *nt*.

stir [stɜːʳ] **1** *n* **(a)** **to give sth a ~** etw rühren; *tea etc* etw umrühren. **(b)** *(fig: excitement)* Aufruhr *m*. **to cause** *or* **create a ~** Aufsehen erregen.

2 *vt* **(a)** umrühren; *cake mixture* rühren. **~ sugar into the mixture** den Zucker darunterrühren. **(b)** *(move)* bewegen; *limbs* rühren; *water, waves* kräuseln. **come on, ~ yourself** *(col)* komm, beweg dich! *(col)*. **(c)** *(fig) emotions* aufwühlen; *passion* wachrufen; *imagination* anregen; *curiosity* erregen; *(incite) person* anstacheln; *(move) person, heart* rühren. **to ~ sb to do sth** jdn bewegen, etw zu tun; *(incite)* jdn dazu anstacheln, etw zu tun; **to ~ sb into action** jdn zum Handeln bewegen.

3 *vi* sich regen; *(person also)* sich rühren;

(leaves, animal etc) sich bewegen.

♦ **stir up** *vt sep (fig) anger* erregen; *memories* wachrufen; *opposition, discord* erzeugen; *hatred* schüren; *revolution* anzetteln; *mob* aufstacheln. **to ~ ~ trouble** Unruhe stiften; **that'll ~ things ~** das kann heiter werden!

stirring ['stɜːrɪŋ] *adj speech, music* bewegend; *(stronger)* aufwühlend.

stirrup ['stɪrəp] *n* Steigbügel *m.*

stitch [stɪtʃ] **1** *n* **(a)** Stich *m*; *(in knitting etc)* Masche *f*; *(kind of ~) (in knitting etc)* Muster *nt*; *(in embroidery)* Stichart *f.* **to put a few ~es in sth** etw mit ein paar Stichen nähen; **he needed ~es in his arm** sein Arm mußte genäht werden; **to have one's ~es out** die Fäden gezogen bekommen; **a ~ in time saves nine** *(Prov)* was du heute kannst besorgen, das verschiebe nicht auf morgen *(Prov).* **(b)** *(col: piece of clothing)* **she hadn't a ~ on** sie war splitter(faser)nackt *(col).* **(c)** *(pain)* Seitenstiche *pl.* **(d) to be in ~es** *(col: from laughing)* sich schieflachen *(col).* **2** *vt (Sew, Med)* nähen; *tear* zunähen.

stoat [stəʊt] *n* Wiesel *nt.*

stock [stɒk] **1** *n* **(a)** *(supply)* Vorrat *m (of* an *+dat)*; *(Comm)* Bestand *m (of* an *+dat).* **to have sth in ~** etw vorrätig haben; **to be in ~/out of ~** *(goods)* vorrätig/nicht vorrätig sein; **to take ~** *(Comm)* Inventur machen; **to take ~ of sb** jdn abschätzen; **to take ~ of the situation** sich *(dat)* über die Situation klarwerden. **(b)** *(live~)* Viehbestand *m.* **(c)** *(Cook)* Brühe *f.* **(d)** *(Fin) (capital)* Aktienkapital *nt*; *(shares held by investor)* Anteil *m*; *(government ~)* Staatsanleihe *f.* **~s and shares** (Aktien und) Wertpapiere *pl*, Effekten *pl.* **(e) to be on the ~s** *(ship)* im Bau sein; *(book etc)* in Arbeit sein. **(f) ~s** *pl (Hist: for punishment)* Stock *m.* **(g)** *(Rail)* rollendes Material.

2 *adj attr phrase etc* Standard-.

3 *vt* **(a)** *(shop etc) goods* führen. **(b)** *cupboard* füllen; *shop also, library* ausstatten; *pond, river* (mit Fischen) besetzen; *farm* mit einem Viehbestand versehen.

♦ **stock up** *vi* sich eindecken *(on* mit*).*

stock: ~broker *n* Börsenmakler *m*; **~ car** *n* **(a)** *(for racing)* Stock Car *nt (frisierter, verstärkter Serienwagen)*; **(b)** *(US Rail: cattle truck)* Viehwaggon *m*; **~ company** *n (US)* **(a)** *(Fin)* Aktiengesellschaft *f*; **(b)** *(Theat)* Repertoiretheater *nt*; **~ exchange** *n* Börse *f*; **~holder** *n* Aktionär(in *f*) *m.*

stocking ['stɒkɪŋ] **1** *n* Strumpf *m.* **2** *vt* **in one's ~ed feet** in Strümpfen.

stock-in-trade [ˌstɒkɪn'treɪd] *n (tools, materials, fig)* Handwerkszeug *nt.*

stockist ['stɒkɪst] *n (Brit)* Händler *m.*

stock: ~ market *n* Börse(nmarkt *m*) *f*; **~pile 1** *n* Vorrat *m (of* an *+dat)*; *(of weapons)* Lager *nt*; **2** *vt* Vorräte an *(+dat)* ... anlegen; *(pej)* horten; **~taking** *n (Brit)* Inventur *f*; *(fig)* Bestandsaufnahme *f.*

stocky ['stɒkɪ] *adj (+er)* stämmig.

stodgy ['stɒdʒɪ] *adj (+er) food* pampig *(col)*, schwer; *subject* trocken; *book* schwer verdaulich.

stoic ['stəʊɪk] **1** *n* Stoiker *m.* **2** *adj* stoisch.

stoical ['stəʊɪkəl] *adj* stoisch.

stoicism ['stəʊɪsɪzəm] *n* stoische Ruhe.

stoke [stəʊk] *vt furnace* (be)heizen; *fire* schüren.

stole *pret of* **steal.**

stolen ['stəʊlən] **1** *ptp of* **steal. 2** *adj* gestohlen. **~ goods** Diebesgut *nt.*

stolid ['stɒlɪd] *adj person* phlegmatisch, stur *(pej).*

stomach ['stʌmək] **1** *n (abdomen)* Magen *m*; *(belly, paunch)* Bauch *m*; *(fig: appetite)* Lust *f (for* auf *+acc).* **to hit sb in the ~** jdn in die Bauchgegend schlagen; **on an empty ~** *drink etc* auf leeren *or* nüchternen Magen; **on an empty/full ~** *swim, drive etc* mit leerem/vollem Magen; **I have no ~ for that** das ist mir zuwider; **he doesn't have the ~ for it** *(guts)* dazu hat er nicht den Mumm *(col).* **2** *vt (col) behaviour, cruelty* vertragen; *person, film etc* ausstehen.

stomach *in cpds* Magen-; **~-ache** *n* Magenschmerzen *pl*; **~ trouble** *n* Magenbeschwerden *pl*; **~ ulcer** *n* Magengeschwür *nt.*

stomp [stɒmp] *vi* stapfen.

stone [stəʊn] **1** *n* **(a)** Stein *m.* **a ~'s throw from the station** nur einen Steinwurf *or* Katzensprung vom Bahnhof entfernt; **to leave no ~ unturned** nichts unversucht lassen. **(b)** *(Brit: weight) = 6.35 kg.* **2** *adj* Stein-, aus Stein. **3** *vt* **(a)** *(throw ~s at)* mit Steinen bewerfen; *(kill)* steinigen. **(b)** *fruit* entsteinen. **(c)** *(col)* **to be ~d (out of one's mind***)* total weg sein *(col).*

stone: S~ Age *n* Steinzeit *f*; **~-cold 1** *adj* eiskalt; **2** *adv* **~-cold sober** stocknüchtern *(col)*; **~-dead** *adj* mausetot *(col)*; **~-deaf** *adj* stocktaub *(col)*; **~mason** *n* Steinmetz *m*; **~wall** *vi (fig: esp Parl)* obstruieren; *(in answering questions)* ausweichen; *(Sport)* mauern *(Sport sl)*; **~ware** *n* Steingut *nt*; **~work** *n* Mauerwerk *nt.*

stony ['stəʊnɪ] *adj (+er) ground* steinig; *(fig) glance, silence* steinern.

stony-broke ['stəʊnɪ'brəʊk] *adj (Brit col)* völlig abgebrannt.

stood [stʊd] *pret, ptp of* **stand.**

stooge [stuːdʒ] *n (col)* Handlanger *m*; *(comedian's)* Stichwortgeber *m.*

stool [stuːl] *n (seat)* Hocker *m*; *(foot ~, kitchen ~, milking ~ also)* Schemel *m*; *(folding)* Klappstuhl *m.* **to fall between two ~s** sich zwischen zwei Stühle setzen; *(be neither one thing nor the other)* weder dem einen noch dem anderen gerecht werden.

stool pigeon *n (col) (decoy)* Lockvogel *m*; *(informer)* Spitzel *m.*

stoop [stuːp] **1** *n* Gebeugtheit *f*; *(deformity)* krummer Rücken, Buckel *m.* **to walk with a ~** gebeugt gehen. **2** *vi* sich beugen *(over* über *+acc)*; *(also* **~ down***)* sich bücken; *(have a ~)* gebeugt gehen. **to ~ to sth/to doing sth** *(fig)* sich zu etw herablassen/sich dazu herablassen, etw zu tun.

stop [stɒp] **1** *n* **(a)** *(act of ~ping)* Halt *m.* **to bring sth to a ~** *(lit)* etw anhalten *or* stoppen; *traffic* etw zum Erliegen bringen; *(fig) meeting, development* einer Sache *(dat)* ein Ende machen; *conversation* etw verstummen lassen; **to come to a ~** *(car, machine)* anhalten; *(traffic)* stocken; *(meeting, rain)* aufhören; *(conversation)* verstummen; **to put a ~ to sth** einer Sache *(dat)* einen Riegel vorschieben.

(b) *(stay)* Aufenthalt *m*; *(break)* Pause *f*; *(Aviat)* Zwischenlandung *f.* **to make a ~** *(bus, train, tram)* (an)halten; *(plane, ship)* (Zwischen)station machen; **to have a ~ for coffee** eine Kaffeepause machen; **to have a ~** haltmachen; **to work without a ~** ohne Unterbrechung arbeiten.

(c) *(~ping place)* Station *f*; *(for bus)* Haltestelle *f.*

(d) *(esp Brit: punctuation mark)* Punkt *m.*

(e) *(stopper) (for door etc)* Sperre *f*; *(on typewriter)* Feststelltaste *f.*

(f) *(on organ)* Registerzug *m.* **to pull out all the ~s** *(fig)* alle Register ziehen.

2 *vt* **(a)** *(when moving) person* anhalten; *engine, machine etc* abstellen; *blow* auffangen; *traffic (hold up)* aufhalten; *(bring to standstill)* zum Erliegen bringen; *(policeman)* anhalten; *(keep out) noise, light* abfangen, auffangen. **~ thief!** haltet den Dieb!

(b) *(from continuing) rumour, crime* ein Ende machen *(+dat)*; *nonsense, noise* unterbinden; *match, conversation, work* beenden; *development, attack* aufhalten; *(temporarily)* unterbrechen; *flow of blood* stillen; *speaker, speech* unterbrechen; *production* zum Stillstand bringen; *(tempo-*

rarily) unterbrechen.

(c) *(cease)* aufhören mit. **to ~ doing sth** aufhören, etw zu tun; **she never ~s talking** sie redet ununterbrochen; **to ~ smoking** mit dem Rauchen aufhören; *(put out cigarette etc)* das Rauchen einstellen; **~ it!** hör auf!

(d) *(suspend)* stoppen; *payments, production etc* einstellen; *cheque, electricity* sperren; *subsidy, grant etc* streichen; *proceedings* abbrechen; *(cancel) subscription* kündigen.

(e) *(prevent from happening) sth* verhindern; *(prevent from doing) sb* abhalten. **to ~ oneself** sich zurückhalten, sich bremsen *(col)*; **there's no ~ping him** *(col)* er ist nicht zu bremsen *(col)*; **to ~ sb (from) doing sth** jdn davon abhalten *or (physically)* daran hindern, etw zu tun; *(put a ~ to)* dafür sorgen, daß jd etw nicht mehr tut; **to ~ sth (from) happening** *(prevent)* (es) verhindern, daß etw geschieht; **how can we ~ the baby (from) crying?** *(prevent)* was können wir tun, damit das Baby nicht schreit?; **to ~ the thief (from) escaping** den Dieb an der Flucht hindern.

(f) *(block)* verstopfen; *(fill) tooth* plombieren; *(fig) gap* füllen; *leak of information* stopfen.

3 *vi* **(a)** *(halt)* anhalten; *(train, car also)* halten; *(traveller)* haltmachen; *(pedestrian, clock)* stehenbleiben; *(engine, machine)* nicht mehr laufen. **~!** halt!, stopp!; **we ~ped for a drink at the pub** wir machten in der Kneipe Station, um etwas zu trinken; **to ~ at nothing (to do sth)** *(fig)* vor nichts haltmachen(, um etw zu tun). **(b)** *(finish, cease)* aufhören; *(pain also)* weggehen; *(heart)* stehenbleiben; *(production, payments)* eingestellt werden; *(show, match, film)* zu Ende sein; *(music, speaker also)* verstummen. **to ~ doing sth** aufhören, etw zu tun, mit etw aufhören; **he never knows when to ~** er weiß nie, wann er aufhören muß. **(c)** *(col: stay)* bleiben *(at* in *+dat, with* bei*)*.

♦ **stop away** *vi (col)* wegbleiben.

♦ **stop by** *vi* kurz vorbeischauen. **to ~ ~ (at) sb's house** bei jdm hereinschauen *(col)*.

♦ **stop in** *vi (col)* drinbleiben *(col)*.

♦ **stop off** *vi* (kurz) haltmachen *(at sb's* bei jdm*)*.

♦ **stop over** *vi* kurz haltmachen; *(on travels)* Zwischenstation machen *(in* in *+dat)*; *(Aviat)* zwischenlanden.

♦ **stop up 1** *vt sep* verstopfen; *crack, hole also* zustopfen. **2** *vi (col: stay up)* aufbleiben.

stop: ~cock *n* Absperrhahn *m*; **~gap** *n (thing)* Notbehelf *m*; *(scheme)* Notlösung *f*; *(person)* Lückenbüßer *m*; **~over** *n* Zwischenstation *f*; *(Aviat)* Zwischenlandung *f*.

stoppage ['stɒpɪdʒ] *n* **(a)** *(in work)* Unterbrechung *f*; *(in traffic)* Stockung *f*; *(because of strike etc)* Stopp *m*; *(strike)* Streik *m*. **(b)** *(of pay, cheque)* Sperrung *f*; *(deduction)* Abzug *m*. **(c)** *(blockage)* Verstopfung *f*, Stau *m*.

stopper ['stɒpəʳ] *n (plug)* Stöpsel *m*.

stop: ~-press *n (esp Brit) (news)* letzte Meldungen *pl*; **~watch** *n* Stoppuhr *f*.

storage ['stɔːrɪdʒ] *n (of goods, food)* Lagerung *f*; *(of books, documents)* Aufbewahrung *f*; *(of electricity, data)* Speicherung *f*, Speichern *nt*. **to put sth into ~** etw unterstellen, etw (ein)lagern.

storage: ~ capacity *n (of computer)* Speicherkapazität *f*; **~ heater** *n* (Nachtstrom)speicherofen *m*; **~ space** *n* Lagerraum *m*; *(in house)* Schränke und Abstellräume *pl*.

store [stɔːʳ] **1** *n* **(a)** *(stock)* Vorrat *m (of* an *+dat)*; *(fig)* Fülle *f*, Reichtum *m (of* an *+dat)*. **~s** *pl (supplies)* Vorräte *pl*; **to lay** *or* **get in a ~ of food** einen Lebensmittelvorrat anlegen; **to be in ~ for sb** jdm bevorstehen; **to have a surprise in ~ for sb** für jdn eine Überraschung auf Lager haben; **what has the future in ~ for us?** was wird uns *(dat)* die Zukunft bringen?; **to set great/little ~ by sth** viel/wenig von etw halten. **(b)** *(esp US: shop)* Laden *m*, Geschäft *nt*; *(department ~)* Kaufhaus *nt*. **2** *vt* lagern; *documents* aufbewahren; *furniture* unterstellen; *(in depository)* einlagern; *information, heat* speichern; *(keep in reserve, collect: also ~* **up***)* Vorräte an *(+dat)* ... anschaffen. **to ~ sth away** etw verwahren.

store: ~house *n* Lager(haus) *nt*; *(fig)* Fundgrube *f*; **~ keeper** *n (in ~house)* Lagerverwalter *m; (esp US: shopkeeper)* Ladenbesitzer(in *f*); **~room** *n* Lagerraum *m*; *(for food)* Vorratskammer *f*.

storey, (US) story ['stɔːrɪ] *n, pl* **-s** *or (US)* **stories** Stock(werk *nt*) *m*, Etage *f*. **a nine-~ building** ein neunstöckiges Gebäude; **on the second ~** im zweiten Stock; *(US)* im ersten Stock.

stork [stɔːk] *n* Storch *m*.

storm [stɔːm] **1** *n* **(a)** Unwetter *nt*; *(thunder~)* Gewitter *nt*; *(strong wind)* Sturm *m*. **there is a ~ blowing** es stürmt; **a ~ in a teacup** *(fig)* ein Sturm im Wasserglas. **(b)** *(fig) (of abuse)* Flut *f (of* von*)*; *(of applause, criticism)* Sturm *m (of gen)*; *(of blows, missiles)* Hagel *m (of* von*)*; *(outcry)* Aufruhr *m*. **~ of protest** Proteststurm *m*. **(c) to take sth/sb by ~** *(Mil, fig)* etw/jdn im Sturm erobern. **2** *vt* stürmen. **3** *vi* **(a)** *(talk angrily)* wüten *(at* gegen*)*. **(b)** *(move violently)* stürmen.

storm: ~ cloud *n (lit, fig)* Gewitterwolke *f*; **~ cone** *n* Sturmkegel *m*; **~ door** *n* äußere Windfangtür; **~ force** *n* Windstärke *f*; **~ troops** *npl* Sturmtruppe *f*.

stormy ['stɔːmɪ] *adj (+er) (lit, fig)* stürmisch; *discussion also, temper* hitzig; *protests* heftig.

story[1] ['stɔːrɪ] *n* **(a)** *(tale, account)* Geschichte *f*; *(Liter also)* Erzählung *f*; *(joke)* Witz *m*. **it's a long ~** das ist eine lange Geschichte; **the ~ of her life** ihre Lebensgeschichte; **that's another ~** das ist eine andere Geschichte; **his ~ is that ...** er behauptet, daß ...; **that's not the whole ~** das ist nicht die ganze Wahrheit; **the marks tell their own ~** die Flecke sprechen für sich; **to cut a long ~ short** um es kurz zu machen, der langen Rede kurzer Sinn; **it's the (same) old ~** es ist das alte Lied; **but it's another ~ now** aber jetzt sieht die Sache anders aus. **(b)** *(Press) (event)* Geschichte *f*; *(newspaper ~)* Artikel *m*. **(c)** *(plot)* Handlung *f*. **(d)** *(col: lie)* Märchen *nt*. **to tell stories** Märchen erzählen.

story[2] *n (US)* = **storey.**

story-book ['stɔːrɪbʊk] **1** *n* Geschichtenbuch *nt*. **2** *adj attr castles, romance etc* märchenhaft.

stout [staʊt] **1** *adj (+er)* **(a)** *(corpulent)* korpulent. **(b)** *(strong) stick, horse etc* kräftig; *door, rope, gate* stark. **(c)** *(brave)* tapfer; *denial* entschieden. **2** *n* Starkbier *nt*; *(sweet ~)* ≈ Malzbier *nt*.

stout-hearted ['staʊt'hɑːtɪd] *adj* tapfer.

stove [stəʊv] *n* Ofen *m*; *(for cooking)* Herd *m*. **electric/gas ~** Elektro-/Gasherd *m*.

stove in *pret, ptp of* **stave in.**

stow [stəʊ] *vt* **(a)** *(Naut) cargo* verladen, (ver)stauen. **(b)** *(put away: also ~* **away***)* verstauen *(in* in *+dat)*.

♦ **stow away** *vi* als blinder Passagier fahren.

stowaway ['stəʊəweɪ] *n* blinder Passagier.

straddle ['strædl] *vt (standing)* breitbeinig stehen über *(+dat)*; *(sitting)* rittlings sitzen auf *(+dat)*; *(jumping)* grätschen über *(+acc)*; *(fig) differences* überbrücken; *two continents* überspannen. **to ~ the border/river** sich über beide Seiten der Grenze/beide Ufer des Flusses erstrecken.

strafe [streɪf] *vt* unter Beschuß nehmen.

straggle ['strægl] *vi (spread untidily) (houses, trees)* verstreut liegen; *(hair)* (unordentlich) hängen; *(plant)* in alle Richtungen wuchern. **to ~ behind** zurückbleiben, hinterherzockeln *(col)*.

straggler ['stræglәʳ] *n* Nachzügler *m*.

straggling ['stræglɪŋ] *adj* **(a)** *children, cattle etc* weit verteilt; *(~ behind)* zurückgeblieben; *village* sich lang hinziehend; *houses* zerstreut liegend; *group, row* auseinandergezogen. **(b)** *(col: also* **straggly***) hair* zottig; *plant* wuchernd.

straight [streɪt] **1** *adj (+er)* **(a)** gerade; *posture also* aufrecht; *hair* glatt; *skirt, trousers* gerade geschnitten. **your tie isn't ~** deine Krawatte sitzt schief; **the picture isn't ~** das Bild hängt schief; **as ~ as a die** kerzengerade; *road* schnurgerade; **to keep a ~ face** keine Miene verziehen; **to be (all) ~** *(in order)* in Ordnung sein; *(fig: clarified also)* (völlig) geklärt sein; **to put things ~** *(tidy)* alles in Ordnung bringen; *(clarify)* alles klären; **to put sb ~ about sth** jdm etw klarmachen; **he soon put me ~!** er hat mich eines Besseren belehrt.

(b) *(frank) answer, talking* offen; *denial, refusal* direkt; *(honest) person, dealings, advice* ehrlich. **to be ~ with sb** offen zu jdm sein.

(c) *(plain) drink* pur; *(Pol) fight* direkt; *choice* einfach; *(col) (heterosexual)* normal, hetero *(col)*; *(conventional)* etabliert, spießig *(pej)*. **to have a ~ choice between ...** nur die Wahl zwischen ... haben.

(d) *(continuous)* ununterbrochen. **~ run** *(Cards)* Sequenz *f*; **our team had ten ~ wins** unsere Mannschaft gewann zehnmal hintereinander.

(e) *(Theat) production* konventionell; *actor* ernsthaft. **a ~ play** ein reines Drama.

2 *adv* **(a)** *hold, walk, shoot* gerade; *stand up also* aufrecht; *leap at, aim for, above, across* direkt. **~ through sth** glatt durch etw; **he came ~ at me** er kam direkt auf mich zu; **it went ~ up in the air** es flog senkrecht in die Luft; **to look ~ ahead** geradeaus sehen; **the town lay ~ ahead of us** die Stadt lag direkt vor uns; **to drive ~ on** geradeaus weiterfahren.

(b) *(directly)* direkt; *(immediately)* sofort. **I went ~ home** ich ging direkt nach Hause; **to look sb ~ in the eye** jdm direkt in die Augen sehen; **~ after this** sofort danach; **~ away** *or* **off** sofort, auf der Stelle; **to come ~ to the point** gleich zur Sache kommen.

(c) *(clearly) think, see* klar; *(frankly)* offen, ohne Umschweife. **~ out** *(col)* rundheraus.

(d) *drink* pur.

3 *n* (*~ part, on race track*) Gerade *f*; *(road, rail)* gerade Strecke. **the final ~** die Zielgerade; **to keep on the ~ and narrow** dafür sorgen, daß man nicht auf die schiefe Bahn kommt; **to cut sth on the ~** etw gerade (ab)schneiden.

straighten ['streɪtn] **1** *vt* **(a)** *hat* gerade aufsetzen; *tie* geradeziehen; *shoulders* straffen. **(b)** *(also* **~ out:** *make straight)* geradermachen; *picture* gerade hinhängen; *road, river* begradigen; *tablecloth* geradeziehen; *wire* geradebiegen; *hair* glätten. **(c)** *(also* **~ up:** *tidy)* in Ordnung bringen. **(d)** *(also* **~ out:** *put right) problem, situation* klären. **2** *vi (also* **~ out:** *road, plant etc)* gerade werden; *(hair)* glatt werden. **3** *vr* **to ~ oneself (up)** sich aufrichten; **the problem will soon ~ itself out** das Problem wird sich bald von selbst erledigen.

straight: ~faced [streɪt'feɪst] **1** *adv* ohne die Miene zu verziehen; **2** *adj* **to be ~faced** keine Miene verziehen; **~forward** *adj (honest) person* aufrichtig; *explanation, look also* offen, freimütig; *(simple) question, problem* einfach.

strain[1] [streɪn] **1** *n* **(a)** *(Mech)* Belastung *f*; *(on beams, floor also)* Druck *m*. **the ~ on a rope** die Seilspannung; **can you take some of the ~?** können Sie mal mit festhalten/mit ziehen?; **to put a (great) ~ on sth** etw (stark) belasten; **to show signs of ~** Zeichen von Überlastung zeigen.

(b) *(fig: mental, economic etc)* Belastung *f (on* für*)*; *(effort)* Anstrengung *f*; *(pressure) (of job etc also)* Beanspruchung *f (of* durch*)*; *(of responsibility)* Last *f*; *(muscle-~)* (Muskel)zerrung *f*; *(on eyes, heart etc)* Überanstrengung *f (on gen)*. **to be under a lot of ~** stark beansprucht sein; **I find her/that a bit of a ~** ich finde sie/das ziemlich anstrengend; **to put a (great) ~ on sb/sth** jdn/etw stark belasten; **to show signs of ~** Zeichen von Überlastung zeigen; **to be under ~** großen Belastungen ausgesetzt sein; **the ~s of modern life** die Belastungen *or* der Streß des heutigen Lebens.

(c) *~s pl (of instrument, tune)* Klänge *pl*; **to the ~s of** zu den Klängen *(+gen)*.

2 *vt* **(a)** *(stretch)* spannen. **(b)** *(put ~ on) rope, relationship, budget* belasten; *nerves, patience also* strapazieren; *(put too much ~ on)* überlasten; *meaning* dehnen. **to ~ one's ears/eyes to ...** angestrengt lauschen/gucken, um zu ...; **to ~ every nerve** jeden Nerv anspannen; **to ~ oneself** sich anstrengen; *(excessively)* sich überanstrengen. **(c)** *(Med) muscle* zerren; *back, eyes, voice* strapazieren; *(excessively)* überanstrengen; *heart* belasten; *(excessively)* überlasten. **(d)** *(filter)* (durch)sieben; *(pour water off) vegetables* abgießen. **to ~ off water** Wasser abgießen.

3 *vi (exert effort)* sich anstrengen; *(pull)* zerren, ziehen; *(fig: strive)* sich bemühen. **to ~ to do sth** sich anstrengen, etw zu tun; **to ~ at sth** sich mit etw abmühen; *(pull)* an etw *(dat)* ziehen.

strain[2] *n* **(a)** *(streak)* Hang, Zug *m*; *(hereditary)* Veranlagung *f*. **a ~ of madness** eine Veranlagung zum Wahnsinn. **(b)** *(breed) (animals)* Rasse *f*; *(of plants)* Sorte *f*; *(of virus etc)* Art *f*.

strained [streɪnd] *adj* **(a)** *muscle* gezerrt; *back, eyes* überanstrengt. **(b)** *expression, style* unnatürlich; *smile, conversation* gezwungen; *meeting* steif; *voice, relations, atmosphere, nerves* (an)gespannt. **he looked rather ~** er sah ziemlich abgespannt aus.

strainer ['streɪnə^r] *n (Cook)* Sieb *nt*.

strait [streɪt] *n (Geog)* Meerenge *f*. **the ~s of Dover** die Straße von Dover; **to be in dire ~s** in großen Nöten sein.

straitened ['streɪtnd] *adj* **in ~ circumstances** in bescheidenen Verhältnissen.

strait: ~jacket *n (lit, fig)* Zwangsjacke *f*; **~-laced** [streɪt'leɪst] *adj* prüde, spießig *(col)*.

strand [strænd] *n* Strang *m*; *(of hair)* Strähne *f*; *(of thread)* Faden *m*; *(of wire)* Litze *f*; *(of beads)* Schnur *f*.

stranded ['strændɪd] *adj* **to be ~** *(ship, fish, shipwrecked person)* gestrandet sein; **to be (left) ~** *(person)* festsitzen; *(without money also)* auf dem trockenen sitzen *(col)*.

strange [streɪndʒ] *adj (+er)* **(a)** seltsam, merkwürdig. **(b)** *(unfamiliar) surroundings* fremd; *(unaccustomed) work* ungewohnt. **I felt rather ~ at first** zuerst fühlte ich mich ziemlich fremd; **I feel ~ in a skirt** ich komme mir in einem Rock komisch vor *(col)*.

strangely ['streɪndʒlɪ] *adv (oddly)* seltsam, merkwürdig; *act, behave also* komisch *(col)*. **~ enough** seltsamerweise, merkwürdigerweise.

stranger ['streɪndʒə^r] *n* Fremde(r) *mf*. **he's a perfect ~ to me** ich kenne ihn überhaupt nicht; **I'm a ~ here myself** ich bin selbst fremd hier; **he is no ~ to London** er kennt sich in London aus; **he is no ~ to misfortune** Leid ist ihm nicht fremd; **hullo, ~!** *(col)* hallo, lange nicht gesehen.

strangle ['stræŋgl] *vt (murder)* erwürgen; *(fig) cry* ersticken.

stranglehold ['stræŋgl,həʊld] *n (fig)* absolute Machtposition *(on* gegenüber*)*. **they have a ~ on us** *(fig)* sie haben uns in der Zange.

strangler ['stræŋglə^r] *n* Würger(in *f*) *m*.

strangulation [,stræŋgjʊ'leɪʃən] *n* Erwürgen *nt*. **death was due to ~** der Tod trat durch Ersticken ein.

strap [stræp] **1** *n* Riemen *m*; *(for safety also)* Gurt *m*; *(watch ~)* Band *nt*; *(shoulder ~)* Träger *m*. **to give sb the ~** jdn verprügeln. **2** *vt* **to ~ sth onto sth** etw auf etw *(acc)* schnallen; **to ~ sb/sth down** jdn/etw festschnallen; **to ~ sb/oneself in** *(in car, plane)* jdn/sich anschnallen.

strap-hanging ['stræp,hæŋɪŋ] *n* Pendeln *nt*.

strapless ['stræplıs] *adj* trägerlos; *dress also* schulterfrei.
strapping ['stræpıŋ] *adj (col)* stramm.
Strasbourg ['stræzbɜːg] *n* Straßburg *nt*.
strata ['strɑːtə] *pl of* **stratum.**
stratagem ['strætıdʒəm] *n (Mil)* Kriegslist *f*; *(artifice)* List *f*.
strategic [strə'tiːdʒık] *adj* strategisch; *(strategically important)* strategisch wichtig; *(fig also)* taktisch.
strategically [strə'tiːdʒıkəlı] *adv* strategisch; *(fig also)* taktisch. **to be ~ placed** eine strategisch günstige Stellung haben.
strategy ['strætıdʒı] *n* **(a)** *(Mil)* Strategie *f*; *(Sport, fig also)* Taktik *f*. **(b)** *(art of ~) (Mil)* Kriegskunst *f*; *(fig)* Taktieren *nt*.
stratosphere ['strætəʊsfıə^r] *n* Stratosphäre *f*.
stratum ['strɑːtəm] *n, pl* **strata** *(Geol, fig)* Schicht *f*.
straw [strɔː] **1** *n* **(a)** *(stalk)* Strohhalm *m*; *(collectively)* Stroh *nt no pl*. **it's the last ~!** *(col)* das ist der Gipfel! *(col)*; **to clutch at ~s** sich an einen Strohhalm klammern. **(b)** *(drinking ~)* Strohhalm *m*. **2** *adj attr* Stroh-; *basket* aus Stroh.
strawberry ['strɔːbərı] *n* Erdbeere *f*.
straw: ~-coloured, ~-colored *(US) adj* strohfarben; *hair* strohblond; **~ hat** *n* Strohhut *m*.
stray [streı] **1** *vi (also* **~ away***)* sich verirren; *(also* **~ about***)* (umher)streunen; *(fig: thoughts, speaker)* abschweifen. **to ~ (away) from sth** *(lit, fig)* von etw abkommen. **2** *adj child, bullet, cattle* verirrt; *cat, dog etc* streunend *attr*; *(ownerless)* herrenlos; *(isolated) remarks, houses* vereinzelt; *(single) remark* einzeln; *(occasional)* gelegentlich; *thoughts* flüchtig. **3** *n (dog, cat)* streunendes Tier; *(ownerless)* herrenloses Tier.
streak [striːk] **1** *n* Streifen *m*; *(of light)* Strahl *m*; *(in hair)* Strähne *f*; *(of fat also)* Schicht *f*; *(fig) (trace)* Spur *f*; *(of jealousy, meanness etc)* Zug *m*; *(of madness, humour)* Anflug *m*. **~ of lightning** Blitz(strahl) *m*; **a winning/losing ~** eine Glücks-/Pechsträhne. **2** *vt* streifen. **the sky was ~ed with red** der Himmel hatte rote Streifen; **~ed with dirt/paint** schmutzverschmiert/mit Farbe beschmiert. **3** *vi* **(a)** *(lightning)* zucken; *(col: move quickly)* flitzen *(col)*. **to ~ along/past** entlang-/vorbeiflitzen *(col)*. **(b)** *(run naked)* blitzen.
streaker ['striːkə^r] *n* Blitzer(in *f*) *m*.
streaky ['striːkı] *adj (+er) bacon* durchwachsen.
stream [striːm] **1** *n* **(a)** *(small river)* Bach *m*; *(current)* Strömung *f*. **to go with/against the ~** *(lit, fig)* mit dem/gegen den Strom schwimmen. **(b)** *(of liquid, people)* Strom *m*; *(of light, tears)* Flut *f*; *(of words, abuse)* Schwall *m*. **(c)** *(Brit Sch)* Leistungsgruppe *f*. **2** *vt* **(a) the walls ~ed water** von den Wänden rann das Wasser; **his face ~ed blood** Blut strömte ihm übers Gesicht. **(b)** *(Brit Sch)* in (Leistungs)gruppen einteilen. **3** *vi (lit, fig)* strömen; *(eyes)* tränen. **the walls were ~ing with water** die Wände trieften vor Nässe; **the rain was ~ing down** es regnete in Strömen; **tears ~ed down her face** Tränen rannen über ihr Gesicht.
♦ **stream in** *vi* herein-/hineinströmen.
♦ **stream out** *vi* heraus-/hinausströmen *(of* aus*)*.
♦ **stream past** *vi* vorbeiströmen *(prep obj* an *+dat)*; *(cars)* in Strömen vorbeifahren *(prep obj* an *+dat)*.
streamer ['striːmə^r] *n (flag)* Banner *nt*; *(made of paper)* Luftschlange *f*.
streamline ['striːmlaın] *vt (lit)* Stromlinienform geben *(+dat)*; *(fig)* rationalisieren.
streamlined ['striːmlaınd] *adj wing* windschlüpfig; *car, plane* stromlinienförmig; *(fig)* rationalisiert.
street [striːt] **1** *n* Straße *f*. **in** *or* **on the ~** auf der Straße; **it's right up my ~** *(fig col)* das ist genau mein Fall *(col)*; **to be ~s ahead of** *or* **better than sb** *(fig col)* jdm haushoch überlegen sein *(col)*; **to take to the ~s** *(demonstrators)* auf die Straße gehen; **to be on the ~s** *(prostitute)* auf den Strich gehen *(col)*; *(homeless)* auf der Straße stehen. **2** *adj attr* Straßen-.
street: ~car *n (US)* Straßenbahn *f*; **~ cleaner** *n* Straßenfeger(in *f*) *m*; **~ lamp** *n* Straßenlaterne *f*; **~ level** *n* **at ~ level** zu ebener Erde; **~ light** *n* Straßenlaterne *f*; **~ lighting** *n* Straßenbeleuchtung *f*; **~ map, ~ plan** *n* Stadtplan *m*; **~ value** *n* Verkaufswert *m*; **~walker** *n* Prostituierte *f*.
strength [streŋθ] *n* **(a)** *(lit, fig)* Stärke *f*; *(of person, feelings)* Kraft *f*; *(of table, wall)* Stabilität *f*; *(of conviction, views)* Festigkeit *f*; *(of argument, evidence)* Überzeugungskraft *f*; *(of mixture)* Konzentration *f*. **~ of character/will** Charakter-/Willensstärke *f*; **on the ~ of sth** auf Grund einer Sache *(gen)*; **his ~ failed him** ihn verließen die Kräfte; **to save one's ~** mit seinen Kräften haushalten; **when she has her ~ back** wenn sie wieder bei Kräften ist; **to go from ~ to ~** einen Erfolg nach dem anderen haben. **(b)** *(numbers)* (An)zahl *f*; *(Mil)* Stärke *f*. **to be up to/below ~** (die) volle Stärke/nicht die volle Stärke haben; **the police were there in ~** ein starkes Polizeiaufgebot war da; **they came in ~** sie kamen in großer Zahl.
strengthen ['streŋθən] **1** *vt* stärken; *building, protest* verstärken; *person (lit)* Kraft geben *(+dat)*; *(fig: in opinion)* bestärken *(in* in *+dat)*; *currency, market* festigen; *affection also, effect* vergrößern. **2** *vi* stärker werden.
strenuous ['strenjʊəs] *adj* **(a)** *(exhausting)* anstrengend; *march, game also* ermüdend. **(b)** *(energetic) supporter, support* unermüdlich; *effort, denial* hartnäckig; *conflict, protest* heftig.
stress [stres] **1** *n* **(a)** *(strain)* Belastung *f*, Streß *m*; *(Med)* Überlastung *f*, Streß *m*. **the ~es and strains of modern life** die Belastungen des heutigen Lebens; **times of ~** Zeiten *pl* großer Belastung; **to be under ~** großen Belastungen ausgesetzt sein; *(as regards work)* unter Streß stehen, im Streß sein. **(b)** *(accent)* Betonung *f*; *(fig: emphasis)* Akzent *m*. **to put** *or* **lay (great) ~ on sth** großen Wert auf etw *(acc)* legen; *on fact, detail* etw (besonders) betonen. **(c)** *(Mech)* Belastung. **2** *vt (lit, fig: emphasize)* betonen; *good manners, subject* großen Wert legen auf *(+acc)*.
stressed [strest] *adj person* gestreßt, überlastet.
stretch [stretʃ] **1** *n* **(a)** *(elasticity)* **to be at full ~** *(lit: material)* bis zum äußersten gedehnt sein; *(fig) (person)* mit aller Kraft arbeiten; *(factory etc)* auf Hochtouren arbeiten *(col)*; *(engine, production, work)* auf Hochtouren laufen; **by no ~ of the imagination** beim besten Willen nicht. **(b)** *(of road etc)* Strecke *f*; *(of river, countryside etc)* Stück *nt*; *(of journey)* Abschnitt *m*. **a straight ~ of road** eine gerade Strecke; **in that ~ of the river** in dem Teil des Flusses; **for a long ~** über eine weite Strecke. **(c)** *(~ of time)* Zeit(raum *m*) *f*. **for a long ~ of time** für (eine) lange Zeit; **for hours at a ~** stundenlang; **three days at a ~** drei Tage an einem Stück; **to do a ~** *(col: in prison)* im Knast sein *(col)*.
2 *adj attr* dehnbar, Stretch-.
3 *vt* **(a)** *(extend)* strecken; *(widen) jumper also, elastic, shoes* dehnen; *(spread) wings etc* ausbreiten; *(tighten) rope* spannen. **to ~ one's legs** *(go for a walk)* sich *(dat)* die Beine vertreten *(col)*. **(b)** *(make go further) money* strecken; *(use fully) resources* voll (aus)nutzen; *credit* voll beanspruchen; *athlete, student etc* fordern; *one's abilities* bis zum äußersten fordern. **(c)** *(strain) meaning* äußerst weit fassen; *truth, rules* großzügig auslegen. **to ~ a point** großzügig sein; **that's ~ing it a bit (far)** das geht fast zu weit.
4 *vi (after sleep etc)* sich strecken; *(be elastic)* sich dehnen, dehnbar sein; *(extend) (time, area, influence)* sich erstrecken *(to* bis, *over* über

+*acc*); *(be enough: food, money)* reichen *(to* für*)*; *(become looser)* weiter werden; *(become longer)* länger werden. **to ~ to reach sth** sich recken, um etw zu erreichen; **the fields ~ed away into the distance** die Felder dehnten sich bis in die Ferne aus; **I can't ~ to that** so viel kann ich mir nicht erlauben.

♦ **stretch out 1** *vt sep arms, wings* ausbreiten; *leg, hand* ausstrecken; *foot* vorstrecken; *rope* spannen; *meeting, essay* ausdehnen. **to ~ oneself ~ (on the ground)** sich auf den Boden legen. **2** *vi* sich strecken; *(col: lie down)* sich hinlegen; *(countryside)* sich ausbreiten; *(in time)* sich erstrecken *(over* über +*acc)*. **he lay ~ed ~ on the bed** er lag ausgestreckt auf dem Bett.

stretcher ['stretʃəʳ] *n (Med)* Trage *f.*

stretcher: ~-bearer *n* Krankenträger *m*; **~ case** *n* Kranke(r) *mf*/Verletzte(r) *mf*, der/die nicht gehen kann; *(Mil)* Schwerverwundete(r) *mf.*

stretch marks *npl* Schwangerschaftsstreifen *pl.*

strew [struː] *ptp* **strewn** [struːn] *or* **~ed** *vt (scatter)* verstreuen; *flowers, sand* streuen. **the floor was ~n with ...** ... lag/lagen überall auf dem Boden verstreut.

stricken ['strɪkən] **1** *(old) ptp of* **strike. 2** *adj (liter: wounded)* verwundet; *(afflicted)* leidgeprüft; *(ill)* leidend *(geh)*; *ship, plane* in Not. **~ with grief/fear** *etc* schmerzerfüllt/von Angst *etc* erfüllt.

strict [strɪkt] *adj (+er)* **(a)** *law, parent etc* streng; *order, discipline also, obedience* strikt; *Catholic* strenggläubig. **(b)** *(precise)* streng; *meaning* genau. **in the ~ sense of the word** genau genommen; **in ~ confidence** streng vertraulich.

strictly ['strɪktlɪ] *adv* **(a)** streng. **smoking is ~ forbidden** Rauchen ist strengstens verboten. **(b)** *(precisely)* genau; *(absolutely)* absolut. **~ confidential** streng vertraulich; **~ speaking** genau genommen; **not ~ true** nicht ganz richtig; **~ between you and me** ganz unter uns.

strictness ['strɪktnɪs] *n* **(a)** Strenge *f.* **(b)** *(preciseness)* Genauigkeit *f.*

stricture ['strɪktʃəʳ] *n usu pl (criticism)* (scharfe) Kritik *no pl.*

stride [straɪd] *(vb: pret* **strode,** *ptp* **stridden** ['strɪdn]*)* **1** *n (step)* Schritt *m*; *(gait also)* Gang *m*; *(fig)* Fortschritt *m.* **to get into one's ~** *(fig)* in Schwung *or* in Fahrt kommen; **to take sth in one's ~** mit etw spielend fertigwerden; *exam, interview* etw spielend schaffen. **2** *vi* schreiten *(geh)*, mit großen Schritten gehen. **to ~ off** davonschreiten *(geh)*; **to ~ up to sb** auf jdn zuschreiten *(geh)*.

strident ['straɪdənt] *adj sound* schrill, durchdringend; *colour* grell; *criticism, tone* scharf; *demand, protest* lautstark.

strife [straɪf] *n* Unfriede *m*; *(in family, between friends)* Zwietracht *f (geh)*. **armed ~** bewaffneter Konflikt; **internal ~** innere Kämpfe *pl.*

strike [straɪk] *(vb: pret* **struck,** *ptp* **struck** *or (old)* **stricken***)* **1** *n* **(a)** Streik *m.* **to be on ~** streiken; **to come out** *or* **go on ~** in den Streik treten. **(b)** *(discovery of oil, gold etc)* Fund *m.* **to make a ~** fündig werden; **a lucky ~** ein Treffer, ein Glücksfall *m.* **(c)** *(Mil: attack)* Angriff *m.* **(d)** *(act of striking)* Schlag *m.*

2 *vt* **(a)** *(hit)* schlagen; *door* schlagen an (+*acc*); *nail, table* schlagen auf (+*acc*); *metal, hot iron etc* hämmern; *(bullet, lightning, misfortune)* treffen; *(disease)* befallen. **to ~ sb/sth a blow** jdm/einer Sache einen Schlag versetzen; **who struck the first blow?** wer hat zuerst (zu)geschlagen?; **to ~ a blow for sth** *(fig)* eine Lanze für etw brechen.

(b) *(collide with, meet) (spade)* stoßen auf (+*acc*); *(car)* fahren gegen; *ground* aufschlagen auf (+*acc*); *(ship)* auflaufen auf (+*acc*); *(sound, light) ears, eyes* treffen. **to ~ one's head against sth** sich *(dat)* den Kopf an etw *(acc)* stoßen; **to ~ difficulties/obstacles** *(fig)* in Schwierigkeiten geraten/auf Hindernisse stoßen; **a terrible sight struck my eyes** plötzlich sah ich etwas Schreckliches.

(c) *(sound) string, chord, note* anschlagen; *(clock)* schlagen.

(d) *(occur to)* in den Sinn kommen (+*dat*). **to ~ sb as unlikely** *etc* jdm unwahrscheinlich *etc* vorkommen; **that ~s me as a good idea** das kommt mir sehr vernünftig vor; **has it ever struck you that ...?** *(occurred to you)* haben Sie je daran gedacht, daß ...?; *(have you noticed)* ist Ihnen je aufgefallen, daß ...?; **to be struck by sth** von etw beeindruckt sein; **how does it ~ you?** was halten Sie davon?; **how does she ~ you?** welchen Eindruck haben Sie von ihr?

(e) *(produce, make) coin* prägen; *(fig) agreement* aushandeln. **to ~ a light/match** Feuer machen/ein Streichholz anzünden; **to be struck dumb** stumm werden; **to ~ fear into sb** jdn mit Angst erfüllen.

(f) *(find) oil* stoßen auf (+*acc*). **to ~ it rich** das große Geld machen.

(g) *(remove)* streichen. **to be struck** *or (US)* **stricken from a list/the record** von einer Liste/aus dem Protokoll gestrichen werden.

3 *vi* **(a)** *(hit)* treffen; *(lightning)* einschlagen; *(snake)* zubeißen; *(tiger)* die Beute schlagen; *(attack, Mil etc)* angreifen; *(disease)* zuschlagen; *(panic)* ausbrechen. **to ~ against sth** gegen etw stoßen; **to ~ at sb/sth** *(lit)* nach jdm/etw schlagen; **to ~ at the roots of democracy** an den Wurzeln der Demokratie rütteln; **they were within striking distance of success** der Erfolg war in greifbarer Nähe. **(b)** *(clock)* schlagen. **(c)** *(workers)* streiken *(for* für*)*. **(d) to ~ on a new idea** auf eine neue Idee kommen.

♦ **strike back** *vi* zurückschlagen; *(fig also)* sich wehren. **to ~ ~ at sb** jds Angriff *(acc)* erwidern; *(fig)* sich gegen jdn wehren.

♦ **strike down** *vt sep* niederschlagen; *(God) enemies* vernichten; *(fig)* zu Fall bringen. **to be struck ~** niedergeschlagen werden; *(by illness)* getroffen werden.

♦ **strike off** *vt sep* **(a)** *(cut off)* abschlagen. **(b)** *(from list)* (aus)streichen; *solicitor* die Lizenz entziehen (+*dat*); *doctor* die Zulassung entziehen (+*dat*).

♦ **strike out 1** *vi* **(a)** *(hit out)* schlagen. **to ~ ~ at sb** *(lit, fig)* jdn angreifen. **(b)** *(change direction)* zuhalten *(for, towards* auf +*acc)*; *(set out)* sich aufmachen *(for* zu*)*. **to ~ ~ on one's own** *(lit)* allein losziehen; *(fig)* eigene Wege gehen; **to ~ ~ in a new direction** *(fig)* neue Wege gehen. **2** *vt sep name, entry* (aus)streichen.

♦ **strike up 1** *vi (band etc)* anfangen (zu spielen). **2** *vt insep* **(a)** *(band) tune* anstimmen. **(b)** *friendship* schließen; *conversation* anfangen.

strike: ~ action *n* Streikmaßnahmen *pl*; **~breaker** *n* Streikbrecher *m*; **~ force** *n (Mil)* Kampftruppe *f.*

striker ['straɪkəʳ] *n* **(a)** *(worker)* Streikende(r) *mf.* **(b)** *(Ftbl)* Stürmer *m.*

striking ['straɪkɪŋ *adj colour, resemblance etc* auffallend; *difference* erstaunlich; *beauty* eindrucksvoll. **a ~ example of sth** ein hervorragendes Beispiel für etw.

string [strɪŋ] *(vb: pret, ptp* **strung***)* **1** *n* **(a)** *(cord)* Schnur *f*, Bindfaden *m*; *(on apron etc)* Band *nt*; *(on anorak)* Kordel *f*; *(of puppet)* Faden *m.* **to pull ~s** *(fig col)* Fäden ziehen, Beziehungen spielen lassen; **with no ~s attached** ohne Bedingungen. **(b)** *(row) (of beads, onions etc)* Schnur *f*; *(of racehorses etc)* Reihe *f*; *(of people, vehicles)* Schlange *f*; *(fig: series)* Reihe *f*; *(of lies, curses)* Serie *f.* **(c)** *(of musical instrument, tennis racket etc)* Saite *f*; *(of bow)* Sehne *f.* **the ~s** *pl (instruments)* die Streichinstrumente *pl*; *(players)* die Streicher *pl*; **to have more than one ~ to one's bow** mehrere Eisen im Feuer haben.

2 *vt* **(a)** *(put on ~)* aufreihen. **to ~ objects/sentences** *etc* **together** Gegenstände zusammenbinden/Sätze *etc* aneinanderreihen; **she can't even ~ two sentences together** sie bringt keinen vernünftigen Satz zusammen. **(b)** *violin etc, tennis racket* (mit Saiten) bespannen. **(c)** *(space out)* aufreihen.

♦ **string along** *(col)* **1** *vt sep* **to ~ sb ~** jdn hinhalten. **2** *vi (go along with)* sich anschließen *(with dat)*.

stringed [strɪŋd] *adj instrument* Saiten-; *(played with bow also)* Streich-.

stringent ['strɪndʒənt] *adj standards, laws* streng; *testing, training etc also* hart; *measures also* energisch. **~ economies** schärfste Sparmaßnahmen *pl*.

string: ~ quartet *n* Streichquartett *nt*; **~ vest** *n* Netzhemd *nt*.

strip [strɪp] **1** *n* **(a)** *(narrow piece)* Streifen *m*; *(of land also)* (schmales) Stück; *(of metal)* Band *nt*. **(b)** *(Brit Sport)* Trikot *nt*. **2** *vt* **(a)** *(remove clothes etc from) person* ausziehen; *bed* abziehen; *wall (remove paint from)* abkratzen; *(remove paper from)* die Tapeten abziehen von; *wallpaper* abziehen; *(remove contents from)* ausräumen. **to ~ a house of its contents** ein Haus ausräumen; **to ~ sth from** *or* **off sth** etw von etw entfernen; **~ped of sth** ohne etw. **(b)** *(fig: deprive of)* berauben *(of gen)*. **(c)** *(Tech: dismantle) engine, car, gun* auseinandernehmen. **3** *vi (remove clothes)* sich ausziehen; *(at doctor's)* sich freimachen; *(perform ~tease)* strippen *(col)*. **to ~ naked** sich ganz ausziehen; **to ~ to the waist** den Oberkörper freimachen.

♦ **strip off** *vi* = **strip 3.**

stripe [straɪp] *n* **(a)** Streifen *m*. **(b)** *(US: kind) (of politics)* Richtung *f*; *(of character, opinion)* Art *f*.

striped [straɪpt] *adj* gestreift.

stripper ['strɪpə^r] *n* **(a)** *(performer)* Stripteasetänzerin *f*. **(b)** *(paint-~)* Farbentferner *m*; *(wallpaper ~)* Tapetenlöser *m*.

striptease ['strɪpti:z] *n* Striptease *m or nt*.

strive [straɪv] *pret* **strove,** *ptp* **striven** ['strɪvn] *vi (exert oneself)* sich bemühen; *(fight)* kämpfen. **to ~ to do sth** bestrebt sein, etw zu tun; **to ~ for sth** nach etw streben; **to ~ against sth** gegen etw (an)kämpfen.

strode [strəʊd] *pret of* **stride.**

stroke [strəʊk] **1** *n* **(a)** *(blow)* Schlag, Hieb *m*. **(b)** *(Cricket, Golf, Rowing, Tennis)* Schlag *m*; *(Swimming) (movement)* Zug *m*; *(type of ~)* Stil *m*. **to put sb off his ~** *(fig)* jdn aus dem Konzept bringen. **(c)** *(of pen etc)* Strich *m*. **he doesn't do a ~ (of work)** er tut keinen Schlag *(col)*; **a ~ of genius** ein genialer Einfall; **a ~ of luck** ein Glücksfall *m*; **we had a ~ of luck** wir hatten Glück; **at a** *or* **one ~** mit einem Schlag. **(d)** *(of clock)* Schlag *m*. **on the ~ of twelve** Punkt zwölf (Uhr). **(e)** *(of piston)* Hub *m*. **two-~ engine** Zweitaktmotor *m*. **(f)** *(Med)* Schlag *m*. **to have a ~** einen Schlaganfall bekommen. **(g)** *(caress)* Streicheln *nt no pl*. **to give sb/sth a ~** jdn/etw streicheln. **2** *vt* streicheln. **he ~d his chin** er strich sich *(dat)* übers Kinn.

stroll [strəʊl] **1** *n* Spaziergang *m*. **to go for a ~, to take a ~** einen Bummel machen. **2** *vi* spazieren. **to ~ along** bummeln; **to ~ along the road** die Straße entlangspazieren; **to ~ up to sb** auf jdn zuschlendern.

stroller ['strəʊlə^r] *n (US: for babies)* Sportwagen *m*.

strong [strɒŋ] **1** *adj (+er)* **(a)** stark; *material, grip also, kick, voice* kräftig; *table, wall* stabil; *shoes* fest; *(Fin) economy* gesund; *(strongly marked) features* ausgeprägt. **you need a ~ stomach to be a nurse** als Krankenschwester muß man allerhand verkraften können. **(b)** *(healthy)* kräftig; *constitution also* robust; *teeth also, eyes, eyesight, heart, nerves* gut. **when you're ~ again** wenn Sie wieder bei Kräften sind.

(c) *(powerful, effective)* stark; *character, views* fest; *country* mächtig; *candidate, case* aussichtsreich; *argument, evidence* überzeugend; *protest* energisch; *measure* drastisch; *letter* geharnischt. **to have ~ feelings/views about sth** in bezug auf etw *(acc)* stark engagiert sein; **to have ~ feelings for sth** eine starke Bindung an etw *(acc)* haben; **to protest in ~ terms** energisch protestieren; **a group 20 ~** eine 20 Mann starke Gruppe; **he is ~ in/on sth** etw ist seine Stärke.

(d) *curry etc* deftig; *(pungent) smell, taste* streng; *colour, light* kräftig; *acid* stark; *solution* konzentriert. **a ~ drink/whisky** ein harter Drink/ein starker Whisky.

2 *adv (+er) (col)* **to be going ~** *(old person, thing)* gut in Schuß sein *(col)*; *(runner)* eine gute Kondition zeigen; *(party, rehearsals)* in Schwung sein *(col)*.

strong: ~-arm *adj (col) tactics etc* brutal, Gewalt-; **~-box** *n* (Geld)kassette *f*; **~hold** *n (castle, fortress)* Festung *f*; *(town etc)* Stützpunkt *m*; *(fig)* Hochburg *f*.

strongly ['strɒŋlɪ] *adv* **(a)** *(physically)* stark; *kick, grip* kräftig; *fight* energisch; *built* stabil; *built (person)* kräftig. **(b)** *influence, suspect, tempt* stark; *interest also* brennend; *believe* fest. **to feel very ~ about sth** in bezug auf etw *(acc)* stark engagiert sein; **I didn't know that you felt so ~ about it** ich habe nicht gewußt, daß Ihnen das so viel bedeutet; *(against it)* ich habe nicht gewußt, daß Sie so dagegen sind. **(c)** *(powerfully)* stark; *protest* heftig, energisch; *plead* inständig; *support* kräftig; *answer, worded* in starken Worten. **I ~ advise you ...** ich möchte Ihnen dringend(st) raten ...

strong: ~ point *n* Stärke *f*; **~room** *n* Stahlkammer *f*; **~-willed** ['strɒŋ'wɪld] *adj* willensstark; *(pej)* eigensinnig.

strontium ['strɒntɪəm] *n* Strontium *nt*.

strove [strəʊv] *pret of* **strive.**

struck [strʌk] **1** *pret, ptp of* **strike. 2** *adj* **(a)** *pred* **to be ~ with sb/sth** *(impressed)* von jdm/etw begeistert *or* angetan sein; **I wasn't very ~ with him** er hat keinen großen Eindruck auf mich gemacht; **to be ~ on sb/sth** *(keen)* auf jdn/etw stehen *(col)*, auf jdn/etw versessen sein. **(b)** *(US attr) (striking) workers* streikend; *factory, employers* vom Streik betroffen.

structural ['strʌktʃərəl] *adj* **(a)** strukturell; *(of building) alterations, damage* baulich; *defect* Konstruktions-. **(b)** *(weight-bearing) wall, beam* tragend.

structure ['strʌktʃə^r] **1** *n* **(a)** Struktur *f*; *(Liter)* Aufbau *m*; *(Tech: of bridge, car etc)* Konstruktion *f*. **(b)** *(thing constructed)* Konstruktion *f*. **2** *vt* strukturieren; *essay, argument* gliedern; *layout, life* gestalten.

struggle ['strʌgl] **1** *n (lit, fig)* Kampf *m (for* um*)*; *(fig: effort)* Anstrengung *f*. **without a ~** *surrender* kampflos; **to put up a ~** sich wehren; **the ~ for survival** der Überlebenskampf; **it was a ~** es war mühsam; **I had a ~ to persuade him** es war gar nicht einfach, ihn zu überreden.

2 *vi* **(a)** *(contend)* kämpfen; *(in self-defence)* sich wehren; *(financially)* in Schwierigkeiten sein; *(fig: strive)* sich sehr anstrengen. **to ~ to do sth** sich sehr anstrengen, etw zu tun; **to ~ for sth** um etw kämpfen; **to ~ with sth** *with problem* sich mit etw herumschlagen; *with language, homework* sich mit etw abmühen; *with doubts, conscience* mit etw ringen. **(b)** *(move with difficulty)* sich quälen. **to ~ to one's feet** mühsam aufstehen; **to ~ on** *(lit)* sich weiterkämpfen; *(fig)* weiterkämpfen.

strum [strʌm] *vt tune* klimpern; *guitar* klimpern auf *(+dat)*.
strung [strʌŋ] *pret, ptp of* **string.**
strut[1] [strʌt] *vi* stolzieren. **to ~ about (the yard)** (auf dem Hof) herumstolzieren; **to ~ past** vorbeistolzieren.
strut[2] *n (horizontal)* Strebe *f*; *(vertical)* Pfeiler *m*.
strychnine ['strɪkniːn] *n* Strychnin *nt*.
stub [stʌb] **1** *n (of candle, pencil, tail, cigarette)* Stummel *m*; *(of cheque, ticket)* Abschnitt *m*; *(of tree)* Stumpf *m*. **2** *vt* **to ~ one's toe (on** *or* **against sth)** sich *(dat)* den Zeh (an etw *dat*) stoßen; **to ~ out a cigarette** eine Zigarette ausdrücken.
stubble ['stʌbl] *n no pl* Stoppeln *pl*.
stubborn ['stʌbən] *adj person, insistence* stur; *animal also, child* störrisch; *refusal, weeds, cough* hartnäckig; *lock* widerspenstig. **to be ~ about sth** stur auf etw *(dat)* beharren.
stubbornness ['stʌbənnɪs] *n see adj* Sturheit *f*; störrische Art; Hartnäckigkeit *f*; Widerspenstigkeit *f*.
stubby ['stʌbɪ] *adj (+er) revolver etc* kurz; *tail* stummelig; *pencil, vase* kurz und dick; *person* gedrungen, untersetzt; *legs* kurz und stämmig.
stucco ['stʌkəʊ] *n, pl* **-(e)s** Stuck *m*.
stuck [stʌk] **1** *pret, ptp of* **stick**[2]. **2** *adj* **(a)** *(baffled)* **to be ~** nicht klarkommen. **(b)** *(col)* **he/she is ~ for sth** es fehlt ihm/ihr an etw *(dat)*; **I'm a bit ~ for cash** ich bin ein bißchen knapp bei Kasse. **(c)** *(col)* **to get ~ into sth** sich in etw *(acc)* richtig reinknien *(col)*; **to be ~ with sb/sth** jdn/etw am Hals haben *(col)*.
stuck-up ['stʌk'ʌp] *adj (col) person* hochnäsig.
stud[1] [stʌd] **1** *n (nail)* Beschlagnagel *m*; *(decorative)* Ziernagel *m*. **2** *vt* **~ded with ...** mit ... übersät; *with jewels* mit ... besetzt.
stud[2] *n (group of horses) (for breeding)* Gestüt *nt*, Zucht *f*; *(for racing etc)* Stall *m*; *(stallion)* (Zucht)hengst *m*.
student ['stjuːdənt] **1** *n (Univ)* Student(in *f*) *m*; *(esp US: at school, night school)* Schüler(in *f*) *m*. **he is a ~ of French** *or* **a French ~** *(Univ)* er studiert Französisch; **medical/law ~s** Medizin-/Jurastudenten *pl*. **2** *adj attr* Studenten-; *activities also, movement* studentisch. **~ driver** *(US)* Fahrschüler(in *f*) *m*.
student: ~ teacher *n* Referendar(in *f*) *m*; **~ union** *n* **(a)** *(organization)* Studentenvereinigung *f*; **(b)** *(building)* Gebäude *nt* der Studentenvereinigung.
studied ['stʌdɪd] **1** *pret, ptp of* **study. 2** *adj reply* wohlüberlegt; *prose* kunstvoll.
studio ['stjuːdɪəʊ] *n* Studio *nt*; *(of painter also)* Atelier *nt*; *(broadcasting ~ also)* Senderaum *m*.
studio: ~ audience *n* Publikum *nt* im Studio; **~ flat** Appartementwohnung *f*.
studious ['stjuːdɪəs] *adj person* fleißig, eifrig; *attention, piece of work* gewissenhaft, sorgfältig.
study ['stʌdɪ] **1** *n* **(a)** *(studying) (esp Univ)* Studium *nt*; *(at school)* Lernen *nt*; *(of situation, evidence, case)* Untersuchung *f*; *(of nature)* Beobachtung *f*. **the ~ of cancer** die Krebsforschung; **African studies** *(Univ)* afrikanische Sprache und Kultur, Afrikanistik *f*; **to make a ~ of sth** etw untersuchen; *(academic)* etw studieren; **during my studies** während meines Studiums. **(b)** *(piece of work)* Studie *f (of* über *+acc)*; *(Art, Phot)* Studie *f (of gen)*; *(Mus)* Etüde *f*. **(c)** *(room)* Arbeitszimmer *nt*. **2** *vt* studieren; *(Sch)* lernen; *nature also, stars* beobachten; *author, text etc* sich befassen mit; *(research into)* erforschen; *(examine also)* untersuchen; *evidence* prüfen. **3** *vi* studieren; *(esp Sch)* lernen. **to ~ to be a teacher/doctor** ein Lehrer-/Medizinstudium machen; **to ~ under sb** bei jdm studieren.
stuff [stʌf] **1** *n* **(a)** Zeug *nt*. **the ~ that heroes are made of** der Stoff, aus dem Helden gemacht sind; **it's poor/good ~** das ist schlecht/gut; **books and ~** Bücher und so *(col)*; **and ~ like that** und so was *(col)*; **all that ~ about how he wants to help us** all das Gerede, daß er uns helfen will; **~ and nonsense** Quatsch *(col)*. **(b)** *(col)* **that's the ~** so ist's richtig!, weiter so!; **to do one's ~** seine Nummer abziehen *(col)*; **he did his ~ well** er hat seine Sache gut gemacht; **to know one's ~** sich auskennen.
2 *vt* **(a)** *(fill)* vollstopfen; *hole* zustopfen; *object* (hinein)stopfen *(into* in *+acc)*; *(into envelope)* stecken *(into* in *+acc)*. **to ~ sth away** etw wegstecken; **he ~ed it away in his pocket** er stopfte es in seine Tasche; **to be ~ed up (with a cold)** verschnupft sein, eine verstopfte Nase haben. **(b)** *(Cook)* füllen. **(c)** *cushion etc* füllen; *toy also* (aus)stopfen; *(in taxidermy)* ausstopfen. **a ~ed toy** ein Stofftier *nt*. **(d)** *(col!)* **~ it** *(be quiet)* halt's Maul! *(col)*; **get ~ed!** du kannst mich mal *(col!)*.
3 *vr* **to ~ oneself (with cakes)** sich (mit Kuchen) vollstopfen *(col)*.
stuffing ['stʌfɪŋ] *n (of pillow, Cook)* Füllung *f*; *(of furniture)* Polstermaterial *nt*; *(in taxidermy, toys)* Füllmaterial *nt*.
stuffy ['stʌfɪ] *adj (+er)* **(a)** *room, atmosphere* stickig, dumpf. **(b)** *(narrow-minded)* spießig; *(prudish)* prüde; *(stiff)* steif; *(dull)* langweilig, öde.
stultify ['stʌltɪfaɪ] *vt mind, person* verkümmern lassen. **to become stultified** verkümmern.
stumble ['stʌmbl] *vi (lit, fig)* stolpern; *(in speech)* stocken. **to ~ against sth** gegen etw stoßen; **to ~ on** *or* **across sth** *(fig)* auf etw *(acc)* stoßen.
stumbling-block ['stʌmblɪŋ'blɒk] *n (fig)* Hindernis *nt*. **to be a ~ to sth** einer Sache *(dat)* im Weg stehen.
stump [stʌmp] **1** *n* **(a)** *(of tree, limb, tooth, candle)* Stumpf *m*; *(of pencil, tail)* Stummel *m*; *(Cricket)* Stab *m*. **(b)** *(US Pol: platform)* Rednertribüne *f*. **~ speaker** Wahlredner(in *f*) *m*. **2** *vt (fig col)* **you've got me ~ed** da bin ich überfragt; **I'm ~ed** ich bin mit meinem Latein am Ende *(col)*; **to be ~ed for an answer** um eine Antwort verlegen sein. **3** *vi (col)* stapfen. **to ~ along/about** entlang-/herumstapfen.
stun [stʌn] *vt (make unconscious)* betäuben; *(daze)* benommen machen; *(fig) (shock)* fassungslos machen; *(amaze)* verblüffen. **he was ~ned by the news** *(bad news)* er war über die Nachricht wie gelähmt; *(good news)* die Nachricht hat ihn überwältigt.
stung [stʌŋ] *pret, ptp of* **sting.**
stunk [stʌŋk] *ptp of* **stink.**
stunning ['stʌnɪŋ] *adj dress, girl etc* toll *(col)*, atemberaubend.
stunt[1] [stʌnt] *n (in film)* Action-Szene *f*; *(publicity ~, trick)* Gag *m*; *(Aviat)* Kunststück *nt*.
stunt[2] *vt (lit, fig) growth, development* hemmen; *trees, mind etc* verkümmern lassen.
stunted ['stʌntɪd] *adj plant, mind* verkümmert; *child* unterentwickelt.
stuntman ['stʌntmæn] *n, pl* **-men** [-ˌmen] *n* Stuntman *m*.
stupefy ['stjuːpɪfaɪ] *vt* benommen machen; *(fig: amaze, surprise)* verblüffen.
stupefying ['stjuːpɪfaɪɪŋ] *adj (amazing)* verblüffend.
stupendous [stjuː'pendəs] *adj* phantastisch; *effort* enorm.
stupid ['stjuːpɪd] *adj* dumm. **don't be ~** sei nicht so blöd *(col)*; **I've done a ~ thing** ich habe etwas ganz Dummes gemacht; **you ~ idiot!** du blöder Idiot!; **that was a ~ thing to do** das war dumm (von dir); **to drink oneself ~** sich sinnlos betrinken.
stupidity [stjuː'pɪdɪtɪ] *n* Dummheit *f*.
stupor ['stjuːpəʳ] *n* Benommenheit *f*. **to be in a drunken ~** im Vollrausch sein.
sturdy ['stɜːdɪ] *adj (+er)* **(a)** *person, plant* kräftig;

material robust; *building, car* stabil. **(b)** *(fig) opposition* standhaft.

sturgeon ['stɜːdʒən] *n* Stör *m.*

stutter ['stʌtəʳ] **1** *n (of person, engine)* Stottern *nt no pl.* **he has a bad ~** er stottert sehr. **2** *vti* stottern.

sty [staɪ] *n (lit, fig)* Schweinestall *m.*

sty(e) [staɪ] *n (Med)* Gerstenkorn *nt.*

style [staɪl] *n* **(a)** Stil *m.* **~ of painting** Malstil *m*; **the ~ of his writing** sein Stil *m*; **~ of life** Lebensstil *m*; **a poem in the Romantic ~** ein Gedicht im Stil der Romantik; **he won in fine ~** er gewann überlegen; **that house is not my ~** so ein Haus ist nicht mein Stil; **hillwalking/flattering people is not his ~** Bergwanderungen liegen ihm nicht/es ist nicht seine Art zu schmeicheln; **the man has ~** der Mann hat Format; **in ~** stilvoll; **to do things in ~** alles im großen Stil tun; **to celebrate in ~** groß feiern. **(b)** *(Fashion)* Stil *m no pl,* Mode *f*; *(cut)* Schnitt *m*; *(hair~)* Frisur *f.* **all the latest ~s** die neueste Mode.

styli ['staɪlaɪ] *pl of* **stylus.**

stylish ['staɪlɪʃ] *adj person* elegant; *car, hotel, district also* vornehm; *furnishings* stilvoll; *(fashionable)* modisch; *way of life* großartig.

stylist ['staɪlɪst] *n (Fashion)* Modeschöpfer(in *f*) *m*; *(hair~)* Friseur *m,* Friseuse *f.*

stylistic [staɪ'lɪstɪk] *adj* stilistisch. **~ device** Stilmittel *nt.*

stylus ['staɪləs] *n, pl* **styli** *(on record-player)* Nadel *f.*

styptic ['stɪptɪk] *adj* **~ pencil** Blutstillstift *m.*

suave ['swɑːv] *adj* weltmännisch, aalglatt *(pej).*

sub [sʌb] = **(a) submarine. (b) subscription. (c) substitute.**

sub- *pref* Unter-, unter-; *(esp with foreign words)* Sub-, sub-.

subaltern ['sʌbltən] *n (Brit Mil)* Subalternoffizier *m.*

sub: **~committee** *n* Unterausschuß *m*; **~conscious 1** *adj* unterbewußt; **2** *n* **the ~conscious** das Unterbewußtsein; **~consciously** *adv* im Unterbewußtsein; **~continent** *n* Subkontinent *m*; **~contract 1** ['sʌbkəntrækt] *vt* (vertraglich) weitervergeben *(to* an *+acc)*; **2** [sʌb'kɒntrækt] *n* Nebenvertrag *m*; **~contractor** *n* Unterkontrahent *m*; **~divide** *vt* unterteilen; **~division** *n (act)* Unterteilung *f*; *(~group)* Unterabteilung *f.*

subdue [səb'djuː] *vt rebels, country* unterwerfen; *rioters* überwältigen; *(fig) anger, desire* unterdrücken; *noise, light, high spirits* dämpfen; *animals, children* bändigen.

subdued [səb'djuːd] *adj colour, lighting, voice* gedämpft; *manner, person* ruhig; *mood, atmosphere* gedrückt; *(submissive) voice, manner, person* fügsam, gehorsam; *(repressed) feelings, excitement* unterdrückt.

sub: **~-editor** *n (esp Brit)* Redakteur(in *f*) *m*; **~group** *n* Unterabteilung *f*; **~heading** *n* Untertitel *m*; **~human** *adj* unmenschlich.

subject ['sʌbdʒɪkt] **1** *n* **(a)** *(Pol)* Staatsbürger(in *f*) *m*; *(of king etc)* Untertan *m,* Untertanin *f.* **(b)** *(Gram)* Subjekt *nt,* Satzgegenstand *m.* **(c)** *(topic, Mus)* Thema *nt.* **to change the ~** das Thema wechseln; **on the ~ of ...** zum Thema *(+gen)* ...; **while we're on the ~** da wir gerade beim Thema sind. **(d)** *(discipline) (Sch, Univ)* Fach *nt*; *(specialist ~)* (Spezial)gebiet *nt.* **(e)** *(object)* Gegenstand *m (of gen)*; *(in experiment) (person)* Versuchsperson *f*; *(animal)* Versuchstier *nt.* **he is the ~ of much criticism** er wird stark kritisiert.

2 *adj* **(a)** *(conquered)* unterworfen. **(b) to be ~ to sth** *to law, change, sb's will* einer Sache *(dat)* unterworfen sein; *to illness* für etw anfällig sein; *to consent, approval* von etw abhängig sein; **northbound trains are ~ to delays** bei Zügen in Richtung Norden muß mit Verspätung gerechnet werden; **prices are ~ to change** *or* **alteration without notice** Preisänderungen sind vorbehalten; **~ to confirmation in writing** vorausgesetzt, es wird schriftlich bestätigt.

3 [səb'dʒekt] *vt* **(a)** *(subjugate)* unterwerfen; *terrorists, guerillas* zerschlagen. **(b) to ~ sb to sth** *to questioning, analysis* jdn einer Sache *(dat)* unterziehen; *to torture, criticism* jdn einer Sache *(dat)* aussetzen; **to ~ sb/a book to criticism** jdn/ein Buch kritisieren.

subjection [səb'dʒekʃən] *n* **(a)** *(state)* Abhängigkeit *f.* **to hold a people in ~** ein Volk unterdrücken. **(b)** *(act)* Unterwerfung *f*; *(of terrorists etc)* Zerschlagung *f.*

subjective [səb'dʒektɪv] *adj* subjektiv.

subject-matter ['sʌbdʒɪkt'mætəʳ] *n (theme)* Stoff *m*; *(content)* Inhalt *m.*

sub judice [ˌsʌb'dʒuːdɪsɪ] *adj* **to be ~** verhandelt werden.

subjugate ['sʌbdʒʊgeɪt] *vt* unterwerfen, unterjochen.

subjunctive [səb'dʒʌŋktɪv] **1** *adj* konjunktivisch. **the ~ mood** der Konjunktiv. **2** *n (mood, verb)* Konjunktiv *m.*

sub: **~let** *pret, ptp* **~let** *vti* untervermieten *(to* an *+acc)*; **~lieutenant** *n (Brit Naut)* Leutnant *m* zur See.

sublimate ['sʌblɪmeɪt] *vt* sublimieren.

sublime [sə'blaɪm] *adj beauty, scenery, thoughts* erhaben; *achievement, genius also* überragend; *indifference, contempt* vollkommen.

subliminal [ˌsʌb'lɪmɪnl] *adj (Psych)* unterschwellig.

submachine gun [ˌsʌbmə'ʃiːn'gʌn] *n* Maschinenpistole *f.*

submarine ['sʌbməˌriːn] *n* Unterseeboot, U-Boot *nt.*

submerge [səb'mɜːdʒ] **1** *vt* untertauchen; *(flood)* überschwemmen. **the house was completely ~d** das Haus stand völlig unter Wasser. **2** *vi (diver, submarine)* tauchen.

submersion [səb'mɜːʃən] *n* Untertauchen *nt*; *(of submarine)* Tauchen *nt*; *(by flood)* Überschwemmung *f.*

submission [səb'mɪʃən] *n* **(a)** *(yielding)* Unterwerfung *f (to* unter *+acc)*; *(submissiveness)* Gehorsam *m*; *(Sport)* Aufgabe *f.* **(b)** *(presentation)* Eingabe *f*; *(documents)* Vorlage *f.*

submissive [səb'mɪsɪv] *adj* demütig, unterwürfig *(pej) (to* gegenüber*).*

submit [səb'mɪt] **1** *vt* **(a)** *(put forward)* vorlegen *(to dat)*; *application etc* einreichen *(to* bei*).* **to ~ that ...** *(esp Jur)* behaupten, daß ... **(b) to ~ sth to scrutiny** *etc* etw einer Prüfung *etc* unterziehen; **to be ~ted to sth** *to sth unpleasant* einer Sache *(dat)* ausgesetzt werden. **2** *vi (yield)* nachgeben; *(Mil)* sich ergeben *(to dat)*; *(Sport)* aufgeben. **to ~ to sth** *to sb's orders, judgement* sich einer Sache *(dat)* beugen; *to indignity* etw erdulden; *to demands, threats* einer Sache *(dat)* nachgeben; **to ~ to blackmail** sich erpressen lassen.

subnormal [ˌsʌb'nɔːməl] *adj intelligence, temperature* unterdurchschnittlich; *person* minderbegabt. **mentally ~** minderbemittelt.

subordinate [sə'bɔːdnɪt] **1** *adj officer* rangniedriger; *position, importance* untergeordnet. **~ clause** *(Gram)* Nebensatz *m*; **to be ~ to sb/sth** jdm/einer Sache untergeordnet sein. **2** *n* Untergebene(r) *mf.* **3** [sə'bɔːdɪneɪt] *vt* unterordnen *(to dat).*

subpoena [səb'piːnə] *(Jur)* **1** *n* Vorladung *f.* **to serve a ~ on sb** jdn vorladen. **2** *vt* vorladen.

subscribe [səb'skraɪb] **1** *vt money* spenden *(to* für*).* **2** *vi* **to ~ to an appeal** sich an einer Spendenaktion beteiligen; **to ~ to a magazine** *etc* eine Zeitschrift *etc* abonnieren; **to ~ to sth** *to proposal* etw gutheißen, etw billigen; *to opinion, theory* etw vertreten.

subscriber [səb'skraɪbəʳ] *n (to paper)* Abonnent(in *f*) *m*; *(to fund)* Spender(in *f*) *m*; *(Telec)* Teilnehmer(in *f*) *m*; *(of shares)* Zeichner *m*. ~ **trunk dialling** *(Brit)* der Selbstwählferndienst.

subscription [səb'skrɪpʃən] *n (money subscribed)* Beitrag *m*; *(to newspaper, concert etc)* Abonnement *nt (to gen)*. **to take out a ~ to sth** etw abonnieren; **to pay one's ~ (to a club)** seinen (Vereins)beitrag bezahlen.

subsection ['sʌb,sekʃən] *n* Unterabteilung *f*; *(Jur)* Paragraph *m*.

subsequent ['sʌbsɪkwənt] *adj* (nach)folgend. ~ **to** *(form)* im Anschluß an *(+acc)*.

subsequently ['sʌbsɪkwəntlɪ] *adv (afterwards)* später; *(from that time also)* von da an.

subservient [səb'sɜːvɪənt] *adj (pej)* unterwürfig *(to* gegenüber*)*.

subside [səb'saɪd] *vi (flood)* sinken; *(land, building)* sich senken, absacken *(col)*; *(storm, wind, anger etc)* nachlassen, sich legen.

subsidence [səb'saɪdəns] *n* Senkung *f*.

subsidiary [səb'sɪdɪərɪ] **1** *adj role, interest, subject* Neben-; *company* Tochter-. **2** *n* Tochtergesellschaft *f*.

subsidize ['sʌbsɪdaɪz] *vt company etc* subventionieren; *(col) person* unterstützen.

subsidy ['sʌbsɪdɪ] *n* Subvention *f*. **there is a ~ on butter** Butter wird subventioniert; **housing subsidies** Wohnungsbaubeihilfen *pl*.

subsist [səb'sɪst] *vi* sich ernähren, leben *(on* von*)*.

subsistence [səb'sɪstəns] *n (living)* Leben *nt (on* von*)*; *(means of ~)* (Lebens)unterhalt *m*.

subsistence: ~ **allowance** *n* Unterhaltszuschuß *m*; ~ **farming** *n* Ackerbau *m* für den Eigenbedarf; ~ **level** *n* Existenzminimum *nt*; **at ~ level** auf dem Existenzminimum; ~ **wage** *n* Minimallohn *m*.

substance ['sʌbstəns] *n* Substanz *f*. **in ~** im wesentlichen; **the argument lacks ~** das Argument hat keine Substanz; **there is some ~ in his claim** seine Behauptung ist nicht unfundiert; **a man of ~** ein vermögender Mann.

substandard [,sʌb'stændəd] *adj work, goods, quality* minderwertig; *housing* unzulänglich.

substantial [səb'stænʃəl] *adj* **(a)** *meal, person, cloth* kräftig; *furniture, building, firm* solide; *book* umfangreich. **(b)** *(considerable) loss, part, improvement, amount* beträchtlich; *sum also* namhaft; *(rich) landowner* vermögend. **(c)** *(weighty)* bedeutend; *proof, argument* überzeugend; *difference* wesentlich.

substantially [səb'stænʃəlɪ] *adv* **(a)** *(solidly)* solide; *(considerably)* erheblich, beträchtlich. ~ **built** *house* solide gebaut; *person* kräftig gebaut. **(b)** *(essentially, basically)* im wesentlichen.

substantiate [səb'stænʃɪeɪt] *vt* erhärten.

substantive ['sʌbstəntɪv] *adj evidence, argument, reason* überzeugend, stichhaltig.

substitute ['sʌbstɪtjuːt] **1** *n* Ersatz *m no pl*; *(representative also)* Vertretung *f*; *(Sport)* Ersatzspieler(in *f*) *m*. **2** *adj attr* Ersatz-. **3** *vt* **to ~ A for B** B durch A ersetzen; *(Sport also)* B gegen A auswechseln. **4** *vi* **to ~ for sb/sth** für jdn einspringen/etw ersetzen.

substitution [,sʌbstɪ'tjuːʃən] *n* Ersetzen *nt (of X for Y* von Y durch X*)*; *(Sport)* Austausch *m (of X for Y* von Y gegen X*)*. **to make a ~** *(Sport)* auswechseln.

subtenant [,sʌb'tenənt] *n (of flat etc)* Untermieter(in *f*) *m*; *(of land)* Unterpächter(in *f*) *m*.

subterfuge ['sʌbtəfjuːdʒ] *n (trickery)* Täuschung *f*; *(trick)* Trick *m*.

subterranean [,sʌbtə'reɪnɪən] *adj* unterirdisch.

subtitle ['sʌb,taɪtl] **1** *n* Untertitel *m*. **2** *vt film* mit Untertiteln versehen; *book etc* einen Untertitel geben *(+dat)*.

subtle ['sʌtl] *adj* fein; *hint* zart; *charm* unaufdringlich; *(not obvious) remark, point* scharfsinnig; *design, proof* raffiniert.

subtlety ['sʌtltɪ] *n see adj* Feinheit *f*; Zartheit *f*; Unaufdringlichkeit *f*; Scharfsinn(igkeit *f*) *m*; Raffiniertheit *f*.

subtly ['sʌtlɪ] *adv* fein; *flavoured also* delikat; *argue, analyse* scharfsinnig; *achieve one's ends* auf raffinierte Weise. ~ **different** auf subtile Weise verschieden.

subtotal ['sʌb,təʊtl] *n* Zwischen- *or* Teilsumme *f*.

subtract [səb'trækt] *vti* abziehen, subtrahieren *(from* von*)*.

subtraction [səb'trækʃən] *n* Subtraktion *f*.

suburb ['sʌbɜːb] *n* Vorort *m*.

suburban [sə'bɜːbən] *adj* Vorort-; *(pej)* kleinbürgerlich. ~ **line** *(Rail)* Vorortbahn *f*.

suburbia [sə'bɜːbɪə] *n (usu pej)* die Vororte *pl*. **to live in ~** am Stadtrand wohnen.

subversion [səb'vɜːʃən] *n no pl* Subversion *f*; *(of rights, freedom etc)* Untergrabung *f*.

subversive [səb'vɜːsɪv] **1** *adj* subversiv. ~ **elements** subversive Kräfte *pl*. **2** *n* Umstürzler(in *f*) *m*.

subway ['sʌbweɪ] *n* Unterführung *f*; *(US Rail)* U-Bahn *f*.

subzero ['sʌb'zɪərəʊ] *adj temperatures* unter Null.

succeed [sək'siːd] **1** *vi* **(a)** *(person)* erfolgreich sein, Erfolg haben; *(plan etc also)* gelingen. **to ~ in business/in a plan** geschäftlich/mit einem Plan erfolgreich sein; **I ~ed in doing it** es gelang mir, es zu tun; **you'll only ~ in making things worse** damit erreichst du nur, daß alles noch schlimmer wird. **(b)** *(come next)* **to ~ to an office** in einem Amt nachfolgen; **he ~ed to his father's position** er trat die Nachfolge seines Vaters an *(geh)*. **2** *vt (come after, take the place of)* folgen *(+dat)*; *(person also)* Nachfolger(in *f*) *m* werden *(+gen)*. **to ~ sb in a post/in office** jds Stelle *(acc)* übernehmen/jdm im Amt nachfolgen.

succeeding [sək'siːdɪŋ] *adj* folgend. ~ **generations** nachfolgende Generationen *pl*.

success [sək'ses] *n* Erfolg *m*. **without ~** ohne Erfolg, erfolglos; **to make a ~ of sth** mit *or* bei etw erfolgreich sein; **to meet with ~** Erfolg haben, erfolgreich sein.

successful [sək'sesfʊl] *adj* erfolgreich. **to be ~** erfolgreich sein, Erfolg haben *(in* mit, bei*)*; **I was ~ in doing it** es gelang mir, es zu tun.

successfully [sək'sesfəlɪ] *adv* erfolgreich, mit Erfolg.

succession [sək'seʃən] *n* **(a)** Folge, Serie *f*; *(with no intervening period)* (Aufeinander)folge *f*. **in ~** hintereinander; **in quick ~** schnell hintereinander. **(b)** *(to post)* Nachfolge *f*. **fourth in ~ to the throne** an vierter Stelle in der Thronfolge.

successive [sək'sesɪv] *adj* **4 ~ days** 4 Tage hintereinander, 4 aufeinanderfolgende Tage; **~ generations have ...** eine Generation nach der anderen hat ...

successively [sək'sesɪvlɪ] *adv* nacheinander.

successor [sək'sesəʳ] *n* Nachfolger(in *f*) *m (to gen)*; *(to throne)* Thronfolger(in *f*) *m*.

succinct [sək'sɪŋkt] *adj* knapp.

succinctly [sək'sɪŋktlɪ] *adv* kurz und bündig; *write* in gedrängtem Stil. **as he very ~ put it** wie er so treffend bemerkte.

succulent ['sʌkjʊlənt] **1** *adj peach, steak* saftig. **2** *n (Bot)* Sukkulente *f (spec)*.

succumb [sə'kʌm] *vi* erliegen *(to dat)*; *(to threats)* sich beugen *(to dat)*.

such [sʌtʃ] **1** *adj* **(a)** *(of that kind)* solche(r, s). **~ a person** so ein Mensch, ein solcher Mensch; **~ people/books** solche Leute/Bücher; **many/all ~ people** viele/all solche Leute; **do you have ~ a book?** haben Sie so ein Buch?; **~ a thing (as)** so etwas (wie); **I said no ~ thing** das habe ich nie gesagt; **no ~ thing** nichts dergleichen; **you'll do no ~ thing** du wirst dich hüten; **there's no ~ thing as a unicorn** so etwas wie ein Einhorn gibt es nicht; **... or some ~ idea** ... oder so etwas, ...

oder so ähnlich; ... **or some ~ name/place** ... oder so (ähnlich); **in ~ a case** in einem solchen Fall; **books ~ as these, ~ books as these** Bücher wie diese, solche Bücher.

(b) *(so much, so great etc)* solche(r, s). **he's ~ a liar** er ist ein derartiger *or* solcher Lügner; **he's not ~ a fool as you think** er ist nicht so dumm, wie Sie denken; **he did it in ~ a way that ...** er machte es so, daß ...; **~ wealth/beauty!** was für ein Reichtum/welche Schönheit!; **he's always in ~ a hurry** er hat es immer so eilig.

(c) *pred* **his surprise was ~ that ...** er war so überrascht, daß ...; **his manner was ~ that ...** er benahm sich so, daß ...

2 *adv* so, solch *(geh)*. **~ a big house** so ein großes Haus; **nobody else makes ~ a good cup of tea as you** niemand kocht so guten Tee wie du; **it's ~ a long time ago** es ist so lange her.

3 *pron* **rabbits and hares and ~** Kaninchen, Hasen und dergleichen; **~ being the case ...** in diesem Fall ...; **~ was not my intention** dies war nicht meine Absicht; **~ is not the case** dies ist nicht der Fall; **~ is life!** so ist das Leben!; **as ~** an sich; **~ as?** zum Beispiel?; **~ as it is** so, wie es nun mal ist.

such-and-such ['sʌtʃən'sʌtʃ] *(col)* **1** *adj* **~ a time/town** die und die Zeit/Stadt. **2** *n* **Mr ~** Herr Soundso.

suchlike ['sʌtʃ,laɪk] *(col)* **1** *adj* solche. **2** *pron* dergleichen.

suck [sʌk] **1** *vt* saugen; *sweet, pastille* lutschen; *lollipop, thumb* lutschen an *(+dat)*. **to ~ sb dry** *(fig)* jdn bis aufs Blut aussaugen. **2** *vi (at* an *+dat)* saugen; *(at lollipop, thumb)* lutschen; *(at pipe, through straw)* ziehen.

♦ **suck down** *vt sep (current etc)* hinunterziehen.

♦ **suck in** *vt sep liquid, dust* aufsaugen; *air (ventilator)* ansaugen; *(person)* in tiefen Zügen einatmen; *cheeks* einziehen.

♦ **suck up 1** *vt sep liquid, dust* aufsaugen. **2** *vi (col)* **to ~ ~ to sb** vor jdm kriechen *(col)*.

sucker ['sʌkəʳ] *n* **(a)** *(col: fool)* Trottel *m (col)*. **to be a ~ for sth** (immer) auf etw *(acc)* hereinfallen; *(be partial to)* eine Schwäche für etw haben. **(b)** *(US col: lollipop)* Lutscher *m*.

suckle ['sʌkl] *vt child* stillen; *animal* säugen.

suction ['sʌkʃən] *n* Saugwirkung *f*. **~-pump** Saugpumpe *f*.

Sudan [sʊ'dɑːn] *n* **(the) ~** der Sudan.

sudden ['sʌdn] **1** *adj* plötzlich; *movement also* jäh, abrupt; *(unexpected) bend, change of direction* unerwartet. **~ death play-off** Entscheidungskampf *m*; *(Ftbl)* Elfmeterschießen *nt*. **2** *n* **all of a ~** (ganz) plötzlich.

suddenly ['sʌdnlɪ] *adv* plötzlich; *move also* abrupt.

suddenness ['sʌdnnɪs] *n* Plötzlichkeit *f*.

suds [sʌdz] *npl* Seifenlauge *f*; *(lather)* (Seifen)schaum *m*.

sue [suː] **1** *vt (Jur)* **to ~ sb for sth** jdn wegen etw verklagen; **to ~ sb for divorce** gegen jdn die Scheidung einreichen; **to ~ sb for damages** jdn auf Schadenersatz verklagen. **2** *vi (Jur)* klagen, Klage erheben. **to ~ for divorce** die Scheidung einreichen.

suede [sweɪd] **1** *n* Wildleder *nt*. **2** *adj* Wildleder-.

suet ['sʊɪt] *n* Nierenfett *nt*.

Suez ['suːɪz] *n* Suez *nt*. **~ Canal** Suezkanal *m*.

suffer ['sʌfəʳ] **1** *vt* **(a)** *pain, setback* erleiden; *hardship also, hunger* leiden; *headache, effects etc* leiden unter *(+dat)*; *shock* haben. **the pound ~ed further losses** das Pfund mußte weitere Einbußen hinnehmen. **(b)** *(tolerate)* dulden, ertragen. **he doesn't ~ fools gladly** Dummheit ist ihm ein Greuel. **2** *vi (physically, mentally, fig)* leiden *(from* unter *+dat, from illness* an *+dat)*; *(as punishment, in hell etc)* büßen. **he was ~ing from shock** er hatte einen Schock (erlitten); **your health will ~** deine Gesundheit wird darunter leiden; **you'll ~ for this!** das wirst du büßen!

sufferance ['sʌfərəns] *n* **he's only here on ~** er wird hier nur geduldet.

sufferer ['sʌfərəʳ] *n (Med)* Leidende(r) *mf (from* an *+dat)*. **diabetes ~s, ~s from diabetes** Diabeteskranke *pl*.

suffering ['sʌfərɪŋ] *n* Leiden *nt*; *(hardship, deprivation)* Leid *nt no pl*.

suffice [sə'faɪs] *(form)* **1** *vi* (aus)reichen. **2** *vt* **~ it to say ...** es reicht wohl, wenn ich sage, ...

sufficient [sə'fɪʃənt] *adj* genügend; *reason, condition* hinreichend. **to be ~** genügen, ausreichen; **thank you, that's ~** danke, das genügt.

sufficiently [sə'fɪʃəntlɪ] *adv* genug. **~ good/warm** *etc* gut/warm *etc* genug *pred*; **a ~ large number** eine ausreichend große Anzahl.

suffix ['sʌfɪks] *n (Ling)* Suffix *nt*, Nachsilbe *f*; *(in code etc)* Zusatz *m*.

suffocate ['sʌfəkeɪt] *vti (lit, fig)* ersticken. **he was ~d by the smoke** er erstickte am Rauch.

suffocating ['sʌfəkeɪtɪŋ] *adj (lit)* erstickend *attr*; *(fig also)* erdrückend *attr*; *heat* drückend *attr*.

suffocation [,sʌfə'keɪʃən] *n (lit, fig)* Ersticken *nt*.

suffrage ['sʌfrɪdʒ] *n* Wahlrecht *nt*.

suffragette [,sʌfrə'dʒet] *n* Suffragette *f*.

sugar ['ʃʊgəʳ] **1** *n* **(a)** Zucker *m*. **(b)** *(col: term of affection)* Schätzchen *nt (col)*. **2** *vt* zuckern, süßen. **to ~ the pill** die bittere Pille versüßen.

sugar *in cpds* Zucker-; **~ beet** *n* Zuckerrübe *f*; **~ bowl** *n* Zuckerdose *f*; **~ candy** *n (US: sweet)* Bonbon *nt or m*; **~ cane** *n* Zuckerrohr *nt*; **~-coated** *adj* mit Zucker überzogen.

sugared ['ʃʊgəd] *adj* gezuckert; *almonds* Zucker-; *words* (honig)süß.

sugary ['ʃʊgərɪ] *adj taste* süß; *(full of sugar)* zuckrig; *(fig) style etc* süßlich.

suggest [sə'dʒest] **1** *vt* **(a)** *(propose)* vorschlagen; *plan, idea also* anregen; *explanation, theory* vorbringen. **I ~ that we go, I ~ going** ich schlage vor, (daß) wir gehen; **what do you ~ we do?** was schlagen Sie vor?; **are you ~ing I should tell a deliberate lie?** soll das heißen, daß ich bewußt lügen soll?; **I am ~ing nothing of the kind** das habe ich nicht gesagt. **(b)** *(indicate, hint at)* andeuten; *(unpleasantly)* unterstellen; *(evoke) (music, poem)* denken lassen an *(+acc)*. **what are you trying to ~?** was wollen Sie damit sagen?; **the symptoms would ~ an operation** die Symptome lassen eine Operation angeraten erscheinen. **2** *vr* **to ~ itself** *(idea, thought)* sich anbieten, naheliegen.

suggestion [sə'dʒestʃən] *n* **(a)** *(proposal)* Vorschlag *m*. **my ~ is that ...** mein Vorschlag lautet ..., ich schlage vor, daß ...; **following your ~** auf Ihren Vorschlag *or* Ihre Anregung hin; **I'm open to ~s** Vorschläge sind willkommen. **(b)** *(insinuation)* Andeutung *f*; *(unpleasant)* Unterstellung *f*. **I resent that ~** ich weise diese Unterstellung zurück; **there is no ~ that he was involved** es gibt keinen Anhaltspunkt dafür, daß er beteiligt war. **(c)** *(hint: of irony etc)* Anflug *m*. **(d)** *(also* **indecent ~)** unsittlicher Antrag.

suggestive [sə'dʒestɪv] *adj* **(a) to be ~ of sth** auf etw *(acc)* hindeuten; *(create impression of)* den Eindruck von etw vermitteln. **(b)** *(indecent) joke, remark etc* zweideutig.

suicidal [,sʊɪ'saɪdl] *adj* selbstmörderisch. **that would be ~** das wäre glatter Selbstmord.

suicide ['sʊɪsaɪd] *n* Selbstmord *m*; *(person)* Selbstmörder(in *f*) *m*. **to commit ~** Selbstmord begehen.

suit [suːt] **1** *n* **(a)** Anzug *m*; *(woman's)* Kostüm *nt*. **~ of clothes** Garnitur *f*. **(b)** *(Jur)* Verfahren *nt*. **to bring a ~ (against sb for sth)** (wegen etw gegen jdn) einen Prozeß anstrengen. **(c)** *(Cards)* Farbe *f*. **to follow ~** *(lit)* Farbe bedienen; *(fig)* jds Beispiel *(dat)* folgen.

2 *vt* **(a)** *(be convenient to) (arrangement, date,*

price) passen *(+dat)*; *(climate, food)* bekommen *(+dat)*; *(occupation)* gefallen *(+dat)*. **that ~s me fine!** *(col)* das ist mir recht; **that would ~ me nicely** *(time, arrangement)* das würde mir gut passen; *(house, job etc)* das wäre genau das richtige für mich; **when would it ~ you to come?** wann wäre es Ihnen recht? **(b)** *(be suitable, right for)* geeignet sein für. **he is very well ~ed to the job** er eignet sich sehr gut für die Stelle; **they are well ~ed (to each other)** sie passen gut zusammen. **(c)** *(clothes, hairstyle)* (gut) stehen *(+dat)*. **(d)** *(adapt)* anpassen *(to dat)*. **(e)** *(please)* gefallen *(+dat)*. **you can't ~ everybody** man kann es nicht jedem recht machen; **~ yourself!** wie du willst!

suitability [ˌsuːtəˈbɪlɪtɪ] *n* Angemessenheit *f*; *(of person for job)* Eignung *f*.

suitable [ˈsuːtəbl] *adj (convenient, practical)* geeignet, passend; *(socially, culturally appropriate)* angemessen. **to be ~ for sb** *(date, place)* jdm passen; *(film, job)* für jdn geeignet sein; **the most ~ man for the job** der am besten geeignete Mann für den Posten; **would 8 o'clock be a ~ time?** wäre Ihnen *etc* 8 Uhr recht?; **Tuesday is the most ~ day** Dienstag ist der günstigste Tag; **she's not ~ for him** sie paßt nicht zu ihm.

suitably [ˈsuːtəblɪ] *adv* angemessen; *behave also, apologize* wie es sich gehört. **he was ~ impressed** er war gehörig beeindruckt.

suitcase [ˈsuːtˌkeɪs] *n* Koffer *m*. **to live out of a ~** aus dem Koffer leben.

suite [swiːt] *n (of furniture)* Garnitur *f*; *(of rooms)* Suite, Zimmerflucht *f*; *(Mus)* Suite *f*. **bedroom ~** Schlafzimmergarnitur *f*; **3-piece ~** dreiteilige Sitzgarnitur.

suitor [ˈsuːtə^r] *n* **(a)** *(old: of woman)* Freier *m (old)*. **(b)** *(Jur)* Kläger(in *f*) *m*.

sulk [sʌlk] **1** *vi* schmollen, beleidigt sein. **2** *n* Schmollen *nt*. **to have the ~s** schmollen.

sulky [ˈsʌlkɪ] *adj (+er)* schmollend.

sullen [ˈsʌlən] *adj* **(a)** *(morose)* mürrisch. **(b)** *sky etc* düster, finster.

sully [ˈsʌlɪ] *vt reputation* besudeln.

sulphate, *(US)* **sulfate** [ˈsʌlfeɪt] *n* Sulfat *nt*.

sulphide, *(US)* **sulfide** [ˈsʌlfaɪd] *n* Sulfid *nt*.

sulphur, *(US)* **sulfur** [ˈsʌlfə^r] *n* Schwefel *m*.

sulphuric, *(US)* **sulfuric** [sʌlˈfjʊərɪk] *adj* Schwefel-. **~ acid** Schwefelsäure *f*.

sultan [ˈsʌltən] *n* Sultan *m*.

sultana [sʌlˈtɑːnə] *n (fruit)* Sultanine *f*.

sultry [ˈsʌltrɪ] *adj weather* schwül; *woman* temperamentvoll; *beauty, look* glutvoll.

sum [sʌm] *n* **(a)** *(total)* Summe *f*; *(of money also)* Betrag *m*. **that was the ~ (total) of his achievements** das war alles, was er geschafft hatte. **(b)** *(esp Brit: calculation)* Rechenaufgabe *f*. **to do ~s (in one's head)** (im Kopf) rechnen.

♦ **sum up 1** *vt sep* **(a)** *(summarize)* zusammenfassen. **(b)** *(evaluate rapidly)* ab- *or* einschätzen. **2** *vi (also Jur)* zusammenfassen. **to ~ ~, we can say that ...** zusammenfassend können wir feststellen, daß ...

summarize [ˈsʌməraɪz] *vt* zusammenfassen.

summary [ˈsʌmərɪ] **1** *n* Zusammenfassung *f*. **he gave us a short ~ of the film** er gab uns eine kurze Inhaltsangabe des Films. **2** *adj* **(a)** *(brief) account* knapp, kurzgefaßt. **(b)** *(fast) treatment* kurz, knapp; *perusal* flüchtig; *(Jur) trial, punishment* summarisch; *dismissal* fristlos.

summer [ˈsʌmə^r] **1** *n* Sommer *m*. **in (the) ~** im Sommer; **two ~s ago** im Sommer vor zwei Jahren; **a ~'s day** ein Sommertag *m*. **2** *adj attr* Sommer-.

summer: ~ house *n* Gartenhaus *nt*; **~time** *n* Sommer(zeit *f*) *m*; *(daylight-saving time)* Sommerzeit *f*.

summery [ˈsʌmərɪ] *adj* sommerlich.

summing-up [ˈsʌmɪŋˈʌp] *n (Jur)* Resümee *nt*.

summit [ˈsʌmɪt] **1** *n* Gipfel *m*; *(fig also)* Höhepunkt *m*; *(~ conference)* Gipfel(konferenz *f*) *m*. **2** *adj attr* Gipfel-.

summon [ˈsʌmən] *vt* **(a)** *servant, police etc* (herbei)rufen; *help* holen; *meeting, Parliament* einberufen. **(b)** *(Jur)* vorladen.

♦ **summon up** *vt sep courage* zusammennehmen; *strength* aufbieten; *enthusiasm, energy* aufbringen.

summons [ˈsʌmənz] **1** *n (Jur)* Vorladung *f*. **to take out a ~ against sb** jdn vorladen lassen. **2** *vt (Jur)* vorladen.

sump [sʌmp] *n (Brit Aut)* Ölwanne *f*.

sumptuous [ˈsʌmptjʊəs] *adj (splendid)* luxuriös; *(costly)* kostspielig; *food etc* üppig, verschwenderisch.

sun [sʌn] **1** *n* Sonne *f*. **I've got the ~ in my eyes** die Sonne blendet mich; **he was up with the ~** er stand in aller Frühe auf; **there is no reason under the ~ why ...** es gibt keinen Grund auf Erden, warum ...; **he's tried everything under the ~** er hat alles Menschenmögliche versucht; **there's nothing new under the ~** *(prov)* es ist alles schon mal dagewesen; **a place in the ~** *(fig)* ein Platz an der Sonne. **2** *vr* **to ~ oneself** sich sonnen.

sun: ~bathe *vi* sonnenbaden; **~bather** *n* Sonnenanbeter(in *f*) *m (col)*; **~bathing** *n* Sonnenbaden *nt*; **~beam** *n* Sonnenstrahl *m*; **~bed** *n* Sonnenliege *f*; **~ blind** *n (awning)* Markise *f*; *(venetian blind)* Jalousie *f*; **~burn** *n* Bräune *f*; *(painful)* Sonnenbrand *m*; **~burnt** *adj* sonnengebräunt; *(painfully)* von der Sonne verbrannt; **to get ~burnt** braun werden; (einen) Sonnenbrand bekommen.

sundae [ˈsʌndeɪ] *n* Eisbecher *m*.

Sunday [ˈsʌndɪ] **1** *n* Sonntag *m*. **a month of ~s** *(col)* eine Ewigkeit; **never in a month of ~s** *(col)* nie im Leben; *see* **Tuesday. 2** *adj attr* Sonntags-. **~ best** Sonntagskleider *pl*; **~ school** Sonntagsschule *f*.

sun: ~ deck *n* Sonnendeck *nt*; **~dial** *n* Sonnenuhr *f*; **~down** *n (esp US)* Sonnenuntergang *m*.

sundry [ˈsʌndrɪ] **1** *adj* verschiedene. **2** *pron* **all and ~** jedermann. **3** *n* **sundries** *pl* Verschiedenes *(+sing vb)*.

sunflower [ˈsʌnˌflaʊə^r] *n* Sonnenblume *f*.

sung [sʌŋ] *ptp of* **sing.**

sun: ~glasses *npl* Sonnenbrille *f*; **~-god** *n* Sonnengott *m*; **~ hat** *n* Sonnenhut *m*.

sunk [sʌŋk] *ptp of* **sink**[1].

sunken [ˈsʌŋkən] *adj ship, treasure* versunken; *garden* tiefliegend *attr*; *bath* eingelassen; *cheeks* hohl; *eyes* eingesunken.

sun: ~ lamp *n* Höhensonne *f*; **~less** *adj garden* ohne Sonne; *room also* dunkel; *day also* trübe; **~light** *n* Sonnenlicht *nt*; **in the ~light** in der Sonne; **~lit** *adj* sonnig.

sunny [ˈsʌnɪ] *adj (+er) place, day etc* sonnig; *(fig) smile, disposition also* heiter. **~ intervals** *(Met)* Aufheiterungen *pl*; **to look on the ~ side (of things)** die Dinge von der angenehmen Seite sehen.

sun: ~rise 1 *n* Sonnenaufgang *m*; **at ~rise** bei Sonnenaufgang; **2** *adj attr (col) industries* der Spitzentechnologie; **~roof** *n (of car)* Schiebedach *nt*; *(of hotel etc)* Sonnenterrasse *f*; **~set** *n* Sonnenuntergang *m*; **at ~set** bei Sonnenuntergang; **~shade** *n* Sonnenschirm *m*; *(awning)* Markise *f*; **~shine** *n* Sonnenschein *m*; **hours of ~shine** Sonnenstunden *pl*; **~spot** *n* **(a)** Sonnenfleck *m*; **(b)** *(col: for holiday)* Ferienparadies *nt*; **~stroke** *n* Sonnenstich *m*; **to get ~stroke** einen Sonnenstich bekommen; **~tan** *n* Sonnenbräune *f*; **to get a ~tan** braun werden; **~tan lotion/oil** *n* Sonnenöl *nt*; **~tanned** *adj* braungebrannt; **~trap** *n* sonniges Eckchen; **~-up** *n (esp US)* Sonnenaufgang *m*; **at ~-up** bei Sonnenaufgang.

super [ˈsuːpə^r] *adj (col)* phantastisch, klasse *inv*

(col). ~! Klasse! *(col)*; **we had a ~ time** es war große Klasse *(col) or* phantastisch.
superabundance [ˌsuːpərə'bʌndəns] *n (of* an *+dat)* großer Reichtum; *(excessive amount)* Überfluß *m*.
superannuation [ˌsuːpəˌrænjʊ'eɪʃən] *n* Rente *f*.
superb [suː'pɜːb] *adj* großartig; *design, painting also* meisterhaft.
supercharger ['suːpəˌtʃɑːdʒə^r] *n* Lader *m*.
supercilious [ˌsuːpə'sɪlɪəs] *adj* hochnäsig.
superficial [ˌsuːpə'fɪʃəl] *adj person, injury* oberflächlich; *characteristics, resemblance* äußerlich.
superficiality ['suːpəˌfɪʃɪ'ælɪtɪ] *n see adj* Oberflächlichkeit *f*; Äußerlichkeit *f*.
superficially [ˌsuːpə'fɪʃəlɪ] *adv see adj* oberflächlich; äußerlich. **~ this may be true** oberflächlich gesehen mag das stimmen.
superfluous [sʊ'pɜːflʊəs] *adj* überflüssig.
super: ~highway *n (US)* ≈ Autobahn *f*; **~human** *adj* übermenschlich.
superimpose [ˌsuːpərɪm'pəʊz] *vt* **to ~ sth on sth** etw auf etw *(acc)* legen; *(Phot)* etw über etw *(acc)* photographieren; *(Film)* etw über etw *(acc)* filmen.
superintend [ˌsuːpərɪn'tend] *vt* überwachen.
superintendent [ˌsuːpərɪn'tendənt] *n* Aufsicht *f*; *(in swimming-pool)* Bademeister *m*; *(of police) (Brit)* ≈ Kommissar(in *f*) *m*; *(US)* ≈ Polizeipräsident *m*.
superior [sʊ'pɪərɪə^r] **1** *adj* **(a)** *(better) quality, equipment* besser *(to* als*)*; *intellect, skill* überlegen *(to sb/sth* jdm/einer Sache*)*. **(b)** *(excellent) work(manship), technique* großartig, hervorragend. **~ quality goods** Waren *pl* bester Qualität. **(c)** *(higher in rank etc)* höher. **~ officer** Vorgesetzte(r) *mf*; **to be ~ to sb/sth** jdm/etw übergeordnet sein. **(d)** *(greater)* überlegen *(to sb/sth* jdm/etw*)*; *forces also* stärker *(to* als*)*; *strength also* größer *(to* als*)*. **they were ~ to us in number(s)** sie waren uns zahlenmäßig überlegen. **(e)** *(snobbish) person* überheblich; *smile also* überlegen; *(smart) restaurant, clientèle* fein, vornehm. **2** *n* **(a)** *(in rank)* Vorgesetzte(r) *mf*. **to be sb's ~** *(in ability)* jdm überlegen sein. **(b)** *(Eccl)* **Mother S~** Mutter Oberin *f*.
superiority [sʊˌpɪərɪ'ɒrɪtɪ] *n* **(a)** *(of cloth etc)* bessere Qualität; *(of technique, ability, in numbers)* Überlegenheit *f*. **(b)** *(in rank)* höhere Stellung. **(c)** *(conceitedness)* Überheblichkeit *f*.
superlative [sʊ'pɜːlətɪv] **1** *adj (excellent)* überragend; *(Gram)* superlativisch. **2** *n* Superlativ *m*.
superman ['suːpəmæn] *n, pl* **-men** [-men] Übermensch *m*. **S~** *(in comics)* Supermann *m*.
supermarket ['suːpəˌmɑːkɪt] *n* Supermarkt *m*.
supernatural [ˌsuːpə'nætʃərəl] *adj* übernatürlich. **the ~** das Übernatürliche.
superpower ['suːpəˌpaʊə^r] *n (Pol)* Supermacht *f*.
supersede [ˌsuːpə'siːd] *vt* ablösen; *person, belief also* an die Stelle treten von. **~d ideas** überholte Ideen.
supersonic [ˌsuːpə'sɒnɪk] *adj* Überschall-.
superstar ['suːpəˌstɑː^r] *n* Superstar *m*.
superstition [ˌsuːpə'stɪʃən] *n* Aberglaube *m no pl*.
superstitious [ˌsuːpə'stɪʃəs] *adj* abergläubisch.
superstructure ['suːpəˌstrʌktʃə^r] *n* Überbau *m*; *(of ship)* Aufbauten *pl*.
supertanker ['suːpəˌtæŋkə^r] *n* Supertanker *m*.
supertax ['suːpəˌtæks] *n* Höchststeuer *f*.
supervise ['suːpəvaɪz] **1** *vt* beaufsichtigen. **2** *vi* Aufsicht führen, die Aufsicht haben.
supervision [ˌsuːpə'vɪʒən] *n* Aufsicht *f*; *(action)* Beaufsichtigung *f*. **under the ~ of** unter der Aufsicht von.
supervisor ['suːpəvaɪzə^r] *n (of work)* Aufseher(in *f*) *m*, Aufsicht *f*; *(of research)* Leiter(in *f*) *m*; *(Brit Univ)* ≈ Tutor(in *f*) *m*; *(for PhD)* Doktorvater *m*.
supervisory ['suːpəvaɪzərɪ] *adj role* beaufsichtigend. **in a ~ post** in einer Aufsichtsposition.
supper ['sʌpə^r] *n (evening meal)* Abendessen *nt*; *(late evening snack)* (später) Imbiß. **to have ~** zu Abend essen.
supplant [sə'plɑːnt] *vt* ablösen, ersetzen; *(forcibly)* verdrängen; *(by ruse) rival* ausstechen.
supple ['sʌpl] *adj (+er)* geschmeidig, elastisch; *shoes* weich; *mind* beweglich.
supplement ['sʌplɪmənt] **1** *n* **(a)** Ergänzung *f (to gen)*; *(of book)* Ergänzungsband *m (to* zu*)*; *(at end of book)* Anhang *m*. **a ~ to his income** eine Aufbesserung seines Einkommens. **(b)** *(colour ~ etc)* Beilage *f*. **2** *vt* ergänzen; *income* aufbessern.
supplementary [ˌsʌplɪ'mentərɪ] *adj* zusätzlich, ergänzend; *volume, report also* Zusatz-, Ergänzungs-. **~ benefit** *(Brit)* ≈ Arbeitslosenhilfe *f*.
supplication [ˌsʌplɪ'keɪʃən] *n* Flehen *nt no pl*.
supplier [sə'plaɪə^r] *n (Comm)* Lieferant(in *f*) *m*.
supply [sə'plaɪ] **1** *n* **(a)** *(supplying)* Versorgung *f*; *(Comm: delivery)* Lieferung *f (to* an *+acc)*; *(Econ)* Angebot *nt*. **electricity ~** Stromversorgung *f*; **the ~ of blood to the brain** die Versorgung des Gehirns mit Blut; **~ and demand** Angebot und Nachfrage *(+pl vb)*. **(b)** *(that supplied)* Lieferung *f*. **to cut off the ~** *(of gas, water etc)* das Gas/ Wasser *etc* abstellen. **(c)** *(stock)* Vorrat *m*. **supplies** *pl (food)* Vorräte *pl*; *(for expedition also, for journey)* Proviant *m*; **to get** *or* **lay in supplies** *or* **a ~ of** sich *(dat)* einen Vorrat an *(+dat)* anlegen; **a month's ~** ein Monatsbedarf *m*; **to be in short ~** knapp sein; **fresh supplies** *(Mil)* Nachschub *m*; **office supplies** Bürobedarf *m*; **medical supplies** Ärztebedarf *m*.

2 *vt* **(a)** *material, food etc* sorgen für; *(deliver) goods* liefern; *evidence, gas* liefern; *(put at sb's disposal)* stellen. **(b)** *(with* mit*)* versorgen; *(Comm)* beliefern. **this supplied me with the chance ...** das gab mir die Chance ...; **we have not been supplied with a radio** wir haben kein Radio bekommen. **(c)** *(satisfy, make good) need* befriedigen; *want* abhelfen *(+dat)*; *(Comm) demand* decken.
supply: ~ industry *n* Zulieferungsindustrie *f*; **~ lines, ~ routes** *npl (Mil, fig)* Versorgungslinien *pl*; **~ ship** *n* Versorgungsschiff *nt*.
support [sə'pɔːt] **1** *n* **(a)** *(lit)* Stütze *f*. **to give ~ to sb/sth** jdn/etw stützen; **to lean on sb for ~** sich auf jdn stützen. **(b)** *(fig) (no pl: moral, financial backing)* Unterstützung *f*; *(person)* Stütze *f*. **in ~ of** zur Unterstützung *(+gen)*; **in ~ of an allegation** zur Untermauerung einer Behauptung; **to speak in ~ of a candidate** einen Kandidaten unterstützen; **there was a lot of ~ for his views** viele stimmten seiner Meinung bei.

2 *attr (Mil) troops, vessel etc* Hilfs-.

3 *vt* **(a)** *(lit)* stützen; *(Tech also)* abstützen; *(bear the weight of)* tragen. **(b)** *(fig)* unterstützen; *plan, motion, sb's application also* befürworten; *party, cause also* eintreten für; *(give moral ~ to also)* beistehen *(+dat)*, Rückhalt geben *(+dat)*; *(corroborate)* erhärten, untermauern; *(financially) family* unterhalten; *party, orchestra* finanziell unterstützen. **he ~s Arsenal** er ist Arsenal-Anhänger *m*; **which team do you ~?** für welche Mannschaft bist du?

4 *vr* **to ~ oneself** *(physically)* sich stützen *(on* auf *+acc)*; *(financially)* seinen Unterhalt (selbst) bestreiten.
supporter [sə'pɔːtə^r] *n* Anhänger(in *f*) *m*; *(of theory, cause also)* Befürworter(in *f*) *m*; *(Sport also)* Fan *m*.
supporting [sə'pɔːtɪŋ] *adj film* Vor-; *part, role* Neben-.
suppose [sə'pəʊz] *vt* **(a)** *(imagine)* sich *(dat)* vorstellen; *(assume, postulate also)* annehmen. **let us ~ that X equals 3** angenommen, X sei gleich 3; **even supposing it were** *or* **was true** (sogar) angenommen, daß es wahr ist; **always supposing he comes** immer vorausgesetzt, (daß) er kommt.

(b) *(believe, think)* annehmen, denken. **I ~ he'll come** ich nehme an, (daß) er kommt; **I don't ~ he'll come** ich glaube kaum, daß er kommt; **I ~ he won't come** ich denke, er wird nicht kommen, er wird wohl nicht kommen; **I ~ that's the best thing** das ist vermutlich das Beste; **I don't ~ you could lend me a pound?** Sie könnten mir nicht zufällig ein Pfund leihen?; **will he be coming? — I ~ so** kommt er? — ich denke schon; **you ought to be leaving — I ~ so** du solltest jetzt gehen — stimmt wohl; **I don't ~ so** ich glaube kaum; **he is generally ~d to be rich** er gilt als reich; **he's ~d to be coming** er soll (angeblich) kommen.

(c) *(in passive: ought)* **to be ~d to do sth** etw tun sollen; **he's the one who's ~d to do it** er müßte es eigentlich tun; **you're ~d to be in bed** du solltest eigentlich im Bett sein; **he isn't ~d to find out** er darf es nicht erfahren; **you're not ~d to (do that)** das darfst du nicht tun.

(d) *(in imper: I suggest)* **~ we have a go?** warum versuchen wir es nicht einmal?; **~ we buy it?** wie wäre es, wenn wir es kauften?

(e) *(presuppose)* voraussetzen. **that ~s unlimited resources** das setzt unbegrenzte Vorräte voraus.

supposed [sə'pəuzd] *adj* vermutet; *date, site, author also* mutmaßlich.

supposedly [sə'pəuzɪdlɪ] *adv* angeblich. **the atom was ~ indivisible** das Atom galt als unteilbar.

supposing [sə'pəuzɪŋ] *conj* angenommen. **but ~ ...** aber wenn ...

supposition [ˌsʌpə'zɪʃən] *n (no pl: hypothesizing)* Mutmaßung, Spekulation *f*; *(thing supposed)* Annahme *f*. **acting on the ~ that you are right** vorausgesetzt, daß Sie recht haben.

suppository [sə'pɒzɪtərɪ] *n* Zäpfchen *nt*.

suppress [sə'pres] *vt* unterdrücken.

suppression [sə'preʃən] *n* Unterdrückung *f*.

supra- ['su:prə-] *pref* über-; *(esp with foreign words)* supra-. **~national** überstaatlich.

supremacy [sʊ'preməsɪ] *n* Vormachtstellung *f*; *(Pol, Eccl, fig)* Supremat *nt or m*. **air/naval ~** Luft-/Seeherrschaft *f*.

supreme [sʊ'pri:m] **1** *adj (highest, ultimate)* höchste(r, s); *court* oberste(r, s); *(very great) courage etc* äußerste(r, s), größte(r, s). **with ~ indifference** völlig unbeteiligt. **2** *adv* **to rule** *or* **reign ~** *(monarch)* absolut herrschen; *(champion, justice)* unangefochten herrschen.

supremely [sʊ'pri:mlɪ] *adv confident* zutiefst.

surcharge ['sɜ:tʃɑ:dʒ] *n* Zuschlag *m*; *(postal)* Nachporto, Strafporto *(col) nt*.

sure [ʃʊəʳ] **1** *adj (+er)* sicher; *proof, facts also* eindeutig; *method also, remedy* zuverlässig, verläßlich. **I'm perfectly ~** ich bin (mir da) ganz sicher; **to be ~ about sth** sich *(dat)* einer Sache *(gen)* sicher sein; **I'm not so ~ about that** da bin ich nicht so sicher; **to be ~ of oneself** sich *(dat)* seiner Sache sicher sein; *(generally self-confident)* selbstsicher sein; **it is ~ that he will come** er kommt ganz bestimmt; **it's ~ to rain** es regnet ganz bestimmt; **be ~ to turn the gas off** vergiß nicht, das Gas abzudrehen; **you're ~ of success** der Erfolg ist Ihnen sicher; **I want to be ~ of seeing him** ich möchte ihn auf jeden Fall sehen; **to make ~** *(check)* nachsehen; **make ~ you get the leads the right way round** achten Sie darauf, daß die Kabel richtig herum sind; **make ~ you take your keys** denk daran, deine Schlüssel mitzunehmen; **it's best to make ~** sicher ist sicher; **to make ~ of one's facts** sicherstellen, daß die Angaben stimmen; **to make ~ of a seat** sich *(dat)* einen Platz sichern; **~ thing!** *(esp US col)* klare Sache! *(col)*; **he'll quit for ~** er kündigt ganz bestimmt; **I'll find out for ~** ich werde das genau herausfinden; **do you know for ~?** wissen Sie das ganz sicher?; **with a ~ hand** mit sicherer Hand.

2 *adv (esp US)* **will you do it? — ~!** machst du das? — klar! *(col)*; **that meat ~ was tough** das Fleisch war vielleicht zäh!; **and ~ enough he did come** und er ist tatsächlich gekommen; **he'll come ~ enough** er kommt ganz bestimmt.

sure: ~-fire *adj (col)* todsicher *(col)*; **~-footed** *adj* (tritt)sicher.

surely ['ʃʊəlɪ] *adv* **(a)** bestimmt, sicher. **~ you don't mean it?** das meinen Sie doch bestimmt nicht (so)?; **~ not!** das kann doch nicht stimmen!; **~ someone must know the answer** irgend jemand muß doch die Antwort wissen. **(b)** *(esp US: gladly)* gern, mit Vergnügen.

sureness ['ʃʊənɪs] *n* **(a)** *(positiveness)* Überzeugung, Sicherheit *f*. **(b)** *(reliability, steadiness)* Sicherheit *f*; *(of method)* Verläßlichkeit *f*; *(of sb's judgement also)* Untrüglichkeit *f*.

surety ['ʃʊərətɪ] *n (sum)* Bürgschaft, Sicherheit *f*; *(person)* Bürge *m*. **to go** *or* **stand ~ for sb** für jdn bürgen.

surf [sɜ:f] **1** *n* Brandung *f*. **2** *vi* surfen.

surface ['sɜ:fɪs] **1** *n* **(a)** *(lit, fig)* Oberfläche *f*; *(of road)* Decke *f*, Belag *m*. **on the ~ it seems that ...** oberflächlich sieht es so aus, als ob ...; **on the ~ he is friendly enough** nach außen hin ist er sehr freundlich. **(b)** *(Math: of cube etc)* Fläche *f*. **(c)** *(Min)* **at/on/up to the ~** über Tage. **2** *adj attr* **(a)** oberflächlich; *measurements* Oberflächen-. **(b)** *travel* auf dem Land-/Seeweg. **(c)** *(Min) worker, job* über Tage. **3** *vt road* mit einem Belag versehen; *wall* verblenden. **4** *vi (lit, fig)* auftauchen.

surface: ~ area *n* Fläche *f*; *(Math)* Flächeninhalt *m*; **~ mail** *n* **by ~ mail** auf dem Land-/Seeweg, nicht per Luftpost; **~-to-air** *adj attr missile* Boden-Luft-.

surfboard ['sɜ:fˌbɔ:d] *n* Surfbrett *nt*.

surfeit ['sɜ:fɪt] *n* Übermaß, Zuviel *nt (of* an *+dat)*.

surfer ['sɜ:fəʳ] *n* Wellenreiter(in *f*), Surfer(in *f*) *m*.

surfing ['sɜ:fɪŋ] *n* Wellenreiten, Surfen *nt*.

surge [sɜ:dʒ] **1** *n (of sea)* Wogen *nt*; *(of floodwater)* Schwall *m*. **a ~ of people** eine wogende Menschenmenge; **he felt a sudden ~ of rage** er fühlte, wie die Wut in ihm aufsstieg. **2** *vi (sea)* branden; *(floods, river)* anschwellen. **blood ~d into her face** ihr Schoß das Blut ins Gesicht; **they ~d towards/round him** sie drängten auf ihn zu/ sie umdrängten ihn; **people ~d in/out** eine Menschenmenge flutete herein/heraus.

surgeon ['sɜ:dʒən] *n* Chirurg(in *f*) *m*.

surgery ['sɜ:dʒərɪ] *n* **(a)** Chirurgie *f*. **to have ~** operiert werden; **to need (heart) ~** (am Herzen) operiert werden müssen. **(b)** *(Brit) (room)* Sprechzimmer *nt*; *(consultation)* Sprechstunde *f*. **~ hours** Sprechstunden *pl*.

surgical ['sɜ:dʒɪkəl] *adj treatment* operativ; *technique, instrument* chirurgisch; *training, skill* Chirurgen-, eines Chirurgen. **~ spirit** Wundbenzin *nt*.

surly ['sɜ:lɪ] *adj (+er)* verdrießlich, mißmutig.

surmise [sɜ:'maɪz] *vt* vermuten, mutmaßen.

surmount [sɜ:'maʊnt] *vt obstacle* überwinden.

surname ['sɜ:neɪm] *n* Nachname *m*. **what is his ~?** wie heißt er mit Nachnamen?

surpass [sɜ:'pɑ:s] **1** *vt* **(a)** *(be better than)* übertreffen. **(b)** *(exceed) comprehension* hinausgehen über *(+acc)*. **2** *vr* **to ~ oneself** sich selbst übertreffen.

surplice ['sɜ:pləs] *n* Chorrock *m*.

surplus ['sɜ:pləs] **1** *n* Überschuß *m (of* an *+dat)*. **2** *adj* überschüssig; *(of countable objects)* überzählig. **sale of ~ stock** Verkauf *m* von Lagerbeständen; **it is ~ to my requirements** das benötige ich nicht.

surprise [sə'praɪz] **1** *n* Überraschung *f*. **in ~** überrascht; **much to my ~, to my great ~** zu meiner großen Überraschung; **with a look of ~** mit überraschtem Gesicht; **what a ~!** was für eine Überraschung!; **to give sb a ~** jdn überraschen;

to take sb by ~ jdn überraschen. **2** *attr attack, visit* Überraschungs-; *parcel etc* überraschend. **3** *vt* überraschen. **I wouldn't be ~d if ...** es würde mich nicht wundern, wenn ...; **don't be ~d if he refuses** wundern Sie sich nicht, wenn er ablehnt; **I'm ~ed at you!** du überraschst mich sehr!

surprising [sə'praɪzɪŋ] *adj* überraschend, erstaunlich. **it's hardly ~ he said no** es ist kaum verwunderlich, daß er nein gesagt hat.

surprisingly [sə'praɪzɪŋlɪ] *adv* **~ (enough), he was right** er hatte erstaunlicherweise recht; **and then ~ he left** und dann ist er zu unserer/ihrer *etc* Überraschung gegangen.

surrealism [sə'rɪəlɪzəm] *n* Surrealismus *m*.

surrealist [sə'rɪəlɪst] **1** *adj* surrealistisch. **2** *n* Surrealist(in *f*) *m*.

surrender [sə'rendə^r] **1** *vi* sich ergeben *(to dat)*; *(to police)* sich stellen *(to dat)*. **I ~!** ich ergebe mich! **2** *vt (Mil)* übergeben; *goods, firearms also* ausliefern; *insurance policy* einlösen; *lease* kündigen; *claim, right* aufgeben. **3** *vr* **to ~ oneself to sth** sich einer Sache *(dat)* hingeben; *to fate* sich in etw *(acc)* ergeben. **4** *n* **(a)** Kapitulation *f (to* vor *+dat)*. **(b)** *see vt* Übergabe *f (to* an *+acc)*; Auslieferung *f (to* an *+acc)*; Einlösen *nt*; Kündigung *f*; Aufgabe *f*. **~ value** *(Insur)* Rückkaufswert *m*.

surreptitious [ˌsʌrəp'tɪʃəs] *adj* heimlich.

surrogate ['sʌrəgɪt **1** *n (substitute)* Ersatz *m*. **2** *attr* Ersatz-. **~ mother** Leihmutter *f*.

surround [sə'raʊnd] **1** *n* Umrandung *f*. **2** *vt* umgeben; *(Mil)* umstellen.

surrounding [sə'raʊndɪŋ] *adj* umliegend. **in the ~ countryside** in der Umgebung.

surroundings [sə'raʊndɪŋz] *npl* Umgebung *f*.

surtax ['sɜːtæks] *n* Steuerzuschlag *m*.

surveillance [sɜː'veɪləns] *n* Überwachung *f*. **to be under ~** überwacht werden; **to keep sb under ~** jdn überwachen.

survey ['sɜːveɪ] **1** *n* **(a)** *(of land)* Vermessung *f*; *(report)* (Vermessungs)gutachten *nt*; *(of house)* Begutachtung *f*; *(report)* Gutachten *nt*. **to have a ~ done on a house** ein Gutachten über ein Haus erstellen lassen. **(b)** *(review: of subject, development)* Überblick *m (of* über *+acc)*. **(c)** *(inquiry)* Untersuchung *f (of, on* über *+acc)*; *(by opinion poll etc)* Umfrage *f (of, on* über *+acc)*.

2 [sɜː'veɪ] *vt* **(a)** *(look at) scene, person, prospects* sich *(dat)* ansehen; *(appraisingly also)* begutachten; *person, goods* mustern. **(b)** *(study) prospects, plans* untersuchen; *events, trends* einen Überblick geben über *(+acc)*. **(c)** *(Surv) site* vermessen; *building* inspizieren.

surveying [sɜː'veɪɪŋ] *n (of land)* Vermessung *f*; *(Brit: of buildings)* Inspektion *f*.

surveyor [sə'veɪə^r] *n (land~)* Landvermesser(in *f*) *m*; *(Brit: building ~)* Bauinspektor(in *f*) *m*.

survival [sə'vaɪvəl] *n* Überleben *nt*; *(of customs)* Weiterleben *nt*. **the ~ of the fittest** das Überleben der Stärkeren; **~ kit** Überlebensausrüstung *f*.

survive [sə'vaɪv] **1** *vi (person, animal etc)* überleben; *(in job)* sich halten (können); *(treasures, play)* erhalten bleiben; *(custom)* fortbestehen. **you'll ~** *(iro)* das wirst du schon überleben! **2** *vt* überleben; *(house, objects) fire etc* überstehen; *(col) heat, boredom etc* aushalten.

survivor [sə'vaɪvə^r] *n* Überlebende(r) *mf*.

susceptibility [səˌseptə'bɪlɪtɪ] *n no pl see adj* Beeindruckbarkeit *f*. **~ to sth** Empfänglichkeit *f* für etw; Ausgesetztsein *nt* gegenüber etw; Anfälligkeit *f* für etw.

susceptible [sə'septəbl] *adj (impressionable)* beeindruckbar. **~ to sth** *to charms etc* für etw empfänglich; *to attack* einer Sache *(dat)* ausgesetzt; *to colds, influence* für etw anfällig.

suspect ['sʌspekt] **1** *adj* verdächtig. **2** *n* Verdächtige(r) *mf*. **3** [sə'spekt] *vt* **(a)** *person* verdächtigen *(of sth* einer Sache *gen)*, in Verdacht haben. **I ~ her of having stolen it** ich habe sie im Verdacht, es gestohlen zu haben; **he ~s nothing** er ahnt nichts. **(b)** *(doubt) truth* anzweifeln; *motive* argwöhnisch sein gegenüber. **(c)** *(think likely)* vermuten. **I ~ed as much** das habe ich doch vermutet.

suspend [sə'spend] *vt* **(a)** *(hang)* (auf)hängen *(from* an *+dat)*. **to hang ~ed from sth/in sth** von/in etw *(dat)* hängen. **(b)** *(stop, defer) publication, payment* (zeitweilig) einstellen; *judgement* aufschieben; *sentence* zur Bewährung aussetzen. **he was given a ~ed sentence** seine Strafe wurde zur Bewährung ausgesetzt. **(c)** *person* suspendieren; *member, pupil* zeitweilig ausschließen; *(Sport)* sperren; *licence* zeitweilig einziehen; *law, privileges* aussetzen. **to ~ from duty** suspendieren.

suspender [sə'spendə^r] *n usu pl* **(a)** *(Brit) (for stockings)* Strumpfhalter, Straps *m*; *(for socks)* Sockenhalter *m*. **~ belt** Strumpf(halter)gürtel *m*. **(b)** *(US)* **~s** *pl* Hosenträger *pl*.

suspense [sə'spens] *n (in book, film etc)* Spannung *f*. **the ~ is killing me** ich bin gespannt wie ein Regenschirm *(hum col)*; **to keep sb in ~** jdn auf die Folter spannen *(col)*.

suspension [sə'spenʃən] *n* **(a)** *see* **suspend (b)** zeitweilige Einstellung; Aufschub *m*; Aussetzung *f* (zur Bewährung). **(b)** *see* **suspend (c)** Suspendierung *f*; zeitweiliger Ausschluß; Sperrung *f*; zeitweiliger Einzug; Aussetzen *nt*. **(c)** *(Aut)* Federung *f*.

suspension bridge *n* Hängebrücke *f*.

suspicion [sə'spɪʃən] *n* Verdacht, Argwohn *(geh) m no pl*; *(trace)* Hauch *m*, Spur *f*. **to arouse sb's ~s** jds Verdacht erregen; **I have a ~ that ...** ich habe den Verdacht, daß ...; **to have one's ~s about sth** seine Zweifel bezüglich einer Sache *(gen)* haben; **to be above (all)/under ~** über jeden Verdacht erhaben sein/unter Verdacht stehen; **to arrest sb on ~/on ~ of murder** jdn wegen Tatverdachts/Mordverdachts festnehmen.

suspicious [sə'spɪʃəs] *adj* **(a)** *(feeling suspicion)* argwöhnisch, mißtrauisch *(of* gegenüber*)*. **to be ~ about sth** etw mit Mißtrauen betrachten. **(b)** *(causing suspicion)* verdächtig.

suspiciously [sə'spɪʃəslɪ] *adv see adj* **(a)** argwöhnisch, mißtrauisch. **(b)** verdächtig. **it looks ~ like measles to me** das sieht mir verdächtig nach Masern aus.

♦ **suss out** ['sʌs'aʊt] *vt sep (Brit col)* **to ~ sb ~** jdm auf den Zahn fühlen *(col)*; **to ~ sth ~** etw herausbekommen; **to ~ things ~** die Lage peilen *(col)*.

sustain [sə'steɪn] *vt* **(a)** *(support) load, weight* aushalten, tragen; *life* erhalten; *family* unterhalten; *(nourish) body* bei Kräften halten. **(b)** *(maintain) pretence, argument* aufrechterhalten; *effort also* nicht nachlassen in *(+dat)*; *(Jur) objection* stattgeben *(+dat)*. **(c)** *(receive) injury* erleiden.

sustained [sə'steɪnd] *adj effort etc* ausdauernd; *applause* anhaltend.

sustenance ['sʌstɪnəns] *n (food and drink)* Nahrung *f*; *(nutritive quality)* Nährwert *m*.

suture ['suːtʃə^r] *(Med)* **1** *n* Naht *f*. **2** *vt* nähen.

swab [swɒb] **1** *n (Med)* Tupfer *m*; *(specimen)* Abstrich *m*. **to take a ~** einen Abstrich machen. **2** *vt* **(a)** *(Med) wound etc* (ab)tupfen. **(b)** *(Naut: also ~ down)* wischen.

swag [swæg] *n (col)* Beute *f*.

swagger ['swægə^r] *vi* **(a)** stolzieren. **(b)** *(boast, act boastfully)* angeben.

swallow[1] ['swɒləʊ] **1** *n* Schluck *m*. **2** *vt food, drink* (hinunter)schlucken; *(fig) story, evidence, insult* schlucken. **to ~ sth whole** *(lit)* etw ganz schlucken; *(fig)* etw ohne weiteres schlucken; **to ~ one's words** *(retract)* seine Worte zurücknehmen. **3** *vi* schlucken. **to ~ hard** *(fig)* kräftig schlucken.

♦ **swallow up** *vt sep (fig)* verschlingen. **the mist seemed to ~ them ~** der Nebel schien sie zu verschlucken; **I wished the ground would open and ~ me ~** ich wäre am liebsten in den Boden versunken.

swallow² *n (bird)* Schwalbe *f.*

swam [swæm] *pret of* **swim.**

swamp [swɒmp] **1** *n* Sumpf *m.* **2** *vt* unter Wasser setzen; *(fig)* überschwemmen.

swampy ['swɒmpɪ] *adj (+er)* sumpfig.

swan [swɒn] **1** *n* Schwan *m.* **2** *vi (col)* **to ~ off** abziehen *(col)*; **to ~ around New York** in New York herumziehen *(col)*.

swank [swæŋk] *vi (col)* angeben *(about* mit*)*.

swansong ['swɒn,sɒŋ] *n (fig)* Schwanengesang *m.*

swap [swɒp] **1** *n* Tausch *m.* **to do a ~ (with sb)** (mit jdm) tauschen. **2** *vt stamps, cars, houses etc* tauschen; *stories* austauschen. **to ~ sth for sth** etw für etw eintauschen; **to ~ places with sb** mit jdm tauschen. **3** *vi* tauschen.

swarm [swɔːm] **1** *n (of insects, birds)* Schwarm *m*; *(of people also)* Schar *f.* **2** *vi (bees, flies, people)* schwärmen. **the place was ~ing with insects/people** es wimmelte von Insekten/Leuten.

swarthy ['swɔːðɪ] *adj (+er) skin* dunkel.

swastika ['swɒstɪkə] *n* Hakenkreuz *nt.*

swat [swɒt] *vt fly* totschlagen.

swathe [sweɪð] *vt* wickeln *(in* in *+acc)*.

sway [sweɪ] **1** *n (influence, rule)* Macht *f (over* über *+acc)*. **to hold ~ over sb** jdn beherrschen, jdn in seiner Macht haben. **2** *vi (trees)* sich wiegen; *(hanging object)* schwingen; *(building, bridge etc, person)* schwanken; *(train, boat)* schaukeln; *(hips)* wackeln. **3** *vt* **(a)** schwenken; *(wind)* hin und her bewegen. **(b)** *(influence)* beeinflussen; *(change sb's mind)* umstimmen.

swear [swɛəʳ] *(vb: pret* **swore,** *ptp* **sworn***)* **1** *vt allegiance* schwören; *oath also* leisten, ablegen. **I ~ it!** ich kann das beschwören!; **to ~ sb to secrecy** jdn schwören lassen, daß er nichts verrät; **I could have sworn that was Louise** *(am almost sure)* ich könnte schwören, daß das Louise war; *(but it wasn't)* ich hätte schwören können, daß das Louise war. **2** *vi* **(a)** *(use solemn oath)* schwören. **to ~ on the Bible** auf die Bibel schwören; **to ~ to sth** etw beschwören. **(b)** *(use swearwords)* fluchen *(about* über + *acc)*. **to ~ at sb/sth** jdn/etw beschimpfen.

♦ **swear by** *vi +prep obj (col)* schwören auf *(+acc)*.

♦ **swear in** *vt sep witness etc* vereidigen.

swearword ['swɛə,wɜːd] *n* Fluch, Kraftausdruck *m.*

sweat [swet] **1** *n* Schweiß *m no pl.* **by the ~ of one's brow** *(fig)* im Schweiße seines Angesichts *(liter)*; **to get into a ~ about sth** *(fig)* wegen etw ins Schwitzen geraten *or* kommen; **no ~** *(col)* kein Problem; **it was a real ~** *(col)* wir haben wirklich geschuftet *(col)*. **2** *vi* schwitzen *(with* vor *+dat)*; *(fig col) (work hard)* sich abrackern *(col) (over* mit*)*; *(worry)* zittern *(with* vor *+dat)*. **to ~ like a pig** *(col)* wie ein Affe schwitzen *(col)*. **3** *vt* **to ~ blood** *(with worry)* Blut und Wasser schwitzen; *(with effort)* sich abrackern *(col)*; **to ~ it out** *(fig col)* durchhalten; *(sit and wait)* abwarten.

sweatband ['swet,bænd] *n* Schweißband *nt.*

sweater ['swetəʳ] *n* Pullover *m.*

sweat: ~shirt *n* Sweatshirt *nt*; *(Sport)* Trainingspullover *m*; **~shop** *n (pej, hum col)* Ausbeuterbetrieb *m (pej)*.

sweaty ['swetɪ] *adj (+er) hands* schweißig; *feet, smell also* Schweiß-; *person, socks* verschwitzt; *weather, work* zum Schwitzen.

swede [swiːd] *n (Brit)* Kohlrübe, Steckrübe *f.*

Swede [swiːd] *n* Schwede *m*, Schwedin *f.*

Sweden ['swiːdn] *n* Schweden *nt.*

Swedish ['swiːdɪʃ] **1** *adj* schwedisch. **2** *n* Schwedisch *nt.*

sweep [swiːp] *(vb: pret, ptp* **swept***)* **1** *n* **(a) to give the floor a ~** den Boden kehren. **(b)** *(chimney ~)* Schornsteinfeger *m.* **(c)** *(of arm, pendulum)* Schwung *m*; *(of sword also)* Streich *m*; *(of dress)* Rauschen *nt no pl*; *(of light, radar)* Strahl *m.* **this magnificent ~ of countryside** diese herrliche Landschaft; **a long ~ of motorway** eine weitgestreckte Autobahn; **at one ~** *(fig)* auf einen Schlag; **to make a clean ~** *(fig)* gründlich aufräumen *(of sth* bei etw*)*.

2 *vt* **(a)** kehren, fegen; *dust, snow* wegfegen. **to ~ sth under the carpet** *(fig)* etw unter den Teppich kehren. **(b)** *(scan)* absuchen *(for* nach*)*; *(lights also, bullets)* streichen über *(+acc)*; *minefield* durchkämmen; *mines* räumen. **(c)** *(move quickly over) (wind, skirt)* fegen über *(+acc)*; *(waves) deck etc* überschwemmen; *(glance)* gleiten über *(+acc)*; *(fig) (violence, fashion)* überrollen; *(disease)* um sich greifen in *(+dat)*. **(d)** *(remove with ~ing movement) (wave)* spülen, schwemmen; *(current)* reißen; *(wind)* fegen; *person* reißen. **to ~ sth off the table/into a bag** etw vom Tisch fegen/etw in eine Tasche raffen; **the crowd swept him into the square** er wurde von der Menge zum Platz hin mitgerissen; **he swept her off her feet** *(fig)* er eroberte sie im Sturm; **to ~ the board** *(fig)* alle Preise/Medaillen gewinnen, abräumen *(col)*.

3 *vi* **(a)** *(with broom)* kehren, fegen. **(b)** *(move) (person)* rauschen; *(vehicle, plane) (quickly)* schießen; *(majestically)* gleiten; *(skier)* fegen; *(road, river)* in weitem Bogen führen. **panic swept through Europe** Panik griff in Europa um sich.

♦ **sweep aside** *vt sep (lit, fig)* beiseite fegen.

♦ **sweep away 1** *vi* davonrutschen; *(car, plane)* davonschießen; *(majestically)* davongleiten; *(skier)* davonfegen. **2** *vt sep dust, leaves etc* wegfegen; *(avalanche)* wegreißen; *(flood etc)* wegspülen; *(fig) old laws* aufräumen mit.

♦ **sweep up 1** *vi (with broom)* zusammenkehren *or* -fegen. **2** *vt sep* zusammenkehren *or* -fegen; *(collect up) objects* zusammenraffen; *person* hochreißen; *hair* hochbinden.

sweeper ['swiːpəʳ] *n (road ~)* Straßenkehrer(in *f*) *m*; *(machine)* Kehrmaschine *f*; *(carpet ~)* Teppichkehrer *m.*

sweeping ['swiːpɪŋ] *adj* **(a)** *gesture* weitausholend. **(b)** *(fig) change* radikal, drastisch; *statement* pauschal; *victory* überragend.

sweepstake ['swiːpsteɪk] *n Rennen nt etc, bei dem die Preise aus den Einsätzen gebildet werden,* Sweepstake *nt.*

sweet [swiːt] **1** *adj (+er)* **(a)** süß. **to have a ~ tooth** gern Süßes essen. **(b)** *(fresh) food, water* frisch; *(fragrant) smell* süß. **(c)** *(fig: pleasant etc)* süß; *(kind also)* lieb. **that's very ~ of you** das ist sehr lieb von dir; **once he caught the ~ smell of success** als erst der Erfolg lockte; **the words were ~ to his ear** die Worte klangen lieblich in seinen Ohren; **in his own ~ way** *(iro)* auf seine unübertroffene Art. **2** *n* **(a)** *(Brit: candy)* Bonbon *nt.* **(b)** *(Brit: dessert)* Nachtisch *m*, Dessert *nt.* **for ~** zum Nachtisch. **(c) yes, (my) ~** ja, (mein) Schätzchen *or* Liebling.

sweet: ~ and sour *adj* süß-sauer; **~ chestnut** *n* Eßkastanie *f*; **~ corn** *n* Mais *m.*

sweeten ['swiːtn] *vt coffee, sauce* süßen; *(fig) temper* bessern; *task* versüßen. **to ~ sb** *(col)* jdn gnädig stimmen.

sweetener ['swiːtnəʳ] *n (Cook)* Süßungsmittel *nt*; *(artificial)* Süßstoff *m.*

sweetheart ['swiːt,hɑːt] *n* Schatz *m*, Liebste(r) *mf.*

sweetness ['swiːtnɪs] *n* Süße *f*; *(of smile, nature)* Liebenswürdigkeit *f*; *(of person)* liebe Art. **now all is ~ and light** *(usu iro)* nun herrscht eitel Freude und Sonnenschein.

sweet: ~ pea *n* Gartenwicke *f*; **~ potato** *n* Süßkartoffel *f*; **~-shop** *n (Brit)* Süßwarenladen *m or* -geschäft *nt*; **~-smelling** *adj* süß riechend *attr*.

swell [swel] *(vb: pret* **~ed,** *ptp* **swollen** *or* **~ed)** **1** *n (of sea)* Wogen *nt no pl*. **there was a heavy ~** es herrschte hoher Seegang. **2** *adj (US col: excellent)* klasse *(col)*, prima *(col)*. **3** *vt river, sound etc* anschwellen lassen; *stomach* (auf)blähen; *wood* (auf)quellen; *sail* blähen; *numbers* anwachsen lassen; *sales* steigern. **to be swollen with pride** stolzgeschwellt sein. **4** *vi* **(a)** *(ankle, arm, eye etc: also ~* **up***)* (an)schwellen; *(balloon etc)* sich füllen. **(b)** *(river, lake, sound etc)* anschwellen; *(sails: also ~* **out***)* sich blähen; *(wood)* quellen; *(in size, number)* anwachsen.

swelling ['swelɪŋ] *n (Med)* Schwellung *f*.

sweltering ['sweltərɪŋ] *adj day, weather* glühend heiß; *heat* glühend. **it's ~ in here** *(col)* hier verschmachtet man ja! *(col)*.

swept [swept] *pret, ptp of* **sweep.**

swerve [swɜːv] **1** *n* Bogen *m*; *(of car etc also)* Schlenker *m (col)*. **2** *vi* einen Bogen machen *(around sth* um etw*)*; *(car, driver)* ausschwenken; *(fig) (from truth)* abweichen; *(from chosen path)* abschwenken. **the car was swerving all over the road** der Wagen schwankte von einer Straßenseite zur anderen.

swift [swɪft] **1** *adj (+er)* schnell; *reaction also, revenge* prompt. **2** *n (bird)* Mauersegler *m*.

swiftness ['swɪftnɪs] *n see adj* Schnelligkeit *f*; Promptheit *f*.

swig [swɪg] *(col)* **1** *n* Schluck *m*. **to have** *or* **take a ~ of beer** einen Schluck Bier trinken. **2** *vt (also ~* **down***) beer* herunterkippen *(col)*.

swill [swɪl] **1** *n (animal food)* (Schweine)futter *nt*; *(garbage, slops) (solid)* Abfälle *pl*; *(liquid)* Schmutzwasser *nt*. **2** *vt* **(a)** *(also ~* **out***)* auswaschen; *cup, dish* ausschwenken. **(b)** *(col) beer etc* kippen *(col)*.

swim [swɪm] *(vb: pret* **swam,** *ptp* **swum)** **1** *n* **(a)** **it's a long ~** es ist weit (zu schwimmen); **to go for a ~** schwimmen gehen; **to have a ~** schwimmen. **(b)** *(col)* **to be in the ~** up to date sein; *(socially active)* mitmischen *(col)*. **2** *vt* schwimmen; *river, Channel* durchschwimmen. **3** *vi* schwimmen. **she can't ~ a stroke** sie kann sich keinen Meter über Wasser halten; **my head is ~ming** mir dreht sich alles; **it was absolutely ~ming in vinegar** es schwamm in Essig.

swimmer ['swɪmə^r] *n* Schwimmer(in *f*) *m*.

swimming ['swɪmɪŋ] **1** *n* Schwimmen *nt*. **do you like ~?** schwimmen Sie gern? **2** *adj (for ~)* Schwimm-; *(dizzy) feeling* schwummrig *(col)*.

swimming: ~ bath *n usu pl (Brit)* = **~ pool;** **~ costume** *n* Badeanzug *m*; **~ pool** *n* Schwimmbad *nt*; *(outdoor also)* Freibad *nt*; *(indoor also)* Hallenbad *nt*; **~ trunks** *npl* Badehose *f*.

swimsuit ['swɪmsuːt] *n* Badeanzug *m*.

swindle ['swɪndl] **1** *n* Schwindel, Betrug *m*. **it's a ~!** das ist (der reinste) Schwindel! **2** *vt person* beschwindeln. **to ~ sb out of sth** *(take from)* jdm etw abgaunern *(col)*; *(withhold from)* jdn um etw betrügen.

swindler ['swɪndlə^r] *n* Schwindler(in *f*) *m*.

swine [swaɪn] *n* **(a)** *pl* **-** *(old, form)* Schwein *nt*. **(b)** *pl* **-s** *(pej col)* Schwein *nt*; *(woman also)* Sau *f*.

swing [swɪŋ] *(vb: pret, ptp* **swung)** **1** *n* **(a)** *(movement)* Schwung *m*; *(to and fro)* Schwingen *nt*; *(of needle)* Ausschlag *m*; *(Boxing etc: blow)* Schwinger *m*; *(fig, Pol)* (Meinungs)umschwung *m (to* zugunsten *+gen, away from* zuungunsten *+gen)*. **to take a ~ at sb** nach jdm schlagen; **a ~ in opinion** ein Meinungsumschwung. **(b)** *(rhythm)* Schwung *m*; *(kind of music, dance)* Swing *m*. **to go with a ~** *(fig)* ein voller Erfolg sein *(col)*; **to be in full ~** voll im Gang sein; **to get into the ~ of things** *(col)* reinkommen *(col)*. **(c)** *(seat for ~ing)* Schaukel *f*. **to have a ~** schaukeln; **it's ~s and roundabouts** *(col)* es ist gehüpft wie gesprungen.

2 *vt* **(a)** schwingen; *(to and fro)* hin und her schwingen; *(on swing)* schaukeln; *arms and legs (vigorously)* schwingen (mit); *(dangle)* baumeln mit; *propeller* einen Schwung geben *(+dat)*. **he swung his racket at the ball** er holte mit dem Schläger aus; **he swung the case (up) onto his shoulder** er schwang sich *(dat)* die Kiste auf die Schulter. **(b)** *(influence) election* beeinflussen; *opinion* umschlagen lassen; *person* umstimmen, herumkriegen *(col)*. **his speech swung the decision in our favour** seine Rede ließ die Entscheidung zu unseren Gunsten ausfallen; **he managed to ~ the deal** *(col)* er hat das Geschäft gemacht *(col)*; **if you can ~ it so that ...** *(col)* wenn du es so hinkriegen kannst, daß ... **(c)** *(turn: also ~* **around***) plane, car* herumschwenken.

3 *vi* **(a)** schwingen; *(to and fro)* (hin und her) schwingen; *(hanging object also)* pendeln; *(pivot)* sich drehen; *(on swing)* schaukeln; *(arms, legs: dangle)* baumeln. **(b)** *(move: into saddle, along rope)* sich schwingen. **to ~ open/shut** aufschwingen/zuschlagen; **to ~ into action** in Aktion treten; **the car swung into the square** der Wagen schwenkte auf den Platz ein; **he swung around on his chair** er drehte sich auf seinem Stuhl herum; **the party has swung to the right** in der Partei hat es einen Rechtsruck gegeben; **he'll ~ for it** dafür wird er hängen *or* baumeln *(col)*.

swing: ~ bridge *n* Drehbrücke *f*; **~-door** *n (Brit)* Pendeltür *f*.

swingeing ['swɪndʒɪŋ] *adj (Brit) blow* hart; *attack* scharf; *defeat* vernichtend; *taxation, price increases* extrem hoch; *cuts* extrem.

swinging ['swɪŋɪŋ] *adj step, music* schwungvoll; *movement* schaukelnd. **the ~ sixties** die „Swinging Sixties".

swipe [swaɪp] **1** *n (blow)* Schlag *m*. **to take a ~ at sb/sth** nach jdm/etw schlagen. **2** *vt* **(a)** *person, ball etc* schlagen. **(b)** *(col: steal)* mopsen *(col)*, klauen *(col)*. **3** *vi* **to ~ at sb/sth** nach jdm/etw schlagen.

swirl [swɜːl] **1** *n* Wirbel *m*. **2** *vti* wirbeln. **to ~ around** herumwirbeln.

swish [swɪʃ] **1** *n see vi* Zischen *nt*; Rascheln *nt*; Rauschen *nt*. **2** *adj (Brit col: plush)* schick. **3** *vt cane* zischen lassen; *tail* schlagen mit; *skirt* rauschen mit; *water* schwenken. **4** *vi (whip, cane, tyres)* zischen; *(grass, skirts)* rascheln; *(water)* rauschen.

Swiss [swɪs] **1** *adj* Schweizer, schweizerisch. **~ roll** Biskuitrolle *f*. **2** *n* Schweizer(in *f*) *m*. **the ~** *pl* die Schweizer *pl*; **~ French/German** *(person)* Französisch-/Deutschschweizer(in *f*) *m*; *(language)* Schweizer Französisch *nt*/Schweizerdeutsch, Schwyzerdütsch *nt*.

switch [swɪtʃ] **1** *n* **(a)** *(Elec etc)* Schalter *m*. **(b)** *(US Rail)* Weiche *f*. **(c)** *(change)* Wechsel *m*; *(in plans, policies)* Änderung *f (in gen)*; *(exchange)* Tausch *m*. **a rapid ~ of plan** eine schnelle Änderung der Pläne; **to make a ~** tauschen. **(d)** *(stick, cane)* Rute, Gerte *f*.

2 *vt* **(a)** *(change)* wechseln; *direction, plans* ändern; *allegiance* übertragen *(to* auf *+acc)*; *attention, conversation* lenken *(to* auf *+acc)*. **(b)** *(move) production* verlegen; *object* umstellen. **(c)** *(exchange)* tauschen; *(transpose: also ~* **over, ~ around***) objects, figures in column* vertauschen. **I ~ed hats with him** ich tauschte meinen Hut mit ihm; **to ~ A for B** A für *or* gegen B (ein)tauschen. **(d)** *(Elec)* (um)schalten. **~ the radio to another programme** schalten Sie auf ein anderes Radioprogramm um. **(e)** *(esp US Rail)* rangieren.

3 *vi (change: also ~* **over***)* (über)wechseln *(to* zu*)*; *(Elec, TV, Rad)* umschalten *(to* auf *+acc)*; *(exchange: also ~* **around, ~ over***)* tauschen. **he ~ed to another line of attack** er wechselte seine Angriffstaktik.

♦ **switch off** **1** *vt sep light* ausschalten; *radio, TV,* *machine also, engine* abschalten. **the oven ~es itself** ~ der Backofen schaltet sich selbsttätig ab. **2** *vi* **(a)** *see vt* ausschalten; abschalten. **(b)** *(col: person)* abschalten.

♦ **switch on 1** *vt sep gas etc* anstellen; *machine, TV also, light* einschalten; *engine also* anlassen. **please leave the TV ~ ed** ~ laß den Fernseher bitte an. **2** *vi see vt* anstellen; einschalten; anlassen; *(automatically)* sich einschalten, angehen *(col)*.

switch: ~back *n* Berg- und Talbahn *f*; *(Brit: roller-coaster also)* Achterbahn *f*; **~board** *n (Telec) (exchange)* Vermittlung *f*; *(in office etc)* Zentrale *f*; *(actual panel, Elec)* Schalttafel *f*; **~board operator** *n (in office)* Telefonist(in *f*) *m*.

Switzerland ['swɪtsələnd] *n* die Schweiz. **to** ~ in die Schweiz; **in** ~ in der Schweiz.

swivel ['swɪvl] **1** *(also* ~ **around***) vt* (herum)drehen. **2** *vi* sich drehen; *(person)* sich herumdrehen.

swollen ['swəʊlən] **1** *ptp of* **swell. 2** *adj ankle, face, glands etc* geschwollen; *stomach* aufgedunsen; *wood* gequollen; *river* angeschwollen. **her eyes were ~ with tears** ihre Augen waren verweint; **he has a ~ head** *(fig)* er ist so aufgeblasen.

swoon [swuːn] **1** *n (old)* Ohnmacht *f*. **2** *vi (old: faint)* in Ohnmacht fallen; *(fig: over pop star etc)* beinahe ohnmächtig werden *(over sb* wegen jdm*)*.

swoop [swuːp] **1** *vi (lit: also* ~ **down***) (bird)* herabstoßen, niederstoßen *(on* auf *+acc)*; *(plane)* einen Sturzflug machen; *(fig) (police)* einen Überraschungsangriff machen *(on* auf *+acc) or* landen *(col) (on* bei*)*; *(person)* sich stürzen *(on* auf *+acc)*. **the plane ~ed (down) low over the village** das Flugzeug flog im Tiefflug über das Dorf hinweg. **2** *n (of bird, plane)* Sturzflug *m*. **at one (fell)** ~ auf einen Schlag.

swop [swɒp] = **swap.**

sword [sɔːd] *n* Schwert *nt*. **to cross ~s with sb** *(lit, fig)* mit jdm die Klinge(n) kreuzen.

swordfish ['sɔːdfɪʃ] *n* Schwertfisch *m*.

swordsman ['sɔːdzmən] *n, pl* **-men** [-mən] Schwertkämpfer *m*; *(fencer)* Fechter *m*.

swore [swɔːʳ] *pret of* **swear.**

sworn [swɔːn] **1** *ptp of* **swear. 2** *adj enemy* eingeschworen; *(Jur) statement* eidlich, unter Eid.

swot [swɒt] *(Brit col)* **1** *vti* büffeln *(col)*, pauken *(col)*. **to ~ up (on) one's maths** Mathe pauken *(col)*. **2** *n (pej: person)* Streber(in *f*) *m*.

swum [swʌm] *ptp of* **swim.**

swung [swʌŋ] *pret, ptp of* **swing.**

sycamore ['sɪkəmɔːʳ] *n* Bergahorn *m*; *(US: plane tree)* nordamerikanische Platane.

sycophant ['sɪkəfənt] *n* Kriecher *m*.

syllable ['sɪləbl] *n* Silbe *f*. **a two-~(d) word** ein zweisilbiges Wort; **in words of one** ~ *(hum)* in einfachen Worten.

syllabus ['sɪləbəs] *n, pl* **-es** *or* **syllabi** [sɪləbaɪ] *(Sch, Univ)* Lehrplan *m*; *(lecture timetable)* Vorlesungsverzeichnis *nt*.

symbiotic [ˌsɪmbɪ'ɒtɪk] *adj* symbiotisch.

symbol ['sɪmbəl] *n* Symbol, Zeichen *nt (of* für*)*.

symbolic [sɪm'bɒlɪk] *adj* symbolisch *(of* für*)*. **to be ~ of sth** etw symbolisieren.

symbolism ['sɪmbəlɪzəm] *n* Symbolik *f*; *(Art, Liter: movement)* Symbolismus *m*.

symbolize ['sɪmbəlaɪz] *vt* symbolisieren.

symmetrical [sɪ'metrɪkəl] *adj* symmetrisch.

symmetry ['sɪmɪtrɪ] *n* Symmetrie *f*.

sympathetic [ˌsɪmpə'θetɪk] *adj (showing pity)* mitfühlend; *(understanding)* verständnisvoll; *(well-disposed)* wohlwollend; *look, smile* freundlich. **to be** *or* **feel ~ to(wards) sb** mit jdm mitfühlen; für jdn Verständnis haben; *(Pol etc)* mit jdm sympathisieren; **a ~ ear** ein offenes Ohr.

sympathize ['sɪmpəθaɪz] *vi (feel compassion)* mitfühlen *(with* mit*)*; *(understand)* Verständnis haben *(with* für*)*; *(agree)* sympathisieren *(with* mit*) (esp Pol)*; *(express sympathy)* sein Mitgefühl aussprechen; *(on bereavement)* sein Beileid aussprechen. **to ~ with sb's views** jds Ansichten teilen; **I really do ~** *(have pity)* das tut mir wirklich leid; *(understand your feelings)* ich habe wirklich vollstes Verständnis.

sympathizer ['sɪmpəθaɪzəʳ] *n* Mitfühlende(r) *mf*; *(with cause)* Sympathisant(in *f*) *m*.

sympathy ['sɪmpəθɪ] *n* **(a)** *(pity, compassion)* Mitgefühl, Mitleid *nt (for* mit*)*; *(at death)* Beileid *nt*. **to feel** *or* **have ~ for sb** Mitleid mit jdm haben; **a letter of** ~ ein mitfühlender Brief, ein Beileidsbrief *m*; **you have my ~!** *(hum)* herzliches Beileid *(hum)*; **you won't get any ~ from me** erwarte kein Mitleid von mir. **(b)** *(understanding)* Verständnis *nt*; *(fellow-feeling, agreement)* Sympathie *f*. **to be in/out of ~ with sb/sth** mit jdm/etw einhergehen/nicht einhergehen; **to come out in** ~ *(Ind)* in Sympathiestreik treten; ~ **strike** Sympathiestreik *m*.

symphonic [sɪm'fɒnɪk] *adj* symphonisch, sinfonisch.

symphony ['sɪmfənɪ] *n* Symphonie, Sinfonie *f*. ~ **orchestra** Symphonie- *or* Sinfonieorchester *nt*.

symposium [sɪm'pəʊzɪəm] *n, pl* **-s** *or* **symposia** [sɪm'pəʊzɪə] Symposium, Symposion *nt*.

symptom ['sɪmptəm] *n (lit, fig)* Symptom *nt*.

symptomatic [ˌsɪmptə'mætɪk] *adj* symptomatisch *(of* für*)*.

synagogue ['sɪnəgɒg] *n* Synagoge *f*.

synchromesh ['sɪŋkrəʊˌmeʃ] *n* Synchrongetriebe *nt*.

synchronize ['sɪŋkrənaɪz] *vt* abstimmen *(with* auf *+acc)*; *two actions, movements* aufeinander abstimmen; *clocks* gleichstellen *(with* mit*)*. **to ~ a film** Bild und Ton eines Films aufeinander abstimmen.

syndicate ['sɪndɪkɪt] *n* Interessengemeinschaft *f*; *(for gambling)* Wettgemeinschaft *f*; *(Comm)* Syndikat *nt*, Verband *m*; *(Press)* (Presse)zentrale *f*; *(crime ~)* Ring *m*.

syndrome ['sɪndrəʊm] *n (Med)* Syndrom *nt*; *(fig, Sociol)* Phänomen *nt*.

synod ['sɪnəd] *n* Synode *f*.

synonym ['sɪnənɪm] *n* Synonym *nt*.

synonymous [sɪ'nɒnɪməs] *adj* synonym. **to be ~ with sth** *(fig)* gleichbedeutend mit etw sein.

synopsis [sɪ'nɒpsɪs] *n, pl* **synopses** [sɪ'nɒpsiːz] Abriß *m* der Handlung; *(of article, book)* Zusammenfassung *f*.

syntax ['sɪntæks] *n* Syntax *f*.

synthesis ['sɪnθəsɪs] *n, pl* **syntheses** ['sɪnθəsiːz] Synthese *f*.

synthesize ['sɪnθəsaɪz] *vt* synthetisieren; *speech* synthetisch bilden; *theories etc* zusammenfassen.

synthesizer ['sɪnθəˌsaɪzəʳ] *n (Mus)* Synthesizer *m*.

synthetic [sɪn'θetɪk] **1** *adj* synthetisch; *fibre, silk* Kunst-. **2** *n* Kunststoff *m*, Synthetik *f*.

syphilis ['sɪfɪlɪs] *n* Syphilis *f*.

syphon *n* = **siphon.**

Syria ['sɪrɪə] *n* Syrien *nt*.

Syrian ['sɪrɪən] **1** *adj* syrisch. **2** *n* Syrer(in *f*) *m*.

syringe [sɪ'rɪndʒ] **1** *n (Med)* Spritze *f*. **2** *vt (Med)* (aus)spülen.

syrup, *(US also)* **sirup** ['sɪrəp] *n* Sirup *m*. **cough ~** *(Med)* Hustensaft *m*.

system ['sɪstəm] *n* System *nt*. **new teaching ~s** neue Lehrmethoden *pl*; **it was a shock to his ~** er hatte schwer damit zu schaffen; **to get sth out of one's ~** *(fig col)* sich *(dat)* etw von der Seele schaffen *(col)*; **you can't beat the ~** gegen das System kommst du einfach nicht an.

systematic [ˌsɪstə'mætɪk] *adj* systematisch; *liar, cruelty* ständig. **he works in a ~ way** er arbeitet mit System.

systems analyst *n (Comp)* Systemanalytiker(in *f*) *m*.

T

T, t [tiː] *n* T, t *nt*. **that's him/it to a T** das ist er, wie er leibt und lebt/genau so ist es.

ta [tɑː] *interj (Brit col)* danke.

TA *(Brit)* = **Territorial Army.**

tab [tæb] *n* **(a)** *(loop on coat etc)* Aufhänger *m*; *(fastener on coat etc)* Riegel *m*; *(name ~) (of owner)* Namensschild *nt*; *(of maker)* Etikett *nt*; *(Mil)* Spiegel *m*; *(on filing cards)* Reiter *m*. **to keep ~s on sb/sth** *(col)* jdn/etw genau im Auge behalten. **(b)** *(US col: bill)* Rechnung *f*.

tabby [tæbɪ] *n (also* **~ cat***)* getigerte Katze; *(female)* weibliche Katze.

table ['teɪbl] **1** *n* **(a)** Tisch *m*; *(banquet ~)* Tafel *f*. **at the ~** am Tisch; **at ~** bei Tisch; **to sit down to** *or* **at ~** sich zu Tisch setzen; **to be under the ~** *(drunk)* unter dem Tisch liegen; **to turn the ~s (on sb)** (gegenüber jdm) den Spieß umdrehen; **the whole ~ laughed** die ganze Runde lachte. **(b)** *(of figures, prices etc, Sport)* Tabelle *f*. **(multiplication) ~s** Einmaleins *nt*; **~ of contents** Inhaltsverzeichnis *nt*. **(c)** *(Geog)* **water ~** Grundwasserspiegel *m*. **2** *vt* **(a)** *motion* einbringen. **(b)** *(US: postpone) bill* zurückstellen.

tableau ['tæbləʊ] *n, pl* **-s** *or* **-x** ['tæbləʊ(z)] *(Art, Theat)* Tableau *nt*; *(fig)* Bild *nt*, Szene *f*.

table: ~ cloth *n* Tischdecke *f or* -tuch *nt*; **~ lamp** *n* Tischlampe *f*; **~ manners** *npl* Tischmanieren *pl*; **~ mat** *n* Untersetzer *m*; *(of cloth)* Set *nt*; **~spoon** *n* Eßlöffel *m*; **~spoonful** *n* Eßlöffel(voll) *m*.

tablet ['tæblɪt] *n* **(a)** *(Pharm)* Tablette *f*. **(b)** *(of wax, clay)* Täfelchen *nt*; *(of soap)* Stückchen *nt*. **(c)** *(on wall etc)* Tafel *f*.

table: ~ tennis *n* Tischtennis *nt*; **~ware** *n no pl* Tafelgeschirr *nt* und -besteck *nt*; **~ wine** *n* Tisch- *or* Tafelwein *m*.

tabloid ['tæblɔɪd] *n (also* **~ newspaper***) kleinformatige Zeitung; (pej)* Boulevardzeitung *f*.

taboo [tə'buː] **1** *n* Tabu *nt*. **2** *adj* tabu *pred*.

tabulate ['tæbjʊleɪt] *vt* tabellarisch darstellen.

tabulation ['tæbjʊleɪʃən] *n* Tabulation *f*.

tachometer [tæ'kɒmɪtə^r] *n* Drehzahlmesser *m*.

tacit ['tæsɪt] *adj* stillschweigend.

taciturn ['tæsɪtɜːn] *adj* schweigsam.

tack [tæk] **1** *n* **(a)** *(nail)* kleiner Nagel; *(with small head also)* Stift *m*; *(esp US: drawing pin)* Heftzwecke *f*. **(b)** *(Brit Sew)* Heftstich *m*. **(c)** *(Naut: course)* Schlag *m*; *(fig)* Richtung *f*, Weg *m*. **to be on the port/starboard ~** auf Backbord-/Steuerbordbug segeln; **to be on the right/wrong ~** *(fig)* auf der richtigen/falschen Spur sein; **to try another ~** *(fig)* es anders versuchen. **2** *vt* **(a)** *(with nail)* annageln *(to* an *+dat or acc)*; *(with clip, pin)* feststecken *(to* an *+dat)*. **(b)** *(Brit Sew)* heften. **3** *vi (Naut)* aufkreuzen.

tackle ['tækl] **1** *n* **(a)** *(lifting gear)* Flaschenzug *m*; *(Naut)* Talje *f*, Takel *nt*. **(b)** *(equipment)* Ausrüstung *f*. **fishing ~** Angelausrüstung *f*. **(c)** *(Sport)* Angriff *m*, Tackling *nt*. **2** *vt* **(a)** *(physically, Sport)* angreifen; *(Rugby)* fassen; *thief also* sich stürzen auf *(+acc)*; *(verbally)* zur Rede stellen *(about* wegen*)*. **(b)** *(undertake) job* in Angriff nehmen; *new challenge* sich versuchen an *(+dat)*; *problem* angehen; *(manage to cope with)* fertig werden mit. **3** *vi* angreifen.

tacky[1] ['tækɪ] *adj (+er)* klebrig. **the paint is still ~** die Farbe klebt noch.

tacky[2] *adj (+er) (col)* verlottert *(col)*; *(cheap)* billig.

tact [tækt] *n no pl* Takt *m*.

tactful ['tæktfʊl] *adj* taktvoll.

tactic ['tæktɪk] *n* Taktik *f*.

tactical ['tæktɪkəl] *adj (Mil, fig)* taktisch.

tactics ['tæktɪks] *n sing (Mil, fig)* Taktik *f*.

tactile ['tæktaɪl] *adj* Tast-; *(tangible)* fühlbar.

tactless ['tæktlɪs] *adj* taktlos.

tadpole ['tædpəʊl] *n* Kaulquappe *f*.

taffy ['tæfɪ] *n (US)* Toffee *nt*.

tag [tæg] **1** *n* **(a)** *(label)* Schild(chen) *nt*; *(on clothes) (maker's name)* Etikett *nt*; *(owner's name)* Namensschild *nt*; *(loop)* Aufhänger *m*. **(b)** *(game)* Fangen *nt*. **2** *vi* **to ~ behind** *or* **after sb** hinter jdm herzockeln *(col)*.

♦ **tag along** *vi* mitzockeln *(col)*. **why don't you ~ ~?** *(col)* warum kommst du nicht mit?

tail [teɪl] **1** *n* **(a)** *(of animal)* Schwanz *m*. **with his ~ between his legs** *(fig)* mit eingezogenem Schwanz *(col)*; **to turn ~** die Flucht ergreifen; **he was right on my ~** er saß mir direkt im Nacken; **to put a ~ on sb** jdn beschatten lassen. **(b)** *(of aeroplane, procession)* Schwanz *m*; *(of comet)* Schweif *m*; *(of shirt)* Zipfel *m*; *(of jacket, coat)* Schoß *m*. **~s** *pl (jacket)* Frack *m*. **(c) ~s** *(on coin)* Rückseite *f*; **~s I win!** bei Zahl gewinne ich. **2** *vt suspect* beschatten *(col)*; *car etc* folgen *(+dat)*.

♦ **tail away** *vi* = **tail off (a).**

♦ **tail back** *vi (Brit: traffic)* sich gestaut haben.

♦ **tail off** *vi* **(a)** *(diminish)* abnehmen; *(interest also)* schwinden; *(sounds)* schwächer werden; *(sentence)* abbrechen. **(b)** *(deteriorate)* sich verschlechtern.

tail: ~back *n (Brit)* Rückstau *m*; **~board** *n* Ladeklappe *f*; **~ coat** *n* Frack *m*; **~ end** *n* Ende *nt*; **~gate** *n (of car)* Hecktür *f*; *(of lorry)* Ladeklappe *f*; **~-light** *n (Aut)* Rücklicht *nt*.

tailor ['teɪlə^r] **1** *n* Schneider *m*. **~'s dummy** *(lit)* Schneiderpuppe *f*. **2** *vt* **(a)** *dress etc* schneidern. **(b)** *(fig) plans* zuschneiden *(to* auf *+acc)*; *products etc* abstimmen *(to* auf *+acc)*. **~ed to meet his needs** auf seine Bedürfnisse abgestimmt.

tailor-made ['teilə'meɪd] *adj (lit, fig)* maßgeschneidert; *role also* zugeschnitten *(for* auf *+acc)*. **~ suit/costume** Maßanzug *m*/Schneiderkostüm *nt*; **the job was ~ for him** die Stelle war ihm wie auf den Leib geschnitten.

taint [teɪnt] **1** *n (lit: of food etc)* Stich *m*; *(fig) (blemish)* Makel *m*; *(trace)* Spur *f*. **2** *vt food* verderben; *air, atmosphere* verpesten; *(fig) reputation* beschmutzen.

take [teɪk] *(vb: pret* **took,** *ptp* **taken***)* **1** *vt* **(a)** nehmen; *(for oneself)* sich *(dat)* nehmen; *(~ away with one)* mitnehmen; *(remove from its place)* wegnehmen. **to ~ sth from sb** jdm etw wegnehmen; *(steal)* jdm etw stehlen; **~ three eggs** *(Cook)* man nehme drei Eier; **~ a seat/chair!** nehmen Sie Platz!; **~ your seats!** nehmen Sie Ihre Plätze ein!; **this seat is ~n** dieser Platz ist besetzt; **I'll ~ a pound of apples** ich nehme ein Pfund Äpfel.

(b) *(transport, accompany)* bringen; *(~ along with one) person, things* mitnehmen. **I'll ~ you to the station** ich bringe Sie zum Bahnhof; **I'll ~ you (with me) to the party** ich nehme dich zur

Party mit; **let me ~ your case** komm, ich nehme *or* trage deinen Koffer; **to ~ sb/the dog for a walk** mit jdm spazierengehen/den Hund ausführen; **to ~ sb to the cinema** *(treat)* jdn ins Kino einladen; *(~ along with one)* mit jdm ins Kino gehen; **this bus will ~ you to the town hall** der Bus fährt zum Rathaus; **this road will ~ you to Paris** diese Straße führt nach Paris.

(c) *(capture) person* fassen; *animal* fangen; *town, country etc* einnehmen; *(Chess etc)* schlagen; *(Cards) trick* machen.

(d) *(accept, receive)* nehmen; *job, dye, perm* annehmen; *command, role* übernehmen; *prize* gewinnen. **I won't ~ less than £200** ich verkaufe es nicht unter £200; **we ~ the Guardian** wir bekommen den „Guardian"; **to ~ things as they come** die Dinge nehmen, wie sie kommen; **~ it from me!** das können Sie mir glauben; **(you can) ~ it or leave it** die Entscheidung liegt bei Ihnen; **he took the blow on his left arm** der Schlag traf ihn am linken Arm; *(in defence)* er wehrte den Schlag mit dem linken Arm ab; **do you ~ my meaning?** verstehen Sie, was ich meine?

(e) *exam, driving test, course, French* machen; *(as optional subject)* wählen; *lessons, tuition* nehmen; *(teach) lesson, subject* geben; *class* unterrichten. **he took his degree in 1965** er hat 1965 Examen gemacht *or* sein Examen abgelegt; **who ~s you for Latin?** wer unterrichtet bei euch Latein?

(f) *(consume) drink, food* zu sich *(dat)* nehmen; *drugs, medicine* nehmen; *(on directions for use)* einnehmen. **to ~ sugar in one's tea** den Tee mit Zucker trinken; **do you ~ sugar?** nehmen Sie Zucker?; **will you ~ coffee or tea?** möchten Sie Kaffee oder Tee?; **not to be ~n (internally)** *(Med)* nur zur äußerlichen Anwendung.

(g) *photo* machen. **he took the whole group** er nahm die ganze Gruppe auf.

(h) *(put up with)* sich *(dat)* gefallen lassen; *(endure) alcohol, climate* vertragen; *long journey* aushalten; *emotional experience, shock* verkraften; *(thing)* aushalten. **I just can't ~ any more** das halte ich nicht mehr aus.

(i) *(respond to, regard) news, blow* aufnehmen; *person* nehmen; *(understand, interpret)* auffassen, verstehen. **she knows how to ~ him** sie versteht es, ihn von der richtigen Seite zu nehmen; **she took his death very badly** sein Tod hat sie sehr mitgenommen; **I would ~ that to mean that ...** ich würde das so auffassen *or* verstehen, daß...; **to ~ sb/sth for** *or* **to be ...** jdn/etw für ... halten; **what do you ~ me for?** wofür hältst du mich eigentlich?; **may I ~ it that ...?** darf ich annehmen, daß ...?

(j) *(require)* brauchen; *clothes size* haben. **it ~s five hours/men ...** man braucht fünf Stunden/Leute ...; **it ~s me five hours ...** ich brauche fünf Stunden ...; **it took ten men to complete the job** zehn Leute waren nötig, um diese Arbeit zu erledigen; **the journey ~s 3 hours** die Fahrt dauert 3 Stunden; **the wound took five weeks to heal** es dauerte fünf Wochen, bis die Wunde verheilt war; **it took a lot of courage/intelligence** dazu gehörte viel Mut/Intelligenz; **it ~s time** es braucht (seine) Zeit, es dauert (eine Weile); **it took a long time** es hat lange gedauert; **it won't ~ long** das dauert nicht lange; **that'll ~ some explaining** das wird schwer zu erklären sein; **she's got what it ~s** *(col)* sie ist nicht ohne *(col)*; *(is capable also)* sie kann was *(col)*; *(for job)* sie hat das Zeug dazu.

(k) *(support) weight* aushalten; *(have capacity or room for) 50 people, 200 books* Platz haben für.

(l) *walk* machen; *trip also* unternehmen; *taxi, train, motorway* nehmen. **to ~ the plane/next plane** fliegen/das nächste Flugzeug nehmen.

(m) to be ~n sick *or* **ill** krank werden; **to be ~n with sb/sth** *(attracted by)* von jdm/etw angetan sein.

2 *vi (fire)* angehen; *(dye, graft)* angenommen werden; *(vaccination)* anschlagen; *(plant)* anwachsen; *(seeds)* kommen; *(fish: bite)* anbeißen.

3 *n* **(a)** *(Film)* Aufnahme *f.* **(b)** *(US col: takings)* Einnahmen *pl.*

♦**take after** *vi +prep obj* nachschlagen *(+dat)*; *(in looks)* ähneln *(+dat)*. **he ~s ~ her** er ist nach ihr geraten.

♦**take along** *vt sep* mitnehmen.

♦**take apart** *vt sep (also fig col)* auseinandernehmen.

♦**take aside** *vt sep* beiseite nehmen.

♦**take away 1** *vi* **to ~ ~ from sth** etw schmälern; *from worth* etw mindern. **2** *vt sep* **(a)** *(subtract)* abziehen. **6 ~ ~ 2** 6 weniger 2. **(b)** *(remove) child, thing, privilege* wegnehmen *(from sb* jdm*)*; *(from school etc)* nehmen *(from* aus*)*; *(lead, transport, carry away)* wegbringen *(from* von*)*; *prisoner* abführen *(to* in *+acc)*. **to ~ ~ sb's pleasure/freedom** *etc* jdm die Freude/Freiheit *etc* nehmen. **(c)** *(Brit) food* mitnehmen. **pizza to ~ ~** Pizza zum Mitnehmen.

♦**take back** *vt sep* **(a)** *(reclaim, get back)* sich *(dat)* zurückgeben lassen; *toy etc* wieder wegnehmen; *(fig: retract) threat, statement* zurücknehmen. **(b)** *(return)* zurückbringen. **he took us ~ (home)** er brachte uns (nach Hause) zurück. **(c)** *(agree to receive again) thing* zurücknehmen; *employee* wieder einstellen. **(d)** *(remind)* **to ~ sb ~ to his childhood** jdn an seine Kindheit erinnern.

♦**take down** *vt sep* **(a)** *(lit) (off shelf etc)* herunternehmen; *curtains, decorations* abnehmen; *picture* abhängen; *flag* einholen **(b)** *(dismantle) scaffolding etc* abbauen; *tent also* abbrechen; *railing, gate* entfernen. **(c)** *(write down)* (sich *dat*) notieren; *notes* (sich *dat*) machen; *letter* aufnehmen; *lecture* mitschreiben.

♦**take home** *vt insep £100 per week* netto verdienen.

♦**take in** *vt sep* **(a)** *(bring in) thing, person* hinein-/hereinbringen; *harvest* einbringen. **when are you taking the car ~ (to the garage)?** wann bringen Sie das Auto in die Werkstatt? **(b)** *(receive in one's home) refugee* (bei sich) aufnehmen; *child* zu sich nehmen; *(for payment) student* vermieten an *(+acc)*. **she ~s ~ lodgers** sie vermietet (Zimmer). **(c)** *(make narrower) dress* enger machen. **(d)** *(usu insep: include, cover)* einschließen. **(e)** *(note)* wahrnehmen; *area, room* überblicken; *(grasp) meaning, lecture, sb's death* begreifen; *impressions, sights etc* aufnehmen; *situation* erfassen. **(f)** *(deceive)* hereinlegen. **to be ~n ~** hereingelegt werden; **to be ~n ~ by sb/sth** auf jdn/etw hereinfallen; **to be ~n ~ by appearances** sich vom äußeren Schein täuschen lassen.

♦**take off 1** *vi (plane, passengers)* starten, abfliegen; *(plane: leave the ground)* abheben; *(Sport)* abspringen; *(fig) (project, sales)* anlaufen; *(film, product)* ankommen.

2 *vt sep* **(a)** *(remove, cut off: person)* abmachen *(prep obj* von*)*; *hat, lid* abnehmen *(prep obj* von*)*; *tablecloth* herunternehmen *(prep obj* von*)*; *coat, gloves etc* ausziehen; *leg* abnehmen; *play* absetzen; *food from menu, bus* streichen *(prep obj* von*)*; *service, tax* abschaffen; *(remove from duty, job) detective etc* abziehen *(prep obj* von*)*; *driver* ablösen. **to ~ sth ~ sb** jdm etw abnehmen; **to ~ the receiver ~ (the hook)** den Hörer abnehmen; **he/she took her dress ~** er zog ihr das Kleid aus/sie zog ihr Kleid aus; **he took his/her clothes off** er zog sich/sie aus; **would you like to ~ your coat ~?** möchten Sie ablegen?

(b) *(deduct)* abziehen *(prep obj* von*)*; *(from price) 5%, 50p* nachlassen.

(c) *(lead away, go away with)* mitnehmen;

(under arrest etc) abführen. **he was ~n ~ to hospital** er wurde ins Krankenhaus gebracht; **to ~ oneself ~** *(col)* sich auf den Weg machen.

(d) *(have free) week, Monday* frei nehmen. **to ~ time ~ work** sich *(dat)* frei nehmen.

(e) *(imitate)* nachmachen.

(f) to ~ sb's mind ~ sth jdn von etw ablenken; **to ~ sb/sth ~ sb's hands** jdm jdn/etw abnehmen.

♦ **take on 1** *vi* **(a)** *(col: become upset)* sich aufregen. **(b)** *(become popular: song, fashion etc)* sich durchsetzen. **2** *vt sep* **(a)** *(undertake) job, work* übernehmen; *responsibility* auf sich *(acc)* nehmen; *bet* annehmen. **(b)** *(Sport etc: accept as opponent)* antreten gegen; *opponent, authorities* sich anlegen mit. **(c)** *(employ)* einstellen; *apprentice* annehmen. **(d)** *(take aboard) (coach, train etc) passengers* aufnehmen; *(plane, ship also)* an Bord nehmen; *cargo, stores* laden; *fuel* tanken. **(e)** *(assume) colour, expression* bekommen, annehmen. **he took ~ an air of importance** er gab sich *(dat)* eine gewichtige Miene.

♦ **take out** *vt sep* **(a)** *(bring or carry out)* (hinaus)bringen *(of* aus*)*; *(out of garage) car* hinaus-/herausfahren *(of* aus*)*; *(for drive etc) car, boat* wegfahren mit.

(b) *(to theatre etc)* ausgehen mit. **to ~ the dog ~ (for a walk)** den Hund ausführen; **to ~ sb ~ to** *or* **for dinner/to the cinema** jdn zum Essen/ins Kino einladen.

(c) *(pull out, extract)* herausnehmen; *tooth also* ziehen; *nail* herausziehen *(of* aus*)*. **to ~ sth ~ of** *or* **from sth** etw aus etw (heraus)nehmen.

(d) *(withdraw from bank etc)* abheben.

(e) *(procure) insurance* abschließen. **to ~ ~ a subscription for sth** etw abonnieren.

(f) to ~ sb ~ of himself jdn auf andere Gedanken bringen; **to ~ sth ~ on sb** *(col)* etw an jdm auslassen *(col)*; **to ~ it ~ on sb** sich an jdm abreagieren; **to ~ it/a lot ~ of sb** *(tire)* jdn ziemlich/sehr schlauchen *(col)*.

♦ **take over 1** *vi (assume government)* an die Macht kommen; *(military junta etc)* die Macht ergreifen; *(party)* an die Regierung kommen; *(new boss etc)* die Leitung übernehmen; *(in a place: tourists, guests etc)* sich breitmachen *(col)*. **to ~ ~ (from sb)** jdn ablösen; **the next shift ~s ~ at 6 o'clock** die nächste Schicht übernimmt um 6 Uhr. **2** *vt sep* **(a)** *(take control or possession of)* übernehmen. **tourists ~ ~ Edinburgh in the summer** im Sommer machen sich die Touristen in Edinburgh breit *(col)*. **(b)** *(escort or carry across) person* hinüberbringen; *(+prep obj)* bringen über *(+acc)*. **(c) to ~ sb ~ sth** *(show round)* jdm etw zeigen.

♦ **take to** *vi +prep obj* **(a)** *(form liking for) person* mögen. **the children soon took ~ their new surroundings** den Kindern gefiel es bald in der neuen Umgebung; **I don't know how she'll ~ ~ him/it** ich weiß nicht, wie sie auf ihn/darauf reagieren wird; **I don't ~ kindly ~ that** ich kann das nicht leiden. **(b)** *(form habit of)* **to ~ ~ doing sth** anfangen, etw zu tun; **to ~ ~ drink** zu trinken anfangen **(c)** *(escape to) hills* sich zurückziehen in *(+acc)*, Zuflucht suchen in *(+dat)*.

♦ **take up** *vt sep* **(a)** *(raise, lift)* aufnehmen; *carpet, floor-boards* hochnehmen; *road* aufreißen; *dress* kürzer machen; *pen* greifen zu.

(b) *(lead or carry upstairs etc) invalid, child* hinauf-/heraufbringen; *visitor* (mit) hinauf-/heraufnehmen.

(c) *time, attention* in Anspruch nehmen; *space* einnehmen.

(d) *(absorb)* (in sich *acc*) aufnehmen.

(e) *matter, point (raise)* zur Sprache bringen *(with sb* bei jdm*)*; *(go into)* eingehen auf *(+acc)*.

(f) *photography, archaeology* zu seinem Hobby machen; *a hobby* sich *(dat)* zulegen; *a language* anfangen zu lernen. **to ~ ~ painting/the guitar** anfangen zu malen/Gitarre zu spielen.

(g) *(adopt) cause* sich einsetzen für; *idea* aufgreifen; *case* sich annehmen *(+gen)*. **to ~ ~ an attitude** eine Haltung einnehmen; **to ~ ~ a position** *(lit)* eine Stellung einnehmen; *(fig)* eine Haltung einnehmen.

(h) *(accept) challenge, invitation, suggestion* annehmen.

(i) *(start) job, employment* annehmen; *new job, post* antreten; *one's duties* übernehmen; *career* einschlagen.

(j) *(continue) story* aufnehmen; *conversation* weiterführen; *(join in) chorus, chant* einstimmen in *(+acc)*.

(k) I'll ~ you ~ on that *(on invitation, offer)* ich werde davon Gebrauch machen; *(on promise etc)* ich nehme Sie beim Wort.

♦ **take upon** *vt +prep obj* **he has ~n it ~ himself to ...** er hat die Verantwortung auf sich genommen, zu ...; **he took it ~ himself to answer for me** er meinte, er müsse für mich antworten.

♦ **take up with** *vi +prep obj person* sich anfreunden mit.

take: ~-away *(esp Brit)* **1** *n* **(a)** *(meal)* Essen *nt* zum Mitnehmen; **(b)** *(restaurant)* Imbißstube *f*; **2** *adj attr meal* zum Mitnehmen; **~-home pay** *n* Nettolohn *m*.

taken ['teɪkən] *ptp of* **take.**

take: ~-off *n* *(Aviat)* Start, Abflug *m*. **~-over** *n* *(Fin, Comm)* Übernahme *f*; **~-over bid** *n* Übernahmeangebot *nt*.

taking ['teɪkɪŋ] **1** *n* **(a) it's yours for the ~** das können Sie (umsonst) haben. **(b) ~s** *pl (Comm)* Einnahmen *pl*. **2** *adj person* anziehend.

talc [tælk], **talcum powder** ['tælkəm,paʊdə^r] *n* Talkumpuder *m*; *(perfumed)* (Körper)puder *m*.

tale [teɪl] *n* **(a)** Geschichte *f*; *(Liter)* Erzählung *f*. **(b) to tell ~s** petzen *(col) (to* bei*)*; **to tell ~s about sb** jdn verpetzen *(col) (to* bei*)*.

talent ['tælənt] *n* **(a)** Talent *nt*. **to have a ~ for drawing/mathematics** Begabung zum Zeichnen/für Mathematik haben. **(b)** *(talented people)* Talente *pl*. **~ scout** Talentsucher *m*.

talented ['tæləntɪd] *adj* begabt, talentiert.

talk [tɔːk] **1** *n* **(a)** Gespräch *nt (also Pol)*; *(conversation also)* Unterhaltung *f*. **to have a ~** ein Gespräch führen/sich unterhalten *(with sb about sth* mit jdm über etw *acc)*; **could I have a ~ with you?** könnte ich Sie mal sprechen?; **to hold** *or* **have ~s** Gespräche führen. **(b)** *no pl (~ing)* Rederei *f*; *(rumour)* Gerede *nt*. **there is some ~ of his returning** es heißt, er kommt zurück; **she's the ~ of the town** sie ist zum Stadtgespräch geworden; **he's all ~** er ist ein Schwätzer. **(c)** *(lecture)* Vortrag *m*. **to give a ~** einen Vortrag halten *(on* über *+acc)*.

2 *vi* sprechen, reden *(of* von, *about* über *+acc)*; *(have conversation also)* sich unterhalten *(of, about* über *+acc)*. **to ~ to** *or* **with sb** mit jdm reden *(about* über *+acc)*; *(converse also)* sich mit jdm unterhalten *(about* über *+acc)*; **could I ~ to Mr Smith please?** kann ich bitte Herrn Smith sprechen?; **it's easy for you to ~** *(col)* du hast gut reden *(col)*; **don't (you) ~ to me like that!** wie redest du denn mit mir?; **he knows/doesn't know what he's ~ing about** er weiß (schon)/weiß nicht, wovon er spricht; **you can ~!** *(col)* du kannst gerade reden!; **to keep sb ~ing** jdn (mit einem Gespräch) hinhalten; **to ~ to oneself** Selbstgespräche führen; **now you're ~ing!** das läßt sich schon eher hören!; **he's been ~ing of going abroad** er hat davon geredet, daß er ins Ausland fahren will; **~ing of films ...** da wir gerade von Filmen sprechen ...; **stop ~ing!** sei/seid ruhig!; **everyone was ~ing about them** sie waren in aller Munde; *(because of scandal)* alle haben über sie geredet; **you're ~ing about at**

least £100 das wird mindestens £ 100 kosten.

3 *vt* **(a)** *a language, slang* sprechen; *nonsense* reden; *(discuss) politics* sich unterhalten über *(+acc)*. **(b)** *(persuade)* **to ~ sb into doing sth** jdn überreden *or* dazu bringen, etw zu tun; *(against better judgement)* jdm einreden, etw zu tun; **to ~ sb out of sth/doing sth** jdm etw ausreden/jdm ausreden, etw zu tun; **he ~ed himself out of trouble** er redete sich (geschickt) heraus.

♦ **talk around** *vt always separate* umstimmen. **I ~ed her ~ to my way of thinking** ich habe sie zu meiner Anschauung bekehrt.

♦ **talk down 1** *vi* **to ~ ~ to sb** mit jdm herablassend sprechen. **2** *vt sep pilot* zur Landung einweisen.

♦ **talk over** *vt sep problem* besprechen.

talkative ['tɔːkətɪv] *adj person* gesprächig.

talked-of ['tɔːktɒv] *adj:* **much ~** berühmt.

talker ['tɔːkəʳ] *n* Redner *m*; *(pej)* Schwätzer *m*.

talking ['tɔːkɪŋ] *n* Reden, Sprechen *nt*. **I'll let you do the ~** ich überlasse das Reden Ihnen; **he did all the ~** er übernahm das Reden.

talking: ~ point *n* Gesprächsthema *nt*; **~ shop** *(pej)* Quasselbude *f*.

tall [tɔːl] *adj (+er)* **(a)** *person* groß; *building, tree* hoch. **how ~ are you?** wie groß sind Sie?; **he is 1 m 80 ~** er ist 1,80 m groß. **(b)** *(col)* **that's a ~ order** das ist ganz schön viel verlangt; **a ~ story** ein Märchen *nt (col)*.

tallboy ['tɔːlbɔɪ] *n (Brit)* hohe Schlafzimmerkommode.

tallow ['tæləʊ] *n* Talg *m*.

tally ['tælɪ] **1** *n* **(a) to keep a ~ of** Buch führen über *(+acc)*. **(b)** *(result of counting)* (An)zahl *f*. **2** *vi* **they don't ~** sie stimmen nicht überein.

talon ['tælən] *n (also fig: of person)* Kralle *f*.

tambourine [ˌtæmbəˈriːn] *n* Tamburin *nt*.

tame [teɪm] **1** *adj (+er)* **(a)** *animal, person* zahm. **(b)** *(dull) person, life, story, film etc* lahm *(col)*. **2** *vt animal, person* zähmen, bändigen; *passion* zügeln.

♦ **tamper with** ['tæmpəˌwɪθ] *vi +prep obj* herumhantieren an *(+dat)*; *(with evil intent)* sich *(dat)* zu schaffen machen an *(+dat)*.

tampon ['tæmpən] *n* Tampon *m*.

tan [tæn] **1** *n* **(a)** *(suntan)* Bräune *f*. **to get a ~** braun werden. **(b)** *(colour)* Hellbraun *nt*. **2** *adj* hellbraun. **3** *vt* **(a)** *skins* gerben. **to ~ sb's hide** *(fig col)* jdm das Fell gerben. **(b)** *(sun) face, body etc* bräunen. **4** *vi* braun werden. **she ~s easily** sie wird schnell braun.

tandem ['tændəm] **1** *n (cycle)* Tandem *nt*. **2** *adv* **in ~** *aligned* hintereinander; *work* zusammen.

tang [tæŋ] *n (smell)* scharfer Geruch; *(taste)* starker Geschmack.

tangent ['tændʒənt] *n (Math)* Tangente *f*. **to go** *or* **fly off at a ~** *(fig)* (plötzlich) vom Thema abschweifen.

tangerine [ˌtændʒəˈriːn] *n* Mandarine *f*.

tangible ['tændʒəbl] *adj (lit, fig)* greifbar; *proof also* handfest; *assets* real.

tangle ['tæŋgl] **1** *n (lit)* Gewirr *nt*; *(fig: muddle)* Durcheinander *nt*. **to get into a ~** *(lit, fig)* sich verheddern; **he got into a ~ with the police** er hat Schwierigkeiten mit der Polizei gehabt. **2** *vt (also* **~ up***) (lit, fig)* durcheinanderbringen; *wool, string also* verheddern. **to get ~d** *(lit, fig)* sich verheddern; *(ropes)* sich verknoten; **a ~d web** ein Gespinst *nt*.

♦ **tangle with** *vi +prep obj (col)* aneinandergeraten mit. **I'm not tangling ~ him** mit ihm laß ich mich (doch) nicht ein.

tango ['tæŋgəʊ] **1** *n* Tango *m*. **2** *vi* Tango tanzen.

tank [tæŋk] *n* **(a)** *(container)* Tank *m*; *(for water also)* Wasserspeicher *m*; *(of boiler also)* Kessel *m*; *(for diver: oxygen ~)* Flasche *f*. **(b)** *(Mil)* Panzer *m*.

♦ **tank up 1** *vi (ship, plane)* auftanken. **2** *vt sep (Brit col)* **to get ~ed ~** sich vollaufen lassen *(col)* *(on* mit*)*; **to be ~ed ~** voll sein.

tankard ['tæŋkəd] *n* Krug *m*.

tanker ['tæŋkəʳ] *n* **(a)** *(boat)* Tanker *m*. **(b)** *(vehicle)* Tankwagen *m*.

tanned [tænd] *adj person* braun(gebrannt).

tanner ['tænəʳ] *n* Gerber *m*.

Tannoy ® ['tænɔɪ] *n* Lautsprecheranlage *f*. **over** *or* **on the ~** über den Lautsprecher.

tantalize ['tæntəlaɪz] *vt* reizen; *(torment)* quälen.

tantalizing ['tæntəlaɪzɪŋ] *adj smell, promise* verlockend, verführerisch.

tantamount ['tæntəmaʊnt] *adj:* **to be ~ to sth** einer Sache *(dat)* gleichkommen.

tantrum ['tæntrəm] *n* Wutanfall, Koller *(col) m*. **to have** *or* **throw a ~** einen Wutanfall bekommen.

tap[1] [tæp] **1** *n (esp Brit)* Hahn *m*. **on ~** *(lit: beer etc)* vom Faß; *(fig)* zur Hand. **2** *vt cask, barrel* anzapfen; *telephone lines* abhören, anzapfen *(col)*; *resources* erschließen. **the wires are ~ped here** die Leitung hier wird abgehört.

tap[2] **1** *n (light knock)* Klopfen *nt*; *(light touch)* Klaps *m*. **2** *vti* klopfen. **he ~ped me on the shoulder** er klopfte mir auf die Schulter; **he ~ped his foot impatiently** er klopfte ungeduldig mit dem Fuß auf den Boden; **to ~ at the door** leise anklopfen.

tap: ~-dance *vi* steppen; **~-dancing** *n* Steppen *nt*.

tape [teɪp] **1** *n* **(a)** Band *nt*; *(sticky paper)* Klebeband *nt*; *(Sellotape ® etc)* Kleb(e)streifen *m*; *(punch~)* Lochstreifen *m*; *(Sport)* Zielband *nt*. **to break** *or* **breast the ~** *(Sport)* durchs Ziel gehen. **(b)** *(magnetic)* (Ton)band *nt*. **on ~** auf Band; **to put** *or* **get sth on ~** etw auf Band aufnehmen. **2** *vt* **(a)** *parcel* (mit Kleb(e)streifen/-band) zukleben. **(b)** *(~-record) song, message* (auf Band) aufnehmen. **(c)** *(col)* **I've got the situation ~d** ich habe die Sache im Griff *(col)*; **I've got him ~d** ich kenne mich mit ihm aus.

tape: ~ deck *n* Tapedeck *nt*; **~ measure** *n* Bandmaß *nt*.

taper ['teɪpəʳ] **1** *n (candle)* (dünne) Kerze. **2** *vt end of plank, stick etc* zuspitzen; *edge* abschrägen; *pair of trousers* (nach unten) verengen. **3** *vi (also* **~ off***)* sich zuspitzen; *(trousers)* nach unten enger werden.

tape: ~-record *vt* auf Band aufnehmen; **~-recorder** *n* Tonbandgerät *nt*; **~-recording** *n* Bandaufnahme *f*.

tapering ['teɪpərɪŋ] *adj* spitz zulaufend.

tapestry ['tæpɪstrɪ] *n* Wandteppich, Gobelin *m*.

tapeworm ['teɪpwɜːm] *n* Bandwurm *m*.

tapioca [ˌtæpɪˈəʊkə] *n* Tapioka *f*.

tappet ['tæpɪt] *n (Aut)* Stößel *m*.

tap water *n* Leitungswasser *nt*.

tar [tɑːʳ] **1** *n* Teer *m*. **2** *vt fence* teeren. **they are all ~red with the same brush** *(fig)* sie sind alle vom gleichen Schlag.

tarantula [təˈræntjʊlə] *n* Tarantel *f*.

tardy ['tɑːdɪ] *adj (+er)* zu spät.

target ['tɑːgɪt] *n* **(a)** *(person, object, Mil)* Ziel *nt*; *(Sport: board, fig: of joke, criticism etc)* Zielscheibe *f*. **his shot was off/on ~** *(Mil)* sein Schuß ist daneben gegangen/hat getroffen; **Apollo III is on ~ for the moon** Apollo III ist auf direktem Kurs zum Mond. **(b)** *(objective, goal)* Ziel *nt*; *(in production)* (Plan)soll *nt*. **production is above/on/below ~** das Produktionssoll ist überschritten/erfüllt/nicht erfüllt; **we set ourselves the ~ of £10,000** wir haben uns £ 10.000 zum Ziel gesetzt.

tariff ['tærɪf] *n* **(a)** Tarif *m*; *(in hotels)* Preisliste *f*. **(b)** *(Econ: tax)* Zoll *m*; *(table)* Zolltarif *m*.

tarmac ['tɑːmæk] *n* Asphalt *m*; *(esp Brit Aviat)* Rollfeld *nt*.

tarn [tɑːn] *n* kleiner Bergsee.

tarnish ['tɑːnɪʃ] **1** *vt* **(a)** *metal* stumpf werden lassen. **(b)** *(fig) reputation* beflecken; *ideals* trüben. **2** *vi (metal)* anlaufen. **3** *n* Beschlag *m*.

tarot card ['tærəʊkɑːd] *n* Tarockkarte *f*.

tarpaulin [tɑːˈpɔːlɪn] *n (waterproof sheet)* Plane *f*; *(Naut)* Persenning *f*.

tarragon [ˈtærəgən] *n* Estragon *m*.

tart[1] [tɑːt] *adj (+er)* **(a)** *flavour, wine* herb, sauer *(pej)*; *fruit* sauer. **(b)** *(fig) remark, manner* scharf.

tart[2] *n (Cook)* Obsttorte *f*; *(individual)* Obsttörtchen *nt*. **apple/jam ~** Apfelkuchen *m*/ Marmeladentörtchen *nt*.

tart[3] *n (col) (prostitute)* Nutte *f (col!)*; *(loose woman)* Flittchen *nt (pej)*.

♦**tart up** *vt sep (esp Brit col)* aufmachen *(col)*; *oneself* auftakeln *(col)*. **there she was, all ~ed ~** da stand sie, aufgetakelt wie eine Fregatte *(col)*.

tartan [ˈtɑːtən] **1** *n (pattern)* Schottenkaro *nt*; *(material)* Schottenstoff *m*. **2** *adj skirt* mit Schottenkaro *or* -muster.

tartar [ˈtɑːtəʳ] *n (of wine)* Weinstein *m*; *(in kettle)* Kesselstein *m*; *(on teeth)* Zahnstein *m*.

Tartar [ˈtɑːtəʳ] *n* Tatar *m*. **t~** *(fig)* Tyrann *m*.

tartar sauce *n* ≈ Remouladensoße *f*.

task [tɑːsk] *n* Aufgabe *f*. **it is the ~ of the politician to ...** es ist Aufgabe des Politikers, zu ...; **to take sb to ~** sich *(dat)* jdn vornehmen *(col) (for, about* wegen*)*.

task: ~ force *n* Spezialeinheit *f*; **~master** *n* (strenger) Arbeitgeber; **he's a hard ~master** er ist ein strenger Meister.

tassel [ˈtæsəl] *n* Quaste, Troddel *f*.

taste [teɪst] **1** *n (lit, fig)* Geschmack *m*; *(small amount, fig: as an example)* Kostprobe *f*; *(of sth in the future)* Vorgeschmack *m*. **I don't like the ~ of it** das schmeckt mir nicht; **a ~ of onions** ein Zwiebelgeschmack *m*; **to have a ~ (of sth)** *(lit)* (etw) probieren; *(fig)* eine Kostprobe (von etw) bekommen; *(of sth to come)* einen Vorgeschmack (von etw) haben; **in good/bad ~** geschmackvoll/ geschmacklos; **to have a ~ for sth** eine Vorliebe für etw haben; **it's an acquired ~** das ist etwas für Kenner; **she has expensive ~s** sie hat einen teuren Geschmack; **my ~ in music has changed** mein musikalischer Geschmack hat sich geändert; **to be to sb's ~** nach jds Geschmack sein; **it is a matter of ~** das ist Geschmack(s)sache; **sweeten to ~** *(Cook)* nach Geschmack süßen.

2 *vt* **(a)** *(perceive flavour of)* schmecken; *(fig) blood* lecken. **(b)** *(test) wine, food products* probieren; *(official)* prüfen. **(c)** *(fig) power, freedom* erleben.

3 *vi* schmecken. **to ~ good** (gut) schmecken; **to ~ of sth** nach etw schmecken.

taste bud *n* Geschmacksknospe *f*.

tasteful [ˈteɪstfʊl] *adj* geschmackvoll.

tasteless [ˈteɪstlɪs] *adj* geschmacklos; *food also* fade.

tastiness [ˈteɪstɪnɪs] *n* Schmackhaftigkeit *f*.

tasty [ˈteɪstɪ] *adj (+er) dish* schmackhaft.

ta-ta [ˈtæˈtɑː] *interj (Brit col)* tschüs *(col)*.

tattered [ˈtætəd] *adj clothes* zerlumpt; *book, sheet* zerfleddert; *(fig) reputation* angeschlagen.

tatters [ˈtætəz] *npl* Lumpen, Fetzen *pl*. **to be in ~** in Fetzen sein; **his jacket hung in ~** sein Jackett war zerrissen.

tattoo[1] [təˈtuː] **1** *vt* tätowieren. **2** *n* Tätowierung *f*.

tattoo[2] *n* **(a)** *(military pageant)* Musikparade *f*. **(b)** *(Mil: on drum or bugle)* Zapfenstreich *m*.

tatty [ˈtætɪ] *adj (+er) (col)* schmuddelig; *clothes* schäbig.

taught [tɔːt] *pret, ptp of* **teach.**

taunt [tɔːnt] **1** *n* Spöttelei *f*, höhnische Bemerkung. **2** *vt person* verspotten *(about* wegen*)*. **to ~ sb with cowardice** jdm höhnisch Feigheit vorwerfen.

Taurus [ˈtɔːrəs] *n (Astron, Astrol)* Stier *m*.

taut [tɔːt] *adj (+er) rope* straff (gespannt); *muscles* gestrafft; *(fig) (tense) nerves, situation* (an)gespannt; *(economical) prose* knapp.

tautological [ˌtɔːtəˈlɒdʒɪkəl] *adj* tautologisch, doppelt gemoppelt *(col)*.

tautology [tɔːˈtɒlədʒɪ] *n* Tautologie *f*.

tavern [ˈtævən] *n (old)* Schenke *f (old)*.

tawdry [ˈtɔːdrɪ] *adj (+er) clothes* billig und geschmacklos; *jewellery, decorations* ordinär; *person* aufgedonnert.

tawny [ˈtɔːnɪ] *adj (+er)* goldbraun.

tax [tæks] **1** *n* **(a)** *(Fin, Econ)* Steuer *f*; *(on a company's profit)* Abgabe *f*. **before/after ~** vor/ nach Abzug der Steuern; **to put a ~ on sb/sth** jdn/etw besteuern. **(b)** *(fig)* Belastung *f (on sth gen, on sb* für jdn*)*. **2** *vt* **(a)** *(Fin, Econ)* besteuern; *country* mit Steuern belegen. **(b)** *(fig) brain, imagination* strapazieren; *one's patience also* auf eine harte Probe stellen; *strength* stark beanspruchen; *resources* angreifen. **(c)** *(accuse)* **to ~ sb with sth** jdn einer Sache *(gen)* beschuldigen.

taxable [ˈtæksəbl] *adj person* steuerpflichtig; *income also* steuerbar *(form)*; *goods* abgabenpflichtig.

taxation [tækˈseɪʃən] *n* Besteuerung *f*; *(taxes also)* Steuern *pl*. **exempt from ~** steuerfrei; **subject to ~** steuerpflichtig.

tax *in cpds* Steuer; **~ avoidance** *n* Steuerumgehung *f*; **~ collector** *n* Steuerbeamte(r) *m*; *(Bibl, Hist)* Zöllner *m*; **~ evasion** *n* Steuerhinterziehung *f*; *(by going abroad)* Steuerflucht *f*; **~ exile** *n* Steuerexil *nt*; **~-free** *adj, adv* steuerfrei; **~ haven** *n* Steuerparadies *nt*.

taxi [ˈtæksɪ] **1** *n* Taxi *nt*. **to go by ~** mit dem Taxi fahren. **2** *vi (Aviat)* rollen. **the plane ~ed to a halt** das Flugzeug rollte aus.

taxidermist [ˈtæksɪˈdɜːmɪst] *n* Präparator *m*.

taxi: ~-driver *n* Taxifahrer(in *f*) *m*; **~ plane** *n (US)* Lufttaxi *nt*; **~ rank** *(Brit)*, **~ stand** *n* Taxistand *m*.

tax: ~payer *n* Steuerzahler *m*; **~ rebate** *n* Steuervergütung *f*; **~ return** *n* Steuererklärung *f*.

TB = **tuberculosis** Tb, Tbc *f*.

T-bone steak [ˈtiːbəʊnˈsteɪk] *n* T-bone-Steak *nt*.

tea [tiː] *n* **(a)** Tee *m*. **to make (the) ~** (den) Tee machen; **a cup of ~** eine Tasse Tee; **not for all the ~ in China** nicht um alles Gold der Welt. **(b)** *(afternoon ~)* ≈ Kaffee und Kuchen; *(meal)* Abendessen *nt*. **we have ~ at five** wir essen um 5 Uhr zu Abend.

tea: ~ bag *n* Teebeutel *m*; **~ break** *n* Pause *f*; **~ caddy** *n* Teedose *f*; *(dispenser)* Teespender *m*; **~ cart** *n (US)* Tee- *or* Servierwagen *m*.

teach [tiːtʃ] *(vb: pret, ptp* **taught***)* **1** *vt subject, person* unterrichten; *animal* abrichten. **to ~ sth to sb** jdm etw beibringen; *(teacher)* jdn in etw *(dat)* unterrichten; **to ~ sb to do sth** jdm beibringen, etw zu tun; **to ~ sb how to do sth** jdm etw beibringen; **he ~es French** er unterrichtet *or* gibt *(col)* Französisch; **to ~ oneself sth** sich *(dat)* etw beibringen; **let that ~ you not to ...** laß dir das eine Lehre sein, nicht zu ...; **that'll ~ you to break the speed limit** das hast du (nun) davon, daß du die Geschwindigkeitsbegrenzung überschritten hast. **2** *vi* unterrichten, Unterricht geben. **he wants to ~** er möchte Lehrer werden.

teacher [ˈtiːtʃəʳ] *n* Lehrer(in *f*) *m*. **she is a German ~** sie ist Deutschlehrerin.

teacher-training [ˈtiːtʃəˈtreɪnɪŋ] *n* Lehrerausbildung *f*. **~ college** *(primary)* pädagogische Hochschule; *(secondary)* Studienseminar *nt*.

tea-chest [ˈtiːtʃest] *n* Kiste *f*.

teaching [ˈtiːtʃɪŋ] *n* **(a)** das Unterrichten; *(as profession)* der Lehrberuf. **to take up ~** Lehrer werden; **she enjoys ~** sie unterrichtet gern. **(b)** *(doctrine: also* **~s***)* Lehre *f*.

teaching: ~ aid *n* Lehrmittel *nt*; **~ hospital** *n* Ausbildungskrankenhaus *nt*; **~ staff** *n* Lehrerkollegium *nt*, Lehrkörper *m (form)*.

tea: ~ cloth *n (Brit)* Geschirrtuch *nt*; **~ cosy** *n* Teewärmer *m*; **~cup** *n* **(a)** Teetasse *f*; **(b)** *(also* **~cupful***)* Tasse *f* (voll).

teak [tiːk] *n* Teak(holz) *nt*; *(tree)* Teakbaum *m*.

tea-leaf ['ti:li:f] *n* Teeblatt *nt.*
team [ti:m] *n* **(a)** Team *nt*; *(Sport also)* Mannschaft *f.* **football ~** Fußballmannschaft *f.* **(b)** *(of horses, oxen etc)* Gespann *nt.*
♦ **team up** *vi* sich zusammentun *(with* mit*)*; *(join group)* sich anschließen *(with sb* jdm, an jdn*)*.
team: ~ game *n* Mannschaftsspiel *nt*; **~ spirit** *n* Gemeinschaftsgeist *m*; *(Sport)* Mannschaftsgeist *m*; **~work** *n* Gemeinschaftsarbeit *f,* Teamwork *nt.*
tea: ~ party *n* Teegesellschaft *f*; **~pot** *n* Teekanne *f.*
tear[1] [tɛəʳ] *(vb: pret* **tore,** *ptp* **torn***)* **1** *vt* **(a)** *paper, dress* zerreißen; *flesh* aufreißen; *hole* reißen. **I've torn a muscle** ich habe mir einen Muskel gezerrt; **to ~ sth to pieces** etw in Stücke reißen; **the critics tore the play to pieces** die Kritiker haben das Stück total verrissen; **to ~ sth open** etw aufreißen; **that's torn it!** *(fig col)* das hat alles verdorben! **(b)** *(pull away)* reißen. **her child was torn from her/her arms** das Kind wurde ihr entrissen/ihr aus den Armen gerissen; **he tore it out of my hand** er riß es mir aus der Hand. **(c)** *(fig: usu pass)* **a country torn by war** ein vom Krieg zerrissenes Land; **to be torn between two things/people** zwischen zwei Dingen/Menschen hin-und hergerissen sein.
2 *vi* **(a)** *(material etc)* (zer)reißen. **her coat tore on a nail** sie zerriß sich *(dat)* den Mantel an einem Nagel; **~ along the dotted line** an der gestrichelten Linie abtrennen. **(b)** *(move quickly)* rasen. **to ~ past** vorbeirasen.
3 *n (in material etc)* Riß *m.*
♦ **tear along** *vi* entlangrasen. **he tore ~ the street** er raste die Straße entlang.
♦ **tear apart** *vt sep house (thieves etc)* völlig durcheinanderbringen; *(bomb etc)* völlig zerstören; *meat, country* zerreißen.
♦ **tear away 1** *vi* davonrasen. **2** *vt sep wrapping* abreißen *(from* von*)*. **if you can ~ yourself ~ from the paper** wenn du dich von der Zeitung losreißen kannst.
♦ **tear down** *vt sep poster* herunterreißen; *house* abreißen.
♦ **tear off 1** *vi* **(a)** wegrasen. **he tore ~ down the street** er raste die Straße hinunter. **(b) the carbon ~s ~** die Durchschrift läßt sich abtrennen. **2** *vt sep label, wrapping, cover* abreißen; *clothes* herunterreißen. **he tore me ~ a strip** *(col)* er hat mich zur Schnecke gemacht *(col).*
♦ **tear out 1** *vi* heraus-/hinausrasen. **he tore ~ through the front door** er raste zur Vordertür hinaus. **2** *vt sep* (her)ausreißen *(of* aus*)*.
♦ **tear up 1** *vi* angerast kommen. **he tore ~ the hill/road** er raste den Berg hinauf/die Straße entlang. **2** *vt sep* **(a)** *paper (fig) contract* zerreißen. **(b)** *stake, plant* (her)ausreißen.
tear[2] [tɪəʳ] *n* Träne *f.* **in ~s** in Tränen aufgelöst; **the news brought ~s to her eyes** als sie das hörte, stiegen ihr die Tränen in die Augen; **you are bringing ~s to my eyes** *(iro)* mir kommen die Tränen *(iro)*; **~ drop** Träne *f.*
tearaway ['tɛərəweɪ] *n (col)* Rabauke *m (col).*
tearful ['tɪəfʊl] *adj look* tränenfeucht; *face* tränenüberströmt. **..., she said in a ~ voice ...,** sagte sie unter Tränen.
teargas ['tɪəgæs] *n* Tränengas *nt.*
tear-jerker ['tɪəˌdʒɜ:kəʳ] *n (col)* Schnulze *f.*
tearoom ['ti:rʊm] *n* Teestube *f*, Café *nt.*
tease [ti:z] **1** *vt person* necken; *animal* reizen; *(torment)* quälen; *(make fun of)* aufziehen, hänseln *(about* wegen*)*; *(have on)* auf den Arm nehmen *(col).* **2** *n (col: person)* Scherzbold *m (col).*
♦ **tease out** *vt sep* **(a)** *fibres* kardieren; *wool* kämmen; *tangles* auskämmen. **(b)** *(fig) information* ablocken *(out of sb* jdm*)*.
teaser ['ti:zəʳ] *n (difficult question)* harte Nuß *(col)*; *(riddle)* Denksportaufgabe *f.*
tea: ~ service, ~ set *n* Teeservice *nt*; **~ shop** *n (Brit)* Teestube *f*; **~spoon** *n* **(a)** Teelöffel *m*; **(b)** *(also* **~spoonful***)* Teelöffel *m* (voll); **~ strainer** *n* Teesieb *nt.*
teat [ti:t] *n (of animal)* Zitze *f*; *(of woman)* Brustwarze *f*; *(Brit: on baby's bottle)* (Gummi)sauger *m.*
tea: ~time *n (for afternoon ~)* Teestunde *f*; *(mealtime)* Abendessen *nt*; **~ towel** *n (Brit)* Geschirrtuch *nt*; **~ tray** *n* Tablett *nt.*
tech [tek] *(Brit)* = **technical college.**
technical ['teknɪkəl] *adj* **(a)** *(concerning technology)* technisch. **~ hitch** technisches Problem. **(b)** *(of particular branch)* fachlich, Fach-; *adviser, dictionary* Fach-; *problems, vocabulary* fachspezifisch; *details* formal. **~ term** Fachausdruck *m*; **~ terminology** Fachsprache *f*; **~ question** *(Jur)* Verfahrensfrage *f*; **for ~ reasons** *(Jur)* aus verfahrenstechnischen Gründen.
technical college *n (Brit)* Technische Fachschule.
technicality [ˌteknɪ'kælɪtɪ] *n* **(a)** *no pl* **the ~ of the language** die Fülle von Fachausdrücken. **(b)** *(technical detail, difficulty)* technische Einzelheit; *(fig, Jur)* Formsache *f.* **that's just a ~** das ist bloß ein Detail.
technically ['teknɪkəlɪ] *adv* **(a)** technisch. **(b)** *(strictly speaking)* **~ you're right** genau genommen haben Sie recht.
technician [tek'nɪʃən] *n* Techniker(in *f*) *m*; *(skilled worker)* Facharbeiter(in *f*) *m.*
technique [tek'ni:k] *n* Technik *f*; *(method)* Methode *f.*
technological [ˌteknə'lɒdʒɪkəl] *adj* technologisch; *details* technisch.
technologist [tek'nɒlədʒɪst] *n* Technologe *m,* Technologin *f.*
technology [tek'nɒlədʒɪ] *n* Technologie *f.* **the ~ of printing** die Drucktechnik; **University/College of T~** Technische Hochschule/Fachschule; **the age of ~** das technische Zeitalter.
teddy (bear) ['tedɪ(ˌbɛəʳ)] *n* Teddy(bär) *m.*
tedious ['ti:dɪəs] *adj* langweilig, öde.
tediousness ['ti:dɪəsnɪs] *n* Lang(e)weile *f.* **his ~** seine Langweiligkeit.
tee [ti:] *(Golf)* **1** *n* Tee *nt.* **2** *vt ball* auf das Tee legen.
♦ **tee off** *vi* einen Ball vom (ersten) Abschlag spielen.
teem [ti:m] *vi* **(a)** *(with people, insects etc)* wimmeln *(with* von*)*. **(b) it's ~ing (with rain)** es regnet *or* gießt *(col)* in Strömen.
teenage ['ti:nˌeɪdʒ] *adj* Jugend-, Teenager-; *child, son* halbwüchsig.
teenager ['ti:nˌeɪdʒəʳ] *n* Teenager *m.*
teens [ti:nz] *npl* Teenageralter *nt.* **to be in one's ~** im Teenageralter sein.
tee-shirt *n* = **T-shirt.**
teeter ['ti:təʳ] *vi* **(a)** taumeln, schwanken. **to ~ on the brink** *or* **edge of sth** *(lit)* am Rand von etw taumeln; *(fig)* am Rand von etw sein. **(b)** *(US: seesaw)* schaukeln.
teeth [ti:θ] *pl of* **tooth.**
teethe [ti:ð] *vi* zahnen.
teething ['ti:ðɪŋ] *n* Zahnen *nt.* **~ troubles** *npl (fig)* Kinderkrankheiten *pl.*
teetotal ['ti:'təʊtl] *adj person* abstinent; *party etc* ohne Alkohol. **to be ~** keinen Alkohol trinken, Antialkoholiker(in *f*) *m* sein.
teetotaller, *(US)* **teetotaler** ['ti:'təʊtləʳ] *n* Abstinenzler(in *f*), Antialkoholiker(in *f*) *m.*
telecommunications [ˌtelɪkəˌmju:nɪ'keɪʃənz] *n* **(a)** *pl* Fernmeldewesen *nt.* **(b)** *sing (science)* Fernmeldetechnik *f.*
telegram ['telɪgræm] *n* Telegramm *nt.*
telegraph: ~ pole *n* Telegrafenmast *m*; **~ wire** *n* Telegrafenleitung *f.*
telepathic [ˌtelɪ'pæθɪk] *adj* telepathisch. **you must be ~!** du mußt Hellseher sein!
telepathy [tɪ'lepəθɪ] *n* Telepathie *f.*

telephone ['telɪfəʊn] **1** *n* Telefon *nt*. **you're wanted on the ~** Sie werden am Telefon verlangt; **are you on the ~**? haben Sie Telefon?; *(can you be reached by ~)* sind Sie telefonisch zu erreichen?; **he's on the ~** *(is using the ~)* er telefoniert gerade; *(wants to speak to you)* er ist am Telefon; **by ~** telefonisch; **I've just been/I'll get on the ~ to him** ich habe eben mit ihm telefoniert/ich werde ihn anrufen. **2** *vt* anrufen; *message, reply* telefonisch übermitteln. **would you ~ the office to say ...** würden Sie im Büro anrufen und sagen ... **3** *vi* anrufen, telefonieren; *(make ~ call)* telefonieren. **to ~ for a taxi** ein Taxi rufen.

telephone *in cpds* Telefon-, Fernsprech- *(form)*; **~ booth** *or* **box** *(Brit) n* Telefonzelle, Fernsprechzelle *f*; **~ call** *n* Telefongespräch *nt*; **~ directory** *n* Telefonbuch *nt*; **~ exchange** *n* Vermittlungsstelle *f (form)*; **~ kiosk** *n (Brit)* Telefonzelle *f*; **~ number** *n* Telefonnummer, Rufnummer *(form) f*; **~ operator** *n* Telefonist(in *f*) *m*.

telephonist [tɪ'lefənɪst] *n (Brit)* Telefonist(in *f*) *m*.

telephoto (lens) ['telɪˌfəʊtəʊ('lenz)] *n* Teleobjektiv *nt*.

teleprinter ['telɪˌprɪntə^r] *n* Fernschreiber *m*.

telescope ['telɪskəʊp] **1** *n* Teleskop *nt*. **2** *vi (also ~ together) (aerial, umbrella)* sich ineinanderschieben lassen.

telescopic [ˌtelɪ'skɒpɪk] *adj aerial etc* ausziehbar.

televise ['telɪvaɪz] *vt* (im Fernsehen) übertragen.

television ['telɪˌvɪʒən] *n* Fernsehen *nt*; *(set)* Fernsehapparat, Fernseher *(col) m*. **to watch ~** fernsehen; **to be on ~** im Fernsehen kommen; *(person)* im Fernsehen sein.

television *in cpds* Fernseh-; **~ camera** *n* Fernsehkamera *f*; **~ personality** *n* bekannte Fernsehpersönlichkeit; **~ screen** *n* Bildschirm *m*, Mattscheibe *f (col)*; **~ set** *n* Fernsehapparat, Fernseher *(col) m*; **~ studio** *n* Fernsehstudio *nt*.

telex ['teleks] **1** *n* Fernschreiben, Telex *nt*; *(machine)* Fernschreiber *m*. **2** *vt message* per Telex mitteilen; *person* ein Telex schicken *(+dat)*.

tell [tel] *pret, ptp* **told 1** *vt* **(a)** *(relate) story, experiences, adventures* erzählen *(sb sth, sth to sb* jdm etw*)*; *(inform, say, announce)* sagen *(sb sth* jdm etw*)*. **to ~ lies/fortunes** lügen/wahrsagen; **to ~ sb about** *or* **of sth** jdm von etw erzählen; **I can't ~ you how pleased I am** ich kann Ihnen gar nicht sagen, wie sehr ich mich freue; **who told you that?** wer hat Ihnen denn das erzählt?; **to ~ sb the way** jdm den Weg sagen; **could you ~ me the way to the station, please?** könn(t)en Sie mir bitte sagen, wie ich zum Bahnhof komme?; **(I'll) ~ you what, let's go to the cinema** weißt du was, gehen wir doch ins Kino!; **don't ~ me you can't come!** sagen Sie bloß nicht, daß Sie nicht kommen können!; **I won't do it, I ~ you!** und ich sage dir, das mache ich nicht!; **let me ~ you ...** lassen Sie sich von mir sagen, daß ...; **it was cold, I can ~ you** ich kann dir sagen, das war vielleicht kalt!; **I told you so** ich habe es (dir) ja gesagt; **~ me another!** wer's glaubt! *(col)*; **don't ~ me, let me guess** sag's mir nicht, laß mich raten; **you're ~ing me!** wem sagen Sie das!

(b) *(distinguish, discern)* **to ~ the time** die Uhr kennen; **to ~ the difference** den Unterschied erkennen; **you can ~ that he's a foreigner** man sieht *or* merkt, daß er Ausländer ist; **to ~ sb/sth by sth** jdn/etw an etw *(dat)* erkennen; **to ~ right from wrong** Recht von Unrecht unterscheiden; **how can/could I ~ that?** wie soll ich das wissen?/wie hätte ich das wissen können?

(c) *(order)* sagen *(sb* jdm*)*. **we were told to bring sandwiches with us** es wurde uns gesagt, daß wir belegte Brote mitbringen sollten; **~ him to stop singing** sagen Sie ihm, er soll aufhören zu singen; **do as** *or* **what you are told!** tu, was man dir sagt!; **I won't ~ you again** ich sage es dir nicht noch einmal.

2 *vi* **(a)** *(discern, be sure)* wissen. **who can ~?** wer weiß?; **how can I ~?** *(how should I know)* woher soll ich das wissen?; **you never can ~** man kann nie wissen. **(b)** *(talk, ~ tales of)* sprechen. **that would be ~ing!** das kann ich nicht verraten; **promise you won't ~** du mußt versprechen, daß du nichts sagst; **it hurt me more than words can ~** es hat mich mehr verletzt, als ich mit Worten ausdrücken kann. **(c)** *(have effect)* sich bemerkbar machen. **his age told against him** *(in applying for job)* sein Alter war ein Nachteil für ihn; *(in competition)* sein Alter machte sich bemerkbar.

♦ **tell off** *vt sep (col: scold)* ausschimpfen *(for* wegen*)*. **he told me ~ for being late** er schimpfte (mich aus), weil ich zu spät kam.

teller ['telə^r] *n* **(a)** *(in bank)* Kassierer(in *f*) *m*. **(b)** *(vote counter)* Stimmenauszähler(in *f*) *m*. **(c)** *(of story)* Erzähler(in *f*) *m*.

telling ['telɪŋ] **1** *adj (effective)* wirkungsvoll; *argument also* schlagend; *blow (lit, fig)* empfindlich; *(revealing)* aufschlußreich. **2** *n* **(a)** *(narration)* Erzählen *nt*. **(b) there is no ~ what he may do** man kann nicht wissen, was er tut.

telling-off ['telɪŋ'ɒf] *n (col)* Standpauke *f (col)*. **to give sb a good ~** jdn kräftig ausschimpfen.

telltale ['telteɪl] **1** *n* Petzer *m*, Petze *f*. **2** *adj attr* verräterisch.

telly ['telɪ] *n (Brit col)* Fernseher *m (col)*.

temerity [tɪ'merɪtɪ] *n* Kühnheit *f*.

temp^1 = **(a) temporary. (b) temperature.**

temp^2 [temp] *(Brit)* **1** *n* Aushilfskraft *f*. **2** *vi* als Aushilfskraft arbeiten.

temper ['tempə^r] **1** *n (disposition)* Wesen, Naturell *nt*; *(angry mood)* Wut *f*. **to be in a ~/good/bad ~** wütend sein/guter/schlechter Laune sein; **she's got a quick/vicious ~** sie kann sehr jähzornig sein/tückisch werden; **to lose one's ~** die Beherrschung verlieren *(with sb* bei jdm*)*; **to keep one's ~** sich beherrschen *(with sb* bei jdm*)*; **to fly into a ~** einen Wutanfall bekommen; **a fit of ~** ein Wutanfall *m*. **2** *vt* **(a)** *metal* tempern. **(b)** *(fig) action, passion* mäßigen; *criticism* mildern.

temperament ['tempərəmənt] *n* Temperament *nt*; *(disposition)* Veranlagung *f*. **he has an artistic ~** er ist eine Künstlernatur.

temperamental [ˌtempərə'mentl] *adj* temperamentvoll, launenhaft *(pej)*; *car* launisch *(hum)*.

temperance ['tempərəns] *n* **(a)** *(moderation)* Mäßigung *f*; *(in speech etc also)* Zurückhaltung *f*; *(in eating, drinking also)* Maßhalten *nt*. **(b)** *(teetotalism)* Enthaltsamkeit *f*.

temperate ['tempərɪt] *adj person, climate* gemäßigt; *(in eating, demands)* maßvoll.

temperature ['temprɪtʃə^r] *n* Temperatur *f*; *(Med: above normal ~ also)* Fieber *nt*. **to take sb's ~** bei jdm Fieber messen; **he has a ~/a slight/high ~** er hat Fieber/erhöhte Temperatur/hohes Fieber; **he has a ~ of 39°C** er hat 39° Fieber.

tempest ['tempɪst] *n (liter)* Sturm *m (also fig)*.

tempestuous [ˌtem'pestjʊəs] *adj (lit liter, fig)* stürmisch; *speech* leidenschaftlich.

template ['templɪt] *n* Schablone *f*.

temple^1 ['templ] *n (Rel)* Tempel *m*.

temple^2 *n (Anat)* Schläfe *f*.

tempo ['tempəʊ] *n (Mus, fig)* Tempo *nt*.

temporal ['tempərəl] *adj* **(a)** zeitlich; *(Gram)* Zeit-, temporal. **(b)** *(Rel)* weltlich.

temporarily [ˌtempə'rɛərɪlɪ] *adv* vorübergehend.

temporary ['tempərərɪ] *adj* vorübergehend; *job also* befristet; *arrangement also, road surface* provisorisch; *powers also* befristet. **he's looking for ~ work** er sucht einen Job *(col)*.

tempt [tempt] *vt* in Versuchung führen; *(successfully)* verführen; *(Rel also)* versuchen. **to ~ sb to do** *or* **into doing sth** jdn dazu verleiten, etw zu tun; **don't ~ me** bring mich nicht in Versuchung!; **to ~ fate** *(fig)* sein Schicksal herausfordern; *(in words)* den Teufel an die Wand malen; **I'm ~ed** es reizt mich.

temptation [temp'teɪʃən] *n* Versuchung *(also Rel)*, Verlockung *f.* **to yield to ~** der Versuchung erliegen.

tempting ['temptɪŋ] *adj* verlockend, verführerisch.

ten [ten] **1** *adj* zehn. **~ to one he won't come** (ich wette) zehn zu eins, daß er nicht kommt; **nine out of ~ people would agree with you** neun von zehn Leuten würden Ihnen zustimmen. **2** *n* Zehn *f.* **~s** *(Math)* Zehner *pl*; *see* **six.**

tenable ['tenəbl] *adj (Mil) position* haltbar; *(fig) opinion, theory also* vertretbar.

tenacious [tɪ'neɪʃəs] *adj* zäh; *character, person also* beharrlich.

tenacity [tɪ'næsɪtɪ] *n see adj* Zähigkeit *f*; Beharrlichkeit *f.* **the ~ of his grip** sein eiserner Griff.

tenant ['tenənt] *n* Mieter(in *f*) *m*; *(of farm)* Pächter(in *f*) *m.* **~ farmer** Pächter *m.*

tend[1] [tend] *vt* sich kümmern um; *sheep* hüten; *sick person* pflegen; *machine* bedienen.

tend[2] *vi* **to ~ to be/do sth** *(have habit)* gern etw sein/tun; *(person also)* dazu neigen *or* tendieren, etw zu sein/tun; **the lever ~s to stick** der Hebel bleibt oft hängen; **I ~ to believe him** ich neige dazu, ihm zu glauben; **to ~ towards** *(incline) (person, views etc)* neigen *or* tendieren zu.

tendency ['tendənsɪ] *n* Tendenz *f (geh)*; *(physical predisposition)* Neigung *f.* **to have a ~ to be/do sth** gern etw sein/tun; *(person, style of writing also)* dazu neigen *or* tendieren, etw zu sein/zu tun; **he had an annoying ~ to forget things** er hatte die ärgerliche Angewohnheit, alles zu vergessen.

tendentious [ten'denʃəs] *adj* tendenziös.

tender[1] ['tendə^r] *n (Naut, Rail)* Tender *m.*

tender[2] **1** *vt money, services* (an)bieten; *thanks* aussprechen; *resignation* einreichen. **"please ~ exact fare"** „bitte Fahrgeld abgezählt bereithalten". **2** *vi (Comm)* sich bewerben *(for* um*)*. **3** *n* **(a)** *(Comm)* Angebot *nt.* **to invite ~s for a job** Angebote *pl* für eine Arbeit einholen; **to put in a ~ for sth** ein Angebot für etw einreichen. **(b) legal ~** gesetzliches Zahlungsmittel.

tender[3] *adj* **(a)** *spot, bruise* empfindlich; *skin, plant also* zart; *(fig) subject* heikel. **(b)** *meat* zart. **(c)** *(affectionate) person, look* zärtlich, liebevoll; *memories* lieb. **to bid sb a ~ farewell** liebevoll(en) Abschied von jdm nehmen.

tender-hearted [,tendə'hɑːtɪd] *adj* gutherzig.

tenderly ['tendəlɪ] *adv* zärtlich, liebevoll.

tenderness ['tendənɪs] *n see adj* **(a)** Empfindlichkeit *f*; Zartheit *f.* **(b)** Zartheit *f.* **(c)** Zärtlichkeit *f.*

tendon ['tendən] *n* Sehne *f.*

tendril ['tendrɪl] *n* Ranke *f.*

tenement ['tenɪmənt] *n* Mietshaus *nt.*

tenet ['tenət] *n* Lehrsatz *m*; *(Rel)* Glaubenssatz *m.*

tenner ['tenə^r] *n (col)* Zehner *m (col).*

tennis ['tenɪs] *n* Tennis *nt.*

tennis *in cpds* Tennis-; **~ club** *n* Tennisclub *m*; **~ court** *n* Tennisplatz *m*; **~ elbow** *n (Med)* Tennisarm *m*; **~ racket** *n* Tennisschläger *m.*

tenor ['tenə^r] **1** *n* **(a)** *(voice)* Tenor(stimme *f*) *m*; *(person)* Tenor *m.* **(b)** *(purport)* Tenor *m*; *(of theory)* Tendenz *f*; *(general nature: of life)* Stil *m.* **2** *adj (Mus)* Tenor-.

tenpin bowling [,tenpɪn'bəʊlɪŋ], *(US)* **tenpins** ['tenpɪns] *n* Bowling *nt.*

tense[1] [tens] *n (Gram)* Zeit *f*, Tempus *nt.*

tense[2] **1** *adj (+er) rope, atmosphere* gespannt; *muscles also, person, expression (through stress etc)* angespannt; *(through fear etc)* verkrampft; *voice* nervös; *(thrilling) scene* spannungsgeladen. **2** *vt* anspannen.

tension ['tenʃən] *n* **(a)** *(lit)* Spannung *f*; *(of muscle)* Anspannung *f*; *(Knitting)* Festigkeit *f.* **(b)** *(nervous strain)* Anspannung *f.* **(c)** *(strain: in relationship)* Spannungen *pl.*

tent [tent] *n* Zelt *nt.* **~ peg** *(Brit) or* **stake** *(US)* Zeltpflock, Hering *m.*

tentacle ['tentəkl] *n* Fangarm *m*; *(fig)* Klaue *f.*

tentative ['tentətɪv] *adj (provisional)* vorläufig; *offer* unverbindlich; *(hesitant) player, movement* vorsichtig; *conclusion, suggestion* vorsichtig.

tenterhooks ['tentəhʊks] *npl*: **to be on ~** wie auf glühenden Kohlen sitzen *(col)*; **to keep sb on ~** jdn zappeln lassen.

tenth [tenθ] **1** *adj (in series)* zehnte(r, s). **2** *n (fraction)* Zehntel *nt*; *(in series)* Zehnte(r, s); *see* **sixth.**

tenuous ['tenjʊəs] *adj* **(a)** *(lit) thread etc* dünn, fein. **(b)** *(fig) connection, argument* schwach.

tenure ['tenjʊə^r] *n* **(a)** *(holding of office)* Anstellung *f*; *(period of office)* Amtszeit *f.* **(b)** *(of property)* **during his ~ of the house** während er das Haus innehat/innehatte *(geh).*

tepid ['tepɪd] *adj (lit, fig)* lau(warm).

term [tɜːm] **1** *n* **(a)** *(period of time)* Zeitraum *m*; *(of contract)* Laufzeit *f*; *(limit)* Frist *f.* **~ of government/office** Regierungszeit *f*/Amtszeit *f*; **in the long/short ~** auf lange/kurze Sicht.

(b) *(Sch: three in one year)* Trimester *nt*; *(Univ)* Semester *nt.* **in ~(-time)** während der Schulzeit/des Semesters; **out of ~(-time)** in den Ferien.

(c) *(expression)* Ausdruck *m.* **in plain ~s** in einfachen Worten; **technical ~s** Fachausdrücke *pl*; **a contradiction in ~s** ein Widerspruch in sich.

(d) *(Math, Logic)* Term *m.* **to express one thing in ~s of another** eine Sache mit einer anderen erklären; **in ~s of production we are doing well** was die Produktion betrifft, stehen wir gut da; **in ~s of money/time** finanziell/zeitlich.

(e) ~s *pl (conditions)* Bedingungen *pl*; **~s of reference** *(of committee etc)* Aufgabenbereich *m*; *(of thesis etc)* Themenbereich *m*; **to buy sth on credit/easy ~s** etw auf Kredit/auf Raten kaufen; **the hotel offered reduced ~s in winter** das Hotel bot ermäßigte Winterpreise an; **on what ~s?** zu welchen Bedingungen?; **to come to ~s (with sb)** sich (mit jdm) einigen; **to come to ~s with sth** sich mit etw abfinden.

(f) ~s *pl (relations)* **to be on good/bad ~s with sb** gut/nicht (gut) mit jdm auskommen; **they are not on speaking ~s** sie reden nicht miteinander.

2 *vt* nennen, bezeichnen.

terminal ['tɜːmɪnl] **1** *adj syllable, station* End-; *cancer, patient* unheilbar. **2** *n* **(a)** *(Rail)* Endbahnhof *m*; *(of buses)* Endstation *f*; *(airport ~, container ~)* Terminal *m.* **(b)** *(Elec)* Pol *m.* **(c)** *(Comp)* Terminal *nt or m.*

terminate ['tɜːmɪneɪt] **1** *vt* beenden; *contract, lease etc* lösen; *pregnancy* unterbrechen. **2** *vi* enden; *(contract, lease)* ablaufen.

termination [,tɜːmɪ'neɪʃən] *n* Ende *nt*; *(bringing to an end)* Beendigung *f*; *(expiry)* Ablauf *m*; *(cancellation)* Lösung *f.*

terminology [,tɜːmɪ'nɒlədʒɪ] *n* Terminologie *f.* **technical ~** Fachausdrücke *pl.*

terminus ['tɜːmɪnəs] *n (Rail, Bus)* Endstation *f.*

termite ['tɜːmaɪt] *n* Termite *f.*

tern [tɜːn] *n (Orn)* Seeschwalbe *f.*

terrace ['terəs] *n* Terrasse *f.* **(a) ~s** *pl (Sport)* Ränge *pl.* **(b)** *(row of houses)* Häuserreihe *f.*

terraced ['terəst] *adj* **(a)** *hillside etc* terrassenförmig angelegt. **(b) ~ house** *(Brit)* Reihenhaus *nt.*

terracotta ['terə'kɒtə] *n* Terrakotta *f.*

terra firma ['terə'fɜːmə] *n* **to be on ~ again** wieder festen Boden unter den Füßen haben.

terrain [te'reɪn] *n* Terrain *(esp Mil)*, Gelände *nt*; *(fig)* Boden *m.*

terrestrial [tɪ'restrɪəl] *adj* **(a)** *(of land) plants, animals* Land-, auf dem Land lebend. **(b)** *(of the planet Earth)* irdisch.
terrible ['terəbl] *adj* schrecklich, furchtbar. **he is ~ at golf** er spielt furchtbar schlecht Golf.
terribly ['terəblɪ] *adv (badly, col: very)* schrecklich, furchtbar.
terrier ['terɪəʳ] *n* Terrier *m*.
terrific [tə'rɪfɪk] *adj shame, shock* unheimlich *(col); person, success, idea also* klasse *inv (col); speed, strength* unwahrscheinlich *(col)*.
terrify ['terɪfaɪ] *vt (person)* in Angst versetzen. **to be terrified of sth** vor etw schreckliche Angst haben.
terrifying ['terɪfaɪɪŋ] *adj film* grauenerregend; *thought, sight* entsetzlich; *speed* angsterregend.
territorial [ˌterɪ'tɔːrɪəl] **1** *adj* territorial, Gebiets-. **~ waters** Territorialgewässer *pl*; **T~ Army** *(Brit)* Territorialheer *nt*. **2** *n* **the T~s** *(Brit)* die Heimatschutztruppe.
territory ['terɪtərɪ] *n* Territorium *nt*; *(of animals also)* Revier *nt*; *(Comm: of agent etc)* Bezirk *m*; *(fig)* Revier, Gebiet *nt*.
terror ['terəʳ] *n* **(a)** *no pl (great fear)* panische Angst *(of* vor *+dat)*. **in ~** in panischer Angst. **(b)** *(col) (person)* Teufel *m*; *(child)* Ungeheuer *nt*. **she's a ~ on the roads** *(hum)* sie ist der Schrecken der Landstraße *(hum)*.
terrorism ['terərɪzəm] *n* Terrorismus *m*; *(acts of ~)* Terror *m*. **an act of ~** ein Terrorakt *m*.
terrorist ['terərɪst] **1** *n* Terrorist(in *f*) *m*. **2** *attr* terroristisch.
terrorize ['terəraɪz] *vt* terrorisieren.
terror-stricken ['terəˌstrɪkən] *adj* starr vor Schreck(en).
terse [tɜːs] *adj (+er)* knapp.
tertiary ['tɜːʃərɪ] *adj* tertiär; *colour* Misch-.
Terylene ® ['terəliːn] *n* ≈ Trevira ®, Diolen ® *nt*.
test [test] **1** *n* **(a)** *(Sch)* Klassenarbeit *f*; *(Univ)* Klausur *f*; *(short)* Test *m*; *(intelligence ~ etc)* Test *m*; *(driving ~)* (Fahr)prüfung *f*. **he gave them a vocabulary ~** er ließ eine Vokabelarbeit schreiben; *(orally)* er hat sie Vokabeln abgefragt; **to put sb/sth to the ~** jdn/etw auf die Probe stellen; **to stand the ~** die Probe bestehen; **to stand the ~ of time** die Zeit überdauern. **(b)** *(of vehicle, product etc, chemical ~)* Test *m*; *(check)* Kontrolle *f*; *(on road also)* Testfahrt *f*.
2 *vt* **(a)** *(examine, check)* testen, prüfen; *(Sch) pupil* prüfen; *(orally)* abfragen; *intelligence etc* testen; *(fig)* auf die Probe stellen. **the teacher ~ed them on that chapter** der Lehrer fragte sie das Kapitel ab; **to ~ sb/sth for accuracy** jdn/etw auf Genauigkeit prüfen. **(b)** *(chemically) gold, water, chemical etc* untersuchen. **to ~ sth for sugar** etw auf seinen Zuckergehalt untersuchen.
3 *vi* Tests/einen Test machen; *(chemically also)* untersuchen *(for* auf *+acc)*.
testament ['testəmənt] *n* **(a)** *(old)* Testament *nt*. **(b)** *(Bibl)* **Old/New T~** Altes/Neues Testament.
test: ~ ban *n* Teststopp *m*; **~ ban treaty** *n* Teststoppabkommen *nt*; **~ card** *n (TV)* Testbild *nt*; **~ case** *n* Musterfall *m*; **~ drive** *n* Probefahrt *f*; **~-drive** *vt* probefahren; **~ flight** *n* Testflug *m*.
testicle ['testɪkl] *n* Hoden *m*.
testify ['testɪfaɪ] **1** *vt* **to ~ that ...** *(Jur)* bezeugen, daß ... **2** *vi (Jur)* eine Zeugenaussage machen, aussagen. **to ~ against/in favour of sb** gegen/für jdn aussagen; **to ~ to sth** *(speak for)* etw bezeugen *(also Jur)*; *(be sign of) sincerity etc* von etw zeugen.
testimonial [ˌtestɪ'məʊnɪəl] *n (character recommendation)* Referenz *f*.
testimony ['testɪmənɪ] *n* Aussage *f*.
testiness ['testɪnɪs] *n* Gereiztheit *f*.
testing ['testɪŋ] *adj* hart. **I had a ~ time** es war hart (für mich).
testing ground *n* Testgebiet *nt*; *(fig)* Versuchsfeld *nt*.
test: ~ match *n (Brit)* Testmatch *nt*; **~ paper** *n (Sch)* Klassenarbeit *f*; *(Chem)* Reagenzpapier *nt*; **~ pattern** *n (US)* = **~ card**; **~ pilot** *n* Testpilot *m*; **~ tube** *n* Reagenzglas *nt*; **~-tube baby** *n* Retortenbaby *nt*.
testy ['testɪ] *adj (+er)* gereizt.
tetanus ['tetənəs] *n* Wundstarrkrampf, Tetanus *m*.
tête-à-tête ['teɪtɑː'teɪt] *n* Tête-à-tête *nt*.
tether ['teðəʳ] **1** *n (lit)* Strick *m*; *(chain)* Kette *f*. **to be at the end of one's ~** *(fig col)* am Ende sein *(col)*. **2** *vt (also ~ up) animal* an- *or* festbinden.
Teutonic [tjʊ'tɒnɪk] *adj (Hist, hum)* teutonisch.
text [tekst] *n* Text *m*; *(of document also)* Wortlaut *m*.
textbook ['tekstbʊk] *n* Lehrbuch *nt*. **~ case** Paradefall *m*.
textile ['tekstaɪl] **1** *adj* Textil-, textil. **2** *n* Stoff *m*. **~s** Textilien *pl*.
textual ['tekstjʊəl] *adj* Text-.
texture ['tekstʃəʳ] *n* Beschaffenheit *f*; *(of food)* Substanz, Textur *f*; *(of material, paper)* Textur *f*; *(of minerals also, fig: of music, poetry etc)* Gestalt *f*.
textured ['tekstʃəd] *adj* strukturiert, Struktur-.
Thai [taɪ] **1** *adj* thailändisch. **2** *n* **(a)** Thailänder(in *f*) *m*, Thai *mf*. **(b)** *(language)* Thai *nt*.
Thailand ['taɪlænd] *n* Thailand *nt*.
Thames [temz] *n* Themse *f*.
than [ðæn, *weak form* ðən] *conj* als. **I'd rather do anything ~ that** das wäre das letzte, was ich tun wollte; **no sooner had I sat down ~ he began to talk** kaum hatte ich mich hingesetzt, als er auch schon anfing zu reden; **who better to help us ~ he?** wer könnte uns besser helfen als er?
thank [θæŋk] *vt* danken *(+dat)*, sich bedanken bei. **I don't know how to ~ you** ich weiß nicht, wie ich Ihnen danken soll; **I'll ~ you to mind your own business** ich wäre Ihnen dankbar, wenn Sie sich nicht einmischen würden; **he has his brother/he only has himself to ~ for this** das hat er seinem Bruder zu verdanken/sich selbst zuzuschreiben; **~ you** danke (schön); **~ you very much** vielen Dank; **no ~ you/yes, ~ you** nein, danke/ja, bitte *or* danke; **~ you for the present** vielen Dank für Ihr Geschenk; **~ you for nothing** *(iro)* ich danke (bestens)!; **~ goodness** *or* **God** *(col)* Gott sei Dank! *(col)*.
thankful ['θæŋkfʊl] *adj* dankbar *(to sb* jdm*)*. **I'm only ~ that it didn't happen** ich bin bloß froh, daß es nicht passiert ist.
thankfully ['θæŋkfəlɪ] *adv* dankbar, voller Dankbarkeit. **~, no real harm has been done** zum Glück ist kein wirklicher Schaden entstanden.
thankless ['θæŋklɪs] *adj* undankbar. **a ~ task** eine undankbare Aufgabe.
thanks [θæŋks] **1** *npl* **(a)** Dank *m*. **to accept sth with ~** etw dankend annehmen; **and that's all the ~ I get** und das ist jetzt der Dank dafür. **(b) ~ to** wegen *(+gen)*; *(with positive cause also)* dank *(+gen)*; **it's all ~ to you that we're so late** bloß deinetwegen kommen wir so spät; **it was no ~ to him that ...** ich hatte/wir hatten *etc* es nicht ihm zu verdanken, daß ... **2** *interj (col)* danke *(for* für*)*. **many ~** vielen Dank; **~ a lot** *or* **a million** vielen *or* tausend Dank; *(iro)* (na,) vielen Dank *(col)*.
thanksgiving ['θæŋksˌgɪvɪŋ] *n* **(a)** Danksagung *f*. **(b)** *(US)* **T~ (Day)** Thanksgiving Day *m*.
that[1] [ðæt, *weak form* ðət] **1** *dem pron, pl* **those (a)** das. **what is ~?** was ist das?; **who is ~?** wer ist das?; **who is ~ speaking?** wer spricht da?; *(on phone)* wer ist am Apparat?; **~'s what they've been told** das hat man ihnen gesagt; **she's not as stupid as all ~** so dumm ist sie nun auch (wieder) nicht; **I didn't think she'd get/be as angry as ~** ich hätte nicht gedacht, daß sie sich so ärgern würde; **... and all ~** ... und so *(col)*; **like ~** so; **with weather like ~ ...** bei so einem Wetter ...; **~ is (to say)** das heißt; **oh well, ~'s ~** nun ja, damit ist

der Fall erledigt; **you can't go and ~'s ~** du darfst nicht gehen, und damit hat sich's; **~'s it!** das ist es!; *(the right way)* richtig!; *(finished)* so, das wär's!; *(the last straw)* jetzt reicht's; **after/below ~** danach/darunter; **you can get it in any supermarket and quite cheaply at ~** man kann es in jedem Supermarkt bekommen, und zwar ganz billig; **with ~ she got up and left** damit stand sie auf und ging.

(b) *(opposed to "this" and "these")* das (da), jenes *(geh)*. **I prefer this to ~** dies ist mir lieber als das (da); **~'s the one I like, not this one** das (dort) mag ich, nicht dies (hier).

2 *dem adj, pl* **those (a)** der/die/das, jene(r, s) *(old, liter)*. **what was ~ noise?** was war das für ein Geräusch?; **~ poor girl!** das arme Mädchen!; **I like ~ one** ich mag das da; **I'd like ~ one, not this one** ich möchte das da, nicht dies hier; **she was rushing this way and ~** sie rannte hierhin und dorthin; **what about ~ plan of yours now?** was ist denn nun mit Ihrem Plan?

3 *dem adv (col)* so. **he was at least ~ much taller than me** er war mindestens soviel größer als ich; **it's not ~ cold** *so* kalt ist es auch wieder nicht; **he was ~ angry** er hat sich *derart*(ig) geärgert.

that[2] *rel pron* **(a)** der/die/das; die. **all/nothing/everything** *etc* **~ ...** alles/nichts/alles *etc*, was ...; **the best** *etc* **~ ...** das Beste *etc*, das *or* was ...; **fool ~ I am** ich Idiot; **the girl ~ I told you about** das Mädchen, von dem ich Ihnen erzählt habe. **(b)** *(with expressions of time)* **the minute ~ he came the phone rang** genau in dem Augenblick, als er kam, klingelte das Telefon; **the day ~ ...** an dem Tag, als ...

that[3] *conj* daß. **~ he should behave like this is quite incredible** daß er sich so benehmen kann, ist kaum zu glauben; **he said ~ it was wrong** er sagte, es sei *or* wäre *(col)* falsch, er sagte, daß es falsch sei *or* wäre *(col)*; **not ~ I want to do it** nicht (etwa), daß ich das tun wollte.

thatch [θætʃ] **1** *n (roof)* Strohdach *nt*. **2** *vt roof* mit Stroh decken.

thatched [θætʃt] *adj roof* Stroh-; *cottage* mit Strohdach.

thaw [θɔː] **1** *vt* auftauen (lassen); *ice, snow also* tauen lassen; *(make warm) person, hands* aufwärmen; *(fig) relations* entspannen. **2** *vi (lit, fig)* auftauen; *(ice, snow)* tauen. **it is ~ing** es taut. **3** *n (lit, fig)* Tauwetter *nt*. **before the ~** bevor das Tauwetter einsetzt.

♦ **thaw out 1** *vi (lit, fig)* auftauen. **2** *vt sep (lit) frozen food etc* auftauen (lassen); *person, hands* aufwärmen; *(fig) person* aus der Reserve locken.

the [ðə, *before vowels, stressed* ðiː] **1** *def art* **(a)** der/die/das. **in ~ room** im *or* in dem Zimmer; **he went up on ~ stage** er ging aufs *or* auf das Podium; **to play ~ piano** Klavier spielen; **all ~ windows** alle Fenster; **have you invited ~ Browns?** haben Sie die Browns *or* die Familie Brown eingeladen?; **in ~ 20s** in den zwanziger Jahren; **Henry ~ Eighth** Heinrich der Achte.

(b) *(with adj used as n)* das; die; *(with comp or superl)* der/die/das. **~ Good** das Gute; **~ poor** die Armen *pl*; **translated from ~ German** aus dem Deutschen übersetzt.

(c) *(distributive use)* **twenty pence ~ pound** zwanzig Pence das *or* pro Pfund; **paid by ~ hour** stundenweise *or* pro Stunde bezahlt.

2 *adv* **~ bigger ~ better** je größer, desto besser.

theatre, (US) theater ['θɪətə^r] *n* **(a)** Theater *nt*; *(esp in names, ~ company also)* Bühne *f*. **to go to the ~** ins Theater gehen; **what's on at the ~?** was wird im Theater gespielt? **(b)** *(Brit: operating ~)* Operationssaal *m*. **(c)** *(scene of events)* Schauplatz *m*. **~ of war** Kriegsschauplatz *m*.

theatre: ~ company *n* Theaterensemble *nt*; *(touring)* Schauspieltruppe *f*; **~goer** *n* Theaterbesucher(in *f*) *m*.

theatrical [θɪ'ætrɪkəl] *adj* Theater-; *company also* Schauspiel-; *experience also* schauspielerisch; *(pej) behaviour etc* theatralisch.

thee [ðiː] *pron (old)* Dich; Dir.

theft [θeft] *n* Diebstahl *m*.

their [ðɛə^r] *poss adj* **(a)** ihr. **(b)** *(his or her)* seine(r, s). **everyone knows ~ rights nowadays** jeder kennt heutzutage seine Rechte.

theirs [ðɛəz] *poss pron* ihre(r, s).

them [ðem, *weak form* ðəm] *pers pron pl* *(dir obj, with prep +acc)* sie; *(indir obj, with prep +dat)* ihnen. **both/neither of ~ saw me** beide haben/keiner von beiden hat mich gesehen; **give me a few of ~** geben Sie mir ein paar davon; **none of ~** keine(r, s) (von ihnen); **it's ~** sie sind's; **it's ~ who did it** *sie* haben es gemacht.

theme [θiːm] *n* **(a)** *(subject)* Thema *nt*. **(b)** *(US Sch: essay)* Aufsatz *m*. **(c)** *(Mus)* Thema *nt*; *(Film, TV also)* Musik *f (from* aus).

theme music, theme tune *n (Film)* Titelmusik *f*; *(TV)* Erkennungsmelodie *f*.

themselves [ðəm'selvz] *pers pron pl* **(a)** *(reflexive)* sich. **(b)** *(emph)* selbst. **the figures ~** die Zahlen selbst *or* an sich; *see* **myself**.

then [ðen] **1** *adv* **(a)** *(next)* dann; *(at this particular time)* da; *(in those days also)* damals. **and ~ what happened?** und was geschah dann?; **it was ~ 8 o'clock** da war es 8 Uhr; **I was/will be on holiday ~** ich war da (gerade) in Urlaub/werde da in Urlaub sein; **he did it there and ~** er hat es auf der Stelle getan.

(b) *(after prep)* **from ~ on(wards)** von da an; **before ~** vorher, zuvor; **but they had gone by ~** aber da waren sie schon weg; **we'll be ready by ~** bis dahin sind wir fertig; **since ~** seitdem; **between now and ~** bis dahin; **(up) until ~ I had never tried it** bis dahin hatte ich es nie versucht.

(c) *(in that case)* dann. **what are you going to do, ~?** was wollen Sie dann tun?; **all right, ~** also *or* dann meinetwegen; **so it's true ~** dann ist es (also) wahr.

(d) *(furthermore, and also)* dann, außerdem. **(and) ~ there's my aunt** und dann ist da noch meine Tante; **but ~ ...** aber ... auch; **but ~ again he is my friend** aber andererseits ist er mein Freund.

2 *adj attr* **the ~ Prime Minister** der damalige Premierminister.

theologian [θɪə'ləʊdʒɪən] *n* Theologe *m*, Theologin *f*.

theological [θɪə'lɒdʒɪkəl] *adj* theologisch. **~ college** Priesterseminar *nt*.

theology [θɪ'ɒlədʒɪ] *n* Theologie *f*.

theorem ['θɪərəm] *n (also Math)* Satz *m*.

theoretic(al) [θɪə'retɪk(əl)] *adj* theoretisch.

theorize ['θɪəraɪz] *vi* theoretisieren.

theory ['θɪərɪ] *n* Theorie *f*. **in ~** theoretisch.

therapeutic(al) [ˌθerə'pjuːtɪk(əl)] *adj* therapeutisch. **to be ~** therapeutisch wirken.

therapist ['θerəpɪst] *n* Therapeut(in *f*) *m*.

therapy ['θerəpɪ] *n* Therapie *f*.

there [ðɛə^r] **1** *adv* **(a)** dort, da; *(with movement)* dorthin, dahin. **it's over/in ~** es liegt da drüben/drin; **put it under/in ~** stellen Sie es da drunter/hinein; **~ and back** hin und zurück; **so ~ we were** da waren wir nun also.

(b) *(fig: on this point)* da. **~ you are wrong** da irren Sie sich.

(c) *(in phrases)* **~ is/are** es *or* da ist/sind; *(~ exists/exist also)* es gibt; **~ is a mouse in the room** es ist eine Maus im Zimmer; **~ was once a castle here** hier war *or* stand einmal eine Burg; **is ~ any wine left? — well, ~ was** ist noch Wein da? — gerade war noch welcher da; **how many mistakes were ~?** wie viele Fehler waren es?; **~ comes a time when ...** es kommt eine Zeit, wo ...;

~ **being no alternative solution** da es keine andere Lösung gibt/gab; ~ **you go again** *(col)* jetzt geht's schon wieder los; ~ **you are** *(giving sb sth)* hier(, bitte)!; *(on finding sb)* da sind Sie ja!; **you press the switch and** ~ **you are!** Sie brauchen nur den Schalter zu drücken, das ist alles.

2 *interj* ~! ~! na, na!; **stop crying now,** ~**'s a good boy** hör auf zu weinen, na komm.

thereabouts [ˌðɛərəˈbaʊts] *adv* **(a)** *(place)* dort in der Nähe, dort irgendwo. **(b) five pounds/fifteen or** ~ so um die fünf Pfund/fünfzehn (herum).

thereafter [ˌðɛərˈɑːftəʳ] *adv (form)* danach, darauf *(geh)*.

thereby [ˌðɛəˈbaɪ] *adv* dadurch, damit.

therefore [ˈðɛəfɔːʳ] *adv* deshalb, daher; *(as logical consequence)* also.

there's [ðɛəz] = **there is; there has.**

thereupon [ˌðɛərəˈpɒn] *adv* **(a)** *(at that point)* darauf(hin). **(b)** *(form: on that subject)* darüber.

thermal [ˈθɛːməl] *adj* **(a)** *(Phys) capacity, unit* Wärme-; *reactor* thermisch. **(b)** ~ **springs** Thermalquellen *pl*.

thermo [ˌθɜːməʊ-]: ~**dynamic** *adj* thermodynamisch; ~**dynamics** *npl* Thermodynamik *f*.

thermometer [θəˈmɒmɪtəʳ] *n* Thermometer *nt*.

thermos ® [ˈθɜːməs] *n (also* ~ **flask** *or* **bottle** *US)* Thermosflasche *f*.

thermostat [ˈθɜːməstæt] *n* Thermostat *m*.

thesaurus [θɪˈsɔːrəs] *n* Thesaurus *m*.

these [ðiːz] *adj, pron* diese; *see* **this.**

thesis [ˈθiːsɪs] *n, pl* **theses** [ˈθiːsiːz] **(a)** *(argument)* These *f*. **(b)** *(Univ) (for PhD)* Dissertation, Doktorarbeit *(col) f*; *(for diploma)* Diplomarbeit *f*.

they [ðeɪ] *pers pron pl* **(a)** sie. ~ **are very good people** es sind sehr gute Leute; **it is** ~ *(form)* sie sind es; ~ **who** wer *(+sing vb)*. **(b)** *(people in general)* ~ **say that ...** man sagt, daß ...; ~ **are going to build a new road** man will *or* sie wollen eine neue Straße bauen. **(c)** *(he or she)* **if anyone reads this,** ~ **will notice ...** wenn jemand das liest, wird er bemerken ...

they'd [ðeɪd] = **they had; they would.**

they'll [ðeɪl] = **they will.**

they're [ðɛəʳ] = **they are.**

they've [ðeɪv] = **they have.**

thick [θɪk] **1** *adj* **(a)** *(+er)* dick; *wall, legs also* stark; *hair, fog, smoke also, forest, hedge, beard* dicht; *liquid, sauce etc* dick(flüssig); *darkness* tief; *crowd* dicht(gedrängt); *air* schlecht. **a wall three feet** ~ eine drei Fuß dicke *or* starke Wand; **the shelves were** ~ **with dust** auf den Regalen lag dick der Staub; **the hedgerows were** ~ **with flowers** die Hecken strotzten von wilden Blumen; **the air was** ~ **with fumes/smoke** die Luft war voller Abgase/Rauch. **(b)** *(col: stupid) person* dumm, doof *(col)*. **(c)** *(col: intimate)* **they are very** ~ sie sind dicke Freunde *(col)*. **(d)** *(col: much)* **that's a bit** ~! das ist ein starkes Stück *(col)*.

2 *n* **in the** ~ **of the crowd/it** mitten in der Menge/mittendrin; **to stick together through** ~ **and thin** zusammen durch dick und dünn gehen.

3 *adv (+er) spread, lie, cut* dick; *grow* dicht. **the snow lay** ~ es lag eine dichte Schneedecke; **offers of help poured in** ~ **and fast** es kam eine Flut von Hilfsangeboten; **to lay it on** ~ *(col)* (zu) dick auftragen *(col)*.

thicken [ˈθɪkən] **1** *vt sauce etc* eindicken. **2** *vi* **(a)** dicker werden; *(fog, hair, crowd, forest)* dichter werden; *(darkness)* sich verdichten; *(sauce)* dick werden. **(b)** *(fig: plot, mystery)* immer undurchsichtiger werden. **aha, the plot** ~**s!** aha, jetzt wird's interessant!

thicket [ˈθɪkɪt] *n* Dickicht *nt*.

thickly [ˈθɪklɪ] *adv spread, cut* dick; *wooded* dicht. **snow was falling** ~ dichter Schnee fiel.

thickness [ˈθɪknɪs] *n* **(a)** *see adj (a)* Dicke *f*; Stärke *f*; Dichte *f*; Dickflüssigkeit *f*. **(b)** *(layer)* Lage, Schicht *f*.

thick: ~**-set** *adj* gedrungen; ~**-skinned** *adj (fig)* dickfellig.

thief [θiːf] *n, pl* **thieves** [θiːvz] Dieb(in*f*) *m*. **to be as thick as thieves** dicke Freunde sein *(col)*.

thieve [θiːv] *vti* stehlen.

thieving [ˈθiːvɪŋ] **1** *adj* diebisch. **keep your** ~ **hands off my cigarettes** laß die Finger weg von meinen Zigaretten *(col)*. **2** *n* Diebstähle *pl*.

thigh [θaɪ] *n* (Ober)schenkel *m*.

thimble [ˈθɪmbl] *n* Fingerhut *m*.

thin [θɪn] **1** *adj (+er)* **(a)** dünn; *vegetation* gering, spärlich; *population, crowd* klein; *fog* leicht; *column* schmal. **his hair is getting** ~ sein Haar lichtet sich; **to be** ~ **on the ground** *(fig)* dünn gesät sein; **to vanish into** ~ **air** *(fig)* sich in Luft auflösen. **(b)** *(fig: weak, poor) voice, smile, disguise, plot* schwach; *excuse also* fadenscheinig. **2** *adv (+er) spread, cut, lie* dünn. **3** *vt paint, sauce* verdünnen; *trees* lichten; *blood* dünner werden lassen. **4** *vi (fog, crowd)* sich lichten; *(hair also)* schütter werden.

♦ **thin out 1** *vi (audience, crowd)* sich lichten. **the houses started** ~**ning** ~ die Häuser wurden immer spärlicher. **2** *vt sep hair, seedlings* ausdünnen; *forest* lichten; *population* verkleinern.

thine [ðaɪn] *(old)* **1** *poss pron* der/die/das deine. **2** *poss adj* Dein/Deine/Dein.

thing [θɪŋ] *n* **(a)** Ding *nt*. **a** ~ **of beauty/great value** etwas Schönes/etwas sehr Wertvolles; **I don't have a** ~ **to wear** ich habe nichts zum Anziehen; **poor little** ~ das arme (kleine) Ding!; **you poor** ~! du Arme(r)!

(b) *(clothes, equipment, belongings)* ~**s** *pl* Sachen *pl*; **have you got your swimming** ~**s?** hast du dein Badezeug dabei?; **they washed up the breakfast** ~**s** sie spülten das Frühstücksgeschirr.

(c) *(non material: affair, subject)* Sache *f*. **the odd/best** ~ **about it is ...** das Seltsame/Beste daran ist, ...; **it's a good** ~ **I came** nur gut, daß ich gekommen bin; **he's on to a good** ~ *(col)* er hat da was Gutes aufgetan *(col)*; **what a (silly)** ~ **to do** wie kann man nur so was (Dummes) tun!; **there is one/another** ~ **I want to ask you** eines/und noch etwas möchte ich Sie fragen; **the** ~**s you do/say!** was du so machst/sagst!; **I must be hearing/seeing** ~**s!** ich glaube, ich höre/sehe nicht richtig; **all the** ~**s I meant to do** alles, was ich tun wollte; **to expect great** ~**s of sb/sth** Großes *or* große Dinge von jdm/etw erwarten; **I must think** ~**s over** ich muß mir die Sache überlegen; ~**s are going from bad to worse** es wird immer schlimmer; **as** ~**s stand at the moment ...** so wie die Dinge im Moment liegen; **how are** ~**s with you?** wie geht's (bei) Ihnen?; **to talk of one** ~ **and another** von diesem und jenem reden; **for one** ~ **it doesn't make sense** erst einmal ergibt das überhaupt keinen Sinn; **to tell sb a** ~ **or two** jdm einiges erzählen; **he knows a** ~ **or two** er hat etwas auf dem Kasten *(col)*; **it's just one of those** ~**s** so was kommt eben vor *(col)*.

(d) *(what is suitable, best)* **that's just the** ~ **for me** das ist genau das richtige für mich; **that's not the** ~ **to do** so was tut man nicht; **the latest** ~ **in ties** der letzte Schrei in der Krawattenmode; **that would be the honourable** ~ **to do** es wäre nur anständig, das zu tun; **I'll do that first** ~ **in the morning** ich werde das gleich morgen früh tun; **I'll do it first** ~ ich werde das als erstes tun; **last** ~ **at night** vor dem Schlafengehen; **the** ~ **is we haven't got enough money** die Sache ist die, wir haben nicht genug Geld; **to do one's own** ~ *(col)* tun, was man will; **she's got this** ~ **about Sartre** *(col) (can't stand)* sie kann Sartre einfach nicht ausstehen; *(is fascinated by)* sie hat einen richtigen Sartrefimmel *(col)*; **she's got a ~ about spiders** *(col)* bei Spinnen dreht sie durch *(col)*.

thingummybob ['θɪŋəmɪ,bɒb], **thingamajig** ['θɪŋəmɪ,dʒɪg], **thingummy** ['θɪŋəmɪ] *n* Dings, Dingsbums, Dingsda *nt or (for people) mf (all col)*.

think [θɪŋk] *(vb: pret, ptp* **thought***)* **1** *vi* denken. **to ~ to oneself** sich *(dat)* denken; **~ before you speak/act** denk nach, bevor du sprichst/handelst; **to act without ~ing** unüberlegt handeln; **~ again!** denk noch mal nach; **well, you'd better ~ again!** das hast du dir (wohl) gedacht!; **it makes you ~** es macht einen nachdenklich; **I need time to ~** ich brauche Zeit zum Nachdenken; **now let me ~** laß (mich) mal überlegen; **it's a good idea, don't you ~?** es ist eine gute Idee, findest du nicht auch?; **just ~** stellen Sie sich *(dat)* bloß mal vor; **listen, I've been ~ing, ...** hör mal, ich habe mir überlegt, ...

2 *vt* **(a)** denken; *(be of opinion also)* glauben, meinen. **I ~ it's too late** ich glaube, es ist zu spät; **I ~ I can do it** ich denke, daß ich es schaffen kann; **well, I *think* it was there!** nun, ich glaube zumindest, daß es da war!; **and what do you ~? asked the interviewer** und was meinen Sie? fragte der Interviewer; **I ~ you'd better go/accept** ich denke, Sie gehen jetzt besser/Sie stimmen lieber zu; **I ~ so** ich denke *or* glaube (schon); **I don't ~ so** ich denke *or* glaube nicht; **I should ~ so/not!** das will ich (aber) auch gemeint haben/das will ich auch nicht hoffen; **I hardly ~ that/~ it likely that ...** ich glaube kaum, daß .../ich halte es nicht für wahrscheinlich, daß ...; **I wouldn't have thought you would do such a thing** ich hätte nie geglaubt, daß Sie so etwas tun würden; **I ~ I'll go for a walk** ich glaube, ich mache einen Spaziergang; **you must ~ me very rude** Sie müssen mich für sehr unhöflich halten; **he ~s he's intelligent, he ~s himself intelligent** er hält sich für intelligent; **they are thought to be rich** man hält sie für reich.

(b) *(imagine)* sich *(dat)* denken, sich *(dat)* vorstellen. **I don't know what to ~** ich weiß nicht, was ich davon halten soll; **that's what you ~!** denkste! *(col)*; **that's what he ~s** hat der eine Ahnung! *(col)*; **who do you ~ you are!** wofür hältst du dich eigentlich?; **anyone would ~ he was dying** man könnte beinahe glauben, er läge im Sterben; **who would have thought it?** wer hätte das gedacht?; **to ~ that she's only ten!** wenn man sich *(dat)* vorstellt, daß sie erst zehn ist; **to ~ how to do sth** sich *(dat)* überlegen, wie man etw macht; **I never thought to ask you** ich habe gar nicht daran gedacht, Sie zu fragen; **I thought as much/I thought so** das habe ich mir schon gedacht.

(c) *(imagine)* sich *(dat)* vorstellen, bedenken. **~ ~ the cost of all that!** denk dir bloß, was das alles kostet.

(d) *(entertain possibility of)* **she'd never ~ ~ getting married** sie denkt gar nicht daran zu heiraten; **he'd never ~ ~ such a thing** so etwas würde ihm nicht im Traum einfallen.

(e) *(devise, suggest) solution, idea, scheme* sich *(dat)* ausdenken. **who thought ~ that idea/plan?** wer ist auf diese Idee gekommen/wer hat sich diesen Plan ausgedacht?

(f) *(have opinion of)* halten von. **what do you ~ ~ it/him?** was halten Sie davon/von ihm?; **to ~ highly ~ sb/sth** viel von jdm/etw halten; **I told him what I thought ~ him** ich habe ihm gründlich die *or* meine Meinung gesagt.

3 *n* **have a ~ about it** denken Sie mal darüber nach.

♦**think about** *vi +prep obj* **(a)** *(reflect on) idea, suggestion* nachdenken über *(+acc)*. **OK, I'll ~ ~ it** okay, ich überlege es mir; **what are you ~ing ~?** woran denken Sie gerade?; **it's worth ~ing ~** das ist überlegenswert, das wäre zu überlegen; **to ~ twice ~ sth** sich *(dat)* etw zweimal überlegen; **that'll give him something to ~ ~** das wird ihm zu denken geben. **(b) we're ~ing ~ a holiday in Spain** wir denken daran, in Spanien Urlaub zu machen. **(c) = think of (a, f).**

♦**think ahead** *vi* vorausdenken; *(anticipate: driver etc)* Voraussicht walten lassen.

♦**think of** *vi +prep obj* **(a)** *(consider)* denken an *(+acc)*. **he has his family to ~ ~** er muß an seine Familie denken; **to ~ ~ sb's feelings** auf jds Gefühle *(acc)* Rücksicht nehmen; **he ~s ~ nobody but himself** er denkt bloß an sich.

(b) *(remember)* denken an *(+acc)*. **will you ~ ~ me sometimes?** wirst du manchmal an mich denken?; **I can't ~ ~ her name** ich kann mich nicht an ihren Namen erinnern.

♦**think out** *vt sep plan* durchdenken; *(come up with) solution* sich *(dat)* ausdenken.

♦**think over** *vt sep offer* sich *(dat)* überlegen.

♦**think through** *vt sep* (gründlich) durchdenken.

♦**think up** *vt sep* sich *(dat)* ausdenken. **who thought ~ that idea?** wer ist auf die Idee gekommen?

thinkable ['θɪŋkəbl] *adj* denkbar.

thinker ['θɪŋkə^r] *n* Denker(in *f*) *m*.

thinking ['θɪŋkɪŋ] **1** *adj* denkend. **all ~ men will agree with me** alle vernünftigen Menschen werden mit mir übereinstimmen. **2** *n* **to my way of ~** meiner Meinung nach; **this calls for some quick ~** hier muß eine schnelle Lösung gefunden werden.

thinly ['θɪnlɪ] *adv* **(a)** dünn; *wooded* spärlich. **(b)** *(fig) disguised* kaum, dürftig; *smile* schwach.

thin-skinned ['θɪnskɪnd] *adj (fig)* dünnhäutig.

third [θɜːd] **1** *adj* dritte(r,s). **she was** *or* **came ~ in her class/in the race** sie war die Drittbeste in der Klasse/sie belegte den dritten Platz beim Rennen; **~ time lucky** beim dritten Anlauf gelingt's! **2** *n* **(a)** *(of series)* Dritte(r,s); *(fraction)* Drittel *nt*. **(b)** *(Mus)* Terz *f*. **(c)** *(Aut: ~ gear)* dritter Gang; *see* **sixth.**

third: ~-class 1 *adv* dritter Klasse; **2** *adj (lit)* dritter Klasse; *(fig)* drittklassig; **~-degree burns** *npl (Med)* Verbrennungen *pl* dritten Grades.

thirdly ['θɜːdlɪ] *adv* drittens.

third: ~ party *n* Dritte(r) *m*, dritte Person; **~-party 1** *adj attr* Haftpflicht-; **2** *adv* **to be insured ~-party** haftpflichtversichert sein; **~ person** *adj* in der dritten Person; **~-rate** *adj* drittklassig; **T~ World 1** *n* Dritte Welt; **2** *attr* der Dritten Welt.

thirst [θɜːst] **1** *n* Durst *m*. **~ for knowledge/revenge/adventure/love** Wissensdurst *m*/Rachsucht *f*/Abenteuerlust *f*/Liebeshunger *m*; **to die of ~** verdursten. **2** *vi (fig)* **to ~ for revenge** *etc* nach Rache *etc* dürsten.

thirsty ['θɜːstɪ] *adj (+er)* durstig. **to be ~** Durst haben; **~ for praise/love** begierig auf Lob/nach Liebe; **it's ~ work** diese Arbeit macht durstig.

thirteen ['θɜː'tiːn] **1** *adj* dreizehn. **2** *n* Dreizehn *f*.

thirteenth ['θɜː'tiːnθ] *adj* dreizehnte(r, s); *see* **sixteenth.**

thirtieth ['θɜːtɪɪθ] *adj* dreißigste(r, s); *see* **sixtieth.**

thirty ['θɜːtɪ] **1** *adj* dreißig. **2** *n* Dreißig *f*; *see* **sixty.**

this [ðɪs] **1** *dem pron, pl* **these** dies, das. **what is ~?** was ist das (hier)?; **who is ~?** wer ist das?; **these are my children** das sind meine Kinder; **~ is where I live** hier wohne ich; **do you like ~?** gefällt dir das?; **I prefer ~** ich mag dies(es) lieber; **~ is to certify that ...** hiermit wird bestätigt, daß ...; **under/in front of** *etc* **~** darunter/davor *etc*; **what's all ~?** was soll das?; **we were talking of ~ and that** wir haben über dies und das geredet; **~, that and the other** alles mögliche; **will you take ~ or that?** nehmen Sie dieses hier oder das da?; **it was like ~** es war so;

~ **is Mary (speaking)** hier (ist) Mary.

2 *dem adj, pl* **these** diese(r, s). ~ **week/month/year** diese Woche/diesen Monat/dieses Jahr; ~ **evening** heute abend; ~ **time last week** letzte Woche um diese Zeit; ~ **time** diesmal, dieses Mal; **these days** heutzutage.

3 *dem adv* so. **it was** ~ **long** es war so lang; ~ **far** *(time)* bis jetzt; *(place)* so weit; ~ **much is certain** soviel ist sicher.

thistle ['θɪsl] *n* Distel *f.*

thong [θɒŋ] *n (of whip)* Peitschenschnur *f; (fastening)* Lederriemen *m.*

thorax ['θɔːræks] *n* Brustkorb *m.*

thorn [θɔːn] *n* Dorn *m; (shrub)* Dornenstrauch *m.* **to be a** ~ **in sb's flesh** *or* **side** *(fig)* jdm ein Dorn im Auge sein.

thorny ['θɔːnɪ] *adj (+er) (lit)* dornig; *(fig)* haarig.

thorough ['θʌrə] *adj* gründlich; *knowledge also* solide; *rascal* ausgemacht.

thorough: ~**bred 1** *n* reinrassiges Tier; *(horse)* Vollblüter *m;* **2** *adj* reinrassig; *horse* Vollblut-; *dog* Rasse-; ~**fare** *n* Durchgangsstraße *f;* **"no ~fare"** „Durchfahrt verboten"; ~**going** *adj changes* gründlich; *revision* grundlegend; *reform* durchgreifend.

thoroughly ['θʌrəlɪ] *adv* **(a)** gründlich. **(b)** *(extremely)* durch und durch, von Grund auf. ~ **boring** ausgesprochen langweilig; **I'm** ~ **ashamed** ich schäme mich zutiefst.

thoroughness ['θʌrənɪs] *n* Gründlichkeit *f.*

those [ðəʊz] *pl of* **that 1** *dem pron* **whose are** ~? wem gehören diese da?; ~ **are the girls** das (da) *or* dies(es) sind die Mädchen; **above** ~ darüber; ~ **who want to go, may** wer möchte, kann gehen; **one of** ~ **who ...** einer/eine von denjenigen, die ...; **two of** ~ **please** zwei davon bitte; **there are** ~ **who say ...** einige sagen ... **2** *dem adj* diese *or* die (da), jene *(old, liter).* **what are** ~ **men doing?** was machen diese Männer da?; **it was just one of** ~ **days/things** das war wieder so ein Tag/so eine Sache.

thou [ðaʊ] *pers pron (old)* Du.

though [ðəʊ] **1** *conj* **(a)** obwohl. **even** ~ obwohl; ~ **poor she is generous** obwohl sie arm ist, ist sie großzügig; **strange** ~ **it may seem ...** so seltsam es auch scheinen mag ... **(b) as** ~ als ob. **2** *adv* **(a)** *(nevertheless)* doch. **he didn't do it** ~ er hat es aber (doch) nicht gemacht; **nice day — rather windy** ~ schönes Wetter — aber ziemlich windig. **(b)** *(really)* **but will he** ~? tatsächlich?, wirklich?

thought [θɔːt] **1** *pret, ptp of* **think.**

2 *n* **(a)** *no pl* Denken *nt.* **to spend hours in** ~ stundenlang in Gedanken (vertieft) sein; **to be lost in** ~ in Gedanken sein; **modern** ~ das moderne Denken.

(b) *(idea, opinion)* Gedanke *m; (sudden)* Einfall *m.* **he didn't express any** ~**s on the matter** er hat keine Ansichten zu diesem Thema geäußert; **that's a** ~! *(amazing)* man stelle sich das mal vor!; *(problem to be considered)* das ist wahr!; *(good idea)* das ist ein guter Gedanke; **what a** ~! was für eine Vorstellung!; **I've just had a** ~ *(col)* mir ist gerade etwas eingefallen; **on second** ~**s** wenn man sich das noch mal überlegt; **his one** ~ **was ...** sein einziger Gedanke war ...; **it's the** ~ **that counts, not how much you spend** es kommt nur auf die Idee an, nicht auf den Preis; **to collect one's** ~**s** sich sammeln; **the very** ~ **of it** der bloße Gedanke (daran).

(c) *no pl (care, consideration)* Nachdenken *nt.* **to give some** ~ **to sth** sich *(dat)* Gedanken über etw *(acc)* machen; **after much** ~ nach langer Überlegung; **without** ~ **for sb/oneself** ohne an jdn/sich selbst zu denken; **I never gave it a** ~ ich habe mir nie Gedanken darüber gemacht.

thoughtful ['θɔːtfʊl] *adj* **(a)** *(full of thought) expression, person* nachdenklich; *remark, analysis, book* gut durchdacht; *present* gut ausgedacht. **(b)** *(considerate)* rücksichtsvoll; *(attentive, helpful)* aufmerksam. **it was very** ~ **of you to ...** es war sehr aufmerksam von Ihnen, zu ...

thoughtfully ['θɔːtfəlɪ] *adv* **(a)** *say, look* nachdenklich. **(b)** *(with much thought)* mit viel Überlegung. **a** ~ **written book** ein wohldurchdachtes Buch. **(c)** *(considerately)* rücksichtsvoll; *(attentively, helpfully)* aufmerksam.

thoughtless ['θɔːtlɪs] *adj* **(a)** gedankenlos; *(inconsiderate also)* rücksichtslos. **(b)** ~ **of the danger, he leapt** ungeachtet der Gefahr sprang er.

thousand ['θaʊzənd] **1** *adj* tausend. **a** ~**/two** ~ (ein)tausend/zweitausend; **a** ~ **times** tausendmal; **a** ~ **and one/two** tausend(und)eins/tausend(und)zwei. **2** *n* Tausend *nt.* **the** ~**s** *(Math)* die Tausender *pl;* **there were** ~**s of people** es waren Tausende (von Menschen) da; **the year three** ~ das Jahr dreitausend; **people arrived in their** ~**s** die Menschen kamen zu Tausenden.

thousandth ['θaʊzəntθ] **1** *adj* tausendste(r, s). **2** *n (in series)* Tausendste(r, s); *(fraction)* Tausendstel *nt; see* **sixth.**

thrash [θræʃ] **1** *vt* **(a)** *(beat)* verprügeln; *donkey etc* einschlagen auf *(+acc).* **(b)** *(Sport col) opponent* (vernichtend) schlagen. **(c)** *(move wildly) arms* schlagen mit; *legs* strampeln mit. **2** *vi* **to** ~ **about** *or* **around** um sich schlagen; *(in bed)* sich herumwerfen; *(fish)* zappeln.

♦ **thrash out** *vt sep problem* ausdiskutieren.

thrashing ['θræʃɪŋ] *n* **(a)** *(beating)* Prügel, Schläge *pl.* **to give sb a good** ~ jdm eine ordentliche Tracht Prügel verpassen. **(b)** *(Sport col)* komplette Niederlage. **to give sb a** ~ jdn vernichtend schlagen.

thread [θred] **1** *n* **(a)** *(Sew)* Garn *nt; (~ of cotton, wool etc)* Faden *m; (strong ~)* Zwirn *m.* **to hang by a** ~ *(fig)* an einem (seidenen) Faden hängen. **(b)** *(fig: of story)* (roter) Faden. **to follow the** ~ **of an argument/a story** dem Gedankengang einer Argumentation/dem roten Faden (in) einer Geschichte folgen; **he lost the** ~ **of what he was saying** er hat den Faden verloren; **to pick up the** ~**s of a conversation** den Gesprächsfaden wiederaufnehmen. **(c)** *(Tech: of screw)* Gewinde *nt.* **2** *vt* **(a)** *needle* einfädeln; *beads* aufreihen *(on* auf *+acc); necklace* aufziehen. **(b) to** ~ **one's way through the crowd/trees** sich durch die Menge/zwischen den Bäumen hindurchschlängeln.

threadbare ['θredbɛəʳ] *adj* abgewetzt; *clothes also* abgetragen; *carpet also* abgelaufen.

threat [θret] *n* Drohung *f; (danger)* Bedrohung *(to gen),* Gefahr *(to* für*) f.* **is that a** ~? soll das eine Drohung sein?; **to make a** ~ drohen *(against sb* jdm*);* **under** ~ **of sth** unter Androhung von etw.

threaten ['θretn] *vt* **(a)** *person* bedrohen, drohen *(+dat); revenge* androhen. **to** ~ **to do sth** (an)drohen, etw zu tun; **to** ~ **sb with sth** jdm mit etw drohen. **(b)** *(put in danger)* bedrohen, gefährden. **the rain** ~**ed to spoil the harvest** der Regen drohte die Ernte zu zerstören.

threatening ['θretnɪŋ] *adj* drohend; *weather, clouds also* bedrohlich. **a** ~ **letter** ein Drohbrief *m;* ~ **behaviour** Drohungen *pl.*

three [θriː] **1** *adj* drei. **2** *n* Drei *f; see* **six.**

three: ~**-D 1** *n* **to be in** ~**-D** dreidimensional sein; **2** *adj (also* ~**-dimensional***)* dreidimensional; *film also* 3-D- *attr;* ~**fold** *adj, adv* dreifach; ~**-piece suit** *n (man's)* Anzug *m* mit Weste; *(lady's)* dreiteiliges Ensemble; ~**-piece suite** *n* dreiteilige Sitzgarnitur; ~**-ply** *attr wool* dreifach, Dreifach-; *wood* dreischichtig; ~**-point turn** *n (Aut)* Wenden *nt* in drei Zügen; ~**quarters 1** *n* Dreiviertel *nt;* **2** *adv* dreiviertel; ~**some** *n* Trio *nt,* Dreiergruppe *f; (Golf)* Dreier *m;* **in a** ~**some** zu dritt; ~**-wheeler** *n (Aut)* dreirädriges Auto; *(tricycle)* Dreirad *nt.*

thresh [θreʃ] *vti* dreschen.

threshing ['θreʃɪŋ] *n* Dreschen *nt*. ~ **machine** Dreschmaschine *f.*

threshold ['θreʃhəʊld] *n (lit, fig, Psych)* Schwelle *f.* **we are on the ~ of a great discovery** wir stehen unmittelbar an der Schwelle zu einer großen Entdeckung.

threw [θruː] *pret of* **throw.**

thrift [θrɪft] *n* Sparsamkeit *f.*

thrifty ['θrɪftɪ] *adj (+er)* **(a)** *(careful, economical)* sparsam, wirtschaftlich. **(b)** *(US: thriving)* blühend.

thrill [θrɪl] **1** *n* Erregung *f.* **the ~ of her touch** der erregende Reiz ihrer Berührung; **it was quite a ~ for me** es war ein richtiges Erlebnis. **2** *vt person (story, crimes)* mitreißen, fesseln; *(experience)* eine Sensation sein für; *(sb's touch, voice etc)* freudig erzittern lassen; *(sexually)* erregen. **I was ~ed to get your letter** ich habe mich riesig über deinen Brief gefreut.

thriller ['θrɪləʳ] *n* Reißer *m (col); (whodunnit)* Krimi, Thriller *m.*

thrilling ['θrɪlɪŋ] *adj* aufregend; *book, film* spannend; *sensation* überwältigend; *music* mitreißend; *(sexually)* erregend.

thrive [θraɪv] *vi (be in good health: animal, plant)* (gut) gedeihen; *(child also)* sich gut entwickeln; *(do well) (business)* blühen, florieren; *(businessman)* erfolgreich sein.

♦ **thrive on** *vi +prep obj* **the baby ~s ~ milk** mit Milch gedeiht das Baby prächtig; **this plant ~s ~ sun and light** bei Sonne und Licht gedeiht diese Pflanze prächtig; **he ~s ~ hard work** harte Arbeit ist sein Lebenselixier.

thriving ['θraɪvɪŋ] *adj plant* prächtig gedeihend; *person, business* blühend; *child* gut gedeihend; *businessman* erfolgreich.

throat [θrəʊt] *n* Kehle *f.* **to grab sb by the ~** jdn bei der Gurgel packen; **to cut sb's/one's ~** jdm/sich die Kehle durchschneiden; **to cut one's own ~** *(fig)* sich *(dat)* selbst das Wasser abgraben; **to clear one's ~** sich räuspern; **to ram** *or* **force one's ideas down sb's ~** *(col)* jdm seine eigenen Ideen aufzwingen.

throaty ['θrəʊtɪ] *adj (+er)* rauh.

throb [θrɒb] **1** *vi (engine, heart, pulse)* klopfen; *(very strongly)* hämmern; *(drums, gunfire)* dröhnen; *(painfully: wound also)* pochen; *(fig: with life, activity)* pulsieren *(with* vor *+dat,* mit*).* **my head is ~bing** ich habe rasende Kopfschmerzen. **2** *n see vi* Klopfen *nt*; Hämmern *nt;* Pochen *nt.*

throes [θrəʊz] *npl* **in the ~ of death** in Todesqualen *pl*; **to be in its final ~** *(fig)* in den letzten Zügen liegen; **we are in the ~ of moving** wir stecken mitten im Umzug.

thrombosis [θrɒm'bəʊsɪs] *n* Thrombose *f.*

throne [θrəʊn] *n* Thron *m; (Eccl)* Stuhl *m.* **to come to the ~** den Thron besteigen.

throng [θrɒŋ] **1** *n* **a ~ of people** Scharen *pl* von Menschen. **2** *vi* sich drängen. **to ~ around sb/sth** sich um jdn/etw scharen. **3** *vt* **people ~ed the streets** die Menschen drängten sich in den Straßen; **to be ~ed with** wimmeln von.

throttle ['θrɒtl] **1** *vt* **(a)** erdrosseln, erwürgen. **(b)** *(fig) opposition* unterbinden. **2** *n (on engine)* Drossel *f; (Aut etc) (lever)* Gashebel *m*; *(valve)* Drosselklappe *f.* **at full ~** mit Vollgas.

through [θruː] **1** *prep* **(a)** *(place)* durch. **he went right ~ the red lights** er ist bei Rot einfach durchgefahren; **we're ~ that stage now** wir sind jetzt durch dieses Stadium hindurch; **to be halfway ~ a book** ein Buch zur Hälfte durchhaben *(col)*; **that happens halfway ~ the book** das passiert in der Mitte des Buches.

(b) *(time)* **all ~ his life** sein ganzes Leben lang; **he worked ~ the night** er hat die Nacht durchgearbeitet; **he slept ~ the film** er hat den ganzen Film hindurch geschlafen; **all ~ the autumn** den ganzen Herbst über.

(c) *(US)* **Monday ~ Friday** von Montag bis (einschließlich) Freitag.

(d) *(means, agency)* durch. **~ the post** mit der Post; **absent ~ illness** abwesend wegen Krankheit; **~ neglect** durch Nachlässigkeit; **to act ~ fear** aus Angst handeln.

2 *adv (time, place)* durch. **he's a liar ~ and ~** er ist durch und durch verlogen; **to sleep all night ~** die ganze Nacht durchschlafen; **did you stay right ~?** sind Sie bis zum Schluß geblieben?; **to let sb ~** jdn durchlassen; **to be wet ~** durch und durch naß sein; **to read sth ~** etw durchlesen; **~ in the other office** (drüben) im anderen Büro; **the train goes ~ to Berlin** der Zug fährt bis nach Berlin durch.

3 *adj pred* **(a)** *(finished)* **to be ~ with sb/sth** mit jdm/etw fertig sein *(col)*; **we're ~** *(have finished relationship)* es ist aus zwischen uns; *(have finished job)* wir sind fertig; **I'm ~ with that kind of work** ich habe genug von dieser Arbeit; **are you ~?** sind Sie fertig? **(b)** *(Brit Telec)* **to be ~ (to sb/London)** mit jdm/London verbunden sein; **to get ~ (to sb/London)** zu jdm/nach London durchkommen; **you're ~** Ihre Verbindung!

through: ~ coach *n (Rail)* Kurswagen *m (for* nach*)*; *(bus)* direkte Busverbindung; **~ flight** *n* Direktflug *m.*

throughout [θrʊ'aʊt] **1** *prep* **(a)** *(place)* überall in *(+dat).* **~ the country/world** im ganzen Land/in der ganzen Welt. **(b)** *(time)* **~ the war** den ganzen Krieg hindurch *or* über; **~ his life** sein ganzes Leben lang. **2** *adv* **(a)** *(in every part)* **the house is carpeted ~** das Haus ist ganz mit Teppichboden ausgelegt; **a house with electric light ~** ein Haus, das in jedem Raum elektrisches Licht hat. **(b)** *(time)* die ganze Zeit hindurch *or* über.

through: ~put *n (Ind)* Leistung *f*; **~ ticket** *n* **can I get a ~ ticket to London?** kann ich bis London lösen?; **~ traffic** *n* Durchgangsverkehr *m*; **~ train** *n* durchgehender Zug; **~ way** *n (US)* Schnellstraße *f.*

throw [θrəʊ] *(vb: pret* **threw,** *ptp* **thrown)** **1** *n (of ball, dice)* Wurf *m.* **it's your ~** du bist dran; **have another ~** werfen Sie noch einmal; **a 30-metre ~** ein Wurf *m* von 30 Metern. **2** *vt* **(a)** *ball, stone* werfen; *rider* abwerfen; *opponent* zu Boden werfen. **to ~ the dice/a six** würfeln/eine Sechs würfeln; **to ~ sth to sb** jdm etw zuwerfen; **to ~ sth at sb** etw nach jdm werfen; *mud, paint etc* jdn mit etw bewerfen; **he threw himself to the floor/out of the window** er warf sich zu Boden/er stürzte sich aus dem Fenster; **to be ~n from the saddle** aus dem Sattel geworfen werden; **to ~ a glance at sb/sth** einen Blick auf jdn/etw werfen; **to ~ sb off the scent** jdn abhängen. **(b)** *switch, lever* betätigen. **(c)** *(fig col: disconcert)* aus dem Konzept bringen. **(d)** *party* geben; *fit* bekommen, kriegen *(col)*. **(e)** *pot etc* formen.

♦ **throw about** *or* **around** *vt always separate* **(a)** *(scatter)* verstreuen; *(fig) money* um sich werfen mit. **(b)** *(toss)* herumwerfen; *one's arms* fuchteln mit; *one's legs* strampeln mit.

♦ **throw away** *vt sep* **(a)** *(discard) rubbish* wegwerfen. **(b)** *(waste)* verschenken; *money* verschwenden *(on sth* auf etw, *on sb* an jdn*).* **(c)** *(say casually) remark* beiläufig sagen.

♦ **throw back** *vt sep ball, head, enemy* zurückwerfen; *curtains* aufreißen. **to be ~n ~ upon sth** auf etw *(acc)* zurückgreifen müssen.

♦ **throw in** *vt sep* **(a)** *extra* (gratis) dazugeben. **with a tour of London ~n ~** mit einer Gratistour durch London extra. **(b)** *(Sport) ball* einwerfen. **(c)** *(fig)* **to ~ ~ one's hand** aufgeben; **to ~ ~ the sponge** *or* **towel** das Handtuch werfen *(col)*. **(d)** *(say casually) remark* einwerfen *(to* in *+acc).*

♦ **throw off** *vt sep* **(a)** *(get rid of) clothes* abwerfen; *disguise, habits* ablegen; *pursuer* abschütteln;

cold loswerden.

♦ **throw out** *vt sep* **(a)** *(discard) rubbish etc* wegwerfen. **(b)** *(reject) suggestion, bill (Parl)* ablehnen. **(c)** *person* hinauswerfen, rauswerfen *(col) (of* aus*)*. **(d)** *(make wrong) calculations etc* über den Haufen werfen *(col)*, durcheinanderbringen. **to ~ sb ~ in his calculations** jdn bei seinen Berechnungen durcheinanderbringen. **(e)** *chest* herausdrücken.

♦ **throw together** *vt sep* **(a)** *(put hastily together) ingredients* zusammenwerfen; *clothes* zusammenpacken; *(make quickly)* hinhauen *(col)*; *essay* runterschreiben *(col)*. **(b)** *(fate) people* zusammenführen.

♦ **throw up 1** *vi* sich übergeben. **2** *vt sep* **(a)** *ball, hands* hochwerfen. **(b)** *(abandon) job* aufgeben; *opportunity etc* verschenken. **(c)** *(produce)* hervorbringen. **the meeting threw ~ several good ideas** bei der Versammlung kamen ein paar gute Ideen zutage.

throw: ~away *adj* **(a)** *(casual) remark* nebenbei gemacht; **(b)** *packet* Wegwerf-; *bottle* Einweg-; **(c)** *(cheap)* **~away prices** Schleuderpreise *pl;* **~-back** *n* **(a) his selfishness is a ~-back to an earlier generation** in ihm schlägt die Selbstsucht seiner Vorfahren wieder durch; **(b)** *(fig)* Rückkehr *(to* zu*)*

throw-in ['θrəʊɪn] *n (Sport)* Einwurf *m.*

thrown [θrəʊn] *ptp of* **throw.**

thru *pref, adv, adj (US)* = **through.**

thrush[1] [θrʌʃ] *n (Orn)* Drossel *f.*

thrush[2] *n (Med)* Soor *m (spec)*, Pilzkrankheit *f.*

thrust [θrʌst] *(vb: pret, ptp ~)* **1** *n* **(a)** Stoß *m*; *(of knife also)* Stich *m*; *(fig: of intellect)* Stoßkraft *f.* **(b)** *(Tech)* Druckkraft *f*; *(in rocket, turbine)* Schub(kraft *f*) *m.* **(c)** *(Mil: also ~* **forward***)* Vorstoß *m.* **2** *vt* **(a)** *(push, drive)* stoßen. **to ~ one's hands into one's pockets** die Hände in die Tasche stecken. **(b)** *(fig)* **to ~ oneself (up)on sb** sich jdm aufdrängen; **I had the job ~ upon me** die Arbeit wurde mir aufgezwungen; **to ~ one's way to the front** sich nach vorne kämpfen. **3** *vi* stoßen *(at* nach*)*; *(with knife)* stechen *(at* nach*)*.

♦ **thrust out** *vt sep leg, hand* ausstrecken; *head* vorstrecken; *chest* wölben. **she ~ her head ~ (of the window)** sie streckte den Kopf (zum Fenster) hinaus.

thud [θʌd] **1** *n* dumpfes Geräusch. **the ~ of his footsteps** seine dumpfen Schritte; **he fell to the ground with a ~** er fiel mit einem Plumps *(col) or* dumpfen Aufschlag zu Boden. **2** *vi* dumpf aufschlagen; *(move heavily)* stampfen. **the heavy door ~ded into place** mit einem dumpfen Knall fiel die Tür zu.

thug [θʌg] *n* Schläger(typ) *m.*

thumb [θʌm] **1** *n* Daumen *m.* **to be under sb's ~** unter jds Fuchtel *(dat)* stehen; **he gave me the ~s up/down** er gab mir zu verstehen, daß alles in Ordnung war/daß es nicht in Ordnung war; **it sticks out like a sore ~** das springt einem direkt ins Auge. **2** *vt* **(a)** *(col)* **to ~ a lift** per Anhalter fahren. **(b) a well ~ed book** ein Buch mit abgegriffenen Seiten.

thumb: ~nail *n* Daumennagel *m;* **~nail sketch** *(drawing)* kleine Skizze; *(description)* kurze Skizze; **~ print** *n* Daumenabdruck *m*; **~-tack** *n (US)* Reiß- *or* Heftzwecke *f.*

thump [θʌmp] **1** *n (blow)* Schlag *m*; *(noise)* (dumpfes) Krachen. **2** *vt table* schlagen auf *(+acc)*; *door* klopfen *or* schlagen an *(+acc)*; *(repeatedly)* trommeln auf/an *(+acc)*; *(accidentally) one's head* sich *(dat)* anschlagen. **he ~ed the box down on my desk** er knallte die Schachtel auf meinen Tisch; **I ~ed him (one) on the nose** *(col)* ich habe ihm eins auf die Nase verpaßt *(col)*. **3** *vi (person)* schlagen *(on the door/table* an die Tür/auf den Tisch*)*; *(heart)* heftig schlagen; *(move heavily)* stapfen; *(object: fall loudly)* plumpsen *(col)*.

♦ **thump out** *vt sep tune* hämmern.

thumping ['θʌmpɪŋ] *adj (also ~* **great***) (col)* kolossal.

thunder ['θʌndə[r]] **1** *n* **(a)** Donner *m.* **there is ~ in the air** es liegt ein Gewitter *nt* in der Luft. **(b)** *(fig) (of applause)* Sturm *m*; *(of cannons)* Donnern *nt*; *(of waves)* Tosen *nt.* **2** *vi (lit, fig)* donnern; *(waves, sea)* tosen. **the horses came ~ing up to the gate** die Pferde kamen aufs Tor zugeprescht. **3** *vt (shout)* brüllen, donnern.

thunderbolt *n (lit)* Blitz *m.* **the news came as something of a ~** *(fig)* die Nachricht schlug wie ein Blitz ein.

thunderous ['θʌndərəs] *adj* stürmisch; *voice* donnernd.

thunderstorm ['θʌndəstɔːm] *n* Gewitter *nt.*

thundery ['θndərɪ] *adj weather* gewittrig.

Thursday ['θɜːzdɪ] *n* Donnerstag *m*; *see* **Tuesday.**

thus [ðʌs] *adv* **(a)** *(in this way)* so, auf diese Art. **~ it was that ...** so kam es, daß ... **(b)** *(consequently)* folglich. **(c)** *(+ptp or adj) reassured, encouraged etc* derart *(geh)*. **~ far** so weit.

thwart [θwɔːt] *vt* vereiteln; *robbery, attack also* verhindern; *person* einen Strich durch die Rechnung machen *(+dat)*. **to ~ sb in sth** jdm etw vereiteln.

thy [ðaɪ] *poss adj (old) (before vowel* **thine***)* Euer/Eure/Euer *(obs)*; *(to God)* Dein/Deine/Dein.

thyme [taɪm] *n* Thymian *m.*

thyroid ['θaɪrɔɪd] **1** *n (also ~* **gland***)* Schilddrüse *f.* **2** *adj* Schilddrüsen-.

tiara [tɪ'ɑːrə] *n* Diadem *nt.*

Tibet [tɪ'bet] *n* Tibet *nt.*

Tibetan [tɪ'betən] **1** *adj* tibetanisch, tibetisch. **2** *n* **(a)** Tibetaner(in *f*) *m.* **(b)** *(language)* Tibetanisch *nt.*

tibia ['tɪbɪə] *n, pl* **-s** Schienbein *nt.*

tic [tɪk] *n (Med)* Tick *m*, nervöses Zucken.

tick[1] [tɪk] **1** *n* **(a)** *(of clock etc)* Ticken *nt.* **(b)** *(col: moment)* Augenblick *m*, Minütchen *nt (col)*. **half a ~** eine Sekunde; **I'll be ready in a ~** *or* **two ~s** bin sofort fertig *(col)*. **(c)** *(mark)* Haken *m.* **to put a ~ against a name/an answer** einen Namen/eine Antwort abhaken. **2** *vi* **(a)** *(clock)* ticken. **the minutes ~ed by** *or* **past** die Minuten verstrichen. **(b)** *(col)* **what makes him ~?** was geht in ihm vor? **3** *vt name, answer* abhaken.

♦ **tick off** *vt sep* **(a)** *name etc* abhaken. **(b)** *(col: scold)* ausschimpfen *(col)*.

♦ **tick over** *vi* **(a)** *(idle: engine)* im Leerlauf sein. **the engine is ~ing ~ nicely** der Motor läuft ganz gut. **(b)** *(fig: business etc)* ganz ordentlich laufen; *(pej)* auf Sparflamme sein *(col)*. **to keep things ~ing ~** die Sache in Gang halten.

tick[2] *n (Zool)* Zecke *f.*

tick[3] *n (Brit col)*: **on ~** auf Pump *(col)*.

ticker [tɪkə[r]] *n (col: heart)* Pumpe *f (col)*.

ticker tape *n* Lochstreifen *m.*

ticket ['tɪkɪt] *n* **(a)** *(rail, bus)* Fahrkarte *f*, Fahrschein *m*; *(plane ~)* Ticket *nt*, Flugschein *m*; *(Theat, for football match etc)* (Eintritts)karte *f*; *(cloakroom)* Garderobenmarke *f*; *(library)* ≃ Buchzettel *m*; *(for dry cleaners etc)* Zettel *m*; *(luggage office)* (Gepäck)schein *m*; *(raffle ~)* Los *nt*; *(price ~)* Preisschild *nt*; *(for car park)* Parkschein *m.* **(b)** *(US Pol)* Wahlliste *f.* **he's running on the Democratic ~** er kandidiert für die Demokratische Partei. **(c)** *(Jur: parking ~)* Strafzettel *m.* **to give sb a ~** jdm einen Strafzettel geben *or* verpassen *(col)*.

ticket: ~ collector *n (Rail)* Fahrkartenkontrolleur *m*; *(on train also)* Schaffner(in *f*) *m*; **~holder** *n* **~holders only through this door** *(Theat etc)* Eingang nur für Besucher mit Eintrittskarten; **~ inspector** *n* (Fahrkarten)kontrolleur *m*; **~ office** *n (Rail)* Fahrkartenschalter *m*; *(Theat)* Kasse *f*; **~ window** *n (Rail)* (Fahrkarten)schalter *m*; *(Theat)*

Kasse *f*.

ticking-off ['tɪkɪŋ'ɒf] *n (col)* Anpfiff *(col) m*. **to give sb a ~** jdm den Marsch blasen *(col)*.

tickle ['tɪkl] **1** *vti* **(a)** kitzeln; *(wool)* kratzen. **this wool ~s my skin** diese Wolle kratzt (auf der Haut). **(b)** *(fig col) person* amüsieren. **to feel/be ~ed** sich gebauchpinselt fühlen *(col)*; **to be ~d pink** sich wie ein Schneekönig freuen *(col)*. **2** *vi* kitzeln. **3** *n* Kitzeln *nt*. **to have a ~ in one's throat** einen Hustenreiz haben.

ticklish ['tɪklɪʃ] *adj (lit) person* kitz(e)lig; *(fig) situation* heikel.

tidal ['taɪdl] *adj river, harbour* Tide-. **~ wave** *(lit)* Flutwelle.

tiddler ['tɪdləʳ] *n (Brit)* **(a)** *(fish)* winziger Fisch. **(b)** *(col: child)* Knirps *m*.

tiddly ['tɪdlɪ] *adj (+er)* **(a)** *(tiny)* winzig, klitzeklein *(col)*. **(b)** *(tipsy)* angesäuselt *(col)*, beschwipst.

tiddlywinks ['tɪdlɪwɪŋks] *n* Floh(hüpf)spiel *nt*. **to play ~** Flohhüpfen spielen.

tide [taɪd] *n* **(a)** *(lit)* Gezeiten *pl*, Tide *(N Ger) f*. **(at) high/low ~** (bei) Hochwasser *nt or* Flut *f*/ Niedrigwasser *nt or* Ebbe *f*; **the ~ is in/out** es ist Flut/Ebbe. **(b)** *(fig: trend)* **the ~ of history** der Lauf der Geschichte; **the ~ of public opinion** der Trend der öffentlichen Meinung; **to go** *or* **swim against/with the ~** *(lit, fig)* gegen den/mit dem Strom schwimmen.

♦ **tide over** *vt always separate* **that will ~ me ~ until tomorrow** damit werde ich bis morgen auskommen.

tidemark ['taɪdmɑːk] *n* Flutmarke *f*; *(man-made)* Pegelstand *m*.

tidily ['taɪdɪlɪ] *adv* ordentlich.

tidiness ['taɪdɪnɪs] *n see adj* Ordentlichkeit *f*; Sauberkeit *f*; Gepflegtheit *f*.

tidings ['taɪdɪŋz] *npl (old, liter)* Botschaft *(liter)*.

tidy ['taɪdɪ] **1** *adj (+er)* **(a)** *(orderly)* ordentlich; *(of ~ habits also)* sauber; *appearance* gepflegt. **to keep sth ~** etw in Ordnung halten; **to get a room ~** ein Zimmer aufräumen; **to make oneself ~** sich zurechtmachen. **(b)** *(col)* **a ~ sum** eine ordentliche Stange Geld *(col)*. **2** *vt hair* in Ordnung bringen; *room also* aufräumen.

♦ **tidy away** *vt sep* wegräumen, aufräumen.

♦ **tidy out** *vt sep* aufräumen, ausmisten *(col)*.

♦ **tidy up 1** *vi* **(a)** *(clear away)* aufräumen. **(b)** *(clean oneself)* sich zurechtmachen. **2** *vt sep books, room* aufräumen; *piece of work* in Ordnung bringen.

tie [taɪ] **1** *n* **(a)** *(also esp US:* **neck ~***)* Krawatte *f*, Schlips *m (col)*. **(b)** *(fig: bond)* Beziehung, Bindung *f*; *(hindrance)* Belastung *f*. **~s of friendship** freundschaftliche Beziehungen *pl*; **business ~s** Geschäftsverbindungen *pl*; **family ~s** familiäre Bindungen *pl*; **I don't want any ~s** ich will keine Bindung; **pets can be a ~** Haustiere können eine Belastung sein. **(c)** *(Sport etc: result of match)* Unentschieden *nt*; *(match, competition ending in a draw)* unentschiedenes Spiel. **the match ended in a ~** das Spiel endete unentschieden; **there was a ~ for second place** es gab zwei zweite Plätze. **(d)** *(esp Ftbl: match)* Spiel *nt*.

2 *vt* **(a)** binden *(to* an *+acc)*; *(fasten also)* befestigen *(to* an *+dat)*. **my hands are ~d** *(fig)* mir sind die Hände gebunden; **to ~ a knot in sth** einen Knoten in etw *(acc)* machen; **we're very ~d in the evenings** wir sind abends sehr gebunden. **(b)** *(fig: unite, link)* verbinden.

3 *vi* **(a)** *(ribbon etc)* **it won't ~ properly** es läßt sich nicht richtig binden; **it ~s at the back** es wird hinten (zu)gebunden. **(b)** *(Sport)* unentschieden spielen; *(in competition, vote)* gleich stehen. **they ~d for the first place** *(Sport, competition)* sie belegten gemeinsam den ersten Platz.

♦ **tie back** *vt sep hair, door* zurückbinden.

♦ **tie down** *vt sep* **(a)** *(lit)* festbinden *(to* an *+dat)*; *tents* verankern *(to* in *+dat)*. **(b)** *(fig: restrict)* binden *(to* an *+acc)*; *meaning* genau bestimmen.

♦ **tie in 1** *vi* dazu passen. **to ~ ~ with sth** zu etw passen; **it all ~s ~** das paßt alles zusammen; **the new evidence didn't ~ ~** das neue Beweismaterial paßte nicht ins Bild. **2** *vt sep plans* in Einklang bringen.

♦ **tie on** *vt sep* anbinden.**to ~ sth ~(to) sth** etw an etw *(dat)* anbinden.

♦ **tie up 1** *vi* **(a) now it all ~s ~** jetzt paßt alles zusammen. **(b)** *(Naut)* festmachen. **2** *vt sep* **(a)** *parcel* verschnüren; *shoelaces* binden; *boat* festmachen; *animal* anbinden *(to* an *+dat)*; *prisoner, hands etc* fesseln. **(b)** *(settle) deal etc* unter Dach und Fach bringen. **to ~ ~ a few loose ends (of sth)** (bei einer Sache) ein paar Lücken schließen. **(c)** *(Fin) capital* (fest) anlegen. **(d)** *(link)* **to be ~d ~ with sth** mit etw zusammenhängen. **(e)** *(keep busy)* beschäftigen; *machines* auslasten. **he's ~d ~ all tomorrow** er ist morgen den ganzen Tag beschäftigt.

tie: ~ breaker *n (Tennis)* Tiebreaker *m*; **~ clip** *n* Krawattennadel *f*; **~-on** *adj attr* Anhänge-, zum Anbinden; **~ pin** *n* Krawattennadel *f*.

tier [tɪəʳ] *n (of cake)* Etage, Stufe *f*; *(Theat, of stadium)* Rang *m*; *(fig: in hierarchy etc)* Stufe *f*, Rang *m*. **a three-~ hierarchy** eine dreigestufte Hierarchie; **to arrange sth in ~s** etw stufenförmig aufbauen.

tiff [tɪf] *n (col)* Krach *m (col)*. **to have a ~ with sb** mit jdm Krach haben *(col)*.

tiger ['taɪgəʳ] *n* Tiger *m*.

tight [taɪt] **1** *adj (+er)* **(a)** *clothes* eng; *join* dicht.

(b) *(stiff, difficult to move) screw, bolt* festsitzend. **the top/cork is (too) ~** der Hahn ist zu fest zu/der Korken sitzt fest; **the drawer is a bit ~** die Schublade klemmt ein bißchen.

(c) *(firm) screw, knot* fest angezogen; *tap, window* dicht; *lid, embrace* fest; *control, discipline* streng; *organization* straff. **to run a ~ ship** *(lit, fig)* ein strenges Regiment führen.

(d) *(taut) rope, skin* straff.

(e) *(leaving little space)* eng; *weave also* dicht.

(f) *timing, race, match, money* knapp; *schedule* knapp bemessen.

(g) *(difficult) situation* schwierig. **in a ~ spot** *(fig)* in der Klemme *(col)*.

(h) *(col: miserly)* knick(e)rig *(col)*, geizig.

(i) *(col: drunk)* voll *(col)*. **to get ~** blau werden *(col)*.

2 *adv (+er) hold, shut, screw* fest; *stretch* straff. **to hold sb/sth ~** jdn/etw festhalten; **to do sth up ~** etw gut befestigen; **sleep ~!** schlaf(t) gut!; **hold ~!** festhalten!; **to sit ~** sich nicht rühren.

3 *adj suf* **water~/air~** wasser-/luftdicht.

tighten ['taɪtn] *(also* **~ up***)* **1** *vt* **(a)** *knot* fester machen; *screw* anziehen; *(re-tighten)* nachziehen; *rope* straffen; *(stretch tighter)* straffer spannen. **(b)** *restrictions* verschärfen. **2** *vi (rope)* sich spannen; *(knot)* sich zusammenziehen.

♦ **tighten up 1** *vi* **(a) = tighten 2. (b)** *(in discipline)* strenger werden, härter durchgreifen. **they've ~ed ~ on security** sie haben die Sicherheitsvorkehrungen verschärft. **2** *vt sep* **(a) = tighten 1 (a). (b)** *organization, procedure* straffen; *discipline, controls* verschärfen.

tight: ~-fisted ['taɪt'fɪstɪd] *adj* knauserig *(col)*; **~-fitting** *adj* eng anliegend; **~-knit** *adj community* eng miteinander verwachsen; **~-lipped** *adj (lit)* mit schmalen Lippen; *(silent)* verschlossen.

tightness ['taɪtnɪs] *n see adj* **(a)** enges Anliegen; Dichtheit *f*. **(b)** Festsitzen *nt*. **(c)** fester Sitz; Dichtheit *f*; Strenge *f*; Straffheit *f*. **(d)** Straffheit *f*. **(e)** Enge *f*; Dichte *f*. **(f)** Knappheit *f*. **(g)** *(with money)* Knick(e)rigkeit *f (col)*, Geiz *m*.

tightrope ['taɪtrəʊp] *n* Seil *nt*. **to walk a ~** *(fig)* einen Balanceakt vollführen; **~ walker**

Seiltänzer(in *f*) *m*.

tights [taɪts] *npl (esp Brit)* Strumpfhose *f*. **a pair of ~** ein Paar *nt* Strumpfhosen.

tile [taɪl] **1** *n (on roof)* (Dach)ziegel *m*; *(ceramic ~)* Fliese *f*; *(on wall)* Kachel *f*; *(lino ~, polystyrene ~ etc)* Platte *f*; *(carpet ~)* (Teppich)fliese *f*. **to have a night on the ~s** *(col)* einen draufmachen *(col)*. **2** *vt roof* (mit Ziegeln) decken; *floor* mit Fliesen/Platten auslegen; *wall, bathroom* kacheln. **~d** *roof* Ziegel-.

till[1] [tɪl] *prep, conj* = **until**.

till[2] *n (cash-register)* Kasse *f*.

till[3] *vt (Agr)* bestellen.

tiller ['tɪləʳ] *n (Naut)* Ruderpinne *f*.

tilt [tɪlt] **1** *n (slope)* Neigung *f*. **2** *vt* kippen, schräg stellen; *head* (seitwärts) neigen. **3** *vi (slant)* sich neigen. **this part of the machine ~s** dieser Teil der Maschine läßt sich kippen.

♦ **tilt back 1** *vi* sich nach hinten neigen. **he ~ed ~ in his chair** er kippte mit seinem Stuhl nach hinten. **2** *vt sep* nach hinten neigen; *chair also, machine part* nach hinten kippen.

♦ **tilt forward 1** *vi* sich nach vorne neigen; *machine part* nach vorn kippen. **he ~ed ~ in his chair** er kippte mit seinem Stuhl nach vorne. **2** *vt sep* nach vorne neigen; *chair also, machine part* nach vorne kippen.

♦ **tilt over 1** *vi (lean)* sich neigen; *(fall)* (um)kippen. **2** *vt sep (slant)* neigen, schräg stellen; *barrel, chair* kippen.

timber ['tɪmbəʳ] *n* **(a)** Holz *nt*; *(for buildings also)* Bauholz *nt*; *(land planted with trees)* (Nutz)wald *m*. **(b)** *(beam)* Balken *m*.

timbered ['tɪmbəd] *adj house* Fachwerk-; *land* Wald-.

timbre ['tɪmbəʳ] *n* Timbre *nt*.

time [taɪm] **1** *n* **(a)** Zeit *f*. **how ~ flies!** wie die Zeit vergeht!; **only ~ will tell whether ...** es muß sich erst herausstellen, ob ...; **it takes ~ to do that** das braucht (seine) Zeit; **to take (one's) ~ (over sth)** sich *(dat)* (bei etw) Zeit lassen; **it took me all my ~ to finish** ich bin gerade noch fertig geworden; **in (the course of) ~** mit der Zeit; **in (next to) no ~** im Nu, im Handumdrehen; **to have a lot of/no ~ for sb/sth** viel/keine Zeit für jdn/etw haben; *(fig: be for/against)* viel/nichts für jdn/etw übrig haben; **to find/make ~ (for sb/sth)** Zeit finden/sich *(dat)* Zeit nehmen (für jdn/etw); **to have ~ on one's hands** viel freie Zeit haben; **he lost no ~ in telling her** er verlor keine Zeit und sagte es ihr sofort; **to be in good ~** rechtzeitig dran sein; **don't rush, do it in your own ~** nur keine Hast, tun Sie es, wie Sie es können; **let me know in good ~** sagen Sie mir rechtzeitig Bescheid; **(for) a long/short ~** lange/kurz; **I'm going away for a long ~** ich fahre für längere Zeit weg; **it's a long ~ (since)** es ist schon lange her (, seit); **what a (long) ~ you have been!** du hast (aber) lange gebraucht!; **a short ~ later/ago** kurz darauf/vor kurzem; **in a short ~ they were all gone** nach kurzer Zeit waren alle gegangen; **for some ~ past** seit einiger Zeit; **all the ~** die ganze Zeit; **in two weeks' ~** in zwei Wochen; **for a ~** eine Zeitlang; **for the ~ being** *(provisionally)* vorläufig; *(temporarily)* vorübergehend; **to do ~** *(col: in prison)* sitzen *(col)*.

(b) *(of clock, moment, season)* **what ~ is it?, what's the ~?** wie spät ist es?, wieviel Uhr ist es?; **my watch keeps good ~** meine Uhr geht genau; **it's ~ (for me/us** *etc***) to go, it's ~ I was/we were** *etc* **going** es wird Zeit, daß ich gehe/wir gehen *etc*; **on ~/ahead of ~/behind ~** pünktlich/zu früh/zu spät; **the project is ahead of ~/behind ~** das Projekt ist dem Zeitplan voraus/zeitlich im Rückstand; **to make good ~** gut vorankommen; **the trains are on ~** die Züge fahren pünktlich; **to be in ~ for sth** rechtzeitig zu etw kommen; **it's about ~ he was here** *(he has arrived)* es wird (aber) auch Zeit, daß er kommt; *(he has not arrived)* es wird langsam Zeit, daß er kommt; **(and) about ~ too!** das wird aber auch Zeit!; **at all ~s** jederzeit; **at any ~ during the day** zu jeder Tageszeit; **not at this ~ of night!** nicht zu dieser nachtschlafenden Zeit!; **there are ~s when ...** es gibt Augenblicke, wo ...; **at the** *or* **that ~** damals, zu der Zeit; **at the present ~** zur Zeit; **at one ~** früher, einmal; **at any/no ~** jederzeit/niemals; **at the same ~** *(lit)* gleichzeitig; **they arrived at the same ~ as us** sie kamen zur gleichen Zeit an wie wir; **but at the same ~, you must admit that ...** aber andererseits müssen Sie zugeben, daß ...; **at ~s** manchmal; **by the ~ it had finished** als es zu Ende war; **by the ~ we arrive, there's not going to be anything left** bis wir ankommen, ist nichts mehr übrig; **by this ~** inzwischen; **by this ~ next year/tomorrow** nächstes Jahr/morgen um diese Zeit; **from ~ to ~** von Zeit zu Zeit; **from that ~ on** von der Zeit an; **since that ~** seit der Zeit; **until such ~ as ...** so lange bis ...; **this ~ of the day/year** diese Tages-/Jahreszeit; **this ~ last year/week** letztes Jahr/letzte Woche um diese Zeit; **to die before one's ~** zu früh sterben; **when the ~ comes** wenn es soweit ist; **the ~ has come (to do sth)** es ist an der Zeit (, etw zu tun); **the ~ has come for us to leave** es ist Zeit für uns zu gehen; **my ~ is (almost) up** meine *or* die Zeit ist (gleich) um; *(fig: life)* meine Zeit ist gekommen.

(c) *(occasion)* **this ~** diesmal, dieses Mal; **(the) next ~** nächstes Mal; **(the) next ~ I see you** wenn ich dich das nächste Mal sehe; **(the) last ~** letztes Mal; **(the) last ~ he was here** das letzte Mal, als er hier war; **every** *or* **each ~ ...** jedesmal, wenn ...; **many a ~, many ~s** viele Male; **for the last ~** zum letzten Mal; **he's not very bright at the best of ~s** er ist sowieso nicht sehr intelligent; **~ and (~) again, ~ after ~** immer wieder; **they came in one/three at a ~** sie kamen einzeln/jeweils zu dritt herein; **four at a ~** vier auf einmal; **for weeks at a ~** wochenlang.

(d) *(multiplication)* **2 ~s 3 is 6** 2 mal 3 ist 6; **it was ten ~s as big** es war zehnmal so groß.

(e) *(rate)* **you're paid ~ and a half for overtime** Sie bekommen 50% Zuschlag für Überstunden.

(f) *(era)* **in Victorian ~s** im Viktorianischen Zeitalter; **in olden ~s** in alten Zeiten; **in my ~** zu meiner Zeit; **he is ahead of his ~** er ist seiner Zeit (weit) voraus; **to be behind the ~s** rückständig sein; **to keep up with the ~s** mit der Zeit gehen; *(keep in touch)* auf dem laufenden bleiben; **~s are hard** die Zeiten sind hart; **~s are changing** es kommen andere Zeiten.

(g) *(experience)* **we had a good ~** es hat uns *(dat)* gut gefallen; **have a good ~!** viel Spaß!; **to have the ~ of one's life** eine herrliche Zeit verbringen; **to have an easy/a hard ~** es leicht/schwer haben; **we had an easy/a hard ~ getting to the finals** es war leicht für uns/wir hatten Schwierigkeiten, in die Endrunde zu kommen; **to have a bad/rough ~ (of it)** viel mitmachen; **to give sb a rough ~** jdm das Leben schwermachen.

(h) *(rhythm)* Takt *m*. **(to be) in ~ (with)** im Takt (sein) (mit); **(to be/get) out of ~** aus dem Takt (sein/kommen); **3/4 ~** Dreivierteltakt *m*; **to keep ~** *(beat ~)* den Takt angeben; *(keep in ~)* (den) Takt halten.

2 *vt* **(a)** *(choose ~ of)* **to ~ sth perfectly** genau den richtigen Zeitpunkt für etw wählen; **he ~d his arrival to coincide with ...** er legte seine Ankunft so, daß sie mit ... zusammenfiel; **the bomb is ~d to explode at ...** die Bombe ist so eingestellt, daß sie um ... explodiert; **you ~d that well** *(also iro)* du hast dir den richtigen Zeitpunkt ausgesucht. **(b)** *(with stop-watch etc)* stoppen; *speed also* messen.

time: ~ **bomb** *n (lit, fig)* Zeitbombe *f*; ~**card** *n (for workers)* Stechkarte *f*; *(US: ~table)* Fahrplan *m*; ~**-consuming** *adj* zeitraubend; ~**-honoured** *or (US)* **-honored** *adj* althergebracht; ~**-lag** *n* Zeitdifferenz *f*; *(delay)* Verzögerung.

timeless ['taɪmlɪs] *adj* zeitlos; *(everlasting)* immerwährend.

time limit *n* zeitliche Begrenzung; *(for the completion of a job)* Frist *f*. **to put a ~ on sth** etw befristen.

timely ['taɪmlɪ] *adj* rechtzeitig. **a ~ piece of advice** ein Rat zur rechten Zeit; **that was very ~** das war genau zur rechten Zeit.

timepiece ['taɪmpiːs] *n* Uhr *f*.

timer ['taɪməʳ] *n* Zeitmesser *m*; *(switch)* Schaltuhr *f*; *(person)* Zeitnehmer *m*.

time: ~**saving** *adj* zeitsparend; ~ **signature** *(Mus) n* Taktvorzeichnung *f*; ~**table** *n (transport)* Fahrplan *m*; *(Brit Sch)* Stundenplan *m*; **to have a busy ~table** ein volles Programm haben; **what's on the ~table?** was steht auf dem Programm?; ~ **warp** *n* **we were in a ~ warp** wir hatten einen Zeitsprung gemacht.

timid ['tɪmɪd] *adj* scheu, ängstlich; *person, behaviour, words also* schüchtern.

timidity [tɪ'mɪdɪtɪ] *n see adj* Scheu *f*; Schüchternheit *f*.

timing ['taɪmɪŋ] *n* **(a)** *(choice of time)* Wahl *f* des richtigen Zeitpunkts *(of* für*)*, Timing *nt*. **perfect ~, I'd just opened a bottle** ihr kommt gerade richtig, ich habe eben eine Flasche aufgemacht. **(b)** *(Aut) (mechanism)* Steuerung *f*; *(adjustment)* Einstellung *f*. **(c)** *(measuring of time)* Zeitmessung *f (of* bei*)*; *(of race etc)* Stoppen *nt*.

timorous ['tɪmərəs] *adj* furchtsam, scheu.

timpani ['tɪmpənɪ] *npl (Mus)* Kesselpauken *pl*.

tin [tɪn] **1** *n* **(a)** Blech *nt*; *(Chem: metal)* Zinn *nt*. **(b)** *(esp Brit: can)* Dose, Büchse *f*. **a ~ of beans/biscuits** ein Dose Bohnen/Kekse. **2** *vt (esp Brit) fruit etc* in Dosen konservieren.

tinfoil ['tɪnfɔɪl] *n (wrapping)* Stanniolpapier *nt*; *(aluminium foil)* Aluminiumfolie *f*.

tinge [tɪndʒ] **1** *n* **(a)** *(of colour)* Hauch *m*, Spur *f*. **(b)** *(fig: hint, trace)* Spur *f*; *(of sadness also)* Anflug *m*. **2** *vt* **(a)** *(colour)* (leicht) tönen. **(b)** *(fig)* ~**d with ...** mit einer Spur von ...; **our happiness was ~d with sorrow** unser Glück war getrübt.

tingle ['tɪŋgl] **1** *vi* kribbeln *(col) (with* vor *+dat)*; *(with blows)* leicht brennen *(with* von*)*. **to ~ with excitement** vor Aufregung beben. **2** *n see vi* Kribbeln *(col) nt*; leichtes Brennen. **she felt a ~ of excitement** sie war ganz kribbelig *(col)*.

tinker ['tɪŋkəʳ] **1** *n* Kesselflicker *m*. **you little ~!** *(col)* du kleiner Zigeuner! *(col)*. **2** *vi (also ~ **about**)* herumbasteln *(with, on* an *+dat)*.

tinkle ['tɪŋkl] **1** *vi (bells etc)* klingen, bimmeln *(col)*; *(on piano)* klimpern; *(breaking glass)* klirren. **2** *n* Klingen, Bimmeln *(col) nt no pl*; *(of breaking glass)* Klirren *nt no pl*. **to give sb a ~** *(Brit col: on telephone)* jdn anbimmeln *(col)*.

tinkling ['tɪŋklɪŋ] **1** *n (of bells etc)* Klingen, Bimmeln *(col) nt*; *(of piano)* Klimpern *nt*; *(of broken glass)* Klirren *nt*. **2** *adj see n* klingend, bimmelnd *(col)*; klimpernd; klirrend.

tinned [tɪnd] *adj (esp Brit)* Dosen-, Büchsen-.

tinny ['tɪnɪ] *adj (+er) sound* blechern; *instrument* blechern klingend; *taste* nach Blech; *(pej) typewriter etc* schäbig.

tin: ~**-opener** *n (esp Brit)* Dosenöffner *m*; ~ **plate** *n* Zinnblech *nt*.

tinsel ['tɪnsəl] *n (foil)* Girlanden *pl* aus Rauschgold *etc*.

tin: ~**smith** *n* Blechschmied *m*; ~ **soldier** *n* Zinnsoldat *m*.

tint [tɪnt] **1** *n* Ton *m*; *(product for hair)* Tönung(smittel *nt*) *f*. **2** *vt* tönen.

tiny ['taɪnɪ] *adj (+er)* winzig, sehr klein; *baby, child* ganz klein. ~ **little** winzig klein; **a ~ mind** *(pej)* ein Zwergenverstand *m*.

tip[1] [tɪp] *n* Spitze *f*; *(of cigarette)* Filter *m*; *(col: cigarette)* Filter(zigarette) *f*. **from ~ to toe** von Kopf bis Fuß; **it's on the ~ of my tongue** es liegt mir auf der Zunge; **it's just the ~ of the iceberg** *(fig)* das ist nur die Spitze des Eisbergs.

tip[2] **1** *n* **(a)** *(gratuity)* Trinkgeld *nt*. **(b)** *(warning, advice, Racing)* Tip *m*. **2** *vt* **(a)** *(give gratuity to)* Trinkgeld geben *(+dat)*. **to ~ sb £1** jdm £1 Trinkgeld geben. **(b)** *(Racing)* tippen *or* setzen auf *(+acc)*. **they are ~ped to win the election** *(fig)* sie sind die Favoriten für die Wahl.

♦ **tip off** *vt sep* einen Tip geben *(+dat) (about* über *+acc)*. **he ~ped ~ the police as to her whereabouts** er verriet der Polizei, wo sie war.

tip[3] **1** *vt (tilt, incline)* kippen; *(overturn)* umkippen; *(pour, empty) liquid, load, sand, rubbish* schütten. **to ~ sth backwards/forwards** etw nach hinten/vorne kippen *or* neigen; **he ~s the scales at 70kg** er bringt 70 kg auf die Waage; **it ~ped the scales in his favour** *(fig)* das hat für ihn den Ausschlag gegeben; ~ **the case upside down** stell die Kiste auf den Kopf; **to ~ sb off his chair** jdn vom Stuhl kippen. **2** *vi (incline)* kippen; *(dump rubbish)* Schutt abladen. **3** *n (Brit) (for rubbish)* Müllkippe *f*; *(for coal)* Halde *f*; *(col: untidy place)* Saustall *m (col)*.

♦ **tip back** *vti sep* nach hinten kippen.

♦ **tip over** *vti sep (overturn)* umkippen.

♦ **tip up** *vti sep (tilt)* kippen; *(overturn)* umkippen; *(folding seat)* hochklappen.

tip-off ['tɪpɒf] *n (col)* Tip, Wink *m*.

tipper ['tɪpəʳ] *n (also ~ **truck**)* Kipplaster, Kipper *m*.

tipple ['tɪpl] *(col)* **1** *n* **he enjoys a ~** er trinkt ganz gerne mal einen. **2** *vi* picheln *(col)*.

tippler ['tɪpləʳ] *n (col)* Schluckspecht *m (col)*.

tipsy ['tɪpsɪ] *adj (+er)* beschwipst *(col)*.

tip: ~**toe** **1** *n* **on ~toe** auf Zehenspitzen. **2** *vi* auf Zehenspitzen gehen; ~**top** *adj (col: first-rate)* tipptopp *pred (col)*, erstklassig.

tirade [taɪ'reɪd] *n* Tirade, Schimpfkanonade *f*.

tire[1] [taɪəʳ] **1** *vt* müde machen. **2** *vi* **(a)** müde werden. **(b)** *(become bored)* **to ~ of sb/sth** jdn/etw satt haben, jds/einer Sache *(gen)* überdrüssig werden *(geh)*; **she never ~s of talking about her son** sie redet ständig über ihren Sohn.

tire[2] *n (US)* = **tyre.**

tired ['taɪəd] *adj* **(a)** *(fatigued)* müde; *cliché* abgegriffen. ~ **out** völlig erschöpft. **(b) to be ~ of sb/sth** jdn/etw leid sein; **to get ~ of sb/sth** jdn/etw satt bekommen; **I'm ~ of telling you** ich habe es satt, dir das zu sagen.

tiredness ['taɪədnɪs] *n* Müdigkeit *f*. **the accident was a result of (his) ~** (seine) Übermüdung war die Unfallursache.

tireless ['taɪəlɪs] *adj* unermüdlich.

tiresome ['taɪəsəm] *adj (irritating)* lästig, leidig; *(boring)* langweilig.

tiring ['taɪərɪŋ] *adj* anstrengend, ermüdend.

tissue ['tɪʃuː] *n* **(a)** *(Anat, Bot, fig)* Gewebe *nt*. **a ~ of lies** ein Lügengespinst *nt*. **(b)** *(handkerchief)* Papier(taschen)tuch *nt*. **(c)** *(also ~ **paper**)* Seidenpapier *nt*.

tit[1] [tɪt] *n (bird)* Meise *f*.

tit[2] *n:* ~ **for tat** wie du mir, so ich dir; **he was repaid ~ for tat** er bekam es mit gleicher Münze heimgezahlt.

tit[3] *n (col!: breast)* Titte *f (col!)*.

titbit ['tɪtbɪt] *n (esp Brit)* Leckerbissen *m*.

titillate ['tɪtɪleɪt] *vt person, senses* anregen; *interest* erregen. **it ~s the palate** es kitzelt den Gaumen.

title ['taɪtl] *n* **(a)** Titel *m (also Sport)*; *(of chapter)* Überschrift *f*; *(form of address)* Anrede *f*. **(b)** *(Jur) (right)* (Rechts)anspruch *(to* auf *+acc)*, Titel *(spec) m*; *(document)* Eigentumsurkunde *f*.

titled ['taɪtld] *adj person, classes* mit (Adels)titel. **is**

he ~? hat er einen Titel?

title: ~ holder *n (Sport)* Titelträger(in*f*) *m*; **~ page** *n (Typ)* Titelseite *f*; **~ role** *n (Theat, Film)* Titelrolle *f*.

titter ['tɪtəʳ] **1** *vti* kichern. **2** *n* Gekicher *nt*.

tittle-tattle ['tɪtl,tætl] *n* Geschwätz *nt*; *(gossip also)* Klatsch *m*.

T-junction ['tiː,dʒʌŋkʃən] *n* **"~ ahead"** „Achtung, Vorfahrtsstraße".

TNT = **trinitrotoluene** TNT *nt*.

to [tuː] **1** *prep* **(a)** *(in direction of, towards)* zu. **to go ~ the station** zum Bahnhof gehen/fahren; **to go ~ the theatre/cinema** *etc* ins Theater/Kino *etc* gehen; **to go ~ France/London** nach Frankreich/ London gehen/fahren; **to go ~ Switzerland** in die Schweiz gehen/fahren; **to to ~ school** zur Schule *or* in die Schule gehen; **to go ~ bed** ins *or* zu Bett gehen; **~ the left** nach links; **~ the west** nach Westen; **I have never been ~ Spain** ich war noch nie in Spanien; **hold it ~ the light** halte es gegen das Licht.

(b) *(as far as, until)* bis. **to count (up) ~ 20** bis 20 zählen; **there were (from) 40 ~ 60 people** es waren 40 bis 60 Leute da; **it's 90 kms ~ Paris** nach Paris sind es 90 km.

(c) *(+indir obj)* **to give sth ~ sb** jdm etw geben; **a present from me ~ you** ein Geschenk für dich von mir; **who did you give it ~?, ~ who(m) did you give it?** wem haben Sie es gegeben?; **what is it ~ you?** was geht dich das an?; **he is kind ~ everyone** er ist zu allen freundlich; **he has been a good friend ~ us** er war uns *(dat)* ein guter Freund; **to address sth ~ sb** etw an jdn adressieren; **"To ..."** *(on envelope etc)* „An *(+acc)* ..."; **to pray ~ God** zu Gott beten; **~ Lorna** *(toast)* auf Lorna *(acc)*.

(d) *(next ~, with position)* **bumper ~ bumper** Stoßstange an Stoßstange; **at right angles/ parallel ~ the wall** im rechten Winkel/parallel zur Wand; **~ the west (of)/the left (of)** westlich/ links (von).

(e) *(with expressions of time)* vor. **20 (minutes) ~ 2** 20 (Minuten) vor 2; **at (a) quarter ~ 2** um Viertel vor 2; **25 ~ 3** 5 nach halb 3; **it was five ~** es war fünf vor.

(f) *(in relation ~)* **3 ~ the 4th** *(Math)* 3 hoch 4; **by a majority of 10 ~ 7** mit einer Mehrheit von 10 zu 7; **they won by 4 goals ~ 2** sie haben mit 4:2 *(spoken:* vier zu zwei*)* Toren gewonnen.

(g) *(per)* pro; *(in recipes, when mixing)* auf *(+acc)*. **one person ~ a room** eine Person pro Zimmer.

(h) *(in comparison ~)* **that's nothing ~ what is to come** das ist gar nichts verglichen mit dem, was noch kommt.

(i) *(concerning)* **there's nothing ~ it** *(it's very easy)* es ist nichts dabei; **that's all there is ~ it** das ist alles.

(j) *(accompanied by)* **to sing ~ the guitar** zur Gitarre singen; **to sing sth ~ the tune of ...** etw nach der Melodie von ... singen.

2 *(in infin)* **(a) ~ begin ~ do sth** anfangen, etw zu tun; **he decided ~ come** er beschloß zu kommen; **I want ~ do it** ich will es tun; **I want him ~ do it** ich will, daß er es tut.

(b) *(in order ~)* **I did it ~ help you** ich tat es, um dir zu helfen.

(c) *(until)* **he lived ~ be 100** er wurde 100 Jahre alt; **the firm grew ~ be the biggest in the world** die Firma wurde zur größten der Welt.

(d) *(other uses)* **~ see him now, one would never think ...** wenn man ihn jetzt sieht, würde man nicht glauben, ...; **~ be honest, ...** ehrlich gesagt, ...; **well, not ~ exaggerate ...** ohne zu übertreiben, ...; **he is not the sort ~ do that** er ist nicht der Typ dazu; **I have done nothing ~ deserve this** ich habe nichts getan, womit ich das verdient hätte; **who is he ~ order you around?** wer ist er denn, daß er dich so herumkommandiert?; **there's no-one ~ help us** es ist niemand da, der uns helfen könnte; **what is there ~ do here?** was gibt es hier zu tun?; **the book is still ~ be written** das Buch muß noch geschrieben werden; **he's a big boy ~ be still in short trousers** er ist so ein großer Junge und trägt noch kurze Hosen; **I arrived ~ find she had gone** als ich ankam, war sie weg; **are you ready ~ go at last?** bist du endlich fertig?; **you are foolish ~ try it** du bist dumm, daß du das versuchst; **is it good ~ eat?** schmeckt es gut?; **it's too heavy ~ lift** es ist zu schwer zum Heben; **I'll try ~** ich werde es versuchen; **you have ~** du mußt; **I should love ~** sehr gerne.

3 *adj (slightly ajar) door* angelehnt; *(shut)* zu.

4 *adv* **~ and fro** hin und her; *walk* auf und ab.

toad [təʊd] *n* Kröte *f*; *(fig: repulsive person)* Ekel *nt*.

toad-in-the-hole ['təʊdɪnðə'həʊl] *n Teigspeise mit Würsten.*

toadstool ['təʊdstuːl] *n* Giftpilz *m*.

toady ['təʊdɪ] **1** *n (pej)* Kriecher *m*. **2** *vi* radfahren *(pej col)*. **to ~ to sb** vor jdm kriechen.

toast[1] [təʊst] **1** *n* Toast *m*. **a piece of ~** eine Scheibe Toast; **on ~** auf Toast; **as warm as ~** *(fig)* mollig warm; **~ rack** Toastständer *m*. **2** *vt bread* toasten; *(on open fire)* rösten.

toast[2] **1** *n* Toast, Trinkspruch *m*. **to drink a ~ to sb** auf jdn trinken; **to propose a ~** einen Toast ausbringen *(to* auf *+acc)*. **2** *vt* **to ~ sb/sth** auf jds Wohl *or* auf jdn/etw trinken.

toaster ['təʊstəʳ] *n* Toaster *m*.

tobacco [tə'bækəʊ] *n* Tabak *m*.

tobacconist [tə'bækənɪst] *n (Brit)* Tabak(waren)-händler *m*; *(shop)* Tabakladen *m*.

to-be [tə'biː] *adj pred* zukünftig. **the mother-/bride-/husband-~** die werdende Mutter/zukünftige Braut/der zukünftige Mann.

toboggan [tə'bɒgən] **1** *n* Rodel(schlitten) *m*. **2** *vi* Schlitten fahren, rodeln. **to go ~ing** Schlitten fahren, rodeln.

today [tə'deɪ] *adv, n* **(a)** heute. **a week/fortnight ~** heute in einer Woche/zwei Wochen; **a year ago ~** heute vor einem Jahr; **~ is Monday** heute ist Montag; **from ~** von heute an, ab heute; **~'s paper/news** die Zeitung/Nachrichten von heute. **(b)** *(these days)* heutzutage. **the cinema/world ~** das Kino/die Welt von heute.

toddle ['tɒdl] *vi* **(a)** wackeln. **the little boy ~d into the room** der kleine Junge kam ins Zimmer gewackelt. **(b)** *(col) (walk)* gehen; *(leave: also* **~ off***)* abzwitschern *(col)*.

toddler ['tɒdləʳ] *n* Kleinkind *nt*.

to-do [tə'duː] *n (col)* Theater *(col)*, Gedöns *(col) nt*. **to make a ~** ein Theater machen *(col) (about* um*)*.

toe [təʊ] **1** *n* **(a)** Zehe *f*, Zeh *m*. **to tread** *or* **step on sb's ~s** *(lit)* jdm auf die Zehen treten; *(fig)* jdm ins Handwerk pfuschen *(col)*; **to keep sb on his ~s** *(fig)* jdn auf Zack halten *(col)*. **(b)** *(of sock, shoe)* Spitze *f*. **2** *vt (fig)* **to ~ the line** spuren *(col)*; **to ~ the party line** *(Pol)* sich nach der Parteilinie richten.

toe: ~cap *n* (Schuh)kappe *f*; **~nail** *n* Zehennagel *m*.

toffee ['tɒfɪ] *n (substance)* Karamel *m*; *(sweet)* Toffee *nt*. **he can't sing for ~** *(col)* er kann überhaupt nicht *or* nicht die Bohne *(col)* singen.

toffee: ~ apple *n* kandierter Apfel; **~-nosed** *adj (Brit col)* hochnäsig.

together [tə'geðəʳ] *adv* zusammen. **to do sth ~** etw zusammen tun; *(jointly) try, achieve sth etc also* etw gemeinsam tun; **to sit/stand** *etc* **~** zusammen *or* beieinander sitzen/stehen *etc*; **to tie/ fit** *etc* **two things ~** zwei Dinge zusammenbinden/-setzen *etc*; **all ~ now!** jetzt alle zusammen!

togetherness [tə'geðənɪs] *n (physical)* Beisammensein *nt*; *(mental, emotional)* Zusammengehörigkeit *f*.

toggle ['tɒgl] n Knebel *m*; *(on clothes)* Knebelknopf *m*. ~ **switch** Kippschalter *m*.

toil [tɔɪl] **1** *vi (liter: work)* sich plagen *(at, over* mit*)*. **2** *n (liter: work)* Mühe, Plage *(geh) f*.

toilet ['tɔɪlɪt] *n (lavatory)* Toilette *f*. **to go to the ~** auf die Toilette gehen; **she's in the ~/~s** sie ist auf der Toilette.

toilet *in cpds* Toiletten-; ~ **bag** *or* **case** *n* Kulturbeutel *m*; ~ **paper** *n* Toilettenpapier *nt*; ~ **requisites** *npl* Toilettenartikel *pl*.

toiletries ['tɔɪlɪtrɪz] *npl* Toilettenartikel *pl*.

toilet: ~ **roll** *n* Rolle *f* Toilettenpapier; ~ **soap** *n* Toilettenseife *f*; ~ **water** *n* Duftwasser, Eau de Toilette *nt*.

to-ing and fro-ing ['tu:ɪŋən'frəʊɪŋ] *n* Hin und Her *nt*.

token ['təʊkən] **1** *n* **(a)** *(sign)* Zeichen *nt*. **as a ~ of/in ~ of** zum Zeichen *(+gen)*; **by the same ~** ebenso; **then by the same ~ you can't object to ...** dann können Sie aber auch nichts gegen ... einwenden. **(b)** *(counter)* Spielmarke *f*. **(c)** *(voucher, gift ~)* Gutschein *m*. **2** *attr* Schein-, pro forma. **it was just a ~ offer** das hat er/sie *etc* nur pro forma *or* so zum Schein angeboten; ~ **gesture** leere Geste; ~ **payment** symbolische Bezahlung; ~ **resistance** Scheinwiderstand *m*; ~ **strike** Warnstreik *m*; ~ **rent/fine** nominelle *or* symbolische Miete/symbolische Strafe.

told [təʊld] *pret, ptp of* **tell. there were 50 people there all ~** es waren alles in allem 50 Leute da.

tolerable ['tɒlərəbl] *adj (lit)* erträglich; *(fig: not too bad also)* annehmbar, passabel *(col)*.

tolerably ['tɒlərəblɪ] *adv* ziemlich. ~ **well** ganz annehmbar, ziemlich gut.

tolerance ['tɒlərəns] *n (also Tech)* Toleranz *f (of, for, towards* gegenüber*)*; *(towards children)* Nachsicht *f (of* mit*)*.

tolerant ['tɒlərənt] *adj (of, towards, with* gegenüber*)* tolerant; *(towards children)* nachsichtig.

tolerate ['tɒləreɪt] *vt pain, noise, weather etc* ertragen; *person* dulden; *ideas* tolerieren; *behaviour, injustice etc also* hinnehmen.

toleration [,tɒlə'reɪʃən] *n* Duldung *f*.

toll[1] [təʊl] **1** *vti (bell)* läuten. **2** *n* Läuten *nt*; *(single stroke)* Glockenschlag *m*.

toll[2] *n* **(a)** *(bridge ~, road ~)* Zoll *m*; *(US Telec)* (Fernsprech)gebühr *f*. **(b)** *(deaths, loss etc)* **the death ~ on the roads** die Zahl der Verkehrsopfer; **the earthquake took a heavy ~ of human life** das Erdbeben forderte viele Menschenleben.

toll: ~ **bridge** *n* gebührenpflichtige Brücke; ~ **call** *n (US)* Ferngespräch *nt*; ~**gate** *n* Schlagbaum *m*; ~ **road** *n* gebührenpflichtige Straße.

Tom [tɒm] *n* **any ~, Dick or Harry** *(col)* jeder x-beliebige.

tom [tɒm] *n (cat)* Kater *m*.

tomato [tə'mɑ:təʊ, *(US)* tə'meɪtəʊ] *n, pl* **-es** Tomate *f*.

tomato *in cpds* Tomaten-; ~ **juice** *n* Tomatensaft *m*; ~ **ketchup** *n* (Tomaten)ketchup *m or nt*; ~ **sauce** *n* Tomatensoße *f*; *(ketchup)* (Tomaten)ketchup *m or nt*.

tomb [tu:m] *n* Grab *nt*; *(building)* Grabmal *nt*.

tombola [tɒm'bəʊlə] *n* Tombola *f*.

tomboy ['tɒmbɔɪ] *n* Wildfang *m*.

tombstone ['tu:mstəʊn] *n* Grabstein *m*.

tomcat ['tɒmkæt] *n* Kater *m*.

tome [təʊm] *n* dickes Buch, Wälzer *m (col)*.

tomfoolery [tɒm'fu:lərɪ] *n* Unsinn *m*.

tomorrow [tə'mɒrəʊ] *adv, n* morgen. **the day after ~** übermorgen; ~ **morning** morgen früh; **(as) from ~** ab morgen, von morgen an; **see you ~!** bis morgen!; ~**'s paper** die Zeitung von morgen.

tomtom ['tɒmtɒm] *n* Tamtam *nt*.

ton [tʌn] *n* **(a)** Tonne *f*. **(b) ~s** *pl (col: lots)* jede Menge *(col)*; **to have ~s of time/friends** jede Menge Zeit/Freunde haben *(col)*; **it weighs a ~** *(fig col)* es ist ganz schön schwer *(col)*.

tone [təʊn] **1** *n* **(a)** *(lit, fig)* Ton *m*; *(of colour also)* Farbton *m (of neighbourhood)* Ansehen *nt*. **don't speak to me in that ~ (of voice)** in diesem Ton kannst du mit mir nicht reden; **Trevor lowered the ~ (of the conversation)** Trevor mußte natürlich wieder ausfallend werden. **(b)** *(Mus)* Ton *m*; *(US: note)* Note *f*. **2** *vt (Phot: tint)* einfärben, tonen *(spec)*.

♦ **tone down** *vt sep (lit, fig)* abmildern; *colour also* abschwächen; *criticism also, language* mäßigen.

♦ **tone in** *vi* (im Farbton) harmonieren.

♦ **tone up** *vt sep muscles* kräftigen; *person* in Form bringen. **cycling keeps you ~d ~** Radfahren hält einen in Form.

tone-deaf [,təʊn'def] *adj* **he's ~** er hat kein Gehör für Tonhöhen.

tongs [tɒŋz] *npl* Zange *f*; **a pair of ~** eine Zange.

tongue [tʌŋ] *n* **(a)** Zunge *f*. **to put** *or* **stick one's ~ out at sb** jdm die Zunge herausstrecken; **to lose one's ~** *(fig)* die Sprache verlieren; **to hold one's ~** den Mund halten; **her remark was ~ in cheek** ihre Bemerkung war ironisch gemeint; **to have a sharp ~** eine scharfe Zunge haben. **(b)** *(liter: language)* Sprache *f*; *(old, Bibl)* Zunge *f*. **(c)** *(of shoe)* Zunge, Lasche *f*; *(of land)* Landzunge *f*.

tongue: ~**-in-cheek** *adj attr remark* witzelnd; ~**-tied** *adj* **to be ~-tied** keinen Ton herausbringen; ~**-twister** *n* Zungenbrecher *m*.

tonic ['tɒnɪk] *n* **(a)** *(Med)* Tonikum *nt*; *(hair ~)* Haarwasser *nt*; *(skin ~)* Lotion *f*. **it was a real ~ to see him again** *(fig)* es hat richtig gutgetan, ihn wiederzusehen. **(b) ~ (water)** Tonic(water) *nt*; **gin and ~** Gin Tonic *m*.

tonight [tə'naɪt] *adv (this evening)* heute abend; *(during the coming night)* heute nacht. **see you ~!** bis heute abend!

tonnage ['tʌnɪdʒ] *n* Tonnage *f*.

tonne [tʌn] *n (Brit)* Tonne *f*.

tonsil ['tɒnsl] *n* Mandel *f*. **to have one's ~s out** sich *(dat)* die Mandeln herausnehmen lassen.

tonsillitis [,tɒnsɪ'laɪtɪs] *n* Mandelentzündung *f*.

too [tu:] *adv* **(a)** zu. **that's ~ difficult a question to answer** diese Frage ist zu schwer zu beantworten; ~ **much/many** zuviel *inv*/zu viele; **it's ~ much for her** es ist zuviel für sie; **don't worry ~ much** mach dir nicht zuviel Sorgen; ~ **right!** *(col)* das kannst du laut sagen *(col)*; **all ~ ...** allzu ...; **only ~ ...** nur zu ...; **none ~ ...** gar nicht ..., keineswegs ...; **not ~/not any ~ ...** nicht zu/nicht allzu ...; **he wasn't ~ interested** er war nicht allzu interessiert; **I'm not/none ~ sure** ich bin nicht ganz/gar nicht sicher; **you're ~ kind** *(iro)* (das ist) wirklich zu nett von Ihnen; **none ~ soon** keineswegs zu früh.

(b) *(also)* auch. ***he* can swim ~, he ~ can swim** er kann *auch* schwimmen; **he can *swim* ~** schwimmen kann er auch.

(c) *(moreover, into the bargain)* auch noch. **it was really cheap, and it works ~!** es war wirklich billig, und es funktioniert sogar!

took [tʊk] *pret of* **take.**

tool [tu:l] *n (lit, fig)* Werkzeug *nt*; *(gardening ~)* (Garten)gerät *nt*. **~s** Werkzeuge *pl*; *(set)* Werkzeug *nt*; **that's one of the ~s of the trade** das gehört zum Handwerkszeug; **to have the ~s for the job** das nötige Werkzeug haben.

tool: ~**box** *n* Werkzeugkasten *m*; ~ **kit** *n* Werkzeug(ausrüstung *f*) *nt*; ~**shed** *n* Geräteschuppen *m*.

toot [tu:t] *vt* **to ~ one's horn** *(driver)* hupen.

tooth [tu:θ] *n, pl* **teeth** *(Anat, Tech)* Zahn *m*. **to have a ~ out/filled** sich *(dat)* einen Zahn ziehen/plombieren lassen; **to get one's teeth into sth** *(lit)* etw zwischen die Zähne bekommen; *(fig)* sich in etw *(dat)* festbeißen; **to show one's teeth** die Zähne zeigen *(also fig)*; **to fight ~ and nail** bis aufs Blut kämpfen; **to kick sb in the teeth** *(fig)* jdn vor den Kopf stoßen; **armed to the teeth** bis an die Zähne bewaffnet; **in the teeth of great opposition** trotz großen Widerstandes.

tooth *in cpds* Zahn-; **~ache** n Zahnschmerzen *pl*; **~brush** *n* Zahnbürste *f*.

toothed [tu:θt] *adj* gezahnt, mit Zähnen.

tooth: ~less *adj* zahnlos; **~paste** *n* Zahnpasta *or* -creme *f*; **~pick** *n* Zahnstocher *m*.

toothy ['tu:θɪ] *adj (+er)* **to be ~** ein Pferdegebiß haben *(col)*.

top[1] [tɒp] **1** *n* **(a)** *(highest part)* oberer Teil; *(of spire, tree etc, fig: of league etc)* Spitze *f*; *(of mountain)* Gipfel *m*; *(of carrots)* Ende *nt*; *(of table, bed)* Kopfende *nt*; *(of road, beach)* oberes Ende. **which is the ~?** wo ist oben?; **the ~ of the milk** die Rahmschicht (auf der Milch); **at the ~** oben; **at the ~ of the page/league/pile/stairs** *etc* oben auf der Seite/in der Tabelle/im Stapel/an der Treppe *etc*; **to be (at the) ~ of the class** der/die Beste in der Klasse sein; **near the ~** (ziemlich) weit oben; **he's near the ~ in English** in Englisch gehört er zu den Besten; **he aims to reach the ~** er will an die Spitze; **five lines from the ~** in der fünften Zeile von oben; **from ~ to bottom** von oben bis unten; **to scream at the ~ of one's voice** aus Leibeskräften brüllen; **they were talking at the ~(s) of their voices** sie haben sich in voller Lautstärke unterhalten; **to go over the ~** *(exaggerate)* zu viel des Guten tun; **to be over the ~** *(exaggerated)* übertrieben sein; *(past it: person)* auf dem absteigenden Ast sein.

(b) *(upper surface)* Oberfläche *f*. **to be on ~** oben liegen; *(fig)* obenauf sein; **it was on ~ of the cupboard** es war oben auf dem Schrank; **put it on ~ of the cupboard** leg es oben auf den Schrank; **on ~ of** *(in addition to)* zusätzlich zu; **things are getting on ~ of me** die Dinge wachsen mir über den Kopf; **and, on ~ of that ...** und zusätzlich ...; **it's just one thing on ~ of another** es kommt eines zum anderen; **he didn't see it until he was right on ~ of it** er sah es erst, als er ganz nah dran war; **to come out on ~** sich durchsetzen; *(over rival)* die Oberhand gewinnen; **to talk off the ~ of one's head** *(col)* nur so daherreden; **to blow one's ~** aus der Haut fahren *(col)*.

(c) *(working surface)* Arbeitsfläche *f*.

(d) *(bikini ~, blouse)* Oberteil *nt*.

(e) *(of jar, suitcase)* Deckel *m*; *(of bottle)* Verschluß *m*; *(of pen)* Hülle *f*; *(of car)* Dach *nt*. **hard/soft ~** Hardtop *nt*/Weichverdeck *nt*.

(f) *(Brit Aut: ~ gear)* höchster Gang. **in ~** im höchsten Gang.

2 *adj (upper)* obere(r, s); *(highest)* oberste(r, s); *branches, note, honours, price* höchste(r, s); *(best) driver, athlete, job* Spitzen-; *pupil, marks* beste(r, s); *entertainer, management* Top-. **~ prices** Höchstpreise *pl*; **on the ~ floor** im obersten Stockwerk; **a ~-floor flat** eine Dachgeschoßwohnung; **the ~ right-hand corner** die obere rechte Ecke; **at ~ speed** mit Höchstgeschwindigkeit; **in ~ form** in Höchstform; **to be ~** *(Sch)* Beste(r) sein; **the ~ people** *(in a company)* die Leute an der Spitze; *(in society)* die oberen Zehntausend.

3 *adv* **to come ~** *(Sch)* Beste(r) werden.

4 *vt* **(a)** *(cover, cap)* bedecken. **~ped by a dome** gekrönt von einer Kuppel.

(b) *(be higher than, fig: surpass)* übersteigen. **that ~s the lot** *(col)* das übertrifft alles; **and to ~ it all ...** *(col)* und um das Maß vollzumachen ...

(c) to ~ a tree die Spitze eines Baumes abschneiden; **to ~ and tail gooseberries** Stachelbeeren putzen.

♦ **top up** *vt sep glass, battery, tank* auffüllen. **to ~ ~ the oil** Öl nachfüllen; **can I ~ you ~?** *(col)* darf ich Ihnen nachschenken?

top[2] *n* Kreisel *m*. **to sleep like a ~** wie ein Murmeltier schlafen.

topaz ['təʊpæz] *n* Topas *m*.

top: ~coat *n* **(a)** *(overcoat)* Mantel *m*; **(b)** *(coat of paint)* Deckanstrich *m*; **~ copy** *n* Original *nt*; **~-flight** *adj* Spitzen-, erstklassig; **~ gear** *n* höchster Gang; **~ hat** *n* Zylinder *m*; **~-heavy** *adj (lit, fig)* kopflastig.

topic ['tɒpɪk] *n* Thema *nt*. **~ of conversation** Gesprächsthema *nt*.

topical ['tɒpɪkəl] *adj problem, speech, event* aktuell.

top: ~less *adj* (mit) oben ohne, Oben-ohne-; **~-level** *adj* Spitzen-; **~most** *adj* oberste(r, s).

topographic(al) [ˌtɒpə'græfɪk(əl)] *adj* topographisch.

topography [tə'pɒgrəfɪ] *n* Topographie *f*.

topping ['tɒpɪŋ] *n (Cook)* **with a ~ of cream/nuts** *etc* mit Sahne/Nüssen *etc* (oben) darauf.

topple ['tɒpl] **1** *vi* wackeln; *(fall)* fallen. **2** *vt* umwerfen; *(from a height)* hinunterkippen; *(fig) government* stürzen.

♦ **topple over** *vi* fallen *(prep obj* über *+acc)*.

top: ~-ranking *adj* von hohem Rang; *civil servant, officer also* hohe(r); *author, singer* Spitzen-; **~-secret** *adj* streng geheim; **~soil** *n (Agr)* Ackerkrume *f*.

topsy-turvy ['tɒpsɪ'tɜ:vɪ] *(col)* **1** *adj (in disorder)* kunterbunt durcheinander *pred; (fig)* auf den Kopf gestellt. **it's a ~ world** es ist eine verkehrte Welt. **2** *adv* **to turn sth ~** *(lit, fig)* etw auf den Kopf stellen.

top-up ['tɒpʌp] *n (col)* **would you like a ~?** darf man Ihnen noch nachschenken?

torch [tɔ:tʃ] *n (lit, fig)* Fackel *f*; *(Brit: flashlight)* Taschenlampe *f*; *(blowlamp)* Schweißbrenner *m*.

tore [tɔ:ʳ] *pret of* **tear**[1].

torment ['tɔ:ment] **1** *n* Qual *f*. **to be in ~** Qualen leiden. **2** [tɔ:'ment] *vt* quälen; *(annoy, tease)* plagen.

tormentor [tɔ:'mentəʳ] *n* Peiniger(in *f*) *m*.

torn [tɔ:n] *ptp of* **tear**[1]

tornado [tɔ:'neɪdəʊ] *n, pl* **-es** Tornado *m*.

torpedo [tɔ:'pi:dəʊ] **1** *n, pl* **-es** Torpedo *m*. **~ boat** Torpedoboot *nt*. **2** *vt* torpedieren.

torpid ['tɔ:pɪd] *adj (lethargic)* träge.

torpor ['tɔ:pəʳ] *n* Trägheit *f*.

torrent ['tɒrənt] *n (river)* reißender Strom. **the rain came down in ~s** der Regen kam in wahren Sturzbächen herunter; **a ~ of abuse** eine Flut von Beschimpfungen.

torrential [tɒ'renʃəl] *adj rain* sintflutartig.

torrid ['tɒrɪd] *adj (lit, fig)* heiß; *heat, air, sun* sengend.

torso ['tɔ:səʊ] *n* Körper *m*; *(Art)* Torso *m*.

tortoise ['tɔ:təs] *n* Schildkröte *f*.

tortuous ['tɔ:tjʊəs] *adj (lit) path* gewunden; *(fig)* verwickelt; *methods also, person* umständlich.

torture ['tɔ:tʃəʳ] **1** *n* Folter *f*; *(fig)* Qual *f*. **~ chamber** Folterkammer *f*. **2** *vt (lit)* foltern; *(fig: torment)* quälen, peinigen *(geh)*; *(fig: distort)* verzerren.

torturer ['tɔ:tʃərəʳ] *n (lit)* Folterknecht *m*; *(fig: tormentor)* Peiniger(in *f*) *m*.

Tory ['tɔ:rɪ] *(Brit Pol)* **1** *n* Konservative(r) *mf*, Tory *m*. **2** *adj* konservativ, Tory-.

toss [tɒs] **1** *n* Wurf *m*. **with a proud ~ of her head** mit einer stolzen Kopfbewegung; **to win/lose the ~** *(esp Sport)* die Seitenwahl gewinnen/verlieren; **there is no point in arguing the ~ (with me)** es hat keinen Sinn, (mit mir) darüber zu streiten. **2** *vt* **(a)** *(throw) ball* werfen; *salad* anmachen; *(Brit) pancake* wenden *(durch Hochwerfen)*; *rider* abwerfen. **to ~ sth to sb** jdm etw zuwerfen. **(b)** *(move: wind)* schütteln, zerren an *(+dat)*. **the boat, ~ed (about) by the waves ...** das Boot, von den Wellen hin und her geworfen, ...; **to ~ (back) one's head** den Kopf zurückwerfen. **(c) to ~ a coin** eine Münze (zum Losen) hochwerfen; **I'll ~ you for it** laß uns darum knobeln. **3** *vi* **(a)** *(ship)* rollen. **to ~ and turn (in bed)** sich (im Bett) hin und her werfen. **(b) to ~ for sth** um etw knobeln.

♦ **toss up 1** *vi* knobeln *(for* um*)*. **2** *vt sep* werfen. **to ~ sth ~ (into the air)** etw hochwerfen.

tot [tɒt] *n* **(a)** *(child: also* **tiny ~***)* Knirps *(col) m.* **(b)** *(esp Brit: of alcohol)* Schlückchen *nt.*

♦ **tot up** *vt sep (esp Brit col)* zusammenzählen.

total ['təʊtl] **1** *adj* völlig, absolut; *sum, loss, number* Gesamt-; *war, eclipse, disaster* total. **what is the ~ number of rooms you have?** wie viele Zimmer haben Sie (insgesamt)?; **to be in ~ ignorance (of sth)** (von etw) überhaupt nichts wissen. **2** *n* Gesamtmenge *f*; *(money, figures)* Endsumme *f*. **a ~ of 50 people** insgesamt 50 Leute. **3** *vt* **(a)** *(amount to)* sich belaufen auf *(+acc)*. **(b)** *(add: also* **~ up***)* zusammenzählen *or* -rechnen.

totalitarian [ˌtəʊtælɪ'tɛərɪən] *adj* totalitär.

totality [təʊ'tælɪtɪ] *n* Gesamtheit *f.*

tote[1] [təʊt] *n (col)* **the ~** der Totalisator.

tote[2] *vt (col: carry) sth heavy* schleppen; *gun* bei sich haben.

totem pole ['təʊtəmˌpəʊl] *n* Totempfahl *m.*

totter ['tɒtəʳ] *vi (wobble before falling)* wanken; *(stagger)* taumeln; *(old man, baby)* tapsen; *(invalid, fig)* schwanken; *(economy)* kränkeln.

tottery ['tɒtərɪ] *adj* wack(e)lig; *person* tatterig. **a ~ old man** ein Tattergreis *m (col)*.

touch [tʌtʃ] **1** *n* **(a)** *(sense of ~)* (Tast)gefühl *nt*. **to be cold/soft to the ~** sich kalt/weich anfühlen.

(b) *(act of ~ing)* Berühren *nt*, Berührung *f*; *(of pianist, typist, piano, typewriter)* Anschlag *m*. **I felt a ~ on my arm** ich spürte, daß jd/etw meinen Arm berührte; **it opens at a ~** es öffnet sich auf leichten Druck.

(c) *(skill)* Hand *f*; *(style also)* Stil *m*. **the ~ of a master** die Hand eines Meisters; **it has the ~ of genius/the professional ~** es hat etwas Geniales/Professionelles; **he's losing his ~** er wird langsam alt; **a personal ~** eine persönliche Note.

(d) *(stroke) (Art)* Strich *m*; *(fig)* Einfall *m*. **a book with humorous ~es** ein stellenweise humorvolles Buch; **a nice ~** eine hübsche Note; *(gesture)* eine nette Geste; **to put the finishing ~es to sth** einer Sache *(dat)* den letzten Schliff geben.

(e) *(small quantity)* Spur *f*; *(of irony, sadness etc also)* Anflug *m*. **a ~ of flu** eine leichte Grippe.

(f) *(contact)* **to be in ~ with sb** mit jdm in Verbindung stehen; **they were** *or* **got in ~ with us yesterday** sie haben sich gestern mit uns in Verbindung gesetzt; **to be/keep in ~ with (political) developments** (politisch) auf dem laufenden sein/bleiben; **I'll be in ~!** ich lasse von mir hören!; **keep in ~!** laß/laßt wieder einmal von dir/euch hören!; **to be out of ~ with sb** keine Verbindung mehr zu jdm haben; **to be completely out of ~ (with sth)** (in bezug auf etw *acc*) überhaupt nicht auf dem laufenden sein; **to lose ~ with sb** den Kontakt zu jdm verlieren.

(g) *(Ftbl)* **to be in ~** im Aus sein.

2 *vt* **(a)** berühren; *(get hold of also)* anfassen; *(press lightly also) piano keys* anschlagen; *brakes* antippen; *(brush against)* streifen. **to ~ glasses** anstoßen; **don't ~ that!** faß das nicht an!; **I was ~ing 100 most of the way** ich fuhr fast ständig 100. **(b)** *(lay hands on)* anrühren. **the police/tax authorities can't ~ me** die Polizei/das Finanzamt kann mir nichts anhaben; **the paintings weren't ~ed by the fire** die Gemälde blieben vom Feuer verschont; **I never ~ whisky** ich rühre keinen Whisky an; **I don't want to ~ my savings** ich will meine Ersparnisse nicht anbrechen; **I wouldn't ~ those shares** ich würde meine Finger von den Aktien lassen. **(c)** *(concern)* berühren. **(d)** *(move emotionally)* rühren, bewegen; *(affect)* berühren; *(wound) pride* treffen. **deeply ~ed** tief gerührt *or* bewegt. **(e)** *(equal)* **nobody can ~ him (for ...)** bei ... kommt keiner an ihn heran.

3 *vi (come into contact)* sich berühren; *(estates etc: be adjacent also)* aneinandergrenzen. **"please do not ~"** „bitte nicht berühren".

♦ **touch down 1** *vi* **(a)** *(Aviat, Space)* aufsetzen. **(b)** *(Rugby, US Ftbl)* einen Versuch erzielen. **2** *vt sep ball* niederlegen.

♦ **touch (up)on** *vi +prep obj subject* kurz berühren, antippen.

touch-and-go ['tʌtʃən'gəʊ] *adj* **to be ~** riskant sein; **it's ~ whether ...** es steht auf des Messers Schneide, ob ...

touchdown ['tʌtʃdaʊn] *n* **(a)** *(Aviat, Space)* Aufsetzen *nt*. **(b)** *(Rugby, US Ftbl)* Versuch *m (Niederlegen des Balles im Malfeld des Gegners)*.

touched [tʌtʃt] *adj pred (moved)* gerührt, bewegt.

touching ['tʌtʃɪŋ] **1** *adj* rührend. **2** *prep (form)* bezüglich *(+gen) (form)*.

touch: ~line *n (Sport)* Seitenlinie *f*; **~paper** *n* Zündpapier *nt*; **~-type** *vti* blindschreiben.

touchy ['tʌtʃɪ] *adj* empfindlich *(about* in bezug auf *+acc)*; *(irritable also)* leicht reizbar; *subject* heikel.

tough [tʌf] *adj (+er)* **(a)** zäh; *resistant* widerstandsfähig; *cloth* strapazierfähig; *(towards others)* hart; *bargaining, opponent, struggle, district, policy, controls* hart. **to get ~ (with sb)** hart durchgreifen (gegen jdn); **~ guy** *(col)* (knall)harter Bursche *(col)*. **(b)** *(difficult) task, problem* hart; *journey* strapaziös, anstrengend. **it was ~ going** *(lit, fig)* es war eine Strapaze; **to have a ~ time of it** nichts zu lachen haben; **it was ~ on the others** das war hart für die andern; **~ (luck)!** Pech!

toughen ['tʌfn] *vt* **(a)** *glass, metal* härten. **(b)** *(fig) person* zäh machen; *(physically)* abhärten.

toughness ['tʌfnɪs] *n see adj* **(a)** Zähigkeit *f*; Widerstandsfähigkeit *f*; Strapazierfähigkeit *f*; Härte *f*. **(b)** *(difficulty)* Schwierigkeit *f*; *(of journey)* Strapazen *pl.*

toupee ['tuːpeɪ] *n* Toupet *nt.*

tour [tʊəʳ] **1** *n (journey, walking ~ etc)* Tour *f*; *(of town, building etc)* Rundgang *m (of* durch*)*; *(also* **guided ~***)* Führung *f (of* durch*)*; *(by bus)* Rundfahrt *f (of* durch*)*. **to go on a ~ of Scotland/the castle** eine Schottlandreise machen/an einer Schloßführung teilnehmen; **to go/be on ~** *(Theat, Sport)* auf Tournee gehen/sein. **2** *vt* **(a)** *country etc* fahren durch; *(on foot)* ziehen durch *(col)*; *(visit) town, building* einen Rundgang machen durch; *(by bus etc)* eine Rundfahrt machen durch. **(b)** *(Theat, Sport)* eine Tournee machen durch. **3** *vi* **(a)** *(on holiday)* eine Reise *or* Tour machen. **we're ~ing (around)** wir reisen herum; **to go ~ing** Touren/eine Tour machen. **(b)** *(Theat, Sport)* eine Tournee machen.

tourism ['tʊərɪzəm] *n* Fremdenverkehr, Tourismus *m.*

tourist ['tʊərɪst] **1** *n (person)* Tourist(in *f*) *m*; *(Sport)* Gast *m*. **2** *attr class, hotel, shop* Touristen-; *guide* Fremden-; *bureau, office, industry* Fremdenverkehrs-. **~ season** Reisezeit *f*; **~ trade** Fremdenverkehrsgewerbe *nt.*

tournament ['tʊənəmənt] *n (Sport, Hist)* Turnier *nt.*

tourniquet ['tʊənɪkeɪ] *n* Aderpresse *f.*

tousled ['taʊzld] *adj hair* zerzaust. **~ head** Wuschelkopf *m (col)*.

tout [taʊt] *(col)* **1** *n (tipster)* Wettberater *m*; *(ticket ~)* Schwarzmarkthändler *m*; *(for business)* Kundenfänger *m*. **2** *vi* **to ~ for business/customers** (aufdringlich) Reklame machen/auf Kundenfang sein *(col)*.

tow [təʊ] **1** *n* **to give sb/a car a ~** jdn/ein Auto abschleppen; **to give sb/a yacht a ~** jdn/eine Jacht ins Schlepptau nehmen; **in ~** *(fig)* im Schlepptau. **2** *vt boat, glider* schleppen; *car also*

abschleppen; *trailer* ziehen.
♦ **tow away** *vt sep* abschleppen.
toward(s) [tə'wɔːd(z)] *prep* **(a)** *(in direction of) (with verbs of motion)* auf *(+acc)* ... zu. **they walked ~ the town** sie gingen auf die Stadt zu; **we sailed ~ China** wir segelten in Richtung China; **it's further north, ~ Dortmund** es liegt weiter im Norden, Richtung Dortmund; **~ the south** nach Süden; **he turned ~ her** er wandte sich ihr zu; **they are working ~ a solution** sie arbeiten auf eine Lösung hin. **(b)** *(in relation to)* ... *(dat)* gegenüber. **what are your feelings ~ him?** was empfinden Sie ihm gegenüber? **(c) ~ ten o'clock** gegen zehn Uhr; **~ the end of the year** gegen Ende des Jahres. **(d) the money will go ~** ... das Geld wird für ... verwendet; **most of my salary goes ~ the rent** der größte Teil meines Gehalts geht für die Miete drauf *(col)*.
towel ['taʊəl] *n* Handtuch *nt*. **~ rail** Handtuchhalter *m*.
tower ['taʊəʳ] *n* **(a)** Turm *m*. **(b)** *(fig: person)* **a ~ of strength** ein starker (Rück)halt.
♦ **tower above** *or* **over** *vi +prep obj* **(a)** *(buildings etc)* emporragen über *(+acc)*. **(b)** *(lit, fig: people)* überragen.
tower block *n (Brit)* Hochhaus *nt*.
towering ['taʊərɪŋ] *adj building* hochragend; *mountain* (steil) aufragend; *tree* hochgewachsen. **one of the ~ giants of literature** eine der einsamen Größen der Literatur.
town [taʊn] *n* Stadt *f*. **the ~ of Brighton** (die Stadt) Brighton; **to go into ~** in die Stadt gehen; **to live in ~** in der Stadt wohnen; **he's out of ~** er ist nicht in der Stadt; **to have a night on the ~** *(col)* die Nacht durchmachen *(col)*; **to go to ~ on sth** *(fig col) (go to great trouble with)* sich bei etw einen abbrechen *(col)*; *(to please)* sich bei etw ins Zeug legen.
town: ~ centre *(Brit) or* **center** *(US) n* Stadtmitte *f*, (Stadt)zentrum *nt*; **~ clerk** *n* Stadtdirektor *m*; *(of bigger town)* Oberstadtdirektor *m*; **~ council** *n* Stadtrat *m*; **~ hall** *n* Rathaus *nt*; **~ planning** *n* Stadtplanung *f*.
townspeople ['taʊnz,piːpl] *npl* Städter, Stadtmenschen *pl*; *(citizens)* Bürger *pl*.
tow: ~path *n* Treidelpfad *m*; **~rope** *n* Abschleppseil *nt*; **~-truck** *n (US)* Abschleppwagen *m*.
toxic ['tɒksɪk] *adj* giftig, Gift-, toxisch.
toy [tɔɪ] **1** *n* Spielzeug *nt*. **~s** Spielsachen *pl*, Spielzeug *nt*. **2** *vi* **to ~ with an object/idea** *etc* mit einer Sache/Idee *etc* spielen; **to ~ with one's food** mit dem Essen (herum)spielen.
toy *in cpds car, soldier* Spielzeug-; **~shop** *(Brit) or* **store** *(US) n* Spielwarenladen *m*.
trace [treɪs] **1** *n (sign, small amount)* Spur *f*. **to vanish without ~** spurlos verschwinden; **to lose ~ of sb/sth** jdn/etw aus den Augen verlieren. **2** *vt* **(a)** *(draw)* zeichnen; *(copy)* nachziehen; *(with tracing paper)* durchpausen. **(b)** *(follow trail of)* verfolgen; *steps* folgen *(+dat)*. **she was ~d to a house in Soho** ihre Spur führte zu einem Haus in Soho. **(c)** *(find)* ausfindig machen, auffinden.
♦ **trace back** *vt sep descent* zurückverfolgen; *rumour* auf seinen Ursprung zurückverfolgen; *neurosis etc* zurückführen *(to* auf *+acc)*.
trace element *n* Spurenelement *nt*.
trachea [trə'kɪə] *n* Luftröhre *f*.
tracing ['treɪsɪŋ] *n (drawing)* Durchpausen *nt*; *(result)* Pause *f*. **~ paper** Pauspapier *nt*.
track [træk] **1** *n* **(a)** *(trail)* Fährte, Spur *f*; *(of tyres)* (Fahr)spur *f*. **to be on sb's ~** jdm auf der Spur sein; **to keep ~ of sb/sth** jdn/etw im Auge behalten; **I can't keep ~ of your girlfriends** du hast so viele Freundinnen, da komme ich nicht mit *(col)*; **no-one can keep ~ of the situation** niemand hat mehr einen Überblick über die Lage; **to lose ~ of sb/sth** *(lose sight of)* jdn/etw aus den Augen verlieren; *(lose count of, be confused about)* über Leute/etw den Überblick verlieren; **we must be making ~s** *(col)* wir müssen uns auf die Socken machen *(col)*; **he stopped dead in his ~s** er blieb abrupt stehen; **to cover (up) one's ~s** seine Spuren verwischen.
(b) *(path)* Weg, Pfad *m*. **off the ~** *(fig)* abwegig; **to be on the right/wrong ~** *(fig)* auf der richtigen/falschen Spur sein.
(c) *(Rail)* Gleise *pl*; *(US: platform)* Bahnsteig *m*. **to leave the ~(s)** entgleisen.
(d) *(Sport)* Rennbahn *f*; *(Athletics)* Bahn *f*; *(Motorsport)* Piste *f*; *(circuit)* Rennstrecke *f*.
(e) *(on tape)* Spur *f*; *(song etc)* Stück *nt*.
(f) *(also* **caterpillar ~***)* Raupenkette *f*.
2 *vt (follow) person, animal* verfolgen; *(Space) rocket* die Flugbahn *(+gen)* verfolgen.
♦ **track down** *vt sep* aufspüren *(to* in *+dat)*; *thing* aufstöbern, auftreiben *(col)*; *reference, source* ausfindig machen.
tracker dog *n* Spürhund *m*.
track: ~ record *n (fig)* **what's his ~ record?** was hat er vorzuweisen?; **~suit** *n* Trainingsanzug *m*.
tract[1] [trækt] *n* **(a)** *(of land)* Gebiet *nt*. **narrow ~** Streifen *m*. **(b)** *(respiratory)* Wege *pl*; *(digestive)* Trakt *m*.
tract[2] *n (pamphlet)* Traktat *nt*, Schrift *f*.
traction ['trækʃən] *n* Zugkraft, Zugleistung *f*; *(of wheels)* Bodenhaftung *f*; *(Med)* Streckverband *m*. **~ engine** Zugmaschine *f*.
tractor ['træktəʳ] *n* Traktor, Trecker *m*.
trade [treɪd] **1** *n* **(a)** *(commerce)* Handel *m*, Gewerbe *nt*; *(turnover: of shop etc)* die Geschäfte *pl*. **to do a good ~** gute Geschäfte machen; **to do a brisk ~ in sth** einen reißenden Absatz an etw *(dat)* haben. **(b)** *(line of business)* Branche *f*, Geschäftszweig *m*; *(job)* Handwerk *nt*. **he's in the wool ~** er ist in der Wollbranche; **he's in the ~** er ist vom Fach; **as we call it in the ~** wie es in unserer Branche heißt; **he's a bricklayer by ~** er ist Maurer von Beruf; **he's a lawyer by ~** *(hum)* er ist Rechtsanwalt. **(c)** *(exchange)* Tausch(handel) *m*. **2** *vt* tauschen. **to ~ sth for sth else** etw gegen etw anderes (ein)tauschen. **3** *vi* **(a)** *(Comm)* Handel treiben, handeln. **to ~ in sth** mit etw handeln; **to ~ with sb** mit jdm Geschäfte machen. **(b)** *(US col)* einkaufen *(at* bei*)*.
♦ **trade in** *vt sep* in Zahlung geben *(for* für*)*.
trade: ~ fair *n* Handelsmesse *f*; **~ figures** *npl* Handelsziffern *pl*; **~ gap** *n* Außenhandelsdefizit *nt*; **~-in** *n* **to take/offer sth as a ~-in** etw in Zahlung nehmen/geben; **~mark** *n (lit)* Warenzeichen *nt*; **honesty was his ~mark** er war für seine Ehrlichkeit bekannt; **~ name** *n* Handelsname *m*.
trader ['treɪdəʳ] *n (person)* Händler *m*.
trades: ~man *n (delivery man)* Lieferant *m*; *(shopkeeper)* Händler *m*; *(plumber, electrician etc)* Handwerker *m*; **~man's entrance** Lieferanteneingang *m*; **~ union** *n* = **trade union; T~ Union congress** (britischer) Gewerkschaftsbund.
trade: ~ union *n* Gewerkschaft *f*; **~ unionism** *n* Gewerkschaftsbewegung *f*; **~ unionist** *n* Gewerkschaft(l)er(in *f*) *m*.
trading ['treɪdɪŋ] *n* Handel *m*, Handeln *nt (in* mit*)*.
tradition [trə'dɪʃən] Tradition *f*. **~ has it that he ...** es ist überliefert, daß er ...
traditional [trə'dɪʃənl] *adj* traditionell; *virtues also* überkommen; *jazz* Old-time-.
traditionally [trə'dɪʃnəlɪ] *adv* traditionell; *(customarily)* üblicherweise.
traffic ['træfɪk] **1** *n* **(a)** Verkehr *m*; *(Aviat)* Flugverkehr *m*. **closed to heavy ~** gesperrt für den Schwerlastverkehr. **(b)** *(business: of port, airport)* Umschlag *m*. **~ in steel** Stahlumschlag *m*. **(c)** *(usu pej: trading)* Handel *m (in* mit*)*; *(in pornography)* Vertrieb *m (in* von*)*. **2** *vi (usu pej)* handeln *(in* mit*)*.

traffic *in cpds* Verkehrs-; ~ **circle** *n (US)* Kreisverkehr *m*; ~ **cop** *n (col)* Verkehrspolizist *m*; ~ **island** *n* Verkehrsinsel *f*; ~ **jam** *n* Verkehrsstauung *f*.
trafficker ['træfɪkə^r] *n (usu pej)* Händler *m*; *(in drugs also)* Dealer *m*.
traffic: ~ **lights** *(Brit) npl,* ~ **light** *n (US)* Verkehrsampel *f*; ~ **policeman** *n* Verkehrspolizist *m*; ~ **warden** *n (Brit)* ≃ Verkehrspolizist *m ohne amtliche Befugnisse; (woman)* ≃ Politesse *f*.
tragedy ['trædʒɪdɪ] *n* Tragödie. *f*. **six killed in holiday crash** ~ tragischer Urlaubsunfall forderte sechs Todesopfer; **the** ~ **of it is that ...** das Tragische daran ist, daß ...
tragic ['trædʒɪk] *adj* tragisch.
tragically ['trædʒɪkəlɪ] *adv* ~, **he was killed before ...** tragischerweise kam er ums Leben, bevor ...
trail [treɪl] **1** *n* **(a)** Spur *f*. ~ **of blood** Blutspur *f*; ~ **of smoke/dust** Rauchfahne *f*/Staubwolke *f*. **(b)** *(track)* Fährte, Spur *f*. **hot on the** ~ dicht auf den Fersen; **to be on the** ~ **of an animal** die Spur eines Tieres verfolgen; **the police are on his** ~ die Polizei ist ihm auf der Spur. **(c)** *(path)* Weg, Pfad *m*; *(nature* ~ *etc)* (Wander)weg *m*. **2** *vt* **(a)** *(follow) person* folgen *(+dat)*; *animal* verfolgen. **(b)** *(drag)* schleppen, schleifen. **the bird** ~**ed its broken wing** der Vogel zog seinen gebrochenen Flügel nach. **(c)** *(US: tow)* ziehen, schleppen. **3** *vi* **(a)** *(on floor)* schleifen. **(b)** *(plant)* sich ranken. **(c)** *(walk)* trotten. **(d)** *(be behind: in competition etc)* weit zurückliegen; *(Sport)* weit zurückgefallen sein.
♦ **trail away** *or* **off** *vi (voice)* sich verlieren *(into* in *+dat)*.
trailer ['treɪlə^r] *n* **(a)** *(Aut)* Anhänger *m*; *(esp US: of lorry)* Sattelauflieger *m*. **(b)** *(US)* Wohnwagen, Caravan *m*. **(c)** *(Film, TV)* Vorschau *f*.
train[1] [treɪn] *n* **(a)** *(Rail)* Zug *m*. **to go/travel by** ~ mit dem Zug *or* der Bahn fahren/reisen; **a** ~ **journey** eine Bahn- *or* Zugfahrt; **to take** *or* **get the 11 o'clock** ~ den Elfuhrzug nehmen; **to change** ~**s** umsteigen; **on the** ~ im Zug. **(b)** *(line)* Kolonne *f*; *(of people)* Schlange *f*; *(retinue)* Gefolge *nt*. **the war brought famine in its** ~ der Krieg brachte eine Hungersnot mit sich. **(c)** *(of events)* Folge, Kette *f*. **he interrupted my** ~ **of thought** er unterbrach meinen Gedankengang. **(d)** *(of dress)* Schleppe *f*.
train[2] **1** *vt* **(a)** ausbilden; *child* erziehen; *animal* abrichten, dressieren; *mind* schulen; *(Sport)* trainieren. **to** ~ **sb as sth** jdn als *or* zu etw ausbilden; **to** ~ **an animal to do sth** ein Tier dazu abrichten, etw zu tun; **this dog has been** ~**ed to kill** dieser Hund ist aufs Töten abgerichtet. **(b)** *(aim) gun* richten *(on* auf *+acc)*. **(c)** *plant* wachsen lassen *(over* über *+acc)*. **2** *vi* **(a)** *(esp Sport)* trainieren *(for* für*)*. **(b)** *(study)* ausgebildet werden. **he** ~**ed as a teacher** er hat eine Lehrerausbildung gemacht.
train driver *n* Zug- *or* Lokführer(in *f*) *m*.
trained [treɪnd] *adj worker* gelernt, Fach-; *nurse, teacher, voice* ausgebildet; *animal* dressiert; *mind, ear, eye* geschult.
trainee [treɪ'niː] *n* Auszubildende(r) *mf*; *(academic, technical)* Praktikant(in *f*) *m*; *(nurse)* Krankenpflegeschüler(in *f*) *m*, Schwesternschülerin *f*; *(management)* Trainee *m*.
trainee: ~ **manager** *n* Management-Trainee *m*; ~ **teacher** *n (in primary school)* ≃ Praktikant(in *f*) *m*; *(in secondary school)* ≃ Referendar(in *f*) *m*.
trainer ['treɪnə^r] *n* **(a)** *(Sport, of racehorse)* Trainer *m*; *(of animals)* Dresseur *m*. **(b)** *(shoe)* Trainingsschuh *m*.
training ['treɪnɪŋ] *n* Ausbildung *f (also Mil)*; *(of staff)* Schulung *f*; *(of animal)* Dressur *f*; *(Sport)* Training *nt*. **to be in** ~ im Training sein, trainieren; *(be fit)* gut in Form *or* durchtrainiert sein; **to be out of** ~ nicht in Form sein, aus dem Training sein.
training: ~**college** *n (for teachers)* ≃ Pädagogische Hochschule; ~ **course** *n* Ausbildungskurs *m*; ~ **shoes** *npl* Trainingsschuhe *pl*.
train: ~**load** *n (of goods)* Zugladung *f*; ~**loads of holidaymakers** ganze Züge voller Urlauber; ~ **service** *n* Zugverkehr *m*; *(between two places)* (Eisen)bahnverbindung *f*; ~ **set** *n* (Spielzeug)eisenbahn *f*; ~**sick** *adj* **he gets** ~ **sick** ihm wird beim Zugfahren schlecht *or* übel; ~**spotter** *n* Eisenbahnfan *m*; ~**spotting** *n Hobby nt, bei dem Züge begutachtet und deren Nummern notiert werden.*
traipse [treɪps] *(col) vi* latschen *(col)*. **to** ~ **around the shops** in den Geschäften rumlatschen *(col)*.
trait [treɪt, treɪ] *n* Eigenschaft *f*.
traitor ['treɪtə^r] *n* Verräter *m*. **to be a** ~ **to one's country** sein Vaterland verraten; **to turn** ~ zum Verräter werden.
trajectory [trə'dʒektərɪ] *n* Flugbahn *f*.
tram [træm] *n (Brit)* Straßenbahn *f*.
tramp [træmp] **1** *vi* **(a)** *(walk heavily, trudge)* stapfen, stampfen. **(b)** *(hike)* wandern; *(as vagabond)* umherziehen. **he** ~**ed all over Europe** er wanderte in ganz Europa umher. **2** *vt* **(a)** *(spread by walking)* herumtreten. **don't** ~ **that mud into the carpet** tritt den Dreck nicht in den Teppich. **(b)** *(walk) streets* latschen durch *(col)*. **3** *n (vagabond)* Landstreicher(in *f*), Tramp *m*; *(in town)* Stadtstreicher(in *f*) *m*.
trample ['træmpl] **1** *vt* niedertrampeln, zertrampeln. **to** ~ **sth underfoot** auf etw *(dat)* herumtrampeln; ~**d to death** zu Tode getrampelt; **to** ~ **sth into the ground** etw in den Boden trampeln. **2** *vi* **he lets his wife** ~ **all over him** *(fig)* er läßt sich *(dat)* von seiner Frau auf dem Kopf herumtanzen.
♦ **trample on** *vi +prep obj* herumtreten auf *(+dat)*. **to** ~ ~ **sb** *(fig)* jdn herumschikanieren; **to** ~ ~ **sb's feelings** *(fig)* jds Gefühle mit Füßen treten.
trampoline ['træmpəlɪn] *n* Trampolin *nt*.
trance [trɑːns] *n* Trance *f*. **to go into a** ~ in einen Trancezustand verfallen.
tranquil ['træŋkwɪl] *adj* ruhig.
tranquillity, *(US)* **tranquility** [træŋ'kwɪlɪtɪ] *n* Ruhe *f*.
tranquillize, *(US)* **tranquilize** ['træŋkwɪlaɪz] *vt* beruhigen.
tranquillizer, *(US)* **tranquilizer** ['træŋkwɪlaɪzə^r] *n* Beruhigungsmittel *nt*.
trans- [trænz-] *pref* trans-, Trans-.
transact [træn'zækt] *vt* abwickeln; *deal* abschließen.
transaction [træn'zækʃən] *n* **(a)** *(act) see vt* Abwicklung *f*; Abschluß *m*. ~ **of business** Geschäftsbetrieb *m*. **(b)** *(piece of business)* Geschäft *nt*; *(Fin, St Ex)* Transaktion *f*. **(c)** ~**s** *pl (of society)* Sitzungsbericht *m*.
transatlantic ['trænʒət'læntɪk] *adj* transatlantisch, Transatlantik-; *customs* auf der anderen Seiten (des Atlantiks); *cousins, accent* amerikanisch; *(for Americans)* britisch.
transcend [træn'send] *vt* übersteigen, überschreiten; *(Philos)* transzendieren.
transcontinental ['trænz,kɒntɪ'nentl] *adj* transkontinental.
transcribe [træn'skraɪb] *vt manuscripts* abschreiben; *(from shorthand)* (in Langschrift) übertragen; *proceedings etc* niederschreiben; *(Mus)* transkribieren.
transcript ['trænskrɪpt] *n (of court proceedings)* Protokoll *nt*; *(of tapes)* Niederschrift *f*; *(copy)* Kopie, Abschrift *f*.
transcription [træn'skrɪpʃən] *n (Mus, Phon)* Transkription *f*; *(copy, of shorthand notes)* Abschrift *f*; *(act)* Abschreiben *nt*; *(of speech,*

proceedings) Niederschrift *f*, Protokoll *nt*; *(Rad, TV: recording)* Aufnahme *f*.

transept ['trænsept] *n* Querschiff *nt*.

transfer [træns'fɜːʳ] **1** *vt* übertragen *(to* auf *+acc)*; *prisoner* überführen *(to* in *+acc)*; *premises, troops, account* verlegen *(to* in *+acc, to town* nach*)*; *soldier, employee* versetzen *(to* in *+acc, to town, country* nach*)*; *(Sport) player* abgeben *(to* an *+acc)*; *(Fin) funds, money* überweisen *(to* auf *+acc)*; *(Jur) property* überschreiben *(to* auf *+acc)*. **he ~red the money from the box to his pocket** er nahm das Geld aus der Schachtel und steckte es in die Tasche.

2 *vi* **(a)** überwechseln *(to* zu*)*; *(to new system, working conditions)* umstellen *(to* auf *+acc)*. **(b)** *(Fin)* umsteigen *(into* auf *+acc)*. **(c)** *(in travelling)* umsteigen *(to* in *+acc)*; *(Univ)* das Studienfach wechseln, umsatteln *(col) (from ... to* von ... auf *+acc)*.

3 ['trænsfɜːʳ] *n* **(a)** *see vt* Übertragung *f*; Überführung *f*; Verlegung *f*; Versetzung *f*; *(of footballer)* Transfer *m*; Überweisung *f*; Überschreibung *f*. **he asked for a ~** *(soldier, employee)* er bat um Versetzung; *(footballer)* er bat, auf die Transferliste gesetzt zu werden. **(b)** *(picture)* Abziehbild *nt*. **(c)** *(~ ticket)* Umsteige(fahr)karte *f*.

transferable [træns'fɜːrəbl] *adj* übertragbar; *money, stocks* transferierbar.

transfix [træns'fɪks] *vt* **(a)** *(fix)* annageln, feststecken *(to* an *+acc)*. **(b)** *(fig)* **to be** *or* **stand ~ed with horror** starr vor Entsetzen sein; **he stood as though ~ed** er stand da wie angewurzelt.

transform [træns'fɔːm] *vt* umwandeln, umformen *(into* zu*)*; *ideas, views* (von Grund auf) verändern; *person, caterpillar* verwandeln; *(Phys)* umwandeln *(into* in *+acc)*; *(Elec)* (um)wandeln *(into* in *+acc)*, transformieren *(into* in *+acc)*. **the old house was ~ed into three flats** aus dem alten Haus wurden drei Wohnungen gemacht.

transformation [ˌtrænsfə'meɪʃən] *n* Umwandlung, Umformung *f*; *(of ideas, views etc)* (grundlegende) Veränderung; *(of person, caterpillar etc)* Verwandlung *f*; *(Phys)* Umwandlung *f*; *(Elec)* Umwandlung, Transformation *f*.

transformer [træns'fɔːməʳ] *n (Elec)* Transformator *m*.

transfusion [træns'fjuːʒən] *n (also* **blood ~***)* Blutübertragung, Transfusion *f*. **to give sb a ~** jdm eine Blutübertragung geben.

transgress [træns'gres] **1** *vt standards* verstoßen gegen, verletzen. **2** *vi* sündigen.

transgression [træns'greʃən] *n* **(a)** *(of law)* Verstoß *m*, Verletzung *f*. **(b)** *(sin)* Sünde *f*, Verstoß *m*.

transience ['trænzɪəns] *n (of life)* Kürze *f*; *(of grief, joy)* Kurzlebigkeit *f*; *(of interest)* Flüchtigkeit *f*.

transient ['trænzɪənt] **1** *adj* **(a)** *life* kurz; *grief, joy* kurzlebig, vorübergehend; *interest* flüchtig. **(b)** *(US)* **~ population** nichtansässiger Teil der Bevölkerung. **2** *n (US)* Durchreisende(r) *mf*.

transistor [træn'zɪstəʳ] *n* **(a)** *(Elec)* Transistor *m*. **(b)** *(also* **~ radio***)* Transistorradio *nt*, Transistor *m (col)*.

transistorized [træn'zɪstəraɪzd] *adj circuit* transistorisiert.

transit ['trænzɪt] *n* Durchfahrt *f*, Transit *m (esp DDR)*; *(of goods)* Transport *m*. **the books were damaged in ~** die Bücher wurden beim Transport beschädigt; **~ camp** Durchgangslager *nt*.

transition [træn'zɪʃən] *n* Übergang *m (from ... to* von ... zu*)*.

transitional [træn'zɪʃənl] *adj* Übergangs-.

transitive ['trænzɪtɪv] *adj* transitiv.

transitory ['trænzɪtərɪ] *adj life* kurz; *grief, joy* kurzlebig, vorübergehend; *interest* flüchtig.

transit visa *n* Transitvisum *nt*.

translate [trænz'leɪt] *vti* **(a)** übersetzen; *work of literature also* übertragen. **to ~ a text from German (in)to English** einen Text aus dem Deutschen ins Englische übersetzen; **it is ~d as ...** es wird mit ... übersetzt; **his novels ~ well (into English)** seine Romane lassen sich gut (ins Englische) übersetzen *or* übertragen. **(b) to ~ words into action** Worte in die Tat umsetzen.

translation [trænz'leɪʃən] *n* Übersetzung *f (from* aus*)*; *(of work of literature also)* Übertragung *f*. **it loses in ~** es verliert bei der Übersetzung.

translator [trænz'leɪtəʳ] *n* Übersetzer(in *f*) *m*.

translucent [trænz'luːsnt] *adj glass etc* lichtdurchlässig; *skin* durchsichtig.

transmission [trænz'mɪʃən] *n* **(a)** *(transmitting)* Übertragung *f*; *(through heredity)* Vererbung *f*; *(of news)* Übermittlung *f*; *(of heat)* Leitung *f*; *(programme also)* Sendung *f*. **(b)** *(Aut)* Getriebe *nt*. **~ shaft** Kardanwelle *f*.

transmit [trænz'mɪt] *vt (convey) message, information* übermitteln; *sound waves, programme, illness* übertragen; *(by heredity)* vererben; *heat etc* leiten.

transmitter [trænz'mɪtəʳ] *n (Tech)* Sender *m*; *(in telephone)* Mikrofon *nt*.

transmute [trænz'mjuːt] *vt* umwandeln *(into* in *+acc)*; *metal* verwandeln *(into* in *+acc)*.

transom ['trænsəm] *n (~ window)* Oberlicht *nt*; *(cross-piece)* Querbalken *m*.

transparency [træns'pærənsɪ] *n* **(a)** Transparenz, Durchsichtigkeit *f*. **(b)** *(of lies, excuses etc)* Durchschaubarkeit *f*. **(c)** *(Brit Phot)* Dia(positiv) *nt*. **colour ~** Farbdia *nt*.

transparent [træns'pærənt] *adj* **(a)** durchsichtig, transparent. **(b)** *(fig) lie, intentions, personality* durchschaubar; *meaning* klar, eindeutig.

transpire [træn'spaɪəʳ] *vi* **(a)** *(become known)* **it now ~s that ...** jetzt hat sich herausgestellt, daß ... **(b)** *(happen)* passieren *(col)*.

transplant [træns'plɑːnt] **1** *vt* **(a)** *(Hort)* umpflanzen. **(b)** *(Med)* verpflanzen. **2** ['traːnsplɑːnt] *n (operation)* Verpflanzung, Transplantation *f*; *(organ)* Transplantat *nt*, verpflanztes Organ. **to have a ~** sich einer Organverpflanzung unterziehen.

transport ['trænspɔːt] **1** *n* **(a)** *(of goods, of troops)* Transport *m*. **Ministry of T~** Verkehrsministerium *nt*; **have you got your own ~?** bist du motorisiert?; **public ~** öffentliche Verkehrsmittel *pl*. **(b)** *(US: shipment)* (Schiffs)fracht, Ladung *f*. **(c)** *(liter)* **it sent her into ~s of delight** es erfüllte sie mit freudigem Entzücken *(liter)*. **2** [træns'pɔːt] *vt* **(a)** *goods* transportieren; *people* befördern; *(Hist) convict* deportieren. **(b)** *(liter)* **to be ~ed with joy** freudig entzückt sein *(liter)*.

transportation [ˌtrænspɔː'teɪʃən] *n* **(a)** Transport *m*; *(means)* Beförderungsmittel *nt*; *(public)* Verkehrsmittel *nt*; *(cost)* Transportkosten *pl*. **Department of T~** *(US)* Verkehrsministerium *nt*. **(b)** *(Hist: of criminal)* Deportation *f*.

transport café *n (Brit)* Fernfahrerlokal *nt*.

transpose [træns'pəʊz] *vt* umstellen; *(Mus)* transponieren.

transship [træns'ʃɪp] *vt* umschiffen.

transverse ['trænzvɜːs] *adj beam, bar, section* Quer-; *position* horizontal; *engine* querstehend.

transvestite [trænz'vestaɪt] *n* Transvestit *m*.

trap [træp] **1** *n* **(a)** *(for animal, fig)* Falle *f*. **to set** *or* **lay a ~ for an animal** eine Falle für ein Tier (auf)stellen; **to set a ~ for sb** *(fig)* jdm eine Falle stellen; **he is caught in a ~** er sitzt in der Falle; **to fall into a ~** in die Falle gehen. **(b)** *(vehicle)* zweirädriger Pferdewagen. **(c)** *(col: mouth)* Klappe *(col)*. **shut your ~!** halt die Klappe! *(col)*.

2 *vt* **(a)** *animal* (mit einer Falle) fangen. **(b)** *(fig) person* in die Falle locken. **he realized he was ~ped** er merkte, daß er in der Falle saß; **to ~ sb into saying sth** jdn dazu bringen, etw zu sagen. **(c)** *(block off, leave no escape)* in die Enge treiben. **the miners are ~ped** die Bergleute sind eingeschlossen; **my arm was ~ped** mein Arm war eingeklemmt. **(d)** *(catch) (Sport) ball* stoppen. **to ~ one's finger in the door** sich *(dat)* den Finger in der Tür einklemmen. **(e)** *gas, liquid* stauen.

trapdoor ['træp'dɔːʳ] *n* Falltür *f*; *(Theat)* Versenkung *f*.

trapeze [trə'piːz] *n (in circus)* Trapez *nt*. **~ artist** Trapezkünstler(in *f*) *m*.

trapper ['træpəʳ] *n* Fallensteller, Trapper *m*.

trappings ['træpɪŋz] *npl* äußeres Drum and Dran *(col)*; *(of power)* Insignien *pl*. **~ of office** Amtsinsignien *pl*.

trash [træʃ] *n* **(a)** *(US: refuse)* Abfall *m*. **(b)** *(goods)* Ramsch *m*; *(book, play etc)* Schund *m*; *(pop group etc)* Mist, Schrott *m (col)*. **don't talk ~** red nicht so einen Quatsch *(col)*.

trash-can ['træʃkæn] *n (US)* Abfalleimer *m*.

trashy ['træʃɪ] *adj (+er) goods* minderwertig; *play also* Schund-.

trauma ['trɔːmə] *n (Psych)* Trauma *nt*.

traumatic [trɔː'mætɪk] *adj* traumatisch.

travel ['trævl] *(vb: pret, ptp (Brit)* **travelled,** *(US)* **traveled)** **1** *vi* **(a)** *(make a journey)* reisen. **he ~s to work by car** er fährt mit dem Auto zur Arbeit; **she is ~ling to London tomorrow** sie fährt morgen nach London; **they ~led for 300 kms** sie fuhren 300 km; **to ~ around a country** ein Land bereisen. **(b)** *(go, move)* sich bewegen; *(sound, light)* sich fortpflanzen. **light ~s at ...** die Lichtgeschwindigkeit beträgt ...; **we were ~ling at 80 kph** wir fuhren 80 km/h; **the electricity ~s along the wire** der Strom fließt durch den Draht; **that's ~ling!** *(col)* das ist aber schnell! **(c)** *(Comm)* Vertreter sein. **he ~s in ladies' underwear** er reist in Damenunterwäsche. **(d)** *(Tech)* **as the piston ~s from A to B** während sich der Kolben von A nach B bewegt.

2 *vt area* bereisen; *distance* zurücklegen; *route* fahren.

3 *n* Reisen *nt*. **to be fond of ~** gerne reisen; **if you meet him on your ~s** wenn Sie ihm auf einer Ihrer Reisen begegnen.

travel: ~ agency *n* Reisebüro *nt*; **~ agent** *n* Reisebürokaufmann *m*; *(of package tours)* Reiseveranstalter *m*; **~ brochure** *n* Reiseprospekt *m*.

travelled, *(US)* **traveled** ['trævld] *adj* **well-~** *person* weitgereist *attr*, weit gereist *pred*; *route* vielbefahren *attr*, viel befahren *pred*.

traveller, *(US)* **traveler** ['trævləʳ] *n* **(a)** Reisende(r) *mf*. **I am a very poor** *or* **bad ~** ich vertrage das Reisen nicht. **(b)** *(also* **commercial ~)** Vertreter *m*.

traveller's cheque, *(US)* **traveler's check** *n* Reisescheck, Travellerscheck *m*.

travelling, *(US)* **traveling** ['trævlɪŋ] *n* Reisen *nt*. **I hate ~** ich hasse das Reisen.

travelling: ~ bag *n* Reisetasche *f*; **~ clock** *n* Reisewecker *m*; **~ expenses** *npl* Reisekosten *pl*; *(on business)* Reisespesen *pl*; **~ salesman** *n* Vertreter *m*.

travelogue ['trævəlɒg] *n* Reisebericht *m*.

travel: ~-sick *adj* reisekrank; **~-sickness** *n* Reisekrankneit *f*.

traverse ['trævɜːs] *vt (cross) land* durchqueren; *(bridge, person) water* überqueren; *(Mountaineering) ice, slope* queren. **the searchlight ~d the sky** der Suchscheinwerfer leuchtete den Himmel ab.

travesty ['trævɪstɪ] *n (Liter)* Travestie *f*. **a ~ of justice** ein Hohn *m* auf die Gerechtigkeit; **the elections were a ~** die Wahlen waren ein Hohn *m or* eine Farce.

trawl [trɔːl] **1** *n (net)* Schleppnetz, Trawl *nt*; *(US:* **~ line)** Grundleine *f*. **2** *vi* mit dem Schleppnetz fischen; *(US)* mit einer Grundleine fischen.

trawler ['trɔːləʳ] *n* Fischdampfer, Trawler *m*.

tray [treɪ] *n* Tablett *nt*; *(of cakes) (small)* Platte *f*; *(big)* Brett *nt*; *(for display)* Auslagekästchen *nt*; *(baking ~)* (Back)blech *nt*; *(for papers, mail)* Ablage(korb *m*) *f*.

treacherous ['tretʃərəs] *adj* **(a)** *person, action* verräterisch. **(b)** *(unreliable)* trügerisch. **(c)** *(dangerous)* tückisch; *ice, smile* trügerisch.

treachery ['tretʃərɪ] *n* Verrat *m*.

treacle ['triːkl] *n (Brit)* Sirup *m*.

tread [tred] *(vb: pret* **trod,** *ptp* **trodden)** **1** *n* **(a)** Schritt *m*. **to walk with a heavy ~** mit schweren Schritten gehen; **I could hear his ~ on the stairs** ich konnte seine Schritte auf der Treppe hören. **(b)** *(of stair)* Stufe *f*; *(of shoe, tyre)* Profil *nt*. **2** *vi* **(a)** *(walk)* gehen. **(b)** *(bring foot down)* treten *(on* auf *+acc)*. **he trod on my foot** er trat mir auf den Fuß; **to ~ softly** leise auftreten; **to ~ carefully** *(lit)* vorsichtig gehen; *(fig)* vorsichtig vorgehen. **3** *vt path (make)* treten; *(follow)* gehen. **it got trodden underfoot** es wurde zertreten; **to ~ grapes** Trauben stampfen; **to ~ water** Wasser treten; **don't ~ that earth into the carpet** treten Sie die Erde nicht in den Teppich.

treadle ['tredl] *n (of sewing machine)* Tretkurbel *f*.

treadmill ['tredmɪl] *n (lit)* Tretwerk *nt*; *(fig)* Tretmühle *f*.

treason ['triːzn] *n* Verrat *m (to* an *+dat)*. **an act of ~** Verrat *m*.

treasure ['treʒəʳ] **1** *n (lit, fig)* Schatz *m*. **2** *vt* (hoch)schätzen. **I shall always ~ this memory** ich werde das immer in lieber Erinnerung behalten.

treasure: ~ house *n* **a ~ house of knowledge** eine Fundgrube des Wissens; **~ hunt** *n* Schatzsuche *f*.

treasurer ['treʒərəʳ] *n (of club)* Kassenwart *m*; *(city ~)* Stadtkämmerer *m*; *(of business)* Leiter *m* der Finanzabteilung.

treasure trove *n* Schatzfund *m*; *(place where treasures are found)* Fundgrube *f*.

treasury ['treʒərɪ] *n* **(a)** *(Pol)* **T~,** *(US also)* **T~ Department** Finanzministerium *nt*. **(b)** *(anthology)* Schatzkästlein *nt*.

treat [triːt] **1** *vi* **(a)** *(behave towards, handle, process, Med)* behandeln; *sewage* klären; *wastepaper* verarbeiten. **the doctor is ~ing him for flu** er ist wegen einer Grippe in Behandlung. **(b)** *(consider)* betrachten *(as* als*)*. **you should ~ your work more seriously** Sie sollten Ihre Arbeit ernster nehmen. **(c)** *(pay for, give)* einladen. **to ~ sb to sth** jdn zu etw einladen, jdm etw spendieren; **I'm ~ing you** ich lade Sie ein; **to ~ oneself to sth** sich *(dat)* etw gönnen.

2 *n* **(a)** besondere Freude. **children's ~** Kinderfest *nt*; **it's my ~** das geht auf meine Kosten; **it's a ~ in store** das ist etwas, worauf wir uns noch freuen können; **it's a (real) ~ to see you again** was für eine Freude, Sie mal wiederzusehen! **(b)** *(col)* **it's coming on a ~** es macht sich prima *(col)*.

treatise ['triːtɪz] *n* Abhandlung *f (on* über *+acc)*.

treatment ['triːtmənt] *n* **(a)** *(of person, object)* Behandlung *f*. **their ~ of foreigners** ihre Art, Ausländer zu behandeln; **to give sb the ~** *(col: violently, sexually)* es jdm ordentlich besorgen *(col)*; **when the delegates visited the factory, they were given the full ~** *(col)* als die Delegierten die Firma besichtigten, wurde eine große Schau abgezogen *(col)*. **(b)** *(Med)* Behandlung *f*. **there are many ~s for rheumatism** es gibt viele Behandlungsarten für Rheumatismus; **to be having ~ for sth** wegen etw in Behandlung sein. **(c)** *(processing)* Behandlung *f*; *(of leather also)* Bearbeitung *f*; *(of sewage)* Klärung *f*; *(of wastepaper)* Verarbeitung *f*. **(d)** *(of subject)* Bearbeitung *f*.

treaty ['triːtɪ] *n* Vertrag *m*.

treble[1] ['trebl] **1** *adj* dreifach. **the country's inflation rate is in ~ figures** das Land hat eine dreistellige Inflationsrate. **2** *adv* **clothes are ~ the price** Kleider kosten dreimal soviel. **3** *vt* verdreifachen. **4** *vi* sich verdreifachen.

treble[2] **1** *n (Mus) (boy's voice)* Knabensopran *m or* -stimme *f*. **2** *adj voice* Knabensopran-; *part* Oberstimmen-. **~ clef** Violinschlüssel *m*.

tree [triː] *n* **(a)** Baum *m*. **an oak/a cherry ~** eine Eiche/ein Kirschbaum *m*; **money doesn't grow on ~s** das Geld fällt nicht vom Himmel. **(b)** *(family ~)* Stammbaum *m*.

tree *in cpds* Baum-; **~ house** *n* Baumhaus *nt*; **~-lined** *adj* baumbestanden; **~top** *n* Baumkrone *f*, Wipfel *m*; **~ trunk** *n* Baumstamm *m*.

trek [trek] **1** *vi* trecken; *(col: traipse)* latschen *(col)*. **they ~ked across the desert** sie zogen durch die Wüste. **2** *n* Treck, Zug *m*; *(col)* anstrengender Marsch.

trellis ['trelɪs] *n* Gitter *nt*.

tremble ['trembl] **1** *vi (person, hand etc)* zittern *(with* vor*)*; *(voice also)* beben *(with* vor*)*; *(ground, building)* beben, zittern. **2** *n* Zittern, Beben *nt*. **to be all of a ~** *(col)* am ganzen Körper zittern.

tremendous [trə'mendəs] *adj* **(a)** gewaltig, enorm; *size, crowd also* riesig; *success* Riesen-. **(b)** *(very good)* klasse *(col)*, toll *(col)*. **we had a ~ time** wir haben uns ganz toll amüsiert.

tremendously [trə'mendəslɪ] *adv* sehr; *fat, tall etc also* enorm; *relieved, grateful, dangerous also* ungeheuer; *intelligent, difficult also* äußerst. **they enjoyed themselves ~** sie haben sich prächtig amüsiert *(col)*.

tremor ['tremәʳ] *n* Zittern, Beben *nt*; *(Med)* Tremor *m*; *(of emotion)* Zucken *nt*; *(earth ~)* Beben *nt*.

tremulous ['tremjʊləs] *adj voice* bebend; *(timid) smile, person* zaghaft.

trench [trentʃ] *n* Graben *m*; *(Mil)* Schützengraben *m*. **in the ~es** *(Mil)* im Schützengraben; **~ warfare** Grabenkrieg *m*.

trenchant ['trentʃənt] *adj language* treffsicher; *style* prägnant; *satire* beißend; *speech* pointiert; *wit, criticism* scharf.

trench coat *n* Trenchcoat, Regenmantel *m*.

trend [trend] **1** *n* **(a)** *(tendency)* Tendenz *f*, Trend *m*. **the ~ towards violence** die Tendenz zur Gewalttätigkeit; **upward ~** steigende Tendenz, Aufwärtstrend *m*; **the downward ~ in the birth rate** die Rückläufigkeit der Geburtenrate; **to set a ~** richtungweisend sein. **(b)** *(fashion)* Mode *f*, Trend *m*. **2** *vi* verlaufen *(towards* nach*)*. **prices are ~ing upwards** die Preise haben eine steigende Tendenz.

trendy ['trendɪ] *adj (+er) in pred (col)*. **to be ~** als schick gelten; *(clothes etc also)* gerade modern sein.

trepidation [ˌtrepɪ'deɪʃən] *n* Beklommenheit, Ängstlichkeit *f*. **full of ~ he knocked on the door** voll ängstlicher Erwartung klopfte er an die Tür.

trespass ['trespəs] **1** *vi (on property)* unbefugt betreten *(on sth* etw *acc)*. **to ~ (up)on sb's privacy** jds Privatsphäre verletzen; **to ~ (up)on sb's time** jds Zeit überbeanspruchen; **"no ~ing"** „Betreten verboten". **2** *n (Jur)* unbefugtes Betreten.

trespasser ['trespəsәʳ] *n* Unbefugte(r) *mf*. **"~s will be prosecuted"** „widerrechtliches Betreten wird strafrechtlich verfolgt".

trestle ['tresl] *n* Bock *m*. **~ table** auf Böcken stehender Tisch; *(decorator's)* Tapeziertisch *m*.

trial ['traɪəl] *n* **(a)** *(Jur)* (Gerichts)verfahren *nt*, Prozeß *m*; *(actual hearing)* Verhandlung *f*. **to be on ~** angeklagt sein; **to be on ~ for theft** des Diebstahls angeklagt sein; **at the ~** bei der Verhandlung; **to bring sb to ~** jdm den Prozeß machen; **~ by jury** Schwurgerichtsverfahren *nt*. **(b)** *(test)* Versuch *m*, Probe *f*. **~s** *(of machine, aeroplane)* Test(s *pl*) *m*; *(Sport)* Qualifikationsspiel *nt*; **horse ~s** Querfeldeinrennen *nt*; **to give sth a ~** etw ausprobieren; **to give sb a ~** *(for job)* jdn auf Probe anstellen; **to take sth on ~** etw zur Probe *or* etw probeweise nehmen; **~ of strength** Kraftprobe *f*; **by ~ and error** durch Ausprobieren. **(c)** *(hardship)* Unannehmlichkeit *f*; *(nuisance)* Plage *f*, Problem *nt (to* für*)*. **he's a ~ to his mother** er macht seiner Mutter sehr viel Kummer; **~s and tribulations** Schwierigkeiten *pl*.

trial: ~ basis *n* **on a ~ basis** auf Probe; **~ offer** *n* Einführungsangebot *nt*; **~ period** *n* Probezeit *f*; **~ run** *n* Generalprobe *f*; *(with car etc)* Probefahrt *f*; *(of machine)* Probelauf *m*; **give the new method a ~ run** probieren Sie die neue Methode einmal aus.

triangle ['traɪæŋgl] *n* Dreieck *nt*; *(set square)* (Zeichen)dreieck *nt*; *(Mus)* Triangel *m*; *(fig: relationship)* Dreiecksbeziehung *f*.

triangular [traɪ'æŋgjʊləʳ] *adj (Math)* dreieckig. **~ relationship** Dreiecksverhältnis *nt*.

tribal ['traɪbəl] *adj customs, dance* Stammes-.

tribe [traɪb] *n* Stamm *m*.

tribesman ['traɪbzmən] *n, pl* **-men** [-mən] Stammesangehörige(r) *m*.

tribulation [ˌtrɪbjʊ'leɪʃən] *n* Kummer *m no pl*. **~s** Sorgen *pl*; *(less serious)* Kümmernisse *pl*.

tribunal [traɪ'bjuːnl] *n* Gericht(shof *m*) *nt*; *(inquiry)* Untersuchungsausschuß *m*; *(held by revolutionaries etc)* Tribunal *nt*.

tributary ['trɪbjʊtərɪ] **1** *adj state* tributpflichtig; *river* Neben-. **2** *n (state)* tributpflichtiger Staat; *(river)* Nebenfluß *m*.

tribute ['trɪbjuːt] *n* Tribut *m*. **to pay ~ to sb/sth** jdm/einer Sache (den schuldigen) Tribut zollen; **in ~ to sb** jdm zu Ehren; **~s have been coming in from all over the world** aus der ganzen Welt kamen Zeichen der Anerkennung.

trice [traɪs] *n*: **in a ~** im Handumdrehen, im Nu.

trick [trɪk] **1** *n* **(a)** *(ruse)* Trick *m*. **be careful, it's a ~** paß auf, das ist eine Falle!; **he knows a ~ or two** *(col)* der kennt sich aus; **he knows all the ~s of the trade** er ist ein alter Hase; *(is crafty)* er ist mit allen Wassern gewaschen. **(b)** *(mischief)* Streich *m*. **to play a ~ on sb** jdm einen Streich spielen; **the car's started playing ~s again** der Wagen fängt wieder an zu mucken *(col)*; **a dirty ~** ein ganz gemeiner Trick; **how's ~s?** *(col)* wie geht's? **(c)** *(skilful act)* Kunststück *nt*. **to teach a dog to do ~s** einem Hund Kunststücke beibringen; **there's a special ~ to it** da ist ein Trick dabei; **that should do the ~** *(col)* das müßte eigentlich hinhauen *(col)*; **he doesn't miss a ~** *(col)* er läßt sich nichts entgehen. **(d)** *(habit)* Eigenart *f*. **to have a ~ of doing sth** die Eigenart haben, etw zu tun. **(e)** *(Cards)* Stich *m*. **to take a ~** einen Stich machen.

2 *attr cigar, spider* als Scherzartikel.

3 *vt* hereinlegen *(col)*. **I've been ~ed!** ich bin hereingelegt *or* übers Ohr gehauen *(col)* worden!; **to ~ sb into doing sth** jdn (mit einem Trick) dazu bringen, etw zu tun.

trickery ['trɪkərɪ] *n* Tricks *pl (col)*. **a piece of ~** ein Trick *m*; **that's just verbal ~** das ist bloß ein raffinierter Trick mit Worten.

trickle ['trɪkl] **1** *vi* **(a)** *(liquid)* tröpfeln, tropfen; *(sand)* rieseln; *(ball)* trudeln *(col)*. **tears ~d down her cheeks** Tränen kullerten ihr über die Wangen; **the rain ~d down his neck** der Regen tropfte ihm in den Kragen. **(b)** *(fig)* **people began to ~ back in** die Leute begannen, vereinzelt wieder hereinzukommen; **reports are beginning to ~ in** so langsam trudeln die Berichte ein *(col)*. **3** *n* **(a)** *(of liquid)* Tröpfeln *nt*; *(stream)* Rinnsal *nt*. **(b)** *(fig)* **a constant ~ of people gradually filled the lecture hall** der Hörsaal füllte sich

langsam aber stetig mit Leuten; **profits have been reduced to a ~** die Gewinne sind spärlich geworden.
trick: ~ photography *n* Trickfotografie *f*; **~ question** *n* Fangfrage *f*.
tricky ['trɪkɪ] *adj (+er)* **(a)** *(difficult)* schwierig; *(fiddly also)* knifflig. **(b)** *situation, problem* heikel, kitzlig. **(c)** *(sly, crafty) person, plan* durchtrieben, gerissen.
tricolour, *(US)* **tricolor** ['trɪkələʳ] *n* Trikolore *f*.
tricycle ['traɪsɪkl] *n* Dreirad *nt*.
tried [traɪd] *adj* erprobt, bewährt.
trifle ['traɪfl] *n* **(a)** Kleinigkeit *f*; *(trivial matter also)* Lappalie *(col)*, Nichtigkeit *f*. **more cake? — just a ~, thank you** noch etwas Kuchen? — bloß ein ganz kleines Stückchen, bitte; **a ~ hot/small** ein bißchen heiß/klein; **a ~ too ...** ein wenig *or* eine Spur zu ... **(b)** *(Cook)* Trifle *nt, geleeartige Süßspeise*.
♦ **trifle with** *vi +prep obj affections* spielen mit. **he is not to be ~d ~** mit ihm ist nicht zu spaßen.
trifling ['traɪflɪŋ] *adj* unbedeutend, geringfügig.
trigger ['trɪgəʳ] **1** *n (of gun)* Abzug *m*; *(of cine-camera, machine)* Auslöser *m*; *(Elec)* Trigger *m*. **to pull the ~** abdrücken. **2** *vt (also* **~ off***)* auslösen.
trigger-happy ['trɪgə,hæpɪ] *adj (col)* schießfreudig *(col)*, schießwütig *(pej)*.
trigonometry [,trɪgə'nɒmɪtrɪ] *n* Trigonometrie *f*.
trilby ['trɪlbɪ] *n (also* **~ hat***)* weicher Filzhut.
trill [trɪl] **1** *n* **(a)** *(of bird)* Trillern *nt*; *(of voice)* Tremolo *nt*. **(b)** *(Mus)* Triller *m*. **2** *vti (birds, Mus)* trillern; *(person)* trällern.
trillion ['trɪljən] *n (Brit)* Trillion *f*; *(US)* Billion *f*.
trilogy ['trɪlədʒɪ] *n* Trilogie *f*.
trim [trɪm] **1** *adj (+er)* sauber; *appearance also* adrett; *haircut* gepflegt. **he keeps his garden very ~** sein Garten ist immer sehr gepflegt. **2** *n* **(a) in good ~** *(house, car etc)* in gutem Zustand; *(person)* gut in Form; **to get into ~** sich in Form bringen. **(b)** *(col)* **to give sth a ~** etw schneiden; *(tree, hedge, beard also)* etw stutzen; **your hair needs a ~** du mußt dir die Haare etwas nachschneiden lassen. **(c)** *(in car)* Innenaustattung *f*. **3** *vt* **(a)** *(cut) hair* nachschneiden; *beard, hedge* stutzen; *dog* trimmen; *wick, roses* beschneiden; *piece of wood* zurechtschneiden. **(b)** *(fig: cut down) budget, essay* kürzen. **(c)** *(decorate) dress* besetzen; *Christmas tree* schmücken. **(d)** *boat, plane* trimmen; *sails* richtig stellen. **(e)** *(US col) (defeat)* schlagen; *(cheat)* übers Ohr hauen *(col)*.
trimming ['trɪmɪŋ] *n* **(a)** *(on clothes)* Besatz *m*. **~s** Verzierung(en *pl*) *f*. **(b) ~s** *pl (cuttings)* Abfälle *pl*; *(of paper also)* Papierschnitzel *pl*. **(c) ~s** *pl (accessories)* Zubehör *nt*; **roast beef with all the ~s** Roastbeef mit allem Drum und Dran *(col)*.
Trinity ['trɪnɪtɪ] *n* Dreifaltigkeit *f*. **~ Sunday** Trinitatis, Dreifaltigkeitsfest *nt*.
trinket ['trɪŋkɪt] *n* Schmuckstück *nt*. **~ box** Schmuckkästchen *nt*.
trio ['trɪəʊ] *n* Trio *nt*.
trip [trɪp] **1** *n* **(a)** *(journey)* Reise *f*; *(excursion)* Ausflug *m*, Tour *f*; *(shorter also)* Trip *m (col)*. **when was your last ~ to the dentist's?** wann waren Sie zuletzt beim Zahnarzt?; **he is away on a ~/a ~ to Canada** er ist auf Reisen/macht zur Zeit eine Reise nach Kanada; **to take a ~** eine Reise machen, verreisen. **(b)** *(col: on drugs)* Trip *m (col)*. **2** *vi* **(a)** *(stumble)* stolpern *(on, over* über *+acc)*. **(b)** *(skip)* trippeln. **to ~ in/out** hinein-/hinaustrippeln. **3** *vt* **(a)** *(make fall)* stolpern lassen; *(deliberately also)* ein Bein stellen *(+dat)*. **(b)** *(Mech) lever* betätigen; *mechanism* auslösen.
♦ **trip over** *vi* stolpern *(+prej obj* über *+acc)*.
♦ **trip up 1** *vi* **(a)** stolpern. **(b)** *(fig)* sich vertun. **2** *vt sep* **(a)** *(make fall)* stolpern lassen. **(b)** *(fig: cause to make mistake)* eine Falle stellen *(+dat)*.
tripartite [,traɪ'pɑːtaɪt] *adj agreement, talks* dreiseitig; *division* Drei-.
tripe [traɪp] *n* **(a)** *(Cook)* Kaldaunen, Kutteln *(S Ger, Aus, Sw) pl*. **(b)** *(fig col)* Quatsch *m*.
triple ['trɪpl] **1** *adj* dreifach. **~ jump** Dreisprung *m*. **2** *adv* dreimal soviel. **it's ~ the distance** es ist dreimal so weit. **3** *n* Dreifache(s) *nt*. **4** *vt* verdreifachen. **5** *vi* sich verdreifachen.
triplet ['trɪplɪt] *n* **(a)** *(baby)* Drilling *m*. **(b)** *(Mus)* Triole *f*.
triplicate ['trɪplɪkɪt] *n*: **in ~** in dreifacher Ausfertigung.
tripod ['traɪpɒd] *n (Phot)* Stativ *nt*.
tripwire ['trɪpwaɪəʳ] *n* Stolperdraht *m*.
trite [traɪt] *adj (+er) (trivial, banal)* banal; *(hackneyed)* abgedroschen.
triumph ['traɪʌmf] **1** *n* Triumph *m (over* über *+acc)*. **in ~** triumphierend, im Triumph; **shouts of ~** Triumphgeschrei *pl*. **2** *vi* den Sieg davontragen *(over* über *+acc)*. **to ~ over sb/sth** über jdn/etw triumphieren.
triumphal [traɪ'ʌmfəl] *adj* triumphal. **~ arch** Triumphbogen *m*.
triumphant [traɪ'ʌmfənt] *adj (victorious)* siegreich; *(rejoicing)* triumphierend; *moment* triumphal. **to be ~ (over sth)** triumphieren *(over* über *+acc)*.
trivia ['trɪvɪə] *npl* triviales Zeug.
trivial [trɪvɪəl] *adj* **(a)** trivial; *objection, loss, details also* belanglos. **(b)** *person* oberflächlich.
triviality [,trɪvɪ'ælɪtɪ] *n see adj (a)* Trivialität *f*; Belanglosigkeit *f*.
trivialize ['trɪvɪəlaɪz] *vt* trivialisieren.
trod [trɒd] *pret of* **tread.**
trodden ['trɒdn] *ptp of* **tread.**
trolley ['trɒlɪ] *n* **(a)** *(Brit: cart) (four wheels)* Handwagen *m*; *(in supermarket)* Einkaufswagen *m*; *(in station)* Gepäckwagen *m*; *(for passengers)* Kofferkuli *m*; *(two wheels) (for golf clubs)* Caddy *m*; *(in station, factory etc)* Sackkarre *f*; *(tea-~)* Teewagen *m*. **(b)** *(Rail)* Lore *f*, Förderkarren *m*.
trolley: ~bus *n* Obus, Oberleitungsomnibus *(form) m*; **~-car** *n (US)* Straßenbahn *f*.
trombone [trɒm'bəʊn] *n (Mus)* Posaune *f*.
troop [truːp] **1** *n* **(a)** *(Mil: of cavalry)* Trupp *m*; *(unit)* Schwadron *f*. **(b)** *(Mil)* **~s** *pl* Truppen *pl*; **200 ~s** 200 Soldaten. **(c)** *(of scouts)* Stamm *m*. **(d)** *(of people)* Horde *(pej)*, Schar *f*. **2** *vi* **to ~ out/in** hinaus-/hineinströmen; **to ~ past sth** an etw *(dat)* vorbeiziehen. **3** *vi (Mil)* **to ~ the colours** die Fahnenparade abhalten.
troop-carrier ['truːp,kærɪəʳ] *n (vehicle)* Truppentransporter *m*.
trooper ['truːpəʳ] *n (Mil)* Kavallerist *m*; *(US: state ~)* Polizist *m*. **to swear like a ~** wie ein Kutscher fluchen.
troop-ship ['truːp,ʃɪp] *n* (Truppen)transportschiff *nt*.
trophy ['trəʊfɪ] *n (Mil, Sport)* Trophäe *f*.
tropic ['trɒpɪk] *n* **(a)** Wendekreis *m*. **T~ of Cancer/Capricorn** Wendekreis des Krebses/Steinbocks. **(b) ~s** *pl* Tropen *pl*.
tropical ['trɒpɪkəl] *adj* tropisch, Tropen-.
trot [trɒt] **1** *n* **(a)** *(pace)* Trab *m*. **to go at a ~** traben; **to go for a ~** einen Ausritt machen; **I've been on the ~ all day** *(fig col)* ich bin schon den ganzen Tag auf Trab. **(b)** *(col)* **for five days on the ~** fünf Tage lang in einer Tour. **2** *vi (horse, person)* traben; *(pony)* zockeln; *(small child)* trippeln.
♦ **trot out** *vt sep excuses, list* aufwarten mit.
trotter ['trɒtəʳ] *n (of animal)* Fuß *m*. **pigs' ~s** *(Cook)* Schweinsfüße *pl*.
trouble ['trʌbl] **1** *n* **(a)** Ärger *m*; *(difficulties)* Schwierigkeiten *pl*. **did you have any ~ (in) getting it?** hatten Sie Schwierigkeiten, es zu bekommen?; **to be in ~** in Schwierigkeiten sein; **to be in ~ with sb** mit jdm Schwierigkeiten *or* Ärger haben; **to get into ~** in Schwierigkeiten geraten; *(with authority)* Ärger bekommen *(with*

mit); **to get sb into ~** jdn in Schwierigkeiten bringen *(with* mit); **to get a girl into ~** *(euph)* ein Mädchen ins Unglück bringen; **to make ~** *(cause a row etc)* Krach schlagen *(col)*, Ärger machen; **that's/you're asking for ~** das kann ja nicht gutgehen; **what's the ~?** was ist los?; *(to sick person)* wo fehlt's?; **the ~ is that ...** das Problem ist, daß ...; **that's the ~** das ist das Problem; **family/money ~s** Familien-/Geldsorgen *pl*; **heart/back ~** Herz-/Rückenleiden *nt*; **engine ~** (ein) Motorschaden *m*.

(b) *(bother, effort)* Mühe *f*. **it's no ~ (at all)!** das mache ich doch gern; **thank you — (it was) no ~** vielen Dank — (das ist) gern geschehen; **it's not worth the ~** das ist nicht der Mühe wert; **nothing is too much ~ for her** nichts ist ihr zuviel; **to go to the ~ (of doing sth), to take the ~ (to do sth)** sich *(dat)* die Mühe machen (, etw zu tun); **to take a lot of ~ (over** *or* **with sth)** sich *(dat)* (mit etw) viel Mühe geben; **to put sb to a lot of ~** jdm viel Mühe machen.

(c) *(unrest, upheaval)* Unruhe *f*. **labour ~s** Arbeiterunruhen *pl*; **he made ~ between them** er hat Unruhe zwischen ihnen gestiftet.

2 *vt* **(a)** *(worry)* beunruhigen; *(disturb, grieve)* bekümmern. **to be ~d by sth** wegen etw besorgt sein; **his eyes ~ him** seine Augen machen ihm zu schaffen. **(b)** *(bother)* bemühen, belästigen. **I'm sorry to ~ you, but could you tell me if ...** entschuldigen Sie die Störung, aber könnten Sie mir sagen, ob ...; **may I ~ you for a light?** darf ich Sie um Feuer bitten?; **I shan't ~ you with the details** ich werde Ihnen die Einzelheiten ersparen; **to ~ to do sth** sich bemühen, etw zu tun; **please don't ~ yourself** bitte bemühen Sie sich nicht.

troubled ['trʌbld] *adj person, look* unruhig, beunruhigt; *(grieved)* bekümmert; *times* unruhig. **the ~ waters of race relations** die gestörten Beziehungen zwischen den Rassen.

trouble: ~-free *adj period, process, car* problemlos; *relationship also* reibungslos; *area* ruhig; *machine* störungsfrei; **~maker** *n* Unruhestifter(in *f*) *m*; **~shooter** *n (Pol, Ind: mediator)* Vermittler(in *f*) *m*; **~some** *adj (bothersome)* lästig; *person, problem* schwierig; **~ spot** *n* Unruheherd *m*; *(in system)* Störung *f*.

trough [trɒf] *n* **(a)** *(container)* Trog *m*. **drinking ~** Wassertrog *m*. **(b)** *(depression)* Rille *f*; *(between waves, on graph)* Tal *nt*; *(Met)* Tiefdruckkeil *m*.

troupe [tru:p] *n (Theat)* Truppe *f*.

trouser ['traʊzə]: **~ leg** *n* Hosenbein *nt*; **~ press** *n* Hosenpresse *f*.

trousers ['traʊzɪz] *npl (esp Brit: also* **pair of ~***)* Hose *f*. **she was wearing ~** sie trug eine Hose; **to wear the ~** *(fig col)* die Hosen anhaben *(col)*.

trouser-suit ['traʊzə,su:t] *n (Brit)* Hosenanzug *m*.

trousseau ['tru:səʊ] *n* Aussteuer *f*.

trout [traʊt] *n* Forelle *f*. **~ fishing** Forellenfang *m*.

trowel ['traʊəl] *n* Kelle *f*. **to lay sth on with a ~** *(fig col)* bei etw dick auftragen.

truancy ['trʊənsɪ] *n* (Schule)schwänzen *nt*.

truant ['trʊənt] *n* (Schul)schwänzer(in *f*) *m*. **to play ~** unentschuldigt fehlen, schwänzen *(col)*.

truce [tru:s] *n (Mil, fig)* Waffenstillstand *m*; *(Mil: interrupting fighting)* Waffenruhe *f*. **~!** Friede!

truck[1] [trʌk] **1** *n* **(a)** *(Rail)* Güterwagen *m*. **(b)** *(barrow)* Karren *m*. **(c)** *(lorry)* Last(kraft)wagen *m*; *(van, pick-up)* Lieferwagen *m*. **2** *vt (US)* transportieren. **3** *vi (US)* Lastwagen fahren.

truck[2] *n* **(a)** *(fig: dealings)* **to have no ~ with sb/sth** mit jdm/etw nichts zu tun haben. **(b)** *(US: garden produce) (für den Verkauf angebautes)* Gemüse.

truck driver *n* Lastwagenfahrer(in *f*) *m*.

trucker ['trʌkə^r] *n (US)* **(a)** *(truck-driver)* Lastwagenfahrer(in *f*) *m*; *(haulage contractor)* Spediteur *m*. **(b)** *(vegetable farmer)* Gemüsegärtner(in *f*) *m*.

truck *(US)*: **~ farm** *n* Gemüsefarm *f*; **~ farmer** *n* Gemüsegärtner(in *f*) *m*.

trucking ['trʌkɪŋ] *n (US)* Transport *m*.

truckload ['trʌkləʊd] *n* Wagenladung *f*.

truculent ['trʌkjʊlənt] *adj* trotzig, aufsässig.

trudge [trʌdʒ] *vi* **to ~ in/out/along** *etc* hinein-/hinaus-/entlangtrotten *etc*.

true [tru:] **1** *adj* **(a)** wahr. **to come ~** *(dream, wishes)* wahr werden; *(prophecy)* sich verwirklichen; *(fears)* sich bewahrheiten; **that's ~** das stimmt, das ist wahr; **the same is** *or* **holds ~ for ...** dasselbe gilt auch für ...; **~!** richtig!; **too ~!** (das ist nur) zu wahr!

(b) *(accurate) description* wahrheitsgetreu; *likeness* (lebens)getreu; *copy* getreu.

(c) *(real, genuine) feeling, friend, opinion* wahr, echt; *reason* wirklich; *antique* echt. **~ love** die wahre Liebe; *(person)* Herzallerliebste(r) *mf (old)*.

(d) *(faithful) friend, follower* treu. **to be ~ to sb** jdm treu sein/bleiben; **to be ~ to one's word** (treu) zu seinem Wort stehen, seinem Wort treu bleiben; **~ to life** lebensnah; *(Art)* lebensecht; **the horse ran ~ to form** das Pferd lief erwartungsgemäß.

(e) *wall, surface* gerade; *join* genau; *circle* rund; *(Mus) note* rein.

2 *n* **out of ~** *beam, wheels* schief.

truffle ['trʌfl] *n* Trüffel *f or m*.

truism ['tru:ɪzəm] *n (obvious truth)* Binsenwahrheit *f*; *(platitude)* Platitüde *f*, Gemeinplatz *m*.

truly ['tru:lɪ] *adv* **(a)** *(genuinely)* wirklich, wahrhaftig. **a ~ great writer** ein wahrhaft großer Schriftsteller. **(b)** *(faithfully) serve* treu; *reflect* wahrheitsgetreu.

trump [trʌmp] **1** *n (Cards, fig)* Trumpf *m*. **spades are ~s** Pik ist Trumpf; **to hold all the ~s** *(fig)* alle Trümpfe in der Hand halten; **~ card** *(Cards)* Trumpf(karte) *f*) *m*; *(fig)* Trumpf *m*; **to play one's ~ card** *(lit, fig)* seinen Trumpf ausspielen; **to turn up ~s** *(col)* die Lage retten. **2** *vt (Cards)* stechen; *(fig)* übertrumpfen.

♦ **trump up** *vt sep* erfinden.

trumpet ['trʌmpɪt] **1** *n (Mus)* Trompete *f*. **to blow one's own ~** sich selbst loben. **2** *vi (elephant)* trompeten.

trumpeter ['trʌmpɪtə^r] *n* Trompeter(in *f*) *m*.

truncate [trʌŋ'keɪt] *vt* beschneiden.

truncheon ['trʌntʃən] *n (esp Brit)* Knüppel *m*; *(esp of riot police)* Schlagstock *m*.

trundle ['trʌndl] **1** *vt (push)* rollen; *(pull)* ziehen. **2** *vi* **to ~ along/down** entlang-/hinunterzockeln; *(clatter)* entlang-/hinunterrumpeln.

trunk [trʌŋk] *n* **(a)** *(of tree)* Stamm *m*; *(of body)* Rumpf *m*. **(b)** *(of elephant)* Rüssel *m*. **(c)** *(case)* Schrankkoffer *m*; *(US Aut)* Kofferaum *m*. **(d) ~s** *pl (for swimming)* Badehose *f*; *(for sport)* Shorts *pl*; **a pair of ~s** ein Badehose/(ein Paar) Shorts.

trunk: ~ call *n (Brit Telec)* Ferngespräch *nt*; **~ road** *n (Brit)* Fernstraße *f*.

truss [trʌs] **1** *n (Med)* Bruchband *nt*. **2** *vt* **(a)** *(tie) hay* bündeln. **(b)** *(Cook) chicken etc* dressieren.

♦ **truss up** *vt sep person* fesseln.

trust [trʌst] **1** *n* **(a)** Vertrauen *nt (in* zu). **I have every ~ in him** ich habe volles Vertrauen zu ihm; **to put** *or* **place one's ~ in sb** Vertrauen in jdn setzen; **to take sth on ~** etw einfach glauben; **position of ~** Vertrauensstellung *f*. **(b)** *(charge)* Verantwortung *f*. **to commit sth to** *or* **place sth in sb's ~** jdm etw anvertrauen. **(c)** *(Jur, Fin)* Treuhand(schaft) *f*; *(property)* Treuhandeigentum *nt*; *(charitable fund)* Fonds *m*, Stiftung *f*. **to hold sth in ~ for sb** etw für jdn treuhänderisch verwalten; **~ fund** Treuhandvermögen *nt*; Stiftungsgelder *pl*. **(d)** *(Comm: also* **~ company***)* Trust *m*.

2 *vt* **(a)** *(have confidence in)* trauen *(+dat)*; *person also* vertrauen *(+dat)*; *words* glauben. **to ~**

sb to do sth jdm vertrauen, daß er etw tut; **to ~ sb with sth, to ~ sth to sb** jdm etw anvertrauen; **can he be ~ed not to lose it?** kann man sich darauf verlassen, daß er es nicht verliert?; **can we ~ him to go shopping alone?** können wir ihn allein einkaufen gehen lassen?; **I wouldn't ~ him an inch** *(col)* ich traue ihm nicht über den Weg *(col)*. **(b)** *(iro col)* **~ you/him!** typisch!; **~ him to break it!** er muß es natürlich kaputtmachen. **(c)** *(hope)* hoffen. **I ~ not** ich hoffe nicht.

3 *vi* **to ~ in sb** auf jdn vertrauen; **to ~ to luck** *or* **chance** sich auf sein Glück verlassen.

trusted [ˈtrʌstɪd] *adj method* bewährt; *friend, servant* getreu.

trustee [trʌsˈtiː] *n* **(a)** *(of estate)* Treuhänder(in *f*) *m*. **(b)** *(of institution)* Verwalter *m*. **~s** Vorstand *m*.

trustful [ˈtrʌstfʊl], **trusting** [ˈtrʌstɪŋ] *adj look* vertrauensvoll; *person also* gutgläubig, arglos.

trustworthy [ˈtrʌstˌwɜːðɪ] *adj person* vertrauenswürdig; *statement, account* glaubwürdig.

trusty [ˈtrʌstɪ] *adj (+er) (liter, hum)* getreu *(liter)*.

truth [truːθ] *n, pl* **-s** [truːðz] *no pl* Wahrheit *f*. **you must always tell the ~** du mußt immer die Wahrheit sagen; **to tell the ~ ...** um ehrlich zu sein ...; **the ~ of the matter is that ...** die Wahrheit ist, daß ...; **there's no ~ in what he says** es ist kein Wort wahr von dem, was er sagt; **there's some ~ in that** da ist etwas Wahres dran *(col)*; **the ~, the whole ~ and nothing but the ~** *(Jur)* die Wahrheit, die reine Wahrheit und nichts als die Wahrheit; **in ~** in Wahrheit, in Wirklichkeit.

truthful [ˈtruːθfʊl] *adj person* ehrlich; *statement* wahrheitsgetreu. **to be ~ about it** ehrlich sein.

truthfully [ˈtruːθfəlɪ] *adv* ehrlich; *say also, explain* wahrheitsgemäß.

try [traɪ] **1** *n* **(a)** Versuch *m*. **to have a ~** es versuchen; **let me have a ~** laß mich mal versuchen!; **to have a ~ at doing sth** versuchen *or* probieren, etw zu tun; **have another ~ (at it)** versuch's noch mal; **I'll give it a ~** *(will attempt it)* ich werde es mal versuchen; *(will test it out)* ich werde es ausprobieren; **it was a good ~** das war schon ganz gut; **it's worth a ~** es ist einen Versuch wert. **(b)** *(Rugby)* Versuch *m*. **to score a ~** einen Versuch erzielen.

2 *vt* **(a)** *(attempt)* versuchen. **to ~ one's hardest** *or* **one's best** sein Bestes tun *or* versuchen; **it's ~ing to rain** *(col)* es fängt an zu regnen; **to ~ one's hand at sth** etw probieren; **just you ~ it!** *(dare)* versuch's bloß!

(b) *(~ out) new product etc* ausprobieren; *job applicant* eine Chance geben *(+dat)*, es versuchen mit *(col)*; *(~ using) glue, aspirin* es versuchen mit; *(~ to buy or get sth at) newsagent, next door* es versuchen bei; *(~ to open) door, window* ausprobieren. **~ this for size** *(fig col)* wie wär's denn damit? *(col)*.

(c) *(sample, taste)* probieren.

(d) *(test) courage, patience* auf die Probe stellen; *(strain) eyes* anstrengen. **(just) ~ me!** *(col)* wetten?; **tried and tested** *(Comm)* erprobt, bewährt.

(e) *(Jur) person* unter Anklage stellen; *case* verhandeln. **he is being tried for theft** er steht wegen Diebstahls vor Gericht.

3 *vi* versuchen. **~ and arrive on time** versuche pünktlich zu sein; **he wasn't even ~ing** er hat sich *(dat)* überhaupt keine Mühe gegeben; *(didn't attempt it)* er hat es überhaupt nicht versucht.

♦ **try for** *vi +prep obj* sich bemühen um.

♦ **try on** *vt sep* **(a)** *clothes* anprobieren; *hat* aufprobieren. **(b)** *(fig col)* **to ~ it ~ with sb** probieren, wie weit man bei jdm gehen kann.

♦ **try out** *vt sep* ausprobieren *(on* bei, an *+dat)*; *person* eine Chance geben *(+dat)*.

trying [ˈtraɪɪŋ] *adj* anstrengend; *experience* schwer. **they've had a ~ time of it recently** sie haben es in letzter Zeit sehr schwer gehabt.

tsar [zɑːʳ] *n* Zar *m*.

tsetse (fly) [ˈtsetsɪ(ˈflaɪ)] *n* Tsetsefliege *f*.

T-shirt [ˈtiːʃɜːt] *n* T-Shirt *nt*.

T-square [ˈtiːskwɛəʳ] *n* Reißschiene *f*.

tub [tʌb] *n* Kübel *m*; *(for rainwater)* Tonne, Traufe *f*; *(for washing)* Zuber, Bottich *m*; *(of ice-cream, margarine)* Becher *m*.

tuba [ˈtjuːbə] *n* Tuba *f*.

tubby [ˈtʌbɪ] *adj (+er) (col)* dick, rundlich.

tube [tjuːb] *n* **(a)** *(pipe)* Rohr *nt*; *(of rubber, plastic)* Schlauch *m*. **(b)** *(of toothpaste etc)* Tube *f*; *(of sweets)* Rolle *f*. **(c)** *(London underground)* U-Bahn *f*. **by ~** mit der U-Bahn; **~ station** U-Bahnstation *f*. **(d)** *(Elec, TV, US Rad)* Röhre *f*. **the ~** *(US col)* die Röhre *(col)*.

tubeless [ˈtjuːblɪs] *adj tyre* schlauchlos.

tuber [ˈtjuːbəʳ] *n (Bot)* Knolle *f*.

tuberculosis [tjʊˌbɜːkjʊˈləʊsɪs] *n* Tuberkulose *f*.

tubing [ˈtjuːbɪŋ] *n* Schlauch *m*.

tubular [ˈtjuːbjʊləʳ] *adj* röhrenförmig.

TUC = Trades Union Congress ≈ DGB.

tuck [tʌk] **1** *n* **(a)** *(Sew)* Saum *m*; *(ornamental)* Biese *f*. **to put a ~ in sth** einen Saum in etw *(acc)* nähen. **(b)** *(Sch sl: food)* Süßigkeiten *pl*. **~ shop** Bonbonladen *m*. **2** *vt (put)* stecken. **he ~ed his umbrella under his arm** er steckte *or* klemmte *(col)* sich *(dat)* den Regenschirm unter den Arm. **3** *vi* **your bag will ~ under the seat** du kannst deine Tasche unter dem Sitz verstauen.

♦ **tuck away** *vt sep (hide)* wegstecken. **he ~ed it ~ in his pocket** er steckte es in die Tasche; **the hut is ~ed ~ among the trees** die Hütte liegt versteckt zwischen den Bäumen.

♦ **tuck in 1** *vi (col)* zulangen, reinhauen *(col)*. **~ ~!** langt zu!, haut rein! *(col)*; **to ~ ~ to sth** sich *(dat)* etw schmecken lassen. **2** *vt sep flap etc* hineinstecken, reinstecken *(col)*. **to ~ one's shirt ~** das Hemd in die Hose stecken; **to ~ sb ~ (to bed)** jdn zudecken.

♦ **tuck up** *vt sep skirt, hair* hochnehmen; *sleeve* hochkrempeln; *legs* unterschlagen. **to ~ sb ~ (in bed)** jdn zudecken.

Tuesday [ˈtjuːzdɪ] *n* Dienstag *m*. **on ~** (am) Dienstag; **~ December 5th** *(in letter)* Dienstag, den 5. Dezember; **on ~s** dienstags; **I met her on a ~** ich habe sie an einem Dienstag kennengelernt; **on ~ morning/evening** (am) Dienstag morgen/abend; **on ~ mornings/evenings** dienstags *or* Dienstag morgens/abends; **last/next/this ~** letzten/nächsten/diesen Dienstag; **a year last/next ~** letzten/nächsten Dienstag vor einem Jahr; **our ~ meeting** *(this week)* unser Treffen am Dienstag; *(every week)* unser Dienstagstreffen.

tuft [tʌft] *n* Büschel *nt*. **a ~ of hair/feathers** ein Haarbüschel *nt*/Federbusch *m*.

tug [tʌg] **1** *vt* zerren, ziehen. **she ~ged his sleeve** sie zog an seinem Ärmel. **2** *vi* ziehen, zerren *(at* an *+dat)*. **3** *n* **(a)** *(pull)* **to give sth a ~** an etw *(dat)* ziehen; **~ of war** *(Sport, fig)* Tauziehen *nt*. **(b)** *(also* **~boat***)* Schlepper *m*.

tuition [tjʊˈɪʃən] *n* Unterricht *m*. **extra ~** Nachhilfeunterricht.

tulip [ˈtjuːlɪp] *n* Tulpe *f*.

tumble [ˈtʌmbl] **1** *n (fall)* Sturz *m*. **to take a ~** stürzen, straucheln; *(fig)* fallen. **2** *vi (fall)* straucheln, (hin)fallen; *(move quickly)* stürzen; *(fig: prices)* fallen. **he ~d off his bicycle** er stürzte vom Fahrrad; **to ~ out of/into bed** aus dem Bett/ins Bett fallen.

tumble: ~down *adj* verfallen, baufällig; **~-drier** *n* Trockenautomat *m*.

tumbler [ˈtʌmbləʳ] *n* **(a)** *(glass)* (Becher)glas *nt*. **(b)** *(tumble drier)* Trockenautomat *m*.

tummy [ˈtʌmɪ] *n (col)* Bauch *m*. **(a) ~ ache** Bauchschmerzen *pl*, Bauchweh *nt*.

tumour, *(US)* **tumor** ['tju:mǝʳ] *n* Geschwulst *f,* Tumor *m.*

tumult ['tju:mʌlt] *n (uproar)* Tumult *m.* **the ~ of battle** das Schlachtgetümmel.

tumultuous [tju:'mʌltjuǝs] *adj* tumultartig; *applause* stürmisch. **they gave him a ~ welcome** sie begrüßten ihn stürmisch.

tuna (fish) ['tju:nǝ('fɪʃ)] *n* Thunfisch *m.*

tune [tju:n] **1** *n* **(a)** *(melody)* Melodie *f.* **sung to the ~ of ...** gesungen nach der Melodie (von) ...; **to change one's ~** *(fig)* seine Meinung ändern; **to the ~ of £100** in Höhe von £ 100. **(b) to sing in ~/out of ~** richtig/falsch singen; **the piano is out of ~** das Klavier ist verstimmt; **to be in/out of ~ with sb/sth** *(fig)* mit jdm/etw harmonieren/nicht harmonieren; **the engine's out of ~** der Motor ist falsch eingestellt; **he's in ~ with young people** er ist auf einer Wellenlänge mit der Jugend *(col)*; **he felt out of ~ with his new environment** er fühlte sich in seiner neuen Umgebung fehl am Platze. **2** *vt* **(a)** *(Mus) instrument* stimmen. **(b)** *(Rad, Aut)* einstellen.

♦**tune in 1** *vi (Rad)* einschalten. **to ~ ~ to Radio London** Radio London einschalten *or* hören. **2** *vt sep radio* einschalten *(to acc)*. **you are ~d ~ to Radio 2** Sie hören Radio 2.

♦**tune up 1** *vi (Mus)* (sein Instrument/die Instrumente) stimmen. **2** *vt sep engine* einstellen.

tuneful ['tju:nfʊl] *adj* melodisch.

tuneless ['tju:nlɪs] *adj* unmelodisch.

tuner ['tju:nǝʳ] *n* **(a)** *(Mus)* Stimmer *m.* **(b)** *(Rad etc)* Tuner *m.*

tungsten ['tʌŋstǝn] *n* Wolfram *nt.*

tunic ['tju:nɪk] *n* Kasack *m,* Hemdbluse *f; (of uniform)* Uniformrock *m.*

tuning ['tju:nɪŋ] *n* **(a)** *(Mus)* stimmen *nt.* **~-fork** Stimmgabel *f.* **(b)** *(Rad)* Einstellen *nt.* **~ knob** Stationswahlknopf *m.* **(c)** *(Aut)* Einstellen *nt.*

Tunisia [tju:'nɪzɪǝ] *n* Tunesien *nt.*

tunnel ['tʌnl] *(vb: pret, ptp (Brit)* **tunnelled,** *(US)* **tunneled***)* **1** *n* Tunnel *m; (Min)* Stollen *m.* **2** *vi (into* in *+acc, through* durch*)* einen Tunnel bauen; *(rabbit)* einen Bau graben; *(mole)* Gänge graben. **3** *vt* **they ~led a passage under the prison wall** sie gruben sich unter der Gefängnismauer durch; **to ~ one's way through sth** sich durch etw hindurchgraben.

tunny (fish) ['tʌnɪ('fɪʃ)] *n* Thunfisch *m.*

tuppence ['tʌpǝns] *n* zwei Pence. **I don't care ~** das interessiert mich nicht für fünf Pfennig *(col)*.

turban ['tɜ:bǝn] *n* Turban *m.*

turbid ['tɜ:bɪd] *adj liquid* trüber.

turbine ['tɜ:baɪn] *n* Turbine *f.*

turbo ['tɜ:bǝʊ]: **~ charger** *n* Turbolader *m;* **~jet** *(engine)* Turbotriebwerk *nt; (aircraft)* Turbojet *m.*

turbot ['tɜ:bǝt] *n* Steinbutt *m.*

turbulence ['tɜ:bjʊlǝns] *n (of emotions)* Aufgewühltheit *f; (of career, period)* Turbulenz *f.* **air ~** Turbulenz *f.*

turbulent ['tɜbjʊlǝnt] *adj* stürmisch; *emotions also* aufgewühlt; *career, period also* turbulent.

tureen [tǝ'ri:n] *n* (Suppen)terrine *f.*

turf [tɜ:f] **1** *n, pl* **-s** *or* **turves (a)** *(no pl: lawn)* Rasen *m; (no pl: squares of grass)* Soden *pl; (square of grass)* Sode *f.* **(b)** *(no pl: peat)* Torf(soden *pl*) *m; (square of peat)* Torfsode *f.* **to cut ~(s)** Torf stechen. **(c)** *(Sport)* **the T~** die (Pferde)rennbahn; **~ accountant** Buchmacher *m.* **2** *vt* **(a) he ~ed the garden** er verlegte (Gras)soden im Garten. **(b)** *(col)* **to ~ sb down the stairs** jdn die Treppe hinunterscheuchen *(col)*; **to ~ sth into the corner** etw in die Ecke werfen.

♦**turf out** *vt sep (col) person* rauswerfen; *plan* umschmeißen *(col)*, verwerfen; *(throw away)* wegschmeißen *(col)*.

turgid ['tɜ:dʒɪd] *adj (swollen)* (an)geschwollen; *(fig) style* schwülstig, überladen.

Turk [tɜ:k] *n* Türke *m,* Türkin *f.*

Turkey ['tɜ:kɪ] *n* die Türkei.

turkey ['tɜ:kɪ] *n* Truthahn *m*/-henne *f,* Pute(r) *mf (esp Cook)*.

Turkish ['tɜ:kɪʃ] **1** *adj* türkisch. **~ bath** türkisches Bad; **~ delight** Lokum *nt.* **2** *n (language)* Türkisch *nt.*

turmoil ['tɜ:mɔɪl] *n* Aufruhr *m; (confusion)* Durcheinander *nt.* **everything is in a ~** alles ist in Aufruhr; **her mind was in a ~** sie war völlig verwirrt.

turn [tɜ:n] **1** *n* **(a)** *(movement)* Drehung *f.* **to give sth a ~** etw drehen.

(b) *(change of direction) (in road)* Kurve *f; (Sport)* Wende *f.* **to make a ~ to the left** nach links einbiegen; *(driver, car also, road)* nach links abbiegen; *(road)* eine Linkskurve machen; **take the left-hand ~** biegen Sie links ab; **"no left ~"** „Linksabbiegen verboten"; **the ~ of the tide** *(lit)* der Gezeitenwechsel; **the tide is on the ~** *(lit)* die Ebbe/Flut setzt ein; *(fig)* es tritt eine Wende ein; **at the ~ of the century** um die Jahrhundertwende; **at every ~** *(fig)* auf Schritt und Tritt; **things took a ~ for the worse/the better** die Dinge wendeten sich zum Schlechten/zum Guten; **the patient took a ~ for the worse/the better** das Befinden des Patienten wendete sich zum Schlechteren/zum Besseren; **things took a new ~** die Dinge nahmen eine neue Wendung; **~ of phrase** Ausdrucksweise *f.*

(c) *(in game, queue, series)* **in ~** der Reihe nach; **out of ~** außer der Reihe; **it's your ~** du bist an der Reihe, du bist dran; **it's your ~ to do the dishes** du bist mit (dem) Abwaschen dran; **it's my ~ next** ich komme als nächste(r) an die Reihe; **wait your ~** warten Sie, bis Sie an der Reihe sind; **your ~ will come** du kommst auch noch mal dran; **sorry, have I spoken out of ~?** Entschuldigung, habe ich etwas Falsches gesagt?; **in ~, by ~s** abwechselnd; **to take ~s at doing sth** etw abwechselnd tun; **to take ~s at the wheel** sich beim Fahren abwechseln; **to take a ~ at the wheel** (für eine Weile) das Steuer übernehmen.

(d) *(service)* **to do sb a good/bad ~** jdm einen guten/schlechten Dienst erweisen; **one good ~ deserves another** *(Prov)* eine Hand wäscht die andere *(prov)*.

(e) *(tendency, talent)* **to have a mathematical ~ of mind** mathematisch begabt sein; **an optimistic/a strange ~ of mind** eine optimistische/seltsame Einstellung; **a melancholy ~ of mind** ein Hang zur Melancholie.

(f) *(Med col)* **he had one of his ~s last night** er hatte letzte Nacht wieder einen Anfall; **you/it gave me quite a ~** du hast/es hat mir einen schönen Schrecken eingejagt.

(g) *(Theat)* Nummer *f.* **they got him to do a ~ at the party** sie brachten ihn dazu, auf der Party etwas zum besten zu geben.

2 *vt* **(a)** *(revolve) key, screw, steering wheel* drehen. **to ~ the key in the lock** den Schlüssel im Schloß herumdrehen; **what ~s the wheel?** wie wird das Rad angetrieben?; **he ~ed the wheel sharply** er riß das Steuer herum.

(b) *(~ over, ~ round) mattress, car, soil* wenden; *page* umblättern; *record, chair, picture etc* umdrehen.

(c) *(transform, make become)* verwandeln *(in(to)* in *+acc)*. **the play was ~ed into a film** das Stück wurde verfilmt; **this hot weather has ~ed the milk (sour)** bei dieser Hitze ist die Milch sauer geworden.

(d) he ~ed his head towards me er wandte mir den Kopf zu; **he ~ed his back to the wall** er kehrte den Rücken zur Wand; **success has ~ed his head** der Erfolg ist ihm zu Kopf gestiegen;

she seems to have ~ed his head sie scheint ihm den Kopf verdreht zu haben; **she can still ~ a few heads** die Männer schauen sich immer noch nach ihr um; **as soon as his back is ~ed** sobald er den Rücken kehrt; **the sight of all that food quite ~ed my stomach** beim Anblick des vielen Essens drehte sich mir regelrecht der Magen um; **without ~ing a hair** ohne mit der Wimper zu zucken; **she ~ed her hand to cooking** sie versuchte sich im Kochen; **to ~ one's thoughts/attention to sth** seine Gedanken/Aufmerksamkeit einer Sache *(dat)* zuwenden; **to ~ a gun on sb** ein Gewehr auf jdn richten; **he has ~ed forty** er ist vierzig geworden; **it is** *or* **has ~ed 2 o'clock** es ist 2 Uhr vorbei; **the car ~ed the corner** das Auto bog um die Ecke; **to have ~ed the corner** *(fig)* über den Berg sein; **nothing will ~ him from his purpose** nichts wird ihn von seinem Vorhaben abbringen; **to ~ a dog on sb** einen Hund auf jdn hetzen.

3 *vi* **(a)** *(revolve, move round: key, wheel)* sich drehen. **he ~ed to me and smiled** er drehte sich mir zu und lächelte; **to ~ upside down** umkippen; **my head is ~ing** in meinem Kopf dreht sich alles.

(b) *(change direction) (to one side) (person, car)* abbiegen; *(plane, boat)* abdrehen; *(~ around)* wenden; *(person: on the spot)* sich umdrehen; *(wind)* drehen. **to ~ and go back** umkehren; **to ~ (to the) left** links abbiegen; **our luck ~ed** unser Glück wendete sich.

(c) *(go)* **to ~ to sb/sth** sich an jdn wenden/sich einer Sache *(dat)* zuwenden; **after her death, he ~ed to his books for comfort** nach ihrem Tod suchte er Trost bei seinen Büchern; **this job would make anyone ~ to drink!** bei dieser Arbeit muß man ja zum Trinker werden!; **the conversation ~ed to the accident** das Gespräch kam auf den Unfall; **I don't know which way to ~** ich weiß nicht, was ich machen soll.

(d) *(leaves)* sich (ver)färben; *(milk)* sauer werden; *(meat)* schlecht werden; *(weather)* umschlagen. **to ~ into sth** sich in etw *(acc)* verwandeln; *(develop into)* sich zu etw entwickeln; **their short holiday ~ed into a three-month visit** aus ihrem Kurzurlaub wurde ein Aufenthalt von drei Monaten; **to ~ to stone** zu Stein werden; **to ~ traitor** zum Verräter werden; **to ~ red** *(leaves etc)* sich rot färben; *(person: blush)* rot werden; *(traffic lights)* auf Rot umspringen; **his hair is ~ing grey** sein Haar wird grau.

♦ **turn against 1** *vi +prep obj* sich wenden gegen. **2** *vt sep +prep obj* **they ~ed him ~ his parents** sie brachten ihn gegen seine Eltern auf; **they ~ed his argument ~ him** sie verwendeten sein Argument gegen ihn.

♦ **turn around 1** *vi (face other way)* sich umdrehen; *(go back)* umkehren. **we ~ed ~ the corner** wir bogen um die Ecke. **2** *vt sep head* drehen; *box* umdrehen. **~ the picture ~ the other way** dreh das Bild andersherum.

♦ **turn aside 1** *vi* sich abwenden *(from* von*)*. **2** *vt sep* abwenden.

♦ **turn away 1** *vi* sich abwenden. **2** *vt sep* **(a)** *(move) head, eyes* abwenden. **(b)** *(send away) person* abweisen; *business* ablehnen.

♦ **turn back 1** *vi* **(a)** *(traveller, aeroplane)* umkehren; *(look back)* sich umdrehen. **there can be no ~ing ~ now** *(fig)* jetzt gibt es kein Zurück mehr. **(b)** *(in book)* **to ~ ~ to page 100** auf Seite 100 zurückblättern. **2** *vt sep* **(a)** *(fold) bedclothes* zurückschlagen; *corner* umknicken; *hem* umschlagen. **(b)** *(send back) person* zurückschicken. **they were ~ed ~ at the frontier** sie wurden an der Grenze zurückgewiesen. **(c)** *clock* zurückstellen. **to ~ the clock ~ fifty years** die Uhr um fünfzig Jahre zurückdrehen.

♦ **turn down 1** *vt sep* **(a)** *(fold down) bedclothes* zurückschlagen; *collar, brim* herunterklappen; *corner of a page* umknicken. **(b)** *gas, heat, lights* herunterdrehen; *volume* leiser stellen. **(c)** *candidate, novel etc* ablehnen; *offer also* zurückweisen; *suitor* abweisen. **2** *vi +prep obj* **he ~ed ~ a side street** er bog in eine Seitenstraße ab.

♦ **turn in 1** *vi* **(a)** *(drive in)* **the car ~ed ~ at the top of the drive** das Auto bog in die Einfahrt ein. **(b)** *(col: go to bed)* sich hinhauen *(col)*. **2** *vt sep (col: to police)* **to ~ sb ~** jdn anzeigen *or* verpfeifen *(col)*.

♦ **turn off 1** *vi* abbiegen *(for* nach, *prep obj* von*)*. **2** *vt sep* **(a)** *light, gas, radio* ausmachen; *tap* zudrehen; *TV* abschalten; *water, electricity, engine, machine* abstellen. **(b)** *(col)* **to ~ sb ~** *(disgust)* jdn anwidern; *(put off)* jdm die Lust verderben.

♦ **turn on 1** *vt sep* **(a)** *gas, heat, engine* anstellen, anmachen; *light, radio, television, the news also* einschalten; *tap, central heating* aufdrehen. **(b)** *(col: appeal to: music, novel etc)* **sth ~s sb ~** jd steht auf etw *(acc) (col)*; **whatever ~s you ~** wenn du das gut findest *(col)*; **he/it doesn't ~ me ~** er/das läßt mich kalt *(also sexually)*; **that ~s me ~** *(sexually)* das macht mich ganz scharf *(col)*. **2** *vi +prep obj* **(a)** *(attack)* angreifen. **(b)** *(depend on)* abhängen von.

♦ **turn out 1** *vi* **(a)** *(firemen)* ausrücken; *(doctor)* einen Krankenbesuch machen. **(b)** *(point)* **his toes ~ ~** er läuft nach außen. **(c) the car ~ed ~ of the drive** das Auto bog aus der Einfahrt. **(d)** *(transpire)* sich herausstellen. **he ~ed ~ to be the murderer himself** es stellte sich heraus, daß er selbst der Mörder war; **as it ~ed ~** wie sich herausstellte. **(e)** *(develop, progress)* sich entwickeln. **everything will ~ ~ all right** es wird sich schon alles ergeben; **it's ~ed ~ nice today** es ist heute wieder schön geworden.

2 *vt sep* **(a)** *light* ausmachen; *gas also* abstellen. **(b)** *(produce)* produzieren; *novel etc* schreiben; *good students* hervorbringen. **(c)** *(expel)* vertreiben *(of* aus*)*, hinauswerfen *(col) (of* aus*)*; *tenant* kündigen *(+dat)*. **(d)** *(tip out) cake* stürzen; *pockets* (aus)leeren. **he ~ed the photos ~ of the box** er kippte die Fotos aus der Schachtel. **(e)** *(clean) room* gründlich saubermachen. **(f)** *guard* antreten lassen. **(g) well ~ed-~** gut gekleidet.

♦ **turn over 1** *vi* **(a)** *(person, stomach)* sich umdrehen; *(car, place etc)* sich überschlagen; *(boat)* kentern. **he ~ed ~ on(to) his back** er drehte sich auf den Rücken. **(b)** *(with pages)* **please ~ ~** bitte wenden. **2** *vt sep* **(a)** umdrehen; *(turn upside down)* umkippen; *page* umblättern; *soil* umgraben; *mattress, steak* wenden. **the police ~ed the whole place ~** *(search)* die Polizei durchsuchte das ganze Haus *etc*; **to ~ an idea ~ in one's mind** sich *(dat)* eine Idee durch den Kopf gehen lassen. **(b)** *(hand over)* übergeben *(to dat)*.

♦ **turn round** *vti* = **turn around.**

♦ **turn up 1** *vi* **(a)** *(arrive)* erscheinen, auftauchen *(col)*. **I was afraid you wouldn't ~ ~** ich hatte Angst, du würdest nicht kommen. **(b)** *(be found)* (wieder) auftauchen *(col)*. **(c)** *(happen)* **something is sure to ~ ~** irgend etwas passiert schon. **(d)** *(point up)* **a ~ed-~ nose** eine Stupsnase; **to ~ ~ at the ends** sich an den Enden hochbiegen. **2** *vt sep* **(a)** *(fold) collar* hochklappen; *hem* umnähen. **to ~ ~ one's nose at sth** *(fig)* die Nase über etw *(acc)* rümpfen. **(b)** *heat, gas* höher drehen; *radio* lauter drehen; *volume* aufdrehen; *light* heller machen.

turn: ~about, ~around *n* Kehrtwendung *f*; **~coat** *n* Überläufer *m*.

turning ['tɜːnɪŋ] *n (in road)* Abzweigung *f*. **take the second ~ on the left** nimm die zweite Abfahrt links.

turning point *n* Wendepunkt *m*.

turnip ['tɜːnɪp] *n* Rübe *f*.

turn-off ['tɜːnɒf] *n* Abzweigung *f*; *(on motorway)* Abfahrt, Ausfahrt *f*. **the Birmingham ~** die Abfahrt *or* Ausfahrt Birmingham.

turnout ['tɜːnaʊt] *n* **(a)** *(attendance)* Teilnahme, Beteiligung *f*. **in spite of the rain there was a big ~ for the match** trotz des Regens war das Spiel gut besucht. **(b)** *(clean)* **to give sth a good ~** etw gründlich säubern. **(c)** *(dress)* Aufmachung *f*.

turnover ['tɜːnˌəʊvəʳ] *n (total business)* Umsatz *m*; *(Comm, Fin: of capital)* Umlauf *m*; *(Comm: of stock)* (Lager)umschlag *m*; *(of staff)* Fluktuation *f*.

turn: ~pike *n (Brit Hist)* Mautschranke *f*; *(US)* gebührenpflichtige Autobahn; **~stile** *n* Drehkreuz *nt*; **~table** *n* Drehscheibe *f*; *(on record player)* Plattenteller *m*; **~-up** *n* **(a)** *(Brit: on trousers)* Aufschlag *m*; **(b)** *(col: event)* **that was a ~-up for the book** das war eine (echte) Überraschung.

turpentine ['tɜːpəntaɪn] *n* Terpentin *nt*.

turquoise ['tɜːkwɔɪz] **1** *n* **(a)** *(gem)* Türkis *m*. **(b)** *(colour)* Türkis *nt*. **2** *adj* türkis(farben).

turret ['tʌrɪt] *n (Archit)* Mauerturm *m*; *(on tank)* Turm *m*; *(on ship)* Gefechtsturm *m*.

turtle ['tɜːtl] *n* (Wasser)schildkröte *f*; *(US also)* (Land)schildkröte *f*. **to turn ~** kentern.

turtle: ~-dove *n (lit, fig col)* Turteltaube *f*; **~-neck (pullover)** *n* Schildkrötenkragenpullover *m*.

tusk [tʌsk] *n (of elephant)* Stoßzahn *m*; *(of walrus)* Eckzahn *m*; *(of boar)* Hauer *m*.

tussle ['tʌsl] **1** *n (lit, fig)* Gerangel *nt*. **2** *vi* sich rangeln *(with sb for sth* mit jdm um etw*)*.

tussock ['tʌsək] *n* (Gras)büschel *nt*.

tutor ['tjuːtəʳ] **1** *n* **(a)** Privatlehrer *m*. **(b)** *(Brit Univ)* Tutor *m*. **2** *vt (as private teacher)* privat unterrichten; *(give extra lessons to)* Nachhilfe(unterricht) geben *(+dat)*. **to ~ sb in Latin** jdm Privatunterricht/Nachhilfe in Latein geben.

tutorial [tjuː'tɔːrɪəl] *n (Brit Univ)* Kolloquium *nt*.

tut-tut ['tʌt'tʌt] *interj (in disapproval)* na, na.

tuxedo [tʌk'siːdəʊ] *n (US)* Smoking *m*.

TV *n (col)* = **television.**

twaddle ['twɒdl] *n (col)* Geschwätz *nt*.

twang [twæŋ] **1** *n (of wire, guitar string)* Doing *nt*; *(of rubber band, bowstring)* scharfer Ton; *(of voice)* Näseln *nt*, näselnder Tonfall. **2** *vt* zupfen; *guitar, banjo also* klimpern auf *(+dat)*. **3** *vi* einen scharfen Ton von sich geben; *(rubber band)* pitschen *(col)*.

tweak [twiːk] **1** *vt* kneifen. **to ~ sb's ear** jdn am Ohr ziehen. **2** *n* **to give sb's ear/nose a ~** jdn am Ohr/an der Nase ziehen.

twee [twiː] *adj (+er) (col)* niedlich; *manner* geziert; *expression* gekünstelt.

tweed [twiːd] **1** *n* **(a)** *(cloth)* Tweed *m*. **(b) ~s** *pl (clothes)* Tweedkleidung *f*. **2** *adj* Tweed-.

tweet [twiːt] **1** *n* Piepsen *nt no pl*. **2** *vi* piepsen.

tweeter ['twiːtəʳ] *n* Hochtonlautsprecher *m*.

tweezers ['twiːzəz] *npl (also* **pair of ~***)* Pinzette *f*.

twelfth [twelfθ] **1** *adj* zwölfte(r, s). **2** *n (in series)* Zwölfte(r, s); *(fraction)* Zwölftel *nt*; *see* **sixth.**

twelve [twelv] *adj* zwölf. **~ noon** zwölf Uhr (mittags); *see* **six.**

twentieth ['twentɪɪθ] **1** *adj* zwanzigste(r, s). **2** *n (in series)* Zwanzigste(r, s); *(fraction)* Zwanzigstel *nt*; *see* **sixtieth.**

twenty ['twentɪ] *adj* zwanzig; *see* **sixty.**

twerp [twɜːp] *n (col)* Einfaltspinsel *(col)*.

twice [twaɪs] *adv* zweimal. **~ as much/many** doppelt *or* zweimal soviel/so viele; **~ as much bread** doppelt soviel Brot; **~ as long as ...** zweimal so lange wie ...; **at ~ the speed of sound** mit doppelter Schallgeschwindigkeit; **she is ~ your age** sie ist doppelt so alt wie du; **~ 2 is 4** zweimal 2 ist 4; **~ a week** zweimal wöchentlich, zweimal pro Woche; **I'd think ~ before trusting him with it** ihm würde ich das nicht so ohne weiteres anvertrauen.

twiddle ['twɪdl] **1** *vt* herumdrehen an *(+dat)*. **she ~d the pencil in her fingers** ihre Finger spielten mit dem Bleistift; **to ~ one's thumbs** *(lit, fig)* Däumchen drehen. **2** *vi* **to ~ with a knob** an einem Knopf herumdrehen.

twig[1] [twɪg] *n (thin branch)* Zweig *m*.

twig[2] *(Brit col)* **1** *vt (realize)* mitkriegen *(col)*, mitbekommen. **he's ~ged it** er hat's kapiert *(col)*. **2** *vi* schalten *(col)*, es mitkriegen *(col)*.

twilight ['twaɪlaɪt] *n* Dämmerung *f*. **at ~** in der Dämmerung; **in the ~** im Zwielicht.

twin [twɪn] **1** *n* Zwilling *m*; *(of vase, object)* Gegenstück, Pendant *nt*. **her ~** ihre Zwillingsschwester/ihr Zwillingsbruder *m*. **2** *vt (Brit) town* verschwistern. **Oxford was ~ned with Bonn** Oxford und Bonn wurden zu Partnerstädten.

twin: ~ beds *npl* zwei (gleiche) Einzelbetten; **~ brother** *n* Zwillingsbruder *m*; **~ carburettors** *(Brit) or* **carburetors** *(US) npl* Doppelvergaser *m*.

twine [twaɪn] **1** *n* Schnur *f*, Bindfaden *m*. **2** *vt* winden. **to ~ one's arms around sb** seine Arme um jdn schlingen. **3** *vi* **to ~ around sth** sich um etw winden.

twinge [twɪndʒ] *n (of pain)* Zucken *nt*, leichtes Stechen. **a ~ of pain** ein zuckender Schmerz; **a ~ of conscience/remorse** Gewissensbisse *pl*.

twinkle ['twɪŋkl] **1** *vi* funkeln; *(stars also)* glitzern. **2** *n* Funkeln, Glitzern *nt*. **there was a ~ in her eye** man sah den Schalk in ihren Augen.

twinkling ['twɪŋklɪŋ] *n* **in the ~ of an eye** im Nu, im Handumdrehen.

twin: ~set *n (Brit)* Twinset *nt*; **~ sister** *n* Zwillingsschwester *f*; **~ town** *n (Brit)* Partnerstadt *f*; **~-tub (washing-machine)** *n* Waschmaschine *f* mit getrennter Schleuder.

twirl [twɜːl] **1** *vt* (herum)wirbeln; *skirt* herumwirbeln; *moustache* zwirbeln. **2** *vi* wirbeln. **3** *n* Wirbel *m*; *(in dance)* Drehung *f*; *(of moustache)* hochstehende Spitze.

twist [twɪst] **1** *n* **(a)** *(action)* **to give sth a ~** etw (herum)drehen; **with a quick ~ of the hand** mit einer schnellen Handbewegung. **(b)** *(bend)* Kurve, Biegung *f*; *(fig: in story etc)* Wendung *f*. **(c)** *(Brit col)* **to be/go round the ~** verrückt sein/werden; **it's driving me round the ~!** das macht mich wahnsinnig! **(d)** *(dance)* Twist *m*.

2 *vt* **(a)** *(wind, turn)* drehen; *(coil)* wickeln *(into* zu *+dat)*. **to ~ threads** *etc* **together** Fäden *etc* zusammendrehen; **to ~ the top off a jar** den Deckel von einem Glas abdrehen. **(b)** *(bend, distort) key* verbiegen; *part of body, (fig) meaning, words* verdrehen. **to ~ sth out of shape** etw verbiegen; **to ~ sb's arm** *(lit)* jdm den Arm verdrehen; *(fig)* jdn überreden; **to ~ one's ankle** sich *(dat)* den Fuß vertreten; **his face was ~ed with pain** sein Gesicht war schmerzverzerrt.

3 *vi* **(a)** sich drehen; *(smoke)* sich ringeln; *(plant)* sich ranken; *(road, river, person: wriggle)* sich schlängeln. **(b)** *(dance)* Twist tanzen.

♦**twist off** *vt sep* abdrehen; *lid* abschrauben; *flowerheads* abknipsen.

twisted ['twɪstɪd] *adj* **(a)** *wires, rope* (zusammen)gedreht; *(bent)* verbogen. **(b)** *ankle* verrenkt. **(c)** *(fig) mind, logic* verdreht.

twit [twɪt] *(Brit col: person)* Trottel *m (col)*.

twitch [twɪtʃ] **1** *n* **(a)** *(tic)* Zucken *nt*; *(individual spasm)* Zuckung *f*. **to give a ~** zucken. **(b)** *(pull)* Ruck *m (of* an *+dat)*. **to give sth a ~** an etw *(dat)* rucken. **2** *vi (face, muscles)* zucken. **the cat's nose ~ed** die Katze schnupperte.

twitter ['twɪtəʳ] **1** *vti (lit, fig)* zwitschern. **2** *n* **(a)** *(of birds)* Gezwitscher *nt*. **(b)** *(col)* **to be all of a ~** ganz aufgeregt sein.

two [tuː] **1** *adj* zwei. **to cut sth in ~** etw in zwei Teile schneiden; **~ by ~, in ~s** zu zweit, zu zweien; **the ~ of them** die beiden; **to put ~ and ~ together** *(fig)* seine Schlüsse ziehen; **~ can play**

that game *(col)* den Spieß kann man auch umdrehen; *see* **six.** **2** *n* Zwei *f.* **just the ~ of us/them** nur wir beide/die beiden.

two: **~-dimensional** *adj* zweidimensional; **~-door** *adj* zweitürig; **~-edged** *adj (lit, fig)* zweischneidig; **~-faced** *adj (lit)* doppelgesichtig; *(fig)* falsch; **~fold 1** *adj* zweifach, doppelt; **a ~fold increase** ein Anstieg um das Doppelte; **2** *adv* **to increase ~fold** um das Doppelte steigern; **~-legged** *adj* zweibeinig; **a ~-legged animal** ein Zweibeiner *m*; **~-party system** *n* Zweiparteiensystem *nt*; **~-piece 1** *adj* zweiteilig; **2** *n (suit)* Zweiteiler *m*; *(swimming costume)* zweiteiliger Badeanzug; **~-pin plug** *n* Stecker *m* mit zwei Kontakten; **~-ply** *adj wool* zweifädig; *wood* aus zwei Lagen bestehend; *tissue* zweilagig; **~seater** *n (car, plane)* Zweisitzer *m*; **~some** *n* **(a)** *(people)* Paar, Pärchen *nt*; **(b)** *(game)* **to have a ~some at golf** zu zweit Golf spielen; **~ star petrol** *(Brit)* Normalbenzin *nt*; **~-stroke 1** *adj* Zweitakt-; **2** *n* Zweitakter *m.* **~-time** *vt (col) boyfriend, accomplice* betrügen; **~-tone** *adj (in colour)* zweifarbig; **~-up ~-down** *n (Brit col)* kleines Reihenhäuschen; **~-way** *adj* **~-way (radio)** Funksprechgerät *nt*; **~-way traffic** Verkehr *m* in beiden Richtungen; **~-wheeler** *n* Zweirad, Fahrrad *nt.*

tycoon [taɪ'kuːn] *n* Magnat *m.*

type[1] [taɪp] *n* **(a)** *(kind)* Art *f*; *(of produce, plant also)* Sorte *f*; *(esp of people)* Typ, Typus *m.* **different ~s of cows/roses** verschiedene Arten von Rindern/verschiedene Rosensorten; **what ~ of car is it?** was für ein Auto(typ) ist das?; **they're totally different ~s of person** sie sind völlig verschiedene Typen; **I object to that ~ of behaviour** ich protestiere gegen ein solches Benehmen; **it's not my ~ of film** diese Art Film gefällt mir nicht; **he's not my ~** er ist nicht mein Typ; **she's my ~ of girl** sie ist mein Typ; **he's not the ~ to hit a lady** er ist nicht der Mensch, der eine Frau schlägt. **(b)** *(col: man)* Typ *m.*

type[2] **1** *n (Typ)* Type *f.* **small/large ~** kleine/große Schrift. **2** *vt* tippen *(col)*, (mit der Maschine) schreiben. **a badly ~d letter** ein schlecht getippter Brief. **3** *vi* maschineschreiben, tippen *(col)*.

♦ **type out** *vt sep letter* schreiben, tippen *(col)*.

type: **~-cast** *vt (Theat)* (auf eine bestimmte Rolle) festlegen; **~face** *n* Schrift *f*; **~script** *n* (mit Maschine geschriebenes) Manuskript; **~setter** *n (person)* Setzer(in *f*) *m.*

typewriter ['taɪpˌraɪtəʳ] *n* Schreibmaschine *f.* **~ ribbon** Farbband *nt.*

typewritten ['taɪpˌrɪtn] *adj* maschinengeschrieben, getippt *(col)*.

typhoid ['taɪfɔɪd] *n (also* **~ fever***)* Typhus *m.*

typhoon [taɪ'fuːn] *n* Taifun *m.*

typhus ['taɪfəs] *n* Fleckfieber *nt*, Flecktyphus *m.*

typical ['tɪpɪkəl] *adj* typisch *(of* für*)*. **a ~ English town** eine typisch englische Stadt; **that's ~ of him** das ist typisch für ihn.

typically ['tɪpɪkəlɪ] *adv see adj.* **~, he did nothing but complain** es war typisch für ihn, daß er sich ständig beschwerte.

typify ['tɪpɪfaɪ] *vt* bezeichnend sein für. **he typifies the reserved Englishman** er verkörpert den Typ des zurückhaltenden Engländers.

typing ['taɪpɪŋ] **1** *n* Maschineschreiben, Tippen *(col) nt.* **his ~ isn't very good** er kann nicht besonders gut maschineschreiben. **2** *attr* Schreibmaschinen-. **~ error** Tippfehler *m*; **~ pool** Schreibzentrale *f.*

typist ['taɪpɪst] *n (professional)* Schreibkraft *f*, Stenotypist(in *f*) *m.*

typographic(al) [ˌtaɪpə'græfɪk(əl)] *adj* typographisch. **~ error** Druckfehler *m.*

tyrannic(al) [tɪ'rænɪk(əl)] *adj* tyrannisch.

tyrannize ['tɪrənaɪz] *vt (lit, fig)* tyrannisieren.

tyranny ['tɪrənɪ] *n (lit, fig)* Tyrannei *f.*

tyrant ['taɪərənt] *n (lit, fig)* Tyrann(in *f*) *m.*

tyre, *(US)* **tire** [taɪəʳ] *n* Reifen *m.* **~ gauge** Reifendruckmesser *m*; **~ pressure** Reifendruck *m.*

Tyrol [tɪ'rəʊl] *n* **the ~** Tirol *nt.*

Tyrolean ['tɪrəlɪən] *adj* Tiroler.

tzar *n* = **tsar.**

U

U, u [juː] *n* U, u *nt.*
ubiquitous [juːˈbɪkwɪtəs] *adj* allgegenwärtig.
U-boat [ˈjuːbəʊt] *n* U-Boot *nt.*
udder [ˈʌdə^r] *n* Euter *nt.*
UFO [ˈjuːfəʊ] = **unidentified flying object** Ufo, UFO *nt.*
Uganda [juːˈgændə] *n* Uganda *nt.*
ugh [ɜːh] *interj* i, igitt.
ugliness [ˈʌglɪnɪs] *n* Häßlichkeit *f.*
ugly [ˈʌglɪ] *adj (+er)* **(a)** *(not pretty)* häßlich. **as ~ as sin** häßlich wie die Nacht. **(b)** *(unpleasant, nasty)* übel; *news, wound also* schlimm; *scenes, vice, clouds* häßlich; *crime also* gemein; *sky* bedrohlich. **an ~ customer** ein übler Kunde.
UHF = **ultra-high frequency** UHF.
UK = **United Kingdom** Vereinigtes Königreich.
ulcer [ˈʌlsə^r] *n (Med)* Geschwür *nt*; *(stomach ~)* Magengeschwür *nt*; *(fig)* Übel *nt.*
Ulster [ˈʌlstə^r] *n* Ulster, Nordirland *nt.* **U~man/woman** Einwohner(in *f*) *m* von Ulster.
ulterior [ʌlˈtɪərɪə^r] *adj* **~ motive** Hintergedanke *m.*
ultimate [ˈʌltɪmɪt] **1** *adj* **(a)** *(final)* letzte(r, s); *destiny, solution, decision* endgültig; *result, outcome, aim* End-; *control* oberste(r, s); *authority* höchste(r, s). **what is your ~ ambition in life?** was streben Sie letzten Endes im Leben an?; **although they had no ~ hope of escape** obwohl im Endeffekt keine Hoffnung auf Flucht bestand.

(b) *(that cannot be improved on)* vollendet, perfekt. **the ~ insult** der Gipfel der Beleidigung; **the ~ deterrent** *(Mil)* das endgültige Abschreckungsmittel; *(fig)* die äußerste Abschreckungsmaßnahme; **the ~ weapon** *(Mil)* die Superwaffe; *(fig)* das letzte und äußerste Mittel; **death is the ~ sacrifice** der Tod ist das allergrößte Opfer.

(c) *(basic)* Grund-; *cause* eigentlich; *explanation* grundsätzlich; *truth* letzte(r, s).

(d) *(furthest)* entfernteste(r, s); *ancestors* früheste(r, s). **the ~ origins of man** die frühesten Ursprünge des Menschen.

2 *n* Nonplusultra *nt.* **the ~ in comfort** das Höchste an Komfort.
ultimately [ˈʌltɪmɪtlɪ] *adv (in the end)* letztlich, letzten Endes; *(eventually)* schließlich; *(fundamentally)* im Grunde genommen. **it's ~ your decision** letztlich müssen Sie das entscheiden.
ultimatum [ˌʌltɪˈmeɪtəm] *n, pl* **-s** *or* **ultimata** *(Mil, fig)* Ultimatum *nt.* **to deliver an ~ to sb** jdm ein Ultimatum stellen.
ultraviolet [ˌʌltrəˈvaɪəlɪt] *adj* ultraviolett.
umbilical [ˌʌmbɪˈlaɪkəl] *adj* **~ cord** Nabelschnur *f.*
umbrage [ˈʌmbrɪdʒ] *n:* **to take ~ at sth** an etw *(dat)* Anstoß nehmen.
umbrella [ʌmˈbrelə] *n* (Regen)schirm *m*; *(sun ~)* (Sonnen)schirm *m.* **collapsible** *or* **telescopic ~** Taschenschirm *m*; **under the ~ of** *(fig)* unter der Kontrolle von.
umbrella: ~ organization *n* Dachorganisation *f*; **~ stand** *n* Schirmständer *m.*
umpire [ˈʌmpaɪə^r] **1** *n (lit, fig)* Schiedsrichter(in *f*) *m.* **2** *vt (Sport)* Schiedsrichter sein bei; *(fig)* schlichten. **3** *vi* Schiedsrichter sein *(in* bei*).*
umpteen [ˈʌmpˈtiːn] *adj (col)* zig *(col)*, x *(col).* **I've told you ~ times** ich habe dir x-mal gesagt *(col).*
umpteenth [ˈʌmpˈtiːnθ] *adj (col)* x-te(r, s). **for the ~ time** zum x-ten Mal.
UN = **United Nations** UNO *f.* **~ troops** UNO-Truppen *pl.*
unabashed [ˌʌnəˈbæʃt] *adj (not ashamed)* dreist; *(not overawed)* unbeeindruckt.
unabated [ˌʌnəˈbeɪtɪd] *adj* unvermindert. **the rain continued ~** der Regen ließ nicht nach.
unable [ˌʌnˈeɪbl] *adj pred* **to be ~ to do sth** etw nicht tun können; *(not be in a position to)* außerstande sein, etw zu tun.
unabridged [ˌʌnəˈbrɪdʒd] *adj* ungekürzt.
unacceptable [ˌʌnəkˈseptəbl] *adj plans, terms* unannehmbar; *excuse, offer, behaviour* nicht akzeptabel; *standard, conditions* untragbar. **it's quite ~ that we should be expected to ...** es kann doch nicht von uns verlangt werden, daß ...; **it's quite ~ for young children to ...** es kann nicht zugelassen werden, daß kleine Kinder ...; **the ~ face of capitalism** die Kehrseite des Kapitalismus.
unaccompanied [ˌʌnəˈkʌmpənɪd] *adj person, child, singing* ohne Begleitung; *instrument* Solo-. **~ luggage** aufgegebenes Reisegepäck.
unaccountable [ˌʌnəˈkaʊntəbl] *adj* unerklärlich.
unaccountably [ˌʌnəˈkaʊntəblɪ] *adv* unerklärlicherweise; *disappear* auf unerklärliche Weise.
unaccounted for [ˌʌnəˈkaʊntɪdˈfɔː^r] *adj* ungeklärt. **the £30 is still ~** es ist noch ungeklärt, wo die £30 geblieben sind; **three of the passengers are still ~** drei Passagiere werden noch vermißt.
unaccustomed [ˌʌnəˈkʌstəmd] *adj* **(a)** *(unusual)* ungewohnt. **(b)** *(of person: unused)* **to be ~ to sth** etw nicht gewohnt sein, an etw *(acc)* nicht gewöhnt sein; **to be ~ to doing sth** nicht daran gewöhnt sein, etw zu tun.
unacquainted [ˌʌnəˈkweɪntɪd] *adj pred* **to be ~ with poverty** die Armut nicht kennen; **to be ~ with the facts** mit den Tatschen nicht vertraut sein.
unadulterated [ˌʌnəˈdʌltəreɪtɪd] *adj* **(a)** unverfälscht, rein; *wine* rein, ungepanscht; *(hum) whisky* unverdünnt. **(b)** *(fig) nonsense* absolut; *bliss* ungetrübt.
unadventurous [ˌʌnədˈventʃərəs] *adj time, life* ereignislos; *tastes* bieder; *style, performance* einfallslos; *person* wenig unternehmungslustig.
unaffected [ˌʌnəˈfektɪd] *adj* **(a)** *(sincere)* ungekünstelt, natürlich; *pleasure, gratitude* echt. **(b)** *(not damaged)* nicht angegriffen *(also Med)*, nicht beeinträchtigt; *(not influenced)* unbeeinflußt; *(not involved)* nicht betroffen; *(unmoved)* ungerührt. **she remained quite ~ by his tears** sie blieb beim Anblick seiner Tränen völlig ungerührt.
unafraid [ˌʌnəˈfreɪd] *adj* furchtlos. **to be ~ of sb/sth** vor jdm/etw keine Angst haben.
unaided [ʌnˈeɪdɪd] **1** *adv* ohne fremde Hilfe. **2** *adj* **his own ~ work** seine eigene Arbeit.
unalterable [ʌnˈɒltərəbl] *adj intention, decision* unabänderlich; *laws* unveränderlich.
unambiguous [ˌʌnæmˈbɪgjʊəs] *adj* eindeutig, unzweideutig.

unambitious [ˌʌnæm'bɪʃəs] *adj person, plan* nicht ehrgeizig (genug); *performance* anspruchslos.
un-American [ˌʌnə'merɪkən] *adj* unamerikanisch.
unanimous [juː'nænɪməs] *adj* einmütig; *decision also, (Jur)* einstimmig. **we were ~ in thinking ...** wir waren einmütig der Ansicht ...; **by a ~ vote** einstimmig.
unanimously [juː'nænɪməslɪ] *adv* einstimmig.
unanswerable [ʌn'ɑːnsərəbl] *adj question* nicht zu beantworten(d *attr) pred; argument, case* unwiderlegbar.
unanswered [ʌn'ɑːnsəd] *adj* unbeantwortet.
unappealing [ˌʌnə'piːlɪŋ] nicht reizvoll; *person* unansehnlich; *prospect, sight* nicht verlockend.
unappetizing [ʌn'æpɪtaɪzɪŋ] *adj* unappetitlich; *prospect, thought* wenig verlockend.
unappreciative [ˌʌnə'priːʃɪətɪv] *adj* undankbar; *audience* verständnislos. **to be ~ of sth** etw nicht zu würdigen wissen.
unapproachable [ˌʌnə'prəʊtʃəbl] *adj place* unzugänglich; *person also* unnahbar.
unarmed [ʌn'ɑːmd] *adj* unbewaffnet. **~ combat** Nahkampf *m* ohne Waffe.
unashamed [ˌʌnə'ʃeɪmd] *adj* schamlos. **his ~ conservatism** sein unverhohlener Konservatismus; **he was quite ~ about it** er schämte sich dessen überhaupt nicht.
unashamedly [ˌʌnə'ʃeɪmɪdlɪ] *adv* unverschämt; *say, admit* ohne Scham; *in favour of, partisan* unverhohlen.
unasked [ʌn'ɑːskt] *adj (unrequested)* unaufgefordert, ungefragt; *(uninvited)* ungebeten.
unassailable [ˌʌnə'seɪləbl] *adj* unangreifbar; *fortress* uneinnehmbar; *position, reputation* unanfechtbar; *conviction* unerschütterlich; *argument* unwiderlegbar, zwingend.
unassisted [ˌʌnə'sɪstɪd] *adj, adv* = **unaided.**
unassuming [ˌʌnə'sjuːmɪŋ] *adj* bescheiden.
unattached [ˌʌnə'tætʃt] *adj* **(a)** *(not fastened)* unbefestigt; *(Mil)* keinem Regiment/keiner Einheit *etc* zugeteilt. **(b)** *(emotionally)* ungebunden.
unattended [ˌʌnə'tendɪd] *adj children* unbeaufsichtigt; *car, luggage* unbewacht; *wound, patient* unbehandelt; *shop* ohne Bedienung; *customer* nicht bedient; *business* unerledigt.
unattractive [ˌʌnə'træktɪv] *adj sight, place* unschön, wenig reizvoll; *offer, woman* unattraktiv; *trait, scar* unschön; *character* unsympathisch.
unauthorized [ʌn'ɔːθəraɪzd] *adj* unbefugt. **no entry for ~ persons** Zutritt für Unbefugte verboten!
unavailable [ˌʌnə'veɪləbl] *adj* nicht erhältlich; *person* nicht zu erreichen *pred; library book* nicht verfügbar.
unavailing [ˌʌnə'veɪlɪŋ] *adj* vergeblich.
unavenged [ˌʌnə'vendʒd] *adj* ungerächt.
unavoidable [ˌʌnə'vɔɪdəbl] *adj* unvermeidlich; *conclusion* zwangsläufig.
unavoidably [ˌʌnə'vɔɪdəblɪ] *adv* notgedrungen. **to be ~ detained** verhindert sein.
unaware [ˌʌnə'weəʳ] *adj pred* **to be ~ of sth** sich *(dat)* einer Sache *(gen)* nicht bewußt sein; **I was ~ of his presence** ich hatte nicht bemerkt, daß er da war; **I was ~ that he was interested** es war mir nicht bewußt, daß er (daran) interessiert war.
unawares [ˌʌnə'weəz] *adv (by surprise)* unerwartet; *(accidentally)* unbeabsichtigt, versehentlich; *(without knowing)* unwissentlich. **to catch** *or* **take sb ~** jdn überraschen.
unbalanced [ʌn'bælənst] *adj* **(a)** unausgewogen; *diet, report also, view* einseitig; *ship etc* nicht im Gleichgewicht. **(b)** *(also* **mentally ~***) (mad)* irre, verrückt; *(slightly crazy)* nicht ganz normal. **(c)** *account* nicht ausgeglichen.
unbearable [ʌn'beərəbl] *adj* unerträglich.
unbeatable [ʌn'biːtəbl] *adj* unschlagbar; *record also* nicht zu überbieten(d *attr) pred.*
unbeaten [ʌn'biːtn] *adj* ungeschlagen; *record* ungebrochen.
unbecoming [ˌʌnbɪ'kʌmɪŋ] *adj behaviour, language etc* unschicklich; *clothes* unvorteilhaft; *beards* unschön.
unbeknown(st) [ˌʌnbɪ'nəʊn(st)] *adv* ohne daß es jemand wußte. **~ to me/his father** ohne mein Wissen/ohne Wissen seines Vaters.
unbelievable [ˌʌnbɪ'liːvəbl] *adj* unglaublich.
unbelievably [ˌʌnbɪ'liːvəblɪ] *adv* unglaublich.
unbeliever [ˌʌnbɪ'liːvəʳ] *n* Ungläubige(r) *mf.*
unbelieving [ˌʌnbɪ'liːvɪŋ] *adj* ungläubig.
unbend [ʌn'bend] *pret, ptp* **unbent 1** *vt (straighten) metal etc* geradebiegen; *arms* strecken. **2** *vi (person, relax)* aus sich herausgehen; *(straighten body)* sich aufrichten.
unbending [ʌn'bendɪŋ] *adj person, attitude* unnachgiebig; *determination* unbeugsam.
unbent [ʌn'bent] *pret, ptp of* **unbend.**
unbias(s)ed [ʌn'baɪəst] *adj* unvoreingenommen; *opinion, report also* unparteiisch.
unblemished [ʌn'blemɪʃt] *adj (lit, fig)* makellos.
unblock [ʌn'blɒk] *vt* frei machen; *sink, pipe* die Verstopfung in *(+dat)* ... beseitigen.
unbolt [ʌn'bəʊlt] *vt* aufriegeln. **he left the door ~ed** er verriegelte die Tür nicht.
unborn [ʌn'bɔːn] *adj* ungeboren. **generations yet ~** kommende Generationen.
unbounded [ʌn'baʊndɪd] *adj* grenzenlos.
unbreakable [ʌn'breɪkəbl] *adj glass, toy* unzerbrechlich; *record* nicht zu brechen(d *attr) pred; rule* unumstößlich; *promise* unverbrüchlich.
unbridled [ʌn'braɪdld] *adj passion* ungezügelt; *anger* hemmungslos; *tongue* lose; *capitalism* ungehemmt.
un-British [ʌn'brɪtɪʃ] *adj* unbritisch.
unbroken [ʌn'brəʊkən] *adj* **(a)** *(intact)* ungeschädigt; *heart, promise* nicht gebrochen. **(b)** *(continuous)* ununterbrochen; *(Mil) ranks* geschlossen; *line of descent* direkt. **an ~ night's sleep** eine ungestörte Nacht. **(c)** *(unbeaten) record* ungebrochen. **(d)** *horse* nicht zugeritten; *pride* ungebeugt. **his spirit remained ~** er war ungebrochen.
unbuckle [ʌn'bʌkl] *vt* aufschnallen.
unburden [ʌn'bɜːdn] *vt* **to ~ oneself/one's heart to sb** jdm sein Herz ausschütten.
unbusinesslike [ʌn'bɪznɪslaɪk] *adj* wenig geschäftsmäßig. **in spite of his ~ appearance ...** obwohl er gar nicht wie ein Geschäftsmann aussieht ...
unbutton [ʌn'bʌtn] *vt* aufknöpfen.
uncalled-for [ʌn'kɔːldfɔːʳ] *adj (unjustified) criticism* ungerechtfertigt; *(unnecessary)* unnötig; *(rude) remark* deplaziert. **that was quite ~** das war nun wirklich nicht nötig.
uncanny [ʌn'kænɪ] *adj* unheimlich.
uncared-for [ʌn'keədfɔːʳ] *adj garden, hands* ungepflegt; *child* vernachlässigt.
uncaring [ʌn'keərɪŋ] *adj* gleichgültig; *parents* lieblos.
unceasing [ʌn'siːsɪŋ] *adj* unaufhörlich.
uncensored [ʌn'sensəd] *adj film* unzensiert.
unceremonious [ˌʌnserɪ'məʊnɪəs] *adj* **(a)** *(abrupt, rude) dismissal* brüsk, barsch; *exit, departure* überstürzt; *haste* unfein. **(b)** *(informal, simple) greeting* zwanglos.
unceremoniously [ˌʌnserɪ'məʊnɪəslɪ] *adv* kurzerhand.
uncertain [ʌn'sɜːtn] *adj* **(a)** *(unsure)* unsicher; *light* undeutlich, schwach. **to be ~ whether** sich *(dat)* nicht sicher sein, ob; **to be ~ of** *or* **about sth** sich *(dat)*einer Sache *(gen)* nicht sicher sein; **I was ~ as to what to do** ich war unsicher, was ich tun sollte. **(b)** *(unknown) date, result* ungewiß; *origins* unbestimmt. **(c)** *(unreliable) weather, prices* unbeständig; *temper* unbere-

chenbar; *judgement* unzuverlässig. **(d)** *(unclear)* vage. **in no ~ terms** klar und deutlich.
uncertainly [ʌn'sɜːtnlɪ] *adv say* unbestimmt; *look, move* unsicher.
uncertainty [ʌn'sɜːtntɪ] *n (state)* Ungewißheit *f*; *(indefiniteness)* Unbestimmtheit *f*; *(doubt)* Unsicherheit *f*. **there is still some ~ as to whether ...** es besteht noch Ungewißheit, ob ...
unchallenged [ʌn'tʃælɪndʒd] *adj* unbestritten; *(Jur) evidence* unangefochten. **to go ~** *(Mil)* ohne Anruf passieren; **the record was** *or* **went ~ for several years** der Rekord wurde jahrelang nicht überboten; **I cannot let that remark go ~** diese Bemerkung kann ich nicht unwidersprochen hinnehmen.
unchanged [ʌn'tʃeɪndʒd] *adj* unverändert.
unchanging [ʌn'tʃeɪndʒɪŋ] *adj* unveränderlich.
uncharitable [ʌn'tʃærɪtəbl] *adj* hartherzig; *remark* unfreundlich, lieblos; *view* herzlos; *criticism* unbarmherzig.
uncharted [ʌn'tʃɑːtɪd] *adj (not explored)* unerforscht; *(not on map)* nicht eingezeichnet.
unchecked [ʌn'tʃekt] *adj* **(a)** *(unrestrained)* unkontrolliert; *advance* ungehindert; *anger* ungezügelt. **to go ~** *(abuse)* geduldet werden; *(advance)* nicht gehindert werden; *(inflation)* nicht eingedämmt werden; **if the epidemic goes ~** wenn der Epidemie nicht Einhalt geboten wird. **(b)** *(not verified)* ungeprüft.
unchristian [ʌn'krɪstjən] *adj* unchristlich.
uncivilized [ʌn'sɪvɪlaɪzd] *adj country, tribe, behaviour* unzivilisiert; *(col) habit* barbarisch.
unclaimed [ʌn'kleɪmd] *adj prize* nicht abgeholt; *property also* herrenlos; *right* nicht geltend gemacht; *social security etc* nicht beansprucht.
uncle ['ʌŋkl] *n* Onkel *m*. **U~ Sam** Onkel Sam; **to say** *or* **cry ~** *(US)* aufgeben.
unclean [ʌn'kliːn] *adj* unsauber *(also Bibl)*; *(Rel) animal* unrein; *thoughts* unkeusch; *(fig: contaminated)* schmutzig.
unclear [ʌn'klɪəʳ] *adj* unklar; *essay etc* undurchsichtig. **to be ~ about sth** sich *(dat)* über etw *(acc)* im unklaren sein.
unclouded [ʌn'klaʊdɪd] *adj sky* unbewölkt; *(fig) happiness, vision* ungetrübt; *mind* klar.
uncoil [ʌn'kɔɪl] **1** *vt* abwickeln. **2** *vir (snake)* sich langsam strecken; *(person)* sich ausstrecken; *(wire etc)* sich abspulen.
uncollected [ˌʌnkə'lektɪd] *adj tax* nicht eingezogen; *fare* nicht kassiert.
uncombed [ʌn'kəʊmd] *adj* ungekämmt.
uncomfortable [ʌn'kʌmfətəbl] *adj* **(a)** unbequem; *chair, position also* ungemütlich. **I feel ~ sitting like this** es ist unbequem, so zu sitzen; **I feel ~ in this jacket** in dieser Jacke fühle ich mich nicht wohl; **it feels ~** es ist unbequem. **(b)** *(uneasy) feeling* unangenehm, ungut; *silence (awkward)* peinlich. **to feel ~** sich unbehaglich fühlen; **I felt ~ about it** mir war nicht wohl dabei. **(c)** *(unpleasant) time, position* unerfreulich. **to make life ~ for sb** jdm das Leben schwer machen.
uncomfortably [ʌn'kʌmfətəblɪ] *adv* **(a)** unbequem. **(b)** *(uneasily)* unbehaglich. **(c)** *(unpleasantly)* unangenehm. **it's getting ~ close** es rückt bedrohlich näher.
uncommitted [ˌʌnkə'mɪtɪd] *adj* nicht engagiert; *party, country* neutral. **we want to remain ~** *(not decide)* wir wollen uns nicht festlegen.
uncommon [ʌn'kɒmən] *adj* **(a)** *(unusual)* ungewöhnlich. **it is not ~ for her to be late** es ist nichts Ungewöhnliches, daß sie zu spät kommt; **a not ~ occurrence** eine häufige Erscheinung. **(b)** *(outstanding)* außergewöhnlich.
uncommunicative [ˌʌnkə'mjuːnɪkətɪv] *adj (by nature)* verschlossen; *(temporarily)* schweigsam.
uncomplaining [ˌʌnkəm'pleɪnɪŋ] *adj* duldsam.
uncomplainingly [ˌʌnkəm'pleɪnɪŋlɪ] *adv* geduldig, klaglos.
uncompleted [ˌʌnkəm'pliːtɪd] *adj* unvollendet.
uncomplicated [ʌn'kɒmplɪkeɪtɪd] *adj* unkompliziert.
uncomplimentary [ˌʌnkɒmplɪ'mentərɪ] *adj* unschmeichelhaft. **to be ~ about sb/sth** sich nicht sehr schmeichelhaft über jdn/etw äußern.
uncomprehending [ˌʌnkɒmprɪ'hendɪŋ] *adj* verständnislos.
uncompromising [ʌn'kɒmprəmaɪzɪŋ] *adj* kompromißlos; *dedication, honesty* rückhaltlos; *commitment* hundertprozentig.
unconcealed [ˌʌnkən'siːld] *adj joy* offen, unverhüllt; *hatred, distaste etc also* unverhohlen.
unconcerned [ˌʌnkən'sɜːnd] *adj (unworried)* unbekümmert; *(indifferent)* gleichgültig. **to be ~ about sth** sich nicht um etw kümmern.
unconditional [ˌʌnkən'dɪʃənl] *adj* vorbehaltlos. **~ surrender** bedingungslose Kapitulation.
unconfirmed [ˌʌnkən'fɜːmd] *adj* unbestätigt.
uncongenial [ˌʌnkən'dʒiːnɪəl] *adj person* unliebenswürdig; *work, surroundings* unerfreulich.
unconnected [ˌʌnkə'nektɪd] *adj* **(a)** *(unrelated)* nicht miteinander in Beziehung stehend *attr*. **the two events are ~** es besteht keine Beziehung zwischen den beiden Ereignissen. **(b)** *(incoherent)* unzusammenhängend.
unconscious [ʌn'kɒnʃəs] **1** *adj* **(a)** *(Med)* bewußtlos. **the blow knocked him ~** durch den Schlag wurde er bewußtlos. **(b)** *pred (unaware)* **to be ~ of sth** sich *(dat)* einer Sache *(gen)* nicht bewußt sein; **I was ~ of the fact that ...** es war mir nicht bewußt, daß ... **(c)** *(unintentional) insult, allusion etc* unbeabsichtigt; *blunder also* ungewollt; *humour* unfreiwillig. **(d)** *(Psych)* unbewußt. **2** *n (Psych)* **the ~** das Unbewußte.
unconsciously [ʌn'kɒnʃəslɪ] *adv* unbewußt. **an ~ funny remark** eine ungewollt lustige Bemerkung.
unconstitutional [ˌʌnkɒnstɪ'tjuːʃənl] *adj* verfassungswidrig.
uncontested [ˌʌnkən'testɪd] *adj* unbestritten; *election, seat* ohne Gegenkandidat. **the chairmanship was ~** in der Wahl für den Vorsitz gab es keinen Gegenkandidaten.
uncontrollable [ˌʌnkən'trəʊləbl] *adj* unkontrollierbar; *child* nicht zu bändigen(d *attr*) *pred*; *horse, dog* nicht unter Kontrolle zu bringen(d *attr*) *pred*; *desire, urge* unwiderstehlich; *(physical)* unkontrollierbar; *twitch* unkontrolliert; *laughter, mirth* unbezähmbar. **to become ~** außer Kontrolle geraten.
uncontrolled [ˌʌnkən'trəʊld] *adj* ungehindert; *dogs, children* unbeaufsichtigt; *laughter* unkontrolliert; *weeping* haltlos. **if inflation is allowed to go ~** wenn die Inflation nicht unter Kontrolle gebracht wird.
unconventional [ˌʌnkən'venʃənl] *adj* unonventionell.
unconvinced [ˌʌkən'vɪnst] *adj* **I remain ~** ich bin noch immer nicht überzeugt.
unconvincing [ˌʌnkən'vɪnsɪŋ] *adj* nicht überzeugend. **rather ~** wenig überzeugend.
uncooked [ʌn'kʊkt] *adj* ungekocht, roh.
uncooperative [ˌʌnkəʊ'ɒpərətɪv] *adj attitude* stur, wenig entgegenkommend; *witness, colleague* wenig hilfreich, nicht hilfsbereit. **the government remained ~** die Regierung war auch weiterhin nicht zur Kooperation bereit.
uncork [ʌn'kɔːk] *vt bottle* entkorken.
uncorroborated [ˌʌnkə'rɒbəreɪtɪd] *adj* unbestätigt; *evidence* nicht bekräftigt.
uncouple [ʌn'kʌpl] *vt train etc* abkoppeln.
uncouth [ʌn'kuːθ] *adj* ungehobelt; *expression, word* unflätig, unfein.
uncover [ʌn'kʌvəʳ] *vt* **(a)** *(remove cover from)* aufdecken; *head* entblößen *(liter)*. **(b)** *scandal, plot* aufdecken; *ancient ruins* zum Vorschein bringen.

uncritical [ʌn'krɪtɪkəl] *adj* unkritisch *(of, about* in bezug auf *+acc).*

unction ['ʌŋkʃən] *n (Rel: anointing)* Salbung *f.* **extreme ~** Letzte Ölung.

uncultivated [ʌn'kʌltɪveɪtɪd] *adj land* unbebaut; *person, behaviour* unkultiviert; *mind* nicht ausgebildet.

uncultured [ʌn'kʌltʃəd] *adj person, mind* ungebildet; *behaviour* unkultiviert.

uncurl [ʌn'kɜːl] **1** *vt* auseinanderrollen. **to ~ oneself** sich strecken. **2** *vi (cat, snake)* sich langsam strecken; *(person)* sich ausstrecken.

undamaged [ʌn'dæmɪdʒd] *adj* unbeschädigt; *(fig) reputation* makellos.

undated [ʌn'deɪtɪd] *adj* undatiert.

undaunted [ʌn'dɔːntɪd] *adj (not discouraged)* nicht entmutigt, unverzagt; *(fearless)* unerschrocken. **he carried on ~** er machte unverzagt weiter.

undecided [ˌʌndɪ'saɪdɪd] *adj* **(a)** *person* unentschlossen. **he is ~ as to whether he should go or not** er ist (sich *dat*) noch unschlüssig, ob er gehen soll oder nicht. **(b)** *question* unentschieden.

undefeated [ˌʌndɪ'fiːtɪd] *adj army, team* unbesiegt; *spirit* ungebrochen.

undefined [ˌʌndɪ'faɪnd] *adj* nicht definiert; *(vague)* undefinierbar.

undelivered [ˌʌndɪ'lɪvəd] *adj mail* nicht zugestellt. **if ~ return to sender** bei Nichtzustellung zurück an Absender.

undemanding [ˌʌndɪ'mɑːndɪŋ] *adj* anspruchslos; *task* wenig fordernd, keine großen Anforderungen stellend *attr.*

undemonstrative [ˌʌndɪ'mɒnstrətɪv] *adj* zurückhaltend.

undeniable [ˌʌndɪ'naɪəbl] *adj* unbestreitbar. **it is ~ that ...** es läßt sich nicht bestreiten, daß ...

undeniably [ˌʌndɪ'naɪəblɪ] *adv* zweifellos; *successful, proud* unbestreitbar.

under ['ʌndəʳ] **1** *prep* **(a)** *(beneath) (place)* unter *(+dat); (direction)* unter *(+acc).* **~ it** darunter; **to come out from ~ the bed** unter dem Bett hervorkommen; **it's ~ there** es ist da drunter *(col);* **~ barley** mit Gerste bebaut. **(b)** *(less than)* unter *(+dat).* **it took ~ an hour** es dauerte weniger als eine Stunde. **(c)** *(subordinate to, ~ influence of etc)* unter *(+dat).* **he had 50 men ~ him** er hatte 50 Männer unter sich; **he studied ~ Popper** er hat bei Popper studiert; **he was born ~ Virgo** *(Astrol)* er wurde im Zeichen Jungfrau geboren; **the matter ~ discussion** der Diskussionsgegenstand; **to be ~ the doctor** in (ärztlicher) Behandlung sein; **it's classified ~ history** es ist unter „Geschichte" eingeordnet. **(d)** *(according to)* nach, gemäß *(+dat).* **~ the terms of the contract** gemäß den Vertragsbedingungen.

2 *adv* **(a)** *(beneath)* unten; *(unconscious)* bewußtlos. **he came to the fence and crawled ~** er kam zum Zaun und kroch darunter durch; **to go ~** untergehen. **(b)** *(less)* darunter.

under- *pref (in rank)* Unter-. **for the ~-twelves/-eighteens/-forties** für Kinder unter zwölf/Jugendliche unter achtzehn/Leute unter vierzig.

under: **~-age** *adj attr* minderjährig; **~-age drinking** Alkoholgenuß *m* Minderjähriger; **~arm** *adj throw* von unten; *hair* Unterarm-; **~carriage** *n (Aviat)* Fahrwerk *nt;* **~charge** *vt* zuwenig berechnen *(sb* jdm*);* **he ~charged me by 10p** er berechnete mir 10 Pence zuwenig; **~clothes** *npl* Unterwäsche *f;* **~coat** *n (paint)* Grundierfarbe *f;* **~cover** *adj agent* Geheim-; **~current** *n (lit, fig)* Unterströmung *f;* **~cut** *pret, ptp* **~cut** *vt competitor* unterbieten; **~developed** *adj* unterentwickelt; *resources* ungenutzt; **~dog** *n* Benachteiligte(r) *m; (in game also)* sicherer Verlierer; **~done** *adj* nicht gar; *(deliberately)* nicht durchgebraten; **~estimate 1** *vt cost, person* unterschätzen; **2** *n* Unterschätzung *f;* **~exposed** *adj (Phot)* unterbelichtet; **~fed** *adj* unterernährt; **~floor heating** *n* Fußbodenheizung *f;* **~foot** *adv* am Boden; **it is wet ~foot** der Boden ist naß; **to trample sb/sth ~foot** *(lit, fig)* auf jdm/etw herumtrampeln; **~go** *pret* **~went,** *ptp* **~gone** *vt suffering* durchmachen; *change also* erleben; *test, treatment, (Med) operation* sich unterziehen *(+dat); (machine) test* unterzogen werden *(+dat);* **~grad** *(col),* **~graduate 1** *n* Student(in *f*) *m;* **2** *attr* Studenten-.

underground ['ʌndəgraʊnd] **1** *adj* **(a)** unterirdisch; *(Min)* Untertage-. **(b)** *(fig) press, movement* Untergrund-. **2** *adv* **(a)** unterirdisch; *(Min)* unter Tage. **3m ~** 3 m unter der Erde. **(b)** *(fig)* **to go ~** untertauchen. **3** *n* **(a)** *(Brit Rail)* U-Bahn, Untergrundbahn *f.* **(b)** *(movement)* Untergrundbewegung *f; (sub-culture)* Underground *m.*

under: **~growth** *n* Gestrüpp *nt; (under trees)* Unterholz *nt;* **~hand** *adj (sly)* hinterhältig; **~insured** *adj* unterversichert; **~lie** *pret* **~lay,** *ptp* **~lain** *vt (lit)* liegen unter *(+dat); (fig: be basis for or cause of)* zugrunde liegen *(+dat);* **~line** *vt (lit, fig)* unterstreichen.

underling ['ʌndəlɪŋ] *n (pej)* Befehlsempfänger(in *f*) *m (pej).*

under: **~lying** *adj* **(a)** *soil, rocks* tieferliegend; **(b)** *cause* eigentlich; *(deeper also)* tiefer; *problem* zugrundeliegend; **~manned** *adj* unterbesetzt; **~mentioned** *adj* untengenannt; **~mine** *vt* **(a)** *(tunnel under)* unterhöhlen; *(Mil)* unterminieren; **(b)** *(fig: weaken) authority, confidence* untergraben; *health* angreifen; **~most** *adj* unterste(r, s).

underneath ['ʌndə'niːθ] **1** *prep (place)* unter *(+dat); (direction)* unter *(+acc).* **~ it** darunter. **2** *adv* darunter. **the ones ~** die darunter. **3** *n* Unterseite *f.*

under: **~nourished** *adj* unterernährt; **~pants** *npl* Unterhose(n *pl*) *f;* **a pair of ~pants** eine Unterhose, ein Paar Unterhosen; **~pass** *n* Unterführung *f;* **~pay** *pret, ptp* **~paid** *vt* unterbezahlen; **~pin** *vt wall, argument* untermauern; *economy etc* stützen; **~play** *vt (Cards) hand* nicht voll ausspielen; **to ~play one's hand** *(fig)* nicht alle Trümpfe ausspielen; **~populated** *adj* unterbevölkert; **~price** *vt* zu billig anbieten, unter Preis anbieten; **to be ~ priced** zu billig gehandelt werden; **~privileged** *adj* unterprivilegiert; **the ~privileged** die Unterprivilegierten *pl;* **~rate** *vt (~estimate) danger, chance, person* unterschätzen; *(~value) qualities* unterbewerten; **~secretary** *n (also* **Parliamentary U~secretary***)* (parlamentarischer) Staatssekretär; **~sell** *pret, ptp* **~sold** *vt (sell at lower price) competitor* unterbieten; *goods* unter Preis verkaufen; **he tends to ~sell himself/his ideas** er kann sich/seine Ideen nicht verkaufen; **~shirt** *n (US)* Unterhemd *nt;* **~shorts** *npl (US)* Unterhose(n *pl*) *f;* **~side** *n* Unterseite *f;* **~signed** *adj (form)* unterzeichnet; **we the ~signed** wir, die Unterzeichneten; **~sized** *adj* klein; *(less than proper size)* zu klein; *(pej) person also* zu kurz geraten *(hum);* **~ skirt** *n* Unterrock *m;* **~sold** *pret, ptp of* **~sell; ~staffed** *adj office* unterbesetzt; **we are very ~staffed at the moment** wir haben momentan zu wenig Leute.

understand [ˌʌndə'stænd] *pret, ptp* **understood 1** *vt* **(a)** verstehen; *action, event, person, difficulty also* begreifen. **I don't ~ Russian** ich verstehe kein Russisch; **I can't ~ his agreeing to do it** es ist mir unbegreiflich, warum er sich dazu bereit erklärt hat; **what do you ~ by "pragmatism"?** was verstehen Sie unter „Pragmatismus"?; **to ~ one another** sich verstehen. **(b)** *(believe)* **we**

understood we were to be paid wir hatten angenommen, daß man uns bezahlt; **I ~ that you are going to Australia** ich höre, Sie gehen nach Australien; **I ~ you've already met** Sie haben sich, soviel ich weiß, schon kennengelernt; **am I/are we to ~ ...?** soll das etwa heißen, daß ...?; **to give sb to ~ that ...** jdm zu verstehen geben, daß ...; **I understood from his speech that ...** ich schloß aus seiner Rede, daß ...
2 *vi* **(a)** verstehen. ~? verstanden?; **you don't ~!** du verstehst mich nicht!; **I quite ~** ich verstehe schon. **(b) so I ~** es scheint so; **he was, I ~, a widower** wie ich hörte, war er Witwer.

understandable [ˌʌndəˈstændəbl] *adj* verständlich.

understandably [ˌʌndəˈstændəblɪ] *adv* verständlicherweise.

understanding [ˌʌndəˈstændɪŋ] **1** *adj* verständnisvoll. **he asked me to be ~** er bat mich um Verständnis. **2** *n* **(a)** *(knowledge)* Kenntnisse *pl*; *(comprehension, sympathy)* Verständnis *nt*. **her ~ of children** ihr Verständnis für Kinder; **my ~ of the situation is that ...** ich verstehe die Situation so, daß ...; **he has a good ~ of the problem** er kennt sich mit dem Problem gut aus; **in order to promote international ~** um die internationale Verständigung zu fördern. **(b)** *(agreement)* Abmachung, Vereinbarung *f*. **to come to** *or* **reach an ~ with sb** eine Vereinbarung mit jdm treffen. **(c)** *(assumption)* Voraussetzung *f*. **on the ~ that ...** unter der Voraussetzung, daß ...

understate [ˌʌndəˈsteɪt] *vt* untertreiben, herunterspielen. **to ~ one's case** untertreiben.

understatement [ˈʌndəˌsteɪtmənt] *n* Untertreibung *f*, Understatement *nt*.

understood [ˌʌndəˈstʊd] **1** *pret, ptp of* **understand. 2** *adj* **(a)** *(clear)* klar. **to make oneself ~** sich verständlich machen; **do I make myself ~?** ist das klar?; **I wish it to be ~ that ...** ich möchte klarstellen, daß ...; **~?** klar?; **~!** gut! **(b)** *(believed)* **he is ~ to have left** es heißt, daß er gegangen ist; **it is ~ that ...** es heißt *or* man hört, daß ...; **he let it be ~ that ...** er gab zu verstehen, daß ....

understudy [ˈʌndəˌstʌdɪ] *n (Theat)* zweite Besetzung.

undertake [ˌʌndəˈteɪk] *pret* **undertook** [ˌʌndəˈtʊk], *ptp* **undertaken** [ˌʌndəˈteɪkn] *vt* **(a)** *job, duty, responsibility* übernehmen; *risk* eingehen, auf sich *(acc)* nehmen. **he undertook to be our guide** er übernahm es, unser Führer zu sein. **(b)** *(agree, promise)* sich verpflichten; *(guarantee)* garantieren.

undertaker [ˈʌndəˌteɪkəʳ] *n (esp Brit)* Beerdigungsunternehmer *m*.

undertaking [ˌʌndəˈteɪkɪŋ] *n* **(a)** *(enterprise)* Unternehmen *nt*; *(Comm: project also)* Projekt *nt*. **(b)** *(promise)* Zusicherung *f*, Wort *nt*. **I give you my solemn ~ that I will never do it again** ich verpflichte mich feierlich, es nie wieder zu tun; **I can give no such ~** das kann ich nicht versprechen.

under: **~tone** *n* **(a)** *(of voice)* **in an ~ tone** mit gedämpfter Stimme; **(b)** *(fig: of criticism, discontent)* Unterton *m*; **an ~tone of racialism** ein rassistischer Unterton; **~took** *pret of* **~take; ~tow** *n* Unterströmung *f*; **~value** *vt antique, artist* unterbewerten; *(price too low)* zu niedrig schätzen; *person* zu wenig schätzen; **~water 1** *adj diving, exploration* Unterwasser-; **2** *adv* unter Wasser; **~wear** *n* Unterwäsche *f*; **~weight** *adj* untergewichtig; **~went** *pret of* **~go; ~world** *n (criminals, Myth)* Unterwelt *f*; **~write** *pret* **~wrote**, *ptp* **~written** *vt (finance) company, loss* tragen, garantieren; *insurance policy* bürgen für; *(insure) shipping* versichern; *(St Ex) shares* zeichnen; **~writer** *n (Insur)* Versicherer *m*.

undeserved [ˌʌndɪˈzɜːvd] *adj* unverdient.

undeserving [ˌʌndɪˈzɜːvɪŋ] *adj person, cause* unwürdig. **to be ~ of sth** *(form)* einer Sache *(gen)* unwürdig sein *(form)*.

undesirable [ˌʌndɪˈzaɪərəbl] **1** *adj policy, effect* unerwünscht; *influence, characters, area* übel. **it is ~ that ...** es wäre höchst unerwünscht, wenn ... **2** *n (person)* unerwünschtes Element.

undetected [ˌʌndɪˈtektɪd] *adj* **to go ~** nicht entdeckt werden.

undeveloped [ˌʌndɪˈveləpt] *adj* unentwickelt; *land, resources* ungenutzt.

undid [ʌnˈdɪd] *pret of* **undo.**

undies [ˈʌndɪz] *npl (col)* (Unter)wäsche *f*.

undignified [ʌnˈdɪgnɪfaɪd] *adj person, behaviour* würdelos; *(inelegant) way of sitting etc* unelegant.

undiluted [ˌʌndaɪˈluːtɪd] *adj* unverdünnt; *(fig) truth, version* unverfälscht; *pleasure* rein, voll.

undiplomatic [ˌʌndɪpləˈmætɪk] *adj* undiplomatisch.

undiscerning [ˌʌndɪˈsɜːnɪŋ] *adj reader, palate* anspruchslos, unkritisch; *critic* unbedarft.

undisciplined [ʌnˈdɪsɪplɪnd] *adj* undiszipliniert.

undiscovered [ˌʌndɪˈskʌvəd] *adj* unentdeckt.

undisguised [ˌʌndɪsˈgaɪzd] *adj* ungetarnt; *(fig) truth* unverhüllt; *dislike, affection* unverhohlen.

undisputed [ˌʌndɪˈspjuːtɪd] *adj* unbestritten.

undistinguished [ˌʌndɪˈstɪŋgwɪʃt] *adj performance* (mittel)mäßig; *appearance* durchschnittlich.

undisturbed [ˌʌndɪˈstɜːbd] *adj* **(a)** *(untouched) papers, dust* unberührt; *(uninterrupted) person, sleep etc* ungestört. **(b)** *(unworried)* unberührt.

undivided [ˌʌndɪˈvaɪdɪd] *adj country, (fig) opinion, attention* ungeteilt; *support* voll; *loyalty* absolut.

undo [ʌnˈduː] *pret* **undid**, *ptp* **undone** *vt* **(a)** *(unfasten)* aufmachen; *button, dress, parcel also* öffnen; *knitting also* aufziehen; *sewing also* auftrennen. **(b)** *wrong* ungeschehen machen; *work* ruinieren. **2** *vi (dress etc)* aufgehen.

undoing [ʌnˈduːɪŋ] *n* Ruin *m*, Verderben *nt*.

undone [ʌnˈdʌn] **1** *ptp of* **undo. 2** *adj* **(a)** *(unfastened)* offen. **to come ~** aufgehen. **(b)** *(neglected) task, work* unerledigt.

undoubted [ʌnˈdaʊtɪd] *adj* unbestritten; *success also* unzweifelhaft.

undoubtedly [ʌnˈdaʊtɪdlɪ] *adv* zweifellos.

undreamed-of [ʌnˈdriːmdɒv], **undreamt-of** [ʌnˈdremtɒv] *adj* ungeahnt. **in their time this was ~** zu ihrer Zeit hätte man sich *(dat)* das nie träumen lassen.

undress [ʌnˈdres] **1** *vt* ausziehen. **to get ~ed** sich ausziehen. **2** *vi* sich ausziehen.

undrinkable [ʌnˈdrɪŋkəbl] *adj* ungenießbar.

undue [ʌnˈdjuː] *adj (excessive)* übermäßig; *(improper)* ungebührlich.

undulating [ˈʌndjʊleɪtɪŋ] *adj movement, line* Wellen-; *waves, sea* wogend; *countryside* hügelig; *hills* sanft.

unduly [ʌnˈdjuːlɪ] *adv* übermäßig; *punished* übermäßig streng. **you're worrying ~** Sie machen sich *(dat)* unnötige Sorgen.

undying [ʌnˈdaɪɪŋ] *adj* unsterblich.

unearned [ʌnˈɜːnd] *adj (Fin, fig)* unverdient. **~ income** Kapitaleinkommen *nt*.

unearth [ʌnˈɜːθ] *vt* ausgraben; *(fig) book etc* aufstöbern; *evidence* ausfindig machen.

unearthly [ʌnˈɜːθlɪ] *adj (eerie) calm, scream* unheimlich; *beauty* überirdisch. **at some ~ hour** *(col)* zu nachtschlafender Stunde; **an ~ din** *(col)* ein Riesenlärm *m*.

uneasily [ʌnˈiːzɪlɪ] *adv sit* unbehaglich; *smile, speak etc also* unsicher; *sleep* unruhig. **to be ~ balanced** sehr prekär sein.

uneasiness [ʌnˈiːzɪnɪs] *n see adj* Unruhe *f*; Unbehaglichkeit *f*; Unsicherheit *f*; *(of person)* Beklommenheit *f*; Unruhe *f*.

uneasy [ʌnˈiːzɪ] *adj sleep, night* unruhig; *conscience* schlecht; *(worried) laugh, look, (awkward) silence,* *atmosphere* unbehaglich; *peace, balance* unsicher; *(worrying) suspicion, feeling* beunruhigend. **to be ~** *(person) (ill at ease)* beklommen sein; *(worried)* beunruhigt sein; **I am ~ about it** mir ist nicht wohl dabei; **to make sb ~** jdn beunruhigen; **I have an ~ feeling that ...** ich habe das ungute Gefühl, daß ...; **to become ~** unruhig werden.

uneaten [ʌn'iːtn] *adj* nicht gegessen. **he left the frogs' legs ~** er ließ die Froschschenkel auf dem Teller; **the ~ food** das übriggbliebene Essen.

uneconomic [ʌn,iːkə'nɒmɪk] *adj* unwirtschaftlich.

uneconomical [ʌn,iːkə'nɒmɪkəl] *adj* unwirtschaftlich; *person* verschwenderisch.

uneducated [,ʌn'edjʊkeɪtɪd] *adj person* ungebildet; *speech also* unkultiviert.

unemotional [,ʌn'ɪməʊʃənl] *adj person, reaction, description* nüchtern; *(without passion)* leidenschaftslos, kühl *(pej)*.

unemployed [,ʌnɪm'plɔɪd] *adj person* arbeitslos; *(unused) machinery* ungenutzt; *(Fin) capital* tot. **the ~** *pl* die Arbeitslosen *pl*.

unemployment [,ʌnɪm'plɔɪmənt] **1** *n* Arbeitslosigkeit *f*. **~ has risen this month** die Arbeitslosenziffer ist diesen Monat gestiegen. **2** *attr* **~ benefit** *(Brit) or* **compensation** *(US)* Arbeitslosenunterstützung *f*; **~ figures** Arbeitslosenziffer *f*; **~ rate** Arbeitslosenquote *f*.

unending [ʌn'endɪŋ] *adj (everlasting)* ewig; *stream* endlos; *(incessant)* unaufhörlich. **it seems ~** es scheint nicht enden zu wollen.

unendurable [,ʌnɪn'djʊərəbl] *adj* unerträglich.

unenterprising [,ʌn'entəpraɪzɪŋ] *adj person, policy* ohne Unternehmungsgeist.

unenthusiastic [,ʌnɪnθuːzɪ'æstɪk] *adj* kühl, wenig begeistert.

unenviable [ʌn'envɪəbl] *adj position, task* wenig beneidenswert.

unequal [ʌn'iːkwəl] *adj* ungleich; *standard, quality* unterschiedlich. **to be ~ to a task** einer Aufgabe *(dat)* nicht gewachsen sein.

unequalled, *(US)* **unequaled** [ʌn'iːkwəld] *adj* unübertroffen; *skill, record also* unerreicht; *ignorance* beispiellos. **he is ~ by any other player** kein anderer Spieler kommt ihm gleich.

unequivocal [,ʌnɪ'kwɪvəkəl] *adj* unmißverständlich, eindeutig. **he was quite ~ about it** er sagte es ganz unmißverständlich *or* klar.

unerring [ʌn'ɜːrɪŋ] *adj judgement, accuracy* unfehlbar; *instinct* untrüglich; *aim* treffsicher.

UNESCO [juː'neskəʊ] = **United Nations Educational, Scientific and Cultural Organization** UNESCO *f*.

unethical [ʌn'eθɪkəl] *adj* unmoralisch; *(in more serious matters)* unethisch.

uneven [ʌn'iːvən] *adj (not level) surface* uneben; *(irregular) line* ungerade; *thickness* ungleich; *pulse* unregelmäßig; *voice* unsicher; *colour, distribution* ungleichmäßig; *quality* unterschiedlich; *temper* unausgeglichen.

unevenly [ʌn'ːvənlɪ] *adv see adj* **the teams were ~ matched** die Mannschaften waren sehr ungleich.

uneventful [,ʌnɪ'ventfʊl] *adj day, meeting* ereignislos; *career* wenig bewegt; *life also* ruhig, eintönig *(pej)*.

unexceptionable [,ʌnɪk'sepʃnəbl] *adj* einwandfrei; *person* solide.

unexceptional [,ʌnɪk'sepʃənl] *adj* durchschnittlich.

unexciting [,ʌnɪk'saɪtɪŋ] *adj time* nicht besonders aufregend.

unexpected [,ʌnɪk'spektɪd] *adj* unerwartet. **this is an ~ pleasure** *(also iro)* welch eine Überraschung!

unexpectedly [,ʌnɪk'spektɪdlɪ] *adv* unerwartet; *arrive, happen also* plötzlich.

unexplainable [,ʌnɪk'spleɪnəbl] *adj* unerklärlich.

unexplained [,ʌnɪk'spleɪnd] *adj phenomenon* ungeklärt; *mystery* unaufgeklärt; *lateness, absence* unbegründet.

unexploded [,ʌnɪk'spləʊdɪd] *adj* nicht explodiert.

unexposed [,ʌnɪk'spəʊzd] *adj* **(a)** *villain* nicht entlarvt; *crime* unaufgedeckt. **(b)** *(Phot)* unbelichtet.

unexpressed [,ʌnɪk'sprest] *adj sorrow, wish* unausgesprochen.

unexpressive [,ʌnɪk'spresɪv] *adj* ausdruckslos.

unfailing [ʌn'feɪlɪŋ] *adj source, interest* unerschöpflich; *remedy* unfehlbar; *friend* treu.

unfailingly [ʌn'feɪlɪŋlɪ] *adv* immer, stets.

unfair [ʌn'fɛə^r] *adj* unfair; *decision, method, remark also* ungerecht; *(Comm) competition also* unlauter. **to be ~ to sb** jdm gegenüber unfair sein.

unfairly [ʌn'fɛəlɪ] *adv* unfair; *treat, criticise etc also* ungerecht; *accuse, dismiss* zu Unrecht.

unfairness [ʌn'fɛənɪs] *n* Ungerechtigkeit *f*.

unfaithful [ʌn'feɪθfʊl] *adj wife, lover* untreu; *friend* treulos. **to be ~ to sb** jdm untreu sein.

unfamiliar [,ʌnfə'mɪljə^r] *adj* **(a)** *experience, sight* ungewohnt; *surroundings also, subject, person* unbekannt. **it is ~ to me** es ist ungewohnt für mich; es ist mir unbekannt. **(b)** *(unacquainted)* **to be ~ with sth** mit etw nicht vertraut sein.

unfashionable [ʌn'fæʃnəbl] *adj* unmodern; *district* unbeliebt; *hotel, habit* nicht in Mode.

unfasten [ʌn'fɑːsn] **1** *vt* aufmachen; *(detach) tag, dog* losbinden; *bonds* lösen. **2** *vi* aufgehen. **how does this dress ~?** wie macht man das Kleid auf?

unfathomable [ʌn'fæðəməbl] *adj* unergründlich.

unfavourable, *(US)* **unfavorable** [ʌn'feɪvərəbl] *adj* ungünstig; *conditions also, wind* widrig; *opinion, reaction, reply* negativ; *trade balance* passiv.

unfavourably, *(US)* **unfavorably** [ʌn'feɪvərəblɪ] *adv see adj* ungünstig; negativ. **to look ~ on sth** einer Sache *(dat)* ablehnend gegenüberstehen.

unfeeling [ʌn'fiːlɪŋ] *adj* gefühllos.

unfinished [ʌn'fɪnɪʃt] *adj* **(a)** *(incomplete)* unfertig; *work of art* unvollendet; *business* unerledigt. **(b)** *(Tech)* unbearbeitet; *cloth* Natur-.

unfit [ʌn'fɪt] *adj* **(a)** *(unsuitable) person, thing* ungeeignet, untauglich; *(incompetent)* unfähig. **~ to drive** fahruntüchtig; **~ to eat** ungenießbar. **(b)** *(Sport: injured)* nicht fit; *(in health also)* schlecht in Form, unfit. **~ (for military service)** untauglich; **to be ~ for work** arbeitsunfähig sein.

unflagging [ʌn'flægɪŋ] *adj person, zeal* unermüdlich; *enthusiasm* unerschöpflich; *devotion, interest* unverändert stark.

unflappable [ʌn'flæpəbl] *adj (col)* unerschütterlich. **to be ~** die Ruhe selbst sein.

unflattering [ʌn'flætərɪŋ] *adj portrait, comments* wenig schmeichelhaft; *dress, light also* unvorteilhaft.

unflinching [ʌn'flɪntʃɪŋ] *adj* unerschrocken; *determination* unbeirrbar.

unfold [ʌn'fəʊld] **1** *vt* **(a)** *paper, cloth* auseinanderfalten; *(spread out) map also, wings* ausbreiten; *arms* lösen; *chair* auseinanderklappen. **(b)** *(fig) story* entwickeln *(to* vor *+dat)*; *plans, ideas also* darlegen *(to dat)*; *secret* enthüllen. **2** *vi (story, plot)* sich abwickeln; *(truth)* an den Tag kommen; *(view, personality)* sich entfalten; *(countryside)* sich ausbreiten.

unforeseeable [,ʌnfɔː'siːəbl] *adj* unvorhersehbar.

unforeseen [,ʌnfɔː'siːn] *adj* unvorhergesehen.

unforgettable [,ʌnfə'getəbl] *adj* unvergeßlich.

unforgivable [,ʌnfə'gɪvəbl] *adj* unverzeihlich.

unforgiving [,ʌnfə'gɪvɪŋ] *adj* unversöhnlich.

unformed [ʌn'fɔːmd] *adj clay, foetus* ungeformt; *character, idea* unfertig.

unfortunate [ʌn'fɔːtʃnɪt] *adj* unglücklich; *person*

glücklos; *day, event, error* unglückselig; *turn of phrase* ungeschickt; *time* ungünstig. **to be ~** *(person)* Pech haben; **it is most ~ that ...** es ist höchst bedauerlich, daß ...; **the ~ Mr Brown** der bedauernswerte Herr Brown.

unfortunately [ʌn'fɔːtʃnɪtlɪ] *adv* leider; *worded* ungeschickt. **an ~ chosen expression** ein unglücklicher Ausdruck.

unfounded [ʌn'faʊndɪd] *adj* unbegründet; *allegations* aus der Luft gegriffen.

unfriendly [ʌn'frendlɪ] *adj* unfreundlich *(to sb* zu jdm*)*; *(hostile also) natives, country, act* feindselig; *territory* unwirtlich.

unfulfilled [ˌʌnfʊl'fɪld] *adj* unerfüllt; *person* unausgefüllt.

unfurl [ʌn'fɜːl] *vt flag* aufrollen; *sail* losmachen; *(peacock) tail* entfalten.

unfurnished [ʌn'fɜnɪʃt] *adj* unmöbliert.

ungainly [ʌn'geɪnlɪ] *adj* unbeholfen; *appearance* unelegant, unschön.

un-get-at-able [ˌʌnget'ætəbl] *adj (col)* unerreichbar.

ungodly [ʌn'gɒdlɪ] *adj* gottlos; *(col) hour* unchristlich *(col)*; *noise* Heiden-.

ungracious [ʌn'greɪʃəs] *adj* unhöflich; *refusal* schroff; *answer* rüde.

ungrammatical [ˌʌngrə'mætɪkəl] *adj* ungrammatisch.

ungrateful [ʌn'greɪtfʊl] *adj* undankbar *(to* gegenüber*)*.

ungrudging [ʌn'grʌdʒɪŋ] *adj help* bereitwillig; *admiration* neidlos; *contribution* großzügig; *praise* von ganzem Herzen kommend *attr*.

unguarded [ʌn'gɑːdɪd] *adj* **(a)** *(undefended)* unbewacht. **(b)** *(fig: careless)* unvorsichtig, unachtsam. **in an ~ moment he ...** als er einen Augenblick nicht aufpaßte, ... er ...

unhappily [ʌn'hæpɪlɪ] *adv (unfortunately)* unglücklicherweise; *(miserably)* unglücklich.

unhappiness [ʌn'hæpɪnɪs] *n* Traurigkeit *f*; *(discontent)* Unzufriedenheit *f (with* mit*)*.

unhappy [ʌn'hæpɪ] *adj (+er)* **(a)** *(sad)* unglücklich; *look, voice also, state of affairs* traurig. **(b)** *(not pleased)* unzufrieden *(about* mit*)*; *(uneasy)* unwohl. **if you feel ~ about it** wenn Sie darüber nicht glücklich sind; *(worried)* wenn Ihnen dabei nicht wohl ist. **(c)** *(unfortunate) coincidence, phrasing* unglücklich; *person* glücklos.

unharmed [ʌn'hɑːmd] *adj person* unverletzt; *thing, reputation* unbeschädigt. **to be ~ by sth** durch etw nicht gelitten haben.

unhealthy [ʌn'helθɪ] *adj* **(a)** *person* nicht gesund; *climate, place, life, complexion,* ungesund; *(col) car* nicht in Ordnung. **(b)** *curiosity, interest* krankhaft; *influence* schädlich. **it's an ~ relationship** das ist eine verderbliche Beziehung. **(c)** *(col: dangerous)* ungesund *(col)*.

unheard-of [ʌn'hɜːdɒv] *adj (unknown)* gänzlich unbekannt; *(unprecedented)* noch nicht dagewesen; *(outrageous)* unerhört.

unheeded [ʌn'hiːdɪd] *adj* unbeachtet. **to go ~** keine Beachtung finden.

unhelpful [ʌn'helpfʊl] *adj person* nicht hilfreich; *advice, book* wenig hilfreich. **that was very ~ of you** das war wirklich keine Hilfe; **you are being very ~** du bist aber wirklich keine Hilfe.

unhesitating [ʌn'hezɪteɪtɪŋ] *adj (immediate) answer, offer* prompt; *help also, generosity* bereitwillig; *(steady) steps, progress* stet; *(undoubting) answer* fest.

unhesitatingly [ʌn'hezɪteɪtɪŋlɪ] *adv* ohne zu zögern; *(undoubtingly also)* ohne zu zweifeln.

unhinge [ʌn'hɪndʒ] *vt* **to ~ sb/sb's mind** jdn aus der Bahn werfen; **his mind was ~d** er hatte den Verstand verloren.

unholy [ʌn'həʊlɪ] *adj (+er) (col) mess* heillos; *din* Riesen-.

unhook [ʌn'hʊk] *vt latch, gate* loshaken; *dress* aufhaken; *(take from hook) picture* abhaken.

unhoped-for [ʌn'həʊptfɔːʳ] *adj* unverhofft.

unhurried [ʌn'hʌrɪd] *adj pace, person* gelassen; *steps, movement* gemächlich; *meal, journey, life* geruhsam.

unhurt [ʌn'hɜːt] *adj* unverletzt.

unhygienic [ˌʌnhaɪ'dʒiːnɪk] *adj* unhygienisch.

unicorn ['juːnɪˌkɔːn] *n* Einhorn *nt*.

unidentified [ˌʌnaɪ'dentɪfaɪd] *adj* unbekannt; *body* nicht identifiziert; *belongings* herrenlos. **~ flying object** unbekanntes Flugobjekt.

unification [ˌjuːnɪfɪ'keɪʃən] *n (of country)* Einigung *f*; *(of system)* Vereinheitlichung *f*.

uniform ['juːnɪfɔːm] **1** *adj (unvarying) length, colour* einheitlich; *treatment also* gleich; *temperature also, pace* gleichbleibend *attr*; *(lacking variation) life, thinking* gleichförmig. **2** *n* Uniform *f*. **in/out of ~** in Uniform/in Zivil.

uniformity [ˌjuːnɪ'fɔːmɪtɪ] *n see adj* Einheitlichkeit *f*; Gleichheit *f*; Gleichmäßigkeit *f*; Gleichförmigkeit *f*.

unify ['juːnɪfaɪ] *vt* einigen, einen *(geh)*; *systems* vereinheitlichen.

unilateral [ˌjuːnɪ'lætərəl] *adj (Jur, Pol)* einseitig; *(Pol also)* unilateral.

unimaginable [ˌʌnɪ'mædʒɪnəbl] *adj* unvorstellbar.

unimaginative [ˌʌnɪ'mædʒɪnətɪv] *adj* phantasielos.

unimpaired [ˌʌnɪm'pɛəd] *adj quality, prestige* unbeeinträchtigt; *health* unvermindert. **to be ~** nicht gelitten haben.

unimpeachable [ˌʌnɪm'piːtʃəbl] *adj reputation, conduct* untadelig; *proof, honesty* unanfechtbar; *source* absolut zuverlässig.

unimportant [ˌʌnɪm'pɔːtənt] *adj* unwichtig.

unimpressed [ˌʌnɪm'prest] *adj* unbeeindruckt, nicht beeindruckt. **I remain ~** das beeindruckt mich überhaupt nicht.

uninhabited [ˌʌnɪn'hæbɪtɪd] *adj* unbewohnt.

uninhibited [ˌʌnɪn'hɪbɪtɪd] *adj person* ohne Hemmungen; *greed, laughter* hemmungslos. **to be ~** keine Hemmungen haben.

uninitiated [ˌʌnɪ'nɪʃɪeɪtɪd] **1** *adj* nicht eingeweiht. **~ members of a tribe** nicht initiierte Mitglieder eines Stammes. **2** *n* **the ~** *pl* Nichteingeweihte *pl*.

uninjured [ʌn'ɪndʒəd] *adj person* unverletzt; *reputation* nicht beeinträchtigt.

uninspired [ˌʌnɪn'spaɪəd] *adj* einfallslos. **to be ~ by a subject** von einem Thema nicht begeistert werden.

unintelligent [ˌʌnɪn'telɪdʒənt] *adj person, remark* unintelligent; *approach* ungeschickt.

unintelligible [ˌʌnɪn'telɪdʒɪbl] *adj person* nicht zu verstehen; *speech, writing* unverständlich.

unintended [ˌʌnɪn'tendɪd], **unintentional** [ˌʌnɪn'tenʃənl] *adj* unbeabsichtigt; *joke also* unfreiwillig.

unintentionally [ˌʌnɪn'tenʃnəlɪ] *adv* unabsichtlich; *funny* unfreiwillig.

uninterested [ʌn'ɪntrɪstɪd] *adj* interesselos. **to be ~ in sth** an etw *(dat)* nicht interessiert sein.

uninteresting [ʌn'ɪntrɪstɪŋ] *adj* uninteressant.

uninterrupted [ˌʌnɪntə'rʌptɪd] *adj (continuous) line* ununterbrochen, kontinuierlich; *noise, rain also* anhaltend; *(undisturbed) rest* ungestört.

uninvited [ˌʌnɪn'vaɪtɪd] *adj guest* ungeladen, ungebeten; *criticism* ungebeten.

uninviting [ˌʌnɪn'vaɪtɪŋ] *adj appearance, atmosphere* nicht (gerade) einladend; *prospect* nicht (gerade) verlockend; *food, sight* unappetitlich.

union ['juːnjən] **1** *n* **(a)** Vereinigung *f*; *(uniting also)* Zusammenschluß *m*; *(Pol also)* Union *f*. **the U~** *(US)* die Vereinigten Staaten; *(in civil war)* die Unionsstaaten *pl*; **U~ of Soviet Socialist Republics** Union *f* der Sozialistischen Sowjetrepubliken. **(b)** *(trade ~)* Gewerkschaft *f*. **(c)** *(association)* Vereinigung *f*; *(customs ~)* Union *f*; *(students' ~ also)* Studentenclub *m (also* *building).* **(d)** *(harmony)* Eintracht, Harmonie *f.* **2** *adj attr (trade ~)* Gewerkschafts-. **~ card** Gewerkschaftsausweis *m.*

unionist ['ju:njənɪst] *n* **(a)** *(trade ~)* Gewerkschaftler(in *f*) *m.* **(b)** *(Pol)* Unionsanhänger(in *f*) *m.*

unionize ['ju:njənaɪz] *vt* gewerkschaftlich organisieren.

union: U~ Jack *n* Union Jack *m*; **~ shop** *n* gewerkschaftspflichtiger Betrieb.

unique [ju:'ni:k] *adj* einzig *attr; (outstanding)* einzigartig, einmalig. **such cases are not ~ to Britain** solche Fälle sind nicht nur auf Großbritannien beschränkt.

uniquely [ju:'ni:klɪ] *adv (solely)* einzig und allein, nur; *(outstandingly)* einmalig.

unisex ['ju:nɪseks] *adj* Unisex-, unisex.

unison ['ju:nɪzn] *n (Mus)* Gleichklang, Einklang *m (also fig).* **in ~** unisono *(form)*, einstimmig.

unit ['ju:nɪt] *n* **(a)** *(section, Mil)* Einheit *f*; *(set of equipment also)* Anlage *f*; *(of furniture, machine)* Element *nt*; *(of organization also)* Abteilung *f.* **x-ray ~** Röntgenanlage *f.* **(b)** *(measure)* Einheit *f.* **~ of length** Längeneinheit *f*; **monetary ~** Währungseinheit *f.* **(c)** *(Math)* Einer *m.*

unit cost *n (Fin)* Kosten *pl* pro (Rechnungs)einheit.

unite [ju:'naɪt] **1** *vt (join)* verbinden; *party, country* (ver)einigen; *(emotions, ties)* (ver)einen. **2** *vi* sich zusammenschließen. **to ~ in doing sth** gemeinsam etw tun; **to ~ in opposition to sth** gemeinsam gegen etw Opposition machen.

united [ju:'naɪtɪd] *adj* verbunden; *group, nation, front* geschlossen; *(unified) people, nation* einig; *efforts* vereint. **to present a ~ front** eine geschlossene Front bieten.

United: ~ Kingdom *n* Vereinigtes Königreich; **~ Nations (Organization)** *n* Vereinte Nationen *pl*; **~ States (of America)** *npl* Vereinigte Staaten *pl* (von Amerika).

unit trust *n (Brit)* Investmentfonds *m.*

unity ['ju:nɪtɪ] *n* Einheit *f*; *(harmony)* Einigkeit *f*; *(of a novel, painting etc)* Einheitlichkeit *f.* **this ~ of purpose** diese gemeinsamen Ziele; **to live in ~ with** in Eintracht leben mit.

Univ = University Univ.

universal [ˌju:nɪ'vɜ:səl] *adj phenomenon, applicability, remedy* universal, universell; *language, remedy also* Universal-; *custom also* allgemein verbreitet; *truth, rule also* allgemein gültig; *approval, peace* allgemein. **~ remedy** Allheilmittel *nt*; **to be a ~ favourite** überall beliebt sein; **to become ~** allgemein verbreitet werden.

universally [ˌju:nɪ'vɜ:səlɪ] *adv* allgemein. **~ applicable** allgemeingültig.

universe ['ju:nɪvɜ:s] *n (cosmos)* (Welt)all, Universum *nt*; *(world)* Welt *f.*

university [ˌju:nɪ'vɜ:sɪtɪ] **1** *n* Universität *f.* **to be at ~/to go to ~** studieren; **to go to London U~** in London studieren. **2** *adj attr town, library* Universitäts-; *qualifications, education also* akademisch. **~ teacher** Hochschullehrer *m.*

unjust [ʌn'dʒʌst] *adj* ungerecht *(to* gegen*).*

unjustifiable [ʌn'dʒʌstɪfaɪəbl] *adj* nicht zu rechtfertigen(d *attr*) *pred.*

unjustifiably [ʌn'dʒʌstɪfaɪəblɪ] *adv expensive, severe, critical* ungerechtfertigt; *rude* unnötig; *criticize* zu Unrecht.

unjustified [ʌn'dʒʌstɪfaɪd] *adj* ungerechtfertigt. **to be ~ in thinking that ...** zu Unrecht denken, daß ...

unjustly [ʌn'dʒʌstlɪ] *adv* zu Unrecht; *judge, treat* ungerecht.

unjustness [ʌn'dʒʌstnɪs] *n* Ungerechtigkeit *f.*

unkempt [ʌn'kempt] *adj hair* ungekämmt; *appearance, garden etc* ungepflegt.

unkind [ʌn'kaɪnd] *adj (+er) person, remark, action (not nice)* unfreundlich; *(cruel)* lieblos, gemein; *remark also* spitz. **~ to the skin** nicht hautfreundlich.

unkindly [ʌn'kaɪndlɪ] *adv* unfreundlich; *(cruelly)* lieblos, gemein. **don't take it ~ if ...** nimm es nicht übel, wenn ...

unkindness [ʌn'kaɪndnɪs] *n* Unfreundlichkeit *f*; *(cruelty)* Lieblosigkeit, Gemeinheit *f.*

unknowing [ʌn'nəʊɪŋ] *adj agent* unbewußt.

unknowingly [ʌn'nəʊɪŋlɪ] *adv* unbewußt, ohne es zu wissen.

unknown [ʌn'nəʊn] **1** *adj* unbekannt. **~ quantity** *(Math, fig)* unbekannte Größe; **~ territory** *(lit, fig)* Neuland *nt*; **to be ~ to sb** *(feeling, territory)* jdm fremd sein; **it's ~ for him to get up for breakfast** man ist es von ihm gar nicht gewohnt, daß er zum Frühstück aufsteht. **2** *n (person)* Unbekannte(r) *mf*; *(factor, Math)* Unbekannte *f.* **a voyage into the ~** *(lit, fig)* eine Fahrt ins Ungewisse. **3** *adv* **~ to me** *etc* ohne daß ich *etc* es wußte.

unladylike [ʌn'leɪdɪlaɪk] *adj* nicht damenhaft.

unlawful [ʌn'lɔ:fʊl] *adj* gesetzwidrig; *means, assembly* illegal; *wedding* ungültig.

unless [ən'les] *conj* es sei denn; *(at beginning of sentence)* wenn ... nicht. **don't do it ~ I tell you to** mach das nicht, es sei denn, ich sage es dir; **~ I tell you to, don't do it** wenn ich es dir nicht sage, mach das nicht; **~ I am mistaken ...** wenn ich mich nicht irre ...; **~ otherwise stated** sofern nicht anders angegeben.

unlicensed [ʌn'laɪsənst] *adj car, dog, TV* nicht angemeldet; *premises* ohne (Schank)konzession; *(unauthorized)* unbefugt.

unlike [ʌn'laɪk] **1** *adj* unähnlich; *poles* gegensätzlich. **2** *prep* **(a)** im Gegesatz zu *(dat)*, anders als. **(b)** *(uncharacteristic of, photo etc)* **to be quite ~ sb** jdm (gar) nicht ähnlich sehen; *(behaviour also)* überhaupt nicht zu jdm passen.

unlikelihood [ʌn'laɪklɪhʊd], **unlikeliness** [ʌn'laɪklɪnɪs] *n* Unwahrscheinlichkeit *f.*

unlikely [ʌn'laɪklɪ] *adj (+er) happening, outcome* unwahrscheinlich; *explanation also* unglaubwürdig; *clothes* komisch. **it is (most) ~/not ~ that ...** es ist (höchst) unwahrscheinlich/es kann durchaus sein, daß ...; **she is ~ to come** sie kommt höchstwahrscheinlich nicht; **it looks an ~ place for mushrooms** es sieht mir nicht nach der geeigneten Stelle für Pilze aus; **in the ~ event that it does happen** in dem unwahrscheinlichen Fall, daß das geschieht.

unlimited [ʌn'lɪmɪtɪd] *adj wealth, time* unbegrenzt; *power also* schrankenlos; *patience* unendlich.

unlined [ʌn'laɪnd] *adj paper* unliniert; *face* faltenlos; *(without lining) dress* ungefüttert.

unlit [ˌʌn'lɪt] *adj road* unbeleuchtet; *lamp* nicht angezündet.

unload [ʌn'ləʊd] *vt* **(a)** *ship, gun* entladen; *car also, luggage* ausladen; *truck, luggage* abladen; *cargo* löschen. **(b)** *(col: get rid of) children, problems* abladen *(on(to)* bei*).*

unlock [ʌn'lɒk] *vt door etc* aufschließen. **the door is ~ed** die Tür ist nicht abgeschlossen; **to leave a door ~ed** eine Tür nicht abschließen.

unloose [ʌn'lu:s] *vt* **(a)** *(also* **~n***) knot, grasp* lösen; *rope also* losmachen. **(b)** *prisoner, dog* losbinden.

unlovable [ʌn'lʌvəbl] *adj* wenig liebenswert, unsympathisch.

unluckily [ʌn'lʌkɪlɪ] *adv* zum Pech, zum Unglück. **~ for him** zu seinem Pech.

unlucky [ʌn'lʌkɪ] *adj (+er)* unglückselig; *choice* unglücklich. **to be ~** *(person)* Pech haben; *(not succeed)* keinen Erfolg haben; **he was ~ enough to meet her** er hatte das Pech, sie zu treffen; **broken mirrors are ~** zerbrochene Spiegel bringen Unglück.

unmanageable [ʌn'mænɪdʒəbl] *adj (unwieldy) vehicle* schwer zu handhaben; *parcel, size* unhandlich; *(uncontrollable) animal, person, hair*

widerspenstig; *situation* unkontrollierbar.
unmanly [ʌn'mænlɪ] *adj behaviour* unmännlich; *(cowardly)* feige; *(effeminate)* weibisch.
unmanned [ʌn'mænd] *adj (not requiring crew) level crossing, space flight* unbemannt; *(lacking crew) telephone exchange, lighthouse* unbesetzt.
unmarked [ʌn'mɑːkt] *adj (unstained)* ohne Flecken, fleckenlos; *(without marking) face* ungezeichnet *(also fig)*; *suitcase etc* ohne Namen *or* Adresse; *police car* nicht gekennzeichnet.
unmarried [ʌn'mærɪd] *adj* unverheiratet. **~ mother** ledige Mutter.
unmask [ʌn'mɑːsk] **1** *vt (lit)* demaskieren; *(fig)* entlarven. **2** *vi* die Maske abnehmen.
unmatched [ʌn'mætʃt] *adj* einmalig, unübertroffen *(for* in bezug auf *+acc)*.
unmentionable [ʌn'menʃnəbl] *adj* tabu *pred*; *word also* unaussprechlich. **to be ~** tabu sein.
unmerciful [ʌn'mɜːsɪfʊl] *adj* erbarmungslos.
unmindful [ʌn'maɪndfʊl] *adj* **to be ~ of sth** nicht auf etw *(acc)* achten, etw nicht beachten.
unmistak(e)able [ˌʌnmɪ'steɪkəbl] *adj* unverkennbar; *(visually)* nicht zu verwechseln.
unmitigated [ʌn'mɪtɪgeɪtɪd] *adj wrath, severity* ungemildert; *(col: complete) disaster* total; *liar, rogue* Erz- *(col)*.
unmoved [ʌn'muːvd] *adj person* ungerührt. **they were ~ by his playing** sein Spiel(en) ergriff sie nicht; **it leaves me ~** das (be)rührt mich nicht.
unmusical [ʌn'mjuːzɪkəl] *adj* unmusikalisch.
unnamed [ʌn'neɪmd] *adj (nameless)* namenlos; *(anonymous)* ungenannt.
unnatural [ʌn'nætʃrəl] *adj* unnatürlich; *(abnormal also) relationship, crime* nicht normal *pred*, widernatürlich.
unnecessarily [ʌn'nesɪ'serɪlɪ] *adv* unnötigerweise; *strict, serious* unnötig, übertrieben.
unnecessary [ʌn'nesɪsərɪ] *adj* unnötig; *(not requisite) visa* nicht notwendig; *(superfluous also)* überflüssig. **really, that was quite ~ of you!** also, das war wirklich überflüssig!
unnerve [ʌn'nɜːv] *vt* entnerven; *(gradually)* zermürben; *(discourage) speaker* entmutigen.
unnoticed [ʌn'nəʊtɪst] *adj* unbemerkt. **to go** *or* **pass ~** unbemerkt bleiben.
UNO = United Nations Organization UNO *f*.
unobjectionable [ˌʌnəb'dʒekʃnəbl] *adj* einwandfrei.
unobservant [ˌʌnəb'zɜːvənt] *adj* unaufmerksam. **to be ~** ein schlechter Beobachter sein.
unobserved [ˌʌnəb'zɜːvd] *adj (not seen)* unbemerkt; *(not celebrated)* nicht (mehr) eingehalten.
unobtainable [ˌʌnəb'teɪnəbl] *adj* nicht erhältlich. **number ~** *(Telec)* kein Anschluß unter dieser Nummer.
unobtrusive [ˌʌnəb'truːsɪv] *adj* unauffällig.
unoccupied [ʌn'ɒkjʊpaɪd] *adj person* unbeschäftigt; *house* unbewohnt; *seat* frei; *(Mil) zone* unbesetzt.
unofficial [ˌʌnə'fɪʃəl] *adj* inoffiziell. **to take ~ action** *(Ind)* inoffiziell streiken.
unofficially [ˌʌnə'fɪʃəlɪ] *adv* inoffiziell.
unopened [ʌn'əʊpənd] *adj* ungeöffnet.
unopposed [ˌʌnə'pəʊzd] *adj* **elected ~** ohne Gegenstimme gewählt; **they marched on ~** sie marschierten weiter, ohne auf Widerstand zu treffen; **~ by the committee** ohne Widerspruch seitens des Ausschusses.
unorganized [ʌn'ɔːgənaɪzd] *adj* unsystematisch; *life* ungeregelt; *(Ind)* nicht (gewerkschaftlich) organisiert. **he is so ~** er hat überhaupt kein System.
unoriginal [ˌʌnə'rɪdʒɪnəl] *adj* wenig originell.
unorthodox [ʌn'ɔːθədɒks] *adj* unkonventionell, unorthodox.
unpack [ʌn'pæk] *vti* auspacken.
unpaid [ʌn'peɪd] *adj* unbezahlt.
unpalatable [ʌn'pælɪtəbl] *adj food, drink* ungenießbar; *(fig) fact, truth, mixture* unverdaulich, schwer zu verdauen.
unparalleled [ʌn'pærəleld] *adj* einmalig, beispiellos. **an ~ success** ein Erfolg ohnegleichen.
unpardonable [ʌn'pɑːdnəbl] *adj* unverzeihlich.
unpatriotic [ˌʌnpætrɪ'ɒtɪk] *adj* unpatriotisch.
unpaved [ʌn'peɪvd] *adj road* nicht gepflastert.
unperturbed [ˌʌnpə'tɜːbd] *adj* nicht beunruhigt *(by* von, durch*)*, gelassen.
unpick [ʌn'pɪk] *vt* auftrennen.
unpin [ʌn'pɪn] *vt dress, hair* die Nadeln entfernen aus; *notice* abnehmen.
unplaced [ʌn'pleɪst] *adj (Sport)* nicht plaziert. **to be ~** sich nicht plaziert haben.
unplanned [ʌn'plænd] *adj* ungeplant.
unpleasant [ʌn'pleznt] *adj* unangenehm; *person, remark* unfreundlich *(to sb* jdm gegenüber*)*.
unpleasantly [ʌn'plezntlɪ] *adv reply* unfreundlich; *warm, smell* unangenehm.
unpleasantness [ʌn'plezntnɪs] *n* **(a)** *(quality) see adj* Unangenehmheit *f*; Unfreundlichkeit *f*. **(b)** *(bad feeling, quarrel)* Unstimmigkeit *f*.
unplug [ʌn'plʌg] *vt radio, lamp* den Stecker herausziehen von.
unpolished [ʌn'pɒlɪʃt] *adj* unpoliert; *stone, (fig) person, manners* ungeschliffen; *performance, style* unausgefeilt.
unpolluted [ˌʌnpə'luːtɪd] *adj* sauber, unverschmutzt.
unpopular [ʌn'pɒpjʊlə^r] *adj person* unbeliebt *(with sb* bei jdm*)*; *decision, move* unpopulär.
unprecedented [ʌn'presɪdəntɪd] *adj* noch nie dagewesen; *profit, step* unerhört. **this event is ~** dieses Ereignis ist bisher einmalig; **an ~ success** ein beispielloser Erfolg.
unpredictable [ˌʌnprɪ'dɪktəbl] *adj* unvorhersehbar; *result* nicht vorherzusagen(d *attr*) *pred; behaviour, person, weather* unberechenbar.
unprejudiced [ʌn'predʒʊdɪst] *adj (impartial)* objektiv, unparteiisch; *(not having prejudices)* vorurteilslos.
unprepared [ˌʌnprɪ'pɛəd] *adj* nicht vorbereitet; *person also* unvorbereitet. **to be ~ for sth** für etw nicht vorbereitet sein; *(be surprised)* auf etw *(acc)* nicht vorbereitet *or* gefaßt sein.
unprepossessing [ˌʌnpriːpə'zesɪŋ] *adj* wenig einnehmend.
unpretentious [ˌʌnprɪ'tenʃəs] *adj* schlicht, bescheiden; *style, book* einfach.
unprincipled [ʌn'prɪnsɪpld] *adj* skrupellos.
unprintable [ʌn'prɪntəbl] *adj* nicht druckfähig; *(fig) answer* nicht druckreif.
unproductive [ˌʌnprə'dʌktɪv] *adj capital* nicht gewinnbringend; *soil* ertragsarm; *meeting* unergiebig.
unprofessional [ˌʌnprə'feʃənl] *adj conduct* berufswidrig; *work* unfachmännisch.
unprofitable [ʌn'prɒfɪtəbl] *adj (financially)* keinen Profit bringend; *mine etc* unrentabel; *(fig)* nutzlos.
unpromising [ʌn'prɒmɪsɪŋ] *adj* nicht sehr vielversprechend.
unpronounceable [ˌʌnprə'naʊnsɪbl] *adj* unaussprechbar.
unprotected [ˌʌnprə'tektɪd] *adj* ohne Schutz, schutzlos; *machine* ungeschützt; *(by insurance)* ohne Versicherungsschutz.
unproved [ʌn'pruːvd] *adj* unbewiesen; *(untested)* noch nicht bewährt. **he's still ~** er hat sich noch nicht bewährt.
unprovoked [ˌʌnprə'vəʊkt] *adj* grundlos.
unpublished [ʌn'pʌblɪʃt] *adj* unveröffentlicht.
unpunished [ʌn'pʌnɪʃt] *adj* unbestraft. **to go ~** ohne Strafe bleiben.
unqualified [ʌn'kwɒlɪfaɪd] *adj* **(a)** unqualifiziert. **to be ~** nicht qualifiziert sein. **(b)** *(absolute) praise, acceptance* uneingeschränkt; *success*

voll(ständig); *(col) idiot, liar* ausgesprochen.
unquestionable [ʌn'kwestʃənəbl] *adj authority* unbestritten, unangefochten; *evidence, fact* unbezweifelbar; *sincerity, honesty* fraglos. **his honesty is ~** seine Ehrlichkeit steht außer Frage.
unquestionably [ʌn'kwestʃənəblɪ] *adv* fraglos, zweifellos.
unquestioning [ʌn'kwestʃənɪŋ] *adj* bedingungslos.
unravel [ʌn'rævəl] *vt knitting* aufziehen; *(lit, fig: untangle)* entwirren; *mystery* lösen.
unreadable [ʌn'ri:dəbl] *adj writing* unleserlich; *book, text* unverständlich.
unrealistic [ˌʌnrɪə'lɪstɪk] *adj* unrealistisch.
unreality [ˌʌnrɪ'ælɪtɪ] *n* Unwirklichkeit *f*.
unreasonable [ʌn'ri:znəbl] *adj demand, price etc* übertrieben; *person* uneinsichtig; *(showing lack of sense)* unvernünftig. **to be ~ about sth** *(not be understanding)* kein Verständnis für etw zeigen; *(be overdemanding)* in bezug auf etw *(acc)* zuviel verlangen; **it is ~ to ...** es ist zuviel verlangt, zu ...; **am I being ~?** verlange ich zuviel?
unrecognizable [ʌn'rekəgnaɪzəbl] *adj* nicht wiederzuerkennen(d *attr*) *pred*. **he was totally ~ in his disguise** man konnte ihn in seiner Verkleidung überhaupt nicht erkennen.
unrecognized [ʌn'rekəgnaɪzd] *adj (not noticed) person, danger, value* unerkannt; *(not acknowledged) government, record* nicht anerkannt; *genius, talent* ungewürdigt, unerkannt.
unrecorded [ˌʌnrɪ'kɔ:dɪd] *adj* nicht aufgenommen; *(Rad, TV)* nicht aufgezeichnet; *(in documents)* nicht schriftlich erfaßt.
unrefined [ˌʌnrɪ'faɪnd] *adj* **(a)** *petroleum etc* nicht raffiniert. **(b)** *person* unkultiviert.
unrehearsed [ˌʌnrɪ'hɜ:st] *adj (Theat etc)* nicht geprobt; *cast* schlecht eingespielt; *(spontaneous) incident* spontan.
unrelated [ˌʌnrɪ'leɪtɪd] *adj (unconnected)* ohne Beziehung *(to* zu); *(by family)* nicht verwandt.
unrelenting [ˌʌnrɪ'lentɪŋ] *adj pressure* unablässig; *opposition, struggle* unerbittlich; *determination* hartnäckig; *pace* unvermindert; *rain* anhaltend *attr*, nicht nachlassend *attr; (not merciful) person, heat* unbarmherzig.
unreliable [ˌʌnrɪ'laɪəbl] *adj* unzuverlässig.
unrelieved [ˌʌnrɪ'li:vd] *adj pain, gloom* ungemindert; *grey* eintönig; *monotony, boredom* tödlich. **a life of ~ drudgery** ein Leben, das eine einzige Schinderei ist; **to be ~ by** nicht aufgelockert sein durch *or* von.
unremitting [ˌʌnrɪ'mɪtɪŋ] *adj efforts, toil* unablässig; *zeal* unermüdlich; *hatred* unversöhnlich.
unrepeatable [ˌʌnrɪ'pi:təbl] *adj words, views* nicht wiederholbar; *offer* einmalig.
unrepentant [ˌʌnrɪ'pentənt] *adj* nicht reumütig, reu(e)los. **he is ~ about it** er bereut es nicht.
unrepresentative [ˌʌnreprɪ'zentətɪv] *adj (Pol) government* nicht frei gewählt; *(untypical)* nicht repräsentativ *(of* für*)*.
unrequited [ˌʌnrɪ'kwaɪtɪd] *adj love* unerwidert.
unreserved [ˌʌnrɪ'zɜ:vd] *adj* **(a)** *(frank) person* nicht reserviert, offen. **(b)** *(complete) approval* uneingeschränkt. **(c)** *(not booked)* nicht reserviert.
unresponsive [ˌʌnrɪ'spɒnsɪv] *adj (physically)* nicht reagierend *attr*; *(emotionally, intellectually)* gleichgültig, unempfänglich. **to be ~** nicht reagieren *(to* auf *+acc)*; *(engine)* nicht ansprechen; **an ~ audience** ein Publikum, das nicht mitgeht; **I suggested it but he was fairly ~** ich habe es vorgeschlagen, aber er zeigte sich nicht sehr interessiert.
unrest [ʌn'rest] *n* Unruhen *pl*; *(discontent)* Unzufriedenheit *f*.
unrestrained [ˌʌnrɪ'streɪnd] *adj* uneingeschränkt; *feelings* offen, ungehemmt; *enthusiasm, atmosphere* ungezügelt; *behaviour* unbeherrscht.
unrestricted [ˌʌnrɪ'strɪktɪd] *adj power, use, growth* unbeschränkt; *access* ungehindert.
unrewarded [ˌʌnrɪ'wɔ:dɪd] *adj* unbelohnt. **to go ~** unbelohnt bleiben; *(not gain recognition)* keine Anerkennung finden.
unrewarding [ˌʌnrɪ'wɔ:dɪŋ] *adj work* undankbar; *(financially)* wenig einträglich.
unripe [ʌn'raɪp] *adj* unreif.
unrivalled, *(US)* **unrivaled** [ʌn'raɪvəld] *adj* unübertroffen. **~ in** *or* **for quality** von unübertroffener Qualität.
unroadworthy [ʌn'rəʊdˌwɜ:ðɪ] *adj* nicht verkehrssicher.
unroll [ʌn'rəʊl] **1** *vt carpet, map* aufrollen. **2** *vi* sich aufrollen; *(fig) (plot)* sich abwickeln; *(landscape)* sich ausbreiten.
unruffled [ʌn'rʌfld] *adj person* gelassen; *sea* ruhig, unbewegt; *hair* ordentlich; *calm* unerschütterlich. **she was quite ~** sie blieb ruhig und gelassen.
unruly [ʌn'ru:lɪ] *adj (+er)* wild, ungebärdig.
unsafe [ʌn'seɪf] *adj ladder, machine, car, person* nicht sicher; *(dangerous) journey, toy, wiring* gefährlich. **to feel ~** sich nicht sicher fühlen.
unsaid [ʌn'sed] *adj* ungesagt, unausgesprochen. **to leave sth ~** etw unausgesprochen lassen; **it's best left ~** das bleibt besser ungesagt.
unsaleable [ʌn'seɪləbl] *adj* unverkäuflich. **to be ~** sich nicht verkaufen lassen.
unsatisfactory [ˌʌnsætɪs'fæktərɪ] *adj* unbefriedigend; *profits etc* nicht ausreichend; *service, hotel* unzulänglich; *(Sch)* mangelhaft. **this is most ~** das läßt sehr zu wünschen übrig.
unsatisfied [ʌn'sætɪsfaɪd] *adj person* unzufrieden; *(not convinced)* nicht überzeugt; *appetite, desire, curiosity* unbefriedigt.
unsatisfying [ʌn'sætɪsfaɪɪŋ] *adj* unbefriedigend; *meal* unzureichend.
unsavoury, *(US)* **unsavory** [ʌn'seɪvərɪ] *adj smell, sight* widerlich; *appearance (repulsive)* abstoßend; *(dishonest, shady etc)* fragwürdig; *subject, details* unerfreulich; *joke* unfein; *district, characters* zwielichtig, übel; *reputation* zweifelhaft.
unscathed [ʌn'skeɪðd] *adj (lit)* unverletzt, unversehrt; *(fig)* unbeschadet; *relationship* heil. **to escape ~** *(fig)* ungeschoren davonkommen.
unscheduled [ʌn'ʃedju:ld] *adj stop etc* außerfahrplanmäßig; *meeting* außerplanmäßig.
unscientific [ˌʌnsaɪən'tɪfɪk] *adj* unwissenschaftlich.
unscrew [ʌn'skru:] **1** *vt (loosen)* losschrauben. **to come ~ed** sich lösen. **2** *vi* sich los- *or* abschrauben lassen; *(become loose)* sich lösen.
unscrupulous [ʌn'skru:pjʊləs] *adj person, behaviour* skrupellos, gewissenlos.
unseasoned [ʌn'si:znd] *adj timber* nicht abgelagert; *food* ungewürzt; *(fig: inexperienced) troops* unerfahren.
unseaworthy [ʌn'si:ˌwɜ:ðɪ] *adj* seeuntüchtig.
unseemly [ʌn'si:mlɪ] *adj* unschicklich.
unseen [ʌn'si:n] **1** *adj* ungesehen; *(invisible)* unsichtbar; *(unobserved) escape* unbemerkt. **2** *n (esp Brit Sch)* unvorbereitete Übersetzung in die Muttersprache.
unselfish [ʌn'selfɪʃ] *adj* uneigennützig, selbstlos.
unserviceable [ʌn'sɜ:vɪsəbl] *adj* unbrauchbar.
unsettle [ʌn'setl] *vt* durcheinanderbringen; *(upset)* aufregen; *(disturb emotionally)* verstören; *animal, (news)* beunruhigen; *(defeat, criticism)* verunsichern.
unsettled [ʌn'setld] *adj* **(a)** *(unpaid)* unbeglichen; *(undecided) question* ungeklärt; *future* unbestimmt, ungewiß. **(b)** *(changeable) weather, (Fin) market* unbeständig; *(Pol) conditions also* unsicher; *life, character* unstet. **to be ~** durchein-

ander sein; *(thrown off balance)* aus dem Gleis geworfen sein; *(emotionally disturbed)* verstört sein. **(c)** *(unpopulated) territory* unbesiedelt.

unsettling [ʌn'setlɪŋ] *adj change* aufreibend; *defeat, knowledge* verunsichernd; *news* beunruhigend.

unshakeable [ʌn'ʃeɪkəbl] *adj* unerschütterlich.

unshaken [ʌn'ʃeɪkən] *adj* unerschüttert. **his nerve was ~** er behielt seine Kaltblütigkeit.

unshaven [ʌn'ʃeɪvn] *adj* unrasiert; *(bearded)* bärtig.

unsightly [ʌn'saɪtlɪ] *adj* unansehnlich; *(stronger)* häßlich.

unskilled [ʌn'skɪld] *adj* **(a)** *work, worker* ungelernt. **(b)** *(inexperienced)* ungeübt, unerfahren.

unsociable [ʌn'səʊʃəbl] *adj* ungesellig.

unsocial [ʌn'səʊʃəl] *adj* **to work ~ hours** außerhalb der normalen Arbeitszeiten arbeiten; **visitors at this ~ hour** Besuch um diese Zeit!

unsold [ʌn'səʊld] *adj* unverkauft.

unsolicited [ˌʌnsə'lɪsɪtɪd] *adj* unerbeten; *manuscript* unverlangt eingesandt.

unsolved [ʌn'sɒlvd] *adj* ungelöst.

unsophisticated [ˌʌnsə'fɪstɪkeɪtɪd] *adj (simple)* einfach; *(naïve)* naiv, simpel; *(undiscriminating)* unkritisch.

unsound [ʌn'saʊnd] *adj heart, teeth* krank; *health* angegriffen; *timber* morsch; *construction, design* unsolide; *foundations, finances* unsicher; *argument* nicht stichhaltig, anfechtbar; *advice* unvernünftig; *judgement* unzuverlässig; *doctrine* unvertretbar; *policy, move* unklug. **of ~ mind** *(Jur)* unzurechnungsfähig; **the book is ~ on some points** das Buch weist an einigen Stellen Schwächen auf.

unsparing [ʌn'spɛərɪŋ] *adj* **(a)** *(lavish)* großzügig, verschwenderisch. **to be ~ with sth** mit etw nicht geizen. **(b)** *criticism* schonungslos.

unspeakable [ʌn'spiːkəbl] *adj* unbeschreiblich.

unspeakably [ʌn'spiːkəblɪ] *adv* unsagbar.

unspecified [ʌn'spesɪfaɪd] *adj time, amount* nicht (genau) genannt.

unspoiled [ˌʌn'spɔɪld], **unspoilt** [ˌʌn'spɔɪlt] *adj countryside* unberührt; *child* nicht verwöhnt.

unspoken [ʌn'spəʊkən] *adj words, thought* unausgesprochen; *agreement, consent* stillschweigend.

unstable [ʌn'steɪbl] *adj structure* nicht stabil; *area, economy* unsicher; *(Chem, Phys)* instabil; *(mentally)* labil.

unstamped [ʌn'stæmpt] *adj letter* unfrankiert; *document, passport* ungestempelt.

unsteady [ʌn'stedɪ] *adj hand* unsicher; *ladder* wack(e)lig; *voice, economy* schwankend; *growth* unregelmäßig. **to be ~ on one's feet** unsicher auf den Beinen sein; **the £ is still ~** das Pfund schwankt noch.

unstinting [ʌn'stɪntɪŋ] *adj person* großzügig; *kindness, generosity, support* uneingeschränkt. **to be ~ in one's efforts** keine Kosten und Mühen scheuen; **he was ~ in his praise** sein Lob war überschwenglich; **to be ~ of one's time** unendlich viel Zeit opfern.

unstressed [ʌn'strest] *adj (Phon)* unbetont.

unstuck [ʌn'stʌk] **1** *pret, ptp of* **unstick. 2** *adj* **to come ~** *(stamp, notice)* sich lösen; *(col) (plan)* schiefgehen *(col)*; *(speaker, actor)* steckenbleiben; *(in exam)* ins Schwimmen geraten.

unsubstantiated [ˌʌnsəb'stænʃɪeɪtɪd] *adj accusation, testimony, rumour* unbegründet.

unsuccessful [ˌʌnsək'sesfʊl] *adj venture, meeting, person etc* erfolglos; *candidate* abgewiesen; *attempt* vergeblich; *marriage, outcome* unglücklich. **to be ~ in doing sth** keinen Erfolg damit haben, etw zu tun; **he is ~ in everything he does** nichts gelingt ihm; **he was ~ in his exam** er hat kein Glück in seinem Examen gehabt.

unsuccessfully [ˌʌnsək'sesfəlɪ] *adv* erfolglos; *try* vergeblich; *apply* vergebens.

unsuitable [ʌn'suːtəbl] *adj* unpassend. **it would be ~ at this moment to ...** es wäre im Augenblick unangebracht, ...; **this film is ~ for children** dieser Film ist für Kinder nicht geeignet; **we're ~ for each other** wir passen nicht zusammen; **he's ~ for the job** er ist für die Arbeit ungeeignet.

unsuited [ʌn'suːtɪd] *adj* **to be ~ for** *or* **to sth** für etw ungeeignet sein.

unsure [ʌn'ʃʊə^r] *adj person* unsicher. **to be ~ of oneself** unsicher sein; **to be ~ (of sth)** sich *(dat)* (einer Sache *gen*) nicht sicher sein; **I'm ~ of him** ich bin mir bei ihm nicht sicher.

unsurpassed [ˌʌnsə'pɑːst] *adj* unübertroffen. **to be ~ by anybody** von niemandem übertroffen werden.

unsuspected [ˌʌnsə'spektɪd] *adj presence etc* unvermutet; *consequences, wealth* ungeahnt.

unsuspecting [ˌʌnsə'spektɪŋ] *adj* ahnungslos, nichtsahnend.

unsweetened [ˌʌn'swiːtnd] *adj* ungesüßt.

unswerving [ʌn'swɜːvɪŋ] *adj loyalty* unwandelbar.

unsympathetic [ˌʌnsɪmpə'θetɪk] *adj* **(a)** *(unfeeling)* gefühllos; *attitude, response* ablehnend, abweisend. **(b)** *(unlikeable)* unsympathisch.

unsystematic [ˌʌnsɪstɪ'mætɪk] *adj* unsystematisch.

untangle [ʌn'tæŋgl] *vt (lit, fig)* entwirren.

untapped [ʌn'tæpt] *adj barrel* unangezapft; *resources, talent* ungenutzt.

untaxed [ʌn'tækst] *adj goods, income* steuerfrei; *car* unversteuert.

untended [ʌn'tendɪd] *adj patient* unbewacht; *garden* ungepflegt.

untested [ʌn'testɪd] *adj* unerprobt.

unthinkable [ʌn'θɪŋkəbl] *adj* undenkbar; *(too horrible)* unvorstellbar.

untidiness [ʌn'taɪdɪnɪs] *n (of room)* Unordnung *f*; *(of person, dress)* Unordentlichkeit *f*.

untidy [ʌn'taɪdɪ] *adj (+er)* unordentlich.

untie [ʌn'taɪ] *vt knot* lösen; *parcel* aufknoten; *person, animal, hands* losbinden.

until [ən'tɪl] **1** *prep* **(a)** bis. **from morning ~ night** von morgens bis abends; **~ now** bis jetzt; **~ then** bis dahin. **(b) not ~** *(in future)* nicht vor *(+dat)*; *(in past)* erst; **I didn't leave him ~ the following day** ich habe ihn erst am folgenden Tag verlassen. **2** *conj* **(a)** bis. **wait ~ I come** warten Sie, bis ich komme. **(b) not ~** *(in future)* nicht bevor, erst wenn; *(in past)* nicht bis, erst als; **he won't come ~ you invite him** er kommt erst, wenn Sie ihn einladen; **they did nothing ~ we came** bis wir kamen, taten sie nichts; **they didn't start ~ we came** sie fingen erst an, als wir da waren.

untimely [ʌn'taɪmlɪ] *adj death* vorzeitig; *(inopportune) moment* unpassend; *remark* zur falschen Zeit.

untiring [ʌn'taɪərɪŋ] *adj work, effort* unermüdlich. **to be ~ in one's efforts** unermüdliche Anstrengungen machen.

untold ['ʌn'təʊld] *adj story* nicht erzählt; *secret* ungelüftet; *wealth* unermeßlich; *agony, delights* unsäglich; *stars etc* unzählig. **~ thousands** unzählig viele.

untouchable [ʌn'tʌtʃəbl] **1** *adj* unberührbar. **2** *n* Unberührbare(r) *mf*.

untouched [ʌn'tʌtʃt] *adj* **(a)** unberührt, unangetastet; *bottle etc also* nicht angebrochen; *(unmentioned)* nicht erwähnt. **~ by human hand** nicht von Menschenhand berührt. **(b)** *(unharmed)* heil, unversehrt; *(unaffected)* unberührt; *(unmoved)* ungerührt. **(c)** *(unequalled)* **~ for quality** in der Qualität unerreicht.

untoward [ˌʌntə'wɔːd] *adj (unfortunate) event* unglücklich, bedauerlich; *(unseemly)* unpassend.

nothing ~ had happened es war nichts Schlimmes passiert.

untrained [ʌn'treɪnd] *adj person, teacher* unausgebildet; *voice* ungeschult; *animal* undressiert. **to the ~ eye** dem ungeschulten Auge.

untranslatable [ˌʌntrænz'leɪtəbl] *adj* unübersetzbar.

untried [ʌn'traɪd] *adj* **(a)** *(not tested)* unerprobt; *(not attempted)* unversucht. **(b)** *(Jur) case* nicht verhandelt; *person* nicht vor Gericht gestellt.

untroubled [ʌn'trʌbld] *adj period* friedlich, ruhig. **the children seemed ~ by the heat** die Hitze schien den Kindern nichts auszumachen.

untrue [ʌn'tru:] *adj* **(a)** *(false)* unwahr. **(b)** *(unfaithful) person* untreu. **to be ~ to sb** jdm untreu sein.

untrustworthy [ʌn'trʌstˌwɜ:ðɪ] *adj (not reliable) book, person* unzuverlässig; *(not worthy of confidence) person* nicht vertrauenswürdig.

untruth [ʌn'tru:θ] *n* Unwahrheit *f*.

untruthful [ʌn'tru:θfʊl] *adj statement* unwahr; *person* unaufrichtig. **you're being ~** was du da sagst, ist nicht ganz wahr.

unusable [ʌn'ju:zəbl] *adj* unbrauchbar.

unused[1] [ʌn'ju:zd] *adj (new)* unbenutzt, ungebraucht; *(not made use of)* ungenutzt; *(no longer used)* nicht mehr benutzt.

unused[2] [ʌn'ju:st] *adj* **to be ~ to sth** etw *(acc)* nicht gewohnt sein; **to be ~ to doing sth** nicht daran gewöhnt sein, etw zu tun.

unusual [ʌn'ju:ʒʊəl] *adj (uncommon)* ungewöhnlich; *(exceptional)* außergewöhnlich. **it's ~ for him to be late** er kommt normalerweise nicht zu spät; **how ~!** das kommt selten vor; **that's ~ for him** das ist sonst nicht seine Art.

unusually [ʌn'ju:ʒʊəlɪ] *adv see adj.* **most ~, he was late** ganz gegen seine Gewohnheit kam er zu spät.

unutterable [ʌn'ʌtərəbl] *adj* unsäglich.

unvaried [ʌn'vɛərɪd] *adj* unverändert; *(pej)* eintönig.

unvarnished [ʌn'vɑ:nɪʃt] *adj wood* unlackiert; *(fig) truth* ungeschminkt.

unveil [ʌn'veɪl] *vt statue, plan* enthüllen; *(Comm) car* vorstellen; *face* entschleiern.

unvoiced [ʌn'vɔɪst] *adj* unausgesprochen.

unwanted [ʌn'wɒntɪd] *adj furniture, clothing* unerwünscht. **he feels ~** er kommt sich unerwünscht vor.

unwarranted [ʌn'wɒrəntɪd] *adj* ungerechtfertigt.

unwary [ʌn'wɜərɪ] *adj* unvorsichtig, unachtsam.

unwashed [ʌn'wɒʃt] *adj* ungewaschen; *dishes* ungespült.

unwavering [ʌn'weɪvərɪŋ] *adj faith, resolve* unerschütterlich; *course* beharrlich.

unwelcome [ʌn'welkəm] *adj visitor* unwillkommen; *news, memories* unerfreulich.

unwell [ʌn'wel] *adj pred* unwohl, nicht wohl. **to be** *or* **feel (a little) ~** sich nicht (recht) wohl fühlen.

unwholesome [ʌn'həʊlsəm] *adj* ungesund; *influence* ungut; *appearance, character* schmierig.

unwieldy [ʌn'wi:ldɪ] *adj tool* unhandlich; *object also* sperrig; *(clumsy) body* schwerfällig.

unwilling [ʌn'wɪlɪŋ] *adj helper, pupil* widerwillig; *accomplice* unfreiwillig. **to be ~ to do sth** nicht bereit *or* gewillt sein, etw zu tun.

unwillingly [ʌn'wɪlɪŋlɪ] *adv* widerwillig.

unwillingness [ʌn'wɪlɪŋnɪs] *n* Widerwilligkeit *f*. **their ~ to compromise** ihre mangelnde Kompromißbereitschaft.

unwind [ʌn'waɪnd] *pret, ptp* **unwound 1** *vt thread, tape* abwickeln; *(untangle)* entwirren. **2** *vi* **(a)** sich abwickeln; *(fig: plot)* sich entwickeln. **(b)** *(col: relax)* abschalten *(col)*.

unwise [ʌn'waɪz] *adj* unklug. **they were ~ enough to believe him** sie waren so töricht, ihm zu glauben.

unwitting [ʌn'wɪtɪŋ] *adj accomplice* unwissentlich; *action also* unabsichtlich; *victim* ahnungslos.

unwittingly [ʌn'wɪtɪŋlɪ] *adv (innocently)* ahnungslos; *(unknowingly)* unbewußt.

unworkable [ʌn'wɜ:kəbl] *adj scheme* undurchführbar; *mine* nicht abbaubar.

unworldly [ʌn'wɜ:ldlɪ] *adj life* weltabgewandt; *(naïve)* weltfremd.

unworthy [ʌn'wɜ:ðɪ] *adj person* nicht wert *(of gen)*; *conduct also* unwürdig *(of gen)*. **this is ~ of you** das ziemt sich nicht für dich.

unwound [ʌn'waʊnd] *pret, ptp of* **unwind.**

unwrap [ʌn'ræp] *vt* auspacken, auswickeln.

unwritten [ʌn'rɪtn] *adj book, law* ungeschrieben; *agreement* stillschweigend.

unyielding [ʌn'ji:ldɪŋ] *adj* unnachgiebig.

unzip [ʌn'zɪp] *vt zip* aufmachen; *dress, case* den Reißverschluß aufmachen an *(+dat)*.

up [ʌp] **1** *adv* **(a)** *(in high or higher position)* oben; *(to higher position)* nach oben. **~ there** dort oben; **~ here on the roof** hier oben auf dem Dach; **on your way ~ (to see us/them)** auf dem Weg (zu uns/ihnen) herauf/hinauf; **he climbed all the way ~ (to us/them)** er ist den ganzen Weg (zu uns/ihnen) hochgeklettert; **to throw sth ~** etw hochwerfen; **it's five floors ~** es ist im fünften Stock; *(higher)* es ist fünf Stockwerke höher; **the road goes ~ and ~** die Straße steigt immer weiter an; **we were 6,000 m ~ when ...** wir waren 6.000 m hoch, als ...; **a little further ~** ein bißchen weiter oben; **the sun/moon is ~** die Sonne/der Mond ist aufgegangen; **with his collar ~** mit hochgeschlagenem Kragen; **the road is ~** die Straße ist aufgegraben; **to be ~ with the leaders** vorn bei den Führenden sein; **then ~ jumps Richard and says ...** und dann springt Richard auf und sagt ...; **~ with the Liberals!** hoch die Liberalen; **from £10 ~** ab £ 10.

(b) *(installed, built)* **to be ~** *(building)* stehen; *(scaffolding)* aufgestellt sein; *(shutters)* zu sein; *(wallpaper, curtains, pictures)* hängen; **they're putting ~ a new cinema** sie bauen ein neues Kino; **stick the notice ~ here** häng den Anschlag hier hin.

(c) *(not in bed)* auf. **to get ~** aufstehen; **to be ~ and about** auf sein; *(after illness also)* auf den Beinen sein; **to be ~ late** lange aufbleiben.

(d) *(geographically)* oben. **~ in Inverness** oben in Inverness; **we are going ~ to Hamburg** wir fahren nach Hamburg (hinauf); **to be/go ~ north** im Norden sein/in den Norden fahren; **we're ~ for the day** wir sind (nur) für heute hier; **he was ~ at Susie's place** er war bei Susie (zu Hause).

(e) *(in price, value)* gestiegen *(on* gegenüber*)*. **potatoes are ~ again** die Kartoffelpreise sind wieder gestiegen.

(f) *(in score)* **to be 3 goals ~** mit 3 Toren führen *or* vorn liegen *(on* gegenüber*)*; **to be one ~ on sb** jdm um einen Schritt voraus sein.

(g) *(col: wrong)* **what's ~?** was ist los?; **there's something ~** *(wrong)* da stimmt irgend etwas nicht; *(happening)* da ist irgend etwas im Gange.

(h) *(knowledgeable)* firm, beschlagen *(in, on* in *+dat)*. **he's well ~ in** *or* **on foreign affairs** in Auslandsfragen ist er firm.

(i) *(finished)* **time's ~** deine Zeit ist um; **the lease is ~ next month** das Mietverhältnis endet nächsten Monat; **to eat/use sth ~** etw aufessen/aufbrauchen; **it's all ~ with him** *(col)* es ist aus mit ihm *(col)*.

(j) ~ to *(as far as)* bis; **~ to now** bis jetzt; **~ to then** bis dann *or* dahin.

(k) ~ to *(col: doing)* **what's he ~ to?** *(actually doing)* was macht er da?; *(planning etc)* was hat er vor?; *(suspiciously)* was führt er im Schilde?; **he's ~ to no good** er führt nichts Gutes im

Schilde.

(l) ~ **to: I don't feel ~ to it** ich fühle mich dem nicht gewachsen; *(not well enough)* ich fühle mich nicht wohl genug dazu; **he's not/it isn't ~ to much** mit ihm/damit ist nicht viel los *(col)*; **it isn't ~ to his usual standard** es entspricht nicht seinem sonstigen Niveau; **it's ~ to us to help him** wir sollten ihm helfen; **if it was ~ to me** wenn es nach mir ginge; **it's ~ to you whether you go or not** es liegt an *or* bei dir, ob du gehst oder nicht; **shall I take it? — that's entirely ~ to you** soll ich es nehmen? — das müssen Sie selbst wissen; **it's ~ to the government to put things right** es ist Sache der Regierung, das richtigzustellen.

(m) ~ **and down** auf und ab; **he's been ~ and down all evening** er hat den ganzen Abend keine Minute stillgesessen; **it was ~ against the wall** es war an die Wand gelehnt; **to be ~ against a difficulty/an opponent** einem Problem/Gegner gegenüberstehen; **I fully realize what I'm ~ against** mir ist völlig klar, womit ich es hier zu tun habe; **they were really ~ against it** sie hatten wirklich schwer zu schaffen.

2 *prep* **further ~ the page** weiter oben auf der Seite; **to live/go ~ the hill** am Berg wohnen/den Berg hinaufgehen; **they live further ~ the hill/street** sie wohnen weiter oben am Berg/weiter die Straße entlang; ~ **the road from me** (von mir) die Straße entlang; **he went off ~ the road** er ging (weg) die Straße hinauf; **he hid it ~ the chimney** er versteckte es (oben) im Kamin; **the water goes ~ this pipe** das Wasser geht durch dieses Rohr; ~ **a tube** *(position)* in einer Röhre; *(motion)* in eine Röhre; **to go/march ~ to sb** auf jdn zugehen/-marschieren.

3 *n* **~s and downs** gute und schlechte Zeiten *pl*; *(of life)* Höhen und Tiefen *pl*; **to be on the ~ and ~** *(col: improving)* auf dem aufsteigenden Ast sein *(col)*; **his career is on the ~ and ~** *(col)* mit seiner Karriere geht es aufwärts.

4 *adj (going up) escalator* nach oben; *(Rail) train, line* zur nächsten größeren Stadt.

5 *vt (col) price, offer* hinaufsetzen; *production* ankurbeln; *bet* erhöhen *(to* auf *+acc)*.

6 *vi (col)* **she ~ped and hit him** sie knallte ihm ganz plötzlich eine *(col)*; **he ~ped and ran** er rannte ganz plötzlich davon.

up-and-coming ['ʌpən'kʌmɪŋ] *adj* Nachwuchs-; *business* aufstrebend.

upbringing ['ʌpbrɪŋɪŋ] *n* Erziehung *f*. **to have a good ~** eine gute Kinderstube haben.

up-country ['ʌp'kʌntrɪ] *adv* landeinwärts.

update [ʌp'deɪt] **1** *vt* auf den neuesten Stand bringen. **2** ['ʌpdeɪt] *n* **to give sb an ~** jdn auf den neuesten Stand bringen.

up-end [ʌp'end] *vt box, sofa* hochkant stellen.

up-front [ˌʌp'frʌnt] *adv* im voraus.

upgrade [ʌp'greɪd] *vt employee* befördern; *job* höher einstufen; *product* verbessern.

upheaval [ʌp'hiːvəl] *n* Aufruhr *m*. **emotional ~** Aufruhr der Gefühle; **social/political ~s** soziale/politische Umwälzungen *pl*.

upheld [ʌp'held] *pret, ptp of* **uphold.**

uphill ['ʌp'hɪl] **1** *adv* bergauf. **to go ~** bergauf gehen; *(car)* den Berg hinauffahren. **2** *adj road* bergauf (führend); *(fig) work, struggle* mühsam, mühselig. **it's ~ all the way** *(lit)* es geht die ganze Strecke bergauf; *(fig)* es ist ein harter Kampf.

uphold [ʌp'həʊld] *pret, ptp* **upheld** *vt (sustain) tradition, honour* wahren; *the law* hüten; *(support) person, decision, objection* (unter)stützen; *(Jur) verdict* bestätigen.

upholstery [ʌp'həʊlstərɪ] *n (interior)* Polsterung *f*; *(cover)* Bezug *m*; *(trade)* Polsterei *f*; *(skill)* das Polstern.

upkeep ['ʌpkiːp] *n (running)* Unterhalt *m*; *(cost)* Unterhaltskosten *pl*; *(maintenance)* Instandhaltung *f*.

uplift ['ʌplɪft] **1** *n (exaltation)* Erhebung *f*; *(moral inspiration)* Erbauung *f*. **2** [ʌp'lɪft] *vt spirit, voice* erheben. **to feel ~ed** sich erbaut fühlen.

up-market ['ʌp'mɑːkɪt] *adj* anspruchsvoll.

upon [ə'pɒn] *prep see* **on 1.**

upper ['ʌpə[r]] **1** *adj* obere(r, s); *lip, arm, jaw, deck* Ober-. **temperatures in the ~ thirties** Temperaturen über 35 Grad; **U~ Egypt/the ~ Loire** Oberägypten *nt*/die obere Loire; **~ storey** *(of house)* oberes Stockwerk; **~ circle** *(Brit Theat)* zweiter Rang; **the ~ ranks of the Civil Service** das gehobene Beamtentum; **~ school** Oberschule *f*; **U~ House** *(Parl)* Oberhaus *nt*. **2** *n* **~s** *pl (of shoe)* Obermaterial *nt*; **to be on one's ~s** *(col)* auf den Hund gekommen sein *(col)*.

upper: **~ case** *n (Typ) (also* **~-case letter***)* Großbuchstabe *m*; **~ class** *n* **the ~ classes** die Oberschicht; **~-class** *adj accent, district, person* vornehm; *sport, expression, attitude* der Oberschicht; **to be ~-class** *(person)* zur Oberschicht gehören; **~classman** *n (US) Mitglied nt einer High School oder eines College;* **~ crust** *n (col)* obere Zehntausend *pl (col)*; **~-crust** *adj (col)* (schrecklich) vornehm *(col);* **~most 1** *adj* oberste(r, s); *(fig) ambition* größte(r, s), höchste(r, s); **safety should be ~most in your minds** Sicherheit sollte für Sie an erster Stelle stehen; **2** *adv* **the blue side ~most** mit der blauen Seite nach oben.

uppish ['ʌpɪʃ] **uppity** ['ʌpɪtɪ] *adj (col: arrogant)* hochnäsig *(col)*. **to get ~ with sb** jdm gegenüber anmaßend werden.

upright ['ʌpraɪt] **1** *adj* **(a)** *(erect)* aufrecht; *(vertical) post* senkrecht. **~ piano** Klavier *nt*; **~ chair** Stuhl *m*. **(b)** *(fig: honest) person* aufrecht. **2** *adv (erect)* aufrecht, gerade; *(vertical)* senkrecht. **to hold oneself ~** sich gerade halten. **3** *n* **(a)** *(post)* Pfosten *m*. **(b)** *(piano)* Klavier *nt*.

uprising ['ʌpraɪzɪŋ] *n* Aufstand *m*, Erhebung *f*.

upriver ['ʌp'rɪvə[r]] *adv* **2 miles ~ from Fen Ditton** 2 Meilen flußaufwärts von Fen Ditton.

uproar ['ʌprɔː[r]] *n* Aufruhr *m*. **in ~** in Aufruhr.

uproarious [ʌp'rɔːrɪəs] *adj meeting* tumultartig; *laughter* brüllend; *success, welcome* überwältigend; *joke* zum Schreien *pred*.

uproot [ʌp'ruːt] *vt plant* entwurzeln; *(fig: eradicate) evil* ausmerzen. **~ed by the war** durch den Krieg entwurzelt; **to ~ sb from his familiar surroundings** jdn aus seiner gewohnten Umgebung herausreißen.

upset [ʌp'set] *(vb: pret, ptp ~)* **1** *vt* **(a)** *(knock over, spill)* umstoßen; *boat* umkippen. **she ~ the milk all over the best carpet** sie stieß die Milch um, und alles lief auf den guten Teppich. **(b)** *(make sad: news, death)* bestürzen, erschüttern; *(question, insolence etc)* aus der Fassung bringen; *(experience, accident etc)* mitnehmen *(col)*; *(distress, excite) patient, parent etc* aufregen; *(offend etc)* verletzen; *(annoy)* ärgern. **(c)** *(disorganize) calculations, balance etc* durcheinanderbringen. **(d)** *(make ill)* **the rich food ~ his stomach** das schwere Essen ist ihm auf den Magen geschlagen.

2 *adj* **(a)** *(about divorce, accident etc)* mitgenommen *(col)*; *(about death, bad news etc)* bestürzt *(about* über *+acc)*; *(sad)* betrübt, geknickt *(col) (about* über *+acc)*; *(distressed)* aufgeregt *(about* wegen*)*; *child* durcheinander *pred*; *(annoyed)* aufgebracht *(about* über *+acc)*; *(hurt)* gekränkt, verletzt *(about* über *+acc)*. **to get ~** sich aufregen *(about* über *+acc)*; *(hurt)* verletzt werden. **(b)** ['ʌpset] *stomach* verdorben *attr*. **to have an ~ stomach** sich *(dat)* den Magen verdorben haben.

3 ['ʌpset] *n* **(a)** *(disturbance)* Störung *f*; *(emotional)* Aufregung *f*; *(col: quarrel)* Verstimmung *f*, Ärger *m*; *(unexpected defeat etc)* böse Überraschung. **(b)** *(of stomach)* Magenverstimmung *f*, verdorbener Magen.

upsetting [ʌp'setɪŋ] *adj (saddening)* traurig; *(stronger)* bestürzend; *(disturbing) changes* störend; *situation* unangenehm; *(offending)* beleidigend; *(annoying)* ärgerlich.

upshot ['ʌpʃɒt] *n (result)* Ergebnis *nt*. **the ~ of it all was that ...** es lief darauf hinaus, daß ...

upside down ['ʌpsaɪd'daʊn] **1** *adv* verkehrt herum. **to turn sth ~** *(lit)* etw umdrehen; *(fig)* etw auf den Kopf stellen *(col)*. **2** *adj* **in an ~ position** verkehrt herum; **to be ~** *(picture)* verkehrt herum hängen; *(world)* kopfstehen.

upstairs [ʌp'stɛəz] **1** *adv* oben; *(with movement)* nach oben. **2** *adj window* im oberen Stock(werk); *room also* obere(r, s). **3** *n* oberes Stockwerk.

upstanding [ʌp'stændɪŋ] *adj (strong)* kräftig; *(honourable)* rechtschaffen.

upstart ['ʌpstɑːt] *n* Emporkömmling *m*.

upstate ['ʌpsteɪt] *(US)* **1** *adj* im Norden (des Bundesstaates). **2** *adv* im Norden (des Bundesstaates); *(with movement)* in den Norden (des Bundesstaates).

upstream ['ʌpstriːm] *adv* flußaufwärts. **3 kms ~ from Henley** 3 km oberhalb Henley.

upsurge ['ʌpsɜːdʒ] *n* Zunahme, Eskalation *(pej) f*. **she felt an ~ of revulsion** sie fühlte Ekel in sich *(dat)* aufwallen.

uptake ['ʌpteɪk] *n (col)*: **to be quick/slow on the ~** schnell verstehen/schwer von Begriff sein *(col)*.

uptight ['ʌp'taɪt] *adj (col) (nervous)* nervös; *(inhibited)* verklemmt *(col)*; *(angry)* sauer *(col)*.

up-to-date ['ʌptə'deɪt] *adj* auf dem neusten Stand; *fashion also, book, news* aktuell; *person, method, technique also* up to date *pred (col)*. **to keep ~ with sth** mit *or* bei etw auf dem laufenden bleiben.

up-to-the-minute ['ʌptəðə'mɪnɪt] *adj news, reports* allerneuste(r, s), allerletzte(r, s). **her clothes are ~** ihre Kleider sind immer der allerletzte Schrei.

uptown ['ʌptaʊn] *(US) adj, adv* im Villenviertel.

upturn [ʌp'tɜːn] **1** *vt* umdrehen. **2** ['ʌptɜːn] *n (fig: improvement)* Aufschwung *m*.

upturned ['ʌptɜːnd] *adj box etc* umgedreht; *face* nach oben gewandt. **~ nose** Stupsnase *f (col)*.

upward ['ʌpwəd] **1** *adj* aufwärts-, nach oben; *glance* nach oben. **~ movement** Aufwärtsbewegung *f*; **~ slope** Steigung *f*. **2** *adv (also* **~s***)* **(a)** *move* aufwärts, nach oben. **to look ~** hochsehen, nach oben sehen; **face ~** mit dem Gesicht nach oben. **(b)** *(with numbers)* **prices from 50p ~** Preise von 50 Pence an, Preise ab 50 Pence; **and ~** und darüber; **~ of 3000** über 3000.

uranium [jʊə'reɪnɪəm] *n* Uran *nt*.

Uranus [jʊə'reɪnəs] *n (Astron)* Uranus *m*.

urban ['ɜːbən] *adj* städtisch. **~ renewal** Stadterneuerung *f*.

urbane [ɜː'beɪn] *adj person, style* weltmännisch; *(civil)* höflich; *manner, words* verbindlich.

urbanization [ˌɜːbənaɪ'zeɪʃən] *n* Urbanisierung, Verstädterung *(pej) f*.

urchin ['ɜːtʃɪn] *n* Gassenkind *nt*; *(mischievous)* Range *f*.

urge [ɜːdʒ] **1** *n (need)* Verlangen, Bedürfnis *nt*; *(drive)* Drang *m no pl*; *(physical, sexual)* Trieb *m*. **to feel an ~ to do sth** das Bedürfnis verspüren, etw zu tun; **I resisted the ~ (to contradict him)** ich habe mich beherrscht (und ihm nicht widersprochen); **come and stay with us if you get the ~** *(col)* komm uns besuchen, wenn du Lust hast. **2** *vt* **(a) to ~ sb to do sth** *(plead with)* jdn eindringlich bitten, etw zu tun; *(earnestly recommend)* darauf dringen, daß jd etw tut; **to ~ sb to accept** jdn drängen, anzunehmen; **he needed no urging** er ließ sich nicht lange bitten. **(b)** *(advocate) caution, acceptance* drängen auf *(+acc)*. **to ~ that sth should be done** darauf drängen, daß etw getan wird.

♦ **urge on** *vt sep* antreiben.

urgency ['ɜːdʒənsɪ] *n* Dringlichkeit *f*; *(of tone, pleas also)* Eindringlichkeit *f*. **it's a matter of ~** es ist dringend; **there's no ~** es eilt nicht; **there was a note of ~ in his voice** es klang sehr dringend.

urgent ['ɜːdʒənt] *adj* dringend; *letter, parcel* Eil-. **to be in ~ need of medical attention** dringend ärztliche Hilfe benötigen.

urgently ['ɜːdʒəntlɪ] *adv required* dringend; *requested also* dringlich; *talk* eindringlich. **he is ~ in need of help** er braucht dringend Hilfe.

urinal ['jʊərɪnl] *n (room)* Pissoir *nt*; *(vessel)* Becken *nt*.

urine ['jʊərɪn] *n* Urin, Harn *m*.

urn [ɜːn] *n* **(a)** Urne *f*. **(b)** *(also* **tea ~, coffee ~***)* Kessel *m*.

US = **United States** USA *pl*.

us [ʌs] *pers pron* **(a)** *(dir and indir obj)* uns. **give it (to) ~** gib es uns; **younger than ~** jünger als wir; **it's ~** wir sind's; **he is one of ~** er ist einer von uns; **this table shows ~ the tides** auf dieser Tafel sieht man die Gezeiten; **~ and them** wir und die. **(b)** *(col: me) (dir obj)* mich; *(indir obj)* mir; *(pl subj)* wir. **give ~ a look** laß (mich) mal sehen; **~ English** wir Engländer.

USA = **United States of America** USA *pl*; **United States Army.**

usable ['juːzəbl] *adj* verwendbar; *ideas* brauchbar. **no longer ~** nicht mehr zu gebrauchen.

USAF = **United States Air Force.**

usage ['juːzɪdʒ] *n* **(a)** *(treatment, handling)* Behandlung *f*. **it's had some rough ~** es ist ziemlich unsanft behandelt worden. **(b)** *(custom, practice)* Brauch *m*, Sitte *f*. **it's common ~** es ist allgemein üblich. **(c)** *(Ling: use, way of using)* Gebrauch *m no pl*, Anwendung *f*. **words in common ~** allgemein gebräuchliche Wörter *pl*.

use[1] [juːz] **1** *vt* **(a)** benutzen, gebrauchen; *means, materials also, personnel, idea* verwenden; *system, force, one's abilities, strength* anwenden; *tact, care* walten lassen; *drugs* einnehmen. **~ only in emergencies** nur im Notfall gebrauchen; **what's this ~d for?** wofür wird das benutzt?; **to ~ sth for sth** etw zu etw verwenden.

(b) *(make use of, exploit) information, talents, resources, chances* (aus)nutzen; *advantage* nutzen; *waste products* verwerten. **you can ~ the leftovers to make a soup** Sie können die Reste zu einer Suppe verwerten.

(c) *(~ up, consume) petrol, electricity etc* verbrauchen.

(d) *(pej: exploit)* ausnutzen. **I feel (I've just been) ~d** ich habe das Gefühl, man hat mich ausgenutzt; *(sexually)* ich komme mir mißbraucht vor.

2 [juːs] *n* **(a)** Verwendung *f*; *(operation: of machines etc)* Benutzung *f*; *(of calculator etc, of word, arms, intelligence)* Gebrauch *m*; *(of method, force)* Anwendung *f*; *(of personnel, truncheons etc)* Einsatz *m*; *(of drugs)* Einnahme *f*. **directions for ~** Gebrauchsanweisung *f*; **for the ~ of** für; **for ~ in case of emergency** für Notfälle; **for external ~** zur äußerlichen Anwendung; **ready for ~** gebrauchsfertig; *(machine)* einsatzbereit; **to make ~ of sth** von etw Gebrauch machen, etw benutzen; **in ~/out of ~** in/außer Gebrauch; *(machines)* in/außer Betrieb; **to be in daily ~/no longer in ~** täglich/nicht mehr benutzt werden.

(b) *(exploitation, making~ of)* Nutzung *f*; *(way of using)* Verwendung *f*; *(of waste products, leftovers etc)* Verwertung *f*. **to make ~ of sth** etw nutzen; **to make good/bad ~ of sth** etw gut/schlecht nutzen; **to have no ~ for** *(lit, fig)* keine Verwendung haben für; **to have no further ~ for sth** etw nicht mehr brauchen.

(c) *(usefulness)* Nutzen *m*. **to be of ~ to sb/for doing sth** für jdn von Nutzen sein/nützlich sein, um etw zu tun; **this is no ~ any more** das ist zu nichts mehr zu gebrauchen; **is this (of) any ~ to you?** können Sie das brauchen?, können Sie damit etwas anfangen?; **can I be of any ~?** kann ich irgendwie behilflich sein?; **this is no ~, we must start work** so hat das keinen Sinn, wir müssen etwas tun; **it's no ~ you** *or* **your protesting** es hat keinen Sinn *or* es nützt nichts, daß du protestierst; **what's the ~ of telling him?** was nützt es, wenn man es ihm sagt?; **it's no ~** es hat keinen Zweck; **ah, what's the ~!** ach, was soll's!

(d) *(right)* Nutznießung *f (Jur).* **to have ~ of a car** einen Wagen benutzen können; **to give sb the ~ of sth** jdn etw benutzen lassen; *(of car also, of money)* jdm etw zur Verfügung stellen; **to have lost the ~ of one's arm** seinen Arm nicht mehr gebrauchen können.

♦**use up** *vt sep food, objects, one's strength* verbrauchen; *(finish also)* aufbrauchen; *scraps, leftovers etc* verwerten. **the butter is all ~d ~** die Butter ist alle *(col) or* aufgebraucht.

use[2] [juːs] *aux as in* **I didn't ~ to like it** *see* **used**[2].

used[1] [juːzd] *adj clothes, car etc* gebraucht; *(soiled) towel etc* benutzt.

used[2] [juːst] *aux only in past* **I ~ to swim every day** ich bin früher täglich geschwommen; **I ~ not to smoke, I didn't use to smoke** ich habe früher nicht geraucht, ich pflegte nicht zu rauchen *(geh)*; **I don't now but I ~ to** früher schon, jetzt nicht mehr; **he ~ to be a good singer** er war einmal ein guter Sänger; **there ~ to be a field here** hier war (früher) einmal ein Feld; **things aren't what they ~ to be** es ist alles nicht mehr (so) wie früher.

used[3] [juːst] *adj* **to be ~ to sth** an etw *(acc)* gewöhnt sein, etw gewohnt sein; **to be ~ to doing sth** es gewohnt sein, etw zu tun; **I'm not ~ to it** ich bin das nicht gewohnt; **to get ~ to sth/doing sth** sich an etw *(acc)* gewöhnen/sich daran gewöhnen, etw zu tun.

useful ['juːsfʊl] *adj* **(a)** nützlich; *person, contribution also* wertvoll; *(handy) tool also* praktisch; *size* zweckmäßig; *discussion* fruchtbar; *life, employment* nutzbringend. **it is ~ for him to be able to ...** es ist günstig *or* praktisch, daß er ... kann; **to make oneself ~** sich nützlich machen; **to come in ~** sich als nützlich erweisen; **he's a ~ man to know** es ist sehr nützlich, ihn zu kennen; **it has a ~ life of 10 years** es hat eine Nutzdauer von 10 Jahren. **(b)** *(col: capable) player* brauchbar, fähig. **he's quite ~ with a gun** er kann ziemlich gut mit der Pistole umgehen.

useless ['juːslɪs] *adj* **(a)** nutzlos; *(unusable)* unbrauchbar; *person also* zu nichts nütze; *remedy also* wirkungslos. **it's ~ without a handle** ohne Griff nützt es nichts; **I'm ~ at languages** Sprachen kann ich überhaupt nicht. **(b)** *(pointless)* zwecklos, sinnlos.

user ['juːzəʳ] *n* Benutzer(in *f*) *m.*

user-friendly ['juːzə'frendlɪ] *adj* benutzerfreundlich.

usher ['ʌʃəʳ] **1** *n (Theat etc)* Platzanweiser *m*; *(Jur)* Gerichtsdiener *m.* **2** *vt* **to ~ sb into a room/to his seat** jdn in ein Zimmer/zu seinem Sitz bringen; **to ~ sb out** jdn hinauskomplimentieren; **to ~ in a new era** ein neues Zeitalter einleiten.

usherette [ˌʌʃə'ret] *n* Platzanweiserin *f.*

USN = United States Navy.

USS = United States Ship; United States Senate.

USSR = Union of Soviet Socialist Republics UdSSR *f.*

usual ['juːʒʊəl] **1** *adj (customary)* üblich; *(normal also)* gewöhnlich, normal. **when shall I come? — oh, the ~ time** wann soll ich kommen? — oh, wie immer; **it's the ~ thing nowadays** das ist heute so üblich; **it's ~ to ask first** normalerweise fragt man erst; **as ~, as per ~** *(col)* wie üblich, wie gewöhnlich; **business as ~** normaler Betrieb; *(in shop)* Verkauf geht weiter; **later/less/more than ~** später/weniger/mehr als sonst; **it's not ~ for him to be late** er kommt normalerweise nicht zu spät. **2** *n (col)* der/die/das Übliche. **the ~ please!** *(drink)* dasselbe wie immer, bitte!

usually ['juːʒʊəlɪ] *adv* gewöhnlich, normalerweise. **do you go to Spain? — ~** fahren Sie nach Spanien — meist(ens); **is he ~ so rude?** ist er immer so unhöflich?

usurer ['juːʒərəʳ] *n* Wucherer *m.*

usurp [juː'zɜːp] *vt* sich *(dat)* widerrechtlich aneignen; *power, title, inheritance also* an sich *(acc)* reißen; *throne* sich bemächtigen *(+gen) (geh)*; *role* sich *(dat)* anmaßen; *person* verdrängen.

usury ['juːʒʊrɪ] *n* Wucher *m.*

utensil [juː'tensl] *n* Gerät, Utensil *nt.*

uterus ['juːtərəs] *n* Gebärmutter *f.*

utilitarian [ˌjuːtɪlɪ'teərɪən] *adj* auf Nützlichkeit ausgerichtet; *qualities* nützlich; *(Philos)* utilitaristisch.

utility [juː'tɪlɪtɪ] *n* **(a)** *(usefulness)* Nützlichkeit *f*, Nutzen *m.* **(b) public ~** *(company)* Versorgungsbetrieb *m*; *(service)* Leistung *f* der Versorgungsbetriebe.

utilization [ˌjuːtɪlaɪ'zeɪʃən] *n see vt* Verwendung *f*; Nutzung *f*; Verwertung *f.*

utilize ['juːtɪlaɪz] *vt* verwenden; *situation, time, opportunity, talent* nutzen; *waste paper etc* verwerten.

utmost ['ʌtməʊst] **1** *adj* **(a)** *(greatest) ease, danger* größte(r, s); *caution, candour also* äußerste(r, s). **they used their ~ skill** Sie taten ihr Äußerstes; **with the ~ speed/care** so schnell/sorgfältig wie nur möglich; **matters of the ~ importance** Angelegenheiten von äußerster Wichtigkeit. **(b)** *(furthest)* äußerste(r, s). **2** *n* **to do/try one's ~** sein möglichstes *or* Bestes tun; **to the ~ of one's ability** so gut man nur kann; **one should enjoy life to the ~** man sollte das Leben in vollen Zügen genießen.

Utopia [juː'təʊpɪə] *n* Utopia *nt.*

Utopian [juː'təʊpɪən] *adj* utopisch, utopistisch *(pej).*

utter[1] ['ʌtəʳ] *adj* total, vollkommen; *rogue* Erz-. **what ~ nonsense!** so ein totaler Blödsinn!

utter[2] *vt* von sich *(dat)* geben; *word* sagen; *cry, threat* ausstoßen.

utterance ['ʌtərəns] *n* Äußerung *f.* **his last ~** seine letzten Worte.

utterly ['ʌtəlɪ] *adv* total, völlig; *depraved also, despise* zutiefst. **~ beautiful** ausgesprochen schön.

uttermost ['ʌtəməʊst] *n, adj* = **utmost.**

U-turn ['juːtɜːn] *n (lit, fig)* Wende *f.* **no ~s** Wenden verboten!; **the government has done a ~ over pensions** die Rentenpolitik der Regierung hat sich um 180 Grad gedreht.

V

V, v [viː] *n* V, v *nt.*
vacancy ['veɪkənsɪ] *n* **(a)** *(emptiness)* Leere *f*; *(of look also)* Ausdruckslosigkeit *f*. **(b)** *(in boarding house)* (freies) Zimmer. **have you any vacancies for August?** haben Sie im August noch Zimmer frei?; **"no vacancies"** „belegt". **(c)** *(job)* offene *or* freie Stelle. **to fill a ~** eine Stelle besetzen; **vacancies** Stellenangebote, offene Stellen.
vacant ['veɪkənt] *adj* **(a)** *post* frei, offen; *WC, seat, hotel room* frei; *chair* unbesetzt; *house* unbewohnt. **to become** *or* **fall ~** frei werden. **(b)** *mind, stare* leer.
vacate [və'keɪt] *vt seat* frei machen; *post* aufgeben; *house* räumen.
vacation [və'keɪʃən] **1** *n* **(a)** *(Univ)* Semesterferien *pl*. **(b)** *(US)* Ferien *pl*, Urlaub *m*. **on ~** im *or* auf Urlaub; **to take a ~** Urlaub machen; **to go on ~** auf Urlaub *or* in die Ferien gehen. **2** *vi (US)* Urlaub machen.
vaccinate ['væksɪneɪt] *vt* impfen.
vaccination [ˌvæksɪ'neɪʃən] *n* (Schutz)impfung *f*.
vaccine ['væksiːn] *n* Impfstoff *m*.
vacillate ['væsɪleɪt] *vi (lit, fig)* schwanken.
vacuous ['vækjʊəs] *adj face, stare* ausdruckslos, leer; *remarks* nichtssagend.
vacuum ['vækjʊəm] *n* **1** *n (Phys, fig)* (luft)leerer Raum, Vakuum *nt*. **cultural ~** kulturelles Vakuum. **2** *vt carpet* saugen.
vacuum: ~ bottle *n (US)* = **~ flask**; **~ cleaner** *n* Staubsauger *m*; **~ flask** *n (Brit)* Thermosflasche *f*; **~-packed** *adj* vakuumverpackt.
vagabond ['vægəbɒnd] *n* Vagabund *m*.
vagary ['veɪgərɪ] *n usu pl* Laune *f*; *(strange idea)* verrückter Einfall.
vagina [və'dʒaɪnə] *n* Scheide, Vagina *f*.
vagrancy ['veɪgrənsɪ] *n* Landstreicherei *f*; Stadtstreicherei *f*.
vagrant ['veɪgrənt] *n* Landstreicher(in *f*) *m*; Stadtstreicher(in *f*) *m*.
vague [veɪg] *adj (+er)* **(a)** *(not clear)* vage, unbestimmt; *outline, shape, photograph* verschwommen; *report, question* ungenau; *murmur* undeutlich. **I haven't the ~st idea** ich habe nicht die leiseste Ahnung; **there's a ~ resemblance** es besteht eine entfernte Ähnlichkeit; **I had a ~ idea she would come** ich hatte so eine (dunkle) Ahnung, daß sie kommen würde; **he was ~ about the time of his arrival** er äußerte sich nur unbestimmt über seine Ankunftszeit. **(b)** *(absent-minded)* geistesabwesend.
vaguely ['veɪglɪ] *adv* vage; *remember also* dunkel; *speak also* unbestimmt; *understand* ungefähr, in etwa. **to look ~ at sb** jdn verständnislos ansehen; **they're ~ similar** sie haben eine entfernte Ähnlichkeit.
vain [veɪn] *adj* **(a)** *(+er) (about looks)* eitel; *(about qualities)* eingebildet. **he's very ~ about his musical abilities** er bildet sich *(dat)* auf sein musikalisches Können viel ein. **(b)** *(useless, empty)* eitel *(liter)*; *attempt also* vergeblich; *hope also* töricht. **in ~** umsonst; **to take God's name in ~** Gott lästern.
vainly ['veɪnlɪ] *adv* **(a)** *(to no effect)* vergeblich, vergebens. **(b)** *(conceitedly) (about looks)* eitel; *(about qualities also)* eingebildet.
valance ['væləns] *n (for bed frame)* Volant *m*; *(on window)* Querbehang *m*; *(wooden)* Blende *f*.
valentine ['væləntaɪn] *n* **St V~'s Day** Valentinstag *m*; **~ (card)** Valentinskarte *f*.
valet ['vælеɪ] *n* Kammerdiener *m*. **~ service** Reinigungsdienst *m*.
valiant ['væljənt] *adj* **(a)** *(liter) soldier, deed* tapfer, kühn *(geh)*. **(b) he made a ~ effort to save him** er unternahm einen kühnen Versuch, ihn zu retten; **she made a ~ effort to smile** sie versuchte tapfer zu lächeln.
valid ['vælɪd] *adj* **(a)** *ticket, passport* gültig; *(Jur) document, marriage* rechtsgültig; *contract* bindend; *claim* begründet. **(b)** *argument* stichhaltig; *excuse, reason* einleuchtend; *objection* begründet. **that's a very ~ point** das ist ein sehr wertvoller Hinweis.
validate ['vælɪdeɪt] *vt document (check validity)* für gültig erklären; *(with stamp, sign)* (rechts)gültig machen; *claim* bestätigen; *(Jur)* Rechtskraft verleihen *(+dat)*.
validity [və'lɪdɪtɪ] *n* **(a)** *(Jur etc: of document)* Rechtsgültigkeit *f*; *(of ticket etc)* Gültigkeit *f*; *(of claim)* Berechtigung *f*. **(b)** *(of argument)* Stichhaltigkeit *f*; *(of excuse etc)* Triftigkeit *f*.
valley ['vælɪ] *n* Tal *nt*; *(big and flat)* Niederung *f*. **up/down the ~** talaufwärts/talabwärts.
valour, *(US)* **valor** ['væləʳ] *n (liter)* Tapferkeit *f*.
valuable ['væljʊəbl] **1** *adj* **(a)** *jewel* wertvoll; *time, oxygen* kostbar. **(b)** *(useful)* wertvoll; *help, advice also* nützlich. **2** *n* **~s** *pl* Wertsachen *pl*.
valuation [ˌvæljʊ'eɪʃən] *n* Schätzung *f*; *(fig: of person's character)* Einschätzung *f*.
value ['væljuː] **1** *n* **(a)** Wert *m*; *(usefulness)* Nutzen *m*. **to be of ~** wertvoll/nützlich sein; **to put a ~ on sth** etw bewerten; *(on leisure etc)* einer Sache *(dat)* (hohen) Wert beimessen; **he attaches no/great ~ to it** er legt keinen/großen Wert darauf; **of little ~** nicht sehr wertvoll/nützlich; **of no ~** wertlos/nutzlos; **of great ~** sehr wertvoll; **what's the ~ of your house?** wieviel ist Ihr Haus wert?; **it's good ~** es ist preisgünstig; **in our shop you get ~ for money** in unserem Geschäft bekommen Sie etwas für Ihr Geld *(col)*; **goods to the ~ of £100** Waren im Wert von £ 100; **they put a ~ of £50 on it** sie haben es auf £ 50 geschätzt. **(b) ~s** *pl (moral standards)* (sittliche) Werte *pl*.
2 *vt* **(a)** *house, jewels* schätzen *(at* auf *+acc)*. **(b)** *friendship, person, opinion, advice* schätzen. **I ~ it (highly)** ich weiß es zu schätzen; **if you ~ my opinion ...** wenn Sie Wert auf meine Meinung legen ...; **if you ~ your life** wenn Ihnen Ihr Leben lieb ist.
value-added tax ['væljuːædɪd'tæks] *n (Brit)* Mehrwertsteuer *f*.
valued ['væljuːd] *adj friend* geschätzt, lieb.
value judgement *n* Werturteil *nt*.
valve [vælv] *n (Anat)* Klappe *f*; *(Tech, on musical instrument)* Ventil *nt*; *(Brit: Rad, TV)* Röhre *f*.
vampire ['væmpaɪəʳ] *n (lit, fig)* Vampir *m*.
van[1] [væn] *n* **(a)** *(Brit Aut)* Transporter *m*. **(b)** *(Rail)* Waggon, Wagen *m*.
van[2] *n* = **vanguard.**
vandal ['vændəl] *n (fig)* Rowdy *m*. **it was damaged by ~s** es ist mutwillig beschädigt worden.
vandalism ['vændəlɪzəm] *n* Vandalismus *m*; *(Jur)* mutwillige Beschädigung.

vandalize ['vændəlaɪz] *vt* mutwillig beschädigen; *building* verwüsten; *(wreck)* demolieren.
vane [veɪn] *n* **(a)** *(also* **weather ~***)* Wetterfahne *f.* **(b)** *(of windmill, propeller)* Flügel *m.*
vanguard ['vængɑːd] *n (Mil, Naut)* Vorhut *f.* **in the ~ of progress** an der Spitze des Fortschritts.
vanilla [və'nɪlə] **1** *n* Vanille *f.* **2** *adj* Vanille-.
vanish ['vænɪʃ] *vi* verschwinden; *(traces also)* sich verlieren; *(fears)* sich legen; *(hopes)* schwinden; *(become extinct)* untergehen. **~ing point** *(fig)* Nullpunkt *m.*
vanity ['vænɪtɪ] *n (concerning looks)* Eitelkeit *f; (concerning own value)* Eingebildetheit *f.*
vanquish ['væŋkwɪʃ] *vt (liter)* bezwingen *(geh).*
vantage ['vɑːntɪdʒ] *n (Tennis)* Vorteil *m.*
vantage point *n (Mil)* (günstiger) Aussichtspunkt. **our window is a good ~ for watching the procession** von unserem Fenster aus hat man einen guten Blick auf die Prozession; **from our modern ~** aus heutiger Sicht.
vapid ['væpɪd] *adj (liter) remark* nichtssagend, geistlos; *style* kraftlos; *taste* schal.
vaporize ['veɪpəraɪz] **1** *vt (by boiling etc)* verdampfen; *(naturally)* verdunsten lassen. **2** *vi see vt* verdampfen; verdunsten.
vapour, *(US)* **vapor** ['veɪpəʳ] *n* Dunst *m; (steamy)* Dampf *m.* **~ trail** Kondensstreifen *m.*
variable ['vɛərɪəbl] **1** *adj* **(a)** veränderlich, variabel; *weather, mood* wechselhaft. **~ winds** wechselnde Winde *pl;* **his work is very ~** er arbeitet sehr unterschiedlich. **(b)** *speed* regulierbar; *salary level* flexibel. **2** *n (Math, Phys, fig)* Variable *f.*
variance ['vɛərɪəns] *n* **(a) to be at ~ with sb** anderer Meinung sein als jd *(about* hinsichtlich *+gen);* **this is at ~ with what he said earlier** dies stimmt nicht mit dem überein, was er vorher gesagt hat. **(b)** *(difference)* Unterschied *m.*
variant ['vɛərɪənt] **1** *n* Variante *f.* **2** *adj (alternative)* andere(r, s). **there are two ~ spellings** es gibt zwei verschiedene Schreibweisen.
variation [ˌvɛərɪ'eɪʃən] *n* **(a)** *(varying)* Veränderung *f; (Sci)* Variation *f; (Met, of temperature, of prices)* Schwankung *f.* **~ in opinions** unterschiedliche Auffassungen. **(b)** *(Mus)* Variation *f.* **~s on a theme** Variationen über ein Thema. **(c)** *(different model, Biol)* Variante *f (on* von*).* **(d)** *(deviation)* Abweichung *f.*
varicose ['værɪkəʊs] *adj:* **~ veins** Krampfadern *pl.*
varied ['vɛərɪd] *adj* unterschiedlich; *career, life* bewegt; *selection* reichhaltig. **a ~ group of people** eine gemischte Gruppe.
variegated ['vɛərɪgeɪtɪd] *adj (coloured)* buntscheckig; *forms etc* verschiedenartig.
variety [və'raɪətɪ] *n* **(a)** *(diversity)* Abwechslung *f.* **to give** *or* **add ~ to sth** Abwechslung in etw *(acc)* bringen; **a job with a lot of ~** eine sehr abwechslungsreiche Arbeit. **(b)** *(assortment)* Vielfalt *f; (Comm)* Auswahl *f (of* an *+dat).* **in a great ~ of ways** auf die verschiedensten Arten; **in a ~ of colours** in den verschiedensten Farben; **for a ~ of reasons** aus verschiedenen Gründen. **(c)** *(type)* Art *f; (of cigarette, potato)* Sorte *f; (of car, chair)* Modell *nt.* **a new ~ of tulip** eine neue Tulpensort. **(d)** *(esp Brit Theat)* Varieté *nt.*
variety: ~ artist *n (esp Brit)* Varietékünstler(in *f*) *m;* **~ show** *n (esp Brit)* Varietévorführung *f; (Rad, TV)* Unterhaltungssendung *f.*
various ['vɛərɪəs] *adj* verschieden.
variously ['vɛərɪəslɪ] *adv* unterschiedlich.
varnish ['vɑːnɪʃ] **1** *n* Lack *m.* **2** *vt* lackieren; *painting* firnissen.
vary ['vɛərɪ] **1** *vi* **(a)** *(diverge, differ)* sich unterscheiden, abweichen *(from* von*).* **they ~ in price from the others** sie unterscheiden sich im Preis von den anderen; **opinions ~ on this point** in diesem Punkt gehen die Meinungen auseinander. **(b)** *(be different)* unterschiedlich sein. **the price varies from shop to shop** der Preis ist von Geschäft zu Geschäft verschieden. **(c)** *(change, fluctuate)* sich (ver)ändern; *(pressure, prices)* schwanken. **to ~ with the weather** sich nach dem Wetter richten. **2** *vt (alter)* verändern, abwandeln; *(give variety)* variieren.
varying ['vɛərɪɪŋ] *adj (changing)* veränderlich; *(different)* unterschiedlich. **with ~ degrees of success** mit unterschiedlichem Erfolg *m.*
vase [vɑːz, *(US)* veɪz] *n* Vase *f.*
vasectomy [væ'sektəmɪ] *n* Sterilisation *f (des Mannes).*
vaseline ® ['væsɪliːn] *n* Vaseline *f.*
vast [vɑːst] *adj (+er)* gewaltig, riesig; *knowledge* enorm; *majority* überwältigend. **a ~ expanse** eine weite Ebene.
vastly ['vɑːstlɪ] *adv* erheblich, bedeutend. **it is ~ different** da besteht ein erheblicher Unterschied.
vat [væt] *n* Faß *nt; (without lid)* Bottich *m.*
VAT ['viːeɪ'tiː, væt] *(Brit)* = **value-added tax** MwSt.
Vatican ['vætɪkən] *n* Vatikan *m.*
vault[1] [vɔːlt] *n* **(a)** *(cellar)* (Keller)gewölbe *nt; (tomb)* Gruft *f; (in bank)* Tresor(raum) *m.* **in the ~s** im Gewölbe *etc.* **(b)** *(Archit)* Gewölbe *nt.*
vault[2] **1** *n* Sprung *m.* **2** *vi* springen. **3** *vt* überspringen.
vaulted ['vɔːltɪd] *adj (Archit)* gewölbt.
vaunt [vɔːnt] *vt* rühmen, preisen *(geh).* **much-~ed** vielgepriesen.
VD = **venereal disease.**
VDU = **visual display unit.**
veal [viːl] *n* Kalbfleisch *nt.*
veer [vɪəʳ] *vi (wind)* (sich) drehen *(to* nach*); (ship)* abdrehen; *(car)* ausscheren; *(road)* scharf abbiegen. **to ~ off course** vom Kurs abkommen; **public opinion ~ed to the right** die öffentliche Meinung ist nach rechts geschwenkt.
vegetable ['vedʒɪtəbl] *n* **(a)** Gemüse *nt.* **cabbage is a ~** Kohl ist eine Gemüsepflanze. **(b)** *(generic term: plant)* Pflanze *f.* **(c) he's just a ~** er vegetiert nur vor sich hin; **she's become a ~** sie ist zum körperlichen und geistigen Krüppel geworden.
vegetable: ~ garden *n* Gemüsegarten *m;* **~ oil** *n* Pflanzenöl *nt.*
vegetarian [ˌvedʒɪ'tɛərɪən] **1** *n* Vegetarier(in *f*) *m.* **2** *adj* vegetarisch.
vegetate ['vedʒɪteɪt] *vi (fig)* dahinvegetieren.
vegetation [ˌvedʒɪ'teɪʃən] *n* Vegetation *f.*
vehemence ['viːɪməns] *n* Vehemenz *f (geh); (of actions, feelings, protests also)* Heftigkeit *f; (of love, hatred)* Leidenschaftlichkeit *f.*
vehement ['viːɪmənt] *adj* vehement *(geh); feelings, speech* leidenschaftlich; *attack, desire, dislike, opposition* heftig.
vehicle ['viːɪkl] *n* Fahrzeug *nt; (fig)* Mittel *nt.*
veil [veɪl] **1** *n* Schleier *m.* **to take the ~** ins Kloster gehen; **under a ~ of secrecy** unter dem Mantel der Verschwiegenheit. **2** *vt (lit, fig)* verschleiern; *feelings* verbergen. **the town was ~ed by mist** die Stadt lag in Nebel gehüllt.
veiled [veɪld] *adj reference* versteckt; *face* verschleiert.
vein [veɪn] *n (Anat, Bot, Min)* Ader *f; (fig: mood)* Stimmung, Laune *f.* **in a humorous ~** in lustiger Stimmung; **in the same ~** in derselben Art.
vellum ['veləm] *n* Pergament *nt.*
velocity [və'lɒsɪtɪ] *n* Geschwindigkeit *f.*
velvet ['velvɪt] **1** *n* Samt *m.* **2** *adj jacket* Samt-; *skin, feel* samtweich, samten *(geh).*
velveteen ['velvɪtiːn] *n* Veloursamt *m.*
velvety ['velvɪtɪ] *adj* samtig.
venal ['viːnl] *adj (liter) person* käuflich; *practices* korrupt.
vendetta [ven'detə] *n* Fehde *f; (in family)* Blutrache *f; (of gangsters)* Vendetta *f.* **to carry on**

a ~ against sb mit jdm in Fehde liegen/an jdm Blutrache üben.
vending machine ['vendɪŋmə'ʃiːn] n Automat *m*.
vendor ['vendɔːʳ] *n (esp Jur)* Verkäufer *m*.
veneer [və'nɪəʳ] *n (lit)* Furnier *nt*; *(fig)* Politur *f*; *(of civilization)* (An)schein *m*. **it's just a ~** es ist nur äußerer Schein.
venerable ['venərəbl] *adj* ehrwürdig.
venerate ['venəreɪt] *vt* verehren, hochachten; *sb's memory* ehren.
venereal disease [vɪ'nɪərɪəldɪ'ziːz] *n* Geschlechtskrankheit *f*.
Venetian blind [vɪ'niːʃən'blaɪnd] *n* Jalousie *f*.
Venezuela [ˌvene'zweɪlə] *n* Venezuela *nt*.
Venezuelan [ˌvene'zweɪlən] **1** *adj* venezolanisch. **2** *n* Venezolaner(in *f*) *m*.
vengeance ['vendʒəns] *n* **(a)** Vergeltung, Rache *f*. **to take ~ (up)on sb** Vergeltung an jdm üben. **(b)** *(col)* **with a ~** gewaltig *(col)*; **to work with a ~** hart *or* mächtig *(col)* arbeiten.
venial ['viːnɪəl] *adj* verzeihlich, entschuldbar.
Venice ['venɪs] *n* Venedig *nt*.
venison ['venɪsən] *n* Reh(fleisch) *nt*.
venom ['venəm] *n (lit)* Gift *nt*; *(fig)* Bosheit, Gehässigkeit *f*. **he spoke with real ~ in his voice** er sprach mit haßerfüllter Stimme.
venomous ['venəməs] *adj (lit, fig)* giftig; *snake* Gift-; *tone also* gehässig; *sarcasm* beißend.
vent [vent] **1** *n (for gas, liquid)* Öffnung *f*; *(in chimney)* Abzug *m*; *(in coat)* Schlitz *m*; *(for feelings)* Ventil *nt*. **to give ~ to sth** *(fig)* einer Sache *(dat)* Ausdruck verleihen; **to give ~ to one's feelings** seinen Gefühlen freien Lauf lassen. **2** *vt feelings, anger* abreagieren *(on an +dat)*.
ventilate ['ventɪleɪt] *vt (control air flow)* belüften; *(let fresh air in)* lüften.
ventilation [ˌventɪ'leɪʃən] *n see vt* Belüftung *f*; Lüften *nt*. **~ shaft** Luftschacht *m*.
ventilator ['ventɪleɪtəʳ] *n* Ventilator *m*.
ventriloquist [ven'trɪləkwɪst] *n* Bauchredner(in *f*) *m*.
venture ['ventʃəʳ] **1** *n* Unternehmen *nt*. **a new ~ in publishing** ein neuer verlegerischer Versuch; **this was a disastrous ~ for the company** dieses Projekt war für die Firma ein Fiasko.
2 *vt* **(a)** *life, reputation* aufs Spiel setzen; *money also* riskieren *(on* bei*)*. **nothing ~d nothing gained** *(Prov)* wer nicht wagt, der nicht gewinnt *(Prov)*. **(b)** *guess, explanation* wagen; *opinion* zu äußern wagen. **if I may ~ an opinion** wenn ich mir erlauben darf, meine Meinung zu sagen.
3 *vi* sich wagen. **to ~ out of doors** sich vor die Tür wagen; **the company ~d into a new field** die Firma wagte sich in ein neues Gebiet vor.
venue ['venjuː] *n (for event)* Schauplatz *m*; *(Sport)* Austragungsort *m*; *(Jur)* Verhandlungsort *m*.
Venus ['viːnəs] *n* Venus *f*.
veracity [və'ræsɪtɪ] *n (of report etc)* Richtigkeit *f*.
veranda(h) [və'rændə] *n* Veranda *f*.
verb [vɜːb] *n* Verb, Zeitwort *nt*.
verbal [vɜːbəl] *adj* mündlich; *error, skills* sprachlich.
verbally ['vɜːbəlɪ] *adv (spoken)* mündlich.
verbatim [vɜː'beɪtɪm] *adj, adv* (wort)wörtlich.
verbiage ['vɜːbɪɪdʒ] *n* Wortfülle *f*, Blabla *nt (col)*.
verbose [vɜː'bəʊs] *adj* wortreich, weitschweifig.
verdict ['vɜːdɪkt] *n* Urteil *nt*; *(of electors)* Entscheidung *f*. **~ of guilty/not guilty** Schuldspruch *m*/Freispruch *m*; **what's the ~?** wie lautet das Urteil?; **to give one's ~ about** *or* **on sth** sein Urteil über etw *(acc)* abgeben.
verge [vɜːdʒ] *n (lit, fig)* Rand *m*. **to be on the ~ of ruin/war** am Rande des Ruins/eines Krieges stehen; **to be on the ~ of a discovery** kurz vor einer Entdeckung stehen; **to be on the ~ of tears** den Tränen nahe sein; **to be on the ~ of doing sth** im Begriff sein, etw zu tun.
♦ **verge on** *vi +prep obj (ideas, actions)* grenzen an *(acc)*. **he's verging ~ bankruptcy** er steht kurz vor dem Bankrott; **she is verging ~ fifty** sie geht auf die Fünfzig zu.
verger ['vɜːdʒəʳ] *n (Eccl)* Küster *m*.
verifiable ['verɪfaɪəbl] *adj* nachprüfbar.
verification [ˌverɪfɪ'keɪʃən] *n (check)* Überprüfung *f*; *(confirmation)* Bestätigung *f*; *(proof)* Nachweis *m*.
verify ['verɪfaɪ] *vt (check)* (über)prüfen; *(confirm)* bestätigen; *theory* beweisen.
veritable ['verɪtəbl] *adj genius* wahr. **a ~ disaster** die reinste Katastrophe.
vermilion [və'mɪljən] *adj* zinnoberrot.
vermin ['vɜːmɪn] *n no pl (animal)* Schädling *m*; *(insects)* Ungeziefer *nt*; *(pej: people)* Pack *nt*.
vermouth ['vɜːməθ] *n* Vermut *m*.
vernacular [və'nækjʊləʳ] *n (dialect)* Mundart *f*; *(not official language)* Landessprache *f*.
versatile ['vɜːsətaɪl] *adj* vielseitig. **he has a very ~ mind** er ist geistig sehr flexibel.
versatility ['vɜːsə'tɪlɪtɪ] *n see adj* Vielseitigkeit *f*; Flexibilität *f*.
verse [vɜːs] *n* **(a)** *(stanza)* Strophe *f*. **(b)** *no pl (poetry)* Dichtung *f*. **in ~** in Versform. **(c)** *(of Bible, Koran)* Vers *m*.
versed [vɜːst] *adj (also* **well ~***)* bewandert, beschlagen *(in* in *+dat)*.
version ['vɜːʃən] *n* **(a)** *(account: of event, of facts)* Darstellung *f*. **(b)** *(variant)* Version *f*; *(of text also)* Fassung *f*; *(of car)* Modell *nt*.
versus ['vɜːsəs] *prep* gegen *(+acc)*.
vertebra ['vɜːtɪbrə] *n, pl* **-e** [-briː] Rückenwirbel *m*.
vertebrate ['vɜːtɪbrət] **1** *n* Wirbeltier *nt*. **2** *adj* Wirbel-.
vertex ['vɜːteks] *n, pl* **vertices** Scheitel(punkt) *m*.
vertical ['vɜːtɪkəl] **1** *adj line* senkrecht, vertikal. **~ cliffs** senkrecht abfallende Klippen; **~ take-off aircraft** Senkrechtstarter *m*. **2** *n (line)* Vertikale, Senkrechte *f*.
vertigo ['vɜːtɪgəʊ] *n* Schwindel *m*; *(Med)* Gleichgewichtsstörung *f*.
verve [vɜːv] *n* Schwung *m*.
very ['verɪ] **1** *adv* **(a)** *(extremely)* sehr. **that's not ~ funny** das ist überhaupt nicht lustig; **it's ~ possible** es ist gut möglich; **~ probably** höchstwahrscheinlich; **he is so ~ lazy** er ist *so* faul; **how ~ odd** wie eigenartig; **~ much** sehr; **I liked it ~ much** es hat mir sehr gut gefallen; **he doesn't work ~ much** er arbeitet nicht sehr viel; **~ much so** sehr (sogar).
(b) *(absolutely)* aller-. **~ best quality** allerbeste Qualität; **~ last/first** allerletzte(r, s)/allererste(r, s); **at the ~ latest** allerspätestens; **to do one's ~ best** sein Äußerstes tun; **at the ~ most/least** allerhöchstens/allerwenigstens.
(c) *(for emphasis)* **he fell ill and died the ~ same day** er wurde krank und starb noch am selben Tag; **he died the ~ same day as Kennedy** er starb genau am selben Tag wie Kennedy; **the ~ same hat** genau der gleiche Hut; **we met again the ~ next day** wir trafen uns am nächsten Tag schon wieder; **the ~ next day he walked under a bus** schon einen Tag später kam er unter einen Bus; **my ~ own car** mein eigenes Auto.
2 *adj* **(a)** *(precise)* genau. **that ~ day** genau an diesem Tag; **in the ~ centre of the picture** genau in der Mitte des Bildes; **at the ~ heart of the organization** direkt im Zentrum der Organisation; **those were his ~ words** genau das waren seine Worte; **you are the ~ person I want to speak to** mit *Ihnen* wollte ich sprechen; **the ~ thing!** genau das richtige!
(b) *(extreme)* äußerste(r, s). **in the ~ beginning/at the ~ end** ganz am Anfang/Ende; **at the ~ back/front** ganz hinten/vorn(e).
(c) *(mere)* **the ~ thought of it** allein schon der

Gedanke daran; **the ~ idea!** nein, so etwas!
vespers ['vespəz] *npl* Vesper *f.*
vessel ['vesl] *n* **(a)** *(Naut)* Schiff *nt.* **(b)** *(form: receptacle)* Gefäß *nt.*
vest[1] [vest] *n* **(a)** *(Brit)* Unterhemd *nt.* **(b)** *(US)* Weste *f.* **~-pocket** *adj (US)* Taschen-.
vest[2] *vt (form)* **to ~ sb with sth, to ~ sth in sb** jdm etw verleihen; **he has ~ed interests in the oil business** er ist (finanziell) am Ölgeschäft beteiligt; **he has a ~ed interest in the play** *(fig)* er hat ein persönliches Interesse an dem Stück.
vestibule ['vestɪbjuːl] *n* Vorhalle *f.*
vestige ['vestɪdʒ] *n* Spur *f.* **there is not a ~ of truth in what he says** es ist kein Körnchen Wahrheit an dem, was er sagt.
vestment ['vestmənt] *n* Ornat *m.*
vestry ['vestrɪ] *n* Sakristei *f.*
vet [vet] **1** *n* = **veterinary surgeon** Tierarzt *m*/-ärztin *f.* **2** *vt* überprüfen.
veteran ['vetərən] *n (Mil, fig)* Veteran(in *f*) *m.* **~ car** Oldtimer *m.*
veterinary ['vetərɪnərɪ] *adj medicine, science* Veterinär-; *training* tierärztlich. **~ surgeon** Tierarzt *m*/-ärztin *f.*
veto ['viːtəʊ] **1** *n, pl* **-es** Veto *nt.* **power of ~** Vetorecht *nt*; **to have a ~** das Vetorecht haben; **to use one's ~** von seinem Vetorecht Gebrauch machen. **2** *vt* sein Veto einlegen gegen.
vex [veks] *vt (annoy)* ärgern, irritieren; *animals* quälen. **to be ~ed with sb** mit jdm böse sein; **to be ~ed about sth** sich über etw *(acc)* ärgern.
vexation [vek'seɪʃən] *n* Ärger *m*; *(act)* Ärgern *nt*; *(of animal)* Quälerei *f.*
vexatious [vek'seɪʃəs] *adj* ärgerlich; *regulations, headache* lästig.
vexed [vekst] *adj* **(a)** *(annoyed)* verärgert. **(b)** *question* peinlich.
vexing ['veksɪŋ] *adj* irritierend; *problem* verzwickt.
VHF *(Rad)* = **very high frequency** UKW.
via ['vaɪə] *prep* über *(+acc)*. **they got in ~ the window** sie kamen durchs Fenster herein.
viability [ˌvaɪə'bɪlɪtɪ] *n* **(a)** *(of life forms)* Lebensfähigkeit *f.* **(b)** *(of plan)* Durchführbarkeit *f*; *(of firm)* Rentabilität *f.* **the ~ of the EEC** die Existenzfähigkeit der EG.
viable ['vaɪəbl] *adj* **(a)** *plant, foetus* lebensfähig. **(b)** *company* rentabel; *economy* lebensfähig; *suggestion* brauchbar; *plan* durchführbar. **not economically ~** unrentabel.
viaduct ['vaɪədʌkt] *n* Viadukt *m.*
vibrant ['vaɪbrənt] *adj personality etc* dynamisch; *voice* volltönend, sonor. **the ~ life of the city** das pulsierende Leben der Großstadt.
vibrate [vaɪ'breɪt] **1** *vi (lit, fig)* zittern, beben *(with* vor *+dat)*; *(machine, string, air)* vibrieren; *(notes)* schwingen. **2** *vt* zum Vibrieren bringen; *string* zum Schwingen bringen.
vibration [vaɪ'breɪʃən] *n (of string, sound waves)* Schwingung *f*; *(of machine)* Vibrieren *nt*; *(of voice, ground)* Beben *nt.* **I get good ~s from him** *(col)* er macht einen guten Eindruck auf mich.
vicar ['vɪkəʳ] *n* Pfarrer *m.*
vicarage ['vɪkərɪdʒ] *n* Pfarrhaus *nt.*
vicarious [vɪ'kɛərɪəs] *adj pleasure* indirekt, nachempfunden; *experience* ersatzweise.
vice[1] [vaɪs] *n* Laster *nt.* **his main ~ is laziness** sein größter Fehler ist die Faulheit; **~ squad** Sittenpolizei *f.*
vice[2], *(US)* **vise** *n* Schraubstock *m.* **to hold sth in a ~-like grip** etw fest umklammern.
vice- *pref* **~-chairman** *n* stellvertretender Vorsitzender; **~-chancellor** *n (Univ)* ≈ Rektor *m*; **~-president** *n* Vizepräsident *m.*
vice versa ['vaɪsɪ'vɜːsə] *adv* umgekehrt.
vicinity [vɪ'sɪnɪtɪ] *n* Umgebung *f.* **in the ~** in der Nähe *(of* von, *gen)*; **in the ~ of £500** um die £ 500.
vicious ['vɪʃəs] *adj* boshaft; *remark* gehässig; *habit* lasterhaft; *animal* bösartig; *dog* bissig; *blow, criminal, murder* brutal; *(col) headache* gemein *(col)*. **~ circle** Teufelskreis, Circulus vitiosus *m (geh)*.
vicissitude [vɪ'sɪsɪtjuːd] *n usu pl* Wandel *m.* **the ~s of life** die Wechselfälle des Lebens.
victim ['vɪktɪm] *n* Opfer *nt.* **he was the ~ of a practical joke** ihm wurde ein Streich gespielt; **to fall ~ to sth** Opfer einer Sache *(gen)* werden.
victimization [ˌvɪktɪmaɪ'zeɪʃən] *n see vt* ungerechte Behandlung; Schikanierung.
victimize ['vɪktɪmaɪz] *vt* ungerecht behandeln; *(pick on)* schikanieren. **she feels ~d** sie fühlt sich ungerecht behandelt.
victor ['vɪktəʳ] *n* Sieger(in *f*) *m.*
Victorian [vɪk'tɔːrɪən] **1** *n* Viktorianer(in *f*) *m.* **2** *adj* viktorianisch; *(fig)* (sitten)streng.
victorious [vɪk'tɔːrɪəs] *adj army* siegreich; *smile* siegesbewußt. **to be ~ over sb/sth** jdn/etw besiegen.
victory ['vɪktərɪ] *n* Sieg *m.* **to win a ~ over sb** einen Sieg über jdn erringen, jdn besiegen.
victuals ['vɪtlz] *npl* Lebensmittel *pl.*
video ['vɪdɪəʊ] **1** *n* **(a)** Video *nt.* **on ~** *see* als Video; *record* auf Video. **(b)** *(US TV)* Fernsehen *nt.* **on ~** im Fernsehen. **2** *vt* auf Video aufnehmen.
video: ~ cassette Videokassette *f*; **~-recorder** Videorecorder *m*; **~-recording** *n* Videoaufnahme *f*; **~tape** *n* Videoband *nt.*
vie [vaɪ] *vi* wetteifern; *(Comm)* konkurrieren. **to ~ with sb for sth** mit jdm um etw wetteifern.
Vienna [vɪ'enə] *n* Wien *nt.*
Viennese [ˌvɪə'niːz] **1** *adj* Wiener, wienerisch. **2** *n* Wiener(in *f*) *m.*
Vietnam [ˌvjet'næm] *n* Vietnam *nt.*
Vietnamese [ˌvjetnə'miːz] **1** *adj* vietnamesisch. **2** *n* **(a)** Vietnamese *m*, Vietnamesin *f.* **(b)** *(language)* Vietnamesisch *nt.*
view [vjuː] **1** *n (range of vision)* Sicht *f*; *(prospect, sight)* Aussicht *f.* **in full ~ of thousands of people** vor den Augen von Tausenden von Menschen; **the ship came into ~** das Schiff kam in Sicht; **to keep sth in ~** etw im Auge behalten; **the house is within ~ of the sea** vom Haus aus ist das Meer zu sehen; **hidden from ~** verborgen, versteckt; **on ~** *(for purchasing)* zur Ansicht; *(of exhibits)* ausgestellt; **there is a splendid ~ from here** von hier hat man einen herrlichen Blick; **a good ~ of the sea** ein schöner Blick auf das Meer; **a room with a ~** ein Zimmer mit schöner Aussicht; **an idealistic ~ of the world** eine idealistische Weltsicht; **a general ~ of a problem** ein allgemeiner Überblick über ein Problem; **in ~ of** angesichts *(+gen)*.

(b) *(photograph etc)* Ansicht *f.*

(c) *(opinion)* Ansicht, Meinung *f.* **in my ~** meiner Ansicht nach; **what are his ~s on this problem?** was meint er zu diesem Problem?; **I have no ~s on that** ich habe keine Meinung dazu; **to take the ~ that ...** die Ansicht vertreten, daß ...; **to take a poor ~ of sth** etw mißbilligen.

(d) *(intention, plan)* **to have sth in ~** etw beabsichtigen; **with a ~ to doing sth** mit der Absicht, etw zu tun.

2 *vt (see)* betrachten; *house* besichtigen; *(consider) problem etc* sehen. **he ~s the prospect with dismay** er sieht dieser Sache mit Schrecken entgegen.
viewer ['vjuːəʳ] *n* **(a)** *(TV)* Zuschauer(in *f*) *m.* **(b)** *(for slides)* Diabetrachter *m.*
view-finder ['vjuːˌfaɪndəʳ] *n* Sucher *m.*
viewpoint ['vjuːpɔɪnt] *n* Standpunkt *m.* **from the ~ of economic growth** unter dem Gesichtspunkt des Wirtschaftswachstums; **to see sth from sb's ~** etw aus jds Sicht *(dat)* sehen.
vigil ['vɪdʒɪl] *n* (Nacht)wache *f.* **to keep ~ over sb** bei jdm wachen.
vigilance ['vɪdʒɪləns] *n* Wachsamkeit *f.*

vigilant ['vɪdʒɪlənt] *adj* wachsam.
vigilante [ˌvɪdʒɪ'læntɪ] *n* ~**s** Bürgerwehr *f.*
vigorous ['vɪgərəs] *adj* kräftig; *prose, tune* kraftvoll; *protest, measures, exercises* energisch; *walk* forsch, flott.
vigour, *(US)* **vigor** [vɪgə^r] *n* Kraft, Energie *f*; *(of protest)* Heftigkeit *f*; *(of prose)* Ausdruckskraft *f.* **youthful** ~ jugendliche Spannkraft; **to speak with** ~ mit Nachdruck sprechen.
vile [vaɪl] *adj* abscheulich; *language also* unflätig; *weather, food also* scheußlich. **that was a** ~ **thing to say** es war gemein, so etwas zu sagen.
vilify ['vɪlɪfaɪ] *vt* diffamieren, verleumden.
villa ['vɪlə] *n* Villa *f.*
village ['vɪlɪdʒ] *n* Dorf *nt.*
village *in cpds* Dorf-; ~ **green** *n* Dorfwiese *f*; ~ **idiot** *n* Dorftrottel *m (col).*
villager ['vɪlɪdʒə^r] *n* Dorfbewohner(in *f*).
villain ['vɪlən] *n (scoundrel)* Schurke *m*; *(col: criminal)* Verbrecher, Ganove *(col) m*; *(in drama, novel)* Bösewicht *m.*
villainous ['vɪlənəs] *adj* böse; *deed* gemein.
villainy ['vɪlənɪ] *n* Gemeinheit *f.*
vindicate ['vɪndɪkeɪt] *vt* **(a)** *opinion, action* rechtfertigen. **(b)** *(from suspicion)* rehabilitieren.
vindication [ˌvɪndɪ'keɪʃən] *n see vt* **(a)** Rechtfertigung *f.* **in** ~ **of** zur Rechtfertigung *(+gen).* **(b)** Rehabilitation *f.*
vindictive [vɪn'dɪktɪv] *adj speech, person* rachsüchtig; *mood* unversöhnlich. **to feel** ~ **towards sb** Rachegefühle gegen jdn haben.
vine [vaɪn] *n (grapevine)* Rebe *f.*
vinegar ['vɪnɪgə^r] *n* Essig *m.*
vine: ~ **grower** *n* Weinbauer *m*; ~**-growing district** *n* Weinbaugebiet *nt*; ~ **harvest** *n* Weinlese *f*; ~**yard** ['vɪnjəd] *n* Weinberg *m.*
vintage ['vɪntɪdʒ] **1** *n* **(a)** *(of wine, fig)* Jahrgang *m*; *(of car)* Baujahr *nt.* **the 1972** ~ der Jahrgang 1972. **(b)** *(harvesting, season)* Weinlese *f.* **2** *adj attr (old)* uralt; *(high quality)* glänzend.
vintage: ~ **car** *n* Oldtimer *m*; ~ **wine** *n* edler Wein; ~ **year** *n*: **a** ~ **year for wine** ein besonders gutes Weinjahr.
vinyl ['vaɪnɪl] *n* Vinyl *nt.*
viola [vɪ'əʊlə] *n (Mus)* Bratsche *f.*
violate ['vaɪəleɪt] *vt* **(a)** *treaty, promise* brechen; *(partialiy)* verletzen; *law, rule* verstoßen gegen; *rights* verletzen. **(b)** *holy place* schänden; *peacefulness* stören. **to** ~ **sb's privacy** in jds Privatsphäre eindringen.
violation [ˌvaɪə'leɪʃən] *n* **(a)** *(of law, rule)* Verstoß *m (of* gegen*)*; *(of rights)* Verletzung *f.* **a** ~ **of a treaty** ein Vertragsbruch *m*; **he did this in** ~ **of the conditions agreed** er verstieß damit gegen die Vereinbarungen. **(b)** *(of holy place)* Schändung *f*; *(of peacefulness)* Störung *f.*
violence ['vaɪələns] *n* **(a)** *(forcefulness, strength)* Heftigkeit *f*; *(of protest also)* Schärfe *f.* **(b)** *(brutality)* Gewalt *f*; *(of people)* Gewalttätigkeit *f*; *(of actions)* Brutalität *f.* **act of** ~ Gewalttat *f*; **robbery with** ~ Raubüberfall *m*; **to use** ~ **against sb** Gewalt gegen jdn anwenden; **was there any** ~? kam es zu Gewalttätigkeiten?; **outbreak of** ~ Ausbruch von Gewalttätigkeiten; **to do** ~ **to sth** *(fig)* etw verletzen.
violent ['vaɪələnt] *adj person, action* brutal, gewalttätig; *feeling, speech* leidenschaftlich; *storm, dislike, attack, pain* heftig; *death* gewaltsam; *contrast* kraß. **to have a** ~ **temper** jähzornig sein; **to get** ~ gewalttätig werden.
violet ['vaɪəlɪt] **1** *n (Bot)* Veilchen *nt*; *(colour)* Violett *nt.* **2** *adj* violett.
violin [ˌvaɪə'lɪn] *n* Geige, Violine *f*; *(player)* Geiger(in *f*) *m.* ~ **case** Geigenkasten *m.*
violinist [ˌvaɪə'lɪnɪst] *n* Geiger(in *f*) *m.*
VIP *n* prominente Persönlichkeit, VIP *m.*
viper ['vaɪpə^r] *n (Zool)* Viper *f*; *(fig)* Schlange *f.*
virgin ['vɜːdʒɪn] **1** *n* Jungfrau *f.* **the (Blessed) V**~ *(Rel)* die (heilige) Jungfrau Maria; **he's still a** ~ er ist noch unschuldig. **2** *adj (fig) forest, snow* unberührt. ~ **birth** unbefleckte Empfängnis.
virginity [vɜː'dʒɪnɪtɪ] *n* Unschuld *f*; *(of girls also)* Jungfräulichkeit *f.*
Virgo ['vɜːgəʊ] *n (Astrol)* Jungfrau *f.*
virile ['vɪraɪl] *adj (lit)* männlich; *(fig)* kraftvoll.
virility [vɪ'rɪlɪtɪ] *n (lit)* Männlichkeit *f*; *(sexual power)* Potenz *f*; *(fig)* Ausdruckskraft *f.*
virtual ['vɜːtjʊəl] *adj attr* **he is the** ~ **leader** er ist praktisch der Führer; **it was a** ~ **disaster** es war geradezu eine Katastrophe.
virtually ['vɜːtjʊəlɪ] *adv* praktisch. **to be** ~ **certain** sich *(dat)* so gut wie sicher sein.
virtue ['vɜːtjuː] *n* **(a)** *(moral quality)* Tugend *f.* **a life of** ~ ein tugendhaftes Leben; **a woman of easy** ~ *(euph)* ein leichtes Mädchen. **(b)** *(advantage, point)* Vorteil *m.* **there is no** ~ **in doing that** es scheint nicht sehr zweckmäßig, das zu tun; **by** ~ **of** aufgrund *(+gen).*
virtuoso [ˌvɜːtjʊ'əʊzəʊ] *n (esp Mus)* Virtuose *m.*
virtuous *adj* ['vɜːtjʊəs] tugendhaft.
virulent ['vɪrʊlənt] *adj* **(a)** *(Med)* bösartig; *poison* stark, tödlich. **(b)** *(fig)* geharnischt, scharf.
virus ['vaɪərəs] *n (Med)* Virus, Erreger *m.*
visa ['viːzə] *n* Visum *nt.*
vis-à-vis ['viːzəviː] *prep* in bezug auf *(+acc).*
viscount ['vaɪkaʊnt] *n* Viscount *m.*
viscous ['vɪskəs] *adj* zähflüssig; *(Phys)* viskos.
vise [vaɪs] *n (US)* = **vice**[2].
visibility [ˌvɪzɪ'bɪlɪtɪ] *n* **(a)** Sichtbarkeit *f.* **(b)** *(Met)* Sichtweite *f.* **poor/good** ~ schlechte/gute Sicht; **low** ~ geringe Sichtweite.
visible ['vɪzəbl] *adj* sichtbar; *(obvious)* sichtlich. ~ **to the naked eye** mit dem bloßen Auge zu erkennen.
visibly ['vɪzəblɪ] *adv* sichtlich; *deteriorate* zusehends.
vision ['vɪʒən] *n* **(a)** *(power of sight)* Sehvermögen *nt.* **within the range of** ~ in Sichtweite. **(b)** *(foresight)* Weitblick *m.* **a man of** ~ ein Mann mit Weitblick. **(c)** *(in dream, trance)* Vision *f*; *(image)* Vorstellung *f.* **I had** ~**s of having to walk all the way home** *(col)* ich sah mich im Geiste schon den ganzen Weg nach Hause laufen.
visionary ['vɪʒənərɪ] **1** *adj (of visions)* vorhersehend; *(unreal)* eingebildet. **2** *n* Seher *m (geh).*
visit ['vɪzɪt] **1** *n* Besuch *m*; *(of doctor)* Hausbesuch *m*; *(of inspector)* Kontrolle *f*; *(stay also)* Aufenthalt *m.* **to pay sb/sth a** ~ jdn/etw besuchen; **to have a** ~ **from sb** von jdm besucht werden; **to be on a** ~ **to London** zu einem Besuch in London sein. **2** *vt* **(a)** *person, museum* besuchen. **3** *vi* **(a)** einen Besuch machen. **(b)** *(US col: chat)* ein Schwätzchen halten.
visiting: ~ **card** *n (Brit)* Visitenkarte *f*; ~ **hours** *npl* Besuchszeiten *pl*; ~ **team** *n* Gäste *pl.*
visitor ['vɪzɪtə^r] *n* Besucher(in *f*) *m*; *(in hotel)* Gast *m.* **to have** ~**s** *or* **a** ~ Besuch haben; ~**s' book** Gästebuch *nt.*
visor ['vaɪzə^r] *n (on helmet)* Visier *nt*; *(on cap)* Schirm *m*; *(Aut)* Blende *f.*
vista ['vɪstə] *n* Aussicht *f*, Blick *m.*
visual ['vɪzjʊəl] *adj field, nerve* Seh-; *memory, impression* visuell. ~ **aids** Anschauungsmaterial *nt*; ~ **display unit** Bildschirm(gerät *nt*) *m.*
visualize ['vɪzjʊəlaɪz] *vt (see in mind)* sich *(dat)* vorstellen; *(foresee)* erwarten.
visually ['vɪzjʊəlɪ] *adv* visuell. ~ **handicapped** sehbehindert.
vital ['vaɪtl] *adj* **(a)** *(of life)* vital, Lebens-; *(necessary for life)* lebenswichtig. ~ **force** Lebenskraft *f*; ~ **organs** lebenswichtige Organe *pl*; ~ **statistics** *(col: of woman)* Maße *pl.* **(b)** *(essential)* unerläßlich. **of** ~ **importance** von größter Wichtigkeit; **this is** ~ das ist unbedingt notwendig; **your support is** ~ **to us** wir brauchen unbedingt Ihre Unterstützung. **(c)** *(critical) error*

schwerwiegend; *problem* Kern-. **at the ~ moment** im entscheidenden Moment. **(d)** *(lively) person* vital; *artistic style also* lebendig.

vitality [vaɪ'tælɪtɪ] *n (energy)* Energie, Vitalität *f*; *(of prose)* Lebendigkeit *f*; *(of company)* Dynamik *f*.

vitally ['vaɪtəlɪ] *adv important* äußerst, ungeheuer.

vitamin ['vɪtəmɪn] *n* Vitamin *nt*.

vitriolic [ˌvɪtrɪ'ɒlɪk] *adj (fig) remark, criticism* beißend; *attack, speech* haßerfüllt.

vivacious [vɪ'veɪʃəs] *adj* lebhaft.

vivacity [vɪ'væsɪtɪ] *n* Lebhaftigkeit *f*.

vivid ['vɪvɪd] *adj light* hell; *colour* kräftig, lebhaft; *(lively) imagination* lebhaft; *description* lebendig; *emotions* stark. **the memory of that day is still ~** der Tag ist mir/uns *etc* noch in lebhafter Erinnerung.

vividness ['vɪvɪdnɪs] *n (of colour, imagination etc)* Lebhaftigkeit *f*; *(of light)* Helligkeit *f*; *(of description)* Lebendigkeit *f*.

vivisection [ˌvɪvɪ'sekʃən] *n* Vivisektion *f*.

vixen ['vɪksn] *n (Zool)* Füchsin *f*.

V-neck ['viːnek] *n* V-Ausschnitt *m*.

vocabulary [vəʊ'kæbjʊlərɪ] *n* Wortschatz *m*, Vokabular *nt (geh)*; *(in textbook)* Wörterverzeichnis *f*. **legal ~** juristisches Vokabular.

vocal ['vəʊkəl] **1** *adj* **(a)** Stimm-. **~ cords** Stimmbänder *pl*. **(b)** *(voicing one's opinions)* lautstark. **2** *n (of pop song)* (gesungener) Schlager.

vocalist ['vəʊkəlɪst] *n* Sänger(in *f*) *m*.

vocation [vəʊ'keɪʃən] *n (Rel etc)* Berufung *f*; *(form: profession)* Beruf *m*. **to have a ~ for teaching** zum Lehrer berufen sein.

vocational [vəʊ'keɪʃənl] *adj* Berufs-. **~ guidance** Berufsberatung *f*; **~ school** *(US)* ≈ Berufsschule *f*; **~ training** Berufsausbildung *f*.

vociferous [vəʊ'sɪfərəs] *adj* laut; *protest* lautstark.

vodka ['vɒdkə] *n* Wodka *m*.

vogue [vəʊg] *n* Mode *f*. **to be in ~** Mode sein; **~ word** Modewort *nt*.

voice [vɔɪs] **1** *n* **(a)** Stimme *f*. **to lose one's ~** die Stimme verlieren; **I've lost my ~** ich habe keine Stimme mehr; **to be in (good)/poor ~** gut/nicht gut bei Stimme sein; **in a deep ~** mit tiefer Stimme; **with one ~** einstimmig; **to give ~ to sth** einer Sache *(dat)* Ausdruck verleihen; **we have no ~ in the matter** wir haben in dieser Angelegenheit kein Mitspracherecht *nt*. **(b)** *(Gram)* **the active/passive ~** das Aktiv/Passiv. **2** *vt opinion* zum Ausdruck bringen.

void [vɔɪd] **1** *n (lit, fig)* Leere *f*. **2** *adj (empty)* leer; *(Jur)* ungültig, nichtig. **~ of hope** hoffnungslos.

volatile ['vɒlətaɪl] *adj* **(a)** *(Chem)* flüchtig. **(b)** *person* impulsiv; *political situation* brisant.

volcanic [vɒl'kænɪk] *adj dust* vulkanisch; *region, eruption* Vulkan-.

volcano [vɒl'keinəʊ] *n* Vulkan *m*.

vole [vəʊl] *n* Wühlmaus *f*; *(common ~)* Feldmaus *f*.

volition [vɒ'lɪʃən] *n* Wille *m*. **of one's own ~** aus freiem Willen.

volley ['vɒlɪ] *n* **(a)** *(of shots)* Salve *f*; *(of arrows, stones)* Hagel *m*; *(fig: of insults)* Flut *f*. **(b)** *(Tennis)* Volley, Flugball *m*.

volleyball ['vɒlɪˌbɔːl] *n* Volleyball *m*.

volt [vəʊlt] *n* Volt *nt*. **~ meter** Voltmeter *nt*.

voltage ['vəʊltɪdʒ] *n* Spannung *f*.

volte-face ['vɒlt'fɑːs] *n (fig)* Kehrtwendung *f*.

voluble ['vɒljʊbl] *adj speaker* redegewandt, redselig *(pej)*; *protest* wortreich.

volume ['vɒljuːm] *n* **(a)** Band *m*. **a six-~ dictionary** ein sechsbändiges Wörterbuch; **to write ~s** ganze Bände *pl* schreiben; **that speaks ~s** *(fig)* das spricht Bände *(for* über *+acc)*. **(b)** *(space occupied by sth)* Volumen *nt*. **(c)** *(size, amount)* Ausmaß *nt (of* an *+dat)*. **the ~ of traffic** das Verkehrsaufkommen; **trade has increased in ~** das Handelsvolumen hat sich vergrößert. **(d)** *(sound)* Lautstärke *f*. **turn the ~ up/down** *(Rad, TV)* stell (das Gerät) lauter/leiser; **~ control** *(Rad, TV)* Lautstärkeregler *m*.

voluminous [və'luːmɪnəs] *adj figure* üppig; *writings* umfangreich; *dress* wallend.

voluntarily ['vɒləntərɪlɪ] *adv* freiwillig.

voluntary ['vɒləntərɪ] *adj* freiwillig. **~ worker** freiwilliger Helfer, freiwillige Helferin; *(overseas)* Entwicklungshelfer(in *f*) *m*; **a ~ organization** ein freiwilliger Wohlfahrtsverband.

volunteer [ˌvɒlən'tɪəʳ] **1** *n (also Mil)* Freiwillige(r) *mf*. **any ~s?** wer meldet sich freiwillig? **2** *vt help* anbieten; *suggestion* machen; *information* geben. **3** *vi* **(a)** sich (freiwillig) melden. **to ~ for sth** sich freiwillig für etw zur Verfügung stellen; **to ~ to do sth** sich anbieten, etw zu tun. **(b)** *(Mil)* sich freiwillig melden *(for* zu, *for places* nach*)*.

voluptuous [və'lʌptjʊəs] *adj woman, movement* sinnlich; *curves* üppig.

vomit ['vɒmɪt] **1** *n* Erbrochene(s) *nt*. **2** *vt* erbrechen; *(fig)* spucken. **3** *vi* sich übergeben.

voracious [və'reɪʃəs] *adj person* gefräßig. **she is a ~ reader** sie verschlingt die Bücher geradezu; **to have a ~ appetite** einen Riesenappetit haben.

vortex ['vɔːteks] *n, pl* **-es** *or* **vortices** ['vɔːtɪsiːz] *(lit)* Wirbel, Strudel *(also fig) m*.

vote [vəʊt] **1** *n* Stimme *f f*; *(act of voting)* Abstimmung *f*; *(result)* Abstimmungsergebnis *nt*. **to put sth to the ~** über etw *(acc)* abstimmen lassen; **the Labour ~** die Labourstimmen *pl*; **to have the ~** das Wahlrecht haben. **2** *vti (elect)* wählen; *(approve)* bewilligen. **he was ~d chairman** er wurde zum Vorsitzenden gewählt; **to ~ Labour** Labour wählen; **to ~ for/against** für/gegen stimmen; **I ~ we leave now** ich schlage vor, daß wir jetzt gehen.

♦ **vote in** *vt sep law* beschließen; *person* wählen.

♦ **vote on** *vi +prep obj* abstimmen über *(+acc)*.

voter ['vəʊtəʳ] *n* Wähler(in *f*) *m*.

voting ['vəʊtɪŋ] *n* Wahl *f*. **~ booth** Wahlkabine *f*; **~ paper** Stimmzettel *m*.

vouch [vaʊtʃ] *vi* **to ~ for sb/sth** sich für jdn/etw verbürgen; *(legally)* für jdn/etw bürgen.

voucher ['vaʊtʃəʳ] *n* **(a)** *(for cash, petrol, meals)* Gutschein *m*; *(cigarette ~)* Coupon *m*. **(b)** *(receipt)* Beleg *m*; *(for debt)* Schuldschein *m*.

vow [vaʊ] **1** *n* Versprechen *nt*; *(Rel)* Gelübde *nt*. **to make a ~ to do sth** geloben, etw zu tun; **to take one's ~s** sein Gelübde ablegen. **2** *vt obedience* geloben.

vowel ['vaʊəl] *n* Vokal, Selbstlaut *m*.

voyage ['vɔɪɪdʒ] *n* Reise, Fahrt; *(by sea also)* Seereise *f*; *(Space also)* Flug *m*. **to go on a ~** auf eine Reise *etc* gehen; **the ~ out** die Hinreise/der Hinflug; **the ~ back** die Rückreise/der Rückflug; **~ of discovery** *(fig)* Entdeckungsreise *f*.

voyager ['vɔɪədʒəʳ] *n* Passagier *m*; *(Space)* Raumfahrer *m*.

vs = versus.

V-sign ['viːsaɪn] *n* **to give sb the ~** ≈ jdm den Vogel zeigen *(col)*.

vulgar ['vʌlgəʳ] *adj (pej)* ordinär; *(tasteless)* geschmacklos. **~ fraction** *(Math)* gemeiner Bruch.

vulgarity [vʌl'gærɪtɪ] *n* Vulgarität *f*; *(of gesture, joke also)* Anstößigkeit *f*; *(of colour etc)* Geschmacklosigkeit *f*.

vulnerable ['vʌlnərəbl] *adj* verwundbar; *(exposed)* verletzlich; *(fig)* verletzbar; *troops, fortress* ungeschützt. **to be ~ to temptation** für Versuchungen anfällig sein.

vulture ['vʌltʃəʳ] *n (lit, fig)* Geier *m*.

W

W, w ['dʌblju:] *n* W, w *nt.*
W = **west** W.
wad [wɒd] *n (compact mass)* Knäuel *m*; *(of cotton wool etc)* Bausch *m*; *(of papers, banknotes)* Bündel *nt.*
wadding ['wɒdɪŋ] *n (for packing)* Material *nt* zum Ausstopfen; *(Sew)* Wattierung *f.*
waddle ['wɒdl] *vi* watscheln.
wade [weɪd] **1** *vt* durchwaten. **2** *vi* waten. **to ~ into sb/sth** *(col: attack)* auf jdn losgehen/etw in Angriff nehmen; **they all ~d in and helped** sie halfen alle mit; **to ~ through a book** sich durch ein Buch kämpfen.
wader ['weɪdəʳ] *n* **(a)** *(Orn)* Watvogel *m.* **(b) ~s** *pl (boots)* Watstiefel *pl.*
wafer ['weɪfəʳ] *n* **(a)** *(biscuit)* Waffel *f.* **a vanilla ~** eine Vanilleeiswaffel. **(b)** *(Eccl)* Hostie *f.* **(c)** *(silicone~)* Wafer *f.*
wafer-thin ['weɪfə'θɪn] *adj* hauchdünn.
waffle[1] ['wɒfl] *n (Cook)* Waffel *f.*
waffle[2] *(Brit col)* **1** *n* Geschwafel *nt (col).* **2** *vi (also ~ on)* schwafeln *(col).*
waft [wɑ:ft] *vti* wehen. **a delicious smell ~ed up from the kitchen** ein köstlicher Geruch zog aus der Küche herauf.
wag[1] [wæg] **1** *n* **with a ~ of its tail** mit einem Schwanzwedeln. **2** *vt tail* wedeln mit; *(bird)* wippen mit. **to ~ one's finger at sb** jdm mit dem Finger drohen. **3** *vi (tail)* wedeln; *(of bird)* wippen. **that'll set the tongues ~ging** dann geht das Gerede los.
wag[2] *n (joker)* Witzbold *m (col).* **a bit of a ~** ein alter Witzbold.
wage[1] [weɪdʒ] *n usu pl* Lohn *m.*
wage[2] *vt war, campaign* führen.
wage *in cpds* Lohn-; **~ demand** *n* Lohnforderung *f*; **~ earner** *n* Lohnempfänger *m*; **~ freeze** *n* Lohnstopp *m*; **~ increase** *n* Lohnerhöhung *f*; **~ packet** *n* Lohntüte *f.*
wager ['weɪdʒəʳ] **1** *n* Wette *f (on* auf *+acc).* **to lay a ~** eine Wette abschließen. **2** *vti* wetten *(on* auf *+acc).*
waggle ['wægl] **1** *vt* wackeln mit; *tail* wedeln mit; *(bird)* wippen mit. **he ~d his finger at me disapprovingly** er drohte mir mißbilligend mit dem Finger. **2** *vi* wackeln; *(tail)* wedeln. **3** *n* **with a ~ of its tail** mit einem Schwanzwedeln.
waggon *(Brit),* **wagon** ['wægən] *n* **(a)** *(horse-drawn)* Wagen *m*; *(covered ~)* Planwagen *m*; *(US: delivery truck)* Lieferwagen *m*; *(US col: police car)* Streifenwagen *m*; *(US col: for transporting prisoners)* grüne Minna *(col).* **(b)** *(Brit Rail)* Waggon *m.* **(c)** *(col)* **I'm on the ~** ich trinke nichts.
wagtail ['wægteɪl] *n (Orn)* Bachstelze *f.*
waif [weɪf] *n* heimatloses Kind. **~s and strays** heimatlose Kinder *pl.*
wail [weɪl] **1** *n (of baby)* Geschrei *nt*; *(of mourner, music)* Klagen *nt*; *(of sirens, wind)* Heulen *nt*; *(col: complaint)* Gejammer *nt (col).* **2** *vi (baby, cat)* schreien; *(mourner, music)* klagen; *(sirens, wind)* heulen; *(col: complain)* jammern *(over* über *+acc).*
waist [weɪst] *n* Taille *f.* **stripped to the ~** mit nacktem Oberkörper.
waist: ~band *n (of trousers)* Hosenbund *m*; *(of dress)* Rockbund *m*; **~coat** *n (Brit)* Weste *f*; **~-deep** *adj* hüfthoch, bis zur Taille reichend; **we stood ~-deep in ...** wir standen bis zur Hüfte im ...; **~line** *n* Taille *f.*
wait [weɪt] **1** *vi* **(a)** warten *(for* auf *+acc).* **to ~ for sb to do sth** darauf warten, daß jd etw tut; **it was definitely worth ~ing for** es hat sich wirklich gelohnt, darauf zu warten; **well, what are you ~ing for?** worauf wartest du denn (noch)?; **let him ~!** laß ihn warten, soll er warten!; **this work will have to ~ till later** diese Arbeit muß bis später warten; **~ a minute** *or* **moment** (einen) Moment (mal); **(just) you ~!** warte nur ab!; *(threatening)* warte nur!; **I can't ~** ich kann's kaum erwarten; *(out of curiosity)* ich bin gespannt; **I can't ~ to see his face** da bin ich (aber) auf sein Gesicht gespannt. **(b) to ~ at table** servieren.

2 *vt* **to ~ one's turn** (ab)warten, bis man an der Reihe ist; **to ~ one's chance** eine günstige Gelegenheit abwarten; **to ~ dinner for sb** mit dem Essen auf jdn warten.

3 *n* **(a)** Wartezeit *f.* **did you have a long ~?** mußten Sie lange warten? **(b) to lie in ~ for sb/sth** jdm/einer Sache auflauern.
♦ **wait behind** *vi* zurückbleiben. **to ~ ~ for sb** zurückbleiben und auf jdn warten.
♦ **wait in** *vi* zu Hause bleiben *(for* wegen*).*
♦ **wait on** *vi +prep obj* **(a)** *(also ~* **upon***) (serve)* bedienen. **(b)** *(US)* **to ~ ~ table** servieren, bei Tisch bedienen.
♦ **wait up** *vi* aufbleiben *(for* wegen, für*).*
waiter ['weɪtəʳ] *n* Kellner, Ober *m.* **~!** (Herr) Ober!
waiting ['weɪtɪŋ] *n* Warten *nt.* **no ~** Halteverbot *nt.*
waiting: ~ game *n* Wartespiel *nt*; **to play a ~ game** ein Wartespiel spielen; **~ list** *n* Warteliste *f*; **~ room** *n* Warteraum *m*; *(at doctor's)* Wartezimmer *nt*; *(in station)* Wartesaal *m.*
waitress ['weɪtrɪs] *n* Kellnerin *f.* **~!** Fräulein!
waive [weɪv] *vt* **(a)** *rights, claim* verzichten auf *(+acc)*; *rule, age limit etc* außer acht lassen. **(b)** *(put aside, dismiss) question, objection* abtun.
waiver ['weɪvəʳ] *n (Jur)* Verzicht *m (of* auf *+acc)*; *(document)* Verzichterklärung *f*; *(of law, contract)* Außerkraftsetzung *f.*
wake[1] [weɪk] *n (Naut)* Kielwasser *nt.* **in the ~ of** *(fig)* nach; **to follow in sb's ~** in jds Kielwasser segeln; **X leaves Y in its ~** X hinterläßt Y; **to bring sth in its ~** etw mit sich bringen.
wake[2] *n (esp Ir: over corpse)* Totenwache *f.*
wake[3] *pret* **woke,** *ptp* **woken 1** *vt* wecken. **2** *vi* aufwachen. **he woke to find himself in prison** als er aufwachte, fand er sich im Gefängnis wieder.
♦ **wake up 1** *vi (lit, fig)* aufwachen. **to ~ ~ to sth** *(fig)* sich *(dat)* einer Sache *(gen)* bewußt werden. **2** *vt sep (lit)* aufwecken; *(fig: rouse from sloth)* aufrütteln. **to ~ sb ~ to sth** *(fig)* jdm etw bewußt machen; **to ~ one's ideas ~** sich zusammenreißen.
wakeful ['weɪkfʊl] *adj (sleepless)* schlaflos; *(alert)* wachsam.
waken ['weɪkən] *vt* (auf)wecken.
waking ['weɪkɪŋ] *adj* **to spend one's ~ hours doing sth** den (ganzen) Tag damit verbringen, etw zu tun.
Wales [weɪlz] *n* Wales *nt.*

walk [wɔːk] **1** *n* **(a)** *(stroll)* Spaziergang *m*; *(hike)* Wanderung *f*; *(charity ~)* Marsch *m (für Wohltätigkeitszwecke)*; *(signposted route)* Wanderweg *m*. **it's only 2 minutes' ~** es sind nur 2 Minuten zu Fuß; **it's a long/short ~ to the shops** zu den Läden ist es weit/nicht weit zu Fuß; **to go for a ~** einen Spaziergang machen; **to take sb/the dog for a ~** mit jdm/dem Hund spazierengehen; **there are some good ~s in the hills** in den Bergen gibt es einige gute Wandermöglichkeiten. **(b)** *(gait)* Gang *m*; *(of horse also)* Gangart *f*. **the horse went at a ~** das Pferd ging im Schritt. **(c) ~ of life** Milieu *nt*; **people from all ~s of life** Leute aus allen Schichten und Berufen. **(d)** *(US: Baseball)* Walk *m*, Freibase *nt*.

2 *vt* **(a)** *(lead) person, horse* (spazieren)führen; *dog* ausführen; *(ride at a ~)* im Schritt gehen lassen. **to ~ sb home/to the bus** jdn nach Hause/zum Bus bringen. **(b)** *distance* laufen, gehen. **I've ~ed this road many times** ich bin diese Straße oft gegangen. **(c) to ~ the streets** *(prostitute)* auf den Strich gehen *(col)*; *(in search of sth)* durch die Straßen irren; *(aimlessly)* durch die Straßen gehen; **let's ~ it** gehen wir doch zu Fuß.

3 *vi* **(a)** gehen, laufen. **~ a little with me** gehen Sie ein Stück mit mir; **to ~ in one's sleep** schlafwandeln. **(b)** *(not ride)* zu Fuß gehen, laufen *(col)*; *(stroll)* spazierengehen; *(hike)* wandern. **you can ~ there in 5 minutes** da ist man in 5 Minuten zu Fuß; **to ~ home** zu Fuß nach Hause gehen.

♦ **walk about** *or* **around** *vi* herumlaufen *(col)*. **to ~ ~ sth** um etw herumgehen; *(about room etc)* in etw *(dat)* herumgehen.

♦ **walk away** *vi* weggehen, davongehen. **he ~ed ~ from the crash unhurt** er ist bei dem Unfall ohne Verletzungen davongekommen; **to ~ ~ with a prize** *etc* einen Preis *etc* kassieren *(col)*.

♦ **walk in** *vi* herein-/hineinkommen; *(casually)* herein-/hineinspazieren *(col)*.

♦ **walk into** *vi +prep obj room* herein-/hineinkommen in *(+acc)*; *person* anrempeln; *wall* laufen gegen. **to ~ ~ sb** *(meet unexpectedly)* jdn zufällig treffen; **to ~ ~ a trap** in eine Falle gehen; **to ~ ~ a job** eine Stelle ohne Schwierigkeiten bekommen; **to ~ right ~ sth** *(lit)* mit voller Wucht gegen etw rennen; **you ~ed right ~ that one, didn't you?** da bist du aber ganz schön reingefallen *(col)*.

♦ **walk off 1** *vt sep* **to ~ ~ one's hangover** einen Spaziergang machen, um seinen Kater loszuwerden. **2** *vi* weggehen. **he ~ed ~ in the opposite direction** er ging in die andere Richtung davon.

♦ **walk off with** *vi +prep obj (col) (take) (unintentionally)* abziehen mit *(col)*; *(intentionally)* abhauen mit *(col)*; *(win easily) prize* kassieren *(col)*.

♦ **walk on** *vi* **(a)** *+prep obj grass etc* betreten. **(b)** *(continue walking)* weitergehen.

♦ **walk out** *vi* **(a)** *(quit)* gehen. **to ~ ~ of a meeting/room** eine Versammlung/einen Saal verlassen; **to ~ ~ on sb** jdn verlassen; *(let down)* jdn im Stich lassen; *on girlfriend etc* jdn sitzenlassen *(col)*; **to ~ ~ on sth** aus etw aussteigen *(col)*. **(b)** *(strike)* streiken, in Streik treten.

♦ **walk over** *vi +prep obj* **(a)** *(defeat)* in die Tasche stecken *(col)*. **(b) to ~ all ~ sb** *(col) (dominate)* jdn unterbuttern *(col)*; *(in competition, match etc)* jdn fertigmachen *(col)*.

♦ **walk up** *vi (go up, ascend)* (zu Fuß) hinaufgehen; *(approach)* zugehen *(to* auf *+acc)*. **a man ~ed ~ to me/her** ein Mann kam auf mich zu/ging auf sie zu; **~ ~!, ~ ~!** treten Sie näher!

walk: ~about *n* Rundgang *m*; **the Queen went (on a) ~about** die Königin machte ein Bad in der Menge; **~away** *n (US)* = **~over.**

walker ['wɔːkəʳ] *n (stroller)* Spaziergänger(in *f*) *m*; *(hiker)* Wanderer *m*, Wanderin *f*; *(Sport)* Geher(in *f*) *m*. **to be a fast ~** schnell gehen.

walkie-talkie ['wɔːkɪ'tɔːkɪ] *n* Walkie-talkie *nt*.

walking ['wɔːkɪŋ] **1** *n* Gehen *nt*; *(as recreation)* Spazierengehen *nt*; *(hiking)* Wandern *nt*. **we did a lot of ~ on holiday** in den Ferien sind wir viel gewandert. **2** *adj attr encyclopaedia, miracle etc* wandelnd; *doll* Lauf-. **at a ~ pace** im Schrittempo; **it's within ~ distance** dahin kann man zu Fuß gehen.

walking: ~ shoes *npl* Wanderschuhe *pl*; **~ stick** *n* Spazierstock *m*; **~ tour** *n* Wanderung *f*.

walk: ~-on *adj part, role* Statisten-; **~out** *n (strike)* Streik *m*; **to stage a ~out** *(from conference)* demonstrativ den Saal verlassen; **~over** *n (easy victory)* spielender Sieg; *(fig)* Kinderspiel *nt*; **~way** *n* Fußweg *m*; **a pedestrian ~way** ein Fuß(gänger)weg *m*.

wall [wɔːl] *n (outside)* Mauer *f*; *(inside, of mountain)* Wand *f*. **a ~ of fire** eine Feuerwand; **a ~ of policemen/troops** eine Mauer von Polizisten/Soldaten; **to go up the ~** *(col)* die Wände hochgehen *(col)*; **he drives me up the ~** *(col)* er bringt mich auf die Palme *(col)*; **to go to the ~** *(firm etc)* kaputtgehen *(col)*.

♦ **wall in** *vt sep* mit einer Mauer umgeben.

♦ **wall off** *vt sep (cut off)* durch eine Mauer (ab)trennen.

♦ **wall up** *vt sep* zumauern.

wallaby ['wɒləbɪ] *n* Wallaby *nt*.

wall: ~bars *npl* Sprossenwand *f*; **~ chart** *n* Wandkarte *f*.

walled [wɔːld] *adj* von Mauern umgeben.

wallet ['wɒlɪt] *n* Brieftasche *f*.

wall: ~flower *n (Bot)* Goldlack *m*; *(fig col)* Mauerblümchen *nt (col)*; **~ hanging** *n* Wandbehang *m*; **~ map** *n* Wandkarte *f*.

wallop ['wɒləp] *(col)* **1** *n (blow)* Schlag *m*. **to give sb/sth a ~** jdm/einer Sache einen Schlag versetzen. **2** *vt (hit)* schlagen; *(punish)* versohlen *(col)*.

walloping ['wɒləpɪŋ] *(col) n* Prügel *pl (col)*; *(defeat)* Schlappe *f*. **to give sb a ~** jdm eine Tracht Prügel geben *(col)*.

wallow ['wɒləʊ] *vi* **(a)** *(lit) (animal)* sich wälzen; *(boat)* rollen. **(b) to ~ in luxury/self-pity** *etc* im Luxus/Selbstmitleid *etc* schwelgen.

wall: ~paper 1 *n* Tapete *f*; **2** *vt* tapezieren; **~-to-~** *adj* **~-to-~ carpeting** Teppichboden *m*.

wally ['wɒlɪ] *n (Brit col)* Idiot *m*.

walnut ['wɔːlnʌt] *n (nut)* Walnuß *f*; *(tree, wood)* Nußbaum *m*.

walrus ['wɔːlrəs] *n* Walroß *nt*.

waltz [wɔːls] **1** *n* Walzer *m*. **2** *vi* **(a)** Walzer tanzen. **(b)** *(col: move, come etc)* walzen *(col)*. **he came ~ing up** er kam angetanzt *(col)*.

wan [wɒn] *adj* bleich; *light, smile, look* matt.

wand [wɒnd] *n (magic ~)* Zauberstab *m*.

wander ['wɒndəʳ] **1** *n* Spaziergang *m*; *(through town, park also)* Bummel *m*. **I'm going for a ~ around the shops** ich mache einen Ladenbummel.

2 *vt hills, world* durchstreifen *(geh)*. **to ~ the streets** durch die Straßen wandern.

3 *vi* **(a)** herumlaufen; *(more aimlessly)* umherwandern *(through, about* in *+dat)*; *(leisurely)* schlendern; *(to see the shops)* bummeln. **he ~ed over to speak to me** er kam zu mir herüber, um mit mir zu reden. **(b)** *(go off, stray)* **to ~ from the path** vom Wege abkommen; **he ~ed too near the edge of the cliff** er geriet zu nahe an den Rand des Abhangs. **(c)** *(fig: thoughts, eye)* schweifen, wandern. **to let one's mind ~** seine Gedanken schweifen lassen; **the old man's mind is beginning to ~ a bit** der alte Mann wird ein wenig wirr; **to ~ from** *or* **off a point/subject** von einem Punkt/vom Thema abschweifen *or* abkommen.

♦ **wander off** *vi* weggehen; *(col: leave)* allmählich gehen.
wanderer ['wɒndərəʳ] *n* Wandervogel *m.*
wandering ['wɒndərɪŋ] **1** *adj tribesman* umherziehend; *minstrel* fahrend; *thoughts* (ab)schweifend; *path* gewunden. **2** *n* **~s** *pl* Herumziehen *nt; (mental)* wirre Gedanken *pl.*
wanderlust ['wɒndəlʌst] *n* Fernweh *nt.*
wane [weɪn] **1** *n* **to be on the ~** *(fig)* im Schwinden sein. **2** *vi (moon)* abnehmen; *(fig) (influence, strength)* schwinden; *(reputation)* verblassen; *(daylight)* nachlassen.
wangle ['wæŋgl] *(col)* **1** *n* Schiebung *(col) f.* **2** *vt job, ticket etc* organisieren *(col),* verschaffen. **to ~ oneself/sb in** sich hineinmogeln *(col)*/jdn einschleusen *(col);* **he'll ~ it for you** er wird das schon für dich drehen *(col).*
wangler ['wæŋgləʳ] *n (col)* Schlawiner *m (col).*
wank [wæŋk] *vi (col!)* wichsen *(col!).*
wanly ['wɒnlɪ] *adv* matt.
want [wɒnt] **1** *n* **(a)** *(lack)* Mangel *m (of* an *+dat).* **for ~ of** aus Mangel an *(+dat);* **for ~ of anything better to do** weil es nichts anderes zu tun gibt/gab *etc;* **though it wasn't for ~ of trying** nicht, daß er sich/ich mich *etc* nicht bemüht hätte. **(b)** *(poverty)* Not *f.* **to be/live in ~** Not leiden. **(c)** *(need)* Bedürfnis *nt; (wish)* Wunsch *m.* **the farm supplied all their ~s** der Bauernhof versorgte sie mit allem Notwendigen; **to be in ~ of sth** etw benötigen; **to be in ~ of help/repair** Hilfe brauchen/reparaturbedürftig sein.
2 *vt* **(a)** *(wish, desire)* wollen. **to ~ to do sth** etw tun wollen; **I ~ you to come here** ich will *or (more polite)* möchte, daß du herkommst; **I ~ it done now** ich will/möchte das sofort erledigt haben; **I don't ~ you interfering** ich will nicht, daß Sie sich einmischen. **(b)** *(need, require)* brauchen. **you ~ to see a doctor** Sie sollten zum Arzt gehen; **you ~ to be careful!** *(col)* du mußt aufpassen; **it ~s cutting** es muß geschnitten werden; **that's all we ~ed!** *(iro col)* das hat uns gerade noch gefehlt!; **it only ~ed the police to turn up ...** das hätte gerade noch gefehlt, daß auch noch die Polizei anrückt ...; **"~ed"** „gesucht"; **he's a ~ed man** er wird (polizeilich) gesucht; **you're ~ed on the phone** Sie werden am Telefon verlangt.
3 *vi* **(a)** *(wish, desire)* wollen. **you can go if you ~ (to)** wenn du willst, kannst du gehen; **I don't ~ to** ich will *or (more polite)* möchte nicht. **(b) he does not ~ for friends** es fehlt *or* mangelt *(geh)* ihm nicht an Freunden; **they ~ for nothing** es fehlt ihnen an nichts.
wanting ['wɒntɪŋ] *adj* fehlend. **humour is ~ in the novel** diesem Roman fehlt es an Humor; **he is ~ in confidence** es fehlt *or* mangelt *(geh)* ihm an Selbstvertrauen; **his courage/the new engine was found ~** sein Mut war nicht groß genug/der neue Motor hat sich als unzulänglich erwiesen; **he was tried and found ~** er konnte sich nicht bewähren.
wanton ['wɒntən] *adj* **(a)** *(licentious) life* liederlich; *behaviour, woman, pleasures* schamlos; *looks, thoughts* lüstern. **(b)** *(wilful) cruelty* mutwillig; *disregard, waste* sträflich.
war [wɔːʳ] **1** *n* Krieg *m.* **this is ~!** *(fig)* das bedeutet Krieg!; **the ~ against poverty** der Kampf gegen die Armut; **~ of nerves** Nervenkrieg *m;* **~ of words** Wortgefecht *nt;* **to be at ~** sich im Krieg(szustand) befinden; **to declare ~** den Krieg erklären *(on dat); (fig also)* den Kampf ansagen *(on dat);* **to make** *or* **wage ~** Krieg führen *(on, against* gegen*);* **he/this car has been in the ~s a bit** er/dieses Auto sieht ziemlich mitgenommen aus. **2** *vi* sich bekriegen; *(fig)* ringen *(geh) (for* um*).*
warble ['wɔːbl] *vti* trällern.
warbler ['wɔːbləʳ] *n (Orn)* Grasmücke *f; (wood~)* Waldsänger *m.*
war cry *n* Kriegsruf *m; (fig)* Schlachtruf *m.*
ward [wɔːd] *n* **(a)** *(part of hospital)* Station *f; (room) (small)* Krankenzimmer *nt; (large)* Krankensaal *m.* **(b)** *(Jur: person)* Mündel *nt.* **~ of court** Mündel unter Amtsvormundschaft. **(c)** *(Admin)* Stadtbezirk *m; (election~)* Wahlbezirk *m.*
♦ **ward off** *vt sep attack, blow, person* abwehren; *danger also* abwenden; *depression* nicht aufkommen lassen.
war dance *n* Kriegstanz *m.*
warden ['wɔːdn] *n (of youth hostel)* Herbergsvater *m,* Herbergsmutter *f; (game ~)* Jagdaufseher *m; (traffic ~)* Verkehrspolizist *m,* ≈ Politesse *f; (of museum etc)* Aufseher *m; (Univ)* Heimleiter(in *f*) *m; (of Oxbridge college)* Rektor *m; (US: of prison)* Gefängnisdirektor *m.*
warder ['wɔːdəʳ] *n (Brit)* Wärter, Aufseher *m.*
wardress ['wɔːdrɪs] *n (Brit)* Wärterin, Aufseherin *f.*
wardrobe ['wɔːdrəʊb] *n* **(a)** *(cupboard)* Kleiderschrank *m.* **(b)** *(clothes)* Garderobe *f.* **(c)** *(Theat) (clothes)* Kostüme *pl; (room)* Kleiderkammer *f.*
wardroom ['wɔːdruːm] *n (Naut)* Offiziersmesse *f.*
-ward(s) [-wəd(z)] *adv suf* -wärts. **town~** in Richtung Stadt.
warehouse ['wɛəhaʊs] *n* Lager(haus) *nt.*
wares [wɛəz] *npl* Waren *pl.*
warfare ['wɔːfɛəʳ] *n* Krieg *m; (techniques)* Kriegskunst *f.*
war: ~ game *n* Kriegsspiel *nt;* **~head** *n* Sprengkopf *m;* **~horse** *n (lit, fig)* Schlachtroß *nt.*
warily ['wɛərɪlɪ] *adv* vorsichtig; *(suspiciously)* mißtrauisch, argwöhnisch. **to tread ~** *(lit, fig)* sich vorsehen.
wariness ['wɛərɪnɪs] *n* Vorsicht *f; (mistrust)* Mißtrauen *nt (of* gegenüber*).*
warlike ['wɔːlaɪk] *adj* kriegerisch; *tone* militant.
warm [wɔːm] **1** *adj (+er)* **(a)** warm. **I am** *or* **feel ~** mir ist warm. **(b)** *(in games)* **am I ~?** ist es (hier) warm?; **you're getting ~** es wird schon wärmer. **(c)** *(hearty) person, welcome* herzlich, warm. **(d)** *(heated) dispute, words* hitzig. **2** *n* **we were glad to get into the ~** wir waren froh, daß wir ins Warme kamen; **to give sth a ~** etw wärmen. **3** *vt* wärmen. **it ~s my heart to ...** mir wird (es) ganz warm ums Herz, wenn ... **4** *vi* **the milk was ~ing on the stove** die Milch wurde auf dem Herd erwärmt; **I ~ed to him** er wurde mir sympathischer; **to ~ to one's work** sich mit seiner Arbeit anfreunden.
♦ **warm up 1** *vi (lit, fig)* warm werden; *(party, game, speaker)* in Schwung kommen; *(Sport)* sich aufwärmen. **things are ~ing ~** es kommt Schwung in die Sache; *(becoming dangerous)* es wird allmählich brenzlig *(col).* **2** *vt sep engine* warmlaufen lassen; *food etc* aufwärmen; *(fig) party* in Schwung bringen; *audience* in Stimmung bringen.
warm-blooded ['wɔːm'blʌdɪd] *adj* warmblütig; *(fig)* heißblütig. **~ animal** Warmblüter *m.*
warm front *n (Met)* Warm(luft)front *f.*
warm-hearted ['wɔːm'hɑːtɪd] *adj person* warmherzig; *gesture* großzügig.
warmly ['wɔːmlɪ] *adv* warm; *welcome* herzlich; *recommend* wärmstens. **we ~ welcome it** wir begrüßen es sehr.
war: ~monger ['wɔːˌmʌŋgəʳ] *n* Kriegshetzer *m;* **~mongering** ['wɔːˌmʌŋgərɪŋ] **1** *adj* kriegshetzerisch; **2** *n* Kriegshetze *f.*
warmth [wɔːmθ] *n (lit, fig)* Wärme *f; (of welcome)* Herzlichkeit *f.*
warm-up ['wɔːmʌp] *n (Sport)* Aufwärmen *nt.*
warn [wɔːn] *vt* warnen *(of, about, against* vor *+dat); (police, judge etc)* verwarnen. **to ~ sb not to do sth** jdn davor warnen, etw zu tun; **be ~ed** sei gewarnt!; **he had ~ed me off** er hatte mich davor gewarnt; **she ~ed us not to be late** sie ermahnte uns, nicht zu spät zu kommen; **to ~ sb**

that ... *(inform)* jdn darauf hinweisen, daß ...
warning ['wɔːnɪŋ] **1** *n* Warnung *f*; *(from police, judge etc)* Verwarnung *f*. **without ~** unerwartet, ohne Vorwarnung; **to give sb a ~** jdn warnen; *(police, judge etc)* jdn verwarnen; **let this be a ~ to you** lassen Sie sich *(dat)* das eine Warnung sein!; **to give sb due ~** *(inform)* jdm rechtzeitig Bescheid sagen. **2** *adj* Warn-; *look, tone* warnend. **a ~ sign** ein erstes Anzeichen; *(signboard etc)* ein Warnzeichen *nt*/-schild *nt*.
warp [wɔːp] **1** *n (in weaving)* Kette *f*; *(in wood etc)* Welle *f*. **2** *vt wood* wellen; *character* entstellen; *judgement* verzerren. **3** *vi (wood)* sich wellen, sich verziehen.
war: **~paint** *n (lit, fig col)* Kriegsbemalung *f*; **~path** *n* Kriegspfad *m*; **on the ~path** auf dem Kriegspfad.
warped [wɔːpt] *adj* **(a)** *(lit)* wellig. **(b)** *(fig) sense of humour* abartig; *character also* verbogen; *judgement* verzerrt.
war plane *n* Kampfflugzeug *nt*.
warrant ['wɒrənt] **1** *n (Comm)* Garantie *f*; *(Mil)* Patent *nt*; *(search ~)* Durchsuchungsbefehl *m*; *(death ~)* Hinrichtungsbefehl *m*. **there is a ~ out for his arrest** gegen ihn ist Haftbefehl erlassen worden *(Jur)*. **2** *vt* **(a)** *(justify) action etc* rechtfertigen. **to ~ sb doing sth** jdn dazu berechtigen, etw zu tun. **(b)** *(merit)* verdienen. **(c)** *(guarantee)* gewährleisten. **it'll work, I ~ you that** es funktioniert, das garantiere ich Ihnen.
warranty ['wɒrəntɪ] *n (Comm)* Garantie *f*. **it's still under ~** darauf ist noch Garantie.
warren ['wɒrən] *n (rabbit ~)* Kaninchenbau *m*; *(fig)* Labyrinth *nt*.
warring ['wɔːrɪŋ] *adj nations* kriegführend; *interests* gegensätzlich; *factions* sich bekriegend.
warrior ['wɒrɪə^r] *n* Krieger *m*.
Warsaw ['wɔːsɔː] *n* Warschau *nt*. **~ Pact** Warschauer Pakt *m*.
warship ['wɔːʃɪp] *n* Kriegsschiff *nt*.
wart [wɔːt] *n* Warze *f*. **~s and all** *(hum col)* mit allen seinen/ihren *etc* Fehlern.
wart-hog ['wɔːthɒg] *n* Warzenschwein *nt*.
wartime ['wɔːtaɪm] **1** *n* Kriegszeit *f*. **in ~** in Kriegszeiten. **2** *adj* Kriegs-. **in ~ England** in England während des Krieges.
wary ['wɛərɪ] *adj (+er)* vorsichtig; *(looking and planning ahead)* umsichtig, klug; *look* mißtrauisch. **to be ~ of sb/sth** vor jdm/einer Sache auf der Hut sein; **to be ~ about doing sth** seine Zweifel haben, ob man etw tun soll.
was [wɒz] *1st, 3rd pers sing pret of* **be**.
wash [wɒʃ] **1** *n* **(a)** *(act of ~ing)* **sth needs a ~** etw muß gewaschen werden; **I need a ~** ich muß mich waschen; **to give sb/sth a (good) ~** jdn/etw (gründlich) waschen; **to have a ~** sich waschen. **(b)** *(laundry)* Wäsche *f*. **to be in the ~** in der Wäsche sein; **it will all come out in the ~** *(fig col) (become known)* es wird schon alles rauskommen; *(work out)* es wird sich schon noch alles regeln. **(c)** *(of ship)* Kielwasser *nt*.

2 *vt* **(a)** waschen; *dishes* spülen; *floor* aufwischen; *hands etc* sich *(dat)* waschen. **to ~ one's hands of sb/sth** mit jdm/etw nichts mehr zu tun haben wollen; **I ~ my hands of it** ich wasche meine Hände in Unschuld; **to ~ sth clean** etw reinwaschen. **(b)** *(sea etc)* umspülen; *cliffs etc* schlagen gegen; *(carry)* spülen. **it was ~ed ashore** es wurde an Land gespült.

3 *vi* **(a)** *(have a ~)* sich waschen. **(b) a material that ~es well/won't ~** ein Stoff, der sich gut wäscht/den man nicht waschen kann; **that excuse won't ~** *(Brit fig col)* diese Entschuldigung kauft dir keiner ab! *(col)*. **(c) the sea ~ed over the promenade** das Meer überspülte die Strandpromenade.
♦ **wash away** *vt sep* (hin)wegspülen. **to ~ ~ sb's sins** jdn von seinen Sünden reinwaschen.
♦ **wash down** *vt sep (clean)* abwaschen; *meal* hinunterspülen.
♦ **wash off** **1** *vi (stain, dirt)* sich herauswaschen lassen. **most of the pattern has ~ed ~** das Muster ist fast ganz verwaschen. **2** *vt sep* abwaschen.
♦ **wash out** **1** *vi* sich auswaschen lassen. **2** *vt sep (clean)* auswaschen; *mouth* ausspülen.
♦ **wash up** **1** *vi* **(a)** *(Brit: clean dishes)* abwaschen, spülen. **(b)** *(US: have a wash)* sich waschen. **2** *vt sep* **(a)** *(Brit) dishes* spülen. **(b)** *(sea etc)* anspülen.
washable ['wɒʃəbl] *adj* waschbar; *wallpaper* abwaschbar.
wash: **~ basin** *n* Waschbecken *nt*; **~ bowl** *n* Waschschüssel *f*; *(in unit)* Waschbecken *nt*; **~ cloth** *n (US)* Waschlappen *m*; **~day** *n* Waschtag *m*.
washed out ['wɒʃt'aʊt] *adj (col)* erledigt *(col)*, schlapp *(col)*. **to look ~** mitgenommen aussehen.
washer ['wɒʃə^r] *n* **(a)** *(Tech)* Dichtung(sring *m*) *f*. **(b)** *(clothes ~)* Waschmaschine *f*; *(dish~)* (Geschirr)spülmaschine *f*.
washhand basin ['wɒʃ,hænd,beɪsn] *n* Handwaschbecken *nt*.
washing ['wɒʃɪŋ] *n* Waschen *nt*; *(clothes)* Wäsche *f*. **to do the ~** Wäsche waschen.
washing: **~ machine** *n* Waschmaschine *f*; **~ powder** *n (Brit)* Waschpulver *nt*; **~-up** *n (Brit)* Abwasch *m*; **to do the ~-up** spülen, den Abwasch machen; **~-up bowl** *n* Spülschüssel *f*; **~-up liquid** *n (Brit)* Spülmittel *nt*.
wash: **~ leather** *n* Waschleder *nt*; **~out** *n (col)* Reinfall *m (col)*; *(person)* Flasche *(col)*, Niete *(col) f*; **~ room** *n* Waschraum *m*.
wasn't ['wɒznt] = **was not**.
wasp [wɒsp] *n* Wespe *f*.
waspish ['wɒspɪʃ] *adj* giftig.
wastage ['weɪstɪdʒ] *n* Schwund *m*; *(action)* Verschwendung *f*; *(amount also)* Materialverlust *m*; *(from container also)* Verlust *m*; *(unusable products etc also)* Abfall *m*.
waste [weɪst] **1** *adj (superfluous)* überschüssig, überflüssig; *(left over)* ungenutzt; *land* brachliegend. **to lay ~** verwüsten; **to lie ~** brachliegen.

2 *n* **(a)** Verschwendung *f*; *(unusable materials)* Abfall *m*. **it's a ~ of time/money** es ist Zeit-/Geldverschwendung; **it's a ~ of effort** das ist nicht der Mühe wert; **to go to ~** *(food)* umkommen; *(money, land, talent)* ungenutzt sein/bleiben, brachliegen. **(b)** *(~ material)* Abfallstoffe *pl*; *(rubbish)* Abfall *m*. **radioactive ~** Atommüll *m*. **(c)** *(land, expanse)* Wildnis *no pl*, Einöde *f*.

3 *vt* verschwenden *(on* an *+acc*, für*)*; *life, time* vergeuden; *opportunity* vertun. **you're wasting your time** das ist reine Zeitverschwendung; **don't ~ my time** stiehl mir nicht meine Zeit; **you didn't ~ much time, did you?** *(col)* das ging aber schnell!; **Beethoven/she is ~d on him** Beethoven ist an den vergeudet/sie ist zu schade für ihn.

4 *vi (food)* umkommen; *(skills)* verkümmern; *(body)* verfallen; *(strength, assets)* schwinden. **~ not, want not** *(Prov)* spare in der Zeit, so hast du in der Not *(Prov)*.
♦ **waste away** *vi (physically)* dahinschwinden *(geh)*, immer weniger werden *(col)*.
waste: **~-bin** *n (Brit)* Abfalleimer *m*; **~ disposal** *n* Müllbeseitigung *f*; **~ disposal unit** *n* Müllschlucker *m*.
wasteful ['weɪstfʊl] *adj* verschwenderisch; *method, process* unwirtschaftlich. **to be ~ with sth** verschwenderisch mit etw umgehen.
waste: **~land** *n* Ödland *nt*; *(fig)* Einöde *f*; **~paper** *n* Papierabfall *m*; *(for recycling)* Altpapier *nt*; **~paper basket** *n (Brit)* Papierkorb *m*; **~ pipe** *n* Abflußrohr *nt*; **~ product** *n* Abfallprodukt *nt*.
waster ['weɪstə^r] *n* **(a) it's a real time-/money-~**

das ist wirklich Zeit-/Geldverschwendung. **(b)** *(good-for-nothing)* Taugenichts *m.*

watch[1] [wɒtʃ] *n* (Armband)uhr *f.*

watch[2] **1** *n* **(a) to be on the ~ for sb/sth** nach jdm/etw Ausschau halten; **to keep ~** Wache halten; **to keep a close ~ on sb/sth** jdn/etw scharf bewachen; **to keep ~ over sb/sth** bei jdm/etw Wache halten; **to set a ~ on sb/sth** jdn/etw überwachen lassen. **(b)** *(period of duty, Naut, people)* Wache *f*; *(people also)* Wachmannschaft *f.* **to be on ~** Wache haben; **officer of the ~** wachhabender Offizier.

2 *vt* **(a)** *(guard)* aufpassen auf *(+acc)*; *(police etc)* überwachen.

(b) *(observe)* beobachten; *match* zusehen *or* zuschauen bei; *film, play, TV programme* sich *(dat)* ansehen. **to ~ TV** fernsehen; **to ~ sb doing sth** jdm bei etw zuschauen; **I ~ed her coming down the street** ich habe sie beobachtet, wie sie die Straße entlang kam; **~ the road in front of you** guck *or* achte auf die Straße!; **~ this!** paß auf!; **we are being ~ed** wir werden beobachtet; **a new actor to be ~ed** ein Nachwuchsschauspieler, den man im Auge behalten sollte.

(c) *(be careful of)* achten auf *(+acc)*, aufpassen auf *(+acc)*. **(you'd better) ~ it!** *(col)* paß (bloß) auf! *(col)*; **~ your manners/language!** bitte benimm dich!/drück dich bitte etwas gepflegter aus!; **~ how you drive, the roads are icy** paß beim Fahren auf, die Straßen sind vereist!

3 *vi (observe)* zusehen, zuschauen. **to ~ for sb/sth** nach jdm/etw Ausschau halten.

♦ **watch out** *vi* **(a)** *(look carefully)* Ausschau halten *(for sb/sth* nach jdm/etw*)*. **(b)** *(be careful)* aufpassen, achtgeben *(for* auf *+acc)*. **~ ~!** Achtung!; **~ ~ for him, he's crafty** nimm dich vor ihm in acht, er ist gerissen.

♦ **watch over** *vi +prep obj* wachen über *(+acc)*.

watchdog ['wɒtʃdɒg] *n (lit)* Wachhund *m*; *(fig)* Aufpasser *(col)*.

watcher ['wɒtʃəʳ] *n* Schaulustige(r) *mf*; *(observer)* Beobachter(in *f*) *m.*

watchful ['wɒtʃfʊl] *adj* wachsam. **to be ~ for** wachsam Ausschau halten nach.

watchfulness ['wɒtʃfʊlnɪs] *n* Wachsamkeit *f.*

watch: ~maker *n* Uhrmacher *m*; **~man** *n (night-~ etc)* (Nacht)wächter *m*; **~strap** *n* Uhrarmband *nt*; **~ tower** *n* Wachtturm *m*; **~word** *n* Parole *f.*

water ['wɔːtəʳ] **1** *n* Wasser *nt.* **the field is under ~** das Feld steht unter Wasser; **to make ~** *(ship)* lecken; **in American ~s** in amerikanischen Hoheitsgewässern; **by ~** auf dem Wasserweg; **to make** *or* **pass ~** Wasser lassen; **to drink** *or* **take the ~s** eine Kur machen; **a lot of ~ has flowed under the bridge since then** *(fig)* seitdem ist viel Wasser den Bach hinuntergeflossen; **to stay above ~** *(fig)* sich über Wasser halten; **to pour cold ~ on sb's idea** jds Vorschlag miesmachen *(col)*; **to get into deep ~(s)** *(fig)* ins Schwimmen kommen; **to hold ~** *(lit)* wasserdicht sein; **that argument won't hold ~** *(col)* dieses Argument ist nicht hieb- und stichfest *(col)*; **to be in/get into hot ~** *(fig col)* in Teufels Küche sein/geraten *(col)* *(over* wegen *+gen)*; **to spend money like ~** *(col)* mit dem Geld nur so um sich werfen *(col)*.

2 *vt* **(a)** *garden* sprengen; *field* bewässern; *plant* (be)gießen. **(b)** *horses, cattle* tränken.

3 *vi (mouth)* wässern; *(eye)* tränen. **the smoke made his eyes ~** ihm tränten die Augen vom Rauch; **my mouth ~ed** mir lief das Wasser im Mund zusammen; **to make sb's mouth ~** jdm den Mund wässerig machen.

♦ **water down** *vt sep (lit, fig pej)* verwässern; *(fig also)* abschwächen; *liquids* verdünnen.

water: ~bed *n* Wasserbett *nt*; **~-bottle** *n* Wasserflasche *f*; *(for troops etc)* Feldflasche *f*; **~ cannon** *n* Wasserwerfer *m*; **~ closet** *n (abbr* **WC***)* Wasserklosett *nt*; **~colour** *(Brit)*, **~color** *(US)* **1** *n* Wasserfarbe, Aquarellfarbe *f*; *(picture)* Aquarell *nt*; **2** *attr* Aquarell-; **~-cooled** *adj* wassergekühlt; **~course** *n (stream)* Wasserlauf *m*; *(bed)* Flußbett *nt*; *(artificial)* Kanal *m*; **~cress** *n* (Brunnen)kresse *f*; **~fall** *n* Wasserfall *m*; **~front 1** *n* Hafenviertel *nt*; **we drove along the ~front/down to the ~front** wir fuhren am Wasser entlang/hinunter zum Wasser; **2** *attr* am Wasser.

watering can ['wɔːtərɪŋˌkæn] *n* Gießkanne *f.*

water: ~ level *n* Wasserstand *m*; *(of river etc also)* Pegelstand *m*; **~lily** *n* Seerose *f*; **~line** *n* Wasserlinie *f*; **~logged** *adj* **the fields are ~logged** die Felder stehen unter Wasser; **the ship was completely ~logged** das Schiff war voll Wasser gelaufen; **~ main** *n* Haupt(wasser)leitung *f*; **~mark** *n* **(a)** *(on wall)* Wasserstandsmarke *f*; **(b)** *(on paper)* Wasserzeichen *nt*; **~melon** *n* Wassermelone *f*; **~-pistol** *n* Wasserpistole *f*; **~-polo** *n* Wasserball *nt*; **~-power** *n* Wasserkraft *f*; **~proof 1** *adj* wasserdicht; *paint* wasserfest; **2** *n (esp Brit)* Regenhaut ® *f*; **3** *vt* wasserundurchlässig machen; **~ rat** *n* Wasserratte *f*; **~shed** *n (Geol)* Wasserscheide *f*; *(fig)* Wendepunkt *m*; **~side 1** *n* Ufer *nt*; *(at sea)* Strand *m*; **2** *attr* am Wasser wachsend/lebend *etc*; **~-ski** *vi* Wasserski laufen; **~-skiing** *n* Wasserskilaufen *nt*; **~ supply** *n* Wasserversorgung *f*; **~table** *n* Grundwasserspiegel *m*; **~tight** *adj (lit)* wasserdicht; *(fig) argument etc also* hieb- und stichfest; **~-tower** *n* Wasserturm *m*; **~ vapour** *(Brit) or* **vapor** *(US)* *n* Wasserdampf *m*; **~way** *n* Wasserstraße *f*; *(channel)* Fahrrinne *f*; **~-wheel** *n (Mech)* Wasserrad *nt*; *(Agr)* Wasserschöpfrad *nt*; **~-wings** *npl* Schwimmflügel *pl*; **~works** *npl or sing* Wasserwerk *nt*; **to turn on the ~works** *(fig col)* zu heulen anfangen; **to have trouble with one's ~works** *(fig col)* ständig laufen müssen *(col)*.

watery ['wɔːtərɪ] *adj soup, colour* wäßrig; *eye* tränend; *(pale) sky* blaß.

watt [wɒt] *n* Watt *nt.*

wave [weɪv] **1** *n* **(a)** *(of water, Phys, Rad, in hair, fig)* Welle *f.* **a ~ of strikes/enthusiasm** eine Streikwelle/Welle der Begeisterung; **the new ~** *(Mus, Film)* die Neue Welle. **(b)** *(movement of hand)* **to give sb a ~** jdm (zu)winken; **with a ~ of his hand** mit einer Handbewegung.

2 *vt* **(a)** *(as a sign or greeting)* winken mit *(at, to sb* jdm*)*; *(~ about)* schwenken. **to ~ one's hand to sb** jdm winken; **to ~ goodbye to sb** jdm zum Abschied winken; **she ~d her umbrella threateningly at him** sie schwang drohend ihren Schirm nach ihm; **he ~d his fist at the intruders** er drohte den Eindringlingen mit der Faust; **he ~d me over** er winkte mich zu sich herüber. **(b)** *hair* wellen.

3 *vi* **(a)** winken. **to ~ at** *or* **to sb** jdm winken; *(greeting)* jdm zuwinken. **(b)** *(flag)* wehen; *(branches)* sich hin und her bewegen; *(corn)* wogen. **(c)** *(hair)* sich wellen.

♦ **wave around** *vt sep* herumfuchteln mit.

♦ **wave aside** *vt sep (lit) person* zur Seite winken; *(fig) person, objection etc* zurückweisen; *help also* ausschlagen.

♦ **wave away** *vt sep* wegwinken.

♦ **wave on** *vt sep* **the policeman ~d us ~** der Polizist winkte uns weiter.

wave: ~band *n (Rad)* Wellenband *nt*; **~length** *n (Rad, fig)* Wellenlänge *f*; **we're not on the same ~length** *(fig)* wir haben nicht dieselbe Wellenlänge.

waver ['weɪvəʳ] *vi* **(a)** *(light, flame, eyes)* flackern; *(voice)* zittern. **(b)** *(courage, self-assurance)* ins Wanken geraten; *(support)* nachlassen. **(c)**

(hesitate) schwanken *(between* zwischen *+dat).*

wavy ['weɪvɪ] *adj (+er) hair, surface* wellig, gewellt. **~ line** Schlangenlinie *f.*

wax[1] [wæks] **1** *n* Wachs *nt; (ear~)* Ohrenschmalz *nt; (sealing ~)* Siegellack *m.* **2** *adj* Wachs-. **3** *vt* wachsen; *floor also* bohnern.

wax[2] *vi* **(a)** *(moon)* zunehmen. **to ~ and wane** *(lit)* ab- und zunehmen; *(fig)* schwanken. **(b)** *(liter: become)* werden. **to ~ enthusiastic** in Begeisterung geraten.

wax(ed) paper *n* Wachspapier *nt.*

wax: ~ work *n* Wachsfigur *f;* **~ works** *n sing or pl* Wachsfigurenkabinett *nt.*

waxy ['wæksɪ] *adj (+er)* wächsern.

way [weɪ] **1** *n* **(a)** *(road)* Weg *m.* **across** *or* **over the ~** gegenüber, vis-à-vis; *(motion)* rüber; **to fall by the ~** *(fig)* auf der Strecke bleiben.

(b) *(route)* Weg *m.* **the ~ to the station** der Weg zum Bahnhof; **by ~ of** *(via)* über *(+acc);* **which is the ~ to the town hall, please?** wo geht es hier zum Rathaus, bitte?; **~ in/out** *(also on signs)* Ein-/Ausgang *m;* **can you find your own ~ out?** finden Sie selbst hinaus?; **on the ~ out/in** beim Hinaus-/Hereingehen; **to be on the ~ in** *(fig col)* im Kommen sein; **to be on the ~ out** *(fig col)* am Verschwinden sein; **there's no ~ out** *(fig)* es gibt keinen Ausweg; **~ up/down** Weg nach oben/ unten; *(climbing)* Aufstieg/Abstieg *m;* **~ up/back** Hinweg/Rückweg *m;* **prices are on the ~ up/ down** die Preise steigen/fallen; **the shop is on the ~** der Laden liegt auf dem Weg; **to stop on the ~** unterwegs anhalten; **on the ~ to London** auf dem Weg nach London; **he's on the ~ to becoming an alcoholic** er ist auf dem besten Weg, Alkoholiker zu werden; **we had to go out of our ~** wir mußten einen Umweg machen; **to go out of one's ~ to do sth** *(fig)* sich *(dat)* die Mühe machen, etw zu tun; **to feel one's ~** sich weiter-/vorwärts-/ entlangtasten; **I know my ~ about town** ich finde mich in der Stadt zurecht; **she knows her ~ about** *(fig col)* sie kennt sich aus, sie weiß Bescheid *(col);* **to lose one's ~** sich verlaufen; *(driving)* sich verfahren; **to make one's ~ to somewhere** sich an einen Ort begeben; **can you make your own ~ to the theatre?** kannst du allein zum Theater kommen?; **to make one's ~ home** nach Hause gehen; *(start)* sich auf den Heimweg begeben; **to push one's ~ through the crowd** sich durch die Menge drängen; **to make one's ~ in the world** seinen Weg machen; **to go one's own ~** *(fig)* eigene Wege gehen; **they went their separate ~s** *(lit, fig)* ihre Wege trennten sich; **to pay one's ~** für sich selbst bezahlen; *(company, machine)* sich rentieren; **the ~ forward** der Weg vorwärts; **to go down the wrong ~** *(food, drink)* in die falsche Kehle kommen; **to prepare the ~** *(fig)* den Weg bereiten *(for sb/ sth* jdm/einer Sache*);* **could you see your ~ to lending me a pound?** wäre es Ihnen wohl möglich, mir ein Pfund zu leihen?; **to get under ~** in Gang kommen; *(Naut)* Fahrt aufnehmen *or* machen; **to be (well) under ~** im Gang/in vollem Gang sein; *(Naut)* in (voller) Fahrt sein; *(with indication of place)* unterwegs sein.

(c) *(room for movement, path)* Weg *m.* **to block the ~** den Weg versperren; **to leave the ~ open** *(fig)* einen Weg frei lassen *(for sth* für etw*);* **to make ~ for sb/sth** *(lit, fig)* für jdn/etw Platz machen; **to be in sb's ~** jdm im Weg sein; **to get in sb's ~** sich jdm in den Weg stellen; **it's in the ~ there** es ist dort im Weg; **I don't want to get in your ~ when you're working** ich will dich nicht beim Arbeiten stören; **to get sth out of the ~** *(move)* etw aus dem Weg räumen; *problem also, work* etw hinter sich *(acc)* bringen; **get out of the/my ~!** weg da!; **to keep out of sb's/the ~** *(not get in the ~)* (jdm) aus dem Weg bleiben; *(avoid)* (jdm) aus dem Weg gehen; **to put difficulties in sb's ~** jdm Hindernisse in den Weg stellen; **to stand in sb's ~** *(lit, fig)* jdm im Weg sein.

(d) *(direction)* Richtung *f.* **this ~, please** hier entlang, bitte; **he went that ~** er ging in diese Richtung; **this ~ and that** hierhin und dorthin; **which ~ are you going?** in welche Richtung gehen Sie?; **she didn't know which ~ to look** *(fig)* sie wußte nicht, wo sie hinsehen sollte; **to look the other ~** *(fig)* wegsehen; **this one is better, there are no two ~s about it** *(col)* dieses hier ist besser, da gibt es gar keinen Zweifel; **it does not matter (to me) one ~ or the other** es ist mir gleich; **either ~, we're bound to lose** (so oder so,) wir verlieren auf jeden Fall; **it's the wrong ~ up** es steht verkehrt herum; **"this ~ up"** „hier oben"; **it's the other ~ around** es ist (genau) umgekehrt.

(e) *(distance)* Weg *m,* Strecke *f.* **it rained all the ~ there** es hat auf der ganzen Strecke (über) geregnet; **I'm behind you all the ~** *(fig)* ich stehe voll (und ganz) hinter Ihnen; **a little/long ~ off** nicht/sehr weit entfernt; **that's a long ~ back** *(in time)* das war schon vor einer ganzen Weile; **he'll go a long ~** *(fig)* er wird es weit bringen; **to have (still) a long ~ to go** (noch) weit vom Ziel entfernt sein; *(with practice)* (noch) viel vor sich haben; **it should go some/a long ~ towards solving the problem** das sollte bei dem Problem schon etwas/ein gutes Stück weiterhelfen; **a little kindness goes a long ~** ein bißchen Freundlichkeit hilft viel; **not by a long ~** bei weitem nicht.

(f) *(method, manners)* Art, Weise *f.* **do it this ~** machen Sie es so; **it's not the right ~ to do it** so kann man das nicht machen; **what's the best ~ to do it?** wie macht man das am besten?; **you could tell by the ~ he was dressed** das merkte man schon an seiner Kleidung; **the ~ she walks/talks** (so) wie sie geht/spricht; **do you remember the ~ it was?** erinnerst du dich noch (daran), wie es war?; **to show sb the ~ to do sth** jdm zeigen, wie *or* auf welche Art und Weise etw gemacht wird; **to do sth the hard ~** etw auf die schwierige Art (und Weise) machen; **to learn the hard ~** aus dem eigenen Schaden lernen; **we'll find a ~** wir werden (schon) einen Weg finden; **I'd rather do it my ~** ich möchte es lieber auf meine (eigene) Art machen; **that's his ~ of saying thank-you** das ist seine Art, sich zu bedanken; **~s and means** Mittel und Wege; **~ of life** Lebensstil *m; (of nation)* Lebensart *f;* **~ of thinking** Denk(ungs)art *f;* **to my ~ of thinking** meiner Meinung *or* Auffassung nach; **a funny ~ of talking** eine komische Art, sich auszudrücken; **there are many ~s of solving the problem** es gibt viele Wege, das Problem zu lösen; **that's the ~ it goes!** so ist das eben, so ist das nun mal; **the ~ things are** so, wie die Dinge liegen; **in one ~ or another** so oder so, irgendwie; **to get** *or* **have one's (own) ~** seinen Willen durchsetzen; **have it your own ~!** wie du willst!; **you can't have it both ~s** beides zugleich geht nicht; **what a ~ to speak!** so spricht man doch nicht!; **the ~s of the Spaniards** die spanische Lebensweise; **the ~ of the world** der Lauf der Dinge; **he has a ~ with children** er versteht es, mit Kindern umzugehen.; **to get out of/into the ~ of sth** sich *(dat)* etw ab-/ angewöhnen.

(g) *(respect)* Hinsicht *f.* **in a ~** in gewisser Hinsicht *or* Weise; **in no ~** in keiner Weise; **no ~!** ausgeschlossen!; **there's no ~ I'm going to agree** ich werde auf keinen Fall zustimmen; **what have you got in the ~ of drink?** was haben Sie an Getränken?; **in every possible ~** auf jede mögliche *or* denkbare Art; **in many/some ~s** in vieler/gewisser Hinsicht; **in a big ~** *(not petty)* im großen Stil; *(on a large scale)* im großen; **in the ordinary ~ we ...** normalerweise ... wir ...

(h) *(state)* Zustand *m.* **he's in a bad ~** er ist in schlechter Verfassung; **things are in a bad ~** die Dinge stehen schlecht.

(i) *(with by)* **by the ~** übrigens; **all this is by the ~** *(irrelevant)* das ist alles nebensächlich; *(extra)* das nur nebenbei; **by ~ of an answer/excuse** als Antwort/Entschuldigung; **by ~ of illustration** zur Illustration.

2 *adv (col)* **~ back/up** weit zurück/oben; **~ back when** vor langer Zeit, als; **since ~ back** seit Urzeiten; **that was ~ back** das ist schon lange her; **his guess was ~ out** seine Annahme war weit gefehlt.

way: ~bill *n* Frachtbrief *m*; **~farer** ['weɪˌfɛərəʳ] *n (liter)* Wanderer *m*; **~lay** *pret, ptp* **~laid** *vt (ambush)* überfallen; *(col)* abfangen; **~-out** *adj (col)* irre *(col)*; **~side 1** *n (of path, track)* Wegrand *m*; *(of road)* Straßenrand *m*; **by the ~side** am Weges-/Straßenrand; **to fall by the ~side** auf der Strecke bleiben; **2** *adj café, inn* am Weg/an der Straße gelegen; **~ward** ['weɪwəd] *adj (self-willed)* eigenwillig; *(capricious)* abwegig.

WC = water closet WC *nt.*

we [wiː] *pron* wir.

weak [wiːk] *adj (+er)* schwach; *character* labil; *tea, solution etc* dünn; *stomach* empfindlich. **the ~er sex** das schwache Geschlecht; **he must be a bit ~ in the head** *(col)* er ist wohl nicht ganz bei Trost *(col).*

weaken ['wiːkən] **1** *vt (lit, fig)* schwächen; *control etc* verringern; *foundations* angreifen; *hold* lockern. **2** *vi (lit, fig)* schwächer werden, nachlassen; *(person)* schwach werden; *(foundations)* nachgeben; *(defence, strength also)* erlahmen. **his grip on my arm ~ed** er hielt meinen Arm nicht mehr ganz so fest.

weak-kneed ['wiːk'niːd] *adj (fig col)* schwach, feige.

weakling ['wiːklɪŋ] *n* Schwächling *m.*

weakly ['wiːklɪ] **1** *adj (dated)* schwächlich. **2** *adv* schwach.

weakness ['wiːknɪs] *n* Schwäche *f*; *(weak point)* schwacher Punkt. **to have a ~ for sth** eine Schwäche für etw haben.

weak-willed ['wiːk'wɪld] *adj* willensschwach.

weal [wiːl] *n (welt)* Striemen *m.*

wealth [welθ] *n* **(a)** Reichtum *m.* **~ tax** Vermögenssteuer *f.* **(b)** *(fig: abundance)* Fülle *f (of* von*).*

wealthy ['welθɪ] *adj (+er)* wohlhabend, reich. **the ~** *pl* die Reichen *pl.*

wean [wiːn] *vt baby* entwöhnen. **to ~ sb from sth** jdn einer Sache *(gen)* entwöhnen *(geh).*

weapon ['wepən] *n (lit, fig)* Waffe *f.*

wear [wɛəʳ] *(vb: pret* **wore,** *ptp* **worn***)* **1** *n* **(a)** *(use)* **I've had a lot of ~ out of this jacket** ich habe diese Jacke viel getragen; **there isn't much ~ left in this carpet** dieser Teppich hält nicht mehr lange; **for casual/evening/everyday ~** für die Freizeit/den Abend/jeden Tag. **(b)** *(clothing)* Kleidung *f.* **(c) ~ and tear** Abnutzung *f*, Verschleiß *m*; **fair ~ and tear** normale Abnutzungserscheinungen; **to show signs of ~** *(lit)* anfangen, alt auszusehen; *(fig)* angegriffen aussehen; **to look the worse for ~** *(lit) (clothes, curtains etc)* verschlissen aussehen; *(clothes)* abgetragen aussehen; *(furniture etc)* abgenutzt aussehen; *(fig)* verbraucht aussehen; **I felt a bit the worse for ~** ich fühlte mich etwas angegriffen.

2 *vt* **(a)** *clothing, jewellery etc* tragen. **what shall I ~?** was soll ich anziehen?; **I haven't a thing to ~!** ich habe nichts anzuziehen. **(b)** *(~ down, ~ out)* abnutzen; *clothes* abtragen; *sleeve etc* durchwetzen; *steps* austreten; *tyres* abfahren; *engine* kaputtmachen. **to ~ holes in sth** etw durchwetzen; *(in shoes)* etw durchlaufen; **to ~ smooth** *(by handling)* abgreifen; *(by walking)* austreten; *rocks* glätten. **(c)** *(col: accept, tolerate)* schlucken *(col).*

3 *vi* **(a)** *(last)* halten; *(dress, shoes etc also)* sich tragen. **she has worn well** *(col)* sie hat sich gut gehalten *(col)*; **the theory has worn well** die Theorie hat sich bewährt. **(b)** *(become worn)* kaputtgehen; *(engine, material also)* sich abnutzen, verbraucht sein; *(tyres also)* abgefahren sein. **to have worn smooth** *(by water)* glattgewaschen sein; *(by weather)* verwittert sein; *(pattern)* abgegriffen sein; **to ~ thin** *(lit)* dünn werden; **my patience is ~ing thin** meine Geduld geht langsam zu Ende.

♦ **wear away 1** *vt sep (erode) steps* austreten; *rock* abschleifen, abtragen; *(hollow out)* aushöhlen; *inscription* tilgen *(geh)*, verwischen; *(fig) determination* untergraben. **2** *vi (rocks, rough edges etc)* sich abschleifen; *(inscription)* verwittern; *(pattern)* verwischen; *(fig: patience etc)* schwinden.

♦ **wear down 1** *vt sep* **(a)** *(reduce by friction)* abnutzen; *heel* ablaufen, abtreten; *tyre tread* abfahren. **(b)** *(fig) person, opposition etc* zermürben. **2** *vi* sich abnutzen; *(heels)* sich abtreten; *(tyre tread)* sich abfahren.

♦ **wear off** *vi* **(a)** *(diminish)* nachlassen. **the novelty has worn ~** der Reiz des Neuen ist vorbei; **don't worry, it'll ~ ~!** keine Sorge, das gibt sich. **(b)** *(paint)* abgehen; *(plating, gilt)* sich abwetzen.

♦ **wear on** *vi* sich hinziehen; *(year)* voranschreiten. **as the evening/year** *etc* **wore ~** im Laufe des Abends/Jahres *etc.*

♦ **wear out 1** *vt sep* **(a)** kaputtmachen; *carpet also* abtreten; *clothes, shoes* kaputttragen; *record, machinery* abnutzen. **(b)** *(exhaust) (physically)* erschöpfen, erledigen *(col)*; *(mentally)* fertigmachen *(col).* **to be worn ~** erschöpft *or* erledigt sein; *(mentally)* am Ende sein *(col)*; **to ~ oneself ~** sich überanstrengen, sich kaputtmachen *(col).* **2** *vi* kaputtgehen; *(clothes, carpets also)* verschleißen. **his patience is rapidly ~ing ~** seine Geduld erschöpft sich zusehends.

♦ **wear through 1** *vt sep* durchwetzen; *soles of shoes* durchlaufen. **2** *vi* sich durchwetzen; *(soles of shoes)* sich durchlaufen.

weariness ['wɪərɪnɪs] *n see adj (a)* Müdigkeit *f*; Lustlosigkeit *f*; Mattheit *f.*

wearing ['wɛərɪŋ] *adj* anstrengend.

wearisome ['wɪərɪsəm] *adj* ermüdend; *(bothersome) questions* lästig; *(tedious) discussion* langweilig.

weary ['wɪərɪ] **1** *adj (+er)* **(a)** *(tired)* müde; *(fed up)* lustlos; *smile, groan* matt. **to feel ~** müde sein; **to be/grow ~ of sth** etw leid sein/werden. **(b)** *(tiring)* ermüdend. **for three ~ hours** drei endlose Stunden (lang). **2** *vt* ermüden. **3** *vi* **to ~ of sth** einer Sache *(gen)* müde werden *(geh).*

weasel ['wiːzl] *n* Wiesel *nt.*

weather ['weðəʳ] **1** *n* Wetter *nt.* **in cold/this ~** bei kaltem/diesem Wetter; **what's the ~ like?** wie ist das Wetter?; **in all ~s** bei jedem Wetter; **to be** *or* **feel under the ~** *(col)* angeschlagen sein *(col)*; **to make heavy ~ of sth** *(col)* sich mit etw fürchterlich anstellen *(col).* **2** *vt* **(a)** *(storms, winds etc)* angreifen. **(b)** *(survive: also* **~ out***) crisis etc* überstehen. **to ~ (out) the storm** *(fig)* den Sturm überstehen. **3** *vi (rock etc)* verwittern; *(paint etc)* verblassen.

weather *in cpds* Wetter; **~-beaten** *adj face* vom Wetter gegerbt; *house* verwittert; *skin* wettergegerbt; **~cock** *n* Wetterhahn *m.*

weathered ['weðəd] *adj* verwittert; *skin* wettergegerbt.

weather: ~ forecast *n* Wettervorhersage *f*; **~man** *n* Mann *m* vom Wetteramt; **~proof** *adj* wetterfest; **~ report** *n* Wetterbericht *m*; **~ vane** *n* Wetterfahne *f.*

weave [wiːv] *(vb: pret* **wove,** *ptp* **woven)** **1** *n (pattern of threads)* Webart *f*; *(fabric)* Gewebe *nt*. **2** *vt* **(a)** *cloth etc* weben *(into* zu); *cane, flowers* flechten *(into* zu); *web* spinnen. **(b)** *(fig) plot* ersinnen, erfinden; *details* einflechten *(into* in *+acc)*. **(c)** *(pret also* **~d)** **to ~ one's way through the traffic** sich durch den Verkehr schlängeln. **3** *vi* **(a)** *(lit)* weben. **(b)** *(pret also* **~d)** *(twist and turn)* sich schlängeln. **to ~ in and out through the traffic** sich durch den Verkehr schlängeln. **(c)** *(col)* **to get weaving** sich ranhalten *(col)*.
weaver ['wiːvəʳ] *n* Weber(in *f*) *m*.
weaving ['wiːvɪŋ] *n* Weberei *f*; *(as craft)* Webkunst *f*.
web [web] *n (lit, fig)* Netz *nt*; *(of lies also)* Gespinst, Gewebe *nt*.
webbed [webd] *adj foot* Schwimm-.
webbing ['webɪŋ] *n* Gurte *pl*; *(material)* Gurtband *nt*.
wed [wed] *(old, form) pret, ptp* **~** *or* **~ded** **1** *vi* sich vermählen *(form)*, trauen. **2** *vt (bride, bridegroom)* sich vermählen mit *(form)*; *(priest)* vermählen *(form)*. **to be ~ded to one's job/an idea** mit seinem Beruf verheiratet sein/einer Idee verfallen sein.
we'd [wiːd] = **we would; we had.**
wedded ['wedɪd] *adj bliss, life* Ehe-.
wedding ['wedɪŋ] *n (ceremony)* Trauung *f*; *(ceremony and festivities)* Hochzeit *f*. **to have a church ~** sich kirchlich trauen lassen.
wedding *in cpds* Hochzeits-: **~ anniversary** *n* Hochzeitstag *m*; **~ breakfast** *n* Hochzeitsessen *nt*; **~ day** *n* Hochzeitstag *m*; **~ dress** *m* Brautkleid *nt*; **~ night** *n* Hochzeitsnacht *f*; **~ present** *n* Hochzeitsgeschenk *nt*; **~ ring** *n* Trauring, Ehering *m*.
wedge [wedʒ] **1** *n (of wood etc, fig)* Keil *m*; *(of cake etc)* Stück *nt*; *(of cheese)* Ecke *f*. **it's the thin end of the ~** so fängt's immer an. **2** *vt* **(a)** verkeilen, (mit einem Keil) festklemmen. **to ~ a door/window open/shut** eine Tür/ein Fenster festklemmen *or* verkeilen. **(b)** *(pack tightly)* **to ~ oneself/sth** sich/etw zwängen *(in* in *+acc)*; **to be ~d between two things/people** zwischen zwei Dingen/Personen eingekeilt sein.
wedge-shaped ['wedʒʃeɪpt] *adj* keilförmig.
Wednesday ['wenzdɪ] *n* Mittwoch *m*; *see* **Tuesday.**
wee [wiː] *adj (+er) (col)* winzig; *(Scot)* klein. **a ~ bit** ein kleines bißchen.
weed [wiːd] **1** *n* **(a)** Unkraut *nt no pl*. **(b)** *(col: person)* Schwächling *m*. **2** *vti (lit)* jäten.
♦ **weed out** *vt sep (fig)* aussondern.
weeding ['wiːdɪŋ] **to do the ~** Unkraut jäten.
weed-killer ['wiːdkɪləʳ] *n* Unkrautbekämpfungsmittel *nt*.
weedy ['wiːdɪ] *adj (+er) (col) person (in appearance)* schmächtig; *(in character)* blutarm.
week [wiːk] *n* Woche *f*. **it'll be ready in a ~** in einer Woche ist es fertig; **~ in, ~ out** Woche für Woche; **twice/£15 a ~** zweimal/£ 15 in der Woche *or* pro Woche; **a ~ today** heute in einer Woche *or* in acht Tagen; **tomorrow ~, a ~ tomorrow** morgen in einer Woche; **for ~s** wochenlang; **a ~'s/a two ~ holiday** ein einwöchiger/zweiwöchiger Urlaub; **in the ~ ending May 15** in der Woche vom 11. Mai; **to knock sb into the middle of next ~** *(col)* jdn windelweich schlagen *(col)*.
week: ~day 1 *n* Wochentag *m*; **2** *attr* Wochentags-, Werktags-; **~end** *n* Wochenende *nt*; **to go/be away for the ~end** übers Wochenende verreisen/nicht da sein; **at** *or* **on the ~end** am Wochenende; **~end case** Reisekoffer *m*.
weekly ['wiːklɪ] **1** *adj* Wochen-; *visit* allwöchentlich. **2** *adv* wöchentlich. **3** *n* Wochenzeitschrift *f*.
weep [wiːp] *(vb: pret, ptp* **wept)** **1** *vi* **(a)** weinen *(over* über *+acc)*. **to ~ for joy/rage** vor Freude/Wut weinen; **I could have wept!** ich hätte heulen mögen. **(b)** *(wound, cut etc)* nässen. **2** *vt tears* weinen. **3** *n* **to have a good ~** sich ausweinen.
weeping ['wiːpɪŋ] *n* Weinen *nt*.
weeping willow *n* Trauerweide *f*.
wee-wee ['wiːwiː] *n (baby-talk)* **to go for a ~** Pipi machen *(col)*.
weft [weft] *n* Einschlagfaden, Schußfaden *m*.
weigh [weɪ] **1** *vt* **(a)** wiegen. **could you ~ these bananas for me?** könnten Sie mir diese Bananen auswiegen? **(b)** *(fig) problem, merits etc* abwägen. **to ~ sth in one's mind** etw erwägen; **to ~ A against B** A und B gegeneinander abwägen. **2** *vi* **(a)** wiegen. **(b)** *(fig: be a burden)* lasten *(on* auf *+dat)*. **it's been ~ing on my mind** es liegt mir auf der Seele. **(c)** *(fig: be important)* gelten. **to ~ with sb** Gewicht bei jdm haben; **his age ~ed against him** sein Alter wurde gegen ihn in die Waagschale geworfen.
♦ **weigh down** *vt sep (lit, fig)* niederbeugen. **she was ~ed ~ with parcels** sie war mit Paketen überladen; **to be ~ed ~ with sorrows** mit Sorgen beladen sein.
♦ **weigh in 1** *vi (Sport)* **he ~ed ~ at 70 kilos** er brachte 70 Kilo auf die Waage. **2** *vt sep luggage* wiegen lassen.
♦ **weigh out** *vt sep* abwiegen.
♦ **weigh up** *vt sep alternatives, situation* abwägen; *person* einschätzen.
weigh: ~bridge *n* Brückenwaage *f*; **~-in** *n (Sport)* Wiegen *nt*.
weighing machine ['weɪɪŋmə'ʃiːn] *n* Waage *f*.
weight [weɪt] **1** *n* **(a)** Gewicht *nt*; *(Sport, esp Boxing)* Gewichtsklasse *f*; *(of blow)* Wucht, Heftigkeit *f*. **3 kilos in ~** ein Gewicht von 3 Kilo; **to put on/lose ~** zunehmen/abnehmen; **I hope the chair takes my ~** ich hoffe, der Stuhl hält mein Gewicht aus; **she's quite a ~** sie ist ganz schön schwer. **(b)** *(fig) (burden)* Last *f*; *(importance)* Bedeutung *f*, Gewicht *nt*. **the ~ of evidence** die Beweislast; **he/his opinion carries no ~** seine Stimme/Meinung fällt nicht ins Gewicht; **to add ~ to sth** einer Sache *(dat)* zusätzliches Gewicht geben; **to pull one's ~** seinen Beitrag leisten; **to throw one's ~ about** *(col)* sein Gewicht geltend machen.
2 *vt* beschweren; *(fig) results* verfälschen. **to be ~ed in favour of/against sb** jdn bevorzugen/benachteiligen.
♦ **weight down** *vt sep person (with parcels etc)* überladen; *corpse* beschweren.
weighting ['weɪtɪŋ] *n (Brit: supplement)* Zulage *f*.
weight: ~less *adj* schwerelos; **~lessness** *n* Schwerelosigkeit *f*; **~lifter** *n* Gewichtheber *m*; **~lifting** *n* Gewichtheben *nt*; **~-watcher** *n* Kalorienbewußte(r) *mf*.
weighty ['weɪtɪ] *adj (+er)* **(a)** *(lit)* schwer. **(b)** *(fig)* gewichtig; *responsibility* schwer.
weir [wɪəʳ] *n (barrier)* Wehr *nt*.
weird [wɪəd] *adj (+er) (uncanny)* unheimlich; *(col: odd)* seltsam.
weirdo ['wɪədəʊ] *n (col)* verrückter Typ *(col)*.
welcome ['welkəm] **1** *n* Willkommen *nt*. **to give sb a warm ~** jdm einen herzlichen Empfang bereiten; **to meet with a cold/warm ~** einen kühlen/herzlichen Empfang bekommen; **to bid sb ~** *(form)* jdn willkommen heißen; **what sort of a ~ will this product get from the public?** wie wird das Produkt von der Öffentlichkeit aufgenommen werden?
2 *adj* willkommen; *visitor also* gerngesehen *attr*; *news also* angenehm. **the money is very ~ just now** das Geld kommt gerade jetzt sehr gelegen; **to make sb ~** jdn sehr freundlich empfangen; **you're ~!** nichts zu danken!, aber gerne!; *(iro)* wenn's Ihnen Spaß macht!; **you're ~ to use my room** Sie können gerne mein Zimmer benutzen.

3 *vt (lit, fig)* begrüßen, willkommen heißen.
4 *interj* ~ **home/to Scotland!** willkommen daheim/in Schottland!

welcoming ['welkəmɪŋ] *adj* zur Begrüßung; *smile, gesture* einladend.

weld [weld] **1** *vt* **(a)** *(Tech)* schweißen. **to ~ parts together** Teile zusammenschweißen *or* verschweißen; **to ~ sth on** etw anschweißen *(to* an *+acc)*. **(b)** *(fig: also* **~ together***)* zusammenschmieden *(into* zu*)*. **2** *n* Schweißnaht *f.*

welder ['weldəʳ] *n (person)* Schweißer(in *f*) *m*; *(machine)* Schweißgerät *nt.*

welding ['weldɪŋ] *n* Schweißen *nt.* **~ torch** Schweißbrenner *m.*

welfare ['welfɛəʳ] *n* **(a)** *(well-being)* Wohl, Wohlergehen *nt.* **(b)** *(~ work, social security)* Fürsorge *f.* **child ~** Kinderfürsorge *f.*

welfare: ~ state *n* Wohlfahrtsstaat *m*; **~ worker** *n* Fürsorger(in *f*) *m.*

well[1] [wel] *n (water ~)* Brunnen *m*; *(oil ~)* Ölquelle *f*; *(fig: source)* Quelle *f*; *(for lift)* Schacht *m*; *(of stairs)* Treppenhaus *nt.*

♦ **well up** *vi (water)* emporsteigen, emporquellen; *(fig)* aufsteigen. **tears ~ed ~ in her eyes** Tränen stiegen ihr in die Augen.

well[2] *comp* **better,** *superl* **best 1** *adv* **(a)** gut. **he did it as ~ as he could** er machte es so gut er konnte; **he's doing ~ at school** er ist gut in der Schule; **he did ~ in the exam** er hat in der Prüfung gut abgeschnitten; **his business is doing ~** sein Geschäft geht gut; **the patient is doing ~** dem Patienten geht es gut; **if you do ~ you'll be promoted** wenn Sie sich bewähren, werden Sie befördert; **he has done ~ for himself** er hat es zu etwas gebracht; **you did ~ to help** es war gut, daß du geholfen hast; **he really did ~ there** das war wirklich eine Leistung von ihm; **~ done!** gut gemacht!, bravo!; **~ played!** gut gespielt!; **to do oneself ~** *(col)* es sich *(dat)* gut gehen lassen; **everything went ~** es ging alles gut; **to speak/think ~ of sb** über jdn Gutes sagen/positiv denken; **to be ~ in with sb** *(col)* auf gutem Fuß mit jdm stehen; **to do ~ out of sth** von etw ganz schön *or* ordentlich profitieren; **we were ~ beaten** wir sind gründlich geschlagen worden; **all** *or* **only too ~** nur (all)zu gut; **~ and truly** (ganz) gründlich; *married, settled in* ganz richtig; **he was ~ away** *(col)* er war in Fahrt *(col)*; *(drunk)* er hatte einen sitzen *(col)*; **it was ~ worth the trouble** das hat sich sehr gelohnt; **~ out of sight** weit außer Sichtweite; **~ within ...** durchaus in *(+dat)* ...; **~ past midnight** lange nach Mitternacht; **he's ~ over fifty** er ist einiges *or* weit über fünfzig; **~ over a thousand** weit über tausend.

(b) *(probably, reasonably)* ohne weiteres, gut, wohl. **I may ~ not come** es kann ohne weiteres sein, daß ich nicht komme; **it may ~ be that ...** es ist gut *or* ohne weiteres möglich, daß ...; **you may ~ be right** Sie mögen wohl recht haben; **she cried, as ~ she might** sie weinte, wozu sie auch allen Grund hatte; **you may ~ ask!** *(iro)* das kann man wohl fragen; **you might as ~ have stayed at home** du hättest genausogut zu Hause bleiben können; **I couldn't very ~ stay** ich konnte schlecht bleiben; **you might as ~ go** du könntest eigentlich ebensogut gehen; **are you coming? — I might as ~** kommst du? — ach, warum nicht.

(c) *(in addition)* **as ~** auch; **x as ~ as y** x sowohl als auch y.

2 *adj* **(a)** *(in good health)* gesund. **get ~ soon!** gute Besserung; **I'm very ~, thanks** danke, es geht mir sehr gut; **she's not been ~ lately** ihr ging es in letzter Zeit (gesundheitlich) gar nicht gut; **I don't feel at all ~** ich fühle mich gar nicht gut *or* wohl.

(b) *(satisfactory)* gut. **all is not ~ with him** mit ihm steht es nicht zum besten; **that's all very ~, but ...** das ist ja alles schön und gut, aber ...; **it's all very ~ for you to say that** Sie haben gut reden; **it would be as ~ to ask first** es wäre wohl besser, sich erst mal zu erkundigen; **it's just as ~ he came** es ist (nur) gut, daß er gekommen ist; **you're ~ out of it** seien Sie froh, daß Sie nichts (mehr) damit zu tun haben; **all's ~ that ends ~** Ende gut, alles gut.

3 *interj* also; *(expectantly also)* na; *(doubtfully)* na ja. **~ ~!, ~ I never** also so was!, na so was!; **~ now** also; **~ then** also (gut); *(in question)* na?, also?; **very ~ then!** na gut, also gut; *(indignantly)* also bitte.

4 *n* Gute(s) *nt.* **to wish sb ~** *(in general)* jdm alles Gute wünschen; *(in an attempt, iro)* jdm Glück wünschen *(in* bei*)*.

we'll [wi:l] = **we shall; we will.**

well *in cpds* gut; **~-advised** *adj* **you'd be ~-advised to ...** du tätest gut daran, zu ...; **~-balanced** *adj person* ausgeglichen; *scheme, diet* (gut) ausgewogen; **~-behaved** *adj child* artig, wohlerzogen; *animal* guterzogen *attr;* **~-being** *n* Wohl, Wohlergehen *nt*; **~-bred** *adj person* wohlerzogen; *accent* distinguiert; **~-built** *adj house* gut *or* solide gebaut; *person* stämmig, kräftig; **~-chosen** *adj words* gut gewählt; **~-developed** *adj muscle* gutentwickelt *attr; sense* (gut) ausgeprägt; **~-disposed** *adj* **to be ~-disposed towards sb/sth** jdm/einer Sache freundlich gesonnen sein; **~-done** *adj steak* durchgebraten, durch *inv;* **~-dressed** *adj* gut angezogen *or* gekleidet; **~-earned** *adj* wohlverdient; **~-educated** *adj person* gebildet; **~-founded** *adj* wohlbegründet *attr;* **~-heeled** *adj* *(col)* betucht; **~-informed** *adj* gutinformiert *attr;* *sources also* gutunterrichtet *attr;* **to be ~-informed about sth** über etw gut informiert sein.

wellington (boot) ['welɪŋtən('bu:t)] *n (Brit)* Gummistiefel *m.*

well: ~-kept *adj garden, hair etc* gepflegt; *secret* streng gehütet; **~-known** *adj* bekannt; **it's ~-known that ...** es ist allgemein bekannt, daß ...; **~-meaning** *adj* wohlmeinend *attr;* **~-meant** *adj action* gutgemeint *attr;* **~-nigh** *adv* nahezu, beinahe; **~-off** *adj (affluent)* reich, gut d(a)ran *(col)*; **you don't know when you're ~-off** *(col)* du weißt (ja) nicht, wann es dir gut geht; **~-preserved** *adj* guterhalten *attr;* **~-read** *adj* belesen; **~-spent** *adj time* gut genützt *or* verbracht; *money* sinnvoll ausgegeben; **~-spoken** *adj* mit gutem Deutsch/Englisch *etc*; **to be ~-spoken** gutes Deutsch/Englisch *etc* sprechen; **~-stocked** *adj* gutbestückt *attr*; *(Comm also)* mit gutem Sortiment; *larder, shelves also* reichlich gefüllt; **~-timed** *adj* (zeitlich) gut abgepaßt; **~-to-do** *adj* wohlhabend, reich; *district* Reichen-; **~-wisher** *n* **our cause has many ~-wishers** unsere Sache hat viele Sympathisanten; **"from a ~-wisher"** „jemand, der es gut mit Ihnen meint"; **~-worn** *adj garment* abgetragen; *carpet etc* abgelaufen; *path* ausgetreten; *saying etc* abgedroschen.

welsh [welʃ] *vi* **to ~ on sb** *(col)* jdn (auf)sitzen lassen.

Welsh [welʃ] **1** *adj* walisisch. **2** *n* **(a)** *(language)* Walisisch *nt.* **(b) the ~** *pl* die Waliser *pl.*

Welsh: ~man *n* Waliser *m*; **~ rarebit** *n* überbackene Käseschnitte; **~woman** *n* Waliserin *f.*

welt [welt] *n (weal)* Striemen *m.*

welterweight ['weltəweɪt] *n* Weltergewicht *nt.*

wend [wend] *vt* **to ~ one's way home** sich auf den Heimweg begeben.

went [went] *pret of* **go.**

wept [wept] *pret, ptp of* **weep.**

were [wɜ:] *2nd pers sing, 1st, 2nd, 3rd pers pl pret of* **be.**

we're [wɪəʳ] = **we are.**

weren't [wɜ:nt] = **were not.**

werewolf ['wɪəwʊlf] *n* Werwolf *m.*

west [west] **1** *n* **(a)** Westen *m*. **in/to the ~** im/nach Westen; **to the ~ of** westlich von, im Westen von; **the wind is blowing from the ~** der Wind kommt von West(en). **(b)** *(western world)* **the W~** der Westen. **2** *adj* West-, westlich. **3** *adv* nach Westen, westwärts. **it faces ~** es geht nach Westen; **~ of** westlich von; **to go ~** *(fig col)* flöten gehen *(col)*.

west *in cpds* West-; **W~ Berlin** *n* Westberlin *nt*; **~-bound** *adj traffic* in Richtung Westen.

westerly ['westəlɪ] *adj* westlich.

western ['westən] **1** *adj* westlich. **W~ Europe** Westeuropa *nt*. **2** *n* Western *m*.

westerner ['westənəʳ] *n* Abendländer(in *f*) *m*.

westernized ['westənaɪzd] *adj culture* vom Westen beeinflußt; *(pej)* verwestlicht.

West: **~ German 1** *adj* westdeutsch, bundesdeutsch; **2** *n* Westdeutsche(r) *mf*; **~ Germany** *n* Westdeutschland *nt*, Bundesrepublik *f* (Deutschland); **~ Indian 1** *adj* westindisch; **2** *n* Westindier(in *f*) *m*; **~ Indies** *npl* Westindische Inseln *pl*.

west: **~ward(s)** [westwəd(z)], **~wardly** [-wədlɪ] **1** *adj* westlich; **in a ~wardly direction** (in) Richtung Westen; **2** *adv* westwärts, nach Westen.

wet [wet] *(vb: pret, ptp* **~** *or* **~ted) 1** *adj (+er)* **(a)** naß. **to be ~ through** durch und durch naß sein, völlig durchnäßt sein; **"~ paint"** „frisch gestrichen"; **to get one's feet ~** sich *(dat)* nasse Füße holen *(col)*. **(b)** *(rainy)* naß, feucht; *climate, country* feucht. **the ~ season** die Regenzeit; **in ~ weather** bei nassem Wetter. **(c)** *(Brit col: weak, spiritless)* weichlich, lasch. **2** *n* **(a)** *(moisture)* Feuchtigkeit *f*. **(b)** *(rain)* Nässe *f*. **it's out in the ~** es ist draußen im Nassen. **(c)** *(Brit col: person)* Waschlappen *m (col)*. **3** *vt* naß machen; *lips, washing* befeuchten. **to ~ the bed/one's pants/oneself** ins Bett/in die Hose(n) machen/ sich naß machen.

wet: **~ blanket** *n (col)* Miesmacher(in *f*) *m (col)*; **~suit** *n* Taucheranzug *m*.

we've [wiːv] = **we have.**

whack [wæk] **1** *n* **(a)** *(blow)* (knallender) Schlag. **(b)** *(col: attempt)* Versuch *m*. **to have a ~ at sth** etw probieren *or* versuchen. **(c)** *(col: share)* (An)teil *m*. **2** *vt* **(a)** *(hit)* schlagen, hauen *(col)*. **(b)** *(col: defeat)* (haushoch) schlagen.

whacked [wækt] *adj (col: exhausted)* kaputt *(col)*.

whacking ['wækɪŋ] *adj (Brit col)*: **a ~ great ...** ein(e) Mords- ... *(col)*.

whale [weɪl] *n* **(a)** Wal *m*. **(b)** *(col)* **to have a ~ of a time** sich prima amüsieren.

whaler ['weɪləʳ] *n (person, ship)* Walfänger *m*.

wharf [wɔːf] *n, pl* **-s** *or* **wharves** [wɔːvz] Kai *m*.

what [wɒt] **1** *pron* **(a)** *(interrog)* was. **~'s the weather like?** wie ist das Wetter?; **~'s that to you?** was geht dich das an?; **~ for?** wozu?, wofür?; **~'s that tool for?** wofür ist das Werkzeug?; **~ did you do that for?** warum hast du das gemacht?; **~'s the German for ...?** wie heißt ... auf deutsch?; **~ did he agree to?** wozu hat er zugestimmt?; **~ about ...?** wie wär's mit ...?; **you know that pub? — ~ about it?** kennst du die Kneipe? — was ist damit?; **~ if ...?** was ist, wenn ...?; **so ~?** *(col)* na und?; **~ does it matter?** was macht das schon?; **~'s-his/-her/-its name** *(col)* der/die/das Dings(da) *(col)*.

(b) *(rel)* was. **that is not ~ I asked for** danach habe ich nicht gefragt; **he agrees with ~ I say** er stimmt mit dem überein, was ich sage; **that's exactly ~ I said** genau das habe ich gesagt; **do you know ~ you are looking for?** weißt du, wonach du suchst?; **come ~ may** komme was wolle; **and ~'s more** und außerdem, und noch dazu; **~ with one thing and another I didn't have time** wie es sich so ergab, hatte ich keine Zeit; **he knows ~'s ~** *(col)* er kennt sich aus, der weiß Bescheid *(col)*; **and ~ have you** *(col)*, **and ~ not** *(col)* und was sonst noch alles; **(I'll) tell you ~** *(col)* weißt du was?; **to give sb ~ for** *(col)* es jdm ordentlich geben *(col)*.

2 *adj* **(a)** *(interrog)* welche(r, s), was für ein/ eine *(col)*. **~ age is he?** wie alt ist er?; **~ good would that be?** *(col)* wozu sollte das gut sein? **(b)** *(rel)* der/die/das. **~ little I had** das wenige, das ich hatte; **buy ~ food you like** kauf das Essen, das du willst. **(c)** *(in set constructions)* **~ sort of** was für ein/eine; **~ else** was noch; **~ more** was mehr. **(d)** *(in interj)* **~ a man!** was für ein Mann!; **~ luck!** was für ein Glück, so ein Glück; **~ a fool I've been/I am!** ich Idiot!; **~ terrible weather** was für ein scheußliches Wetter.

3 *interj* was!

whatever [wɒt'evəʳ] **1** *pron* **(a) ~ you like** was (immer) du (auch) möchtest; **... or ~ they're called** ... oder wie sie sonst heißen; **or ~** oder sonst (so) etwas. **(b)** *(interrog)* **~ does he want?** was will er wohl?; *(impatiently)* was, zum Kuckuck, will er denn?; **~ do you mean?** was meinst du denn bloß? **2** *adj* **(a)** welche(r, s) (auch). **~ book you choose** welches Buch Sie auch wählen; **for ~ reasons** aus welchen Gründen auch immer. **(b)** *(with neg)* überhaupt, absolut. **nothing/no man ~** überhaupt gar nichts/niemand überhaupt; **it's of no use ~** es hat absolut keinen Sinn. **(c)** *(interrog)* **~ reason can he have?** was für einen Grund kann er bloß *or* wohl haben?; **~ else will he do?** was wird er wohl noch alles machen?

what's [wɒts] = **what is; what has.**

whatsit ['wɒtsɪt] *n (col)* Dingsbums *nt (col)*.

whatsoever [,wɒtsəʊ'evəʳ] *pron, adj see* **whatever 1 (a), 2 (a, b).**

wheat [wiːt] **1** *n* Weizen *m*. **2** *attr* **~germ** Weizenkeim *m*.

wheedle ['wiːdl] *vt* **to ~ one's way into sth** *into organization, sb's confidence* sich in etw einschleichen; *into position* sich in etw hineinmanövrieren; **to ~ sth out of sb** jdm etw abschmeicheln.

wheel [wiːl] **1** *n* **(a)** Rad *nt*; *(steering ~)* Lenkrad *nt*; *(Naut)* Steuer(rad) *nt*; *(roulette ~)* Drehscheibe *f*; *(potter's ~)* (Töpfer)scheibe *f*. **at the ~** *(lit)* am Steuer; *(fig also)* am Ruder; **to take the ~** das Steuer übernehmen; **~ of fortune** Glücksrad *nt*. **(b)** *(Mil)* Schwenkung *f*. **2** *vt* **(a)** *(push) bicycle, pram* schieben; *(pull)* ziehen; *(invalid) wheelchair* fahren. **(b)** *(cause to turn)* drehen. **3** *vi (turn)* drehen; *(birds, planes)* kreisen; *(Mil)* schwenken. **to ~ left** nach links schwenken.

♦ **wheel around** *vi* sich (rasch) umdrehen; *(troops)* (ab)schwenken.

wheel: **~barrow** *n* Schubkarre *f*, Schubkarren *m*; **~base** *n* Rad(ab)stand *m*; **~chair** *n* Rollstuhl *m*.

wheeler-dealer ['wiːlə'diːləʳ] *n (col)* Schlitzohr *nt (col)*; *(in finance also)* Geschäftemacher *m*.

wheeze [wiːz] *vi* pfeifend atmen; *(machines, asthmatic)* keuchen.

whelk [welk] *n* Wellhornschnecke *f*.

when [wen] **1** *adv* **(a)** wann. **since ~ have you been here?** seit wann sind Sie hier?; **say ~!** *(col)* sag' halt! **(b)** *(rel)* **on the day ~** an dem Tag, an dem; **at the time ~** zu der Zeit, als *or* wo *(col)*; **during the time ~ he was in Germany** während der Zeit, als *or* wo er in Deutschland war; **that's ~ it's important** genau dann ist es wichtig.

2 *conj* **(a)** wenn; *(with past reference)* als. **you can go ~ I have finished** du kannst gehen, sobald *or* wenn ich fertig bin; **~ I was in London** als ich in London war; **each time ~ I was in London** jedesmal, wenn ich in London war. **(b) be careful ~ crossing the road** seien Sie vorsichtig, wenn Sie über die Straße gehen; **the Prime Minister is coming here in May, ~ he'll ...** der Premier kommt im Mai hierher und wird dann

... **(c)** *(although, whereas)* wo ... doch. **why do you do it that way ~ it would be much easier like this?** warum machst du es denn auf die Art, wo es doch so viel einfacher wäre?

whence [wens] *adv (old)* woher.

whenever [wen'evəʳ] *adv* **(a)** *(each time)* jedesmal wenn. **(b)** *(at whatever time)* wann (auch) immer; *(as soon as)* sobald. **~ you like!** wann du willst! **(c)** *(emph)* **~ can he have done it?** wann kann er das nur *or* wohl getan haben?

where [wɛəʳ] **1** *adv* wo. **~ (to)** wohin, wo ... hin; **~ (from)** woher, wo ... her; **~ are you going (to)?** wohin gehst du, wo gehst du hin?; **~ to, sir?** wohin (wollen Sie) bitte?; **~ are you from?** wo kommen Sie her?; **from ~ I'm sitting I can see the church** von meinem Platz aus kann ich die Kirche sehen; **~ should we be if ...?** was wäre nur, wenn ...?

2 *conj* wo; *(in the place where)* da, wo ..., an der Stelle, wo ... **go ~ you like** geh, wohin du willst; **the bag is ~ you left it** die Tasche ist da, wo du sie liegengelassen hast; **this is ~ we got out** hier sind wir ausgestiegen; **that's ~ Nelson fell/I used to live** hier *or* an dieser Stelle fiel Nelson/hier *or* da habe ich (früher) gewohnt; **I've read up to ~ the king ...** ich habe bis dahin gelesen, wo der König ...; **we succeeded ~ we expected to fail** wir hatten da Erfolg, wo wir ihn nicht erwartet hatten; **~ money is concerned** wo es ums Geld geht.

whereabouts [ˌwɛərə'baʊts] **1** *adv* wo, in welcher Gegend. **2** ['wɛərəbaʊts] *n sing or pl* Verbleib *m*; *(of people also)* Aufenthaltsort *m*.

whereas [wɛər'æz] *conj (whilst)* während; *(while on the other hand)* wohingegen.

whereby [wɛə'baɪ] *adv (form)* **the sign ~ you will recognize him** das Zeichen, an dem *or* woran Sie ihn erkennen; **the rule ~ it is not allowed** die Vorschrift, wonach es verboten ist.

wherever [wɛər'evəʳ] **1** *conj* **~ it came from** egal, woher es kommt, woher es auch kommt; **we'll go ~ you like** wir gehen, wohin Sie wollen; **~ you see this sign** überall, wo Sie dieses Zeichen sehen. **2** *adv* **~ have I seen that before?** wo habe ich das nur *or* bloß schon gesehen?; **in London or Liverpool or ~** in London oder Liverpool oder sonstwo.

wherewithal ['wɛəwɪðɔːl] *n (money)* nötiges Kleingeld; *(implements)* Utensilien *pl*.

whet [wet] *vt knife* wetzen; *axe* schleifen, schärfen; *appetite, curiosity* anregen.

whether ['weðəʳ] *conj* ob. **I am not certain ~ or not they're coming** ich bin nicht sicher, ob sie kommen oder nicht; **~ they come or not, we'll ...** ob sie kommen oder nicht, wir ...; **he's not sure ~ to go or stay** er weiß nicht, ob er gehen oder bleiben soll.

whew [hwuː] *interj* puh, uff.

whey [weɪ] *n* Molke *f*.

which [wɪtʃ] **1** *adj* **(a)** *(interrog)* welche(r, s). **~ one?** welche(r, s)?; *(of people also)* wer? **(b)** *(rel)* welche(r, s). **... by ~ time I was asleep** ... und zu dieser Zeit schlief ich bereits; **look at it ~ way you will ...** man kann es sehen, wie man will ...

2 *pron* **(a)** *(interrog)* welche(r, s); *(of people also)* wer. **~ of the children?** welches Kind?; **~ is ~?** *(of people)* wer ist wer? *(of things)* welche(r, s) ist welche(r, s)? **(b)** *(rel)* der/die/das, welche(r, s) *(geh)*. **the bear ~ I saw** der Bär, den ich sah; **at ~ he remarked ...** worauf er bemerkte, ...; **it rained hard, ~ upset her** es regnete stark, was sie aufregte; **from ~ we deduce that ...** woraus wir ableiten, daß ...; **after ~ we went to bed** worauf *or* wonach wir zu Bett gingen; **the shelf on ~ I put it** das Brett, auf das *or* worauf ich es gelegt habe.

whichever [wɪtʃ'evəʳ] **1** *adj* welche(r, s) auch immer; *(no matter which)* ganz gleich *or* egal welche(r, s). **2** *pron* welche(r, s) auch immer. **~ (of you) has the most money** wer immer (von euch) das meiste Geld hat.

whiff [wɪf] *n (puff)* Zug *m*; *(wisp)* kleine Fahne, Wolke *f*; *(smell)* Hauch *m*; *(fig: trace)* Spur *f*. **to catch a ~ of sth** den Geruch von etw wahrnehmen.

while [waɪl] **1** *n* Weile *f*, Weilchen *nt (col)*. **for a ~** (für) eine Weile, eine Zeitlang; *(a short moment)* (für) einen Moment; **a good** *or* **long ~** eine ganze Weile *or* Zeitlang; **for/after quite a ~** ziemlich lange/nach einer ziemlich langen Zeit; **a little** *or* **short ~** ein Weilchen *(col)*, kurze Zeit; **it'll be ready in a short ~** es wird bald fertig sein; **a little/long ~ ago** vor kurzem/vor längerer *or* langer Zeit; **some ~ ago** vor einiger Zeit; **all the ~** die ganze Zeit (über); **to be worth (one's) ~ to ...** sich (für jdn) lohnen, zu ...; **we'll make it worth your ~** es soll ihr Schaden nicht sein.

2 *conj* **(a)** während; *(as long as)* solange. **she fell asleep ~ reading** sie schlief beim Lesen ein. **(b)** *(although)* **~ one must admit there are difficulties ...** man muß zwar zugeben, daß es Schwierigkeiten gibt, trotzdem ...; **~ the text is not absolutely perfect, nevertheless ...** obwohl der Text nicht einwandfrei ist, ... trotzdem ... **(c)** *(whereas)* während. **I always drink tea ~ she drinks coffee** ich bin Teetrinker, während sie Kaffeetrinkerin ist.

♦ **while away** *vt sep time* sich *(dat)* vertreiben.

whilst [waɪlst] *conj* = **while 2.**

whim [wɪm] *n* Laune *f*. **her every ~** jede ihrer Launen.

whimper ['wɪmpəʳ] **1** *n (of dog)* Winseln *nt no pl*; *(of person)* Wimmern *nt no pl*. **without a ~** ohne einen (Klage)laut. **2** *vti (dog)* winseln; *(person)* wimmern.

whimsical ['wɪmzɪkəl] *adj* wunderlich; *look, remark* neckisch; *idea, tale* schnurrig.

whine [waɪn] **1** *n (of dog)* Jaulen, Heulen *nt no pl*; *(complaining cry)* Jammern, Gejammer *nt no pl*; *(of child)* Quengelei *f no pl*; *(of siren, jet engine)* Heulen *nt no pl*; *(of bullet)* Pfeifen *nt no pl*. **2** *vi (dog)* jaulen; *(person: speak, complain)* jammern, klagen; *(child)* quengeln; *(siren, jet engine)* heulen; *(bullet)* pfeifen. **don't come whining to me if ...** du brauchst mir nichts vorzujammern, wenn ...

whinny ['wɪnɪ] **1** *n* Wiehern *nt no pl*. **2** *vi* wiehern.

whip [wɪp] **1** *n* **(a)** Peitsche *f*; *(riding ~)* Reitgerte *f*. **(b)** *(Parl)* *(person)* Fraktionsführer *m*; *(call)* Anordnung *f* des Fraktionsführers. **three-line ~** Fraktionszwang *m*. **(c)** *(Cook)* Creme, Speise *f*. **2** *vt* **(a)** *(with whip) people* auspeitschen; *horse* peitschen; *(with stick etc)* schlagen. **(b)** *(Cook)* schlagen. **(c)** *(fig: move quickly)* **he ~ped the book off the desk** er schnappte sich *(dat)* das Buch vom Schreibtisch; **he ~ped his hand out of the way** er zog blitzschnell seine Hand weg; **he ~ped a gun out of his pocket** er zog rasch eine Pistole aus der Tasche. **(d)** *(col: steal)* mitgehen lassen *(col)*. **3** *vi* **he ~ped around when he heard ...** er fuhr herum, als er hörte ...; **he's just ~ped out for a minute** *(col)* er ist nur schnell mal rausgegangen *(col)*.

♦ **whip up** *vt sep* **(a)** *(pick up)* schnappen. **(b)** *(set in motion) horses* antreiben; *(Cook) cream* schlagen; *mixture* verrühren; *(col: prepare quickly) meal* hinzaubern; *(fig: stir up) feeling* anheizen, entfachen; *support* finden; *audience, crowd* mitreißen.

whip: ~cord *n (rope)* Peitschenschnur *f*; *(fabric)* Whipcord *m*; **~ hand** *n* **to have the ~ hand (over sb)** (über jdn) die Oberhand haben; **~lash** *n* (Peitschen)riemen *m*; *(Med)* Peitschenhiebverletzung *f*.

whipped cream ['wɪpt'kriːm] *n* Schlagsahne *f*.

whippet ['wɪpɪt] *n* Whippet *m (eine Hundeart)*.

whipping ['wɪpɪŋ] *n (beating)* Tracht *f* Prügel; *(col: defeat)* Niederlage *f*; *(fig: in debate etc)* Pleite *f (col)*.

whipping: ~ boy *n* Prügelknabe *m*; **~ cream** *n* Schlagsahne *f*.

whip-round ['wɪpraʊnd] *n (esp Brit col)* **to have a ~** den Hut herumgehen lassen.

whirl [wɜːl] **1** *n (spin)* Wirbeln *nt no pl*; *(of dust, water etc, also fig)* Wirbel *m*; *(of cream etc)* Tupfer *m*. **to give sb/sth a ~** *(fig col: try out)* jdn/etw ausprobieren; **the social ~** das gesellschaftliche Leben; **my head is in a ~** mir schwirrt der Kopf. **2** *vt (make turn)* wirbeln. **to ~ sb/sth around** jdn/etw herumwirbeln. **3** *vi (spin)* wirbeln; *(water)* strudeln. **to ~ around** herumwirbeln; *(water)* strudeln; *(person: turn quickly)* herumfahren; **my head is ~ing** mir schwirrt der Kopf; **to ~ past** *(time, countryside)* vorbeirauschen.

whirlpool ['wɜːlpuːl] *n* Strudel *m*.

whirlwind ['wɜːlwɪnd] *n* Wirbelwind *m*. **like a ~** wie der Wirbelwind; **a ~ romance** eine stürmische Romanze.

whirr [wɜːʳ] **1** *n (of wings)* Schwirren *nt*; *(of wheels, machine) (quiet)* Surren *nt*; *(louder)* Dröhnen *nt*. **2** *vi see n* schwirren; surren; dröhnen.

whisk [wɪsk] **1** *n (Cook)* Schneebesen *m*; *(electric)* Rührgerät *nt*. **give the eggs a good ~** schlagen Sie die Eier gut durch; **with a ~ of its tail** mit einem Schwanzschlag. **2** *vt (Brit Cook)* schlagen; *eggs* verquirlen. **to ~ the eggs into the mixture** die Eier unter die Masse einrühren.

♦ **whisk away** *vt sep* **the magician ~ed ~ the tablecloth** der Zauberer zog das Tischtuch schnell weg; **the kidnappers ~ed him ~** die Entführer sausten mit ihm davon.

whisker ['wɪskəʳ] *n* Schnurrhaar *nt*; *(of people)* Barthaar *nt*. **~s** *(moustache, Zool)* Schnurrbart *m*; *(side ~s)* Backenbart *m*. **to win/miss sth by a ~** etw fast gewinnen/etw um Haaresbreite verpassen.

whisky, *(US, Ir)* **whiskey** ['wɪskɪ] *n* Whisky *m*. **two whiskies, please** zwei Whisky, bitte.

whisper ['wɪspəʳ] **1** *n* **(a)** Geflüster, Flüstern *nt no pl*; *(of wind)* Wispern *nt no pl*; *(mysterious)* Raunen *nt no pl*. **to speak in a ~** im Flüsterton sprechen. **(b)** *(rumour)* Gerücht *nt*. **there are ~s (going around) that ...** es geht das Gerücht, daß ... **2** *vt* **(a)** flüstern, wispern. **to ~ sth to sb** jdm etw zuflüstern. **(b)** *(rumour)* **it's (being) ~ed that ...** es geht das Gerücht, daß ..., man munkelt, daß ... **3** *vi* flüstern, wispern *(also fig)*; *(wind)* säuseln; *(schoolchildren)* tuscheln. **to ~ to sb** jdm zuflüstern; mit jdm tuscheln.

whist [wɪst] *n* Whist *nt*.

whistle ['wɪsl] **1** *n* **(a)** *(sound)* Pfiff *m*; *(of wind)* Pfeifen *nt*; *(of kettle)* Pfeifton *m*. **to give a ~** einen Pfiff ausstoßen. **(b)** *(instrument)* Pfeife *f*. **to blow a ~** pfeifen; **they searched him but he was as clean as a ~** *(col)* sie durchsuchten ihn, aber er war blitzsauber *(col)*; **it broke off as clean as a ~** *(col)* es ist ganz glatt abgebrochen. **2** *vti* pfeifen. **the boys ~d at her** die Jungen pfiffen ihr nach; **the crowd ~d at the referee** die Menge pfiff den Schiedsrichter aus; **the refereee ~d for a foul** der Schiedsrichter pfiff ein Foul; **he can ~ for it** *(col)* da kann er lange warten.

whistle-stop ['wɪsl,stɒp] *adj* **~ tour** *(US Pol)* Wahlreise *f*; *(fig) Reise f mit Kurzaufenthalten an allen Orten*.

whit [wɪt] *n* **not a ~** keine Spur; *(of truth, common sense)* kein Gramm *or* Körnchen.

white [waɪt] **1** *adj* weiß; *(with fear, anger etc)* blaß, kreidebleich. **to go** *or* **turn ~** *(thing)* weiß werden; *(person)* bleich *or* blaß werden. **2** *n (colour)* Weiß *nt*; *(person)* Weiße(r) *mf*; *(of egg)* Eiweiß *nt*; *(of eye)* Weiße(s) *nt*. **~s** *(household)* Weißwäsche *f*; *(Sport)* weiße Kleidung.

white: ~bait *n, pl* **~bait** Breitling *m*; **~ coffee** *n (Brit)* Kaffee *m* mit Milch; **~-collar** *adj* **~-collar worker** Angestellte(r) *mf*; **~-collar crime** Wirtschaftskriminalität *f*; **~-collar job** Angestelltenstelle *f*, Büroposten *m*; **~ elephant** *n* nutzloser Gegenstand; *(waste of money)* Fehlinvestition *f*; **~ elephant stall** *n* Stand *m* mit allerlei Krimskrams; **~-haired** *adj* weißhaarig; **W~hall** *n* **if W~hall decides ...** wenn London beschließt ...; **~ horse** *n* Schimmel *m*; *(wave)* Welle *f* mit einer Schaumkrone; **~-hot** *adj* weißglühend; *(fig)* glühend; **the W~ House** *n* das Weiße Haus; **~ lie** *n* kleine Unwahrheit, Notlüge *f*; **~ man** *n* Weiße(r) *m*; **~ meat** *n* helles Fleisch.

whiten ['waɪtn] **1** *vt* weiß machen. **2** *vi* weiß werden.

whiteness ['waɪtnɪs] *n* Weiße *f*; *(of skin)* Helligkeit *f*; *(due to illness etc)* Blässe *f*.

whitening ['waɪtnɪŋ] *n* weiße Farbe, Schlämmkreide *f*.

white: ~ paper *n (Pol)* Weißbuch *nt*; **~ sauce** *n* Mehlsoße *f*, helle Soße; **~ spirit** *n* Terpentinersatz *m*; **~wash 1** *n* Tünche *f*; *(fig)* Schönfärberei *f*; **2** *vt walls* tünchen; *(fig)* beschönigen; **~ wedding** *n* Hochzeit *f* in Weiß; **~ wine** *n* Weißwein *m*. **~ woman** *n* Weiße *f*.

whither ['wɪðəʳ] *adv* **(a)** *(old)* wohin. **(b)** *(journalese)* **~ socialism?** Sozialismus, was nun?

whiting ['waɪtɪŋ] *n, pl* **-** Weißling, Weißfisch *m*.

whitish ['waɪtɪʃ] *adj colour* weißlich.

Whit Monday [,wɪt'mʌndɪ] *n* Pfingstmontag *m*.

Whitsun ['wɪtsən] **1** *n* Pfingsten *nt*. **2** *attr* Pfingst-.

whittle ['wɪtl] *vt* schnitzen.

♦ **whittle away** *vt sep* **(a)** *bark etc* wegschneiden. **(b)** *(gradually reduce)* allmählich abbauen; *rights, power etc also* allmählich beschneiden.

♦ **whittle down** *vt sep* **(a)** *piece of wood* herunterschneiden. **to ~ ~ to size** zurechtschneiden. **(b)** *(reduce)* kürzen, stutzen; *gap, difference* verringern. **to ~ sth ~ to sth** etw auf etw *(acc)* reduzieren; **to ~ sb ~ to size** *(fig)* jdn zurechtstutzen.

whiz(z) [wɪz] **1** *n* **(a)** *(of arrow)* Schwirren *nt*. **(b)** *(col)* Kanone *f (col)*. **2** *vi (arrow)* schwirren. **the cars ~ed past** die Autos sausten vorbei.

whi(z)z-kid ['wɪz'kɪd] *n (col: in career)* Senkrechtstarter *m*. **financial ~** Finanzgenie *nt*.

WHO = World Health Organization Weltgesundheitsorganisation *f*.

who [huː] *pron* **(a)** *(interrog)* wer; *(acc)* wen; *(dat)* wem. **~ do you think you are?** was glaubst du, wer du bist?, für wen hältst du dich eigentlich?; **~ are you looking for?** wen suchen Sie?; **~ did you stay with?** bei wem haben Sie gewohnt?; **you'll soon find out ~'s ~** Sie werden bald alle kennenlernen. **(b)** *(rel)* der/die/das, welche(r, s). **any man ~ ...** jeder (Mensch), der ...; **he ~ wishes/those ~ wish to go ...** wer gehen will ...

who'd [huːd] = **who had; who would.**

whodun(n)it [huː'dʌnɪt] *n (col)* Krimi *m*.

whoever [huː'evəʳ] *pron* wer (auch immer); *(acc)* wen (auch immer); *(dat)* wem (auch immer); *(no matter who)* ganz gleich wer/wen/wem. **~ told you that?** wer hat dir das denn (bloß) gesagt?

whole [həʊl] **1** *adj* ganz; *truth* voll. **but the ~ purpose was to ...** aber der ganze Sinn der Sache war, daß ...; **three ~ weeks** drei volle *or* ganze Wochen; **the ~ lot** das Ganze; *(of people)* alle, der ganze Verein *(col)*; **a ~ lot of people** eine ganze Menge Leute; **a ~ lot better** *(col)* ein ganzes Stück besser; **not a cup was left ~** nicht eine Tasse blieb heil; **she swallowed it ~** sie schluckte es ganz (hinunter). **2** *n* Ganze(s) *nt*. **the ~ of the month/London** der ganze Monat/ganz London; **nearly the ~ of our production** fast unsere gesamte Produktion; **as a ~** als Ganzes; **on the ~** im großen und ganzen, alles in allem.

whole: ~food *n* Reformkost, Biokost *f*; **~hearted**

adj völlig, uneingeschränkt; **~hearted thanks to X** X *(dat)* danken wir von ganzem Herzen; **~heartedly** *adv* voll und ganz; **~ hog** *n*: **to go the ~ hog** *(col)* aufs Ganze gehen; **~meal** *(Brit)* **1** *adj* Vollkorn-; **2** *n* feiner Vollkornschrot; **~ milk** *n* Vollmilch *f*; **~ note** *n (esp US Mus)* ganze Note; **~ number** *n* ganze Zahl.

wholesale ['həʊlseɪl] **1** *n* Großhandel *m*. **2** *adj attr* **(a)** *(Comm)* Großhandels-. **(b)** *(fig: widespread)* umfassend, massiv; *slaughter, redundancies* Massen-; *(indiscriminate)* wild, generell. **3** *adv* **(a)** im Großhandel. **(b)** *(fig)* in Bausch und Bogen; *(in great numbers)* massenhaft; *(without modification)* (so) ohne weiteres.

wholesaler ['həʊlseɪlə^r] *n* Großhändler *m*.

wholesome ['həʊlsəm] *adj* gesund.

wholewheat ['həʊlwiːt] *n, adj (US)* = **wholemeal.**

who'll [huːl] = **who will; who shall.**

wholly ['həʊlɪ] *adv* völlig, gänzlich.

whom [huːm] *pron* **(a)** *(interrog) (acc)* wen; *(dat)* wem. **(b)** *(rel) (acc)* den/die/das; *(dat)* dem/der/dem. **..., all of ~ were drunk** ..., die alle betrunken waren; **none/all of ~** von denen keine(r, s)/alle.

whoop [huːp] **1** *n* Ruf, Schrei *m*. **2** *vi* rufen, schreien; *(with whooping cough)* pfeifen; *(with joy)* jauchzen.

whooping cough ['huːpɪŋ,kɒf] *n* Keuchhusten *m*.

whoosh [wuːʃ] **1** *n (of water)* Rauschen *nt*; *(of air)* Zischen *nt*. **2** *vi* rauschen; zischen.

whopper ['wɒpə^r] *n (col) (sth big)* Brocken *m (col)*; *(lie)* faustdicke Lüge.

whopping ['wɒpɪŋ] *adj (col)* Mords- *(col)*, Riesen-.

whore [hɔː^r] *n* Hure *f*.

whorl [wɜːl] *n* Kringel *m*; *(of shell)* (Spiral)windung *f*.

who's [huːz] = **who has; who is.**

whose [huːz] *poss pron* **(a)** *(interrog)* wessen. **~ is this?** wem gehört das?; **~ car did you go in?** in wessen Auto sind Sie gefahren? **(b)** *(rel)* dessen; *(after f and pl)* deren. **the man ~ wife ...** der Mann, dessen Frau ...

why [waɪ] **1** *adv* warum, weshalb; *(asking for the purpose)* wozu; *(how come that ...)* wieso. **~ not ask him?** warum fragst du/fragen wir *etc* ihn nicht?; **~ wait?** wozu (noch) warten?; **~ do it this way?** warum denn so?; **that's ~** darum, deswegen; **that's exactly ~ ...** genau deshalb *or* deswegen ... **2** *interj* **are you sure? — ~ yes** sind Sie sicher?; — (aber) ja; **~ that's easy!** na, das ist doch einfach!; **who did it? ~ it's obvious** wer das war? also, das ist doch klar. **3** *n*: **the ~s and (the) wherefores** das Warum und Weshalb.

wick [wɪk] *n* Docht *m*. **to get on sb's ~** *(col)* jdm auf den Wecker gehen *(col)*.

wicked ['wɪkɪd] *adj person etc* böse; *(immoral)* schlecht, gottlos; *(indulging in vices)* lasterhaft; *(col: scandalous) price etc* unverschämt; *smile, look, grin* frech, boshaft; *satire* boshaft; *blow, frost also* gemein *(col)*. **that was a ~ thing to do** das war aber gemein (von dir/ihm *etc*); **he/the dog has a ~ temper** er ist unbeherrscht *or* aufbrausend/der Hund ist bösartig; **he has a ~ sense of humour** er hat eine böse Art von Humor.

wickedness ['wɪkɪdnɪs] *n (of person)* Schlechtigkeit *f*; *(immorality)* Verderbtheit *f*; *(indulgence in vices)* Lasterhaftigkeit *f*; *(of look etc)* Boshaftigkeit *f*; *(mischievousness)* Bosheit *f*.

wicker ['wɪkə^r] **1** *n* Korbgeflecht *nt*. **2** *adj attr* Korb-.

wicker: ~ basket *n* (Weiden)korb *m*; **~work** *n* *(material)* Korbgeflecht *nt*; *(articles)* Korbwaren *pl*.

wicket ['wɪkɪt] *n (Cricket) (stumps: also* **~s***)* Mal, Pfostentor *nt*; *(pitch)* Spielbahn *f*.

wicket-keeper ['wɪkɪt'kiːpə^r] *n (Cricket)* Torwächter *m*.

wide [waɪd] **1** *adj* **(a)** *road, smile* breit; *skirt, plain* weit; *eyes* groß. **it is three metres ~** es ist drei Meter breit; **the big ~ world** die (große) weite Welt. **(b)** *variety* groß; *experience, choice* reich; *public, knowledge, range* breit; *interests* vielfältig; *coverage of report* umfassend; *network* weitverzweigt *attr*; *circulation* weit, groß; *question* weitreichend. **~ reading is the best education** viel zu lesen ist die beste Art der Erziehung; **his ~ reading** seine große Belesenheit. **(c)** *(missing the target)* daneben *pred*. **you're a bit ~ there** da liegst du etwas daneben; **~ of the truth** nicht ganz wahrheitsgetreu.

2 *adv* **(a)** *(extending far)* weit. **they are set ~ apart** sie liegen weit auseinander. **(b)** *(fully)* weit. **open ~!** bitte weit öffnen; **~ open** *(door)* weit offen; **the law is ~ open to criticism** das Gesetz bietet viele Ansatzpunkte für Kritik; **the game is still ~ open** der Spielausgang ist noch völlig offen; **to be ~ awake** hellwach sein; *(alert)* wach sein. **(c)** *(far from the target)* daneben. **to go ~ of sth** an etw *(dat)* vorbeigehen.

wide: ~-angle (lens) *n (Phot)* Weitwinkel(objektiv *nt*) *m*; **~-awake** *adj (fully awake)* hellwach; *(alert)* wach; **~-eyed** *adj* mit großen Augen; **in ~-eyed amazement** mit großen, erstaunten Augen.

widely ['waɪdlɪ] *adv* weit; *(by or to many people)* weit und breit, allgemein; *differing* völlig. **the opinion is ~ held ...** es herrscht in weiten Kreisen die Ansicht ...; **it is ~ believed that ...** es wird allgemein angenommen, daß ...; **he became ~ known as ...** er wurde überall *or* in weiten Kreisen bekannt als ...; **a ~ read student** ein sehr belesener Student.

widen ['waɪdn] **1** *vt road* verbreitern; *passage, knowledge* erweitern. **2** *vi* breiter werden; *(interests etc)* sich ausweiten.

♦ **widen out** *vi (valley etc)* sich erweitern *(into* zu*)*.

wide: ~-ranging *adj* weitreichend; **~spread** *adj* weitverbreitet *attr*; **to become ~spread** weite Verbreitung erlangen.

widow ['wɪdəʊ] **1** *n* Witwe *f*. **golf ~** *(hum)* Golfwitwe *f*. **2** *vt* zur Witwe/zum Witwer machen. **she was twice ~ed** sie ist zweimal verwitwet.

widower ['wɪdəʊə^r] *n* Witwer *m*.

width [wɪdθ] *n* Breite *f*; *(of trouser legs etc)* Weite *f*; *(of interests also)* Vielfalt *f*. **six centimetres in ~** sechs Zentimeter breit.

widthways ['wɪdθweɪz] *adv* der Breite nach.

wield ['wiːld] *vt pen, sword* führen; *axe* schwingen; *power* ausüben.

wife [waɪf] *n, pl* **wives** Frau, Gattin *(form) f*.

wifely ['waɪflɪ] *adj* **~ duties** Pflichten *pl* als Ehefrau; **~ devotion** Hingabe *f* einer Ehefrau.

wig [wɪg] *n* Perücke *f*.

wiggle ['wɪgl] **1** *n* Wackeln *nt no pl*. **give it a ~ and it might come free** wackeln Sie mal daran, dann geht es vielleicht raus. **2** *vt* wackeln mit. **3** *vi* wackeln.

wiggly ['wɪglɪ] *adj* wackelnd; *line* Schlangen-.

wigwam ['wɪgwæm] *n* Wigwam *m*.

wild [waɪld] **1** *adj* **(a)** *(not domesticated)* wild; *people* unzivilisiert; *garden, wood* verwildert; *flowers* wildwachsend *attr*. **the W~ West** der Wilde Westen; **~ animals** Tiere *pl* in freier Wildbahn; **the plant in its ~ state** die Pflanze im Naturzustand. **(b)** *(stormy) weather, wind, sea* rauh, stürmisch. **(c)** *(excited, riotous)* wild *(with* vor *+dat)*; *(disordered) hair also* wirr, unordentlich; *children also, desire* unbändig. **I'm not ~ about the idea** *(col)* auf die Idee bin ich nicht gerade versessen *(col)*; **to be ~ about sb** *(col)* verrückt nach jdm sein *(col)*; **the audience went ~** das Publikum raste. **(d)** *(col: angry)* wütend *(with, at* mit, auf *+acc)*, rasend. **it drives me ~** das macht mich ganz wild *or* rasend; **to get ~** wild werden *(col)*.

(e) *(rash, extravagant)* verrückt; *exaggeration, allegation* maßlos, wild; *fluctuations* stark; *expectations* kühn; *shot* Fehl-. **never in my ~est dreams** auch in meinen kühnsten Träumen nicht.

2 *adv grow* wild; *run* frei. **to let one's imagination run ~** seiner Phantasie *(dat)* freien Lauf lassen; **the roses/the children have run ~** die Rosen/die Kinder sind verwildert.

3 *n* Wildnis *f*. **in the ~** in der Wildnis, in freier Wildbahn; **out in the ~s of Berkshire** *(hum)* im hintersten Berkshire.

wildcat ['waɪldkæt] *n (Zool)* Wildkatze *f*. **~ strike** wilder Streik.

wilderness ['wɪldənɪs] *n* Wildnis *f*; *(fig)* Wüste *f*.

wild: ~fire *n* **to spread like ~fire** sich wie ein Lauffeuer ausbreiten; **~fowl** *n no pl* Wildgeflügel *nt*; **~-goose chase** *n* fruchtloses Unterfangen; **to send sb out on a ~-goose chase** jdn für nichts und wieder nichts losschicken; **~ life** *n* die Tierwelt; **~life sanctuary** Wildreservat *nt*.

wildly ['waɪldlɪ] *adv* **(a)** wild. **(b)** *(in disorder)* wirr. **(c)** *(extravagantly) guess* drauflos, ins Blaue hinein; *talk* unausgegoren; *exaggerated* stark, maßlos. **not ~ enthusiastic** nicht allzu begeistert.

wildness ['waɪldnɪs] *n* Wildheit *f*; *(of storm etc also)* Heftigkeit *f*; *(of allegation)* Maßlosigkeit *f*.

wiles [waɪlz] *n pl* Schliche *pl*.

wilful, *(US)* **willful** ['wɪlfʊl] *adj* **(a)** *(self-willed)* eigenwillig. **(b)** *(deliberate) neglect, damage* mutwillig; *murder* vorsätzlich; *disobedience* wissentlich.

will[1] [wɪl] *pret* **would 1** *modal aux* **(a)** *(forming future)* werden. **I'm sure that he ~ come** ich bin sicher, daß er kommt; **you ~ come to see us, won't you** Sie kommen uns doch besuchen, ja?; **I'll be right there** komme sofort!, bin gleich da!; **he'll be there — he won't** er wird dort sein — nein; **I ~ have finished by Tuesday** bis Dienstag bin ich fertig; **you won't lose it, ~ you?** du wirst es doch nicht verlieren, oder?

(b) *(emphatic)* **I ~ not have it!** das kommt nicht in Frage *(col)*; **~ you be quiet!** bist du *or* sei jetzt endlich ruhig!; **well, if you won't take advice** wenn du (eben) keinen Rat annimmst, na bitte; **he ~ interrupt all the time** er muß ständig dazwischenreden.

(c) *(expressing willingness, capability etc)* wollen. **he won't sign** er will nicht unterschreiben; **wait a moment, ~ you?** warten Sie bitte einen Moment; *(impatiently)* jetzt warte doch mal einen Moment!; **the car won't start** das Auto springt nicht an; **the cut won't heal** die Schnittwunde will nicht (ver)heilen; **the car ~ do up to 120 mph** das Auto fährt bis zu 120 Meilen pro Stunde.

(d) *(in questions)* **~ you have some more tea?** möchten Sie noch Tee?; **~ you accept these conditions?** akzeptieren Sie diese Bedingungen?

(e) *(assumption)* **he'll be there by now** jetzt ist er schon da *or* dürfte er schon da sein; **this ~ be the bus** das wird *or* dürfte unser Bus sein.

(f) *(tendency)* **sometimes he ~ sit in his room for hours** manchmal sitzt er stundenlang in seinem Zimmer; **accidents ~ happen** Unfälle passieren nun (ein)mal.

2 *vi* wollen. **say what you ~** du kannst sagen, was du willst; **as you ~!** wie du willst!

will[2] **1** *n* **(a)** Wille *m*. **to have a ~ of one's own** einen eigenen Willen haben; *(hum)* so seine Mucken haben *(col)*; **the ~ to win** der Wille, zu gewinnen; **(to go) against sb's ~** gegen jds Willen (handeln); **at ~** nach Belieben; **of one's own free ~** aus freien Stücken *or* freiem Willen; **with the best ~ in the world** beim (aller)besten Willen; **where there is a ~ there is a way** *(Prov)* wo ein Wille ist, ist auch ein Weg *(Prov)*. **(b)** *(testament)* Letzter Wille, Testament *nt*. **the last ~ and testament of ...** der Letzte Wille *or* das Testament des/der ...; **to make one's ~** sein Testament machen.

2 *vt (urge by willpower)* (durch Willenskraft) erzwingen. **to ~ sb to do sth** jdn durch die eigene Willensanstrengung dazu bringen, daß er etw tut; **he ~ed himself to stay awake** er hat sich (dazu) gezwungen, wach zu bleiben; **he ~ed the ball into the net** er hat den Ball ins Netz hypnotisiert *(col)*; **the crowd were ~ing him on** das Publikum feuerte ihn an.

willie ['wɪlɪ] *n (hum: penis)* Pimmel *m (col)*.

willies ['wɪlɪz] *npl (col)* **it/he gives me the ~** da/bei ihm wird mir ganz anders *(col)*.

willing ['wɪlɪŋ] *adj* **(a)** *(prepared)* **to be ~ to do sth** bereit *or* gewillt *(geh)* sein, etw zu tun; **God ~** so Gott will; **he was ~ for me to take it** es war ihm recht, daß ich es nahm; **he was not ~ for us to go** er war nicht gewillt, uns gehen zu lassen. **(b)** *workers, assistance* bereitwillig. **there were plenty of ~ hands** es gab viele, die helfen wollten; **to show ~** Bereitschaft zeigen.

willingly ['wɪlɪŋlɪ] *adv* bereitwillig, gerne. **will you help? — yes, ~** wollen Sie helfen? — (ja,) gerne.

willingness ['wɪlɪŋnɪs] *n see adj* **(a)** Bereitschaft *f*. **(b)** Bereitwilligkeit *f*.

will-o'-the-wisp ['wɪləðə'wɪsp] *n* Irrlicht *nt*; *(fig)* Trugbild *nt*.

willow ['wɪləʊ] *n (also ~* **tree***)* Weide *f*; *(wood)* Weidenholz *nt*.

willow pattern *n* chinesisches Weidenmotiv *(auf Porzellan)*.

willowy ['wɪləʊɪ] *adj* gertenschlank.

willpower ['wɪl,paʊə^r] *n* Willenskraft *f*.

willy-nilly ['wɪlɪ'nɪlɪ] *adv* wohl oder übel; *(at random, without plan)* nur einfach so.

wilt [wɪlt] *vi* **(a)** *(flowers)* welken, verwelken. **(b)** *(person: after exercise)* schlapp werden; *(enthusiasm, energy)* abflauen.

wily ['waɪlɪ] *adj (+er)* schlau, hinterlistig *(pej)*.

win [wɪn] *(vb: pret, ptp* **won***)* **1** *n* Sieg *m*. **to have a ~** *(money)* einen Gewinn machen; *(victory)* einen Sieg erzielen. **2** *vt* gewinnen; *reputation* erwerben; *scholarship, contract* bekommen; *victory* erringen. **land won from the sea** dem Meer abgewonnenes Land. **3** *vi* gewinnen, siegen. **OK, you ~, I was wrong** okay, du hast gewonnen, ich habe mich geirrt.

♦ **win back** *vt sep* zurück- *or* wiedergewinnen.

♦ **win over** *or* **round** *vt sep* für sich gewinnen. **to ~ sb ~ to one's way of thinking** jdn überzeugen.

♦ **win through** *vi (patient)* durchkommen. **we'll ~ ~ in the end** wir werden es schon schaffen *(col)*.

wince [wɪns] **1** *n* **to give a ~ (of pain)** (vor Schmerz) zusammenzucken. **2** *vi* zusammenzucken *(at* bei*)*.

winch [wɪntʃ] **1** *n* Winde *f*. **2** *vt* winden. **to ~ sth up** etw hochwinden.

wind[1] [wɪnd] **1** *n* **(a)** Wind *m*. **the ~ is from the east** der Wind kommt von Osten; **(to run) like the ~** (rennen) wie der Wind; **a ~ of change** *(fig)* ein frischer Wind; **there's something in the ~** (irgend) etwas liegt in der Luft; **to get/have the ~ up** *(col) (nervous)* Angst *or* Schiß *(col)* kriegen/haben; **to put the ~ up sb** *(col)* jdm Angst machen; **to see which way the ~ blows** *(fig)* sehen, woher der Wind weht; **to take the ~ out of sb's sails** *(fig)* jdm den Wind aus den Segeln nehmen; **to get ~ of sth** von etw Wind bekommen; **to throw caution to the ~s** Bedenken in den Wind schlagen; **to sail close to the ~** *(fig)* sich hart an der Grenze des Erlaubten bewegen.

(b) *(Med)* Blähung *f*. **to break ~** einen Wind entweichen lassen.

(c) *(breath)* Atem *m*, Luft *f (col)*. **to be short of**

~ außer Atem sein; **to get one's ~ back** wieder zu Atem kommen.
2 *vt (knock breathless)* den Atem nehmen *(+dat).*

wind[2] [waınd] *(vb: pret, ptp* **wound***)* **1** *vt* **(a)** *wool, bandage* wickeln; *(once round)* winden; *(on to a reel)* spulen. **(b)** *handle* drehen; *clock etc* aufziehen. **(c) to ~ one's way** sich schlängeln. **2** *vi (river etc)* sich winden *or* schlängeln.

♦ **wind down** *vt sep* **(a)** *car windows etc* herunterkurbeln. **(b)** *operations* reduzieren; *production* zurückschrauben.

♦ **wind in** *vt sep fish* einholen; *rope* aufspulen.

♦ **wind on** *vt sep film* weiterspulen.

♦ **wind up 1** *vt sep* **(a)** *bucket* heraufholen; *car window* hinaufkurbeln. **(b)** *clock* aufziehen. **to be wound ~ about sth** *(fig)* wegen einer Sache *(gen)* erregt sein. **(c)** *meeting, speech* beschließen, zu Ende bringen. **(d)** *company* auflösen; *service, series* auslaufen lassen. **2** *vi* **(a)** *(col: end up)* enden. **to ~ ~ in hospital** im Krankenhaus landen. **(b) to ~ ~ for the government** die abschließende Rede für die Regierung halten. **(c)** *(road)* sich hinaufschlängeln.

wind ['wınd-]: **~bag** *n (col)* Schwätzer(in *f*) *m*; **~break** *n* Windschutz *m*; **~breaker** ® *(US),* **~cheater** *(Brit) n* Windjacke.

winder ['waındəʳ] *n (of watch)* Rädchen *nt*; *(of alarm clock, toy etc)* Aufziehschraube *f.*

windfall ['wındfɔːl] *n* Fallobst *nt*; *(fig)* unverhoffter Glücksfall.

winding ['waındıŋ] **1** *adj river* gewunden; *road also* kurvenreich. **2** *n (Elec)* Wicklung *f.*

wind instrument *n* Blasinstrument *nt.*

windlass ['wındləs] *n (winch)* Winde *f*; *(Naut)* Ankerwinde *f.*

wind ['wınd-]: **~less** *adj* windstill; **~mill** *n* Windmühle *f.*

window ['wındəʊ] *n* Fenster *nt*; *(shop~)* (Schau)fenster *nt*; *(of bank etc)* Schalter *m.*

window: ~ box *n* Blumenkasten *m*; **~-cleaner** *n* Fensterputzer *m*; **~-dressing** *n* Schaufensterdekoration *f*; *(fig)* Schau *(col),* Augenwischerei *(pej) f*; **~ ledge** *n* = **~sill; ~ seat** *n (in house)* Fensterbank *f or* -sitz *m*; *(Rail etc)* Fensterplatz *m*; **~-shopping** *n* Schaufensterbummel *m*; **to go ~-shopping** einen Schaufensterbummel machen; **~sill** *n* Fensterbank *f.*

wind ['wınd-]: **~pipe** *n* Luftröhre *f*; **~screen,** *(US)* **~shield** *n* Windschutzscheibe *f*; **~screen** *or (US)* **~shield wiper** *n* Scheibenwischer *m*; **~sock** *n* Luft- *or* Windsack *m*; **~swept** *adj plains* über den/die/das der Wind fegt; *person, hair* (vom Wind) zerzaust; **~-tunnel** *n* Windkanal *m.*

windy ['wındı] *adj (+er)* windig.

wine [waın] **1** *n* Wein *m.* **2** *vt* **to ~ and dine sb** jdn gut bewirten.

wine: ~ cellar *n* Weinkeller *m*; **~glass** *n* Weinglas *nt*; **~-grower** *n* Winzer, Weinbauer *m*; **~-growing 1** *adj district* Wein(an)bau-; **2** *n* Wein(an)bau *m*; **~ list** *n* Weinkarte *f*; **~-taster** *n* Weinprüfer *m*; **~-tasting** *n* Weinprobe *f*; **~ waiter** *n* Getränkekellner *m.*

wing [wıŋ] *n* **(a)** *(of bird, plane, building, Mil, Pol, Sport)* Flügel *m*; *(Brit Aut)* Kotflügel *m.* **on the ~** im Flug(e); **to take sb under one's ~** *(fig)* jdn unter seine Fittiche nehmen; **to spread one's ~s** *(fig: children)* flügge werden. **(b) ~s** *pl (Theat)* Kulisse *f*; **to wait in the ~s** *(lit, fig)* in den Kulissen warten.

winger ['wıŋəʳ] *n (Sport)* Flügelspieler(in *f*) *m.*

wing: ~mirror *n* Außenspiegel *m*; **~ nut** *n* Flügelmutter *f*; **~span** *n* Flügelspannweite *f*; **~spread** *n* Spannweite *f.*

wink [wıŋk] **1** *n (with eye)* Zwinkern, Blinzeln *nt.* **to give sb a ~** jdm zuzwinkern; **to tip sb the ~** *(col)* jdm einen Wink geben; **I didn't sleep a ~** ich habe kein Auge zugetan. **2** *vi (meaningfully)* zwinkern, blinzeln; *(light, star etc)* blinken, funkeln. **to ~ at sb** jdm zuzwinkern.

winker ['wıŋkəʳ] *n (Brit Aut col)* Blinker *m.*

winkle ['wıŋkl] **1** *n* Strandschnecke *f.* **2** *vt* **to ~ a secret out of sb** jdm ein Geheimnis entlocken.

winner ['wınəʳ] *n (in race, competition)* Sieger(in *f*) *m*; *(of bet, pools etc)* Gewinner(in *f*) *m*; *(col: sth successful)* Renner *(col),* Schlager *m.* **to be onto a ~** *(col)* das große Los gezogen haben *(col).*

winning ['wınıŋ] **1** *adj* **(a)** *person, entry* der/die gewinnt; *horse, team* siegreich; *goal* Sieges-; *point, stroke* entscheidend. **~ ticket** Gewinnlos *nt*; **the ~ time** die beste Zeit; **~ post** Zielpfosten *m.* **(b)** *(charming) smile, ways* gewinnend, einnehmend. **2** *n* **~s** *pl* Gewinn *m.*

winter ['wıntəʳ] **1** *n (lit, fig)* Winter *m.* **2** *adj attr* Winter-. **~ sports** Wintersport *m*; **~time** Winter *m*; *(for clocks)* Winterzeit *f.*

winterize ['wıntəraız] *vt (esp US)* winterfest machen.

wint(e)ry ['wınt(ə)rı] *adj* winterlich; *(fig) look* eisig.

wipe [waıp] **1** *n* Wischen *nt.* **to give sth a ~** etw abwischen. **2** *vt* wischen; *floor* aufwischen; *hands, feet* abwischen, abputzen. **to ~ sb/sth clean** jdn/etw säubern; **to ~ sth with/on a cloth** etw mit/an einem Tuch abwischen; **to ~ one's brow/nose** sich *(dat)* die Stirn abwischen/die Nase putzen; **to ~ one's feet** sich *(dat)* die Füße abwischen; **to ~ the tears from one's eyes** sich *(dat)* die Tränen aus den Augen wischen; **to ~ the floor with sb** *(fig col)* jdn fertigmachen *(col).*

♦ **wipe away** *vt sep (lit, fig)* wegwischen.

♦ **wipe off** *vt sep mark* weg- *or* abwischen. **to be ~d ~ the face of the earth** von der Erdoberfläche verschwinden.

♦ **wipe out** *vt sep* **(a)** *(clean)* auswischen. **(b)** *(erase)* (aus)löschen; *guilt* verschwinden lassen. **(c)** *(cancel) debt* bereinigen; *gain* zunichte machen. **(d)** *(destroy) disease, village* ausrotten; *enemy* aufreiben.

♦ **wipe up 1** *vt sep liquid* aufwischen; *dishes* abtrocknen. **2** *vi* abtrocknen.

wiper ['waıpəʳ] *n* (Scheiben)wischer *m.*

wiping-up ['waıpıŋ'ʌp] *n* **to do the ~** abtrocknen.

wire [waıəʳ] **1** *n* **(a)** Draht *m*; *(cable, on appliance)* Leitung *f*; *(in circus: high ~)* (Hoch)seil *nt.* **you've got your ~s crossed there** *(col)* Sie verwechseln da etwas; **to get in under the ~** *(US col)* etwas gerade (eben) noch rechtzeitig schaffen. **(b)** *(Telec)* Telegramm *nt.* **2** *vt* **(a)** *(put in wiring) house* die (elektrischen) Leitungen verlegen in *(+dat)*; *(connect to electricity)* (an das Stromnetz) anschließen. **(b)** *(Telec)* telgrafieren. **(c)** *(fix with ~)* mit Draht zusammenbinden.

♦ **wire up** *vt sep lights, battery, speakers* anschließen; *house* elektrische Leitungen verlegen in *(+dat).*

wire: ~-cutters *npl* Drahtschere *f*; **~-haired** *adj terrier* Drahthaar-.

wireless ['waıəlıs] *(esp Brit dated) n* **(a)** *(also ~ set)* Radio, Rundfunkgerät *nt.* **(b)** *(radio)* Rundfunk *m*; *(also ~* **telegraphy***)* drahtlose Telegrafie.

wire: ~ netting *n* Maschendraht *m*; **~-pulling** *n (col)* Drahtziehen *nt*; **~-tapping** *n* Abhören *nt,* Anzapfen *nt* von Leitungen.

wiring ['waıərıŋ] *n* elektrische Leitungen *pl.*

wiring diagram *n* Schaltplan *m.*

wiry ['waıərı] *adj (+er)* drahtig; *hair also* borstig.

wisdom ['wızdəm] *n* Weisheit *f*; *(prudence)* Einsicht *f.*

wisdom tooth *n* Weisheitszahn *m.*

wise [waız] *adj (+er)* weise; *move etc* klug, vernünftig; *(col: smart)* klug, schlau. **a ~ choice** eine kluge *or* gute Wahl; **the Three W~ Men** die drei Weisen; **to be ~ after the event** hinterher gut reden haben; **I'm none the ~r** *(col)* ich bin nicht klüger als zuvor; **nobody will be any the ~r** *(col)* niemand wird etwas (davon) merken; **to get ~ to sb/sth** *(col)* dahinterkommen, wie jd/etw ist; **to put sb ~ to sb/sth** *(col)* jdn über jdn/etw aufklären.

wise: ~crack *(esp US) n* Witzelei *f*; *(pej)* Stichelei *f*; **~guy** *n (esp US col)* Klugschwätzer *(col)*, Klugscheißer *(col!) m.*

wisely ['waɪzlɪ] *adv* weise; *(sensibly)* klugerweise.

wish [wɪʃ] **1** *n* **(a)** Wunsch *m (for* nach*)*. **your ~ is my command** dein Wunsch ist mir Befehl; **I have no great ~ to see him** ich habe keine große Lust, ihn zu sehen; **to make a ~** sich *(dat)* etwas wünschen; **you shall have your ~** dein Wunsch soll in Erfüllung gehen. **(b) ~es** *pl (in greetings)* **with best ~es** mit den besten Grüßen; **please give him my good ~es** bitte grüßen Sie ihn (vielmals) von mir.

2 *vt* wünschen. **he ~es to be alone** er möchte allein sein; **I ~ you to be present** ich wünsche, daß Sie anwesend sind; **do you ~ more coffee, sir?** *(Scot, form)* hätten Sie gern noch Kaffee?; **~ you were here** ich wünschte, du wärest hier; **I ~ he'd be quiet** ich wollte *or* wünschte, er wäre still; **to ~ sb well/ill** jdm Glück *or* alles Gute/Schlechte wünschen; **to ~ sb a pleasant journey/a happy Christmas** jdm eine gute Reise/frohe Weihnachten wünschen; **he ~ed himself anywhere but there** er wünschte sich nur möglichst weit weg.

3 *vi (make a wish)* sich *(dat)* etwas wünschen.

♦ **wish for** *vi +prep obj* **to ~ ~ sth** sich *(dat)* etw wünschen; **she had everything she could ~ ~** sie hatte alles, was man sich nur wünschen kann.

wishbone ['wɪʃbəʊn] *n* Gabelbein *nt.*

wishful ['wɪʃfʊl] *adj* **that's just ~ thinking** das ist reines Wunschdenken.

wishy-washy ['wɪʃɪˌwɒʃɪ] *adj soup* labberig *(col)*, wäßrig; *person* farblos, lasch; *colour* verwaschen; *argument* schwach *(col)*; *story* ungenau, wischiwaschi *pred (col)*.

wisp [wɪsp] *n (of straw, hair etc)* kleines Büschel; *(of cloud)* Fetzen *m*; *(of smoke)* Wölkchen *nt.*

wistful ['wɪstfʊl] *adj* wehmütig; *song also* schwermütig.

wit [wɪt] *n* **(a)** *(understanding)* Verstand *m.* **a battle of ~s** ein geistiges Kräftemessen; **to be at one's ~s' end** am Ende seiner Weisheit sein, mit seinem Latein am Ende sein *(hum col)*; **to scare sb out of his ~s** jdn zu Tode erschrecken; **to keep one's ~s about one** seine (fünf) Sinne beisammenhalten, einen klaren Kopf behalten; **to live by one's ~s** sich schlau durchs Leben schlagen. **(b)** *(humour)* Geist, Witz *m.* **full of ~** geistreich; **there's a lot of ~ in the book** es ist sehr viel Geistreiches in dem Buch. **(c)** *(person)* geistreicher Kopf.

witch [wɪtʃ] *n (lit, fig)* Hexe *f.*

witch: ~craft *n* Hexerei, Zauberei *f*; **~ doctor** *n* Medizinmann *m.*

witch-hunt ['wɪtʃˌhʌnt] *n (lit, fig)* Hexenjagd *f.*

with [wɪð, wɪθ] *prep* **(a)** mit. **are you pleased ~ it?** bist du damit zufrieden?; **bring a book ~ you** bring ein Buch mit; **~ no ...** ohne ...; **put it ~ the rest** leg es zu den anderen; **how are things ~ you?** wie geht's?

(b) *(at house of, in company of etc)* bei. **I'll be ~ you in a moment** einen Augenblick bitte, ich bin gleich da; **10 years ~ the company** 10 Jahre bei *or* in der Firma.

(c) *(on person, in bag etc)* bei. **I haven't got my cheque book ~ me** ich habe mein Scheckbuch nicht bei mir.

(d) *(cause)* vor *(+dat)*. **to shiver ~ cold** vor Kälte zittern; **the hills are white ~ snow** die Berge sind weiß vom Schnee; **to be ill ~ measles** die Masern haben.

(e) *(in the case of)* bei, mit. **it's always the same ~ you** es ist (doch) immer dasselbe mit dir; **the trouble ~ him is that he ...** die Schwierigkeit bei *or* mit ihm ist (die), daß er ...; **I cannot concentrate ~ all this noise going on** bei diesem Lärm kann ich mich nicht konzentrieren; **~ the window open** bei offenem Fenster; **~ her being ill** da sie krank ist/war; **it varies ~ the temperature** es verändert sich je nach Temperatur; **wine improves ~ age** Wein wird mit zunehmendem Alter immer besser; **~ all his faults** bei allen seinen Fehlern, trotz aller seiner Fehler.

(f) *(expressing agreement, comprehension)* **I'm ~ you there** *(col)* da stimme ich dir zu; **are you ~ me?** verstehen Sie?, kapierst du? *(col)*.

withdraw [wɪθ'drɔː] *pret* **withdrew,** *ptp* **withdrawn 1** *vt object, motion, charge* zurückziehen; *troops, team also* abziehen; *ambassador* zurückbeordern; *coins* einziehen, aus dem Verkehr ziehen; *(from bank) money* abheben; *words, comment* zurücknehmen, widerrufen; *privileges* entziehen. **the workers withdrew their labour** die Arbeiter legten ihre Arbeit nieder. **2** *vi* sich zurückziehen; *(Sport also)* zurücktreten *(from* von*)*, nicht antreten *(from* von/bei*)*; *(move away)* zurücktreten *or* -gehen. **to ~ in favour of sb else** zu Gunsten eines anderen zurücktreten; **to ~ into oneself** sich in sich *(acc)* selbst zurückziehen.

withdrawal [wɪθ'drɔːəl] *n (of objects, charge)* Zurückziehen *nt*; *(of ambassador)* Abziehen *nt*; *(of coins)* Einziehen *nt*; *(of money)* Abheben *nt*; *(of words)* Zurücknahme *f*; *(of troops)* Rückzug *m*; *(from drugs)* Entzug *m.* **to make a ~ from the bank** von einer Bank etwas *or* Geld abheben; **~ symptoms** Entzugserscheinungen *pl.*

withdrawn [wɪθ'drɔːn] **1** *ptp of* **withdraw. 2** *adj person* verschlossen; *manner also* zurückhaltend.

withdrew [wɪθ'druː] *pret of* **withdraw.**

wither ['wɪðəʳ] *vi* **(a)** verdorren, ausdorren; *(limb)* verkümmern. **(b)** *(fig)* welken; *(religion)* dahinschwinden.

withered ['wɪðəd] *adj plant* verdorrt, vertrocknet; *skin, person* verschrumpelt; *limb* verkümmert.

withering ['wɪðərɪŋ] *adj look* vernichtend.

withhold [wɪθ'həʊld] *pret, ptp* **withheld** [wɪθ'held] *vt* vorenthalten; *truth also* verschweigen; *(refuse) consent, help* verweigern, versagen *(geh)*. **to ~ sth from sb** jdm etw vorenthalten/verschweigen/verweigern; **~ing tax** *(US)* (vom Arbeitgeber) einbehaltene Steuer.

within [wɪð'ɪn] *prep* innerhalb *(+gen)*; *(temporal also)* binnen *(+dat)*. **a voice ~ him** seine innere Stimme; **we were/came ~ 100 m of the summit** wir waren auf den letzten 100 Metern vor dem Gipfel/wir kamen bis auf 100 Meter an den Gipfel heran; **accurate to ~ 10 mm** auf 10 mm genau; **~ his power** in seiner Macht; **to keep ~ the law** sich im Rahmen des Gesetzes bewegen; **to live ~ one's income** im Rahmen seiner finanziellen Möglichkeiten leben.

with it ['wɪðɪt] *adj (col)* **(a)** *(attr* **with-it***)* *(trendy)* up to date. **(b)** *pred (awake, alert)* **to be ~** da sein *(col)*.

without [wɪð'aʊt] *prep* ohne. **~ a tie** ohne Krawatte; **~ speaking** ohne zu sprechen, wortlos; **~ my noticing it** ohne daß ich es bemerke/bemerkte; **he left ~ telling us** er ging, ohne es uns zu sagen.

withstand [wɪθ'stænd] *pret, ptp* **withstood** [wɪθ'stʊd] *vt cold* standhalten *(+dat)*; *climate, attack also* trotzen *(+dat)*; *persuasion etc* widerstehen *(+dat)*.

witness ['wɪtnɪs] **1** *n* **(a)** *(person: Jur, fig)* Zeuge *m*, Zeugin *f.* **~ for the defence/prosecution** Zeuge/Zeugin der Verteidigung/Anklage; **to call sb as a ~** jdn als Zeugen vorladen. **(b)** *(evidence)* Zeugnis *nt.* **to give ~ for/against sb** für/gegen jdn aussagen; **to bear ~ to sth** *(lit, fig)* Zeugnis über

etw *(acc)* ablegen. **2** *vt* **(a)** *(see) accident* Zeuge sein bei *or +gen; scenes also* (mit)erleben; *changes* erleben. **(b)** *(testify)* bezeugen; *(attest by signature)* bestätigen. **3** *vi (testify)* bezeugen. **to ~ to sth** etw bezeugen.
witness box *or (US)* **stand** *n* Zeugenstand *m.*
witticism ['wɪtɪsɪzəm] *n* geistreiche Bemerkung.
witty ['wɪtɪ] *adj (+er)* witzig, geistreich.
wives [waɪvz] *pl of* **wife.**
wizard ['wɪzəd] *n* Zauberer, Hexenmeister *m; (col)* Genie *nt.* **a financial ~** ein Finanzgenie *nt.*
wizened ['wɪznd] *adj* verhutzelt, verschrumpelt.
wk = week Wo.
wobble ['wɒbl] **1** *n* Wackeln *nt.* **the chair has a ~** der Stuhl wackelt. **2** *vi* wackeln; *(cyclist)* schwanken; *(voice, hand, compass needle)* zittern; *(wheel)* eiern *(col); (chin, jelly etc)* wabbeln.
wobbly ['wɒblɪ] *adj (+er)* wacklig; *voice also, hand* zitterig, zitternd; *jelly* wabbelig; *wheel* eiernd *(col).* **to be ~** *(col: after illness)* wacklig auf den Beinen sein *(col).*
woe [wəʊ] *n* **(a)** *(liter, hum: sorrow)* Jammer *m.* **~ betide him who ...!** wehe dem, der ...! **(b)** *(esp pl: trouble)* Kummer *m.* **to tell sb one's ~s** jdm sein Leid klagen.
woebegone ['wəʊbɪˌgɒn] *adj* kläglich, jämmerlich.
woeful ['wəʊfʊl] *adj (sad)* traurig; *neglect also, ignorance* beklagenswert.
wog [wɒg] *n (Brit pej col!)* Kaffer *m (pej col).*
woke [wəʊk] *pret of* **wake.**
woken ['wəʊkn] *ptp of* **wake.**
wolf [wʊlf] **1** *n, pl* **wolves** Wolf *m; (col: womanizer)* Don Juan *m.* **a ~ in sheep's clothing** ein Wolf im Schafspelz; **to cry ~** blinden Alarm schlagen; **to keep the ~ from the door** sich über Wasser halten. **2** *vt (also ~* **down***) food* hinunterschlingen.
wolf-whistle ['wʊlfˌwɪsl] *n* **they gave her a ~** sie pfiffen ihr nach.
wolves [wʊlvz] *pl of* **wolf.**
woman ['wʊmən] **1** *n, pl* **women** Frau *f; (domestic help)* (Hautshalts)hilfe *f; (mistress)* Geliebte *f.* **women's rights** die Rechte *pl* der Frau; **women's page** Frauenseite *f;* **women's lib** *(col)* Frauenrechtsbewegung *f;* **women's libber** *(col)* Frauenrechtlerin, Emanze *(esp pej col) f;* **women's hurdles** Hürdenlauf *m* der Damen. **2** *adj attr* **~ doctor** Ärztin *f;* **~ driver** Frau *f* am Steuer.
womanize ['wʊmənaɪz] *vi* hinter den Frauen her sein.
womanizer ['wʊmənaɪzə[r]] *n* Schürzenjäger *m.*
womanly ['wʊmənlɪ] *adj figure, person* fraulich; *qualities* weiblich.
womb [wuːm] *n* Mutterleib *m,* Gebärmutter *f (Med); (fig)* Schoß *m.*
women ['wɪmɪn] *pl of* **woman.**
womenfolk ['wɪmɪnfəʊk] *npl* Frauen *pl.*
won [wʌn] *pret, ptp of* **win.**
wonder ['wʌndə[r]] **1** *n* **(a)** *(feeling)* Staunen *nt,* Verwunderung *f.* **in ~** voller Staunen. **(b)** *(object or cause of ~)* Wunder *nt.* **the ~ of electricity** das Wunder der Elektrizität; **the seven ~s of the world** die sieben Weltwunder; **it is a ~ that ...** es ist ein Wunder, daß ...; **it is no** *or* **little ~** (es ist) kein Wunder; **no ~ (he refused)!** kein Wunder(, daß er abgelehnt hat)!; **to work ~s** Wunder wirken.

2 *vt* **I ~ what he'll do now** ich bin gespannt, was er jetzt tun wird *(col);* **I ~ who first said that** ich wüßte (zu) gern, wer das zuerst aufgebracht hat; **I was ~ing about going to the cinema** ich habe vielleicht vor, ins Kino zu gehen; **I was ~ing if you'd like to come too** möchten Sie nicht vielleicht auch kommen?; **I was ~ing if I could come tomorrow** könnte ich vielleicht morgen kommen?

3 *vi* **(a)** *(ask oneself, speculate)* **why do you ask? — oh, I was just ~ing** warum fragst du? — ach, nur so; **what will happen next, I ~?** ich bin gespannt, was als nächstes kommt; **I was ~ing about that** ich habe mich das auch schon gefragt; **I've been ~ing about him** ich habe mir auch schon über ihn Gedanken gemacht; **could you possibly help me, I ~** könnten Sie mir vielleicht helfen? **(b)** *(be surprised)* sich wundern. **I ~ (that) he didn't tell me** es wundert mich, daß er es mir nicht gesagt hat; **to ~ at sth** sich über etw *(acc)* wundern, über etw *(acc)* erstaunt sein; **she'll be married by now, I shouldn't ~** es würde mich nicht wundern, wenn sie inzwischen verheiratet wäre.
wonder *in cpds* Wunder-; **~ boy** *n* Wunderknabe *m;* **~ drug** *n* Wunderheilmittel *nt.*
wonderful ['wʌndəfʊl] *adj* wunderbar.
wondering ['wʌndərɪŋ] *adj (astonished) tone, look* verwundert, erstaunt; *(doubtful)* fragend.
wonderland ['wʌndəˌlænd] *n (fairyland)* Wunderland *nt; (wonderful place)* Paradies *nt.*
wonky ['wɒŋkɪ] *adj (+er) (Brit col) table, marriage, grammar* wackelig; *machine* nicht (ganz) in Ordnung. **your hat's a bit ~** dein Hut sitzt ganz schief.
won't [wəʊnt] = **will not.**
woo [wuː] *vt* **(a)** *(dated: court) woman* den Hof machen *(+dat),* umwerben; *(fig) person* umwerben. **(b)** *(fig) stardom etc* suchen.
wood [wʊd] **1** *n* **(a)** *(material)* Holz *nt.* **touch ~!** dreimal auf Holz geklopft!; **beer from the ~** Bier vom Faß. **(b)** *(small forest)* Wald *m.* **~s** Wald *m;* **we're not out of the ~ yet** *(fig)* wir sind noch nicht über den Berg *or* aus dem Schneider *(col);* **he can't see the ~ for the trees** *(prov)* er sieht den Wald vor lauter Bäumen nicht *(prov).* **(c)** *(Bowls)* Kugel *f; (Golf)* Holz *nt.* **2** *adj attr* **(a)** *(made of ~)* Holz-. **(b)** *(living etc in a ~)* Wald-.
wood: ~ carving *n* (Holz)schnitzerei *f;* **~cock** *n no pl* Waldschnepfe *f;* **~cut** *n* Holzschnitt *m;* **~cutter** *n* **(a)** Holzfäller *m; (of logs)* Holzhacker *m;* **(b)** *(Art)* Holzschnitzer *m.*
wooded ['wʊdɪd] *adj* bewaldet; *countryside also* Wald-.
wooden ['wʊdn] *adj* **(a)** Holz-. **~ leg** Holzbein *nt.* **(b)** *(fig) expression, manner* hölzern; *personality* steif.
wood: ~land *n* Waldland *nt;* **~pecker** *n* Specht *m;* **~pigeon** *n* Ringeltaube *f;* **~pulp** *n* Holzschliff *m;* **~shed** *n* Holzschuppen *m.*
woodsman ['wʊdzmən] *n, pl* **-men** [-mən] Waldarbeiter *m.*
wood: ~wind *n* Holzblasinstrument *nt;* **the ~wind(s), the ~wind section** die Holzbläser *pl;* **~work** *n* **(a)** Holzarbeit *f; (craft)* Tischlerei *f;* **(b)** *(wooden parts)* Holzteile *pl;* **~worm** *n* Holzwurm *m;* **it's got ~worm** da ist der Holzwurm drin.
woof [wʊf] *interj* **~, ~!** wau, wau!
woofer ['wʊfə[r]] *n* Tieftöner *m.*
wool [wʊl] **1** *n* Wolle *f; (cloth also)* Wollstoff *m.* **pure new ~** reine Schurwolle; **to pull the ~ over sb's eyes** *(col)* jdm Sand in die Augen streuen *(col).* **2** *adj* Woll-.
woollen, *(US)* **woolen** ['wʊlən] **1** *adj* Woll-, wollen. **2** *n* **~s** *pl (garments)* Wollsachen *pl; (fabrics, blankets)* Wollwaren *pl.*
woolly, *(US)* **wooly** ['wʊlɪ] **1** *adj (+er)* wollig; *(soft also)* flauschig; *(fig) outline* verschwommen; *(pej) mind, thinking* verworren, wirr. **2** *n (col: sweater etc)* Pulli *m (col).* **winter woollies** *(esp Brit: sweaters etc)* dicke Wollsachen *(col); (esp US: underwear)* Wollene *pl (col).*
woozy ['wuːzɪ] *adj (+er) (col)* benommen.
word [wɜːd] **1** *n* **(a)** Wort *nt.* **~s** Wörter *pl; (meaningful sequence)* Worte *pl;* **foreign ~s** Fremdwörter *pl;* **the W~ of God** das Wort

Gottes; ~ **for** ~ Wort für Wort; **cold isn't the** ~ **for it** kalt ist gar kein Ausdruck (dafür); **too funny for** ~**s** unbeschreiblich komisch; **to put one's thoughts into** ~**s** seine Gedanken in Worte fassen; ~**s fail me** mir fehlen die Worte; **in a** ~ mit einem Wort, kurz gesagt; **in so many** ~**s** direkt, ausdrücklich; **in other** ~**s** mit anderen Worten; **the last** ~ *(fig)* der letzte Schrei *(in an +dat)*; **he had the last** ~ er hatte das letzte Wort; **in the** ~**s of Goethe** um mit Goethe zu sprechen; **a** ~ **of advice** ein Rat(schlag) *m*; **a** ~ **of warning** eine Warnung; **fine** ~**s** schöne Worte *pl*; **a man of few** ~**s** ein Mann, der nicht viele Worte macht; **by** ~ **of mouth** durch mündliche Überlieferung; **to take sb at his** ~ jdn beim Wort nehmen; **to have a** ~ **with sb (about sth)** mit jdm (über etw) sprechen; *(reprimand, discipline)* jdn ins Gebet nehmen; **you took the** ~**s out of my mouth** du hast mir das Wort aus dem Mund genommen; **I wish you wouldn't put** ~**s into my mouth** ich wünschte, Sie würden mir nicht das Wort im Munde herumdrehen; **to put in a (good)** ~ **for sb** für jdn ein gutes Wort einlegen; **without a** ~ ohne ein Wort; **don't say** *or* **breathe a** ~ **about it** sag aber bitte keinen Ton davon; **to have** ~**s with sb** mit jdm eine Auseinandersetzung haben; ~ **of honour** Ehrenwort *nt*; **to keep one's** ~ sein Wort halten; **I give you my** ~ ich gebe dir mein (Ehren)wort; **to go back on one's** ~ sein Wort nicht halten; **to break one's** ~ sein Wort brechen; **take my** ~ **for it** das kannst du mir glauben; **my** ~! meine Güte!; **to give the** ~ **(to do sth)** das Kommando geben(, etw zu tun); **just say the** ~ sag nur ein Wort.

(b) ~**s** *pl (text, lyrics)* Text *m*.

(c) *no pl (message, news)* Nachricht *f*. ~ **went around that ...** es ging die Nachricht um, daß ...; *(rumour)* es ging das Gerücht um, daß ...; **to leave** ~ **(with sb/for sb) that ...** (bei jdm/für jdn) (die Nachricht) hinterlassen, daß ...; **is there any** ~ **from John yet?** schon Nachrichten von John?; **to send** ~ Nachricht geben; **to send** ~ **to sb** jdn benachrichtigen; **to send sb** ~ **of sth** jdn von etw benachrichtigen.

2 *vt* formulieren, in Worte fassen; *letter* formulieren; *speech* abfassen.

word: ~**-blind** *adj* wortblind; ~ **game** *n* Buchstabenspiel *nt*.

wording ['wɜːdɪŋ] *n* Formulierung *f*; *(text)* Text *m*; *(on label)* Aufschrift *f*.

word: ~ **order** *n* Wortstellung *f*; ~**-perfect** *adj* sicher im Text; ~ **processing** *n* Textverarbeitung *f*; ~ **processor** *n (machine)* Textverarbeitungsanlage *f*.

wordy ['wɜːdɪ] *adj (+er)* wortreich, langatmig *(pej)*.

wore [wɔːʳ] *pret of* **wear**.

work [wɜːk] **1** *n* **(a)** *(labour, task)* Arbeit *f*. **he doesn't like** ~ er arbeitet nicht gern; **that's a good piece of** ~ das ist gute Arbeit; **is this all your own** ~? haben Sie das alles selbst gemacht?; **to be at** ~ **(on sth)** (an etw *dat*) arbeiten; **you need to do some more** ~ **on your accent** Sie müssen noch an Ihrem Akzent arbeiten; **to put a lot of** ~ **into sth** eine Menge Arbeit in etw *(acc)* stecken; **to get on with one's** ~ sich (wieder) an die Arbeit machen; **to make short** ~ **of sth** mit etw kurzen Prozeß machen; **the medicine had done its** ~ die Arznei hatte ihre Wirkung getan; **the forces at** ~ **here** die Kräfte, die hier am Werk sind; **it was hard** ~ **for the old car to get up the hill** das alte Auto hatte beim Anstieg schwer zu schaffen.

(b) *(employment, job)* Arbeit *f*. **to be (out) at** ~ arbeiten sein; **to go out to** ~ arbeiten gehen; **to be out of/in** ~ arbeitslos sein/eine Stelle haben; **he travels to** ~ **by car** er fährt mit dem Auto zur Arbeit; **at** ~ am Arbeitsplatz; **what is your** ~? was tun Sie (beruflich)?; **to put sb out of** ~ jdn arbeitslos machen; **to be off** ~ (am Arbeitsplatz) fehlen.

(c) *(product)* Arbeit *f*; *(Art, Liter)* Werk *nt*. ~ **of art/reference** Kunstwerk *nt*/Nachschlagewerk *nt*; **a** ~ **of literature** ein literarisches Werk; **good** ~**s** gute Werke *pl*.

(d) ~**s** *pl (Mil)* Befestigungen *pl*; *(Mech)* Getriebe, Innere(s) *nt*; *(of watch, clock)* Uhrwerk *nt*.

(e) ~**s** *sing or pl (factory)* Betrieb *m*, Fabrik *f*; **gas** ~**s/steel** ~**s** Gas-/Stahlwerk *nt*.

(f) *(col)* **the** ~**s** *pl* alles Drum und Dran; **to give sb the** ~**s** *(treat harshly)* jdn gehörig in die Mangel nehmen *(col)*; *(treat generously)* jdn nach allen Regeln der Kunst verwöhnen *(col)*.

2 *vi* **(a)** arbeiten *(at* an *+dat)*. **to** ~ **towards/for sth** auf etw *(acc)* hin/für etw arbeiten; **to** ~ **for better conditions** *etc* sich für bessere Bedingungen *etc* einsetzen. **(b)** *(function, operate)* funktionieren; *(marriage, plan also, be successful)* klappen *(col)*; *(medicine, spell)* wirken. **it won't** ~ das klappt nicht; **to get sth** ~**ing** etw in Gang bringen; **it** ~**s by electricity** es läuft auf Strom; **it** ~**s both ways** es trifft auch andersherum zu. **(c)** *(mouth, face)* zucken; *(jaws)* mahlen. **(d)** *(move gradually)* **to** ~ **loose/along** sich lockern/sich entlangarbeiten.

3 *vt* **(a)** *(make* ~*) employees* arbeiten lassen, schinden *(pej)*. **to** ~ **oneself to death** sich zu Tode arbeiten.

(b) *(operate) machine* bedienen; *lever, brake* betätigen. **to** ~ **sth by hand** etw mit Hand betreiben.

(c) *change, cure* bewirken. **to** ~ **mischief** Unheil anrichten; **to** ~ **it (so that ...)** *(col)* es so deichseln(, daß ...) *(col)*; **to** ~ **one's passage** seine Überfahrt abarbeiten; **to** ~ **one's hands free** seine Hände freibekommen; **to** ~ **sth loose** etw losbekommen; **to** ~ **sth into the conversation** etw in das Gespräch einfließen lassen; **to** ~ **oneself into a rage** fürchterlich wütend werden; **to** ~ **one's way through a book** sich durch ein Buch arbeiten; **to** ~ **one's way to the top** sich nach oben arbeiten *or* kämpfen; **he** ~**ed his way across the rock-face** er überquerte die Felswand; **he had to** ~ **his way through college** er mußte sich sein Studium durch eigene Arbeit finanzieren.

(d) *(shape) wood, metal* bearbeiten; *dough, clay also* kneten, durcharbeiten. **he** ~**ed the clay into a human shape** er formte den Ton zu einer menschlichen Gestalt.

(e) *(exploit) mine* ausbeuten, abbauen; *land* bearbeiten; *smallholding* bewirtschaften; *(salesman) area* bereisen.

♦ **work around to** *vi +prep obj* **what are you** ~**ing** ~ ~? worauf wollen Sie hinaus?

♦ **work in** *vt sep* **(a)** *(rub in)* einarbeiten; *lotion* einmassieren. **(b)** *(in book, speech) reference* einbauen, einarbeiten. **(c)** *(in schedule etc)* einschieben.

♦ **work off** *vt sep debts, fat* abarbeiten; *energy* loswerden; *feelings* abreagieren *(on* an *+dat)*.

♦ **work on 1** *vi* weiterarbeiten. **2** *vi +prep obj* **(a)** *car, accent* arbeiten an *(+dat)*. **who's** ~**ing** ~ **this case?** wer bearbeitet diesen Fall?; **we haven't solved it yet but we're still** ~**ing** ~ **it** wir haben es noch nicht gelöst, aber wir sind dabei. **(b)** *evidence* ausgehen von; *principle (person)* ausgehen von; *(machine)* arbeiten nach. **if we** ~ ~ **the assumption that ...** wenn wir von der Annahme ausgehen, daß ...

♦ **work out 1** *vi* **(a)** *(amount to)* **that** ~**s** ~ **at £105** das gibt *or* macht £ 105; **how much does that** ~ ~ **at?** was macht das? **(b)** *(succeed: plan, marriage)* funktionieren, klappen *(col)*. **how's your new job** ~**ing** ~? was macht die neue Arbeit?; **I hope it** all ~s ~ for you ich hoffe, daß dir alles gelingt; things didn't ~ ~ that way es kam ganz anders. (c) *(in gym etc)* trainieren.

2 *vt sep* (a) *(solve, calculate)* herausbringen; *code* entschlüsseln; *mathematical problem* lösen; *problem* fertig werden mit *(+dat)*; *sum* ausrechnen. you can ~ that ~ for yourself das kannst du dir (doch) selbst denken; things will always ~ themselves ~ Probleme lösen sich stets von selbst. (b) *(devise) scheme* (sich *dat*) ausdenken; *(in detail)* ausarbeiten. (c) *(understand) person* schlau werden aus *(+dat)*. I can't ~ ~ why it went wrong ich kann nicht verstehen, wieso es nicht geklappt hat. (d) *(exhaust) mine* ausbeuten; *minerals* abbauen.

♦ **work up** *vt sep* (a) *(develop) business* zu etwas bringen, entwickeln; *enthusiasm (in oneself)* aufbringen; *appetite* sich *(dat)* holen. to ~ one's way ~ von der Pike auf dienen. (b) *(stimulate) audience* aufstacheln. to ~ ~ feelings against sb gegen jdn Stimmung machen; to get ~ed ~ sich aufregen.

♦ **work up to** *vi +prep obj question etc* zusteuern auf *(+acc)*. I know what you're ~ing ~ ~ ich weiß, worauf Sie hinauswollen.

workable ['wɜːkəbl] *adj mine* abbaufähig; *land* bebaubar; *clay* formbar; *plan* durchführbar.

workaday ['wɜːkədeɪ] *adj* Alltags-.

work: ~**bench** *n* Werkbank *f*; ~**day** *n (esp US)* Arbeitstag *m*; *(day of week)* Werktag *m*.

worker ['wɜːkə^r] *n* (a) Arbeiter(in *f*) *m*. (b) *(also* ~ **ant/bee)** Arbeiterin *f*.

work: ~ **force** *n* Arbeiterschaft *f*; ~**house** *n (Brit Hist)* Armenhaus *nt*.

working ['wɜːkɪŋ] 1 *adj* (a) *population* arbeitend, berufstätig. ~ **man/woman** *(worker)* Arbeiter(in *f*) *m*; **I'm a ~ man!** ich gehöre zur arbeitenden Bevölkerung. (b) *day, conditions, clothes* Arbeits-. ~ **capital** Betriebskapital *nt*; ~ **hours** Arbeitszeit *f*; ~ **party** (Arbeits)ausschuß *m*; ~ **week** *(~ hours)* Wochenarbeitszeit *f*. (c) *hypothesis, model* Arbeits-; *(sufficient) majority* arbeitsfähig. **in ~ order** in betriebsfähigem Zustand; ~ **knowledge** Grundkenntnisse *pl*. 2 *n* (a) *(work)* Arbeiten *nt*, Arbeit *f*. (b) ~**s** *pl (way sth works)* Arbeitsweise *f*; **the ~s of his mind** seine Gedankengänge; ~**s of fate** Wege *pl* des Schicksals. (c) ~**s** *pl (Min)* Schächte *pl*; *(of quarry)* Grube *f*.

working class *n (also* ~ ~**es)** Arbeiterklasse *f*.

working-class ['wɜːkɪŋ'klɑːs] *adj* der Arbeiterklasse, Arbeiter-; *(pej)* ordinär, proletenhaft. **to be ~** zur Arbeiterklasse gehören.

work: ~ **load** *n* Arbeit(slast) *f*; ~**man** *n* Handwerker(in *f*) *m*; ~**manlike** ['wɜːkmən'laɪk] *adj attitude, job* fachmännisch; *product* fachmännisch gearbeitet; ~**manship** ['wɜːkmənʃɪp] *n* Arbeit(squalität) *f*; ~**out** *n (Sport)* **to have a ~out** trainieren; ~ **permit** *n* Arbeitserlaubnis *f*; ~**shop** *n* Werkstatt *f*; **a music ~shop** ein Musik-Workshop *m*; ~**shy** *adj* arbeitsscheu; ~ **surface,** ~ **top** *n* Arbeitsfläche *f*; ~**-to-rule** *n* Dienst *m* nach Vorschrift; ~**week** *n (esp US)* Arbeitswoche *f*.

world [wɜːld] *n* Welt *f*. **in the ~** auf der Welt; **all over the ~** auf der ganzen Welt; **he sails all over the ~** er segelt in der Weltgeschichte herum; **it's the same all the ~ over** es ist (doch) überall das Gleiche; **to go around the ~** eine Weltreise machen; **to feel on top of the ~** sich glänzend fühlen; **it's a small ~** die Welt ist klein; **it's not the end of the ~!** *(col)* davon geht die Welt nicht unter! *(col)*; **to live in a ~ of one's own** in seiner eigenen (kleinen) Welt leben; **the New/Third W~** die Neue/Dritte Welt; **the business/literary ~** die Geschäftswelt/die literarische Welt; **man/woman of the ~** Mann *m*/Frau *f* von Welt; **to come down in the ~** herunterkommen; **to go up in the ~** es (in der Welt) zu etwas bringen; **to lead the ~ in sth** in etw *(dat)* in der Welt führend sein; **to have the best of both ~s** das eine tun und das andere nicht lassen; **out of this ~** *(col)* phantastisch; **not for (all) the ~** nicht um alles in der Welt; **what/who in the ~** was/wer in aller Welt; **it did him a ~ of good** es hat ihm (unwahrscheinlich) gut getan; **a ~ of difference** ein himmelweiter Unterschied; **they're ~s apart** sie sind total verschieden; **for all the ~ like ...** beinahe wie ...; **to think the ~ of sb/sth** große Stücke auf jdn halten/etw über alles stellen; **she/it means the ~ to him** sie/es bedeutet ihm alles.

world *in cpds* Welt-; ~**-beater** *n* **to be a ~-beater** führend in der Welt sein; ~ **champion** *n* Weltmeister(in *f*) *m*; **W~ Cup** *n* Fußballweltmeisterschaft *f*; *(cup)* Weltmeisterschaftspokal *m*; ~**-famous** *adj* weltberühmt.

worldly ['wɜːldlɪ] *adj (+er)* weltlich; *person* weltlich gesinnt. ~**-wise** weltklug.

world: ~ **record** *n* Weltrekord *m*; ~ **record holder** *n* Weltrekordinhaber(in *f*) *m*; ~ **war** *n* Weltkrieg *m*; **W~ War One/Two** der Erste/Zweite Weltkrieg; ~**-wide** *adj, adv* weltweit.

worm [wɜːm] 1 *n (lit, fig col)* Wurm *m*; *(wood ~)* Holzwurm *m*. ~**s** *(Med)* Würmer *pl*. 2 *vt* zwängen. **to ~ one's way into sth** sich in etw *(acc)* hineinzwängen; **to ~ one's way into sb's confidence** sich in jds Vertrauen einschleichen; **to ~ sth out of sb** jdm etw entlocken.

worn [wɔːn] 1 *ptp of* **wear.** 2 *adj (~-out) coat* abgetragen; *book* zerlesen; *carpet* abgetragen; *tyre* abgefahren; *person* angegriffen. **to look ~** *(with care)* besorgt aussehen.

worn-out *adj attr,* **worn out** ['wɔːn,aʊt] *adj pred coat* abgetragen; *carpet* abgetreten; *phrase* abgedroschen; *(exhausted) person* erschöpft.

worried ['wʌrɪd] *adj* besorgt *(about, by* wegen*)*; *(anxious also)* beunruhigt. **to be ~ sick** krank vor Sorge(n) sein.

worrier ['wʌrɪə^r] *n* Pessimist *m*. **he's a terrible ~** er macht sich ständig Sorgen.

worry ['wʌrɪ] 1 *n* Sorge *f*. **what's your ~?** was drückt dich?; **that's the least of my worries** das macht mir noch am wenigsten Sorgen. 2 *vt* (a) *(cause concern)* beunruhigen, Sorgen machen *(+dat)*. **to ~ oneself sick (about sth)** sich krank machen vor Sorge (um *or* wegen etw). (b) *(bother)* **to ~ sb with sth** jdn mit etw stören. (c) *(dog etc) sheep* nachstellen *(+dat)*; *(bite)* reißen. 3 *vi* sich sorgen, sich *(dat)* Sorgen machen *(about, over* um, wegen*)*. **don't ~!, not to ~!** keine Angst *or* Sorge!; **don't ~, I'll do it** laß mal, das mach ich schon.

worrying ['wʌrɪɪŋ] *adj problem* beunruhigend. **it's very ~** es macht mir große Sorge.

worse [wɜːs] 1 *adj, comp of* **bad** schlechter; *(morally, with bad consequences)* schlimmer, ärger. **it gets ~ and ~** es wird immer schlimmer; **and to make matters ~** und zu allem Übel; **it could have been ~** es hätte schlimmer kommen können; ~ **luck!** (so ein) Pech!; **the patient is getting ~** der Zustand des Patienten verschlechtert sich; **to be the ~ for drink** betrunken sein; **he's none the ~ for it** es ist ihm nichts dabei passiert; **you'll be none the ~ for it** das wird dir nicht schaden; **I don't think any the ~ of you for it** ich halte deswegen aber nicht weniger von dir.

2 *adv, comp of* **badly** schlechter; schlimmer. **to be ~ off than ...** schlechter dran sein *(col) or* in einer schlechteren Lage sein als ...; **I could do a lot ~ than accept their offer** es wäre bestimmt kein Fehler, wenn ich das Angebot annähme.

3 *n* Schlechteres *nt*; Schlimmeres *nt*. **there is ~ to come** es kommt noch schlimmer; **it's changed for the ~** es hat sich zum Schlechteren gewendet.

worsen ['wɜːsn] 1 *vt* verschlechtern. 2 *vi* sich

verschlechtern, schlechter werden.

worship ['wɜːʃɪp] **1** *n* **(a)** Verehrung *f*. **place of ~** Andachtsstätte *f*; *(non-Christian)* Kultstätte *f*. **(b)** *(Brit: in titles)* **Your W~** *(to judge)* Euer Ehren; *(to mayor)* (sehr geehrter) Herr Bürgermeister. **2** *vt (lit, fig)* anbeten. **3** *vi (Rel)* den Gottesdienst abhalten; *(RC)* die Messe feiern.

worshipper ['wɜːʃɪpəʳ] *n* Kirchgänger(in *f*) *m*.

worst [wɜːst] **1** *adj, superl of* **bad** schlechteste(r, s); *(morally, in consequence)* schlimmste(r, s). **the ~ possible time** die ungünstigste Zeit. **2** *adv, superl of* **badly** am schlechtesten; am schlimmsten. **3** *n* **the ~ is over** das Schlimmste *or* Ärgste ist vorbei; **at ~** schlimmstenfalls; **the ~ of it is ...** das Schlimmste daran ist, ...; **if the ~ comes to the ~** wenn alle Stricke reißen *(col)*; **to get the ~ of it** den kürzeren ziehen.

worsted ['wɜːstɪd] *n* Kammgarn *nt*.

worth [wɜːθ] **1** *adj* **(a)** wert. **it's ~ £5** es ist £ 5 wert; **it's not ~ £5** es ist keine £ 5 wert; **what's this ~?** was *or* wieviel ist das wert?; **it's ~ a great deal to me** es ist mir viel wert; *(sentimentally)* es bedeutet mir sehr viel; **what's it ~ to me to do that?** was springt für mich dabei heraus? *(col)*; **he was ~ a million** er besaß eine Million; **for all one is ~** so sehr man nur kann; **that's my opinion for what it's ~** das ist meine bescheidene Meinung; **it's more than my job is ~ to tell you** ich sage es dir nicht, dazu liegt mir zu viel an meiner Stelle.

(b) to be (well) ~ it sich (sehr) lohnen; **to be ~ sth** etw wert sein; **it's not ~ it** es lohnt sich nicht; **it's not ~ the trouble** es ist der Mühe nicht wert; **the book is ~ reading** das Buch ist lesenswert; **is there anything ~ seeing in this town?** gibt es in dieser Stadt etwas Sehenswertes?; **it's a film ~ seeing** es lohnt sich, diesen Film anzusehen; **hardly ~ mentioning** kaum der Rede wert.

2 *n* Wert *m*. **£10's ~ of books** Bücher im Werte von £ 10; **to show one's true ~** seinen wahren Wert zeigen; **to increase in ~** im Wert steigen.

worthless ['wɜːθlɪs] *adj* wertlos.

worthwhile ['wɜːθ'waɪl] *adj* **(a)** lohnend *attr*. **to be ~** sich lohnen; *(worth the trouble also)* der Mühe *(gen)* wert sein. **(b)** *(useful) contribution* wertvoll. **to do sth ~ with one's life** etwas Nützliches mit seinem Leben anfangen.

worthy ['wɜːðɪ] *adj (+er)* **(a)** ehrenwert, achtbar; *opponent* würdig; *motive, cause* lobenswert. **(b)** *pred* wert, würdig. **~ of mention** erwähnenswert; **to be ~ of sb/sth** jds/einer Sache würdig sein *(geh)*.

would [wʊd] *pret of* **will**[1] *modal aux vb* **(a)** *(conditional)* **if you asked him he ~ do it** wenn du ihn fragtest, würde er es tun; **if you had asked him he ~ have done it** wenn du ihn gefragt hättest, hätte er es getan; **I thought you ~ want to know** ich dachte, du würdest es gerne wissen; **you ~ think ...** man sollte meinen ...

(b) *(in indirect speech)* **she said she ~ come** sie sagte, sie würde kommen *or* sie käme.

(c) *(emph)* **you ~ be the one to get hit** typisch, daß ausgerechnet du getroffen worden bist; **I ~n't know** keine Ahnung; **you ~!** das sieht dir ähnlich!; **he ~ have to come right now** ausgerechnet jetzt muß er kommen.

(d) *(insistence)* **I warned him, but he ~ do it** ich habe ihn gewarnt, aber er mußte es ja unbedingt tun; **he ~n't listen** er wollte partout nicht zuhören.

(e) it ~ seem so es sieht wohl so aus; **it ~ have been about 8 o'clock** es war (wohl) so ungefähr 8 Uhr; **you ~n't have a cigarette, ~ you?** Sie hätten nicht zufällig eine Zigarette?; **what ~ you have me do?** was soll ich tun?; **~ you mind closing the window?** würden *or* könnten Sie bitte das Fenster schließen?; **~ you care for some tea?** möchten Sie gerne etwas Tee?

(f) *(habit)* **he ~ paint it each year** er strich es jedes Jahr.

would-be ['wʊdbiː] *adj attr* **(a)** *(pej) salesman, contract, improvements* angeblich. **a ~ poet** ein Möchtegern-Dichter. **(b)** *(training as, wanting to be)* angehend.

wouldn't ['wʊdnt] = **would not.**

wound[1] [wuːnd] **1** *n (lit)* Wunde *f*; *(fig also)* Kränkung *f*. **2** *vt (lit, fig)* verletzen. **the ~ed** *pl* die Verwundeten *pl*; **~ed pride/vanity** verletzter Stolz/gekränkte Eitelkeit.

wound[2] [waʊnd] *pret, ptp of* **wind**[2].

wove [wəʊv] *pret of* **weave.**

woven ['wəʊvən] *ptp of* **weave.**

wow [waʊ] *interj* hui *(col)*, Mann *(col)*.

wrangle ['ræŋgl] *vi* streiten, rangeln *(about* um*)*; *(in bargaining)* feilschen.

wrap [ræp] **1** *n* **(a)** *(garment)* Umhangtuch *nt*; *(for child)* Wickeltuch *nt*; *(cape)* Cape *nt*; *(coat)* Mantel *m*. **(b) to be under ~s** *(fig)* geheimgehalten werden. **2** *vt* einwickeln. **shall I ~ it for you?** soll ich es Ihnen einpacken *or* einwickeln?; **to ~ sth around sth** etw um etw wickeln; **he ~ped his car around a lamppost** *(col)* er hat sein Auto an einen Laternenpfahl gesetzt *(col)*; **to be ~ped in sth** *(fig)* in etw *(acc)* gehüllt sein.

♦ **wrap up 1** *vt sep* **(a)** *(lit, fig)* einwickeln, verpacken. **(b)** *(col: finalize) deal* unter Dach und Fach bringen. **that just about ~s it ~ for today** das wäre alles für heute. **(c)** *(be involved)* **to be ~ped ~ in sb/sth** in jdm/etw aufgehen. **2** *vi* **(a)** *(dress warmly)* sich warm einpacken *(col)*. **(b)** *(col!: be quiet)* den Mund halten *(col)*.

wrapper ['ræpəʳ] *n* Verpackung *f*; *(of sweets)* Papier(chen) *nt*; *(of cigar)* Deckblatt *nt*; *(of book)* (Schutz)umschlag *m*; *(postal)* Streifband *nt*.

wrapping ['ræpɪŋ] *n* Verpackung *f*. **~ paper** Packpapier *nt*; *(decorative)* Geschenkpapier *nt*.

wrath [rɒθ] *n* Zorn *m*; *(liter: of storm)* Wut *f*.

wreak [riːk] *vt destruction* anrichten; *chaos also* stiften; *(liter) vengeance* üben *(on* an *+dat)*.

wreath [riːθ] *n, pl* **-s** [riːðz] Kranz *m*; *(of smoke etc)* Kringel *m*.

wreathe [riːð] *vt (encircle)* (um)winden; *(clouds, mist)* umhüllen. **his face was ~d in smiles** er strahlte über das ganze Gesicht.

wreck [rek] **1** *n (ship~)* Schiffbruch *m*; *(ship itself)* Wrack *nt*; *(US: car crash etc)* Zusammenstoß *m*; *(fig) (old bicycle etc)* Trümmerhaufen *m*; *(person)* Wrack *nt*; *(of hopes, life etc)* Trümmer, Ruinen *pl*. **2** *vt* **(a)** *ship, train* zum Wrack machen; *car* kaputtfahren *(col)*, zu Schrott fahren *(col)*; *machine, furniture* zerstören; *(person)* kurz und klein schlagen *(col)*. **to be ~ed** *(Naut)* Schiffbruch erleiden; **~ed ship/car** wrackes Schiff/zu Schrott gefahrenes Auto. **(b)** *(fig) hopes, plans* zunichte machen; *marriage* zerrütten; *career, health* zerstören, ruinieren; *person* kaputtmachen *(col)*; *holiday* verderben.

wreckage ['rekɪdʒ] *n (lit, fig: remains)* Trümmer *pl*; *(washed ashore)* Strandgut *nt*; *(of house, town also)* Ruinen *pl*.

wrecker ['rekəʳ] *n* **(a)** *(Naut: salvager)* Bergungsarbeiter *m*; *(vessel)* Bergungsschiff *nt*. **(b)** *(US: breaker, salvager)* Schrotthändler *m*; *(for buildings)* Abbrucharbeiter *m*; *(breakdown truck)* Abschleppwagen *m*.

wren [ren] *n* Zaunkönig *m*.

wrench [rentʃ] **1** *n* **(a)** *(tug)* Ruck *m*; *(Med)* Verrenkung *f*. **(b)** *(tool)* Schraubenschlüssel *m*. **(c)** *(fig)* **to be a ~** weh tun. **2** *vt* **(a)** reißen. **to ~ sth (away) from sb** jdm etw entwinden *or* entreißen; **to ~ a door open** eine Tür aufzwingen. **(b)** *(Med)* **to ~ one's ankle** sich *(dat)* den Fuß verrenken.

wrest [rest] *vt* **to ~ sth from sb** jdm etw entreißen.

wrestle ['resl] **1** *n* Ringkampf *m*. **to have a ~ with sb** mit jdm ringen. **2** *vt* ringen mit. **3** *vi (lit, fig)* ringen.

wrestler ['reslə[r]] *n* Ringkämpfer *m*; *(modern)* Ringer(in *f*) *m*.

wrestling ['reslɪŋ] *n* Ringen *nt*. ~ **match** Ringkampf *m*.

wretch [retʃ] *n* **(a)** *(miserable)* armer Teufel. **(b)** *(contemptible)* Schuft *m*; *(child)* Schlingel *m*.

wretched ['retʃɪd] *adj* elend; *conditions, clothing etc also* erbärmlich; *(unhappy)* (tod)unglücklich; *housing, weather* erbärmlich, miserabel *(col)*; *(col: damned)* verflixt *(col)*, Mist- *(col)*. **I feel** ~ *(ill)* mir geht es miserabel *(col)*.

wrick [rɪk] *vt* **to** ~ **one's neck/shoulder** sich *(dat)* den Hals/die Schulter ausrenken.

wriggle ['rɪgl] **1** *vt toes, ears* wackeln mit. **to** ~ **one's way through sth** sich durch etw (hin)durchwinden. **2** *vi (also* ~ **about** *or* **around***)* *(snake)* sich schlängeln; *(fish)* sich winden, zappeln; *(person) (restlessly)* zappeln; *(in embarrassment)* sich winden. **to** ~ **along/down** sich vorwärts schlängeln/sich nach unten schlängeln; **she managed to** ~ **free** es gelang ihr, sich loszuwinden.

♦ **wriggle out** *vi (lit)* sich herauswinden *(of* aus*)*; *(fig also)* sich herausmanövrieren *(of* aus*)*. **he's** ~**d (his way)** ~ **of it** er hat sich gedrückt.

wring [rɪŋ] *(vb: pret, ptp* **wrung***)* *vt* **(a)** *(also* ~ **out***)* *clothes etc* auswringen, auswinden. **do not** ~ *(on washing instructions)* nicht wringen. **(b)** *hands (in distress)* ringen. **I could have wrung his neck** ich hätte ihm den Hals umdrehen können. **(c)** *(extract)* **to** ~ **sth out of sb** etw aus jdm herausquetschen *(col)*, jdm etw abringen.

wringer ['rɪŋə[r]] *n* (Wäsche)mangel *f*.

wringing ['rɪŋɪŋ] *adj (also* ~ **wet***)* tropfnaß.

wrinkle ['rɪŋkl] **1** *n (in clothes, paper)* Knitter(falte *f*) *m*; *(on face, skin, in stocking)* Falte *f*. **2** *vt fabric, paper* zerknittern; *skin* faltig machen. **to** ~ **one's nose/brow** die Nase rümpfen/die Stirn runzeln. **3** *vi (material)* knittern; *(stockings)* Falten schlagen; *(skin etc)* Falten bekommen.

wrinkled ['rɪŋkld] *adj sheet, paper* zerknittert; *stockings* Ziehharmonika- *(col)*; *skin* faltig; *brow* gerunzelt; *apple, old lady* verschrumpelt.

wrist [rɪst] *n* Handgelenk *nt*.

wristband ['rɪst,bænd] *n* Armband *nt*; *(Sport)* Schweißband *nt*.

wristwatch ['rɪst,wɒtʃ] *n* Armbanduhr *f*.

writ [rɪt] *n (Jur)* Verfügung *f*. **to issue a** ~ **against sb** jdn vorladen *(for* wegen*)*.

write [raɪt] *pret* **wrote,** *ptp* **written** **1** *vt* schreiben; *cheque also* ausstellen; *notes* sich *(dat)* machen. **he wrote me a letter** er schrieb mir einen Brief; **he wrote five sheets of paper** er schrieb fünf Seiten voll; **how is that written?** wie schreibt man das?; **to be writ(ten) large** *(fig)* klar zu erkennen sein; **it was written all over his face** es stand ihm im Gesicht geschrieben. **2** *vi* schreiben. **to** ~ **to sb** jdm schreiben; **we** ~ **to each other** wir schreiben uns; **that's nothing to** ~ **home about** *(col)* das ist nichts Weltbewegendes; **I'll** ~ **for it at once** *(order)* ich bestelle es sofort.

♦ **write away** *vi* schreiben. **to** ~ ~ **for sth** etw anfordern.

♦ **write back** *vi* zurückschreiben, antworten.

♦ **write down** *vt sep (make a note of)* aufschreiben; *(put in writing)* niederschreiben.

♦ **write in 1** *vt sep word etc* hineinschreiben, einfügen *(prep obj* in *+acc)*. **2** *vi* schreiben *(to* an *+acc)*. **to** ~ ~ **for sth** etw anfordern.

♦ **write off 1** *vi* = **write away. 2** *vt sep debt, losses, (fig: regard as failure)* abschreiben; *car etc (driver)* zu Schrott fahren; *(insurance company)* als Totalschaden abschreiben.

♦ **write out** *vt sep notes* ausarbeiten; *name etc* ausschreiben; *cheque* ausstellen.

♦ **write up** *vt sep notes* ausarbeiten; *report, diary* schreiben; *event* schreiben über *(+acc)*; *(review) play, film* eine Kritik schreiben über *(+acc)*.

write-off ['raɪtɒf] *n (car etc)* Totalschaden *m*; *(Comm)* Abschreibung *f*.

writer ['raɪtə[r]] *n* Schriftsteller(in *f*) *m*; *(of report etc)* Autor(in *f*) *m*; *(of music)* Komponist(in *f*) *m*. **he's a very poor** ~ er schreibt sehr schlecht; *(correspondent)* er ist kein großer Briefschreiber; ~**'s cramp** Schreibkrampf *m*.

write-up ['raɪtʌp] *n* Pressebericht *m*; *(of play etc)* Kritik *f*.

writhe [raɪð] *vi* sich krümmen, sich winden *(with, in* vor *+dat)*.

writing ['raɪtɪŋ] *n* Schrift *f*; *(act, profession)* Schreiben *nt*; *(inscription)* Inschrift *f*. **in** ~ schriftlich; **permission in** ~ schriftliche Genehmigung; **his** ~**s** seine Werke *or* Schriften; **in sb's own** ~ *(not typewritten)* handgeschrieben; *(not written by sb else)* in jds eigener (Hand)schrift *(dat)*; **the** ~ **is on the wall for them** ihre Stunde hat geschlagen; **he had seen the** ~ **on the wall** er hatte die Zeichen erkannt.

writing *in cpds* Schreib-; ~ **case** Schreibmappe *f*; ~ **desk** *n* Schreibtisch *m*; ~ **pad** *n* Notizblock *m*; ~ **paper** *n* Schreibpapier *nt*.

written ['rɪtn] **1** *ptp of* **write. 2** *adj examination, statement* schriftlich; *language* Schrift-; *word* geschrieben.

wrong [rɒŋ] **1** *adj* **(a)** falsch; *(when choice is given also)* verkehrt. **to be** ~ nicht stimmen; *(person)* unrecht haben; *(answer also)* falsch *or* verkehrt sein; *(watch)* falsch gehen; **it's all** ~ **that I should have to ...** das ist doch nicht richtig, daß ich ... muß; **I was** ~ **about him** ich habe mich in ihm geirrt; **you were** ~ **in thinking he did it** du hast unrecht gehabt, als du dachtest, er sei es gewesen; **I took a** ~ **turning** ich habe eine falsche Abzweigung genommen; **to say/do the** ~ **thing** das Falsche sagen/tun; **the** ~ **side of the fabric** die linke Seite des Stoffes; **to do sth the** ~ **way** etw falsch *or* verkehrt machen.

(b) *(morally)* schlecht, unrecht; *(unfair)* ungerecht, unfair. **it's** ~ **to steal** es ist unrecht zu stehlen; **you were** ~ **to do that** es war nicht richtig von dir, das zu tun; **what's** ~ **with a drink now and again?** was ist schon (Schlimmes) dabei, wenn man ab und zu einen trinkt?

(c) *pred (amiss)* **something is** ~ (irgend) etwas stimmt nicht *or* ist nicht in Ordnung; *(suspiciously)* irgend etwas stimmt da nicht *or* ist da faul *(col)*; **is anything** ~? ist was? *(col)*; **there's nothing** ~ (es ist) alles in Ordnung; **what's** ~? was ist los?; **what's** ~ **with you?** was fehlt Ihnen?; **something's** ~ **with my watch** mit meiner Uhr stimmt (et)was nicht.

2 *adv* falsch. **you did** ~ **to do it** es war unrecht *or* nicht richtig von dir, das zu tun; **to get sth** ~ sich mit etw vertun; **to get one's sums** ~ sich verrechnen; **don't get me** ~ verstehen Sie mich nicht falsch; **to go** ~ *(on route)* falsch gehen/fahren; *(plan)* schiefgehen; *(affair etc)* schieflaufen; **my washing-machine has gone** ~ meine Waschmaschine ist nicht in Ordnung; **you can't go** ~ du kannst gar nichts verkehrt machen; *(in telling sb the way)* du kannst dich nicht verlaufen/verfahren.

3 *n* Unrecht *nt no pl*. **(social)** ~**s** (soziale) Ungerechtigkeiten *pl*; **to be in the** ~ im Unrecht sein; **to put sb in the** ~ jdn ins Unrecht setzen; **two** ~**s don't make a right** ein zweites Unrecht hebt das erste nicht auf; **she, of course, can do no** ~ sie macht natürlich nie einen Fehler.

4 *vt* **to** ~ **sb** jdm unrecht tun; **to be** ~**ed** ungerecht behandelt werden.

wrongdoer ['rɒŋ,duːə[r]] *n* Übeltäter(in *f*) *m*.

wrongful ['rɒŋfʊl] *adj* ungerechtfertigt.

wrongly ['rɒŋlɪ] *adv* **(a)** *(unjustly, improperly)* unrecht; *punished* zu Unrecht. **(b)** *(incorrectly)* falsch, verkehrt; *maintain* zu Unrecht; *believe*

fälschlicherweise.
wrote [rəʊt] *pret of* **write.**
wrought [rɔːt] **1** *vt* **(a)** *(obs, liter) pret, ptp of* **work. (b) great changes have been** ~ große Veränderungen wurden herbeigeführt; **the storm** ~ **great destruction** der Sturm richtete große Verheerungen an. **2** *adj iron* Schmiede-; *silver* gehämmert.
wrought: ~**-iron** *adj* schmiedeeisern *attr,* aus Schmiedeeisen; ~**-up** *adj* **to be** ~**-up** aufgeregt sein.
wrung [rʌŋ] *pret, ptp of* **wring.**
wry [raɪ] *adj (ironical)* ironisch; *joke, humour etc* trocken.
wryly ['raɪlɪ] *adv* ironisch.
wt = **weight** Gew.

X

X, x [eks] *n* X, x *nt.* ~ **pounds** x Pfund; ~ **marks the spot** die Stelle ist mit einem Kreuz gekennzeichnet; ~**-certificate film** nicht jugendfreier Film.

Xerox ® ['zɪərɒks] *vt* xerokopieren.

Xmas ['eksməs, 'krɪsməs] *n* = **Christmas** Weihnachten *nt.*

X-ray ['eks'reɪ] **1** *n* Röntgenstrahl *m*; *(also ~* **photograph***)* Röntgenaufnahme *f.* **to have an** ~ geröntgt werden. **2** *vt person, heart* röntgen; *envelope* durchleuchten.

xylophone ['zaɪləfəʊn] *n* Xylophon *nt.*

Y

Y, y [waɪ] *n* Y, y *nt.*

yacht [jɒt] *nt* Jacht, Yacht *f.* ~ **club** Jacht- *or* Segelklub *m*; ~ **race** (Segel)regatta *f.*

yachting ['jɒtɪŋ] *n* Segeln *nt.* **to go ~ing** segeln gehen.

yachtsman ['jɒtsmən] *n, pl* **-men** [-mən] Segler *m.*

yachtswoman ['jɒtswʊmən] *n, pl* **-women** [-wɪmɪn] Seglerin *f.*

yak [jæk] *n (Zool)* Jak, Grunzochse *m.*

yam [jæm] *n* **(a)** *(plant)* Yamswurzel *f.* **(b)** *(US: sweet potato)* Süßkartoffel *f.*

yank [jæŋk] **1** *n* Ruck *m.* **give it a good** ~ zieh mal kräftig dran. **2** *vt* **to ~ sth** mit einem Ruck an etw *(dat)* ziehen.

♦ **yank out** *vt sep* ausreißen; *tooth* ziehen.

Yank [jæŋk] **1** *n* Ami *m (col).* **2** *adj attr* Ami- *(col).*

yap [jæp] *vi (dog)* kläffen; *(talk noisily)* quatschen *(col)*, labern *(col).*

yard[1] [jɑːd] *n (Measure)* Yard *nt.* **to buy cloth by the** ~ ≃ Stoff im Meter kaufen.

yard[2] *n* **(a)** Hof *m.* **back** ~ Hinterhof *m*; **in the** ~ auf dem Hof. **(b)** *(worksite)* Werksgelände *nt*; *(for storage)* Lagerplatz *m.* **builder's** ~ Bauhof *m*; **shipbuilding** ~ Werft *f*; **naval (dock)~, navy** ~ Marinewerft *f.* **(c)** *(US: garden)* Garten *m.*

yard: ~-arm *n (Naut)* Nock *f*; **~stick** *n (measuring rod)* Elle *f*; *(fig)* Maßstab *m.*

yarn [jɑːn] *n* **(a)** *(Tex)* Garn *nt.* **(b)** *(tale)* Seemannsgarn *nt.* **to spin a** ~ Seemannsgarn spinnen; **to spin sb a ~ about sth** jdm eine Lügengeschichte über etw *(acc)* erzählen.

yawn [jɔːn] **1** *vt (lit, fig)* gähnen. **to ~ one's head off** fürchterlich gähnen *(col).* **2** *n* Gähnen *nt.* **to give a** ~ gähnen; **to be a** ~ *(col)* langweilig sein.

yawning ['jɔːnɪŋ] *adj chasm etc* gähnend.

yd = **yard(s).**

yea [jeɪ] **1** *adv (obs: yes)* ja. **2** *n* **the ~s and the nays** die Jastimmen und die Neinstimmen.

yeah [jɛə] *adv (col)* ja.

year [jɪə^r] *n* **(a)** Jahr *nt.* **last** ~ letztes Jahr; **this** ~ dieses Jahr; **every other** ~ jedes zweite Jahr; **in the ~ 1969** im Jahr(e) 1969; ~ **after** ~ Jahr für Jahr; ~ **by ~, from ~ to** ~ von Jahr zu Jahr; ~ **in, ~ out** jahrein, jahraus; **all (the) ~ round** das ganze Jahr über; **~s (and ~s) ago** vor (langen) Jahren; **I haven't seen her in ~s** ich habe sie jahrelang *or* seit Jahren nicht mehr gesehen; **a ~ last January** (im) Januar vor einem Jahr; **a ~ from now** nächstes Jahr um diese Zeit; **a hundred-~-old tree** ein hundertjähriger Baum; **he is six ~s old** er ist sechs Jahre (alt); **it costs £100 a** ~ es kostet £100 pro *or* im Jahr; **it has put ~s on me** es hat mich (um) Jahre älter gemacht; **it takes ~s off you** es macht dich um Jahre jünger; **he looks old for his ~s** er sieht älter aus als er ist; **well on in ~s** im vorgerückten Alter; **to get on in ~s** in die Jahre kommen.

(b) *(Univ, Sch, of wine)* Jahrgang *m.* **first-~ student** Student(in *f*) *m* im ersten Jahr; *(in first term)* ≃ Erstsemester *nt.*

yearbook ['jɪəbʊk] *n* Jahrbuch *nt.*

yearling ['jɪəlɪŋ] *n (animal)* Jährling *m*; *(racehorse also)* Einjährige(r) *mf.*

yearly ['jɪəlɪ] **1** *adj* jährlich. **2** *adv* jährlich, einmal im Jahr. **twice** ~ zweimal im Jahr.

yearn [jɜːn] *vi* sich sehnen *(after, for* nach*).* **to ~ to do sth** sich danach sehnen, etw zu tun.

yearning ['jɜːnɪŋ] **1** *n* Sehnsucht *f*, Verlangen *nt (to do sth* etw zu tun, *for* nach*).* **2** *adj desire, look* sehnsüchtig.

yeast [jiːst] *n no pl* Hefe *f.*

yell [jel] **1** *n* Schrei *m.* **to let out a** ~ einen Schrei ausstoßen, schreien. **2** *vt (also ~* **out***)* schreien, brüllen *(with* vor *+dat).* **he ~ed at her** er schrie *or* brüllte sie an; **he ~ed abuse at the teacher** er beschimpfte den Lehrer wüst.

yellow ['jeləʊ] **1** *adj (+er)* **(a)** gelb. **to turn** ~ gelb werden; *(paper)* vergilben; ~ **pages** Branchenverzeichnis *nt*, Gelbe Seiten *pl.* **(b)** *(col: cowardly)* feige. **2** *n (colour)* Gelb *nt*; *(of egg)* Eigelb *nt.* **3** *vi* gelb werden; *(pages)* vergilben.

yellowish ['jeləʊɪʃ] *adj* gelblich.

yelp [jelp] **1** *n (of animal)* Jaulen *nt no pl*; *(of person)* Aufschrei *m.* **2** *vi (animal)* (auf)jaulen; *(person)* aufschreien.

yen[1] [jen] *n (Fin)* Yen *m.*

yen[2] *n (col)* Lust *f (for* auf *+acc).* **to have a ~ to do sth** Lust haben, etw zu tun.

yeoman ['jəʊmən] *n, pl* **-men** [-mən] **(a)** *(Hist: small landowner)* Freibauer *m.* **(b) Y~ of the Guard** königlicher Leibgardist.

yes [jes] **1** *adv* ja; *(answering neg question)* doch. **to say ~ to a demand** einer Forderung *(dat)* nachkommen; **if management says ~ to an increase** wenn die Betriebsleitung eine Lohnerhöhung bewilligt; ~ **sir!** jawohl, mein Herr; *(Mil)* jawohl,

Herr General/Leutnant *etc*; **I didn't say that — oh ~, you did** das habe ich nicht gesagt — o doch, das hast du. **2** *n* Ja *nt*.

yes man ['jesmæn] *n, pl* ~ **men** [-men] Jasager *m*.

yesterday ['jestədeɪ] **1** *n* Gestern *nt*. **the fashions of** ~ die Mode von gestern. **2** *adv (lit, fig)* gestern. ~ **morning/evening** gestern morgen/abend; **he was at home all (day)** ~ er war gestern den ganzen Tag zu Hause; **the day before** ~ vorgestern; **a week ago** ~ gestern vor einer Woche; **~'s paper** die Zeitung von gestern.

yet [jet] **1** *adv* **(a)** *(still)* noch; *(thus far)* bis jetzt, bisher. **they haven't returned** ~ sie sind noch nicht zurückgekommen; **this is his best book** ~ das ist sein bisher bestes Buch; **as** ~ *(with present tenses)* bis jetzt, bisher; *(with past)* bis dahin; **no, not** ~ nein, noch nicht; **not just** ~ jetzt noch nicht; **they have a few days** ~ sie haben noch ein paar Tage; **I've** ~ **to learn how to do it** ich muß erst noch lernen, wie man es macht; **he may** ~ **come** er kann noch kommen; **I may** ~ **go to Italy** ich fahre vielleicht noch nach Italien; **I'll do it** ~ ich schaffe es schon noch.

(b) *(with interrog)* schon. **has he arrived** ~? ist er schon angekommen?; **do you have to go just** ~? müssen Sie jetzt schon gehen?

(c) *(with comp)* noch. **this is** ~ **more difficult** dies ist (sogar) noch schwieriger; **he wants** ~ **more money** er will noch mehr Geld.

(d) *(in addition)* **(and)** ~ **again** und wieder, und noch einmal; **another arrived and** ~ **another** es kam noch einer und noch einer.

2 *conj* doch, dennoch, trotzdem. **and** ~ und doch *or* dennoch; **it's strange** ~ **true** es ist seltsam, aber wahr.

yeti ['jetɪ] *n* Yeti, Schneemensch *m*.

yew [juː] *n (also* ~ **tree***)* Eibe *f*; *(wood)* Eibe(nholz *nt) f*.

Yiddish ['jɪdɪʃ] **1** *adj* jiddisch. **2** *n (language)* Jiddisch *nt*.

yield [jiːld] **1** *vt* **(a)** *crop, result* hervorbringen; *(tree) fruit* tragen; *(mine)* bringen; *(shares) interest* (ein)bringen. **the information ~ed by the poll** die Information, die die Meinungsumfrage ergeben hat. **(b)** *(surrender)* aufgeben. **to ~ sth to sb** etw an jdn abtreten; **to ~ ground to the enemy** vor dem Feind zurückweichen.

2 *vi* **(a)** *(surrender, give way)* **they ~ed to us** sie haben nachgegeben; *(Mil)* sie haben sich uns *(dat)* ergeben; **to ~ to force** der Gewalt nachgeben; **to ~ to reason** sich der Vernunft beugen; **to ~ to sb's entreaties/threats** jds Bitten *(dat)* nachgeben/sich jds Drohungen *(dat)* beugen; **to ~ to temptation** der Versuchung erliegen. **(b)** *(give way: branch, ground)* nachgeben. **(c)** *(Mot)* **to ~ to oncoming traffic** den Gegenverkehr vorbeilassen; **"~"** *(US, Ir)* „Vorfahrt gewähren!"

3 *n (of land, tree)* Ertrag *m*; *(of work also)* Ergebnis *nt*; *(of mine, well)* Ausbeute *f*; *(of industry: goods)* Produktion *f*; *(profit)* Gewinne, Erträge *pl*; *(Fin: of shares, business)* Ertrag, Gewinn *m*.

yippee [jɪ'piː] *interj* juchhu, hurra.

YMCA = **Young Men's Christian Association** CVJM *m*.

yob(bo) ['jɒb(əʊ)] *n (Brit col)* Halbstarke(r), Rowdy *m*.

yodel ['jəʊdl] *vti* jodeln.

yoga ['jəʊgə] *n* Joga, Yoga *m or nt*.

yog(h)urt ['jɒgət] *n* Joghurt *m or nt*.

yoke [jəʊk] **1** *n (for oxen)* Joch *nt*; *(for carrying pails)* Schultertrage *f*. **to throw off the** ~ *(fig)* das Joch abschütteln. **(b)** *pl* - *(pair of oxen)* Joch, Gespann *nt*. **2** *vt* **(a)** *(also* ~ **up***) oxen* (ins Joch) einspannen. **(b)** *(fig: join together)* zusammenschließen.

yokel ['jəʊkəl] *n (pej)* Bauerntölpel *m*.

yolk [jəʊk] *n (of egg)* Eigelb *nt*.

yonder ['jɒndəʳ] *(poet, dial)* **1** *adv* **(over)** ~ dort drüben. **2** *adj* **from** ~ **house** von dem Haus (dort) drüben.

you [juː] *pron* **(a)** *(German familiar form, in letter-writing usu with a capital) (sing) (nom)* du; *(acc)* dich; *(dat)* dir; *(pl) (nom)* ihr; *(acc, dat)* euch; *(German polite form: sing, pl) (nom, acc)* Sie; *(dat)* Ihnen. **all of** ~ *(pl)* ihr alle/Sie alle; **if I were** ~ wenn ich du/Sie wäre; ~ **Germans** ihr Deutschen; **is that** ~? bist du's/seid ihr's/sind Sie's?; **it's** ~ du bist es/ihr seid's/Sie sind's; **that hat just isn't** ~ *(col)* der Hut paßt einfach nicht zu dir/zu Ihnen; **now there's a car for** ~! das ist mal ein tolles Auto. **(b)** *(indef) (nom)* man; *(acc)* einen; *(dat)* einem. ~ **never know** man kann nie wissen, man weiß nie; **it's not good for** ~ es ist nicht gut.

you'd [juːd] = **you would; you had.**

you'd've ['juːdəv] = **you would have.**

you'll [juːl] = **you will; you shall.**

young [jʌŋ] **1** *adj (+er)* jung; *wine, grass also* neu. ~ **people** junge Leute *pl*; ~ **people's fashions** Jugendmoden *pl*; ~ **lady/man** junge Dame/junger Mann; **they have a** ~ **family** sie haben kleine Kinder; **he is** ~ **at heart** er ist innerlich jung geblieben; ~ **Mr Brown** der junge Herr Brown; **Pitt the Y~er** Pitt der Jüngere; **he's a very** ~ **forty** er ist ein jugendlicher Vierziger. **2** *npl* **(a)** *(people)* **the** ~ die Jugend, die jungen Leute; **books for the** ~ Jugendbücher *pl*. **(b)** *(animals)* Junge *pl*. **with** ~ trächtig.

youngster ['jʌŋstəʳ] *n (boy)* Junge *m*; *(child)* Kind *nt*.

your [jɔːʳ] *poss adj* **(a)** *(German familiar form, in letter-writing usu with a capital) (sing)* dein/deine/dein; *(pl)* euer/eure/euer; *(German polite form: sing, pl)* Ihr/Ihre/Ihr. **(b) the climate here is bad for** ~ **health** das Klima hier ist nicht gut für die Gesundheit; ~ **typical American** der typische Amerikaner.

you're [jʊəʳ] = **you are.**

yours [jɔːz] *poss pron (German familiar form, in letter-writing usu with a capital) (sing)* deiner/deine/deins; *(pl)* eurer/eure/euers; *(German polite form: sing, pl)* Ihrer/Ihre/Ihr(e)s. **this is my book and that is** ~ dies ist mein Buch und das (ist) deins/Ihres; **the idea was** ~ es war deine/Ihre Idee, die Idee stammt von dir/Ihnen; **she is a cousin of** ~ sie ist deine Kusine, sie ist eine Kusine von dir; **that is no business of** ~ das geht dich/Sie nichts an; **that dog of** ~! dein/Ihr blöder Hund!; ~ *(in letter writing)* Ihr/Ihre; ~ **faithfully,** ~ **truly** *(on letter)* mit freundlichen Grüßen, hochachtungsvoll *(form)*; **what's** ~? *(to drink)* was trinkst du/was trinken Sie?; ~ **truly** *(col: I, me)* meine Wenigkeit.

yourself [jə'self] *pron, pl* **yourselves (a)** *(reflexive) (German familiar form) (sing) (acc)* dich; *(dat)* dir; *(pl)* euch; *(German polite form: sing, pl)* sich. **have you hurt** ~? hast du dir/haben Sie sich weh getan?; **you never speak about** ~ du redest nie über dich (selbst)/Sie reden nie über sich (selbst). **(b)** *(emph)* selbst. **you told me** ~ du hast/Sie haben es mir selbst gesagt; **you will see for** ~ du wirst/Sie werden selbst sehen; **did you do it by** ~? hast du/haben Sie das allein gemacht?

youth [juːθ] *n* **(a)** *no pl* Jugend *f*. **in my** ~ in meiner Jugend(zeit); **she has kept her** ~ sie ist jung geblieben. **(b)** *pl* **-s** [juːðz] *(young man)* junger Mann, Jugendliche(r) *m*. **(c)** ~ *pl (young men and women)* Jugend *f*. **she likes working with (the)** ~ sie arbeitet gerne mit Jugendlichen; ~ **club** Jugendklub *m*; ~ **hostel** Jugendherberge *f*; ~ **movement** Jugendbewegung *f*.

youthful ['juːθfʊl] *adj* jugendlich.

youthfulness ['juːθfʊlnɪs] *n* Jugendlichkeit *f*.

you've [juːv] = **you have.**

yowl [jaʊl] **1** *n (of person)* Heulen *nt no pl*; *(of dog)* Jaulen *nt no pl*; *(of cat)* klägliches Miauen *no pl*. **2**

vi (person) heulen; *(dog)* jaulen; *(cat)* kläglich miauen.
yo-yo ['jəʊjəʊ] *n* Jo-Jo *nt.*
Yugoslav ['juːgəʊ'slɑːv] **1** *adj* jugoslawisch. **2** *n* Jugoslawe *m*, Jugoslawin *f.*
Yugoslavia ['juːgəʊ'slɑːvɪə] *n* Jugoslawien *nt.*
Yule [juːl] *n (old)* Weihnachten *nt.* **~tide** Weihnachtszeit *f.*
yummy ['jʌmɪ] **1** *adj (+er) (col) food* lecker; *man* toll. **2** *interj* ~!, ~ ~! lecker!, hm! *(col).*
YWCA = **Young Women's Christian Association** CVJF *m.*

Z

Z, z [*(Brit)* zed, *(US)* ziː] *n* Z, z *nt.*
Zambia [zæmbɪə] *n* Sambia *nt.*
zany ['zeɪnɪ] *adj (+er) humour* verrückt; *person also* irrsinnig komisch.
zap [zæp] *vt (col) (hit)* schlagen; *(kill)* ausradieren *(col)*; *(erase) data* löschen.
♦ **zap up** *vt sep (col)* aufmotzen *(col).*
zeal [ziːl] *n no pl* Eifer *m.* **to work with great ~** mit Feuereifer arbeiten.
zealot ['zelət] *n* Fanatiker(in *f*) *m*; *(religious also)* (Glaubens)eiferer(in *f*) *m.*
zealous ['zeləs] *adj worker* eifrig, emsig. **~ for sth** eifrig um etw bemüht; **to be ~ to begin** erpicht darauf sein, anzufangen.
zebra ['zebrə] *n* Zebra *nt.* **~ crossing** *(Brit)* Zebrastreifen *m.*
zenith ['zenɪθ] *n (Astron, fig)* Zenit *m.*
zeppelin ['zeplɪn] *n* Zeppelin *m.*
zero ['zɪərəʊ] **1** *n, pl* **-(e)s** Null *f*; *(point on scale)* Nullpunkt *m.* **15 degrees below ~** 15 Grad unter Null. **2** *adj* **~ degrees** null Grad; **~ gravity** Schwerelosigkeit *f*; **at ~ gravity** unter Schwerelosigkeit; **~ hour** *(Mil, fig)* die Stunde X; **~-rated** *(for VAT)* mehrwertsteuerfrei.
♦ **zero in on** *vi +prep obj main point etc* herausgreifen.
zest [zest] *n (enthusiasm)* Begeisterung *f*; *(in style, of food etc)* Pfiff *(col)*, Schwung *m.* **~ for life** Lebensfreude *f*; **a story full of ~** eine Geschichte mit Schwung.
zigzag ['zɪgzæg] **1** *n* Zickzack *m or nt.* **the river cuts a ~ through the rocks** der Fluß bahnt sich im Zickzack einen Weg durch die Felsen. **2** *adj course, line* Zickzack-; *road, path* zickzackförmig. **3** *adv* zickzackförmig, im Zickzack. **4** *vi* im Zickzack laufen/fahren *etc.*
zinc [zɪŋk] *n* Zink *nt.* **~ ointment** Zinksalbe *f*; **~ oxide** Zinkoxyd *nt.*
Zionism ['zaɪənɪzəm] *n* Zionismus *m.*
Zionist ['zaɪənɪst] **1** *adj* zionistisch. **2** *n* Zionist(in *f*) *m.*
zip [zɪp] **1** *n* **(a)** *(Brit: fastener)* Reißverschluß *m.* **(b)** *(col: energy)* Schwung *m.* **2** *vi (col: car, person)* flitzen *(col).* **to ~ past/along** *etc* vorbei-/daherflitzen *etc (col).*
♦ **zip up 1** *vt sep* **to ~ ~ a dress** den Reißverschluß eines Kleides zumachen. **2** *vi* **the dress ~s ~** das Kleid hat einen Reißverschluß.
zip: ~ code *n (US)* Postleitzahl *f*; **~ fastener** *n* Reißverschluß *m.*
zipper ['zɪpəʳ] *n* Reißverschluß *m.*
zit [zɪt] *n (esp US col)* Pickel *m.*
zither ['zɪðəʳ] *n* Zither *f.*
zodiac ['zəʊdɪæk] *n* Tierkreis *m.* **signs of the ~** Tierkreiszeichen *pl.*
zombie ['zɒmbɪ] *n* **(a)** *(lit: revived corpse)* Zombie *m.* **(b)** *(fig)* Idiot *(col)*, Schwachkopf *(col) m.* **like a ~/like ~s** wie im Tran.
zone ['zəʊn] **1** *n* **(a)** Zone *f*; *(fig also)* Gebiet *nt.* **no-parking ~** Parkverbot *nt*; **time ~** Zeitzone *f.* **(b)** *(US: postal ~)* Postbezirk *m.* **2** *vt* **(a)** *town* in Zonen aufteilen. **(b) to ~ a district for industry** einen Bezirk zur Industriezone erklären.
zonked [zɒŋkt] *adj (col) (drunk, high)* total ausgeflippt *(col)*; *(tired)* total geschafft *(col).*
zoo [zuː] *n* Zoo, Tierpark *m.* **~ keeper** Tierpfleger(in *f*), Wärter(in *f*) *m.*
zoological [ˌzuə'lɒdʒɪkəl] *adj* zoologisch. **~ gardens** zoologischer Garten.
zoologist [zʊ'ɒlədʒɪst] *n* Zoologe *m*, Zoologin *f.*
zoology [zʊ'ɒlədʒɪ] *n* Zoologie *f.*
zoom [zuːm] **1** *n* **(a)** *(sound of engine)* Surren *nt.* **(b)** *(Phot: also* **~ lens***)* Zoom(objektiv) *nt.* **2** *vi (engine)* surren; *(col)* sausen *(col).* **the car ~ed past us** der Wagen sauste an uns vorbei *(col)*; **to ~ off** davonrasen.
♦ **zoom in** *vi* **to ~ ~ on sth** *(Phot)* etw heranholen.
zucchini [zuː'kiːnɪ] *n (US)* Zucchini *f.*
Zulu ['zuːluː] **1** *adj* Zulu-. **2** *n* Zulu *mf*; *(language)* Zulu *nt.*

IRREGULAR GERMAN VERBS

Infinitive	Present Indicative 2nd pers sing; 3rd pers sing	Imperfect Indicative	Past Participle
backen	bäckst, backst; bäckt, backt	backte	gebacken
befehlen	befiehlst; befiehlt	befahl	befohlen
beginnen	beginnst; beginnt	begann	begonnen
beißen	beißt; beißt	biß	gebissen
bergen	birgst; birgt	barg	geborgen
bersten	birst; birst	barst	geborsten
bewegen[2]	bewegst; bewegt	bewog	bewogen
biegen	biegst; biegt	bog	gebogen
bieten	bietest; bietet	bot	geboten
binden	bindest; bindet	band	gebunden
bitten	bittest; bittet	bat	gebeten
blasen	bläst; bläst	blies	geblasen
bleiben	bleibst; bleibt	blieb	geblieben
braten	brätst; brät	briet	gebraten
brechen	brichst; bricht	brach	gebrochen
brennen	brennst; brennt	brannte	gebrannt
bringen	bringst; bringt	brachte	gebracht
denken	denkst; denkt	dachte	gedacht
dreschen	drischst; drischt	drosch	gedroschen
dringen	dringst; dringt	drang	gedrungen
dürfen	*1st* darf; *2nd* darfst; *3rd* darf	durfte	gedurft; *(after infin)* dürfen
empfangen	empfängst; empfängt	empfing	empfangen
empfehlen	empfiehlst; empfiehlt	empfahl	empfohlen
empfinden	empfindest; empfindet	empfand	empfunden
erschrecken	erschreckst; erschreckt	erschrak	erschrocken
essen	ißt; ißt	aß	gegessen
fahren	fährst; fährt	fuhr	gefahren
fallen	fällst; fällt	fiel	gefallen
fangen	fängst; fängt	fing	gefangen
fechten	fichtst, fichst *(col)*; ficht	focht	gefochten
finden	findest; findet	fand	gefunden
flechten	flichtst, flichst *(col)*; flicht	flocht	geflochten
fliegen	fliegst; fliegt	flog	geflogen
fliehen	fliehst; flieht	floh	geflohen
fließen	fließt; fließt	floß	geflossen
fressen	frißt; frißt	fraß	gefressen
frieren	frierst; friert	fror	gefroren
gebären	gebierst; gebiert	gebar	geboren
geben	gibst; gibt	gab	gegeben
gedeihen	gedeihst; gedeiht	gedieh	gediehen
gehen	gehst; geht	ging	gegangen
gelingen	gelingt	gelang	gelungen
gelten	giltst; gilt	galt	gegolten
genesen	genest; genest	genas	genesen
genießen	genießt; genießt	genoß	genossen
geschehen	geschieht	geschah	geschehen
gewinnen	gewinnst; gewinnt	gewann	gewonnen
gießen	gießt; gießt	goß	gegossen
gleichen	gleichst; gleicht	glich	geglichen
gleiten	gleitest; gleitet	glitt	geglitten
glimmen	glimmst; glimmt	glomm	geglommen
graben	gräbst; gräbt	grub	gegraben
greifen	greifst; greift	griff	gegriffen
haben	hast; hat	hatte	gehabt
halten	hältst; hält	hielt	gehalten
hängen	hängst; hängt	hing	gehangen
hauen	haust; haut	haute	gehauen
heben	hebst; hebt	hob	gehoben
heißen	heißt; heißt	hieß	geheißen
helfen	hilfst; hilft	half	geholfen
kennen	kennst; kennt	kannte	gekannt

klingen	klingst; klingt	klang	geklungen
kneifen	kneifst; kneift	kniff	gekniffen
kommen	kommst; kommt	kam	gekommen
können	*1st* kann; *2nd* kannst; *3rd* kann	konnte	gekonnt; *(after infin)* können
kriechen	kriechst; kriecht	kroch	gekrochen
laden	lädst; lädt	lud	geladen
lassen	läßt; läßt	ließ	gelassen; *(after infin)* lassen
laufen	läufst; läuft	lief	gelaufen
leiden	leidest; leidet	litt	gelitten
leihen	leihst; leiht	lieh	geliehen
lesen	liest; liest	las	gelesen
liegen	liegst; liegt	lag	gelegen
lügen	lügst; lügt	log	gelogen
mahlen	mahlst; mahlt	mahlte	gemahlen
meiden	meidest; meidet	mied	gemieden
melken	melkst; melkt	melkte	gemolken
messen	mißt; mißt	maß	gemessen
mißlingen	mißlingt	mißlang	mißlungen
mögen	*1st* mag; *2nd* magst; *3rd* mag	mochte	gemocht; *(after infin)* mögen
müssen	*1st* muß; *2nd* mußt; *3rd* muß	mußte	gemußt; *(after infin)* müssen
nehmen	nimmst; nimmt	nahm	genommen
nennen	nennst; nennt	nannte	genannt
pfeifen	pfeifst; pfeift	pfiff	gepfiffen
preisen	preist; preist	pries	gepriesen
quellen	quillst; quillt	quoll	gequollen
raten	rätst; rät	riet	geraten
reiben	reibst; reibt	rieb	gerieben
reißen	reißt; reißt	riß	gerissen
reiten	reitest; reitet	ritt	geritten
rennen	rennst; rennt	rannte	gerannt
riechen	riechst; riecht	roch	gerochen
ringen	ringst; ringt	rang	gerungen
rinnen	rinnst; rinnt	rann	geronnen
rufen	rufst; ruft	rief	gerufen
salzen	salzt; salzt	salzte	gesalzen
saufen	säufst; säuft	soff	gesoffen
saugen	saugst; saugt	sog, saugte	gesogen, gesaugt
schaffen	schaffst; schafft	schuf	geschaffen
scheiden	scheidest; scheidet	schied	geschieden
scheinen	scheinst; scheint	schien	geschienen
scheißen	scheißt; scheißt	schiß	geschissen
schelten	schiltst; schilt	schalt	gescholten
scheren	scherst; schert	schor	geschoren
schieben	schiebst; schiebt	schob	geschoben
schießen	schießt; schießt	schoß	geschossen
schinden	schindest; schindet	schindete	geschunden
schlafen	schläfst; schläft	schlief	geschlafen
schlagen	schlägst; schlägt	schlug	geschlagen
schleichen	schleichst; schleicht	schlich	geschlichen
schleifen	schleifst; schleift	schliff	geschliffen
schließen	schließt; schließt	schloß	geschlossen
schlingen	schlingst; schlingt	schlang	geschlungen
schmeißen	schmeißt; schmeißt	schmiß	geschmissen
schmelzen	schmilzt; schmilzt	schmolz	geschmolzen
schneiden	schneid(e)st; schneidet	schnitt	geschnitten
schreiben	schreibst; schreibt	schrieb	geschrieben
schreien	schreist; schreit	schrie	geschrie(e)n
schreiten	schreitest; schreitet	schritt	geschritten
schweigen	schweigst; schweigt	schwieg	geschwiegen
schwellen	schwillst; schwillt	schwoll	geschwollen
schwimmen	schwimmst; schwimmt	schwamm	geschwommen

schwinden	schwindest; schwindet	schwand	geschwunden
schwingen	schwingst; schwingt	schwang	geschwungen
schwören	schwörst; schwört	schwor	geschworen
sehen	siehst; sieht	sah	gesehen; *(after infin)* sehen
sein	*1st* bin; *2nd* bist; *3rd* ist; *pl 1st* sind; *2nd* seid; *3rd* sind	war	gewesen
senden *(send)*	sendest; sendet	sandte	gesandt
singen	singst; singt	sang	gesungen
sinken	sinkst; sinkt	sank	gesunken
sinnen	sinnst; sinnt	sann	gesonnen
sitzen	sitzt; sitzt	saß	gesessen
sollen	*1st* soll; *2nd* sollst; *3rd* soll	sollte	gesollt; *(after infin)* sollen
spalten	spaltest; spaltet	spaltete	gespalten, gespaltet
speien	speist; speit	spie	gespie(e)n
spinnen	spinnst; spinnt	spann	gesponnen
sprechen	sprichst; spricht	sprach	gesprochen
sprießen	sprießt; sprießt	sproß, sprießte	gesprossen
springen	springst; springt	sprang	gesprungen
stechen	stichst; sticht	stach	gestochen
stecken *(vi)*	steckst; steckt	steckte, stak	gesteckt
stehen	stehst; steht	stand	gestanden
stehlen	stiehlst; stiehlt	stahl	gestohlen
steigen	steigst; steigt	stieg	gestiegen
sterben	stirbst; stirbt	starb	gestorben
stieben	stiebst; stiebt	stob, stiebte	gestoben, gestiebt
stinken	stinkst; stinkt	stank	gestunken
stoßen	stößt; stößt	stieß	gestoßen
streichen	streichst; streicht	strich	gestrichen
streiten	streitest; streitet	stritt	gestritten
tragen	trägst; trägt	trug	getragen
treffen	triffst; trifft	traf	getroffen
treiben	treibst; treibt	trieb	getrieben
treten	trittst; tritt	trat	getreten
trinken	trinkst; trinkt	trank	getrunken
trügen	trügst; trügt	trog	getrogen
tun	*1st* tue; *2nd* tust; *3rd* tut	tat	getan
verderben	verdirbst; verdirbt	verdarb	verdorben
verdrießen	verdrießt, verdrießt	verdroß	verdrossen
vergessen	vergißt; vergißt	vergaß	vergessen
verlieren	verlierst; verliert	verlor	verloren
verschleißen	verschleißt; verschleißt	verschliß	verschlissen
verzeihen	verzeihst; verzeiht	verzieh	verziehen
wachsen	wächst; wächst	wuchs	gewachsen
wägen	wägst; wägt	wog	gewogen
waschen	wäschst; wäscht	wusch	gewaschen
weben	webst; webt	webte, wob *(liter, fig)*	gewebt, gewoben *(liter, fig)*
weichen	weichst; weicht	wich	gewichen
weisen	weist; weist	wies	gewiesen
wenden	wendest; wendet	wendete, wandte	gewendet, gewandt
werben	wirbst; wirbt	warb	geworben
werden	wirst; wird	wurde	geworden; *(after ptp)* worden
werfen	wirfst; wirft	warf	geworfen
wiegen	wiegst; wiegt	wog	gewogen
winden	windest; windet	wand	gewunden
winken	winkst; winkt	winkte	gewinkt, gewunken
wissen	*1st* weiß; *2nd* weißt; *3rd* weiß	wußte	gewußt
wollen	*1st* will; *2nd* willst; *3rd* will	wollte	gewollt; *(after infin)* wollen
wringen	wringst; wringt	wrang	gewrungen
ziehen	ziehst; zieht	zog	gezogen
zwingen	zwingst; zwingt	zwang	gezwungen

UNREGELMÄSSIGE ENGLISCHE VERBEN

Präsens	Imperfekt	Partizip Perfekt
arise	arose	arisen
awake	awoke	awaked
be (am, is, are; being)	was, were	been
bear	bore	born(e)
beat	beat	beaten
become	became	become
befall	befell	befallen
begin	began	begun
behold	beheld	beheld
bend	bent	bent
beset	beset	beset
bet	bet, betted	bet, betted
bid	bid, bade	bid, bidden
bind	bound	bound
bite	bit	bitten
bleed	bled	bled
blow	blew	blown
break	broke	broken
breed	bred	bred
bring	brought	brought
build	built	built
burn	burnt, burned	burnt, burned
burst	burst	burst
buy	bought	bought
can	could	(been able)
cast	cast	cast
catch	caught	caught
choose	chose	chosen
cling	clung	clung
come	came	come
cost	cost; costed	cost; costed
creep	crept	crept
cut	cut	cut
deal	dealt	dealt
dig	dug	dug
do (3rd person: he/she/ it does)	did	done
draw	drew	drawn
dream	dreamed, dreamt	dreamed, dreamt
drink	drank	drunk
drive	drove	driven
dwell	dwelt	dwelt
eat	ate	eaten
fall	fell	fallen
feed	fed	fed
feel	felt	felt
fight	fought	fought
find	found	found
flee	fled	fled
fling	flung	flung
fly	flew	flown
forbid	forbad(e)	forbidden
forecast	forecast	forecast
forget	forgot	forgotten
forgive	forgave	forgiven
forsake	forsook	forsaken
freeze	froze	frozen
get	got	got, *(US)* gotten
give	gave	given
go (goes)	went	gone
grind	ground	ground
grow	grew	grown
hang	hung, hanged	hung, hanged
have	had	had
hear	heard	heard
hide	hid	hidden
hit	hit	hit
hold	held	held
hurt	hurt	hurt
keep	kept	kept
kneel	knelt, kneeled	knelt, kneeled
know	knew	known
lay	laid	laid
lead	led	led
lean	leant, leaned	leant, leaned
leap	leapt, leaped	leapt, leaped
learn	learnt, learned	learnt, learned
leave	left	left
lend	lent	lent
let	let	let

lie (lying)	lay	lain
light	lit, lighted	lit, lighted
lose	lost	lost
make	made	made
may	might	—
mean	meant	meant
meet	met	met
mistake	mistook	mistaken
mow	mowed	mown, mowed
must	(had to)	(had to)
pay	paid	paid
put	put	put
quit	quit, quitted	quit, quitted
read	read	read
rid	rid	rid
ride	rode	ridden
ring	rang	rung
rise	rose	risen
run	ran	run
saw	sawed	sawed, sawn
say	said	said
see	saw	seen
seek	sought	sought
sell	sold	sold
send	sent	sent
sew	sewed	sewn
set	set	set
shake	shook	shaken
shear	sheared	shorn, sheared
shed	shed	shed
shine	shone	shone
shoot	shot	shot
show	showed	shown
shrink	shrank	shrunk
shut	shut	shut
sing	sang	sung
sink	sank	sunk
sit	sat	sat
slay	slew	slain
sleep	slept	slept
slide	slid	slid
sling	slung	slung
slit	slit	slit
smell	smelt, smelled	smelt, smelled
sow	sowed	sown, sowed
speak	spoke	spoken
speed	sped, speeded	sped, speeded
spell	spelt, spelled	spelt, spelled
spend	spent	spent
spill	spilt, spilled	spilt, spilled
spin	spun	spun
spit	spat	spat
spoil	spoiled, spoilt	spoiled, spoilt
spread	spread	spread
spring	sprang	sprung
stand	stood	stood
steal	stole	stolen
stick	stuck	stuck
sting	stung	stung
stink	stank	stunk
stride	strode	stridden
strike	struck	struck, stricken
strive	strove	striven
swear	swore	sworn
sweep	swept	swept
swell	swelled	swollen, swelled
swim	swam	swum
swing	swung	swung
take	took	taken
teach	taught	taught
tear	tore	torn
tell	told	told
think	thought	thought
throw	threw	thrown
thrust	thrust	thrust
tread	trod	trodden
wake	woke, waked	woken, waked
wear	wore	worn
weave	wove, weaved	woven, weaved
wed	wedded, wed	wedded, wed
weep	wept	wept
win	won	won
wind	wound	wound
wring	wrung	wrung
write	wrote	written

WEIGHTS AND MEASURES — MASSE UND GEWICHTE

1 Metric System — Metrisches System

Linear measures — Längenmaße

1 millimetre (Millimeter)	=	0.03937 inch
1 centimetre (Zentimeter)	=	0.3937 inch
1 metre (Meter)	=	39.37 inches
	=	1.094 yards
1 kilometre (Kilometer)	=	0.6214 mile ($\frac{5}{8}$ mile)

Square measures — Flächenmaße

1 square centimetre (Quadratzentimeter)	=	0.155 square inch
1 square metre (Quadratmeter)	=	10.764 square feet
	=	1.196 square yards
1 square kilometre (Quadratkilometer)	=	0.3861 square mile
	=	247.1 acr
1 are (Ar) = 100 square metres	=	119.6 square yards
1 hectare (Hektar) = 100 ares	=	2.471 acres

Measures of capacity — Hohlmaße

1 litre (Liter)	=	1.76 pints
	=	0.22 gallon

Weights — Gewichte

1 gramme (Gramm)	=	15.4 grains
1 kilogramme (Kilogramm)	=	2.2046 pounds
1 metric ton (Tonne) = 1000 kilogrammes	=	0.9842 ton

2 Non-metric system — Nicht-metrisches System

Linear measures — Längenmaße

1 inch (Zoll)	=	2,54 Zentimeter
1 foot (Fuß) = 12 inches	=	30,48 Zentimeter
1 yard (Yard) = 3 feet	=	91,44 Zentimeter
1 furlong = 220 yards	=	201,17 Meter
1 mile (Meile) = 1760 yards	=	1,609 Kilometer

Square measures — Flächenmaße

1 square inch (Quadratzoll)	=	6,45 cm²
1 square foot (Quadratfuß) = 144 square inches	=	929.03 cm²
1 square yard (Quadratyard) = 9 square feet	=	0,836 m²
1 square rod = 30.25 square yards	=	25,29 m²
1 acre = 4840 square yards	=	40,47 Ar
1 square mile (Quadratmeile) = 640 acres	=	2,59 km²

Liquid measures — Flüssigkeitsmaße

1 gill	=	0,142 Liter
1 pint = 4 gills	=	0,57 Liter
1 quart = 2 pints	=	1,136 Liter
1 gallon (Gallone) = 4 quarts	=	4,546 Liter

Weights — Avoirdupois system — Handelsgewichte

1 ounce (Unze)	=	28,35 Gramm
1 pound (britisches Pfund) = 16 ounces	=	453,6 Gramm
	=	0,453 Kilogramm
1 stone = 14 pounds	=	6,348 Kilogramm
1 quarter = 28 pounds	=	12,7 Kilogramm
1 hundredweight = 112 pounds	=	50,8 Kilogramm
1 ton (Tonne) = 2240 pounds = 20 hundredweight	=	1016 Kilogramm

3 US Measures — Amerikanische Maße

Liquid measures — Flüssigkeitsmaße

1 US liquid gill	=	0,118 Liter
1 US liquid pint = 4 gills	=	0,473 Liter
1 US liquid quart = 2 pints	=	0,946 Liter
1 US gallon = 4 quarts	=	3,785 Liter

Weights — Gewichte

1 hundredweight (*or* short hundredweight) = 100 pounds	=	45,36 Kilogramm
1 ton (*or* short ton) = 2000 pounds = 20 short hundredweights	=	907,18 Kilogramm